~~FOR REFERENCE~~

~~Do Not Take From This Room~~

VAN BURE
DECATU

W9-AEZ-841

DISCARDED

ENCARTA® WEBSTER'S DICTIONARY OF THE ENGLISH LANGUAGE

ENCARTA® WEBSTER'S DICTIONARY OF THE ENGLISH LANGUAGE

BLOOMSBURY

423
ubb

A BLOOMSBURY REFERENCE BOOK
Created from the Bloomsbury Dictionary Database
www.wordadvisory.com

© Bloomsbury Publishing Plc 1999, 2004

First US edition published 1999
Second US edition published 2004

All rights reserved. No part of this publication may be reproduced, stored in a retrieval system, or transmitted by any means, electronic, mechanical, photocopying, or otherwise, without the prior written permission of the Publisher. For information contact Bloomsbury, 175 Fifth Avenue, New York, NY 10010

Published by Bloomsbury, New York and London
Distributed to the trade by Holtzbrinck Publishers

This Dictionary includes words on the basis of their usage in the English language today. Words that are known to have current trademark, service mark, or proprietary registrations are identified as such. The inclusion of any such word or identification in this Dictionary is not, however, to be regarded as an expression of the Publisher's opinion as to whether or not it is subject to proprietary rights. Neither the presence nor absence of any such word or identification in the Dictionary is to be regarded as affecting in any way whatever the validity or status of any trademark or other proprietary rights throughout the world.

Microsoft® and Encarta® are either registered trademarks or trademarks of Microsoft Corp. in the United States and/or other countries. Other product and company names herein may be trademarks of their respective owners.
Except where indicated all illustrations are copyright Bloomsbury Publishing Plc 1999, 2004

Library of Congress Cataloging-in-Publication Data is available on request

ISBN 1-58234-510-4

All papers used by Bloomsbury Publishing are natural, recyclable products made from wood grown in well-managed forests. The manufacturing processes conform to the environmental regulations of the country of origin.

Typeset by Selwood Systems, Midsomer Norton, United Kingdom
Printed in the United States of America

Contents

US General Editor
Anne H. Soukhanov

Editor-in-Chief
Dr. Kathy Rooney

Publisher
Nigel Newton

Dictionaries Publisher
Faye Carney

Executive Editor
Susan Jellis

Database Manager
Edmund Wright

Senior Lexicographer
Lesley Brown

Project Manager
Katy McAdam

Project Coordinator
Joel Adams

Chief Etymologist
John Ayto

Chief Phonetician
Dinah Jackson

Production Director
Penny Edwards

Production Editor
Nicky Thompson

EDITORIAL CONTRIBUTORS TO THE SECOND EDITION

Lexicographers
David Barnett
Carol Braham
Robert Clevenger
Dewayne Crawford
Steve Curtis
Rosalind Fergusson
Scott Forbes
Jennifer Goss Duby
David Hallworth
Ruth Hein
Georgia Hole
Ann-Marie Imbornoni
Barbara Kelly
Imogen Kerr
Duncan Marshall
Michael Munro
Julie Plier
Jane Rogoyska
Howard Sargeant
Karen Stern
Fraser Sutherland
Megan Thomson
Donald Watt
Pamela White

Science And Technical Editors
Rich Cutler
Pam England
Robert Hine
Alan D. Levy
James E. Shea
Tom Shields

Etymologies
Lesley Brown
Martha Mayou
Susan Sigalas Ph.D.
David M. Weeks Ph.D.

Usage And Language Heritage Notes
John Ayto
Lesley Brown
Rosalind Fergusson
Anne H. Soukhanov

Proofreaders
Sandra Anderson
Pat Bulhosen
Christina Gleeson
Isabel Griffiths
Ruth Hillmore
Irene Lakhani
Jill Leatherbarrow
Clea McEnery
Mark Miller
Vanessa Mitchell
Susan Turner

ADDITIONAL CONTRIBUTORS

Editorial, Keyboarding, and Administrative Assistance
Sara Al-Bader
Simon Arnold
Heather Bateman
Emma Harris
Sarah Lusznat
Rebecca McKee
Simone Potter
Charlotte Regan
Darren Treend

Illustrations
Wendy Bramwell
Chris Lyon
Annabel Milne
Sylvie Rabbe
Beatriz Waller
David Wood

Tables
Nigel Partridge
Jeffrey Petts
Ruth Bateson
Anthony Duke

Annotations
Andrew Clarke

Maps
Digital Wisdom Publishing Ltd.

Design
William Webb
Fiona Knowles
Mercer Design

Jacket Design
William Webb
Yeti McCaldin

ADVISERS AND CONSULTANTS TO THE BLOOMSBURY DICTIONARY DATABASE

Clark Adams Ph.D.,
Professor, Department of Wildlife and Fisheries Sciences, Texas A&M University (Hunting)

Michael Allaby,
Writer and science consultant (Life Sciences)

Robert Allen,
Editor and lexicographer (English Language)

Christopher Arnison Ph.D.,
Professor, Royal Agricultural College (Agriculture)

Michele Aina Barale Ph.D.,
Professor of English and of Women's and Gender Studies, Amherst College, Massachusetts (English Language)

Tallis Barker Ph.D.,
(Music)

Alan Barnard Ph.D.,
Professor, University of Edinburgh (Anthropology)

LynnDianne Beene Ph.D.,
Professor, Department of English, University of New Mexico (English Language)

Stephen C. Behrendt Ph.D.,
George Holmes Distinguished Professor of English, University of Nebraska (English Language)

Philip D. Beidler Ph.D.,
Professor, University of Alabama (English Language)

Joseph J. BelBruno Ph.D.,
Professor, Dartmouth College, Hanover, New Hampshire (Chemistry)

Erin Belieu M.F.A.,
Assistant Professor, Department of English, Ohio State University (English Language)

Bethan Benwell Ph.D.,
Department of English Studies, University of Stirling (English Language)

Teresa Bevin Ph.D.,
Author and Professor, Montgomery College (Hispanic English)

David F. Bjorklund,
Professor, Department of Psychology, Florida Atlantic University (Psychology)

Donald Black,
Professor, College of Food and Natural Resources, University of Massachusetts (Agriculture)

David Blair,
Senior Research Fellow, Department of English, Macquarie University (Australian English)

Sheila S. Blair Ph.D.,
Norma Jean Calderwood University Professor of Islamic and Asian Art, Boston College (Arabic Words and Places)

Clive Bloom Ph.D.,
Professor, Middlesex University (Media)

Joseph Donald Blount Ph.D.,
Professor, Department of English, University of South Carolina Aiken (English Language)

Suzanne Bordelon Ph.D.,
Assistant Professor, Department of Rhetoric and Writing Studies, San Diego State University (English Language)

Robert H. Brinkmeyer Jr. Ph.D.,
Professor and Chair, Department of English, University of Arkansas (English Language)

Allan Brooks,
Editor and writer; member, US Government Technical committees, Sr. VP Electro-Lite Corp. (Engineering)

Charles Butcher,
Specialist writer and editor (Chemical Engineering)

Col. John A. Calabro,
US Army, Retired. Adjunct Professor of English, US Military Academy, West Point (Military)

Colin Callander,
Freelance journalist and former editor of *Golf Monthly* (Golf)

Paul A. Carling,
Professor, University of Lancaster (Geography)

Teena A. M. Carnegie Ph.D.,
Assistant Professor, Department of English, University of Iowa (English Language)

Ronald Carter,
Professor of Modern English Language, University of Nottingham (English Language)

Christopher Chippindale Ph.D.,
Reader in Archaeology & curator for British archaeology collections, Cambridge University Museum of Archaeology & Anthropology (Archaeology)

William Leon Coburn Ph.D.,
Associate Professor, Department of English, University of Nevada, Las Vegas (English Language)

N. J. Collar,
Leventis Fellow in Conservation Biology, BirdLife International and Cambridge University (Ornithology)

Timothy Collings,
Motor racing correspondent, Reuters and *Daily Telegraph* (Motor Sports)

Peter Colvin,
Faculty Librarian for Languages and Cultures, School of Oriental and African Studies (Islamic Culture)

Nikolas Coupland,
Professor, Centre for Applied English Language Studies, University of Wales (English in Wales)

Helen Cowie,
Professor, Director of UK Observatory for the Promotion of Nonviolence, University of Surrey, Guildford (Psychology)

Michael Crane,
Director, British Isles Backgammon Association (Backgammon)

Andrew Dalby Ph.D.,
Honorary Fellow, Institute of Linguists, author of *Dictionary of Languages* and *Language in Danger* (Languages)

Robert Day,
Chairman, Suffolk Advanced Motorcyclists Club (DIY, Motorcycles)

Scott Delancey Ph.D.,
Department of Linguistics, University of Oregon (Native American English)

Col. Michael Dewar,
Formerly Deputy Director, Institute of Strategic Studies (Military)

Robert Ditton,
Professor, Department of Wildlife and Fisheries Sciences, Texas A&M University (Ecology, Recreational Fishing)

Paul B. Diehl Ph.D.,
Associate Professor, Department of English, University of Iowa (English Language)

Kenneth L. Donelson Ph.D.,
Professor, Department of English, Arizona State University (English Language)

Bethany K. Dumas,
Professor, Department of English, University of Tennessee (Law)

Stephen Dundas M.A.,
Teacher of English, St. Bede's School, Redhill, Surrey (English Language)

Catherine Emmott Ph.D.,
Senior Lecturer, Department of English Language, University of Glasgow (English Language)

Roy Evans Ph.D.,
Formerly Faculty of Education, Roehampton Institute, London (Education)

Alan Ewart Ph.D.,
University of Northern British Columbia (Mountaineering / Climbing)

Margery Fee,
Professor, Department of English, University of British Columbia; co-author, *Oxford Guide to Canadian Usage* (Canadian English)

Joshua Fishman,
Professor, City University of New York (Yiddish)

Nancy Flynn Ph.D.,
Cornell University (Botany)

Tom Gallagher,
Writer (Baseball)

Bruce Ganem,
Professor, Department of Chemistry and Chemical Biology, Cornell University (Chemistry)

Shirley Nelson Garner Ph.D.,
Professor and Associate Dean of the Graduate School, University of Minnesota (English Language)

Andrew Goldsbrough Ph.D.,
St. John's Innovation Centre, Cambridge, UK (Biotechnology)

Lynne Goldstein,
Professor and Chair, Department of Anthropology, Michigan State University (Anthropology / Archaeology)

David Graddol,
The English Company (UK) Ltd. (World English)

James Gramann,
Professor, Department of Recreation, Park and Tourism Sciences, Texas A&M University (Leisure)

Jeremy Gray,
Open University (Mathematics)

Dr. A. C. Grayling,
Reader in Philosophy, Birkbeck College, London (Philosophy)

Eugene Green Ph.D.,
Professor, Department of English, Boston University (English Language)

Jonathon Green,
Writer, broadcaster, author of a history of lexicography *Chasing the Sun: Dictionary Makers and the Dictionaries They Made*, and leading slang lexicographer; author, *Cassell Dictionary of Slang*

Fayal Greene,
Gardening writer and editor (Gardening)

Steven Griffiths,
UK civil servant (Transport / Environment)

Trevor Griffiths,
Professor and Programme Director, Department of Humanities, Arts and Languages, London Metropolitan University (Theater)

Anthea Fraser Gupta Ph.D.,
School of English, University of Leeds (English Language)

Eva Hertel Ph.D.,
English Language and Linguistics, TU Chemnitz (East Africa)

David Hoover Ph.D.,
Associate Professor of English, New York University (English Language)

Andrew Howard,
Middlesex University (Politics)

Alastair Hudson,
Reader in Equity and Law, Queen Mary, University of London (Law)

Philip Johansson,
Managing Editor, Earthwatch Institute (Zoology)

Bridget Jones,
Cookery editor and writer, member of the Guild of Food Writers (Food)

Darlene Juschka,
Professor, University of Toronto (World Religions)

Kathryn Kavanagh,
Formerly Executive Director, Dictionary Unit for South African English, Rhodes University (South African English)

David Kemp,
VP and Euro Director, London, ABN-AMRO Bank N. V. (Currencies)

Alison Kervin,
Editor, *Rugby World* (Rugby)

Kate Kiefer,
Professor, Colorado State University (English Language)

Betty Kirkpatrick,
Editor, author, and lexicographer (English Language)

Ira Konigsberg,
Professor, University of Michigan, Ann Arbor; author, *Complete Film Dictionary* (Cinema)

Tracy Lake,
Head of English, Skegness Grammar School, Skegness (English Language)

Jacqueline Lam Ph.D.,
Language Centre, Hong Kong University of Science & Technology (Hong Kong English)

John Laurence Ph.D.,
Boyce Thomson Institute, Cornell University (Botany)

Bryan Lawson,
Professor and Dean, Faculty of Architectural Studies, University of Sheffield (Architecture)

Andrew Leclair,
Professor, Newman Laboratory, Cornell University (Physics)

Becky Lee Ph.D.,
Associate Professor, Division of Humanities and School of Women's Studies, York University, Toronto (Christianity and The Bible)

Naomi C. Losch,
Assistant Professor in Hawaiian, Department of Hawaiian and Indo-Pacific Languages, University of Hawaii at Manoa (Hawaiian English)

Caroline Macafee Ph.D.,
University of Aberdeen (Scottish, Northern Irish)

Carolyn Marcus,
Gardening writer and editor, ESOL lecturer (Gardening)

Donald G. Marshall Ph.D.,
Professor and Fletcher Jones Chair of Great Books, Humanities and Teacher Education Division, Pepperdine University (English Language)

Aya Matsuda Ph.D.,
Assistant Professor, Department of English, University of New Hampshire (English Language)

Tom McArthur Ph.D.,
Editor, *English Today: The International Review of the English Language* (1985-) and *The Oxford Companion to the English Language* (1992-); author, *The Oxford Guide to World English* (2002)

Joy McEntee Ph.D.,
Lecturer, Discipline of English, University of Adelaide, Australia (English Language)

Alastair McIver,
Editor, *Tennis World* (Tennis)

Jeffrey McQuain,
Writer and researcher, *New York Times*; word columnist and researcher for William Safire; author, *Power Language* (Politics)

Anthony Middleton,
Formerly editor, RAF in-house publications service; formerly Technical Publications Editor, GEC-Marconi (Engineering)

Mark Miller,
Editor (Literature)

Frank Molloy Ph.D.,
Senior Lecturer, Department of English, School of Humanities, Charles Sturt University, New South Wales, Australia (English Language)

Martyn Moore,
Editor, *Practical Photography* (Photography)

Philip D. Morehead,
Lyric Opera of Chicago (Music)

David Morton,
Professor, School of Biomedical Science and Ethics, University of Birmingham (Veterinary Science)

Bruce Murphy,
Professor, Faculty of Veterinary Medicine, University of Montreal (Biology)

Adrian Napper,
Formerly Department of Architecture, Edinburgh College of Art (Building and Construction)

Mark Newbrook Ph.D.,
Honorary Research Associate in Linguistics, Monash University; Honorary Research Associate in Linguistics, University of Sheffield (English in Malaysia and Singapore)

Ronald B. Newman Ph.D.,
Associate Professor of English, University of Miami (English Language)

Susan North,
Textiles and Fashion, Victoria and Albert Museum (Fashion)

Kathleen O'Grady,
Trinity College, University of Cambridge (Religion and Mythology)

Thomas S. Oliver Jr. Ph.D.,
Former Chair, Department of English, University of the District of Columbia (English Language)

Alex Orenstein,
Professor, City University of New York (Philosophy)

Lee Pederson,
Charles Howard Professor of English Language, Emory University, Atlanta GA (US regionalisms, History of US English)

Anthony Pellegrini Ph.D.,
Professor, Department of Educational Psychology, University of Minnesota (Education)

Sandra Poulton,
Teacher of English Language, Weald of Kent Grammar School, Tonbridge, Kent (English Language)

Terry K. Pratt Ph.D.,
Professor Emeritus, Department of English Language and Literature, University of Prince Edward Island (English Language)

Verbie Lovorn Prevost Ph.D.,
Katharine Pryor Professor of English, University of Tennessee at Chattanooga (English Language)

Michael Quinion,
Lexicographer and editor (New Words)

Lilita Rodman,
Assistant Professor Emerita, University of British Columbia (Canadian English)

John Ross,
Writer and editor (Computing)

Edward Ruddell Ph.D.,
Department of Parks, Recreation and Tourism, University of Utah (Martial Arts)

M. Elizabeth (Betsy) Sargent Ph.D.,
Associate Professor, Department of English, University of Alberta (English Language)

Mary Scott M.A.,
Former Head of English, Hills Road Sixth Form College, Cambridge (English Language)

Mark Sebba Ph.D.,
Department of Linguistics, Lancaster University (British Black English)

Robert N. Smead Ph.D.,
Associate Professor of Spanish Linguistics, Brigham Young University (Hispanic English)

Geneva Smitherman,
University Distinguished Professor; Director, African American Language and Literacy Program; Director, "My Brother's Keeper" Program, Department of English, Michigan State University (African American English)

Richard Soffe,
University of Plymouth Business School (Agriculture and Countryside)

Ian M. Spackman,
Editor (Computer Games)

Tony Spybey,
Professor, Department of Sociology, Staffordshire University (Sociology)

Kamal Keskar Sridhar,
Associate Professor, India Studies and Linguistics and Director, Center for India Studies, State University of New York (South Asian English)

Peter N. Stearns,
Professor and Dean, College of Humanities and Social Sciences, Carnegie Mellon University; author, *Encyclopedia of World History* (History)

James M. Steele,
Professor, School of Architecture, University of Southern California (Architecture and Building)

Sol Steinmetz,
Formerly Editorial Director, Random House Dictionaries (English Language)

Rebecca Stott Ph.D.,
Professor and director of the Speak-Write Project, Department of English, Anglia Polytechnic University, Cambridge (English Language)

Robert Strong,
Professor of Finance, Maine Business School, University of Maine (Finance)

Bruce Thom,
Professor Emeritus, Visiting Professor, University of New South Wales (Geography)

Peter Timmer Ph.D.,
Bisant Interactive Ltd. (Computing)

Loreto Todd Ph.D.,
Professor, Academy for Irish Cultural Heritages, University of Ulster (Irish English, UK regional English, World English)

Diane Tolomeo Ph.D.,
Associate Professor, Department of English, University of Victoria, British Columbia (English Language)

Roger Trigg C.Chem. F.R.S.C.,
Formerly Principal Pharmaceutical Officer, British Pharmacopoeia Commission (Pharmacy)

Amos Turk Ph.D.,
Professor Emeritus, Department of Chemistry, City College of New York (Chemical Engineering)

Heather Valencia Ph.D.,
University of Stirling (Judaism)

Robert Veltman M.A.,
Lecturer in Applied Linguistics, Department of English Language and Linguistics, University of Kent at Canterbury, Kent (English Language)

Gregory A. Waller Ph.D.,
Professor and Chair, Department of English, University of Kentucky (English Language)

Barbara Wallraff,
Usage columnist, *The Atlantic*, author, *Word Court* (2000) and *Your Own Words* (2004)

Michael J. Walsh,
Editor of *The Heythrop Journal* and archivist, Heythrop College, University of London (The Bible)

John Wells,
Professor of Phonetics, University College, London (Phonetics)

Rosemary Wilkinson,
Crafts publisher (Crafts and Design)

Gillian Williams,
Editor, *Ski and Board Magazine* (Skiing)

John Williams,
Sir Norman Chester Centre for Football Research, University of Leicester (Soccer)

Deborah Wills Ph.D.,
Associate Professor, Department of English, Mount Allison University, New Brunswick (English Language)

Lise Winer Ph.D.,
Faculty of Education, McGill University (Caribbean English)

Ellen Wohl,
Professor, Colorado State University (Geography)

Susan J.Wolfe Ph.D.,
Professor, Department of English, University of South Dakota (English Language)

Jill Wolvaardt,
Director, Dictionary Unit for South African English, Rhodes University (South African English)

Shawn H. Wong,
Professor and Director of the University Honors Program at the University of Washington (English Language)

Alison Wray Ph.D.,
Reader, Centre for Language and Communication Research, Cardiff University (English Language)

Philip C. Wright,
Professor, University of New Brunswick (Business and Management)

Ben Yagoda,
Professor, Department of English, University of Delaware (English Language)

Robert Youngson M.B., Ch.B.
Author, *Royal Society of Medicine Encyclopedia of Family Health* and *Collins Medical Dictionary*, formerly consultant advisor on ophthalmology to British Army (Medicine and Pharmacology)

Foreword

Anne H. Soukhanov
US General Editor

If George Washington was "the Father of His Country," Noah Webster was "the Father of American Lexicography." Indeed, in the public mind, 176 years after publication of his *American Dictionary of the English Language* in 1828, *Webster* equals "dictionary" just as *Roget* equals "thesaurus." Noah Webster's enduring legacy was his use of US, not British spellings in his work, his inclusion of US words denoting things found only on this continent, and his establishment of principles underlying the ways US dictionary editors define and illustrate words to this day. The *Encarta® Webster's Dictionary of the English Language*—a new lexicon of 432,042 entry words, meanings, variant spellings, inflections, idioms, phrases, derivative words, and self-explanatory list words—adheres to those principles, and in so doing, joins the great Webster tradition of North America.

"The defining part of a dictionary is by far the most important," wrote Webster, and he was a brilliant purveyor of meaning. He was a master of concision and clarity in defining words, often adding full-sentence encyclopedic extensions to his phrasal meanings in an effort to impart important supplementary information about the entries. The editors of the *Encarta Webster's*, committed to the very same clarity and concision, have included thousands of similar extensions to meanings. The editors have included "quick definitions," or brief summaries of full meanings, at longer entries to help readers easily find the meanings they seek. And the editors have worded all the meanings so that readers can understand them without navigating innumerable cross-references and deciphering complex defining language. In doing all this, the editors have set down the core vocabulary of North American English, most particularly US English, in the breadth and depth required by twenty-first century users, in the firm belief that our language is our most precious—and essential—communications tool in an increasingly complex, often dangerous, world. Though this world is radically different from that of Webster, our mission in recording Standard English is identical to his.

Noah Webster entered scientific and technical words new to his age because, as he put it in the Preface to his 1828 dictionary, he had "found almost insuperable difficulties, from the want of a dictionary, for explaining many new words, which recent discoveries in the ... sciences had introduced into use." The editors of the *Encarta Webster's* have included thousands of words and meanings from science, medicine, high technology, and e-communications; among the newer are *chemoprotective, coagulating bandage, darmstadtium, hypernova, nanoscience, qubit, SARS, blogware, DDR SDRAM, jumpstation, killfile, SIM card, spim,* and *spyware*.

Noah Webster is most memorable because his was the first authentically *American* dictionary. For example, his US-oriented definitions for *congress* differed totally from meanings of the word in British dictionaries. Moreover, he included a great number of words designating North American plants, animals, environmental features, and implements, many making first-time appearances in a dictionary. Notable was his inclusion of words of Native North American origin, e.g., *skunk*, and words that we now know are of African origin, e.g., *yam*. The *Encarta Webster's* not only follows this principle, it expands upon it in its broad coverage of Native North American words, supplemented by a Native North American Language Heritage essay encapsulating this culture's influence on US and Canadian English, e.g., in place names, environmental features, and the names of plants and animals. Going even further, the new dictionary explores, as does no other, the vast array of words of Hispanic origin that have entered US English. The Hispanic-labeled entries and meanings, e.g., *camel* (a Cuban public conveyance), *carnitas, chilaquiles, corte de honor, fonda, madrina, mojito, La Migra, nortec, pila, pipa, quinceañera, refresco,* and *sobremesa*, plus the Usage essays at *Amexican* and *Hispanic*, are illustrative. Included too are words directly related to US-Mexican trade and immigration, e.g., *Amexica, bridge town, laser visa,* and *matricula consular*, a part of the Hemispheric English used in the US Southwest. Others are, e.g., *acequia madre*, *altiplano*, and *majordomo* (an irrigation canal caretaker). These entries are associated with our regional US English coverage of 4,446 words and meanings used only in certain areas of the United States, augmented by 246 Regional essays.

In an additional effort to emphasize the role of language as a mirror on culture within the sphere of the Americas, the editors have entered many Caribbean terms, e.g., *breakfast shed*, *Demerara window*, and *rake-and-scrape band*. Moving farther north, the dictionary contains 5,150 Canadian words and meanings, e.g., *cabbagetown*, *francize*, *Lunenberg bump*, *pond hockey*, and *sovereigntist*. (See also the essay at *Canadian English*.)

Just as Noah Webster created examples showing defined words in commonly used contexts, so too does the *Encarta Webster's*. This dictionary, whose content is based on the over 200-million-word Bloomsbury Corpus, contains 27,005 examples and citations (quoted usages). Moreover, attached to the 4,908 biographical entries of well-known people are 1,653 quotations by those people, bringing a living dimension to their personas and times. As an example, the entry for *Noah Webster* contains this quotation from the preface to his *American Dictionary*—a remark that resonates in the minds of all dictionary editors today: "This Dictionary, like all others of the kind, must be left, in some degree, imperfect; for what individual is competent to trace to their source, and define in all their various applications, popular, scientific, and technical, *seventy* or *eighty thousand* words!"

Noah Webster is also inextricably associated with his best-selling "Blue-Backed Speller," part of *A Grammatical Institute of the English Language* (1783). In consonance with Webster's interest in spelling and grammar, this dictionary includes entries for 980 commonly misspelled words, lined through with cross-references to the correct spellings, 443 Spellchecks delineating the differences between often confused words such as *horde* and *hoard*, and 870 Usage essays intended to assist readers in using English concisely, precisely, clearly, and accurately in writing and speaking. The essays at *nuclear*, *issue*, *irregardless*, *passive*, and *apostrophe* are examples. In a further effort to help readers use the language with felicity, we include 133 Synonym essays exploring the meanings of 819 synonyms.

Coming almost two centuries after Webster enunciated his view of a changing language ("To arrest the progress of language ... is impossible, and, if possible, would be a misfortune"), the *Encarta Webster's* contains 9,660 new entries and meanings, such as *Amber Alert*, *belt bomber*, *bling-bling*, *deskfast*, *casevac*, *cell yell*, *commentariat*, *commitment ceremony*, *FISA Court*, *527 committee*, *make-nice*, *metrosexual*, *microhistory*, *NASCAR dad*, *9/11*, *no-fly list*, *Patriot Act*, *pedway*, *rondo* (a condominium formerly a rental unit), *scratchbook*, *September 10th*, *silver ceiling*, *speed dating*, *stovepiping*, *tipping point*, *UCAV*, *unlawful combatant*, *urban exploration*, and *yuzu*. New meanings often reflect our times, however fraught they may be, e.g., *embed* in combat journalism and an additional meaning of *Gulf War*.

Unlike Noah Webster, who recorded a developing American English on a developing North American continent, we live in a globalized world, and so this new dictionary espouses a world view. The A-Z list includes 9,254 World English words and meanings—ones used by English speakers from, e.g., the United Kingdom and Ireland, Southeast Asia, Australia, New Zealand, Africa, and Southwest Asia. Examples are *chatterati*, *chair class*, *Cantopop*, *Viet kieu*, *mbalax*, *shroud waving*, *shedload*, and *Blairism*. Thirty-three World English essays explore the characteristics of these English varieties.

The *Encarta Webster's* has 33,698 etymologies containing many century-dates of the words' first occurrence in print, along with 210 Word Origin essays. Forty-three Language Heritage essays, unique to this dictionary, explore the numerous international borrowings accepted by English over the ages, e.g., at *Yiddish*, *Japanese*, *Chinese*, *Arabic*, *Hindi*, and *Italian*. They explain, for instance, that *cashew* comes from Tupi-Guarani, *forlorn hope* from Dutch, *teak* from Dravidian, *cider* from Hebrew, and *giraffe* from Arabic. They show that words travel with the people who use them, often transiting the languages of various countries and undergoing structural changes before finally landing in English—there, to undergo still more changes until their ultimate ancestries become almost unrecognizable.

Still other important features of this dictionary are 300 Cultural Notes showing linkages between the meanings of certain words with literature, drama, art, music, and films (see *Catch-22*, *shrew*, *scream*, *enigma*, and *full monty*).

In addition to strictly lexical items, the editors have included, aside from the previously mentioned biographical entries, 6,220 geographic entries with more than 4,000 individual items illustrated in maps, photographs, tables, and line drawings. The biographical and geographic entries and the graphic illustrations should not be viewed as exhaustive, for the core of the Dictionary is, as it always has been, and always will be, the

English wordlist and the definitions *per se*. The biographical and geographic entries, also called "nonlexical items," merely represent quick-reference snapshots of important people and places that the editors feel readers are likely to look up as a first resort, not as a thorough, last resort. For full and in-depth coverage of peoples and places, readers are urged to consult biographical dictionaries and atlases.

If Noah Webster could view twenty-first-century lexicography, he would, no doubt, be fascinated by the ability of an e-mail-linked international staff of lexicographers, specialists, and consultants to compile a dictionary according to his principles, supported by an ever changing computerized Corpus and Internet resources for vocabulary acquisition. Surely he would be glad that this technology has enabled us to obey yet another of his imperatives: "to collect, arrange, and define, as far as possible *all* the words that belong to the language" insofar as the words' frequency of occurrence indicates permanence.

And if, as Webster said, "Language is the expression of ideas," then the *Encarta Webster's Dictionary of the English Language*—with its comprehensive wordlist, its focus on the diverse cultural strands constituting the texture of North American and World English, its inclusion of the newest words, its concentration on excellent spelling, usage, and grammar, its inventive use of quotations, and its deep sense of sociolinguistic history—is the twenty-first century's most comprehensive record of the people's diverse ideas, captured in the words they created in explicating those ideas. This dictionary is, therefore, the People's Dictionary, by and for a richly diverse population.

Anne H. Soukhanov
May 2004

Introduction

Dr. Kathy Rooney

English can be called the world's favorite language. Approximately 375 million people speak English as their first language. Over 375 million people speak English as their second language. Unlike Chinese, Arabic, Spanish, and other major world languages, English is the language in which speakers of other languages choose to communicate with one another. English is the main international language of science and technology, business, pop music, sports, advertising, academic conferences, travel, airports, air-traffic control, diplomacy, and the military. English is the main language of the Internet as about 70 percent of the information stored on the Web is in English. It is estimated that by the year 2050 over 50 percent of the world's population will have some competence in English, an increase of almost 20 percent in 50 years.

The *Encarta® Webster's Dictionary of the English Language*, the second, totally revised edition of the *Encarta World English Dictionary*, reflects this worldwide status of English, having been compiled in the two main spelling forms of the language (American English and British English), while also covering the other main varieties of our language, from Canada, Australia, New Zealand, Africa, Asia, the Caribbean, and the Pacific Rim, as well as regional variations within both the UK and US. This gives the Dictionary a truly world perspective that accurately reflects the worldwide presence of the English language today.

This Dictionary is first and foremost a dictionary of the English language of today. The audience for this dictionary is diverse, worldwide, encompassing a wide range of ages and backgrounds. It is also a multimedia audience, for the Dictionary appears in both print and electronic forms. For this reason we have made the language of the definitions as natural as possible, avoiding jargon where feasible. We have tried to create clear, informative, and readable definitions that readers will understand without difficulty. Our definitions identify and focus clearly on the characteristics that distinguish and differentiate a word from related terms and include features that are picked up in extended usage.

Where some other dictionaries might be described as literary, based on historical principles, or scientific, the *Encarta Webster's Dictionary of the English Language* should be described as modern, for it focuses on the language needs of general dictionary users today. These needs encompass definitions of both the newest scientific and slang terms, and of literary or historical language that users of the Dictionary may encounter especially in their reading. Our guiding principle has been to define the language that our readers are likely to encounter in their everyday lives. Part of the role of our dictionary editors is to monitor where specialized terms move over into everyday usage, where technical jargon becomes part of the mainstream. This can happen, for example, through television shows that bring medical or law-enforcement vocabulary into the homes of millions.

Traditionally, dictionaries have provided definitions of terms, information on how to pronounce words, explanations of where words have come from and, in some instances, information on how to use words. The *Encarta Webster's Dictionary of the English Language* is no exception to these conventions. We include over 100,000 headwords (the words you look up), and almost four million words of text.

But what else should readers reasonably expect from a dictionary aimed at the language needs of the twenty-first century? The stance of this Dictionary is both to define today's English and to offer clear advice and guidance on how to use our language well. Research with our advisors and readers has shown that this is what readers want from their dictionaries. Problems with spelling and how to use English correctly are perceived as increasing problems for many. Our dictionaries pay particular attention to these issues. This Dictionary includes over 900 frequently misspelled words together with their correct spellings. In our highly computerized era people increasingly find it difficult to distinguish between words that sound or look alike and that a computer spellchecker will not detect as potential errors. Examples include *hoard/horde* or *principal/principle*. To help our readers avoid errors of this type we have included in this Dictionary several hundred Spellcheck notes that explain the difference between such terms. We give further advice on frequent grammatical and language problems in our Usage essays, while our Synonym essays help readers distinguish between words of similar meaning.

Dictionary editors require hard data to make sure that the definitions they write are based on good linguistic evidence. For earlier dictionary writers such evidence was garnered and stored on cards or slips of paper. In recent years the advent of the computer has meant that such cumbersome and time-consuming methods have been replaced by computerized corpora. A corpus is like a huge filing cabinet, filled with millions of words of real language (taken from fiction, nonfiction, and journalism, for example). Software developed specifically for this project has enabled our editors to call up examples of the use of any term at the touch of a computer key. The Internet is also a huge repository of information about language and how it is used today—but one that our editors must analyze with great care as the material available is not always reliable.

People use dictionaries to find out what words mean, and often these words are scientific or technical. However, many dictionaries define such terms in ways that can seem just as technical as the term itself. In writing this Dictionary we have tried to bring the same criteria of clarity, concision, and transparency to our scientific and technical definitions that have characterized our approach to other definitions. We have applied these criteria across all our specialized entries. In doing so, we combined the skills of our technical definers with contributions from our many subject advisers who checked the accuracy of our definitions and patiently answered thousands of queries. Thus, the Dictionary tries to paint a word picture that the reader can understand by keeping use of specialist terminology to a minimum.

Our research has also indicated that today's dictionary users want to find the information they are seeking quickly. In response to that need, we developed the "quick definition" feature that is unique to this Dictionary. Quick definitions appear in small capital letters at all entries with more than two senses. They provide a brief gloss of the headword for the user who does not want, or need, the full picture, providing a thumbnail sketch rather than a full analysis of the meaning. The quick definitions are also important in helping readers to navigate through the many senses of a long entry.

When deciding on the order of sense categories, our general principle has been "most frequent first, least frequent last" as judged by current usage and evidence from our Corpus and language research. This is to make certain that the most common senses occur early in the entry, to enable readers to find what they want quickly. We have, however, in some instances overridden this principle where more frequent senses clearly develop out of a less frequent (probably more technical) sense. Senses within the same part of speech are grouped together in an entry. Informal and slang senses usually come before dated or archaic senses but after stylistically neutral senses.

In sense division, we have tried to strike a balance midway between broad and narrow categorization of senses. The primary consideration has always been ease of use by the reader. We have applied a similar priority when deciding which words and senses should be expanded by example phrases and sentences. We have tried to include these wherever they will help the reader grasp the meaning more easily.

The pronunciation system has been specially developed for this Dictionary to provide a system that speakers of English will find easy to decode. Rather than using the International Phonetic Alphabet (IPA), an excellent system for learners of our language, we felt that we should provide a more up-to-date system that our users, mainly speakers of the English language, would find easier to understand.

Language is a powerful tool, one that can hurt and offend. We have endeavored to write definitions that convey the meaning of the word in an appropriately clear but sensitive way. Since the Dictionary is a snapshot of the language today, we include some terms that some users may find offensive or even highly offensive. It has been our policy throughout to indicate clearly when such terms are likely to cause offense. A number of lexical entries labeled *offensive* or *taboo* must be defined as entries in any adult dictionary that attempts to cover the whole range of the language. However, in writing the Dictionary, we have tried to avoid sexist, ethnic, ethnocentric, ethnophobic, ageist, racist, and physiologically or otherwise offensively stereotypical language in the Dictionary text. This thoroughly modern editorial policy reflects the standards of changing times during which a great many people deplore what they deem a "coarsening of the language" by some users, especially ones who, having seen a questionable word in a dictionary, justify their use of the word by dint of the mere fact that it is neither labeled nor stigmatized.

Since the English language has a multifaceted history, we have paid particular attention to tracing the histories of words (etymologies). These are written in clear language, using as few symbols and abbreviations as possible. We have also included hundreds of extended word history essays. In addition to extended paragraphs on word histories, we have included similar brief essays on World English, regional English, Cultural Notes, and key quotations from leading figures that appear at our biographical entries. The essays form a stepping stone from the dictionary text into the wider world of cultural reference. Language Heritage essays, a new feature for this edition, trace the words that have been absorbed into English from the world's other main language traditions, such as Arabic, German, Italian, and Yiddish.

This Dictionary and its first edition were compiled by a team of over 320 dictionary editors (lexicographers), word history experts (etymologists), pronunciation specialists (phoneticians), and over 120 special subject and World English consultants. Our team was drawn from around the world and included, for example, a Canadian poet and a professor from a major suburban Maryland college with a large international student population. I would like to thank sincerely everyone who has contributed to this Dictionary and our Dictionary Database.

It is estimated that there are in the region of one million words in the English language ranging from the most frequently used everyday vocabulary to the most highly specialized technical jargon, the most informal slang, and the most arcane regional terminology. This total continues to grow, especially in science, technology, business, media, sports, and food.

Since it absorbed thousands of French words after the Norman Conquest of 1066, English has always welcomed the new. The 9,600 new words and senses added to this Dictionary since our first edition only five years ago bear witness to this.

The most exciting challenge for dictionary editors today is to keep up with the changes in our language as new words come in and linguistic norms and conventions change and develop in response to technological and cultural innovation. The work of the lexicographer has never been more exciting—defining an ever-evolving language and providing clear advice to readers on how to use English.

Kathy Rooney
May 2004

How to Use the Dictionary

INTRODUCTION

Structurally, a dictionary is a detailed, complex mosaic of different elements relating to what you want from such a reference book—spelling, pronunciation, meanings, examples of use, advice on grammar or usage, and an explanation of the origins of words. This section outlines briefly the different elements in the text, so that you can find what you want in the *Encarta® Webster's Dictionary of the English Language* quickly and easily.

How the dictionary page is laid out

Guide words

Each page has two **guide words** that show, on the left, the first **boldface** dictionary entry on that page, and, on the right, the last, so that you can quickly find the word you are looking for.

Layout of the text

The text is designed in three columns for maximum coverage and legibility. Important elements of the text appear in **boldface** type. Quick definitions appear in **SMALL CAPITALS.** Full definitions appear in roman type and examples and citations in *italic* type. Quotations by key figures appear after the entries for those people, in roman type and within quotation marks.

Graphic illustrations and tables

Illustrations appear as close as possible to the entries to which they refer. An explicit cross-reference is given if an illustration or table falls on a different page from its entry.

guide word—first entry

guide word—last entry

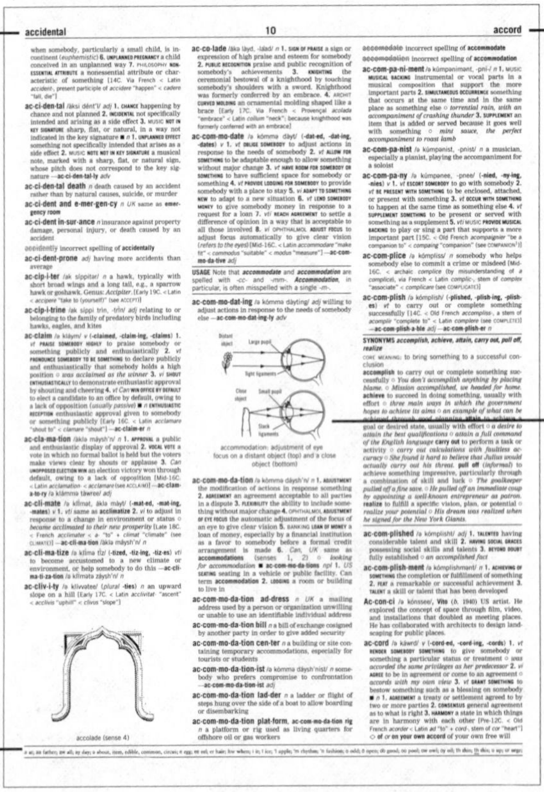

illustration

pronunciation key

Finding the word you are looking for

This Dictionary contains over 400,000 individual elements that you might want to look up. Here is a guide to finding the different types of information quickly.

Headwords

The *Encarta Webster's Dictionary of the English Language* contains over 100,000 **headwords** (the words you look up), including approximately 10,000 entries about people and places—the biographical and geographic entries (see page xxiii for a discussion of these "nonlexical" biographical and geographic entries). There are also over 3,700 "list words"—words beginning with a common prefix such as *anti-* or *non-* that are entered without definitions because their meanings are self-explanatory.

Headwords are listed in strict alphabetical order, ignoring internal or end punctuation and other characters:

brand·ing i·ron *n* an iron tool that is heated and pressed onto a surface, especially an animal's hide, in order to leave a permanent identifying mark

bran·dish /brándish/ (**-dished, -dish·ing, -dish·es**) *vt* to wave something about, especially a weapon, in a menacing, theatrical, or triumphant way [14C. < French *brandiss-*, stem of *brandir* < *brand* "sword"] —**bran·dish·er** *n*

brand lead·er *n* the best-selling product in a particular category

brand·ling /brándling/ *n* a small reddish brown earthworm that is often used as bait by anglers. Latin name: *Eisenia foetida*. [Mid-17C. Because of its coloring, like a burning brand]

brand loy·al·ty *n* the tendency to buy a particular brand of a product

brand name *n* a trade name for a product or service produced by a particular company. It may or may not be a registered trademark. ○ *A computer with a brand name can cost 10 percent more.* —**brand-named** *adj*

brand-new *adj* completely new and unused [As if newly made in a furnace]

Words with the same spelling

Words with the same spelling (**homographs**) but with different pronunciations or origins (**etymologies**) are listed with superscript, or raised, numbers to differentiate them. The order of these numbers broadly reflects usage and frequency of occurrence:

baste^1 /bayst/ (**bast·ed, bast·ing, bastes**) *vt* to moisten meat or fish at intervals during cooking with a liquid such as melted fat or cooking juices [15C. Origin ?]

baste^2 /bayst/ (**bast·ed, bast·ing, bastes**) *vt* to sew fabric with long loose stitches in order to hold pieces of material together temporarily [14C. Via Old French *bastir* < Germanic, "join together with bast"]

baste^3 /bayst/ (**bast·ed, bast·ing, bastes**) *vt* **1.** to beat somebody severely (*dated informal*) **2.** to scold somebody vigorously [Mid-16C. Origin ?]

Alternate spellings of headwords

The Dictionary recognizes instances when a word has more than one possible spelling (**variant**). Such entries appear in **boldface** type following their headwords:

fa·la·fel /fə laáf'l/, **fe·la·fel** *n* a deep-fried ball of ground chickpeas seasoned with onions and spices, originating in Southwest Asia [Mid-20C. Via Egyptian Arabic *falāfil* < Arabic *fulful* "pepper"]

At the entry for the alternate spelling, a cross-reference directs you back to the entry where the word is defined:

fe·la·fel *n* FOOD another spelling of **falafel**

Inflections

Inflections are grammatical forms of headwords that include the principal tenses of verbs, the comparative and superlative forms of adjectives and adverbs, and irregular plurals of nouns. These forms are shown after the pronunciation where the inflection applies to the whole headword, or at a specific sense or group of senses where appropriate:

a·dieu /ə dyoó, ə doó/ *interj*, *n* (*plural* **a·dieux** /ə dyoóz, ə doóz/ or **a·dieus**) used to say goodbye (*literary*) ○"*...the more gentle adieus of her sisters were uttered without being heard*" (Jane Austen, *Pride And Prejudice*; 1813) [14C. < French, "(I commend you) to God"]

shoo /shoo/ *interj* used to tell a child or animal to go away ■ *vti* (**shooed, shoo·ing, shoos**) to say shoo and gesture to a child or animal to go away ○ *shooed the pigeons away* [15C. Natural exclamation]

ca·gey /káyjee/ (**-gi·er, -gi·est**), **ca·gy** *adj* secretive and refusing to be open, frank, or direct (*informal*) [Late 19C. Origin ?] —**ca·gi·ly** *adv* —**ca·gi·ness** *n*

fly^1 /flī/ *v* (**flew** /floo/, **flown** /flōn/, **fly·ing, flies**) **1.** *vi* MOVE THROUGH AIR to travel through the air using wings or an engine ... **21.** (*past and past participle* **flied**) *vi* BASEBALL HIT FLY in baseball, to hit a fly ball ○ *She flied twice in the second inning.*

When a headword has a plural form with the same spelling, this is indicated by the label *plural same*:

air·craft /ér kràft/ (*plural same*) *n* any vehicle capable of flight.

Important irregular inflections also appear as headwords in their own right, cross-referred back to their main entries:

ca·ly·ces BOT plural of **calyx**

fled past participle, past tense of **flee**

Abbreviations and acronyms

Abbreviations and acronyms are included in the alphabetical headword list, grouped together according to their punctuation and their status as either an abbreviation or symbol. Our Corpus of World English has shown that punctuation within abbreviations varies considerably. This Dictionary gives the most common form; important alternate forms are also shown. Meanings are ordered alphabetically:

C. *abbr* **1.** CHR Catholic **2.** POL Chancellor **3.** chief **4.** city **5.** Companion **6.** POL Congress **7.** POL Conservative **8.** SPORTS court

C2B /seè tə beé/ *abbr* E-COMMERCE consumer-to-business

C3I /seè three ī/ *n* command, control, communications, and intelligence, which are the operational aspects of military science, as opposed to training or logistics

ca *abbr* Canada (*used in Internet addresses*) See table at **domain name**

Ca *symbol* CHEM ELEM calcium

CA *abbr* **1.** MAIL California **2.** ONLINE certificate authority (*used in e-mails*)

ca. *abbr* HIST circa (*used before dates*)

c.a. *abbr* **1.** chartered accountant **2.** chronological age

C.A. *abbr* **1.** Central America **2.** Central American **3.** ACCT chartered accountant **4.** chronological age

C/A *abbr* FIN **1.** capital account **2.** credit account

CAAT *abbr* E-COMMERCE certificate authority administration tool

When an abbreviation is more frequently used than its full form, we give the definition at the abbreviation:

BSE *n* a disease that affects the nervous system of cattle, believed to be caused by a transmissible protein particle (**prion**) and related to Creutzfeldt-Jakob disease in humans. Full form **bovine spongiform encephalopathy**

Foreign words and phrases

Based on information in our Corpus of World English, foreign words and phrases are included in the A-Z list as entries if they have established English pronunciations and are used, without being explained, in contemporary literature, journalism, general writing, or general conversation:

> **du jour** /doo zhŏŏr/ *adj* **1.** offered or served today ○ *the soup du jour* **2.** being the latest in a series, sequence, or trend [< French, "of the day"]

Two- and three-word verbs (phrasal verbs)

Phrasal verbs are two- or three-word verbs, each consisting of a common verb plus an adverb or preposition such as *out* or *up*, whose meaning is not self-explanatory, for example, *do up, put up with*. These are listed after the entries for their root verbs:

> **keel** /keel/ *n* **1.** NAUT **SHIP'S STRUCTURAL ELEMENT** the main structural element of a ship, stretching along the center line of its bottom from the bow to the stern. It sometimes extends farther downward into the water to provide extra stability. **2.** AVIAT **AIRCRAFT'S STRUCTURAL ELEMENT** a structure that looks or acts like a ship's keel, e.g., the main structural element of an aircraft's fuselage **3.** BIRDS **PART OF BIRD'S BREASTBONE** a ridge-shaped part in the breastbone of a bird to which the flight muscles are anchored. Technical name **carina** **4.** BIOL **PART LIKE RIDGE** any ridge-shaped part of an organism **5.** same as **ship** (*literary*) ■ *vti* (**keeled, keel·ing, keels**) NAUT **CAPSIZE** to capsize a vessel, or capsize [14C. < Old Norse *kjölr*] ◇ **on an even keel** in a stable steady condition
>
> **keel over** *v* **1.** *vi* to collapse or fall over, often through exhaustion or illness (*informal*) **2.** *vti* NAUT same as **keel**

Idiomatic phrases

Idiomatic phrases such as *on the run* and *let the cat out of the bag* are shown at the ends of many entries, introduced by the symbol ◇:

> **game**[1] /gaym/ *n* **1. SOMETHING PLAYED FOR FUN** an activity that people participate in, together or on their own, for fun ... [Old English *gamen* < Germanic, "people participating together"] —**game·ly** *adv* —**game·ness** *n* ◇ **ahead of the game** anticipating and reacting more promptly than others to new developments ◇ **give the game away** to reveal a secret, usually without intending to ◇ **play the game** to follow the rules of a given situation, even if they are unspoken ◇ **the game's up** the plan or trick has failed or been discovered (*informal*) ◇ **the only game in town** the only possibility ◇ **game the system** to manipulate and take unfair advantage of loopholes in rules and regulations in order to make that system of rules and regulations work to your own advantage in risky, typically illegal, schemes

Incorrect spellings

This Dictionary includes in its A-Z text over 900 frequently misspelled words, which are entered at their own alphabetical places where users are most likely to look them up. This list of misspellings was compiled using the help of our advisers on English usage and the evidence in our own Corpus of World English and Internet research. In order to avoid reinforcing an erroneous idea of the spelling of a word, we have shown the incorrect form with a line through it:

> ~~**Carribean**~~ incorrect spelling of **Caribbean**

See also the section titled "Spellchecks," on page xxii.

Cross-references

Cross-references in this Dictionary serve various purposes. They take the place of definitions, and indicate that the information you need is given at other entries with the same meanings as the words you have looked up:

> **a·bele** /ə beel/ *n* TREES same as **white poplar** (sense 1) [13C. Directly or via Dutch *abeel* < Old French *a(u)bel* < Latin *albus* "white"]
>
> **ban·nis·ter** *n* ARCHIT another spelling of **banister**
>
> **ar·mour** *n* Can, UK spelling of **armor**

Cross-references in the form of *plural of, past tense of*, and so on, refer from inflected forms to their root words:

> **chil·dren** plural of **child**

Full form of refers from the expanded form of an abbreviation or acronym to its abbreviation, where a definition is given:

> **disc jock·ey** *n* MUSIC, MEDIA full form of **DJ** (sense 1)
>
> **DJ** *n* **1.** somebody who plays records or other recorded music, e.g., at a live dance or on the radio. Full form **disc jockey** **2.** somebody who composes rap or techno music using samples of recorded music [Abbreviation of DISC JOCKEY] —**DJ** *vi*

The boldface symbol ➧ directs you to another nonlexical, i.e., geographic or biographical entry, where you will find a definition:

> **Bo·na·parte** /bṓnə paart/ ➧ **Napoleon I**
>
> **Da·ko·ta**[2] /də kṓtə/ ➧ **North Dakota, South Dakota** —**Da·ko·tan** *n, adj*

A lightface arrow ◊ after a definition directs you to a related lexical entry where you will find additional relevant information:

> **Cel·si·us** /sélssee əss, sélshəss/ *adj* using or measured on an international metric temperature scale on which water freezes at 0° and boils at 100° under normal atmospheric conditions. The term "Celsius" is usually preferred to "centigrade," especially in technical contexts. ◊ **Fahrenheit** [Mid-19C. After Anders *Celsius* (1701–44), Swedish astronomer]
>
> **cold·boot** /kṓld bòot/ (**-boot·ed, -boot·ing, -boots**) *vt* to restart a computer by turning it off and on. ◊ **warmboot**

Derivative words

At the ends of many entries there are additional boldface words with no definitions (**undefined runons**). These consist of the headwords plus common suffixes such as *–able, –ly*, or *–ness*, or the headwords shown in other parts of speech. They do not require definitions because they correlate predictably in usage and meaning with their headwords. Where appropriate, these derivative words have been given pronunciations, for example, when their stress patterns differ significantly from those of their headwords:

> **change·a·ble** /cháynjəb'l/ *adj* capable of changing, or liable to change or vary —**change·a·bil·i·ty** /chàynjə bíllətee/ *n* —**change·a·ble·ness** *n* —**change·a·bly** *adv*

Words beginning with common prefixes

The Dictionary includes several lists of self-explanatory words (**list words**) made up of a word defined elsewhere in the text and a common prefix, such as *anti-, non-*, or *un-*. These words do not need definitions, as their meanings can be easily deduced from their elements. Here we show the first and last pairs of words of the list at *ultra*:

> **ultra-** *prefix* **1.** more than normal, excessively, completely ○ *ultrasophisticated* **2.** outside the range of ○ *ultrasound* [< Latin *ultra* "beyond" < Indo-European]
>
> **ul·tra·care·ful** *adj*
> **ul·tra·ca·su·al** *adj*
> [etc.]
> **ul·tra·thin** *adj*
> **ul·tra·vi·o·lent** *adj*
>
> **ul·tra·ba·sic** /ùltrə báyssik/ *adj* describes igneous rock that is high in iron and magnesium and contains no free quartz ■ *n* a rock of ultrabasic composition

Similar lists of self-explanatory words can be found at the following prefixes: *anti-, co-, cyber-, e-, hyper-, ill-, inter-, mis-, multi-, neo-, non-, out-, over-, post-, pre-, pro-, pseudo, quasi-, re-, self-, semi-, sub-, super-, ultra-, un-, under-* and *well-*.

Finding the meaning you are looking for

Entries with more than one meaning

Many words have more than one meaning, or definition. The different meanings are indicated by numbers that appear in **boldface** type. Meanings are ordered according to usage and frequency, with the most frequent sense given first:

> **pu·er·ile** /pyóorəl, pyóor ìl, pyóo ərəl/ *adj* **1.** regarded as childishly silly or immature **2.** relating to or characteristic of childhood (*formal*) [Late 16C. Directly or via French < Latin *puerilis* < *puer* "child, boy"] —**pu·er·ile·ly** *adv* —**pu·er·il·i·ty** /pyoor rílləteé/ *n*

Parts of speech

Part-of-speech labels, in *italic type*, indicate whether the headword functions as a noun, adjective, verb, and so on. If an entry contains meanings that have different parts of speech, they are grouped together (all noun meanings together, all verb meanings, and so on). A change of part of speech within an entry is introduced by the symbol ■:

> **bod·y·check** /bóddee chèk/ *n* in some sports, especially hockey or soccer, an illegal act of using the body to obstruct an opposing player ■ *vt* (**-checked, -check·ing, -checks**) in some sports, especially hockey or soccer, to use the body to obstruct an opposing player illegally

The part-of-speech labels used in the Dictionary are:

abbr	abbreviation
adj	adjective
adv	adverb
aux v	auxiliary verb
conj	conjunction
contr	contraction
det	determiner
interj	interjection
modal v	modal verb
n	noun
npl	plural noun
prefix	prefix
prep	preposition
pron	pronoun
symbol	symbol
suffix	suffix
vt	verb
vi	intransitive verb
vr	reflexive verb
vt	transitive verb
vti	transitive / intransitive verb

The label *tdmk* indicates trademarks.

Quick definitions

The **Quick Definitions** are a unique feature of this Dictionary and are designed to guide you through longer entries. They appear in **SMALL CAPITALS** and act as brief summaries of the full definitions, so that you can easily find your way to the appropriate sense:

> **ex·trem·i·ty** /ik strémmətee/ *n* (*plural* **-ties**) **1.** **HAND OR FOOT** a limb of a person or animal, or the part of a limb that is farthest from the body, especially somebody's hand or foot (*often used in the plural*) **2.** **FARTHEST POINT** a point that is the farthest out, especially from the center ○ *the southernmost extremity of the continent* **3.** **HIGHEST DEGREE** the highest degree or greatest intensity of something ○ *in the extremity of her grief* **4.** **DANGER** a situation or state of great danger or distress ○ *They prayed for help in their extremity.* ■ **ex·trem·i·ties** *npl* **DRASTIC MEASURES** drastic or unreasonable measures (*formal*)

Specialist meanings

The Dictionary includes the main specialized meanings you are likely to encounter in general publications and consumer magazines. **Subject labels** such as COMP (computing) and FIN (finance) signal meanings belonging to specialist subject areas and help you identify them readily in an entry (a full list of the subject labels used in the Dictionary is given on p. xxiv):

> **ex·port** *v* /ik spáwrt, ék spàwrt/ (**-port·ed, -port·ing, -ports**) **1.** *vti* COMM **SEND GOODS ABROAD** to send goods for sale or exchange to other countries **2.** *vt* SOC SCI **SPREAD ONE SOCIETY'S CULTURE TO ANOTHER** to cause the spread of ideas, values, or a way of life from one society, culture, or nation to another **3.** *vt* COMPUT **ALTER FORMAT OF COMPUTER DATA** to convert data from a computer program into a form suitable for a different program or environment ■ *n* /ék spàwrt/ COMM **1.** **SELLING OF GOODS ABROAD** the selling of goods to other countries **2.** **PRODUCT SOLD ABROAD** a product sold and transported to another country [15C. < Latin *exportare* "carry away" < *portare* "carry"] —**ex·port·a·bil·i·ty** /ik spàwrtə bíllətee/ *n* —**ex·port·a·ble** *adj* —**ex·por·ta·tion** /èk spawr táysh'n/ *n* —**ex·port·er** *n*

Some information that occurs routinely in scientific and technical definitions, for example, the sources of minerals or the uses to which chemicals are put, is shown in a concise form for greater accessibility and consistency:

> **be·ta-block·er** *n* a drug that regulates the activity of the heart. Use: treatment of high blood pressure.

> **cal·ci·um car·bon·ate** *n* a white crystalline solid that is one of the most common natural substances. Source: chalk, limestone, marble, animal shells, bones. Use: antacids, paint, cement, toothpaste. Formula: $CaCO_3$.

> **gar·de·nia** /gaar deényə/ *n* an evergreen tree or bush with shiny leaves. Flowers: white, fragrant. Native to: Africa, Asia. Genus: *Gardenia*. [Mid-18C. < modern Latin, after Alexander *Garden* (1730–91), Scottish-American naturalist]

Information on how a word is used

Illustrative examples

The Dictionary has thousands of illustrative examples that clarify the definitions and place them in context. These are drawn from our 200-million-word Corpus of World English. The symbol ○ introduces examples:

> **be·lieve** /bi léev/ (**-lieved, -liev·ing, -lieves**) *v* **1.** *vt* **ACCEPT SOMETHING AS TRUE** to accept that something is true or real ○ *I don't know which story to believe.* **2.** *vt* **ACCEPT SOMEBODY AS TRUTHFUL** to accept that somebody is telling the truth ○ *Nobody will believe you!* ○ *I don't believe him.* **3.** *vt* **CREDIT SOMEBODY WITH SOMETHING** to accept that somebody or something has a particular quality or ability ○ *No one believed her capable of such a malicious remark.* **4.** *vi* **THINK THAT SOMETHING EXISTS** to be of the opinion that something exists or is a reality, especially when there is no absolute proof of its existence or reality ○ *believe in reincarnation* **5.** *vi* **HAVE TRUST** to be confident that somebody or something is worthwhile or effective ○ *We all believe in you.* **6.** *vi* **THINK SOMETHING IS GOOD** to be of the opinion that something is right or beneficial and, usually, to act in accordance with that belief ○ *believed strongly in freedom of expression* **7.** *vi* **HAVE RELIGIOUS FAITH** to have a belief in God or in a religion's gods [Old English *belyfan*, alteration of *gelēfan* < Germanic, "to love, trust"] —**be·liev·er** *n* ◇ **make believe** to pretend, especially in play

Quoted citations

The Dictionary also includes many quotations taken from written sources (**citations**) such as fiction, nonfiction, and journalism. These citations are also drawn from our Corpus of World English:

> **min·gy** /mínjee/ (**-gi·er, -gi·est**) *adj* **1.** **SMALL IN QUANTITY** very small or tiny in quantity or degree ○ *tried to live on a mingy salary* **2.** **STINGY** ungenerous or stingy (*informal*) ○ *a mingy roommate who wouldn't share living expenses* **3.** **SHODDY IN QUALITY** creating a negative impression on others because of being shoddy

(*informal*) ○*"Finally, they will have to change the mingy, defensive, consultant-driven style of recent campaigns."* (Joe Klein *Newsweek*; May 19, 2003) [Early 20C. Origin ?]

Mit·tel·eu·ro·pe·an /mitt'l yoorə peé ən/ *adj* relating to Central Europe, its culture, and its various inhabitants ○*"A master of wild, at times uproarious, plots and characters whose Eastern and Mitteleuropean accents he renders with perfect pitch, the author has until now remained very much offstage."* (Elizabeth Frank, professor of literature, Bard College *New York Times Book Review*; July 20, 2003) —**Mit·tel·eu·ro·pe·an** *n*

Style levels, registers of usage, and currency

The Dictionary uses *italic* labels to give information on the style, register, and currency of a word or meaning. If a label applies to all meanings of a word, it appears before the first numbered meaning; if it applies to a specific meaning, it appears after that meaning:

back-seat driv·er *n* (*informal*) **1.** a passenger in a vehicle who continually pesters the driver with unwanted advice or criticism **2.** somebody who gives unwanted advice or criticism while somebody else does something

gat[2] /gat/ *n* same as **handgun** (*dated slang*) [Early 20C. Shortening of GATLING GUN]

The following labels are used in the Dictionary to indicate stylistic level or degree of currency:

Currency

archaic	not used since before World War II
dated	used at some stage between 1945 and 1990 but no longer part of the current idiom

Register

literary	used in literature and poetry and for special effect, but not used in everyday contexts
formal	used in formal situations and formal writing, but inappropriate in everyday contexts
technical	marks specialist terms that have an everyday equivalent
informal	used in relaxed conversation or writing but avoided in more formal contexts
humorous	pompous or formal or dated terms typically used self-consciously for humorous effect
disapproving	marks a derogatory attitude on the part of the speaker
slang	highly informal language, completely inappropriate in formal contexts, and often with a crude edge
babytalk	used by adults when talking to young children and babies
nonstandard	not considered part of correct or educated usage, though current in spoken usage

Offensiveness

insult	a pejorative term that would be likely to insult or upset somebody if said directly to the person
offensive	likely to be offensive to many people, for example, because of being racist or sexual
taboo	marks classic taboo words referring to sex and bodily functions

Some lexical entries commonly regarded as offensive or taboo require inclusion in a dictionary of this size and scope. However, the editors have attempted to ensure that these and other offensive or potentially offensive lexical items and areas of reference are not used in the defining language and other elements of the text.

Words not universally regarded as offensive but likely to give offense in varying degrees are qualified accordingly: *often considered offensive, sometimes considered offensive*, and *offensive in some contexts.*

Offensive terms have been defined by glosses rather than substitutable definitions.

Regional varieties of English: global and domestic

In the Dictionary, we give a global and domestically regional view of the English language. Globally, we have included information on the two main spelling forms of English—American and British—and have differentiated the main varieties of World English when alternate terms are preferred. American usage is explicitly labeled only where it differs from other varieties of World English:

main·street·ing /máyn streèting/ *n Can* the practice of walking around a town or city to meet and talk with its inhabitants as a way of soliciting votes during an election campaign —**main·street** *vi*

pam·pa·lam /pàmpə lám/ *n Carib* confusion, fuss, or uproar [Late 20C. An imitation of the sound of noisy activity, perhaps after Twi *pam* "sound of a gun," *pam pam* "drive away"]

film·i /fílmee/ *S Asia adj* **1.** OF INDIAN MOVIE INDUSTRY relating to the Indian motion picture industry **2.** SENSATIONAL melodramatic or exaggerated ■ *n* MOVIE STAR a star of the Indian motion picture industry [Late 20C. < FILM + Hindi *-i*, adjective suffix]

Can·to·pop /kántō pòp/ *n SE Asia* pop music of Southeast Asia, originally sung in Hong Kong's Cantonese but now also in Mandarin, English, and Japanese. It is characterized by a decorous balladic style sung by musicians who are neatly dressed.

sup·ply teach·er *n UK* same as **substitute teacher**

ha·ku /haá koo/ *n Hawaii* a crown made of fresh flowers

pre·sa /práyssə/ (*plural* **-se** /práy sày/) *n Southwest US* a dam that diverts water from a river into an irrigation canal (**acequia**) [Early 18C. < Italian, "taking up"]

pro·mo·to·ra /prò mō tṓrə/ *n Hispanic* an outreach worker in a Hispanic community who is responsible for raising awareness of health and educational issues [Via American Spanish < Spanish, "promoter"]

The Dictionary accords special extra coverage of terms labeled *Hispanic* in US English.

The Dictionary uses the following *italic* labels to indicate the geographic area where a word is used:

ANZ	Australian and New Zealand English
Aus	Australian English
Can	Canadian English
Carib	Caribbean English
E Africa	East African English
Hawaii	Hawaiian English
Hispanic	Hispanic English (in US)
Hong Kong	Hong Kong English
Ireland	Irish English
Malaysia	Malaysian English
Midwest	Midwestern United States
N Am	North American English (US and Canada)
N England	Northern England
NZ	New Zealand English
New England	New England
Northeast US	Northeastern United States
Northwest US	Northwestern United States
Philippines	Philippines English
Quebec	Quebec
Rocky Mountains	Rocky Mountains
S Africa	South African English
S Asia	South Asian English
S Atlantic US	South Atlantic United States
S England	Southern England
Scot	Scottish English

Singapore	Singapore
Southeast US	Southeastern United States
Southern US	Southern United States
Southwest England	Southwestern England
Southwest US	Southwestern United States
UK	British English
US	American English
W Africa	West African English
Wales	Welsh English
Western US	Western United States

The label *regional* indicates that a word or meaning has widespread use in English dialects. The labels *US regional* and *UK regional* indicate dialectal use in American English and British English, respectively. See also the section titled "World English and regional essays" on page xxii.

Other restrictions on usage

Other restrictions on the usage of words are shown by italic comments in brackets. These Usage notes spell out useful syntactic information beyond the basic part of speech, for example, *takes a singular verb*; they give information on the typical users of a word or phrase, for example, *used mainly by children*; and they give information on the speaker's attitude or tone of voice, for example, *often used ironically*:

> **cit·y slick·er** *n* a worldly resident of a city (*informal disapproving*)
>
> **fine**[1] /fīn/ *adj* (**fin·er, fin·est**) **1. VERY WELL OR SATISFACTORY** in a good, acceptable, or comfortable condition (*informal*) ○ *Everything's fine, thank you. ...* **9. UNPLEASANT** extremely unsuitable or undesirable (*informal; used ironically*) ○ *This is a fine mess!*
>
> **hard·en·ing of the ar·ter·ies** *n* MED same as **atherosclerosis** (*not in technical use*)

Trademarks, trade names, and proprietary terms

The Dictionary includes words on the basis of their usage in the English language today. Words that are known to have current trademark or proprietary registrations have been given the label *tdmk*. They are defined with glosses, not substitutable definitions.

Graphic illustrations and tables

The Dictionary illustrates over 4,000 items with photographs, drawings, and maps. Their main function is to help you by adding to and complementing the text, providing additional contexts for the definitions, and placing the definitions in their context. The Dictionary contains 24 tables. Cross-references to illustrations and tables are shown after their definitions:

> **ce·si·um** /seézee əm/ *n* a rare ductile silver-white element of the alkali metals group that is the most reactive of the elements. Use: photoelectric cells. Symbol **Cs**. See table at **element** [Mid-19C. < modern Latin < Latin *caesius* "bluish gray"; from its blue spectral lines]

Special features of the dictionary entry

In addition to definitions, the Dictionary includes information on the pronunciation of headwords and the origin and development of headwords. It also contains additional features that give information on a specific aspect of a word, going beyond the scope of the standard dictionary entry. These features include extended notes on spelling, grammar, and usage; regionalisms; varieties of World English; notes on Amexican English and the contributions by Native North American languages to American English; sets of synonyms; cultural notes incorporating cultural references; and quotations at key biographical entries.

Pronunciation

Our pronunciation system has been developed specifically for the *Encarta Webster's Dictionary of the English Language*. It relies on familiar combinations of letters of the alphabet, so that you can use it without constant reference to a table of explanations and symbols. An abbreviated pronunciation key appears at the bottom of each page, and the entire pronunciation system is explained in full on pp. xxvi–xxvii.

Word origins

The principal intent of the word origins (**etymologies**) in the Dictionary is to present the etymologies of the entries with as much accuracy as present-day knowledge permits, in a way that is accessible and interesting to general readers. As far as possible, etymologies have been written in plain English, with few abbreviations or technical terms. Whenever possible, etymologies include the century when the headword was first recorded, an account of the word's origin, and other relevant information likely to be of interest to you. The symbol < , meaning "from," indicates the various stages in a word's development. A question mark [?] is used after the word "Origin" when the ultimate origin of a word is not definitely known:

> **ca·peesh** /ka peésh/ *interj* do you understand? [Mid-20C. < Italian *capisce* "he or she understands," form of *capire* "understand"]
>
> **grav·lax** /graáv laàks/ *n* a Scandinavian dish consisting of thin slices of dried salmon marinated in sugar, salt, pepper, and herbs, especially dill, and usually served as an appetizer [Mid-20C. < Swedish or Norwegian *gravlaks* "buried salmon" (because originally marinated in a hole in the ground)]
>
> **han·ker** /hángkər/ (**-kered, -ker·ing, -kers**) *vi* to want something very badly and persistently ○ *hankers after something she can't have* [Early 17C. Origin ?]

At some entries we explain why a word is used with a particular meaning. This may be because of a development of a meaning in English or in a source language, or an association with a person or place, or a visual image or stereotype:

> **Ru·ri·ta·ni·a** /ro͝orə táynee ə/ *n* a place of romance, adventure, and intrigue [Late 19C. After a fictional central European kingdom in novels by Anthony Hope (1863–1933)] —**Ru·ri·ta·ni·an** *adj, n*

In addition, over 200 short word history essays, titled **ORIGIN**, give additional information of etymological interest that applies to more than one headword, for example, at *ocular*:

> **oc·u·lar** /ókyələr/ *adj* relating to, perceived by, or performed by the eye ■ *n* an eyepiece in an optical instrument [Late 16C. Via French *oculaire* < late Latin *ocularis* < Latin *oculus* "eye"]
>
> **ORIGIN** The Indo-European word from which ***ocular*** is derived is also the ancestor of English *atrocious, eye, ferocious, inoculate, optic*, and *window*.

Finally, a unique series of 28 extended essays titled **LANGUAGE HERITAGE** trace the influence of languages such as Arabic, Dutch, Spanish, and Hebrew on English vocabulary over the centuries:

> **Tu·pi-Gua·ra·ni** *n* a Native South American language family whose principal members are Tupi and Guarani. It is itself a branch of the Andean-Equatorial family of languages. —**Tu·pi-Gua·ra·ni** *adj*
>
> **LANGUAGE HERITAGE** ***Tupi-Guarani*** Much of English is made up of words from other languages, and the ***Tupi-Guarani*** group of South American languages is a small but significant contributor in this respect. Names of unfamiliar animals and birds reached English relatively soon after Europeans discovered the New World (usually via Portuguese, Spanish, or sometimes French): the ***agouti*** and the ***toucan*** in the mid-16th century, the ***capybara, eyra, jaguar***, and ***tanager*** in the early 17th, followed later by, for example, ***cougar, jabiru, piranha***, and ***tapir***. Foodstuffs were adopted: ***manioc*** (mid-16th century), ***cashew*** (late 16th), ***cayenne pepper***, and ***tapioca***, for

example. Valuable products and their sources became known and used, for instance, ***ipecac*** (a plant from whose dried roots an emetic is made, early 17th century), ***jacaranda*** (a tree with a valuable wood), and ***jaborandi*** (a bush whose dried leaves yield the drug pilocarpine). Tupi also gave us (via Portuguese) the sound of the ***maraca*** (early 17th century).

Usage essays

The Usage essays complement the Usage notes by providing more extended information on particularly thorny usage problems. Meanings that may be challenged as to the legitimacy of their usage are signaled by a lightface triangle ⚠. Usage essays appear after the heading **USAGE**:

non·plussed /nòn plúst/ *adj* **1.** surprised, confused, and uncertain what to do or say **2.** ⚠ calm and unperturbed (*informal*)

USAGE The adjective ***nonplussed*** means "surprised, confused, and uncertain what to do or say." It is increasingly used in the almost opposite sense of "untroubled," especially in US English (*Nonplussed by the criticism, she continued to direct her films in the very same offbeat manner for which she was famed.*). This new meaning is not yet accepted as standard, and it may cause ambiguity in sentences such as *He seemed nonplussed by the news*. It possibly derives from a misunderstanding of the *non-* element, perhaps also influenced by *nonchalant* which does mean "calm and unconcerned." But ***nonplussed*** goes back to Latin *non plus* "no more," and does not have a positive or affirmative form *plussed.*

Spellchecks

A common spelling problem today is confusion over homophones, or words with similar sounds but different meanings or spellings such as *ware, wear, were,* and *where.* Although this confusion has always existed, it is our belief that increasing reliance on automatic spellcheckers, which do not, of course, distinguish homophones as errors, has exacerbated the problem in recent years. For this reason the Dictionary features pairs or sets of common homophones that are routinely confused in written texts, after the heading **SPELLCHECK.** The Spellcheck notes are entered at the first word of the pair or set, regardless of relative frequency, with cross-references from the other homophones to the entries with the Spellchecks. Unlike incorrect spellings, Spellcheck terms are all valid forms:

ware[1] /wer/ *n* **1.** SIMILAR THINGS similar things, or things that are made of the same material (*usually used in combination*) ○ *flatware* **2.** CERAMICS ceramic articles of a particular kind or made by a particular manufacturer (*often used in combination*) ○ *delftware* ■ **wares** *npl* **1.** THINGS FOR SALE articles offered for sale **2.** MARKETABLE SKILLS skills or talents offered as a service or a commodity [Old English *waru*]

SPELLCHECK ware, wear, were, or **where**? Do not confuse the spelling of ***ware, wear, were,*** and ***where,*** which sound similar. ***Ware*** (referring to similar things, or things made of the same material), is most likely to be confused with ***wear*** (referring to clothing) in compound words such as *software, tableware, footwear,* and *knitwear.* ***Were*** is the past tense of *are* (as in *We were all young once.*), and ***where*** is used to ask about or indicate the place that somebody or something is in, at, going to, or coming from: *Where were you last night? They still live in the town where they were born.*

Synonym essays

Synonym essays distinguish between sets of words that are close in meaning. Examples help to clarify nuances of meaning, and cross-references from individual synonyms direct you from them to the Synonym essays at which they appear:

an·noy /ə nóy/ (**-noyed, -noy·ing, -noys**) *v* **1.** *vt* IRRITATE SOMEBODY to make somebody feel impatient or mildly angry **2.** *vt* HARASS SOMEBODY to harass somebody repeatedly **3.** *vi* BE IRRITATING to be a source of irritation ○ *Barking dogs are bound to annoy.* [13C. Via Old French *anoier* < late Latin *inodiare* "make loathsome" < Latin *in odio* "in hatred"]

SYNONYMS *annoy, irritate, exasperate, vex, irk*

CORE MEANING: to cause a mild degree of anger in somebody

annoy to make somebody feel impatient or mildly angry ○ *His constant complaining annoys everyone.* ○ *We're annoyed that no-one told us how long the alterations would take.* **irritate** to annoy somebody slightly ○ *The loud humming quickly started to irritate her.* ○ *We were irritated to find that everyone had left early.* **exasperate** to make somebody angry or frustrated, often by repeatedly doing something annoying ○ *The frequent breakdowns and delays exasperated even loyal customers.* ○ *We soon became exasperated with his laziness and excuses.* **vex** to make somebody slightly annoyed or upset, especially over a relatively unimportant matter ○ *The mistake vexed him but did not worry him unduly.* ○ *It vexed her that she had almost wanted to laugh at his remark.* **irk** to annoy somebody slightly by being tiresome or tedious ○ *What irked her more than anything else was that Jo was probably right.* ○ *He also irked his colleagues with frequent TV appearances and public pronouncements.*

irk /urk/ (**irked, irk·ing, irks**) *vt* to annoy somebody slightly, especially by being tedious [14C. Perhaps < Old Norse *yrkja* "to work"; originally N English, "grow weary or vexed"]

SYNONYMS See ***annoy*** and ***bother.***

World English and regional essays

The World English coverage in the Dictionary is underpinned by a number of essays on specific varieties of English, both domestically regional and global:

ham·burg /hám bùrg/ *n regional* FOOD same as **hamburger** [Late 19C. Shortening]

REGIONAL NOTE The term ***hamburg*** is used in New England and the North Central States, as far west as Michigan. The Northern usage contrasts with the general-currency terms *hamburger* and *hamburger steak* used elsewhere in the United States. And in the North, especially among the young, the ***hamburg*** forms are less frequent than the primary American terms.

Phil·ip·pine Eng·lish *n* a variety of English spoken in the Philippines. See panel on next page

WORLD ENGLISH *Philippine English,* also Filipino English, is the variety of English used in the Philippines. It has some co-official status with Filipino. English is the second western colonial language, after Spanish; the United States took the territory in 1898 from Spain, whose colony it had been since 1521. The nation is diverse, with a Malay majority, a Chinese minority, and many people of mixed Malay, Chinese, Spanish, and US backgrounds. Because English is used in varying degrees by over half the population of about 60 million, the Philippines rightly claims to be a major English-speaking country.

Like US English, Philippine English pronounces *r* in words such as *art, door,* and *worker.* Also, *h* is pronounced with the tip of the tongue curled back and raised. Vowels tend to be full in all syllables (e.g., *seven* being pronounced "seh-ven," not "sev'n"). An "s" or "sh" sound may serve instead of a "z" or "zh," as in "carss" (cars), "pleshure" (pleasure). In grammar, the present progressive is commonly used for habitual behavior, rather than the simple present ("We are doing this work all the time" for "We do this work all the time"), the present perfect may be used rather than the simple past ("We have done it yesterday" for "We did it yesterday"), and the past perfect rather than the present perfect ("They had already been there" for "They have already been there").

Distinctive vocabulary includes: (1) Hispanicisms, unchanged or adapted, e.g., *asalto* (surprise party), *querida* (mistress); (2) words from Tagalog, e.g., *boondock* (mountain) – whence "the boondocks," *kundiman* (love song), *tao* (man) – as in "the common tao"; (3) local coinages, e.g., *carnap* (to steal a car), formed by analogy with *kidnap,* and *jeepney* (small bus), blending *jeep* and *jitney,* a jeep adapted for passengers.

Cultural notes

Cultural Notes form stepping stones from particular senses of words to their wider cultural contexts. Cultural Notes typically refer to titles of books, films, plays, works of art, and musical pieces, especially those that have passed into the language:

> **Catch-22** /-twentee tóo/ (*plural* **Catch-22's** or **Catch-22s**), **catch-22** *n* a situation or predicament from which it is impossible to extricate yourself because of built-in illogical rules and regulations [After the novel *Catch-22* by Joseph Heller]
>
> **CULTURAL NOTE** ***Catch-22***, a novel (1961) by Joseph Heller. The title of this dark satire relates to the skewed military logic that entraps the protagonist, Yossarian, a pilot serving in Italy during World War II. He tries to get himself grounded by being pronounced insane, but is told that only an insane person would want to fly, and his desire not to fly proves that he is, in fact, sane, and so must continue to fly. The term ***Catch-22*** eventually came to have a more general meaning of a situation in which somebody is trapped by illogical conditions and restrictions.
>
> **e·nig·ma** /i nígmə, e-/ *n* somebody or something that is not easily explained or understood [Mid-16C. Via Latin < Greek *ainigma* < *ainos* "fable"]
>
> **CULTURAL NOTE** ***The Enigma Variations***, an orchestral work (1899) by British composer Edward Elgar. Elgar's most popular and widely performed work, it was originally entitled *Variations on an Original Theme*. Each of the variations is a musical portrait of a friend of Elgar, identified in the score only by his or her initials or nickname. The title of Elgar's piece influenced the Berlin engineer who built the now-famed German military cipher machine known as *Enigma*, a typewriter-like device capable of producing an infinite number of ciphers.

"Nonlexical" entries for people and places

The Dictionary contains thousands of entries for people (biographical entries) and places (geographic entries) in the A-Z list. Though the Dictionary does not presume to be an exhaustive source of such items because its primary mission is recording North American and World English words, it nevertheless includes a representative, broad sampling of some of the more important people and places you might have occasion to look up as a very first step in a reference search.

Entries for people and places

Biographical entries for people and geographic entries for place names are listed alphabetically. Whenever one biographical surname appears in more than one entry, the entries appear in alphabetical order following the comma, with a pronunciation at the first occurrence of the name:

> **Wash·ing·ton** /wóshingtən, wáwsh-/ state in the northwestern United States, bordered by British Columbia, Idaho, Oregon, and the Pacific Ocean. Capital: Olympia. Population: 6,068,996 (2002 estimate). Area: 70,637 sq. mi./182,949 sq. km. — **Wash·ing·to·ni·an** /wòshing tṓnee ən/ *n, adj*
>
> **Wash·ing·ton, Booker T.** (1856–1915) US educator. As the first principal of Alabama's Tuskegee Institute (1881–1915), he urged African Americans to attempt to gain advancement through educational attainments. Full name **Washington, Booker Taliaferro**
>
> **Washington, D.C.** capital city of the United States. The city of Washington has the same boundaries as the District of Columbia, a federal territory established in 1790 as the site of the new nation's permanent capital. Located at the confluence of the Potomac and Anacostia rivers, it is bordered by Maryland and Virginia. Population: 570,898 (2002 estimate).
>
> **Wash·ing·ton, Denzel** (*b.* 1954) US actor. His movies include *Malcolm X* (1992) and *Training Day* (2001), for which he won the Academy Award for best actor.
>
> **Wash·ing·ton, George** (1732–99) 1st president of the United States (1789–97). Commander in chief of the American forces during the American Revolution (1775–83) and president of the second Constitutional Convention, he was the first president of the newly independent United States.
>
> **Wash·ing·ton, Martha Dandridge Custis** (1731–1802) US First Lady. The widow of Daniel Parke Custis, she married George Washington in 1759 and as his wife later became the first of a long line of first ladies.
>
> **Wash·ing·ton's birth·day** *n US* the birthday of George Washington. Date: February 22.

Biographical Quotations

At some biographical entries, quotations by or about the people have been included when it is felt that their words characterize them or serve to validate their historical or cultural significance:

> **Gra·ham, Katharine** (1917–2001) US newspaper executive. She was publisher of *The Washington Post* (1969–79). Born **Meyer, Katharine**
>
> "If we had failed to pursue the facts as far as they led, we would have denied the public any knowledge of an unprecedented scheme of political surveillance and sabotage."
> [Katharine Graham. On the *Washington Post*'s investigative reportage of the Watergate scandal, *The Washington Post*; March 5, 1973]
>
> **Paine, Thomas** (1737–1809) British-born American writer, political philosopher, and revolutionary. His pamphlet *Common Sense* (1776) influenced the move toward American independence. Known as **Tom Paine**
>
> "Government, even in its best state, is but a necessary evil; in its worst state, an intolerable one."
> [Thomas Paine, *Common Sense*; 1776]
>
> "These are the times that try men's souls. The summer soldier and the sunshine patriot will, in this crisis, shrink from the service of their country; but he that stands it *now*, deserves the love and thanks of men and women."
> [Thomas Paine, Introduction, *The Crisis*; December 1776]

Subject Labels for Specialist Areas

ACCT	Accounting
ACOUSTICS	Acoustics
AEROSP	Aerospace
AGRIC	Agriculture
AIR FORCE	Air force
ALPHA	Alphabet
ALTERN MED	Alternative medicine
AMPHIB	Amphibians
ANAT	Anatomy
ANCIENT HIST	Ancient history
ANTHROP	Anthropology
ARCHAEOL	Archaeology
ARCHERY	Archery
ARCHIT	Architecture
ARMS	Arms and weapons
ARMY	Armed forces
ART	Art
ARTS	Arts
ASTROL	Astrology
ASTRON	Astronomy
AUTOMOT	Automotive
AVIAT	Aviation
BALLET	Ballet
BANKING	Banking
BASEBALL	Baseball
BASKETBALL	Basketball
BEVERAGES	Beverages
BIBLE	Biblical terms
BIOCHEM	Biochemistry
BIOL	Biology
BIOTECH	Biotechnology
BIRDS	Birds
BOARD GAMES	Board games
BOATING	Boating
BOT	Botany
BOXING	Boxing
BREED	Breed of animal
BROADCAST	Broadcasting
BUDDHISM	Buddhism
BUILDINGS	Buildings
BUSINESS	Business
CALENDAR	Calendar terms
CAMPING	Camping
CANOEING	Canoeing
CARDS	Card games
CARS	Cars
CERAMICS	Ceramics and pottery
CHEM	Chemistry
CHEM ELEM	Chemical elements
CHESS	Chess
CHR	Christianity
CIV ENG	Civil engineering
CLIMBING	Climbing
CLOTHING	Clothing and costume
COINS	Coins and coin collecting
COLLECTING	Collecting
COLORS	Colors
COMM	Commerce
COMMUNICATION	Communication
COMPASS	Compass points
COMPUT	Computing
COMPUT GAMES	Computer games
CONSTR	Construction
COOK	Cooking
COSMETICS	Cosmetics
COVERINGS	Coverings
CRICKET	Cricket
CRIME	Crime
CRYSTALS	Crystals
CUE GAMES	Cue games
CULTL ANTHROP	Cultural anthropology
CYCLING	Cycling
DANCE	Dance
DENT	Dentistry
DESIGN	Design
DRUGS	Drugs
ECOL	Ecology
E-COMMERCE	E-commerce
ECON	Economics
EDUC	Education
ELEC	Electricity
ELEC ENG	Electrical engineering
ELECTRONICS	Electronics
EMERGENCIES	Emergencies
ENG	Engineering
ENVIRON	Environment
ETHICS	Ethics
EXTREME SPORTS	Extreme sports
FASHION	Fashion
FENCING	Fencing
FIELD HOCKEY	Field hockey
FIN	Finance
FISH	Fish
FISHERIES	Fisheries
FISHING	Fishing
FITNESS	Fitness
FOOD	Food
FOOD INDUST	Food industries
FOOTBALL	Football
FORESTRY	Forestry
FREIGHT	Freight
FUNGI	Fungi
FURNITURE	Furniture
GAMBLING	Gambling
GARDENING	Gardening
GENETICS	Genetics
GEOG	Geography
GEOL	Geology
GLASS	Glassware
GOLF	Golf
GOV	Government
GRAM	Grammar
GYM	Gym
GYMNASTICS	Gymnastics
HAIR	Hairdressing
HANDICRAFT	Handicraft
HEALTH	Health
HEALTH SERVICES	Health services
HERALDRY	Heraldry
HINDUISM	Hinduism
HIST	History
HOBBIES	Hobbies
HOCKEY	Hockey
HOME MAINTENANCE	Home maintenance
HORSERACING	Horseracing
HOUSEHOLD	Household items
HR	Human resources
HUNTING	Hunting
ICE SKATING	Ice skating
IMMUNOL	Immunology
INDUST	Industry
INFO SCI	Information science
INSECTS	Insects
INSUR	Insurance
INTERNAT REL	International relations
ISLAM	Islam
JEWELRY	Jewelry
JUDAISM	Judaism
JUD-CHR	Judeo-Christian religion
LANG	World languages
LANGUAGE	Language
LAW	Law
LAWN BOWLING	Lawn bowling
LEISURE	Leisure
LIBRARIES	Libraries
LING	Linguistics
LITERAT	Literature
LOGIC	Logic
MAIL	Mail
MANAGEMT	Management
MANUF	Manufacturing
MAPS	Maps
MARINE BIOL	Marine biology
MARKETING	Marketing
MARTIAL ARTS	Martial arts
MATH	Mathematics
MEASURE	Measurements
MECH ENG	Mechanical engineering
MED	Medicine
MEDIA	Media
METALL	Metallurgy
METEOROL	Meteorology
MICROBIOL	Microbiology
MIL	Military
MIN EXTRACT	Mineral extraction
MINERALS	Minerals and mineralogy
MONEY	Currencies
MOTOR SPORTS	Motor sports
MOTORCYCLES	Motorcycles
MOVIES	Movies
MUSIC	Music
MYTHOL	Mythology
NAUT	Nautical
NAVIG	Navigation
NAVY	Navy
OCCUPATIONS	Occupations
OCEANOG	Oceanography
ONLINE	Online
OPHTHALMOL	Ophthalmology
OPTICS	Optics
PALEONT	Paleontology
PAPER	Papermaking
PARANORMAL	Paranormal
PARAPSYCHOL	Parapsychology
PEOPLES	Peoples
PHARM	Pharmacology
PHILOSOPHY	Philosophy
PHON	Phonetics
PHOTOGRAPHY	Photography

PHYS	Physics
PHYSIOL	Physiology
PLANES	Planes
PLANTS	Plants
POL	Politics
POLICE	Police
PREHIST	Prehistory
PRINTING	Printing
PSYCHIAT	Psychiatry
PSYCHOANAL	Psychoanalysis
PSYCHOL	Psychology
PUBL	Publishing
PUBLIC ADMIN	Public administration
QUANTUM PHYS	Quantum physics
RACKET GAMES	Racket games
RAIL	Railroads
RECORDING	Recording
RELIG	Religions
REPT	Reptiles
RIDING	Riding
RIFLERY	Riflery
ROADS	Roads
ROLLER SKATING	Roller skating
ROWING	Rowing
RUGBY	Rugby
SAFETY	Safety
SAILING	Sailing
SCI	Science
SCULPTURE	Sculpture
SEISMOL	Seismology
SHIPPING	Shipping
SHOW JUMPING	Show jumping
SKIING	Skiing
SOC SCI	Social sciences
SOC WELFARE	Social welfare
SOCCER	Soccer
SOCIOL	Sociology
SOFTBALL	Softball
SPORTS	Sports in general
STAMPS	Stamps
STATS	Statistics
SURFING	Surfing
SURG	Surgery
SWIMMING	Swimming
TECH	Technology
TELECOM	Telecommunications
TENNIS	Tennis
TEXTILES	Textiles
THEATER	Theater
TIME	Time
TRACK AND FIELD	Track and field sports
TRANSP	Transportation
TRAVEL	Travel
TREES	Trees
URBAN PLAN	Urban planning
UTIL	Public utilities
VEHICLES	Vehicles
VERTEB	Vertebrates
VET	Veterinary medicine
WATER SKIING	Waterskiing
WINE	Wine and winemaking
WOODWORK	Woodwork
WRESTLING	Wrestling
YOUTH ORG	Youth organizations
ZODIAC	Astrology
ZOOL	Zoology

Abbreviations and Symbols

C	century (in etymologies)
cgs	centimeter-gram-second
cl	centiliter(s)
cm	centimeter(s)
cu.	cubic
e.g.	for example
fl.	fluid
ft.	foot/feet
gal.	gallon(s)
in.	inch(es)
kg	kilogram(s)
km	kilometer(s)
kmph	kilometers per hour
l	liter(s)
lb.	pound(s)
m	meter(s)
mi.	mile(s)
ml	milliliter(s)
mm	millimeter(s)
mph	miles per hour
oz	ounce(s)
sq.	square
pt.	pint(s)
yd.	yard(s)

■	precedes new part of speech
○	precedes illustrative example
◇	precedes idiomatic phrase
⇨	precedes cross-reference to related entry
➧	precedes cross-reference to geographic or biographical entry where meaning is given
⚠	marks a contraindicated usage

Pronunciation Guide

Pronunciations in the *Encarta® Webster's Dictionary of the English Language* are given in a pronunciation system specially developed for the Dictionary. It relies on familiar combinations of letters of the alphabet so that it can be interpreted without constant reference to a table of explanations. The only symbol taken from outside the ordinary alphabet is the *schwa* /ə/, which stands for the sound represented by **a** in **approve** and **megabyte**. In the Dictionary the pronunciations follow the headword or sense number and appear between forward slashes / /.

PRONUNCIATION KEY

a	at
aa	father
aw	all
ay	day
b, bb	but, ribbon
ch	chin
d, dd	do, ladder
ə	about, edible, item, common, circus
e	egg, hair, tear
ee	eel, happy, medium
f, ff	fond, differ
g, gg	go, giggle
h	hot
hw	when
i	it
ī	ice
j, jj	juice, pigeon
k	key, thick
l, ll	let, silly
m, mm	mother, hammer
n, nn	not, funny
ng	song
o	odd
ō	open
o͝o	good
oo	school
ow	owl
oy	oil
p, pp	pen, happy
r, rr	road, carry, hard
s, ss	say, lesson
sh	sheep
th	thin
t̲h̲	this
t, tt	tell, butter
u	up
ur	urge
v, vv	very, savvy
w	wet
y	yes
z, zz	zoo, blizzard
z̲h̲	vision

´ over a vowel indicates the syllable with the strongest (primary) stress, e.g., **depend** /di pénd/.
` over a vowel indicates the syllable with medium (secondary) stress, e.g., **territory** /térrə tàwree/.
' before /l/, /m/, or /n/ shows that the consonant is syllabic (takes the function of a vowel), e.g., **bottle** /bótt'l/.

I. Consonants

The following are used to describe the sound they usually stand for in ordinary spelling:

/b d f g h j k l m n p r s t v w y z/

befriend	/bi frénd/
hug	/hug/
strap	/strap/
milk	/milk/
jazz	/jaz/
yes	/yess/

The following two-consonant combinations also denote the sound they stand for in ordinary spelling:

/ch ng th/

church	/church/
thing	/thing/
shop	/shop/

For the sound in "**this**" (**voiced dental fricative**) we have used /t̲h̲/:

mother	/mút̲h̲ər/
that	/t̲h̲at/

For the central sound in "**vision**" (**voiced palatoalveolar fricative**) we have used /z̲h̲/:

vision	/víz̲h̲'n/
pleasure	/plézh̲ər/

Double consonants

This Dictionary uses double consonants to show many sounds in the middle of words because English spelling normally doubles letters in these positions. Consonants are doubled when they are preceded by the stressed vowels /á, é, í, ó, ú, ó͝o/ or /à, è, ì, ò, ù, ò͝o/ and followed by either a vowel or a syllabic consonant, or by /l, r, y, or w/:

rubber	/rúbbər/
metric	/méttrik/
travel	/trávv'l/
inward	/ínnwərd/
deputy	/déppyətee/
supposi-tion	/sùppə zísh'n/

In order to show clearly that /s/ is required, not /z/, we double the /s/ additionally at the end of a syllable and with voiced consonants:

face	/fayss/
miscue	/mìss kyo͞o/
mincer	/mínssər/

But not with voiceless consonants:

wasp	/wosp/
first	/furst/
tax	/taks/

The consonant /k/ is not doubled:

flicker	/flíkər/
tackle	/ták'l/

There is no doubling of the two-consonant combinations /ch, sh, th, ng, t̲h̲, z̲h̲/:

touching	/túching/
passion	/pásh'n/
rhythm	/rít̲h̲'m/
measure	/méz̲h̲ər/
hanger	/hángər/

II. Vowels

The traditional short vowels /a, e, i, o, u/ denote the sounds they usually stand for in ordinary spelling:

cat	/kat/
head	/hed/
myth	/mith/
swan	/swon/
double	/dúbb'l/

For the short vowel as in "**put**" we use /o͝o/:

good	/go͝od/
could	/ko͝od/
full	/fo͝ol/

For the weak vowel as in the first syllable of "**along**" and the second syllable of "**butter**" we use the symbol /ə/ (schwa):

along	/ə lóng/
butter	/búttər/
flattering	/fláttəring/

For the vowel in "**goose**" and "**soup**" we use /oo/:

food	/food/
move	/moov/
rude	/rood/

When this is preceded by a y-sound we use /yoo/:

music	/myŏŏ́zik/
acute	/ə kyŏŏ́t/
sinuous	/sínnyoo əss/

In words such as "sure" and "pure" we have used /oor/ and /yoor/ respectively:

poor	/poor, pawr/
cure	/kyoor/
during	/dŏŏ́ring/

For the diphthongs in "gray," "flee," and "boy," the respellings /ay/, /ee/, and /oy/ are used:

great	/grayt/
niece	/neess/
voice	/voyss/

For the diphthongs in "high," "low," and "cow" we use /ī/, /ō/, and /ow/ respectively:

write	/rīt/
goat	/gōt/
micro	/mī́krō/
loud	/lowd/
frown	/frown/

For the vowel of "nurse" we use /ur/:

turn	/turn/
stern	/sturn/
first	/furst/

For the stressed vowel of "father" we use /aa/:

father	/faáthər/
bravado	/brə vaádō/

For the vowel of "start" in words where there is an "r" in the spelling we have used /aar/:

farm	/faarm/
starry	/staáree/

We have used /aw/ for the vowel of "thought":

thought	/thawt/
tall	/tawl/

For the vowel of "north" in words where there is an "r" in the spelling we have used /awr/:

short	/shawrt/
war	/wawr/
sport	/spawrt/
story	/stáwree/

For the vowels in "near" and "square" we have used /eer/ and /er/ respectively:

beer	/beer/
beard	/beerd/
weary	/weéree/
declare	/di klér/
scarce	/skerss/
vary	/vérree/

For the vowels in "fire" and "sour", we have used /īr/ and /owr/:

inspire	/in spī́r/
virus	/vī́rəss/
flour	/flówr/
dowry	/dówree/

Consonants that take the place of a vowel in a syllable (**syllabic consonants**) are preceded by /'/:

apple	/ápp'l/
garden	/gaárd'n/
station	/stáysh'n/
dental	/dént'l/

In the vowel at the end of words such as "happy" we have used /ee/. The same applies to vowels such as the central one in "various":

happy	/háppee/
coffee	/káwfee, kóffee/
various	/vérree əss/
radiate	/ráydee àyt/

III. Stress

Single syllable words (**monosyllables**) have no stress marks. In words with more than one syllable (**polysyllables**) we have indicated the primary (main) stress with an acute accent /´/:

another	/ə núthər/
collide	/kə lī́d/
cosmetic	/koz méttik/

There are two types of secondary stress. We have used a grave accent /`/ to show those that occur **after** the main stress (**posttonic stresses**) as well as those that occur **before** the main stress (**pretonic stresses**):

agriculture	/ággri kùlchər/
seventeen	/sèvv'n teén/

IV. When are pronunciations given?

The *Encarta Webster's Dictionary of English* shows pronunciations at headwords except where the headword is made up of separate or hyphenated words that are given pronunciations elsewhere in the Dictionary. Thus we include pronunciations for all entries that are different headwords with the same spelling (**homographs**) such as *bank* or *bow.*

Capitalized forms of common names are not given a pronunciation unless they are geographic or biographical entries. In geographic and biographical entries where the names are repeated, the first occurrence only is given a pronunciation. Important variants in pronunciation are covered in the Dictionary, as are changes in pronunciation or stress in undefined entries (**runons**) and pronunciations of plural or other forms where the pronunciation or stress changes from that of the headword.

V. Spacing

As it is easier to work out the pronunciation of a word if longer respellings are broken up into easily processed pieces, we have inserted spaces within the respelling of a word in the following cases:

(i) before a stressed syllable or other syllable containing a strong vowel (for this purpose, any vowel other than /ə i ō oo yoo ŏŏ/):

allow	/ə lów/
detect	/di tékt/
unknown	/ùn nṓn/
celebrate	/séllə bràyt/
cucumber	/kyŏŏ́ kùmbər/

(ii) between the elements of a compound in which each element retains its usual pronunciation:

bedtime	/béd tīm/
teakettle	/teé kètt'l/

(iii) between any two successive vowel or diphthong symbols:

payee	/pay eé/
chaos	/káy òss/
radiate	/ráydee àyt/

(iv) between /ng/ and a following /g/:

anger	/áng gər/

VI. Foreign pronunciations

In occasional cases—particularly proper names—we have used the following to indicate non-English sounds:

/hl/ as in Welsh **Llangollen**
/kh/ as in Scottish loch, German Bach, Spanish Gijón
/N/ to show nasalization of the preceding vowel as in the French pronunciation of **un bon vin blanc** /öN boN vaN blaaN/
/ö/ as in French **boeuf**, German **schön**
/ü/ as in French **rue**, German **gemütlich**

English: the Word Web

John Ayto

English is a member of the Indo-European family of languages, which is over 7,000 years old. We do not know for certain where this language family originated, but good evidence suggests that it had its beginnings in the general area to the north of the Black Sea. Over the millennia the people of those lands migrated northwestward and southeastward, into Europe and the northern part of India. As the people spread more and more widely, their language became differentiated into distinct groups, which form the basis of the languages spoken today in the areas where they settled. Immediately to the south and southeast are the Iranian languages, including Farsi (Modern Persian), Pashto (spoken in Afghanistan), and Kurdish. In India, ancient Sanskrit evolved into a multiplicity of modern languages, including Bangla (Bengali), Gujarati, Hindi, Punjabi, Sinhalese, Urdu, and also Romany. Also among these easterly branches are Armenian and the now extinct Hittite and Tocharian.

To the west and north, fragmentation produced the Slavic languages (Russian, Polish, Czech, Slovak, Bulgarian, Serbo-Croat, etc.) in eastern Europe; the Baltic languages (Latvian and Lithuanian, which of all these modern languages most closely resembles its Indo-European ancestor); Greek in Greece; Albanian in Albania; the Romance languages (French, Provençal, Italian, Spanish, Catalan, Portuguese, Romanian, Rhaeto-Romance—descendants of Latin) further west; and the Celtic languages (Welsh, Irish and Scottish Gaelic, Breton, Cornish, Manx) at the very western edge of Europe.

One particular group of migrants had settled in northern Europe, in the area around the Elbe River, about 3,000 years ago. Around the second century B.C. the language they spoke, known as Common Germanic, began to split up into three different dialects, one of which was East Germanic. (The only written evidence we have of this is in the now extinct Gothic language.) The second was North Germanic, which has evolved into modern Swedish, Danish, Norwegian, Icelandic, and Faroese. And lastly there was West Germanic, the ancestor of modern German, Dutch (and Afrikaans), Flemish, Frisian, Yiddish—and English.

The ancestor of modern English crossed the English Channel, in the form of a set of mutually intelligible Germanic dialects, in the fifth and sixth centuries A.D., brought by peoples from the northeastern corner of the European mainland, around Jutland and modern Denmark—the Angles, Saxons, and Jutes. The story of its subsequent development is told in **A Brief History of the English Language** (see p. xxx)

English has never abandoned its roots, but it has changed almost beyond recognition over the past millennium and a half. The lexicon of English is now probably larger and more eclectic than that of any other language; as the Language Heritage notes in this dictionary show, there is not a major language in the world that has not over the past 500 years made some contribution to English. There was a huge influx of French vocabulary after the Norman Conquest and of Latin and Greek words during and after the Renaissance; the spread of English speakers around the world later sucked in thousands of words from sources as diverse as Nahuatl (*tomato*), Tibetan (*lama*), Maori (*kiwi*), Finnish (*sauna*), Swahili (*safari*), Inuit (*kayak*), Czech (*pistol*), and Hawaiian (*ukulele*); and new words continue to pour into the language at the rate of over a thousand a year.

All down these centuries of development and assimilation runs a complicated web of descent—often muddled, interrupted, canceling itself out, or losing itself in dead ends. Many of the word history essays in this dictionary show how one ancestor can be responsible for a surprising number of English words: for example, the Latin *gradus* "step" is the source of *grade*, *gradation*, *gradient*, *gradual*, and *graduate*, but also of *aggression*, *congress*, *degrade*, *degree*, *digress*, *ingredient*, *progress*, *regress*, *retrograde*, and *transgress*.

Often, too, the unseen web of interconnections conceals patterns that link the unlikeliest of English partners. It seems scarcely plausible, for instance, that *symphony* and *fate* should be related, or *acrobat* and *oxygen*, but they are, as the diagrams opposite prove. Both *symphony* and *fate* go back to the same Indo-European root *bha-*, meaning "speak," *symphony* being derived from the Greek *phōnē* "voice, sound," and *fate* from Latin *fatum*, "destiny"—more literally, "that which is spoken (by the gods)." The family of *acrobat* and *oxygen* is linked by the idea of "pointed" or "sharp": an *acrobat* is literally someone who walks on tiptoe, on the "points" of the feet, while *oxygen* literally means "acid producer."

The Dictionary, and the word history essays in it, uncover more of the unexpected connections between English words, revealing the links in the word web that centuries of language change have obscured.

Routes into English

The diagrams below take two related groups of English words and trace them back to their Indo-European sources, namely *ak-* meaning "sharp" and *bha-* meaning "speak." The complex web of links shows how these two roots evolved into seemingly unconnected English words, and traces the stages of their development via languages such as French and Latin.

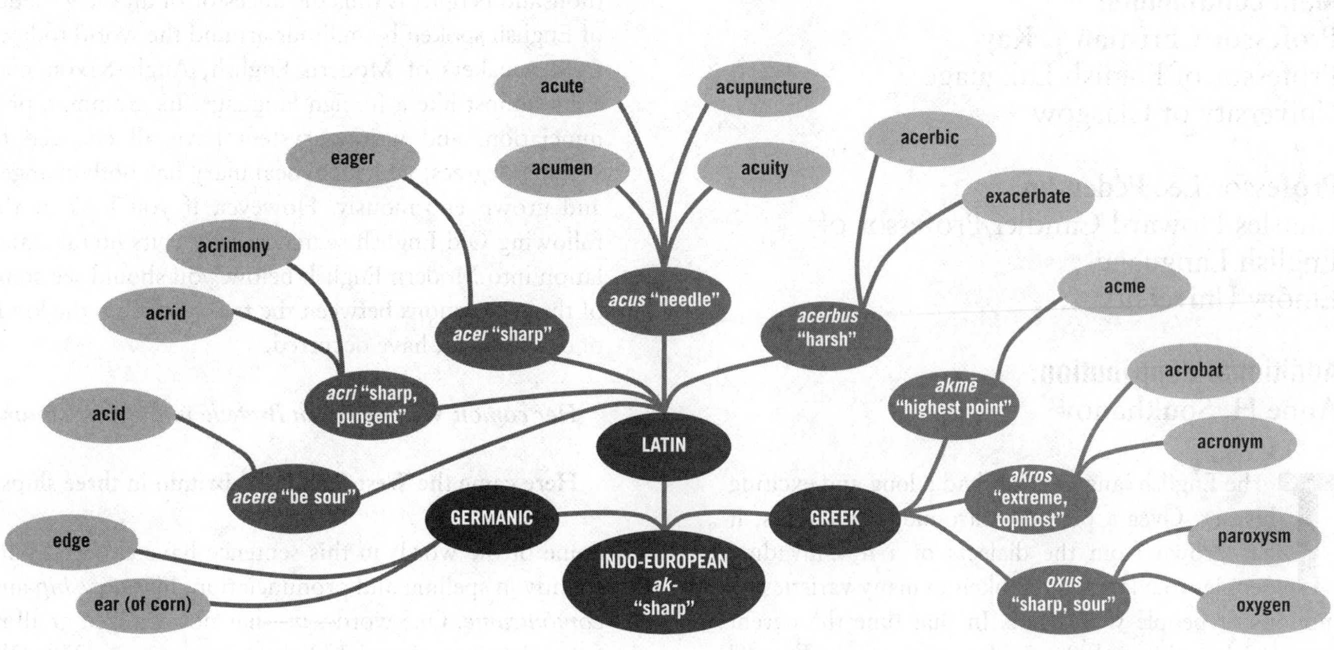

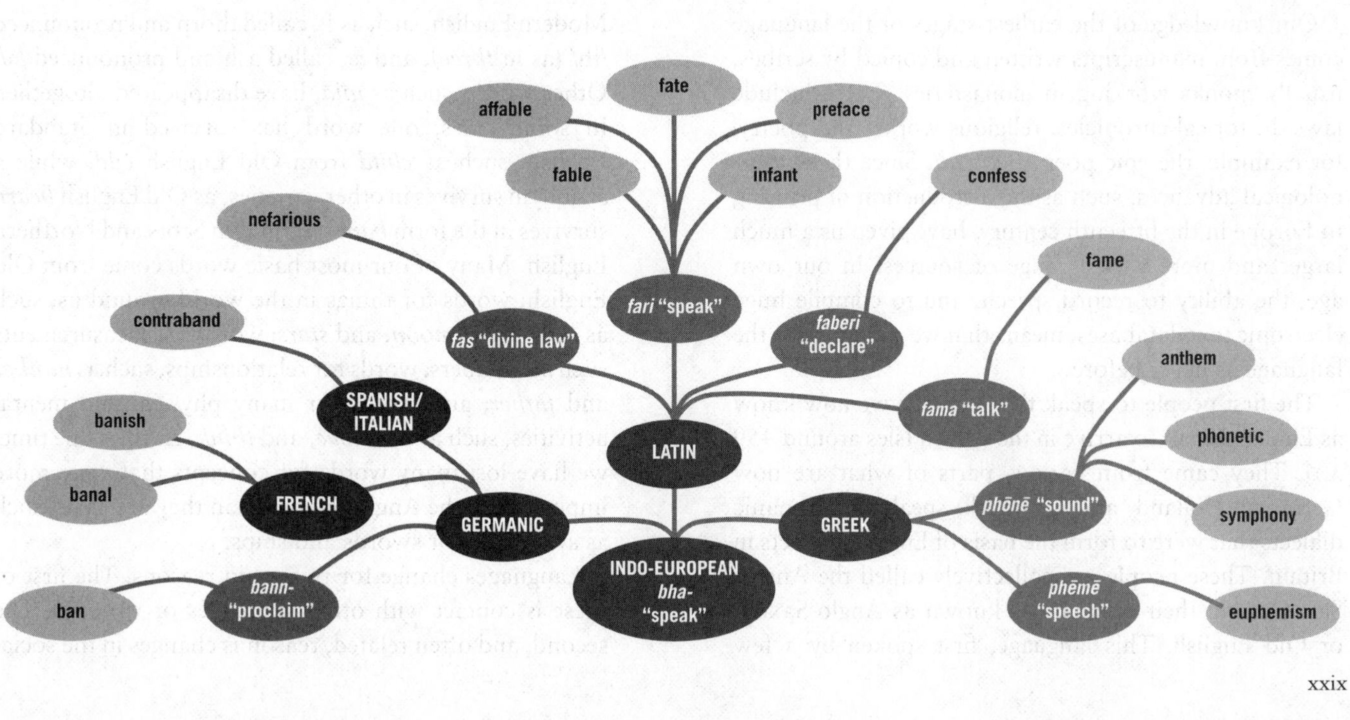

A Brief History of the English Language

Main contributors:
Professor Christian J. Kay
Professor of English Language
University of Glasgow

Professor Lee Pederson
Charles Howard Candler Professor of
English Language
Emory University

Additional contribution:
Anne H. Soukhanov

The English language has had a long and exciting history. Over a period of around 1,500 years, it has grown from the dialects of a few invading peoples to a language spoken in many varieties by millions of people worldwide. In that time the parent language has changed almost, but not entirely, beyond recognition.

Our knowledge of the earliest stages of the language comes from manuscripts written and copied by scribes, usually monks working in monasteries. These include laws, historical chronicles, religious works, and poetry, for example, the epic poem *Beowulf*. Since then, technological advances, such as the introduction of printing to Europe in the fifteenth century, have given us a much larger and more varied range of sources. In our own age, the ability to record speech, and to compile huge electronic text databases, means that we can monitor the language as never before.

The first people to speak the language we now know as English began to arrive in the British Isles around 450 A.D. They came from various parts of what are now Germany, Holland, and Denmark, speaking Germanic dialects that were to form the basis of English dialects in Britain. These people are collectively called the Anglo-Saxons, and their language is known as Anglo-Saxon, or Old English. This language, first spoken by a few thousand people, is thus the ancestor of all the varieties of English spoken by millions around the world today.

To speakers of Modern English, Anglo-Saxon may seem almost like a foreign language. Its grammar, pronunciation, and writing system have all changed to varying degrees, while its vocabulary has both changed and grown enormously. However, if you look at the following Old English sentence, and at its literal translation into Modern English below, you should see some of the connections between the two as well as the kinds of changes that have occurred.

Her comon West-seaxe in Bretene mid Þrim scipum.

Here came the West-Saxons to Britain in three ships.

Some of the words in this sentence have changed only slightly in spelling and pronunciation, like *scip/ship* and *comon/came*. One word—*in*—has not changed at all in form, but has changed slightly in meaning. The Old English alphabet had letters that have disappeared from Modern English, such as Þ, called thorn and pronounced /th/ (as in *three)*, and *æ*, called ash and pronounced /a/. Other words, such as *mid*, have disappeared altogether. In some cases, one word has survived in Standard English, such as *child* from Old English *cild,* while a synonym survives in other varieties, as Old English *bearn* survives in the form *bairn* (=child) in Scots and Northern English. Many of our most basic words come from Old English: words for things in the world around us, such as *earth*, *sun*, *moon*, and *stars*; words for measurements such as numbers; words for relationships, such as *mother* and *father*; and words for many physical and mental activities, such as *run, love,* and *think*. At the same time, we have lost many words for concepts that were more important to the Anglo-Saxons than they are to us, such as synonyms for swords and ships.

Languages change for two main reasons. The first of these is contact with other languages or varieties. The second, and often related, reason is changes in the social and cultural context in which speakers operate. Even before they came to England, the Germanic peoples had made contact with the Romans, borrowing such words as *cheese* and *copper*. In England they encountered the Celtic peoples, whose language is still spoken in parts of Ireland, Wales, and Scotland. Many Celtic place names and geographic terms survive, as in *Dunedin*, the Celtic name for Anglo-Saxon Edinburgh. More important for the general development of English were the waves of invasions by Scandinavian Vikings that started in the late eighth century. Some came simply to plunder, but others settled down. Unlike the Celts, their language was quite similar to that of the Anglo-Saxons, making communication between the two groups possible. They added many everyday words to English, such as *sky*, *egg*, and *law*, the verb *to take*, and the pronoun *they*. Grammatical changes, such as the *-s* ending in such forms as *she walks*, spread into English from Scandinavian areas.

By far the most important contact, however, was the Norman Conquest of 1066, when the Norman-French Duke William defeated the Anglo-Saxon King Harold at the Battle of Hastings and became King William I of England. The Anglo-Saxon aristocracy was destroyed and their lands given to William's nobles, who built many of the castles that still dominate the British landscape. French became the language of government, although the bulk of the population continued to work on the land and speak English. Communication between French and English speakers became increasingly necessary, and, as in any bilingual situation, the languages influenced each other. French words were used in English and its grammar was simplified. By the end of this period, generally known as Middle English, English was much more recognizably the language we know today. Thus in the late fourteenth century, the poet Geoffrey Chaucer wrote of one of his characters:

He was a verray parfit gentil knyght.

He was a very perfect gentle knight.

The words *he*, *was*, *a*, and *knyght* are Old English in origin, but *verray*, *parfit*, and *gentil* were borrowed into English from French and from there can be traced back to Latin. *Knyght* has changed in meaning since Old English, where it meant "boy" or "servant," while the use of *gentle* to mean "noble" or "courteous" differs somewhat from its modern meaning. Such changes in the meanings of words are typical of the way languages develop. These Middle English borrowings from French show the beginnings of one of the most characteristic features of modern English—its large and varied vocabulary. French words come from many vocabulary areas, such as government, law, religion, cooking, the arts, and courtly life. Sometimes words from both sources survive side by side, as with *kingly* (Old English) and *royal* (French). Sometimes their meanings are differentiated, as in *calf* (Old English) and *veal* (French), originally the animal, but developing to mean only the meat.

Time Life Picture/Getty Images

Detail from an early illuminated manuscript of Chaucer's *The Canterbury Tales*, showing Chaucer as a pilgrim on horseback.

Because French and Latin were the official languages during the early Middle English period, English was slow to develop a standard form in speech or writing. There was considerable diversity in the dialects people spoke, as there still is in their modern descendants in Britain or elsewhere. When English began to be written again, the scribes tended to write the words as they were pronounced, which is helpful to modern scholars interested in reconstructing the language of the past.

From the point of view of Modern English, continuing changes in grammar are also significant. In Old English grammatical relationships between words were expressed mainly by changing their endings, as were distinctions such as past/present or singular/plural. The majority of the world's languages have this kind of grammar. This system began to break down through contact with Scandinavian speakers, whose language had a similar system but different endings, and the process was accelerated by the contact with French. In the course of this process English began to move toward its present system of expressing grammatical relationships largely through word order and the use of prepositions. It also lost its system of grammatical gender and began to develop the complex system of verb forms that we know today.

By the end of the Middle English period, generally put at around 1500, a more uniform written language was emerging, based on the dialect of London. This development was promoted both by the greater physical and social mobility of the population and by the rapid spread of printed books. The printers were less tolerant of spelling variation than the medieval scribes had been, and a standardized system began to emerge. Unfortunately for modern users of English, this system predated various changes in the pronunciation of vowels, especially a series known as the Great Vowel Shift. This situation led to apparently illogical spelling variations such as *made/maid*, *flood/food*, or *great/dream*; in the first pair, the vowels used to be pronounced differently, whereas in the others they were once the same. However illogical English spelling seems, there is usually a reason for it!

Early Modern English saw major grammatical patterns being established. Shakespeare and his contemporaries in the late sixteenth century could use either older forms such as "Why go you?" or "He speaks not," or newer ones such as "Why do you go?" and "He does not speak." They could choose between the older "Thou goest, he goeth" or the more modern "You go, he goes." They could express wishes through the old subjunctive form, "Long live the Queen," or the newer "May the Queen live long." In all these cases the older forms were in decline and died out as modern English progressed. At the same time, the verbal group developed, producing forms unavailable to Shakespeare, such as "When are you going?" or "He would have been surprised." An indicator of social change was the fact that speakers gradually ceased to use the singular and plural pronouns *thou* and *you* to distinguish between those of lower and higher rank.

Vocabulary has also continued to grow throughout Modern English. Partly as a result of the renaissance of learning in Europe, the Early Modern period saw an upsurge in Latin borrowings in order to develop terminologies for new approaches to subjects such as science, philosophy, and medicine. National pride increasingly demanded that English, not Latin, should be used in all kinds of writing. Formal prose styles developed, often favoring Latinate words above native ones: *fraternal* might be considered more elegant than the native *brotherly*, or *illuminate* preferred to *light up*. English thus acquired a multilayered vocabulary, able to express a concept at different stylistic levels. This process of borrowing, changing, or inventing words to accommodate new intellectual developments continues to this day, as can be seen from the vocabulary of industrialization in the nineteenth century or of computers or space travel in the twentieth into the twenty-first century.

During the Early Modern period English-speaking traders and adventurers were also setting out to explore the world, reaching the Americas, Africa, India, the Far East, and later Australia and New Zealand. Exotic objects were collected or described, and words such as *chocolate*, *wigwam*, *banana*, *gorilla*, *tea*, and *outback* were added to the language. Like their ancestors before them, some of the invaders settled down, thus laying the foundations of English as a world language and contributing to its continual development.

The same factors of contact and context underlie the process of linguistic change that formed American speech and writing. Through four centuries of cultural evolution, American English developed its distinctive pattern, reflecting the unique social experience of a people. As Horace Gregory explained in his preface to William Carlos Williams's *In the American Grain*, "Our nationality which answers to the name of American is neither at the center of a huge continent nor is it floating loosely around its East, West, and Tropical coastlines and harbors. It is a language." The Colonial American period of the seventeenth century marked the settlements of the Atlantic Seaboard communities, the focal areas of major regional dialects: Northern (Boston 1630), Midland (Philadelphia 1701), Greater New York (New York City 1644), and Southern (Newport News 1621; Charleston 1670). All these varieties began with the same energetic, fluid, and unsettled code called Early Modern English, but each American dialect selected somewhat differently among the alternatives provided in the source language. From these early options came such distinctive forms as Northern *broom*, *roof*, and *root*, and Midland *poke* ("sack"). With these English forms emerged the loanwords from Native American such as *moose*, *hickory*, *squash*, and *terrapin*; from Dutch *coleslaw*, *cruller*, *sleigh*, and *snoop*; and from French *bateau*, *portage*, *prairie*, and *rapids*.

The Frontier period of the eighteenth century extended American speech westward to include the Old Frontier de-

Mr. WILLIAM
SHAKESPEARES
COMEDIES,
HISTORIES, &
TRAGEDIES.
Publifhed according to the True Originall Copies.

Bettmann/Corbis

Title page of the original Bodleian copy of the First Folio edition of Shakespeare (1623).

limited by Pittsburgh in the northwest and Knoxville in the southwest. This period framed the greatest variety of cultural interaction and the most remarkable demographic movement in American history, including the settlement of the Interior South through the Shenandoah Valley and, later, of Kentucky and the Ohio Valley through the Cumberland Gap. This process carried Midland (East Pennsylvania) speech across the Appalachian Highlands to the Piedmont and then south and westward. During this period, the German and Scottish-Irish influences combined with earlier French and Native American loans, especially along the Frontier. Familiar forms from this period reflect sources in German: *clook* "brood hen," *flitch* "fritter," *pannhas* "scrapple," and *smearcase* "cottage cheese"; and Scottish-Irish: *brickle* "brittle," *donsie* "sick, peaked," *redd up* "clean up (the house)," and *scoot over* "make room for."

The nineteenth century began with the Louisiana Purchase and ended with the Spanish-American War. Between those events the divisiveness of Sectionalism emerged across the country, but nowhere more ominously than in those conflicts that led to the American Civil War. But the isolation of the South had a profound impact on its dialects. Immediately after the Civil War, technology developed equipment that made agriculture possible in the arid sections of the West and Southwest. The period also witnessed the rise of regional literature, from Harriet Beecher Stowe in the Northeast, George Washington Harris in the South Midlands of Tennessee, Joel Chandler Harris in the South, and Mark Twain in the West, a literary progression that began with local colorists and concluded with *The Adventures of Huckleberry Finn*. Interaction with Mexico began with the acquisition of Texas and much of the Southwest. Although Spanish loanwords appeared in the previous eras, the largest number occurred in the nineteenth and twentieth centuries. Among the earlier forms are Louisiana French *bayou*, *levee*, and *picayune*; and Spanish *buckaroo* (from *vaquero*), *lariat* (from *la reata*), *pronto*, and *stampede*. English has continued to take in a great many words from Spanish, especially the Spanish spoken in Mexico, clearly illustrating the way languages influence one another via the instrument of human contact and interaction. One obvious example is the contribution of Spanish to the culinary lexicon of American English. Consider *burrito*, *carnitas*, *embutido*, *empanada*, *enchilada*, *fajitas*, *frijole*, *huevos rancheros*, *quesadilla*, *taco*, and *tamale*. And words such as *maquiladora* signify US-Mexican business interactions.

The language of twentieth-century America combines the resources of its past with the factors of contact and context in an urban setting. Here, linguistic change reflects the reorganization of inner cities, from Boston to Los Angeles, involving the emergence of the rural Southern-based Black English and Latino dialects from several sources including Puerto Rico, Cuba, and Mexico. The process also involves a sharp contrast between rural and urban varieties, resulting in a national suburban speech community. This means that the language and culture of suburban New York, Chicago, and San Francisco have more in common with one another in speech and society than they have with any immediate rural communities. These developments explain the emergence of social dialects based on social class. Although most of the old regional dialects endure, most have fewer speakers today as megalopolitan areas have emerged from Massachusetts to Washington, D.C. or Gary, Indiana, through Chicago to Milwaukee, Wisconsin. Contrary to the assumption that it obliterates differences of language and culture, modern American urbanization expands and unifies communities by bringing together formerly discrete locations. Such new social contexts make linguistic change inevitable.

The same patterns of a heritage gained from a country's first settlers, borrowings from local languages and peoples, and continuing development and change in response to geographic, cultural, social, and other factors characterize the continuing changes to the English language in its many manifestations today. Australian and New Zealand Englishes have been enriched by words from Aboriginal and Maori traditions; the English of South Asia bears testament to the many local languages and varied cultural heritage of that vast subcontinent. South Africa's Anglo-Dutch heritage yields a multiplicity of words from that dual background as well as from local languages. In the many territories of the Pacific Rim the same process has given rise to a continuing enrichment of English with new words and senses.

In the early years of this new millennium English can reasonably be regarded as the first worldwide *lingua franca* since Latin. This Dictionary has been written to reflect this phenomenon. It will fall to our dictionary editors to monitor the continuing development of the English language in its manifold forms around the world.

The Formation of New Words in English

John Ayto

The vocabulary of English is in a state of continuous, accelerating expansion. On average, nearly a thousand new items found a place for themselves in our lexicon each year in the twentieth century, and there is no reason to suppose that the language will stop growing at a comparable rate in the foreseeable future. What drives it on?

For one thing, many more people are using English as each decade passes. There are now almost 375 million native speakers of English in the world, approximately three times as many as there were a hundred years ago, and the numbers of second-language English users are growing even faster. It would be surprising if more speakers did not produce more words.

The effect is multiplied by the fragmentation of the language into a number of regional, ethnic, and national varieties (for example, Singapore English, East African English), each of which increasingly feels sanctioned to revitalize its own vocabulary.

And then, of course, with every passing year, new things in the world need names—from the *hot dog* in 1895 to the *webcam* in 1995 to *SARS* in 2002. (Indeed, human beings' ability to conceptualize something that does not yet exist means that not a few words predate the objects they name—the term *atomic bomb*, for instance, is first recorded in 1917.) Nor is the phenomenon limited to "things": a growing perception in the mid-twentieth century that English lacked a title common to married and unmarried women led to the emergence of the use of *Ms* for both.

Language also has a key role in cementing and defining social groups, and the need to maintain its exclusionary power is a considerable spur to the introduction of new vocabulary—hence the rapid turnover of words in many areas of slang, baffling to outsiders.

These are all the forces of the external world operating on the language. The changes they cause can be termed "socially triggered." But alterations within the language can produce new vocabulary, too. Change in meaning, a major contributor to lexical evolution, is very often attributable to gradual, unconscious shifts in the application of a word. For example, in the thirteenth century *nice* meant "ignorant, stupid, or foolish." By the fourteenth century it had taken on yet another pejorative meaning, "wanton or lascivious." Over centuries of various changes, *nice* has lost its original meanings, now coming to mean, among other things, "pleasing and agreeable." The obverse can happen to a meaning of a word: *silly*, which once meant "blessed, innocent, helpless," has lost that meaning and has taken on the pejorative one we are all familiar with. And what might originally have been described (and condemned) as a wrong interpretation of a word's inner structure can easily survive to become an accepted form: *umpire*, for instance, was once *numpire* but evolved into the spelling we use today by the process of *false division*.

The vocabulary of English takes in new words by any of five basic methods: combining existing words or word parts; shortening existing words; using existing words with new meanings; taking words from other languages; and coining entirely new words.

Combination. By far the most common way of forming words in present-day English is to take words or word parts that already exist and join them together. Combination accounts for at least three quarters of the new vocabulary that comes into the language. It usually involves either adding one word to another (a process called *compounding*), so that *sail* + *board* becomes *sailboard*; or adding a prefix or suffix to a word (a process called *affixation* or *derivation*), so that *bio-* + *terrorism* becomes *bioterrorism*. One particular type of compound that became especially popular in the twentieth century is the *blend*. It involves merging the beginning of the first word into the end of the second, so that the two form a new whole: thus *camera* + *recorder* becomes *camcorder* and *casualty evacuation* becomes *casevac*. Sometimes more than one developmental process is involved: *blog*, formed from *(we)b* + *log*, involves combining two words and then shortening the result. Such is the inventiveness of word formation.

Shortening or **abbreviation**. The most straightforward way of shortening a word is to remove its final or first element or elements: so *discotheque* becomes *disco*, and *magazine* becomes *zine*. More specifically, a word containing a suffix can have its suffix removed, usually resulting in a change in its word class; thus the noun *destruction* gives rise to the verb *destruct* in a process linguists call *back-formation*. More radically, all the latter part of a word can be removed, leaving only the first letter. Sequences of such letters are known as *initialisms*: *DVT* for *deep vein thrombosis*, *CEO* for *chief executive officer*. When the letters are pronounced as an ordinary word, the sequence is called an *acronym*: *NAFTA* for *North American Free Trade Agreement*, *NIMBY* for *not in my back yard*, and *SARS*, mentioned above, for *severe acute respiratory syndrome*.

Change in meaning. Words are constantly being redeployed to new uses. So, for example, an *attack dog* becomes "an aggressive political partisan," *plastic* becomes "credit card," *radioactive* becomes "so controversial as to be avoided altogether," and, *mail* becomes "an e-mail, or e-mail generally." Included in this category is the use of trademarks and surnames, altered or not, in such a way that they take on their own distinct meanings; thus, the all-too-familiar *Teflon* presidency, *Churchillian* oratory, and *Bushism*.

A particular type of verbal reassignment is *functional shift*, also known as *conversion* or *zero derivation*. A word is taken from its existing word class (say, a noun) and is put into a new one. In essence, the word changes its grammatical function; hence, the technical descriptor *functional shift*. When this happens, for example, *access* becomes a verb, meaning "to retrieve data or a computer file" and *embed* becomes a noun, meaning "a journalist who travels with troops in a combat zone and files reports on operations."

Borrowing. From its earliest days, English has enriched itself by taking words from other languages, and in the centuries after the Norman Conquest, its entire nature was changed by the huge number of French words it took in. The "borrowing" frenzy has never reached quite that height again, but English now gets a healthy five percent of its new vocabulary from foreign sources. The borrowing tends to be concentrated on areas of cultural contact (for example, assimilation of foreign cuisines has provided English with terms as diverse as *focaccia*, *taco*, and *sushi*) and on areas in which another language is dominant (for instance, France's lead in aviation technology at the beginning of the twentieth century means that many English aeronautical terms are French in origin: *aileron, fuselage, hangar*, and so on).

Coinage. It is comparatively rare that new words are simply dreamed up out of nothing, unconnected to any existing English word, with the exception of many proprietary product names. Such coinages account for less than one percent of twentieth-century neologisms. The practice is not uncommon, though, as can be seen in these genuine scientific and technical coinages: *byte, dongle, googol*. Writers of science fiction and fantasy are fond of inventing words, too (*munchkin, hobbit, Muggle*).

This unceasing surge of words presents a problem to dictionary makers. Clearly, not all new words can be included in "the dictionary": the existing vocabulary would be swamped. Some sort of selection process must be followed. How does it work?

For one thing, some items exclude themselves: for example, highly technical terms of very limited circulation would be wasted in a dictionary for the general user; and, where space is at a premium, terms whose meaning can be easily deduced (such as *leg brace*) are unlikely to gain entry. But the main flood of new words and meanings must be passed through a series of filters, designed to trap only those that the dictionary editor thinks are suitable for entry. The raw material—the lexical evidence—nowadays comes mainly in the form of a database of texts that can be read and analyzed by a computer. All sorts of information useful in the description and definition of words—for example, which prepositions are most typically used with a particular verb—can be extracted from these databases by increasingly sophisticated computer programs. Decisions on what to include and exclude, however, rest mainly on three simpler calculations.

First, and most basic, how common is this word or meaning? Are there large numbers of examples of it in our database, or a thin trickle? Then, what is its chronological profile? Has it only just appeared, or have we got evidence for it going back over several years? And how consistent is that evidence—is its timeline fairly level, or was there a brief explosion of popularity to begin with, followed by years in the doldrums? Third, how even is the word's distribution? Has it been in reasonably general use, or, when we examine the evidence more closely, does it turn out that it is the preferred usage of only a small group, or even of a single individual, and that it has never spread widely throughout the language community?

There is no single right answer to these three questions, no magic number of citations collected or years passed that will guarantee a word's admission to the dictionary—not least because different types and sizes of dictionaries will dictate different criteria. It is the overall profile presented by the various statistics that determines the lexicographer's decision: in or out.

There is evidently an assumption underlying these calculations, and it is this: the more clearly it can be demonstrated that a given usage has established a long-term place for itself in the language, the more likely it is to be included in the dictionary. This has always been an assumption lexicographers have followed, and it underpins the whole notion of dictionaries as normative, standard-setting texts. But it is a slightly slippery one. After all, if the question is asked, "How can we tell if a word is 'established' in the language?", many people's reply is likely to be "It's established if it's in the dictionary"—closing a perilous logical circle.

Such caution made commercial sense in the days of hot-metal printing, when a new edition of a large dictionary represented a major capital investment and each new entry had to prove its stamina, chiefly by maintaining its staying power over a period of roughly 10 to 12 years in a broad group of publications. But nowadays, with computerized typesetting, new entries can be put in and with ease taken out again next time around, and the advent of the online dictionary offers at least the prospect of a constantly updated flow of new entries (that could, if desired, be unfiltered). This situation would mirror quite accurately the lexical mobility of English, but it would put a severe strain on the dictionary's traditional role as a repository of "standard" usage.

Modern data-gathering techniques mean that dictionaries can be based on a far wider range of evidence than in the past. Until the late twentieth century their standard evidence base was printed books, newspapers, and journals: language carefully considered and revised. Now we can access far more spontaneous language—spoken English, for example, and the English of the Internet. This too will challenge the traditional standard-setting role of "the dictionary."

The general perception of what is a "dictionary word," a word or expression fit to be entered in the lexicon, will probably broaden out over the coming century, but as long as we have dictionaries in book form (as we assuredly will) there will be several thousand hopefuls that fail the audition each time around. So, in this edition of the *Encarta® Webster's Dictionary of the English Language* we might have had, for example, *Bladerunneresque* "reminiscent of the bleak futuristic vision of the science-fiction film *Blade Runner*," but it missed the cut.

A Brief History of Dictionaries and Dictionary Makers

Jonathon Green

The first dictionary, a very distant ancestor of today's CD-ROMs, online dictionaries, and spellcheckers, was a list of words committed to a clay tablet around 2000 B.C. The conquest of Sumeria (roughly in the region of today's Iraq) by the neighboring territory Akkad required, as such things do, that the conquerors absorb the language of the conquered. In this case the Akkadians were particularly anxious to take on board the sophistication of the Sumerian legal system. So the tablets were filled with glossaries of legal, and soon other, words offering the Sumerian term followed by the Akkadian term.

Such early compilations, however, remained isolated. It was only in the fourth century B.C. that the Greeks took up dictionary making. They feared that the language of Homer was becoming "dead," even to scholars, and began to compile glossaries of his more obscure vocabulary. This same process was repeated later by the Romans, who also were seeking to preserve the language of their "dead" authorities and authors.

From then through the scholars of Byzantium, of the Middle Ages, and of the Renaissance, the flow of dictionaries was maintained, mainly as bilingual glossaries that translated words from one language into another. One of the most ambitious was the *Calepine*, first created by the monk Ambrosio Calepino in 1502. Edition followed edition, and at its peak its massive folio pages encompassed words in no fewer than 11 discrete languages for every single entry.

Precursors to today's English dictionaries first appeared in the eighth century. Four glossaries (the *Corpus*, the *Leiden*, the *Epinal*, and the *Erfurt* (named for the libraries that now hold them) are each dedicated to translating the vocabulary of a single text and were written to give scholars access to what were seen as the harder words of specific, usually ecclesiastical texts, by translating the original Latin into Anglo-Saxon English.

ALPHABETICAL ORDER

Early glossaries were usually based only on "A-order." This meant that all the words starting with the same letter were listed together, but with no attempt to refine the order further. It would take several centuries before full alphabetization was finally in place.

Over subsequent centuries the production of such text-specific lists began to be amalgamated, offering scholars translations of more than one work in the same list. Such lists, it should be noted, were rudimentary. All these dictionaries—some 20 major works between 1440 and 1600—were bilingual, the usual mix being Latin-English, although some involved European languages. One of these, John Florio's *A World of Words* (1598), introduced so many new English words in his translations that it provided a huge step in English dictionary making in itself.

WORDS FOR WORD BOOKS

Among the titles given to word books have been an *abecedarium* (an alphabetical order), an *alveary* (beehive), a *catholicon* (cure-all), an *ortus* (garden), a *medulla* (marrow or pith), a *glossary*, a *manipulus* (a handful), a *sylva* (wood), a *promptuarium*, a *vocabulary*, and a *vulgar* (common thing).

By 1700 *dictionary*, from the medieval Latin *dictionarius*, a repertory of words, had won out, and ever since it has been the predominant term.

In 1604 the first dictionary that defined rather than translated words appeared. Robert Cawdrey's *Table Alphabeticall, Contayning and Teaching the True Writing and Understanding of Hard Usuall English Words* was the first true English–English dictionary. It contained barely 3,000 entries, and its goal was to explain the meanings of difficult words.

Cawdrey had many successors who formed major way stations in the development of lexicography in English. Among the "hard words" lexicographers were John Bullokar (in 1616), Henry Cockeram (1623), Thomas Blount (1656), Edward Philips (1658), and Elisha Coles, whose dictionary, appearing in 1676, would be the first mainstream English work to include slang (the dedicated collection of which had begun in Copland's *Hye Way to the Spittel House* in 1531). These were in response to the emergence in the seventeenth century of a middle class and thus a surge in literacy.

If the seventeenth century had reflected the expansion of literacy beyond the universities and churches, then the eighteenth reflected that of England itself beyond its own territorial borders. The century that saw the expansion and consolidation of the British colonies demanded new efforts to establish English as a major language, specifically as a rival to French. The creation in 1635 of the *Académie Française* and the publication in 1694 of its authoritative *Dictionnaire* promoted much comment across the English Channel. Such literary figures as John Dryden, Robert Hooke, Daniel Defoe, and Jonathan Swift variously called for some form of English Academy and suggested that its primary task would be to produce a purified version of truly standard English.

These ruminations led in 1746 to the commissioning by a group of booksellers (who, as was the custom, were also publishers) of one Samuel Johnson, then best known as an essayist and parliamentary writer for the *Gentleman's Magazine*, to prepare a *Dictionary of the English Language*. That dictionary, which appeared in 1755, represents a great turning point in English-language dictionary making.

Lexicography is an ever developing craft, for the language does not reform and reappear mint-new in time for every successive lexicon. Johnson used his predecessors, especially Nathaniel Bailey, whose own major work, the *Universal Etymological English Dictionary* (published in 1730), provided massive assistance in compiling the basic word lists. Nor did Johnson invent any of the processes seen to such advantage in his work, namely etymology, illustrative citations, and basic guides to pronunciation. All of these had been attempted before, but Johnson brought them together and did so more skillfully than had ever been done before.

Johnson did not, however, fix the language, as he and his publishers had once felt was feasible. Instead, recognizing reality, he would declare that such fantasies were "the dreams of a poet doomed at last to wake a lexicographer" and that thus to pursue perfection was reminiscent of ancient tribes who would "chace the sun, which, when they had reached the hill where he seemed to rest, was still beheld at the same distance from them." Language changes and lexicographers, now as much as then, must reflect such changes in their work. Johnson's decision to accept such a reality has influenced the growth of English ever since.

Corbis
Samuel Johnson

In a nice twist of coincidence, the very first US dictionary, *The School Dictionary* (1798), was written by one Samuel Johnson, a teacher. And others would follow, among them titles from this Johnson and his coeditor the Reverend John Elliott (1800), from another preacher Caleb Alexander (1800), from Richard Coxe (1813) and, in 1807, from Sarah Rowson, a British actor who had quit London and gained a new reputation as a best-selling US novelist.

The first major US dictionary, Noah Webster's two-volume *American Dictionary of the English Language*, appeared in 1828, a little over 20 years after the appearance of his *Compendious Dictionary of the English Language* (1806), which contained 5,000 more words than Johnson's volume. A year later, Webster began work on his 1828 magnum opus. Webster was a New England schoolteacher whose *American Spelling Book*, popularly dubbed the "Blue-Backed Speller" (1783) sold over 70 million copies within a century of its publication, an astounding feat. He was a great pioneer of US English, as opposed to British English. For him the establishment of a national language, based upon but independent of its source, was as politically important as the American Revolution itself. In fact, he called US English "Federal English." In *Dissertations on the English Language* (1789), Webster wrote: "Several circumstances render a

Noah Webster

future separation of the American tongue from the English necessary and unavoidable." The respelling of terms such as *theater* for "theatre" and *color* for "colour" is Webster's legacy, as is his inclusion of meanings of words that applied specifically, and only, to life in North America, for example, *plantation* and *senate*.

The *Oxford English Dictionary* (*OED*) is arguably still the world's greatest dictionary on historical principles (offering the usage history and development of a word as well as definition and highly detailed etymology). Conceived in 1857, it would override a false start (in 1865) to begin once more in 1878 with the appointment of James Murray, a self-educated schoolteacher and philologist, as its editor. The first 352-page section, offering words from *A* to *Ant*, appeared in 1884 and the dictionary was eventually completed in 1928 after Murray's death.

With the exception of Webster, lexicography has never really been a solo craft. Even Johnson had his assistants, the eight "harmless drudges" who did the basic work of compilation, while the *OED* lists dozens of individuals, from Murray's coeditors through to the ranks of subeditors and readers, all enlisted on the great work. Today's dictionaries, the products of publishers (whether academic or popular), are rarely associated with a single individual. Modern lexicography is in every sense a corporate endeavor – the large number of lexicographers and consultants enlisted for this project are typical. Such a finely tuned exercise may have sacrificed a degree of idiosyncrasy (after all, is not the decision by one individual to compile a dictionary, "chasing the panting syllable" as one poet had it, somewhat eccentric in itself?), but has gained an infinity of expertise. It may be less romantic, but today's user wants accuracy and information first.

And not only have dictionaries become available on computer, but computers are central to every stage of the production. The great dictionaries of the past depended on armies of amateur readers, scanning texts for examples of usage. Today's compilers have the great corpora, literally "bodies" of real language, available for consultation. Such a corpus was compiled for this dictionary, ensuring that every nuance of a word's existence can be laid down, and backed up with illustrative quotations. Not only that, but the keyboarding of a great dictionary into a permanent, if evolving, database, renders the great consumers of the lexicographer's time—inserting new and updating old entries and inserting and verifying cross-references—infinitely simpler than the most sophisticated of pre-electronic systems could ever manage.

Perhaps the most important aspect of lexicographic change, and never more so than as illustrated here, is the change in the word list itself. All these earlier dictionaries tried to be language-specific; not so today. World English is the name of the modern game. This dictionary, like its predecessor, is aimed at a worldwide audience. Incorporating multinational expertise in its compilation and in the entries that have been produced, it is proof in itself of the extent to which English has long since burst through its territorial confines.

The Internet, the globally encompassing electronic forum, presents a special challenge for lexicography and its potential enhancement. While the old identity of the "information superhighway" seems to have vanished with the dot-com boom that spawned it, the Internet remains an unrivaled source of language. At its worst it is no more than a vast library still lacking a proper index, but at its best it is a superb repository of infinitely wide-ranging (and continually expanding) source material. And it is undeniable, and telling, that its primary language is English. Setting aside its role as a marketplace, the Net has speeded up the proliferation of language, rendered the formerly arcane massively accessible, and in every way, and quite literally, "spread the word."

For dictionary makers this proliferation is undoubtedly challenging. To assess the state of a globally reaching language is hard enough with no more than the printed word and the visual media to analyze. With the countless "documents" of whatever sort on offer via the Net—be they century-old newspapers or yesterday's hip-hop lyrics—that task is rendered even harder. Yet simultaneously it is hugely empowering. Indeed, some lexicographers suggest that this generation will be the last to go searching among terrestrial libraries for usage examples, with the inevitable pursuit of "first use." In a few decades, with everything digitized, one will need to do no more than perform a search, and every example will be there, first to most recent, online. Whether this will prove optimistic—it will require both dedication and, equally important, extensive funding—remains to be seen. But for anyone working on language, and especially language reference, the potential is hugely exciting. The lexicographer is not and never has been, in Johnson's ironic, now hackneyed phrase, a "harmless drudge." Lexicographers hold a strange position, employed in an unglamorous task, yet occupying a position of power and influence by virtue of defining what the words in our language mean. That those words, once confined to a small elite of scholars, are now the property of many differing millions and available in myriad variations is both a challenge and a reward to the dictionary maker.

ENGLISH AROUND THE WORLD

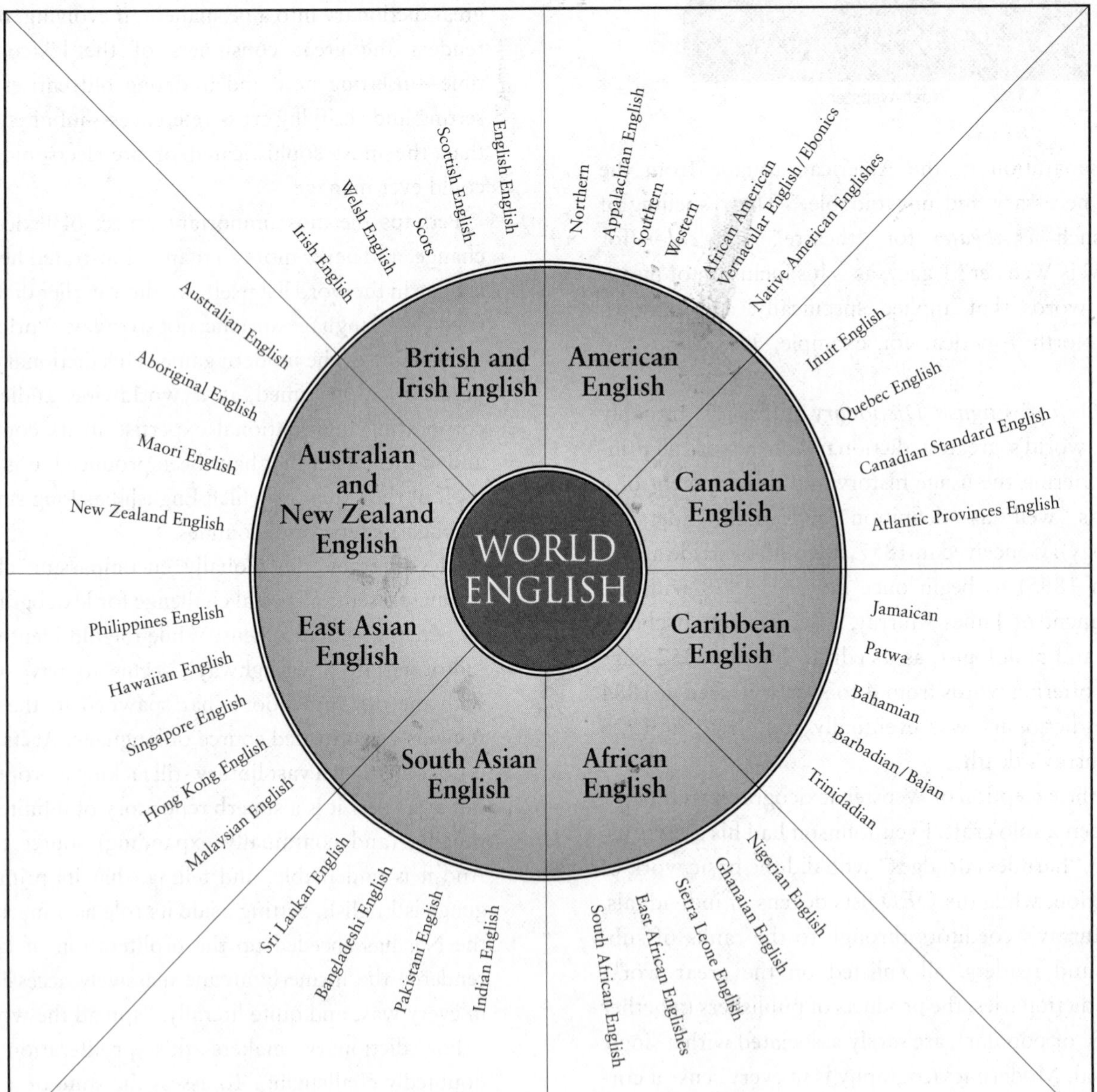

There are many varieties of World English; some of the main ones are included in this diagram.

World English

Tom McArthur

In the early years of a new century and a new millennium, English is the most used—and studied—language in the history of the human race. At the beginning of the twentieth century, it was already one of the foremost languages of the world, because it was the main language of both the British Empire and the United States of America. At that time it had significant competition from other widespread European languages such as French, German, Russian, and Spanish and, beyond Europe, from Mandarin Chinese, Arabic, and Swahili that all still belong, with English, in the prestigious club of world languages. However, since World War II, although all the other world languages have continued to be widely used, English has been alone in becoming—ever more notably with each passing decade—the sole universal language, the world's *lingua franca*.

Noting its growing role, scholars and other observers have for some time been giving distinctive labels to this runaway language. Increasingly, since occasional use in the 1930s, it has come most commonly to be known as "World English." Since around 1980, this term has also been put into the plural, as "World Englishes," so as to highlight proliferating varieties that are often called simply "the Englishes," and, in Asia and Africa, "the New Englishes." Since at least the 1970s, the language complex has also been called "International English," and, in the 1990s, the term "Global English" has proved fashionable, to accompany and blend in with the current economic buzzword *globalization*.

Describing and cataloging any language is difficult, but in the past the relatively limited scope and roles of the world's languages have allowed us to suppose that the grammars, dictionaries, and other works associated with them are comprehensive. But the scale and variety of present-day English do not permit any such comfortable illusion. Even the population statistics of World English are uncertain, ranging hazily from over three hundred million people who are assumed to be native speakers to over a billion users of English of all kinds, from the most informed and fluent to the most casual and halting. The unnumbered varieties and uses of this language (whether thought, spoken, written, typed, printed, broadcast, taped, telephoned, faxed, e-mailed, texted, or disseminated on the World Wide Web) are so complex that no individual, group, or system can catch them all. Even the most extensive and flexible computer corpus currently imaginable cannot encompass all the registers and usages of the standard language, let alone all the rest.

Even so, however, and paradoxically, there is a manifest need to say something as comprehensive as possible about World English, including its immense wealth of words, past, present, and potential. Although the task is fraught with difficulty, publishers of dictionaries must inevitably respond to the challenge, part of which is to acknowledge the nature and impact of the phenomenon being described, and this has been the primary goal of the *Encarta® Webster's Dictionary.*

The *study* of English is an international industry. Tens of thousands of scholars and teachers engage in it throughout the world, instructing a student population of hundreds of millions while producing innumerable books, periodicals, dissertations, articles, reports, conference proceedings, class notes, textbooks, newsletters, and Internet materials. Their total output is more than any of them can digest; indeed, few will see—or even be informed about—every proceeding or document that touches on their special interests *within* the language and its literatures. But again, simply to say this and turn away is not enough. If anything, we now need more guidance and discrimination from the makers of dictionaries than ever: the challenge is now to make even fuller, clearer, and more appropriate dictionaries of English, both benefiting from the technological revolution that has accompanied and helped drive the enlargement of English and acknowledging that English is larger than any of the communities in which it is used.

One outcome of this unique and often unnerving state of affairs is that no one can even think today about who "owns" the language or its many varieties. The English language has become a global resource. As such, it does not owe its existence—or its future—to any nation, group, or individual. Inasmuch as a language belongs to any individual or community, English is the possession of every individual and community that wishes to use it, wherever they are in the world. It is in effect as democratic and universal an institution as humankind has ever possessed.

Aa

a[1] /ay/ (*plural* **a's**), **A** (*plural* **A's** or **As**) *n* **1.** the first letter of the English alphabet, representing a vowel sound **2.** a written representation of the letter "a"

a[2] *symbol* **1.** PHYS acceleration **2.** used to refer to the first vertical row of squares from the left on a chessboard

a[3] *abbr* **1.** about **2.** MEASURE acre **3.** MEASURE are[2]

a[4] *stressed* /ay/; *unstressed* /ə/ CORE MEANING: the indefinite article, used before a singular countable noun to refer to one person or thing not previously known or specified, in contrast with "the," referring to somebody or something known to the listener ○ *I need a new car.*
indef art **1. INDICATES TYPE** used before a noun to indicate that somebody or something has some of the same qualities as the person or thing mentioned ○ *a Hercules* ○ *He's a genius.* **2. ONE** used instead of "one" with words of measurement ○ *a teaspoonful of salt* **3. PER** in each or in every ○ *twice a day* **4. INDICATES SOMEBODY NOT KNOWN PERSONALLY** used to indicate somebody not personally known, but known of ○ *There's a Mr. O'Flynn here to see you.* **5. ANY** used in negative structures to emphasize a complete absence of something ○ *He doesn't have a hope!* [Old English, shortening of *ān* (see ONE)]

USAGE a or **an**? ***A*** is the form of the indefinite article used before words that are pronounced with an initial consonant sound (even if the spelling does not begin with a consonant): *a banana*; *a hunk*; *a ewe*. ***An*** is used before words that begin with a vowel sound (even if an unpronounced consonant comes first): *an elephant*; *an heir*. The same rule regarding sound rather than spelling applies to abbreviations: *a CD* but *an LP*. The practice of using ***an*** before words beginning with *h* and an unstressed syllable (for example, *an hotel*, *an historic occasion*) is falling out of use, and it is much more usual now to hear *a hotel* and *a historic occasion*, with the *h* sounded.

A[1] *symbol* **1.** CHEM activity **2.** BIOCHEM adenine **3.** MEASURE ampere **4.** PHYS mass number **5.** COMPUT 10 (*used in hexadecimal notation*)

A[2] *abbr* **1.** academy **2.** adult **3.** answer

A[3] /ay/ (*plural* **A's** or **As**) *n* **1. "A"-SHAPED OBJECT** something shaped like a letter "A" **2.** MUSIC **6TH NOTE IN C MAJOR** the sixth note of a scale in C major. The A above middle C is often used to tune instruments and is standardized at a frequency of 440 hertz. **3.** MUSIC **SOMETHING THAT PRODUCES A** a string, key, or pipe tuned to produce the note A **4.** MUSIC **SCALE BEGINNING ON A** a scale or key that starts on the note A **5.** MUSIC **WRITTEN SYMBOL OF A** a graphic representation of the tone of A **6.** EDUC **HIGHEST GRADE** the highest grade in a series, e.g., a top grade for academic work ○ *solid As for the semester.* **7.** MED **HUMAN BLOOD TYPE** a human blood type of the ABO system, containing the A antigen. Somebody with this type of blood can donate to people of the same group or of the AB group, and can receive blood from people with this type or with type O. ◇ **from A to B** from one place to another ◇ **from A to Z 1.** extremely thoroughly **2.** all the way from the beginning to the end

A., Å *symbol* MEASURE angstrom

a-[1] *prefix* in a particular place, condition, or manner ○ *abed* ○ *adrift* ○ *aloud* [Old English, < *an*, alternative for *on* (see ON)]

a-[2] *prefix* without, not ○ *agnostic* ○ *amoral* [< Greek]

A1, A-1, A-one *adj* **1.** in excellent or first-rate condition (*informal*) **2.** describes a boat as being well equipped and in excellent condition [Mid-19C. < Lloyd's Register, an annual British shipping list; *A* indicated a hull in first-class condition, *1* that the ship was well-provisioned and well-equipped]

aa /aa aa/ *n* solidified lava with a rough jagged surface and sharp angular features [Mid-19C. < Hawaiian *a-'a*]

AA *abbr* **1.** EDUC achievement age **2.** ARMS air-to-air

A.A. *abbr* **1.** Alcoholics Anonymous **2.** ARMS antiaircraft **3.** *US* EDUC Associate of Arts

AAA *abbr* /trìpp'l áy/ **1.** American Automobile Association **2.** antiaircraft artillery

AAAL *abbr US* American Academy of Arts and Letters

AAAS *abbr US* American Association for the Advancement of Science

AAF *abbr US* Army Air Forces

AAFC *abbr* GOV Agriculture and Agri-Food Canada

aah *interj, vi, n* another spelling of **ah**

aa·jaa *n Carib* another spelling of **aja**

aa·jee *n Carib* another spelling of **aji**

Aal·to /aaltō/, **Alvar** (1898–1976) Finnish architect. He designed the Helsinki Hall of Culture (1958) and was noted for his use of organic materials and forms. Full name **Aalto, Hugo Alvar Henrik**

AAM *abbr* ARMS air-to-air missile

A & M *abbr* EDUC Agricultural and Mechanical

A & R *abbr* MUSIC, RECORDING artists and repertoire

aa·pa /aapə/ *n S Asia* somebody's elder sister (*used by Muslims*) [< Urdu *āpa*]

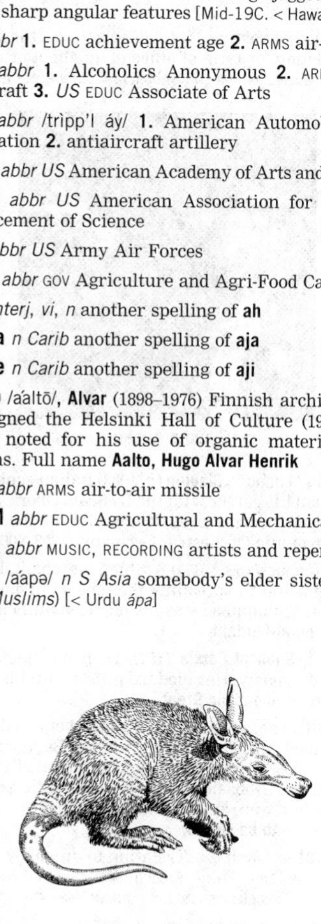

aardvark

aard·vark /aard vaark/ *n* a burrowing mammal with a long snout, powerful claws, long tongue, and heavy tail. Native to: southern Africa. Latin name: *Orycteropus afer*. [Late 18C. < Afrikaans, "earth pig"]

aard·wolf /aard wòolf/ (*plural* **-wolves** /-wòolvz/) *n* a striped nocturnal mammal, related to the hyena, that feeds mainly on termites. Native to: southern Africa. Latin name: *Proteles cristatus*. [Mid-19C. < Afrikaans, "earth wolf"]

aargh /aa/ *interj* used to express annoyance or disgust at something or somebody (*informal; often used humorously*) [Late 18C. Lengthened form of AH]

Aar·hus another spelling of **Århus**

Aar·on /érrən/ *n* in the Bible, the first Jewish high priest and elder brother of Moses. With Moses, he led the Israelites out of Egypt but died before reaching the Promised Land.

Aar·on /érrən/, **Hank** (*b.* 1934) US baseball player. He broke many batting records, including Babe Ruth's career total of home runs, during a 23-year career with the Milwaukee Braves, Atlanta Braves, and Milwaukee Brewers. Full name **Aaron, Henry Louis**

> "I've got a bat...I let the fellow with the ball do the fretting."
> [Attributed to Hank Aaron]

Aar·on's beard *n* PLANTS same as **rose of Sharon** (sense 2) [After AARON, who had a long beard (Psalms 133:2), because of the flower's prominent hairy stamens]

Aar·on's rod *n* a tall smooth-stemmed plant. Flowers: yellow. Native to: Asia, Europe, North America. [After the rod belonging to AARON, said to have flowered (Numbers 17:8)]

AARP *n US* an organization that promotes the interests of people over 50 years old [Abbreviation of its former name *American Association of Retired Persons*]

aar·ti *n, v* HINDUISM another spelling of **arti**

AAS *abbr US* **1.** American Academy of Sciences **2.** EDUC Associate in Applied Sciences

AAU *abbr US* Amateur Athletic Union

AAUP *abbr* American Association of University Professors

AAVE *abbr* African American Vernacular English

Ab *n* CALENDAR, JUDAISM same as **Av**

AB[1] *abbr* Alberta

AB[2] *n* a human blood type of the ABO system, containing the A and B antigens. Somebody with this type of blood can donate to people of the same group and receive blood from people with this type or with type O, A, or B.

a.b. *abbr* BASEBALL at bat

A.B. *abbr US* EDUC Bachelor of Arts

ab- *prefix* away from, off ○ *aboral* ○ *abaxial* [< Latin < Indo-European, "off, away"]

a·ba /ə baa, a-/ *n* **1.** a cloth made in Syria using hair from goats or camels **2.** a loose sleeveless outer garment worn by boys and men in North Africa and Southwest Asia [Early 19C. < Arabic *'abā*]

ABA *abbr* **1.** *also* **A.B.A.** American Bar Association **2.** American Basketball Association **3.** American Booksellers Association

ab·a·ca /àbbə kaa, ábbəkə/ *n* **1.** TEXTILES same as **Manila hemp 2.** a large plant from whose leaves Manila hemp is produced. It is related to bananas. Latin name: *Musa textilis*. [Mid-18C. Via Spanish < Tagalog *abaká*]

ab·a·ci MATH, ARCHIT plural of **abacus**

a·back /ə bák/ *adv* **1.** SAILING **WITH WIND BLOWING TOWARD BOW** with the wind blowing against the forward part of a sail or sails, so that a vessel cannot move ahead **2. BACKWARD** backward or toward the back (*archaic*) **3.** *Carib* **FORMERLY** in the past [Old English *on bæc* "toward the back, backward"] ◇ **aback of** *Carib* in back of ◇ **take somebody aback** to surprise somebody and make him or her unsure how to react

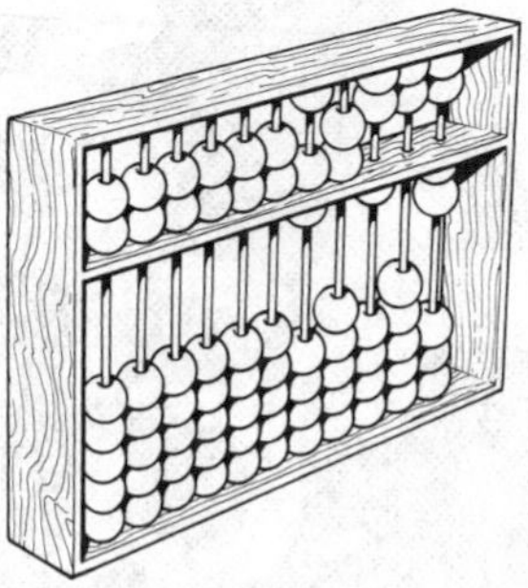

abacus

ab·a·cus /ábbəkəss/ (*plural* **-cus·es** or **-ci** /-sī, -kī/) *n* **1.** a mechanical device for making calculations consisting of a frame mounted with rods along which beads or balls are moved **2.** a flat slab at the top of an architectural column [14C. Via Latin < Greek *abakos* "board strewn with dust on which to draw or write" (later "slab, table")]

A·ba·dan /aàbə daán, àbbə dán/, **Ā·bā·dān** city in southwestern Iran. It is a major petroleum-refining and shipping center. Population: 296,081 (1996).

a·baft /ə báft/ *adv* toward the rear of a boat ■ *prep* to the rear of an area on a boat [14C. < Old English *an* + *be* (see BY[1]) + *æftan* "behind"]

A·ba·kan /aàbə kaán/ capital of the autonomous republic of Khakassia in eastern Russia. Population: 168,047 (1999).

ab·a·lo·ne /àbbə lṓnee, ábbə lṓnee/ *n* an edible invertebrate ocean animal that breathes through holes in its ear-shaped shell. The pearly interior of the shell is used for making jewelry. Genus: *Haliotis*. [Mid-19C. Via American Spanish *abulón* < Shoshonean *aulun*]

ab·am·pere /ab ám pair/ *n* the centimeter-gram-second unit of electromagnetic current equal to ten amperes

a·ban·don /ə bándən/ *v* (**-doned, -don·ing, -dons**) **1.** *vt* LEAVE SOMEBODY BEHIND to leave somebody or something behind for others to look after, especially somebody or something meant to be a personal responsibility ○ *pets abandoned by their owners* **2.** *vt* LEAVE PLACE BECAUSE OF DANGER to leave a place or vehicle, especially for reasons of safety and without intending to return soon ○ *had to abandon their vehicles in the snow* **3.** *vt* RENOUNCE SOMETHING to renounce or reject something previously done or used ○ *The practice was abandoned long ago.* **4.** *vt* GIVE UP CONTROL OF SOMETHING to surrender control of something completely to somebody else ○ *As troops closed in the town was abandoned to its fate.* **5.** *vt* HALT SOMETHING IN PROGRESS to stop doing something before it is completed, usually because of difficulty or danger ○ *abandoning the rescue attempt* **6. a·ban·don your·self** *vr* GIVE IN TO EMOTION to give yourself over to a powerful emotion ○ *He abandoned himself to his grief.* ■ *n* LACK OF RESTRAINT complete lack of inhibition or self-restraint [14C. < Old French *abandoner* < *a bandon* "under control" < Latin *bannum* "proclamation"] —**a·ban·don·ment** *n*

a·ban·doned /ə bándənd/ *adj* **1.** EMPTY left empty because of not being used or lived in anymore **2.** ALONE left alone without being cared for or supported **3.** UNRESTRAINED without restraint or self-control

a·ban·don·ment op·tion *n* in a contract, a clause relating to the possibility of abandoning a project and terminating the contract earlier than originally planned

a·ban·don·ment val·ue *n* the value that can be realized by terminating a business project or disposing of a business before its anticipated maturity

a·base /ə báyss/ (**a·based, a·bas·ing, a·bas·es**) *v* **1.** *vt* to make somebody feel belittled or degraded **2. a·base your·self** *vr* to behave in a way that lowers your sense of dignity or self-esteem [14C. < Old French *abaissier* < *baissier* "to lower" < Latin *bassus* "short of stature"] —**a·base·ment** *n*

a·bash /ə básh/ (**a·bashed, a·bash·ing, a·bash·es**) *vt* to make somebody feel ashamed, embarrassed, or uncomfortable [14C. < Anglo-Norman *abaiss-* < Old French *baïr* "astound"] —**a·bash·ment** *n*

a·bate /ə báyt/ (**a·bat·ed, a·bat·ing, a·bates**) *v* **1.** *vti* BECOME LESS to lessen or make something lessen gradually (*formal or literary*) **2.** *vti* LAW END to suppress or end a nuisance, act, or writ, or be suppressed or ended **3.** *vt* FIN REDUCE SOMETHING to lower the amount or rate of something such as a tax (*formal*) [13C. < Old French *abatre* "beat down" < Latin *batt(u)ere* "fight, beat"] —**a·bate·ment** *n*

ab·a·tis /ábbə teè, ábbətiss, ə báttiss/ (*plural* **-tis** /ábbə teèz/ or **-tis·es** /ábbətissəz, ə báttissəz/) *n* a rampart made of felled trees placed so that their bent or sharpened branches face out toward the enemy [Mid-18C. < French < Old French *abatre* "beat down, fell" (see ABATE)]

ab·at·toir /ábbə twaàr, -twaár/ *n* FOOD INDUST same as **slaughterhouse** [Early 19C. < French < *abattre* "fell" < Old French *abatre* (see ABATE)]

ab·ax·i·al /ab áksee əl/ *adj* used to describe the underside of a leaf or other surface that faces away from the stem

Ab·ba /ábbə/ *n* **1.** in the Bible, a name used to address God **2.** in the Syrian Orthodox and Coptic Churches, a title given to bishops and patriarchs [14C. Via ecclesiastical Latin and New Testament Greek < Aramaic *'abbā* "father"]

ab·ba·cy /ábbəssee/ (*plural* **-cies**) *n* the rank, jurisdiction, or term of office of an abbot or abbess [15C. < ecclesiastical Latin *abbacia* < *abbat-* (see ABBOT)]

AKG London

Claudio Abbado

Ab·ba·do /ə baádō/, **Claudio** (*b.* 1933) Italian conductor. He began his career with the La Scala Opera, Milan, Italy, and became artistic director of the Berlin Philharmonic Orchestra, Germany (1989–2002).

Ab·bas /ábbəss/ (566?–653) Arabian merchant. He was instrumental in spreading the tenets of Islam. The prophet Muhammad was his nephew. Full name **Al-Abbas ibn al-Muttalib**

Ab·bas I, Shah of Persia (1571–1629) member of the Safavid dynasty. He ruled from 1588 until his death. Known as **Abbas the Great**

Ab·ba·sid /ə bássid, ábbə sìd/ *n* a member of a dynasty that ruled an Islamic empire from Baghdad from 750 to 1258. Descended from Muhammad's uncle, Abbas, the Abbasids often wielded little political power but were great patrons of Islamic art and culture. —**Ab·ba·sid** *adj*

ab·ba·tial /ə báysh'l/ *adj* relating to an abbey, abbot, or abbess [Late 17C. < French, or < medieval Latin *abbatialis*, both < ecclesiastical Latin *abbat-* (see ABBOT)]

~~**abbatoir**~~ incorrect spelling of **abattoir**

ab·bé /á bay/ *n* an abbot or member of a religious order in a French-speaking area [Mid-16C. Via French < ecclesiastical Latin *abbat-* (see ABBOT)]

ab·bess /ábbəss/ *n* the nun in charge of a convent [13C. < Old French *abbesse* < ecclesiastical Latin *abbat-* (see ABBOT)]

Ab·be·ville /ábbə vìl, -veèl/ city in southwestern Louisiana, southwest of Baton Rouge. Population: 11,778 (2002 estimate).

Ab·be·vil·le·an /ab víllee ən, àbbə-/ *adj* relating to or typical of early Lower Paleolithic culture in Europe [Mid-20C. < French *Abbevillien*, after the town of *Abbeville* in N France]

ab·bey /ábbee/ (*plural* **-beys**) *n* **1.** a building or buildings occupied by monks under an abbot, or nuns under an abbess, especially the church building **2.** a church that is or was used by a community of monks or nuns [13C. < Old French *ab(b)eïe* < ecclesiastical Latin *abbat-* (see ABBOT)]

Ab·bey /ábbee/, **Edwin Austin** (1852–1911) US painter and illustrator who produced panels for the Boston Public Library (1890–1902) and murals at the Pennsylvania state capitol (1911)

ab·bot /ábbət/ *n* the monk in charge of a monastery [Pre-12C. Via ecclesiastical Latin *abbat-*, stem of *abbas* < Aramaic *'abbā* "father"] —**ab·bot·ship** *n*

Ab·bott /ábbət/, **Berenice** (1898–1991) US photographer who was known especially for her portrait photography and who documented New York City for the Federal Art Project in the 1930s

> "Photography can never grow up if it imitates some other medium. It has to walk alone; it has to be itself."
> [Berenice Abbott, "It Has to Walk Alone," *Infinity*, 1951]

Ab·bott, George Francis (1887–1995) US playwright, producer, and director. He was a major figure in the Broadway theater, and his productions included *Call Me Madam* (1950), *The Pajama Game* (1954), and *Damn Yankees* (1955).

> "Very few plays are any good and *no* first plays are any good."
> [George Francis Abbott, *Saturday Evening Post*, 1955]

Ab·bott, Sir John (1821–93) Canadian politician. He was prime minister of Canada (1891–92) and the mayor of Montreal (1887–88). Full name **Abbott, Sir John Joseph Caldwell**

abbr, abbr., abbrev. *abbr* abbreviation

ab·bre·vi·ate /ə breèvee ayt/ (**-at·ed, -at·ing, -ates**) *vt* **1.** to shorten a word by leaving out some of its letters or sounds **2.** to shorten a piece of text by cutting sections or paraphrasing it [15C. < Latin *abbreviat-*, past participle of *abbreviare* "shorten" < *brevis* "short"] —**ab·bre·vi·a·tor** *n*

ab·bre·vi·a·tion /ə breèvee áysh'n/ *n* **1.** a shortened form of a word or phrase **2.** the shortening of a word or phrase to be used to represent the full form

USAGE Types of **abbreviations**: There are four main kinds of abbreviations: shortenings, contractions, initialisms, and acronyms. **1 Shortenings** of words usually consist of the first few letters of the full form and are usually spelled with a final period when they are still regarded as abbreviations, for example, *cont.* = continued, *in* = inch. In the cases when they form words in their own right, the period is omitted, for example, *hippo* = hippopotamus, *limo* = limousine. Such shortenings are often but not always informal. Some become the standard forms, and the full forms are then regarded as formal or technical, for example, *bus* = omnibus, *taxi* = taxicab, *deli* = delicatessen, *zoo* = zoological garden. Sometimes shortenings are altered to facilitate their pronunciation or spelling: *bike* = *bicycle* **2 Contractions** are abbreviated forms in which letters from the middle of the full form have been omitted, for example, *Dr.* = doctor, *St.* = saint or street. Such forms are invariably followed by a period. Another kind of contraction is the type with an apostrophe marking the omission of letters: *can't* = cannot, *didn't* = did not, *you've* = you have. **3 Initialisms** are made up of the initial letters of words and are pronounced as separate letters: *CIA* (or *C.I.A.*), *NYC*, *pm* (or *p.m.*), *U.S.* (or *US*). Practice varies with regard to periods, with current usage increasingly in favor of omitting them, especially when the initialism consists entirely of capital letters. **4 Acronyms** are initialisms that have become words in their own right, or similar words formed from parts of several words. They are pronounced as words rather than as a series of letters, for example, *AIDS*, *laser*, *scuba*, *UNESCO*, and do not have periods. In many cases the acronym becomes the standard term and the full form is only used in explanatory contexts.

ABC[1] *n UK* same as **ABCs** ◇ **as easy as ABC** extremely easy

ABC[2] *abbr* **1.** Advanced Booking Charter **2.** American Broadcasting Company **3.** ARMS atomic, biological, and chemical

ab·cou·lomb /ab kōō lòm, -kōō lȫm/ *n* the centimeter-gram-second unit of electrical charge equal to ten coulombs

ABCs *npl* **1.** the alphabet, especially in referring to the basic aspects of reading and writing ○ *learned her ABCs* **2.** the basic facts or essential parts of a subject ○ *the ABCs of carpentry*

ABD *n* a doctoral candidate who has completed all requirements for a degree except the submission of a completed thesis. Full form **all but dissertation**

Abd al-Ha·mid /àb daal hámmid/ ➧ **Abdulhamid II**

ab·di·cate /ábdi kàyt/ (**-cat·ed, -cat·ing, -cates**) *v* **1.** *vti* to give up a high office formally or officially, especially the throne **2.** *vt* to fail to fulfill a duty or responsibility ○ *The company seems to have abdicated all responsibility for the damage.* [Mid-16C. < Latin *abdicat-*, past participle of *abdicare* "renounce" < *dicare* "proclaim"] —**ab·di·ca·tion** /àbdi káysh'n/ *n* —**ab·di·ca·tor** *n*

ab·do·men /ábdəmən/ *n* **1.** BODY SECTION CONTAINING STOMACH the part of the body of a vertebrate that contains the stomach, intestines, and other organs. In mammals it is situated between the pelvis and the thorax. **2.** BELLY the surface of the body of a vertebrate around the stomach **3.** INSECTS REAR PART OF INSECT the elongated portion of the body of an arthropod, located behind the thorax. It is usually segmented. [Mid-16C. < Latin] —**ab·dom·i·nal** /ab dómmin'l/ *adj*

ab·du·cens nerve /ab dóoss'nz-, ab dyóoss'nz-/, **ab·duc·ent nerve** /ab dóoss'nt-, ab dyóoss'nt-/ *n* a nerve conveying impulses from the brain to the muscle that moves the eye laterally in its socket, one of a pair of cranial nerves [*Abducens* < modern Latin, present participle of *abducere* (see ABDUCT)]

ab·duct /ab dúkt/ (**-duct·ed, -duct·ing, -ducts**) *vt* **1.** to take somebody away by force or deception **2.** to pull something, e.g., a muscle, away from the midpoint or midline of the body or of a limb [Early 17C. < Latin *abduct-*, past participle of *abducere* "lead out" < *ducere* "lead"] —**ab·duc·tion** *n*

ab·duc·tor /ab dúktər/ *n* **1.** somebody who takes somebody else away by force or deception **2.** a muscle that pulls the body or a limb away from a midpoint or midline

Ab·dul·ha·mid II /àbdòol hámmid/ (1842–1918) Ottoman sultan. He suspended the constitution (1877) and fought Western influences. He was deposed by the Young Turks' revolt (1909).

Ab·dul-Jab·bar /ab dòol jə báar/, **Kareem** (*b.* 1947) US basketball player. He retired in 1989 as the NBA's all-time leading scorer. Born **Alcindor, Ferdinand Lewis, Jr.**

> "I've had enough success for two lifetimes. My success is talent put together with hard work and luck."
> [Kareem Abdul-Jabbar, *Star*; May 1986]

Ab·dul·lah /ab dóollə/ (*b.* 1939) prime minister of Malaysia. A member of the United Malays National Organization party, he entered parliament in 1978, became deputy prime minister in 1999, and prime minister in 2003. Full name **Datak Seri Abdullah Ahmad Badani**

Ab·dul·lah II /ab dóollə/ (*b.* 1962) king of Jordan. He was commander of the Jordanian army's Special Forces and succeeded his father Hussein in 1999. Full name **Abdullah bin Hussein**

Ab·dul·lah et Taa·i·sha /-et taa eésha/ (1846–99) Sudanese nationalist resistance leader who led the uprising against the Egyptian administration of Sudan and was defeated by Lord Horatio Kitchener (1898)

Ab·dul·lah ibn Hu·sein /ab dóollə ib'n hōo sáyn/ (1882–1951) king of Jordan. He was emir of Transjordan (1921–46) and the first king of the modern state of Jordan (1946–51).

Ab·dul Rah·man /ab dòol ráamən/, **Tunku** (1903–90) Malayan politician. He was the first prime minister of the Federation of Malaya (1957–63) and of Malaysia (1963–70).

a·beam /ə beém/ *adv* to or at the side of a boat or aircraft, especially at right angles to its length

a·be·ce·dar·i·an /ày bee see dérree ən/ *n* somebody learning the basics of literacy or a subject [Early 17C. < medieval Latin *abecedarium* "book containing the alphabet" < the names of the first four letters of the alphabet]

a·bed /ə béd/ *adv* in or confined to bed (*archaic*)

A·bed·ne·go /ə bédnə gṓ/ *n* in the Bible, one of Daniel's companions thrown into the furnace of Nebuchadnezzar II (Daniel 3:12–20)

a·beer *n* HINDUISM another spelling of **abir**

A·bel /áyb'l/ *n* in the Bible, a shepherd and the second son of Adam and Eve, who was killed by his brother Cain (Genesis 4)

Ab·e·lard /ábbə laàrd, aàbə laár/, **Peter** (1079–1142) French philosopher and theologian whose correspondence with his pupil and lover Héloïse became a literary classic

> "We call the intention good which is right in itself, but the action is good, not because it contains within it some good, but because it issued from a good intention."
> [Peter Abelard, *Abailard's Ethics*; 1935, tr. J. McCallum]

a·bele /ə beél/ *n* TREES same as **white poplar** (sense 1) [13C. Directly or via Dutch *abeel* < Old French *a(u)bel* < Latin *albus* "white"]

a·be·li·a /ə beélee ə/ *n* a widespread ornamental bush. Flowers: white to purple, tubular. Native to: East Asia. Genus: *Abelia.* [Mid-19C. < modern Latin, after Clarke *Abel* (1780–1826), English botanist]

A·be·lian group /ə beélyən-/ *n* an algebraic group in which the result of the operation is independent of the sequence of the operands, e.g., ab = ba or a+b = b+a [Mid-19C. After Niels *Abel* (1802–29), Norwegian mathematician]

a·bel·mosk /áyb'l mòsk/ *n* a tropical plant of the mallow family with yellow-and-red flowers. Native to: Asia. Latin name: *Abelmoschus moschatus.* [Late 18C Via modern Latin *abelmoschus* < Arabic *abu'l misk* "father of musk"]

Ab·e·na·ki /aàbə naákee, àbbə nákee/ (*plural same* or **-kis**), **Ab·na·ki** /aàb naákee, àb nákee/ *n* a member of a Native North American people who once lived throughout New England and southeastern Canada, but who now live in Maine and southern Quebec [Early 18C. Via French *Abénaqui* < Montagnais *ou-abanăkionek* "people of the eastern country"] —**Ab·e·na·ki** *adj*

ABEND /áb ènd/ *n* **1.** *also* **ab·end** a sudden failure of a computer program. Full form **abnormal end 2.** used in the subject line of e-mails to warn correspondents of an imminent loss of Internet access. Full form **absent by enforced Net deprivation**

A·be·o·ku·ta /àybee ō kóotə/ city and port in southwestern Nigeria. It is the capital of Ogun state. Population: 416,800 (1995).

Ab·er·deen /ábbər deén, àbbər deén/ **1.** town northeast of Baltimore, Maryland, near Aberdeen Proving Ground, a military testing base. Population: 14,018 (2002 estimate). **2.** city in northeastern South Dakota in the James River valley. Population: 24,312 (2002 estimate). **3.** city and port in western Washington, situated where the Chehalis River flows into Grays Harbor. Population: 16,271 (2002 estimate). **4.** city, port, and industrial center in northeastern Scotland, located at the mouth of the Dee and Don rivers. It is known as the Granite City as many of its buildings are constructed of granite. Population: 212,125 (2001). —**Ab·er·don·i·an** /àbbər dṓnee ən/ *n, adj*

Ab·er·deen An·gus (*plural same* or **Ab·er·deen An·gus·es**) *n Can, UK* a cow belonging to a shorthaired, black, hornless breed of beef cattle. US term **Angus**[1] [Mid-19C. After *Aberdeenshire* and *Angus*, counties in Scotland where the breed originated]

Ab·er·deen·shire /ábbər deén sheér, àbbər deén-/ Scottish administrative county since 1998. The county headquarters are in Aberdeen. Area: 1,971 sq. mi./5,103 sq. km.

Ab·er·nath·y /ábbər nàthee/, **Ralph David** (1926–90) US civil rights leader who succeeded Martin Luther King, Jr. as leader of the Southern Christian Leadership Conference (SCLC) (1968–77).

ab·er·rant /ə bérrənt/ *adj* deviating from what is normal or desirable [Mid-16C. < Latin *aberrant-*, present participle of *aberrare* (see ABERRATION)] —**ab·er·rance** *n* —**ab·er·rant·ly** *adv*

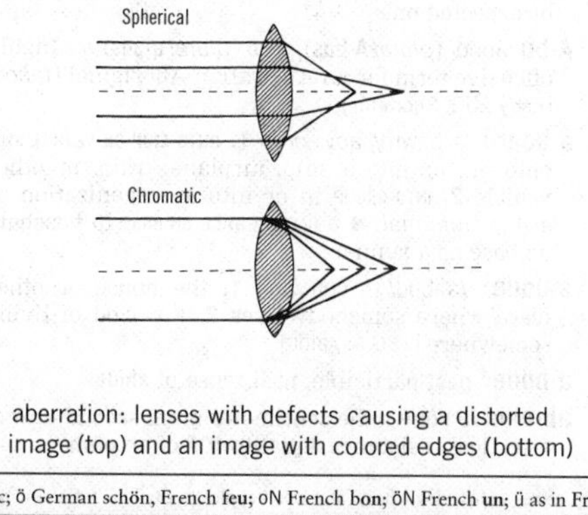

aberration: lenses with defects causing a distorted image (top) and an image with colored edges (bottom)

ab·er·ra·tion /àbbə ráysh'n/ *n* **1.** DEVIATION a departure from what is normal or desirable ○ *in a moment of aberration* **2.** LAPSE a temporary departure from somebody's normal mental state **3.** OPTICS OPTICAL DEFECT a defect in a lens or mirror, causing a distorted image or one with colored edges **4.** ASTRON APPARENT DISPLACEMENT IN STAR'S POSITION a small periodic change in the apparent position of a star or other astronomical object, caused by the motion of the Earth around the Sun [Late 16C. < Latin *aberration-* < *aberrare* "go astray" < *errare* "wander, err"] —**ab·er·ra·tion·al** *adj*

A·ber·yst·wyth /àbbə ríst wìth/ seaside resort and university city in Ceredigion, Wales. Population: 11,154 (1991).

a·bet /ə bét/ (**a·bet·ted, a·bet·ting, a·bets**) *vt* to assist somebody to do something, especially something illegal [14C. < Old French *abeter* "urge, stimulate" < *beter* "hound, drive on"] —**a·bet·tor** *n*

a·bey·ance /ə báy ənss/ *n* **1.** temporary inactivity or nonoperation ○ *a law that has been in abeyance for some time* **2.** a condition in which legal ownership of an estate has not been established [Late 16C. < Old French *abeance* "expectation, desire" < *abaer* "desire" < *baer* "gape" < medieval Latin *batare*] —**a·bey·ant** *adj*

ab·far·ad /ab fárr ad, -əd/ *n* the centimeter-gram-second unit of electrical capacitance equal to 10^9 farads

ab·hen·ry /ab hénree/ (*plural* **-ries**) *n* the centimeter-gram-second unit of electrical conductance equal to 10^{-9} of a henry

ab·hor /ab háwr/ (**-horred, -hor·ring, -hors**) *vt* to disapprove of or reject something very strongly [15C. < Latin *abhorrere* "shrink back in horror" < *horrere* "shudder, bristle"] —**ab·hor·rer** *n*

ab·hor·rence /ab háwrənss/ *n* **1.** a feeling of intense disapproval of something **2.** somebody or something that is strongly disapproved of ○ *The mere idea was an abhorrence to her.*

SYNONYMS See *dislike.*

ab·hor·rent /ab háwrənt/ *adj* **1.** arousing strong feelings of repugnance or disapproval ○ *a practice abhorrent to nearly everyone* **2.** incompatible with or conflicting with something (*literary*) —**ab·hor·rent·ly** *adv*

a·bide /ə bíd/ (**a·bode** /ə bṓd/ or **a·bid·ed, a·bode** or **a·bid·ed, a·bid·ing, a·bides**) *v* **1.** *vt* TOLERATE SOMETHING to find somebody or something acceptable or bearable ○ *couldn't abide his superior attitude* **2.** *vi* DWELL to live or reside in a place (*archaic*) **3.** *vt* AWAIT SOMETHING to wait for somebody or something (*archaic*) **4.** *vt* WITHSTAND SOMETHING to endure or withstand something (*archaic*) [Old English *ābīdan* "wait for, expect" < *bīdan* "wait" (see BIDE)] —**a·bid·ance** *n* —**a·bid·er** *n*
abide by *vt* to comply with or act in accordance with something such as a decision or rule ○ *Applicants must agree to abide by the rules.*

a·bid·ing /ə bíding/ *adj* permanent or long-lasting ○ *my abiding memory of her* —**a·bid·ing·ly** *adv*

Ab·i·djan /àbbi jaán/ cultural and commercial capital of the Côte d'Ivoire, in the southeastern part of the country. Population: 1,929,079 (1988).

ab·i·et·ic ac·id /àbbee èttik-/ *n* a naturally occurring yellowish powder. Source: rosin. Use: varnishes, lacquers, soaps. Formula: $C_{20}H_{30}O_2$. [< Latin *abiet-* "fir," from which rosin is obtained]

Ab·i·gail /ábbi gàyl/ *n* in the Bible, a woman who averted an attack by David and his followers by taking provisions to them. She later married David (1 Samuel 25).

ABIL *abbr Can* FIN allowable business investment loss

Ab·i·lene /ábbə leén/ **1.** city in east-central Kansas on the banks of the Great Smoky Hill River. Population: 6,438 (2002 estimate). **2.** city in central Texas. It is a center for agriculture and the oil industry. Population: 115,225 (2002 estimate).

a·bil·i·ty /ə bíllətee/ (*plural* **-ties**) *n* **1.** BEING ABLE a natural tendency to do something successfully or well ○ *The vehicle has the ability to perform well on really rough terrain.* **2.** INTELLIGENCE OR COMPETENCE a high degree of intelligence or competence ○ *We need people of your ability.* **3.** NATURAL GIFT FOR SOMETHING a particular gift for doing something well ○ *a student with impressive musical abilities* [14C. Via Old French *ablete* < Latin *habilitas* "suitability, aptness" < *habilis* (see ABLE)]

SYNONYMS ***ability, skill, competence, aptitude, talent, capacity, capability***

CORE MEANING: the necessary skill, knowledge, or experience to do something

ability a natural tendency to do something successfully or well ○ *an event open to people of all ages and abilities* ○ *Honeybees show a remarkable ability to respond collectively to external stimuli.* **skill** the ability to do something well gained through training or experience ○ *She made all the arrangements with consummate skill and professionalism.* ○ *good communication skills* **competence** the ability to do something well, measured against a standard, especially ability acquired through experience or training ○ *the professional competence built up over the preceding 20 years* ○ *has reached a high level of competence in arithmetic* **aptitude** a natural tendency to do something well, especially one that can be further developed ○ *These students show a natural aptitude for mechanical construction.* **talent** an unusual natural ability to do something well, especially in artistic areas that can be developed by training ○ *had considerable talent as a teacher, as well as in music* ○ *a talent for modeling with clay* **capacity** mental or physical ability for something or to do something ○ *his youthful energy and capacity for hard work* ○ *a limited capacity to sustain interest in politics* **capability** the power or practical ability necessary for doing something ○ *It is beyond our official capability to influence these things.* ○ *the relationship between a company's size and its technological capabilities*

ab in·i·ti·o /àbbi níshee ō/ *adv* **1.** from the beginning (*formal*) **2.** without any previous knowledge of a subject being studied ○ *study Spanish ab initio* [Early 17C. < Latin]

a·bi·o·gen·e·sis /ày bī ō jénnəsiss/ *n* the hypothesis that life can come into being from nonliving materials [Late 19C. < Greek *abios* "without life" < *bios* "life"] —**a·bi·o·ge·net·ic** /ày bī ō jə néttik/ *adj* —**a·bi·o·ge·net·i·cal** *adj* —**a·bi·o·ge·nist** /-jénnist/ *n*

a·bi·ot·ic /ày bī óttik/ *adj* **1.** describes the physical and chemical aspects of an organism's environment **2.** not containing or supporting life —**a·bi·o·sis** /-ōssiss/ *n* —**a·bi·ot·ic·al·ly** *adv*

a·bir /a beér/, **a·beer** *n* the red-purple dye thrown on people during the Hindu Holi festival [Late 20C. Via Hindi < Arabic, "mica powder"]

ab·ject /áb jèkt, ab jékt/ *adj* **1.** MISERABLE allowing no hope of improvement or relief ○ *abject poverty* **2.** HUMBLE extremely or excessively humble, e.g., in making an apology or request ○ *an abject apology* **3.** DESPICABLE utterly despicable or contemptible ○ *abject cruelty* [15C. < Latin *abjectus*, past participle of *abjicere* "throw away, reject" < *jacere* "throw"] —**ab·jec·tion** /ab jéksh'n/ *n* —**ab·ject·ly** *adv* —**ab·ject·ness** *n*

ab·jure /ab jóor/ (**-jured, -jur·ing, -jures**) *vt* **1.** to give up a previously held belief, especially formally or solemnly **2.** to abstain from, reject, or avoid something (*literary*) [15C. < Latin *abjurare* "deny on oath" < *jurare* "swear"] —**ab·ju·ra·tion** /àbjə ráysh'n/ *n* —**ab·jur·er** *n*

Ab·khaz /ab kaáz/ *n* an Abkhaz-Adyghean language spoken in the Republic of Georgia. Native speakers: 80,000–100,000. [Mid-19C. After a territory in the Caucasus] —**Ab·khaz** *adj*

Ab·khaz-Ad·y·ghe·an /-aadee gáy ən/ *n* a group of Caucasian languages spoken in Georgia and southern Russia —**Ab·khaz-Ad·y·ghe·an** *adj*

Ab·kha·zi·a /ab káyzhə, -zhee ə/ autonomous republic in the Republic of Georgia, bordered to the north by Russia and to the southwest by the Black Sea. Area: 3,300 sq. mi./8,600 sq. km. Population: 537,500 (1990).

ab·late /ə bláyt/ (**-lat·ed, -lat·ing, -lates**) *vt* **1.** to remove diseased or unwanted tissue from the body by surgical or other means **2.** to remove or reduce snow and ice from a glacier by melting and evaporation [15C. < Latin *ablat-* (see ABLATIVE)]

ab·la·tion /ə bláysh'n/ *n* **1.** MED REMOVAL OF TISSUE the removal of diseased or unwanted tissue from the body by surgical or other means **2.** AEROSP MELTING OF SPACECRAFT'S OUTER SURFACE the melting or erosion of the protective outer surface of a spacecraft during reentry through the Earth's atmosphere **3.** GEOL MELTING OF SNOW AND ICE the removal of snow and ice by melting and sublimation from a glacier or iceberg

ab·la·tive /ábblətiv/ *n* **1.** a grammatical form (**case**) that identifies the source, agent, or instrument of action of the verb in some inflected languages and affects nouns, pronouns, and adjectives **2.** a word or phrase in the ablative [15C. Directly or via French *ablatif* < Latin *ablativus* < *ablat-*, past participle of *auferre* "carry away"] —**ab·la·tive** *adj*

ab·la·tor /ə bláytər/ *n* a heat shield on a spacecraft

ab·laut /áb lòwt/ *n* in Indo-European languages, a regular change of vowels in a related series of words or forms, e.g., "sing," "sang," "sung" [Mid-19C. < German < *ab* "off" + *Laut* "sound"]

a·blaze /ə bláyz/ *adj* **1.** ON FIRE burning strongly **2.** BRIGHTLY LIT very brightly lit **3.** SHOWING STRONG EMOTION displaying great emotion or excitement, especially in the face

a·ble /áyb'l/ *adj* (**a·bler, a·blest**) **1.** IN POSITION TO DO SOMETHING physically or mentally equipped to do something, especially because of circumstances and timing ○ *Were you able to reach her before she left?* **2.** CAPABLE OR TALENTED having the necessary resources or talent to do something ○ *a very able administrator* **3.** EDUC GOOD AT LEARNING quick to learn in an educational environment ○ *schoolwork to challenge able children* ■ *vt* (**a·bled, a·bling, a·bles**) *Carib* **1.** BE ABLE TO DO SOMETHING to be able or have the ability to do something **2.** TOLERATE SOMETHING to put up with something [14C. Via Old French *(h)able* < Latin *habilis* "easy to hold or handle" < *habere* "have, hold"]

SYNONYMS See ***intelligent***.

-able *suffix* **1.** capable of or fit for ○ *readable* **2.** tending to ○ *changeable* [< Latin *-abilis*] —**-ability** *suffix*

a·ble-bod·ied /àyb'l bóddeed/ *adj* healthy and physically strong

a·ble-bod·ied sea·man *n* NAUT same as **able seaman** (sense 1)

a·bled /áyb'ld/ *adj* **1.** having particular abilities **2.** *US* having all physical or mental functions

a·ble·ism /áyb'l ìzzəm/ *n* discrimination in favor of those who are not physically or mentally challenged —**a·ble·ist** *adj, n*

a·ble sea·man *n* **1.** a member of a ship's crew, especially the crew of a merchant ship, who possesses basic skills and qualifications **2.** a sailor in the British Royal or Canadian navy of a rank above ordinary seaman

a·bloom /ə blóom/ *adj* blooming or flowering

ab·lu·tion /ə blóosh'n/ *n* the ritual cleansing of a priest's hands or body, or of sacred vessels, during a religious ceremony ■ **ab·lu·tions** *npl* the act of washing the hands or the whole of the body (*formal or humorous*) [14C. Directly or via French < Latin *ablution-* < *abluere* "wash away, wash clean" < *luere* "wash"] —**ab·lu·tion·ar·y** *adj*

a·bly /áyblee/ *adv* in a skillful or competent way

ABM *abbr* ARMS antiballistic missile

Ab·na·ki *n, adj* PEOPLES another spelling of **Abenaki**

ab·ne·gate /ábnə gàyt/ (**-gat·ed, -gat·ing, -gates**) *vt* to give up or renounce something (*formal*) [Early 17C. < Latin *abnegat-*, past participle of *abnegare* "refuse, reject" < *negare* "deny"] —**ab·ne·ga·tion** /ábnə gáysh'n/ *n* —**ab·ne·ga·tor** *n*

ab·nor·mal /ab náwrm'l, əb-/ *adj* unusual or unexpected, especially in a way that causes alarm or anxiety ○ *X-rays of the lung showed nothing abnormal.* [Mid-19C. < French *anormal* < Latin *abnormis* "deviating from a rule"] —**ab·nor·mal·ly** *adv*

ab·nor·mal·i·ty /àb nawr mállətee/ (*plural* **-ties**) *n* **1.** a variation from the usual structure or function of the mind or body ○ *The blood test detected no abnormalities.* **2.** any condition that is not the usual or expected one

A·bo /ábbō/ (*plural* **A·bos**), **a·bo** (*plural* **a·bos**) *n* a highly offensive term for an Australian Aboriginal (*taboo*) [Early 20C. Shortening]

a·board /ə báwrd/ *adv, prep* **1.** ONTO SHIP OR VEHICLE on, onto, in, or into a ship, airplane, train, or other vehicle **2.** INTO GROUP in or into an organization or group (*informal*) ■ *adv* BASEBALL ON BASE in baseball, on base as a runner

a·bode[1] /ə bṓd/ *n* (*literary*) **1.** the house or other place where somebody lives **2.** a period of living somewhere [13C. < ABIDE]

a·bode[2] past participle, past tense of **abide**

ab·ohm /a bṓm/ *n* the centimeter-gram-second unit of electrical resistance equal to 10^{-9} of an ohm

a·boi·teau /àb waa tṓ/ (*plural* **-teaux** /*pronunc. same*/) *n Can* a sluice gate in a dike that prevents sea water from flowing in but allows flood water to flow out

a·bol·ish /ə bóllish/ (**-ished, -ish·ing, -ish·es**) *vt* to put an end to something such as a law ○ *"Critics of advertising usually forget that if it were eliminated or abolished, other methods would necessarily be substituted for it."* (Daniel Starch, *Principles of Advertising*; 1923) [15C. < French *aboliss-*, stem of *abolir* < Latin *abolere* "destroy"] —**a·bol·ish·a·ble** *adj* —**a·bol·ish·er** *n* —**a·bol·ish·ment** *n*

ab·o·li·tion /àbbə lísh'n/ *n* **1.** the act of officially ending a law, regulation, or practice **2.** *also* **Ab·o·li·tion** the official ending of the practice of slavery [Early 16C. Directly or via French < Latin *abolition-* < *abolere* "destroy"] —**ab·o·li·tion·ar·y** *adj*

ab·o·li·tion·ist /àbbə lísh'nist/ *n* **1.** *also* **Ab·o·li·tion·ist** an antislavery campaigner in the 18th and 19th centuries **2.** a supporter of the abolition of something —**ab·o·li·tion·ism** *n*

ab·o·ma·sum /àbbə máyssəm/ (*plural* **-sa** /-sə/) *n* the fourth and final chamber of the digestive system of cattle and other ruminants, where enzymatic or true digestion takes place

A-bomb *n* ARMS same as **atomic bomb** [Mid-20C. Contraction]

a·bom·i·na·ble /ə bómminəb'l, ə bómnəb'l/ *adj* **1.** extremely repugnant or offensive **2.** of very bad quality, or very unpleasant to experience [14C. Via Old French < Latin *abominabilis* < *abominari* "shun something as being a bad omen" < *omen* "omen"] —**a·bom·i·na·bly** *adv*

ORIGIN Between the 14th and the 17th centuries ***abominable*** was often spelled *abhominable* because of a widely held belief that it was derived from Latin *ab hominem*, literally "away from humankind," hence "unnatural, beastly." Shakespeare puns on this sense when Hamlet speaks of incompetent actors who "imitate humanity abominably."

A·bom·i·na·ble Snow·man *n* same as **yeti**

a·bom·i·nate /ə bómmi nàyt/ (**-nat·ed, -nat·ing, -nates**) *vt* to dislike and disapprove of somebody or something intensely (*formal*) [Mid-17C. < Latin *abominat-*, past participle of *abominari* (see ABOMINABLE)] —**a·bom·i·na·tor** *n*

a·bom·i·na·tion /ə bòmmi náysh'n/ *n* **1.** SOMETHING HORRIBLE an object of intense disapproval or dislike **2.** SOMETHING SHAMEFUL something that is immoral, disgusting, or shameful **3.** INTENSE DISLIKE a feeling of intense dislike or disapproval toward somebody or something (*literary*)

ab·o·ral /ab áwrəl/ *adj* situated away from or opposite the mouth ○ *the aboral surface of a starfish*

ab·o·rig·i·nal /àbbə ríjjənəl/ *adj* existing in a place from the earliest known times ■ *n* a member of a people who have lived in an area from the earliest known times [Mid-17C. < Latin *aborigines* (see ABORIGINE)] —**ab·o·rig·i·nal·i·ty** /àbbə rijə nállətee/ *n* —**ab·o·rig·i·nal·ly** *adv*

SYNONYMS See ***native***.

Ab·o·rig·i·nal *n* **1.** a descendant of any of the indigenous peoples who inhabited Canada before the arrival of European settlers **2.** a member of any of the indigenous peoples who inhabited Australia before the arrival of European settlers —**Ab·o·rig·i·nal** *adj*

ab·o·rig·i·ne /àbbə ríjjənee/ *n* **1.** ⚠ a member of a people who has lived in an area from the earliest known times (*often offensive*) **2.** an animal or plant that has existed in a place since earliest times [16C. Back-formation < Latin *aborigines*, the pre-Roman inhabitants of Latium < *ab origine* "from the beginning"]

USAGE Avoid the use of ***aborigine*** without a capital letter to refer to a person who has lived in an area from the earliest known times.

Ab·o·rig·i·ne *n* a member of any of the indigenous peoples who inhabited Australia before the arrival of European settlers

a·born·ing /ə báwrning/ *adv* while being born, created, or realized

a·bort /ə báwrt/ (**a·bort·ed, a·bort·ing, a·borts**) *v* **1.** *vt* REMOVE FETUS to remove an embryo or fetus from the womb in order to end a pregnancy **2.** *vi* HAVE MISCARRIAGE to give birth to an embryo or fetus before its independent survival is possible. Survival is usually possible at about 24 weeks for human fetuses. (*technical*) **3.** *vti* **END SOMETHING PREMATURELY** to bring something to an end or come to an end at an early stage **4.** *vti* **ABANDON MISSION** to end a space flight or similar mission before it is completed **5.** *vti* COMPUT **QUIT COMPUTER PROGRAM** to abandon a computer program, command, or operation before it has finished [Mid-16C. < Latin *abort-*, past participle of *aboriri* "miscarry" < *oriri* "come into being"]

a·bor·ti·fa·cient /ə bàwrtə fáysh'nt/ *adj* describes a drug or device that causes abortion —**a·bor·ti·fa·cient** *n*

a·bor·tion /ə báwrsh'n/ *n* **1. OPERATION TO END PREGNANCY** an operation or other intervention to end a pregnancy by removing an embryo or fetus from the womb **2.** MED same as **miscarriage** (sense 1) (*technical*) **3. OFFENSIVE TERM** an offensive term for something so badly done or made that it is a complete failure **4.** AEROSP **CANCELLATION OF MISSION** the ending of a flight or mission before it is completed

a·bor·tion doc·tor *n* a doctor whose job is to perform abortions

a·bor·tion·ist /ə báwrsh'nist/ *n* somebody who performs abortions. The term, used in the past often in contexts reflecting the former illegality of the procedure in the United States, is still used disapprovingly by some, but not by all, groups.

a·bor·tion pill *n* a drug that induces an abortion at a very early stage of pregnancy

a·bor·tion trau·ma syn·drome *n* a set of symptoms associated with the period following an abortion including guilt, anxiety, depression, low self-esteem, eating and sleeping disorders, and suicidal thoughts

a·bor·tive /ə báwrtiv/ *adj* **1.** failing to reach completion **2.** describes an organ that has had its development terminated —**a·bor·tive·ly** *adv*

ABO sys·tem *n* a system that classifies human blood by dividing it into the four groups A, B, AB, and O. Classification is based on the presence or absence of two chemical groups (**antigens**), A and B, on the red blood cells.

A·bou·kir, Bay of ➧ **Abukir, Bay of**

a·bou·li·a *n* PSYCHOL another spelling of **abulia**

a·bound /ə bównd/ (**a·bound·ed, a·bound·ing, a·bounds**) *vi* **1.** to be present in large numbers or quantities **2.** to contain something in large numbers or amounts [14C. Via Old French *abunder* < Latin *abundare* "overflow" < *undare* "surge" < *unda* "wave"] —**a·bound·ing** *adj* —**a·bound·ing·ly** *adv*

a·bout /ə bówt/ CORE MEANING: a grammatical word that refers to different sides or aspects of something from some point of orientation ○ (prep) *a book about a dog*

1. *prep* **IN CONNECTION WITH** in connection with or relating to ○ *think about problems* **2.** *prep* **APPROXIMATELY** close to in number, time, or degree ○ *inviting about fifteen people* **3.** *prep* **DOING OR ATTENDING TO** with or in an activity ○ *go about your business* **4.** *prep, adv UK* **AT HAND** somewhere in a place or on a person ○ *I don't have any cash about me.* ○ *She must be about. I saw her a minute ago.* **5.** *adv* **ALL AROUND** on every side of or all the way around ○ *"He proceeded to the banks of the Hudson, and looked about among the vessels."* (Jules Verne, *Around the World in 80 Days*; 1873) **6.** *adv* **ADDS EMPHASIS** used to emphasize a statement, usually when expressing impatience or anger (*informal*) ○ *Well, it's about time you showed up!* **7.** *adv* SAILING **TO OPPOSITE TACK** on or to the opposite tack **8.** *prep, adv UK* same as **around** (senses 5, 11, 13–14) [Old English *onbūtan* "on or around the outside of" < *on* (see ON) + *būtan* (see BUT)] ◇ **be about** to have something as an essential characteristic ○ *Being successful is all about energy, drive, and commitment.* ◇ **be about to** to be on the point of doing something ○ *The game was about to start.* ◇ **be what something or somebody is (all) about** to be what something or somebody involves or has as a purpose (*informal*) ◇ **not about to** used to emphasize that somebody is certainly not going to do something (*informal*) ○ *I'm not about to apologize!*

a·bout-face *n* **1. REVERSAL** a sudden and complete reversal of a previous opinion or policy **2. TURN** a turn to face in the opposite direction ■ *vi* **TURN AROUND** to turn to face in the opposite direction (*usually used as a command*)

a·bout-ship (**a·bout-shipped, a·bout-ship·ping, a·bout-ships**) *vi* in sailing, to turn to a new tack

a·bout-turn *vi* (**a·bout-turned, a·bout-turn·ing, a·bout-turns**), *n UK* MIL same as **about-face**

a·bove /ə búv/ CORE MEANING: a grammatical word indicating a position directly overhead, on top of, or higher than something ○ (prep) *The bird flew up above the trees.* ○ (adv) *gazing at the sky above*

1. *prep* **OVER** over, higher than, or on top of ○ *hanging over the fireplace* **2.** *prep, adv* **MORE THAN** greater than an amount or level ○ *100 pounds above the ideal body weight* **3.** *prep, adv* **SUPERIOR TO** higher in status or power ○ *A general is above a colonel.* **4.** *prep* **TOO GOOD FOR** too good or important to be affected by or involved in something ○ *They felt they were above small town gossip.* **5.** *prep* **BEYOND** not subject to something negative such as criticism or reproach ○ *"He wanted her to know that here too his conduct should be above suspicion."* (George Eliot, *Middlemarch*; 1872) **6.** *prep* **IN MORE RESPECTED POSITION THAN** in a position that is valued more or considered more important than other people or things ○ *We put your needs above everything else.* **7.** *prep* **TOO DIFFICULT FOR** outside or beyond somebody's understanding ○ *The lecture was completely above me.* **8.** *prep* **LOUDER THAN** louder than or over another sound ○ *She couldn't hear him above the roar of the band.* **9.** *prep* **NORTH OF** lying north of a place ○ *a small town just above Seattle* **10.** *prep* **UPSTREAM FROM** lying upstream from a place **11.** *adv, adj* **IN PREVIOUS PLACE IN WRITING** appearing previously in a piece of writing (*often used in hyphenated compounds*) ○ *using the information from the table above* **12.** *adv* RELIG **IN HEAVEN** to or in heaven (*literary*) **13.** *adv* **ON TOP** overhead, in a higher position, or on top [Old English *abufan* < *an* (see ON) + *bufan* "above" < Indo-European] ◇ **above all** used to indicate the most important thing or the main point of a statement

a·bove·board /ə bùv báwrd/ *adj* honest, legal, and without deception ■ *adv* honestly, legally, and without deception [Late 16C. Originally a gambling term indicating that the player's hands were above the gaming table and nothing was being concealed]

a·bove·ground /ə búv gròwnd/ *adj* **1.** on or above the surface of the ground ○ *aboveground plant parts* ○ *aboveground tests* **2.** produced within or acceptable to the mainstream of society

a·bove-men·tioned *adj* written or listed above, or referred to previously ■ *n* a person previously referred to in a text

a·bove-the-fold *adj* relating to the portion of a webpage that can be seen without scrolling downward. Commercially this is the most valuable portion of the page, as it is seen by everybody who calls it up.

a·bove-the-line *adj* **1.** describes the profit after taxation that a company makes on its ordinary activities **2.** used to describe the advertising for which payment is made and for which a commission is paid to an advertising agency

a·bove-the-ti·tle *adj* shown in movie credits before the title is seen, and therefore in a starring role ○ *an above-the-title mention*

ab o·vo /àb ṓvō/ *adv* from the very beginning [Late 16C. < Latin, "from the egg"]

ab·ra·ca·dab·ra /àbbrəkə dábbrə/ *interj* **MAGIC WORD** used to ensure the supposed success of a magic trick (*used by magicians and conjurors*) ■ *n* **1. MAGIC SPELL** a supposedly magical charm or spell **2. GIBBERISH** deliberately nonsensical language [Mid-16C. Via Latin < Greek]

a·brade /ə bráyd/ (**a·brad·ed, a·brad·ing, a·brades**) *vti* to wear something away or be worn away by friction [Late 17C. < Latin *abradere* < *radere* "scrape"]

A·bra·ham /áybrə hàm/, **A·bram** /áybrəm/ *n* in the Bible, the first patriarch, seen by Jews as the father of the Israelites through his son Isaac, and by Muslims, who call him Ibrahim, as the father of Arab peoples through his son Ishmael

A·bra·ham, Plains of /áybrə hàm/ plateau in eastern Canada, in the city of Quebec, on the St. Lawrence River. It was the scene of a battle between British and French forces in 1759.

A·bra·hams /áybrə hàmz/, **Harold** (1899–1978) British athlete. His victory in the 100 meters at the 1924 Paris Olympic Games was featured in the motion picture *Chariots of Fire* (1981).

A·bram *n* BIBLE another spelling of **Abraham**

ab·ra·sion /ə bráyzh'n/ *n* **1. WEARING AWAY** the process of wearing away by friction **2.** MED **SCRAPED AREA OF SKIN** an area on the skin, or some other surface of the body, that has been damaged by scraping or rubbing ○ *dental abrasion* **3.** GEOG **WEARING AWAY OF ROCK** the erosion of bedrock by continuous friction caused by rock fragments in water, wind, or ice [Mid-17C. < Latin *abrasion-* < *abras-* (see ABRASIVE)]

ab·ra·sive /ə bráyssiv, -ziv/ *adj* **1. USING FRICTION** using friction and roughness of texture to smooth or clean a surface ○ *an abrasive cleaner* **2. HARSH IN MANNER** aggressively direct and insensitive ■ *n* **SMOOTHING SUBSTANCE** a substance such as pumice or emery that is used to smooth or polish a surface by grinding or scraping [Mid-19C. < Latin *abras-*, past participle of *abradere* (see ABRADE)]

ab·re·act /àbbree ákt/ (**-act·ed, -act·ing, -acts**) *vt* to release unconscious psychological tension by talking about or reliving the events that caused it —**ab·re·ac·tion** *n*

a·breast /ə brést/ *adv* side by side and facing the front ■ *adj* up to date with something

~~**abreviation**~~ incorrect spelling of **abbreviation**

a·bridge /ə bríj/ (**a·bridged, a·bridg·ing, a·bridg·es**) *vt* **1. SHORTEN SOMETHING** to shorten a text, e.g., by cutting or summarizing it ○ *abridged for television* **2. CUT SOMETHING SHORT** to reduce something in scope or extent ○ *trying to abridge First Amendment rights* **3. RESTRICT SOMEBODY'S RIGHTS** to deprive somebody of rights or privileges (*archaic*) [14C. Via Old French *abreg(i)er* < Latin *abbreviare* "shorten" < *brevis* "short"] —**a·bridg·a·ble** *adj* —**a·bridged** *adj* —**a·bridg·er** *n* —**a·bridg·ment** *n*

a·broad /ə bráwd/ *adv* **1. AWAY FROM YOUR OWN COUNTRY** in or to another country or other countries **2. IN CIRCULATION** in public or into general circulation **3. EVERYWHERE** over a wide area ■ *n* **OTHER COUNTRIES** countries other than a specific one

~~**abroard**~~ incorrect spelling of **abroad**

ab·ro·gate /ábbrə gàyt/ (**-gat·ed, -gat·ing, -gates**) *vt* to repeal or abolish something formally and publicly (*formal*) [Early 16C. < Latin *abrogat-*, past participle of *abrogare* "repeal a law" < *rogare* "ask, propose a law"] —**ab·ro·ga·tion** /àbbrə gáysh'n/ *n*

SYNONYMS See ***nullify***.

a·brupt /ə brúpt/ *adj* **1. SUDDEN** sudden and unexpected **2. BRUSQUE** brief and making no effort to be friendly **3. DISCONNECTED** not passing smoothly from topic to topic **4. STEEP** with a sudden steep slope [Late 16C. < Latin *abruptus* "broken off, steep," past participle of *abrumpere* "break off" < *rumpere* "break"] —**a·brupt·ly** *adv* —**a·brupt·ness** *n*

a·brup·tion /ə brúpsh'n/ *n* the sudden breaking off of a part from a larger mass (*formal*) [Early 17C. < Latin *abruption-* < *abruptus* (see ABRUPT)]

A·bruz·zi /aa brŏŏtsee, ə-/ agricultural region of central southern Italy consisting of the provinces of L'Aguila, Chieti, Pescara, and Teramo. Area: 4,168 sq. mi./10,795 sq. km. Population: 1,279,016 (2000).

abs /abz/ *npl* the abdominal muscles (*informal*) [Late 20C. Shortening]

ABS[1] *n* a type of strong plastic (**copolymer**). Use: molded casings, pipes, car parts. Full form **acrylonitrile-butadiene-styrene**

ABS[2] *n* a system of electronically controlled brakes that prevents a vehicle's wheels locking if the driver brakes suddenly. Full form **antilock braking system**

Ab·sa·lom /ábssə lòm/ *n* in the Bible, the third son of David, King of Israel. He rebelled against his father and was killed by Joab (2 Samuel 13–18).

ab·scess /áb sèss/ *n* a pus-filled cavity resulting from inflammation and usually caused by bacterial infection ■ *vi* (**-scessed, -scess·ing, -scess·es**) to form an abscess or be the site where one develops [Mid-16C. < Latin *abscessus* < *abscedere* "go away" (referring to bodily humors going away in the pus) < *cedere* "go"]

ab·scis·ic ac·id /ab sìssik-/ *n* a plant hormone that promotes leaf and fruit fall, and dormancy in seeds and buds

ab·scis·sa /ab síssə/ (*plural* **-sas** or **-sae** /-síssee/) *n* in mathematics, the horizontal coordinate or x-coordinate of a point in a two-dimensional system of Cartesian coordinates. It is the distance from the vertical axis or y-axis measured along a line parallel to the horizontal axis or x-axis. [Late 17C. < modern Latin *abscissa linea* "line cut off"]

ab·scis·sion /ab sízh'n/ *n* **1.** the act of suddenly cutting something off **2.** the natural process by which leaves or other parts are shed from a plant [Early 17C. < Latin *abscission-* < *abscindere* "cut off" < *scindere* "cut up, divide"]

ab·scond /ab skónd, əb-/ (**-scond·ed, -scond·ing, -sconds**) *vi* **1.** to run away secretly, especially in order to avoid arrest or prosecution **2.** to escape from a place of detention [Mid-16C. < Latin *abscondere* "hide or put away" < *condere* "stow"] —**ab·scond·er** *n*

ab·seil /áb sàyl/ *UK* CLIMBING *vi* (**-seiled, -seil·ing, -seils**) same as **rappel** ■ *n* same as **rappel** [Mid-20C. < German *abseilen* < *ab* "down" + *Seil* "rope"] —**ab·seil·er** *n* —**ab·seil·ing** *n*

ab·sence /ábs'nss/ *n* **1.** NOT BEING PRESENT the fact of somebody's not being in a specific place ○ *took note of certain people's absence* **2.** TIME AWAY a period during which somebody is away ○ *returning after a short absence* **3.** NONEXISTENCE the lack or nonexistence of a quality or feature ○ *in the absence of any fresh information* [14C. Via French < Latin *absentia* < *abesse* (see ABSENT[1])] ◇ **absence makes the heart grow fonder** separation makes love or affection for somebody grow stronger

~~**absense**~~ incorrect spelling of **absence**

ab·sent[1] /ábs'nt/ *adj* **1.** NOT PRESENT not attending a place or event, especially when expected to ○ *absent from school* **2.** INATTENTIVE not paying attention ○ *His face took on an absent expression.* ■ *prep* WITHOUT in the absence of ○ *Absent a definite refusal, I decided to proceed.* [14C. < Latin *absent-*, present participle of *abesse* "be away" < *esse* "be"]

ab·sent[2] /ab sént/ (**-sent·ed, -sent·ing, -sents**) *vr* **ab·sent your·self** to stay away from or leave something such as an event or occasion ○ *absented themselves from the meeting* [14C. Directly or via French *absenter* < Latin *absentare* "keep or be away" < *absent-* (see ABSENT[1])]

ab·sen·tee /àbs'n tée/ *n* somebody who is not present at an event

ab·sen·tee bal·lot *n* a ballot sent by somebody who is unable to attend to vote in person at the voting place

ab·sen·tee·ism /àbs'n tée ìzzəm/ *n* persistent absence from work or some other place without good reason

ab·sen·tee land·lord *n* a landlord who lives away from the accommodations rented out, especially one who neglects the needs of tenants

ab·sen·tee vot·er *n* a voter who cannot visit the voting place and votes by mail

ab·sent·ly /ábs'ntlee/ *adv* in an inattentive or absent-minded way

ab·sent-mind·ed *adj* tending to be preoccupied or forgetful —**ab·sent-mind·ed·ly** *adv* —**ab·sent-mind·ed·ness** *n*

ab·sent with·out leave *adj* absent from military duties without permission, but not assumed to have deserted

ab·sinthe /ábsinth/, **ab·sinth** *n* **1.** a highly alcoholic liqueur tasting of aniseed and made from wormwood and herbs. Absinthe is now banned in many countries because of its toxicity. **2.** PLANTS same as **wormwood** (sense 1) [Early 17C. Via French < Greek *apsinthion* "wormwood"]

ab·so·lute /ábssə lòot, àbsə lóot/ *adj* **1.** ADDS EMPHASIS used to give strong emphasis to what is being said ○ *an absolute disaster* **2.** POSSESSING UNLIMITED POWER having total power and authority ○ *an absolute monarch* **3.** UNEQUIVOCAL completely unequivocal and not capable of being viewed as partial or relative ○ *absolute proof* **4.** INDEPENDENT AND UNMODIFIABLE not depending on or qualified by anything else ○ *absolute truth* **5.** GRAM GRAMMATICALLY INDEPENDENT not syntactically dependent on the main clause of a sentence, e.g., "It being sunny" in the sentence "It being sunny, they went to the pool" **6.** GRAM WITHOUT DIRECT OBJECT used without an explicit direct object. The usage of "satisfy" is absolute in the sentence "We aim to satisfy." **7.** GRAM USED AS NOUN used without an explicit noun. "The rich and the poor" are absolute adjectival usages. **8.** PHYS MEASURED RELATIVE TO VACUUM involving or relating to measurements made relative to the vacuum state **9.** PHYS ACCORDING TO STANDARDIZED MEASURES relating to or using basic units of length, time, mass, and charge **10.** PHYS MEASURED RELATIVE TO ABSOLUTE ZERO measured on or relating to a scale that has as its lowest temperature absolute zero, the point at which all molecular motion ceases **11.** LAW FULL AND UNCONDITIONAL complete and in no way conditional on any future evidence or behavior ○ *an absolute pardon* **12.** LAW OWNED OUTRIGHT having unconditional ownership of a title or property, unrestricted by trusts or entails (*often used after a noun*) **13.** MATH CONSTANT IN VALUE not changing in value in varying mathematical expressions **14.** MATH ALWAYS TRUE ALGEBRAICALLY true for all values of a variable in an algebraic expression **15.** MATH WITHOUT VARIABLES not containing an algebraic variable ■ *n* **1.** UNQUESTIONABLE RULE a principle or value that is held to be always true or valid **2.** *also* **Ab·so·lute** PHILOSOPHY ULTIMATE REALITY in some schools of philosophy, the one ultimate reality that does not depend on anything, and is not relative to anything else [14C. < Latin *absolutus*, past participle of *absolvere* "set free" (see ABSOLVE)]

ab·so·lute ceil·ing *n* the maximum height above sea level at which an aircraft can maintain horizontal flight

ab·so·lute·ly /ábssə lòotlee, àbssə lóot-/ *adv* **1.** ⚠ ADDS EMPHASIS used to give strong emphasis to what is being said **2.** ⚠ THAT'S RIGHT used in speech or dialogue as an emphatic way of agreeing with the other speaker **3.** LAW UNCONDITIONALLY with no conditions or restrictions, especially constitutional or legal ones **4.** GRAM WITH NO GRAMMATICAL OBJECT used syntactically with an implied direct object or noun head **5.** NOT IN RELATIVE WAY in a way that is independent of circumstances and never variable or modified

USAGE Some people dislike the use of ***absolutely*** to give strong emphasis (*That is absolutely disgraceful!*), and regard it as an affectation. Also controversial is its use to express agreement. It retains some meaning in uses such as *"Do you like it?"-"Yes, absolutely,"* but is simply an intensifier when used with answers that are factual rather than an expression of opinion: *"Have you been to Paris?"-"Yes, absolutely."*

ab·so·lute ma·jor·i·ty *n* the winning total of votes that amounts to more than half of the votes available

ab·so·lute mu·sic *n* music whose meaning is derived solely from the music itself and that does not evoke another source, e.g., a visual scene

ab·so·lute pitch *n* **1.** the ability to identify the pitch of a single note without reference to any other sound **2.** the exact pitch a tone is expected to have, measured by its number of vibrations per second

ab·so·lute tem·per·a·ture *n* temperature derived from the laws of thermodynamics rather than being primarily derived from properties of substances

ab·so·lute val·ue *n* **1.** the magnitude of a number, irrespective of whether it is positive or negative, symbolized by placing the number within vertical bars, thus $|7| = |-7| = 7$ **2.** MATH same as **modulus**

ab·so·lute ze·ro *n* the temperature at which hypothetically all molecular motion ceases, equal to 0 degrees K and equivalent to -273.16°C or -459.69°F

ab·so·lu·tion /àbssə lóosh'n/ *n* **1.** forgiveness for somebody's sins, especially when formally given in a Christian church **2.** a spoken blessing used in a Christian church to grant absolution to somebody [13C. Via French < Latin *absolution-* "acquittal, perfection" < *absolutus* (see ABSOLUTE)]

ab·so·lut·ism /ábssə lòot ìzzəm/ *n* **1.** POLITICAL SYSTEM a political system in which the power of a ruler is unchecked and absolute **2.** PHILOSOPHY THEORY OF OBJECTIVE VALUES a philosophical theory in which values such as truth or morality are absolute and not conditional upon human perception **3.** SOMETHING ABSOLUTE a standard, principle, or theory that is absolute —**ab·so·lut·ist** *n, adj*

ab·solve /əb zólv, -sólv/ (**-solved, -solv·ing, -solves**) *vt* **1.** PRONOUNCE SOMEBODY BLAMELESS to state publicly or officially that somebody is not guilty and not to be held responsible **2.** RELIEVE SOMEBODY OF OBLIGATION to release somebody from an obligation or requirement **3.** FORGIVE SOMEBODY to forgive somebody's sins, especially formally in a Christian church service or sacrament [15C. < Latin *absolvere* "set free" < *solvere* "loosen"] —**ab·solv·a·ble** *adj* —**ab·solv·er** *n*

ab·sorb /əb sáwrb, -záwrb/ (**-sorbed, -sorb·ing, -sorbs**) *vt* **1.** TAKE SOMETHING UP OR IN to soak up a liquid or take in nutrients or chemicals gradually **2.** NOT TRANSMIT SOMETHING to take up light, noise, or energy and not transmit it at all ○ *built to absorb the shock of a collision* **3.** TAKE SOMETHING IN MENTALLY to see, read, or hear something and understand it fully ○ *He hasn't yet absorbed the news.* **4.** ENGROSS SOMEBODY to hold somebody's attention or occupy somebody's time completely **5.** INCORPORATE SOMETHING INTO WHOLE to incorporate something into a larger entity in such a way that it loses much of its own identity ○ *The islands were later absorbed into the Roman Empire.* **6.** ADAPT TO SOMETHING to adapt to a changing situation without being adversely affected **7.** NOT PASS COSTS ON to accept increased costs without passing them on to somebody else ○ *forced to absorb the cost of tax increases* **8.** REQUIRE SOMETHING IN QUANTITY to require something in considerable quantities, usually without significant results ○ *absorbing a huge amount of money* [15C. Via French *absorber* < Latin *absorbere* "swallow" < *sorbere* "suck in"] —**ab·sorb·a·ble** *adj* —**ab·sorbed** *adj* —**ab·sorb·er** *n*

ab·sorb·ance /əb sáwrbənss, -záwrb-/ *n* the capacity of a substance to absorb radiation. Symbol **A**

ab·sorb·ent /əb sáwrbənt, -záwrb-/ *adj* **1.** capable of soaking up liquid **2.** capable of absorbing light, noise, or energy instead of reflecting it (*often used in combination*) ○ *shock-absorbent* [Early 18C. < Latin *absorbent-*, present participle of *absorbere* "swallow" (see ABSORB)] —**ab·sorb·en·cy** *n*

ab·sorb·ent cot·ton *n* cotton that has had the natural wax removed, making it absorbent and suitable for medical and cosmetic use as dressings or swabs

ab·sorb·ing /əb sáwrbing, -záwrb-/ *adj* extremely interesting and therefore occupying the attention completely —**ab·sorb·ing·ly** *adv*

~~**absorbtion**~~ incorrect spelling of **absorption**

ab·sorp·tance /əb sáwrptənss, -záwrp-/ *n* a measure of the ability of an object or substance to absorb radiant energy, equal to the ratio of the absorbed energy to the total energy reaching the object or substance. Symbol α [Mid-20C. < Latin *absorptus* (see ABSORPTION)]

ab·sorp·tion /əb sáwrpsh'n, -záwrp-/ *n* **1.** PREOCCUPATION a state in which the whole attention is occupied **2.** SOAKING UP the uptake of liquid into the fibers of a substance **3.** INCORPORATION the incorporation of something into a larger group or entity **4.** PHYSIOL ASSIMILATION BY BODY the passage of material through the lining of the intestine into the blood or through a cell membrane into a cell **5.** PHYS ABILITY OF SUBSTANCE TO ABSORB ENERGY the ability of a substance to absorb light, noise, or energy, or the fact that it does so **6.** PHYS REDUCTION IN RADIATED ENERGY the reduction in the intensity of radiated energy within a medium, caused by converting some or all of the energy into another form **7.** IMMUNOL REMOVAL OF ANTIBODIES the elimination of antibodies or antigens by the use of a chemical reagent [Late 16C. < Latin *absorption-* < *absorptus*, past participle of *absorbere* "swallow" (see ABSORB)] —**ab·sorp·tive** *adj* —**ab·sorp·tiv·i·ty** /əb sàwrp tívvətee, -zàwrp-/ *n*

ab·sorp·tion spec·trum *n* the pattern of dark bands that is seen when electromagnetic radiation passes through an absorbing medium and is observed with a spectroscope. It is the result of unequal absorption of the radiation as it passes through the medium.

ab·squat·u·late /əb skwóchə làyt/ (**-lat·ed, -lat·ing, -lates**) *vi US* to leave, especially in a hurry or under suspicious circumstances (*archaic or humorous*) [Mid-19C. < Latin *ab* "away" + SQUAT[1] + *-ulate* (as in CONGRATULATE)]

ab·stain /əb stáyn/ (**-stained, -stain·ing, -stains**) *vi* **1.** not to vote for or against a proposal when a vote is held **2.** to choose not to do something [14C. Via Old French *abstenir* < Latin *abstinere* "hold yourself away" < *tenere* "hold"] —**ab·stain·er** *n*

ab·ste·mi·ous /əb stéemee əss/ *adj* not indulging in or characterized by excessive eating or drinking [Early 17C. < Latin *abstemius* < *abs-* "away from" + *temetum* "intoxicating liquor"] —**ab·ste·mi·ous·ly** *adv* —**ab·ste·mi·ous·ness** *n*

ab·sten·tion /əb sténsh'n/ *n* **1.** a refusal to vote either for or against a proposal **2.** the deliberate choice not to do something [Early 16C. < late Latin *abstention-* < Latin *abstentus*, past participle of *abstinere* (see ABSTAIN)]

ab·sti·nence /ábstənənss/ *n* restraint from indulging a desire for something, e.g., alcohol or sexual relations [14C. Via Old French < Latin *abstinentia* < *abstinent-*, present participle of *abstinere* (see ABSTAIN)] —**ab·sti·nent** *adj* —**ab·sti·nent·ly** *adv*

ab·stract *adj* /áb stràkt, ab strákt/ **1.** NOT CONCRETE not relating to concrete objects but expressing something that can only be appreciated intellectually **2.**

THEORETICAL based on general principles or theories rather than on specific instances ○ *abstract arguments* **3.** ARTS **NONREPRESENTATIONAL** not aiming to depict an object but composed with the focus on internal structure and form **4.** MUSIC **CONCEPTUAL** describes music that is intended to have no programmatic or emotional content **5. IRREGULARLY PATTERNED** decorated with irregular areas of color that do not represent anything concrete **6. IMPERSONAL** emotionally detached or distanced from something ■ *n* /áb stràkt, ab strákt/ **1. SUMMARY** a summary of a longer text, especially of an academic article **2. INTELLECTUAL CONCEPT** a concept or term that does not refer to a concrete object but denotes a quality, emotion, or idea **3.** ARTS **ABSTRACT ARTWORK** a work of art, especially a painting, in an abstract style ■ *vt* /əb strákt/ (**-stract·ed, -stract·ing, -stracts**) **1. CONCEPTUALIZE SOMETHING** to develop a line of thought from a concrete reality to a general principle or an intellectual idea **2. SUMMARIZE SOMETHING** to make a summary of the main points of an argument or text **3. EXTRACT SOMETHING** to remove something from a place, usually with some difficulty **4. STEAL SOMETHING** to steal something by taking it unobtrusively (*used euphemistically*) **5.** ENVIRON **PUMP WATER** to remove water from a river or other source for industrial use [14C. < Latin *abstractus*, past participle of *abstrahere* "drag away" < *trahere* "drag"] —**ab·stract·ed** *adj* —**ab·stract·ed·ly** *adv* —**ab·stract·er** *n* —**ab·stract·ly** *adv* —**ab·stract·ness** *n*

ab·stract ex·pres·sion·ism *n* a school of painting, originating in New York in the 1940s, that combined abstract forms with spontaneity of artistic expression

ab·strac·tion /ab stráksh'n/ *n* **1. GENERALIZED CONCEPT** a generalized idea or theory developed from concrete examples of events **2. GENERALIZING PROCESS** the formation of general ideas or concepts from concrete examples **3. PREOCCUPATION** a state in which somebody is deep in thought and not concentrating on his or her surroundings **4.** PHILOSOPHY **CONCEPTUALIZATION** the philosophical process by which people develop concepts either from experience or from other concepts **5.** ART **ABSTRACT ART** an abstract painting or sculpture **6. EXTRACTION** the removal or theft of something, usually with some difficulty **7.** ENVIRON **PUMPING OF WATER FROM RIVER** the removal of water from a river or other source for industrial use

ab·strac·tion·ism /ab stráksh'n ìzzəm/ *n* the principles and practice of abstract art —**ab·strac·tion·ist** *n*

ab·stract noun *n* a noun signifying a concept, quality, or other abstract idea

ab·stract of ti·tle *n* a summary of the details of the ownership of a piece of land

ab·struse /ab stróoss/ *adj* difficult to understand [Late 16C. Directly or via French < Latin *abstrusus*, past participle of *abstrudere* "thrust away" < *trudere* "thrust"] —**ab·struse·ly** *adv* —**ab·struse·ness** *n*

SYNONYMS See ***obscure***.

ab·surd /əb súrd, -zúrd/ *adj* **1. LUDICROUS** ridiculous because of being irrational, incongruous, or illogical ○ *an absurd notion* **2.** PHILOSOPHY **MEANINGLESS** lacking any meaning that would give purpose to life ○ *the notion that existence is absurd* ■ *n also* **Ab·surd MEANINGLESSNESS** the condition of living in a meaningless universe where life has no purpose, especially as a concept in some 20th-century philosophical movements [Mid-16C. Via French < Latin *absurdus* "inharmonious," literally "away from the (right) sound"] —**ab·surd·ly** *adv* —**ab·surd·ness** *n*

ab·surd·ism /əb súrd ìzzəm, -zúrd-/, **Ab·surd·ism** *n* the idea that the universe is without meaning or rational order and that human beings, in attempting to find a sense of order, conflict with it —**ab·surd·ist** *n, adj*

ab·surd·i·ty /əb súrdətee, -zúrd-/ (*plural* **-ties**) *n* **1.** ridiculousness because of being irrational, incongruous, or illogical **2.** something that is ridiculous because of being irrational, incongruous, or illogical

ABT *abbr US* BALLET American Ballet Theater

A·bu Ba·kr /áaboo baákər/ (570?–634) Arabian religious leader who was the first caliph of Islam. He was responsible for uniting Arabia and spreading Islam.

A·bu Dha·bi /áaboo daábee/ capital of the United Arab Emirates, on the island of Abu Dhabi in the Persian Gulf. Population: 904,000 (1999).

a·build·ing /ə bílding/ *adj US* in the process of being built

A·bu·ja /aa bóo jaa/ official capital of Nigeria since December 1991. It is located in the Federal Capital Territory in central Nigeria. Population: 403,000 (1999).

A·bu·kir, Bay of /ábboo keér, aáboo-/, **A·bou·kir, A·bū Qīr** bay in the Nile Delta that was the site of Lord Nelson's defeat of the French fleet in 1798

a·bu·li·a /ə bóolee ə, ə boólyə/, **a·bou·li·a** *n* a lack of will or motivation, usually manifested as an inability to make decisions or to set goals [Mid-19C. < Greek < *a-* "without, not" + *boulē* "will"] —**a·bu·lic** *adj*

a·bun·dance /ə búndənss/ *n* **1. LARGE AMOUNT** a more than plentiful quantity of something ○ *the abundance of art treasures in Florence* ○ *food and drink in abundance* **2. AFFLUENCE** a lifestyle with more than adequate material provisions ○ *living in careless abundance* **3. FULLNESS** a fullness of spirit that overflows ○ *the abundance of her soul* **4.** CHEM, GEOL **RATE OF INCIDENCE** the extent to which an element is present in the earth or in a rock **5.** PHYS **PROPORTION OF ISOTOPE ATOMS** the proportion of one isotope of an element, expressed by number of atoms, to the total quantity of the element [14C. Via Old French < Latin *abundantia* < *abundant-* (see ABUNDANT)]

a·bun·dant /ə búndənt/ *adj* **1.** present in great quantities **2.** providing a more than plentiful supply of something ○ *abundant in natural resources* [14C. < Latin *abundant-*, present participle of *abundare* "overflow" (see ABOUND)] —**a·bun·dant·ly** *adv*

~~**abundent**~~ incorrect spelling of **abundant**

A·bū Qīr, Bay of ➧ **Abukir, Bay of**

a·buse *n* /ə byóoss/ **1. MALTREATMENT** the physical, psychological, or sexual maltreatment of a person or animal **2. IMPROPER USE** the illegal, improper, or harmful use of something ○ *allegations of abuse of government powers* **3. IMPROPER PRACTICE** an illegal, improper, or harmful practice ○ *human rights abuses* **4. INSULTS** insulting or offensive language **5.** **DRUG USE** the harmful use of drugs or alcohol ■ *v* /ə byóoz/ (**a·bused, a·bus·ing, a·bus·es**) **1.** *vt* **MALTREAT SOMEBODY** to treat a person or animal cruelly, whether physically, psychologically, or sexually, especially on a regular or habitual basis **2.** *vt* **MISUSE SOMETHING** to use something in an improper, illegal, or harmful way **3.** *vt* **INSULT SOMEBODY** to speak insultingly or offensively to somebody **4. a·buse your·self** *vr* **MASTURBATE** to masturbate (*disapproving*) [15C. Via French *abus* < Latin *abusus*, past participle of *abuti* "use up, misuse" < *uti* "use"] —**a·bus·er** /ə byóozər/ *n*

SYNONYMS See ***mistreat*** and ***misuse***.

Great Temple of Rameses II

A·bu Sim·bel /áaboo símbəl, aáboo sím bèl/ site of two carved rock temples in southern Egypt, built in the reign of Rameses II in the 13th century B.C. They were moved to higher ground in the 1960s to avoid possible damage from the construction of the Aswan High Dam.

a·bu·sive /ə byóossiv/ *adj* **1. INSULTING** intended to insult or offend somebody ○ *abusive language* **2. HARMFUL** involving physical, psychological, or sexual maltreatment ○ *an abusive relationship* **3. WRONGFUL** involving illegal, improper, or harmful activities ○ *using abusive methods to secure power* —**a·bu·sive·ly** *adv* —**a·bu·sive·ness** *n*

a·but /ə bút/ (**a·but·ted, a·but·ting, a·buts**) *vti* to touch or be adjacent to something along one side [15C. Partly < Anglo-Latin *abuttare* < *butta* "ridge or strip of land"; partly < Old French *aboter* "aim at" < *boter* "strike" < Germanic] —**a·but·ter** *n*

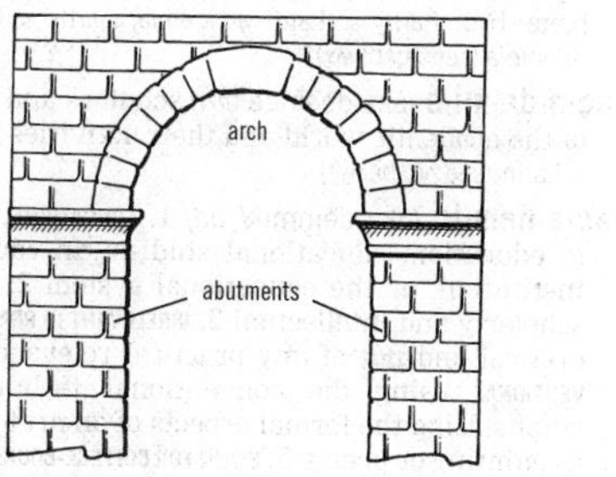

abutment (sense 4)

a·but·ment /ə bútmənt/ *n* **1. ADJACENCY** the state of touching or being adjacent to an object or piece of land along one side **2. MEETING POINT** the point at which two things abut **3. MAKING THINGS ABUT** the positioning of two things so that they abut **4. SUPPORT STRUCTURE** a structure that supports or bears the thrust of something

a·but·tals /ə bútt'lz/ *npl* the boundaries of a piece of land in relation to an adjoining piece of land

a·buzz /ə búz/ *adj* filled with buzzing or a sound like it, often as a result of lively conversation or activity

ab·volt /áb vōlt/ *n* the centimeter-gram-second unit of electromotive force or potential difference equal to 10^{-8} of a volt [Mid-20C. < *ab-*, abbreviation of ABSOLUTE + VOLT[1]]

ab·watt /áb wòt/ *n* the centimeter-gram-second unit of electrical power, equal to 10^{-7} of a watt

a·bys·mal /ə bízm'l/ *adj* **1.** extremely bad or severe **2.** similar in depth to that of an abyss [Mid-17C. < *abysm*, via Old French < medieval Latin *abysmus*, alteration of late Latin *abyssus* (see ABYSS)] —**a·bys·mal·ly** *adv*

a·byss /ə bíss/ *n* **1. CHASM** a chasm or gorge so deep that its extent is not visible **2. ENDLESS SPACE** something that is immeasurably deep or infinite **3. TERRIBLE SITUATION** a situation of apparently unending awfulness **4. HELL** hell thought of as a bottomless pit [14C. Via late Latin *abyssus* < Greek *abussos* "bottomless" < *bussos* "bottom"]

a·bys·sal /ə bíss'l/ *adj* found in the very deepest areas of the oceans or on the deep ocean floor

a·bys·sal plain *n* a broad flat area of seafloor at the deepest part of an ocean basin

Ab·ys·sin·i·a /àbbə sínnee ə/ former name for **Ethiopia** —**Ab·ys·sin·i·an** *adj, n*

Ab·ys·sin·i·an cat *n* a shorthaired domestic cat belonging to a breed with dark brown or black markings on its brown coat

ab·ys·so·pe·la·gic /ə bìssōpə lájjik/ *adj* relating to or living in the water just above the deep ocean floor [< Greek *abussos* "abyss" (see ABYSS) + *pelagikos* "of the sea" (see PELAGIC)]

Ab·zug /áb tsòog/, **Bella** (1920–98) US feminist, lawyer, and politician. She was an outspoken critic of the Vietnam War and an advocate for civil and minority rights and feminism, an agenda she vigorously pursued as a Democratic US Representative (1970–76). Born **Savitsky, Bella**

ac *abbr* (*used in Internet addresses*) **1.** academic organization **2.** Ascension Island ▶ see table at **domain name**

Ac[1] *symbol* CHEM ELEM actinium

Ac[2] *abbr* BIBLE Acts of the Apostles

AC *abbr* **1.** air conditioning **2.** ELEC ENG alternating current **3.** WINE appellation contrôlée

ac. *abbr* MEASURE acre

ac- *prefix* same as **ad-** (*used before c, k, and q*)

-ac *suffix* person affected with a particular condition ○ *amnesiac* [Via modern Latin *-acus* < Greek *-akos*]

a/c *abbr* **1.** account **2.** account current

A/C *abbr* **1.** ACCT account **2.** ACCT account current **3.** air conditioning

a·ca·cia /ə káyshə/ (*plural* **-cias** *or same*) *n* **1.** a bush or tree that has narrow leaves and dark fruit pods. Flowers: small, yellow. Native to: tropics, subtropics. Genus: *Acacia*. **2.** a tree or plant similar to the acacia **3.** INDUST same as **gum arabic** [14C. Via Latin < Greek *akakia*]

ac·a·deme /ákə deēm/ *n* **1.** EDUC same as **academia 2.** a place of learning, especially a college or university [Late 16C. Partly < Latin *academia*, partly < Greek *Akadēmeia* (see ACADEMY)]

ac·a·de·mi·a /àkə deēmee ə/ *n* scholars and students of the academic world and their activities [Mid-20C. < Latin (see ACADEMY)]

ac·a·dem·ic /àkə démmik/ *adj* **1. EDUCATIONAL** relating to education, educational studies, an educational institution, or the educational system **2. SCHOLARLY** scholarly and intellectual **3. IRRELEVANT IN PRACTICE** theoretical and not of any practical relevance **4. CONVENTIONAL** using the conventional techniques or emphasizing the formal aspects of an art form such as painting or poetry **5.** EDUC **FOR COLLEGE-BOUND STUDENTS** designed for students who intend to study at a college after high school, or attending a school with such courses ○ *She's taking the academic track.* ■ *n* **1. UNIVERSITY TEACHER** somebody teaching or conducting research at an institution of higher learning **2. SCHOLARLY PERSON** somebody with a scholarly background or attitudes —**ac·a·dem·i·cal** *adj* —**ac·a·dem·i·cal·ly** *adv*

ac·a·de·mi·cian /àkədə mísh'n, ə kàddə-/ *n* a member of an academy or society concerned with the arts or sciences

ac·a·dem·i·cism /àkə démmə sìzzəm/, **a·cad·e·mism** /ə káddə mìzzəm/ *n* a reliance on conventional artistic techniques or an emphasis on the formal aspects of an art form such as painting or poetry

ac·a·dem·ic year *n* the annual cycle of teaching and study at an educational institution. It usually starts more than halfway through the calendar year and is divided into semesters or quarters.

a·cad·e·mism *n* ARTS same as **academicism**

a·cad·e·my /ə káddəmee/ (*plural* **-mies**) *n* **1. SOCIETY** a formal society whose purpose is to promote a particular aspect of knowledge or culture **2. SPECIALIZED SCHOOL** an educational institution devoted to a particular subject **3. PRIVATE HIGH SCHOOL** a secondary or high school, usually a private one (*usually used in school names*) **4. ACADEMIC WORLD** the academic community, especially scholars at colleges and universities [Mid-16C. Via Latin *academia* < Greek *Akadēmeia*, the school of philosophy founded by Plato, after the park on the outskirts of Athens where he taught]

A·cad·e·my *n* the school Plato founded to teach his philosophy

A·cad·e·my A·ward *n* an award given annually by the Academy of Motion Picture Arts and Sciences for work in filmmaking or acting

A·ca·di·a /ə káydee ə/ *n* former French colony in North America that encompassed present-day New Brunswick, Nova Scotia, Prince Edward Island, and parts of Quebec and New England —**A·ca·di·an** *n, adj*

A·ca·di·a Na·tion·al Park /ə kàydee ə-/ national park in Northeastern Maine, partially on Mount Desert Island. Established in 1919 as Lafayette National Park, its name changed in 1929. Area: 76 sq. mi./193 sq. km.

A·ca·di·an French *n Can* the form of French spoken in the Canadian provinces of New Brunswick, Nova Scotia, and Prince Edward Island —**A·ca·di·an French** *adj*

A·ca·di·an o·rog·e·ny *n* the stage of mountain formation that occurred in the Appalachian Mountains during the Devonian Period

a·cal·cu·li·a /ày kal kyoōlee ə/ *n* an inability, or the loss of the ability, to carry out basic arithmetic calculations [Early 20C. < A-[2] + Latin *calculare* (see CALCULATE)]

a·can·thi PLANTS, ARCHIT plural of **acanthus**

acantho- *prefix* thorn ○ *acanthopterygian* [< Greek *akanthos* "thorn plant" (see ACANTHUS)]

a·can·tho·ceph·a·lan /ə kànthə séffələn/ *n* ZOOL same as **spiny-headed worm** [Mid-19C. < ACANTHO- + Greek *kephalē* "head" (see CEPHALO-)] —**a·can·tho·ceph·a·lan** *adj*

ac·an·thop·ter·yg·i·an /àkən thòptə ríjjee ən/ *n* a fish with toothed scales and spiny rays on the fins, e.g., a mackerel, perch, or bass. Superorder: Acanthopterygii. [Mid-19C. < Greek *akantha* "thorn" + *pterugion* "fin," literally "small wing" < *pterux* "wing"] —**ac·an·thop·ter·yg·i·an** *adj*

acanthus

a·can·thus /ə kánthəss/ (*plural* **-thus·es** or **-thi** /-thī/ or *same*) *n* **1.** a spiny-leaved bush or perennial plant. Flowers: white, purple. Native to: Mediterranean. Genus: *Acanthus*. **2.** a design characteristic of the capital of a Corinthian column, representing acanthus leaves [Mid-16C. Via Latin < Greek *akanthos* < *akantha* "thorn"]

a cap·pel·la /aàkə péllə, àkə péllə/ *adv, adj* unaccompanied by musical instruments [Late 19C. < Italian, "in chapel style," that is, "in the style of church music"]

Ac·a·pul·co /àkə poōlkō, aàkə poōl-/ seaport and resort on the Pacific coast in southern Mexico. Population: 722,499 (2000).

ac·a·ri ZOOL plural of **acarus**

ac·a·ri·a·sis /àkə rī́ əssiss/ *n* infestation of the skin with mites or ticks

a·car·i·cide /ə kárrə sīd/ *n* a substance that kills mites or ticks

ac·a·rid /ákərid/ *n* a mite or tick. Order: Acarina.

ac·a·roid res·in /àkə royd-/, **ac·a·roid gum** *n* a red resin exuded by some grass trees. Use: varnishes, coatings for paper.

ac·a·rol·o·gy /àkə róllәjee/ *n* the study of mites and ticks —**ac·a·rol·o·gist** *n*

ac·a·ro·pho·bi·a /àkərə fṓbee ə/ *n* an irrational fear of mites or ticks

ac·a·rus /ákərəss/ (*plural* **-ri** /-rī/) *n* a mite or tick (*technical*) [Mid-17C. Via modern Latin < Greek *akari* "mite," literally "too short to cut, tiny" < *kar-* "cut"]

a·cat·a·lec·tic /ay kàttə léktik/ *adj* having the full number of syllables in the final foot of a line of verse ■ *n* a line of verse that has the full number of syllables in the final foot [Late 16C. Via late Latin *acatalecticus* < Greek *akatalēktos* "complete" < *katalēktos* "incomplete"]

a·cau·dal /ay káwd'l/, **a·cau·date** /-dayt/ *adj* without a tail (*technical*)

a·cau·les·cent /ày kaw léss'nt, à kaw-/ *adj* having no stem or one that is very short

acc. *abbr* **1.** ACCT account **2.** GRAM accusative

~~**accademic**~~ incorrect spelling of **academic**

ac·cede /ak seēd/ (**-ced·ed, -ced·ing, -cedes**) *vi* **1. ASSENT** to give consent or agreement to something **2. COME TO POWER** to attain an important and powerful position **3. SIGN TREATY** to become a party to an international agreement or treaty [15C. < Latin *accedere* "come to" < *cedere* "come"] —**ac·ced·ence** *n* —**ac·ced·er** *n*

SPELLCHECK accede or **exceed**? Do not confuse the spelling of ***accede*** and ***exceed***, which sound similar. ***Accede*** is usually followed by *to*, as in *accede to our requests, accede to the throne.* ***Exceed*** means "be greater than" or "go beyond": *Income exceeds expenditure. Do not exceed the speed limit.*

accel. *abbr* MUSIC accelerando

ac·cel·er·an·do /ak sèllə rándō, aa chèllə raándō/ *adv, adj* with gradually increasing speed (*used as a musical direction*) [Early 19C. < Italian, "accelerating"]

ac·cel·er·ant /ak séllərənt/ *n* **1.** a substance that is used to intensify a fire **2.** CHEM same as **accelerator** (sense 3)

ac·cel·er·ate /ak séllə ràyt/ (**-at·ed, -at·ing, -ates**) *vti* **1.** to move increasingly quickly, or cause something to do this **2.** to happen or develop faster, or cause something to do this [Early 16C. < Latin *acceleratus*, past participle of *accelerare* "quicken" < *celer* "quick"] —**ac·cel·er·at·ed** *adj* —**ac·cel·er·a·tive** *adj*

ac·cel·er·at·ed graph·ics port *n* a computer interface that allows the display of three-dimensional graphics

ac·cel·er·a·tion /ak sèllə ráysh'n/ *n* **1. INCREASE IN SPEED** the rate at which something increases in velocity **2. INCREASE IN RATE OF PROGRESS** an increase in the rate at which something happens or develops **3. ACT OF ACCELERATING** the act of accelerating, or the process of being accelerated **4.** PHYS **MEASURE OF INCREASE IN VELOCITY** a measure of the rate of increase in the velocity of something per unit of time. Symbol *a*

ac·cel·er·a·tion clause *n* a clause in the terms of a loan or mortgage stipulating that payments must be made earlier in specific circumstances

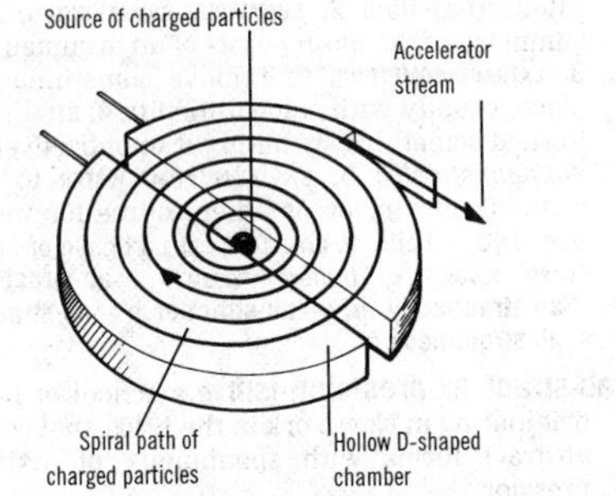

accelerator (sense 2)

ac·cel·er·a·tor /ak séllə ràytər/ *n* **1. SPEED-INCREASING CONTROL** a pedal or other control mechanism used to cause a vehicle to increase speed **2.** PHYS **DEVICE FOR GIVING PARTICLES HIGH VELOCITIES** a machine used to increase the velocity, and hence the kinetic energy, of subatomic particles or nuclei, usually in preparation for collision with a target **3.** CHEM **CHEMICAL THAT SPEEDS UP REACTION** a substance that speeds up chemical reactions

ac·cel·er·a·tor card, ac·cel·er·a·tor board *n* a circuit board that adds a faster central processing unit to a computer

ac·cel·er·om·e·ter /ak sèllə rómmətər/ *n* an instrument or device for measuring acceleration, especially one in which a sensor converts acceleration into an electrical signal

ac·cent *n* /ák sènt/ **1. MANNER OF PRONUNCIATION** a way of pronouncing words that indicates the place of origin or social background of the speaker ○ *a Southern accent* **2. INTONATION** a way of using intonation or inflection to convey the speaker's mood or character ○ *He answered with an accent of bitterness.* **3. STRESS ON SYLLABLE** a greater emphasis in pronouncing a syllable within a word or a word within a phrase **4. MARK ABOVE LETTER** a symbol used in print or writing to indicate stress or the pronunciation of a vowel **5. MAIN EMPHASIS** an aspect of a situation or issue that is emphasized ○ *The accent is on safety.* **6. CONTRASTING DETAIL** a contrasting decorative feature used to add interest ○ *a blue room with green accents in the furnishings* **7. STYLE** a distinctive style that is characteristic of a particular person, region, or artistic school **8.** MUSIC **STRESS ON NOTES** stress placed on specific notes in a piece of music, or the symbol printed above the notes to indicate this stress **9.** MATH, MEASURE same as **prime**[1] *n* (sense 3) ■ *vt* /ák sènt, ak sént/ (**-cent·ed, -cent·ing, -cents**) **1. EMPHASIZE SOMETHING** to stress or emphasize something, e.g., to pronounce a word or syllable more prominently than those surrounding it or play a musical note or beat with greater volume or attack **2. MARK SOMETHING WITH ACCENT** to mark something such as a letter or word with a written or printed accent [Early 16C. Via French < Latin *accentus* < *ad* "to" + *cantus* "singing," literal translation of Greek *prosōidia* "accompanied song"]

ac·cent·ed /ák sentəd/ *adj* **1.** written or printed with an accent above the character **2.** having a way of pronouncing words that is characteristic of a particular native language or region of birth

USAGE Inflected or **accented**? In terms of speech, ***inflected*** means, among other things, "modulated or modified in pitch or loudness" as in *a monologue inflected*

with tag questions and funny exclamations. By contrast, ***accented*** means, among other things, "having a way of pronouncing words that is characteristic of a particular native language or region of birth," as in *the accented speech patterns of people from Maine.* Recently some writers have started using ***inflected*** where ***accented*** is the word of choice, as in *He grew up in non-English-speaking lands, but spent more time in England than elsewhere. You can hear that in his barely inflected English, full of idioms.* This usage, which has not gained acceptance in Standard English, should be avoided.

ac·cent light·ing *n* lighting that highlights an area or feature of a room, e.g., a painting or an alcove

ac·cen·tu·al /ak sénchoo əl/ *adj* **1.** involving or associated with accent or stress **2.** employing a structure based on the number of stresses in a poetic line instead of the number of syllables —**ac·cen·tu·al·ly** *adv*

ac·cen·tu·ate /ak sénchoo àyt/ (**-at·ed, -at·ing, -ates**) *vt* **1.** to make a feature of something more noticeable **2.** to emphasize a syllable, word, or phrase when saying it [Mid-18C. < medieval Latin *accentuatus*, past participle of *accentuare* "emphasize" < Latin *accentus* (see ACCENT)] —**ac·cen·tu·a·tion** /ak sènchoo áysh'n/ *n*

ac·cept /ak sépt/ (**-cept·ed, -cept·ing, -cepts**) *v* **1.** *vt* **TAKE SOMETHING OFFERED** to take something that is offered, e.g., a gift or payment **2.** *vti* **SAY YES TO INVITATION** to reply in the affirmative to an invitation or offer **3.** *vt* **COME TO TERMS WITH SOMETHING** to acknowledge a fact or truth and come to terms with it **4.** *vt* **ENDURE SITUATION** to tolerate something without protesting or attempting to change it **5.** *vt* **BELIEVE SOMETHING** to acknowledge that something is true **6.** *vt* LAW **AGREE TO TERMS** to indicate formal agreement to the terms and conditions in a contract **7.** *vt* **TAKE BLAME FOR SOMETHING** to admit the blame or responsibility for something **8.** *vti* **TAKE ON DUTY** to agree to take on a duty, responsibility, or position **9.** *vt* **PROCESS SOMETHING** to be able to process something or be operated by something ○ *old machines that won't accept the new cards* **10.** *vt* **ALLOW SOMEBODY TO JOIN** to allow somebody to join an organization or attend an institution **11.** *vt* **BE WELCOMING TO SOMEBODY** to treat somebody as a member of a group or social circle **12.** *vt* **RECEIVE FOR REVIEW** to receive something such as a report for official action or review [14C. Via French *accepter* < Latin *acceptare* < *accipere* "take to (yourself)" < *capere* "take"] —**ac·cept·ed** *adj*

USAGE accept or **except**? Do not confuse these two, even though they have similar pronunciations. ***Accept*** is a verb only; it means variously "to take something offered," "to believe something," and "to agree to something," as in *We cannot accept* [not *except*] *such a lame excuse.* ***Except*** can work as a preposition meaning "to the exclusion of," "excluding," as in *All students except* [not *accept*] *the freshmen are eligible.* It is also a conjunction meaning "if it were not for the fact that" and "otherwise than," as in *I would have finished the course except* [not *accept*] *that I became ill at the end of the semester. The demonstrators did not quiet down except* [not *accept*] *to regroup and plan their next move.* Finally, it is a verb used most often in the passive voice in the meaning "to leave out or exclude," as in *Only children were excepted* [not *accepted*] *from attendance.*

ac·cept·a·ble /ak séptəb'l/ *adj* **1.** **ADEQUATE** considered to be satisfactory **2.** **APPROVED OF** likely to gain somebody's approval **3.** **WELCOME** likely to please the person who receives it —**ac·cept·a·bil·i·ty** /ak sèptə bíllətee/ *n* —**ac·cept·a·ble·ness** *n* —**ac·cept·a·bly** *adv*

ac·cept·a·ble dai·ly in·take *n* the highest daily intake level of a chemical that, if continued over the whole life of a person, is considered to pose no health risk

ac·cep·tance /ak séptənss/ *n* **1.** **AGREEMENT TO INVITATION OR OFFER** a written or verbal indication that somebody agrees to an invitation or offer **2.** **ACT OF WILLINGLY TAKING GIFT** the willing receipt of a gift or payment **3.** **WILLINGNESS TO BELIEVE** willingness to believe that something is true **4.** **COMING TO TERMS WITH SOMETHING** the realization of a fact or truth and the process of coming to terms with it **5.** **TOLERATION** the toleration of something without protest **6.** **SOCIAL TOLERANCE** willingness to treat somebody as a member of a group or social circle **7.** **POSITIVE RESPONSE TO APPLICATION** an offer to allow somebody to join an organization or attend an institution **8.** LAW **AGREEMENT TO TERMS** formal written or verbal agreement showing that somebody assents to the terms and conditions in a contract **9.** LAW **AGREEMENT TO PAY** a formal agreement by a debtor to pay a draft or bill of exchange when it becomes payable

ac·cep·ta·tion /àk sep táysh'n/ *n* **1.** a generally favorable reception of something **2.** the sense in which a word or phrase is generally understood

ac·cept·er /ak séptər/ *n* **1.** somebody or something that accepts something **2.** LAW another spelling of **acceptor** (sense 1)

ac·cept·ing /ak sépting/ *adj* able to endure something difficult or unpleasant without complaint or protest ○ *Illness brought many restrictions, but he was very accepting of them.* —**ac·cept·ing·ly** *adv*

ac·cept·ing house *n* a financial institution that guarantees bills of exchange

ac·cep·tor /ak séptər/ *n* **1.** somebody who accepts liability for a bill of exchange **2.** an atom or group of atoms that accepts electrons to form a coordinate bond during the formation of a chemical compound

ac·cess /ák sèss/ *n* **1.** **ENTRY OR APPROACH** a means of entering or approaching a place ○ *Thieves gained access to the premises via a side door.* **2.** **OPPORTUNITY FOR USE** the opportunity or right to experience or make use of something **3.** **RIGHT TO MEET SOMEBODY** the opportunity to meet somebody **4.** **OUTBURST** a sudden strongly felt burst of emotion (*literary*) ○*"With a sudden access of tenderness he flung his arm about me."* (Rider Haggard, *She*; 1887) **5.** COMPUT **RIGHT TO USE COMPUTER** the right or ability to log on to a computer system or use a computer program ○ *software that allows network access* ■ *vt* (**-cessed, -cess·ing, -cess·es**) **1.** **ENTER PLACE** to find a means of entering or approaching a place **2.** ⚠ **GET INFORMATION** to have the opportunity or right to experience or make use of something **3.** COMPUT **CALL UP DATA** to retrieve data or a computer file ○ *The program can be accessed using the correct password.* [14C. Directly or via Old French *acces* < Latin *accessus*, past participle of *accedere* "come near" (see ACCEDE)]

SPELLCHECK access or **excess**? Do not confuse the spelling of ***access*** and ***excess***, which sound similar. ***Access*** refers to a right or opportunity for approach, entry, contact, or use: *gain access to secret information, to access a computer program.* ***Excess*** refers to something extra or more than enough: *temperatures in excess of 100 degrees, excess baggage.* Note also the literary use of ***access*** to mean "an outburst of emotion," as in *an access of tenderness*, and do not confuse it with ***excess*** meaning "a surplus of emotion," as in *an excess of enthusiasm.*

USAGE access as a verb: It is entirely appropriate to use ***access*** as a verb in computing contexts, as in *had to access several complex spreadsheets*, but some critics resist its use in general contexts such as accessing bank accounts or biographical information.

~~accessable~~ incorrect spelling of **accessible**

ac·ces·sa·ry *n, adj* LAW another spelling of **accessory** *n* (sense 3), *adj* (sense 2)

USAGE See ***accessory.***

ac·cess bro·ker *n US* somebody with connections to high officials in a political administration who uses those connections for lobbying

ac·cess code *n* a sequence of letters or numbers that have to be keyed in to allow somebody access to a restricted area, e.g., a building or a computerized network

ac·ces·si·ble /ak séssəb'l/ *adj* **1.** **EASILY REACHED** easy to enter or reach physically **2.** **EASILY UNDERSTOOD** able to be appreciated or understood without specialist knowledge **3.** **EASILY AVAILABLE** able to be obtained, used, or experienced without difficulty **4.** **APPROACHABLE** not aloof and not difficult to talk to or meet with **5.** **SUSCEPTIBLE** susceptible to or likely to be influenced by something **6.** **EASY FOR PHYSICALLY CHALLENGED PEOPLE TO USE** suitable or adapted for people with physical challenges **7.** LOGIC **OBSERVABLE FROM ANOTHER WORLD** able to be referred to from another possible world, so that the truth value of statements about it can be given —**ac·ces·si·bil·i·ty** /ak sèssə bíllətee/ *n* —**ac·ces·si·bly** *adv*

ac·ces·sion /ak sésh'n/ *n* **1.** **TAKING UP OF POSITION** the assumption of an important position, usually a position of power **2.** LAW **ACCEPTANCE OF TREATY** the formal acceptance by a state of an international treaty or convention **3.** **ASSENT** agreement or consent, usually when given unwillingly **4.** **ADDITION TO COLLECTION** an item added to a collection **5.** **SUDDEN MOOD** a sudden and unexpected display of a particular mood or emotion (*literary*) **6.** LAW **INCREASE TO PROPERTY** addition to property by natural growth or improvement **7.** LAW **RIGHT TO INCREASE IN PROPERTY** the right of an owner to add to a property by natural growth or improvement ■ *vt* (**-sioned, -sion·ing, -sions**) **CATALOG ADDITIONS TO COLLECTION** to make a formal record of an addition to a collection —**ac·ces·sion·al** *adj*

ac·cess num·ber *n* the telephone number used to link to an Internet service provider or other network provider using a dial-up connection

ac·ces·sor·ize /ak séssə rīz/ (**-ized, -iz·ing, -iz·es**) *v* **1.** *vti* to wear or use items such as gloves, hats, and handbags to complete an outfit of clothing **2.** *vt* to fit accessories to something

ac·ces·so·ry /ak séssəree/ *n* (*plural* **-ries**) **1.** **OPTIONAL PART** an optional part that may be fitted to something to perform an additional function or enhance performance **2.** **FASHION ARTICLE** an item of clothing that is worn or used for a fashionable effect with an outfit ○*"designers who create neckties as fashion accessories"* (*International Herald Tribune*; June 1997) **3.** *also* **ac·ces·sa·ry** LAW **SOMEBODY WHO HELPS CRIMINAL** somebody who aids somebody else in committing a crime or avoiding arrest but who does not participate in the crime itself ■ *adj* **1.** **ADDITIONAL** supplementary or subsidiary to something more important **2.** *also* **ac·ces·sa·ry** LAW **ASSISTING IN CRIME** aiding a criminal act although not participating in the crime itself —**ac·ces·so·ri·al** /àk se sáwree əl/ *adj* —**ac·ces·so·ri·ly** *adv* —**ac·ces·so·ri·ness** *n*

USAGE ***Accessory*** is the usual spelling. ***Accessary*** is an older form that is still occasionally used, especially in some legal contexts.

ac·ces·so·ry af·ter the fact (*plural* **ac·ces·so·ries af·ter the fact**) *n* somebody who helps a criminal after a crime

ac·ces·so·ry a·part·ment *n US* a self-contained apartment within a family home, usually used as an in-law suite or for rental

ac·ces·so·ry be·fore the fact (*plural* **ac·ces·so·ries be·fore the fact**) *n* somebody who incites or helps a criminal before a crime

ac·ces·so·ry min·er·al *n* a mineral in igneous rock that occurs in small quantities

ac·ces·so·ry nerve *n* the eleventh cranial nerve, associated with the pharynx and muscles in the throat, larynx, palate, neck, and back

ac·cess point *n* a transceiver in a wireless local area network that connects a wired local area network to wireless devices or that connects wireless devices to each other

ac·cess pro·file *n* the details identifying a computer user held on a server or other computer, specifying the name and password and the areas of a computer system the user is authorized to access

ac·cess time *n* the time a computer takes to locate and retrieve data

ac·ciac·ca·tu·ra /aa chaàkə tóorə/ (*plural* **-ras** or **-re** /-ray/) *n* a brief note (**grace note**) added to a piece of music and played quickly at the same time as or just before a principal note [Early 19C. < Italian, "crushed"]

ac·ci·dence /áksidənss/ *n* the area of traditional grammar dealing with the inflections of words [15C. < late Latin *accidentia* (plural) "things that happen" (taken as singular) < Latin *accident-* (see ACCIDENT)]

ac·ci·dent /áksidənt, áksi dènt/ *n* **1.** **CRASH** a collision or similar incident involving a moving vehicle, resulting in property damage, personal injury or death **2.** **MISHAP** an unplanned and unfortunate event that results in damage, injury, or upset of some kind **3.** **CHANCE** the way things happen without any planning, apparent cause, or deliberate intent ○ *I met him by accident.* **4.** **CHANCE HAPPENING** an event that happens completely by chance, with no planning or deliberate intent **5.** **INSTANCE OF INCONTINENCE** an incident when somebody, particularly a small child, is incontinent (*euphemistic*) **6. UNPLANNED PREGNANCY** a child conceived in an unplanned way **7.** PHILOSOPHY **NONESSENTIAL ATTRIBUTE** a nonessential attribute or characteristic of something [14C. Via French < Latin *accident-*, present participle of *accidere* "happen" < *cadere* "fall, die"]

ac·ci·den·tal /àksi dént'l/ *adj* **1. CHANCE** happening by chance and not planned **2. INCIDENTAL** not specifically intended and arising as a side effect **3.** MUSIC **NOT IN KEY SIGNATURE** sharp, flat, or natural, in a way not indicated in the key signature ■ *n* **1. UNPLANNED EFFECT** something not specifically intended that arises as a side effect **2.** MUSIC **NOTE NOT IN KEY SIGNATURE** a musical note, marked with a sharp, flat, or natural sign, whose pitch does not correspond to the key signature —**ac·ci·den·tal·ly** *adv*

ac·ci·den·tal death *n* death caused by an accident rather than by natural causes, suicide, or murder

ac·ci·dent and e·mer·gen·cy *n UK* same as **emergency room**

ac·ci·dent in·sur·ance *n* insurance against property damage, personal injury, or death caused by an accident

~~**accidently**~~ incorrect spelling of **accidentally**

ac·ci·dent-prone *adj* having more accidents than average

ac·cip·i·ter /ak síppitər/ *n* a hawk, typically with short broad wings and a long tail, e.g., a sparrow hawk or goshawk. Genus: *Accipiter*. [Early 19C. < Latin < *accipere* "take to (yourself)" (see ACCEPT)]

ac·cip·i·trine /ak síppi trìn, -trīn/ *adj* relating to or belonging to the family of predatory birds including hawks, eagles, and kites

ac·claim /ə kláym/ *v* (**-claimed, -claim·ing, -claims**) **1.** *vt* **PRAISE SOMEBODY HIGHLY** to praise somebody or something publicly and enthusiastically **2.** *vt* **PRONOUNCE SOMEBODY TO BE SOMETHING** to declare publicly and enthusiastically that somebody holds a high position ○ *was acclaimed as the winner* **3.** *vi* **SHOUT ENTHUSIASTICALLY** to demonstrate enthusiastic approval by shouting and cheering **4.** *vt Can* **WIN OFFICE BY DEFAULT** to elect a candidate to an office by default, owing to a lack of opposition (*usually passive*) ■ *n* **ENTHUSIASTIC RECEPTION** enthusiastic approval given to somebody or something publicly [Early 16C. < Latin *acclamare* "shout to" < *clamare* "shout"] —**ac·claim·er** *n*

ac·cla·ma·tion /àklə máysh'n/ *n* **1. APPROVAL** a public and enthusiastic display of approval **2. VOCAL VOTE** a vote in which no formal ballot is held but the voters make views clear by shouts or applause **3.** *Can* **UNOPPOSED ELECTION WIN** an election victory won through default, owing to a lack of opposition [Mid-16C. < Latin *acclamation-* < *acclamare* (see ACCLAIM)] —**ac·clam·a·to·ry** /ə klámmə tàwree/ *adj*

ac·cli·mate /ə klīmət, áklə màyt/ (**-mat·ed, -mat·ing, -mates**) *v* **1.** *vti* same as **acclimatize 2.** *vi* to adjust in response to a change in environment or status ○ *became acclimated to their new prosperity* [Late 18C. < French *acclimater* < *a-* "to" + *climat* "climate" (see CLIMATE)] —**ac·cli·ma·tion** /àklə máysh'n/ *n*

ac·cli·ma·tize /ə klīmə tīz/ (**-tized, -tiz·ing, -tiz·es**) *vti* to become accustomed to a new climate or environment, or help somebody to do this —**ac·cli·ma·ti·za·tion** /ə klīmətə záysh'n/ *n*

ac·cliv·i·ty /ə klívvətee/ (*plural* **-ties**) *n* an upward slope on a hill [Early 17C. < Latin *acclivitat-* "ascent" < *acclivis* "uphill" < *clivus* "slope"]

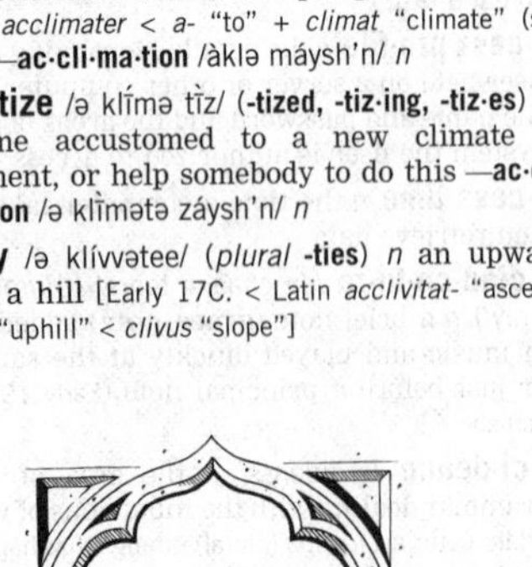

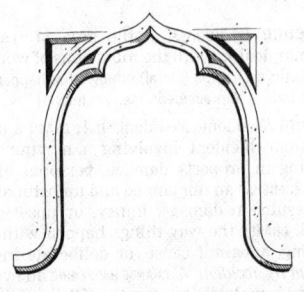

accolade (sense 4)

ac·co·lade /ákə làyd, -laad/ *n* **1. SIGN OF PRAISE** a sign or expression of high praise and esteem for somebody **2. PUBLIC RECOGNITION** praise and public recognition of somebody's achievements **3. KNIGHTING** the ceremonial bestowal of a knighthood by touching somebody's shoulders with a sword. Knighthood was formerly conferred by an embrace. **4.** ARCHIT **CURVED MOLDING** an ornamental molding shaped like a brace [Early 17C. Via French < Provençal *acolada* "embrace" < Latin *collum* "neck"; because knighthood was formerly conferred with an embrace]

ac·com·mo·date /ə kómmə dàyt/ (**-dat·ed, -dat·ing, -dates**) *v* **1.** *vt* **OBLIGE SOMEBODY** to adjust actions in response to the needs of somebody **2.** *vt* **ALLOW FOR SOMETHING** to be adaptable enough to allow something without major change **3.** *vt* **HAVE ROOM FOR SOMEBODY OR SOMETHING** to have sufficient space for somebody or something **4.** *vt* **PROVIDE LODGING FOR SOMEBODY** to provide somebody with a place to stay **5.** *vi* **ADAPT TO SOMETHING NEW** to adapt to a new situation **6.** *vt* **LEND SOMEBODY MONEY** to give somebody money in response to a request for a loan **7.** *vti* **REACH AGREEMENT** to settle a difference of opinion in a way that is acceptable to all those involved **8.** *vi* OPHTHALMOL **ADJUST FOCUS** to adjust focus automatically to give clear vision (*refers to the eyes*) [Mid-16C. < Latin *accommodare* "make fit" < *commodus* "suitable" < *modus* "measure"] —**ac·com·mo·da·tive** *adj*

USAGE Note that ***accommodate*** and ***accommodation*** are spelled with *-cc-* and *-mm-*. ***Accommodation,*** in particular, is often misspelled with a single *-m-*.

ac·com·mo·dat·ing /ə kómmə dàyting/ *adj* willing to adjust actions in response to the needs of somebody else —**ac·com·mo·dat·ing·ly** *adv*

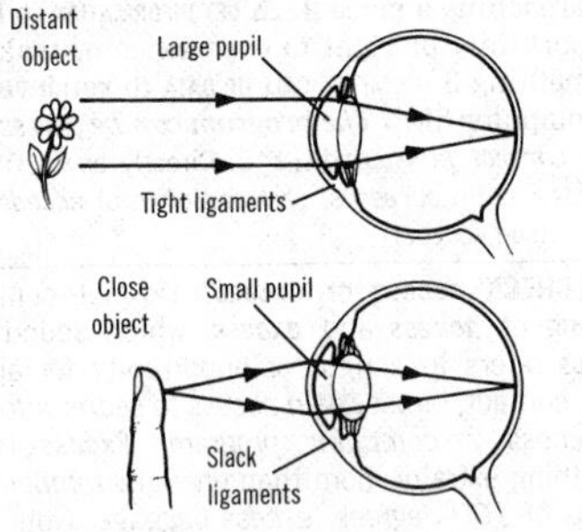

accommodation: adjustment of eye focus on a distant object (top) and a close object (bottom)

ac·com·mo·da·tion /ə kòmmə dáysh'n/ *n* **1. ADJUSTMENT** the modification of actions in response something **2. AGREEMENT** an agreement acceptable to all parties in a dispute **3. FLEXIBILITY** the ability to include something without major change **4.** OPHTHALMOL **ADJUSTMENT OF EYE FOCUS** the automatic adjustment of the focus of an eye to give clear vision **5.** BANKING **LOAN OF MONEY** a loan of money, especially by a financial institution as a favor to somebody before a formal credit arrangement is made **6.** *Can, UK* same as **accommodations** (senses 1, 2) ○ *looking for accommodation* ■ **ac·com·mo·da·tions** *npl* **1.** *US* **SEATING** seating in a vehicle or public facility. Can term **accommodation 2. LODGING** a room or building to live in

ac·com·mo·da·tion ad·dress *n UK* a mailing address used by a person or organization unwilling or unable to use an identifiable individual address

ac·com·mo·da·tion bill *n* a bill of exchange cosigned by another party in order to give added security

ac·com·mo·da·tion cen·ter *n* a building or site containing temporary accommodations, especially for tourists or students

ac·com·mo·da·tion·ist /ə kòmmə dáysh'nist/ *n* somebody who prefers compromise to confrontation —**ac·com·mo·da·tion·ist** *adj*

ac·com·mo·da·tion lad·der *n* a ladder or flight of steps hung over the side of a boat to allow boarding or disembarking

ac·com·mo·da·tion plat·form, ac·com·mo·da·tion rig *n* a platform or rig used as living quarters for offshore oil or gas workers

~~**accomodate**~~ incorrect spelling of **accommodate**

~~**accomodation**~~ incorrect spelling of **accommodation**

ac·com·pa·ni·ment /ə kúmpənimənt, -pni-/ *n* **1.** MUSIC **MUSICAL BACKING** instrumental or vocal parts in a musical composition that support the more important parts **2. SIMULTANEOUS OCCURRENCE** something that occurs at the same time and in the same place as something else ○ *torrential rain, with an accompaniment of crashing thunder* **3. SUPPLEMENT** an item that is added or served because it goes well with something ○ *mint sauce, the perfect accompaniment to roast lamb*

ac·com·pa·nist /ə kúmpənist, -pnist/ *n* a musician, especially a pianist, playing the accompaniment for a soloist

ac·com·pa·ny /ə kúmpənee, -pnee/ (**-nied, -ny·ing, -nies**) *v* **1.** *vt* **ESCORT SOMEBODY** to go with somebody **2.** *vt* **BE PRESENT WITH SOMETHING** to be enclosed, attached, or present with something **3.** *vt* **OCCUR WITH SOMETHING** to happen at the same time as something else **4.** *vt* **SUPPLEMENT SOMETHING** to be present or served with something as a supplement **5.** *vti* MUSIC **PROVIDE MUSICAL BACKING** to play or sing a part that supports a more important part [15C. < Old French *acompaignier* "be a companion to" < *compaing* "companion" (see COMPANION[1])]

ac·com·plice /ə kómpliss/ *n* somebody who helps somebody else to commit a crime or misdeed [Mid-16C. < archaic *complice* (by misunderstanding of *a complice*), via French < Latin *complic-*, stem of *complex* "associate" < *complicare* (see COMPLICATE)]

ac·com·plish /ə kómplish/ (**-plished, -plish·ing, -plish·es**) *vt* to carry out or complete something successfully [14C. < Old French *accompliss-*, a stem of *acomplir* "complete to" < Latin *complere* (see COMPLETE)] —**ac·com·plish·a·ble** *adj* —**ac·com·plish·er** *n*

SYNONYMS *accomplish, achieve, attain, carry out, pull off, realize*

CORE MEANING: to bring something to a successful conclusion

accomplish to carry out or complete something successfully ○ *You don't accomplish anything by placing blame.* ○ *Mission accomplished, we headed for home.* **achieve** to succeed in doing something, usually with effort ○ *three main ways in which the government hopes to achieve its aims* ○ *an example of what can be achieved through good planning* **attain** to achieve a goal or desired state, usually with effort ○ *a desire to attain the best qualifications* ○ *attain a full command of the English language* **carry out** to perform a task or activity ○ *carry out calculations with faultless accuracy* ○ *She found it hard to believe that Julius would actually carry out his threat.* **pull off** (*informal*) to achieve something impressive, particularly through a combination of skill and luck ○ *The goalkeeper pulled off a fine save.* ○ *He pulled off an immediate coup by appointing a well-known entrepreneur as patron.* **realize** to fulfill a specific vision, plan, or potential ○ *realize your potential* ○ *His dream was realized when he signed for the New York Giants.*

ac·com·plished /ə kómplisht/ *adj* **1. TALENTED** having considerable talent and skill **2. HAVING SOCIAL GRACES** possessing social skills and talents **3. BEYOND DOUBT** fully established ○ *an accomplished fact*

ac·com·plish·ment /ə kómplishmənt/ *n* **1. ACHIEVING OF SOMETHING** the completion or fulfillment of something **2. FEAT** a remarkable or successful achievement **3. TALENT** a skill or talent that has been developed

Ac·con·ci /ə kónssee/, **Vito** (*b.* 1940) US artist. He explored the concept of space through film, video, and installations that doubled as meeting places. He has collaborated with architects to design landscaping for public places.

ac·cord /ə káwrd/ *v* (**-cord·ed, -cord·ing, -cords**) **1.** *vt* **RENDER SOMEBODY SOMETHING** to give somebody or something a particular status or treatment ○ *was accorded the same privileges as her predecessor* **2.** *vi* **AGREE** to be in agreement or come to an agreement ○ *accords with my own view* **3.** *vt* **GRANT SOMETHING** to bestow something such as a blessing on somebody ■ *n* **1. AGREEMENT** a treaty or settlement agreed to by two or more parties **2. CONSENSUS** general agreement as to what is right **3. HARMONY** a state in which things are in harmony with each other [Pre-12C. < Old French *acorder* < Latin *ad* "to" + *cord-*, stem of *cor* "heart"] ◇ **of** *or* **on your own accord** of your own free will

ac·cor·dance /ə káwrd'nss/ *n* **1.** CONSENSUS consensus as to the right course of action **2.** ADHERENCE TO CORRECT PROCESS conformity with specific procedures or actions ○ *in accordance with official guidelines* **3.** BESTOWAL the bestowal of a particular status or treatment on somebody or something

ac·cord·ing as /ə káwrding-/ *conj* depending on whether, or corresponding to the extent to which ○ *were deemed approved or unapproved, according as each matched the specification*

ac·cord·ing·ly /ə káwrdinglee/ *adv* **1.** in a way that is appropriate **2.** in accordance with what has been said or with a principle or practice

ac·cord·ing to *prep* **1.** ON SOMEBODY'S OR SOMETHING'S AUTHORITY as stated by somebody or indicated by something ○ *the gospel according to St. Luke* **2.** RELATED TO depending on and corresponding in extent to something ○ *salary according to experience* **3.** AS DETERMINED BY on the basis of and in line with a method or principle ○ *arranged according to alphabetical order* **4.** AS LAID DOWN BY in the way that a plan or system stipulates ○ *done exactly according to the instructions*

ac·cor·di·on /ə káwrdee ən/ *n* a musical instrument with a keyboard or buttons on one side, buttons on the other, and a bellows in the middle that forces air through metal reeds [Mid-19C. < German *Akkordion* < *Akkord* "chord" < Italian *accordare* "tune (an instrument)"]

ac·cor·di·on pleats *npl* sharp pleats in a garment or piece of fabric, like the folds in an accordion's bellows

ac·cost /ə káwst/ (**-cost·ed, -cost·ing, -costs**) *vt* to approach and stop somebody in order to speak to that person, especially in an aggressive, insistent, or suggestive way [Late 16C. Via French < Latin *accostare* "adjoin" < *costa* "rib, side"] —**ac·cost·er** *n*

ac·count /ə kównt/ *n* **1.** REPORT a written or spoken report of something **2.** EXPLANATION an explanation of something that has happened, especially one given to somebody in authority **3.** BANKING BANK ARRANGEMENT an arrangement in which a customer keeps money in a bank or other financial institution and is offered financial services in exchange **4.** BANKING MONEY IN BANK the money that a customer keeps in a bank **5.** FIN FINANCIAL ARRANGEMENT an arrangement with a store, company, stockbroker, or other business, in which financial services are provided, e.g., credit **6.** ONLINE NETWORK ACCESS CONTRACT a contractual agreement between a user and an Internet or e-mail service provider establishing a directory and other system information and giving the user access to a network, e.g., the Internet, in return for a fee or other consideration **7.** BUSINESS CUSTOMER a customer who has a regular business relationship with a company ■ **ac·counts** *npl* ACCT LIST OF FINANCIAL INFORMATION a detailed list of everything that a person or company earns or spends, kept primarily for tax purposes ■ *vt* (**-count·ed, -count·ing, -counts**) CONSIDER to consider somebody or something to have a particular quality (*formal*) ○ *We would account it a privilege to serve you.* [14C. < Old French *aconte* "a counting up" < *aconter* < Latin *computare* "sum up"] ◇ **by all accounts** according to what most people say ◇ **call somebody to account** to demand that somebody explain what he or she has done ◇ **give a good account of yourself** to do something in a way that does justice to your abilities or character ◇ **of no account** of no importance ◇ **on account** on credit ◇ **on account of** because of ◇ **on no account** for no reason, whatever the circumstances ◇ **on somebody's account** out of concern for somebody's well-being ◇ **take account of somebody or something, take somebody or something into account** to consider somebody or something when making a decision ◇ **turn something to good account** to use or deal with something in a way that puts it to good use

account for *vt* **1.** EXPLAIN SOMETHING to provide an explanation for something ○ *And how do you account for his behavior?* **2.** BE RESPONSIBLE FOR SOMETHING to be responsible for something or be an important factor in something ○ *Export sales account for at least half of our total business.* **3.** KILL OR DESTROY SOMEBODY OR SOMETHING to be responsible for killing, destroying, or neutralizing somebody or something

ac·count·a·ble /ə kówntəb'l/ *adj* **1.** responsible to somebody or for something **2.** capable of being explained (*formal*) —**ac·count·a·bil·i·ty** /ə kòwntə bíllətee/ *n* —**ac·count·a·ble·ness** *n* —**ac·count·a·bly** *adv*

ac·count·an·cy /ə kówntənsee/ *n* the work or profession of an accountant

ac·count·ant /ə kówntənt/ *n* somebody who maintains the business records of a person or organization and prepares forms and reports for tax or other financial purposes

ac·count ex·ec·u·tive *n* an employee, especially in an advertising or public relations company, who handles all of a client's business

ac·count·ing /ə kównting/ *n* the activity, practice, or profession of maintaining the business records of a person or organization and preparing forms and reports for tax or other financial purposes

ac·count·ing rate of re·turn (*plural* **ac·count·ing rates of re·turn**) *n* a calculation of the anticipated net profit from an investment in an asset or project, expressed as a percentage of the money invested

ac·counts pay·a·ble *npl* a record that shows how much a company owes suppliers for the purchase of goods or services on credit

ac·counts re·ceiv·a·ble *npl* a record that shows how much is owed to a company by customers who have purchased goods or services on credit

~~**accoustic**~~ incorrect spelling of **acoustic**

ac·cou·ter /ə kóotər/ (**-tered, -ter·ing, -ters**), **ac·cou·tre** (**-tred, -tring, -tres**) *vt* to equip and clothe somebody, especially for military purposes [Mid-16C. < French *accoutrer* "equip with something, especially clothes" < assumed Latin *consutura* "sewn together" < *sutura* "sewn"]

ac·cou·ter·ment /ə kóotərmənt/, **ac·cou·tre·ment** /ə kóotrə-/ *n* **1.** an accessory or piece of equipment associated with a specific object, task, or role **2.** a piece of military equipment carried by soldiers in addition to their standard uniform and weapons

ac·cou·tre *vt* MIL another spelling of **accouter**

ac·cou·tre·ment *n* MIL another spelling of **accouterment**

ac·cra *n* another spelling of **akara**

Ac·cra /ə kraá, ákrə/ capital of Ghana. It is located on the Gulf of Guinea in southeastern Ghana. Population: 1,904,000 (1999).

ac·cred·it /ə kréddət/ (**-it·ed, -it·ing, -its**) *vt* **1.** GIVE OFFICIAL RECOGNITION TO SOMEBODY to officially recognize a person or organization as having met a standard or criterion (*usually passive*) ○ *The hospital is fully accredited.* **2.** APPOINT SOMEBODY AS ENVOY to appoint somebody as an envoy or ambassador to another country **3.** GIVE SOMEBODY AUTHORITY to give somebody the authority to perform a function (*usually passive*) **4.** ATTRIBUTE QUALITY TO SOMEBODY to regard somebody as having a particular quality ○ *accredited them with more intelligence than they have* **5.** ASCRIBE SOMETHING TO SOMEBODY to consider something as belonging to or attributable to somebody ○ *We cannot accredit all the problems to immigration.* [Early 17C. < French *accréditer* "believe (firmly)" < *crédit* (see CREDIT)] —**ac·cred·i·ta·tion** /ə krèddə táysh'n/ *n*

ac·crete /ə kreét/ (**-cret·ed, -cret·ing, -cretes**) *vti* to increase in size, or increase the size of something, especially by accumulation or the growing together of separate things [Late 18C. < Latin *accret-*, past participle of *accrescere* < *crescere* "grow"]

ac·cre·tion /ə kreésh'n/ *n* **1.** INCREASE an increase in size as a result of accumulation or the growing together of separate things **2.** SOMETHING ACCUMULATED something formed by or resulting from accretion **3.** FIN ADDITION something added to something such as a fund of money from an external source **4.** ASTRON ATTRACTION OF MATTER BY GRAVITY a process in which matter revolving around an astronomical object is gradually pulled in and added to the body's mass **5.** GEOL INCREASE IN LANDMASS a process by which a body of rock or a landmass increases in size as a result of material accumulating on or around it **6.** GEOL INCREASE IN SIZE OF CONTINENTS a process by which the size of a continent increases as a result of the moving together and deforming of tectonic plates —**ac·cre·tion·ar·y** *adj*

ac·cre·tion disk *n* a band of matter revolving around and being pulled toward an astronomical object with an intense gravitational field, e.g., a star or black hole

~~**accross**~~ incorrect spelling of **across**

ac·cru·al /ə kroó əl/ *n* something that has accrued

ac·cru·al meth·od *n* a method of accounting that counts income or expenses at the time they are earned or incurred, irrespective of when money is received or paid out

ac·crue /ə kroó/ (**-crued, -cru·ing, -crues**) *v* **1.** *vi* INCREASE to increase in amount or value ○ *The money had started to accrue in my account.* **2.** *vt* ACCUMULATE AMOUNT to gather together an amount, especially over a period of time ○ *investments accruing interest* **3.** *vi* COME AS A RESULT to come as a result or consequence of something, especially over a period of time ○ *environmental benefits that will accrue to the area* **4.** *vi* LAW BECOME ENFORCEABLE to become legally enforceable (*refers to claims or rights*) [15C. Via Anglo-Norman < Latin *accrescent-*, present participle of *accrescere* (see ACCRETE)] —**ac·crue·ment** *n*

acct. *abbr* ACCT, BANKING, FIN account

ac·cul·tur·ate /ə kúlchə ràyt/ (**-at·ed, -at·ing, -ates**) *v* **1.** *vi* to absorb and assimilate the culture of another group of people or another person **2.** *vt* to change somebody's cultural behavior and thinking through contact with another culture [Mid-20C. Back-formation < ACCULTURATION] —**ac·cul·tur·a·tive** *adj*

ac·cul·tur·a·tion /ə kùlchə ráysh'n/ *n* **1.** a change in the cultural behavior and thinking of a person or group of people through contact with another culture **2.** the process by which somebody absorbs the culture of a society from birth onward [Late 19C. < AC- + CULTURE + -ATION] —**ac·cul·tur·a·tion·al** *adj*

ac·cu·mu·late /ə kyoómyə làyt/ (**-lat·ed, -lat·ing, -lates**) *v* **1.** *vti* to collect or obtain a large amount of something over a period of time ○ *The magazines she had accumulated over 20 years filled the shelves.* ○ *The report suggests that the herbicide accumulates in the soil.* **2.** *vi* to gather, grow, or increase over a period of time [15C. < Latin *accumulat-*, past participle of *accumulare* "heap up in addition" < *cumulus* "heap"] —**ac·cu·mu·la·ble** /ə kyoómyələb'l/ *adj*

SYNONYMS See ***collect***[1].

ac·cu·mu·la·tion /ə kyoòmyə láysh'n/ *n* **1.** PROCESS OF GATHERING the process of gathering together and increasing in amount over a period of time **2.** COLLECTION OF THINGS a number of things that have collected or been collected over a period of time **3.** FIN GROWTH THROUGH INTEREST the growth of a sum by the addition of earned interest

ac·cu·mu·la·tive /ə kyoómyələtiv, -myə làytiv/ *adj* **1.** growing by gradual additions **2.** tending to gather or collect things —**ac·cu·mu·la·tive·ly** *adv* —**ac·cu·mu·la·tive·ness** *n*

ac·cu·mu·la·tor /ə kyoómyə làytər/ *n* **1.** a section of short-term memory in a computer or calculator **2.** *UK* same as **storage battery**

ac·cu·ra·cy /ákyərəssee/ *n* **1.** the correctness or truthfulness of something **2.** the ability to be precise and avoid errors

ac·cu·rate /ákyərət/ *adj* **1.** CORRECT giving a correct or truthful representation of something ○ *Their account of the incident was not entirely accurate.* **2.** FREE FROM ERRORS precise or free from errors ○ *an accurate typist* **3.** PROVIDING INFORMATION TO ACCEPTED STANDARD capable of providing information in accordance with an accepted standard ○ *an accurate watch* [Late 16C. < Latin *accuratus* "done with care" < *cura* "care"] —**ac·cu·rate·ly** *adv* —**ac·cu·rate·ness** *n*

ac·curs·ed /ə kúrssed, ə kúrst/, **ac·curst** /ə kúrst/ *adj* **1.** horrible or hateful (*dated*) **2.** enduring the effects of a curse (*archaic or literary*) [12C. < *a-* "on" (< Old English *ar-*) + CURSE] —**ac·curs·ed·ly** /-ədlee/ *adv* —**ac·curs·ed·ness** /-ədnəss/ *n*

ac·cu·sa·tion /àkyə záysh'n/ *n* **1.** a claim that somebody has done something illegal or wrong **2.** the accusing of somebody, or the state of having been accused of something

ac·cu·sa·tive /ə kyoózətiv/ *n* **1.** a grammatical case that identifies the direct object of a verb or other grammatical parts in some inflected languages and that affects nouns, pronouns, and adjectives **2.** a word or phrase in the accusative [15C. < Latin *ac-*

cusativus < *accusare* (see ACCUSE)] —**ac·cu·sa·tive** *adj* —**ac·cu·sa·tive·ly** *adv*

ac·cu·sa·to·ri·al /ə kyo͞ozə táwree əl/ *adj* **1.** describes a legal system in which the prosecution is required to provide proof of guilt beyond a reasonable doubt, with the evidence being assessed by an impartial judge and jury **2.** same as **accusatory** (*formal*) —**ac·cu·sa·to·ri·al·ly** *adv*

ac·cu·sa·to·ry /ə kyo͞ozə tàwree/ *adj* containing or making an accusation (*formal*)

ac·cuse /ə kyo͞oz/ (**-cused, -cus·ing, -cus·es**) *v* **1.** *vti* to confront somebody with a charge of having done something illegal, wrong, or undesirable **2.** *vt* to charge somebody formally with having committed a crime [14C. Via French < Latin *accusare* "call somebody to account" < *ad causa* "to the (legal) case"] —**ac·cus·er** *n*

ac·cused /ə kyo͞ozd/ *n* somebody being charged with wrongdoing in a criminal case

ac·cus·ing /ə kyo͞ozing/ *adj* containing or suggesting a claim that somebody has done something wrong —**ac·cus·ing·ly** *adv*

ac·cus·tom /ə kústəm/ (**-tomed, -tom·ing, -toms**) *vt* to make yourself or somebody else used to something through frequent or prolonged contact or use [15C. < Anglo-Norman *acustomer* < *custome* "habit" (see CUSTOM)]

ac·cus·tomed /ə kústəmd/ *adj* habitual or usual ◇ **accustomed to USED TO** used to or familiar with something or somebody ○ *I've grown accustomed to life in a small town.*

AC/DC *adj* **1.** able to be powered by battery or by connection to an electrical outlet. Full form **alternating current/direct current 2.** an offensive term meaning bisexual (*slang*)

ace /ayss/ *n* **1.** PLAYING CARD a playing card that has a single mark on it, or the single mark itself **2.** SINGLE-SPOTTED SIDE a single-spotted side of a die or domino, or the single spot itself **3.** TENNIS **WINNING SERVE** in tennis, a serve that an opponent cannot reach **4.** GOLF **HOLE IN ONE** the hitting of a golf ball from the tee into a hole in one stroke, or a score resulting from such a stroke **5.** AIR FORCE **FIGHTER PILOT** a top fighter pilot, especially one who has shot down five or more enemy aircraft **6.** SOMEBODY WITH EXCEPTIONAL SKILL somebody who is outstandingly good at something, e.g., a sport (*informal*) ■ *vt* (**aced, ac·ing, ac·es**) **1.** TENNIS **BEAT WITH SERVE** in tennis, to beat an opponent by serving an ace **2.** GOLF **PLAY HOLE IN SINGLE STROKE** to play a golf hole with only one stroke **3.** DEFEAT SOMEBODY SOUNDLY to defeat an opponent decisively (*slang*) **4.** SCORE HIGH GRADE to score an A in a course or examination (*slang*) ○ *aced all her finals* ■ *adj* EXCELLENT very good (*informal*) [14C. Via French *as* < Latin, "unit, unity"] ◇ **ace in the hole** an advantage that is reserved for use until it is most needed (*informal*) ◇ **be coming up aces** to be flourishing or successful (*informal*) ○ *She's hot, coming up aces with every movie she makes.* ◇ **have an ace up your sleeve** to have a hidden advantage (*informal*) ◇ **hold all the aces** to have all the advantages (*informal*) ◇ **within an ace of** very close to

Ace *tdmk* a trademark for a type of elastic bandage

ACE[1] /ayss/ *n* an enzyme that increases blood pressure. Full form **angiotensin-converting enzyme**

ACE[2] *abbr* American Council on Education

-acean *suffix* same as **-aceous**

ac·e·bu·to·lol /àssə byo͞otə làwl/ *n* a drug that reduces the heart rate and the force of heart muscle contraction. Use: treatment of high blood pressure and irregular heart rhythms. [Mid-20C. < ACETYL + BUTYL]

a·ce·dap·sone /àssə dáp sōn/ *n* a sulfur-containing drug. Use: treatment of malaria and leprosy. [Mid 20C. Blend of *acetylated* + DAPSONE]

ACE in·hib·i·tor *n* a drug that blocks an enzyme that raises blood pressure

a·cen·tric /ay séntrik/ *adj* **1.** without a center **2.** describes a chromosome that lacks the structure at which the two arms of a chromosome join (**centromere**)

-aceous, -acean *suffix* resembling or related to ○ *herbaceous* [< Latin *-aceus*]

a·ceph·a·lous /ay séffələss/ *adj* describes an animal that has no head [Mid-18C. Via medieval Latin < Greek *akephalos* "without a head" < *kephalē* "head"]

a·ce·pro·ma·zine /àyssə prṓmə zeen/ *n* an antipsychotic drug, often used as a tranquilizer in veterinary medicine [< *aceprom-* + *-azine*, INN stem]

a·ce·qui·a /aa sáykee ə/ *n Southwest US* an irrigation canal or ditch [Mid-19C. Via Spanish < Arabic *sāqīah* "irrigation stream"]

a·ce·qui·a mad·re /aa sàykee ə maadray/ *n Southwest US* a main irrigation canal from which smaller ones flow [< American Spanish, "mother irrigation canal"]

ac·er /áyssər/ *n* a deciduous tree or bush grown for its ornamental foliage. Native to: Europe, Asia, North America. Genus: *Acer*. [Late 19C. < Latin, "maple"]

a·cerb /ə súrb/ *adj* same as **acerbic** [Early 17C. < Latin *acerbus* (see ACERBIC)]

ac·er·bate /ássər bàyt/ (**-bat·ed, -bat·ing, -bates**) *vt* (*formal*) **1.** to annoy or irritate somebody **2.** to make something taste bitter [Mid-18C. < Latin *acerbat-*, past participle of *acerbare* "make harsh" < *acerbus* (see ACERBIC)]

a·cer·bic /ə súrbik/ *adj* bitter or sharp in tone, taste, or manner ○ *an acerbic remark* [Mid-19C. < Latin *acerbus* "harsh" < Indo-European] —**a·cer·bi·cal·ly** *adv*

a·cer·bi·ty /ə súrbətee/ *n* bitterness or sharpness in tone, taste, or manner [Late 16C. Directly or via French *acerbité* < Latin *acerbitas* < *acerbus* (see ACERBIC)]

~~**acessory**~~ incorrect spelling of **accessory**

acet- *prefix* same as **aceto-** (*used before vowels*)

ac·e·tab·u·lum /àssə tábbyələm/ (*plural* **-lums** or **-la** /-lə/) *n* **1.** the curved cavity on the side of the hipbone where the end of the thighbone fits **2.** a round cup-shaped sucker found on flatworms, leeches, and mollusks such as the octopus [14C. < Latin, "vinegar cup, cup-shaped cavity" < *acetum* "vinegar"] —**ac·e·tab·u·lar** *adj*

ac·e·tal /ássət'l, ássə tàl/ *n* **1.** a colorless volatile liquid. Use: solvent, perfumes. Formula: $C_6H_{14}O_2$. **2.** an organic compound similar to acetal that contains the chemical group -$CH(OR_1)OR_2$

ac·et·al·de·hyde /àssə táldə hīd/ *n* a colorless volatile liquid with a pungent smell. Use: manufacture of acetic acid, acetic anhydride, and butanol. Formula: C_2H_4O.

a·cet·a·mide /ə séttə mīd, àssət á-/ *n* a white crystalline solid that absorbs water readily. Use: solvent, manufacture of organic chemicals. Formula: CH_3CONH_2.

a·cet·a·min·o·phen /ə seetə mínnəfən, àssətə-/ *n* **1.** a drug that relieves pain and reduces fever **2.** a tablet or capsule containing acetaminophen

ac·et·an·i·lide /àssə tánn'l īd/ *n* a white crystalline compound. Use: manufacture of chemicals, dyes, and rubber. Formula: C_8H_9NO. [Mid-19C. < ACETYL + ANILINE + -IDE]

ac·e·tate /ássə tàyt/ *n* **1.** a salt or ester of acetic acid **2.** CHEM same as **cellulose acetate 3.** a product made of or containing acetate

a·ce·tic /ə seetik/ *adj* containing, producing, or made from vinegar or acetic acid [Late 18C. < French *acétique* < Latin *acetum* "vinegar"]

a·ce·tic ac·id /ə seetik-/ *n* a colorless liquid with a pungent odor that is the main component of vinegar. Use: manufacture of drugs, dyes, plastics, and fibers. Formula: CH_3COOH.

a·ce·tic an·hy·dride *n* a colorless liquid with a pungent odor. Use: manufacture of aspirin and plastics. Formula: $C_4H_6O_3$.

a·ce·ti·fy /ə seetə fī, -séttə-/ (**-fied, -fy·ing, -fies**) *vti* to turn into, or cause something to turn into, acetic acid or vinegar —**a·ce·ti·fi·ca·tion** /ə seetəfə káysh'n, -sèttə-/ *n* —**a·ce·ti·fi·er** *n*

aceto- *prefix* acetic acid ○ *acetify* [< Latin *acetum* "vinegar"]

a·ce·to·hex·a·mide /ə seetō héksə mīd/ *n* a sulfur-containing drug. Use: treatment of diabetes. [< ACETO- + HEXA- + AMIDE]

ac·e·tone /ássə tōn/ *n* a colorless flammable liquid with a slightly sweet smell. Use: paint and nail polish solvent, manufacture of organic chemicals. Formula: C_3H_6O.

ac·e·tone bod·y *n* BIOCHEM same as **ketone body**

a·ce·to·phe·none /ə seetō fə nṓn, -fee nṓn/ *n* a colorless liquid with a sweet pungent smell and taste. Use: perfumes, solvent, flavoring. Formula: C_8H_8O. [Mid-19C. < ACETO- + PHENYL + -ONE]

a·ce·tous /ə seetəss, ássə-/ *adj* like, containing, or producing acetic acid or vinegar [14C. < late Latin *acetosus* < Latin *acetum* "vinegar"]

a·ce·tyl /ə seet'l, ássə-/ *adj* relating to or containing the chemical group CH_3CO-

a·cet·y·late /ə sétt'l àyt/ (**-lat·ed, -lat·ing, -lates**) *vt* to introduce the acetyl group into a compound —**a·cet·y·la·tion** /ə sètt'l áysh'n/ *n*

a·ce·tyl·cho·line /ə seet'l kō leen, àssət'l-/ *n* a white crystalline compound released from the ends of nerve fibers and involved in the transmission of nerve impulses. Formula: $C_7H_{17}NO_3$.

a·ce·tyl·cho·lin·es·ter·ase /ə seet'l kōlən éstə rayss, -ràyz/ *n* an enzyme, present in blood and some nerve endings, that aids the breakdown of acetylcholine and suppresses its stimulatory effect on nerves

a·ce·tyl co·en·zyme A, a·ce·tyl CoA *n* a coenzyme produced during metabolism of carbohydrates, fatty acids, and amino acids

a·cet·y·lene /ə sétt'lən, -l een/ *n* a colorless gaseous flammable hydrocarbon. Use: welding, manufacture of organic chemicals. Formula: C_2H_2. —**a·cet·y·len·ic** /ə sètt'l énnik/ *adj*

a·cet·y·lide /ə sétt'l īd/ *n* any acetylene-derived compound containing a metal atom, often very explosive

a·ce·tyl·sal·i·cyl·ic ac·id /ə seet'l sàlli sìllik-, àssət'l-/ *n* the drug aspirin (*technical*)

ac·ey-deuc·y /àyssee do͞ossee/ *n* a version of backgammon in which a dice throw of one or two wins an additional turn [< ACE, DEUCE[1]]

ACH *n* in e-commerce, a wholesale payment network for interbank clearing and payment settlement, accessible through points of sale or automated teller machine systems. Full form **automated clearinghouse**

A·chae·a /ə kee ə/, **A·cha·ia** /ə kī ə, ə káy ə/ **1.** administrative area in the Northern Peloponnesus, Greece. Area: 1,239 sq. mi./3,209 sq. km. Population: 300,078 (1991). **2.** in ancient Greece, province in the northern Peloponnesus

A·chae·an /ə kee ən/, **A·chai·an** /ə kī ən, ə káy ən/ *n* **1.** a member of an ancient Hellenic people thought to have founded the Mycenaean civilization on the Peloponnesus **2.** somebody who comes from the modern Greek administrative area of Achaea —**A·chae·an** *adj*

A·cha·ia, etc. another spelling of **Achaea, etc.**

ach·a·la·sia /àkə láyzhə, -láyzhee ə/ *n* a failure of smooth muscle bands such as those in the gullet to relax [Early 20C. < A-[2] + Greek *khalasis* "relaxation" < *khalan* "loosen"]

a·char /ə cha'ar/ *n* FOOD same as **anchar** [Late 16C. Via Hindi < Persian *āchār*]

a·char·y·a /ə chaaree ə/ *n S Asia* a learned religious teacher and guide

ach·cha /úchə/ *interj S Asia* **1.** used to express agreement **2.** used to express surprise or doubt [< Hindi *acchā*]

ache /ayk/ *n* CONSTANT PAIN a feeling of constant dull pain ■ *vi* (**ached, ach·ing, aches**) **1.** FEEL PAIN to feel or be the site of a dull constant pain **2.** YEARN to yearn for the presence of somebody or something **3.** WANT BADLY to want something very much (*informal*) ○ *aching to tell her the news* [Old English *æce* (noun), *acan* (verb), origin ? The *ch* spelling arose from a mistaken association with Greek *akhos* "pain"] —**ach·ing·ly** *adv*

A·che·be /ə cháy bay, aa-/, **Chinua** (*b.* 1930) Nigerian novelist. He is the author of *Things Fall Apart* (1958) and *Anthills of the Savannah* (1987).

> "I feel that English will be able to carry the weight of my African experience. But it will have to be a new English, still in communion with its ancestral home but altered to suit its new African surroundings."
> [Chinua Achebe, *Morning Yet on Creation Day*; 1964]

~~**acheive**~~ incorrect spelling of **achieve**

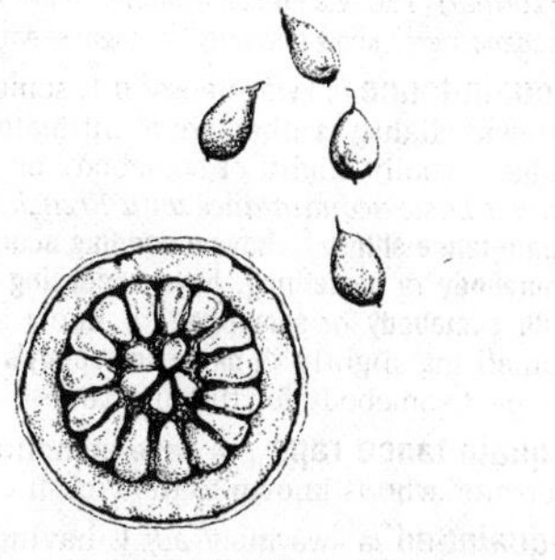

achene: cross section of the fruit of the dog rose

a·chene /ə kéen/, **a·kene** *n* a dry single-seeded fruit that does not open to release its seed. Dandelions and sunflowers have achenes. [Mid-19C. < modern Latin *achaenium* "not gaping" < Greek *khainein* "gape"]

Ach·er·on /ákə rŏn/ *n* in Greek mythology, one of the rivers that ran through Hades

Ach·e·son /áchəss'n/, **Dean** (1893–1971) US secretary of state (1949–52). He played an important role in the development of the Truman Doctrine, the Marshall Plan, and NATO. Full name **Acheson, Dean Gooderham**

> "A memorandum is written not to inform the reader but to protect the writer."
> [Dean Acheson, Quoted in *Wall Street Journal*; September 8, 1977]

A·cheu·li·an /ə shóolee ən/ *n* a period of the Paleolithic era during which people made symmetrical stone hand axes [Early 20C. After the French village of Saint-*Acheul* near Amiens] —**A·cheu·li·an** *adj*

a·chieve /ə chéev/ (**a·chieved, a·chiev·ing, a·chieves**) *vt* to succeed in doing or gaining something, usually with effort [14C. < French *achever* "bring to an end or head" < *a chief* "to a head" (see CHIEF)] —**a·chiev·a·bil·i·ty** /ə chéevə bíllətee/ *n* —**a·chiev·a·ble** *adj* —**a·chiev·a·bly** *adv*

SYNONYMS See ***accomplish***.

a·chieved /ə chéevd/ *adj* showing great skill or accomplishment

a·chieved sta·tus *n* social importance within a culture that somebody gains through personal effort rather than by inheriting it

a·chieve·ment /ə chéevmənt/ *n* **1. SUCCESS** something that somebody has succeeded in doing, usually with effort **2. FINISHING WELL** the act or process of finishing something successfully **3.** HERALDRY **FULL COAT OF ARMS** a full coat of arms that includes standing figures such as lions or unicorns (**supporters**), the family symbol (**crest**), and the family motto **4.** SOCIOL **EARNED SOCIAL STATUS** social status gained through personal merit rather than as a result of the circumstances into which somebody is born

a·chieve·ment age *n* the age at which a child should be able to perform a specific task successfully

a·chiev·er /ə chéevər/ *n* **1.** a successful and motivated person **2.** somebody who succeeds in an activity ○ *low achievers*

A·chil·les /ə kílleez/ *n* in Greek mythology, the principal hero of the Trojan War, made invulnerable by being dipped in the river Styx as a baby, except for the heel he was held by. He killed the Trojan hero Hector before being fatally wounded in the heel with an arrow fired by Paris.

A·chil·les heel /ə kìllee-/ *n* a weakness that seems small but makes somebody or something fatally vulnerable

A·chil·les jerk *n* a reflex action of the foot, which jerks downward when the lower leg muscles contract

A·chil·les ten·don *n* the tendon that connects the heel bone to the calf muscles

a·chir·al /ay kīrəl/ *adj* describes a molecule having neither left-handed nor right-handed configuration

a·chlor·hy·dri·a /ày klawr hīdree ə/ *n* an absence of or reduction in hydrochloric acid in the gastric juice —**a·chlor·hy·dric** *adj*

a·chon·drite /ay kón drīt/ *n* a stony meteorite that does not contain rounded grains (**chondrules**) —**a·chon·drit·ic** /ày kon dríttik/ *adj*

a·chon·dro·pla·sia /ày kondrə pláyzhə, -zhee ə/ *n* a genetic disorder in which cartilage fails to develop into bone during early stages of development, resulting in dwarfism [Late 19C. < Greek *akhondros* "without cartilage"] —**a·chon·dro·plas·tic** /ày kondrə plástik/ *adj*

a·choo /ə chóo/ *interj* a representation of the sound of somebody sneezing [Late 19C. An imitation of the sound]

ach·ro·mat /ákrə màt/ *n* **1.** PHYS same as **achromatic lens 2.** OPHTHALMOL same as **monochromat** [Early 20C. Back-formation < ACHROMATIC]

ach·ro·mat·ic /àkrə máttik/ *adj* **1. WITHOUT COLOR** without color and therefore white, gray, or black in appearance **2.** PHYS **WITHOUT SPECTRUM COLORS** able to reflect or refract light without spectral color separation **3.** BIOL **NOT EASILY STAINED** describes cells of organisms that cannot easily be stained with standard dyes **4.** MUSIC **WITHOUT SHARPS OR FLATS** using a musical scale with no sharps or flats —**ach·ro·mat·i·cal·ly** *adv* —**ach·ro·ma·tic·i·ty** /àkrəmə tíssətee/ *n* —**a·chro·ma·tism** /aykrṓmə tìzzəm/ *n*

ach·ro·mat·ic col·or *n* a color with no hue or chromatic component

ach·ro·mat·ic lens *n* a composite lens in which two or more lenses with different properties are combined to prevent distortion (**chromatic aberration**)

ach·ro·mat·ic prism *n* a composite prism in which two or more prisms deflect, but do not disperse, light

a·chro·ma·top·si·a /ày krōmə tópsee ə/ *n* MED same as **monochromatism** [Mid-19C. < Greek *akhrōmatos* "without color" < *a-* "without, not" + *khrōmato-* (see CHROMATO-) + *-opsia* (see -OPSY)]

ach·y /áykee/ (**-i·er, -i·est**) *adj* feeling or being the site of a constant dull pain —**ach·i·ness** *n*

a·ci·clo·vir /ay sīklə veer/, **a·cy·clo·vir** *n* an antiviral drug. Use: treatment of herpes cold sores.

a·cic·u·la /ə síkyələ/ (*plural* **-lae** /-lèe, -lī/) *n* a needle-shaped part, e.g., a spine, bristle, or crystal (*technical*) [Mid-19C. < late Latin, "little needle"] —**a·cic·u·late** /ə síkyələt, -làyt/ *adj* —**a·cic·u·lat·ed** *adj*

ac·id /ássid/ *n* **1.** CHEM **CORROSIVE SUBSTANCE** a sour-tasting compound that releases hydrogen ions to form a solution with a pH of less than 7, reacts with a base to form a salt, and turns blue litmus red **2.** CHEM **COMPOUND FORMING COVALENT BOND WITH BASE** a compound that can donate a proton or accept a pair of electrons to form a covalent bond with a base **3.** DRUGS same as **LSD** (*slang*) **4. SHARPNESS** a sharp, bitter, or sarcastic quality in speech or writing ■ *adj* **1. HAVING ACIDIC PROPERTIES** with the properties of or containing an acid **2. SARCASTIC** sharp, bitter, or sarcastic in tone ○ *acid comments* **3.** METEOROL **POLLUTED** describes rain or snow that contains dilute acid resulting from pollution **4.** GEOL **HIGH IN SILICA** describes igneous rocks that have a high silica content [Late 17C. Directly or via French < Latin *acidus* < *acere* "be sour"] —**a·cid·i·ty** /ə síddətee/ *n* —**ac·id·ly** *adv*

ORIGIN The Indo-European word from which ***acid*** is ultimately derived is also the ancestor of English *acme, acrid, acrobat, acute, alacrity, eager, edge, oxygen,* and *vinegar.*

ac·id an·hy·dride *n* CHEM same as **anhydride**

ac·id chlo·ride *n* CHEM same as **acyl chloride**

ac·id dep·o·si·tion *n* a deposit of water vapor formed in the atmosphere, e.g., dew, rain, snow, hail, or fog, that is high in acid content because of atmospheric pollution

ac·id house *n UK* electronic dance music of the late 1980s, using pulsating rhythms and associated with the use of the drug ecstasy

a·cid·ic /ə síddik/ *adj* **1. SOUR-TASTING** sour or bitter in taste **2.** CHEM **CONTAINING ACID** containing or having the properties of an acid **3.** CHEM **FORMING ACID IN WATER** forming an acid in water

a·cid·i·fy /ə síddə fī/ (**-fied, -fy·ing, -fies**) *vti* to turn something acid, or become acid —**a·cid·i·fi·a·ble** *adj* —**a·cid·i·fi·ca·tion** /ə sìddəfi káysh'n/ *n* —**a·cid·i·fi·er** *n*

ac·i·dim·e·ter /àssə dímmətər/ *n* an instrument for measuring the amount of acid in a solution —**a·cid·i·met·ric** /ə sìddə méttrik/ *adj* —**ac·i·dim·e·try** /àssə dímmətree/ *n*

a·cid·i·ty /ə síddətee/ (*plural* **-ties**) *n* **1.** the concentration of acid in a substance, of which pH is a measure **2.** MED same as **hyperacidity**

ac·id jazz *n* a mixture of funk, jazz, and soul music that first appeared in the 1980s

a·cid·o·phil /ə síddə fìl, ə síddə-/, **a·cid·o·phile** *n* **1.** a microorganism or plant that flourishes in an acid environment **2.** a cell that stains readily with acidic dyes

ac·i·do·phil·ic /àssidō fíllik, ə sìddə-/ *adj* **1.** describes cells that are easily stained by an acid dye **2.** describes microorganisms or plants that flourish in an acid environment

ac·i·doph·i·lus /àssi dóffiləss/ (*plural* **a·ci·doph·i·li** /-lī/) *n* a bacterium with slender rod-shaped cells, usually in chains, that thrives in acidic conditions and is beneficial to the intestinal tract. Use: yogurt manufacture. Latin name: *Lactobacillus acidophilus.* [Mid-19C. < modern Latin, "acid-loving"]

ac·i·doph·i·lus milk *n* milk to which acidophilus culture has been added but which has not fully fermented as has yogurt. Use: treatment of digestive disorders.

ac·i·do·sis /àssi dṓsiss/ *n* a failure of the mechanism that controls the acidity of the blood, other body fluids, or body tissues, commonly caused by untreated diabetes

ac·id pro·te·ase *n* a protein-digesting enzyme activated in stomach acid

ac·id rain *n* rain that contains dilute acid derived from burning fossil fuels and that is potentially harmful to the environment

ac·id re·flux *n* upward ejection of acid from the stomach into the esophagus, causing pain known as heartburn

ac·id rock *n* electric rock music popular in the late 1960s, with instrumental effects and lyrics suggesting or promoting psychedelic experiences

ac·id test *n* a decisive test that establishes the worth or credibility of something ○ *"The treatment accorded Russia by her sister nations in the months to come will be the acid test of their good will."* (Woodrow Wilson, *Speech on the Fourteen Points*; 1918) [< the use of nitric acid to test gold]

a·cid·u·late /ə síjjə làyt/ (**-lat·ed, -lat·ing, -lates**) *vti* to make something slightly acid, or become slightly acid —**a·cid·u·la·tion** /ə sìjjə láysh'n/ *n*

a·cid·u·lous /ə síjjələss/ *adj* **1.** slightly sour in taste (*formal*) **2.** cutting and sharp in speech or tone [Mid-18C. < Latin *acidulus* < *acidus* (see ACID)]

ac·i·du·ri·a /àssi dóoree ə/ *n* a condition in which there is a higher level of acidity of the urine than is usual or desirable

ac·i·nus /ássənəss/ (*plural* **-ni** /-n ī/) *n* **1.** ANAT a rounded sac containing secretory cells, found at the ends of the ducts in an exocrine gland **2.** ANAT same as **alveolus** (sense 1) **3.** BOT any of the small globes (**drupelets**) that make up an aggregate fruit such as a blackberry or raspberry [Mid-18C. < Latin, "berry growing in a cluster, kernel"] —**ac·i·nar** *adj* —**ac·i·nous** *adj*

ack-ack /ák àk, àk ák/ *n* (*informal*) **1.** ARMS same as **antiaircraft gun 2.** antiaircraft fire [Representing *AA* "antiaircraft" in a former system of spelling out messages]

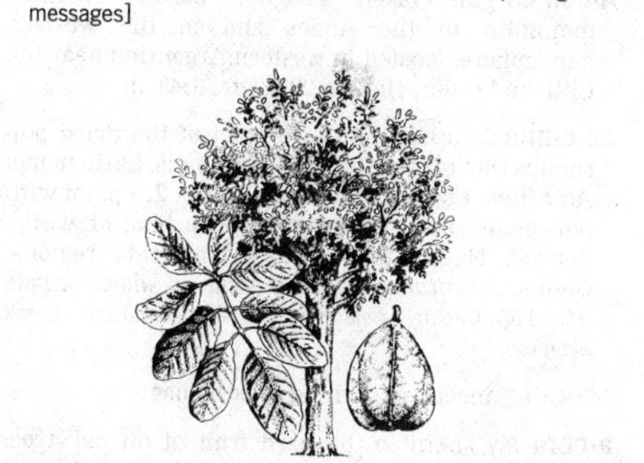

ackee

ack·ee /ákee, a keé/ (*plural* **-ees** or *same*), **ak·ee** *n* **1.** a red pear-shaped fruit with poisonous seeds, edible when ripe but poisonous at other times **2.** an evergreen tree cultivated in the Caribbean and Florida for ackees. Native to: tropical western Africa. Latin name: *Blighia sapida*. ▶ See illustration on previous page [Late 18C. Perhaps < Kru]

ac·knowl·edge /ək nóllij/ (**-edged, -edg·ing, -edg·es**) *v* **1.** *vti* ADMIT SOMETHING to admit or accept that something exists, is true, or is real **2.** *vti* SHOW AWARENESS OF SOMETHING to respond to something such as a greeting or message to show it has been noticed or received **3.** *vt* SHOW APPRECIATION OF SOMETHING to show appreciation or express thanks for something such as a letter or gift **4.** *vt* RECOGNIZE SOMEBODY OR SOMETHING LEGALLY to recognize or admit the existence, rights, or authority of somebody or something, especially in a legal context **5.** *vt* THANK SOMEBODY OFFICIALLY to officially or publicly recognize somebody's help or work [15C. Probably < KNOWLEDGE after obsolete *aknow* "recognize, acknowledge" (< KNOW)] —**ac·knowl·edg·a·ble** *adj* —**ac·knowl·edged** *adj* —**ac·knowl·edg·er** *n*

ac·knowl·edg·ment /ək nóllijmənt/, **ac·knowl·edge·ment** *n* **1.** ACCEPTANCE OF FACTS the act of accepting the truth or existence of something **2.** SIGN OF RECOGNITION a sign showing that somebody has seen or heard somebody else **3.** OFFICIAL RECOGNITION official or public recognition of somebody's help or work **4.** INDICATION OF RECEIPT a letter or message sent to say that something has been received **5.** THANKS an expression of thanks or appreciation for something ■ **ac·knowl·edg·ments** *npl* AUTHOR'S THANKS a section in a book or other piece of writing where an author thanks those who have helped

aclaim incorrect spelling of **acclaim**

ac·la·rub·i·cin /àklə ro͝obəssin/ *n* an antibiotic that is toxic to dividing cells. Use: treatment of leukemia.

a·clin·ic line /ay klínnik-/ *n* GEOG same as **magnetic equator** [< Greek *aklinēs* "not leaning" < *klinein* "to lean"]

ACLU *abbr* American Civil Liberties Union

ACM *abbr* COMPUT Association for Computing Machinery

ac·me /ákmee/ *n* the highest point of perfection or achievement [Late 16C. < Greek *akmē* "highest point"]

ac·ne /áknee/ *n* a disease of the oil-secreting glands of the skin that often affects adolescents, producing eruptions on the face, neck, and shoulders that can leave pitted scars [Mid-19C. < Latin, misreading of Greek *akmē* "highest point"] —**ac·ned** *adj*

ac·ne ro·sa·cea *n* MED same as **rosacea**

a·coe·lo·mate /ə seélə màyt/ *n* an organism with no cavity (**coelom**) between its digestive tract and outer wall, e.g., a flatworm or jellyfish

ac·o·lyte /ákə lìt/ *n* **1.** a follower or assistant ○ *the acolytes of this powerful leader* **2.** somebody, especially a young person, who assists a member of the clergy in the performance of rites [14C. Directly or via Old French < ecclesiastical Latin *acolytus* < Greek *akolouthos* "follower" < *a-* "together" + *keleuthos* "path"]

acommodate incorrect spelling of **accommodate**

acommodation incorrect spelling of **accommodation**

acompany incorrect spelling of **accompany**

A·con·ca·gua /àkən kaágwə, aakən-/ highest mountain in the Andes and in the western hemisphere, located in western Argentina near the Chilean border. Height: 22,834 ft./6,960 m.

ac·o·nite /ákə nìt/ *n* **1.** an extract of the dried poisonous root of some plants of the genus. Latin name: *Aconitum*. Use: homeopathic remedy. **2.** a plant with poisonous roots. Flowers: purplish blue or white, hooded. Native to: northern temperate regions. Genus: *Aconitum*. **3.** PLANTS same as **winter aconite** [Mid-16C. Directly or via French < Latin *aconitum* < Greek *akoniton*]

acording incorrect spelling of **according**

a·corn /áy kàwrn/ *n* the hard fruit of an oak tree, consisting of a smooth single-seeded nut that is set in a cup-shaped base and ripens from green to brown [Old English *æcern*, perhaps < *æcer* "open land"; later interpreted as "oak-corn"]

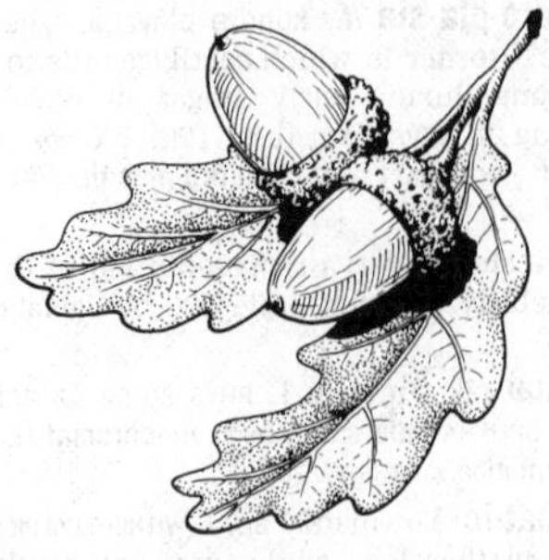

acorn

a·corn bar·na·cle *n* an invertebrate ocean animal with a conical shell that attaches itself to rocks and catches food using tendrils. Latin name: *Balanus balanoides*.

acorn squash

a·corn squash *n* an acorn-shaped winter squash with a ridged dark green rind and yellow or orange flesh

a·corn worm *n* a burrowing invertebrate ocean animal resembling a worm with an acorn-shaped snout that it uses to dig for food. Native to: shallow coastal waters. Phylum: Chordata.

a·cou·chi /ə ko͞oshee/ (*plural* **-chis** or **-chies**), **a·cou·chy** (*plural* **-chies**) *n* an agile rodent similar to an agouti. Native to: South America. Genus: *Myoprocta*. [Late 18C. Via French < Tupi]

a·cous·tic /ə ko͞ostik/, **a·cous·ti·cal** /-stik'l/ *adj* **1.** OF SOUND relating to sound, hearing, or the study of sound **2.** DESIGNED FOR USE WITH SOUND designed to control, absorb, or carry sound **3.** MUSIC NOT AMPLIFIED describes music or a musical instrument that is not electronically amplified, e.g., a guitar ■ *n* **1.** MUSICAL INSTRUMENT WITHOUT AMPLIFICATION a musical instrument that is not electronically amplified, usually a guitar (*informal*) **2.** MUSIC same as **acoustics** *npl* [Early 18C. < Greek *akoustikos* < *akouein* "hear" < Indo-European] —**a·cous·ti·cal·ly** *adv*

a·cous·tic nerve *n* MED same as **auditory nerve**

a·cous·tic neur·o·ma *n* a benign tumor that develops on the auditory nerve causing hearing loss, loss of balance, and headaches

a·cous·tic rock *n* rock music intended to be played mainly on unamplified instruments

a·cous·tics /ə ko͞ostiks/ *n* the scientific study of sound (*takes a singular verb*) ■ *npl* the characteristic way in which sound carries or can be heard within an enclosed space such as an auditorium (*takes a plural verb*) —**ac·ous·ti·cian** /àkoo stísh'n/ *n*

a·cous·tic tile *n* a ceiling or wall tile designed to stop or diminish the transmission of sound

a·cous·tic trau·ma *n* physical damage or changes in the body caused by sound waves, e.g., hearing loss, disorientation, motion sickness, and dizziness

a·cous·to·e·lec·tric /ə ko͞ostō i léktrik/ *adj* ACOUSTICS same as **electroacoustic** —**a·cous·to·e·lec·tric·al·ly** *adv*

ac·quaint /ə kwáynt/ (**-quaint·ed, -quaint·ing, -quaints**) *vt* **1.** to make somebody, or yourself, aware of or familiar with something **2.** to introduce somebody or make somebody known to somebody else (*dated or formal*) [13C. Via French *acointier* "make known" < Latin *accognoscere* "know perfectly" < *cognoscere* "know"]

ac·quain·tance /ə kwáyntənss/ *n* **1.** somebody who is known slightly rather than intimately **2.** knowledge, usually slight, of something or something ○ *only a basic acquaintance with French theater* —**ac·quain·tance·ship** *n* ◇ **have a nodding acquaintance with somebody** *or* **something, have a passing acquaintance with somebody** *or* **something** to know somebody or something slightly ◇ **make somebody's acquaintance** to meet somebody for the first time

ac·quain·tance rape *n* a rape committed by a perpetrator who is known to the victim

ac·quaint·ed /ə kwáyntəd/ *adj* **1.** having some, often not very much, knowledge of something ○ *not acquainted with this software* **2.** known to somebody or to each other from a previous introduction

ac·qui·esce /àkwee éss/ (**-esced, -esc·ing, -esc·es**) *vi* to agree or comply with something in a passive or reserved way [Early 17C. < Latin *acquiescere* "remain resting," hence "agree tacitly" < *quiescere* "to rest"] —**ac·qui·es·cence** *n* —**ac·qui·es·cent** *adj* —**ac·qui·es·cent·ly** *adv*

SYNONYMS See ***agree***.

ac·quire /ə kwír/ (**-quired, -quir·ing, -quires**) *vt* **1.** GET SOMETHING to get or obtain possession of something **2.** DEVELOP SOMETHING to learn or develop something ○ *a habit I acquired in the army* **3.** LOCATE SOMETHING BY RADAR to locate an object such as an aircraft or ship by the use of radar or other detector [15C. Via Old French *acquerre* < Latin *acquirere* "get something extra" < *quaerere* "try to get or obtain"] —**ac·quir·a·ble** *adj* —**ac·quired** *adj*

SYNONYMS See ***get***[1].

ac·quired char·ac·ter, **ac·quired char·ac·ter·is·tic** *n* a characteristic that an organism develops in response to its environment and that cannot be passed on to the next generation

ac·quired im·mune de·fi·cien·cy syn·drome, **ac·quired im·mu·no·de·fi·cien·cy syn·drome** *n* MED full form of **AIDS**

ac·quired taste *n* a liking that develops for something that seems unpleasant at first

ac·quire·ment /ə kwírmənt/ *n* **1.** the act or process of acquiring something **2.** something learned or attained, especially a skill

ac·quir·er /ak kwírər/ *n* **1.** somebody or something that acquires something **2.** a financial institution that processes transactions paid for by credit or debit card, supplying payment to the retailer and notifying the card issuer of the debt incurred by the purchaser

ac·qui·si·tion /àkwi zísh'n/ *n* **1.** ACQUIRING the act of acquiring something **2.** NEW POSSESSION something that has recently been bought or obtained **3.** SKILL DEVELOPMENT the development of a new skill, practice, or way of doing things ○ *language acquisition* **4.** LOCATING BY RADAR the location of an object such as an aircraft or ship by the use of radar or other detector [14C. < Latin *acquisition-* < *acquisit-*, past participle of *acquirere* (see ACQUIRE)]

ac·qui·si·tions /àkwi zísh'nz/ *n* (*takes a singular verb*) **1.** the department of a library or museum responsible for obtaining and taking care of new items **2.** the department in a company responsible for taking over other businesses ○ *I work in acquisitions and mergers.*

ac·quis·i·tive /ə kwízzətiv/ *adj* **1.** eager to acquire things, especially possessions **2.** curious, eager, and quick to learn ○ *an acquisitive mind* [Mid-17C. < Latin *acquisit-* (see ACQUISITION), after French *acquisitif*] —**ac·quis·i·tive·ly** *adv* —**ac·quis·i·tive·ness** *n*

ac·quit /ə kwít/ (**-quit·ted, -quit·ting, -quits**) *v* **1.** *vt* LAW DECLARE SOMEBODY INNOCENT to declare officially that somebody is not guilty of a charge **2. ac·quit yourself** *vr* BEHAVE to conduct yourself in a particular way (*formal*) ○ *The band acquitted itself well at the performance.* **3.** *vt* FREE SOMEBODY FROM OBLIGATION to free somebody from a duty or obligation (*formal*) **4.** *vt* REPAY SOMETHING to repay something such as a debt (*archaic*) [13C. Via Old French *a(c)quiter* < assumed Latin *acquitare* "bring to rest," hence "set free" < *quies* "quiet"] —**ac·quit·ter** *n*

ac·quit·tal /ə kwítt'l/ *n* a judgment given by a judge or jury that somebody is not guilty of a charge

ac·quit·tance /ə kwítt'nss/ *n* release from a debt or obligation, or a record of this (*dated*)

a·cre /áykər/ *n* UNIT OF AREA a unit of area used in some countries, including the United States and the United Kingdom, equal to 4,840 sq. yd./4,046.86 sq. m ■ **a·cres** *npl* **1.** LAND land, especially a large amount of land **2.** LARGE AMOUNT a large amount or area of something (*informal*) ○ *acres of space in the new headquarters* [Old English *æcer*. Ultimately probably "area over which plowing oxen can be driven in a day" < Indo-European, "drive"]

CULTURAL NOTE *A Thousand Acres*, a novel (1991) by US writer Jane Smiley. A retelling of *King Lear* set in the Midwest, it exposes the tragedies of alcoholism and emotional and environmental abuse behind the rural idyll of a family farm. The novel won the Pulitzer Prize in literature and a National Book Critics' Circle Award, and was made into a movie in 1997.

A·cre /áykər/ industrial seaport in northern Israel. Population: 44,800 (1999).

a·cre·age /áykərij, áykrij/ *n* land, or an area of land, measured in acres

a·cre-foot *n* the volume of water that would cover an area of one acre to a depth of one foot, equal to 43,560 cu. ft./1,233.5 cu. m

a·cre-inch *n* the volume of water that would cover an area of one acre to a depth of one inch, equal to one-twelfth of an acre-foot or 3,630 cu. ft./102.8 cu. m

ac·rid /ákrəd/ *adj* **1.** unpleasantly strong and bitter in smell or taste **2.** sharp or bitter in tone or character [Early 18C. < Latin *acri-* "sharp, pungent," after ACID] —**a·crid·i·ty** /ə kríddətee/ *n* —**ac·rid·ly** *adv* —**ac·rid·ness** *n*

ac·ri·dine /ákrə deen, -din/ *n* a colorless crystalline solid. Source: coal tar. Use: manufacture of dyes and pharmaceuticals. Formula: $C_{13}H_9N$. [Late 19C. < German *Acridin* < Latin *acri-* "sharp, pungent"]

ac·ri·fla·vine /ákrə fláy veen, -fláyvin/ *n* an orange-brown crystalline solid. Use: as an antiseptic in solution. Formula: $C_{14}H_{14}N_3Cl$.

~~**acrilic**~~ incorrect spelling of **acrylic**

ac·ri·mo·ni·ous /ákrə mṓnee əss/ *adj* full of or displaying anger and resentment —**ac·ri·mo·ni·ous·ly** *adv* —**ac·ri·mo·ni·ous·ness** *n*

ac·ri·mo·ny /ákrə mṓnee/ *n* bitterness and resentment, especially in speech, attitude, or tone [Mid-16C. Directly or via French < Latin *acrimonia* < *acri-* "sharp, pungent"]

a·cri·va·stine /a krívvə steen/ *n* a drug that inhibits the production of histamine. Use: treatment of rhinitis, urticaria, and eczema. [Late 20C. < ACRYLIC ACID + *-astine*, INN stem]

acro- *prefix* top, tip, height ○ *acrocentric* ○ *acrophobia* [< Greek *akros* "extreme, topmost" < Indo-European]

ac·ro·bat /ákrə bàt/ *n* **1.** a performer of gymnastic feats as entertainment **2.** somebody whose opinions or positions change readily to suit the circumstances [Early 19C. Via French < Greek *akrobatos* "walking on tiptoe" < *akros* (see ACRO-) + *bainein* "to walk"] —**ac·ro·bat·ic** /àkrə báttik/ *adj* —**ac·ro·bat·i·cal·ly** *adv*

ac·ro·bat·ics /àkrə báttiks/ *n* **1.** MOVEMENTS OF ACROBAT the skill or performance routines of an acrobat (*takes a singular or plural verb*) **2.** ACTIVITY REQUIRING AGILITY an activity that requires great skill or agility (*takes a plural verb*) ○ *mental acrobatics* **3.** VIRTUOSO PERFORMANCE performance of something that is marked by skill and artistry (*takes a plural verb*) ○ *verbal acrobatics in her closing argument*

ac·ro·cen·tric /àkrō séntrik/ *adj* describes a chromosome that has arms of unequal length, because the structure at which the two arms join (**centromere**) is located toward one end

ac·ro·ceph·a·ly /àkrō séffəlee/ *n* MED same as **oxycephaly** —**ac·ro·ce·phal·ic** /àkrō sə fállik/ *adj* —**ac·ro·ceph·a·lous** *adj*

ac·ro·cy·a·no·sis /àkrō sī ə nṓssiss/ *n* a disorder affecting the fingers and toes causing them to become blue and cold at low temperatures. Acrocyanosis is a feature of Raynaud's disease.

ac·ro·dont /ákrə dònt/ *adj* describes the teeth of some reptiles that have no roots and are joined to the jawbone ■ *n* a reptile with acrodont teeth

ac·ro·lect /ákrə lèkt/ *n* the language variety among a group of related varieties that is closest to the standard form of the language

a·cro·le·in /ə krṓlee in/ *n* a colorless poisonous pungent aldehyde. Use: manufacture of chemicals and pharmaceuticals. Formula: CH_2CHCHO. [Mid-19C. < ACRID + Latin *oleum* "oil"]

ac·ro·lith /ákrə lìth/ *n* a statue, especially in ancient Greece, with a wooden body and hands, feet, and head of stone

ac·ro·meg·a·ly /àkrō méggəlee/ *n* overproduction of growth hormones, resulting in enlarged bones in the hands, feet, jaw, nose, and ribs of adults —**ac·ro·me·gal·ic** /àkrō mə gállik/ *adj*

a·cro·mi·on /ə krṓmee òn, -ən/ (*plural* **a·cro·mi·a** /-mee ə/) *n* a bony projection from the outer end of the spine of the shoulder blade, to which the collarbone is attached [Late 16C. < Greek *akrōmion* < *akros* (see ACRO-) + *ōmos* "shoulder"]

ac·ro·nym /ákrə nìm/ *n* a word formed from the initials or other parts of several words, e.g., "NATO," from the initial letters of "North Atlantic Treaty Organization" [Mid-20C < ACRO- + *-nym* < Greek *onuma* "name," after SYNONYM etc] —**ac·ro·nym·ic** /àkrə nímmik/ *adj* —**a·cron·y·mous** /ə krónnəməss/ *adj*

USAGE See ***abbreviation***.

a·crop·e·tal /ə króppət'l/ *adj* describes leaves or flowers that grow in order from the base of a plant or stem toward the apex —**a·crop·e·tal·ly** *adv*

ac·ro·pho·bi·a /àkrə fṓbee ə/ *n* an irrational fear of being in high places —**ac·ro·pho·bic** *adj*

a·crop·o·lis /ə króppəliss/ *n* in ancient Greece, the fortified citadel of a city [Early 17C. < Greek *akropolis*]

A·crop·o·lis *n* the ancient citadel of Athens in Greece that was the religious focus of the city. It contains the remains of several classical temples, including the Parthenon.

ac·ro·some /ákrə sṑm/ *n* a structure at the end of a sperm cell that releases enzymes to digest the cell membrane of an egg, enabling the sperm to penetrate the egg

a·cross /ə kráwss, -króss/ CORE MEANING: a grammatical word indicating that somebody or something is on the opposite side of something or moves or reaches from one side to the other ○ (prep) *I live across the street from you.* ○ (adv) *a bridge wide enough to walk across*

1. *prep* IN SPITE OF BOUNDARIES in such a way that boundaries or borders are transcended ○ *united across cultures* **2.** *adj, adv* SO AS TO CROSS SOMETHING in such a way as to intersect or form a cross with something ○ *placed one board across the other* **3.** *prep* THROUGHOUT all over something or somewhere ○ *all across the state* **4.** *adv* MEASURED IN WIDTH as measured from one side of something to the other ○ *about an inch across* **5.** *adv* HORIZONTALLY ON CROSSWORD in a horizontal position in a crossword puzzle ○ *couldn't find the solution to 3 across* [13C. < Old French *à croix* or *en croix* "transversely" < Latin *crux* "cross"]

a·cross-the-board *adj, adv* affecting everyone or everything equally or proportionally ■ *adj* wagering an equal amount to win if a horse or other competitor finishes first, second, or third —**a·cross the board** *adv*

a·cros·tic /ə króstik/ *n* a number of lines of writing, especially a poem or word puzzle, in which a combination of letters from each line spells a word or phrase [Late 16C. Via French *acrostiche* < Greek *akrostikhis* < *akros* "outermost" + *stikhos* "line of verse" (< *steikhein* "go")] —**a·cros·ti·cal·ly** *adv*

a·cryl·a·mide /ə kríllə mīd, àkrə lá mīd/ *n* **1.** a poisonous colorless crystalline solid. Use: manufacture of polymers. Formula: $C_{17}H_{10}O$. **2.** a polymer made with acrylamide [Late 19C. < ACRYLIC]

ac·ryl·ate /ákrə làyt, -lət/ *n* **1.** a salt or ester of acrylic acid **2.** CHEM same as **acrylate resin** [Mid-19C. < ACRYLIC]

ac·ry·late res·in *n* a resin derived from acrylic or other related acids. Use: paints, sizing, adhesives, plastics.

a·cryl·ic /ə kríllik, a-/ *n* **1.** SYNTHETIC FIBER a synthetic textile fiber produced from acrylonitrile **2.** SOMETHING MADE FROM ACRYLIC ACID something containing or made from acrylic acid **3.** PAINT a paint containing acrylate resin, used especially in painting pictures [Mid-19C. < ACROLEIN + -YL] —**a·cryl·ic** *adj*

a·cryl·ic ac·id *n* a colorless corrosive acid. Use: manufacture of acrylate resins. Formula: $C_3H_4O_2$.

a·cryl·ic re·sin *n* CHEM same as **acrylate resin**

ac·ry·lo·ni·trile /àkrəlō nítrəl, -nī tril/ *n* a colorless toxic liquid. Use: manufacture of acrylic fibers and resins, rubbers, and thermoplastics. Formula: C_3H_3N. [Late 19C. < ACRYLIC]

act /akt/ *n* **1.** SOMETHING DONE something that somebody does **2.** DOING SOMETHING the action of carrying something out **3.** PART OF PLAY one of the main sections of a play or other dramatic performance **4.** ONE OF SEVERAL PERFORMANCES a short performance, especially one that is part of a varied program or show ○ *The next act is a barbershop quartet.* **5.** PERFORMER the performer or performers who take part in an act **6.** PERSONAL BEHAVIOR somebody's actions or behavior considered as entertainment or used as an assessment of that person's worth (*informal*) ○ *a class act* **7.** PRETENSE behavior that is intended to impress or deceive other people ○ *He's just putting on an act.* **8.** POL RECORD REGARDING LAW a record or statement of the decision made by a legislative or judicial body **9.** FORMAL RECORD a formal written record of the proceedings of a society, committee, or elected group **10.** PHILOSOPHY SOMETHING DONE INTENTIONALLY something brought about by human will ■ *v* (**act·ed, act·ing, acts**) **1.** *vi* DO SOMETHING to do something to change a situation, e.g., to solve a problem or prevent one arising ○ *need to act at once* **2.** *vti* BEHAVE IN PARTICULAR WAY to adopt a particular way of behaving ○ *You've been acting funny all morning.* ○ *Stop acting like a fool.* ○ *"I even liked him when he was "difficult" and official, because I thought I knew why he acted like that."* (Paul Scott, *The Jewel in the Crown*; 1966) **3.** *vi* PRETEND to behave in a way intended to impress or deceive other people **4.** *vi* FUNCTION AS SOMETHING to serve a particular purpose or perform a particular function ○ *The ozone layer acts as a barrier against harmful radiation.* **5.** *vi* REPLACE SOMEBODY to be a substitute for somebody or something else ○ *Since the director cannot attend, his deputy will act for him.* **6.** *vi* HAVE EFFECT to create, produce, or bring about an effect or result ○ *Once the medicine acts, you'll feel better.* **7.** *vti* PLAY ROLE to play the part of a character in a dramatic performance ○ *a chance to act Othello* **8.** *vi* BE ACTOR to pursue a career in movies or drama **9.** *vti* PERFORM SOMETHING, OR BE PERFORMED to stage a dramatic performance, or be capable of being staged ○ *The company will act a different play tomorrow night.* [14C. Directly or via French *acte* < Latin *actus*, *actum* "public transaction" < past participle of *agere* "do"] —**act·a·ble** *adj* ◇ **a hard** *or* **tough act to follow** somebody or something that sets a standard difficult to reach by others who come later (*informal*) ◇ **catch somebody in the act** to see or meet somebody just as he or she is doing something, especially something wrong ◇ **clean up your act** to improve your behavior (*slang*) ◇ **get in on the act** to join in something in order to share in its success or profit (*informal*) ◇ **get your act together** to do something to become more organized (*slang*)

act on, act upon *vt* **1.** to be guided by somebody's advice or suggestion **2.** to have an effect on something

act out *v* **1.** *vt* to perform something or portray it in action **2.** *vti* to express a negative feeling or impulse by behaving in a socially unacceptable way

act up *vi* to cause trouble or pain

ACT *abbr* Australian Capital Territory

Act·ae·on /ak tée ən/ *n* in Greek mythology, a hunter who was turned into a stag after inadvertently seeing the goddess Artemis bathing

ACTH *n* a pituitary hormone that stimulates the adrenal cortex to produce steroid hormones. Full form **adrenocorticotropic hormone**

ac·tin /áktin/ *n* a protein present in all cells and in muscle tissue where it plays a role in contraction [Mid-20C. < Latin *actus* (see ACT)]

actin- *prefix* same as **actino-** (*used before vowels*)

ac·ti·nal /áktənəl/ *adj* **1.** describes the side of an invertebrate ocean animal such as a jellyfish or sea anemone from which the arms or tentacles radiate, or on which the mouth area is situated **2.** having rays or tentacles

act·ing /ákting/ *n* PERFORMING IN PLAYS the art, profession, or performance of an actor ■ *adj* **1.** TEMPORARY carrying out particular duties or doing somebody else's job temporarily ○ *the acting manager* **2.** WITH DIRECTIONS FOR STAGING including directions in a play's text to be used in staging a performance ○ *a copy of the acting edition of the play*

ac·tin·i·an /ak tínnee ən/ *n* MARINE BIOL same as **sea anemone** (*technical*) [Late 19C. < modern Latin *Actinia* < Greek *aktin-* "ray"]

ac·tin·ic /ak tínnik/ *adj* relating to radiation such as ultraviolet radiation that produces a chemical effect —**ac·tin·i·cal·ly** *adv*

ac·tin·ide /áktə nīd/ *n* an element in the series of radioactive elements beginning with actinium and ending with lawrencium [Mid-20C. < ACTINIUM, after LANTHANIDE]

ac·tin·ism /áktə nìzzəm/ *n* the property of radiation that makes photochemical change possible

ac·tin·i·um /ak tínnee əm/ *n* a radioactive silvery white metallic element. Source: pitchblende. Use: source of alpha rays. Symbol **Ac**. See table at **element** [Early 20C. < Greek *aktin-* "ray"]

actino- *prefix* **1.** radial ○ *actinomorphic* **2.** radiation [< Greek *aktin-*, stem of *aktis* "ray"]

ac·tin·o·lite /ak tínnə līt/ *n* a green or grayish green silicate mineral of the amphibole group, containing calcium, magnesium, and iron

ac·ti·nom·e·ter /àktə nómmətər/ *n* a device for measuring the intensity of radiation, especially that from the Sun —**ac·ti·no·met·ric** /àktənō méttrik/ *adj* —**ac·ti·nom·e·try** /àktə nómmətree/ *n*

ac·ti·no·mor·phic /àktənō máwrfik/, **ac·ti·no·mor·phous** /-máwrfəss/ *adj* spreading out symmetrically around a central point and so making identical halves when divided along any vertical axis. Tulips and starfish are actinomorphic. —**ac·ti·no·mor·phy** *n*

ac·ti·no·my·cete /àktənō mī seet, -mī seet/ *n* a rod-shaped or filamentous bacterium belonging to a large group that includes some that cause diseases and some that are the sources of antibiotics. Order: Actinomycetales. [Early 20C. Back-formation < modern Latin *actinomycetes*, plural of *actinomyces* < ACTINO- + Greek *mukēs* "fungus"] —**ac·ti·no·my·ce·tous** *adj*

ac·ti·no·my·cin /àktənō mīssin/ *n* an antibiotic. Use: treatment of childhood cancers.

ac·ti·no·u·ra·ni·um /àktənō yoo ráynee əm/ *n* the only naturally occurring, naturally fissile, radioactive isotope of uranium. Use: nuclear reactors, weapons.

ac·tion /ákshən/ *n* **1.** DOING SOMETHING TOWARD GOAL the process of doing something in order to achieve a purpose **2.** SOMETHING DONE something that somebody or something does **3.** MOVEMENT the way somebody or something moves or works, or the movement itself ○ *the action of a piston* **4.** VERVE energetic activity ○ *a woman of action* **5.** LAW LEGAL PROCEEDINGS legal proceedings in a court to obtain compensation for something or to enforce a right ○ *decided not to take action* **6.** EVENTS the important events in a narrative composition such as a novel or film **7.** FUNCTION OR INFLUENCE the way in which something functions, or the effect it produces ○ *the action of water on stone* **8.** FIGHTING DURING WAR a small battle, or the fighting that takes place during a war ○ *wounded in action* ○ *a campaign of brief actions* **9.** EXCITING OR PROFITABLE ACTIVITY involvement in something that brings excitement, profit, or pleasure (*slang*) ○ *a piece of the action* **10.** OPERATING MECHANISM the operating parts of a mechanism or instrument, e.g., a watch or piano **11.** MUSIC SPACE UNDER STRINGS the space between the fingerboard and strings of a string instrument such as a violin or a guitar **12.** PHYS FORCE the force applied to a body **13.** PHYS PROPERTY OF SYSTEM USED IN DYNAMICS twice the average kinetic energy of a system in a given time multiplied by the time ■ *interj* MOVIES START PERFORMING a command from a film director telling actors to begin acting as filming has begun [14C. Directly or via Old French < Latin *action-* < *actus* (see ACT)] ◇ **missing in action** absent after combat and not known to be captured, injured, or dead

ac·tion·a·ble /ákshənəb'l/ *adj* **1.** giving a basis for somebody to take legal action **2.** able or ready to be acted upon or put into action ○ *A marketing consultancy must provide actionable and effective marketing solutions.*

ac·tion·er /ákshənər/ *n* a movie that features a great deal of usually extreme action (*informal*) ○ *a made-for-TV actioner with a little-known cast*

ac·tion fig·ure *n* a small usually plastic doll with movable legs and arms, often based on a character from an action adventure

ac·tion game *n* a computer game that simulates exciting or violent action, especially shooting

ac·tion group *n* a group of people formed to achieve a social or political objective ○ *a pro-merger action group*

act·ion man *n UK* a man who takes part in many energetic and exciting activities (*informal*)

action officer *n* a military officer responsible for a project

ac·tion-packed *adj* involving or containing a large number of exciting events

ac·tion paint·ing *n* a technique used by artists of the Abstract Expressionism movement in which paintings are created by splashing, dripping, spattering, or smearing paint

ac·tion po·ten·tial *n* a temporary change in electrical potential that occurs between the inside and the outside of a nerve or muscle fiber when a nerve impulse is transmitted

ac·tion re·play *n UK* SPORTS, MEDIA same as **instant replay**

ac·tion sta·tions *Can, UK npl* MIL POST FOR COMBAT the posts assigned to people during or in readiness for combat ■ *interj* **1.** MIL GO TO COMBAT POSTS used as a command ordering people to take up the posts assigned to them during or in readiness for combat **2.** GET READY used to warn people to get ready to carry out their assigned tasks (*informal*) ▶ US term (all senses) **battle stations**

ac·ti·vate /áktə vàyt/ (**-vat·ed, -vat·ing, -vates**) *v* **1.** *vti* MAKE SOMETHING CAPABLE OF ACTION to make something active or operational, or become active or operational ○ *Any sound in the room will activate the alarm.* ○ *The detonator will activate in 30 seconds.* **2.** *vt US* MIL MOBILIZE MILITARY to set up or mobilize a military unit ○ *activate the National Guard* **3.** *vt* PHYS MAKE SOMETHING RADIOACTIVE to make a substance radioactive **4.** *vt* CHEM MAKE SOMETHING REACTIVE to increase the rate of a chemical reaction, e.g., by applying heat **5.** *vt* CHEM INCREASE POWER OF ADSORPTION OF SOMETHING to treat a substance such as charcoal so as to increase its capacity for adsorption **6.** *vt* INDUST PURIFY SEWAGE WITH AIR to purify sewage by aerating it —**ac·ti·va·tion** /àktə váysh'n/ *n* —**ac·ti·va·tor** *n*

ac·ti·vat·ed car·bon, ac·ti·vat·ed char·coal *n* a highly adsorbent powdered or granular form of carbon. Use: liquid and gas purification, chemical extraction, solvent recovery, poison antidote.

ac·ti·vat·ed sludge *n* aerated sewage containing microorganisms, added to untreated sewage to purify it by accelerating its bacterial decomposition

ac·ti·va·tion en·er·gy *n* the energy needed to make molecules of a substance take part in a chemical reaction

ac·tive /áktiv/ *adj* **1.** MOVING ABOUT moving about, working, or doing something, and not resting or sleeping **2.** BUSY full of or involved in busy activity ○ *an active life* **3.** DOING SOMETHING carrying out, or able to carry out, an action or process ○ *an active ingredient* **4.** CHEM, BIOL HAVING AN EFFECT having a chemical or biological effect on something, or able to have one **5.** SHOWING INVOLVEMENT OR ENERGY characterized by involvement, energy, or action ○ *played an active part* **6.** NEEDING AND USING ENERGY requiring a lot of energy and movement ○ *active pastimes* **7.** COMPUT READY FOR INPUT FROM COMPUTER OPERATOR describes the part of a computer screen or window that is currently in use or ready to accept input from the user ○ *active cell* ○ *active window* **8.** GEOL NOT EXTINCT describes a volcano that is not extinct and still erupts occasionally **9.** GRAM RELATING TO ROLE OF VERB'S SUBJECT describes a verb whose subject is the person or thing performing the action described by the verb **10.** ASTRON SHOWING VARIABLE SURFACE FEATURES describes the Sun when it is displaying large numbers of dark patches (**sunspots**) and bright patches (**faculae**), and high variability in radio-wave emissions **11.** COMM USED TO PRODUCE PROFIT producing or being used to produce profits or dividends ○ *an active account* **12.** FIN TRADING IN LARGE VOLUME bought and sold in large quantities ○ *the ten most active stocks* **13.** ELECTRONICS WITH POWER SOURCE describes electronic networks and components that contain a power source and are capable of operating ■ *n* GRAM VERB VOICE the active voice, or a verb in the active voice [14C. Directly or via Old French < Latin *activus* < *actus* (see ACT)] —**ac·tive·ly** *adv* —**ac·tive·ness** *n*

ac·tive cell *n* a spreadsheet cell in which values or formulas may be entered

ac·tive du·ty *n* full-time service in the armed forces with full pay and benefits

ac·tive im·mu·ni·ty *n* immunity generated by the production of antibodies by the body when it is exposed to antigens

ac·tive-life·style wag·on *n* AUTOMOT same as **sport tourer** [Early 21C]

ac·tive-ma·trix dis·play *n* a flat liquid-crystal display with high color resolution that is particularly suitable for use in laptop and notebook computers

ac·tive pack·ag·ing *n* food packaging that interacts chemically or biologically with its contents to extend shelf-life or modify the product during storage

ac·tive ser·ver page *n* a page in HyperText Markup Language with scripts that are processed on a server before being sent to a user

ac·tive ser·vice *n* MIL same as **active duty**

ac·tive site *n* the part of an enzyme molecule that binds the substance the enzyme acts on (**substrate**)

ac·tive trans·port *n* the movement of substances across cell membranes from low to high concentrations, requiring energy and proteins that act as carriers

ac·tive vo·cab·u·lar·y *n* the range of words that somebody normally uses in speech or writing, as opposed to words he or she understands when used by others

ac·tiv·ism /áktə vìzzəm/ *n* vigorous and sometimes aggressive action in pursuing a political or social end —**ac·tiv·ist** *n, adj* —**ac·tiv·is·tic** /àktə vístik/ *adj*

ac·tiv·i·ty /ak tívvətee/ (*plural* **-ties**) *n* **1.** SOMETHING SOMEBODY DOES something that somebody takes part in or does (*often used in the plural*) ○ *leisure activities* **2.** PHYSICAL EXERCISE energetic physical movement or exercise **3.** STATE OF DOING SOMETHING the state or process of doing something or being active ○ *Activity in the newsroom has reached fever pitch.* **4.** CHEM POTENTIAL FOR CHEMICAL REACTION the ability of a substance to undergo a chemical reaction **5.** BIOL NATURAL PROCESS a process or function that takes place naturally in a living organism ○ *activities such as eating or sleeping* **6.** EDUC LEARNING EXPERIENCE an educational exercise designed to provide direct experience of something ○ *an activity to accompany the geography lesson* **7.** PHYS RADIOACTIVITY the emission of radiation from a radioactive substance (*technical*) Symbol *A*

act of con·tri·tion *n* a short prayer of penitence

act of faith *n* an action motivated by belief in something for which there is no concrete evidence

act of God *n* a sudden uncontrollable event produced by natural forces, e.g., an earthquake or a tornado

Act of Un·ion *n* **1.** the 1707 Act of Parliament by which Scotland was united with England to form Great Britain **2.** the 1801 Act of Parliament by which Ireland was united with Great Britain to form the United Kingdom

ac·to·my·o·sin /àktə mī əssən/ *n* a complex of actin and myosin formed in muscle cells during contraction [Mid-20C. < ACTIN]

ac·tor /áktər/ *n* **1.** somebody who acts in plays, movies, or television **2.** somebody who pretends to be somebody else or to feel something so as to impress or deceive

ac·tress /áktrəss, -triss, -tress/ *n* **1.** a woman or girl who acts in plays, movies, or television **2.** a woman or girl who pretends to be somebody else or to feel something so as to impress or deceive

USAGE Many actresses now prefer to refer to themselves as actors.

Acts of the A·pos·tles *n* a book of the Bible that describes the early history of the Christian Church (*takes a singular verb*) See table at **Bible**

ac·tu·al /ákchoo əl/ *adj* **1. REAL** real and existing as fact ○ *Is that her actual title?* **2.** ⚠ **USED FOR EMPHASIS** used for emphasis, e.g., to stress that somebody or something being referred to is genuinely the person or thing involved ○ *This is the actual place where Lincoln stood.* **3. EXISTING NOW** existing or occurring at the moment ○ *actual as opposed to projected income* [14C. Via Old French < late Latin *actualis* < Latin *actus* (see ACT)]

USAGE ***Actual*** is often overused as a mere emphatic term without any real meaning, as in: *He wanted to know if any (actual) damage had been done.* In this sentence ***actual*** could be removed without any significant change to the sense. In the sentence *The actual total was much higher than we had expected,* ***actual*** is legitimately used to mark a contrast with projected or estimated totals.

ac·tu·al·i·ty /àkchoo álləteе/ (*plural* **-ties**) *n* **1.** something that is real, as opposed to what is expected, intended, or feared ○ *Let's deal with actualities.* **2.** everything that does or could exist or happen in real life

ac·tu·al·ize /ákchoo ə lìz/ (**-ized, -iz·ing, -iz·es**) *vt* **1.** to make something actual or real, or make something come about ○ *expectations actualized by deeds* **2.** to portray or represent something realistically —**ac·tu·al·i·za·tion** /àkchoo əli záysh'n/ *n*

ac·tu·al·ly /ákchoo əlee/ *adv* **1.** ⚠ used to emphasize that something really is so or really exists, e.g., when it may be hard to believe or when it contrasts with what has already been said ○ *He's actually over 35, although he looks much younger.* **2.** used to express an opinion, often a contradictory one, or to change the subject ○ *Actually, I'd prefer it if you left right now.* ○ *He's in India – he's always wanted to go there, actually.*

USAGE ***Actually***, like ***actual***, is used most effectively when it contrasts with what is theoretical or only apparent: *It sounds difficult, but it's actually quite straightforward.* It is regarded as poor style to use it as a sentence filler with no real meaning, although this practice is common in informal conversation: *Actually, I prefer her to her cousin.*

ac·tu·ar·i·al /àkchoo érree əl, àkshoo-/ *adj* **1.** relating to the statistical calculation of risk or life expectancy for insurance purposes **2.** relating to actuaries and their work

ac·tu·ar·i·al sci·ence *n* the branch of statistics that deals with the calculation of risk, life expectancy, and insurance premiums

ac·tu·ar·y /ákchoo èrree, ákshoo-/ (*plural* **-ies**) *n* a statistician who calculates insurance premiums, risks, dividends, and annuity rates [Mid-16C. < Latin *actuarius* < *actus* (see ACT)]

ac·tu·ate /ákchoo àyt/ (**-at·ed, -at·ing, -ates**) *vt* **1.** to make somebody act or behave in a specific way (*often used in the passive*) ○ *was actuated by self-interest* **2.** to make a device move or start working (*formal*) [Late 16C. < medieval Latin *actuatus*, past participle of *actuare* "cause something to be done" < Latin *actus* (see ACT)] —**ac·tu·a·tion** /àkchoo áysh'n/ *n* —**ac·tu·a·tor** *n*

ACT-UP /ákt ùp/ *n* an AIDS activist organization in the United States and United Kingdom. Full form **AIDS Coalition To Unleash Power**

ACU *abbr* MONEY Asian currency unit

a·cu·i·ty /ə kyoó ətee/ *n* keenness of hearing, sight, or intellect [Mid-16C. Directly or via French *acuité* < medieval Latin *acuitas* < Latin *acuere* (see ACUTE)]

a·cu·le·ate /ə kyoólee ət/ *adj* **1.** describes an insect that has a sting **2.** describes a plant or plant part that has prickles [Mid-17C. < Latin *aculeatus* < *aculeus* "small needle" < *acus* (see ACUTE)]

a·cu·men /ə kyoómən, ákyə-/ *n* the ability to make quick accurate intelligent judgments about people or situations ○ *political acumen* [Late 16C. < Latin, "point, sharpness" < *acuere* (see ACUTE)]

a·cu·mi·nate /ə kyoómənət, -nàyt/ *adj* describes leaves that taper to a sharp point [Late 16C. < late Latin *acuminatus*, past participle of *acuminare* "sharpen to a point" < Latin *acumen* (see ACUMEN)]

~~acumulate~~ incorrect spelling of **accumulate**

ac·u·pres·sure /ákyoo prèshər/ *n* a form of alternative therapy similar to acupuncture that uses manual pressure instead of needles [Mid-19C. *Acu-* < ACUPUNCTURE]

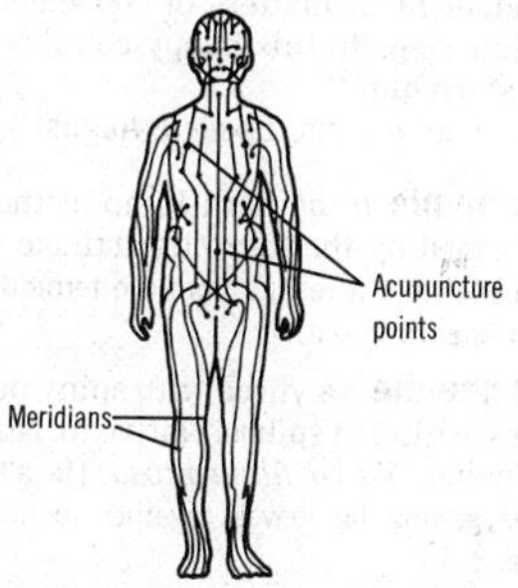

acupuncture: points and energy flow paths (meridians) in the human body

ac·u·punc·ture /ákyoo pùngkchər/ *n* the treatment of disorders by inserting needles into the skin at points where the flow of energy is thought to be blocked (**meridians**) [Late 17C. < Latin *acus* "needle"] —**ac·u·punc·tur·ist** *n*

~~acurate~~ incorrect spelling of **accurate**

a·cute /ə kyoót/ *adj* **1. VERY GREAT OR BAD** extremely serious, severe, or painful ○ *an acute financial crisis* **2. PERCEPTIVE** keenly perceptive and intelligent ○ *an acute grasp of foreign affairs* **3. SENSITIVE** very powerful and sensitive to detail ○ *acute eyesight* **4.** MATH **LESS THAN 90 DEGREES** describes an angle that is less than 90 degrees **5.** MATH **WITH ANGLES LESS THAN 90 DEGREES** describes a triangle that has three internal angles each of less than 90 degrees **6.** MED **SEVERE AND OF SHORT DURATION** describes a disease that is brief, severe, and quickly comes to a crisis **7.** BOT **POINTED** describes leaves that end in a short narrow point ■ *n also* **a·cute ac·cent** LANGUAGE **ACCENT OVER LETTER** in some languages, a mark placed above a letter to show that it is sounded in a specific way, as in *é, ó*. In Spanish, the acute indicates a stressed syllable, as in *cupón*; in French, a specific pronunciation of *e*, as in *blé*; and in classical Greek, a vowel sounded at a higher pitch. See table at **diacritic** [14C. < Latin *acutus*, past participle of *acuere* "sharpen" < *acus* "needle"] —**a·cute·ly** *adv* —**a·cute·ness** *n*

a·cute dose *n* a fatal amount of radiation received over a short period

a·cute lym·pho·cyt·ic leu·ke·mi·a *n* a form of leukemia affecting mainly children, characterized by anemia, weight loss, bone pain, and fatigue

a·cute non·lym·pho·cyt·ic leu·ke·mi·a *n* a form of leukemia affecting mainly adults, characterized by anemia, fatigue, and weight loss

a·cy·clic /ay síklik, -síklik/ *adj* **1.** having a molecular structure in which the atoms are arranged in a string whose ends do not meet (**open chain**) **2.** describes flowers that have their parts arranged in a spiral, not a whorl

a·cy·clo·vir *n* PHARM another spelling of **aciclovir**

ac·yl /áyss'l/ *adj* relating to or containing a chemical group derived from a carboxylic acid by removal of a hydroxyl group [Late 19C. < ACID]

a·cyl·a·tion /àyssə láysh'n/ *n* the introduction of an acyl group into a chemical compound

a·cyl chlo·ride *n* a chemical group containing the compound -COCl

ad[1] /ad/ *n* MARKETING same as **advertisement** (*informal*) [Mid-19C. Shortening]

ad[2] *abbr* TENNIS advantage

ad[3] *abbr* Andorra (*used in Internet addresses*) See table at **domain name**

AD *abbr* MED Alzheimer's disease

A.D., A.D. *adv* used to indicate a date that is a particular number of years after the birth of Jesus Christ. Full form **anno Domini**

USAGE Because of its literal Latin meaning, "in the year of the Lord," ***A.D.*** is traditionally put before the numeral to which it relates, so that it makes grammatical sense if understood in its expanded form: *A.D. 1453*. In practice, A.D. is usually put after the numeral, and it is also acceptable to put it after the identification of a century, as in *the fifth century A.D.* Some writers prefer to use P.E. (Present Era) or C.E. (Common Era) as alternatives in order to avoid the association with Christianity.

ad- *prefix* **1.** to, toward ○ *adsorb* ○ *advance* **2.** near ○ *adrenal* [< Latin *ad* "toward, near" < Indo-European]

-ad *suffix* to, toward ○ *cephalad* [< Latin *ad* (see AD-)]

A·da /áydə/ *n* a high-level computer programming language used for military and other complex applications [Late 20C. After Augusta *Ada* Byron, Countess of Lovelace (1815–52), British mathematician]

ADA *abbr US* **1.** American Dental Association **2.** Americans with Disabilities Act

ADA de·fi·cien·cy *n* a genetic disease resulting from the deficiency of a metabolic enzyme (**adenosine deaminase**), characterized by low numbers of some lymphocytes and increased susceptibility to lymphomas and chronic infections [*ADA* contraction of ADENOSINE DEAMINASE]

ad·age /áddij/ *n* a traditional saying that expresses something considered to be a general truth ○ *"Oysters are said to be best in months containing the letter R, according to an old adage."* (Barbara Sturm, *Living Page*; 1997) [Mid-16C. Via French < Latin *adagium* < *ad* "to" + variant of *aio* "I say"]

a·da·gio /ə daájee ō, -zhee ō, -jō/ *adv* slowly, but faster than lento (*used as a musical direction*) ■ *n* (*plural* **-gios**) a movement or piece of music played or marked adagio [Late 17C. < Italian, "at ease"] —**a·da·gio** *adj*

Ad·am /áddəm/ *n* in the Bible, the first man, created by God ◇ **not know somebody from Adam** to have never met or seen somebody before

Ad·am /aa daán/, **Adolphe** (1803–56) French composer who wrote 60 operas and the ballet *Giselle* (1841). Full name **Adam, Adolphe Charles**

Ad·am /áddəm/, **Robert** (1728–92) British architect and interior designer who built grand neoclassical country and townhouses, including Kenwood House (1768) and Osterley Park (1761–80)

ad·a·mant /áddəmənt, -mànt/ *adj* very determined and not influenced by appeals to reconsider a position or decision ○ *"They did their best to persuade her, but Mother was adamant."* (Gerald Durrell, *Birds, Beasts and Relatives*; 1969) ■ *n* a legendary, extremely hard stone, sometimes identified as diamond or lodestone (*archaic*) [Pre-12C. Via Old French *adamaunt* and Latin *adamant-* "adamant, steel, diamond" < Greek *adamas* "unbreakable" < *daman* "break down"] —**ad·a·mant·ly** *adv*

ad·a·man·tine /àddə mán teen, -tìn, -tin/ *adj* (*literary*) **1.** extremely hard or unyielding **2.** like a diamond in hardness and brilliance

Ad·am·a·wa-East·ern /àddə maáwə-/ *n* one of the major branches of the Niger-Congo family of African languages. Native speakers: 12 million. [Mid-20C. After the *Adamawa* Massif in Cameroon] —**Ad·am·a·wa-East·ern** *adj*

Ad·am·ov /áddə mòv/, **Arthur** (1908–70) Russian poet and dramatist. He was one of the chief exponents of the Theater of the Absurd. His plays include *Professeur Taranne* (1953) and *Ping Pong* (1955).

Ad·ams /áddəmz/, **Abigail** (1744–1818) US first lady and early feminist. She married John Adams, 2nd president of the United States. Her letters to him were published by her grandson. Born **Smith, Abigail**

> "Whilst you are proclaiming peace and good will to men, emancipating all nations, you insist upon retaining absolute power over your wives. But you must remember that arbitrary power is

Abigail Adams

most like other things which are very hard, very liable to be broken."
[Abigail Adams, *Letter to John Adams*; May 7, 1776]

Ad·ams, Ansel (1902–84) US photographer, noted for his dramatic photographs of the North American wilderness landscape

Ad·ams, Gerry (*b.* 1948) Northern Irish politician and president of Sinn Fein, the political wing of the Irish Republican Army. He was elected to the British Parliament (1983–92, 1997) but declined to take his seat. He is seen as having played an important part in the negotiations to end violence in Northern Ireland. Full name **Adams, Gerard**

Ad·ams, Henry (1838–1918) US historian. His works include *History of the United States during the Administrations of Jefferson and Madison* (1889–91). His autobiography *The Education of Henry Adams* was published privately (1907) and later for a general readership (1918) and won a posthumous Pulitzer Prize (1919).

> "Politics, as a practice, whatever its professions, has always been the systematic organization of hatreds."
> [Henry Adams, *The Education of Henry Adams*; 1907]

John Adams

Ad·ams, John (1735–1826) 2nd president of the United States (1797–1801). He served as the first vice president (1789–97) and succeeded Washington to the presidency in 1797. He was a member of the committee that drafted the Declaration of Independence (1776). See table at **president**

> "English is destined to be in the next and succeeding centuries more generally the language of the world than Latin was in the last or French is in the present age."
> [John Adams, *A Letter to the President of Congress*; 1780]

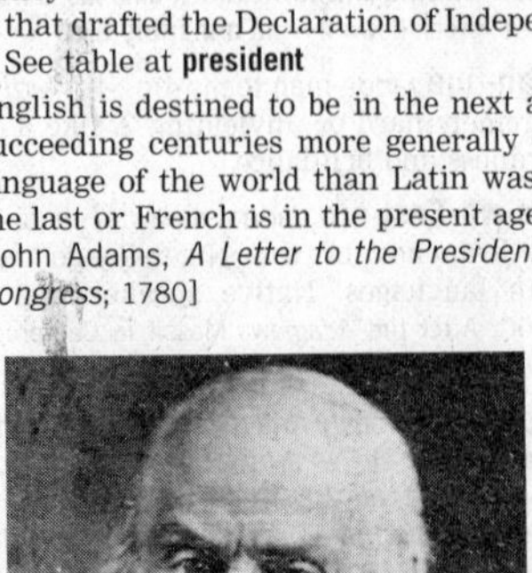

John Quincy Adams

Ad·ams, John Quincy (1767–1848) 6th president of the United States (1825–29). As secretary of state to President James Monroe (1817–25), he helped to formulate the Monroe Doctrine opposing foreign intervention in the American continents. See table at **president**

Ad·ams, Samuel (1722–1803) American revolutionary leader. He was a signatory to the Declaration of Independence (1776), and governor of Massachusetts (1794–97).

> "Driven from every corner of the earth, freedom of thought and the right of private judgment in matters of conscience direct their steps to this happy country as their last asylum."
> [Samuel Adams, *Speech*; August 1, 1776]

Ad·am's ap·ple *n* the hard lump at the front of the neck formed by the thyroid cartilage of the larynx [< the belief that it results from the forbidden apple being stuck in Adam's throat]

Ad·am's nee·dle *n* a yucca with spiny pointed leaves. Flowers: white, in spikes. Native to: North America. Latin name: *Yucca filamentosa*. [In allusion to Adam and Eve sewing fig leaves together to cover themselves (Genesis 3:7)]

A·da·na /áadənə, ə daánə/ city in southern Turkey and capital of the province of the same name. Population: 1,131,198 (1997).

a·dapt /ə dápt/ (**a·dapt·ed, a·dapt·ing, a·dapts**) *v* **1.** *vti* CHANGE TO MEET REQUIREMENTS to change something to suit different conditions or a different purpose, or be changed in this way **2.** *vti* ADJUST TO SOMETHING to become, or make somebody or something become, used to a new environment or different conditions **3.** *vt* REWRITE BOOK OR PLAY to rewrite a book or a play in order to make it into a film or television program [15C. Via French *adapter* < Latin *adaptare* "fit to" < *aptus* "attached"]

USAGE adapt or **adopt**? ***Adapt*** means "to change something to meet requirements," "to adjust to something," or "to rewrite something," as in *adapted* [not *adopted*] *the cottage to a year-round dwelling; flora and fauna that had adapted* [not *adopted*] *to an arid climate; adapted* [not *adopted*] *the novel for television.* ***Adopt*** means "to legally raise another's child," "to choose and decide to use something," and "to assume a behavior pattern," as in *adopted* [not *adapted*] *two boys; adopted* [not *adapted*] *a new ideology; adopted* [not *adapted*] *an attitude of superiority.*

a·dapt·a·ble /ə dáptəb'l/ *adj* **1.** able to adjust easily to a new environment or different conditions **2.** capable of being modified to suit different conditions or a different purpose ○ *adaptable for different voltages* —**a·dapt·a·bil·i·ty** /ə dàptə bíllətee/ *n* —**a·dapt·a·ble·ness** *n* —**a·dapt·a·bly** *adv*

ad·ap·ta·tion /à dap táysh'n, àddəp-/, **ad·ap·tion** /ə dápshən/ *n* **1.** ADAPTING the process or state of changing to fit a new environment or different conditions, or the resulting change **2.** SOMETHING ADAPTED TO FIT NEED something that has been modified to suit different conditions or a different purpose ○ *a film adaptation of a novel* **3.** BIOL CHANGE TO SUIT ENVIRONMENT the development of physical and behavioral characteristics that allow organisms to survive and reproduce in their habitats **4.** PHYSIOL DIMINISHING SENSORY RESPONSE the diminishing response of a sense organ to a sustained stimulus [Early 17C. Via French < late Latin *adaptation-* < Latin *adaptare* (see ADAPT)] —**ad·ap·ta·tion·al** *adj* —**ad·ap·ta·tion·al·ly** *adv*

a·dapt·er /ə dáptər/, **a·dapt·or** *n* **1.** ELECTRIC CONNECTOR a device used to connect an electrical appliance to a power source with a different voltage or a different plug shape, or to connect several appliances to one outlet **2.** DEVICE FOR CONNECTING UNLIKE PARTS a device for connecting two nonmatching parts **3.** SOMEBODY OR SOMETHING THAT ADAPTS somebody or something that changes something or is able to adjust to suit different conditions

a·dap·tion *n* same as **adaptation**

a·dap·tive /ə dáptiv/ *adj* able to be adjusted for use in different conditions —**a·dap·tive·ly** *adv*

a·dap·tive ra·di·a·tion *n* the developmental diversification of a group of organisms from an ancestral form into several different forms that adapt to different environments

a·dap·tive re·use *n* a use of a building that is different from its original or previous use, often involving conversion work

a·dap·tor *n* ELEC another spelling of **adapter**

A·dar /ə daár/ *n* in the Jewish calendar, the 12th month of the religious year, lasting 29 or 30 days and falling about the same time as February to March. ◊ **Adar Rishon**. See table at **calendar** [14C. < Hebrew *ădār*]

A·dar Rish·on /-rísh on/ *n* in the Jewish calendar, the name given to the month of Adar during a leap year, when an additional month (**Adar Sheni**) follows it [*Rishon* < Hebrew *ri'šōn*, "first"]

A·dar She·ni /-sháynee/ *n* in the Jewish calendar, a thirteenth month, lasting 29 days, added after Adar in leap years and falling around March to April. See table at **calendar** [*Sheni* < Hebrew *šēnî* "second"]

a·dax·i·al /ad áksee əl/ *adj* describes the upper side of a leaf or other surface that faces toward the stem

ADC *abbr* **1.** SOC WELFARE Aid to Dependent Children **2.** MIL Air Defense Command **3.** ELECTRONICS analog-to-digital converter

a.d.c. *abbr* MIL Air Defense Command

Ad·cock /ád kòk/, **Fleur** (*b.* 1934) New Zealand poet, author of *The Inner Harbour* (1979). Full name **Adcock, Kareen Fleur**

A-D con·ver·sion *n* an electronic process that converts an analog signal to a multilevel digital signal

add /ad/ (**add·ed, add·ing, adds**) *v* **1.** *vt* UNITE OR COMBINE THINGS to put something into or join something onto something else ○ *I'll add your name to the list.* **2.** *vti* CALCULATE TOTAL OF SOMETHING to calculate the total of two or more numbers or amounts **3.** *vt* PUT IN INGREDIENT to mix in an ingredient that is part of a recipe ○ *Add six eggs to the flour.* **4.** *vt* INTRODUCE QUALITY to give something a particular quality or more of a particular quality ○ *The flowers add a touch of cheerfulness.* **5.** *vi* INTENSIFY SOMETHING to increase the effect of something ○ *This adds to our problems.* **6.** *vt* SUPPLEMENT SPEECH OR WRITING to say or write something as a further remark ○ *"Don't forget your umbrella," she added.* [14C. < Latin *addere* < *dare* "give"] —**add·a·ble** *adj*

add up *v* **1.** *vti* MAKE TOTAL to calculate the total of two or more numbers or amounts, or reach a total **2.** *vi* MAKE SENSE to make a sensible or believable story or explanation ○ *His story just doesn't add up.* **3.** *vi* FORM LARGE AMOUNT to make a large total or amount ○ *If everyone gives a little, it soon adds up.*

add up to *vt* to amount to or result in a particular sum or thing

ADD *abbr* MED attention deficit disorder

add. *abbr* **1.** addendum **2.** MATH addition **3.** address

ad·da /ə daá/ *n S Asia* informal talk among several people [< Hindi, "perch for birds"]

Ad·dams /áddəmz/, **Charles Samuel** (1912–88) US cartoonist, noted for his humorous and macabre drawings in *The New Yorker* magazine

Ad·dams, Jane (1860–1935) US reformer and feminist. She founded Hull House, Chicago, (1889) the largest settlement house. She was awarded the Nobel Peace Prize (1931).

> "Civilization is a method of living, an attitude of equal respect for all men."
> [Jane Addams, *Speech, Honolulu*; 1933]

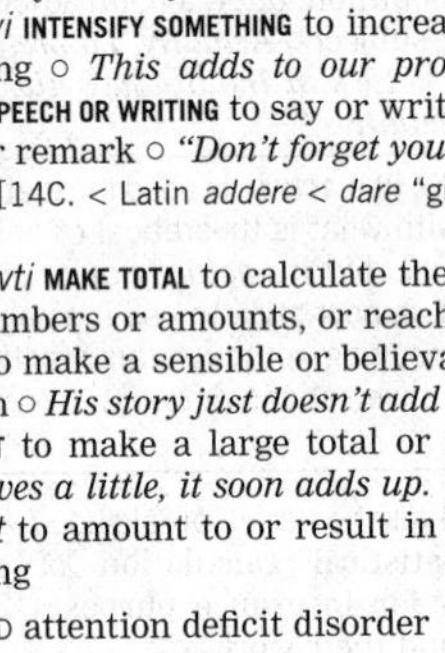

addax

ad·dax /ád àks/ (*plural* **-dax·es** or *same*) *n* an antelope that has long spiraling horns. Native to: desert regions of North Africa. Latin name: *Addax nasomaculatus*. See illustration on previous page [Late 17C. < Latin < an African word]

ad·dend /ád ènd, ə dénd/ *n* a number that is to be added [Late 17C. Shortening of ADDENDUM]

ad·den·dum /ə déndəm/ (*plural* **-da** /-də/) *n* **1.** something that is or has been added **2.** a supplement to a book or magazine [Late 17C. < Latin < *addere* (see ADD)]

adder

add·er[1] /áddər/ *n* somebody or something that adds, especially an electronic device that adds numbers [Late 16C. < ADD]

ad·der[2] /áddər/ *n* a small venomous snake that is dark gray with a black zigzag pattern on its back. Native to: Europe. Latin name: *Vipera berus*. [Old English *nǣd(d)re* "snake" < Germanic. The initial *n* was lost when "a nadder" was misanalyzed as "an adder"]

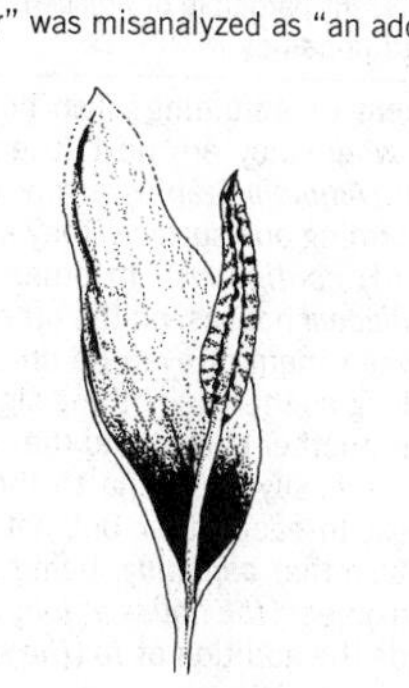

adder's tongue

ad·der's tongue *n* **1.** a fern with a spore-bearing stalk at the base of a pointed frond. Native to: northern hemisphere. Genus: *Ophioglossum*. **2.** PLANTS same as **dogtooth violet**

ad·dict /áddikt/ *n* **1.** somebody who is physiologically or psychologically dependent on a potentially harmful drug **2.** somebody who is very interested in a particular thing and devotes a lot of time to it ○ *soap opera addicts* [Mid-16C. < Latin *addictus*, past participle of *addicere* "award, devote" < *dicere* "say"]

ad·dict·ed /ə díktəd/ *adj* **1.** physiologically or psychologically dependent on a potentially harmful drug **2.** very interested in a particular thing and devoting a lot of time to it ○ *addicted to football*

ad·dic·tion /ə díksh'n/ *n* **1.** a state of physiological or psychological dependence on a potentially harmful drug **2.** great interest in a particular thing to which a lot of time is devoted ○ *Internet addiction*

ad·dic·tion·ol·o·gy /ə dìksh'n óllәjee/ *n* the study and treatment of addictions —**ad·dic·tion·ol·o·gist** *n*

ad·dic·tive /ə díktiv/ *adj* making or likely to make somebody an addict —**ad·dic·tive·ly** *adv*

ad·dic·tive per·son·a·li·ty *n* a personality predisposed toward becoming addicted to something

add-in *n* COMPUT same as **add-on**

Ad·dis Ab·a·ba /àddiss ábbəbə/ capital of Ethiopia. Population: 2,424,100 (1999).

Ad·di·son /áddiss'n/ village in northeastern Illinois, west of Chicago. Population: 36,378 (2002 estimate).

Ad·di·son, Joseph (1672–1719) English essayist and politician. An originator of the modern essay, he was cofounder (with Richard Steele) of *The Spectator* (1711).

> "Thus I live in the world rather as a Spectator of mankind, than as one of the species, by which means I have made myself a speculative statesman, soldier, merchant, and artisan, without ever meddling with any practical part of life."
> [Joseph Addison, *Spectator (London)*; March 1, 1711]

Ad·di·son, Thomas (1793–1860) British physician who correctly ascribed the symptoms of Addison's disease to adrenal malfunction

Ad·di·son's dis·ease *n* a wasting disease caused by failure of the adrenal glands to function normally and characterized by bronzing of the skin, low blood pressure, and weakness [Mid-19C. After Thomas ADDISON]

ad·di·tion /ə dísh'n/ *n* **1.** PUTTING IN OR ON the act of adding something onto or into something else **2.** ADDED PERSON OR THING somebody or something that is added **3.** MATH CALCULATION the process of calculating the sum of two or more numbers or amounts **4.** BUILDINGS ANNEX a part added to a building **5.** CHEM CHEMICAL REACTION a chemical reaction in which two or more compounds combine to produce a new compound ○ *an addition-type reaction* [14C. Directly or via French < Latin *addition-* < *additus*, past participle of *addere* (see ADD)] ◇ **in addition 1.** used to introduce an additional point or relevant fact **2.** also ◇ **in addition to** as well as

ad·di·tion·al /ə díshən'l, -díshnəl/ *adj* added on to something else

ad·di·tion·al·ly /ə díshən'lee, -díshnəlee/ *adv* **1.** FURTHER further to what has just been said ○ *Additionally, each machine is checked hourly.* **2.** TOO also **3.** EVEN MORE to an even greater extent (*literary*) ○*"The atmosphere of the place was heavy and moldy, being rendered additionally oppressive by the closing of the door which led into the church."* (Wilkie Collins, *The Woman in White*; 1860)

ad·di·tive /áddətiv/ *n* something added to something else to alter or improve it in some way, e.g., to change the color or texture of food ■ *adj* involving or produced by addition or by the addition of something (*formal*) [Late 17C. < late Latin *additivus* < *additus* (see ADDITION)]

ad·di·tive i·den·ti·ty *n* a quantity that, when added to another, leaves it unchanged. For ordinary numbers this is zero.

ad·di·tive in·verse *n* a number or quantity that gives zero when added to another. For example, the additive inverse of 3 is –3.

ad·di·tive print·ing *n* a printing process in which colors are produced by adding proportionate amounts of three primary colors

ad·dle /ádd'l/ (**-dled, -dling, -dles**) *vti* **1.** to confuse or muddle somebody, or become confused or muddled **2.** to make something rotten or spoiled, or become rotten or spoiled [Old English *adela* "filth, liquid manure" < Germanic]

add-on, **add-in** *n* a piece of computer equipment added to another to expand its capabilities

ad·dress *n* /ə dréss, á drèss/ **1.** PHYSICAL LOCATION the number, street name, and other information that describes where a building is or where somebody lives **2.** WRITTEN FORM OF ADDRESS the address of a person or organization when written on a letter or an item of mail **3.** /ə dréss/ FORMAL TALK a formal speech or report **4.** COMPUT NUMBER FOR LOCATION a number that specifies a location in a computer's memory ■ **ad·dress·es** *npl* COURTSHIP attention paid to somebody that is intended as courtship (*archaic*) ■ *v* /ə dréss/ (**-dressed, -dress·ing, -dress·es**) **1.** *vt* WRITE DIRECTIONS ON MAIL to write or print on an item of mail details of where it is to be delivered **2.** *vt* SPEAK OR MAKE SPEECH TO SOMEBODY to say something to somebody, or make a speech to an audience **3.** *vt* USE CORRECT TITLE FOR SOMEBODY to use the proper name or title in speaking or writing to somebody ○ *You should address him by his last name.* **4.** *vr* BEGIN TASK to set about doing some task ○*"Through this program of action we address ourselves to putting our own national house in order."* (Franklin D. Roosevelt, *First Inaugural Address*; 1933) **5.** *vt* DEAL WITH ISSUE to face up to and deal with a problem or issue ○ *failure to address the main issue* **6.** *vt* FACE SOMEBODY OR SOMETHING to stand facing a dance partner or an archery target **7.** *vt* GOLF PREPARE TO HIT GOLF BALL to take up the correct stance beside a golf ball before hitting it [14C. Via Old French *adresser* < assumed Vulgar Latin *addrictiare* "direct to" < Latin *directus* (see DIRECT)] —**ad·dress·a·ble** /ə dréssəb'l/ *adj*

ad·dress·ee /à dre sée, ə drèss ée/ *n* a person or organization to whom an item of mail is to be delivered

ad·dress har·vest·er *n* a computer program that collects e-mail addresses from the Internet

ad·duce /ə dóoss, ə dyóoss/ (**-duced, -duc·ing, -duc·es**) *vt* to offer something as evidence, a reason, or proof (*formal*) [15C. < Latin *adducere* "bring forward" < *ducere* "lead"] —**ad·duc·i·ble** *adj*

ad·duct /ə dúkt, a-/ *vt* (**-duct·ed, -duct·ing, -ducts**) to pull a leg or arm toward the central line of the body or a toe or finger toward the axis of a leg or arm ■ *n* a chemical compound formed by an addition reaction between two or more different compounds or elements [Mid-19C. Back-formation < *adduction*, directly or via French < Latin *adduction-* < *adductus*, past participle of *adducere* (see ADDUCE)] —**ad·duc·tion** *n* —**ad·duc·tive** *adj*

ad·duc·tor /ə dúktər/ *n* a muscle that pulls a leg or arm toward the central line of the body or a toe or finger toward the axis of a leg or arm [Early 17C. < modern Latin < Latin *adductus* (see ADDUCT)]

Ade /ayd/, **George** (1866–1944) US writer. He wrote a dozen popular Broadway plays (1900–10), but is best remembered for his satirical fables, written in Midwestern vernacular and published in several collections including *People You Know* (1903).

-ade *suffix* **1.** a sweetened drink ○ *orangeade* **2.** an action ○ *cannonade* [Via Old French < Latin *-ata*, feminine of *-atus* (see -ATE)]

Ad·e·laide /ádd'l àyd/ city in southeastern Australia, on the Gulf of St. Vincent. It is the state capital and main port of South Australia. Population: 1,088,400 (1998). —**A·de·lai·di·an** /àdd'l áydee ən/ *n, adj*

A·den /áad'n, áyd'n/ **1.** port and second largest city of Yemen, situated on a peninsula that juts into the Gulf of Aden. Population: 400,783 (1993 estimate). **2.** former British colony and protectorate that became part of South Yemen in 1967 and is Now part of Yemen

aden- *prefix* same as **adeno-** (*used before vowels*)

Ad·en·au·er /ádd'n òw ər/, **Konrad** (1876–1967) chancellor of the Federal Republic of Germany (1949–63). He also served as foreign minister (1951–55) and led West Germany into NATO in 1955.

> "We must free ourselves from thinking in terms of nation states."
> [Konrad Adenauer, *Speech*; May 1953]

ad·e·nec·to·my /àddə néktəmee/ (*plural* **-mies**) *n* the surgical removal of a gland

ad·e·nine /áddə neen, -nin/ *n* a purine base found in DNA, RNA, and energy-carrying molecules such as ATP. Symbol **A**

ad·e·ni·tis /àddə nítiss/ *n* inflammation of a gland or a lymph node

adeno- *prefix* gland ○ *adenovirus* [< Greek *adēn*]

ad·e·no·car·ci·no·ma /àddənō kaarssə nṓmə/ (*plural* **-mas** or **-ma·ta** /-nṓmətə/) *n* **1.** a malignant tumor in glandular tissue. Breast cancers are often adenocarcinomas. **2.** a malignant tumor with cells arranged in patterns similar to those of a gland —**ad·e·no·car·ci·nom·a·tous** *adj*

ad·e·noid /áddə nòyd/ *adj* **1.** RELATING TO GLANDS relating to or similar to a gland **2.** CONCERNING LYMPHOID TISSUE relating to lymphoid tissue **3.** MED same as **adenoidal** (sense 1) ■ **ad·e·noids** *npl* THROAT TISSUE a mass of tissue at the back of the nose and throat that can restrict breathing if enlarged. See illustration on next page

ad·e·noi·dal /àddə nóyd'l/ *adj* **1.** displaying symptoms caused by enlarged adenoids, e.g., a nasal voice or breathing difficulties **2.** relating to the adenoids

ad·e·noi·dec·tom·y /àddə noy déktəmee/ (*plural* **-ies**) *n* the surgical removal of adenoids

ad·e·no·ma /àddə nṓmə/ (*plural* **-mas** or **-ma·ta** /-mətə/)

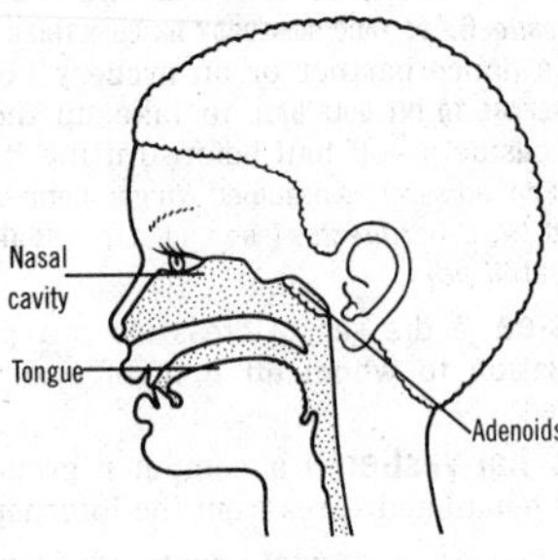

adenoids

n **1.** a benign tumor in glandular tissue **2.** a benign tumor with cells arranged in patterns similar to those of a gland —**ad·e·nom·a·toid** *adj*

ad·e·no·ma seb·a·ceum /-sə báyshəm/ *n* a skin condition of the face characterized by raised red vascular bumps, usually beginning in late childhood or early adolescence [< modern Latin, "sebaceous adenoma"]

ad·e·nop·ath·y /àddə nóppəthee/ *n* a diseased condition in a gland or lymph node, e.g., inflammation or enlargement

a·den·o·sine /ə dénnə seen/ *n* **1.** a compound of adenine and a ribose found in nucleic acids and energy-carrying molecules such as ATP **2.** a drug used to treat irregular heartbeat [Early 20C. Blend of ADENINE + RIBOSE]

a·den·o·sine de·a·mi·nase *n* an enzyme that catalyzes the removal of an amino group from adenosine to form inosine during purine metabolism. Lack of adenosine deaminase marks ADA deficiency.

a·den·o·sine di·phos·phate BIOCHEM full form of **ADP**[1]

a·den·o·sine mon·o·phos·phate *n* BIOCHEM full form of **AMP**

a·den·o·sine tri·phos·pha·tase *n* BIOCHEM full form of **ATPase**

a·den·o·sine tr·iphos·phate BIOCHEM full form of **ATP**

ad·en·o·sis /àddə nṓssiss/ *n* **1.** the unusual enlargement or development of a gland **2.** a disease characterized by adenosis

ad·e·no·vi·rus /àddənō vī́rəss/ *n* a virus that causes respiratory infections in humans [< its occurrence in adenoid tissue]

a·den·yl·ate cy·clase /ə dénnələt-/, **a·den·yl cy·clase** /àddə nīl-/ *n* an enzyme involved in the formation of cyclic AMP from ATP

a·dept *adj* /ə dépt/ highly proficient or expert at something ■ *n* /ádd ept/ somebody who is highly proficient or expert at something [Mid-17C. < Latin *adeptus*, past participle of *adipisci* "acquire" < *apisci* "pursue"] —**a·dept·ly** *adv* —**a·dept·ness** *n*

ad·e·quate /áddəkwət/ *adj* **1.** sufficient in quality or quantity to meet a need or qualify for something **2.** just barely sufficient in quality or quantity to meet a need or qualify for something [Late 16C. < Latin *adaequatus*, past participle of *adaequare* "make equal, match" < *aequus* "equal"] —**ad·e·qua·cy** *n* —**ad·e·quate·ly** *adv* —**ad·e·quate·ness** *n*

~~**adequatly**~~ incorrect spelling of **adequately**

A·der /aa dér/, **Clément** (1841–1926) French engineer who constructed a steam-powered aircraft and made the first heavier-than-air powered flight (1890)

à deux /aa dṓ/ *adv, adj* involving only two people and therefore private [Late 19C. < French]

ADH *abbr* BIOCHEM antidiuretic hormone

ADHD *abbr* MED attention deficit hyperactivity disorder

ad·here /əd heér, ad-/ (**-hered, -her·ing, -heres**) *vi* **1.** OBEY to be conscientious in supporting or following somebody or something ○ *adhere to the rules* **2.** SUPPORT to hold firmly to a belief, idea, or opinion ○ *on account of the opinion to which they consistently adhere* **3.** STICK FIRMLY to stick firmly to a surface or an object [15C. Directly or via French *adhérer* < Latin *adhaerere* < *haerere* "to stick"] —**ad·her·ence** *n*

ad·her·ent /əd heérənt, ad-, əd hérrənt/ *n* a supporter of a cause or of a leader ■ *adj* able to stick firmly to a surface or an object (*formal*)

ad·he·sion /əd heézh'n, ad-/ *n* **1.** STICKING POWER the ability to stick firmly to something **2.** ABSENCE OF SLIPPERINESS the ability to make firm contact with a surface without slipping **3.** SUPPORT loyal support for a cause or for a leader **4.** MED JOINING OF BODY PARTS the joining of normally unconnected body parts by bands of fibrous tissue **5.** PHYS INTERMOLECULAR ATTRACTION intermolecular attraction between substances that are unlike and in surface contact, causing them to cling together [15C. Directly or via French < Latin *adhaesion-* < *adhaes-*, past participle of *adhaerere* (see ADHERE)]

ad·he·sive /əd heéssiv, ad-, -heéziv/ *n* a substance used to stick things together ■ *adj* able to stick to something or to stick things together [Late 17C. < Latin *adhaes-* (see ADHESION)] —**ad·he·sive·ly** *adv* —**ad·he·sive·ness** *n*

ad hoc /ad hók, -hṓk/ *adj* done or set up solely in response to a specific situation or problem, without considering wider or longer-term issues ○ *ad hoc measures* [Mid-17C. < Latin, "to this"] —**ad hoc** *adv*

ad hoc com·mit·tee *n* **1.** a temporary committee formed for a specific need **2.** a congressional committee that is not permanent but is formed by members of various other committees to address a specific issue or problem

ad hoc·ism /ad hók ìzzəm, -hṓk-/, **ad hock·er·y** /ad hókəree, -hṓkəree/ *n* the making of decisions or the implementation of measures solely in response to a specific situation or problem, without considering wider or longer-term issues (*disapproving*)

ad·hoc·ra·cy /ad hókrəssee/ (*plural* **-cies**) *n* an organization that does not have a fixed bureaucratic structure and can adapt to changing circumstances [Late 20C. Blend of AD HOC + BUREAUCRACY]

ad hom·i·nem /ad hómmə nèm, -hómmənəm/ *adj* appealing to people's emotions and prejudices instead of their ability to think (*formal*) [Late 16C. < Latin, "to the person"] —**ad hom·i·nem** *adv*

ad·i·a·bat·ic /àddee ə báttik, àydee-, ày dī-/ *adj* describes a thermodynamic process that happens without loss or gain of heat [Late 19C. < Greek *adiabatos* "impassable" < *a-* "not" + *diabainein* "go through"] —**ad·i·a·bat·i·cal·ly** *adv*

ad·i·a·phor·ism /àddee áffə rìzzəm/ *n* especially in Protestant Christianity, the view that things not specifically forbidden by the Scriptures may be treated with indifference [Early 17C. < Greek *adiaphoros* "indifferent" < *a-* "not" + *diaphoros* "different"] —**ad·i·a·phor·is·tic** /-àffə rístik/ *adj*

~~**adict**~~ incorrect spelling of **addict**

A·die's pu·pil /áydeez-/ *n* a condition of the eyes in which one pupil is much larger than the other and less responsive to light [Early 20C. After William John *Adie* (1886–1935), Australian-born British neurologist]

a·dieu /ə dyṑo, ə dṑo/ *interj, n* (*plural* **a·dieux** /ə dyṑoz, ə dṑoz/ or **a·dieus**) used to say goodbye (*literary*) ○ *"...the more gentle adieus of her sisters were uttered without being heard"* (Jane Austen, *Pride And Prejudice*; 1813) [14C. < French, "(I commend you) to God"]

A·di Granth /aádi grúnt/ *n* the principal Sikh scripture, which contains the teachings of the first five gurus and also poems and hymns [< Sanskrit *ād-igrantha* "first book" < *grantha* "tying, work of literature"]

ad in·fi·ni·tum /ad ìnfə nī́təm/ *adv* endlessly, or for so long as to seem endless [Early 17C. < Latin, "to infinity"]

ad in·ter·im /ad íntərim/ *adv* for the meantime ■ *adj* done or created for the meantime only [< Latin, "to the meanwhile"]

ad·i·os /àddee ṓss, aàdee-/ *interj* used to say goodbye (*informal*) [Mid-19C. < Spanish, "(I commend you) to God"]

ad·ip·ic ac·id /ə dìppik-/ *n* a white crystalline solid. Use: making nylon, production of chemicals. Formula: $C_6H_{10}O_4$. [< Latin *adip-* "fat" (see ADIPO-), because the acid was originally made by oxidizing fats]

adipo- *prefix* fat, fatty ○ *adipocyte* [< Latin *adip-*, stem of *adeps* "fat"]

ad·i·po·cyte /áddipə sī̀t/ *n* a cell that synthesizes and stores fat [Mid-20C. < modern Latin *adiposus* (see ADIPOSE)]

ad·i·pose /áddə pṑss/ *adj* containing fat ■ *n* fat under the skin and surrounding major organs, providing stored energy, insulation, and protection [Mid-18C. < modern Latin *adiposus* "fatty" < Latin *adip-* (see ADIPO-)] —**ad·i·pose·ness** *n* —**ad·i·pos·i·ty** /àddə póssətee/ *n*

ad·i·pose tis·sue *n* connective tissue in human or animal bodies that contains fat

a·dip·sin /ə dípsin/ *n* a protein that is believed to control appetite. Use: obesity treatment. [Late 20C. < A[2] + Greek *dipsa* "thirst"]

Ad·i·ron·dack chair /àddə rón dak-/ *n* a wooden armchair usually used outdoors, having wide slats and a slanted seat and back [After their early use in the ADIRONDACK MOUNTAINS]

Ad·i·ron·dack Moun·tains /àddə rón dak-/, **Ad·i·ron·dacks** /-daks/ mountain chain in northeastern New York State, known for spectacular scenery and recreational activities. The highest peak is Mount Marcy 5,344 ft./1,629 m.

ad·it /áddət/ *n* a nearly horizontal shaft used for giving access to a mine or for drainage [Early 17C. < Latin *aditus* "approach, entrance" < past participle of *adire* "go toward" < *ire* "go"]

adj, **adj.** *abbr* **1.** GRAM adjective **2.** MATH adjoint **3.** LOGIC adjunct **4.** BANKING, INSUR adjustment **5.** MIL adjutant

Adj, **Adj.** *abbr* adjutant

ad·ja·cent /ə jáyss'nt/ *adj* **1.** situated near or close to something or each other, especially without touching **2.** describes either a pair of vertices in a graph that have common edges or a pair of edges in a graph that have a common vertex [15C. < Latin *adjacent-*, present participle of *adjacere* "lie near" < *jacere* "to lie"] —**ad·ja·cen·cy** *n*

USAGE adjacent or **adjoining**? Two houses are said to be ***adjoining*** when they are next to each other with a common wall. ***Adjoining*** tables are next to each other, end to end, forming one surface (they are, to use a more technical word, *contiguous*). In other words, ***adjoining*** items *join*. ***Adjacent*** houses, on the other hand, can have a space between them or even be on opposite sides of the road, as long as there is nothing significant between them (such as another house) and they are close enough for you to pass easily from one to the other. ***Adjacent*** tables are next to each other but not necessarily touching. Note also that ***adjoining***, being a form of a verb, can govern an object (*the house adjoining ours*), whereas ***adjacent*** needs the addition of *to* (*the house adjacent to ours*).

ad·ja·cent an·gle *n* either of the two angles that are formed by the intersection of two straight lines and lie on the same side of one line

ad·jec·tive /ájjəktiv/ *n* GRAM WORD DESCRIBING NOUN a word that describes or qualifies a noun or pronoun ■ *adj* **1.** GRAM ACTING AS ADJECTIVE relating to, forming, or functioning as an adjective **2.** LAW PRACTICED IN COURT relating to court practice and procedure rather than the principles of law [14C. Via French *adjectif* < Latin *adjectivus* < *adjicere* "throw to" < *jacere* "to throw"] —**ad·jec·ti·val** /àjjək tī́v'l/ *adj* —**ad·jec·ti·val·ly** *adv* —**ad·jec·tive·ly** *adv*

USAGE See ***adverb***.

ad·join /ə jóyn/ (**-joined, -join·ing, -joins**) *v* **1.** *vti* to be next to or share a common border with something, especially an area of land ○ *The two properties adjoin.* **2.** *vt* to attach or add on something (*archaic*) [14C. < Old French *ajoin-*, stem of *ajoindre* < Latin *adjungere* "join to" < *jungere* "to join"]

ad·join·ing /ə jóyning/ *adj* situated next to and touching something or each other

USAGE See ***adjacent***.

ad·joint /á jòynt/ *n* a matrix formed from a given square matrix, each element being derived from its cofactors, the determinants of the given matrix obtained by removing the row and column containing the element [Late 16C. < French, past participle of *ajoindre* (see ADJOIN)]

ad·journ /ə júrn/ (**-journed, -journ·ing, -journs**) *v* **1.** *vti* SUSPEND PROCEEDINGS to suspend the business of a court, legislature, or committee temporarily or indefinitely, or become suspended temporarily or indefinitely ○ *The court adjourned at one o'clock.* **2.** *vti* POSTPONE MEETING to postpone a meeting to another time, or become postponed **3.** *vt* DEFER SOMETHING to defer a matter or an action to another time **4.** *vi* MOVE AS GROUP to move together from one place to another ○ *We adjourned to the lounge.* **5.** *vi* STOP DOING SOMETHING to stop the current activity (*informal*) ○ *Time to adjourn for today.* [14C. < Old French *ajourner* < *à jorn (nomé)* "to an (appointed) day"] —**ad·journ·ment** *n*

Adjt., adjt. *abbr* MIL adjutant

ad·judge /ə jŭj/ (**-judged, -judg·ing, -judg·es**) *vt* **1.** MAKE JUDGMENT ABOUT SOMEBODY OR SOMETHING to judge somebody or something in a particular way ○ *She was adjudged to be an accomplished musician.* **2.** DETERMINE SOMETHING JUDICIALLY to decide something in a judicial proceeding **3.** DECREE SOMETHING LEGALLY to pronounce something by law [14C. Via Old French *ajuger* < Latin *adjudicare* (see ADJUDICATE)]

ad·ju·di·cate /ə jo͞odi kàyt/ (**-cat·ed, -cat·ing, -cates**) *vti* **1.** to reach a judicial decision on something **2.** to make an official decision about a problem or dispute [Early 18C. < Latin *adjudicat-*, past participle of *adjudicare* "award in arbitration" < *judic-* "a judge"] —**ad·ju·di·ca·tion** /ə jo͞odi káysh'n/ *n* —**ad·ju·di·ca·tive** /ə jo͞odi kàytiv, -kətiv/ *adj* —**ad·ju·di·ca·tor** *n*

ad·junct /á jùngkt/ *n* **1.** SOMETHING ADDED ON AS EXTRA something inessential added to something else **2.** ASSISTANT an assistant or subordinate **3.** INESSENTIAL PART OF SENTENCE a part of a sentence that is not the subject or predicate ■ *adj* ATTACHED TEMPORARILY TO STAFF assigned temporarily or as an auxiliary member to the staff of an institution ○ *an adjunct professor of art history* [Early 16C. < Latin *adjunctus*, past participle of *adjungere* (see ADJOIN)] —**ad·junc·tion** /ə júngksh'n/ *n* —**ad·junc·tive** *adj*

ad·jure /ə jo͝or/ (**-jured, -jur·ing, -jures**) *vt* **1.** to order somebody to do something, especially under oath **2.** to make an earnest appeal to somebody [14C. < Latin *adjurare* "swear by oath" < *jurare* "swear" (see JURY)] —**ad·ju·ra·tion** /àjjə ráysh'n/ *n* —**ad·jur·er** *n*

ad·just /ə júst/ (**-just·ed, -just·ing, -justs**) *v* **1.** *vt* to make slight changes in something to make it fit or function better **2.** *vti* to adapt to a new environment or condition [Early 17C. Via obsolete French *adjuster* < assumed Vulgar Latin *adjuxtare* "put close to" < Latin *juxta* "close"] —**ad·just·a·bil·i·ty** /ə jùstə bíllətee/ *n* —**ad·just·a·ble** *adj* —**ad·just·ment** *n*

ad·just·a·ble-rate mort·gage *n* a mortgage on which interest is payable at a rate that varies according to a predetermined formula. The interest is typically tied to the prime rate or another interest rate.

ad·just·able wrench *n* a wrench with a head that can be adjusted by means of a screw to fit different sizes of nuts and bolts

ad·just·er /ə jústər/, **ad·jus·tor** *n* somebody who assesses the validity of an insurance claim on behalf of an insurance company and authorizes appropriate payment, repairs, or other action

ad·ju·tant /ájjətənt/ *n* **1.** a military officer who acts as an administrative assistant to a commanding officer **2.** BIRDS same as **adjutant stork** [Early 17C. < Latin *adjutant-*, present participle of *adjutare* "keep on helping" < *adjuvare* (see ADJUVANT)]

ad·ju·tant gen·er·al (*plural* **ad·ju·tants gen·er·al**) *n* **1.** an army general responsible for administration and personnel **2.** the adjutant of a military unit commanded by a general staff

adjutant stork

ad·ju·tant stork *n* a large, often carrion-eating stork with a naked yellow head and neck, black wings, and white undersides. Native to: Southeast Asia. Latin name: *Leptoptilos dubius* or *Leptoptilos javanicus*. [< the similarity of its walk to that of a military staff officer]

ad·ju·vant /ájjəvənt/ *n* **1.** PHARM DRUG-ENHANCING AGENT a drug or agent added to another drug or agent to enhance its medical effectiveness **2.** PHARM ANTIGEN-ENHANCING DRUG a substance injected along with an antigen to enhance the immune response stimulated by the antigen **3.** HELPING AGENT something that helps or assists ■ *adj* ASSISTING helping by supplementing [Late 16C. Directly or via French < Latin *adjuvant-*, present participle of *adjuvare* "give help to" < *juvare* "to help"]

Ad·ler /áddlər/, **Alfred** (1870–1937) Austrian psychiatrist who stressed the importance of the inferiority complex. His books include *The Neurotic Constitution* (1912).

Ad·ler, Stella (1901–92) US actor who taught Method acting at her school, the Stella Adler Conservatory of Acting

ad lib /àd líb/ *adj, adv* **1.** without any advance preparation **2.** MUSIC same as **ad libitum** [Early 19C. Shortening of AD LIBITUM]

ad-lib /àd líb/ *vti* (**ad-libbed, ad-lib·bing, ad-libs**) IMPROVISE SPEECH OR PERFORMANCE to make up a speech or a musical or dramatic performance on the spot without a fixed text or score ■ *adj* UNPLANNED improvised or made up on the spot ■ *n* IMPROVISED PART OF PERFORMANCE something said by an actor or other performer that is not in the script —**ad-lib·ber** *n*

ad li·bi·tum /àd líbbətəm/ *adj, adv* to be performed in the way the performer chooses [Early 17C. < Latin, "at your pleasure"]

ad lit·em /àd lītəm/ *adj* appointed by a court to represent a minor [Mid-18C. < Latin, "for the purpose of a lawsuit"]

Adm. *abbr* **1.** Admiral **2.** Admiralty

ad·man /ád màn/ (*plural* **-men** /-mèn/) *n* a man who works in advertising (*informal*)

ad·meas·ure /ad mézhər/ (**-ured, -ur·ing, -ures**) *vt* to divide something up to be shared out (*formal*) [14C. Via Old French *amesurer* < medieval Latin *admensurare* "apply a measure to"] —**ad·meas·ure·ment** *n*

ad·min /ád mìn/ *n* (*informal*) **1.** the administrative work involved in running a business or organization **2.** an administrative assistant [Mid-20C. Shortening]

ad·min·is·ter /əd mínnəstər/ (**-tered, -ter·ing, -ters**) *v* **1.** *vt* BE IN CHARGE OF AFFAIRS to manage the affairs of a business, organization, or institution **2.** *vt* DISPENSE SOMETHING to preside over the dispensation of something ○ *He administered justice in the fairest possible manner.* **3.** *vt* GIVE MEDICATION to give somebody a measured amount of a medication, often by physically introducing it into the body **4.** *vt* PERFORM RITUAL to carry out a set ritual or religious ceremony on behalf of a person or group of people **5.** *vi* SUPERVISE TAKING OF OATH to oversee the taking of an oath by somebody **6.** *vi* LOOK AFTER SOMEBODY to look after and tend to the needs of somebody **7.** *vt* LAW ORGANIZE HANDOVER OF PROPERTY to manage the distribution of a deceased person's property in accordance with the law [14C. Via Old French *aministrer* < Latin *administrare* "serve, manage" < *ministrare* "serve"] —**ad·min·is·tra·ble** *adj* —**ad·min·is·trant** *n, adj*

ad·min·is·trate /əd mínnə stràyt/ (**-trat·ed, -trat·ing, -trates**) *vti* to oversee or organize the affairs of something, especially a business, organization, or institution [Mid-16C. < Latin *administrat-*, past participle of *administrare* (see ADMINISTER)]

ad·min·is·tra·tion /əd mìnnə stráysh'n/ *n* **1.** MANAGEMENT OF BUSINESS the management of the affairs of a business, organization, or institution **2.** MANAGEMENT STAFF the staff of a business, organization, or institution whose task is to manage its affairs **3.** MANAGEMENT OF GOVERNMENT the management of public affairs or the affairs of a government **4.** STAFF OF GOVERNMENT a government's staff whose task is to manage its affairs **5.** TERM OF OFFICE the duration of a term of office, usually a political one **6.** GOVERNMENT a government, especially its executive branch **7.** *US* GOV US GOVERNMENT AGENCY a United States government agency or board **8.** LAW LEGAL DISPOSAL OF ESTATE the legal disposal or management of a deceased person's estate or an estate held in trust **9.** ADMINISTERING OF SOMETHING TO SOMEBODY the act of administering something such as an oath, medicine, or sacrament

ad·min·is·tra·tive /əd mínnə stràytiv/ *adj* relating to the administration of a business, organization, or institution —**ad·min·is·tra·tive·ly** *adv*

ad·min·is·tra·tive as·sis·tant *n* an employee whose task is to assist a superior with the day-to-day affairs of running a business or department

ad·min·is·tra·tive law *n* the area of law dealing with the affairs of agencies of the executive branch of a government, and with the judicial review of public bodies generally

ad·min·is·tra·tor /əd mínnə stràytər/ *n* **1.** somebody whose job is to manage the affairs of a business, organization, or institution **2.** somebody appointed by a court to manage the estate of a deceased person, especially when there is no competent executor

ad·mi·ra·ble /ádmərəb'l/ *adj* deserving to be admired [15C. < Latin *admirabilis* < *admirari* (see ADMIRE)] —**ad·mi·ra·ble·ness** *n* —**ad·mi·ra·bly** *adv*

admiral (sense 3)

ad·mi·ral /ádmərəl/ *n* **1.** NAVAL COMMANDER an officer in the US Navy or Coast Guard of a rank above vice admiral **2.** NAVAL OFFICER a high-ranking naval officer entitled to fly a personal flag **3.** INSECTS BRIGHTLY COLORED BUTTERFLY a brightly colored butterfly of temperate regions. Family: Nymphalidae. [13C. Via French *amiral* < Arabic *amir-al* "commander of" in such phrases as *amir-al-bahr* "commander of the sea"] —**ad·mi·ral·ship** *n*

Ad·mi·ral of the Fleet *n* an officer in the British Royal Navy of the highest rank

Ad·mi·ral's Cup *n* **1.** an international yacht race held every two years off the southern coast of England between teams of three yachts **2.** the trophy awarded to the winning team in the Admiral's Cup

ad·mi·ral·ty /ádmərəltee/ *n* the office or jurisdiction of an admiral

Ad·mi·ral·ty Is·lands /ádmərəltee-/ island group in the Bismarck Archipelago, north of New Guinea in the western Pacific Ocean, part of Papua New Guinea. The group's largest island is Manus. Area: 800 sq. mi./2,072 sq. km.

ad·mi·ra·tion /àdmə ráysh'n/ *n* **1.** warm approval, appreciation, or respect ○ *was filled with admiration for her courage* **2.** somebody or something regarded with approval, appreciation, or respect ○ *a house that was the admiration of the neighborhood*

SYNONYMS See ***regard***.

ad·mire /əd mīr/ (**-mired, -mir·ing, -mires**) *vt* **1.** to regard somebody or something with approval, appreciation, or respect ○ *I admire your determination.* **2.** to look at somebody or something beautiful or attractive with enjoyment ○ *admired the view from the summit* [Late 16C. Directly or via French *admirer* < Latin *admirari* "wonder at" < *mirari* "to wonder"] —**ad·mir·er** *n*

ad·mir·ing /əd mīring/ *adj* full of admiration for somebody or something —**ad·mir·ing·ly** *adv*

~~**admision**~~ incorrect spelling of **admission**

~~**admissable**~~ incorrect spelling of **admissible**

ad·mis·si·ble /əd míssəb'l/ *adj* **1.** ALLOWABLE allowed to be done **2.** ALLOWED TO COME IN able or deserving to enter **3.** ALLOWED TO BE USED IN COURT accepted as evidence in court [Early 17C. Directly or via French < medieval Latin *admissibilis* < Latin *admiss-* (see ADMISSION)] —**ad·mis·si·bil·i·ty** /əd mìssə bíllətee/ *n* —**ad·mis·si·ble·ness** *n* —**ad·mis·si·bly** *adv*

ad·mis·sion /əd mísh'n/ *n* 1. **ENTRY** the right, ability, or permission to enter a place or an organization or institution ○ *Admission is by invitation only.* 2. **FEE FOR ENTRY** a fee paid for entrance to a place or event 3. **CONFESSION** a confession to having committed a crime or having made a mistake ○ *an admission of guilt* 4. **DECLARATION** an acknowledgment that something is true ○ *The letter contained a clear admission of the error.* ■ **ad·mis·sions** *npl* 1. **PROCESS OF ACCEPTING STUDENTS** the process of accepting students for study at a university or college ○ *a new system of admissions* 2. **NUMBER OF STUDENTS ACCEPTED** the number of students accepted into a university or college ○ *a drop in admissions* [15C. < Latin *admission-* < *admiss-*, past participle of *admittere* (see ADMIT)]

ad·mit /əd mít/ (**-mit·ted, -mit·ting, -mits**) *v* 1. *vti* **ACKNOWLEDGE TRUTH** to acknowledge that something is true ○ *You must admit it is a tempting offer.* 2. *vt* **ALLOW SOMEBODY TO ENTER** to allow somebody or something entrance or access ○ *"Admits one"* 3. *vti* **CONFESS** to confess to having committed a crime or having made a mistake 4. *vti* **OFFER POSSIBILITY** to permit the possibility of something ○ *Their conduct admits of only one explanation.* [14C. < Latin *admittere* "let go into" < *mittere* "let go"]

ad·mit·tance /əd mítt'nss/ *n* 1. **PERMISSION TO GO IN** the permission or right to enter a place 2. **ENTRANCE TO PLACE** physical entry to a place 3. PHYS **MEASURE OF FLOW OF CURRENT** the reciprocal of impedance, a measure of the ability of an electrical current to flow. Symbol *Y*

ad·mit·ted·ly /əd míttədlee/ *adv* as must be acknowledged

ad·mix /əd míks, ad-/ (**-mixed, -mix·ing, -mix·es**) *vt* to mix something into something else [Early 16C. Probably back-formation < ADMIXTURE]

ad·mix·ture /əd míkschər, ad-/ *n* 1. **PRODUCT OF MIXING** something produced by incorporating an item into something else 2. **INGREDIENT** something added to something else by mixing 3. **PROCESS OF MIXING INGREDIENTS** the mixing of something into something else [Early 17C. < AD- + MIXTURE]

ad·mon·ish /əd mónnish/ (**-ished, -ish·ing, -ish·es**) *vt* 1. to rebuke somebody mildly but earnestly 2. to advise somebody to do or, more often, not to do something [14C. < Old French *amonester* < assumed Vulgar Latin *admonere* < Latin *monere* "warn"] —**ad·mon·ish·er** *n* —**ad·mon·ish·ment** *n*

ad·mo·ni·tion /àdmə nísh'n/ *n* 1. a mild but earnest rebuke 2. advice for or against doing something —**ad·mon·i·to·ry** /əd mónnə tàwree/ *adj*

ad nau·se·am /ad náwzee əm/ *adv* to an extreme or annoying extent [Mid-17C. < Latin, "to sickness"]

~~ad nauseum~~ incorrect spelling of **ad nauseam**

ad·nex·a /ad néksə/ *npl* adjoining structural parts of the body [Late 19C. < Latin < *adnectere* "tie together" < *nectere* "to tie"] —**ad·nex·al** *adj*

ad·nom·i·nal /ad nómmən'l/ *n* a word that modifies a noun [Mid-19C. < Latin *adnomen*, alteration of *agnomen* (see AGNOMEN)]

a·do /ə dóo/ *n* excited activity or bother [14C. Contraction of N English dialect *at do* < Old Norse *at* "to" + DO[1]] ◇ **without further ado** without wasting any time

CULTURAL NOTE ***Much Ado About Nothing***, a play (1598?) by English dramatist William Shakespeare. A comedy set in the court of the Duke of Messina in Sicily, it tells of the love of a soldier, Claudio, for the Duke's daughter, Hero, and the eventually unsuccessful attempts of Claudio's enemy, Don John, to prevent their marriage.

a·do·be /ə dóbee/ *n* 1. **EARTHEN BRICK** brick made from earth and straw and dried by the sun 2. **BUILDING MADE OF ADOBE** a structure made with adobe bricks 3. **EARTH THAT FORMS ADOBE** earth used to make adobe bricks [Mid-18C. Via Spanish < Arabic *at-tūb* "the bricks"]

a·do·be flat *n* a gently sloping plain of clay soil deposited by desert floods

a·do·bo /aa dó bò, ə-/ (*plural* **-bos**) *n SE Asia* a Philippine dish of marinated meat or fish seasoned with vinegar, garlic, soy sauce, and spices [Mid-20C. < Spanish]

ad·o·les·cence /àddə léss'nss/ *n* 1. the period from puberty to adulthood in human beings 2. the stage in the development of something such as a civilization before it reaches maturity

ad·o·les·cent /àddə léss'nt/ *n* **SOMEBODY IN PERIOD PRECEDING ADULTHOOD** somebody who has reached puberty but is not yet an adult ■ *adj* 1. **EXPERIENCING ADOLESCENCE** going through the period of adolescence ○ *adolescent males* 2. **HAPPENING DURING ADOLESCENCE** typically occurring during the period of adolescence 3. **IMMATURE** involving, relating to, or meant for somebody who is immature [15C. Via French < Latin *adolescent-*, present participle of *adolescere* "be nourished, grow up" < *alere* "nourish"]

~~adolesent~~ incorrect spelling of **adolescent**

Ad·o·nai /àadō ní, -nóy/ *n* a name used in Judaism instead of the unspeakable name of God [14C. < Hebrew *'ădōnay*]

A·don·is /ə dónniss, -dó-/ *n* 1. in Greek mythology, a handsome youth loved by Aphrodite and Persephone. He was killed while hunting boar, but was allowed by Zeus to divide his time between Aphrodite on earth and Persephone in the underworld. 2. *also* **a·don·is** an extremely handsome young man [Late 16C. < Greek *Adōnis* < Phoenician *ædōnī* "my lord"]

a·dopt /ə dópt/ (**a·dopt·ed, a·dopt·ing, a·dopts**) *vt* 1. **LEGALLY RAISE ANOTHER'S CHILD** to raise a child of other biological parents as if it were your own, in accordance with formal legal procedures 2. **CHOOSE AND DECIDE TO USE SOMETHING** to take up something such as a plan, idea, cause, or practice and use or follow it ○ *decided to adopt a wait-and-see policy* 3. **ASSUME WAY OF ACTING** to assume an attitude or way of behaving ○ *adopted an air of innocence* 4. **START USING NEW NAME** to take on and use a new name or title ○ *plans to adopt a pseudonym* 5. POL **VOTE IN FAVOR OF SOMETHING** to vote to accept something such as a committee's decision or a congressional bill 6. *US* **CHOOSE SOMETHING AS REQUIREMENT** to officially select something as a requirement [15C. Directly or via French *adopter* < Latin *adoptare* "choose for yourself" < *optare* "choose"] —**a·dopt·a·ble** *adj* —**a·dopt·ed** *adj* —**a·dop·tee** /ə dòp tée/ *n* —**a·dopt·er** *n*

USAGE adopted or **adoptive**? Parents who adopt a child have an ***adopted*** child, and the child has ***adoptive*** parents. Any children related to the parents by birth have an ***adopted*** brother or sister; the ***adopted*** child has ***adoptive*** siblings.

USAGE See ***adapt.***

a·dop·tion /ə dópsh'n/ *n* 1. a formal legal process to adopt a child 2. an instance of adopting somebody or something such as an idea, name, or attitude [14C. Directly or via French < Latin *adoption-* < *adoptare* (see ADOPT)]

a·dop·tive /ə dóptiv/ *adj* describes a parent who adopts a child, or somebody who is related to somebody else by adoption ○ *her adoptive sister*

USAGE See ***adopt.***

a·dor·a·ble /ə dáwrəb'l/ *adj* charming, lovable, and usually very attractive —**a·dor·a·bil·i·ty** /ə dàwrə bíllətee/ *n* —**a·dor·a·ble·ness** *n* —**a·dor·a·bly** *adv*

a·dore /ə dáwr/ (**a·dored, a·dor·ing, a·dores**) *vt* 1. **LOVE SOMEBODY DEEPLY** to love somebody intensely 2. **LIKE SOMETHING VERY MUCH** to like something or somebody very much (*informal*) 3. **WORSHIP GOD** to worship God, a god, or a spirit [14C. Via Old French < late Latin *adorare* "pray to" < Latin *orare* "pray"] —**ad·o·ra·tion** /àddə ráysh'n/ *n* —**a·dor·er** *n*

a·dor·ing /ə dáwring/ *adj* showing love or admiration for somebody —**a·dor·ing·ly** *adv*

a·dorn /ə dáwrn/ (**a·dorned, a·dorn·ing, a·dorns**) *vt* 1. to add decoration or ornamentation to something 2. to add to the beauty or glory of something or somebody [14C. Via Old French < Latin *adornare* "embellish with ornaments" < *ornare* "embellish"] —**a·dorn·er** *n* —**a·dorn·ment** *n*

ADP[1] *n* a chemical compound (**nucleotide**) involved in energy transfer reactions in living cells. Full form **adenosine diphosphate**

ADP[2] *abbr* COMPUT automatic data processing

ADR *abbr US* FIN American depositary receipt

A·dras·te·a /ə drástee ə/ *n* a small natural satellite of Jupiter, discovered in 1979

ad rem /ad rém/ *adv* to the point or purpose (*formal*) [Late 16C. < Latin, "to the matter or business"] —**ad rem** *adj*

adren- *prefix* same as **adreno-** (*used before vowels*)

ad·re·nal /ə drée n'l/ *adj* 1. relating to or on the kidneys 2. describes parts or effects of the adrenal glands ■ *n* ANAT same as **adrenal gland** [Late 19C. < AD- + RENAL, because the adrenal glands are next to the kidneys] —**ad·re·nal·ly** *adv*

ad·re·nal·ec·to·my /ə drée n'l éktəmee/ (*plural* **-mies**) *n* the surgical removal of one or both of the adrenal glands

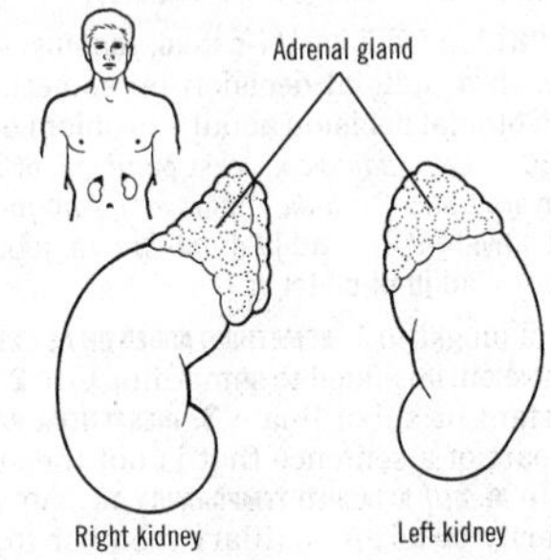

adrenal gland

ad·re·nal gland *n* an endocrine gland located above each kidney. The inner part (**medulla**) of each gland secretes epinephrine and the outer part (**cortex**) secretes steroids.

A·dren·a·lin /ə drénn'lən/ *tdmk* a trademark for epinephrine

a·dren·a·line /ə drénn'lən/ *n* a hormone secreted by the adrenal glands and by some nerve endings, that increases the speed and force of heart contraction (*often nontechnical*) ○ *get the adrenaline pumping* [Early 20C. < ADRENAL + -INE]

ad·re·nal·ize /ə drénn'l ìz/ (**-ized, -iz·ing, -iz·es**) *vt US* to get somebody stirred up and ready for action

ad·re·ner·gic /àddrə núrjik/ *adj* producing or activated by epinephrine or a similar substance [Mid-20C. < ADREN- + Greek *ergon* "work"] —**ad·re·ner·gi·cal·ly** *adv*

adreno- *prefix* relating to adrenaline or the adrenal glands ○ *adrenochrome* [< ADRENAL or ADRENALINE]

ad·re·no·chrome /ə drée nə krōm/ *n* a naturally occurring mixture of quinones, brick red in color, produced by the oxidation of epinephrine, that reduces the permeability of small blood vessels. Use: control of bleeding.

ad·re·no·cor·ti·cal /ə drée nō káwrtək'l/ *adj* involving, located in, or produced by the cortex of the adrenal glands

ad·re·no·cor·ti·co·ster·oid /ə drée nō kàwrtikō stéer òyd, -stér-/ *n* 1. any steroid hormone released from the adrenal cortex 2. a drug that mimics steroids produced by the adrenal cortex

ad·re·no·cor·ti·co·trop·ic /ə drée nō káwrtikō tróppik/, **ad·re·no·cor·ti·co·troph·ic** /-tróffik/ *adj* describes hormones or drugs that stimulate the adrenal cortex to produce corticosteroids

ad·re·no·cor·ti·co·trop·ic hor·mone *n* BIOCHEM full form of **ACTH**

ad·re·no·cor·ti·co·trop·in /ə drée nō kàwrtikō trṓpin/, **ad·re·no·cor·ti·co·troph·in** /-trṓfin/ *n* BIOCHEM same as **ACTH**

ad·re·no·leu·ko·dys·tro·phy /ə drée nō lóokə dístrəfee/ *n* a hereditary disorder of the nervous system in boys that affects the adrenal glands

ad·re·no·lyt·ic /ə drée n'l íttik/ *adj* blocking the action of the adrenergic nerves or inhibiting the response to epinephrine ■ *n* an adrenolytic drug or agent

ad·re·no·re·cep·tor /ə drée nō ri séptər/ *n* a nerve ending that is activated by epinephrine or related substances

~~adress~~ incorrect spelling of **address**

A·dri·an /áydree ən/ city in southeastern Michigan, southwest of Detroit. Population: 21,359 (2002 estimate).

A·dri·a·tic /àydree áttik/ *adj* relating to the area that borders on the Adriatic Sea, or islands in that sea ■ *n* same as **Adriatic Sea**

A·dri·at·ic Sea /àydree áttik-/ arm of the Mediterranean Sea, east of Italy. Area: 51,000 sq. mi./132,000 sq. km.

a·drift /ə dríft/ *adj, adv* **1.** floating freely without being steered in a specific direction **2.** living life without a goal

a·droit /ə dróyt/ *adj* displaying physical or mental skill [Mid-17C. < French *à droit* "by right, properly"] —**a·droit·ly** *adv* —**a·droit·ness** *n*

ADSL *abbr* asymmetrical digital subscriber line

ad·sorb /əd sáwrb, -záwrb/ (**-sorbed, -sorb·ing, -sorbs**) *vti* to undergo, or cause something to undergo, adsorption [Late 19C. Back-formation < ADSORPTION] —**ad·sorb·a·ble** *adj*

ad·sor·bate /əd sáwrbət, -záwrbət, -sáwr bàyt/ *n* a substance that is adsorbed

ad·sor·bent /əd sáwrbənt, -záwr-/ *adj* able to adsorb ■ *n* a substance capable of adsorbing

ad·sorp·tion /əd sáwrpsh'n, -záwrp-/ *n* the adhesion of a thin layer of molecules of some substance to the surface of a solid or liquid [Late 19C. Blend of AD- + ABSORPTION] —**ad·sorp·tive** *adj*

ad·speak /ád speek/ *n* the language thought of as typical of advertisements, especially characterized as misleading or exaggerated

ad·spend /ád spènd/ *n* the amount of money spent on advertising for a product or activity

ADT *abbr* TIME Atlantic Daylight Time

a·du·ki bean *n* PLANTS, FOOD same as **adzuki bean**

ad·u·lar·i·a /àjjə lérree ə/ *n* a white or transparent precious stone that is a variety of orthoclase. Use: gems. [Late 18C. < French *adulaire* < *Adula*, mountains in the Swiss Alps]

ad·u·late /ájjə làyt/ (**-lat·ed, -lat·ing, -lates**) *vt* to admire or flatter somebody excessively [Mid-18C. Back-formation < ADULATION] —**ad·u·la·tor** *n* —**ad·u·la·to·ry** /ájjələ tàwree/ *adj*

ad·u·la·tion /àjjə láysh'n/ *n* excessive flattery or admiration [14C. Directly or via French < Latin *adulation-* < *adulari* "flatter"]

a·dult /ə dúlt, á dùlt/ *n* **1.** FULLY GROWN LIFE FORM a fully mature person, animal, plant, or other form of life **2.** SOMEBODY LEGALLY ADULT somebody who has reached the age of legal majority, generally 18 years of age in the United States ■ *adj* **1.** COMPLETELY GROWN fully developed and mature ○ *an adult male* ○ *adult life* **2.** FOR SOMEBODY MATURE involving, relating to, or meant for mature people ○ *adult education* **3.** UNSUITABLE FOR CHILDREN considered unsuitable for young people because of pornography, violence, or sexually explicit language [Mid-16C. < Latin *adultus*, past participle of *adolescere* (see ADOLESCENT)] —**a·dult·hood** *n* —**a·dult·ness** *n*

a·dult ed·u·ca·tion *n* EDUC same as **continuing education** (sense 1)

a·dul·ter·ant /ə dúltərənt/ *n* something that makes something else less pure —**a·dul·ter·ant** *adj*

a·dul·ter·ate /ə dúltə ràyt/ *vt* (**-at·ed, -at·ing, -ates**) to make something less pure by adding inferior or unsuitable elements or substances to it ■ *adj* **1.** made less pure **2.** same as **adulterous** (*literary*) [Mid-16C. < Latin *adulterat-*, past participle of *adulterare* "change, corrupt, commit adultery" < *alterare* (see ALTER)] —**a·dul·ter·a·tion** /ə dùltə ráysh'n/ *n* —**a·dul·ter·a·tive** /-ràytiv, -rətiv/ *adj* —**a·dul·ter·a·tor** *n*

a·dul·ter·ine /ə dúltə rīn, -reen, -rin/ *adj* **1.** IMPURE characterized by adulteration **2.** ILLEGAL not within the law **3.** BORN FROM ADULTERY born from an adulterous relationship (*literary*)

a·dul·ter·ous /ə dúltərəss/ *adj* relating to or involved in adultery [Early 17C. < obsolete *adulter* "adulterer" < Latin *adulterare* (see ADULTERATE)] —**a·dul·ter·ous·ly** *adv*

a·dul·ter·y /ə dúltəree/ *n* voluntary sexual relations between a married person and somebody other than his or her spouse [15C. Directly and via Old French *avout(e)rie* < Latin *adulterare* (see ADULTERATE)] —**a·dul·ter·er** *n*

a·dul·to·les·cent /àddultə léss'nt/, **a·dul·tes·cent** /àddul téss'nt/ *n* a young person, aged 25–34, who enjoys entertainment such as computer games or books intended for a much younger audience [Early 21C. < ADULT + ADOLESCENT]

a·dult-on·set di·a·be·tes *n* a form of diabetes mellitus that develops slowly in some adults as the body becomes unable to use insulin effectively

~~adultry~~ incorrect spelling of **adultery**

ad·um·brate /áddəm bràyt, ə dúm-/ (**-brat·ed, -brat·ing, -brates**) *vt* **1.** to give an incomplete or faint outline or indication of something **2.** to give a vague indication or warning of something to come [Late 16C. < Latin *adumbrat-*, past participle of *adumbrare* "overshadow" < *umbra* "shade"] —**ad·um·bra·tion** /àddəm bráysh'n/ *n* —**ad·um·bra·tive** /áddəm bràytiv, ə dúmbrətiv/ *adj* —**ad·um·bra·tive·ly** *adv*

adv, adv. *abbr* **1.** GRAM adverb **2.** adverbial

ad val. *abbr* FIN ad valorem

ad va·lo·rem /àd və láwrəm/ *adj, adv* in proportion to the value of something [Late 17C. < Latin, "according to value"]

ad·vance /əd vánss/ *v* (**-vanced, -vanc·ing, -vanc·es**) **1.** *vti* MOVE AHEAD to move, or move somebody or something, forward in position **2.** *vt* SUGGEST SOMETHING to put something forward as a proposal **3.** *vt* GIVE SOMETHING AHEAD OF TIME to supply something or part of something, especially money, before it is due **4.** *vt* LEND MONEY OR GOODS to supply money or goods on credit **5.** *vti* RISE IN STATUS to rise, or make or help somebody rise, in rank or position **6.** *vt* BRING SOMETHING FORWARD IN TIME to make something happen earlier than originally expected **7.** *vti* PROGRESS to further the progress or improvement of something such as a cause, or undergo progress or improvement **8.** *vti* RISE IN AMOUNT to increase in price, rate, or amount, or increase the price, rate, or amount of something ■ *n* **1.** DEVELOPMENT progress or improvements **2.** FIN PAYMENT AHEAD OF TIME a sum of money paid before it is due **3.** MOVEMENT AHEAD a forward movement in position **4.** FRIENDLY APPROACH an approach made to somebody in an attempt to form a relationship or come to an agreement (*often used in the plural*) **5.** COMM PROVIDING SOMETHING BEFORE BEING PAID the act of supplying money or goods before payment is received **6.** COMM SOMETHING RECEIVED BEFORE BEING PAID FOR a quantity of money or goods supplied before payment is made or repayments begin **7.** FIN LOAN a loan of money **8.** FIN PRICE RISE an increase in price or rate ■ *adj* **1.** AHEAD OF TIME made, given, or sent ahead of time **2.** GOING IN FRONT going ahead of the main group [13C. Via Old French *avancer* < assumed Vulgar Latin *abantiare* < *abante* "(from) before" < Latin *ante* "before"] —**ad·vanc·er** *n* ◇ **in advance** before an event takes place

ad·vanced /əd vánst/ *adj* **1.** LATEST employing the newest ideas or techniques **2.** FAR ALONG at a point late in the progress or development of something **3.** MORE HIGHLY DEVELOPED at a higher stage of development or progress than other similar people or things ○ *an advanced class*

ad·vanced de·gree *n* a university degree higher than a bachelor's

ad·vanced green *n Can* a flashing green traffic light indicating that oncoming traffic is held back and that it is safe to turn left

ad·vanced stand·ing *n* the status of a college student who has been granted credit for courses taken or demonstrated knowledge acquired elsewhere

ad·vance guard *n* a body of troops sent ahead of a main force to prepare an area for operations

ad·vance man *n US* a man employed by a politician or other public figure to travel ahead on trips to organize schedules, publicity, security, and other arrangements

ad·vance·ment /əd vánssmənt/ *n* **1.** PROMOTION a promotion in rank or position **2.** ADVANCING an act or instance of moving ahead **3.** IMPROVEMENT the progress or development of something **4.** LAW USE OF LEGACY BEFORE DUE the use of money from a legacy by or on behalf of its beneficiary before that person is strictly entitled to it

ad·vance par·ty (*plural* **ad·vance par·ties**) *n* **1.** a group of soldiers or units sent ahead of a larger force to prepare an area for operations **2.** a small group sent on ahead of any main party, e.g., on an expedition

ad·vance per·son *n* somebody employed by a politician or other public figure to travel ahead on trips to organize schedules, publicity, security, and other arrangements

ad·vance poll *n* in Canada, an early vote held for voters who will be absent from their regular polling place on election day

ad·vance wo·man *n* a woman employed by a politician or other public figure to travel ahead on trips to organize schedules, publicity, security, and other arrangements

ad·van·tage /əd vántij/ *n* **1.** SUPERIOR POSITION a superior or favorable position in relation to somebody or something ○ *hoping to gain an advantage in the negotiations* **2.** FACTOR FAVORING SOMEBODY a circumstance or factor that places somebody in a favorable position in relation to others ○ *have the advantage of a stable home* **3.** PROFIT a benefit or gain ○ *Their mistakes worked to our advantage.* **4.** TENNIS POINT AFTER DEUCE in tennis, the point scored after deuce ■ *vt* (**-taged, -tag·ing, -tag·es**) BENEFIT SOMEBODY to put somebody in a superior or favorable position in relation to others [14C. < Old French *avantage* < *avant* "before" < assumed Vulgar Latin *abante* (see ADVANCE)] ◇ **take advantage of somebody** to use somebody in a selfish way in order to achieve a personal benefit, usually by exploiting a weakness ◇ **take advantage of something 1.** to make use of something that is available for personal benefit **2.** use somebody or something in a selfish way in order to achieve a personal benefit ◇ **to advantage** in a way that emphasizes the positive aspects of somebody or something

ad·van·ta·geous /àdvən táyjəss/ *adj* **1.** giving an advantage **2.** of use or benefit —**ad·van·ta·geous·ly** *adv* —**ad·van·ta·geous·ness** *n*

ad·vect /əd vékt/ (**-vect·ed, -vect·ing, -vects**) *vt* to transfer something by advection [Mid-20C. Back-formation < ADVECTION]

ad·vec·tion /əd véksh'n/ *n* the horizontal transfer of a property such as heat, caused by air movement [Early 20C. < Latin *advection-* < *advehere* "carry to" < *vehere* "carry"]

ad·vent /ád vènt/ *n* the arrival of something important or awaited [Mid-18C, < ADVENT]

Ad·vent *n* **1.** the four-week period leading up to Christmas, beginning on the fourth Sunday before Christmas Day **2.** in Christian theology, the coming of Jesus Christ [Pre-12C. < Latin *adventus* "arrival" < *advenire* "come to" < *venire* "come"]

Ad·vent·ist /ád vèntist, ad véntist/ *n* a member of a Christian denomination such as the Seventh-Day Adventists who believes that the Second Coming of Jesus Christ is imminent —**Ad·vent·ism** *n*

ad·ven·ti·tia /àdvən tíshə/ *n* the outer covering of an organ or body part, especially that of a blood vessel [Late 19C. < medieval Latin < neuter plural of *adventitius* (see ADVENTITIOUS)]

ad·ven·ti·tious /àdvən tíshəss/ *adj* **1.** added from an outside and often unexpected source rather than intrinsic **2.** developing in an unusual position, as does a root growing downward from a branch [Early 17C. < medieval Latin *adventitius* "coming from outside," alteration of Latin *adventicius* < *adventus* (see ADVENT)] —**ad·ven·ti·tious·ly** *adv*

ad·ven·tive /əd véntiv/ *adj* describes a plant or animal found in an environment where it is not native and is not fully established ■ *n* an adventive plant or animal —**ad·ven·tive·ly** *adv*

Ad·vent Sun·day *n* the fourth Sunday before Christmas, marking the start of Advent. It is regarded as the beginning of the Christian ecclesiastical year.

ad·ven·ture /əd vénchər/ *n* **1.** EXCITING EXPERIENCE an exciting or extraordinary event or series of events **2.** BOLD UNDERTAKING an undertaking involving uncertainty and risk **3.** INVOLVEMENT IN BOLD UNDERTAKINGS the participation or willingness to participate in things that involve uncertainty and risk ○ *Where's your sense of adventure?* **4.** FINANCIAL SPECULATION a risky or speculative financial undertaking ■ *v* (**-tured, -tur·ing, -tures**) **1.** *vt* RISK SAYING SOMETHING to risk saying something that other people may disagree with or find offensive **2.** *vt* PUT SOMETHING AT RISK to put something at risk or in danger **3.** *vi* RISK DANGER to dare to go somewhere new or engage in something dangerous [13C. Via French *aventure* < Latin *adventurus* "about to arrive," future participle of *advenire* (see ADVENT)]

CULTURAL NOTE ***The Adventures of Huckleberry Finn***, a novel by Mark Twain (1884). Conceived as a sequel to *Tom Sawyer*, it focuses on subsequent events in the life of Tom's friend Huckleberry Finn. With its realistic portrayal of frontier life, it is generally seen as a more adult book than its predecessor.

ad·ven·ture game *n* a puzzle-solving computer game in which players take on the role of characters in the game world but that generally lacks the numerical characteristics of role-play games

ad·ven·tur·er /əd vénchərər/ *n* **1.** SOMEBODY IN SEARCH OF ADVENTURE somebody who enjoys exciting or risky activities **2.** SOMEBODY PURSUING MONEY OR POSITION somebody who is unscrupulous in trying to gain wealth or status **3.** SPECULATOR a financial speculator

ad·ven·ture·some /əd vénchərssəm/ *adj* willing or eager to participate in exciting or risky activities —**ad·ven·ture·some·ly** *adv* —**ad·ven·ture·some·ness** *n*

ad·ven·ture sport *n* a sport involving strenuous physical activity with an element of risk, e.g., bungee jumping

ad·ven·tur·ess /əd vénchərəss/ *n* a woman who uses unscrupulous means in order to gain wealth or social position (*dated*)

ad·ven·ture trav·el *n* a type of vacationing involving strenuous and often risky outdoor activities in remote areas

ad·ven·tur·ism /əd vénchər ìzzəm/ *n* reckless intervention by one government in the affairs of another —**ad·ven·tur·ist** *n*

ad·ven·tur·ous /əd vénchərəss/ *adj* **1.** willing or eager to participate in risky or exciting activities **2.** involving risk —**ad·ven·tur·ous·ly** *adv* —**ad·ven·tur·ous·ness** *n*

ad·verb /ád vùrb/ *n* a word that modifies a verb, an adjective, another adverb, or a sentence, e.g., "happily," "very," or "frankly" [15C. Directly or via French < Latin *adverbium* (after Greek *epirrhēma* "added word")]

USAGE adjective or **adverb**? Some adjectives are used as adverbs without changing their form: *a fast car. You're driving too fast.* Other adjectives can be used as adverbs, instead of the *-ly* adverb form, in a restricted range of contexts: *Hold on tight* [or *tightly*]. *He spelled my name wrong* [or *wrongly*]. In most cases, however, it is incorrect to use an adjective as an adverb: *I want it badly* [not *bad*]. *She was really* [not *real*] *pleased.*

ad·ver·bi·al /ad vúrbee əl/ *adj* relating to or functioning as an adverb ■ *n* an adverb, or a phrase or clause that functions as an adverb —**ad·ver·bi·al·ly** *adv*

ad ver·bum /ad vúrbəm/ *adv* word for word (*formal*) [< Latin, "in accordance with the word"]

ad·ver·sar·i·al /ádvər sérree əl/ *adj* **1.** relating to conflict or adversaries **2.** *UK* same as **adversary**

USAGE adversarial or **adversative**: Not until the 20th century did ***adversarial*** begin to come into use: *He took an adversarial position at the hearing.* Formerly, ***adversative*** was the only possible choice. Now, however, ***adversarial*** is standard usage and ***adversative*** is rarely used except in reference to grammar and such *adversative conjunctions* as *but* and *yet*, and in connection with the stringent methods employed by certain military schools: *"This 'adversative education,' as they call it, is designed to break the cadet of flabby, undisciplined habits acquired early in life and to remake him into a soldier."*

ad·ver·sar·y /ádvər sèrree/ *n* (*plural* **-ies**) an opponent in a conflict, contest, or debate ■ *adj* involving conflicting parties or interests, in relation to a legal proceeding [14C. Via Old French < Latin *adversarius* "enemy" < *adversus* (see ADVERSE)]

ad·ver·sa·tive /əd vúrssətiv/ *adj* **1.** EXPRESSING OPPOSITION expressing opposition or contrast **2.** *US* MIL STRICT employing stringent methods ■ *n* WORD EXPRESSING OPPOSITION a word, phrase, or clause that expresses opposition or contrast, e.g., "but" or "although" [Mid-16C. Directly or via French < late Latin *adversativus* "opposed" < Latin *adversus* (see ADVERSE)] —**ad·ver·sa·tive·ly** *adv*

USAGE See ***adversarial***.

ad·verse /ad vúrss, ád vùrss/ *adj* **1.** UNFAVORABLE creating unfavorable, undesirable, or harmful results ○ *adverse conditions* **2.** ANTAGONISTIC acting with or characterized by opposition or antagonism ○ *adverse publicity* **3.** CONTRARY creating momentum in a direction away from that desired **4.** BOT FACING STEM describes a leaf or flower that faces the main stem [14C. Via Old French < Latin *adversus* "turned against, hostile" < past participle of *advertere* (see ADVERT[1])] —**ad·verse·ly** /ad vúrslee/ *adv* —**ad·verse·ness** *n*

USAGE adverse or **averse**? Both words mean "opposed" in different ways. ***Adverse*** is normally used before an abstract noun such as *circumstances* or *conditions* when they are unfavorable or likely to cause difficulties: *An adverse action was filed against him.* ***Averse*** describes people who are disinclined to do something or have a strong dislike specified by the word that follows *to*: *As an actor he is not averse to publicity.* ***Averse*** is never used before a noun, as ***adverse*** normally is, and is most often accompanied by *not*.

ad·verse pos·ses·sion *n* the possession or occupation of land or property without the owner's permission as a method of acquiring legal ownership

ad·ver·si·ty /ad vúrssətee/ (*plural* **-ties**) *n* **1.** hardship and suffering **2.** an extremely unfavorable experience or event

ad·vert[1] /ad vúrt/ (**-vert·ed, -vert·ing, -verts**) *vi* to call attention or make reference to something [15C. Via Old French *advertir* "notice" < Latin *advertere* "turn toward" < *vertere* "to turn"] —**ad·ver·tence** /əd vúrt'nss/ *n*

ad·vert[2] /ád vùrt/ *n* *UK* MARKETING same as **advertisement** (sense 2) (*informal*) [Mid-19C. Shortening]

ad·ver·tise /ádvər tīz/ (**-tised, -tis·ing, -tis·es**) *v* **1.** *vti* PRAISE COMMERCIAL PRODUCT to publicize the qualities of a product, service, business, or event in order to encourage people to buy or use it **2.** *vti* PUBLICLY ANNOUNCE AVAILABILITY OR NEED to publicize something such as a job opening or item for sale ○ *advertise for a new roommate* **3.** *vt* TELL OTHERS ABOUT SOMETHING to make something known to others ○ *She advertised her arrival with a shout.* [15C. < Old French *advertiss-*, stem of *advertir* (see ADVERT[1])] —**ad·ver·tis·er** *n*

ad·ver·tise·ment /ádvər tīzmənt, ádvər tīz-, əd vúrtəss-/ *n* **1.** a public announcement in a newspaper or on the radio, television, or Internet advertising something such as a product for sale or an event **2.** the act of advertising something

ad·ver·tis·ing /ádvər tīzing/ *n* **1.** PUBLIC PROMOTION OF SOMETHING the public promotion of something such as a product, service, business, or event in order to attract or increase interest in it **2.** INDUSTRY THAT CREATES ADVERTISEMENTS the business of producing advertisements **3.** ADVERTISEMENTS advertisements considered collectively

~~advertisment~~ incorrect spelling of **advertisement**

ad·ver·tor·i·al /ádvər táwree əl/ *n* an advertisement in a publication that looks like one of its normal articles [Mid-20C. Blend of ADVERTISEMENT + EDITORIAL]

ad·vice /əd víss/ *n* **1.** somebody's opinion about what another person should do ○ *May I give you some advice?* **2.** formal or official information about something, usually received from a distance (*often used in the plural*) [13C. < French *avis* "opinion" < Latin *ad (meum) visum* "in (my) view or opinion" (*visum*, past participle of *videre* "to see")]

USAGE advice or **advise**? ***Advice*** is a noun only, spelled with a *-c-*: *He followed the doctor's advice;* ***advise*** is a verb only, spelled with an *-s-*: *She advised me to seek a doctor's advice.*

ad·vice col·umn *n* a section of a newspaper or magazine in which advice and answers to questions or problems sent in by readers are printed

~~advid~~ incorrect spelling of **avid**

ad·vis·a·ble /əd vízəb'l/ *adj* being a sensible or desirable thing to do —**ad·vis·a·bil·i·ty** /əd vīzə bíllətee/ *n* —**ad·vis·a·ble·ness** *n* —**ad·vis·a·bly** *adv*

ad·vise /əd vīz/ (**-vised, -vis·ing, -vis·es**) *v* **1.** *vti* OFFER ADVICE to offer a personal opinion to somebody ○ *I won't choose until somebody can advise me.* **2.** *vt* RECOMMEND SOMETHING to suggest or recommend a course of action to somebody ○ *We were advised against staying longer.* **3.** ⚠ *vt* INFORM SOMEBODY to tell somebody about something **4.** *vi* *US* SEEK ADVICE to seek advice or information [14C. < French *aviser* < *avis* "opinion" (see ADVICE)]

USAGE The use of the verb ***advise*** to mean "tell somebody about something" is often regarded as jargon and is best avoided in formal usage: *Please advise us of* [better: *let us know*] *your new address. I will advise them* [better: *inform them*] *of the new time of the meeting.*

SYNONYMS See ***recommend***.

ad·vis·ed·ly /əd vīzədlee/ *adv* after careful consideration

ad·vi·see /əd vī zée/ *n* **1.** somebody who receives advice **2.** a student who receives advice on academic matters from an adviser

ad·vise·ment /əd vīzmənt/ *n* **1.** careful consideration or deliberation ○ *will take it under advisement* **2.** the act of giving advice [14C. < French *avisement* < *aviser* (see ADVISE)]

ad·vis·er /əd vīzər/, **ad·vi·sor** *n* **1.** GIVER OF ADVICE somebody who gives advice **2.** SOMEBODY ADVISING STUDENTS somebody who advises students on academic matters such as course choices **3.** *UK* SUBJECT SPECIALIST a teacher who is a specialist in a subject and advises other teachers on teaching it

ad·vi·so·ry /əd vīzəree/ *adj* **1.** GIVING ADVICE providing or of the nature of advice **2.** HAVING FUNCTION OF GIVING ADVICE having the function of giving advice, usually with the implication that the advice given need not be followed ○ *an advisory committee* ■ *n* (*plural* **-ries**) *US* **1.** INFORMATIONAL BULLETIN a report that gives facts or data and sometimes advice about a subject, e.g., about economic conditions **2.** WARNING OF SOMETHING TO COME an advance notice of something, e.g., a warning of impending severe weather ○ *a small craft advisory*

ad·vi·so·ry teach·er *n* *UK* EDUC same as **adviser** (sense 3)

ad·vo·caat /ádvō kaát/ *n* an alcoholic beverage similar to eggnog, containing eggs, sugar, and brandy [Mid-20C. < Dutch, "advocate," because supposed to help clear the throat]

ad·vo·ca·cy /ádvəkəssee/ (*plural* **-cies**) *n* active verbal support for a cause or position [14C. Via Old French *advocacie* < medieval Latin *advocatia* < Latin *advocatus* (see ADVOCATE)]

ad·vo·ca·cy group *n* a group of people working together to promote a cause

ad·vo·cate *vt* /ádvə kàyt/ (**-cat·ed, -cat·ing, -cates**) RECOMMEND OR SUPPORT SOMETHING to support or speak in favor of something ■ *n* /ádvəkət, -kàyt/ **1.** SOMEBODY GIVING SUPPORT somebody who supports or speaks in favor of something ○ *a tireless advocate of social reform* **2.** HELPER somebody who acts or intercedes on behalf of another **3.** LAW LEGAL REPRESENTATIVE somebody such as a lawyer, who pleads another's case in a legal forum [14C. Via Old French *avocat* "advocate" < Latin *advocatus* < *advocare* "call to" < *vocare* "to call"] —**ad·vo·ca·tor** *n* —**ad·voc·a·to·ry** /ad vókə tàwree, ádvə kàytəree/ *adj*

SYNONYMS See ***recommend***.

ad·wo·man /ád wòommən/ (*plural* **-wo·men** /-wìmmin/) *n* a woman who works in advertising (*informal*)

A·dy·ghe /aádi gay, aàdi gáy/, **A·dy·gei** *n* an Abkhaz-Adyghean language spoken in the northwestern region of the Republic of Georgia. Native speakers: 100,000. —**A·dy·ghe** *adj*

a·dy·na·mic /ày dī námmik/ *adj* characterized by loss of normal function ○ *adynamic ileus*

ad·y·tum /áddətəm/ (*plural* **-ta** /-tə/) *n* the most sacred part in an ancient temple, restricted to priests [Early 17C. < Latin < Greek *adutos* "not to be entered" < *duein* "enter"]

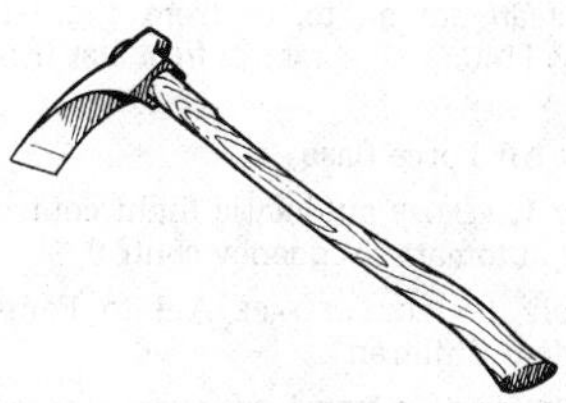

adz

adz /adz/, **adze** *n* a tool similar to an ax, with an arched blade set at right angles to the handle. Use: trimming and shaping wood. [Old English *adesa*, *eadesa*, origin ?]

ad·zu·ki bean /ad zóokee-/, **a·du·ki bean** /a dóokee-/, **a·zu·ki bean** /a zóokee-/ *n* **1.** a small slightly sweet red-brown bean. Use: in vegetarian dishes in Europe and North America, in sweet dishes in East Asian cooking. **2.** a plant that produces adzuki beans. Latin name: *Vigna angularis*. [< Japanese *azuki* "red bean"]

AEC *abbr US* Atomic Energy Commission

ae·ci·a FUNGI plural of **aecium**

ae·cid·i·a FUNGI plural of **aecidium**

ae·cid·i·o·spore /ee síddee ə spàwr/ *n* FUNGI same as **aeciospore** [Late 19C. < AECIDIUM]

ae·cid·i·um /ee síddee əm/ (*plural* **-i·a** /-ee ə/) *n* FUNGI same as **aecium** [Mid-19C. < modern Latin < Greek *aikia* (see AECIUM)]

ae·ci·o·spore /éessee ə spàwr, -shee-/ *n* a spore produced in the reproductive organ **(aecium)** of a rust fungus with two genetically distinct nuclei [Early 20C. < AECIUM]

ae·ci·um /éeshee əm, éessee əm/ (*plural* **-ci·a** /-shee ə, -see ə/) *n* a cup-shaped reproductive organ **(fruiting body)** produced by some rust fungi in the tissue of their host plant, in which spores **(aeciospores)** are formed [Early 20C. Via modern Latin < Greek *aikia* "injury"; from the harm caused by the fungi]

a·e·des /ay ée deez/ (*plural same*) *n* a mosquito that can transmit serious diseases such as yellow fever and dengue. Native to: tropics and subtropics. Latin name: *Aedes aegypti*. [Early 20C. < modern Latin < Greek *aēdēs* "unpleasant"; because it carries diseases]

ae·dile /ée dīl/ *n* in ancient Rome, a magistrate responsible for public works and buildings, games, markets, and the grain and water supplies [Mid-16C. < Latin *aedilis* < *aedes* "building"]

Ae·ge·an Sea /i jée ən-/ arm of the Mediterranean Sea, situated between Greece and Turkey, containing numerous islands divided into three main groups, the Cyclades, Dodecanese, and Sporades. Area: 80,000 sq. mi./207,200 sq. km.

ae·gis /éejiss/, **e·gis** *n* in Greek mythology, the shield of Zeus or Athena [Early 17C. Via Latin < Greek *aigis* "goatskin shield of Zeus"] ◇ **under the aegis of somebody** *or* **something** with the support or protection of somebody or something (*formal*)

Ael·fric /álfrik/ (955?–1020?) Anglo-Saxon monk and writer. As abbot of Eynsham from 1005 he wrote several works, including *Lives of the Saints* (993–998) and a Latin grammar.

-aemia *suffix* another spelling of **-emia**

Ae·ne·as /i née əss/ *n* in Greek and Roman mythology, a Trojan hero who escaped after the fall of Troy and spent seven years traveling before settling near the site of Rome in Italy. His travels are the subject of Virgil's *Aeneid*.

Ae·o·li·a ♦ **Aeolis**

ae·o·li·an *adj* METEOROL another spelling of **eolian**

Ae·o·li·an /ee óolee ən, -ólyən/, **E·o·li·an** *n* **1.** MEMBER OF HELLENIC PEOPLE a member of an ancient Hellenic people who lived in Aeolis and Lesbos about 1100 B.C. **2.** LANG same as **Aeolic** ■ *adj* **1.** OF AEOLIS relating to Aeolis, or its people, language, or culture **2.** OF AEOLUS relating to Aeolus [Late 16C. < Latin *Aeolius*]

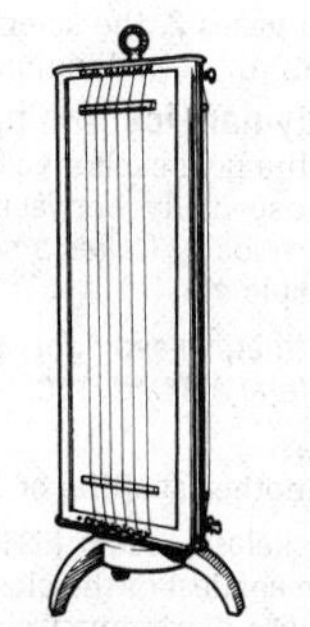

aeolian harp: 18th-century French three-sided aeolian harp

ae·o·li·an harp, **Ae·o·li·an harp** *n* a box-shaped musical instrument with strings of equal length that are tuned in unison and sounded when the wind blows over them

Ae·o·li·an Is·lands ♦ **Lipari Islands**

Ae·o·li·an mode *n* a medieval scale of notes that consists of the eight notes of the diatonic scale rising from A to A, corresponding to the modern minor scale

Ae·ol·ic /ee óolik/, **E·ol·ic** *n* a dialect of Ancient Greek spoken mainly in Aeolis, Thessaly, and Boeotia

Ae·o·lis /ée ə liss/, **Ae·o·li·a** /ee óolee ə/ ancient region on the northwestern coast of Asia Minor, settled by the Aeolian Greeks about 1100 B.C.

Ae·o·lus /ée ələss/ *n* in Greek mythology, the god of wind

ae·on *n* TIME another spelling of **eon**

ae·py·or·nis /éepee áwrniss/ (*plural* **-nis·es** *or same*) *n* a giant extinct flightless bird that lived in Madagascar. It reached a height of 9 ft./2.7 m and weighed up to 1,000 lb./450 kg. Genus: *Aepyornis*. [Mid-19C. < modern Latin < Greek *aipus* "high" + *ornis* (see ORNITHO-)]

aer- *prefix* same as **aero-** (*used before vowels*)

aer·ate /ér ràyt/ (**-at·ed**, **-at·ing**, **-ates**) *vt* **1.** to allow circulating air to reach or penetrate something **2.** to charge a liquid with a gas, especially when using carbon dioxide to make carbonated drinks **3.** PHYSIOL same as **oxygenate** [Late 18C. < Latin *aer* "air" < Greek *aēr*] —**aer·a·tion** /er ráysh'n/ *n* —**aer·a·tor** *n*

aer·en·chy·ma /er réngkəmə/ *n* the spongy tissue in some water plants that keeps them afloat and helps in the exchange of gases [Late 19C. < Greek *aēr* "air" + *egkhuma* "infusion"]

aeri- *prefix* same as **aero-**

aer·i·al /éree əl/ *adj* **1.** INVOLVING AIRCRAFT done by or involving aircraft ○ *an aerial bombardment* **2.** IN AIR living, happening, or moving in the air ○ *a plant with aerial roots* **3.** RELATING TO AIR consisting of, typical of, or relating to the air **4.** LIGHT IN WEIGHT like the air in being light and insubstantial (*literary*) ■ *n* **1.** *UK* BROADCAST same as **antenna** (sense 2) **2.** FIELD HOCKEY HIGH BALL IN FIELD HOCKEY in field hockey, a ball passed by being raised off the ground ■ **aer·i·als** *npl* SKIING MID-AIR SKI-JUMP ACROBATICS acrobatic movements that a ski-jumper performs while in the air (*informal*) [Early 17C. < Latin *aerius* < Greek *aerios* < *aēr* "air"]

aer·i·al·ist /éree əlist/ *n* an acrobat who performs on a tightrope or trapeze

aer·i·al lad·der *n* a mechanically extending ladder used to reach high places, especially one on a fire engine

aer·i·al per·spec·tive *n* the use in painting of gradations in color and definition to suggest distance

aer·ie /éree, éer-/, **eyr·ie**, **aer·y** (*plural* **-ies**), **eyr·y** *n* **1.** the nest of an eagle or other bird of prey, usually built in a high inaccessible place **2.** a building, especially a stronghold, in a high inaccessible place [15C. Via medieval Latin *aeria* < Old French *airie* < Latin *area* "level ground"]

aer·i·form /érrə fàwrm/ *adj* **1.** existing as air or gas **2.** having no substance or material form

ae·ro[1] /érrō/ *adj* used in aircraft or aeronautics

aero[2] *abbr* aviation industry (*used in Internet addresses*) See table at **domain name**

aero-, **aeri-** *prefix* **1.** air, atmosphere, gas ○ *aerodynamic* **2.** aviation ○ *aerospace* [< Greek *aēr* "air"]

aer·o·bal·lis·tics /èrrō bə lístiks/ *n* the branch of ballistics that deals with projectiles fired or dropped from aircraft (*takes a singular verb*) —**aer·o·bal·lis·tic** *adj*

aer·o·bat·ics /èrrō báttiks/ *n* the flying of an aircraft in daring maneuvers, often as an entertainment (*takes a singular or plural verb*) [Early 20C. < AERO-, after ACROBATICS] —**aer·o·bat·ic** *adj*

aer·obe /ér ōb/ *n* a microorganism that requires oxygen for metabolism [Late 19C. < AERO- + Greek *bios* "life"]

aer·o·bic[1] /e róbik, ə-/ *adj* **1.** living or taking place only in the presence of oxygen **2.** having or providing oxygen [Late 19C. < French *aérobie*, coined by Louis Pasteur < Greek *aēr* "air" + *bios* "life"] —**aer·o·bic·al·ly** *adv*

aer·o·bic[2] /e róbik, ə-/ *adj* **1.** increasing respiration and heart rates ○ *aerobic exercise* **2.** used in or relating to aerobics [Mid-20C. < AEROBICS]

aer·o·bic res·pi·ra·tion *n* the breakdown of foodstuffs to create energy in the presence of oxygen

aer·o·bics /e róbiks, ə-/ *n* (*takes a singular or plural verb*) **1.** an active exercise program done to music, often in a class **2.** exercises such as walking, jogging, cycling, and swimming that increase respiration and heart rates [Mid-20C. < AEROBIC[1], after GYMNASTICS]

aer·o·bi·ol·o·gy /èrrō bī óllәjee/ *n* the study of airborne biological materials and organisms such as allergens and disease-causing microorganisms —**aer·o·bi·o·log·i·cal** /èrrō bī ə lójjik'l/ *adj* —**aer·o·bi·o·log·i·cal·ly** *adv*

aer·o·bi·o·sis /èrrō bī óssiss/ *n* life in the presence of oxygen [Early 20C. < modern Latin < Greek *aēr* "air" + *biōsis* (see -BIOSIS)]

aer·o·drome /érrə drōm/ *n Can, UK* a small airfield with limited facilities. US term **airdrome** [Early 20C. < AERO- + -DROME]

aer·o·dy·nam·ic /èrrō dī námmik/ *adj* **1.** designed to reduce air resistance, especially to increase fuel efficiency or maximum speed **2.** involving or typical of aerodynamics —**aer·o·dy·nam·i·cal·ly** *adv*

aer·o·dy·nam·ics /èrrō dī námmiks/ *n* the study of moving gases, especially the study of the forces experienced by objects moving through air (*takes a singular verb*) ■ *npl* the aerodynamic properties of an object (*takes a plural verb*) —**aer·o·dy·nam·i·cist** /-əssist/ *n*

aer·o·dyne /érrō dīn/ *n* an aircraft such as an airplane or helicopter that is heavier than air and whose lift in flight results from forces caused by its motion through the air [Early 20C. Back-formation < AERODYNAMIC]

aer·o·em·bo·lism /èrrō émbə lìzzəm/ *n* MED same as **air embolism**

aer·o·foil /érrə fòyl/ *n UK* same as **airfoil**

aer·o·gel /érrō jèl/ *n* a highly porous, extremely lightweight solid formed by replacing the particles in a gel with a gas

aer·o·gram /érrō gràm/, **aer·o·gramme** *n* a single sheet of lightweight paper for airmail use that, once written on, can be folded and sealed to form its own envelope [Late 19C. After TELEGRAM]

aer·og·ra·phy /e róggrəfee/ *n* the study of atmospheric conditions —**aer·og·ra·pher** *n* —**aer·og·ra·phic** /èrrə gráffik/ *adj*

aer·o·lite /érrō līt/ *n* a meteorite with a high silicate content —**aer·o·lit·ic** /èrrō líttik/ *adj*

aer·o·li·za·tion /èrrəli záysh'n/ *n* the airborne transmission of a substance in the form of a vapor or fine particles —**aer·o·lize** /érrə līz/ *vt*

aer·ol·o·gy /e rólləjee/ *n* the study of the lower layers of the Earth's atmosphere —**aer·o·log·ic** /èrrə lójjik/ *adj* —**aer·o·log·i·cal** *adj* —**aer·ol·o·gist** *n*

aer·o·mag·net·ic /èrrō mag néttik/ *adj* relating to the study or measurement of the Earth's magnetic field from aircraft —**aer·o·mag·net·i·cal·ly** *adv* —**aer·o·mag·net·ics** *n*

aer·o·me·chan·ics /èrrō mə kánniks/ *n* the study of gases in motion and in equilibrium, including the study of the mechanical effects of gases upon objects (*takes a singular verb*) —**aer·o·me·chan·i·cal** *adj* —**aer·o·me·chan·i·cal·ly** *adv*

aer·o·med·i·cine /érrō médəssin/ *n* MED, AVIAT same as **aviation medicine** —**aer·o·med·i·cal** /-méddik'l/ *adj*

aer·o·me·te·or·o·graph /èrrō meetee áwrə gràf/ *n* an instrument on board an aircraft that records temperature, atmospheric pressure, and humidity

aer·om·e·ter /e rómmətər/ *n* an instrument for measuring the mass or density of air or another gas [Late 18C. < French *aéromètre*]

aer·o·naut /érrə nàwt/ *n* somebody who flies in a blimp or balloon [Late 18C. < French *aéronaute* < *aéro-* (< Greek *aēr* "air") + Greek *nautēs* "sailor"]

aer·o·nau·ti·cal /èrrə náwtik'l/, **aer·o·nau·tic** /èrrə náwtik/ *adj* relating to aircraft or their flight [Early 19C. < French *aéronautique* < *aéronaute* (see AERONAUT)] —**aer·o·nau·ti·cal·ly** *adv*

aer·o·nau·tics /èrrə náwtiks/ *n* the science, art, theory, and practice of designing, building, and operating aircraft (*takes a singular verb*)

aer·o·neu·ro·sis /èrrō nŏŏ rṓssiss/ *n* anxiety and fatigue in airline pilots brought on by prolonged periods of flying

aer·on·o·my /er ónnəmee/ *n* the study of the upper atmosphere of the Earth above 31 mi./50 km, including its reaction with cosmic and ionizing radiation —**aer·on·o·mer** *n* —**ae·ro·nom·ic** /èrrə nómmik/ *adj* —**ae·ro·nom·i·cal** *adj* —**aer·on·o·mist** *n*

aer·o·pause /érrə pàwz/ *n* the part of the Earth's upper atmosphere above which air is too thin for aircraft to fly

aer·o·pha·gy /e róffəjee/, **aer·o·pha·gia** /èrrə fáyjə/ *n* the spasmodic swallowing of air, a common cause of flatulence and belching [Late 19C. After French *aérophagie*]

aer·o·pho·bi·a /èrrə fṓbee ə/ *n* an unusual fear of drafts of air —**aer·o·pho·bic** *adj*

aer·o·phyte /érrə fìt/ *n* BOT same as **epiphyte**

aer·o·plane /érrə plàyn/ *n UK* same as **airplane**

aer·o·pon·ics /èrrə pónniks/ *n* the growing of plants without soil, their nutrients being supplied in a water spray (*takes a singular verb*) [Late 20C. After HYDROPONICS]

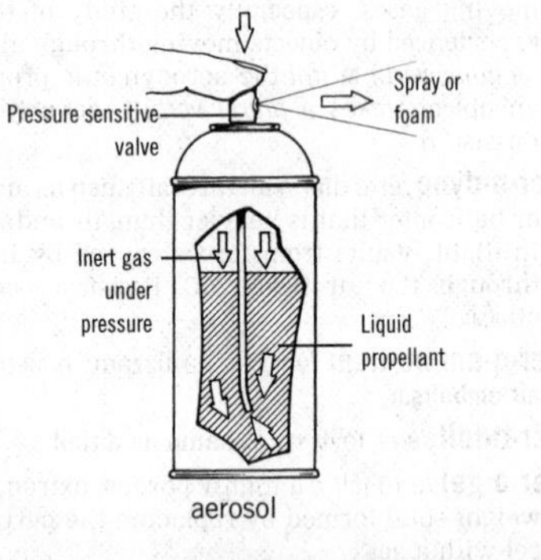

aerosol

aer·o·sol /érrə sòl/ *n* **1.** CONTAINER WITH GAS UNDER PRESSURE a small container holding a substance that can be dispensed under pressure by a propellant as a spray **2.** SUBSTANCE SPRAYED a substance held in a small container from which it can be dispensed under pressure by a propellant as a spray **3.** SUSPENSION OF PARTICLES IN GAS a suspension of solid or liquid particles in a gaseous medium

aer·o·sol bomb *n US* same as **aerosol** (sense 1)

aer·o·sol·ize /érrəssə lìz/ (**-ized, -iz·ing, -iz·es**) *vt* to convert a substance into a fine spray or colloidal suspension

aer·o·space /érrō spàyss/ *n* the Earth's atmosphere and outer space ■ *adj* relating to the design, manufacture, and flight of vehicles or missiles that fly in and beyond the Earth's atmosphere

aer·o·stat /érrō stàt/ *n* a hot-air or gas-filled aircraft, e.g., a blimp or balloon [Late 18C. < French *aérostat* < *aéro-* (< Greek *aēr* "air") + Greek *statos* "standing"] —**aer·o·stat·ic** /èrrō státtik/ *adj*

aer·o·stat·ics /èrrō státtiks/ *n* (*takes a singular verb*) **1.** the study of gases in equilibrium and objects in equilibrium in gases **2.** the science of aircraft that are lighter than air, e.g., dirigibles and balloons

aer·o·ther·mo·dy·nam·ics /èrrō thùrmō dì námmiks/ *n* the study of the heat exchange between gases and solid objects, especially between air and aircraft flying at high velocity (*takes a singular verb*) —**aer·o·ther·mo·dy·nam·ic** *adj*

aer·y[1] /érree/ (**-i·er, -i·est**) *adj* insubstantial and unworldly (*literary*) [Late 16C. < Latin *aerius* (see AERIAL)]

aer·y[2] *n* BIRDS another spelling of **aerie**

Aes·chy·lus /éskələss, éess-/ (525?–456 B.C.) Greek dramatist. The earliest of the classical Greek tragic dramatists whose work survives, he is believed to have written 90 plays. Seven survive, including his great trilogy *The Oresteia*, first performed in 458 B.C.

Aes·cu·la·pi·an /èskyə láypee ən/ *adj* relating to medicine and the healing arts [Early 17C. < Latin *Aesculapius*, the Roman god of medicine]

aes·cu·la·pi·an snake *n* a long slender brown nonvenomous snake. Native to: forests of Europe and western Asia. Latin name: *Elaphe longissima*. [< the common depiction of Aesculapius (see AESCULAPIAN) in antiquity with such a snake]

Ae·sop /éessəp, ée sòp/ (620?–560? B.C.) Greek writer, reputedly a former slave. His fables were popularized by the Roman poet Phaedrus (A.D. 1st century). See Cultural note at **fable**

aes·the·sia /es théezhə/, **es·the·sia** /es théezee ə/ *n* the ability to feel or experience through the senses [Early 18C. Via modern Latin < Greek *aisthēsis* "perceiving" < *aisthesthai* "perceive"]

aes·thete /és thèet/, **es·thete** *n* somebody who has or affects a highly developed appreciation of beauty, especially in the arts [Late 19C. Back-formation < AESTHETIC, after ATHLETE]

aes·thet·ic /es théttik/, **es·thet·ic** *adj* **1.** BEAUTIFUL pleasing in appearance **2.** ARTS APPRECIATING BEAUTY sensitive to or appreciative of art or beauty **3.** PHILOSOPHY RELATING TO AESTHETICS relating to the philosophical principles of aesthetics ■ *n* ARTS SET OF PRINCIPLES a set of principles about art ○ *the modernist aesthetic* [Early 19C. < Greek *aisthētikos* "perceptual" < *aisthesthai* "perceive"] —**aes·thet·i·cal·ly** *adv*

aes·the·ti·cian /èsthə tísh'n/, **es·the·ti·cian** *n* **1.** a student or devotee of the principles of art or beauty **2.** somebody whose job is to give people beauty treatments

aes·thet·i·cism /es thétti sìzzəm/, **es·thet·i·cism** *n* **1.** ARTS BELIEF IN IMPORTANCE OF AESTHETICS the belief that the principles of aesthetics are of the highest importance in the arts **2.** PHILOSOPHY DERIVATION OF MORAL PRINCIPLES FROM BEAUTY the philosophical doctrine that all moral principles are derived from beauty **3.** LOVE OF BEAUTY appreciation of and devotion to beauty

aes·thet·i·cize /es thétti sìz/ (**-cized, -ciz·ing, -ciz·es**), **es·thet·i·cize** *vt* to show something in its best or most artistic light

aes·thet·ics /es théttiks/, **es·thet·ics** *n* **1.** OUTWARD APPEARANCE the way something looks, especially when considered in terms of how pleasing it is (*takes a singular or plural verb*) **2.** IDEA OF BEAUTY an idea of what is beautiful or artistic (*takes a singular or plural verb*) **3.** ARTS STUDY OF ART the study of the rules and principles of art (*takes a singular verb*) **4.** PHILOSOPHY STUDY OF BEAUTY the branch of philosophy dealing with the study of aesthetic values, e.g., the beautiful and the sublime (*takes a singular verb*) [Early 19C. Via modern Latin *aesthetica* < Greek *aisthētikos* (see AESTHETIC), perhaps after ATHLETICS]

aes·thet·ic sur·ge·ry *n* SURG same as **cosmetic surgery**

aes·ti·val, etc. BIOL another spelling of **estival, etc.**

Aeth·el·red another spelling of **Ethelred**

ae·ti·ol·o·gy *n* another spelling of **etiology**

af *abbr* Afghanistan (*used in Internet addresses*) See table at **domain name**

AF *abbr* **1.** AIR FORCE air force **2.** Anglo-French **3.** PHOTOGRAPHY autofocus

Af. *abbr* **1.** Africa **2.** African

a.f. *abbr* ELECTRONICS audio frequency

af- *prefix* same as **ad-** (*used before f*)

AFAIK *abbr* as far as I know (*used in e-mails or text messages*)

a·far /ə fáar/ *adv* at, to, or from a great distance (*literary*) [14C. < A-[1] + FAR] ◇ **from afar** from a place far away

AFB *abbr* Air Force Base

AFC *abbr* **1.** AEROSP automatic flight control **2.** ELECTRONICS automatic frequency control

AFDC *abbr US* SOC WELFARE Aid to Families with Dependent Children

a·feard /ə féerd/, **a·feared** *adj regional* same as **afraid** (*archaic*) [Old English *āfǣred*, past participle of *āfǣren* "frighten" < *fǣren* "to fear"]

a·feb·rile /ay féb rìl, -féeb-/ *adj* having no fever, or marked by absence of fever

af·fa·ble /áffəb'l/ *adj* good-natured, friendly, and easy to talk to [15C. Via French < Latin *affabilis* "easy to speak to" < *(af)fari* "speak (to)"] —**af·fa·bil·i·ty** /àffə bíllətee/ *n* —**af·fa·bly** *adv*

af·fair /ə fér/ *n* **1.** OCCURRENCE an event or occurrence that has been referred to or is known about ○ *that odd affair at work last year* **2.** MATTER OF CONCERN a concern of a particular person or group ○ *What he does with the information is his own affair.* **3.** SOCIAL EVENT a social event or gathering **4.** SOMETHING OF PARTICULAR KIND an object or item of a particular kind ○ *The house is a ramshackle affair.* **5.** SEXUAL RELATIONSHIP a sexual relationship between two people not married to each other **6.** SCANDALOUS INCIDENT an incident that attracts public attention or notoriety ■ **af·fairs** *npl* **1.** PUBLIC MATTERS OF BUSINESS public, government, or professional business or activities ○ *affairs of state* ○ *consumer affairs* **2.** PERSONAL DUTIES personal responsibilities or business ○ *He must settle his affairs in Paris before returning home.* ○ *the family's financial affairs* [12C. < Anglo-Norman *afere*, Old French *afaire* < *à faire* "to do"]

af·faire de coeur /ə fér də kúr/ (*plural* **af·faires de coeur** /*pronunc. same*/), **af·faire** *n* a love affair or romantic attachment (*literary*) [Early 19C. < French, "affair of the heart"]

af·fect[1] /ə fékt/ (**-fect·ed, -fect·ing, -fects**) *vt* **1.** INFLUENCE SOMEBODY OR SOMETHING to act upon or have an effect on somebody or something **2.** STIR SOMEBODY'S EMOTIONS to move somebody emotionally **3.** CAUSE SOMEBODY TO HAVE DISEASE to infect or harm somebody or something with disease [14C. < Latin *affect-*, past participle of *afficere* "act on" < *facere* "do"]

USAGE affect or **effect**? In general use, ***affect*** is only used as a verb, whereas ***effect*** is commonly used as a noun and only in formal contexts as a verb. What causes confusion is that they have very similar pronunciations and closely related meanings. If one thing ***affects*** [acts upon] another, it has an ***effect*** on it [causes it to change]. Notice also that you can ***affect*** [cause a change in] people as well as things, but you can only ***effect*** [bring about] things such as changes: *The election has affected our entire society, for it has effected major changes in the government. The bad weather has a bad effect* [not *affect*] *on him.*

---

af·fect[2] /ə fékt/ (**-fect·ed, -fect·ing, -fects**) *vt* **1.** PRETEND TO BE SOMETHING to give the appearance or pretense of something **2.** ADOPT SOMETHING to adopt a use, style, or manner of doing something **3.** ACT LIKE SOMEBODY to imitate somebody else's style or character **4.** COME TO BE OR HAVE SOMETHING to assume a particular form or state ○ *affect a liquid state* [15C. Directly or via French *affecter* < Latin *affectare* "strive for" < *affect-* (see AFFECT[1])] —**af·fect·er** *n*

af·fect[3] /á fèkt/ *n* an emotion or mood associated with an idea or action, or the external expression of such a feeling [Late 19C. < German *Affekt*]

af·fec·ta·tion /à fek táysh'n/ *n* **1.** feigned or unnatural behavior that is often meant to impress others **2.** an appearance or manner assumed as a show or pretense, often to impress others [Mid-16C. Directly or via French < Latin *affectation-* "influence" < *affectare* < *affect-* (see AFFECT[1])]

af·fect·ed /ə féktəd/ *adj* **1.** INFLUENCED BY SOMETHING acted upon or influenced by somebody or something **2.** MOVED EMOTIONALLY emotionally moved by something **3.** INFECTED OR DAMAGED infected or harmed by disease **4.** TRYING TO IMPRESS behaving in an unnatural way intended to impress others **5.** INTENDED TO IMPRESS done or assumed with the intention of impressing others —**af·fect·ed·ly** *adv* —**af·fect·ed·ness** *n*

af·fect·ing /ə fékting/ *adj* able to stir the emotions —**af·fect·ing·ly** *adv*

af·fec·tion /ə fékshən/ *n* fond or tender feeling toward somebody or something ■ **af·fect·ions** *npl* feelings of fondness or tenderness, sometimes as opposed to reason [12C. Via Old French, "emotion" < Latin *affection-* "inclination" < *afficere* (see AFFECT[1])] —**af·fec·tion·al** *adj* —**af·fec·tion·al·ly** *adv*

SYNONYMS See ***love***.

af·fec·tion·ate /ə fékshənət/ *adj* feeling or showing affection [15C. Directly or via French < Latin *affectionatus* "devoted" < *affection-* (see AFFECTION)] —**af·fec·tion·ate·ly** *adv* —**af·fec·tion·ate·ness** *n*

af·fec·tive /ə féktiv/ *adj* **1.** relating to an external expression of emotion associated with an idea or action **2.** same as **affecting** [15C. Via French < late Latin *affectivus* < Latin *affect-* (see AFFECT[1])] —**af·fec·tive·ly** *adv* —**af·fec·tiv·i·ty** /à fek tívvətee/ *n*

af·fec·tive dis·or·der *n* a psychiatric disorder with a central emotional component, e.g., depression

af·fect·less /ə féktləss/ *adj* feeling or showing no emotion —**af·fect·less·ness** *n*

affenpinscher

af·fen·pin·scher /áffən pìnchər/ *n* a small dog with wiry hair and a tufted muzzle, belonging to a breed developed in Europe [Early 20C. < German, "ape terrier"]

af·fer·ent /áffərənt/ *adj* describes nerves that carry impulses from the body toward the brain or spinal cord, or blood vessels that carry blood to an organ [Mid-19C. < Latin *afferent-*, present participle of *afferre* "bring toward"] —**af·fer·ent·ly** *adv*

af·fet·tu·o·so /ə fèchoo ṓssō/ *adv, adj* played or sung musically with feeling (*used as a musical direction*) [Early 18C. < Italian < Latin *affect-* (see AFFECT[1])]

af·fi·ance /ə fī́ ənss/ (**-anced, -anc·ing, -anc·es**) *vt* to promise somebody or yourself in marriage to somebody else (*literary; often passive*) [14C. < Old French *afiancer* < *afiance* "trust" < medieval Latin *affidare* "to trust"]

af·fi·da·vit /àffi dáyvit/ *n* a written declaration made on oath before somebody authorized to administer oaths, usually setting out the statement of a witness for court proceedings [Late 16C. < medieval Latin, "he or she has sworn," form of *affidare* "trust, affirm" < *fidus* "faithful"]

af·fil·i·ate *v* /ə fíllee àyt/ (**-at·ed, -at·ing, -ates**) **1.** *vti* **COMBINE ORGANIZATIONS** to come, or bring a person or group, into a close relationship with another, usually larger group **2.** *vt* **DETERMINE SOMETHING'S ORIGIN** to determine the origin of something ■ *n* /ə fíllee ət, -àyt/ **ASSOCIATE** a group that is closely connected with a larger group, or a person who joins with others to form a group [Mid-18C. < Latin *affiliat-*, past participle of *affiliare* "adopt as a son" < *filius* "son"] —**af·fil·i·at·ed** *adj* —**af·fil·i·a·tion** /ə fìllee áysh'n/ *n*

af·fil·i·ate mar·ket·ing *n* the use of a central website to market the products and services of other sites

af·fine /ə fī́n, a-/ *n* **1.** MATH a geometric transformation that maps points and parallel lines to points and parallel lines **2.** ANTHROP a relative by marriage [Early 20C. < Latin *affinis* (see AFFINITY)] —**af·fi·nal** *adj*

af·fin·i·ty /ə fínnətee/ (*plural* **-ties**) *n* **1. FEELING OF IDENTIFICATION** a natural liking for or identification with somebody or something **2. CONNECTION** a similarity or connection between people or things **3. SOMEBODY ATTRACTIVE** somebody to whom somebody else is attracted **4.** CULTL ANTHROP **KINSHIP BY MARRIAGE** a relationship by marriage, not by blood **5.** BIOL, LANGUAGE **SIMILARITY IN STRUCTURE** a similarity in structure, e.g., in species or languages, that may suggest a common origin **6.** CHEM **LIKELIHOOD OF CHEMICAL REACTION** a measure of the likelihood of a chemical reaction taking place between two substances **7.** IMMUNOL **ANTIGEN-ANTIBODY ATTRACTION** the attraction between an antigen and an antibody [14C. < Old French *afinité* "close relationship" < Latin *affinis* "bordering on something" < *finis* "border"]

af·firm /ə fúrm/ (**-firmed, -firm·ing, -firms**) *v* **1.** *vt* **DECLARE SOMETHING TO BE TRUE** to declare positively that something is true ○ *affirmed that the rumor is true* **2.** *vt* **DECLARE SUPPORT FOR SOMETHING** to declare support or admiration for somebody or something ○ *affirmed their commitment to peace* **3.** *vt* LAW **CONFIRM SOMETHING** to confirm something as binding or valid **4.** *vi* LAW **MAKE FORMAL STATEMENT** to make a statement formally but not under oath [13C. Via Old French < Latin *affirmare* "strengthen" < *firmus* "firm"] —**af·firm·a·ble** *adj* —**af·firm·a·bly** *adv* —**af·fir·mant** *n* —**af·firm·er** *n*

af·fir·ma·tion /àffər máysh'n/ *n* **1. ACT OF AFFIRMING** an assertion of support or agreement **2. SOMETHING AFFIRMED** a positive statement or declaration of the truth or existence of something ○ *an affirmation of his love* **3.** LAW **FORMAL LEGAL DECLARATION** a formal declaration acceptable in a court, usually made by somebody who has a conscientious objection to taking an oath **4.** PSYCHOL **POSITIVE STATEMENT OF ACHIEVEMENT** a positive thought or statement affirming that a desired goal has been reached or is within reach [15C. Directly or via French < Latin *affirmation-* < *affirmare* (see AFFIRM)]

af·fir·ma·tive /ə fúrmətiv/ *adj* **1. TRUE** confirming or asserting that something is true **2. INDICATING AGREEMENT** indicating agreement or giving assent **3.** LOGIC **RELATING TO TYPE OF PROPOSITION** relating to or consisting of a categorical proposition in which the predicate's extension is contained partially or wholly within the subject, as in "All humans are mammals" ■ *n* **1. POSITIVE ASSERTION** an emphatic statement that something is true **2. WORD CONVEYING AGREEMENT** a word or statement conveying agreement or approval **3. SIDE SUPPORTING PROPOSITION IN DEBATE** the side in a debate that supports a proposition ■ *interj* **YES** a signal code word expressing agreement or compliance —**af·fir·ma·tive·ly** *adv*

af·fir·ma·tive ac·tion *n* a policy or program aimed at countering discrimination against minorities and women, especially in employment and education

af·fix *vt* /ə fíks/ (**-fixed, -fix·ing, -fix·es**) **1. FASTEN SOMETHING** to fasten something to something else **2. ADD SOMETHING AT END** to add something at the end of something, e.g., a signature to a document **3. ATTRIBUTE SOMETHING** to ascribe something such as responsibility or blame, to somebody ■ *n* /áffiks/ **1.** GRAM **PART ADDED TO WORD** a form added to the beginning, middle, or end of another word that creates a derivative word or inflection **2. SOMETHING ATTACHED** an attachment or addition to something [Mid-16C. Directly or via French *affixer* < medieval Latin *affixare* "keep on fastening to" < Latin *affigere* "fasten to" < *figere* "fasten"] —**af·fix·a·ble** *adj* —**af·fix·er** *n*

af·fix·a·tion /àffik sáysh'n/ *n* the addition of a prefix, suffix, or infix to a word in order to create a new word or an inflected form

af·fla·tus /ə fláytəss/ *n* creative inspiration, usually thought of as divine (*formal*) [Mid-17C. < Latin, "act of blowing on" < *flare* "to blow"]

af·flict /ə flíkt/ (**-flict·ed, -flict·ing, -flicts**) *vt* to cause severe physical or mental distress to somebody [14C. < Latin *afflict-*, past participle of *affligere* "strike down, cause to suffer" < *fligere* "to strike"] —**af·flict·er** *n* —**af·flic·tive** *adj* —**af·flic·tive·ly** *adv*

USAGE afflict or **inflict**? The chief difference is in the grammatical construction: you ***inflict*** something unpleasant *on* somebody, whereas you ***afflict*** somebody *with* something unpleasant (or, more usually, somebody is ***afflicted*** *with* or *by* something unpleasant): *They promoted measures to avoid inflicting further harm on the environment. The population was afflicted by a series of natural disasters.*

af·flic·tion /ə flíkshən/ *n* **1.** a condition of great physical or mental distress **2.** something that causes great physical or mental distress [14C. Via Old French < Latin *affliction-* < *afflict-* (see AFFLICT)]

af·flu·ent /áffloo ənt, a flóo-/ *adj* having an abundance of material wealth ■ *n* GEOG a stream or river that flows into another [15C. Via Old French < Latin *affluent-*, present participle of *affluere* "flow toward" < *fluere* "flow"] —**af·flu·ence** *n* —**af·flu·ent·ly** *adv*

CULTURAL NOTE ***The Affluent Society***, a book (1958) by US economist John Kenneth Galbraith. One of Galbraith's most widely read works, it attacks what he views as the American obsession with production and material goods, and urges greater government expenditure on the country's infrastructure and public services.

af·flux /á flùks/ *n* a flow inward or toward a point, e.g., of blood toward a body organ [Early 17C. < medieval Latin *affluxus* < Latin *affluere* (see AFFLUENT)]

af·ford /ə fáwrd/ (**-ford·ed, -ford·ing, -fords**) *vt* **1. BE ABLE TO BUY SOMETHING** to be able to meet the cost of something without unacceptable difficulty **2. BE ABLE TO DO SOMETHING** to be able to do or provide something without unacceptable or disadvantageous consequences ○ *We can't afford to be late.* **3. BE ABLE TO SPARE SOMETHING** to be able to spare something without unacceptable or disadvantageous consequences ○ *I'd like to come but I can't afford the time.* **4. PROVIDE SOMETHING** to supply or provide something (*formal*) ○ *The film will afford you much pleasure.* [Old English *geforian* "accomplish" < *forian* "to further"] —**af·ford·a·ble** *adj*

af·ford·able hous·ing *n* subsidized housing for people on lower incomes in which rent or mortage costs do not exceed a specific percentage, usually 30%, of the gross annual household income

af·for·est /ə fáwrəst/ (**-est·ed, -est·ing, -ests**) *vt* to convert land not previously forested into forest by planting trees [Early 16C. < medieval Latin *afforestare* < *foresta* "forest"] —**af·for·es·ta·tion** /ə fàwrə stáysh'n/ *n*

af·fray /ə fráy/ *n* a fight or noisy disturbance in a public place [14C. Via Anglo-Norman *afrayer* "disturb" < assumed Vulgar Latin *exfridare* "take out of peace"]

af·fri·cate /áffrikət/, **af·fri·ca·tive** /ə fríkətiv/ *n* a composite speech sound made up of a stop immediately followed by a fricative [Late 19C. < Latin *affricat-*, past participle of *affricare* "rub against" < *fricare* "rub"] —**af·fri·ca·tive** *adj*

af·fright /ə frī́t/ (*archaic or literary*) *vt* (**-fright·ed, -fright·ing, -frights**) to overwhelm somebody with sudden fear ■ *n* sudden overwhelming fear [Late 16C. < obsolete *fright* "frighten" < Old English *fryhtan* < Germanic] —**af·fright·ment** *n*

af·front /ə frúnt/ *n* an open insult or giving of offense to somebody ■ *vt* (**-front·ed, -front·ing, -fronts**) to insult or offend somebody openly [14C. Via Old French < Vulgar Latin *affrontare* "strike in the face" < *ad frontem* "to the face"]

af·ghan /áf gàn/ *n* **1.** a knitted or crocheted blanket or shawl, often with geometric designs **2.** a large carpet woven in a geometric design [Mid-19C. < AFGHAN]

Af·ghan /áf gàn/ *n* **1.** somebody who comes from Afghanistan **2.** LANG same as **Pashto** (sense 1) **3.** DOGS same as **Afghan hound** [Early 18C. < Pashto *afghānī* "of Afghanistan"] —**Af·ghan** *adj*

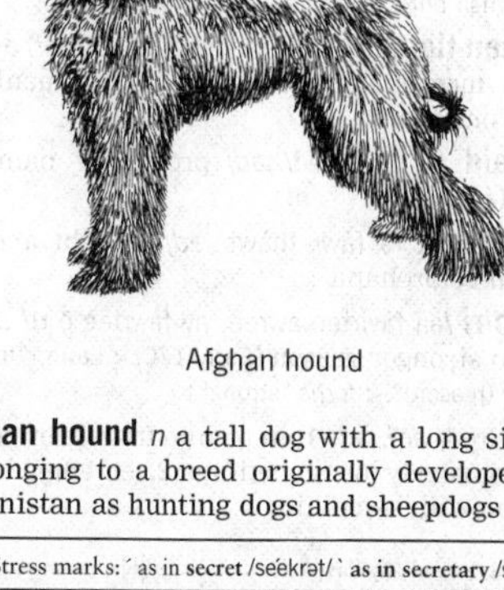

Afghan hound

Af·ghan hound *n* a tall dog with a long silky coat, belonging to a breed originally developed in Afghanistan as hunting dogs and sheepdogs

af·ghan·i /af gánnee, -gaánee/ (*plural* **-is**) *n* the main unit of Afghan currency. See table at **currency** [Early 20C. < Pashto *afghānī*]

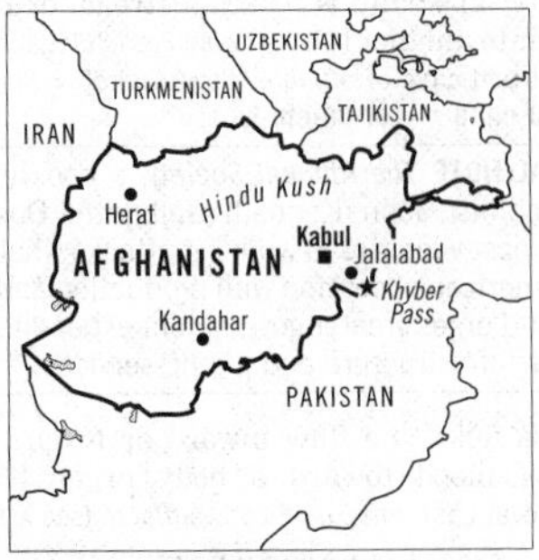

Afghanistan

Af·ghan·i·stan /af gánni stàn/ landlocked country in Southwest Asia, between Iran and Pakistan. Language: Pashto, Dari (Persian). Currency: afghani. Capital: Kabul. Population: 28,717,213 (2003). Area: 251,825 sq. mi./652,225 sq. km. Official name **Islamic State of Afghanistan**

a·fi·cio·na·da /ə fìshə naádə, ə fìshee ə-/ *n* a woman who is enthusiastic and knowledgeable about something

a·fi·cio·na·do /ə fìshə naádō, ə fìshee ə-/ (*plural* **-dos**) *n* **1.** somebody who is enthusiastic and knowledgeable about something **2.** a devotee of bullfighting [Mid-19C. < Spanish, "somebody who likes something" < Latin *affection-* (see AFFECTION)]

a·field /ə féeld/ *adv, adj* **1.** distant from home ○ *wandered far afield* **2.** off the point or subject

a·fi·ko·men /aáfi kṓmən/ *n* in Judaism, the unleavened bread that completes the festive meal (**Seder**) on the first night of Passover [Late 19C. Via Hebrew *aphīqōmān* < Greek *epikōmion* "festival"]

a·fire /ə fír/ *adj, adv* **1.** on fire or blazing **2.** passionately interested in something

AFL *abbr* **1.** American Federation of Labor **2.** American Football League

a·flame /ə fláym/ *adj* **1.** in flames or blazing **2.** highly aroused or impassioned

af·la·tox·in /àfflə tóksin/ *n* a toxin produced by some molds in crops, especially peanuts [Mid-20C. < modern Latin *Aspergillus flavus* + TOXIN]

AFL-CIO *abbr* American Federation of Labor and Congress of Industrial Organizations

a·float /ə flṓt/ *adj, adv* **1.** FLOATING floating on water **2.** ON BOARD SHIP on board a ship or at sea **3.** FLOODED covered with water **4.** WITHOUT PURPOSE lacking purpose or guidance **5.** IN CIRCULATION circulating among the public **6.** FINANCIALLY SOLVENT free of debt or financial problems

AFLP *abbr* BIOTECH amplified fragment length polymorphism

a·flut·ter /ə flúttər/ *adj, adv* **1.** in a state of agitation or excitement **2.** flapping or waving, e.g., as a flag does in the breeze

AFM *abbr* PHYS atomic force microscope

AFO *abbr* CRIME assault on a federal officer

a·foot /ə fŏŏt/ *adj, adv* **1.** in the process of happening **2.** on foot or by walking [13C. Partly after Old Norse *á fótum* "on foot"]

a·fore /ə fáwr/ *adv, prep, conj regional* same as **before** [Old English *onforan* < *foran* "in front, before"]

a·fore·men·tioned /ə fáwr mènshənd/ (*formal*) *adj* previously mentioned ■ *n* the previously mentioned person or people

a·fore·said /ə fáwr sèd/ *adj* previously named or stated (*formal*)

a·fore·thought /ə fáwr thàwt/ *adj* thought about or planned beforehand

a for·ti·o·ri /aa fàwrtee áwree, ay fàwrtee ō rí/ *adv* for an even stronger reason [Early 17C. < Latin, "from the stronger (reason)" < *fortis* "strong"]

a·foul /ə fówl/ *adj, adv* **1.** in or into trouble or conflict with somebody or something **2.** entangled or in collision with something

Afr. *abbr* **1.** Africa **2.** African

a·fraid /ə fráyd/ *adj* **1.** FRIGHTENED frightened or apprehensive about something **2.** RELUCTANT feeling hesitation or disinclination toward something **3.** REGRETFUL feeling regret about something [14C. Originally past participle of AFFRAY, after Anglo-Norman *affrayé*]

CULTURAL NOTE ***Who's Afraid of Virginia Woolf?***, a play (1962) by US dramatist Edward Albee. Albee's first full-length play examines the sour relationship between a middle-aged underachieving academic and his embittered wife. A dinner party with a younger, not dissimilar couple forces them to confront the reality of their past and present.

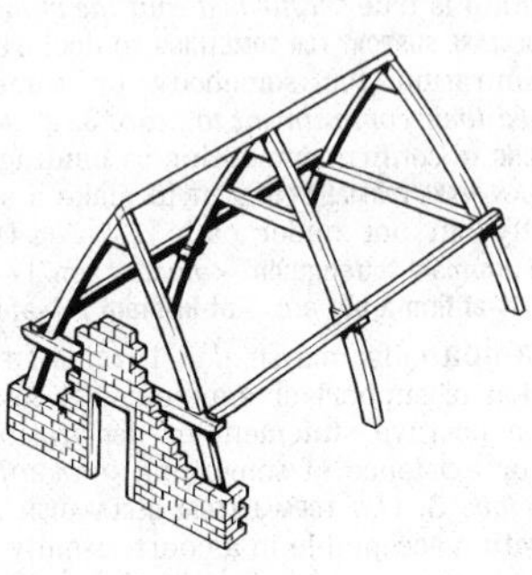
A-frame

A-frame *adj* built in the shape of a capital letter A ■ *n* a building shaped like a capital letter A, with a triangular front and back, and a roof that slopes to the ground to form the sides of the building

af·reet /á freèt, ə freèt/, **af·rit** *n* in Arabian mythology, an evil spirit or powerful monster [Late 18C. < Arabic *afrīt*]

a·fresh /ə frésh/ *adv* once again, especially from the beginning

Af·ri·ca /áffrikə/ the second largest continent, lying south of Europe, with the Atlantic Ocean to the west and the Indian Ocean to the east. Population: 875,027,307 (2004). Area: 11,677,239 sq. mi./30,243,910 sq. km.

Af·ri·can /áffrikən/ *adj* OF AFRICA relating to any part of the African continent, or its peoples, languages, or culture ■ *n* **1.** SOMEBODY FROM AFRICA somebody who comes from Africa **2.** SOMEBODY OF AFRICAN DESCENT somebody descended from a people of Africa [Pre-12C. < Latin *Africanus* < *Afri* "the ancient inhabitants of N Africa"]

Af·ri·can A·mer·i·can *n* an American of African descent —**Af·ri·can A·mer·i·can** *adj*

USAGE African American, Afro-American, or **Black?** ***African American*** has vigorously overtaken ***Afro-American*** as a term descriptive of Black Americans. Similarly, *Chinese American* is now more common than *Sino-American*, and *Italian American* than *Italo-American*. Unlike the other compounds, of course, ***African American***, along with *Asian American*, refers to a continent, not a country, and this perhaps explains why ***African American*** and *Asian American* seldom appear in discussions of international relations. Other limitations on the use of ***African American*** have to do with the stress it lays on African heritage. Although Blacks with Caribbean or Hispanic backgrounds may be able to trace their ancestry to Africa, they do not necessarily regard themselves as ***African Americans***, any more than the descendants of Spanish immigrants to Argentina consider themselves Spanish. ***Black*** is broader in application, referring as well to people who are not American. *People of color* is broader still, referring to people who are not Caucasian of whatever origin and nationality. *Colored people* should be avoided except in its long-established use in the full form of the abbreviation *NAACP*.

Af·ri·can A·mer·i·can Ver·nac·u·lar Eng·lish *n* the variety of English spoken by many African Americans. See panel on next page

Af·ri·can buf·fa·lo *n* a reddish brown to black wild buffalo, either the Cape buffalo or the smaller forest or dwarf buffalo. Native to: Africa. Latin name: *Synceros caffer* or *Synceros nanus*.

Af·ri·can Ca·na·di·an *n* a Canadian of African descent —**Af·ri·can Ca·na·di·an** *adj*

Af·ri·can Car·ib·be·an *n* somebody of African descent who lives in or comes from the Caribbean —**Af·ri·can Ca·rib·be·an** *adj*

Af·ri·can dai·sy *n* a plant of the composite family that resembles a daisy. Flowers: colorful, large. Native to: Africa. Genera: *Dimorphotheca* or *Gerbera or Lonas*.

Af·ri·can Eng·lish *n* the variety of English spoken in Africa

Af·ri·can·ism /áffrikən ìzzəm/ *n* a cultural feature associated with Africa or Africans, especially a linguistic feature found in a language that is not itself African

Af·ri·can·ist /áffrikənist/ *n* a specialist in African affairs, cultures, or languages

Af·ri·can·ized bee *n* an aggressive honeybee that was accidentally hybridized in Brazil from African and European strains and has spread north into Mexico and southern Texas

Af·ri·can lil·y *n US* a plant of the lily family. Flowers: blue or white, funnel-shaped. Native to: southern Africa. Latin name: *Agapanthus africanus*. Can term **agapanthus**

Af·ri·can ma·hog·a·ny *n* **1.** a hard wood similar in appearance to that of tropical American mahogany. Use: furniture-making. **2.** a tree that produces African mahogany. Native to: Africa. Genera: *Khaya* or *Entandrophragma*.

Af·ri·can Na·tion·al Con·gress *n* a South African political party founded in 1912 that fought against apartheid and formed South Africa's first multiracial, democratically elected government in 1994

Af·ri·can sleep·ing sick·ness *n* MED same as **sleeping sickness**

Af·ri·can Un·ion *n* an organization of African states founded in 2002 for mutual cooperation, superseding the Organization of African Unity

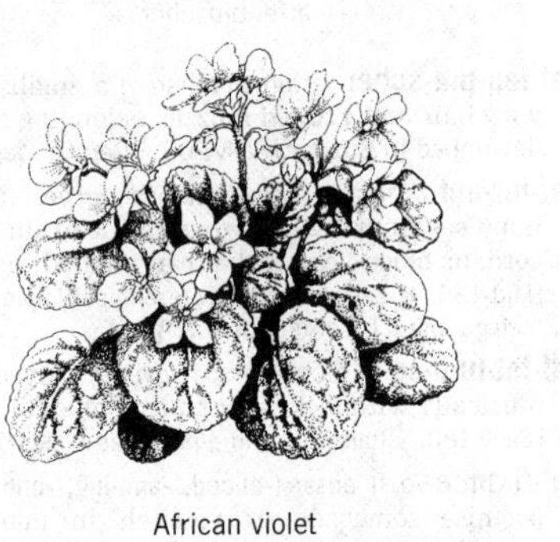
African violet

Af·ri·can vi·o·let *n* a tropical plant with fleshy leaves, grown as a houseplant. Flowers: violet, white, or pink. Native to: Africa. Genus: *Saintpaulia*.

Af·ri·kaans /àffri kaánss, -kaánz/ *n* an official language of South Africa, also spoken in Namibia, that is descended from the Dutch spoken by 17th-century settlers. Native speakers: 10 million. ■ *adj* relating to the Afrikaner people, or their language or culture [Early 20C. < Dutch, "African"]

LANGUAGE HERITAGE See ***Dutch***.

Af·ri·ka·ner /àffri kaánər/ *n* a South African whose first language is Afrikaans, usually descended from 17th-century settlers (**Boers**) [Early 19C. < Afrikaans < *Afrikaan* "African person," after *Hollander* "Dutch person"] —**Af·ri·ka·ner** *adj*

af·rit *n* MYTHOL same as **afreet**

Af·ro /áffrō/ *n* (*plural* **-ros**) a hairstyle with thick tight curls ■ *adj* African in origin or style [Mid-20C. < AFRO-AMERICAN or AFRO-]

Afro- *prefix* Africa, African ○ *Afro-Cuban* [< Latin *Afr-*, stem of *Afer* "an African"]

Af·ro-A·mer·i·can *n* same as **African American** (*dated*) —**Af·ro-A·mer·i·can** *adj*

USAGE See ***African American***.

WORLD ENGLISH ***African American Vernacular English***, or **AAVE**, is the term used by scholars for the widespread and varied African American usages of the English Language, also called *Ebonics, Afro-American English, American Black English, Black English, Black English Vernacular*, and *Black Vernacular English*. Originating in the pidgin of the slave trade and Plantation Creole in the US Southern states, African American Vernacular English considerably influenced US Southern English and, in the late 19th and the 20th centuries, spread by migration through much of the nation. It therefore has both rural and urban components. It has also come to be associated with the language of blues, jazz, and rap music.

As with African English, African American Vernacular English does not pronounce *r* in words such as *art, door*, and *worker*. Other characteristics, some going back to similar features of African languages, are: (1) the use of *d* and *t* instead of *th*, as in *dem* for *them* and *tree* for *three*; (2) the dropping of *l*, as in *hep* for *help, sef* for *self*, and *too* for *tool*; (3) consonant reduction at the ends of some words (including tense endings), as in *wha* for *what, jus* for *just*, and *pas* for *past*; (4) use of *-n* for *-ing*, as in *runnin* for *running*; (5) multiple negatives, as in *no way nobody can do it*; (6) verb aspects marked for intermittent, momentary, or continuous action rather than tense per se, the tense time being apparent from the contexts, as in *he be laughin* for *he is always laughing* and *he run* for *he runs*; and (7) dropping of the verb in some constructions, as in *she sick* and *he gone* for *she is sick* and *he has gone*.

African American Vernacular English expressions have contributed to the rich texture of American English, these terms being typical: *yam* (sweet potato), *goober* (peanut), *okra, gumbo* (the soup and the river mud), *tote* (carry), *juke, mumbo jumbo, hep/hip*, and *boogie woogie*. All these are rooted in African languages. In its more urban settings, African American Vernacular English's contributions are also many, these few examples making the point: *dis* (to disrespect), *igg* (to ignore), *chill out* (to stop behaving stupidly), *'tude* (attitude), *the Man* (the police), *hang-up* (a problem), *rap* (to talk), *make it* (succeed), *kicks* (pleasure), and the sense of *bad* meaning variously "good," "extraordinary," and "beautiful."

Af·ro-A·mer·i·can Eng·lish *n* LANG same as **African American Vernacular English**

WORLD ENGLISH See ***African American Vernacular English.***

Af·ro-A·sian *adj* relating to the continents of Africa and Asia, or to their peoples or shared cultural phenomena

Af·ro-A·si·at·ic *n* a large family of languages spoken across North Africa and Southwest Asia. Native speakers: 250 million. —**Af·ro-A·si·at·ic** *adj*

Af·ro-Car·ib·be·an *n* PEOPLES same as **African Caribbean**

Af·ro·cen·tric /àffrō séntrik/ *adj* centered on or originating in Africa or African culture

Af·ro-Cu·ban *adj* relating to Cuban culture as influenced by Africa, especially a style of jazz based on Cuban interpretations of African rhythms

Af·ro-La·ti·na *n* a woman of African and Latin American ancestry

Af·ro-La·ti·no *n* a man of African and Latin American ancestry ■ *adj* relating to people of African and Latin American ancestry

aft /aft/ *adv, adj* toward or at the rear of a ship, submarine, or aircraft [Early 17C. Shortening of ABAFT]

AFT *abbr US* American Federation of Teachers

af·ter /áftər/ *prep* **1. LATER THAN** later in time than **2. BEHIND** behind in order or place **3. IN PURSUIT OF** in pursuit of or looking for **4. REGARDING** about or regarding **5. FOLLOWING FROM** subsequent to and considering **6. LIKE** in imitation or in the manner of ○ *a painting after the style of Cézanne* **7. AGREEING WITH** in agreement with or in conformity to **8. PAST HOUR OF** later than a particular hour ○ *a quarter after seven* ■ *adv* **1. LATER** later in time or place **2.** NAUT, AVIAT **FARTHER BACK** farther toward the rear of a ship, submarine, or aircraft ■ *conj* **FOLLOWING TIME WHEN** following a time when, and sometimes as a result ○ *You'll miss me after I've gone.* ■ *adj* **1. SUBSEQUENT** later in time **2.** NAUT, AVIAT **REAR** situated farther toward the rear of a ship, submarine, or aircraft [Old English *æfter*. Assumed to be a comparative form, "farther away" < Indo-European, "away, off"] ◇ **after all 1.** used to emphasize something that should be taken into consideration in spite of what has happened or been said **2.** used to show that in the end something happened, was done, or was recognized in spite of expectations to the contrary or efforts to prevent it

af·ter·beat /áftər bēet/ *n* MUSIC same as **backbeat**

af·ter·birth /áftər bùrth/ *n* the placenta and fetal membranes expelled from the uterus after a birth [Late 16C. Perhaps after German *Aftergeburt*]

af·ter·burn·er /áftər bùrnər/ *n* **1.** a system for increasing the thrust of an aircraft jet engine by feeding fuel into the hot exhaust gases **2.** a device in the exhaust system of an internal combustion engine for burning or catalytically destroying potentially harmful unburned or incompletely burned carbon compounds

af·ter·care /áftər kèr/ *n* **1.** HEALTH SERVICES **CARE AFTER LEAVING HOSPITAL** care or support that somebody receives after leaving a hospital, often provided by a home nurse or social worker **2.** HEALTH SERVICES **CARE AFTER ILLNESS** care given in a hospital to a patient who is recovering from an illness or operation **3.** *US* PSYCHOL **COUNSELING OF BEREAVED** counseling of bereaved clients by funeral home staff after a death and the funeral

af·ter·clap /áftər klàp/ *n* a belated, unexpected, and usually adverse consequence of something thought to be over and done with

af·ter·damp /áftər dàmp/ *n* gaseous fumes remaining in a mine after an explosion of firedamp

af·ter·deck /áftər dèk/ *n* the part of the main open deck of a boat that extends from the bridge or midships to the stern

af·ter·ef·fect /áftər i fèkt/ *n* **1. DELAYED RESULT** an effect, usually unpleasant, that follows its cause after an interval of time (*usually used in the plural*) ○ *The stock markets are still showing the aftereffects of last month's rise in interest rates.* **2.** PHYSIOL **SECONDARY REACTION** a secondary response that follows the primary response to a physiological stimulus **3.** PSYCHOL **DELAYED REACTION** a delayed reaction to a psychological stimulus

af·ter·glow /áftər glō/ *n* **1.** radiated light that remains visible after a source of light or energy has been removed, e.g., the glow sometimes seen in the sky after sunset **2.** a feeling of pleasure or a favorable impression that remains after a positive experience ○ *basking in the afterglow of victory*

af·ter·im·age /áftər ìmmij/ *n* a visual image that remains briefly after light stimulation has ended

af·ter·life /áftər lìf/ *n* **1. LIFE AFTER DEATH** a form of existence believed to continue after death **2. LATER STAGE OF LIFE** the period of somebody's life that follows a specific event or role ○ *Is there an afterlife for retired football players?* **3. REPUTATION AFTER DEATH** a well-known person's reputation that persists after he or she has died (*literary*)

af·ter·mar·ket /áftər maàrkət/ *n* subsequent sales opportunities resulting from an original sale, especially the demand for parts and services that follows the purchase of something such as a car

af·ter·math /áftər màth/ *n* **1.** the consequences of an event, especially a disastrous one, or the period of time during which these consequences are felt ○ *in the aftermath of the war* **2.** a second crop or growth of grass in the same season, after the first harvest or mowing [15C. < *math* "mowing" < Old English *mæ*]

af·ter·most /áftər mōst/, **aft·most** /áft mōst/ *adj* nearest to the stern of a boat

af·ter·noon /àftər noōn/ *n* **1. DAYTIME BETWEEN MIDDAY AND EVENING** the period of the day between noon and evening **2. LATTER PART** the latter part of something, especially of somebody's life (*literary*) ■ *interj* **GREETING** a greeting used to say "good afternoon" (*informal*)

af·ter·noons /àftər noōnz/ *adv* in any or during every afternoon (*informal*)

af·ter·pains /áftər pàynz/ *npl* pains experienced by some women just after giving birth, similar to labor pains and caused by contractions of the uterus

af·ter·piece /áftər peèss/ *n* a short entertainment, usually comic, performed after a play

af·ter-school *adj* occurring after school, especially from the end of the school day until the end of the normal working day ○ *an after-school club*

af·ter·sen·sa·tion /áftər sen sàysh'n/ *n* a sense impression that remains after the immediate stimulus has been removed

af·ter·shave /áftər shàyv/ *n* a liquid applied after shaving to soothe and scent the skin of the face

af·ter·shock /áftər shòk/ *n* **1.** a small earthquake, usually one of several, that follows a larger one **2.** a delayed psychological or physical reaction to a serious event or trauma

af·ter·taste /áftər tàyst/ *n* **1.** a taste left in the mouth by food or drink after swallowing **2.** a feeling or sensation, especially an unpleasant one, left behind after an experience

af·ter-tax *adj* remaining after paying or deducting money for taxes ○ *after-tax earnings*

af·ter·thought /áftər thàwt/ *n* something not thought of, said, or done originally, but added afterward

af·ter·ward /áftərwərd/, **af·ter·wards** /-wərdz/ *adv* at a later time or after an event that has been mentioned previously ○ *Let's have breakfast now and go skiing afterward.*

USAGE See ***toward.***

af·ter·word /áftər wùrd/ *n* a short concluding section added at the end of a literary work as an epilogue or a commentary of some kind

af·ter·world /áftər wùrld/ *n* in some religions, a world that people are believed to go to and live in after death

aft·most *adj* NAUT same as **aftermost**

AFTRA /áftrə/ *abbr US* American Federation of Television and Radio Artists

ag *abbr* Antigua and Barbuda (*used in Internet addresses*) See table at **domain name**

Ag *symbol* CHEM ELEM silver [Shortening of Latin *argentum* "silver"]

Ag. *abbr* CALENDAR August

A.G., AG *abbr* **1.** ARMY Adjutant General **2.** LAW Attorney General

ag- *prefix* same as **ad-** (*used before g*)

a·ga /aágə, ággə/, **a·gha** *n* used as a title for a military commander or important official in Islamic countries, especially during the Ottoman Empire ○ *the Aga Khan* [Mid-16C. < Turkish *aghā* "chief, master, lord"]

A·ga·dir /aágə deér/ port and city in Morocco. Population: 550,200 (1994).

a·gain /ə gén/ *adv* **1. AT ANOTHER TIME** at another time or on another occasion, repeating what has happened or been done before ○ *I hope to come here again some day.* **2. AS BEFORE** to the place, person, or state where somebody or something was earlier ○ *Will I ever be able to walk again?* **3. DIFFERENTLY** on the other hand ○ *You may be right, but again you may be wrong.* **4. IN ADDITION** in addition to a previously mentioned quantity ○ *You'll need all that and half as much again.* **5. MOREOVER** similarly and in addition ○ *Again, that is something that the court must take into account.* **6.** *Carib* **THESE DAYS** nowadays or any longer ○ *He doesn't live here again.* **7.** *Carib* **AFTER ALL** used to indicate that what has happened or been done represents a change of plan or is contrary to expectations ○ *What happen, you not doing Accounting again?* **8.** *Carib* **MORE** in addition ○ *How long again do you have to go?* [Old English *ongēan* "in a direct line with, facing" or "back to a starting point" < Germanic] ◇ **again and again** repeatedly

a·gainst /ə génst/ CORE MEANING: a preposition indicating opposition to or conflict with somebody or something, either physically or intellectually ○ (prep) *a battle against cancer*

prep **1. IN COMPETITION WITH** with somebody or something as an opponent in a competitive situation, especially in sports ○ *Iowa against UCLA in the Rose Bowl* **2. IN CONTACT WITH BY LEANING** in a position such that part or all of something touches another object or surface, by leaning or resting on the side of it ○ *I leaned against a tree.* **3.** INTO SUDDEN CONTACT OR COLLISION WITH so as to briefly touch or suddenly collide with a usually stationary object while in movement ○ *banged his head against the beam* **4.** IN OPPOSITE DIRECTION TO in the opposite direction to the movement, angle, or position of something or somebody ○ *to swim against the current* **5.** SEEN IN CONTRAST WITH seen in contrast with physical surroundings ○ *The dark green pines are lovely against the blue sky.* **6.** IN RELATION TO EVENTS in relation to, or contrasted with, a set of events or circumstances ○ *Government action makes sense against the background of rising tensions.* **7.** AS PROTECTION FROM in order to prevent or avoid something, or to be protected from something ○ *vaccinate against disease* **8.** IN PAYMENT OF in partial or total payment of, or as a charge on ○ *I'd like to put this money against the amount I owe you.* **9.** AS DISADVANTAGE TO to the disadvantage of somebody or something ○ *Will you hold it against me if I don't come to your party?* **10.** COMPARED WITH in comparison with something ○ *weighed the cost of hiring someone against that of promoting existing staff* **11.** CONTRARY TO contrary to, or not approved or allowed by somebody or something ○ *It's against the law.* **12.** IN PREPARATION FOR in preparation for something, usually an expected unpleasant event (*dated*) ○ *to save against hard times* [14C. < AGAIN + adverbial suffix *-es* + *-t*, after such words as AMIDST]

A·ga Khan III /aàgə kaán/ (1877–1957) religious leader, born in Karachi, India, now Pakistan. He was imam of the Ismaili Muslim religious group and president of the League of Nations Assembly (1937).

A·ga Khan IV (*b.* 1936) Swiss-born Muslim leader. He became imam of the Ismaili religious group in 1957. Born **Karim al Hussaini Shah**

a·ga·ma /ə gáymə, ággə-/ *n* **1.** a small, long-tailed, often colorful lizard. Native to: tropical Africa, Asia. Genus: *Agama.* **2.** REPT same as **agamid** [Late 18C. < modern Latin and Spanish, probably < Carib *mami* "lizard"]

Ag·a·mem·non /ággə mém nòn, -nən/ *n* in Greek mythology, the commander of the Greek army in the Trojan War. When Agamemnon returned from the war, he was murdered by his wife Clytemnestra and her lover Aegisthus. His death was later avenged by his son Orestes.

a·gam·ic /ay gámmik/, **ag·a·mous** /ággəməss/ *adj* describes an organism that multiplies asexually [Mid-19C. < Greek *agamos* "unmarried" < *gamos* "marriage"] —**a·gam·i·cal·ly** *adv*

a·ga·mid /ággəmid/ *n* a small long-tailed insect-eating lizard. Native to: tropical Africa, Asia. Family: Agamidae. [Late 19C. < modern Latin *Agamidae* < *agama* (see AGAMA)]

a·gam·o·gen·e·sis /ay gàmmə jénnəssiss, àggəmō-/ *n* asexual reproduction, e.g., by cell division or budding [Mid-19C. < Greek *agamos* "unmarried" + -GENESIS]

a·gam·o·sper·my /ay gámmə spùrmee, ággəmō-/ *n* the asexual formation of seeds without fertilization [Mid-20C. < Greek *agamos* "unmarried" + SPERM[1] + -Y[1]]

ag·a·mous *adj* BIOL same as **agamic**

ag·a·pan·thus /àggə pánthəss/ (*plural same* or **-thus·es**) *n Can, UK* a plant of the lily family. Flowers: bluish or white, funnel-shaped, in ball-shaped clusters. Native to: southern Africa. Genus: *Agapanthus.* US term **African lily** [Late 18C. < modern Latin < Greek *agapē* "brotherly love" + *anthos* "flower"]

a·gape[1] /ə gáyp/ *adv, adj* (*literary*) **1.** with the mouth wide open, usually in surprise or wonder **2.** opened widely ○ *The door to the room was agape.* [Mid-17C. < A-[1]]

a·ga·pe[2] /aa gaá pay/ *n* **1.** NONSEXUAL LOVE love that is wholly selfless and spiritual **2.** CHR CHRISTIAN LOVE selfless love felt by Christians for their fellow human beings **3.** CHR CHRISTIAN COMMUNAL MEAL a communal meal held by a Christian community, especially in early Christian times, in commemoration of the Last Supper [Mid-17C. < Greek *agapē* "brotherly love"]

a·gar /áagər, áy-/, **a·gar-a·gar** *n* **1.** a powdered seaweed extract. Use: gelling agent, thickener. **2.** a culture medium based on a seaweed extract. Use: growing microorganisms in laboratories. [Late 19C. < Malay *agar-agar* "jelly"]

ag·ar·bat·ti /úggər bùttee/ (*plural same* or **-tis**) *n S Asia* same as **joss stick** [< Hindi]

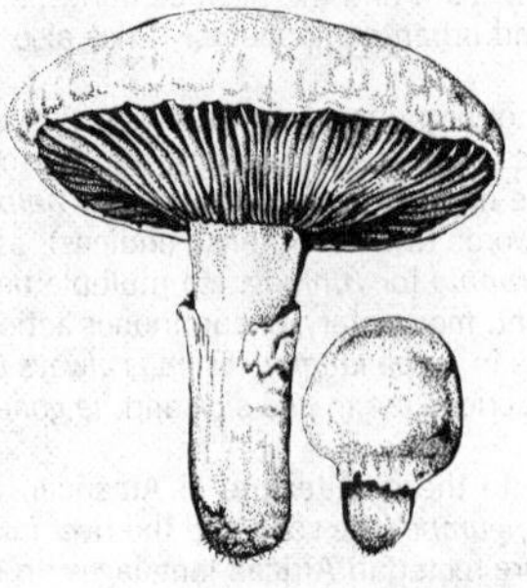

agaric

ag·a·ric /ággərik, ə gárrik/ *n* a fungus with a large cap resembling an umbrella with numerous radiating gills on the underside. Some types are edible and some are poisonous. Family: Agaricaceae. [15C. Directly or via French < Latin *agaricum* < Greek *agarikon* "tree fungus"]

ag·a·rose /ággə rōss, -rōz/ *n* a complex carbohydrate (**polysaccharide**) obtained from agar. Use: as a medium in chromatography and electrophoresis.

Ag·ar·ta·la /aárgətə laà/ capital city of Tripura state in northeastern India. Population: 158,000 (1991).

Ag·as·si /ággəssee/, **Andre** (*b.* 1970) US tennis player. He won Wimbledon in 1992, the US Open in 1994 and 1999, and a gold medal in the Atlanta Olympics in 1996.

Ag·as·siz /ággəssee/, **Louis** (1807–73) Swiss-born US naturalist and glaciologist who became Professor of Natural History at Harvard (1848), and developed theories on the occurrence of Ice Ages. Full name **Agassiz, Jean Louis Rodolphe**

> "Every great scientific truth goes through three stages. First, people say it conflicts with the Bible. Next they say it had been discovered before. Lastly, they say they always believed it."
> [Louis Agassiz. Quoted in *Science-Week*, January 9, 1998]

ag·ate /ággət/ *n* **1.** a hard fine-grained semiprecious stone with variously colored bands, markings, and areas of clouding that is a form of chalcedony. Use: gems. **2.** a playing marble made of agate or of glass that looks like agate [Late 16C. Via French < Greek *akhatēs*, perhaps after *Achates*, river in Sicily]

ag·ate line *n US* a measure of page space, e.g., in classified advertising, one column wide and 1.8 mm deep

ag·ate·ware /ággət wèr/ *n* **1.** decorative pottery made using a cross section of layers of clay of contrasting colors **2.** metalware, e.g., pots and pans, with an enamel surface decorated to resemble agate

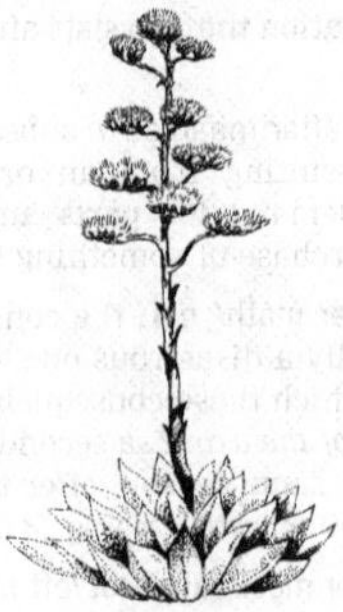

agave

a·ga·ve /ə gaávee, -gáy-/ (*plural* **-ves** or *same*) *n* a spiny-leaved plant with a single tall flower stalk. Use: fiber, alcoholic drinks, especially tequila. Native to: America. Genus: *Agave.* [Late 18C. Via Latin < Greek *Agauē*, mother of Pentheus in Greek mythology]

A·ga·wam /ággə waàm/ city in southwestern Massachusetts, situated on the western bank of the Connecticut River. Population: 28,391 (2002 estimate).

ag·bi·o·tech /ag bī ō tèk/, **ag·bi·o·tech·nol·o·gy** /ag bī ō tek nólləjee/ *n* agriculture or an agricultural industry using products and processes developed through biotechnology [Late 20C. Shortening of *ag-biotechnology* < shortening of AGRICULTURAL or AGRICULTURE]

age /ayj/ *n* **1.** LENGTH OF SOMEBODY'S OR SOMETHING'S EXISTENCE the length of time that somebody or something has existed, usually expressed in years **2.** STAGE OF LIFE a stage or phase in the lifetime of somebody or something ○ *at an early age* **3.** LEGAL ADULTHOOD the age at which somebody is legally considered to be an adult **4.** STATE OF HAVING LIVED LONG the condition of having lived many years ○ *the wisdom of age* **5.** *also* **Age** HISTORICAL ERA a period in history, especially a long period or one associated with and named for a distinctive characteristic, achievement, or influential person ○ *the space age* **6.** *also* **Age** GEOL GEOLOGIC ERA a relatively short division of recent geologic time, shorter than an epoch ○ *the Ice Age* **7.** EDUC LEVEL OF DEVELOPMENT a level of development equivalent to that of an average person of a particular age ○ *a reading age of 7* **8.** GENERATION a generation of people (*literary*) ○ *the greatest writer of her age* ■ **ag·es** *npl* **1.** LONG TIME a very long time (*informal*) **2.** HISTORY human history ○ *People have warred with one another throughout the ages.* ■ *v* (**aged, ag·ing** or **age·ing, ag·es**) **1.** *vti* GROW OR CAUSE TO GROW OLD to become old, develop the characteristics of being old, or cause somebody or something to become or seem old ○ *Too much sun ages the skin.* **2.** *vti* FOOD IMPROVE OVER TIME to cause a food or wine to mature, develop a desired flavor, or become more tender, or to become improved in this way over time ○ *The wine is aged in oak barrels.* **3.** *vt* ELECTRONICS STABILIZE DEVICE THROUGH USE to stabilize an electronic device by using it [13C. Via Old French *aage* < Latin *aetat-* "period of life" < Indo-European] ◇ **come of age** to reach the age when people are legally considered to be adults ◇ **of a certain age** no longer young (*humorous*)

-age *suffix* **1.** action or result of an action ○ *breakage* ○ *coinage* **2.** collection of things ○ *signage* ○ *mileage* **3.** housing ○ *orphanage* **4.** condition, office ○ *brigandage* ○ *peerage* **5.** charge ○ *dockage* ○ *postage* [Via French < assumed Vulgar Latin *-aticum* < Latin *-aticus*, suffix forming adjectives]

age brack·et *n* the range of ages included between two particular ages ○ *the 30–40 age bracket*

ag·ed *adj* **1.** /áyjəd/ OLD very advanced in years **2.** /ayjd/ OF PARTICULAR AGE of a particular age ○ *a person aged 50* **3.** /ayjd/ IMPROVED WITH TIME stored for a period of time in order to mature, develop a desired flavor, or become more tender ○ *well-aged wine* **4.** /ayjd/ GEOL ERODED showing evidence of advanced erosion ■ /áyjəd/ *npl* SENIOR CITIZENS people of advanced years, especially those whose physical or mental health has diminished [15C. Probably after French *âgé*] —**ag·ed·ly** /áyjədlee/ *adv* —**ag·ed·ness** /-nəss/ *n*

age dis·crim·i·na·tion *n* same as **ageism**

age di·ver·sit·y *n* the inclusion of people of all age groups, especially in the workplace

A·gee /áyjee/, **James** (1909–55) US poet, novelist, screenwriter, and movie critic. He cowrote *Let Us Now Praise Famous Men* with Walker Evans (1941) and wrote the screenplay for *The African Queen* (1951).

age gap *n* the difference in age between two people

age-grade *n* a group of people in a society who are the same sex and approximately the same age. Age-grades and the relationships between them are an important part of the organization of some cultures.

age group *n* a group of people whose ages are approximately the same or fall within a particular range

age·ing *n, adj* another spelling of **aging**

age·ism /áyj ìzzəm/, **ag·ism** *n* discrimination or prejudice against people of specific ages, especially in employment —**age·ist** *adj*

age·less /áyjləss/ *adj* **1.** never growing or seeming to grow older **2.** not typical of or confined to a specific period of time ○ *the ageless search for the truth* —**age·less·ly** *adv* —**age·less·ness** *n*

age lim·it *n* a restriction limiting participation in an activity to people above or below a particular age

a·gen·cy /áyjənssee/ (*plural* **-cies**) *n* **1.** BUSINESS, MANAGEMT **COMPANY ACTING AS AGENT** an organization, especially a company, that acts as the agent, representative, or subcontractor of a person or another company ○ *an employment agency* **2.** GOV **GOVERNMENT ORGANIZATION** an administrative division of a government or international organization ○ *a United Nations agency* **3. AGENCY OFFICES** the building or offices where an agency is located **4. MEANS** the action, medium, or means by which something is accomplished **5.** LAW **LEGAL RELATIONSHIP** a legal relationship involving a person (**the principal**) and another who acts for the person (**the agent**), or the area of the law concerned with such relationships ○ *The case hinges on a question of agency.* [Mid-17C. < medieval Latin *agentia* < Latin *agent-* (see AGENT)]

a·gen·cy shop *n US* a workplace in which a union represents both union and nonunion workers and requires payments from nonunion workers

a·gen·da /ə jéndə/ *n* **1. LIST OF THINGS TO DO** a formal list of things to be done in a specific order, especially a list of things to be discussed at a meeting **2. MATTERS NEEDING ATTENTION** the various matters that somebody needs to deal with at a specific time ○ *What's your agenda for today?* **3. PERSONAL MOTIVATION** an underlying personal viewpoint or bias ○ *Of course she's in favor, but then she has her own agenda.* ■ plural of **agendum** [Early 17C. < Latin, plural of *agendum* "thing to be done" < *agere* "to do"] ◇ **set the agenda** to be the major influence or force affecting something ○ *It is the environmental lobby that is setting the agenda in this round of negotiations.*

USAGE Although ***agenda*** is strictly speaking a plural noun meaning "things to be done," the singular form *agendum* is no longer used; ***agenda*** is used in the singular as if it were "a list of things to be done," with a plural form ***agendas***: *The agenda for tomorrow's meeting has been changed. This item has appeared on a number of previous agendas.* The use of ***agenda*** as a verb meaning "to put an item on an agenda" (*We will agenda that for the next meeting*) is criticized and is better avoided.

A·gen·da 21 *n* the global environmental program and statement of principles emphasizing sustainable development agreed to at the Earth Summit in Rio de Janeiro in 1992

a·gen·dum /ə jéndəm/ (*plural* **-dums** or **-da** /-də/) *n* an item on an agenda (*formal*) [Early 17C. < Latin (see AGENDA)]

USAGE See ***agenda***.

a·gen·e·sis /ay jénnəssiss/ *n* the incomplete development or total absence of a body part ○ *ovarian agenesis*

a·gent /áyjənt/ *n* **1.** BUSINESS **SOMEBODY REPRESENTING ANOTHER** somebody who officially represents somebody else in business **2. SOMEBODY PROVIDING SERVICE** somebody who provides a particular service for another ○ *a travel agent* **3.** *US* **GOVERNMENT EMPLOYEE** an investigator or representative employed by a government or other organization ○ *a federal agent* **4. CAUSATIVE SUBSTANCE** something such as a chemical substance, organism, or natural force that causes an effect ○ *a cleansing agent* **5. MEANS EFFECTING RESULT** the means by which an effect or result is produced ○ *As C.E.O. you will be expected to be the main agent of change.* **6. SPY** a spy or agent provocateur (*informal*) **7.** COMPUT **COMPUTER PROGRAM** a program that works automatically on routine tasks such as sorting e-mail or gathering information [15C. < Latin *agent-*, present participle of *agere* "drive, lead, act, do"] —**a·gen·tial** /ay jénshəl/ *adj*

ORIGIN The Latin word *agere* "to drive, act, do" from which ***agent*** is derived is also the source of English *act, active, actual, agile, agitate, ambiguous, cogent, essay, exact, examine*, and *prodigal*.

a·gent-gen·er·al (*plural* **a·gents-gen·er·al**) *n* a representative of a Canadian province or Australian state in a foreign country

A·gent Or·ange *n* a toxic herbicide sprayed by the US military during the Vietnam War to defoliate jungle areas and expose enemy forces [< the orange stripe on its storage drums]

a·gent pro·vo·ca·teur /a zhaaN praw vàwkə tőr/ (*plural* **a·gents pro·vo·ca·teurs** /*pronunc. same*/) *n* somebody employed to gain the trust of suspects and then tempt them to do something illegal so that they can be arrested and punished [< French, "provocative agent"]

a·gent·ry /áyjəntree/ *n* an agent's office or work

Age of A·quar·i·us *n* an astrological era in which increased spirituality and harmony are said to characterize people's lives

age of con·sent *n* the age at which somebody is legally old enough to consent to marriage or sexual intercourse

Age of Rea·son *n* the period from the middle to the end of the 18th century during which there was an emphasis on rationalism in philosophy, religion, and society

age-old *adj* dating from a very long time ago and still in existence

ag·er·a·tum /àjjə ráytəm/ (*plural same* or **-tums**) *n* a low-growing garden plant. Flowers: blue, white, or purplish, in thick clusters. Genus: *Ageratum*. [Mid-16C. < modern Latin < Greek *agēratos* "ageless, everlasting" < *gēras* "old age"]

age-re·lat·ed *adj* relating to or typical of the age that somebody has reached ○ *a normal age-related risk*

Ag·ga·dah *n* JUDAISM same as **Haggadah**

ag·gie[1] /ággee/ *n* LEISURE same as **agate** (sense 2) (*informal*)

ag·gie[2] /ággee/ *n* (*informal*) **1.** a student at an agricultural school, college, or university **2.** an agricultural school, college, or university

ag·gior·na·men·to /ə jàwrnə méntō/ *n* the process of modernizing the ritual and policy of the Roman Catholic Church [Mid-20C. < Italian < *aggiornare* "bring up to date"]

ag·glom·er·ate *vti* /ə glómmə ràyt/ (**-at·ed, -at·ing, -ates**) **COLLECT IN ROUND MASS** to gather something or form into a rounded mass ■ *n* /ə glómmərət/ **1. JUMBLED COLLECTION** a jumbled mass or collection of something (*formal*) **2.** GEOL **VOLCANIC ROCK** rock produced by a volcanic eruption, consisting of fragments of different rock types, sizes, and shapes set in fine-grained solidified volcanic ash ■ *adj* /ə glómmərət/ **IN ROUND MASS** gathered into or forming a rounded mass [Mid-17C. < Latin *agglomerat-*, past participle of *agglomerare* "heap up" < *glomer-* "ball"] —**ag·glom·er·a·tion** /ə glòmmə ráysh'n/ *n* —**ag·glom·er·a·tive** /ə glómmə ràytiv, -rətiv/ *adj* —**ag·glom·er·a·tor** *n*

ag·glu·ti·nate /ə gloot'n àyt/ (**-nat·ed, -nat·ing, -nates**) *vti* **1. ADHERE OR CAUSE TO ADHERE** to be joined or glued together, or cause things to do this **2. CLUMP OR CAUSE CELLS TO CLUMP** to cause cells such as red blood cells or bacteria to form clumps, or gather together in clumps **3.** LING **FORM COMPOUND WORD** to combine simple words without changing their form to make a new word, or be combined in a new word in this way [Mid-16C. < Latin *agglutinat-*, past participle of *agglutinare* "fasten with glue" < *gluten* "glue"] —**ag·glu·tin·a·bil·i·ty** /ə gloot'nə bíllətee/ *n* —**ag·glu·tin·a·ble** *adj* —**ag·glu·ti·nant** *n, adj* —**ag·glu·ti·na·tion** /ə gloot'n áysh'n/ *n*

ag·glu·ti·na·tive /ə gloot'n àytiv, ə gloot'nətiv/ *adj* **1.** able or likely to agglutinate **2.** LING forming new words by combining simple words without changing their form ○ *an agglutinative language*

ag·glu·ti·nin /ə gloot'nin/ *n* a substance that causes cells to clump together, e.g., an antibody or lectin

ag·glu·tin·o·gen /àggloo tínnəjən, ə gloot'nəjən/ *n* an antigen responsible for the formation of an agglutinin

ag·grade /ə gráyd/ (**-grad·ed, -grad·ing, -grades**) *vt* to build up a land surface or streambed through the natural deposition of material [Early 20C. Back-formation < *aggradation* < AG- + DEGRADATION] —**ag·gra·da·tion** /àggrə dáysh'n/ *n* —**ag·gra·da·tion·al** *adj*

~~aggragate~~ incorrect spelling of **aggregate**

ag·gran·dize /ə grán dīz, ággrən-/ (**-dized, -diz·ing, -diz·es**) *vt* **1. ENLARGE OR EXTEND SOMETHING** to increase the size or scope of something **2. IMPROVE STATUS OF SOMETHING** to increase or improve the power, wealth, influence, or status of somebody or something, especially by a deliberate plan **3. EXAGGERATE GREATNESS OF SOMEBODY** to make somebody or something seem bigger or better than is actually the case, especially through exaggerated praise (*formal*) ○ *aggrandizing the value of her accomplishments* [Mid-17C. < French *agrandiss-*, stem of *agrandir* < *grandir* "increase" < Latin *grandis* "great"] —**ag·gran·dize·ment** /ə grándizmənt, -dīzmənt/ *n* —**ag·gran·diz·er** *n*

ag·gra·vate /ággrə vàyt/ (**-vat·ed, -vat·ing, -vates**) *vt* **1.** ⚠ to irritate or anger somebody, especially with a continuing or trivial annoyance (*informal*) **2.** to make something become even worse or even more severe than before [Mid-16C. Probably via Old French < Latin *aggravat-*, past participle of *aggravare* "make heavier" < *gravis* "heavy"] —**ag·gra·vat·ing** *adj* —**ag·gra·vat·ing·ly** *adv* —**ag·gra·va·tor** *n*

USAGE aggravate meaning "annoy": Many people still dislike the use of ***aggravate*** to mean "irritate," despite a history of usage dating back to the 17th century: *We were aggravated by the continuous loud noise from the street. Their bad behavior is very aggravating.* Except in informal conversation, it is usually better to use another word such as *annoy, exasperate,* or *irritate*.

ag·gra·vat·ed /ággrə vàytəd/ *adj* having features that make something a worse criminal offense ○ *aggravated assault*

ag·gra·va·tion /àggrə váysh'n/ *n* **1. IRRITATION** a feeling of irritation or anger, especially when caused by a continuing or trivial annoyance **2. SOURCE OF IRRITATION** somebody or something that causes continuing irritation or anger **3. WORSENING** the worsening of an already bad situation, or somebody or something that makes a bad situation even worse ○ *Exercising before you have fully recovered may lead to an aggravation of your condition.* **4.** *UK* **TROUBLE** annoyance or bother, often aggressive in nature (*informal*) ○ *I get a lot of aggravation from dissatisfied customers.*

ag·gre·gate *adj* /ággrəgət, -gàyt/ **1. FORMING WHOLE** collected together from different sources and considered as a whole (*formal*) **2.** GEOL **RESEMBLING ROCK** describes a mixture of minerals or rock fragments that resembles rock ○ *an aggregate structure* ■ *n* /ággrəgət, -gàyt/ **1. SUM TOTAL** a total or whole made up of different parts from often disparate sources (*formal*) ○ *The political party was an aggregate of many diverse groups.* **2.** *UK* SPORTS **TOTAL OF SCORES** the overall score gained by a team or player in a series of games in a competition **3.** CONSTR **INGREDIENTS OF CONCRETE** broken stone, gravel, and sand used in road construction and, when mixed with cement and water, for making concrete **4.** GEOL **MINERAL MIXTURE RESEMBLING ROCK** a mixture of minerals or rock fragments that resembles rock ■ *v* /ággrə gàyt/ (**-gat·ed, -gat·ing, -gates**) **1.** *vti* **UNITE** to come together, or bring different things together, into a total, mass, or whole ○ *Aggregate the different totals to get the overall cost.* **2.** *vt* MATH **ADD UP TO NUMBER** to amount or add up to a number ○ *The company's earnings aggregate $175,000.* [15C. < Latin *aggregat-*, past participle of *aggregare* "add to" < *greg-* "flock"] —**ag·gre·gate·ly** *adv* —**ag·gre·ga·tion** /àggrə gáysh'n/ *n* —**ag·gre·ga·tive** *adj* —**ag·gre·ga·tor** *n* ◇ **in the aggregate** considered or taken together as a whole

ag·gress /ə gréss/ (**-gressed, -gress·ing, -gress·es**) *vi* to attack first, or begin a war, fight, or argument (*formal*) [Late 16C. Via obsolete French *aggresser* < Latin *aggress-*, past participle of *aggredi* "approach, attack" < *gradi* "walk"]

ag·gres·sion /ə grésh'n/ *n* **1.** threatening behavior or actions **2.** hostile action, especially a physical or military attack, directed against another person or country, often without provocation [Early 17C. Directly or via French < Latin *aggression-* < *aggress-* (see AGGRESS)]

ag·gres·sive /ə gréssiv/ *adj* **1. LIKELY TO ATTACK** showing a readiness or having a tendency to attack or do harm to others **2. ATTACKING** attacking or taking action without provocation or without waiting for an enemy to make the first move **3.** ⚠ **ASSERTIVE** characterized by or exhibiting determination, energy, and initiative ○ *an aggressive investment policy* **4.** MED **SPREADING QUICKLY** describes a disease or a pathological growth such as a tumor that spreads or grows quickly **5.** EXTREME SPORTS **EMPHASIZING STUNTS** describes a type of in-line skating, skateboarding, or snowboarding that focuses on performing stunts —**ag·gres·sive·ly** *adv* —**ag·gres·sive·ness** *n*

USAGE Note that the correct spelling of ***aggressive*** and ***aggression*** is with *-gg-* and *-ss-*.

ag·gres·sive growth fund *n* a mutual stock fund that takes risks in the hope of making large long-term gains by investing in companies that are expected to grow fast

ag·gres·sor /ə gréssər/ *n* a person or country that attacks or starts a war, fight, or argument, often without being provoked [Mid-17C. < late Latin < Latin *aggress-* (see AGGRESS)]

ag·grieve /ə gre͞ev/ (**-grieved, -griev·ing, -grieves**) *vt* **1.** to cause somebody pain, trouble, or distress (*formal*) **2.** LAW to inflict an actionable injury on somebody [13C. Via Old French *agrever* "make heavier" < Latin *aggravare* (see AGGRAVATE)] —**ag·grieved** *adj*

ag·gro /ággrō/ *n UK* (*slang*) **1.** threatening behavior, especially troublemaking or fighting ○ *We don't want any aggro.* **2.** trouble or difficulty ○ *He's having a lot of aggro with that car.* [Mid-20C. Shortening of AGGRAVATION or AGGRESSION]

a·gha *n* POL another spelling of **aga**

A·gha Mo·ham·mad Khan /a̋agə mə hàmməd ka̋an/, **Shah** (1742–97) Iranian ruler who was self-proclaimed Shah (1796–97). He founded the Qajar dynasty, which reigned from 1794 until 1925.

a·ghast /ə gást/ *adj* overcome with shock and dismay [13C. < the past participle of obsolete *agast* "frighten" < Old English *gǣst* "spirit, ghost"]

AGI *abbr* FIN adjusted gross income

ag·ile /ájj'l/ *adj* **1.** able to move quickly and with suppleness, skill, and control **2.** able to think quickly and intelligently [Late 16C. Via French < Latin *agilis* "able to be moved easily, nimble, quick" < *agere* "move, do"] —**ag·ile·ly** *adv* —**ag·ile·ness** *n* —**a·gil·i·ty** /ə jíllətee/ *n*

a·gin /ə gín/ *prep regional* same as **against**

ag·ing /áyjing/, **age·ing** *n* **1.** PROCESS OF GROWING OLD the process of growing old, especially of acquiring the physical and mental characteristics of old age **2.** MATURING PROCESS the natural or chemically assisted process of bringing foods to maturity or of making materials like wood appear older ■ *adj* BECOMING OLD growing old, especially by acquiring the physical and mental characteristics of old age

ag·i·o /ájjee ō/ (*plural* **-os**) *n UK* FIN **1.** an amount charged as a premium or percentage for changing one country's currency into that of another **2.** an allowance or discount given when paying in a foreign currency to compensate for the costs of exchanging the currency [Late 17C. Via Italian < medieval Greek *allagion* "exchange" < *allagē* "change" < *allos* "other"]

ag·i·o·tage /ájjee ə tìj/ *n UK* **1.** the business of exchanging currencies between countries **2.** speculation in stocks, securities, or foreign currencies [Late 18C. < French < Italian *agio* (see AGIO)]

ag·ism *n* SOC SCI another spelling of **ageism**

ag·i·ta /ájjitə/ *n US* acid indigestion

ag·i·tate /ájji tàyt/ (**-tat·ed, -tat·ing, -tates**) *v* **1.** *vt* MAKE SOMEBODY ANXIOUS to make somebody feel anxious, nervous, or disturbed **2.** *vi* AROUSE PUBLIC INTEREST to attempt to arouse public feeling, interest, or support for or against something **3.** *vt* MOVE SOMETHING VIOLENTLY to cause something to move vigorously or violently, e.g., by shaking or blowing it ○ *Agitate the mixture until the sediment is thoroughly dispersed.* [Late 16C. < Latin *agitat-*, past participle of *agitare* "move to and fro" < *agere* "drive, move"] —**ag·i·tat·ed** *adj* —**ag·i·tat·ed·ly** *adv* —**ag·i·ta·tive** *adj*

ag·i·ta·tion /àjji táysh'n/ *n* **1.** ANXIETY nervous anxiety **2.** PUBLIC CAMPAIGNING actions intended to arouse public feeling, interest, or support for or against something **3.** SHAKING vigorous or violent shaking, stirring, or other disturbance of something, especially a liquid ○ *Observe the mixture after agitation.* —**ag·i·ta·tion·al** *adj*

ag·i·ta·to /àjji ta̋atō/ *adj, adv* in a restless, tense, or excited manner (*used as a musical direction*) [Early 19C. Via Italian < Latin *agitat-* (see AGITATE)]

ag·i·ta·tor /ájji tàytər/ *n* **1.** somebody who attempts to arouse feeling about something, especially a political cause **2.** a machine or machine part that causes vigorous movement in a liquid or other substance

ag·it·prop /ájjit pròp/ *n* **1.** political propaganda, especially when disseminated through literature, drama, music, or art **2.** artistic work or works serving as a vehicle for political propaganda [Early 20C. < Russian < *agitatsiya* "agitation" + *propaganda* "propaganda"]

A·gla·ia /ə gláy ə, ə glī ə/ *n* in Greek mythology, one of the three Graces who lived on Mount Olympus and tended the goddess Aphrodite. Aglaia was the daughter of Zeus and Euronyme.

a·gleam /ə gle͞em/ *adj* emitting or seeming to emit light (*literary*) ○ *She was laughing, her eyes agleam.*

ag·let /ágglət/ *n* **1.** a plain or ornamental metal or plastic sheath covering the end of a shoelace or ribbon **2.** a metallic ornament such as a stud, cord, or pin worn on clothing [15C. < French *aiguillette* (see AIGUILLETTE)]

a·gley /ə gláy, ə glī/ *adv, adj N England, Scotland* awry or askew ○ *"The best laid schemes o' mice and men/ Gang aft agley"* (Robert Burns, *To a mouse*; 1785) [Late 18C. < A-[1] + *gley* "squint," origin ?]

a·glim·mer /ə glímmər/ *adj* glimmering with light (*literary*)

a·glit·ter /ə glíttər/ *adj* glittering with light (*literary*)

ag·loo *n* OCEANOG another spelling of **aglu**

a·glow /ə glṓ/ *adj* radiating light, warmth, excitement, or happy emotion

ag·lu /ággloo/ (*plural* **-lus**), **ag·loo** (*plural* **-loos**) *n Can* a breathing hole that a seal has made in sea ice [Late 19C. < Inuktitut]

ag·ma /ágmə/ *n* in phonetics, the symbol (ŋ) used to represent a velar nasal consonant, as in the final sound of "long" [Mid-20C. < Greek, "fragment"]

ag·nail /ág nàyl/ *n* **1.** ANAT same as **hangnail** **2.** a painful swelling near the nail of a toe or finger [Old English *angnægl* < *ang-* "narrow, painful" + *nægl* "nail"]

ag·nate /ág nàyt/ (*formal*) *n* a relative who is descended from a man who is also the ancestor of other relatives, especially through the male line ■ *adj* **1.** ANTHROP same as **patrilineal** **2.** related or similar in any way [15C. < Latin *agnatus* "born in addition" < Old Latin *gnatus*, past participle of *gnasci* "be born"] —**ag·nat·ic** /ag náttik/ *adj* —**ag·nat·i·cal·ly** *adv* —**ag·na·tion** /ag náysh'n/ *n*

Ag·nes /ágnəss/, **St.** (*d.* 304?) Roman Christian martyr and saint. As a young woman she rejected marriage because of her devotion to Jesus Christ, and was put to death for her faith.

Ag·new /ág no͞o/, **Spiro T.** (1918–96) vice president of the United States (1969–73). He was Richard Nixon's vice president and was forced to resign as a result of charges of illegal financial dealings during his period as governor of Maryland (1966–68). Full name **Agnew, Spiro Theodore**

Ag·ni /ágnee, úgnee/ *n* in Hinduism, the god of fire [< Sanskrit, "fire, the fire god"]

ag·no·lot·ti /ànnyə lóttee, àgnə-/ *npl* small pieces of semicircular pasta stuffed with meat, cheese, or other filling and sealed at the edges [Late 20C. < Italian dialect, alteration of Italian *anellotto* "little ring"]

ag·no·men /ag nṓmən/ (*plural* **-nom·i·na** /-nómmənə/ or **-no·mens**) *n* in ancient Rome, a fourth name that was occasionally bestowed on somebody as an honor [Mid-17C. < Latin, "additional name" < *(g)nomen* "name"]

Ag·non /a̋ag nàwn/, **Shmuel Yosef** (1888–1970) Austrian-born Israeli author whose novels include *The Bridal Canopy* (1919) and *The Day Before Yesterday* (1945). Born **Czaczkes, Shmuel Yosef**

ag·no·sia /ag nṓzhə/ *n* the total or partial loss of the ability to recognize familiar people or objects, usually caused by brain damage [Early 20C. < Greek, "lack of knowledge" < *gnōsis* (see GNOSIS)]

ag·nos·tic /ag nóstik/ *n* **1.** somebody who believes that it is impossible to know whether or not God exists **2.** somebody who doubts that a question has one correct answer or that something can be completely understood ○ *I'm an agnostic concerning space aliens.* [Mid-19C. < A-[2] + GNOSTIC] —**ag·nos·tic** *adj* —**ag·nos·ti·cal·ly** *adv*

ag·nos·ti·cism /ag nóstə sìzzəm/ *n* the belief that it is impossible to know whether or not God exists

ag·nus cas·tus /ágnəss kástəss/ *n* a preparation of the dried fruit of the chaste tree. Use: in alternative medicine, to treat various disorders of the female reproductive system. [14C. < Latin *agnus* < Greek *agnos*, the tree + *castus* "chaste"]

Ag·nus Dei /a̋agno͝oss dáy ée, a̋agnəss-, àg-/ *n* **1.** LAMB AS SYMBOL OF CHRIST a lamb, usually depicted with a halo and holding a cross and banner, symbolizing Jesus Christ **2.** CHRISTIAN PRAYER a Christian prayer that begins in Latin with the words "Agnus Dei," or "Lamb of God," part of the liturgy of the Mass **3.** MUSIC MUSIC FOR AGNUS DEI PRAYER a musical setting of the Christian prayer beginning "Agnus Dei" [15C. < Latin, "Lamb of God"]

a·go /ə gṓ/ *adv, adj* before the present time ○ *He only left about five minutes ago.* [14C. < the past participle of Old English *āgān* "go away, pass by" < *gān* "go"]

USAGE ago and **since**: If ***ago*** is used, it should be followed by *that* and not ***since*** in a following clause: *It was several weeks ago that I saw them.* If ***ago*** is left out, then ***since*** is used: *It is several weeks since I saw them.*

a·gog /ə góg/ *adj* intensely interested, excited, or eager ○ *agog at the new twist to the scandal* [15C. Probably based on Old French *en gogues* "enjoying yourself," literally "in enjoyment"]

-agog *suffix* another spelling of **-agogue**

à go·go /ə gṓ gṓ/ *adj* (*dated informal*) **1.** in a whirl of activity ○ *The club was completely à gogo by nine in the evening.* **2.** as much as anybody could want ○ *caviar à gogo* [Mid-20C. < French, "joyfully" < *en gogues* (see AGOG) by repeating the *go-*]

-agogue, **-agog** *suffix* substance promoting the flow of something ○ *galactagogue* [Via French < Greek *agōgos* "a drawing off" < *agein* "lead"]

ag·o·nist /ággənist/ *n* **1.** COMPETITOR somebody involved in a struggle, contest, or competition with somebody else (*formal*) **2.** ANAT MUSCLE ACTING AGAINST ANOTHER a muscle whose action is balanced by that of another associated muscle **3.** BIOCHEM DRUG MIMICKING BODILY CHEMICAL a hormone, neurotransmitter, or drug that triggers a response by binding to specific cell receptors [Early 17C. < Greek *agōnistēs* "contestant, actor" < *agōn* "contest"]

ag·o·nis·tic /àggə nístik/, **ag·o·nis·ti·cal** /àggə nístik'l/ *adj* **1.** TRYING FOR EFFECT striving to achieve an effect but appearing contrived or exaggerated (*literary*) **2.** ARGUMENTATIVE tending to argue and eager to win an argument (*literary*) **3.** OF GREEK CONTESTS relating to the ancient Greek sports, musical, or theatrical contests **4.** ZOOL AGGRESSIVE characteristic of aggressive interaction between individuals, usually of the same species [Mid-17C. Via late Latin < Greek *agōnistikos* < *agōnistēs* (see AGONIST)] —**ag·o·nis·ti·cal·ly** *adv*

ag·o·nize /ággə nīz/ (**-nized, -niz·ing, -niz·es**) *v* **1.** *vi* SPEND TIME WORRYING to think about something intensely and anxiously, usually in great detail and for a long time, before making a decision ○ *to agonize over the answer to every question* **2.** *vti* SUFFER OR CAUSE SOMEBODY PAIN to suffer, or cause somebody to suffer, extreme pain or mental anguish **3.** *vi* STRUGGLE to make a desperate or strenuous effort (*literary*) [Late 16C. Directly or via French < late Latin *agonizare*, after Greek *agōnizesthai* "take part in a contest" < *agōn* "contest"]

ag·o·nized /ággə nīzd/ *adj* expressing or characterized by severe pain or anxiety ○ *an agonized scream* ○ *an agonized search for the missing person*

ag·o·niz·ing /ággə nīzing/ *adj* **1.** extremely painful **2.** causing much difficulty or unpleasantness ○ *an agonizing decision* —**ag·o·niz·ing·ly** *adv*

ag·o·ny /ággənee/ (*plural* **-nies**) *n* **1.** GREAT PAIN OR ANGUISH intense physical pain or mental anguish **2.** INTENSE EMOTION a consuming emotion ○ *an agony of indecision* **3.** SUFFERING PRECEDING DEATH a period of struggle or suffering immediately preceding death (*literary*) ○ *last agony* [14C. Directly or via French < Latin *agonia* < Greek *agōnia* "(mental) struggle, anguish" < *agōn* "contest"] —**ag·o·nal** *adj* ◇ **prolong the agony** to make a period of misfortune or anxiety last longer than necessary

ag·o·ny aunt *n UK* a woman who gives personal advice to readers in a regular column in a newspaper or magazine or to callers on a radio or television program

ag·o·ny col·umn *n* a newspaper column of personal advertisements, usually inquiring about missing relatives or friends (*archaic*)

ag·o·ny un·cle *n UK* a man who gives personal advice to readers in a regular column in a newspaper or magazine or to callers on a radio or television program

ag·o·ra[1] /ággərə, ə gáwrə/ (*plural* **ag·o·ras** or **a·go·rae** /-ree/) *n* in ancient Greece, an open space in a town where people gathered, especially a marketplace [Late 16C. < Greek, "marketplace, place of assembly" < *ageirein* "assemble"]

a·go·ra[2] /àagə ráa/ (*plural* **-rot** /-rṓt/) *n* a subunit of Israeli currency. See table at **currency** [Mid-20C. < Hebrew *agōrāh* "small coin"]

ag·o·rae ANCIENT HIST plural of **agora**[1]

ag·o·ra·pho·bi·a /àggərə fóbee ə/ *n* a condition characterized by an irrational fear of public or open spaces [Late 19C. < Greek *agora* "open place" (see AGORA[1])] —**ag·o·ra·pho·bic** *adj, n*

a·go·rot MONEY plural of **agora**[2]

a·gou·ti /ə gόotee/ (*plural* **-tis** or **-ties**) *n* **1.** a rabbit-sized rodent with short ears and clawed feet. Native to: tropical Central and South America. Genus: *Dasyprocta*. **2.** an irregularly striped pattern in the individual hairs of the fur of an agouti [Mid-16C. Via French or Spanish < Tupi-Guarani *akuti*]

AGP *abbr* COMPUT accelerated graphics port

Ag·ra /áagrə/, **Āg·ra** city in Uttar Pradesh state, northern India. It is famous as the site of the Taj Mahal. Population: 1,321,410 (2001).

~~**agragate**~~ incorrect spelling of **aggregate**

Ag·ra·hay·a·na /àggrəhī áanə/ *n* HINDUISM, CALENDAR same as **Margasirsa**

a·gran·u·lo·cy·to·sis /ay grànnyəlō sī tṓssiss/ *n* a sometimes fatal acute illness characterized by a decrease in granular white blood cells and by lesions of the throat, gastrointestinal tract, and skin. The condition often occurs as a toxic effect of specific drugs. [Early 20C. < A-[2] + GRANULOCYTE]

ag·ra·pha /ággrəfə/ *npl* sayings of Jesus Christ not recorded in the Bible but found in other early Christian writings [Late 19C. < Greek, plural of *agraphon* "unwritten"]

a·graph·i·a /ə gráffee ə, ay-/ *n* loss of the ability to write, resulting from neurological damage such as a brain lesion [Mid-19C. < A[3] + Greek *graphia* "writing"] —**a·graph·ic** *adj*

a·grar·i·an /ə grérree ən/ *adj* **1. PRO-FARMER** promoting the interests of farmers, especially by seeking a more equitable basis of land ownership ○ *an agrarian political party* **2. OF RURAL LIFE** dominated by or relating to farming or rural life **3. OF LAND** relating to land, especially its ownership and cultivation ■ *n* **LAND REFORMER** somebody, often a member of an agrarian political movement, who believes in the fair distribution of land, especially the redistribution of large amounts of land owned by the rich [Early 17C. < Latin *agrarius* < *agr-* "field, land"] —**a·grar·i·an·ism** *n*

a·grar·i·an·ism /ə grérree ə nìzzəm/ *n* a political movement or philosophy that promotes the interests of the farmer, especially the redistribution of land owned by the rich or government

a·gree /ə grée/ (**a·greed, a·gree·ing, a·grees**) *v* **1.** *vi* **BE IN ACCORD** to have the same opinion about something as somebody else ○ *Scientists don't agree about what causes these reactions.* **2.** *vi* **CONSENT** to consent to or approve a course of action ○ *They agreed on a postponement.* **3.** *vti* **ADMIT AS TRUE** to admit that something is true ○ *I had to agree that the room looked better with a coat of paint.* **4.** *vti* **DECIDE** to come to an understanding or reach a settlement regarding something ○ *Do you think we can agree on a plan?* **5.** *vi* **BE CONSISTENT** to be consistent with something in content, meaning, or characteristics ○ *The witnesses' stories agree in most details with the accused's.* **6.** *vi* **BE SUITABLE** to suit or be good for somebody ○ *The climate doesn't agree with me.* **7.** *vi* GRAM **MATCH EACH OTHER GRAMMATICALLY** to have the same grammatical number, case, person, or gender, especially in the same sentence [14C. < French *agréer* "please" < Latin *ad* "to" + *gratus* "pleasing"] ◇ **agree to disagree** to stop arguing and accept that the opposing viewpoints are irreconcilable

SYNONYMS ***agree, concur, acquiesce, consent, assent***

CORE MEANING: to accept an idea, plan, or course of action that has been put forward

agree to have the same opinion as somebody else ○ *We agreed on an appointment at nine o'clock the next morning.* ○ *They have agreed in principle to lease the land.* **concur** to have the same opinion as somebody else, or reach agreement independently on a specific point ○ *I'd like to concur with my colleague's comment.* ○ *Do both sides in the negotiations concur that a settlement needs to be achieved very soon?* **acquiesce** to agree or comply with something in a passive or reserved way ○ *Peter refused at first, but later acquiesced.* ○ *The ministers acquiesced in a decision to seek funding for the project.* **consent** to give formal permission for something to happen ○ *consented to the marriage* **assent** to accept something formally ○ *a nation in which everyone assented to a common identity*

a·gree·a·ble /ə grée əb'l/ *adj* **1. PLEASING** pleasing to the senses or to somebody's taste ○ *The climate here is very agreeable.* **2. FRIENDLY** pleasant, friendly, and ready to please others ○ *an agreeable companion* **3. WILLING TO COMPLY** willing to consent to or consider something ○ *If the committee is agreeable, you can start work straight away.* **4. SATISFACTORY** good enough or suitable for somebody (*formal*) ○ *Let us make an arrangement agreeable to both sides.* —**a·gree·a·bil·i·ty** /ə grèe ə bíllətee/ *n* —**a·gree·a·ble·ness** *n* —**a·gree·a·bly** *adv*

a·greed /ə gréed/ *adj* **1. DETERMINED BY CONSENSUS** previously decided and assented to by two or more people ○ *the agreed procedure* **2. SHARING OPINION** sharing the same view as somebody else or others ○ *Are we all agreed on the proposal?* ■ *interj* **YES** used to confirm agreement with somebody else

a·gree·ment /ə gréemənt/ *n* **1. FORMAL CONTRACT** a contract or arrangement, either written or verbal and sometimes enforceable by law **2. SITUATION OR ACT OF CONSENT** the state of having come to the same opinion or having made the same decision as somebody else, or an expression of this state ○ *There is general agreement about the need for better transport.* ○ *Do we have your agreement on this issue?* **3. CONSENSUS OF OPINION** a situation in which everyone accepts the same terms or has the same opinion ○ *everyone is in agreement* **4.** GRAM **GRAMMATICAL CORRESPONDENCE** correspondence of the number, case, gender, or person of one word with that of another word, especially in the same sentence

~~**agression**~~ incorrect spelling of **aggression**

~~**agressive**~~ incorrect spelling of **aggressive**

~~**agressor**~~ incorrect spelling of **aggressor**

agri- *prefix* same as **agro-**

ag·ri·busi·ness /àggri bìznəss/ *n* the operations and businesses that are associated with large-scale farming

ag·ri·chem·i·cal *n* AGRIC same as **agrochemical**

A·gric·o·la /ə gríkələ/, **Gnaeus Julius** (40–93) Roman colonial administrator and governor of Britain (78–84). He encouraged Romanization, and was recalled to Rome and retirement in 85.

ag·ri·cul·tur·al /àggri kúlchərəl/ *adj* **1.** involving or relating to agriculture ○ *agricultural equipment* ○ *agricultural college* **2.** with farming as the dominant way of life ○ *one of the earliest agricultural communities* —**a·gri·cul·tur·al·ist** *n* —**ag·ri·cul·tur·al·ly** *adv*

ag·ri·cul·ture /ággri kùlchər/ *n* the occupation, business, or science of cultivating the land, producing crops, and raising livestock [15C. Directly or via French < Latin *agricultura* < *agri* "of the land" (< *agr-* "field, land") + *cultura* "cultivation"] —**ag·ri·cul·tur·ist** /àggri kúlchərist/ *n*

Ag·ri·cul·ture and Agri-Food Can·a·da *n* a department of the Canadian federal government that conducts research and develops policies and programs to ensure the security of the country's food system

ag·ri·food /ággri-/ *adj* describes industries involved in the mass production, processing, and inspection of food products made from agricultural commodities

ag·ri·mo·ny /ággrə mōnee/ (*plural same* or **-nies**) *n* **1.** a perennial plant with compound leaves and spiny fruits. Flowers: small, yellow, in spikes. Genus: *Agrimonia*. **2.** PLANTS same as **hemp agrimony** [Pre-12C. Via Old French < Latin *agrimonia*, misreading of *argemonia* < Greek *argemōnē* "poppy"]

A·grip·pa /ə gríppə/, **Marcus Vipsanius** (63–12 B.C.) Roman general and a principal aide of the Emperor Augustus. He won the naval battle of Actium (31 B.C.).

Ag·rip·pi·na (the Elder) /àggrə pínə, -péenə/ (13? B.C.–A.D. 33) Roman noblewoman. The daughter of Agrippa and the granddaughter of Augustus, she married the general Germanicus, by whom she became the mother of Caligula and Agrippina the Younger. Renowned for her virtue and heroism, she starved herself to death after being banished by Tiberius.

Ag·rip·pi·na (the Younger) (A.D. 15–59) Roman noblewoman. The daughter of Agrippina the Elder and Germanicus, she was the mother of Nero. She ensured Nero's accession to the throne by poisoning her third husband, the emperor Claudius, and ruled the empire through her son until she was murdered at his order.

ag·ri·ter·ror·ism /àggri térrə rìzzəm/, **ag·ro·ter·ror·ism** /àggrō-/ *n* terrorism against a nation that involves the poisoning of agricultural livestock, meats, grains, and vegetables

agro-, **agri-** *prefix* **1.** soil ○ *agronomy* **2.** agriculture ○ *agroindustrial* [< Latin *agri* (form of *ager*) and Greek *agros* "field" < Indo-European]

ag·ro·bi·ol·o·gy /àggrō bī óllәjee/ *n* the branch of biology concerned with agricultural production, especially crop growth —**ag·ro·bi·o·log·i·cal** /àggrō bī ə lójjik'l/ *adj* —**ag·ro·bi·o·log·i·cal·ly** *adv* —**ag·ro·bi·ol·o·gist** *n*

ag·ro·chem·i·cal /àggrō kémmik'l/, **ag·ri·chem·i·cal** /àggri-/ *n* **1.** a chemical used in farming, e.g., a fertilizer or pesticide **2.** a chemical that is extracted or derived from an agricultural product

ag·ro·for·est·ry /àggrō fáwrəstree/ *n* **1.** the method or practice of integrating the raising of trees into farming to provide fuel, fruits, forage, shelter for animals or crops, and other benefits **2.** forestry conducted purely to produce timber, without any regard for sporting or recreational pursuits

ag·ro·in·dus·tri·al /àggrō in dústree əl/ *adj* **1.** relating to the production or provision of materials needed by both agriculture and industry, e.g., water **2.** used in, produced by, or involved in the industrial processing of agricultural products

ag·ro·in·dus·try /àggrō ìndəstree/ *n* **1.** AGRIC same as **agribusiness** **2.** the operations and businesses that are associated with the industrial processing of agricultural products

ag·ro·nom·ic /àggrə nómmik/, **ag·ro·nom·i·cal** /-nómmik'l/ *adj* **1.** relating to the scientific study of soil management, land cultivation, and crop production **2.** describes plant characteristics that are important during growth and development of a crop, e.g., height and stem strength

ag·ro·nom·ics /àggrə nómmiks/ *n* the branch of economics that is concerned with the use and productivity of land (*takes a singular verb*) [Mid-19C. < AGRO- + ECONOMICS]

a·gron·o·my /ə grónnəmee/ *n* the science of soil management, land cultivation, and crop production [Early 19C. < French *agronomie* < Greek *agronomos* "overseer of land" < *agros* "land" + *-nomos* "dispensing, administering"] —**a·gron·o·mist** *n*

a·ground /ə grównd/ *adj, adv* onto or on ground, especially a shore, a reef, rocks, or the bottom of shallow water

a·gua fres·ca /áagwaa fréskə/ (*plural same*) *n Hispanic* a cold drink that is a mixture of fruit juice, water, and sugar [< Spanish, literally "cool water"]

a·guar·di·en·te /àa gwaardee éntee, àa gwaard yén tày/ *n Hispanic* rough brandy distilled in Spain, Portugal, or Latin America, sometimes flavored with anise [Early 19C. < Spanish < *agua* "water" + *ardiente* "fiery"]

A·guas·ca·lien·tes /àa gwaass kaal yéntess/ **1.** state in central Mexico on the Anahuac Plateau. The resort city of Aguascalientes is its capital. Population: 944,285 (2000). Area: 2,007 sq. mi./5,197 sq. km. **2.** capital city of Aguascalientes State and a popular health resort in central Mexico. Population: 643,360 (2000).

a·gue /áy gyoo/ *n* **1.** a feverish condition involving alternating hot, cold, and sweating stages, especially as a symptom of malaria **2.** a fever or shivering fit (*archaic*) [14C. Via French < medieval Latin *acuta*, short for *febris acuta* "sharp fever"] —**a·gu·ish** *adj* —**a·gu·ish·ly** *adv* —**a·gu·ish·ness** *n*

A·gui·nal·do /àa gee náaldō/, **Emilio** (1869–1964) Filipino nationalist resistance leader. He led the fight for independence from Spain (1896–98) and fought against US occupation (1899–1901). Nominated president of the new republic (1898) and head of the provisional government (1899), he was captured and swore allegiance to the United States in 1901.

ah /aa/, **aah** *interj also* **aah** *or* **ahh** **1.** EXPRESSING EMOTION used to express emotions ranging from blissful contentment to acute discomfort to disgust, depending on the speaker's tone of voice ○ *Ah, Mom, do I have to?* **2.** EXPRESSING RECOGNITION used to express surprise or recognition and understanding ○ *Ah, I see.* ■ *vi* (**ahed, ah·ing, ahs; aahed, aah·ing, aahs**) SAY "AH" to say "ah" ■ *n* UTTERANCE OF "AH" an exclamation of "ah" expressing any of various emotions [13C. < Old French *a(h)*, natural exclamation]

AH, **A.H.** *adv* CALENDAR used to indicate a date that is a particular number of years after the Hegira (A.D. 622), a key date in the Islamic calendar. Full form **anno Hegirae**

A.h. *abbr* MEASURE ampere-hour

a·ha /aa háa/ *interj* used when discovering something, especially to express triumphant satisfaction or excitement ○ *Aha, I caught you in the act!* [14C. < AH + HA[1]]

AHA *abbr* CHEM alpha-hydroxy acid

A·hab /áy hàb/ (*fl* 9th century B.C.) king of Israel. He ruled Israel from 869 B.C. to 850 B.C.

a·head /ə héd/ *adv, adj* **1.** IN FRONT in front of somebody or something ○ *They are in the white car just ahead.* **2.** FORWARD onward or in a forward direction ○ *Keep walking straight ahead and it'll be on your left.* **3.** TO FUTURE in or into the future ○ *We expect more news in the weeks ahead.* **4.** EARLIER before or in advance of something or somebody ○ *You need to learn to plan ahead!* **5.** BETTER in or into a more advanced or desirable state ○ *Our company is definitely ahead compared to competition.* **6.** IN FIRST PLACE in a winning position in a contest or competition ○ *They were ahead by 6 points.* ◇ **ahead of 1.** in front of **2.** at an earlier time than **3.** in a more advanced or advantageous position than ◇ **get ahead** to succeed, do well, or advance financially (*informal*)

a·hem /ə hém/ *interj* used in writing to indicate the sound of a quiet cough made to attract attention, express disapproval or doubt, or gain time [Mid-18C. An imitation of the sound]

A·hern /ə húrn/, **Bertie** (*b.* 1951) Irish politician who became leader of the Fianna Fáil political party in 1994 and was elected Irish prime minister in 1997

> "It is an observable phenomenon in Northern Ireland—and elsewhere—that tension and violence tend to rise when compromise is in the air."
> [Attributed to Bertie Ahern]

ahh *interj US* another spelling of **ah**

a·him·sa /ə hím saa/ *n* the Hindu, Buddhist, and Jain philosophy of revering all life and refraining from harm to any living thing [Late 19C. < Sanskrit < *a-* "without" + *hiṁsā* "injury"]

a·his·tor·i·cal /ày hi stáwrik'l/, **a·his·tor·ic** /-stáwrik/ *adj* not concerned with or not taking into account history or historical development, especially when examining a phenomenon that changes over time

AHL *abbr* American Hockey League

a·hold /ə hṓld/ *n US* a firm grasp on something, usually with the hand (*informal*) ◇ **get ahold of** (*informal*) **1.** get somebody or something or reach somebody by phone or similar means **2.** *US* to regain emotional control after a shock or state of distress, fear, anxiety, or excitement

a·ho·le·ho·le /ə hōlee hōlee/ (*plural same or* **-les**) *n* a silvery tropical fish with spiny fins that is caught for food in the Pacific and Indian oceans. Family: Kuhlidae. [< Hawaiian]

-aholic *suffix* dependent on or with an extreme fondness for ○ *workaholic* [< ALCOHOLIC]

A-ho·ri·zon *n* the uppermost layer of soil containing humus, topsoil, and organic debris

a·hoy /ə hóy/ *interj* **1.** used by sailors to greet another ship or person or to attract attention ○ *Ahoy there!* **2.** used by sailors to announce that something, usually another ship or land, is in sight ○ *Land ahoy!* [Mid-18C. Probably blend of AHA + *hoy* < Middle Dutch *hoei* "barge, ship"]

Ah·ri·man /áarimən/ *n* the spirit of evil in Zoroastrianism, and the opponent of Ahura Mazda [Via Persian < Avestan *angrō mainiiuš* "evil spirit"]

A·hu·ra Maz·da /ə hoorə mázdə/ *n* the creator god in Zoroastrianism, and the opponent of Ahriman [< Avestan *ahurō mazdå* "wise lord"]

ah we, **ah·wee** *pron Carib* another spelling of **awe**[2]

ai *abbr* Anguilla (*used in Internet addresses*) See table at **domain name**

AI *abbr* **1.** artificial insemination **2.** COMPUT artificial intelligence

AIB *abbr US* American Institute of Banking

aid /ayd/ *vti* (**aid·ed, aid·ing, aids**) GIVE HELP TO SOMEBODY to provide somebody or something with help or with what is needed to achieve something ○ *Better sewage systems aid in the fight against cholera.* ■ *n* **1.** MONEY OR SUPPLIES financial or material assistance, e.g., that provided by a government or international organization, especially in times of crisis **2.** ASSISTANCE anything done or provided that assists somebody or something ○ *I wouldn't have made it without the aid of my friends.* **3.** SOMEBODY OR SOMETHING HELPFUL a person, device, resource, or material that helps or assists with something ○ *visual aids such as maps* ○ *This book is an aid to using the Internet for research.* **4.** ASSISTANT an assistant or aide **5.** *US* MIL same as **aide-de-camp** **6.** HIST PAYMENT TO LORD a monetary payment by a vassal to an English feudal lord **7.** HIST SUBSIDY FOR ENGLISH KING a special subsidy formerly granted to the English king by parliament. Aids for extraordinary expenses were granted from the time of the Norman Conquest into the 18th century. [15C. Via French < Latin *adjutare* "to help"] ◇ **aid and abet** to assist somebody in commission of a crime

AID *abbr* **1.** MED acute infectious disease **2.** INTERNAT REL Agency for International Development **3.** MED artificial insemination by donor (*dated*)

aid a·gen·cy *n* a usually charitable organization that gives money, food, or other material assistance to a country or area at a time of crisis

aide /ayd/ *n* **1.** an assistant to somebody in public office or to somebody providing a professional service, who may also offer advice ○ *a congressional aide* **2.** MIL same as **aide-de-camp** [Late 18C. Shortening of AIDE-DE-CAMP]

SYNONYMS See ***assistant***.

aide-de-camp /àyd də kámp/ (*plural* **aides-de-camp** /àydz-/) *n* a military officer acting as a confidential assistant to a general or senior officer [Late 17C. < French, "camp assistant"]

aide-mé·moire /àyd mem waar/ (*plural* **aide-mé·moires** /*pronunc. same*/ *or* **aides-mé·moire** /*pronunc. same*/) *n* (*formal*) **1.** a brief written summary or outline of the items on an agenda for a meeting or on which agreement was reached in a meeting **2.** something, e.g., a mnemonic device, book, or document, that is an aid to remembering something else [Mid-19C. < French, "help-memory"]

AIDS /aydz/ *n* a disease of the immune system caused by infection with the retrovirus HIV, which destroys some types of white blood cells and is transmitted through blood or bodily secretions such as semen. Patients lose the ability to fight infections, often dying from secondary causes such as pneumonia or kaposi's sarcoma. [Late 20C. Acronym < *Acquired Immune Deficiency Syndrome*]

AIDS de·men·tia *n* a dementia caused by HIV infection of the brain and characterized by neurologic and psychiatric symptoms, e.g., severe cognitive impairment and degeneration of motor nerves and the spinal cord

AIDS-re·lat·ed com·plex *n* the set of symptoms associated with infection by HIV, including weight loss and fever

aid sta·tion *n US* a military medical installation for troops in the field

aid work·er *n* somebody who works for an aid agency either as an employee or volunteer

ai·grette /ay grét, áy gret/, **ai·gret** *n* **1.** a tuft of long upright plumes, especially the tail feathers of an egret, worn on the head or on a hat for decoration **2.** a piece of jewelry that resembles a plume of feathers, usually worn on the head or on a hat [Mid-17C. < French, "egret, heron"]

aiguille: Teton Mountains, Jackson Hole, Wyoming

ai·guille /ay gweel/ *n* a mountain peak or large rock that is tall and sharply pointed [Early 19C. < French, "needle"]

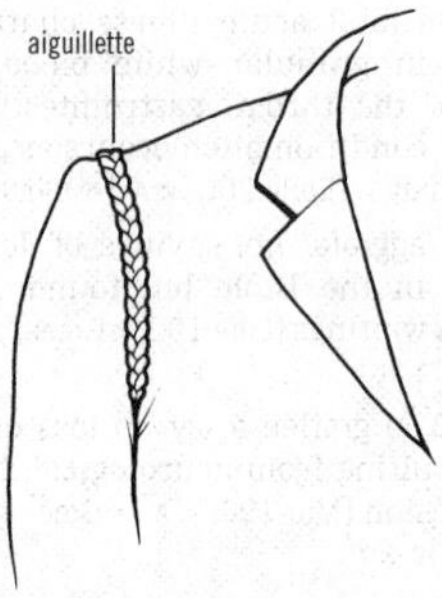

aiguillette

ai·guil·lette /àygwi lét/ *n* a decorative cord with hanging points worn on the shoulder of some military uniforms [Mid-16C. < French, "little needle" < *aiguille* "needle"]

AIH *abbr* MED artificial insemination by husband

Ai·ken /áykən/ city in west central South Carolina. It was the site of a Civil War battle in 1865. Population: 26,047 (2002 estimate).

Ai·ken, Conrad (1889–1973) US writer, poet, and critic. He won the Pulitzer Prize (1930) for *Selected Poems* (1929). Full name **Aiken, Conrad Potter**

> "All lovely things will have an ending / All lovely things will fade and die / And youth that's now so bravely spending, / Will beg a penny by and by."
> [Conrad Aiken, "All Lovely Things"; 1916]

ai·ki·do /ī kee dō, ī kée-/ *n* a martial art originating in Japan that is similar to judo but incorporates blows made with the hands and feet [Mid-20C. < Japanese *aikidō* < *ai* "mutual" + *ki* "spirit" (< Middle Chinese *khi*) + *dō* "art" (< Middle Chinese *daw*)]

ail /ayl/ (**ailed, ail·ing, ails**) *vt* to cause pain or discomfort to somebody or something (*archaic or literary*) ○ *"Oh what can ail thee, knight at arms/Alone and palely loitering"* (John Keats, *La Belle Dame Sans Merci*; 1820) [Old English *eglian* < Indo-European, "be afraid or distressed"]

SPELLCHECK Do not confuse the spelling of ***ail*** and ***ale*** ("beer"), which sound similar.

ai·lan·thus /ay lánthəss/ *n* a tree or bush with long feathery leaves, winged fruit, and dense flower clusters. Native to: Asia. Genus: *Ailanthus*. [Early 19C. Via modern Latin < Ambonese *ai lanto* "tree of heaven," influenced by plant names ending in *-anthus*]

ai·le·ron /áylə ròn/ *n* a hinged flap on the trailing edge of an aircraft wing, used to control banking movements [Early 20C. < French, "small wing" < *aile* "wing" < Latin *ala*]

Ai·ley /áylee/, **Alvin** (1931–89) US dancer and choreographer. He founded the Alvin Ailey American Dance Theater (1958). His works, known for their fusion of ballet, jazz, modern dance, and African American dance influences, include *Revelations* (1960).

ail·ing /áyling/ *adj* **1.** performing below an expected standard ○ *the nation's ailing steel industry* **2.** affected or weakened by an illness

ail·ment /áylmənt/ *n* a mild illness or injury, especially a persistent one

ai·lu·ro·phile /ī lŏŏrə fìl, ay-/ *n* somebody who loves cats [Mid-20C. < Greek *ailuros* "cat"]

ai·lu·ro·phobe /ī lŏŏrə fòb, ay-/ *n* somebody who hates or fears cats [Early 20C. < Greek *ailuros* "cat"] —**ai·lu·ro·pho·bi·a** /ī lŏŏrə fóbee ə, ay-/ *n*

aim /aym/ *v* (**aimed, aim·ing, aims**) **1.** *vti* POINT OBJECT to point a weapon or object or direct a blow at somebody or something **2.** *vi* PLAN TO DO SOMETHING to intend or plan to do something **3.** *vt* DIRECT MESSAGE to target words, a message, an action, or a product at a person or group ■ *n* **1.** INTENTION a plan to do or achieve something **2.** ACT OF AIMING an act or manner of aiming ○ *Take aim and fire.* **3.** SKILL IN AIMING skill at hitting a target ○ *Her aim was perfect.* **4.** DEGREE OF ACCURACY the level of accuracy of a weapon ○ *A rifle has more precise aim than a shotgun.* [14C. < Old French *esmer* "estimate," *aesmer* "aim at" < Latin *aestimare* (see ESTIMATE)] —**aim·er** *n*

AIM *abbr* American Indian Movement

aim·less /áymləss/ *adj* without purpose or direction —**aim·less·ly** *adv* —**aim·less·ness** *n*

ain't /aynt/ *contr* ⚠ a contraction of "am not," "is not," "are not," "have not," or "has not" (*nonstandard*)

USAGE ***Ain't*** is one of the most informal verb contractions in English, and its use in formal contexts may be criticized because it is associated with careless speech. It is, however, accepted in folk and popular song lyrics, show titles, direct quotations, and fictional dialogue. Otherwise ***ain't*** is best avoided, except as a deliberate rhetorical device and in allusive expressions such as *You ain't seen nothing yet.*

Ai·nu /ī nŏŏ/ (*plural same* or **-nus**) *n* **1.** a member of a Japanese people who now live in the north of the Japanese island of Hokkaido, and on the Kurile Islands and the island of Sakhalin **2.** a language spoken by the Ainu on Hokkaido that is considered to be unrelated to any other language [Early 19C. < Ainu, "person"] —**Ai·nu** *adj*

ai·o·li /ī ólee/ *n* mayonnaise flavored with garlic, used especially to garnish fish and vegetables [Early 20C. Via French < Provençal < *ai* "garlic" + *oli* "oil"]

air /er/ *n* **1.** GASES FORMING ATMOSPHERE the mixture of gases, mainly nitrogen and oxygen, that forms the Earth's atmosphere **2.** ATMOSPHERE IN OPEN SPACE the atmosphere of an open space as opposed to that of an enclosed space ○ *I need to get some air.* ○ *in the open air* **3.** ATMOSPHERE WE BREATHE the atmosphere in a place or enclosed space ○ *The air in here is too stuffy.* **4.** SKY the sky or the empty space above the Earth ○ *It flew through the air and landed at our feet.* **5.** TRAVEL IN AIRCRAFT travel in or transportation by aircraft (*often used before a noun*) ○ *sending the package by air* ○ *an air terminal* **6.** SOMEBODY'S DISTINCTIVE QUALITY a distinctive quality in somebody's appearance or manner ○ *her air of superiority* ○ *an air of sadness about him* **7.** MUSIC MELODY a melody or tune, especially a light or cheerful one **8.** same as **air conditioning** **9.** LIGHT WIND a very light wind **10.** AERIAL SKATING OR BOARDING TRICK in skateboarding, in-line skating, and snowboarding, a trick performed with the whole board off the ground ■ **airs** *npl US* AFFECTATION affected manners or conduct meant to impress others ○ *He's always putting on airs.* ■ *adj* OF ZODIAC SIGNS relating to the Aquarius, Gemini, or Libra signs of the zodiac ■ *v* (**aired, air·ing, airs**) **1.** *vti* BROADCAST OR BE BROADCAST to broadcast something or be broadcast on radio or television ○ *will be aired in the spring* **2.** *vt* MAKE SOMETHING KNOWN to express something such as an opinion or complaint ○ *air your views* **3.** *vti* EXPOSE TO AIR to be exposed to the air, or expose something to the air in order to dry it, cool it, or ventilate it [13C. Partly via Old French and Latin < Greek *aēr* "air, atmosphere," partly via French, "nature, place of origin" < Latin *ager* "field," *area* "open space"] ◇ **clear the air** to remove the tension, uncertainty, or misunderstanding from a situation ◇ **give air to something** to express something verbally ◇ **in the air** happening or about to happen ○ *The rumor is that a merger is in the air.* ◇ **off (the) air** not being broadcast on radio or television, e.g., because a person or program has stopped or finished broadcasting ◇ **on (the) air** being broadcast on radio or television ◇ **punch the air** to thrust your arm upward or outward with your fist clenched as a gesture of triumph ◇ **take the air** to go for a walk (*formal*) ◇ **up in the air** undecided or uncertain ◇ **vanish into thin air** to disappear completely ◇ **walk on air** to be extremely happy

SPELLCHECK **air, ere, err,** and **heir.** Do not confuse the spelling of ***air, ere, err,*** and ***heir,*** which sound similar. ***Air*** is the most common of the four words, as in *the air that we breathe, an air of superiority, to air an opinion.* ***Ere*** is a literary word meaning "before" (as in *ere long*), ***err*** is a verb meaning "make a mistake" (as in *to err is human, err on the side of caution*), and ***heir*** is a noun meaning "legal inheritor" (as in *the heir to the throne*).

air bag *n* **1.** a safety device in an automobile consisting of a bag that automatically inflates on impact to protect the occupant of the seat **2.** a strong inflatable bag used to bring sunken items to the surface or by rescue workers to lift heavy machinery or debris under which somebody is trapped

air ball *n* a shot in basketball that misses not only the net but the rim and backboard (*informal*)

air base *n* a place from which military aircraft operate

air bed *n* an inflatable mattress, especially a plastic or rubber one used by sunbathers

air blad·der *n* **1.** an air-filled sac above the alimentary canal in most fishes that regulates buoyancy and, in some, aids in respiration **2.** an air-filled sac that aids buoyancy in some types of seaweed

air·boat /ér bòt/ *n* same as **swamp boat** [Because it is driven with a propellor and steered with a rudder like an airplane's]

air·borne /ér bàwrn/ *adj* **1.** CARRIED BY AIR carried along by movements of air ○ *airborne infections* **2.** BY AIRCRAFT carried out or transported by aircraft ○ *airborne troops* **3.** IN FLIGHT in flight or in the air ○ *A meal will be served once we are airborne.*

air brake *n* **1.** a brake operated by compressed air, especially in a heavy motor vehicle **2.** a flap or small parachute on an aircraft operated to increase drag and thus slow the aircraft

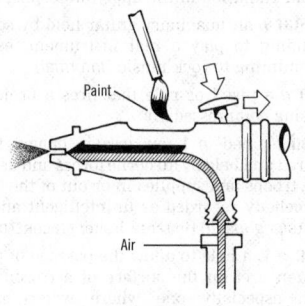

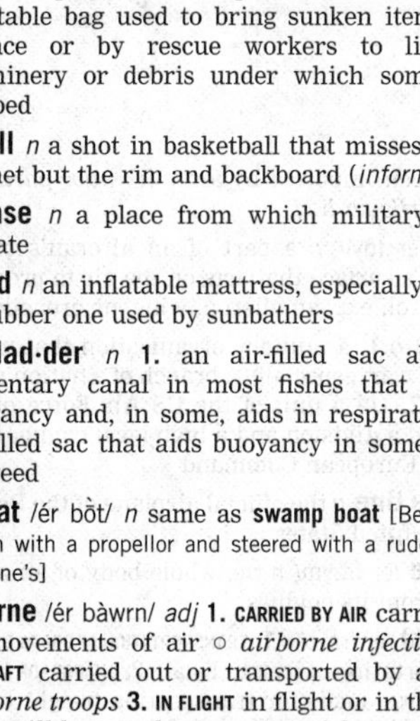

airbrush

air·brush /ér brùsh/ *n* a device for spraying paint using compressed air ■ *vt* (**-brushed, -brush·ing, -brush·es**) to paint something or alter or improve a picture using an airbrush ○ *The blemish had been airbrushed out.*

air·burst /ér bùrst/ *n* an explosion of a bomb, shell, or missile in the air

Air·bus /ér bùss/ *tdmk* a trademark for a large passenger jet aircraft manufactured by aerospace companies from different European countries working as a consortium

air cham·ber *n* **1.** an enclosed space with air in it **2.** a chamber in a hydraulic system in which air expands and compresses to control the flow of a fluid

air-con·di·tion (**air-con·di·tioned, air-con·di·tion·ing, air-con·di·tions**) *vt* to cool and control the humidity and purity of the air circulating in a space with an air conditioner —**air con·di·tioned** *adj*

air con·di·tion·er *n* a device for cooling and controlling the humidity and purity of the air circulating in a space

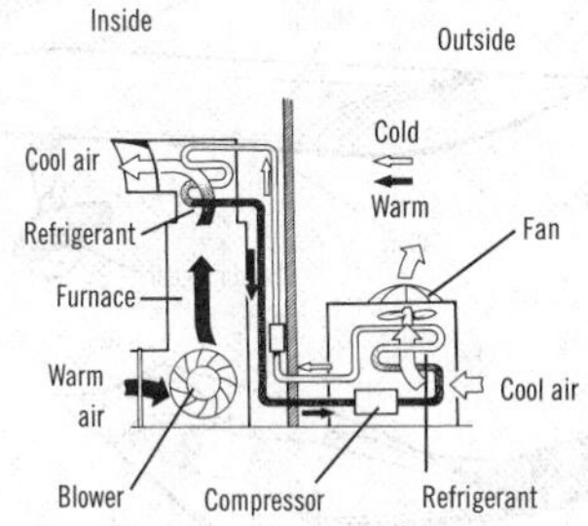

air conditioning

air con·di·tion·ing *n* a system for cooling and controlling the humidity and purity of the air circulating in a space

air-cool (**air-cooled, air-cool·ing, air-cools**) *vt* to cool something, especially an engine, by a flow of air rather than a water system —**air-cooled** *adj*

air cool·er *n* a device, e.g., a portable air-conditioning unit, for cooling the air inside a building, room, or vehicle

Air Corps *n* the airborne division of the US Army that later became the US Air Force

air cor·ri·dor *n* a defined route that aircraft should take through airspace in which flying is restricted

air cov·er *n* the provision of an airborne defense for ground forces against an enemy air attack, or the aircraft providing the defense

air·craft /ér kràft/ (*plural same*) *n* any vehicle capable of flight. See illustration on next page

air·craft car·ri·er *n* a warship with a long flat deck designed to allow aircraft to take off and land on it

air·crew /ér krŏŏ/ *n* the pilot, navigator, and other crew members of an aircraft

air cur·tain *n* a stream of air directed across a doorway, especially to prevent drafts

air cush·ion *n* **1.** the pocket of air that is forced down to support a hovercraft **2.** a type of suspension that uses enclosed air to absorb shocks —**air-cush·ioned** *adj*

air cush·ion ve·hi·cle *n US* VEHICLES same as **hovercraft**

air dam *n* a device for reducing the air resistance of a vehicle, especially a strip of metal or plastic fitted across the width of a car below the front bumper

air·date /ér dàyt/ *n* the date on which a radio or television program is scheduled to be broadcast

air di·vi·sion *n* a unit of the US Air Force of a size between a wing and an air force

air door *n* a strong current of air directed upward in an entrance to take the place of a door

air·drome /ér dròm/ *n US* a small airfield with limited facilities. Can term **aerodrome** [Early 20C. < AIR + -DROME]

air·drop /ér dròp/ *n* a landing of troops or supplies by parachute from an aircraft ■ *vt* (**-dropped, -drop·ping, -drops**) to land troops or supplies by parachute from an aircraft

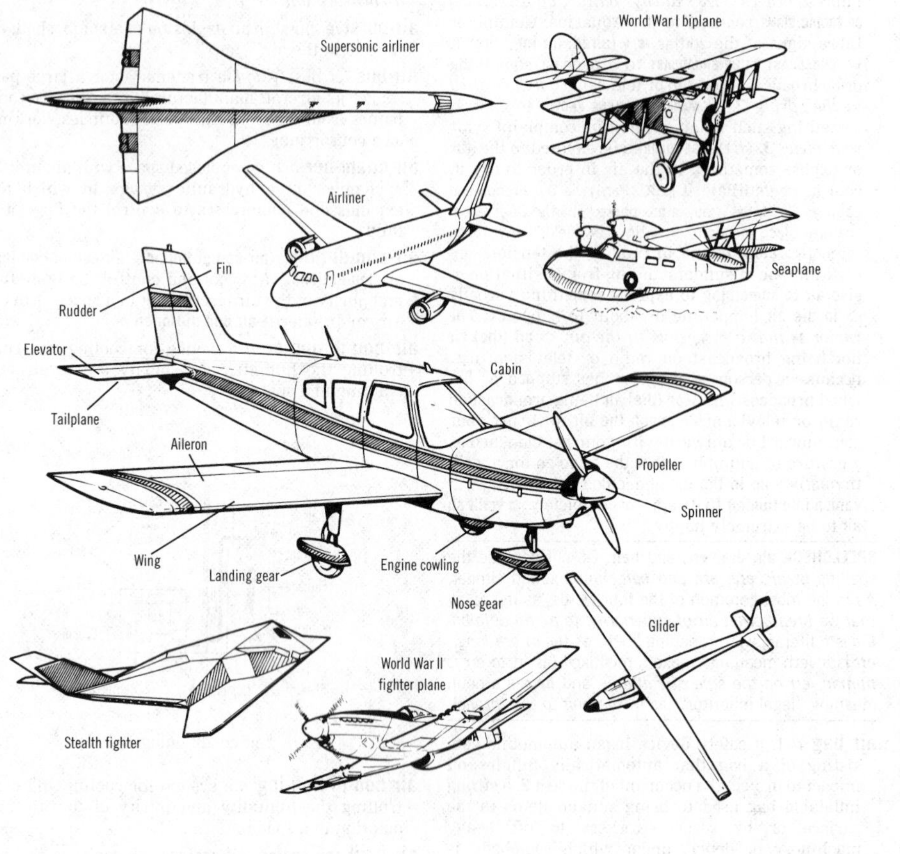

aircraft

air-dry *v* (**air-dried, air-dry·ing, air-dries**) to dry something by exposing it to air ■ *adj* dry to the point where continued exposure to air will remove no further moisture

Airedale

Aire·dale /ér dàyl/, **Aire·dale ter·ri·er** *n* a large terrier belonging to a breed with rough tan-colored hair and a black patch on the back [Late 19C. After a district in W Yorkshire, England]

air em·bo·lism *n* the presence of air in a blood vessel resulting from injury, from moving too rapidly from high to lower atmospheric pressure, or from using a heart-lung machine during cardiopulmonary bypass

air·er /érrər/ *n UK* a frame on which to hang clothes to dry indoors

air ex·chang·er *n* a device that expels stale air from a room and brings in fresh air from outside, and may also heat or cool the incoming air

air·fare /ér fèr/ *n* the price of a trip in an aircraft

air·field /ér fèeld/ *n* **1.** an area where aircraft can take off and land **2.** an airport or air base

air·flow /ér flò/ *n* a flow of air, especially around a moving vehicle

air·flown /ér flòn/ *adj Malaysia* describes goods that have been imported by air ○ *We have particularly good airflown beef.*

air·foil /ér fòyl/ *n* a part of an aircraft's or other vehicle's surface that acts on the air to provide lift or control, e.g., an aileron, wing, or propeller

air force *n* **1.** a military organization that uses aircraft in war, especially a branch of a nation's armed forces **2.** *US* a unit of the US Air Force of a size between a division and a high-level command, e.g., the US European Command

Air Force One *n* the official airplane of the President of the United States

air·frame /ér fràym/ *n* the whole body of an aircraft, apart from its engines

air·freight /ér fràyt/ *n* **1.** TRANSPORTATION OF GOODS BY AIR the transportation of freight by air **2.** CHARGE FOR AIRFREIGHT the charge made for transporting freight by air ■ *vt* (**-freight·ed, -freight·ing, -freights**) TRANSPORT GOODS BY AIR to transport goods by air

air gas *n* CHEM same as **producer gas**

air·glow /ér glò/ *n* a faint light observed in the night sky caused by photochemical reactions generated by solar radiation in the upper atmosphere

air gui·tar *n* an imaginary guitar held by somebody pretending to play a real instrument, especially when miming to rock music (*informal*)

air gun *n* a pistol or rifle that fires a projectile by releasing compressed air

air·head /ér hèd/ *n* **1.** an area in enemy territory captured and held by airborne forces and used when flying troops and supplies in or out of the territory **2.** somebody regarded as unintelligent and superficial (*slang insult*) [In sense 1 after BEACHHEAD]

air hole *n* **1.** a hole to allow the passage of air **2.** an unfrozen area in the surface of a frozen body of water, especially one where water mammals surface to breathe **3.** METEOROL same as **air pocket** (sense 1)

air·i·ly /érrilee/ *adv* **1.** in a carefree or light-hearted way as if something was unimportant **2.** in a delicate or light way

air·ing /érring/ *n* **1.** DRYING exposure to air or heat, especially for drying, removal of dampness, or ventilation **2.** MAKING SOMETHING KNOWN the exposure to public attention of somebody's opinions or ideas **3.** RADIO OR TELEVISION BROADCAST a radio or television broadcast

air in·take *n* an opening through which air enters a duct, a confined space, or a fuel-burning engine

air·ish /érrish/ *adj regional* chilly, or cold enough to be uncomfortable

air jack·et *n* **1.** an air-filled casing around a machine to insulate it against heat loss or gain **2.** SAFETY same as **life jacket**

air-kiss (**air-kissed, air-kiss·ing, air-kiss·es**) *vt* greet somebody by making a kissing gesture near to, but not actually making contact with, his or her cheek (*informal*) ○ *The guests were welcomed in a flurry of air-kissing and delighted squeals.* —**air kiss** *n*

air lane *n* a regular route used in air travel

air lay·er·ing *n* a plant propagation method in which a growing branch is cut or stripped of bark and the area wrapped in moist compost to encourage root formation

air·less /érləss/ *adj* **1.** WITH STALE AIR with stale rather than fresh air ○ *an airless room* ○ *an airless night* **2.** STILL without wind or movement of air **3.** WITHOUT AIR completely lacking any air —**air·less·ness** *n*

air·lift /ér lìft/ *n* the transport of people or things by air, especially when alternative means cannot be used ■ *vt* (**-lift·ed, -lift·ing, -lifts**) to transport people or things by air, especially when alternative means cannot be used

air·line /ér līn/ *n* **1.** a system of commercial scheduled flights transporting people and goods, or a company that operates such a system **2.** a tube through which air is passed under pressure

air·lin·er /ér līnər/ *n* a large commercial passenger-carrying aircraft

air·lock /ér lòk/ *n* **1.** an airtight chamber between two areas of differing air pressure in which air pressure can be altered to match that of either area **2.** an obstruction to the flow of a liquid in a pipe, caused by a bubble of air

air·mail /ér màyl/ *n* **1.** SENDING OF MAIL BY AIR the system of transporting letters and packages in aircraft **2.** MAIL SENT BY AIR mail transported in aircraft ■ *adj* SENT BY AIR sent by airmail ■ *vt* (**-mailed, -mail·ing, -mails**) SEND BY AIR to send a letter or package by airmail

air·man /érmən/ (*plural* **-men** /-mən/) *n* **1.** an enlisted person in the US Air Force, of a rank above airman basic **2.** a pilot, especially of a military aircraft

air·man ba·sic (*plural* **air·men ba·sic**) *n* an enlisted person in the US Air Force of the lowest rank

air·man first class (*plural* **air·men first class**) *n* an enlisted person in the US Air Force of a rank above airman

air mar·shal *n* TRAVEL same as **sky marshal**

air mass *n* a large body of air with temperature, pressure, and moisture uniform throughout its mass but changed by the environment through which it passes

Air Med·al *n* a decoration for meritorious conduct in the air awarded by the US Army, Navy, or Air Force

air mile *n* a unit of distance used in air travel, equal to one international nautical mile

air·mo·bile /ér mṑb'l, -beel, -bīl/ *adj* able to be transported into a combat zone by air, especially by helicopter

air·pack /ér pàk/ *n* a device consisting of a portable supply of oxygen connected to a face mask that allows somebody to enter an area where the air is unsafe to breathe

air·park /ér paàrk/ *n US* a small airport, usually close to a business or industrial center

air·per·son /ér pùrss'n/ (*plural* **-per·sons** or **-peo·ple** /-peèp'l/) *n* **1.** a member of an aircrew **2.** an enlisted person in the US Air Force

air pis·tol *n* a pistol that fires a projectile by releasing compressed air or another gas

air·plane /ér plàyn/ *n* a vehicle with wings and a jet

engine or propellers that is heavier than air and is able to fly [Late 19C. < French *aéroplane* < *aéro-* (< Greek *aēr* "air") + *-plane*]

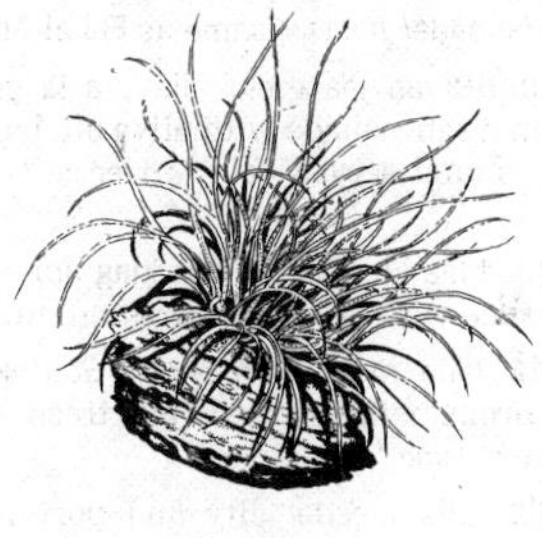

air plant

air plant *n* a plant that obtains nutrients and moisture from the air and rain, especially one grown as a houseplant for the novelty value of its requiring no soil or compost

air·play /ér plày/ *n* the playing on radio of a piece of recorded music

air pock·et *n* **1.** a small area of lower air density or a downward air current that makes an aircraft abruptly lose height **2.** an air bubble that impedes the flow of liquid or gas in a pipe

air po·lice *n US* the military police of an air force

air pop·per *n* a container for cooking popcorn that uses heated air

air·port /ér pàwrt/ *n* an area where civil aircraft may take off and land, especially one equipped with surfaced runways and facilities for handling passengers and cargo

air·port tax *n* a tax levied on passengers departing on a flight from an airport, sometimes included in the cost of the airline ticket

air·pow·er /ér pòwr/ *n* military capability in terms of combat power delivered from the air

air pres·sure *n* METEOROL same as **atmospheric pressure**

air pump *n* a device for compressing air or forcing it into or out of something

air qua·li·ty in·dex *n* a numerical scale that indicates how polluted the air is

air rage *n* disruptive or aggressive behavior by passengers aboard an aircraft that is liable to endanger the safety of other passengers

air raid *n* an attack by aircraft on something on the ground, especially a nonmilitary target

air ri·fle *n* a rifle that fires a projectile by releasing compressed air or another gas

air rights *npl* rights to build in or otherwise use space above an existing structure

air sac *n* **1.** ANAT same as **alveolus** (sense 1) **2.** BIRDS an air-filled cavity in a bird, formed as an extension of the respiratory system and growing into the bones, that aids respiration and decreases bone mass **3.** INSECTS a thin-walled bulge **(diverticulum)** that aids respiration, located in the tubes that transport air through the bodies of some insects

air·screw /ér skroō/ *n UK* a propeller on an aircraft

air-sea res·cue *n* a rescue at sea in which aircraft are used

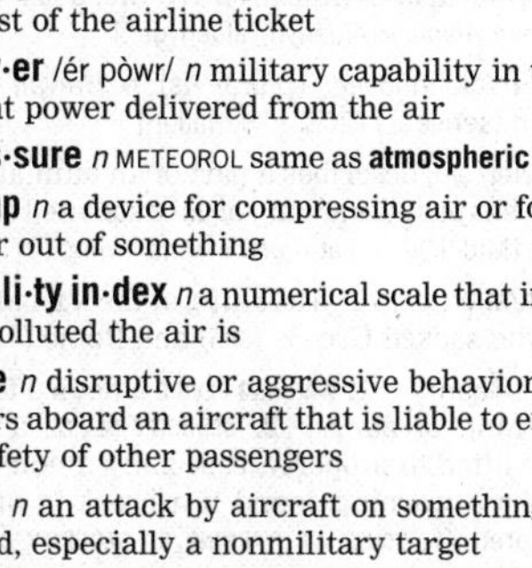

airship

air·ship /ér shìp/ *n* an aircraft that is lighter than air, powered, and navigable

air·show /ér shō/ *n* a public exhibition at an airfield of aircraft in flight and on the ground

air show·er *n* a device in which jets of air are used to remove dust or particles from the clothes of people who work in a clean environment

air·sick·ness /ér sìknəss/ *n* motion sickness caused by air travel —**air·sick** *adj*

air·side /ér sīd/ *n* the area of an airport where the aircraft take off and land, load, or unload

air sign *n* each of the three signs of the zodiac, Gemini, Libra, and Aquarius, traditionally associated with thought, communication, and social interaction

air sock *n* AVIAT same as **windsock**

air·space /ér spàyss/ *n* **1.** the part of the atmosphere directly above an area of land or water, especially a part over which a state claims jurisdiction **2.** the space in the air that a flying aircraft occupies or needs to maneuver

air speed *n* the speed of an aircraft in relation to the air through which it moves

air splint *n* a splint consisting of an inflatable cylinder that surrounds an injured limb

air spray *n* same as **aerosol** (senses 1–2)

air sta·tion *n* a small airfield with facilities for maintenance of aircraft

air·stream /ér streēm/ *n* **1.** a wind, especially one blowing at a high altitude **2.** AEROSP same as **airflow**

air strike *n* an attack by aircraft on something on the ground, especially an enemy position or formation —**air·strike** /ér strīk/ *vt*

air·strip /ér strìp/ *n* a place for aircraft to take off and land that has no facilities and is often temporary

air strip·ping *n* a technique for removing pollutants from water by breaking the water into minute particles

air tax·i *n* a small commercial aircraft used for brief flights between places that do not have regularly scheduled flights

air ter·mi·nal *n* an airport building with facilities for passengers, where disembarking passengers are received and outward-bound passengers leave to board an aircraft

air ter·ror·ism *n* the use of skyjacking, aircraft bombing, and other terrorist acts involving airplanes in an attempt to achieve a political objective or get international publicity

air·tight /ér tīt/ *adj* **1.** IMPERMEABLE BY AIR not allowing air in or out **2.** FLAWLESS without flaws or vulnerable points ○ *an airtight alibi* ■ *n W Africa* METAL BOX a metal box

air·time /ér tīm/ *n* **1.** the amount of time given to a program or subject in radio or television broadcasting **2.** the time at which an item is scheduled to be broadcast

air-to-air *adj* moving or passing from one aircraft to another while in flight

air-to-sur·face *adj* moving or passing from a flying aircraft to a point on the ground

air traf·fic *n* the movement of aircraft in an area

air-traf·fic con·trol *n* the system or organization responsible for directing the movement of aircraft over an area, operated by ground staff in radio contact with pilots —**air-traf·fic con·trol·ler** *n*

air ves·i·cle *n* same as **air bladder**

air walk *n US* a high-level passageway connecting two buildings, usually made from a transparent material

air·waves /ér wàyvz/ *npl* radio waves as used in broadcasting

air·way /ér wày/ *n* **1.** BREATHING PASSAGE a passage for air from the nose or mouth to the lungs **2.** TUBE TO KEEP AIRWAY OPEN a device for keeping an unconscious person's airway open, incorporating a tube inserted into the throat **3.** VENTILATION PASSAGE a passage for ventilation in a mine or tunnel **4.** AIR ROUTE an air route, especially one used by regular commercial flights (*often used in the plural*)

air·wo·man /ér wòommən/ (*plural* **-wo·men** /-wìmmin/) *n* **1.** a woman who is a member of an aircrew **2.** a woman who is an enlisted person in the US Air Force

air·wor·thy /ér wùrthee/ *adj* in good enough condition to be safe to fly [Early 19C. After SEAWORTHY] —**air·wor·thi·ness** *n*

air·y /érree/ (**-i·er, -i·est**) *adj* **1.** ROOMY well ventilated and having plenty of space **2.** LOFTY positioned or performed high in the air **3.** CAREFREE lighthearted and unconcerned ○ *an airy wave of her hand* **4.** ETHEREAL ethereal or illusory ○ *airy concepts* **5.** GRACEFUL light and graceful in movement (*literary*) ○ *an airy step* **6.** HIGH IN AIR at a great height in the sky (*literary*) —**air·i·ness** *n*

A·i·sha /aā ee shaā/, **A·ye·sha** (614?–678) wife of the prophet Muhammad. She was the daughter of the prophet Muhammad's chief adviser Abu Bakr and was Muhammad's favorite among his nine wives. Her political maneuvering led to her exile in 656.

aisle /īl/ *n* **1.** PASSAGEWAY BETWEEN SEATS a passageway between areas of seating, especially in a church, theater, or passenger vehicle **2.** PASSAGEWAY BETWEEN GOODS a passageway between stacks or displays of goods, especially in a supermarket or warehouse **3.** DIVISION IN CHURCH an area of a church separated from the nave or central area by pillars, especially one forming a passage between seats [14C. < Old French *ele* "wing" < Latin *ala*, influenced by ISLE and, later, French *aile* "wing"] ◇ **rolling in the aisles** laughing very heartily (*informal*)

SPELLCHECK aisle or **isle**? Do not confuse the spelling of ***aisle*** and ***isle***, which sound similar. An ***aisle*** is a passageway, for example, in a church or supermarket: *The bride walked down the aisle.* ***Isle*** is a literary word for a small island that is also sometimes used in place names: *the Isle of Wight.*

aitch /aych/ *n* the letter "h," or its sound [Mid-16C. < French *hache*, via late Latin *ach* < Latin *ah*, alteration of *ha*]

Aix-en-Pro·vence /àyk saaN prō vaāNs, èk-/ city in the Bouches-du-Rhône Department in the Provence-Alpes-Côte d'Azur Region of southeastern France. It was the first Roman settlement in Gaul. Population: 134,222 (1999).

Ai·zawl /ī jàwl/ capital city of Mizoram state in northeastern India. Population: 155,240 (1991).

a·ja /ájə/, **aa·jaa** *n Carib* the father of somebody's father [Late 20C. < Hindi *daadaa*]

A·jac·cio /aa yaāchō/ main port and capital of Corsica. Population: 52,880 (1999).

a·jar /ə jaār/ *adj, adv* neither shut nor wide open ○ *left the door ajar* [Late 17C. < later form of Old English *cierr* "turn"]

A·jax /áy jàks/ *n* in Greek mythology, a powerful warrior who fought in the Trojan War as leader of the Salamis forces. He was stricken by madness by the goddess Athena and killed himself when he was not awarded the armor of the dead Achilles.

a·ji /ájee/, **aa·jee** *n Carib* the mother of somebody's father [Late 20C. < Hindi *daadii* "grandmother"]

a·jou·pa /ə joōpə/, **a·ju·pa** *n Carib* a simple shelter or house with a thatched roof [Mid-20C. < Carib *ajouppa*]

AK *abbr* Alaska

a.k.a., **aka** *abbr* also known as

A·kan /aā kaān/ (*plural same* or **A·kans**) *n* **1.** a member of a people who live in southern Ghana, southeastern Ivory Coast, and parts of Togo **2.** a language spoken in Ghana and Ivory Coast, belonging to the Kwa group of Niger-Congo languages. Native speakers: 8 million. [Late 17C. < Twi *akan*] —**A·kan** *adj*

a·ka·ra /ákərə/, **ac·cra** /ákrə/ *n* in Caribbean countries and western Africa, a fritter made from black-eyed peas or another pulse, or sometimes from fish [Late 19C. < Yoruba *àkàrà* "bean cake"]

a·kar·y·ote /ay kárree ōt/ *n* a cell that has no nucleus [< A-[2] + Greek *karuon* "kernel"] —**a·kar·y·ot·ic** /ày kàrree óttik/ *adj*

Ak·bar /ák baar/ (1542–1605) emperor of India. During his reign (1556–1605), he conquered a vast realm in the north of the Indian subcontinent. Regarded as the most important of the Mughal emperors, he established a modern administrative system and promoted religious tolerance, economic development, and the arts. Known as **Akbar the Great**

AKC *abbr US* American Kennel Club

ak·ee *n* TREES another spelling of **ackee**

A·ke·la /aa káylə/ *n Can, UK* the adult leader of a Cub Scout pack [Early 20C. After a wolf in Kipling's *Jungle Book*]

a·kene *n* BOT another spelling of **achene**

a·kha·ra /ə ka̅arə/ *n S Asia* same as **gymnasium** (sense 1) [< Hindi]

A·khe·na·ton /a̅akə na̅at'n, a̅ak-/, **Ikh·na·ton** /ik-/ (*fl* 14th century B.C.) Egyptian pharaoh. He ruled from about 1353 to 1337 B.C. and introduced a monotheistic religion based on the worship of the sun god Aton. He was married to Nefertiti.

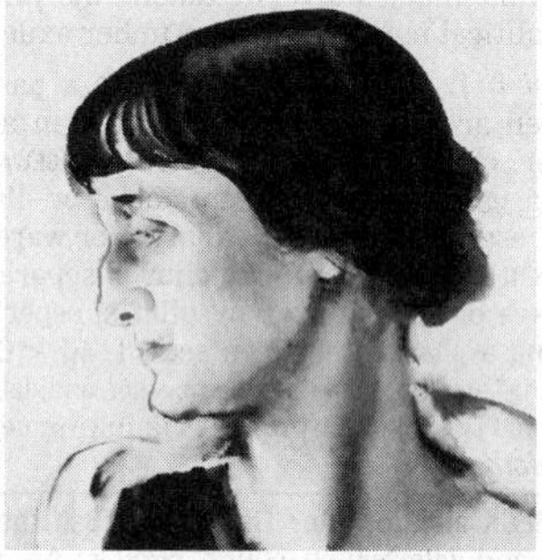

Anna Akhmatova: detail of a portrait (1928) by Nikolai Tyrsa

Akh·ma·to·va /ak ma̅atəvə, àkmə tṓvə/, **Anna** (1889–1966) Russian poet. She was a leading figure in an early 20th-century movement that advocated precision and brevity in poetic language. Pseudonym of **Gorenko, Anna Andreyevna**

> "And the stone word fell / Upon my still living breast. / Never mind, I was prepared for this. / Somehow, I shall stand the test."
> [Anna Akhmatova, "The Sentence"; June 22, 1939]

A·ki·ba ben Jo·seph /aa ke̅e baa bən jṓzəf, -jóssəf/ (A.D. 50?–135?) Palestinian Jewish rabbi. He lived near Jaffa and was executed by the Romans for teaching Judaism.

Ak·i·hi·to /a̅akee he̅etō/ (*b.* 1933) emperor of Japan. He succeeded his father, Hirohito, in 1989

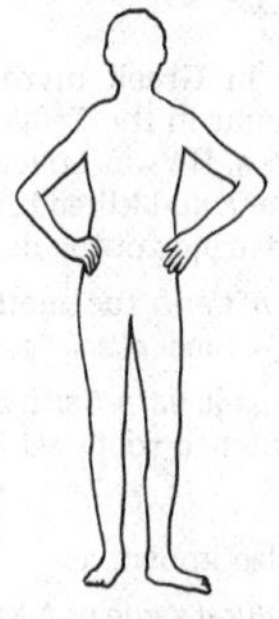
akimbo

a·kim·bo /ə kímbō/ *adj, adv* **1.** with the hands on the hips and the elbows turned outward **2.** bent or arched [14C. Origin ?]

a·kin /ə kín/ *adj* **1.** SIMILAR similar or closely related to something **2.** RELATED related by blood **3.** SHARING COMMON ORIGIN describes languages that share a common origin or ancient forms [Mid-16C. < *a*, reduced form of OF]

a·ki·ne·sia /ày kə ne̅ezhə, ày kī-/ *n* the loss or reduction of the usual power of movement [Mid-19C. < Greek *akinēsia* "lack of movement" < *kinein* "to move"] —**a·ki·net·ic** /-néttik/ *adj*

A·ki·ra Yo·shi·mu·ra /a ke̅erə yṓshi mo͝orə/ (*b.* 1927) Japanese writer. His prize-winning novels and nonfiction works include *Journey to the Stars* (1966) and *Von Siebold's Daughter* (1978)

A·ki·ta[1] /ə ke̅etə/ capital city of Akita Prefecture on the Sea of Japan (East Sea), northwestern Honshu Island, Japan. Population: 312,926 (2002).

A·ki·ta[2] /ə ke̅etə/ *n* a large powerful dog with a broad head, deep muzzle, and curled tail, belonging to a Japanese breed

Ak·kad /á kàd, a̅a ka̅ad/ ancient city and region of the same name situated in central Northern Mesopotamia. It was most influential during the third millennium B.C.

Ak·ka·di·an /ə káydee ən/ *n* **1.** somebody who came from the ancient city or region of Akkad **2.** the extinct Semitic language of Mesopotamia, written in cuneiform [Mid-19C. < *Akkad*, city in ancient Babylonia] —**Ak·ka·di·an** *adj*

Ak·mol·insk /ak móllinsk, ak máwlinsk/ former name for **Astana** (1824–1960)

~~**aknowledge**~~ incorrect spelling of **acknowledge**

ak·ra·sia /ə kráyzhə/ *n* weakness of will, especially a failure to act according to a sense of moral obligation [< Greek, variant of *akrateia* "powerlessness" < *kratos* "strength" (see -CRACY)] —**ak·rat·ic** /ə kráttik/ *adj*

Ak·ron /ákrən/ city in northeastern Ohio. Population: 214,349 (2002 estimate).

A·ku·ta·ga·wa Ry·u·no·su·ke /a̅a kootə ga̅awə ro̅onə sṓkee/, **A·ku·ta·ga·wa Ry·ū·no·su·ke** (1892–1927) Japanese author. He is noted for stories set in Japan's feudal era, e.g., *Rashomon* (1915).

ak·va·vit *n* BEVERAGES same as **aquavit**

al *abbr* Albania (*used in Internet addresses*) See table at **domain name**

Al *symbol* aluminum

AL *abbr* **1.** Alabama **2.** *US* FOOTBALL American League

al. *abbr* **1.** alcohol **2.** alcoholic

-al[1] *suffix* **1.** relating to or characterized by ○ *delusional* **2.** action, process ○ *disposal* [Via French < Latin *-alis, alia*]

-al[2] *suffix* aldehyde ○ *chloral* [< ALDEHYDE]

à la /a̅a laa, állə/, **a la** *prep* in the style of somebody or something [Late 16C. < French, shortening of *à la mode de* "in the fashion of"]

Ala. *abbr* Alabama

Alabama

Al·a·bam·a /àllə bámmə/ **1.** state in the southeastern United States, bordered by Georgia, the Gulf of Mexico, Mississippi, and Tennessee. Capital: Montgomery. Population: 4,486,508 (2002 estimate). Area: 52,237 sq. mi./135,293 sq. km. **2.** river flowing from central Alabama southwest to the Tombigbee River north of Mobile. Length: 310 mi./500 km. —**Al·a·ba·man** *adj, n* —**Al·a·ba·mi·an** /-báymee ən/ *adj, n*

al·a·bas·ter /àllə bástər/ *n* **1.** TYPE OF GYPSUM a white or transparent form of gypsum. Use: decorative carving. **2.** TYPE OF CALCITE a hard semitranslucent type of calcite, occasionally with banding ■ *adj* **1.** OF ALABASTER made of alabaster ○ *alabaster ornaments* **2.** WHITE white and translucent like alabaster ○ *her alabaster skin* [14C. Via Old French < Greek *alabastros*]

à la carte /a̅a laa ka̅art, àllə-/, **a la carte** *adj, adv* with each dish on a menu priced separately [Early 19C. < French, "by the menu"]

a·lack /ə lák/ *interj* used to express regret (*archaic or literary*) [15C. < LACK, after ALAS]

a·lac·ri·ty /ə lákrətee/ *n* promptness or eager and speedy readiness [Early 16C. < Latin *alacritas* < *alacer* "lively"] —**a·lac·ri·tous** *adj*

A·lad·din's cave /ə làdd'nz-/ *n* a suddenly discovered place containing great riches

al-Ad·ha /àl a̅adə/ *n* ISLAM same as **Eid al-Adha**

à la grecque /a̅a laa grék, àllə-/, **a la grecque** *adj* cooked in a sauce made with olive oil, lemon, wine, and herbs, and served cold [< French, "in the Greek style"]

à la king /a̅a laa kíng, àllə-/, **a la king** *adj* cooked in a cream sauce with green peppers and mushrooms

a·la·me·da /àllə me̅edə, -máy-/ *n Southwest US* a public promenade shaded by trees [Late 18C. < Spanish < *álamo* "poplar tree"]

A·la·me·da /àllə me̅edə/ city and port in western California, situated on islands and a peninsula in San Francisco Bay. Population: 72,927 (2002 estimate).

Al·a·mein, El ♦ **El 'Alamein**

al·a·mo /állə mṑ/ *n Southwest US* a poplar tree, especially a cottonwood [Mid-19C. < Spanish]

Al·a·mo /állə mṑ/ chapel in San Antonio, Texas, besieged by Mexican forces in 1836 when all 187 Texan defenders were killed

a·la·mode /a̅alə mṓd, àllə-/ *n US* a light silk. Use: shawls. [Mid-17C. < French (see À LA MODE)]

à la mode /a̅a laa mṓd, àllə-/, **a la mode** /a̅a laa mṓd/ *adj* **1.** served with ice cream ○ *apple pie à la mode* **2.** in the latest fashion (*dated*) [Late 16C. < French, "in the style"]

Al·a·mo·gor·do /àlləmə gáwrdō/ city in southern New Mexico, northeast of White Sands Missile Range, the site of the first atomic bomb explosion, on July 16, 1945. Population: 35,107 (2002 estimate).

al·a·nine /állə ne̅en/ *n* an amino acid found in protein foods and also synthesized by the body [Mid-19C. < German *Alanin* < *Aldehyd* "aldehyde"]

a·la·nu·i /álə no̅o ee/ (*plural* **-is**) *n Hawaii* same as **street** *n* (sense 1) [20C. < Hawaiian]

a·lar /áylər/ *adj* describes a part of an animal or plant that is shaped like a wing or is associated with such a part [Mid-19C. < Latin *alaris* < *ala* "wing"]

Al·ar·ic /állərik/ (370?–410?) king of the Visigoths (395–410) who sacked Greece (395) and Rome (410)

a·larm /ə la̅arm/ *n* **1.** WARNING DEVICE a device for giving a warning of danger **2.** SECURITY DEVICE a security device fitted to property, especially a house or car, to make a warning sound if a break-in or theft is attempted **3.** SOUND OF WARNING OR SECURITY DEVICE the sound made by a warning or security device **4.** same as **alarm clock** **5.** FEAR fear caused by perception of imminent danger **6.** CALL TO ARMS a summons to prepare to fight (*archaic*) **7.** FENCING CHALLENGE MADE BY STAMPING a warning or challenge to a fencer made by stamping the leading foot ■ *vt* (**a·larmed, a·larm·ing, a·larms**) **1.** FRIGHTEN SOMEBODY to make somebody frightened or apprehensive **2.** FIT SOMETHING WITH SECURITY DEVICE to fit property, especially a building or vehicle, with a security device that sounds a warning if a break-in or theft is attempted **3.** WARN SOMEBODY to give somebody warning of danger [Early 16C. < archaic *alarm* adverb, via French < Italian *all' arme* "to arms!"] —**a·larmed** *adj*

a·larm clock *n* a clock that can be set to sound a buzzer or bell at a desired time, especially to wake somebody

a·larm·ing /ə la̅arming/ *adj* frightening or disturbing —**a·larm·ing·ly** *adv*

a·larm·ist /ə la̅armist/ *n* **1.** somebody who spreads unnecessary fear or warnings of danger **2.** somebody who becomes afraid easily —**a·larm·ism** *n* —**a·larm·ist** *adj*

a·larm re·ac·tion *n* the initial response of a person or animal to stress, including increased heart rate and hormonal activity

a·la·rum /ə la̅arəm, ə lérrəm/ *n* same as **alarm** *n* (sense 6) (*archaic*) [Variant]

a·las /ə láss/ *interj* used to express sorrow or pity ■ *adv* unfortunately or regrettably [13C. Via French *hélas* < Latin *lassus* "weary"]

Alas. *abbr* Alaska

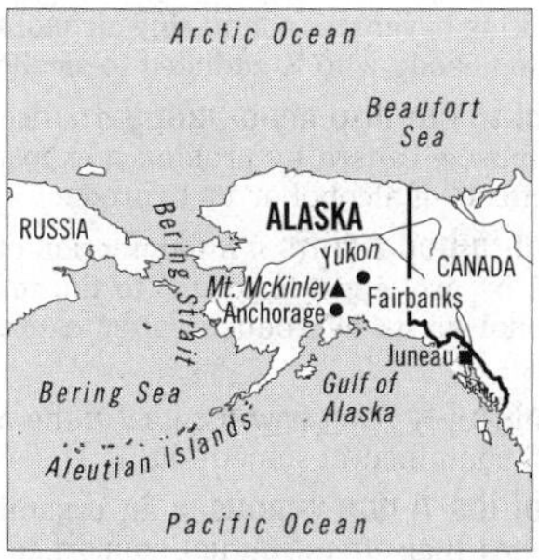

Alaska

A·las·ka /ə láskə/ US state of northwestern North America, bordered by Canada and the Pacific and Arctic Oceans. Capital: Juneau. Population: 643,786 (2002 estimate). Area: 615,230 sq. mi./1,593,438 sq. km. —**A·las·kan** *adj, n*

A·las·ka High·way *n* a road built in 1942 from Dawson Creek, British Columbia, to Fairbanks, Alaska. Former name **Alcan Highway**

A·las·ka Na·tive *n US* a member of any of the original peoples of Alaska

A·las·kan king crab *n* MARINE BIOL same as **king crab** (sense 1)

A·las·kan mal·a·mute *n* DOGS same as **malamute**

A·las·kan Pen·in·su·la peninsula of southern Alaska separating the Pacific Ocean from the Bering Sea to the northwest. Length: 400 mi./644 km.

A·las·ka Range mountain range in southern Alaska, extending in a 400 mi./640 km semicircle north of Anchorage. It includes the highest peak in North America, Mount McKinley 20,320 ft./6,194 m.

A·las·ka Stan·dard Time, A·las·ka Time *n* the standard time in the time zone centered on longitude 135° W, which includes Alaska, apart from the western Aleutian Islands. It is nine hours behind Universal Time.

a·las·trim /ə lástrəm/ *n* a mild form of smallpox, found especially in South America and West Africa [Early 20C. < Portuguese < *alastrar* "spread"]

a·late /áy lày̆t/, **a·lat·ed** /-təd/ *adj* describes insects with wings, or seeds with parts resembling wings [Mid-17C. < Latin *alatus* < *ala* "wing"]

alb /alb/ *n* a long white robe with long sleeves worn by priests [Pre-12C. Via ecclesiastical Latin *(vestis) alba* "white (garment)" < Latin *albus* "white"]

Alb. *abbr* **1.** Albania **2.** Albanian

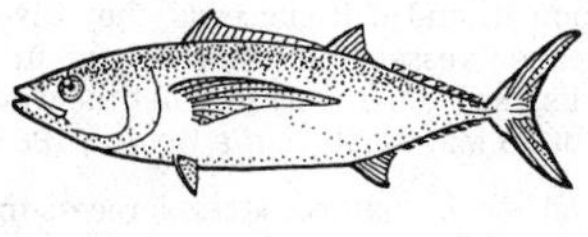
albacore

al·ba·core /álbə kàwr/ (*plural same* or **-cores**) *n* **1.** a large tuna with a long pectoral fin. Native to: warm waters of the Atlantic and Pacific. Latin name: *Thunnus alalunga.* **2.** the flesh of an albacore used as food [Late 16C. < Portuguese *albacor*]

Al·ba·ni·a /al báynee ə/ country in southeastern Europe, bordering the Adriatic Sea. A former Communist state, it became a parliamentary democracy in 1991. Language: Albanian. Currency: lek. Capital: Tirana. Population: 3,582,205 (2003). Area: 11,100 sq. mi./28,748 sq. km. Official name **Republic of Albania**

Al·ba·ni·an /al báynee ən/ *n* **1.** the official language of Albania that is also spoken in parts of nearby

Albania

countries and is a branch of the Indo-European languages. Native speakers: 4 million. **2.** somebody who comes from Albania —**Al·ba·ni·an** *adj*

Al·ba·ny /áwlbənee/ **1.** capital of New York State, situated on the western bank of the Hudson River. Population: 93,779 (2002 estimate). **2.** city in west-central Oregon, on the east bank of the Willamette River, south of Salem. Population: 42,190 (2002 estimate). **3.** city in southwestern Georgia, situated on the Flint River. Population: 76,325 (2002 estimate). **4.** river in Ontario, Canada, flowing northeast into James Bay. Length: 610 mi./982 km.

albatross

al·ba·tross /álbə tròss/ (*plural* **-tross·es** or *same*) *n* **1.** a large long-winged seabird that spends most of its life in flight. Native to: cool southern oceans. Family: Diomedeidae. **2.** an oppressive burden or hindrance **3.** *UK* GOLF same as **double eagle** (sense 2) [Late 17C. Alteration (after Latin *albus* "white") of Spanish and Portuguese *alcatraz* < Arabic *al-ġaṭṭās* "the diver"] ◇ **an albatross around somebody's neck** a burden from which somebody cannot escape

al·be·do /al beédō/ (*plural* **-dos**) *n* the fraction of light hitting an object that is reflected by that object, especially a planet reflecting the Sun's light [Mid-19C. < ecclesiastical Latin, "whiteness" < Latin *albus* "white"]

Al·bee /áwlbee, ál-/, **Edward** (*b.* 1928) US playwright and author of *Who's Afraid of Virginia Woolf?* (1962). His play *Three Tall Women* (1991) won him his third Pulitzer Prize for drama. Full name **Albee, Edward Franklin**

> "Sometimes a person has to go a very long distance out of his way to come back a short distance correctly."
> [Edward Albee, *The Zoo Story*; 1960]

al·be·it /awl beé it/ *conj* used to introduce a statement that modifies a statement just made ○ *a difficult, albeit rewarding job* [14C. < ALL + BE[1] + IT[1], "all though it may be"]

Al·be·marle Sound /álbər maàrl-/ inlet of the Atlantic Ocean, in northeastern North Carolina. Kitty Hawk, where the Wright brothers first flew, is on the barrier island that separates the shallow sound from the ocean. Length: 50 mi./80 km.

al·ben·da·zole /álbəndə zōl/ *n* a veterinary drug used to prevent parasitic worms [Mid-20C. < ALBUMEN + ENDO- + AZOLE]

Al·be·rich /álbərikh/ *n* in medieval Germanic mythology, king of the dwarves and guardian of the treasures of the Nibelung

Al·bers /álbərz, áwl-/, **Josef** (1888–1976) German-born US painter and designer. He taught at the Bauhaus school of design. After 1933 he worked in the United States.

Al·bert /álbərt/ (1819–61) German-born prince consort to Queen Victoria. A supporter of technological innovation and patron of the arts, he organized the Great Exhibition (1851). The proceeds financed the building of several museums and the Royal Albert Hall (1871).

Al·bert, Lake lake in east central Africa, on the border between Uganda and the Democratic Republic of the Congo, in the north of the Rift Valley system. Area: 2,160 sq. mi./5,600 sq. km. Length: 99 mi./160 km.

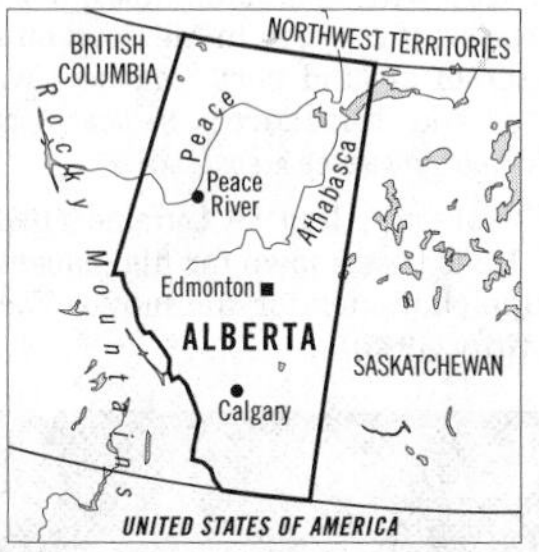

Alberta

Al·ber·ta /al búrtə/ Canada's westernmost Prairie Province and a leading producer of oil and natural gas. Capital: Edmonton. Population: 3,113,600 (2002). Area: 255,541 sq. mi./661,848 sq. km.

Al·bert Ed·ward Ny·an·za /-nee ánzə, -nī ánzə/ former name for **Edward, Lake**

Al·ber·ti /al bértee/, **Leon Battista** (1404–72) Italian architect and writer. His architectural designs are characterized by a pure classical style. His treatise *On Painting* (1436) expounded the principles of perspective and was an important source for artists of his and future generations.

al·ber·tite /álbər tīt/ *n* a solid black variety of bitumen found in oil-bearing rock strata [Mid-19C. After *Albert County*, New Brunswick, Canada]

Al·ber·tus Mag·nus /al bùrtəss mágnəss/, **St.** (1200?–80) German cleric and philosopher. He wrote on logic, natural and moral sciences, and theology. He taught St. Thomas Aquinas.

al·bes·cent /al béss'nt/ *adj* becoming white or whitish (*technical or literary*) [Early 18C. < Latin *albescent-* < *albus* "white"]

Al·bi·gen·ses /àlbi jén seèz/ *npl* a heretical Christian religious group in southern France during the 12th and 13th centuries. They believed that everything in the material world is evil. [Early 17C. < medieval Latin < *Albiga* "Albi," city in S France] —**Al·bi·gen·sian** /àlbi jénshən/ *adj* —**Al·bi·gen·sian·ism** *n*

al·bi·nism /álbi nìzzəm/ *n* congenital lack of pigmentation in the skin and hair of a person or animal or in the coloration of a plant —**al·bi·nis·tic** /álbi nístik/ *adj*

Dorling Kindersley Ltd, London/Corbis
albino: dwarf Russian hamsters with albino shown right

al·bi·no /al bīnō/ (*plural* **-nos**) *n* **1.** a person or animal whose skin and hair lack pigmentation and whose irises are pink because of a hereditary condition (**albinism**) **2.** a plant that lacks pigmentation in its coloration because of a hereditary condition (**albinism**) [Early 18C. < Portuguese < Latin *albus* "white"]

Al·bi·on /álbee ən/ ancient name for England or the island of Britain

al·bite /ál bīt/ *n* a usually white form of feldspar. Use: glass, ceramics. [Early 19C. < Latin *albus* "white"] —**al·bit·ic** /al bíttik/ *adj*

al·bon·di·ga /al bón digə/ *n Hispanic* a meatball made of ground pork and beef, usually served with a spicy tomato-serrano chili sauce, or in Mexican cuisine, soup with meatballs (*usually used in the plural*) [Via Spanish *albóndiga* "meatball" < Arabic *al-bunduga* "hazelnut, ball the size or shape of a hazelnut"]

al·bon·di·gas /al bón digəss/ *n Hispanic* in Mexican cuisine, soup with meatballs (*takes a singular verb*) ■ *npl Southwest US* FOOD in Mexican cuisine, meatballs made of ground pork and beef with a spicy tomato-serrano chili sauce [< Mexican Spanish < plural of Spanish *albóndiga* (see ALBONDIGA)]

Al·bright /áwl brīt/, **Ivan Le Lorraine** (1897–1983) US painter. He is best known for his macabre painting of the title character for the movie *The Picture of Dorian Gray* (1945).

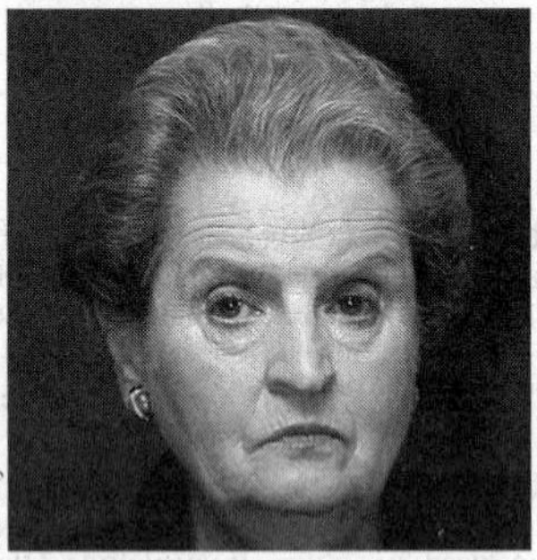

Madeleine Albright

Al·bright, Madeleine (*b.* 1937) Czech-born US secretary of state (1997–2001). A Democrat, she was appointed US ambassador to the United Nations in 1993 and later became the first woman to hold the post of US secretary of state. Full name **Albright, Madeleine Korbel**

> "Words are cheap; actions are the coin of the realm."
> [Madeleine Albright. On Iraq's massing of 80,000 troops while accusing the US of harboring ill will, *Time*; October 31, 1994]

al·bum /álbəm/ *n* **1.** BLANK BOOK a book or binder with blank pages or pockets for keeping collected items such as postage stamps, photographs, mementos, and autographs **2.** MUSIC RECORDING a music recording, sometimes including more than one CD, cassette, or record, issued as a single item **3.** RECORD HOLDER a cardboard holder for phonograph records, similar to a book in shape **4.** *UK* COLLECTION a collection in book form of short literary or musical pieces or pictures (*dated*) [Early 17C. < Latin, "blank tablet" < *albus* "white"]

ORIGIN The Latin word *albus* "white," from which ***album*** is derived, is also the source of English *alb, albino, albumen, auburn,* and *daub.*

al·bum·blatt /álbəm blàt/ (*plural* **-blatts** or **-blät·ter** /-blèttər/) *n* a short light instrumental piece popular in the 19th century, usually bound together in a set with other similar pieces [< German, "page from an album"]

al·bu·men /al byóomən/ *n* **1.** the clear water-soluble protein that surrounds the yolk of an egg and provides nutrition for the embryo (*technical*) **2.** the protein component of egg white, which includes albumin [Late 16C. < Latin < *albus* "white"]

al·bu·min /al byóomin/ *n* a common water-soluble protein coagulated by heat, found in egg white, blood plasma, and milk —**al·bu·mi·nous** *adj*

al·bu·mi·noid /al byóomə nòyd/ *adj* resembling albumin ■ *n* BIOCHEM same as **scleroprotein** —**al·bu·mi·noi·dal** /al byòomə nóyd'l/ *adj*

al·bu·mi·nu·ri·a /àl byoomə nóoree ə/ *n* the presence of albumin in urine, usually an indication of kidney disease

Al·bu·quer·que /álbə kùrkee/ city and tourist resort on the Rio Grande and the largest city in New Mexico. Population: 463,874 (2002 estimate).

al·bu·te·rol /al byóotə ràwl/ *n US* a drug that relaxes and dilates the bronchi. Use: asthma treatment. Can term **salbutamol**

alc. *abbr US* **1.** BEVERAGES, CHEM alcohol **2.** MED alcoholic

alc·a·h·est *n* HIST another spelling of **alkahest**

Al·ca·ic /al káy ik/ *adj* describes lyric poetry written in the metrical form of a stanza of four lines, each containing four feet ■ *n* a lyric poem or line written in the Alcaic form (*often used in the plural*) [Mid-17C. < late Latin *alcaicus* < Greek *Alkaios* "Alcaeus," lyric poet credited with inventing the form]

al·cai·de /al kīdee/, **al·cay·de** *n Hispanic* **1.** the commander of a fortress in a Spanish-speaking area **2.** the governor of a prison in a Spanish-speaking area [Early 16C. Via Spanish < Arabic *al-kā-'id* "the commander"]

al·cal·de /al kaáldee/ *n Hispanic* the mayor or chief magistrate of a town in a Spanish-speaking area [Mid-16C. Via Spanish < Arabic *al-kādī* "the judge"]

Al·can High·way /ál kàn/ *n* former name for **Alaska Highway** [Contraction of *Alaska-Canada*]

Al·ca·traz /álkə tràz/ island in San Francisco Bay, California, site of a federal prison from 1933 to 1963. It has been part of Golden Gate National Recreation Area since 1972.

al·cay·de *n* MIL, CRIME another spelling of **alcaide**

al·caz·ar /al kázzər, álkə zaàr, aàlkə zaàr/ *n* in Spain, a fortress or palace, especially one built by the Moors [Early 17C. Via Spanish < Arabic *al-kaṣr* "the castle" < Latin *castrum* "camp"]

Al·ces·tis /al séstiss/ *n* in Greek mythology, the daughter of Pelias and wife of Admetus, King of Pherae. She agreed to die to save her husband's life, but was later rescued from Hades by Heracles.

al·che·mist /álkəmist/ *n* somebody who practices alchemy —**al·che·mis·tic** /àlkə místik/ *adj*

al·che·mize /álkə mīz/ (**-mized, -miz·ing, -miz·es**) *vt* to transform something into gold or into a much purer or brighter form by alchemy

al·che·my /álkəmee/ *n* **1.** an early, unscientific form of chemistry that sought to change base metals into gold and discover a life-prolonging elixir, a universal cure for disease, and a universal solvent (**alkahest**) **2.** a power supposedly like alchemy, especially of enchantment or transformation [14C. Via Old French *alquemie* and medieval Latin *alchimia* < Arabic *al-kīmiyā* "the chemistry" < Greek *khēmeia*] —**al·chem·ic** /al kémmik/ *adj* —**al·chem·i·cal** /al kémmik'l/ *adj*

~~**alchol**~~ incorrect spelling of **alcohol**

Al·ci·bi·a·des /àlssi bī ə deez/ (450?–404 B.C.) Athenian general and political leader. His command contributed to the defeat of Athens in the Peloponnesian War.

al·clo·met·a·sone /àlklō méttə sōn/ *n* a synthetic steroid drug. Use: treatment of dermatosis. [Late 20C. < *alclo-* + *-metasone*, INN stem]

Alc·me·ne /alk meénee/ *n* in Greek mythology, wife of Amphitryon and mother of Heracles and Iphicles

Al·cock /áwl kòk, aál-/, **Sir John William** (1892–1919) British aviator. With Arthur Brown, he made the first transatlantic flight, from Newfoundland to Ireland, which took 16 hours 12 minutes.

al·co·hol /álkə hàwl/ *n* **1.** LIQUID FOR DRINKS OR SOLVENTS a colorless liquid, produced by the fermentation of sugar or starch, that is the intoxicating agent in fermented drinks. Formula: C_2H_5OH. **2.** DRINKS WITH ALCOHOL intoxicating drinks containing alcohol **3.** ORGANIC COMPOUND an organic compound containing one or more hydroxyl groups bound to carbon atoms [Mid-16C. Via medieval Latin, "fine powder, distilled essence" < Arabic *al-kuḥl* "the antimony powder"]

al·co·hol de·hy·drog·e·nase *n* an enzyme found in the liver and stomach that promotes the conversion of alcohols to aldehydes

al·co·hol·ic /àlkə háwlik/ *adj* **1.** CONTAINING ALCOHOL relating to or containing alcohol ○ *alcoholic beverages* **2.** CAUSED BY ALCOHOL caused by alcohol consumption ○ *alcoholic dehydration* **3.** ADDICTED TO ALCOHOL addicted to drinking beverages containing alcohol ■ *n* ALCOHOL ADDICT somebody who is addicted to alcohol

al·co·hol·ic car·di·o·my·o·path·y *n* a disease of the heart muscle caused by prolonged exposure to the toxic effects of alcohol or its byproduct

al·co·hol·ic hep·a·ti·tis *n* inflammation of the liver caused by prolonged exposure to the toxic effects of alcohol or its byproducts, often a precursor to cirrhosis

al·co·hol·ic·i·ty /àlkə haw líssətee/ *n* the amount of alcohol contained in something

Al·co·hol·ics A·non·y·mous *n* an organization for alcoholics that offers mutual support to members to help them overcome their dependency

al·co·hol·ism /álkə haw lìzzəm/ *n* **1.** dependence on alcohol consumption to an extent that adversely affects social and work-related functioning and produces withdrawal symptoms when intake is stopped or greatly reduced **2.** a physical disorder caused by the toxic effects of excessive alcohol consumption

al·co·pop /álkō pòp/ *n UK* a drink made of a soft drink, e.g., lemonade, mixed with alcohol [Late 20C. < ALCOHOL + POP[1]]

Al·co·ran /àlkə rán/ *n* ISLAM same as **Koran** —**Al·co·ran·ic** /àlkə ránnik/ *adj*

Al·cott /áwlkət, ál-/, **Amos Bronson** (1799–1888) US transcendentalist and writer who founded the Concord Summer School of Philosophy and Literature in 1879

> "The true teacher defends his pupils against his own personal influence."
> [Amos Bronson Alcott, "The Teacher," *Orphic Sayings. From The Dial*; July 1840]

Louisa May Alcott

Al·cott, Louisa May (1832–88) US novelist. Her novels include her most famous book, *Little Women* (1868–69). See Cultural note at **woman**

> "When women are the advisers, the lords of creation don't take the advice till they have persuaded themselves that it is just what they intended to do; then they act upon it, and if it succeeds, they give the weaker vessel half the credit of it; if it fails, they generously give her the whole."
> [Louisa May Alcott, *Little Women*; 1868–69]

al·cove /ál kōv/ *n* **1.** INTERNAL RECESS a recess in the wall of a room **2.** EXTERNAL RECESS a recess in an exterior wall, usually with a roof or other covering structure **3.** SECLUDED PLACE a shady or secluded place in a garden [Late 16C. Via French *alcôve* and Spanish *alcoba* < Arabic *al-kubba* "the vault, the arch"]

al·cu·ro·ni·um /àlkyə rṓnee əm/ *n* a drug used as a muscle relaxant [Late 20C. < ALLYL + CURARE]

Al·da·bra /al dábbrə/ group of four islands in the Seychelles in the Indian Ocean. Area: 59 sq. mi./154 sq. km.

Al·deb·a·ran /al débbərən/ *n* the brightest star in the constellation Taurus and one of the brightest stars in the sky

al·de·hyde /áldə hīd/ *n* an organic compound containing a carbon atom connected to an oxygen atom by a double bond and to a hydrogen atom ■ *adj* relating to the chemical group composed of a carbon atom connected to an oxygen atom by a double bond and to a hydrogen atom [Mid-19C. Contraction of modern Latin *alcohol dehydrogenatum* "dehydrogenated alcohol"] —**al·de·hy·dic** /àldə híddik/ *adj*

Al·den /áwldən/, **John** (1599?–1687) English-born American colonist. He emigrated to New England on the *Mayflower* in 1620 and was a founder of the Plymouth Colony. He married Priscilla Mullens, but there is no historical basis for the tale of his proxy courtship of her related in Henry Wadsworth Longfellow's famous poem "The Courtship of Miles Standish" (1858).

al den·te /àl dén tay, àl déntee/ *adj* cooked just long enough to be still firm, and not too soft [< Italian, "to the tooth"]

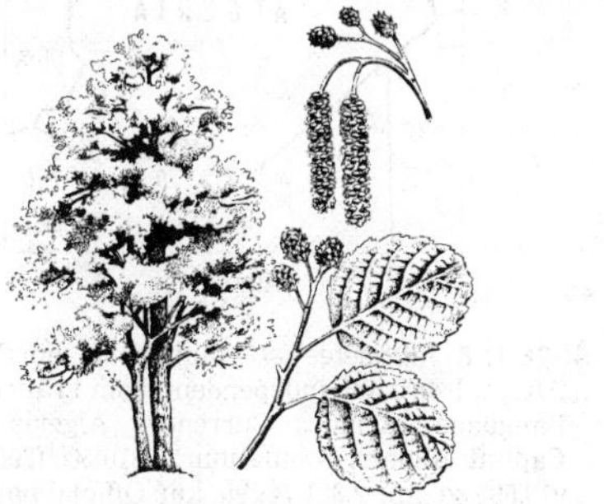

alder

al·der /áwldər/ *n* **1.** a deciduous tree or bush with male catkins and cone-shaped fruits, common in wet places. Native to: northern temperate areas. Genus: *Alnus*. **2.** the rot-resistant wood of an alder tree. Use: in underwater structures, carving, furniture making. [Old English *alor* < Indo-European, "reddish brown"]

al·der·man /áwldərmən/ (*plural* **-men** /-mən/) *n* **1.** a man who is a member of the legislating body of some towns or cities in the United States and Canada **2.** a man who was a senior member of an English or Welsh local council before the local government reorganization of 1974 **3.** HIST another spelling of **ealdorman** [Old English *ealdorman* < *ealdor* "an elder" + MAN] —**al·der·man·cy** *n* —**al·der·man·ic** /àwldər mánnik/ *adj*

Al·der·ney[1] /áwldərnee/ third largest and most northerly of the Channel Islands. Population: 2,297 (1991). Area: 3 sq. mi./18 sq. km.

Al·der·ney[2] /áwldərnee/ *n* a cow belonging to a breed of small dairy cattle originally from the Channel Islands

al·der·per·son /áwldər pùrss'n/ (*plural* **-per·sons** or **-peo·ple** /-peep'l/) *n* a member of the legislating body of some towns or cities in the United States and Canada

Al·der·shot /áwldər shòt/ city and military center in Hampshire, southern England. Population: 51,356 (1991).

al·der·wom·an /áwldər wòòmmən/ (*plural* **-wom·en** /-wìmmin/) *n* **1.** a woman who is a member of the legislating body of some towns or cities in the United States and Canada **2.** a woman who was a senior member of an English or Welsh local council before the local government reorganization of 1974

al·des·leu·kin /ál dez lòokin/ *n* a genetically engineered drug. Use: treatment of cancer. [Late 20C. < *aldes-* + *-leukin*, INN stem]

Al·ding·ton /áwlding tòn/, **Richard** (1892–1962) British writer. He was a founder member of the imagist movement with Ezra Pound and his first wife, Hilda Doolittle. Much of his writing was influenced by his experiences as a soldier in Europe in World War I.

Al·dis lamp /áwldiss-/ *n* a signaling device in the form of a portable lamp used to flash messages in Morse code [Early 20C. After A. C. W. *Aldis* (1878–1953), British inventor]

al·do·hex·ose /àldō hék sōss/ *n* a sugar containing six carbon atoms and an aldehyde group, e.g., glucose or mannose [Early 20C. Contraction of ALDEHYDE + HEXOSE]

al·dol /ál dàwl/ *n* **1.** a colorless or pale yellow oily liquid. Use: catalyst in the vulcanization of rubber, solvent, perfumes. **2.** an organic compound containing an aldehyde group and an alcohol group on neighboring carbon atoms

al·dol·ase /áldə làyss, -làyz/ *n* an enzyme that aids the breakdown of fructose [Mid-20C. < German]

al·dose /ál dōss/ *n* a sugar (**monosaccharide**) that contains an aldehyde group

al·dos·ter·one /al dóstə rōn/ *n* a steroid hormone, secreted by the adrenal cortex, that controls mineral and water balance

al·dos·ter·on·ism /al dóstərə nìzzəm/ *n* a condition caused by excessive secretion of aldosterone by the adrenal cortex, characterized by weakness, high blood pressure, and large fluid intake and urinary output

Al·drich /áwldrich/, **Thomas Bailey** (1836–1907) US writer. The editor of *The Atlantic Monthly* (1881–90) and the author of stories and poems, he is best remembered for the autobiographical novel *The Story of a Bad Boy* (1870).

> "We vivisect the nightingale / To probe the secret of his note."
> [Thomas Bailey Aldrich, "Realism," *The Poems of Thomas Bailey Aldrich*; 1907]

Al·drin /áwldrin/, **Buzz** (*b.* 1930) US astronaut. He was the second man to walk on the Moon (1969). Full name **Aldrin, Jr., Edwin Eugene**

> "Magnificent desolation!"
> [Buzz Aldrin. Message to NASA upon walking with Neil Armstrong on the Moon; July 20, 1969]

ale /ayl/ *n* an alcoholic drink made from rapidly fermented malt to which hops have been added [Old English *ealu* < Germanic, perhaps "intoxicating drink"]

SPELLCHECK See *ail*.

a·le·a·to·ry /áylee ə tàwree/ *adj* **1.** depending on chance or contingency **2.** *also* **a·le·a·to·ric** /áylee ə táwrik/ having the sequence of given notes or passages in a piece of music chosen at random by the performer or left to chance [Late 17C. < Latin *aleatorius* < *alea* "dice"]

A·lec·to /ə léktō/ *n* in Greek mythology, one of the three Furies

a·lee /ə lée/ *adv, adj* on or to the leeward side

a·lef *n* another spelling of **aleph**

ale·house /áyl hòwss/ *n* a place where ale was sold and served (*archaic*)

~~**alein**~~ incorrect spelling of **alien**

Al·e·man·ni /àllə mánnee/ *npl* a group of Germanic peoples who settled in areas around the Rhine, Main, and Danube rivers at the beginning of the 4th century A.D. [< Latin < Germanic, perhaps "all the peoples"]

Al·e·man·nic /àllə mánnik/ *n* **1.** GERMAN DIALECTS a group of High German dialects spoken in Alsace, Switzerland, and southwestern Germany **2.** ANCIENT GERMANIC LANGUAGE the language of the Alemanni ■ *adj* **1.** OF ALEMANNI relating to the Alemanni, or their language or culture **2.** OF ALEMANNIC relating to Alemannic

A·lem·bert /àlləm bér, à laaN bér/, **Jean le Rond d'** (1717–83) French philosopher, mathematician, and encyclopedist. He formulated d'Alembert's principle, a landmark in the study of mechanics, in 1743, and collaborated with Denis Diderot on the great *Encyclopédie* (1751–80).

> "The imagination in a mathematician who creates makes no less difference than in a poet who invents…Of all the great men of antiquity, Archimedes may be the one who most deserves to be placed beside Homer."
> [Jean le Rond d'Alembert, *Discours preliminaire de l'encyclopédie* (*Preliminary Discourse to the Encyclopedia*); 1751]

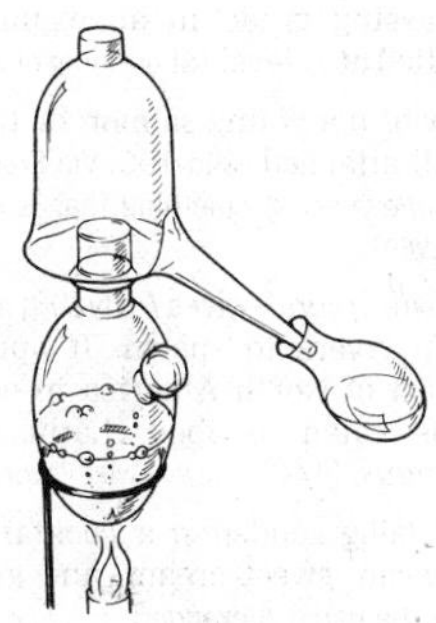

alembic

a·lem·bic /ə lémbik/ *n* an apparatus formerly used in distillation [14C. Via Old French and medieval Latin *alembicus* < Arabic *al-'anbīk* "the still" < Greek *ambix* "cup"]

a·len·dron·ic ac·id /àllən dronic-/ *n* a drug used as its sodium salt. Use: treatment of osteoporosis and Paget's disease.

a·leph /áa lèf, áaləf/, **a·lef** *n* the first letter of the Hebrew alphabet, transliterated as an apostrophe and pronounced as a glottal stop. See table at **alphabet** [14C. < Hebrew and Phoenician *āleph* "first letter of the alphabet, ox"]

A·lep·po /ə léppō/ city in northwestern Syria, northeast of Homs, an important center on an ancient trade route to the East. Population: 1,582,930 (1994). Former name **Beroea**

a·lert /ə lúrt/ *adj* **1.** WATCHFUL watchful and ready to deal with whatever happens **2.** MENTALLY LIVELY clear-headed and responsive ■ *n* **1.** WARNING OF DANGER an alarm or warning of danger **2.** TIME OF DANGER a period of time during which an alert remains in force ■ *vt* (**a·lert·ed, a·lert·ing, a·lerts**) WARN SOMEBODY to make somebody aware of a possible danger or difficulty ○ *Police have alerted the public to the danger.* [Late 16C. Via French *alerte* < Italian *all'erta* "on the lookout"] —**a·lert·ly** *adv* —**a·lert·ness** *n* ◇ **on the alert** watchful and ready to deal with whatever happens

à l'es·pa·gnole *adj* prepared in a style inspired by Spanish cookery, usually containing tomatoes, sweet peppers, onions, and garlic, and fried in olive oil [< French, "in the Spanish style"]

Al·es·san·dri Pal·ma /àllə sàndree pálmə, -sàandree páalmə/, **Arturo** (1868–1950) president of Chile (1920–24, 1925, and 1932–38). Elected president in 1920 on a reform platform, he resigned in 1924 when a military junta seized power. In his second and third terms, he drafted a long-standing constitution and established a central bank.

a·leth·ic /ə léthik, -léeth-/ *adj* relating to the philosophical concepts of truth and possibility and especially to the branch of logic that formalizes them [Late 20C. < Greek *alētheia* "truth" < *alēthēs* "true"]

al·eu·rone /állyə rōn/, **al·eu·ron** /-ròn/ *n* a protein occurring as granules in some plants, especially in seeds [Mid-19C. Alteration of Greek *aleuron* "wheat flour"] —**al·eu·ron·ic** /àllyə rónnik/ *adj*

A·leut /ə lóot, àllee óot/ (*plural same* or **A·leuts**) *n* **1.** a member of an indigenous people who live in the Aleutian Islands and coastal southwestern Alaska **2.** an Eskimo-Aleut language spoken in the Aleutian Islands and coastal parts of Alaska. Native speakers: 500. [Late 18C. < Russian] —**A·leut** *adj* —**A·leu·tian** /ə lóosh'n/ *adj*

A·leu·tian Is·lands /ə lóosh'n-/ chain of islands stretching westward for about 1,100 mi./1,800 km from the tip of the Alaska Peninsula and separating the Pacific Ocean from the Bering Sea to the north

A·leu·tian Range mountain range on the eastern coast of the Alaska Peninsula that includes the Katmai National Park and Preserve. The highest peak is Mount Redoubt 10,197 ft./3,108 m.

A·leu·tian Trench ocean trench at the western end of the Aleutian Islands. Depth: 26,574 ft./8,100 m.

A lev·el *n* **1.** *UK* in England, Wales, and Northern Ireland, the advanced level of any subject studied to gain a General Certificate of Education qualification. It is divided into two levels, AS level and

A2. **2.** a passing grade in an examination in a subject studied at A level [Shortening of *Advanced level*]

a·lev·in /állәvin/ *n* a young salmon or trout with the yolk sac still attached [Mid-19C. Via French < assumed Vulgar Latin *allevamen* "something that is raised" < Latin *levare* (see LEVER)]

ale·wife /áyl wīf/ (*plural* **-wives** /-wīvz/) *n* a herring that migrates up rivers to spawn. It appears off the Atlantic coast of North America in early summer and can be eaten as food. Latin name: *Alosa pseudoharengus.* [14C. < ALE + WIFE "woman"]

a·lex·an·der /àllig zándәr/ *n* a cocktail made from crème de cacao, sweet cream, and gin or brandy [Early 20C. < the name *Alexander*]

A·lex·an·der II /àllig zándәr/ (1818–81) tsar of Russia. He emancipated the serfs in 1861 and sold the Russian lands in North America (now Alaska) to the United States in 1867

A·lex·an·der III, Pope (1105?–81) He was pope from 1159 to 1181, during which time he imposed penance on Henry II of England for the murder of St. Thomas à Becket. Born **Bandinelli, Rolando**

A·lex·an·der, Grover Cleveland (1887–1950) US baseball player who pitched for various teams (1911–30) and was voted into the Baseball Hall of Fame in 1938

A·lex·an·der tech·nique *n* a method of improving the posture that involves developing awareness of it [Mid-20C. After Frederick *Alexander* (1869–1955), Australian physiotherapist]

A·lex·an·der the Great (356–323 B.C.) king of Macedonia. He conquered most of the ancient world from Asia Minor to Egypt and parts of India.

A·lex·an·dra /àllig zándrә/, **Empress of Russia** (1872–1918) The wife of Tsar Nicholas II, she was executed by the Bolsheviks at Ekaterinberg

A·lex·an·dria /àllig zándree ә/ **1.** city in eastern Virginia on the Potomac River, south of Washington, D.C. Population: 130,804 (2002 estimate). **2.** city and Mediterranean seaport in northern Egypt, on the delta of the Nile River. Founded by Alexander the Great in 332 B.C., it was a major cultural center of the ancient world, renowned for its library. Population: 3,328,000 (1998). —**Al·ex·an·dri·an** *adj*

al·ex·an·drine /àllig zándrin, -zán dreen/ *n* **1.** ENGLISH VERSE FORM in English poetry, a line of verse that has six iambic feet and usually a caesura after the third foot **2.** FRENCH VERSE FORM in French poetry, a line of verse that has twelve syllables and usually a caesura after the sixth syllable ■ *adj* LIKE OR IN ALEXANDRINES typical of or written in alexandrines [Late 16C. < French, after the romance *Alexandre* about Alexander the Great, which was written in this meter]

al·ex·an·drite /àllig zán drīt/ *n* a precious stone that is a green chrysoberyl. Use: gems. [Mid-19C. < German *Alexandrit*, after *Alexander* II (1818–81), tsar of Russia, because it was discovered on the day of his majority]

a·lex·i·a /ә léksee ә/ *n* a loss of the ability to read, caused by a disorder of the central nervous system [Late 19C. < A[3] + Greek *lexis* "speech"; meaning influenced by Latin *legere* "read"]

A·lex·is Mi·khail·o·vich /ә lèksiss mi kīlәvich/ (1629–76) tsar of Russia (1645–76). Ruling from 1645 to 1676, he legitimized serfdom (1649) and suppressed a peasant revolt (1670–71).

al·fa *n, adj* another spelling of **alpha**

~~**alfabet**~~ incorrect spelling of **alphabet**

al·fa·cal·cid·ol /àlfә kálssә dàwl/ *n* a derivative of vitamin D used by the body in the regulation of calcium and phosphate, and as a drug in the treatment of vitamin D deficiency [Late 20C. < *alfa* + *calcidol*, INN stem]

al·fal·fa /al fálfә/ *n* a plant of the pea family. Use: hay, forage crop. Native to: Europe, Asia. Latin name: *Medicago sativa.* [Mid-19C. Via Spanish < Arabic *al-faṣfaṣa* "the best kind of fodder"]

Al Fa·tah /àl fáttә/ *n* a Palestinian political group that seeks to establish an independent Palestinian state. Formed in the 1950s, it became part of the Palestine Liberation Organization in 1968. [Late 20C. < Arabic *al* "the" + acronym < *Ḥ(arakat) T(aḥrīr) F(ilastīn)* "Movement for the Liberation of Palestine" (resembling *fataḥ* "conquer")]

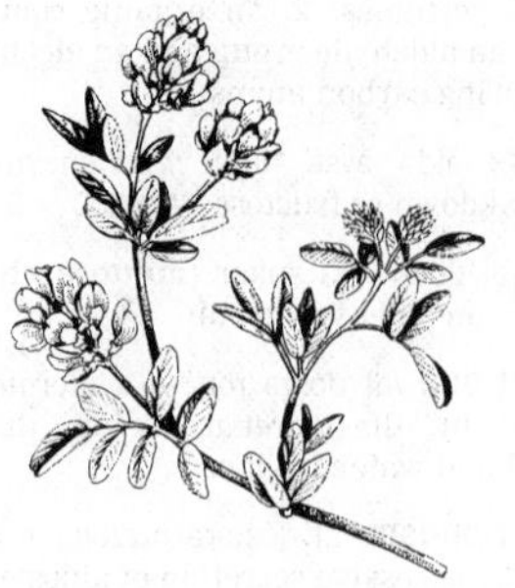

alfalfa

al·fen·tan·il hyd·ro·chlo·ride /al fèntәnil-/ *n* a drug that is an opium derivative. Use: general anesthesia. [< *al-* + *-fentanil*, INN stem]

al·fil·a·ri·a /al fillә rée ә/, **al·fil·e·ri·a** *n* a plant of the geranium family grown for forage in the western United States. Flowers: pink, purple. Native to: Europe. Latin name: *Erodium cicutarium.* [Mid-19C. Alteration of American Spanish *alfilerillo* "little pin" < Spanish *alfiler* "pin" < Arabic *al-ḵilāl* "thorn"]

al-Fit·r /al fíttәr/ *n* ISLAM same as **Eid al-Fitr**

Al·fon·so XIII /al fónssō/ (1886–1941) king of Spain. His reign (1886–1931) was marked by riots and revolts. He was forced into exile when Spain became a republic.

al·for·ja /al fáwr haà/ *n Southwest US* same as **saddlebag** [Early 17C. Via Spanish < Arabic *al-ḵurj* "the saddlebag"]

Al·fre·do /al fréddō/ *adj* served with a rich sauce made from cream, butter, and Parmesan cheese [Late 20C. Origin ?]

Al·fred the Great /álfrәd/ (849–901) king of Wessex. He reigned from 871 until his death, reconquering Danish territories in England. He also translated several Latin works into English.

al·fres·co /al fréskō/ *adv* outdoors or in the open air ■ *adj* taking place or located outdoors [Mid-18C. < Italian, "in the fresh (air)"]

Alf·ven /aal váyn/, **Hannes Olof Gosta** (1908–95) Swedish theoretical physicist who worked on the harnessing of nuclear fusion power and was awarded the Nobel Prize in physics (1970)

Alf·ven wave *n* a magnetic disturbance that travels along magnetic field lines in a plasma

Alg. *abbr* **1.** Algeria **2.** Algerian

al·ga /álgә/ (*plural* **-gae** /-jee/ or **-gas**) *n* a photosynthetic organism of a group that lives mainly in water and includes the seaweeds. Algae differ from plants in not having true leaves, roots, or stems. [Mid-16C. < Latin, "seaweed"] —**al·gal** *adj* —**al·goid** /ál gòyd/ *adj*

USAGE alga or **algae**? ***Alga*** is singular and ***algae*** is plural; it is generally regarded as incorrect to use ***algae*** as a singular noun.

---

al·gal bloom *n* an excessive growth of algae on or near the surface of water, occurring naturally or as a result of an excess of nutrients from organic pollution

al·gar·ro·ba /àlgә róbә/, **al·ga·ro·ba** *n* **1.** TREES same as **carob 2.** TREES same as **honey mesquite 3.** the edible fruit of the carob or the mesquite [Late 16C. Via Spanish < Arabic *al-ḵarrūba* "the carob"]

Al·gar·ve /aal gaárvә/ region in southern Portugal. Its coastline is the country's leading vacation area.

al·ge·bra /áljәbrә/ *n* **1.** the branch of mathematics in which symbols, usually letters of the alphabet, represent unknown numbers **2.** the study of structures in mathematics such as groups, rings, fields, and categories [Mid-16C. Via Italian and medieval Latin < Arabic *al-jabr* "the reuniting," in the title of a treatise by the mathematician al-Khwarizmi] —**al·ge·bra·ist** /àlji bráy ist/ *n*

al·ge·bra·ic /àljә bráy ik/ *adj* **1.** relating to or involving algebra **2.** relating to or using only finite numbers, expressions, and operations —**al·ge·bra·i·cal·ly** *adv*

Al·ge·cir·as /àljә seérәss/ port and resort near the southern tip of Spain. Population: 106,710 (2002).

Al·ger /áljәr/, **Horatio** (1834–99) US writer and cleric. He wrote many novels, including *Ragged Dick* (1867) and *Tattered Tom* (1871). His works feature boys born into poverty who, through hard work, achieve wealth and success.

Algeria

Al·ge·ri·a /al jéeree ә/ country in northwestern Africa. It became independent from France in 1962. Language: Arabic. Currency: Algerian dinar. Capital: Algiers. Population: 32,818,500 (2003). Area: 919,595 sq. mi./2,381,741 sq. km. Official name **Democratic and Popular Republic of Algeria** —**Al·ge·ri·an** *adj, n*

al·ge·sia /al jéezee ә, al jéezhә/ *n* sensitivity to or perception of pain [< modern Latin < Greek *algēsis* < *algos* "pain"]

-algia *suffix* pain ○ *neuralgia* [< Greek *algos* "pain"]

al·gi·cide /álji sīd/ *n* a substance that kills algae or prevents their growth —**al·gi·ci·dal** /àlji sīd'l/ *adj*

al·gid /áljid/ *adj* describes an episode during a severe fever when the patient's body temperature suddenly drops to an unusually low level [Early 17C. < Latin *algidus* < *algere* "be cold"] —**al·gid·i·ty** /al jíddәtee/ *n*

Al·giers /al jéerz/ capital, chief port, and largest city of Algeria. Population: 2,561,992 (1998).

al·gin /áljin/ *n* a viscous liquid, especially alginic acid or an alginate. Source: seaweed. Use: thickener or emulsifier in plastics or food. [Late 19C. < ALGA + -IN]

al·gi·nate /áljә nàyt, áljәnәt/ *n* a salt or ester of alginic acid. Use: thickener or emulsifier in plastics or food.

al·gin·ic ac·id /al jìnnik-/ *n* an insoluble powdery acid. Source: brown seaweed. Use: thickener in foods; adjuvant in pharmaceuticals; in antacid preparations, cosmetics, textiles. Formula: $(C_6H_8O_6)_n$.

algo- *prefix* pain ○ *algophobia* [< Greek *algos* "pain"]

ALGOL /ál gòl/, **Al·gol** *n* a high-level computer programming language that uses algebraic symbols in solving mathematical and scientific problems. Full form **algorithm-oriented language** [Mid-20C. Contraction of *algorithm-oriented language*]

al·go·lag·ni·a /àlgō lágnee ә/ *n* sexual pleasure experienced through inflicting or experiencing pain [Early 20C. < Greek *algos* "pain" + *lagneia* "lust"] —**al·go·lag·nic** *adj* —**al·go·lag·nist** *n*

al·gol·o·gy /al góllәjee/ *n* the branch of botany concerned with the scientific study of algae —**al·go·log·i·cal** /àlgә lójjik'l/ *adj* —**al·gol·o·gist** *n*

Al·gon·ki·an *n, adj* LANG, PEOPLES another spelling of **Algonquian**

Al·gon·kin *n, adj* LANG, PEOPLES another spelling of **Algonquin**[1]

Al·gon·qui·an /al gŏngkee әn, -kwee-/ (*plural same* or **-ans**), **Al·gon·ki·an** /-kee-/ *n* **1.** a group of Native North American languages that are, or were, spoken in central and eastern Canada and parts of the central and eastern United States. Algonquian includes the languages of the Arapaho, Blackfoot, Cheyenne, Delaware, Fox, Ojibwa, Sauk, and Shawnee peoples. **2.** a member of an Algonquian-speaking people [Late 19C. < ALGONQUIN[1]] —**Al·gon·qui·an** *adj*

LANGUAGE HERITAGE See ***Native North American.***

Al·gon·qui·an-Wa·kash·an *n* a family of over 40 Native American languages spoken throughout wide areas of Canada and in the central, eastern, and southern United States. Its three main branches are Algonquian, Salishan, and Wakashan.

Al·gon·quin[1] /al góngkin, -kwin/ (*plural same* or **-quins**), **Al·gon·kin** /-kin/ (*plural same* or **-kins**) *n* **1.** a member of a group of Native North American peoples living along the Ottawa and St. Lawrence rivers in eastern Canada. Historically, the Algonquin were allies of the French against the Iroquois people. **2.** a Native North American language spoken in Quebec and Ontario. Native speakers: 3,000. [Early 17C. Via Canadian French < Algonquian] —**Al·gon·quin** *adj*

Al·gon·quin[2] /al góngkin, -kwin/ village in northeastern Illinois. Population: 26,362 (2002 estimate).

al·go·pho·bi·a /àlgə fṓbee ə/ *n* an unusually intense fear of pain

al·go·rithm /álgə rìthəm/ *n* **1.** a logical step-by-step procedure for solving a mathematical problem in a finite number of steps, often involving repetition of the same basic operation **2.** a logical sequence of steps for solving a problem, often written out as a flow chart, that can be translated into a computer program [Late 17C. Alteration, after Greek *arithmos* "number," of *algorism*, via Old French and medieval Latin < Arabic *al-Kwārizmī*, name of the 9C mathematician who introduced algorithms to the West] —**al·go·rith·mic** /àlgə ríthmik/ *adj*

Al·gren /áwlgrin/, **Nelson** (1909–81) US writer. His gritty fiction, often set in his native Chicago, includes the novels *The Man with the Golden Arm* (1949) and *A Walk on the Wild Side* (1956), both of which were made into successful movies. Born **Abraham, Nelson Ahlgren**

al·gua·cil /àlgwaa seél/, **al·gua·zil** *n Hispanic* in Latin America, a law enforcement officer [Early 16C. Via Spanish < Arabic *al-wazīr* "the vizier"]

Al·ham·bra[1] /al hámbrə/ *n* a citadel and palace in Granada, Spain, built for Moorish kings in the 12th and 13th centuries

Al·ham·bra[2] city in southwestern California, northeast of Los Angeles. Population: 87,655 (2002 estimate).

Al·ha·zen /àl hə zén/ (965–1040) Arab scientist. He made important contributions in optics, astronomy, and mathematics. Arabic name **Abu Ali al-Hasan ibn al-Haytham**

A·li /aa leé/ cousin and son-in-law of Muhammad. He became the fourth caliph. After his assassination in A.D. 661 following a civil war, Islam divided into two branches, the Sunni and the Shia.

Muhammad Ali

A·li, Muhammad (*b.* 1942) US boxer, three times world heavyweight champion (1964–71, 1974–78, 1978–80). Born **Clay, Cassius Marcellus**

> "At home I am a nice guy: but I don't want the world to know. Humble people, I've found, don't get very far."
> [Muhammad Ali, *The Sunday Express (London)*; January 13, 1963]

A·li·a /aálee ə/, **Ramiz** (*b.* 1925) president of Albania (1982–92). He succeeded Enver Hoxha as leader of the communist party in 1985 and paved the way for general elections in 1990. He resigned in 1992 after his party was defeated at the polls.

a·li·as /áylee əss, áylyəss/ *n* **1.** FALSE NAME an assumed name that somebody uses **2.** FILE OR DIRECTORY NAME a name assigned to a computer file or directory, e.g., to make it more convenient to locate or manipulate ■ *adv* ALSO KNOWN AS otherwise or also known as [15C. < Latin, "otherwise"]

al·i·bi /állə bī/ *n* (*plural* **-bis**) **1.** ACCUSED'S CLAIM OF HAVING BEEN ELSEWHERE a form of defense against an accusation in which the accused person claims or proves that he or she was somewhere else at the time that a crime was committed **2.** SOMEBODY OR SOMETHING GIVING ALIBI somebody or something used by an accused person to prove that he or she was somewhere else at the time that a crime was committed **3.** ⚠ EXCUSE an explanation offered to justify something (*informal*) ■ *vt* (**-bied, -bi·ing, -bis**) GIVE ALIBI FOR SOMEBODY to provide an alibi or excuse for somebody [Late 17C. < Latin, "elsewhere"]

USAGE alibi meaning "excuse": ***Alibi*** should only be used informally in the weakened meaning "an explanation offered to justify something," because it has a precise legal meaning that is in danger of being compromised. Avoid overuse when *excuse* is the more natural word to use: *He used his illness as an excuse* [not *as an alibi*] *for leaving work early.*

Al·i·can·te /àlli kaántee, -tày/ city and port in southeastern Spain. Population: 293,629 (2002).

A·lice /álliss/ city in southeastern Texas, west of Corpus Christi. Population: 19,104 (2002 estimate).

Al·ice-in-Won·der·land /àlliss in wúndərland/ *adj* absurd, fantastic, or completely at odds with reality [Early 20C. < *Alice's Adventures in Wonderland* (1865), fantasy by Lewis CARROLL]

Al·ice Springs /àlliss-/ town in the southern part of Australia's Northern Territory, a center of tourism. Population: 26,306 (2002 estimate).

al·i·cy·clic /àllee síklik, -sík-/ *adj* describes organic compounds that have carbon atoms joined in a string (**open chain**) as well as in rings [Late 19C. Blend of ALIPHATIC + CYCLIC]

al·i·dade /állə dàyd/ *n* an instrument consisting of a rule with sights at both ends, used in surveying for measuring angles and directions [14C. Via French and Spanish < Arabic *al-idada* "the revolving radius"]

a·li·en /áylyən, -lee ən/ *n* **1.** EXTRATERRESTRIAL BEING a being from another planet or another part of the universe, especially in works of science fiction **2.** NONCITIZEN RESIDENT OF COUNTRY a citizen of a country other than the one he or she is currently in **3.** OUTSIDER somebody who does not belong to or does not feel accepted by a group or society ■ *adj* **1.** STRANGE outside somebody's normal or previous experience and seeming strange and sometimes threatening ○ *an alien practice* **2.** INCONSISTENT WITH SOMEBODY OR SOMETHING not in keeping or totally incompatible with the nature of somebody or something ○ *ideas that were alien to her philosophy* **3.** NOT FROM COUNTRY not a citizen of, or not belonging to, the country in question **4.** EXTRATERRESTRIAL from another world or part of the universe, or relating to extraterrestrial beings, especially in works of science fiction ○ *an alien spacecraft* ■ *vt* (**-ened, -en·ing, -ens**) LAW same as **alienate** (sense 4) [14C. Directly or via Old French < Latin *alienus* < *alius* "other"]

al·ien·a·ble /áylyənəb'l, áylee ən-/ *adj* capable of being transferred by a legal process to another owner —**al·ien·a·bil·i·ty** /àylyənə bíllətee, àylee ənə-/ *n*

a·li·en ab·scond·er *n* an illegal foreign visitor to the United States who has final orders to leave the country but has not done so, has refused to do so, or has disappeared

al·ien·ate /áylyə nàyt, áylee ə-/ (**-at·ed, -at·ing, -ates**) *vt* **1.** MAKE SOMEBODY UNFRIENDLY to cause somebody to change his or her previously friendly or supportive attitude and become unfriendly, unsympathetic, or hostile ○ *His selfishness alienated all of his friends.* **2.** MAKE SOMEBODY FEEL DISAFFECTED to make somebody feel that he or she does not belong to or share in something, or is isolated from it (*often passive*) ○ *People like that often feel alienated from society.* **3.** TURN SOMETHING AWAY to cause something, especially somebody's affections, to be directed toward somebody or something else **4.** LAW TRANSFER OWNERSHIP TO SOMEBODY to transfer the ownership of property or a right to somebody [15C. < Latin *alienat-*, past participle of *alienare* "make somebody else's, alienate" < *alienus* (see ALIEN)] —**al·ien·a·tion** /àylyə náysh'n, àylee ə-/ *n* —**al·ien·a·tor** *n*

al·ien·ee /àylyə neé, àylee ə-/ *n* somebody to whom property or a right is transferred by a legal process

al·ien·ist /áylyənist, áylee ə-/ *n* **1.** *US* an expert witness, usually a psychiatrist, who is accepted by a court of law as qualified to assess the psychological state of somebody appearing in court **2.** same as **psychiatrist** (*archaic*) [Mid-19C. < French *aliéniste* < Latin *alienare* "estrange, make irrational" (see ALIENATE)]

al·ien·or /áylyə nàwr, -lee ə-/ *n* somebody who transfers property or a right to somebody else by a legal process

a·li·form /áylə fàwrm, állə-/ *adj* shaped like a wing (*technical*) [Early 18C. < Latin *ala* "wing"]

A·li·ghie·ri /alli gyérree/ ➧ **Dante**

a·light[1] /ə lít/ (**a·light·ed** or **a·lit** /ə lít/, **a·light·ing, a·lights**) *vi* **1.** GET OUT OF VEHICLE to step down or dismount from something onto the ground or a platform ○ *The VIPs alighted from their train.* **2.** LAND to land or settle after a flight ○ *A crow alighted on a branch.* **3.** FIND BY CHANCE to happen to find, spot, or come to rest on something ○ *alighted on a suitable candidate* [Old English *alīhtan* < *a-* "away, up, out" + *līhtan* "make lighter in weight"]

a·light[2] /ə lít/ *adj* **1.** FULL OF ENERGY filled with or radiating energy, excitement, interest, or pleasure ○ *His face was alight with joy.* **2.** LIT UP lit up or full of light ○ *The sky was alight with fireworks.* **3.** ON FIRE on fire or burning ○ *set the bonfire alight* [Old English *aliht* "illuminated," past participle of *alihtan* "light up"]

a·lign /ə lín/ (**a·ligned, a·lign·ing, a·ligns**), **a·line** (**a·lined, a·lin·ing, a·lines**) *v* **1.** *vti* BRING SOMETHING INTO LINE to place something in a straight line or in an orderly position in relation to something else, or be placed in this way **2.** *vti* BRING OR COME INTO CORRECT POSITION to bring something such as different parts of a machine or structure, into the correct position with respect to each other or something else, or come into this position **3.** *vti* DECLARE SUPPORT FOR SOMEBODY OR SOMETHING to declare your support, or the support of somebody or something you represent, for a person, group, argument, or point of view ○ *The country aligned itself with NATO.* **4.** *vi* FORM LINE to become arranged in a line ○ *The marching band aligned behind the drum major.* [15C. < Old French *alignier* < Latin *linea* "line"] —**a·lign·er** *n*

a·lign·ment /ə línmənt/, **a·line·ment** *n* **1.** LINEAR OR ORDERLY ARRANGEMENT the arrangement of something in a straight line or in an orderly position in relation to something else **2.** POSITIONING OF SOMETHING FOR PROPER PERFORMANCE the correct position or positioning of different components with respect to each other or something else, so that they perform properly ○ *The wheels are out of alignment.* **3.** SUPPORT OR ALLIANCE support for, or a political alliance with, a person, group, argument, or point of view ○ *shifting alignments within the legislature* **4.** GROUND PLAN a ground plan, especially one showing the course of a road or railroad track

a·like /ə lík/ *adj* similar in appearance or character ○ *They're so alike, it's difficult to tell them apart.* ■ *adv* in a similar or the same way ○ *The film will please young and old alike.* [Old English *gelīc* "alike, similar" < Germanic, "body, form"] —**a·like·ness** *n*

al·i·ment /álləmənt/ *n* something that feeds, sustains, or supports something else (*formal*) [15C. Via French < Latin *alimentum* < *alere* "nourish"] —**al·i·ment** *vt* —**al·i·men·tal** /àllə mént'l/ *adj* —**al·i·men·tal·ly** *adv*

al·i·men·ta·ry /àllə méntəree/ *adj* (*formal*) **1.** OF FOOD OR NUTRITION relating to food or nutrition **2.** PROVIDING NOURISHMENT providing food or nourishment **3.** PROVIDING SUPPORT providing support or maintenance

al·i·men·ta·ry ca·nal *n* the tubular passage between the mouth and the anus, including the organs through which food passes for digestion and elimination as waste

al·i·men·ta·tion /àllәmәn táysh'n/ *n* (*formal*) **1.** the providing of food or nourishment **2.** the providing of support or maintenance —**al·i·men·ta·tive** /àllə méntətiv/ *adj*

al·i·mo·ny /állə mōnee/ *n* **1.** money paid regularly by one marriage partner to the other as ordered by a court after a legal separation or divorce, or during proceedings for divorce or separation **2.** something that provides somebody with a living [Early 17C. < Latin *alimonia* "subsistence" < *alere* "nourish"]

a·line *vti* another spelling of **align**

A-line *adj* resembling the outline of the letter A, especially in a garment by flaring out from the top to the bottom ○ *an A-line dress*

a·line·ment *n* another spelling of **alignment**

al·i·phat·ic /àllə fáttik/ *adj* describes organic compounds that have carbon atoms joined in a string (**open chain**) [Late 19C. < Greek *aleiphat-* "fat," because originally applied to fatty acids]

al·i·quant /állə kwònt, -kwənt/ *adj* describes a number or quantity that cannot divide another number or quantity without leaving a remainder [Late 17C. < Latin *aliquantum* "somewhat"]

al·i·quot /állə kwòt, -kwət/ *adj* describes a number or quantity that will divide another number or quantity without leaving a remainder ■ *n* an aliquot part [Late 16C. Via French < Latin, "a certain number"]

A list *n* the people most sought after or most in demand for an activity such as a social function or for recruitment to a team or organization (*informal; hyphenated when used before a noun*)

a·lit past participle, past tense of **alight**[1]

a·lit·er·ate /ay líttərət/ *n* somebody who, though usually able to read, is completely uninterested in reading or literature —**a·lit·er·acy** *n* —**a·lit·er·ate** *adj*

a·live /ə lív/ *adj* **1.** LIVING living, especially still living, and not dead **2.** OF ALL PEOPLE LIVING of all people currently living (*usually used with a superlative*) ○ *the luckiest person alive* **3.** STILL IN EXISTENCE still existing, continuing, or functioning ○ *The movement remained alive by going underground.* **4.** FULL OF LIFE full of energy and vigor, and with a zest for and interest in life ○ *He feels alive only when he is writing his book.* **5.** ANIMATED active or animated, especially full of busy activity or a sense of excitement ○ *The place doesn't come alive till after midnight.* **6.** STILL INTERESTING still interesting, relevant, or vividly imaginable for people in the present day ○ *Her brief was to make the subject come alive for a modern audience.* **7.** SWARMING WITH SOMETHING full of or swarming with people or animals ○ *The floor of the tent was alive with ants.* **8.** AWARE OF SOMETHING sensitive to or aware of things ○ *alive to the danger involved in the operation* [Old English *on līfe* "in life"] —**a·live·ness** *n* ◇ **alive and kicking** still active, healthy, or functioning vigorously (*informal*)

SYNONYMS See *living*.

a·li·yah /aa lée yaà, àalee yaá/ *n* travel to Israel by somebody who is Jewish in order to take up residence [Mid-20C. < Hebrew, "ascent"]

a·liz·a·rin /ə lízzərin/ *n* an orange-red or brownish yellow crystalline compound. Source: coal tar, formerly madder root. Use: dyes. Formula: $C_{14}H_8O_4$. [Mid-19C. < French *alizarine*, probably < Arabic *alizari* "madder"]

Al Ja·zee·ra /àl jə zéerə/, **Al Je·ze·ra** *n* an independent Arab television station in Qatar [< Arabic *Al-Jazīrah*, literally "the peninsula"]

al-Kadr *n* ISLAM same as **Lailat ul-Qadr**

al·ka·hest /álkə hèst/, **al·ca·hest** *n* a hypothetical universal solvent sought by alchemists [Mid-17C. Coined by Paracelsus, in imitation of Arabic]

al·ka·les·cent /àlkə léss'nt/ *adj* slightly alkaline, or becoming alkaline —**al·ka·les·cence** *n*

al·ka·li /álkə lī/ (*plural* **-lis** *or same*) *n* **1.** ACID-NEUTRALIZING CHEMICAL SUBSTANCE a water-soluble chemical that reacts with acids to form salts, has a pH above 7, and turns red litmus paper blue **2.** SOLUBLE SALT HARMFUL TO CROPS a soluble mineral salt found in some dry soils and natural waters at levels harmful to agriculture **3.** SOLUBLE PLANT ASH the water-soluble material in the ash of burnt plants [14C. Via medieval Latin < Arabic *al-ḳalī* "the ashes of saltwort," from which it was first obtained]

al·ka·li met·al *n* a metallic element belonging to group 1 of the periodic table, either lithium, sodium, potassium, rubidium, cesium, or francium, characterized by being soft, white, and highly reactive

al·ka·lim·e·ter /àlkə límmətər/ *n* an instrument used for measuring the concentration of alkalis in a solution —**al·ka·li·met·ric** /àlkəli méttrik/ *adj* —**al·ka·li·met·ri·cal·ly** *adv* —**al·ka·lim·e·try** *n*

al·ka·line /álkəlin, -līn/ *adj* having the properties of an alkali, or containing an alkali or alkalis

al·ka·line-earth met·al, **al·ka·line earth** *n* a metallic element belonging to group 2 of the periodic table, either beryllium, magnesium, calcium, strontium, barium, or radium, characterized by having a valence of two

al·ka·line phos·pha·tase *n* an enzyme that controls hydrolysis. Use: in clinical diagnosis of many illnesses.

al·ka·lin·i·ty /àlkə línnətee/ *n* the concentration of alkali in a solution, measured in terms of pH

al·ka·lize /álkə līz/ (**-lized, -liz·ing, -liz·es**) *vti* to make something alkaline, or become alkaline

al·ka·loid /álkə lòyd/ *n* a group of nitrogen-containing compounds that are physiologically active as poisons or drugs [Early 19C. < ALKALI, because their chemical properties are similar to it] —**al·ka·loid·al** /àlkə lóyd'l/ *adj*

al·ka·lo·sis /àlkə lóssiss/ *n* an unusually high level of alkalinity in the blood, other body fluids, or body tissues, causing a high blood pH —**al·ka·lot·ic** /àlkə lóttik/ *adj*

al·kane /ál kàyn/ *n* an open-chain hydrocarbon containing only carbon-to-carbon or carbon-to-hydrogen single bonds and belonging to a series whose members all have the same general chemical formula. Formula: C_nH_{2n+2}.

al·ka·net /álkə nèt/ (*plural* **-nets** *or same*) *n* **1.** RED DYE a red dye obtained from the roots of a European plant **2.** EUROPEAN DYE PLANT a plant related to borage with red roots that produce alkanet. Flowers: small, blue. Native to: Europe. Latin name: *Alkanna tinctoria*. **3.** PLANT RELATED TO ALKANET a bristly plant related to alkanet. Flowers: blue. Native to: Europe, Asia, Africa. Genus: *Anchusa*. [14C. Probably via Old Spanish *alcaneta* < Arabic *al-ḥinnā'* "the henna"]

al·kap·to·nu·ri·a /al kàptə nóoree ə/ *n* a rare genetic disease characterized by arthritis and the destruction of connective tissue and bone [Late 19C. < German *Alkapton*, an acid + -URIA]

al·kene /ál keen/ *n* an open-chain hydrocarbon containing one carbon-to-carbon double bond and belonging to a series whose members all have the same general chemical formula. Formula: C_nH_{2n}.

al·kie *n* SOC SCI another spelling of **alky** (*slang offensive*)

al·kox·ide /al kók sīd/ *n* a salt formed by replacing the hydroxyl ion of an alcohol with a metal [Late 19C. < ALKALI + OXY- + -IDE]

al·ky /álkee/ (*plural* **-kies**), **al·kie** *n* an offensive term for somebody who is an alcoholic or who drinks to excess (*slang*) [Mid-20C. Shortening]

al·kyd /ál kid/, **al·kyd res·in** *n* a sticky resin that is prepared from phthalic acid and glycerol and becomes liquid or plastic when heated. Use: paints, lacquer. [Early 20C. < ALKYL + ACID]

al·kyl /álkəl/ *adj* describes a hydrocarbon group derived from an alkane, e.g., the ethyl group [Late 19C. < German < *Alkohol* "alcohol" + -YL]

al·kyl·a·tion /àlkə láysh'n/ *n* the addition of an alkyl group to a chemical compound through the replacement of a hydrogen atom

al·kyne /ál kīn/ *n* an open-chain hydrocarbon containing one carbon-to-carbon triple bond and belonging to a series whose members all have the same general chemical formula. Formula: C_nH_{2n-2}.

all /awl/ CORE MEANING: a grammatical word used to indicate that the whole of a particular thing, amount, group, or area is involved or affected ○ (adj) *all men and all women* ○ (pron) *All of the computers are down.* ○ (pron) *All that glitters is not gold.*

1. *adj* WHOLE OF used to indicate that the whole of an amount, area, quantity, or thing is involved or affected ○ *All Europe was in the grip of freezing temperatures.* **2.** *adj* EVERY every one of ○ *all employees over 30* **3.** *adj* ANY any whatever (*used after a negative word such as "refuse" or "deny"*) ○ *Deny all connection with the plot.* **4.** *adj* MOST the greatest possible ○ *with all speed* **5.** *adj* CHARACTERIZED BY dominated in mood or character by something (*informal*) ○ *He was all smiles.* **6.** *adj regional* USED UP finished or used up, especially of food or drink **7.** *adv* VERY very, completely, or totally (*informal*) ○ *I got all confused.* **8.** *adv* APIECE to or for each one ○ *The score was thirty all.* **9.** *pron* EVERY ONE OR WHOLE the whole number or amount (*takes a plural verb*) ○ *All of us are going to the game.* **10.** *pron* EVERYONE OR EVERYTHING the whole quantity or group ○ *All that glitters is not gold.* **11.** *n* SOMEBODY'S BEST EFFORT the greatest amount of somebody's ability or effort ○ *He gave his all in the performance.* [Old English *eall* < Germanic] ◇ **all along** from the beginning, or for the whole time that something else was taking place ○ *I knew all along he was lying.* ◇ **all but** almost ○ *I was all but asleep when the phone rang.* ◇ **(all) in all** when everything has been taken into account ○ *All in all, it was a good party.* ◇ **all of** only, or no more than (*informal*) ○ *It took us all of three hours to get here.* ◇ **all or nothing** used to indicate that only complete success or obtaining everything counts, and that anything less than that has no value ◇ **all that 1.** very, particularly, or to that extent (*informal; usually used in negative statements or questions*) ○ *I'm not all that worried about it.* **2.** *US* extraordinarily good or admirable (*slang*) ○ *She is definitely all that!* ◇ **all the same 1.** none the less ○ *It rained a bit but the children enjoyed their day out all the same.* **2.** used to indicate that it is unimportant to the speaker which of two or more things is done or chosen ○ *I'd rather go by train, if it's all the same to you.* ◇ **all there** fully alert, aware of what is going on, and able to deal with it (*informal*) ◇ **all very well** used to indicate that there is some kind of objection or drawback, despite the fact that somebody else is apparently satisfied with the situation ○ *That's all very well, but it's still my responsibility.* ◇ **be all over somebody** to be extremely or excessively friendly or effusive toward somebody (*informal*) ◇ **be all over something** to have something, especially a project or a problem, completely under control (*informal*) ◇ **in all** in total ○ *That makes 52 votes in all for our candidate.*

SPELLCHECK Do not confuse the spelling of ***all*** and ***awl*** ("a sharp-pointed tool"), which sound similar.

USAGE all or all of? You have a choice between ***all*** and ***all of*** when the following noun is qualified by *the, this, that, these, those*, or a possessive adjective such as *my* and *your*: *All my life I've wanted to be a singer. All of my life I've wanted to be a singer. All these things worried them. All of these things worried them.* Generally ***all*** is preferred, but the balance and flow of a particular sentence also plays a part.

REGIONAL NOTE On its own meaning "finished or used up," ***all*** is a German loanword that occurs primarily in the territory of the Pennsylvanian Dutch (southeastern Pennsylvania) and neighboring states. It is used especially of quantifiable amounts of food and drink: *the meat is all; potatoes are yet*, indicates that the meat is all gone, but the potatoes remain.

al·la breve /àllə brév, àalə bré vày/ MUSIC *n* same as **cut time** ■ *adv* at twice the normal speed (*used as a musical direction*) [< Italian, "according to the breve"] —**al·la breve** *adj*

all-age *adj* intended or suitable for all age groups

all-age per·son·als *npl* advertisements by people of all ages who have an interest in finding romantic partners, usually placed with an online dating service

Al·lah /állə, aálə/ *n* in Islam, the name of God [Late 16C. < Arabic *'allāh*]

Al·la·ha·bad /aáləhə bàd, álləhə-/ city in northern India in Uttar Pradesh State. Located at the confluence of the Yamuna and Ganges rivers, it is an important pilgrimage destination for Hindus. Population: 858,213 (1991). Former name **Prayag**

al·la·man·da /àllə mándə/ (*plural* **-das** *or same*) *n* an evergreen bush. Flowers: yellow, purple, trumpet-shaped. Native to: tropical America. Genus: *Allamanda*. [Late 18C. After J. N. S. *Allamand* (1713–87), Swiss scientist]

all-A·mer·i·can *adj* **1.** OF OR ABOUT UNITED STATES of or about the United States, its people, or their way of life, or representing them at their best **2.** BEST IN UNITED STATES selected and honored as the best amateur player or athlete in the United States in a position or event ○ *an all-American linebacker* **3.** MADE OF US COMPONENTS made up entirely of people, materials, or components from the United States **4.**

OF ALL AMERICAS including all the countries of North and South America, or representatives from them ○ *an all-American agreement* ■ *n* 1. BEST US ATHLETE a player or athlete chosen as being the best in the United States in a position or event 2. TEAM OF BEST US PLAYERS a team made up of the best US players or athletes

Al·lan /állən/, **Sir Hugh** (1810–82) Scottish-born Canadian businessman and shipping magnate. He was head of the company that built Canada's transcontinental railroad.

al·lan·to·in /ə lántō in/ *n* a drug used in the treatment of skin disorders [Mid-19C. < ALLANTOIS, because first found in the allantoic fluid of cows]

al·lan·to·is /ə lántō iss/ (*plural* **-i·des** /állən tṓ ideez/) *n* a membranous sac that grows from the lower gut in mammal, bird, and reptile embryos. In mammals, it combines with the chorion to form the umbilical cord and placenta. [Mid-17C. Via modern Latin < Greek *allantoeidēs* "sausage-like," because of its shape] —**al·lan·to·ic** /állən tṓ ik/ *adj*

al·lar·gan·do /àa laar gáandō/ *adv* at a gradually slower tempo, with a broadening stately sound (*used as a musical direction*) ■ *n* (*plural* **-dos** or **-di** /-gáandee/) a section of a piece of music played allargando [Late 19C. < Italian, "broadening"] —**al·lar·gan·do** *adj*

all-a·round *adj* 1. WITH MANY ABILITIES able to do many things well, or useful in a number of different ways, and not specialized ○ *the best all-around player for both offense and defense* 2. ALL-INCLUSIVE broad or comprehensive in scope ○ *for all-around news coverage* 3. IN ALL DIRECTIONS in all directions

al·lay /ə láy/ (**-layed, -lay·ing, -lays**) *vt* 1. to calm a strong emotion such as anger, or diminish and set at rest somebody's fears or suspicions 2. to relieve or reduce the severity of pain or a painful emotion [Old English *ālecgan* "lay aside" (see LAY[1]). The meaning was influenced by Old French *aleger* "lighten" and *aleier* "moderate"] —**al·lay·er** *n*

all-can·di·dates meet·ing *n Can* a public meeting during which all candidates for an elected office explain their policies and answer questions from the audience

all-choice *adj US* describes a school system that allows people to choose a school to attend

all clear *n* 1. a signal that a period of danger is over, especially one sounded on a siren after an air raid 2. a signal or notification that something may proceed ○ *We've got the all clear to start building.*

all-com·ers *npl* everyone who wants to participate in a competition or sport

all-con·sum·ing *adj* absorbing somebody's attention, time, or energy to the exclusion of everything else

~~**alledged**~~ incorrect spelling of **alleged**

al·le·ga·tion /állə gáysh'n/ *n* 1. UNPROVED ASSERTION an assertion, especially relating to wrongdoing or misconduct on somebody's part, that has yet to be proved or supported by evidence 2. ALLEGING the alleging of something, especially wrongdoing 3. DECLARATION an assertion made as a plea or excuse

al·lege /ə léj/ (**-leged, -leg·ing, -leg·es**) *vt* 1. ASSERT SOMETHING WITHOUT PROOF to state or assert something, especially by accusing somebody of wrongdoing without offering proof of it or with a view to proving it later ○ *The prosecutor alleged that Simmons knew about the planned robbery.* 2. AFFIRM SOMETHING to state something positively ○ *allege that a watch has been stolen* 3. GIVE SOMETHING AS REASON to put something forward as a reason or excuse for your actions or conduct (*formal*) ○ *He declined the invitation, alleging a prior appointment.* [14C. Via Anglo-Norman, "declare before a legal tribunal" < assumed Vulgar Latin *exlitigare* "clear of charges" < Latin *litigare* (see LITIGATE)] —**al·lege·a·ble** *adj* —**al·leg·er** *n*

al·leged /ə léjd/ *adj* asserted but not yet proven to have taken place, have been committed, or be as described —**al·leg·ed·ly** /ə léjjədlee/ *adv*

Al·le·ghe·nies same as **Allegheny Mountains**

Al·le·ghe·ny /állə gáynee/ river in Pennsylvania and New York, flowing north from its headwaters in Pennsylvania into New York before turning south again to join the Monongahela River at Pittsburgh to create the Ohio River. Length: 325 mi./523 km.

Al·le·ghe·ny Moun·tains, Al·le·ghe·nies /állə gáyneez/ western mountain range of the Appalachian Mountains, in Pennsylvania, Maryland, West Virginia, and Virginia. The range is the divide between those rivers emptying into the Gulf of Mexico and those flowing into the Atlantic Ocean. The highest peak is Spruce Knob 4,861ft./1,482 m.

Al·le·ghe·ny Pla·teau high plateau region of the eastern United States, stretching from Mohawk Valley, in New York State, southward through Pennsylvania, Maryland, West Virginia, and Virginia to the Cumberland Plateau

Al·le·ghe·ny spurge *n* a low-growing creeping evergreen plant of the box family grown for ground cover. Native to: southern United States. Latin name: *Pachysandra procumbens.*

al·le·giance /ə léejənss/ *n* 1. LOYALTY TO RULER OR STATE a subject's or citizen's loyalty to a ruler or state, or the duty of obedience and loyalty owed by a subject or citizen 2. DEVOTED SUPPORT loyalty to or support for a person, cause, or group ○ *The game was a treat for all fans, whatever their allegiance.* 3. FEUDAL OBLIGATION the feudal obligation of a vassal to a liege lord [14C. < Anglo-Norman variant of Old French *ligeance* < *lige* (see LIEGE)] —**al·le·giant** *adj*

~~**allegience**~~ incorrect spelling of **allegiance**

al·le·gor·i·cal /állə gáwrik'l/, **al·le·gor·ic** /-gáwrik/ *adj* 1. expressing something through an allegory 2. relating to or used in allegory —**al·le·gor·i·cal·ly** *adv*

al·le·go·rize /állə gaw rīz, állәgə-/ (**-rized, -riz·ing, -riz·es**) *v* 1. *vti* to express something in the form of an allegory 2. *vt* to interpret or treat something as an allegory —**al·le·go·ri·za·tion** /állə gaw rə záysh'n, àllәgərə-/ *n* —**al·le·go·riz·er** *n*

al·le·go·ry /állə gàwree/ (*plural* **-ries**) *n* 1. SYMBOLIC WORK a work in which the characters and events are to be understood as representing other things and symbolically expressing a deeper, often spiritual, moral, or political meaning 2. SYMBOLIC EXPRESSION OF MEANING IN STORY the symbolic expression of a deeper meaning through a story or scene acted out by human, animal, or mythical characters ○ *the poet's use of allegory* 3. GENRE allegories considered as a literary or artistic genre 4. SYMBOLIC REPRESENTATION a symbolic representation of something [14C. < Latin *allegoria* < Greek *allegorein* "say otherwise" < *allos* "other" + *agoreuein* "speak in public"] —**al·le·go·rist** *n*

al·le·gret·to /állə gréttō/ *adv* at a fairly quick tempo (*used as a musical direction*) ■ *n* (*plural* **-tos**) a piece of music, or a section of a piece, played allegretto [Mid-18C. < Italian, "less than allegro"] —**al·le·gret·to** *adj*

al·le·gro /ə léggrō/ *adv* at a quick and lively tempo (*used as a musical direction*) ■ *n* (*plural* **-gros**) a piece of music, or a section of a piece, played allegro [Late 17C. < Italian, "lively"] —**al·le·gro** *adj*

al·lele /ə léel/ *n* one of two or more alternative forms of a gene, occupying the same position (**locus**) on paired chromosomes and controlling the same inherited characteristic [Mid-20C. < German *Allel*, shortening of *Allelomorph* "allelomorph"] —**al·le·lic** *adj* —**al·le·lism** *n*

allelo- *prefix* one another ○ *allelopathy* [< Greek *allēlōn* < *allos* "other" (see ALLO-)]

al·le·lo·chem·i·cal /ə léelə kémmik'l/ *n* a chemical produced by one plant that is toxic to another

al·le·lo·morph /ə léelə màwrf, -léllə-/ *n* GENETICS same as **allele** —**al·le·lo·mor·phic** /ə léelə máwrfik, -lèllə-/ *adj* —**al·le·lo·mor·phism** *n*

al·le·lop·a·thy /állə lóppəthee/ *n* the release into the environment by one plant of a substance that inhibits the germination or growth of other potential competitor plants of the same or another species —**al·lelo·path·ic** /ə léelə páthik, -lèllə-/ *adj*

al·le·lo·tox·in /ə léelə tóksin/ *n* BOT same as **allelochemical**

al·le·lu·ia *interj, n* same as **hallelujah**

al·le·mande /állə mànd, àllə maánd/ *n* 1. DANCE MOVEMENT a movement used in country dancing that involves partners changing positions, often by interlinking arms 2. MUSICAL MOVEMENT FORMING PART OF SUITE a stately piece of music in moderate tempo and four-four time, often used as the opening movement of a baroque or classical suite 3. POPULAR 18C DANCE a stately dance of German origin popular in France in the 18th century [Late 17C. < French, "German"]

all-em·brac·ing *adj* including all or everything without discrimination

Al·len /állən/ city in northeastern Texas. It is a suburb of Dallas. Population: 57,216 (2002 estimate).

Al·len ♦ **Van Allen, James**

Al·len, Ethan (1738–89) American soldier from Connecticut who led the Green Mountain Boys to victory at Fort Ticonderoga (1775) during the American Revolution

Al·len, Fred (1894–1956) US comedian and comic writer who was known for his satirical radio show *Allen's Alley* (1932–49). Born **Allen, John Florence Sullivan**

> "A celebrity is a person who works hard all his life to become known, then wears dark glasses to avoid being recognized."
> [Fred Allen, *Treadmill to Oblivion*; 1954]

Al·len, Paul (*b.* 1953) US business executive. He was a cofounder of Microsoft Corporation (1975) and after his retirement in 1983 extended his business interests to multimedia and communications companies and sports teams.

Al·len, Woody (*b.* 1935) US movie director, actor, screenwriter, playwright, and humorous essayist. His movies include the Academy Award-winning *Annie Hall* (1977). Born **Konigsberg, Allen Stewart**

Al·len·by /állənbee/, **Edmund Henry Hynman, 1st Viscount** (1861–1936) British soldier who commanded the Third Army in France in World War I and also took Jerusalem from the Turks (1917)

all-en·com·pass·ing *adj* including or affecting everyone or everything

A·llen·de /aa yén day/, **Isabel** (*b.* 1942) Chilean author. She fled to Venezuela in 1973 when her uncle, Salvador Allende, president of Chile, died during a military coup. Her novel *La casa de los espíritus* (1982) (*The House of Spirits* (1985)) combines elements of magic, realism, and intensely personal material.

A·llen·de Gos·sens /aa yèn day gṓ senss/, **Salvador** (1908–73) president of Chile (1970–73). A founder of the Chilean socialist party, he died during the military coup led by General Pinochet that ended his presidency.

al·lene /ál een/ *n* a colorless unstable gas. Use: manufacture of chemicals. Formula: C_3H_4. [Late 19C. Contraction of *allylene*, a gaseous hydrocarbon]

Al·len key *n Can, UK* ENG same as **Allen wrench**

Al·len screw *n* a screw with a hexagonal recess in its head that allows it to be turned using an Allen wrench [Mid-20C. After the *Allen* Manufacturing Company of Hartford, Connecticut]

Al·len·town /állən tòwn/ city in east central Pennsylvania. It is home to Muhlenberg College. Population: 106,105 (2002 estimate).

Al·len wrench *n* a tool in the form of an L-shaped rod, hexagonal in cross section, made in different sizes to turn corresponding sizes of Allen screws [See ALLEN SCREW]

al·ler·gen /állərjən/ *n* any substance that causes an allergic reaction —**al·ler·gen·ic** /állər jénnik/ *adj*

al·ler·gic /ə lúrjik/ *adj* 1. HAVING ALLERGY having an allergy to a substance ○ *allergic to cat hair* 2. CAUSED BY ALLERGY typical of or caused by an allergy ○ *an allergic reaction* 3. HAVING DISLIKE having a strong aversion to something or somebody (*informal*) ○ *allergic to loud music*

al·ler·gic pur·pur·a *n* a form of the skin condition purpura caused by inflammation of blood vessels, found most often in children

al·ler·gist /állərjist/ *n* a physician who specializes in allergies and their treatment

al·ler·gy /állərjee/ (*plural* **-gies**) *n* 1. unusual sensitivity to a normally harmless substance that provokes a strong reaction from a person's body. The body is sensitized by the immune system's response to the first exposure to the substance, and the reaction takes place only upon subsequent exposures. 2. a strong aversion to something (*informal*) ○ *an allergy to housework* [Early 20C.

< German *Allergie* < Greek *allos* "other" (see ALLO-), after *Energie* "energy"]

al·le·thrin /állə thrìn/ *n* a clear or amber-colored viscous liquid. Use: insecticide. Formula: $C_{19}H_{26}O_3$. [Mid-20C. Blend of ALLYL + PYRETHRIN]

al·le·vi·ate /ə léevee àyt/ (**-at·ed, -at·ing, -ates**) *vt* to make something such as pain or hardship more bearable or less severe [Early 16C. < late Latin *alleviat-*, past participle of *alleviare* "lighten" < Latin *levis* "light (in weight)"] —**al·le·vi·a·tion** /ə léevee áysh'n/ *n* —**al·le·vi·a·tive** *adj* —**al·le·vi·a·tor** *n* —**al·le·vi·a·to·ry** /-ə tàwree/ *adj*

al·ley[1] /állee/ (*plural* **-leys**) *n* **1. NARROW PASSAGE** a narrow passageway or lane, especially one running between or behind buildings **2.** BOWLING same as **bowling alley** (sense 2) **3. SMALL STREET** a short or narrow street **4.** BASEBALL **OUTFIELD ZONE IN BASEBALL** in baseball, the zones between the normal position of the center fielder and those of the right and left fielders **5.** TENNIS **PART OF TENNIS COURT** either of the two spaces, one on each side of a court, between the singles and doubles sidelines **6. PATH IN GARDEN OR PARK** a path in a garden or park, especially one between trees or bushes [14C. < Old French *alee* "a walk" < Latin *ambulare* (see AMBULATE)] ◇ **up** *or* **down somebody's alley** *US* completely suited to somebody's interest, expertise, or line of work

al·ley[2] /állee/ *n* a large playing marble [Early 18C. Shortening of ALABASTER, from which they were originally made]

al·ley ball *n US* the game of basketball as played informally in urban neighborhoods (*slang*)

al·ley cat *n* **1.** a stray cat, usually in bad condition or half wild, that lives on the streets **2.** *US* somebody thought to be disreputable or fierce-tempered, or thought to have loose morals

al·ley-oop /állee óop/ *interj* **ENCOURAGEMENT ON GETTING UP** used as a word of encouragement to somebody who is getting up, being helped up, or lifting something (*dated*) ■ *n* **1.** BASKETBALL **TYPE OF MOVE IN BASKETBALL** in basketball, a play in which a player jumps up to receive a pass over the basket and immediately puts the ball into the net from above **2.** BASKETBALL **TYPE OF PASS IN BASKETBALL** in basketball, a pass aimed to allow a player to jump up to receive it over the basket **3.** EXTREME SPORTS **SNOWBOARDING AND SURFING MANEUVER** in snowboarding and surfing, a rotation of 180 degrees or more made in the air while moving in an uphill or upward direction (*slang*) **4.** EXTREME SPORTS **SKATEBOARDING MANEUVER** in skateboarding, a trick performed in the opposite direction to which the skateboarder is moving (*slang*) [Early 20C. < French *allez* "come on!" + *houp* "upsadaisy!"]

al·ley·way /állee wày/ *n* an alley or narrow passageway

all-fired *adv US* in an excessive or inordinate way (*informal*) ○ *Don't act so all-fired high and mighty.* [Early 19C. Alteration of *hell-fired*]

All Fools' Day *n* CALENDAR same as **April Fools' Day**

all fours *n* CARDS same as **seven-up** ◇ **on all fours** crawling along or crouched down on the hands and knees

All·hal·lows /àwl hállōz/ (*plural same*), **All·hal·low·mas** /-hállōməss/ *n* CALENDAR same as **All Saints' Day** (*archaic; takes a singular verb*) [Old English *ealra hālgena* "of all saints" < *hālga* "saint" < *hālig* "holy" (see HOLY)]

All·hal·lows' Eve *n* CALENDAR same as **Halloween** (*archaic*)

all·heal /áwl heèl/ (*plural* **-heals** or *same*) *n* a plant traditionally believed to have healing powers, e.g., valerian or selfheal

all how *adv Carib* **1.** no matter how **2.** completely

al·li·ance /ə lī́ ənss/ *n* **1. ASSOCIATION OF GROUPS WITH COMMON AIM** an association of groups, people, or nations who agree to cooperate to achieve a common goal **2. FORMING OF ALLIANCE** the establishment of or participation in an alliance **3. MEMBERS OF ALLIANCE** the nations, people, or groups that make up an alliance ○ *the enemy alliance* **4. CLOSE RELATIONSHIP** a close relationship, based on similar objectives or characteristics ○ *the first university to emphasize research in alliance with teaching* **5. MARRIAGE** a marriage uniting family interests ○ *an alliance between the king's daughter and the emperor* [13C. < Old French *aliance* < *alier* "to ally" (see ALLY)]

Al·li·ance /ə lī́ ənss/ city in northeastern Ohio, on the Mahoning River, southeast of Cleveland. Population: 22,922 (2002 estimate).

al·lied /ə lī́d, ál ī̀d/ *adj* **1. JOINED WITH OTHERS IN ALLIANCE** joined in an alliance with other nations, people, or groups **2. ASSOCIATED** in a close relationship ○ *allied banks* **3. OF SIMILAR TYPE** of a similar or related type ○ *sociology and allied studies*

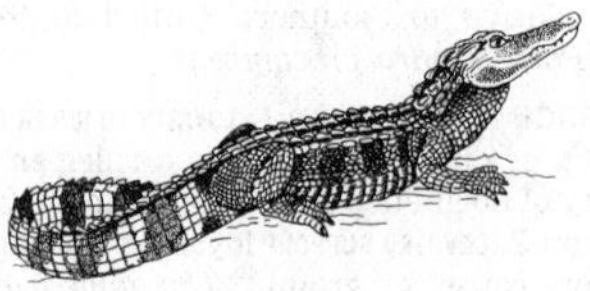

alligator

al·li·ga·tor /álli gàytər/ *n* **1.** (*plural* **al·li·ga·tors** or *same*) **LARGE REPTILE** a large reptile that lives near water, has thick scaly skin, powerful jaws, a long tail, and a shorter and broader snout than a crocodile. Native to: southern United States, China. Genus: *Alligator*. **2. LEATHER** leather made from alligator skin **3. TOOL OR MACHINE WITH MOVABLE JAW** a tool or machine with a strong, movable, often toothed jaw for gripping or crushing ■ *vi* (**-tored, -tor·ing, -tors**) *US* **CRACK** to develop cracks or blisters ○ *Paint alligators in hot sun.* [Mid-16C. Alteration of Spanish *el lagarto* "the lizard" < Latin *lacertus*]

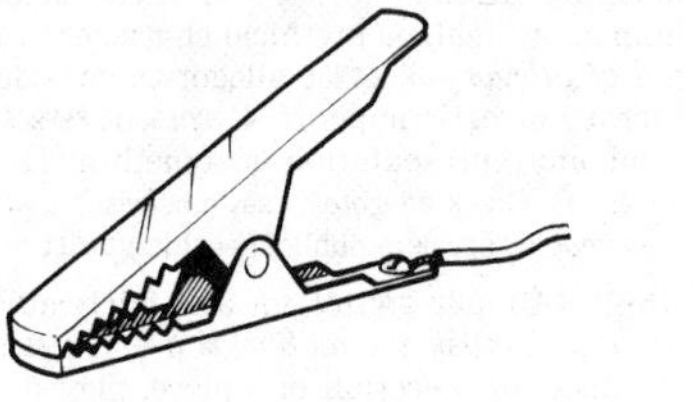

alligator clip

al·li·ga·tor clip *n* a narrow clasp with a spring and serrated jaws for making temporary electrical connections [Because it resembles an alligator's jaws]

al·li·ga·tor pear *n* FOOD same as **avocado** (sense 1) [Mid-18C. Alteration of American Spanish *aguacate* "avocado," perhaps because of the rough dark skin of some varieties]

al·li·ga·tor snap·ping tur·tle, al·li·ga·tor snap·per *n* a large freshwater snapping turtle. Native to: Gulf States of the United States. Latin name: *Macroclemys temmincki*.

all-im·por·tant *adj* vitally important or necessary

all in *adj* extremely tired (*informal*) ○ *We were all in by the time we got back to the hotel.*

all-in·clu·sive *adj* including or encompassing everything that is expected or appropriate —**all-in·clu·sive·ness** *n*

all-in-one *adj* **1.** performing two or more functions, or made up of two or more things **2.** describes a single-piece garment —**all-in-one** *n*

all-in wres·tling *n UK* a style of professional wrestling with relatively few restrictions on the permissible types of holds, blows, or throws

al·lit·er·ate /ə líttə ràyt/ (**-at·ed, -at·ing, -ates**) *v* **1.** *vi* to begin consecutive or neighboring words with the same consonant sound, or contain such sound matches **2.** *vti* to use alliteration in speaking or writing, or arrange words or construct sentences so as to achieve the effect of alliteration [Late 18C. Back-formation < ALLITERATION] —**al·lit·er·a·tive** /ə líttə ràytiv, -rətiv/ *adj* —**al·lit·er·a·tive·ly** *adv*

al·lit·er·a·tion /ə líttə ráysh'n/ *n* a poetic or literary effect achieved by using several words that begin with the same or similar consonants, as in "Whither wilt thou wander, wayfarer?" [Early 17C. < medieval Latin *alliteration-* < Latin *littera* "letter of the alphabet"]

~~**allmost**~~ incorrect spelling of **almost**

all-night *adj* lasting, open, or available throughout the night, or throughout a specific night ○ *all-night negotiations*

all-night·er *n* a study or work session, entertainment, or other event that lasts throughout an entire night (*informal*)

all now *adv Carib* **1.** same as **still**[2] **2.** right away **3.** by this time

allo- *prefix* other, different, alternate ○ *allosteric* ○ *allophone* [< Greek *allos* "other" < Indo-European, "other of more than two"]

al·lo·cate /állə kàyt/ (**-cat·ed, -cat·ing, -cates**) *vt* to give something to or set something aside for a person or purpose ○ *Each team member has been allocated a specific task.* [Mid-17C. < medieval Latin *allocat-*, past participle of *allocare* "put in place" < Latin *locus* "place"] —**al·lo·cat·a·ble** /állə káytəb'l/ *adj* —**al·lo·ca·tor** *n*

SYNONYMS See ***share***[1].

al·lo·ca·tion /állə káysh'n/ *n* **1.** the assignment or earmarking of something ○ *allocation of duties* **2.** a thing, amount, or share allocated to somebody or something ○ *The department has already used its entire allocation.*

al·loch·thon·ous /ə lókthənəss/ *adj* **1.** describes features of the landscape or elements of its geologic structure that have been moved to their current position by tectonic forces **2.** describes flora, fauna, or inhabitants that have moved to the region in which they are found from elsewhere [Early 20C. < Greek *allochthon* < *allo-* "other" + *khthōn* "soil"]

al·lo·cu·tion /állə kyóosh'n/ *n* **1.** a formal speech or address, especially one that contains an authoritative statement on a subject or an exhortation to somebody **2.** a traditional formal question directed by a court to a defendant convicted of a felony before sentencing, asking whether or not the defendant has anything to say regarding why the sentence should not be pronounced against him or her [Early 17C. < Latin *allocution-* < *alloqui* "speak to" < *loqui* "speak"]

al·log·a·my /ə lóggəmee, a-/ *n* the process of cross-fertilization in flowering plants —**al·log·a·mous** *adj*

al·lo·ge·ne·ic /álləjə neé ik/, **al·lo·gen·ic** /állə jénnik/ *adj* describes tissues that are genetically different and therefore incompatible when transplanted [Mid-20C. < ALLO- + Greek *genea* "race, generation"] —**al·lo·ge·ne·ic·al·ly** *adv*

al·lo·graft /állə gràft/ *n* a graft of tissue from one member of a species to a genetically different member of the same species

al·lo·graph /állə gràf/ *n* **1.** something, especially a signature, written by one person on another's behalf **2.** a letter or combination of letters that is one of a set that can be used to represent the same speech sound (**phoneme**), e.g., "s," "ss," and "c" in English

al·lom·er·ism /ə lómmə rìzzəm/ *n* similarity in the crystal structure of substances that are chemically different —**al·lom·er·ous** *adj*

al·lom·e·try /ə lómmətree/ *n* measurement of the rate of growth of a part or parts of an organism relative to the growth of the whole organism. This rate determines the organism's final shape. —**al·lo·met·ric** /állə méttrik/ *adj*

al·lo·mone /állə mṓn/ *n* a chemical substance produced by a plant in response to attack by other organisms [Late 20C. < ALLO- + PLANT HORMONE]

al·lo·morph /állə màwrf/ *n* **1.** a letter or combination of letters that is part of a set used to represent the same basic grammatical element (**morpheme**) of a language. "-ed" and "-t" both form the English past tense and are allomorphs. **2.** a different crystal form of the same mineral, chemical compound, or element [Mid-20C. < ALLO- + MORPHEME] —**al·lo·mor·phic** /állə máwrfik/ *adj* —**al·lo·mor·phism** *n*

al·lop·a·thy /ə lóppəthee/ *n* the treatment of a disease by using remedies whose effects differ from those produced by that disease. This is the principle of mainstream medical practice, as opposed to that of homeopathy. —**al·lo·path** /állə pàth/ *n* —**al·lo·path·ic** /állə páthik/ *adj* —**al·lo·path·i·cal·ly** *adv*

al·lo·pat·ric /állə páttrik/ *adj* describes species or populations that do not interbreed because they are geographically isolated from one another [Mid-20C. < ALLO- + Greek *patra* "homeland" < *patēr* "father"] —**al·lo·pat·ri·cal·ly** *adv* —**al·lop·a·try** /ə lóppətree/ *n*

al·lo·phane /állə fàyn/ *n* an amorphous, variously colored, hydrated aluminosilicate mineral [Early 19C. < Greek *allophanēs* "appearing otherwise" (because it changes color when heated) < *allos* "other" + *phainesthai* "appear"]

al·lo·phone /állə fōn/ *n* **1.** one of the slightly differing forms that the same single speech sound (**phoneme**) can take **2.** *Can* an immigrant in Quebec who speaks neither English nor French as a first language [Mid-20C. < ALLO- + PHONEME] —**al·lo·phon·ic** /állə fónnik/ *adj* —**al·lo·phon·i·cal·ly** *adv*

al·lo·pu·ri·nol /àllō pyŏŏrə nàwl/ *n* a drug that blocks production of uric acid. Use: gout treatment. [Mid-20C. < ALLO- + PURINE]

all-or-none *adj US* functioning or taking effect either completely or not at all

all-or-noth·ing *adj* **1.** bound to result either in complete success or total failure **2.** unwilling to accept anything less than all ○ *an all-or-nothing approach to negotiating*

al·lo·saur·us /állə sáwrəss/ *n* a very large carnivorous theropod dinosaur of the late Upper Jurassic period. Native to: North America. Genus: *Allosaurus.* [Late 19C. < modern Latin < Greek *allos* "other"+ *sauros* "lizard"]

al·lo·ster·ic /állə stérrik/ *adj* describes a binding site on an enzyme at which interaction induces altered activity at another site —**al·lo·ster·i·cal·ly** *adv* —**al·los·ter·y** /ə lóstəree/ *n*

al·lot /ə lót/ (**-lot·ted, -lot·ting, -lots**) *vt* **1.** to give something to somebody as a share of what is available or what has to be done ○ *I was allotted the task of sweeping up.* **2.** to earmark or reserve something for a purpose ○ *allotting ten shelves for books* [15C. < Old French *aloter* < *lot* "portion" < Germanic] —**al·lot·tee** /ə lò tée, àllə tée/ *n* —**al·lot·ter** *n*

USAGE See ***lot.***

SYNONYMS See ***share***[1].

al·lot·ment /ə lótmənt/ *n* **1.** a thing or amount allotted to somebody or something **2.** the assignment or earmarking of something ○ *the allotment of shares*

al·lo·trans·plant /àllō tráns plànt/ *vt* (**-plant·ed, -plant·ing, -plants**) to transplant an organ or body tissue from one member of a species to a genetically different member of the same species ■ *n* an organ or piece of body tissue transplanted from one member of a species to a genetically different member of the same species

al·lo·trope /állə trōp/ *n* one of many forms in which a chemical element occurs, each differing in physical properties, e.g., diamonds and coal as forms of carbon —**al·lo·trop·ic** /állə tróppik, -trōpik/ *adj* —**al·lo·trop·i·cal·ly** *adv*

al·lot·ro·py /ə lóttrəpee/, **al·lot·ro·pism** /ə lóttrə pìzzəm/ *n* the existence of a chemical element in more than one form (**allotrope**), each having different physical but the same chemical properties

all'ot·ta·va /állə taávə/ *adv* to be played an octave higher or lower than written (*used as a musical direction*) [Early 19C. < Italian, "on the octave"] —**all'ot·ta·va** *adj*

al·lot·tee /ə lò tée, àllə tée/ *n* somebody to whom something is allotted

all out *adv* with maximum effort, at full power, or at top speed

all-out *adj* involving the maximum possible effort or every available resource ○ *an all-out attempt to break the record*

all o·ver *adv* (*informal*) **1.** same as **everywhere 2.** used to stress that a description or action is characteristic of a particular person or type of person ○ *That's Jack all over: late again!*

all-o·ver *adj* covering the whole surface area of something ○ *an all-over tan*

al·low /ə lów/ (**-lowed, -low·ing, -lows**) *v* **1.** *vt* LET SOMETHING HAPPEN to permit something to happen or somebody to do something ○ *I can't allow you to throw this chance away.* ○ *He's allowed the toast to burn.* **2.** *vt* LET SOMEBODY ENTER OR BE PRESENT to let somebody or something enter or be present in a place ○ *Children are not allowed after nine o'clock.* **3.** *vt* LET SOMEBODY HAVE SOMETHING to let somebody or yourself have something, often a benefit or pleasure of some kind ○ *Allow yourself a few minutes to catch your breath.* **4.** *vt* CREDIT SOMEBODY MONEY FOR SOMETHING to give or credit somebody with an amount of money as a discount or in exchange for something ○ *How much will you allow on our old machine?* **5.** *vti* MAKE PROVISION FOR SOMETHING to take something into consideration or make provision for it when making a plan or decision ○ *We allowed an extra 20 minutes but were still late.* ○ *allow for shrinkage* **6.** *vt* ADMIT SOMETHING to admit something or accept it to be true or valid (*formal*) ○ *You must allow that it was rather harsh.* **7.** *vi* PRESENT AS POSSIBLE to present something as possible or reasonable ○ *The events allow of only one interpretation.* **8.** *vt Southern US* SAY OR THINK to state or suppose ○ *He allowed it was time to go.* [14C. Via Old French *allouer* < Latin *allaudare* "to praise" and medieval Latin *allocare* "assign" (see ALLOCATE)] —**al·low·a·ble** *adj* —**al·low·a·bly** *adv* —**al·lowed** *adj*

al·low·ance /ə lów ənss/ *n* **1.** MONEY GIVEN TO CHILD BY PARENTS a small sum of money paid regularly by parents to a child so that the child can make his or her own purchases **2.** PERMITTED AMOUNT the amount of something that is allowed, especially according to regulations ○ *We're going to exceed the baggage allowance when we go home.* **3.** BUDGETED AMOUNT an amount of something given out at regular intervals or for a specific purpose ○ *a mileage allowance as well as expenses* **4.** DISCOUNT money deducted from the selling price of something by the seller as a discount or in exchange for something **5.** TOLERATION the allowing of something to happen, or the toleration of it **6.** *US* HANDICAP a handicap or advantage in some sports, especially horseracing **7.** MECH ENG AMOUNT OF VARIATION ALLOWED a small amount of variation permitted in the dimensions of closely fitting machine parts ■ *vt* (**-anced, -anc·ing, -anc·es**) **1.** *US* GIVE SOMEBODY ALLOWANCE to restrict somebody to a fixed regular amount of something **2.** HAND SOMETHING OUT to supply something, especially an amount of money, in limited amounts (*archaic*) ◇ **make allowance** *or* **allowances (for somebody** *or* **something) 1.** to take a charitable view of somebody or something and take mitigating circumstances into account **2.** to take something into consideration when making a plan, decision, or judgment

al·low·ed·ly /ə lówədlee/ *adv* admittedly or by general agreement ○ *Allowedly, the salary is modest.*

al·loy *n* /á lòy/ **1.** METALL MIXTURE OF METALS a substance that is a mixture of two or more metals, or of a metal with a nonmetallic material **2.** DEBASING ADDITION something that detracts from the value or quality of the thing it is added to or mixed with ○ *The movie is weakened by the alloy of sentimentality.* **3.** BLEND any mixture, amalgam, or compound of different materials ■ *vt* /ə lóy, á lòy/ (**-loyed, -loy·ing, -loys**) **1.** METALL MIX METALS to mix one metal with another, or mix a metal with a nonmetallic material **2.** DEBASE SOMETHING to detract from the quality, purity, or value of something by the addition of something inferior ○ *principles alloyed with cynicism* **3.** COMBINE SOMETHING to mix or combine different things [Mid-17C. Via Old French dialect *allai* (noun), *allayer* (verb) < Latin *alligare* "bind to" < *ligare* "bind"]

SYNONYMS See ***mixture.***

all-par·ty *adj UK* involving all political parties ○ *all-party talks*

all-per·vad·ing *adj* spread or present throughout everything ○ *a sense of all-pervading gloom*

all-points bul·le·tin *n US* a message broadcast to all police in an area, usually containing urgent information or a warning

all-pow·er·ful *adj* possessing unlimited authority or power —**all-pow·er·ful·ness** *n*

all-pur·pose *adj* suitable for a wide variety of uses

all-pur·pose flour *n* flour that has had no baking powder added to it

~~**allready**~~ incorrect spelling of **already**

all right *adj* **1.** SATISFACTORY generally good, satisfactory, or pleasing (*hyphenated when used before a noun*) ○ *Everything's going to be all right.* **2.** JUST ADEQUATE just about acceptable or adequate, but not very good ○ *The new job's all right, I guess.* **3.** UNINJURED not injured or unwell **4.** IN GOOD CONDITION in good condition or order, and not defective or damaged ■ *interj* YES used to express agreement or approval ○ *"Will you come along?" "All right."* ■ *adv* **1.** SATISFACTORILY in a generally good, satisfactory, or pleasing way ○ *My old drill still works all right.* **2.** CERTAINLY without any doubt ○ *He's his father's son all right.* ◇ **it's all right for some** *UK* some people are more privileged or have more advantages than others (*used humorously*)

USAGE all right or **alright**? ***Alright*** has never gained wide acceptance even though it is to be seen in the prose of many well-known writers such as Langston Hughes, Gertrude Stein, and James Joyce. It is generally regarded as nonstandard, and so should be avoided in formal writing unless it is purposely included in fictional dialogue or another special context in which a particular effect is sought by the writer. Use instead ***all right***, which has all the meanings, including "satisfactory," associated with ***alright.***

all round *adv* **1.** in every respect or taking everything into consideration ○ *I think, all round, it was a pretty successful effort, don't you?* **2.** for, from, or involving everyone

all-round *adj UK* same as **all-around**

All Saints' Day, All Saints *n* the day in the Christian calendar set aside to celebrate the lives of saints. Date: November 1.

all-sea·son *adj* usable in every season of the year, regardless of weather conditions

all-see·ing *adj* seeing or appearing to see everything

All Souls' Day, All Souls *n* the day set aside in the Roman Catholic Church calendar for prayer for the souls of those who have died and are believed to be in purgatory. Date: November 2.

allspice

all·spice /áwl spìss/ *n* **1.** the ground dried berries of a tropical evergreen tree, used as a spice **2.** (*plural* **all·spices** or *same*) an evergreen tree whose aromatic berries make allspice. Native to: tropical America. Latin name: *Pimenta dioica.* [Because it is thought to combine the flavors of cinnamon, cloves, and nutmeg]

all-star *adj* made up of very famous and talented performers or players ■ *n* a member of an all-star team

All-Star game *n* a baseball game between teams composed of the best professional players, played every summer in the United States

All·ston /áwlstən/, **Washington** (1779–1843) US artist and writer, author of the Gothic novel *Monaldi* (1841)

all-suite *adj* describes a hotel room that has a sitting room and kitchenette as well as the standard features of hotel accommodations

all-ter·rain bike *n* a bicycle or motorcycle designed for use in open country as well as on roads

all-ter·rain board·ing *n* a form of skateboarding using a modified board with larger wheels that enables the rider to travel over all types of terrain, especially down mountain slopes —**all-ter·rain board** *n*

all-ter·rain ve·hi·cle *n* a motor vehicle designed for use on rough, sandy, or marshy ground, as well as on roads. It usually has only one seat.

~~**allthough**~~ incorrect spelling of **although**

all-time *adj* having never yet been bettered, or the best, greatest, or most popular ever (*informal*) ○ *an all-time record for this distance*

all told *adv* when everything or everyone is included or taken into account ○ *A dozen people made it, all told.*

al·lude /ə lo͞od/ (**-lud·ed, -lud·ing, -ludes**) *vi* to refer to something or somebody indirectly, without giving a precise name or explicit identification ○ *I presume you are alluding to the alleged financial discrepancy.* [Mid-16C. < Latin *alludere* "play to" < *ludere* < *ludus* "play"]

SPELLCHECK allude or **elude**? Do not confuse the spelling of ***allude*** and ***elude***, which sound similar. ***Allude*** is usually followed by *to*, as in *alluding to the disappearance of her husband.* ***Elude*** means "escape from," "avoid," or "be beyond": *He eluded his pursuers. Her name eludes me.*

USAGE allude or **refer**? The sentence *She alluded to her husband by name* is a self-contradiction, because ***allude*** means "to mention indirectly." When the reference is direct, the word to use is ***refer.*** So if she mentioned "the man at home looking after the children," she was ***alluding*** to her husband, whereas if she mentioned "George" or "my husband" directly, she was ***referring*** to him: *She referred to her husband frequently.*

al·lure /ə lo͝or/ *n* an attractive or tempting quality ○ *They couldn't resist the allure of the big city.* ■ *vti* (**-lured, -lur·ing, -lures**) to exert a very powerful and often dangerous attraction on somebody [15C. < Anglo-Norman *alurer,* Old French *aloirrier, aleurier* "bring to the bait" < *leure* "bait" (see LURE)] —**al·lure·ment** *n*

al·lur·ing /ə lo͝oring/ *adj* extremely attractive, tempting, or glamorous, and able to arouse strong desire in people —**al·lur·ing·ly** *adv*

al·lu·sion /ə lo͞ozh'n/ *n* **1.** an indirect reference to somebody or something ○ *He made an allusion to marital problems.* **2.** the act of making an indirect reference to somebody or something [Early 17C. Directly or via French < late Latin *allusion-* < Latin *allus-,* past participle of *alludere* (see ALLUDE)]

USAGE allusion, delusion, or **illusion**? ***Allusion*** and ***illusion*** are the closest in sound but the furthest apart in meaning: an ***allusion*** is an indirect reference to a person, thing, or event: *The story contained an allusion to her childhood in Africa.* An ***illusion*** is something that deceives the senses or mind: *The shimmering effect on a hot road is an optical illusion. By shutting himself in his room for hours he kept up an illusion of studying hard.* ***Illusion*** and ***delusion*** are similar in meaning, but ***delusion*** denotes something falsely believed, often harmfully, rather than a wrong impression received: *Visitors often suffer under the delusion that the weather is always hot here.*

al·lu·sive /ə lo͞ossiv, -ziv/ *adj* **1.** making or containing an indirect reference to something or somebody **2.** characterized by the use of indirect references or subtle suggestion —**al·lu·sive·ly** *adv* —**al·lu·sive·ness** *n*

SPELLCHECK See ***elusive.***

al·lu·vi·a GEOL plural of **alluvium**

al·lu·vi·al /ə lo͞ovee əl/ *adj* relating to, consisting of, or formed by sediment deposited by flowing water

al·lu·vi·al fan *n* a fan-shaped deposit of sediment formed at the point where a stream enters a valley or plain or another, larger stream

al·lu·vi·on /ə lo͞ovee ən/ *n* **1.** the flow or wash of the sea or other body of water against a shore **2.** the expansion of a land area through the buildup of alluvial deposits or the receding of a body of water [Mid-16C. Via French < Latin *alluvion-* < *alluvius* (see ALLUVIUM)]

al·lu·vi·um /ə lo͞ovee əm/ (*plural* **-vi·ums** or **-vi·a** /-vee ə/) *n* sediment deposited by flowing water, especially soil formed in river valleys and deltas from material washed down by the river [Mid-17C. < Latin, form of *alluvius* "washed against" < *lavare* "to wash"]

~~**allways**~~ incorrect spelling of **always**

all-weath·er *adj* usable in or able to stand up to all types of weather

al·ly /ə lī, á lī/ *n* (*plural* **-lies**) **1.** MEMBER OF ALLIANCE a person, group, or state that is joined in an association with another or others for a common purpose **2.** BIOL RELATED ORGANISM an organism that is closely related to another ■ *v* (**-lied, -ly·ing, -lies**) **1.** *vti* JOIN IN MUTUALLY SUPPORTIVE ASSOCIATION to join, or enlist somebody, in an association with one or more other states, organizations, or people for a common purpose **2.** *vt* RELATE THINGS to connect something with something else through similarity or common features (*usually passive*) ○ *These plants are allied to lilies.* **3.** *vti* CONNECT PEOPLE, OR BE CONNECTED to connect people or families, or form a connection with another person or family, especially through marriage [14C. Via Old French *al(e)ier* < Latin *alligare* "bind to" (see ALLOY)]

al·lyl /állәl/ *adj* describes a compound containing the chemical group C_3H_5– [Mid-19C. < Latin *allium* "garlic" (because first obtained from garlic)]

al·lyl al·co·hol *n* a colorless, strong-smelling liquid. Use: manufacture of resins, plasticizers.

Al·ma-A·ta /aalmə aatə, əl maa ə taa/ former name for **Almaty**

Al·ma·gest /álmə jèst/ *n* **1.** a text on astronomy written by Ptolemy in the 2nd century A.D. setting out his view of the universe with the Earth at its center surrounded by spheres **2.** *also* **al·ma·gest** an important medieval treatise on a subject, especially on astronomy, astrology, or alchemy [14C. Via Old French < Arabic *al-mijistī* "the greatest" < Greek *megistē* "greatest," superlative of *megas* "great" (see MEGA-)]

Al Ma·hal·lah al Ku·brá /al mə haalə al kō braa/ industrial city in the central Nile delta, northern Egypt. Population: 408,000 (1992).

al·ma ma·ter /aalmə maatər, àl-/, **Al·ma Ma·ter** *n* **1.** the school, college, or university that somebody formerly attended **2.** a song used as the anthem of a school, college, or university [< Latin, "bounteous mother," title given by the Romans to several goddesses]

al·ma·nac /áwlmə nàk, álmə-/ *n* **1.** CALENDAR an annual publication that includes a calendar for the year as well as astronomical information and details of anniversaries and events **2.** BOOK OF DATA an annually published book of information relating to a subject or activity ○ *a sports almanac* **3.** PRACTICAL GUIDEBOOK a book, often but not always published annually, containing practical information on a subject ○ *a home winemaker's almanac* [14C. < medieval Latin *almanac(h)*]

al·man·dine /álmən deen/, **al·man·dite** /-dīt/ *n* a precious stone colored deep red by iron that is a variety of garnet. Use: gems. [15C. Via French < Latin *alabandina (gemma)* "(gem) of Alabanda" (city in Asia Minor where the gem was originally cut and polished)]

Al·ma·ty /aalmə tee/ city and former capital of Kazakhstan, in the southeastern part of the country, east of Bishkek in Kyrgyzstan. Population: 1,135,000 (2000). Former name **Alma-Ata, Verny**

al·might·y /awl mītee/ *adj* **1.** ALL-POWERFUL having supreme unquestionable power over everything ○ *almighty God* **2.** EXTREME extreme or excessive of its kind (*informal*) ○ *an almighty quarrel* ■ *adv* EXTREMELY to an extreme or excessive degree (*informal*) ○ *almighty proud* [Old English *ælmeahtig* < *æl* "completely" (see ALL) + *meahtig* (see MIGHTY)] —**al·might·i·ness** *n*

Al·might·y *n* RELIG same as **God** ○ *pray to the Almighty*

Al-Min·ya /al mínyə/ city and trading center in eastern Egypt, in the Nile valley. Population: 208,000 (1992).

Al·mo·dó·var /álmə dṓ vaar/, **Pedro** (*b.* 1951) Spanish movie director of comedies such as *Women on the Verge of a Nervous Breakdown* (1988) and *All About My Mother* (1999)

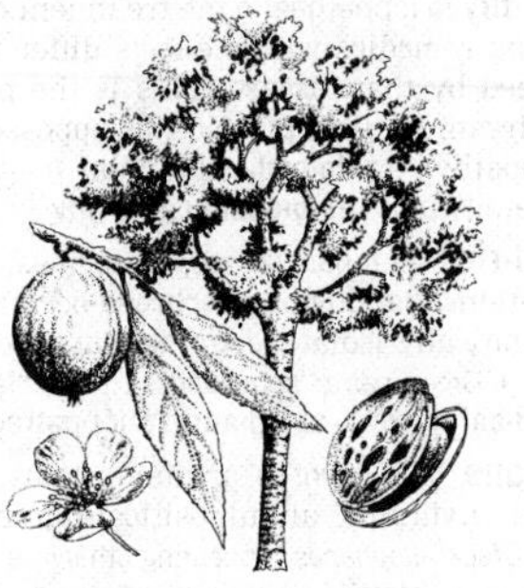

almond

al·mond /aamənd, aal-, ám-, ál-/ *n* **1.** EDIBLE OVAL NUT an edible, oval-shaped, brown-skinned nut that is widely used in cooking **2.** SMALL TREE PRODUCING ALMONDS a tree that bears almonds. Native to: western Asia. Latin name: *Prunus dulcis.* **3.** YELLOWISH GRAY a yellowish gray color, like that of an almond kernel **4.** ALMOND-SHAPED OBJECT something oval and pointed in shape like an almond ■ *adj* **1.** ALMOND-SHAPED oval and pointed in shape like an almond **2.** OF YELLOWISH GRAY yellowish gray in color, like an almond kernel [14C. Via Old French *alemande, a(l)mande* < Greek *amugdalē*]

al·mo·ner /álmənər, aam-/ *n* **1.** in former times, somebody who distributed alms to the needy, especially on behalf of a church, monastery, or wealthy family **2.** *UK* formerly, somebody affiliated with a hospital as a social worker for its patients [15C. Alteration of obsolete *aumener,* via Old French *aumoner* < ecclesiastical Latin *eleemosynarius* "connected with alms" < *eleemosyna* (see ALMS)]

al·most /áwl mṓst, awl mṓst/ *adv* not exactly, not yet, or not in fact, but very close to being or happening as described ○ *I almost wrecked the car.*

USAGE most for **almost**? Though ***most*** is often used in oral and informal settings as a synonym for ***almost,*** it is best to avoid this use in formal writing because many critics regard it as much too informal. Thus, it is wise to write *Almost everyone was invited* rather than *Most everyone was invited.*

alms /aamz, aalmz/ *npl* in former times, money or other assistance given to people in need as charity [Pre-12C. Via assumed Vulgar Latin *alimosina* < ecclesiastical Latin *eleemosyna* < Greek *eleēmosynē* "compassionateness" < *eleos* "compassion, mercy"]

alms·house /aamz hòwss, aalmz-/ (*plural* **-hous·es** /-hòwzəz/) *n* SOC WELFARE, HIST same as **poorhouse**

al·ni·co /álni kṓ/ *n* an alloy of iron, aluminum, and nickel together with one or more of cobalt, copper, and titanium. Use: strong permanent magnets. [Mid-20C. < ALUMINUM + NICKEL + COBALT]

al·o·ca·sia /àllə káyzhə/ *n* a plant of the arum family, grown as a houseplant for its large heart-shaped or arrow-shaped leaves. Native to: tropical Asia. Genus: *Alocasia.* [Mid-19C. Alteration of *colocasia,* a related plant < Greek *kolokasia* "Egyptian water lily"]

aloe

al·oe /állō/ *n* a plant with fleshy toothed leaves. Flowers: red, yellow. Native to: southern Africa. Genus: *Aloe.* [14C. Via Latin < Greek *aloē,* probably of Asian origin]

al·oes /állōz/ *n* (*takes a singular verb*) **1.** a bitter-tasting aloe leaf extract. Use: laxative. **2.** *also* **al·oes wood**

the fragrant wood of the eaglewood tree from which a resin is obtained. Use: making perfumes.

al·oe ver·a /-véerə/ *n* **1.** a soothing, moisturizing extract made from the leaves of a species of aloe. Use: drugs, cosmetics. **2.** the Mediterranean species of aloe from which aloe vera is extracted. Latin name: *Aloe barbadensis.* [< modern Latin, "true aloe"]

a·loft /ə láwft/ *adv* **1.** upward, high up, or in a higher position (*literary*) **2.** in or into the rigging of a sailing ship [13C. < Old Norse *á lopt(i)* "in the air" < *lopt* "air, sky" (see LOFT)]

a·log·i·cal /ay lójjik'l/ *adj* unable to be dealt with by, or having nothing to do with, logic —**a·log·i·cal·ly** *adv* —**a·log·i·cal·ness** *n*

a·lo·ha /ə lṓ aa, -haa, aa-/ *interj Hawaii* used as a greeting or farewell [Early 19C. < Hawaiian, "love, affection"]

a·lo·ha par·ty *n Hawaii* **1.** a party held to welcome somebody to a place or into a community **2.** a party held to welcome somebody to a place or into a community **2.** a party held to welcome somebody who is arriving or to say farewell to somebody who is leaving

A·lo·ha State *n* a nickname for the state of Hawaii

al·o·in /állō in/ *n* a bitter-tasting aloe derivative. Use: manufacture of laxatives. [Mid-19C. < ALOE + -INE]

a·lone /ə lṓn/ CORE MEANING: a grammatical word meaning without any other person or thing nearby ○ (adj) *I like to be alone sometimes.* ○ (adv) *wandering alone in the wilderness*

1. *adv* WITHOUT HELP FROM OTHERS without help or support from anybody or anything else ○ *I can't do this job alone.* **2.** *adv, adj* WITHOUT COMPANY without any other person or thing nearby or in attendance, for company, or to give assistance ○ *She left with the others but returned alone.* **3.** *adj* UNIQUE IN SOME RESPECT being the only one of a group to do, achieve, or think something ○ *Am I alone in thinking this?* **4.** *adj* DONE WITHOUT OTHERS carried out by somebody or assigned to somebody without the assistance or company of others ○ *an assignment that was too much for one person alone* [13C. < *all one* "completely by yourself"] —**a·lone·ness** *n*

a·long /ə láwng/ CORE MEANING: a preposition indicating that something is situated or moves over all or part of the length of something ○ *came racing along the path*

1. *prep* PARALLEL WITH following a course or line parallel with or beside ○ *freighters sailing along the coastline* **2.** *adv* WITH SOMEBODY with you, with somebody, or with the rest of the group when going somewhere ○ *I asked if I could come along.* ○ *Next time you come, bring your guitar along.* **3.** *prep* SIMILAR TO in accordance with or similar to ○ *new questions along the same lines* **4.** *adv* FORWARD forward, onward, or in a particular direction ○ *Move along there!* **5.** *adv* AT OR TO PLACE arriving at or coming or going to a place ○ *There'll be a bus along in a minute.* [14C. < Old English *andlang* "against the long" < *lang* "long"] ◇ **along with** together with, or as well as

---

USAGE See ***with***.

---

a·long·shore /ə láwng shàwr, -shawr/ *adv* near to, beside, or along a shore ○ *The water was too shallow to bring the ship alongshore.* ■ *adj* located on or near a shore or moving along a shore

a·long·side /ə láwng sī̀d, ə làwng sī́d/ *prep also* **a·long·side of** close up against, near, or parallel to the side of ○ *pulled the boat alongside the pier* ■ *adv* in or into a position along or by the side of something ○ *anchored alongside*

A·lon·so /ə lónzō/, **Alicia** (*b.* 1921) Cuban ballerina, choreographer, and dance teacher who was instrumental in establishing the National Ballet of Cuba

a·loo /áa lo͞o/, **a·lu** *n S Asia* cooked potato in South Asian cuisine [Via Hindi, Urdu < Sanskrit *ālū*]

a·loof /ə ló͞of/ *adj* **1.** uninvolved or unwilling to become involved with other people or events ○ *always courteous but aloof* ○ *tried to stay aloof of the infighting and scandals* **2.** physically distant or apart [Mid-16C. Probably < *a luff* "in a windward direction," hence "away from the shore," after Dutch *te loef*] —**a·loof·ly** *adv* —**a·loof·ness** *n*

al·o·pe·cia /àllə péesh ə, -péeshee ə/ *n* loss or the absence of hair, especially from the human head [14C. Via Latin < Greek *alōpekia* "baldness, fox mange" < *alōpek-* "fox"] —**al·o·pe·cic** *adj*

al·o·pe·cia ar·e·a·ta /-ari áttə/ *n* a reversible patchy hair loss of the scalp and beard caused by inflammation [< modern Latin, "alopecia with patches"]

a·loud /ə lówd/ *adv* **1.** using an audible speaking voice ○ *reading aloud* **2.** in a loud voice ○ *cried aloud for mercy*

al·ox·i·prin /ə lóksə prìn/ *n* a compound of aluminum hydroxide and aspirin. Use: analgesic. [Blend of ALUMINUM + OXY- + ASPIRIN]

alp /alp/ *n* a high mountain, especially one capped with snow [15C. Via French *Alpes* "Alps" < Latin < Greek *Alpeis*]

alpaca

al·pac·a /al pákə/ *n* **1.** (*plural* **al·pac·as** or *same*) S AMERICAN MAMMAL a domesticated, longhaired South American animal of the camel family, related to the llama and similar in appearance. Latin name: *Lama pacos.* **2.** WOOL FROM ALPACA wool or cloth made from the long shaggy hair of the alpaca **3.** GLOSSY CLOTH a thin glossy cotton, wool, or rayon fabric made to simulate alpaca cloth [Late 18C. Via Spanish < Aymara *alpako* < *pako* "reddish brown," from the color of its hair]

al·pen·glow /álpən glṑ/ *n* a reddish glow on snow-covered mountain peaks at sunset or sunrise, caused by reflected weak sunlight [Late 19C. Partial translation of German *Alpenglühen* "glowing of the Alps"]

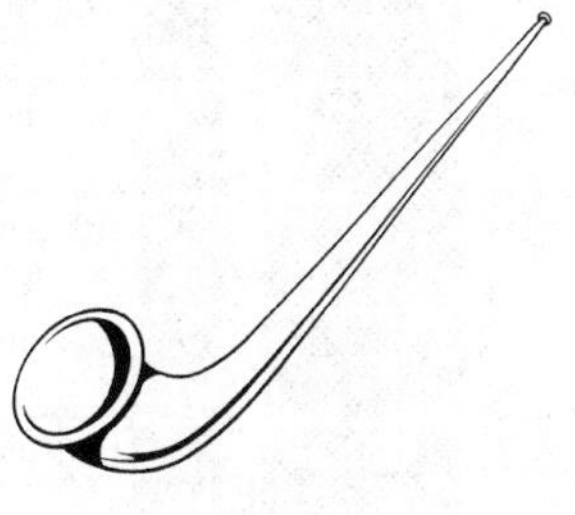

alpenhorn

al·pen·horn /álpən hàwrn/, **alp·horn** /álp-/ *n* a traditional wooden wind instrument with a long tube that rests on the ground and curves up at the end [Late 19C. < German, "horn of the Alps"]

al·pen·stock /álpən stòk/ *n* a long staff with an iron spike at one end, formerly used by mountain climbers [Early 19C. < German, "staff of the Alps"]

al·pes·trine /al péstrin/ *adj* describes a plant that grows at high altitudes [Late 19C. < Latin *alpestris* "alpine" < *Alpes* (see ALP)]

al·pha /álfə/, **al·fa** *n* 1ST LETTER OF GREEK ALPHABET the first letter of the Greek alphabet represented in the English alphabet as "a." See table at **alphabet** ■ *adj* **1.** ALPHABETICAL relating to or being in alphabetical order ○ *in alpha order* **2.** COMPUT OF FIRST TEST VERSION describes the first working version of a new hardware or software product or upgrade. Some features of the product may not be implemented in the alpha version and the discovery of significant bugs is usually anticipated. **3.** CHEM RELATING TO NEAREST ATOM describes the atom nearest to a particular atom or group of atoms in an organic molecule **4.** CHEM RELATING TO MAJOR FORM OF ELEMENT describes the major form of a chemical element with more than one physical form (**allotrope**) [13C. Via Latin < Greek, related to Hebrew and Phoenician *āleph* (see ALEPH)]

Al·pha *n* **1.** a code word for the letter "A," used in international radio communications **2.** the brightest or main star in a constellation (*followed by the Latin genitive*) ○ *Alpha Centauri*

al·pha and o·me·ga *n* **1.** the beginning and end of something **2.** the most important aspect of something [< their being the first and last letters of the Greek alphabet]

al·pha·bet /álfə bèt/ *n* **1.** LETTERS USED TO REPRESENT LANGUAGE a set of letters, usually listed in a fixed order, used in writing a language and representing its basic speech sounds ○ *the Cyrillic alphabet.* See table on next page **2.** SYMBOLS FOR COMMUNICATING a set of symbols representing units used in communication, especially speech sounds or words ○ *the alphabet in Braille* **3.** BASIC PRINCIPLES the basic principles of something (*formal*) [Early 16C. Via late Latin *alphabetum* < Greek *alphabētos* < Greek *alpha* and *bēta*, the first and second letters of the alphabet]

al·pha·bet·i·cal /àlfə béttik'l/, **al·pha·bet·ic** /-béttik/ *adj* **1.** ordered like the letters of the alphabet **2.** based on, typical of, or relating to an alphabet —**al·pha·bet·i·cal·ly** *adv*

al·pha·bet·ize /álfəbət ī̀z/ (**-ized, -iz·ing, -iz·es**) *vt* **1.** to arrange words or items in alphabetical order **2.** to provide a language with an alphabet —**al·pha·bet·i·za·tion** /àlfə beti záysh'n/ *n* —**al·pha·bet·iz·er** *n*

al·pha·bet soup *n* a confusing mass of letters, especially with unintelligible abbreviations (*informal*)

al·pha-block·er *n* a drug that prevents the constriction of blood vessels. Use: treatment of high blood pressure.

Al·pha Cen·tau·ri /-sen táwree/ *n* a multiple star that is the brightest star in the constellation Centaurus. It consists of two bright stars and a red dwarf in orbit around each other.

al·pha-chy·mo·tryp·sin /àlfə kī̀mō trípsin/ *n* a hydrolytic enzyme (**chymotrypsin**), synthesized in the pancreas, that has an unusually reactive serine residue in the active site

al·pha de·cay *n* a radioactive decay process in which an alpha particle is emitted from a nucleus

al·pha e·mis·sion *n* the emission of alpha particles from an atomic nucleus —**al·pha e·mit·ter** *n*

al·pha-fe·to·pro·tein *n* **1.** a protein in the liver of a human fetus, the presence of which in very high or low quantities in the amniotic fluid may indicate spina bifida or Down syndrome **2.** a blood protein produced in the liver, yolk sac, and gastrointestinal tract of a fetus and used as an indicator of cancer and other diseases in adults

al·pha he·lix *n* a helical protein structure consisting of amino acids stabilized by hydrogen bonds

al·pha-hy·drox·y ac·id *n* an organic acid in which a hydroxyl acid is bonded to a carbon atom. Use: skin care products.

al·pha male *n* **1.** a male in a pack of wolves, or a similar pack or troop of animals, that other members submit to and follow and that takes priority in mating with females **2.** a man who controls the activities of a group and to whom others defer (*informal*)

al·pha·nu·mer·ic /àlfənoo mérrik/, **al·pha·nu·mer·i·cal** /-mérrik'l/, **al·pha·mer·ic** /àlfə mérrik/ *adj* using both letters and numbers ○ *an alphanumeric code* [Mid-20C. Blend of ALPHABET + *numeric*] —**al·pha·nu·mer·i·cal·ly** *adv*

al·pha par·ti·cle *n* a particle consisting of two neutrons and two protons that is identical to the helium nucleus and is emitted during some radioactive transformations

al·pha ray *n* a stream of alpha particles

al·pha-re·cep·tor *n* a protein molecule in the cell membrane that specifically binds epinephrine or norepinephrine, triggering a response in the cell

al·pha rhythm *n* the pattern of electrical activity in the brain of somebody awake but relaxed or drowsy,

MAJOR ALPHABETS OF THE WORLD

Phoenician
20 letters, no cases

sound	name
[']	'aleph
[b]	bēth
[g]	gaml, gimel
[d]	dag, dāleth
[h]	hē
[w]	wāw
[z]	zayin
[ḥ]	ḥēth
[y]	yōdh
[k]	kaph
[l]	lāmedh
[m]	mēm
[n]	nahš, nūn
[s]	samekh
[']	'ayin
[p]	pē
[q]	qōph
[r]	rōsh, rēsh
[th,š]	thann, shin
[t]	tāw

Early Greek
21 letters, no cases

sound	name
[a]	alpha
[b]	beta
[g]	gamma
[d]	delta
[ĕ]	e (psilon)
[w]	wau, digamma
[z]	zēta
[h,ē]	ēta
[i,y]	iōta
[k]	kappa
[l]	lambda
[m]	mu
[n]	nu
[ks]	xi
[ŏ]	o (micron)
[p]	pi
[q]	koppa
[r]	rhō
[s]	sigma
[t]	tau
[ū,w]	u (psilon)

Hebrew
23 letters, no cases

	sound	name
א	[']	aleph
ב	[b,bh]	beth
ג	[g,gh]	gimel
ד	[d,dh]	daleth
ה	[h]	he
ו	[w]	vav
ז	[z]	zayin
ח	[ḥ]	heth
ט	[t]	teth
י	[y]	yod
כ ך	[k,kh]	kaph
ל	[l]	lamedh
מ ם	[m]	mem
נ ן	[n]	nun
ס	[s]	samekh
ע	[']	ayin
פ ף	[p,ph]	pe
צ ץ	[ṣ]	sadhe
ק	[q]	qoph
ר	[r]	resh
שׂ	[ś]	sin
שׁ	[šh]	shin
ת	[t,th]	tav

Classical Roman
23 letters, capitals only

A
B
C
D
E
F
G
H
I
K
L
M
N
O
P
Q
R
S
T
V
X
Y
Z

Modern Greek
24 letters[1]

	sound	name
Αα	[a]	alpha
Ββ	[b]	beta
Γγ	[g,n]	gamma
Δδ	[d]	delta
Εε	[e]	epsilon
Ζζ	[z]	zēta
Ηη	[ē]	ēta
Θθ	[th]	thēta
Ιι	[i]	iota
Κκ	[k]	kappa
Λλ	[l]	lambda
Μμ	[m]	mu
Νν	[n]	nu
Ξξ	[x]	xi
Οο	[o]	omicron
Ππ	[p]	pi
Ρρ	[r,rh]	rhō
Σσς	[s]	sigma[4]
Ττ	[t]	tau
Υυ	[y,u]	upsilon
Φφ	[ph]	phi
Χχ	[kh]	chi/khi
Ψψ	[ps]	psi
Ωω	[ō]	ōmega

Cyrillic
31 letters[2]

	sound
Аа	[a]
Бб	[b]
Вв	[v]
Гг	[g]
Дд	[d]
ЕеЁё	[e,ё][5]
Жж	[zh]
Зз	[z]
ИиЙй	[i][6]
Кк	[k]
Лл	[l]
Мм	[m]
Нн	[n]
Оо	[o]
Пп	[p]
Рр	[r]
Сс	[s]
Тт	[t]
Уу	[u]
Фф	[f]
Хх	[kh]
Цц	[ts]
Чч	[ch]
Шш	[sh]
Щщ	[shch]
Ъъ	["]
Ыы	[y]
Ьь	[']
Ээ	[e]
Юю	[yu]
Яя	[ya]

Modern Arabic
28 letters[3]

forms	sound	name
ا ـا	[']	alif
ب ـب ـبـ بـ	[b]	bā
ت ـت ـتـ تـ	[t]	tā
ث ـث ـثـ ثـ	[ṯ]	thā
ج ـج ـجـ جـ	[j]	jīm
ح ـح ـحـ حـ	[ḥ]	ḥā
خ ـخ ـخـ خـ	[kh]	khā
د ـد	[d]	dāl
ذ ـذ	[dh]	dhāl
ر ـر	[r]	rā
ز ـز	[z]	zāy
س ـس ـسـ سـ	[s]	sīn
ش ـش ـشـ شـ	[sh]	shīn
ص ـص ـصـ صـ	[ṣ]	ṣād
ض ـض ـضـ ضـ	[ḍ]	ḍād
ط ـط ـطـ طـ	[ṭ]	ṭā
ظ ـظ ـظـ ظـ	[ẓ]	ẓā
ع ـع ـعـ عـ	[']	'ayn
غ ـغ ـغـ غـ	[ġ]	ghayn
ف ـف ـفـ فـ	[f]	fā
ق ـق ـقـ قـ	[q]	qāf
ك ـك ـكـ كـ	[k]	kāf
ل ـل ـلـ لـ	[l]	lām
م ـم ـمـ مـ	[m]	mīm
ن ـن ـنـ نـ	[n]	nūn
ه ـه ـهـ هـ	[h]	hā
و ـو	[w]	wāw
ي ـي ـيـ يـ	[y]	yā

Notes

1 In the modern Greek alphabet, each letter has an uppercase and lowercase form.
2 In the Cyrillic alphabet, each letter has an uppercase and lowercase form.
3 In the modern Arabic alphabet, each letter has between two and four forms each.
4 The classical and modern Greek letter *sigma* has two lowercase forms.
5 The Cyrillic letter *e* has two forms, each with uppercase and lowercase.
6 The Cyrillic letter *i* has two forms, each with uppercase and lowercase.

registering on an electroencephalograph at a reading between 8 and 13 hertz

al·pha source *n* a radioactive atom that emits alpha particles, e.g., polonium

al·pha test *n* a first test by the manufacturer of new or upgraded software or hardware [< the idea of being first in a series] —**al·pha-test** *vt*

al·pha·to·coph·e·rol /álfə tō kóffə ràwl/ *n* BIOCHEM same as **vitamin E**

alp·horn *n* MUSIC same as **alpenhorn**

al·pine /ál pīn/ *adj* **1. TYPICAL OF HIGH MOUNTAINS** relating to, typical of, or found in high mountains ○ *an alpine climate* **2. USED IN MOUNTAINEERING** used in or involving mountain climbing **3.** BOT **SITUATED OR GROWING ABOVE TIMBERLINE** describes the zone of vegetation on high mountains between the timberline and snow line and any plant that grows in or originates from that zone **4.** SKIING, EXTREME SPORTS another spelling of **Alpine** (senses 2–3) ■ *n* **MOUNTAIN PLANT** a plant that originates from or can grow in the alpine zone on mountains, above the timberline [15C. < Latin *alpinus* < *Alpes* (see ALP)]

Al·pine *adj* **1. OF ALPS** relating to the Alps **2.** SKIING **RELATING TO DOWNHILL SKIING** describes competitive skiing on steep downhill courses, especially downhill and slalom events **3. DESCRIBES SNOWBOARD AND SNOWBOARDING STYLE** describes a type of snowboard that is thinner than average and more like a standard ski, or a type of snowboarding that concentrates on fast runs and freecarving

al·pine-style *adj* describes a type of mountaineering in which the climbers carry all the necessary equipment with them on a single ascent to a mountain summit —**al·pine-style** *adv*

al·pin·ist /álpənist/ *n* a mountain climber, especially one who climbs in the Alps or mountains of similar height [Late 19C. < French *alpiniste* < Latin *alpinus* (see ALPINE)] —**al·pin·ism** *n*

Al·port's syn·drome /ál pàwrts-/, **Al·port syn·drome** *n* a genetic disease characterized by kidney disease and hearing and sight loss

al·pros·ta·dil /al próstəd'l/ *n* a drug that dilates blood vessels. Use: treatment of impotence, prevention of coagulation, treatment of neonates. [Late 20C. < *al-* + *-prost-*, INN stem + *-a-* + VASODILATOR]

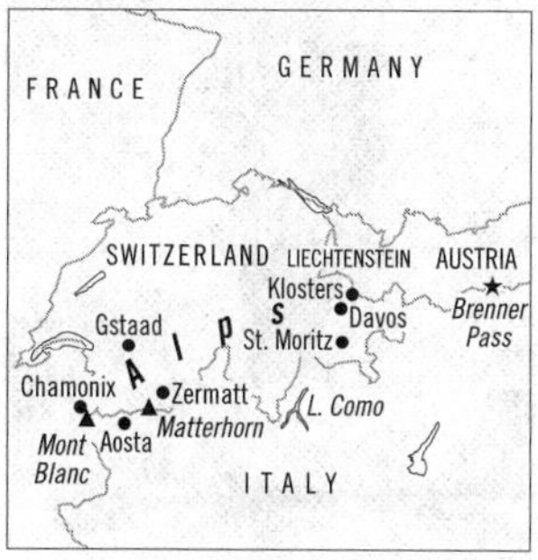

Alps

Alps /alps/ mountain range in southern Europe, extending about 500 mi./800 km from southeastern France to Austria. The highest peak is Mont Blanc. Height: 15,771 ft./4,807 m.

al Qae·da /al kīdə/, **al Qai·da**, **al-Qae·da**, **al-Qai·da** *n* an international Islamic fundamentalist organization associated with several terrorist incidents, including the attack on the World Trade Center, New York (2001). Al-Qaeda was established by Osama bin Laden in 1989 and was based in Afghanistan until driven out by US and coalition forces in 2001. [Late-20C. < Arabic "the base"]

al-Quds /al kŏŏdz/ *n* ISLAM Arabic name for **Jerusalem**

al·read·y /awl réddee, áwl redee/ CORE MEANING: an adverb indicating that something has happened before now, happened in the past before a particular time, or will have happened by or before a particular time in the future ○ *I already know what you're going to say.* ○ *She had already left when I arrived.*

adv **1.** by or at an earlier time than expected ○ *Have you finished already?* **2.** used after a command, exclamation, or other statement to give it emphasis or express exasperation (*informal*) ○ *Enough already!* [14C. < *all ready* "completely ready"]

USAGE already or **all ready**? These words do not mean the same thing, and so they are not interchangeable. ***Already***, an adverb, means "by or at an earlier time than expected," as in *Have they already* [not *all ready*] *left?* ***All ready*** means "all or totally prepared," as in *Is everything all ready* [not *already*] *for tomorrow?*

al·right /awl rít, áwl rít/ (*nonstandard*) *adv* ⚠ in a generally good, satisfactory, or pleasing way ■ *adj* ⚠ generally good, satisfactory, or pleasant

USAGE See ***all right***.

ALS *abbr* MED amyotrophic lateral sclerosis

A.L.S. *abbr* autograph letter, signed

Al·sace /al sáss/ region and former province of France, situated west of the River Rhine. Capital: Strasbourg. Population: 1 734 145 (1999). Area: 3,197 sq. mi./8,280 sq. km.

Al·sace-Lor·raine /-lə ráyn/ area of France on the German border, Now divided into two administrative regions, Alsace and Lorraine. The area was disputed by France and Germany between 1871 and 1945. Population: 3,930,100 (1990). Area: 12,288 sq. mi./31,827 sq. km.

Al·sa·tian /al sáysh'n/ *n* **1.** somebody who comes from Alsace **2.** *UK* same as **German shepherd** ■ *adj* relating to Alsace, or its people, language, or culture [Late 19C. < medieval Latin *Alsatia* "Alsace"]

al se·gno /aal sáyn yō/ *adv* used in a musical score to indicate that the performer should continue playing to a point marked elsewhere in the score by a sign [Late 18C. < Italian, "to the sign"]

al·sike clo·ver /ál sak-, -sīk-/ *n* a perennial clover widely grown for forage. Flowers: white or pink. Native to: Europe. Latin name: *Trifolium hybridum.* [Mid-19C. After *Alsike*, town in Sweden]

al·so /áwlssō/ *adv* **1. IN ADDITION** used to indicate that something is true or is the case in addition ○ *got his picture in the paper and also won a prize* **2. LIKEWISE OR SIMILARLY** like or in the same way as somebody or something else ○ *Her niece was also called Jean.* ○ *When they withdraw their forces, we shall also withdraw ours.* **3. MOREOVER** and in addition to that (*used to modify a whole sentence or clause*) ○ *Also, you must complete the task in one hour.* [Old English *ealswā, allswā* (see ALL, SO[1])]

Al·sop /áwlssəp, ólssəp/, **Joseph, Jr.** (1910–89) US journalist. His nationally syndicated political column "Matter of Fact" ran from 1946 to 1974. Full name **Alsop, Jr., Joseph Wright**

> "Gratitude, like love, is never a dependable international emotion."
> [Joseph Alsop, Jr., *Observer (London)*; November 1952]

al·so-ran *n* **1. LOSING RUNNER** a horse or other entrant in a race that does not finish in any of the winning places **2. LOSING COMPETITOR** a losing entrant in any contest **3. SOMEBODY UNIMPORTANT** somebody of little or no consequence or significance [Because newspaper racing results formerly listed horses that finished fourth or lower under the heading "Also Ran"]

al·stroe·me·ri·a /àlstrə méeree ə/ (*plural* **-as** or *same*) *n* a tuberous plant of the amaryllis family. Flowers: long-lasting, variously colored. Native to: South America. Genus: *Alstroemeria.* [Late 18C. < modern Latin, after Klas von *Alstroemer* (1736–96), Swedish naturalist]

Alt *abbr* COMPUT Alt key

alt. *abbr* **1.** alteration **2.** BOT alternate **3.** ASTRON, MEASURE, MATH altitude **4.** MUSIC alto

alt- *prefix* same as **alto-** (*used before vowels*)

Alta. *abbr* Alberta

Al·ta·de·na /àltə déenə/ urban community in southwestern California, in the San Gabriel Mountains. Population: 42,610 (2000).

Al·ta·ic /al táy ik/ *n* a family of languages that consists of Turkic, Mongolic, and Tungusic, sometimes considered as part of a wider Ural-Altaic family [Mid-19C. After the ALTAI MOUNTAINS] —**Al·ta·ic** *adj*

Al·tai Moun·tains /áltī-/ mountains in Central Asia, on the Kazakhstan-Mongolia border, south of Russia and north of China. The highest peak is Mount Belukha 15,157 ft./4,620 m.

Al·ta·mon·te Springs /áltə mont-/ city in east-central Florida, near Orlando. Population: 40,976 (2002 estimate).

altar: Roman Catholic Church altar

al·tar /áwltər/ *n* **1.** a raised, typically flat-topped structure or area where religious ceremonies are performed **2.** the table or other raised structure in a Christian church on which the bread and wine of Communion are prepared [Pre-12C. < Latin *altare* < *altaria* "burnt offerings," probably < *adolere* "burn up"] ◇ **lead somebody to the altar** to marry somebody (*dated informal*)

SPELLCHECK altar or **alter**? Do not confuse the spelling of ***altar*** and ***alter***, which sound similar. ***Altar*** is a noun referring to a ceremonial structure where religious ceremonies take place, and ***alter*** is a verb meaning "change," as in *I had to alter the wording of the document.*

al·tar boy *n* a boy who assists the priest during services, especially in the Roman Catholic Church

al·tar call *n* an appeal by an evangelist for worshipers to come forward and make a profession of faith

al·tar·piece /áwltər pèess/ *n* a work of art, usually a painting, placed above and behind an altar

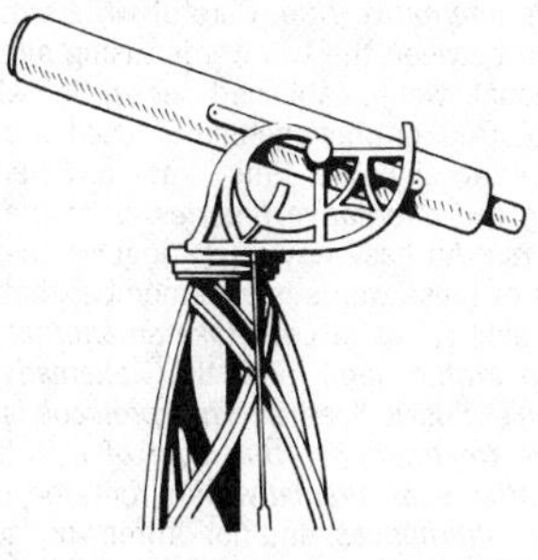

altazimuth

alt·az·i·muth /al tázməth, -tázzə-/ *n* **1.** an instrument, incorporating a telescope that can move vertically and horizontally, used to measure the altitude and azimuth of an astronomical object **2.** an instrument similar to a theodolite used in surveying to measure horizontal and vertical angles [Mid-19C. Blend of ALTITUDE + AZIMUTH]

al·te·plase /áltə plàyss, -plàyz/ *n* a tissue plasminogen activator produced by recombinant DNA technology. Use: treatment of heart failure.

al·ter /áwltər/ (**-tered, -ter·ing, -ters**) *v* **1.** *vti* **CHANGE** to make changes to something or somebody, or be changed or become different ○ *We'll have to alter our plans.* **2.** *vt* **ADJUST GARMENT FOR BETTER FIT** to make adjustments to a piece of clothing so that it fits better ○ *The pants are fine, but the jacket will have to be altered.* **3.** *vt* **CASTRATE ANIMAL** to castrate or spay an animal (*informal*) [14C. Via French < late Latin *alterare* < Latin *alter* "other"] —**al·ter·a·bil·i·ty** /àwltərə bíllətee/ *n* —**al·ter·a·ble** *adj*

SPELLCHECK See *altar.*

SYNONYMS See *change.*

al·ter·a·tion /àwltə ráysh'n/ *n* **1.** CHANGE a change, modification, or adjustment made to something, especially a garment **2.** DIFFERENCE a difference in something resulting from change ○ *I don't see any alteration in the patient's condition.* **3.** PROCESS OF CHANGING the process of changing something or of being changed ○ *undergoing alteration*

al·ter·ca·tion /àwltər káysh'n/ *n* a heated argument, quarrel, or confrontation [14C. Via French < Latin *altercation-* < *altercari* "to dispute" < *alter* "other"] —**al·ter·cate** /áwltər kàyt/ *vi*

al·ter e·go /àwltər éegō/ (*plural* **al·ter e·gos**) *n* **1.** a second side to somebody's personality, different from the one that most people know **2.** a very close and trusted friend [< Latin, "other self"]

al·ter·nate *vi* /áwltər nàyt/ (**-nat·ed, -nat·ing, -nates**) **1.** FOLLOW IN INTERCHANGING PATTERN to follow each other and take each other's place in a regular pattern ○ *as night alternates with day* **2.** FLUCTUATE to shift back and forth, especially regularly or constantly, between one state and another ○ *Her mood alternates between elation and despair.* **3.** BE UNDERSTUDY to act as an understudy for another performer ■ *adj* /áwltərnət/ **1.** ARRANGED IN ALTERNATING PATTERN arranged or happening in a regular pattern in which the one thing alternates with the other ○ *alternate spells of sun and showers* **2.** EVERY OTHER every other or second of a series ○ *They babysit for each other on alternate weekends.* **3.** SERVING AS BACKUP different from and serving, or able to serve, as a substitute for something else ○ *The band decided to go with the song's alternate title.* **4.** BOT NOT ALIGNED describes flowers, buds, or leaves that are arranged singly and at different levels on either side of the stem of a plant, as opposed to being in pairs or groups ■ *n* /áwltərnət/ **1.** SOMEBODY WHO FILLS IN somebody who substitutes for somebody else ○ *An alternate for the first-string quarterback played the entire first half.* **2.** same as **alternative** *n* (sense 1) [Early 16C. < Latin *alternat-*, past participle of *alternare* "do things one after another" < *alternus* "one after another" < *alter* "other"]

USAGE alternate or **alternative**? The adjective ***alternative*** is often used instead of ***alternate*** to mean "different from, and serving, or able to serve, as a substitute for something else," as in *The band decided to go with the song's alternative title.* Careful writers maintain a distinction between the two words, using ***alternative*** in its traditional, well-established sense, "of which only one can be true, or only one can be used or chosen, or take place at any one time," as in *Scientists are examining two alternative theories as to the origin of the universe.* An easy way to distinguish the separate meanings of these words is to remember that ***alternate*** means "backup," as in *Let's take an alternate route to avoid the traffic jam,* and that ***alternative*** means "mutually exclusive," as in *This protocol is the sole alternative treatment for this type of infection.* Note that, in strict use, ***alternative*** may only be used with "two" (*two alternatives*) and not "three" or "several."

al·ter·nate an·gle *n* one of a pair of angles on opposite sides and at opposite ends of a line that cuts two other lines

al·ter·nate·ly /áwltərnətlee/ *adv* **1.** by following one immediately after the other in a regular repeated pattern or sequence ○ *Driving downtown was restricted to cars with odd and even license plate numbers alternately by day of the month.* **2.** same as **alternatively**

al·ter·nat·ing cur·rent *n* an electric current that regularly reverses direction

al·ter·na·tion /àwltər náysh'n/ *n* **1.** a process of change in which one thing follows, or is made to follow, another in a regular repeated pattern **2.** LOGIC a proposition of the form "p or q," that is, either sentence "p" is true or sentence "q" is true

al·ter·na·tion of gen·er·a·tions *n* the existence in the life cycle of an organism of two or more alternating forms or reproductive modes, e.g., sexual and asexual cycles

al·ter·na·tive /awl túrnətiv/ *n* **1.** OTHER POSSIBILITY something different from, and able to serve as a substitute for, something else ○ *You could take the bus as an alternative to driving.* **2.** POSSIBILITY OF CHOOSING the possibility of choosing between two different things or courses of action ○ *We gave you the alternative; you decided to stay.* **3.** ⚠ OPTION either one of two, or one of several, things or courses of action to choose between ○ *I can't decide which of the two alternatives is worse.* ■ *adj* **1.** *Can, UK* same as **alternate** *adj* (sense 3) **2.** MUTUALLY EXCLUSIVE of which only one can be true, or only one can be used or chosen, or take place at any one time ○ *There are two alternative theories as to why this phenomenon occurs.* **3.** UNCONVENTIONALLY NONTRADITIONAL outside the establishment or mainstream, and often presented as being less institutionalized or conventional, or more natural or economical with resources ○ *alternative methods of painting* **4.** LOGIC same as **disjunctive** *adj* (sense 3)

USAGE See *alternate.*

al·ter·na·tive com·e·dy *n* any form of comedy characterized by subject matter and a style of presentation deliberately made different from mainstream comedy —**al·ter·na·tive co·me·di·an** *n*

al·ter·na·tive en·er·gy *n* any form of energy obtained from the Sun, wind, waves, or another natural renewable source, in contrast to energy generated from fossil fuels

al·ter·na·tive life·style *n* a way of living adopted by people who reject the prevailing lifestyle, often because they consider it to be too materialistic or too dependent on technology

al·ter·na·tive·ly /awl túrnətivlee/ *adv* or instead of that ○ *Alternatively, you could drive there.*

al·ter·na·tive med·i·cine *n* the treatment of illness using remedies such as homeopathy or naturopathy that are not considered part of mainstream medicine

al·ter·na·tive press *n* newspapers and periodicals that reflect nontraditional viewpoints and lifestyles

al·ter·na·tive school *n* an educational establishment with a curriculum and methods that are nontraditional

al·ter·na·tor /áwltər nàytər/ *n* a device that generates alternating current, especially in a car

~~alternitive~~ incorrect spelling of **alternative**

al·tho /awl thṓ/ *conj US* another spelling of **although** (*informal*)

althorn

alt·horn /ált hàwrn/ *n* an alto brass wind instrument of either the saxhorn or the flügelhorn family, used mainly in brass or military bands [Mid-19C. < German < *Alt* "alto" + *Horn* "horn"]

al·though /awl thṓ/ *conj* granting or in spite of the fact that ○ *Although the children were sleepy, they kept watching the movie.* [14C. < ALL in the sense "even" + THOUGH]

USAGE although or **though**? In many uses ***although*** and ***though*** are interchangeable, but ***though*** is generally more versatile, in that it can occupy different positions in a sentence with more grammatical flexibility. It is the only choice in the phrases *as though* and *even though,* and in the following types of uses: *I don't like them, though. It is true, though, that they have been kind to us. The chair, though damaged, could still be used. We enjoyed the day outside, cold though it was.*

USAGE although or **however**? Do not use the conjunction ***although*** as a substitute for the adverb ***however. However*** is used to add contrasting and surprising information, and, unlike ***although***, is followed by a comma when it is used as a conjunction, e.g., *We were from different backgrounds. However, we got along really well.* and *We got along very well, although we were from different backgrounds.*

alti- *prefix* same as **alto-**

al·tim·e·ter /al tímmətər, áltə meetər/ *n* an instrument that shows height above sea level, especially one mounted in an aircraft and incorporating an aneroid barometer that senses differences in pressure caused by changes in altitude —**al·ti·met·ric** /àltə méttrik/ *adj* —**al·tim·e·try** /al tímmətree/ *n*

al·ti·pla·no /àalti plaánō/ (*plural* **-nos**) *n Southwest US* especially in Mexico or the Andes of South America, a high plateau [Early 20C. < American Spanish, "high plain"]

Al·ti·pla·no /àalti plaánō/ region of the Andes Mountains extending from southwestern Bolivia to southern Peru. Height: about 12,000 ft./3,650 m.

al·tis·si·mo /aal tíssəmō/ *adv* [Late 18C. < Italian, "highest," superlative of *alto* (see ALTO)] ◇ **in altissimo** in the octave beginning on the G one octave above the G at the top of the treble staff

al·ti·tude /áltə tood/ *n* **1.** HEIGHT ABOVE SEA LEVEL the height of something above a specific level, especially above sea level or the Earth's surface **2.** HIGH PLACE a place or region situated high above sea level (*often used in the plural*) **3.** MATH DISTANCE in a geometrical figure, the perpendicular distance from the vertex to the base **4.** ASTRON ANGLE OF ASTRONOMICAL OBJECT ABOVE HORIZON the angle of an astronomical object above an observer's horizon, measured from the horizon along the circle passing through the object and the point above the observer **5.** HIGH RANK OR POSITION a high rank or high position in a society or group [14C. < Latin *altitudo* < *altus* "high"] —**al·ti·tu·di·nal** /àltə tood'nəl/ *adj*

al·ti·tude sick·ness *n* a condition caused by low levels of oxygen in the air at high altitudes, resulting in nausea and breathlessness

Alt key /áwlt-/ *n* a computer key that is pressed together with another key to change its function

Robert Altman

Alt·man /áwltmən/, **Robert** (*b.* 1925) US movie director and screenwriter. His movies include *M*A*S*H* (1970) and *The Player* (1992).

"What's a cult? It just means not enough people to make a minority."
[Robert Altman, *Observer (London)*; April 11, 1981]

al·to /áltō/ (*plural* **-tos**) *n* **1.** MUSIC same as **contralto** (sense 1) **2.** HIGHEST MAN'S VOICE the highest singing voice for a man, achieved by using falsetto **3.** ALTO SINGER a singer with an alto or contralto voice **4.** INSTRUMENT BETWEEN SOPRANO AND TENOR in a family of instruments, the instrument whose size and pitch fall between the soprano and tenor instruments [Late 16C. Via Italian, "high" < Latin *altus*]

alto-, **alti-** *prefix* high, altitude ○ *altocumulus, altimeter* [< Latin *altus* "high, deep" < Indo-European, "grow"]

al·to clef *n* the C clef indicating that middle C is on the third line of the staff

al·to·cu·mu·lus /àltō kyoómyələss/ (*plural* **-li** /-lī/) *n* white or gray patchy cloud with a rounded outline

al·to·geth·er /àwltə gé*th*ər, áwltə gè*th*ər/ *adv* **1. WITH EVERYTHING INCLUDED** when everything is included or taken into account ○ *Altogether, your bill comes to $75.99.* **2. TOTALLY** entirely or utterly ○ *I'm not altogether satisfied.* **3. ON THE WHOLE** considered as a whole ○ *Altogether, it's been a good day.* [12C. < ALL "the whole group" + TOGETHER] ◇ **in the altogether** naked (*informal*)

USAGE altogether or **all together**? These words mean different things. ***Altogether*** means "with everything included," "totally," or "on the whole" and is an adverb (*It was an altogether spectacular tennis championship; Altogether seventeen people are missing.*). ***All together*** means "everyone together," "all at the same place or time"; it functions as an adjectival phrase. Usually the word *all* can be removed without affecting the grammar or the sense: *They arrived (all) together at nine. The plates are (all) together on a separate shelf.*

al·to·ist /áltō ist/ *n* a musician who plays an alto saxophone

Al·ton /áwlt'n/ city on the eastern bank of the Mississippi River, in southwestern Illinois. Population: 30,190 (2002 estimate).

Al·too·na /al tóonə/ city in south central Pennsylvania, in the heart of the state's coal-mining region. Population: 48,490 (2002 estimate).

al·to-re·lie·vo /àltō ri lée vō/ (*plural* **al·to-re·lie·vos** or **al·to-re·lie·vi** /-vee/), **al·to-ri·lie·vo** /-ril yáy vō/ (*plural* **al·to-ri·lie·vos** or **al·to-ri·lie·vi**) *n* SCULPTURE same as **high relief** [Mid-17C. < Italian *alto-rilievo*]

al·to·stra·tus /àltō stráytəss, -stráttəss/ (*plural* **-ti** /-tī/) *n* grayish cloud in thin sheets or layers of uniform appearance, through which the Sun can be seen

al·tri·cial /al tríshəl/ *adj* describes birds or mammals that are helpless when young and dependent on their parents for food ■ *n* a bird or mammal that produces young that are unable to move or feed themselves without help [Late 19C. < modern Latin *Altrices* (former division of birds), plural of Latin *altrix* "female nourisher" < *alere* "nourish"]

alt rock /áwlt-/ *n* MUSIC rock music played by lesser known performers and considered an alternative to the music promoted by large record companies [< shortening of ALTERNATIVE]

al·tru·ism /áltroo ìzzəm/ *n* **1.** an attitude or way of behaving marked by unselfish concern for the welfare of others **2.** the belief that acting for the benefit of others is right and good [Mid-19C. < French *altruisme* < Italian *altrui* "that which belongs to other people" < Latin *alter* "other"] —**al·tru·ist** *n* —**al·tru·is·tic** /àltroo ístik/ *adj* —**al·tru·is·ti·cal·ly** *adv*

ALU *abbr* COMPUT arithmetic logic unit

al·u·la /állyələ/ (*plural* **-lae** /-lee/) *n* the part of a bird's wing that corresponds to a thumb and contains a few short feathers [Late 18C. < modern Latin, "little wing" < Latin *ala* "wing"] —**al·u·lar** *adj*

al·um[1] /álləm/ *n* **1.** a colorless crystalline solid that turns white in air. Use: astringents, pigments, dyes, water purification, leather dressing. Formula: $KAl(SO_4)_2.12H_2O$. **2.** an inorganic chemical having a structure like alum [14C. Via French < Latin *alumen*]

a·lum[2] /ə lúm/ *n* a graduate of a school, college, or university (*informal*) [Mid-20C. Shortening of ALUMNUS, ALUMNA]

a·lu·mi·na /ə lóomənə/ *n* a white or colorless oxide of aluminum. Source: corundum, bauxite. Use: catalysts, abrasives, manufacture of artificial rubies and sapphires. Formula: Al_2O_3. [Late 18C. < Latin *alumin-* (see ALUMINUM), after words such as SODA and MAGNESIA]

a·lu·mi·nate /ə lóomənət/ *n* any salt of aluminum and a metallic oxide

a·lu·mi·nif·er·ous /ə lòomə níffərəss/ *adj* containing or being a source of alumina or aluminum

al·u·min·i·um /àllə mínnee əm/ *n UK* CHEM ELEM same as **aluminum**

a·lu·mi·nize /ə lóomə nīz/ (**-nized, -niz·ing, -niz·es**) *vt* to treat or coat something with aluminum

a·lu·mi·no·sil·i·cate /ə lòomənō sílli kàyt, -síllikət/ *n* a silicate that contains aluminum. The minerals feldspar and beryl are aluminosilicates.

a·lu·min·o·ther·my /ə lòomənō thúrmee/ *n* a process for extracting a metal from its oxide that involves burning the oxide together with aluminum powder

a·lu·mi·nous /ə lóomənəss/ *adj* **1.** resembling aluminum or alum **2.** CHEM same as **aluminiferous** [15C. < Latin *aluminosus* < *alumin-* (see ALUMINUM)]

a·lu·mi·num /ə lóomənəm/ *n* a silvery white, light metallic element that is ductile, malleable, and resistant to corrosion. Source: bauxite. Use: lightweight construction, corrosion-resistant materials. Symbol **Al**. See table at **element** [Early 19C. < Latin *alumin-*, stem of *alumen* "alum"]

a·lu·mi·num chlo·ride *n* a white or yellowish crystalline powder. Use: medicines, cosmetics, pigments, antiperspirants. Formula: $AlCl_3$ or Al_2Cl_6.

a·lu·mi·num hy·drox·ide *n* a white solid. Use: antacid, catalyst, drying agent, glass and ceramics manufacturing. Formula: $Al(OH)_3$ or $Al_2O_3.3H_2O$.

a·lu·mi·num ox·ide *n* CHEM same as **alumina**

a·lu·mi·num sid·ing *n* aluminum used as a protective surface on the outer walls of frame buildings

a·lu·mi·num sul·fate *n* a white crystalline solid. Use: paper, textiles, water purification. Formula: $Al_2(SO_4)_3$.

a·lum·na /ə lúmnə/ (*plural* **-nae** /-nī/) *n* a female graduate or former student of a school, college, or university [Late 19C. < Latin, feminine form of ALUMNUS]

a·lum·nus /ə lúmnəss/ (*plural* **-ni** /-nī/) *n* a male graduate or former student of a school, college, or university [Mid-17C. < Latin, "pupil, foster child" < *alere* "nourish"]

al·um·root /álləm ròot/ *n* a plant of the saxifrage family with dark green round or heart-shaped leaves and astringent roots. Flowers: small, bell-shaped. Native to: North America. Genus: *Heuchera*. [< the astringency of the roots]

al·u·nite /állyə nīt/ *n* a white, gray, or reddish mineral composed of hydrated potassium aluminum sulfate. Source: altered volcanic rocks. Use: fertilizers. [Mid-19C. < French < *alun* "alum" < Latin *alumen* (see ALUMINUM)]

Al·va·ra·do /àlvə ráadō/, **Pedro de** (1486–1541) Spanish explorer who served with Hernán Cortés in the conquest of Mexico (1519) and became governor of Guatemala (1530)

Al·va·rez /álvə rèz/, **Luis W.** (1911–88) US physicist. He developed the first proton linear accelerator and liquid hydrogen bubble chamber, and won the Nobel Prize in physics (1968) for his work on subatomic particles. Full name **Alvarez, Luis Walter**

al·ve·o·lar /al vée ələr, -vée lər, -vee ṓlər/ *adj* **1.** ANAT **RELATING TO AIR SAC IN LUNG** relating to the air sacs in the lungs (**alveoli**) **2.** ANAT **RELATING TO JAWBONE** relating to the part of the upper or lower jaw that contains the roots of the teeth **3.** PHON **WITH TONGUE NEAR UPPER TEETH RIDGE** describes a consonant that is sounded with the tongue touching or close to the ridge behind the teeth of the upper jaw ■ *n* PHON **CONSONANT** an alveolar consonant, e.g., "t," "d," or "s" in English —**al·ve·o·lar·ly** *adv*

al·ve·o·lar ridge *n* a hard ridge in the mouth immediately behind the roots of the teeth

al·ve·o·lec·to·my /àlvee ə léktəmee/ (*plural* **-mies**) *n* surgical excision of a portion of the tooth socket or ridge

al·ve·o·li ANAT plural of **alveolus**

al·ve·o·li·tis /àlvee ə lítiss/ *n* inflammation of the air sacs of the lungs

al·ve·o·lus /al vée ələss/ (*plural* **-li** /-lī/) *n* **1.** a tiny thin-walled air sac found in large numbers in each lung, through which oxygen enters and carbon dioxide leaves the blood **2.** a socket in the jaw bone in which a tooth is rooted [Late 17C. < Latin, "little cavity" < *alveus* "cavity" < *alvus* "belly"]

Al·vin /álvin/ city in eastern Texas, south of Houston. Population: 22,025 (2002 estimate).

al·ways /áwl wayz, -wiz/ *adv* **1. AT ALL TIMES** used to indicate that something happens or is done continuously, repetitively, or on every occasion ○ *She's always very polite.* **2. THROUGH ALL PAST OR FUTURE TIME** throughout all past time or all future time, or for as long as anyone can remember and as long as anyone can foresee ○ *I will always love you.* **3. IF NECESSARY** if necessary, or if there is no other or no better option ○ *I could always stay an extra day if you need help.* [14C. < Old English *ealne weg* "all the way"] ◇ **for always** for all time

al·ways-on *adj* **1.** describes a home or business with several computers and mobile phones, in which Internet access is not restricted to specific times **2.** describes a modem that is continuously switched on

Al·yce clo·ver /àlləss-/ *n* a low-growing spreading tropical plant grown as a pasture and hay crop in the southern United States. Latin name: *Alysicarpus vaginalis.* [Mid-20C. *Alyce* probably (by association with the forename *Alice*) < modern Latin *Alysicarpus* < Greek *halusis* "chain" + *karpos* "fruit"]

a·lys·sum /ə líssəm/ *n* **1.** PLANTS same as **sweet alyssum** **2.** *Can, UK* a perennial plant with oval hairy gray-green leaves. Flowers: bright yellow. Native to: Europe. Latin name: *Aurinia saxatilis.* US term **basket-of-gold** [Mid-16C. Via modern Latin < Greek *alysson* "madwort" (believed to cure rabies) < *a-* "without" + *lyssa* "rabies"]

Alz·heim·er's dis·ease /áalts hīmərz-/, **Alzheimer's** *n* a degenerative disorder that affects the brain and causes dementia, especially late in life [Early 20C. After Alois *Alzheimer* (1864–1915), German neurologist]

am[1] *abbr* **1.** TELECOM amplitude modulation **2.** Armenia (*used in Internet addresses*) See table at **domain name**

am[2] *stressed* /am/; *unstressed* /əm/ 1st person singular present of **be**[1] [Old English *eom* < Indo-European]

Am[1] *abbr* BIBLE Amos

Am[2] *symbol* CHEM ELEM americium

Am. *abbr* American

a.m., A.M. *adj, adv* in the period between midnight and noon. Full form **ante meridiem**

A.M. *abbr* **1.** MEDIA amplitude modulation **2.** EDUC Master of Arts [In sense 2 Latin *Artium Magister*]

AMA *abbr* HEALTH SERVICES American Medical Association

A·ma·do /ə maádō, ə maádoo/, **Jorge** (1912–2001) Brazilian novelist and Communist politician. His works include *Dona Flor and Her Two Husbands* (1966, English version 1969).

a·mah /aámə, -maa, aa maá/ *n* in East and South Asia, a woman employed as a children's nurse, domestic servant, office cleaner, or attendant [Mid-19C. Via Portuguese *ama* "nurse" < medieval Latin *amma* "mother"]

a·mal·gam /ə málgəm/ *n* **1.** a combination of two or more characteristics ○ *an amalgam of liberal and socialist ideas* **2.** a substance used as filling for tooth cavities, consisting of a paste of powdered mercury, silver, and tin that quickly hardens [15C. Directly or via French < medieval Latin *amalgama*]

SYNONYMS See ***mixture***.

a·mal·ga·mate /ə málgə màyt/ (**-mat·ed, -mat·ing, -mates**) *vti* **1.** to combine two or more organizations or things into one unified whole, or take the form of one unified whole **2.** to alloy a metal with mercury, or be alloyed with mercury —**a·mal·ga·ma·tive** *adj* —**a·mal·ga·ma·tor** *n*

a·mal·ga·ma·tion /ə màlgə máysh'n/ *n* **1.** BUSINESS **BUSINESS MERGER** a combination of two or more business concerns so as to form one **2. RESULT OF COMBINING THINGS** something that is a combination of different things or results from their amalgamation **3. COMBINING THINGS** the process of amalgamating things into a unified whole **4.** METALL **METAL EXTRACTION FROM ORE** a method of extracting a precious metal from an ore by using mercury to form an amalgam with the metal

Am·al·the·a /àmm'l thée ə/ *n* a natural satellite of Jupiter, discovered in 1892

a·man·dine /aamən déen, -déen, ámmən-/ *adj* filled, cooked, or served with almonds ○ *salmon amandine* [Mid-19C. < French < *amande* "almond"]

a·man·ta·dine /ə mántə déen/ *n* an antiviral drug that is also used to treat Parkinson's disease [Mid-20C. Blend of AMINE + *adamantane*]

a·man·u·en·sis /ə mànnyoo énssiss/ (*plural* **-en·ses** /-én seez/) *n* (*literary*) **1.** somebody employed by a person to write from his or her dictation or to copy manuscripts **2.** a writer's assistant with research and secretarial duties [Early 17C. < Latin < *a manu* "by hand" (in *servus a manu* "enslaved servant with secretarial duties")]

am·a·ranth /ámmə rànth/ (*plural* **-ranths** or *same*) *n* **1.** PLANT WITH DROOPING FLOWERS a plant grown for ornament and sometimes as a grain crop or leafy vegetable. Flowers: green, red, or purple, in long drooping heads. Genus: *Amaranthus.* **2.** LEGENDARY FLOWER according to legend, a flower that never fades **3.** FOOD DYE a synthetic red food dye [Mid-16C. Via French *amarante* or modern Latin *amaranthus* < Latin *amarantus* < Greek *amarantos* "not corruptible, not fading"]

am·a·ran·thine /àmmə ránthən, -thīn/ *adj* **1.** undying or unfading, like the legendary amaranth (*literary*) **2.** of a dark reddish purple color

am·a·ret·ti /àmmə rétte/ *npl* small crisp Italian cookies flavored with almonds [< Italian, plural of *amaretto* (see AMARETTO)]

am·a·ret·to /àmmə réttō/ *n* an Italian almond-flavored liqueur [Mid-20C. < Italian, "little bitter (one)" < *amaro* "bitter" < Latin *amarus*]

Am·a·ril·lo /àmmə ríllō/ city in northwestern Texas, near the center of the Texas Panhandle. Population: 177,010 (2002 estimate).

amaryllis

am·a·ryl·lis /àmmə ríllәss/ (*plural* **-lis·es** or *same*) *n* **1.** a plant grown from a bulb. Flowers: large, red, pink, or white, trumpet-shaped, at the head of a single stalk. Native to: southern Africa. Latin name: *Amaryllis belladonna.* **2.** a tropical American plant related to the southern African amaryllis. Genus: *Hippeastrum.* [Late 18C. Via modern Latin < Greek *Amarullis*, shepherdess in pastorals]

a·mass /ə máss/ (**a·massed, a·mass·ing, a·mass·es**) *vt* to bring a large quantity of things together over time ○ *amassed a fortune in the 1950s* [15C. < French *amasser* < *masser* "gather into a mass" < Latin *massa* (see MASS)] —**a·mass·a·ble** *adj* —**a·mass·er** *n* —**a·mass·ment** *n*

SYNONYMS See ***collect***[1].

am·a·teur /ámmə tùr, -tər, -choor/ *n* **1.** SOMEBODY DOING SOMETHING FOR PLEASURE somebody who does something for pleasure rather than payment ○ *a competition open only to amateurs* **2.** UNSKILLED PERSON somebody with limited skill in, or knowledge of, an activity ○ *Whoever fixed your car must have been an amateur.* **3.** SOMEBODY WHO LOVES SOMETHING somebody who loves or is greatly interested in something (*literary*) ○ *She is an amateur of classical sculpture.* ■ *adj* **1.** BEING AMATEUR engaging in something as an amateur ○ *a talented amateur golfer* **2.** BY AMATEURS for, by, or consisting of amateurs **3.** NOT DONE WITH SKILL done in an unskillful or unprofessional way [Late 18C. Via French < Latin *amator* "lover" < *amare* "to love"]

am·a·teur·ish /àmmə túrish, -choor-/ *adj* lacking the skill of a professional, or unskillfully or unprofessionally done —**am·a·teur·ish·ly** *adv* —**am·a·teur·ish·ness** *n*

am·a·teur·ism /ámmətər ìzzəm, -choor-/ *n* amateur status, participation by amateurs, or the principle that something should be reserved for amateurs ○ *one of the last bastions of true amateurism in sports*

A·ma·ti /ə maátee/ family of Italian violin makers including **Andrea** (*d.* 1578), his son **Girolamo** (1556?–1630?), and grandson **Nicolò** (1596–1684), the most eminent of the Amati family, known for the extreme elegance of his instruments

am·a·tol /ámmə tàwl/ *n* an explosive made from ammonium nitrate and TNT. Use: bombs. [Early 20C. < AMMONIUM + TOLUENE]

am·a·to·ry /ámmə tàwree/, **am·a·to·ri·al** /àmmə táwree əl/ *adj* relating to, involving, expressing, or typical of physical love (*formal*) ○ *amatory adventures* [Late 16C. < Latin *amatorius* < *amator* (see AMATEUR)]

~~**amatuer**~~ incorrect spelling of **amateur**

am·au·ro·sis /àmmaw rṓssiss/ *n* partial or complete vision impairment, especially when there is no obvious damage to the eye [Mid-17C. < Greek *amaurōsis* < *amauroun* "darken" < *amauros* "dark"] —**am·au·rot·ic** /-róttik/ *adj*

am·au·ro·sis fu·gax /-fyoó gàks/ *n* a brief episode of partial blindness occurring when there is no obvious damage to the eye [*Fugax* < Latin < *fugere* "flee"]

a·mau·tik /ə mówtik/, **a·mau·ti** /-tee/ *n Can* among the Inuit, a woman's jacket that has a fur-lined hood for carrying an infant or small child [< Inuktitut]

a·maze /ə máyz/ (**a·mazed, a·maz·ing, a·maz·es**) *vt* to fill somebody with wonder or astonishment [Old English *āmasian* "stupefy, stun," origin ?] —**a·mazed** *adj* —**a·maz·ed·ly** /ə máyzədlee/ *adv* —**a·maz·ed·ness** /-nəss/ *n*

a·maze·ment /ə máyzmənt/ *n* a strong feeling of wonder or surprise at the extraordinariness of something

a·maz·ing /ə máyzing/ *adj* **1.** so extraordinary or wonderful as to be barely believable or to cause extreme surprise ○ *an amazing escape* **2.** outstandingly good, skillful, or admirable (*informal*) ○ *an amazing concert* —**a·maz·ing·ly** *adv* —**a·maz·ing·ness** *n*

am·a·zon /ámmə zòn, -əzən/ *n* a medium-sized parrot that typically has green feathers and a short tail. Native to: tropical America. Genus: *Amazona.* [Late 19C. After the AMAZON[2]]

Am·a·zon[1] /ámmə zòn, -əzən/ *n* **1.** in Greek mythology, a member of a group of women warriors who lived in Scythia, an area of present-day Ukraine, or elsewhere at the northern limits of the world. According to one version, they fought in the Trojan war on the side of Troy. **2.** *also* **am·a·zon** a notably tall, physically strong, or strong-willed woman [14C. Via Latin < Greek *Amazōn*] —**Am·a·zo·ni·an** /àmmə zṓnee ən/ *adj*

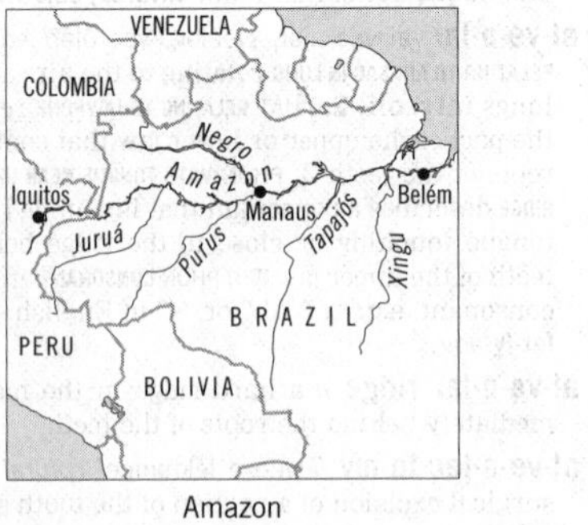

Amazon

Am·a·zon[2] /ámmə zòn, -əzən/ world's second longest river. It flows east from northern Peru, traversing northern South America and emptying into the Atlantic Ocean in Brazil. Length: 4,000 mi./6,400 km. —**Am·a·zo·ni·an** /àmmə zṓnee ən/ *adj*

Am·a·zon·as /àmmə zṓnəss/ state in Northwestern Brazil. Capital: Manaus. Population: 2,389,279 (1996). Area: 609,200 sq. mi./1,577,820 sq. km.

Am·a·zon dol·phin *n* a freshwater dolphin with a long snout. Native to: upper Amazon and Orinoco rivers. Latin name: *Inia geoffrensis.*

am·a·zon·ite /ámmə zo nīt/ *n* a green or bluish green precious stone that is a variety of microcline. Use: gems. [After the AMAZON[2], where similar green stones were formerly found]

am·bas·sa·dor /am bássədər, -dàwr/ *n* **1.** DIPLOMATIC REPRESENTATIVE a diplomatic official of the highest rank sent by one country as its long-term representative to another **2.** OFFICIAL REPRESENTATIVE an official representative of an organization or movement ○ *visiting this country as an ambassador for a fund dedicated to saving endangered species* **3.** UNOFFICIAL REPRESENTATIVE somebody or something regarded as an unofficial representative or a symbol of something ○ *The swallow is an ambassador of spring.* [14C. Via French *ambassadeur* < Italian *ambasciator* < Latin *ambactus* "vassal" < Gaulish, "servant"] —**am·bas·sa·do·ri·al** /am bàssə dáwree əl/ *adj* —**am·bas·sa·dor·ship** *n*

CULTURAL NOTE ***The Ambassadors***, a novel (1903) by Henry James. Sometimes regarded as James's masterpiece, it tells the story of Lambert Strether, a middle-aged editor sent by his wealthy New England patron and fiancée to Paris to persuade her expatriate son Chad to return home.

am·bas·sa·dor at large (*plural* **am·bas·sa·dors at large**) *n* an ambassador not assigned to one specific country

am·beer /ám beer/ *n Southern US* saliva in the mouth containing the juice of chewed tobacco [Mid-19C. Origin ?]

REGIONAL NOTE In its original sense, "water stained with tobacco refuse," the term ***ambeer*** is limited to the tobacco-producing regions of the southeastern United States. But its main meaning, given here, is commonplace throughout the rural South.

am·ber /ámbər/ *n* **1.** YELLOW FOSSIL RESIN a hard translucent fossil resin varying in color from yellow to light brown. Use: jewelry, ornaments. **2.** BROWNISH YELLOW COLOR a yellow to brown color **3.** SIGNAL FOR CAUTION in a system of road traffic lights or railway signaling, the yellow-colored light that advises caution [14C. Via French *ambre* < Arabic *anbar* "ambergris," from a perceived similarity between the two] —**am·ber** *adj*

Am·ber a·lert *n* a system of bulletins issued by police to the media and sometimes on electronic highway signs, requesting vital information leading to the rapid rescue of a kidnapped child [Early 21C. After *Amber* Hagerman, a child kidnapped and murdered in Texas in 1996]

am·ber·gris /ámbər grìss, -greess/ *n* a gray waxy substance, consisting mainly of cholesterol, secreted from the intestines of the sperm whale. It is found floating in tropical waters or on beaches. Use: perfume-making. [15C. < French *ambre gris* "gray amber"]

am·ber·jack /ámbər jàk/ (*plural* **-jacks** or *same*) *n* a large sea fish that has golden markings. Native to: warm waters. Genus: *Seriola.*

am·ber·oid /ámbər òyd/ *n* a synthetic form of amber made by heating and compressing valueless small pieces of amber with other resins

ambi- *prefix* both ○ *ambiversion* [< Latin *ambi* "around, on both sides" < Indo-European]

am·bi·ance /ámbee ənss/, **am·bi·ence** *n* the typical atmosphere or mood of a place ○ *a restaurant with a welcoming ambiance* [Mid-20C. < French *ambiance* < *ambiant* < Latin *ambient-* (see AMBIENT)]

am·bi·dex·ter·i·ty /àmbi dek stérrətee/ *n* **1.** ABILITY TO USE EACH HAND EQUALLY WELL the ability to use each hand with equal skill **2.** SKILLFULNESS general skillfulness, especially with the hands **3.** DECEIT dishonesty, deceit, or double-dealing (*literary*)

am·bi·dex·trous /àmbi dékstrəss/ *adj* **1.** able to use the right and the left hand with equal skill **2.** very skillful and versatile [Mid-17C. < late Latin *ambidexter* "right-handed on both sides" < Latin *dexter* "right-handed"] —**am·bi·dex·trous·ly** *adv*

am·bi·ence *n* another spelling of **ambiance**

am·bi·ent /ámbee ənt/ *adj* in the immediately surrounding area ○ *ambient temperature* ■ *n* MUSIC same as **ambient music** [Late 16C. Directly or via French < Latin *ambient-*, present participle of *ambire* "go around" (see AMBITION)]

am·bi·ent music *n* music that is usually instrumental and repetitive and often contains soothing electronic sounds, used to create an atmosphere of calm or relaxation

am·bi·gu·i·ty /àmbi gyoō ətee/ (*plural* **-ties**) *n* **1.** a situation in which something can be understood in more than one way and it is not clear which meaning is intended **2.** an expression or statement that has more than one meaning

am·big·u·ous /am bíggyoo əss/ *adj* **1.** having more than one possible meaning or interpretation ○ *an ambiguous response* **2.** causing uncertainty or confusion ○ *an ambiguous result* [Early 16C. < Latin *ambiguus* "undecided" < *ambigere* "wander around" < *agere* "to lead"] —**am·big·u·ous·ly** *adv* —**am·big·u·ous·ness** *n*

USAGE ambiguous or **ambivalent**? Both words describe uncertainty in understanding what is meant. The principal difference is that ***ambivalent*** is used of people and their attitudes, whereas ***ambiguous*** refers to information or context. If people are ***ambivalent*** about disarmament, they are unsure about the advantages and disadvantages and cannot easily decide between the various arguments, whereas if a political leader makes an ***ambiguous*** statement about disarmament, then the statement has more than one possible interpretation.

am·bi·gu·ous gen·i·ta·lia *n* a congenital condition in which the outer genitals do not have the typical appearance of either sex (*takes a singular verb*) ■ *npl* outer genitals that do not have the typical appearance of either sex (*takes a plural verb*)

am·bi·sex·u·al /àmbi sékshoo əl/ *adj* **1.** describes secondary sexual characteristics that are common to both sexes **2.** sexually responsive or attracted to both sexes —**am·bi·sex·u·al·i·ty** /-sèkshoo állətee/ *n*

am·bi·son·ics /àmbi sónniks/ *n* a recording and reproduction system that uses separate channels and speakers to create the effect of being surrounded by sound (*takes a singular verb*) —**am·bi·son·ic** *adj*

am·bit /ámbit/ *n* the scope, extent, or limits of something ○ *within the ambit of the court's jurisdiction* [Late 16C. < Latin *ambitus* "circuit" < *ambire* (see AMBITION)]

am·bi·tion /am bísh'n/ *n* **1.** a strong feeling of wanting to be successful in life and achieve great things ○ *She lacks ambition.* **2.** a goal or objective that somebody is trying to achieve [14C. Via French < Latin *ambition-* < *ambire* "canvass for votes, go around" < *ire* "go"]

am·bi·tious /am bíshəss/ *adj* **1.** HAVING STRONG DESIRE FOR SUCCESS having a strong desire to be successful in life **2.** NEEDING GREAT EFFORT TO SUCCEED sounding impressive but difficult to achieve because very high standards have been set or a great deal of work is required ○ *an ambitious plan to increase market share* **3.** STRONGLY DESIROUS with a strong desire to have or do something ○ *ambitious to be the youngest person ever to win the championship* —**am·bi·tious·ly** *adv* —**am·bi·tious·ness** *n*

am·biv·a·lence /am bívvələnss/ *n* **1.** the presence of two opposing ideas, attitudes, or emotions at the same time **2.** a feeling of uncertainty about something due to a mental conflict [Early 20C. < German *Ambivalenz*, after *Äquivalenz* "equivalence"]

am·biv·a·lent /am bívvələnt/ *adj* having mixed, uncertain, or conflicting feelings about something

USAGE See ***ambiguous***.

am·bi·ver·sion /àmbi vúrzhən/ *n* a personality pattern that has characteristics of both introversion and extroversion —**am·bi·vert** /ámbi vùrt/ *n*

am·ble /ámb'l/ *vi* (**-bled, -bling, -bles**) to walk slowly in a relaxed way ○*"I took off shoes and socks and ambled along carrying them, enjoying the evening sun."* (Dick Francis, *The Danger*; 1983) ■ *n* a slow and relaxed walk or style of walking [14C. Via French *ambler* < Latin *ambulare* "walk"] —**am·bler** *n*

am·blyg·o·nite /am blíggə nìt/ *n* a white or grayish green mineral. Use: source of lithium. [Early 19C. < Greek *amblugōnios* "obtuse-angled"]

am·bly·o·pi·a /àmbli ṓpee ə/ *n* an impairment of the vision in one eye that does not have a physical cause [Early 18C. Via modern Latin < Greek *ambluōpia* "dim-sightedness"] —**am·bly·o·pic** *adj*

am·bo /ám bṑ/ (*plural* **-bos** or **-bo·nes** /am bṓ neez/) *n* a lectern or pulpit in early Christian churches [Mid-17C. Via medieval Latin < Greek *ambōn* "raised edge (of a dish)"]

Am·boi·nese *n, adj* PEOPLES, LANG same as **Ambonese**

am·bo·nes CHR plural of **ambo**

Am·bo·nese /àmbə neéz, -neéss/ (*plural same*), **Am·boi·nese** /-boy-/ *n* **1.** somebody who was born or raised on the island of Ambon in eastern Indonesia **2.** the form of Malay spoken on the island of Ambon [Mid-19C. < *Ambon*] —**Am·bo·nese** *adj*

am·brette /am brét/ (*plural same* or **-brettes**) *n* PLANTS same as **abelmosk** [Mid-19C. < French, "a little ambergris" < *ambre* (see AMBER)]

Am·brose /ám brṑz/, **St.** (340?–397) Roman priest and theologian. As bishop of Milan from 374 he combated Arianism and introduced much Greek theology to the West.

am·bro·sia /am brṓzhə/ *n* **1.** FOOD OF CLASSICAL GODS in classical mythology, the food of the deities, which was supposed to make those who ate it immortal **2.** FRUIT AND COCONUT DISH a dessert or salad made from oranges, bananas, and coconut **3.** SOMETHING DELICIOUS a substance that tastes or smells delicious (*literary*) [Mid-16C. Via Latin < Greek < *ambrotos* "immortal"] —**am·bro·sial** *adj*

am·bry /ámbree/ (*plural* **-bries**), **aum·bry** /áwmbree/ *n* **1.** a small recess near the altar in a church, where sacred vessels are kept **2.** *UK* a small cupboard or pantry (*archaic*) [14C. Via French *armarie* < Latin *armarium* (see ARMOIRE)]

ambs·ace /áymz àyss/, **ames·ace** *n* (*archaic*) **1.** the lowest throw at dice, with the single spot uppermost on both dice **2.** bad luck or worthlessness [13C. Via Old French *ambes as* "both aces" < Latin *ambas as*]

am·bu·lac·rum /àmbyə láykrəm/ (*plural* **-ra** /-rə/) *n* in a starfish, sea urchin, or similar animal, each of the five radial areas on the underside of the body along which the blood vessels and nerves run and through which the feet extend [Early 19C. < Latin, "avenue" < *ambulare* "to walk"] —**am·bu·lac·ral** *adj*

am·bu·lance /ámbyələnss/ *n* a vehicle designed and equipped for carrying people to and from a hospital [Mid-19C. < French < *hôpital ambulant* "field hospital," literally "walking hospital" < Latin *ambulant-*, present participle of *ambulare* "walk"]

am·bu·lance chas·er *n* **1.** a lawyer who, in order to earn large fees, seeks out accident victims and encourages them to claim heavy damages (*slang disapproving*) **2.** a lawyer considered to be overly aggressive and perhaps unethical (*slang*) —**am·bu·lance chas·ing** *n*

am·bu·lant /ámbyələnt/ *adj* **1.** moving around from place to place **2.** MED same as **ambulatory** *adj* (sense 3) [Early 17C. Via French < Latin *ambulant-* (see AMBULANCE)]

am·bu·late /ámbyə làyt/ (**-lat·ed, -lat·ing, -lates**) *vi* to walk or move from one place to another (*formal*) [Early 17C. < Latin *ambulat-*, past participle of *ambulare* "walk"] —**am·bu·la·tion** *n*

am·bu·la·to·ry /ámbyələ tàwree/ *adj* **1.** RELATING TO WALKING relating to or equipped for walking (*formal*) **2.** WALKING OR MOVING walking or moving around, or done while walking or moving (*formal*) ○ *ambulatory activities* **3.** MED NOT CONFINED TO BED describes a patient who is able to walk and does not have to be kept in bed ○ *an ambulatory patient* **4.** LAW REVOCABLE able to be revoked ○ *an ambulatory will* ■ *n* (*plural* **-ries**) WALKWAY IN CHURCH OR CLOISTER an aisle at the end of a choir or chancel in a church, or a covered walkway of a cloister —**am·bu·la·to·ri·ly** /àmbyələ táwrəlee/ *adv*

am·bus·cade /ámbə skàyd/ (*literary*) *n* an ambush set for somebody ■ *vt* (**-cad·ed, -cad·ing, -cades**) to ambush somebody [Late 16C. Via French *embuscade* and Italian *imboscata* < assumed Vulgar Latin *imboscare* (see AMBUSH)] —**am·bus·cad·er** *n*

am·bush /ámboŏsh/ *n* **1.** SURPRISE ATTACK an unexpected attack from a concealed position **2.** CONCEALMENT BEFORE ATTACK concealment before a surprise attack ○ *They lay in ambush and waited for their victims.* **3.** SOMEBODY WAITING IN AMBUSH one or more people concealed in order to make a surprise attack **4.** PLACE OF CONCEALMENT BEFORE ATTACK a hiding place used in an ambush ■ *vt* (**-bushed, -bush·ing, -bush·es**) ATTACK SOMEBODY OR SOMETHING to attack somebody or something suddenly from a concealed position [14C. Via Old French *embusche* < assumed Vulgar Latin *imboscare* "hide in a bush" < assumed *boscus* "bush"] —**am·bush·er** *n*

a·me·ba *n* MICROBIOL another spelling of **amoeba**

am·e·bi·a·sis /àmmə bī́ əssiss/, **am·oe·bi·a·sis** *n* an infection or disease affecting the bowel, caused by the amoeba *Entamoeba histolytica*

a·me·bic dys·en·ter·y, **a·moe·bic dys·en·ter·y** *n* an inflammation of the colon causing diarrhea of varying degrees of severity and resulting from infection by the amoeba *Entamoeba histolytica*

a·me·bo·cyte *n* BIOL another spelling of **amoebocyte**

a·me·jo /a méjō/ (*plural same*) *n* an offensive term for a young Okinawan woman who dates male members of the US armed forces, typically whites [< AMERICAN[1] + Japanese *jo* "woman"]

am·e·lan·chi·er /àmmə lángkee ər/ (*plural* **-ers** or *same*) *n* a small tree or bush of the rose family that produces small, edible, dark blue fruits. A common variety is the serviceberry. Flowers: white, in clusters. Native to: North America. Genus: *Amelanchier*. [Mid-18C. < Savoy dialect *amelancier* "medlar"]

a·me·lio·rate /ə meélee ə ràyt/ (**-rat·ed, -rat·ing, -rates**) *vti* to make something better, or become better (*formal*) [Mid-18C. Alteration of MELIORATE, after French *améliorer*] —**a·me·lio·ra·ble** /-rəb'l/ *adj* —**a·me·lio·rant** *n* —**a·me·lio·ra·tion** /ə meélee ə ráysh'n/ *n* —**a·me·lio·ra·tive** *adj* —**a·me·lio·ra·tor** *n*

a·men /ay mén, aa-/ *interj* **1.** SO BE IT said or sung at the end of a prayer or hymn to affirm its content **2.** EXPRESSING STRONG AGREEMENT used to express strong agreement ○ *amen to that* ■ *n* AFFIRMATION IN PRAYER an indication, at the end of a prayer or hymn, that the person praying or singing affirms its content [Pre-12C. Via late Latin and Greek < Hebrew *'āmēn* "truly" < *'āman* "confirm"]

a·me·na·ble /ə meénəb'l/ *adj* **1.** WILLING TO COOPERATE responsive to suggestion and likely to cooperate **2.** ABLE TO BE AFFECTED susceptible to being affected in a particular way ○ *The tumor is not amenable to treatment.* **3.** ACCOUNTABLE required to account for your behavior to an authority **4.** LIABLE TO BE JUDGED likely or available to be tested or judged [Late 16C. < Anglo-Norman < Old French *amener* "bring to" < Latin *minari* "threaten" < *minae* "threats"] —**a·me·na·bil·i·ty** /ə meenə bíllətee/ *n* —**a·me·na·ble·ness** *n* —**a·me·na·bly** *adv*

a·men cor·ner *n* **1.** the part of some Protestant churches where the most fervent worshipers sit **2.** a group of supporters or followers who tend to agree with everything their leader says (*informal*) ○ *As usual, enthusiastic support for the bill came from the sponsoring senator's amen corner.* [< the practice of responding to the preacher's prayers by saying "amen"]

a·mend /ə ménd/ (**a·mend·ed, a·mend·ing, a·mends**) *v* **1.** *vt* IMPROVE OR CORRECT SOMETHING to make changes to something, especially a piece of text, in order to improve or correct it **2.** *vt* REVISE LEGISLATION to revise or alter formally a motion, bill, or constitution **3.** *vi* BEHAVE BETTER THAN BEFORE to behave in a more acceptable way than in the past [13C. Via French *amender* < Latin *emendare* "to correct" < *menda* "error"] —**a·mend·a·ble** *adj* —**a·men·da·to·ry** *adj*

USAGE amend or **emend**? The word to use in general contexts involving change for the better or legislative alterations is **amend**: *We amended the rules so that we could admit 20 more members to the club. Has the Senate amended the House bill?* ***Emend*** is normally restricted to the correction of errors in a printed or written text: *The text was emended after proofreaders found several serious errors in it.*

a·mend·ment /ə méndmənt/ *n* **1.** ALTERATION TO SOMETHING a change, correction, or improvement to something **2.** CHANGE TO LEGAL DOCUMENT an addition or alteration to a motion, bill, or constitution **3.** PROCESS OF ALTERING SOMETHING the process of changing, correcting, or improving something ○ *The bill was passed without amendment.*

a·mends /ə méndz/ *n* something done or given as compensation for a wrong (*takes a singular or plural verb*) ○ *a desire to make amends after the misunderstanding* ○ *No amends were forthcoming even after we had proven that they were in the wrong.* [14C. < Old French *amendes*, plural of *amende* "reparation" < *amender* (see AMEND)]

A·men·ho·tep III /aà men hṓ tep, aàmən-/ (*fl* 15th-14th century B.C.) king of Egypt (1417–1379 B.C.). His reign was characterized by the building of monuments and other architectural works.

A·men·ho·tep IV ➧ **Akhenaton**

a·men·i·ties /ə ménnə teez, -me͞en-/ *npl* **1. SOCIAL PLEASANTRIES** any gestures and words of courtesy or pleasantness ○ *The secretary of state and the foreign minister engaged in the usual diplomatic amenities before signing the treaty.* **2. ATTRACTIVE EXTRAS** the features that, when taken together, make a place such as a hotel or resort attractive to guests or customers ○ *among the usual amenities such as hair dryers in every room of the hotel* **3. TOILET** a toilet, especially one in a public building (*euphemistic*)

a·men·i·ty /ə ménnə tee, -me͞en-/ (*plural* **-ties**) *n* **1.** a useful or attractive feature or a service, e.g., leisure facilities (*often used in the plural*) ○ *the amenities of a luxury hotel* **2.** the experience of a place as pleasant or attractive ○ *thoroughly enjoyed the amenity of the clean mountain air in the summer* [14C. Directly or via French *aménité* < Latin *amoenitas* < *amoenus* "pleasant"]

a·men·or·rhe·a /ay mènnə rée ə/, **a·men·or·rhoe·a** *n* the suppression or unusual absence of menstruation —**a·men·or·rhe·ic** *adj*

a·men·sa·lism /ay ménssə lìzzəm/ *n* an interaction between populations of two species that harms one but not the other [Probably < COMMENSALISM]

a·ment /ámmənt, áy-/ *n* BOT same as **catkin** (*technical*) [Mid-18C. < Latin *amentum* "strap"]

Amer. *abbr* American[1]

Am·er·a·sian /ámmə ráyzh'n/ *n* somebody of mixed American and Asian parentage ■ *adj* having mixed American and Asian parentage [Mid-20C. Blend of AMERICAN[1] + ASIAN]

a·merce /ə múrss/ (**a·merced, a·merc·ing, a·merc·es**) *vt* (*archaic*) **1.** to punish somebody with a fine **2.** to punish somebody in an arbitrary way [14C. < Anglo-Norman *amercier* "place at somebody's mercy (as to the amount of a fine)" < Old French *a merci* "at (your) mercy"] —**a·merce·a·ble** *adj* —**a·merce·ment** *n*

A·mer·i·ca /ə mérrikə/ *n* **1.** ⚠ **UNITED STATES** the United States of America **2. N, S, AND CENTRAL AMERICA** a landmass comprising North America, South America, and Central America **3.** ⚠ **N. AMERICA** North America (*informal*) [Early 16C. < *Americus*, Latinized form of *Amerigo* Vespucci (1454–1512), Italian navigator]

USAGE The use of ***America*** to mean the United States may cause offense to people from Canada and Central and South America, and should be avoided. The term ***North America*** may be used to refer to the United States and Canada together.

A·mer·i·can[1] /ə mérrikən/ *n* **SOMEBODY FROM UNITED STATES** somebody who comes from the United States ■ *adj* **1. OF UNITED STATES** relating to the United States, or its people, languages, or cultures **2. OF N, S, OR CENTRAL AMERICA** relating to North, South, or Central America or the landmass comprising them [Mid-16C. < modern Latin *Americanus* < AMERICA] —**A·mer·i·can·ness** *n*

A·mer·i·can[2] /ə mérrikən/ river in north central California flowing southward to join the Sacramento River at Sacramento. Gold discovered along the river in 1848 spurred the California Gold Rush. Length: 30 mi./48 km.

A·mer·i·ca·na /ə mèrri kaánə, -kánnə/ *n* **1.** things from or about the United States, especially items that are valued by collectors (*takes a singular or plural verb*) **2.** the culture of the United States (*takes a singular verb*)

A·mer·i·can al·oe *n* PLANTS same as **century plant**

A·mer·i·can ash *n* TREES same as **white ash**

A·mer·i·can Black Eng·lish *n* LANG same as **African American Vernacular English**

WORLD ENGLISH See ***African American Vernacular English.***

A·mer·i·can cha·me·leon *n* REPT same as **anole**

A·mer·i·can cheese *n* a smooth processed cheese with a mild taste similar to cheddar

A·mer·i·can dream, A·mer·i·can Dream *n* the idea that everyone in the United States has the chance to achieve success and prosperity

WORLD ENGLISH ***American English*** is the variety of English used in the United States. With a population of over 260 million, the United States is the largest and most influential English-speaking country in the world, and English has been in use within its present borders for over 400 years. American English can be described in terms of three groups: (1) the dialect divisions Northern, Coastal Southern, Midland, and Western; (2) distinctive urban varieties, as in New York and New Orleans; (3) vernacular forms, for example, African American English and Jewish English. Because many, especially immigrant, Americans have at least one language other than English, they may casually mix English with those languages, as in the remark *Sometimes I start a sentence in English y termino en español* ("... and end in Spanish").

Spanish is the most prominent other language, and the hybrid variety *Spanglish* has distinctive forms in New York, Florida, Texas, California, and Puerto Rico. Although English is the administrative language of the nation, is culturally dominant, and is the statutory official language in many states, it is not statutory at the federal level – a situation that has engendered no small controversy.

The history of American English falls into three broad periods: (1) *colonial* 1607–1776, dominated by British English norms; (2) *national* 1776–1898, exhibiting a vigorous and growing independence that included dictionaries and style guides; and (3) *international* 1898–, marked by a steadily increasing worldwide influence and prestige. American English tends to be nasal and, apart from three areas (eastern New England, New York City, and the Southern states), the *r* sound is pronounced in words such as *art, door,* and *worker*; it is also pronounced with the tip of the tongue curled back and raised. The spelling, punctuation, grammar, vocabulary, and idiom of standard American English have been established since the late 19th century; they differ in many ways from British English and other varieties, with the exception of Philippine English, which follows the US model, and Canadian English, which has features of both American English and British English.

Although standard American and British English are similar, there are significant differences in pronunciation, grammar, and vocabulary. With pronunciation, the two Englishes differ chiefly in vowel quality, stress, and voice timbre. For example, Americans pronounce the *a* in words such as *ask, grass,* and *path* in a flat short manner, as in *gasoline*, whereas British English speakers use a broad *a*, as in *father*, when saying these words. American English speakers rather clearly articulate certain unaccented syllables, such as *-ary* in *secretary*, whereas British English speakers clip them to yield pronunciations such as *secret'ry*. American English often places stress on the first syllables of certain words, for example, *laboratory* and *excess*, whereas British English moves the stress to medial or terminal positions, as in their pronunciations /lə bórrətri/ and /ek séss/. The reverse is also true with words such as *garage*, in which the US stress is on the last syllable, whereas the UK stress is on the first syllable.

As for spelling, Americans use, for example, *center, anemia, color, fulfill,* and *tire* whereas British speakers use *centre, anaemia, colour, fulfil,* and *tyre*. In terms of vocabulary, the two Englishes can and do diverge markedly: American English uses *molasses, snow pea, truck stop,* and *zucchini*, while British English uses *treacle, mangetout, transport café,* and *courgette* for the same things.

By preference or established convention, American English tends to prefer *store, defog, visor,* and *rooster*, while British English prefers *shop, demist, peak,* and *cock*. American and British English are also set apart by sets of words sharing elements in common, yet being distinctively different words for the same things. American English speakers say *talk show, fish stick, substitute teacher,* and *moving van*, while speakers of British English say *chat show, fish finger, supply teacher,* and *removal van*. The two Englishes also have sets of words covering the same subject matter, yet not having the same specific meanings. A prime example is the food term *biscuit*, which, in British English, is the equivalent of US *cookie*, while *biscuit* in American English is a small round light pastry.

There are also words mutually exclusive to each English, based upon historical, social, and cultural differences: for example, *inside the Beltway* referring to people, opinions, and issues close to the nation's capital, is US English only, whereas *Questions in the Commons* or *Question Time*, the period when members of the British Parliament may question government ministers, is British English only. Finally, the idiomatic expressions used in both varieties of English can and do differ: *a tempest in a teapot* is American English; *a storm in a teacup* is British English. See ***African American Vernacular English, Canadian English, Hawaiian English, Philippine English.***

A·mer·i·can ea·gle *n* BIRDS same as **bald eagle**

A·mer·i·can elm *n* an elm tree with large spreading branches, formerly grown for shade or ornament but now reduced by disease. Native to: North America. Latin name: *Ulmus americana*.

A·mer·i·can Eng·lish *n* the variety of English spoken in the United States

A·mer·i·can Falls waterfall forming part of Niagara Falls, on the Niagara River, on the US side of the boundary with Canada. About two-thirds of the water volume for Niagara Falls passes over American Falls. Height: 182 ft./55 m.

A·mer·i·can foot·ball *n Can, UK* a game played in the United States by two teams of 11 players who carry, throw, or kick an oval ball. Points are scored by carrying the ball across the opposing team's goal line or by kicking it through open-topped goal posts. US term **football**

A·mer·i·can Fork city in northern Utah, beside Utah Lake, southeast of Salt Lake City and northwest of Provo. Population: 22,501 (2002 estimate).

A·mer·i·can fox·hound *n* a small dog with drooping ears and a smooth black, tan, and white coat, belonging to a US breed. It is smaller than the English foxhound.

A·mer·i·can fries, A·mer·i·can fried po·ta·toes *npl* boiled potatoes, sliced and pan-fried

A·mer·i·can gold·finch *n* a goldfinch with yellow and black markings. Native to: United States and Canada. Latin name: *Carduelis tristis*.

American Gothic (1930) by Grant Wood

A·mer·i·can goth·ic, A·mer·i·can Goth·ic *adj* depicting or representing hard work, frugality, and conservative social attitudes associated with rural and small-town United States

CULTURAL NOTE ***American Gothic*** was initially criticized as a cruel caricature of country folk, but is now one of the best-known and most popular of all American paintings. A generic term, American gothic is one of the relatively few such terms whose meaning derives not merely from the title of a painting but from the visual representation in the painting.

A·mer·i·can In·di·an *n, adj* ANTHROP same as **Native American** (*sometimes considered offensive*)

USAGE See ***Indian.***

A·mer·i·can·ism /ə mérrikə nìzzəm/ *n* **1.** a word, phrase, or custom that originated in, or is regarded as characteristic of, the United States **2.** strong affection or support for the United States

A·mer·i·can·ist /ə mérrikənist/ *n* **1.** an expert on the life, history, language, or culture of the United States **2.** a student of or specialist in the languages and cultures of Native Americans

A·mer·i·can·ize /ə mérrikə nīz/ (**-ized, -iz·ing, -iz·es**) *vti* to give something the form, style, or qualities associated with or used in the United States, or take on such qualities —**A·mer·i·can·i·za·tion** /ə mèrrikəni záysh'n/ *n*

A·mer·i·can kes·trel *n* BIRDS same as **sparrow hawk** (sense 1)

A·mer·i·can Le·gion *n* an organization of veterans of the US armed services, founded in 1919

a·mer·i·ca·no /ə mèrri kaánō/ (*plural* **-nos**) *n* an espresso coffee diluted with hot water and containing no milk [Late 20C. < Italian, "American"]

A·mer·i·can pit bull ter·ri·er *n* DOGS same as **pit bull terrier**

A·mer·i·can plan *n* a pricing system used in hotels and resorts in which there is a fixed per-day charge for room and meals

A·mer·i·can Re·vised Ver·sion *n* BIBLE same as **American Standard Version**

A·mer·i·can Rev·o·lu·tion *n* the war in which the American colonies won independence from Great Britain (1775–83)

A·mer·i·can sad·dle horse *n* a high-stepping saddle horse originally bred in Kentucky and trained to walk, trot, canter, gallop, and pace

A·mer·i·can Sa·mo·a US territory, consisting of a group of South Pacific islands, in the Samoan island chain. Pago Pago is the seat of government. Population: 67,084 (2001). Area: 75 sq. mi./195 sq. km.

A·mer·i·can short·hair *n* a shorthaired domestic cat belonging to a breed with a broad head and thick coat

A·mer·i·can Sign Lan·guage *n* a system of communication used by people with impaired hearing that uses motions or gestures of the hands

A·mer·i·can Span·ish *n* the form of Spanish that is spoken in the United States

A·mer·i·can Staf·ford·shire ter·ri·er *n* DOGS same as **pit bull terrier**

A·mer·i·can Stan·dard Code for In·for·ma·tion In·ter·change *n* COMPUT full form of **ASCII**

A·mer·i·can Stan·dard Ver·sion *n* a US revision of the King James Bible, published in 1901

A·mer·i·can War of In·de·pend·ence *n UK* same as **American Revolution**

A·mer·i·can wa·ter span·iel *n* a dog with a tightly curled brown coat belonging to a breed that swims strongly, using the tail as a rudder, and is used for hunting

A·mer·i·cas /ə mérrikəz/ *npl* same as **America** (sense 2)

am·er·i·ci·um /àmmə ríshee əm/ *n* a white radioactive metallic element. Source: beta decay of plutonium. Use: alpha particle source for research. Symbol **Am**. See table at **element** [Mid-20C. After AMERICA]

A·me·ri·cus /ə mérrikəss/ city southeast of Columbus, in southwestern Georgia. It is an agricultural trading center. Population: 161,918 (2002 estimate).

Am·er·in·di·an /àmmə ríndee ən/ *n* same as **Native American** (*sometimes considered offensive*) [Contraction of AMERICAN INDIAN] —**Am·er·in·di·an** *adj* —**Am·er·in·dic** *adj*

USAGE See ***Indian***.

Ames /aymz/ city in central Iowa, home to Iowa State University of Science and Technology. Population: 50,913 (2002 estimate).

ames·ace *n* LEISURE same as **ambsace**

Am·es·lan /ámmə slàn/ *n* LANG same as **American Sign Language** [Late 20C. Acronym]

Ames test /áymz-/ *n* a test used to determine the cancer-causing potential of a chemical or other agent by measuring its effect on bacteria [Late 20C. After Bruce N. *Ames* (1928–), US biochemist]

a·meth·o·caine /ə méthō kàyn/ *n* MED same as **tetracaine** [Mid-20C. Origin ?]

am·e·thop·ter·in /àmmi thóptərin/ *n* PHARM same as **methotrexate**

am·e·thyst /ámmithəst/ *n* **1.** VIOLET QUARTZ a translucent violet precious stone that is a variety of quartz. Use: gems. **2.** PURPLE SAPPHIRE a purple variety of corundum. Use: gems. **3.** BLUISH PURPLE a bluish purple color [13C. Via French and Latin < Greek *amethustos* "not intoxicating" < *methu* "wine"] —**am·e·thyst** *adj* —**am·e·thys·tine** /àmmə thíst īn/ *adj*

am·e·tro·pi·a /àmmə trṓpee ə/ *n* a condition such as myopia or astigmatism in which a refractive error prevents the eye from focusing light on the retina [Mid-19C. < Greek *ametros* "irregular" < *metron* (see METER³)] —**am·e·trop·ic** /àmmə trṓppik/ *adj*

Amex /ámmeks/, **AMEX** *abbr* FIN American Stock Exchange

A·mex·i·ca /ə méhee kaá/ *n* (*informal*) **1.** the US–Mexican border from the Pacific Coast to the Gulf Coast and the cities adjacent to it **2.** the Mexican presence on the US—Mexican border, in other nonborder western states, and in large Midwest urban centers [Late 20C. Blend of AMERICA + MEXICO]

A·mex·i·can /ə méhee kən/ *n* English as influenced by Latin American, especially Mexican, Spanish and spoken in the southwestern United States and in Latin American communities elsewhere in the country

USAGE Approximately 65% of the 35 million plus Hispanics, or Latinos, in the United States are of Mexican origin. Traditionally, it was thought that the Mexican influence on American English and culture was confined to the border region and the five southwestern states with large Mexican-origin populations: California, Arizona, Texas, New Mexico, and Colorado. (Northern New Mexico and Southern Colorado are distinguished by the rapidly diminishing presence of another group of Spanish ancestry, known as ***Hispanos***, many of whom are descendants of people who lived in this area prior to annexation by the United States). Today, however, the Mexican presence is not limited to the traditional Southwest since significant Mexican-origin populations can be found in other western states and in large urban centers in the Midwest. Such regions have been labeled by the term ***Amexica*** and the resulting language contact variety has been termed ***Amexican***.
Perhaps the most noteworthy feature of Amexican is the presence of numerous borrowings from Spanish, which can be divided into two distinct periods. The early period, prior to 1910, consists of terms related to cowboys and their work (e.g., ***chaps*** "leggings," ***taps*** "stirrup coverings," ***conchas*** "silver shell-shaped ornaments," ***hackamore*** "a bridle part fitting around a horse's head," and ***dally*** "a turn of the rope around the saddle horn when roping another animal"). Other words of this period relate to mining, e.g., ***placer*** "(gold) flakes or nuggets deposited by rivers or glaciers," ***bonanza*** "a vein of ore of considerable extension." Still others are common terms relating to Spanish/Mexican food and drink, e.g., ***enchilada*** and ***tequila***, customs, institutions, and flora, e.g., ***mesquite***.
The modern period, from 1910 to the present, is characterized by terms relating to a variety of Mexican foods and dishes, e.g., ***fajitas*** "strips of marinated steak," ***huevos rancheros*** "fried eggs smothered in salsa," and ***pan dulce*** "Mexican-style pastries," as well as some words having to do with commerce, e.g., ***maquiladora*** "an assembly plant in Mexico run by foreigners." Others of this period, mock, or so-called "junk," Spanish borrowings, are terms used in a derogatory or jocular fashion, e.g., ***mano a mano***, literally "hand to hand," but sometimes used as "man to man," and ***macho*** "exaggerated masculinity or tough-guy image," as well as words relating to Mexican customs, e.g., ***luminaria*** "a small outdoor light made of a candle inside a weighted paper bag," and ***jalapeño*** "a small hot pepper."

am·fet·a·mine /am féttə meen/ DRUGS same as **amphetamine** (*technical*)

Am·har·ic /am hárrik/ *n* the official language of Ethiopia, belonging to the Semitic branch of Afro-Asiatic languages and written in Ethiopic script. Native speakers: 15 million. [Early 19C. < *Amhara*, province in NW Ethiopia] —**Am·har·ic** *adj*

Am·herst /ámərst, ámhərst/ **1.** town north of Springfield, in southwestern Massachusetts. It is home to Amherst College and the University of Massachusetts. Population: 34,417 (2002 estimate). **2.** city west of Cleveland, near Lake Erie, in northern Ohio. Population: 111,718 (2002 estimate).

Am·herst /ámərst/, **Jeffrey, Baron** (1717–97) British-born American colonial administrator. He was governor-general of the British-held American territories (1760–63).

a·mi·a·ble /áymee əb'l/ *adj* **1.** friendly and pleasant to be with **2.** characterized by friendly feelings [14C. Via French < late Latin *amicabilis* (see AMICABLE), influenced in meaning by French *aimable* "lovable"] —**a·mi·a·bil·i·ty** /àymee ə bíllətee/ *n* —**a·mi·a·ble·ness** *n* —**a·mi·a·bly** *adv*

am·i·an·thus /àmmee ánthəss/ *n* a type of asbestos with thin silky fibers [Early 17C. Via Latin < Greek *amiantos* "undefiled" < *miainein* "defile"]

am·i·ca·ble /ámmikəb'l/ *adj* characterized by or done in friendliness, without anger or bad feelings ○ *an amicable divorce* [15C. < late Latin *amicabilis* < Latin *amicus* "friend" < *amare* "to love"] —**am·i·ca·bil·i·ty** /àmmikə bíllətee/ *n* —**am·i·ca·ble·ness** *n* —**am·i·ca·bly** *adv*

am·ice /ámmiss/ *n* a length of white fabric worn by a Christian priest around the neck [13C. Probably via Old French *amit* < Latin *amictus* "cloak" < *amicire* "to cover" < *iacere* "throw"]

am·i·cus cu·ri·ae /ə meékəss kyoóree ī/ (*plural* **am·i·ci cu·ri·ae** /ə meékee-/), **a·mi·cus** (*plural* **-ci**) *n* somebody whose counsel provides information to a court on legal issues involved in a case [Early 17C. < modern Latin, "friend of the court"]

a·mid /ə míd/, **a·midst** /ə mídst/ *prep* **1.** surrounded by things or people ○ *a small lake amid the hills* **2.** used to indicate the circumstances or events around or accompanying something ○ *I sat down amid roars of laughter.* [12C. < A¹ + MID]

A·mi·da /a meédə/ *n* BUDDHISM same as **Amitabha** [< Sanskrit *amita* "immeasurable, unlimited"]

am·ide /á mīd, ámmid/ *n* **1.** any inorganic compound derived from ammonia and containing the NH_2 ion **2.** any organic compound derived from ammonia, formed by the replacement of one or more hydrogen atoms with acyl groups [Mid-19C. < AMMONIA] —**a·mid·ic** /ə míddik/ *adj*

am·i·dol /ámmi dòl/ *n* a colorless water-soluble crystalline compound. Use: photographic developer. Formula: $C_6H_3(NH_2)_2OH{\cdot}HC$. [Late 19C. < German, a trademark]

a·mid·ships /ə mídships/, **a·mid·ship** *adv, adj* near or in the middle of a boat or ship

a·midst *prep* same as **amid**

a·mi·go /ə meégō/ (*plural* **-gos**) *n* a friend, or somebody thought likely to be friendly (*used especially in Spanish-speaking regions*) [Mid-19C. Via Spanish < Latin *amicus* "friend"]

am·i·ka·cin /àmmi káyssin/ *n* a synthetic antibiotic. Use: treatment of infections caused by aerobic bacteria. [Late 20C. < *ami-* + *-kacin*, INN stem]

A·min /aa meén/, **Idi** (1925–2003) Ugandan president. Under his presidency (1971–79), approximately 70,000 Asians were expelled from Uganda, and perhaps as many as 300,000 Ugandans were killed.

a·mine /ə meén, á meén/ *n* any organic derivative of ammonia formed by the replacement of hydrogen with one or more alkyl groups [Mid-19C. < AMMONIA]

-amine *suffix* amine ○ *tryptamine* [< AMINE]

a·mi·no /ə meénō/ *adj* describes a chemical compound containing the NH_2 group of atoms [Independent use of AMINO-]

amino- *prefix* containing an NH_2 group combined with a nonacid radical ○ *aminophenol* [< AMINE]

a·mi·no ac·id *n* a compound belonging to a class that contains an amino group. Amino acids make up proteins and are important components of cells. Some can be synthesized by the body (**nonessential amino acids**) and others must be obtained through the diet (**essential amino acids**).

a·mi·no·ben·zo·ic ac·id /ə meénō ben zō ik ássid/ *n* a crystalline solid derived from benzoic acid, especially PABA. Use: sunscreen lotions. Formula: $C_7H_7NO_2$.

a·mi·no ca·pro·ic ac·id /ə meénō kap rō ik ássid/, **a·mi·noca·pro·ic ac·id** *n* a type of amino acid. Use: treatment of excessive bleeding.

a·mi·no·glu·teth·i·mide /ə meénō gloo téthə mīd/ *n* a drug that acts on the adrenal cortex, affecting the production of steroids. Use: treatment of breast cancer.

a·mi·no·gly·co·side /ə meénō glīkə sīd/ *n* an antibiotic belonging to a group in which amino sugars are linked as glycosides, e.g., streptomycin. Source: species of *Streptomyces* or *Micromonospora*. Use: treatment of aerobic bacterial infections.

a·mi·no·pep·ti·dase /ə meénō péptə dàyss, -dàyz/ *n* an enzyme that breaks down dietary peptides into amino acids

a·mi·no·phe·nol /ə meénō feé nawl/ *n* a white soluble organic compound. Use: dyes, photographic developers. Formula: C_6H_7NO.

a·mi·no·phyl·line /ə meénō fíllin/ *n* a drug that causes widening of the bronchial tubes. Use: treatment of asthma. [Mid-20C. < AMINO- + THEOPHYLLINE]

a·mi·no·quin·o·lone /ə meénō kwínnə lōn/ *n* a drug belonging to a group used in the prevention of malaria

a·mi·no·trans·fer·ase /ə meénō tránsfə ràyss, -ràyz/ *n* BIOCHEM same as **transaminase**

am·i·od·a·rone /àmmee óddə rōn/ *n* a drug that blocks the displacement of calcium ions from active cell membranes. Use: treatment of irregular heartbeat.

a·mir *n* POL, ISLAM same as **emir**

A·mis /áymiss/, **Sir Kingsley** (1922–95) British novelist. He received critical acclaim for his first novel, *Lucky Jim* (1954), and was awarded the Booker Prize in 1986 for *The Old Devils*.

A·mish /aámish/ *npl* members of a Protestant group who migrated from Europe to North America in the 18th century. The Amish seek to maintain a lifestyle based on the Bible. [Late 19C. Probably < German *amisch*] —**A·mish** *adj*

a·miss /ə míss/ *adj* incorrect, inappropriate, or not as it should be ○ *We knew immediately from the disorder in the house that something was amiss.* ■ *adv* incorrectly or inappropriately ○ *Things began to go amiss after she left.* [13C. < Old Norse *á mis* "so as to miss"] ◇ **take something amiss** to be upset or offended by something, even though no offense was intended

A·mit·ab·ha /àmmi taábə/ *n* an incarnation of Buddha as lord of paradise, into which the souls of the pure are reborn [< Sanskrit, "infinite light"]

a·mi·to·sis /ày mī tṓssiss/ *n* cell division by simple division of the nucleus and cytoplasm, without the appearance of chromosomes [Late 19C. < A-[2] + MITOSIS] —**a·mi·tot·ic** /-tóttik/ *adj*

am·i·trip·tyl·ine /àmmi tríptə leén/ *n* a sedative drug. Use: treatment of depression and chronic pain. [Mid-20C. < AMINE + *triptyline*, INN stem]

am·i·ty /ámmətee/ *n* friendliness and peaceful relations (*formal*) [15C. Via French *amitié* < medieval Latin *amicitas* < Latin *amicus* "friend" (see AMICABLE)]

am·lo·di·pine /am lṓdə peén/ *n* a drug that blocks the displacement of calcium ions from active cell membranes. Use: treatment of hypertension and angina. [Late 20C. < *amlo* + *-dipine*, INN stem]

am·ma /ámmə/ *n S Asia* same as **mother**[1] *n* (sense 1) (*informal; often used as a form of address*) [Probably < children's first attempts at speaking, influenced by AMAH]

Am·man /aa maán/ capital of the Hashemite Kingdom of Jordan, in the northwestern part of the country, northeast of the Dead Sea. Population: 1,147,447 (2000).

~~**ammendment**~~ incorrect spelling of **amendment**

am·me·ter /ám meétər/ *n* an instrument used for measuring electric current in amperes [Late 19C. < AMPERE + -METER]

am·mine /ámmeen/ *n* a compound containing one or more ammonia molecules attached to a salt or similar compound through coordinate bonds [Late 19C. < AMMONIA]

am·mo /ámmō/ *n* ARMS same as **ammunition** (*informal*) [Early 20C. Shortening]

am·mo·coete /ámmə seét/, **am·mo·cete** *n* the filter-feeding larva of the lamprey [Mid-19C. < modern Latin *Ammocoetes* < Greek *ammos* "sand" + *koitē* "bed"]

am·mo·nate /ámmə nàyt/ *n* CHEM same as **ammine**

am·mo·nia /ə mṓnyə/ *n* **1.** a colorless pungent gas that is highly soluble in water. Use: refrigerant, manufacture of fertilizers, explosives, and plastics. Formula: NH_3. **2.** a solution of ammonia in water. Use: household cleaner, manufacture of fertilizers and textiles. [Late 18C. < modern Latin < Latin *sal ammoniacus* "salt of Ammon" < Greek *Ammōn* "Ammon," Egyptian god near whose temple ammonia and ammoniac were said to be obtained]

am·mo·ni·ac /ə mṓnee àk/ *n* a strong-smelling brownish yellow gum resin. Source: Asian plant of the carrot family. Use: medicine, porcelain, cement. ■ *adj* CHEM same as **ammoniacal** [14C. Via French < Latin *ammoniacus* (see AMMONIA)]

am·mo·ni·a·cal /àmmə nī́ ək'l/ *adj* containing or resembling ammonia

am·mo·ni·ate /ə mṓnee àyt/ (**-at·ed, -at·ing, -ates**) *vt* to treat or combine something with ammonia or an ammonia compound —**am·mo·ni·a·tion** /ə mṓnee áysh'n/ *n*

am·mo·nia wa·ter *n* CHEM same as **ammonia** (sense 2)

am·mon·i·fi·ca·tion /ə mònnəfə káysh'n/ *n* **1.** treatment with ammonia or an ammonium compound **2.** the formation of ammonia or ammonium compounds through the bacterial decomposition of organic matter

am·mon·i·fy /ə mónnə fī/ (**-fied, -fy·ing, -fies**) *vti* to treat something with ammonia, or to undergo ammonification —**am·mon·i·fi·er** *n*

am·mo·nite[1] /ámmə nīt/ *n* **1.** an extinct invertebrate ocean animal with a flat partitioned spiral shell, belonging to the ammonoids **2.** the fossilized shell of an ammonite [Mid-18C. < modern Latin *ammonites* < medieval Latin *cornu Ammonis* "horn of Ammon"] —**am·mo·nit·ic** /àmmə níttik/ *adj*

am·mo·nite[2] /ámmə nīt/ *n* **1.** a mixture of dried animal wastes, used as a fertilizer **2.** an explosive consisting of ammonium nitrate and TNT [Mid-20C. < AMMONIUM + NITRATE]

Am·mon·ite /ámmə nīt/ *n* a member of an ancient Semitic people in the Bible who lived between the Syrian desert and the Jordan River from the 13th to the 6th centuries B.C. They were constant enemies of the Israelites. [Mid-16C. < late Latin < Hebrew *'Ammōn* "Ammon (son of Lot)"]

am·mo·ni·um /ə mṓnee əm/ *adj* relating to or containing the NH_4+ ion derived from ammonia [Early 19C. < AMMONIA]

am·mo·ni·um bi·car·bon·ate *n* a white crystalline solid. Use: baking powder. Formula: NH_4HCO_3.

am·mo·ni·um car·bon·ate *n* a white crystalline solid. Use: smelling salts, baking powder. Formula: $(NH_4)_2CO_3$.

am·mo·ni·um chlo·ride *n* a white crystalline solid. Use: expectorant, soldering flux, dry cell electrolyte. Formula: NH_4Cl.

am·mo·ni·um hy·drox·ide *n* a solution of ammonia in water

am·mo·ni·um ni·trate *n* a white crystalline solid. Use: fertilizers, herbicides, insecticides, explosives. Formula: NH_4NO_3.

am·mo·ni·um sul·fate *n* a white crystalline solid. Use: fertilizer, water purification. Formula: $(NH_4)_2SO_4$.

am·mo·noid /ámmə nòyd/ *n* an extinct cephalopod mollusk with a partitioned shell [Mid-19C. < modern Latin *Ammonoidea* < *ammonites* (see AMMONITE[1])]

Am·mons /ámmənz/, **Archie Randolph** (1926–2001) US poet, an important exponent of the poetic tradition of transcendentalism

> "One must write and / rewrite till one writes it right."
> [Archie Randolph Ammons, *Garbage*; 1993]

am·mu·ni·tion /àmmyə nísh'n/ *n* **1.** BULLETS AND MISSILES bullets, shells, missiles, and other projectiles used as weapons **2.** EXPLOSIVE MATERIAL bombs, grenades, and other explosive devices or substances used as weapons **3.** SUPPORTING FACTS facts and information that can be used to support a point of view in an argument [Late 16C. < French, alteration (due to mistaking *la munition* for *l'amunition*) of *munition* (see MUNITION)]

am·ne·sia /am neézhə/ *n* loss of memory as a result of shock, injury, psychological disturbance, or medical disorder [Late 18C. < Greek *amnēsia*, alteration of *amnēstia* "forgetfulness" < *amnēstos* "not remembered" < *mnasthai* "remember"] —**am·ne·si·ac** /-àk/ *n, adj* —**am·nes·tic** /-néstik/ *adj*

am·nes·ty /ámnəstee/ *n* (*plural* **-ties**) **1.** PARDON a general pardon, especially for those who have committed political crimes **2.** PROSECUTION-FREE PERIOD a period during which crimes can be admitted or illegal weapons handed in without prosecution ■ *vt* (**-tied, -ty·ing, -ties**) PARDON SOMEBODY to grant an amnesty to somebody [Late 16C. Via French < Greek *amnēstia* (see AMNESIA)]

Am·nes·ty In·ter·na·tion·al *n* an international human rights organization concerned with prisoners of conscience under any type of political regime

am·ni·a ANAT plural of **amnion**

am·ni·o /ámnee ō/ (*plural* **-os**) *n* MED same as **amniocentesis** (*informal*) [Late 20C. Shortening]

am·ni·o·cen·te·sis /àmnee ō sen teéssiss/ (*plural* **-te·ses** /-teé seez/) *n* a test performed to determine the health, sex, or genetic constitution of a fetus by taking a sample of amniotic fluid through a needle inserted into the womb of the mother [Mid-20C. < AMNION + Greek *kentēsis* "pricking" (from *kentein* "prick")]

am·ni·og·ra·phy /àmnee óggrəfee/ *n* an X-ray of the womb, taken after a substance that will be shown up by the X-rays has been injected into the bloodstream [Mid-20C. < AMNION + -GRAPHY]

am·ni·on /ámnee òn/ (*plural* **-ni·ons** or **-ni·a** /-nee ə/) *n* **1.** the inner of the two membranes enclosing the embryo of a bird, reptile, or mammal and its surrounding fluid **2.** the fluid-filled sac within which the embryo of a bird, reptile, or mammal develops [Mid-17C. < Greek, "caul" < *amnos* "lamb"] —**am·ni·ot·ic** /àmnee óttik/ *adj*

am·ni·ote /ámnee ōt/ *n* a vertebrate that develops from an embryo within an amnion, e.g., a bird, reptile, or mammal [Early 20C. < modern Latin *Amniota* < AMNION]

am·ni·ot·ic flu·id *n* the fluid that surrounds a fetus while it is developing. It flows out in the "breaking of the water" before a baby is born.

am·ni·ot·ic sac *n* ANAT, MED same as **amnion** (sense 2)

am·o·bar·bi·tal /àmmō baárbi tàl/ *n* a barbiturate drug. Use: sedative, hypnotic. [Mid-20C. < AMYL + BARBITAL]

am·o·di·a·quine /àmmō dī́ ə kwīn/ *n* a bitter yellow crystalline solid. Use: prevention of malaria.

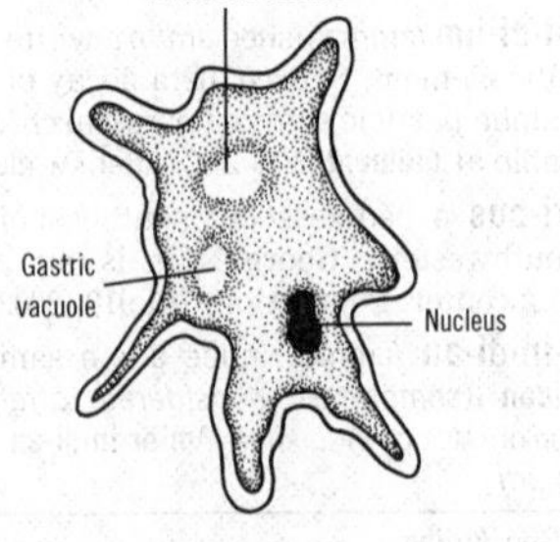

amoeba

a·moe·ba /ə meébə/ (*plural* **-bas** or **-bae** /-bee/), **a·me·ba** (*plural* **-bas** or **-bae**) *n* a single-celled organism found in water and in damp soil on land, and as a parasite of other organisms. Lacking a fixed form and supporting structures, an amoeba consists of a protoplasmic mass in a thin membrane, and forms temporary projections (**pseudopodia**) in order to move. Genus: *Amoeba*. [Mid-19C. Via modern Latin < Greek *amoibē* "change" < *ameibein* "to change"] —**a·moe·bic** *adj* —**a·moe·boid** *adj*

am·oe·bi·a·sis *n* MED another spelling of **amebiasis**

a·moe·bic dys·en·ter·y *n* MED another spelling of **amebic dysentery**

a·moe·bi·cide /ə méebə sīd/ *n* a chemical agent used to kill amoebas

a·moe·bo·cyte /ə méebə sīt/, **a·me·bo·cyte** *n* a cell that moves like an amoeba, e.g., a blood cell that can engulf particles

a·mok /ə múk, ə mók/, **a·muck** /ə múk/ *adv* **1.** OUT OF CONTROL in a very frenzied way **2.** CONFUSEDLY in or into a confused or disorganized state ■ *adj* OUT OF CONTROL frenzied and out of control [Early 16C. Directly or via Portuguese *am(o)uco* < Malay *amuk* "fighting frenziedly"] ◇ **run amok, go amok** to be or become out of control, especially in a frenzied way

a·mo·le /ə mṓ lay/ *n* **1.** the root or other part of some North American plants, used as a substitute for soap **2.** (*plural* **a·mo·les** or *same*) a plant of which the roots or other parts can be used as a substitute for soap. Agave and yucca are amoles. [Mid-19C. Via Mexican Spanish < Nahuatl *ahmōlli* "soap"]

a·mong /ə múng/, **a·mongst** /ə múngst/ CORE MEANING: a preposition indicating that something or somebody is surrounded by people, things, ideas, or circumstances ○ *You're among friends here.*

prep **1.** OF GROUP belonging to a particular group or class ○ *Her carvings are among the world's finest.* **2.** IN GROUP in or by a particular group ○ *a widely-held notion among physicists* **3.** BETWEEN GROUP MEMBERS by, between, or to each person or thing in a group ○ *divided among six of us* **4.** IN ADDITION TO in addition to other things or people ○ *The photos showed, among other things, a birthday party.* [Old English *on (ge)mong* < *on* "in" + *(ge)mong* "crowd" < Indo-European]

USAGE See ***between.***

a·mon·til·la·do /ə mòntə laádō/ *n* a pale medium-dry sherry from Spain [Early 19C. < Spanish]

a·mor·al /ay máwrəl/ *adj* **1.** not concerned with or amenable to moral judgments **2.** not caring about good behavior or morals (*disapproving*) —**a·mor·al·ism** *n* —**a·mor·al·i·ty** /ày mə rállətee/ *n* —**a·mor·al·ly** *adv*

am·o·ret·to /àmmə réttō/ (*plural* **-ti** /-tee/) *n* an artistic representation of a small naked boy or winged cherub as a symbol of love [Early 17C. < Italian, "small cupid" < *amore* "love" < Latin *amor*]

am·o·rist /ámmərist/ *n* somebody who writes about love or is in love (*literary*) [Late 16C. < French *amour* "love" or Latin *amor*]

Am·o·rite /ámmə rīt/ *n* a member of an ancient Semitic people who lived in Mesopotamia, Syria, and Palestine between about 2600 and 1200 B.C. [Mid-16C. < Hebrew *'ĕmōrī* < Akkadian *Amurru(m)*, the land inhabited by the Amorites] —**Am·o·rite** *adj*

am·o·rous /ámmərəss/ *adj* showing or feeling romantic love or sexual attraction [14C. Via Old French < medieval Latin *amorosus* < Latin *amor* "love"] —**am·or·ous·ly** *adv* —**am·or·ous·ness** *n*

a·mor·phism /ə máwr fìzzəm/ *n* **1.** lack of shape, form, structure, or classifying features **2.** CHEM, GEOL lack of crystalline structure, e.g., in chemical compounds or rocks

a·mor·phous /ə máwrfəss/ *adj* **1.** WITHOUT SHAPE without any clear shape, form, or structure **2.** NOT CLASSIFIABLE not obviously belonging to any category or type **3.** CHEM, GEOL NOT CRYSTALLINE without a crystalline structure [Mid-18C. Via modern Latin < Greek *amorphos* "without shape" < *morphē* "shape"] —**a·mor·phous·ly** *adv* —**a·mor·phous·ness** *n*

am·or·tize /ámmər tīz/ (**-tized, -tiz·ing, -tiz·es**) *vt* **1.** REDUCE DEBT BY INSTALLMENTS to reduce a debt by making payments against the principal balance in installments or regular transfers **2.** WRITE OFF COST OF ASSET to write off the cost of an asset over a period of time in a statement of accounts **3.** TRANSFER PROPERTY to transfer land or other assets to an ecclesiastical body (*archaic*) [14C. Via French *amortiss-* "alienate in mortmain" < assumed Vulgar Latin *admortire* "deaden" < Latin *mort-* "death"] —**am·or·tiz·a·ble** *adj* —**am·or·ti·za·tion** /àmmərti záysh'n/ *n*

A·mos /áyməss/ *n* **1.** in the Bible, a Hebrew prophet who lived in the 8th century B.C. and delivered judgments against Judah, Samaria, and Israel **2.** a book of the Bible that contains the prophecies traditionally attributed to Amos. See table at **Bible**

a·mo·ti·va·tion·al syn·drome /ày mōtə váyshən'l-/ *n* a psychological condition characterized by a loss of the motivation to carry out socially accepted behaviors and tasks, usually associated with the use of marijuana

a·mount /ə mównt/ *n* a quantity or degree of something, considered as a unit or total [14C. < Old French *amonter* "rise" < *amont* "upward" < Latin *ad montem* "to the mountain"]

USAGE amount or **number**? ***Amount*** is normally used with singular words that have no plural, that is, so-called uncountable or mass nouns like *coal, happiness,* and *warfare*: *a large amount of coal; any amount of happiness.* In contrast, ***number*** is used with plural nouns such as *books, questions, ships,* and *cheeses* (= *types of cheese*): *a large number of books; an excessive number of questions; a goodly number of cheeses.* In everyday speech, ***amount*** is sometimes used when ***number*** is strictly called for: *a large amount of books.* Avoid this usage in formal speaking and writing. See ***number.***

amount to *vt* **1.** to come to a total when added up **2.** to be equivalent to something ○ *Their statement amounts to nothing more than a slick evasion.*

a·mour /ə mо́or/ *n* a love affair, especially one that is clandestine (*dated*) [14C. Via French < Latin *amor* "love"]

a·mour-pro·pre /àmmoor prṓprə/ *n* self-respect or estimation of your true worth (*formal*) [Late 18C. < French, "self-love"]

a·mox·a·pine /ə móksə peen/ *n* an antidepressant drug taken orally. Use: treatment of neurotic and psychotic depressive disorders. [Late 20C. < *amox-* + *-apine*, INN stem]

a·mox·i·cil·lin /ə mòksi síllin/ *n* an antibiotic with properties similar to those of ampicillin, used to treat a broad range of conditions [Late 20C. < *amoxi-* + *-cillin*, INN stem]

A·moy /ə móy/ *n* the dialect of Chinese spoken on the island of Xiamen and in neighboring areas in southeastern China [Mid-19C. After *Amoy* (XIAMEN)] —**A·moy** *adj*

amp /amp/ *n* **1.** same as **ampere 2.** same as **amplifier** (sense 1) (*informal*) [Late 19C. Shortening]

AMP *n* a compound (**nucleotide**) involved in energy transfer reactions in living cells. Full form **adenosine monophosphate**

amped /ampt/, **amped up** *adj* feeling or showing great excitement or agitation (*slang*) [Late 20C. < AMP, literally "amplified, powered up"]

am·per·age /ámpərij/ *n* the number of amperes measured in an electric current

am·pere /ám peer/ *n* the basic unit of electric current in the SI system, equal to a current that produces a force of $2x10^{-7}$ newtons per meter between two parallel conductors in a vacuum. Symbol **A** [Late 19C. After André-Marie *Ampère* (1775–1836), French physicist]

am·pere-hour *n* a measure of quantity of electricity equal to the amount of electricity that passes in one hour through a conductor with a current of one ampere

am·per·sand /ámpər sànd/ *n* the symbol "&," meaning "and" [Mid-19C. < *and per se and* "(the character) '&' by itself (means) and"]

am·phet·a·mine /am féttə meen/ *n* a drug formerly used to treat depression and as an appetite suppressant, or any of its derivatives. Technical name **amfetamine** [Mid-20C. Contraction of *alpha-methyl-phenethylamine*]

amphi- *prefix* both ○ *amphibious* [Via Latin < Greek *amphi* "on both sides" < Indo-European]

am·phi·ar·thro·sis /àmfee aar thrṓssiss/ (*plural* **-thro·ses** /-thrṓ seez/) *n* a joint that permits only a small amount of movement, e.g., a joint between vertebrae

am·phib·i·an /am fíbbee ən/ *n* **1.** a cold-blooded vertebrate that spends some time on land but must breed and develop into an adult in water. Frogs, salamanders, and toads are amphibians. Class: Amphibia. **2.** an aircraft or vehicle designed to operate on land or water [Mid-19C. < modern Latin *Amphibia* < Greek *amphibion* "amphibious being" < *amphibios* (see AMPHIBIOUS)] —**am·phib·i·an** *adj*

am·phib·i·ous /am fíbbee əss/ *adj* **1.** LIVING ON LAND AND IN WATER describes an animal that lives in water during early development and on land as an adult **2.** OPERATING ON LAND AND IN WATER taking place or operating both on land and in water ○ *made an amphibious assault on the island* ○ *amphibious vehicles* **3.** OF MIXED TYPE with two different qualities or features resulting in a mixed type [Mid-17C. < Greek *amphibios* "living on both (land and water)" < *bios* "life"] —**am·phib·i·ous·ly** *adv* —**am·phib·i·ous·ness** *n*

am·phi·bole /ámfə bōl/ *n* a hydrous silicate mineral containing varying amounts of aluminum, calcium, iron, magnesium, and sodium [Early 19C. < French < Greek *amphibolos* "ambiguous" < *ballein* "to throw"; because the mineral is able to appear in a variety of forms] —**am·phi·bol·ic** /àmfə bóllik/ *adj*

am·phib·o·lite /am fíbbə līt/ *n* a metamorphic rock consisting mainly of amphibole with some plagioclase

am·phib·ol·o·gy /àmfi bólləjee/ (*plural* **-gies**), **am·phib·o·ly** /am fíbbəlee/ (*plural* **-lies**) *n* a phrase or sentence that can be interpreted in two ways, usually because of the grammatical construction rather than the meanings of the words themselves. The phrase "the boy on the chair with a broken leg" is an amphibology. [Late 16C. < late Latin *amphibologia* "ambiguity" < Latin *amphibolia* + Greek *-logia* "speech"] —**am·phib·o·log·i·cal** /àm fibbə lójjik'l/ *adj* —**am·phib·o·log·i·cal·ly** *adv* —**am·phib·o·lous** /am fíbbələss/ *adj*

am·phi·brach /ámfə bràk/ *n* a metrical foot of three syllables with the stress on the second syllable, or of one long syllable between two short syllables. The word "contentment" and the phrase "a mushroom" are amphibrachs. [Late 16C. Via Latin *amphibrachys* < Greek *amphibrakhus* "short on both sides" < *brakhus* "short"] —**am·phi·brach·ic** /àmfə brákik/ *adj*

am·phic·ty·o·ny /am fíktee ənee/ (*plural* **-nies**) *n* in ancient Greece, a group of neighboring states or communities that shared responsibility for shrines and temples. The amphictyony maintaining the shrine of Apollo at Delphi is a famous example. [Mid-19C. < Greek *amphiktuones*, literally "dwellers around" < *ktizein* "to found"] —**am·phic·ty·on·ic** /am fiktee ónnik/ *adj*

am·phi·ge·net·ic /àmfijə néttik/ *adj* produced by or involving both sexes ○ *amphigenetic reproduction*

am·phi·go·ry /ámfə gàwree, am fíggəree/ (*plural* **-ries**), **am·phi·gou·ri** /ámfə goo reé/ (*plural* **-ris**) *n* a nonsensical piece of writing, usually in verse [Early 19C. < French *amphigouri*]

am·phim·a·cer /am fímməssər, ámfə màyssər/ *n* a metrical foot of three syllables with the stress on the first and third syllables, or of one short syllable between two long syllables. The phrase "happy days" is an amphimacer. [Late 16C. Via Latin < Greek *amphimakros* "long on both sides" < *makros* "long"]

am·phi·mix·is /àmfə míksiss/ *n* sexual reproduction involving the fusion of reproductive cells (**gametes**) from two organisms [Late 19C. < modern Latin < Greek *amphi-* "on both sides" + *mixis* "mingling" < *mignunai* "to mix"] —**am·phi·mic·tic** *adj*

am·phi·ox·us /àmfee óksəss/ (*plural* **-ox·i** /-ók sī/ or **-ox·us·es**) *n* MARINE BIOL same as **lancelet** [Mid-19C. < modern Latin, "sharp at both sides" < Greek *amphi-* "at both sides" + *oxus* "sharp"]

am·phi·pod /ámfə pòd/ *n* a small fresh or saltwater crustacean with a thin body and without a carapace. Beach fleas are amphipods. Order: Amphipoda. [Mid-19C. < modern Latin *Amphipoda* < Greek *amphi-* "both" + *pod-*, stem of *pous* "foot," because there are two types of feet in this order] —**am·phi·po·dous** /am fíppədəss/ *adj*

am·phi·pro·style /ámfə prṓ stīl/ *n* a classical temple or other building with a set of columns at each end but not at the sides [Early 18C. Via French and Latin < Greek *amphiprostulos* "with pillars at both ends" < *prostulos* "having pillars" (see PROSTYLE)]

am·phi·pro·tic /àmfi prṓtik/ *adj* producing and reacting with protons as a solvent and therefore having properties of both an acid and an alkali [Mid-20C. < AMPHI- + PROTON]

am·phis·bae·na /àmfiss beénə/ (*plural* **-nae** /-nee/ or **-nas**) *n* **1.** a legless lizard with a rounded tail resembling a second head. Native to: tropical America. Family: Amphisbaenidae. **2.** in classical mythology, a poisonous snake with a head at each end of its body, allowing it to move in either direction [14C. Via Latin < Greek *amphisbaina* "going both ways" < *amphis* "both ways" + *bainein* "go"] —**am·phis·bae·nic** *adj*

am·phi·sty·lar /àmfə stī́lər/ *adj* describes a building, especially a classical temple, that has a set of columns on both ends or sides [19C. < AMPHI- + Greek *stulos* "column"]

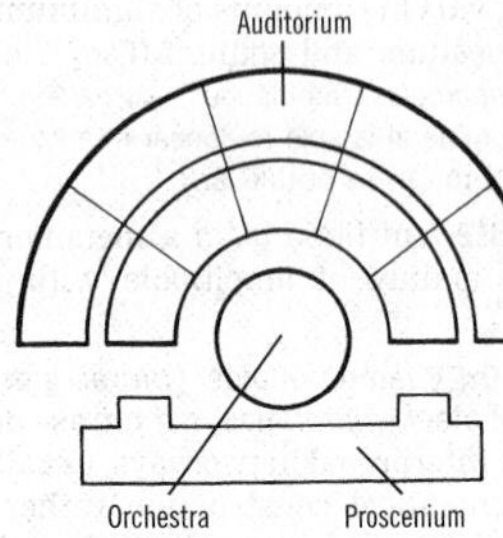

amphitheater

am·phi·the·a·ter /ámfə theè ətər, ámpə-/ *n* **1.** CIRCULAR BUILDING a round or oval building without a roof that has a central open space surrounded by tiers of seats, especially one used by the ancient Romans for public entertainments **2.** PLACE FOR SPORTS a large enclosure where sporting activities or public entertainments take place **3.** SEATING FOR SPECTATORS a gallery of seats arranged in semicircular tiers for the audience in a theater or lecture room **4.** LECTURE ROOM a lecture hall or operating room where seating is arranged in semicircular tiers [Mid-14C. Via Latin < Greek *amphitheatron*, "theater on both sides" (because the typical classical Greek theater had seating on one side only) < *theatron* (see THEATER)] —**am·phi·the·at·ric** /àmfə thee áttrik/ *adj* —**am·phi·the·at·ri·cal·ly** *adv*

am·phi·the·a·tre *n* THEATER Can, UK spelling of **amphitheater**

amphora

am·pho·ra /ámfərə/ (*plural* **-rae** /-ree/ or **-ras**) *n* in ancient Greece and Rome, a jar, usually made of clay, with a narrow neck and two handles, used for holding oil or wine [15C. Via Latin < Greek *amphiphoreus* < *amphi-* "on both sides" + *phoreus* "bearer" < *pherein* "to bear"; from its two handles] —**am·pho·ral** *adj*

am·pho·ter·ic /àmfə térrik/ *adj* able to react chemically as either an acid or a base [Mid-19C. < Greek *amphoteroi* "both of two," comparative form of *amphō* "both"]

am·pho·ter·i·cin /àmfə térrəssin/ *n* a mixture of two antibiotic drugs used intravenously. Use: treatment of fungal infections.

am·pi·cil·lin /àmpə síllin/ *n* a semisynthetic form of penicillin. Use: treatment of respiratory infections. [Mid-20C. < AMINO- + *-cillin*, INN stem]

am·ple /ámp'l/ (**-pler, -plest**) *adj* **1.** as much or as many as required, usually with some left over **2.** large, especially in physical size (*often used euphemistically*) [15C. Via French < Latin *amplus* "large, plentiful"] —**am·ple·ness** *n*

am·plex·us /am pléksəss/ *n* the mating posture of a pair of frogs or toads, in which the male clasps the female from behind during egg release and fertilization [Mid-20C. < Latin < past participle of *amplecti* "embrace"]

am·pli·con /ámpli kòn/ *n* a nucleic acid fragment that is the product of the artificial large-scale reproduction of genetic material [Late 20C. < AMPLIFICATION]

am·pli·dyne /ámplə dīn/ *n* a specialized direct-current generator in which small changes in power input produce large changes in output. It is used especially in servo systems. [Mid-20C. Blend of AMPLIFIER + Greek *dynamis* "power" (see DYNAMIC)]

am·pli·fi·ca·tion /àmpləfi káysh'n/ *n* **1.** PROCESS OF MAKING LOUDER the act or process of making something louder **2.** ENLARGEMENT OF SOMETHING the act or process of making something larger, greater, or stronger **3.** ADDITION OF DETAIL the act or process of making a spoken or written account fuller or clearer **4.** ELECTRONICS INCREASE IN SIGNAL MAGNITUDE the increase in the magnitude of a signal produced by an amplifier **5.** DETAIL ADDED a detail, explanation, or illustration added to a spoken or written account to make it fuller or clearer **6.** GENETICS GENE REPRODUCTION the production of many copies of a section of DNA, naturally or by technological means

am·pli·fied frag·ment length po·ly·mor·phism *n* a rapid method for detecting variations in DNA sequences between individuals, using the polymerase chain reaction technique

am·pli·fi·er /ámplə fīr/ *n* **1.** a device that makes sounds louder, especially one increasing the sound level of musical instruments **2.** an electronic device that increases the magnitude of a signal, voltage, or current

am·pli·fy /ámplə fī/ (**-fied, -fy·ing, -fies**) *v* **1.** *vti* MAKE LOUDER to become louder, or make a sound become louder, by electronic or other means **2.** *vti* INCREASE to become, or make something become, greater in scope or stronger **3.** *vti* ADD DETAIL to make a spoken or written account fuller, clearer, or more detailed **4.** *vt* EXAGGERATE to make something seem greater or larger than it is **5.** *vti* ELECTRONICS INCREASE SIGNAL to increase the magnitude of a signal using an amplifier, or undergo such an increase [15C. Via French *amplifier* < Latin *amplificare* "enlarge" < *amplus* "large" + *fic-*, a stem of *facere* "make"] —**am·pli·fi·a·ble** /ámplə fī əb'l/ *adj*

SYNONYMS See *increase*.

am·pli·tude /ámplə toòd/ *n* **1.** LARGENESS largeness in size, volume, or extent **2.** BREADTH breadth of range **3.** ABUNDANCE an amount that is more than required **4.** PHYS DISTANCE FROM MEAN POINT the farthest distance that a vibrating or oscillating system such as a pendulum travels from a mean or zero point **5.** ELECTRONICS MAXIMUM VALUE OF SIGNAL the maximum value of an alternating signal **6.** MATH ANGLE OF VECTOR REPRESENTING COMPLEX NUMBER the angle between a vector representing a complex number and the positive real axis **7.** SPORTS HEIGHT REACHED BY SNOWBOARDER in snowboarding, the degree of height a rider can attain above the lip of a pipe [Mid-16C. Via French < Latin *amplitudo* "size, greatness, grandeur" < *amplus* "large"]

am·pli·tude mod·u·la·tion *n* the modulation of the amplitude of a radio wave in such a way as to encode the wave with audio or visual information

am·ply /ámplee/ *adv* to a more than adequate degree

am·poule /ám pyoòl/, **am·pule, am·pul** *n* a small sealed glass container that holds a measured amount of a medicinal substance to be injected [Early 20C. Via French < Latin *ampulla* (see AMPULLA); the spelling may be a revival of an earlier form of the word, borrowed < Old French in the 13C]

am·pul·la /am poòllə, -púllə/ (*plural* **-lae** /-lee/) *n* **1.** a small container for a consecrated substance, especially oil, water, or the wine used in the Christian Communion **2.** in ancient Rome, a round two-handled bottle to hold wine, oil, or perfume [Late 14C. < Latin, "little amphora" < *ampora*, variant of *amphora* (see AMPHORA)]

am·pu·tate /ámpyə tàyt/ (**-tat·ed, -tat·ing, -tates**) *vti* to cut off a limb or other appendage of the body, especially in a surgical operation [Mid-16C. < Latin *amputat-*, past participle of *amputare* "cut around" < *ambi-* "around" + *putare* "cut"] —**am·pu·ta·tion** /àmpyə táysh'n/ *n* —**am·pu·ta·tor** *n*

am·pu·tee /àmpyə teé/ *n* somebody who has had a limb or part of a limb cut off

am·ri·ta /am reétə/, **am·ree·ta** *n* **1.** in Hinduism, a substance prepared by the deities that makes those who drink it immortal **2.** in Hinduism, immortality gained by drinking amrita [Late 18C. < Sanskrit *amṛta* "without death" < *mṛta* "death"]

Am·rit·sar /əm rítsər/ city in Punjab State in northwestern India. It is a holy city for Sikhs. Population: 1,011,327 (2001).

Am·ster·dam /ámstər dàm/ **1.** capital and commercial center in the Netherlands, situated where the River Amstel flows into the Ijsselmeer. Population: 735,328 (2002). **2.** city in east central New York, on the Mohawk River. Population: 18,065 (2002 estimate).

am·trac /ám tràk/, **am·track** *n* a flat-bottomed motor vehicle that can move on land or water, used to transport troops from ship to shore in preparation for an attack [Mid-20C. Blend of AMPHIBIOUS + TRACTOR]

amu *abbr* atomic mass unit

a·muck *adv, adj* same as **amok**

A·mu Dar·ya /aàmoo daáryə/ the longest river in Central Asia, flowing from the Pamir plateau toward the Aral Sea. Length: 879 mi./1,415 km.

am·u·let /ámmyələt/ *n* **1.** a piece of jewelry that supposedly protects its wearer against evil, injury, disease, or bad luck **2.** an ordinary object that is supposed to provide protection against bad luck or negative forces [Late 16C. < Latin *amuletum*]

A·mun /aámən/ *n* in Egyptian mythology, the supreme god. Amun was originally a local god of Thebes, but was elevated during the eighteenth dynasty.

A·mund·sen /ámməndssən/, **Roald** (1872–1928) Norwegian explorer. He was the first person to reach the South Pole (1911).

A·mund·sen Gulf body of water in Canada between Banks and Victoria islands and the Northwest Territories coast. Length: 250 mi./400 km.

A·mur /aa moór/ river in east central Asia that forms the boundary between Manchuria and Siberia before flowing north into the Tatar Strait. Length: 2,700 mi./4,345 km. Chinese name **Heilong Jiang**

a·muse /ə myoóz/ (**a·mused, a·mus·ing, a·mus·es**) *vt* **1.** to make somebody smile or laugh or think that something is funny **2.** to keep somebody occupied or entertained by providing entertainment or an interesting task [15C. < French *amuser* "cause to stare stupidly" < *muser* "stare stupidly"] —**a·mused** *adj*

ORIGIN The history of the word ***amuse*** is very similar to that of *distract* and *divert*: all three have moved from the notion of "leading the mind astray" in a negative sense to the notion of "entertainment."

a·muse·ment /ə myoózmənt/ *n* **1.** FEELING SOMETHING IS FUNNY the feeling that something is funny or entertaining **2.** RECREATIONAL ACTIVITY an enjoyable activity such as a game, hobby, or form of entertainment **3.** RIDE OR GAME a ride, game, or other attraction found in an amusement park or a video arcade **4.** KEEPING SOMEBODY HAPPILY OCCUPIED the act of keeping somebody occupied or entertained

a·muse·ment ar·cade *n UK* LEISURE same as **arcade** *n* (sense 3)

a·muse·ment park *n* an outdoor area with a variety of mechanical rides, games, and other attractions that people pay to use

a·muse·ment tax *n* a tax, often levied locally, on various forms or places of amusement

a·mus·ing /ə myoózing/ *adj* causing somebody to smile or laugh or be amused, often in a subdued way —**a·mus·ing·ly** *adv* —**a·mus·ing·ness** *n*

SYNONYMS See *funny*.

Am·vets /ám vèts/, **AMVETS** *n* a private organization of veterans of World War II and the Korean and Vietnam wars

a·myg·da·la /ə mígdələ/ (*plural* **-lae** /-lee/) *n* an almond-shaped mass of gray matter, one in each hemisphere of the brain, associated with feelings of fear and aggression and important for visual learning and memory [Pre-12C. Via Latin < Greek *amugdalē* "almond"]

a·myg·da·lin /ə mígdəlin/, **a·myg·da·line** /-lin, -līn/ *n* a white crystalline bitter-tasting sugar derivative (**glycoside**). Source: almond, apricot, and peach seeds. Use: expectorant. [Mid-19C. < Latin *amygdala* "almond" (see AMYGDALA)]

am·yl /ámm'l/ *adj* CHEM same as **pentyl** [Mid-19C. < Latin *amylum* < Greek *amulon* "finely ground meal" < *mulē* "mill"]

amyl- *prefix* CHEM same as **amylo-** (*used before vowels*)

am·y·la·ceous /ámmə láyshəss/ *adj* having or resembling starch (*technical*)

am·yl ac·e·tate *n* a colorless volatile liquid that smells like pears. Use: flavoring agent, solvent. Formula: $CH_3CO_2C_5H_{11}$.

am·yl al·co·hol *n* a colorless alcohol or mixture of any of the eight related amyl alcohols. Use: solvent, manufacture of organic chemicals and drugs. Formula: $C_5H_{12}O$.

am·y·lase /ámmə làyss, -làyz/ *n* an enzyme in saliva and pancreatic juice that breaks down starch into simple sugars

am·yl·met·a·cre·sol /ámm'l mèttə kreé sàwl/ *n* an antiseptic. Use: treatment of minor infections of the mouth and throat.

am·yl ni·trite *n* a pale yellow fragrant liquid. Use: inhalant to dilate blood vessels. Formula: $C_5H_{11}NO_2$.

amylo- *prefix* starch ○ *amylopectin* [< Latin *amylum* (see AMYL)]

am·y·lo·bar·bi·tone /àmməlō baárbə tōn/ *n* PHARM former name for **amobarbital**

am·y·loid /ámmə lòyd/ *n* **1. WAXY PROTEIN** a waxy translucent substance composed of complex protein fibers and polysaccharides that is formed in body tissues in some degenerative diseases, e.g., Alzheimer's disease **2. STARCHY SUBSTANCE** a substance that resembles starch in composition or function ■ *adj* **STARCHY** resembling a starch (*technical*)

am·y·loid·o·sis /àmmə loy dṓsiss/ *n* a condition marked by the accumulation of a protein-based substance (**amyloid**) in the body's organs and tissues

am·y·lo·pec·tin /àmməlō péktin/ *n* a branched polysaccharide that is an insoluble component of starch

am·y·lose /ámmə lṑss, -lṑz/ *n* an unbranched polysaccharide that is a soluble component of starch

a·my·o·to·ni·a /ày mī ə tṓnee ə/ *n* a medically noteworthy lack of muscle tension [< A-[2] + MYO- + Greek *tonos* "tension, tone"]

a·my·o·tro·phic /àmmee ə trṓfik/ *adj* characterized by degeneration of the muscles (**amyotrophy**)

a·my·o·tro·phic lat·er·al scle·ro·sis *n* a fatal degenerative disease of the nervous system marked by progressive muscle weakness and atrophy. It is a form of motor neuron disease.

a·my·o·tro·phy /ày mī óttrəfee/ *n* a degeneration of the muscles caused by nerve disease [Late 19C. < A-[2] + MYO- + -TROPHY]

an[1] *stressed* /an/; *unstressed* /ən/ *adj* used instead of "a," the indefinite article, in front of words with an initial vowel sound [Old English, unstressed form of *ān* "one"]

USAGE See *a*[4].

an[2] /an, ən/, **an'** *conj* same as **if** (*archaic*) [12C. Reduced form of AND "if"]

an[3] *abbr* Netherlands Antilles (*used in Internet addresses*) See table at **domain name**

AN *abbr* airman, Navy

an. *abbr* **1.** anno **2.** ante

an- *prefix* same as **a-**[2] (*used before vowels*) [< Greek]

-an[1] *suffix* **1.** of or relating to ○ *Minoan* ○ *agrarian* **2.** somebody of or resembling a particular kind ○ *librarian* [Via French < Latin *-anus*]

ORIGIN English words in which the original form of the Old French suffix *-an* is preserved include *captain*, *chamberlain*, *chaplain*, and *fountain*. English *sovereign* is descended from a Latin word with the suffix *-anus*.

-an[2] *suffix* an unsaturated carbon compound ○ *dextran* [Alteration of -ANE]

an·a[1] /ánnə, aánə/ (*plural same* or **-as**) *n* **1.** a collection of things connected with a famous person, place, or period, especially spoken or written information, anecdotes, or sayings **2.** an item in an ana [Mid-18C. < -ANA]

an·a[2] /ánnə/ *adv* of each of the ingredients specified in a medical prescription in equal amounts [< Greek *ana-* (see ANA-)]

ana- *prefix* **1.** up, upward ○ *anamorphic* **2.** back, backward, away ○ *anaphase* **3.** again ○ *anaplastic* [< Greek < *ana* < Indo-European, "on"]

-ana *suffix* a collection of objects or information about a topic, person, or place ○ *Shakespeareana* [Via modern Latin < Latin, neuter plural of *-anus* "relating to"]

an·a·bap·tism /ánnə báp tìzzəm/ *n* the advocacy of adult baptism on the grounds that only as adults can people responsibly accept and declare their faith [See ANABAPTISM]

An·a·bap·tism /ánnə báptìzzəm/ *n* the doctrines or beliefs of the Anabaptists [Mid-16C. Via ecclesiastical Latin *anabaptismus* < Greek *anabaptismos* "second baptism" < *baptismos* "baptism"]

An·a·bap·tist /ánnə báptist/ *n* a member of a 16th-century Protestant movement promoting the doctrine of adult baptism on the grounds that only adults can accept and declare their faith on their own behalf [Mid-16C. < ecclesiastical Latin *anabaptista* < Greek *ana-* "again, afresh" + *baptistēs* "baptizer" < *baptizein* (see BAPTIZE)] —**An·a·bap·tist** *adj*

a·nab·a·sis /ə nábbəsiss/ (*plural* **-a·ses** /-ə seéz/) *n* the advance of an army, especially a large-scale march or expedition moving inland from the coast [Early 18C. < Greek, "going up, ascent" < *anabainein* (see ANABATIC); originally the unsuccessful advance of Greek mercenaries led by Cyrus the Younger across Asia Minor in 401–400 B.C.]

an·a·bat·ic /ánnə báttik/ *adj* describes winds that move or blow upward during the daytime as warm air rises up mountain slopes [Mid-20C. < Greek *anabatikos* "relating to mounting" < *anabainein* "go up, mount" < *bainein* "go"]

an·a·bol·ic /ánnə bóllik/ *adj* promoting tissue growth [Late 19C. Blend of ANA- + METABOLIC]

an·a·bol·ic ster·oid *n* **1.** a synthetic steroid hormone. Use: to increase muscle mass and strength. **2.** a naturally occurring hormone that promotes tissue growth

a·nab·o·lism /ə nábbə lìzzəm/ *n* a metabolic process in which energy is used to make compounds and tissues from simple molecules [Late 19C. Blend of ANA- + METABOLISM]

a·nab·o·lite /ə nábbə lìt/ *n* a substance resulting from anabolism

a·na·branch /ánnə braànch/ *n* a stream that separates from a river and follows its own course before reentering the same river farther downstream [Mid-19C. Blend of *anastomosing* (< ANASTOMOSE) + BRANCH]

a·nach·ro·nism /ə nákrə nìzzəm/ *n* **1. CHRONOLOGICAL MISTAKE** something from a different period of time, e.g., a modern idea or invention wrongly placed in a historical setting in fiction or drama **2. SOMETHING FROM DIFFERENT HISTORICAL PERIOD** a person, thing, idea, or custom that seems to belong to a different time in history **3. MAKING OF CHRONOLOGICAL MISTAKE** the representation of somebody or something out of chronological order or in the wrong historical setting [Mid-17C. < French *anachronisme* < late Greek *anakhronizesthai* "be timed backward" < *khronos* "time"] —**a·nach·ro·nous** /ə nákrənəss/ *adj* —**a·nach·ro·nous·ly** *adv*

a·nach·ro·nis·tic /ə nàkrə nístik/ *adj* **1.** belonging to a time other than the one being represented, especially in fiction or drama **2.** out-of-date or inappropriate at the time in question —**a·nach·ro·nis·ti·cal·ly** *adv*

an·a·clit·ic /ànnə klíttik/ *adj* characterized by strong emotional dependence on a mother or other nurturing person, especially to the extent of exhibiting or causing serious developmental and psychological disturbances [Early 20C. < Greek *anaklitos* "for reclining" < *anaklinein* "lean upon" < *klinein* "lean"] —**an·a·cli·sis** /-klīssis, ə nákləssis/ *n*

an·a·co·lu·thon /ànnəkə lóo thòn/ (*plural* **-tha** /-thə/) *n* an instance of abandoning a grammatical construction in speech or writing before it is complete and continuing with another. The sentence "The subject of the lecture was – I didn't really understand it" contains an anacoluthon. [Early 18C. Via late Latin < Greek *anakolouthon* "illogicality, inconsistency" < *anakolouthos* "not following" < *akolouthos* "following"] —**an·a·co·lu·thic** *adj*

anaconda

an·a·con·da /ànnə kóndə/ *n* a nonvenomous snake that lives in or near water and in trees. It is the largest snake in the boa family. Native to: South America. Latin name: *Eunectes murinus*. [Mid-18C. Origin ?]

An·a·con·da /ànnə kóndə/ city northwest of Butte, in southwestern Montana. It was home to the world's largest ore-smelting plant until 1980. Population: 9,069 (2002).

A·nac·re·on /ə nákree ən/ (570?–478 B.C.) Greek lyric poet. He is well known for celebrating love and wine in his verse.

A·nac·re·on·tic /ə nàkree óntik/, **a·nac·re·on·tic** *adj* written in the style or treating the subjects of the Greek poet Anacreon ■ *n* an Anacreontic poem [Early 17C. < Latin *Anacreonticus* < Greek *Anakreont-*, stem of *Anakreōn* "Anacreon"]

an·a·cru·sis /ànnə kroóssiss/ (*plural* **-cru·ses** /-kroó seez/) *n* **1.** one or more unstressed syllables at the beginning of a line of verse that are not considered part of the metrical pattern of the line **2.** one or more unaccented notes immediately before the first downbeat of a bar of music [Mid-19C. < modern Latin < Greek *anakrouein* "strike up (a tune)" < *krouein* "strike"] —**a·na·crus·tic** /kroóstik/ *adj*

an·a·da·ma bread /ánnə dámmə-/ *n* yeast-raised corn bread that was originally made in New England [Origin ?]

an·a·di·plo·sis /ànnədə plṓsiss/ (*plural* **-plo·ses** /-plṓ seez/) *n* the rhetorical repetition of the last word or words of one phrase or sentence at the beginning of the next. The sentence "He was tormented by fears – fears that were soon to be realized" uses anadiplosis. [Late 16C. < Latin < Greek *anadiploein* "double back" < *diploein* "to double"]

a·nad·ro·mous /ə náddrəməss/ *adj* describes fish such as salmon and shad that return from the sea to the rivers where they were born in order to breed [Mid-18C. < Greek *anadromos* "running up (a river from the sea)" < *dromos* "a running"]

a·nae·mi·a *n* MED another spelling of **anemia**

a·nae·mic *adj* MED another spelling of **anemic**

an·aer·obe /ánnə rṓb/ *n* a microorganism that does not require oxygen for metabolism [Late 19C. Back-formation < French *anaérobie* "living without air" < Greek *an-* "not" + French *aéro-* "air" + Greek *bios* "life"]

an·aer·o·bic /ànnə rṓbik/ *adj* **1.** living or taking place in the absence of oxygen, especially not requiring oxygen for metabolism **2.** having or providing no oxygen —**an·aer·o·bic·al·ly** *adv*

an·aer·o·bic proc·ess *n* a chemical or biological process such as decay or decomposition that does not require oxygen. Such processes are often used to dispose of wastes while generating useful gases.

an·aer·o·bic res·pi·ra·tion *n* the production of energy without the presence of oxygen. Anaerobic respiration occurs in some yeasts and bacteria, and in muscle tissue during strenuous exercise when there is insufficient oxygen.

an·aer·o·bi·o·sis /ànnərō bī óssiss/ *n* life in the absence of free or atmospheric oxygen [Late 19C. < ANAEROBIC + -BIOSIS] —**an·aer·o·bi·ot·ic** /ànnərō bī óttik/ *adj*

an·aes·the·sia, etc. MED another spelling of **anesthesia, etc.**

an·aes·thet·ics /ànnəss théttiks/ *n Can, UK* the medical study and application of anaesthetic substances (*takes a singular verb*) US term **anesthesiology**

an·a·glyph /ánnə glìf/ *n* **1.** a decoration carved in low relief, so that the shape of the design projects only slightly from the background **2.** a three-dimensional visual effect created by dyeing each of two images a different color, usually red and green, and then viewing them through complementary-colored filters, one over each eye [Late 16C. < Greek *anagluphē* "low-relief sculpture" < *gluphein* "carve"] —**an·a·glyph·ic** /-glíffik/ *adj* —**an·a·glyp·tic** /-glíptik/ *adj*

an·a·go·ge /ánnə gōjee/, **an·a·go·gy** /-gōjee/ (*plural* **-gies**) *n* **1.** a spiritual or mystical interpretation of a word or passage, especially in a sacred text, in contrast to a literal or moral interpretation **2.** an allegorical interpretation of a passage in the Bible as an allusion to or foreshadowing of people or events in the New Testament [Mid-16C. Via Latin < Greek *anagōgē* "reference" < *anagein* "take back" < *agein* "take"] —**an·a·gog·ic** /ànnə gójjik/ *adj* —**an·a·gog·i·cal** *adj* —**an·a·gog·i·cal·ly** *adv*

an·a·gram /ánnə gràm/ *n* **1.** a word or phrase that contains all the letters of another word or phrase in a different order. "Astronomers" is an anagram of "no more stars." **2.** a word game that involves the forming of anagrams [Late 16C. Directly or via French *anagramme* < modern Latin *anagramma*, probably < Greek *anagrammatismos* "transposition of letters" < *anagrammatizein* (see ANAGRAMMATIZE)] —**an·a·gram·mat·ic** /ànnəgrə máttik/ *adj* —**an·a·gram·mat·i·cal·ly** *adv*

an·a·gram·ma·tize /ànnə grámmə tìz/ (**-tized, -tiz·ing, -tiz·es**) *vt* to rearrange the letters of a word or phrase to form a different word or phrase [Late 16C. Perhaps < Greek *anagrammatizein* "rearrange the letters of a word" < *gramma* "letter"]

An·a·heim /ánnə hìm/ city in southwestern California. It is home to the Disneyland™ amusement park. Population: 332,642 (2002 estimate).

a·nal /áyn'l/ *adj* **1.** ANAT **RELATING TO ANUS** relating to or situated near the anus **2.** PSYCHOANAL **RELATING TO CHILDHOOD INTEREST IN DEFECATION** in Freudian theory, relating to a stage of childhood psychosexual development during which the focus is on the anal region and functions **3.** PSYCHOANAL **OBSESSIVELY SELF-CONTROLLED** in Freudian theory, relating to adult personality traits that are considered to have originated during or be characteristic of the anal stage of development, e.g., obsessive neatness, stubbornness, and frugality [Mid-18C. < modern Latin *analis* < *anus* (see ANUS)] —**a·nal·ly** *adv*

anal. *abbr* **1.** analogous **2.** analogy **3.** analysis **4.** analytic

a·nal·cime /ə nál seēm/, **a·nal·cite** /ə nál sìt/ *n* a white or light-colored form of the mineral zeolite composed of hydrated sodium aluminum silicate. Source: igneous rocks. [Early 19C. < French < Greek *analkimos* "not strong" (in reference to the mineral's weak electric current) < *alkimos* "strong" < *alkē* "strength"] —**a·nal·cim·ic** /ànn'l símmik/ *adj*

an·a·lects /ánnə lèkts/, **an·a·lec·ta** /ànnə léktə/ *npl* passages selected from one or more literary or philosophical works, especially when published as a collection [Early 17C. Via Latin < Greek *analekta* "collected, or selected, things" < *analegein* "gather up" < *legein* "gather"] —**an·a·lec·tic** /ànnə léktik/ *adj*

an·a·lem·ma /ànnə lémmə/ (*plural* **-mas** or **-ma·ta** /-mətə/) *n* a scale, found on some sundials and globes, that is shaped like a figure eight and marked to indicate the declination of the Sun and to allow the calculation of apparent solar time [Mid-17C. Via Latin, "sundial, pedestal of a sundial" < Greek *analēmma* "pedestal, support" < *analambanein* "take up, support" < *lambanein* "take"]

an·a·lep·tic /ànnə léptik/ *adj* describes a type of medication that is restorative or invigorating, especially after an illness ■ *n* a drug that stimulates the central nervous system [Mid-17C. Via Latin < Greek *analēptikos* "restorative" < *analambanein* (see ANALEMMA)]

a·nal fin *n* a single fin on the underside of some fish, behind the anus

an·al·ge·si·a /ànn'l jeēzee ə, -jeēzhə/ *n* **1.** the lack of sensibility to pain while somebody is conscious **2.** treatment to control pain [Early 18C. Via modern Latin < Greek *analgēsia* "lack of feeling, insensibility" < *algeein* "feel pain" < *algos* "pain"] —**an·al·get·ic** /ànn'l jéttik/ *adj*

an·al·ge·sic /ànn'l jeēzik, -jeēssik/ *adj* describes a type of medication that alleviates pain without loss of consciousness —**an·al·ge·sic** *n*

a·nal in·ter·course *n* a form of sexual intercourse in which a man puts his penis into the anus of a man or woman

an·a·log /ánnə lòg/ *n US* CHEM a chemical with a similar structure to another but differing slightly in composition. Can term **analogue** ■ *adj* COMPUT relating to a system or device that represents data variation by a measurable physical quality [Mid-20C. Variant]

an·a·log clock, **an·a·logue clock** *n* a clock that shows the time by means of hands on a dial

an·a·log com·put·er, **an·a·logue com·put·er** *n* a computer that uses a variable physical quantity such as voltage to represent data

an·a·log·i·cal /ànnə lójjik'l/ *adj* relating to or working by means of analogy [Late 16C. Directly or via French *analogique* < Latin *analogicus* < Greek *analogikos* < *analogos* (see ANALOGOUS)] —**an·a·log·i·cal·ly** *adv*

a·nal·o·gize /ə nállə jìz/ (**-gized, -giz·ing, -giz·es**) *v* **1.** *vt* to compare two things that are similar in some respects, especially in order to explain something or to support an argument **2.** *vi* to make use of an analogy

a·nal·o·gous /ə nálləgəss/ *adj* **1.** similar in some respects, allowing an analogy to be drawn **2.** describes body parts and organs that have equivalent functions but that have evolved independently of one another in different plants or animals. The wings of birds, bats, and insects are analogous. [Mid-17C. < French *analogue* or Latin *analogus* < Greek *analogos* < *analogon* "in due ratio" < *ana* "according to" + *logos* "ratio"] —**a·nal·o·gous·ly** *adv* —**a·nal·o·gous·ness** *n*

USAGE ***Analogous***, correctly used, should include a notion of *analogy*, that is, of similarity in some particular respects: *The Commission has set up guidelines for defense attorneys that are analogous to those for prosecutors.* It is better to avoid it when the comparison is only general and when more straightforward words like *similar, equivalent, comparable,* or *corresponding* serve just as well, as in *The new system is comparable* [not *analogous*] *to that used in the electronics industry.*

---

an·a·logue /ánnə làwg/ *n* **1. CORRESPONDING THING** a thing, idea, or institution that is similar to or has the same function as another ○*"They had no exact analogue for our word 'home,' any more than they had for our Roman-based 'family.'"* (Charlotte Perkins Gilman, *Herland*; 1915) **2.** BIOL **EQUIVALENT BUT INDEPENDENT ORGAN** a body part or organ that has an equivalent function to one in a different plant or animal but that evolved independently. The wings of birds, bats, and insects are analogues. **3.** FOOD **FOOD SUBSTITUTE** a food or dish made to resemble another by the substitution of inferior ingredients **4.** *Can, UK* CHEM same as **analog** ■ *adj UK* COMPUT same as **analog** [Early 19C. Via French < Greek *analogon* (see ANALOGOUS)]

a·na·logue clock *n* another spelling of **analog clock**

an·a·logue com·put·er *n* COMPUT another spelling of **analog computer**

an·a·log watch *n* a watch that shows the time by means of hands on a dial

a·nal·o·gy /ə nálləjee/ (*plural* **-gies**) *n* **1. COMPARISON** a comparison between two things that are similar in some way, often used to help explain something or make it easier to understand **2. SIMILARITY** a similarity in some respects **3.** BIOL **EQUIVALENCE BETWEEN INDEPENDENT PARTS** equivalence in biological function between body parts or organs that have appeared independently in different plants and animals **4.** LOGIC **FORM OF REASONING** a form of logical inference, reasoning that if two things are taken to be alike in one way, they are alike in other ways **5.** LING **STANDARDIZATION OF LINGUISTIC FORMS** the development or production of linguistic forms and patterns that resemble those already predominating in a language [15C. Via French *analogie* or Latin *analogia* < Greek *analogia* "proportion" < *analogos* (see ANALOGOUS)]

an·al·pha·bet·ic /a nàlfə béttik/ (*formal*) *adj* **1. NOT ALPHABETICAL** not in alphabetical order **2. ILLITERATE** not knowing how to read or write ■ *n* **ILLITERATE PERSON** somebody who cannot read or write [Late 19C. < Greek *analphabētos* "not knowing the alphabet" < *alphabētos* "alphabet"]

a·nal-re·ten·tive *adj* PSYCHOANAL same as **anal** (sense 3) —**a·nal re·ten·tion** *n* —**a·nal-re·ten·tive** *n* —**a·nal-re·ten·tive·ness** *n*

a·nal sex *n* same as **anal intercourse**

a·nal·y·sand /ə nállə sànd, -zànd/ *n* somebody who is undergoing psychoanalysis [Mid-20C. < ANALYZE, after *operand*]

an·a·lyse *vt* UK spelling of **analyze**

a·nal·y·sis /ə nálləssiss/ (*plural* **-y·ses** /-ə seēz/) *n* **1. CLOSE EXAMINATION** the examination of something in detail in order to understand it better or draw conclusions from it **2. SEPARATION INTO COMPONENTS** the separation of something into its constituents in order to find out what it contains, to examine individual parts, or to study the structure of the whole **3. ASSESSMENT** an assessment, description, or explanation of something, usually based on careful consideration or investigation **4.** MATH **BRANCH OF MATHEMATICS** the branch of mathematics dealing with differential calculus, functions, and limits **5.** LING **WAY OF EXPRESSING GRAMMATICAL RELATIONSHIPS** the use of function words or word order, rather than inflectional forms, to express grammatical relationships in a language **6.** PSYCHIAT same as **psychoanalysis** (sense 2) [Late 16C. Via medieval Latin < Greek *analusis* "a breaking up into elements" < *analuein* "unloose, dissolve into elements" < *luein* "loosen"] ◇ **in the final** *or* **last analysis** used to introduce or indicate a summary conclusion to a complex subject

a·nal·y·sis of var·i·ance *n* in statistics, the analysis of the difference in outcomes of an experiment to determine the factors contributing to the variations

an·a·lyst /ánn'list/ *n* **1.** somebody with specialist knowledge or skill who studies or examines something by separating it into its constituent parts and gives an assessment, description, or explanation of it **2.** somebody who practices psychoanalysis [Mid-17C. < French *analyste* < *analyse* "analysis" (see ANALYZE)]

~~analysys~~ incorrect spelling of **analysis**

an·a·lyte /ánnə lìt/ *n* the substance being identified and measured in a chemical analysis [Late 20C. Irregularly < ANALYSIS]

an·a·lyt·ic /ànnə líttik/, **an·a·lyt·i·cal** /-líttik'l/ *adj* **1. OF ANALYSIS** connected with or involving analysis **2. USING ANALYSIS** able or inclined to separate things into their constituent parts in order to study or examine them, draw conclusions, or solve problems **3.** LOGIC **TRUE BY MEANING ALONE** true by definition or by virtue of the meaning of the words used **4.** MATH **DIFFERENTIABLE AT ALL POINTS IN DOMAIN** describes a function of a complex variable that is differentiable at all points in its domain **5.** GRAM **USING FUNCTION WORDS** expressing grammatical relationships by means of function words or word order rather than inflections [Late 16C. Via late Latin < Greek *analutikos* < *analuein* (see ANALYSIS)] —**an·a·lyt·i·cal·ly** *adv*

an·a·lyt·i·cal bal·ance *n* an accurate scale used in laboratories for weighing minute objects or quantities

an·a·lyt·i·cal en·gine *n* a programmable calculating machine, the forerunner of the modern computer, invented by Charles Babbage in 1833

an·a·lyt·i·cal re·a·gent *n* a chemical almost free of impurities

an·a·lyt·ic ge·om·e·try *n* a branch of mathematics dealing with geometric properties using algebraic operations and notation to locate points within a coordinate system

an·a·lyt·ic phi·los·o·phy *n* a 20th-century philosophy primarily concerned with resolving philosophical problems through the analysis and clarification of language

an·a·lyt·ic psy·chol·o·gy *n* a system of psychoanalysis based on the psychological theories of Carl Jung

an·a·lyt·ics /ànnə líttiks/ *n* the branch of logic involved with the analysis of propositions (*takes a singular verb*)

an·a·lyze /ánn'l ìz/ (**-lyzed, -lyz·ing, -lyz·es**) *vt* **1. STUDY SOMETHING CLOSELY** to examine something in great detail in order to understand it better or discover more about it **2. BREAK SOMETHING DOWN INTO COMPONENTS** to find out what something is made up of by identifying its constituent parts **3. EXAMINE STRUCTURE** to study the structure of something or how its constituent parts are put together **4.** GRAM **EXPRESS SOMETHING USING FUNCTION WORDS** to express grammatical relationships by using function words or word order rather than inflectional endings **5.** PSYCHIAT same as **psychoanalyze** [Early 17C. Perhaps back-formation < ANALYSIS, or < French *analyse* "analysis" used as a verb; reinforced by French *analyser* "analyze"] —**an·a·lyz·a·ble** *adj* —**an·a·ly·za·tion** /ànn'li záysh'n/ *n* —**an·a·lyz·er** *n*

an·am·ne·sis /àn am néessiss/ (*plural* **-ne·ses** /-née seez/) *n* **1.** a recollection of events, especially from a supposed past existence (*technical*) **2.** the medical history of a patient, especially in the patient's own words [Late 16C. < Greek, "remembrance" < *anamimnēskein* "call back to mind" < *mimnēskein* "call to mind"]

an·am·nes·tic /àn am néstik/ *adj* showing a secondary immunological response to an antigen at some time after initial immunization [Early 18C. < Greek *anamnēstikos* < *anamimnēskein* (see ANAMNESIS)] —**an·am·nes·ti·cal·ly** *adv*

an·a·mor·phic /ànnə máwrfik/ *adj* relating to or producing image distortion caused by unequal magnification along different perpendicular axes

an·a·mor·pho·sis /ànnə mawr fóssiss, -máwrfəssiss/ (*plural* **-pho·ses** /-fō seez/) *n* **1.** a distorted image or drawing of a distorted image that appears normal when viewed with or reflected from a special device **2.** the process of making distorted images by means of special mirrors or other devices [Mid-18C. < Greek, "transformation" < *anamorphoein* "change shape again" < *morphoein* "change shape" < *morphē* "shape"]

a·nan·da /ə nándə/ *n* in Hinduism, a state of bliss that is considered the highest state of being and results from a release from all sense of the body and its demands [Mid-19C. < Sanskrit *ānanda* "joy"]

An·an·ke /ə nángkee/ *n* a small natural satellite of Jupiter, discovered in 1951

A·nan·si /ə nánssee/ *n* in West African folk tales, a popular spider god who is both devious and very wise [< Twi *ananse* "spider"]

an·a·pest /ánnə pèst/, **an·a·paest** *n* a metrical foot of three syllables with the stress on the third syllable, or of two short syllables followed by a long syllable. The word "unconcerned" and the phrase "up the hill" are anapests. [Late 16C. Via Latin < Greek *anapaistos* "struck backward" (from its being a reversed dactyl), past participle of *anapaiein* < *paiein* "strike"] —**an·a·pes·tic** /ànnə péstik/ *adj*

an·a·phase /ánnə fàyz/ *n* a late stage of cell division during which chromosomes move to the poles of the spindle

a·naph·o·ra /ə náffərə/ *n* **1. REPETITION FOR EFFECT** the use of the same word or phrase at the beginning of several successive clauses, sentences, lines, or verses, usually for emphasis or rhetorical effect. "She didn't speak. She didn't stand. She didn't even look up when we came in" is an example of anaphora. (*formal*) **2. REFERRING BACK** reference to a word or phrase used earlier, especially to avoid repeating the word or phrase by replacing it with something else such as a pronoun. In the sentence "I told Paul to close the door and he did so," the clause "he did so" makes use of anaphora. **3.** CHR **PART OF COMMUNION** the offering of the bread and wine in the Christian Communion [Late 16C. Via Latin < Greek, "reference, repetition" < *anapherein* "carry back" < *pherein* "carry"] —**a·naph·o·ric** /ànnə fáwrik/ *adj* —**a·naph·or·i·cal·ly** *adv*

a·naph·o·re·sis /ànnəfə réessiss/ *n* the movement toward the anode of suspended particles in solution

an·aph·ro·dis·i·a /ə nàffrə dízzee ə, -dí*zh*ə/ *n* absence or reduction of sexual desire [20C. < Greek, "inability to inspire love" < *aphrodisia* (see APHRODISIAC)]

an·aph·ro·dis·i·ac /ə nàffrə dízzee àk/ *adj* tending to reduce sexual desire —**an·aph·ro·dis·i·ac** *n*

an·a·phy·lac·tic /ànnəfə láktik/ *adj* relating to or caused or characterized by extreme sensitivity to a substance (**anaphylaxis**) —**an·a·phy·lac·ti·cal·ly** *adv*

an·a·phy·lac·tic shock *n* a sudden severe and potentially fatal allergic reaction in somebody sensitive to a substance, marked by a drop in blood pressure, difficulty in breathing, itching, and swelling

an·a·phy·lax·is /ànnəfə láksiss/ *n* **1.** extreme sensitivity to a substance such as a protein or drug **2.** MED same as **anaphylactic shock** [Early 20C. < modern Latin < Greek *ana-* "again" (because a substance is reintroduced) + *-phylaxis* "guarding, watching"] —**an·a·phy·lac·toid** *adj*

an·a·pla·sia /ànnə pláy*zh*ə/ *n* the reversion of cells, usually within a tumor, to a simpler or less differentiated form

an·a·plas·tic /ànnə plástik/ *adj* relating to or characterized by the loss of distinctive cell features (**anaplasia**)

an·a·ptyx·is /ànnəp tíksiss, ànap-/ *n* the insertion of a weak vowel sound between two consonants in order to make a word or phrase easier to pronounce. Saying "go thataway" rather than "go that way" is an example of anaptyxis. [Late 19C. Via modern Latin < Greek *anaptuxis* "an unfolding" < *anaptussein* "unfold" < *ptussein* "fold"]

an·ar·chic /a náarkik, ə-/, **an·ar·chi·cal** /-kik'l/ *adj* **1. LAWLESS** showing no respect for established laws, rules, institutions, or authority **2. CHAOTIC** characterized by a lack of organization or control **3. ENCOURAGING ANARCHY** likely to cause the overthrow of a formal system of government or a breakdown of law and order —**an·ar·chi·cal·ly** *adv*

an·ar·chism /ánnər kìzzəm/ *n* **1. DOCTRINE REJECTING GOVERNMENT** an ideology that rejects the need for a system of government in society and proposes its abolition **2. ACTIONS OF ANARCHISTS** behavior intended to overthrow or weaken a society's formal system of government **3. RESISTANCE TO CONTROL** resistance to all forms of authority or control

an·ar·chist /ánnərkist/ *n* **1.** somebody who believes that governments should be abolished as unnecessary **2.** somebody who tries to overthrow a government or behaves in a lawless way —**an·ar·chis·tic** /ànnər kístik/ *adj*

an·ar·chy /ánnərkee/ *n* **1.** a situation in which there is a total lack of organization or control **2.** the absence of any formal system of government in a society [Mid-16C. Via medieval Latin < Greek *anarkhia* < *anarkhos* "without a ruler" < *arkhos* "ruler"]

an·ar·thri·a /a náarthree ə/ *n* the loss of the ability to articulate words [Late 19C. Via modern Latin < Greek < *anarthros* (see ANARTHROUS)] —**an·ar·thric** *adj*

an·ar·throus /a náarthrəss/ *adj* used or occurring without a definite or indefinite article [Early 19C. < Greek *anarthros* "not joined or articulated, inarticulate" < *arthron* "article, joint"]

an·a·sar·ca /ànnə sáarkə/ *n* the accumulation of watery fluid in connective tissue and cavities, resulting in swelling (**edema**) [14C. Via medieval Latin < Greek *anasarx*, describing edema, < *ana sarka* "throughout the flesh"] —**an·a·sar·cous** *adj*

A·na·sa·zi /áanə sáazee, ànnə-/ (*plural* **-zis** or *same*) *n* a member of an ancient Native North American people [Mid-20C. < Navajo *anaasází* "enemy ancestors"]

A·na·sa·zi cul·ture *n* a highly developed ancient culture of the region that is now the southwestern United States. It was centered in the broad plateau where present-day Arizona, New Mexico, Colorado, and Utah meet.

A·na·sta·sia /ànnə stáy*zh*ə/ (1901–18) Russian grand duchess. Daughter of Tsar Nicholas II, she died when the Bolsheviks executed the Romanovs (July 1918), but the obscurity of her death led to many women claiming to be her. Born **Romanova, Anastasia Nikolaevna**

an·as·tig·mat /a nástig màt, ànnə stíg màt/ *n* a lens or combination of lenses free from astigmatism [Late 19C. < German, back-formation < *anastigmatisch* "anastigmatic" < Greek *stigmat-* "point"]

an·as·tig·mat·ic /ànnə stig mátik, a nàstig máttik/ *adj* describes a lens that is corrected for or free from astigmatism

a·nas·to·mose /ə nástə mòz, -mòss/ (**-mosed, -mos·ing, -mo·ses**) *vt* to join blood vessels or other tubular parts in a surgical operation (**anastomosis**) [Late 17C. Probably back-formation < ANASTOMOSIS]

a·nas·to·mo·sis /ə nàstə móssiss/ (*plural* **-mo·ses** /-mó seez/) *n* **1. NATURAL JOINT** the connection or place of connection of two or more parts of a natural branching system, e.g., of blood vessels, leaf veins, stems of woody plants, or rivers **2.** SURG **SURGICAL UNION OF TUBULAR PARTS** the surgical union of two hollow organs, e.g., blood vessels or parts of the intestine, to ensure continuity of the passageway **3.** FUNGI **FUSING OF FUNGAL FILAMENTS** a fusion between fungal filaments (**hyphae**) to form a network [Early 17C. Via modern Latin < Greek, "outlet, opening, interconnection of openings" < *anastomoein* "supply with a mouth or opening" < *stoma* "mouth"] —**a·nas·to·mot·ic** /ə nàstə móttik/ *adj*

a·nas·tro·phe /ə nástrəfee/ *n* an alteration of the normal order of words or phrases in a grammatical construction, usually for rhetorical effect. Coleridge's "The helmsman steered; the ship moved on; yet never a breeze up blew" ends with an anastrophe. [Mid-16C. < Greek, "a turning back, inversion" < *stroph-*, stem of *strephein* "to turn"]

anat. *abbr* MED **1.** anatomical **2.** anatomy

an·a·tase /ánnə tàyss, -tàyz/ *n* a blue or yellowish brown mineral consisting of titanium dioxide. Source: igneous rocks. [Early 19C. Via French < Greek *anatasis* "extension" (from the elongated crystals) < *teinein* "to stretch"]

a·nath·e·ma /ə náthəmə/ *n* **1. OBJECT OF LOATHING** somebody or something that is greatly disliked or detested and is therefore shunned **2.** RELIG **SOMEBODY OR SOMETHING FORMALLY DENOUNCED** somebody or something cursed, denounced, or excommunicated by a religious authority **3. GENERAL CURSE** a forceful curse or denunciation **4.** RELIG **ECCLESIASTICAL CURSE** a curse from a religious authority that denounces something or excommunicates somebody [Early 16C. Via ecclesiastical Latin < Greek, "something devoted to evil" < *anatithenai* "set up"]

a·nath·e·ma·tize /ə náthəmə tìz/ (**-tized, -tiz·ing, -tiz·es**) *vti* to formally curse, denounce, or excommunicate somebody or something [Mid-16C. Via ecclesiastical Latin *anathematizare* "ban, curse" < Greek *anathematizein* "dedicate to evil" < *anathemat-*, stem of *anathema* (see ANATHEMA)] —**a·nath·e·ma·ti·za·tion** /ə nàthəməti záysh'n/ *n*

An·a·to·li·a /ànnə tólee ə/ Asian part of Turkey, forming the westernmost peninsula of Asia

An·a·to·li·an /ànnə tólee ən/ *n* **1.** somebody who comes from Anatolia **2.** a group of extinct Indo-European languages spoken more than 3,000 years ago in central and western Turkey —**An·a·to·li·an** *adj*

An·a·to·li·an Pla·teau /ànnə tólee ən-/ mountainous region extending across much of Turkey. The highest peak is Mount Erciyes 12,848 ft./3,916 m.

an·a·tom·i·cal /ànnə tómmik'l/, **an·a·tom·ic** /-tómmik/ *adj* relating to or showing the physical structure of animals or plants —**an·a·tom·i·cal·ly** *adv*

an·a·tom·i·cal·ly cor·rect *adj* describes a doll, model, or other representation of the human body that has an accurate representation of the genitals and other bodily details

an·a·tom·i·cal po·si·tion *n* the standard position of the body in the study of anatomy from which all directions and positions are derived. In it the body is assumed to be standing, the feet together, the arms to the side, and the head, eyes, and palms facing forward.

a·nat·o·mize /ə náttə mīz/ (**-mized, -miz·ing, -miz·es**) *vt* **1.** BIOL same as **dissect** (sense 1) **2.** to analyze or examine something in great detail, thus revealing features that are not obvious —**a·nat·o·mi·za·tion** /ə nàttəmi záysh'n/ *n*

a·nat·o·my /ə náttəmee/ (*plural* **-mies**) *n* **1. STUDY OF STRUCTURE OF BODY** the branch of science that studies the physical structure of animals, plants, and other organisms **2. PHYSICAL STRUCTURE OF ORGANISM** the physical structure, especially the internal structure, of an animal, plant, or other organism, or of any of its parts **3. BOOK ABOUT ANATOMY** a book or other written work about the physical structure of animals, plants, or other organisms **4. BODY** the human body (*informal*) **5. ANALYSIS** a detailed analysis of something [14C. Via French *anatomie* and late Latin *anatomia* < Greek *anatomē* "cutting up" < *temnein* "to cut"] —**a·nat·o·mist** *n*

ORIGIN From the 16th century to the early 19th century ***anatomy*** was used to mean "skeleton," and in this sense it was often misinterpreted as *an atomy*, as if the initial *an-* were the indefinite article: "My bones...will be taken up smooth, and white, and bare as an atomy," Tobias Smollett (1755).

An·ax·ag·o·ras /àn ak sággərəss/ (500?–428 B.C.) Greek philosopher. He stated that matter was infinitely divisible and was the first person to explain solar eclipses.

A·nax·i·man·der /ə nàksə mándər/ (611?–547? B.C.) Greek philosopher. He put forward an evolutionary theory of the origins of life, claiming that human beings evolved from more primitive species.

An·ax·i·me·nes /à nak símmə neez/ (570?–500? B.C.) Greek philosopher. He believed that the universe consisted of air or vapor in various stages of condensation, and that the movement of air changed the structure of physical objects.

ANC *abbr* POL African National Congress

-ance *suffix* **1.** action ○ *utterance* **2.** *also* **-ancy** state or condition ○ *elegance*

an·ces·tor /án sèstər, ánsəstər/ *n* **1. DISTANT RELATION SOMEBODY IS DESCENDED FROM** somebody from whom somebody else is directly descended, especially somebody more distant than a grandparent **2. FORERUNNER** a predecessor of somebody, e.g., in the development of an art form **3.** BIOL **EARLIER SPECIES** an animal or plant from which a species has evolved **4. EARLIER MODEL** a device that was an earlier form of a modern invention or was used as a basis for developing it [14C. Via Old French *ancestre* < Latin *antecessor* "somebody who goes before" < *cess-*, past participle of *cedere* "give way"]

an·ces·tral /an séstrəl/ *adj* relating to something belonging to former generations of somebody's family [15C. < Old French *ancestrel* < *ancestre* (see ANCESTOR)] —**an·ces·tral·ly** *adv*

an·ces·try /án sèstree, ánsès-/ *n* the former generations of somebody's family ○ *was rumored to have a buccaneer in his ancestry* [14C. Alteration of Old French *ancesserie* < *ancessour* < Latin *antecessor* (see ANCESTOR)]

an·char /án chaar/ *n* a pungent pickle made of mango, lemon, and ginger, used in South Asian and Caribbean cooking [Late 20C. Alteration of ACHAR after Hindi *aam* "mango"]

An·chi·ses /an kī seez/ *n* in Greek and Roman mythology, a Trojan prince and the father of Aeneas by the goddess Aphrodite. In later life, Anchises was saved during the Greek sack of Troy when Aeneas carried him from the burning city on his back.

an·chor /ángkər/ *n* **1. DEVICE TO HOLD SHIP IN PLACE** a heavy, traditionally double-hooked, device for keeping a ship or floating object in place **2. DEVICE KEEPING OBJECT IN PLACE** any device that keeps an object in place **3.** BROADCAST **ANNOUNCER OF NEWS PROGRAM** an announcer on a news program, providing links between the studio and reporters on location **4. SOMETHING DEPENDABLE** somebody who or something that provides stability ○ *She was my anchor during the crisis.* **5.** COMM same as **anchor store** **6.** TRACK AND FIELD **SOMEBODY POSITIONED**

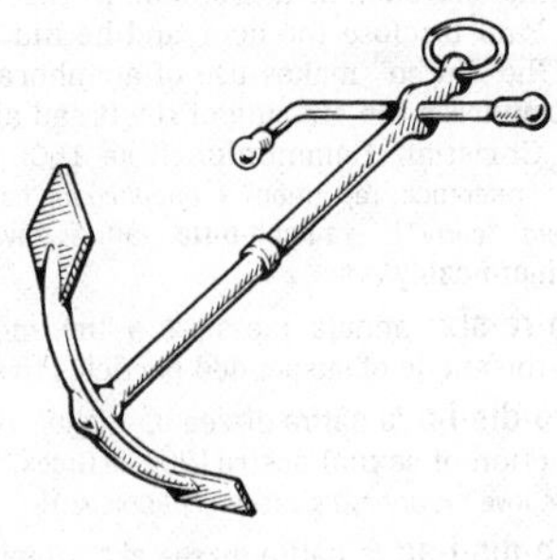

anchor

LAST the team member who is responsible for the last leg in a relay race or farthest to the rear in a tug of war **7.** CLIMBING **CLIMBER'S ROPE ATTACHMENT** a point to which a climber's rope is attached, e.g., on a rock face or in ice ■ *adj* **ATTACHING** used for securing or connecting something ■ *v* (**-chored, -chor·ing, -chors**) **1.** *vt* **HOLD SOMETHING IN PLACE** to hold something securely in place **2.** *vti* NAUT **PUT DOWN ANCHOR** to moor a ship by lowering its anchor so that it remains stationary in a place ○ *anchored off the Nigerian coast* **3.** *vt* BROADCAST **BE ANNOUNCER OF NEWS PROGRAM** to be the announcer on a news program [Pre-12C. Via Latin *ancora* < Greek *agkura*] ◇ **at anchor** held on the water by an anchor

an·chor·age /ángkərij/ *n* **1. PLACE TO HOLD BOATS SECURE** a place in or near a harbor where boats are moored **2. CHARGE FOR ANCHORING BOAT** a charge for anchoring a boat in a harbor **3. SOMETHING HOLDING OBJECT IN PLACE** a device used to hold an object in place **4. ANCHORING** the securing of a ship with an anchor **5. SECURITY** a source of stability, or a stable condition

An·chor·age /ángkərij/ city and port in southern Alaska, at the eastern end of Cook Inlet. Population: 268,983 (2002 estimate).

an·cho·rite /ángkə rīt/ *n* somebody who lives a reclusive life of prayer [15C. Via medieval Latin *anc(h)orita* < ecclesiastical Greek *anakhōrētēs* < Greek *anakhōrein* "withdraw" < *ana-* "away" + *khōrein* "move"]

an·chor·man /ángkər màn/ (*plural* **-men** /-mèn/) *n* **1.** a man who is an anchor for a news program **2.** a man or boy who is the anchor in a relay race or for a tug-of-war team

an·chor·per·son /ángkər pùrss'n/ (*plural* **-per·sons** or **-peo·ple** /-peep'l/) *n* BROADCAST, TRACK AND FIELD same as **anchor** *n* (senses 3, 6)

an·chor store *n* a large retail store such as a department store that is a major store in a shopping mall and is intended to attract shoppers who will patronize the smaller stores

an·chor·wom·an /ángkər wòommən/ (*plural* **-wom·en** /-wìmmin/) *n* **1.** a woman who is an anchor for a news program **2.** a woman or girl who is the anchor in a relay race or for a tug-of-war team

an·cho·vy /án chòvee, an chóvee/ (*plural* **-vies** or *same*) *n* **1.** a small silvery ocean fish that travels in large schools. Family: Engraulidae. **2.** the flesh of an anchovy as food, often sold salted and canned in oil [Late 16C. < Spanish *anchova*]

an·cien ré·gime /aaN syaaN ray zheem/ (*plural* **an·ciens ré·gimes** /*pronunc. same*/) *n* **1.** the political and social system of France before the revolution of 1789 **2.** an outmoded system, method, or way of life [Late 18C. < French, "old regime"]

an·cient /áynshənt/ *adj* **1. OLD** very old **2. OF DISTANT PAST** belonging to the distant past, especially to the time before the collapse of the Western Roman Empire in A.D. 476 ■ *n* **1. SOMEBODY FROM PAST CIVILIZATION** a member of a civilization of the distant past **2. SOMEBODY OF ADVANCED YEARS** a very mature or venerable person ■ **an·cients** *npl* **1. PEOPLE OF ANCIENT WESTERN CIVILIZATIONS** the people who lived in one of the ancient civilizations, especially Greece and Rome **2. ANCIENT GREEK AND ROMAN AUTHORS** the authors of ancient Greece and Rome, whose writings form the basis of the classics as a subject of study [14C. Via French *ancien* < assumed Vulgar Latin *anteanus* < Latin *ante* "before"] —**an·cient·ly** *adv* —**an·cient·ness** *n*

An·cient Greek *n* the forms of the Greek language spoken from about 1500 B.C. to about A.D. 500

an·cient his·to·ry *n* **1.** the study of the civilizations that flourished in the distant past, especially those of Greece and Rome **2.** things that happened a long time ago (*informal*)

An·cient Mar·i·ner *n* somebody who tends to talk at length (*informal humorous*) [< the title of a poem by Samuel Taylor Coleridge]

an·cil·la·ry /ánssə lèrree/ *adj* **1. SUBORDINATE** in a position of lesser importance **2. PROVIDING SUPPORT** providing support for somebody or something, e.g., nontechnical assistance to people who work in an industry or profession ■ *n* (*plural* **-ries**) **1. SUBORDINATE PART** a subordinate part or element, e.g., a branch of an organization **2. EMPLOYEE PROVIDING NONTECHNICAL SUPPORT** a worker who provides nontechnical assistance or support to the core workers in an industry or profession [Mid-17C. < Latin *ancillaris* < *ancilla* "handmaid," feminine of *anculus* "manservant"]

anc·the·a /ángk thee ə/ *n* in African cuisine, a plant that grows in a way similar to the eggplant but whose leaves, as opposed to its fruit, are eaten. They are sliced, parboiled, and then cooked with meat and ground seeds, e.g., those of the pumpkin.

an·cy·lo·sto·mi·a·sis /àngkə lōstə mī əssiss, ànssə-/, **an·ky·lo·sto·mi·a·sis** /àngkə-/ *n* a tropical disease caused by infestation of the small intestine by hookworms, with symptoms of anemia and tiredness [Late 19C. < modern Latin *Ancyclostoma*, genus of hookworms < Greek *agkulos* "hooked" + *stoma* "mouth"]

and *stressed* /and/; *unstressed* /ənd, ən/ CORE MEANING: a conjunction used to indicate an additional thing, situation, or fact. "And" in this case links words and phrases of the same grammatical value. ○ *a sister and two brothers* ○ *We need to clean the house and pack our suitcases.* ○ *switching back and forth between different systems*

conj **1. THEN** used to link two verbs or statements about events to indicate that the second follows the first ○ *Just add water and stir.* **2. AS RESULT** used to introduce a situation or event that is a consequence of something just mentioned ○ *Their work was excellent and won several awards.* **3. USED TO STRESS REPETITION OR CONTINUITY** used to link identical words or phrases in order to emphasize repetition or continuity ○ *It gets better and better.* **4. PLUS** used to link two numbers or quantities to indicate that they are to be added together ○ *One and one are two.* **5. BUT** used to introduce a contrasting statement ○ *My dentist says to eat fruit and avoid refined sugar.* **6. MOREOVER** used to introduce a statement that continues or adds weight to a statement just made ○ *The kids needed clothes, and I hadn't been paid in weeks.* **7. USED TO CONNECT IDEAS** used to connect clauses or sentences, especially in spoken conversation ○ *I like the head waiter, but the work's hard. And the hours are very long.* **8. INDICATES INFINITIVE VERB** used instead of "to" before an infinitive verb, usually with verbs such as "try," "go," and "come" (*informal*) ○ *I usually try and visit her once a week.* **9. IF** used to introduce a conditional clause (*archaic*) ○ *and it please you* [Old English *and, ond* < Germanic] ◇ **and (all) that** and everything else that is similar or included (*informal*) ○ *I've painted the doors and window frames and all that.* ◇ **and how** used to show strong agreement with or to emphasize something that has just been said (*informal*)

USAGE The notion that ***and*** should not be used at the beginning of a sentence arose from too literal an understanding of the "joining" function of conjunctions. The same objection is also raised with regard to *but.* If initial ***and*** is overdone, the effect is of poor style, but it is not a matter of grammatical correctness. Using ***and*** at the beginning of a sentence often can be an effective way of drawing attention to what follows: *"You can't get away with this," he threatened. And we knew he meant it.*

AND /and/ *n* **1.** a binary operator in Boolean algebra whose result is true only if both its operands are true **2.** a logic circuit, used especially in computers, that gives a high-voltage output if its input carries a low voltage and a low-voltage output otherwise [Mid-20C. < AND]

An·da·lu·sia /àndə lóozhə, -shee ə/ autonomous region of southern Spain bordered by the

Mediterranean Sea and the Atlantic Ocean. It contains the historic cities of Seville, Granada, and Cadiz and many examples of Moorish architecture. Population: 7,357,558 (2001). Area: 33,822 sq. mi./87,599 sq. km. Spanish name **Andalucía** —**An·da·lu·si·an** *adj, n*

an·da·lu·site /àndə lóo sìt/ *n* a variously colored precious stone that is composed of aluminum silicate. Use: gems. [Early 19C. After ANDALUSIA]

An·da·man and Nic·o·bar Is·lands /ándəmən ənd níkə baar-/ union territory of eastern India, comprising two island groups in the Bay of Bengal between India and Myanmar. Capital: Port Blair. Population: 356,265 (2001). Area: 3,185 sq. mi./8,249 sq. km. —**An·da·man·ese** *n*

An·da·man Is·lands northern part of the Indian union territory of the Andaman and Nicobar Islands, situated between the Bay of Bengal and the Andaman Sea. The Andaman Islands consist of five large islands and over 200 islets. Population: 240,089 (1991). Area: 2,500 sq. mi./6,500 sq. km.

an·dan·te /aan daan tay, -tee, an dántee/ *adj, adv* at a moderate musical tempo but slower than moderato (*used as a musical direction*) ■ *n* a title given to musical pieces or movements that are to be played andante [Early 18C. < Italian, "walking," present participle of *andare* "go, walk"]

an·dan·ti·no /aan daan teénō, àn dan-/ *adj, adv* at a moderate musical tempo slightly faster than andante (*used as a musical direction*) ■ *n* (*plural* **-nos**) a title given to musical pieces or movements that are to be played andantino [Early 19C. < Italian, "little andante"]

AND cir·cuit *n* ELECTRONICS same as **AND** (sense 2)

An·de·an /ándee ən/ *adj* relating to the Andes ■ *n* somebody who lives in the Andes

An·de·an-E·qua·to·ri·al *n* a family of Native South American languages, one of whose main branches is Tupi-Guarani —**An·de·an-E·qua·to·ri·al** *adj*

An·de·an mar·gin *n* an area of tectonic plate convergence along the Andes Mountain Range, characterized by thicker than normal crust and high mountains

An·der·sen /ándərssən/, **Hans Christian** (1805–75) Danish writer. His fairy tales include "The Ugly Duckling" (1843) and "The Snow Queen" (1844).

"It doesn't matter about being born in a duckyard, as long as you're hatched from a swan's egg."
[Hans Christian Andersen, "The Ugly Duckling," *Fairy Tales*; 1843]

An·der·son /ándərssən/ **1.** city in east central Indiana. It is the site of Native American burial mounds. Population: 58,853 (2002 estimate). **2.** city in northwestern South Carolina. Population: 25,690 (2002 estimate).

An·der·son, Laurie (*b.* 1947) US composer and performance artist. She combines speech, song and other vocal techniques, dance, film and projection, and unusual instruments in works such as *United States* (1984).

"I think a Benedictine convent is very close to the art world in a lot of ways. The nuns are isolated, but these are people who think and feel and have a relationship to—to a kind of ideal, a spiritual or intellectual ideal."
[Laurie Anderson. Quoted in "Laurie Anderson," *View*, Robin White (interviewer); January 1990]

An·der·son, Marian (1897–1993) US contralto. She was the first African American singer to appear at the Metropolitan Opera in New York City (1955).

"Where there is money, there is fighting."
[Marian Anderson, *Marian Anderson, A Portrait*, Kosti Verhanen; 1941]

An·der·son, Maxwell (1888–1959) US playwright and screenwriter. He wrote the plays *Elizabeth the Queen* (1930) and *Mary of Scotland* (1933) in blank verse.

"If you practice an art, be proud of it and make it proud of you..."

Marian Anderson

[Maxwell Anderson, *New York Herald Tribune*; March 7, 1959]

An·der·son, Philip W. (*b.* 1923) US physicist. He shared the Nobel Prize in physics (1977). Full name **Anderson, Philip Warren**

"You never understand everything. When one understands everything, one has gone crazy."
[Attributed to Philip W. Anderson]

An·der·son, Sherwood (1876–1941) US writer. His most famous work is the short-story collection *Winesburg, Ohio* (1919).

"The idea is very simple, so simple that if you are not careful you will forget it. It is this—that everyone in the world is Christ and they are all crucified."
[Sherwood Anderson, *Winesburg, Ohio*; 1919]

An·der·son·ville /ándərssən vìl/ site of a Confederate prison in central Georgia where approximately 14,000 Union soldiers died during the Civil War. It was made a national historic site in 1970.

Andes

An·des /ándeez/ huge South American mountain system that extends north to south along the west coast from Panama to Tierra del Fuego. It consists of several ranges and has its highest peak at Aconcagua 22,835 ft./6,960 m.

an·de·sine /ándə zeen/ *n* a hard colorless mineral of the feldspar group. Source: andesite. [Because found in the ANDES]

an·de·site /ándə zìt/ *n* a fine-grained grayish volcanic rock characterized by feldspar minerals [Because found in the ANDES] —**an·de·sit·ic** /àndə zíttik/ *adj*

And·hra Pra·desh /aandrə prə désh/ Indian state in the southeast of the country on the Bay of Bengal. Capital: Hyderabad. Population: 75,727,541 (2001). Area: 106,195 sq. mi./275,045 sq. km.

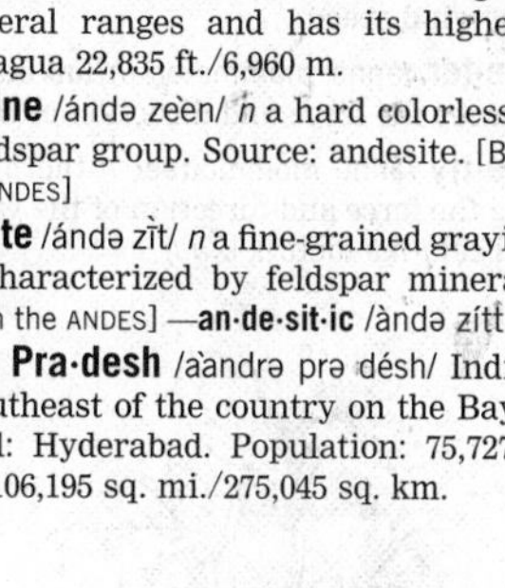

andiron

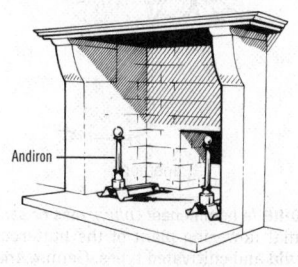

and·i·ron /ánd ìrn/ *n* either of a pair of metal stands used to hold logs in a fireplace [14C. Alteration (influenced by IRON) of Old French *andier* < Celtic]

and/or /ánd áwr/ *conj* a short way of saying that either or both of two options may be valid ○ *Bring mosquito netting and/or bug repellent.*

USAGE When to use **and/or**? ***And/or*** is a useful device to express three possibilities in a concise form: *A and/or B* gives the three possibilities A only, B only, or both A and B. On the other hand, since ***and/or*** is not a particularly elegant expression, it is best restricted to legal and business contexts. An often preferable alternative in general contexts is *A or B or both*, as in *Sarah or Anne or both will participate in the chess championship.*

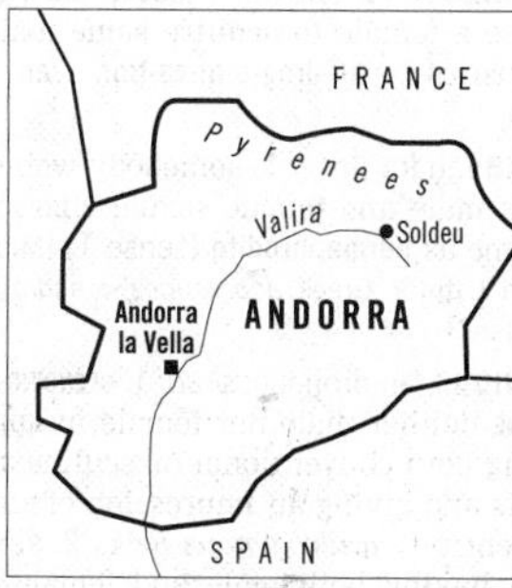

Andorra

An·dor·ra /an dáwrə/ principality in the Pyrenees Mountains between France and Spain. Language: Catalan. Currency: Euro. Capital: Andorra la Vella. Population: 69,150 (2003). Area: 181 sq. mi./468 sq. km. Official name **Principality of Andorra** —**An·dor·ran** *adj, n*

An·dor·ra la Vel·la /-lə véllə/ capital of the Principality of Andorra. Population: 25,000 (1999).

an·dou·ille /aan dóo ee, awn dweé, aaN dweé/ *n* **1.** a long spicy smoked pork sausage used in Cajun cooking **2.** a black-skinned French sausage [Early 17C. < French]

An·do·ver /án dōvər, ándəvər/ town in northeastern Massachusetts, north of Boston. It is home to Phillips Academy, one of the oldest preparatory schools in the United States. Population: 31,818 (2002 estimate).

andr- *prefix* same as **andro-** (*used before vowels*)

an·dra·dite /an draa dìt/ *n* a variously colored precious stone that is a variety of garnet and is composed of calcium iron silicate. Use: gems. [Mid-19C. After José Bonifácio de *Andrada* e Silva (1763?–1838), Brazilian geologist and independence leader]

An·dre /aan dràỳ/, **Carl** (*b.* 1935) US sculptor. He is known for abstract minimalist sculptures made of mass-produced objects such as bricks and metal plates.

An·dré /aan dràỳ/, **John** (1750–80) British soldier and spy in the American Revolution. He conspired to turn over West Point to the British (1780), but was captured and hanged.

An·dre·a del Sar·to /aan dràỳ ə del saartō/ (1486–1530) Italian High Renaissance painter based in Florence. He is best known for his series of frescoes depicting the life of John the Baptist.

An·dre·a·nof Is·lands /ándree ánnəf-, aandree aanəf-/ group of islands in southwestern Alaska, forming part of the Aleutian Islands

An·drees·sen /an dráyss'n/, **Marc** (*b.* 1971) US computer scientist. He developed and commercialized Internet browser software.

An·drew /ándroo/, **St.** (*d.* A.D. 60) one of the 12 apostles of Jesus Christ. He preached the Gospel in Scythia and was crucified in Achaea. He is the patron saint of Russia, Greece, and Scotland.

An·drews /ándrooz/, **Julie** (*b.* 1935) British-born US actor and singer. She made her Broadway debut in the musical *My Fair Lady* (1956) and starred in the popular films *Mary Poppins* (1964) and *The Sound of Music* (1965). Born **Wells, Julia Elizabeth**

andro- *prefix* male, masculine ○ *androgen* [< Greek < *andr-*, stem of *anēr* "man"]

An·dro·cles /ándrə kleez/ *n* in Roman legend, a slave who was forced to fight a lion, which spared his life after recognizing Androcles as the man who had once removed a thorn from its paw

an·droe·ci·um /an dreeshee əm, -shəm/ (*plural* **-ci·a** /-shee ə, -shə/) *n* the set of stamens in a single flower [Mid-19C. < modern Latin < Greek *andro-* "man, male" + *oikion* "house"] —**an·droe·cial** *adj*

an·dro·gen /ándrəjən/ *n* a natural or artificial male sex hormone responsible for the development of male sexual characteristics. Testosterone and androsterone are androgens. —**an·dro·gen·ic** /àndrə jénnik/ *adj*

an·drog·e·nize /an drójjə nīz/ (**-nized, -niz·ing, -niz·es**) *vt* to cause a female to acquire some male sexual characteristics —**an·drog·e·ni·za·tion** /an dròjjəni záysh'n/ *n*

an·dro·gyne /ándrə jīn/ *n* **1.** somebody who seems to have both male and female sexual characteristics **2.** BIOL same as **hermaphrodite** (sense 1) [Mid-16C. Via French and Latin < Greek *androgunos* < *andro-* "man" + *gunē* "woman"]

an·drog·y·nous /an drójjənəss/ *adj* **1. BLENDING MASCULINE AND FEMININE** neither male nor female in appearance but having both conventional masculine and feminine traits and giving an impression of ambiguous sexual identity ○ *androgynous looks* **2.** PHYSIOL **HERMAPHRODITE** having both male and female physical characteristics **3.** BOT **WITH BOTH MALE AND FEMALE FLOWERS** describes a plant species in which both male and female flowers occur in the same flower head [Early 17C. < Latin *androgynus* "hermaphrodite" (see ANDROGYNE)] —**an·drog·y·nous·ly** *adv* —**an·drog·y·ny** *n*

an·droid /án dròyd/ *n* in science fiction, a robot that looks and behaves like a human being [Early 18C. < modern Latin *androides* < Greek *andro-* "man"]

An·drom·a·che /an drómmәkee/ *n* in Greek mythology, a princess of Troy and the wife of Hector, who led the Trojan women throughout the Trojan War

an·drom·e·da /an drómmədə/ (*plural same* or **-das**) *n* an evergreen bush of the heath family. Flowers: pink, drooping in clusters. Genera: *Andromeda* or *Pieris*. [Mid-18C. < modern Latin, after ANDROMEDA (sense 1)]

Andromeda Galaxy: photographed from the Palomar Observatory, California Institute of Technology

An·drom·e·da /an drómmədə/ *n* **1.** in Greek mythology, the daughter of Cassiopeia, who was saved from a sea monster by her future husband, Perseus **2.** a constellation of the northern hemisphere containing a spiral galaxy (**Andromeda Galaxy**) that can be seen with the naked eye. See illustration at **constellation**

an·dro·pause /ándrō pàwz/ *n* PSYCHOL same as **male menopause** [Late 20C. After MENOPAUSE] —**an·dro·paus·al** /àndrō páwz'l/ *adj*

An·dro·pov /an dróppov/, **Yuri** (1914–84) president of the former Soviet Union (1983–84). He was chairman of the KGB (1967–82), general secretary of the Communist Party from 1982, and succeeded Brezhnev as president in 1983. Full name **Andropov, Yuri Vladimirovich**

An·dros /án dròss, ándrəss/, **Sir Edmund** (1637–1714) English-born American colonial administrator. He governed the English North American colonies of New York (1674–81), New England (1686–89), Virginia (1692–98), and Maryland (1693–94).

an·dro·sten·e·di·one /àndrō steén dīōn/ *n* a dietary supplement that increases testosterone production, energy, strength, and muscle development. Unwanted side effects include disruption of hormonal balance, leading to aggressive behavior and mood swings, and hair loss. [Mid-20C. < ANDROSTERONE + -ENE + DI-1 + -ONE]

an·dros·ter·one /an dróstə rōn/ *n* a weak male sex hormone produced by males and females [Mid-20C. < ANDRO- + STEROL + -ONE]

-andry *suffix* **1.** the condition of having a particular number of males or husbands ○ *polyandry* **2.** the condition of having a particular number of stamens ○ *monandry* [< Greek *-andria* < *andr-*, stem of *anēr* "man"] —**-androus** *suffix*

-ane *suffix* a saturated hydrocarbon ○ *methane* [After -ENE, -ONE]

a·near /ə neér/ (*archaic or literary*) *prep* near to ○ *"I wouldn't ever go anear that house again"* (Mark Twain, *The Adventures of Huckleberry Finn*; 1884) ■ *adv* nearby

an·ec·dot·al /ànnək dṓt'l/ *adj* **1.** consisting of or based on secondhand accounts rather than firsthand knowledge or experience or scientific investigation ○ *anecdotal evidence* **2.** relating to anecdotes or in the form of anecdotes —**an·ec·do·tal·ly** *adv*

an·ec·dote /ánnək dōt/ *n* a short personal account of an incident or event [Early 18C. Directly or via French < modern Latin *anecdota* < Greek *anekdota* "things unpublished" < *an-* "not" + *ekdidonai* "publish"]

an·ec·dot·ic /ànnək dóttik/ *adj* same as **anecdotal**

an·e·cho·ic /ànnə kṓ ik/ *adj* producing or characterized by few or no echoes (*technical*)

a·ne·mi·a /ə neémee ə/, **a·nae·mi·a** *n* **1.** a blood condition in which there are too few red blood cells or the red blood cells are deficient in hemoglobin, resulting in poor health. Common causes include a lack of dietary iron, heavy blood loss, or the production of too few red blood cells due to disorders such as leukemia. **2.** lack of vitality or courage [Early 19C. Via modern Latin < Greek *anaimia* "being without blood" < *haima* "blood"]

a·ne·mic /ə neémik/, **a·nae·mic** *adj* **1.** MED **HAVING ANEMIA** having some form of anemia **2. SICK-LOOKING** pale and not looking well **3. WEAK** lacking vitality, strength, or courage —**a·ne·mic·al·ly** *adv*

anemo- *prefix* wind ○ *anemography* [< Greek *anemos* "wind" < Indo-European, "breathe"]

a·nem·o·chore /ə némmə kàwr/ *n* a plant that depends on the wind to disperse its seeds or fruits

an·e·mog·ra·phy /ànnə móggrəfee/ *n* the process of measuring wind speed

an·e·mom·e·ter /ànnə mómmətər/ *n* an instrument that measures the force and direction of the wind

an·e·mom·e·try /ànnə mómmətree/ *n* the process of measuring the force and direction of the wind —**an·e·mo·met·ri·cal** /-mə méttrik'l/ *adj*

anemone

a·nem·o·ne /ə némmənee/ (*plural* **-nes** or *same*) *n* **1.** a perennial flowering plant of the buttercup family with wild and cultivated types. Genus: *Anemone*. **2.** MARINE BIOL same as **sea anemone** [Mid-16C. Via Latin < Greek *anemōnē*]

a·nem·o·ne fish *n* a small colorful damselfish with stinging cells, found in close association with sea anemones. Native to: tropical coral reefs. Genus: *Amphiprion*.

an·e·moph·i·lous /ànnə móffələss/ *adj* describes a plant species that is pollinated by the wind —**an·e·moph·i·ly** *n*

an·en·ceph·a·ly /àn en séffəlee/ *n* the absence of all or a part of the brain and part of the skull at birth —**an·en·ce·phal·ic** /àn enssə fállik/ *adj*

~~anenome~~ incorrect spelling of **anemone**

an·er·gy /á nurjee, ánnə-/ *n* decreased immunity or lack of immunity to an antigen [Late 19C. < modern Latin *anergia* < Greek *an-* "without" + *ergon* "work"] —**an·er·gic** /a núrjik/ *adj*

an·er·oid /ánnə ròyd/ *adj* not containing or using liquid [Mid-19C. < French *anéroïde* < Greek *a-* "without" + *nēron* "water, liquid"]

an·er·oid ba·rom·e·ter *n* an instrument for indicating atmospheric pressure on a circular dial

an·es·the·sia /ànnəss theézhə/, **an·aes·the·sia** *n* **1.** MEDICALLY **INDUCED INSENSITIVITY TO PAIN** induced loss of sensitivity to pain in all or a part of the body for medical reasons. Methods include drugs, acupuncture, and hypnosis. The procedure may render the patient unconscious (**general anesthesia**) or merely numb a body part (**local anesthesia**). **2. LOSS OF SENSATION** the loss of sensation caused by damage to a nerve **3. APATHY** a state of apathy or mindlessness [Early 18C. Via modern Latin < Greek *anaisthēsia* "lack of sensation" < *aisthēsis* "feeling, sensation" (see AESTHESIA)]

an·es·the·si·ol·o·gist /ànnəss theezee óllәjist/, **an·aes·the·si·ol·o·gist** *n US* a doctor qualified to administer anesthetics to patients. ◊ **anesthetist** (sense 1).

an·es·the·si·ol·o·gy /ànnəss theezee óllәjee/, **an·aes·the·si·ol·o·gy** *n US* the branch of medicine that deals with the study and use of anesthetic substances. Can term **anaesthetics**

an·es·thet·ic /ànnəss théttik/, **an·aes·thet·ic** *n* a substance that reduces sensitivity to pain and may cause unconsciousness, especially a drug used in medicine [Mid-19C. < Greek *anaisthētos* "without feeling" < *aisthētos* "capable of feeling" < *aisthesthai* "perceive"] —**an·es·thet·ic** *adj* —**an·es·thet·ic·al·ly** *adv*

a·nes·the·tist /ə nésthətist/, **a·naes·the·tist** *n* **1.** somebody qualified to administer anesthetics, especially a nurse or technician **2.** *Can, UK* a senior doctor who specializes in administering anaesthetics. US term **anesthesiologist**

a·nes·the·tize /ə nésthə tīz/ (**-tized, -tiz·ing, -tiz·es**), **a·naes·the·tize** (**-tized, -tiz·ing, -tiz·es**) *vt* to administer an anesthetic to somebody —**an·es·the·ti·za·tion** /ə nèsthətə záysh'n/ *n*

an·es·trous /an éstrəss/ *adj* **1.** describes a female mammal that is sexually inactive between breeding periods **2.** describes the period of sexual inactivity between breeding periods in some female mammals

an·es·trus /an éstrəss/ *n* the period of sexual inactivity between the breeding periods of some female mammals

an·eu·ploid /ánnyə plòyd/ *adj* describes a cell or organism with fewer or more chromosomes than usual —**an·eu·ploid** *n* —**an·eu·ploid·y** *n*

an·eu·rysm /ánnyə rìzzəm/, **an·eu·rism** *n* a fluid-filled sac in the wall of an artery that can weaken the wall [15C. < Greek *aneurusma* "dilation, swelling" < *aneurunein* "widen out" < *ana-* "through" + *eurus* "wide"] —**an·eu·rys·mal** /ànnyə rízm'l/ *adj*

a·new /ə noó/ *adv* **1.** once more **2.** in a new way or form that is unlike the previous one [14C. < *a-* (reduced form of *of*) + NEW; probably after Old French *de neuf, de nouveau*]

ANFO /án fō/ *n* a binary explosive made of ammonium nitrate and fuel oil. Use: in mining. Full form **ammonium nitrate and fuel oil**

an·frac·tu·os·i·ty /àn frakchoo óssətee/ (*plural* **-ties**) *n* (*literary*) **1.** a twist or turn, e.g., in a road or in the plot of a novel **2.** the twisting turning nature of something [Late 16C. < French *anfractuosité* < late Latin *anfractuosus* < Latin *anfractus* "bending"] —**an·frac·tu·ous** /an frákchoo əss/ *adj*

Ang. *abbr* Angola

an·gel /áynjəl/ *n* **1.** HEAVENLY BEING in some religions, a divine being who acts as a messenger of God **2.** PICTURE OF HEAVENLY BEING a depiction of an angel as a human figure with wings **3.** KIND PERSON somebody who is kind or beautiful **4.** GUARDIAN AND GUIDE a spirit that protects and offers guidance **5.** FIN FINANCIAL BACKER somebody who provides financial support for an enterprise, e.g., a theatrical venture (*informal*) **6.** CHR MEMBER OF LOWEST ANGELIC ORDER an angel of the first of the nine orders of angels in the traditional Christian hierarchy. The nine orders are, in ascending order, angels, archangels, principalities, powers, virtues, dominations, thrones, cherubim, and seraphim. **7.** MONEY OLD ENGLISH COIN a gold coin that was a unit of currency in England between the 15th and early 17th centuries [13C. Via Old French and ecclesiastical Latin < Greek *aggelos* "messenger"]

SYNONYMS See *backer.*

an·gel cake *n UK* same as **angel food cake**

an·gel dust *n* the illegal hallucinogenic drug phencyclidine (*slang*)

An·ge·le·no /ànjə léenō/ (*plural* **-nos**) *n Hispanic* somebody who comes from Los Angeles, California [Late 19C. < American Spanish *angeleño*]

REGIONAL NOTE The term ***Angeleno*** was formerly restricted to southern California, but is now widespread across the United States.

An·gel Falls /áynjəl fàwlz/ the world's highest waterfall, located in southeastern Venezuela in the Guiana Highlands. Height: 3,212 ft./979 m.

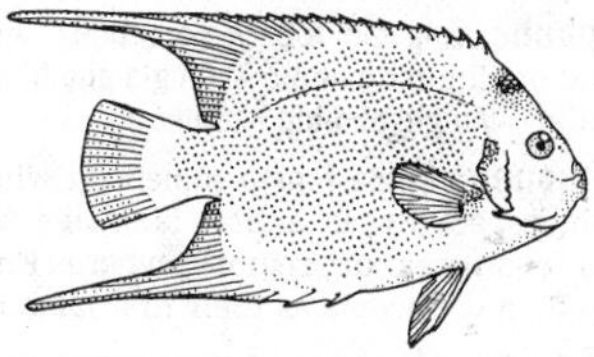

angelfish

an·gel·fish /áynjəl fish/ (*plural same* or **-fish·es**) *n* **1.** a freshwater fish with a broad striped body and large fins that is often kept in aquariums. Native to: the tropical rivers of South America. Latin name: *Pterophyllum scalare.* **2.** a brightly colored ocean fish that has a broad flat body. Native to: tropics. Family: Chaetodontidae *or* Pomacanthidae. **3.** FISH same as **angel shark**

an·gel food cake *n* a whitish light-textured cake made with egg whites but without yolks

an·gel·ic /an jéllik/, **an·gel·i·cal** /-jéllik'l/ *adj* **1.** KIND OR BEAUTIFUL very kind or beautiful **2.** WELL-BEHAVED not disturbing or annoying other people **3.** OF ANGELS relating to angels —**an·gel·i·cal·ly** *adv*

an·gel·i·ca /an jéllikə/ (*plural* **-cas** or *same*) *n* **1.** bright green, candied plant stems. Use: decorating cakes and cookies. **2.** a tall hollow-stemmed plant of the carrot family that is the source of angelica. Native to: Europe, Asia. Genus: *Angelica.* [Early 16C. < medieval Latin, short for *herba angelica* "angelic plant"]

an·gel·i·cal *adj* same as **angelic**

An·gel·i·co /an jélli kō/, **Fra** (1400?–55) Italian religious painter. He became a Dominican monk. He is noted for his frescoes in Florence, including the *Annunciation* and the *Coronation of the Virgin.* Born **Guido di Pietro**

an·gel of mer·cy *n* somebody who brings welcome assistance

An·ge·lou /ánjə lòo/, **Maya** (*b.* 1928) US writer. Her novels and poetry are notable for their depiction of assertive African American women.

Barnaby's

Maya Angelou

"History, despite the wrenching pain, / Cannot be unlived, but if faced / With courage, need not be lived again."
[Maya Angelou, poem read at President Bill Clinton's Inauguration; January 20, 1993]

an·gel shark *n* a small shark with a flat body, broad head, and enlarged pectoral fins, giving it the appearance of a ray. Genus: *Squatina.* [< its winglike pectoral fins]

An·ge·lus /ánjələss/, **an·ge·lus** *n* **1.** in the Roman Catholic Church, a set of prayers to commemorate the Annunciation and the Incarnation **2.** a bell rung to announce the time for the Angelus [Mid-17C. < Latin *Angelus domini* "the angel of the Lord," the first words of the prayers]

an·ger /áng gər/ *n* a strong feeling of grievance and displeasure ■ *vti* (**-gered, -ger·ing, -gers**) to become or make somebody extremely annoyed [13C. < Old Norse *angr* "trouble, sorrow"]

CULTURAL NOTE ***Look Back in Anger,*** a play (1956) by British dramatist John Osborne. Seen at the time of its first performances as a landmark play that reflected the disaffection of many young people, this domestic drama focuses on Jimmy Porter, a working-class graduate who feels stifled by the middle-class family into which he has married and trapped by social conventions.

SYNONYMS ***anger, annoyance, irritation, resentment, indignation, fury, rage, ire, wrath***

CORE MEANING: a feeling of strong displeasure in response to an assumed injury

anger a strong feeling of grievance and displeasure ○ *His face turned white with anger.* ○ *She could feel the anger bubbling up inside her.* **annoyance** mild anger and impatience ○ *Her untidiness was a source of annoyance to him.* ○ *I couldn't find my credit card, much to the annoyance of the people in line behind me.* **irritation** a feeling of impatience or exasperation ○ *replied with ill-concealed irritation* ○ *a sign of his intense irritation with his distant superiors* **resentment** aggrieved feelings caused by a sense of having been badly treated ○ *The policy provoked bitter resentment throughout the police force.* ○ *Try to overcome your feelings of resentment at being denied this experience.* **indignation** anger because something seems unfair or unreasonable ○ *The woman protested in righteous indignation at the idea.* **fury** violent anger ○ *Their eyes were fixed on each other in cold fury.* ○ *Fury at the rejection welled up in him.* **rage** sudden and extreme anger ○ *jealous rage* ○ *Toby flew into a rage.* **ire** (*literary*) strong anger ○ *a change that raised the ire of union members* ○ *This decision drew the ire of rights activists.* **wrath** strong anger, often with a desire for revenge ○ *the wrath of God* ○ *I don't want to incur the wrath of my manager by changing the plan.*

An·gers /aaN zháy/ capital of Maine-et-Loire Department in the Pays de la Loire Region in western France. Population: 151,279 (1999).

An·ge·vin /ánjəvin/ *adj* **1.** relating to the Anjou region in France **2.** relating to the House of Anjou, especially the branch that includes the Plantagenet kings of England [Mid-17C. Via French < medieval Latin *Andegavinus* < *Andegavia* "Anjou"]

an·gi·na /an jīnə, ánjənə/, **an·gi·na pec·to·ris** /-péktəriss/ *n* a medical condition in which lack of blood to the heart causes severe chest pains [Mid-16C. < Latin, "quinsy," alteration (after *angere* "to squeeze") of Greek *agkhonē* "strangling" < *agkhein* "to squeeze, strangle"]

angio- *prefix* **1.** blood or lymph vessel ○ *angiogram* **2.** pericarp ○ *angiosperm* [< modern Latin < Greek *aggeion* "blood vessel" < *aggos* "vessel"]

an·gi·o·car·di·og·ra·phy /ànjee ō kaardee óggrəfee/ *n* X-ray examination of the heart and related blood vessels after a substance that will show up when X-rayed has been injected into the bloodstream —**an·gi·o·car·di·o·graph·ic** /-kaardee ə gráffik/ *adj*

an·gi·o·gen·e·sis /ànjee ō jénnəssəss/ *n* the formation of new blood vessels, e.g., in an embryo or as a result of a tumor

an·gi·o·gram /ánjee ə gràm/ *n* an X-ray photograph of a blood vessel

an·gi·og·raph·y /ànjee óggrəfee/ *n* X-ray examination of blood vessels after a substance that will show up when X-rayed has been injected into the bloodstream —**an·gi·o·graph·ic** /ànjee ə gráffik/ *adj*

an·gi·ol·o·gy /ànjee óllәjee/ *n* the branch of medicine that deals with blood vessels and the lymphatic system

an·gi·o·ma /ànjee ṓmə/ (*plural* **-mas** or **-ma·ta** /-mətə/) *n* a benign tumor made up of blood or lymph vessels —**an·gi·o·ma·tous** *adj*

an·gi·op·a·thy /ànjee óppəthee/ (*plural* **-thies**) *n* a disease of the blood vessels or lymph vessels

an·gi·o·plas·ty /ánjee ə plàstee/ (*plural* **-ties**) *n* a surgical operation to clear a narrowed or blocked artery

an·gi·o·sar·co·ma /ànjee ō saar kṓmə/ (*plural* **-mas** or **-ma·ta** /-mətə/) *n* a malignant tumor consisting of vascular cells, often in the liver

an·gi·o·scope /ánjee ə skōp/ *n* a long fine surgical viewing instrument threaded into a patient's blood vessels to allow surgeons to observe and perform operations without large incisions —**an·gi·os·co·py** /ànjee óskəpee/ *n*

an·gi·o·spasm /ánjee ə spàzzəm/ *n* a spasmodic contraction of a blood vessel

an·gi·o·sperm /ánjee ə spùrm/ *n* a plant in which the sex organs are within flowers and the seeds are in a fruit [Early 19C. < ANGIO- + Greek *sperma* "seed"] —**an·gi·o·sper·mous** /ànjee ə spúrməss/ *adj* —**an·gi·o·sper·my** *n*

an·gi·o·stat·in /ánjee ə stàttin/ *n* a naturally occurring protein in the body that plays a role in inhibiting the formation of new blood vessels

an·gi·o·ten·sin /ànjee ō ténssən/ *n* a hormone that causes blood pressure to rise, formed in the blood by a series of processes that can be influenced by drugs [Mid-20C. < ANGIO- + HYPERTENSION + -IN]

an·gi·o·ten·sin-con·vert·ing en·zyme in·hib·i·tor *n* PHARM full form of **ACE inhibitor**

Barnaby's

Angkor

Ang·kor /áng kàwr/, **Âng·kôr** ancient capital city of early Khmer civilization, now deserted but noted for its temples and monuments, built 850–900. It is in present-day northwestern Cambodia. Area: 5 sq. mi./13 sq. km.

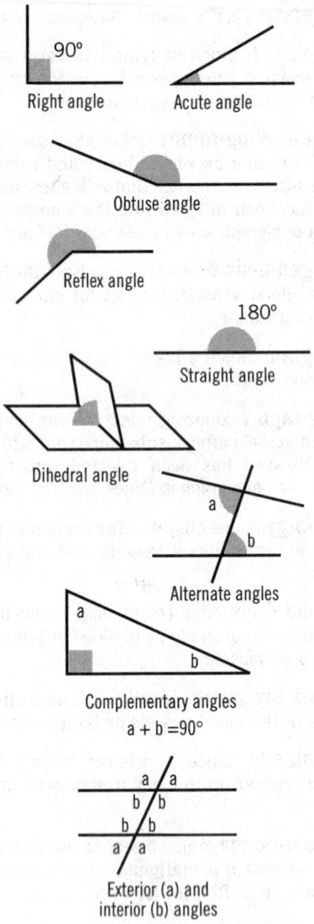

angle

an·gle[1] /áng g'l/ *n* **1.** SPACE BETWEEN DIVERGING LINES the space between two diverging lines or planes, or a measure of the space **2.** FIGURE FORMED BY DIVERGING LINES a figure formed by two lines diverging from a common point or two planes diverging from a common line **3.** MATH same as **solid angle 4.** PART THAT STICKS OUT a projecting part of something **5.** POSITION FOR VIEWING SOMETHING a position from which somebody can look at something ○ *a sculpture seen from three angles* **6.** WAY OF CONSIDERING SOMETHING a way of looking at a situation ○ *Consider the matter from this angle.* ■ *v* (**-gled, -gling, -gles**) **1.** *vti* PLACE SOMETHING, OR BE PLACED, OBLIQUELY to direct or place something obliquely, or move or be placed obliquely **2.** *vt* PRESENT SOMETHING WITH BIAS to present something with a particular audience in mind or in order to express a particular point of view **3.** *vi* CHANGE DIRECTION SHARPLY to turn in a sharply different direction [14C. Directly or via French < Latin *angulus* "corner"]

an·gle[2] /áng g'l/ (**-gled, -gling, -gles**) *vi* **1.** to fish with a hook, line, and rod **2.** to attempt to obtain a compliment or an advantage (*informal*) [Old English *angul* "fishhook" < Indo-European, "to bend, hook"]

An·gle /áng g'l/ *n* a member of a Germanic people who invaded and settled eastern and northern England in the 5th and 6th centuries A.D. [Pre-12C. < Latin *Angli* "people from Angul" (in N Germany)] —**An·gli·an** /áng glee ən/ *adj, n*

an·gle bar *n* CONSTR same as **angle iron**

an·gle brack·et *n* either of a pair of marks (< or >) used to enclose text

an·gle i·ron *n* an iron or steel bar that is L-shaped in cross section

an·gle of at·tack *n* the acute angle between the direction of airflow and the line linking the leading and trailing edges of an aircraft wing

an·gle of in·ci·dence *n* the angle between an incoming ray of light and the line perpendicular to the surface at the point of arrival

an·gle of re·flec·tion *n* the angle between a reflected ray of light and the line perpendicular to the surface at the point of reflection

an·gle of re·frac·tion *n* the angle between a refracted ray of light and the line perpendicular to the surface at the point of refraction

an·gle of re·pose *n* the maximum slope or angle at which unconsolidated material such as sand can be made into a mound before it begins to slide

an·gle plate *n* an L-shaped metal plate used to support a framework

an·gler /áng glər/ *n* **1.** somebody who fishes with a hook, line, and rod **2.** FISH same as **anglerfish**

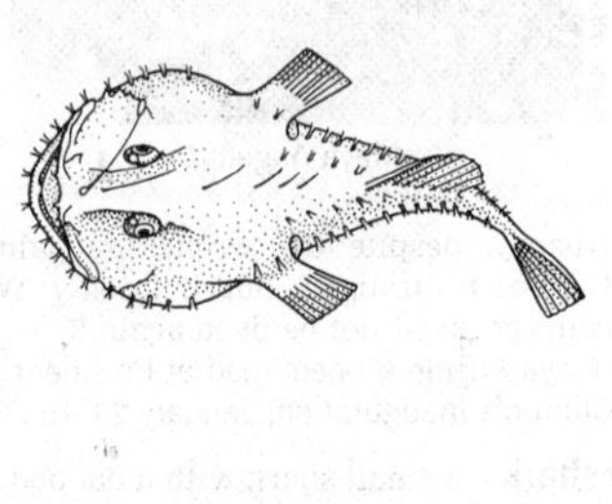
anglerfish

an·gler·fish /áng glər fish/ (*plural same* or **-fish·es**) *n* an ocean fish that uses a long dorsal fin extending over its mouth to attract prey. Order: Lophiiformes.

An·gle·sey /áng g'lssee/ island off the coast of northwestern Wales, the largest island in England and Wales. Population: 66,829 (2001). Area: 261 sq. mi./676 sq. km.

an·gle·site /áng g'l sīt/ *n* a colorless, white, or lightly tinted lead sulfate mineral [Mid-19C. < ANGLESEY]

An·gli·can /áng gləkən/ *adj* relating to the Anglican Church ■ *n* a member of an Anglican Church [Early 17C. < medieval Latin *Anglicanus* "English" < Latin *Angli* "the Angles"; from its originally denoting the Church of England]

An·gli·can Church *n* a group of Christian churches including the Churches of England and Ireland, as well as the Protestant Episcopal Church

An·gli·can Com·mu·nion *n* a worldwide association of churches related to the Church of England, e.g., the Protestant Episcopal Church, with the Archbishop of Canterbury at its head

An·gli·can·ism /áng glәkә nìzzəm/ *n* the doctrines of the Church of England and other Anglican churches

An·gli·cism /áng glə sizzəm/, **an·gli·cism** *n* **1.** a term that is peculiar to British English as opposed to other varieties of English **2.** an English word or phrase used in a foreign language [Mid-17C. < medieval Latin *Anglicus* "English" < Latin *Angli* "the Angles"]

An·gli·cize /áng glə sīz/ (**-cized, -ciz·ing, -ciz·es**), **an·gli·cize** (**-cized, -ciz·ing, -ciz·es**) *vti* to become or make somebody or something more English [Early 18C. < medieval Latin *Anglicus* (see ANGLICISM)] —**An·gli·ci·za·tion** /áng gləssi záysh'n/ *n*

An·glin /áng glin/, **Margaret** (1876–1958) Canadian actor. She was a stage performer in Canada, Australia, and the United States.

an·gling /áng gling/ *n* the sport of catching fish with a hook, line, and rod

An·glo /áng glō/ (*plural* **-glos**), **an·glo** *n* (*informal*) **1.** *Hispanic* an English-speaking white person in the United States who is not of Hispanic origin **2.** *Can* an English-speaking person in Canada, especially in Quebec [Early 19C. < ANGLO-]

USAGE ***Anglo*** is the counterpart of *Latino/Latina* or *Hispanic*. In one sense it refers to any white person whose first language is English and whose descent is not Latin American or Hispanic. In another sense ***Anglo*** refers to any Canadian person whose first language is English and whose descent is British, not French.

Anglo- *prefix* England, the English, British ○ *Anglophile* ○ *Anglo-American* [< Latin *Angli* "the Angles"]

An·glo-A·mer·i·can *n* a citizen of the United States or Canada whose ancestors were originally from Great Britain and whose language and culture derive from Great Britain

An·glo-A·sian *n* somebody from the United Kingdom whose family originally came from South Asia

An·glo·bal·i·za·tion /àng glōb'li záysh'n/ *n* POL, INTERNAT REL the British imperial process and network of emigration, trade, and rule that eventually broke down starting in 1914 but reappeared in 1989 after the end of the Cold War, with the central sphere of influence moving from London to Washington, DC

An·glo-French *adj* relating to the links that exist between France and Great Britain

An·glo-In·di·an *adj* FROM SOUTH ASIAN LANGUAGE introduced into English from a South Asian language ■ *n* **1.** SOMEBODY WITH BRITISH AND INDIAN ANCESTRY somebody of both British and South Asian descent **2.** BRITISH PERSON RESIDENT IN INDIA a British person who lived or has lived a long time in South Asia, especially during the time of former British India, from 1765 to 1947

An·glo-I·rish *npl* IRISH PEOPLE WITH ENGLISH ANCESTRY people of English descent who were born or who live in Ireland ■ *adj* **1.** ENGLISH AND IRISH relating to the United Kingdom and Ireland or the Republic of Ireland **2.** OF THE ANGLO-IRISH of English descent but from or living in Ireland

An·glo-Lat·in *n* a form of Latin used in medieval England, having some English loanwords and forms

An·glo-Nor·man *adj* ENGLISH AND NORMAN relating to the 11th-century Norman conquerors of England ■ *n* **1.** HIST NORMAN IN ENGLAND a Norman inhabitant of England after 1066 **2.** LANG FRENCH SPOKEN IN MEDIEVAL ENGLAND the variety of Norman French spoken in medieval England

An·glo·phile /áng glə fīl/ *n* an admirer of England or English people —**An·glo·phil·i·a** /àng glə fíllee ə/ *n* —**An·glo·phil·ic** /àng glə fíllik/ *adj*

An·glo·phobe /áng glə fōb/ *n* somebody who hates England or English people —**An·glo·pho·bi·a** /àng glə fōbee ə/ *n* —**An·glo·pho·bic** /-fōbik/ *adj*

an·glo·phone /áng glə fōn/ *n* somebody who speaks English, especially as a first language ■ *adj* describes countries or regions where English is spoken by most people as their first language

An·glo-Sax·on *n* **1.** PEOPLES MEMBER OF GERMANIC PEOPLE a member of a West Germanic people who settled in Britain from the 5th century A.D. and were dominant until 1066. They included the Angles, Saxons, and Jutes. **2.** LANG same as **Old English** (sense 1) **3.** ENGLISH NATIVE SPEAKER a white speaker of English as a first language ■ *adj* **1.** LANG FROM OLD ENGLISH describes a word in Modern English that comes from Old English **2.** OF ENGLISH SPEAKERS relating to white English speakers

An·glo·sphere /áng glō sfeer/ *n* English-speaking nations such as Britain, Australia, and New Zealand and their lands, territories, heritages, and common political, economic, and security interests

ang mo /àng mṓ/ (*plural* **ang mos**) *n Malaysia, Singapore* an inhabitant of the West, especially western Europe or North America (*informal*) [< Hokkien, "red hair"]

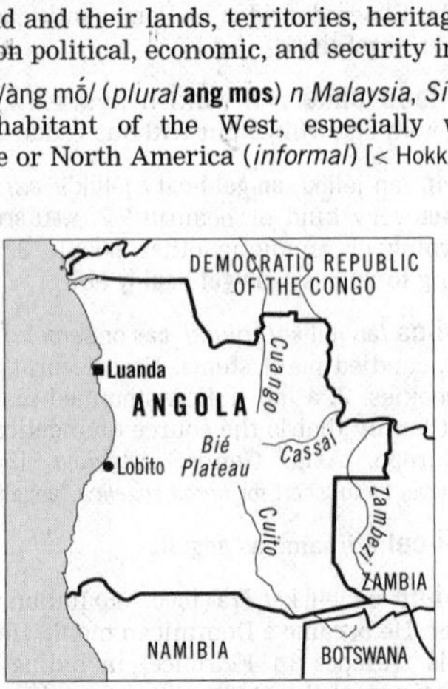

Angola

An·go·la /ang gṓlə/ country in west central Africa that gained its independence from Portugal in 1975. Language: Portuguese. Currency: kwanza. Capital: Luanda. Population: 10,766,471 (2003 estimate).

Area: 481,530 sq. mi./1,246,700 sq. km. Official name **Republic of Angola** —**An·go·lan** *adj, n*

an·go·ra /ang gáwrə/ *n* **1.** wool made from the hair of an angora goat or rabbit (*often used before a noun*) **2.** a rabbit, goat, or cat belonging to a breed with long silky fur [Early 19C. < ANGORA]

An·go·ra /ang gáwrə/ former name for **Ankara** (until 1930)

an·gos·tu·ra /àng gə stóorə/, **an·gos·tu·ra bark** *n* the bitter aromatic bark of either of two South American citrus trees. Use: flavoring in bitters and formerly to relieve fever. [After *Angostura* (now Ciudad Bolívar), Venezuela]

an·gri·ly /áng grəlee/ *adv* **1.** in a way that conveys extreme annoyance or displeasure **2.** in a stormy threatening way

an·gry /áng gree/ (**-gri·er, -gri·est**) *adj* **1. FEELING VERY ANNOYED** feeling extremely annoyed, often about an insult or a wrong **2. EXPRESSING ANNOYANCE** expressing extreme annoyance ○ *"Low growls and angry snarls assailed our ears on every side..."* (Edgar Rice Burroughs, *The Gods of Mars*; 1913) **3. STORMY** stormy-looking **4. INFLAMED** inflamed and painful-looking ○ *an angry bruise* [14C. < ANGER]

an·gry young man *n* **1.** *also* **An·gry Young Man** a member of a group of British men writing in the 1950s who were hostile to authority. The setting for their works is typically working-class, and the central character typically a lone man. (*often used in the plural*) **2.** a young man who is hostile to authority

angst /angkst, aangkst/ *n* **1.** in existentialist philosophy, a feeling of dread arising from an awareness of free choice **2.** any feeling of dread or anxiety [Early 20C. < German]

SYNONYMS See *worry.*

angst·rid·den *adj* dominated by a feeling of dread or anxiety

ang·strom /ángstrəm/ *n* **1.** *also* **ang·strom u·nit** a unit of length equal to one ten-billionth of a meter (10^{-10} m), used to measure the wavelengths of electromagnetic radiations. Symbol **Å** **2.** the letter "a" with a mark (°) placed above it, used in some Scandinavian languages to indicate a change in pronunciation from "a" to "aw." See table at **diacritic** [Late 19C. After Anders Jonas *Ångström* (1814–74), Swedish physicist]

An·guil·la /ang gwíllə/ one of the Leeward Islands, in the eastern Caribbean, east of Puerto Rico. Area: 35 sq. mi./91 sq. km. Population: 12,446 (2002 estimate)

an·guish /áng gwish/ *n* extreme anxiety or emotional torment ■ *vti* (**-guished, -guish·ing, -guish·es**) to feel or cause somebody to feel anguish [12C. < Old French *anguis* < Latin *angustus* "narrow, tight"]

an·guished /áng gwisht/ *adj* feeling or producing extreme anxiety or torment

an·gu·lar /áng gyələr/ *adj* **1. SHARPLY DEFINED** describes an object with a lot of angles **2. THIN** thin and bony **3. AWKWARD AND UNGAINLY** stiff, awkward, and ungainly **4.** MATH **MEASURED BY ANGLES** measured by an angle or rate of change of an angle [14C. < Latin *angularis* < *angulus* "corner"] —**an·gu·lar·ly** *adv*

an·gu·lar ac·cel·er·a·tion *n* the rate at which the rotation of a rotating body changes. Symbol α

an·gu·lar dis·place·ment *n* the angle through which something has been rotated about an axis, usually measured in radians

an·gu·lar fre·quen·cy *n* the frequency of a repeating rotation expressed in radians per second and multiplied by 2π. Symbol ω

an·gu·lar·i·ty /àng gyə lárrətee/ (*plural* **-ties**) *n* **1.** the thin and bony appearance of somebody's body **2.** a sharp corner or angle (*often used in the plural*)

an·gu·lar mo·men·tum *n* the momentum that a body has due to its rotation about an axis, calculated as the product of its mass and its angular velocity. Symbol *L*

an·gu·lar sto·ma·ti·tis *n* a condition of the lips, mouth, and cheeks characterized by cracks and fissures and caused by a bacterial infection

an·gu·lar ve·loc·i·ty *n* the rate of rotation of a body around an axis. Symbol ω

An·gus[1] /áng gəss/ (*plural* **same** or **-gus·es**) *n US* a cow belonging to a shorthaired, black, hornless breed of beef cattle that originally came from the Aberdeen region of Scotland. Can term **Aberdeen Angus**

An·gus[2] /áng gəss/ historic Scottish county

an·hin·ga /an híng gə/ (*plural* **-gas** or *same*) *n US* a fish-eating diving bird with a long neck and sharp beak. Native to: warmer freshwater regions of North and South America, Africa, Asia, and Australia. Family: Anhingidae. Can term **darter** [Mid-18C. Via Portuguese < Tupi *áyinga*]

An·hui /áan hwée/, **An·hwei** province in east central China bordered by the provinces of Jiangsu, Zhejiang, Jiangxi, Hubei, and Henan. Capital: Hefei. Population: 60,700,000 (1997). Area: 54,015 sq. mi./139,899 sq. km.

an·hy·dride /an hī drīd, -drid/ *n* a compound formed from another by the removal of water [Mid-19C. < ANHYDROUS]

an·hy·drite /an hī drīt/ *n* a colorless or lightly tinted anhydrous calcium sulfate mineral. Use: cement, fertilizers. [Early 19C. < ANHYDROUS]

an·hy·drous /an hīdrəss/ *adj* describes compounds that contain no water, or crystals that lack chemically bound water (**water of crystallization**) [Early 19C. < Greek *anudros* "waterless" < *hudōr* "water"]

a·ni /aa née/ (*plural* **a·nis** or *same*) *n* a glossy black long-tailed bird that has a heavy arched beak and lays eggs in a communal nest. Native to: tropical America. Genus: *Crotophaga*. [Early 19C. Via Spanish or Portuguese < Tupi *anū*]

An·i·ak·chak Na·tion·al Mon·u·ment and Pre·serve /ànnee ák chàk-/ national park in southwestern Alaska. One of its outstanding natural features is the Aniakchak Crater, a volcanic crater 2,000 ft./610 m deep.

an·ic·ca /ə níkə/ *n* in Buddhism, the cycle of birth, life, and death [Via Pali < Sanskrit *anitya-* "not eternal" < *nitya-* "constant, perpetual"]

~~**anihilation**~~ incorrect spelling of **annihilation**

an·il /ánnil/ (*plural* **-ils** or *same*) *n* a bush that is the source of indigo dye. Native to: Caribbean. Latin name: *Indigofera suffruticosa*. [Late 16C. Via French and Portuguese < Arabic *an-nīl* "the indigo" < Arabic and Persian *nīl* < Sanskrit *nīla-* "dark blue"]

an·ile /á nīl, áy-/ *adj* resembling a woman of advanced years (*literary*) [Mid-17C. < Latin *anilis* < *anus* "venerable woman"]

an·i·line /ánn'lən/ *n* a colorless poisonous oily liquid. Use: manufacture of dyes, resins, pharmaceuticals, explosives. Formula: $C_6H_5NH_2$. [Mid-19C. < ANIL, because first obtained by distilling indigo with alkali]

an·i·line dye *n* a synthetic dye derived from aniline

a·ni·lin·gus /àyni líng gəss/ *n* the act of sexually stimulating the anus with the tongue or mouth [Mid-20C. < modern Latin < Latin *anus* "anus," after CUNNILINGUS]

an·i·ma /ánnəmə/ *n* **1.** in Jungian psychology, the true inner self as opposed to the outer persona **2.** in Jungian psychology, the feminine aspect of a man's personality [Early 20C. < Latin, "breath, soul, spirit"]

an·i·mad·ver·sion /ànnə mad vúrzh'n/ *n* a critical comment or comments, especially those reproaching somebody (*formal*)

an·i·mad·vert /ànnə mad vúrt, -məd-/ (**-vert·ed, -vert·ing, -verts**) *vi* to comment critically or unfavorably (*formal*) [Mid-17C. < Latin *animadvertere* "turn the mind toward" < *animus* "mind" + *advertere* (see ADVERT[1])]

an·i·mal /ánnəm'l/ *n* **1. LIVING ORGANISM WITH INDEPENDENT MOVEMENT** a living organism that is distinguished from plants by independent movement and responsive sense organs **2. MAMMAL** a land mammal other than a human being **3. BRUTISH PERSON** somebody regarded as vulgar or brutish **4. INSTINCT-DRIVEN INNER SELF** the instinctive inner self as opposed to the one subject to self-restraint **5. TYPE OF PERSON OR THING** somebody or something of a particular type (*informal*) ○ *The laser printer is a completely different animal.* ■ *adj* **1. FROM ANIMALS** derived from animals ○ *animal fats* **2. INSTINCTIVE** belonging to the realm of instincts and urges ○ *animal urges* [14C. < Latin *animal(e)* < *animalis* "living, breathing" < *anima* "breath, life, soul"]

an·i·mal crack·er *n* a small cookie in the shape of an animal

an·i·mal·cule /ànnə mál kyóol/, **an·i·mal·cu·lum** /ànnə málkyələm/ (*plural* **-la** /-málkyələ/) *n* a microscopic organism such as an amoeba that moves about, eats other microbes, or resembles an animal in some other way (*archaic*) [Late 16C. < modern Latin *animalculum* "little animal" < Latin *animal(e)* (see ANIMAL)] —**an·i·mal·cu·lar** *adj*

an·i·mal hus·band·ry *n* the branch of agriculture concerned with breeding and rearing farm animals

an·i·mal·ism /ánnəm'l ìzzəm/ *n* **1. PREOCCUPATION WITH PHYSICAL SIDE OF LIFE** preoccupation with physical rather than spiritual needs **2. THEORY OF HUMANS' NONSPIRITUAL NATURE** the theory that human beings are driven by physical appetites rather than spiritual needs **3. TYPICAL ANIMAL BEHAVIOR** behavior that is typical of animals —**an·i·mal·is·tic** /ànnəmə lístik/ *adj*

an·i·mal·ist /ánnəm'l ist/ *n* **1. SOMEBODY PREOCCUPIED WITH PHYSICAL NEEDS** somebody who is preoccupied with physical rather than spiritual needs **2. SOMEBODY DENYING HUMANS' SPIRITUAL NATURE** somebody who holds that humans are driven by physical rather than spiritual needs **3. ANIMAL RIGHTS SUPPORTER** a supporter of animal rights, especially a militant one (*informal*)

an·i·mal·i·ty /ànnə mállətee/ *n* **1.** the characteristics of animals, as opposed to those of plants **2.** the physical needs of human beings, as opposed to the spiritual needs

an·i·mal·ize /ánnəm'l īz/ (**-ized, -iz·ing, -iz·es**) *vt* to bring out somebody's brutish or instinctive nature —**an·i·mal·i·za·tion** /ànnəməli záysh'n/ *n*

an·i·mal lib·er·a·tion *n* the movement to free animals from what is held to be human exploitation (*often used before a noun*)

an·i·mal mag·net·ism *n* somebody's strong physical attractiveness (*informal humorous*)

an·i·mal rights *npl* basic rights for animals, e.g., the right to live free from human-inflicted suffering ○ *an animal rights activist*

an·i·mal spir·its *npl* natural energy and high spirits

an·i·mal wel·far·ist *n* a supporter of animal rights

an·i·mate *vt* /ánnə màyt/ (**-mat·ed, -mat·ing, -mates**) **1. MAKE SOMEBODY OR SOMETHING LIVELY** to make a person, subject, or event lively **2. INSPIRE SOMEBODY** to rouse or inspire somebody to take action or to have strong feelings **3.** MOVIES **PRESENT SOMETHING USING ANIMATION TECHNIQUES** to present or record something in the form of a sequence of moving still images **4. MAKE SOMEBODY ACTIVE** to arouse somebody or something into activity or motion ○ *leaves animated by a stiff breeze* **5. CAUSE TO LIVE** to bring somebody or something to life ■ *adj* /ánnəmət/ **1. PHYSICALLY ALIVE** in a physically live state, as opposed to being dead or inert **2. LIVELY** full of liveliness or energy [14C. < Latin *animat-*, past participle of *animare* "give life to" < *anima* "breath, soul, spirit"] —**an·i·mat·ed** *adj*

an·i·ma·tion /ànnə máysh'n/ *n* **1.** MOVIES **PRODUCTION OF ANIMATED FILMS** the making of movies by filming a sequence of slightly varying drawings or models so that they appear to move and change when the sequence is shown **2.** MOVIES **ANIMATED MOVIES** a movie or movies consisting of a series of drawn, painted, or modeled scenes **3.** COMPUT **COMPUTER GRAPHICS** the production of moving images by computer techniques, or the image produced ○ *smooth and realistic animations* **4. LIVELINESS** liveliness in the way somebody speaks or behaves

a·ni·ma·to /àanə maátō/ *adj, adv* to be played in a lively animated manner (*used as a musical direction*) [Early 18C. < Italian < Latin *animare* (see ANIMATE)]

a·ni·ma·tor /ánnə màytər/ *n* **1.** a maker of animated movies **2.** somebody who or something that makes things lively, exciting, or interesting

an·i·ma·tron·ics /ànnəmə trónniks/ *n* the use of computer technology and a form of radio control to animate puppets or other models, e.g., for a movie (*takes a singular verb*) [Late 20C. Blend of ANIMATE + ELECTRONICS] —**an·i·ma·tron·ic** *adj*

an·i·me /ánni mày, ánnimə/ *n* a Japanese style of animated cartoon, often with violent or sexually explicit content [Late 20C. < Japanese < English ANIMATION]

an·i·mé /ánni mày/ *n* resin obtained from various tropical American trees. Use: varnishes, perfumes. [Late 16C. Via French < Tupi *wana'ni*]

an·i·mism /ánnə mìzzəm/ *n* **1.** BELIEF THAT NATURE HAS SOUL the belief that things in nature, e.g., trees, mountains, and the sky, have souls or consciousness **2.** BELIEF IN ORGANIZING FORCE IN UNIVERSE the belief that a supernatural force animates and organizes the universe **3.** BELIEF IN EXISTENCE OF SEPARATE SPIRIT the belief that people have spirits that do or can exist separately from their bodies [Mid-19C. < Latin *anima* "soul"] —**an·i·mist** *adj, n* —**an·i·mis·tic** /ánnə místik/ *adj*

an·i·mos·i·ty /ánnə mόssətee/ (*plural* **-ties**) *n* a feeling or spirit of hostility and resentment [15C. Directly or via French *animosité* < late Latin *animositas* "spiritedness" < *animosus* "spirited" < *animus* "mind, spirit"]

SYNONYMS See ***dislike***.

an·i·mus /ánnəməss/ *n* **1.** HOSTILITY a feeling or display of animosity **2.** MOTIVATION an attitude or feeling that motivates somebody's actions **3.** PSYCHOL WOMAN'S MASCULINE SIDE in Jungian psychology, the masculine aspect of a woman's personality [Early 19C. < Latin, "mind, spirit"]

an·i·on /á nī ən/ *n* a negatively charged ion, especially one that is attracted to an anode, either during electrolysis or within a vacuum tube [Mid-19C. Blend of ANODE + ION] —**an·i·on·ic** /àn ī ónnik/ *adj* —**an·i·on·i·cal·ly** *adv*

an·i·on-ex·change res·in *n* a solid resin in which the functional group is positive and thus attracts negative ions. Use: chemical and radioactive waste cleanup, chemical separation.

an·ise /ánniss/ *n* **1.** FOOD same as **aniseed 2.** an aromatic plant with licorice-flavored seeds (**aniseed**). Use: medicines, flavoring for food and drinks. Native to: Mediterranean. Latin name: *Pimpinella anisum*. [13C. Via French *anis* and Latin *anisum* < Greek *anison*]

an·i·seed /ánni sèed/ *n* the licorice-flavored seeds of anise, used whole or in ground spice mixtures as a flavoring in foods and drinks

an·i·sei·ko·ni·a /an ī sī kónee ə/ *n* a condition in the lens of one eye that results in its seeing an image that differs in size and shape from the image seen by the other eye [Mid-20C. < ANISO- + Greek *eikōn* "image"]

an·i·sette /ánni sét, -zét/ *n* a sweet liqueur flavored with aniseed [Mid-19C. < French, "little anise" < *anis* (see ANISE)]

A·nish·na·be /a nísh naàbee/ (*plural same*) *n Can* PEOPLES same as **Ojibwa** (sense 1) (*used by members of the Ojibwa people*) [< Ojibwa, "the people"]

aniso- *prefix* differing, not equal ○ *anisogamy* [< Greek *anisos* < *an-* "not" + *isos* "equal"]

an·i·so·gam·ete /an īssō gámmeet, -gə mèet/ *n* BIOL same as **heterogamete** (sense 1)

an·i·sog·a·my /àn ī sóggəmee/ *n* BIOL same as **heterogamy** (sense 1) —**an·i·so·gam·ic** /àn īssə gámmik/ *adj* —**an·i·sog·a·mous** *adj*

an·i·sole /ánni sōl/ *n* a colorless liquid with a pleasant smell. Use: solvent, perfume, flavoring. Formula: $C_6H_5OCH_3$. [Mid-19C. < ANISE + -OLE]

an·i·so·mer·ic /an īssə mérrik/ *adj* describes a compound that does not form structurally different molecules (**isomers**)

an·i·so·met·ric /an īssə méttrik/ *adj* **1.** not isometric or symmetrical ○ *an anisometric particle* **2.** describes a crystal that does not have three perpendicular axes of equal length and is therefore not regular

an·i·so·me·tro·pi·a /an īssəmə trṓpee ə/ *n* lack of balance between each eye's ability to refract light [Late 19C. < ANISO- + Greek *metron* "measure" + -OPIA] —**an·i·so·me·trop·ic** /-tróppik/ *adj*

an·i·so·trop·ic /an īssə tróppik/ *adj* describes something with physical properties that are different in different directions, e.g., crystals that measure differently along each of two or more axes —**an·i·so·trop·i·cal·ly** *adv* —**an·i·sot·ro·pism** /àn ī sóttrə pìzzəm/ *n* —**an·i·sot·ro·py** /-pee/ *n*

a·nis·tre·plase /a nístrə plàyss, -plàyz/ *n* a drug that breaks down fibrous tissue. Use: to dissolve blood clots blocking arteries. [Late 20C. < *anistre-* + *-plase*, INN suffix]

An·jou[1] /ánzhoo, -joo/, **An·jou pear** *n* a variety of pear with green skin and firm flesh [After ANJOU[2]]

An·jou[2] /án jòo, oN zhòo/ former province in western France in the lower Loire valley. Once ruled by the English kings, it was claimed for France in 1481.

An·ka·ra /ángkərə/ capital of Turkey, in the north central part of the country, on the Ankara River, northwest of Adana and southeast of Bursa. Population: 3,023,000 (2000). Former name **Angora**

an·ker·ite /ángkə rīt/ *n* a white, gray, brown, or reddish carbonate mineral containing calcium, magnesium, iron, and sometimes manganese [Mid-19C. < German *Ankerit*, after M. J. *Anker* (1772–1843), Austrian mineralogist]

ankh /angk/ *n* a symbol consisting of a cross with a loop for the top extension and a short crossbar, used in ancient Egypt to signify life [Late 19C. < Egyptian, "life"]

an·kle /ángk'l/ *n* **1.** the joint that connects the leg bones with the highest bone in the foot **2.** the slender part of the leg immediately above the ankle [14C. < assumed Old Norse *ankula*, which replaced related Old English *anclēow*, < Indo-European]

an·kle·bone /ángk'l bōn/ *n* ANAT same as **talus**[1]

an·kle boot *n* a boot that extends up to the ankle but not much beyond

an·kle-length *adj* reaching up to or down to the ankles

an·kle sock *n Can, UK* same as **anklet** (sense 2)

an·klet /ángklət/ *n* **1.** a piece of jewelry or some other ornament worn around the ankle **2.** *US* a sock that extends up to the ankle but not much beyond. Can term **ankle sock**

an·kle·warm·er /ángk'l wàwrmər/ *n* a knitted tube that covers the ankles and sometimes also the calves and top of the foot

an·ky·lo·saur /ángkələ sàwr/ *n* a plant-eating dinosaur with short legs, a heavy thickset body, and bony dorsal plates. It lived during the Cretaceous period. [Late 20C. < modern Latin *Ankylosaurus* < Greek *agkulōsis* (see ANKYLOSIS) + *sauros* "lizard"]

an·ky·lose /ángkə lòss, -lòz/ (**-losed, -los·ing, -los·es**) *vti* to cause bones to fuse and a joint to become stiff as a result of injury or disease, or intentionally through surgery, or to fuse and become stiff [Late 18C. Back-formation < ANKYLOSIS]

an·ky·los·ing spon·dy·li·tis /àngkə lòssing-, -lòz-/ *n* a disease of the spine that causes the vertebrae to form a solid inflexible column

an·ky·lo·sis /àngkə lṓssiss/ (*plural* **-los·es** /-lṓ sèez/) *n* **1.** the fusion of bones of a joint, often as a result of disease or injury, or intentionally through surgery **2.** stiffness or immobility in a joint caused by bones fusing as a result of disease or injury, or intentionally through surgery [Early 18C. Via modern Latin < Greek *agkulōsis* "stiffening of the joints" < *agkuloun* "bend" < *agkulos* "bent"] —**an·ky·lot·ic** /àngkə lóttik/ *adj*

an·ky·lo·sto·mi·a·sis *n* MED another spelling of **ancylostomiasis**

an·lage /áan laàgə/ (*plural* **-la·gen** /-laàgən/ or **-la·ges**) *n* **1.** something, often a principle, on which something else is based or founded (*literary*) **2.** BIOL a part or organ in its earliest stage of development [Late 19C. < German, "layout"]

ANLL *abbr* MED acute nonlymphocytic leukemia

Ann, Cape /an/ cape on a peninsula of northeastern Massachusetts, jutting 9 mi./14 km into the Atlantic Ocean at the northern edge of Massachusetts Bay

ANN *abbr* COMPUT artificial neural network

ann. *abbr* **1.** annals **2.** annual **3.** FIN annuity

an·na /áanə, ánnə/ *n* a copper coin formerly used in South Asia, worth one-sixteenth of a rupee [Early 17C. < Hindi *ānā*]

An·na I·van·ov·na /áanə ee vaánəvnə/, **Empress of Russia** (1693–1740) She was the niece of Peter the Great. While she was empress (1730–40), her German advisers administered the country.

an·nal·ist /ánn'list/ *n* somebody who compiles annals

an·nals /ánn'lz/ *npl* **1.** ANNUAL RECORDS a record of events arranged chronologically by year **2.** RECORDED HISTORY history in general, as it is recorded in books and other documents ○ *Her achievements have secured her place in the annals of our nation.* **3.** LEARNED JOURNAL a periodical that records events and reports in a field of research [Mid-16C. Directly or via French < Latin *annales* < *annalis* (see ANNUAL)]

~~**annalysis**~~ incorrect spelling of **analysis**

An·nam /ə nám, á nàm/ region in Vietnam forming a narrow strip along the South China Sea. It became a protectorate of France in 1883, gaining autonomy after World War II until Vietnam was partitioned in 1954. —**An·na·mese** /ànnə mèez, -mèess/ *adj, n*

An·nan /a naán, ánnən/, **Kofi** (*b.* 1938) Ghanaian secretary-general of the United Nations. As the United Nations special envoy to the former Yugoslavia, he oversaw the Dayton Accords in 1995 that ended the Bosnian-Croatian-Serbian war. He was appointed secretary-general of the United Nations in 1996 and awarded the Nobel Peace Prize in 2001.

"The best way of using force is to show it in order not to have to use it."
[Attributed to Kofi Annan]

An·nan·dale-on-Hud·son /ánnən dàyl-/ village in New York State, situated on the Hudson River. It is home to Bard College. Population: 35,500.

An·nap·o·lis /ə náppəliss/ capital of Maryland, situated near the Chesapeake Bay. Population: 36,196 (2002 estimate). ■ *n* the US Naval Academy, which is located in Annapolis

An·na·pur·na /ànnə pòornə, -púrnə/ mountain in the Himalaya range in north central Nepal, one of the world's highest peaks. Height: 26,545 ft./8,091 m.

Ann Ar·bor /àn aárbər/ city in southeastern Michigan, home to the main campus of the University of Michigan. Population: 115,213 (2002 estimate).

an·nat·to /ə náttō/ (*plural* **-tos**) *n* **1.** a yellowish red dye made from the pulp around the seeds of a tropical tree. Use: food coloring, fabric dye. **2.** the tree from whose seeds annatto dye is made. Native to: tropical America. Latin name: *Bixa orellana*. [Early 17C. < Carib]

Anne /an/ (1665–1714) queen of Great Britain and Ireland. The daughter of James II, she inherited the English throne from William III. She ruled from 1702 to 1714 and provided for the Hanoverian succession after her death.

Anne, the Princess Royal (*b.* 1950) The daughter of Queen Elizabeth II and Prince Philip, Duke of Edinburgh, she became president of the Save the Children Fund in 1970. Full name **Anne Elizabeth Alice Louise**

Anne (of Aus·tri·a) (1601–66) queen of France. She was the wife of Louis XIII of France and became queen regent for her son Louis XIV in 1643.

Anne (of Cleves) /-kleevz/ (1515–57) German-born queen of England. She married Henry VIII of England in a match made for political expediency (1540). He divorced her the same year.

Anne (of Den·mark) (1574–1619) queen of England, Scotland, and Ireland. She married James VI of Scotland (later James I of England) in 1589 and was the mother of Charles I.

an·neal /ə nèel/ *v* **1.** *vt* MAKE SOMETHING MORE RESOLUTE to make something, especially an opinion, a feeling, or an intention, stronger, firmer, or more resolute (*literary*) **2.** *vti* METALL, GLASS MAKE SOMETHING STRONGER THROUGH HEATING to subject an alloy, metal, or glass to a process of heating and slow cooling to make it tougher and less brittle **3.** *vti* BIOL SEPARATE STRANDS OF NUCLEIC ACID to subject nucleic acid to a process of heating and cooling in order to separate its strands [Old English *onǣlan* < *ǣlan* "burn" < Germanic]

an·ne·lid /ánnəlid/ *n* an invertebrate organism with a flat body that is divided into segments. Earthworms and leeches are annelids. Phylum: Annelida. [Mid-

19C. < modern Latin *Annelida* < French *annelés* "ringed" < Latin *an(n)ulus* (see ANNULUS)]

an·nex *vt* /ə néks, a-, á nèks/ (**-nexed, -nex·ing, -nex·es**) **1.** **TAKE OVER TERRITORY** to take over territory and incorporate it into another political entity, e.g., a country or state **2.** **ADD SOMETHING TO SOMETHING** to attach something subsidiary to a larger thing (*usually passive*) ○ *The new pool will be annexed to the gymnasium.* **3.** **ATTACH QUALITY TO SOMETHING** to add something such as a consequence, quality, or condition (*usually passive*) ○ *Annexed to his feeling of guilt was a sense of having let everybody down.* **4.** **STEAL SOMETHING** to take something without permission (*informal*) ○ *He returned to find that his assistant had annexed his chair.* ■ *n* /á nèks/ **1.** **AUXILIARY BUILDING** a building added on to another building or serving as an auxiliary building to a larger one **2.** *US* **ATTACHED DOCUMENT** an appendix, epilogue, or other additional material attached to a larger document. Can term **annexe** [14C. Via French *annexer* < Latin *annectere* "tie together" < *nectere* "to tie"] —**an·nex·a·tion** /à nek sáysh'n/ *n*

an·nexe /á nèks/ *n* **1.** *UK* same as **annex** *v* (sense 4) **2.** *Can, UK* same as **annex** *n* (sense 2)

An·nie Oak·ley /ànnee ṓklee/ *n* a free ticket for something [Early 20C. After Annie OAKLEY]

an·ni·hi·late /ə nī́ ə làyt/ (**-lat·ed, -lat·ing, -lates**) *v* **1.** *vt* **DESTROY SOMETHING** to destroy something completely, especially so that it ceases to exist **2.** *vt* **DEFEAT SOMEBODY** to defeat somebody easily and decisively (*slang*) **3.** *vi* PHYS **BE DESTROYED IN PARTICLE COLLISION** to be mutually destroyed when a particle collides with a corresponding antiparticle [Early 16C. < late Latin *annihilat-*, past participle of *annihilare* "reduce to nothing" < Latin *nihil* "nothing"] —**an·ni·hi·la·ble** /ə nī́ ələb'l/ *adj* —**an·ni·hi·la·tive** *adj* —**an·ni·hi·la·tor** *n*

an·ni·hi·la·tion /ə nī̀ ə láysh'n/ *n* **1.** **DESTRUCTION** the complete destruction of something **2.** **DEFEAT OF OPPONENT** the decisive defeat of an opponent (*informal*) **3.** PHYS **DESTRUCTIVE COLLISION OF PARTICLE AND ANTIPARTICLE** the process in which a particle combines with its antiparticle, destroying both and releasing their energy in the form of radiation or other particles ○ *annihilation radiation*

An·ning /ánning/, **Mary** (1799–1847) British pioneer of fossil collecting. She discovered the first complete plesiosaur skeleton (1810) and the first Early Jurassic pterosaur (1828).

An·nis·ton /ánnistən/ city in northeastern Alabama, south of Gadsden. Population: 23,792 (2002 estimate).

an·ni·ver·sa·ry /ànnə vúrssəree/ (*plural* **-ries**) *n* **1.** a date that is observed on an annual basis because it is the same date as an important event in a past year, e.g. the date of somebody's wedding **2.** a celebration or other commemorative ritual marking the date of an important event [13C. Directly or via French *anniversaire* < medieval Latin *anniversarium* < Latin *anniversarius* "returning yearly" < *annus* "year" + *versus*, past participle of *vertere* "turn"]

an·no Dom·i·ni /ànnō dómmi nī, -dómminee/ *adv* CALENDAR full form of **A.D.** [Mid-16C. < Latin, "in the year of the Lord"]

anno He·gi·rae /ànnō hə jī́ree, ànnō héjjəree/ *adv* CALENDAR, ISLAM full form of **AH** [Late 19C. < Latin, "in the year of the Hegira"]

~~**annoint**~~ incorrect spelling of **anoint**

~~**annonymous**~~ incorrect spelling of **anonymous**

an·no·tate /ánnə tàyt/ (**-tat·ed, -tat·ing, -tates**) *vt* to add critical or explanatory notes to a text (*often passive*) [Mid-18C. < Latin *annotat-*, past participle of *annotare* "note down" < *nota* "mark"] —**an·no·ta·tive** *adj* —**an·no·ta·tor** *n*

an·no·ta·tion /ànnə táysh'n/ *n* **1.** the addition of explanatory or critical comments to a text **2.** an explanatory or critical comment that has been added to a text

an·nounce /ə nównss/ (**-nounced, -nounc·ing, -nounc·es**) *v* **1.** *vt* **TELL SOMETHING PUBLICLY** to declare or report something publicly **2.** *vt* **SAY SOMETHING** to say something in a formal, forceful, or aggressive way ○ *the day they announced to the children they were selling the house* **3.** *vt* **DECLARE ARRIVAL OF SOMEBODY OR SOMETHING** to tell others formally that somebody or something has arrived **4.** *vt* **SIGNIFY OR FORETELL SOMETHING** to be a sign that something has arrived or is imminent **5.** *vti* **SERVE AS ANNOUNCER OF SOMETHING** to act as an announcer of something, e.g., a television or radio show **6.** *vti* **DECLARE CANDIDACY** to declare an intention to run for a public office **7.** *vi* BROADCAST **BE ANNOUNCER** to act as an announcer on television or radio [15C. Directly or via French *annoncer* < Latin *annuntiare* < *nuntius* "messenger"]

an·nounce·ment /ə nównssmənt/ *n* **1.** a public statement giving people information or news, or the making of the statement **2.** a formal written notice, often a card or newspaper item, giving the news of a birth, wedding, or other event

an·nounc·er /ə nównssər/ *n* **1.** a television or radio commentator who gives news bulletins, commentary on sports, or program information **2.** somebody who makes announcements, e.g., on a public address system at an airport

an·noy /ə nóy/ (**-noyed, -noy·ing, -noys**) *v* **1.** *vt* **IRRITATE SOMEBODY** to make somebody feel impatient or mildly angry **2.** *vt* **HARASS SOMEBODY** to harass somebody repeatedly **3.** *vi* **BE IRRITATING** to be a source of irritation ○ *Barking dogs are bound to annoy.* [13C. Via Old French *anoier* < late Latin *inodiare* "make loathsome" < Latin *in odio* "in hatred"]

SYNONYMS ***annoy, irritate, exasperate, vex, irk***

CORE MEANING: to cause a mild degree of anger in somebody

annoy to make somebody feel impatient or mildly angry ○ *His constant complaining annoys everyone.* ○ *We're annoyed that no-one told us how long the alterations would take.* **irritate** to annoy somebody slightly ○ *The loud humming quickly started to irritate her.* ○ *We were irritated to find that everyone had left early.* **exasperate** to make somebody angry or frustrated, often by repeatedly doing something annoying ○ *The frequent breakdowns and delays exasperated even loyal customers.* ○ *We soon became exasperated with his laziness and excuses.* **vex** to make somebody slightly annoyed or upset, especially over a relatively unimportant matter ○ *The mistake vexed him but did not worry him unduly.* ○ *It vexed her that she had almost wanted to laugh at his remark.* **irk** to annoy somebody slightly by being tiresome or tedious ○ *What irked her more than anything else was that Jo was probably right.* ○ *He also irked his colleagues with frequent TV appearances and public pronouncements.*

---

an·noy·ance /ə nóy ənss/ *n* **1.** feelings of mild anger and impatience **2.** something that causes somebody to be mildly angry or impatient ○ *Living in this neighborhood is not without its annoyances.*

SYNONYMS See ***anger***.

---

an·noy·ing /ə nóy ing/ *adj* causing mild anger or impatience —**an·noy·ing·ly** *adv*

an·nu·al /ánnyoo əl/ *adj* **1.** **ONCE A YEAR** happening once a year **2.** **FOR PERIOD OF ONE YEAR** based on or accumulating over one year **3.** BOT **DYING AFTER ONE SEASON** describes a plant that flowers, produces seed, and dies in one growing season ■ *n* **1.** BOT **PLANT THAT DIES AFTER ONE SEASON** a plant that flowers, produces seed, and dies in one growing season **2.** EDUC same as **yearbook** (sense 2) **3.** PUBL **YEARLY BOOK OR MAGAZINE** a book or magazine published once a year, especially one for children [14C. Directly or via French *annuel* < late Latin *annualis*, blend of Latin *annuus* + *annalis* "yearly" < *annus* "year"]

an·nu·al gen·er·al meet·ing *n Can, UK* a yearly gathering of members of an organization, at which officers are elected and the year's activities, including financial dealings, are discussed. US term **annual meeting**

an·nu·al·ize /ánnyoo ə lī̀z/ (**-ized, -iz·ing, -izes**) *vt* **1.** to calculate or adjust figures so that they reflect a period of a year **2.** to put something on, or change something to, a once-a-year schedule ○ *Let's annualize the newsletter.*

an·nu·al·ly /ánnyoo əlee/ *adv* every year or once a year

an·nu·al meet·ing *n US* a yearly meeting of the stockholders of a corporation or members of a foundation. At an annual meeting the officers usually report on matters such as the financial health of the organization. Can term **annual general meeting**

an·nu·al re·port *n* a document that outlines and analyzes the activities, especially the financial dealings, of a company or other organization over the past year

an·nu·al ring *n* TREES same as **growth ring**

an·nu·i·tant /ə nóo itənt/ *n* somebody who receives an annuity

an·nu·i·ty /ə nóo ətee/ (*plural* **-ties**) *n* **1.** **MONEY PAID AT REGULAR INTERVALS** an amount of money paid to somebody yearly or at some other regular interval **2.** **INVESTMENT PAYING ANNUAL SUM** an investment that pays the investor a set amount of money each year for a number of years, often the investor's lifetime **3.** **CONTRACT FOR ANNUAL PAYMENT** the right to receive or the obligation to pay an annuity [15C. Via French *annuité* < medieval Latin *annuitas* < Latin *annuus* (see ANNUAL)]

an·nul /ə núl/ (**-nulled, -nul·ling, -nuls**) *vt* **1.** **MAKE SOMETHING INVALID** to render a legal document or agreement invalid **2.** **DECLARE MARRIAGE INVALID** to declare that a marriage was never a true marriage in the eyes of a church, e.g., because one of the parties was not completely committed to it **3.** **DESTROY SOMETHING** to wipe out or destroy the effect or existence of something ○ *not able to annul my fears* [14C. Via Old French *anuller* < late Latin *annullare* "make into nothing" < Latin *nullus* "nothing"] —**an·nul·ment** *n*

SYNONYMS See ***nullify***.

---

an·nu·lar /ánnyələr/ *adj* shaped like or forming a ring (*technical*) [Late 16C. Directly or via French *annulaire* < Latin *an(n)ularis* < *an(n)ulus* (see ANNULUS)]

an·nu·lar e·clipse *n* a solar eclipse in which all but the outermost rim of the Sun is blocked by the Moon, leaving a ring of sunlight visible around the Moon

an·nu·lar lig·a·ment *n* a ring-shaped ligament that surrounds an ankle joint or a wrist joint and holds other ligaments in place

an·nu·late /ányələt, -làyt/, **an·nu·lat·ed** /-làytəd/ *adj* with ring-shaped parts, or consisting of rings [Early 19C. < Latin *an(n)ulatus* < *an(n)ulus* (see ANNULUS)]

an·nu·la·tion /ànnyə láysh'n/ *n* **1.** the formation of rings or ring-shaped parts **2.** any part that is shaped like a ring

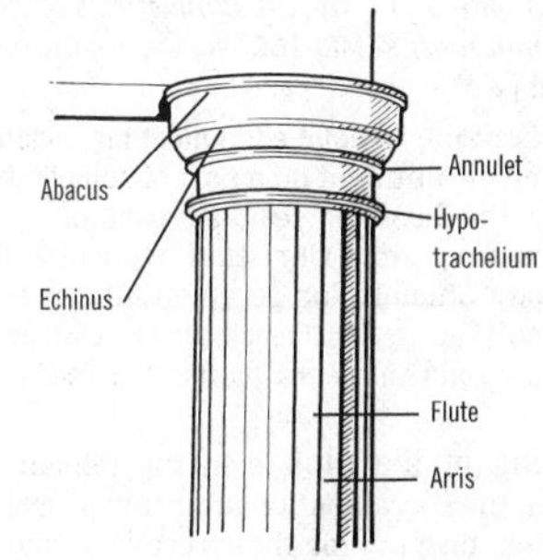

annulet

an·nu·let /ánnyələt/ *n* in architecture, a ring-shaped molding around a column [Late 16C. < Latin *an(n)ulus* (see ANNULUS)]

an·nu·lus /ánnyələss/ (*plural* **-li** /-lī/ or **-lus·es**) *n* **1.** BIOL a ring-shaped part or arrangement of parts in a plant or animal, e.g., a growth ring on fish scales **2.** MATH the area bounded by two concentric circles [Mid-16C. < Latin *an(n)ulus* "small ring" < *anus* "ring"]

an·nun·ci·ate /ə núnssee àyt/ (**-at·ed, -at·ing, -ates**) *vt* to announce or proclaim something (*archaic*) [14C. < Latin *annuntiat-*, past participle of *annuntiare* (see ANNOUNCE)]

an·nun·ci·a·tion /ə nùnssee áysh'n/ *n* the announcing of something, or an announcement (*archaic*) [14C. Via Old French < late Latin *annuntiation-* < Latin *annuntiare* (see ANNOUNCE)]

AKG London

Annunciation (1513?) by Lucas Cranach the Elder

An·nun·ci·a·tion *n* **1.** in the Bible, the archangel Gabriel's visit to the Virgin Mary to announce that she had been chosen to be the mother of Jesus Christ (Luke 1:26–38) **2.** the Christian festival known as the feast of the Annunciation. Date: March 25.

an·nun·ci·a·tor /ə núnssee àytər/ *n* an electronic signaling device, e.g., a switchboard device that indicates the source of incoming telephone calls

an·nus mi·rab·i·lis /ánnəss mi rábbəliss/ (*plural* **an·ni mi·rab·i·les** /ánnī mi rábbə lèez/) *n* a year that is remarkable for its great events [Mid-17C. < Latin, "wonderful year"]

an·ode /á nōd/ *n* **1.** the negative terminal of a battery **2.** the positive electrode in an electrolytic cell [Mid-19C. < Greek *anodos* "way up" < *hodos* "way"]

an·o·dize /ánnə dīz/ (**-dized, -diz·ing, -diz·es**) *vt* to coat a metal, e.g., aluminum, with a protective or decorative oxide by making the metal the anode of an electrolytic cell —**an·o·di·za·tion** /ànnədi záysh'n/ *n*

an·o·don·tia /ànnə dónshə, -shee ə/ *n* the absence of some or all teeth, because the teeth have never developed

an·o·dyne /ánnə dīn/ *n* **1.** PHARM **PAINKILLER** a medication that relieves pain, e.g., aspirin or codeine **2. COMFORTING THING** something that soothes, comforts, or relaxes (*literary*) ■ *adj* **1.** PHARM **PAINKILLING** bringing relief from pain or discomfort **2. BLAND** harmless, inoffensive, or uncontroversial to the point of being dull ○ *a rather anodyne speech, given the nature of the crisis* **3. SOOTHING** serving to soothe, relax, or comfort (*literary*) ○ *the anodyne effects of a weekend in the mountains* [Mid-16C. Via Latin < Greek *anōdunos* "without pain" < *odunē* "pain"]

a·noint /ə nóynt/ (**a·noint·ed, a·noint·ing, a·noints**) *vt* **1.** to rub oil or ointment on a part of somebody's body, usually the head or feet, as part of a religious ceremony, e.g., in a Christian baptism **2.** to install somebody officially or ceremonially in a position or office [14C. < Old French *enoint*, past participle of *enoindre* < Latin *inungere* < *ungere* "to smear"] —**a·noint·ment** *n*

a·noint·ing of the sick *n* in the Roman Catholic Church, the sacrament of anointing people who are very sick, praying for their recovery, and offering confession and absolution of sins

a·no·le /ə nṓlee/ *n* a tree-climbing lizard that can change color. Genus: *Anolis*. [Early 18C. Via modern Latin *Anolis* < Carib *anoli*]

a·nom·a·lis·tic month /ə nòmmə lìstik-/ *n* the average time taken by the Moon to orbit the Earth once, starting from the point in its orbit at which it is nearest the Earth, measured as 27.554 days

a·nom·a·lis·tic year *n* the time taken by the Earth to orbit the Sun once, starting from the point in its orbit at which the Earth is nearest the Sun, measured as 365.26 days

a·nom·a·lous /ə nómmələss/ *adj* **1.** deviating from the norm or from what people expect ○ *We're getting anomalous readings on the heart monitor.* **2.** strange and difficult to identify or classify ○*"Individuals would occasionally give rise to new species having anomalous habits."* (Charles Darwin, *On the Origin of Species*; 1859) [Mid-17C. < late Latin *anomalus* < Greek *anōmalos* "uneven" < *homalos* "even"]

a·nom·a·ly /ə nómmalee/ (*plural* **-lies**) *n* **1. IRREGULARITY** something that deviates from the norm or from expectations ○ *looking for anomalies in the blood tests* **2. PECULIARITY** something strange and difficult to identify or classify ○ *The space probe has encountered an anomaly.* **3.** ASTRON **ANGLE IN PLANET'S ORBIT** the angle between a planet's position, the Sun, and the point in the planet's orbit when it is closest to the Sun

an·o·mic /ə nómmik, ə nṓmik/ *adj* **1.** SOCIOL **UNSTABLE BECAUSE OF MORAL BREAKDOWN** unstable because moral and social codes have been eroded or abandoned ○ *an anomic society* **2.** PSYCHOL **AFFECTED BY ALIENATION** feeling alienated from society and disoriented by the perceived absence of a social or moral framework ■ *n* PSYCHOL **SOMEBODY AFFECTED BY ALIENATION** somebody who feels alienated and disoriented because of the lack of a social and moral framework

an·o·mie /ánnəmee/, **an·o·my** *n* **1.** instability in society caused by the erosion or abandonment of moral and social codes **2.** a feeling of disorientation and alienation from society caused by the perceived absence of a supporting social or moral framework [Late 16C. Via French < Greek *anomia* "lawlessness" < *anomos* "lawless" < *nomos* "law"]

a·non /ə nón/ *adv* (*archaic or literary*) **1.** at an unspecified future time ○ *I'll see you anon.* **2.** in a short while ○ *more of these grotesque escapades anon* [Old English *on ān* "in one"]

anon. /ə nón/ *abbr* anonymous

an·o·nym /ánnə nìm/ *n* **1.** an author whose name is not known or not given **2.** a name used by somebody to hide his or her identity [Early 19C. < French *anonyme* < Greek *anōnumos* (see ANONYMOUS)]

an·o·nym·i·ty /ànnə nímmətee/ (*plural* **-ties**) *n* **1. FREEDOM FROM IDENTIFICATION** the state of not being known or identified by name, e.g., as the author or donor of something ○ *preserve the anonymity of your informant* **2. LACK OF DISTINCTIVENESS** a lack of distinctive features that makes things seem bland or interchangeable ○ *detested the anonymity of the downtown hotels* **3. STATE OF BEING UNNOTICED** the state of blending into a crowd and going unnoticed ○ *I always preferred the anonymity of the big city.* **4. UNNAMED PERSON** an unnamed or unacknowledged person

a·non·y·mi·zer /ə nónnə mīzər/ *n* a website through which a person browsing can visit the World Wide Web without leaving any identity traces

a·non·y·mous /ə nónnəməss/ *adj* **1. UNNAMED** whose name is not known or not given ○ *the anonymous author* **2. WITH NAME WITHHELD** with the performer's, maker's, or creator's identity withheld ○ *an anonymous letter* **3. INDISTINCTIVE** lacking individuality or distinctiveness ○ *a quirkiness unsuited to an anonymous shopping mall* **4. PREVENTING IDENTIFICATION** obscuring somebody's identity, or allowing somebody to go unnoticed ○ *a thief who lost his pursuers in an anonymous crowd* [Early 17C. < late Latin *anonymus* < Greek *anōnumos* "unnamed" < *onuma* "name"] —**a·non·y·mous·ness** *n*

a·non·y·mous FTP *n* a type of Internet file transfer in which no password is needed, used by some organizations to make their file archives publicly accessible

a·non·y·mous·ly /ə nónnəməsslee/ *adv* without being named or acknowledged

a·noph·e·les /ə nóffə lèez/ (*plural same*) *n* a mosquito belonging to a genus that includes some that can carry and transmit malaria to humans. Genus: *Anopheles*. [Late 19C. Via modern Latin < Greek *anōphelēs* "useless"]

an·o·rak /ánnə ràk/ *n* **1.** a warm thick waterproof hip-length jacket with a hood **2.** *UK* a boring, unfashionable, or studious person, especially somebody who is excessively devoted to a hobby or interest (*humorous*) ○ *You can be into something without becoming a total anorak about it.* [Early 20C. < (Greenlandic) Inuit *annoraaq*]

an·o·rec·tic /ànnə réktik/ *adj* relating to pathological loss of appetite ■ *n* a medicine that suppresses the appetite [Late 19C. < Greek *anorektos* "without appetite" < *orexein* "to desire"]

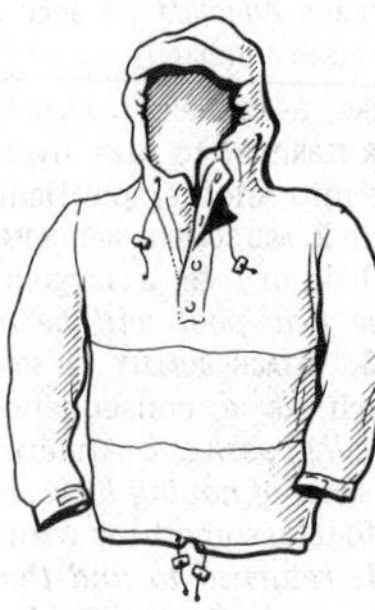

anorak

an·o·rex·i·a /ànnə réksee ə/ *n* **1.** PSYCHIAT same as **anorexia nervosa 2.** persistent loss of appetite [Late 16C. Via modern Latin < Greek, "lack of appetite" < *orexis* "appetite" < *orexein* "to desire"]

an·o·rex·i·a nerv·o·sa /-nər vṓssə/ *n* an eating disorder, marked by an extreme fear of becoming overweight, that leads to excessive dieting to the point of serious ill-health and sometimes death [< modern Latin, "nervous anorexia"]

an·o·rex·ic /ànnə réksik/ *adj* **1. OF ANOREXIA NERVOSA** relating to or affected by anorexia nervosa **2. VERY THIN** extremely thin, especially unhealthily or unattractively so (*informal*) ■ *n* **SOMEBODY WITH ANOREXIA NERVOSA** somebody who is affected by anorexia nervosa

an·or·thite /a náwr thīt/ *n* a rare white, gray, or reddish gray feldspar mineral. Source: mainly in igneous rocks. Use: glass, ceramics. —**an·or·thi·tic** /à nawr thíttik/ *adj*

an·or·tho·site /a náwrthə sīt/ *n* a coarse-grained igneous rock composed of at least 90% feldspar [Mid-19C. < French *anorthose*, type of feldspar < Greek *anorthos* "not straight"; from its crystals] —**an·or·tho·si·tic** /a nàwrthə síttik/ *adj*

an·os·mi·a /an ózmee ə/ *n* absence or loss of the sense of smell [Early 19C. < AN- + Greek *osmē* "smell"] —**an·os·mic** *adj*

an·oth·er /ə nú<u>th</u>ər/ *adj, pron* **1. ONE MORE** an additional ○ *need another person to help* ○ *May I have another?* **2. ONE THAT IS DIFFERENT** somebody or something that is separate or different ○ *We need another accountant because ours is moving.* ○ *This one is too dark; I would prefer another.* **3. SOME OTHER** some other one, or any other one ○ *at one time or another*

A·nou·ilh /aa nóo ee/, **Jean** (1910–87) French dramatist. His plays include *Antigone* (1942), *Ring Round the Moon* (1947), and *Becket* (1959).

> "There will always be a lost dog somewhere that will prevent me from being happy."
> [Jean Anouilh, *La Sauvage (The Restless Heart)*; 1938]

an·ov·u·lant /a nóvvyələnt/ *n* a drug that prevents ovulation, e.g., a birth-control pill [Mid-20C. < AN- + OVULATE] —**an·ov·u·lant** *adj*

an·o·vu·la·tion /a nòvvyə láysh'n, -ōv yə-/ *n* the state of not ovulating because of a medical condition, suppression by drugs, or menopause —**an·o·vu·la·to·ry** /a nóvvyələ tàwree, -nṓv-/ *adj, n*

an·ox·e·mi·a /à nok séemee ə/ *n* a deficiency of oxygen in the blood flowing through the arteries —**an·ox·e·mic** *adj*

an·ox·i·a /a nóksee ə/ *n* MED same as **hypoxia** —**an·ox·ic** *adj*

an·sate /án sàyt/ *adj* with a handle or a part shaped like a handle [Late 19C. < Latin *ansatus* < *ansa* "handle"]

an·sate cross *n* same as **ankh**

An·selm /án selm/, **St.** (1033?–1109) Italian theologian and philosopher. His most famous work is his ontological proof of God's existence, completed in 1078. His tenure as Archbishop of Canterbury (1093–1109) was marked by conflict with England's kings.

> "I do not seek to understand so that I may believe, but I believe so that I may understand."
> [St. Anselm, *Proslogion*; 1078]

ANSI /ánssee/ *abbr* American National Standards Institute

An·so·ni·a /an sṓnee ə, -sṓnyə/ city in southern Connecticut, on the Naugatuck River. Population: 18,739 (2002 estimate).

an·swer /ánssər/ *n* **1.** RESPONSE TO QUESTION the information requested by a spoken or written question **2.** WAY OF SOLVING SOMETHING the solution to a problem ○ *trying to find an answer to our ecological problems* **3.** RESPONSE TO ACTION a reaction intended to deal with something that somebody says or does ○ *She had no answer to her opponent's lethal backhand.* **4.** RESPONSE TO CALL a response to a summons, e.g., a ringing telephone, a doorbell, or somebody calling your name ○ *I tried phoning him, but there was no answer.* **5.** CORRESPONDING THING something designed to match or correspond to something else ○ *The Space Needle is Seattle's answer to the Eiffel Tower.* **6.** LAW PLEA IN COURT a defendant's plea in response to a charge, lawsuit, or summons ■ *v* (**-swered, -swer·ing, -swers**) **1.** *vti* REPLY TO SOMETHING to reply to something written or spoken ○ *answered with a stinging rebuttal* **2.** DO SOMETHING IN REACTION to do something as a reaction to something that somebody says or does **3.** *vti* RESPOND TO CALL to respond to a summons such as a ringing telephone, a doorbell, or somebody calling your name **4.** *vti* CORRESPOND TO SOMETHING to match or correspond to something ○ *nobody who answers to that description* **5.** *vti* MEET NEED to fulfill a need or wish ○ *Her arrival answered our need for an experienced radiologist.* **6.** *vi* SERVE PURPOSE to be adequate in serving a purpose ○ *an upturned box that answers for a seat* **7.** *vt* LAW RESPOND TO CHARGE IN COURT to offer a plea in response to a charge, lawsuit, or summons ○ *The defendant will now answer the charges.* [Old English *andswaru* < Germanic, "swear against"] —**an·swer·er** *n* ◇ **know** *or* **have all the answers** to be admirably knowledgeable about a subject

SYNONYMS ***answer, reply, response, retort, riposte, rejoinder***

CORE MEANING: something said, written, or done in acknowledgment of a question or remark, or in reaction to a situation

answer the information requested by a spoken or written question ○ *He wasn't sure he had given the right answer to Question 3a.* ○ *She searched for an appropriate answer to Jason's question about job prospects.* **reply** a reaction, usually written or spoken, to a question, letter, or situation ○ *a written reply to our letter* ○ *"How do you know that?" she asked, but her friend only giggled in reply.* **response** a spoken or written answer, or a reaction to a situation ○ *Could I have your response by Wednesday?* ○ *His comments sparked an angry response in the press.* ○ *a steady improvement in ambulance response times* **retort** a sharp spoken reply, often to criticism ○ *Polly managed to suppress a cutting retort.* **riposte** a quick or witty reply, usually spoken ○ *You can never manage to deliver a witty riposte at the time, but always think of one later.* **rejoinder** (*formal*) a sharp, critical, angry, or clever reply, usually spoken ○ *"Of course the school is to blame," came the parents' angry rejoinder.*

answer back *vti* to reply to somebody impudently or disrespectfully

answer for *vt* **1.** BE ACCOUNTABLE FOR SOMETHING to be accountable or responsible for something ○ *You'll have to answer for this broken window.* **2.** RECEIVE PUNISHMENT FOR SOMETHING to be punished for a wrongdoing ○ *They'll answer for their carelessness when the case comes to trial.* **3.** GUARANTEE SOMEBODY'S RELIABILITY to give an assurance about the good character of somebody ○ *She can be trusted, but I can't answer for the rest of the team.*

answer to *vt* to be accountable to somebody for something

an·swer·a·ble /ánssərəb'l/ *adj* **1.** ACCOUNTABLE responsible or accountable to somebody for something ○ *You're answerable to your boss for any losses you incur.* **2.** SOLVABLE having a possible solution or a correct response **3.** ABLE TO BE DENIED able to be argued against or disproved ○ *Is the charge answerable?* —**an·swer·a·bil·i·ty** /ànssərə bíllətee/ *n* —**an·swer·a·bly** *adv*

an·swer·back /ánssər bàk/ *n* a response in a two-way radio transmission

an·swer·ing ma·chine *n* a recording device that is connected to or part of a telephone and can be activated to play a message to callers and record messages from them

an·swer·ing ser·vice *n* a business that receives telephone calls on behalf of other people or organizations and takes messages for them

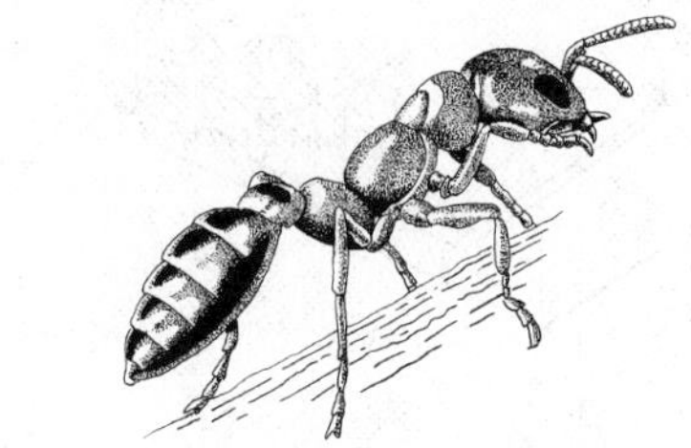

ant

ant /ant/ *n* **1.** an insect that lives in complex well-organized colonies and is noted for its ability to carry objects heavier than itself. Male ants have wings, as do fertile females (**queens**) after mating. Family: Formicidae. **2.** a smuggler who makes repeated trips across a border carrying such things as cigarettes, liquor, or weapons (*slang*) [Old English *æmette* < Germanic, "cut off"] ◇ **have ants in your pants** to be excited or impatient about something (*informal*)

ant. *abbr* **1.** antiquarian **2.** antiquity **3.** LING antonym

Ant. *abbr* Antarctica

ant- *prefix* same as **anti-** (*used before vowels*)

-ant *suffix* **1.** performing a particular action ○ *coolant* **2.** being in a particular condition ○ *hesitant* [< Latin *-ant-*, stem of *-ans*, a present participle ending]

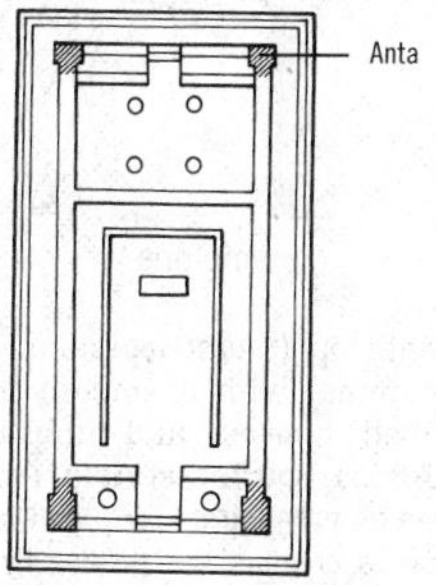

anta

an·ta /ántə/ (*plural* **-tas** *or* **-tae** /-tee/) *n* a thicker end of the side wall of a Greek temple that forms one side of a porch [Mid-18C. Back-formation < Latin *antae* "square pilasters"]

ant·ac·id /ant ássid/ *n* a drug that reduces or neutralizes stomach acid ■ *adj* preventing, counteracting, or neutralizing acidity, especially in the stomach

an·tae plural of **anta**

an·tag·o·nism /an tággə nìzzəm/ *n* **1.** HOSTILITY hostility or hatred causing opposition and ill will **2.** OPPOSITION opposition between forces or principles ○ *the antagonism between good and evil* **3.** BIOCHEM NEUTRALIZING INTERACTION BETWEEN CHEMICALS the interaction between two or more chemical substances in the body that diminishes the effect that each of them has individually **4.** PHYSIOL OPPOSITION BETWEEN MUSCLES the opposing force that usually exists between pairs of muscles

an·tag·o·nist /an tággənist/ *n* **1.** OPPONENT somebody or something opposing or in conflict with another ○ *a former supporter turned antagonist* **2.** CHARACTER IN CONFLICT WITH HERO a major character in a book, play, or movie whose values or behavior are in conflict with those of the protagonist or hero **3.** PHARM NEUTRALIZING AGENT a drug that neutralizes the effect of a substance on the body **4.** PHYSIOL OPPOSING MUSCLE a muscle that acts with and limits the action of another muscle

an·tag·o·nis·tic /an tàggə nístik/ *adj* showing or expressing hostility or opposition —**an·tag·o·nis·ti·cal·ly** *adv*

an·tag·o·nize /an tággə nīz/ (**-nized, -niz·ing, -niz·es**) *vt* to cause a person or animal to become hostile [Mid-17C. < Greek *antagōnizesthai* "struggle against" < *agōnizesthai* "struggle" < *agōn* "contest"]

An·ta·kya /aan taákyə/ city in southern Turkey on the Orontes River. Founded in 301 B.C., it was the capital of the eastern Roman Empire from 64 B.C. to A.D. 260. Population: 123,871 (1990). Former name **Antioch**

An·tal·ya /aan taályə/ city in southwestern Turkey, situated on the Gulf of Antalya. Population: 564,914 (1997).

An·ta·na·na·ri·vo /àntə nànnə réevō, aàntə naà-/ capital of Madagascar, located in the central part of the island. Population: 1,689,000 (2001). Former name **Tananarive** (until 1977)

Ant·arc·tic /an taárktik, -taártik/ region lying south of the Antarctic Circle —**Ant·arc·tic** *adj*

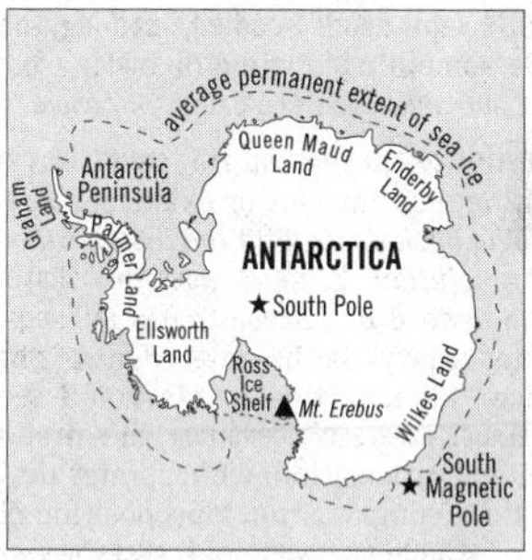

Antarctica

Ant·arc·ti·ca /an taárktikə, -taártik-/ uninhabited continent surrounding the South Pole, consisting of an ice-covered plateau and high mountain peaks. Area: 5,400,000 sq. mi./14,000,000 sq. km.

Ant·arc·tic Cir·cle *n* parallel of latitude at 66°30'S, encircling Antarctica and its surrounding seas, marking the Northern limit of the area in which the sun does not set during the summer solstice and does not rise during the winter solstice

Ant·arc·tic Cur·rent ocean current circling Antarctica. Moving eastward, it circulates water from one ocean to another.

Ant·arc·tic O·cean the waters that surround the South Pole and Antarctica, consisting of the waters of the southern Atlantic, Indian, and Pacific oceans. Depths exceed 20,000 ft./6,000 m.

~~**Antartic**~~ incorrect spelling of **Antarctic**

an·taz·o·line /an tázzə leen/ *n* a white odorless compound. Use: control of allergic reactions. [Late 20C, < *ant-* + *-azoline*, INN stem]

ant bear *n* ZOOL same as **aardvark**

ant·bird /ánt bùrd/ *n* a bird that follows army ants and feeds on insects, frogs, and lizards disturbed by the ants. Native to: South America. Family: Formicariidae.

an·te /ántee/ *n* **1.** STAKE the amount a card player puts into the gambling pot before cards are dealt **2.** AMOUNT PAID a sum of money or price to be paid (*informal*) ■ *vti* (**-ted, -te·ing, -tes**) CONTRIBUTE TO GAMBLING POT to put forward betting stakes before cards are dealt [Early 19C. < Latin (see ANTE-)] ◇ **up the ante** (*informal*) **1.** to increase the amount of money required to do something **2.** to demand more in a situation, especially in an extortionate way

ante up *vti* to pay money that is owed (*informal*) ○ *We know you've got the cash, so ante up now!*

ante- *prefix* before, in front ○ *antechamber* [< Latin *ante* "before" < Indo-European, "front"]

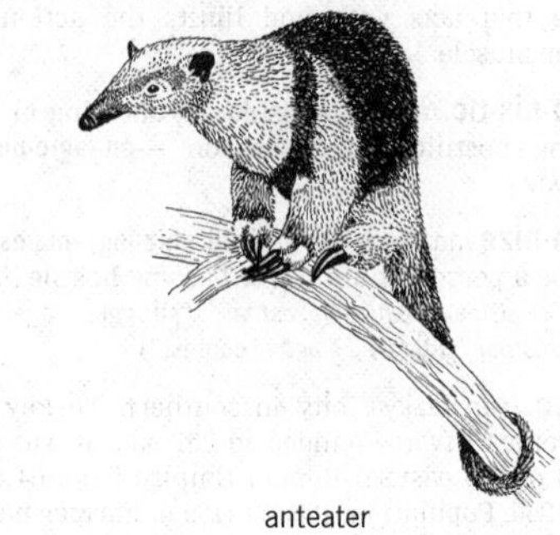

anteater

ant·eat·er /ánt eetər/ *n* **1.** a long-snouted toothless mammal that has long claws and a sticky tongue for catching prey, usually ants and termites. Native to: Central and South America. Family: Myrmecophagidae. **2.** ZOOL same as **pangolin 3.** ZOOL same as **echidna 4.** ZOOL same as **aardvark**

an·te·bel·lum /ántee bélləm/ *adj* **1.** belonging or relating to the time before the Civil War **2.** preceding a war, or characteristic of the time preceding a war [Mid-19C. < Latin *ante bellum* "before the war"]

an·te·cede /ànti seed/ (**-ced·ed, -ced·ing, -cedes**) *vt* to precede something in time or order (*formal*) [Early 17C. < Latin *antecedere* "go before" < *cedere* "give way"]

an·te·ce·dent /ànti seed'nt/ *n* **1.** SOMETHING COMING BEFORE something that happens or exists before something else ○ *The book deals with the historical antecedents of the revolution.* **2.** GRAM WORD THAT SUBSEQUENT WORD REFERS TO a word or phrase that a subsequent word refers to. "Mary" is the antecedent of "her" in the sentence "I'll give this to Mary if I see her." **3.** LOGIC CLAUSE EXPRESSING CONDITION the first part of a conditional proposition, which states the condition and is the p component in a proposition phrased "if p then q" ■ **an·te·ce·dents** *npl* **1.** ANCESTORS somebody's ancestors **2.** SOMEBODY'S PERSONAL HISTORY the events or circumstances in somebody's past ○ *He's done pretty well for himself, considering what we know of his antecedents.* ■ *adj* OCCURRING EARLIER IN TIME happening or existing before something else (*formal*) [14C. Directly or via French < Latin *antecedent-*, present participle of *antecedere* (see ANTECEDE)] —**an·te·ce·dence** *n* —**an·te·ce·dent·ly** *adv*

USAGE Antecedents *Relative clauses* need something such as *nouns* to refer to, and the relationship ought to be clear. Avoid constructions like these where the antecedents (words or phrases that subsequent material refers to) are either absent or unclear: *I'd sign up for advanced calculus if I were smart, which I'm not.* The clause *which I'm not* has no antecedent; also, *if I were smart* already tells the reader that I am not smart. Don't try to make an entire clause an antecedent for a *relative clause*, as in *I need to purchase an entirely new computer system, which upsets me.* Say instead *I need to purchase an entirely new computer system, and this [or that] upsets me.* Similarly, avoid relative clause constructions with vague antecedents: *She crashed the ultralight aircraft into the freeway, which was her own fault.* Since the freeway was definitely not her own fault but the crash indeed was, reword the sentence: *Crashing the ultralight aircraft into the freeway was her own fault* or *She crashed the ultralight aircraft into the freeway in an accident that was her own fault.*

an·te·cham·ber /ántee chàymbər/ *n* a small room leading into a larger room and often used as a waiting area [Mid-17C. < French *antichambre*, translation of Italian *anticamera* "room in front"]

an·te·choir /ánti kwīr/ *n* an area at the entrance to the choir in a church, reserved for clergy and choir members

an·te·date /ánti dàyt/ *vt* (**-dat·ed, -dat·ing, -dates**) **1.** OCCUR EARLIER THAN SOMETHING to exist or happen at an earlier date than something else ○ *These tapestries antedate the development of synthetic dyes.* **2.** PUT EARLIER DATE ON SOMETHING to assign something a date that is earlier than its true or original date ○ *This vase was mistakenly antedated to the Ming dynasty.* ■ *n* EARLIER DATE a date assigned to something that is earlier than its true or original date

an·te·di·lu·vi·an /ànti də lóovee ən/ *adj* **1.** extremely old-fashioned or out-of-date (*humorous*) **2.** in or from the time before the biblical Flood [Mid-17C. < ANTE- + Latin *diluvium* "flood"]

SYNONYMS See ***old-fashioned.***

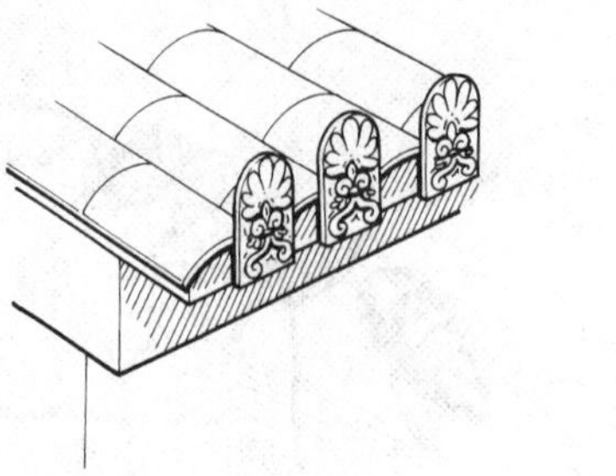

antefix

an·te·fix /ántee fiks/ (*plural* **-fix·es** or **-fix·a** /-fiksə/ or **-fix·ae** /-seè/) *n* an ornamental edging on the eaves of an ancient building with a tiled roof that hides the joints of the roof tiles [Mid-19C. < Latin *antefixum* < *antefigere* "fasten before" < *figere* "fasten"] —**an·te·fix·al** /ántee fíksəl/ *adj*

an·te·grade am·ne·sia /ántə grayd-/ *n* a form of amnesia in which the memory loss relates to events occurring after a traumatic event [After RETROGRADE]

antelope

an·te·lope /ántə lōp/ (*plural* **-lopes** or *same*) *n* **1.** a cud-chewing mammal with a smooth brown or gray coat, two-toed hooves, and unbranched horns. Native to: Africa, Southwest Asia. Family: Bovidae. **2.** ZOOL same as **pronghorn** [15C. Via Old French *antelop* "mythical horned creature said to live by the Euphrates" < medieval Greek *antholops*]

an·te·me·rid·i·an /ántee mə ríddee ən/ *adj* relating to or taking place in the morning

an·te me·rid·i·em /-mə ríddee əm/ *adj, adv* full form of **a.m.** [Mid-16C. < Latin, "before noon"]

an·te·mor·tem /ántee máwrtəm/ *adj* existing or happening before death (*formal*) [Late 19C. < Latin *ante mortem* "before death"] —**an·te mor·tem** *adv*

an·te·na·tal /ántee náyt'l/ *adj UK* same as **prenatal** —**an·te·na·tal·ly** *adv*

an·ten·na /an ténnə/ (*plural* **-nae** /-nee/ or **-nas**) *n* **1.** THIN SENSOR ON ORGANISM'S HEAD a thin movable sensory organ found in pairs on the heads of some organisms, including insects and crustaceans **2.** DEVICE FOR SENDING AND RECEIVING RADIO WAVES a metallic piece of equipment of variable shape, used in the sending and receiving of television or radio signals **3.** INQUIRING SENSE somebody's inquisitive or inquiring sense (*informal; often used in the plural*) [Mid-17C. < Latin, "pole supporting a sail"] —**an·ten·nal** *adj*

an·ten·na head *n* a person, especially a child, who spends a great deal of time watching television (*slang*)

an·te·par·tum /ánti paártəm/ *adj* relating to the period before birth, especially the period of labor before a baby is delivered [Late 19C. < Latin *ante partum* "before birth"]

an·te·pen·di·um /àntee péndee əm/ (*plural* **-di·ums** or **-di·a** /-dee ə/) *n* a decorative cloth that hangs on the front of an altar or lectern [Late 16C. < medieval Latin < Latin *ante* "before" + *pendere* "hang"]

an·te·pe·nult /àntee peé nùlt, àntee pi núlt/ *n* the third from last syllable in a word ○ *The antepenult is stressed in the word "superfluous."*

an·te·pe·nul·ti·mate /àntee pi núltəmət/ *adj* third from last in a series ○ *the antepenultimate word in the paragraph* ■ *n* GRAM same as **antepenult**

an·te·ri·or /an teéree ər/ *adj* **1.** IN FRONT at, near, or from the front of something (*formal*) ○ *an anterior view of the building* **2.** EARLIER existing or happening before something else (*formal*) **3.** ANAT NEAR FRONT OF BODY situated at or near the front of the body or of a body part **4.** BOT SITUATED AWAY FROM STEM describes a leaf or flower part that is situated farthest away or facing away from the stem of a plant [Mid-16C. Directly or via French < Latin, "earlier" < *ante* "before"] —**an·te·ri·or·i·ty** /an teèree áwratee/ *n* —**an·te·ri·or·ly** *adv*

an·te·room /ántee ròom, -ròom/ *n* a subsidiary room that opens into a larger room, often used as a waiting area

an·te·type /ántee tīp/ *n* an earlier form of something

an·te·ver·sion /àntee vúrzh'n/ *n* an unusual tilting forward of an organ, especially the uterus

ant·he·li·on /ant heélyən, an theé-/ (*plural* **-li·a** /-lyə/ or **-li·ons**) *n* a luminous spot appearing occasionally in the sky opposite the Sun [Late 17C. < Greek, "opposite the Sun" < *hēlios* "Sun"]

ant·he·lix /ant heéliks, an theé-/ (*plural* **-lix·es** or **-li·ces** /-lə seèz/), **an·ti·he·lix** /ántī heéliks, àntee-/ (*plural* **-lix·es** or **-li·ces**) *n* a ridge of cartilage located behind the folded edge (**helix**) of the outer ear and running more or less parallel to it

ant·hel·min·tic /ànt hel míntik, àn thel-/, **ant·hel·min·thic** /ànt hel mínthik, àn thel-/ *adj* describes a natural or pharmaceutical substance that destroys or expels intestinal parasitic worms ■ *n* a natural or pharmaceutical substance that kills or expels intestinal parasitic worms [Late 17C. < Greek *anti* "against" + *helminth-* "worm"]

an·them /ánthəm/ *n* **1.** SONG OF ALLEGIANCE a song praising and declaring loyalty to something, e.g., a country, school, or organization ○ *a national anthem* **2.** SHORT HYMN FOR CHOIR a short hymn with words from the Bible, sung by a choir as part of a Christian church service **3.** RELIGIOUS SONG WITH PARTS a religious song with parts for different singers or groups, especially a hymn sung in a Christian church with parts sung by different members of the congregation **4.** ROUSING POPULAR SONG a stirring, often commercially popular, song that has become associated with a group, period, or cause and celebrates a sense of solidarity with it ○ *rock anthems* [Pre-12C. < late Latin *antiphona* "antiphon" < Greek *antiphōnos* "responsive" < *phōnē* "sound"]

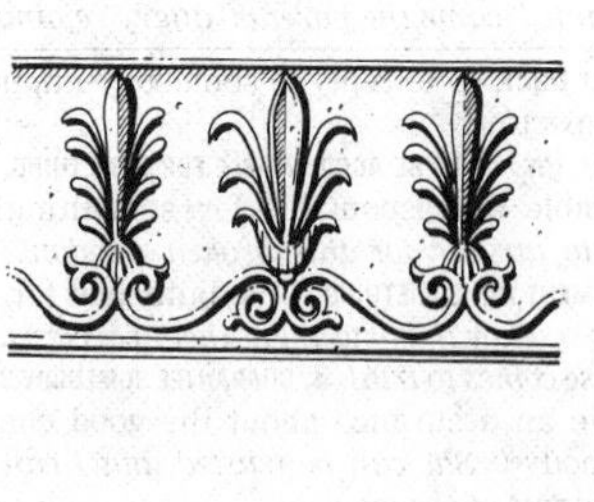

anthemion

an·the·mi·on /an theémee ən/ (*plural* **-mi·a** /-mi ə, -mee ə/) *n* a motif of radiating leaves found in classical Greek art and design [Mid-19C. < Greek, "small flower" < *anthos* "flower"]

an·ther /ánthər/ *n* a male flower part forming the top part of a stamen and bearing the pollen in sacs [Early 18C. Via Latin, "medicine made from (the pollen-bearing part of) flowers" < Greek *anthēra* "flowery" < *anthos* "flower"]

an·ther·id·i·um /ànthə ríddee əm/ (*plural* **-i·a** /-ee ə/) *n* the male reproductive organ in algae, ferns, fungi, and mosses

an·the·sis /an thḗessiss/ *n* **1.** the opening of a flower bud **2.** the period of time between the opening of a flower and the formation of the fruit [Mid-19C. Via modern Latin < Greek *anthēsis* "bloom" < *anthein* "to flower" < *anthos* "flower"]

ant·hill /ánt hìl/ *n* a mound of earth formed by ants during the construction of their nest

antho- *prefix* flower ○ *anthozoan* [< Greek *anthos*]

an·tho·cy·a·nin /ànthō sí ənin/ *n* a water-soluble pigment that produces blue, violet, and red colors in plants [Mid-19C. < ANTHO- + CYANINE]

an·thol·o·gize /an thóllə jìz/ (**-gized, -giz·ing, -giz·es**) *v* **1.** *vt* to gather works from different writers, musicians, or artists, into a collection ○ *O. Henry's stories are often anthologized.* ○ *a much anthologized writer* **2.** *vi* to compile or publish an anthology —**an·thol·o·gist** *n*

an·thol·o·gy /an thólləjee/ (*plural* **-gies**) *n* **1.** COLLECTION OF DIFFERENT WRITERS' WORKS a book that consists of essays, stories, or poems by different writers **2.** COLLECTION OF MUSICAL OR ARTISTIC WORKS a collection of works from different musicians or artists **3.** COLLECTION OF THINGS a collection of various things or ideas ○ *an anthology of complaints* [Mid-17C. Via medieval Latin < medieval Greek *anthologia* "collection of flowers" < Greek *anthos* "flower"]

An·tho·ny (of Pa·du·a) /ánthənee/, **St.** (1195–1231) Italian friar. He joined the Franciscan order in 1227. A renowned preacher, he taught theology in Italy and France. Born **Fernando**

Library of Congress

Susan B. Anthony

An·tho·ny, Susan B. (1820–1906) US social reformer. She helped to found the National Woman Suffrage Association (1869). Full name **Anthony, Susan Brownell**

> "The true republic: men their rights and nothing more; women their rights and nothing less."
> [Susan B. Anthony. Motto on the front of her newspaper, *The Revolution*; 1868–70]

an·tho·phi·lous /an thóffələss/ *adj* describes an insect that feeds on or lives among flowers

an·tho·zo·an /ànthə zṓ ən/ *n* an invertebrate ocean animal with a roundish hollow body, e.g., a coral or sea anemone. Class: Anthozoa. [Late 19C. < modern Latin *Anthozoa* < ANTHO- + Greek *zōia* "animals"] —**an·tho·zo·ic** *adj*

an·thra·cene /ánthrə seen/ *n* an aromatic crystalline solid with a faint blue glow. Source: coal tar. Use: manufacture of dyes, organic chemicals. Formula: $C_{14}H_{10}$. [Mid-19C. < Greek *anthrax* "coal"]

an·thra·ces plural of **anthrax**

an·thra·cite /ánthrə sìt/ *n* a hard shiny black coal that is clean-burning, high in carbon content, and low in volatile matter [Early 19C. Via Latin < Greek *anthrakitēs* < *anthrax* "coal"] —**an·thra·cit·ic** /ànthrə síttik/ *adj*

an·thrac·nose /an thrák nòss/ *n* a fungal disease of beans and vines that produces dark sunken spots on fruit, stems, and leaves [Late 19C. < French < Greek *anthrax* "coal" + *nosos* "disease"]

an·thra·co·sis /ànthrə kṓssiss/ *n* a disease of the lungs caused by long-term inhalation of coal dust [Mid-19C. < Greek *anthrax* "coal"]

an·thra·qui·none /ànthrə kwí nōn, -kwi nṓn/ *n* a yellow crystalline chemical. Use: manufacture of dyes. Formula: $C_{14}H_8O_2$. [Late 19C. Blend of ANTHRACENE + QUINONE]

an·thrax /án thràks/ (*plural* **-thra·ces** /-thrə seez/) *n* **1.** a highly infectious, often fatal, bacterial disease of mammals, especially cattle and sheep, that is transmissible to humans and causes skin ulcers (**cutaneous anthrax**) or a form of pneumonia when inhaled (**pulmonary anthrax**) **2.** an open sore on the skin that results from infection with anthrax [14C. Via Latin, "carbuncle" < Greek, "coal, carbuncle"]

an·thro·bot·ics /ànthrō bóttiks/ *n* the study and development of robots that are intended to behave like or resemble human beings (*takes a singular verb*) [Late 20C. Blend of ANTHROPO- + ROBOTICS]

anthrop. *abbr* **1.** anthropological **2.** anthropology

anthropo- *prefix* human being ○ *anthropology* [< Greek *anthrōpos*]

an·thro·po·cen·tric /ànthrəpə séntrik/ *adj* **1.** regarding humans as the universe's most important entity **2.** seeing things in human terms, especially judging things according to human perceptions, values, and experiences ○ *anthropocentric responses to the condition of animals* —**an·thro·po·cen·tri·cal·ly** *adv* —**an·thro·po·cen·trism** *n*

an·thro·po·gen·e·sis /ànthrəpə jénnəssiss/, **an·thro·po·gen·y** /ànthrə pójjənee/ *n* the scientific study of the origin of humankind and how it has developed

an·thro·po·gen·ic /ànthrəpə jénnik/, **an·thro·po·ge·ne·tic** /ànthrəpəjə néttik/ *adj* **1.** relating to or resulting from the influence that humans have on the natural world **2.** relating to the origin and development of human beings —**an·thro·po·gen·i·cal·ly** *adv*

an·thro·po·gen·y *n* ANTHROP same as **anthropogenesis**

an·thro·poid /ánthrə pòyd/ *adj* **1.** OF APES AND MONKEYS relating to the group of animals that includes monkeys, gibbons, great apes, and humans **2.** LIKE HUMANS physically resembling human beings or human parts **3.** CLUMSY OR UNINTELLIGENT rough-mannered, clumsy, ugly, or unintelligent, as apes are sometimes characterized (*informal*) ■ *n* **1.** PRIMATE an animal belonging to the group that includes monkeys, gibbons, great apes, and humans. Suborder: Anthropoidea. **2.** ZOOL same as **anthropoid ape** —**an·thro·poid·al** /ànthrə póyd'l/ *adj*

an·thro·poid ape *n* a tailless animal with long arms and a highly developed brain that belongs to the family that includes the gorillas, chimpanzees, orangutans, and gibbons

an·thro·po·log·i·cal /ànthrəpə lójjik'l/ *adj* relating to the study of humankind, especially the study of cultures —**an·thro·po·log·i·cal·ly** *adv*

an·thro·po·log·i·cal lin·guis·tics *n* a branch of linguistic research that investigates the relationship between language and culture (*takes a singular verb*)

an·thro·pol·o·gy /ànthrə póllәjee/ *n* **1.** the study of humankind in all its aspects, especially human culture or human development. It differs from sociology in taking a more historical and comparative approach. **2.** the parts of Christian doctrine that are concerned with the nature, origin, and destiny of humankind —**an·thro·pol·o·gist** *n*

an·thro·pom·e·try /ànthrə pómmətree/ *n* the study of human body measurements. The uses of anthropometry include the creation of ergonomic furniture designs and the examination and comparison of populations. —**an·thro·po·met·ric** /ànthrəpə méttrik/ *adj* —**an·thro·po·met·ri·cal** *adj* —**an·thro·po·met·ri·cal·ly** *adv* —**an·thro·pom·e·trist** *n*

an·thro·po·mor·phism /ànthrəpə máwr fìzzəm/ *n* the attribution of a human form, human characteristics, or human behavior to nonhuman things, e.g., deities in mythology and animals in children's stories —**an·thro·po·mor·phic** *adj* —**an·thro·po·mor·phi·cal·ly** *adv*

an·thro·po·mor·phize /ànthrəpə máwr fìz/ (**-phized, -phiz·ing, -phiz·es**) *vt* to give a nonhuman thing a human form, human characteristics, or human behavior ○ *our tendency to anthropomorphize wild animals* —**an·thro·po·mor·phi·za·tion** /ànthrəpə mawrfi záysh'n/ *n*

an·thro·po·mor·phous /ànthrəpə máwrfəss/ *adj* **1.** having the shape of the human body or a human body part **2.** relating to the attribution of human characteristics to nonhuman things

an·thro·pop·a·thism /ànthrə póppə thìzzəm/, **an·thro·pop·a·thy** /-thee/ *n* the attribution of human emotions to a nonhuman thing, e.g., a deity or an object of worship [Mid-19C. < ANTHROPO- + -PATHY]

an·thro·poph·a·gus /ànthrə póffəgəss/ (*plural* **-gi** /-jì/) *n* somebody who eats human flesh (*technical*) [Mid-16C. < Latin < Greek *anthrōpophagos* "eating humans" < *anthrōpos* "human being"] —**an·thro·po·phag·ic** /ànthrəpə fájjik/ *adj* —**an·thro·poph·a·gous** *adj* —**an·thro·poph·a·gy** /-póffəjee/ *n*

an·thur·i·um /an thṓoree əm/ *n* a tropical evergreen plant with showy foliage. Flowers: glossy, heart-shaped, red or white, enclosing a spike of yellow florets. Native to: America. Genus: *Anthurium*. [Mid-19C. < modern Latin < Greek *anthos* "flower" + *oura* "tail"]

an·ti /ántee, -tì/ (*informal*) *adj* expressing or holding an opposing view, especially with regard to a political issue or moral principle ■ *n* (*plural* **-tis**) somebody with an opposing view, particularly on a political issue or moral principle ○ *Are you a pro or an anti?* [Late 18C. < ANTI-]

anti- *prefix* **1.** against or preventing ○ *anticlerical* ○ *anticoagulant* **2.** opposite ○ *anticlimax* ○ *antiparticle* [Via Latin < Greek *anti* "opposite, against"]

an·ti·a·bor·tion *adj*
an·ti·a·bor·tion·ist *n*
an·ti·ac·a·dem·ic *adj*
an·ti·ag·gres·sion *adj*
an·ti·ag·ing *adj*
an·ti·al·ler·gic *adj*
an·ti·an·xi·e·ty *adj*
an·ti·a·part·heid *adj*
an·ti·asth·ma *adj*
an·ti·bac·ter·i·al *adj, n*
an·ti-Bol·she·vik *adj, n*
an·ti·bour·geois *adj*
an·ti-Brit·ish *adj*
an·ti·bu·reau·crat·ic *adj*
an·ti·bur·glar *adj*
an·ti·busi·ness *adj*
an·ti·cak·ing *adj*
an·ti·can·cer *adj*
an·ti-Cath·o·lic *adj, n*
an·ti-Cath·ol·i·cism *n*
an·ti·cen·sor·ship *adj*
an·ti-Chris·tian *adj*
an·ti·clas·si·cal *adj*
an·ti·clot·ting *adj*
an·ti-Com·mu·nism *n*
an·ti·cor·ro·sive *adj*
an·ti·cor·rup·tion *n*
an·ti·crime *adj*
an·ti-Dar·win·i·an *adj*
an·ti-Dar·win·ism *n*
an·ti·dem·o·crat·ic *adj*
an·ti·di·ar·rhe·al *adj, n*
an·ti·dis·crim·i·na·tion *adj*
an·ti-Eng·lish *adj*
an·ti·es·tab·lish·ment *adj*
an·ti·fem·i·nism *n*
an·ti·fem·i·nist *n, adj*
an·ti·fric·tion *adj*
an·ti·fun·gal *adj, n*
an·ti·gam·bling *adj*
an·ti·gov·ern·ment *adj*
an·ti·in·flam·ma·to·ry *adj, n*
an·ti·i·so·la·tion·ist *n*
an·ti·ma·lar·i·al *adj, n*
an·ti·mar·ket *adj*
an·ti·mi·cro·bi·al *adj, n*
an·ti·par·a·sit·ic *adj, n*
an·ti·plaque *adj*
an·ti·pol·lu·tion *adj*
an·ti·pov·er·ty *adj*
an·ti·ra·cism *n*
an·ti·ra·cist *adj, n*
an·ti·ra·dar *adj*
an·ti·sat·el·lite *adj*
an·ti·slav·er·y *adj*
an·ti·smog *adj*
an·ti·smok·ing *adj*
an·ti·stat·ic *adj*
an·ti·sub·ma·rine *adj*
an·ti·tank *adj*
an·ti·theft *adj*
an·ti·vi·ral *adj*
an·ti·vi·rus *adj*
an·ti·war *adj*
an·ti·wrin·kle *adj*

an·ti·ad·re·ner·gic /àntee àddrə núrjik, àntì-/ *adj* counteracting the physiological effects of epinephrine ■ *n* a drug that counteracts the physiological effects of epinephrine

an·ti·air·craft /àntee ér kràft, àntì-/ *adj* designed and used to destroy enemy aircraft

an·ti·air·craft gun *n* a piece of artillery designed and used to destroy enemy aircraft

an·ti·a·li·as·ing /àntee áylee əssing, àntì-/ *n* the technique of smoothing the jagged edges of diagonal lines in computer graphics by varying the color at the edges

an·ti·an·gi·na /àntee an jínə, àntì-/ *adj* controlling or preventing the symptoms of angina

an·ti·ar·rhyth·mic /àntee ə ríthmik, àntì-/ *adj* counteracting irregular heart action ■ *n* a drug that counteracts irregular heart action

an·ti·art /ántì aàrt, ántee aàrt/ *n* the art of the Dada movement, begun during World War I, that rejected conventional artistic practices and tastes ■ *adj* rejecting conventional artistic practices and tastes

an·ti·at·om /ántee àttəm, ántì-/ *n* an atom made up of antiparticles

an·ti·bal·lis·tic mis·sile /àntee bə lístik-, àntì-/ *n* a missile used to prevent a ballistic missile from reaching its target by destroying it in flight

An·tibes /oN teéb/ port and resort southwest of Nice in the Alpes-Maritimes Department in the Provence-Alpes-Côte d'Azur Region of France. Population: 72,412 (1999).

an·ti·bi·o·sis /àntee bī óssiss, àntī-/ *n* a relationship between organisms that is harmful to one of them, e.g., the production by one microorganism of chemicals that harm another [Late 19C. < ANTI-, after *symbiosis*]

an·ti·bi·ot·ic /ànti bī óttik, àntī-/ *n* a naturally produced substance that kills or inactivates bacteria, but has no effect against viruses, used as a medication ■ *adj* able to kill or inactivate bacteria —**an·ti·bi·ot·i·cal·ly** *adv*

an·ti·bod·y /ánti bòddee, ántī-/ (*plural* **-ies**) *n* a protein produced by B cells in the body in response to the presence of an antigen, e.g., a bacterium or virus. Antibodies are a primary form of immune response in resistance to disease and act by attaching themselves to a foreign antigen and weakening or destroying it. [Early 20C. Translation of German *Antikörper*, contraction of *anti-toxischer Körper* "antitoxic body" or a similar phrase]

an·tic /ántik/ *n* **CLOWN** an actor or performer playing a comic role requiring ludicrously eccentric behavior (*archaic*) ■ **an·tics** *npl* **SILLY PRANKS** amusing, frivolous, or eccentric behavior ■ *adj* **STRANGE** ludicrously eccentric (*archaic*) [Early 16C. Via Italian *antico* "old, old-fashioned" < Latin *anticus, antiquus*]

an·ti·cat·a·lyst /àntee kátt'list, àntī-/ *n* **1.** CHEM same as **inhibitor** (sense 1) **2.** a substance that inhibits or prevents the action of a catalyst

an·ti·cath·ode /àntee ká thōd, àntī-/ *n* the anode in a vacuum tube, e.g., an X-ray tube, toward which electrons flow

an·ti·choice /àntī chóyss, ànti chóyss/ *adj* opposed to the principle or practice of legal abortion

an·ti·cho·lin·er·gic /àntee kōlə núrjik, àntī-/ *adj* blocking nerve impulses that are part of the stress response ■ *n* a drug of a group used to control stress

an·ti·cho·lin·es·ter·ase /àntee kōlə néstə ràyss, àntī-, -ràyz/ *n* a substance that blocks the activity of the enzyme cholinesterase, increasing the concentration of acetylcholine in the body

An·ti·christ /ántee krīst, ántī-/ *n* **1.** an antagonist of Jesus Christ, expected by the early Christians to spread evil throughout the world, but then to be overcome by the second coming of Christ **2.** *also* **an·ti·christ** a person or power opposed to Jesus Christ [Pre-12C. Via ecclesiastical Latin < Greek *antikhristos*]

an·tic·i·pate /an tíssi pàyt/ (**-pat·ed, -pat·ing, -pates**) *vt* **1. EXPECT SOMETHING** to think or be fairly sure that something will happen ○ *We anticipate a few problems in the early stages.* **2. LOOK FORWARD TO SOMETHING** to feel excited, hopeful, or eager about something that is going to happen ○ *anticipating Saturday's concert* **3. ACT BEFOREHAND TO ADDRESS SOMETHING IMMINENT** to imagine or consider something before it happens and make any necessary preparations or changes ○ *anticipate flooding next week* **4. PREVENT SOMETHING** to succeed in preventing or avoiding something by acting in advance **5. START SOMETHING AHEAD OF OTHERS** to say or do something before it becomes common or fashionable (*formal*) **6. ACT IN HOPE OF SOMETHING HAPPENING** to act on the promise or expectation of something, before it has been given or confirmed (*formal*) ○ *frequently anticipated his salary* [Mid-16C. < Latin *anticipat-*, past participle of *anticipare* "catch beforehand" < *capere* "seize, take"] —**an·tic·i·pa·tive** /-pàytiv, -pətiv/ *adj* —**an·tic·i·pa·tor** *n*

USAGE Anticipating trouble: If you ***anticipate*** trouble, it often just means that you are expecting or foreseeing trouble; the word's more traditional meaning is that you are taking steps to prevent trouble, that is, forestalling rather than expecting it. Both these meanings are acceptable; however, some critics object to *unanticipated* as used in *seven unanticipated overnight guests*, where *unexpected* is the preferred choice.

an·tic·i·pa·tion /an tìssi páysh'n/ *n* **1. EXPECTANT WAITING** the feeling of looking forward, usually excitedly or eagerly, to something that is going to happen **2.** FIN **PREMATURE USE OF FUNDS** the seizure or use of funds before they are legally available, especially from a trust fund **3.** MUSIC **NOTE PLAYED BEFORE CHORD** a note related to a chord that is played just before the chord itself

an·tic·i·pa·to·ry /an tíssipə tàwree/ *adj* experienced or done in the expectation of a future event

an·ti·cler·i·cal /àntee klérrik'l, àntī-/ *adj* opposed to the involvement of the church or clergy in politics or public affairs —**an·ti·cler·i·cal·ism** *n*

an·ti·cli·max /àntee klī màks, àntī-/ *n* **1.** an ordinary or unsatisfying event that follows an increasingly exciting, dramatic, or unusual series of events or a period of increasing anticipation and excitement **2.** an unexpected change in tone or subject matter from the high-minded, serious, or compelling to the trivial, comic, or dull —**an·ti·cli·mac·tic** /àntee klī máktik, àn tī -/ *adj* —**an·ti·cli·mac·ti·cal·ly** *adv*

an·ti·cline /ánti klīn/ *n* an arch-shaped formation of layers of sedimentary rock folded upward by movements in the Earth's crust [Mid-19C < ANTI- + Greek *klinein* "to lean," after INCLINE] —**an·ti·cli·nal** /àntee klīn'l, àntī-/ *adj*

an·ti·clock·wise /àntī klók wīz, àntee-/ *adj, adv UK* same as **counterclockwise**

an·ti·co·ag·u·lant /àntee kō ággyələnt, àntī-/ *n* a natural or synthetic agent that prevents blood clots from forming ■ *adj* preventing blood from clotting

an·ti·co·don /àntee kō dòn, àntī-/ *n* a set of three nucleotides in transfer RNA involved in the formation of a protein

an·ti·co·in·ci·dence /àntee kō ínssidənss, àntī-/ *adj* describes an electronic circuit that produces an output pulse if one, but not both, of its input terminals receives a pulse within a specific time frame

an·ti·com·pet·i·tive /àntee kəm péttitiv, àntī-/ *adj* likely or certain to discourage competition

an·ti·con·vul·sant /àntī kən vúlsənt, àntee-/ *adj* preventing or reducing seizures ■ *n* a drug that prevents or reduces seizures. Use: epilepsy control. —**an·ti·con·vul·sive** *n, adj*

An·ti·cos·ti Is·land /àntee kòstee-/ island in the Gulf of St. Lawrence, Quebec, Canada. Its abundant forests shelter diverse wildlife. Area: 3,066 sq. mi./7,941 sq. km.

an·ti·cy·clone /àntee sī klōn, àntī-/ *n* a large system of atmospheric high pressure marked by circulating winds moving clockwise from the center in the northern hemisphere and counterclockwise in the southern hemisphere, bringing generally settled weather —**an·ti·cy·clon·ic** /àntee sī klónnik, àntī-/ *adj*

an·ti·de·pres·sant /àntee di préss'nt, àntī-/ *n* a drug used to prevent or reduce depression ■ *adj* acting to prevent or reduce depression —**an·ti·de·pres·sive** *adj*

an·ti·di·a·bet·ic /àntee dī ə béttik, àntī-/ *adj* reducing the effects of diabetes

an·ti·di·u·ret·ic /àntee dī ə réttik, àntī-/ *adj* preventing the excessive output of urine ○ *an antidiuretic hormone* ○ *antidiuretic drugs* ■ *n* a drug for preventing the excessive output of urine

an·ti·di·u·ret·ic hor·mone *n* BIOCHEM same as **vasopressin**

an·ti·dote /ánti dōt/ *n* **1.** a substance that counteracts the effects of a toxin **2.** something that will take away or reduce the bad effects of something unpleasant or undesirable ○ *an antidote to boredom* [15C. Via Latin < Greek *antidoton* < *antididonai* "give against" < *didonai* "give"] —**an·ti·dot·al** /ànti dṓt'l/ *adj*

an·ti·dump·ing /àntee dúmping, àntī-/ *adj* opposed to or restricting the importation of cheaply produced goods that undercut domestic producers' prices

an·ti·e·met·ic /àntee i méttik, àntī-/ *adj* preventing vomiting ■ *n* a drug that prevents vomiting

An·tie·tam /an teétəm/ village in northwestern Maryland, southeast of Sharpsburg. On September 17, 1862, Robert E. Lee's army crossed nearby Antietam Creek and was repelled by George McClellan's forces in one of the bloodiest battles of the Civil War. In the South, the engagement is usually called the Battle of Sharpsburg.

an·ti·fed·er·al·ist /àntee féddərəlist, àntī-/ *n* **1.** *also* **An·ti·fed·er·al·ist** HIST **HISTORICAL OPPONENT OF US CONSTITUTION** somebody who opposed the US Constitution when it was being drawn up **2. SOMEBODY OPPOSED TO FEDERALISM** an opponent of the division of power between a central government and regional governments ■ *adj* **AGAINST FEDERALISM** opposed to the idea or practice of federalism —**an·ti·fed·er·al·ism** *n*

an·ti·fer·ro·mag·net·ic /àntee fèrrō mag néttik, àntī-/ *adj* describes substances that behave like paramagnetic substances with respect to their permeability but behave like ferromagnetic substances when their temperature is changed —**an·ti·fer·ro·mag·net** /àntee fèrrō mágnət, àntī-/ *n* —**an·ti·fer·ro·mag·net·ism** *n*

an·ti·fer·til·i·ty /àntee fər tíllətee, àntī-/ *adj* acting to reduce or destroy the ability to reproduce

an·ti·foul·ing paint /àntee fówling-, àntī-/ *n* a poisonous paint used to prevent barnacles and other organisms from growing on the bottom of a boat or ship

an·ti·freeze /ánti freéz/ *n* a substance added to a liquid to lower its freezing point. An antifreeze such as ethylene glycol is added to or substituted for the water in a vehicle's radiator to stop it from freezing in winter.

an·ti·gen /ántijən/ *n* a substance, usually a protein, on the surface of a cell or bacterium that stimulates the production of an antibody [Early 20C. Via German < French *antigène* < *anti-* "anti-" + Greek *-genēs* (see -GEN)] —**an·ti·gen·ic** /ànti jénnik/ *adj* —**an·ti·gen·i·cal·ly** *adv* —**an·ti·ge·nic·i·ty** /ànti jə níssətee/ *n*

an·ti·gen feed·ing *n* the oral administration of a protein antigen to encourage immune-system tolerance to it

an·ti·gen·ic drift *n* changes of a minor nature in the antigenic structure of a virus strain. Antigenic drift is the result of natural selection after mixing with a partially immune population.

an·ti·gog·lin /ànti gógglin/ *regional adj* **1. ASKEW** crooked or askew **2. DIAGONAL** in a diagonal position or arrangement ■ *adv* **DIAGONALLY** in a diagonal direction [Late 19C. Perhaps < ANTI- + *goggle* in British dialect sense "tremble, shake"]

REGIONAL NOTE Both the "askew" and "diagonal(ly)" senses of ***antigoglin*** are common in the southern, South Midland, and western United States. These regions share several synonyms, none of which is easily distinguished in meaning from the others: *angly, antigoglin, blasy, catawampus, crossways,* and *diagonally.*

An·tig·o·ne /an tíggənee/ *n* in Greek mythology, the daughter of Oedipus and his mother and wife Jocasta. Sentenced to death for defying an order that her brother should not be buried, she committed suicide.

An·tig·o·nus I /an tíggənəss/ (382?–301 B.C.) Greek general and king of Macedonia (306–301 B.C.). He secured a large part of Asia Minor from the empire of Alexander the Great broke up in 323 B.C.

an·ti·grav·i·ty /àntee grávvətee, àntī-/ *n* a hypothetical force that would counteract the effects of gravity or of high acceleration ■ *adj* counteracting the effects of gravity or of high acceleration

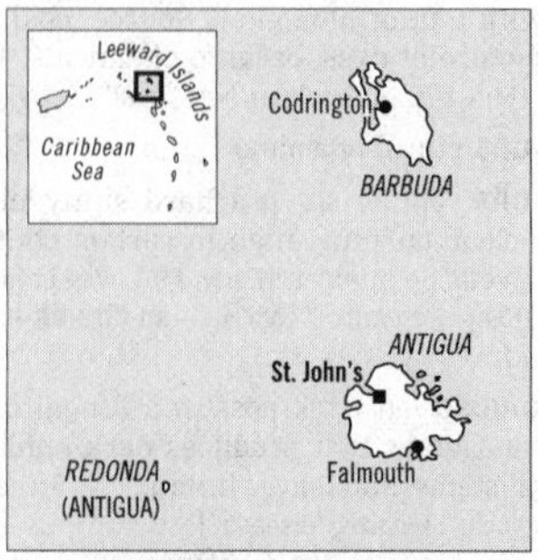

Antigua and Barbuda

An·ti·gua and Bar·bu·da /an teégə ənd baar bóódə/ island nation in the Leeward Islands, east of Puerto

Rico and north of Venezuela in the Caribbean Sea. It became a member of the British Commonwealth in 1981. Language: English. Currency: East Caribbean dollar. Capital: St John's. Population: 67,897 (2001). Area: 171 sq. mi./442 sq. km. —**An·ti·guan** *adj, n*

an·ti·he·lix *n* ANAT same as **anthelix**

an·ti·he·ro /ántee hèerō, ántī-/ (*plural* **-roes**) *n* the central character in a story who is not a traditionally brave or good hero —**an·ti·her·o·ic** /àntee hi rṓ ik, àntī-/ *adj*

an·ti·his·ta·mine /àntee hístəmin, àntī-, -meen/ *n* a drug that blocks the action of histamine. Use: to control allergies. (*often used before a noun*) —**an·ti·his·ta·min·ic** /àntī hístə mínnik, àntee-/ *adj*

an·ti·hy·per·ten·sive /àntee hīpər ténssiv, àntī-/ *adj* controlling high blood pressure ■ *n* an agent or means to control high blood pressure

an·ti·knock /ánti nòk/ *n* a substance added to gasoline. Use: to reduce or stop faulty fuel combustion associated with a knocking sound.

An·ti-Leb·a·non Moun·tains /àntee lébbənən-/ mountain range in southwestern Syria and eastern Lebanon, parallel to the Mediterranean coast. Highest peak: Mount Hermon 9,232 ft./2,814 m.

an·ti·lep·ton /àntee lép tòn, àntī-/ *n* the antiparticle of a lepton

an·ti·life /àntee līf, ántī-/ *adj* regarded as preventing or opposed to living life fully in tune with the natural world (*informal*) ○ *antilife legislation* ○ *It is absurd and antilife to have to sit in an office all day.*

An·til·les ♦ **Greater Antilles, Lesser Antilles**

an·ti·lock /àntee lók, àntī-/ *adj* describes an electronically controlled braking system or brakes that prevent the vehicle's wheels from locking if the driver brakes very suddenly

an·ti·log·a·rithm /àntee lóggə rìthəm, àntī-/, **an·ti·log** /àntee lòg, àntī-/ *n* a number for which the logarithm is a given number, so for logarithm$_a$b = c, then antilogarithm$_a$c = b

an·ti·ma·cas·sar /àntee mə kássər/ *n* a piece of fabric placed over the back of an armchair to keep it clean [Mid-19C. < ANTI- + *Macassar*, brand of hair oil]

an·ti·mag·net·ic /àntee mag néttik, àntī-/ *adj* describes a material that does not become permanently magnetized in a magnetic field

an·ti·masque /ánti màsk/, **an·ti·mask** *n* an interlude in or prelude to a 17th-century masque that contrasts with the main performance and often involves grotesque costumes and dancing

an·ti·mat·ter /ánti màttər, ántī-/ *n* a hypothetical form of matter composed of subatomic particles (**antiparticles**) that correspond to and can annihilate other elementary particles

an·ti·mere /ánti mèer/ *n* a part of a radially symmetrical animal that is the opposite of a corresponding part of the animal —**an·ti·mer·ic** /ànti mérrik/ *adj*

an·ti·me·tab·o·lite /àntee mə tábbə līt, àntī-/ *n* a synthetic substance similar to one needed for normal cell growth that disrupts cell development by replacing the natural metabolite. Antimetabolites may be used in cancer therapy.

an·ti·mis·sile mis·sile /àntee míss'l-, àntī-/ *n* a missile used to prevent another missile from reaching its target by destroying it in flight

an·ti·mi·tot·ic /àntī mī tóttik, àntee-/ *adj* preventing cell division (**mitosis**) —**an·ti·mi·tot·ic** *n*

an·ti·mo·ny /ántə mōnee/ *n* a toxic crystalline element that occurs in metallic and nonmetallic forms. Source: ores, e.g., stibnite. Use: alloys, electronics. Symbol **Sb**. See table at **element** [15C. < medieval Latin *antimonium*]

an·ti·my·cot·ic /àntee mī kóttik, àntī-/ *adj* **1.** preventing, killing, or reducing the growth of fungi **2.** a drug for preventing, killing, or reducing the growth of fungi [< ANTI- + Greek *mukētes* "fungi"]

an·ti·ne·o·plas·tic /àntee nee ō plástik, àntī-/ *adj* preventing or inhibiting the growth of cancers —**an·ti·ne·o·plas·tic** *n*

an·ti·neu·tri·no /àntee noo treenō, àntī-/ (*plural* **-nos**) *n* the antiparticle of a neutrino. When a neutrino and an antineutrino are brought together, mutual annihilation occurs.

an·ti·neu·tron /àntee noo tròn, àntī-/ *n* the antiparticle of a neutron. When a neutron and an antineutron are brought together, mutual annihilation occurs.

an·ti·no·ci·cep·tion /àntinō si sépshən/ *n* a reduction in pain sensitivity produced within neurons when an endorphin or similar opium-containing substance (**opioid**) combines with a receptor —**an·ti·no·ci·cep·tive** *adj*

an·ti·node /ánti nōd/ *n* a point of maximum amplitude of a wave characteristic in a system in which the wave form is stationary in time

an·ti·no·mi·an /ànti nṓmee ən/ *n* CHRISTIAN BELIEVING SALVATION DEPENDS ON FAITH a Christian who believes that faith and divine grace bring about salvation and that it is therefore not necessary to accept established moral laws ■ *adj* **1.** HAVING ANTINOMIAN BELIEFS holding antinomian Christian beliefs **2.** REJECTING FIXED MORAL LAWS refusing to accept established moral laws that apply to everybody [Mid-17C. < medieval Latin *Antinomi* "antinomians" < Latin *antinomia* (see ANTINOMY)]

an·ti·no·mi·an·ism /ànti nṓmee ə nìzzəm/ *n* **1.** in Christian doctrine, the belief that Christians are not bound by established moral laws, but should rely on faith and divine grace for salvation **2.** the belief that it is impossible to apply a universal moral code because it will have a different meaning for different people

an·tin·o·my /an tínnəmee/ (*plural* **-mies**) *n* **1.** PHILOSOPHY a contradictory and illogical conclusion produced by two apparently correct and reasonable statements or facts **2.** LAW a contradiction between two laws, principles, or authorities [Late 16C. Via Latin *antinomia* < Greek, literally "against law" < *nomos* "law, rule"] —**an·ti·nom·ic** /ànti nómmik/ *adj*

an·ti·nov·el /àntee nòvv'l, ántī-/ *n* a work of fiction that lacks the features traditionally used in a novel, e.g., consistent characters, a coherent plot, and a constant authorial perspective —**an·ti·nov·el·ist** /àntee nóvv'list, àntī-/ *n*

an·ti·nu·cle·ar /àntī nooklee ər, àntee-/ *adj* **1.** opposed to nuclear weapons or power **2.** reactive with or destructive to cell nuclei

an·ti·nu·cle·on /àntee nooklee òn, àntī-/ *n* an antiproton or antineutron. When a nucleon and an antinucleon are brought together, mutual annihilation occurs.

an·ti·nuke /àntee nook, àntī-/ *adj* same as **antinuclear** (sense 1) (*informal*) ○ *an antinuke demonstration*

An·ti·och /ántee òk/ **1.** city in northwestern California, on the San Joaquin River. Population: 99,870 (2002 estimate). **2.** former name for **Antakya**

an·ti·on·co·gene /àntee óngkə jeen, àntī-/ *n* a recessive gene that is thought to suppress cancers by limiting cell multiplication

an·ti·ox·i·dant /àntee óksid'nt, àntī-/ *n* a substance that inhibits the destructive effects of oxidation, e.g., in the body or in foodstuffs or plastics

an·ti·par·al·lel /àntee párrə lèl, àntī-/ *adj* parallel but opposite in linear or rotational direction

an·ti·par·ti·cle /àntee paartik'l, àntī-/ *n* an elementary particle with the same mass as its corresponding particle but with opposite values for other properties such as charge. When an antiparticle and its particle interact, mutual annihilation occurs.

an·ti·pas·to /àntee paastō, -pástō, aantee-/ (*plural* **-ti** /-tee/) *n* a food served at the beginning of an Italian meal or as a snack [Early 17C. < Italian, "before food"]

an·tip·a·thet·ic /àntipə théttik, an tìppə-/ *adj* **1.** feeling or expressing anger, hostility, strong opposition, or disgust toward somebody or something **2.** causing anger, hostility, strong opposition, or disgust [Early 17C. < ANTIPATHY, after PATHETIC] —**an·tip·a·thet·i·cal·ly** *adv*

an·tip·a·thy /an típpəthee/ (*plural* **-thies**) *n* **1.** strong hostility or opposition toward somebody or something **2.** somebody or something that causes anger, hostility, strong opposition, or disgust [Late 16C. Via French *antipathie* < Greek *antipathēs* "feeling the opposite" < *pathos* "feeling"]

SYNONYMS See ***dislike***.

an·ti·pe·ri·od·ic /àntee peeree óddik, àntī-/ *adj* preventing the periodic recurrence of symptoms or of a disease such as malaria —**an·ti·pe·ri·od·ic** *n*

an·ti·pe·ri·stal·sis /àntee peri stáwlssiss, àntī-, -perri stólsiss/ (*plural* **-stal·ses** /-stáwl seez/) *n* contractions of the intestine in the reverse direction to what is usual, tending to cause vomiting —**an·ti·pe·ri·stal·tic** *adj*

an·ti·per·son·nel /àntee pùrssə nél, àntī-/ *adj* intended to injure and kill enemy personnel rather than to destroy buildings, structures, arsenals, or missiles

an·ti·per·spi·rant /àntee púrspərənt, àntī-/ *n* an astringent preparation applied especially under the arms to reduce or prevent perspiration. Antiperspirants are produced in many forms, including aerosols, roll-ons, and sticks. ■ *adj* used to reduce or prevent perspiration

an·ti·phase /ántee fàyz, ántī-/ *adj* relating to a boundary, e.g., in an alloy, where an ordered pattern of atoms meets a random pattern

an·ti·phon /ántə fòn/ *n* **1.** MUSIC SUNG IN ALTERNATING PARTS a hymn or psalm performed by two groups of singers chanting alternate sections **2.** SECTION OF FORMAL CHURCH SERVICE a short piece of biblical or devotional text that is chanted or sung before or after a psalm verse in a Roman Catholic or Anglican church service **3.** RESPONSE a response or reply (*literary*) [15C. < ecclesiastical Latin *antiphona* < Greek *antiphōnos* "sounding in response" < *phōnē* "sound"]

an·tiph·o·nar·y /an tíffə nèrree/ (*plural* **-ies**) *n* a book, often large and richly decorated, containing antiphons or anthems to be sung or chanted responsively

an·tiph·o·ny /an tíffənee/ (*plural* **-nies**) *n* **1.** CHR same as **antiphon** (sense 1) **2.** responsive chanting, recitation, or singing, e.g., of liturgical antiphons **3.** a musical response or answering phrase —**an·tiph·o·nal** *adj*

an·tiph·ra·sis /an tíffrəssiss/ *n* the use of a word or phrase to mean the opposite of its usual or literal sense, e.g., saying on a rainy day, "What a great day for a picnic!" [Mid-16C. < late Latin < Greek *antiphrazein* "express oppositely" < *phrazein* "declare"]

an·ti·pode /ánti pōd/ *n* an exact or diametrical opposite [Early 17C. Back-formation < ANTIPODES]

an·tip·o·de·an /an tìppə dee ən/, **An·tip·o·de·an** *adj* coming from or relating to Australia or New Zealand

an·tip·o·des /an típpə deez/ *npl* **1.** places at opposite sides of the world from each other, or the areas at the side of the world opposite from a given place **2.** two points, places, or things that are diametrically opposite each other [14C. Via French or late Latin < Greek *antipodes* "those who have their feet opposite" < *pod-*, stem of *pous* "foot"] —**an·tip·o·dal** *adj*

An·tip·o·des *npl* Australia and New Zealand, from the perspective of the United Kingdom or Europe (*informal*)

an·ti·pope /ánti pōp/ *n* an alternative pope elected in opposition to a standing pope [15C. Via French *antipape* < medieval Latin *antipapa* < *papa* "pope," after *antichristus* "Antichrist"]

an·ti·pros·ta·glan·din /àntee pròstə glánd'n, àntī-/ *n* a drug or agent used to limit the release of prostaglandins

an·ti·pro·ton /àntee prṓ tòn, àntī-/ *n* the antiparticle of a proton. When a proton and an antiproton are brought together, mutual annihilation occurs.

an·ti·pru·rit·ic /àntee proo ríttik, àntī-/ *adj* alleviating the symptoms of itching ■ *n* a drug or other agent that controls itching

an·ti·pso·ri·a·sis /àntee sə rī́əsiss, àntī-/ *adj* alleviating the symptoms of psoriasis —**an·ti·pso·ri·at·ic** /àntī sàwree áttik, àntee-/ *adj*

an·ti·psy·chi·a·try /ànti sī kī́ ətree, àntī-/ *n* a way of treating people with psychiatric disorders that is derived from psychoanalysis and is opposed to conventional medication

an·ti·psy·chot·ic /àntī sī kóttik, àntee-/ *adj* relieving the symptoms of psychosis ■ *n* a drug that relieves the symptoms of a psychiatric disorder

an·ti·py·ret·ic /àntee pī réttik, àntī-/ *adj* reducing fever ■ *n* a drug or other agent that reduces fever —**an·ti·py·re·sis** /àntī pī reéssiss, àntee-/ *n*

antiq. *abbr* **1.** antiquarian **2.** antiquity

an·ti·quar·i·an /ànti kwérree ən/ *adj* relating to or dealing with antiques or antiquities, especially rare and old books ■ *n* same as **antiquary** —**an·ti·quar·i·an·ism** *n*

an·ti·quark /àntee kwàwrk, àntī-/ *n* the antiparticle of a quark. When a quark and an antiquark are brought together, mutual annihilation occurs.

an·ti·quar·y /ánti kwèrree/ (*plural* **-ies**) *n* a collector, scholar, or seller of antiques or antiquities [Mid-16C. < Latin *antiquarius* < *antiquus* "old"]

an·ti·quate /ánti kwàyt/ (**-quat·ed, -quat·ing, -quates**) *vt* **1.** to cause something to become out of date or old **2.** HANDICRAFT same as **antique** [Late 16C. < ecclesiastical Latin *antiquat-*, past participle of *antiquare* "make old" < Latin *antiquus* "old"]

an·ti·quat·ed /ánti kwàytəd/ *adj* out of date, old-fashioned, or in need of updating or replacing

SYNONYMS See ***old-fashioned.***

an·tique /an teék/ *n* **1. COLLECTIBLE OLD ITEM** a collectible decorative or household object that is valued because of its age **2. CLASSICAL ART** the style, traditions, and qualities of ancient times, especially the art and sculpture of ancient Greece and Rome (*formal*) ■ *adj* **1. MADE LONG AGO** old and often valuable, of interest to collectors, and characteristic of a period and style of manufacture **2. FROM CLASSICAL TIMES** derived from a period of ancient history, especially ancient Greece and Rome, or stylistically typical of such a period (*formal*) **3. ANCIENT** very old or old-fashioned (*informal*) ■ *vt* (**-tiqued, -tiqu·ing, -tiques**) HANDICRAFT **MAKE SOMETHING APPEAR OLD** to treat something, especially a new object, so that it looks antique or worn with time [15C. Via French < Latin *antiquus* "old"]

an·tiq·ui·ty /an tíkwətee/ (*plural* **-ties**) *n* **1. ANCIENT HISTORY** ancient history, especially the period of time during which the ancient Greek and Roman civilizations flourished **2. PEOPLE OF ANCIENT TIMES** the people of ancient civilizations, especially those of ancient Greece and Rome **3. OLDNESS** the state of being very old or ancient ○ *a sculpture of great antiquity* **4. OLD OBJECT** an object, especially something collectible, decorative, valuable, or interesting, that dates from a previous era

an·ti·re·jec·tion /àntee ri jéksh'n, àntī-/ *adj* designed to prevent the immune system from rejecting a newly grafted organ or tissue

an·ti·ret·ro·vir·al /àntee rèttrō vīrəl, àntī-/ *adj* effective against retroviruses —**an·ti·ret·ro·vir·al** *n*

an·ti·rheu·ma·toid /àntee roómə tòyd, àntī-/ *adj* preventing or relieving the symptoms of rheumatism

an·ti·roll bar /àntī rōl-, ànti-/ *n* a cross-mounted metal bar incorporated in the suspension system of a motor vehicle, designed to prevent the vehicle from swinging dangerously or overturning

an·tir·rhi·num /ànti rīnəm/ *n UK* PLANTS same as **snapdragon** [Mid-16C. Via Latin < Greek *antirrhinon*, literally "counterfeiting a nose" < *rhin-* "nose"; from the flower's shape]

an·ti-Se·mit·ic *adj* hating or discriminating against Jews

an·ti-Sem·i·tism *n* policies, views, or actions that harm or discriminate against Jews —**an·ti-Sem·ite** *n*

an·ti·sense /àntee sénss, àntī-/ *adj* relating to or having a strand of DNA complementary to other genetic material, so that the expression of a trait can be regulated

an·ti·sep·sis /ànti sépsiss/ *n* **1.** the reduction or prevention of infection, especially by the elimination or reduction of the growth of microorganisms that cause disease or decay **2.** the condition of being free from microorganisms

an·ti·sep·tic /ànti séptik/ *adj* **1. CONTROLLING INFECTION** reducing or preventing infection, especially by the elimination or reduction of the growth of microorganisms that cause disease or decay **2. DULL** unexciting and unimaginative **3. UNCONTENTIOUS** not contentious, controversial, or offensive in any way ■ *n* **AGENT FOR CONTROLLING INFECTION** an agent that reduces or prevents infection, especially by eliminating or reducing the growth of microorganisms that cause disease or decay —**an·ti·sep·ti·cal·ly** *adv*

an·ti·se·rum /ànti seérəm/ (*plural* **-rums** or **-ra** /-seérə/) *n* an animal or human blood serum containing one or more ready-made antibodies that can provide immunity against a disease or counteract a venom

an·ti·so·cial /àntee sṓsh'l, àn tī-/ *adj* **1.** preferring not to spend time with other people **2.** hostile or indifferent to the comfort or needs of other members of a community or society as a whole —**an·ti·so·cial·ly** *adv*

USAGE See ***unsociable.***

an·ti·spas·mod·ic /àntī spaz móddik, àntee-/ *adj* controlling spasms ■ *n* a drug or other agent that controls muscle spasms

An·tis·the·nes /an tísthə neéz/ (444?–371? B.C.) Greek philosopher. He believed that happiness depends on moral virtue and founded the Cynic school of philosophy.

an·tis·tro·phe /an tístrəfee/ *n* **1. SECOND PART OF GREEK CHORAL ODE** in a classical Greek drama, the second section of an ode sung by the chorus after the first section (**strophe**) **2. RETURN MOVEMENT IN ANCIENT GREEK DRAMA** in a classical Greek drama, the second of two movements made by the chorus, back in the opposite direction to that of the first movement (**strophe**) **3.** LITERAT **SECOND METRICAL FORM IN POEM** the second type of metrical form in a poem that alternates two contrasting metrical forms [Mid-16C. Via late Latin < Greek *antistrophē* < *antistrephein* "turn back" < *strophē* (see STROPHE)] —**an·ti·stroph·ic** /ànti strṓffik/ *adj* —**an·ti·stroph·i·cal·ly** *adv*

an·ti·sway bar /àntī swáy-, ànti-/ *n* AUTOMOT same as **antiroll bar**

an·ti·ter·ror·ism /àntī térrə rìzzəm, àntee-/ *n* the combating of terrorists in their attempts to carry out violent and illegal activities against society or property (*often used before a noun*)

an·tith·e·sis /an títhəssiss/ (*plural* **-e·ses** /-ə seéz/) *n* **1. DIRECT OPPOSITE** the complete or exact opposite of something **2. FIGURE OF SPEECH** a use of words or phrases that contrast with each other to create a balanced effect **3.** PHILOSOPHY **CONTRASTING PROPOSITION** a proposition that is the opposite of another already proposed (**thesis**) [Early 16C. < late Latin < Greek *antithithenai* "set against" < *tithenai* "set"]

an·ti·thet·i·cal /ànti théttik'l/, **an·ti·thet·ic** /-théttik/ *adj* **1.** expressing or constituting the complete or exact opposite (*formal*) ○ *policies that are antithetical to the prevailing mood of the country* **2.** relating to or consisting of a proposition that is the opposite of another already proposed [Late 16C. < Greek *antithetikos* < *antitithenai* (see ANTITHESIS)] —**an·ti·thet·i·cal·ly** *adv*

an·ti·thy·roid /àntee thī ròyd, àntī-/ *adj* counteracting thyroid overactivity, especially in the production of thyroid hormone

an·ti·tox·ic /àntee tóksik/ *adj* acting to counteract toxins

an·ti·tox·in /àntee tóksin/ *n* **1.** an antibody produced in response to a specific toxin **2.** PHARM same as **antiserum**

an·ti·trade /ánti tràyd/ *n* a wind in the planetary wind system that is above the trade winds and blows in the opposite direction from them

an·ti·tra·gus /an títtrəgəss, ànti tráygəss/ (*plural* **-gi** /-jī, -gī/) *n* a bump of cartilage just below the opening of the external ear

an·ti·trust /àntee trúst, àn tī-/ *adj* intended to oppose trusts and cartels, e.g., by preventing them from using monopolistic business practices to make unfair profits ○ *antitrust legislation*

an·ti·tu·ber·cu·lo·sis /àntee tə burkyə lṓssiss, àntī-/ *adj* effective against tuberculosis

an·ti·tus·sive /àntee tússiv, àntī-/ *adj* controlling coughing ■ *n* a drug that controls coughing

an·ti·type /ánti tīp/ *n* **1.** in the Bible, somebody or something foreshadowed by or having striking similarities to an earlier person or thing (**type**) **2.** an opposite or contrasting type [Early 17C. Via late Latin < Greek *antitupos* "corresponding as an impression (to the die in which it was cast)" < *tupos* (see TYPE)] —**an·ti·typ·i·cal** /ànti típpik'l/ *adj*

an·ti·u·to·pi·a *n* a place, society, or state that is the opposite of perfect in every way —**an·ti·u·to·pi·an** *adj*

an·ti·ven·in /àntee vénnin, àntī-/, **an·ti·ven·om** /-vénnəm/ *n* **1.** an antitoxin to a specific venom **2.** an antiserum containing antibodies to a specific venom [Early 20C. < ANTI- + VENOM + -IN]

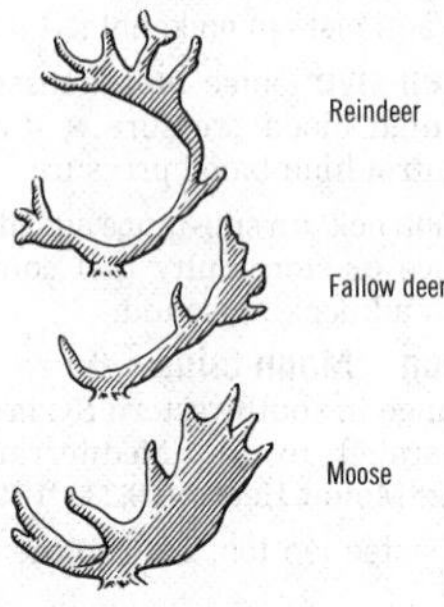

antler

ant·ler /ántlər/ *n* a solid bony branched horn found in pairs on the head of an animal, especially a male, of the deer family, including caribou and elk. Antlers are shed each year. [14C. < Anglo-Norman variant of Old French *antoillier*] —**ant·lered** *adj*

Ant·li·a /ántlee ə/ *n* a faint constellation of the southern hemisphere near Centaurus and Hydra

ant li·on *n* a nocturnal insect that resembles a damselfly when adult. The larvae lie buried under sand at the bottom of a cone-shaped pit and trap insects such as ants. Family: Myrmeleontidae. [Translation of Greek *murmēkoleōn*; from its usual prey and its fierce-looking jaws]

An·to·fa·gas·ta /àantō fə gaástə/ city in northern Chile, on the fringes of the Atacama Desert. Population: 251,429 (1998).

An·to·nel·lo da Mes·si·na /àntə néllō daa mə seénə/ (1430?–79) Sicilian painter who was influenced by Flemish realism

An·to·ni·nus Pi·us /àntə nīnəss pī əss/ (A.D. 86–161) Roman emperor. He succeeded Hadrian and enjoyed a peaceful and prosperous reign (A.D. 138–161). Full name **Titus Aurelius Fulvus Boionius Arrius Antoninus**

An·to·ni·on·i /an tṓnee ṓnee/, **Michelangelo** (*b.* 1912) Italian movie director whose movies include *L'Avventura* (1960) and *Zabriskie Point* (1970)

> "I don't work from a written script. My work begins when I look through the viewfinder of the camera—that for me is the moment of creation."
> [Michelangelo Antonioni, *Interview, Times (London)*; November 29, 1960]

an·to·no·ma·sia /àntənə máyzhə/ *n* **1.** the use of a title or formal description such as "Your Highness" or "His Excellency" in place of somebody's proper name **2.** the use of a proper name as a common noun to refer to somebody or something with associated characteristics, e.g., when a strong young man is called "a Hercules" [Mid-16C. < Latin < Greek *antonomazein* "name instead" < *anti-* "against, instead" + *onoma* "name"]

An·to·ny /ántənee/, **Mark** (83?–30 B.C.) Roman politician and general. He fought in Republican Rome's last civil war in alliance with Cleopatra and was defeated by Octavian. Latin name **Marcus Antonius**

an·to·nym /ántənìm/ *n* a word that means the opposite of another word. For example, "hot" is the antonym of "cold." [Mid-19C. < French *antonyme* < Greek *anti-* "against, opposite" + *onuma* "name"] —**an·to·nym·ic** /àntə nímmik/ *adj* —**an·ton·y·mous** /an tónnəməss/ *adj* —**an·ton·y·my** /an tónnə mee/ *n*

an·tra plural of **antrum**

An·trim /ántrim/ **1.** historic town in County Antrim, Northern Ireland. Population: 20,878 (1991). **2.** historic county in Ulster Province, Northern Ireland

an·tros·to·my /an tróstəmee/ (*plural* **-mies**) *n* the surgical creation of an opening into an antrum, usually for drainage purposes [< ANTRUM]

an·trum /ántrəm/ (*plural* **-tra** /-trə/) *n* a cavity within a bone, especially a sinus cavity [Early 19C. Via Latin, "cave" < Greek *antron*]

ant·sy /ántsee/ (**-si·er, -si·est**) *adj* (*informal*) **1.** feeling nervous, apprehensive, or tense **2.** moving or squirming around in a restless, bored, or impatient way [Mid-20C. Probably < *have ants in your pants*]

Ant·werp /ántwərp/ leading port of Belgium, situated on the Schelde river estuary 55 mi./88 km from the sea. Population: 447,632 (1999).

a·ñu /aá nōō, -nyōō, á-/, **an·yu** /aá nyōō, á-/ *n* **1.** the edible tuber of a twining plant, eaten in Peru, Bolivia, and Chile **2.** a twining plant of the nasturtium family that produces añus. Flowers: large, yellow with red spurs. Native to: Andes. Latin name: *Tropaeolum tuberosum*. [Mid-20C. Via American Spanish *añú* < Quechua *áñu*]

~~**anual**~~ incorrect spelling of **annual**

A·nu·bis /ə nóobiss/ *n* in Egyptian mythology, a god represented with the head of a jackal, who leads the dead to judgment

a·nu·ran /ə nóorən/ *n* an amphibian such as a frog or toad that does not have a tail as an adult and has long powerful hind legs. Order: Anura. [Late 19C. < modern Latin *Anura* < Greek *an-* "without" + *oura* "tail"]

a·nu·ri·a /ə nyóoree ə, -nóoree-/ *n* inability of the kidneys to form urine, so that toxic waste builds up in the blood —**a·nu·ric** *adj*

a·nu·rous /ə nóorəss/ *adj* without a tail

a·nus /áynəss/ *n* the opening at the lower end of the alimentary canal through which feces are released [15C. < Latin, "ring"]

An·u·szkie·wicz /ànnə skáyvich/, **Richard** (*b.* 1930) US artist. A former student of Josef Albers, he is considered one of the major figures of the Op Art movement. His works often feature geometric designs and bold color blocks in two or, in *Spiral* (1967), three dimensions.

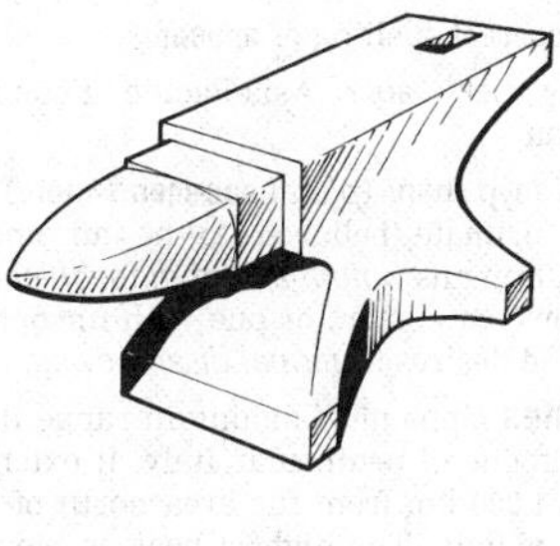

anvil

an·vil /ánvil/ *n* **1.** a sturdy piece of iron onto which heated metal is placed to be beaten into the required shape, especially by a blacksmith **2.** ANAT same as **incus** [Old English *anfilte, anfealt* < Indo-European, "to beat"]

an·vil tech·nique *n* a prehistoric method of making chipped stone tools that involves striking a stone repeatedly against a static boulder used as an anvil

anx·i·e·ty /ang zí ətee/ (*plural* **-ties**) *n* **1.** FEELING OF WORRY nervousness or agitation, often about something that is going to happen **2.** SOMETHING THAT WORRIES SOMEBODY a subject or concern that causes worry **3.** STRONG WISH TO DO SOMETHING the strong wish to do something, especially if the wish is unnecessarily or unhealthily strong ○ *his anxiety to please* **4.** PSYCHIAT EXTREME APPREHENSION a medical condition marked by intense apprehension or fear of real or imagined danger [Early 16C. < French *anxiété* < Latin *anxius* (see ANXIOUS)]

SYNONYMS See *worry*.

anx·i·e·ty dis·or·der *n* a psychiatric disorder causing feelings of persistent anxiety, e.g., panic disorder or post-traumatic stress disorder

anx·i·e·ty neu·ro·sis *n* a persistent panic disorder characterized by emotional distress, constant worry, and a strong tendency to avoid specific situations

anx·i·o·lyt·ic /àngzee ə líttik/ *adj* relieving anxiety ■ *n* a drug that relieves anxiety [Mid-20C. < ANXIETY + *-lytic*]

anx·ious /ángkshəss/ *adj* **1.** FEELING NERVOUS worried or afraid, especially about something that is going to happen or might happen **2.** ⚠ EAGER wanting to do something very much, or in a tense or uneasy way **3.** PRODUCING ANXIETY producing feelings of nervousness or agitation ○ *a few anxious moments* [Early 17C. < Latin *anxius* < *anx-*, past participle of *angere* "torment," literally "strangle"] —**anx·ious·ly** *adv* —**anx·ious·ness** *n*

USAGE anxious or **eager**? In formal writing avoid using ***anxious*** to mean ***eager***, as in *I am anxious to attend the concert.* Say instead: *I am eager to attend the concert.*

an·y /énnee/ CORE MEANING: a grammatical word used to indicate one, some, or several, when the quality, type, or number is not important. It is also used as an intensifier with comparative adjectives and adverbs and a few other words. ○ (adj) *Do you have any books on gardening?* ○ (pron) *for any who wish to enter* ○ (adv) *I'm not getting any younger.*

1. *adj, pron* EVEN ONE OR LITTLE even one or even the least amount (*used in negative statements*) ○ *I don't want any dessert.* ○ *I didn't see any.* ○ *This isn't any of your business.* **2.** *adj, pron* EVERY every person or thing of a particular category or description, no matter who or what ○ *Any financial adviser would agree.* **3.** *adj* WITHOUT LIMIT an unlimited or indefinite amount or number of ○ *any number of foods including soups, stews, and salads* **4.** *adv* IN SOME DEGREE to even the smallest extent or degree (*before adjectives and adverbs*) ○ *Is it getting any louder?* ○ *You don't look any different.* **5.** ⚠ *adv* AT ALL used after a verb to add emphasis (*informal*) ○ *I still don't like him any.* ○ *Her manners haven't improved any.* [Old English *ænig* < Indo-European, "one of a kind"]

USAGE Singular or plural? ***Any*** used as a pronoun is followed by a singular or plural verb depending on the intended meaning: *Any of these suggestions is acceptable.* [i.e., any one of the suggestions is acceptable]. *Are any of the children* [i.e. more than one of several children] *coming?* (*Is any of the children coming?* implies that one is expected, with uncertainty as to which). In formal writing, avoid use of the adverb ***any*** alone after a verb, as in *The criticism was harsh, but we didn't complain any*, where ***any*** can be dropped or replaced by "at all."

USAGE Do not use ***any old*** as an emphatic form of *any* in formal writing: *You can use any* [not *any old*] *glue, provided that it is not soluble in water. Old* should be added only when *old* is meant, as in *Any old rag from the attic will do.*

an·y·bod·y /énnee bòddee, -bùddee/ *pron* same as **anyone**

USAGE See *anyone*.

an·y·cast /énnee kàst/ *n* an act of sending data across a computer network from a single user to the nearest receiver

an·y·how /énnee hòw/ *adv* **1.** IN ANY CASE no matter what the situation is or no matter what may be true ○ *What does it matter, anyhow?* **2.** IN CARELESS WAY in a haphazard, careless, or untidy way ○ *ideas produced anyhow* **3.** IN ANY MANNER in any manner or by any means whatever ○ *Just do it anyhow.* **4.** NEVERTHELESS in spite of something ○ *I asked him to wait, but he left anyhow.*

an·y·more /ènnee máwr/, **an·y more** *adv* **1.** STILL at present and continuing from a point in the past (*used in negative statements and questions*) ○ *They sure don't make them like this anymore!* **2.** FROM NOW ON from the present and ongoing (*used in negative statements and questions*) ○ *I'm not tolerating this anymore.* **3.** NOWADAYS these days (*nonstandard or regional; used in positive sentences*) ○ *We always use a taxi anymore.*

USAGE anymore or **any more**? ***Anymore*** is an adverb: *She doesn't live here anymore. Don't you eat out anymore?* The two-word form ***any more*** refers to any unspecified additional amount, as in *Is there any more pasta left?* The two should not be confused.

REGIONAL NOTE The use of ***anymore*** in the positive sense of "nowadays," as in *Asparagus is expensive anymore*, occurs over much of the United States. It is most frequent in the South Midland states of Kentucky and Indiana, but is also fairly common in the Upper and Lower Midwest, from Minnesota to Oklahoma, and in the Blue Ridge region of Virginia.

an·y·one /énnee wùn/ CORE MEANING: an indefinite pronoun used to mean one or more people, when exactly which person or which people is not known or not important ○ *Can I get anyone more coffee?* ○ *Did anyone show up?* ○ *There isn't anyone home.*

pron **1.** EVERY PERSON any or every person who could be named or thought of ○ *more qualified than anyone in the business* **2.** EVEN ONE PERSON used to emphasize the unlikelihood of finding even one person to match a description or criteria ○ *Why would anyone want to hurt me?* **3.** UNIMPORTANT PERSON an unimportant and unknown person ○ *It's not just anyone, it's your sister!*

USAGE anyone or **any one**? ***Anyone*** is somewhat more common than *anybody* (which has the same meaning). ***Anyone*** and *anybody* are used only of human beings after a negative or a question: *Has anyone seen my pen?* The words *any* and *one* are written separately when they mean any one particular person or thing: *Any one of them could have started the fire. The tables are all free, so you can sit at any one you like.*

an·y·place /énnee plàyss/, **an·y place** *adv* at, in, or to any place (*informal*)

an·y·thing /énnee thìng/ *pron* any object, event, action, situation, or fact ○ *Is there anything I need to know?* ■ *adv* in any way (*used in negative statements and questions*) ○ *He isn't anything like his brother.* ◇ **anything but** used as an emphatic way of contradicting or negating a statement

an·y·time /énnee tìm/ *adv* at some undecided time, or whenever seems convenient or appropriate (*informal*)

an·yu *n* PLANTS same as **añu**

an·y·way /énnee wày/ CORE MEANING: an adverb meaning no matter what the situation is ○ *Anyway, we have to pay whether it was accidental or not.* ○ *Recycling, according to some anyway, is the best way of teaching respect for the environment.*

adv **1.** IN ANY CASE no matter what ○ *Don't worry about the damage; I was going to buy a new one anyway.* **2.** REGARDLESS OF SOMETHING in spite of the situation ○ *I knew it would be a sad movie but I went anyway.* **3.** IN CARELESS WAY in a careless, haphazard, or lazy way ○ *According to my mother, packing is a skilled operation, not throwing your clothes into a case just anyway.* **4.** *also* **an·y way** BY ANY MEANS in any manner or way (*informal*) ○ *We have to teach our children moral values anyway we can.*

an·y·ways /énnee wàyz/ *adv* same as **anyway** (*nonstandard or regional*)

USAGE anyways Avoid using this regional word in formal writing, as it is not regarded as Standard English. Similarly, avoid other words of the type, for example, *anywheres* and *somewheres*. Use instead *anyway, anywhere,* and *somewhere*.

an·y·wear /énnee wèr/ *n* clothing that can be worn for both casual and more formal occasions (*informal*)

an·y·where /énnee wèr, -hwèr/ CORE MEANING: an indefinite pronoun and adverb referring to one or many places unknown or unspecified ○ (pron-indef) *Is there anywhere you prefer?* ○ (pron-indef) *Anywhere we live now will seem warm.* ○ (adv) *She can sleep anywhere.*

1. *pron* SOME UNIDENTIFIED PLACE one or many places unknown or unspecified **2.** *adv* TO ANY PLACE to one or many places unknown or unspecified ○ *I'll follow you anywhere!* **3.** *adv* AT OR IN ANY PLACE in, at, or to any place ○ *We couldn't find her anywhere.* ○ *will live anywhere with a beach* ◇ **anywhere from...to...** used to indicate an approximate measurement of something by giving the smallest and largest possible measurements ○ *weighing anywhere from six to ten pounds*

an·y·wheres /énnee wàirz, -hwàirz/ *adv US* anywhere (*nonstandard*)

USAGE See ***anyways***.

an·y·wise /énnee wìz/ *adv US regional, Can* in any way or in any case (*nonstandard; usually used in negative statements*)

An·zac /án zàk/ *n* **1.** a soldier who served in the Australian and New Zealand Army Corps in World War I **2.** any Australian soldier [Early 20C. Acronym]

An·zi·o /ánzee ō/ port and resort on the western coast of Italy 37 mi./60 km south of Rome. Heavy fighting occurred there during World War II when Allied forces secured a beachhead in January 1944. Population: 36,952 (2001).

ANZUS /ánzəss/ *n* a defense treaty negotiated between Australia, New Zealand, and the United States in 1951. Full form **Australia, New Zealand, & United States**

ao *abbr* Angola (*used in Internet addresses*) See table at **domain name**

a/o, A/O, a.o. *abbr* ACCT account of

AOB *abbr* any other business

AOC *abbr* appellation d'origine contrôlée

A-OK /āy ō káy/, **A-o·kay** *adj* in excellent condition or working order (*informal*) [Mid-20C. < *all (systems) OK*]

AONB *n* in the United Kingdom, an area of countryside officially designated for the purposes of town and country planning as being special and deserving of protection. Full form **Area of Outstanding Natural Beauty**

AOR *abbr* MUSIC adult-oriented rock

a·o·rist /áy ərist/ *n* a verb tense used to express a past action in an unqualified way, without specifying whether that action was repeated, continuing, or completed or how long it lasted, found especially in classical Greek [Late 16C. < Greek *aoristos* "indefinite" < *a-* "not" + *horistos* "delimited" < *horizein* "delimit" (see HORIZON)] —**a·o·ris·tic** /āy ə rístik/ *adj* —**a·o·ris·ti·cal·ly** *adv*

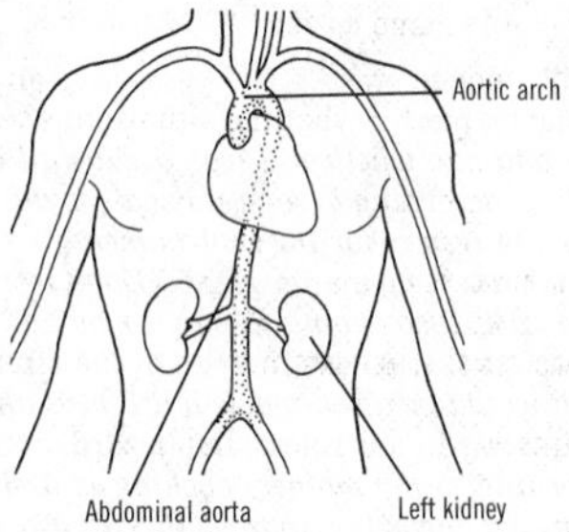

aorta

a·or·ta /ay áwrtə/ (*plural* **-tas** or **-tae** /-tee/) *n* the main artery in mammals that carries blood from the left ventricle of the heart to all the branch arteries in the body except those in the lungs [Mid-16C. Via modern Latin < Greek *aortē* < *aeirein* "raise"; perhaps from the notion that the heart was held up by the aorta] —**a·or·tal** *adj* —**a·or·tic** *adj*

a·or·tic arch *n* **1.** the section of the largest artery (**aorta**) in the body that forms the curve between the ascending and descending parts. As it leaves the heart, the aorta goes upward and then bends back on itself to form the arch. **2.** a set of paired curved arteries, one of several in the vertebrate embryo that begin in the aorta, rise through the pharynx, and join with the dorsal arterial system

a·or·tic valve *n* the valve in the largest artery (**aorta**) in the body at the point where it leaves the heart. It allows the blood to flow out but not back into the heart.

a·or·tog·ra·phy /āy awr tóggrəfee/ *n* X-ray examination of the largest artery (**aorta**) in the body —**a·or·to·graph·ic** /āy awrtə gráffik/ *adj*

A·o·te·a·ro·a /àa ō tee ə rṓ ə/ *n* the preferred Maori name for New Zealand (*often used in combination*) ○ *Aotearoa-New Zealand* [< Maori, "land of the long white cloud," < *ao* "cloud" + *tea* "white" + *roa* "long, tall"]

a·ou·dad /ów dàd, àa oo-/ *n* a wild sheep that has long curved horns and a long fringe of hair on the neck and forelegs. Native to: North Africa. Latin name: *Ammotragus lervia*. [Early 19C. Via French < Berber *udād*]

A·oui·ta /ow éetə/, **Said** (*b.* 1960) Moroccan runner who set many world records, including 1,500 and 5,000 meters (1985), 2,000 and 5,000 meters (1987), and 3,000 meters (1989)

AP *abbr* **1.** EDUC advanced placement **2.** MIL Air Police **3.** TRAVEL American plan **4.** MIL antipersonnel **5.** PUBL Associated Press

a.p. *abbr* **1.** FIN additional premium **2.** PUBL author's proof **3.** PHARM before a meal (*used in prescriptions*)

ap-[1] *prefix* same as **ad-** (*used before p*)

ap-[2] *prefix* same as **apo-** (*used before vowels and h*)

a·pace /ə páyss/ *adv* **1.** at a good or fast pace **2.** at a sufficient rate to keep up with or be alongside somebody or something [14C. < Old French *a pas* "on step"]

A·pach·e /ə páchee/ (*plural same* or **-es**) *n* **1.** a member of a Native North American people who formerly lived throughout the present-day southwestern United States and northern Mexico, but now live in Arizona, New Mexico, and Oklahoma **2.** an Athabaskan language spoken in parts of Arizona, New Mexico, and Oklahoma. Native speakers: 50,000. [Mid-18C. < American Spanish] —**A·pach·e** *adj* —**A·pach·e·an** *adj*

Ap·a·lach·i·co·la /àppə làchi kṓlə/ river in western Florida, formed at the Georgia border by the confluence of the Chattahoochee and Flint rivers. It flows southward into the Gulf of Mexico at Apalachicola Bay. Length: 90 mi./140 km.

Ap·a·lach·i·co·la Na·tion·al For·est national forest in the panhandle of western Florida. It includes Bradwell Bay Wilderness. Area: 881 sq.mi./2,283 sq.km.

~~apalling~~ incorrect spelling of **appalling**

ap·a·nage *n* HIST another spelling of **appanage**

~~aparatus~~ incorrect spelling of **apparatus**

ap·a·re·jo /àppə ráy hō, -ō/ (*plural* **-jos**) *n Southwest US* a padded leather saddle used for carrying goods on a horse or mule [Mid-19C. < American Spanish, "equipment" < Latin *apparare* "prepare" (see APPARATUS)]

~~aparent~~ incorrect spelling of **apparent**

~~aparently~~ incorrect spelling of **apparently**

a·part /ə páart/ CORE MEANING: a grammatical word meaning separated in space or time ○ (adv) *scheduled appointments a month apart* ○ (adv) *living apart* ○ (adj) *hard to be apart* ○ (adj) *sitting with legs apart*

1. *adv* NOT TOGETHER separated in space or time ○ *She placed the chairs some distance apart.* **2.** *adv* INTO PIECES into separate parts or sections ○ *take the machine apart* ○ *pulled the two scuffling children apart* **3.** *adv* MOVING AWAY AFTER BEING TOGETHER away from somebody or something after previously being together ○ *We've drifted apart over the years.* **4.** *adv* REMOVED FROM CONSIDERATION set aside or excluded from consideration, or taken as an exception ○ *The orange-flowered tie apart, it was a pretty cool outfit.* **5.** *adv* INTO DIFFICULTY into a bad or difficult condition ○ *ripped the peace process apart* **6.** *adv* OF SEPARATE KIND different and consequently separate from others ○ *a world apart* **7.** *adj* SEPARATED away from each other in position or location ○ *I think of her all the time we're apart.* [14C. < Old French *a part* "to the side"] —**a·part·ness** *n* ◇ **apart from** same as **aside from** (sense 1)

a·part·heid /ə páart hìt, -hàyt/ *n* a political system in South Africa from 1948 to the early 1990s that separated the different peoples living there and gave privileges to those of European origin [Mid-20C. < Afrikaans, "separateness" < Dutch *apart* "separate" < French]

a·part·ment /ə páartmənt/ *n* **1.** HOME IN LARGER BUILDING a self-contained residence, situated with other similar units in a larger building **2.** BUILDINGS same as **apartment building** **3.** LARGE ROOM a single room in a residential building (*formal*) ■ **a·part·ments** *npl UK* SPECIAL ROOMS IN BIG BUILDING a suite of adjoining rooms, e.g., an office, entertainment suite, or place to live (*formal*) [Mid-17C. < French *appartement* < Italian *a parte* "apart," literally "to the side"]

a·part·ment build·ing, a·part·ment house, a·part·ment block *n* a building containing a number of separate apartments

a·part·ment com·plex *n* a group of several apartment buildings

a·part·ment house *n* BUILDINGS same as **apartment building**

ap·a·thet·ic /àppə théttik/ *adj* not taking any interest in anything, or not bothering to do anything [Mid-18C. < APATHY, after *pathetic*] —**ap·a·thet·i·cal·ly** *adv*

SYNONYMS See ***impassive***.

ap·a·thy /áppəthee/ *n* **1.** lack of interest in anything, or the absence of any wish to do anything **2.** inability to feel normal or passionate human feelings or to respond emotionally [Early 17C. < French *apathie* < Greek *apathēs* "without feeling" < *pathos* "feeling"]

ap·a·tite /áppə tìt/ *n* a glassy, variously colored calcium phosphate mineral. Use: fertilizers, source of phosphorus. [Early 19C. < Greek *apatē* "deceit"; from its diversity of form and color]

a·pa·to·saur·us /ə pàttə sáwrəss/, **a·pa·to·saur** /ə páttə sàwr/ *n* a large plant-eating dinosaur that lived in North America during the Jurassic period and had a small head, short front legs, and a long neck and tail. Genus: *Apatosaurus*. Former name **brontosaurus** [Late 19C. < modern Latin < Greek *apatē* "deceit" + *sauros* "lizard"]

APB *abbr* all-points bulletin

ape /ayp/ *n* **1.** TAILLESS PRIMATE a tailless primate such as a chimpanzee, gorilla, or orang-utan. Family: Pongidae. **2.** PRIMATE a primate of any type (*informal*) **3.** IMITATOR an imitator or mimic of somebody or something **4.** CLUMSY PERSON somebody regarded as clumsy or unintelligent (*informal insult*) ■ *vt* (**aped, ap·ing, apes**) MIMIC SOMEBODY OR SOMETHING to act like somebody else in an absurd or grotesque way [Old English *apa* < Germanic] ◇ **go ape** to lose self-control, because of either anger or excitement (*slang*)

SYNONYMS See ***imitate***.

a·peak /ə péek/ *adj, adv* in a vertical position or direction [Late 16C. < French *à pic* "at the peak"]

~~apear~~ incorrect spelling of **appear**

APEC /áy pek/ *abbr* Asia-Pacific Economic Cooperation

ape-man /áyp màn/ (*plural* **ape-men** /-mèn/) *n* **1.** any extinct primate believed to be an ancestor of modern humans (*informal; not in technical use*) **2.** a rough or coarse man, or one with unsophisticated urges and desires (*informal disapproving*)

Ap·en·nines /áppə nìnz/ mountain range that forms the backbone of peninsular Italy. It extends about 800 mi./1,290 km from the area north of Genoa to the toe of Italy. The highest peak is Monte Corno 9,554 ft./2,912 m.

a·per·çu /àapər sóo, -syóo/ *n* (*formal*) **1.** a revealing glimpse or insight **2.** a concise outline or summary [Early 19C. < French, "something perceived"]

a·pe·ri·ent /ə péeree ənt/ *n* a mild laxative [Early 17C. < Latin *aperient-*, present participle of *aperire* "to open"] —**a·pe·ri·ent** *adj*

a·pe·ri·od·ic /āy peeree óddik/ *adj* **1.** happening at irregular intervals ○ *aperiodic floods* **2.** describes a mechanical or electrical system that does not exhibit resonance when a periodic disturbance is applied —**a·pe·ri·od·i·cal·ly** *adv* —**a·pe·ri·o·dic·i·ty** /-ə díssətee/ *n*

a·pe·ri·tif /aa pèrrə téef, ə-/ *n* an alcoholic beverage drunk before a meal [Late 19C. < French *apéritif* < Latin *apertus*, past participle of *aperire* "to open"]

ap·er·ture /áppər chòor/ *n* **1.** NARROW OPENING a small narrow opening **2.** OPENING THROUGH LENS OR MIRROR a fixed or adjustable opening in a piece of equipment such as a camera or microscope that lets light pass through a lens or mirror **3.** SIZE OF APERTURE the diameter of an aperture in a piece of equipment such as a camera [Mid-17C. < Latin *apertura* < *apert-*, past participle of *aperire* "to open"] —**ap·er·tur·al** *adj*

ap·er·ture card *n* a card for mounting microfilmed pages

ap·er·ture pri·or·i·ty *n* the system in a semiautomatic camera in which the user sets the lens aperture and the camera then selects the appropriate shutter speed automatically

ap·er·ture stop *n* PHOTOGRAPHY same as **f-stop**

ape·shit /áyp shìt/ *adj* an offensive term meaning unreasonably angry or excited (*taboo slang*)

~~apetite~~ incorrect spelling of **appetite**

a·pex /áy pèks/ (*plural* **a·pex·es** or **a·pi·ces** /áppə seez, áy-/) *n* **1.** HIGHEST POINT the highest point of something **2.** MOST SUCCESSFUL POINT the most successful part of something, especially somebody's career or life ○ *at the apex of his career* **3.** TIP OF SOMETHING the tip or top of something, especially something that is pointed, e.g., a triangle [Early 17C. < Latin]

A·pex /áy pèks/, **APEX** *n* a system whereby air tickets are available at a reduced price when bought a specific period of time in advance [Acronym < *advance-purchase excursion*]

Ap·gar score /áp gaar-/ *n* a score that is given after assessing the condition of a newborn baby in the five areas of heart rate, breathing, skin color, muscle tone, and reflex response. Each area has a maximum of two points. [After Virginia *Apgar* (1909–74), US physician]

a·phaer·e·sis /ə férrəssəss/, **a·pher·e·sis** *n* the loss of a syllable from the beginning of a word, e.g., in "coon" for "raccoon" [Mid-16C. Via late Latin < Greek *aphairesis* < *aphairein* "take away" < *hairein* "take"] —**aph·ae·ret·ic** /àffə réttik/ *adj*

a·pha·gi·a /ə fáyjee ə, -jə/ *n* the inability or refusal to swallow

a·pha·ki·a /ə fáykee ə/ *n* a medical condition in which the internal crystalline lens of the eye is absent [Mid-19C. < A[3] + Greek *phakos* "lentil," because of the lens's shape]

aph·a·nite /áffə nìt/ *n* an igneous rock with mineral components that are too fine to be seen by the naked eye [Early 19C. < Greek *aphanēs* "unseen" < *phan-*, stem of *phainein* (see PHENOMENON)] —**aph·a·nit·ic** /àffə níttik/ *adj*

a·pha·sia /ə fáyzhee ə, -zhə/ *n* the partial or total inability to produce and understand speech as a result of brain damage caused by injury or disease [Mid-19C. < Greek < *aphatos* "speechless" < *phanai* "speak"] —**a·pha·sic** /ə fáyzik/ *adj*

a·phe·lan·dra /àffə lándrə/ *n* an evergreen bush with shiny leaves and brightly colored flowers, often grown as a houseplant. Native to: tropical America. Genus: *Aphelandra*.

a·phe·li·on /ə féelyən/ (*plural* **-li·a** /-lyə/) *n* the point in the orbit of a planet, comet, or other astronomical object that is farthest from the Sun [Mid-17C. < modern Latin *aphelium* < Greek *apo-* "away" + *hēlios* "sun"] —**a·phe·li·an** *adj*

a·pher·e·sis /ə férrəssəss/ *n* **1.** the retransfusion of a donor's or patient's own blood from which some constituents have been removed **2.** LING same as **aphaeresis** [Variant of APHAERESIS]

aph·e·sis /áffəssəss/ *n* the loss of an unstressed vowel at the beginning of a word, e.g., in "squire" for "esquire" [Late 19C. < Greek, "letting go" < *aphienai* "send away" < *hienai* "send"] —**a·phet·ic** /ə féttik/ *adj* —**a·phet·i·cal·ly** *adv*

a·phid /áy fid/ *n* an insect that has specially adapted mouthparts for piercing and sucking the sap from plants. Many aphids transfer viruses from plant to plant as they feed. Family: Aphididae. [Late 19C. < modern Latin *aphid-*, stem of *Aphis*, genus name] —**a·phid·i·an** /ə fíddee ən/ *adj* —**a·phid·i·ous** /ə fíddee əss/ *adj*

a·pho·ni·a /ay fṓnee ə, ə-/ *n* loss of the power of speech. This may be as a result of injury or disease of the larynx or mouth or may arise from various psychological conditions. [Late 17C. < Greek < *aphōnos* "having no voice" < *phōnē* "sound"] —**a·phon·ic** /ay fónnik/ *adj*

aph·o·rism /áffə rìzzəm/ *n* a succinct statement expressing an opinion or a general truth ○ *Jerome Kern's famous aphorism "Irving Berlin has no place in American music – he is American music"* [Early 16C. < French *aphorisme* < Greek *aphorizein* "define" < *horizein* "delimit" (see HORIZON)] —**aph·o·rist** *n* —**aph·o·ris·tic** /àffə rístik/ *adj* —**aph·o·ris·ti·cal·ly** *adv*

aph·o·rize /áffə rìz/ (**-rized, -riz·ing, -riz·es**) *vi* to speak or write using aphorisms

a·pho·tic /ay fṓtik/ *adj* describes those parts of the ocean that are not reached by sunlight, or plants that grow there without photosynthesizing

aph·ro·dis·i·ac /àffrə dízzee àk, -déez-/ *n* something that arouses or intensifies sexual desire [Early 18C. < Greek *aphrodisiakos* "arousing sexual desire" < *aphrodisia* "sexual pleasures" < *Aphroditē* "Aphrodite"] —**aph·ro·dis·i·ac** *adj* —**aph·ro·di·si·a·cal** /àffrədi zí ək'l/ *adj*

Aph·ro·di·te /àffrə dítee/ *n* in Greek mythology, the goddess of love and beauty. She was the daughter of Zeus. Roman equivalent **Venus**

aph·tha /áfthə/ (*plural* **-thae** /-thee/) *n* a small white ulcer that appears in groups in the mouth and on the tongue as a result of the fungal condition thrush (*technical; usually used in the plural*) [Mid-17C. Via Latin < Greek] —**aph·thous** *adj*

A·pi·a /ə pée ə, aapee ə/ capital of Samoa, on northern Upolu Island in the South Pacific Ocean, northeast of Nuku'alofa in Tonga. Population: 35,000 (2000 estimate).

a·pi·an /áypee ən/ *adj* relating to or resembling bees [Early 19C. < Latin *apianus* < *apis* "bee"]

a·pi·a·rist /áypee ərist/ *n* somebody who keeps bees, often for commercial purposes

a·pi·ar·y /áypee èrree/ (*plural* **-ies**) *n* a place where beehives are kept and bees are raised for their honey [Mid-17C. < Latin *apiarium* "beehive" < *apis* "bee"] —**a·pi·ar·i·an** /àypee érree ən/ *adj*

ap·i·cal /áppək'l, áy-/ *adj* **1.** situated at the top or tip of something **2.** describes a consonant that is pronounced with the tip of the tongue, e.g., "t" or "d" [Early 19C. < Latin *apic-*, stem of *apex* "apex"] —**ap·i·cal·ly** *adv*

ap·i·cal dom·i·nance *n* the inhibition exerted on the growth of lateral buds by the terminal bud of a growing plant shoot

ap·i·cal mer·i·stem *n* the zone of actively dividing tissue at the tip of a shoot or root that produces new tissue, mainly to increase length

a·pi·ces plural of **apex**

a·pic·u·late /ə píkyələt/ *adj* describes a leaf that has a short broad tip [Early 19C. < modern Latin *apiculus* "little apex" < *apic-* "apex"]

a·pi·cul·ture /áypi kùlchər/ *n* the keeping of bees, especially for commercial purposes [Mid-19C. < Latin *apis* "bee"] —**a·pi·cul·tur·al** /àypi kúlchərəl/ *adj* —**a·pi·cul·tur·ist** /àypi kúlchərist/ *n*

a·piece /ə péess/ *adv* to or for each one ○ *gold watches, from $150 to $550 apiece* [Mid-16C. < A[4] + PIECE]

ap·ish /áypish/ *adj* **1.** silly, ridiculous, or boorish **2.** imitating somebody else or somebody's style —**ap·ish·ly** *adv* —**ap·ish·ness** *n*

a·pla·cen·tal /àyplə sént'l/ *adj* used to describe mammals such as marsupials that do not develop a placenta

ap·la·nat·ic /àpplə náttik/ *adj* describes a lens that does not have, or is corrected for, spherical aberration and so produces a clear undistorted image [Late 18C. < Greek *aplanētos* "without error" < *planasthai* "wander"]

a·pla·sia /ə pláyzh ə, -zhee ə/ *n* the absence or partial development of an organ, part of an organ, or tissue

a·plas·tic /ay plástik/ *adj* unable to develop new cells or tissue

a·plas·tic a·ne·mia *n* severe anemia in which the capacity of bone marrow cells to generate red blood cells is diminished. The condition can be congenital or it can be caused by exposure to radiation, toxic chemicals, or drugs.

a·plen·ty /ə pléntee/ *adj* in large or excessive amounts ○ *There are apples aplenty for all of you.*

ap·lite /áp lìt/ *n* a light-colored fine-grained igneous rock [Late 19C. < German *Aplit* < Greek *haplous* "single"] —**ap·lit·ic** /ap líttik/ *adj*

a·plomb /ə plóm, -plúm/ *n* confidence, skill, and poise, especially in difficult or challenging circumstances [Early 19C. < French *à plomb* "perpendicular"]

ap·ne·a /ápnee ə/, **ap·noe·a** *n* a temporary suspension or absence of breathing [Early 18C. Via modern Latin < Greek *apnoia* "not breathing" < *pnein* "breathe"]

ap·neu·sis /ap nóossiss/ *n* a form of breathing, caused by brain damage, in which each full inhalation is held for a prolonged period —**ap·neus·tic** *adj*

ap·noe·a *n* MED another spelling of **apnea**

APO *abbr* ARMY Army Post Office

apo- *prefix* away from, detached ○ *apolune* ○ *apocarpous* [< Greek *apo* "off, away" < Indo-European]

Apoc. *abbr* BIBLE **1.** Apocalypse **2.** Apocrypha

a·poc·a·lypse /ə pókə lìps/ *n* **1.** the destruction or devastation of something, or an instance of this **2.** a revelation made concerning the future [13C. Via late Latin < Greek *apokalupsis* "revelation" < *apokaluptein* "uncover" < *kaluptein* "to cover"]

CULTURAL NOTE ***Apocalypse Now***, a movie (1979) by Francis Ford Coppola. This surreal, hallucinatory account of the Vietnam War is based loosely on Joseph Conrad's *Heart of Darkness*. It follows a US captain on his mission to assassinate a rebel officer, played by Marlon Brando, conducting his own independent war in the heart of the jungle.

A·poc·a·lypse *n* BIBLE same as **Revelation**

a·poc·a·lyp·tic /ə pòkə líptik/ *adj* **1.** PREDICTING DISASTER warning about a disastrous future or outcome ○ *an apocalyptic scenario of global warming* **2.** INVOLVING DESTRUCTION involving widespread destruction and devastation **3.** BIBLE RELATING TO APOCALYPSE relating to the events in the Book of Revelation in the Bible —**a·poc·a·lyp·ti·cal·ly** *adv*

ap·o·car·pous /àppə kaárpəss/ *adj* describes a flower that has separate carpels [Mid-19C. < APO- + Greek *karpos* "fruit"] —**ap·o·car·py** /áppə kaarpee/ *n*

a·po·chro·mat /àppə krṓmət/ *n* a lens that is corrected for chromatic aberration by incorporating different types of glass

ap·o·chro·mat·ic /àppəkrō máttik/ *adj* describes a lens that has been corrected for chromatic aberration —**a·po·chro·ma·tism** /àppə krṓmə tìzzəm/ *n*

a·poc·o·pe /ə pókəpee/ *n* the loss or omission of one or more sounds from the end of a word, e.g., the shortening of "kind of" to "kinda" [Mid-16C. Via late Latin < Greek *apokopē* "cutting off" < *koptein* "to cut"] —**a·poc·o·pate** /ə pókə pàyt/ *vt*

ap·o·crine /áppəkrin, áppə krìn, -kreen/ *adj* describes glands that secrete part of their secreting cells with the secretory products [Early 20C. < APO- + Greek *krinein* "to separate"]

a·poc·ry·pha /ə pókrəfə/ *n* writings or reports that are not regarded as authentic [14C. Via ecclesiastical Latin, < Greek *apokruphos* "hidden away" < *kruptein* "to hide"]

A·poc·ry·pha *n* **1.** books of the Bible that are included in the Vulgate and Septuagint versions of the Christian Bible, but not in the Protestant Bible or the Hebrew canon (*takes a singular or plural verb*) See table at **Bible 2.** a group of Christian writings dating from the early centuries A.D. that are not included in the Bible

a·poc·ry·phal /ə pókrəf'l/ *adj* **1.** probably not true, but widely believed to be true **2.** *also* **A·poc·ry·phal** relating to the Apocrypha —**a·poc·ry·phal·ly** *adv*

ap·o·dal /áppəd'l/, **ap·o·dous** /-dəss/ *adj* without limbs, feet, or pelvic fins. Eels and snakes are apodal organisms. [Mid-18C. < Greek *apod-* "footless" < *pous* "foot"]

ap·o·dic·tic /àppə díktik/, **ap·o·deic·tic** /-díka-/ *adj* demonstrably or indisputably true [Mid-17C. < Latin *apodicticus* < Greek *apodeiknunai* "demonstrate" < *deiknunai* "to show" (see DEICTIC)] —**ap·o·dic·ti·cal·ly** *adv*

a·pod·o·sis /ə póddəssiss/ (*plural* **-o·ses** /-ə seez/) *n* the main clause explaining the consequence in a conditional statement, e.g., "we can watch the film" in "If you come early, we can watch the film." In logic, the apodosis is the "q" component of propositions of the form "if p then q." [Early 17C. < late Latin, < Greek *apodidonai* "give back" < *didonai* (see DOSE)]

ap·o·dous *adj* ZOOL same as **apodal**

ap·o·en·zyme /àppō én zìm/ *n* the inactive protein component of an enzyme that has no physiological effect without attachment of a specific molecule (**coenzyme**)

a·pog·a·my /ə póggəmee/ *n* the development of an embryo without prior fertilization. Apogamy occurs in some ferns, algae, and fungi. —**ap·o·gam·ic** /àppə gámmik/ *adj*

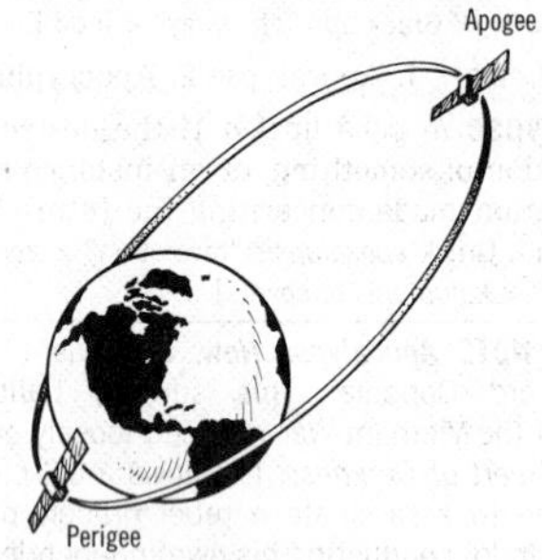

apogee (sense 2)

ap·o·gee /áppə jèe/ *n* **1.** the best or greatest point **2.** the point at which a satellite orbiting an astronomical object is farthest from the center of the object being orbited [Late 16C. < French < Greek *apogaios* "away from the Earth" < *gaia* "Earth"] —**ap·o·ge·an** /àppə jée ən/ *adj*

ap·o·lip·o·pro·tein /àppə lipō prṓ teen/ *n* a protein that combines with a lipid to form a constituent of lipoproteins

a·po·lit·i·cal /àypə líttək'l/ *adj* having no interest in politics, or not concerned with politics —**a·po·lit·i·cal·ly** *adv*

A·pol·li·naire /ə pòlli nér/, **Guillaume** (1880–1918) Italian-born French poet. His verse includes *Les Alcools* (1913) and *Calligrammes* (1918). His play *Les Mamelles de Tirésias* (1917) coined the word "surrealist."

> "A structure becomes architecture and not sculpture when its elements no longer have their justification in nature."
> [Guillaume Apollinaire. Quoted in *The Cubist Painters*; 1944]

A·pol·lo /ə póllō/ *n* **1.** in Greek and Roman mythology, the god of prophecy, sunlight, music, and healing. He was the son of Zeus and Leto, and Artemis was his twin sister. **2. A·pol·lo** (*plural* **-los**), **a·pol·lo** a very handsome young man (*literary*) [Via Latin < Greek *Apollōn*] —**Ap·ol·lo·ni·an** /àppə lṓnee ən/ *adj*

a·pol·o·get·ic /ə pòllə jéttik/ *adj* **1.** expressing apology or contrition for something **2.** defending something in speech or writing [Mid-17C. Via French and Latin < Greek *apologētikos* < *apologeisthai* "speak in your own defense" < *apologia* (see APOLOGY)] —**a·pol·o·get·i·cal·ly** *adv*

a·pol·o·get·ics /ə pòllə jéttiks/ *n* a branch of theology that is concerned with proving the truth of Christianity (*takes a singular verb*)

ap·o·lo·gi·a /àppə lṓjee ə, ə pṑlə jée ə/ *n* a formal, usually written, defense or justification of a belief, theory, or policy (*formal*) [Late 18C. < Latin (see APOLOGY)]

a·pol·o·gist /ə póllәjist/ *n* somebody who defends a doctrine or ideology

a·pol·o·gize /ə póllə jìz/ (**-gized, -giz·ing, -giz·es**) *vi* **1. EXPRESS REMORSE FOR SOMETHING** to say that you are sorry for something that has upset or inconvenienced somebody else **2. ACKNOWLEDGE THAT SOMETHING IS NOT IDEAL** to acknowledge that something is not as it should be, especially when you feel embarrassed or guilty about it **3. DEFEND SOMETHING FORMALLY** to defend something formally in writing or speech [Late 16C. < Greek *apologizesthai* < *apologia* (see APOLOGY)] —**a·pol·o·giz·er** *n*

ap·o·logue /áppə lòg/ *n* a fable that is intended to teach a moral lesson, especially one that has animals as characters [Mid-16C. Via French or late Latin < Greek *apologos* "story" < *logos* "speech" (see LOGOS)]

a·pol·o·gy /ə póllәjee/ (*plural* **-gies**) *n* **1. STATEMENT EXPRESSING REMORSE** a written or spoken statement expressing remorse for something **2. INFERIOR EXAMPLE** an inferior or bad example of something (*humorous*) ○ *I can't work in this apology for an office!* **3. FORMAL JUSTIFICATION** a formal defense or justification of something [Mid-16C. Via French *apologie* and Latin *apologia* < Greek, "speech in defense" < *logos* "speech" (see LOGOS)]

a·po·lune /áppə lòon/ *n* the point at which a spacecraft orbiting the moon is farthest from the Moon's center [Mid-20C. < APO- + Latin *luna* "moon" (see LUNAR), after APOGEE]

ap·o·mic·tic /àppə míktik/ *adj* describes an organism that reproduces asexually —**ap·o·mict** /áppə mìkt/ *n* —**ap·o·mic·tic·al·ly** *adv*

ap·o·mix·is /àppə míksiss/ *n* asexual reproduction in organisms that are also able to reproduce sexually, in which embryos are formed without fertilization or the creation of specialized reproductive cells [Early 20C. < APO- + Greek *mixis* "mingling" (see AMPHIMIXIS)]

ap·o·neu·ro·sis /àppō nòo rṓssiss/ (*plural* **-ro·ses** /-rṓ sèez/) *n* a broad sheet of fibrous tissue or expanded tendon that joins muscles together or connects muscle to bone [Late 17C. < modern Latin < Greek *aponeurousthai* "become like a tendon" < *neuron* "sinew"] —**ap·o·neu·rot·ic** /-róttik/ *adj*

a·poph·a·sis /ə póffəssəss/ *n* the rhetorical device of alluding to something by denying that it will be mentioned, as in "I will not bring up the question of age now that you are forty" [Mid-17C. < late Latin < Greek *apophanai* "deny" < *phanai* "say" (see -PHASIA)]

ap·o·phthegm *n* LANGUAGE same as **apothegm**

a·poph·y·ge /ə póffəjee/ *n* the outward curve at the top of an architectural column where it joins the capital, or at the bottom where it joins the base [Mid-16C. < Greek *apophugē* "fleeing away" < *pheugein* "flee"]

a·poph·yl·lite /ə póffə lìt, àppə fíl lìt/ *n* a white, pale pink, or pale green hydrated silicate mineral containing potassium, calcium, and fluorine [Early 19C. < APO- + Greek *phullon* "leaf," because it peels when heated]

a·poph·y·sis /ə póffəssiss/ (*plural* **-y·ses** /-ə sèez/) *n* **1.** a natural swelling or outgrowth on an animal or plant, e.g., a bony protuberance on a vertebra **2.** a small offshoot or network of veins from a large mass of igneous rock such as granite [Late 16C. Via modern Latin < Greek *apophuein* "grow out" < *phuein* "grow"] —**a·poph·y·sate** *adj* —**a·poph·y·si·al** /ə pòffə sée əl/ *adj*

ap·o·plec·tic /àppə pléktik/ *adj* **1.** overcome with anger **2.** having the symptoms of a stroke (*archaic*) [Early 17C. Via French or late Latin < Greek *apoplēktikos* < *apoplēxia* (see APOPLEXY)] —**ap·o·plec·ti·cal·ly** *adv*

ap·o·plex·y /áppə plèksee/ *n* **1.** a fit of anger **2.** a cerebral stroke, usually caused by a hemorrhage in the brain (*archaic*) [14C. Via French and Latin < Greek *apoplēxia* < *apoplēssein* "strike completely" < *plēssein* "to strike"]

ap·o·pro·tein /àppō prṓ teen/ *n* the protein part of a protein molecule that also contains a nonprotein component

a·po·ri·a /ə páwree ə/ *n* a confusion in establishing the truth of a proposition [Mid-16C. Via late Latin < Greek < *aporos* "without passage" < *poros* "passage" (see PORE[1])] —**a·po·ret·ic** /àppə réttik/ *adj*

a·port /ə páwrt/ *adv, adj* on or toward the left side of a boat as somebody faces forward

ap·o·se·mat·ic /àppə se máttik/ *adj* describes natural colors and bright markings on an animal that warn predators that it is poisonous ○ *aposematic coloration*

ap·o·si·o·pe·sis /àppə sì ə péessiss/ (*plural* **-pe·ses** /-pee sèez/) *n* a sudden break in speaking, giving the impression that the speaker does not want to or cannot continue, e.g., in the sentence "On Tuesday morning I came in just as I always do, and I saw – I can't go on" [Late 16C. Via Latin < Greek *aposiōpēsis* < *aposiopan* "stop speaking" < *siopē* "silence"] —**ap·o·si·o·pet·ic** /-péttik/ *adj*

ap·o·spor·y /áppə spàwree, ə póspəree/ *n* the process of asexual reproduction in some ferns and mosses without the occurrence of cell division (**meiosis**) or spore formation [Late 19C. < APO- + SPORE + -Y[2]]

a·pos·ta·sy /ə póstəssee/ *n* the renunciation of a religious or political belief or allegiance [14C. Via French < Greek *apostasis* "standing away" < *histasthai* "to stand"]

a·pos·tate /ə pós tàyt, -stət/ *n* somebody who renounces a belief or allegiance [14C. Via French and Latin < Greek *apostatēs* "somebody caused to stand away" < *stat-*, related to *histanai* "cause to stand"]

a·pos·ta·tize /ə póstə tìz/ (**-tized, -tiz·ing, -tiz·es**) *vi* to renounce a religious faith, a political party, a set of principles, or a moral allegiance (*formal*)

a pos·te·ri·o·ri /àa po steeree áw ree, ày po steeree áw rì/ *adj, adv* reasoning from observed facts or events back to their causes [< Latin, "from what comes later"]

a·pos·tle /ə póss'l/ *n* **1. PROMOTER OF IDEA OR CAUSE** somebody who tries to persuade others to share an idea or cause ○ *an apostle of free trade* **2. PROMINENT CHRISTIAN MISSIONARY** a prominent Christian missionary, especially one who is responsible for first converting a people **3. MORMON OFFICIAL** a member of the 12-person administrative council of the Church of Jesus Christ of Latter-Day Saints [Pre-12C. Via ecclesiastical Latin *apostolus* < Greek *apostolos* "somebody sent out" < *stellein* "send"] —**a·pos·tle·ship** *n*

A·pos·tle *n* any of the 12 followers of Jesus Christ chosen by him to preach the news about Christianity

A·pos·tles' Creed *n* a statement of Christian belief ascribed to the Apostles and dating from around A.D. 500. It is frequently used in services in Eastern Orthodox, Episcopalian, and Lutheran churches.

a·pos·to·late /ə póstə làyt, ə póstələt/ *n* **1.** the duties or mission of an apostle **2.** a group involved in converting new followers to a religion or doctrine [Mid-17C. < ecclesiastical Latin *apostolatus* < *apostolus* (see APOSTLE)]

ap·os·tol·ic /àppə stóllik/ *adj* **1.** relating to, given by, or on behalf of the pope **2.** relating to the Apostles or their teachings [Mid-16C. Via French and ecclesiastical Latin < Greek *apostolos* (see APOSTLE)] —**ap·os·tol·i·cal** *adj* —**ap·os·tol·i·cal·ly** *adv*

ap·os·tol·ic del·e·gate *n* a representative of the pope who is sent to a country that has no formal diplomatic relations with the Vatican

Ap·os·tol·ic Fa·ther *n* a Christian church leader of the first or second century A.D. who was contemporary with or lived shortly after the Apostles

Ap·os·tol·ic See *n* the area of jurisdiction (**see**) of the pope

ap·os·tol·ic suc·ces·sion *n* the doctrine of some Christian denominations that the ordination of bishops follows in an unbroken line of succession from the Apostles, providing the basis of their spiritual authority

a·pos·tro·phe[1] /ə póstrəfee/ *n* the punctuation mark (') used to show where letters are omitted from a word, to mark the possessive, and sometimes to form the plural of numbers, letters, and symbols [Mid-16C. < French < Greek *apostrophos* "turned away" < *apostrephein* "turn away" < *strephein* "to turn"]

USAGE The ***apostrophe*** is used in contractions such as *we've, it's, hadn't, 'em,* and some literary words such as *e'en* and *ne'er* to show that a letter or letters have been omitted. Do not confuse the contraction *it's*, meaning *it is* or *it has*, with the possessive *its*, which does not have an apostrophe: *It's* [= it has] *lost all its hair.* When used to mark the possessive form of nouns, the apostrophe is followed by *s* unless the noun is plural and already ends in *s*: *the cat's tail; London's theaters; my children's computer; the companies' accounts; the boys' behavior.* For singular nouns ending in *s* it is often acceptable to use either ' or *'s*: *Dickens' best-loved novel* or *Dickens's best-loved novel.* Note that the possessives *its, hers, yours,* and *theirs* do not have an apostrophe. An apostrophe may also be used to indicate relationships of description (*a summer's day*) or measurement (*ten days' absence*). The use of an apostrophe in forming the plural of numbers and letters is optional: *the word has two Ts/T's; in the 1990s/1990's*. However, *'s* is preferable where confusion may arise, especially in showing plural forms of lowercase letters: *dot the i's and cross the t's*.

a·pos·tro·phe[2] /ə póstrəfee/ *n* a rhetorical passage in which an absent or imaginary person or an abstract or inanimate entity is addressed directly [Mid-16C. Via Latin < Greek *apostrophē* < *apostrephein* (see APOSTROPHE[1])] —**ap·os·troph·ic** /àppə stróffik/ *adj*

a·pos·tro·phize /ə póstrə fìz/ (**-phized, -phiz·ing, -phiz·es**) *vti* to address an absent or imaginary person or a personified abstraction

a·poth·e·car·ies' meas·ure *n* a system of liquid measures formerly used in pharmacy

a·poth·e·car·ies' weight *n* a system of weights formerly used in pharmacy and based on a troy ounce equal to 480 grains and a pound equal to 12 ounces

a·poth·e·car·y /ə póthə kèrree/ (*plural* **-ies**) *n* (*archaic*) **1.** OCCUPATIONS same as **pharmacist 2.** COMM same as **pharmacy** (sense 2) [14C. Via French < late Latin *apothecarius* "storekeeper" < Greek *apothēkē* "storehouse" < *apotithenai* "put away" < *tithenai* "put"]

ap·o·the·ci·um /àppə théeshee əm, -ssee əm/ (*plural* **-ci·a** /-shee ə, -ssi ə/) *n* a disk-shaped or cup-shaped spore-bearing structure found in some fungi, including the fungal component of most lichens [Early 19C. < modern Latin < Greek *apothēkē* (see APOTHECARY)] —**ap·o·the·cial** /àppə théesh'l/ *adj*

ap·o·thegm /àppə thèm/, **ap·o·phthegm** *n* a terse saying that embodies an important truth, e.g., "Haste makes waste" [Mid-16C. < Greek *apophthegma* < *apophtheggesthai* "speak plainly" < *phtheggesthai* "speak"] —**ap·o·theg·mat·ic** /àppə theg máttik/ *adj* —**ap·o·theg·mat·i·cal·ly** *adv*

a·poth·e·o·sis /ə pòthee óssiss/ (*plural* **-o·ses** /-ó seez/) *n* **1.** HIGHEST LEVEL OF GLORY OR POWER the highest point of glory, power, or importance **2.** BEST EXAMPLE OF SOMETHING the best or most glorious example of something ○ *the apotheosis of Romantic music* **3.** TRANSFORMATION INTO DEITY the supposed transformation of a human being into a deity [Late 16C. Via late Latin < Greek *apotheōsis* < *apotheoun* "make into a god completely" < *theos* "god"]

ap·o·the·o·size /àppə thée ə sìz, ə póthee ə sìz/ (**-sized, -siz·ing, -siz·es**) *vt* **1.** to glorify or exalt somebody or something **2.** to elevate somebody to the status of a deity

ap·o·tro·pa·ic /àppətrə páy ik/ *adj* intended to ward off evil or bad luck [Late 19C. < Greek *apotropaios* < *apotrepein* "turn away" < *trepein* "to turn"] —**ap·o·tro·pa·i·cal·ly** *adv* —**ap·o·tro·pa·ism** *n*

app /ap/ *n* a computer application (*informal*)

app. *abbr* **1.** apparatus **2.** PUBL appendix **3.** appointed **4.** apprentice

Ap·pa·la·chi·a /àppə láychee ə, -láchə/ part of the United States that includes the southern Appalachian Mountains, extending roughly from southwestern Pennsylvania through West Virginia and parts of Kentucky and Tennessee to Northwestern Georgia

Ap·pa·la·chi·an /àppə láychee ən, -láchən/ *adj* **1.** OF APPALACHIAN MOUNTAINS relating to the Appalachian Mountains **2.** OF APPALACHIA relating to Appalachia, or its people or culture ■ *n* SOMEBODY FROM APPALACHIA somebody who comes from Appalachia [Late 17C. < *Apalachee*, Native North American people]

Ap·pa·la·chi·an Moun·tains /àppə làychee ən-, àppə làchən-/, **Ap·pal·a·chi·ans** North American mountain system, stretching from southeastern Canada to central Alabama. Major ranges include the White, Green, Catskill, Allegheny, Blue Ridge, Great Smoky, and Cumberland mountains. The highest peak is Mount Mitchell 6,684 ft./2,037 m.

Ap·pa·la·chi·an tea *n* TREES same as **withe rod**

Ap·pa·la·chi·an Trail *n* a hiking path in the eastern United States, extending about 2,050 mi./3,298 km from Mount Katahdin in central Maine to Springer Mountain in northern Georgia. It is one of the longest continuous mountain trails in the world.

ap·pall /ə páwl/ (**-palled, -pall·ing, -palls**) *vt* to make somebody feel shock, horror, or disgust [Mid-16C. < Old French *apallir* "grow pale or faint" < *pale* (see PALE[1])]

ap·palled /ə páwld/ *adj* feeling or appearing to be shocked by something dreadful or awful ○ *an appalled look*

ap·pall·ing /ə páwling/ *adj* **1.** causing shock or horror **2.** causing dismay —**ap·pall·ing·ly** *adv*

Ap·pa·loo·sa /àppə lóossə/, **ap·pa·loo·sa** *n* a saddle horse with white hair and dark patches, belonging to a breed originating in northwestern North America and formerly much used by Native Americans [Mid-19C. Origin ?]

ap·pa·nage /áppənij/, **ap·a·nage** *n* **1.** a source of revenue set aside for children, especially land given by a sovereign for the maintenance of a younger member of the royal family **2.** something that naturally or usually accompanies something else [Early 17C. < French < medieval Latin *appanare* "provide with subsistence" < *panis* "bread"]

~~apparantly~~ incorrect spelling of **apparently**

ap·pa·rat /àppə ráat, áap-/ *n* the administrative organization or staff of the Communist Party in the former Soviet Union and other Communist states [Mid-20C. Via Russian < German, "apparatus"]

ap·pa·ra·tchik /àppə ráachik, áap-/ *n* **1.** a subordinate who is unquestioningly loyal to a powerful political leader or organization **2.** a member of the administrative organization or staff (**apparat**) of the Communist Party in the former Soviet Union and other Communist states [Mid-20C. < Russian]

ap·pa·ra·tus /àppə ráttəss, -ráy-/ (*plural* **-tus·es** or *same*) *n* **1.** EQUIPMENT a piece of machinery, a tool, or a device used for a specific purpose ○ *breathing apparatus* **2.** SYSTEM ALLOWING SOMETHING TO FUNCTION the system or structure in which a process occurs or an organization functions ○ *a complex bureaucratic apparatus* **3.** ANAT SYSTEM OF ORGANS a group or system of organs that work together to perform a specific function [Early 17C. < Latin, past participle of *apparare* "prepare" < *parare* "prepare"]

ap·par·el /ə párrəl/ *n* **1.** CLOTHING clothing, especially outer or decorative clothing ○ *sports apparel* **2.** NAUT SHIP'S EQUIPMENT a ship's gear and equipment ■ *vt* (**-eled, -el·ing, -els**) CLOTHE SOMEBODY to dress somebody, especially in formal clothes (*archaic*) [13C. < Old French *apareil* "preparation" < Latin *apparare* (see APPARATUS)]

ap·par·ent /ə párrənt/ *adj* **1.** CLEAR clearly seen or understood ○ *From the type of clay used, it's apparent that pottery in Miletus was made locally.* **2.** SEEMING appearing to be shown as a quality, feeling, or attribute but perhaps not genuine ○ *her apparent indifference* **3.** PHYS DIRECTLY OBSERVED BUT NEGLECTING MODIFYING FACTORS directly observed or measured but not taking into account factors or effects that should be allowed for, e.g., distortion caused by the measuring instruments themselves [14C. < Old French *aparant*, present participle of *aparoir* (see APPEAR)] —**ap·par·ent·ness** *n*

ap·par·ent ho·ri·zon *n* GEOG same as **horizon** (sense 1)

ap·par·ent·ly /ə párrəntlee/ *adv* according to what seems to be the case but may not actually be so

ap·par·ent mag·ni·tude *n* ASTRON same as **magnitude** (sense 6)

ap·par·ent wind /-wínd/ *n* a combination of the actual wind and the wind created by a ship's motion

ap·pa·ri·tion /àppə rísh'n/ *n* **1.** an appearance of a supposed ghost or something ghostly **2.** an appearance of something or somebody unexpected or strange [15C. Directly or via French < Latin *apparition-*, < *apparere* (see APPEAR)] —**ap·pa·ri·tion·al** *adj*

~~appartment~~ incorrect spelling of **apartment**

ap·pas·sion·a·to /ə pàssyə náa tō/ *adj, adv* to be performed in an impassioned way (*used as a musical direction*) [< Italian, "impassioned"]

ap·peal /ə péel/ *n* **1.** EARNEST OR URGENT REQUEST an earnest or urgent request to somebody for something ○ *an emotional appeal for forgiveness* **2.** CAMPAIGN TO RAISE MONEY a campaign to raise money or resources ○ *The hospital has launched an appeal for funds.* **3.** ATTRACTION the quality that makes somebody or something pleasant or desirable ○ *The movie's appeal lies in its humor and charm.* **4.** FORMAL REQUEST a formal request to a higher authority requesting a change in or confirmation of a decision ○ *An appeal to the boss might solve the matter.* **5.** LAW HEARING OF CASE BEFORE SUPERIOR COURT the hearing by a superior court of part or the whole of a previously tried case, a request for such a hearing, or the right to have such a hearing ■ *v* (**-pealed, -peal·ing, -peals**) **1.** *vi* EARNESTLY REQUEST SOMETHING to make an earnest or urgent request for something ○ *We are appealing to the public to let us know if they see anything suspicious.* **2.** *vi* REQUEST MONEY to ask for or campaign to raise money or resources ○ *The charity is appealing for books and toys.* **3.** *vi* MAKE FORMAL REQUEST TO SUPERIOR to make a formal request to a higher authority for a change in or confirmation of a decision ○ *You will have to appeal to a senior officer.* **4.** *vi* ATTRACT OR FASCINATE SOMEBODY to be interesting or desirable ○ *Starting up my own business really appeals to me.* **5.** *vti* LAW APPLY TO SUPERIOR COURT FOR HEARING to apply to a superior court for a hearing of the whole or part of a case previously tried in a lower court **6.** *vi* CHALLENGE UMPIRE'S DECISION to challenge the decision of an umpire or referee [14C. Via Old French *apeler* < Latin *appellare* "address, entreat," related to *pellere* "push"] —**ap·peal·a·ble** *adj* —**ap·peal·er** *n* ◇ **on appeal** at the stage of a court case that involves reconsideration of the decision made at a previous trial

ORIGIN The Latin word *pellere* "to push," from which *appeal* is derived, is also the source of English *compel*, *dispel*, *expel*, *impel*, *propel*, *pulse*[1], *push*, *repeal*, and *repel*.

ap·peal·ing /ə péeling/ *adj* **1.** having pleasing or attractive qualities **2.** appearing to request help or sympathy ○ *a timid appealing glance* —**ap·peal·ing·ly** *adv*

ap·peals court *n* same as **court of appeals**

ap·pear /ə péer/ (**-peared, -pear·ing, -pears**) *v* **1.** *vi* COME INTO VIEW to come into view, or become visible ○ *The main menu will appear whenever you turn on the computer.* **2.** *vi* BEGIN TO EXIST to come into existence ○ *When did this rash appear?* **3.** *vi* BECOME AVAILABLE to become available, especially as a product for sale ○ *Cheaper and better printers have appeared on the market.* **4.** *vti* SEEM LIKELY to seem likely or true ○ *The three men appear to have left the city.* **5.** *vi* BE SEEN IN PUBLIC to come before the public, especially to perform a duty or to act ○ *His dream was to appear on Broadway.* **6.** *vi* LAW BE IN LAW COURT OFFICIALLY to be present in a court of law as a defendant, plaintiff, witness, or legal adviser ○ *due to appear in court next week* **7.** *vi* FORMALLY PRESENT YOURSELF TO SOMEBODY to present yourself formally to somebody after receiving an official request ○ *He was ordered to appear in the police chief's office.* [13C. Via Old French *aparoir* < Latin *apparere* "show, become visible to" < *parere* "show"]

ap·pear·ance /ə péerənss/ *n* **1.** COMING INTO EXISTENCE the act of emerging, arriving, or coming into existence ○ *the appearance of the first spring flowers* **2.** WAY SOMEBODY OR SOMETHING LOOKS the way somebody or something looks or seems to other people ○ *a youthful appearance* **3.** OUTWARD ASPECT an outward aspect of somebody or something that creates a particular impression (*often used in the plural*) ○ *The place gives the appearance of prosperity.* ○ *Don't be fooled by appearances.* **4.** PERFORMANCE OR EXHIBITION IN PUBLIC a performance or exhibition before a public audience ○ *It was the band's first US appearance.* **5.** ATTENDANCE IN COURT attendance in court as a defendant, plaintiff, witness, or legal adviser ○ *The prospect of an appearance in court was daunting.* ◇ **keep up appearances** to maintain an appearance of well-being despite difficulties ◇ **put in an appearance (at something)** to attend something, often only for a short time or to fulfill an obligation

~~appearence~~ incorrect spelling of **appearance**

ap·pease /ə péez/ (**-peased, -peas·ing, -peas·es**) *vt* **1.** to say or do something in order to make somebody less angry or aggressive, especially by giving in to demands that have been made **2.** to satisfy a need for something, especially a physical appetite ○ *appeased their thirst with a long cool drink* [14C. < Old French *apaisier* < *pais* "peace")] —**ap·peas·a·ble** *adj* —**ap·peas·a·bly** *adv* —**ap·peas·er** *n*

ap·pease·ment /ə péezmənt/ *n* **1.** the political strategy of pacifying a potentially hostile nation in the hope of avoiding war, often by granting concessions **2.** an attempt to stop complaints or reduce difficulties by making concessions

ap·pel /ə pél/ *n* **1.** a stamp of the foot that signals a fencer's intention to start attacking **2.** in fencing, a sharp blow with the blade made to procure an opening [< French, "call"]

ap·pel·lant /ə péllənt/ *n* a person or group of people in a legal action who appeal a judicial decision in a higher court or a different jurisdiction [Late 16C. < Old French *apelant*, present participle of *apeler* (see APPEAL)]

ap·pel·late /ə péllət/ *adj* having the jurisdiction to hear appeals and review the decisions of lower courts [Mid-18C. < Latin *appellatus*, past participle of *appellare* (see APPEAL)]

ap·pel·late court *n* a court with the power to review and reverse the decisions of lower courts

ap·pel·late ju·ris·dic·tion *n* the power vested in an appellate court authorizing it to review the decisions of lower courts

ap·pel·la·tion /àppə láysh'n/ *n* the name or title by which something or somebody is known (*formal*) [15C. Via French "naming" < Latin *appellation-* < *appellare* (see APPEAL)]

ap·pel·la·tion con·trô·lée /aa pellaa syawN kawNtrō láy/ (*plural* **ap·pel·la·tions con·trô·lées** /*pronunc. same*/), **ap·pel·la·tion d'or·i·gine con·trô·lée** /-dòrrijeen-/ (*plural* **ap·pel·la·tions d'or·i·gine con·trô·lées**) *n* a certification for French wine that guarantees its origin and verifies that it meets production regulations [< French, "controlled name (of origin)"]

ap·pel·la·tive /ə péllətiv/ *n* **1.** same as **appellation** (*formal*) **2.** GRAM same as **common noun** ■ *adj* **1.** connected with a name or title **2.** used as a common noun to describe a class of things —**ap·pel·la·tive·ly** *adv*

ap·pend /ə pénd/ (**-pend·ed, -pend·ing, -pends**) *vt* **1.** ADD EXTRA INFORMATION to add extra information to something, especially to a document **2.** ADD AUTHORIZED SIGNATURE to add an authorized signature to a bill or an official agreement as a final part of the ratification or agreement process (*formal*) ○ *All principals to the sale must append their signatures.* **3.** ATTACH SOMETHING to attach or fasten something to something else [Mid-17C. < Latin *appendere* "hang upon" < *pendere* "hang"]

ap·pend·age /ə péndij/ *n* **1.** a body part or organ that projects from the main part of the body, e.g., a tail, wing, or fin **2.** something fastened to something else as a small or secondary attachment ○ *feeling like an appendage of a large company*

ap·pen·dant /ə péndənt/ *n* **1.** ATTACHMENT something that is attached or added to something larger or more important **2.** LAW SOMETHING ADDED TO LEGAL DOCUMENT a secondary document that is attached to the main body of a legal document, e.g., a codicil altering the terms of a will ■ *adj* ATTACHED attached or added to something larger or more important [Early 16C. < Old French *apendant*, present participle of *apendre* < Latin *appendere* (see APPEND)]

ap·pen·dec·to·my /àppən déktəmee/ (*plural* **-mies**) *n* a surgical operation to remove the appendix [Late 19C. < Latin *appendic-*, stem of *appendix* (see APPENDIX)]

ap·pen·di·ces ANAT, PUBL plural of **appendix**

ap·pen·di·ci·tis /ə pèndə sítiss/ *n* inflammation of the appendix, causing severe pain

ap·pen·dic·u·lar /àppən díkyələr/ *adj* **1.** describes body parts that are associated with the limbs ○ *appendicular muscles* **2.** describes the appendix [Mid-17C. < Latin *appendicula* "small appendix" < *appendix* (see APPENDIX)]

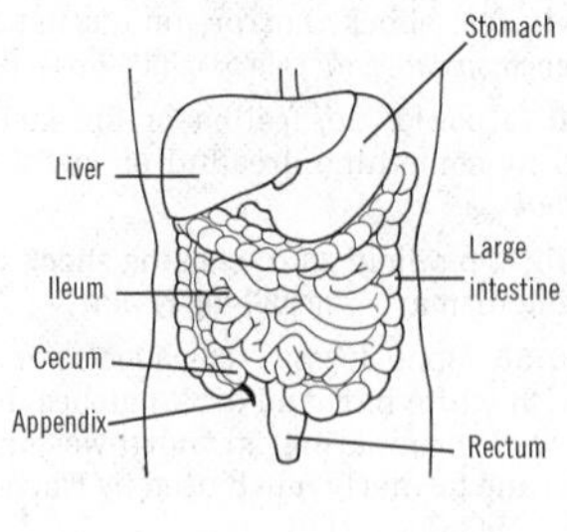

appendix

ap·pen·dix /ə péndiks/ (*plural* **-dix·es** or **-di·ces** /-di sèez/) *n* **1.** SMALL OUTGROWTH FROM LARGE INTESTINE a blind-ended tube leading from the large intestine (**cecum**), near its junction with the small intestine. In humans it is small, occurs in the lower right-hand part of the abdomen, and contains cells of the immune system. **2.** ADDITIONAL INFORMATION a collection of separate material at the end of a book or document **3.** PROJECTING PART a part that projects from something larger [Mid-16C. < Latin < *appendere* (see APPEND)]

ap·per·ceive /àppər sèev/ (**-ceived, -ceiv·ing, -ceives**) *vt* to comprehend or assimilate something such as a new idea in terms of previous experiences or perceptions [Late 19C. < APPERCEPTION]

ap·per·cep·tion /àppər sépsh'n/ *n* the comprehension or assimilation of something such as a new idea, in terms of previous experiences or perceptions [Mid-18C. < modern Latin *apperception-* < Latin *perception-* (see PERCEPTION)] —**ap·per·cep·tive** *adj*

ap·per·tain /àppər táyn/ (**-tained, -tain·ing, -tains**) *vi* to belong or relate to something (*formal*) ○ *another issue that appertains to the policy under discussion* [14C. Via Old French *apartenir* < late Latin *appertinere* "belong completely to" < *pertinere* "belong to" (see PERTAIN)]

ap·pe·stat /áppə stàt/ *n* the region of the brain that controls appetite and eating [< APPETITE + -STAT]

ap·pe·tence /áppət'nss/, **ap·pe·ten·cy** /-tənssee/ (*plural* **-cies**) *n* a desire or longing for something (*technical or literary*) [Early 17C. Via French < Latin *appetentia* < *appetent-*, present participle of *appetere* (see APPETITE)]

ap·pe·tite /áppə tīt/ *n* **1.** a natural desire for food **2.** a strong desire or craving for something [14C. Via French < Latin *appetitus* "desire" < *appetere* "seek after" < *petere* "seek" (see PETITION)] —**ap·pe·ti·tive** /áppə tītiv, ə péttətiv/ *adj*

ap·pe·tiz·er /áppə tīzər/ *n* **1.** a small dish of food served at the beginning of a meal to stimulate the appetite **2.** a sample of something that is meant to stimulate an interest [Mid-19C. Back-formation < APPETIZING]

ap·pe·tiz·ing /áppə tīzing/ *adj* appealing to or stimulating the appetite [Mid-17C. Anglicization of French *appétissant* < *appétit* (see APPETITE)] —**ap·pe·tiz·ing·ly** *adv*

ap·pla·na·tion to·nom·et·ry /àpplə náysh'n tə nómmətree/ *n* a technique for measuring the force per unit area required to flatten the cornea, used in diagnosing glaucoma [< modern Latin *applanare* "flatten, level" < Latin *planus* "flat"]

ap·plaud /ə pláwd/ (**-plaud·ed, -plaud·ing, -plauds**) *v* **1.** *vti* to clap hands as a sign of welcome, enjoyment, appreciation, or approval **2.** *vt* to praise somebody or something ○ *applauded the students' achievement* [15C. Directly or via French < Latin *applaudere* "clap at" < *plaudere* "clap"] —**ap·plaud·a·ble** *adj* —**ap·plaud·er** *n*

ap·plause /ə pláwz/ *n* the clapping of hands as a sign of welcome, enjoyment, appreciation, or approval [Late 16C. < Latin *applausus* < *applaus-*, past participle of *applaudere* (see APPLAUD)]

ap·ple /ápp'l/ *n* **1.** a firm round fruit with a central core, red, green, or yellow skin, and white or yellow flesh **2.** a tree that bears apples. Latin name: *Malus pumila*. [Old English *æppel* < Indo-European] ◇ **the apple of somebody's eye** somebody or something very much loved and favored by another person

Ap·ple·baum /ápp'l bòwm/, **Louis** (1918–2000) Canadian composer and conductor. He was a prolific composer for film, theater, television, and radio.

ap·ple but·ter *n* a smooth spread made of stewed apples flavored with spices

ap·ple·cart /ápp'l kaart/ ◇ **upset the applecart** to spoil a plan or arrangement

ap·ple green *n* a bright yellowish green color —**ap·ple-green** *adj*

ap·ple·jack /ápp'l jàk/ *n* **1.** a type of brandy distilled from cider **2.** an alcoholic beverage made from the liquid remaining after cider has been frozen

ap·ple of Pe·ru *n* an ornamental annual plant. Flowers: pale violet-blue, bell-shaped. Native to: Peru. Latin name: *Nicandra physaloides*.

ap·ple pear *n Can* FOOD, TREES same as **Asian pear**

ap·ple pie *n* a dessert made by cooking sliced apples in a pastry case

ap·ple-pie *adj* characteristic of or embodying the virtues that Americans believe to be characteristic of US culture, e.g., neighborliness, civic pride, and honesty (*informal*) ○ *apple-pie generosity* ◇ **in apple-pie order** neat and tidy

ap·ple-pol·ish (**ap·ple-pol·ished, ap·ple-pol·ish·ing, ap·ple-pol·ish·es**) *vti* to try to win favor by flattering somebody (*slang*) —**ap·ple pol·ish·er** *n*

ap·ple·sauce /ápp'l sàwss/ *n* **1.** a sauce of sweetened stewed apples, often served with pork **2.** silly nonsense (*informal*)

ap·plet /ápplət/ *n* **1.** a simple computer program that performs a single task, run from within a larger application **2.** a small piece of computer code, often embedded in a webpage, that is transferred over the Internet and executed by the recipient's computer [Late 20C. < APPLICATION + -LET]

Ap·ple·ton /ápp'ltən/ city in east central Wisconsin, on the Fox River. Population: 70,633 (2002 estimate).

Ap·ple·ton, Edward Victor (1892–1965) British physicist. He discovered the F region of ionized gas in the upper atmosphere.

Ap·ple·ton lay·er *n* METEOROL same as **F region**

Ap·ple Val·ley /ápp'l-/ city in southeastern Minnesota, south of the city of St. Paul. Population: 48,480 (2002 estimate).

ap·pli·ance /ə plī́ ənss/ *n* **1.** DOMESTIC ELECTRICAL MACHINE an electrical device or machine that is used for a specific purpose in the home, e.g. a vacuum cleaner or washing machine **2.** DEVICE FOR STRAIGHTENING TEETH a device made of metal bands or wires that is connected to the teeth and tightened in order to make them straighter **3.** DOING SOMETHING the act of putting something into effect

ap·pli·ca·ble /ápplikəb'l, ə plíkəb'l/ *adj* affecting, connected with, or relevant to a person, group of people, or situation [Mid-16C. < French < Latin *applicare* (see APPLY)] —**ap·pli·ca·bil·i·ty** /àpplikə bíllətee, ə plìkə-/ *n* —**ap·pli·ca·bly** /ə plíkəblee/ *adv*

ap·pli·cant /ápplәkənt/ *n* somebody who has formally applied for something such as a job, a grant of money, or admission to a school or college [Early 19C. < Latin *applicant-*, present participle of *applicare* (see APPLY)]

SYNONYMS See ***candidate***.

ap·pli·ca·tion /àpplə káysh'n/ *n* **1.** FORMAL REQUEST FOR SOMETHING a formal and usually written request for something such as a job, a grant of money, or admission to a school or college **2.** USE OF SOMETHING the use something is put to or the process of putting it to use **3.** RELEVANCE the relevance or value that something has, especially when it is applied to a specific field or area ○ *the industrial applications of biochemical research* **4.** SPREADING LIQUID ON SURFACE the act of spreading a liquid such as paint or medicine on a surface **5.** HARD WORK concentration and hard work **6.** COMPUTER SOFTWARE a computer program or piece of software designed to perform a specific task [15C. Via French < Latin *application-* < *applicare* (see APPLY)]

ap·pli·ca·tion ser·vice pro·vid·er *n* a company that provides one or more program functions such as accounting on behalf of an enterprise, freeing it to concentrate on its primary business

ap·pli·ca·tive /ápplə kàytiv, ə plíkətiv/ *adj* capable of being applied [Mid-17C. < Latin *applicat-* (see APPLICATOR)] —**ap·pli·ca·tive·ly** *adv*

ap·pli·ca·tor /ápplə kàytər/ *n* a device used to apply a liquid or powder to a surface [Mid-17C. < Latin *applicat-*, past participle of *applicare* (see APPLY)]

ap·pli·ca·to·ry /ápplikə tàwree, ə plíkə tàwree/ *adj* easily or suitably applied [Mid-17C. < Latin *applicat-* (see APPLICATOR)]

ap·plied /ə plīd/ *adj* able to be put to practical use, especially as a branch of a subject that has both practical and theoretical aspects

ap·pli·qué /àppli káy/ *n* shaped pieces of fabric sewn on a foundation fabric to form a design or pattern [Mid-18C. < French, "applied"] —**ap·pli·qué** *vt*

ap·ply /ə plī/ (**-plied, -ply·ing, -plies**) *v* **1.** *vi* **FORMALLY REQUEST SOMETHING** to make a formal, usually written, request for something ○ *How do I apply for the job?* **2.** *vt* **USE SOMETHING** to make use of something to achieve a result ○ *applied his first-aid skills to help the accident victims* **3.** *vi* **BE RELEVANT** to be relevant to somebody or something ○ *The requirement applies only if you are over 65.* **4.** *vt* **SPREAD SOMETHING** to spread a liquid or other material over a surface ○ *Apply a thin layer of cream to the face and neck.* **5. ap·ply your·self** *vr* **WORK HARD** to work hard or spend a significant amount of time on something ○ *I could have done better if I'd applied myself a little more.* [14C. Via Old French *aplier* < Latin *applicare* "fold toward" < *plicare* "to fold" (see PLY²)] —**ap·pli·er** *n*

ap·pog·gia·tu·ra /ə pòjjə tóorə/ (*plural* **-ras** or **-re** /-ray/) *n* in music, an ornamental dissonant note resolving, usually downward by a step, into a principal note [Mid-18C. < Italian, "something supported by another"]

ap·point /ə póynt/ (**-point·ed, -point·ing, -points**) *vt* **1. SELECT SOMEBODY FOR POSITION OR JOB** to select a person or a group of people for an official position or to do a job ○ *She's been appointed director.* **2. AGREE ON TIME OR PLACE** to fix or agree on a time or place for something to happen (*formal*) **3.** LAW **EMPOWER TRUSTEE** to authorize a trustee to transfer trust property to beneficiaries [14C. < Old French *apointier* "arrange, settle" < *a point* "to a point"] —**ap·point·ee** /ə pòyn tée, ə póyntee/ *n* —**ap·point·er** *n*

ap·point·ed /ə póyntəd/ *adj* **1.** previously agreed on ○ *met at the appointed time* **2.** decorated, furnished, or equipped (*usually used in combination*) ○ *a well-appointed apartment*

ap·point·ive /ə póyntiv/ *adj* **1.** describes a position to which somebody is appointed rather than elected ○ *an appointive board* **2.** describes trust property that is managed by a trustee with the power to transfer it to beneficiaries ○ *legally sufficient to dispose of the appointive property*

ap·point·ment /ə póyntmənt/ *n* **1. ARRANGEMENT TO MEET SOMEBODY** an arrangement to have a meeting or be somewhere at a specific time **2. CHOICE OF SOMEBODY FOR JOB** the selection of somebody for a position, office, or job **3. POSITION OR JOB** a position, office, or job to which somebody is appointed **4. SOMEBODY APPOINTED TO JOB** somebody who has been appointed to a position, office, or job **5.** LAW **SELECTION OF TRUSTEE** the selection of a trustee to whom power is given to transfer trust property to beneficiaries ■ **ap·point·ments** *npl* **FURNITURE AND FITTINGS** the furniture, accessories, and equipment belonging to a place

ap·point·ment book *n US* a book, usually with pages labeled according to the days of a calendar year, used to keep notes of appointments. Can term **diary**

ap·poin·tor /ə póyntər/ *n* somebody responsible for selecting a trustee to supervise and transfer trust property

~~**appologize**~~ incorrect spelling of **apologize**

~~**appology**~~ incorrect spelling of **apology**

Ap·po·mat·tox /àppə máttəks/ **1.** river in southeastern Virginia that flows eastward into the James River at Hopewell. Length: 135 mi./217 km. **2.** city in central Virginia. The courthouse there was the site of the 1865 Confederate surrender to the Union Army that ended the Civil War. Population: 1,733 (2002 estimate).

ap·port /ə páwrt/ *n* **1.** the production of objects at a spiritualist's seance, supposedly by paranormal means **2.** an object produced at a spiritualist's seance, supposedly by paranormal means [15C. < French *aport* "bringing to" < *aporter* "carry to" < *porter* "carry"]

ap·por·tion /ə páwrsh'n/ (**-tioned, -tion·ing, -tions**) *vt* to divide and allocate something among different people or groups [Late 16C. Directly or via French < medieval Latin *apportionare* < Latin *portion-* (see PORTION)]

ap·por·tion·ment /ə páwrsh'nmənt/ *n* **1. ALLOCATION** the division and allocation of something among different people or groups **2. DISTRIBUTION OF LEGISLATIVE SEATS** the distribution of seats in the US House of Representatives or a state legislature, based proportionally on the population of states or electoral districts **3. ALLOCATION OF TAXES** the distribution of direct federal taxes to the states in proportion to their population

ap·pose /ə pṓz/ (**-posed, -pos·ing, -pos·es**) *vt* to be placed near something, or place or move something next to something else (*formal*) [Late 16C. < Latin *apponere* (see APPOSITE), after COMPOSE and EXPOSE]

ap·po·site /áppəzit/ *adj* especially well suited to the circumstances [Early 17C. < Latin *appositus*, past participle of *apponere* "add to, put near" < *ponere* "put" (see POSITION)] —**ap·po·site·ly** *adv* —**ap·po·site·ness** *n*

ap·po·si·tion /àppə zísh'n/ *n* **1. JUXTAPOSITION** the relative position of two things that are next to each other **2.** GRAM **RELATIONSHIP BETWEEN NOUN PHRASES** the relationship between two usually consecutive nouns or noun phrases that refer to the same person or thing and have the same relationship to other sentence elements. In the sentence "My son, an actor, lives with me," the phrase "My son, an actor" is an example of apposition. **3.** PHYSIOL **CELL GROWTH IN LAYERS** cell growth in which layers of material are deposited on existing ones —**ap·po·si·tion·al** *adj* —**ap·po·si·tion·al·ly** *adv*

ap·pos·i·tive /ə pózzətiv/ *adj* describes words or phrases that refer to the same person or thing and have the same relationship to other sentence elements —**ap·pos·i·tive** *n* —**ap·pos·i·tive·ly** *adv*

ap·prais·al /ə práyz'l/ *n* **1.** an estimate of how much money something is worth, especially one given by an expert **2.** a judgment or opinion of something or somebody, especially one that assesses effectiveness or usefulness

ap·praise /ə práyz/ (**-praised, -prais·ing, -prais·es**) *vt* **1. VALUATE SOMETHING** to make or give an estimate of how much money something is worth **2. ASSESS MERITS OR QUALITY** to form or give an opinion of somebody's merits or something's quality **3.** HR **ASSESS SOMEBODY FORMALLY** to make a formal assessment of an employee or an employee's performance following an agreed set of criteria [15C. Alteration of APPRIZE, after PRAISE] —**ap·prais·a·ble** *adj* —**ap·praise·ment** *n* —**ap·prais·er** *n*

USAGE appraise or **apprise**? ***Appraise***, meaning "to evaluate," is used with reference to people or (more usually) the things they do or achieve: *She appraised their work at the end of each week.* ***Apprise***, meaning "to inform," is a more formal word, and is used with reference to people: *He apprised them of the decisions.*

ap·pre·cia·ble /ə préeshəb'l/ *adj* large or important enough to be noticed ○ *There is no appreciable difference between them.* —**ap·pre·cia·bly** *adv*

ap·pre·ci·ate /ə préeshee àyt/ (**-at·ed, -at·ing, -ates**) *v* **1.** *vt* **VALUE SOMEBODY OR SOMETHING HIGHLY** to recognize and like the qualities in somebody or something ○ *I don't feel appreciated.* **2.** *vt* **UNDERSTAND SOMETHING** to understand fully the meaning or significance of a situation ○ *I hadn't appreciated how upset he felt.* **3.** *vt* **FEEL GRATITUDE** to feel grateful for something ○ *I'd appreciate it if you didn't repeat this to anyone.* **4.** *vt* **ACKNOWLEDGE SOMETHING** to accept something as valid ○ *We appreciate that these people have rights as well.* **5.** *vi* **GAIN IN VALUE** to increase in value, especially over time [Mid-17C. < late Latin *appretiare* "value, estimate, rate, appraise" < *pretium* "money spent, worth, value"]

USAGE Opinions on ***appreciate*** vary widely. Some people, explaining that the word's history has to do with accurate valuation, consider that it should be used only in neutral contexts (*I appreciate your position*). Others, pointing out that ***appreciation*** is admiration or gratitude, counter that it should be used only in favorable contexts (*I appreciate your frankness*). Still others argue that the object of this verb should always be a noun (*I appreciate your annoyance*), not a clause (*I don't appreciate what you just said*). Certainly it is worth remembering the verb's continuing ties to the ideas of valuation and gratitude, and worth remembering, too, that no one objects to *recognize*, *realize*, or *understand* in negative contexts or before clauses.

ap·pre·ci·a·tion /ə préeshee áysh'n/ *n* **1. GRATEFULNESS** a feeling or expression of gratitude ○ *a token of my appreciation* **2. POSITIVE OPINION** a favorable opinion of something ○ *clapped and cheered their appreciation* **3. VALUING SOMETHING HIGHLY** recognition and liking of something's qualities ○ *a course in music appreciation* **4. STATEMENT OF PRAISE** a written or spoken statement of somebody's qualities **5. FULL UNDERSTANDING** a full understanding of the meaning and importance of something ○ *an appreciation of our funding problems* **6. GROWTH IN VALUE** an increase in value, especially over time ○ *the rapid appreciation of real estate*

ap·pre·cia·tive /ə préeshətiv/ *adj* expressing or feeling gratitude or approval —**ap·pre·cia·tive·ly** *adv* —**ap·pre·cia·tive·ness** *n*

ap·pre·hend /àppri hénd/ (**-hend·ed, -hend·ing, -hends**) *vt* **1. ARREST SOMEBODY** to take somebody suspected of wrongdoing into legal custody **2. UNDERSTAND SOMETHING** to grasp the importance, significance, or meaning of something **3. BECOME AWARE OF SOMETHING** to become aware of something by use of the senses (*formal*) [14C. Directly or via French < Latin *apprehendere* "take hold of" < *prehendere* "seize"]

ap·pre·hen·si·ble /àppri hénssəb'l/ *adj* capable of being understood

ap·pre·hen·sion /àppri hénsh'n/ *n* **1. DREAD** a feeling of anxiety or fear that something bad or unpleasant will happen **2. ARREST** the taking of a criminal suspect into custody (*formal*) **3. ABILITY TO UNDERSTAND** the power or ability to grasp the importance, significance, or meaning of something (*formal*) **4. IDEA** an idea formed by observation or experience (*formal*) [14C. Directly or via French < late Latin *apprehension-* < Latin *apprehens-*, past participle of *apprehendere* (see APPREHEND)]

ap·pre·hen·sive /àppri hénssiv/ *adj* **1.** worried that something bad will happen **2.** aware or cognizant of something nonphysical such as implications or results (*formal*) —**ap·pre·hen·sive·ly** *adv* —**ap·pre·hen·sive·ness** *n*

ap·pren·tice /ə préntiss/ *n* **1. TRAINEE** somebody being trained by a skilled professional in an art, craft, or trade **2. INEXPERIENCED PERSON** a novice or amateur ■ *vt* (**-ticed, -tic·ing, -tic·es**) **TAKE ON SOMEBODY AS TRAINEE** to give somebody work as an apprentice to a skilled professional ○ *apprenticed to a licensed electrician* [14C. < Old French *aprentis* < *aprendre* "learn" < Latin *apprehendere* (see APPREHEND)] —**ap·pren·tice·ship** *n*

SYNONYMS See ***beginner.***

ap·pressed /ə prést/ *adj* describes a part of a plant that is pressed closely against another part without being joined to it ○ *appressed leaves* [Late 18C. < Latin *appressus*, past participle of *apprimere* "press to" < *premere* "press"]

ap·prise /ə prīz/ (**-prised, -pris·ing, -pris·es**) *vt* to inform or give notice to somebody about something (*formal*) [Late 17C. < French *appris*, past participle of *apprendre* "make learn, teach" (see APPRENTICE)]

USAGE See ***appraise.***

ap·prize /ə prīz/ (**-prized, -priz·ing, -priz·es**) *vt* to value something very highly, e.g., because of its monetary worth (*archaic*) [15C. Via Old French *aprisier* < Latin *appretiare* (see APPRECIATE)]

ap·proach /ə prṓch/ *v* (**-proached, -proach·ing, -proach·es**) **1.** *vti* **MOVE CLOSER** to move closer to somebody or something ○ *He motioned to us to approach.* **2.** *vt* **ASK SOMEBODY** to speak to somebody with a view to asking for something ○ *approached me about volunteering* **3.** *vt* **TREAT SOMETHING IN PARTICULAR WAY** to deal with something in a particular way ○ *How did she approach the problem?* **4.** *vt* **COME CLOSE TO BEING SOMETHING** to be almost at a particular level or state ○ *statements approaching libel* **5.** *vti* **COME CLOSER IN**

TIME to come nearer in time to something ○ *As spring approaches I notice people smiling more.* **6.** *vi* GOLF **HIT BALL TOWARD GREEN** in golf, to make a shot from the fairway toward a green ■ *n* **1. COMING NEARER** a coming nearer in space or time **2. METHOD** a way of doing or solving something ○ *an incremental approach to reform* **3. REQUEST OR PROPOSAL** an informal request, offer, suggestion, or proposal made to somebody (*often used in the plural*) ○ *had several approaches from Hollywood agents* **4. APPROXIMATION** one thing that is very similar in its nature or qualities to another ○ *the nearest approach to natural slate* **5. ACCESS** a way of reaching or gaining access to a building or place **6.** AVIAT **AIRCRAFT'S COURSE** the path that an aircraft follows as it prepares to land **7.** GOLF **SHOT TOWARD GREEN** a shot made from the fairway toward a green **8.** BOWLING **MOVEMENT TO RELEASE BALL** in bowling, the steps a bowler takes before releasing the ball, or the part of the bowling alley used for doing this [14C. Via Old French *aproch(i)er* < late Latin *appropiare* "go nearer to" < *prope* "near"]

ap·proach·a·ble /ə próchəb'l/ *adj* **1. INVITINGLY FRIENDLY** friendly and easy to talk to **2. EASILY ACCESSIBLE** able to be reached with ease, especially in terms of transportation **3. USER-FRIENDLY** easy for nonspecialists to understand —**ap·proach·a·bil·i·ty** /ə prōchə bíllətee/ *n* —**ap·proach·a·ble·ness** *n* —**ap·proach·a·bly** *adv*

ap·proach·ing /ə próching/ *adj* coming near in space or time

ap·proach shot *n* **1.** in tennis, a shot hit deep into the opponent's court, designed to give the player time to approach the net for the next shot **2.** GOLF same as **approach** *n* (sense 7)

ap·pro·ba·tion /àpprə báysh'n/ *n* **1.** a favorable opinion about something or somebody **2.** the official approving, authorizing, or sanctioning of something —**ap·pro·ba·tive** /ápprə bàytiv, ə próbətiv/ *adj* —**ap·pro·ba·to·ry** /ə próbə tàwree/ *adj*

~~approch~~ incorrect spelling of **approach**

ap·pro·pri·a·cy /ə própree əssee/ *n* the precise suitability of a word to its context

ap·pro·pri·ate *adj* /ə própree ət/ **FITTING** suitable for the occasion or circumstances ■ *vt* /ə própree àyt/ (**-at·ed, -at·ing, -ates**) **1. USE MONEY FOR PURPOSE** to set aside an amount of money for a particular use **2. TAKE SOMETHING FOR OWN USE** to take something that belongs to or is associated with somebody else for yourself, especially without permission ○ *She soon appropriated the role of chief confidante.* [15C. < Latin *appropriatus*, past participle of *appropriare* "make your own" < *propius* "own"] —**ap·pro·pri·a·ble** *adj* —**ap·pro·pri·ate·ly** *adv* —**ap·pro·pri·ate·ness** *n* —**ap·pro·pri·a·tive** /-àytiv/ *adj* —**ap·pro·pri·a·tor** /-àytər/ *n*

ap·pro·pri·a·tion /ə pròpree áysh'n/ *n* **1.** a sum of money that has been set aside from a budget, especially a government budget, for a specific purpose (*often used in the plural*) **2.** the taking of something that belongs to or is associated with somebody else, especially without permission

ap·prov·al /ə próov'l/ *n* **1.** a favorable opinion or feeling about something **2.** formal or official agreement or permission ◇ **on approval** with the opportunity to try something before deciding whether you really want to buy it

ap·prove /ə próov/ (**-proved, -prov·ing, -proves**) *v* **1.** *vi* to have a favorable opinion of somebody or something **2.** *vt* to give formal confirmation that something is satisfactory [14C. Via Old French < Latin *approbare* "assent to as good" < *probus* "good"] —**ap·prov·a·ble** *adj* —**ap·proved** *adj* —**ap·prov·ing** *adj* —**ap·prov·ing·ly** *adv*

approx. *abbr* **1.** approximate **2.** approximately

ap·prox·i·mal /ə próksim'l/ *adj* used to describe teeth that are side by side or set close together

ap·prox·i·mate *adj* /ə próksəmət/ **1. NEARLY EXACT** not quite exact, but only slightly more or less in number or quantity ○ *giving an approximate value* **2. SIMILAR** similar in nature, appearance, or characteristics to something else ○ *gives you an approximate idea* ■ *v* /ə próksə màyt/ (**-mat·ed, -mat·ing, -mates**) **1.** *vti* **BE SIMILAR** to be or become similar to something in nature, size, or extent ○ *a line approximating the original boundary* **2.** *vt* **ESTIMATE SOMETHING** to make or provide an estimate, usually a rough estimate, of something **3.** *vti* **COME OR BRING CLOSE** to come or bring something close to something else [15C. < late Latin *approximatus*, past participle of *approximare* "draw near to" < Latin *proximus* "near"] —**ap·prox·i·mate·ness** *n* —**ap·prox·i·ma·tion** /ə pròksə máysh'n/ *n*

ap·prox·i·mate·ly /ə próksəmətlee/ *adv* not exactly, but nearly or roughly

~~approximatly~~ incorrect spelling of **approximately**

appt. *abbr* appointment

ap·pulse /ə púlss/ *n* a near approach of two astronomical objects that does not result in a partial concealment or an eclipse [Early 17C. < Latin *appulsus*, past participle of *appellere* "drive to, force toward" < *pellere* "drive"]

ap·pur·te·nance /ə púrt'nənss/ *n* **1. ACCESSORY** an accompanying part or feature of something (*formal; often used in the plural*) ○ *an athletic club with all the usual appurtenances* **2.** LAW **PROPERTY RIGHT** a legal right or privilege attached to a property and inherited with it ■ **ap·pur·te·nan·ces** *npl* **EQUIPMENT** the equipment needed for an activity (*formal*) [14C. < Anglo-Norman < late Latin *appertinere* (see APPERTAIN)] —**ap·pur·te·nant** *adj*

APR *abbr* FIN annual percentage rate

Apr. *abbr* April

a·prax·i·a /ay práksee ə/ *n* the inability to perform complex movements, often as a result of brain damage, e.g., following a stroke [Late 19C. Via German < Greek, "inaction"] —**a·prax·ic** *adj*

~~apreciate~~ incorrect spelling of **appreciate**

a·près /àa pràY, aa práy/ *prep* after an activity [Mid-20C. < French, "after"]

a·près-ski /àa pray skée/ *n* social activities taking place after skiing ■ *adj* taking place during or appropriate to the period of time after skiing [Mid-20C. < French, "after skiing"]

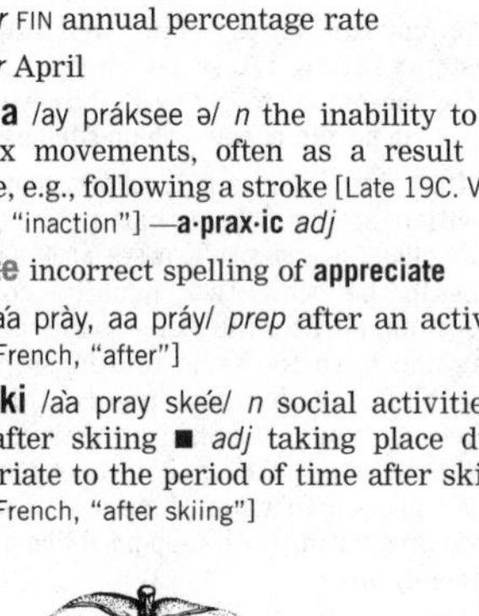

apricot

a·pri·cot /áppri kòt, áy-/ *n* **1. FRUIT** a small round fruit with a soft furry yellowish orange skin and a single pit **2. FRUIT TREE** a fruit tree that produces apricots. Latin name: *Prunus armeniaca.* **3. YELLOWISH ORANGE COLOR** a pale yellowish orange color [Mid-16C. Via obsolete Catalan *abrecoc* < Arabic *al-barqūq* "the apricot"] —**a·pri·cot** *adj*

ORIGIN The ***apricot*** got its name because the Romans regarded it as a type of early ripening peach. They therefore applied to it the epithet *praecocus* (a variant of *praecox*, from which English gets *precocious*). This passed via Byzantine Greek *berikokkia* into Arabic where, with the definite article *al*, it became *al-birqūq* or *al-barqūq*. Catalan adopted this as *abrecoc*, which is how English acquired the word (the earliest recorded English spelling is *abrecock*). The final *-t* came soon after, from French.

A·pril /áyprəl/ *n* in the Gregorian calendar, the fourth month of the year, lasting 30 days. See table at **calendar** [14C. < Latin *Aprilis* < Etruscan *apru* < Greek *Aphrō*, shortening of *Aphroditē* "Aphrodite"]

A·pril fool *n* **1. JOKE** a practical joke played on somebody on April Fools' Day **2. TARGET OF JOKE** the target of a practical joke on April Fools' Day ■ *interj* **REVEALING JOKE** used to tell somebody that he or she has been the target of an April Fools' Day joke

A·pril Fools' Day *n* a day on which people play practical jokes on other people. Date: April 1.

a pri·o·ri /àa pree áwree, ày prī áwrī/ *adj* **1.** working from something that is already known or self-evident to arrive at a conclusion **2.** known or assumed without reference to experience [Mid-17C. < Latin, "from the previous (one, cause, hypothesis)"] —**a pri·o·ri** *adv* —**a·pri·or·i·ty** /àa pree áwrətee, ày prī-/ *n*

a·pron /áyprən/ *n* **1. PROTECTIVE GARMENT TIED OVER CLOTHES** a garment worn over the front of clothes to keep them clean during working, especially cooking **2.** AVIAT **PAVED AREA AT AIRPORT** the paved area immediately in front of airport buildings, on which aircraft are loaded and unloaded **3. PROJECTING EDGE** the projecting edge of a platform such as a theater stage, dock, or loading bay **4. PROTECTIVE PART** a shield or plate attached to a machine that protects the user from flying debris **5.** GOLF **BORDER AROUND GREEN** in golf, the outer edge of a putting green **6.** BOXING **AREA OUTSIDE BOXING RING** in boxing, the part of the floor of a boxing ring that is outside the ropes **7.** GEOG **LOW-ANGLED SURFACE** a gently sloping surface of sand, gravel, or bare rock, usually in front of a mountain range **8.** ENG same as **skirt** *n* (sense 4) [14C. < Old French *naperon* "small cloth" < *nape* "tablecloth" < Latin *mappa* "napkin"; by interpreting "a napron" as "an apron"]

a·pron strings *npl* the strings that secure an apron ◇ **be tied to somebody's apron strings** to be dependent on and controlled by a woman, especially a wife or mother

ap·ro·pos /àpprə pó/ (*formal*) *adj* **JUST RIGHT** appropriate in a specific situation ■ *prep* **IN REGARD TO** on the subject of ○ *Apropos tomorrow's event, I'll see how I feel.* ■ *adv* **INCIDENTALLY** by the way ○ *Apropos, do you think we should delay the announcement?* [Mid-17C. < French *à propos* "to the purpose"]

~~apropriate~~ incorrect spelling of **appropriate**

a·pro·tic /ay prótik/ *adj* describes a solvent that is unable to donate protons [Mid-20C. < A-[2] + PROTON]

a·pro·ti·nin /ay prótinin/ *n* a polypeptide obtained from animal organs. Use: treatment of pancreatitis.

~~aproximately~~ incorrect spelling of **approximately**

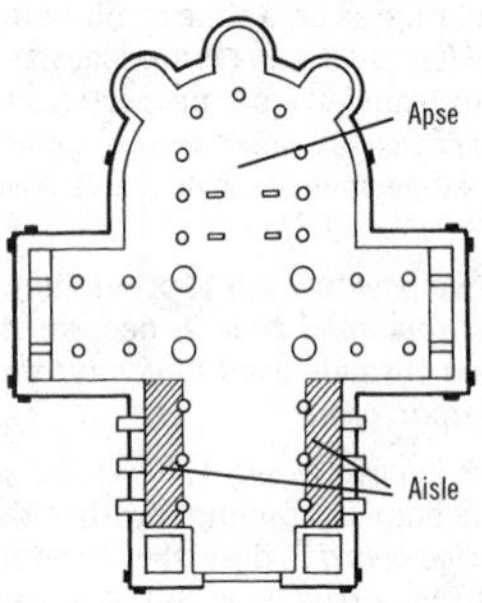

apse

apse /aps/ *n* **1.** a semicircular projecting part of a building, especially the east end of a church, which contains the altar **2.** ASTRON same as **apsis** (sense 1) [Early 19C. < Latin *apsis* (see APSIS)]

ap·si·dal /ápsid'l/ *adj* **1.** relating to the apse of a building **2.** relating to an apsis or the apsides of an orbit [Mid-19C. < Latin *apsid-*, stem of *apsis* (see APSIS)]

ap·sis /ápsiss/ (*plural* **-si·des** /-si dèez/) *n* **1.** either of the two points in an orbit that are nearest to and farthest from the center of gravitational attraction **2.** BUILDINGS same as **apse** (sense 1) [Late 16C. Via Latin < Greek *(h)apsis* "rim of a wheel, wheel, arch, vault"]

apt /apt/ *adj* **1. VERY APPROPRIATE** especially suited to the circumstances ○ *an apt comment* **2. LIKELY** often doing something and likely to do it again ○ *apt to get angry* **3. QUICK TO LEARN** enthusiastic and quick to learn new things ○ *an apt pupil* [14C. Directly or via Old French < Latin *aptus*, past participle of *apere* "fit, fasten, join"] —**apt·ly** *adv* —**apt·ness** *n*

ORIGIN The Latin word *apere* "to fit, fasten," from which ***apt*** is derived, is also the source of English *adapt, attitude,* and *inept.* Its Indo-European ancestor is in turn the source of English *copulate* and *couple.*

apt. *abbr* apartment

ap·ter·al /áptərəl/ *adj* **1.** describes a classical temple that has no columns along its sides **2.** describes a church that has no aisles [Mid-19C. < Greek *apteros* "wingless" < *pteron* "wing, feather"]

ap·ter·ous /áptərəss/ *adj* describes an insect that has no wings [Late 18C. < Greek *apteros* (see APTERAL)]

ap·ti·tude /ápti to͞od/ *n* **1.** a natural tendency to do something well, especially one that can be further developed ○ *a natural aptitude for teaching* **2.** quickness and ease in learning

SYNONYMS See ***ability*** and ***talent***.

ap·ti·tude test *n* a test to determine whether somebody is likely to be able to develop the skills required for a specific kind of work

Ap·u·lei·us /àppyə lée əss/, **Lucius** (125?–200?) Numidian-born Roman philosopher and writer. His most famous work, the satirical *Metamorphoses* or *The Golden Ass*, influenced many later writers including Boccaccio and Henry Fielding.

A·pus /áypəss/ *n* a faint constellation near the south celestial pole. See illustration at **constellation**

APWU *abbr* American Postal Workers Union

ap·y·rase /áppə ràyss, -ràyz/ *n* an enzyme that aids the breakdown of ATP, producing energy [Mid-20C. Contraction of *adenypyrophosphatase*]

a·py·rex·i·a /ày pī réksee ə, àppə-/ *n* absence of fever, or a period during which a patient experiences no fever [Mid-17C. Via modern Latin < Greek *apurexia* < *purexis* (see PYREXIA)] —**a·py·ret·ic** *adj* —**a·py·rex·i·al** *adj*

aq *abbr* Antarctica (*used in Internet addresses*) See table at **domain name**

aq. *abbr* **1.** PHARM aqua **2.** GEOL, CHEM aqueous

A·qa·ba, Gulf of /áakəbə/ northeastern arm of the Red Sea, bordered by Egypt's Sinai Peninsula on the east, Israel on the north, and Saudi Arabia on the west. It is of great strategic importance, as it provides Israel with its only access to the Red Sea. Length: 99 mi./160 km.

Aq·mo·la /àakmō làa/ former name for **Astana** (1991–98)

aq·ua /áakwə, ák-/ *n* **1.** COLORS same as **aquamarine** (sense 2) **2.** water, especially when used in the pharmaceutical industry as a solvent (*technical*) [14C. < Latin, "water"] —**aq·ua** *adj*

aqua- *prefix* water ○ *aquanaut* [< Latin *aqua*]

aq·ua·crop /ákwə kròp/ *n* a crop produced by cultivating organisms that live in the ocean or fresh water, e.g., fish produced by fish-farming [Late 20C. < AQUACULTURE + CROP]

aq·ua·cul·ture /ákwə kùlchər, áakwə-/, **aq·ui·cul·ture** /ákwi-, áakwi-/ *n* **1.** the farming of ocean and freshwater plants and animals for human consumption **2.** BOT same as **hydroponics** [Mid-19C. After AGRICULTURE] —**aq·ua·cul·tur·al** /àkwə kúlchərəl, àakwə-/ *adj* —**aq·ua·cul·tur·ist** /áakwə kúlchərist, àkwə-/ *n*

~~aquaduct~~ incorrect spelling of **aqueduct**

aq·ua·dy·na·mic /àkwə dī námmik/ *adj* having a smooth or streamlined surface in order to reduce drag when passing through water [Late 20C. After AERODYNAMIC]

~~aquaint~~ incorrect spelling of **acquaint**

~~aquaintance~~ incorrect spelling of **acquaintance**

Aq·ua-Lung /ákwə lùng/ *tdmk* a trademark for an underwater breathing apparatus used by divers

aq·ua·ma·rine /àkwə mə réen, àak-/ *n* **1.** a precious stone that is a greenish blue variety of beryl. Use: gems. **2.** a greenish blue color [Late 16C. < Latin *aqua marina* "sea water"] —**aq·ua·ma·rine** *adj*

aq·ua·naut /ákwə nàwt, áak-/ *n* somebody with training and equipment to spend long periods working or swimming underwater [Late 19C. < AQUA- + Greek *nautēs* "sailor," after ARGONAUT]

aq·ua·pho·bi·a /àkwə fṓbee ə, àak-/ *n* an irrational fear of water

aq·ua·plane /ákwə plàyn, áak-/ *n* a water-skiing board on which somebody stands while being towed by a motorboat ■ *vi* (**-planed, -plan·ing, -planes**) **1.** to be towed by a motorboat on an aquaplane **2.** *UK* same as **hydroplane** *v* (sense 2)

aq·ua re·gi·a /ákwə réejee ə, -réejə/ *n* a fuming, highly corrosive mixture of nitric and hydrochloric acids. Use: dissolving gold and other metals. [Early 17C. < Latin, "royal water"; because it can dissolve "noble" metals]

aq·ua·relle /àkwə rél, àak-/ *n* **1.** a painting technique that uses transparent washes of watercolor **2.** a painting produced using the aquarelle technique [Mid-19C. Via French < obsolete Italian *acquarella* "watercolor" < *acqua* "water"] —**aq·ua·rel·list** *n*

a·quar·i·a plural of **aquarium**

a·quar·ist /ə kwérrist/ *n* somebody who takes care of an aquarium as a hobby or a profession

a·quar·i·um /ə kwérree əm/ (*plural* **-i·ums** or **-i·a** /-ee ə/) *n* **1.** a water-filled transparent container, often box-shaped, in which fish and other water animals and plants are kept **2.** a building in which fish and other water animals are kept and shown to the public [Mid-19C. < Latin *aquarius* (see AQUARIUS) after VIVARIUM]

A·quar·i·us /ə kwérree əss/ *n* **1.** CONSTELLATION IN SOUTHERN HEMISPHERE a zodiacal constellation of the southern hemisphere between Pisces and Capricornus. See illustration at **constellation** **2.** 11TH SIGN OF ZODIAC the 11th sign of the zodiac, represented by a man pouring water, and lasting from approximately January 20 to February 18. Aquarius is classified as an air sign and its ruling planets are Saturn and Uranus. **3.** SOMEBODY BORN UNDER AQUARIUS somebody whose birthday falls between January 20 and February 18 [14C. < Latin, "water carrier" < *aquarius* "of water" < *aqua* "water"] —**A·quar·i·an** *n* —**A·quar·i·us** *adj*

aq·ua·ro·bics /àkwə rṓbiks/ *n* aerobic exercises done to music in a swimming pool (*takes a singular or plural verb*) [Late 20C. Blend of AQUA- + AEROBICS]

a·quat·ic /ə kwáatik/ *adj* **1.** OF WATER connected with, consisting of, or dependent on water **2.** LIVING IN WATER living or growing in water **3.** DONE IN WATER played or performed in or on water ○ *aquatic sports* ■ *n* WATER PLANT OR ANIMAL a plant or animal that lives or grows in water —**a·quat·i·cal·ly** *adv*

a·quat·ics /ə kwáatiks/ *n* sports played in or on water (*takes a singular or plural verb*)

aq·ua·tint /ákwə tint, áak-/ *n* **1.** a method of etching a copper plate in which the prints produced from it resemble watercolors in the shading of different areas **2.** an etching produced by the aquatint process [Late 18C. Via French *aquatinte* < Italian *acquatinta* "tinted water"] —**aq·ua·tint·er** *n* —**aq·ua·tint·ist** *n*

a·qua·vit /áakwə vèet, ákwə-/, **ak·va·vit** /áakvə vèet, ákvə-/ *n* a potato- or grain-based liquor flavored with caraway seeds, produced in Scandinavia [Late 19C. Via Danish, Norwegian, Swedish *akvavit* < Latin *aqua vitae* "water of life"]

aq·ua vi·tae /ákwə vítee/ *n* a strong liquor, especially brandy [14C. < Latin, "water of life"]

Barnaby's

aqueduct: ancient Roman aqueduct in Tarragona, Spain

aq·ue·duct /ákwə dùkt/ *n* **1.** CHANNEL FOR WATER a pipe or channel for moving water to a lower level, often across a great distance **2.** STRUCTURE CARRYING CANAL a structure in the form of a bridge that carries a canal across a valley or river **3.** ANAT CHANNEL CARRYING FLUID IN BODY a channel in an organ or body part through which fluid passes [Mid-16C. Via medieval Latin *aqueductus* < Latin *aquae ductus* "water conveyance"]

a·que·ous /áykwee əss, ákwee-/ *adj* **1.** containing, dissolved in, or consisting mostly of water **2.** describes rocks or deposits that are formed from material carried by water [Mid-17C. < medieval Latin *aqueus* < Latin *aqua* "water"]

a·que·ous hu·mor *n* the transparent fluid that circulates in the eye chamber between the back of the cornea and the front of the iris and pupil and permeates the vitreous humor behind the lens

aqui- *prefix* water ○ *aquifer* [< Latin *aqua*]

aq·ui·clude /ákwi klo͞od/ *n* a layer of rock, sediment, or soil through which ground water cannot flow [Late 20C. < AQUI- + EXCLUDE]

aq·ui·cul·ture *n* AGRIC same as **aquaculture**

aq·ui·fer /ákwifər/ *n* a layer of permeable rock, sand, or gravel through which ground water flows, containing enough water to supply wells and springs

A·qui·la /ákwələ, ə kwíllə/ *n* a constellation near the celestial equator containing the bright star Altair. See illustration at **constellation**

aq·ui·le·gi·a /àkwi léejee ə, -léej ə/ (*plural* **-as** or *same*) *n UK* PLANTS same as **columbine**[1] [Late 16C. < medieval Latin]

aq·ui·line /ákwi līn/ *adj* **1.** thin, curved, and pointed like an eagle's beak ○ *an aquiline nose* **2.** resembling or connected with eagles [Mid-17C. < Latin *aquilinus* < *aquila* "eagle"] —**aq·ui·lin·i·ty** /àkwi línnətee/ *n*

A·qui·nas /ə kwínəss/, **Thomas, St.** (1225–74) Italian philosopher and theologian. He sought to reconcile the philosophy of Aristotle with the theology of St. Augustine.

> "Whatever is in motion must be moved by something else. Moreover, this something else...must itself be moved by something else, and that in turn by yet another thing...So we reach a first mover which is not moved by anything. And this all men think of as God."
> [Thomas Aquinas, *Summa Theologica*; 1266–73]

A·qui·no /ə kéenō/, **Corazón** (*b.* 1933) Filipino politician. She was president of the Philippines (1986–92) after the uprising against Ferdinand Marcos. Born **Cojuangco, Maria Corazón**

> "One must be frank to be relevant."
> [Corazón Aquino, chiding the UN for its non-support of the opposition to the Ferdinand Marcos regime; September 22, 1986]

~~aquire~~ incorrect spelling of **acquire**

~~aquit~~ incorrect spelling of **acquit**

Aq·ui·taine /ákwi tàyn/ region of southwestern France. It includes the departments of Dordogne, Gironde, Landes, Lot-et-Garonne, and Pyrénées-Atlantiques. It corresponds roughly to the Roman administrative region of Aquitania. Capital: Bordeaux. Population: 2,908,359 (1999). Area: 15,949 sq. mi./41,309 sq. km.

~~aquittal~~ incorrect spelling of **acquittal**

a·quiv·er /ə kwívvər/ *adj* quivering, especially from excitement or agitation

Ar *symbol* CHEM ELEM argon

AR *abbr* Arkansas

ar. *abbr* **1.** arrival **2.** arrive

Ar. *abbr* **1.** Arabia **2.** Arabian **3.** Arabic

-ar *suffix* of, relating to, or resembling ○ *nebular* [Via Old French *-ar* < Latin *-aris*, alternative for *-alis*]

A·ra /árrə/ *n* a faint constellation of the southern hemisphere lying in the Milky Way near Scorpius. See illustration at **constellation**

a·ra-A /àrrə áy/ *n* PHARM same as **vidarabine** [Late 20C. < contraction of *arabinoside* (< ARABINOSE) + A[1] (sense 2)]

Ar·ab /árrəb/ *n* a member of a Semitic Arabic-speaking people who live throughout North Africa and Southwest Asia ■ *adj* PEOPLES same as **Arabian** [14C. Via French and Latin < Greek *Arab-* < Arabic *'arab*]

USAGE Arab, Arabic, or **Arabian**? ***Arab*** denotes a person, and is also used before nouns as a modifier (*the Arab world; Arab customs*). ***Arabian*** is an adjective referring to *Arabia* in geographic terms (*the Arabian Peninsula*). ***Arabic*** is a noun and an adjective meaning the language of the ***Arab*** people (*She speaks Arabic and knows Arabic* *literature*). ***Arabic*** is written with a capital initial letter in *Arabic numerals* (1, 2, 3, etc.), and with a small initial letter in the term *gum arabic*, a substance obtained from African acacia trees.

Arab. *abbr* **1.** Arabia **2.** Arabian **3.** Arabic

ar·a·besque /àrrə bésk/ *n* **1. BALLET POSTURE** a ballet position in which the dancer stands on one leg with the other extended back and both arms stretched out, usually one forward and the other backward **2. ORNATE DESIGN** an intricate and often symmetrical design incorporating curves, geometric patterns, leaves, flowers, and animal shapes **3. MUSIC WITH ORNATE MELODY** a piece of classical music characterized by decorative melodies, especially one written for solo piano [Early 17C. Via French < Italian *arabesco* "in the Arabian style"]

A·ra·bi·a /ə ráybee ə/, **A·ra·bi·an Pen·in·su·la** peninsula of Southwest Asia, bordering the Persian Gulf, the Arabian Sea, and the Red Sea. It includes the nations of Saudi Arabia, Yemen, Oman, the United Arab Emirates, Qatar, Kuwait, and the island state of Bahrain. Area: 1,158,306 sq. mi./3,000,000 sq. km.

A·ra·bi·an /ə ráybee ən/ *adj* relating to Arabia, or its peoples or cultures ■ *n* **1.** somebody who comes from a country of the Arabian Peninsula **2. BREED** same as **Arabian horse**

USAGE See *Arab*.

A·ra·bi·an cam·el *n* ZOOL same as **dromedary**

A·ra·bi·an Des·ert /ə ràybee ən-/ mountainous dry region of eastern Egypt, between the Nile and the Red Sea. Area: 86,870 sq. mi./225,000 sq. km.

A·ra·bi·an Gulf same as **Persian Gulf**

A·ra·bi·an horse *n* a horse belonging to a breed known for its intelligence, graceful build, and speed. Native to: Arabia.

A·ra·bi·an Pen·in·su·la ➧ **Arabia**

A·ra·bi·an Sea part of the Indian Ocean, extending from the Arabian Peninsula to South Asia

Ar·a·bic /árrəbik/ *n* **SEMITIC LANGUAGE** a Semitic language that is the official language of several countries of North Africa and Southwest Asia. Native speakers: 150 million. Other speakers: 175 million. ■ *adj* **1. OF ARABIA** relating to Arabia, or its peoples, language, or cultures **2. OF ARABIC** relating or belonging to the language Arabic

USAGE See *Arab*.

a·rab·i·ca /ə rábbikə/ *n* **1.** a widely grown species of coffee bush producing high-quality coffee. Latin name: *Coffea arabica*. **2.** coffee made with arabica coffee beans [Early 20C. < modern Latin, "Arabic"]

Ar·a·bic nu·mer·al *n* a symbol of the type 0, 1, 2, 3, 4, 5, 6, 7, 8, and 9 that is used to represent a number

a·rab·i·nose /ə rábbi nòss, árrəbi nòss/ *n* a sugar (**aldose**) derived from various plant gums. Use: biological culture medium. Formula: $C_5H_{10}O_5$. [Late 19C. < GUM ARABIC + -IN + -OSE[1]]

A·rab·ism /árrəbizzəm/ *n* **1. ARAB IDENTITY** Arab cultural identity **2. ARAB NATIONALISM** support for Arab causes or political positions **3. ARABIC EXPRESSION** an Arabic word or phrase

Ar·ab·ist /árrəbist/ *n* **1.** a student of or expert on the Arabs, their language, or their culture **2.** somebody who favors Arab causes or political positions

Ar·ab·ize /árrə bīz/ (**-ized, -iz·ing, -iz·es**) *vti* to conform, or make something conform, to Arab customs or culture —**Ar·ab·i·za·tion** /àrrəbi záysh'n/ *n*

ar·a·ble /árrəb'l/ *adj* describes land that can be cultivated for growing crops ■ *n* land that is fit for planting crops [15C. Via French < Latin *arabilis* < *arare* "to plough"] —**ar·a·bil·i·ty** /àrrə bíllətee/ *n*

Ar·ab League *n* a political and economic association of Arab states, formed in 1945

a·ra·ca·ri /àrrə sáaree, àrrə kàaree/ (*plural* **-ris** or *same*) *n* a toucan that has a long, slim, gently curved beak with serrated edges. Native to: South America. Genus: *Pteroglossus*.

ar·a·chi·don·ic ac·id /àrrəki dónnik-/ *n* an essential fatty acid found in most animal fats that is a precursor of prostaglandins [< modern Latin *arachid-* "peanut" (< Greek *arakhos* "type of leguminous plant") + -ONE]

LANGUAGE HERITAGE ***Arabic*** Much of English is made up of words from other languages, and Arabic is an important contributor in this respect. It has, for example, contributed a word to US regional English: ***alforja***, used in the Southwest to mean "saddlebag," the same meaning held by its Arabic ancestor. First recorded in the early 17th century, ***alforja*** migrated into US dialect from Arabic *al-ḵurj* "the saddlebag," via Spanish. Arabic is also the ultimate source, via American Spanish, of ***alfilaria***, also called "pin clover" and "pin grass," a forage grass grown in the Southwest. First recorded in the late 19th century, it is an alteration of American Spanish *alfilerillo*, a diminutive of Spanish *alfiler* "pin," from Arabic *al-khilāl* "the thorn, the pin."
Moreover, Arabic is an intermediate, direct, or ultimate ancestor of many other English words opening with *al-*, where the definite article in Arabic becomes a formative element in English and in other languages, for example, Spanish, Portuguese, Latin, French, and Italian, through which many Arabic words transited into English. Among these borrowings are, for example, ***albatross*** (ultimately from Arabic *al-ġaṭṭās* "the diver"), ***alcaide*** ("the commander"), ***alcazar*** ("the castle"), ***alchemy***, ***alcohol***, ***alcove***, ***alembic***, ***alfalfa*** ("the best kind of fodder"), ***algarroba***, ***algebra***, ***alkali***, and ***alguacil*** or ***alguazil***, a law enforcement officer in Latin American regions under Spanish influence (ultimately from *al-wazīr* "the vizier").
Arabic is also the direct or ultimate source of some very common English words, for example, ***ghoul***, ***sash*** (from Arabic *šāš* "muslin"), ***candy*** (via French), ***cotton*** (via French), ***lemon*** (via French), ***lime*** (via French and Spanish), ***giraffe*** (via French or Italian, both words from Arabic *zarāfa*), ***magazine*** (via French and Italian), and ***zero*** (via French and Italian, ultimately from Arabic *ṣifr* "emptiness," the source of English ***cipher***).
Another émigré with an interesting history is ***mohair***. Going back in English to the late 16th century, it was respelled from *mocayre* because English speakers, unfamiliar with *-ayre*, likened it to *hair*, a familiar English form, which they substituted for *-ayre*, in a process called "folk etymology." *Mocayre* is ultimately from Arabic *mukayyar* "cloth of goat's hair," literally "select, choice," the past participle of the Arabic verb *kayyara* "prefer."
Arabic has also been an intermediate transport medium in migrations of words from other languages into English. For instance, ***sugar***, first recorded in English in the 13th century, came into English via an early form of French *sucre*, which itself came via medieval Latin from Arabic *sukkar*, and finally from Sanskrit *śarkarā* "grit, ground sugar." ***Elixir*** entered English in the 14th century via medieval Latin from Arabic *al-iksir*, from Greek *xērion* "dry powder for treating wounds," from *xēros* "dry."
Arabic occasionally combines with English to yield compound words, for example, ***seif dune***, first recorded in English in the early 20th century, denoting an enormous desert dune formed in parallel ridges, *seif* coming from Arabic *sayf* "sword." Some Arabic borrowings have taken on English affixes: ***jihadist***, ***Islamism***, and ***Islamize*** are examples.
English also contains a number of direct borrowings from Arabic: for example, ***hashish*** (16th century, from *ḥašīš* "dry herb, powdered hemp," also the source of English ***assassin***), ***fatwa*** (early 17th), ***shrub***, a fruit-and-alcohol drink (early 18th), ***loofa*** (late 19th), and ***intifada*** (late 20th, from *intifāḍa* "a shaking off").
Aside from other direct borrowings readily recognizable as Arabic émigrés, for example, ***falafel***, ***kebab***, ***imam***, ***madrasa***, and ***wadi***, a few derive from place names. For example, ***saluki***, the name of a breed of dog, going back in English to the early 19th century, comes from Arabic *salūkī*, from *Salūk*, a town in Yemen. And ***tabby***, the fabric and striped pattern of cat's fur, first recorded in the late 16th century, came into English via French *tabis* from Arabic *'attābī*. It was named for *al-'Attābiyya*, a quarter of Baghdad, Iraq, where the fabric, originally with stripes, was made.

ar·a·chis oil /árrəkiss-/ *n* FOOD same as **peanut oil**

a·rach·nid /ə ráknid/ *n* an animal with four pairs of legs and a body with two segments, belonging to a large class that includes spiders, scorpions, and mites. Class: Arachnida. [Mid-19C. < modern Latin *Arachnida* < Greek *arakhnē* "spider, spider's web"] —**a·rach·ni·dan** *adj*

a·rach·no·dac·ty·ly /ə ráknō dákt'lee/ *n* a condition characterized by unusually long fingers and toes

a·rach·noid /ə rák nòyd/ *n* **1.** ANAT the middle of the three membranes that envelop the brain and spinal cord **2.** ZOOL same as **arachnid** ■ *adj* ZOOL resembling or related to an arachnid [Mid-18C. Via modern Latin < Greek *arakhnoeidēs* "like a spider's web" < *arakhnē* "spider's web"]

a·rach·nol·o·gy /ə ràk nóllәjee/ *n* the branch of zoology concerned with the study of spiders and other arachnids [Mid-19C. < Greek *arakhnē* "spider"] —**a·rach·nol·o·gist** *n*

a·rach·no·pho·bi·a /ə ràknə fōbee ə/ *n* an unusually strong fear of spiders [Early 20C. < Greek *arakhnē* "spider"] —**a·rach·no·phobe** /ə ráknə fōb/ *n* —**a·rach·no·pho·bic** *adj*

Ar·a·fat /árrə fàt/, **Yasir** (*b.* 1929) president of the Palestinian National Authority (1996–). He became chairman of the Palestine Liberation Organization (1968) and shared the Nobel Peace Prize with Itzhak Rabin (1994).

Barnaby's
Yasir Arafat

A·ra·fu·ra Sea /àarə fòorə-/ area of the Pacific Ocean between the northern coast of Australia, New Guinea, and eastern Indonesia

A·ra·gón /àrrə gón/ autonomous region and former kingdom in northeastern Spain. It contains the provinces of Huesca, Zaragoza, and Teruel. Capital: Zaragoza. Population: 1,188,817 (1991). Area: 18,405 sq. mi./47,669 sq. km.

a·rag·o·nite /ə rággə nīt/ *n* a colorless, blue to violet, or yellow mineral consisting of calcium carbonate [Late 18C. After ARAGÓN]

A·ra·ka·wa Shu·sa·ku /aarə kàawə shoo sàakoo/ (*b.* 1936) Japanese artist whose Western-style paintings influenced early conceptual art. He moved to the United States in 1961.

a·ra·li·a /ə ráylee ə/ (*plural* **-as** or *same*) *n* a plant widely grown as a houseplant for its ornamental leaves. Genera: *Aralia* or *Polyscias*. [Mid-18C. < modern Latin]

Ar·al Sea /árrəl-/ inland sea straddling the Kazakhstan-Uzbekistan border in Central Asia, east of the Caspian Sea. Area: 12,050 sq. mi./31,220 sq. km.

Ar·a·ma·ic /àrrə máy ik/ *n* a Semitic language of the ancient Near East, dating from about 300 B.C. and still spoken in the region. Native speakers: 50,000–100,000. [Mid-19C. < Greek *Aramaios* "of Aram" (ancient Syria)] —**Ar·a·ma·ic** *adj*

Ar·an Is·lands /árrən-/ group of three islands, Inishmoor, Inishmaan, and Inisheer, situated at the mouth of Galway Bay in western Ireland. Population: 1280 (2002). Area: 18 sq. mi./47 sq. km.

A·rap·a·ho /ə ráppə hō/ (*plural same* or **-hos**), **A·rap·a·hoe** (*plural same* or **-hoes**) *n* **1.** a member of a Native North American people who formerly lived on the Great Plains, and now live in Colorado, Wyoming, and Montana **2.** an Algonquian language of western North America. Native speakers: 1,500. [Early 19C. < Crow *alappahó* "many tattoo marks"] —**A·rap·a·ho** *adj*

Ar·a·rat, Mount /árrə ràt/ mountain in eastern Turkey, which rises in two peaks, Great Ararat 16,854 ft./5,137 m and Little Ararat 12,840 ft./3,914 m. According to the Bible, it was the landing place of Noah's Ark.

Ar·au·ca·ni·an /à raw káynee ən/ *n* 1. a member of a Native South American people who live in central Chile and western Argentina 2. a South American language spoken in parts of Chile and western Argentina. Native speakers: 300,000. [Early 19C. < Spanish *Araucanía*, region of Chile] —**Ar·au·ca·ni·an** *adj*

ar·au·car·i·a /àrraw kérree ə/ (*plural* **-as** or *same*) *n* an evergreen coniferous tree with stiff sharp leaves. Monkey-puzzle is a species of araucaria. Native to: southern hemisphere. Genus: *Araucaria*. [Mid-19C. < modern Latin < *Arauco*, province in Chile]

Ar·a·wak /árrə waák/ (*plural same* or **-waks**) *n* 1. a member of a Native South American people who live in Guyana, Suriname, and French Guiana 2. a South American language of the Arawakan family, spoken in Guyana and neighboring countries [Mid-18C. < Carib *aruac*] —**Ar·a·wak** *adj*

Ar·a·wa·kan /árrə waákən/ (*plural same* or **-kans**) *n* 1. a member of a Native South American people who live in northeastern South America 2. a family of Native South American languages, spoken by widely scattered peoples in South America. Native speakers: 300,000. —**Ar·a·wa·kan** *adj*

arb /aarb/ *n* FIN same as **arbitrageur** (*slang*) [Late 20C. Shortening]

ar·ba·lest /aárbəlist/, **ar·ba·list** *n* a large medieval crossbow used to propel stones, arrows, and other missiles [Pre-12C. Via Old French *arbaleste* < late Latin *arcuballista* < *arcus* "bow" + *ballista* (see BALLISTA)] —**ar·ba·lest·er** /-lèstər/ *n*

Ar·benz Guz·man /aárbənz go͝ozmən/, **Jacobo** (1913–71) president of Guatemala (1951–54). He pursued a policy of radical land reform and was ousted by a coup in 1954.

ar·bi·ter /aárbətər/ *n* 1. somebody who can settle a dispute or decide an issue 2. somebody with great influence over what people say, think, or do [14C. Directly or via French < Latin, "judge, umpire"] —**ar·bi·tral** *adj*

ar·bi·trage /aárbə traàzh/ *n* the simultaneous buying and selling of the same negotiable financial instruments or commodities in different markets in order to make an immediate profit without risk ■ *vi* (**-traged, -trag·ing, -trag·es**) to engage in arbitrage [Mid-19C. < French < *arbitrer* "to judge" < Latin *arbitrari* (see ARBITRATE)]

ar·bi·tra·geur /aárbi traa zhúr/ *n* somebody who engages in arbitrage [Mid-19C. < French < *arbitrage* (see ARBITRAGE)]

ar·bi·trar·y /aárbə trèrree/ *adj* 1. **BASED ON WHIM** based solely on personal wishes, feelings, or perceptions, rather than on objective facts, reasons, or principles ○ *an arbitrary decision* 2. **RANDOM** chosen or determined at random ○ *the arbitrary order of the entries* 3. **AUTHORITARIAN** with unlimited power ○ *arbitrary government* 4. LAW **NOT ACCORDING TO RULE** based on the decision of a judge or court rather than in accordance with any rule or law ○ *arbitrary arrest* [15C. < Latin *arbitrarius* "uncertain, depending on the judgment of an arbiter" < *arbiter* "judge"] —**ar·bi·trar·i·ly** /aárbə tráirrəlee/ *adv* —**ar·bi·trar·i·ness** *n*

ar·bi·trate /aárbi tràyt/ (**-trat·ed, -trat·ing, -trates**) *v* 1. *vti* to act as a judge in a dispute between others 2. *vt* to submit a dispute to be decided by a third party [Late 16C. < Latin *arbitrat-*, past participle of *arbitrari* "judge, decide" < *arbiter* "judge"] —**ar·bi·tra·ble** *adj*

ar·bi·tra·tion /aárbi tráysh'n/ *n* the process of resolving disputes between people or groups by referring them to a third party, either agreed on by them or provided by law, who makes a judgment —**ar·bi·tra·tion·al** *adj*

ar·bi·tra·tor /aárbi tràytər/ *n* somebody designated to hear both sides of a dispute and make a judgment

ar·bor[1] /aárbər/ *n* 1. a shaded place formed by the leaves and branches of trees and plants that interweave naturally or are trained to grow around a trellis 2. a trellis or other structure used to support plants that form an arbor [14C. Via Old French *(h)erb(i)er* < late Latin *herbarium* (see HERBARIUM)]

ar·bor[2] /aárbər/ *n* 1. **AXLE ON MACHINE OR POWER TOOL** a shaft, axle, or spindle on a machine or a power tool 2. **SUPPORTING PIECE** a machine part that holds an object being worked on 3. **REINFORCING PART OF MOLD** a part that reinforces the core of a mold used to cast metal [Mid-17C. Via French < Latin, "tree, mast, lever, shaft"]

Ar·bor Day *n* a day set aside for the planting and appreciation of trees. Date: typically the last Friday in April, but varying from state to state.

ar·bo·re·al /aar báwree əl/ *adj* 1. describes a species that lives in trees 2. relating to, resembling, or consisting of trees —**ar·bo·re·al·ly** *adv*

ar·bo·re·ous /aar báwree əss/ *adj* covered with trees (*formal*)

ar·bo·res·cent /aárbə réss'nt/ *adj* resembling a tree, especially in developing branches or similar parts [Mid-17C. < Latin *arborescent-*, present participle of *arborescere* "grow into a tree" < *arbor* "tree"] —**ar·bo·res·cence** *n*

ar·bo·re·tum /aárbə reétəm/ (*plural* **-tums** or **-ta** /-tə/) *n* an area planted with many types of trees for study, display, and preservation [Mid-19C. < Latin, "place grown with trees, plantation of trees" < *arbor* "tree"]

ar·bo·ri·cul·ture /aárbəri kùlchər, aar báwri-/ *n* the cultivation of trees and bushes for study, ornamentation, or profit [Mid-19C. Blend of Latin *arbor* "tree" + AGRICULTURE] —**ar·bo·ri·cul·tur·al** *adj* —**ar·bo·ri·cul·tur·ist** *n*

ar·bor·i·o /aar báwree ō/, **ar·bor·i·o rice** *n* a short-grained rice used to make risotto and other Italian dishes [Late 20C. < Italian]

ar·bor·ist /aárbərist/ *n* an expert in the cultivation and care of trees

ar·bo·rize /aárbə rīz/ (**-rized, -riz·ing, -riz·es**) *vi* to develop many branching parts or formations —**ar·bo·ri·za·tion** /aárbəri záysh'n/ *n*

ar·bor·vi·tae /aárbər vítee, -veé tī/, **ar·bor vi·tae** *n* an ornamental coniferous tree with flat leaves that fit closely like scales. Native to: Asia, North America. Genus: *Thuja*. [Mid-17C. < Latin, "tree of life"]

ar·bour *n* Can, UK spelling of **arbor**[1]

ar·bo·vi·rus /aárbə vīrəss/ *n* a virus transmitted by bloodsucking arthropods such as ticks and fleas. Arboviruses contain RNA, exist in over 500 species, and include the viruses that cause encephalitis, yellow fever, and dengue. [Mid-20C. Contraction of *arthropod-borne virus*] —**ar·bo·vi·ral** /aárbə vīrəl/ *adj*

Ar·bus /aárbəss/, **Diane** (1923–71) US photographer, known for her unconventional and occasionally morbid portraits of unusual characters

> "There are things nobody would see if I didn't photograph them."
> [Diane Arbus. Quoted in *Diane Arbus*; 1972]

ar·bu·tus /aar byo͞otəss/ (*plural* **-tus·es** or *same*) *n* 1. PLANTS same as **trailing arbutus** 2. a bush or tree that bears reddish fruits. Flowers: white, pink. Native to: southern Europe. Genus: *Arbutus*. [Mid-16C. < Latin, "wild strawberry"]

arc /aark/ *n* 1. **CURVE** a curved or semicircular line, direction of movement, or arrangement of items ○ *swung in a high arc overhead* ○ *an arc of children around their teacher* 2. MATH **SECTION OF CIRCLE** a section of a circle, ellipse, or other curved figure 3. ASTRON **VISIBLE PART OF ASTRONOMICAL OBJECT'S PATH** a section of the path that a planet or other astronomical object appears to follow, especially that seen above the horizon 4. ELEC ENG **ELECTRIC DISCHARGE** a luminous discharge caused by an electric current flowing across a gap in an electrical circuit 5. GEOL same as **island arc** ■ *vi* (**arced, arc·ing, arcs**) 1. **FORM OR MOVE IN ARC** to form a curve or move along a curved path 2. ELEC ENG **SPARK ACROSS GAP** to produce a luminous discharge across a gap in an electrical circuit [14C. Via French < Latin *arcus* "bow, curve"]

ARC *abbr* MED AIDS-related complex

ar·cade /aar káyd/ *n* 1. **PASSAGEWAY WITH ARCHES** a passageway or building with a series of arches and supporting columns 2. **AVENUE OF STORES** a covered passage with stores on both sides 3. **ENCLOSED AREA WITH GAME MACHINES** an enclosed area where people can play on coin-operated game machines such as pinball machines or video games 4. **SERIES OF ARCHES** a series of arches and the columns supporting them 5. COMPUT GAMES same as **video arcade** ■ *adj* COMPUT GAMES **OF VIDEO GAMES** relating to or typical of video arcade games [Mid-18C. Via French < Italian *arcata* < Latin *arcus* "bow, curve, arch"]

ar·cade game *n* a coin-operated game played in amusement arcades, e.g., a slot machine, pinball machine, or video game

Ar·ca·di·a[1] /aar káydee ə/, **ar·ca·di·a** *n* a place in which people are imagined or believed to enjoy a perfect life of rustic simplicity [Late 19C. Via Latin < Greek *Arkadia*, mountainous district in Peloponnesus]

Ar·ca·di·a[2] /aar káydee ə/ 1. mountainous region in the central Peloponnesus, southwestern Greece 2. city in southwestern California, a suburb of Los Angeles. Population: 54,904 (2002 estimate).

Ar·ca·di·an /aar káydee ən/ *adj* 1. *also* **ar·ca·di·an OF IMAGINED ARCADIA** relating to the perfect life of rustic simplicity of Arcadia 2. **OF ARCADIA IN GREECE** relating to the region of Arcadia in southwestern Greece 3. **OF ARCADIA IN CALIFORNIA** relating to the city of Arcadia in southwestern California —**Ar·ca·di·an** *n*

ar·ca·na /aar káynə/ *n* either of two divisions of a pack of tarot cards ■ plural of **arcanum**

ar·cane /aar káyn/ *adj* 1. difficult or impossible to understand 2. requiring secret knowledge to be understood [Early 16C. < Latin *arcanus* "closed, secret" < *arca* "box"] —**ar·cane·ly** *adv* —**ar·cane·ness** *n*

SYNONYMS See ***obscure***.

ar·ca·num /aar káynəm/ (*plural* **-na** /-nə/) *n* (*usually used in the plural*) 1. a secret known only to the members of a small select group 2. a secret of nature, of the kind that was formerly sought by alchemists [Late 16C. < Latin, form of *arcanus* (see ARCANE)]

AKG London

Arc de Triomphe, Paris, France

Arc de Tri·omphe /aárk də treé ōNf/ *n* a triumphal arch at the end of the Avenue des Champs Elysées in Paris, France, completed in 1835. It was commissioned by Napoleon to commemorate military victories, and is now used as a war memorial.

arc fur·nace *n* a furnace in which an electric arc supplies the heat

arch[1] /aarch/ *n* 1. **CURVED STRUCTURE** a curved structure that forms the upper edge of an open space such as a window, a doorway, or the space between a bridge's supports 2. **PASSAGE UNDER ARCH** an entrance or passageway under an arch 3. **ARCH SHAPE** the shape of an arch, resembling an inverted "U," or an object with such a shape ○ *the arch of his eyebrows* 4. ANAT **CURVED BODY PART** a body part with the shape of an arch, especially the bony structure in the foot ■ *v* (**arched, arch·ing, arch·es**) 1. *vt* **FORM CURVED SHAPE** to form something into the shape of an arch ○ *Arch your back and let your arms take your weight.* 2. *vi* **MOVE IN CURVING LINE** to follow a trajectory in the shape of an arch 3. *vt* **SPAN** to extend across something 4. *vt* **BUILD ARCH** to build something in the shape of an arch or with arch-shaped supports [13C. Via Old French *arche* < Latin *arcus* "bow, curve, arch"] —**arched** *adj*

arch[2] /aarch/ *adj* 1. expressing playfulness, mischief, or shared humor in a knowing way 2. greatest, especially most hostile [Mid-16C. < ARCH-] —**arch·ly** *adv* —**arch·ness** *n*

arch. *abbr* 1. archaic 2. archaism 3. CHR archbishop 4. archery 5. GEOG archipelago 6. architect 7. architecture

arch- *prefix* **1.** chief, most important ○ *archrival* **2.** extreme ○ *archconservative* [Via Old French and Latin *arche* < Greek *arkhi-* "first, chief" (see ARCHI-)]

-arch *suffix* leader, ruler ○ *matriarch* [Via French and late Latin < Greek *arkhos* < *arkhein* "to rule"] —**-archic** *suffix* —**-archy** *suffix*

archae- *prefix* same as **archaeo-** (*used before vowels*)

ar·chae·a /aar kée ə, áarkee ə/ *npl* members of one of two distinct groups of the most primitive living single-celled organisms, similar in size to bacteria but different in molecular organization [Late 20C. Shortening of ARCHAEBACTERIA]

Ar·chae·an *n, adj* GEOL another spelling of **Archean**

ar·chae·bac·te·ri·a /áarki bak téeree ə/ *npl* MICROBIOL same as **archaea** [Late 20C. Because believed to be of ancient origin] —**ar·chae·bac·te·ri·al** *adj*

archaeo-, archeo- *prefix* ancient ○ *archaeobotany* [Via modern Latin < Greek *arkhaios*]

ar·chae·o·as·tron·o·my /áarkee ō ə strónnəmee/, **ar·che·o·as·tron·o·my** *n* the study of the astronomical beliefs, practices, and discoveries of prehistoric and ancient cultures —**ar·chae·o·as·tron·o·mer** *n* —**ar·chae·o·as·tro·nom·i·cal** /áarkee ō astrə nómmik'l/ *adj*

ar·chae·o·bot·a·ny /áarkee ō bótt'nee/, **ar·che·o·bot·a·ny** *n* the scientific study of excavated plant remains from ancient times —**ar·chae·o·bot·a·nist** *n*

ar·chae·o·log·i·cal /áarkee ə lójjik'l/, **ar·che·o·log·i·cal, ar·chae·o·log·ic** /-lójjik/, **ar·che·o·log·ic** *adj* relating to archaeology, or carried out for the purposes of archaeology —**ar·chae·o·log·i·cal·ly** *adv*

ar·ch·ae·o·log·i·cal dat·ing *n* the use of the decay rates of biological specimens to determine the age of an archaeological site, effective back to about 50,000 years

ar·chae·ol·o·gy /áarkee óllәjee/, **ar·che·ol·o·gy** *n* the scientific study of ancient cultures through the examination of their material remains such as buildings, graves, tools, and other artifacts usually dug up from the ground —**ar·chae·ol·o·gist** *n*

ar·chae·o·mag·net·ism /áarkee ō mágnət ìzzəm/, **ar·che·o·mag·net·ism** *n* a method of dating excavated artifacts by measuring the degree of their magnetization

ar·chae·om·e·try /áarkee ómmətree/, **ar·che·om·e·try** *n* the systematic dating of archaeological objects —**ar·chae·o·met·ri·cal** /áarkee ə méttrik'l/ *adj* —**ar·chae·o·met·ri·cal·ly** *adv* —**ar·chae·om·e·trist** *n*

archaeopteryx

ar·chae·op·ter·yx /áarkee óptəriks/ *n* an extinct bird of the Jurassic period that had the feathers of modern birds but the jaw and sharp teeth of reptiles. It is considered to be a link between reptiles and birds. Latin name: *Archaeopteryx lithographica.* [Mid-19C. < ARCHAEO- + Greek *pterux* "wing"]

ar·cha·ic /aar káy ik/ *adj* **1.** OUTMODED no longer useful or efficient **2.** NO LONGER IN ORDINARY LANGUAGE describes a word or phrase that is no longer in general use but is still encountered in older literature and still sometimes used for special effect **3.** ANCIENT belonging or relating to a much earlier period [Mid-19C. Via French < Greek *arkhaikos* < *arkhaios* "old, ancient" < *arkhē* "beginning"] —**ar·cha·i·cal·ly** *adv*

SYNONYMS See ***old-fashioned.***

ar·cha·ism /áarkee ìzzəm/ *n* **1.** a word, expression, practice, or method from an earlier time that is no longer used **2.** the use of expressions, techniques, and fashions from an earlier period [Mid-17C. Via modern Latin < Greek *arkhaismos* < *arkhaizein* "copy the ancients, give an archaic air to" < *arkhaios* (see ARCHAIC)] —**ar·cha·ist** *n* —**ar·cha·is·tic** /áarkee ístik/ *adj*

ar·cha·ize /áarkee ìz/ (**-ized, -iz·ing, -iz·es**) *vt* to make something seem much older than it is by using old forms or styles —**ar·cha·iz·er** *n*

arch·an·gel /áark àynjəl/ *n* **1.** a chief or principal angel **2.** an angel of the second of the nine orders of angels in the traditional Christian hierarchy [Pre-12C. Via Anglo-Norman < ecclesiastical Greek *arkhaggelos* < Greek *arkhi-* "chief" (see ARCHI-) + *aggelos* "messenger"] —**arch·an·gel·ic** /áark an jéllik/ *adj*

Arch·an·gel /áark àynjəl/ English name for **Arkhangelsk**

arch·bish·op /aarch bíshəp/ *n* a bishop of the highest rank, who heads an archdiocese or an ecclesiastical province

arch·bish·op·ric /aarch bíshəprik/ *n* **1.** the area of an archbishop's jurisdiction **2.** the status or term of office of an archbishop [Pre-12C. < ARCHBISHOP + Old English *rice* "realm"]

arch bridge *n* a bridge whose span curves in the shape of an arch

arch·con·ser·va·tive /áarch kən súrvətiv/ *n* somebody with strong conservative views

archd. *abbr* **1.** CHR archdeacon **2.** archduke

arch·dea·con /aarch déekən/ *n* a member of the clergy who ranks just below a bishop and assists the bishop with ceremonial and administrative duties —**arch·dea·con·ate** *n* —**arch·dea·con·ship** *n*

arch·dea·con·ry /aarch déekənree/ *n* the status or term of office of an archdeacon

arch·di·o·cese /aarch dī əssəss/ *n* the area for which an archbishop has ecclesiastical responsibility —**arch·di·oc·e·san** /áarch dī óssəss'n/ *adj*

arch·du·cal /aarch dóok'l/ *adj* relating or belonging to archdukes, archduchesses, or archduchies

arch·duch·ess /aarch dúchəss/ *n* **1.** an archduke's wife or widow **2.** a princess of the former Austrian imperial family

arch·duch·y /aarch dúchee/ (*plural* **-ies**) *n* the land ruled by an archduke or archduchess

arch·duke /aarch dóok/ *n* a senior duke in some countries, especially Austria [Early 16C. Via Old French *archeduc* < late Latin *archidux* < *archi-* "chief, first" + *dux* "leader"]

Ar·che·an /aar kée ən/, **Ar·chae·an** *n* the earliest eon of geologic time, dating from about four billion years ago. See table at **geologic time** [Late 19C. < Greek *arkhaios* "old, ancient" + AN²] —**Ar·che·an** *adj*

ar·che·go·ni·a BOT plural of **archegonium**

ar·che·go·ni·ate /áarki gṓnee ət/ *adj* bearing archegonia ■ *n* a plant that bears archegonia

ar·che·go·ni·um /áarki gṓnee əm/ (*plural* **-ni·a** /-nee ə/) *n* the female reproductive organ of mosses, ferns, liverworts, and most gymnosperms. It contains a single egg cell. [Mid-19C. < modern Latin < Greek *arkhegonos* < *arkhe-* "chief, first" + *gonos* "people"] —**ar·che·go·ni·al** *adj*

arch·en·e·my /aarch énnəmee/ (*plural* **-mies**) *n* **1.** somebody's main or worst enemy **2.** *also* **Arch·en·e·my** the devil

ar·chen·ter·on /aar kéntə ròn, -tərən/ *n* a digestive cavity in animal embryos that develops into the gut [Late 19C. < Greek *arkhē* "beginning"+ *enteron* "intestine"] —**ar·chen·ter·ic** /áarkən térrik/ *adj*

archeo-, etc. another spelling of **archaeo-, etc.**

arch·er /áarchər/ *n* somebody who uses a bow and arrow [13C. < Anglo-Norman *archer,* Old French *archier* < Latin *arcus* "bow, curve"]

Arch·er *n* ZODIAC same as **Sagittarius** (sense 2)

arch·er·fish /áarchər fish/ (*plural same* or **-fish·es**) *n* a freshwater fish that hunts insects by spitting water at them. Native to: Australia, Southeast Asia. Family: Toxotidae.

arch·er·y /áarchəree/ *n* **1.** USE OF BOW AND ARROW the activity of shooting with a bow and arrow **2.** TROOP OF ARCHERS a troop of soldiers armed with bows and arrows **3.** ARCHERS' WEAPONS the bows and arrows used by archers

Arch·es Na·tion·al Park /áarchəz-/ park in southeastern Utah noted for its natural stone arches. Established as a national monument in 1929, it became a national park in 1971. Area: 115 sq. mi./297 sq. km.

ar·che·spo·ri·um /áarki spáwree əm/ (*plural* **-ri·a** /-ree ə/) *n* the tissue that gives rise to spore-producing cells in a sporangium in fungi [Late 19C. < *arche-*, alteration of ARCHI- + SPORE + -IUM]

ar·che·type /áarki tīp/ *n* **1.** TYPICAL SPECIMEN a typical, ideal, or classic example of something ○ *It was described as an archetype of the interior design of the period.* **2.** ORIGINAL MODEL something that serves as the model or pattern for other things of the same type ○ *The movie was one of the archetypes of the American Western.* **3.** PSYCHOANAL IMAGE FROM COLLECTIVE UNCONSCIOUS in Jungian psychology, an inherited memory represented in the mind by a universal symbol and observed in dreams and myths **4.** ARTS RECURRING SYMBOL an image or symbol that is used repeatedly in art or literature [Mid-16C. Via Latin *archetypum* < Greek *arkhetupon* "first molded as a model" < *arkhe-* "first, chief" + *tupon* "mold, model"] —**ar·che·typ·al** /áarki tīp'l/ *adj* —**ar·che·typ·ic** /áarki típpik/ *adj* —**ar·che·typ·i·cal** *adj* —**ar·che·typ·i·cal·ly** *adv*

arch·fiend /áarch féend/ *n* **1.** an extremely wicked person or being **2.** *also* **Arch·fiend** the devil

archi- *prefix* **1.** chief, most important ○ *archimandrite* **2.** primitive, primary ○ *archenteron* [Via French < Greek *arkhi-* < *arkhein* "be first, rule"]

ar·chi·di·ac·o·nal /áarki dī ákən'l/ *adj* relating to the work or position of an archdeacon [15C. < Latin *archidiaconus* < *diaconus* (see DEACON)]

ar·chi·di·ac·o·nate /áarki dī ákənət, -ákə nàyt/ *n* an archdeacon's position, area of jurisdiction, or term of office [Mid-18C. < Latin *archidiaconus* (see ARCHIDIACONAL)]

Ar·chie /áarchee/ *n* an Internet database used to search for files and programs that can be downloaded using FTP. The master server is at McGill University in Montreal. [Late 20C. < ARCHIVE + -IE, after the name *Archie*]

ar·chi·e·pis·co·pal /áarkee ə pískəp'l/ *adj* relating to an archbishop or an archdiocese [Early 17C. < ecclesiastical Latin *archiepiscopus* "archbishop" < ecclesiastical Greek *arkhiepiskopos* < *episkopos* (see BISHOP)] —**ar·chi·e·pis·co·pal·i·ty** /áarkee ə pìskə pállətee/ *n* —**ar·chi·e·pis·co·pal·ly** *adv* —**ar·chi·e·pis·co·pate** *n*

ar·chi·man·drite /áarkə mán drīt/ *n* in the Eastern Orthodox Church, a senior priest who heads a monastery or group of monasteries [Mid-17C. Directly or via French < ecclesiastical Latin *archimandrita* < ecclesiastical Greek *arkhimandritēs* < *arkhi-* "first, chief" + *mandra* "enclosure, monastery"]

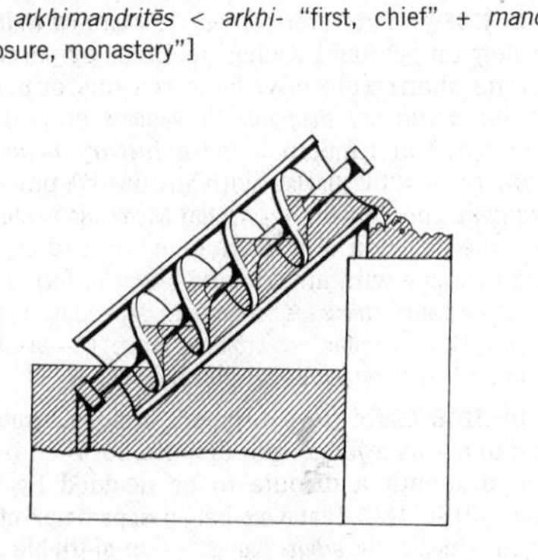

Archimedean screw

Ar·chi·me·de·an screw /áarkə méedee ən-/ *n* an ancient method of raising water, using either a large screw inside a sloping tube or a spiral tube curling around a sloping axis, that causes water to flow upward when the screw or tube is turned [After ARCHIMEDES]

Ar·chi·me·des /áarkə mée deez/ (287–212 B.C.) Greek mathematician. He wrote on geometry, arithmetic, and mechanics.

Ar·chi·me·des' prin·ci·ple *n* the principle that an object immersed in a liquid experiences an upward thrust equal to the weight of liquid it displaces, so that light objects float and heavy objects sink

Ar·chi·me·des' screw *n* ENG same as **Archimedean screw**

ar·chi·pel·a·go /aarkə péllə gō/ (*plural* **-gos** or **-goes**) *n* **1.** a group or chain of islands (*often used in place names*) **2.** an area of sea with many islands [Early 16C. < Italian *arcipelago* < Greek *arkhi-* "chief, main" + *pelagos* "sea"] —**ar·chi·pe·lag·ic** /aarkəpə lájjik/ *adj*

ar·chi·tect /aarkə tèkt/ *n* **1.** BUILDING DESIGNER somebody whose job is to design buildings and advise on their construction **2.** CREATOR somebody who creates or invents something ○ *the architect of her own fortune* **3.** COMPUTER SYSTEM DESIGNER the developer of the structure of a computer system or program [Mid-16C. Directly or via French and Italian < Latin *architectus* < Greek *arkhitektōn* "chief builder" < *tektōn* "builder"]

ar·chi·tec·ton·ic /aarkə tek tónnik/ *adj* **1.** relating to architecture or the qualities such as design and structure that architecture requires **2.** relating to the classification of knowledge used in metaphysics [Mid-17C. Via Latin < Greek *arkhitektonikos* < *arkhitektōn* (see ARCHITECT)] —**ar·chi·tec·ton·i·cal·ly** *adv*

ar·chi·tec·ton·ics /aarkə tek tónniks/ *n* **1.** SCIENCE OF ARCHITECTURE the science of architecture (*takes a singular verb*) **2.** STRUCTURAL DESIGN OF COMPLEX THING the way in which the parts of a complex object or system fit together (*takes a plural verb*) ○ *the architectonics of a good novel* **3.** PHILOSOPHY CLASSIFICATION OF KNOWLEDGE in metaphysics, the classification of knowledge (*takes a singular verb*)

ar·chi·tec·ture /aarki tèkchər/ *n* **1.** BUILDING DESIGN the art and science of designing and constructing buildings **2.** BUILDING STYLE a style or fashion of building, especially one that is typical of a period of history or of a particular place **3.** STRUCTURE OF COMPUTER SYSTEM the design, structure, and behavior of a computer system, microprocessor, or system program, including the characteristics of individual components and how they interact ○ *network architecture* —**ar·chi·tec·tur·al** /aarki tékchərəl/ *adj* —**ar·chi·tec·tur·al·ly** *adv*

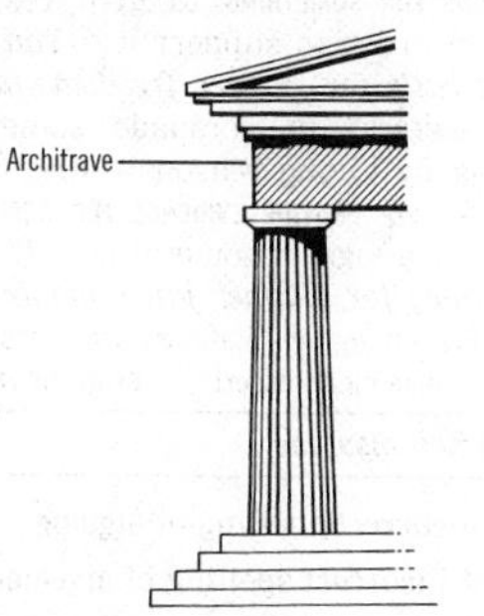

architrave

ar·chi·trave /aarki tràyv/ *n* **1.** in classical architecture, the lowest section of an entablature, which comes into contact with the top of the columns **2.** a decorative strip of wood or plaster forming a frame around a door or window [Mid-16C. Via French < Italian, "main beam" < *trave* "beam" < Latin *trab-*]

ar·chive /aar kīv/ *n* **1.** COLLECTION OF DOCUMENTS a collection of documents such as letters, official papers, photographs, or recorded material, kept for their historical interest (*often used in the plural*) ○ *We'll have to check the archives.* **2.** PLACE WHERE ARCHIVES ARE HELD a building or room that houses archives **3.** COMPUT BACKUP OF COMPUTER FILES a copy of computer files stored, often in compressed form, on tape or disk **4.** COMPUT FILE OF COMPRESSED FILES a computer file containing other compressed files **5.** ONLINE INTERNET DIRECTORY a directory of files that Internet users can access using anonymous File Transfer Protocol ■ *vt* (**-chived, -chiv·ing, -chives**) **1.** PUT DOCUMENT IN ARCHIVE to store a document in an archive **2.** COMPUT STORE DATA EXTERNALLY to transfer data from a computer's hard disk to a disk or, formerly, a tape for storage. Optical disks are used to archive files as they are more reliable than floppy disks for long-term storage. **3.** COMPUT COMBINE COMPUTER FILES to store compressed copies of computer files in a single file [Early 17C. Via French < Latin *archiva, archia* < Greek *arkheia* "things kept at the public office," plural of *arkheion* "ruler's house, public office" < *arkhē* "beginning, government"] —**ar·chi·val** /aar kīv'l/ *adj*

ar·chi·vist /aarkəvist, aar kīvist/ *n* somebody employed to collect, catalog, and take care of the items in an archive

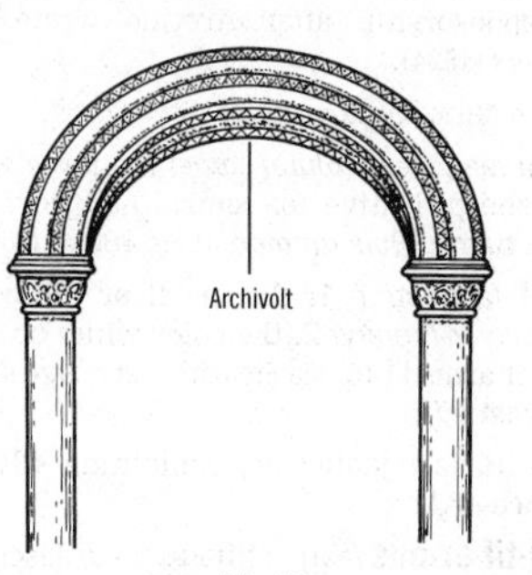

archivolt

ar·chi·volt /aarkə vōlt/ *n* **1.** a decorative molding or band on the face of an arch **2.** the underside of an arch [Mid-17C. Directly or via French *archivolte* < Italian *archivolto* < Latin *arcus* "arch" + *volta* "vault"]

ar·chon /aar kòn/ *n* in ancient Greece, one of the nine chief Athenian magistrates [Late 16C. < Greek *arkhōn* < *arkhein* "to rule"] —**ar·chon·ship** *n*

arch·priest /aarch préest/ *n* **1.** HIGH-RANKING EASTERN ORTHODOX PRIEST in the Eastern Orthodox Church, a married priest of the highest rank **2.** ROMAN CATHOLIC PRIEST WITH SPECIFIC DUTY in the Roman Catholic Church, a title given to a priest who has a specific important duty or function **3.** ROMAN CATHOLIC BISHOP'S SENIOR ASSISTANT formerly, a title given to the senior Roman Catholic priest in a cathedral chapter, who acted as the bishop's principal assistant [14C. Via Old French *archeprestre* < late Latin *archipresbyter* "chief priest"]

arch·ri·val /aarch rīv'l/ *n* somebody's main or most dangerous rival

arch·way /aarch wày/ *n* an entrance or passage under one or more arches, or an arch that forms an entrance

Ar·chy·tas /aar kītəss/ (*fl* early 4th century B.C.) Greek mathematician. He calculated the mathematical relationships of musical notes and scales.

Ar·cim·bol·do /aarchim báwldō/, **Giuseppe** (1530?–93) Italian painter and designer. He produced pictures of fantastic heads composed of items such as vegetables and animals.

arc light, arc lamp *n* an intensely bright electric light with numerous uses, e.g., in floodlights and spotlights on film sets. The light is generated by passing electric current through ionized gas.

ar·co /aarkō/ *adv* played using the bow of a stringed instrument, usually after a passage played by plucking the strings (**pizzicato**) (*used as a musical direction*) [Mid-18C. < Italian, "bow"] —**ar·co** *adj*

arc·tic /aarktik, aartik/ *adj* extremely cold (*informal*) ■ *n* a high waterproof overshoe with a warm lining [14C. Via Old French *artique* < Greek *arktikos* < *arktos* "bear," also "the constellation Ursa Major (the Great Bear)"]

Arc·tic /aarktik, aartik/ region that lies around the North Pole, inside the Arctic Circle —**Arc·tic** *adj*

arc·tic char *n* a fish of the salmon family, similar to a trout. Native to: northern hemisphere. Latin name: *Salvelinus alpinus.*

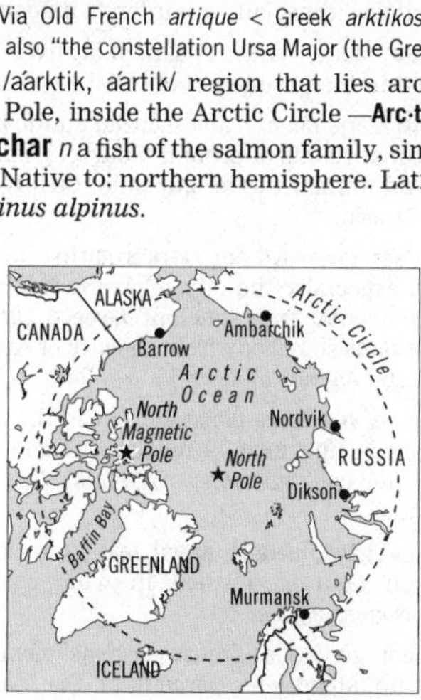

Arctic Circle

Arc·tic Cir·cle *n* the line of latitude at 66°30'N that marks the boundary of the Arctic. North of this latitude there are periods of continuous night in the winter and continuous day in the summer.

arc·tic fox *n* a small fox with thick fur that is brownish gray in summer and white or blue in winter. Native to: Arctic. Latin name: *Alopex lagopus.*

arc·tic hare *n* a large hare with white fur that in southern regions turns brown in the summer. Native to: Arctic North America, Greenland. Latin name: *Lepus arcticus.*

Arc·tic O·cean the world's smallest ocean, mostly ice-covered, situated north of the Arctic Circle and surrounding the North Pole. Area: 5,427,100 sq. mi./14,056,000 sq. km. Depth: 17,880 ft./5,500 m.

arc·tic tern *n* a black-headed seabird that breeds in Arctic regions and migrates to southern Africa, South America, and the Antarctic. Latin name: *Sterna paradisaea.*

arc·ti·id /aarktee id/ (*plural* **-ids** or *same*) *n* a small-to medium-sized moth. There are 8,000 species of arctiid, including the tiger moth. Family: Arctiidae. [< modern Latin *arctiidae* < Greek *arktos* "bear"]

Arc·tu·rus /aark tòorəss/ *n* the brightest star in the constellation Boötes and the fourth brightest star in the sky

ar·cu·ate /aarkyoo ət, -àyt/ *adj* in the shape of an arc or a bow [15C. < Latin *arcuatus* < *arcus* "bow, arch"] —**ar·cu·ate·ly** *adv*

arc weld·ing *n* the joining of metal components by fusing them with heat from an electrical arc struck between two electrodes

ARD *abbr* acute respiratory disease

-ard, -art *suffix* somebody characterized by a given quality ○ *sluggard* [< Old French < Germanic]

Ar·dennes /aar dén/ forested and thinly populated plateau in southeastern Belgium, extending into Luxembourg and northeastern France. The Battle of the Bulge took place in the Ardennes in 1944. The highest peak is Botrange, near Belgium's border with Germany, with a height of 2,277 ft./694 m.

ar·dent /aard'nt/ *adj* **1.** PASSIONATE feeling great passion, or felt very passionately **2.** ENTHUSIASTIC feeling or showing great enthusiasm or eagerness ○ *one of his most ardent supporters* **3.** GLOWING shining or glowing brightly, with a fiery quality (*literary*) ○ *ardent embers* [14C. Via Old French *ardant* < Latin *ardent-*, present participle of *ardere* "to burn"] —**ar·dent·ly** *adv*

ar·dent spir·its *npl* distilled alcoholic beverages such as whiskey and rum

Ard·more /aard màwr/ city north of Lake Murray, in southern Oklahoma. Population: 23,939 (2002 estimate).

ar·dor /aardər/ *n* great passion, enthusiasm, or eagerness ○ *repeated attempts to dampen their revolutionary ardor* [14C. Via French < Latin *ardor* < *ardere* "to burn"]

ar·dour *n* Can, UK spelling of **ardor**

ar·du·ous /aarjoo əss/ *adj* **1.** requiring hard work or continuous physical effort **2.** very difficult to traverse, endure, or overcome [Mid-16C. < Latin *arduus* "steep, difficult"] —**ar·du·ous·ly** *adv* —**ar·du·ous·ness** *n*

SYNONYMS See ***hard.***

are[1] *stressed* /aar/; *unstressed* /ər/ *v* 1st person plural present of **be**[1]. 2nd person singular present of **be**[1]. 2nd person plural present of **be**[1]. 3rd person plural present of **be**[1] [Old English *earon* < Germanic]

are[2] /er, aar/ *n* a metric unit of area, equal to 100 sq. m. There are 100 ares in a hectare. [Late 18C. Via French < Latin *area* (see AREA)]

ar·e·a /érree ə/ *n* **1.** MEASUREMENT OF SURFACE the extent of part of a surface enclosed within a boundary, or the extent of the surface of all or part of a solid. The area of a square or rectangle can be calculated by multiplying together the lengths of two adjacent sides. **2.** PART OF SURFACE a distinct part of the surface of something, especially a piece of land ○ *The storms resulted in flooding over a large area.* **3.** SPACE OR PART WITH SPECIFIC FUNCTION a space, part, or surface of something, especially when intended for a specific use ○ *an area of the brain used for memory* **4.** REGION OR DISTRICT a region or district, either a distinct political or administrative division or a place that has specific qualities or features **5.** SUBJECT a subject of study, field of knowledge, or sphere of activity ○ *in the area of genetic research* **6.** SOCCER same as **penalty area** [Mid-16C. < Latin, "flat piece of unoccupied land"]

ar·e·a code *n* digits indicating a specific area of a country that are dialed before the local number in calls from outside that area. In the United States and Canada, area codes have three digits.

ar·e·a rug *n* a rug covering only part of a floor

ar·e·a·way /érree ə wày/ *n* an area of lowered ground outside a basement, created to allow more light into basement windows or direct access to the basement from outside

a·re·ca /ə réékə, árri-/ *n* a tall palm tree with white flowers. Native to: Southeast Asia. Genus: *Areca.* [Late 16C. Via Portuguese < Malayalam *aṭekka*]

A·re·ci·bo /àarə séébō/ port, commercial and industrial center in northern Puerto Rico. Population: 93,385 (1990).

a·reg GEOG plural of **erg**[2]

a·re·na /ə réénə/ *n* **1.** STADIUM an indoor or outdoor area surrounded by seating for spectators, where shows or sports events take place **2.** SCENE OF ACTIVITY a place or situation where there is conflict or intense activity ○ *A new contestant has entered the political arena.* **3.** CENTER OF ROMAN AMPHITHEATER the open area inside a Roman amphitheater, in which gladiatorial contests and other entertainments were staged [Early 17C. < Latin, "sand, sand-strewn place"]

ar·e·na·ceous /àrrə náyshəss/ *adj* **1.** describes rocks or deposits that are composed of sand grains or have a sandy texture **2.** describes plants that grow best in sandy soil [Mid-17C. < Latin *arenaceus* "of sand" < *arena* "sand"]

a·re·na the·a·ter *n* THEATER same as **theater-in-the-round**

A·rendt /árrənt, áar-/, **Hannah** (1906–75) German-born US philosopher and political theorist. Her major works include *Origins of Totalitarianism* (1951) and *Eichmann in Jerusalem* (1963).

> "It was as though in those last minutes he [Eichmann] was summing up the lessons that this long course in human wickedness had taught us — the lesson of the fearsome, word-and-thought-defying *banality of evil.*"
> [Hannah Arendt, *Eichmann in Jerusalem: A Report on the Banality of Evil*; 1963]

ar·ene /á reen/ *n* an aromatic hydrocarbon [Mid-20C. < AROMATIC]

ar·e·nic·o·lous /àrrə níkələss/ *adj* living, burrowing, or thriving in sand [Mid-18C. < Latin *arena* "sand" + *-cola* "inhabiting"]

aren't /aarnt/ *contr* (*informal*) **1.** are not ○ *They aren't coming.* **2.** am not (*only used in questions*) ○ *I'm allowed to go too, aren't I?*

a·re·o·la /ə réé ələ/ (*plural* **-lae** /-lèe/ or **-las**) *n* **1.** the small circular dark area around the nipple in humans **2.** a small circular reddened area such as an inflamed ring around a spot [Mid-17C. < Latin, "little area"] —**a·re·o·lar** *adj* —**a·re·o·late** /ə réé ələt/ *adj* —**a·re·o·la·tion** /ə rèe ə láysh'n/ *n*

ar·e·ole /árree ōl/ *n* **1.** a small clearly defined space, e.g., that between veins on a leaf **2.** a depression on the surface of a cactus that the spines, hairs, or flowers grow from [Mid-19C. Via French < Latin *areola* "little area"]

A·re·qui·pa /àrrə kéépə, àa-/ city in southern Peru in the Andes. It is an important commercial center. Population: 710,103 (1998).

A·res /érreez/ *n* in Greek mythology, the god of war and the son of Zeus and Hera. Roman equivalent **Mars**

a·rête /ə ráyt, a-, ə rét, a-/ *n* a narrow ridge of bare rock situated between two or more deep smooth-sided semicircular areas (**cirques**), found in a mountainous area that has been glaciated [Early 19C. Via French < Latin *arista* "ear of grain, fish bone, spine," from its shape]

ar·e·thu·sa /àrree thóozə/ *n* PLANTS same as **swamp pink** [After *Arethusa*, mythical Greek nymph]

A·re·ti·no /àarə téénō/, **Pietro** (1492–1556) Italian poet. He served under various nobles including Giovanni de Medici, who became Pope Leo X and withdrew his sponsorship after Aretino wrote his *Lewd Sonnets* (1524).

ar·gal *n* CHEM same as **argol**

ar·ga·li /áargəlee/ (*plural same*) *n* a large wild mountain sheep. Native to: central and northern Asia. Latin name: *Ovis ammon.* [Late 18C. < Mongolian]

ar·gent /áarjənt/ *n* **1.** the metal or the color silver (*archaic or literary*) **2.** the color white or silver on a coat of arms [14C. Via French < Latin *argentum* "silver"] —**ar·gent** *adj*

ar·gen·tic /aar jéntik/ *adj* containing silver with a valence of 2

ar·gen·tif·er·ous /àarjən tíffərəss/ *adj* describes rocks or deposits containing silver

Argentina

Ar·gen·ti·na /àarjən téénə/ country that occupies most of the southern tip of South America. It was settled by the Spanish in the 16th century and became independent in 1816. Language: Spanish. Currency: peso argentino. Capital: Buenos Aires. Population: 38,740,807 (2003). Area: 1,073,518 sq. mi./2,780,400 sq. km. Official name **Argentine Republic** —**Ar·gen·tine** /áarjən tīn, -tèen/ *adj, n* —**Ar·gen·tin·e·an** /àarjən tínnee ən/ *adj, n*

Ar·gen·ti·na, La ♦ **La Argentina**

ar·gen·tine /áarjən tīn, -tèen/ *adj* silvery in color (*archaic or literary*) ■ *n* the metal silver, or a material that looks like silver

ar·gen·tite /áarjən tīt/ *n* a gray to black silver sulfide mineral, forming cubic crystals [Mid-19C. < Latin *argentum* "silver"]

ar·gil /áarjəl/ *n* clay, especially potter's clay [14C. Via Old French *argille* < Greek *argillos* "clay"]

ar·gil·la·ceous /àarjə láyshəss/ *adj* describes sedimentary rock that is made up of clay or silt particles

ar·gil·lite /áarjə līt/ *n* rock that is made up of clay or silt particles, especially a hardened mudstone

ar·gi·nase /áarjə nàyss, -nàaz/ *n* a liver enzyme involved in the production of urea

ar·gi·nine /áarjə neen/ *n* an essential amino acid, one of the constituents of protein. Source: guanidine in plant and animal tissue. Formula: $C_6H_{14}N_4O_2$. [Late 19C. < German]

Ar·give /áar gīv, -jīv/ *adj* GREEK relating to ancient Greece, especially the city of Argos ■ *n* **1.** ANCIENT GREEK somebody from ancient Greece (*literary*) **2.** CITIZEN OF ARGOS somebody from the city of Argos [Mid-16C. < Latin *Argivus* "of Argos"]

Ar·go /áargō/ *n* a large constellation in the southern hemisphere, now usually regarded as consisting of the smaller constellations of Puppis, Vela, Carina, and Pyxis

ar·gol /áar gàwl, áarg'l/, **ar·gal** /áarg'l/ *n* potassium hydrogen tartrate, formed in wine casks [14C. < Anglo-Norman *argoile*]

ar·gon /áar gòn/ *n* an inert gaseous element that makes up about one percent of the Earth's atmosphere. Use: electric lights, gas shield in welding. Symbol **Ar**. See table at **element** [Late 19C. < Greek < *argos* "inactive, idle" < *a-* "without" + *ergon* "work"]

ar·go·naut /áargə nàwt/ *n* ZOOL same as **paper nautilus** [Mid-19C. < modern Latin *Argonauta* (see ARGONAUT)]

Ar·go·naut /áargə nàwt/ *n* **1.** in Greek mythology, one of the heroes who sailed with Jason in his ship, the Argo, to find the Golden Fleece **2.** *also* **ar·go·naut** an adventurer, especially somebody who took part in the California gold rush of 1849 [Late 16C. Via Latin *argonauta* < Greek *argonautēs* "sailor in the ship Argo"]

Ar·gonne /aar gón, áar gon/ wooded highland region in northeastern France, forming a natural barrier between Champagne and Lorraine

ar·go·sy /áargəssee/ (*plural* **-sies**) *n* a large richly laden merchant ship, or a fleet of such ships (*literary*) [Late 16C. Probably < Italian *Ragusea* "(ship from the port of) Ragusa"]

ar·got /áargət, -gō/ *n* the special language used by a particular group of people [Mid-19C. < French] —**ar·got·ic** /aar góttik/ *adj*

SYNONYMS See *jargon*[1].

ar·gu·a·ble /áargyoo əb'l/ *adj* **1.** able to be supported or proved with evidence or arguments ○ *an arguable case for global warming* **2.** not obviously true or accurate, and therefore likely to be questioned or argued about ○ *It's arguable whether he really is the world's best guitarist.*

ar·gu·a·bly /áargyoo əblee/ *adv* used to mean that a statement is open to dispute but could be defended in an argument ○ *This is arguably the best restaurant in town.*

USAGE arguably or **debatably**? ***Arguably***, the most common of the two words, suggests that the speaker assumes widespread but not universal agreement with what is being said: *arguably the most influential legislator in the county.* ***Debatably*** is more neutral: *It was a debatably rude thing to do.*

ar·gue /áargyoo/ (**-gued, -gu·ing, -gues**) *v* **1.** *vi* EXPRESS DISAGREEMENT to express disagreement with somebody, especially continuously or angrily **2.** *vti* GIVE REASONS FOR SOMETHING to give reasons for an opinion in order to support it ○ *You could argue that this calls for greater freedom, not less.* **3.** *vt* PERSUADE SOMEBODY to persuade somebody to do something by giving reasons ○ *argued her out of leaving* **4.** *vti* PROVIDE EVIDENCE FOR SOMETHING to be evidence or a sign of something ○ *The increase in crime argued for tougher jail sentences, said some.* [14C. Via French *arguer* < Latin *argutari* "assert repeatedly" < *arguere* "make clear, assert"] —**ar·gu·er** *n*

SYNONYMS See *disagree*.

~~**argueing**~~ incorrect spelling of **arguing**

~~**arguement**~~ incorrect spelling of **argument**

ar·gu·fy /áargyə fī/ (**-fied, -fy·ing, -fies**) *vi Southern US* to argue about something that is unimportant (*informal*)

ar·gu·ment /áargyəmənt/ *n* **1.** DISAGREEMENT a disagreement in which different views are expressed, often angrily **2.** REASON a reason put forward in support of or in opposition to a point of view ○ *the arguments for and against the planned development* **3.** STATED POINT OF VIEW the main point of view expressed in a book, report, or speech **4.** DISCUSSION debate or discussion about whether something is correct **5.** GRAM NOUN ELEMENT IN CLAUSE a noun element in a clause that relates directly to the verb, e.g., the subject or object **6.** COMPUT FEATURE CONTROLLING COMPUTER PROGRAM a value that modifies how a command or function operates in a computer program

ar·gu·men·ta LOGIC plural of **argumentum**

ar·gu·men·ta·tion /àargyəmən táysh'n, -men-/ *n* **1.** the process of debating or discussing something **2.** reasoning that proceeds methodically from a statement to a conclusion

ar·gu·men·ta·tive /àargyə méntətiv/ *adj* **1.** tending to disagree and argue **2.** characterized by disagreement or argument —**ar·gu·men·ta·tive·ly** *adv* —**ar·gu·men·ta·tive·ness** *n*

ar·gu·men·tum /àargyə méntəm/ (*plural* **-ta** /-tə/) *n* a series of statements or a demonstration that leads to a logical conclusion (*formal*) [Mid-17C. < Latin, "argument, rationale" < *arguere* "make clear, assert"]

Ar·gus /áargəss/ *n* **1.** in Greek mythology, a giant with 100 eyes. He was sent by the jealous Hera to watch over her husband Zeus's lover, Io, but was later lulled to sleep and killed by Hermes. **2.** an alert watchful person (*literary*)

argyle

ar·gyle /áar gīl, aar gī́l/, **ar·gyll** *adj* knitted with a pattern of colored diamond shapes ■ *n* a sock or sweater made in an argyle design [Mid-20C. < being based on the tartan of Campbells from Argyll in Scotland]

ar·gyll *adj, n* HANDICRAFT another spelling of **argyle**

ar·hat /áarhət/ *n* a Buddhist who has reached the highest state of peace and enlightenment [Late 19C. Via Pali < Sanskrit, "deserving, meritorious"] —**ar·hat·ship** *n*

År·hus /áwr hòoss, áar-/, **Aar·hus** city, port, and seat of Århus County on the Jutland Peninsula and Århus Bay in eastern Jutland, Denmark. Population: 216,564 (1999).

a·ri·a /áaree ə/ *n* a melody sung solo or as a duet in an opera, oratorio, or cantata [Early 18C. Via Italian < Latin *aer* "air" (see AIR)]

Ar·i·ad·ne /àrree ádnee/ *n* in Greek mythology, the daughter of King Minos of Crete. She gave Theseus the ball of thread that he used to find his way out of the labyrinth after killing the Minotaur.

Ar·i·an[1] /érree ən/ *n* ZODIAC same as **Aries** (sense 3) —**Ar·i·an** *adj*

Ar·i·an[2] /érree ən/ *n* a follower of the ancient Greek Christian theologian Arius, who argued that Jesus Christ was the highest created being, but was not divine. This doctrine was pronounced heretical in the 4th century A.D. —**Ar·i·an·ism** *n*

A·ri·as /áaree àass/, **Arnulfo** (1901–88) Panamanian national leader. As president of Panama (1940–41, 1949–51, and 1968), he was noted for his authoritarian policies.

A·ri·as Sán·chez /áaree aass sáan chez/, **Oscar** (*b.* 1941) president of Costa Rica (1986–90). He was awarded the Nobel Peace Prize (1987) for his contribution to the restoration of peace in Central America.

a·ri·bo·fla·vi·no·sis /ay rībə flayvə nṓssiss/ *n* a condition caused by a dietary deficiency of vitamin B_2 (**riboflavin**). The symptoms are mouth lesions and excessive oiliness of the skin and hair. [Mid-20C. < A-[2] + RIBOFLAVIN]

ar·id /árrid/ *adj* **1.** describes a region in which annual rainfall is less than 10 in./25 cm **2.** completely lacking in interest or excitement [Mid-17C. Directly or via French < Latin *aridus* < *arere* "be dry"] —**a·rid·i·ty** /ə ríddətee/ *n* —**ar·id·ly** *adv* —**ar·id·ness** *n*

SYNONYMS See *dry*.

ar·id zone *n* either of two zones of latitude that are between 15° and 30° north and south of the equator, consisting mostly of desert or semidesert

Ar·i·el /érree əl/ *n* a natural satellite of Uranus with a radius of 580 km, discovered in 1851

Ar·ies /é rèez, -ree èez/ *n* **1.** ASTRON **CONSTELLATION IN NORTHERN HEMISPHERE** a zodiacal constellation of the northern hemisphere lying between Pisces and Taurus. See illustration at **constellation 2.** ZODIAC **FIRST SIGN OF ZODIAC** the first sign of the zodiac, represented by a ram and lasting from approximately March 21 to April 19. Aries is classified as a fire sign and its ruling planet is Mars. **3.** ZODIAC **SOMEBODY BORN UNDER ARIES** somebody whose birthday falls between March 21 and April 19 [Pre-12C. < Latin *aries* "ram"] —**Ar·ies** *adj*

a·ri·et·ta /àaree éttə, àrree-/ *n* a short simple aria in an opera, oratorio, or cantata [Early 18C. < Italian, "little aria"]

a·right /ə rī́t/ *adv* in the correct or proper way (*archaic*)

A·rik·a·ra /ə ríkərə/ (*plural* **-ras** or *same*) *n* a member of a Native North American people who once lived in the Missouri River valley, but who now live in western North Dakota

ar·il /árrəl/ *n* a fleshy, often brightly colored seed covering in some plants. Its function is to draw attention to the seed to aid its dispersal by birds. [Mid-18C. Via modern Latin *arillus* < medieval Latin *arilli* "dried grape pips"] —**ar·iled** *adj* —**ar·il·late** /árrə làyt, -lət/ *adj*

a·ri·o·so /àaree ṓzō, -ṓssō/ *adj, adv* with intense lyricism or feeling (*used as a musical direction*) ■ *n* (*plural* **-sos**) a short lyrical aria or instrumental work [Early 18C. < Italian, "like an aria"]

A·ri·os·to /àaree óstō/, **Ludovico** (1474–1533) Italian poet. His best-known work is the epic poem *Orlando Furioso* (1532).

> "Nature made him, and then broke the mold."
> [Ludovico Ariosto, *Orlando Furioso*; 1532]

a·rise /ə rī́z/ (**a·rose** /ə rṓz/, **a·ris·en** /ə rízz'n/, **a·ris·ing**, **a·ris·es**) *vi* **1. OCCUR** to appear or come into existence ○ *When did the problem arise?* **2. BE CAUSED BY SOMETHING** to happen or exist as a result of something ○ *a shortage of qualified staff arising from a lack of investment in training* **3. BECOME ACTIVE OR VOCAL** to rise from a quiet, inactive, or subjugated state to become active, vocal, or rebellious (*literary*) **4. STAND UP** to stand up from a sitting, lying, or kneeling position (*literary*) [Old English *arisan* "rise up" < Germanic]

a·ris·ta /ə rístə/ (*plural* **-tae** /-tay, -tee/) *n* **1.** BOT same as **awn 2.** a bristly part of the antennae of some flies [Late 17C. < Latin, "ear of grain"]

Ar·is·tar·chus of Sa·mos /àrri stáarkəss-/ (310?–250? B.C.) Greek astronomer. He proposed that the Earth rotates on its axis and orbits the Sun.

Ar·is·tide /àari stéed/, **Jean-Bertrand** (*b.* 1953) Haitian politician. He was elected president of the independent republic of Haiti (1991) in Haiti's first free elections since 1804, but was forced into exile by a military coup. He returned to power (1994–96) and was re-elected president in 2001, but was deposed in 2004.

> "The first Black republic on earth...is marching resolutely...toward establishment of a democratic society."
> [Jean-Bertrand Aristide, speech to the UN General Assembly, *New York Times*; October 5, 1994]

Ar·is·ti·des the Just /àrri stī́ deez-/ (530–468 B.C.) Athenian general. He took part in the battles of Marathon (490 B.C.), Salamis (480 B.C.), and Plataea (479 B.C.) against the Persians.

Ar·is·tip·pus /àrri stíppəss/ (435?–360? B.C.) Greek philosopher. A student of Socrates, he founded the Cyrenaic school of hedonism, believing that pleasure is the highest good.

a·ris·to /ə rístō/ (*plural* **-tos**) *n* same as **aristocrat** (sense 1) (*informal*) [Mid-19C. < French, abbreviation of *aristocrate* "aristocrat"]

ar·is·toc·ra·cy /àrri stókrəssee/ (*plural* **-cies**) *n* **1. PEOPLE OF HIGHEST SOCIAL CLASS** people of noble families or the highest social class **2. SUPERIOR GROUP** a group believed to be superior to all others of the same kind **3. GOVERNMENT BY ELITE** government of a country by a small group of people, especially a hereditary nobility **4. STATE RUN BY ELITE** a state governed by an aristocracy [15C. Via French *aristocratie* < Greek *aristokratia* "rule by the best" < *aristos* "best" + *kratos* "power, rule" (see -CRACY)]

a·ris·to·crat /ə rístə kràt/ *n* **1. MEMBER OF HIGHEST SOCIAL CLASS** a member of the nobility or the highest social class in a country **2. SUPPORTER OF ARISTOCRATIC RULE** a member of a governing aristocracy, or somebody who supports government by an aristocracy **3. SUPERIOR PERSON** a person, thing, or group believed to be superior to all others of the same kind

a·ris·to·crat·ic /ə rìstə kráttik/ *adj* **1.** characteristic of noble or wealthy families, e.g., in having a grand lifestyle or elegant manners **2.** relating or belonging to the highest social class, especially the nobility —**a·ris·to·crat·i·cal·ly** *adv*

Ar·is·toph·a·nes /àrri stóffə neez/ (448?–385 B.C.) Greek dramatist. He satirized social and intellectual pretensions in comedies such as *The Birds* (414 B.C.) and *The Clouds* (423 B.C.).

Ar·is·to·te·li·an /àrristə téelee ən/ *adj* expressing or based on the ideas of the Greek philosopher Aristotle ■ *n* a follower of Aristotle's philosophy

Ar·is·to·te·li·an log·ic *n* the system of logic developed by Aristotle, based on the kind of reasoning (**syllogism**) that reaches a conclusion from two independent statements with a common factor

Ar·is·tot·le /àrri stòtt'l/ (384–322 B.C.) Greek philosopher and scientist. He was one of the most influential philosophers in Western history.

a·rith·me·tic *n* /ə ríthmə tìk/ **1. BASIC MATH** the branch of mathematics that deals with addition, subtraction, multiplication, and division **2. CALCULATION** one or more calculations using basic mathematics **3. USE OF NUMBERS** the use of numbers in calculation, or educational exercises involving this **4. ABILITY TO DO ARITHMETIC** somebody's ability to add, subtract, multiply, and divide (*informal*) ■ *adj* /àrrith méttik/ **RELATING TO ARITHMETIC** relating to, using, or based on arithmetic [13C. Via Old French *arismetique* < Greek *arithmētikē (tekhnē)* "counting (art)" < *arithmein* "reckon" < *arithmos* "number"] —**ar·ith·met·i·cal** /àrrith méttik'l/ *adj* —**ar·ith·met·i·cal·ly** *adv* —**a·rith·me·ti·cian** /ə rìthmə tísh'n/ *n*

ar·ith·met·ic log·ic u·nit *n* the circuit in a computer's central processing unit that makes decisions based on the results of calculations

ar·ith·met·ic mean *n* the average of a set of numbers, calculated by adding them together and then dividing their sum by the number of terms

ar·ith·met·ic pro·gres·sion *n* a sequence of numbers in which a constant figure (**common difference**) is added to each term to give the next. For example, 3, 8, 13, 18 is an arithmetic progression in which the common difference is 5.

-arium *suffix* a place or device for or relating to something ○ *herbarium* [< Latin]

Ariz. *abbr* Arizona

Arizona

Ar·i·zo·na /àrri zṓnə/ state in the southwestern United States, bordered by New Mexico, Mexico, California, Nevada, and Utah. Capital: Phoenix. Population: 5,456,453 (2002 estimate). Area: 114,006 sq. mi./295,274 sq. km. —**Ar·i·zo·nan** *adj, n* —**Ar·i·zo·ni·an** *adj, n*

Ar·i·zo·na cloud·burst *n* *regional* a dust storm (*humorous*)

Ar·ju·na /áarjənə/ *n* a major character in the *Mahabharata*. Krishna, serving as his charioteer, explains Hindu doctrine to him.

ark /aark/ *n* **1.** BIBLE in the Bible, the ship that Noah was instructed to build by God to save his family and the animals from the Flood **2.** *also* **Ark** JUDAISM in a synagogue, a cupboard in a synagogue in which the scrolls of the Torah are kept **3.** *also* **Ark** JUD-CHR same as **Ark of the Covenant** [Old English *ærc*, via Germanic < Latin *arca* "chest, box"] ◇ **out of the ark** extremely old or old-fashioned (*informal*)

CULTURAL NOTE ***Schindler's Ark***, a novel (1982) by Thomas Keneally. It tells the true story of a German industrialist, Oskar Schindler, who helped thousands of Jews avoid the Nazi death camps by employing them in his factories. It was made into a movie called *Schindler's List* by Steven Spielberg in 1993.

Ark. *abbr* Arkansas

Ar·ka·del·phi·a /aárkə délfee ə/ town in southwestern Arkansas, on the Ouachita River. Population: 11,043 (2002 estimate).

Ar·kan /aárkan/ ➧ **Raznatovic, Zeljko**

Arkansas

Ar·kan·sas /aárkən sàw/ **1.** state in the southern United States, bordered by Missouri, Tennessee, Mississippi, Louisiana, Texas, and Oklahoma. Capital: Little Rock. Population: 2,710,079 (2002 estimate). Area: 53,182 sq. mi./137,741 sq. km. **2.** major river of the central United States, rising in central Colorado and flowing south and eastward to join the Mississippi River in southeastern Arkansas. The main cities along its course are Tulsa, Oklahoma, and Little Rock, Arkansas. Length: 1,460 mi./2,350 km. —**Ar·kan·san** /aar kánz'n/ *n, adj*

Ar·kan·sas Post Na·tion·al Me·mo·ri·al national park in east central Arkansas. It is situated on the site of the first permanent French settlement established in 1686 in the lower Mississippi River valley. Area: 389 acres/157 hectares.

Ar·kan·saw·yer /aárkən sàw yər/ *n regional* somebody who comes from Arkansas [Early 20C. < ARKANSAS + *-yer* in SAWYER]

REGIONAL NOTE ***Arkansawyer*** is, apparently, preferred by natives of Arkansas to the more familiar *Arkansan.*

Ark·han·gelsk /aar kán gelsk/, **Arch·an·gel** /aárk àynjəl/ city in northwestern Russia, capital of Arkhangelsk Oblast, on the Northern Dvina (Severnaya Dvina) River, near its mouth on the White Sea. It was Russia's chief seaport in the 17th century. Population: 367,200 (1999).

Ark of the Cov·e·nant, **Ark of the Tes·ti·mo·ny** *n* in the Bible, the chest in which Moses placed the two stone tablets containing the Ten Commandments. The Hebrews treasured it as the most sacred sign of God's presence among them.

ark·ose /aárk ōss, -ōz/ *n* a coarse-grained sedimentary rock rich in feldspar and quartz [Mid-19C. < French, probably < Greek *arkhaios* "ancient"]

Ark·wright /aárk rīt/, **Sir Richard** (1732–92) British industrialist. He invented the cotton spinning frame (1768) and introduced steam power into his works in Nottingham, England (1790).

Ar·len /aárlən/, **Harold** (1905–86) US composer. He wrote the scores for many Broadway musicals and movies including *The Wizard of Oz* (1939).

Arles /aarl/ city in the Bouches-du-Rhône Department in the Provence-Alpes-Côte-d'Azur region in France, situated northwest of Marseilles. It was a major Roman city and, after the 10th century, was the capital of a kingdom of the same name. Population: 50,513 (1999).

Ar·ling·ton /aárlingtən/ **1.** city in northeastern Virginia, near Washington, D.C. It is home to Arlington National Cemetery and the Pentagon. Population: 189,927 (2002 estimate). **2.** city situated between Fort Worth and Dallas in northeastern Texas. Population: 349,944 (2002 estimate).

Ar·ling·ton Heights city in northeastern Illinois, a northern suburb of Chicago. Population: 76,421 (2002 estimate).

arm[1] /aarm/ *n* **1.** UPPER HUMAN LIMB a limb attached to the shoulder of the human body **2.** CLOTHING PART OF GARMENT the part of a piece of clothing that covers the arm **3.** FURNITURE PART OF CHAIR a side piece of a seat designed to support the arms of somebody sitting in it **4.** ZOOL ANIMAL'S LIMB a part of an animal's body that is similar to the human arm **5.** ZOOL INVERTEBRATE'S LIMB a flexible limb in an invertebrate such as an octopus **6.** PROJECTING PART a long thin part projecting from something larger ○ *an arm of the sea* **7.** DIVISION OF LARGER GROUP a branch of an organization, especially a section of the armed forces ○ *infantry as a combat arm* [Old English *arm, earm* < Indo-European, "fit, join"] —**arm·ful** *n* ◇ **arm in arm** holding each other affectionately by linking arms ◇ **at arm's length** in a position or situation that avoids involvement or familiarity ◇ **put the arm on somebody 1.** to try to force somebody to do something (*slang*) **2.** to borrow money from somebody (*informal*) ◇ **the long arm of the law** the far-reaching power of the police (*humorous*) ◇ **twist somebody's arm** to try to persuade somebody to do something against his or her will (*informal*) ◇ **with open arms** in a friendly and welcoming way ◇ **would give your right arm for something** would be willing to do or give almost anything to get something that you want (*informal*)

arm[2] /aarm/ *v* (**armed, arm·ing, arms**) **1.** *vti* MIL EQUIP SOMEBODY WITH WEAPONS to equip a person or a country with weapons **2.** *vt* MIL MAKE WEAPON READY FOR USE to prepare a weapon so that it is ready to use **3.** *vt* PROVIDE SOMEBODY WITH INFORMATION OR TOOLS to provide somebody with the information or equipment needed to do something ○ *armed myself with statistics before the meeting* ■ *n* MIL WEAPON a weapon, especially one used in warfare (*often used in the plural*) ■ **arms** *npl* **1.** MIL WARFARE fighting or military activity **2.** HERALDRY HERALDIC BADGE the coat of arms of a family, university, or town [12C. Via Old French *armer* < Latin *armare* < *arma* (plural) "weapons"] ◇ **be up in arms** to protest or complain angrily ◇ **lay down your arms** to stop fighting ◇ **take up arms** to enter, or prepare to enter, a battle

ARM *abbr* adjustable rate mortgage

ar·ma·da /aar maádə/ *n* a large fleet of ships [Mid-16C. Via Spanish < medieval Latin *armata* (see ARMY)]

armadillo

ar·ma·dil·lo /aármə díllō/ (*plural* **-los** or *same*) *n* a burrowing mammal whose body is covered in hard plates, related to the anteater and sloth. Native to: temperate and tropical Americas. Family: Dasypodidae. [Late 16C. < Spanish, "little armed man" < Latin *armare* (see ARM[2])]

ar·ma·ged·don /aármə gédd'n/ *n* a final and decisive war or conflict, e.g., a worldwide nuclear war [Early 19C. < ARMAGEDDON]

Ar·ma·ged·don /aármə gédd'n/ *n* in the Bible, the battle between the forces of good and evil that is predicted to mark the end of the world and precede the Day of Judgment. (Revelation 16:16). [Via late Latin < Hebrew *har megiddōn* "hill of Megiddo"]

Ar·magh /aar maá/ **1.** town in the province of Ulster, southern Northern Ireland. Population: 14,640 (1991). **2.** historic county of Northern Ireland, in the province of Ulster. Area: 258 sq. mi./667 sq. km.

Ar·ma·gnac /aármə nyàk/ *n* a brandy made in southwestern France [Mid-19C. After a historical region]

ar·ma·ment /aármәmənt/ *n* **1.** the guns and other weapons on a military aircraft, vehicle, or ship (*often used in the plural*) **2.** the provision of weapons and equipment in preparation for war [Late 17C. < Latin *armamentum* < *armare* (see ARM[2])]

ar·ma·men·tar·i·um /aármə men térree əm/ (*plural* **-i·ums** or **-i·a** /-ee ə/) *n* the complete range of equipment, medications, and techniques that a medical practitioner has at his or her disposal [Late 19C. < Latin, "arsenal, armory" < *armare* (see ARM[2])]

Ar·ma·ni /aar maánee/, **Giorgio** (*b.* 1934) Italian fashion designer. He founded the Giorgio Armani fashion house in 1975.

> "I realized that fashion was moving in a very brutal, nostalgic and sometimes vulgar direction, and I refused it."
> [Giorgio Armani, *The Fashion Conspiracy*; 1989]

ar·ma·ture /aármәchər, -choor/ *n* **1.** KEEPER FOR MAGNET a bar of soft iron or steel placed across the poles of a magnet to maintain its strength **2.** ELEC ENG MOVING PART IN ELECTROMAGNETIC DEVICE the moving part in an electromagnetic device, wound with coils that carry a current. In a generator, an electric current is induced in the coils when they revolve through a magnetic field. **3.** BIOL PROTECTIVE PART a protective outer covering or structure, e.g., quills on a porcupine or spines on a plant **4.** SCULPTURE FRAMEWORK FOR SCULPTURE a framework that supports a sculpture while it is being modeled [15C. Via French < Latin *armatura* < *armat-*, past participle of *armare* (see ARM[2])]

arm·band /aárm bànd/ *n* a band of fabric worn around the upper arm

arm can·dy *n* somebody good-looking whom a person takes to a public event in order to impress others and enhance his or her status (*slang offensive*)

arm·chair /aárm chèr/ *n* a chair with arms, especially a comfortable upholstered chair ■ *adj* having no direct experience, only secondhand or theoretical knowledge ○ *an armchair tourist*

armed /aarmd/ *adj* **1.** EQUIPPED WITH WEAPON equipped with one or more weapons ○ *armed robbers* **2.** INVOLVING WEAPONS involving the use of weapons ○ *armed conflict* **3.** WITH EXPLODING MECHANISM ACTIVE prepared and ready for use as a weapon, especially with a fuse or detonator activated **4.** PROVIDED WITH NECESSARY INFORMATION OR TOOLS equipped with the information or tools needed to achieve something ○ *armed with the latest statistics*

armed forc·es *npl* the combined bodies of troops of a country, who fight on land, at sea, or in the air

Armenia

Ar·me·ni·a /aar meénee ə/ country in western Asia between the Black Sea and the Caspian Sea, bordered by Azerbaijan, Azerbaijan-Nakcivan enclave, Iran, Turkey, and Georgia. Language: Armenian. Currency: dram. Capital: Yerevan. Population: 3,326,448 (2003). Area: 11,500 sq. mi./29,800 sq. km. Official name **Republic of Armenia**

Ar·me·ni·an /aar meénee ən/ *n* **1.** somebody who comes from Armenia **2.** the national language of Armenia, also spoken in Turkey and in other parts of the world, that forms a branch of Indo-European. Native speakers: 4 million. —**Ar·me·ni·an** *adj*

arm·hole /a͡arm hōl/ *n* either of the holes at the top of a garment for the wearer's arms to go through

armillary sphere

ar·mil·lar·y sphere /a͡armə lèrree-, aar mìlləree-/ *n* a spherical model of the universe, first used by early Greek astronomers, in which the relative positions of the Earth and other astronomical objects are represented by intersecting metal rings [< modern Latin *armillaris* < Latin *armilla* "arm bracelet" < *armus* "shoulder"]

Ar·min·i·an /aar mínnee ən/ *adj* relating to or following the Protestant theologian Arminius or his doctrines, which rejected the Calvinist view of absolute predestination ■ *n* a follower of Arminius or his doctrines [Early 17C. < *Arminius*, Latinized surname of Jakob Hermandszoon (1560–1609)] —**Ar·min·i·an·ism** *n*

ar·mi·stice /a͡armistiss/ *n* a truce in a war to discuss terms for peace [Early 18C. Directly or via French < modern Latin *armistitium* "stoppage of weapons" < Latin *arma* "weapons"]

Ar·mi·stice Day *n* the former annual celebration of the armistice that ended World War I on November 11 1918. In 1954 it was incorporated into the observance of Veterans Day.

arm·let /a͡armlət/ *n* **1.** a short narrow arm of a lake or the sea **2.** a band worn on the upper arm

arm·lock /a͡arm lòk/ *n* a tight immobilizing grip around one or both of somebody's upper arms, e.g., in wrestling or judo

ar·moire /aar mwa͡ar/ *n* a tall cupboard or wardrobe, often ornately decorated. Originally, an armoire was used for storing weapons. [Late 16C. Via French < Latin *armarium* "chest" < *arma* "weapons"]

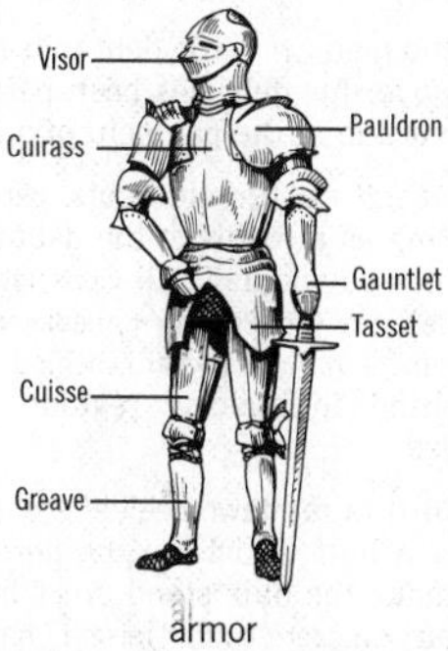

armor

ar·mor /a͡armər/ *n* **1.** MIL, HIST **PROTECTION FOR SOLDIERS** protective clothing of metal or leather worn in battle by soldiers in former times **2.** MIL **PROTECTION FOR MILITARY VEHICLES** the protective layer of metal covering military vehicles, ships, and aircraft **3.** BIOL **COVERING ON PLANTS OR ANIMALS** a protective layer covering a plant or animal **4. PROTECTION** something that gives protection or acts as a safeguard **5.** GEOG **GRAVEL ON RIVER BED** a surface layer of gravel on a river bed preventing erosion of the material below **6.** HERALDRY **COATS OF ARMS** coats of arms, or the symbols and designs used on them [13C. < French *armure* < Latin *armatura* (see ARMATURE)]

ar·mored /a͡armərd/ *adj* **1.** MIL **HAVING PROTECTIVE METAL COVERING** equipped with a protective metal covering against bullets or missiles **2.** MIL **USING ARMORED VEHICLES** equipped with and using armored vehicles **3.** BIOL **HAVING NATURAL PROTECTIVE COVERING** having a natural protective covering such as a shell

ar·mored car *n* **1.** a vehicle such as a security van with an extra layer of thick metal to protect the occupants from bullets or other weapons **2.** a lightly armored military vehicle used mainly for reconnaissance

ar·mor·er /a͡armərər/ *n* **1. MAKER OF ARMS** somebody who makes armor and weapons **2. SOMEBODY MAINTAINING SMALL ARMS** somebody who repairs and maintains small arms **3. SOMEBODY LOADING WEAPONS FOR TRANSPORTATION** a soldier, sailor, or airman who loads weapons onto vehicles, aircraft, or missiles

ar·mo·ri·al /aar máwree əl/ *adj* relating to or decorated with a coat of arms ○ *armorial bearings* [Late 16C. < obsolete *armory* "heraldry" < Old French *armoi(e)rie* < *armoier* "to blazon" < *armes* "weapons" < Latin *arma*]

ar·mor plate *n* MIL same as **armor** (sense 2) —**ar·mor-plat·ed** *adj*

ar·mor·y /a͡armərее/ (*plural* **-ies**) *n* **1. STORE FOR WEAPONS** a building in which weapons are stored **2. US BUILDING FOR MILITARY TRAINING** a building used for drilling and training US National Guard units **3. COLLECTION OF WEAPONS** a store or collection of weapons **4. ARMS FACTORY** a factory where arms are manufactured **5. RESOURCES AVAILABLE FOR DEALING WITH OPPONENT** a range of equipment and skills available to somebody, used especially in dealing with opponents [14C. < Old French *armoi(e)rie* "weaponry" (see ARMORIAL)]

ar·mour *n* Can, UK spelling of **armor**

Ar·mour /a͡armər/, **Philip Danforth** (1832–1901) US business executive. He revolutionized the meat-packing business and founded Armour & Company in 1870.

ar·mour·y /a͡arməree/ *n* (*plural* **-ies**) MIL Can, UK spelling of **armory** ■ **ar·mour·ies** *npl Can* a building used for drilling and training militia [Variant]

arm·pit /a͡arm pìt/ *n* **1.** the hollow area under the arm where it joins the body **2.** a place that is the worst of its kind (*slang*)

arm·rest /a͡arm rèst/ *n* a projecting part on a seat, designed to support the arm of somebody sitting down

arms con·trol *n* reduction or limitation in the number or type of weapons held by some countries, especially as a result of mutual agreement

arm's-length *adj* without close contact or an intimate relationship ○ *the companies' arm's-length trading arrangement*

arms race *n* a competition between countries for superiority in the number and power of weapons held

Arm·strong /a͡arm stràwng/, **Edwin Howard** (1890–1954) US engineer. He invented electronic circuitry, which became the basis of radio and television transmission.

Arm·strong, Lance (*b.* 1971) US bicycle racer. He won the Tour de France in five consecutive years (1999–2003).

Louis Armstrong

Arm·strong, Louis (1901–71) US jazz musician. He was known for his trumpet playing and gravelly singing voice. Full name **Armstrong, Daniel Louis**. Known as **Satchmo**

> "Folk music? Why, daddy, I don't know no other kind of music *but* folk music. I ain't never heard a horse sing a song."
> [Louis Armstrong. Quoted in *The Jazz Book*, Joachim E. Berendt; 1983]

Neil Armstrong

Arm·strong, Neil (*b.* 1930) US astronaut. He was the first person to set foot on the Moon (1969).

> "That's one small step for man, one giant leap for mankind."
> [Neil Armstrong. Message to NASA; July 20, 1969]

arm-twist·ing *n* heavy-handed or unfair pressure on somebody to do something (*informal*)

arm wres·tling *n* a contest of strength between two people in which they sit opposite each other with one elbow each on a table, clasp hands, and try to force the other's hand onto the table

ar·my /a͡armee/ (*plural* **-mies**) *n* **1. BRANCH OF ARMED FORCES** the branch of a country's armed forces trained to fight on land **2. LARGE ARMED GROUP** a trained or armed fighting force **3. LARGE ORGANIZED GROUP** a large group of people, especially one that has been organized to do a specific thing ○ *an army of volunteers cleared the wasteland* **4. LARGE GROUP OF THINGS** a very large number of similar things [14C. Via French *armée* < medieval Latin *armata* < past participle of Latin *armare* (see ARM²)]

ar·my ant *n* a nomadic tropical ant that forages in large groups

ar·my brat *n* somebody who is born into, or grows up in, the family of a member of the army (*informal*) ○ *As an army brat, she's lived all over the world.*

ar·my post *n* a piece of land owned and occupied by the army, used for housing and training personnel

ar·my·worm /a͡armee wùrm/ *n* the larva of an insect that travels in large migratory groups destroying vegetation and crops

Arne /aarn/, **Thomas** (1710–78) British composer. He wrote operas, composed songs for the theater, and wrote *Rule Britannia* (1740). Full name **Arne, Thomas Augustine**

Arn·hem /a͡arn hèm, a͡arnəm/ city in the eastern Netherlands. It was the scene of a major battle in World War II, when Allied airborne troops fought unsuccessfully to secure Rhine bridges in September 1944. Population: 138,020 (2000).

Arn·hem Land region in Northern Australia, situated between the Roper and South Alligator rivers in the Northern Territory, and the site of one of Australia's largest Aboriginal reserves

ar·ni·ca /a͡arnikə/ (*plural* **-cas** or *same*) *n* **1.** a liquid preparation made from the dried flower heads of a perennial herb. Use: treating bruises and sprains in alternative medicine. **2.** a perennial plant from which arnica is prepared. Flowers: yellow, resembling daisies. Native to: northern Europe. Genus: *Arnica*. [Mid-18C. < modern Latin]

Ar·no /a͡arnō/ chief river of the Tuscany region in central Italy. It rises in the Tuscan Apennines and flows through Florence and Pisa. Length: 150 mi./240 km.

Ar·nold /a͡arn'ld/, **Benedict** (1741–1801) American officer who later betrayed the American cause by planning to surrender West Point to the British (1780) during the American Revolution

Ar·nold, Sir Malcolm (*b.* 1921) British composer. He wrote symphonies, concertos, operas, ballets, and movie scores, including that for *The Bridge on the River Kwai* (1957).

Ar·nold, Matthew (1822–88) British poet and critic. He was professor of poetry at Oxford (1857), and in addition to poetry wrote critical and religious works.

> "And we are here as on a darkling plain / Swept with confused alarms of struggle and flight, / Where ignorant armies clash by night."
> [Matthew Arnold, "Dover Beach"; 1867]

ar·oid /á ròyd/ *adj* relating to or belonging to the arum family of perennial plants [Late 19C. < ARUM]

a·ro·ma /ə rṓmə/ *n* **1.** a smell, especially a pleasant one **2.** a subtle impression or quality ○ *an aroma of scandal* [12C. Via Latin < Greek *arōma* "spice"]

SYNONYMS See *smell*.

a·ro·ma·tase /ə rṓmə tàyss, -tàyz/ *n* an enzyme that converts androgens to estrogens

a·ro·ma·tase in·hib·i·tor *n* a chemical belonging to a group that block the action of the substance that converts androgens into estrogens. Use: control of breast cancer.

a·ro·ma·ther·a·py /ə rṑmə thérrəpee/ *n* the use of oils extracted from plants to alleviate physical and psychological disorders, usually through massage or inhalation [Mid-20C. < French *aromathérapie*] —**a·ro·ma·ther·a·pist** *n*

ar·o·mat·ic /àrrō máttik/ *adj* **1.** HAVING FRAGRANT SMELL giving off a distinctive and pleasant smell **2.** CHEM OF CLASS OF ORGANIC COMPOUNDS describes organic compounds that contain one or more rings of carbon atoms and undergo chemical reactions that are characteristic of benzene. About half of all organic compounds are aromatic. ■ *n* FRAGRANT SUBSTANCE OR PLANT a substance or plant that has a distinctive pleasant smell [14C. Via French < Greek *arōmatikos* < *arōma* "spice"] —**ar·o·mat·i·cal·ly** *adv*

a·ro·ma·tize /ə rṓmə tìz/ (**-tized, -tiz·ing, -tiz·es**) *vt* **1.** to make something fragrant, or release the fragrance of something **2.** to convert a nonaromatic (**aliphatic**) chemical compound to an aromatic compound —**a·ro·ma·ti·za·tion** /ə rṑmati záysh'n/ *n*

A·roos·took /ə rṓostək, -rṓos-/ river in northern Maine. It flows northeastward into New Brunswick, Canada, and empties into the St. John River. It is a source of hydroelectric power. Length: 140 mi./225 km.

a·rose past tense of **arise**

a·round /ə równd/ CORE MEANING: a grammatical word used to indicate that something surrounds a place or object or is situated on or moves from place to place on all sides of it ○ (prep) *She came in and looked at the mess all around her.* ○ (prep) *A crumbling wall still stood around the old town.* ○ (adv) *From this spot you could see the countryside for miles around.*

1. *prep* TO OTHER SIDE OF moving or looking to the other side of ○ *There is a drugstore around the corner.* **2.** *prep* SURROUNDING so as to surround or be on all sides of ○ *a belt around his waist* ○ *A crowd gathered around them.* **3.** *prep, adv* TURNING ON AXIS revolving round a center or axis ○ (prep) *satellites moving around the planet* **4.** *adv, adj* ALIVE OR EXISTING present, alive, or in existence (*informal*) ○ *What's amazing is that nearly everyone from that era is still around.* **5.** *prep, adv* IN ALL DIRECTIONS situated, moving, or happening in all directions from a central point of reference ○ (adv) *The area was built up for several miles around.* **6.** *prep* REGARDING with regard to ○ *There is a great deal of controversy swirling around the issue of national identity cards.* **7.** *prep* NEAR in the near vicinity of ○ *She lives around the Boston area.* **8.** *prep* SO AS TO AVOID so as to sidestep or otherwise avoid something unpleasant or difficult ○ *finally found a way around the problem* **9.** *prep, adv* TO EVERYONE to all members in a group, from person to person ○ (adv) *passed the plate of sandwiches around* **10.** *adv* TO REVERSED POSITION in or to a different or the opposite direction ○ *wheeled around and jogged off* **11.** *adv* PRESENT in existence ○ *since computers have been around* **12.** *adv, prep* IN VARIOUS PLACES positioned here and there ○ *There were vases of flowers around the room.* **13.** *adv, prep* AT HAND in the vicinity, sometimes with no definite purpose or intent ○ *lounged around in the hotel lobby* ○ *Is the boss around?* **14.** *adv, prep* IN VARIOUS DIRECTIONS from place to place in different directions or in no particular direction ○ *rushing around* **15.** *adv* IN CIRCULATION available, prevalent, or in circulation ○ *There's lots of illness around at the moment.* **16.** *adv, prep* APPROXIMATELY close to in number, time, or degree ○ *around $600 a month* [13C. < A-[1] "on" + ROUND[1], probably after Old French *a la reond* "in the round, roundabout"] ◇ **have been around** to have had enough experience of life and the ways of the world not to be easily deceived (*informal*)

a·round-the-clock *adj* happening constantly, with no breaks, for 24 hours a day

a·rouse /ə rówz/ (**a·roused, a·rous·ing, a·rous·es**) *v* **1.** *vt* STIMULATE SOMETHING to evoke a feeling, response, or desire ○ *aroused their interest* **2.** *vt* STIMULATE SEXUAL DESIRE IN SOMEBODY to cause feelings of sexual desire in somebody **3.** *vt* ANNOY SOMEBODY to make somebody angry **4.** *vti* WAKE UP to wake up, or wake somebody up, from sleep or unconsciousness (*formal*) [Late 16C. < ROUSE] —**a·rous·al** *n*

AKG London

Jean Arp

Arp /aarp/, **Jean** (1887–1966) French sculptor. A cofounder of the Dada movement (1916), he produced organic abstract sculptures based on natural forms.

> "I love nature but not its substitutes. Naturalistic, illusionistic art is a substitute."
> [Jean Arp. Quoted in *On My Way, Poetry and Essays. 1912...1947*, Ralph Manheim (tr.); 1948]

ARP /aarp/ *abbr* air-raid precautions

ARPA·net /áarpə nèt/ *n* a wide area computer network of the late 1960s linking US government, academic, business, and military sites

ar·peg·gi·o /aar péjjee ō, -péjjō/ (*plural* **-os**) *n* a sounding of the notes of a chord one after the other in rapid succession, instead of simultaneously [Early 18C. < Italian < *arpeggiare* "play on the harp" < *arpa* "harp"]

ar·pent /aar paàN/ *n* in Canada and some parts of the United States where French-settlement influences are still prevalent, especially Louisiana, a unit used to measure land area, approximately equal to 0.85 acres/0.4 hectares. It was originally a French unit of length. (*regional*) [Mid-16C. < French]

ar·que·bus *n* ARMS same as **harquebus**

arr. *abbr* **1.** MUSIC arranged **2.** TRAVEL arrival **3.** TRAVEL arrived **4.** TRAVEL arrives

ar·raign /ə ráyn/ (**-raigned, -raign·ing, -raigns**) *vt* to bring somebody to court to answer a criminal charge (*usually passive*) [14C. Via Anglo-Norman *arainer* < assumed Vulgar Latin *adrationare* "call to account" < Latin *ratio* "reason"] —**ar·raign·er** *n* —**ar·raign·ment** *n*

ar·range /ə ráynj/ (**-ranged, -rang·ing, -rang·es**) *v* **1.** *vt* PUT SOMEBODY OR SOMETHING IN ORDER to put people or things in a position or order ○ *All the CDs were arranged alphabetically.* **2.** *vt* PREPARE FOR SOMETHING to do what is necessary to make something happen in the future ○ *arrange a meeting* **3.** *vti* MAKE AGREEMENT FOR SOMETHING TO HAPPEN to make an agreement so that something can happen or somebody can have something ○ *She's arranged for the painters to start next week.* **4.** *vti* MUSIC ADAPT MUSIC to adapt a piece of music for playing or singing in a different manner (*often passive*) [Mid-18C. < Old French *arangier* "put in a line to" < *rangier* (see RANGE)] —**ar·range·a·ble** *adj* —**ar·ranged** *adj* —**ar·rang·er** *n*

ar·ranged mar·riage *n* a marriage in which the parents choose a bride or bridegroom for their son or daughter

ar·range·ment /ə ráynjmənt/ *n* **1.** PREPARATION something that has to be done so that something else can happen in the future, or the making of such preparations (*often used in the plural*) **2.** AGREEMENT an agreement made with somebody to do something, or the making of such an agreement **3.** PLEASING DISPLAY a group of things organized in a way that is meant to be pleasing to look at, or the arranging of such a group **4.** ORGANIZATION the way in which something is organized **5.** MUSIC MUSICAL ADAPTATION a version of a piece of music adapted for playing or singing in a different manner, or the scoring of such a version

ar·rant /árrənt/ *adj* used to emphasize that somebody or something is an extreme example of something disapproved of ○ *an air of arrant self-importance* [Mid-16C. Alteration of ERRANT "wandering"] —**ar·rant·ly** *adv*

ar·ras /árrəss/ *n* a tapestry used as a wall hanging or hanging screen [15C. < Anglo-Norman *draps d'Arras* "cloth of Arras" (French town famous for its woolens and tapestry)]

ar·ray /ə ráy/ *n* **1.** COLLECTION a large number or wide range of people or things ○ *a dazzling array of talent* **2.** STRIKING ARRANGEMENT a group of things arranged in an impressive or structured way ○ *an array of Greek sculptures* **3.** TELECOM GROUP OF ANTENNAS a group of antennas arranged to increase their effectiveness **4.** CLOTHING FINE CLOTHES fine, expensive, or impressive clothes (*literary*) **5.** MATH ORDERED SET OF NUMBERS a set of numbers or symbols, e.g., experimental data, usually arranged in a specific order **6.** COMPUT DATA STRUCTURE an arrangement of items of computerized data in tabular form for easy reference. A computer program references an item by naming the array and the position of the item in it. **7.** LAW JURORS a panel of jurors, or the group of people from whom a jury is selected ■ *vt* (**-rayed, -ray·ing, -rays**) **1.** ARRANGE SOMETHING to arrange something for display or in readiness for use (*formal; usually passive*) **2.** MIL DEPLOY TROOPS to arrange troops for battle (*literary; usually passive*) **3.** CLOTHING CLOTHE SOMEBODY to clothe somebody in particular attire (*literary; often passive*) ○ *was arrayed in ermine and diamonds* [14C. Via Anglo-Norman < Old French *arei* < *areer* "to array" < assumed Vulgar Latin *arredare* "arrange" < Latin *ad* "to" + a Germanic word, "prepare"]

ar·ré /ú ràyl/ *interj S Asia* used to attract another person's attention, or to express emotions such as interest, surprise, or irritation [Via Hindi < Sanskrit *are*, used to summon somebody of inferior rank]

ar·rear·age /ə reérij/ *n* **1.** the debt that remains after part of an overdue debt has been paid **2.** the state of being overdue in the payment of a debt

ar·rears /ə reérz/ *npl* unpaid debts, especially debts accumulating as a result of the debtor's failure to make regular payments [15C. < obsolete *arrear* "to the rear, overdue," via Old French < medieval Latin *adretro* < Latin *ad* "to" + *retro* "backward, behind"] ◇ **in** *or* **into arrears** behind in making regular payments of money owed

ar·rec·tor pi·li /a rèk tawr peélee/ *n* a small muscle connecting a hair follicle to the dermis that contracts to make the hair stand erect in response to cold or fear [< modern Latin, "raiser of hair"]

ar·rest /ə rést/ *vt* (**-rest·ed, -rest·ing, -rests**) **1.** LAW TAKE SOMEBODY INTO CUSTODY to seize and take somebody into legal custody **2.** STOP SOMETHING to stop or slow something (*formal*) ○ *a mechanism that arrests the motion of the flywheel* **3.** TAKE HOLD OF SOMETHING to suddenly capture and hold something, especially somebody's attention (*formal*) ○ *an astonishing sight that arrested our attention* **4.** SEIZE SOMETHING LEGALLY to seize or detain something by legal authority (*formal*) ■ *n* **1.** LAW TAKING OF SOMEBODY INTO CUSTODY the seizure of somebody and the taking of that person into legal custody ○ *a case of wrongful arrest* **2.** LAW CUSTODY the state of being held in legal custody ○ *You're under arrest!* **3.** STOPPING OF SOMETHING the stopping or slowing of something **4.** LAW LEGAL SEIZURE OF SOMETHING the legal seizure or detention of something (*formal*) ○ *the arrest of the suspect merchant ship by customs officers* [14C. Via Old French < assumed Vulgar Latin *arrestare* "cause to stop" < Latin *restare* "stay behind" (see REST[2])] —**ar·rest·ee** /ə rès tée/ *n* —**ar·rest·ment** *n*

ar·rest·er /ə réstər/, **ar·res·tor** /ə réstər, -àwr/ *n* **1.** somebody who takes a suspect into legal custody **2.** somebody or something that is arresting, e.g., causing something to stop or somebody to pause **3.** NAVY same as **arresting cable**

ar·rest·ing /ə résting/ *adj* so good-looking or so unusual that people's attention is immediately caught —**ar·rest·ing·ly** *adv*

ar·rest·ing ca·ble *n* one of a set of cables strung across the deck of an aircraft carrier to catch the tail hook of a landing aircraft and bring it to a halt (*usually used in the plural*)

ar·rest of judg·ment *n* the withholding of judgment in a legal action if there appears to be a good reason to question its appropriateness, e.g., because of a lack of jurisdiction

ar·res·tor *n* same as **arrester**

Ar·rhe·ni·us /ə réenee əss/, **Svante August** (1859–1927) Swedish chemist. His theory of ions carrying electrical charges became one of the cornerstones of modern physical chemistry and electrochemistry.

Ar·rhe·ni·us e·qua·tion *n* an equation in physical chemistry that relates the increase in the rate of a chemical reaction to a rise in temperature

ar·rhyth·mi·a /ə ríthmee ə, ay-/ *n* an irregularity in the rhythm of the heartbeat [Late 19C. < Greek < *arruthmos* "without measure" < *rhuthmos* (see RHYTHM)]

ar·rhyth·mic /ə ríthmik, ay-/ *adj* **1.** describes an irregular rhythmic action of a heartbeat or breathing **2.** without a regular or recognizable rhythm ○ *an arrhythmic tapping on the glass* —**ar·rhyth·mi·cal·ly** *adv*

ar·ri·ère-pen·sée /àrree air poN sáy/ (*plural* **ar·ri·ère-pen·sées** /*pronunc. same*/) *n* (*formal*) **1.** a mental reservation **2.** an unspoken intention [Early 19C. < French, literally "behind-thought"]

ar·ris /árrəss/ (*plural same* or **-ris·es**) *n* a sharp edge or ridge made by the meeting of two surfaces on an architectural column or molding [Late 17C. Via French *areste* "sharp edge" < Latin *arista* (see ARÊTE)]

ar·ri·val /ə rív'l/ *n* **1.** ARRIVING the reaching of a place after coming from another place ○ *Her arrival caused a buzz of comment.* **2.** NEWCOMER somebody or something recently arriving at a place or joining a group ○ *a late arrival* **3.** PASSENGER VEHICLE ARRIVING SOMEWHERE an aircraft, train, or bus arriving at an airport or station **4.** BEGINNING the moment when something begins or becomes important ○ *The arrival of television changed the world.* **5.** BIRTH the birth of a baby **6.** REACHING OF SOMETHING the achieving or reaching of something after much work or effort ○ *Their arrival at a decision seems unlikely.*

ar·rive /ə rív/ (**-rived, -riv·ing, -rives**) *vi* **1.** GET TO PLACE to reach a place after coming from another place **2.** BE DELIVERED to be delivered or brought to somebody or something ○ *She's waiting for the mail to arrive.* **3.** BECOME AVAILABLE to become available or common **4.** BEGIN to begin or happen after a period of time or waiting ○ *We've got to finish the work before summer arrives.* **5.** WORK OUT SOLUTION to reach a decision after thinking about or discussing a problem ○ *How did you arrive at the idea of using strings?* **6.** ENTER LIFE to be born **7.** SUCCEED to become successful or famous (*informal*) ○ *You haven't arrived until you've eaten in this restaurant.* [12C. Via French < assumed Vulgar Latin *arripare* "come to shore" < Latin *ripa* "shore"] —**ar·riv·er** *n*

ar·ri·ve·der·ci /àrrivə dérchee, ə reéve-/ *interj* goodbye for now [Late 20C. < Italian *a rivederci* "until we see each other again" < *rivedere* "see again"]

ar·ri·viste /àrree veést, -víst/ *n* somebody who has recently become influential or socially prominent and is regarded as an upstart [Early 20C. < French, "somebody who arrives"]

ar·ro·gant /árrəgənt/ *adj* feeling or showing self-importance and contempt or disregard for others [14C. Via French < Latin *arrogant-*, present participle of *arrogare* "claim for yourself" < *rogare* "ask"] —**ar·ro·gance** *n* —**ar·ro·gant·ly** *adv*

SYNONYMS See *proud.*

ar·ro·gate /árrə gàyt/ (**-gat·ed, -gat·ing, -gates**) *vt* (*formal*) **1.** to take or claim something for yourself without the right to do so ○ *arrogating the powers of the General* **2.** to assign or attribute something to another in a way that is not warranted [Mid-16C. < Latin *arrogat-*, past participle of *arrogare* (see ARROGANT)] —**ar·ro·ga·tion** /àrrə gáysh'n/ *n* —**ar·ro·ga·tor** *n*

ar·ron·disse·ment /ə róndissmənt, -mòN/ (*plural* **-ments** /*pronunc. same*/) *n* **1.** an administrative area in France that is a major subdivision of an administrative district **2.** an administrative area in some large cities in France, including Paris [Early 19C. < French < *arrondiss-*, stem of *arrondir* "make round"]

ar·row /árrō/ *n* **1.** MISSILE SHOT FROM BOW a long thin missile pointed at one end and usually with feathers at the other, fired from a bow **2.** DIRECTION SIGN a direction sign consisting of a horizontal stroke finishing in the middle of a V shape **3.** *Carib* FLOWER ON STALK a sugar cane flower and its stalk ■ *v* (**-rowed, -row·ing, -rows**) **1.** *vt Malaysia* SELECT SOMEBODY to choose somebody to do something unpleasant (*informal*) ○ *The teacher arrowed me because I was dreaming in class.* **2.** *vi Carib* PRODUCE BLOOMS to come into flower (*refers to sugar cane*) [Old English *arwe* < Old Norse *örv-* < Indo-European] —**ar·row·y** *adj*

ar·row ar·um *n* a perennial plant with arrow-shaped leaves. Native to: eastern North America. Latin name: *Peltandra virginica.*

ar·row·head /árrō hèd/ *n* **1.** a sharp pointed tip attached to an arrow **2.** a water plant with arrow-shaped leaves. Flowers: white, in clusters. Native to: Asia, North America. Genus: *Sagittaria.*

ar·row key *n* one of four computer keys marked with an up, down, left, or right arrow, used to move the cursor

ar·row-poi·son frog *n* a brightly colored frog whose skin glands produce poison that is used by local peoples for smearing on arrow tips. Native to: South America. Family: Dendrobatidae.

ar·row·root /árrō ròot/ (*plural same* or **-roots**) *n* **1.** STARCH edible starch obtained from the rhizomes of a tropical plant. Use: thickener for clear sauces, in cookies. **2.** CENTRAL AMERICAN PLANT a plant with rhizomes that yield arrowroot. Native to: tropical Central America. Latin name: *Maranta arundinacea.* **3.** EDIBLE RHIZOME the edible rhizome of the arrowroot plant [Late 17C. By folk etymology < Arawak *aru-aru* "meal of meals"; from its use to absorb poison from arrow wounds]

ar·row-wood (*plural* **ar·row-woods** or *same*) *n* a bush with tough straight stems. Use: formerly, by Native Americans, to make arrows. Genus: *Viburnum.*

ar·row worm *n* an invertebrate ocean animal that has an arrow-shaped body and spines on its head for catching prey. Phylum: Chaetognatha. [< the spines on its head]

ar·roy·o /ə róy ō/ (*plural* **-os**) *n Southwest US* **1.** a steep-sided dry gulch in a desert area that is wet only after heavy rain **2.** a small stream of running water [Mid-19C. Via Spanish < Latin *arrugia* "mineshaft"]

Ar·roy·o /a róy ō/, **Gloria** (*b.* 1947) president of the Philippines (2001–). Elected to the senate in 1992 and 1995 and as vice president in 1998, she was sworn in as president when her predecessor was forced to resign following allegations of corruption. Full name **Arroyo, Maria Gloria Macapagal**

arse /aars/ *n UK* same as **ass**[2] (sense 1) (*taboo offensive*) [Old English *ærs, ears* < Indo-European]

arse lick·er *n UK* same as **ass kisser** (*taboo offensive*) —**arse-lick·ing** *n*

ar·se·nal /áarssən'l, -nəl/ *n* **1.** WEAPONS STOREHOUSE a building where weapons and military equipment are stored **2.** ARMAMENTS a stockpile of weapons and military equipment **3.** RESOURCES a supply of methods or resources ○ *an arsenal of teaching strategies* [Early 16C. Directly or via French < Italian *arzanale* < Venetian Italian *arzanà* < Arabic *dār-(aṣ-)ṣinā'a* "workshop, factory"]

ORIGIN *Arsenal* is derived from an Arabic word *dār-(aṣ-)ṣinā'a,* meaning "workshop" or "factory." When the original Arabic word was borrowed into Venetian Italian, the initial *d* was lost, possibly because it was misinterpreted as the Italian preposition *di* "of." The word came to mean "dock possessing naval stores," and in Venice, the leading naval power in the Mediterranean in the 15th century, the dockyard is known to this day as the *Arzenale.* The Romance languages retain this meaning in words from the same ancestor that still show the Arabic *d,* in Italian *darsena* "dock," for example; in English too, "dockyard" was the original sense, giving way from the late 16th century to "military storehouse."

ar·se·nate /áarssənət, áarssnət, -ə nàyt/ *n* any salt of arsenic acid [Early 19C. < ARSENIC]

ar·se·nic /áarssnik, áarssənik/ *n* **1.** a steel-gray poisonous solid element that is a brittle crystalline metalloid. Source: realgar, arsenopyrite. Use: in glass manufacture to remove impurities of color, in alloys to harden lead. Symbol **As.** See table at **element** **2.** CHEM same as **arsenic trioxide** ■ *adj* relating to or containing arsenic, especially with a valence of 5 [14C. Via French < Greek *arsenikon* "yellow orpiment" < Arabic *az-zarnīk* "the orpiment" < Persian *zar* "gold"]

ORIGIN The term *arsenic* was originally applied to a lemon-yellow mineral that is a compound of arsenic, hence its origin in *zar,* the Persian word for gold. The Arabic derivative of this word was misinterpreted by foreign listeners as including the definite article *al,* and in Greek the supposed beneficial effects on virility led the term to be associated by folk etymology with the similar-sounding words *arsenikos,* "masculine," and *arsēn,* "manly." In English the word still referred to the mineral at first (for which *orpiment* was the other current name), and it was not until the early 17th century that it was applied to white arsenic or arsenic trioxide. The element arsenic itself was isolated and so named at the start of the 19th century.

ar·sen·ic ac·id /aar sènnik ássid/ *n* a white poisonous crystalline solid containing arsenic. Use: manufacture of pigments and insecticides. Formula: H_3AsO_4.

ar·sen·i·cal /aar sénnik'l/ *adj* relating to or containing arsenic ■ *n* a substance that contains arsenic, e.g., a drug or insecticide

ar·sen·ic tri·ox·ide /áarssnik trī ók sīd, aar sènnik-/ *n* a white poisonous solid that contains arsenic. Use: insecticide, rodenticide, herbicide, manufacture of glass and pigments. Formula: As_2O_3.

ar·se·nide /áarssə nīd/ *n* a chemical compound of arsenic and a metal [Mid-19C. < ARSENIC]

ar·se·ni·ous /aar seénee əss/ *adj* relating to or containing arsenic, especially with a valence of 3 [Early 19C. < ARSENIC]

ar·se·no·py·rite /áarssənō pír īt, aar sènnō-/ *n* a gray-to-white metallic mineral consisting of a sulfide of iron and arsenic [Mid-19C. < ARSENIC]

ar·se·no·ther·a·py /áarssənō thérrəpee/ *n* the treatment of disease with arsenic or one of its derivatives or preparations [< ARSENIC]

ar·ses LITERAT plural of **arsis**

ar·sine /aar seén, áar seen/ *n* a colorless, very poisonous gas with an odor like garlic. Use: manufacture of organic chemicals, transistors, chemical weapons. Formula: AsH_3. [Late 19C. < ARSENIC]

ar·sis /áarssiss/ (*plural* **ar·ses** /áar seez/) *n* **1.** in classical Greek and Roman verse, the short syllable or syllables in a metrical foot **2.** in modern verse, the accented syllable in a metrical foot [14C. Via late Latin, "raising of the voice to greater force, accented part of the metrical foot" < Greek, "raising (of the foot in beating time)"]

ar·son /áarss'n/ *n* the burning of a building or other property for a criminal or malicious reason [Late 17C. < legal Anglo-Norman *arsoun* < Latin *arsus,* past participle of *ardere* "to burn"] —**ar·son·ist** *n*

art[1] /aart/ *n* **1.** CREATION OF BEAUTIFUL THINGS the creation of beautiful or thought-provoking works, e.g., in painting, music, or writing **2.** BEAUTIFUL OBJECTS beautiful or thought-provoking works produced through creative activity **3.** BRANCH OF ART a branch or category of art, especially one of the visual arts **4.** ARTISTIC SKILL the skill and technique involved in producing visual representations **5.** STUDY OF ART the study of a branch of the visual arts **6.** CREATION BY HUMANS creation by human endeavor rather than by nature

7. TECHNIQUES OR CRAFT the set of techniques used by somebody in a particular field, or the use of those techniques ○ *the art of the typographer* **8.** ABILITY the skill or ability to do something well ○ *the art of conversation* **9.** CUNNING the ability to achieve things by deceitful or cunning methods (*literary*) ■ **arts** *npl* **1.** FORMS OF CREATIVE BEAUTY activities enjoyed for the beauty they create or the way they present ideas, e.g., painting, music, and literature **2.** NONSCIENTIFIC SUBJECTS nonscientific and nontechnical subjects at school or college [13C. Via French < Latin *art-* "skill"] ◇ **have something down to a fine art** to be able to do something very skillfully

ORIGIN The Latin stem *art-* "skill," from which ***art*** is derived, is also the source of English *artificial*, *artisan*, and *inert*.

art[2] /aart/ 2nd person singular present of **be**[1] (*archaic or literary*)

ART *abbr* MED assisted reproductive technology

art. *abbr* **1.** article **2.** artificial **3.** MIL artillery **4.** artist

-art *suffix* same as **-ard**

ar·tal MEASURE plural of **rotl**

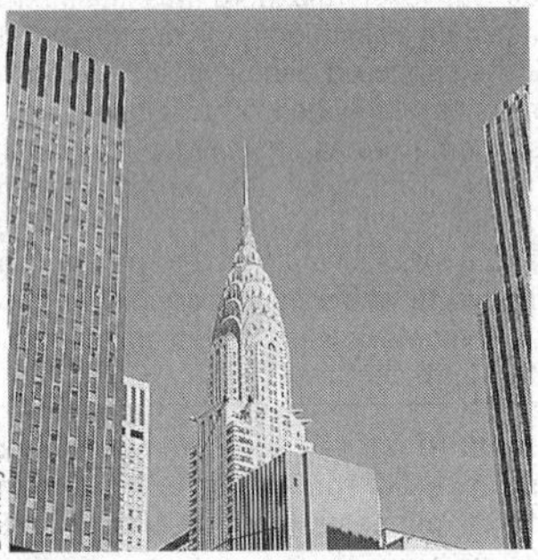
Barnaby's

art deco: Chrysler Building, New York City (1930), designed by William van Alen

art dec·o /-dékō/, **Art Dec·o** *n* a style of architecture, interior design, and jewelry most popular in the 1930s that used geometric designs and bold colors and outlines [Mid-20C. < French, shortening of *arts décoratifs* "decorative arts"]

art di·rec·tor *n* the person in charge of the sets and costumes when something is being filmed or photographed

ar·tee *n*, *v* HINDUISM another spelling of **arti**

ar·te·fact *n* another spelling of **artifact**

ar·tel /aar tél/ *n* a workers' or producers' cooperative in imperial Russia or the Soviet Union [Late 19C. < Russian]

Ar·te·mis /áartəmiss/ *n* in Greek mythology, the goddess of hunting and the Moon, and of childbirth. She was the daughter of Zeus and the sister of Apollo. Roman equivalent **Diana**

ar·te·mis·i·a /àartə mízhee ə/ (*plural* **-as** or *same*) *n* an aromatic plant with grayish green leaves. Flowers: profuse, small. Native to: northern hemisphere. Genus: *Artemisia*. [14C. Via Latin < Greek, "wormwood" < *Artemis* "Artemis," to whom it was sacred]

ar·te·ri·al /aar téeree əl/ *adj* **1.** OF ARTERIES relating to, affecting, or used in arteries **2.** OXYGENATED describes the bright red blood in the arteries that has absorbed oxygen **3.** MAIN constituting a main route in a road, rail, or river system —**ar·te·ri·al·ly** *adv*

ar·te·ri·al·ize /aar téeree ə lìz/ (**-ized, -iz·ing, -iz·es**) *vt* to convert venous blood into arterial blood by replenishing its oxygen —**ar·te·ri·al·i·za·tion** /aar tèeree əli záysh'n/ *n*

arterio- *prefix* artery, arterial ○ *arteriovenous* [< Greek *artēria* "artery"]

ar·te·ri·o·gram /aar téeree ə gràm/ *n* an X-ray of the arteries made after a substance that shows up on an X-ray has been injected into the bloodstream

ar·te·ri·og·ra·phy /aar tèeree óggrəfee/ *n* X-ray examination of the arteries —**ar·te·ri·o·graph·ic** /aar tèeree ə gráffik/ *adj*

ar·te·ri·ole /aar téeree ōl/ *n* a blood vessel that branches off from an artery [Mid-19C. < French *artériole* "little artery" < *artère* "artery" < Latin *arteria* (see ARTERY)] —**ar·te·ri·o·lar** /aar tèeree ṓlər/ *adj*

ar·te·ri·o·scle·ro·sis /aar tèeree ō sklə rṓssiss/ *n* MED same as **atherosclerosis** —**ar·te·ri·o·scle·rot·ic** /-sklə róttik/ *adj*

ar·te·ri·o·ve·nous /aar tèeree ō véenəss/ *adj* involving both a vein and an artery

ar·te·ri·tis /àartə rítiss/ *n* inflammation of the walls of an artery

ar·ter·y /áartəree/ (*plural* **-ies**) *n* **1.** a blood vessel that is part of the system carrying blood under pressure from the heart to the rest of the body **2.** a main route in a road, rail, or river system [14C. Via Latin < Greek *artēria*]

ar·te·sian aq·ui·fer /aar tée̱zh'n-/ *n* an aquifer that has an impermeable bed both above and below it and is under enough pressure for water to be forced upward [See ARTESIAN WELL]

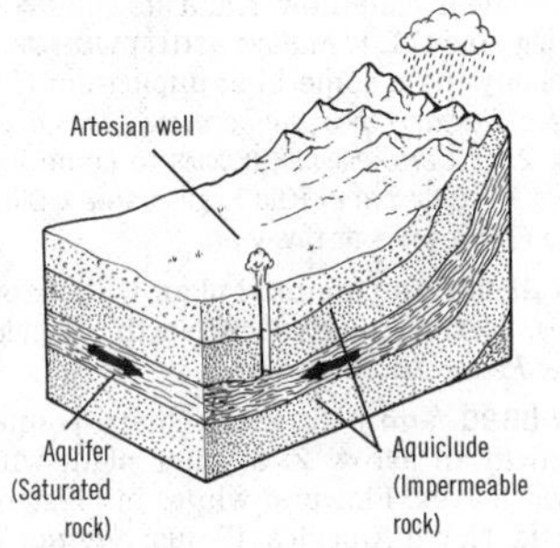

artesian well

ar·te·sian well /aar tée̱zh'n-/ *n* a well drilled through impermeable rocks into strata where water is under enough pressure to force it to the surface without pumping [Mid-19C. < French *artésien* "of Artois" (*Arteis* in Old French), region in NE France where such wells were first drilled]

art film *n* a serious, independently made film that is not aimed at a mass audience

art form *n* **1.** a creative activity or type of artistic expression that is intended to be beautiful or thought-provoking **2.** something that is done in such a sophisticated or skillful way that it can be seen as artistic ○ *He's turned the answering of questions without actually saying anything into an art form.*

art·ful /áartf'l/ *adj* **1.** using clever, subtle, and sometimes dishonest means to achieve things **2.** done skillfully or with taste ○ *an artful arrangement of blue and green ceramics* —**art·ful·ly** *adv* —**art·ful·ness** *n*

art·ful dod·ger *n* somebody skilled at avoiding difficult situations and having to answer questions [After a young pickpocket in *Oliver Twist* by Charles Dickens]

art gal·ler·y *n* **1.** a building where works of art are displayed **2.** an establishment that displays and sells works of art

art house *n* a theater where art films are shown

arthr- *prefix* same as **arthro-** (*used before vowels*)

ar·thral·gia /aar thráljə, -jee ə/ *n* pain in a joint —**ar·thral·gic** *adj*

ar·threc·to·my /aar thréktəmee/ (*plural* **-mies**) *n* a surgical operation to remove a joint

ar·thri·tis /aar thrítiss/ *n* a medical condition affecting a joint or joints, causing pain, swelling, and stiffness [Mid-16C. Via Latin < Greek, "joint disease" < *arthron* "joint" (see ARTHRO-)] —**ar·thrit·ic** /aar thríttik/ *adj*, *n*

arthro- *prefix* joint of the body ○ *arthroscopic* [< Greek *arthron* < Indo-European, "fit together"]

ar·thro·gram /áarthrə gràm/ *n* an X-ray of the inside of a damaged joint made after a substance that shows up on an X-ray has been injected into the joint

ar·throg·ra·phy /aar thróggrəfee/ *n* X-ray examination of the inside of a damaged joint

ar·throp·a·thy /aar thróppəthee/ *n* a disease or medically noteworthy condition of a joint

ar·thro·plas·ty /áarthrə plàstee/ (*plural* **-ties**) *n* surgical repair of a joint, or replacement of a joint or part of one by metal or plastic parts

ar·thro·pod /áarthrə pòd/ *n* an invertebrate animal that has jointed limbs, a segmented body, and an exoskeleton made of chitin, e.g., an insect, arachnid, centipede, or crustacean. Phylum: Arthropoda. [Late 19C. < modern Latin *Arthropoda* < Greek *arthron* "joint" (see ARTHRO-) + *pod-* "foot" (see -POD)] —**ar·thro·pod** *adj* —**ar·throp·o·dal** /aar thróppəd'l/ *adj*

ar·thros·co·py /aar thróskəpee/ (*plural* **-pies**) *n* inspection of the inside of a joint of the body using an endoscope —**ar·thro·scope** /áarthrə skōp/ *n* —**ar·thro·scop·ic** /àarthrə skóppik/ *adj* —**ar·thro·scop·ic·al·ly** *adv*

ar·thro·sis /aar thrṓssiss/ (*plural* **-thro·ses** /-thrṓ seez/) *n* **1.** a degenerative disease of a joint **2.** a joint between two bones (*technical*) [Mid-17C. Via Latin < Greek *arthrōsis* < *arthroun* "to articulate" < *arthron* "joint" (see ARTHRO-)]

ar·throt·o·my /aar thróttəmee/ (*plural* **-mies**) *n* a surgical operation that involves cutting into a joint of the body

Ar·thur /áarthər/ *n* in medieval legend, a king of the Britons whose court was based at Camelot. He was the leader of the Knights of the Round Table. —**Ar·thu·ri·an** /aar thóoree ən/ *adj*

Bettmann/Corbis

Chester A. Arthur

Ar·thur /áarthər/, **Chester A.** (1829–86) 21st president of the United States. A Republican president (1881–85), he enacted sweeping civil service reforms (1883) that lost him the support of his party. Full name **Arthur, Chester Alan.** See table at **president**

Ar·thur, Owen (*b.* 1949) prime minister of Barbados (1994–). A member of the Barbados Labor Party, he became leader of the opposition in 1993 and won general election victories in 1994 and 1999. Full name **Arthur, Owen Seymour**

> "A rising tide can also overturn small boats."
> [Owen Arthur, *New York Times*; December 12, 1994]

ar·ti /áartee/, **aar·ti, ar·tee** *n* a Hindu ritual in which a small fire in a flat container or lamp is moved in a circular motion in front of a god or person during a puja ■ *vt* (**-tied, -ti·ing, -ties; -teed, -tee·ing, -tees**) *Carib* to give a blessing to somebody, or receive a blessing from somebody [Late 20C. Via Hindi < Sanskrit *aartrika*]

~~**artic**~~ incorrect spelling of **arctic**

~~**artical**~~ incorrect spelling of **article**

ar·ti·choke /áartə chōk/ (*plural* **-chokes** or *same*) *n* **1.** a large flower bud with parts that can be eaten after cooking **2.** a plant that produces artichokes. Native to: Europe, Asia. Latin name: *Cynara scolymus*. **3.** FOOD same as **Jerusalem artichoke** (sense 1) [Mid-16C. < N Italian *articiocco, arciciocco* < Italian *arcicioffo*, via Spanish *alcarchofa* < Arabic *al-karšūf(a)*]

ar·ti·cle /áartik'l/ *n* **1.** NEWSPAPER OR REFERENCE PIECE a piece of nonfiction writing in a newspaper, magazine, or reference book ○ *an article on ecology* **2.** ITEM an object or item, especially one that is part of a group ○ *articles of clothing* **3.** GRAM WORD BEFORE NOUN a word used with a noun that specifies whether the noun is definite or indefinite. In English the indefinite articles are "a" and "an," and the definite article is "the." **4.** ONLINE NEWSGROUP MESSAGE a message or posting to a newsgroup **5.** LAW LEGAL PARAGRAPH a

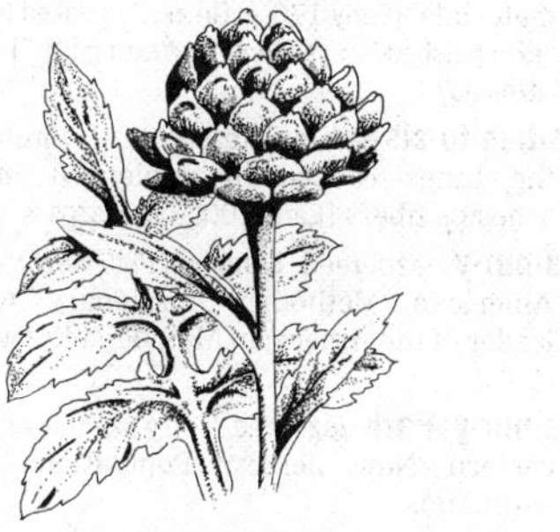

artichoke

section of a legal document that deals with a specific point ■ *vt* (**-cled, -cling, -cles**) LAW **BIND SOMEBODY BY CONTRACT** to bind somebody by the articles of a contract, especially somebody training in the legal profession [12C. Via French < Latin *articulus* "joint, section" < *artus* "joint, limb"]

ar·ti·cle of faith *n* **1.** any one of the items that must be believed as part of a creed or statement of faith **2.** something that somebody believes completely

ar·ti·cles of in·cor·po·ra·tion *npl* a document that, once approved by an appropriate state authority, creates a corporation

ar·tic·u·lar /aar tíkyələr/ *adj* relating to or involving a joint of the body [15C. < Latin *articularis* < *articulus* "joint" (see ARTICLE)] —**ar·tic·u·lar·ly** *adv*

ar·tic·u·lar fac·et *n* a small surface of a bone such as a vertebra that articulates with another bone such as a rib

ar·tic·u·late *v* /aar tíkyə làyt/ (**-lat·ed, -lat·ing, -lates**) **1.** *vt* **COMMUNICATE SOMETHING** to express thoughts, ideas, or feelings coherently ○ *unable to articulate his grief* **2.** *vti* **SPEAK DISTINCTLY** to pronounce something or speak clearly **3.** *vti* **JOIN TO ALLOW MOVEMENT** to form the kind of joint or connection that allows movement **4.** *vi* **SPEAK INTELLIGIBLY** to utter intelligible speech ■ *adj* /aar tíkyələt/ **1. ELOQUENT** able to express thoughts, ideas, or feelings coherently **2. COHERENT** spoken or expressed clearly **3. ABLE TO SPEAK** possessing the power of speech **4. JOINTED** with joints or jointed segments, as in the bodies of higher vertebrates and arthropods (*technical*) [Mid-16C. < Latin *articulatus*, past participle of *articulare* "divide into joints, speak distinctly" < *articulus* "joint" (see ARTICLE)] —**ar·tic·u·la·ble** *adj* —**ar·tic·u·la·cy** *n* —**ar·tic·u·late·ly** *adv*

ar·tic·u·lat·ed /aar tíkyə làytəd/ *adj* made up of two or more sections connected by a joint that can pivot ○ *an articulated bus*

ar·tic·u·lat·ed lor·ry *n UK* VEHICLES same as **tractor-trailer**

ar·tic·u·la·tion /aar tìkyə láysh'n/ *n* **1. COMMUNICATION** the coherent expression of thoughts, ideas, or feelings **2. SPEECH** the pronouncing of words, or the manner in which they are pronounced **3. JOINTING** the connection of the different parts of something by joints, or the way the parts fit together **4. ANIMAL'S JOINT** a joint in an animal (*technical*) **5. PLANT NODE** a node of a plant, or the space on a stem between two nodes (*technical*) —**ar·tic·u·la·tive** /aar tíkyələtiv/ *adj* —**ar·tic·u·la·to·ry** /-tíkyələ tàwree/ *adj*

ar·tic·u·la·tor /aar tíkyə làytər/ *n* **1.** somebody who communicates clearly **2.** a part of the vocal organs that helps form speech sounds. Active articulators include the pharynx, soft palate, lips, and tongue, while the passive articulators include the upper teeth, the alveolar ridge, and the hard palate.

ar·ti·fact /áarti fàkt/, **ar·te·fact** *n* **1. OBJECT MADE BY HUMAN** an object made by a human being, e.g., a tool or ornament, especially one that has archaeological or cultural interest **2. METHOD-DEPENDENT RESULT** something that appears to exist because of the way an object or data is examined, e.g., a form of behavior that is indicated by a behavioral test **3. FOREIGN SUBSTANCE** something in a biological specimen that is not present naturally but has been introduced or produced during a procedure [Early 19C. < Latin *arte*, a form of *ars* "skill" (see ART[1]) + *factum* "thing made" (see FACT)]

ar·ti·fice /áartəfəss/ *n* (*formal*) **1. CLEVER TRICK** a clever trick or stratagem **2. CLEVERNESS** the use of clever stratagems or tricks **3. INSINCERE BEHAVIOR** the deception of people using cleverness or subtlety [Early 17C. Via French < Latin *artificium* "craft, art, cunning" < *artific-* "artisan, contriver" < *art-* "skill" + *facere* "make"]

ar·tif·i·cer /aar tíffəssər/ *n* (*dated*) **1.** somebody whose work requires manual skill **2.** same as **inventor** [14C. < Anglo-Norman, probably < Old French *artificien* < Latin *artificium* "craft, cunning" (see ARTIFICE)]

ar·ti·fi·cial /àartə físh'l/ *adj* **1. MADE BY HUMANS** made by human beings rather than occurring naturally **2. SYNTHETIC** made in imitation of something natural **3. INSINCERE** without sincerity or spontaneity ○ *an artificial smile* **4. CREATED BY CULTURE** produced as a result of political or cultural forces ○ *artificial barriers to promotion* [14C. Directly or via French < Latin *artificialis* < *artificium* "craft, cunning" (see ARTIFICE)] —**ar·ti·fi·ci·al·i·ty** /àartəfishee állətee/ *n* —**ar·ti·fi·cial·ly** *adv*

ar·ti·fi·cial climb·ing *n* climbing on indoor or other humanmade environments such as walls specifically designed and built for this activity

ar·ti·fi·cial feed·ing *n* the feeding of somebody by means that do not occur naturally, e.g., feeding a patient on life support intravenously or bottle-feeding a baby

ar·ti·fi·cial ho·ri·zon *n* an instrument that displays, usually pictorially, the amount of pitch or bank of an aircraft relative to the horizon

ar·ti·fi·cial in·sem·i·na·tion *n* a method of inducing pregnancy in a woman or other female mammal by injecting sperm into the womb

ar·ti·fi·cial in·tel·li·gence *n* **1.** a branch of computer science that develops programs to allow machines to perform functions normally requiring human intelligence **2.** the ability of computers to perform functions that normally require human intelligence

ar·ti·fi·cial·ize /àartə físhə lìz/ (**-ized, -iz·ing, -iz·es**) *vt* to give something an artificial appearance or quality —**ar·ti·fi·cial·i·za·tion** /àartəfishəli záysh'n/ *n*

ar·ti·fi·cial lan·guage *n* a language that has been invented for international communication or for use with computers. The best-known artificial language is Esperanto.

ar·ti·fi·cial life *n* the use of computer systems to embody and simulate aspects of natural human behavior such as learning and reproduction

ar·ti·fi·cial neu·ral net·work *n* an information processing system with interconnected components analogous to neurons, based on mathematical models that mimic some features of biological nervous systems and the ability to learn through experience

ar·ti·fi·cial res·pi·ra·tion *n* any method of forcing air into the lungs of somebody who has stopped breathing, especially the method that involves blowing air into the mouth

ar·ti·fi·cial se·lec·tion *n* selection by humans of animals and plants with desirable characteristics for use in breeding over several generations

ar·ti·fi·cial sweet·en·er *n* a synthetic sugar substitute

ar·ti·gi *n Can* CLOTHING same as **atigi**

ar·til·ler·y /aar tílləree/ *n* **1. POWERFUL GUNS** large-caliber guns, e.g., cannons, howitzers, missile launchers, and mortars **2. SOLDIERS USING POWERFUL GUNS** soldiers who specialize in operating large powerful firearms, regarded as a group or unit **3. CATAPULTS** catapults and other large mechanical weapons once used by armies (*archaic*) [14C. < French *artillerie* < *artiller*, variant of *atillier* "equip, arm," influenced by *art* "skill"]

ar·til·ler·y·man /aar tílləreemən/ (*plural* **-men** /-mən/) *n* a soldier in an artillery unit

ar·til·ler·y plant *n* a plant with fleshy leaves and stamens that discharge their pollen by exploding. Native to: tropical America. Latin name: *Pilea microphylla*.

ar·ti·o·dac·tyl /àartee ō dákt'l/ *n* a herbivorous hoofed mammal with an even number of toes on each foot, e.g., a cow or deer. Order: Artiodactyla. [Mid-19C. < modern Latin *artiodactyla* < Greek *artios* "even, fitting" + *dactylos* "finger, toe"] —**ar·ti·o·dac·tyl** *adj* —**ar·ti·o·dac·ty·lous** *adj*

ar·ti·san /áartəz'n/ *n* somebody who is skilled at a craft [Mid-16C. Via French < Italian *artigiano* < Latin *artit-*, past participle of *artire* "instruct in the arts" < *art-* "skill"] —**ar·ti·san·ship** *n*

art·ist /áartist/ *n* **1. CREATOR OF ART** somebody who creates art, especially paintings or sculptures **2. PERFORMER** a member of the performing arts ○ *a well-known recording artist* **3. SKILLED PERSON** somebody who does something skillfully and creatively ○ *an artist with a basketball* **4. CUNNING PERSON** somebody who is very good at a particular thing, especially something cunning (*slang*) ○ *a rip-off artist* [Late 16C. Via French *artiste* < Italian *artista* < *arte* "art"]

ar·tiste /aar tēēst/ *n* **1.** a professional entertainer, especially a singer or dancer **2.** somebody who aspires to being artistic (*humorous*) [Early 19C. < French (see ARTIST)]

ar·tis·tic /aar tístik/ *adj* **1. GOOD AT ART** good at a form of creative expression **2. OF ART** involving or relating to art or artists ○ *the artistic tradition of a nation* **3. TASTEFUL** showing taste, skill, and imagination ○ *artistic flower arrangements* **4. APPRECIATIVE OF ART** able to appreciate the beauty and worth of art ○ *lacking an artistic eye* —**ar·tis·ti·cal·ly** *adv*

ar·tis·tic di·rec·tor *n* somebody responsible for the artistic content of an enterprise in one of the performing arts

art·ist·ry /áartəstree/ *n* **1.** the creative ability and skill of an artist, or the expression of this **2.** great ability and skill in doing something

art·less /áartləss/ *adj* **1. WITHOUT DECEPTION** without guile or deception **2. TOTALLY NATURAL** completely natural and unforced **3. INELEGANT** lacking skill, knowledge, or elegance —**art·less·ly** *adv* —**art·less·ness** *n*

art nou·veau /àart noo vṓ, àar-/, **Art Nou·veau** *n* a style of art, architecture, and decoration popular in the 1890s that used stylized natural forms and flowing lines [Early 20C. < French, "new art"]

art run·ner *n* an art dealer who acts as a broker by bringing prospective buyers and sellers together

arts and crafts *n* the hand production of decoratively designed everyday objects, especially as a skilled craft or as part of an educational or rehabilitation program (*takes a singular or plural verb*)

Arts and Crafts *n* a movement in the late 19th and early 20th centuries in Britain and the United States that stressed the value of artisanship

arts med·i·cine *n US* a medical specialty that deals with the disorders and injuries sustained by performers, e.g., musicians

art song *n* a lyric song composed in the classical tradition

art·sy /áartsee/ (**-si·er, -si·est**), **art·y** /áartee/ (**-i·er, -i·est**) *adj* pretentiously or self-consciously artistic (*informal*)

art·sy-craft·sy /áartsi kráftee/ *adj* (*informal*) **1.** relating to handicrafts or objects decorated by hand **2.** decorated in a pretentiously artistic or cute way [Early 20C. < ARTS AND CRAFTS]

art·sy-fart·sy /áartsi fáartsee/ *adj* pretentiously artistic in a elitist or self-indulgent way (*slang*)

art ther·a·py *n* a form of psychotherapy that encourages the expression of emotions in artistic media such as paint or sculpture

art·work /áart wùrk/ *n* **1.** a work or works of art **2.** the illustrations that are to be printed in a publication

art·y *adj* same as **artsy** (*informal*)

arty. *abbr* MIL artillery

art·y-craft·y /-kráftee/ *adj UK* same as **artsy-craftsy** (*informal*) [Early 20C. < ARTS AND CRAFTS]

art·y-fart·y /-fáartee/ *adj UK* same as **artsy-fartsy** (*slang*)

A·ru·ba /ə rōōbə/ island off the Venezuelan coast, formerly a Dutch dependency and since 1986 a self-governing part of the Netherlands. Language: Dutch, Papamiento. Capital: Orangestad. Population: 70,007 (2001). Area: 75 sq. mi./193 sq. km.

a·ru·gu·la /ə rōōgyələ/ (*plural* **-las** or *same*) *n* an herb with pungently flavored leaves that are eaten in salads. Native to: Mediterranean. Latin name:

Eruca vesicaria. [Mid-20C. Probably related to dialectal Italian (Lombard) *arigola* and Venetian Italian *rucola*]

arum

ar·um /érrəm/ (*plural* **-ums** or *same*) *n* a perennial plant that grows from tubers and has arrow-shaped leaves. Native to: Europe. Genus: *Arum.* [14C. Via Latin < Greek *aron*]

ar·um lil·y *n UK* PLANTS same as **calla lily** (sense 1)

A·ru·na·chal Pra·desh /àarə naák'l prə désh/, **A·ru·nā·chal Pra·desh** union state of India. Situated in Northeastern India, it has borders with China and Myanmar. A portion of this state's territory is claimed by China. Capital: Itanagar. Population: 1,091,117 (2001). Area: 32,333 sq. mi./83,743 sq. km.

a·run·do /ə rúndō/ *n* a giant reed that grows in warm climates and is considered invasive in some areas. Use: for reeds in woodwind instruments, ornament. Native to: Mediterranean. Latin name: *Arundo donax.* [< Latin *(h)arundo* "reed"]

a·rus·pex *n* ANCIENT HIST same as **haruspex**

ARV *abbr US* BIBLE American Revised Version

-ary *suffix* of or relating to ○ *functionary* [Via Old French *-arie* < Latin *-arius*]

Ar·y·an /érree ən/ *n* **1.** HIST, POL **NAZI IDEAL** in Nazi ideology, a white person of non-Semitic descent regarded as racially superior **2.** LANG **INDO-EUROPEAN LANGUAGE** the hypothetical parent language of the Indo-European languages (*dated*) **3.** PEOPLES **INDO-EUROPEAN ANCESTOR** somebody who spoke the hypothetical parent language of Indo-European languages (*dated*) [Mid-19C. < Sanskrit *ārya* "noble, of good family"] —**Ar·y·an** *adj*

ar·yl /árrəl/ *adj* describes a chemical group derived from an aromatic hydrocarbon

ar·y·te·noid /àrrə tée nòyd, ə rítt'n òyd/, **ar·y·te·noid·al** /àrrəti nóyd'l/ *adj* **1.** describes either of the two small cartilages of the larynx to which the vocal cords are attached **2.** describes any of the small muscles of the larynx [Early 18C. Via modern Latin < Greek *arutainoeidēs* "ladle-shaped" < *arutaina* "ladle, funnel" < *aruein* "draw water"] —**ar·y·te·noid** *n*

as[1] *stressed* /az/; *unstressed* /əz/ CORE MEANING: a grammatical word indicating simultaneity, causality, comparison, or the identity or function of somebody or something ○ (conj) *Once again, as I started my interview, the telephone rang.* ○ (conj) *I'll drop the book off, as I'll be passing your house anyway.* ○ (conj) *Here, take this pencil as it's sharper than yours.* ○ (prep) *Data is stored on the disk as magnetic patterns.* ○ (conj) *It is stored much as music is stored on an audiotape or cassette.*

1. *conj* **AT TIME THAT** used to indicate that something happens at the same time as something else ○ *A woman stands near the water's edge as two large golden retrievers frolic in the river.* **2.** *conj* **WHAT** that which ○ *Do as you like!* **3.** *conj* **BECAUSE** seeing that ○ *I'm not sure where we are in math, as I've been absent for the last week.* **4.** *conj* **USED FOR COMPARISON** used to compare things, people, or situations ○ *He is almost as tall as she.* ○ *I'm working as hard as before but getting less done.* **5.** *conj* **EMPHASIZES AMOUNTS** used to indicate that an amount is small or large **6.** *conj* **INTRODUCES CLAUSE** used to introduce a short clause referring to a previous or subsequent statement ○ *As you know, I have been in this job for a long time.* **7.** *conj* **IN WAY THAT** used to indicate the way that something happens or exists ○ *Did everything go as planned?* **8.** *conj* **IN SAME WAY THAT** used to indicate that something happens or exists in the same way as something else ○ *Her attitude to life was very practical, as her mother's had been.* **9.** *conj* **THOUGH** in spite of the fact that ○ *Hard-working as she is, she can't compete with the others.* **10.** *prep* **AT TIME WHEN** used to indicate a stage in somebody's life ○ *As a teenager I was quite shy.* **11.** *prep* **IN CAPACITY OF** used to indicate the capacity in which somebody or something exists or acts ○ *uses it as a shortcut* [12C. Contraction of earlier form of ALSO] ◇ **as against** used to indicate comparison or contrast between two facts or amounts ◇ **as ever** used to indicate that a situation is the same as usual ◇ **as far as** to the extent to which a situation holds or is relevant ◇ **as for** used to refer back to a topic and introduce further information about it or comment on it ◇ **as how 1.** used to mean "that" in the phrases "seeing as how" and "allowed as how" (*informal*) ○ *Seeing as how they were almost finished, I waited.* ○ *She allowed as how I had helped her more than anybody.* **2.** *Carib* because **3.** *Carib* seeing that **4.** *Carib* in the same way as ◇ **as if 1.** in a way that suggests something ○ *He looked as if he'd been crying.* **2.** used to indicate that the speaker is saying something ridiculous ○ *As if I'd say a thing like that!* ◇ **as is** in the present condition, with whatever faults there may be ◇ **as it were** used to indicate qualification, uncertainty, or lack of definiteness in a statement ◇ **as long as 1.** provided that ○ *You can go, as long as you're home by midnight.* **2.** because or seeing that ○ *As long as we're here we may as well look around.* ◇ **as much again** twice as much ◇ **as of** on and after a particular date or time ◇ **as per** in accordance with ◇ **as such 1.** used to indicate that a word or phrase does not apply exactly to a situation (*often used with a negative*) ○ *I have no qualifications as such, but I feel I could do the job.* **2.** used to indicate that something is being considered separately ○ *After the earthquake, the village as such virtually ceased to exist.* ◇ **as though** same as **as if** ◇ **as to** same as **as for** ◇ **as yet** used to indicate that a situation has lasted up to the present time ○ *She has never once mentioned the terrible accusation nor has she, as yet, said that she is sorry.* ◇ **as you were** a military command to return to the same position as before

USAGE As meaning "in the capacity of": In this use, the preposition ***as*** shows the capacity in which a person or thing exists or acts: *She has a job as a copywriter. As a doctor I understand these problems.* Avoid making false links with the ***as*** clause when they result in ambiguity or apparent absurdity: *As a judge, you know I do not like being asked such questions* (which one is the judge?).

USAGE See ***because***.

as[2] *abbr* American Samoa (*used in Internet addresses*) See table at **domain name**

As *symbol* CHEM ELEM arsenic

AS *abbr* **1.** BANKING after sight **2.** *also* **A.S.** LANG, PEOPLES Anglo-Saxon **3.** ARMS antisubmarine **4.** EDUC Associate in Science

As. *abbr* **1.** Asia **2.** Asian

ASA[1] *adj* used to indicate the speed of photographic film [< ASA[2]]

ASA[2] *abbr* American Standards Association

As·ad·ha /áash udə/ *n* in the Hindu calendar, the fourth month of the year, lasting 31 days and falling about the same time as June to July. See table at **calendar**

as·a·fet·i·da /àssə féttədə, -féet-/, **as·a·foet·i·da** *n* **1.** a bitter brownish acrid-smelling plant resin. Use: South Asian cuisine. **2.** a plant of the parsley family that produces asafetida. Latin name: *Ferula assafoetida.* [14C. < medieval Latin < *asa* (< Persian *āzā* "mastic") + *fetida* "fetid," form of *fetidus* (see FETID)]

a·sal·to /ə sáltō/ (*plural* **-tos**) *n Philippines* a party given as a surprise for somebody [< Spanish, "attack, assault"]

a·sa·na /áassənə/ *n* a posture used in yoga [Mid-20C. < Sanskrit *āsana* "manner of sitting" < *āste* "he sits"]

ASAP, **asap** *abbr* as soon as possible

ASAT, **Asat** *abbr* MIL antisatellite

as·bes·tos /ass béstəss, az-/ *n* a fibrous carcinogenic silicate mineral. Use: formerly, heat-resistant materials. [Early 17C. < Greek, "unslaked lime" < *sbestos* "extinguished" < *sbennunai* "extinguish"] —**as·bes·tine** /-tin/ *adj*

as·bes·to·sis /àss bes tṓsiss, àz-/ *n* inflammation of the lungs caused by prolonged inhalation of asbestos fibers [Early 20C. < ASBESTOS + -OSIS]

As·bur·y /ázbəree/, **Francis** (1745–1816) British-born American Methodist missionary who became leader of the American Methodist Episcopal Church (1785)

As·bur·y Park /ázbəree-/ city and tourist resort in eastern New Jersey. Population: 16,795 (2002 estimate).

ASCAP *abbr* ARTS American Society of Composers, Authors, and Publishers

a·scared /ə skérd/ *adj Southern US* frightened

as·ca·ri·a·sis /àskə rī́ əssiss/ *n* infestation of the intestines by common roundworms or related nematode worms (**ascarids**) [Late 19C. < ASCARID + -IASIS]

as·ca·rid /áskərid/ *n* a parasitic nematode worm, e.g., a common roundworm. Family: Ascaridae. [Late 17C. Back-formation < modern Latin *ascarides,* plural of *ascaris* < Greek *askaris* "intestinal worm" < *askarizein* "to jump"]

ASCE *abbr US* American Society of Civil Engineers

as·cend /ə sénd/ (**-cend·ed, -cend·ing, -cends**) *v* **1.** *vi* **MOVE UPWARD** to go upward, usually vertically or into the air **2.** *vti* **CLIMB SOMETHING** to climb up something such as a hill or stairway ○ *The climber let down a rope so the others could ascend.* **3.** *vi* **LEAD UPWARD** to rise or lead to a higher level **4.** *vi* **RISE TO HIGHER CAREER POSITION** to rise through the ranks to a higher status ○ *She ascended through the ranks all the way to general.* **5.** *vt* **TAKE UP POSITION** to succeed to an important position, especially as a monarch (*formal*) ○ *ascend the throne* [14C. < Latin *ascendere* "climb to" < *scandere* "to climb"] —**as·cend·a·ble** *adj*

as·cen·dance /ə séndənss/, **as·cen·dence** *n* **1.** succeeding or rising to a powerful position **2.** same as **ascendancy**

as·cen·dan·cy /ə séndənssee/, **as·cen·den·cy** *n* a position of power or domination over others

as·cen·dant /ə séndənt/, **as·cen·dent** *adj* **1.** **MOVING UPWARD** moving into a higher position (*literary*) **2.** **DOMINANT** having a position of power or domination over others (*formal*) **3.** BOT same as **ascending** (sense 2) ■ *n* **POINT ON ECLIPTIC** in astrology, the point on the ecliptic or the sign of the zodiac that is rising in the east at a specific time

as·cen·dence, etc. another spelling of **ascendance, etc.**

as·cend·er /ə séndər/ *n* **1.** **SOMEBODY OR SOMETHING THAT GOES UP** somebody or something that moves upward **2.** **LETTER PART EXTENDING UPWARD** the part of a lowercase letter such as h, d, or b that projects above the body of the letter **3.** **LETTER WITH ASCENDER** a lowercase letter with an ascender

as·cend·ing /ə sénding/ *adj* **1.** moving upward, especially on a scale **2.** describes a plant part that grows upward

as·cen·sion /ə sénsh'n/ *n* an act of ascending something (*formal*) [14C. Via French < Latin *ascension-* < *ascens-*, present participle of *ascendere* (see ASCEND)] —**as·cen·sion·al** *adj*

As·cen·sion *n* in Christian belief, the rising of Jesus Christ from earth to heaven after the Resurrection

As·cen·sion Day *n* the day when Christians celebrate the rising of Jesus Christ from earth to heaven after the Resurrection. Date: Thursday, forty days after Easter Day.

As·cen·sion Is·land /ə sénsh'n-/ island in the South Atlantic Ocean to the northwest of Saint Helena, by which it is administered as a British dependency. Population: 1,007 (1988). Area: 34 sq. mi./88 sq. km.

as·cent /ə sént/ *n* **1.** **CLIMB** an act of climbing a mountain or hill ○ *the ascent of Everest* **2.** **UPWARD MOVEMENT** an upward vertical movement **3.** **UPWARD SLOPE** a slope in an upward direction **4.** **WAY UP MOUNTAIN** a climbers' route up a mountain or hill **5.** **RISE TO IMPORTANCE** the process by which somebody becomes more important, successful, or powerful [Late 16C. < ASCEND, after DESCEND, DESCENT]

SPELLCHECK ascent or **assent**? Do not confuse the spelling of ***ascent*** and ***assent***, which sound similar. ***Ascent*** is only used as a noun, denoting an upward movement or slope, as in *the elevator's rapid ascent.* ***Assent*** can be used as a noun or verb, referring to agreement or acceptance: *She nodded in assent. He assented to our request.*

as·cer·tain /àssər táyn/ (**-tained, -tain·ing, -tains**) *vti* to find out something with certainty (*formal*) [Late 16C. < Old French *acertain-*, stem of *acertener* < *certain* (see CERTAIN)] —**as·cer·tain·a·ble** *adj* —**as·cer·tain·a·bly** *adv* —**as·cer·tain·ment** *n*

as·cet·ic /ə séttik/ *adj* choosing or reflecting austerity and self-denial as personal or religious discipline ■ *n* somebody who is self-denying and lives with minimal material comforts [Mid-17C. Directly or via medieval Latin < Greek *askētikos* < *askētēs* "monk, hermit" < *askein* "to exercise"] —**as·cet·i·cal·ly** *adv*

as·cet·i·cism /ə séttə sìzzəm/ *n* austerity and self-denial, especially as a principled way of life

Asch /ash/, **Sholem** *or* **Shalom** (1880–1957) Russian-born US writer. He wrote in Hebrew and later primarily in Yiddish. Many of his works, including *Salvation* (1934), were translated into English.

As·cham /áskəm/, **Roger** (1515–68) English humanist and scholar. The tutor to Princess Elizabeth (1548–50), his works include the treatise *The Scholemaster* (1570).

> "There is no such whetstone, to sharpen a good wit and encourage a will to learning, as is praise."
> [Roger Ascham, *The Scholemaster*; 1570]

as·ci FUNGI plural of **ascus**

as·cid·i·a BOT plural of **ascidium**

as·cid·i·an /ə síddee ən/ (*plural* **-ans** or *same*) *n* MARINE BIOL same as **sea squirt** (*technical*) [Mid-19C. < modern Latin *Ascidia* < Greek *askidion* "little wineskin" < *askos* "wineskin, leather bag"]

as·cid·i·um /ə síddee əm/ (*plural* **-i·a** /-ee ə/) *n* a part of a plant or fungus shaped like a pitcher [Mid-18C. Via modern Latin < Greek *askidion* (see ASCIDIAN)]

ASCII /áskee/ *n* a standard that identifies letters, numbers, and various symbols by code numbers for exchanging data between different computer systems. Full form **American Standard Code for Information Interchange**

ASCII art *n* illustrations using only ASCII characters, often used in e-mails

ASCII file *n* a computer file that contains only ASCII characters

as·ci·tes /ə sī́ teez/ *n* an accumulation of fluid (**serous fluid**) in the peritoneal cavity, causing abdominal swelling [14C. Via late Latin < Greek *askitēs* "edema" < *askos* "wineskin, leather bag"] —**as·cit·ic** /ə síttik/ *adj*

asco- *prefix* ascus ○ *ascocarp* [Via modern Latin < Greek *askos* "wineskin, leather bag"]

as·co·carp /áskə kaàrp/ *n* a fleshy structure in specific fungi (**ascomycetes**) containing sexually produced spores (**ascospores**) in a membranous spore case (**ascus**)

as·co·go·ni·um /àskə gṓnee əm/ (*plural* **-ni·a** /-nee ə/) *n* a female reproductive part in specific fungi (**ascomycetes**)

a·sco·ma /ə skṓmə/ (*plural* **-ma·ta** /-mətə/) *n* FUNGI same as **ascocarp**

as·co·my·cete /àskō mī séet, -mī́ seet/ *n* a fungus that produces spores sexually inside a membranous spore case (**ascus**), e.g., a yeast or truffle. Class: Ascomycetes. —**as·co·my·ce·tous** /àskō mī séetəss/ *adj*

a·scor·bate /ə skáwrbət/ *n* any salt of ascorbic acid

a·scor·bic ac·id /ə skàwrbik-/ *n* BIOCHEM same as **vitamin C** [< A-[2] + SCORBUTIC]

as·co·spore /áskə spàwr/ *n* a fungal spore produced sexually inside a membranous spore case (**ascus**) —**as·co·spor·ic** /àskə spáwrik, -spórrik/ *adj*—**as·co·spo·rous** /àskə spáwrəss, as kóspərəss/ *adj*

as·cot /áskət, ás kòt/ *n* a broad cravat with square ends, often held in place with an ornamental stud

As·cot /áskət, ás kòt/ town in southern England where horseraces are held. Population: 13,500.

as·cribe /ə skrī́b/ (**-cribed, -crib·ing, -cribes**) *vt* (*formal*) **1.** GIVE SOMETHING AS CAUSE to believe or say that something was caused by a particular thing ○ *ascribed the defeat to a series of tactical errors* **2.** GIVE SOMEBODY AS AUTHOR to believe or say that something was originally written or said by a particular person ○ *a poem no longer ascribed to Shakespeare* **3.** GIVE SOMETHING AS CHARACTERISTIC to believe that something belongs to or characterizes a person or group ○ *to ascribe contentment to the unambitious* [15C. < Latin *ascribere* "add to in writing" < *scribere* "write"] —**as·crib·a·ble** *adj*

as·cribed sta·tus /ə skrī̀bd-/ *n* the status that somebody possesses by reason of age, sex, ethnic background, family background, or another factor outside personal control

as·crip·tion /ə skrípsh'n/ *n* **1.** ATTRIBUTION the attributing of a relationship between something and somebody or something else (*formal*) **2.** STATEMENT OF ATTRIBUTION a statement that assigns or attributes something to somebody or something else (*formal*) **3.** SOCIAL STATUS BY BIRTH the social status derived from the circumstances into which somebody is born [Late 16C. < Latin *ascription-* < *ascript-*, past participle of *ascribere* (see ASCRIBE)]

ASCU *abbr US* Association of State Colleges and Universities

as·cus /áskəss/ (*plural* **-ci** /-sī, -kee/) *n* a membranous spore case formed by specific fungi (**ascomycetes**) that contains eight sexually produced spores (**ascospores**) [Mid-19C. Via modern Latin < Greek *askos* "wineskin, leather bag"]

ASDE *abbr* Airport Surface Detection Equipment

ASE *abbr US* American Stock Exchange

-ase *suffix* enzyme ○ *polymerase* [< DIASTASE]

ASEAN /ássee àn/ *abbr* Association of Southeast Asian Nations

a·seis·mic /ay sī́zmik/ *adj* **1.** not subject to earthquakes **2.** built to withstand earthquakes

a·seis·mic creep *n* movement of tectonic plates below the Earth's crust that is not caused by earthquakes or other seismic disturbance

a·seis·mic ridge *n* a long linear mountainous ridge in an ocean basin, usually the result of volcanic activity generated as an ocean plate travels over a hot spot in the Earth's mantle

a·sep·sis /ay sépsiss/ *n* **1.** a condition in which no living disease-causing microorganisms are present **2.** the process or methods of bringing about a condition in which no disease-causing microorganisms are present

a·sep·tic /ay séptik/ *adj* **1.** free of disease-causing microorganisms **2.** designed to prevent infection from pathogenic microorganisms ○ *aseptic techniques* —**a·sep·ti·cal·ly** *adv* —**a·sep·ti·cism** /-sizzəm/ *n*

a·sex·u·al /ay sékshoo əl, -sh'l/ *adj* **1.** SEXUALLY INACTIVE without sexual desire or activity **2.** WITHOUT SEX-LINKED FEATURES lacking any apparent sex or sex organs **3.** WITHOUT SEXUAL FUSION describes reproduction in which there is no fusion of male and female sex cells (**gametes**), e.g., vegetative reproduction or budding —**a·sex·u·al·i·ty** /ay sèkshoo állətee/ *n* —**a·sex·u·al·ly** *adv*

asg. *abbr US* **1.** assigned **2.** assignment

As·gard /áz gaàrd, áss-/ *n* in Norse mythology, the home of the deities and of heroes killed in battle

ash[1] /ash/ *n* **1.** REMAINS OF FIRE the powdery substance that is left when something has been burned (*often used in the plural*) ○ *fireplace ashes* **2.** VOLCANIC DUST fine-grained lava that erupts or flows from a volcano before settling on the ground ■ **ash·es** *npl* BURNED REMAINS OF BODY the remains of somebody's body after it has been cremated ■ *adj* SILVERY GRAY of a silvery gray color [Old English *æsce* < Indo-European, "burn, be dry"] ◇ **rise (like a phoenix) from the ashes** to come into existence or popularity again, seemingly from a state of ruin or destruction

ash

ash[2] /ash/ *n* **1.** (*plural* **ash·es** or *same*) DECIDUOUS TREE a deciduous tree that has compound leaves with paired leaflets and winged fruits. Native to: temperate regions. Genus: *Fraxinus.* **2.** WOOD OF ASH the hard durable wood of an ash tree. Use: furniture, tool handles. **3.** SYMBOL FOR VOWEL SOUND the character "æ," representing the vowel sound of the modern English word "pad," used in Old English and the International Phonetic Alphabet [Old English *æsc* < Germanic]

a·shamed /ə sháymd/ *adj* **1.** feeling full of shame **2.** embarrassed or regretful ○ *I'm ashamed to say I didn't acknowledge their invitation.* [Old English *āscamod* < *sceamu* "shame"] —**a·sha·med·ly** /-mədlee/ *adv*

A·shan·ti[1] /ə shántee, -shaán-/ (*plural same* or **-tis**), **A·shan·te** (*plural same* or **-tes**) *n* **1.** somebody who comes from Ashanti in central Ghana **2.** a language spoken in central Ghana, often regarded as a form of Akan [Early 18C. < Twi *Asante*] —**A·shan·ti** *adj*

A·shan·ti[2] /ə shántee, -shaán-/ former kingdom and present-day administrative area in central Ghana

ash blond, **ash blonde** *adj* light or whitish blond in color ■ *n* somebody with ash blond hair

Ash·bur·ton /ásh bùrt'n/ river in northwestern Western Australia. Length: 404 mi./650 km.

ash·cake /ásh kàyk/ *n regional* a small cornmeal patty that is cooked over an open fire or in hot ashes

ash·can /ásh kàn/ *n* **1.** a large can or barrel for ashes and trash **2.** *US* MIL same as **depth charge** (*slang*)

Ash·can School *n* an early 20th-century school of US painters whose works focused on the everyday life of cities and city dwellers, depicted realistically

Barnaby's

Dame Peggy Ashcroft

Ash·croft /ásh kròft/, **Dame Peggy** (1907–91) British actor who played leading theatrical roles from the 1930s to the 1950s. Her films include *A Passage to India* (1984). Born **Ashcroft, Edith Margaret Emily**

Ashe /ash/, **Arthur** (1943–93) US tennis player who was the first African American to become men's tennis champion. Full name **Ashe, Jr., Arthur Robert**

> "The ideal attitude is to be physically loose and mentally tight."
> [Arthur Ashe, *New York Times*; February 8, 1993]

ash·en[1] /ásh'n/ *adj* **1.** extremely pale in appearance **2.** resembling or consisting of ashes [15C. < ASH[1]]

ash·en[2] /ásh'n/ *adj* relating to the ash tree or its wood (*archaic*) [12C. < ASH[2]]

Ashe·ville /ásh vìl/ city in western North Carolina, near the foothills of the Great Smoky Mountains. It is the site of Biltmore, a large mansion and estate built by the agriculturist and philanthropist George W. Vanderbilt. Population: 69,193 (2002 estimate).

ash flow *n* **1.** an avalanche of hot volcanic ash and debris down the sides of a volcano **2.** a deposit of volcanic ash and debris resulting from an ash flow

Ash·ga·bat /áashgə baat/ capital of Turkmenistan, located in the southern part of the country near the Turkmenistan-Iran border and the Kara Kum desert. Population: 605,000 (1999).. Former name **Ashkhabad**

Ash·ke·naz·i /aashka naazee, àshkə-/ (*plural* **-naz·im** /-naazim/) *n* a member of a Jewish people originating in Germany and northern Europe [Mid-19C. < modern Hebrew < medieval Hebrew *Ashkenaz* "Germany" < Hebrew *Ashkĕnāz*, a grandson of Noah] —**Ash·ke·naz·i** *adj* —**Ash·ke·naz·ic** *adj*

Ash·kha·bad /áashkə baad/ former name for **Ashgabat**

Ash·land /áshlənd/ **1.** city in northeastern Kentucky, on the Ohio River. Population: 21,601 (2002 estimate). **2.** city in north central Ohio. Population: 21,132 (2002 estimate).

ash·lar /áshlər/, **ash·ler** *n* **1.** a thin slab of squared stone, used for facing walls or in building **2.** masonry using thin slabs of squared stone as facing material [14C. Via Old French *aisselier* "plank" < medieval Latin *axicellus* < Latin *axis* "plank, axletree"]

ash·lar·ing /áshləring/ *n* the construction of a building using ashlars

ash·ler *n* CONSTR another spelling of **ashlar**

Ash·more and Car·tier Is·lands /ásh mawr ən kaart yáy-/ external territory lying 323 mi./500 km off the northwestern coast of Australia. It comprises Ashmore Reef and the Cartier Islands. Area: 2 sq. mi./5 sq. km.

Ash·or·a /ə sháwrə/, **Ash·ur·a** /ə shoorə/ *n* an Islamic festival associated by Shia Muslims with the death of Muhammad's grandson Husain. Date: tenth day of Muharram. [Mid-19C. < Arabic *'āšūrā* "tenth"]

a·shore /ə sháwr/ *adv* to the land from the water, or on land as opposed to on a ship or boat ○ *All but the captain went ashore.*

~~**ashphalt**~~ incorrect spelling of **asphalt**

ash·ram /áashrəm/ *n* **1.** a retreat for the practice of yoga or other Hindu disciplines **2.** a commune or communal house whose members share spiritual goals and practices [Early 20C. < Sanskrit *āśramaḥ* "hermitage"]

Ash·ta·bu·la /àshtə byoolə/ city in the extreme northeast of Ohio, beside Lake Erie. Population: 20,482 (2002 estimate).

Ash·ton /áshtən/, **Sir Frederick** (1904–88) British dancer and choreographer. He helped found the Ballet Rambert and Sadlers Wells, which became the Royal Ballet, London, England. Full name **Ashton, Sir Frederick William Mallandaine**

Ash·ton-un·der-Lyne /áshtən undər lín/ engineering town in Greater Manchester, northwestern England. Population: 43,906 (1991).

Ash·to·reth /áshtə rèth/ *n* MYTHOL ➧ **Ishtar**

ash·tray /ásh tràyl/ *n* an open receptacle for the ash from a cigarette, cigar, or pipe and for cigarette butts

Ash·ur·a *n* CALENDAR, ISLAM same as **Ashora**

A·shur·ba·ni·pal /àashoor baanə paal/ (*fl* 7th century B.C.) king of Assyria. He ruled the Assyrian empire from 669 to 627 B.C. and founded the first library in Southwest Asia in his capital at Nineveh.

Ash Wednes·day *n* a Christian holy day marking the first day of Lent [Because of the Roman Catholic custom of marking the heads of penitents with ashes on this day]

ash·y /áshee/ (**-i·er, -i·est**) *adj* **1.** extremely pale or grayish in appearance (*literary*) **2.** resembling or covered in ash

A·sia /áyzhə, áyshə/ the world's largest continent, bordered by the Ural and Caucasus mountains and the Arctic, Pacific, and Indian oceans. Population: estimated 3,460,000,000 (2001 estimate). Area: 17,139,400 sq. mi./44,391,000 sq. km.

A·sia·dol·lar /áyzhə dòllər, áyshə-/ *n* a US dollar used in Asian banks and currency markets

A·sia Mi·nor historic region in the extreme west of Asia, roughly corresponding to Asian Turkey

A·sian /áyzh'n, -sh'n/ *adj* relating to Asia, or its peoples, languages, or cultures ■ *n* somebody who comes from Asia, or is of Asian descent [15C. Via Latin < Greek *Asianos* < *Asia* "Asia"]

A·sian A·mer·i·can *n* an American of Asian descent —**A·sian A·mer·i·can** *adj*

USAGE See *African American.*

A·sian flu, A·sian in·flu·en·za *n* influenza that occurs in sporadic worldwide epidemics, caused by a strain of virus thought to have originated in China in the mid-1950s and related strains

A·sian·ize /áyzh'n ìz, -sh'n-/ (**-ized, -iz·ing, -iz·es**) *vt US* **1.** to make somebody or something Asian, e.g., in cultural characteristics **2.** to bring something under Asian ownership or control —**A·sian·i·za·tion** /àyzh'ni záysh'n, -sh'ni-/ *n*

A·sian pear *n* **1.** a fruit resembling a brownish yellow apple with crisp juicy flesh **2.** *UK* a tree that produces Asian pears. Genus: *Pyrus.* ▶ Can term **apple pear**

A·sia-Pa·ci·fic *n* a commercial region encompassing some of the countries of East and Southeast Asia and the Pacific Rim

A·si·at·ic /àyzhee áttik, àyzee-/ *adj* describes things relating to Asia or of Asian origin such as flora, fauna, or climatic conditions ○ *Asiatic plants and animals* ○ *parts of the Asiatic steppes* [Early 17C. Via Latin < Greek *Asiatikos* < *Asia* "Asia"]

A·si·at·ic chol·er·a *n* MED same as **cholera**

a·side /ə síd/ *adv* **1.** AWAY OR TO ONE SIDE to one side of somebody or something ○ *Stand aside and let the people through.* **2.** OUT OF WAY out of the way, or away from the area of main concern ○ *brush aside all criticism* **3.** IGNORED ignored for the sake of argument ○ *Budget constraints aside, is the deadline feasible?* **4.** FOR FUTURE USE for special or future use ○ *put aside some money each week* ■ *n* **1.** ACTOR'S COMMENT a remark made by an actor, usually to the audience, that the other characters on stage supposedly cannot hear **2.** CONFIDENTIAL COMMENT IN UNDERTONE a spoken remark not directed to all listeners and usually made in a quiet voice **3.** DIGRESSION a digression from a main point ◇ **aside from 1.** in addition to or besides somebody or something ○ *Aside from his medical practice he is also a lawyer.* **2.** except for or not considering something ○ *Aside from the cold weather, I love it here.*

As·i·mov /ázzi mòf, -màwf/, **Isaac** (1920–92) Russian-born US scientist and writer, author of around 500 books, including textbooks and science fiction

> "The good earth is dying; so in the name of humanity let us move. Let us make our hard but necessary decisions. Let us do it quickly. Let us do it now."
> [Isaac Asimov, *The Roving Mind: A Panoramic View of Fringe Science, Technology, and the Society of the Future*; 1987]

as·i·nine /áss'n ìn/ *adj* **1.** utterly ridiculous or lacking sense **2.** relating to or resembling an ass [15C. < Latin *asininus* < *asinus* "ass"] —**as·i·nine·ly** *adv* —**as·i·nin·i·ty** /àss'n ínnətee/ *n*

a·si·ty /ássitee/ *n* a small round-bodied bird with a short tail and rounded wings that feeds on fruit. Native to: Madagascar. Family: Philepittidae.

ask /ask/ (**asked, ask·ing, asks**) *v* **1.** *vti* QUESTION SOMEBODY to communicate with somebody in order to get information ○ *Ask them how long it will take.* **2.** *vti* MAKE REQUEST to make a request for something ○ *They asked me for my opinion.* **3.** *vt* INVITE SOMEBODY to invite somebody to a social event ○ *Only close friends were asked to dinner.* **4.** *vt* REQUIRE SOMETHING to require somebody to give or contribute something ○ *The job asks a lot more of me than I expected.* **5.** *vt* NAME PRICE to name an amount as an acceptable price ○ *They're asking $100,000 for the house.* [Old English *āscian* < Indo-European, "to wish"] —**ask·er** *n* ◇ **for the asking** available at no cost ○ *apples for the asking*

ask after *vt* to inquire about somebody's welfare ○ *She asks after the children whenever we meet.*

ask for *v* **1.** *vti* REQUEST SOMETHING to request that something be provided ○ *I asked for a cup of coffee.* **2.** *vt* REQUEST SOMEBODY'S APPEARANCE to request somebody's appearance ○ *A visitor is asking for you.* **3.** *vt* REQUEST TELEPHONE CONVERSATION WITH SOMEBODY to request that somebody be called to the telephone ○ *The caller is asking for the manager.* **4.** *vt* INVITE SOMETHING UNPLEASANT to behave in a way that deserves something unpleasant ○ *You're asking for a lot of problems if you do that.* ○ *just asking for it*

ask out *vt* to invite somebody to go on a date

a·skance /ə skánss/ *adv* with doubt or suspicion ○*"They surveyed each other askance, feeling that they were rivals, and mentally calculating each other's chances."* (Horatio Alger, Jr., *Ragged Dick*; 1868) [15C. Origin ?]

as·ka·ri /áskaree, ə skaaree/, **as·kar** /áskər/ *n* a soldier or police officer in various Islamic countries of eastern Africa [Late 19C. < Arabic *askarī* "soldier"]

a·skew /ə skyoo/ *adj, adv* at an angle ○ *with his hat askew*

ask·ing price *n* the price set by a seller before any negotiation

ASL *abbr* LANG American Sign Language

a·slant /ə slánt/ *adv* at an angle ○ *books all aslant on the shelves*

a·sleep /ə sleep/ *adj* **1.** NOT AWAKE in or into a state of sleep ○ *After tossing and turning for some hours I eventually fell asleep.* **2.** NOT ALERT not alert enough to function or operate properly ○ *asleep on the job* **3.** NUMB describes part of the body that has become numb ○ *My arm's gone asleep.*

a·slope /ə slóp/ *adj, adv* at a sloping angle (*archaic or literary*)

ASM *abbr* MIL air-to-surface missile

As·ma·ra /aaz maarə/ capital and largest city of Eritrea. It is also the name of one of the ten provinces within Eritrea. Population: 514,000 (1999).

a·so·cial /ay sósh'l/ *adj* **1.** UNWILLING TO MIX SOCIALLY averse to human social interaction **2.** UNSUITED TO SOCIETY not conforming to normal social standards, or showing a lack of consideration for others ○ *asocial behavior* **3.** NOT INTERACTING SOCIALLY describes animals that do not interact socially

~~**asociation**~~ incorrect spelling of **association**

A·so·ka /ə sókə/, **king of Maghada** (291?–232 B.C.) After conquering most of the Indian subcontinent, he renounced violence and converted to Buddhism, actively propagating that faith in his own kingdom and abroad. His reign (273?–232 B.C.) was marked by religious tolerance and public and charitable works.

asp /asp/ *n* **1.** a small poisonous snake that caused the death of Cleopatra, thought to have been a member of the cobra family. Native to: Africa, Asia, Europe. Latin name: *Naja haje.* **2.** a snake of the viper family, resembling a small adder. Native to: southern Europe. **3.** REPT same as **horned viper** [14C. Directly or via Old French < Latin *aspis* < Greek]

ASP *abbr* COMPUT **1.** active server page **2.** application service provider

as·par·a·gin·ase /ə spárrəjə nàyss, -nàyz/ *n* an enzyme that catalyzes the breakdown of asparagine

as·par·a·gine /ə spárrə jeen/ *n* an amino acid found in many plant seeds that can also be produced by humans and other animals. Formula: $C_4H_8N_2O_3$. [Early 19C. < ASPARAGUS, from which it was first obtained]

as·par·a·gus /ə spárrəgəss/ *n* **1.** spear-shaped young plant shoots, eaten cooked as a vegetable **2.** a perennial plant that produces asparagus. Latin name: *Asparagus officinalis.* ▶ See illustration on next page [Pre-12C. Via Latin < Greek *asparagos*]

as·par·tame /áspər tàym, ə spaar-/ *n* a protein produced from aspartic acid. Use: synthetic sweetener. [Late 20C. < ASPARTIC ACID]

a·spar·tate /ə spaar tàyt, áspər-/ *n* a salt or ester of aspartic acid

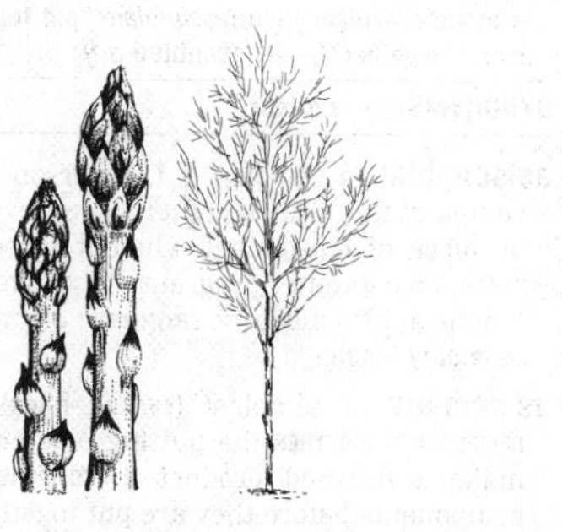
asparagus

aspergillum

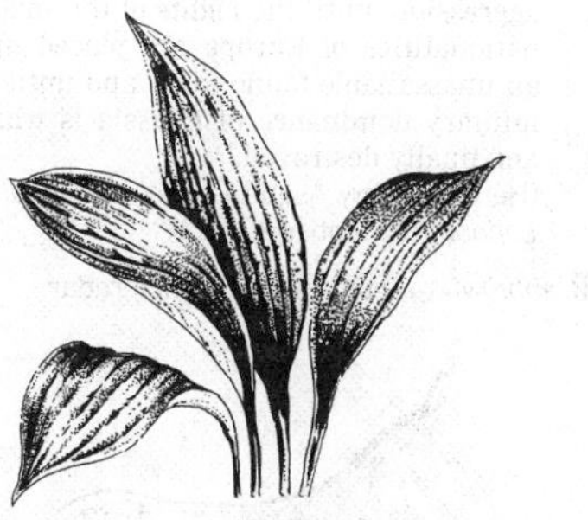
aspidistra

as·par·tic ac·id /ə spaártik-/ *n* an amino acid occurring in many plant proteins that can also be produced by humans and other animals. Formula: $C_4H_7NO_4$. [Mid-19C. < French *aspartique* < Latin *asparagus* (see ASPARAGUS)]

A.S.P.C.A. *abbr* American Society for the Prevention of Cruelty to Animals

as·pect /á spèkt/ *n* **1.** ONE SIDE OR PART a facet, phase, or part of a whole ○ *consider the various aspects of the problem* **2.** APPEARANCE the appearance of something to the mind or eye ○ *The stone has a greenish aspect in this light.* **3.** VIEWPOINT a view or point of view ○ *the aspect of the mountain from the river* ○ *seeing life from a new aspect* **4.** EXPOSURE exposure to a particular direction, weather, or other influence ○ *This plant requires a sunny aspect.* **5.** ASTRON ANGLE BETWEEN ASTRONOMICAL OBJECTS the apparent angular separation of two astronomical objects, especially as observed from Earth **6.** ASTROL POSITIONS OF PLANETS in astrology, the relative positions of the stars and planets, believed to influence human affairs **7.** GRAM GRAMMATICAL CATEGORY a grammatical category of verbs that considers qualities of action independent of tense, e.g., the progressive and perfect aspects in English [14C. < Latin *aspectus*, past participle of *aspicere* < *specere* "look at"]

as·pect ra·tio *n* **1.** in television and the movies, the ratio of the width of the picture on the screen to its height. This ratio was 4:3 until the 1950s, when it increased in the movies to 1.85:1 in the United States and 5:3 in Europe. **2.** the ratio of the length of an aircraft's wing to the mean distance between the front and back edge of the wing. Aircraft operating at low speeds, e.g., gliders, need a high aspect ratio and have long narrow wings while for supersonic flight a low aspect ratio is created by swinging the wings back.

as·pec·tu·al /a spékchoo əl/ *adj* relating to the aspects of a verb

as·pen /áspən/ (*plural* **-pens** or *same*) *n* a poplar with leaves that rustle and flutter in the breeze. Native to: northern United States, Europe. Latin name: *Populus tremens* or *Populus tremuloides*. [14C. < *asp* "aspen" < Germanic]

As·pen /áspən/ city in the Rocky Mountains, at an altitude of 7,900 ft./2,410 m, in west central Colorado. It is a popular ski resort. Population: 5,902 (2002 estimate).

As·per·ger's syn·drome /ás pùrjərz-/, **As·per·ger syn·drome** /ás pùrjər-/ *n* a severe developmental disorder, similar to autism, characterized by difficulties with social relations, strange behavior patterns, concentration on details of objects, and often a heightened ability to memorize [After Hans *Asperger* (1906–80), Austrian pediatrician]

as·per·ges /ə spúrjiz/ *n* a religious ceremony of the Roman Catholic Church in which holy water is sprinkled over the altar, clergy, and congregation before High Mass [Late 16C. < Latin, "you will sprinkle," the first word of the rite]

as·per·gill *n* CHR same as **aspergillum**

as·per·gil·la CHR plural of **aspergillum**

as·per·gil·lo·sis /àspərji lṓssiss/ *n* a disease affecting mucous membranes, lungs, and sometimes bones that is caused by infection with the fungus *Aspergillus*

as·per·gil·lum /àspər jílləm/ (*plural* **-la** /-lə/ or **-lums**), **as·per·gill** /àspər jíl/ *n* a brush or perforated container for sprinkling holy water [Mid-17C. < modern Latin, "little sprinkler" < Latin *aspergere* "to sprinkle"]

as·per·i·ty /a spérrətee/ (*plural* **-ties**) *n* **1.** HARSHNESS OR SEVERITY harshness or severity of manner or tone (*formal*) **2.** HARDSHIP something that is hard to bear because of its harshness or severity (*formal*) **3.** ROUGHNESS the roughness of a surface (*literary*) **4.** PHYS AREA WHERE SURFACES TOUCH a region of contact between two load-bearing flat surfaces [13C. Via French *aspérité* < Latin *asperitas* < *asper* "rough"]

a·sper·mi·a /ay spúrmee ə/ *n* a medical condition in which no spermatozoa are present in the seminal fluid [Mid-19C. < A³ + Greek *sperma* "seed"] —**a·sper·mic** *adj*

as·per·sion /ə spúrzh'n, -sh'n/ *n* **1.** a statement that attacks somebody's character or reputation (*often used in the plural*) ○ *cast aspersions on his integrity* **2.** the making of defamatory remarks

as·per·so·ri·um /àspər sáwree əm/ (*plural* **-ri·a** /-ree ə/) *n* CHR same as **aspergillum** [Mid-19C. < medieval Latin < Latin *aspers-*, past participle of *aspergere* "to sprinkle"]

as·phalt /ás fàwlt/ *n* **1.** SEMISOLID BITUMINOUS SUBSTANCE a brownish black solid or semisolid substance. Source: oil-bearing rocks, byproduct of petroleum distillation. Use: paving, waterproofing, fungicides. **2.** MATERIAL USED FOR SURFACING ROADS paving material composed mainly of asphalt and gravel that hardens on cooling and is used for making roads and sidewalks ■ *vt* (**-phalt·ed, -phalt·ing, -phalts**) COVER SOMETHING WITH ASPHALT to surface a roadway, sidewalk, or other area with asphalt [14C. Via late Latin < Greek *asphaltos*] —**as·phal·tic** /as fáwltik/ *adj*

as·phal·tite /as fáwl tìt, às-/ *n* a solid organic compound resembling asphalt and belonging to a group that occurs naturally in veins and beds below ground

as·phalt jun·gle *n* a big city or urban area with much paving and little natural landscape

a·spher·ic /ay sfeérik, ay sférr-/, **a·spher·i·cal** /-k'l/ *adj* not perfectly spherical

as·pho·del /ásfə dèl/ (*plural* **-dels** or *same*) *n* **1.** FLOWERING PLANT a perennial plant of the lily family. Flowers: white, pink, yellow, in clusters. Native to: southern Europe. Genera: *Asphodelus* or *Asphodeline*. **2.** PLANT RESEMBLING ASPHODEL a plant similar to the true asphodel, e.g., bog asphodel **3.** MYTHOL FLOWER OF HADES in Greek mythology, the flower of Hades that was sacred to Persephone [15C. Via Latin < Greek *asphodelos*]

as·phyx·i·a /as fíksee ə, əs-/ *n* suffocation as a result of physical blockage of the airway or inhalation of toxic gases, causing a lack of oxygen and unconsciousness [Early 18C. Via modern Latin < Greek *asphuxia* "lack of pulse" < *sphuxis* "heartbeat" < *sphuzein* "to throb"] —**as·phyx·i·ant** *adj, n*

as·phyx·i·ate /as fíksee àyt, əs-/ (**-at·ed, -at·ing, -ates**) *vti* to deprive a person or animal of oxygen, or be deprived of oxygen, usually leading to unconsciousness or death —**as·phyx·i·a·tion** /as fìksee áysh'n, əs-/ *n* —**as·phyx·i·a·tor** *n*

as·pic /áspik/ *n* a jelly made from meat or fish stock and often used to form a mold of fish, meat, eggs, or vegetables [Late 18C. < French, "asp," alteration of Old French *aspe* (see ASP)]

as·pi·dis·tra /àspi dístrə/ *n* a common houseplant of the lily family with large glossy leaves. Flowers: small, brownish. Native to: Asia. Genus: *Aspidistra*. [Early 19C. < modern Latin < Greek *aspid-*, stem of *aspis* "shield"; from the shape of the leaves]

as·pi·rant /áspərənt, ə spírənt/ *n* somebody who is hoping to achieve distinction or advancement ○ *an aspirant to the presidency* ■ *adj* seeking or hoping to attain something

SYNONYMS See ***candidate***.

as·pi·rate *vt* /áspə ràyt/ (**-rat·ed, -rat·ing, -rates**) **1.** PRONOUNCE WHILE BREATHING OUT to pronounce a sound or word while breathing out, e.g., the letter "h" at the beginning of words such as "house" and "hat" in standard English **2.** INHALE SOMETHING to inhale something, especially a liquid, into the lungs **3.** REMOVE LIQUID to remove liquid or gas by suction, especially from a body cavity (*technical*) ○ *using a syringe to aspirate the fluid from the cyst* ■ *n* /áspərət/ **1.** BREATHY LETTER a sound pronounced while breathing out, e.g., the sound of the letter "h" at the beginning of many English words **2.** MATTER REMOVED matter removed by aspirating ■ *adj* PRONOUNCED WITH BREATH pronounced while breathing out [Late 17C. < Latin *aspirat-*, past participle of *aspirare* "breathe toward" < *spirare* "breathe"]

as·pi·ra·tion /àspə ráysh'n/ *n* **1.** AMBITION a desire or ambition to achieve something **2.** BREATHY PRONUNCIATION pronunciation accompanied by breathing out **3.** SUCTION the withdrawal by suction of fluids or gases from the body or a body cavity **4.** INHALATION drawing matter into the lungs along with the breath —**as·pir·a·to·ry** /ə spírə tàwree/ *adj*

as·pi·ra·tion·al /àspi ráyshən'l, -shnəl/ *adj* showing a desire or ambition to achieve something, especially self-improvement or material success ○ *the aspirational working class*

as·pi·ra·tion pneu·mo·nia *n* pneumonia caused by foreign matter such as food entering the lungs

as·pi·ra·tor /áspə ràytər/ *n* an apparatus for drawing out fluids or gases from the body or a body cavity by suction

as·pire /ə spír/ (**-pired, -pir·ing, -pires**) *vi* **1.** to seek to attain a goal ○ *aspire to public office* **2.** to soar to a great height (*literary*) [14C. < Latin *aspirare* "breathe toward" (see ASPIRATE)] —**as·pir·er** *n* —**as·pir·ing** *adj*

as·pi·rin /áspirin, -prin/ (*plural* **-rins** or *same*) *n* **1.** a drug that relieves pain and inflammation, lowers fever, and reduces blood clotting **2.** a pill containing aspirin [Late 19C. < German < contraction of *acetylierte Spirsäure* "acetylated spiraeic acid" (former name of salicylic acid)]

~~**asprin**~~ incorrect spelling of **aspirin**

a·squint /ə skwínt/ *adv* from the corner of the eye, as if suspiciously

As·quith /áskwith/, **Herbert Henry** (1852–1928) British prime minister (1908–16). His government introduced retirement pensions and national insurance, and passed the Parliament Act (1911) that removed the power of veto from the House of Lords. See table at **prime minister**

"We shall never sheath the sword which we have not lightly drawn until Belgium recovers in full measure all and more than she has sacrificed, until France is adequately secured against the menace of

aggression, until the rights of the smaller nationalities of Europe are placed upon an unassailable foundation, and until the military dominance of Prussia is wholly and finally destroyed."
[Herbert Henry Asquith, *Speech, Guildhall, London*; November 9, 1914]

ASR *abbr* AVIAT airport surveillance radar

ass

ass[1] /ass/ *n* **1.** an animal resembling a small horse with long ears, sometimes used as a beast of burden. The donkey is a domesticated descendant of the wild ass. Genus: *Equus*. **2.** an offensive term that deliberately insults somebody's intelligence, consideration for others, or general value (*slang insult*) [Old English *assa*, via Celtic < Latin *asinus*]

ass[2] /ass/ *n* **1.** an offensive term for the buttocks or anus **2.** a highly offensive term for sexual intercourse (*taboo*) [Mid-19C. Euphemistic alteration of ARSE] ◇ **cover your ass** a highly offensive phrase meaning to behave in a way that ensures you will not be blamed for something later (*taboo*) ◇ **haul ass** a highly offensive phrase meaning to move or start to move quickly (*taboo*) ◇ **have somebody's ass in a sling** *or* **bind** a highly offensive phrase meaning to get somebody into trouble (*taboo*) ◇ **kick (some) ass** a highly offensive phrase meaning to behave aggressively or ruthlessly in order to achieve a goal (*taboo*) ◇ **kiss ass** a highly offensive phrase meaning to flatter or obediently carry out the orders of a superior in order to gain favor (*taboo*) ◇ **not know your ass from your elbow** a highly offensive phrase meaning to be very ignorant (*taboo*)

As·sad /aa sa'ad/, **Bashar al-** (*b.* 1965) president of Syria (2000–). The second son of Hafez al-Assad, he studied ophthalmology in Damascus and London (1988–94) before reaching the rank of colonel at a military academy in 1999.

As·sad, Hafez al- (1928–2000) Syrian politician. He served as minister of defense (1966–70) before being elected president of Syria (1971–2000).

as·sa·gai *n* ARMS another spelling of **assegai**

as·sail /ə sáyl/ (**-sailed, -sail·ing, -sails**) *vt* **1.** to attack somebody vigorously with words or actions ○ *assailed by furious criticism* **2.** to overwhelm the mind or senses of somebody ○ *"Low growls and angry snarls assailed our ears on every side."* (Edgar Rice Burroughs, *The Gods of Mars*; 1913) [13C. Via Old French *asaill-*, stem of *asalir* < assumed Vulgar Latin *assalire* "leap at" < Latin *salire* "leap"] —**as·sail·a·ble** *adj* —**as·sail·er** *n* —**as·sail·ment** *n*

as·sail·ant /ə sáylənt/ *n* somebody who violently attacks somebody else, usually causing physical injury

As·sam /a sám/ state in northeastern India. Capital: Dispur. Population: 26,638,407 (2001). Area: 30,285 sq. mi./78,438 sq. km. Language: Assamese.

As·sam·ese /àssə méez, -méess/ (*plural same*) *n* **1.** somebody who comes from Assam, India **2.** an Indic language spoken in Assam and in Bangladesh that shares a script with Bangla. Native speakers: 11 million. —**As·sam·ese** *adj*

~~**assasin**~~ incorrect spelling of **assassin**

as·sas·sin /ə sássʼn/ *n* a killer, especially of a political leader or other public figure [Mid-16C. Via French < Arabic *ḥašāšīn* "hashish users"]

as·sas·si·nate /ə sássʼn àyt/ (**-nat·ed, -nat·ing, -nates**) *vt* **1.** to kill somebody, especially a political leader or other public figure, by a sudden violent attack **2.** to harm or destroy something such as somebody's reputation maliciously or treacherously —**as·sas·si·na·tor** *n*

SYNONYMS See ***kill***[1].

as·sas·si·na·tion /ə sàssʼn áyshʼn/ *n* **1.** the killing of somebody, especially a political leader or other public figure, by a sudden violent attack ○ *an unsuccessful assassination attempt* **2.** the destruction of something such as somebody's reputation by malicious or treacherous means

as·sas·sin bug *n* a large long-legged insect with powerful mouthparts that kills and sucks the blood of other animals. Family: Reduviidae.

As·sa·teague Is·land /ássə teeg-/ barrier island in the Atlantic Ocean off the US coast, divided between Maryland and Virginia. It is noted for its wild ponies, whose young are traditionally rounded up each July. Area: 62 sq. mi./161 sq. km.

as·sault /ə sáwlt/ *n* **1.** PHYSICAL OR VERBAL ATTACK a violent physical or verbal attack **2.** LAW THREAT OF BODILY HARM an unlawful threat or attempt to do violence or harm to somebody else **3.** LAW RAPE the crime of raping somebody **4.** ATTEMPT TO DESTROY SOMETHING a campaign or series of actions that aims to challenge or destroy something ○ *The proposals are under assault by various special interest groups.* ■ *vt* (**-sault·ed, -sault·ing, -saults**) **1.** ATTACK SOMEBODY to attack somebody physically or verbally in a violent way **2.** MIL MAKE MILITARY ATTACK to attack a place with a military force [13C. Via Old French *assaut* < assumed Vulgar Latin *assaltus*, past participle of *assalire* (see ASSAIL)]

as·sault and bat·ter·y *n* the crime of doing bodily harm to somebody

as·sault course *n UK* MIL same as **obstacle course** (sense 1)

as·sault·er /ə sáwltər/ *n* **1.** POLICE OFFICER TRAINED IN WEAPONS a member of a police or FBI SWAT or hostage rescue team **2.** MIL ATTACKER OF ENEMY POSITION a soldier or other fighter who takes part in a military assault on an enemy position **3.** LAW VIOLENT ATTACKER somebody who attacks another person physically or verbally in a violent way

as·saul·tive /ə sáwltiv/ *adj* extremely aggressive or disposed to attack

as·sault weap·on *n* a weapon designed for use in warfare, especially when used in noncombat situations such as terrorism

as·say *n* /á sày, a sáy/ **1.** ANALYSIS OF SOMETHING an examination and analysis of something **2.** CHEM CHEMICAL ANALYSIS OF SUBSTANCE chemical testing carried out to determine the composition of a substance or the concentration of its components **3.** SAMPLE OF MATERIAL a sample of material for analysis **4.** ATTEMPT AT SOMETHING an attempt to do something (*archaic*) ■ *vt* /a sáy, á sày/ (**-sayed, -say·ing, -says**) **1.** EXAMINE SOMETHING to examine or test something with a view to evaluating it **2.** ATTEMPT SOMETHING to make an attempt to do something (*formal*) **3.** CHEM ANALYZE SUBSTANCE to analyze a substance such as an ore in order to discover its components and their concentration [14C. < Old French *assai* "test" and its source *assaier* "to test," variant of *essaier* (see ESSAY)] —**as·say·a·ble** /a sáyəb'l/ *adj* —**as·say·er** *n*

ass-back·ward *adj, adv* an offensive term meaning wrong, unusual, or irregular, or in a wrong, unusual, or irregular way (*slang*) —**ass-back·wards** *adv*

as·se·gai /ássə gī/, **as·sa·gai** *n* a slender hardwood spear with an iron tip, used especially by the Zulu peoples of southern Africa [Early 17C. Via obsolete French *azagaie* < Berber *zaḡāya* "spear"]

as·sem·blage /ə sémblij/ *n* **1.** a gathering of things or people at one point ○ *an assemblage of world-famous actors* **2.** a work of art made from a collection of different objects

as·sem·blag·ist /ə sémblijist/ *n* a sculptor who creates assemblages

as·sem·ble /ə sémb'l/ (**-bled, -bling, -bles**) *v* **1.** *vt* to fit the parts of something together to make a finished whole ○ *assembled a model* **2.** *vti* to bring people or things together, or gather together in one place ○ *A crowd began to assemble.* [13C. Via French *assembler* < assumed Vulgar Latin *assimulare* "put together" < Latin *simul* "together"] —**as·sem·bled** *adj*

SYNONYMS See ***collect***[1].

as·sem·bler /ə sémblər/ *n* **1.** a person, machine, or company that puts together the parts of a machine or piece of equipment when it is being built **2.** COMPUT a computer program that converts assembly language into machine language **3.** COMPUT same as **assembly language**

as·sem·bly /ə sémblee/ (*plural* **-blies**) *n* **1.** FITTING COMPONENTS TOGETHER the putting together of parts to make a finished product **2.** COMPONENTS a set of components before they are put together to make a finished product **3.** SCHOOL MEETING a regular formal gathering of all the students in a school for a special program **4.** *also* **As·sem·bly** LEGISLATIVE MEETING a group of people meeting as a deliberative or lawmaking body **5.** GATHERING the coming together of people for a common purpose ○ *freedom of assembly* **6.** MILITARY GATHERING the gathering together of a military unit prior to an event or operation **7.** MILITARY SIGNAL a signal for soldiers or other personnel to gather **8.** COMPUT TRANSLATION OF COMPUTER LANGUAGE the translation of assembly language into machine language [14C. < French *assemblée*, feminine past participle of *assembler* (see ASSEMBLE)]

as·sem·bly lan·guage *n* a low-level computer language consisting of mnemonic codes and symbolic addresses corresponding to machine-language instructions

as·sem·bly line *n* a series of workstations at which individual steps in the assembly of a product are carried out by workers or machines as the product is moved along

as·sem·bly·man /ə sémbleemən/ (*plural* **-men** /-mən/) *n* a man who is a member of a legislative assembly

As·sem·bly of God *n* an evangelical Christian Church founded in the United States in 1914

as·sem·bly·per·son /ə sémbli pùrss'n/ (*plural* **-per·sons** or **-peo·ple** /-pèep'l/) *n* a member of a legislative assembly

as·sem·bly·wom·an /ə sémblee wòomman/ (*plural* **-wom·en** /-wìmmin/) *n* a woman who is a member of a legislative assembly

as·sent /ə sént/ *n* a formal expression of agreement or acceptance ■ *vi* (**-sent·ed, -sent·ing, -sents**) to accept a concept or course of action formally ○ *She will never assent to their marriage.* [13C. Via French < Latin *assentire* "feel toward" < *sentire* "feel"] —**as·sent·er** *n* —**as·sent·ing·ly** *adv*

SPELLCHECK See ***ascent***.

SYNONYMS See ***agree***.

as·sent·ed /ə séntəd/ *adj* describes securities that are bought or held with the understanding that proposed changes may affect their status or number

as·sen·ti·ent /ə sénshee ənt/ (*formal*) *adj* agreeing or accepting ■ *n* a person or party that agrees [Mid-19C. < Latin *assentient-*, present participle of *assentire* (see ASSENT)]

as·sent·ing /ə sénting/ *adj* FIN same as **assented**

as·sert /ə súrt/ (**-sert·ed, -sert·ing, -serts**) *v* **1.** *vt* STATE SOMETHING to state something as being true ○ *She asserted that she had never seen the man before.* **2.** *vt* INSIST ON RIGHTS to insist on or exercise your rights ○ *He asserted his Fifth Amendment rights and refused to testify.* **3. as·sert your·self** *vr* BEHAVE FORCEFULLY to exercise your power, influence, and prerogatives in an obvious way ○ *The new management quickly began to assert itself after the takeover.* **4.** *vr* BECOME KNOWN OR EFFECTIVE to start to have an effect or become noticeable ○ *The relationship went well until their age difference began to assert itself.* [Early 17C. < Latin *assert-*, past participle of *asserere* "join to" < *serere* "join, connect"] —**as·sert·a·ble** *adj* —**as·sert·er** *n*

as·ser·tion /ə súrsh'n/ *n* **1.** a strong statement that something is true **2.** the act of stating emphatically that something is true ○ *the assertion of their rights*

as·ser·tive /ə súrtiv/ *adj* **1.** confident in stating a position or claim ○ *Modern education encourages the assertive student.* **2.** forcefully strong and noticeable ○ *an assertive flavor* —**as·ser·tive·ly** *adv* —**as·ser·tive·ness** *n*

USAGE See *aggressive.*

as·ser·tive·ness train·ing *n* teaching people how to overcome shyness and assert themselves

as·sess /ə séss/ (**-sessed, -sess·ing, -sess·es**) *vt* **1. JUDGE SOMETHING** to examine something in order to judge or evaluate it ○ *not enough information to assess whether the event occurred* **2. DETERMINE AMOUNT** to calculate a value based on various factors ○ *Insurance adjusters are assessing the damage.* **3.** FIN **CALCULATE VALUE FOR TAX** to calculate the value of something in order to establish how much tax must be paid ○ *property assessed at $300,000* **4.** LAW **CHARGE AS AMOUNT** to present a demand for payment, e.g., of a fine or penalty ○ *We were assessed $750 in court costs.* [15C. < Old French *assesser* < Latin *assess-*, past participle of *assidere* "sit beside" < *sedere* "sit"] —**as·sess·a·ble** *adj*

as·sessed val·ue *n* the value of a property that serves as the basis for tax calculation

as·sess·ment /ə séssmənt/ *n* **1. EVALUATION** a judgment about something based on an understanding of the situation ○ *a fair assessment of the project* **2. PROPERTY VALUATION** a calculation of the value of something, made especially for tax or insurance purposes **3. AMOUNT CALCULATED** an amount assessed, e.g., on property **4. EDUCATIONAL EVALUATION** a method of evaluating student performance and attainment

as·ses·sor /ə séssər/ *n* **1.** somebody who calculates amounts to be paid or assessed, especially for tax or insurance purposes **2.** a judge's or magistrate's assistant in some jurisdictions, typically somebody with specialized expertise in a subject

as·set /á sèt/ *n* **1. SOMEBODY OR SOMETHING USEFUL** somebody or something that is useful and contributes to the success of something ○ *Good health is a great asset.* **2. VALUABLE THING** a property to which a value can be assigned ■ **as·sets** *npl* **1. OWNED ITEMS** the property that is owned by a person or organization **2.** LAW **SEIZABLE PROPERTY** the property of a person that can be taken by law for the settlement of debts or that forms part of a dead person's estate **3.** ACCT **BALANCE SHEET ITEMS** the items on a balance sheet that constitute the total value of an organization [Mid-16C. Via Anglo-Norman *assetz* "sufficient goods" (to settle an estate) < Latin *ad satis* "sufficiency"]

as·set de·mand *n* the desire of a person or organization to acquire money, property, or other assets

as·set-strip·ping *n* the practice of buying a company cheaply and making a profit by selling all its assets individually —**as·set-strip·per** *n*

as·sev·er·ate /ə sévvə ràyt/ (**-at·ed, -at·ing, -ates**) *vt* to state something earnestly or solemnly (*formal*) [Mid-16C. < Latin *asseverat-*, past participle of *asseverare* < *severus* "serious"] —**as·sev·er·a·tion** /ə sèvvə ráysh'n/ *n*

ass·hole /áss hòl/ *n* **1.** a highly offensive term that deliberately insult's somebody's value or importance (*taboo insult*) **2.** a highly offensive term for the anus (*taboo*)

as·sib·i·late /ə síbbi làyt/ (**-lat·ed, -lat·ing, -lates**) *v* **1.** *vt* to utter something with a hissing sound like that of the letter "s" or "z" **2.** *vi* to be transformed into a hissing sound (**sibilant**) [Mid-19C. < Latin *assibilat-*, past participle of *assibilare* "hiss at" < *sibilare* (see SIBILANT)] —**as·sib·i·la·tion** /ə sìbbi láysh'n/ *n*

as·si·du·i·ty /àssi dóo ətee/ *n* great care and attention in doing something ■ **as·si·du·i·ties** *npl* constant attentiveness shown toward somebody

as·sid·u·ous /ə síjjoo əss/ *adj* showing persistent and hard-working effort in doing something [Mid-16C. < Latin *assiduus* < *assidere* (see ASSESS), in a late sense "apply yourself"] —**as·sid·u·ous·ly** *adv* —**as·sid·u·ous·ness** *n*

SYNONYMS See *careful.*

as·sign /ə sín/ *vt* (**-signed, -sign·ing, -signs**) **1. GIVE SOMEBODY TASK OR DUTY** to give somebody a job to do ○ *assign homework* **2. SEND SOMEBODY TO DO SOMETHING** to send somebody to work in a particular place or with a particular group of people ○ *I assigned him to the maintenance department.* **3. DETERMINE QUALITY OF SOMETHING** to determine that somebody or something has a particular quality, name, use, or category ○ *The words are assigned a rating based on frequency.* **4. SET SOMETHING ASIDE FOR SOMETHING** to designate something for a particular use ○ *The new radio station has been assigned a frequency by the authorities.* **5.** MIL **ORDER SOLDIER** to put a soldier or military unit under a particular command **6.** LAW **TRANSFER PROPERTY** to transfer property or rights to another person by an official act **7.** COMPUT **PLACE VALUE** to designate a value for a computer memory location corresponding to a named variable ■ *n* **1.** LAW same as **assignee** (sense 1) **2.** LAW same as **assignee** (sense 2) [14C. Via French < Latin *assignare* < *signare* "mark out, designate" < *signum* "mark"] —**as·sign·a·bil·i·ty** /ə sìnə bílləteе/ *n* —**as·sign·a·ble** *adj* —**as·sign·a·bly** *adv* —**as·sign·er** *n* —**as·sign·or** *n*

as·sig·na·tion /àssig náysh'n/ *n* **1.** an appointment to meet with a lover, especially secretly **2.** the act of giving somebody a specific job or designating something for a specific use **3.** LAW same as **assignment** (sense 5) [14C. Via French < Latin *assignation-* < *assignare* (see ASSIGN)]

as·signed coun·sel /ə sìnd-/ *n* a lawyer who has been appointed by the court to represent a defendant

as·signed risk *n* a risk assigned to one of a pool of insurers by state law, the risk being otherwise unacceptable

as·sign·ee /ə sì neé, à sī-/ *n* **1. SOMEBODY RECEIVING RIGHT OVER PROPERTY** somebody to whom a right over property is given or transferred **2. PROXY** somebody who is appointed to act for another **3. INHERITOR** a person or a generation that inherits something, e.g., a set of values, a culture, or a group of problems

as·sign·ment /ə sínmənt/ *n* **1. TASK** a task that is assigned or undertaken ○ *All team members have received their assignments.* **2. APPOINTMENT** a position, duty, or job for which somebody is chosen ○ *an assignment in Japan* **3. PROCESS OF ASSIGNING** the process of giving a value, use, task, or position to somebody or something **4.** LAW **LEGAL TRANSFER DOCUMENT** a document such as a deed that effects a legal transfer of rights **5.** LAW **LEGAL TRANSFER** the transfer of a right in or over property to another person

SYNONYMS See *job.*

as·sim·i·late /ə símmi làyt/ (**-lat·ed, -lat·ing, -lates**) *v* **1.** *vti* SOC SCI **INTEGRATE** to integrate somebody into a larger group, so that differences are minimized or eliminated, or become integrated in this way **2.** *vt* **ABSORB INFORMATION** to integrate new knowledge or information with what is already known **3.** *vt* PHYSIOL **ABSORB NUTRIENTS** to incorporate digested food materials into the cells and tissues of the body ○ *assimilate protein* **4.** *vti* PHON **MAKE SPEECH SOUND LIKE ADJACENT SOUND** to make a speech sound similar to an adjacent sound, or to become similar to an adjacent sound [15C. < Latin *assimilat-*, past participle of *assimilare* "make the same" < *similis* "like"] —**as·sim·i·la·ble** /-ləb'l/ *adj* —**as·sim·i·la·tor** *n* —**as·sim·i·la·to·ry** /-lə tàwree/ *adj*

as·sim·i·la·tion /ə sìmmi láysh'n/ *n* **1. ACT OF BECOMING PART OF SOMETHING** the process of becoming part of or more like something greater **2. INTEGRATION INTO GROUP** the process in which one group takes on the cultural and other traits of a larger group **3. LEARNING PROCESS** the integration of new knowledge or information with what is already known **4.** PHYSIOL **NUTRIENT CONVERSION** the incorporation of nutrients into the cells and tissues of plants and animals involving digestion, photosynthesis, and root absorption **5.** PHON **SPEECH SOUND CHANGE** the changing of a speech sound under the influence of an adjacent sound

as·sim·i·la·tion·ism /ə sìmmi láysh'n ìzzəm/ *n* a policy of assimilating differing ethnic or cultural groups —**as·sim·i·la·tion·ist** *n, adj*

As·sin·i·boin /ə sínnə bòyn/ (*plural same* or **-boins**), **As·sin·i·boine** (*plural same* or **-boines**) *n* **1.** a member of a Native North American people who once lived in the northern Great Plains, and who now live mainly in Saskatchewan, Alberta, and Montana **2.** a Siouan language spoken in southern and western Canada and in Montana by the Assiniboin [Late 17C. Via Canadian French < Ojibwa *assini:-pwa:n* "stone Sioux"] —**As·sin·i·boin** *adj*

As·sin·i·boine /ə sínni bòyn/ river flowing from southeastern Saskatchewan, Canada, southwestward into Manitoba and the Red River at Winnipeg. Length: 665 mi./1,070 km.

As·si·si /ə seé seé, -zeé/ town in central Italy, famous as the birthplace of St. Francis in 1182. The Basilica of St. Francis suffered considerable earthquake damage in 1997. Population: 25,304 (2001).

As·si·si em·broi·der·y *n* embroidery in which designs are outlined, some design areas are left open, and the background is filled in with cross-stitch

as·sist /ə síst/ *vti* (**-sist·ed, -sist·ing, -sists**) **HELP SOMEBODY** to help somebody to do or accomplish something ○ *a program to assist new parents* ■ *n* **1. HELP BY TEAM PLAYER** an act by a player in a sport that enables a teammate to score or achieve a successful defensive play **2. ACT OF HELPING** an act or series of actions helping another person [15C. Via French < Latin *assistere* "stand beside" < *sistere* < *stare* "to stand"] —**as·sist·er** *n*

as·sis·tance /ə sístənss/ *n* help given or made available to another ○ *technical assistance*

as·sis·tant /ə sístənt/ *n* **HELPER** somebody who works to somebody else's instructions, often in a paid capacity ■ *adj* **1. HELPING** subordinate to or helping another person ○ *an assistant teacher* **2. HELPFUL** serving to help or be useful

SYNONYMS ***assistant, helper, deputy, aide***

CORE MEANING: somebody who helps another person in carrying out a task

assistant somebody who works to somebody else's instructions, often in a paid capacity ○ *Each supervisor usually works with an assistant.* ○ *She was appointed assistant to the Director of Education.* **helper** somebody who helps with something, often in an informal or voluntary capacity ○ *volunteer helpers* ○ *He had a helper in the shape of his daughter, Celestine.* **deputy** an assistant who is authorized to act in a superior's place ○ *decided to appoint a deputy to take over some tasks* ○ *a committee headed by a chairperson with three deputies with different responsibilities* **aide** an assistant to somebody in public office or to somebody providing a professional service, who may also offer advice ○ *a teacher's aide* ○ *a close aide to the President*

as·sis·tant pro·fes·sor *n* a member of a college or university faculty ranking typically above an instructor and below an associate professor

as·sis·tant·ship /ə sístənt shìp/ *n* an academic position that provides financial support in exchange for teaching or research services, typically for a graduate student

as·sist·ed con·cep·tion /ə sìstəd-/ *n* MED same as **assisted reproduction**

as·sist·ed liv·ing *n* **1.** the provision of independent residential care in a home environment for seniors needing some help with their daily living and medications **2.** a freestanding facility, or a part of a nursing home, where residents live with varying degrees of independence

as·sist·ed re·pro·duc·tion, **as·sist·ed con·cep·tion** *n* the use of a technique such as in vitro fertilization to aid human reproduction in cases where this is problematic

as·sist·ed su·i·cide *n* the suicide of a patient, usually somebody who is terminally ill, that is aided by a caregiver or especially a physician, by the express wish and consent of the patient

as·size /ə síz/ *n* a judicial inquest, or the verdict of the jurors involved ■ **as·siz·es** *npl* periodic judicial proceedings held until 1971 in the counties of England and Wales and presided over by itinerant judges. They were replaced by the Crown Courts. [14C. < Old French *assise*, past participle of *asseoir* "settle" < Latin *assidere* (see ASSESS)]

ass kis·ser *n* a highly offensive term for somebody who flatters or obediently carries out the orders of a superior in order to gain favor (*taboo*) —**ass-kiss·ing** *n*

assn., **assoc.** *abbr* association

as·so·ci·ate *v* /ə sṓshee àyt, ə sṓssee-/ (**-at·ed, -at·ing,**

-ates) **1.** *vt* CONNECT THINGS IN MIND to connect one thing with another in the mind **2.** *vi* PASS TIME WITH SOMEBODY to spend time together with somebody ○ *Before the race she associated only with other skiers.* **3.** *vi* MIX SOCIALLY OR PROFESSIONALLY to be involved with somebody or something in a personal or professional capacity ○ *associates with members of the legal profession* **4. as·so·ci·ate your·self** *vr* BE CONNECTED WITH SOMEBODY OR SOMETHING to allow yourself to be connected with somebody or something, or voluntarily connect yourself with somebody or something ○ *refused to associate herself with the petition* ■ *n* /ə sṓshee ət, -àyt, ə sṓssee-/ **1.** PARTNER a partner in a business or other undertaking ○ *my associates in the firm* **2.** CONNECTED PERSON somebody who is known to spend time with another person ○ *I couldn't identify any of his associates.* **3.** MEMBER a member of an organization such as a club or a law firm, especially a newly licensed lawyer, who does not have full status, rights, or privileges **4.** HOLDER OF DEGREE a holder of an associate degree ■ *adj* /ə sṓshee ət, -àyt, ə sṓssee-/ **1.** ALLIED joined with others on an equal or nearly equal basis **2.** SECONDARY with subordinate status or less than full membership in an organization ○ *an associate member* [14C. < Latin *associat-*, past participle of *associare* < *socius* "ally, companion"] **—as·so·ci·a·ble** /ə sṓshee əb'l, -shəb'l/ *adj* **—as·so·ci·ate·ship** *n* ◇ **be associated with somebody** *or* **something 1.** to be involved with somebody or something considered undesirable **2.** to join a person or people in a professional relationship, or belong to an organization in a professional capacity **3.** to connect with or result from something else ○ *The swelling is associated with inflammation of the joint.*

as·so·ci·ate de·gree *n* a degree earned on completion of a two-year program of study at a community college, junior college, technical school, or other institution of higher education

as·so·ci·at·ed state·hood /ə sṓshee aytid-/ *n* the status of several former British colonies, mostly in the Caribbean, after dissolution of direct rule from Britain but before full independence

as·so·ci·ate jus·tice *n* **1.** a judge of a court, other than the presiding judge or chief justice **2.** a judge on any of several high state courts

as·so·ci·ate pro·fes·sor *n* a member of a college or university faculty ranking typically above an assistant professor and below a professor

as·so·ci·a·tion /ə sṓssee áysh'n, ə sṓshee-/ *n* **1.** GROUP a group of people or organizations joined together for a purpose ○ *form an association to represent dairy farmers* **2.** CONNECTION a linking or joining of people or things ○ *She hasn't profited from her association with him.* **3.** COMING TOGETHER coming together and social interaction between people ○ *freedom of association* **4.** PSYCHOL PSYCHOLOGICAL CONNECTION a connection of ideas, memories, or feelings with each other, or with events **5.** LINKED IDEA a thought, idea, or feeling that is linked with an event **6.** CHEM GROUPING OF MOLECULES the formation of groups of loosely bound molecules **7.** ECOL GROUPING OF ORGANISMS a major ecological community dominated by one or more species, e.g., oak and hickory in a deciduous forest **—as·so·ci·a·tion·al** *adj*

as·so·ci·a·tion foot·ball *n* UK same as **soccer** (*formal*)

as·so·ci·a·tion·ism /ə sṓssee áysh'n ìzzəm, ə sṓshee-/ *n* a psychological theory that explains complex thoughts and feelings in terms of associations with simpler elements **—as·so·ci·a·tion·ist** *n* **—as·so·ci·a·tion·is·tic** /ə sṓssee àysh'n ístik, ə sṓshee-/ *adj*

as·so·ci·a·tive /ə sṓshee àytiv, ə sṓssee-, -ətiv/ *adj* **1.** relating to the association of ideas, events, or experiences **2.** MATH, LOGIC giving the same result irrespective of the order taken, thus since a + (b + c) = (a + b) + c, addition is associative. Multiplication is also associative but subtraction and division are not. **—as·so·ci·a·tive·ly** *adv*

as·so·ci·a·tive learn·ing *n* a learning process in which separate ideas and beliefs are linked in order to increase learning effectiveness

as·so·ci·a·tive mem·o·ry *n* computer memory organization in which stored information is accessed by content rather than memory address

as·so·nance /ássənənss/ *n* the similarity of two or more vowel sounds or the repetition of two or more consonant sounds, especially in words that are close together in a poem [Early 18C. < French < Latin *assonare* "respond to" < *sonare* "to sound"] **—as·so·nant** *adj*

as·sort /ə sáwrt/ (**-sort·ed, -sort·ing, -sorts**) *v* **1.** *vt* to sort things by type or category **2.** *vi* to fit into a group [15C. < Old French *assorter* < *sorte* "a sort" (see SORT)] **—as·sort·er** *n*

as·sort·ed /ə sáwrtəd/ *adj* **1.** consisting of various kinds ○ *arrived with assorted excuses* **2.** arranged in groups

as·sort·ment /ə sáwrtmənt/ *n* a collection of various kinds ○ *an assortment of drawings*

A.S.S.R., ASSR *abbr* POL Autonomous Soviet Socialist Republic

asst. *abbr* assistant

asstd. *abbr* **1.** assisted **2.** assorted

as·suage /ə swáyj/ (**-suaged, -suag·ing, -suag·es**) *vt* to provide relief from something distressing or painful (*formal*) ○ *Constant reassurance could not assuage their fears.* [13C. Via Old French *assuagier* < assumed Vulgar Latin *assuaviare* "sweeten" < Latin *suavis* "sweet"] **—as·suage·ment** *n* **—as·suag·er** *n* **—as·sua·sive** /ə swáyssiv, -ziv/ *adj*

as·sume /ə sóom/ (**-sumed, -sum·ing, -sumes**) *vt* **1.** SUPPOSE SOMETHING to accept that something is true without checking or confirming it ○ *Don't assume that all has been revealed.* **2.** TAKE RESPONSIBILITY FOR SOMETHING to start being responsible for something ○ *She assumed all of her brother's debts when he died.* **3.** ADOPT SOMETHING to adopt or take on a quality ○ *The task facing them assumed Herculean proportions.* **4.** UNDERTAKE ROLE to undertake a role or function ○ *assume a new role as sales director* **5.** PRETEND SOMETHING to put on a pretense of something, usually in order to hide true feelings ○ *He assumed an air of indifference.* [15C. < Latin *assumere* "take up" < *sumere* (see SUMPTUARY)] **—as·sum·a·ble** *adj* **—as·sumed** *adj* **—as·sum·er** *n*

SYNONYMS See ***deduce.***

as·sumed name /ə sóomd-/ *n* a false name, especially one used by somebody doing something illegal

as·sum·ing /ə sóoming/ *adj* expecting too much of other people ■ *conj* if it is assumed that **—as·sum·ing·ly** *adv*

as·sump·sit /ə súmpsit/ *n* LAW **1.** an oral or written agreement, contract, or promise that exists without being on the record or under seal **2.** an attempt to recover damages from a breached assumpsit [Late 16C. < Latin, "he or she has undertaken"]

as·sump·tion /ə súmpshən/ *n* **1.** SOMETHING TAKEN FOR GRANTED something that is believed to be true without proof ○ *Make no assumptions before looking at the evidence.* ○ *"Cruelty will be slyly advocated by the assumption that its only opposite is sentimentality."* (C. S. Lewis, *Reflections on the Psalms*; 1961) **2.** BELIEF WITHOUT PROOF the belief that something is true without having any proof **3.** ACT OF UNDERTAKING SOMETHING the act of taking something upon yourself ○ *With the assumption of power comes responsibility.* **4.** ACCEPTANCE OF RESPONSIBILITY FOR SOMETHING the act of taking over responsibility for something **5.** INCLINATION TO HIGH EXPECTATIONS the tendency to expect too much **6.** LOGIC UNPROVED STARTING POINT something taken as a starting point of a logical proof rather than given as a premise [13C. < Latin *assumption-* < *assumpt-*, past participle of *assumere* (see ASSUME)]

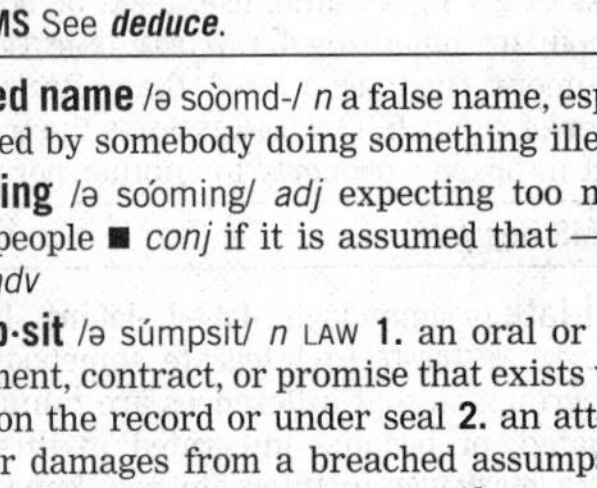

Assumption (1649–50) by Nicolas Poussin

As·sump·tion, As·sump·tion of the Vir·gin Mar·y *n* **1.** the ascent of the Virgin Mary to heaven at her death, as believed by some Christians **2.** a Christian feast that celebrates the Assumption. Date: August 15.

as·sump·tive /ə súmptiv/ *adj* based on an assumption or a set of assumptions

as·sur·ance /ə shóorənss/ *n* **1.** PLEDGE OR PROMISE a declaration that inspires or is intended to inspire confidence ○ *They gave us every assurance it would arrive on time.* **2.** CONFIDENCE confidence in personal ability or status ○ *He steered the ungainly machine with smooth assurance.* **3.** CERTAINTY freedom from uncertainty ○ *took heart in the assurance that the problem was solved* **4.** MAKING SOMETHING CERTAIN making something certain or overcoming doubt **5.** UK INSUR INSURANCE AGAINST CERTAINTY insurance against something that is certain to happen such as death, rather than something that might happen such as loss of or damage to property ○ *life assurance*

as·sure /ə shóor/ (**-sured, -sur·ing, -sures**) *vt* **1.** CONVINCE SOMEBODY to convince somebody of something ○ *assured us of her sincerity* **2.** MAKE SOMEBODY CONFIDENT to overcome somebody's doubt or disbelief about something ○ *I can assure you that every word is true.* **3.** MAKE SOMETHING CERTAIN to make something certain to happen ○ *Proper planning assures that the job will be done right.* **4.** UK INSUR INSURE AGAINST CERTAINTY to insure somebody against something that is certain to happen, e.g., death, rather than something that might happen, e.g., loss of or damage to property [14C. Via French *assurer* < assumed Vulgar Latin *assecurare* "make secure" < Latin *securus* (see SECURE)] **—as·sur·a·ble** *adj* **—as·sur·er** *n*

USAGE assure, ensure, or **insure?** You use ***assure*** when you are referring to somebody else being made sure about something; ***insure*** is used chiefly in connection with insurance (that is, financial protection); ***ensure*** is a variant spelling for this but is also used when you are referring to something that you want to be sure of: *I assure you it doesn't hurt. She wanted to ensure that it wouldn't hurt. I have insured my jewelry.*

as·sured /ə shóord/ *adj* **1.** certain to happen ○ *an assured victory* **2.** confident about personal abilities or other qualities ○ *the most assured conductor the orchestra had ever seen* **—as·sur·ed·ly** /ə shóorədlee/ *adv* **—as·sur·ed·ness** /ə shóorədnəss/ *n*

As·syr·i·a /ə sírree ə/ ancient Mesopotamian kingdom with a large empire extending southward and eastward, at its height from the ninth to the seventh centuries B.C.

As·syr·i·an /ə sírree ən/ *n* **1.** the Akkadian language, especially as recorded in cuneiform tablets from Assyria **2.** somebody who lived in Assyria **—As·syr·i·an** *adj*

AST *abbr* TIME **1.** Alaska Standard Time **2.** Atlantic Standard Time

a·sta·ble /ay stáyb'l/ *adj* **1.** lacking stability **2.** ELEC oscillating between two unstable states

Fred Astaire

A·staire /ə stér/, **Fred** (1899–1987) US dancer and actor who was known for his performances in Broadway musicals and movies. He famously partnered Ginger Rogers. Born **Austerlitz, Frederick**

"At the risk of disillusionment, I must admit that I don't like to wear top hats, white ties, and tails."

[Fred Astaire. Quoted in *Starring Fred Astaire*, Stanley Green and Burt Goldblatt; 1973]

As·ta·na /ə staánə/ capital of Kazakhstan. It is situated in the northern part of the country, on the Ishim River. Population: 312,965 (1999). Former name **Aqmola** (1991–98), **Tselinograd** (1960–91), **Akmolinsk** (1824–1960)

As·tar·te /ə staártee/ *n* MYTHOL ➧ **Ishtar**

a·stat·ic /ay státtik/ *adj* unsteady because of poor muscle coordination [Early 19C. < Greek *astatos* "unstable" < *statos* "standing"] —**a·stat·i·cal·ly** *adv* —**a·stat·i·cism** /ay státti sìzzəm/ *n*

a·stat·ic gal·va·nom·e·ter *n* an instrument for measuring electric current that is not significantly affected by the Earth's magnetic field

as·ta·tine /ástə teèn/ *n* an unstable radioactive element, the heaviest in the halogen series. Source: bombardment of bismuth with alpha particles. Use: in medicine as a tracer element. Symbol **At**. See table at **element** [Mid-20C. < Greek *astatos* (see ASTATIC)]

as·ter /ástər/ *n* **1.** PLANTS an annual plant of the daisy family. Flowers: white, pink, violet. **2.** a star-shaped structure seen during cell division **(mitosis)** [Early 18C. Via Latin < Greek *astēr* "star"]

-aster *suffix* one that is inferior ○ *poetaster* [< Latin]

as·te·ri·at·ed /ə steèree aytəd/ *adj* describes a crystal that reflects light in a star shape [Early 19C. < Greek *asterios* "starry" < *astēr* "star"]

~~**asterick**~~ incorrect spelling of **asterisk**

as·ter·isk /ástərisk/ *n* **1.** STAR-SHAPED SYMBOL a star-shaped symbol (*) used in printing **2.** ASTERISK AS LINGUISTIC SYMBOL in linguistics, an asterisk used to mark a sound, form, or structure that is believed to have existed but is unrecorded, or that is wrong or ungrammatical ■ *vt* **(-isked, -isk·ing, -isks)** MARK SOMETHING WITH ASTERISK to mark a printed or written item with an asterisk, especially to call attention to it [14C. Via late Latin < Greek *asteriskos* "little star" < *astēr* "star"]

as·ter·ism /ástər ìzzəm/ *n* **1.** PRINTING PRINTER'S MARK OF THREE ASTERISKS a triangle formed of three asterisks that calls the reader's attention to a following passage **2.** ASTRON STAR CLUSTER a cluster of stars smaller than a constellation **3.** CRYSTALS STAR-SHAPED REFLECTION IN CRYSTALS an optical effect appearing as a star in the light reflected from some crystals [Late 16C. < Greek *asterismos* "constellation" < *astēr* "star"]

a·stern /ə stúrn/ *adv* **1.** IN OR TO STERN in, on, to, or toward the stern of a ship or boat ○ *The deck hand walked astern.* **2.** WITH STERN FOREMOST into a position with the stern pointing in the direction of motion ○ *Bring the captain's gig astern.* ■ *adj* BEHIND BOAT positioned behind a boat ○ *The astern line has been cut.*

as·ter·oid /ástə ròyd/ *n* **1.** an irregularly shaped rock that orbits the Sun, mostly occurring in a band **(asteroid belt)** between the orbits of Mars and Jupiter. Asteroids range in size from the largest, Ceres, with a diameter of 580 mi./930 km, down to dust particles. **2.** ZOOL same as **starfish** (*technical*) [Early 19C. < Greek *asteroeidēs* "starlike" < *astēr* "star"] —**as·ter·oid·al** /ástə róyd'l/ *adj*

as·ter·oid belt *n* a region of space where the density of asteroids is high, located between the orbits of Mars and Jupiter

as·the·ni·a /as theènee ə/ *n* a condition marked by loss of strength in the body [Late 18C. < modern Latin < Greek *asthenēs* (see ASTHENIC)]

as·then·ic /as thénnik/ *adj* **1.** showing marked physical weakness **2.** having a slender and lightly muscled build [Late 18C. < Greek *asthenikos* < *asthenēs* "without strength" < *sthenos* "strength"]

as·then·o·sphere /as thénnə sfeèr/ *n* a weak zone in the upper part of the Earth's mantle where rock can be deformed in response to stress, resulting in movement of the overlying crust [Early 20C. < Greek *asthenēs* (see ASTHENIC)]

asth·ma /ázmə/ *n* a disease of the respiratory system, sometimes caused by allergies, with symptoms including coughing, sudden difficulty in breathing, and a tight feeling in the chest [14C. Via medieval Latin < Greek < *azein* "breathe hard"]

asth·mat·ic /az máttik/ *adj* **1.** WITH ASTHMA affected with or prone to attacks of asthma **2.** OF ASTHMA relating to the respiratory difficulties associated with asthma ■ *n* SOMEBODY WITH ASTHMA somebody who is affected by asthma [Early 16C. Via Latin < Greek *asthmatikos* < *asthma* (see ASTHMA)] —**asth·mat·i·cal·ly** *adv*

As·ti /aástee/ *n* WINE same as **Asti Spumante** [Mid-19C. After a province in NW Italy]

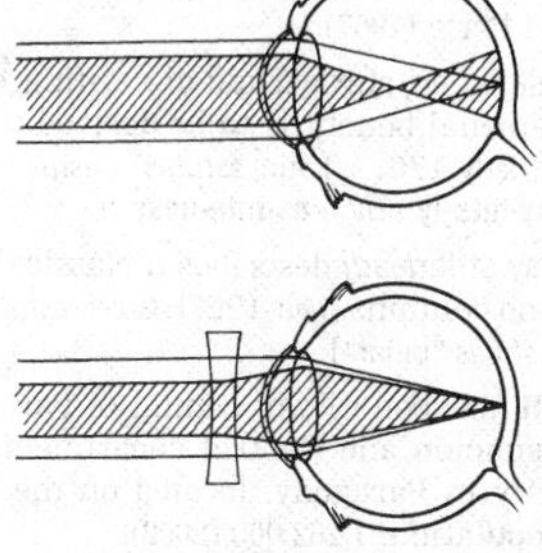

astigmatism: eye condition causing blurred vision (top) and corrected with a concave lens (bottom)

a·stig·ma·tism /ə stígmə tìzzəm/ *n* **1.** an unequal curving of one or more of the refractive surfaces of the eye, usually the cornea. It prevents light rays lying in specific planes from coming to a focus on the retina, thus producing blurred vision. **2.** a defect in a lens or mirror that prevents light rays from meeting at a single point, producing an imperfect image [Mid-19C. < A[3] + Greek *stigmat-* "point"] —**as·tig·mat·ic** /ástig máttik/ *adj* —**as·tig·mat·i·cal·ly** *adv*

a·stil·be /ə stílbee/ (*plural* **-bes** or *same*) *n* a perennial plant widely cultivated in shady damp gardens. Flowers: plume-shaped. Native to: East Asia. Genus: *Astilbe*. [Mid-19C. < modern Latin, "not glittering" < Greek *a-* "not" + *stilbos* "glittering"]

a·stir /ə stúr/ *adj* **1.** awake and moving around, especially out of bed ○ *The children were astir early as usual.* **2.** moving around ○ *leaves astir in the breeze*

As·ti Spu·man·te /aástee spoo maántee/ *n* sparkling white wine from northwestern Italy [< Italian, "sparkling Asti"]

as·told·to *adj* describes an autobiography written by a professional author using conversations with the person whose life is documented (*informal*) ○ *another as-told-to book* [< the phrase sometimes used in the subtitles of such books]

a·ston·ish /ə stónnish/ **(-ished, -ish·ing, -ish·es)** *vt* to amaze somebody to a great degree [Early 16C. < *astone* (see ASTOUND)] —**a·ston·ish·ing** *adj* —**a·ston·ish·ing·ly** *adv*

a·ston·ish·ment /ə stónnishmənt/ *n* great amazement, often eliciting shock ○ *He was on time, to my astonishment.*

As·tor /ástər/, **John Jacob** (1763–1848) German-born US fur trader and property millionaire. Founder of the Astor family and fortune, he endowed the Astor Library, now part of the New York Public Library.

As·tor, Nancy, Viscountess (1879–1964) US-born British politician. She was the first woman member of Parliament (elected 1919). Born **Langhorne, Nancy Witcher**

"Superiority we've always had; all we ask is equality."
[Nancy Astor, on becoming the first woman to sit in the House of Commons, recalled upon her death, press reports; May 2, 1964]

As·to·ri·a /ə stáwree ə/ city and port in northwestern Oregon. The Lewis and Clark expedition ended here in 1806. Population: 9,730 (2002 estimate).

a·stound /ə stównd/ **(a·stound·ed, a·stound·ing, a·stounds)** *vt* to overwhelm and stun somebody with sudden surprise ○ *was astounded by the viciousness of the attacks* [14C. Alteration of *astoned*, past participle of *astone* "stun," via Old French *estoner* < assumed Vulgar Latin *extonare* "thunder out"] —**a·stound·ing** *adj* —**a·stound·ing·ly** *adv*

astr- *prefix* same as **astro-** (*used before vowels*)

a·strad·dle /ə strádd'l/ *prep, adv* with one leg or part on each side of something

as·tra·gal /ástrəg'l/ *n* **1.** a narrow convex molding, often taking the form of beads **2.** a small convex molding attached to double doors to prevent drafts or the passage of light, noise, or smoke [Mid-17C. Via French < Latin *astragalus* (see ASTRAGALUS)]

as·trag·a·lus /ə strággələss/ (*plural* **-li** /-lī/) *n* ANAT same as **talus**[1] [Mid-16C. Via Latin < Greek *astragalos*]

as·tra·khan /ástrə kàn, -kən/ *n* **1.** fur fabric made from the curly dark fleece of lambs from Astrakhan, southern Russia, or an acrylic imitation. Use: hats, trims on coats. **2.** a brimless hat rising to a ridge, made of astrakhan or similar material

as·tral /ástrəl/ *adj* **1.** relating to, characteristic of, or consisting of stars **2.** in theosophical belief, belonging to the ethereal region that is believed to exist throughout and at a higher level than the material world, in which personal auras are said to be perceived [Early 17C. < late Latin *astralis* < Greek *astron* (see ASTRO-)] —**as·tral·ly** *adv*

as·tral bod·y *n* in theosophical belief, a second body, not directly perceivable by the human senses, believed to coexist with and survive the death of the physical body

as·tral plane *n* in theosophical belief, a level of existence where the counterpart of the human body **(astral body)** goes between death and entry into the spirit world

as·tral pro·jec·tion *n* in theosophical belief, the ability to send the astral body outside the physical body, while both remain connected

a·stray /ə stráy/ *adv* **1.** away from the right path ○ *went astray and ended up lost* **2.** in or into an evil or undesirable course of life ○ *led astray by questionable companions* [13C. < Old French *estraie*, past participle of *estraier* "to stray"] ◇ **go astray** to be mislaid or missing

a·stride /ə stríd/ *prep* **1.** WITH LEGS AROUND on top of and with a leg on each side of something ○ *astride a horse* **2.** EXTENDING ACROSS extending across in terms of influence or power ○ *a military colossus astride the world* ■ *adv* WITH LEGS APART with legs spread wide apart ○ *He stood with arms folded and legs astride.*

as·trin·gent /ə strínjənt/ *n* a substance that draws tissue together ■ *adj* speaking or writing in a manner that is critical and hurtful in tone and content [Mid-16C. < Latin *astringent-*, present participle of *astringere* "bind to" < *stringere* "bind"] —**as·trin·gen·cy** *n* —**as·trin·gent·ly** *adv*

astro- *prefix* **1.** star, the stars, outer space ○ *astrobiology* **2.** aster of a cell ○ *astrocyte* [< Greek < *astron* "star" < *astēr* (see ASTER)]

as·tro·bi·ol·o·gy /ástrō bī óllәjee/ *n* same as **exobiology** —**as·tro·bi·o·log·i·cal** /-bī ə lójjik'l/ *adj* —**as·tro·bi·ol·o·gist** *n*

as·tro·bleme /ástrə bleèm/ *n* a depression, usually circular, on the surface of the Earth that is caused by the impact of a meteorite [Mid-20C. < ASTRO- + Greek *blēma* "wound from a missile"]

as·tro·chem·is·try /ástrō kémmistree/ *n* the chemistry of astronomical objects and interstellar space —**as·tro·chem·ist** *n*

as·tro·com·pass /ástrō kùmpəss/ *n* a nonmagnetic navigational instrument used to determine the position of true north relative to an astronomical object

as·tro·cyte /ástrə sìt/ *n* a star-shaped cell in the central nervous system's supportive tissue **(neuroglia)**

as·tro·cy·to·ma /ástrō sī tṓmə/ (*plural* **-mas** or **-ma·ta** /-mətə/) *n* a commonly occurring malignant brain tumor made up of star-shaped cells **(astrocytes)**

as·tro·dome /ástrə dṑm/ *n* a transparent dome on an aircraft or spacecraft through which astronomical observations are made in order to navigate

as·tro·dy·nam·ics /ástrō dī námmiks/ *n* the study of the effects of gravitational and other forces on the motion of natural and artificial bodies in outer space (*takes a singular verb*) —**as·tro·dy·nam·ic** *adj*

as·tro·ge·ol·o·gy /àstrō jee óllәjee/ *n* the study of the origin, history, and structure of cosmic bodies other than Earth —**as·tro·ge·ol·o·gist** *n*

astrol. *abbr* ASTROL **1.** astrologer **2.** astrological **3.** astrology

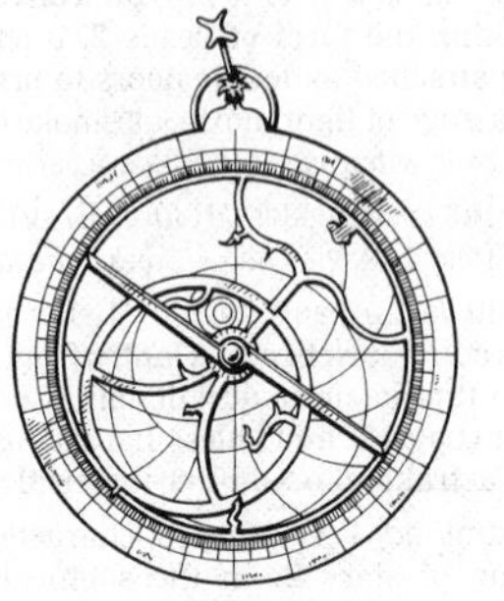

astrolabe

as·tro·labe /ástrә làyb/ *n* an early instrument used to observe the position and determine the altitude of the Sun or other astronomical object. The astrolabe was used for navigation from the Middle Ages until the 18th century when it was replaced by the sextant. [14C. Via Old French and medieval Latin < Greek *astrolabon*, literally "take a star"]

as·trol·o·gy /ә stróllәjee/ *n* the study of the positions of the Moon, Sun, and other planets in the belief that their motions affect human beings [14C. Via French < Greek *astrologia* "account of the stars" < *astron* (see ASTRO-) + *-logia* (see -LOGY)] —**as·trol·o·ger** *n* —**as·tro·log·i·cal** /àstrә lójjik'l/ *adj* —**as·tro·log·i·cal·ly** *adv* —**as·trol·o·gist** *n*

as·trom·e·try /ә strómmәtree/ *n* the measurement of the real and apparent motions and the positions of astronomical objects —**as·tro·met·ri·cal** /àstrә méttrik'l/ *adj*

astron. *abbr* ASTRON **1.** astronomer **2.** astronomical **3.** astronomy

as·tro·naut /ástrә nàwt/ *n* **1.** somebody trained to travel and perform tasks in space **2.** an East or Southeast Asian immigrant whose family is settled in Canada, the United States, Australia, or New Zealand but who frequently travels to Asia to work (*informal*) [Early 20C. < ASTRO-, after *aeronaut*]

as·tro·nau·tics /àstrә náwtiks/ *n* **1.** the science and technology of designing and building spacecraft (*takes a singular verb*) **2.** the skills and activities associated with the operation of a spacecraft (*takes a plural verb*) [Early 20C. < ASTRO-, after *aeronautics*] —**as·tro·nau·tic** *adj* —**as·tro·nau·ti·cal·ly** *adv*

as·tro·nav·i·ga·tion /àstrō navi gáysh'n/ *n* **1.** the navigation of a spacecraft among astronomical objects, especially stars **2.** ASTRON same as **celestial navigation** —**as·tro·nav·i·gate** /àstrō návvi gàyt/ *vti* —**as·tro·nav·i·ga·tor** *n*

as·tro·nom·i·cal /àstrә nómmik'l/, **as·tro·nom·ic** /-nómmik/ *adj* **1.** relating to astronomy **2.** immeasurably numerous, high, or great (*informal*) ○ *reached astronomical proportions* —**as·tro·nom·i·cal·ly** *adv*

as·tro·nom·i·cal clock *n* a clock that shows astronomical information such as the phases of the Moon

as·tro·nom·i·cal tel·e·scope *n* a telescope used to view astronomical objects

as·tro·nom·i·cal twi·light *n* the period of time during which the Sun is at 18° below the horizon

as·tro·nom·i·cal u·nit *n* a unit of astronomical distances, especially within the solar system, equal to the mean distance between the Earth and the Sun, about 93 million mi./150 million km

as·tro·nom·i·cal year *n* ASTRON same as **solar year**

as·tron·o·my /ә strónnәmee/ *n* the scientific study of the universe, especially of the motions, positions, sizes, composition, and behavior of astronomical objects. These objects are studied and interpreted from the radiation they emit and from data gathered by interplanetary probes. [13C. Via Old French and Latin < Greek *astronomia* "star-arranging" < *astron* (see ASTRO-) + *-nomia* (see -NOMY)] —**as·tron·o·mer** *n*

as·tro·pho·tog·ra·phy /àstrō fә tóggrәfee/ *n* the art of photographing astronomical objects and events for astronomical studies

as·tro·phys·ics /àstrō fízziks/ *n* the study of the physical properties, origin, and development of astronomical objects and events (*takes a singular verb*) —**as·tro·phys·i·cal** *adj* —**as·tro·phys·i·cal·ly** *adv* —**as·tro·phys·i·cist** *n*

As·tro·Turf /ástrō tùrf/ *tdmk* a trademark for synthetic turf resembling grass

As·tu·ri·as /a stóoree әss, ә-/, **Miguel Ángel** (1899–1974) Guatemalan writer, author of anti-imperialist novels rooted in Native American tradition. He won the Nobel Prize (1967).

as·tute /ә stóot/ *adj* shrewd and discerning, especially where personal benefit is to be derived ○ *an astute investor* [Early 17C. < Latin *astutus* < *astus* "cleverness, skill"] —**as·tute·ly** *adv* —**as·tute·ness** *n*

a·sty·lar /ay stílәr/ *adj* describes a classical building that has no columns [Mid-19C. < Greek *astulos* "without pillars" < *stulos* "pillar"]

A·sun·ción /aa soon syáwn/ capital of Paraguay and of the Asunción and Central departments and the largest city in Paraguay, located on the Paraguay River. Population: 1,262,000 (2002).

a·sun·der /ә súndәr/ *adv* into separate parts, pieces, or places (*literary*) [Old English *onsundran* "into parts" < *on* "into" + *sundran* "parts" < Germanic]

a·su·ra /ússoorә/ *n* in Hindu mythology, a member of a class of nonhuman beings who are enemies of heavenly beings [< Sanskrit, "demon"]

ASV *abbr* BIBLE American Standard Version

As·vi·na /ásh vìnnә/ *n* in the Hindu calendar, the seventh month of the year, lasting 30 days and falling about the same time as September to October. See table at **calendar**

As·wan /a swaán, á swaan/ city on the Nile River in southern Egypt. The Aswan High Dam, south of the city, holds back Lake Nasser. Population: 220,000 (1992).

a·swarm /ә swáwrm/ *adj* full of moving living things

a·swirl /ә swúrl/ *adj* moving with a swirling or twirling motion

a·swoon /ә swóon/ *adj* experiencing a swoon or faint (*literary*)

a·syl·lab·ic /àyssi lábbik/ *adj* describes a speech sound that does not constitute a syllable

a·sy·lum /ә sílәm/ *n* **1.** PROTECTION FROM EXTRADITION protection and immunity from extradition granted by a government to somebody who has fled another country, e.g., because of political oppression **2.** SHELTER AND PROTECTION protection from danger or imminent harm provided by a sheltered place **3.** OFFENSIVE TERM an offensive term for an institution for people with psychiatric disorders (*dated*) **4.** HIST PLACE OF SANCTUARY a place that once offered shelter to criminals and debtors, especially a church [15C. Via Latin < Greek *asulon* "refuge" < *asulos* "without right of seizure" < *sulon* "right of seizure"]

a·sy·lum seek·er *n* somebody who applies for asylum as a refugee

a·sym·met·ric /ày si méttrik/, **a·sym·met·ri·cal** /-méttrik'l/ *adj* **1.** NOT SYMMETRICAL not balanced or regularly arranged on opposite sides of a line or around a central point ○ *an asymmetric flower arrangement* **2.** NOT EQUAL lacking equality, balance, or harmony ○ *two countries wholly asymmetric in their relations* **3.** CHEM WITH ALTERNATIVE ATOMIC ARRANGEMENTS describes a carbon atom bonded to four different atoms or radicals whose arrangement in space may occur in two different configurations (**stereoisomerism**) **4.** ELEC ENG WITH VARYING CONDUCTIVITY describes a substance or a device that exhibits varying or different conductivities for currents flowing through it in different directions **5.** AEROSP WITH UNEQUAL THRUST describes an aircraft that is unbalanced because of unequal thrust from two or more sources, e.g., when one engine of a pair is not functioning properly **6.** LOGIC, MATH NOT INTERCHANGEABLE describes a relation between two things in which the first has a relation to the second, but the second cannot have the same relation to the first —**a·sym·met·ri·cal·ly** *adv*

a·sym·met·ri·cal dig·i·tal sub·scrib·er line *n* a high-speed telephone line that can transmit voice and video data over copper wires

a·sym·met·ric war·fare *n* highly decentralized unconventional warfare perpetrated on nation-states and civilians by paramilitaries, guerrillas, and terrorists

a·sym·me·try /ay símmәtree/ *n* **1.** the condition of being asymmetric in arrangement ○ *some asymmetry in the design* **2.** LOGIC, MATH a relation between two things in which the first has a relation to the second, but the second cannot have the same relation to the first. Asymmetry is illustrated in the statement "A is the father of B," since B cannot be the father of A.

a·symp·to·mat·ic /ay sìmptә máttik/ *adj* not showing or producing indications of a disease or other medical condition ○ *The surgery was successful, and she has remained asymptomatic ever since.* —**a·symp·to·mat·i·cal·ly** *adv*

as·ymp·tote /ássimp tòt, ássim-/ *n* a line that draws increasingly nearer to a curve without ever meeting it [Mid-17C. Via modern Latin < Greek *asumptōtos* "not adapted to fall together" < *sun-* "together" + *ptōtos* "adapted to fall"] —**as·ymp·tot·ic** /àssimp tóttik, àssim-/ *adj* —**as·ymp·tot·i·cal·ly** *adv*

a·syn·ap·sis /àyssi nápsiss/ *n* the failure of chromosomes that are alike (**homologous**) to pair during cell division (**meiosis**)

a·syn·chro·nism /ay síngkrә nìzzәm/ *n* in computing and electronics, the occurrence of two or more processes at different times

a·syn·chron·ous /ay síngkrәnәss/ *adj* relating to or using an electronic communication method that sends data in one direction, one character at a time —**a·syn·chro·nous·ly** *adv*

a·syn·chro·ny /ay síngkrәnee/ *n* TECH same as **asynchronism**

a·syn·de·ton /ә síndi tòn/ (*plural* **-ta** /-tә/) *n* the omission of conjunctions in sentence constructions in which they would usually be used [Mid-16C. < late Latin < Greek *asundetos* "not bound together" < *sundein* "bind together"] —**as·yn·det·ic** /àssin déttik/ *adj* —**as·yn·det·i·cal·ly** *adv*

a·syn·er·gy /ay sínnәrjee/, **a·sy·ner·gia** /ày si núrjә/ *n* a failure of coordination between different muscle groups so that delicate, skilled, or rapid movements become impossible [Mid-19C. < A-[2] + Greek *sunergia* (see SYNERGY)] —**a·syn·er·gic** /ay sínnәrjik/ *adj*

a·sys·to·le /ay sístәlee/ *n* the absence of any heartbeat —**a·sys·tol·ic** /ày si stóllik/ *adj*

at[1] *stressed* /at/; *unstressed* /әt/ CORE MEANING: a preposition used to indicate general position or location. In order to be more precise about exact physical location, other prepositions such as "on," "over," "under," and "by" are used instead. ○ *a conference at the school* ○ *Someone's at the door.* ○ *I work at home.*

prep **1.** ATTENDING attending regularly ○ *not at school yet* **2.** FROM INTERVAL OF used to describe the position of something by indicating its distance or angle ○ *She followed them at a distance.* **3.** INDICATES WHEN SOMETHING HAPPENS used to indicate the time or age when something happens ○ *Lunch is at noon.* **4.** DURING EVENT while present during an event ○ *had a good time at the carnival* **5.** INDICATES RATE OR FREQUENCY used to indicate the rate, frequency, level, or price of something ○ *driving at 65 miles per hour* **6.** TOWARD to or in the direction of somebody or something ○ *He glanced over at her.* **7.** AS REACTION TO used to indicate what somebody is reacting to ○ *amazed at what had happened* **8.** IN STATED ACTIVITY used to indicate an activity or subject that a judgment about somebody relates to ○ *an expert at windsurfing* **9.** IN CONDITION OR STATE indicating the condition or state that somebody or something is in ○ *at risk of infection* **10.** DOING engaged or occupied in ○ *hard at work* **11.** IN MANNER OF used to indicate how something is done ○ *set off at a run* **12.** INDICATES REPEATED ACTIONS used to indicate the object of a repeated action ○ *She just picks at her food.* **13.** ACCORDING TO SOMEBODY'S WISHES in response to or based on somebody's wish or decision ○ *Spend this money at your discretion.* **14.** *Carib* AT OR TO THE HOUSE OF used to indicate location at somebody's house ○ *I'm living at my aunt.* ○ *I'm going at Eugene.*

[Old English *æt* < Indo-European] ◇ **at all** in any way, to any extent, or under any conditions ○ *don't like it at all* ◇ **at that 1.** in addition ○ *It was a coincidence, and a happy one at that.* **2.** nevertheless, or in spite of something else ○ *It just might work at that.* **3.** at a specific point or place ○ *I think we'll leave it at that for today.* ◇ **where it's** *or* **something is at** where all the action and excitement is happening (*slang*)

USAGE The symbol @ means "at," and until the 1990s it was mainly used in commercial or technical contexts: *25 lbs @ $3.50 per lb; 150 miles @ 30 mph.* Its most familiar use today, however, is in e-mail addresses, where it usually comes between the user's personal screen name and the domain name of his or her organization or Internet service provider: *rtjackson@scotrack.com.*

at[2] *abbr* Austria (*used in Internet addresses*) See table at **domain name**

At *symbol* CHEM ELEM astatine

AT *abbr* **1.** MIL antitank **2.** TIME Atlantic Time **3.** AUTOMOT automatic transmission

at. *abbr* **1.** airtight **2.** PHYS, MEASURE atmosphere **3.** PHYS, ARMS atomic

at- *prefix* same as **ad-** (*used before t*)

A·ta·ca·ma De·sert /àatə kaàmə-/ barren, dry, and sparsely populated plateau in northern Chile known for its once enormously abundant nitrate and copper resources. Area: 140,000 sq. mi./363,000 sq. km.

at·a·ghan *n* ARMS same as **yataghan**

A·ta·hual·pa /àatə waàlpə/ (1500?–33) Inca king. The last ruler of the Inca Empire (1532–33), he was executed for having his coruler, his brother Huascar, assassinated.

at·a·man /áttə màn/ *n* a Cossack chieftain [Mid-19C. Via Russian < Turkic, "great father"]

at·a·mas·co lil·y /àttə máskō-/ *n* a plant that grows from a bulb. Flowers: single, usually white or pinkish, on a tall stalk. Native to: southeastern United States. Latin name: *Zephyranthes atamasco.* [Mid-18C. < Virginia Algonquian *attamusco*]

A·tan·a·soff /ə tánnə sòf/, **John V.** (1903–95) US mathematical physicist

at·ar *n* PHARM another spelling of **attar**

at·a·rac·tic /àttə ráktik/, **at·a·rax·ic** /-ráksik/ *adj* describes a drug or other agent that tranquilizes ■ *n* a tranquilizer (*technical*) [Mid-20C. < Greek *ataraktos* "not disturbed" < *tarassein* "disturb"]

at·a·rax·i·a /àttə ráksee ə/ *n* freedom from worry or any other preoccupation [Mid-19C. < Greek < *ataraktos* (see ATARACTIC)]

at·a·rax·ic *adj, n* MED same as **ataractic**

AKG London
Mustafa Kemal Atatürk

A·ta·türk /áttə tùrk/, **Mustafa Kemal** (1881–1938) Turkish politician. He was the founder and the first president of the republic of Turkey (1923–38). Born **Pasha, Mustafa Kemal**

"If a society consisting of men and women is content to apply progress and education to one half of itself, such a society is weakened by half."
[Mustafa Kemal Atatürk, *Speech*; 1926]

at·a·vism /áttə vìzzəm/ *n* **1.** the recurrence of a genetically controlled feature in an organism after it has been absent for several generations, usually because of an accidental recombination of genes **2.** *also* **at·a·vist** /áttəvist/ an organism showing atavism [Mid-19C. < French *atavisme* < Latin *atavus* "beyond a grandfather" < *avus* "grandfather"]

at·a·vis·tic /àttə vístik/ *adj* **1.** relating to or displaying the recurrence of a genetic feature that has been absent for several generations **2.** relating to or displaying the kind of behavior that seems to be a product of impulses long since suppressed by society's rules —**at·a·vis·ti·cal·ly** *adv*

a·tax·i·a /ə táksee ə/, **a·tax·y** /ə táksee/ *n* the inability to coordinate the movements of muscles [Late 19C. Via modern Latin < Greek, "without order" < *taxis* (see TAXIS)] —**a·tax·ic** *adj*

ATB *abbr* **1.** VEHICLES all-terrain bike **2.** EXTREME SPORTS all-terrain boarding

At·chi·son /áchiss'n/ city on the Missouri River northeast of Topeka, in northeastern Kansas. Population: 10,106 (2002 estimate).

ate past tense of **eat**

-ate *suffix* **1.** having, characterized by ○ *lobate* **2.** office, rank ○ *archdeaconate* **3.** to act on in a particular way ○ *fluoridate* **4.** a chemical compound derived from a particular element or compound ○ *borate* [< Latin *-atus*, past participle ending of verbs in *-are*]

A-team *n* **1.** a unit of 12 soldiers in the US Special Forces **2.** a group of people who are the very best of their type (*informal*)

at·e·lec·ta·sis /àtt'l éktəssiss/ *n* **1.** a partial or total collapse of a lung **2.** a condition in which the lungs fail to expand completely at birth [Mid-19C. < Greek *atelēs* "incomplete" + *ektasis* "extension"]

at·el·ier /átt'l yáy, ə tèl-/ *n* a studio or workshop where an artist works [Late 17C. < French, "carpenter's workshop" < late Latin *astella* "board"]

a·te·moy·a /àatə móy ə, àttə-/ *n* **1.** a cone-shaped or heart-shaped green tropical fruit with sweet white flesh **2.** a tree, a cross between cherimoya and sweetsop, that bears atemoya fruit. Native to: Philippines. [Early 20C. Blend of Philippine English *ate* "sweetsop" + CHERIMOYA]

a tem·po /aa témpō/ *adv, adj* in or back into a previous musical tempo (*used as a musical direction*) [< Italian, "in time"]

a·tem·po·ral /ay témpərəl, -témprəl/ *adj* independent of or unaffected by time

~~**atempt**~~ incorrect spelling of **attempt**

a·ten·ol·ol /ə ténnə làwl/ *n* a drug. Use: blood pressure and angina management. [Late 20C. < *anten-* + *-olol*, INN stem]

ATF *abbr* **1.** GOV (Bureau of) Alcohol, Tobacco, and Firearms **2.** AUTOMOT automatic transmission fluid

Ath·a·bas·ca /àthə báskə/ river flowing northeast from the Rocky Mountains in Alberta, Canada, into Lake Athabasca. Length: 765 mi./1,231 km.

Ath·a·bas·ca, Lake fourth largest lake in Canada, bridging the border of Alberta and Saskatchewan. Area: 3,064 sq. mi./7,935 sq. km.

Ath·a·bas·kan /àthə báskən/, **Ath·a·pas·kan** /àthə páskən/ *n* **1.** a group of Na-Dene languages spoken in northwestern Canada and parts of Alaska, Oregon, and California. Native speakers: 180,000. **2.** a member of an Athabaskan-speaking people [Mid-19C. After Lake ATHABASCA] —**Ath·a·bas·kan** *adj*

Ath·a·na·sian Creed /àthə náyzh'n-, -náysh'n-/ *n* a 5th-century Christian statement of belief of unknown authorship, formerly attributed to St. Athanasius, Greek patriarch of Alexandria

Ath·a·na·sius /àthə náyshəss/, **St.** (293?–373?) Greek theologian. He was patriarch of Alexandria and Primate of Egypt and wrote on the threefold nature of God.

Ath·a·pas·kan *n, adj* LANG, PEOPLES same as **Athabaskan**

a·the·ism /áythee ìzzəm/ *n* disbelief in the existence of God or deities [Late 16C. < French *athéisme* < Greek *atheos* "godless" < *theos* "god"]

a·the·ist /áythee ist/ *n* somebody who does not believe in God or deities

a·the·is·tic /àythee ístik/, **a·the·is·ti·cal** /-tik'l/ *adj* relating to or characteristic of atheists or atheism —**a·the·is·ti·cal·ly** *adv*

~~**athelete**~~ incorrect spelling of **athlete**

ath·e·ling /áthəling/ *n* an Anglo-Saxon nobleman or prince, usually the heir to a throne [Old English *æeling* < Germanic, "noble"]

A·thel·stan /áth'l stàn/ (895?–939) king of Wessex and Mercia. The grandson of Alfred the Great, he was the first monarch to claim the title "King of all Britain" (926?). He defeated an alliance of Scots, Welsh, and Vikings at the battle of Brunanburh (937).

a·the·mat·ic /ày thi máttik/ *adj* describes music that is not based on themes or tunes

A·the·na /ə theénə/, **A·the·ne** /ə theénee/ *n* in Greek mythology, the goddess of wisdom and warfare, and the patron goddess of Athens. She was born from Zeus's head. Roman equivalent **Minerva**

ath·e·nae·um /àthə neé əm/, **ath·e·ne·um** *n* **1.** an institution that encourages learning, e.g., an academy of science **2.** an institution where reading materials are made available to the public, e.g., a library [Mid-18C. Via Latin < Greek *Athēnaion*, the temple of Athena in Athens, used for teaching]

A·the·na·go·ras I /ə theénə gáwrəss/ (1886–1972) Greek religious leader. He was patriarch of the Eastern Orthodox Church (1948–72).

A·the·ne *n* MYTHOL same as **Athena**

Ath·ens /áthənz/ **1.** capital and largest city of Greece, situated in the southeastern part of the country. Population: 571,702 (2001). **2.** city in northeastern Georgia, on the Oconee River. It is a commercial and agricultural center and home to the country's oldest chartered state university. Population: 103,881 (2002 estimate). **3.** city in southeastern Ohio, on the south bank of the Hocking River, southeast of Columbus. Population: 21,545 (2002 estimate). —**A·the·ni·an** /ə theénee ən/ *adj, n*

a·the·o·ret·i·cal /àythee ə réttik'l/ *adj* without a theoretical basis

ath·er·o·gen·e·sis /àthərō jénnəssiss/ *n* the origination and formation of fatty deposits (**atheromas**) in arteries [Mid-20C. < ATHEROMA] —**ath·er·o·gen·ic** *adj* —**ath·er·o·gen·i·ci·ty** /àthərōjə nissətee/ *n*

ath·er·o·ma /àthə rṓmə/ (*plural* **-mas** *or* **-ma·ta** /-mətə/) *n* an accumulation in the inner lining of an artery of a plaque of cholesterol and other constituents (**atheromatous plaque**) [Late 16C. Via Latin < Greek *athērōma* < *athērē* "porridge," from its texture] —**ath·er·o·ma·to·sis** /-tṓssiss/ *n* —**ath·er·om·a·tous** /-rómmətəss, -rṓmətəss/ *adj*

ath·er·o·scle·ro·sis /àthərōsklə rṓssiss/ *n* a common arterial disease in which raised areas of degeneration and cholesterol deposits (**plaques**) form on the inner surfaces of the arteries obstructing blood flow [Early 20C. < ATHEROMA] —**ath·er·o·scle·rot·ic** /àthərōsklə róttik/ *adj* —**ath·er·o·scle·rot·i·cal·ly** *adv*

ath·et·o·sis /àthə tṓssiss/ *n* a condition characterized by involuntary slow movements of the fingers, toes, hands, and feet and usually caused by a brain lesion [Late 19C. < Greek *athetos* "without a place" < *tithenai* "to place"]

~~**athiest**~~ incorrect spelling of **atheist**

a·thirst /ə thúrst/ *adj* **1.** eager or longing for something (*literary*) **2.** same as **thirsty** (*archaic*) [Old English *ofyrst* < past participle of *ofyrstan* "thirst greatly" < *urst* (see THIRST)]

ath·lete /áth leèt/ *n* somebody with the abilities to participate in physical exercise, especially in competitive games and races [15C. Via Latin < Greek *athlētēs* < *athlein* "contend for a prize"]

USAGE Pronunciation of **athlete**: ***Athlete*** is pronounced with two syllables, not three: áth leèt, not áthə leèt.

ath·lete's foot *n* a contagious fungal infection affecting the feet

ath·let·ic /ath léttik/ *adj* **1.** relating to athletes, athletics, or other sports activities ○ *athletic uniforms* **2.** possessing a large skeletal structure and having strong muscles ○ *an athletic build* [Early 17C. Via

French and Latin < Greek *athlētikos* < *athlētēs* (see ATHLETE)] —**ath·let·i·cal·ly** *adv* —**ath·let·i·cism** /-léttissiz'm/ *n*

ath·let·ics /ath léttiks/ *n* **1.** activities such as sports and exercises that require physical skill and strength (*takes a singular or plural verb*) **2.** the methods, systems, or principles of training and practice for athletic activities (*takes a plural verb*) **3.** *UK* same as **track and field**

ath·let·ic shoe *n* a shoe designed to be worn during athletic activities or exercising, but worn with casual clothing for any activity

ath·let·ic sup·port·er *n* CLOTHING same as **jockstrap**

ath·o·dyd /áthədid/ *n* a simple tubular jet engine [Mid-20C. Contraction of *aero-thermodynamic duct*]

at-home, **at home** *n* an informal social gathering in somebody's own home

-athon *suffix* activity or event lasting a long time, especially done for charity ○ *talkathon* [< MARATHON]

a·thwart /ə thwáwrt/ *prep* **1.** so as to be across or positioned crosswise over something **2.** so as to oppose or obstruct something

a·thwart·ships /ə thwáwrt ships/ *adv* from one side of a boat to the other

at·i·gi /áttəgee, ə téegee/ (*plural* **-gis**), **ar·ti·gi** /aártəgee, aar téegee/ *n Can* a traditional Inuit knee-length hooded inner garment, made from animal skins worn with the hair side next to the body [Late 19C. < Inuit]

a·tilt /ə tílt/ *adv, adj* in or into a slanting position ○ *Her hat was atilt on her head.*

a·tin·gle /ə tíng g'l/ *adj* feeling a tingling sensation, often associated with excitement ○ *atingle with anticipation*

-ation *suffix* an action or process, or the result of it ○ *alienation* ○ *presentation* [Via French < Latin *-ation-*, forming nouns from verbs in *-are*]

~~atitude~~ incorrect spelling of **attitude**

-ative *suffix* having a particular characteristic ○ *argumentative* [Via French < Latin *-ativus* < *-atus* (see -ATE)]

At·kins di·et /átkənz-/ *n* a weight loss program that advocates a high protein, high fat, low carbohydrate diet [After Robert C. *Atkins* (1930–2003), US physician]

At·kin·son /átkinssən/, **Brooks** (1894–1984) US theater critic. He was the drama critic for *The New York Times* from 1925 to 1960.

> "It takes most men five years to recover from a college education, and to learn that poetry is as vital to thinking as knowledge."
> [Brooks Atkinson, "August 31," *Once Around the Sun*; 1951]

At·lan·ta /at lántə, ət-/ capital of Georgia, United States, and its largest city. It was an important Civil War battle site. Population: 424,868 (2002 estimate).

at·lan·tes ARCHIT plural of **atlas** (sense 3)

At·lan·tic /ət lántik/ *adj* **1.** OF ATLANTIC OCEAN relating to or situated in or near the Atlantic Ocean **2.** OF EAST COAST OF US relating to the eastern coast of the United States ■ *n* **1.** same as **Atlantic Ocean 2.** WEST AFRICAN LANGUAGE GROUP a group of West African languages, often considered to belong to the Niger-Congo language family [15C. Via Latin < Greek *Atlantikos* < *Atlas*, the Titan Atlas]

At·lan·tic Cit·y city in southeastern New Jersey, on the Atlantic Ocean, noted for its beaches and gambling casinos. Population: 40,172 (2002 estimate).

At·lan·tic In·tra·coas·tal Wa·ter·way /-intrə cṓst'l-/ system of protected inland waterways along the Atlantic Ocean coast, stretching from Cape Cod, Massachusetts, to southern Florida. It is mostly used by pleasure boats.

At·lan·ti·cism /ət lánti sìzzəm/ *n* a doctrine assuming that both Western Europe and the United States can benefit politically and economically from cooperation, especially in military matters

At·lan·tic O·cean the world's second largest ocean, which separates Europe and Africa from North and South America. Area: 31,800,000 sq. mi./82,400,000 sq. km.

At·lan·tic Prov·in·ces Canadian provinces of New Brunswick, Nova Scotia, Prince Edward Island, and Newfoundland

At·lan·tic Rim *n* the countries that border the Atlantic Ocean, especially the northern Atlantic

At·lan·tic salm·on *n* **1.** a species of salmon that lives in northern Atlantic waters and swims up rivers in northern America and Europe to spawn. Latin name: *Salmo salar*. **2.** the flesh of an Atlantic salmon as food

At·lan·tic Stan·dard Time, **At·lan·tic Time** *n* the standard time in the time zone centered on longitude 60° W, which includes Puerto Rico and the Canadian Maritime Provinces. It is four hours behind Universal Time.

At·lan·tic yam *n regional* the wild yam, the tuberous roots of which are cooked and eaten as a vegetable like potatoes. Genus: *Dioscorea*.

REGIONAL NOTE ***Atlantic yam*** in the sense of "wild yam" is recorded only in Kansas.

At·lan·tis /at lántiss, ət-/ *n* in Greek mythology, an idyllic island that sank below the sea in an earthquake

at·las /áttləss/ *n* **1.** MAP BOOK a book containing maps and vital statistics relating to geographic regions **2.** ANAT TOP BONE IN NECK the vertebra that is at the top of the spinal column and supports the skull. The atlas locks with the skull on rotation and turns with the head. **3.** (*plural* **at·lan·tes** /ət lán teez, at-/) ARCHIT FIGURE OF MAN USED AS SUPPORT a figure of a man, either standing or kneeling, used as a support for the upper part of a classical building [Late 16C. Via Latin < Greek]

At·las /áttləss/ *n* **1.** in Greek mythology, a Titan who was forced by Zeus to support the heavens on his shoulders as a punishment **2.** a small natural satellite of Saturn, discovered in 1980

At·las ce·dar *n* an evergreen tree widely grown as an ornamental for its green to silvery-blue foliage. Native to: northern Africa. Latin name: *Cedrus atlantica*. [After the ATLAS MOUNTAINS]

at·las moth *n* a large moth with a wingspan of 10 in./25 cm or more and strongly hooked and boldly patterned wings. Native to: tropical Asia and Australia. Latin name: *Attacus atlas*.

At·las Moun·tains /áttləss-/ system of mountain ranges that extends through Morocco, Algeria, and Tunisia. The highest peak is Jebel Toubkal in Morocco. Height: 13,665 ft./4,165 m.

~~atlass~~ incorrect spelling of **atlas**

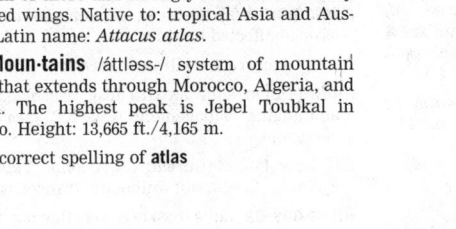

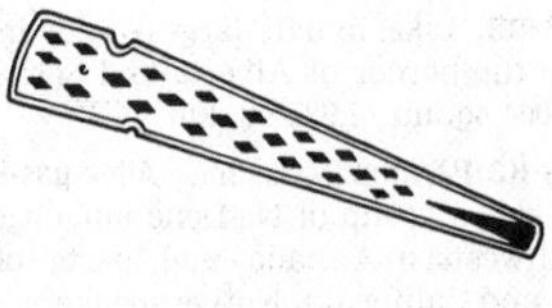

atlatl

at·la·tl /át latt'l, aát laat'l/ *n* a spear-throwing device, usually a stick equipped with a thong or socket, used to steady the butt of the spear during the throwing motion [Late 19C. < Nahuatl *ahtlatl*]

ATM *n* an electronic machine that enables customers to withdraw paper money or carry out other banking transactions on insertion of an encoded plastic card [Acronym < *automated teller machine*]

USAGE Risk of redundancy: Relatively new and conceivably puzzling acronyms, for example, ***ATM***, ***GPS***, and ***PIN***, tempt the user to orient the listener or reader with a redundant additional word such as *machine*, *system*, or *number*. However, *ATM machine* is equivalent to "automated teller machine machine." Whenever it seems likely the acronym alone will not be understood, it may be accompanied by the full form: ***ATM*** (*automated teller machine*) or the full form may be used alone instead.

atm. *abbr* METEOROL, PHYS **1.** atmosphere **2.** atmospheric

at·man /aátmən/ *n* in Hinduism, a person's essence or real self [Late 18C. < Sanskrit *ātman* "breath, spirit"]

At·man *n* in Hinduism, Brahman regarded as the Universal Soul

atmo- *prefix* gas, vapor [< Greek *atmos* "breath, vapor" < Indo-European, "to blow"]

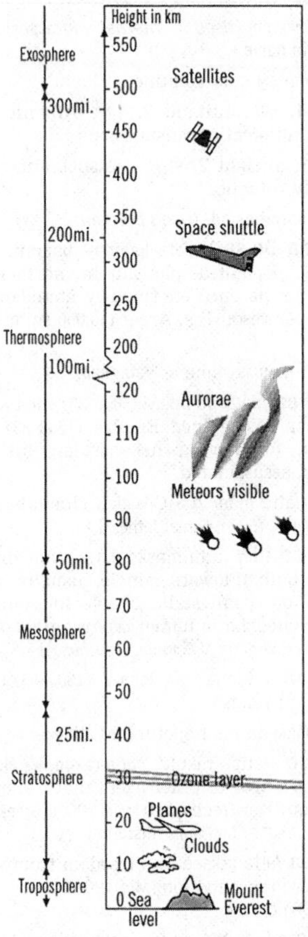

atmosphere: divisions of the Earth's atmosphere

at·mos·phere /átmə sfeer/ *n* **1.** GAS AROUND ASTRONOMICAL OBJECT the mixture of gases that surrounds an astronomical object such as Earth **2.** AIR OR CLIMATE the air or climate in a given place **3.** MOOD OR TONE a prevailing emotional tone or attitude, especially one associated with a specific place or time ○*"The atmosphere of the place was heavy and moldy, being rendered additionally oppressive by the closing of the door which led into the church."* (Wilkie Collins, *The Woman in White*; 1860) **4.** MOOD OR TONE OF ARTWORK the prevailing tone or mood of a work of art **5.** INTERESTING MOOD OF PLACE an interesting or exciting mood characteristic of a place ○ *a jazz club with lots of atmosphere* **6.** PHYS UNIT OF PRESSURE a unit of pressure defined as the pressure that will support a 760 mm column of mercury at 0°C at sea level, equal to 1.01325 x 10^5 newtons per square meter [Mid-17C. < modern Latin *atmosphaera* "sphere of vapor" < Greek *atmos* (see ATMO-) + Latin *sphaera* (see SPHERE)]

at·mos·pher·ic /átməs férrik, -féerik/, **at·mos·pher·i·cal** /-férrik'l, -féerik'l/ *adj* **1.** relating to the atmosphere of an astronomical object such as Earth ○ *atmospheric pollution* **2.** evoking or producing an emotional tone or aesthetic quality ○ *a mural with a misty atmospheric effect* —**at·mos·pher·i·cal·ly** *adv*

at·mos·pher·ic pres·sure *n* the downward pressure exerted by the weight of the overlying atmosphere.

It has a mean value of one atmosphere at sea level but decreases as elevation increases.

at·mos·pher·ics /àtməs férriks, -féeriks/ *n* **1.** STUDY OF ATMOSPHERIC INTERFERENCE the study of electromagnetic radiation emanating from natural sources in the atmosphere (*takes a singular verb*) **2.** ATMOSPHERIC INTERFERENCE WITH ELECTRONIC SIGNALS static on a radio or flickering white spots (**snow**) on a television screen caused by electromagnetic radiation from natural sources in the atmosphere (*takes a singular verb*) **3.** PREVAILING MOOD the mood or atmosphere suffusing a situation, group, or place (*takes a plural verb*)

at. no. *abbr* CHEM atomic number

a·to·le /a tóllay/ *n Hispanic* a hot sweet drink thickened with a powder made from corn dough and sometimes flavored with crushed fruit, sugar, or honey

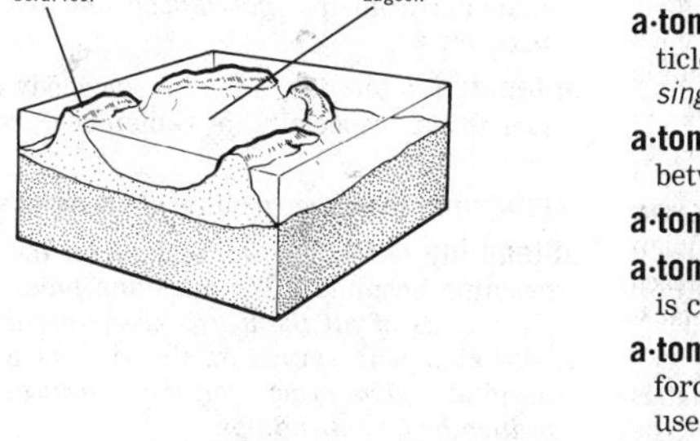

atoll

a·toll /á tòl/ *n* a ring-shaped coral reef and small island that encloses a lagoon and is surrounded by open sea (*often used in place names*) ○ *Bikini Atoll* [Early 17C. < Maldivian *atolu*]

at·om /áttəm/ *n* **1.** SMALLEST PART OF ELEMENT the smallest portion into which an element can be divided and still retain its properties, made up of a dense, positively charged nucleus surrounded by a system of electrons. Atoms usually do not divide in chemical reactions except for some removal, transfer, or exchange of specific electrons. **2.** VERY SMALL AMOUNT a very small part or amount ○ *not an atom of truth* **3.** PARTICLE OF MATTER IN GREEK PHILOSOPHY the basic particle of matter, indestructible and indivisible, first proposed by ancient Greek philosophers as the fundamental component of the universe [16C. < Latin *atomus* < Greek *atomos* "unable to be cut" < *temnein* "to cut"]

at·om bomb *n UK* same as **atomic bomb**

a·tom·ic /ə tómmik/ *adj* **1.** BASED ON NUCLEAR ENERGY based on or using nuclear energy **2.** RELATING TO ATOM relating to an atom or atoms ○ *atomic theory* **3.** TINY extremely small **4.** LOGIC UNANALYZABLE describes a proposition, sentence, or formula that cannot be analyzed into a coherent structure —**a·tom·i·cal·ly** *adv*

A·tom·ic Age *n* the present era, starting with 1945 and the first use of atomic weaponry, considered in terms of the discovery, uses, and social implications of nuclear energy

a·tom·ic bomb *n* an explosive device whose destructive power is due to the uncontrollable release of energy from the fission of heavy nuclei, usually uranium-235 or plutonium-239, by neutrons sustaining a rapid chain reaction

a·tom·ic clock *n* an extremely accurate timekeeping device regulated by the natural regular oscillations of an atom or molecule. An atomic clock powered by a hydrogen atom (**maser**) is accurate to 1 part in 2 quadrillion.

a·tom·ic cock·tail *n* a radioactive substance in liquid form, used to diagnose or treat cancer (*informal*)

a·tom·ic dem·o·li·tion mu·ni·tion *n* a 60–100 lb. tactical nuclear weapon.

a·tom·ic en·er·gy *n* PHYS same as **nuclear energy**

a·tom·ic force mi·cro·scope *n* a microscope that measures forces at the atomic level using a very sensitive crystal-tipped cantilever to probe a sample surface —**a·tom·ic force mi·cros·co·py** *n*

a·tom·ic heat *n* a value obtained by multiplying the specific heat of an element by its relative atomic mass

at·o·mic·i·ty /àttə míssətee/ *n* **1.** the number of atoms in a molecule of a chemical element **2.** the state of being composed of atoms **3.** CHEM same as **valence** (sense 1)

a·tom·ic mass *n* PHYS same as **relative atomic mass**

a·tom·ic mass u·nit *n* a unit used to express the masses of atoms and molecules, equal to one-twelfth of the mass of a carbon-12 atom or about 1.660 x 10^{-27} kg. Symbol **u**

a·tom·ic num·ber *n* the number of protons in the nucleus of an atom of an element and its isotopes, used to determine that element's position in the periodic table ○ *The atomic number of carbon is 6.* Symbol **Z**

a·tom·ic par·ti·cle *n* a particle that is a part of an atom, e.g., a proton, electron, or neutron

a·tom·ic phys·ics *n* the physics of elementary particles and their interactions and processes (*takes a singular verb*)

a·tom·ic ra·di·us *n* a length equal to half the distance between the nuclei of two covalently bonded atoms

a·tom·ic re·ac·tor *n* a nuclear reactor (*dated*)

a·tom·ic the·o·ry *n* any theory proposing that matter is composed of atoms

a·tom·ic vet·er·an *n* a former member of the armed forces who was exposed to radioactivity during the use or testing of nuclear weapons in or after World War II

a·tom·ic weight *n* MEASURE same as **relative atomic mass**

at·om·ism /áttə mìzzəm/ *n* the theory that all matter in the universe is made up of small, individual, finite, and indivisible particles —**at·om·ist** *n*

at·om·ize /áttə mīz/ (**-ized, -iz·ing, -iz·es**) *v* **1.** *vt* SEPARATE SOMETHING INTO ATOMS to reduce something to atoms or separate something into free atoms **2.** *vt* DESTROY SOMETHING to destroy something with atomic weapons **3.** *vti* MAKE INTO SPRAY to convert a liquid into fine particles, or to spray particles converted in this way —**at·om·i·za·tion** /àttəmi záysh'n/ *n*

at·om·iz·er /áttə mīzər/ *n* a device that converts a liquid into fine particles

at·om smash·er *n* a device that speeds up subatomic particles (*informal*)

a·to·nal /ay tṓn'l/ *adj* describes music in which the notes are not related by any mode or key —**a·to·nal·ly** *adv*

a·to·nal·ism /ay tṓn'l ìzzəm/ *n* the process of composing music in an atonal style or using atonality —**a·to·nal·ist** *n, adj*

a·to·nal·i·ty /ày tō nállətee/ *n* in music, the fact of consisting of notes that are not related by any mode or key

a·tone /ə tṓn/ (**a·toned, a·ton·ing, a·tones**) *vi* to make reparation for a sin or a mistake (*formal*) ○ *atoned for his misdeeds* [Mid-16C. < *at one* "in agreement," as in *(set) at one* "reconcile"] —**a·ton·a·ble** *adj* —**a·ton·er** *n*

a·tone·ment /ə tṓnmənt/ *n* **1.** the making of reparation for a sin or a mistake **2.** *also* **A·tone·ment** in Christian belief, the reconciliation between God and people brought about by the death of Jesus Christ

a·ton·ic /ay tónnik/ *adj* **1.** describes a syllable or sound that is not accented or stressed **2.** relating to, caused by, or showing a lack of muscle tone [Mid-18C. < ATONY, after TONIC] —**at·o·nic·i·ty** /àytə níssətee, àytō-, àtt'n íssətee/ *n*

at·o·ny /átt'nee/ *n* **1.** lack of stress or accent **2.** lack of normal muscle tone [Late 17C. Via French or late Latin *atonia* "weakness" < Greek < *atonos* "lacking tone" < *tonos* (see TONE)]

a·top /ə tóp/ *prep, adv* on or at the top of something

a·top·ic /ay tóppik, ə-/ *adj* describes a medical condition that is caused by a hereditary tendency to react to specific allergens, as in hay fever, some skin irritations, and asthma [Early 20C. < Greek *atopia* "unusualness" < *atopos* "out of place" < *topos* "place"] —**at·o·py** /áttəpee/ *n*

-ator *suffix* something or somebody that acts in a given way ○ *demonstrator* —**-atory** *suffix*

a·tor·vast·at·in /ə tòrvə stát'n/ *n* a drug that blocks the biosynthesis of cholesterol, reducing the level present in the blood, and is effective in reducing heart attacks and strokes

A to Z *n* **1.** a book containing maps and alphabetical lists of street names and map references for a town or city **2.** an alphabetically arranged reference work ○ *an A to Z of cooking terms*

ATP *n* a chemical compound (**nucleotide**) in living organisms that releases energy for cellular reactions when it converts to ADP. Full form **adenosine triphosphate**

ATP·ase /ày tee pée ayss, -ayz/ *n* an enzyme that aids the breakdown of ATP into ADP with a release of energy. Full form **adenosine triphosphatase**

at·ra·bil·ious /àttrə bíllee əss, -bíllyəss/ *adj* (*literary*) **1.** tending to feel very sad **2.** inclined to peevishness and irritability [Mid-17C. < Latin *atra bilis* "black bile" (translation of Greek *melankholia*), the bodily fluid formerly thought to cause sadness and irritability] —**at·ra·bil·ious·ness** *n*

at·ra·cur·i·um be·sil·ate /àttrə kyooree əm béssilət/, **at·ra·cur·i·um be·syl·ate** *n* a drug administered intravenously that acts as a neuromuscular blocking agent. Use: anesthesia. [< *atra-* + *-curium*, INN stem for substances resembling curare]

at·ra·zine /áttrə zèen/ *n* a white compound. Use: agricultural herbicide. Formula: $C_8H_{14}N_5Cl$. [Mid-20C. < Latin *atr-* "black" (because it prevents photosynthesis) + TRIAZINE]

a·trem·ble /ə trémb'l/ *adj* shaking or trembling from a strong emotion such as fear or excitement (*literary*)

a·tre·sia /ə tréezhə/ *n* the often hereditary absence of a usual body opening such as the anus or ear canal [Early 19C. < A[3] + Greek *trēsis* "perforation"]

A·treus /áy tròoss, áytree əss/ *n* in Greek mythology, king of Mycenae and father of Agamemnon and Menelaus

a·tri·a BUILDINGS, ANAT plural of **atrium**

at·ri·al fib·ril·la·tion /àytree əl-/ *n* an irregularity in heartbeat (**arrhythmia**) caused by involuntary contractions of small areas of heart-wall muscle

a·tri·o·ven·tric·u·lar /àytree ō ven tríkyələr/ *adj* relating to the atria and ventricles of the heart or to their interconnection [Mid-19C. < ATRIUM]

at-risk *adj* exposed to danger or harm of some kind

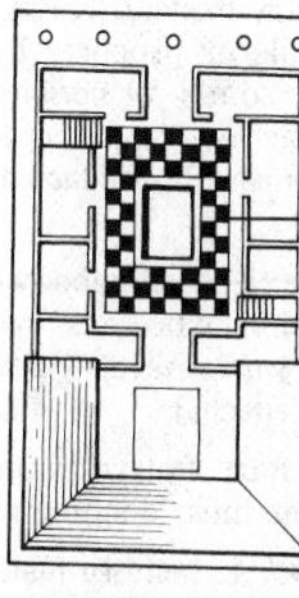

atrium (sense 2)

a·tri·um /áytree əm/ (*plural* **a·tri·ums** or **a·tri·a** /áytree ə/) *n* **1.** CENTRAL HALL WITH SKYLIGHT a central hall usually with a glass roof or skylight and extending the full height or several stories of a building **2.** ROMAN COURTYARD the open central courtyard of an ancient Roman house **3.** ANAT BODY CAVITY a cavity of the body, especially one of the upper chambers of the heart that takes blood from the veins and pumps it into a ventricle [Late 16C. < Latin]

a·tro·cious /ə trṓshəss/ *adj* **1.** VERY BAD appallingly bad ○ *atrocious manners* **2.** VERY CRUEL extremely evil or cruel ○ *atrocious crimes* **3.** UGLY TO LOOK AT ugly in taste or appearance ○ *an atrocious hat* [Mid-17C. < Latin *atroc-* "fierce, cruel" < *ater* "dark"] —**a·tro·cious·ly** *adv* —**a·tro·cious·ness** *n*

a·troc·i·ty /ə tróssətee/ (*plural* **-ties**) *n* **1.** SHOCKINGLY CRUEL ACT a shockingly cruel act, especially an act of wanton violence against an enemy in wartime ○ *to* *deplore the atrocities of war* 2. EXTREME CRUELTY extreme evil or cruelty ○ *an act of atrocity* 3. SOMETHING VERY BAD something repellent or extremely bad of its kind ○ *That design is an atrocity!* [Mid-16C. Directly or via French < Latin *atrocitas* < *atroc-* (see ATROCIOUS)]

a·troph·ic /ə trŏffik/ *adj* relating to or affected by atrophy

a·troph·ic gas·tri·tis *n* inflammation of the stomach caused by the inability to secrete sufficient acid to kill bacteria

a·troph·ic vag·i·ni·tis *n* inflammation of the vagina caused by estrogen deficiency and characterized by thinning and shrinking of the tissues of the vagina

at·ro·phy /áttrəfee/ *n* 1. WASTING AWAY the shrinking in size of some part or organ of the body, usually caused by injury, disease, or lack of use ○ *muscle atrophy* 2. LESSENING OF ABILITY weakening or lessening of some ability ■ *vi* (**-phied, -phy·ing, -phies**) WEAKEN to weaken or waste away through disuse or the effects of disease [Early 17C. Via late Latin *atrophia* < Greek, "lack of food" < *trophē* "food"]

at·ro·pine /áttrə peen, -pìn/, **at·ro·pin** /-pìn/ *n* a poisonous alkaloid obtained from the belladonna plant. Use: muscle relaxant. [Mid-19C. < modern Latin *Atropa*, genus name of belladonna]

At·ro·pos /áttrə pòss/ *n* in Greek mythology, one of the three Fates who influenced human destiny. Atropos was known as the Inexorable, and carried the shears that cut the thread of life.

att. *abbr* 1. attached 2. attention 3. LAW attorney

at·ta·boy /áttə bòy/ (*slang*) *interj* used to express enthusiastic encouragement or approval to a man or boy ■ *n* an act or an instance of congratulating somebody on an achievement ○ *received several attaboys from top management after the sales presentation* [Early 20C. Alteration of *That's the boy!*]

at·tach /ə tách/ (**-tached, -tach·ing, -ta·ches**) *v* 1. *vt* SECURE SOMETHING TO SOMETHING ELSE to secure one thing to another ○ *attached the door to the frame* 2. *vt* ADD SOMETHING TO SOMETHING ELSE to append or fasten one thing to another ○ *attached copies of the contracts* 3. *vt* ASCRIBE SOMETHING to assign a character or quality to something under consideration ○ *I attach no importance whatsoever to their claims.* 4. *vi* BE ASSOCIATED WITH SOMETHING to have a close inherent relationship to something ○ *little prestige attached to this post* 5. *vt* BIND SOMEBODY EMOTIONALLY to bind somebody emotionally to somebody else or to something (*usually passive*) 6. *vt* MIL PLACE SOMEBODY ON TEMP DUTY to assign military personnel to a military group on a temporary basis 7. *vt* LAW SEIZE SOMETHING LEGALLY to seize people or property by legal writ ○ *They've attached her salary for nonpayment of taxes.* [14C. < Old French *atachier*, alteration of *estachier* "fasten with a stake" < Germanic] —**at·tach·a·ble** *adj* —**at·tach·er** *n*

at·ta·ché /áttə sháy, a tà-/ *n* somebody on the staff of a diplomatic mission who has specific responsibilities ○ *a military attaché* [Early 19C. < French, past participle of *attacher* "attach"]

at·ta·ché case *n* a hard flat rectangular briefcase used for carrying business documents

at·tached /ə tácht/ *adj* 1. ENCLOSED fastened to or enclosed with something else ○ *Please see the attached documents and call with any questions.* 2. COMMITTED EMOTIONALLY TO SOMEBODY committed to an emotional relationship with somebody else (*informal*) 3. DEVOTED devoted to or fond of somebody or something 4. TOUCHING ANOTHER STRUCTURE sharing a wall with another building, and thus not standing alone 5. *Malaysia, Singapore* EMPLOYED having a permanent job with a person or organization ○ *My brother is attached to the Ministry.*

~~attachement~~ incorrect spelling of **attachment**

at·tach·ment /ə táchmənt/ *n* 1. EMOTIONAL BOND an emotional bond or tie to somebody or something 2. ONLINE ATTACHED TEXT a document or file attached to another or to an e-mail message 3. ACT OF ATTACHING the action of attaching one thing to another 4. PART ATTACHED an accessory attached or designed to be attached to a machine 5. MEANS OF ATTACHING SOMETHING a means by which something is attached to something else 6. LAW LEGAL SEIZURE the legal seizure of people or property, especially to acquire jurisdiction over them or it

at·tach·ment of earn·ings *n* a court order directing a third party, usually an employer, to withhold somebody's wages in order to satisfy unpaid debts

at·tack /ə ták/ *v* (**-tacked, -tack·ing, -tacks**) 1. *vti* HARM USING VIOLENCE to use violence to try to harm somebody or to defeat an enemy or capture an enemy position 2. *vt* CRITICIZE SOMEBODY OR SOMETHING to subject somebody or something to strong or vehement criticism ○ *The press has repeatedly attacked his plan.* 3. *vti* INFECT SOMEBODY OR DAMAGE SOMETHING to cause an infection, illness, or damage in somebody or something ○ *The disease can attack at any age.* 4. *vt* MAKE VIGOROUS START ON SOMETHING to begin something such as work with enthusiasm or determination and deal vigorously with it 5. *vti* TRY TO WIN to attempt to defeat, or score against, an opponent in a competition or team sport ○ *The chess game began sluggishly, with both sides slow to attack.* ■ *n* 1. ACTION OF ATTACKING the process or an instance of attacking ○ *The proposals have come under attack.* 2. BOUT OF ILLNESS an occurrence of something such as a medical disorder that is temporarily debilitating ○ *an attack of asthma* 3. ATTACKING MEMBERS OF TEAM the offensive players on a team, especially the forwards on a soccer team (*takes a singular verb*) 4. MUSIC ENERGETIC WAY OF PLAYING the decisive or energetic way in which a musician begins to play a piece or passage [Early 17C. Via French *attaquer* < Italian *attacare battaglia* "join battle"] —**at·tack·er** *n*

at·tack dog *n* 1. a powerful dog of a breed that is naturally fierce and aggressive, or is trained to be so 2. an aggressive, often unscrupulous partisan used by a politician or political party to denigrate an opponent or opposing party (*slang*)

at·ta·girl /áttə gùrl/ *interj* used to express enthusiastic encouragement or approval to a woman or girl (*slang*) [Early 20C. Alteration of *That's the girl!*]

at·tain /ə táyn/ (**-tained, -tain·ing, -tains**) *vt* 1. to achieve a goal or desired state, usually with effort 2. to reach an age, speed, or size [13C. Via Old French *ataindre* < Latin *attingere* "reach to" < *tangere* "to touch"] —**at·tain·a·bil·i·ty** /ə tàynə bílləte e/ *n* —**at·tain·a·ble** *adj* —**at·tain·a·ble·ness** *n*

SYNONYMS See ***accomplish***.

at·tain·der /ə táyndər/ *n* formerly, the loss of civil rights or property as a result of being outlawed or sentenced to death for having committed a serious crime, often treason [15C. < Anglo-Norman, variant of Old French *ataindre* "affect, dishonor" (see ATTAIN)]

at·tain·ment /ə táynmənt/ *n* 1. the achievement of the goals that somebody has set 2. a skill, accomplishment, or distinction, especially one achieved through effort (*often used in the plural*)

at·taint /ə táynt/ (**-taint·ed, -taint·ing, -taints**) *vt* formerly, to take away the civil rights of somebody outlawed or sentenced to death for having committed a serious crime, often treason (*archaic; often passive*) [14C. < Old French *atainte*, feminine past participle of *ataindre* "affect, dishonor" (see ATTAIN)]

at·ta·pul·gite /áttə púl gìt/ *n* a hydrated silicate of aluminum and magnesium. Use: in filters, an absorbent in medicine.

at·tar /áttər, á taar/, **at·ar** *n* essential oil extracted from flowers, especially rose petals ○ *attar of roses* [Mid-17C. < Arabic dialect *aṭar*]

at·tempt /ə témpt/ *vti* (**-tempt·ed, -tempt·ing, -tempts**) TRY TO DO SOMETHING to try to do something, especially without much expectation of success ■ *n* 1. EFFORT TO DO SOMETHING an act of trying to do something ○ *a successful attempt at cooking* 2. ATTACK an attack or assault ○ *an attempt on her life* [14C. Via Old French < Latin *attemptare* "try for" < *temptare* "to try, test"] —**at·tempt·a·ble** *adj* —**at·tempt·er** *n*

SYNONYMS See ***try***.

at·tend /ə ténd/ (**-tend·ed, -tend·ing, -tends**) *v* 1. *vti* GO TO EVENT to go to or be present at an event ○ *Hundreds attended the wedding.* 2. *vti* REGULARLY GO TO PARTICULAR ESTABLISHMENT to go regularly to an institution such as a school or church for instruction or worship 3. *vi* LISTEN OR WATCH CAREFULLY to listen or pay close attention to somebody or something (*formal*) 4. *vt* OCCUR ALONG WITH SOMETHING to accompany something or be associated with it (*formal; usually passive*) 5. *vt* BE SOMEBODY'S ATTENDANT to escort somebody or act as an attendant to somebody (*formal; usually passive*) 6. *vi* RESULT FROM SOMETHING to be the consequence of something (*literary*) [14C. Via Old French *atendre* < Latin *attendere* "reach toward" < *tendere* "to stretch"] —**at·tend·er** *n*

attend to *vt* to deal with or look after somebody or something ○ *patients to attend to* ○ *attend to business*

at·ten·dance /ə téndənss/ *n* 1. an instance of being at an event, or the practice of regularly going to a school, church, or other institution 2. the number of people who are present at an event or institution

at·ten·dant /ə téndənt/ *n* 1. SOMEBODY SERVING IN PUBLIC PLACE somebody employed to serve or help members of the public in a public institution or place ○ *a museum attendant* 2. ESCORT somebody who escorts or serves another person ■ *adj* OCCURRING ALONG WITH SOMETHING associated with something, or resulting or following from it ○ *parenthood and its attendant anxieties*

at·ten·dee /ə tèn dée, à ten-/ *n* somebody attending something, especially a conference, course, or seminar

~~attendence~~ incorrect spelling of **attendance**

at·tend·ing /ə ténding/ *adj* serving on the staff of a teaching hospital ○ *The attending physician made the rounds of all the wards every morning.* ■ *n* a physician who serves on the staff of a teaching hospital ○ *The orders for these medications were written by two attendings.*

at·ten·tion /ə ténsh'n/ *n* 1. CONCENTRATION mental focus, serious consideration, or concentration ○ *pay attention* 2. INTEREST notice or interest ○ *media attention* ○ *a letter for the attention of Mr. Brown* 3. APPROPRIATE TREATMENT care, tending, or appropriate treatment 4. AFFECTIONATE ACT a polite, considerate, or affectionate act (*formal; often used in the plural*) 5. MIL FORMAL MILITARY POSTURE a formal standing attitude assumed by members of the armed forces in drill and often when receiving orders, with feet together, eyes forward, and arms at the sides ■ *interj* MIL MILITARY ORDER a shouted military order to assume a posture of attention [14C. < Latin *attention-* < stem of *attendere* (see ATTEND)]

at·ten·tion def·i·cit dis·or·der, **at·ten·tion def·i·cit hy·per·ac·tiv·i·ty dis·or·der** *n* a condition, occurring mainly in children, characterized by hyperactivity, inability to concentrate, and impulsive or inappropriate behavior

at·ten·tion e·con·o·my *n* a view of the economy in the late 20th century that suggests that people's attention to websites is a valuable and tradable commodity

at·ten·tion-grab·bing *adj* attracting notice or interest, especially by being sensational or lurid ○ *attention-grabbing headlines*

at·ten·tion line *n* a line in a formally addressed letter or on an envelope addressed to an organization indicating for whom the letter is intended

at·ten·tion-seek·er *n* somebody who tries to attract attention, especially from somebody whose notice is craved —**at·ten·tion-seek·ing** *n*

at·ten·tion span *n* the length of time that somebody can concentrate effectively on a task or activity

at·ten·tive /ə téntiv/ *adj* 1. listening or watching carefully and with concentration 2. behaving toward somebody in a way that shows special regard or affection [14C. < French *attentif* < *atendre* (see ATTEND)] —**at·ten·tive·ly** *adv* —**at·ten·tive·ness** *n*

at·ten·u·ate /ə ténnyoo àyt/ (**-at·ed, -at·ing, -ates**) *v* 1. *vti* to reduce the size, strength, or density of something, or become thinner, weaker, or less dense 2. *vt* to reduce the virulence of a bacterium or virus, e.g., by exposing it to heat or producing a culture of it in a special medium. Attenuated bacteria or viruses are used in some vaccines. [Mid-16C. < Latin *attenuat-*, past participle of *attenuare* "make thin" < *tenuis* "thin"] —**at·ten·u·a·tion** /ə tènnyoo áysh'n/ *n*

at·ten·u·at·ed /ə ténnyoo àytəd/ *adj* long, narrow, and sometimes tapering

at·ten·u·a·tor /ə ténnyoo àytər/ *n* a device for reducing the strength of a wave, especially an electrical signal

at·test /ə tést/ (**-test·ed, -test·ing, -tests**) *vti* **1.** to show that something exists or is true or valid **2.** to state that something is true, especially in a formal written statement [15C. Via French < Latin *attestari* "to witness to" < *testis* "witness"] —**at·test·ant** *n* —**at·tes·ta·tion** /à te stáysh'n, àttə-/ *n* —**at·tes·tor** *n*

at·tic /áttik/ *n* a room or the area that occupies the space under a pitched roof ○ *boxes in the attic* [Late 17C. Via French *attique* "Attic" < Latin *Atticus* (see ATTIC)]

At·tic /áttik/ *adj* **1. OF ATTICA** relating to the ancient Greek territory of Attica or to the modern Greek department of Attica **2. ELEGANTLY WITTY** elegantly succinct or drily witty ■ *n* **ANCIENT GREEK DIALECT** a dialect of ancient Greek that was spoken in Attica [Late 16C. Via Latin < Greek *Attikos* < *Attikē* "Attica"]

At·ti·ca /áttikə/ **1.** department of east central Greece. Capital: Athens. Area: 5,466 sq. mi./14,257 sq. km. **2.** peninsula region of ancient Greece that was divided into 12 states

At·ti·cism /áttə sìzzəm/, **at·ti·cism** *n* a witty or elegantly simple and concise turn of phrase [Late 16C. < Greek *Attikismos* < *Attikos* (see ATTIC]

At·ti·la /átt'lə, ə tíllə/ (406?–453?) Hunnish warrior king who led an army of Mongolian nomads and subdued lands from the Rhine to the frontiers of China

at·tire /ə tír/ (*formal*) *n* clothing worn on a specific occasion ■ *vt* (**-tired, -tir·ing, -tires**) to dress yourself or somebody else, especially in clothes of a particular type [13C. < Old French *atirier* "to array" < *tire* "order" (see TIER)]

at·ti·tude /áttə tòod/ *n* **1. PERSONAL VIEW OF SOMETHING** an opinion or general feeling about something ○ *a positive attitude to change* **2. BODILY POSTURE** a physical posture, either conscious or unconscious, especially while interacting with others **3. CHALLENGING MANNER** an arrogant or assertive manner or stance assumed as a challenge or for effect (*informal*) ○ *a streetwise teenager with attitude* **4.** AVIAT **ORIENTATION OF AIRCRAFT'S AXES** the angle of an aircraft in relation to the direction of the airflow or to the horizontal plane **5.** AEROSP **ORIENTATION OF SPACECRAFT** the angle of a spacecraft in relation to its direction of movement [Late 17C. Via French < late Latin *aptitudo* "disposition" < Latin *aptus* (see APT)]

at·ti·tu·di·nal /àttə tòod'nəl/ *adj* **1.** insisting strongly on your rights **2.** relating to or involving personal attitudes toward specific issues or things in general ○ *attitudinal and behavioral changes* —**at·ti·tu·di·nal·ly** *adv*

at·ti·tu·di·nize /àttə tòod'n ìz/ (**-nized, -niz·ing, -niz·es**) *vi* to strike exaggerated or unspontaneous poses, or adopt extreme opinions, for effect

At·tle·bor·o /átt'l bùrrō/ city in southeastern Massachusetts, northwest of Providence, Rhode Island. Population: 43,164 (2002 estimate).

Att·lee /áttlee/, **Clement, 1st Earl Attlee** (1883–1967) British prime minister (1945–51). He served as deputy prime minister in Churchill's wartime coalition government. His postwar government, the first majority Labor government, introduced the welfare state and granted independence to India (1947). See table at **prime minister**

> "We believe in a League system in which the whole world should be ranged against an aggressor."
> [Clement Attlee, *Speech to the British Parliament, Hansard*; March 11, 1935]

attn. *abbr* attention

atto- *prefix* one quintillionth (10^{-18}) [< Danish or Norwegian *atten* "eighteen"]

at·tor·ney /ə túrnee/ (*plural* **-neys**) *n* **1.** a qualified lawyer, especially one who represents clients in court proceedings **2.** somebody legally empowered by a document (**power of attorney**) to make decisions and act on behalf of somebody else [14C. < Old French *atorne*, past participle of *atorner* "appoint" < *torner* < Latin *tornare* (see TURN)] —**at·tor·ney·ship** *n*

at·tor·ney at law (*plural* **at·tor·neys at law**) *n* LAW same as **attorney**

at·tor·ney gen·er·al (*plural* **at·tor·ney gen·er·als** or **at·tor·neys gen·er·al**) *n* **1. COUNTRY'S CHIEF LEGAL OFFICER** a country's chief legal officer, and its government's chief legal adviser. In the United States, the attorney general is a member of the president's cabinet. **2. STATE'S CHIEF LEGAL OFFICER** the chief law officer of a state, and its government's chief legal adviser **3. CHIEF LAW OFFICER OF CANADA** the chief law officer of a Canadian province, and its government's chief legal adviser

~~**attornies**~~ incorrect spelling of **attorneys**

at·tract /ə trákt/ (**-tract·ed, -tract·ing, -tracts**) *v* **1.** *vt* **ENTICE SOMEBODY** to be appealing enough to make people visit a place or spend their money **2.** *vt* **GET RESPONSE** to win or elicit a response from people, especially support or encouragement **3.** *vt* **DRAW SOMEBODY'S ATTENTION** to draw or secure somebody's attention, or become the focus of somebody's attention ○ *"It takes a big idea to attract the attention of consumers and get them to buy your product."* (David Ogilvy, *Ogilvy on Advertising*; 1985) **4.** *vt* **APPEAL TO PEOPLE** to appeal to people or awaken a response in them **5.** *vti* **BE OBJECT OF SEXUAL FEELINGS** to be the focus or object of sexual interest **6.** *vt* **DRAW SOMETHING CLOSER** to draw objects nearer, e.g., as a magnet draws iron objects toward it [15C. < Latin *attract-*, past participle of *attrahere* "draw toward" < *trahere* "to draw, pull"] —**at·tract·a·ble** *adj* —**at·tract·er** *n*

at·tract·ant /ə tráktənt/ *n* a substance or other agent that attracts something, especially one that attracts animals to food or members of the opposite sex

at·trac·tion /ə trákshən/ *n* **1. POWER OF ATTRACTING** the power of attracting or the feeling of being attracted ○ *"Our mutual attraction was immediate, and we enjoyed one another's company."* (Peter Ustinov, *Dear Me*; 1977) **2. APPEALING QUALITY OR FEATURE** a quality or feature that attracts somebody ○ *The idea has its attractions.* **3. THING OR PLACE THAT DRAWS TOURISTS** something such as a historic site or building that people, especially tourists, like to see or visit

at·trac·tive /ə tráktiv/ *adj* **1. GOOD-LOOKING** good-looking or sexually desirable **2. AGREEABLE** pleasing in appearance or manner **3. INTERESTING** interesting or appealing because of the probable advantages ○ *an attractive proposition* —**at·trac·tive·ness** *n*

SYNONYMS See ***good-looking***.

---

at·trac·tive·ly /ə tráktivlee/ *adv* in a pleasing, appealing, or sexually interesting way ○ *attractively priced furnishings* ○ *attractively situated a few minutes from the beach*

at·tract·or /ə tráktər/ *n* a fixed point or state of equilibrium that the behavior of a system is attracted to and tends to imitate

at·trib·ute *vt* /ə tríbbyoot/ (**-ut·ed, -ut·ing, -utes**) **1. ASCRIBE CAUSE TO SOMETHING** to think of something as caused by a particular circumstance ○ *To what do you attribute your success?* **2. CREDIT SOMEBODY WITH SOMETHING** to give credit for something such as a work of art or a saying to a particular person, often wrongly ○ *It's a bon mot that is often wrongly attributed to Saki.* **3. ASSIGN QUALITIES TO SOMEBODY OR SOMETHING** to regard somebody or something as having particular qualities ○ *the wisdom that she attributes to her favorite writers* ■ *n* /áttri byòot/ **QUALITY OR PROPERTY** a quality, property, or characteristic of somebody or something [14C. Directly or via French < Latin *attribut-*, past participle of *attribuere* "allot to" < *tribuere* (see TRIBUTE)] —**at·trib·ut·a·ble** *adj* —**at·trib·ut·er** *n*

at·tri·bu·tion /àttrə byóosh'n/ *n* the ascribing of something to somebody or something, e.g., a work of art to a specific artist or circumstances to a specific cause

at·trib·u·tive /ə tríbbyətiv/ *adj* forming part of a noun phrase and typically preceding the noun. For example, the adjective "tiny" in the noun phrase "one tiny problem" is in the attributive position. —**at·trib·u·tive·ly** *adv* —**at·trib·u·tive·ness** *n*

at·trit /ə trít/ (**-trit·ted, -trit·ting, -trits**) *vt* to wear something down little by little, especially enemy forces by persistent attacks (*informal*) [Mid-20C. Back-formation < ATTRITION]

at·tri·tion /ə trísh'n/ *n* **1. LOSS OF PERSONNEL** the gradual reduction of the size of a work force that occurs when personnel lost through retirement or resignation are not replaced **2. WEARING AWAY OF SURFACE** the wearing away of a surface, typically by friction or abrasion **3. WEAKENING BY PERSISTENT ATTACK** the gradual wearing away of morale and the powers of resistance by persistent attacks **4. SORROW FOR SIN** remorse for sin engendered by the fear of damnation [15C. < French < Latin *attrit-*, past participle of *atterere* "rub away" < *terere* "rub"]

At·tu /á tòo/ the most western of the Aleutian Islands, Alaska. It is rocky and barren. During World War II it was taken by the Japanese in June 1942 and retaken by US and Canadian forces in June 1943. Area: 390 sq. mi./1,010 sq. km.

At·tucks /áttəks/, **Crispus** (1723?–70) American patriot. He was a sailor who perhaps escaped from slavery, and who was killed in the Boston Massacre.

at·tune /ə tóon/ (**-tuned, -tun·ing, -tunes**) *vt* to adjust or accustom something to be receptive or responsive to something else

atty. *abbr* LAW attorney

Atty. Gen. *abbr* LAW, GOV Attorney General

ATV *abbr* VEHICLES all-terrain vehicle

At·wa·ter /át wàwtər/ city in central California, east of San Jose. Population: 24,677 (2002 estimate).

Margaret Atwood

At·wood /át wòod/, **Margaret** (*b.* 1939) Canadian writer. Her works include poems and novels such as *The Handmaid's Tale* (1986) and *The Blind Assassin*, which won the Booker Prize in 2000.

at. wt. *abbr* CHEM atomic weight

a·typ·i·cal /ay típpik'l/ *adj* not conforming to the usual type or expected pattern

au *abbr* Australia (*used in Internet addresses*) See table at **domain name**

Au *symbol* gold [< Latin *aurum*]

A.u. *abbr* PHYS angstrom unit

A.U. *abbr* ASTRON astronomical unit

au·bade /ō baád/ *n* a song, poem, or piece of instrumental music celebrating or greeting the dawn [Late 17C. Via French < Provençal *albada* < *alba* "dawn" < Latin *albus* "white"]

au·ber·gine /ṓbər zheen/ *n* **1.** *UK* same as **eggplant** (senses 1–2) **2.** a dark reddish purple color [Late 18C. Via French, Catalan, and Arabic < Persian *bādingān*]

Au·bert de Gas·pé /ō bèr də gas páy/, **Philippe Joseph** (1786–1871) French-Canadian novelist, author of *Les Anciens Canadiens* (1863)

Au·brey /áwbree/, **John** (1626–97) English antiquary whose biographical anecdotes were collected as *Brief Lives* (1813)

au·burn /áwbərn/ *adj* dark coppery red or reddish brown ○ *auburn hair* [15C. < Old French (influenced in sense by the similarity of the variant spelling *abrun* to *brun* "brown") < medieval Latin *alburnus* "whitish" < Latin *albus* "white"] —**au·burn** *n*

Au·burn /áwbərn/ **1.** city northwest of Phenix City, in east central Alabama. Population: 45,389 (2002 estimate). **2.** city in southwestern Maine, on the western bank of the Androscoggin River, north of Lewiston. Population: 23,142 (2002 estimate). **3.** town in central Massachusetts. It is a southeastern suburb of Worcester. Population: 16,287 (2002 estimate). **4.** city in central New York, north of Lake Owasco. It is a southwestern suburb of Syracuse. Population: 28,186 (2002 estimate). **5.** city in west central Washington State, south of Seattle. Population: 44,132 (2002 estimate).

A.U.C. *abbr* ab urbe condita (*used by Roman classical writers to specify the dates of events in terms of the number of years since Rome's foundation in 753* B.C.)

Auck·land /áwklənd/ **1.** administrative region of New Zealand, located in the northwest of the North Island and including the city of Auckland. Population: 1,158,891 (2001). Area: 6,287 sq. mi./16,282 sq. km. **2.** largest city in New Zealand, located in the northwest of the North Island. Founded in 1840, it is a commercial and industrial center and port. Population: 367,737 (2001).

au con·traire /ō kòn trér/ *adv* used to suggest that the opposite is really the case (*literary or humorous*) [< French, "to the contrary"]

au cou·rant /ō kōō ròN/ *adj* abreast of the latest developments [< French, "in the current"]

auc·tion /áwksh'n/ *n* **1.** SALE BY BIDDING a sale of goods or property at which intending buyers bid against one another for individual items, each of which is sold to the bidder offering the highest price ○ *an Internet auction* **2.** CARDS BIDDING IN GAME OF BRIDGE the bidding phase in a game of bridge, during which players contract to win a specific number of tricks if a specific suit is trumps ■ *vti* (**-tioned, -tion·ing, -tions**) SELL THINGS BY AUCTION to sell goods to the highest bidder [Late 16C. < Latin *auction-* "increase" < *augere* "to increase"] —**auc·tion·a·ble** *adj*

auc·tion bridge *n* a form of bridge in which all tricks won count toward the score, as distinct from contract bridge, in which only those tricks contracted to win count

auc·tion·eer /àwkshə néer/ *n* somebody who is in charge of an auction —**auc·tion·eer·ing** *n*

aud. *abbr* **1.** ACCT audit **2.** ACCT, OCCUPATIONS auditor

au·da·cious /aw dáyshəss/ *adj* bold, daring, or fearless, especially in challenging assumptions or conventions [Mid-16C. < Latin *audac-*, stem of *audax* "bold" < *audere* "to dare" < *avidus* (see AVIDITY)] —**au·da·cious·ly** *adv* —**au·da·cious·ness** *n*

au·dac·i·ty /aw dássətee/ *n* **1.** daring or willingness to challenge assumptions or conventions or tackle something difficult or dangerous **2.** lack of respect in somebody's behavior toward another person

AKG London

W. H. Auden

Au·den /áwd'n/, **W. H.** (1907–73) British-born US poet and dramatist. One of the most influential poets of his generation, he wrote numerous works including "September 1939" and "Lullaby," and won the Pulitzer Prize for *The Age of Anxiety* (1947). Full name **Auden, Wystan Hugh**

> "Some books are undeservedly forgotten; none are undeservedly remembered."
> [W. H. Auden, "Reading," *The Dyer's Hand*; 1963]

au·di·al /áwdee əl/ *adj* relating to hearing or sounds [Mid-20C. < AUDIO]

audiance incorrect spelling of **audience**

au·di·ble /áwdəb'l/ *adj* loud or clear enough to be heard ○ *an audible gasp from the crowd* ■ *n* in football, a new play called out in coded form by the quarterback at the line of scrimmage [15C. < late Latin *audibilis* < Latin *audire* "hear"] —**au·di·bil·i·ty** /àwdə bíllətee/ *n* —**au·di·ble·ness** *n* —**au·di·bly** *adv*

au·di·ence /áwdee ənss/ *n* **1.** PEOPLE WATCHING PERFORMANCE a group of people assembled to watch and listen to a show, concert, movie, or speech **2.** PEOPLE WATCHING OR LISTENING TO BROADCAST the viewers of a movie or a television program, or the listeners to a radio program **3.** AUTHOR'S READERSHIP the people who read a writer's books **4.** FORMAL INTERVIEW a formal, usually prearranged, interview with somebody important [14C. Via French < Latin *audientia* "a hearing" < *audire* "hear"]

au·dile /áw dīl/ *adj* PHYSIOL same as **auditory** [Late 19C. < Latin *audire* "hear"]

au·di·o /áwdee ō/ *n* the recording and reproduction of sound [Early 20C. < AUDIO-]

audio- *prefix* sound, hearing ○ *audiogram* [< Latin *audire* "hear"]

au·di·o book *n* a commercial recording, usually on a cassette tape, of somebody reading the text of a popular book

au·di·o·cas·sette /áwdee ō kə sét/ *n* a cassette containing an audiotape, for use in a tape recorder

au·di·o clip *n* an extract from a longer sound recording, e.g., from a movie soundtrack, that can be listened to on a personal computer

au·di·o·con·fer·enc·ing /áwdee ō kònfərənssing/ *n* the holding of a conference, meeting, or discussion in which the participants are linked by telephone

au·di·o fre·quen·cy *n* a frequency that is audible to the human ear, between 20 and 20,000 hertz in people with normal hearing

au·dio·gram /áwdee ō gràm/ *n* a tracing produced by an audiometer, recording the sharpness of somebody's hearing

au·di·ol·o·gy /àwdee óllәjee/ *n* the scientific study of hearing, especially for diagnosing and treating hearing loss —**au·di·o·log·i·cal** /àwdee ə lójjik'l/ *adj* —**au·di·ol·o·gist** *n*

au·di·om·e·ter /àwdee ómmətər/ *n* an instrument for testing the ability of a human ear to detect sounds over a range of frequencies and intensities —**au·di·o·met·ric** /àwdee ō méttrik/ *adj* —**au·di·om·e·try** *n*

au·di·o·phile /áwdee ō fīl/ *n* somebody who has an enthusiasm for sound reproduction, especially high-fidelity music recordings

au·di·o·tape /áwdee ō tàyp/ *n* **1.** magnetic tape for recording sound, or a length of this, typically in a cassette **2.** a sound recording on magnetic tape, especially for use in a tape recorder

au·di·o·vis·u·al /àwdee ō vízhoo əl/ *adj* **1.** OF SOUND AND VISION relating to sound and vision, especially when combined, e.g., in a presentation using both film and sound recordings **2.** OF HEARING AND SIGHT relating to the faculties of hearing and seeing ■ *n* TEACHING AID USING SOUND AND VISION a teaching or lecture aid that combines sound and vision, e.g., in the form of video equipment, software programs, or slides accompanied by sound recordings (*often used in the plural*)

au·di·o·vi·sual aid *n UK* same as **audiovisual** (*often used in the plural*)

au·dit /áwdət/ *n* **1.** CHECK OF FINANCIAL ACCOUNTS a formal examination, correction, and official endorsing of financial accounts, especially those of a business, undertaken annually by an accountant **2.** EFFICIENCY CHECK a systematic check or assessment, especially of the efficiency or effectiveness of an organization or a process, typically carried out by an independent assessor ■ *vt* (**-dit·ed, -dit·ing, -dits**) **1.** CHECK FINANCIAL ACCOUNTS to carry out an audit of the financial accounts of a business, department, or organization to establish accuracy or efficiency **2.** SIT IN ON CLASS to attend a class without asking for or receiving academic credit for it, usually attending all the sessions but not doing the assignments [15C. < Latin *auditus* "hearing" < *audit-*, past participle of *audire* "hear"] —**au·dit·a·ble** *adj*

au·di·tee /àwdi tée/ *n* a person or organization that is being audited

au·di·tion /aw dísh'n/ *n* **1.** TEST PERFORMANCE BY CANDIDATE a test in the form of a short performance, e.g., by an actor applying for a role in a movie or play **2.** HEARING the sense, faculty, or process of hearing ■ *vti* (**-tioned, -tion·ing, -tions**) GIVE AUDITION to do an audition, or give somebody an audition for a role [Late 16C. < Latin *audition-* "hearing" < *audire* "hear"]

au·di·tive /áwdətiv/ *adj* PHYSIOL same as **auditory** [Early 17C. < French < Latin *audire* "hear"]

au·di·tor /áwdətər/ *n* **1.** SOMEBODY CHECKING ACCOUNTS OR SYSTEMS somebody who checks accounts or conducts an audit of an organization **2.** STUDENT SITTING IN ON CLASS a student who attends a class without asking for or receiving academic credit for it **3.** HEARER a hearer or listener, e.g., a member of an audience or somebody listening to somebody who is talking (*formal*) [14C. Via Anglo-Norman < Latin, "hearer" < *audire* "hear"]

au·di·tor-gen·er·al (*plural* **au·di·tor-gen·er·als** *or* **au·di·tors-gen·er·al**) *n* in Canada, an independent auditor who prepares annual reports on federal government spending, including the spending of some Crown corporations

au·di·to·ri·um /àwdi táwree əm/ (*plural* **-ri·ums** or **-ri·a** /-ree ə/) *n* **1.** a hall or a building with a hall that is used for lectures, concerts, and other events **2.** the area of a theater or concert hall where the audience sits [Early 17C. < Latin, "place for hearing" < *audire* "hear"]

au·di·to·ry /áwdə tàwree/ *adj* relating to the organs of hearing or the process of hearing [Late 16C. < late Latin *auditorius* < Latin *audire* "hear"]

au·di·to·ry ca·nal *n* a passage from the outer ear drum along which sound waves travel

au·di·to·ry nerve *n* a nerve that conveys impulses relating to hearing and balance from the inner ear to the brain

au·dit trail *n* **1.** a sequential record of financial transactions, calculations, and other evidence examined by an auditor **2.** a record showing what operations a computer or computer user has performed in a specific period of time

Au·du·bon /áwdə bòn/, **John James** (1785–1851) Haitian-born US ornithologist, naturalist, and artist. An outstanding wildlife artist, he is best known for *The Birds of America* (1827–38), which contains life-size, hand-colored illustrations of more than 1,000 American birds.

au fait /ō fáy/ *adj* familiar with the latest developments in or facts about something [< French, "to the fact"]

Auf·bau prin·ci·ple /ówf bòw-/ *n* a principle that each successive chemical element in a sequence can be created by adding a proton to the nucleus and an electron to an orbital of the preceding element [< German, "construction"]

Aug. *abbr* CALENDAR August

Au·ge·an /aw jée ən/ *adj* **1.** disgustingly dirty, like the Augean stables **2.** extremely difficult and unpleasant

Au·ge·an sta·bles *npl* in Greek mythology, the stables owned by King Augeas that had not been cleaned in 30 years. One of Heracles' tasks was to clean them in one day, which he achieved by diverting two rivers through them.

au·ger /áwgər/ *n* a hand tool with a corkscrew-shaped bit for boring holes, or a larger tool, using the same principle, for boring holes in the ground [Old English *nafogār* < NAVE[2] + *gār* "spear" (see GORE[1]); *n* lost in 16C by false division of *a nauger* as *an auger*]

SPELLCHECK auger or **augur**? Do not confuse the spelling of ***auger*** and ***augur***, which sound similar. ***Auger*** is only used as a noun, denoting a tool for boring holes. ***Augur*** can be used as a noun, denoting a foreteller of the future, or as a verb, meaning "indicate what will happen in the future": *This does not augur well for the company's expansion plans.*

Au·ger ef·fect /ō zháy-/, **Au·ger proc·ess** *n* the emission of an electron from an excited positive ion resulting in a doubly charged ion [Mid-20C. After Pierre *Auger* (1899–1993), French physicist]

aught /awt/ *pron* anything whatever (*literary or archaic*) [Old English *āwiht* "ever a thing" < Germanic]

au·gite /áw jīt, áwgīt/ *n* a dark green mineral of the pyroxene group, containing aluminum, calcium, iron, and magnesium. Source: igneous rocks. [Early 19C. Via Latin *augites*, a precious stone (possibly turquoise) < Greek *augitēs* < *augē* "luster"]

aug·ment /awg mént/ *v* (**-ment·ed, -ment·ing, -ments**) **1.** *vti* INCREASE to add to something in order to make it larger or more substantial, or to grow in this way (*formal*) **2.** *vt* MUSIC **ENLARGE MUSICAL INTERVAL** in music, to enlarge a perfect or major interval by a semitone ■ *n* GRAM **PREFIXED VOWEL** in Greek or Sanskrit grammar, a vowel prefixed to a verb, or added to its initial vowel so as to lengthen it into a diphthong, to form a past tense [14C. < French *augmenter* < Latin *augere* "to increase" < Indo-European] —**aug·ment·ed** *adj* —**aug·ment·er** *n*

SYNONYMS See *increase*.

aug·men·ta·tion /àwgmən táysh'n, -men-/ *n* **1.** the increasing, or growth, of something in number, amount, size, strength, or intensity, or the amount by which something grows or is added to ○ *augmentation in costs* **2.** in music, the technique of varying a theme by increasing its note values proportionally

aug·men·ta·tion mam·mo·plas·ty *n* surgical enlargement of the breasts

aug·men·ta·tive /awg méntətiv/ *adj* **1. CAUSING INCREASE** tending to add to or increase something or to enable something to grow or increase (*formal*) **2.** GRAM **DENOTING GREAT SIZE OR IMPORTANCE** describes an affix that signifies great size or importance, or a word to which an affix of this kind has been added. Spanish "-ote" and Italian "-one" are augmentative affixes. ■ *n* GRAM **AUGMENTATIVE AFFIX OR WORD** an affix signifying great size or importance, or a word to which an affix of this kind has been added

au gra·tin /ō graát'n, ō grátt'n, ō graa taáN/ *adj* sprinkled with breadcrumbs, sometimes mixed with grated cheese, and browned before serving [< French, "with a gratin crust"]

Augs·burg /ówgz bùrg/ city in Bavaria in southern Germany, situated northwest of Munich. Population: 262,110 (1997).

au·gur /áwgər/ *n* **1. INTERPRETER OF MESSAGES FROM ROMAN DEITIES** in ancient Rome, a religious official who interpreted natural phenomena as signs that the deities favored or disapproved of actions proposed by the city **2. SOOTHSAYER OR PROPHET** any soothsayer, prophet, or diviner ■ *vti* (**-gured, -gur·ing, -gurs**) **INDICATE WHAT WILL HAPPEN** to suggest or indicate what will happen in the future or how well or badly things will turn out ○ *Recent events do not augur well for world peace.* ○ *Every circumstance augured success.* [14C. < Latin] —**au·gu·ral** /áwgyərəl, -gə-/ *adj*

SPELLCHECK See *auger*.

au·gu·ry /áwgyəree, -gə-/ (*plural* **-ries**) *n* **1.** the art, activity, prophecies, or pronouncements of an augur, soothsayer, or diviner **2.** an indication of what will happen in the future

au·gust /aw gúst/ *adj* full of solemn splendor and dignity (*formal*) [Mid-17C. Directly or via French < Latin *augustus*] —**au·gust·ly** *adv*

Au·gust /áwgəst/ *n* in the Gregorian calendar, the eighth month of the year, lasting 31 days. See table at **calendar** [Pre-12C. < Latin *augustus*, after the Roman emperor AUGUSTUS]

Au·gus·ta /aw gústə, ə-/ **1.** city on the western bank of the Savannah River, in east central Georgia. It was previously known as Fort Cornwallis. Population: 197,842 (2002 estimate). **2.** capital city of Maine and vacation resort, in the southwest of the state, on the Kennebec River. Population: 18,551 (2002 estimate).

Au·gus·tan /aw gústən/ *adj* **1. OF AUGUSTUS OR HIS TIME** relating to the Roman emperor Augustus, to his reign, or to the classical writers, including Virgil, Ovid, and Horace, who flourished during this period **2. CHARACTERIZED BY CLASSICAL WRITING** relating or belonging to a period during which writing in the classical style flourished, especially the 17th century in France or the 18th century in England ■ *n* **AUGUSTAN WRITER OR STUDENT** a writer from an Augustan period, or somebody who studies Augustan literature

Au·gus·tine /áwgə steén, aw gústin/, **St.** (354–430) Roman priest and theologian. His masterpiece, *The City of God*, greatly influenced the development of Christianity. He was bishop of Hippo, North Africa, from 395 until his death. Known as **St. Augustine of Hippo**

Au·gus·tine, St. (*d.* 604) Roman priest. Sent by Pope Gregory I to convert the Anglo-Saxons, he became the first Archbishop of Canterbury (597–604). Known as **St. Augustine of Canterbury**

Au·gus·tin·i·an /àwgə stínnee ən/ *adj* relating to St. Augustine of Hippo, his teachings, or any of the Christian religious orders living according to his rule or system of monastic life. ■ *n* a follower of St. Augustine of Hippo, especially a member of one of the religious orders living according to his rule.

Au·gus·tus /aw gústəss/ (63 B.C.–A.D. 14) Roman emperor. The founder of the Roman Empire, he was the adopted son of Julius Caesar. He succeeded his adoptive father as absolute ruler in 27 B.C. after a period of civil war.

au jus /ō zhóoss, ō zhóo/ *adj* describes meat that is served in its own cooking juices ○ *roast beef au jus* [< French, "with the juice"]

auk

auk /awk/ *n* a small black-and-white heavy-bodied seabird. Native to: cool northern seas. Family: Alcidae. [Late 17C. Via Norwegian *alk* < Old Norse *álka*]

auk·let /áwklət/ *n* a small auk that nests in burrows or rock slides. Native to: northern Pacific. Family: Alcidae.

auld lang syne /àwld lang zín/ *n Scotland* old times, or times long gone (*archaic*) [Literally "old long since," "old long ago"]

Aum *n* RELIG, BUDDHISM another spelling of **Om**

aum·bry *n* CHR same as **ambry**

au na·tu·rel /ō nàchə rél/ *adv, adj* **1.** served simply and plainly, e.g., uncooked or without seasoning or salt **2.** wearing no clothes (*humorous*) [< French, "in the natural state"]

Aung San /àwng sán/, **U** (1914?–47) Burmese nationalist leader. He became prime minister of British Burma (1945–47) and successfully negotiated Burmese independence, but was assassinated before independence was achieved.

Popperfoto

Aung San Suu Kyi

Aung San Suu Kyi /àwng san soo cheé/, **Daw** (*b.* 1945) Burmese human rights activist. She established Myanmar's National League for Democracy (NLD) party, and won the Nobel Peace Prize (1991).

> "Development requires democracy, the genuine empowerment of the people."
> [Daw Aung San Suu Kyi, *Times (London)*; November 22, 1994]

aunt /ant, aant/ *n* the sister of somebody's mother or father, or the wife of somebody's uncle [13C. Via Anglo-Norman < Latin *amita* "father's sister"] —**aunt·hood** *n*

Aunt *n* used, before a name or alone, as a form of address or reference to an aunt

aunt·ie /ántee, aántee/, **aunt·y** (*plural* **-ies**) *n* an aunt, or a close woman friend of a child's parents (*informal*)

Aun·tie, **Aunt·y** *n* (*informal*) **1. FORM OF ADDRESS TO PARENTS' FRIEND** used, before a name or alone, as a form of address or reference to an aunt or a close woman friend of a child's parents **2.** *UK* **BBC** a nickname for the BBC, or British Broadcasting Corporation, in reference to its image as a kindly and well-intentioned, if old-fashioned, guardian of standards **3.** *Malaysia, S Asia, Singapore* **FORM OF ADDRESS TO WOMAN** used as a form of address or reference to an unfamiliar woman of middle age or beyond ○ *Auntie, do you want to buy some?*

aunt·y *n* another spelling of **auntie**

au pair /ō pér/ *n* a young person from another country living with a family to learn the language, and helping with childcare and domestic work in return for room and board [< French, "on equal terms"]

au·ra /áwrə/ (*plural* **-ras** or **-rae** /-reé/) *n* **1. DISTINCTIVE QUALITY** a characteristic or distinctive impression created by somebody or something ○ *an aura of mystery* **2.** PARANORMAL **FORCE EMANATING FROM SOMEBODY OR SOMETHING** a force that is said to surround all people and objects, discernible, often as a bright glow, only to people of unusual psychic sensitivity **3.** MED **WARNING SENSATION BEFORE EPILEPTIC EPISODE** a distinctive sensation or visual disturbance that may signal the beginning of an epileptic episode or a migraine headache [Mid-18C. Via Latin, "gentle breeze" < Greek]

au·ral /áwrəl/ *adj* relating to the ear or hearing, or to receptiveness and response to speech or other sounds ○ *the extent to which our visual and aural perceptions of painting and music depend on our prior knowledge of the pieces* [Mid-19C. < Latin *auris* "ear"] —**au·ral·ly** *adv*

USAGE aural or **oral**? These two words are often confused because they are pronounced in a similar way and have meanings that are close. Essentially, ***aural*** has to do with hearing, whereas ***oral*** has to do with speaking or the mouth. An *aural test* is an examination testing comprehension by listening, whereas in an *oral test* the answers are spoken rather than written.

au·ran·o·fin /aw ránnə fin/ *n* a pharmaceutical compound containing gold, taken orally. Use: treatment of arthritis.

au·rar MONEY plural of **eyrir**

au·rate /áwr àyt/ *n* a salt containing an anionic grouping of gold and another element

au·re·ate /áwree ət, -àyt/ *adj* **1.** made of, containing, covered with, or colored like gold **2.** expressed or written in a highly or excessively ornamented, florid, or elaborate style [15C. < Latin *aureatus* < *aureus* "golden" < *aurum* "gold"]

au·re·i MONEY plural of **aureus**

Au·re·li·an /aw reélyən, -lee ən/ (215?–275) Roman emperor. Elected Roman emperor by the army (270–75), he recovered Gaul and made the Danube the empire's frontier.

Au·re·li·us /aw reéliee əss/, **Marcus** (121–180) Roman emperor and philosopher. Much of his time as emperor (161–180) was spent fighting on the empire's northern and eastern fronts. While on campaign he wrote *Meditations*, a 12-volume work that shows his interest in Stoic philosophy. Full name **Aurelius Antoninus, Marcus Aelius**

> "Time is like a river made up of the events which happen, and its current is strong; no sooner does anything appear than it is swept away, and another comes in its place, and will be swept away too."
> [Marcus Aurelius, *Meditations*; 170–180]

au·re·ole /áwree ōl/, **au·re·o·la** /aw reé ələ/ *n* **1.** a painted or carved representation of a circle of light around the head of a divine being or a saint **2.** METEOROL same as **corona** (sense 2) [Mid-19C. Via French < late Latin *corona aureola* "golden crown"]

au·re·us /áwree əss/ (*plural* **-re·i** /-ree ī/) *n* a gold coin that was a unit of currency in the Roman Empire between 30 B.C. and A.D. 310 [Early 17C. < Latin, noun use of *aureus* "golden" (see AUREATE)]

au re·voir /ăw rə vwaár, ō-/ *interj* goodbye till we see each other again [< French, "until seeing again"]

auri-[1] *prefix* ear, hearing ○ *auriform* [< Latin *auris* "ear"]

auri-[2] *prefix* gold ○ *auriferous* [< Latin *aurum*]

au·ric /áwrik/ *adj* containing gold with a valence of three ○ *auric oxide* [Early 19C. < Latin *aurum* "gold"]

Au·ric /aw reék/, **Georges** (1899–1983) French composer who produced orchestral works, ballets, and movie scores. He was a member of the Paris-based group of composers known as "Les Six," and was director of the Paris Opera and the Opéra Comique in Paris, France (1962–68).

au·ri·cle /áwrək'l/ *n* **1.** the part of the external ear that projects outward from the head **2.** an ear-shaped muscular part that sticks out from the surface of each upper chamber **(atrium)** of the heart **3.** ANAT same as **atrium** (*dated*) [Mid-17C. < Latin *auricula* "little ear" < *auris* "ear"] —**au·ri·cled** *adj*

au·ric·u·la /aw ríkyələ/ (*plural* **-las** or **-lae** /-leè, -lī/) *n* an alpine primrose with leaves shaped like a bear's ear. Flowers: yellow. Latin name: *Primula auricula*. [Mid-17C. < Latin (see AURICLE)]

au·ric·u·lar /aw ríkyələr/ *adj* **1.** EAR-SHAPED shaped like an ear **2.** OF ORGANS OF HEARING relating to the ear or the sense of hearing **3.** OF HEART CHAMBERS relating to the ear-shaped muscular part **(auricle)** on the surface of each upper chamber **(atrium)** of the heart

au·ric·u·late /aw ríkyələt, -làyt/ *adj* **1.** describes leaves that have an attachment at the base that is shaped like an ear **2.** describes an animal that has ears, auricles, or extensions that resemble earlobes

au·rif·er·ous /aw ríffərəss/ *adj* describes rock or minerals that contain gold

Au·ri·ga /aw rígə/ *n* a prominent constellation of the northern hemisphere containing the bright star Capella. See illustration at **constellation**

Au·rig·na·cian /àwrig náysh'n, àwrin yáysh'n/ *adj* belonging to a prehistoric culture associated with Cro-Magnon people in Europe around the period 30,000 to 22,000 B.C. [Early 20C. After *Aurignac*, France]

Au·ri·ol /àwree áwl/, **Vincent** (1884–1966) first president of the French Fourth Republic (1947–54). He served as finance minister (1936–37) and minister of justice (1937–38) before World War II. He was imprisoned (1940–43) for his opposition to the Vichy government and joined the Free French cabinet in 1945.

au·rochs /ów ròks, áw-/ (*plural same*) *n* a long-horned wild ox, now extinct but thought to be an ancestor of modern domestic cattle. Native to: North Africa, Europe, Southwest Asia. [Late 18C. < German, variant of *Auerochs* "original ox"]

au·ro·ra /aw ráwrə, ə-/ (*plural* **-ras** or **-rae** /-reé/) *n* **1.** a phenomenon occurring in the night sky around the polar regions, caused by atmospheric gases interacting with solar particles to create streamers, folds, or arches of colored light **2.** the dawn, usually personified (*literary*) [15C. < Latin, "dawn"] —**au·ro·ral** *adj*

Au·ro·ra[1] /aw ráwrə, ə-/ *n* in Roman mythology, the goddess of the dawn. Greek equivalent **Eos**

Au·ro·ra[2] /aw ráwrə, ə-/ **1.** city in northeastern Colorado. It is a northern suburb of Denver. Population: 286,028 (2002 estimate). **2.** city southwest of Chicago in northeastern Illinois, on the eastern bank of the Fox River. Population: 156,974 (2002 estimate).

au·ro·ra aus·tra·lis /-aw stráyliss/ *n* the colored lights seen in the skies around the South Pole [< modern Latin, "southern aurora"]

au·ro·ra bo·re·al·is /-bawree álliss/ *n* the colored lights seen in the skies around the North Pole [< modern Latin, "northern aurora"]

AUS *abbr* MIL Army of the United States

Aus. *abbr* **1.** Australia **2.** Australian **3.** Austria **4.** Austrian

Ausch·witz /ów shwìts/ site of the largest Nazi concentration camp, where between 1.5 and 4 million people were murdered between 1941 and 1945. Situated in southern Poland, it is now a museum and archive.

aus·cul·ta·tion /àwskəl táysh'n/ *n* the act of listening to the sounds made by a patient's internal organs, especially the heart, lungs, and abdominal organs, usually with a stethoscope, in order to make a diagnosis [Mid-17C. < Latin *auscultation-* < *auscultare* "listen to"] —**aus·cul·tate** /áwskəl tàyt/ *vt*

aus·land·er /ówss làndər/ *n* somebody from another country or area or who is an outsider [Mid-20C. < German *Ausländer* "outlander"]

Aus·le·se /ówss làyzə/ *n* the grade of high-quality German table wine above Spätlese, made from selected late-picked grapes and typically medium sweet to sweet [Mid-19C. < German, "selection"]

aus·pice /áwspəss/ *n* a sign or token for the future, especially a happy or promising one [Mid-17C. Via French < Latin *auspicium* "taking omens" < *auspex* "soothsayer," originally "somebody who foretells the future by studying the flight pattern of birds" < *avis* "bird" + *specere* "to look"] ◇ **under the auspices of somebody** *or* **something** with the help or support of a person or organization

aus·pi·cious /aw spíshəss/ *adj* marked by lucky signs or good omens, and therefore by the promise of success or happiness —**aus·pi·cious·ly** *adv* —**aus·pi·cious·ness** *n*

Aus·sie /áwssee/ *n* PEOPLES same as **Australian** *n* (sense 1) (*informal*) [Early 20C. Shortening] —**Aus·sie** *adj*

Aust. *abbr* **1.** Australia **2.** Australian **3.** Austria **4.** Austrian

Jane Austen

Aus·ten /áwstən/, **Jane** (1775–1817) British novelist, writer of elegant, satirical fiction, including *Pride and Prejudice* (1813). See Cultural note at **park, pride, sense**

> "A woman, especially if she have the misfortune of knowing anything, should conceal it as well as she can."
> [Jane Austen, *Northanger Abbey*; 1818]

> "For what do we live, but to make sport for our neighbors, and laugh at them in our turn?"
> [Jane Austen, *Pride and Prejudice*; 1813]

aus·ten·ite /áwstə nīt/ *n* a solid solution of carbon in iron that occurs as a component of steel at a specific stage of manufacture [Early 20C. After Sir William Roberts-*Austen* (1843–1902), British metallurgist] —**aus·ten·it·ic** /àwstə níttik/ *adj*

aus·tere /aw steér/ *adj* **1.** SUGGESTING PHYSICAL HARDSHIP imposing or suggesting physical hardship **2.** UNSMILING grimly unsmiling, humorless, or suggesting strict self-denial **3.** PLAIN AND WITHOUT LUXURY plain and simple, without luxury or self-indulgence ○ *lived an austere life on the frontier* **4.** PLAIN IN STYLE OR DESIGN severely plain in design or lines, without distractions or decoration [14C. Via French and Latin < Greek *austēros*] —**aus·tere·ly** *adv* —**aus·tere·ness** *n*

aus·ter·i·ty /aw stérrətee/ (*plural* **-ties**) *n* **1.** SEVERITY OR PLAINNESS severity of discipline, regime, expression, or design **2.** ECONOMY MEASURE a saving, economy, or act of self-denial, especially in respect of something regarded as a luxury **3.** ECON ENFORCED THRIFT thrift imposed as government policy, with restricted access to or availability of consumer goods

Aus·ter·litz /áwstər lìts, ów-/ site of a major battle in 1805 in what is now the eastern Czech Republic, at which Napoleon defeated Russian and Austrian forces

Aus·tin /áwstin/ capital of Texas and university city in the south of the state, on the Colorado River. Population: 671,873 (2002 estimate).

Aus·tin, Stephen Fuller (1793–1836) US political leader. He encouraged the settlement of Texas and became the first secretary of state of the Texas Republic.

aus·tral /áwstrəl/ *adj* relating to, belonging to, or coming from the south [15C. < Latin *australis* < *auster* "south"]

Austral. *abbr* **1.** Australasia **2.** Australia **3.** Australian

Aus·tral·a·sia /àwstrəl áyzhə/ region consisting of Australia, New Zealand, New Guinea, and neighboring islands of the South Pacific —**Aus·tral·a·sian** *adj, n*

Aus·tra·lia /aw stráylyə/ **1.** the world's smallest continent, situated between the Pacific and Indian oceans. Population: 19,401,800 (2003). Area: 2,939,974 sq. mi./7,614,500 sq. km. **2.** country encompassing the continent of Australia and the island of Tasmania. It is the sixth largest country in the world. It became an independent member of the British Commonwealth in 1931. Language: English. Currency: Australian dollar. Capital: Canberra. Population: 19,881,500 (2003). Area: 2,966,200 sq. mi./7,682,300 sq. km. Official name **Commonwealth of Australia**

Aus·tra·lian /aw stráylyən/ *adj* **1.** OF AUSTRALIA relating to Australia, or its people, languages, or cultures **2.** OF ABORIGINAL LANGUAGES OF AUSTRALIA relating to the family of languages spoken in Australia before European settlement. Most Australian languages are now extinct or approaching extinction. ■ *n* **1.** SOMEBODY FROM AUSTRALIA somebody who comes from Australia **2.** AUSTRALIAN ENGLISH the variety of English spoken in Australia

Aus·tra·lian Alps /aw stràylyən-/ mountain range in southeastern Australia, straddling the border between New South Wales and Victoria and forming part of the Great Dividing Range. It includes Australia's highest peak, Mount Kosciuszko, 7,310 ft./2,228 m.

Aus·tra·lian bal·lot *n* POL same as **secret ballot**

Aus·tra·lian Cap·i·tal Ter·ri·to·ry internal federal territory in southeastern Australia, which incorporates Canberra, the national capital. Capital: Canberra. Population: 322,900 (2003). Area: 930 sq. mi./2,400 sq. km.

Aus·tra·lian Eng·lish *n* the form of English spoken in Australia as distinct from other forms of English. See panel on next page

Aus·tra·lian·ism /aw stráylee ə nìzzəm/ *n* a word or expression that originated in, or is used mainly in, Australia

Aus·tra·lian Na·tion·al Gal·ler·y *n* former name for **National Gallery of Australia**

Aus·tra·lian Rules, Aus·tra·lian Rules foot·ball *n* an Australian game resembling rugby, played on an oval field with 18 to a team and a large oval ball that can be punched, kicked, or carried (*takes a singular verb*)

Aus·tra·lian ter·ri·er *n* a short stocky terrier with erect ears and a straight wiry coat that is normally blue- or silver-gray with brown patches on the muzzle and feet

Aus·tra·loid /áwstrə lòyd/ *adj* relating to Australian Aboriginals and some other Southeast Asian and Pacific peoples —**Aus·tra·loid** *n*

aus·tra·lo·pith·e·cine /àwstrəlō píthə seén/ *adj* describes or relating to a prehistoric primate of southern and eastern Africa whose fossilized remains resemble those of humans [Mid-20C. < modern Latin *Australopithecus* < Latin *australis* "southern" + Greek *pithēkos* "ape"] —**aus·tra·lo·pith·e·cine** *n*

Aus·tra·sia /aw stráyzhə/ eastern part of the medieval kingdom of the Franks, consisting of what are now parts of France, Germany, and the Netherlands

Aus·tri·a /áwstree ə/ country in central Europe. Lan-

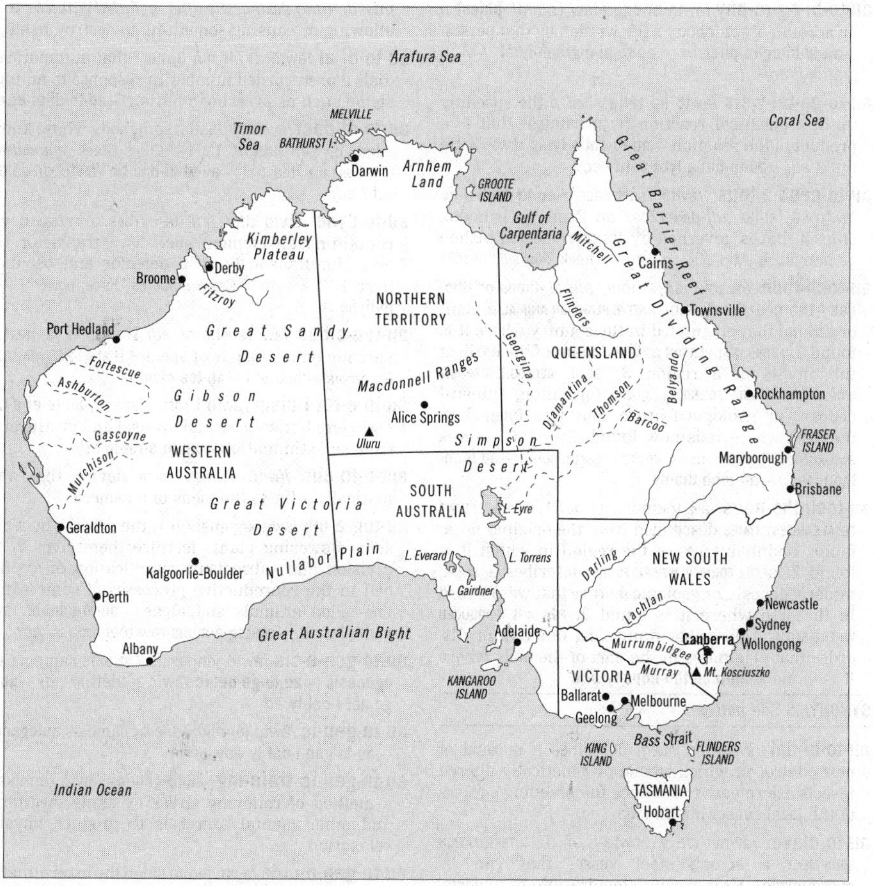

Australia

WORLD ENGLISH ***Australian English*** is the English language as used in the Commonwealth of Australia, population over 19 million, which is, with Canada, third in size and distinctness among the primary English-speaking countries. English has been used in Australia for about 200 years.
Australian English is markedly homogeneous, with three kinds of accent: (1) *Cultivated Australian*, similar to Received Pronunciation in the United Kingdom, and formerly highly regarded; (2) *Broad Australian*, often compared with British Cockney; and (3) *General Australian*, the majority variety, occupying the social middle ground. Australian English does not pronounce *r* in words such as *art, door,* and *worker.* The vowel in *can't dance* is closer to that in "kent dense" than in "cahnt dahnce" or "kaynt dayncе," and the Broad version of *I'm going there today* sounds to some ears like "I'm going there to die."
Australian English and British English spelling are generally identical (with some ambivalence in the *-or/our* endings, most notably in US-style *Labor,* the name of a political party). Grammar is comparable to general usage in both Britain and the United States, but Australian English has a large and distinctive home-grown vocabulary that includes: (1) Adoptions from Aboriginal languages, with a penchant for spelling with double letters (as in *corroboree* and *kookaburra*) and mainly relating to animals, plants, objects, and localities (as, for example, *billabong, boomerang, didgeridoo, dingo, koala, Murrumbidgee, Woomera*), a process similar to American English's adoption from Native American languages; (2) Extensions in meaning of everyday words, for example, *to feel crook* "to feel ill," *to farewell somebody* "to give somebody a farewell party," *mob* "a flock or group (of sheep, kangaroos, etc.)," *station* "a ranch," as in *sheep station*; (3) Extensions or shifts in the meaning of British dialect words, for example, *cobber* "a friend, mate," *dinkum* "reliable, genuine"; (4) Distinctive informal word endings, for example, *-o* in abbreviations such as *arvo* "afternoon" and *journo* "journalist," and *-ie* in names for workers such as *truckie* "truck-driver" and *wharfie* "stevedore." See ***New Zealand English.***

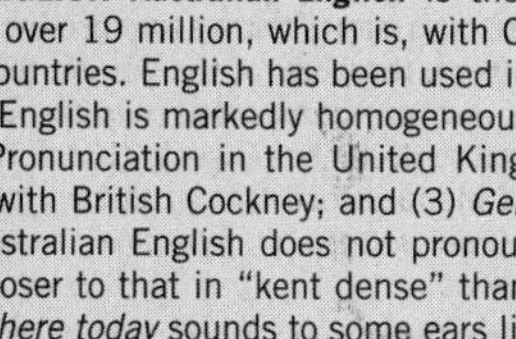

Austria

guage: German. Currency: euro. Capital: Vienna. Population: 8,188,207 (2003). Area: 32,378 sq. mi./83,858 sq. km. Official name **Republic of Austria** —**Aus·tri·an** *adj, n*

Aus·tri·an blind *n* a fabric window blind with panels that can be gathered up vertically into loose folds

Austro- *prefix* southern ○ *Austroasiatic* [< Latin *auster*]

Aus·tro·a·si·at·ic /àwstrō ayzhee áttik/ *n* a large family of languages spoken in Southeast Asia and eastern India. Native speakers: 70 million. —**Aus·tro·a·si·at·ic** *adj*

Aus·tro·ne·sia /àwstrō neézhə, -neéshə/ region consisting of Indonesia, Melanesia, Micronesia, Polynesia, and neighboring islands in the Pacific Ocean

Aus·tro·ne·sian /àwstrō neézh'n, -neésh'n/ *adj* relating to Austronesia, or its peoples, languages, or cultures ■ *n* a family of languages spoken in Taiwan, parts of Southeast Asia, the Pacific Islands, New Zealand, and Madagascar. Native speakers: 250 million.

aut- *prefix* same as **auto-** (*used before vowels*)

au·tar·chy /áw taarkee/ (*plural* **-chies**) *n* **1. UNLIMITED POLITICAL POWER** absolute power, especially such power wielded by a despotic ruler **2. SELF-GOVERNMENT** self-government of a country by representatives drawn from among its own citizens **3. COUNTRY WITH DESPOTIC RULER** a country governed by a ruler who has absolute power **4. SELF-GOVERNING COUNTRY** an independent country with its own government, as distinct from a colony or dependency [Mid-17C. < Greek *autarkhos* "self-governing" < *arkhein* "rule"] —**au·tar·chic** /aw taarkik/ *adj* —**au·tar·chi·cal** *adj* —**au·tar·chist** *n*

au·tar·ky /áw taarkee/ (*plural* **-kies**) *n* **1.** an economic policy or situation in which a nation is independent of international trade and not reliant upon imported goods **2.** a nation that is economically self-sufficient [Early 17C. < Greek *autarkeia* "self-sufficiency" < *autarkēs* "self-sufficient" < *arkein* "be sufficient"] —**au·tar·kic** /aw taarkik/ *adj* —**au·tar·ki·cal** *adj*

au·te·col·o·gy /àwtə kólləjee/ *n* the study of individuals or populations of a single species and their relationship to their environment —**au·te·co·log·i·cal** /àwtekə lójjik'l/ *adj*

au·teur /aw túr/ *n* a film director whose films are so distinctive that he or she is perceived as a film's creator [Mid-20C. < French, "author"]

au·teur·ism /aw túr ìzzəm/ *n* belief in or practice of auteur theory —**au·teur·ist** *adj*

au·teur the·o·ry *n* film criticism that considers the director of a film to be its primary creator

auth. *abbr* **1.** authentic **2.** author **3.** authority **4.** authorized

au·then·tic /aw théntik, ə-/ *adj* **1. NOT FALSE OR COPIED** genuine and original, as opposed to being a fake or reproduction **2. TRUSTWORTHY** shown to be true and trustworthy **3.** LAW **VALID** legally valid because all necessary procedures have been followed correctly **4.** MUSIC **IN STYLE OF ORIGINAL PERIOD** performed in the musical style current at the time of composition, and on instruments similar to those of the time **5.** MUSIC, CHR **WITH UPWARD RANGE FROM MAIN NOTE** describes church music such as Gregorian chant that has an upward range from the keynote of the scale [14C. Via French < Greek *authentikos* "genuine" < *authentes* "master, doer" < *autos* "self"] —**au·then·ti·cal·ly** *adv*

au·then·ti·cate /aw théntə kàyt/ (**-cat·ed, -cat·ing, -cates**) *vt* **1.** to establish that something is genuine or that an account is true **2.** to establish something such as a deed or document as legally valid —**au·then·ti·ca·tor** *n*

au·then·ti·ca·tion /aw thèntə káysh'n/ *n* **1.** the act of proving something to be genuine or valid, or the evidence used in so doing **2.** a security measure using data encryption that identifies the user and verifies that the message was not tampered with (*used in e-commerce*)

au·then·tic·i·ty /àw then tíssətee, àwthən-/ *n* **1.** the genuineness or truth of something **2.** the legal validity or correctness of a legal document

au·thor /áwthər/ *n* **1. WRITER** somebody who writes a book or other text such as a literary work or a report **2. PROFESSIONAL WRITER** somebody who writes books as a profession **3. CREATOR OR SOURCE** the creator or cause of something ■ *vt* (**-thored, -thor·ing, -thors**) **1. WRITE SOMETHING** to write or be responsible for the final form of a book, report, or other text **2. WRITE COMPUTER PROGRAM** to create a computer application such as a multimedia document, usually using special software ○ *authoring systems* **3. CAUSE SOMETHING** to be the cause, creator, or originator of something [14C. Via French < Latin *auctor* "creator, originator" < *augere* "originate, increase"] —**au·thor·i·al** /aw tháwree əl/ *adj* —**au·thor·ship** *n*

USAGE Although the verb ***author*** has been around for over 400 years, many people dislike it in contexts such as *She has authored several books,* because it does not simply imply "to write," but "to be responsible for the content of a printed or published document." However, there is no problem with the use of the verb ***author*** in computing contexts, where it refers specifically to the creation of databases, multimedia products, and other applications.

au·thor·ing /áwthəring/ *n* the creation of computer applications such as multimedia documents, usually done by nonprogrammers using special software (*often used before a noun*) ○ *authoring systems*

au·thor·ing lan·guage *n* a software development system that lets users develop applications without using formal programming language

au·thor·i·tar·i·an /aw thàwrə térree ən/ *adj* **1.** favoring strict rules and established authority **2.** belonging to or believing in a political system in which obedience to the ruling person or group is strongly enforced —**au·thor·i·tar·i·an** *n* —**au·thor·i·tar·i·an·ism** *n*

au·thor·i·ta·tive /ə tháwrə tàytiv/ *adj* **1.** RELIABLE convincing, reliable, backed by evidence, and showing deep knowledge **2.** BACKED BY AUTHORITY backed by an established and accepted authority **3.** SHOWING AUTHORITY showing confidence in or the expectation of being obeyed —**au·thor·i·ta·tive·ly** *adv* —**au·thor·i·ta·tive·ness** *n*

au·thor·i·ty /ə tháwrətee/ (*plural* **-ties**) *n* **1.** RIGHT TO COMMAND the right or power to enforce rules or give orders **2.** HOLDER OF POWER somebody or something with official power **3.** POWER GIVEN TO SOMEBODY power to act on behalf of somebody else, or official permission to do something **4.** SOURCE OF RELIABLE INFORMATION a source of reliable information on a subject **5.** ADMINISTRATIVE BODY an official body that is set up by a government to administer an area of activity (*often used in the plural*) ○ *the local port authority* **6.** JUSTIFICATION a statement that makes somebody believe something is true **7.** QUALITY THAT IS RESPECTED the ability to gain the respect of other people and to influence or control what they do **8.** OBVIOUS KNOWLEDGE AND EXPERIENCE knowledge, skill, or experience worthy of respect **9.** LAW SOURCE OF PRECEDENT OR PRINCIPLE a law or legal decision that is cited as establishing a precedent or a principle **10.** LEGITIMATE POWER a form of rule that is seen as legitimate [13C. Via French < Latin *auctoritas* < *auctor* (see AUTHOR)]

au·thor·i·ty fig·ure *n* somebody who is, or appears to be, strong and powerful and able to command and influence others

au·thor·i·za·tion /àwthəri záysh'n/ *n* **1.** PERMISSION official power or permission to do something **2.** DOCUMENT GIVING PERMISSION a letter or document that confirms that somebody has permission to do something or be somewhere **3.** E-COMMERCE TRANSACTION RISK ASSESSMENT the process of assessing the degree of risk involved in an e-commerce transaction in terms of a customer's debt limits and available credit

au·tho·rize /áwthə rīz/ (**-rized, -riz·ing, -riz·es**) *vt* to give somebody or something power, permission, or authorization to do something or be somewhere [14C. Via French < medieval Latin *auctorizare* < Latin *auctor* (see AUTHOR)] —**au·thor·ized** *adj* —**au·thor·iz·er** *n*

Au·thor·ized Ver·sion /áwthə rīzd-/ *n UK* same as **King James Bible**

au·tism /áw tìzzəm/ *n* a disturbance in psychological development in which use of language, reaction to stimuli, interpretation of the world, and the formation of relationships are not fully established and follow unusual patterns [Early 20C. < Greek *autos* "self"]

au·tis·tic /aw tístik/ *adj* showing evidence of autism, e.g., failure to use language and perceive surroundings in the expected way —**au·tis·ti·cal·ly** *adv*

au·tis·tic sa·vant *n* somebody who has a learning disability or psychiatric disorder but who is exceptionally gifted in one specific area, e.g., rapid mathematical calculation or music

au·to /áwtō/ (*plural* **-tos**) *n* CARS same as **automobile** (*informal*) [Late 19C. Shortening]

auto. *abbr* **1.** automatic **2.** MECH ENG automotive

auto- *prefix* **1.** self ○ *autograft* **2.** automatic ○ *autopilot* [< Greek *autos* "self"]

au·to·an·ti·bod·y /àwtō ánti bòddee/ (*plural* **-ies**) *n* an antibody that reacts against normal substances present in the organism producing it and is present in autoimmune diseases

au·to·bahn /áwtō baan, áwtə-/ *n* an expressway in a German-speaking country or region [Mid-20C. < German, "automobile track"]

au·to·bi·og·ra·phy /àwtō bī óggrəfee/ (*plural* **-phies**) *n* an account of somebody's life written by that person —**au·to·bi·og·ra·pher** *n* —**au·to·bi·o·graph·i·cal** /-bī ə gráffik'l/ *adj*

au·to·ca·tal·y·sis /àwtō kə tálləsiss/ *n* the speeding up of a chemical reaction by a catalyst that is a product of the reaction —**au·to·cat·a·lyt·ic** /àwtō kàttə líttik/ *adj* —**au·to·cat·a·lyt·i·cal·ly** *adv*

au·to·ceph·a·lous /àwtō séffələss/, **au·to·ceph·a·lic** /àwtō sə fállik/ *adj* describes an Eastern Orthodox church that is governed by its own elected bishop or patriarch [Mid-19C. < AUTO- + Greek *kephalē* "head"]

au·toch·thon /aw tókthən, -thòn/ (*plural* **-thons** or **-tho·nes** /-thə neez/) *n* **1.** BIOL NATIVE PLANT OR ANIMAL a plant or animal that originated in the country where it is found **2.** ABORIGINAL PERSON a descendant of the earliest inhabitants of a region **3.** GEOL GEOLOGIC DEPOSIT ORIGINATING WHERE FOUND a rock formation, mineral deposit, or geologic feature that was formed in the area where it is now found [Early 19C. < Greek *autokhthōn* "indigenous" < *khthōn* "earth, soil"] —**au·toch·thon·ism** *n* —**au·toch·tho·ny** *n*

au·toch·tho·nous /aw tókthənəss/ *adj* **1.** BIOL PRESENT FROM EARLIEST TIMES descended from the original flora, fauna, or inhabitants of the region in which it is found **2.** GEOL FORMED WHERE FOUND describes a rock, mineral deposit, or geologic feature that was formed in the area where it is found **3.** PHYSIOL PRODUCED WHERE SITUATED describes a physical function or disorder that originates in the part of the body where it is found —**au·toch·tho·nous·ly** *adv*

SYNONYMS See ***native***.

au·to·ci·dal /àwtō sīd'l/ *adj* describes a method of pest control in which sterile or genetically altered insects are released to reduce the breeding success of the local insect population

au·to·clave /áwtō klàyv, áwtə-/ *n* **1.** STERILIZATION EQUIPMENT a strong steel vessel that can be pressurized. Use: steam sterilization of objects, pressurized chemical reactions at high temperature. **2.** STEAMER FOR CONCRETE an apparatus with which newly cast concrete is cured by steam under pressure ■ *vt* (**-claved, -clav·ing, -claves**) PLACE SOMETHING IN AUTOCLAVE to use an autoclave to steam something [Late 19C. < French < Greek *autos* "self" + Latin *clavus* "nail" or *clavis* "key"; because self-fastening]

au·to·cor·re·la·tion /àwtō kawrə láysh'n/ *n* in statistics, a property displayed by some sequences of adjacent items not being independent of each other

au·toc·ra·cy /aw tókrəssee/ (*plural* **-cies**) *n* **1.** RULE BY ONE PERSON a government in which somebody holds unlimited power **2.** RULER'S ABSOLUTE POWER the unlimited political power of a single ruler **3.** PLACE RULED BY ONE PERSON a country governed by a single ruler who has unlimited power [Mid-17C. < Greek *autokrateia* < *autokratēs* (see AUTOCRAT)]

au·to·crat /áwtə kràt/ *n* **1.** a ruler who holds unlimited power and is answerable to no other person **2.** somebody who dominates others [Early 19C. Via French *autocrate* < Greek *autokratēs* "independent authority" < *kratos* "power"] —**au·to·crat·ic** /àwtə kráttik/ *adj* —**au·to·crat·i·cal·ly** *adv*

CULTURAL NOTE ***The Autocrat of the Breakfast Table***, a book of essays and poems by Oliver Wendell Holmes (1858). One of a series of works that also includes *The Professor at the Breakfast Table* and *The Poet at the Breakfast Table*, this humorous collection satirizes, among other targets, Calvinism and medical bigotry.

au·to·cross /áwtō kràwss/ *n* an automobile competition testing the drivers' speed and skill [Mid-20C. Contraction of AUTOMOBILE + CROSS-COUNTRY]

au·to·da·fé /àwtō də fáy, òwtō-/ (*plural* **au·tos-da-fé** /àwtō-, òwtō-/) *n* a sentence of death pronounced on a heretic by a court of the Spanish Inquisition and carried out by the civil authorities. The condemned person was burned at the stake. [Early 18C. < Portuguese, "act of the faith"]

au·to·de·con·struc·tion /àwtō deekən strúkshən/ *n* critical analysis of artistic works that is done by the artists themselves rather than critics

au·to·de·struct /àwtō di strúkt/ *vi* (**-struct·ed, -struct·ing, -structs**) to undergo self-destruction ○ *The missile auto-destructed after a failed launch.* ■ *adj* allowing or causing something to destroy itself

au·to·di·al /áwtō dī əl/ *n* a device that automatically dials a prerecorded number in response to an input signal such as pressing a button —**au·to·di·al·er** *n*

au·to·di·dact /àwtō dī dàkt/ *n* somebody whose knowledge is self-taught [Mid-18C. < Greek *autodidaktos* < *didaskein* "teach"] —**au·to·di·dac·tic** /àwtō dī dáktik, -di-/ *adj*

au·to·dyne /áwtō dīn/ *adj* describes a radio device containing an element such as a transistor that acts simultaneously as a detector and oscillator [Early 20C. < AUTO- + Greek *dunamis* "force, power"] —**au·to·dyne** *n*

au·toe·cious /aw téeshəss/ *adj* living as a pest or parasite on a single host species [Late 19C. < AUTO- + Greek *oikia* "house"] —**au·toe·cism** *n*

au·to·e·rot·i·cism /àwtō i rótti sìzzəm/, **au·to·er·o·tism** /àwtō érrə tìzzəm/ *n* sexual arousal and gratification from self-stimulation —**au·to·e·rot·ic** *adj*

aut·o·fo·cus /áwtō fòkəss/ *n* a device that automatically adjusts the focus of a camera

au·tog·a·my /aw tóggəmee/ *n* **1.** the process by which some flowering plants fertilize themselves **2.** the division and subsequent reunification of a single cell in the reproductive processes of some simple one-celled animals and algae —**au·to·gam·ic** /àwtə gámmik/ *adj* —**au·tog·a·mous** /aw tóggəməss/ *adj*

au·to·gen·e·sis /àwtō jénnəssiss/ *n* BIOL same as **abiogenesis** —**au·to·ge·net·ic** /àwtō jə néttik/ *adj* —**au·to·ge·net·i·cal·ly** *adv*

au·to·gen·ic /àwtō jénnik/ *adj* BIOL same as **autogenous** —**au·to·gen·i·cal·ly** *adv*

au·to·gen·ic train·ing, **au·to·gen·ics** /àwtō jénniks/ *n* a method of relieving stress by using meditation and other mental exercises to produce physical relaxation

au·to·gen·o·cide /àwtō jénnə sīd/ *n* the extermination of people by members of their own society

au·tog·e·nous /aw tójjənəss/ *adj* **1.** PRODUCED INSIDE SOMETHING produced or created within something itself, without external help or influence **2.** MED PRODUCED FROM SOMETHING FROM RECIPIENT'S BODY produced in, or with tissue from, the body of the person to whom it will be given ○ *an autogenous vaccine* **3.** INSECTS NOT NEEDING BLOOD describes insects that do not require a meal of blood in order to produce viable eggs [Mid-19C. < Greek *autogenēs* < *gignesthai* "be born"] —**au·tog·e·nous·ly** *adv*

au·to·gi·ro /àwtō jīrō/ (*plural* **-ros**) *n* an aircraft that uses a propeller for forward motion and an unpowered horizontal rotor for lift and stability [Early 20C. < Spanish, "self-turning" < *giro* "gyration"]

au·to·graft /áwtə gràft/ *n* **1.** a graft of skin or other tissue obtained from a patient's own body **2.** SURG same as **autotransplant**

au·to·graph /áwtə gràf/ *n* **1.** SOMEBODY'S SIGNATURE a signature, especially the signature of a famous person **2.** HANDWRITTEN TEXT a copy of a document or text handwritten by its creator (*technical*) ■ *vt* (**-graphed, -graph·ing, -graphs**) WRITE SIGNATURE ON SOMETHING to write your signature on something such as a book or photograph ○ *autographing pictures of the band* [Early 17C. Via French or late Latin < Greek *autographon* "written with your own hand" < *graphein* "write"]

au·to·graph hunt·er, **au·to·graph hound** *n* somebody who collects the signatures of famous people (*informal*)

Au·to·harp /áwtō haarp/ *tdmk* a trademark for a many-stringed musical instrument on which simple chords are strummed and the strings that are not to be sounded are held down by a button-controlled damper

au·to·hyp·no·sis /àwtō hip nóssiss/ *n* a process by which somebody hypnotizes himself or herself —**au·to·hyp·not·ic** /àwtō hip nóttik/ *adj*

au·to·im·mune /àwtō i myóon/ *adj* caused by the reaction of an antibody to substances that occur naturally in the body —**au·to·im·mun·i·ty** *n* —**au·to·im·mu·ni·za·tion** /àwtō ìmmyənə záysh'n/ *n*

au·to·im·mune dis·ease *n* a disease caused by the reaction of antibodies to substances occurring naturally in the body. Three common autoimmune diseases are lupus erythematosus, Addison's disease, and rheumatoid arthritis.

au·to·im·mune he·mo·lyt·ic a·ne·mi·a *n* a form of anemia involving autoantibodies of red cell antigens

au·to·in·fec·tion /àwtō in féksh'n/ *n* infection caused by an organism already present in another part of the body or by the larval reproduction of a parasite already present in the body

au·to·in·oc·u·la·tion /àwtō i nòkyə láysh'n/ *n* a disease that occurs when an infection spreads from one part of the body to another —**au·to·in·oc·u·la·ble** /-nókyələb'l/ *adj*

au·to·in·tox·i·ca·tion /àwtō in tòksə káysh'n/ *n* poisoning by a substance that has been produced within the body of the person who is poisoned

au·to·load /áwtō lōd/ *adj* ARMS same as **semiautomatic** *adj* (sense 1) —**au·to·load·er** *n*

au·tol·o·gous /aw tólləgəss/ *adj* derived from a patient's own body [Early 20C. < AUTO- + *-logous* < -LOGY]

au·tol·y·sate /aw tóllə sayt, -sət/ *n* a product of the process (**autolysis**) by which cells are broken down by enzymes produced in the cells themselves

au·tol·y·sin /aw tólləsin, àwtə lī́sin/ *n* an enzyme that causes autolysis

au·tol·y·sis /aw tólləssiss/ *n* the digestion of cells by their own enzymes —**au·to·lyt·ic** /àwtə líttik/ *adj*

au·to·mak·er /áwtō màykər/ *n* a manufacturer of motor vehicles

au·tom·a·ta ENG plural of **automaton**

au·to·mate /áwtə màyt/ (**-mat·ed, -mat·ing, -mates**) *vti* to convert a process or workplace to automation, or utilize the techniques of automation [Mid-20C. Back-formation < AUTOMATION]

au·to·mat·ed clear·ing·house /àwtə maytəd-/ *n* BANKING full form of **ACH**

au·to·mat·ed tel·ler ma·chine *n* BANKING full form of **ATM**

au·to·mat·ic /àwtə máttik/ *adj* **1. STARTING OR FUNCTIONING BY ITSELF** started, operated, or regulated by a process or mechanism without human intervention **2. DONE BY PRIOR ARRANGEMENT** beginning when specific conditions are fulfilled, without the need for a decision or action **3. DONE WITHOUT THOUGHT** done without conscious thought as the result of habit or custom ○ *gave an automatic answer to the child* **4. INDEPENDENT OF SOMEBODY'S WILL** done without intention, especially as the result of a physical reflex ○ *automatic blinking of the eyes* ■ *n* **1. MACHINE OPERATING WITHOUT HUMAN INTERVENTION** a machine that controls its own operating process, e.g., a washing machine **2. MOTOR VEHICLE NOT REQUIRING MANUAL GEAR** a motor vehicle that has a built-in mechanism (**automatic transmission**) for changing gears without requiring the driver to do it **3. GUN THAT FIRES CONTINUOUSLY** a gun that continues to fire and eject used cartridges for as long as the trigger is pressed [18C. < Greek *automatos* "acting by itself"] —**au·to·mat·i·cal·ly** *adv*

au·to·mat·ic drip *n* a machine that heats water, drips it through ground coffee in a filter, and keeps the resulting coffee warm in a pot

au·to·mat·ic ex·po·sure *n* a control system in a camera that sets the lens aperture and shutter speed according to the amount of light that is present

au·to·mat·ic fre·quen·cy con·trol *n* a control system in a radio or television receiver that keeps it tuned to a signal in spite of minor variations in the signal's frequency

au·to·mat·ic gain con·trol *n* a radio receiver control system by which the amplifier is adjusted to compensate for variations in the volume of the signal, so that the volume of the output is constant

au·to·ma·tic·i·ty /àwtəmə tíssətee/ *n* the processing of information in response to stimuli by an organism in a way that is automatic and involuntary, occurring without conscious control

au·to·mat·ic pi·lot *n* **1. AUTOMATIC STEERING SYSTEM** a control in the steering system of a ship, aircraft, or spacecraft that can be set to put or keep it on a steady course **2. PRESET OR INSTINCTIVE BEHAVIOR** a condition in which somebody is not fully aware of what he or she is doing but is acting in a habitual and unthinking way, e.g., because of stress **3. OPERATION WITHOUT GUIDANCE OR CONTROL** a state in which something is operating without guidance or control ○ *The company has been on automatic pilot since she resigned.*

au·to·mat·ic trans·mis·sion *n* a transmission system for motor vehicles in which changes of gear are made automatically in response to the speed of the vehicle

au·to·mat·ic weap·on *n* ARMS same as **automatic** *n* (sense 3)

au·to·mat·ic writ·ing *n* the production of writing while in a trance or similar state as an attempt to make contact with the writer's unconscious or telepathically with a supposed spirit

au·to·ma·tion /àwtə máysh'n/ *n* **1.** a system in which a workplace or process has been converted to one that replaces or minimizes human labor with mechanical or electronic equipment **2.** the act of automating something, or the state of being automated [Mid-20C. < AUTOMATIC]

au·tom·a·tism /aw tómmə tìzzəm/ *n* **1.** PHYSIOL **INVOLUNTARY ORGANIC FUNCTION** a physical reflex or involuntary activity of the body **2.** PHILOSOPHY, LAW **THEORY THAT ACTIONS ARE PERFORMED AUTOMATICALLY** the philosophical theory that all bodily actions have involuntary physical or physiological causes, or the legal defense that an action had such a cause **3.** PSYCHOL **ACTIVITY NOT CONSCIOUSLY CAUSED** behavior that is not consciously motivated, e.g., sleepwalking or involuntary repetitive actions **4.** ARTS **ARTISTIC METHOD** an artistic approach, associated with the surrealists, in which the painter or writer empties the mind and allows the unconscious to direct the work —**au·tom·a·tist** *n*

au·tom·a·tize /aw tómmə tī̀z/ (**-tized, -tiz·ing, -tiz·es**) *vti* **1.** INDUST same as **automate** **2.** to make or become automatic —**au·tom·a·ti·za·tion** /aw tòmməti záysh'n/ *n*

au·tom·a·ton /aw tómmətən, -tòn/ (*plural* **-tons** or **-ta** /-tə/) *n* **1.** a machine that contains its own power source and can perform a complicated series of actions, including responses to external stimuli, without human intervention **2.** somebody who behaves like a machine in emotionlessly obeying instructions and performing repetitive actions [Early 17C. Via Latin < Greek, neuter of *automatos* "acting by itself"] —**au·tom·a·tous** *adj*

au·to·mo·bile /àwtə mō béel, -mṓ bèel/ *n* a road vehicle, usually with four wheels and powered by an internal-combustion engine, designed to carry a small number of passengers [Late 19C. < French, "self-mobile"]

au·to·mo·bil·i·a /àwtə mə béelee ə/ *npl* things to do with automobiles or driving that appeal to collectors and enthusiasts [Late 20C. < AUTOMOBILE, after MEMORABILIA]

au·to·mo·tive /àwtə mṓtiv/ *adj* **1.** relating to or involving motor vehicles **2.** propelled by its own motor or engine

au·to·nom·ic /àwtə nómmik/ *adj* **1. CONTROLLED BY AUTOMATIC RESPONSES** describes functions of the nervous system not under voluntary control, e.g., the regulation of heartbeat or gland secretions **2. WITHOUT THOUGHT** describes an action or response that occurs without conscious control **3. FROM INTERNAL STIMULI** produced or caused by internal stimuli —**au·to·nom·i·cal·ly** *adv*

au·to·nom·ic nerv·ous sys·tem *n* the part of the nervous system in humans and other vertebrates that controls involuntary activity such as the action of the heart and glands, breathing, digestive processes, and reflex actions

au·ton·o·mous /aw tónnəməss/ *adj* **1. SELF-GOVERNING** politically independent and self-governing **2. ABLE TO CHOOSE** able to make decisions and act on them as a free and independent moral agent **3. SELF-SUFFICIENT** existing, reacting, or developing as an independent, self-regulating organism —**au·ton·o·mous·ly** *adv*

au·ton·o·mous re·pub·lic *n* a division of the Russian Federation that has more rights than the other administrative regions. The 21 autonomous republics have their own constitutions and state languages.

au·ton·o·my /aw tónnəmee/ *n* **1.** POL **SELF-GOVERNMENT** political independence and self-government **2.** PHILOSOPHY **EXISTENCE AS INDEPENDENT MORAL AGENT** personal independence and the capacity to make moral decisions and act on them **3.** LITERAT **INDEPENDENCE OF TEXT** the status of a text as an aesthetic object not to be judged or commented on in the light of external knowledge such as the biography of the author [Early 17C. < Greek *autonomia* < *autonomos* "having its own laws" < *nomos* "law"] —**au·ton·o·mist** *n*

au·to·pi·lot /áwtō pī̀lət/ *n* NAVIG, PHYSIOL, PSYCHOL same as **automatic pilot**

au·to·pis·ta /àwtə péestə/ *n* in a Spanish-speaking country or region, an expressway [Mid-20C. < Spanish, "automobile track"]

au·to·plas·ty /áwtə plàstee/ (*plural* **-ties**) *n* the repair of a patient's body using tissue, e.g., skin, taken from another part of the patient's body —**au·to·plas·tic** /àwtə plástik/ *adj*—**au·to·plas·ti·cal·ly** *adv*

au·to·poi·e·sis /àwtō poy éessiss/ *n* a process whereby a system, organization, or organism produces and replaces its own components and distinguishes itself from its environment —**au·to·poi·et·ic** /-poy éttik/ *adj*

au·top·sy /áw tòpsee/ *n* (*plural* **-sies**) **1. EXAMINATION TO FIND CAUSE OF DEATH** the medical examination of a dead body in order to establish the cause and circumstances of death **2. EXHAUSTIVE EXAMINATION** an exhaustive critical examination of something ■ *vt* (**-sied, -sy·ing, -sies**) **PERFORM AUTOPSY ON BODY** to perform an autopsy on a person or organ [Mid-17C. Via French or modern Latin < Greek *autopsia* "seeing with your own eyes" < *autoptēs* "eyewitness"]

au·to rac·ing *n US* racing in motor vehicles, especially in cars that are specially designed to travel at high speeds. Can term **motor racing**

au·to·ra·di·o·graph /àwtō ráydee ə gràf/, **au·to·ra·di·o·gram** /-gràm/ *n* a photograph that reveals how radioactivity is distributed in a specimen or sample, made by exposing a photographic plate to the radiation —**au·to·ra·di·o·graph·ic** /-raydee ə gráffik/ *adj* —**au·to·ra·di·og·ra·phy** /-óggrəfee/ *n*

au·to·res·pond·er /áwtō ri spòndər/ *n* an e-mail software application that enables Internet users to indicate automatically that they are unavailable to respond to incoming e-mail

au·to·rick·shaw /àwtō rík shaw/ *n* a vehicle with three wheels, like a covered motor scooter with a back seat for passengers, that is used as a taxi in South Asia

au·to·ro·ta·tion /àwtō rō táysh'n/ *n* the continuous rotation of an object such as a propeller caused by aerodynamic forces only

au·to·route /áwtō ròot/ *n* in a French-speaking country or region, an expressway [Mid-20C. < French, "automobile route"]

au·to·save /áwtō sàyv/ *n* a computer program feature in which data is saved automatically at predetermined intervals to minimize data loss in the event of a crash

au·to·some /áwtə sōm/ *n* a chromosome other than one that determines sex —**au·to·so·mal** /àwtə sṓm'l/ *adj*—**au·to·so·mal·ly** *adv*

au·to·stra·da /ówtō stràadə, áwtō-/ *n* an expressway in an Italian-speaking country or region [Early 20C. < Italian, "automobile road"]

au·to·sug·ges·tion /àwtō sə jéschən/ *n* the process by which somebody's perceptions, behavior, or physical condition may be altered by means of his or her power of suggestion —**au·to·sug·gest** *vt* —**au·to·sug·gest·i·bil·i·ty** /-jestə bíllətee/ *n* —**au·to·sug·gest·i·ble** *adj*—**au·to·sug·ges·tive** *adj*

au·to·tel·ic /àwtō téllik/ *adj* **1.** done for its own sake rather than to gain a material reward or avoid a punishment **2.** PHILOSOPHY describes an entity or event that has within itself the purpose of its existence or occurrence [Early 20C. < Greek *autotelēs* < *autos* "self" + *telos* "end"] —**au·to·tel·ism** *n*

au·to·tim·er /áwtō tī̀mər/ *n* an automatic timing device, e.g., on a stove

au·tot·o·my /aw tóttəmee/ *n* the casting off of part of the body by an animal when it is caught or attacked by a predator. Lizards, snakes, worms, and crustaceans, e.g., can escape by autotomy. —**au·to·tom·ic** /àwtə tómmik/ *adj*

au·to·tox·e·mi·a /àwtō tok séemee ə/ *n* MED same as **autointoxication**

au·to·tox·in /àwtə tóksən/ *n* a substance that poisons the system within which it is formed

au·to·trans·form·er /àwtō trans fáwrmər/ *n* a transformer in which the primary and secondary coils share all or some windings

au·to·trans·fu·sion /àwtō trans fyóozh'n/ *n* a blood transfusion using the patient's own blood

au·to·trans·plant /àwtō tràns plant/ *n* a surgical procedure in which tissue from one area of a living organism is removed and grafted to another site

au·to·troph·ic /àwtə tróffik, -trṓfik/ *adj* describes organisms, especially green plants, that are capable of making nutrients from inorganic materials [Late 19C. < Greek *autos* "self" + -TROPHIC[1]] —**au·to·troph** /áwtə trṑf, -tròf/ *n* —**au·to·troph·i·cal·ly** *adv* —**au·to·tro·phy** /aw tóttrəfee/ *n*

au·to·wind·er /áwtō wìndər/ *n* a device that automatically winds the film in a camera forward after a photograph is taken

au·tox·i·da·tion /aw tòksi dáysh'n/ *n* **1.** oxidation at normal temperatures due to contact with air **2.** oxidation that occurs only in the presence of another substance undergoing oxidation

~~autum~~ incorrect spelling of **autumn**

au·tumn /áwtəm/ *n* **1.** *Can, UK* the season occurring between summer and winter. Autumn traditionally lasts from September 22 to December 21 in the northern hemisphere, and from March 21 to June 21 in the southern hemisphere. US term **fall 2.** a time in the development of something that follows its most vigorous and successful phase, before its decline ○ *in the autumn of his career as a cellist* [14C. < Latin *autumnus*] —**au·tum·nal** /aw túmn'l/ *adj*

au·tum·nal e·qui·nox *n* **1.** the first day of autumn, when the Sun crosses the plane of the Earth's equator and makes day and night approximately of equal length. It occurs about September 22 in the northern hemisphere and March 21 in the southern hemisphere. **2.** the position of the Sun during the autumnal equinox

au·tumn cro·cus *n* an autumn-flowering plant. Flowers: crocus-shaped, purple or pink, growing directly from the ground after the leaves have died down. Latin name: *Colchicum autumnale.*

au·tun·ite /ṓtə nìt, áwtə-/ *n* a yellow radioactive fluorescent mineral consisting of hydrated calcium uranium phosphate [Mid-19C. After *Autun*, France]

aux. *abbr* auxiliary

aux·e·sis /awg zéessiss, awk séessiss/ *n* growth in animals or plants caused by an increase in the size of cells, not by cellular division [Mid-19C. Via late Latin < Greek] —**aux·et·ic** /awg zéttik, awk séttik/ *adj* —**aux·et·i·cal·ly** *adv*

aux·il·ia·ry /awg zíllyəree, -zílləree/ *adj* **1.** GIVING SUPPORT acting to support or supplement a group of people **2.** HELD IN RESERVE available as backup for a system, process, or piece of equipment **3.** SECONDARY secondary to something larger **4.** NAUT WITH MOTOR AND SAILS describes a boat with an engine to supplement or replace the sails ■ *n* (*plural* **-ries**) **1.** SUPPORTING PERSON OR THING somebody who or something that has a supporting or supplementary role **2.** GRAM same as **auxiliary verb 3.** MIL MEMBER OF SUPPORTING TROOPS a member of a separate troop, often from another country, that fights with an army as allies or mercenaries and has its own command structure ○ *the Coast Guard Auxiliary* **4.** NAUT BOAT WITH SAILS AND ENGINE a boat with an engine to supplement or replace the sails **5.** NAVY NAVAL SUPPORT VESSEL a naval vessel such as a tug or transport ship that does not engage in combat [Early 17C. < Latin *auxiliarius* < *auxilium* "help, assistance"]

aux·il·ia·ry de·vice *n* a peripheral piece of computer hardware, e.g., a printer or scanner

aux·il·ia·ry lan·guage *n* a language that is used by speakers of other languages in order to communicate

aux·il·ia·ry note *n* in music, a note that falls between two adjacent notes of the same pitch and is not an overtone

aux·il·ia·ry ro·tor *n* the tail rotor of a helicopter

aux·il·ia·ry verb *n* a verb that is used with another verb to indicate person, number, mood, tense, or aspect

~~auxillary~~ incorrect spelling of **auxiliary**

aux·in /áwksən/ *n* a natural plant hormone or synthetic substance that affects the growth and development of all plant parts [Mid-20C. < Greek *auxein* "to increase"] —**aux·in·ic** /awk sínnik/ *adj* —**aux·in·i·cal·ly** *adv*

aux·o·ton·ic /àwksə tónnik/ *adj* occurring against increasing force as part of a muscle contraction [< Greek *auxein* "to increase" + TONIC]

aux·o·troph /áwksə trṑf/ *n* a mutant strain of an organism, e.g., a bacterium, that has lost the ability to synthesize a specific nutrient (**growth factor**) and must obtain it from its environment to survive [Mid-20C. < Greek *auxein* "to increase"] —**aux·o·troph·ic** /àwksə tróffik/ *adj*

Au·yu·it·tuq Na·tion·al Park /ów yoo ée tóok-/ the first national park in Canada north of the Arctic Circle, located on eastern Baffin Island in Nunavut Territory. Area: 8,290 sq. mi./21,471 sq. km.

Av /aav/, **Ab** /aab/ *n* in the Jewish calendar, the fifth month of the religious year, lasting 30 days and falling about the same time as July to August. See table at **calendar** [Late 18C. < Hebrew *āḇ*]

AV *abbr* **1.** MEDIA audiovisual **2.** *also* **A.V.** BIBLE Authorized Version

av. *abbr* **1.** avenue **2.** average **3.** MEASURE avoirdupois

Av. *abbr* avenue

a.v., a/v, A/V *abbr* FIN ad valorem

av·a·da·vat /àvvədə vàt/ *n* a songbird of the waxbill family often kept as a cagebird. The male of one species is green and the male of the other species is red. Native to: South Asia. Genus: *Amandava.* [Late 17C. Alteration of *Ahmadabad*, city in W India where these birds were sold]

a·vail /ə váyl/ *v* (**a·vailed, a·vail·ing, a·vails**) **1. a·vail your·self** *vr* USE SOMETHING to make use of something useful or helpful while you have the opportunity ○ *avail yourself of the facilities* **2.** *vti* HELP to help somebody or something succeed, or be helpful or useful (*formal*) ○ *Negotiation could not avail the deadlocked diplomats.* ■ *n* HELP OR ADVANTAGE help, advantage, or success in achieving something (*used in negative statements*) ○ *His defense was of no avail: a conviction was secured.* [14C. < Old French *vail-*, stem of *valoir* "be worth" < Latin *valere* "be strong"]

a·vail·a·ble /ə váyləb'l/ *adj* **1.** ABLE TO BE GOTTEN able to be used, obtained, or relied on ○ *The government intends to make more land available for development.* **2.** UNATTACHED not currently involved in a romantic or sexual relationship but free to engage in one (*informal*) **3.** POL ELIGIBLE FOR OFFICE eligible and willing to undertake a public office or run for election —**a·vail·a·bil·i·ty** /ə vàylə bíllətee/ *n* —**a·vail·a·bly** *adv*

~~availible~~ incorrect spelling of **available**

av·a·lanche /ávvə lànch/ *n* **1.** DOWNHILL FALL OF SNOW a rapid downhill flow of a large mass of something dislodged from a mountainside or the top of a precipice, especially snow or ice **2.** OVERWHELMING QUANTITY a sudden overwhelming quantity of something **3.** PHYS INCREASE IN NUMBER OF IONS an increase in the number of ions or electrons, usually within a medium exposed to an applied electromagnetic field, caused by collisions of the ions or electrons with the medium ■ *v* (**-lanched, -lanch·ing, -lanch·es**) **1.** *vti* FLOW DOWN IN LARGE QUANTITY to descend in a large mass on somebody or something **2.** *vt* INUNDATE SOMEBODY OR SOMETHING to overwhelm somebody or something by arriving in large numbers or quantities [Late 18C. Via French < Romansh *avalantze*]

av·a·lanche lil·y *n* a lily that grows on mountains near the snow line. Flowers: white, yellow. Native to: North America. Genus: *Erythronium.*

Av·a·lon /ávvə lòn/ *n* in Celtic mythology, an island paradise in the west. King Arthur is said to have been taken to Avalon after being apparently mortally wounded.

a·vant-garde /àavaant gáard/ *n* ARTISTS WITH NEW IDEAS AND METHODS writers, artists, filmmakers, or musicians whose work is innovative, experimental, or unconventional, considered as a group ■ *adj* **1.** ARTISTICALLY NEW artistically innovative, experimental, or unconventional **2.** OF AVANT-GARDE ARTISTS belonging to the group of writers, artists, filmmakers, or musicians whose work is innovative, experimental, or unconventional [Early 20C. < French, "before the guard"] —**a·vant-gard·ism** *n* —**a·vant-gard·ist** *n*

A·var /áa vaar/ *n* a North Caucasian language spoken in Dagestan. Native speakers: 601,000. [Late 18C. < Avar] —**A·var** *adj*

av·a·rice /ávvərəss/ *n* an unreasonably strong desire to obtain and keep money [13C. Via French < Latin *avaritia* < *avarus* "greedy" < *avere* "to desire"]

av·a·ri·cious /àvvə ríshəss/ *adj* showing an unreasonably strong desire to obtain and keep money —**av·a·ri·cious·ly** *adv* —**av·a·ri·cious·ness** *n*

a·vas·cu·lar /ay váskyələr/ *adj* lacking blood vessels in body tissue —**a·vas·cu·lar·i·ty** /ay vàskyə lárrətee/ *n*

a·vas·cu·lar ne·cro·sis *n* the death of cells in tissue or organs as a result of deficient blood supply

a·vast /ə vást/ *interj* used by sailors as a command to stop doing something or to ignore a previous order [Early 17C. Alteration of Dutch *hou'vast*, shortening of *houd vast* "hold fast"]

av·a·tar /ávvə taàr/ *n* **1.** INCARNATION OF HINDU DEITY an incarnation of a Hindu deity in human or animal form, especially one of the incarnations of Vishnu such as Rama and Krishna **2.** EMBODIMENT OF SOMETHING somebody who embodies an idea or concept **3.** ONLINE IMAGE OF SOMEBODY IN VIRTUAL REALITY a movable three-dimensional image used to represent somebody in cyberspace **4.** COMPUT GAMES COMPUTER GAME PERSONA in computer games, a character or persona of a player with a graphical representation [Late 18C. < Sanskrit *avatāra* "descent" (of a god to earth)]

avdp. *abbr* MEASURE avoirdupois

a·ve /áa vày/, **A·ve** *n* **1.** CHR same as **Hail Mary** (sense 1) **2.** TIME FOR PRAYER the time when the Hail Mary is to be said, marked by the ringing of a bell **3.** ROSARY BEAD a small bead on a rosary, used for keeping track of how many times the Hail Mary has been said ■ *interj* GREETING OR FAREWELL used as a greeting or farewell (*archaic*) [13C. < Latin, imperative of *avere* "be or fare well"]

Ave., ave. *abbr* avenue (sense 1)

Ave·bu·ry /áyvbəree/ village in Wiltshire, southwestern England, the site of the largest ancient stone circle in the country

A·ve·don /ávvə dòn/, **Richard** (*b.* 1923) US photographer. He is best known for his pictures of political and literary figures and celebrities.

> "Beauty can be as isolating as genius, or deformity. I have always been aware of a relationship between madness and beauty."
> [Richard Avedon. Quoted in *Model: The Ugly Business of Beautiful Women*, Michael Gross; 1995]

A·ve Ma·ri·a /àav ay mə rée ə, àavee-/ *n* CHR same as **Hail Mary** (sense 1) [13C. < Latin]

a·venge /ə vénj/ (**a·venged, a·veng·ing, a·veng·es**) *vt* **1.** to inflict punishment because of a wrong done ○ *swore to avenge his death* **2.** to retaliate on behalf of yourself or somebody else for a wrong done ○ *determined to avenge his brother* [14C. < Old French *avengier* < *vengier* < Latin *vindicare* (see VINDICATE)] —**a·veng·er** *n* —**a·veng·ing·ly** *adv*

USAGE avenge or **revenge**? Both words are about repaying a wrong. The differences between them have to do with grammar and shades of meaning, though there is considerable overlap in meaning, dictated by usage over time. Grammatically speaking, ***avenge*** is a verb only; ***revenge*** is a verb and more usually a noun. ***Avenge*** traditionally relates not only to repaying a wrong but to getting justice on somebody else's behalf as a remedy for that wrong (*They vowed to avenge their sister's murder* [or *their murdered sister*]). ***Revenge***, often connoting malice, traditionally relates to getting even with an adversary by inflicting punishment or harm (*In an act of revenge for the bombing of our ship, our navy shelled the terrorists' training camps; Bands of irregular soldiers set out to revenge their leader's assassination*). Though both ***avenge*** and ***revenge*** can be used as transitive verbs with reflexive pronouns, ***revenge*** is commoner in this use: *The dictatorship revenged itself on the partisans' radio station by burning it to the ground; As a victim of a hate crime, she finally avenged herself on the perpetrators.*

av·ens /ávvənz/ (*plural same*) *n* PLANTS same as **mountain avens** [12C. < Old French *avence*]

a·ven·tu·rine /ə vénchə reen, -rin/, **a·ven·tu·rin** /-rin/ *n* **1.** dark brown or green glass that contains sparkling mineral particles **2.** a variety of quartz or feldspar containing minute particles of mica or hematite. Use: gems. [Early 18C. Via French < Italian *avventurino* "chance" (because discovered accidentally)]

av·e·nue /ávvə noo/ *n* **1.** a wide street or road in a town **2.** a course of action to be taken in order to approach, attain, or gain access to somebody or something ○ *need to explore all avenues* [Early 17C. < French, "approach," feminine past participle of *avenir* "arrive" < Latin *advenire* (see ADVENT)]

a·ver /ə vúr/ (**a·verred, a·ver·ring, a·vers**) *vt* (*formal*) **1.** to assert something confidently **2.** to state or allege that something is true [14C. < French *avérer* < Latin *verus* "true"] —**a·ver·ment** *n* —**a·ver·ra·ble** *adj*

av·er·age /ávvərij, ávvrij/ *n* **1.** TYPICAL AMOUNT the level, amount, or degree of something that is typical of a group or class of people or things **2.** MATH **NUMBER CONSIDERED TYPICAL OF NUMBER GROUP** a number regarded as typical of a group of numbers, obtained by adding each member of the group and dividing the total by the number of members **3.** SPORTS **MEASURE OF PLAYING PERFORMANCE** a measure of a player's or team's achievement, reached by dividing the number of opportunities for successful performances by how many times a successful performance was achieved **4.** LAW **LOSS AT SEA** in maritime law, the loss or damage of a ship and its cargo, or the division of the costs of this loss or damage among the owner or partners involved **5.** FIN **INTERMEDIATE PRICE** a measure of stock exchange performance based on the total of prices for a group or class of securities divided by the number of securities ■ *adj* **1.** TYPICAL lacking any extraordinary, untypical, or exceptional characteristic ○ *just an average person* **2.** NOT VERY GOOD not bad, but not very good either ○ *The performance was no better than average.* **3.** MATH **CALCULATED AS TOTAL DIVIDED BY MEMBERS** obtained by adding the numerical value for each member of a group and dividing the total by the number of members ■ *vt* (**-aged, -ag·ing, -ag·es**) **1.** DO SOMETHING AS AVERAGE to do, produce, or receive a particular number or amount of something as an average ○ *She averages one trip to Asia each year.* **2.** HAVE SOMETHING AS AVERAGE to have or show a particular number or amount as an average **3.** MATH **CALCULATE NUMERICAL AVERAGE OF SOMETHING** to calculate the average of a group of numbers by adding each member of the group and dividing the total by the number of members [15C. Alteration, after DAMAGE, of French *avarie* < Arabic *'awār* "damage to goods"] —**av·er·age·ly** *adv* —**av·er·age·ness** *n*

average down *vi* to purchase more shares of a stock when its price is falling, in the hope of reducing costs and increasing profits

average out *v* **1.** *vi* to result in a particular average number or amount ○ *My earnings average out at 400 dollars a week.* **2.** *vt* to calculate the numerical average of something

average up *vi* to purchase more shares of a stock when its price is rising, in the hope of increasing profits

av·er·age de·vi·a·tion *n* STATS same as **mean deviation**

a·verse /ə vúrss/ *adj* **1.** strongly opposed to or disliking something (*formal*) ○ *The board is not averse to the idea of further talks.* ○ *risk-averse* **2.** describes a leaf or flower that is turned away from the main stem or axis [Late 16C. < Latin *aversus* "turned away," past participle of *avertere* (see AVERT)] —**a·verse·ly** *adv* —**a·verse·ness** *n*

USAGE See ***adverse***.

SYNONYMS See ***unwilling***.

a·ver·sion /ə vúrzh'n/ *n* **1.** a strong feeling of dislike of somebody or something **2.** somebody or something strongly disliked

SYNONYMS See ***dislike***.

a·ver·sion ther·a·py *n* **1.** a method of therapy that attempts to eliminate undesired behavior by associating it repeatedly with painful or unpleasant effects **2.** therapy aimed at eliminating an irrational fear or dislike by making somebody experience the thing feared or disliked in remote or indirect ways that gradually become closer and more direct

a·ver·sive /ə vúrssiv/ *adj* inducing dislike of something —**a·ver·sive·ly** *adv* —**a·ver·sive·ness** *n*

a·vert /ə vúrt/ (**a·vert·ed, a·vert·ing, a·verts**) *vt* **1.** to prevent something from occurring, especially something harmful **2.** to turn your eyes away from something [14C. Via French < Latin *avertere* "turn away" < *vertere* "turn"] —**a·vert·i·ble** *adj*

A·ver·y /áyvəree/, **Milton Clark** (1893–1965) US artist. His work typically uses broad sections of color on large canvases.

A·ver·y, Oswald (1877–1955) Canadian-born US bacteriologist and geneticist. He discovered that genetic information was transferred through DNA and not through proteins. Full name **Avery, Oswald Theodore**

A·ves·ta /ə véstə/ *n* the sacred book of the Zoroastrian religion [Early 16C. < Middle Persian *Avastāk* "original text"]

A·ves·tan /ə véstən/, **A·ves·tic** /ə véstik/ *n* an ancient Iranian language that was spoken in various parts of Southwest Asia. The sacred writings of the Zoroastrians are written in Avestan. —**A·ves·tan** *adj*

avg. *abbr* average

avi *abbr* a file extension for a multimedia video format file. Full form **audio/video interleaved**

a·vi·an /áyvee ən/ *adj* relating to, belonging to, or characteristic of birds [Late 19C. < Latin *avis* "bird"]

a·vi·an flu *n* MED same as **bird flu**

a·vi·ar·y /áyvee èrree/ (*plural* **-ies**) *n* an enclosure or large cage for birds [Late 16C. < Latin *aviarium* < *avis* "bird"]

a·vi·a·tion /àyvee áysh'n/ *n* the design, manufacture, use, or operation of aircraft [Mid-19C. < French < Latin *avis* "bird"]

a·vi·a·tion med·i·cine *n* the branch of medicine concerned with the physical and psychological effects of flying in aircraft

a·vi·a·tor /áyvee àytər/ *n* the pilot of an aircraft

a·vi·a·tor glass·es *npl* eyeglasses with oval tinted lenses and a metal frame

a·vi·a·trix /àyvee áytriks/ (*plural* **-tri·ces** /-triseez/) *n* a woman pilot of an aircraft (*dated*) [Early 20C. Feminine of AVIATOR]

a·vi·cul·ture /áyvi kùlchər, ávvi-/ *n* the care and rearing of birds in cages, aviaries, or enclosures [Late 19C. < Latin *avis* "bird"] —**a·vi·cul·tur·ist** *n*

av·id /ávvid/ *adj* eager for or enthusiastic about something [Mid-18C. Back-formation < AVIDITY] —**av·id·ly** *adv* —**av·id·ness** *n*

av·i·din /ávvədin/ *n* a protein found in egg white that inactivates the vitamin biotin [Mid-20C. < AVID, because of its "avidity" for BIOTIN]

a·vid·i·ty /ə víddətee/ *n* **1.** great eagerness or enthusiasm for something **2.** CHEM same as **affinity** (sense 6) **3.** IMMUNOL a measure of the strength with which an antibody binds to an antigen [15C. Directly or via French < Latin *aviditas* < *avidus* < *avere* "to desire"]

a·vi·fau·na /àyvə fáwnə, àvvə-/ (*plural* **-nas** or **-nae** /-nee/) *n* all the birds present in a region, environment, or period of time [Late 19C. < Latin *avis* "bird"] —**a·vi·fau·nal** *adj*

A·vi·gnon /áavee nyóN/ capital of the Vaucluse Department in the Provence-Alpes-Côte d'Azur Region in southeastern France. Population: 85,935 (1999).

a·vi·on·ics /àyvee ónniks/ *n* the development and use of electric and electronic equipment for aircraft and spacecraft (*takes a singular verb*) ■ *npl* the electrical and electronic equipment of an aircraft or spacecraft (*takes a plural verb*) [Mid-20C. Blend of AVIATION + ELECTRONICS] —**a·vi·on·ic** *adj*

a·vir·u·lent /ay vírrələnt, -vírryələnt/ *adj* describes microorganisms that are not likely to cause disease in another organism —**a·vir·u·lence** *n*

a·vi·ta·min·o·sis /ày vītəmə nṓssiss/ (*plural* **-o·ses** /-ṓ seez/) *n* a disease caused by deficiency of a specific vitamin —**a·vi·ta·min·ot·ic** /-nóttik/ *adj*

A·viv /ə véev/ *n* JUDAISM same as **Nisan**

AVM *abbr UK* AIR FORCE Air Vice-Marshal

a·vo /áavoo/ (*plural* **a·vos**) *n* a subunit of currency in Macau. See table at **currency** [Early 20C. < Portuguese, shortened < *oitavo* "eighth" < Latin *octavus* < *octo* "eight"]

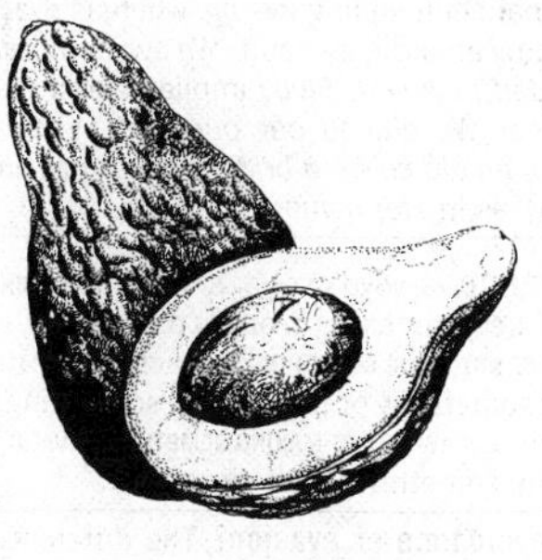

avocado

av·o·ca·do /àvvə káadō, àavə-/ (*plural* **-dos**) *n* **1.** *also* **av·o·ca·do pear** GREEN-FLESHED EDIBLE FRUIT a fruit with a leathery dark green or blackish skin, a large stony seed, and soft smooth-tasting pale green flesh, eaten raw in salads or dips **2.** TREE ON WHICH AVOCADOS GROW a tropical tree that bears avocados. Latin name: *Persea americana*. **3.** CREAMY GREEN a creamy green color, like that of the flesh of an avocado [Mid-17C. < Spanish, alteration of *aguacate* < Nahuatl *ahuacatl* "testicle" (because of the shape of the fruit)] —**av·o·ca·do** *adj*

av·o·ca·tion /àvvə káysh'n/ *n* (*formal*) **1.** a calling or occupation **2.** a hobby or pastime [Early 17C. < Latin *avocation-* "distraction" < *vocare* "to call"] —**av·o·ca·tion·al** *adj* —**av·o·ca·tion·al·ly** *adv*

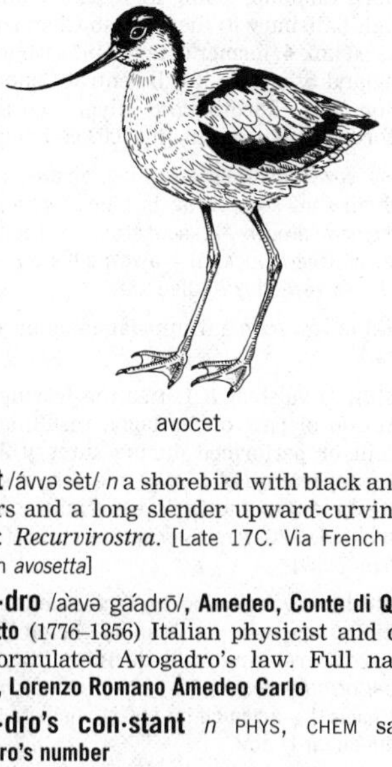

avocet

av·o·cet /ávvə sèt/ *n* a shorebird with black and white feathers and a long slender upward-curving beak. Genus: *Recurvirostra*. [Late 17C. Via French *avocette* < Italian *avosetta*]

A·vo·ga·dro /àavə gáadrō/, **Amedeo, Conte di Quaregna e Ceretto** (1776–1856) Italian physicist and chemist who formulated Avogadro's law. Full name **Avogadro, Lorenzo Romano Amedeo Carlo**

A·vo·ga·dro's con·stant *n* PHYS, CHEM same as **Avogadro's number**

A·vo·ga·dro's law *n* a principle in physics stating that equal volumes of different gases at the same temperature and pressure contain the same number of molecules [Late 19C. After Amedeo AVOGADRO]

A·vo·ga·dro's num·ber, **A·vo·ga·dro's con·stant** *n* the number of atoms or molecules, 6.022 x 10^{23}mole$_{-1}$, contained in one mole of a substance. Symbol N_A [Late 19C. After Amedeo AVOGADRO]

a·void /ə vóyd/ (**a·void·ed, a·void·ing, a·voids**) *v* **1.** *vt* **NOT GO NEAR SOMEBODY OR SOMETHING** to keep away from somebody or something ○ *a place to be avoided* **2.** *vti* **NOT DO SOMETHING OR PREVENT SOMETHING** to manage not to do something, or manage to stop something from happening ○ *I narrowly avoided colliding with it.* **3.** *vt* LAW **STATE SOMETHING IS NOT VALID** to say that something is void or invalid [14C. < Anglo-Norman < Old French *vuide, voide* "empty" (see VOID)] —**a·void·a·ble** *adj* —**a·void·a·bly** *adv* —**a·void·er** *n*

USAGE avoid, **evade**, or **elude**? All three words involve keeping away from a person or thing or keeping a person or thing away from you. The main difference between ***avoid*** and ***evade*** is that ***avoid*** is neutral in tone, whereas ***evade*** implies dishonesty or deception, or at least some sort of ulterior motive. If you ***avoid*** a responsibility, you take measures to prevent it from being necessary, whereas if you ***evade*** a responsibility you get out of it in an underhanded or deceitful way. ***Avoid*** can be followed by a verbal noun ending in *-ing*, whereas ***evade*** must be followed by an ordinary noun: *We avoided having to pay. We evaded payment.* ***Elude*** implies clever or ingenious avoidance: *We eluded our pursuers by hiding in the rafters of an old covered bridge.* It also has an extended meaning, as in *Her name eludes me.*

a·void·ance /ə vóyd'nss/ *n* **1. ACT OF NOT GOING NEAR** the act of keeping away from somebody or something **2. ACT OF NOT DOING SOMETHING** the act of refraining from doing something or preventing something from happening **3.** LAW **ACT OF MAKING SOMETHING INVALID** the act of making something void or invalid

USAGE avoidance or **evasion**? The difference between these two nouns corresponds to the difference between *avoid* and *evade*. In particular, *tax avoidance* means a legal method of reducing a liability to pay taxes, whereas *tax evasion* means an illegal method.

av·oir·du·pois /àvvər də póyz/ *n* **1.** MEASURE same as **avoirdupois weight 2.** the amount that somebody weighs (*humorous*) [14C. < Old French *aveir de peis* "goods of weight"]

av·oir·du·pois weight *n* a system for measuring weights based on the pound

A·von /áy vòn, -vən/ **1.** river in central England, rising in Northamptonshire and flowing through Stratford to join the Severn River. Length: 96 mi./154 km. **2.** river in southwestern England, rising in Gloucestershire and flowing through Bristol to the Bristol Channel. Length: 75 mi./120 km. **3.** river in southern England, rising in Wiltshire and flowing through Salisbury to the English Channel. Length: 60 mi./96 km. **4.** former county (1974–98) in the west of England **5.** city in north central Connecticut. It lies on the Farmington River, northwest of Hartford. Population: 16,346 (2002 estimate).

a·vow /ə vów/ (**a·vowed, a·vow·ing, a·vows**) *vt* to state or affirm that something is true (*formal*) [13C. Via Old French *avouer* "acknowledge" < Latin *advocare* "summon" (see ADVOCATE)] —**a·vow·a·ble** *adj* —**a·vow·a·bly** *adv* —**a·vow·ed·ly** /-ədlee/ *adv*

a·vow·al /ə vów əl/ *n* a frank statement or admission (*formal*)

a·vul·sion /ə vúlsh'n/ *n* **1.** MED the tearing away or separation of part of the body, resulting from an accident or performed during surgery **2.** LAW the sudden separation of part of one person's land and its attachment to another's, especially as a result of a flood [Early 17C. Directly or via French < Latin *avulsion-* < *vellere* "pull"]

a·vun·cu·lar /ə vúngkyələr/ *adj* **1.** resembling an uncle, especially one who is friendly, helpful, or good-humored **2.** relating to or deriving from an uncle (*formal or humorous*) [Mid-19C. < Latin *avunculus* "maternal uncle"] —**a·vun·cu·lar·i·ty** /ə vùngkyə lárrətee/ *n* —**a·vun·cu·lar·ly** *adv*

a·vun·cu·late /ə vúngkyələt/ *n* in some patrilineal societies, a special relationship similar to that of father and son that exists between a man and his sister's sons —**a·vun·cu·late** *adj*

aw /aw/ *interj N Am, Scotland* used to express surprise, disappointment, or pity (*informal*) [Mid-19C. Natural exclamation]

A/W *abbr* MEASURE actual weight

AWACS /áy wàks/ *n* a radar and computer system carried in an aircraft to track large numbers of low-flying aircraft. Full form **Airborne Warning and Control System**

a·wait /ə wáyt/ (**a·wait·ed, a·wait·ing, a·waits**) *v* **1.** *vti* to wait for, expect, or look for somebody or something **2.** *vt* to be going to happen to or be given to somebody ○ *"Where we find a difficulty we may always expect that a discovery awaits us."* (C. S. Lewis, *Reflections on the Psalms*; 1961) [13C. < Anglo-Norman *awaitier* < Old French *guaitier* < Germanic]

USAGE await, await for, wait, or **wait for**? You ***await*** or **wait for** test results or the arrival of a professor, and you travel to exotic lands where great adventures ***wait*** or ***await***. You do not *await for* anybody: *Let's take a break as we wait for* [not *await for*] *the judge to arrive in the courtroom*, or *...while we await the judge's arrival.*

A·wak·a·bal /a wáakə bàl/ (*plural same* or **-bals**) *n* **1.** a member of an Australian Aboriginal people of New South Wales **2.** the language of the Awakabal people, now extinct [Early 19C. < an Aboriginal language] —**A·wak·a·bal** *adj*

a·wake /ə wáyk/ *adj* **1. NOT ASLEEP** fully conscious and not asleep **2. ALERT** alert and vigilant about what is going on all around you ○ *"The color had come back to his face, and his eyes were clear, and fully awake and aware."* (J. R. R. Tolkien, *The Fellowship of the Ring*; 1954) **3. AWARE OF SOMETHING** fully aware of something ○ *awake to all the possibilities* ■ *vti* (**a·woke** /ə wṓk/ or **a·waked, a·waked** or **a·wok·en** /ə wṓkən/, **a·wak·ing, a·wakes**) **1. EMERGE FROM SLEEP** to rouse somebody, or be roused, from sleep **2. BECOME OR MAKE AWARE** to become, or make somebody become, aware of something **3. AROUSE FROM DAZE OR DREAM** to arouse somebody, or be aroused, from a dazed or dreaming state **4. AROUSE FEELINGS** to arouse feelings or memories, or be aroused [Old English *āwæcnan* < *wacian* "be awake" and assumed *wacen* "wake up" < Germanic]

USAGE awake, awaken, wake, or **waken**? Although all four verbs are interchangeable in both the transitive and the intransitive meanings, in practice ***awake*** and ***awaken*** are preferred in figurative meanings: *At last we awoke to the dangers that faced us.* When used in literal meanings ***awake*** and ***awaken*** are normally used intransitively or in the passive: *He awoke at four in the morning. I was awakened by shouts in the street. Will you wake us at four?* ***Wake*** is the only one of these verbs that can be followed by *up*: *I woke up at six this morning.*

a·wak·en /ə wáykən/ (**-ened, -en·ing, -ens**) *vti* to wake up from sleep or a similar state [Old English *āwæcnian* < *wæcnan* "waken" < Germanic] —**a·wak·en·er** *n*

USAGE See ***awake***.

a·wak·en·ing /ə wáykəning/ *adj* **JUST BEGINNING** just beginning or growing ■ *n* **1. AROUSAL FROM SLEEP** the act or process of waking from sleep **2. RENEWED ATTENTION TO SOMETHING** a revival or renewal of interest in something, especially religion **3. SUDDEN AWARENESS** a sudden recognition or realization of something

a·ward /ə wáwrd/ *n* **1. SOMETHING GIVEN FOR ACHIEVEMENT** something such as a prize that is given in recognition of somebody's merit or an achievement **2.** LAW **SOMETHING GRANTED BY LAW COURT** something bestowed, granted, or assigned to somebody by a court of law or by arbitration ■ *vt* (**a·ward·ed, a·ward·ing, a·wards**) **1. GIVE SOMETHING FOR MERIT** to give somebody something in recognition of merit or an achievement ○ *awarded the prize to the whole class* **2.** LAW **BESTOW AS RESULT OF COURT'S DECISION** to bestow, grant, or assign something to somebody by a judicial decision or by arbitration [14C. Via Anglo-Norman, "decide a legal case" < Old French *warder* "judge" < Germanic] —**a·ward·a·ble** *adj* —**a·ward·ee** /ə wàwr dée/ *n* —**a·ward·er** *n*

a·ware /ə wér/ *adj* **1. KNOWING SOMETHING** having knowledge of something from having observed it or been told about it ○ *We are already aware of the problem, and we are dealing with it.* **2. NOTICING OR REALIZING SOMETHING** knowing that something exists because you notice it or realize that it is happening ○ *He became aware of a pain in his left side.* **3. KNOWLEDGEABLE** well-informed about what is going on in the world or about the latest developments in a sphere of activity ○ *More financially aware investors were starting to sell their stock.* [Old English *gewær* "very watchful" < *wær* "watchful" < Indo-European, "perceive, watch out for"] —**a·ware·ness** *n*

SYNONYMS ***aware, conscious, mindful, cognizant, sensible***

CORE MEANING: having knowledge of the existence of something

aware having knowledge of something from having observed it or been told about it ○ *I wasn't aware of any problem.* ○ *The leadership has been made well aware of the current position.* **conscious** fully appreciating the importance of something ○ *conscious of the need to make progress* ○ *He was conscious that his predecessor had not lasted long in the job.* **mindful** actively attentive, or deliberately keeping something in mind ○ *mindful of the need to proceed cautiously* ○ *mindful that the current license expires in early May* **cognizant** (*formal*) having knowledge about something ○ *making people cognizant of the fact that their decision will be final* **sensible** (*formal*) very aware of something ○ *We are sensible of the liberality of your offer.*

a·wash /ə wósh, ə wáwsh/ *adj* **1. COVERED IN WATER** covered in water or another liquid **2. OVERSUPPLIED** having more of something than is desirable or manageable ○ *an office awash with letters of complaint* **3.** NAUT **WITH WATER RUNNING OVER SIDES** describes a boat that has sunk so low that water is able to come in over the sides

a·way /ə wáy/ CORE MEANING: a grammatical word used to indicate that somebody or something moves so as to leave a particular place ○ *I really need to spend some time away for a while.* ○ *The truck drove away leaving us stranded.* ○ *The cat scampered away.* ○ *We have an away game next week.*

1. *adv* **UNINVOLVED** separated or far from somebody or something ○ *I try to stay away from trouble.* **2.** *adv* **IN DIFFERENT DIRECTION** in a different direction from the one somebody was originally facing or looking in ○ *He turned his face away.* **3.** *adv* **INTO DISTANCE** toward the distance ○ *pine groves stretching away toward the sea* **4.** *adv* **IN FUTURE** at a particular time in the future (*follows a span of time*) ○ *Thanksgiving is only a week away.* **5.** *adv* **INTO STORAGE OR SAFEKEEPING** into the place where something is normally stored or kept safe ○ *We filed the valuable papers away.* **6.** *adv* **OFF SOMETHING** so as to remove or separate something, or so as to be removed or separated (*follows a verb*) ○ *a tool to chip away the old paint* **7.** *adv* **TO OR FROM SOMEBODY** into or out of the possession of somebody or something (*follows the verb or object of the verb*) ○ *stopped them from stealing away our clients* **8.** *adv* **UNTIL SOMETHING IS USED UP** so as to make something disappear or be expended (*follows a verb and precedes the object*) ○ *frittered away his inheritance* **9.** *adv* **GRADUALLY** gradually until something ceases or is no longer noticed ○ *The music gradually died away.* **10.** *adv* **SO AS TO SHOW CHANGE** so that a perceptible change from one thing to another occurs ○ *a shift away from heavier taxation* **11.** *adv* **WITHOUT STOPPING** continuously and usually energetically over a period of time ○ *hammering away in the garage* **12.** *adv, adj* **IN ANOTHER PLACE** not in a specific place or the place where somebody usually is, especially at home or at work ○ *I'll be away until Thursday.* ○ *She works away from the office.* **13.** *adv, adj* **IN DISTANCE OR TIME** as measured in distance or time from here (*follows a measure or indication of distance or time*) ○ *He works about 10 minutes away.* ○ *The mountains are not far away.* **14.** *adv, adj* **ON OPPOSING TEAM'S FIELD** played on an opponent's home field ○ *Their next three games will be played away.* ○ *Their away record has been very bad this season.* **15.** *adj* GOLF **FARTHEST FROM HOLE** in golf, placed farthest from the hole [Old English *aweg* < *on weg* "on (your) way"]

awe[1] /aw/ *n* **1. MIXTURE OF WONDER AND DREAD** a feeling of amazement and respect mixed with fear that is often coupled with a feeling of personal insignificance or powerlessness ○ *Filled with awe, they gazed at the ruins of the massive temple.* ○ *I was completely in awe of her.* **2. ABILITY TO INSPIRE DREAD** the ability to inspire dread or reverence (*archaic*) ■ *vt* (**awed, aw·ing, awes**) **CAUSE AWE IN SOMEBODY** to make somebody feel awe (*usually passive*) ○ *The visiting ambassadors were awed by this display of military might.* [13C. < Old Norse *agi*]

a·we[2] /áwee/, **a-wee, ah·wee, ah we** *pron Carib* **1.** same as **we 2.** same as **us**[1] (sense 1) **3.** same as **our** [Mid-20C. Contraction of ALL + WE]

a·wea·ry /ə wéeree/ *adj* feeling very tired (*archaic or literary*) ○ *"By my troth, Nerissa, my little body is aweary of this great world!"* (Shakespeare, *The Merchant of Venice*; 1596)

a·weath·er /ə wéthər/ *adv* toward the windward side

~~aweful~~ incorrect spelling of **awful**

a·weigh /ə wáy/ *adj* hanging clear of the bottom of a body of water ○ *Anchors aweigh!*

awe-in·spir·ing *adj* so impressive as to make a person feel humble or slightly afraid

aw·en·daw /áwin dàw/ *n Southern US* spoon bread made from hominy or cornmeal [After a South Carolina hamlet < a Native N American name]

a·wen·do /ə wéndō/ *n Southern US* corn bread made with eggs and milk

awe·some /áwssəm/ *adj* **1.** so impressive or overwhelming as to inspire a strong feeling of admiration or fear ○ *the awesome destructive power of a tornado* **2.** used as a general term of enthusiastic approval (*slang*) ○ *The second track on this CD is totally awesome.* —**awe·some·ly** *adv* —**awe·some·ness** *n*

awe·struck /áw strùk/, **awe·strick·en** /-strìkən/ *adj* filled with a feeling of awe

aw·ful /áwf'l/ *adj* **1.** EXTREMELY BAD very bad or unpleasant ○ *an awful smell* **2.** CAUSING SHOCK OR SADNESS extremely shocking, saddening, or unpleasant ○ *an awful accident* **3.** SICK in poor health ○ *I feel awful this morning.* **4.** VERY GREAT enormous in size, amount, number, or extent (*informal*) ○ *We spent an awful lot of money on furniture.* **5.** AWE-INSPIRING so impressive as to inspire awe (*literary*) ■ *adv* EXTREMELY to an extreme degree or extent (*informal*) ○ *It's awful hot this morning.* [13C. < AWE[1]] —**aw·ful·ness** *n*

aw·ful·ly /áwflee, -fəlee/ *adv* **1.** to an extremely great degree ○ *I'm awfully grateful to you for helping me out.* **2.** in a very bad or unpleasant way ○ *treated them awfully*

a·while /ə wíl, ə hwíl/ *adv* for a short time

USAGE awhile or **a while**? Both expressions are derived from the word *while*, but they have different roles in sentences. ***Awhile*** is an adverb: *Let us wait awhile* [not *for awhile*]. ***A while*** – written as two words – is a noun phrase and is normally preceded by *for*: *I'm going to be away for a while.* Sometimes, however, the word *for* is left out, making ***a while*** look more like an adverbial phrase, though it is still strictly a noun phrase: *We had to wait quite a while.* This use is fairly easy to identify because *while* is qualified in some way, for example, *quite a while* or *a long while.*

a·whirl /ə wúrl, ə hwúrl/ *adj* **1.** in a dizzy state of excitement or confusion ○ *Her mind was awhirl with new ideas.* **2.** moving around and around (*literary*) ○ *red and golden leaves awhirl in the autumn breeze*

awk·ward /áwkwərd/ *adj* **1.** EMBARRASSING embarrassing and requiring great tact or skill to resolve ○ *I find myself in an awkward situation.* **2.** DIFFICULT OR UNCOMFORTABLE TO USE difficult to use because requiring the body to be moved into an uncomfortable position ○ *I find the gear shift very awkward to use when I move the seat forward.* **3.** PERFORMED GRACELESSLY performed in a way that lacks grace and looks uncomfortable ○ *walked with an awkward gait* **4.** WITHOUT GRACEFUL COORDINATION lacking physical coordination and grace ○ *an awkward, gangling adolescent* **5.** SHYLY UNCOMFORTABLE shy, uncomfortable, and embarrassed ○ *He was always awkward around kids.* [Mid-16C. < obsolete *awk* "turned the wrong way" (< Old Norse *afugr* "turned backward") + -WARD] —**awk·ward·ly** *adv* —**awk·ward·ness** *n*

awl /awl/ *n* a tool consisting of a handle and a slim metal shaft with a sharp point, used for punching small holes in leather or wood [Old English *æl*, origin ?]

SPELLCHECK See *all.*

awn /awn/ *n* a stiff bristle projecting from the tip of a plant organ such as the sheath surrounding a cereal

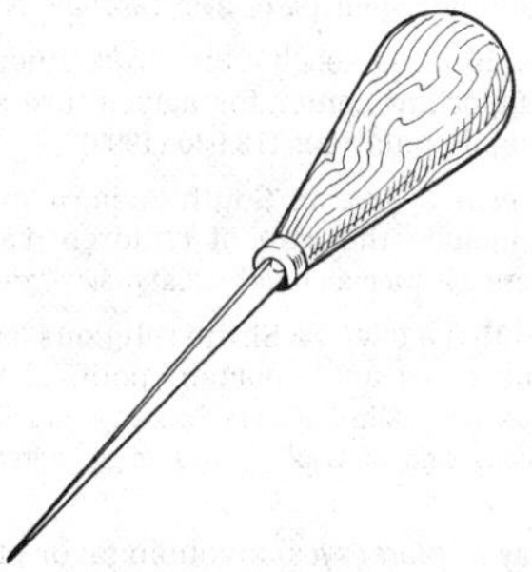

awl

or grass seed [12C. < Old Norse *agn-* "chaff"] —**awned** *adj* —**awn·less** /áwnləss/ *adj*

awn·ing /áwning/ *n* a plastic, canvas, or metal porch or shade supported by a frame and often foldable, placed over a storefront, doorway, window, or the side of a recreational vehicle [Early 17C. Origin ?]

a·woke past tense of **awake**

a·wok·en past participle of **awake**

AWOL /áy wàwl/, **a.w.o.l.** *adj* absent from a post, especially a military position assigned, without official permission ■ *n* a member of the armed forces who is absent from his or her place of assignment without official permission [< *a(bsent) w(ith)o(ut) l(eave)*]

A·wol·o·wo /ə wóllәwə/, **Obafemi** (1909–87) Nigerian Yoruba chief and political leader. He became leader of the opposition in the Nigerian federal parliament (1960–62) and was imprisoned until the coup of 1966.

> "In honest hands, literacy is the surest and the most effective means to true education. In dishonest hands, it may be a most dangerous, in fact a suicidal, acquisition."
> [Obafemi Awolowo, *Voice of Reason: Selected Speeches of Chief Obafemi Awolowo* (1981), vol. 2]

a·wry /ə rí/ *adj* **1.** not in the proper position, but turned or twisted to one side ○ *The cushions were awry and there was mud on the carpet.* **2.** not in keeping with plans or expectations ○ *Our plans have gone awry.* [14C. < *on wry* "in a twist"]

aw-shucks *adj* modest, self-conscious, and unpretentious in manner (*informal*)

ax /aks/, **axe** *n* (*plural* **ax·es**) **1.** TOOL FOR CUTTING a tool consisting of a flat heavy metal head with a sharpened edge attached to a long handle, used to chop wood or fell trees **2.** JOB LOSS an abrupt dismissal from a job (*slang*) ○ *Her secretary got the ax yesterday.* **3.** TERMINATION the termination of something such as a service or series of television programs, usually without prior warning or discussion (*slang*) ○ *The tractor plant is slated for the ax.* **4.** MUSICAL INSTRUMENT a rock guitar or a jazz saxophone (*slang*) ■ *vt* (**axed, ax·ing, ax·es; ax·es**) (*slang*) **1.** TERMINATE SOMETHING to end something such as a service or series of television programs, usually without prior warning or discussion (*usually passive*) ○ *The show was axed after only five episodes.* **2.** FIRE SOMEBODY to dismiss somebody from a job, especially abruptly **3.** REDUCE SOMETHING DRASTICALLY to cut something such as expenditures or services drastically ○ *Most of the welfare provisions were axed from the budget.* [Old English *æcs* < Indo-European] ◇ **an ax to grind** a personal consideration or motivation, especially one involving a grievance ○ *It was clear from their hostile questioning that certain reporters had an ax to grind on this issue.*

ax·el /áks'l/ *n* a figure-skating jump in which the skater takes off from the forward outside edge of one skate, turns in midair, and lands on the rear outside edge of the other skate [Mid-20C. After *Axel* Rudolph Paulser (1885–1938), Norwegian skater]

Ax·el Hei·berg Is·land /áks'l hí burg-/ the easternmost and largest of the Sverdrup Islands, west of Ellesmere Island, in Nunavut Territory, Canada. Area: 16,671 sq. mi./43,178 sq. km.

a·xen·ic /ay zénnik, -zéen-/ *adj* describes a culture of an organism that is free from contamination by other living organisms [Mid-20C. < Greek *a-* "not" + *xenikos* "alien, strange"]

ax·es SCI, POL plural of **axis**[1]

ax·i·al /áksee əl/ *adj* **1.** MATH OF AXIS relating to or forming an axis **2.** CRYSTALS LOCATED ALONG PLANE OF AXIS located on or in the plane of an axis of a crystal **3.** ANAT OF AXIS OF ORGANISM relating to or located in the axis of an organism —**ax·i·al·ly** *adv*

ax·i·al plane *n* a plane that intersects the crest or trough of a geologic fold in such a way that the sides of the fold are symmetrical about the plane

ax·i·al skel·e·ton *n* the bones that make up the vertebral column and skull

ax·il /áks'l/ *n* the space between a leaf or branch and the stem to which it is attached [Late 18C. < Latin *axilla* (see AXILLA)]

ax·il·la /ak síllə/ (*plural* **-lae** /-lee/) *n* **1.** a person's armpit (*technical*) **2.** the hollow underneath the wing of a bird [Early 17C. < Latin, "little wing" < *ala* "wing, upper arm"]

ax·il·lar /ak síllər, áksələr/ *n* a feather growing from the hollow (**axilla**) under a bird's wing

ax·il·lar·y /áksə lérree/ *adj* **1.** ANAT relating to or near the armpit **2.** BOT relating to or growing in the space (**axil**) between a leaf or branch and the stem ■ *n* (*plural* **-ies**) BIRDS same as **axillar**

ax·i·nite /áksi nìt/ *n* a brilliant brown borosilicate mineral containing calcium and aluminum, occurring in wedge-shaped crystals [Early 19C. < Greek *axinē* "ax"]

ax·i·ol·o·gy /àksee óllәjee/ *n* the study of the nature, types, and governing criteria of values and value judgments [Early 20C. < French *axiologie* < Greek *axia* "value"] —**ax·i·o·log·i·cal** /àksee ə lójjik'l/ *adj* —**ax·i·o·log·i·cal·ly** *adv* —**ax·i·ol·o·gist** *n*

ax·i·om /áksee əm/ *n* **1.** a statement or idea that people accept as self-evidently true **2.** MATH, LOGIC a basic proposition of a system that, although unproven, is used to prove the other propositions in the system [15C. Directly or via French < Latin *axioma* < Greek *axiōma* "something worthy" < *axios* "weighty, worthy"]

ax·i·o·mat·ic /áksee ə máttik/ *adj* **1.** self-evidently true, or universally accepted as being true **2.** MATH, LOGIC consisting of or based on axioms [Late 18C. < Greek *axiōmatikos* < stem of *axiōma* (see AXIOM)] —**ax·i·o·mat·i·cal·ly** *adv*

ax·is[1] /áksiss/ (*plural* **ax·es** /ák seez/) *n* **1.** MATH LINE AROUND WHICH OBJECT ROTATES an imaginary straight line around which an object such as Earth rotates **2.** MATH LINE AROUND WHICH SHAPE IS SYMMETRICAL a straight line around which a geometric figure or three-dimensional object is symmetrical **3.** MATH LINE FOR MEASURING COORDINATES one of two or more lines on which coordinates are measured. Often on a graph two axes form its left and lower margins. **4.** ALLIANCE an alliance or association between two or more people, organizations, or countries that is thought of as forming a center of power or influence ○ *the Paris-Bonn axis* **5.** AVIAT LINE DEFINING DIRECTION OF AIRCRAFT one of the three mutually perpendicular lines in an aircraft that define its orientation **6.** ANAT SECOND VERTEBRA IN NECK the second vertebra in the neck, which acts as the pivot on which the head and first vertebra turn **7.** BOT CENTRAL PART OF PLANT the main part of a plant, usually the stem and the root, from which all subsidiary parts develop **8.** OPTICS LINE PERPENDICULAR TO LENS OR MIRROR the axis of symmetry of an optical system, especially a line perpendicular to the surface of a lens or mirror **9.** GEOL LINE AT MAXIMUM CURVATURE an imaginary line along the crest of an anticline or the trough of a syncline at the point of maximum curvature **10.** CRYSTALS LINE PASSING THROUGH CRYSTAL an imaginary line, one of three or four that pass through the center of a crystal and are used to define its symmetry and the arrangement of its atoms [14C. < Latin, "axle, pivot"]

ax·is[2] /áksiss/ *n* ZOOL same as **axis deer** [Early 17C. < Latin, an unidentified wild animal in S Asia]

Ax·is /áksiss/ *n* the military and political alliance of Germany, Italy, and, later, Japan that fought the Allies in World War II [Mid-20C. < Mussolini's idea of "an axis around which nations could assemble"]

ax·is deer *n* a deer with a reddish brown, white-spotted coat. Native to: South Asia. Latin name: *Axis axis.*

ax·is of ro·ta·tion *n* MATH same as **axis**[1] (sense 1)

ax·is of sym·me·try *n* MATH same as **axis**[1] (sense 2)

ax·i·sym·met·ric /àksee sə méttrik/, **ax·i·sym·met·ri·cal** /-méttrik'l/ *adj* symmetrical with respect to an axis —**ax·i·sym·met·ri·cal·ly** *adv*

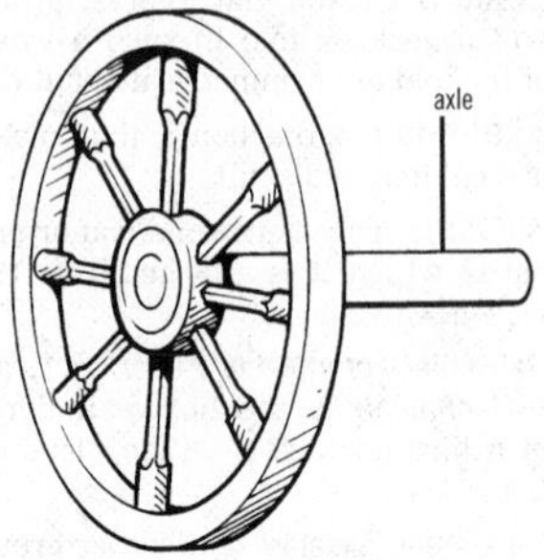

axle

ax·le /áks'l/ *n* **1.** a shaft on which a wheel or set of wheels revolves, especially a shaft under the body of a vehicle that connects a pair of wheels **2.** the spindle on which one or more wheels revolve [Late 16C. Shortening of AXLETREE]

ax·le·tree /áks'l treè/ *n* a shaft that runs underneath the body of a vehicle such as a cart or carriage and connects a pair of wheels [13C. < Old Norse *öxultré* < *öxull* "axle" + *tré* "tree, beam"]

ax·man /áks màn, -mən/ (*plural* **-men** /-mèn, -mèn/) *n* **1.** a man who carries or uses an ax either as a tool or a weapon **2.** a rock guitarist or jazz saxophone player (*slang*)

Ax·min·ster /áks mìnstər/ *n* a high-quality carpet with a cut pile that is usually woven into a colorful pattern [Early 19C. After *Axminster,* SW England]

ax·o·lem·ma /àksə lémmə/ *n* the membranous sheath that encloses the long thin extension of a nerve cell (**axon**) [Late 19C. < Greek *axōn* "axis" + *lemma* "skin, husk"]

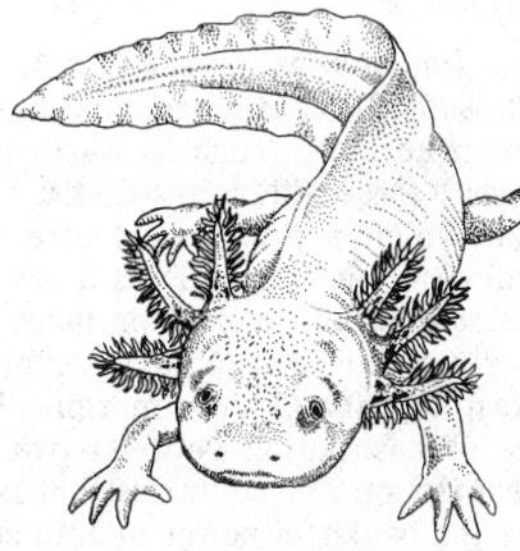

axolotl

ax·o·lotl /áksə lòtt'l/ (*plural* **-lotls** or *same*) *n* a salamander that lives in water and often retains its external gills as an adult. Native to: Mexico, western United States. Genus: *Ambystoma.* [Late 18C. < Nahuatl < *atl* "water" + *xolotl* "servant"]

ax·on /ák sòn/ *n* an extension of a nerve cell, similar in shape to a thread, that transmits impulses outward from the cell body [Late 19C. < Greek *axōn* "axis"]

ax·o·neme /áksə neèm/ *n* a bundle of fibrils that form the central core of a cilium or flagellum. It consists of nine pairs of microtubules surrounding a central pair. [Early 20C. < Greek *axōn* "axis" + *nēma* "thread"]

ax·o·no·met·ric /àksənə méttrik, àksənō-/ *adj* describes a method of drawing a three-dimensional object so that the vertical and horizontal axes are drawn to scale but the curves and diagonals appear distorted

ax·o·plasm /áksə plàzzəm/ *n* the cytoplasm of a nerve cell extension (**axon**) —**ax·o·plas·mic** /àksə plázmik/ *adj*

ay[1] *n, adv, interj* another spelling of **aye**[1]

ay[2] *adv* another spelling of **aye**[2] (*archaic or regional*)

A·ya·cu·cho /àayə koòchō/ city in southern Peru. It is an important center for agriculture and manufacturing. Population: 118,960 (1998).

a·yah /ī ə/ *n S Asia* in South Asia, a maid whose duties include the care of children [Late 18C. Via Portuguese *aia* "woman tutor" < Latin *avia* "grandmother"]

a·ya·tol·lah /ī ə tṓlə/ *n* a Shiite religious leader, often one who takes an important political as well as religious role [Mid-20C. Via Persian < Arabic *'āyatu-llāh* "miraculous sign of God" < *'āya* "sign, miracle" + *allāh* "God"]

aye[1] /ī/, **ay** *n* (*plural* **ayes**) a vote in favor of a motion, or somebody who casts a vote in favor ■ *adv, interj* used to say yes (*archaic or regional*) [Late 16C. Origin ?]

aye[2] /ī/, **ay** *adv* always or forever (*archaic or regional*) [13C. < Old Norse *ei, ey*]

aye-aye

aye-aye /ī ì/ *n* a small nocturnal primate that lives in trees and has a long bushy tail, long bony fingers, and teeth resembling those of a rodent. Native to: Madagascar. Latin name: *Daubentonia madagascariensis.* [Late 18C. Via French < Malagasy *aiay*; probably an imitation of its cry]

Ayer /er/, **A. J.** (1910–89) British philosopher. He was a logical positivist whose works include *Language, Truth, and Logic* (1936). Full name **Ayer, Sir Alfred Jules**

> "In nature one thing just happens after another. Cause and effect have their place only in our imaginative arrangements and extensions of these primary facts."
> [A. J. Ayer, *The Central Questions of Philosophy*; 1973]

Ayers Rock /èrz-/ former name for **Uluru**

A·ye·sha another spelling of **Aisha**

AYH *abbr* American Youth Hostels

a·yin /àa yin/ *n* the 16th letter of the Hebrew alphabet, transliterated as a reversed apostrophe and pronounced approximately like an "o." See table at **alphabet** [Early 19C. < Hebrew *'ayin* "eye"]

Ayl·mer ➧ **Whitworth-Aylmer, Matthew**

Ay·ma·ra /īmə raá/ (*plural same* or **-ras**) *n* **1.** a member of a Native South American people who live around Lake Titicaca in Bolivia and Peru. The great ruins at Tiahuanaco are believed to have been built by the Aymara around A.D. 500. **2.** a language of Bolivia and Peru, related to Quechua. Native speakers: 2 million. [Mid-19C. < Bolivian Spanish] —**Ay·ma·ra** *adj* —**Ay·ma·ran** *adj*

a·yo /áyō/ *Carib adj* describes a kite when the string is cut and it flies away quickly ■ *vti* (**ay·oed, ay·o·ing, ay·oes**) to leave or finish something, especially quickly [Late 20C. Via French Creole, "goodbye" < French *adieu*]

Ayr /er/ historic town in South Ayrshire, Scotland. Population: 47,962 (1991).

A·yur·ved·a /àayər vá ydə, -veèdə/ *n* ALTERN MED same as **Ayurvedic medicine** [Early 20C. < Sanskrit *āyur-veda* "medicine" < *āyur-* "life, vital power" + *veda* "knowledge"] —**A·yur·ved·ic** *adj*

A·yur·ved·ic med·i·cine /àa yoor váydik-, -veèdik-/ *n* a traditional Hindu system of healing that assesses somebody's constitution and lifestyle, and recommends treatment based on herbal preparations, diet, yoga, and purification

az *abbr* Azerbaijan (*used in Internet addresses*) See table at **domain name**

az. *abbr* **1.** ASTRON azimuth **2.** HERALDRY azure

A·zad Kash·mir /àa zad-/ section of western Kashmir that is under the control of Pakistan. Area: 650 sq. mi./1,680 sq. km.

azalea

a·zal·ea /ə záylyə/ (*plural* **-eas** or *same*) *n* a flowering bush related to the rhododendron. Some azaleas are deciduous and some are evergreen, and they range in size from very low-growing plants to small trees. Flowers: pink, purple, white, yellow, or orange, sometimes fragrant. Genus: *Rhododendron.* [Mid-18C. Via modern Latin < Greek *azaleos* "dry"]

a·zan /aa zaán/ *n* the Islamic call to prayer that a muezzin repeats five times a day from the minaret of a mosque [Mid-19C. < Arabic *aḏān* "announcement"]

A·za·ni·a /ə záynee ə/ *n S Africa* a name for South Africa used by resistance movements in the apartheid era

A·za·po /ə záppō/ *n* a Socialist political movement in South Africa [Late 20C. Acronym < *Azanian People's Organization*]

az·a·prop·a·zone /àzzə próppə zṑn/ *n* a ketone derivative of pyrazole with analgesic and anti-inflammatory properties. Use: treatment of rheumatoid arthritis.

a·za·ta·dine /ày záttə deèn/ *n* an antihistamine taken orally. Use: treatment of allergic rhinitis, urticaria.

az·a·thi·o·prine /àzzə thī ə preèn/ *n* a drug that suppresses the immune response. Use: after transplant surgery to prevent rejection. [Mid-20C. < *aza-* + THI- + PURINE]

az·e·la·ic ac·id /àzzə lày ik-/ *n* a dicarboxylic acid that is a yellowish to white powder. Use: treatment of skin cancer and other skin disorders. [< AZO- + Greek *elaion* "oil"]

az·e·las·tine /àzzə lá steèn/ *n* an antihistamine drug inhaled through the nose [Late 20C. < *azel* + *-astine,* INN stem]

a·ze·o·trope /áyzee ə trōp/ *n* a mixture of liquids that has a different boiling point from any of its components and retains its composition as a vapor [Early 20C. < A[3] + Greek *zeo-,* form of *zein* "to boil" + *-tropos* "turning, changing"] —**a·ze·o·trop·ic** /àyzee ə tróppik/ *adj* —**a·ze·ot·ro·py** /àyzee óttrəpee/ *n*

A·zer·bai·jan /àzzər bī jaán, -zhaán/ country of

Azerbaijan

Southwest Asia bisected by Armenia. It is also surrounded by the Caspian Sea, Russia, Georgia, and Iran. Language: Azeri. Currency: manat. Capital: Baku. Population: 7,830,764 (2003). Area: 33,400 sq. mi./86,600 sq. km. Official name **Azerbaijani Republic** —**A·zer·bai·ja·ni** *n, adj*

A·ze·ri /ə zérree/ *n, adj* the Turkic official language of the country of Azerbaijan, also spoken in the province of Azerbaijan in northwestern Iran, belonging to the Altaic family of languages. Native speakers: 14 million.

a·zer·ty /ə zúrtee/, **AZERTY** *adj* describes a computer or typewriter keyboard layout in continental Europe, where the top row of letters, beginning from the left, runs A, Z, E, R, T, Y

az·ide /á zīd, áy-/ *n* a chemical compound containing a group of three adjacent nitrogen atoms. Formula: N_3. [Early 20C. < AZO- + -IDE]

a·zi·do·thy·mi·dine /ə zīdō thímə deen/ *n* PHARM full form of **AZT**

A·zi·ki·we /aazee kee wày/, **Nnamdi** (1904–96) president of Nigeria. He became Nigeria's first president in 1963, but was overthrown by a military coup in 1966.

> "Tell a man whose house is on fire to give a moderate alarm; tell a man moderately to rescue his wife from the arms of a ravisher; tell a mother to extricate gradually her babe from the fire into which it has fallen; but do not ask me to use moderation in a cause like the present."
> [Nnamdi Azikiwe. Quoted in *Zik: A Selection from the Speeches of Nnamdi Azikiwe*; 1961]

A·zil·ian /ə zíllee ən/ *n* a prehistoric culture that existed in Spain and southwestern France from around 10,000 to 8,000 B.C. The distinctive artifacts produced by this culture include flat bone harpoons and painted pebbles. [Late 19C. After Mas d'*Azil* in the French Pyrenees]

az·i·muth /ázzəməth/ *n* **1.** the angle measured from north, eastward along the horizon, to the point where a vertical circle through an astronomical object intersects the horizon **2.** the angular distance along the horizon between a point of reference, usually the observer's bearing, and another object [Early 17C. Via French *azimut* < Arabic *as-samūt*, plural of *as-samt* "the way" < *samt* "way, direction"] —**az·i·muth·al** /àzzə múth'l/ *adj* —**az·i·muth·al·ly** *adv*

az·i·muth·al e·qui·dis·tant pro·jec·tion *n* a method of map projection in which a straight line from the center to any given point represents the shortest distance to that point and can be measured to scale

az·ine /á zeen, áy-/ *n* an organic chemical compound with a six-sided ring structure containing one or more atoms of nitrogen [Late 19C. < AZO- + -INE]

az·i·thro·my·cin /àzzi thrō mīssən/ *n* an antibiotic taken in combination with other drugs. Use: treatment of toxoplasmosis, heart disease, AIDS.

Az·nar /àth naar, àss naar/, **José María** (*b.* 1953) prime minister of Spain (1996–2004). Elected president of the newly formed center-right Popular Party in 1990, he won a narrow election victory in 1996 and an absolute majority in 2000.

az·o /ázzō/ *adj* relating to or containing two adjacent nitrogen atoms. Formula: –N=N–. [Late 19C. < AZO-]

azo- *prefix* containing a nitrogen group ○ *azole* [< French *azote* "nitrogen" < Greek *a-* "not" + *zōē* "life"; because living creatures cannot breathe it]

az·o·ben·zene /àzzō bén zeen, àyzō bén zeen/ *n* a yellow or orange crystalline solid. Use: making dyes. Formula: $C_6H_5N{=}NC_6H_5$.

az·o com·pound *n* a compound containing two adjacent nitrogen atoms attached to aromatic groups

az·o dye *n* an artificial dye, usually orange, yellow, or brown, containing an azo group. Source: amines.

a·zo·ic /ay zō ik, ə-/ *adj* **1.** relating to or belonging to a geologic period before the appearance of living organisms on Earth **2.** exhibiting no trace of life or organic remains [Mid-19C. < Greek *azōos* "without life" < *zōē* "life"]

az·ole /á zōl, áy-/ *n* an organic chemical compound with a ring of five linked atoms, of which at least one is nitrogen [Late 19C. < AZO- + -OLE]

a·zon·al /ay zōn'l/ *adj* **1.** not divided into zones **2. a·zo·nal, a·zo·nic** /-zónnik, -zōnik/ not restricted to a specific zone or geographic area

A·zores /áy zàwrz/ archipelago in the North Atlantic Ocean, west of Portugal, of which it is an autonomous region. There are nine main islands. Capital: Ponta Delgada. Population: 237,800 (1993). Area: 868 sq. mi./2,247 sq. km.

az·o·te·mi·a /àzzə teemee ə/ *n* MED same as **uremia** [Early 20C. < obsolete *azote* "nitrogen" (see AZO-) + -EMIA] —**az·o·te·mic** /àzzə témmik, -teemik/ *adj*

az·ot·ic /a zóttik, ə-/ *adj* relating to or containing nitrogen [Late 18C. < obsolete *azote* < French (see AZO-)]

a·zo·to·bac·ter /a zōtə bàktər, ə-/ *n* a rod-shaped or spherical bacterium found in soil and water that converts atmospheric nitrogen to a stable or biologically available form. Family: Azotobacter. [Early 20C. < modern Latin < French *azote* "nitrogen" (see AZO-) + *bacterium*]

A·zov, Sea of /á zàwf/ shallow inland sea in southern Russia, linked with the Black Sea by the Kerchenskiy Strait. Area: 14,500 sq. mi./37,555 sq. km.

AZT *n* an antiviral drug used in the treatment of AIDS. It works by inhibiting the enzyme reverse transcriptase, which the AIDS virus requires to reproduce. Full form **azidothymidine**

Az·tec /áz tèk/ *n* **1.** a member of a Native Middle American people whose empire dominated central Mexico during the 14th and 15th centuries. As well as having highly developed artistic, musical, astronomical, and mathematical skills, the Aztecs were excellent engineers and architects. **2.** LANG same as **Nahuatl** (sense 2) ■ *adj also* **Az·tec·an** /àz ték'n/ relating to the Aztecs or their language or culture [Late 18C. Via French *Aztèque* or Spanish *Azteca* < Nahuatl *aztecatl* "somebody from Aztlan"]

Az·tec-Ta·no·an *n* a family of Native North and Central American languages, one of whose main branches is Uto-Aztecan —**Az·tec-Ta·no·an** *adj*

az·tre·o·nam /az tree ə nàm/ *n* an antibiotic administered intravenously, effective against a broad range of infections

a·zu·ki bean *n* FOOD same as **adzuki bean**

az·ure /ázhər/ *adj* **1. DEEP BLUE** deep blue, like the color of a clear sky (*literary*) ○ *the azure depths of the ocean* **2.** HERALDRY **BLUE** colored blue on a coat of arms ■ *n* (*literary*) **1. BLUE SKY** a clear blue sky **2. DEEP BLUE HUE** a deep blue color, like that of a clear sky ○ *the azure of her eyes* [13C. Via Old French *azur* < medieval Latin *azzurum* < Arabic *al-lāzaward* "the lapis lazuli" < Persian *lāžward* "lapis lazuli"]

az·ur·ite /ázhə rīt/ *n* a deep blue semiprecious stone that is composed of hydrated copper carbonate. Use: source of copper, gems.

A·zu·sa /ə zóossə/ town in southwestern California. It lies east of Los Angeles, near San Gabriel Canyon. Population: 46,323 (2002 estimate).

a·zy·gos /ázzəgəss/ *adj* occurring as a single muscle or vein, and not as a pair [Mid-17C. < Greek *azugos* "without yoke" < *zugon* "yoke"]

Bb

b[1] /bee/ (*plural* **b's**), **B** (*plural* **B's** or **Bs**) *n* **1.** the second letter of the English alphabet, representing a consonant sound **2.** a written representation of the letter "b"

b[2] *symbol* used to refer to the second vertical row of squares from the left on a chessboard

b[3] *abbr* **1.** PHYS barn **2.** ACOUSTICS bel

B[1] /bee/ (*plural* **B's** or **Bs**) *n* **1. "B"-SHAPED OBJECT** something shaped like a letter "B" **2.** MUSIC **7TH NOTE IN C MAJOR** the seventh note of a scale in C major **3.** MUSIC **SOMETHING THAT PRODUCES B NOTE** a string, key, or pipe tuned to produce the note B **4.** MUSIC **SCALE BEGINNING ON B** a scale or key that starts on the note B **5.** MUSIC **WRITTEN SYMBOL OF B** a graphic representation of the tone of B **6.** EDUC **2ND HIGHEST GRADE** the second highest grade in a series, e.g., an above-average grade for academic work **7.** MED **HUMAN BLOOD TYPE** a human blood type of the ABO system, containing the B antigen. Somebody with this type of blood can donate to people of the same group or of the AB group, and can receive blood from people with this type or with type O.

B[2] *symbol* **1.** CHEM ELEM boron **2.** COMPUT eleven (*used in hexadecimal notation*) **3.** PHYS magnetic flux density

B[3] *abbr* **1.** ACOUSTICS bel **2.** CHESS bishop

b. *abbr* **1.** BASEBALL base[1] **2.** BASEBALL baseman **3.** MUSIC bass[1] **4.** MUSIC basso **5.** billion **6.** book **7.** born **8.** breadth

B. *abbr* **1.** EDUC bachelor (*used in degree titles*) **2.** MICROBIOL bacillus **3.** FIN baht **4.** FIN balboa **5.** Baumé scale **6.** MUSIC bass[1] **7.** MUSIC basso **8.** GEOG bay[1] (*used on maps*) **9.** CHR Bible **10.** MONEY bolivar **11.** book **12.** MEASURE breadth

B2B *abbr* E-COMMERCE business-to-business (*used in e-mails or text messages*)

B2C *abbr* E-COMMERCE business-to-consumer (*used in e-mails or text messages*)

B4 *abbr* before (*used in e-mails or text messages*)

B4N *abbr* bye for now (*used in e-mails or text messages*)

Ba *symbol* CHEM ELEM barium

BA, **B.A.** *abbr* **1.** EDUC Bachelor of Arts **2.** BASEBALL batting average

baa /ba, baa/ *vi* (**baaed, baa·ing, baas**) to make the long wavering cry characteristic of a sheep or lamb ■ *n* (*plural* **baas**) the long wavering cry characteristic of a sheep or lamb [Early 16C. An imitation of the sound]

Ba·al /báy əl, baal/ (*plural* **-al·im** /báy əlim, báalim/ or **-als**) *n* **1.** a fertility or nature god worshiped by the Canaanites and the Phoenicians, and considered a false god by the ancient Hebrews **2.** *also* **ba·al** (*plural* **-al·im** or **-als**) an idol or false god

Baal·bek /báal bèk, báy əl-/ city in eastern Lebanon between the Litani and Asi rivers. It is the site of the ancient ruins of Heliopolis. Population: 50,000 (1981).

baal te·shu·vah /-tə shóovə, -chóovə/ (*plural* **baa·lei te·shu·vah** /bày ə lay-/), **baal tsh·u·va** (*plural* **baa·lei tsh·u·va**) *n* somebody who returns to Orthodox Jewish practice after abandoning it [< Hebrew, "master of return"]

baap /baap/ *n S Asia* same as **father** *n* (sense 1) [< Hindi]

Baath /baath/, **Ba'ath** /baa áath/ *n* a Socialist party in several Arab countries, including Iraq and Syria, founded in 1943 [Mid-20C. < Arabic *ba't* "resurrection"]

Baath·ism /báath ìzzəm/ *n* the ideology of the Baath Party that combines pan-Arabism, state control, institutionalized anti-Semitism, and the cult of a single authoritarian ruler. Baathism was predominant in Iraq until the overthrow of Saddam Hussein in 2003, but it remains predominant in Syria. —**Baath·ist** *n, adj*

Bab /baab, bab/ *n* the title of the Persian religious leader, Mirza Ali Muhammad (1819–50), who founded Babism as a reform of Shiite Islam in Persia in the 19th century [Mid-19C. Via Persian < Arabic *bāb* "gate, intermediary"]

ba·ba[1] /báabə/ (*plural* **-bas**) *n* a dessert made of leavened dough soaked in a rum-flavored syrup and baked in a pan [Early 19C. Via French < Polish, "married (peasant) woman"]

ba·ba[2] /báa baa/ *n S Asia* **1. RESPECTFUL ADDRESS FOR OLDER MAN** a respectful form of address for an older man (*informal*) **2. TITLE FOR HOLY MAN** a title and form of address for a holy man **3.** same as **father** *n* (sense 1) (*informal; often a form of address*) **4. CHILD** a child, especially a boy (*informal; often an endearment or form of address*) [< Hindi *bābā*]

Ba·ba /bábbə/ *n Malaysia* a man of Chinese origin who was born in Melaka and speaks Malay as a first language [Mid-19C. < Malay]

Ba·ban·gi·da /bə báng gèedə/, **Ibrahim** (*b.* 1941) Nigerian soldier and politician. He was president of Nigeria from 1985 to 1993.

ba·bas·su /bàabə sóo/ (*plural* **-sus** or *same*) *n* a tall palm tree that produces oil. Use: manufacture of soap, margarine, cosmetics, cooking oil. Genus: *Orbignya*. [Early 20C. < Brazilian Portuguese *babaçú* < Tupi *ybá* "fruit" + *guasu* "large"]

Bab·bage /bábbij/, **Charles** (1791–1871) British mathematician and inventor. He designed and attempted to build mechanical calculating machines that were forerunners of the computer.

bab·bitt /bábbit/ *n* a bearing made of babbitt metal ■ *vt* (**-bit·ted, -bit·ting, -bitts**) to cover or line a surface with babbitt metal or a similar alloy [Late 19C. See BABBITT METAL]

Bab·bitt /bábbit/ *n* a self-satisfied narrow-minded man who cannot see beyond his own business and social interests ○ *"His name was...Babbitt, and...he was nimble in the calling of selling houses for more than people could afford to pay."* (Sinclair Lewis, *Babbitt*; 1922) [Early 20C. After the main character in the novel *Babbitt* (1922) by Sinclair Lewis] —**Bab·bitt·ry** *n*

Bab·bitt /bábbit/, **Irving** (1865–1933) US humanist and scholar. He was a leader of the New Humanism movement, which was influential in literary studies in the first decades of the 20th century.

Bab·bitt, Milton (*b.* 1916) US composer. He was a leader in the development of serialism and electronic music. Full name **Babbitt, Milton Byron**

bab·bitt met·al *n* a soft alloy originally consisting of tin, copper, and antimony, but now often containing lead. Use: in manufacture of antifriction bearings. [Late 19C. After Isaac *Babbitt* (1799–1862), US inventor]

bab·ble /bább'l/ *v* (**-bled, -bling, -bles**) **1.** *vti* **SAY OR SPEAK INCOHERENTLY** to say something rapidly and incoherently without pausing, usually because of excitement or fear ○ *She babbled something I didn't catch and then dashed out.* **2.** *vi* **SPEAK IRRELEVANTLY** to talk rapidly or at length about things that seem irrelevant or foolish ○ *He babbled on about the importance of some new gadget.* **3.** *vti* **BLURT SOMETHING OUT** to reveal something thoughtlessly or impulsively that is supposed to be secret or confidential ○ *immediately babbled the whole story to the neighbors* **4.** *vi* **MURMUR CONTINUOUSLY** to make a continuous low murmuring or bubbling sound ○ *a brook babbling through the pasture* ■ *n* **1. SOUND OF LOUD UNINTELLIGIBLE VOICES** the sound of voices speaking too excitedly and rapidly to be heard properly ○ *the babble of guests in the hallway* **2. FOOLISH TALK** irrelevant or foolish chatter **3. SOUND OF RUNNING WATER** the low continuous murmuring or bubbling sound made by water as it flows along [13C. Probably < Middle Low German or Middle Dutch *babbelen*, an imitation of the sound, or a similar formation in English] —**bab·ble·ment** *n* —**bab·bler** *n*

babe /bayb/ *n* **1. LOVER** used as an affectionate term of address to a lover or somebody loved (*slang*) **2. YOUNG WOMAN CONSIDERED GOOD-LOOKING** a young woman who is considered good-looking (*slang; sometimes considered offensive*) **3. HANDSOME YOUTH** an attractive young man (*slang*) **4. BABY** a baby or small child (*literary or archaic*) [14C. Probably < obsolete *baban* "baby," an imitation of childish utterances] ◇ **a babe in the woods** a naive excessively trusting person

babe in arms (*plural* **babes in arms**) *n* **1.** a baby too young to walk who needs to be carried **2.** a very inexperienced or naive person who may be incapable of handling a difficult situation or easily duped ○ *We were simply babes in arms when it came to dealing with a real professional.*

ba·bel /báyb'l, bább'l/ *n* (*literary*) **1.** a confused noise, especially the noise of loud unintelligible voices all talking at once **2.** a scene or place of noisy confusion [Early 16C. < the TOWER OF BABEL]

Ba·bel /báyb'l, bább'l/ BIBLE ➧ **Tower of Babel**

babe mag·net *n* a man or possession considered irresistible to good-looking young women (*slang*)

ba·be·si·o·sis /bə bèezee óssiss/, **bab·e·si·a·sis** /bàbbi zī́ əssiss/ *n* a disease of humans and animals caused by protozoan infection of red blood cells and transmitted by a tick bite [Early 20C. < modern Latin *Babesia*, after Victor *Babès* (1854–1926), Romanian bacteriologist]

Ba·bi /báabee/ (*plural* **-bis**) *n* a follower of the Bab or of Babism [Mid-19C. Via Persian < Arabic < *bāb* (see BAB)]

Ba·bin·ski re·flex /bə bìnskee-/, **Ba·bin·ski's re·flex** *n* a curling upward of the big toe when the sole of the foot is stroked. It is a normal reflex in children up to two years old but an indicator of disease of the brain or spinal cord in older people. [Early 20C. After J. F. F. *Babinski* (1857–1932), French neurologist]

bab·i·ru·sa /bàbbə róossə, bàabə-/ (*plural* **-sas** or *same*), **bab·i·rus·sa**, **bab·i·rou·sa** *n* a wild boar that has almost hairless skin and very large curved tusks. Native to: Indonesia, Malaysia. Latin name: *Babyrousa babyrussa*. [Late 17C. < Malay < *babi* "pig" + *rusa* "deer"]

Ba·bism /báa bìzzəm/ *n* a religion founded by the Bab as a reform of Shiite Islam in Persia in the 19th century

ba·boo *n* another spelling of **babu**

baboon

ba·boon /ba bo͞on/ *n* **1.** a large ground-dwelling monkey with a prominent snout resembling a dog's muzzle, large teeth, and bare pink patches on the buttocks. Native to: Africa, Asia. Genus: *Papio*. **2.** somebody regarded as rude or oafishly clumsy (*insult*) [15C. < French *babuin* "gaping figure, baboon" or medieval Latin *babewynus*]

Bab·son /bábss'n/, **Roger** (1875–1967) US statistician. He lectured and wrote about statistics as applied to investments, and founded Babson College, Massachusetts, in 1919. Full name **Babson, Roger Ward**

ba·bu /baábboo/, **ba·boo** *n S Asia* **1.** a courtesy title or form of address in Hindi equivalent to "Mr" **2.** an offensive term for a bureaucrat (*insult*) [Late 18C. < Hindi *bābū* "father"]

ba·bul /bə bo͞ol/ (*plural* **-buls** or *same*) *n* a tree that produces gum arabic, tannin, and hardwood. Native to: North Africa, South Asia. Latin name: *Acacia nilotica*. [Early 19C. Via Hindi *babūl*, Bangla *bābul* < Sanskrit *babbūla*]

ba·bush·ka /bə bo͞oshkə/ *n* **1.** a headscarf folded and tied under the chin in the style of Russian peasant women **2.** a traditional Russian grandmother figure [Mid-20C. < Russian, "grandmother"]

Ba·bu·yan Is·lands /baà boo yaán-/ island group in the northern Philippines. Area: 230 sq. mi./595 sq. km. Population: 24,500

ba·by /báybee/ *n* (*plural* **-bies**) **1. VERY YOUNG CHILD** a very young child who is not yet able to walk or talk **2. UNBORN CHILD** a child who is still in the womb **3. CHILDISH PERSON** somebody regarded as childish or overly dependent ○ *told him not to be such a baby* **4. YOUNGEST MEMBER** the youngest member of a family or group ○ *the baby of the team* **5. IMMATURE ANIMAL** a very young animal **6. TERM OF ENDEARMENT** an affectionate term of endearment, especially for a woman (*slang; sometimes considered offensive*) **7. OBJECT OF AFFECTION OR PRIDE** the object of somebody's affection, pride, or admiration (*slang*) ○ *That baby is ten years old and still like new.* ■ *adj* **SMALLER AND YOUNGER** describes vegetables that are smaller and younger than usual ○ *baby carrots* ■ *vt* (**-bied, -by·ing, -bies**) **TREAT SOMEBODY WITH GREAT CARE** to show a great or inordinate amount of care to something or somebody [14C. Pet form of BABE] —**ba·by·hood** *n* ◇ **throw out the baby with the bathwater** to reject something in its entirety without discriminating between good and bad parts

ORIGIN In Old English, the term for what we would now call a ***baby*** was *child*, and it seems only to have been from about the 11th century that *child* began to extend its range to the slightly more mature age that it now covers. Then when the word ***baby*** came into the language in the 14th century, it was also used in this developed sense of "child," and only gradually came to refer to infants not yet capable of speech or walking.

ba·by blue *n* a pale blue color —**ba·by-blue** *adj*

ba·by-blue-eyes *n* a spreading annual plant with serrated gray-green leaves. Flowers: small, bowl-shaped, blue with white centers. Latin name: *Nemophila menziesii*. [< the imagined resemblance of its flowers to eyes]

ba·by blues *n* PSYCHIAT same as **postpartum depression** (*informal; takes a singular or plural verb*)

ba·by bond *n* **1.** a bond issued for an amount lower than $1,000, usually between $25 and $500 **2.** a tax-free savings scheme for children and young people

ba·by bo·nus *n Can* same as **child tax benefit**

ba·by book *n* a book in which to keep photographs of somebody as a baby and record notable first actions such as smiling and walking

ba·by boom *n* a sudden large increase in the birthrate over a specific period, especially the 15 years after World War II

ba·by boom·er *n* somebody born during a baby boom, especially the one following the end of World War II

baby boomlet *n* an increase in the birthrate smaller than a baby boom

ba·by bug·gy *n* a baby carriage or a young child's stroller

ba·by bust *n* a sudden large decrease in the birthrate over a given period

ba·by car·riage *n* a small carriage, usually consisting of a rectangular body on four wheels with a folding hood and a handle, designed for pushing an infant, especially outdoors

Ba·by Doc ➧ **Duvalier, Jean-Claude**

ba·by-dolls *npl* women's sleepwear consisting of a short loose top and loose shorts [Because worn in the movie *Baby Doll* (1956)]

ba·by face *n* **1.** a smooth round face that gives somebody a childlike innocent look **2.** somebody with a baby face

ba·by fat *n* the plumpness that some children develop when they are young but that disappears as they mature

ba·by food *n* food that has been prepared or manufactured in such a way that it can be fed to a baby

ba·by grand *n* a small grand piano about 5 ft./1.5 m. long

ba·by·ish /báybee ish/ *adj* **1.** like a baby in appearance, sound, or behavior **2.** suitable for a baby or for a younger child ○ *Clothes like these are too babyish for a child his age.* —**ba·by·ish·ly** *adv* —**ba·by·ish·ness** *n*

Bab·y·lon[1] /bábbələn, -lòn/ **1.** capital of ancient Babylonia, sited on the Euphrates River in modern Iraq. It was known for its opulence, and the Hanging Gardens there were one of the Seven Wonders of the World. **2.** town and vacation spot on Long Island, New York. Population: 12,713 (2002 estimate).

Bab·y·lon[2] *n* **1. PLACE OF IMMORALITY** a place of great luxury or immorality **2. PLACE OF EXILE** a place of exile or captivity **3. OFFENSIVE TERM** an offensive term for the police (*slang; used in Black English*) **4. OFFENSIVE TERM** an offensive term for the Establishment, regarded as dominated by white people (*slang; used in Black English*) **5.** RELIG same as **hell** *n* (sense 1) (*slang; used in Black English*)

Bab·y·lo·ni·a /bàbbə lṓnee ə, -lṓnyə/ empire in Mesopotamia that flourished from the first half of the second millennium B.C. until its conquest by Persia in 539 B.C.

Bab·y·lo·ni·an /bàbbə lṓnee ən/ *n* **1.** somebody who lived in ancient Babylon or Babylonia **2.** the Akkadian language, especially as recorded in cuneiform texts from Babylonia —**Bab·y·lo·ni·an** *adj*

Bab·y·lo·ni·an cap·tiv·i·ty *n* the period of time that the Jews spent in exile in Babylonia in the 6th century B.C.

ba·by milk *n* a preparation that imitates the composition of human breast milk and that may be used for feeding babies. It can be a liquid, or a powder to be mixed with water.

ba·by mind·er *n UK* somebody whose job is to look after other people's babies or very young children, especially while their parents are at work

ba·by oil *n* a gentle oil used to moisturize the skin, especially that of a baby

ba·by's breath (*plural same* or **ba·by's breaths**) *n* **1.** a plant with a mass of delicate branched stems, often used in bouquets and floral arrangements. Flowers: small, fragrant, white or pink. Latin name: *Gypsophila paniculata*. **2.** a perennial plant with a mass of tiny flowers, especially a plant of the madder family [< the delicate scent]

ba·by show·er *n* a party given by the women friends of somebody who is pregnant, at which she is given presents for the baby

ba·by-sit, **ba·by·sit** /báybee sìt/ (**-sat** /-sàt/, **-sit·ting, -sits**) *v* **1.** *vti* to take care of a child or children in the child's home while the parents are out **2.** *vt* to take care of somebody or something unable to be left unsupervised or needing constant attention (*informal*) ○ *Would you babysit my plants next week?* —**ba·by-sit·ter** *n*

ba·by-sit·ting /báybee sìtting/ *n* the activity of looking after children in their own home while their parents are out

ba·by-sit·ting co-op *n* a child-care arrangement by which about 30 parents agree to watch one another's children in their own homes for points instead of money, with the accrued points serving as payment for others in the group to take care of the sitters' children

ba·by snatch·er *n* somebody who steals a baby (*slang*)

ba·by's tears (*plural same*) *n* an evergreen plant that has many small roundish leaves and tiny flowers. Native to: Corsica, Sardinia. Latin name: *Soleirolia solerolii*.

ba·by talk *n* **1.** the sounds and words used by babies when they are learning to talk **2.** the simplified or specially modified language and exaggerated intonation that adults use when talking to very small children

ba·by tooth *n* DENT same as **milk tooth**

ba·by walk·er *n UK* same as **walker** (sense 2)

ba·by·ware /báybee wèr/ *n* clothes and equipment for babies

ba·by·wear /báybee wèr/ *n* clothing designed to be worn by babies

BAC *abbr* **1.** BIOTECH bacterial artificial chromosome **2.** MED blood-alcohol concentration

Ba·call /bə káwl/, **Lauren** (*b.* 1924) US actor. She starred in musicals and movies including *To Have and Have Not* (1944) and *The Big Sleep* (1946). Her first husband was Humphrey Bogart. Born **Perske, Betty Joan**

"I think your whole life shows in your face and you should be proud of that."
[Lauren Bacall, *Remark*; 1988]

Ba·cău /bə ków/ city in eastern Romania. It is the capital of Bacău County, and a major rail hub. Population: 209,689 (1997).

bac·ca·lau·re·ate /bàkə láwree ət/ *n* a bachelor's degree (*formal*) [Mid-17C. Directly or via French < medieval Latin *baccalaureatus* < *baccalaureus* "bachelor"]

bac·ca·lau·re·ate ser·mon *n* a farewell sermon delivered to a graduating class, usually at a high school, college, or university

bac·ca·rat /baàkə raá, bàkə-/ *n* a gambling card game in which the winning hand is the one that totals nine points or is closest to nine points without exceeding it [Mid-19C. < French *baccara*]

bac·cate /bák àyt/ *adj* resembling a berry in shape [Early 19C. < Latin *baccatus* < *bacca* "berry"]

Bac·chae /bákee/ *npl* in ancient Greek and Roman religion, the priestesses and women who participated in the orgiastic rites of Bacchus [Early 20C. Via Latin < Greek *Bakkhai*, plural of *Bakkhē* "priest of Bacchus" < *Bakkhos* "Bacchus"]

bac·cha·nal /bàkə nál, -naál, bákənəl/ *n* **1. PARTICIPANT IN ORGIASTIC RITES** a participant in the orgiastic rites of Bacchanalia **2. LOUD DRUNK** a riotous drunken reveler (*literary*) **3. DRUNKEN PARTY** a noisy drunken celebration or spree (*literary*) **4.** *Carib* **LIVELY PARTY** an enjoyably riotous party or occasion, especially with vigorous dancing, drinking, and activities **5.** *Carib* **OUT-OF-CONTROL EVENT** an event or an occasion that has become uncontrolled and argumentative **6.** *Carib* **PUBLIC OUTCRY** scandal or uproar over immoral behavior ■ *adj* **OF BACCHUS** relating to Bacchus or the worship of Bacchus [Mid-16C. < Latin *bacchanalis* "of Bacchus" < *Bacchus* "Bacchus"]

bac·cha·na·lia /bàkə náylyə, -lee ə/ *n* riotous drunken revels (*takes a singular or plural verb*) [Late 16C.

< Latin, plural of *bacchanalis* (see BACCHANAL)] —**bac·cha·na·lian** *adj*

Bac·cha·na·lia *n* in ancient Rome, festivities in honor of Bacchus that involved orgiastic rites (*takes a singular or plural verb*) —**Bac·cha·na·lian** *adj*

bac·chant /bə kánt, bə ka̋ant, bákənt/ *n* in ancient Greece or Rome, a priest or other devotee of Bacchus [Late 16C. Via French *bacchante* < Latin *bacchant-*, present participle of *bacchari* "celebrate the feast of Bacchus" < *Bacchus* "Bacchus"]

bac·chan·te /bə kántee, -ka̋antee, -kánt, -ka̋ant/ *n* in ancient Greece or Rome, a priestess or woman devotee of Bacchus [Late 18C. < French *bacchante* (see BACCHANT)]

bac·chan·tic /bə kántik, -ka̋an-/ *adj* relating to the worship of Bacchus and the orgiastic rites associated with it

bac·chic /bákik/ *adj* characterized by riotous drunkenness (*literary*)

Bac·chic /bákik/ *adj* relating to Bacchus

bac·chi·us /ba kí̄ əss, bə-/ (*plural* **-i** /-ī/) *n* a metrical foot of one short syllable followed by two long ones [Late 16C. Via Latin < Greek *bakkheios (pous)* "Bacchic (foot)" < *Bakkhos* "Bacchus"]

Bac·chus /bákəss, ba̋akəss/ *n* in Greek and Roman mythology, the god of wine, identified with the Greek god Dionysus and the Roman god Liber. He was worshiped with orgiastic and ecstatic rites. [Via Latin < Greek *Bakkhos*]

bac·cif·er·ous /bak síffərəss/ *adj* describes plants that produce berries [Mid-17C. < Latin *baccifer* "bearing berries" < *bacca* "berry"]

bach /bach/ (**bached, bach·ing, bach·es**), **batch** (**batched, batch·ing, batch·es**) *vi US* to live alone as a single man and keep house for yourself (*informal*) [Mid-19C. Shortening of BACHELOR]

Bach /baakh, baak/, **C. P. E.** (1714–88) German composer. The son of Johann Sebastian Bach, he composed numerous concertos and sonatas as well as chamber and church music. He also wrote *The True Art of Clavier Playing* (1753). Full name **Bach, Carl Philipp Emanuel**. Known as **Berlin Bach, Hamburg Bach**

Bach, J. C. (1735–82) German composer. The youngest son of Johann Sebastian Bach and a composer of church music and operas, he settled in London (1762) and was musician to Queen Charlotte. Full name **Bach, Johann Christian**. Known as **London Bach, English Bach**

Johann Sebastian Bach

Bach, Johann Sebastian (1685–1750) German composer and organist. Known as a supreme master of counterpoint, he wrote many organ works, chamber and keyboard works, and oratorios, and over 295 cantatas. His works include the *Brandenburg Concertos* (1720–21) and *St. Matthew Passion* (1727).

Bach, W. F. (1710–84) German composer. He led a dissolute life despite being a gifted organist and composer. He was the eldest son of Johann Sebastian Bach. Full name **Bach, Wilhelm Friedemann**. Known as **Halle Bach**

ba·chac /bá chàk/, **bat·chac, bah-chak** *n Carib* INSECTS same as **leafcutter ant**

bach·cha /búchə/ *n S Asia* **1.** a child or young adult **2.** a naive or immature person [< Hindi *baccā* "child"]

bach·e·lor /báchələr, báchlər/ *n* **1.** UNMARRIED MAN a man who is not or has never been married **2.** HIST YOUNG KNIGHT a young knight in feudal times who served under the banner of another knight or a great lord **3.** MARINE BIOL YOUNG MALE SEAL a young male seal, especially a fur seal, that older male seals keep from having access to breeding grounds [13C. Via Old French *bacheler* "young man aspiring to knighthood" < assumed Vulgar Latin *baccalaris*] —**bach·e·lor·dom** *n* —**bach·e·lor·hood** *n* —**bach·e·lor·ship** *n*

bach·e·lor a·part·ment *n* **1.** an apartment in which a bachelor lives **2.** *Can* an apartment consisting of a large single room, a small kitchen, and a bathroom

bach·e·lor·ette /bàchələ rét/ *n* **1.** *Can* a small bachelor apartment **2.** a young woman who has never been married

bach·e·lor·ette par·ty *n* a party that is given for a woman on the night before her wedding and that is usually attended only by women

bach·e·lor girl *n* a young unmarried woman, usually one who is self-supporting (*dated*)

Bach·e·lor of Arts *n* a college or university degree awarded to somebody who has successfully completed an undergraduate course in an aspect of the arts or humanities

Bach·e·lor of Let·ters *n* a university degree awarded to somebody who has successfully completed a postgraduate course in an aspect of the arts or humanities [Translation of Latin *Baccalaureus Litterarum*]

Bach·e·lor of Lit·er·a·ture *n* **1.** EDUC same as **Bachelor of Letters 2.** especially in South Asia, a college or university degree awarded to somebody who has successfully completed an undergraduate course in literary studies

Bach·e·lor of Sci·ence *n* a college or university degree awarded to somebody who has successfully completed an undergraduate course in an aspect of the sciences or technology

bach·e·lor pad *n UK* same as **bachelor apartment** (sense 1)

bach·e·lor par·ty *n* a party that is given for a man on the night before his wedding and that is usually attended only by men

bach·e·lor's but·ton *n* an ornamental plant with small round double flowers, especially a cornflower (*takes a singular or plural verb*)

bach·e·lor's de·gree *n* a degree awarded on the successful completion of an undergraduate course at a college or university

Bach flow·er rem·e·dies /bách-/ *npl* a healing method using extracts of 38 flowers, each treating a different emotional disorder, to promote physical health [Late 20C. After Edward *Bach* (1886–1936), British physician]

Bach trum·pet /baakh-/ *n* a modern valve trumpet, smaller than an ordinary trumpet, especially designed for playing the high-pitched trumpet parts in baroque music [After J. S. BACH]

bac·il·lar·y /bássə lèrree, bə sílləree/ *adj* **1.** relating to or caused by rod-shaped bacteria (**bacilli**) **2.** shaped like a small rod, or consisting of small rod-shaped parts

ba·cil·lus /bə sílləss/ (*plural* **-li** /-síl ì/) *n* an aerobic, rod-shaped, spore-producing bacterium. Bacilli occur mainly in chains and include many saprophytes, some parasites, and the bacterium that causes anthrax. Genus: *Bacillus*. [Late 19C. < late Latin, "little rod" < *baculus* "rod, stick"]

bac·i·tra·cin /bàssi tráyss'n/ *n* an antibiotic produced by a strain of bacterium. Use: topically, in the treatment of skin infections. [Mid-20C. < BACILLUS + Margaret *Tracy*, in whom the substance was discovered in a wound]

back /bak/ *n* **1.** ANAT REAR PART OF BODY the rear part of the human body between the neck and the pelvis ○ *carrying a baby on her back* ○ *back pain* **2.** ANAT SPINE the spinal column **3.** ANAT AREA OF VERTEBRATE'S BODY the area of a vertebrate animal's body on each side of the backbone **4.** PART AT REAR the part that is at the rear of something or is farthest from the front ○ *Someone at the back of the crowd called out.* **5.** SIDE NOT USUALLY SEEN the side of something such as a sheet of paper or a photograph that carries less information or is away from the viewer **6.** PART OF GARMENT the part of a garment designed to cover the wearer's back **7.** PART OF PIECE OF FURNITURE the part of a seat designed to support somebody's spine **8.** PART TO WHICH PAGES ARE FIXED the part of a book where the pages are glued or stitched to the binding **9.** SPORTS DEFENSIVE PLAYER a player in sports such as soccer or hockey whose role is mainly to prevent the other team from scoring **10.** SPORTS PLAYER BEHIND LINE a player positioned behind the offensive or defensive line, especially in football ■ *adv* **1.** IN REVERSE DIRECTION in the opposite direction from the one in which somebody or something was previously facing or traveling ○ *She looked back over her shoulder.* **2.** AT DISTANCE at a distance from where something is situated or taking place ○ *Stay back, the dog might bite.* **3.** IN RESERVE as a reserve or supply kept for future use ○ *I kept back part of the proceeds.* **4.** SO AS TO UNCOVER SOMETHING away from something so as to leave something else uncovered or revealed ○ *roll back the carpet* **5.** SO AS TO RECLINE in or into a reclining position ○ *Sit back and relax.* **6.** IN OR INTO PAST used to indicate a time in the past ○ *It happened about three weeks back.* **7.** TO MORE DISTANT TIME used to indicate movement in time away from the present ○ *will put the clocks back* ○ *postponed the wedding and moved it back to next year* **8.** TO ORIGINAL OWNER to or into the keeping of the original or former owner or possessor ○ *You can have it back now, because I'm finished with it.* **9.** IN RETURN as a reaction or response to something ○ *She called me while I was out, so I called her back.* **10.** INDICATES DIRECTION AND DISTANCE in the distance behind something, especially somebody's present position ○ *We passed it about two miles back.* **11.** RETURNED TO CONDITION OR TOPIC used to indicate a return to a state, situation, or subject of discussion ○ *to get back to your point* **12.** INTO POPULARITY AGAIN into fashion or popularity again ○ *The 1960s are back.* ○ *Do you think Depression glass will ever come back?* ■ *adj* **1.** LOCATED AT REAR located at the rear of something, or at the part farthest from the front ○ *Use the back entrance.* ○ *a back room* **2.** ISSUED EARLIER published or issued at an earlier date ○ *a back issue* **3.** REMAINING FROM EARLIER TIME due at or owed from an earlier date ○ *paid the back taxes in full* **4.** LOCATED AWAY FROM MAIN ROADS located away from the main roads or the center of a town ○ *a quiet back street* **5.** REMOTE situated away from the main centers of population or activity ○ *explored the back areas of the canyon* **6.** REVERSE moving in an opposite direction from the usual one **7.** PHON FORMED AT REAR OF MOUTH formed at or toward the rear of the mouth, as the vowel in "ball" is ○ *a back vowel* ■ *v* (**backed, back·ing, backs**) **1.** *vti* MOVE BACKWARD to move backward, or make somebody or something move backward ○ *The vehicle in front backed into me.* **2.** *vt* SUPPORT PERSON OR CAUSE to give a person or cause financial, political, or moral support **3.** *vt* BET ON OUTCOME OF RACE to bet money on the person, team, or animal thought likely to win a race or competition **4.** *vt* PROVIDE PROOF TO SUPPORT SOMETHING to provide evidence or proof in support of a statement ○ *But can they back their allegations?* **5.** *vt* REINFORCE SOMETHING to reinforce something by adding a support or backing (*often passive*) ○ *colored paper backed with cardboard* **6.** *vt* BE BEHIND SOMETHING to be situated behind something (*usually passive*) ○ *a lake backed by a range of mountains* **7.** *vt* MUSIC PROVIDE MUSICAL ACCOMPANIMENT FOR SOMEBODY to provide an instrumental or vocal accompaniment for the main performer of a piece of popular music or jazz **8.** *vi* METEOROL CHANGE DIRECTION to change direction, moving in a counterclockwise direction (*refers to winds*) **9.** *vt regional* ADDRESS ENVELOPE to write an address on an envelope or letter [Old English *bæc* < Germanic] ◇ **back and fill 1.** to adjust the sails of a vessel to allow the wind to move in and out of them in an alternating manner while maneuvering in a narrow channel **2.** to dither or vacillate in actions or decision-making ◇ **back of** at the back of or behind something ◇ **behind somebody's back** when somebody is not present ◇ **be** *or* **get on somebody's back** to criticize or pressure somebody (*slang*) ◇ **get off somebody's back** to stop criticizing or pressuring somebody (*slang*) ◇ **get your back up** to become annoyed or angry (*informal*) ◇ **have your back to the wall** to be in a very difficult situation, with little chance of getting out of it ◇ **in back (of something)** at the back of or behind something (*informal*) ◇ **know something like the back of your hand** to know something extremely well ○ *He knew the city like the back of his hand, having lived* *there for nearly 50 years.* ◇ **put somebody's back up** to annoy or antagonize somebody (*informal*) ◇ **put your back into something** to put effort, especially physical strength, into doing something ◇ **stab somebody in the back** to do or say something harmful to somebody after pretending to be a friend ○ *After promising not to tell anyone, he stabbed me in the back and went to the press.* ◇ **the back of beyond** a remote inaccessible place that has few amenities ○ *They bought a small cabin in the back of beyond, just to get away from it all.* ◇ **turn your back on somebody** *or* **something** to ignore or reject somebody or something ◇ **you scratch my back and I'll scratch yours** if you help me, I will help you in return (*often refers to unofficial or dishonest business dealings*)

USAGE back of and **in back of**: The phrase ***back of*** is standard and ***in back of*** is its informal variant. Both mean "behind," and ***in back of*** is formed on the direct analogy of *in front of*: *There was a swimming pool (in) back of the house.*

USAGE Movement in time: ***Back*** as it applies to the past refers to a change to an earlier time. *They have moved the estimate of its date of origin back a hundred years* would mean a change from, say, A.D. 1000 to A.D. 900. As the word applies to the future, however, it usually signifies a change to a later time: *The forecast is for rain, so let's move the picnic back a week.* What the two uses have in common is movement in time away from the present. *Up* is the opposite of ***back*** in this sense: *Let's move the date up* means moving the date closer to the present, and thus in future contexts changing it to an earlier one. *Forward* in future contexts is used less consistently than either ***back*** or *up*; it is best avoided. All these words become particularly confusing when the subject is, for example, a decision, now in the past, about what was at the time the future: *Last month she told me she wanted to move my appointment back.* In a context like this, *make earlier* or *make later* is clearer.

REGIONAL NOTE In the sense "to write an address on an envelope or letter," ***back*** is a mainly Southern and South Midland term, being found from Tennessee and Georgia to Texas, with scattered instances of use in New England, the Midwest, and the West.

back away *vi* **1.** to walk backward away from somebody or something, usually because of fear **2.** to withdraw from a situation or previous position ○ *We think they'll back away from any direct confrontation over sanctions.*
back down *vi* to abandon a claim, opinion, or commitment because of the degree of opposition it arouses
back off *vi* **1. MOVE BACK** to move away backward **2. WITHDRAW** to withdraw from a previous commitment, claim, or position **3. EASE PRESSURE ON SOMEBODY** to stop putting pressure on somebody to do something
back out *v* **1.** *vi* to withdraw from a previous commitment ○ *The buyer backed out before the papers were signed.* **2.** *vti* to move out backward, or cause something to move out backward
back up *v* **1.** *vt* **SUPPORT SOMEBODY** to provide support for a person or idea ○ *I'm sure you'll back me up on this.* **2.** *vt* **PROVE STATEMENT** to supply proof that a statement is true ○ *Evidence of growth is backed up by recent economic statistics.* **3.** *vt* COMPUT **COPY COMPUTER FILES** to make a copy of computer data to keep in case anything goes wrong with the original **4.** *vti* **GO BACKWARD** to go or move something backward **5.** *vti* **ACCUMULATE** to build up, or cause something to build up, especially because normal flow is obstructed ○ *Traffic was backed up three miles from the accident.*

Back /bak/, **Sir George** (1796–1878) British-born Canadian explorer. He helped map the North American coastline, accompanied Sir John Franklin's Arctic expeditions, and searched for Sir John Ross.

back·ache /bák àyk/ *n* an ache or pain affecting the back, most commonly the lower back

back-al·ley *adj* performed illegally or secretly by an unskilled or untrained person

back-and-forth *n* the repeated exchange of ideas, opinions, or information

back ba·con *n Can* relatively fat-free bacon from the loin or rib-end of a pig

back·beat /bák bèet/ *n* a loud rhythmic beat occurring on the off beats of a bar of music, used especially in rock

back·bench /bák bènch/ *n Can, UK* **1.** a rear bench in a legislative assembly reserved for backbenchers (*usually used in the plural*) **2.** the group of backbenchers in a legislative assembly (*often used in the plural*)

back·bench·er /bák bènchər/ *n Can, UK* a junior member of the lower house of a legislative assembly who is not a government minister or an official Opposition spokesperson

back·bend /bák bènd/ *n* an exercise in gymnastics in which somebody bends over backward from a standing position until the hands touch the floor

back·bite /bák bìt/ (**-bit** /-bìt/, **-bit·ten** /-bìtt'n/, **-bit·ing**, **-bites**) *vti* to make spiteful or slanderous comments about somebody who is not present —**back·bit·er** *n*

back·board /bák bàwrd/ *n* **1. BOARD BEHIND BASKET** in basketball, the vertical board situated behind the basket that serves to rebound the ball into the basket or onto the court **2. BOARD USED TO SUPPORT INJURED BACK** a board that is used to support the back after injury or as aid to recovery after surgery **3. BOARD FORMING BACK OF SOMETHING** a board that forms the back of something such as a cart or boat

back·bone /bák bòn/ *n* **1.** ANAT same as **spinal column** **2. SOMETHING SIMILAR TO SPINAL COLUMN** something that is similar in shape or position to a spinal column ○ *the Andes, the backbone of South America* **3. CENTRAL SUPPORTING PART** the part of an organization or system that is its strongest unifying factor and main support ○ *People like her form the backbone of this nation.* **4. FORTITUDE** strength of character and determination ○ *He doesn't have the backbone to stand up to his critics.* **5.** ONLINE **HIGH-SPEED RELAY** a high-speed relay that feeds smaller channels in corporate computer networks and the Internet **6.** COMPUT **CORE OF ELECTRONIC NETWORK** the core of an electronic network, e.g., a physical cable connection or a routing protocol

back bound·a·ry line *n* on a badminton court, either of two lines parallel to the net that mark the rear limit of the playing area

back·break·er /bák bràykər/ *n* **1.** in wrestling, a hold in which somebody's back is bent backward over the opponent's knee or shoulder **2.** an exhausting or physically demanding task (*informal*)

back·break·ing /bák bràyking/ *adj* involving enormous physical effort

back burn·er ◇ **put something on the back burner** to assign something a lower priority or give something less prominence ○ *The project has been put on the back burner.*

back ca·ta·log *n* the complete collection of recordings, films, or books made by an artist or a company to date

back chan·nel *n* a covert way of exchanging sensitive information in politics or diplomacy that circumvents the usual procedures

back·chat /bák chàt/ *n UK* same as **back talk**

back·check /bák chèk/ (**-checked**, **-check·ing**, **-checks**) *vti* in ice hockey, to skate back toward your own goal while trying to block an opponent with your body or stick, or block an opponent while doing this —**back·check·er** *n*

back·cloth /bák klàwth, -klòth/ *n* THEATER same as **backdrop** (sense 2)

back·comb /bák kòm/ (**-combed**, **-comb·ing**, **-combs**) *vt UK* to comb hair with quick short movements toward the roots so that it stands up away from the head and can be brushed into a bouffant hairstyle. Same as **tease** *v* (sense 5). Can term **tease**

back con·ces·sion *n Can* a piece of land that is sparsely populated or remote from well-traveled roads

back cop·y *n* same as **back issue**

back coun·try *n* a remote, sparsely populated rural area, often used for various forms of outdoor recreation, including backpacking and camping

back·coun·try snow·board·ing *n* snowboard riding that, like off-piste skiing, is done away from resorts or marked terrain

back·court /bák kàwrt/ *n* **1. REAR OF COURT** in tennis, the area between the baseline and the service line of a court, or in similar games, the area of a court nearest the back boundary line or back wall **2. DEFENDED HALF OF BASKETBALL COURT** in basketball, the half of a court where the basket being defended is located **3. DEFENSIVE PLAYERS** in basketball, the players who defend the backcourt

back crawl *n* SWIMMING same as **backstroke** (sense 1)

back·cross /bák kràwss/ *vt* (**-crossed**, **-cross·ing**, **-cross·es**) **CROSS HYBRID WITH PARENT** to cross an organism, especially a hybrid, with one of its parents or an individual genetically identical to that parent ■ *n* **1. HYBRID OBTAINED BY BACKCROSSING** a hybrid obtained by backcrossing organisms **2. ACT OF BACKCROSSING** the act or the process of backcrossing organisms

back·dam /bák dàm/ *n Carib* **1.** a dam marking the rear boundary of a plantation **2.** an area beyond the plantation fields used by laborers to grow crops

back·date /bák dàyt/ (**-dat·ed**, **-dat·ing**, **-dates**) *vt* to put a date on a document that is earlier than the actual date of its writing or signing

back dive *n* a dive made when the diver's back is facing the water

back door *n* **1. REAR DOOR** a door or entrance at the rear of a building **2. DISHONEST ADVANTAGE** underhand or indirect access that gives somebody an unfair advantage **3.** COMPUT **DELIBERATE GAP IN SECURITY SYSTEM** an opening deliberately left in a security system to allow access for technicians

back·door /bák dàwr/ *adj* carried out in secrecy or in a surreptitious way ○ *There's been a lot of backdoor pressure on her to step down.*

back·down /bák dòwn/ *n* the abandonment of a course of action or an opinion in the face of opposition from other people

back·drop /bák dròp/ *n* **1.** a setting or context ○ *The ski-jumping took place against the backdrop of jagged mountain peaks.* **2.** a large painted cloth hung at the back of a stage that usually depicts the setting in which the action of a scene takes place

backed /bakt/ *adj* having a back or backing

back emf *n* an electromagnetic force that opposes any change of current in an inductive circuit

back e·mis·sion *n* the production of electrons from the anode of a vacuum tube

back end *n* **1.** a main processing computer, often with a smaller interactive computer **2.** a software program that controls operations not specified by the user **3.** *UK regional* same as **fall** *n* (sense 6)

back end load *n* a mutual fund sales charge paid when shares are sold

back·er /bákər/ *n* **1.** somebody who gives moral or financial support to somebody or something **2.** somebody who bets on somebody or something

SYNONYMS ***backer, angel, guarantor, patron, sponsor***
CORE MEANING: somebody who provides financial support
backer a person who gives moral or financial support ○ *The project's main backer has withdrawn his support.* **angel** a person who provides financial support for an enterprise such as a theatrical venture ○ *Business angels pump money into private companies in return for shares.* **guarantor** a person who gives a legal undertaking to be responsible for somebody else's debts or obligations ○ *My father acted as guarantor for the loan.* **patron** a person who gives financial or moral support to a person, institution, or charity, especially in the arts ○ *kings who were great patrons of the arts* ○ *a 21-year-old architect who apparently spent all his patron's money* **sponsor** a person or organization that contributes money to help fund an event, usually in return for publicity, or gives money to a person taking part in a fundraising activity ○ *looking for sponsors for her next project* ○ *We would like to thank our sponsors for donating the prizes.*

back·field /bák fèeld/ *n* **1. AREA OF FIELD** in football, the area of the playing field behind the line of scrimmage **2. PLAYERS** the football players who line up behind the line of scrimmage **3. POSITIONS** the positions of the football players who line up behind the line of scrimmage

back·fill /bák fìl/ *vt* (**-filled, -fill·ing, -fills**) to refill a trench or other excavation with the soil dug out of it ■ *n* the soil used to refill a trench

back·fire /bák fìr/ *vi* (**-fired, -fir·ing, -fires**) **1.** HAVE OPPOSITE EFFECT to have an effect opposite to the one intended ○ *The policy of mandatory testing may well backfire and do more harm than good.* **2.** AUTOMOT MAKE EXPLOSION IN EXHAUST PIPE to produce an explosion of prematurely ignited fuel in an internal-combustion engine, or of unburned exhaust gases in the exhaust pipe **3.** FORESTRY START FIRE TO CREATE FIREBREAK to start a fire in the path of an advancing wildfire in a forest in order to halt its advance ■ *n* **1.** AUTOMOT EXPLOSION IN CAR EXHAUST an explosion of prematurely ignited fuel in an internal-combustion engine or of unburned exhaust gases in the exhaust pipe **2.** FORESTRY FIRE STARTED TO CREATE FIREBREAK a fire deliberately started in a forest in order to clear the ground in front of an advancing wildfire to halt its advance

back·flip /bák flìp/ *n* a backward midair somersault with the arms and legs extended, performed in gymnastics, diving, and board sports such as skateboarding and snowboarding

back·flow /bák flò/ *n* the flowing back of something toward the source

back·for·ma·tion *n* **1.** a process of word formation in which a new word is coined by removing a real or imagined affix from an existing word **2.** a word formed by back-formation, e.g., "greed" from "greedy," or "televise" from "television"

back for·ty *n* a remote, usually unused part of a farm or ranch

back four *n* in soccer, a defensive formation that consists of two wing backs and two center backs deployed in a straight line across the field

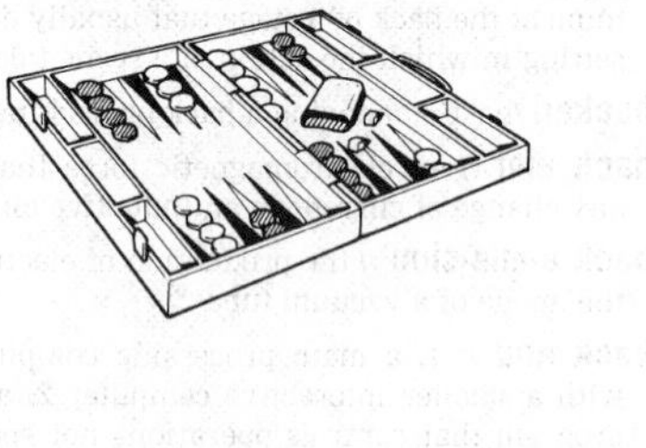

backgammon

back·gam·mon /bák gàmmən/ *n* **1.** a board game for two players who move counters according to throws of a pair of dice, the object being to remove all one player's counters from the board **2.** the most complete form of victory in backgammon. It occurs when a player removes all 15 pieces while the other still has a piece furthest from the point at which he or she can remove pieces from the board. [Mid-17C. < BACK + *gamen*, early form of GAME[1]; probably from the pieces sometimes being put "back" on the table]

back·ground /bák grὸwnd/ *n* **1.** PERSONAL CIRCUMSTANCES AND EXPERIENCES the personal circumstances and experiences that shape somebody's life, e.g., ethnic and social origins, upbringing, education, and work experience ○ *a group of people from very different backgrounds* **2.** CAUSES OF EVENT the circumstances leading up to an event that explain its cause ○ *The meeting takes place against a background of rising tension.* **3.** AREA BEHIND SOMETHING the area that is behind something, forming the setting for it ○ *A silvery lake shone against a background of tall dark firs.* **4.** PART OF PICTURE the part of a picture or pattern that appears to be in the distance or behind the most important part **5.** INFORMATION information that helps to explain what somebody or something is like or why something is happening **6.** INCONSPICUOUS POSITION a position of relative inconspicuousness or unimportance ○ *working tirelessly in the background* **7.** COMPUT LOW-PRIORITY COMPUTER ENVIRONMENT the low-priority environment in computers that can perform multiple tasks **8.** PHYS same as **background radiation** **9.** ELECTRONICS, ACOUSTICS SIGNAL CAUSING DISTORTION OR INTERFERENCE an extraneous signal, often in the form of electronic or acoustic noise, that can cause distortion or affect an instrument reading (*often used before a noun*) ○ *background interference* ■ *adj* **1.** AS PART OF BACKGROUND situated or depicted in, or forming part of, the background to something **2.** ACCOMPANYING functioning or suitable as an accompaniment to something else ◇ **on background** on conditions of anonymity and in an effort to provide the press with nonattributable information, usually sensitive in nature ○ *addressed the issue on background only*

back·ground·er /bák grὸwndər/ *n* an informal meeting or press conference in which a government spokesperson provides journalists with background information on condition that the informant is not identified as the source

back·ground mu·sic *n* music used as an accompaniment to action or dialogue in a movie, or to create a pleasant atmosphere for an activity or a public place

back·ground noise *n* noise that is sufficiently loud to be heard but not so loud as to obscure what is actually being listened to

back·ground pro·cess·ing *n* execution of computer tasks that continues while the user is working with another application. Once started, background tasks such as printing or copying data take place without user input.

back·ground ra·di·a·tion *n* low-level radiation occurring naturally as a result of radioactivity present in the air, soil, and buildings and other structures

back·hand /bák hànd/ *n* **1.** RACKET GAMES BACKHANDED STROKE in tennis and other racket games, a stroke made with the back of the hand turned toward the ball or shuttlecock as the arm moves outward from a position across the body **2.** RACKET GAMES SIDE FOR BACKHANDS the side of a tennis or other racket court, or of the body, on which a player would naturally play a backhand. It is the left-hand side for a right-handed player. **3.** BASEBALL CATCH MADE ON BACKHAND SIDE in baseball, a catch made with the catcher's hand, in a mitt, held across his or her body **4.** HANDWRITING SLOPING LEFTWARD a style of handwriting in which the letters slope to the left ■ *adj* **1.** RACKET GAMES WITH BACK OF HAND TOWARD BALL in tennis and other racket games, used to describe a stroke carried out with the back of the hand toward the ball or shuttlecock, usually with the arm across the body **2.** DONE WITH BACKHANDED MOVEMENT carried out with the back of the hand turned toward the direction of any movement ■ *adv* WITH BACKHAND STROKE with the back of the hand facing in the direction in which a stroke, movement, or blow is made ■ *vt* (**-hand·ed, -hand·ing, -hands**) **1.** SPORTS CONTACT BALL WITH BACKHAND to strike a ball with a backhand stroke, or catch it with the hand held across the body ○ *She backhanded the ball just over the net.* **2.** HIT SOMEBODY WITH BACK OF HAND to hit somebody or something with the back of the hand ○ *accidentally backhanded an opponent*

back·hand·ed /bák hàndəd/ *adj* **1.** WITH BACK OF HAND carried out with the back of the hand, or with the back of the hand facing in the direction in which the stroke, movement, or blow is made ○ *a backhanded return* **2.** WITH DOUBLE MEANING with a doubtful or double meaning, especially one that can be understood equally as a compliment or as an insult ○ *a backhanded compliment* **3.** WRITTEN WITH LETTERS SLOPING LEFTWARD written in a style of handwriting in which the letters slope to the left ■ *adv* WITH BACKHANDED STROKE with the back of the hand, or with the back of the hand facing in the direction in which a stroke, movement, or blow is made —**back·hand·ed·ly** *adv* —**back·hand·ed·ness** *n*

back·hand·er /bák hàndər/ *n* **1.** BACKHANDED BLOW a blow struck with the back of the hand ○ *caught the opposing team member with a terrific backhander across the face during hard play* **2.** RACKET GAMES same as **backhand** *n* (sense 1) **3.** *UK* BRIBE an illicit payment made as a bribe (*informal*) **4.** *UK* BACKHANDED COMPLIMENT a backhanded compliment or veiled verbal attack on somebody (*informal*)

back·hoe /bák hò/ *n* a digging machine or attachment consisting of a hinged scoop attached to a jointed mechanical arm that drags the scoop back toward the cab from which it is operated

back·ing /báking/ *n* **1.** SUPPORT OR HELP active approval, support, or help, often in financial form, given to a person, organization, or cause **2.** SUPPORTERS the people or organizations giving support to a person or cause **3.** REAR SURFACE material forming or covering the back of something, especially to strengthen, stiffen, or protect it **4.** MUSICAL ACCOMPANIMENT the music or singing that accompanies the playing or singing of the main performer of a piece of popular music or jazz

back·ing track *n* a recorded musical accompaniment for use by a solo performer

back is·sue *n* a previous issue of a magazine or newspaper

back kitch·en *n* a pantry or other small room off a kitchen (*informal*)

back·lash /bák làsh/ *n* **1.** STRONG REACTION a strong adverse reaction among a group of people to an event, development, or trend, especially one that benefits another group **2.** VIOLENT BACKWARD MOVEMENT a sudden violent backward jerking movement, e.g., when a cable breaks under strain **3.** MECH ENG RECOIL BETWEEN MACHINE PARTS a jarring recoil that sometimes occurs when worn or badly fitting parts of a mechanism come together **4.** MECH ENG PLAY BETWEEN MACHINE PARTS excessive play between adjacent parts in a mechanism such as a set of gears, usually as a result of the parts being worn or badly fitted **5.** FISHING FISHING LINE TANGLE a tangle in a fishing line wound on a reel

back·less /bákləss/ *adj* with the back cut very low ○ *a backless dress*

back·light /bák lìt/ *n* light that illuminates the subject of a photograph or painting from behind ■ *vt* (**-light·ed** or **-lit** /-lìt/, **-light·ing, -lights**) to illuminate a subject from behind —**back·light·ing** *n*

back·list /bák lìst/ *n* the range of books already published by a publisher that are still in print ○ *The departing editor had built up a highly respectable backlist.*

back·lit past participle, past tense of **backlight**

back·log /bák lòg, -làwg/ *n* **1.** THINGS STILL TO BE DONE a quantity of unfinished business or work that has built up over a period of time and must be dealt with before progress can be made ○ *She faced a backlog of unanswered letters when she came back.* **2.** LARGE LOG ON FIRE a large log placed at the back of an open fire ■ *vti* (**-logged, -log·ging, -logs**) ACCUMULATE to accumulate work or material that needs to be dealt with ○ *Order fulfillment got backlogged when nearly everyone in the department came down with the flu.*

back mat·ter *n* the parts of a book that appear after the main text, e.g., the index or an appendix

back mu·ta·tion *n* the reversion of a mutated gene to its original form

back num·ber *n UK* same as **back issue**

back of·fice *n* **1.** BUSINESS OPERATIONS OTHER THAN POLICYMAKING the business operations performed by people who do not make policy, or the place where they work **2.** SECURE AREA OF SOFTWARE a secure area of e-commerce software where details of store properties, tax tables, and products are held ■ *adj* RELATING TO INTERNAL MATTERS relating to or concerned with the administration and internal workings of a business organization rather than its contacts with the public

back·pack /bák pàk/ *n* **1.** HIKERS' KNAPSACK a large sturdy fabric bag, often on a metal frame, worn on the back and used by hikers **2.** STUDENTS' BOOK BAG a knapsack used to carry schoolbooks, school supplies, or personal items **3.** EQUIPMENT CARRIED ON BACK a carrier for a piece of equipment such as an astronaut's personal life-support system that is designed to be strapped on the user's back ■ *v* (**-packed, -pack·ing, -packs**) **1.** *vi* HIKE WITH BACKPACK to travel, especially hike, carrying belongings or supplies in a backpack ○ *She spent a month backpacking in the Rockies.* **2.** *vt* CARRY SOMETHING ON BACK to transport something, usually equipment or supplies, in a pack on the

backpack

back ○ *astronauts backpacking oxygen during a spacewalk* —**back·pack·er** *n*

back pain *n* persistent pain in part of the back

back pass *n* in soccer, a pass from an outfield player back to the goalkeeper. Goalkeepers are forbidden to handle back passes with their hands.

back pay *n* pay that is owed to an employee for work done before the current payment period and is either overdue or results from a backdated pay increase

back·ped·al /bák pèdd'l/ (**-aled, -al·ing, -als**) *v* **1.** *vti* **PEDAL BACKWARD** to turn the pedals of a bicycle backward in order to operate a brake **2.** *vi* **MOVE BACKWARD** in sports, to move quickly backward in order to get away from an opponent or to catch a ball **3.** *vi* **RETRACT STATEMENT** to try to escape the consequences of a statement or action by retracting it, modifying it, or toning it down

back·plate /bák plàyt/ *n* a piece of armor protecting the back

back pres·sure *n* **1. RESISTANT PRESSURE** resistant pressure exerted by a solid, liquid, or gas to the forward motion of a system, especially the pressure opposing the exhaust stroke of a piston in an internal-combustion engine **2.** INDUST **OIL OR GAS PRESSURE** the pressure exerted by fluids in the bore of an oil well on the oil and gas in the reservoir. Careful control of this pressure ensures an even supply of oil. **3.** MED **PRESSURE DUE TO OBSTRUCTION** pressure within a blood vessel or the urinary system that builds up when there is an obstruction to the flow of fluid

back pro·jec·tion *n* the cinematic technique of projecting a film onto a translucent screen from behind, usually to provide a moving background against which other action can be filmed

back·rest /bák rèst/ *n* a part of a seat designed to support the user's back

back·room /bák ro͝om, -ro͞om/ *n* **1.** *also* **back room ROOM AT BACK** a room at or toward the back of a building **2.** *also* **back room MEETING PLACE OF POWER ELITE** the supposed meeting place of a group that exercises a powerful behind-the-scenes influence on events or an organization ■ *adj also* **back-room UNOBTRUSIVE OR CLANDESTINE** taking place unobtrusively, but usually important or influential nonetheless ○ *The tax law was hammered out in a backroom deal between Republicans and Democrats.*

back·saw /bák sàw/ *n* a small saw stiffened and strengthened by a strip of metal on its noncutting edge

back·scat·ter /bák skàttər/ *n* **1.** the deflection of radiation or particles through angles of greater than 90 degrees measured with respect to the original direction of travel through a medium **2.** radiation or particles deflected more than 90 degrees while passing through a medium

back·scratch·ing /bák skràching/ *n* the doing of favors for other people in return for similar favors from them (*informal*) —**back·scratch** *vi*

back seat *n* **1.** a seat at the back of a vehicle **2.** a less important or active role ◇ **take a back seat (to somebody)** to allow somebody else to direct or control something while taking on a relatively less important role yourself

back-seat driv·er *n* (*informal*) **1.** a passenger in a vehicle who continually pesters the driver with unwanted advice or criticism **2.** somebody who gives unwanted advice or criticism while somebody else does something

back·set /bák sèt/ *n* an eddy or a current flowing against the direction of the main current in a body of water

back shift *n UK* HR same as **swing shift**

back·shore /bák shàwr/ *n* the area of a shore that is above the high-water mark except in very severe weather

back·side /bák sīd/ *n* **1. BUTTOCKS** a person's buttocks (*informal*) **2.** *S Asia* **BACK** a person's back **3.** *Malaysia* **REAR OF SOMETHING** the rear part of a vehicle or building

back·sight /bák sīt/ *n* **1.** an aiming device on the part of a firearm nearest to the aimer's eye **2.** a reading taken by a surveyor back toward a position from which a previous reading has been made

back slang *n* slang in which words are disguised by being pronounced as if spelled backward

back·slap /bák slàp/ (**-slapped, -slap·ping, -slaps**) *vti* to treat somebody, or treat each other, in a hearty, jovial, and enthusiastically complimentary way, with or without physical slaps on the back ○ *a political candidate who backslapped his way across the country* —**back·slap·per** *n*

back·slash /bák slàsh/ *n* a keyboard character (\) with various uses in computing and computer programming

back·slide /bák slīd/ (**-slid** /-slìd/, **-slid** /-slìd/, **-slid·ing, -slides**) *vi* to fall back into wrongdoing or a bad habit after an attempt to act in a better way —**back·slid·er** *n*

back·space /bák spàyss/ (**-spaced, -spac·ing, -spac·es**) *vi* to move the cursor of a computer or the carriage of a typewriter back one or more spaces using the key designed for this purpose

back·spin /bák spìn/ *n* spin that makes a ball rotate in the opposite direction to its line of movement so that when it lands or strikes something its forward momentum will be reduced

back·splash /bák splàsh/ *n* a vertical waterproof surface, usually tiled, that protects the area above a sink or bath from splashes

back·stab /bák stàb/ (**-stabbed, -stab·bing, -stabs**) *vt* to do or say something harmful to somebody after pretending to be a friend [Early 20C. < *stab somebody in the back*] —**back·stab·ber** *n* —**back·stab·bing** *n*

back·stage /bàk stáyj/ *adv* **1.** behind the area of a theater stage that is visible to an audience, e.g., in the areas where stage technicians work or in the dressing rooms ○ *Journalists were allowed backstage to interview the star.* **2.** in private, or out of the view of the general public —**back·stage** /bák stàyj/ *adj*

back·stairs /bák stèrz/ *npl* a set of stairs in a private part of a house, often originally for the use of servants ■ *adj* carried on secretly or furtively

back·stay /bák stày/ *n* **1.** something that supports or strengthens the back of something else, e.g., a piece of leather covering the back seam of a shoe **2.** a rope leading backward from the top of a ship's mast to the side or stern and giving support to the mast

back·stick /bák stìk/ *n regional* a large log at the back of a fire or campfire

REGIONAL NOTE The term ***backstick*** is most common today in Tennessee, Mississippi, Arkansas, and Upper Alabama. It is now essentially an upcountry folk term.

back·stitch /bák stìch/ *n* a method of stitching in which each new stitch starts from the middle of the previous stitch —**back·stitch** *vti*

back·stop /bák stòp/ *n* **1. ADDITIONAL SUPPORT** somebody or something providing additional support or protection in case somebody or something else fails **2. SCREEN TO STOP BALL** a screen or barrier to stop a ball traveling out of the playing area, especially behind home plate on a baseball field **3.** BASEBALL same as **catcher** (sense 1) **4.** MECH ENG **CATCH STOPPING BACKWARD MOVEMENT** a catch on a mechanism often designed as a safeguard to prevent it from moving back too far ■ *vt* (**-stopped, -stop·ping, -stops**) **GIVE SUPPORT TO SOMEBODY** to give support or backing to somebody or something, or to reinforce somebody or something

back·sto·ry *n* **1.** the events that are supposed to have taken place before the action of a movie, television program, or novel begins (*informal*) **2.** MEDIA same as **prequel**

back straight *n UK* SPORTS same as **back stretch**

back·street /bák strèet/ *n also* **back street MINOR STREET** a small street off the main highways in a city or town ■ *adj also* **back-street 1. IN BACKSTREET** situated or taking place in a backstreet **2. ILLICIT** carried out furtively or illicitly in a place where it is unlikely to attract public attention

back stretch *n* the straight section of a racing circuit opposite the home stretch

back·stroke /bák strōk/ *n* **1.** SWIMMING a method of swimming on the back in which the swimmer makes circular backward movements with each arm alternately while kicking the legs rhythmically up and down **2.** MECH ENG a stroke or movement in the opposite direction to that of the original or forward one **3.** RACKET GAMES same as **backhand** *n* (sense 1) —**back·stroke** *vi* —**back·strok·er** *n*

back·swept /bák swèpt/ *adj* angled, slanting, or brushed backward ○ *a backswept hairstyle*

back·swim·mer /bák swìmmər/ *n* a water bug that swims lying on its back and propelled by its broad hind legs. Native to: North America. Family: Notonectidae.

back·swing /bák swìng/ *n* the backward movement of a player's club, bat, or racket away from the eventual point of contact with the ball in preparation for making the actual stroke

back·sword /bák sàwrd/ *n* **1.** a sword with a cutting edge on one side of the blade only **2.** a stick with a basket-shaped hilt used in fencing practice

back talk *n* rude or impertinent answers or comments

back tax *n* tax due at or owed from an earlier date

back-to-back *adj* **1.** standing or sitting with backs turned to, and sometimes touching, one another **2.** following immediately one after the other ○ *We had back-to-back meetings prior to the product launch.* —**back to back** *adv*

back-to-back loan *n* a loan in which two companies in separate countries borrow each other's currency for a particular period, and repay each other's currency at an agreed rate upon maturity

back to front *adv UK* with the back part at the front, or in reverse order ○ *I hadn't noticed I'd put my sweater on back to front.*

back-to-na·ture *adj* relating to or adopting a simple self-sufficient way of life using little modern technology

back·track /bák tràk/ (**-tracked, -track·ing, -tracks**) *vi* **1.** to go back in the direction from which you have come **2.** to change, or distance yourself from, a previous action, opinion, statement, or policy, especially as a result of other people's opposition to it ○ *After enormous public outrage, the government backtracked on its proposed ban.*

back·up /bák ùp/ *n* **1. SUPPORT** support or assistance from other people, e.g., support from the supplier of a product when it breaks down **2. REINFORCEMENTS** reinforcements to help personnel already committed, especially police officers ○ *The officers at the scene are calling for a backup.* **3. SUBSTITUTE OR RESERVE** a substitute or reserve that can be used if the thing normally used fails **4. SECURITY COPY** a copy of computer data that is stored, e.g., a copy stored on a floppy disk **5. COPYING** the procedure for copying computer data with which somebody is working ○ *The backup is done automatically every morning.* **6. OVERFLOW** an overflow from a pipe caused by a blockage ○ *a backup of water* **7. TRAFFIC HOLDUP** a buildup or stoppage of traffic caused by an obstruction, e.g., an accident or road construction **8. ACCOMPANIMENT** instrumental music or singing forming an accompaniment to the main performer of a piece of popular music or jazz **9. BUILDUP OF SOMETHING** an excess quantity of something that builds up when normal flow is obstructed —**back·up** *adj*

back·up light *n* a light on the back of a motor vehicle that comes on when the vehicle is in reverse

back·ward /bákwərd/ *adj* 1. TOWARD REAR facing or turned in the opposite direction to somebody or something 2. REVERSED positioned the opposite way around, arranged in the opposite order, or proceeding in the opposite direction to the normal one 3. NOT ACHIEVING USUAL OR EXPECTED STANDARD lagging behind the progress and development of others of comparable status (*sometimes considered offensive*) ○ *a backward economy* 4. RETROGRADE causing or representing a return to a previous or less advanced, and usually less satisfactory, state ○ *a backward step developmentally* 5. TOWARD PAST directed toward the past ○ *a backward look over the city's progress during the last century* 6. SHY shy or lacking in self-confidence ■ *adv also* **back·wards** /-wərdz/ 1. BACK FIRST so as to have the back facing in the direction of movement ○ *She walked backward out of the room.* 2. TOWARD REAR behind somebody or in a direction away from the front of something ○ *I reached backward until I felt my fingers touch the wall.* 3. WRONG WAY AROUND in the reverse order or direction from the usual ○ *You've got your shirt on backward.* 4. TOWARD PAST toward or into the past ○ *Critics accused the report of going backward in time* 5. INTO WORSE CONDITION into a state that is worse or less advanced than the previous or original one ○ *Everything's gone backward since the new committee took over.* —**back·ward·ly** *adv* —**back·ward·ness** *n* ◇ **bend** *or* **fall** *or* **lean over backward** TRY HARD TO DO SOMETHING to make an exceptional effort to do something, especially to help or please somebody ○ *I felt uncomfortable although everybody bent over backward to make me feel welcome.*

USAGE backward or **backwards**? ***Backward*** is the only form available for the adjective: *a backward glance.* ***Backward*** is more common in adverbial use as well, but in other parts of the English-speaking world ***backwards*** is more usual for the adverb. *The vehicle moved slowly backward/backwards.*

back·ward com·pa·ti·ble *adj* describes a computer hardware or software product that is compatible with its predecessors to the extent that it can use interfaces and data from earlier versions

back·ward-look·ing *adj* more concerned with or relevant to a past state of affairs than the present

back·wards *adv* same as **backward**

back·wash /bák wòsh, -wàwsh/ *n* 1. RETREATING WAVE the movement of water back down a beach after a wave has broken 2. WATER PUSHED BACKWARD a backward movement or flow in water produced by a ship's propeller or by oars 3. AIR PUSHED BACKWARD a backward rush of air produced by an aircraft propeller or jet engine 4. CONSEQUENCES the consequential effects of an event or action, especially unpleasant or unsettling ones

back·wa·ter /bák wàwtər/ *n* 1. SMALL STAGNANT BRANCH OF RIVER a still body of water connected to a river but not affected by its current 2. STILL WATER a still body of water held back by a dam, obstruction, or prevailing countercurrent 3. DULL PLACE a place or situation regarded as cut off from the mainstream of activity and consequently regarded as quiet or unimportant

back·wind /bák wìnd/ (**-wind·ed, -wind·ing, -winds**) *vt* to divert wind from one sail into the back of another

back·woods /bák wŏŏdz/ *n* (*takes a singular or plural verb*) 1. a sparsely inhabited forested area distant from the main centers of population 2. an area regarded as remote, rustic, and culturally unsophisticated —**back·woods** *adj*

back·woods·man /bák wŏŏdzmən/ (*plural* **-men** /-mən/) *n* somebody who lives in the backwoods

back yard *n* 1. a yard or garden behind a house 2. somebody's immediate neighborhood, or the area considered as somebody's home ground ○ *The gangs know better than to cause trouble in each other's back yards.* ◇ **not in my back yard** used to object to something unpleasant or dangerous taking place or being located in your neighborhood

ba·cla·va *n* FOOD another spelling of **baklava**

ba·con /báykən/ *n* meat from the back and sides of a hog that has been salted, dried, and often smoked [14C. < Old French < Germanic, "back meat"] ◇ **bring home the bacon** to earn the money on which a family lives (*informal*) ◇ **save somebody's bacon** to save somebody from serious trouble, punishment, injury, or danger (*informal*)

Ba·con /báykən/, **Sir Francis, 1st Baron Verulam and Viscount St. Albans** (1561–1626) English philosopher, lawyer, and politician. A pioneer of modern scientific thought, he wrote *The Advancement of Learning* (1605) and *Essays* (1597–1625). He was Lord Chancellor (1618–21), but was dismissed for bribery.

> "Knowledge itself is power."
> [Sir Francis Bacon, "De Haeresibus" ("Of Heresies"), *Meditationes Sacrae (Religious Meditations)*; 1597]

> "He that will not apply new remedies must expect new evils: for time is the greatest innovator."
> [Sir Francis Bacon, "Of Innovations," *Essays*; 1597–1625]

Ba·con, Francis (1909–92) Irish-born British painter. A major late-20th century artist, he often used gory and shocking imagery, as in *Head Surrounded by Sides of Beef (Study After Velázquez)* (1954).

> "How can I take an interest in my work when I don't like it?"
> [Attributed to Francis Bacon]

Ba·con, Nathaniel (1647–76) English-born American colonist. He led a rebellion of farmers against Sir William Berkeley's government of Virginia (1676), twice capturing and then burning the city of Jamestown.

Ba·con, Roger (1214?–94) English philosopher and scientist. A Franciscan monk, he published works on mathematics, philosophy, and logic, including his *Great Work* (1266–67). He was imprisoned by the Franciscans for his "novelties." Known as **Doctor Mirabilis ("Wonderful Doctor")**

> "Reasoning draws a conclusion and makes us grant the conclusion, but does not make the conclusion certain, nor does it remove doubt."
> [Roger Bacon, *Opus Majus (Great Work)*; 1266–67]

Ba·co·ni·an /bay kṓnee ən/ *adj* OF WORKS OF SIR FRANCIS BACON relating to or based on the philosophy of Sir Francis Bacon, particularly his method of inductive reasoning in which the emphasis is placed on collecting instances rather than testing theories ■ *n* 1. PHILOSOPHY FOLLOWER OF SIR FRANCIS BACON a student or follower of the philosophy of Sir Francis Bacon 2. LITERAT BELIEVER IN BACON AS AUTHOR OF SHAKESPEARE'S PLAYS somebody who believes that Shakespeare's plays were actually written by Sir Francis Bacon

bact. *abbr* 1. bacteria 2. bacteriology

bac·te·rae·mi·a *n* MED UK spelling of **bacteremia**

bac·te·re·mi·a /bàktə reémee ə/ *n* the presence of bacteria in the blood —**bac·te·re·mic** *adj* —**bac·te·re·mi·cal·ly** *adv*

bacteri- *prefix* same as **bacterio-** (*used before vowels*)

bac·te·ri·a MICROBIOL plural of **bacterium**

bac·te·ri·al /bak teéree əl/ *adj* consisting of, caused by, or connected with bacteria —**bac·te·ri·al·ly** *adv*

bac·te·ri·al ar·ti·fi·cial chro·mo·some *n* a sequence of DNA taken from another organism and expressed in a bacterium to reveal its function

bac·te·ri·cide /bak teéri sīd/ *n* a substance or agent that destroys bacteria —**bac·te·ri·cid·al** /bak teéri sīd'l/ *adj*

bacterio- *prefix* bacteria, bacterial ○ *bacteriostat* [< BACTERIUM]

bacteriol. *abbr* bacteriology

bac·te·ri·ol·o·gy /bak teéree óllәjee/ *n* the scientific study of bacteria, especially in relation to medicine and agriculture —**bac·te·ri·o·log·i·cal** /bak teéree ə lójjik'l/ *adj* —**bac·te·ri·o·log·i·cal·ly** *adv* —**bac·te·ri·ol·o·gist** *n*

bac·te·ri·ol·y·sis /bak teéree óllississ/ *n* the dissolution or destruction of a bacterial cell, e.g., as a result of the use of a bactericidal agent during disinfection —**bac·te·ri·o·lyt·ic** /bak teéree ə líttik/ *adj*

bac·te·ri·o·phage /bak teéree ə fàyj/ *n* a virus that infects bacteria and may integrate into the genetic material of its host cell. Bacteriophages are used as vectors in gene cloning and have other biotechnological uses. —**bac·te·ri·o·phag·ic** /bak teéree ə fájjik/ *adj* —**bac·te·ri·oph·a·gous** /bak teéree óffәgəss/ *adj* —**bac·te·ri·oph·a·gy** /bak teéree óffəjee/ *n*

bac·ter·i·o·plank·ton /bak teéree ō plángktən/ *n* the component of plankton consisting of bacteria —**bac·ter·i·o·plank·ton·ic** /-plangk tónnik/ *adj*

bac·te·ri·o·sta·sis /bak teéree ō stáyssiss/ *n* inhibition of bacterial growth and multiplication by a chemical agent

bac·te·ri·o·stat /bak teéree ə stàt/ *n* a substance that restricts the growth and activity of bacteria without killing them —**bac·te·ri·o·stat·ic** /bak teéree ə státtik/ *adj* —**bac·te·ri·o·stat·i·cal·ly** *adv*

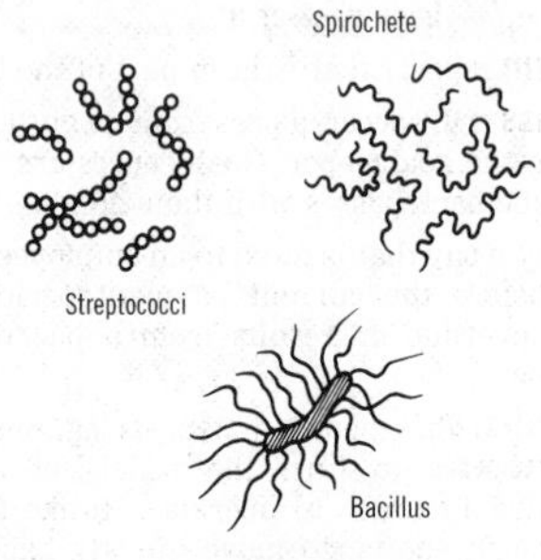

bacterium

bac·te·ri·um /bak teéree əm/ (*plural* **-ri·a** /-ree ə/) *n* a single-celled, often parasitic microorganism without distinct nuclei or organized cell structures. Various species are responsible for decay, fermentation, nitrogen fixation, and many plant and animal diseases. Kingdom: *Eubacteria.* [Mid-19C. < Greek *baktērion* "little rod" (because the first ones discovered were rod-shaped) < *baktron* "rod"] —**bac·te·roid** /báktə ròyd/ *adj*

USAGE bacterium or **bacteria**? ***Bacterium*** is singular and ***bacteria*** is plural. The word is more commonly found in the plural, which can lead to its being wrongly treated as a singular noun taking a singular verb.

bac·te·ri·u·ri·a /bak teéri yŏŏree ə/ *n* the presence of bacteria in urine

Bac·tri·a /báktree ə/ ancient country in Central Asia, in what is now part of Afghanistan, Uzbekistan, and Tajikistan. It was an eastern province of the Persian Empire before its conquest by Alexander the Great in 328 B.C. After his death it became a state ruled by his successors, the Seleucids.

Bactrian camel

Bac·tri·an cam·el /báktree ən-/ *n* a two-humped camel. Native to: Gobi Desert. Latin name: *Camelus bactrianus.* [Early 17C. < Latin *Bactrianus* < *Bactria*, ancient country in central Asia]

bac·u·li·form /bákyələ fàwrm, bə kyóolə-/ *adj* shaped like a rod [< Latin *baculum* "rod"]

bad /bad/ *adj* (**worse** /wurss/, **worst** /wurst/) 1. OF POOR QUALITY below an acceptable standard in quality or performance ○ *bad driving* 2. UNSKILLFUL lacking the skill or competence to perform a task adequately ○ *I've always been bad at remembering dates.* 3. NOT FUNCTIONING PROPERLY not functioning properly because of a fault ○ *bad TV reception* 4. INCORRECT incorrect according to the normal rules, especially those governing the use of language ○ *used bad grammar in the essay* **5.** **WICKED** morally evil, blameworthy, or unacceptable ○ *It's how you tell the good guys from the bad guys.* **6.** **MISBEHAVING AND DISOBEDIENT** troublesome or annoying, usually through rudeness, disobedience, or mischievousness ○ *Bad dog!* **7.** **ANGRY AND UNPLEASANT** characterized by anger and unpleasantness toward other people ○ *in a bad mood* **8.** **OFFENSIVE** likely to cause offense to other people because it deals with a taboo subject or expresses violent feelings ○ *swearing and other bad language* **9.** **HARMFUL** liable to damage health or cause injury ○ *Reading in a dim light is bad for the eyes.* **10.** **ROTTEN** deteriorated in quality to the point of being unfit to eat or drink ○ *This milk is bad.* **11.** **INJURED OR DISEASED** affected by an injury or disease, or not functioning properly, and often causing pain ○ *She's got a bad tooth.* **12.** **UNWELL** unwell or in pain ○ *I've been feeling bad for a couple of days.* **13.** **UNEASY** uneasy or regretful about something, or causing somebody to feel this way ○ *I feel really bad about having had to reprimand you.* **14.** **MORE UNPLEASANT THAN USUAL** possessing an unpleasant, painful, or troublesome quality to a higher degree than usual ○ *Was the pain very bad?* ○ *a bad headache* **15.** **DISTRESSING** likely to cause unhappiness or disappointment ○ *I'm afraid the news is bad.* **16.** **UNFAVORABLE** containing or indicating an unfavorable assessment of somebody's performance, work, or character ○ *received a bad job evaluation* **17.** (*comparative* **bad·der**, *superlative* **bad·dest**) **VERY GOOD** extremely good (*slang; originally used in Black English*) ○ *the baddest outfit at the party* ■ *n* **1.** **EVIL** wrong or immoral behavior ○ *You're old enough to know good from bad.* **2.** **UNSATISFACTORY OR UNPLEASANT THINGS** things or events that are unsatisfactory or unpleasant ○ *You've got to take the good with the bad.* ■ *adv* (*informal*) **1.** **BADLY** in an unsatisfactory manner ○ *We didn't do too bad.* **2.** **VERY MUCH** to an intense or extreme degree ○ *He's got it bad!* [13C. Perhaps < Old English *bǣddel* "effeminate man"] —**bad·ness** *n* ◇ **go bad** to become rotten or unfit to eat ◇ **go from bad to worse** to become even more unpleasant, unsatisfactory, or morally unacceptable than before ◇ **my bad** used to acknowledge that something is your own fault or error (*slang*) ◇ **not (half** *or* **so** *or* **that** *or* **too) bad** fairly good or of a standard that is admitted to be satisfactory, sometimes grudgingly or cautiously, but often in a positive or definitely approving way ○ *That's not bad for a first attempt.*

USAGE See ***badly.***

bad ac·tor *n* somebody or something that causes trouble or has a harmful effect, e.g., a persistent wrongdoer

ba·dam /bə daam/ (*plural same*) *n S Asia* an almond, or almonds processed for use in cooking [< Hindi *badām*]

bad ap·ple *n* somebody thought to be a bad influence on others (*informal*) [< the idea that one bad apple can spoil a whole batch]

bad·ass /bád àss/ *n* a highly offensive term for somebody who is regarded as bad-tempered or aggressive (*taboo insult*) ■ *adj* **1.** a highly offensive term meaning bad-tempered or aggressive (*taboo*) **2.** a highly offensive term meaning tough, intimidating, or powerful (*slang*)

Ba·da·wi /bə daáwee/ ➧ **Abdullah**

bad blood *n* an intense and usually long-lasting feeling of hatred, anger, or resentment

bad breath *n* unpleasant-smelling breath

bad check *n* a check that is invalid because there are insufficient funds in the account to cover it

bad debt *n* a sum of money owed that is unlikely to be repaid

bad·die /báddee/, **bad·dy** (*plural* **-dies**) *n* somebody, especially a character in a movie or a novel, who does evil or criminal things (*informal*)

bade past tense of **bid**

Ba·den-Ba·den /baad'n baad'n/ resort and spa city in the Black Forest in Baden-Württemberg State, southwestern Germany. Population: 52,570 (1997).

Ba·den-Pow·ell /bàyd'n pṓ əl, -pów əl/, **Agnes** (1858–1945) British founder of the Girl Guides Association. Together with her brother Robert, she set up the Girl Guides (1910) as the companion organization to the Boy Scouts.

Ba·den-Pow·ell, Robert, 1st Baron Baden-Powell of Gilwell (1857–1941) British soldier and founder of the Boy Scout Movement. Full name **Baden-Powell, Robert Stephenson Smyth**

> "Be Prepared...the meaning of the motto is that a Scout must prepare himself by previous thinking out and practicing how to act on any accident or emergency so that he is never taken by surprise; he knows exactly what to do when anything unexpected happens."
> [Robert Baden-Powell, *Scouting for Boys*; 1908]

Ba·den-Würt·tem·berg /baad'n wúrtəm bùrg, -vúrtəm-/ state in southwestern Germany. It is bordered to the west by France and to the south by Switzerland. Capital: Stuttgart. Population: 10,426,040 (1998). Area: 13,804 sq. mi./35,752 sq. km.

bad faith *n* insincerity, especially as evidenced by actions that do not accord with somebody's stated intentions

bad feel·ing *n* same as **ill feeling**

badge /baj/ *n* **1.** **EMBLEM** a small distinctive piece of fabric, metal, or plastic worn on clothing to show rank or membership **2.** **IDENTIFYING FEATURE** a characteristic or identifying mark of a particular brand, quality, or type of person ■ *vt* (**badged, badg·ing, badg·es**) **1.** **PUT IDENTIFYING MARK ON SOMETHING** to put a badge or a distinctive identifying mark on something **2.** **PUT BRAND NAME ON SOMETHING** to market a product under different badges or brand names [14C. < Old French *bage*]

badger

badg·er /bájjər/ *n* a medium-sized burrowing animal that is related to the weasel and has short legs, strong claws, and a thick coat. It usually has black and white stripes on the sides of its head. Subfamily: Melinae. ■ *vt* (**-ered, -er·ing, -ers**) to pester or annoy somebody continually ○ *kept badgering me to go shopping* [Early 16C. Perhaps < BADGE, because of the markings on its head]

Bad·ger /bájjər/ *n* somebody who comes from Wisconsin [Because the badger is the state animal of Wisconsin]

Badg·er State *n* a nickname for Wisconsin

bad guy *n* same as **baddie** (*informal*)

bad hair *n Carib* hair that is regarded as too tightly curly

bad hair day *n* a day during which somebody experiences a series of difficulties or annoyances (*slang*)

bad·i·nage /bàdd'n aázh/ *n* the exchange of playful or joking remarks between people in conversation [Mid-17C. < French < *badin* "fool, joker" < assumed Vulgar Latin *badare* "yawn, gape"]

bad·lands /bád làndz/ *npl* a barren area of gullies and bare mountain peaks or mesas formed by erosion

Bad·lands Na·tion·al Park /bàd landz-/ national park in South Dakota and Nebraska. It incorporates a dry region where wind erosion has caused unusual rock formations. Area: 379 sq. mi./982 sq. km.

bad·ly /báddlee/ (**worse, worst**) *adv* **1.** **POORLY** in an unsatisfactory, incompetent, or incorrect way ○ *The paint job had been badly done.* **2.** **UNHAPPILY** in such a way as to cause suffering, sorrow, or disappointment to the people involved ○ *felt badly about the mistake* **3.** **SEVERELY** to a degree that causes serious concern for the person or thing involved ○ *Two of the survivors were very badly burned.* **4.** **VERY MUCH** to a great extent ○ *We're badly in need of new ideas.* **5.** **WICKEDLY** in a way that is immoral, or that causes trouble, offense, or annoyance to other people ○ *had been behaving badly* **6.** **REMORSEFUL** full of remorse or regret ○ *feel badly about it*

USAGE badly or **bad**? ***Bad*** is an adjective; it is also a highly informal adverb meaning "badly," a usage that has never gained acceptance in formal writing. Substitute ***badly*** for ***bad*** in sentences like these: *The sacked quarterback was hurting bad. The Southeast needs rain bad. My back ached so bad that I had to lie down.* Another problem is whether or not to use ***bad*** or ***badly*** after the verb *feel*. After this verb, use the adjective ***bad***, not the adverb ***badly***, if you mean that you are experiencing, or feeling, physical distress: *After chemotherapy, I felt bad.* On the other hand, if you are experiencing or feeling emotional – not physical – distress, use the adverb ***badly***, not the adjective ***bad***: *I feel badly about the accident because it was entirely my fault.* In the last example, ***badly*** works just like some other *-ly* adverbs, such as *strongly* or *emphatically*, in conveying the idea of emotions, as in *The President feels strongly* [not *strong*] *about the need for both sides of the armed conflict to return to the negotiating table. The leaders feel emphatically* [not *emphatic*] *that each side must prove good faith before they will resume their talks.*

USAGE See ***good*** and ***well***[2].

bad·ly off (**worse off, worst off**) *adj* poorly or inadequately supplied with something ○ *We're badly off for good singers at the moment.*

bad man, Bad Man *n regional* same as **devil** *n* (sense 1)

REGIONAL NOTE The ***bad man*** is a euphemism for the devil that is often capitalized, suggesting importance to religion or superstition. The term is most common in Tennessee and the Lower South, with scattered instances of use from New York to California.

bad·mash /búd maash/ *n S Asia* **1.** somebody considered to be aggressive, violent, or evil **2.** used as a term of mock reproof, especially when scolding children ○ *What badmash could have made all this mess?* [Mid-19C. < Urdu < Persian *bad* "evil" + Arabic *ma'āš* "means of livelihood"]

bad·min·ton /bád mìntən/ *n* a game similar to tennis, using rackets to strike a shuttlecock back and forth across a high net [Mid-19C. After *Badminton*, village in SW England that is the seat of the Duke of Beaufort]

bad·mouth /bád mòwth, -mòwth/ (**-mouthed, -mouth·ing, -mouths**) *vt* to make disparaging remarks about somebody (*slang*)

bad news *n* somebody or something that is likely to cause trouble and should be avoided (*slang*) ○ *Something tells me this guy's bad news.*

bad off *adj* having a low income or very little money (*hyphenated before a noun*)

bad-pay *vt Carib* to fail to pay a debt or fulfill a financial obligation

bad-talk (**bad-talked, bad-talk·ing, bad-talks**) *vt Carib* to speak ill of somebody (*informal*)

bad-tem·pered *adj* characterized by anger and unpleasantness toward other people —**bad-tem·pered·ly** *adv* —**bad-tem·pered·ness** *n*

Bae·da /beéda/ ➧ **Bede**

Bae·de·ker /báydəkər/, **bae·de·ker** *n* a guidebook for travelers [Mid-19C. After Karl BAEDEKER]

Bae·de·ker /báydəkər/, **Karl** (1801–59) German publisher. His *Rhine Handbook* (1839) was the first of the famous guidebooks that still bear his name.

Bae·ke·land /báykələnd, -lànd/, **Leo** (1863–1944) Belgian-born US chemist. A pioneer of the modern plastics industry, he invented Bakelite™, a plastic resin, and founded the General Bakelite Corporation (1909). Full name **Baekeland, Leo Hendrik**

Bae·yer /báy ər/, **Johann** (1835–1917) German chemist. He explained the mechanism of photosynthesis and synthesized indigo dye. He received the Nobel Prize in chemistry (1905). Full name **Baeyer, Johann Friedrich Wilhelm Adolf von**

Ba·ez /bī éz, bī̆ èz/, **Joan** (*b.* 1941) US folk singer and activist. From the 1960s, she was widely known for her folk and protest songs and for her human rights campaigning.

> "You don't get to choose how you're going to die. Or when. You can only decide how you're going to live. Now."
> [Joan Baez, *Daybreak*; 1970]

Baf·fin /báffin/, **William** (1584–1622) English navigator. While trying to find the Northwest Passage (1612–16), he explored the Hudson Strait and Baffin Island.

Baf·fin Bay large bay separating Greenland and Canada. It is bordered by the Atlantic Ocean to the south and the Arctic Ocean to the north and west, and is covered by ice most of the year.

Baff·in Is·land Canada's largest island, located in the northeast of the country, forming part of Nunavut. Area: 195,928 sq. mi./507,451 sq. km.

baf·fle /báff'l/ *vt* (**-fled, -fling, -fles**) **1. PUZZLE SOMEBODY** to prove too difficult or complicated for somebody to understand, solve, or deal with, causing a feeling of confusion or helplessness **2. FRUSTRATE SOMETHING** to hinder or thwart an action or intention (*formal*) **3.** TECH **CONTROL SOMETHING** to impede or control the movement of a fluid or gas or the emission of sound or light waves ■ *n* **1.** TECH **RESTRAINING DEVICE** a device used to control or impede the flow or emission of something, e.g., a flap behind a zipper that retains heat or a silencing device in a vehicle's exhaust system **2.** ACOUSTICS **PARTITION IN LOUDSPEAKER** a partition in a loudspeaker or microphone intended to prevent sound waves of different frequencies from interfering with one another [Mid-16C. Perhaps blend of French *bafouer* "ridicule" + Scots *bauchle* "revile"] —**baf·fle·ment** *n*

baf·fle·gab /báff'l gàb/ *n* pretentious and obscure talk full of technical terminology or circumlocutions (*slang*)

baf·fling /báffling/ *adj* impossible for the mind to understand, and causing a feeling of confusion or helplessness —**baf·fling·ly** *adv*

bag /bag/ *n* **1. FLEXIBLE CONTAINER** a flexible container that opens at one end and is used for carrying things **2. AMOUNT IN FLEXIBLE CONTAINER** the amount that can be contained in a bag, often used as a measure **3. PORTABLE CONTAINER FOR EQUIPMENT OR BELONGINGS** a portable container made of strong flexible material for carrying somebody's belongings or equipment ○ *I threw everything into a bag and rushed out.* **4. ITEM OF BAGGAGE** an item of traveler's baggage that can be carried by hand, e.g., a suitcase (*often used in the plural*) ○ *Did you check the bags before coming to the departure gate?* **5. PURSE** a woman's purse **6.** HUNTING **NUMBER OF ANIMALS SHOT** the number of animals shot or captured by a hunter or hunting party **7. OFFENSIVE TERM** an offensive term deliberately insulting a woman's age and appearance (*slang insult*) **8. SOMEBODY'S SPECIALTY** something that somebody is particularly interested in or good at (*slang*) **9.** BASEBALL same as **base**[1] *n* (sense 7) **10.** DRUGS **SMALL QUANTITY OF ILLEGAL DRUG** a small quantity of an illegal drug in a piece of folded paper, a plastic bag, or a similar container (*slang*) ■ **bags** *npl* **LOOSE SKIN UNDER EYES** prominent folds of skin beneath the eyes, often caused by fatigue ■ *v* (**bagged, bag·ging, bags**) **1.** *vt* **PUT SOMETHING IN BAG** to put something into a bag ○ *He spent the afternoon bagging groceries at the local supermarket.* **2.** *vti* **BULGE** to bulge or become baggy, or cause something to do this **3.** *vt* HUNTING **SHOOT OR CAPTURE ANIMAL** to shoot or capture a game animal or bird ○ *He bagged a six-point buck.* **4.** *vt* **OBTAIN SOMETHING** to take, catch, seize, or steal something, usually in an opportunistic way (*informal*) ○ *They've gotten hold of our mailing list and are using it to try to bag some of our customers.* [13C. < Old Norse *baggi*] —**bag·ful** *n* —**bag·ger** *n* ◇ **bag and baggage** with all your belongings ◇ **bag of tricks 1.** the resources available to achieve a goal (*informal*) ○ *He reached into his bag of tricks one last time, trying to shame his team into playing better.* **2.** a magician's collection of equipment and props ◇ **bags of** a huge amount or number of something (*informal*) ◇ **be left holding the bag** to be left in a situation in which you are solely responsible for something because other people have abdicated their own responsibility ◇ **in the bag** certain to be achieved or obtained (*informal*)

Ba·gan·da /bə gaándə/ *npl* a people living in East Africa, mainly in Uganda [Late 19C. < Bantu]

ba·gasse /bə gáss/ *n* **1.** the pulp or dry refuse left after the juice has been extracted from sugar cane, grapes, or sugar beets. Use: fuel, cattle feed, making paper. **2.** paper made from bagasse [Early 19C. Via French < Spanish *bagazo* "dregs" < Latin *baca* "berry"]

bag·a·telle /bàggə tél/ *n* **1.** MUSIC **SHORT PLAYFUL PIECE OF MUSIC** a short piece of classical music, usually for piano, written in a playful style **2. BOARD GAME** a game played on a board or table, in which balls have to be propelled by a cue or spring-loaded launcher past obstacles and into numbered holes **3. SOMETHING UNIMPORTANT** a thing of little importance (*formal*) ○ *a mere bagatelle* [Mid-17C. Via French < Italian *bagatella*]

Bag·dad ➧ **Baghdad**

ba·gel /báyg'l/ *n* a glazed ring-shaped bread roll with a slightly chewy texture [Early 20C. < Yiddish *beygl* < Old High German *boug* "ring"]

bag·gage /bággij/ *n* **1. PACKED SUITCASES AND BAGS** suitcases and other containers holding the belongings of people who are traveling **2. PRECONCEIVED IDEAS** ideas, beliefs, or practices retained from somebody's previous life experiences, especially insofar as they affect a new situation in which they may be no longer relevant or appropriate (*informal*) ○ *emotional baggage* **3.** MIL **PORTABLE EQUIPMENT** the equipment and supplies that a military force carries with it on campaign (*dated*) **4. IMPUDENT GIRL OR WOMAN** a girl or woman who is thought of as impudent or obstinate (*often considered offensive*) **5. PROSTITUTE** an immoral woman, especially a prostitute [15C. < French *bagage* < Old French *bague* "bundle"]

bag·gage car *n* a car on a train reserved for transporting passengers' baggage

bag·gage check *n* a room in a train or bus station where baggage can be temporarily deposited

bag·gage claim *n* the area in an airport where arriving passengers collect their luggage

bag·gage han·dler *n* somebody whose job it is to load and unload baggage onto and off airplanes

bag·gage re·claim *n UK* same as **baggage claim**

bag·gage room *n* a room in a railroad or bus station where luggage can be temporarily deposited

bag·ga·ta·way /bə gáttə way/ *n* an early form of lacrosse played by the Native American peoples of eastern North America [Early 19C. < Ojibwa *paka'towe* "(he) plays lacrosse"]

bag·gies /bággeez/ *npl* (*informal*) **1.** clothing that is cut extra large for the size of the wearer and hangs loosely on the body **2.** very baggy men's pants cut low at the crotch and worn hanging loosely from the hips

Bag·gies /bággeez/ *tdmk* a trademark for a brand of small plastic storage bags

bag·ging /bágging/ *n* coarse material used for making bags

bag·gy /bággee/ (**-gi·er, -gi·est**) *adj* hanging loosely, puffed out, or bulging, either as a deliberate style or as a result of being too big for the wearer or having stretched while being worn —**bag·gi·ly** *adv* —**bag·gi·ness** *n*

bagh /baag/ *n S Asia* same as **garden** *n* (sense 1) [Via Hindi < Persian *bāg*]

Bagh·dad /bág dàd/, **Bag·dad, Bagh·dād** capital of Iraq in the eastern part of the country, on the Tigris River, northwest of Basra. Population: 4,797,000 (2000).

bag job *n* CRIME same as **black bag job** (*slang*)

bag la·dy *n* a homeless woman who carries her possessions in shopping bags (*informal*)

bag·man /bágmən/ (*plural* **-men** /-mən/) *n* **1.** *US* somebody who delivers or collects money for criminals (*slang*) **2.** *Can* a fundraiser for a political party

bagn·a cau·da /bànnyə kówdə/ *n* a warm sauce of olive oil, garlic, and anchovies, served as a dip for raw vegetables [< Italian dialect, literally "hot bath"]

ba·gnio /bánnyō, baán-/ (*plural* **-gnios**) *n* **1.** same as **brothel** (*literary*) **2.** a prison, especially in Asian Turkey (*archaic*) [Late 16C. Via Italian *bagno* "bath" < Latin *balneus*]

Bag·nold /bág nòld/, **Enid** (1889–1981) British author and playwright. She is best known as the author of *National Velvet* (1935).

bag per·son *n* a homeless person who carries his or her possessions in shopping bags (*informal*)

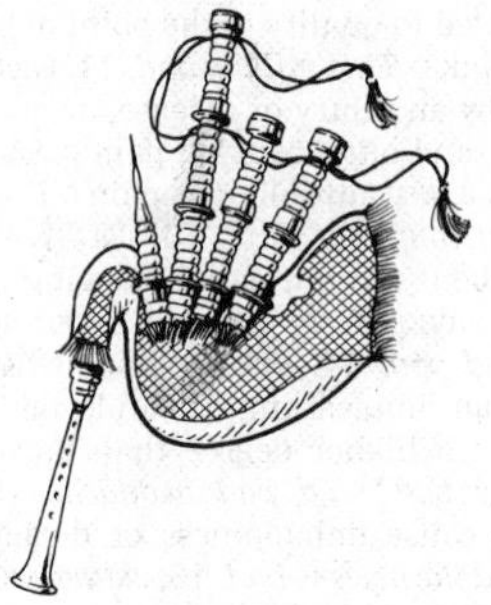

bagpipe

bag·pipe /bág pīp/ *n* a wind instrument consisting of an inflatable bag with an inlet pipe and one or more outlet pipes that produce either one fixed note or several notes. The player squeezes the inflated bag under his or her arm, forcing the air out through the speaking pipes and using finger holes to control the pitch of the note. (*usually used in the plural*) —**bag·pip·er** *n*

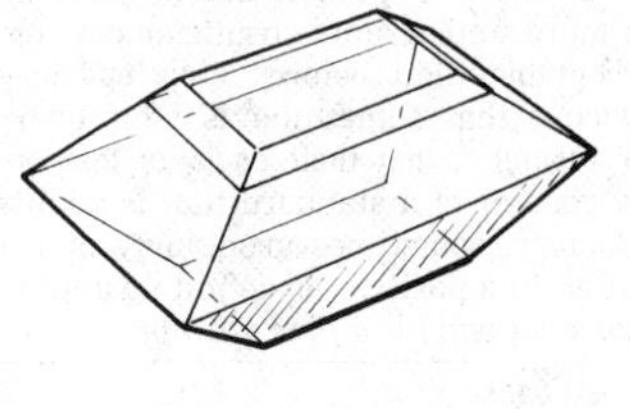

baguette (sense 2)

ba·guette /ba gét/ *n* **1.** FOOD **STICK-SHAPED LOAF** a long thin loaf of French bread **2. RECTANGULAR GEM** a gem cut into a long rectangular shape **3. RECTANGULAR SHAPE** the shape of a baguette gem **4.** ARCHIT **CONVEX MOLDING** a small narrow rounded convex molding on a wall or column [Early 18C. < French < Latin *baculum* "rod"]

ba·guette bag *n* a purse that is relatively long from side to side and small from top to bottom

Bag·ui·o /baágee ō/ city on Luzon Island, the Philippines. It is the country's summer capital. Population: 268,772 (1999).

bag·wom·an /bág wŏŏmmən/ (*plural* **-wom·en** /-wimmin/) *n* **1.** *also* **bag wom·an** same as **bag lady** (*informal*) **2.** *US* a woman who delivers or collects money for criminals (*slang*) **3.** *Can* a woman who is a fundraiser for a political party

bah /baa, ba/ *interj* expresses scornful irritation, disgust, or contempt

ba·ha·dur /bə haádər/ *n S Asia* a Nepalese surname [Late 18C. Via Urdu and Persian *bahādur* < Mongolian, "brave man"]

Ba·ha'i /baa haá ee, bə hī́/ (*plural* **-ha'is**) *n* **1.** a religion founded in Iran in 1863 that maintains that the teachings of all religions are of value and humankind is spiritually one, and advocates world peace **2.** somebody whose religion is Baha'i [Late 19C. Via Persian *bahā'ī* < Arabic *bahā'* "splendor"] —**Ba·ha'i** *adj* —**Ba·ha'ism** *n* —**Ba·ha'ist** *n*

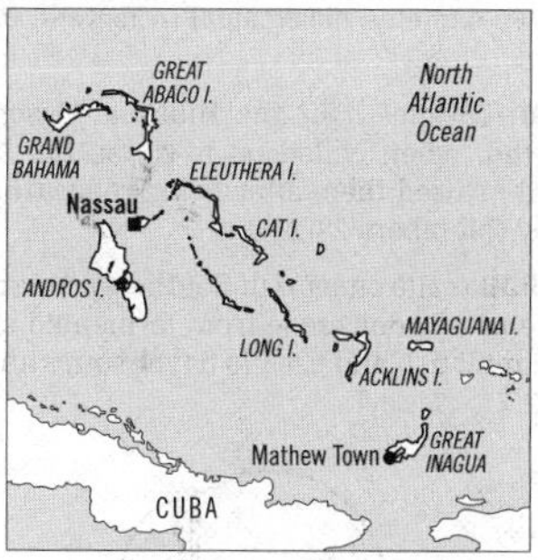

Bahamas

Ba·ha·mas /bə ha̅a̅məz, -hāyməz/ nation consisting of hundreds of islands, islets, and keys in the Atlantic Ocean southeast of Florida and north of Cuba. It was settled by the British in the 17th century and became an independent member of the British Commonwealth in 1973. Language: English. Currency: Bahamian dollar. Capital: Nassau. Population: 297,852 (2001). Area: 5,382 sq. mi./13,939 sq. km. Official name **Commonwealth of the Bahamas** —**Ba·ha·mi·an** /bə háymee ən, bə haa-/ *n, adj*

Ba·ha·sa In·do·ne·sia /baa haassə-/ *n* the form of Malay that is the official language of Indonesia [< Malay, "language of Indonesia"]

Ba·ha·sa Ma·lay·sia /baa haassə-/ *n* the form of Malay that is the official language of Malaysia [< Malay, "language of Malaysia"]

Ba·ha·wal·pur /bə haawəl poor/ city, district, and division of Punjab Province, Pakistan, situated on the Sutlej River. Population: 180,263 (1981).

Ba·hi·a /bə hée ə, baa ée ə/ **1.** state in eastern Brazil on the Atlantic coast. Capital: Salvador. Population: 12,541,675 (1996). Area: 219,034 sq. mi./567,295 sq. km. **2.** former name for **Salvador**

Ba·hí·a Blan·ca /-blángkə, -blaangkə/ city and port in Buenos Aires Province, eastern Argentina. It is an important transport and commercial center. Population: 260,096 (1991).

Ba·hi·a grass *n* a perennial American grass, grown in the southern United States. Native to: Central and South America. Use: lawns, forage. Latin name: *Paspalum notatum.*

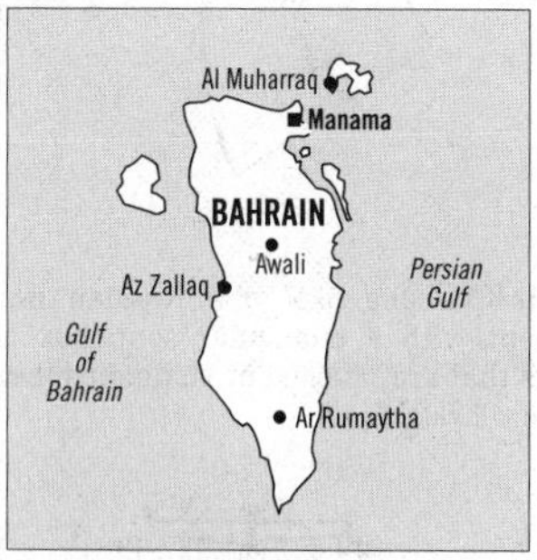

Bahrain

Bah·rain /baa ráyn/, **Bah·rein** independent island state on the Persian Gulf off the coast of Saudi Arabia, northwest of Qatar. Language: Arabic, English, Farsi, Urdu. Currency: Bahraini dinar. Capital: Manama. Population: 667,238 (2003). Area: 273 sq. mi./707 sq. km. Official name **State of Bahrain** —**Bah·rain·i** *n, adj*

baht /baat/ (*plural* **bahts** or *same*) *n* the main unit of Thai currency. See table at **currency** [Early 19C. < Thai *bāt*]

ba·hu·vri·hi /baahoo vrée hee/ (*plural* **-his**) *n* a compound word in which the first part describes the second or governs it grammatically, and the second element cannot be substituted for the whole, e.g., "yellowhammer" or "afternoon" [Mid-19C. < Sanskrit *bahuvrīhi* "possessing much rice," a typical example of this class]

bai /bī/ *S Asia n* in Bihar and Uttar Pradesh, a prostitute ■ *suffix* **-bai** in Maharashtra and parts of Karnataka, a respectful form of address added after a woman's name [< Marathi, "lady"]

bai·gan *n Carib* FOOD another spelling of **bhaigan**

Bai·kal, Lake /bī kaal/ lake in southern Siberia, Russia. It is the world's deepest lake and the largest freshwater lake in Europe and Asia. Area: 12,200 sq. mi./31,500 sq. km. Depth: 5,371 ft./1,637 m.

bail[1] /bayl/ *n* **1.** SECURITY FOR APPEARANCE IN COURT a sum of money deposited to secure an accused person's temporary release from custody and to guarantee that person's appearance in court at a later date. If the person fails to appear in court on the date set, the money is forfeited. **2.** RELEASE UNDER SECURITY temporary release from custody after bail has been paid ○ *Her brother was out on bail.* **3.** SOMEBODY WHO PAYS BAIL somebody who pays bail ■ *v* (**bailed, bail·ing, bails**) **1.** *vt* FREE SOMEBODY BY PAYING BAIL to release an accused person from custody after bail has been paid (*usually passive*) **2.** *vi* CRASH in snowboarding, to crash or fall (*slang*) [14C. < Old French, "temporary custody" < *baillier* "take charge of" < Latin *bajulus* "somebody who carries (responsibility)"] —**bail·a·ble** *adj* ◇ **jump** *or* **skip bail** to fail to appear in court as promised at the end of a bail period (*informal*)

bail out *vt* to secure somebody's release from legal custody by paying bail

bail[2] /bayl/ (**bailed, bail·ing, bails**) *vti* to empty water out of a boat, using a bucket or similar container ○ *We bailed the sinking boat for an hour.* [Early 17C. < obsolete *bail* "bucket," via French < assumed Vulgar Latin *bajula* "water carrier"] —**bail·er** *n*

bail out *v* **1.** *vti* EMPTY WATER OUT OF BOAT to empty water out of a boat, using a bucket or similar container ○ *bailing water out as the boat slowly sank* **2.** *vi* PARACHUTE FROM PLANE to escape from a plane that is in danger of crashing by making a parachute jump **3.** *vi* ESCAPE FROM DIFFICULT SITUATION to abandon hurriedly and unceremoniously a situation that is dangerous or difficult (*informal*) ○ *When the company hit the skids, she was the first to bail out.* **4.** *vt* HELP SOMEBODY OUT OF TROUBLE to help somebody out of a difficult situation (*informal*)

bail[3] /bayl/ *n* in cricket, either of the two short pieces of wood laid on top of the stumps to make the wicket [Mid-18C. Probably via Old French < Latin *baculum* "rod"]

bail[4] /bayl/ *n* **1.** HINGED BAR a hinged bar on a typewriter or printer that holds the paper against the platen **2.** SEMICIRCULAR HANDLE a semicircular handle, e.g., a bucket handle **3.** SEMICIRCULAR SUPPORT a semicircular support, e.g., one that holds up the canopy on a covered wagon [15C. Probably < Old Norse]

bail ban·dit *n UK* an accused person released on bail who commits a crime while awaiting trial for the original offense, or who fails to appear in court on the date set (*informal*)

bail bar *n* PRINTING same as **bail**[4] (sense 1)

bail bond *n* a document in which the prisoner released on bail and the person who pays the bail money promise that the prisoner will appear in court at a set time

bail bonds·man *n* a man engaged in the business of providing bail money, or acting as surety, for an accused person

bail bonds·per·son *n* somebody engaged in the business of providing bail money, or acting as surety, for an accused person

bail bonds·wo·man *n* a woman engaged in the business of providing bail money, or acting as surety, for an accused person

bai·ley /báylee/ (*plural* **-leys**) *n* **1.** the outermost wall surrounding a castle **2.** a courtyard inside the walls, especially the outermost walls, of a castle [13C. Probably alteration of BAIL[3], influenced by medieval Latin *ballium*]

Bai·ley bridge *n* a temporary steel bridge made of prefabricated parts and designed for quick construction [Mid-20C. After Sir D. Coleman *Bailey* (1901–85), British engineer]

bail·iff /báylif/ *n* **1.** LAW COURT OFFICIAL a court official whose tasks include supervising prisoners and keeping order in court during a trial **2.** *UK* LAW SHERIFF'S OFFICER a legal officer who serves under a sheriff and is empowered to take possession of a debtor's property, forcibly if necessary, to serve writs, and to make arrests **3.** *UK* STEWARD a steward or agent of a landowner or landlord [13C. Via Old French *baillif-* "overseer" < assumed medieval Latin *bajulivus* < Latin *bajulus* "somebody who carries (responsibility)"]

bail·i·wick /báyli wìk/ *n* an area of activity in which somebody has specific responsibility, knowledge, or ability ○ *Export permits are her bailiwick.* [15C. < BAILIFF + obsolete *wick* "town" (via Germanic < Latin *vicus* "village, homestead")]

bail·ment /báylmənt/ *n* the granting of bail to somebody in custody

bail·out /báyl òwt/ *n* an intervention by a person or company to help another person or company out of financial difficulties

bails·man /báylzmən/ (*plural* **-men** /-mən/) *n* LAW same as **bail bondsman**

Bai·ly's beads /bàyleez-/ *npl* bright points of sunlight that briefly appear around the Moon immediately before and after a total eclipse of the Sun. They are caused by sunlight shining through valleys on the Moon. [Mid-19C. After Francis *Baily* (1774–1844), British astronomer]

bain-marie

bain-ma·rie /bàN mə rée/ (*plural* **bain-ma·ries** /-mə rée/) *n* a cooking utensil containing hot water into which another container is placed to keep food warm or cook it gently [Early 19C. < French, via medieval Latin translation < Greek *kaminos Marias* "alchemist's apparatus," literally "furnace of Maria" (alchemist and sister of Moses)]

Bai·ram /bī raam/ *n* either of two Islamic festivals, the **Lesser Bairam** marking the end of Ramadan or the **Greater Bairam** seventy days later, marking the end of the Islamic year [Late 16C. Via Turkish *bayram* < Persian *bazrām*]

Baird /berd/, **John Logie** (1888–1946) British inventor. He demonstrated an electromechanical television system in 1926. He also researched radar and fiber optics.

Bai·ri·ki /bī réekee/ administrative center of Kiribati, situated on Tarawa atoll in the western Pacific Ocean. Population: 25,000 (1990).

bairn /bern/ *n N England, Scotland* a young child [Old English *bearn* < Indo-European, "carry, bear children"]

Bai·sak·hi /bī saakee/ *n* a Sikh festival commemorating the founding of the Khalsa order by Gobind Singh in 1699 and marking the New Year. Date: April 13.

bait[1] /bayt/ *n* **1.** FOOD FOR ATTRACTING ANIMALS a piece of food used as a lure in fishing or trapping ○ *fishing with live bait* **2.** ENTICEMENT something used to lure a person or animal into being caught ■ *vt* (**bait·ed, bait·ing, baits**) **1.** PUT FOOD ON HOOK to put a food attractant on a hook or in a trap ○ *This line's baited with a minnow.* **2.** HARASS SOMEBODY to persecute, tease, or harass somebody ○ *Stop baiting the dog, please.* **3.** ATTACK ANIMAL WITH DOGS to set dogs onto a chained animal, usually a bear or bull, for sport [13C. < Old Norse *beit* "food," *beita* "hunt with dogs"] —**bait·er** *n* ◇ **fish or cut bait** to do what needs to be done or else step aside and allow somebody else to do it ◇ **rise to the bait** to react to something, especially to temptation or provocation, in precisely the way that somebody wants you to, e.g., by getting angry when somebody teases you

bait[2] /bayt/ *vi* another spelling of **bate**

bait and switch, bait ad·ver·tis·ing *n* a tactic used in sales in which buyers are tempted by an advertised bargain but are then persuaded to buy a more expensive item instead

bait cast·ing, bait cast *n* a fishing rod with a line to which live or dead bait is attached

bai·za /bī zaa/ (*plural* **-zas** or *same*) *n* a subunit of Omani currency. See table at **currency** [Late 20C. Via Arabic < Hindi *paisā*]

baize /bayz/ *n* a green woolen cloth, similar to felt. Use: tops of pool and card tables. [Late 16C. < French *baies*, plural of *bai* "bay-colored" (see BAY³), probably because of its original color]

Ba·ja Cal·i·for·nia /baá haa-/ **1.** peninsula in Northwestern Mexico between the Gulf of California and the Pacific Ocean, divided into the states of Baja California and Baja California Sur. Length: 760 mi./1,200 km. **2.** state in northwestern Mexico in the northern part of the Baja California peninsula. Capital: Mexicali. Population: 2,486,367 (2000). Area: 27,636 sq. mi./71,576 sq. km.

Ba·ja Cal·i·for·ni·a Sur /-súr/ state in western Mexico in the southern part of the Baja California peninsula. Capital: La Paz. Population: 424,041 (2000). Area: 27,579 sq. mi./71,428 sq. km.

ba·ja·da /bə haádə/ *n* a broad plain formed at the base of a mountain or mountain range resulting from the coalescing of sedimentary deposits from a number of streams [Mid-19C. < Spanish, "slope, descent"]

Ba·ja·zet same as **Bayazid I**

ba·jee *n* FOOD another spelling of **bhaji**

baj·ra /baájrə/, **baj·ri** /-ree/, **baj·ree** *n S Asia* grain such as pearl millet [Early 19C. < Hindi *bājrā, bājrī*]

bak *abbr* a file extension for a backup file

bake /bayk/ *v* (**baked, bak·ing, bakes**) **1.** *vti* **COOK FOOD IN OVEN** to cook food in an oven by dry heat, or be cooked in this way **2.** *vti* **HARDEN BY HEAT** to become hardened, or harden something, by exposing it to dry heat **3.** *vi* **BE VERY HOT** to be or feel very hot (*informal*) ○ *You must be baking in that heavy coat.* ■ *n* **1. AMOUNT BAKED** a number of things baked at the same time **2. PARTY WITH BAKED FOOD** a party at which baked food is served (*informal; often used in combination*) ○ *an oyster bake on the shore* [Old English *bacan* < Indo-European, "to warm"]

baked A·las·ka *n* a dessert of cake that is topped with ice cream, covered with meringue, and then quickly browned in a very hot oven

baked beans *npl* baked navy beans with onion and bacon in a tomato-based sauce

baked po·ta·to *n* a potato that has been baked in the skin, served plain or with a topping

Ba·ke·lite /báykə līt/ *tdmk* a trademark for any of various synthetic resins used in many manufacturing applications

Bake-Off a service mark for a cooking contest during which contestants prepare their own recipes, especially baked goods, with the winners receiving prizes

bak·er /báykər/ *n* **1.** somebody who makes baked foods, especially bread and cakes **2.** a portable oven

Ba·ker /báykər/, **Dame Janet** (*b.* 1933) British mezzo-soprano. After performing as a soloist for Sir John Barbirolli in the 1960s, she moved on to opera, and is associated especially with English music. Born **Abbott, Janet**

Ba·ker, Josephine (1906–75) US-born French dancer and entertainer. She performed as a singer and dancer in New York before settling in Paris in 1925. Highly popular in Europe, she campaigned for racial equality in the United States in the 1950s and 1960s. Born **McDonald, Freda Josephine**

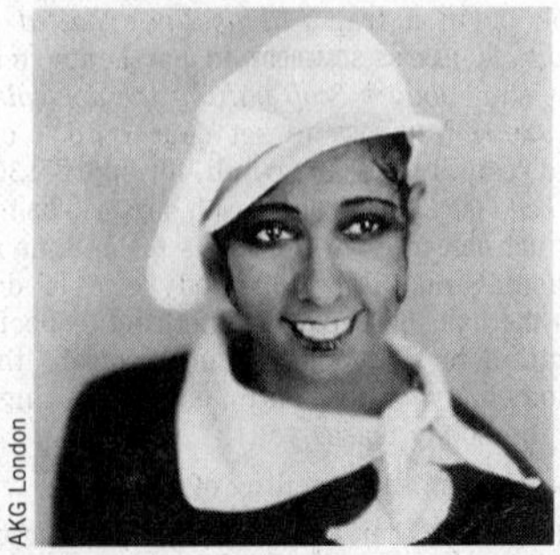

Josephine Baker

"A violinist had his violin, a painter his palette. All I had was myself. *I* was the instrument that I must care for."
[Josephine Baker, *Josephine*; 1976]

Bak·er /báykər/, **Sir Samuel** (1821–93) British explorer. He searched for the sources of the Nile and reached present-day Lake Mobutu Sese Seko, which he called Lake Albert (1864). Full name **Baker, Sir Samuel White**

bak·er's doz·en *n* a set of thirteen items [Because retailers of bread formerly received an extra loaf with each dozen from the baker, which they were entitled to keep as profit]

Ba·kers·field /báykərz feéld/ city in south central California in the valley of the San Joaquin River. Population: 260,969 (2002 estimate).

bak·er·sheet /báykər sheét/ *n New England* a drip pan used in cooking

bak·er·y /báykəree/ (*plural* **-ies**) *n* **1.** a building or part of a building where items of food, especially bread and cakes, are baked **2.** a store or part of a store where items of baked food, especially bread and cakes, are sold

bake·shop /báyk shòp/ *n* a small bakery, especially one forming part of a larger store such as a supermarket

Bakh·ta·ran /baáktə raán/, **Bākh·ta·rān** city in western Iran and capital of Bakhtaran Province. Population: 692,986 (1996).

bak·ing /báyking/ *n* **1. COOKING OF BREAD AND CAKES** the cooking of bread, cakes, and other foods by dry heat in an oven ○ *did the baking early in the morning* **2. AMOUNT BAKED AT ONE TIME** a quantity of items baked at one time ○ *a baking of 46 rolls* ■ *adj* **VERY HOT** very hot and dry ○ *a baking sun*

bak·ing pow·der *n* a mixture containing sodium bicarbonate, or sometimes ammonium bicarbonate or ammonium carbonate, starch, and acids. Use: leavening agent, especially for cakes.

bak·ing sheet *n* a flat metal tray used for baking food in an oven

bak·ing so·da *n* sodium bicarbonate. Use: leavening agent, antacid.

bak·ing tray *n UK* HOUSEHOLD same as **baking sheet**

Bak·ke de·ci·sion /bákee-/ *n* a US Supreme Court ruling that made it unlawful for universities to reserve a specific number of places for students from minority groups, and so prevent applicants who are not from minority groups from competing for those places [After Allan *Bakke*, who was denied a place at medical school in spite of having higher qualifications than others admitted]

ba·kla·va /baáklə vaá, baáklə vaá/, **ba·cla·va** *n* a dessert of phyllo pastry layered with nuts, with syrup or honey poured over it after baking. It originated in southwestern Asia. [Mid-17C. < Turkish]

bak·ra /bákrə/ *n Carib* a white person, especially one from the British Isles [Mid-18C. < Ibibio and Efik *(m)bakara* "European, master"]

bak·sheesh /bák sheésh, bak sheésh/ *n* money given as a tip or bribe, or as charity, especially in North Africa and southwestern Asia [Mid-18C. Ultimately < Persian *bakšīš*]

Ba·ku /baa koó/ capital of Azerbaijan, on the shores of the Caspian Sea, in the center of an oil-producing region in the eastern part of the country. Population: 1,708,000 (1999).

Ba·ku·nin /bə koónin, -koónyin/, **Mikhail** (1814–76) Russian anarchist. Born an aristocrat, he was sent into exile in Siberia in 1857, but escaped to England in 1861 to spread his anarchistic views throughout Europe. Full name **Bakunin, Mikhail Aleksandrovich**

"The urge for destruction is also a creative urge!"
[Mikhail Bakunin, *Die Reaktion in Deutschland (The Reaction in Germany)*; 1842]

BAL *n* MED same as **dimercaprol** [Acronym < *British anti-lewisite*]

Ba·laam /báyləm/ *n* in the Bible, a Mesopotamian seer who, when called on to curse the Israelites, instead praised them after being reproached by his donkey (Numbers 22–24)

bal·a·chan /bàllə chán/ *n* in Southeast Asian cuisine, a paste or powder made from fermented shrimp or other small fish and used to flavor soups and curries [Early 20C. < Malay]

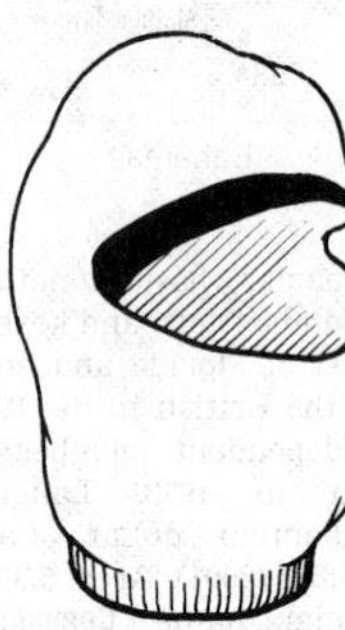
balaclava

bal·a·cla·va /bàllə klaávə/ *n* a close-fitting knitted covering for the head and neck that leaves only the face or eyes exposed [Late 19C. After the village of *Balaklava* in the Crimea, probably because worn by infantry in the campaign there]

Bal·a·guer /baálə gér/, **Joaquín** (1907–2002) president of the Dominican Republic (1960–62, 1966–78, and 1986–96). He went into exile from 1962 to 1965 after his first presidency was ended by a military coup. A veteran of Dominican politics, he was defeated in the 2000 presidential election. Full name **Balaguer, Joaquín Vidella**

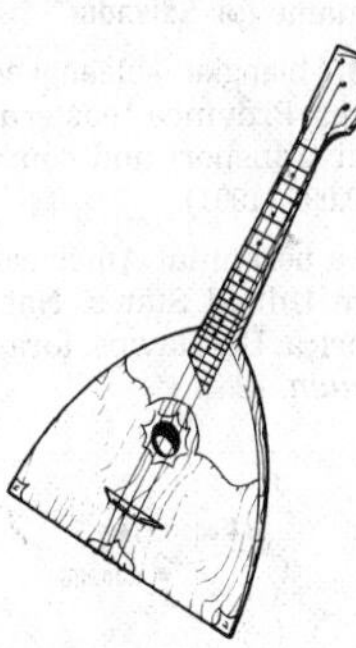
balalaika

bal·a·lai·ka /bàllə līkə/ *n* a Russian musical instrument with a triangular soundbox and three strings that are plucked or strummed [Late 18C. Via Russian < Turkic]

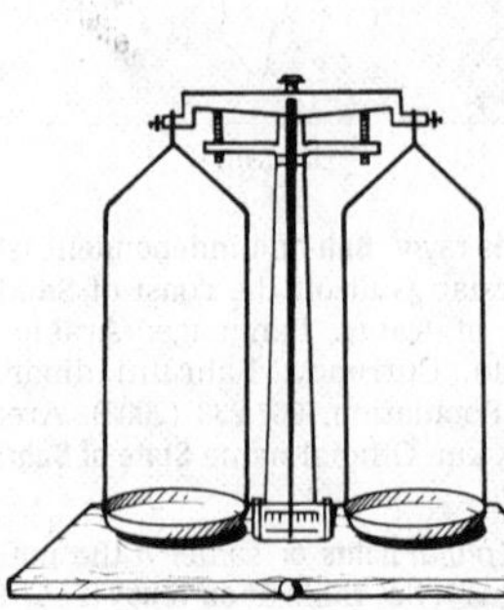
balance (sense 5)

bal·ance /bálləns/ *n* **1. STEADY STATE ON NARROW BASE** a state in which a body or object remains reasonably steady in a particular position while resting on a base that is narrow or small relative to its other dimensions. For human beings, this most commonly involves remaining upright and steady on the feet. ○ *He lost his balance and fell from the beam.* **2. OPPOSITION OF EQUAL FORCES** a state in which two opposing forces or factors are of equal strength or importance so that they effectively cancel each other out and stability is maintained **3.** **HARMONY** a state in which various parts form a satisfying and harmonious whole and nothing is out of proportion or unduly emphasized at the expense of the rest **4.** **EMOTIONAL STABILITY** a state of emotional and mental stability in which somebody is calm and able to make rational decisions and judgments **5.** **WEIGHING MACHINE** a simple mechanical device for weighing objects, often consisting of a pivoted horizontal beam with a pan suspended from each end. Material to be weighed is put in one pan and weights of a fixed value are gradually added to the other until the beam returns to the horizontal. **6.** **COUNTERWEIGHT** something that offsets or counters the weight or influence of another element ○ *a system of checks and balances* **7.** **GREATER PART** a significant or influential amount of something ○ *The balance of evidence was in her favor.* **8.** **REMAINDER** a remaining or outstanding amount, e.g., the amount remaining in a bank account after a withdrawal or the amount still to be paid to settle a bill **9.** ACCT **EQUAL DEBIT AND CREDIT** a position where the amounts on the debit and credit sides of an account are equal and cancel each other out **10.** ACCT **DIFFERENCE BETWEEN DEBIT AND CREDIT** the amount by which the debit and credit sides of an account differ **11.** MATH, CHEM **EQUALITY OF ELEMENTS IN EQUATION** a state in which the elements of a mathematical or chemical equation are equal on both sides ■ *v* (**-anced, -anc·ing, -anc·es**) **1.** *vti* **REMAIN IN OR GIVE SOMETHING EQUILIBRIUM** to achieve or maintain, or cause somebody or something to achieve or maintain, a position of steadiness while resting on a narrow base ○ *balanced precariously on a branch* **2.** *vti* **PLACE IN PRECARIOUS POSITION** to place an object in a position where it is or seems to be in imminent danger of falling, or to be in such a position (*often passive*) **3.** *vt* **ASSESS SOMETHING** to compare the relative importance of different factors or alternatives before making a choice or decision ○ *balanced the pros and cons of the plan before moving ahead with it* **4.** *vt* **WEIGH SOMETHING IN BALANCE** to weigh something in a balance or by an action or method that resembles the working of a balance **5.** *vti* **EQUAL OR CANCEL OUT** to be equal to something in force, weight, or importance, or cancel it out **6.** *vt* ARTS **BRING ELEMENTS INTO HARMONY** to arrange the different parts of something so that they form a harmonious and well-proportioned whole **7.** *vt* MATH, CHEM **BRING EQUATION INTO EQUALITY** to bring the elements of a chemical or mathematical equation into a state of equality **8.** *vt* ACCT **ASSESS ACCOUNT** to assess the relative positions of the debit and credit sides of an account **9.** *vt* ACCT **EQUALIZE ACCOUNT** to make the debit and credit sides of an account equal [13C. Via Old French < Latin *(libra) bilanx* "(scales) with two pans" < *lanx* "plate, pan"] —**bal·ance·a·ble** *adj* —**bal·anc·er** *n* ◇ **hang in the balance** to be in a critical situation in which two diametrically opposed outcomes are possible and the possibility of an unfavorable one is real and greatly feared ◇ **hold the balance 1.** to have the power to decide in which way a situation will develop or which of two opposing sides will prevail **2.** to control the key to maintaining an existing state of equilibrium between two opposing forces ◇ **on balance** having taken all the relevant factors into consideration and assessed their relative significance ○ *The situation, on balance, is relatively hopeful.* ◇ **strike a balance** to reach a compromise between two extremes ◇ **throw somebody off balance** to surprise or confuse somebody

balance out *v* **1.** *vti* to act as an equal and opposing weight, force, or value to something and either neutralize or complement its effect ○ *This gain balances out last month's losses.* **2.** *vi* to arrive at a state of equality or harmony, usually over a period of time ○ *These things tend to balance out in the end.*

Bal·ance *n* ZODIAC same as **Libra** (sense 2)

bal·ance beam *n* a narrow horizontal wooden bar on legs that women gymnasts stand on to perform balancing exercises, or the event involving this

bal·anced /bállənst/ *adj* **1.** **EVEN-HANDED** taking into account all sides on their merits without prejudice or favoritism ○ *a balanced assessment* **2.** **HEALTHY** containing different parts in suitable quantities or suitably arranged to produce a satisfying and effective whole ○ *a balanced diet* **3.** **MENTALLY STABLE** in a state of mental and emotional stability and able to make rational judgments

bal·ance of pay·ments *n* the difference between the amount paid by a national government to other countries and the amount it receives from them

bal·ance of pow·er *n* **1.** the distribution of power among two or more nations, where the pattern of force and dominance among them is balanced in such a way that no single nation has dominance over the others **2.** the power of a single country, group, or person to affect a situation decisively by supporting either of two opposing sides whose powers are equally balanced

bal·ance of trade *n* the difference between the value of the total imports and total exports of a country as assessed over a fixed period

bal·ance sheet *n* a statement showing the assets and liabilities of a company or institution at a particular time

bal·ance weight *n* a weight used to counterbalance a moving part in a machine

bal·ance wheel *n* a wheel in a machine, especially in a clock, that regulates the rate of movement of the main mechanism

Bal·an·chine /bállən cheen, bàllən cheen/, **George** (1904–83) Russian-born US dancer and choreographer. Cofounder of the New York City Ballet (1948), he revolutionized classical ballet with his innovative choreography. Born **Balanchivadze, Georgy Melitonovich**

> "Dance has to look like the music. If you see music simply as an accompaniment, then you don't hear it. I occupy myself with how not to interfere with the music."
> [George Balanchine. Quoted in *Portrait of Mr. B.*, Lincoln Kirstein; 1984]

bal·anc·ing act *n* **1.** a skillful or precarious attempt to deal with opposing groups or opinions or with a large variety of tasks (*informal*) **2.** an entertainment in which the performer balances or keeps objects balanced in precarious positions

bal·an·i·tis /bàllə nītiss/ *n* inflammation of the head of the penis, usually caused by an infection [Mid-19C. < Greek *balanos* "acorn, glans penis"]

bal·as /bálləss/, **bal·as ru·by** *n* a ruby that is a red spinel. Use: gems. [15C. Via Old French *balais*, Spanish *balax* < Arabic *balakš* < Persian *Badakšān*, region of Afghanistan]

ba·la·ta /bə laátə/ *n* **1.** a gum made from tree sap and resembling rubber. Use: gaskets, chewing gum, gutta percha substitute. **2.** *Can, UK* a tropical tree that yields the sap from which balata is made. Latin name: *Manilkara bidentata*. US term **bully tree** [Early 17C. < Carib *balatá*]

Bal·a·ton, Lake /bállə tòn, baalə tòn/ largest lake in central Europe and resort center in west central Hungary. Area: 232 sq. mi./601 sq. km.

bal·bo·a /bal bṓ ə/ *n* the main unit of Panamanian currency. See table at **currency** [Early 20C. After Vasco Núñez de BALBOA]

Bal·bo·a /bal bṓ ə/ town and port in Panama where the Panama Canal flows into the Gulf of Panama. Population: 1,214 (1990).

Bal·bo·a, Vasco Núñez de (1475?–1519) Spanish explorer. He was the first European to reach the Pacific Ocean (1513).

bal·brig·gan /bal bríggən/ *n* a knitted unbleached cotton fabric. Use: making underwear. [Late 19C. After the town of *Balbriggan*, Ireland]

bal·chan *n* FOOD same as **balachan**

bal·co·ny /bálkənee/ (*plural* **-nies**) *n* **1.** a platform projecting from the interior or exterior wall of a building, usually enclosed by a rail or parapet **2.** an area of seating raised entirely above the ground level in a theater, movie theater, or concert hall [Early 17C. Via Italian *balcone* < Old Italian, "scaffold" < Germanic] —**bal·co·nied** *adj*

bald /bawld/ *adj* **1.** **WITH HAIRLESS HEAD** having little or no hair on the head **2.** **WITHOUT NATURAL COVERING** having little or no hair, fur, grass, or other natural covering ○ *a bald patch on the grass* **3.** **WORN** describes tires with a very worn tread **4.** **PLAIN** plain and direct, with no attempt to elaborate or explain ○ *a bald statement of the facts* **5.** *Can* **TREELESS** treeless or nearly treeless ○ *a bald prairie* **6.** **UNORNAMENTED** plain, bare, and without ornamentation, often to the point of seeming dull or prosaic **7.** ZOOL **WITH WHITE MARKINGS** describes birds and mammals that have white markings on the face or head [14C. Perhaps < obsolete *bal* "white spot or streak, especially on a horse's face"] —**bald·ness** *n*

bal·da·chin /báwldəkin, báld-/ *n* **1.** **CANOPY** a canopy made of cloth or stone erected over an altar, shrine, or throne in a Christian church **2.** **PORTABLE CANOPY** a canopy carried above a priest or venerated object during a religious procession **3.** TEXTILES **BROCADE** a rich silk and gold brocade [Late 16C. < Italian *baldacchino* < *Baldacco* "Baghdad"]

bald cy·press *n* a deciduous coniferous tree, often found in swamps or near water, that yields a hard timber. Native to: North America. Latin name: *Taxodium distichum.* [*Bald* because the tree sheds its needles, unlike most members of its family]

bald eagle

bald ea·gle *n* a large eagle, the adult of which has a white head and tail. Native to: lakes and rivers of North America. Latin name: *Haliaeetus leucocephalus.*

Bal·der /báwldər/ *n* in Norse mythology, one of Odin's sons, who was god of the summer sun. He was vulnerable only to mistletoe, by which he was killed.

bal·der·dash /báwldər dàsh/ *n* senseless or pointless talk or writing [Late 16C. Origin ?]

bald-faced *adj* same as **barefaced** (sense 1)

bald·head /báwld hèd/ *n* an offensive term for somebody with a bald head (*informal insult*)

bald·ing /báwlding/ *adj* in the process of losing the hair on the head

bald·ly /báwldlee/ *adv* in a simple and blunt way ○ *To put it baldly, she did a lousy job.*

bal·dric /báwldrik/ *n* a sash or belt worn from one shoulder to the opposite hip, used to support a sword [13C. Directly and via Old French *baudre* < Middle High German *balderich*]

Bald·win /báwldwin/ borough in southwestern Pennsylvania on the Monongahela River. It is a southeastern suburb of Pittsburgh. Population: 19,648 (2002 estimate).

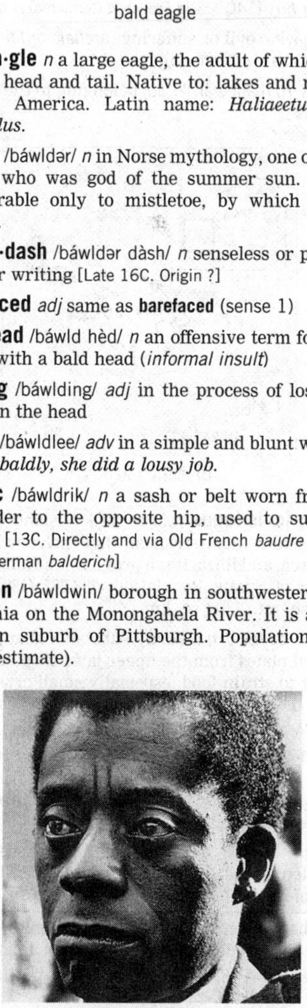

Bob Adelman

James Baldwin

Bald·win, James (1924–87) US writer. His novels and essays addressed racism in the United States, and include *Go Tell It on the Mountain* (1953) and *Notes* *of a Native Son* (1955). Full name **Baldwin, James Arthur**

> "There is never a time in the future in which we will work out our salvation. The challenge is in the moment, the time is always now."
> [James Baldwin, "Faulkner and Desegregation," *Nobody Knows My Name*; 1961]

Bald·win, Robert (1804–58) prime minister of the united Province of Canada (1842–43, 1848–51). He supported the union of Upper and Lower Canada, and became joint prime minister with Louis Lafontaine.

Bald·win, Stanley, 1st Earl Baldwin of Bewdley (1867–1947) British Conservative party leader and prime minister (1923–24, 1924–29, 1935–37). He retired from politics in 1937 amid criticism that he had ignored Germany's preparations for World War II. See table at **prime minister**

> "I would rather be an opportunist and float than go to the bottom with my principles around my neck."
> [Attributed to Stanley Baldwin]

Bald·win Park city in southwestern California, in the San Gabriel Valley. It is an eastern suburb of Los Angeles. Population: 77,828 (2002 estimate).

bald·y /báwldee/ (*plural* **-ies**) *n* an offensive term for somebody who is bald or balding (*informal insult*)

bale[1] /bayl/ *n* a large bundle or package of hay or a raw material such as cotton, tightly bound with string or wire to keep it in shape during transportation or storage ■ *vti* (**baled, bal·ing, bales**) to gather and fasten material or goods into bales ○ *baling hay* [14C. < Old French < Germanic] —**bal·er** *n*

bale[2] /bayl/ *n* evil or suffering (*archaic or literary*) [Old English *bealu* < Germanic]

Bal·e·ar·ic /bàllee árrik/ *adj* belonging to the Balearic Islands

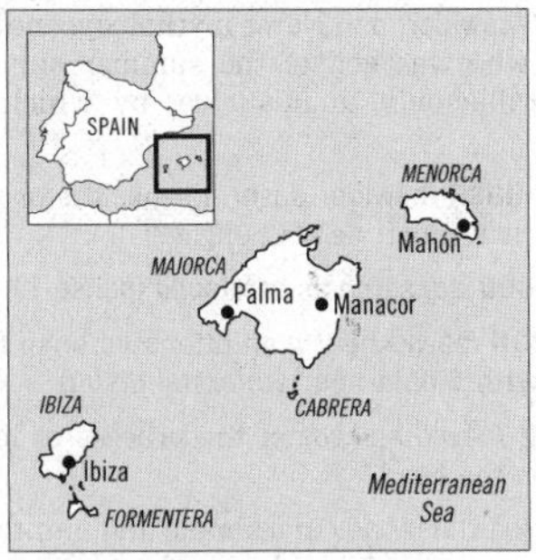

Balearic Islands

Bal·e·ar·ic Is·lands /bàllee árrik-/ island group in the western Mediterranean that includes Majorca, Menorca, and Ibiza. It is a province and autonomous region of Spain. Population: 736,865 (1991). Area: 1,936 sq. mi./5,014 sq. km.

ba·leen /bə léen/ *n* a horny substance that grows as fringed plates from the upper jaws of some whales, acting to strain food, especially small crustaceans, from the water [14C. Via Old French *balaine* < Latin *balaena* "whale" < Greek *phalaina*]

ba·leen whale *n* a large whale that has two blowholes and a set of horny fringed plates instead of teeth. Blue, gray, and right whales are baleen whales. Suborder: Mysticeti.

bale·ful /báylfəl/ *adj* threatening, or seeming to threaten, harm or misfortune ○ *a baleful stare* —**bale·ful·ly** *adv* —**bale·ful·ness** *n*

USAGE baleful or **baneful**? ***Baleful***, meaning "causing harm," is a much more common term than ***baneful***, meaning "causing destruction," which is largely confined to literary use.

~~**balence**~~ incorrect spelling of **balance**

Bal·four /bálfər, -fàwr/, **Arthur James, 1st Earl of Balfour** (1848–1930) British Conservative prime minister (1902–05) and author of the Balfour Declaration (1917), supporting a Jewish homeland in Palestine. See table at **prime minister**

> "History does not repeat itself. Historians repeat each other."
> [Attributed to Arthur James Balfour]

Ba·li /baálee/ mountainous island east of Java, Indonesia, that is a popular vacation destination. Capital: Denpasar. Population: 3,102,400 (2001). Area: 2,171 sq. mi./5,623 sq. km.

bal·i·bun·tal /bàlli búnt'l/ *n* **1.** fine straw woven into material. Use: hat making. **2.** a hat made from balibuntal [Early 20C. < *Baliuag* in the Philippines + Tagalog *buntal* "straw from the talipot palm tree"]

Ba·lik·pa·pan /baálik paà paan/ city and port in Indonesia, situated on the island of Borneo, on the Makassar Strait. Population: 433,494 (1997).

Ba·li·nese /baàlə néez, -néess/ *n* **1.** somebody who comes from Bali **2.** an Austronesian language spoken on Bali. Native speakers: 2–3 million. [Early 19C. < Dutch *Balinees* < *Bali* "Bali"] —**Ba·li·nese** *adj*

Ba·li·ol /báylee əl/, **Bal·li·ol, John de** (1250?–1314) king of Scots. He rebelled against English rule, but was defeated by Edward I at Dunbar, Scotland (1296) and deposed.

balk /bawk/, **baulk** *v* (**balked, balk·ing, balks; baulked, baulk·ing, baulks**) **1.** *vi* BE RELUCTANT OR TURN AWAY to hesitate over something or be unwilling to do something, usually because of moral scruples or a natural aversion ○ *I balked at getting down on my hands and knees to wipe the floor.* ○ *They balked at the asking price.* **2.** *vti* REFUSE TO DEAL WITH SOMETHING to refuse to deal with something that presents a difficulty **3.** *vi* STOP SHORT to stop suddenly and refuse to go on, especially when faced with an obstacle ○ *The horse balked and refused the jump.* **4.** *vt* FOIL SOMEBODY to prevent somebody from carrying out a plan or intention (*often passive*) ○ *acted like a lion balked of its prey* **5.** *vi* BASEBALL MAKE ILLEGAL PITCHING MOTION in baseball, to make an illegal motion by pretending to pitch but not actually throwing the ball ■ *n* **1.** OBSTACLE something that hinders or frustrates ○ *a balk to further progress in the peace negotiations* **2.** BASEBALL ILLEGAL PITCHING MOVE in baseball, an illegal motion in which the pitcher pretends to throw the ball toward the plate or to a base but does not release it **3.** CONSTR LARGE PIECE OF WOOD a large squared wooden beam **4.** ARCHIT WOODEN BEAM IN HOUSE ROOF a wooden tie beam in the roof of a house **5.** AGRIC UNPLOWED RIDGE a ridge of land left unplowed to serve as a boundary or to counter erosion **6.** CUE GAMES AREA BEHIND BALKLINE the area between the balkline and the bottom cushion on a billiard table, or in balkline billiards between any balkline and the cushion [< Old English *balca* "ridge" and Old Norse *bálkr* "beam, bar" < Indo-European, "beam"] —**balk·er** *n*

Bal·kan /báwlkən/ *adj* relating to the states of the Balkan Peninsula, or their peoples, languages, or cultures [Mid-19C. < Turkish, a mountain chain]

Bal·kan·i·za·tion /bàwlkəni záysh'n/, **bal·kan·i·za·tion** *n* division of an area, region, or group into smaller and often mutually hostile units [Early 20C. < the political fragmentation of the Balkan States between the Treaty of Berlin (1878) and the Balkan Wars (1912–13)] —**Bal·kan·ize** *vt*

Bal·kan Moun·tains /báwlkən-/ mountain range running across eastern Yugoslavia and central Bulgaria. The highest point is Botev Peak 7,795 ft./2,376 m.

Bal·kan Pen·in·su·la mountainous peninsula in southeastern Europe between the Adriatic and Ionian seas in the west and the Aegean and Black seas in the east

Bal·kan States, Bal·kans /báwlkənz/ the countries in the Balkan Peninsula, including Albania, Bosnia-Herzegovina, Bulgaria, Croatia, Greece, Macedonia, the European part of Turkey, and the Federal Republic of Yugoslavia

balk·line /báwk lìn/ *n* **1.** a straight line parallel to the end of a billiard table, from behind which opening shots with the cue ball are made **2.** one of four lines parallel to the edges of a billiard table that divide it into the central area and eight smaller compartments that are used in a particular variety of billiards —**balk·line** *adj*

balk·line bil·li·ards *n* the variety of billiards in which balklines are used to divide up the table

balk·y /báwkee/ (**-i·er, -i·est**) *adj* difficult and uncooperative ○ *a balky mule that stopped dead in its tracks* —**balk·i·ly** *adv* —**balk·i·ness** *n*

ball[1] /bawl/ *n* **1.** ROUND OBJECT PLAYED WITH an object, usually round in shape and often hollow and flexible, used in many games and sports in which it is thrown, struck, or kicked **2.** ROUNDED THING something spherical or almost spherical, especially a spherical mass or arrangement of material ○ *a ball of wool* **3.** GAME WITH BALL a game, especially one played by children, in which a ball may be thrown from one player to another in various ways ○ *Who's coming out to play ball?* **4.** BALL PLAYED IN PARTICULAR WAY a particular use, movement, or way of transferring the ball to another player in the course of a game ○ *a long ball into the end zone* **5.** BASEBALL PITCH THAT IS NOT STRIKE in baseball, any pitch that does not pass through the strike zone and at which the batter does not swing **6.** ARMS SOLID PROJECTILE a solid non-explosive and usually round projectile shot from an old-fashioned pistol, musket, or cannon **7.** ARMS SOLID PROJECTILES COLLECTIVELY a collective term for the solid projectiles fired from old-fashioned guns ○ *The gunners were ordered to change from ball to case-shot.* **8.** ROUNDED BODY PART a rounded part of the body, e.g., at the base of the thumb or just behind the toes ○ *the ball of the foot* **9.** TABOO TERM a highly offensive term for a testicle (*taboo*) ■ *vti* (**balled, ball·ing, balls**) **1.** MAKE INTO OR FORM BALL to mold, gather, or wind something into a ball, or become a ball-shaped mass ○ *She balled her fists.* **2.** TABOO TERM a highly offensive term meaning to have sexual intercourse (*taboo*) [13C. < Old Norse *bǫllr* or assumed Old English *beall* < Germanic] ◇ **carry the ball** to be in charge of getting something done (*slang*) ○ *We're looking for a fund-raiser, and so we need a good organizer to carry the ball.* ◇ **drop the ball** to abandon responsibility for or botch something suddenly (*slang*) ○ *The project was going ahead full speed until he dropped the ball.* ◇ **get** *or* **set** *or* **start the ball rolling** to start something off, especially a conversation or project ◇ **keep the ball rolling** to ensure that an activity continues ◇ **on the ball** aware of what is going on and quick to respond and take action (*informal*) ◇ **have a lot on the ball** to have a high level of knowledge, competence, or skill to offer in a particular situation (*informal*) ○ *She has a lot on the ball; let's give her the opportunity to chair the committee.* ◇ **play ball (with somebody)** to cooperate together or with somebody (*slang*) ◇ **the ball is in somebody's court** used to say that it is somebody's turn to take action ◇ **the whole ball of wax** the whole affair (*slang*) ○ *We only wanted a plane ticket, but the travel agent wanted to sell us the whole ball of wax.*

ball up *vt* to make a complete mess of something by mistake or through lack of skill (*slang*) [< BALL[1] "become clogged"]

ball[2] /bawl/ *n* a large-scale formal social event at which the main activity is dancing [Early 17C. < French *bal* < late Latin *ballare* "to dance" < Greek *ballizein*] ◇ **have a ball** to enjoy yourself very much (*slang*) ○ *It was a great party; we really had a ball!*

Ball /bawl/, **Hugo** (1886–1927) German poet and musician. An important figure in the Dadaist movement, he moved to Switzerland at the start of World War I and founded the Cabaret Voltaire in Zurich in 1916.

bal·lad /bálləd/ *n* **1.** a song or poem, especially a traditional one or one in a traditional style, telling a story in a number of short regular stanzas, often with a refrain ○ *The Ballad of Bonnie and Clyde* **2.** a slow romantic popular song ○ *two up-tempo numbers followed by a ballad* [15C. < French *ballade* < late Latin *ballare* (see BALL[2])] —**bal·lad·ic** /bə láddik, ba-/ *adj* —**bal·lad·ist** *n* —**bal·lad·ry** *n*

bal·lade /bə laád, ba-/ *n* **1.** a poem consisting of three stanzas of eight or ten lines and a short concluding explanatory stanza (**envoy**), all of which end with the same refrain **2.** an instrumental piece of music, usually for piano, intended to suggest the telling of a story as in a ballad. The best-known ballades in the classical repertoire are by Chopin and Brahms. [14C. Variant of BALLAD]

bal·lad·eer /bàllə déer/ *n* a ballad singer

bal·lad op·er·a *n* a form of opera with spoken dialogue and popular tunes made into songs. The most famous example is John Gay's *The Beggar's Opera.*

ball and chain *n* something considered to be a great hindrance or restraint ○ *Censorship can be a ball and chain fettering artistic freedom of expression.*

ball-and-claw *adj* having a foot or another part modeled in the shape of an animal's claw holding a ball ○ *a ball-and-claw bathtub*

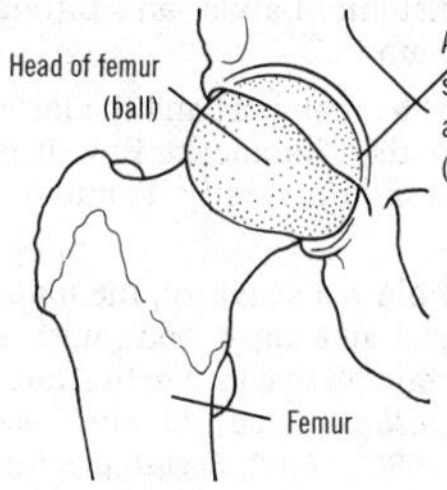

ball and socket joint

ball and sock·et joint, ball joint *n* **1.** a joint such as the hip joint in which a bone with a rounded end fits into a concave area of the adjoining bone, allowing a wide range of movement **2.** a junction between two moving parts of a mechanism in which the rounded end of one part fits into a cup-shaped socket on the other

Bal·la·rat /bállə ràt/ city in southern Victoria, Australia. It was a major gold-mining town in the mid-19th century and is now an industrial center. Population: 84,846 (2002 estimate).

bal·last /bálləst/ *n* **1. STABILIZING HEAVY WEIGHTS** heavy material carried in the hold of a ship, especially one that has no cargo, in the keel of a sailing boat, or in the gondola of a balloon, to give the craft increased stability **2. SOMETHING THAT GIVES BULK OR STABILITY** anything that serves no particular purpose except to give bulk or weight to something or that provides additional stability **3. FOUNDATION MATERIAL** stones or gravel when used as a foundation for a road or railroad track **4.** INDUST **GRAVEL USED IN MAKING CONCRETE** gravel used in making concrete and in earthworks **5.** ELEC ENG **CIRCUIT LIMITING CURRENT FLOW** a circuit that limits the current flow in a fluorescent lamp ■ *vt* **(-last·ed, -last·ing, -lasts) 1. PUT BALLAST ON SOMETHING** to load ballast onto something **2. STABILIZE SOMETHING** to give stability to something [Mid-16C. Probably < Old Danish, "mere weight" < *bar* "bare, mere" + *last* "load"]

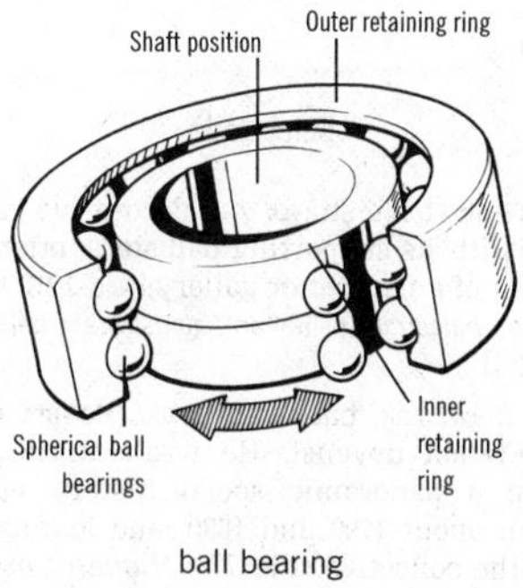

ball bearing

ball bear·ing *n* **1.** a metal ball used to reduce friction between moving parts **2.** a bearing containing a number of metal balls that rotate freely to reduce friction between moving parts

ball boy *n* **1.** a boy who retrieves balls that go out of play during a tennis match and delivers them to the server when required **2.** a boy who takes care of the balls that are out of play during a baseball game or practice

ball·break·er /báwl bràykər/ *n* a highly offensive term that deliberately insults a woman who is regarded as aggressive toward men (*taboo*)

ball·bust·er /báwl bùstər/ *n* **1.** an offensive term for a difficult and unpleasant job (*taboo*) **2.** same as **ballbreaker** (*taboo offensive*)

ball car·ri·er *n* in football, a player who carries the ball toward or across the opposing team's goal line

ball clay *n* a sedimentary clay containing kaolin, mica, other minerals, and organic matter. Use: ceramics. [< an obsolete mining process in which clay was handled as rounded cubes ("balls")]

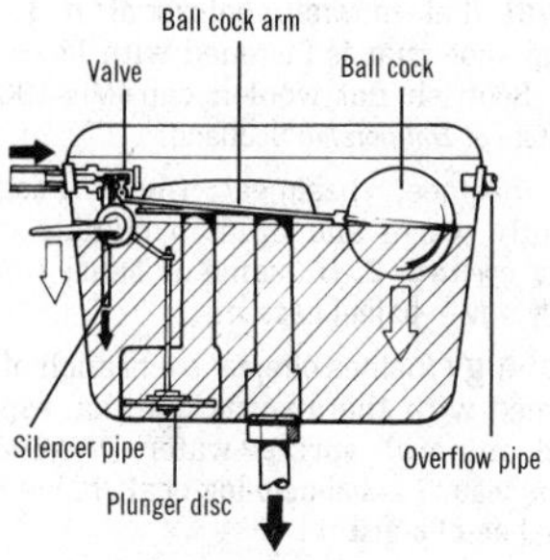

ball cock

ball cock *n* a floating ball on the end of an arm that is connected to a valve controlling the water level in a tank. The valve opens as the ball falls and closes as it rises.

bal·le·ri·na /bàllə réenə/ *n* **1.** a woman ballet dancer **2.** a woman dancer in a ballet company who is regularly given principal parts [Late 18C. < Italian, "woman dancing teacher" < *ballare* "to dance" < Greek *ballizein*]

Bal·les·ter·os /bàllə stérrōss/, **Severiano** (*b.* 1957) Spanish golfer. He won the British Open three times (1979, 1984, and 1988) and in 1980 became the youngest player ever to win the US Masters Tournament.

> "I look into their eyes, shake their hand, pat their back and wish them luck, but I am thinking, I am going to bury you."
> [Severiano Ballesteros, *The Guardian (London)*; October 14, 1989]

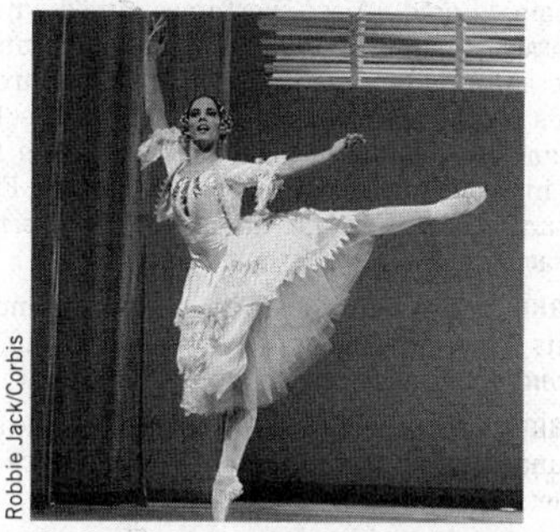

Ballet: Darcy Bussell performing in the ballet *Laurencia* (1990)

bal·let /ba láy, bá lày/ *n* **1. FORM OF DANCE** a form of dance characterized by conventional steps, poses, and graceful movements including leaps and spins **2. STORY PERFORMED BY DANCERS** a choreographed presentation of a story or theme performed to music by ballet dancers, or the musical score written for this **3. GROUP OF DANCERS** a company of ballet dancers who perform together [Mid-17C. Via French < Italian *balletto* < *ballo* "ball (with dancing)"]

bal·let flats *npl* light flat hard-soled shoes resembling those worn by a ballet dancer

bal·let·ic /ba léttik, bə-/ *adj* with the grace of somebody dancing in a ballet

bal·let·o·mane /bə léttə màyn/ *n* a lover of ballet — **bal·let·o·ma·ni·a** /bə lèttə máynee ə/ *n*

bal·let shoe, ballet slipper *n* **1.** a flat light flexible slipper made of silk or leather, worn by ballet dancers for performing and practice **2.** same as **toe shoe**

ball game, ball·game /báwl gàym/ *n* **1.** a game of baseball **2.** a team game with religious significance, played with a ball on walled courts by the Maya and other Mesoamerican peoples ◇ **a whole new ball game** a completely new or different set of circumstances (*slang*)

ball girl *n* **1.** a girl who retrieves balls that go out of play during a tennis match and delivers them to the server when required **2.** a girl who takes care of balls that are out of play during a baseball game or practice

ball gown /báwl gòwn/, **ball·gown** *n* a full-length formal dress suitable for wearing to a ball

ball hock·ey *n Can* hockey played on a rink without ice and with a hard plastic ball instead of a puck

bal·li·cat·ter /bàlli káttər/ *n Can* a ridge of ice formed along a shoreline by waves and freezing spray [Alteration of BARRICADE]

Bal·li·ol another spelling of **Baliol**

bal·lis·ta /bə lístə/ (*plural* **-tae** /-tee/) *n* a piece of military equipment that was used in ancient times to hurl stones and other missiles over a distance [Early 16C. < Latin < Greek *ballein* "throw"]

bal·lis·tic /bə lístik/ *adj* relating to the movements of objects propelled through the air [Mid-18C. < BALLISTA] —**bal·lis·ti·cal·ly** *adv* ◇ **go ballistic** to become extremely angry (*slang*)

bal·lis·tic mis·sile *n* a missile that maintains a course determined by its initial orientation and engine thrust, rather than one calculated by guidance systems during flight

bal·lis·tics /bə lístiks/ *n* **1. STUDY OF PROJECTILES** the study of the movements and forces involved in the propulsion of objects through the air (*takes a singular verb*) **2. STUDY OF FIREARMS** the study of firearms and ammunition (*takes a singular verb*) **3. FIRING CHARACTERISTICS OF WEAPON** the characteristics of a firearm that affect the way missiles are fired (*takes a plural verb*)

ball joint *n* ANAT, MECH ENG same as **ball and socket joint**

ball light·ning *n* a rare form of lightning that takes the shape of a moving glowing ball, typically disappearing without explosion

ball of fire *n* an extremely energetic and dynamic person (*informal*)

bal·lon d'es·sai /baa làwn de sáy/ (*plural* **bal·lons d'es·sai** /baa làwn-/) *n* same as **trial balloon** [< French]

bal·loon /bə lóon/ *n* **1.** LEISURE **GAS-FILLED BAG USED AS TOY** a small colored bag made of thin rubber or plastic that is inflated with air or helium and used as a toy or decoration **2. GAS-FILLED BAG USED IN AIR TRANSPORT** an extremely large bag filled with a lighter-than-air gas and used as a form of air transport, carrying passengers or equipment in a suspended basket or gondola **3. SPEECH CIRCLE IN CARTOON** a rounded outline with a point directed toward a character in a cartoon that encloses the text of the character's speech or thought **4. BRANDY GLASS** a glass with a large rounded bowl, used for drinking brandy ■ *vi* **(-looned, -loon·ing, -loons) 1. SWELL** to form a large round swollen shape **2. INCREASE IN AMOUNT** to increase in amount suddenly and rapidly [Late 16C. < French *ballon* or Italian *ballone* "large (round) ball"] ◇ **go over like a lead balloon** to be completely unsuccessful (*slang*)

bal·loon an·gi·o·plas·ty *n* the use of a balloon catheter to widen a narrowed artery

bal·loon cath·e·ter *n* a tube that can be inserted into a blood vessel or other body part and inflated while inside, e.g., to widen a narrowed artery

bal·loon·ing /bə lóoning/ *n* the sport of riding in or piloting a balloon

bal·loon·ist /bə lóonist/ *n* the pilot of a balloon

bal·loon loan *n* a loan that is repaid with a series of regular payments and one much larger payment at the end

bal·loon mort·gage *n* a mortgage that is paid off in a series of regular payments with one much larger payment at the end

bal·loon pay·ment *n* a final payment of a loan, especially a mortgage, that is significantly larger than a regular payment and pays off the debt

bal·loon sail *n* a large balloon-shaped foresail, used to replace or assist the jib in light winds

bal·loon tire *n* a pneumatic tire with a wide tread inflated to a low pressure, used to drive on soft surfaces such as deep sand

bal·loon vine *n* a vine with ornamental pods shaped like balloons. Native to: tropics. Latin name: *Cardiospermum halicacabum.*

bal·loon whisk *n* a hand-held whisk made of stiff wires that form a loop at one end and are gathered into a covered handle at the other

bal·lot /bállət/ *n* **1. PAPER OR CARD** a piece of paper or card on which somebody can record a vote **2. VOTING SYSTEM** a system in which eligible people vote, usually in secret, to determine the outcome of an election or make some other collective decision **3. TOTAL VOTES** the total number of votes that have been cast in an election ■ *v* (**-lot·ed, -lot·ing, -lots**) **1.** *vt* **ASK PEOPLE TO VOTE** to carry out a ballot on members of an organization or an electorate **2.** *vi* **VOTE** to vote in a ballot [Mid-16C. < Italian *ballotta* "little ball" < *balla* "(round) ball"] —**bal·lot·er** *n*

bal·lot box *n* **1.** a box in which voters put their ballots after marking them **2.** the system in which leaders are elected or decisions are made using a ballot ○ *The people will decide at the ballot box.*

bal·lot rig·ging *n* the use of dishonest or illegal methods of voting to ensure victory for a particular candidate or party in an election

ball·park /báwl paark/ *n* **1. PARK FOR PLAYING BALL GAMES** a stadium or area of land for playing ball games, especially baseball **2.** AEROSP **TOUCHDOWN AREA FOR SPACECRAFT** the approximate area within which a spacecraft is intended to touch down ■ *adj* **APPROXIMATE** rough or approximate (*informal*) ○ *a ballpark figure* ◇ **in the (right) ballpark** within the right general range or scope (*slang*)

ball-pen *n Malaysia* same as **ballpoint**

ball play·er, ball·play·er /báwl plày ər/ *n* somebody who plays baseball, softball, football, or basketball

ball·point /báwl pòynt/, **ball·point pen** *n* a pen with a small rotating ball at its tip that transfers the ink from an inner tube onto the writing surface

ball·room /báwl ro͝om, -ro͞om/ *n* a very large room with a smooth floor and a high ceiling, used for formal dances

ball·room danc·ing *n* formal dancing with a partner in dances such as the foxtrot, quickstep, and waltz that use a set pattern of steps

balls /bawlz/ *npl* a highly offensive term for the testicles ■ *n* (*taboo*) **1.** a highly offensive term meaning courage and determination **2.** *UK* a highly offensive term meaning nonsense

Balls·ton Spa /bàwlstən-/ village southwest of Saratoga Springs in eastern New York, noted for its mineral springs. Population: 5,598 (2002 estimate).

balls·y /báwlzee/ (**-i·er, -i·est**) *adj* a highly offensive term meaning unusually tough, courageous, or determined (*slang taboo*) [Mid-20C. < BALL[1]]

ball valve *n* a valve in which a ball moves in and out of a spherical socket in response to changes in fluid or mechanical pressure

Ball·win /báwl wìn/ city in eastern Missouri, a western suburb of St. Louis. Population: 31,265 (2002 estimate).

bal·ly·hoo /bállee ho͞o/ *n* **1. SENSATIONAL ADVERTISING** sensational, loud, or sustained advertising **2. UPROAR** a noisy argument or disturbance ■ *vt* (**-hooed, -hoo·ing,** -hoos) **ADVERTISE SOMETHING LOUDLY** to advertise or publicize something loudly and insistently [Mid-19C. Origin ?]

bal·ly·rag *vt* same as **bullyrag**

balm /baam, baalm/ *n* **1. SOOTHING OIL** a fragrant oily substance obtained as a resin from various trees. Use: soothing ointments. **2. SOMETHING THAT SOOTHES** something that has the effect of calming, soothing, or comforting ○ *balm to his wounded ego* **3. NICE SMELL** a pleasant scent (*literary*) **4. PLANT OF MINT FAMILY** a plant of the mint family, e.g., bee balm or horse balm **5.** PLANTS same as **lemon balm** [13C. Via French *bame* < Latin *balsamum* (see BALSAM)]

Bal·main bug /bàl mayn-/ *n* a shellfish with a flat wide body, eaten as a delicacy. Native to: Australia. Latin name: *Ibacus peronii.*

Bal·mer se·ries /bálmər-/ *n* a series of lines in the visible part of the atomic spectrum of hydrogen [Early 20C. After J. J. *Balmer* (1825–98), Swiss physicist]

balm of Gil·e·ad /-gíllee əd, -ad/ *n* **1.** TREES same as **balsam fir 2.** a hybrid poplar tree that has heart-shaped leaves and resinous buds. Genus: *Populus.* **3.** a fragrant resin produced by various trees

Bal·mor·al /bal máwrəl/, **bal·mor·al** *n* **1.** a strong walking shoe that is fastened with laces **2.** a traditional Scottish flat woolen cap [Mid-19C. After the royal estate of *Balmoral* in Scotland]

balm·y /baámee, baálmee/ (**-i·er, -i·est**) *adj* **1.** pleasantly warm and mild in climate ○ *a balmy summer evening* **2.** *UK* same as **barmy** (*informal*) —**balm·i·ly** *adv* —**balm·i·ness** *n*

bal·ne·ol·o·gy /bàlnee óllәjee/ *n* a branch of medicine concerned with therapeutic bathing, especially in natural mineral spring water [Mid-19C. < Latin *balneum* "bath"] —**bal·ne·o·log·i·cal** /bàlnee ə lójjik'l/ *adj* —**bal·ne·ol·o·gist** *n*

bal·ne·o·ther·a·py /bàlnee ə thérrəpee/ *n* the medical practice of treatment by immersion in baths, especially those in spas containing water with a high mineral content [Late 19C. < Latin *balneum* "bath"]

Ba·lo·chi *n, adj* PEOPLES, LANG another spelling of **Baluchi**

ba·lo·ney /bə lṓnee/ (*plural* **-neys**) *n* (*informal*) **1.** FOOD same as **bologna** (sense 1) **2.** nonsense or lies ○ *That's nonsense. It's baloney.* [Early 20C. Origin ?]

~~**baloon**~~ incorrect spelling of **balloon**

Bal·qash, Lake /baal kaásh, bal kásh/ shallow lake in southeastern Kazakhstan into which the Ili River flows. Area: 7,030 sq. mi./18,200 sq. km.

bal·sa /báwlssə, baál-/ (*plural* **-sas** or *same*) *n* **1.** *also* **bal·sa wood** a lightweight softwood. Use: rafts, toy models, insulation. **2.** a tree that yields balsa. Native to: South America. Genus: *Ochroma.* [Early 17C. < Spanish, "raft"]

bal·sam /báwlsəm, baál-/ *n* **1. OILY PLANT SUBSTANCE** an oily resinous substance (**oleoresin**) obtained from plants, especially one containing benzoic acid or cinnamic acid. Use: perfumes, medicines. **2. PREPARATION CONTAINING BALSAM** a preparation containing or resembling balsam **3. TREE YIELDING RESIN** a tree that yields a fragrant resinous substance, especially a balsam fir **4. FLOWERING PLANT** a plant of the family that includes impatiens and garden balsam. Family: Balsaminaceae. [Pre-12C. Via Latin < Greek *balsamon*] —**bal·sam·ic** /bawl sámmik, baal-/ *adj*

bal·sam ap·ple *n* a tropical vine grown ornamentally for its yellow flowers and orange fruit. Latin name: *Mormordica balsamina.*

bal·sam fir *n* a pyramid-shaped tree that is the source of canada balsam. Native to: North America. Latin name: *Abies balsamea.*

bal·sam·ic vin·e·gar *n* vinegar made from the juice of white grapes matured in wood for 10 to 50 years, giving it a characteristic dark color and rich sweet-sour taste

bal·sam of Pe·ru *n* **1.** an aromatic resin obtained from trees. Use: perfumes, skin lotions. **2.** a tree that produces high-quality timber and yields balsam of Peru. Native to: South America. Latin name: *Myroxylon balsamum* var. pareirae.

bal·sam pop·lar *n* a tree with broad leaves and sticky resinous buds. Native to: North America. Latin name: *Populus balsamifera.*

Balt /bawlt/ *n* **1.** somebody who comes from Lithuania, Latvia, or Estonia **2.** somebody whose native language is Lithuanian, Latvian, or Estonian [Late 19C. < late Latin *balthae*]

Bal·tha·zar /bal tháyzər, bàlthə zaár/, **Bal·tha·sar** *n* traditionally one of the three magi who the Bible says brought gifts to Bethlehem to honor the birth of Jesus Christ (Matthew 2:1–12)

bal·ti /báwltee, baál-, bál-/ *n* a spicy dish originally from Pakistan that is traditionally served in the bowl-shaped pan it is cooked in [< Urdu *bāltī*, literally "pull"]

Bal·ti /báwltee, baál-, bál-/ *n* a Tibetan language spoken in northern Kashmir [Early 20C. < Ladakhi dialect] —**Bal·ti** *adj*

Bal·tic[1] /báwltik/ *n* a group of Indo-European languages in northeastern Europe, closely related to the Slavic group. Native speakers: 5 million. [Late 16C. < late Latin *Balticus*]

Bal·tic[2] /báwltik/ **1.** ➧ **Baltic Sea 2.** ➧ **Baltic States**

Bal·tic Sea /báwltik-/ sea in northern Europe. Nearly landlocked, it borders Sweden, Finland, Russia, Estonia, Latvia, Lithuania, Poland, Germany, and Denmark. Area: 163,000 sq. mi./422,000 sq. km.

Bal·tic States Estonia, Latvia, and Lithuania, considered as a group

Bal·ti·more /báwltə màwr/ port and the largest city in Maryland, near the Chesapeake Bay. It is home to the Johns Hopkins University. Population: 638,614 (2002 estimate).

Bal·ti·more o·ri·ole *n* a songbird, the male of which has a black head and upper body with an orange underside and tail. Native to: North America. Latin name: *Icterus galbula.* [Late 17C. After George Calvert, Lord *Baltimore* (1580?–1632), English proprietor of Maryland]

Bal·to-Sla·vic /bàwl tō-/, **Bal·to-Sla·von·ic** *n* the Baltic and Slavic branches of the Indo-European language family, sometimes considered to form a unified grouping —**Bal·to-Sla·vic** *adj*

Ba·lu·chi /bə lo͞ochee/ (*plural* **-chis** or *same*), **Ba·lo·chi** *n* **1.** somebody who comes from Baluchistan **2.** an Eastern Iranian language spoken in Baluchistan. Native speakers: 5 million. [Early 17C. < Persian *Balučī*] —**Ba·lu·chi** *adj*

Ba·lu·chi·stan /bə lo͞ochi stán/ dry mountainous region in southwestern Pakistan and southeastern Iran

bal·us·ter /bálləstər/ *n* **1.** an upright post supporting a handrail, e.g., in the banister of a staircase **2.** a support that is shaped like a long narrow vase, e.g., a chair leg or the stem of a glass [Early 17C. Via French *balustre* < Italian *balaustro* < Greek *balaustion* "blossom of the wild pomegranate," because early balusters resembled its shape]

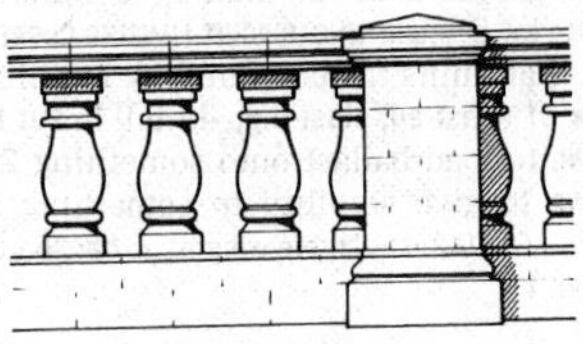

balustrade

bal·us·trade /bállə stràyd/ *n* a decorative railing together with its supporting balusters, often used at the front of a parapet or gallery [Mid-17C. Via French < Spanish *balastrada* or Italian *balaustrata* < *balaustro* (see BALUSTER)]

Bal·zac /báwl zàk, bál-, baal zaák/, **Honoré de** (1799–1850) French novelist. He wrote 90 novels that provide a panoramic social history of France between about 1790 and 1830, and arranged them under the collective title *The Human Comedy.* See Cultural note at **human**. Born **Balssa, Honoré** —**Bal·zac·i·an** /bawl zákee ən, bal-, -záysh'n/ *adj*

> "Equality may perhaps be a right, but no power on earth can ever turn it into a fact."
> [Honoré de Balzac, *La Duchesse de Langeais (The Duchess of Langeais)*; 1834]

bam /bam/ *vti* (**bammed, bam·ming, bams**) **MAKE LOUD NOISE** to make a loud hammering or thudding noise ○ *bammed on the door* ■ *n* **LOUD NOISE** a loud thudding or hammering noise ○ *fell to the floor with a bam* ■ *interj* **USED TO INDICATE SUDDEN IMPACT** used to indicate sudden impact, the result of such impact, or the sudden occurrence of an event of great significance (*informal*) ○ *All of a sudden, bam! I was 30!* [Early 20C. An imitation of the sound]

Ba·ma·ko /baámə kṓ/ capital and largest city of Mali, situated on the Niger River. Population: 1,016,167 (1998).

bam·bam /bám bàm/ *n Carib* same as **batty**[2]

Bam·ba·ra /baam baá raa/ (*plural same* or **-ras**) *n* **1.** a member of an African people living mainly in Mali, western Africa **2.** a Niger-Congo language spoken in Mali, Senegal, Burkina Faso, and Côte d'Ivoire. Native speakers: 1–2 million. [Late 19C. < Bambara] —**Bam·ba·ra** *adj*

Bam·berg /baám bùrg/ city and river port north of Nuremberg in Bavaria, Germany. Population: 70,216 (1997).

bam·bi·no /bam beénō, baam-/ (*plural* **-nos** or **-ni** /-nee/) *n* **1.** a baby or young child (*informal*) **2.** a representation of Jesus Christ as a baby [Early 18C. < Italian, "baby" < *bambo* "silly"]

bam·boo /bam boó/ *n* **1.** the strong hollow stems of a tropical plant. Use: building, furniture, canes, fishing rods. **2.** a plant with long woody, often hollow, stems that grows in dense clumps and produces bamboo. Native to: tropical and semitropical areas. Family: Bambusaceae. [Late 16C. Via Dutch *bamboes*, modern Latin *bambusa* < Malay *mambu*]

bam·boo cur·tain *n* the political, military, and ideological barrier that effectively isolated China from Western countries from the Communist revolution of 1949 until China's relaxation of trade barriers in 1979 [After IRON CURTAIN]

bam·boo shoot *n* an edible young shoot of the bamboo plant that is eaten sliced and cooked, particularly in East Asian dishes

bam·boo·zle /bam boóz'l/ (-zled, -zling, -zles) *vt* (*informal*) **1.** to trick or deceive somebody through misleading statements or falsehoods **2.** to make somebody confused [Early 18C. Origin ?] —**bam·boo·zler** *n*

ban[1] /ban/ *vt* (**banned, ban·ning, bans**) **1.** FORBID SOMETHING to forbid something officially or legally so that it cannot be done, used, seen, or read **2.** STOP SOMEBODY FROM DOING SOMETHING to forbid somebody from doing something or going somewhere **3.** HIST RESTRICT RIGHTS IN SOUTH AFRICA during the apartheid era in South Africa, to punish somebody suspected of breaking the apartheid laws by preventing the person from moving around freely and having contact with other people ■ *n* **1.** ORDER FORBIDDING SOMETHING an order officially or legally forbidding something so that it cannot be done, used, seen, or read **2.** PUBLIC REVILEMENT public condemnation of somebody or something (*archaic*) **3.** CURSE a powerful curse on somebody (*archaic*) [Old English *bannan* "summon, proclaim" < Germanic; noun via Old French *ban* "summons for military duty, proclamation" < same Germanic word]

ban[2] /baan/ (*plural* **ba·ni** /baánee/) *n* a subunit of currency in Romania and Moldova. See table at **currency** [Late 19C. Via Romanian < Serbo-Croatian *bān* "lord" < Turkic *bayan* "very rich person" < *bay* "rich gentleman"]

Ba·na·ba /baa naábə/ one of the 33 islands of Kiribati in the western Pacific Ocean. Population: 284 (1990). Area: 2.2 sq. mi./5.7 sq. km. Former name **Ocean Island**

ba·nal /bə nál, báyn'l, bə naál/ *adj* boringly ordinary and lacking in originality [Mid-19C. < French < *ban* (see BAN[1])] —**ba·nal·ly** *adv*

ba·nal·i·ty /bə nállətee, bay-/ (*plural* **-ties**) *n* **1.** conventional or dull ordinariness **2.** an ordinary remark or feature that lacks originality

ba·nan·a /bə nánnə/ (*plural* **-as** or *same*) *n* **1.** a long and slightly curved fruit with creamy colored soft flesh and a skin that turns from green to yellow when ripe **2.** a large-leaved tropical plant that bears bananas. Genus: *Musa*. [Late 16C. Via Spanish and Portuguese < Mande] ◇ **go bananas** to become uncontrollably or unreasonably angry or excited (*slang*)

ba·nan·a re·pub·lic *n* a small country with an unstable government and an economy dependent on the export of a single product or on outside financial help (*disapproving*)

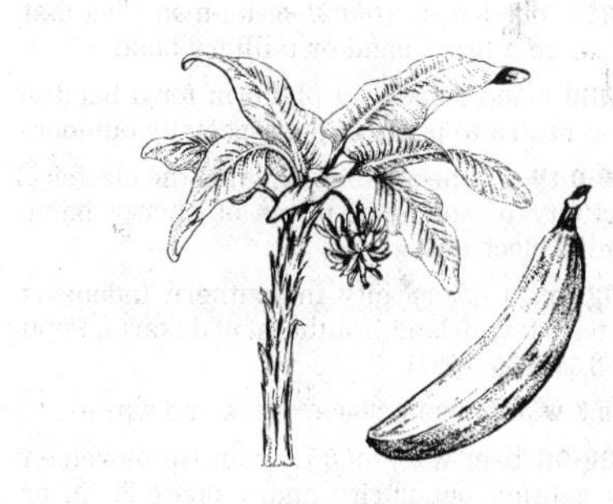

banana

ba·nan·a slug *n* a large slug that often has a yellow body with black spots on it. Native to: forests of northwestern North America. Latin name: *Ariolimax columbianus*.

ba·nan·a split *n* a dessert of peeled banana cut in half lengthwise, typically topped with ice cream, syrup, chopped nuts, pieces of fruit, and whipped cream

ba·nau·sic /bə náwssik, -zik/ *adj* **1.** with no art, creativity, or imagination **2.** practical or materialistic rather than uplifting or inspiring [Mid-19C. < Greek *banausikos* "of or for artisans"]

banc /bangk/ *n* a meeting held by all the judges of a court [Early 18C. < Anglo-French *banc* "bench" < Latin *in banco* "on the bench"]

ban·co /bángkō, baáng-/ *interj* used in baccarat and chemin de fer to declare that a player wishes to place a bet equivalent to the total worth of the bank ■ *n* (*plural* **-cos**) in baccarat and chemin de fer, a bet placed equivalent to the total worth of the bank [Late 18C. Via French < Italian, variant of *banca* (see BANK[1])]

Ban·croft /bán krawft, -kròft, báng-/, **Anne** (*b.* 1931) US actor. She won an Academy Award for her part in the movie *The Miracle Worker* (1962) and gained fame as Mrs. Robinson in *The Graduate* (1967). Born **Italiano, Anna Maria Louise**

Ban·croft, George (1800–91) US historian and diplomat. He founded the US Naval Academy at Annapolis (1845), was ambassador to several nations, and wrote the 10-volume *History of the United States* (1834–40, 1852–74).

~~bancrupcy~~ incorrect spelling of **bankruptcy**

band[1] /band/ *n* **1.** MUSICIANS PLAYING TOGETHER a group of musicians who play together, particularly a group playing popular or rock music **2.** GROUP WITH SAME BELIEFS OR PURPOSE a group of people who have the same ideas or beliefs or who are pursuing the same activity together ○ *a growing band of supporters* **3.** CULTL ANTHROP SMALL GROUP WITH SIMPLE SOCIAL STRUCTURE a subdivision of a people that has a relatively simple social structure **4.** ZOOL ANIMALS TOGETHER a group of animals [15C. < French *bande*] ◇ **to beat the band** to a very great extent or degree (*dated*)
band together *vi* to form a group in order to achieve a goal

band[2] /band/ *n* **1.** STRIP OR LOOP OF MATERIAL a strip of fabric, metal, or elastic placed around something to strengthen it or around several things to hold them together **2.** CONTRASTING STRIPE a long narrow area that is different in material, color, or texture from the adjacent parts **3.** STRIP OR CIRCLE OF MATERIAL a strip or circle of fabric or elastic used for decoration, identification, or absorbing sweat on the forehead or hands **4.** RING a plain ring worn on a finger ○ *a wedding band* **5.** MOVING BELT a moving belt in a piece of machinery **6.** RANGE OF RADIO FREQUENCIES a range of frequencies or wavelengths assigned to a radio station or radio broadcaster **7.** PHYS RANGE OF ENERGIES the range of energies possessed by electrons in a solid **8.** GEOL ORE OR MINERAL LAYER a layer of rock with a different composition or texture from the adjacent layers ■ *vt* (**band·ed, band·ing, bands**) PUT BAND ON OR AROUND SOMETHING to put a strip on or around something to decorate or identify it or to hold a number of things together [13C. < Old Norse < Germanic; reinforced by French *bande* < the same Germanic word]

ban·da /bándə/ *n* a military band used on occasion in operas as an ensemble on or off stage or to provide a contrast to the main orchestra [< Italian, "band, group"]

Ban·da /bándə/, **Hastings** (1906?–97) Malawian politician. He was prime minister (1964–66), then president (1966–94), of Malawi. Full name **Banda, Hastings Kamazu**

> "I wish I could bring Stonehenge to Nyasaland to show there was a time when Britain had a savage culture."
> [Hastings Banda, *Observer (London)*; March 10, 1963]

band·age /bándij/ *n* a long strip of thin or elasticized fabric that is wrapped around a wound or injured part of the body to protect or support it [Late 16C. < French < *bande* (see BAND[2])] —**band·age** *vt* —**band·ag·er** *n*

Band-Aid *tdmk* a trademark for an adhesive bandage with a central gauze pad

ban·dan·na /ban dánnə/, **ban·dan·a** *n* a large square of brightly colored cotton or silk cloth worn over the hair or around the neck [Mid-18C. Probably via Portuguese < Hindi *bāndhnū*, method of tie-dyeing < *bāndhnā* "to tie"]

Ban·da·ra·nai·ke /baán dəraa níkee/, **Sirimavo** (1916–2000) Sri Lankan politician. She succeeded her husband S.W.R.D. Bandaranaike to become the world's first woman prime minister (1960–65, 1970–77, 1994–2000). She nationalized schools and foreign-owned plantations in Sri Lanka. Born **Ratwatte Dias, Sirimavo**

Ban·da·ra·nai·ke, **S.W.R.D.** (1899–1959) prime minister of Sri Lanka (1956–59). He was assassinated by a Buddhist monk. Full name **Bandaranaike, Solomon West Ridgeway Dias**

Ban·dar Se·ri Be·ga·wan /bùndər sèrree bə gaáwən/ capital of Brunei, in the northern part of the country, on Brunei Bay. Population: 49,902 (1997 estimate).

Ban·da Sea /bándə-, baándə-/ sea in the Pacific Ocean in eastern Indonesia, north of the island of Timor and southeast of Sulawesi. Area: 285,000 sq. mi./738,147 sq. km.

B & B *abbr* bed and breakfast (*informal*)

band·box /bánd bòks/ *n* a round lightweight box for carrying accessories such as hats [Mid-17C. Because originally used to carry neckbands]

ban·deau /bàn dṓ/ (*plural* **-deaux** /-dṓz/ or **-deaus**) *n* **1.** a ribbon or band of material worn around the head to keep the hair in place **2.** a piece of material worn around the chest to cover the breasts [Early 18C. < French < Old French *bandel* "little band" < *bande* (see BAND[2])]

band·ed /bándəd/ *adj* marked with bands of different or contrasting colors ○ *banded agate*

band·ed-i·ron for·ma·tion *n* a thin, extremely old, iron-rich layer of sedimentary material of unknown origin, deposited on all continents and containing hematite, magnetite, goethite, and limonite

ban·de·ri·lla /bàndə reé ə, -reélyə/ *n* in a bullfight, a long decorated barbed dart that is thrust into the neck or shoulder of a bull by a bullfighter's assistant [Late 18C. < Spanish, "little banner" < *bandera* "banner"]

ban·de·ri·lle·ro /bàndə ree érrō, -reel yérrō/ (*plural* **-ros**) *n* a bullfighter's assistant who sticks a banderilla into the bull during a bullfight [Late 18C. < Spanish < *banderilla* (see BANDERILLA)]

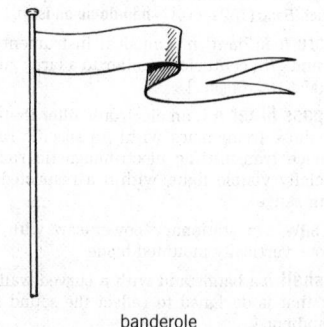

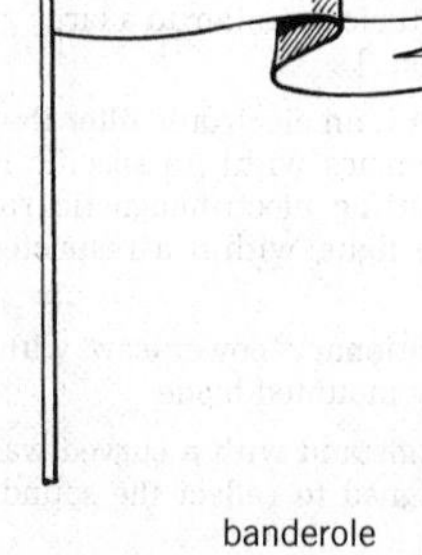

banderole

ban·de·role /bándə rōl/, **ban·de·rol**, **ban·ner·ol** /bánnə-/ *n* **1.** a long narrow flag with a divided end that is flown on a ship's masthead. See illustration on previous page **2.** a sculpted scroll or band bearing an inscription [Mid-16C. Via French < Italian *banderuola* "small banner" < *bandiera* "banner"]

bandicoot

ban·di·coot /bándi ko͞ot/ *n* a marsupial that has a long nose, strong hind legs, and a long tail and eats mainly insects and plants. Native to: Australia, Tasmania, New Guinea. Family: Peramelidae. [Late 18C. < Telugu *pandikokku* "pig-rat"]

ban·di·coot rat *n* a large rodent that is a serious pest to farmers. Native to: South Asia. Latin name: *Bandicota indica.*

ban·di·do /ban dēedō/ (*plural* **-dos**) *n Hispanic* CRIME same as **bandit** (sense 1) [Mid-20C. Via Spanish < Italian *bandito* (see BANDIT)]

ban·dit /bándit/ (*plural* **-dits** or **-dit·ti** /ban dìttee/) *n* **1.** **ARMED ROBBER** an armed robber who steals from travelers and other people, usually at gunpoint **2.** **GANGSTER** a member of a gang of violent criminals **3.** **EXPLOITATIVE PERSON** a swindler or cheat **4.** AIR FORCE **ENEMY AIRCRAFT** an enemy aircraft sighted by a crew while flying (*informal*) ○ *Bandits at twelve o'clock high!* [Late 16C. < Italian *bandito* < *bandire* "to ban"] ◇ **make out like a bandit** *or* **bandits** to be extremely successful, especially by making a lot of money in a short period of time (*slang*)

ban·dit·ry /bánditree/ *n* the occurrence or prevalence of armed robbery and violent crime

ban·dit·ti CRIME plural of **bandit**

Band·jar·ma·sin ➧ **Banjarmasin**

band·lead·er /bánd lēedər/ *n* the conductor of a band, especially of a dance band

band list *n Can* a list of members of a Native North American community that is recognized by the federal government

band·mas·ter /bánd màstər/ *n* the conductor of a band, especially of a brass band or a military band

ban·dog /bán dòg/ *n* an aggressive dog produced by cross-breeding a pit bull terrier with a mastiff, Rottweiler, or Rhodesian ridgeback [15C. Blend of BAND² + DOG; originally a dog that was chained up or bound]

ban·do·leer /bàndə lēer/, **ban·do·lier** *n* a soldier's belt with loops or small pockets for storing cartridges, worn over the shoulder and across the chest [Late 16C. < French, probably either < Spanish *bandolera* < *banda* "sash," or < Catalan *bandolera* < *bandoler* "bandit"]

ban·do·ne·on /ban dónee òn/ *n* a square concertina, used especially in Argentina [Early 20C. Via Spanish *bandoneón* < German *Bandonion*, after its German inventor Heinrich *Band* (1821–60)] —**ban·do·ne·on·ist** *n*

ban·dore /bán dàwr/ *n* a musical instrument of the 16th and 17th centuries, similar to a large guitar or lute [Mid-16C. Origin ?]

band-pass fil·ter *n* **1.** an electronic filter that passes only those frequencies within a specific range **2.** a device transmitting electromagnetic radiation, especially visible light, within a restricted wavelength range

band saw *n* a stationary power saw with a continuous vertically mounted blade

band shell *n* a bandstand with a curved wall at the back that is designed to reflect the sound toward the audience

bands·man /bándzmən/ (*plural* **-men** /-mən/) *n* a man who plays in a brass band or military band

band·stand /bánd stànd/ *n* a platform for a band or small orchestra to perform on, especially outdoors

band the·o·ry *n* a theory that explains the electrical conductivity of solids in terms of energy bands containing electrons

Ban·dung /ba͡an do͝ong/ city in southern Indonesia, on western Java Island, southeast of Jakarta. Population: 3,557,665 (1997).

B & W, **b & w** *abbr* PHOTOGRAPHY black-and-white

band·wag·on /bánd wàggən/ *n* **1.** a cause or movement that is gaining popularity and support **2.** an ornately decorated wagon that musicians perform on during a parade ◇ **jump** *or* **climb on the bandwagon** to join in something only because it is fashionable or likely to be profitable

band·width /bánd wìdth/ *n* **1.** TELECOM **RANGE OF RADIO FREQUENCIES** a range of radio frequencies used in radio or telecommunications transmission and reception **2.** ONLINE **COMMUNICATIONS CAPACITY** the capacity, often measured in bits per second, of a communications channel, e.g., a connection to the Internet **3.** **ABILITY TO PERFORM MULTIPLE TASKS** the ability of somebody to deal with more than one task at a time (*slang*) ○ *Have you got enough bandwidth to do this?*

ban·dy /bándee/ *vt* (**-died, -dy·ing, -dies**) to toss words back and forth casually, often without caring whether they are true or what effect they may have ○ *I've heard the name being bandied about.* ■ *adj* (**-di·er, -di·est**) describes legs that curve outward so that the knees cannot meet [Late 16C. Perhaps < French *bander* "take sides at tennis"]

ban·dy-leg·ged *adj* having legs that curve outward, so that the knees do not touch

bane /bayn/ *n* **1.** **SOMETHING THAT CAUSES MISERY** something that continually causes problems or misery ○ *It's the bane of my life.* **2.** **SOMETHING THAT CAUSES RUIN** something that causes death, destruction, or ruin (*literary or archaic*) **3.** **DEADLY POISON** a fatal poison (*often used in combination in the names of poisonous plants*) [Old English *bana* < Germanic] ◇ **the bane of somebody's existence** *or* **life** somebody or something that is a constant source of trouble or annoyance

bane·ber·ry /báyn bèrree/ (*plural* **-ries**) *n* **1.** a poisonous fleshy red or white berry of a baneberry plant **2.** a plant that bears baneberries. Native to: North America, Europe, Asia. Genus: *Rubus fruticosus.*

bane·ful /báynfəl/ *adj* causing ruin or destruction (*literary or archaic*) —**bane·ful·ly** *adv*

USAGE See *baleful.*

Banff Na·tion·al Park /bànf-/ national park in the Rocky Mountains, southwestern Alberta, Canada. Area: 2,564 sq. mi./6,641 sq. km.

bang¹ /bang/ *n* **1.** **SUDDEN LOUD NOISE** a sudden loud noise, e.g., the sound of a gun firing or a door slamming shut **2.** **SHARP HIT** a sharp blow or hit ○ *a bang on the head* **3.** **PLEASURE** a great deal of pleasure (*informal*) ○ *got a real bang out of it* **4.** **ENERGY BURST** a burst of energy or activity (*informal*) ○ *start with a bang* **5.** **INJECTION OF DRUG** an injection of an illegal drug such as heroin (*slang*) **6.** PRINTING **EXCLAMATION POINT** in typesetting, the character ! ■ **bangs** *npl* **FRINGE OF HAIR** the hair falling over the forehead when it is cut square above the eyes ■ *v* (**banged, bang·ing, bangs**) **1.** *vti* **HIT** to hit something hard, or slam something against a surface ○ *He banged his fist on the table.* **2.** *vti* **HIT SOMETHING ACCIDENTALLY** to hit something unintentionally ○ *bang into the furniture* **3.** *vti* **CLOSE HARD AND NOISILY** to close suddenly and loudly, or make something close with a sudden loud noise ○ *The door banged shut.* **4.** *vi* **MAKE LOUD NOISE** to make a sudden loud noise ○ *children banging on pots and pans* **5.** *vi* **MOVE AROUND NOISILY** to move around making a lot of noise ○ *bang sulkily around the house* **6.** *vti* **OFFENSIVE TERM** an offensive term meaning to have sexual intercourse with somebody (*slang*) **7.** *vi* DRUGS **INJECT DRUG** to inject an illegal drug such as heroin (*slang*) ■ *adv* **1.** **PRECISELY** exactly or precisely ○ *Our hotel is bang in the center of the town.* **2.** **SUDDENLY** suddenly and unexpectedly ○ *I turned around and bang, there he was!* ■ *interj* **IMITATING EXPLOSIVE SOUND** used especially by children to imitate the sound of a gun firing (*informal*) ○ *Bang! You're dead!* [Mid-16C. An imitation of the sound] ◇ **bang for your buck** value for money spent or effort expended (*slang*) ◇ **bang on** *Can, UK* exactly right (*informal*) ◇ **go out with a bang** to end or finish something in a dramatic way (*informal*) ◇ **go over with a bang** to be very successful (*informal*) ○ *His new novel really went over with a bang.* ◇ **go (off) with a bang** *UK* to be very successful

bang away *vi* to keep doing something persistently and determinedly

bang out *vt* (*informal*) **1.** to play a tune on a musical instrument, especially a piano, loudly and coarsely **2.** to produce something speedily ○ *bang out a term paper overnight*

bang up *vt* to damage something badly, or be damaged badly (*informal*) ○ *banged up my car pretty badly*

bang² *n* DRUGS another spelling of **bhang**

Ban·ga·lore /bàng gə láwr/ capital of Karnataka State in southern India. Population: 5,686,844 (2001).

ban·ga·lore tor·pe·do *n* an explosive device in a metal tube, used to blow holes in barbed-wire fences or to detonate land mines [Early 20C. After BANGALORE]

bang·er /bángər/ *n UK* **1.** **SAUSAGE** a fried or broiled sausage (*informal*) **2.** **OLD CAR** an old car that is not in very good condition (*informal*) **3.** **LOUD FIREWORK** a firework that explodes very noisily

Ban·ghā·zī ➧ **Benghazi**

Bang·ka /ba͡ang kaa/, **Ban·ka** island in western Indonesia forming part of the Malay Archipelago. Pangkalpinang is the largest town. Area: 4,609 sq. mi./11,940 sq. km.

Bang·kok /báng kòk/ capital city and port on the Chao Phraya River, just north of the Gulf of Thailand, southern Thailand. Population: 7,358,300 (1998).

Bang·la¹ /ba͡ang glə/ *n S Asia* the Indic national language of Bangladesh and state language of Bangla, India, also spoken in other parts of the world. Native speakers: 170 million. [< Bengali *bāṅglā*] —**Bang·la** *adj*

Bang·la² /báng glə/ state in Northeastern India. It consists of the western part of the former Indian state of Bengal. Capital: Kolkata. Population: 80,221,171 (2001). Area: 33,920 sq. mi./87,853 sq. km. Former name **West Bengal**

Bangladesh

Ban·gla·desh /ba͡ang glə désh, bàng-/ country in south central Asia, formerly part of India and then, from 1947 to 1971, Pakistan. It became a separate nation following a civil war in 1971 and became an independent member of the British Commonwealth in 1972. Language: Bangla. Currency: taka. Capital: Dhaka. Population: 138,448,210 (2003). Area: 56,977 sq. mi./147,570 sq. km. Official name **People's Republic of Bangladesh** —**Bang·la·desh·i** *n, adj*

ban·gle /báng g'l/ *n* **1.** a stiff metal, plastic, or wooden bracelet that is worn around the arm, wrist, or ankle **2.** a decorative disk, charm, or other ornament that hangs from a bracelet [Late 18C. < Hindi *baṅglī* "colored glass bracelet"]

Ban·gor /báng gawr, -gər/ city and port on the Penobscot River, northeast of Belfast, in south central Maine. Population: 31,541 (2002 estimate).

Bang's dis·ease /bángz-/ *n* brucellosis in animals, especially in cattle [Early 20C. After Bernhard L. F. *Bang* (d. 1932), Danish veterinarian]

bang·tail /báng tàyl/ *n* **1.** a horse that is run in races **2.** an envelope with a detachable section that can be used as an order form or to provide marketing information

Ban·gui /baàng geé/ capital city and major port on the Ubangi River, southern Central African Republic. Population: 524,000 (1996).

bang-up *adj* of an excellent quality or standard (*slang*)

ba·ni MONEY plural of **ban**[2]

ban·ia /búnnyə/ *n S Asia* **1.** a merchant or trader **2.** a member of the merchant (**Vaisya**) caste [Late 18C. < Hindi]

ban·ian CLOTHING another spelling of **banyan**

ban·ish /bánnish/ (**-ished, -ish·ing, -ish·es**) *vt* **1.** to exile somebody from a place **2.** to put something out of your mind ○ *I simply couldn't banish my anxieties.* [14C. < French *baniss-*, stem of *banir* "proclaim" < assumed Vulgar Latin *bannire* < Germanic] —**ban·ish·er** *n* —**ban·ish·ment** *n*

ban·is·ter /bánnəstər/, **ban·nis·ter** *n* a handrail supported by posts running up the outside edge of a staircase [Mid-17C. Alteration of BALUSTER]

Ban·ja Lu·ka /bànnyə lo͝okə/ city in northern Bosnia and Herzegovina, on the Vrbas River. Population: 142,644 (1991).

Ban·jar·ma·sin /baànjər maáss'n/, **Band·jar·ma·sin** city in southeastern Borneo, Indonesia. It is the capital of South Kalimantan Province. Population: 546,466 (1997).

ban·jo /bánjō/ (*plural* **-jos** or **-joes**) *n* a musical instrument that has a round sound box covered with parchment, a long neck, and five strings that are plucked or strummed [Mid-18C. Probably < an African language]

Ban·jul /baàn jo͞ol/ capital and largest city of the Gambia. It is situated at the mouth of the Gambia River. Population: 418,000 (2001).

bank[1] /bangk/ *n* **1.** BUSINESS OFFERING FINANCIAL SERVICES a business that keeps money for individual people or companies, exchanges currencies, makes loans, and offers other financial services **2.** BANK'S LOCAL OFFICE a local office of a bank **3.** FUND OF MONEY OR TOKENS the fund of money, tokens, chips, or other pieces that players can draw out in some gambling games, or the player who holds the fund **4.** SOMETHING STORED a supply of something stored, ready for immediate use, e.g., data, food, or blood ■ *v* (**banked, bank·ing, banks**) **1.** *vt* DEPOSIT MONEY IN BANK to pay money into a bank ○ *banked the check immediately* **2.** *vi* HAVE ACCOUNT WITH FINANCIAL INSTITUTION to have an account with or use a particular bank ○ *always banks locally* [15C. Directly or via French *banque* < Italian *banca* "bank, bench, table" < Germanic] ◇ **break the bank 1.** GAMBLING to win more money than is available **2.** to leave somebody very short of or without money (*informal*)

bank on *vt* to count on something happening ○ *We're banking on your support.*

bank[2] /bangk/ *n* **1.** SIDE OF WATERWAY the steep side of a river, stream, lake, or canal **2.** EARTH OR SNOW WITH SLOPING SIDE a pile of earth, snow, or sand, or a raised area of ground with a sloping side **3.** RAISED AREA OF LAND BELOW WATER a ridge of sand or other sedimentary deposit in a river or coastal sea that decreases the depth of the water above it and may become visible at low tide **4.** METEOROL MASS OF CLOUD a large dense area of cloud or fog **5.** SLOPE AT BEND IN RACETRACK an upward slope at a bend in a road or racetrack, designed to reduce the likelihood of drivers going off the road or track when traveling around the bend at speed **6.** AVIAT TURNING ANGLE OF PLANE the tilt of one wing higher than the other made by an airplane as it turns **7.** CUE GAMES CUSHION OF POOL TABLE the cushion of a billiard or pool table **8.** MIN EXTRACT MOUTH OF MINE SHAFT the area around the mouth of a mine shaft **9.** *regional* AGRIC PILE OF VEGETABLES a heap of vegetables, usually potatoes, covered with earth and mulch and sometimes stored in a shed ■ *v* **1.** *vti* FORM INTO PILE to make something into a pile or a large heap or form a pile or heap ○ *snow banked against the fence* **2.** *vt* COVER FIRE to cover a fire with ashes or fuel so that it will continue to burn slowly for a long time **3.** *vti* AVIAT TILT WHILE TURNING PLANE to tilt an airplane with one wing higher than the other while turning **4.** *vti* TILT WHILE DRIVING to tilt a vehicle, especially a motorcycle, while traveling around a bend at speed, or travel around a bend like this **5.** *vt* BUILD SLOPE INTO ROAD OR RACETRACK to build a slope into a road or racetrack at a bend **6.** *vt* CUE GAMES HIT BALL INTO CUSHION in billiards or pool, to hit a ball into the cushion [12C. < assumed Old Norse *banki* "ridge, bank" < Germanic]

REGIONAL NOTE In the sense "a heap of potatoes," ***bank*** is most common in the Lower South, where it competes with potato *bunk*, potato *hill*, potato *hole*, potato *house*, potato *kiln*, and potato *pump*.

---

bank[3] /bangk/ *n* **1.** ROW OF SIMILAR THINGS a row or several rows of things of one type ○ *a bank of switches* **2.** NAUT GALLEY ROWERS' BENCH a bench for rowers in a galley **3.** NAUT GALLEY OARS a row of oars in a galley **4.** MEDIA SECONDARY PART OF HEADLINE a secondary part of a headline running below the main headline in smaller type ■ *vt* (**banked, bank·ing, banks**) PUT THINGS INTO ROWS to arrange things in rows or tiers [13C. < French *banc* "bench" < Germanic]

Ban·ka another spelling of **Bangka**

bank·a·ble /bángkəb'l/ *adj* **1.** likely to become financially profitable ○ *a bankable movie star* **2.** readily and legally acceptable to a bank —**bank·a·bil·i·ty** /bàngkə bíllətee/ *n*

bank ac·count *n* an arrangement according to which a bank accepts deposits of money and keeps that money available for withdrawal by the named account holder or holders

bank an·nu·i·ties *npl UK* FIN same as **consols**

bank bal·ance *n* the amount of money in a bank account at any given time

bank barn *n* a two-story barn built into a hillside that has an entrance to the first story at the front and an entrance to the second story at the back

bank bill *n* BANKING same as **banknote**

bank·book /bángk bo͝ok/ *n* BANKING same as **passbook** (sense 1)

bank card *n* a credit or debit card

bank dis·count *n* the interest on a loan that is deducted from the amount borrowed at the time the loan is taken out

bank draft *n* a bill of exchange drawn by one bank on another

bank·er /bángkər/ *n* **1.** an owner or senior employee of a bank **2.** the player in charge of the bank in a gambling game [Mid-16C. < BANK[1]] —**bank·er·ly** *adj*

bank·er's draft *n* same as **bank draft**

bank·ers' hours, **bank·er's hours** *npl* a short working day (*informal*)

bank·er's or·der *n UK* BANKING same as **standing order** (sense 2)

Bank·head /bángk hèd/, **Tallulah** (1903–68) US actor. She was famous for her husky voice and extravagant acting style on stage in such plays as Lillian Hellman's *The Little Foxes* (1939) and in movies including *Lifeboat* (1944). Born **Brockman, Tallulah**

> "In the theater only one man can count on steady work—the night watchman."
> [Tallulah Bankhead, on a revival of Maeterlinck's *Aglavaine and Selysette*, recalled on her death in press reports; December 12, 1968]

bank hol·i·day *n UK* a weekday public holiday on which banks, government offices, and stores are closed

bank·ing[1] /bángking/ *n* the work carried out by banks or bankers

bank·ing[2] /bángking/ *n Can, New England* in rural areas of New England and the Maritime Provinces, seaweed or hay piled against the side of a house as a form of insulation

bank In·ter·net pay·ment sys·tem *n* a number that uniquely identifies a financial institution for the purposes of Internet transactions

bank·mail /bángk màyl/ *n* an agreement by a bank with a company that is attempting a takeover not to finance any competing bid [Late 20C. After BLACKMAIL]

bank·note /bángk nòt/ *n* a piece of paper money issued by a bank that may be freely exchanged for goods or services

Bank of Can·a·da *n* the federal central bank of Canada

Bank of Eng·land *n* the central bank of England and Wales

bank rate *n* the annual rate of interest set by a country's central bank

bank·roll /bángk ròl/ *n* **1.** ROLL OF PAPER MONEY a roll of banknotes **2.** FUND OF MONEY a fund of money used to finance a project ■ *vt* (**-rolled, -roll·ing, -rolls**) FINANCE SOMETHING to provide the money needed to finance a project on a continuing basis (*slang*) —**bank·roll·er** *n*

bank·rupt /bángk rùpt/ *adj* **1.** UNABLE TO PAY DEBTS judged legally to be unable to pay off personal debts **2.** WITHOUT QUALITIES completely lacking in a particular quality, especially in good or ethical qualities ○ *morally bankrupt* ■ *n* **1.** SOMEBODY WHO CANNOT PAY DEBTS somebody who is unable to pay his or her debts **2.** SOMEBODY WITHOUT QUALITY somebody who completely lacks a particular quality ■ *vt* (**-rupt·ed, -rupt·ing, -rupts**) DEPLETE SOMEBODY'S FUNDS to cost so much that a person or business will have hardly any money left or will be declared bankrupt [Mid-16C. < Italian *banca rotta* "broken table" < *banca* (see BANK[1]) + *rotto* < Latin *ruptus* "broken"]

bank·rupt·cy /bángk rùptsee/ *n* **1.** the state of having been legally declared bankrupt **2.** the complete lack of a particular quality, especially good or ethical qualities ○ *moral bankruptcy*

Banks /bangks/, **Sir Joseph** (1743–1820) British naturalist. A member of Captain Cook's expedition around the world (1768–71), he helped to establish botany as a science and was instrumental in developing Kew Gardens in London.

bank·si·a /bángksee ə/ (*plural* **-as** or *same*) *n* a small evergreen bush or tree with leathery narrow leaves and cylindrical flowers. Native to: Australia. Family: Proteaceae. [Early 19C. < modern Latin, after Sir Joseph BANKS]

Banks Is·land island in the Inuvik Region, Northwest Territories, Canada. It has a predominantly Inuit population. Area: 27,038 sq. mi./70,028 sq. km.

bank state·ment *n* a document showing all the transactions in a bank account over a specific period of time

Ban·ne·ker /bánnəkər/, **Benjamin** (1731–1806) American mathematician and astronomer. He published an annual almanac (1792–1802) and helped plan the District of Columbia (1791–93).

ban·ner /bánnər/ *n* **1.** CLOTH SUSPENDED BETWEEN TWO POLES a long piece of cloth, often bearing a symbol or slogan, and attached at each end to a pole or hanging from the top of a pole **2.** GUIDING PRINCIPLE a guiding principle, cause, or philosophy ○ *under the banner of the labor movement* **3.** ONLINE WEBSITE ADVERTISEMENT a rectangular graphic across a webpage, used as an advertisement, heading, or link **4.** NATION'S OR ARMY'S FLAG the flag of a country or army **5.** MEDIA same as **banner headline** ■ *adj* ESPECIALLY GOOD especially good or successful ○ *a banner year for sales* ■ *vt* (**-nered, -ner·ing, -ners**) MEDIA HEAD ARTICLE WITH BIG HEADLINE to give a newspaper article a banner headline [13C. < Anglo-Norman *banere*, Old French *banière* < medieval Latin *bandum* "standard"]

CULTURAL NOTE ***The Star-Spangled Banner***, a patriotic song (1814) with lyrics by writer Francis Scott Key set to music by English composer John Stafford Smith. Penned by Key after he had witnessed the successful defense of the city of Baltimore by US troops against a British attack in 1814, it soon became a popular patriotic song. It was adopted as the national anthem of the United States on March 3, 1931.

---

ban·ner ad *n* an advertisement displayed full-width at the top or bottom of a printed page or a screen on a webpage

ban·ner·et /bánnərət, -ret, bànnə rét/ *n* formerly, a knight of high rank who was entitled to lead his own men into battle [13C. < Old French *baneret* "bannered" < *banière* (see BANNER)]

ban·ner head·line *n* a headline in large letters that runs across an entire page of a newspaper

ban·ner·ol *n* NAUT, HIST same as **banderole**

ban·nis·ter *n* ARCHIT another spelling of **banister**

Ban·nis·ter /bánnistər/, **Sir Roger** (*b.* 1929) British athlete. He was the first person to run the mile in under four minutes (1954). Full name **Bannister, Sir Roger Gilbert**

ban·nock /bánnək/ *n* **1.** *New England* corn bread baked on a griddle **2.** *Can* a dough of flour, water, lard, and sometimes baking powder cooked on a griddle or in a frying pan, often over a campfire [Old English *bannuc* < Celtic]

ban·nock ball *n Can* a team sport popular among early Native Americans in which points were scored by throwing or carrying a heavy ball into an opponent's goal [Origin ?]

Ban·nock·burn /bánnək bùrn/ town in central Scotland, where the Scots, led by Robert the Bruce, defeated Edward II of England in 1314. Population: 5,799 (1991).

banns /banz/ *npl* an announcement of a forthcoming marriage, proclaimed in the church of the engaged couple on three successive Sundays [14C. < BAN[1]]

ba·ño /baányō/ (*plural* **-ños** /baányōs/) *n Hispanic* a bathroom with or without a toilet [< Spanish]

ban·quet /bángkwit/ *n* **1.** an elaborate formal meal attended by many guests, often held in honor of a particular person or occasion and followed by speeches **2.** an elaborate or lavish meal of many courses [15C. < French, "little bank" < *banc* (see BANK[3])] —**ban·quet** *vi* —**ban·quet·er** *n*

ban·quet hall *n* a room large enough to accommodate a banquet, usually in a palace, castle, or stately home

ban·quet room *n* a room large enough to accommodate a banquet in a hotel, resort, or restaurant

ban·quette /bàng két/ *n* **1.** UPHOLSTERED BENCH an upholstered bench along a wall, especially in a restaurant **2.** RAISED STEP FOR GUNNER a raised step in a trench or behind a parapet on which a soldier may stand to fire or a gun may be mounted **3.** *Southern US* ROADS same as **sidewalk 4.** RAISED BUFFET SHELF a raised ledge at the back of a buffet, used as a shelf for dishes and utensils [Early 17C. Via French < Italian *banchetta* "little bench" < *banca* (see BANK[1])]

ban·shee /bán shee/ *n* in Gaelic folklore, a spirit of a woman who appears, wailing, to signal that somebody in the household is going to die [Late 17C. < Irish *bean sidhe* < Old Irish *ben* "woman" + *side* "of the fairy world"]

ban·tam /bántəm/ *n* **1.** SMALL DOMESTIC FOWL a bird belonging to a breed of small domestic fowl **2.** BOXING same as **bantamweight** (sense 1) **3.** *Can* HOCKEY, SOFTBALL JUNIOR PLAYER in hockey and softball, a category of players from 13 to 15 years of age, or a player in this category ■ *adj* **1.** MINIATURE small in size **2.** OVERCONFIDENT overconfident and slightly aggressive [Mid-18C. After the town of *Bantam* in Java]

ban·tam·weight /bántəm wàyt/ *n* **1.** WEIGHT CATEGORY IN PROFESSIONAL BOXING in professional boxing, a weight category for competitors who weigh between 112 and 118 lb./51 and 53.5 kg **2.** WEIGHT CATEGORY IN AMATEUR BOXING in amateur boxing, a weight category for competitors who weigh between 112 and 119 lb./51 and 54 kg **3.** BOXER COMPETING AT BANTAMWEIGHT a professional or amateur boxer who competes at bantamweight **4.** WEIGHT CATEGORY IN WRESTLING in wrestling, a weight category for competitors who weigh between 115 and 126 lb./52 and 57 kg **5.** WRESTLER COMPETING AT BANTAMWEIGHT a wrestler who competes at bantamweight

ban·ter /bántər/ *n* lighthearted teasing or amusing remarks that are exchanged between people ■ *vi* (**-tered, -ter·ing, -ters**) to exchange lighthearted teasing remarks [Late 17C. Origin ?] —**ban·ter·er** *n*

Ban·ting /bánting/, **Sir Frederick Grant** (1891–1941) Canadian physician. He codiscovered insulin with Charles Best (1922), for which he shared the Nobel Prize in physiology or medicine (1923).

Ban·tu /bántoo/ (*plural same* or **-tus**) *n* **1.** a large group of Niger-Congo languages, spoken in central, eastern, and southern Africa. Native speakers: 150 million. **2.** ⚠ a member of a large group of peoples living in equatorial and southern Africa (*sometimes considered offensive*) [Mid-19C. In some Bantu languages the plural of *-ntu* "person"] —**Ban·tu** *adj*

USAGE In South Africa after the apartheid era, ***Bantu*** is considered highly offensive when used with reference to people, especially in the singular, and *Black* or *African* is the normally accepted term. In technical contexts outside South Africa, for example, academic discussions of anthropology and language, ***Bantu*** continues in use.

ban·tus·tan /bántoo stàn/, **Ban·tus·tan** *n* in South Africa during the apartheid era from the 1950s until 1994, an area where Black people lived with limited self-government [Mid-20C. < BANTU, after such names as HINDUSTAN]

banyan

ban·yan /bánnyən, -yan/ *n* **1.** a tree with roots that grow down from the branches into the ground to form new secondary trunks. Native to: South Asia. Latin name: *Ficus benghalensis.* **2.** *also* **ba·ni·an** *or* **ba·ni·yaan** in parts of South Asia, a cotton shirt worn by men as an undershirt, or in summer as the only shirt [Late 16C. Via Portuguese < Gujarati *vāṇiyo* "man of the trading class" < Sanskrit *nāṇija* "merchant"]

ban·zai /baan zī, báan zì/ *interj* in Japan, used as a patriotic battle cry or shout of enthusiasm ■ *adj* reckless and utterly ferocious in a military attack [Late 19C. < Japanese, "(may you live) ten thousand years" < *ban* "ten thousand" (< Middle Chinese *muanh*) + *zai* "year" (< Middle Chinese *swiajh*)]

ba·o·bab /báy ō bàb, baá-/ *n* a tree with a thick short trunk and edible fruit. Native to: southern Africa and northwestern Australia. Latin name: *Adansonia digitata.* [Mid-17C. Origin ?]

Bao Dai /bòw dī/, **Emperor of Annam** (1913–97) The last emperor (1926–45) of the Nguyen dynasty in Indochina, he renounced his title and headed Vietnam under French rule (1949–55) before being deposed and forced into exile. Born **Nguyen Vinh Thuy**

Bao·tou /bòw tố/ city in Inner Mongolia, northern China, on the Huang He west of Hohhot. Population: 1,340,000 (1995).

bap·tism /báp tìzzəm/ *n* **1.** a religious ceremony in which somebody is sprinkled with or immersed in water to symbolize purification. In some Christian baptisms, the person is named as well as being accepted into the Christian faith. **2.** a ceremony that serves as an initiation or naming ritual —**bap·tis·mal** /bap tízməl/ *adj* —**bap·tis·mal·ly** *adv*

bap·tism of fire *n* **1.** a difficult or dangerous first experience in a new situation **2.** a soldier's first experience of battle

Bap·tist /báptist/ *n* a member of a Protestant denomination that baptizes people by total immersion when they are old enough to understand and declare their faith —**Bap·tist** *adj*

bap·tis·ter·y /báptistree/ (*plural* **-ies**), **bap·tis·try** (*plural* **-tries**) *n* **1.** a part of a Christian church used for baptisms **2.** a tank or pool in a Baptist church used for baptisms by total immersion

bap·tize /bap tīz, báp tīz/ (**-tized, -tiz·ing, -tiz·es**) *v* **1.** *vti* to sprinkle somebody with or immerse somebody in water as a sign that the person has been accepted into the Christian faith **2.** *vt* to give a personal name to somebody during the Christian ceremony of baptism [13C. Via French *baptiser* and ecclesiastical Latin *baptisare* < Greek *baptizein* "baptize" < *baptein* "dip"] —**bap·tiz·er** *n*

bar[1] /baar/ *n* **1.** LENGTH OF SOLID MATERIAL a length of metal, wood, or other solid material used as a barrier, or as part of a structure **2.** SMALL BLOCK a small, solid, usually rectangular, block of some substance ○ *a bar of soap* **3.** PLACE FOR DRINKING a place where alcoholic drinks can be bought and drunk **4.** DRINKS COUNTER a counter at which alcoholic drinks and sometimes food are served **5.** PLACE PROVIDING PRODUCT OR SERVICE a commercial establishment, or a counter inside one, where a product or service is provided ○ *a heel bar* **6.** BARRIER something that blocks or hinders progress ○ *Aloofness is a bar to making friends easily.* **7.** NARROW BAND a narrow stripe or band of color or light **8.** SOMETHING USED AS STANDARD something referred to as an authority or standard ○ *Their redesigned model raises the bar for workstation computing.* **9.** LAW LAWYERS OR THEIR PROFESSION lawyers considered collectively, or the profession of a lawyer ○ *the federal and state Bars* **10.** LAW PART OF LAW COURT the railing in a law court that separates the judge, jury, lawyers, people on trial, and witnesses from the public **11.** LAW TRIBUNAL a tribunal or court of law **12.** LAW DEFEAT OF LEGAL ACTION the defeat, prevention, or nullification of an action or claim, or the process by which this is achieved **13.** MUSIC UNIT OF TIME IN MUSIC in music, a fundamental unit of time into which a musical work is divided, according to the number of beats **14.** MUSIC VERTICAL LINE SEPARATING MUSICAL UNITS in music, any one of the vertical lines on a score that separates each unit of musical time. Can term **bar line 15.** MIL METAL STRIP SHOWING RANK a metal strip worn on a military uniform to show rank or a service distinction **16.** same as **crossbar** (sense 1) **17.** GYMNASTICS same as **horizontal bar** (sense 1) **18.** BALLET another spelling of **barre 19.** GEOG RIDGE OF SAND a low ridge of sand or shingle in the shallow part of the bed of a body of water **20.** GEOG RIVER'S CRESCENT-SHAPED SAND DEPOSIT a crescent-shaped area of alluvium deposited on the convex bend of a river bed **21.** HERALDRY LINE ACROSS SHIELD a horizontal line on a shield, usually one of two or three parallel lines **22.** BOARD GAMES STRIP IN BACKGAMMON BOARD the central dividing strip on a backgammon board ■ *vt* (**barred, bar·ring, bars**) **1.** FIX SOMETHING WITH BAR to fasten something with a bar ○ *barred the door* **2.** BLOCK SOMETHING to block something by means of bars or barriers **3.** NOT ALLOW SOMEBODY ENTRY to refuse somebody entry to a place ○ *He was barred from the club.* **4.** MARK SOMETHING WITH BARS to mark something with stripes or bands of color (*usually passive*) **5.** LAW HALT COURT CASE to prevent a court case from going ahead by making a legal objection to it ■ *prep* EXCLUDING except for ○ *the best speech I've ever heard, bar none.* [12C. Via Old French *barre* < Vulgar Latin *barra*] ◇ **behind bars** in prison ○ *spent 20 years behind bars*

bar[2] /baar/ *n* a centimeter-gram-second unit of pressure that can be used in combination with SI units and prefixes, equal to 10^5 newtons per square meter [Early 20C. < Greek *baros* "weight"]

BAR *abbr* Browning automatic rifle

bar. *abbr* **1.** METEOROL barometer **2.** METEOROL barometric **3.** MEASURE barrel

B.Ar. *abbr* Bachelor of Architecture

Bar·a /bárrə/, **Theda** (1890?–1955) US actor. She was one of the first women to become a movie star, and is best remembered for the line "Kiss me, my fool!". Born **Goodman, Theodosia.** Known as **the Vamp**

Ba·rab·bas /bə rábbəss/ *n* in the Bible, a condemned thief who was freed by Pilate at Passover instead of Jesus Christ (Matthew 27)

ba·ra·chois /bárrə shwaá/ *n Can* a tidal pond separated from a beach by a sandbar [< Canadian French]

Ba·rak /bə rák/, **Ehud** (*b.* 1942) Israeli soldier and prime minister (1999–2001). He served as chief of general staff (1991–95), minister of the interior (1995–96), and foreign minister (1996–97) before becoming chairman of the Labor Party in 1997. As prime minister he implemented the 1998 Wye Accord and held talks with Syria.

Ba·ra·nof Is·land /bárrə nàwf-, -nòf-/ island off southeastern Alaska, part of the Alexander Archipelago. It is named for the first governor of the Russian colony of Alaska, Aleksandr Baranov (1746–1819). Population: 9,000. Area: 1,607 sq. mi./4,162 sq. km.

bar·a·the·a /bàrrə thée ə/ *n* a fabric made from a combination of silk, cotton, wool, or synthetic material. Use: coats. [Mid-19C. Origin ?]

ba·ra·za /bə raázə/ *n* in eastern Africa, a public meeting or a place where meetings are held [Late 19C. < Kiswahili]

barb

barb[1] /baarb/ *n* **1. POINTED TIP** a sharp point facing away from the head of an arrow, fishhook, or harpoon, designed to make it difficult to remove **2. HURTFUL COMMENT** a wounding remark **3.** BIRDS **PART OF FEATHER** a stiff spine that forms the framework of a feather. The barbs stick out on each side of the main shaft. **4.** ZOOL **WHISKER ON ANIMAL'S HEAD** a growth on an animal's head like a beard or whisker **5.** BOT **BRISTLE OF PLANT** a hooked projection on some plants and fruits **6.** (*plural* **barbs** or *same*) **AQUARIUM FISH** a small fish often kept in aquariums. Genera: *Barbus* or *Puntius*. **7.** CLOTHING **MEDIEVAL HEADDRESS** a white cloth headdress covering the chin and throat, worn by women in the Middle Ages ■ *vt* (**barbed, barb·ing, barbs**) **FIT SOMETHING WITH BARB** to provide something with a barb or barbs [14C. Via Old French *barbe* "beard, appendage like a beard" < Latin *barba* "beard"]

barb[2] /baarb/ (*plural* **barbs** or *same*) *n* a horse noted for speed and stamina, belonging to a breed originally from North Africa [Mid-17C. Via French *barbe* < Italian *barbero* "of Barbary"]

barb[3] /baarb/ *n* PHARM same as **barbiturate** (*slang*) [Mid-20C. Shortening]

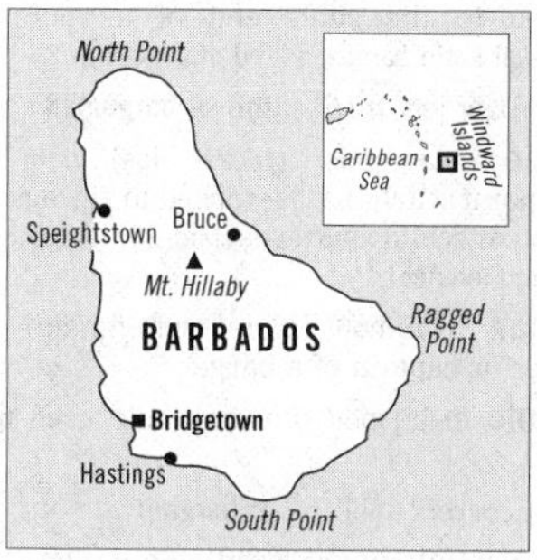

Barbados

Bar·ba·dos /baar báydōss, -báydəss/ island nation of the Windward Islands in the eastern Caribbean off northeastern South America. Settled by the English in the 17th century, it has been an independent state within the British Commonwealth since 1966. Language: English. Currency: Barbados dollar. Capital: Bridgetown. Population: 277,264 (2003). Area: 166 sq. mi./430 sq. km. —**Bar·ba·di·an** *n, adj*

Bar·ba·dos cher·ry *n* **1.** an edible fruit of a tropical tree. Use: jellies and desserts. **2.** a tropical tree that bears Barbados cherries. Latin name: *Malpighia glabra*.

Bar·ba·dos goose·ber·ry *n* **1.** an edible yellow fruit of a cactus, usually eaten in preserves **2.** a broad-leafed cactus with spiny, climbing or trailing shoots, and fragrant flowers, that produces Barbados gooseberries. Native to: tropical America. Latin name: *Pereskia aculeata*.

bar·bar·i·an /baar bérree ən/ *n* **1. UNCIVILIZED PERSON** especially in ancient times, a member of a people whose culture and behavior was considered uncivilized (*sometimes considered offensive*) **2. UNCULTURED PERSON** somebody with no interest in culture **3. AGGRESSIVE PERSON** an extremely aggressive or violent person [14C. < Old French *barbarien* or Latin *barbarianus* < *barbarus* (see BARBAROUS)] —**bar·bar·i·an·ism** *n*

bar·bar·ic /baar bárrik/ *adj* **1.** cruel or extremely brutal **2.** uncivilized or unsophisticated when compared to highly developed civilizations (*sometimes considered offensive*) [14C. Directly or via French < Latin *barbaricus* < Greek *barbarikos* < *barbaros* (see BARBAROUS)] —**bar·bar·i·cal·ly** *adv*

bar·ba·rism /baárbə rìzzəm/ *n* **1. CRUEL ACT** a cruel or brutal act **2. UNCIVILIZED QUALITY** the uncivilized nature of a culture or civilization (*sometimes considered offensive*) **3. UNCONVENTIONAL OR UNACCEPTABLE THING** something that breaks rules of convention or good taste **4.** GRAM **UNGRAMMATICAL WORD** a word or expression considered to be grammatically incorrect [15C. Via French < Latin *barbarismus* < Greek *barbarismos* < *barbarizein* (see BARBARIZE)]

bar·bar·i·ty /baar bárrətee/ (*plural* **-ties**) *n* **1.** a cruel act **2.** an uncivilized condition [Mid-16C. < Latin *barbarus* (see BARBAROUS)]

bar·ba·rize /baárbə rìz/ (**-rized, -riz·ing, -riz·es**) *vti* **1.** to become, or make somebody, cruel or brutal **2.** to become less civilized or less cultured, or reduce something to this state [15C. Via late Latin < Greek *barbarizein* "act or speak like a foreigner, speak gibberish" < *barbaros* (see BARBAROUS)] —**bar·ba·ri·za·tion** /baàrbəri záysh'n/ *n*

Bar·ba·ros·sa /baàrbə róssə/ (1483?–1546) Greek-born Ottoman admiral and pirate. Admiral of the Ottoman fleet after 1533, he was feared as a pirate on the Barbary coast. He defeated Holy Roman Emperor Charles V (1538) and sacked Gibraltar (1540). Born **Khair ad-Din**

bar·ba·rous /baárbərəss/ *adj* **1. EXTREMELY CRUEL** showing extreme cruelty **2. UNCIVILIZED** characterized by an uncivilized culture (*sometimes considered offensive*) **3. NOT SOPHISTICATED** lacking sophistication or refinement **4.** GRAM **UNGRAMMATICAL** using ungrammatical language [15C. Via Latin *barbarus* < Greek *barbaros* "non-Greek, foreign, ignorant, uncivilized"] —**bar·ba·rous·ly** *adv* —**bar·ba·rous·ness** *n*

Bar·ba·ry /baárbəree/ former region of North Africa stretching from the Atlantic coast to western Egypt. It included the Barbary States of Morocco, Algeria, Tripolitania, Tunisia, and Moorish Spain.

Bar·ba·ry ape *n* a tailless monkey with greenish brown hair. Native to: northwestern Africa, introduced to Gibraltar. Latin name: *Macaca sylvana*.

Bar·ba·ry Coast formerly, the Mediterranean coast of North Africa. It was an important base for pirates between the 16th and 19th centuries. ■ the waterfront area of San Francisco, California, between the 1849 gold rush and the 1906 earthquake. It was Notorious for its gambling dens, brothels, and saloons.

Bar·ba·ry sheep *n* ZOOL same as **aoudad**

Bar·beau /baar bṓ/, **Charles Marius** (1883–1969) Canadian anthropologist and folklorist. He collected folk traditions and pioneered professional folklore studies in Canada.

bar·be·cue /baárbə kyoo/, **bar·be·que** *n* **1. OUTDOOR PARTY WITH FOOD COOKED OUTDOORS** an outdoor party where people eat food cooked on a grill **2. FOOD COOKED ON GRILL** food, especially meat, poultry, and fish, cooked on a grill **3. EQUIPMENT FOR COOKING OUTDOORS** an apparatus, including a grill and fuel, used for cooking food outdoors [Mid-17C. < American Spanish *barbacoa*, probably < Arawak *barbakoa* "frame of sticks"] —**bar·be·cue** *vt*

bar·be·cue sauce *n* a sweet-sour and spicy sauce, sometimes with chili, used to marinate meat or served as an accompaniment to meat

barbed /baarbd/ *adj* **1.** with one or more backward-facing points **2.** critical or biting ○ *a barbed comment*

barbed wire *n* strong wire with pointed projections along its length. Use: fences and barriers.

bar·bel /baárb'l/ *n* **1.** a slender feeler resembling a whisker on the lips or jaws of some fishes **2.** a toothless European fish with barbels that resembles the carp. Genus: *Barbus*. [14C. < Latin *barba* "beard"]

bar·bell /baár bèl/ *n* a metal bar with removable weights at each end, used in weightlifting [Late 19C. Blend of BAR[1] + DUMBBELL] —**bar·bel·ler** *n*

bar·be·que *n* another spelling of **barbecue**

bar·ber /baárbər/ *n* **SOMEBODY WHO CUTS HAIR** somebody whose profession it is to cut men's hair and shave their beards ■ *v* (**-bered, -ber·ing, -bers**) **1.** *vt* **CUT SOMEBODY'S HAIR** to cut or shave somebody's hair, especially a man's **2.** *vi* **BE BARBER** to work as a barber [13C. < Anglo-Norman *barbour* < French *barbe* (see BARB[1])]

CULTURAL NOTE ***The Barber of Seville***, an opera (1816) by Italian composer Gioacchino Antonio Rossini. A comedy based on a play (1775) by French dramatist Pierre Augustin Caron de Beaumarchais, it tells of the attempts of Count Almaviva, disguised as a poor student called Lindoro, to woo Rosina, ward of Doctor Bartolo. Almaviva is assisted in his eventful courtship by the wily local barber, Figaro.

Bar·ber /baárbər/, **Samuel** (1910–81) US composer. His neo-Romantic works, which include *Adagio for Strings* (1936), won two Pulitzer Prizes.

> "I have always believed that I need a circumference of silence. As to what happens when I compose, I really haven't the faintest idea."
> [Samuel Barber. Quoted in *American Composers*, David Ewen; 1982]

bar·ber·ry /baár bèrree/ (*plural* **-ries**) *n* a thorny flowering bush widely grown as a garden or hedge plant, especially a yellow-flowered variety that has orange or red berries. Native to: Asia. Genus: *Berberis*. [14C. < Old French *berberis* < medieval Latin *barbaris*, influenced by BERRY]

bar·ber·shop /baárbər shòp/ *n* **1.** the business place of a barber **2.** a style of popular music for unaccompanied single-sex voices in close harmony, originally for four male voices. There are now many female barbershop groups and larger barbershop choirs.

bar·ber's itch *n* a rash or skin eruption on the face and neck, especially around the beard, caused by a fungal infection

bar·ber's pole *n* a short pole with red and white stripes found outside a barbershop

bar·ber's rash *n* MED same as **barber's itch**

Bar·ber·ton /baárbərtən/ city in NE Ohio, a suburb of Akron. Population: 27,663 (2002 estimate).

bar·bet /baárbət/ *n* a small brightly colored forest bird with a large head and a thick beak with bristles at its base. Native to: tropics. Family: Capitonidae. [Late 16C. < French, "small beard" < *barbe* (see BARB[1])]

bar·bi·cel /baárbi sèl/ *n* a tiny projection linking the filaments (**barbules**) of feathers [Mid-19C. < Italian or modern Latin *barbicella* "small beard" < Latin *barba* "beard"]

bar·bie /baárbee/ *n* *UK* a barbecue (*informal*) [Late 20C. Shortening]

Bar·bie /baárbee/, **Klaus** (1913–91) German SS officer. In occupied France during World War II, he deported thousands of Jews to Auschwitz and killed French Resistance workers. He was tried in France after extradition from Bolivia (1983) and imprisoned for life. Known as **The Butcher of Lyons**

bar·bi·tal /baárbi tòl, -tàwl/ *n* a barbiturate with a long-lasting sedative or hypnotic effect. Formula: $C_8H_{12}N_2O_3$. [Early 20C. < BARBITURIC ACID]

bar·bi·tu·rate /baar bíchərət, -ràyt/ *n* a drug with sedative and hypnotic properties belonging to a group of derivatives of barbituric acid [Late 19C. < BARBITURIC ACID]

bar·bi·tu·ric ac·id /baàrbə choorik-/ *n* a white crystalline solid. Use: manufacture of barbiturates. Formula: $C_4H_4N_2O$. [< French *acide barbiturique*, translating German *Barbitursäure* < the name *Barbara*]

Bar·bi·zon School /baárbə zòn-/ *n* a group of mid-19th-century French painters, which included Corot, Millet, Daubigny, and Rousseau, noted for their realistic depictions of landscapes [Late 19C. After the village of *Barbizon* in France]

Bar·bu·da /baar bóodə/ coral island forming part of the independent state of Antigua and Barbuda, in the Caribbean Sea. Population: 1,280 (1995). Area: 161 sq. mi./417 sq. km. ◊ **Antigua and Barbuda** —**Bar·bu·dan** *n, adj*

bar·bule /baar byool/ *n* a slender filament attached to the thicker spines (**barbs**) on a feather's central shaft and interlocking with others [Mid-19C. < Latin *barbula* "little beard" < *barba* "beard"]

barb·wire /baarb wīr/ *n* CONSTR same as **barbed wire**

bar·ca·role /baarkə rōl/, **bar·ca·rolle** *n* **1.** a song traditionally sung by Venetian gondoliers **2.** a piece of instrumental music that imitates a gondolier's song, made popular especially by Chopin and Mendelssohn [Early 17C. Via French < Venetian Italian *barcaruola* < *barcarolo* "gondolier" < late Latin *barca* "bark"]

Bar·ce·lo·na /baarssə lṓnə/ second largest city of Spain and a major seaport on the northern Mediterranean coast. It is capital of Barcelona Province and the autonomous region of Catalonia. Population: 1,527,190 (2002).

B.Arch. *abbr* Bachelor of Architecture

bar chart *n* STATS same as **bar graph**

bar code *n* a sequence of numbers and vertical lines identifying an item and often its price when interpreted by an optical scanner

bard[1] /baard/ *n* **1.** in ancient Celtic culture, a poet who composed and recited epic poems describing important events **2.** a poet, especially one of national importance (*literary or humorous*) [15C. < Gaelic *bàrd* < Celtic] —**bard·ic** *adj*

bard[2] /baard/ *n* ARMOR FOR HORSE a piece of armor for a horse ■ *vt* (**bard·ed, bard·ing, bards**) **1.** PUT BARD ON HORSE to put a bard on a horse **2.** COOK COVER MEAT WITH FAT to cover meat with fat before roasting it to prevent it from drying out [15C. Via French *barde* < Arabic *barda'a* "saddle cloth, padded saddle"]

Bard, Bard of A·von *n* William Shakespeare

Bar·deen /baar déen/, **John** (1908–91) US physicist. He shared two Nobel Prizes in physics, for developing the transistor (1956) and for his research in superconductivity (1972).

Bard of A·von *n* same as **Bard**

Bar·dot /baar dṓ/, **Brigitte** (*b.* 1934) French actor and activist. She became an international sex symbol in movies such as *And God Created Woman* (1956). She retired from movies in 1973 to devote herself to campaigning for animal welfare. Born **Javal, Camille**

> "I gave my beauty and my youth to men. I am going to give my wisdom and experience to animals."
> [Brigitte Bardot, *Guardian (London)*; 1987]

bare /ber/ *adj* (**bar·er, bar·est**) **1.** LACKING CLOTHING not covered by clothing ○ *bare legs* **2.** LACKING PLANTS having no vegetation ○ *a bare hillside* **3.** UNDECORATED lacking the usual furnishings or decorations ○ *The room was bare except for an iron bedstead.* **4.** BASIC simple or essential ○ *the bare facts* **5.** EMPHASIZING SMALLNESS used to emphasize how small something is ○ *the bare minimum of supplies* **6.** MINIMUM only just sufficient ○ *the bare essentials* ■ *vt* (**bared, bar·ing, bares**) **1.** UNCOVER SOMETHING to remove a covering from something ○ *The dog bared its teeth.* **2.** EXPOSE SOMETHING to reveal or expose something secret or concealed ○ *an investigative report that bared the details of the conspiracy* [Old English *bær* < Germanic] —**bare·ness** *n* ◇ **lay something bare** to expose something that has been concealed or hidden ○ *finally laid bare the whole sorry tale of mismanagement*

SPELLCHECK bare or **bear**? Do not confuse the spelling of ***bare*** and ***bear***, which sound similar. ***Bare*** is an adjective meaning "not covered or decorated" (as in *bare walls*) or "minimum" (as in *the bare essentials*). ***Bear*** is a noun denoting an animal (as in *polar bear, teddy bear*) or a verb meaning "carry" or "endure": *I can't bear this oppressive heat.*

SYNONYMS See ***naked.***

bare·back /bér bàk/, **bare·backed** /-bàkt/ *adv, adj* on the back of a horse that has no saddle

bare bones *npl* the essential structure of something, without any elaboration (*informal*)

bare·bones /bèr bṓnz/ *adj* containing only the basic components (*informal*) ○ *the cost of a barebones computing system*

bare·faced /bèr fáyst/ *adj* **1.** shamelessly undisguised ○ *a barefaced lie* **2.** with an uncovered or clean-shaven face —**bare·fac·ed·ly** /-fáystlee, -fáyssəd-/ *adv* —**bare·fac·ed·ness** /-fáystnəs, -fáysədnəs/ *n*

bare·foot /bér fòot/, **bare·foot·ed** /bèr fóottəd, bér fóottəd/ *adj, adv* wearing nothing on the feet

bare·foot doc·tor *n* an auxiliary health-care worker, especially in rural areas of China

bare·foot·ed *adj, adv* same as **barefoot**

bare·hand·ed /bèr hándəd/ *adj, adv* **1.** without weapons **2.** with hands not protected by gloves —**bare·hand·ed·ness** *n*

bare·head·ed /bèr héddəd/ *adj, adv* wearing nothing on the head —**bare·head·ed·ness** *n*

Ba·reil·ly /bə ráylee/ city in Uttar Pradesh State, northern India. Population: 729,800 (2001).

bare·knuck·le /bér nùk'l/, **bare·knuck·led** /-nùk'ld/ *adv* WITHOUT BOXING GLOVES not wearing boxing gloves ■ *adj* **1.** USING BARE HANDS using hands not protected by boxing gloves ○ *He was a great bareknuckle champion in his time.* **2.** AGGRESSIVE OR COMPETITIVE characterized by open aggression or competitiveness ○ *a bareknuckle exchange on the Senate floor*

bare·leg·ged /bèr légd, -léggəd/ *adj, adv* with nothing covering the legs —**bare·leg·ged·ness** /-léggədnəss/ *n*

bare·ly /bérlee/ *adv* **1.** scarcely or almost not ○ *They had barely enough money to pay the rent.* ○ *She had barely sat down when the phone rang.* **2.** sparsely or simply, with no adornments ○ *a barely furnished office*

USAGE See ***hardly.***

Bar·en·boim /bárrən bòym/, **Daniel** (*b.* 1942) Argentine-born Israeli pianist and conductor. A noted performer of the classical repertoire, he has regularly conducted major international orchestras, and in 1991 became music director of the Chicago Symphony Orchestra.

Ba·rents /bárrənts/, **Ba·rentz, Willem** (1550?–97) Dutch explorer. In his search for a Northeast Passage to Asia, he discovered Spitsbergen. Barents Sea is named for him.

Ba·rents Sea shallow part of the Arctic Ocean, north of Norway, Finland, and Russia and south of Franz Josef Land. Area: 529,096 sq. mi./1,370,350 sq. km.

Ba·rentz another spelling of **Barents**

barf /baarf/ (*informal*) *vti* (**barfed, barf·ing, barfs**) VOMIT to vomit the contents of the stomach ■ *n* **1.** VOMITING OF FOOD an act of vomiting the contents of the stomach **2.** SOMETHING VOMITED vomited food [Mid-20C. Probably an imitation of the sound] —**barf·y** *adj*

bar·fi *n* FOOD another spelling of **burfi**

bar·fly /baar flī/ (*plural* **-flies**) *n* a frequent drinker in bars (*slang*) [Early 20C. Because regarded as a pest]

bar·gain /baargən/ *n* **1.** CHEAP PURCHASE something offered or bought at less than the usual price **2.** PACT an agreement between two people or groups in which each promises to carry out an obligation **3.** PRICE AGREEMENT a commercial agreement between two parties that fixes the price of something **4.** THINGS RECEIVED BY AGREEMENT goods or services obtained by a commercial agreement ■ *v* (**-gained, -gain·ing, -gains**) **1.** *vi* NEGOTIATE WITH SOMEBODY to negotiate the terms of an agreement with somebody **2.** *vt* EXCHANGE SOMETHING to exchange one thing for another [14C. < Old French *bargaignier* "trade, negotiate, dispute," probably < Germanic] —**bar·gain·er** *n* ◇ **in** *or* **into the bargain** as well ○ *hard-working and very intelligent in the bargain*

bargain away *vt* to lose something by giving it away as part of an agreement that is ultimately disadvantageous

bargain for *vt* to expect or believe something to be of a particular nature, and prepare for it accordingly ○ *The bill was a lot more than we'd bargained for.*

bargain on *vt* to expect or believe that something will happen, and prepare for it accordingly ○ *We hadn't bargained on the train arriving early.*

bar·gain base·ment *n* an area of a store, often in the basement, selling merchandise cheaply

bar·gain-base·ment *adj* lower than usual in quality or price ○ *at bargain-basement prices*

bar·gain hunt·er *n* somebody who enjoys finding bargains —**bar·gain hunt·ing** *n*

bar·gain·ing chip *n* something that can be used as leverage in negotiations

bar·gain·ing po·si·tion *n* the ability of somebody to achieve a desired end in a negotiation, as determined by his or her relative strengths or weaknesses ○ *must band together to ensure a better bargaining position*

barge /baarj/ *n* **1.** FREIGHT BOAT a long narrow flat-bottomed boat used for transporting freight on rivers or canals **2.** OPEN BOAT USED CEREMONIALLY a large open boat used in ceremonies **3.** SMALL NAVAL BOAT a motorboat used by a high-ranking naval officer for ceremonial occasions ○ *an admiral's barge* ■ *v* (**barged, barg·ing, barg·es**) **1.** *vti* MOVE ROUGHLY to move roughly, colliding with other people ○ *barged his way through the crowd* **2.** *vi* PUSH to push somebody or something roughly **3.** *vt* MOVE SOMETHING IN BARGE to transport freight by barge [13C. < Old French *barge* or medieval Latin *bargia*]

barge in *vt* to enter or intrude suddenly or rudely ○ *Don't just barge in here without knocking.*

barge in on *vt* to interrupt somebody in a clumsy or rude manner ○ *Don't barge in on them: they are having a private meeting.*

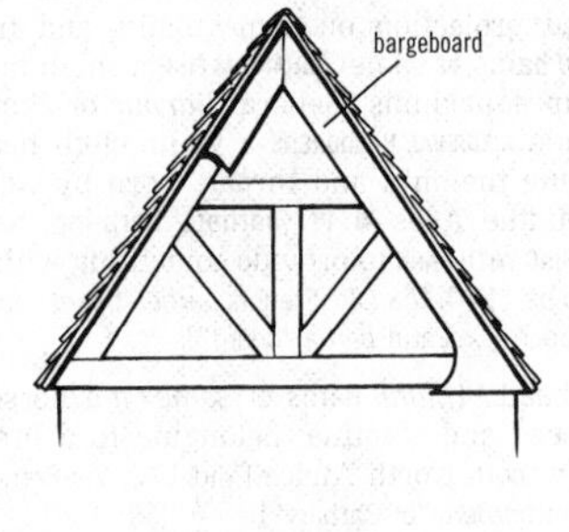

bargeboard

barge·board /baarj bàwrd/ *n* an ornamental board attached to the gable end of a roof [Mid-19C. < medieval Latin *bargus*, a kind of gallows]

barg·ee /baar jée/ *n UK* same as **bargeman**

bar·gel·lo /baar jéllō/ (*plural* **-los**) *n* a straight needlepoint stitch that is worked in zigzags to create chevron or scallop patterns [Mid-20C. After the *Bargello* Palace in Florence]

barge·man /baarjmən/ (*plural* **-men** /-mən/) *n* a crew member or captain of a barge

barge·pole /baarj pōl/ *n* a long pole used to propel barges

~~**bargin**~~ incorrect spelling of **bargain**

bar girl *n* COMM same as **B-girl**[1]

bar graph *n* a graph consisting of a series of vertical or horizontal bars representing statistical data

Bar Har·bor /baar haarbər/ town and tourist spot on Mount Desert Island, southeastern Maine. It is near Acadia National Park. Population: 2,768 (1996).

bar·hop /baar hòp/ (**-hopped, -hop·ping, -hops**) *vi* to visit a number of different bars during an evening (*informal*)

Ba·ri /baaree/ city and port on the southeastern coast of Italy. It is the capital of Apulia region. Population: 316,532 (2001).

bar·i·at·rics /bàrree áttriks/ *n* the branch of medicine concerned with the treatment of obesity (*takes a singular verb*) [Mid-20C. < BARO- + -IATRICS] —**bar·i·at·ric** *adj*

bar·ic /bérrik/ *adj* **1.** relating to or containing barium **2.** relating to barometric pressure

ba·ris·ta /bə rístə/ *n* somebody employed to operate an espresso machine in a coffee bar [Late 20C < Italian, "worker in or owner of a bar"]

bar·ite /bér īt/ *n* barium sulfate in the form of a yellow, white, or colorless mineral, the main ore from which barium is obtained. Formula: $BaSO_4$. [Mid-19C. < BARIUM]

bar·i·tone /bárrə tōn/ *n* **1.** a man's singing voice with a range lower than a tenor and higher than a bass, or a singer with this voice **2.** a wind instrument with the second lowest range in its family [Early 17C. Via Italian *baritono* < Greek *barutonos* "deep-sounding, baritone"]

bar·i·um /bérree əm/ *n* a soft silver-white toxic chemical element. Use: alloys. Symbol **Ba**. See table at **element** [Early 19C. < BARYTA + -IUM]

bar·i·um en·e·ma *n* the introduction of a barium salt suspension into the rectum and colon before an X-ray is taken

bar·i·um meal *n* a barium salt suspension, given by mouth before X-raying the esophagus, stomach, and upper intestine

bar·i·um sul·fate *n* a white or yellowish odorless powder. Use: pigment, contrast medium for X-ray photography. Formula: $BaSO_4$.

bark[1] /baark/ *n* **1.** DOG'S SOUND the characteristic loud abrupt sound made by a dog or fox **2.** ABRUPT SOUND a loud abrupt sound ○ *the bark of guns in the distance* ■ *v* **(barked, bark·ing, barks) 1.** MAKE DOG'S SOUND to make the loud abrupt sound characteristic of a dog or fox **2.** *vi* MAKE ABRUPT SOUND to make a loud abrupt sound **3.** *vti* UTTER SOMETHING ABRUPTLY to say something in a loud abrupt manner ○ *He barked out an order.* [Old English *(ge)beorc* (noun), *beorcan* (verb) < Germanic]

bark[2] /baark/ *n* TREES OUTER LAYER OF TREE the rough outer covering of the woody stems of trees or bushes ■ *vt* **(barked, bark·ing, barks) 1.** GRAZE SKIN to have the skin rubbed off a part of the body through abrasive contact with another object ○ *I barked my shins climbing the fence.* **2.** REMOVE OUTER LAYER FROM TREE to remove the bark from a tree or log **3.** TAN LEATHER USING BARK to tan leather using tannins derived from bark [13C. < Old Norse *bǫrkr*] —**bark·y** *adj*

bark[3] /baark/, **barque** *n* **1.** a small sailing ship with masts whose sails are fixed breadthways **(square)** except for the last mast, which has its sail running lengthwise **(fore-and-aft) 2.** a small sailing ship [15C. Via French *barque* < late Latin *barca*]

bark bee·tle *n* a beetle that burrows under the bark of trees. Family: Scolytidae.

bar·keep·er /báar keépər/ *n* **1.** somebody who runs a bar **2.** COMM same as **bartender**

bark·er[1] /baárkər/ *n* **1.** somebody who stands outside a fair or carnival and shouts out its attractions **2.** a dog that barks a lot

bark·er[2] /baárkər/ *n* a person or machine that strips bark off trees and logs or prepares bark for tanning

Bar·kley /baárklee/, **Alben W.** (1877–1956) 35th vice president of the United States. He was a member of the US Senate and was Truman's vice president (1949–53). Full name **Barkley, Alben William**

Bar·kly Ta·ble·land /baárklee táyb'l lànd/ plateau region situated on the Northern Territory-Queensland border in Australia. Area: 50,200 sq. mi./130,000 sq. km.

bar·ley /baárlee/ *n* **1.** the grain from a cereal plant. Use: food, malt production, livestock feed. **2.** a cereal plant with a long head of whiskered grains. Latin name: *Hordeum vulgare.* [Old English *bærlic* "barley-like" < *bære, bere* "barley" < Indo-European]

bar·ley sug·ar *n* a clear hard orange yellow candy made from boiled-down sugar

bar line *n Can, UK* a vertical line on a sheet of music that separates each unit of musical time. US term **bar**[1]

Bar·low /baárlō/, **Joel** (1754–1812) US diplomat and poet. He is best known for his poem "Hasty Pudding" (1796).

Bar·low knife /baárlō-/ *n* a pocketknife with one blade for cutting and another for poking or gouging [Late 18C. After a family of flatware makers in Sheffield, England]

barm /baarm/ *n* the foam that rises to the surface during the fermentation of malt liquor [Old English *beorma* < Germanic]

barm·brack /baárm bràk/, **barn·brack** /baárn bràk/ *n Ireland* a rich sweet bread with currants in it [Mid-19C. < Irish *bairin breac* "speckled cake"]

bar mitz·vah /baar mítsvə/ *n* **1.** the ritual ceremony that marks the 13th birthday of a Jewish boy, after which he takes full responsibility for his moral and spiritual conduct **2.** a Jewish boy who has reached the age of 13, the age of religious responsibility [Early 19C. < Hebrew *bar miṣwāh* "son of the commandment"]

barm·y /baármee/ **(-i·er, -i·est)** *adj UK (informal)* **1.** unconventional or slightly irrational in behavior **2.** completely lacking in good sense or reason ○ *That's a barmy idea and you know it.* [15C. < *barm* "froth"]

barn[1] /baarn/ *n* **1.** LARGE FARM OUTBUILDING a large outbuilding on a farm used to store grain or shelter livestock **2.** LARGE BUILDING OR ROOM a large building or room, especially one that is plain and functional ○ *walked into a great barn of a living room* **3.** VEHICLE STORAGE BUILDING a large building for housing railroad cars, trucks, or other vehicles [Old English *ber(e)n* "barley house" < *bere* "barley" + *ærn* "house, place"]

barn[2] /baarn/ *n* a unit of area equal to 10^{-28} square meters, used in nuclear physics [Mid-20C. < *as big as a barn door*]

Bar·na·bas /baárnəbəss/, **St.** *(fl* 1st century A.D.) Cypriot missionary. He was a companion of St. Paul during Paul's early ministry, and is traditionally thought to have founded the Cypriot church.

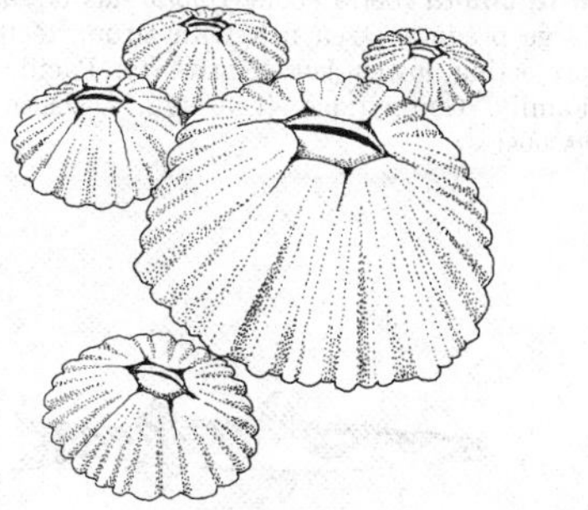

barnacle

bar·na·cle /baárnək'l/ *n* **1.** MARINE BIOL a small invertebrate animal with a shell that clings to rocks and ships and draws food to itself by using slender hairs **(cirri)**. Subclass: Cirripedia. **2.** BIRDS same as **barnacle goose 3.** a clinging or dependent person or thing [12C. < medieval Latin *berneca*]

bar·na·cle goose *n* a wild goose with gray wings and a black-and-white head and body. Native to: northern Europe, Greenland. Latin name: *Branta leucopsis.*

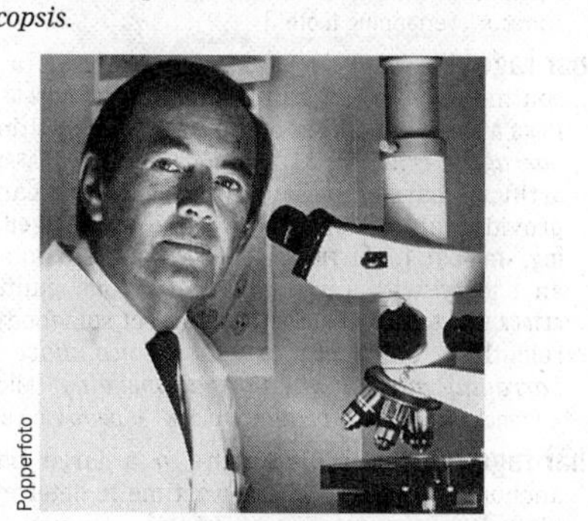

Christiaan Barnard

Bar·nard /baár naárd/, **Christiaan** (1922–2001) South African surgeon. He performed the world's first successful human heart transplant operation in 1967. Full name **Barnard, Christiaan Neethling**

> "The prime goal is to alleviate suffering, and not to prolong life. And if your treatment does not alleviate suffering, but only prolongs life, that treatment should be stopped."
> [Attributed to Christiaan Barnard]

Bar·nard /baárnərd/, **Edward** (1857–1923) US astronomer. He discovered comets, stars and moons, including Amalthea, a moon of Jupiter, (1892) and Barnard's star (1916). He was also a pioneering astrophotographer. Full name **Barnard, Edward Emerson**

Bar·nard /baár naárd/, **Henry** (1811–1900) US educator and legislator. A tireless reformer of public education, he was the first US commissioner of education (1867–70).

Bar·nard's star /baárnərdz-, baár naardz-/ *n* a red dwarf star in the constellation Ophiuchus [Early 20C. After Edward Emerson BARNARD]

Bar·na·ul /baárnə oól/ capital city of Attay Territory, southwestern Siberia, Russia. Population: 616,299 (1995).

barn·brack *n* FOOD same as **barmbrack**

barn dance *n* a party, originally held in a barn, with square dancing

Bar·ne·gat Bay /baárnə gàt-, -nəgət-/ inlet on the coast of New Jersey, separated from the Atlantic Ocean by Long Beach Island and Island Beach Peninsula

barn owl *n* an owl with white and pale brown feathers that often nests in barns. Latin name: *Tyto alba.*

barn rais·ing *n* the construction of a wooden barn by a team of people, traditionally a small rural community, often presented as a symbol of bygone community fellowship

Barns·ley /baárnzlee/ industrial city in South Yorkshire, northern England. Population: 218,063 (2001).

Barn·sta·ble /baárnstəb'l/ tourist resort in SE Massachusetts on an inlet of Cape Cod Bay. Population: 48,854 (2002 estimate).

barn·storm /baárn stàwrm/ **(-stormed, -storm·ing, -storms)** *v* **1.** *vti* MAKE PERFORMING TOUR OF RURAL AREAS to travel from place to place giving performances **2.** *vi* DO FLYING STUNTS to perform exhibitions of aerial acrobatics at shows and fairs **3.** *vti* POL TOUR RURAL AREAS MAKING POLITICAL SPEECHES to go on a whistle-stop tour of rural areas making political speeches as part of an election campaign —**barn·storm·er** *n* —**barn·storm·ing** *n*

barn·storm·ing /baárn stàwrming/ *adj* performing or done in a strikingly enthusiastic and effective way

Bar·num /baárnəm/, **P. T.** (1810–91) US showman, known for his spectacular circuses, including "The Greatest Show on Earth" (1871). With James Bailey (1847–1906) he originated the Barnum and Bailey Circus (1881). Full name **Barnum, Phineas Taylor**

> "There's a sucker born every minute."
> [Attributed to P. T. Barnum]

barn·yard /baárn yaárd/ *n* the area around a barn, where small farm animals roam ■ *adj* crude or vulgar *(informal)* ○ *barnyard humor*

barn·yard grass *n* a coarse weedy grass with spiky clusters of flowers, sometimes grown as forage. Latin name: *Echinochloa crusgalli.*

baro- *prefix* pressure, weight ○ *barometer* [< Greek *baros* "weight"]

bar·o·cep·tor /bárrə sèptər/ PHYSIOL same as **baroreceptor**

Ba·ro·da /bə rṓdə/ former name for **Vadodara** (until 1976)

bar·o·gram /bárrə gràm/ *n* a record of atmospheric pressure produced by a barograph or other meteorological instrument

bar·o·graph /bárrə gràf/ *n* a barometer that gives a continuous printed record of variations in atmospheric pressure —**bar·o·graph·ic** /bàrrə gráffik/ *adj*

Ba·ro·lo /bə rṓlō, ba-/ *n* a full-bodied red wine from northwestern Italy [Late 19C. After a region in NW Italy]

ba·rom·e·ter /bə rómmətər/ *n* **1.** an instrument measuring changes in atmospheric pressure, used in weather forecasting. See illustration on next page **2.** something that indicates an atmosphere or mood ○ *the barometer of public opinion* —**bar·o·met·ric**

/bàrrə méttrik/ *adj* —**bar·o·met·ri·cal** *adj* —**bar·o·met·ri·cal·ly** *adv* —**ba·rom·e·try** *n*

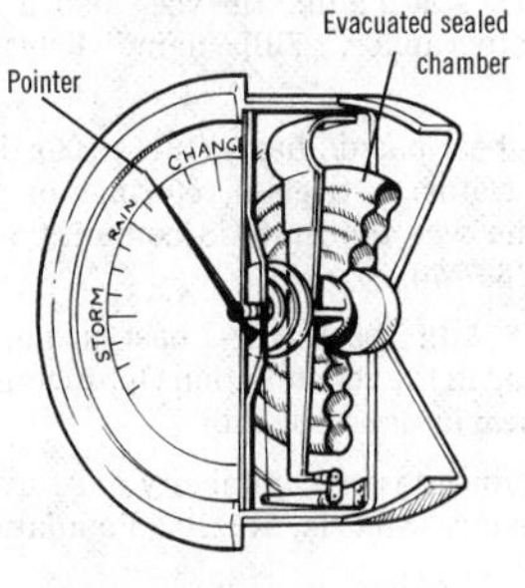

barometer

bar·o·met·ric pres·sure *n* atmospheric pressure as recorded by a barometer

bar·on /bárrən/ *n* **1. NOBLEMAN** a nobleman who belongs to the lowest rank of British or Japanese nobility, or to various ranks in some European countries **2. SOMEBODY POWERFUL** somebody with power or influence ○ *an oil baron* **3. MEDIEVAL NOBLEMAN** in the Middle Ages, a nobleman who was given land in return for loyal service **4. CUT OF MEAT** a cut of beef consisting of a double sirloin, joined at the backbone [12C. Via Anglo-Norman *barun*, Old French *baron* < medieval Latin *baron-* "man"]

SPELLCHECK baron or **barren**? Do not confuse the spelling of ***baron*** and ***barren***, which sound similar. ***Baron*** is a noun denoting a nobleman or a powerful person, as in *an oil baron*. ***Barren*** is an adjective meaning "not productive," as in *barren land*.

bar·on·age /bárrənij/ *n* **1.** barons considered collectively **2.** a baron's rank or position

bar·on·ess /bárrənəss, bárrə nèss/ *n* **1.** a noblewoman who belongs to the lowest rank of British or Japanese nobility, or to various ranks in some European countries **2.** a baron's wife or widow

bar·on·et /bárrənət, bárrə nèt/ *n* a British nobleman who holds the lowest hereditary rank

bar·on·et·age /bárrənətij/ *n* **1.** baronets collectively **2.** same as **baronetcy**

bar·on·et·cy /bárrənətsee/ *n* a baronet's rank or position

ba·rong /bə ráwng, -róng/ *n* a large knife with a broad blade, used by the Moro people of the Philippines [Late 19C. < Austronesian]

ba·ro·ni·al /bə rṓnee əl/ *adj* **1.** relating to or associated with a baron **2.** large, imposing, or sumptuous ○ *a baronial fireplace*

bar·o·ny /bárrənee/ (*plural* **-nies**) *n* **1.** a baron's rank or position, or the land held by a baron **2.** a powerful businessperson's area of influence ○ *a newspaper tycoon zealously guarding his barony*

bar·o·phil·ic /bàrrə fíllik/ *adj* describes an organism that can tolerate high atmospheric pressure —**bar·o·phile** /bárrə fīl/ *n*

ba·roque /bə rṓk, -rók/ *adj* **1.** relating to or in a highly ornamental style of European architecture and art that lasted from the mid-16th to the early 18th centuries **2.** extravagantly or excessively ornamented or complicated [Mid-18C. Via French, applied to ornate architecture < Italian *barocco*, Portuguese *barroco* "irregularly shaped pearl"] —**ba·roque·ly** *adv*

Ba·roque *n* **1.** the baroque style of architecture and art, or its period in European history **2.** highly ornamented music of the 17th century written by composers such as Bach, Handel, Vivaldi, and Telemann

bar·o·re·cep·tor /bárrō ri sèptər/ *n* a nerve ending that is sensitive to blood pressure changes

bar·o·ther·mo·graph /bàrrə thúrmə gràf/ *n* an instrument that records atmospheric pressure and temperature simultaneously

bar·o·ti·tis /bàrrə tītiss/ *n* pain in the ear caused by pressure differences, e.g., during air travel

bar·o·trau·ma /bárrō tràwmə/ *n* pain and possible damage caused to an organ by changes in atmospheric pressure

ba·rouche /bə ro͞osh/ *n* a four-wheeled horse-drawn carriage with two facing double seats, a retractable hood, and a box seat at the front for the driver [Early 19C. Via German dialect *Barutsche* < Italian *baroccio* "two-wheeled" < Latin *birotus* < *rota* "wheel"]

bar·per·son /ba͈ar pùrss'n/ (*plural* **-per·sons** or **-peo·ple** /-pe͈ep'l/) *n* somebody who serves in a bar

bar point *n* the seventh point on a large backgammon board, near the bar

barque *n* another spelling of **bark**[3]

Bar·qui·si·me·to /ba͈arkəssə máytō/ city in northwestern Venezuela and the capital of Lara State, on the Turbio River. Population: 602,622 (1991).

bar·rack[1] /bárrək/ *n* MIL same as **barracks** (sense 1) ■ *vt* (**-racked, -rack·ing, -racks**) **1.** to house soldiers in a barracks **2.** to house a group of people in temporary accommodations (*often passive*) [Late 17C. < BARRACKS]

bar·rack[2] /bárrək/ (**-racked, -rack·ing, -racks**) *vti UK* to shout at somebody in criticism or protest (*informal*) [Late 19C. Probably < N Irish dialect *barrack* "brag"] —**bar·rack·er** *n*

bar·racks /bárrəks/ *n* (*takes a singular or plural verb*) **1.** a building used to accommodate military personnel **2.** temporary accommodations for nonmilitary personnel such as people working away from home [Late 17C. Via French *baraque* < Italian *baracca* or Spanish *barraca* "soldier's tent, barracks"]

bar·ra·cou·ta /bàrrə ko͞otə/ (*plural* **-tas** or *same*) *n* a large predatory sea fish with strong teeth and a projecting lower jaw. Native to: Pacific Ocean. Family: Gempylidae. [Late 17C. Alteration of BARRACUDA]

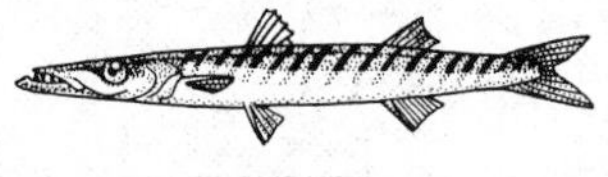

barracuda

bar·ra·cu·da /bàrrə ko͞odə/ (*plural* **-das** or *same*) *n* a predatory sea fish with a long body and protruding jaws and teeth. Native to: tropics. Genus: *Sphyraena*. [Late 17C. Via American Spanish < Spanish dialect *barraco* "overlapping tooth"]

bar·rage /bə ra͈azh/ *n* **1.** ARMS **GUNFIRE BURSTS** a long, continuous burst of gunfire **2. ATTACKING FLOW OF SOMETHING** a rapid attacking outpouring of something ○ *a barrage of criticism* **3.** /ba͈arij/ CIV ENG **RIVER BARRIER** an artificial barrier built across a river or canal to provide water or prevent flooding ■ *vt* (**-raged, -rag·ing, -rag·es**) **1.** MIL **FIRE CONTINUOUSLY ON ENEMY** to attack an enemy with rapid and continuous gunfire **2. ATTACK SOMEBODY CONTINUOUSLY** to subject somebody to a relentless onslaught ○ *Those two have been barraging me with questions all morning.* [Mid-19C. < French, "barrier" < *barrer* "to block" < *barre* (see BAR[1])]

bar·rage bal·loon /bə ra͈azh-/ *n* a large balloon anchored to the ground in wartime to deter enemy aircraft

bar·ra·mun·di /bàrrə múndee/ (*plural* **-dis** or **-dies** or *same*), **bar·ra·mun·da** /-múndə/ (*plural* **-das** or *same*) *n* an edible fish of the perch family. Native to: Australia. Latin name: *Lates calcarifer*. [Late 19C. Probably < a Queensland Aboriginal word]

bar·ran·ca /bə rángkə/, **bar·ran·co** /-kō/ (*plural* **-cos**) *n* *Southwest US* a ravine or steep bank [Late 17C. < Spanish]

Bar·ran·quil·la /ba͈a raan ke͈e yə/ river port and capital of Atlántico Department, northern Colombia. It is situated on the Magdalena River, about 8 mi./13 km inland from the Caribbean Sea. Population: 1,226,000 (1999).

bar·ra·try /bárrətree/ *n* **1. BRINGING OF UNREASONABLE LAWSUITS** the illegal action of persistently bringing lawsuits for little or no reason **2. UNLAWFUL SHIPPING PRACTICE** an unlawful practice committed by a ship's master or crew that harms its owner or charterer **3. BUYING OF CHURCH OR GOVERNMENT POSITION** the sale or purchase of a position in government or the church [15C. < French *baraterie* "combat, deceit" < *barater* "fight, cheat" < Greek *prattein* "do"] —**bar·ra·tor** *n* —**bar·ra·trous** *adj* —**bar·ra·trous·ly** *adv*

Barr bod·y /ba͈ar-/ *n* an inactive X chromosome present in the cells of women and female animals, used in a test to determine sex [Mid-20C. After Murray L. *Barr* (1908–95), Canadian anatomist]

barre /baar/ *n* a rail attached to a wall at about hip height, used by ballet dancers when exercising [Mid-20C. < French (see BAR[1])]

bar·ré /baa ráy/ *n* **1.** the placing of the index finger over all the strings of a guitar or similar string instrument to raise the pitch of each string simultaneously **2.** a chord played on a guitar or similar string instrument in a barré fashion [Late 19C. < French, past participle of *barrer* (see BARRAGE)]

Bar·re /bárree/ town in east central Vermont noted for its granite quarries. Population: 9,245 (2002 estimate).

barred /baard/ *adj* **1. WITH STRIPES** having strips of color **2. HAVING BARS ATTACHED** made of or equipped with bars **3. CLOSED** closed off

barred spi·ral gal·ax·y *n* a galaxy in which the stars form a spiral with a bright bar across the center

bar·rel /bárrəl/ *n* **1. LARGE CASK** a cylindrical container with a flat top and bottom, used to store liquids **2. QUANTITY IN BARREL** the amount held by a barrel **3.** MEASURE **UNIT OF VOLUME IN OIL INDUSTRY** a unit of liquid volume used in the oil industry, usually taken to be 42 US gallons (approximately 159 liters) **4.** MEASURE **UNIT OF VOLUME IN BREWING INDUSTRY** a unit of liquid volume used in the brewing industry, equal to 43 US gallons (approximately 164 liters) **5.** ARMS **TUBE-SHAPED PART OF GUN** the tube-shaped part of a gun through which bullets are fired **6.** MECH ENG **CYLINDRICAL PART** a hollow cylindrical device that forms part of a mechanism, e.g., in clocks ■ *vi* (**-reled** or **-relled, -rel·ing** or **-rel·ling, -rels**) **TRAVEL FAST** to move somewhere at high speed (*informal*) [13C. Via Old French *barril* < medieval Latin *barriclus* "small cask"] —**bar·rel·ful** *n* ◇ **over a barrel** in a situation of powerlessness ◇ **scrape the (bottom of the) barrel** to use the least desirable person or thing because no one or nothing else is available

bar·rel cac·tus *n* a cactus with unbranched spiny stems. Native to: Mexico, southwestern United States. Genera: *Ferocactus* or *Echinocactus*.

bar·rel chair *n* an upholstered chair with a high curved solid back that looks like part of a barrel

bar·rel-chest·ed *adj* having a large rounded chest

bar·rel·head /bárrəl hèd/ *n* the flat circular top of a barrel

bar·rel·house /bárrəl hòwss/ (*plural* **-houses** /-hòwzəz/) *n* **1.** a cheap disreputable bar, especially one where there is music and dancing (*dated*) **2.** a loud rough style of jazz characterized by a heavy two-beat rhythm [Late 19C. < the barrels of liquor along the walls]

bar·rel or·gan *n* a mechanical musical instrument consisting of a cylinder turned by a handle to pass air through a set of pipes

bar·rel roll *n* a flight maneuver in which an aircraft makes one complete sideways revolution

bar·rel vault *n* a ceiling in the shape of a half cylinder

bar·ren /bárrən/ *adj* **1. BARE OF VEGETATION** having no trees or other growing plants **2. NOT FRUITING** producing no fruit or seed **3. UNABLE TO HAVE CHILDREN** not able to bear children (*archaic or literary*) **4. WITH NO USEFUL RESULT** producing no valuable results or interesting effects ○ *It was a barren period in his career.* **5. LACKING IN SOMETHING** completely lacking in a particular thing (*literary*) ○ *Our writers seem somewhat barren of new ideas.* ■ *n* GEOG **FLAT SCRUBLAND** an area of flat, scrubby, unproductive land (*often used in the plural*) [12C. < Old French *baraigne*] —**bar·ren·ly** *adv* —**bar·ren·ness** *n*

SPELLCHECK See *baron*.

bar·ret /bárrət/ *n* a flat hat similar in shape to a biretta, worn in the Middle Ages by members of the clergy and soldiers [Early 19C. Via French *barrette* < Italian *berretta* (see BIRETTA)]

bar·rette /bə rét/ *n* a metal or plastic clasp used by women and girls to keep their hair in place [Early 20C. < French, "small bar" < *barre* (see BAR[1])]

bar·ri·cade /bárri kàyd, bàrri káyd/ *n* a barrier that protects defenders or blocks a route ■ *vt* (**-cad·ed, -cad·ing, -cades**) to obstruct or protect something, or protect yourself, using a barricade [Late 16C. < French < *barrique* "barrel"]

bar·ri·cade tape *n* yellow tape with a repeated warning printed on it in large black letters, used to cordon off, e.g., a crime scene or construction area

Bar·rie /bárree/, **Sir J. M.** (1860–1937) British author. He wrote *Peter Pan* (1904) and numerous other plays including *The Admirable Crichton* (1902). Full name **Barrie, Sir James Matthew**

> "God gave us our memories so that we might have roses in December."
> [Sir J. M. Barrie, *Rectorial address, St. Andrews University*; May 3, 1922]

bar·ri·er /bárree ər/ *n* **1. STRUCTURE BLOCKING ACCESS** a structure such as a fence that is intended to prevent access or keep one place separate from another **2. SOMETHING THAT OBSTRUCTS** something that obstructs or separates, often by emphasizing differences ○ *Impatience can act as a barrier to learning.* **3. LIMIT OR STANDARD** something considered to be a limit, standard, or boundary ○ *sprinters who break the 10-second barrier* **4.** GEOG **ICE SHELF** the part of the Antarctic ice shelf that extends over the sea and partly rests on the ocean floor [14C. < Old French *barriere* < Vulgar Latin *barra* "bar"]

bar·ri·er is·land *n* a long sandy island that runs parallel to a coastline and serves to protect the shore from erosion

bar·ri·er meth·od *n* a method of contraception in which access of sperm to the womb is blocked by the use of protection such as a condom or diaphragm

bar·ri·er reef *n* a narrow ridge of coral lying parallel and close to a coastline and separated from it by a wide deep lagoon

bar·ring /baáring/ *prep* excepting or except for something ○ *Barring delays, we'll arrive this afternoon.*

bar·ri·o /baáree ō/ (*plural* **-os**) *n Hispanic* **1.** a Spanish-speaking quarter in a city or town in the United States **2.** an area of a town in a Spanish-speaking country [Mid-19C. Via Spanish < Arabic *barr* "open area, outskirts"]

bar·ris·ter /bárrəstər/ *n* **1.** *Can* in Canada, a lawyer who represents clients in any court **2.** *UK* a lawyer who is qualified to represent clients in the higher law courts in England and Wales [15C. < BAR[1], probably after words such as *minister, chorister*]

bar·room /baár ròom, -ròom/ *n* a bar for serving drinks, especially one inside a larger establishment such as a hotel or club

bar·row[1] /bárrō/ *n* **1.** GARDENING, CONSTR same as **wheelbarrow 2.** *UK* same as **pushcart** [Old English *bearwe* "stretcher, bier" < Germanic, "to bear"]

bar·row[2] /bárrō/ *n* a large mound of earth above a prehistoric tomb [Old English *beorg* "hill, tumulus" < Germanic, "hide, protect"]

bar·row[3] /bárrō/ *n* a pig that has been castrated before sexual maturity [Old English *b(e)arg* < Germanic]

Bar·row /bárrō/ town in northwestern Alaska with a predominantly Inuit population. It is southwest of Point Barrow, the northernmost point of the United States. Population: 4,469 (2002 estimate).

Bar·row, Clyde (1909–34) US outlaw. He and Bonnie Parker robbed banks and killed 12 people (1932–34) before being killed by Louisiana police.

Bar·ry /bárree/, **Philip James** (1896–1949) US playwright. He is known for sophisticated comedies such as *The Philadelphia Story* (1939).

Bar·ry·more /bárri màwr/, **Ethel** (1879–1959) US actor. The sister of John and Lionel Barrymore, she had a long stage career and won an Academy Award for *None but the Lonely Heart* (1944).

> "For an actress to be a success she must have the face of Venus, the brains of Minerva, the grace of Terpsichore, the memory of Macaulay, the figure of Juno, and the hide of a rhinoceros."
> [Ethel Barrymore, *The Theater in the Fifties*, George Jean Nathan; 1953]

Bar·ry·more, John (1882–1942) US actor. A handsome leading man, he made numerous films, but was most famous for his performance of Hamlet. He was the brother of Ethel and Lionel Barrymore.

> "Audiences? No, the plural is impossible. Whether it be in Butte, Montana, or Broadway, it's an audience. The same great hulking monster with four thousand eyes and forty thousand teeth."
> [John Barrymore, *Letter to playwright Ashton Stevens*; April 1906]

Bar·ry·more, Lionel (1878–1954) US actor. The brother of Ethel and John Barrymore, he won an Academy Award for *Free Soul* (1931) and appeared in the original *Dr Kildare* films.

> "Half the people in Hollywood are dying to be discovered and the other half are afraid they will be."
> [Lionel Barrymore. Quoted in *Hollywood, Babble On*, Bose Hadleigh; 1994]

Bar·sac /baár sàk/ *n* a sweet white wine from western France [Early 18C. After a district in W France]

bar sin·is·ter (*plural* **bars sin·is·ter**) *n* **1.** HERALDRY same as **bend sinister 2.** evidence suggesting that somebody is of illegitimate birth

bar tack *n* a straight stitch that crosses a piece of cloth at a right angle to a slit, e.g., at the end of a buttonhole

bar·tend·er /baár tèndər/ *n* somebody who serves in a bar

bar·ter /baártər/ *v* (**-tered, -ter·ing, -ters**) **1.** *vti* **EXCHANGE GOODS OR SERVICES** to exchange goods or services in return for other goods or services **2.** *vi* **NEGOTIATE TERMS OF AGREEMENT** to negotiate or argue over the terms of a transaction ■ *n* **1. EXCHANGE OF GOODS OR SERVICES** the practice or system of exchanging goods and services **2. THINGS BARTERED** goods or services that are exchanged [15C. Probably < Old French *barater* (see BARRATRY)] —**bar·ter·er** *n*

Barth /baarth/, **John** (*b.* 1930) US writer. He is known for his experimentation in literary form in fictional works such as *Giles Goat-Boy* (1966) and *Tidewater Tales* (1987). Full name **Barth, John Simmons**

Barth /baart, baarth/, **Karl** (1886–1968) Swiss theologian. He was a leading theorist of Reformed theology. His numerous writings include *The Epistle to the Romans* (1919) and the monumental *Church Dogmatics* (1932–62).

> "Men have never been good, they are not good, they never will be good."
> [Karl Barth, *Time*; April 12, 1954]

Barthes /baart/, **Roland** (1915–80) French philosopher and writer. He was a leading proponent of structuralism and author of the seminal critical work *Writing Degree Zero* (1953). He formulated the literary theory that the "meaning" of a text lies not in its author's intentions but in its underlying structure. Full name **Barthes, Roland Gérard**

Bar·thol·di /baar thóldee, -táwldee/, **Frédéric-Auguste** (1834–1904) French sculptor. His best-known work is the *Statue of Liberty* (1886).

Bar·tho·lin's gland /baárt'linz-, -thəlinz-/ *n* a small gland found on each side of the lower vagina that secretes a lubricating mucus during sexual stimulation [Early 20C. After Kaspar *Bartholin* (1655–1738), Danish anatomist]

Bar·tho·lo·mew /baar thóllə myoò/, **St.** (*fl* 1st century A.D.) one of the 12 apostles of Jesus Christ. He is traditionally believed to have been martyred by being flayed alive.

bartizan

bar·ti·zan /baártizən, baártə zàn/ *n* a small turret that projects from a tower or wall of a fortress or castle, used as a lookout or a defensive position [Mid-16C. Scots variant of *bratticing* "timberwork" < BRATTICE] —**bar·ti·zaned** *adj*

Bar·tles·ville /baárt'lz vìl/ town in northeastern Oklahoma, on the Caney River, in an agricultural and oil-producing region. Population: 34,765 (2002 estimate).

Bart·lett[1] /baártlət/, **Bart·lett pear** *n* a variety of pear with juicy white flesh and yellow skin [Mid-19C. After Enoch *Bartlett* (1779–1860), US merchant]

Bart·lett[2] /baártlət/ town in southwestern Tennessee, a northeastern suburb of Memphis. Population: 41,869 (2002 estimate).

Bart·lett, John (1820–1905) US publisher and compiler. Best known for his *Bartlett's Familiar Quotations* (1855), for many years he owned the University Book Store at Harvard (1849–63).

Bart·lett, Josiah (1729–95) American politician. A physician and delegate to the Continental Congress, he signed the Declaration of Independence and was New Hampshire's first governor (1793–94).

Bar·tók /baár tòk, -tàwk/, **Béla** (1881–1945) Hungarian composer. Influenced by Hungarian folk music, he wrote piano concertos, string quartets, and the opera *Bluebeard's Castle* (1911).

Bar·ton /baárt'n/, **Clara** (1821–1912) US philanthropist. A battlefield humanitarian during the Civil War, she founded the American Red Cross and was its first president (1881–1904). Full name **Barton, Clarissa Harlowe**

> "It is wise statesmanship that suggests that in time of peace we must prepare for war, and it is no less a wise benevolence that makes preparation in the hour of peace for assuaging the ills that are sure to accompany war."
> [Clara Barton, *The Red Cross*; 1898]

Bar·tram /baártrəm/, **John** (1699–1777) American botanist. He collected plants native to North America, made plant maps, and experimented with hybrids.

Bar·uch /bə ròok/ *n* a book of the Roman Catholic Bible and the Protestant Apocrypha traditionally attributed to Baruch, a disciple of the prophet Jeremiah. See table at **Bible**

Bar·uch /bə ròok/, **Bernard** (1870–1965) US financier and economist. An adviser to US presidents from Wilson through Kennedy, he participated in the Paris Peace Conference (1919). Full name **Baruch, Bernard Mannes**

> "Let us not be deceived—we are today in the midst of a cold war."
> [Bernard Baruch, *Speech to the South Carolina legislature*; April 16, 1947]

bar·ware /baár wèr/ *n* glassware and other items used to prepare and serve drinks

bar·y·cen·ter /bárri sèntər/ *n* the center of the mass of a system, especially a system of astronomical objects [Late 19C. < Greek *barus* "heavy"] —**bar·y·cen·tric** /bàrri séntrik/ *adj*

bar·y·on /bárree òn/ *n* a subatomic particle belonging to a group that undergoes strong interactions, has a mass greater than or equal to that of the proton, and consists of three quarks [Mid-20C. < Greek *barus* "heavy" + -ON[1]] —**bar·y·on·ic** /bàrree ónnik/ *adj*

Popperfoto

Mikhail Baryshnikov

Ba·rysh·ni·kov /bə rishni kàwf/, **Mikhail** (*b.* 1948) Russian-born US dancer and choreographer. He defected from the Soviet Union (1974) and danced for and directed (1980–89) the American Ballet Theatre. Full name **Baryshnikov, Mikhail Nikolayevich**

ba·ry·ta /bə rítə/ *n* barium oxide or hydroxide [Early 19C. < BARYTES, after SODA] —**ba·ry·tic** /bə ríttik/ *adj*

ba·ry·tes /bə ríteez, bárrə téez/ *n UK* same as **barite** [Late 18C. < Greek *barutēs* "weight"]

Bar·zun /baárzən/, **Jacques** (*b.* 1907) French-born US historian and educator. A distinguished language and literary critic, he worked as a teacher and administrator at Columbia University (1928–75). Full name **Barzun, Jacques Martin**

> "That is the triumph of history—truth absolute is not at hand; the original with which to match the copy does not exist."
> [Jacques Barzun, *Clio and the Doctors*; 1974]

bas·al /báyss'l/ *adj* **1.** at or forming the bottom of something **2.** basic or fundamental —**bas·al·ly** *adv*

bas·al bod·y *n* a structure found near the base of cells that have projecting threads (**cilia**)

bas·al cell *n* a cell forming the deepest layer of the skin

bas·al cell car·ci·no·ma *n* a slow-growing malignant tumor that typically affects the facial skin of senior citizens. It rarely spreads to other parts, and is generally curable by surgery or radiotherapy.

bas·al gan·gli·on *n* a mass of gray matter that lies in the white matter near the base of each cerebral hemisphere of the brain. The basal ganglia help to regulate the body's voluntary movements.

bas·al met·a·bol·ic rate *n* the rate at which an organism consumes oxygen while awake but at rest, measured in calories per square meter of body surface per hour

bas·al me·tab·o·lism *n* the amount of energy consumed by a resting organism simply in maintaining its basic functions

ba·salt /bə sáwlt, báy sàwlt/ *n* **1.** a hard, black, often glassy, volcanic rock. It was produced by the partial melting of the Earth's mantle. **2.** a hard black unglazed pottery [Early 17C. Via Latin *basaltes*, variant of *basanites* < Greek *basanitēs* "very hard stone, touchstone" < Egyptian *bakhan* "slate"] —**ba·sal·tic** /bə sáwltik/ *adj*

ba·salt plat·eau *n* an extensive continental deposit of basaltic volcanic rock

ba·salt·ware /bə sáwlt wèr, báy sawlt-/ *n* a hard black stoneware pottery made in England and parts of continental Europe in the 18th century

ba·san·ite /bássə nīt/ *n* a volcanic basaltic rock containing olivine and additional alkaline minerals [Mid-18C. < Latin *basanites* (see BASALT)]

bas·cule /báskyool/ *n* **1.** a counterbalanced device that pivots on a central axis so that the unweighted end rises as the weighted end is allowed to fall **2.** *also* **bas·cule bridge** a bridge with a roadway that can be raised to allow tall boats and ships to pass through [Late 17C. < French, "seesaw" < *battre* "to batter" + *cul* "buttocks"]

base[1] /bayss/ *n* **1.** LOWEST PART the lowest, bottom, or supporting part or layer of something **2.** MAIN SUPPORTING ELEMENT the main source of an important component in an economy or sphere of influence ○ *improve our customer base* **3.** FUNDAMENTAL PRINCIPLE the main principle or starting point of a system or theory **4.** CENTER FROM WHICH ACTIVITIES START a center from which activities start or are coordinated **5.** ARMED FORCES INSTALLATION a fort, reservation, proving ground, port, air base, or other facility owned and used by the armed forces **6.** MAIN INGREDIENT a main ingredient to which others are added **7.** BASEBALL FIELD MARKER one of the four corners of the diamond-shaped infield that a batter must touch in order to score a run **8.** ARCHIT LOWER PART OF BUILT STRUCTURE the lower part of a built structure such as a wall, pillar, or column **9.** ANAT ATTACHMENT AREA OF BODY ORGAN the part of an organ or body part by which it is attached to a more central structure of an organism **10.** HERALDRY LOWER PART OF HERALDIC SHIELD the lower part of a heraldic shield **11.** MATH REFERENCE NUMBER the number that is the basis for a system of calculation, represented by the total countable digits in the system. The base 10 system contains the ten digits 0–9. **12.** MATH LOGARITHM REFERENCE a number raised to a power denoted by a superscript. In the equation $10^2 = 100$, 10 is the base. Natural logarithms have a base e (= 2.718). **13.** MATH LOWER SIDE OF FIGURE the lower side or face of a geometric figure **14.** MEASURE same as **baseline** (sense 1) **15.** SOLVENT a medium in which ingredients or constituents may be dissolved or carried **16.** FIN LOWEST STOCK PRICE the lowest recorded price level of a tradable commodity or security **17.** CHEM CHEMICAL COMPOUND a compound that releases hydroxyl ions to form a solution with a pH greater than 7, reacts with acids to form salts, and turns red litmus paper blue **18.** CHEM CHEMICAL COMPOUND FORMING COVALENT BOND a compound that can accept a proton or donate a pair of electrons to form a covalent bond with an acid **19.** PHOTOGRAPHY FILM FOUNDATION an inert medium supporting the photographic emulsion of films **20.** ELEC ENG MIDDLE REGION OF TRANSISTOR the middle region of a transistor between the emitter and the collector ■ *vt* (**based, bas·ing, bas·es**) **1.** MAKE BASE FOR SOMETHING to create or provide a base for something ○ *Top management decided to base the new subsidiary in San Antonio.* **2.** ASSIGN SOMEBODY TO BASE to station, post, or assign somebody to a base ○ *Troops have been based in Munich since the end of Word War II.* **3.** USE SOMETHING AS BASIS to use something as a base or basis for something else ○ *His report is based on the research he carried out in Peru.* [14C. Directly or via French < Latin *basis* < Greek *basis* (see BASIS)] ◇ **have all bases covered** to have made preparations to insure that every eventuality is provided for ◇ **off base** wrong or inexact (*informal*) ○ *Your calculations are all off base.* ◇ **touch base (with somebody)** to communicate briefly with somebody, e.g., to move a project forward or exchange current information

USAGE ***base*** or ***bass***? Do not confuse ***base*** and ***bass***, which sound similar. Both words refer to something low, but ***bass*** is used only of sound, as in *a bass voice* or *a bass guitar.* ***Base*** has a much wider range of meanings and uses, as in *the base of the statue, a base unit, base metals, tried to curb his base instincts*, etc.

base[2] /bayss/ (**bas·er, bas·est**) *adj* **1.** LACKING MORALS lacking proper social values or moral principles **2.** OF POOR QUALITY inferior in value or quality **3.** COUNTERFEIT describes a coin that contains a higher proportion of common inexpensive metals than usual **4.** OFFENSIVE TERM an offensive term meaning of humble or illegitimate birth (*archaic*) **5.** HIST RELATING TO PEASANT relating to a peasant (**villein**) renting land from a feudal lord (*archaic*) [14C. Via French *bas* < medieval Latin *bassus* "short, low"] —**base·ly** *adv* —**base·ness** *n*

USAGE See ***base***[1].

SYNONYMS See ***mean***[2].

base·ball /báyss bàwl/ *n* **1.** a game played with a bat and ball by two teams of nine players on a field with four bases marking the course the batters must take to score runs. Each team fields and bats alternately, and the goal is to score the most runs. **2.** a hard leather-covered ball about 9 in./23 cm in circumference, used in the game of baseball

Popperfoto

baseball: a batter swings at the ball

base·ball cap *n* a close-fitting cap with a visor, originally worn by baseball players

base·board /báyss bàwrd/ *n* **1.** a board that serves as the base of something **2.** a narrow board, attached to the base of an interior wall, that covers the joint between the wall and the floor

base·born /báyss bàwrn/ *adj* (*archaic*) **1.** OFFENSIVE TERM an offensive term meaning born of poor parents or of parents regarded as having been disgraced **2.** OFFENSIVE TERM an offensive term meaning born of unmarried parents **3.** CONSIDERED AS IGNOBLE regarded as dishonorable or unworthy

base burn·er *n* a stove into which fuel is fed automatically from a hopper as needed

base camp *n* a place used as a temporary store for supplies and from which an activity, especially a mountaineering expedition, starts

base cur·ren·cy *n* a currency in which a business maintains its accounts and that it uses for buying and selling

Bas·e·dow's dis·ease /bázzədōz-/ *n* MED same as **Graves' disease** [Late 19C. After Karl Adolph von *Basedow* (1799–1854), German physician]

Base Ex·change a service mark for stores on US Air Force and US Navy bases that sell merchandise to military personnel, their dependents, and authorized civilians

base hit *n* in baseball, a hit that enables the batter to reach a base safely without causing an error, a force play, or a fielder's choice

base house *n* a place where people go to smoke (**freebase**) illegal drugs (*slang*)

base jump·ing *n* the extreme sport of parachuting from the tops of very tall natural objects or constructions such as cliffs, towers, or buildings [Acronym < *building, antenna tower, span, earth*, because jumpers use high buildings, bridges, and cliffs] —**base-jump** *vi*

Ba·sel /baáz'l/, **Bas·le** /baal/ city in northwestern Switzerland, situated on the highest navigation point of the Rhine. Population: 168,735 (1998).

base·less /báyssləss/ *adj* **1.** without grounds or a factual basis **2.** lacking a base or foundation

base lev·el *n* the lowest level to which moving water can erode a land surface such as the bed of a stream, lake, or sea

base·line /báyss līn/ *n* **1.** MEASURE MEASURING LINE a line used as a basis for measurement, calculation, or location, e.g., in surveying or navigation **2.** STANDARD OF VALUE a standard of value to which other similar things are compared **3.** REFERENCE DATA the data used as a reference with which to compare future observations or results **4.** BOUNDARY LINE AT END OF COURT a boundary line at each end of a court that marks the limit of play in tennis, badminton, or basketball **5.** BASEBALL LINE BETWEEN BASES on a baseball field, a line running from home plate to first base and from home plate to third base, and extending into the outfield as foul lines **6.** BASEBALL RUNNER'S REFERENCE LINE in baseball, the area within which a base runner must stay when running between bases

base·lin·er /báyss līnər/ *n* a tennis player who prefers to play on or near the baseline and only occasionally moves to the net

base load *n* the average demand placed on an electrical power supply system

base·man /báyssmən/ (*plural* **-men** /-mən/) *n* in baseball, a fielder positioned near first, second, or third base

base·ment /báyssmənt/ *n* **1.** ARCHIT **UNDERGROUND STORY OF BUILDING** a story of a building that is wholly or partly below ground level **2.** BUILDINGS **LOWEST PART OF WALL OR BUILDING** the foundation, substructure, or lowest part of a wall or building **3.** GEOL **PART OF EARTH'S CRUST** the highly folded igneous or metamorphic layer of rocks that lies beneath more recent, softer sedimentary rocks **4.** *New England* **TOILET OR WASHROOM** a toilet or washroom, especially in a school [Mid-18C. Probably via Dutch < Italian *basamento* "base of a column" < *basare* "to base"]

base met·al *n* a common inexpensive metal

ba·sen·ji /bə sénjee/ *n* a small dog belonging to a curly-tailed African breed that rarely barks and has a short smooth coat varying from black to chestnut [Mid-20C. < Bantu]

base on balls *n* in baseball, an advance to first base awarded to a batter who receives four pitches outside the strike zone at which the batter does not swing

base pair *n* a chemical unit linking complementary strands of DNA or RNA. It consists of a purine linked to a pyrimidine by hydrogen bonds.

base pair·ing *n* the hydrogen bonding between complementary bases that holds together the two strands of the double helix of DNA and RNA

base path *n* BASEBALL same as **baseline** (sense 6)

base pay *n* the pay for a job or position excluding additional payments or allowances

base·per·son /báyss pùrss'n/ (*plural* **-per·sons** or **-peo·ple** /-peèp'l/) *n* in baseball, a fielder positioned near first, second, or third base

base rate *n* **1.** the rate of pay set for a unit of work before anything extra is added **2.** *UK* same as **bank rate**

base run·ner *n* in baseball, a player on the team at bat who is on a base or is trying to get to one safely

ba·ses plural of **basis**

base u·nit *n* a fundamental unit within a system of measurement from which other units in the system are derived

base·wom·an /báyss wo͝omman/ (*plural* **-wom·en** /-wìmmin/) *n* in baseball, a woman who is a fielder positioned near first, second, or third base

bash /bash/ (*informal*) *v* (**bashed, bash·ing, bash·es**) **1.** *vt* **STRIKE SOMEBODY OR SOMETHING HEAVILY** to strike somebody or something with a heavy blow **2.** *vt* **SMASH SOMETHING** to smash or strike something violently or damagingly **3.** *vt* **DENT SOMETHING** to make a dent in something **4.** *vi* **COLLIDE WITH SOMETHING** to crash into or collide with something **5.** *vt* **CRITICIZE SOMEBODY OR SOMETHING HARSHLY** to criticize somebody or something harshly and usually publicly ■ *n* **1. CELEBRATION** a party or celebration **2. HEAVY BLOW** a heavy blow dealt to somebody or something **3. DENT** a dent made in something [Mid-17C. Probably an imitation of the sound of hitting]

bash·ful /báshfəl/ *adj* behaving in a shy, self-conscious, or modest way [15C. < shortened form of ABASH] —**bash·ful·ly** *adv* —**bash·ful·ness** *n*

bash·ing /báshing/ *n* (*slang; usually used in combination*) **1. PHYSICAL ASSAULT** mugging or violence, especially when directed at a particular group of people **2. CRITICISM** hostile comment directed at a specific person or group **3.** *UK* **EXCESSIVE USE** the exposure of something to repetitive or prolonged use

Ba·shir /bə sheér/, **Omar Hassan al-** (*b.* 1944?) president of Sudan (1989–). He came to power in a military coup and was elected president (1993) and twice reelected (1996 and 2000) by the Revolutionary Command Council. He presides over a government dominated by members of the National Islamic Front.

Bash·kor·to·stan /baash kàwrtə stán/ autonomous republic in central Russia, west of the Ural Mountains, bordering the republic of Tatarstan to the Northwest and the republic of Udmurtia to the North. Capital: Ufa. Population: 4,134,000 (1997). Area: 55,440 sq. mi./143,600 sq. km. Former name **Bashkiria** (until 1992)

bash·o /baáshō, baa shṓ/ (*plural* **-os**) *n* a sumo wrestling tournament [Late 20C. < Japanese]

Ba·sho /baáshō/, **Ba·shō** (1644–94) Japanese poet, considered an expert in the haiku form. His work was strongly influenced by Zen Buddhism. Pseudonym of **Matsuo Munefusa**

basi- *prefix* same as **baso-**

ba·sic /báyssik/ *adj* **1. MOST IMPORTANT** most important or essential ○ *a few basic guidelines* **2. ELEMENTARY** serving as a starting point or minimum **3. WITHOUT EXTRA** without or before the addition of anything extra ○ *a basic salary* **4. PLAIN** plain and utilitarian rather than luxurious or fancy (*informal*) **5.** CHEM **RELATING TO CHEMICAL BASE** containing, relating to, or being a chemical base **6.** CHEM **ALKALINE** having an alkaline reaction **7.** CHEM **CONTAINING HYDROXIDE OR OXIDE GROUPS** describes a salt that contains hydroxide or oxide anions **8.** GEOL **LOW IN SILICA** describes rock that contains 45–53 percent total silica by weight, e.g., basalt **9.** METALL **USING BASE IN MAKING STEEL** describes a process of making steel in which the furnace is lined with a base that combines with acidic impurities in the ore to produce basic slag ■ *n* MIL same as **basic training** ■ **ba·sics** *npl* **MOST IMPORTANT THINGS** the most important or fundamental parts of something —**ba·sic·i·ty** /bay sísstee/ *n* ◇ **go** *or* **get back to basics** to return to the fundamental parts or principles of something, especially when problems are encountered at a more advanced or complex stage ○ *a movement to get back to basics in education*

BA·SIC /báyssik/, **Ba·sic** *n* a high-level computer programming language that uses common English terms and algebra. Full form **Beginners All-purpose Symbolic Instruction Code**

ba·si·cal·ly /báysikəlee/ *adv* **1.** ⚠ used to emphasize the most important aspect of something, or to give a simplified account of something more complicated ○ *Basically, I'm not interested.* **2.** in a simple way, using only essentials

USAGE Basically as a sentence adverb: This use, in which ***basically*** is reduced to adding emphasis (*Basically it's a waste of time*), is common in informal conversation but should be avoided otherwise. So too should the meaning "essentially," as in *His role is basically to supervise operations.*

ba·sic ed·u·ca·tion *n* the formal education deemed necessary for somebody to function properly in society

Ba·sic Eng·lish *n* a simplified form of English intended as an introductory version of the language for nonnative speakers and for use as an auxiliary international language. It consists of a vocabulary of 850 words for general needs, plus additional international and scientific words.

ba·sic in·put-out·put sys·tem *n* COMPUT full form of **BIOS**

~~**basicly**~~ incorrect spelling of **basically**

ba·sic rate *n* the standard cost or rate of pay excluding any discounts or additions

ba·sic slag *n* the phosphate-rich slag from making steel using a basic process. Use: fertilizer.

ba·sic train·ing *n* the initial training of a military recruit

ba·sid·i·o·my·cete /bə sìddee ō mī́ seèt, -mī seét/ *n* FUNGI former name for **basidiomycote** [Late 19C. < modern Latin *Basidiomycetes* < *basidium* (see BASIDIUM) + Greek *mukētes* "fungi"] —**ba·sid·i·o·my·ce·tous** /-mī seétəss/ *adj*

ba·sid·i·o·my·cote /bə sìddee ō mī́ kōt/ *n* a fungus that produces its spores in a characteristic club-shaped cell (**basidium**). Mushrooms, puffballs, rusts, bracket fungi, and smuts are basidiomycotes. Division: *Basidiomycota.* —**ba·sid·i·o·my·cote** *adj*

ba·sid·i·o·spore /bə síddee ə spàwr/ *n* a spore produced by a basidiomycote fungus such as a mushroom, puffball, smut, or rust —**ba·sid·i·o·spo·rous** /bə sìddee ə spáwrəss/ *adj*

ba·sid·i·um /bə síddee əm/ (*plural* **-i·a** /-ee ə/) *n* a club-shaped cell found in some fungi from which external sexual spores are produced [Mid-19C. < modern Latin, "small base" < Greek *basis* "step, base"] —**ba·sid·i·al** *adj*

Ba·sie /báyssee/, **Count** (1904–84) US composer and bandleader. He was one of the most enduring popular American musicians as the leader of his own big-band swing ensembles for over four decades, and composed numbers including "One O'Clock Jump." Born **Basie, William**

> "I don't think that a band can really swing on just a kick-off, you know; I think you've got to set the tempo first. If you can do it the other way, that's something else...Anyway we do it our way."
> [Count Basie. Quoted in *Count Basie*, Alun Morgan; 1984]

ba·si·fy /báyssi fī/ (**-fied, -fy·ing, -fies**) *vt* **1.** to change a chemical into a base **2.** to make something alkaline —**ba·si·fi·ca·tion** /bàyssəfi káysh'n/ *n*

bas·il /báyz'l, bázz'l/ *n* an herb with aromatic leaves. Use: seasoning. Latin name: *Ocimum basilicum.* [15C. Via Old French *basile* < Latin *basilicum* < Greek *basilikon (phuton)* "royal (herb)"]

Bas·il /bázz'l, báy-/, **St.** (329?–379) Greek prelate and scholar. He studied at Byzantium and Athens, became Bishop of Caesarea (370), and defended Christian philosophy against heresies such as Arianism. Known as **Basil the Great**

bas·i·lar /bássələr/ *adj* relating to or situated at the base of a body part such as the skull [Mid-16C. < modern Latin *basilaris* < Latin *basis* (see BASIS)]

Bas·il·don /bázz'ldən/ city in Essex, southeastern England. Population: 165,661 (2001).

ba·sil·i·ca /bə síllikə, -zíllikə/ *n* **1. PRIVILEGED ROMAN CATHOLIC CHURCH** a Roman Catholic church or cathedral given ceremonial privileges by the Pope **2. ANCIENT ROMAN BUILDING** in ancient Rome, a building with a central nave, a columned aisle on each side, and typically a terminal semicircular apse. It was used as a court of justice, an assembly hall, or an exchange. **3. LARGE CHRISTIAN CHURCH** a Christian church building formed from a Roman basilica or built to a similar design [Mid-16C. Via Latin, "royal palace" < Greek *basilikē* < *basilikos* "royal" < *basileus* "king"] —**ba·sil·i·can** *adj*

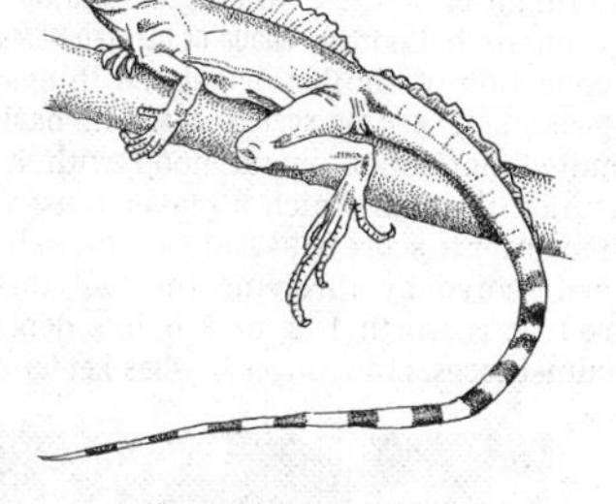

basilisk (sense 2)

bas·i·lisk /bássəlisk, bázz-/ *n* **1.** a legendary reptile, said to have been hatched by a serpent from a rooster's egg, whose look or breath was supposed to be fatal **2.** a lizard, related to the iguana, that is able to run upright on its long hind legs. Native to: Central and South America. Genus: *Basiliscus.* [14C. Via Latin < Greek *basiliskos* "minor king, kind of serpent" < *basileus* "king"]

ba·sin /báyss'n/ *n* **1.** GEOG **LAND DRAINING INTO RIVER OR LAKE** a broad area of land drained by a single river and its tributaries, or draining into a lake **2. DOCK NEAR SEA** a dock built in a harbor or river that opens to the sea **3.** GEOG **DEPRESSION IN LAND FILLED WITH WATER** a depression in the Earth's surface that contains water **4. OPEN CONTAINER FOR WASHING** an open metal, ceramic, or plastic container with sloping sides, typically used for holding water or washing **5. BASIN CONTENTS** the contents of or amount contained in a basin **6.** GEOL **BOWL-SHAPED DEPRESSION** a bowl-shaped depression on land or on the ocean floor into which sediments may be deposited **7.** GEOL **CIRCULAR FORMATION OF SLOPING ROCK STRATA** a large circular outcrop of rock in which strata dip inward toward the center [13C.

Via Old French < medieval Latin *ba(s)cinus* < *bacca* "water container"] —**bas·in·ful** *n*

bas·i·net /bássə nét, bássə nèt/ *n* a lightweight steel helmet, sometimes with a visor, worn in medieval times [14C. < Old French *bacinet* "little basin," from its shape]

Ba·sing·stoke /báyzing stōk/ town in Hampshire, southern England. Population: 77,837 (1991).

ba·sip·e·tal /bay síppit'l/ *adj* developing from the top of a stem toward the base so that the oldest leaves or flowers are at the top —**ba·sip·e·tal·ly** *adv*

ba·sis /báyssiss/ (*plural* **ba·ses** /báy seez/) *n* **1. FOUNDATION** something that acts as a support or foundation, especially of an idea or argument ○ *Are you sure there is no basis to this rumor?* **2. STARTING POINT** the point from which something starts or is developed ○ *find the basis on which to begin negotiations* **3. WAY OF PROCEEDING** the basic method or system according to which something is done or organized ○ *work on a part-time basis* **4. MAIN COMPONENT** the main component or ingredient of something **5.** MATH **SET OF VECTORS** in a vector space, the minimal set of vectors necessary to define all other vectors in the space [Late 16C. Via Latin < Greek, "step, base" < *bainen* "go"]

USAGE ***Basis*** does a number of jobs that other words can do better or that need not be done at all. Expressions such as *on a continuing basis, on a daily basis,* and *on a regular basis* are sometimes only wordier ways of saying *continually, daily,* and *regularly.* By the same token, *providing expert resources on a global basis* means providing them everywhere. Careful writers should avoid the unnecessary use of ***basis***.

ba·sis point *n* one hundredth of one percent, used to express interest rates and bond yields

bask /bask/ (**basked, bask·ing, basks**) *vi* **1.** to lie in or expose yourself to enjoyable warmth, especially from the sun **2.** to derive great satisfaction or pleasure from something [14C. Probably < Old Norse *bathask* "bathe yourself" < Germanic]

Bas·ker·ville /báskər vìl/ *n* a typeface characterized by serifs [Early 19C. After John *Baskerville* (1706–79), British type founder and printer]

bas·ket /báskət/ *n* **1. WOVEN CONTAINER** a container made of woven strips of material, often with a handle or handles **2. BASKET CONTENTS** the contents of or amount contained in a basket **3. CONTAINER** a container resembling a basket, e.g., the open gondola attached to a hot-air balloon **4. GROUP OF RELATED ITEMS** a group or collection of similar or related things or ideas **5.** BASKETBALL **NET FOR SCORING GOALS** in basketball, a mounted horizontal metal hoop with a hanging open net, through which a player must throw the ball in order to score **6.** BASKETBALL **GOAL** in basketball, a goal scored by throwing the ball through the basket. It is worth 1, 2, or 3 points depending on circumstances. [14C. Origin ?] —**bas·ket·ful** *n*

basketball: two players attempt to block a pass

bas·ket·ball /báskət bàwl/ *n* **1.** a game played by two teams of five players, who score points by throwing a ball through a basket mounted at the opponent's end of a rectangular court **2.** a ball of the type used in the game of basketball

bas·ket case *n* **1.** an offensive term for somebody who is affected by severe nervous strain (*insult*) **2.** a nation or organization with serious financial problems (*informal*) ○ *transformed from an economic basket case into a prosperous state*

bas·ket chair *n* a deep chair made of wicker or cane

bas·ket hilt *n* a sword hilt with a guard made of interwoven strips —**bas·ket-hilt·ed** *adj*

Bas·ket Mak·er *n* a member of an ancient Native North American culture of southwestern North America, preceding the Pueblo periods. The culture is noted for skill in basketry and for farming with little water.

bas·ket of cur·ren·cies *n* a group of currencies of which the average value is used as a basis for comparison with another currency

bas·ket-of-gold *n US* a European perennial plant with oval hairy gray-green leaves. Flowers: bright yellow. Latin name: *Aurinia saxatilis.* Can term **alyssum**

bas·ket·ry /báskətree/ *n* **1.** the art or craft of making baskets **2.** baskets collectively

bas·ket star *n* an invertebrate ocean animal that has thin branching interlaced arms and is related to the starfish. Genus: *Gorgonocephalus.*

bas·ket weave *n* a textile weave like the checkered pattern of a woven basket

bas·ket·work /báskət wùrk/ *n* HANDICRAFT same as **basketry**

bask·ing shark *n* a large plankton-eating shark measuring up to 43 ft./13 m that often floats on the surface of the sea. Native to: temperate waters. Genus: *Cetorhinus.*

Basle ♦ **Basel**

bas·ma·ti /ba smaátee, baa-/ *n* a long-grained aromatic rice [Mid-19C. < Hindi *bāsmatī* "fragrant"]

bas mitz·vah *n* JUDAISM same as **bat mitzvah**

baso-, basi- *prefix* **1.** bottom, base ○ *basipetal* **2.** chemical base ○ *basophil* [< Latin *basis* (see BASIS)]

ba·so·phil /báyssə fil, -zə-/ *n* a white blood cell with granules that are readily stained by basic dyes, occurring in some blood diseases

ba·so·phil·i·a /bàyssə fíllee ə, bàzzə \fíllee ə/ *n* **1.** the property of some microorganisms and white blood cells of being readily stained with basic dyes **2.** an increase in the blood of the type of cells that stain with basic dyes, occurring in some blood diseases

ba·so·phil·ic /bàyssə fíllik, bàzzə-/, **ba·soph·i·lous** /bə sóffələss/ *adj* describes cells or cell components that are readily stained by basic dyes

Ba·sot·ho /bə sṓtō, -sóotoo/ *npl* a Sotho people who live in Lesotho in southern Africa [Mid-19C. < Sesotho]

basque /bask/ *n* **1.** a woman's tight-fitting corset that covers the area from the breasts to the top of the thighs **2.** a part of the bodice of a woman's jacket that extends below the waist [Mid-19C. Origin ?]

Basque /bask/ *n* **1.** a member of a people of unknown origin living in the western Pyrenees, in northwestern Spain and southwestern France **2.** the language spoken by the Basques, having no known relationship with another language. Native speakers: 700,000. [Early 19C. Via French < Latin *Vasco*] —**Basque** *adj*

Basque Coun·try /básk-/ autonomous region of northern Spain, consisting of the provinces of Álava, Guipúzcoa, and Vizcaya. The regional capital is Vitoria. Population: 2,082,587 (2001). Area: 2,793 sq. mi./7,234 sq. km. Basque name **Euskadi**. Spanish name **País Vasco**

Bas·ra /baázrə/ city and port in southeastern Iraq, at the northern end of the Shatt al Arab waterway. Population: 406,296 (1987).

bas-re·lief /baá-/ *n* **1.** sculpture in which the design projects slightly from a flat background, but without any part being totally detached from the background **2.** an example or piece of bas-relief sculpture [Early 17C. < BASSO-RELIEVO, altered after French]

bass[1] /bayss/ *n* **1. LOWEST SINGING VOICE** a singing voice of the lowest range, or somebody with that voice **2. LOWEST PITCHES** the lower half of all the pitches produced by a voice or a musical instrument **3. LOWEST MUSICAL PART** the lowest part in instrumental or vocal part music **4. LOWEST INSTRUMENT IN FAMILY** the instrument with the lowest range in a family of musical instruments **5. LOW FREQUENCY IN AUDIO REPRODUCTION** the low-frequency sound output from an electric amplifier **6. BASS CONTROL** a knob on a piece of audio equipment that controls low-frequency sound output ■ *adj* **1. DEEP IN TONE** deep or grave in tone **2. LOW IN PITCH** low in pitch **3. OF BASS** relating to a bass [15C. Via French *bas* < medieval Latin *bassus,* influenced by Italian *basso* (see BASSO)]

USAGE See ***base***[1].

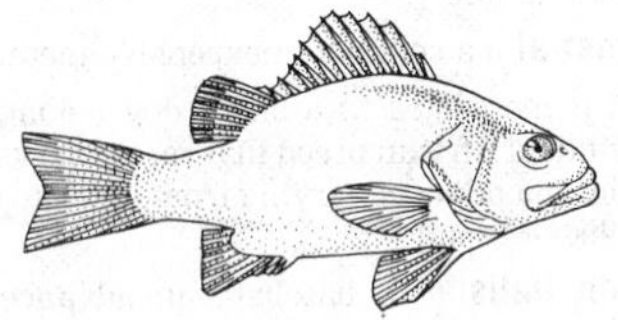

bass

bass[2] /bass/ (*plural same* or **bass·es**) *n* **1.** a spiny-finned fish found in rivers, lakes, and seas that is caught for food. Families: Centrarchidae or Percichthyidae or Serranidae. **2.** bass as food [15C. Alteration of Old English *bærs, bears* < Germanic]

bass[3] /bass/ *n* **1.** TEXTILES same as **bast fiber** **2.** TREES same as **basswood** (sense 1) [Late 17C. Alteration of BAST]

Bass /bass/, **Sam** (1851–78) US outlaw. He robbed trains and stagecoaches with organized gangs, and was shot dead in Texas (1878).

bass-bar·i·tone /bàyss-/ *n* a singing voice between baritone and bass, or somebody with that voice

bass clef /bàyss-/ *n* **1.** a symbol on a musical staff indicating that a note on the fourth line from the bottom represents the F a fifth below middle C **2.** the musical staff on which the bass part of a composition is written. It is identified by a bass clef symbol.

bass drum /bàyss-/ *n* a large drum that has a cylindrical body, two drumheads, and a low indefinite pitch

Bas·sein /bə sáyn/ city in southern Myanmar, about 85 mi./137 km west of the capital, Yangon (Rangoon). Population: 144,096 (1983).

Basse·terre /bass tér, baass-/ capital of St. Kitts and Nevis, in the Leeward Islands. It is situated on the southwestern coast of St. Kitts island. Population: 12,220 (1994).

bas·set horn /bássət-/ *n* an alto clarinet in F, used in classical music [Mid-19C. < German, translating French *cor de basset* < Italian *corno di bassetto,* literally "cello-horn"]

bas·set hound *n* a dog with short legs, long ears, and a shorthaired, white, black, and tan coat, belonging to a breed originally developed for hunting [Early 17C. < French < *bas* "low," from its short legs]

bass gui·tar /bàyss-/ *n* a four-string guitar, usually electric, that has the same pitch and tuning as a double bass

bas·si·net /bàssə nét, bássə nèt/ *n* a baby's bed in the shape of a basket, commonly made of wood or wicker [Mid-19C. < French, "little basin"]

bass·ist /báyssist/ *n* somebody who plays a bass guitar or a double bass

bas·so /bássō, baássō/ (*plural* **-sos** or **-si** /-see/) *n* a bass singer, especially of opera [Early 18C. Via Italian < medieval Latin *bassus* "low"]

bas·so con·tin·u·o /bàssō kən tínnyoo ō, baássō-/ *n* MUSIC same as **continuo**

bas·soon /bə sóon, ba-/ *n* a low-pitched double-reed instrument of the oboe family. Its wooden body is a long U-shaped tube, attached to the mouthpiece by means of a thin metal pipe. [Early 18C. Via French < Italian *bassone* "large bass" < *basso* (see BASSO)] —**bas·soon·ist** *n*

bas·so pro·fun·do /-prə fúndō, -prō fo͞on-/ (*plural* **bas·so pro·fun·dos**) *n* a bass singer with an exceptionally low range [Mid-19C. < Italian, "deep bass"]

bas·so-re·lie·vo /-ri le͞evō/, **bas·so-ri·lie·vo** /-ril yáy vō/ *n* SCULPTURE same as **bas-relief** (sense 1) [Mid-17C. < Italian *basso-rilievo* "low relief"]

Bass Strait /báss-/ area of ocean situated between mainland Australia and Tasmania. It is approximately 140 mi./225 km wide.

bass vi·ol /bàyss-/ *n* MUSIC **1.** same as **viola da gamba 2.** same as **double bass**

bass·wood /báss wo͝od/ *n* **1.** the soft light-colored wood of a linden tree. Use: boxes, carving. **2.** a linden tree, often grown as a shade tree, that yields basswood. Native to: North America. Latin name: *Tilia americana*. [< BASS[3]]

bast /bast/ *n* **1.** BOT same as **phloem 2.** *Can, UK* same as **bast fiber** [Old English *bæst*, origin ?]

bas·tard /bástərd/ *n* **1.** OFFENSIVE TERM an offensive term for somebody regarded as obnoxious and disagreeable (*slang insult*) **2.** OFFENSIVE TERM an offensive term for somebody born to unmarried parents (*archaic or offensive*) **3.** OFFENSIVE TERM an offensive term for something that is extremely difficult, trying, or unpleasant (*slang*) **4.** INFERIOR THING something that is inferior, debased, or of questionable or mixed origin (*sometimes considered offensive*) ■ *adj* **1.** OFFENSIVE TERM an offensive term meaning born to unmarried parents (*archaic; sometimes considered offensive*) **2.** NOT GENUINE not the real thing ○ *bastard quartz* **3.** MIXED of mixed origin or in a mixture of styles **4.** UNUSUAL unusual or irregular in shape, size, or appearance (*sometimes considered offensive*) **5.** ZOOL, BOT SIMILAR AND USUALLY INFERIOR describes plants and animals that are similar but not identical to, and usually slightly inferior to, a particular kind or species ○ *bastard trout* ○ *bastard pine* [14C. Via Old French *bastart* < medieval Latin *bastardus*, probably < *bastum* "pack saddle," the idea probably being of a child produced from a relationship with a traveler] —**bas·tard·ly** *adj*

bas·tard·ize /bástər dīz/ (**-ized, -iz·ing, -iz·es**) *vt* **1.** to lower the value or quality of something by combining it with something else **2.** to prove or declare somebody to be illegitimate (*archaic*) —**bas·tard·i·za·tion** /bàstərdi záysh'n/ *n*

bas·tard ti·tle *n* PUBL same as **half title**

bas·tard wing *n* BIRDS same as **alula**

bas·tard·y /bástərdee/ *n* the state of being a child with unmarried parents (*archaic; sometimes considered offensive*)

baste[1] /bayst/ (**bast·ed, bast·ing, bastes**) *vt* to moisten meat or fish at intervals during cooking with a liquid such as melted fat or cooking juices [15C. Origin ?]

baste[2] /bayst/ (**bast·ed, bast·ing, bastes**) *vt* to sew fabric with long loose stitches in order to hold pieces of material together temporarily [14C. Via Old French *bastir* < Germanic, "join together with bast"]

baste[3] /bayst/ (**bast·ed, bast·ing, bastes**) *vt* **1.** to beat somebody severely (*dated informal*) **2.** to scold somebody vigorously [Mid-16C. Origin ?]

bast·er /báystər/ *n* a cooking utensil, consisting of a long tube with a rubber bulb attached at one end, with which to draw up cooking juices from the pot and release them over the food [Early 16C. < BASTE[1]]

bast fi·ber *n US* a strong woody fibrous material obtained chiefly from the phloem of plants such as flax, hemp, and jute. Use: ropes, mats, textiles. Can term **bast**

Bas·tia /bástyə/ city and capital of Haute-Corse Department on the northeastern coast of the French island of Corsica. Population: 37,884 (1999).

bas·tille /ba ste͞el/ *n* a fortress or fortified tower [14C. < French, alteration of *bastide* < Provençal *bastir* "build"]

Bas·tille /ba ste͞el/ *n* a prison in Paris that was stormed and destroyed by a mob on July 14, 1789 at the beginning of the French Revolution

Bas·tille Day *n* a French national holiday marking the storming of the Bastille in 1789 at the start of the French Revolution. Date: July 14.

bas·ti·na·do /bàsti náydō, -naá-/ *n* (*plural* **-does**) **1.** PUNISHMENT BY BEATING FEET a punishment or torture in which the soles of the victim's feet are beaten with a stick **2.** THRASHING a beating or a blow with a club **3.** CLUB a stick or club ■ *vt* (**-doed, -do·ing, -does**) BEAT WITH STICK to beat somebody with a stick, especially on the soles of the feet [Late 16C. < Spanish *bastonada* < *bastón* "cudgel"]

bast·ing /báysting/ *n* loose or temporary stitches, often used to align seams in preparation for final sewing

bas·tion /báschən, bástee ən/ *n* **1.** STRONG SUPPORTER somebody or something regarded as providing strong defense or support, especially for a belief or cause, or a place where there are such people ○ *The northeastern part of the state is a liberal bastion.* **2.** FORTIFICATION a fortified place **3.** PROJECTING PART a projecting part of a wall, rampart, or other fortification [Mid-16C. Via French < Italian *bastione* < *bastire* "build"]

bast·naes·ite /bástnə sīt/, **bast·na·site** *n* a rare yellow to reddish brown mineral containing lanthanum and cerium. Use: source of rare-earth elements. [Late 19C. After *Bastnäs* in Sweden]

bat[1] /bat/ *n* **1.** CLUB USED IN SPORTS in sports such as baseball and cricket, a club used to strike the ball, usually wooden but sometimes made of metal or plastic **2.** HEAVY STICK OR CLUB a heavy stick or wooden club **3.** BLOW FROM STICK a blow from a heavy stick or club ■ *v* (**bat·ted, bat·ting, bats**) **1.** *vt* STRIKE WITH BAT to strike somebody or something with a bat **2.** *vi* SPORTS HAVE TURN AT BATTING in sports such as baseball and cricket, to come to bat **3.** *vt* BASEBALL HOLD PARTICULAR BATTING AVERAGE in baseball, to have a particular batting average **4.** *vt* BASEBALL ADVANCE RUNNER in baseball, to advance a runner to the next base by making a base hit [Old English *batt*, origin ?] ◇ **be at bat** to be the person on whom success or failure depends (*informal*) ◇ **go to bat for somebody** to support or assist somebody (*informal*) ◇ **(right) off the bat** immediately (*informal*)

bat[2] /bat/ *abbr* a file extension for a batch file. Full form **batch**

bat around *v* **1.** *vt* to discuss or consider something at length (*informal*) **2.** *vi* in baseball, to have all nine batters up, especially in one inning

bat out *vt* to produce or compose something, especially in a casual or rushed manner (*informal*) ○ *bat out three news items in an hour*

bat

bat[3] /bat/ *n* a small nocturnal flying mammal with leathery wings stretching from the forelimbs to the rear legs and tail. Bats eat fruit or insects, usually hang upside down when resting, and often use echolocation to detect prey and to navigate. Order: Chiroptera. [Late 16C. Alteration of *backe* < N Germanic] ◇ **have bats in the belfry** to be slightly but harmlessly eccentric (*informal*) ◇ **like a bat out of hell** extremely fast (*slang*)

bat[4] /bat/ (**bat·ted, bat·ting, bats**) *vt* to wink or flutter something, especially the eyes or eyelids [Early 19C. Variant of BATE]

bat. /bat/ *abbr* **1.** COMPUT batch **2.** MIL battalion

Ba·taan /bə tán, -taán/ peninsula of Luzon Island in the Philippines, the scene of intense Japanese-American World War II combat. Area: 530 sq. mi./1,400 sq. km.

Ba·tak /bə taák, baá taák/ *n* a group of Austronesian languages spoken in Sumatra, Indonesia. Native speakers: 3 million. [Early 19C. < Batak] —**Ba·tak** *adj*

~~**batallion**~~ incorrect spelling of **battalion**

Ba·tan·gas /bə taáng gaáss/ city and port on Luzon Island in the Philippines. It is the capital of Batangas Province. Population: 227,099 (1999).

Ba·tan Is·lands /bə taán-/ most Northerly island group in the Philippines. Area: 76 sq. mi./197 sq. km. Population: 15,000.

Ba·ta·vi·a /bə táyvee ə/ **1.** city in western New York. It is the site of the Tonawanda Indian Reservation. Population: 15,940 (2002 estimate). **2.** former name for **Jakarta**

bat·boy /bát bòy/ *n* in baseball, a person employed to look after the team's equipment, especially the bats

batch[1] /bach/ *n* **1.** QUANTITY REGARDED AS GROUP a quantity of people or things treated or regarded as a group, especially when subdivided from a larger group **2.** AMOUNT FOR ONE OPERATION the amount of material prepared or needed for, or produced in, one operation **3.** COOK AMOUNT BAKED the amount of something baked at one time or produced at one baking **4.** COMPUT PROGRAMS PROCESSED TOGETHER a set of programs or jobs processed on a computer at one time ■ *vt* (**batched, batch·ing, batch·es**) PROCESS ITEMS AS BATCH to process or assemble items as a batch or in batches [15C. < assumed Old English *bæcce* "something baked" < *bacan* (see BAKE)]

batch[2] *vi* another spelling of **bach**

bat chay·il /baat khaáyil/, **bat hay·ill** *n* JUDAISM same as **bat mitzvah** (sense 2) [Late 20C. < Hebrew, "daughter of valor"]

~~**batchelor**~~ incorrect spelling of **bachelor**

batch file *n* a computer file containing a series of commands to be processed by a computer as if they were entered from the keyboard consecutively. Most personal computers execute a batch file at the start of each operating session to prepare the system for use.

batch proc·ess·ing *n* a mode of computer operation in which programs are executed without the user being able to influence processing while it is in progress

bate /bayt/ (**bat·ed, bat·ing, bates**), **bait** (**bait·ed, bait·ing, baits**) *vi* to beat the wings wildly or impatiently in an attempt to fly off a perch or a falconer's fist when still attached by a leash (*refers to falcons or other hunting birds*) [13C. < Old French *batre* (see BATTER[1])]

ba·teau /ba tṓ/ (*plural* **-teaux** /-tṓz, -tṓ/) *n* **1.** FLAT-BOTTOMED RIVERBOAT a light flat-bottomed riverboat with sharply tapering stern and bow, used in New England and Canada **2.** *Southern US* SMALL MOTORBOAT FOR FISHING a motorboat used on the Virginia coast of the United States for fishing and catching shellfish **3.** *Southern US* FLAT-BOTTOMED ROWBOAT a small, light, flat-bottomed rowboat, used in the Gulf and South Atlantic states of the United States [Early 18C. < French, "boat"]

ba·teau bridge /báttō-/ *n* CIV ENG same as **pontoon bridge**

bat·ed /báytəd/ ◇ **with bated breath** in anxious or excited anticipation

Ba·tei Din *n* JUDAISM plural of **Beth Din**

ba·te·leur /bátt'lər/, **ba·te·leur ea·gle** *n* a black eagle that has a red beak, red legs, almost no tail and often eats carrion. Native to: Africa. Latin name: *Terathopius ecaudatus*. [Mid-19C. < French, "juggler, rogue"]

Bates /bayts/, **Katherine Lee** (1859–1929) US educator and writer. She wrote *America the Beautiful* (1893).

> "O beautiful for spacious skies, / For amber waves of grain, / For purple mountain majesties / Above the fruited plain! / America! America! / God shed His grace on thee / And crown thy good with brotherhood / From sea to shining sea!"
> [Katherine Lee Bates, "America the Beautiful"; 1893]

Bates·i·an mim·ic·ry /bàytsee ən-/ *n* mimicry in which a harmless species is protected from predators by its resemblance to a species that is harmful or unpalatable to them [Late 19C. After H. W. *Bates* (1825–92), British naturalist]

bat·fish /bát fìsh/ (*plural same* or **-fish·es**) *n* an anglerfish that has a flattened head and body and waddles on the sea bottom using pectoral and pelvic fins. Family: Ogcocephalidae.

bat·fowl /bát fòwl/ (**-fowled, -fowl·ing, -fowls**) *vi* to catch roosting birds at night by temporarily blinding them with a light and netting or hitting them

bath /bath/ *n* (*plural* **baths** /baths, ba*th*z/) **1. IMMERSION OF BODY** the act of immersing all or part of the body in a bathtub in order to wash it **2. WATER IN TUB** water used for bathing in a tub **3.** *UK* HOUSEHOLD same as **bathtub 4.** BUILDINGS same as **bathroom** (sense 2) **5. BODY TREATMENT** the act of immersing all or part of the body in mud or other substance, usually for therapeutic reasons **6.** CHEM **LIQUID** a liquid, or a liquid and its container, in which something is immersed ■ **baths** *npl* **1.** BUILDINGS same as **bathhouse** (sense 1) **2. WATER SPA** a spa where patrons avail themselves of the water from natural mineral springs (*often in place names*) ■ *vi* (**bathed, bath·ing, baths** /baths/) *Can, UK* HOUSEHOLD same as **bathe** (sense 1) [Old English *bæ* < Germanic] ◇ **take a bath** to suffer a severe financial setback (*slang*)

USAGE bath or **bathe**? There are major differences between the United States and other parts of the English-speaking world in the use of these words. In the United States, ***bath*** cannot be used as a verb and ***bathe*** cannot be used as a noun, whereas in British English they can. *Shall I bath the baby?* and *I'm going for a bathe*, in which the difference between the two words is that the first refers to washing and the second to swimming in the sea, are not American uses. In most varieties of English, ***bathe*** is also used of immersing things in water to clean or moisten them. In the United States, ***bathe*** means "to wash yourself or somebody else in a bathtub": *I'm going to bathe. I'm going to bathe the baby.*

Bath /bath/ city on the Avon River in Somerset, England. It is the site of the only natural hot springs in England and has been a spa since Roman times. Population: 84,100 (1994).

bat hay·ill *n* JUDAISM another spelling of **bat chayil**

bath chair *n* an old-fashioned type of wheelchair, often with a hood [After BATH, England]

bathe /bay*th*/ (**bathed, bath·ing, bathes**) *v* **1.** *vti* **WASH IN BATHTUB** to wash yourself or somebody else in a bathtub **2.** *vt* **CLEANSE WOUND** to apply water or another liquid to a wound or part of the body in order to cleanse, heal, or soothe it **3.** *vt* **DIP SOMETHING IN LIQUID** to immerse something in liquid **4.** *vt* **COVER SOMETHING** to cover or surround something with light, color, or a substance ○ *bathed in a golden glow* **5.** *vt* **FLOW ALONG EDGE OF SOMETHING** to flow along the edge of something **6.** *vi* **SWIM OR PADDLE IN OPEN WATER** to swim or paddle, especially for pleasure, in an area of open water such as the sea or a river [Old English *baian* < Germanic]

USAGE See *bath.*

bath·er /báy*th*ər/ *n* somebody who is swimming

ba·thet·ic /bə théttik/ *adj* **1.** showing or characterized by bathos **2.** trite, commonplace, or absurdly sentimental [Late 18C. < BATHOS, after *pathos, pathetic*] —**ba·thet·ic·al·ly** *adv*

bath·house /báth hòwss/ (*plural* **-houses** /-hòwzəz/) *n* **1.** a building equipped with baths, especially for public use **2.** a building near a swimming pool, equipped with showers and locker rooms

bath·ing /báy*th*ing/ *n* the activity of swimming in the sea, a river, or a lake

bath·ing suit /báy*th*ing-/ *n* CLOTHING same as **swimsuit**

bath·mat /báth màt/ *n* **1.** a mat that is placed beside a bathtub or shower for somebody to step out onto **2.** a mat, often made of rubber, that is placed in a bathtub or shower to prevent somebody from slipping

bath mitz·vah *n* JUDAISM another spelling of **bat mitzvah**

batho- *prefix* deep, depth ○ *bathometer* [< Greek *bathos* "depth"]

bath·o·chrom·ic /bàthə krṓmik/ *adj* describes a shift toward the red end in a chemical compound's absorption spectrum

bath·o·lith /báthə lìth/, **bath·o·lite** /-lìt/ *n* a large mass of igneous rock, composed of granite or gabbro, formed deep in the Earth's crust and intruded in a molten state —**bath·o·lith·ic** /bàthə líthik/ *adj*

ba·thom·e·ter /bə thómmətər/ *n* an instrument for measuring the depth of a body of water —**bath·o·met·ric** /bàthə méttrik/ *adj* —**ba·thom·e·try** *n*

ba·thoph·i·lous /bə thóffiləss/ *adj* describes organisms that are adapted to living in very deep water

ba·thos /báy thòss, -thàwss/ *n* **1.** insincere and excessively sentimental pathos **2.** in writing or speech, a sudden descent in style or manner from the elevated to the commonplace, producing a ludicrous effect [Early 18C. < Greek, "depth" < *bathus* "deep"]

bath·robe /báth rṑb/ *n* a loose-fitting garment with a belt, worn before or after having a bath or shower, or for lounging

bath·room /báth ròom, -rȍom/ *n* **1.** a room with a toilet **2.** a room containing a bathtub or shower and, usually, a sink and a toilet

bath·room scale *n* a step-on device for people to weigh themselves on at home, usually kept in a bathroom

bath salts *npl* soluble mineral salts used to perfume and soften bathwater

Bath·she·ba /bath shéebə, báthshəbə/ *n* in the Bible, the wife of Uriah and later of David, by whom she became the mother of Solomon (II Samuel 11–12)

bath·tub /báth tùb/ *n* a large container, often oblong in shape and usually made of enameled metal or plastic, in which somebody sits to bathe

bath·tub gin *n* homemade spirits consisting of alcohol mixed with flavoring (*slang*)

bath·tub ring *n* a ring of grime deposited on the inside of a bathtub at the high-water mark of bathwater

Bath·urst /báthərst/ **1.** summer resort city in northeastern New Brunswick, Canada. Population: 16,427 (1996). **2.** former name for **Banjul**

Bath·urst Is·land island in the Timor Sea off the northern coast of the Northern Territory, Australia. Population: 1,000. Area: 799 sq. mi./2,070 sq. km.

bath·wa·ter /báth wàwtər/ *n* the water used for a bath

bathy- *prefix* deep, depth ○ *bathysphere* [< Greek *bathus* "deep"]

bath·y·al /báthee əl/ *adj* relating to or living in ocean depths between 650 and 6,550 ft./200 and 2,000 m

ba·thym·e·try /bə thímmətree/ *n* **1.** the measurement of the depth of lakes, oceans, and seas **2.** the data obtained by the use of bathymetry —**bath·y·met·ric** /bàthə méttrik/ *adj* —**bath·y·met·ri·cal·ly** *adv*

bath·y·pe·lag·ic /bàthəpə lájjik/ *adj* relating to or living in the depths of the ocean, especially between 2,000 and 12,000 ft./600 and 3,600 m

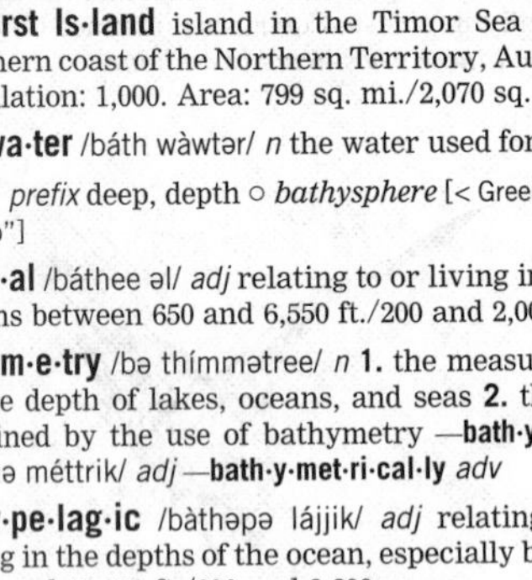

bathyscaphe

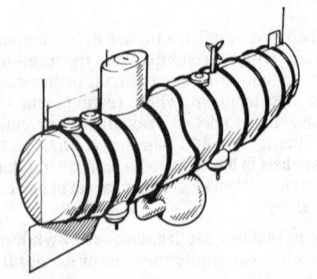

bath·y·scaphe /báthə skàf, -skàyf/, **bath·y·scaph** /-skàf/ *n* a deep-sea research vessel that has a large flotation hull and an observation cabin attached to its underside, and can dive to depths over 6.2 mi./10,000 m [Mid-20C. < BATHY- + Greek *skaphos* "ship"]

bath·y·sphere /báthə sfeer/ *n* a strong steel diving sphere that can be lowered by cable to depths of 3,000 ft./900 m

ba·ti·do /baa téedo/ (*plural* **-dos**) *n Southwest US* a fruit-flavored milk shake, e.g., one containing guava, mangos, or pineapple [Late 20C. < Spanish, literally "beaten, whipped"]

ba·tik /bə téek, báttik/, **bat·tik** *n* **1. FABRIC PRINTING TECHNIQUE** a method of hand-printing a fabric by covering with removable wax the parts that will not be dyed **2. HAND-DYED FABRIC** fabric that has been hand-dyed by the batik method **3. DESIGN IN BATIK** a design produced by batik [Late 19C. < Javanese, "painted"]

Ba·tis·ta y Zal·dí·var /bə téestə ee zaal dée vaar/, **Fulgencio** (1901–73) Cuban soldier and head of state. His presidency of Cuba (1940–44, 1952–59) was ended by Fidel Castro's revolution (1959).

ba·tiste /bə téest, ba-/ *n* a fine soft plain-woven cotton or linen fabric. Use: clothing. [Early 19C. < French]

Bat·lle y Or·dó·ñez /baatye ee awr dáwn yàyss/, **José** (1856–1929) Uruguayan president (1903–07, 1911–15). He helped to modernize Uruguay's society, economy, and government.

bat·man /bátmən/ (*plural* **-men** /-mən/) *n UK* a British military officer's personal servant [Mid-18C. Via Old French < medieval Latin *bastum* "pack saddle"]

bat mitz·vah /baat mítsvə/, **bath mitz·vah, bas mitz·vah** /baass-/ *n* **1.** the ritual that marks the 13th birthday of a Jewish girl, after which she takes full responsibility for her moral and spiritual conduct **2.** a Jewish girl who has reached the age of 13, the age of religious responsibility [Mid-20C < Hebrew *baṯ miṣwāh* "daughter of the commandment"]

BATNEEC /bát neek/ *n* a principle applied to the control of emissions into the air, land, and water from polluting processes, minimizing pollution without requiring technology or methods that are not yet available or unreasonably expensive. Full form **best available technology not entailing excessive cost**

ba·ton /bə tón, bátt'n/ *n* **1.** MUSIC **CONDUCTING STICK** a short thin stick used by a conductor to direct musical performers **2.** POLICE **POLICE STICK** a short thick stick used as a weapon, especially by police ○ *a side-handled baton* **3.** SPORTS **RELAY TEAM STICK** a short stick or hollow cylinder passed by each runner in a relay team to the next runner **4. DRUM MAJOR'S STICK** a long stick with a knob at one or each end, carried and twirled by a drum major or majorette **5. OFFICIAL STAFF** a staff carried by an official such as a field marshal as a symbol of office **6.** HERALDRY **DIAGONAL LINE ON COAT OF ARMS** a shortened narrow diagonal line on a coat of arms, especially one signifying bastardy [Early 16C. Via French < late Latin *bastum* "stick"]

Bat·on Rouge /bátt'n ròo*zh*/ capital of Louisiana, situated on the Mississippi River in the southeastern part of the state. Population: 225,702 (2002 estimate).

ba·tra·chi·an /bə tráykee ən/ *n* a tailless amphibian, e.g., a frog or toad [Mid-19C. < modern Latin *Batrachia* < Greek *batrakhos* "frog"] —**ba·tra·chi·an** *adj*

bats /bats/ *adj* harmlessly eccentric (*informal*) [Early 20C. < *have bats in the belfry*]

bats·man /bátsmən/ (*plural* **-men** /-mən/) *n* a baseball or cricket player who bats or is batting

bats·wom·an /báts wòomman/ (*plural* **-wom·en** /-wìmmin/) *n* in cricket, a woman who bats or is batting

batt /bat/ *n* TEXTILES same as **batting** (sense 2) [Late 19C. Shortening]

bat·tal·ion /bə tállyən/ *n* **1. MILITARY UNIT** a military unit typically consisting of a headquarters and three or more companies, batteries, or other subunits of similar size **2. LARGE BODY OF SOLDIERS** a large body of soldiers organized to act together **3. LARGE NUMBER** a large group or number (*often used in the plural*) [Late 16C. Via French < Italian *bataglione* "great battle" < late Latin *bat(t)uere* "to beat"]

~~**battallion**~~ incorrect spelling of **battalion**

batte·ment /bat maaN, bátmənt/ *n* a ballet movement in which one leg is extended, either once or repeatedly, to the front, side, or back, and then beat against the supporting foot [Mid-19C. < French, "beating"]

bat·ten /bátt'n/ *n* **1.** SAILING **STRIP FOR KEEPING SAILS IN SHAPE** a thin flexible strip of wood or plastic inserted in pockets in a sail to keep it in shape or support the edge **2.** NAUT **SLAT FOR FASTENING DOWN TARPAULIN** a narrow metal or wooden slat used to fasten down the edges of a tarpaulin covering a boat's raised hatch in poor weather **3.** THEATER **LIGHTS IN THEATER** a row of lights in a theater, or the strip or bar that holds it ■ *vt* **(-tened, -ten·ing, -tens) PROVIDE WITH BATTENS** to provide, strengthen, or secure something with battens [Late 16C. < Old Norse *batna* "improve, get better" < Germanic]

bat·ter[1] /báttər/ *vt* **(-tered, -ter·ing, -ters) 1. HIT REPEATEDLY** to hit or beat something repeatedly using heavy blows in order to break, bruise, or damage it **2. SUBJECT TO ATTACK** to subject somebody to persistent attack or violence **3. DAMAGE BY HEAVY BLOWS OR WEAR** to damage or injure something by hard blows or heavy wear (*often passive*) ■ *n* PRINTING **1. DAMAGED TYPE** a damaged or worn printing type or plate **2. FAULTY IMPRESSION** a defective impression produced by a faulty printing plate [14C. Via Old French *batre* < late Latin *bat(t)uere* "to beat"] —**bat·tered** *adj* —**bat·ter·er** *n*

bat·ter[2] /báttər/ *n* a liquid mixture of flour, milk, and eggs used in making cakes and pancakes, and for coating foods before frying ■ *vt* **(-tered, -ter·ing, -ters)** to cover food with batter before frying [14C. < Old French *bateüre* "act of beating" < *batre* (see BATTER[1]); from the idea of beating the mixture]

bat·ter[3] /báttər/ *n* especially in baseball, a player who bats [Late 18C. < BAT[1]]

bat·ter[4] /báttər/ *vt* **(-tered, -ter·ing, -ters)** to build a wall or similar structure in a way that forms an upwardly receding slope ■ *n* a receding upward slope of the outer face of a wall, hedge, or similar structure [Mid-16C. Origin ?]

bat·ter bread *n Southern US* corn bread made with eggs and milk

REGIONAL NOTE ***Batter bread***, also called *baby bread*, is a Virginian term for corn bread that competes with *awendaw*, *egg bread*, *spoon bread*, and dozens of other terms across the Southern states. See also ***egg bread***.

bat·ter·cake /báttər kàyk/ *n Southern US* FOOD **1.** same as **pancake** *n* (sense 1) **2.** same as **johnnycake**

bat·ter·ie /báttəree, ba trée/ *n* a ballet movement in which the dancer beats the feet or calves together during a leap [Early 18C. < French, "battery"]

bat·ter·ie de cui·sine /bat rée də kwi zéen/ (*plural* **bat·ter·ies de cui·sine** /bat rée-/) *n* a set of cooking utensils, pots, and pans [Late 18C. < French, "set (of implements) for cooking"]

bat·ter·ing ram *n* **1.** a large heavy beam used in ancient times to break down the walls and doors of a fortification under siege **2.** a heavy metal bar used by police officers and firefighters to break down doors

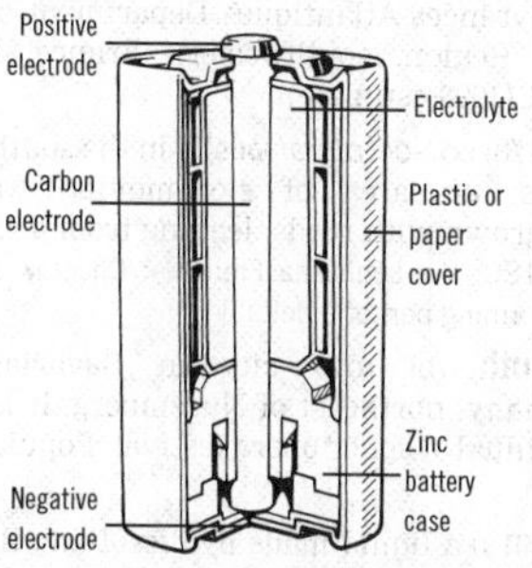

battery: cutaway view of a simple battery

bat·ter·y /báttəree/ (*plural* **-ies**) *n* **1. POWER SOURCE** a number of connected electric cells that produce a direct current through the conversion of chemical energy into electrical energy **2. GROUPING OF SIMILAR THINGS** an array or grouping of similar things intended to be used or considered together **3.** LAW **UNLAWFUL USE OF FORCE ON SOMEBODY** the unlawful use of any physical force on another person, including beating or offensive touching without the person's consent **4.** BASEBALL **BASEBALL PITCHER AND CATCHER** the pitcher and catcher of a baseball team **5.** MIL **ARTILLERY GROUPING** a group of artillery pieces such as guns or missile launchers that function as a single tactical unit **6.** MIL **GUN EMPLACEMENT** a prepared position for artillery **7.** MIL **ARMY ARTILLERY UNIT** an army artillery unit corresponding to a company in an infantry regiment **8.** MUSIC **PERCUSSION SECTION** the percussion section of an orchestra **9. ACT OF BATTERING** the act of battering, beating, or pounding something [Mid-16C. < Old French *baterie* < *batre* (see BATTER[1])] ◇ **recharge your batteries** to restore your level of energy and strength (*informal*)

bat·ter·y charg·er *n* a device for restoring power to electrical batteries

bat·te·ry pack *n* a rechargeable high-capacity battery used for powering portable electrical equipment such as laptop computers and video cameras

bat·tik *n* HANDICRAFT, TEXTILES another spelling of **batik**

bat·ting /bátting/ *n* **1.** especially in baseball or cricket, the action or ability of a player or team that hits with a bat **2.** bulky material made from fabric or other fibers. Use: padding, stuffing. [Early 17C. < BAT[1]; in sense 2 from the beating out of impurities from cotton]

bat·ting av·er·age *n* in baseball, a measure of a batter's performance, calculated by dividing the total of base hits gained in a given period by the number of times at bat

bat·tle /bátt'l/ *n* **1. ARMED FIGHT** a large-scale fight between armed forces involving combat between armies, warships, or aircraft **2. STRUGGLE** a drawn-out conflict between adversaries, or against powerful forces ○ *the battle against malaria* ■ *v* **(-tled, -tling, -tles) 1.** *vti* **FIGHT** to fight in a battle **2.** *vi* **STRIVE** to strive or contend in order to overcome or achieve something ○ *continues to battle to save her career* **3.** *vt* **STRUGGLE AGAINST SOMEBODY OR SOMETHING** to fight or contend with somebody or something, in or as if in a battle ○ *determined to battle terrorism* [13C. Via French *bataille* < late Latin *battualia* "military or gladiatorial exercises" < *bat(t)uere* "to beat"] ◇ **be half the battle** to be an important first part of a difficult task ○ *Shipping the books on time is only half the battle; we have to sell them too.* ◇ **do battle (with somebody** *or* **something)** to fight or struggle against somebody or something ◇ **fight a losing battle** to try hard with no prospect of success

USAGE The use of ***battle*** with a direct object, as in *The people of South Carolina have been battling a hurricane*, instead of with a preposition, as in *battle against* or *battle with something*, is a feature of North American usage that has begun to enter other varieties of English also. This is partly a revival of an older use that died out in the 19th century.

SYNONYMS See ***fight***.

Bat·tle /bátt'l/ town in East Sussex, southeastern England, the site of the Battle of Hastings in 1066. Population: 5,235 (1991).

Bat·tle, Kathleen (*b.* 1948) US soprano. An internationally renowned concert and opera singer, she sang with the Metropolitan Opera Company in New York City (1977–94).

bat·tle·ax /bátt'l àks/ *n* **1.** a large heavy broad-headed ax used as a weapon **2.** an offensive term for a woman who is considered domineering and fearsome (*insult*)

Bat·tle Born State *n* a nickname for Nevada

Bat·tle Creek city in southern Michigan, southwest of Lansing. It is a major producer of breakfast cereals. Population: 53,650 (2002 estimate).

bat·tle cruis·er *n* a heavily armed warship with lighter armor, fewer guns, greater maneuverability, and a faster speed than a battleship

bat·tle cry *n* **1.** a rallying or encouraging shout that soldiers make when going into battle **2.** a slogan used by supporters of a cause to rally fellow supporters

bat·tle·dore /bátt'l dàwr/ *n* **1. EARLY RACKET GAME** an early racket game played by two people with flat wooden rackets and a shuttlecock. It is the ancestor of badminton. **2. RACKET USED IN BATTLEDORE** a light racket, smaller than a tennis racket, used for hitting the shuttlecock in battledore **3. WOODEN BAT** a wooden bat formerly used to beat clothes when washing them [15C. Probably < Provençal *batedor* "beater" < *battre* "to beat" < late Latin *bat(t)uere*]

bat·tle dress *n* the ordinary uniform worn by a soldier

bat·tle fa·tigue *n Can, UK* a psychological disorder resulting from the stress of being involved in a battle and characterized by acute anxiety, depression, and loss of motivation. US term **combat fatigue**

bat·tle·field /bátt'l fèeld/ *n* **1.** the place where a battle is fought **2.** an area of conflict or contention

bat·tle·field de·tain·ee *n* a captured and imprisoned unlawful combatant in a war or other conflict

bat·tle·front /bátt'l frùnt/ *n* an area or sector in which combat between armed forces takes place

bat·tle·ground /bátt'l grównd/ *n* MIL same as **battlefield** (sense 1)

bat·tle group *n* **1.** a US army unit that usually consists of five companies **2.** a naval force made up of warships and other vessels

bat·tle line *n* a position along which a battle takes place (*usually plural*) ◇ **draw (up) the battle lines** to prepare for a fight, quarrel, or contest

bat·tle·ment /bátt'lmənt/ *n* a defensive or decorative parapet with indentations [14C. < French *bateiller* "fortify"] —**bat·tle·ment·ed** *adj*

bat·tle·ments /bátt'lmənts/ *npl* a series of indentations forming a defensive or decorative parapet

Bat·tle of Brit·ain *n* an aerial battle fought in World War II in 1940 between the German Luftwaffe, which carried out extensive bombing in Britain, and the British Royal Air Force, which offered successful resistance

Bat·tle of the At·lan·tic *n* the struggle during World War II for control of the routes used to bring supplies to Britain across the Atlantic

bat·tle plan *n* **1.** a strategy for fighting a battle **2.** a strategy for any operation or contest

bat·tler /bátt'lər/ *n* somebody who is courageous or indomitable in a battle or conflict

bat·tle roy·al (*plural* **bat·tles roy·al** or **bat·tle roy·als**) *n* **1.** a battle involving many combatants, especially a fight to the finish **2.** a passionate conflict, especially one that unfolds in public

bat·tle·ship /bátt'l shìp/ *n* the largest type of warship, which carries the heaviest armor

bat·tle·ship gray *adj* of a medium gray color tinged with blue, like the color in which battleships are commonly painted —**bat·tle·ship gray** *n*

bat·tle sta·tions *US npl* MIL **POST FOR COMBAT** the posts assigned to people during or in readiness for combat ■ *interj* **1.** MIL **GO TO COMBAT POSTS** used as a command ordering people to take up the posts assigned to them during or in readiness for combat **2. GET READY** used to warn people to get ready to carry out their assigned tasks (*informal*) ► Can term (all senses) **action stations**

bat·tle·wag·on /bátt'l wàggən/, **bat·tle wag·on** *n* NAVY same as **battleship** (*informal*)

bat·tue /ba tóo/ *n* **1. DRIVING OF GAME IN HUNT** the beating of bushes, brush, and underbrush in order to drive game toward hunters **2. HUNT USING BATTUE** a hunt in which battue is used **3. SLAUGHTER** a wholesale massacre or indiscriminate slaughter [Early 19C. < French, past participle of *battre* (see BATTER[1])]

bat·ty[1] /báttee/ **(-ti·er, -ti·est)** *adj* slightly eccentric (*informal*) [Early 20C. < *have bats in the belfry*] —**bat·ti·ness** *n*

bat·ty[2] /báttee/ (*plural same*) *n Carib* the buttocks (*slang*) [Mid-20C. Alteration of BOTTY]

ba·tu /báttoo/ (*plural* **-tus**) *n Philippines* a tablet of the recreational drug methamphetamine [< Malay, "rock"]

Ba·tu·mi /bə tóomee/, **Ba·tum** /-tóom/ city and port in southwestern Georgia on the Black Sea, and the capital of Ajaria autonomous region. Population: 137,000 (1990).

bat·wing sleeve /bát wing-/ *n* a sleeve that is wide at the armhole and tight at the wrist

bau·ble /báwb'l/ *n* **1.** something that is small and decorative but of little real value **2.** a mock scepter of office carried by a court jester (*archaic*) [14C. < Old French, "plaything"]

baud /bawd/ *n* a unit of data transmission speed, equal to one unit element per second [Mid-20C. After J. M. E. *Baudot* (1845–1903), French engineer]

Baude·laire /bōd lér/, **Charles** (1821–67) French critic and poet. His symbolist verse, notably *The Flowers of Evil* (1857), explored his sense of melancholy, isolation, and the attractions of evil and vice. Full name **Baudelaire, Charles Pierre**

> "The poet is like the prince of the clouds, / Who rides out the tempest and laughs at the archer. / But when he is exiled on the ground, amidst the clamor, / His giant's wings prevent him from walking."
> [Charles Baudelaire, "L'Albatross" ("The Albatross"), *Les Fleurs du mal (The Flowers of Evil)*; 1857]

Bau·douin I /bō dwáN/, **King of the Belgians** (1930–93) He spent five years in voluntary exile in Switzerland before ascending the throne on the abdication of his father, Leopold III, in 1951. Full name **Baudouin Albert Charles Leopold Axel Marie Gustave**

> "It takes twenty years or more of peace to make a man, it takes only twenty seconds of war to destroy him."
> [Baudouin I, *Address to US Congress*; May 12, 1959]

Bau·haus /bów hòwss/ *n* an influential German school of architecture and design, founded in 1919 by Walter Gropius. It attempted to synthesize technology, craftsmanship, design, and art, and was noted for a style of functional architecture. [Early 20C. < German < *Bau* "building" + *Haus* "house"]

bau·hin·i·a /baw hínnee ə, bō-/ *n* an ornamental climbing plant of the pea family that has flattened stems. Flowers: various bright colors. Native to: tropics, subtropics. Genus: *Bauhinia*. [Late 18C. < modern Latin, after the brothers *Bauhin*, Jean (1541–1613) and Gaspard (1560–1624), Swiss botanists]

baulk *v, n* another spelling of **balk**

Baum /bawm, baam/, **L. Frank** (1856–1919) US writer. He wrote about the fairy-tale land of Oz in 14 volumes starting with *The Wonderful Wizard of Oz* (1900). Full name **Baum, Lyman Frank**

> "This doesn't look like Kansas, Toto."
> [L. Frank Baum, *The Wonderful Wizard of Oz*; 1900]

Bau·mé scale /bō máy-, bṓ may-/ *n* a scale for calibrating hydrometers that are used to ascertain the relative density of liquids [Mid-19C. After Antoine *Baumé* (1728–1804), French chemist]

Bausch /bowsh/, **Pina** (*b.* 1940) German dancer and choreographer. One of the foremost modern dance choreographers, she created expressionist works, and founded the Wuppertal Dance Theater in Wuppertal, Germany (1973). Full name **Bausch, Philippine**

baux·ite /báwk sìt/ *n* a rock containing aluminum hydroxides that is the principal ore of aluminum [Mid-19C. After the S French village of Les *Baux*]

Ba·var·i·a /bə vérree ə/ the largest state of Germany. It is situated in the southeastern part of Germany and has borders with Baden-Württemberg, Hesse, Thringen and Saxony states, and the Czech Republic and Austria. Capital: Munich. Population: 12,086,548 (1998). Area: 27,239 sq. mi./70,548 sq. km. —**Ba·var·i·an** *n, adj*

bav·a·rois /bàvvər waá/ *n UK* a dessert of rich flavored set custard, eaten cold [Mid-19C. < French, "Bavarian"]

bawd /bawd/ *n* **1.** a woman who runs a brothel (*archaic*) **2.** same as **prostitute** *n* (sense 1) [14C. Probably < Old French *baude* "bold, lively" < Germanic]

bawd·ry /báwdree/ *n* coarse or obscene language (*archaic*)

bawd·y /báwdee/ (**-i·er, -i·est**) *adj* ribald in a frank, humorous, and often crude way —**bawd·i·ly** *adv* —**bawd·i·ness** *n*

bawd·y·house /báwdee hòwss/ (*plural* **-hous·es** /-hòwzəz/) *n* same as **brothel** (*archaic*)

bawl /bawl/ *vti* (**bawled, bawl·ing, bawls**) **1.** SHOUT to shout something in a loud and usually aggressive voice **2.** CRY NOISILY to cry very loudly and energetically (*informal*) ■ *n* LOUD SHOUT a loud cry or shout [15C. Origin ?] —**bawl·er** *n*

bawl out *v* **1.** *vti* to shout or cry something out loudly **2.** *vt* to tell somebody off loudly and angrily (*informal*)

bay[1] /bay/ *n* **1.** an area of sea enclosed by a wide inward-curving stretch of coastline **2.** a lowland area with curving hills partly surrounding it [14C. Via French *baie* < Spanish *bahía*]

bay[2] /bay/ *n* **1.** SPECIAL AREA OR COMPARTMENT an area that is divided off and used for a particular purpose, e.g., in a building, bus station, or aircraft **2.** SPACE BETWEEN TWO PILLARS a section of a wall or building between two vertical structures such as pillars or buttresses **3.** RECESS a recess or alcove in a wall **4.** same as **bay window** (sense 1) [14C. < French *baie* "opening" < *bayer* "gape, stand open" < assumed Vulgar Latin *batare* "yawn, gape"]

bay[3] /bay/ *n* **1.** an animal with a reddish brown coat, especially a horse **2.** a reddish brown color [14C. Via Old French *bai* < Latin *badius* "chestnut-colored"] —**bay** *adj*

bay[4] /bay/ *n* **1.** a small evergreen tree of the laurel family with stiff dark green aromatic leaves. Use: flavoring in cooking. Native to: Mediterranean. Latin name: *Laurus nobilis*. **2.** PLANTS same as **laurel** (sense 2) ■ **bays** *npl* a wreath woven out of laurel leaves, presented to poets and victors in classical antiquity, or the honor conferred by this (*literary*) [14C. Via Old French *baie* < Latin *baca* "berry"]

bay[5] /bay/ *v* (**bayed, bay·ing, bays**) **1.** *vi* HOWL to make the howling sound of a hunting dog on the trail of an animal **2.** *vi* MAKE LOUD OUTCRY FOR SOMETHING to call noisily and aggressively for something bad to happen to somebody ○ *an outraged public baying for blood* **3.** *vt* CORNER HUNTED ANIMAL to corner or exhaust a hunted animal so that it must turn and face its hunters ○ *hounds baying a fox* ■ *n* POSITION OF NO ESCAPE the position in which a hunted animal or a person being pursued has to face the hunters or pursuers [13C. Via Old French *(a)baier* < assumed Vulgar Latin *abbaiare*; an imitation of the sound] ◇ **keep somebody** *or* **something at bay** to keep somebody or something unpleasant at a distance to avoid difficulty or harm

ba·ya·dere /bī́ ə deer, -dèr/ *n* a fabric with horizontal stripes of bold contrasting colors [Mid-19C. Via French < Portuguese *bailladeira* "woman dancer" < *bailar* "to dance"]

Ba·ya·món /bī̀ aa mṓn/ city in northeastern Puerto Rico, west of the Bayamón River, and west of San Juan. Population: 220,262 (1990).

Bay·a·zid I /bī́ əzid/, **Bay·e·zit I** /-əzit/, **Ba·ja·zet I** /-zèt/ (1360?–1403?). Sultan of the Ottoman Empire. During his reign (1389–1402) he conquered much of the Balkans and Asia Minor, but was eventually defeated by the Tatar Timur. Known as **Yilderim ("Lightning")**

Bay·a·zid II, **Bay·e·zit II**, **Ba·ja·zet II** (1448–1512). Sultan of the Ottoman Empire. During his reign (1481–1512) he constructed the mosque of Bayazid in Constantinople (1505)

Bay·bars I /bī́ baars/ (1233?–77). Sultan of Egypt and Syria. During his reign (1260–77) he extended his control into Armenia, Asia Minor, Nubia, and Arabia.

bay·ber·ry /báy bèrree/ (*plural* **-ries**) *n* **1.** a fruit covered with a waxy substance, borne by a North American bush. Use: making candles. **2.** a bush that bears bayberries. Native to: coast of eastern North America. Genus: *Myrica*. **3.** same as **bay rum tree**

Bay Cit·y /bày síttee/ **1.** city and port in eastern Michigan, situated where the Saginaw River flows into Saginaw Bay. Population: 35,844 (2002 estimate). **2.** city in southeastern Texas, near the Colorado River, southwest of Houston. Population: 18,450 (2002 estimate).

Bayes' the·o·rem /báyz-/ *n* a theorem of conditional probability that allows estimates of probability to be revised continually on the basis of observations of occurrences of events [Mid-19C. After Thomas *Bayes* (1702–61), British mathematician]

Ba·yeux /bay óo, baa yóo/ town in Calvados Department, northern France. Population: 14,961 (1999).

Ba·yeux tap·es·try *n* a linen embroidery from the 11th century that hangs in Bayeux, France, and depicts the Norman conquest of England in 1066

Bay·e·zit another spelling of **Bayazid**

bay lau·rel *n* TREES same as **bay**[4] (sense 1)

Bayle /bayl, bel/, **Pierre** (1647–1706) French philosopher. His *Dictionary* (1697) and his controversial proposition that morality is independent of religion were major influences on the 18th-century European Enlightenment.

> "If an historian were to relate truthfully all the crimes, weaknesses, and disorders of mankind, his readers would take his work for satire rather than for history."
> [Pierre Bayle, *Historical and Critical Dictionary*; 1697]

bay leaf *n* the aromatic leaf of the Mediterranean bay tree. Use: flavoring in cooking.

bay lynx *n* VERTEB same as **bobcat** [< BAY[3]]

bay·man /báymən, -màn/ (*plural* **-men** /-mən, -mèn/) *n* FISHING a fisherman who lives near, and works on, a bay, catching shellfish and other fish for a living [Mid-17C. < BAY[1]]

Bay of Pigs bay on the southwestern coast of Cuba that was the site of an abortive attempt by US-backed Cuban exiles to overthrow the government of Fidel Castro in 1961

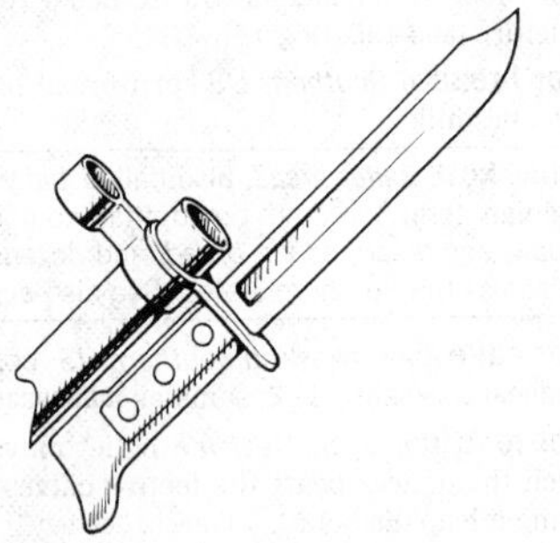

bayonet

bay·o·net /báy ənət, bày ə nét/ *n* a blade that can be attached to the end of a rifle and used for stabbing ■ *vt* (**-net·ed** or **-net·ted, -net·ing** or **-net·ting, -nets**) to stab or kill somebody with a bayonet [Early 17C. < French *baïonnette*, after BAYONNE, in France]

Bay·onne /bay ṓn/ **1.** city in northeastern New Jersey, on a peninsula connected to Staten Island by a bridge. Population: 61,605 (2002 estimate). **2.** city in the Pyrénées-Atlantiques Department of the Aquitaine Region, southwestern France. Population: 61,051 (1998 estimate).

bay·ou /bī́ oo, -ō/ (*plural* **-ous**) *n* in the southern United States, an area of slow-moving water, often overgrown with reeds, leading from a river or lake [Mid-18C. Via Louisiana French < Choctaw *bayuk* "small river forming part of a delta"]

Bay·reuth /bī róyt/ city in Bavaria, southern Germany, northeast of Nuremberg. It is the site of an annual Wagner opera festival. Population: 72,840 (1997).

bay rum *n* a liquid made by dissolving the oil of the leaves of the bay rum tree and other fragrant oils in alcohol and water. Use: men's cosmetics. [Because originally made by distilling the oil with rum]

bay rum tree *n* a tree whose leaves produce fragrant oil. Use: bay rum, soaps. Native to: Central and South America. Latin name: *Pimenta racemosa*.

Bay Shore one of approximately 20 communities comprising the town of Islip, on Long Island, New York

Bay State *n* a nickname for Massachusetts

Bay Street *n* **1.** the street in Toronto on which

Canada's largest stock exchange is located **2.** the controlling financial interests of Toronto, Canada

Bay·town /báy tòwn/ city and port in southeastern Texas, on the northern shore of Galveston Bay, north of Galveston. Population: 67,360 (2002 estimate).

bay win·dow *n* **1.** a rounded or three-sided window that sticks out from an outside wall and forms a recess on the inside **2.** a large bulging belly (*slang*)

bay·wood /báy wòod/ *n* a light variety of mahogany from southern Mexico and Central America [After the *Bay* of Campeche, Mexico]

ba·zaar /bə zaár/ *n* **1.** STREET MARKET a street market in North Africa or southwestern Asia **2.** CHARITY SALE a sale of goods to raise money for charity, often held outdoors **3.** VARIETY STORE a retail store that sells a wide variety of items [Late 16C. Via Italian and Turkish < Persian *bāzār* "market"]

~~**bazar**~~ incorrect spelling of **bazaar**

ba·zil·lion /bə zíllyən/, **bi·zil·lion** *n* a very large indefinite number (*slang*) [*Ba-* expressing emphasis]

ba·zil·lion·aire /bə zìllyə nér, bə zíllyə nèr/ *n* a person of monumentally great wealth (*slang*)

ba·zo·dee /bə zṓdee/ *adj Carib* unable to think clearly, either because of psychological turmoil or because of some physical condition or effect (*slang*) [Mid 20C. Via French Creole < French *abasourdi* "stunned, bewildered"]

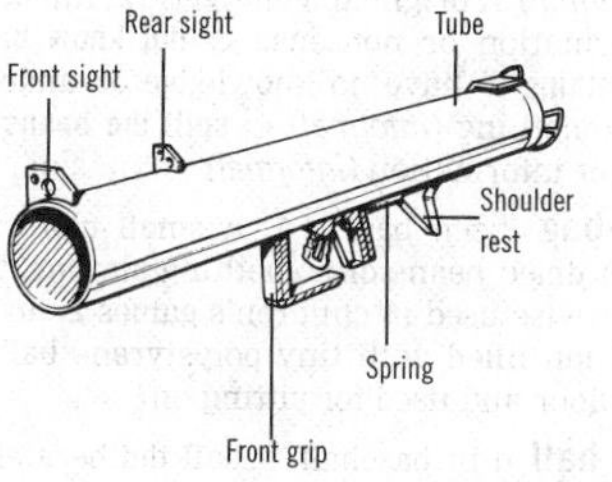

bazooka

ba·zoo·ka /bə zóokə/ *n* a tube-shaped weapon, fired from the shoulder, that launches a missile that can disable a tank [Mid-20C. Origin ?]

bb[1], **b.b.** *abbr* ball bearing

bb[2] *abbr* Barbados (*used in Internet addresses*) See table at **domain name**

BB[1] *n* a pellet fired from a shotgun or air rifle [Late 19C. < the official designation of shot that is 0.18 in]

BB[2] *abbr* **1.** BASEBALL base on balls **2.** *also* **B.B.** JUDAISM B'nai B'rith **3.** bye-bye (*used in e-mails or text messages*)

B.B.A. *abbr* Bachelor of Business Administration

BBB *abbr* COMM Better Business Bureau

BBC *n* in the United Kingdom, the publicly funded organization that provides radio and television services. Full form **British Broadcasting Corporation**

BBC En·glish *n UK* a form of English used by newscasters and announcers on BBC television and radio

BB gun *n* an air rifle that has a spring-loaded plunger rather than a lever for compressing air inside the barrel [< BB[1]]

bbl, bbl. *abbr* MEASURE barrel

BBQ *abbr* FOOD barbecue

BBS *abbr* ONLINE bulletin board system

BC *abbr* **1.** because (*used in e-mails or text messages*) **2.** British Columbia

B.C., B.C. *adv* used to indicate a date that is a particular number of years before the traditional date of the birth of Jesus Christ (*used after dates*) Full form **before Christ**

BCD *abbr* COMPUT binary coded decimal

B.C.E.[1] *abbr* **1.** Bachelor of Chemical Engineering **2.** Bachelor of Civil Engineering

B.C.E.[2], **BCE** *adv* used after a date as the non-Christian equivalent of B.C. Full form **before the Common Era**

B cell *n* a white blood cell (**lymphocyte**), formed in bone marrow in mammals and present in blood and lymph, that creates antibodies in response to a specific antigen

BCG *n* an antituberculosis vaccine made from a weakened strain of the tubercle bacillus. Full form **bacillus Calmette-Guérin (vaccine)**

B.Ch. *abbr* Bachelor of Surgery [Latin *Baccalaureus Chirurgiae*]

bck *abbr* a file extension for a backup file

BCNU *abbr* be seeing you (*used in e-mails or text messages*)

B com·plex *n* BIOCHEM same as **vitamin B complex**

BC soil *n* soil made up of two distinct layers

bd *abbr* Bangladesh (*used in Internet addresses*) See table at **domain name**

BD *abbr* **1.** bank draft **2.** bomb disposal

B/D, b/d *abbr* BANKING **1.** bank draft **2.** bills discounted

bdel·li·um /déllee əm/ *n* **1.** a transparent yellowish resin. Use: perfumes. **2.** a tree that produces bdellium resin. Native to: Africa, western Asia. Genus: *Commiphora*. [14C. Via Latin < Greek < Semitic]

bd. ft. *abbr* MEASURE board foot

bdl. *abbr* bundle

be[1] *stressed* /bee/; *unstressed* /bi/ (*1st person singular past indicative* **was** *stressed* /woz, wuz/; *unstressed* /wəz/, *2nd person singular past indicative* **were** *stressed* /wur/; *unstressed* /wər/, *3rd person singular past indicative* **was**, *1st person plural past indicative* **were**, *2nd person plural past indicative* **were**, *3rd person plural past indicative* **were**, *past subjunctive* **were**, *past participle* **been** /bin/, *present subjunctive* **be**, *1st person present singular* **am** *stressed* /am/; *unstressed* /əm/, *2nd person present singular* **are** *stressed* /aar/; *unstressed* /ər/, *3rd person present singular* **is** /iz/, *1st person present plural* **are**, *2nd person present plural* **are**, *3rd person present plural* **are**) CORE MEANING: a verb used most commonly to link the subject of a clause to a complement in order to give more information about the subject, e.g., its identity, nature, attributes, position, or value ○ *This is my coworker.* ○ *He's a very sweet person.* ○ *Her new car is blue.* ○ *The supermarket is on the left.* ○ *The clock was worth $3,000.*

1. *vi* GIVING DESCRIPTION used after "it" as the subject of the clause, to give a description or judgment of something ○ *It is a good thing that we left early.* **2.** *vi* EXIST OR BE TRUE used after "there" to indicate that something exists or is true ○ *There are many problems with her research.* **3.** *vi* EXIST to exist, have presence, or live ○ *I think, therefore I am.* **4.** *vi* HAPPEN to happen or take place ○ *The meeting was at four o'clock.* **5.** *vi* STAY to stay or visit ○ *I was in Italy during the summer.* **6.** *vi* HAVE PARTICULAR QUALITY to have a particular quality or attribute ○ *This sentence is concise.* **7.** *vi* REMAIN used to indicate that a particular situation remains ○ *The facts are these: it is cold and unhealthy here.* **8.** *aux v* EXPRESSING CONTINUATION used as an auxiliary verb with the present participles of other verbs to express continuation ○ *My legs are getting tired.* ○ *I am leaving on the next train.* **9.** *aux v* FORMING PASSIVE used as an auxiliary verb with the past participles of transitive verbs to form the passive voice ○ *She was sent on the mission.* **10.** *aux v* EXPRESSING FUTURE used as an auxiliary verb to indicate that something is planned, expected, intended, or supposed to happen in the future (*used with an infinitive*) ○ *The meeting is to take place tomorrow.* ○ *What am I to do?* **11.** *aux v* EXPRESSING UNPLANNED ACTION IN PAST used as an auxiliary verb when reporting past events to indicate that something happened later than the time reported and was unplanned or uncertain at the time (*used with an infinitive*) ○ *It was to be the last time he ever saw her.* **12.** *aux v* FORMING PERFECT TENSE used as an auxiliary verb with the past participles of some intransitive verbs to form a perfect tense (*archaic*) ○ *She is come back.* **13.** *vi* INTRODUCING SENTENCE used to introduce a full, often quoted sentence, especially a sentence or quotation encapsulating an idea or opinion (*informal*) [Old English *bēon*, via Germanic, "exist, dwell" < Indo-European, "exist, grow"] ◇ **been there, done that (bought the T-shirt)** used to indicate a blasé attitude to a situation (*slang*) ◇ **be off** to leave somewhere ○ *It's already seven o'clock; I'm off.*

ORIGIN The prehistoric Germanic word from which ***be*** is derived, is also the ancestor of English *boor, booth, build, husband*, and *neighbor*, and perhaps also of *bylaw*.

---

be[2] *abbr* Belgium (*used in Internet addresses*) See table at **domain name**

Be *symbol* CHEM ELEM beryllium

B.E. *abbr* **1.** Bachelor of Education **2.** Bachelor of Engineering **3.** *also* **BE** EDUC Board of Education

be- *prefix* **1.** thoroughly, excessively ○ *bedazzle* ○ *bespatter* **2.** on, over, about ○ *bewail* **3.** to surround or cover with ○ *befog* ○ *bedew* **4.** to supply with ○ *befriend* **5.** to make ○ *belittle* [Old English *be-*, *bi-* < Indo-European, "around"]

B/E *abbr* bill of exchange

beach /beech/ *n* COASTAL SAND a strip of sand or pebbles at the point where land meets the sea or a lake ■ *vti* (**beached, beach·ing, beach·es**) **1.** HAUL BOAT ASHORE to pull or run a boat onto a beach, or be pulled onto a beach **2.** STRAND OR BECOME STRANDED to strand or become stranded on shore (*usually passive*) ○ *a whale that had been beached during a storm* [Mid-16C. Origin ?]

SPELLCHECK beach or **beech**? Do not confuse the spelling of ***beach*** and ***beech***, which sound similar. The word ***beach*** can be used as a noun, meaning "sandy shore" (as in *sunbathing on the beach*), or as a verb, meaning "haul ashore or be stranded ashore" (as in *to beach a boat, a beached whale*). The word ***beech*** is only used as a noun denoting a tree or its wood.

---

beach ball *n* a large light easily inflated ball, often brightly colored, for playing with on a beach

beach bug·gy *n UK* same as **dune buggy**

beach bum *n* somebody with no regular occupation who spends time idly on beaches (*informal*)

beach chair *n* a collapsible adjustable outdoor chair with a wooden or metal framework and a seat made from strong fabric

beach·comb·er /beéch kṑmər/ *n* **1.** somebody who looks for useful or valuable things on beaches **2.** *Can, UK* a long high wave that crashes onto a beach. US term **comber**

beach drift *n* debris and sediment transported by waves breaking on the shore at an angle and returning to the ocean in a direction determined by the slope of a beach

beached /beecht/ *adj* stranded on a beach or out of the water

beach flea *n* MARINE BIOL same as **sand flea** (sense 2)

beach·front /beéch frùnt/ *n* a strip of land that adjoins a beach

beach grass *n* a thick grass with strong roots that grows along sandy shores. It is often planted to stop beach erosion. Native to: North America. Genus: *Ammophila*.

beach·head /beéch hèd/ *n* **1.** a part of an enemy shoreline that troops have captured and are using as a base for launching an attack **2.** an initial success that lays the groundwork for achieving an objective [After BRIDGEHEAD]

Beach-la-Mar /beéch lə maár/ *n* a pidgin based on English that developed in Vanuatu, Fiji, and other nearby islands as a trading lingua franca. The modern form that is the national language of Vanuatu is known as Bislama. [Early 19C. < Portuguese *bicho do mar* "sea cucumber," by association with BEACH] —**Beach-la-Mar** *adj*

beach·mo·bile /beéch mō beél/ *n* a vehicle used to transport surfing equipment onto the beach

beach plum *n* **1.** a dark purple edible plum **2.** a small bushy plum tree with large white flowers that bears beach plums. Native to: coast of northeastern North America. Latin name: *Prunus maritima*.

beach·side /beéch sīd/ *adj* on or next to a beach

beach vol·ley·ball *n* volleyball played on a beach or sandy surface with only two players on each side

beach·wear /beéch wèr/ *n* casual clothing designed to be worn on a beach

Beach·y Head /béechee-/ chalk headland on the English Channel near Eastbourne, East Sussex, southern England. Height: 570 ft./171 m.

bea·con /béekən/ *n* **1.** NAUT **FLASHING LIGHT FOR SHIPS** a lighthouse or signaling buoy that produces a flashing light to warn or guide ships **2.** NAVIG **RADIO TRANSMITTER PRODUCING NAVIGATION SIGNAL** a radio transmitter that continuously broadcasts a signal that aircraft use for guidance **3. SIGNALING FIRE ON HILL** a fire lit on a hilltop or tower as part of a national celebration or, formerly, as a signal or warning **4. SOURCE OF INSPIRATION** somebody or something that inspires or guides others (*literary*) **5. HILL SUITABLE FOR SIGNALING FIRES** a prominent hill on which fires were formerly lit as a signal (*often used in place names*) [Old English *bēacen* "signal, sign" < Germanic]

Bea·con /béekən/ city in southeastern New York, on the Hudson River. Population: 13,945 (1998).

bead /beed/ *n* **1. BALL FOR NECKLACE** a small gemstone or glass, plastic, or wooden ball, pierced for stringing on a cord or sewing onto fabric **2. DROP OF MOISTURE** a drop of moisture, especially of sweat **3.** ARCHIT, FURNITURE **BUILDING OR FURNITURE TRIM** an edge or rim that sticks out on a building or a piece of furniture, traditionally with a pattern of rounded knobs **4.** ARMS **GUN SIGHT** a knob sticking up on the end of the barrel of a gun, forming the front part of the gun's sight **5.** AUTOMOT **SEAL ON TIRE** a projecting lip on the tire of a motor vehicle that forms a seal to the wheel rim **6.** METALL **DEPOSIT OF METAL** a deposit of metal used in welding ■ **beads** *npl* **1. NECKLACE** a necklace made of beads **2.** RELIG same as **rosary** (senses 2–3) ■ *v* (**bead·ed, bead·ing, beads**) **1.** *vt* **DECORATE SOMETHING WITH BEADS** to trim or ornament something with beads **2.** *vi* **FORM INTO BEADS** to form drops of moisture [Old English *gebed* "prayer" < Germanic] —**bead·ed** *adj* ◇ **draw** *or* **get a bead on somebody** *or* **something 1.** to take careful aim at somebody or something **2.** to single out somebody or something for special consideration ◇ **tell** *or* **say** *or* **count your beads** to say prayers recited in sequence and counted using a rosary

bead·ing /béeding/ *n* **1.** an edge or rim that sticks out on a building or a piece of furniture, traditionally with a pattern of rounded knobs **2.** a rounded piece of molding, e.g., on a door

bea·dle /béed'l/ *n* **1.** an official who acts as caretaker of a synagogue and oversees the running of the service **2.** a minor parish official formerly employed in the Church of England to usher and keep order [13C. < Old French *bedel* "proclaimer, messenger" < Germanic]

Bea·dle /béed'l/, **George Wells** (1903–89) US geneticist. He won the Nobel Prize in physiology or medicine (1958) for his pioneering research into the role of genes in synthesis of cellular substances. Full name **Beadle, George Wells**

bead·work /béed wùrk/ *n* **1.** decorative wooden edging, e.g., on a door or window frame **2.** decoration using beads to form a design, e.g., on furniture or knitwear

bead·y /béedee/ (**-i·er, -i·est**) *adj* **1.** small, round, and shiny like a bead **2.** covered or ornamented with beads —**bead·i·ly** *adv* —**bead·i·ness** *n*

bea·gle /béeg'l/ *n* a small smooth-haired dog, belonging to a breed with a white, tan, and black coat and long drooping ears, often used for hunting [15C. Origin ?]

Bea·gle Chan·nel /béeg'l-/ strait in the Tierra del Fuego archipelago, at the southernmost tip of South America. Length: 150 mi./240 km.

bea·gling /béegling/ *n UK* hunting, especially for rabbits or hares, using beagles —**bea·gler** *n*

beak /beek/ *n* **1. BIRD'S MOUTH PARTS** the feeding apparatus of a bird, consisting of two pointed jaws protected by a horny covering. Beaks take many different shapes according to the eating habits of individual bird species. **2. PROJECTING PART** a part that sticks out, e.g., the lip of a container **3. SOMEBODY'S NOSE** somebody's nose, especially when it is long or hooked (*slang*) **4.** ZOOL **PROTRUDING PART OF ANIMAL'S MOUTH** a projecting part of the mouth or jaw of animals other than birds, e.g., the sucking mouthpart of an insect or the bony jaw projection of a fish **5.** ZOOL **PART OF INVERTEBRATE ANIMAL SHELL** the oldest part of the shell of an invertebrate animal with a hinged shell, found nearest the hinge **6.** ARCHIT **CURVED CORNICE OR MOLDING** a cornice or molding with a downward-curving edge [13C. Via Old French *bec* < Latin *beccus*] —**beaked** *adj* —**beak·less** *adj*

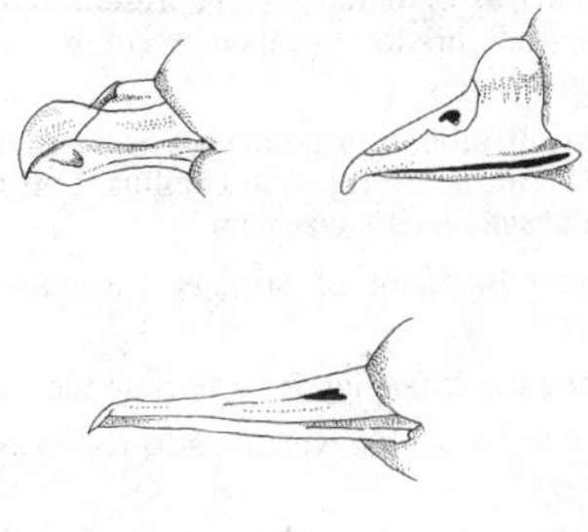

beak

beaked whale *n* a widely found, medium-sized, toothed whale with a long snout. Family: Ziphiidae.

beak·er /béekər/ *n* **1.** a flat-bottomed glass container used in laboratories **2.** a wide-mouthed cup, especially a plastic one without a handle [14C. Via Old Norse *bikarr* < assumed Vulgar Latin *bicarium*, perhaps < Greek *bikos* "wine jar, earthen vessel"]

Beak·er folk *npl* a prehistoric people who lived throughout Central Europe during the period 2000 to 1000 B.C. The remains of pottery beakers are often found in areas where they lived.

be-all ◇ **the be-all and end-all** the thing that is most important

beam /beem/ *n* **1. HORIZONTAL STRUCTURAL SUPPORT** a horizontal structural member, e.g., a long piece of timber, metal, or concrete that spans a gap and supports a floor, roof, or other structure above **2. LINE OF LIGHT** a narrow line of light, e.g., from a flashlight **3. BROAD SMILE** a broad smile of happiness or satisfaction **4.** NAUT **STRUCTURAL CROSSPIECE IN SHIP** a structural member of a ship or boat that joins the sides and supports the deck **5.** NAUT **SHIP'S BREADTH** the full breadth of a ship **6.** NAUT **SIDE OF SHIP** either of the sides of a ship **7.** PHYS **FLOW OF RADIATION** a narrow stream of radiation or particles flowing in one direction **8.** NAVIG **GUIDING SIGNAL** a radio or radar signal intended to guide a ship or aircraft, or the direction indicated by this signal **9.** *UK* GYMNASTICS same as **balance beam 10. HORIZONTAL PART OF BALANCE** the pivoted horizontal bar of a balance on which the two scales hang **11. MAIN SUPPORTING SHAFT** a main bar or shaft, e.g., either of the main stems of a deer's antlers or the central shaft of a plow **12.** MECH ENG **CONNECTING LEVER IN ENGINE** a lever connecting the piston rod and crankshaft in an engine **13.** MANUF **ROLLER IN LOOM** a cylinder in a loom on which either the warp or the cloth is wound ■ *v* (**beamed, beam·ing, beams**) **1.** *vti* **SMILE BROADLY** to smile broadly with happiness or satisfaction, or express feelings by smiling broadly **2.** *vt* BROADCAST **SEND RADIO OR TV SIGNAL** to send or transmit a program to a distant place in the form of a radio or television signal **3.** *vti* **SHINE** to shine, or shine something, in a particular direction **4.** *vti* **CHANGE CIRCUMSTANCES SUDDENLY** to move between completely different places or situations in a sudden and disorienting way, or make somebody or something move in this way (*slang; used with "up" or "down"*) [Old English *bēam* "tree, piece of timber, column, ray" < Germanic] ◇ **broad** *or* **wide in the beam** having wide hips (*informal; sometimes considered offensive*) ◇ **off the beam** missing the point or irrelevant (*informal*) ◇ **on the beam 1.** using a beam for guidance **2.** on track or working effectively (*informal*)

beam aer·i·al *n UK* same as **beam antenna**

beam an·ten·na *n* a radio or television antenna designed to transmit or receive signals in or from a particular direction

beam bridge *n* a bridge, usually with a short span, supported on beams whose ends rest on piers or abutments

beam com·pass *n* a tool for drawing very large circles or arcs, consisting of a horizontal bar with sliding legs

beam-ends *npl* the ends of the beams supporting the deck of a vessel ◇ **on her** *or* **its beam-ends** used to describe a ship leaning so far to one side that its deck is vertical

beam·let /béemlət/ *n* a small amount of low-level radiation, used in noninvasive radiation treatments of cancer

Bea·mon /béemən/, **Bob** (*b.* 1946) US athlete. He set a world long jump record of 29 ft. 2.5 in./8.9 m at the 1968 Olympic Games in Mexico City that stood for 23 years. Full name **Beamon, Robert**

beam split·ter *n* a device used in holography to divide a laser light into two beams by means of a prism and mirror so as to produce a three-dimensional image

beam·y /béemee/ (**-i·er, -i·est**) *adj* **1.** describes a ship with a broad beam **2.** sending out beams of light (*literary*)

bean /been/ *n* **1. EDIBLE GREEN POD** a long thin usually green seedpod eaten cooked whole as a vegetable **2. SMALL ROUND VEGETABLE** a small round or kidney-shaped seed of various colors that is eaten as a vegetable and can be dried to preserve it **3. PLANT WITH EDIBLE PODS AND SEEDS** a tall climbing or small bushy plant that produces beans. Genus: *Phaseolus*. **4. SEED USED IN FOOD OR DRINK** a coffee, cocoa, or carob seed that is processed and used in food or drink **5. HEAD** a person's head or brain (*slang*) ■ **beans** *npl* **NOTHING** nothing at all (*informal*) ■ *vt* (**beaned, bean·ing, beans**) **HIT SOMEBODY ON HEAD** to hit somebody on the head (*slang*) [Old English *bēan* < Germanic] ◇ **full of beans** (*informal*) **1.** bright and energetic **2.** full of incorrect information or nonsense ◇ **not know beans about something** to have no knowledge or understanding of something (*informal*) ◇ **spill the beans** to reveal secret information (*informal*)

bean·bag /béen bàg/ *n* **1.** a small cloth bag filled with dried beans or something similar, thrown or otherwise used in children's games **2.** an oversized cushion filled with tiny polystyrene balls, laid on the floor and used for sitting on

bean ball *n* in baseball, a ball deliberately pitched at the batter's head (*informal*)

bean bee·tle *n* INSECTS same as **Mexican bean beetle**

bean count·er *n* an accountant (*slang insult*)

bean curd *n* tofu, especially as used in Chinese cooking

bean·er·y /béenəree/ (*plural* **-ies**) *n* a cheap restaurant (*informal*)

Bean·head /béen hèd/ *n* a first-year cadet at the United States Military Academy at West Point (*slang*)

bean·ie /béenee/ *n* a round tight-fitting hat like a skullcap, formerly worn by schoolboys and young college students

bean·o /béenō/ *n* the game of bingo, sometimes played with beans as markers, and often considered illegal gambling (*informal*)

bean·pole /béen pōl/ *n* **1.** somebody tall and thin (*informal insult*) **2.** a stick or pole for supporting a climbing bean plant

bean sprouts *npl* long pale shoots of sprouted bean seeds, particularly of the mung bean, harvested while crisp and eaten raw or very lightly cooked

bean·stalk /béen stàwk/ *n* the stem of a bean plant

Bean·town /béen tòwn/ *n* a nickname for Boston (*informal*)

bear[1] /ber/ *n* **1. LARGE FURRY ANIMAL** a large strong omnivorous four-legged animal that has thick shaggy fur and sharp claws, and walks on the flat of its paws. Family: Ursidae. **2. MEDIUM-SIZED FURRY ANIMAL** an animal that resembles but is unrelated to the true bear, e.g., the koala **3. SOMEBODY EASILY ANNOYED** somebody regarded as ill-tempered (*informal*) **4.** FIN **SOMEBODY WHO ANTICIPATES FALLING PRICES** somebody who sells stocks or commodities in anticipation of falling prices **5.** FIN **SOMEBODY WHO ANTICIPATES BAD BUSINESS CONDITIONS** somebody who anticipates unfavorable business conditions **6. DIFFICULT THING** something difficult to experience or endure (*slang*) [Old English *bera* < Germanic, "the brown one"]

SPELLCHECK See *bare.*

bear[2] /ber/ (**bore** /bawr/, **borne** /bawrn/ or **born** /bawrn/, **bear·ing, bears**) *v* **1.** *vti* TOLERATE to be able to endure something without great distress or annoyance (*used in questions and negative statements*) ○ *I can't bear this heat.* **2.** *vt* SUPPORT SOMETHING to hold or support a weight or something heavy **3.** *vti* BE FIT FOR SOMETHING to withstand being subjected to a particular action ○ *Will her theories bear scrutiny?* **4.** *vt* MERIT SOMETHING to be worthy of an action ○ *bear further investigation* **5.** *vt* ACCEPT SOMETHING AS RESPONSIBILITY to accept something as a duty or responsibility ○ *bear the expense* **6.** *vt* BE CHARACTERIZED BY SOMETHING to have something as a quality, characteristic, or permanent attribute ○ *bears no relation to reality* **7.** *vt* BE MARKED BY SOMETHING to show physical signs of something ○ *bears a likeness to his uncle* **8.** *vt* CARRY SOMETHING to hold or support and transport somebody or something ○ *The spores are borne on the wind.* **9.** *vt* PRODUCE SOMETHING to yield something by a natural process, or produce something desirable or valuable ○ *the tree that bore fruit* **10.** *vt* GIVE BIRTH TO CHILD to give birth to a child or young **11.** *vt* THINK SOMETHING to hold a particular thought, feeling, or idea in the mind ○ *I bore him no ill will.* **12.** *vi* HEAD IN PARTICULAR DIRECTION to move or turn in a particular direction ○ *Bear right when the road divides.* **13.** *vt* BEHAVE IN PARTICULAR WAY to conduct or carry yourself in a particular way ○ *bore himself well* **14.** *vt* TRANSMIT SOMETHING to hold something in mind and communicate it to others (*formal*) ○ *I will bear your message.* [Old English *beran* < Indo-European] ◇ **bring something to bear (on something)** to use something to force a desired outcome

ORIGIN The prehistoric Germanic word from which ***bear*** is derived is also the ancestor of English *barrow*[1], *berth, bier, birth,* and *burden*[1]. Its Indo-European ancestor is in turn the source of English *amphora, fertile,* and *suffer.*

bear down *vi* to push with the vaginal muscles during childbirth
bear down on *vt* **1.** to move quickly and menacingly toward somebody or something **2.** to exert downward pressure on somebody or something
bear on, bear upon *vt* **1.** to relate to or affect something **2.** to be a problem for or a burden to somebody or something
bear out *vt* to prove something or somebody to be true or justified ○ *This bears out my theory.*
bear up *vi* **1.** to remain true or undamaged after being examined or criticized **2.** to remain cheerful and determined in spite of problems
bear upon *vt* same as **bear on**
bear with *vt* to be patient with somebody who is trying to do something

Bear /ber/ river that rises in Utah and flows through Wyoming and Idaho before entering Utah and emptying into the Great Salt Lake. Length: 350 mi./563 km.

bear·a·ble /bérəb'l/ *adj* not too unpleasant to put up with or accept —**bear·a·bly** *adv*

bear·bait·ing /bér bàyting/ *n* the setting of fierce dogs onto a chained bear, once a popular form of public entertainment

bear·ber·ry /bér bèrree/ (*plural* **-ries**) *n* a trailing evergreen bush with red berries. Native to: northern America, Europe, Asia. Latin name: *Arctostaphylos uva-ursi.* [Early 17C. < BEAR[1]]

bear·cat /bér kàt/ *n* ZOOL same as **red panda**

beard /beerd/ *n* **1.** HAIR GROWING ON MAN'S CHIN the hair on a man's chin and, often, his neck and cheeks **2.** ZOOL TUFTS GROWING ON ANIMAL OR PLANT a growth of longer hair on an animal, e.g., on a goat's chin, or a long slender growth on plants, e.g., on barley and wheat heads **3.** ATTENTION-DIVERTING PERSON OR THING somebody or something that diverts attention or suspicion from another ■ *vt* (**beard·ed, beard·ing, beards**) OPPOSE SOMEBODY OR SOMETHING to oppose or confront somebody or something confidently or disrespectfully ○ *bearded him in his office* [Old English, < Indo-European] —**beard·ed** *adj* —**beard·less** *adj*

beard·ed col·lie /be͞erdid-/ *n* a medium-sized gray or brown-and-white dog with a long coat, drooping ears, and a tuft of hair on its chin, belonging to a breed used for herding animals

beard·ed drag·on, beard·ed liz·ard *n* a large lizard with a pouch under its chin that inflates to ward off attackers. Native to: Australia. Latin name: *Amphibolus barbatus.*

beard·ed i·ris *n* an iris that has large flowers, with numerous hairs, often colored, along the center of each drooping lower petal

beard·ed liz·ard *n* REPT same as **bearded dragon**

beard·ed vul·ture *n* BIRDS same as **lammergeier**

Beards·ley /be͞erdzlee/, **Aubrey** (1872–98) British artist and illustrator. One of the "Decadents" in the 1890s, he produced art nouveau illustrations in a distinctive black-and-white style, including series for *Morte d'Arthur* (1893–4) and *Salomé* (1894). Full name **Beardsley, Aubrey Vincent**

beard·tongue /be͞erd tùng/ *n* PLANTS same as **penstemon** [Early 19C. < the tufts on one of its stamens]

bear·er /bérrər/ *n* **1.** BRINGER somebody who brings or carries something **2.** FIN HOLDER OF REDEEMABLE NOTE somebody possessing a document redeemable for payment **3.** same as **pallbearer 4.** PORTER a local person employed to carry equipment on an expedition

bear·er bond *n* a bond payable only to the party that presents it

bear·er in·stru·ment *n* a negotiable instrument that may be converted to cash by whoever holds it

bear hug *n* **1.** TIGHT EMBRACE an enthusiastic or energetic embrace **2.** TIGHT WRESTLING HOLD in wrestling, a tight, squeezing hold around an opponent's chest and arms **3.** WARNING OF INTENDED CORPORATE TAKEOVER a warning given by one company to another of its intention to assume control of the other

bear·ing /bérring/ *n* **1.** WAY OF MOVING OR STANDING somebody's way of moving, standing, or behaving generally ○ *her dignified bearing* **2.** MECH ENG HOUSING FOR MOVING MACHINE PART the part of a machine that supports a sliding or rotating part **3.** NAVIG CALCULATION OF DIRECTION OR GEOGRAPHIC POSITION the location or direction of movement of somebody or something, calculated using a map or compass **4.** RELEVANCE a relation to something ○ *This has no bearing on the matter under discussion.* **5.** ARCHIT SUPPORT FOR BEAM a support for a beam or girder **6.** HERALDRY HERALDIC DEVICE a heraldic device or charge ◇ **find** *or* **get your bearings 1.** to learn exactly where you are and in which direction you should proceed **2.** to become familiar with a new environment ◇ **lose your bearings 1.** to become uncertain about where you are and in which direction you should proceed **2.** to become unable to react in a normal manner

bear·ing rein *n Can, UK* a short rein joining a horse's bit to a hook on the saddle, used to keep the horse's head up. US term **checkrein**

bear·ish /bérrish/ *adj* **1.** FIN ANTICIPATING FALLING PRICES conducive to or characterized by selling rather than buying stocks or commodities in anticipation of falling prices **2.** FIN ANTICIPATING BAD BUSINESS CONDITIONS anticipating unfavorable business conditions **3.** BAD-TEMPERED surly or ill-tempered toward people **4.** CLUMSY moving or behaving roughly or clumsily

bear mar·ket *n* a situation in a stock or commodity market in which stockholders are selling in anticipation of falling prices

Bear Mount·ain mountain in southeastern New York State on the western bank of the Hudson River. Height: 1,305 ft./398 m.

bé·ar·naise sauce /bèr náyz-, bày aar-/ *n* a sauce for meat, thickened with egg yolk and flavored with tarragon [Late 19C. < French < *Béarn,* district in SW France]

bear raid *n* an attempt to lower a stock or commodity price by selling large numbers of shares, usually in order to buy them back at a lowered price

bear's breech *n* a large garden plant with spiky leaves. Flowers: whitish, purple-streaked. Latin name: *Acanthus mollis.*

bear's ear *n* PLANTS same as **auricula**

bearskin: two British soldiers wearing bearskins

bear·skin /bér skìn/ *n* **1.** a bear's skin with the fur still attached, stripped from the animal **2.** a tall fur hat worn as part of the ceremonial uniform of soldiers in some British army regiments and by drum majors

beast /beest/ *n* **1.** LARGE ANIMAL an animal, especially a large four-footed mammal **2.** IRRATIONAL SIDE OF SOMEBODY'S PERSONALITY the instinctive, irrational, or aggressive part of somebody's personality **3.** SOMEBODY BRUTAL somebody cruel or aggressive **4.** SOMETHING UNPLEASANT something that is difficult or unpleasant (*informal*) ○ *This is truly a beast of a job!* **5.** SOMETHING WITH PARTICULAR QUALITY something that has a particular quality (*informal*) ○ *The basic beginner's windsurfing board is a hardy beast.* [12C. Via Old French *beste* < Latin *bestia*]

beast·ie /be͞estee/ *n N Am, Scotland* a small animal, especially an insect or small crawling animal (*informal or humorous*)

beast·ings *n* ZOOL another spelling of **beestings**

beast·ly /be͞estlee/ *adj* thoroughly unpleasant or objectionable —**beast·li·ness** *n*

beast of bur·den *n* an animal used to carry or pull things or do other heavy work, e.g., a donkey or an ox

beast of prey *n* an animal that hunts other animals for food

beat /beet/ *v* (**beat, beat·en** /be͞et'n/, **beat·ing, beats**) **1.** *vt* DEFEAT SOMEBODY IN CONTEST to defeat somebody in a contest, race, or competition ○ *She was beaten in the semifinal.* **2.** *vt* HIT SOMEBODY OR SOMETHING REPEATEDLY to hit somebody or something with repeated heavy blows **3.** *vi* KNOCK AGAINST SOMETHING REPEATEDLY to knock or strike against something repeatedly ○ *waves beating against the rocks* **4.** *vt* SURPASS SOMETHING to surpass a previous best performance ○ *beat the long jump record* **5.** *vti* BE BETTER THAN SOMETHING to be or do better than a particular thing, activity, or quality (*informal*) ○ *Sitting by the pool sure beats working.* **6.** *vti* MUSIC HIT DRUM to hit a drum repeatedly to produce a musical rhythm or a signal **7.** *vt* MUSIC SET MUSICAL RHYTHM to show or establish a musical rhythm, e.g., with a conductor's baton or by clapping hands ○ *beating time with her hand* **8.** *vi* PULSATE to make natural short rhythmic movements (*refers to the heart or pulse*) **9.** *vt* COOK STIR INGREDIENTS VIGOROUSLY to mix moist ingredients vigorously to combine them, make them smooth, or incorporate air into them ○ *Now beat the eggs.* **10.** *vt* ARRIVE AHEAD OF SOMEBODY to arrive or finish something sooner than somebody else or before a time limit ○ *She beat me to the office.* **11.** *vt* OVERCOME OBSTACLES IN SOMETHING to overcome the difficulties or obstacles created by something ○ *You can't beat the system.* **12.** *vti* BIRDS FLAP WINGS to move the wings up and down in flight, or be moved in this way ○ *The vulture beat its wings.* **13.** *vt* MAKE SOMETHING BY HITTING to shape or make something by pounding or trampling ○ *beat silver into jewelry* **14.** *vti* HUNTING DRIVE GAME FROM BRUSH to move through or disturb bushes and undergrowth in order to frighten animals and birds for hunting **15.** *vi* SAILING SAIL INTO WIND to sail a boat or ship as nearly as possible in the direction from which the wind is blowing ■ *n* **1.** STEADY THROBBING a rhythmic sound or movement made by something throbbing or pulsating (*often used in combination*) ○ *could hear the beat of his heart* **2.** STROKE an act of striking one thing against another, especially repeatedly and rhythmically, or the sound of one thing striking against another in this way ○ *a drum beat* **3.** MUSIC **SET RHYTHM** a single element of measured time in a musical piece or poem. Beats occur at regular intervals and are the rhythmic and metrical foundations of music. **4.** MUSIC **DOMINANT RHYTHM** the dominant rhythm in a piece of music, especially a strong rhythm in rock music **5. USUAL ROUTE** a regular route followed or area covered while working, e.g., a police officer's route or reporter's usual subject ○ *covering her regular beat* **6. AREA SOMEBODY USUALLY GOES TO** the places somebody usually frequents, especially somebody's usual hunting or fishing area ■ *adj* **1. TIRED OUT** completely exhausted (*slang*) **2. PUZZLED** unable to understand or think how to proceed (*informal*) ○ *It has me beat.* **3.** *also* **Beat OF BEAT GENERATION** relating to or produced by members of the Beat Generation [Old English *bēatan*, via Germanic < Indo-European, "to strike"] ◇ **beat it!** used to tell somebody to go away (*slang*) ◇ **beat somebody to something** to succeed in doing something before somebody else can do it (*informal*) ◇ **beat something to death** to repeat something, e.g., a story or idea, so often that people become bored with it (*informal*) ◇ **it beats me** used to indicate that you do not understand something (*informal*) ◇ **not miss a beat** to show no sign of surprise or upset ◇ **take some beating** to be so good as to be difficult to improve on ○ *Her track record will take some beating.*

SPELLCHECK beat or **beet**? Do not confuse the spelling of ***beat*** and ***beet***, which sound similar. The word ***beat*** can be used as a verb, meaning "defeat," "surpass," "hit repeatedly," or "pulsate" (as in *beat the world record, beat a drum, his heart was beating*), or as a noun, meaning "rhythm" or "usual route" (as in *music with a steady beat, a police officer's beat*). The word ***beet*** is only used as a noun denoting a root vegetable.

SYNONYMS See ***defeat.***

beat down *v* **1.** *vi* **COME DOWN STRONGLY** to shine intensely or fall heavily from the sky (*refers to sun or rain*) **2.** *vt* **EXHAUST SOMEBODY** to make somebody feel completely exhausted **3.** *vt* **PERSUADE SOMEBODY TO SELL FOR LESS** to persuade somebody to charge less than the intended selling price (*informal*)

beat off *v* **1.** *vt* to stop an attack or challenge by vigorous action **2.** *vi* a highly offensive term meaning to masturbate (*slang taboo*)

beat up *vt* to injure somebody badly by repeated punches or kicks (*informal*)

beat up on *vt* same as **beat up** (*informal*)

beat·box /bēet bòks/ *n* an electronic drum used mainly in hip-hop and rap music to provide accompanying rhythm and sounds (*informal*)

beat-'em-up *n* a video or computer game involving a large amount of simulated hand-to-hand fighting (*informal*)

beat·en past participle of **beat**

beat·en-up *adj* damaged or in bad condition after long use

beat·er /bēetər/ *n* **1. TOOL FOR BEATING** a tool for beating something, e.g., an electric food mixer for beating eggs (*often used in combination*) **2.** HUNTING **HUNTER'S ASSISTANT FOR DRIVING BIRDS OUT** somebody who flushes out game for hunters to shoot, usually by hitting bushes **3. SOMEBODY WHO BEATS METAL** somebody who hammers metal **4. OLD CAR** an old rusty automobile in poor running condition (*informal*)

Beat Gen·er·a·tion *n* **1.** young people in the 1950s who rejected the traditional values, customs, and dress of Western society and experimented with Eastern philosophies, communal living, and illegal drugs **2.** a group of writers associated with the attitudes of the Beat Generation, including Jack Kerouac and Allen Ginsberg

be·a·tif·ic /bee ə tíffik/ *adj* (*literary*) **1.** expressing or radiating great happiness and serenity **2.** bringing or expressing the perfect happiness and inner peace supposed to be enjoyed by the soul in heaven [Mid-17C. Directly or via French *béatifique* < Latin *beatificus* < *beatus* "blessed"] —**be·a·tif·i·cal·ly** *adv*

~~**beatiful**~~ incorrect spelling of **beautiful**

be·at·i·fy /bee átti fī/ (**-fied, -fy·ing, -fies**) *vt* **1.** in the Roman Catholic Church, to state officially that a dead person lived a holy life, usually as the first step toward making the person a saint **2.** to make somebody extremely happy (*literary*) [Mid-16C. Directly or via French *béatifer* < ecclesiastical Latin *beatificare* < Latin *beatificus* (see BEATIFIC)] —**be·at·i·fi·ca·tion** /bee àttəfi káysh'n/ *n*

beat·ing /bēeting/ *n* **1.** an attack or punishment in which somebody is repeatedly hit **2.** a severe defeat or setback, e.g., in a competition or in business

beat·ing reed *n* a reed in woodwind instruments that vibrates as air passes over it

be·at·i·tude /bee áttə tòod/ *n* (*literary*) **1.** the perfect happiness and inner peace supposed to be enjoyed by the soul in heaven **2.** extreme happiness and serenity [15C. Directly or via French < Latin *beatitud-* < *beatus* "blessed"]

Be·at·i·tude *n* **1.** in the Bible, one of the sayings of Jesus Christ in the Sermon on the Mount about the eight groups of people who will receive blessing in heaven (Matthew 5:3–11) **2.** a title given to a senior bishop in non-Orthodox Christian churches of the eastern Mediterranean

The Beatles

Beat·les /bēet'lz/ (1959–70) British pop music group. This group of musicians from Liverpool, Paul McCartney, John Lennon, George Harrison, and Ringo Starr, revolutionized popular music in the 1960s.

beat·nik /bēetnik/ *n* somebody who rejects conventional ideas, dress, and social conventions, especially a member of the Beat Generation of the 1950s

Bea·ton /bēet'n/, **Sir Cecil** (1904–80) British photographer and designer. He was a fashion and high-society photographer. He also designed scenery and costumes for *My Fair Lady, Gigi,* and other productions. Full name **Beaton, Sir Cecil Walter Hardy**

> "Be daring, be different, impractical, anything that will assert integrity of purpose and imaginative vision against the play-it-safers."
> [Sir Cecil Beaton, *Theater Arts*; 1957]

Be·a·trix /báy ə trìks, bēe ə-/, **queen of the Netherlands** (*b.* 1938) She acceded to the throne on the abdication of her mother, Queen Juliana, in 1980. Full name **Beatrix Wilhelmina Armgard**

Beat·tie /bēetee/, **Ann** (*b.* 1947) US writer. She wrote the novel *Chilly Scenes of Winter* (1976) and the short-story collection *Where You'll Find Me* (1986).

> "There are things that get whispered about that writers are there to overhear."
> [Ann Beattie, *New York Times*; November 1, 1987]

beat-up *adj* in bad condition because of overuse (*informal*)

beau /bō/ (*plural* **beaus** or **beaux** /bōz/) *n* **1.** a boyfriend or male admirer (*dated*) **2.** a man always smartly dressed in the most fashionable clothes (*archaic*) [Late 17C. < French < *beau* "beautiful" < Latin *bellus* (see BEAUTY)]

beau·coup /bō kòo/ *adj* very many or very much (*slang*) ○ *His new suit cost beaucoup dollars.* [Early 20C. < French]

Beau·fort /bōfərt/, **Henry, Cardinal** (1377?–1447) English prelate and diplomat. He became a cardinal in 1426 and in the 1430s was the real power behind the government of the young King Henry VI of England.

Beau·fort scale /bōfərt-/ *n* an international scale of wind speeds indicated by numbers ranging from 0 for calm to 12 for hurricane. Each force is recognized by its effects on things such as flags and trees and on the surface of the sea. [Mid-19C. After Sir Francis *Beaufort* (1774–1857), Irish admiral and hydrographer]

Beau·fort Sea section of the Arctic Ocean northwest of Canada and north of Alaska. Area: 170,000 sq. mi./450,000 sq. km. Depth: 15,360 ft./4,682 m.

beau geste /bō zhést/ (*plural* **beaux gestes** /*pronunc. same*/) *n* a kind or magnanimous act [Early 20C. < French, "fine gesture"]

Beau·har·nais /bō aar náy/, **Alexandre, Vicomte de** (1760–94) French soldier and politician. He embraced the French Revolution and became president of the Constituent Assembly (1791), but was later guillotined.

Beau·har·nais, Joséphine de ♦ **Joséphine**

beau i·de·al /bō ī dēe əl/ (*plural* **beaux i·de·als** /bō ī dēe əlz, bōz ī dēe əl/) *n* **1.** somebody's idea of perfection or beauty **2.** somebody or something considered to be a perfect example of its kind [Early 19C. < French, "ideal beauty" (but usually taken as meaning "beautiful ideal")]

Beau·jo·lais /bōzhə láy/ *n* a light usually red wine from central France [Mid-19C. After a district in central France]

Beau·jo·lais Nou·veau *n* Beaujolais sold in the November and December of the year of its production

Beau·mar·chais /bō maar sháy/, **Pierre Augustin Caron de** (1732–99) French dramatist. He wrote the comedies *The Barber of Seville* (1775) and *The Marriage of Figaro* (1784). These were made into operas by Gioacchino Rossini and Wolfgang Amadeus Mozart respectively. Born **Caron, Pierre Augustin**

beau monde /bō mónd, -máwnd/ *n* the part of society made up of the richest and most fashionable people [Late 17C. < French, "beautiful world"]

Beau·mont /bō mònt/ city and port in southeastern Texas connected to the Gulf of Mexico by the Neches River ship canal. Population: 112,871 (2002 estimate).

Beau·mont, Francis (1584–1616) English dramatist. He cowrote plays with John Fletcher, including *Philaster* (1610?) and *A King and No King* (1611).

> "All your better deeds / Shall be in water writ, but this in marble."
> [Francis Beaumont, *The Nice Valor*; 1616?]

Beau·mont, William (1785–1853) US physician. His principal work was a study of the digestive system (1833).

> "Of all the lessons which a young man entering upon the profession of medicine needs to learn, this is perhaps the first—that he should resist the fascination of doctrines and hypotheses till he has won the privilege of such studies by honest labor and faithful pursuit of real and useful knowledge."
> [William Beaumont, *Notebook*; 1833?]

Beaune /bōn/ town on the Bouzaise river at the heart of the Burgundy wine-producing region in east central France. Population: 22,171 (1990).

Beau·re·gard /bōrə gaard/, **P. G. T.** (1818–93) US Confederate general. He led troops from the first engagement at Charleston, South Carolina (1861), throughout the Civil War. Full name **Beauregard, Pierre Gustave Toutant**

~~**beaurocracy**~~ incorrect spelling of **bureaucracy**

beaut /byoot/ *n* a fine or impressive thing (*slang*) [Mid-19C. Shortening of BEAUTY or BEAUTIFUL]

beau·te·ous /byóotee əss/ *adj* beautiful to look at —**beau·te·ous·ly** *adv* —**beau·te·ous·ness** *n*

beau·ti·cian /byoo tísh'n/ *n* somebody trained to give beauty treatments such as manicures or facials

beau·ti·ful /byóotəf'l/ *adj* **1.** very pleasing and impressive to look at, listen to, touch, smell, or taste **2.** very good or enjoyable —**beau·ti·ful·ly** *adv* —**beau·ti·ful·ness** *n*

BEAUFORT SCALE

The Beaufort scale was devised in 1805 by Sir Francis Beaufort, a captain (later admiral) in the British Royal Navy, to measure the observable effects of wind force at sea. It was later adapted to include effects on land, and wind speed equivalents were officially incorporated in 1926.

Sailors and forecasters use the Beaufort scale as a standardized way to rate wind speed. Warnings of potentially dangerous conditions for people in small boats are usually issued at a rating of six on the scale. The Beaufort number is also referred to as a "Force" number, for example, "Force 10 Gale."

Beaufort number	Wind speed km/h	Wind speed mph	Description
0	below 1	below 1	Calm
1	1 – 6	1 – 3	Light air
2	7 – 12	4 – 7	Light breeze
3	13 – 19	8 – 12	Gentle breeze
4	20 – 30	13 – 18	Moderate breeze
5	31 – 39	19 – 24	Fresh breeze
6	40 – 50	25 – 31	Strong breeze
7	51 – 62	32 – 38	Moderate gale
8	63 – 74	39 – 46	Fresh gale
9	75 – 87	47 – 54	Strong gale
10	88 – 102	55 – 63	Whole gale
11	103 – 117	64 – 72	Storm
12	above 118	above 73	Hurricane

SYNONYMS See ***good-looking***.

beau·ti·ful peo·ple *npl* **1.** rich fashionable people **2.** in the 1960s, hippies collectively

beau·ti·fy /byóoti fī/ (**-fied, -fy·ing, -fies**) *vt* to make something pleasing and impressive to look at —**beau·ti·fi·ca·tion** /byóotəfi káysh'n/ *n* —**beau·ti·fi·er** *n*

beau·ty /byóotee/ (*plural* **-ties**) *n* **1. PLEASING AND IMPRESSIVE QUALITIES OF SOMETHING** the combination of qualities that make something pleasing and impressive to look at, listen to, touch, smell, or taste **2. PLEASING PERSONAL APPEARANCE** personal physical attractiveness, especially with regard to the use of cosmetics and other methods of enhancing it **3. BEAUTIFUL WOMAN** a beautiful woman or girl ○ *her reputation as a great beauty* **4. FINE EXAMPLE** something very good, attractive, or impressive of its kind ○ *That long pass was a beauty.* **5. EXCELLENT ASPECT** an attractive, useful, or satisfying feature ○ *one of the beauties of working from home* [13C. Via Old French *bealte* < Vulgar Latin *bellitat-* < Latin *bellus* "handsome, fine" < *bonus* "good"]

CULTURAL NOTE ***Sleeping Beauty***, a ballet (1889) by Russian composer Peter Ilich Tchaikovsky. Based on Charles Perrault's fairy tale *La belle au bois dormant*, it tells the story of Princess Aurora, who is condemned to death by the wicked fairy Carabosse. Her sentence is commuted to a hundred years' sleep, from which she is eventually awakened by the handsome Prince Florimund.

beau·ty·bush /byóotee bòosh/ *n* a bush grown for its pink flowers and fruit with hairy knobby skin. Native to: China. Latin name: *Kolkwitzia amabilis*.

beaut·y con·test *n* **1.** same as **beauty pageant 2.** same as **beauty parade 3.** in the United States, a primary election in which the votes serve simply to indicate to the political parties which candidate is the most popular (*informal*)

beau·ty mark *n* same as **beauty spot** (sense 2)

beau·ty pag·eant *n* a competition for women in which a panel of judges decides who is the most beautiful of all the candidates

beaut·y pa·rade *n* a situation in which several organizations in turn compete in order to persuade another organization to use their services (*informal*)

beau·ty par·lor *n US* a business where beauty treatments are provided. Can term **beauty salon**

beau·ty quark *n* QUANTUM PHYS same as **bottom quark**

beau·ty queen *n* a woman judged to be the most beautiful of all the candidates in a competition for beautiful women

beau·ty sa·lon, beau·ty shop *n Can, UK* a business where beauty treatments are provided. US term **beauty parlor**

beau·ty sleep *n* deep restful sleep, especially before midnight, supposed to preserve youthful good looks (*informal*)

beau·ty spot *n* **1. POPULAR SCENIC PLACE** a place that people often visit because of its pleasing scenery **2. SMALL NATURAL MARK ON FACE** a mole or other small round mark on somebody's face **3. DOT WORN ON FACE** a small black or brown dot of silk or makeup on somebody's face used to emphasize the skin's paleness or hide a blemish. Beauty spots were especially popular among aristocratic women in 18th-century Europe.

AKG London

Simone de Beauvoir

Beau·voir /bō vwaár/, **Simone de** (1908–86) French writer. She wrote the feminist classic, *The Second Sex* (1949) and the novel *The Mandarins* (1954). She was the lifelong companion of Jean-Paul Sartre.

> "Man is defined as a human being and woman as a female—whenever she behaves as a human being she is said to imitate the male."
> [Simone de Beauvoir, *The Second Sex*; 1949]

beaux plural of **beau**

beaver

bea·ver[1] /beévər/ *n* **1.** (*plural* **bea·vers** or *same*) **FURRY FLAT-TAILED WATER ANIMAL** a water rodent with a broad flat tail and webbed hind feet. Beavers fell trees to build dams and partially submerged dens called lodges. Native to: North America, Europe, Asia. Genus: *Castor*. **2. FUR FROM BEAVER** the valuable fur of the beaver **3. MAN'S FUR HAT** a man's hat made of beaver fur, felt, or a fabric imitating beaver fur **4. THICK FABRIC** a thick woolen or cotton fabric **5. TABOO TERM** a highly offensive term for a woman's outer sex organs and pubic hair (*taboo*) ■ *vi* (**-vered, -ver·ing, -vers**) **WORK HARD AND CONTINUOUSLY** to work hard with unflagging energy and attention (*informal*) [Old English *beofor* < Indo-European, "brown animal"]

bea·ver[2] /beévər/ *n* the guard for the lower part of the face on a medieval helmet [15C. < French *baviere*, originally "child's bib" < *baver* "to slaver"]

bea·ver·board /beévər bàwrd/ *n* a thick board made of compressed wood fibers. Use: ceilings, inner walls.

Bea·ver·brook /beévər bròok/, **Max Aitken, 1st Baron** (1879–1964) Canadian-born British newspaper owner and politician. His news empire included the London newspapers the *Daily Express*, the *Sunday Express*, and the *Evening Standard*. Full name **William Maxwell Aitken**

Bea·ver State *n* a nickname for Oregon

Bea·ver·ton /beévərtən/ city in northwestern Oregon. It is a western suburb of Portland. Population: 79,768 (2002 estimate).

be·bee·ru /bə beéroo/ *n* TREES same as **greenheart** (sense 2) [Mid-19C. Via Spanish *bibirú* < Carib]

Be·bel /báyb'l/, **August** (1840–1913) German politician. He helped to found the German social democratic movement (1869) and wrote on socialism and the status of women. Full name **Bebel, Ferdinand August**

> "The nature of business is swindling."
> [Attributed to August Bebel]

be·bop /beé bòp/ *n* fast jazz music with complex harmonies and melodies. Charlie Parker was the most famous exponent of the style. [Mid-20C. An imitation of either the two-beat phrase of such music or the nonsense syllables of scat singing] —**be·bop·per** *n*

be·calm /bi kaám/ (**-calmed, -calm·ing, -calms**) *vt* (*usually passive*) **1.** to cause a sailing ship to stop moving because of lack of wind **2.** to bring peace and quiet to a person or a particular situation

be·came past tense of **become**

be·cause /bi káwz, -kúz/ *conj* **1.** for the reason that follows ○ *I like her because she's always so friendly.* **2.** on the basis of or taking into account what follows ○ *It must have been raining, because the sidewalk is wet.* [14C. < *by cause* "for the reason (that)," after Old French *par chance*] ◇ **because of** indicating the reason or cause of something

USAGE because, as, for, or **since**? The conjunctions ***since, because,*** and ***as*** may be used at the beginning of a sentence, when the reason is already well known or when the reason is considered not as important as the main statement: *As you're only staying a little while, we'd better eat now.* ***Because*** puts a greater emphasis on the cause: *Because she was witty and lively, she was often invited to be the keynote speaker.* ***Because*** and ***for*** are both used to introduce reasons that justify a statement as distinct from giving a reason for it, though ***for*** is more literary in style: *You must have forgotten to invite them, because they didn't turn up. He blushed, for he knew he had been caught out.* ***For*** as a conjunction is never used at the beginning of a sentence. ***As*** can also be understood to mean "at the time that" as well as "because": *As Luisa went back to work, Tony stayed home to take care of the baby.* In this case, it is better to avoid ambiguity and use either ***because*** or *while* as appropriate. Avoid using ***being as*** in place of ***because*** in formal writing: *They left for the game late, because* [not *being as*] *the car wouldn't start.*

USAGE See ***due*** and ***reason***.

bé·cha·mel sauce /bàyshə mél-/ *n* a rich sauce made from milk thickened with butter and flour and served hot [Late 18C. After Louis, Marquis de *Béchamel* (1630–1703), steward to Louis XIV of France]

bêche-de-mer /bèsh də mér/ (*plural* **bêches-de-mer** /*pronunc. same*/ or *same*) *n* MARINE BIOL same as **trepang** [Early 19C. < pseudo-French form of Portuguese *bicho do mar* "sea cucumber"]

Bech·u·a·na·land /bech wa̍anə lànd/ former name for **Botswana**

beck /bek/ *n* a nod, wave, or similar gesture to attract attention (*literary*) [14C. Shortening of BECKON] ◇ **at somebody's beck and call** always available and ready to carry out somebody's wishes

Beck·er /békər/, **Boris** (*b.* 1967) German tennis player. The youngest ever men's singles champion at Wimbledon (1985), he won again in 1986 and 1989.

> "It's all about self-belief and a sense of proportion. I say to myself that the worst thing that I can do is lose a tennis match."
> [Boris Becker, *Daily Telegraph (London)*; November 4, 1989]

beck·et /békət/ *n* a rope with a knot at one end and a small loop or hook at the other. Use: tying down loose equipment on a ship or boat. [Mid-18C. Origin ?]

Beck·et /békət/, **Thomas à, St.** (1118?–70) English saint and martyr. He became Archbishop of Canterbury in 1162 and was assassinated by knights of Henry II. In 1155 he became the first Englishman to hold the office of Chancellor since the Norman Conquest. His strong views on religious prerogative brought him into conflict with Henry II.

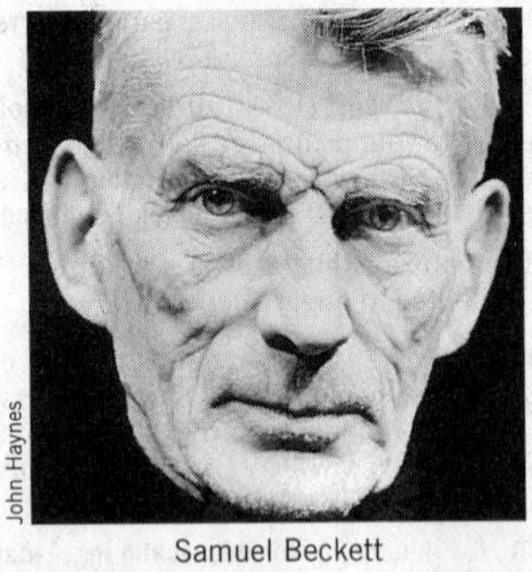

John Haynes

Samuel Beckett

Beck·ett /békət/, **Samuel** (1906–89) Irish-born writer. His bleak dramas of the absurd include *Waiting for Godot* (1952) and *Not I* (1973). He won a Nobel Prize in literature (1969). Beckett settled in Paris in 1937, and produced novels, plays, and poems in both English and French. Full name **Beckett, Samuel Barclay**

> "We are all born mad. Some remain so."
> [Samuel Beckett, *Waiting for Godot*, Act I; 1952]

Beck·ford /békfərd/, **William** (1760–1844) British writer and art collector. Best known for his Gothic novel, *Vathek: An Arabian Tale* (1782; English version, 1786), he built a celebrated Gothic mansion at Fonthill Abbey (1816) in Wiltshire, England.

> "He did not think...that it was necessary to make a hell of this world to enjoy paradise in the next."
> [William Beckford, *Vathek*; 1782]

Beck·ham /békəm/, **David** (*b.* 1975) British soccer player. An outstanding midfielder and crosser of the ball, he played for Manchester United before moving to Real Madrid in 2003. He became captain of the English national team in 2000.

beck·on /békən/ (**-oned, -on·ing, -ons**) *vti* **1.** to signal to somebody to approach with a movement of the hand or head **2.** to be an attraction or temptation to somebody (*literary*) [Old English *bēcnan* < Germanic] — **beck·on·er** *n* —**beck·on·ing·ly** *adv*

be·cloud /bi klówd/ (**-cloud·ed, -cloud·ing, -clouds**) *vt* (*literary*) **1.** to cover or conceal something with cloud or mist **2.** to make something confused or difficult to understand

be·come /bi kúm/ (**-came** /-káym/, **-come, -com·ing, -comes**) *v* **1.** *vi* COME TO BE SOMETHING to change or develop into something ○ *The caterpillar will soon become a moth.* **2.** *vt* SUIT SOMEBODY to suit the appearance or personality of somebody ○ *That color really becomes you.* **3.** *vt* BE APPROPRIATE FOR SOMEBODY to be an appropriate or socially acceptable thing for somebody to do or say (*formal*) [Old English *becuman* < Germanic]

be·com·ing /bi kúmming/ *adj* **1.** attractively suitable for somebody's appearance **2.** appropriate or fitting for somebody —**be·com·ing·ly** *adv*—**be·com·ing·ness** *n*

~~becouse~~ incorrect spelling of **because**

bec·que·rel /be krél, békə rèl/ *n* the SI unit for measuring radioactivity, equal to the activity resulting from the decay of one nucleus of radioactive matter in one second. Symbol **Bq** [Late 19C. After Antoine Henri *Becquerel* (1852–1908), French physicist]

bed /bed/ *n* **1.** FURNITURE ON WHICH TO SLEEP a piece of furniture on which to sleep, usually consisting of a rectangular frame with a mattress on top **2.** MATTRESS a mattress, especially with its coverings **3.** PLACE FOR SLEEPING a place in which to sleep, or an object on which to sleep ○ *looking for a bed for the night* **4.** ACCOMMODATIONS FOR GUEST OR PATIENT a place for one person to stay or sleep as a guest in a hotel or a patient in a hospital **5.** SLEEP sleep or rest in bed, or the time for this ○ *time for bed* **6.** STATE OF INTIMACY the state of sexual intimacy associated with being in bed with somebody ○ *the marriage bed* **7.** PATCH OF SOIL an area of soil prepared for plants, especially flowers, or an area where particular plants are growing ○ *a rose bed* **8.** GROUND UNDER WATER the ground at the bottom of the sea, a river, or a lake **9.** FISHERIES AREA OF WATER WITH SHELLFISH an area of the sea, a river, or a lake, where a particular kind of shellfish is found or cultivated ○ *oyster beds* **10.** CONSTR SURFACE ON WHICH TO BUILD a prepared surface on which something is built or laid, e.g., the foundation of a road or a railroad track **11.** COOK LAYER OF FOOD a layer of food on which another item of food is placed for serving **12.** GEOL LAYER OF ROCK a layer of rock, normally sedimentary, that is generally homogeneous and was deposited more or less continuously without erosion ■ *v* (**bed·ded, bed·ding, beds**) **1.** *vt* FIX SOMETHING INTO SURROUNDING SURFACE to embed something firmly in a surrounding mass of a substance such as rock or concrete **2.** *vti* FORM LAYER to arrange something, or be arranged, in a layer or stratum **3.** *vt* HAVE SEXUAL INTERCOURSE WITH SOMEBODY to have sexual intercourse with somebody (*informal*) [Old English *bedd* < Germanic] ◇ **a bed of nails** an extremely difficult situation or existence ◇ **a bed of roses** an easy, comfortable situation or existence ◇ **get up on the wrong side of the bed** to be in an irritable or angry mood right from the start of the day ◇ **go to bed with somebody** to have sexual intercourse with somebody ◇ **put something to bed** to finish something, such as a project (*informal*)

ORIGIN ***Bed*** meant both "sleeping place" and "garden plot" in Old English, and if the latter is the original sense, it could mean that the word comes ultimately from a prehistoric Germanic ancestor meaning "dig" (which is also the ancestor of English *fossil*), and that the underlying notion of a ***bed*** was originally of a sleeping place dug or scraped in the ground, like an animal's lair.

bed down *v* **1.** *vi* to settle down somewhere, not usually in a bed, ready for sleep ○ *I'll bed down on the sofa.* **2.** *vt* to put a person to bed or an animal in a place with bedding for the night

bed in *vti* to settle something firmly into place, or fit firmly into place

bed out *vt* to put young plants raised indoors into their final growing position outside

B.Ed. /bee éd/ *abbr* EDUC Bachelor of Education

bed and board *n* accommodation and meals provided for somebody

bed and break·fast *n* **1.** a small hotel or, more often, a private home that offers overnight accommodations and breakfast for paying guests **2.** overnight accommodations and breakfast provided for paying guests

be·daub /bi dáwb/ (**-daubed, -daub·ing, -daubs**) *vt* to smear a surface thickly or carelessly with something that spoils it or makes it dirty (*literary*)

be·daz·zle /bi dázz'l/ (**-zled, -zling, -zles**) *vt* (*literary*) **1.** to astonish somebody by being immediately impressive (*usually passive*) **2.** to make somebody temporarily unable to see by shining a bright light

bed bath *n UK* same as **sponge bath**

bed·bug /béd bùg/ *n* a small wingless bloodsucking insect that infests the bedding and furnishings of houses and the nests of animals. Family: Cimicidae.

bed·cham·ber /béd chàymbər/ *n* same as **bedroom** (*archaic*)

bed check *n* an inspection to see if all the members of a group of people under supervision, e.g., students or soldiers, are in bed after lights out

bed·clothes /béd klō<u>th</u>z, -klōz/ *npl* the sheets, blankets, and any other similar coverings on a bed

bed·cov·er /béd kùvvər/ *n* any of the coverings for a bed, e.g., a sheet or blanket

bed·da·ble /béddəb'l/ *adj* considered desirable enough to make a good sexual partner (*informal*)

bed·der /béddər/ *n* GARDENING same as **bedding plant**

bed·ding /bédding/ *n* **1.** BED COVERINGS the mattress, pillows and coverings such as sheets, quilts, and blankets used to prepare a bed **2.** BED FOR ANIMALS material such as straw put down for animals to lie on **3.** CONSTR UNDER LAYER a layer of material put down under something else, especially to serve as a foundation **4.** GEOL ARRANGEMENT OF ROCK STRATA the arrangement of a group of rock strata (**beds**) in an area or outcrop

bed·ding plant *n* a plant suitable for planting in a flower bed for one season's display

Bede /beed/, **St.** (673?–735) English theologian and historian. He wrote many grammatical and historical works, including his *Ecclesiastical History of the English People* (completed in 731). Known as **the Venerable Bede**

> "No reptile is found there [Ireland] nor could a serpent survive; for although serpents have often been brought from Britain, as soon as the ship approaches land they are affected by the scent of the air and quickly perish."
> [Bede, *Ecclesiastical History*; 731]

be·deck /bi dék/ (**-decked, -deck·ing, -decks**) *vt* to make something look pretty or festive, especially by decorating it with colorful ornaments ○ *trees bedecked with colored lights*

be·dev·il /bi dévv'l/ (**-iled, -il·ing, -ils**) *vt* to be a continual source of problems or irritation to something or somebody —**be·dev·il·ment** *n*

be·dew /bi do͞o/ (**-dewed, -dew·ing, -dews**) *vt* to wet or cover something with dew or drops of liquid (*literary*)

bed·fel·low /béd fèllō/ *n* **1.** somebody or something paired or allied with another person or thing **2.** somebody who shares a bed with somebody else (*archaic*)

Bed·ford /bédfərd/ **1.** city on the Ouse River in Bedfordshire, south central England. Population: 137,451 (1996 estimate). **2.** city in northeastern Texas situated between Fort Worth and Dallas. Population: 48,378 (2002 estimate).

Bed·ford cord *n* a heavy ribbed fabric like corduroy [After *Bedford*, city in south-central England]

Bed·ford·shire /béddfərd sheer, -shər/ county in central England. Population: 381,572 (2001). Area: 477 sq. mi./1,235 sq. km.

bed·head /béd hèd/ *n* the upper end of a bed, often with a headboard or rail

bed·hop·ping *n* casual sex with successive partners (*informal*)

be·dim /bi dím/ (**-dimmed, -dim·ming, -dims**) *vt* (*literary*) **1.** to make the eyes or mind less able to perceive things clearly **2.** to make something appear less bright or distinct

be·di·zen /bi dī́z'n, -dízz'n/ (**-zened, -zen·ing, -zens**) *vt* to dress or decorate somebody or something in a way that seems exaggeratedly or vulgarly showy (*literary*) [Mid-17C. < BE- + *dizen* "put flax onto a rod"] —**be·di·zen·ment** *n*

bed jack·et *n* a woman's short light jacket worn over a nightgown when sitting up in bed

bed·lam /béddləm/ *n* **1.** a place or situation full of noise, frenzied activity, and confusion **2.** same as **psychiatric hospital** (*archaic; sometimes offensive*) [15C. Alteration of BETHLEHEM]

bed lin·en *n* the sheets, pillowcases, and other fabric coverings that go on a bed

bed·lin·er /béd lī̀nər/ *n* a molded covering, usually made of rigid synthetic material, used to protect the floor of the open rear area of a pickup truck

Bed·ling·ton ter·ri·er /bèddlingtən-/, **Bed·ling·ton** *n* a dog belonging to a breed of English terriers that have a tapering head and fleecy coat that makes them look similar to lambs [Mid-19C. After a town in N England]

bed load *n* the loose sand and gravel carried by a stream at or just above its bed

Bed·loe's Is·land /béddlōz-/ former name for **Liberty Island**

bed mold·ing *n* in classical architecture, the lowest section of a cornice, protruding less than the topmost part

Bed·ou·in /béddoo ən, béddwin/ (*plural* **-ins** or *same*), **Bed·u·in** *n* a nomadic Arab of the desert regions of Arabia and North Africa [15C. Via Old French *beduin* < Arabic *badw* "desert, nomadic desert people"] —**Bed·ou·in** *adj*

bed·pan /béd pàn/ *n* a shallow container into which a sick or frail person can urinate or defecate while lying in bed

bed·plate /béd plàyt/ *n* a heavy metal base or platform to which the frame of an engine or machine is attached

bed·post /béd pōst/ *n* one of the posts at the corners of a bed, especially a four-poster bed

be·drag·gled /bi drágg'ld/ *adj* wet, dirty, and unkempt, or with hair or clothes in this state

bed·rail /béd ràyl/ *n* a rail at the head, foot, or side of a bed

bed rest *n* a period of time spent in bed in order to rest and recover when not well

bed·rid·den /béd ridd'n/ *adj* forced to remain in bed because of illness, weakness, or injury [14C. < Old English *bedrida* "bed-rider"]

bed·rock /béd ròk/ *n* **1. UNDERLYING FACTS OR PRINCIPLES** the facts or principles on which something is based **2. UNDERLYING ROCK** the solid rock beneath a layer of soil, rock fragments, or gravel **3. LOWEST POINT** the lowest point, especially in a time of hardship or unhappiness

bed·roll /béd rōl/ *n* a roll of bedding carried by somebody who is hiking or camping

bed·room /béd rōom, -rŏom/ *n* a room that has a bed in it and is used mainly for sleeping ■ *adj* involving, depicting, or suggesting sexual activity ○ *a bedroom comedy*

bed·room com·mu·ni·ty, bed·room sub·urb *n* a town or suburb inhabited mainly by people who travel to work in a nearby city

bed·room eyes *npl* a look that seems to indicate a desire to have sex (*informal*)

beds. *abbr* bedrooms (*used in advertisements*)

bed·side /béd sīd/ *n* the side of a bed, or the space next to a bed —**bed·side** *adj*

bed·side man·ner *n* a doctor's way of talking to and dealing with patients

bed·sit·ter *n UK* a combined bedroom and living room, especially one that is rented and serves as somebody's residence [*sitter* < SITTING ROOM]

bed·sore /béd sàwr/ *n* an ulcer on the skin caused by pressure and friction from bedding when somebody is confined to bed for a long time

bed·spread /béd sprèd/ *n* a decorative covering placed on top of bedding

bed·stead /béd stèd/ *n* the structural framework of a bed, excluding the mattress and coverings [Originally the place where a bed stood]

bed·time /béd tīm/ *n* the time when somebody normally goes to bed, or should go to bed

Bed·u·in *n, adj* PEOPLES another spelling of **Bedouin**

bed·warm·er /béd wàwrmər/ *n* a covered metal container for hot coals, formerly used to warm a bed

bed-wet·ting *n* urination in bed during sleep, especially by a child —**bed-wet·ter** *n*

bee

bee /bee/ *n* **1.** a flying insect with a furry body that makes a buzzing sound as it flies. Some species of bees have stingers, and some live in hives and produce honey. Superfamily: Apoidea. **2.** a gathering at which people combine work or a friendly competition with socializing ○ *a sewing bee* [Old English *bēo* < Germanic] ◇ **have a bee in your bonnet about something** to be so interested in or concerned about something that you rarely stop thinking or talking about it

Beeb /beeb/ *n* the British Broadcasting Corporation (*informal humorous*) [Mid-20C. Shortening of the pronunciation of BBC]

bee balm *n US* a plant with aromatic leaves. Flowers: variously colored, in spikes. Native to: North America. Latin name: *Monarda didyma.* Can term **bergamot**

bee·bread /bée brèd/ *n* a yellow-brown pollen stored by bees and mixed with honey as food for their larvae

beech /beech/ *n* **1.** a tall tree with smooth gray bark and glossy deciduous leaves. Native to: temperate regions. Genus: *Fagus.* **2.** the wood of the beech tree. Use: furniture. [Old English *bēce* < Germanic]

SPELLCHECK See *beach.*

beech·drops /béech drὸps/ *n* a low-growing, brownish-colored plant of the broomrape family that lives as a parasite on the roots of beech trees. Flowers: white, tube-shaped. Native to: North America. Latin name: *Epifagus virginiana.*

Bee·cher /béechər/, **Henry Ward** (1813–87) US cleric and orator. The son of Lyman Beecher, he was a popular revivalist preacher, abolitionist, and supporter of women's suffrage. He was acquitted of an adultery charge after a sensational trial (1874).

> "Laws and institutions are constantly tending to gravitate. Like clocks, they must be occasionally cleansed, and wound up, and set to true time."
> [Henry Ward Beecher, *Life Thoughts*; 1863]

Bee·cher, Lyman (1775–1863) American Presbyterian cleric. A popular Presbyterian preacher in New England, he was the first president of Lane Theological Seminary near Cincinnati (1832–50). He was the father of Henry Ward Beecher and Harriet Beecher Stowe.

beech mar·ten *n* ZOOL same as **stone marten** (sense 1)

beech mast *n* the hard fruit of a beech tree enclosed in a prickly case, especially when the fallen fruits form a covering on the ground

beech·nut /béech nùt/ *n* the small triangular hard edible fruit of a beech tree

bee-eat·er *n* a brightly colored bird that eats flying insects, especially bees and wasps. Native to: Europe, Asia. Family: Meropidae.

beef /beef/ *n* **1. MEAT FROM CATTLE** meat from a cow, heifer, bull, or steer **2.** (*plural* **beeves** /beevz/ or *same*) **ANIMAL USED FOR BEEF** a cow, heifer, bull, or steer being raised for meat **3. STRENGTH** muscular strength or effort (*informal*) **4.** same as **complaint** (senses 1–2) (*slang*) ■ *vi* (**beefed, beef·ing, beefs**) same as **complain** (sense 1) (*slang*) [12C. Via Anglo-Norman *boef* < stem of Latin *bos* "ox"]

beef up *vt* to make something stronger or more effective (*informal*) ○ *beef up the article with some statistics* —**beefed-up** *adj*

beef·a·lo /béefə lō/ (*plural same* or **-loes**) *n* a cross between the North American bison and domestic cattle that has high resistance to disease. Raised for: lean meat. [Late 20C. Blend of BEEF + BUFFALO]

beef·burg·er /béef bùrgər/ *n* FOOD same as **hamburger** (senses 1, 3)

beef·cake /béef kàyk/ *n* a muscular man, considered from the point of view of physical appearance, or pictures of such men (*informal*) [After CHEESECAKE]

Barnaby's

beefeater: a Yeoman of the Guard at the Tower of London, with Tower Bridge in the background

beef·eat·er /béef eetər/ *n* one of the Yeomen of the Guard of a British monarch, a group who act as warders of the Tower of London wearing a uniform of Tudor dress

bee fly *n* a fly that resembles a bee, eats pollen and nectar, and whose larvae develop as parasites on insect larvae. Family: Bombyliidae.

beef·steak /béef stàyk/ *n* a slice of lean beef that can be broiled or fried

beef·steak fun·gus, beef·steak mush·room *n* an edible bracket fungus with a large reddish cap that grows especially on oak and ash trees. Latin name: *Fistulina hepatica.*

beef·steak to·ma·to *n* a large, firm-fleshed tomato

beef stro·ga·noff /béef strṓgə nawf/ *n* a dish consisting of thin strips of sautéed beef cooked with onions and mushrooms in a sour cream sauce [After Count Paul *Stroganoff*, 19C Russian diplomat]

beef to·ma·to *n UK* same as **beefsteak tomato**

beef Wel·ling·ton *n* a dish consisting of a fillet of beef covered in pâté de foie gras, wrapped in pastry, and baked

beef·wood /béef wŏod/ *n* **1.** the hard red wood of an Australian tree. Use: construction, cabinetmaking.

2. an evergreen hardwood tree that is the source of beefwood. Native to: Australia. Genus: *Casuarina*.

beef·y /béefee/ (**-i·er, -i·est**) *adj* **1. MUSCULAR** strong and muscular **2. LIKE BEEF** containing, produced by, or resembling beef **3. POWERFUL** having strength, power, or substance (*informal*) ○ *a novel with a really beefy plot* —**beef·i·ly** *adv* —**beef·i·ness** *n*

bee gum *n Midwest, Southern US* a beehive, especially in a hollow tree or log [Originally a hive in a gum tree]

bee·hive /bée hīv/ *n* **1. HIVE FOR BEES** a structure housing a colony of bees **2. TALL HAIRSTYLE** a hairstyle for women, popular around 1960, in which the hair is arranged in a high rounded shape on top of the head ■ *adj* **BEEHIVE-SHAPED** shaped like a beehive, with a round base rising in a cone to a domed top

bee·hive house *n* a round prehistoric house with a domed roof

Bee·hive State *n* a nickname for Utah

bee·keep·er /bée keepər/ *n* somebody who keeps bees for honey or to pollinate crops —**bee·keep·ing** *n*

bee·line /bée līn/ *n* a very direct line, path, or other course from one point to another ○ *The kids made a beeline for the swimming pool as soon as we reached the motel.* [< the belief that bees return to their hives in a straight line]

Be·el·ze·bub /bee élzə bùb/ *n* the devil, or one of the chief devils in hell [Pre-12C. Via Latin < Hebrew *ba'al zĕbūb* "Lord of Flies," a Philistine god]

been past participle of **be**[1]

bee or·chid *n* a European orchid. Flowers: resembling a bee on a flower. Latin name: *Ophrys apiphera*.

beep /beep/ *n* **SHORT HIGH NOISE** a short high-pitched noise emitted as a signal by a piece of electronic equipment or the horn of a vehicle ■ *v* (**beeped, beep·ing, beeps**) **1.** *vti* **MAKE BEEP** to make a beep, or cause a vehicle horn or other device to make a beep **2.** *vt* **PAGE SOMEBODY** to try to contact somebody on his or her pager [Early 20C. An imitation of the sound]

beep·er /béepər/ *n* COMMUNICATION same as **pager** (*informal*)

bee plant *n* any plant that is particularly attractive to bees

beer /beer/ *n* **1. DRINK BREWED FROM MALT** an alcoholic drink brewed by fermenting malt with sugar and yeast and flavoring it with hops **2. QUANTITY OF BEER** a drink or glass of beer **3. HERBAL DRINK** a carbonated or slightly fermented drink made from or flavored with the roots, leaves, or seeds of a plant ○ *root beer* [Old English *bēor* < late Latin *biber* "drink" < *bibere* "to drink"]

SPELLCHECK beer or **bier**? Do not confuse the spelling of ***beer*** and ***bier***, which sound similar. ***Beer*** is a drink (as in *a glass of beer, ginger beer*), whereas a ***bier*** is a stand for a casket.

beer bel·ly *n* an extended stomach often associated with regularly drinking too much beer (*slang*)

Beer·bohm /béer bōm/, **Sir Max** (1872–1956) British writer and caricaturist. He wrote *Zuleika Dobson* (1911), a satire on Oxford undergraduate life, and much drama criticism. He also drew witty caricatures of leading literary and political figures. Full name **Beerbohm, Sir Henry Maximilian**. Known as **the Incomparable Max**

> "Great men are but life-sized. Most of them, indeed, are rather short."
> [Sir Max Beerbohm, *And Even Now*; 1921]

beer gar·den *n* an open space or garden, often attached to a tavern, where beer and other alcoholic drinks can be purchased and drunk in the open air

beer gut *n* same as **beer belly** (*slang*)

beer·mat /béer màt/ *n UK* a small cardboard mat, often displaying brewery advertising, to be placed under a glass to protect a surface in a bar or restaurant

beer par·lour *n Can* a bar where beer is served

Beer·she·ba /beer shéebə, bər-/ city on the edge of the Negev Desert, southwest of Jerusalem, Israel. In biblical times it was in the extreme southern part of Palestine. Population: 163,700 (1999).

beer·y /béeree/ (**-i·er, -i·est**) *adj* **1.** characteristic of somebody who is slightly inebriated from having drunk too much beer **2.** smelling or tasting of beer —**beer·i·ly** *adv* —**beer·i·ness** *n*

bee·stings /bée stingz/, **bea·stings** *n* the first milk secreted by a mammal, especially a cow or goat, after it has given birth [Old English *bȳsting* < Germanic]

bee-stung *adj* full and rounded, as if stung by a bee (*informal*) ○ *bee-stung lips*

bees·wax /béez wàks/ *n* **1. WAX MADE BY BEES** the dark yellow substance secreted by honeybees and used for building honeycombs **2. COMMERCIALLY PROCESSED BEESWAX** wax produced by bees that has been commercially processed for use in furniture polishes, candles, and crayons ■ *vt* (**-waxed, -wax·ing, -wax·es**) **WAX SOMETHING** to polish something with beeswax

bees·wing /béez wing/ *n* a thin shiny sediment that forms in port and some other wines when they are kept for a long time after bottling

beet

beet /beet/ *n* **1. PLANT WITH SWOLLEN ROOT** a plant with a large swollen root. Use: as a vegetable, as animal feed, for sugar production. Genus: *Beta*. **2.** PLANTS **BEET PLANT WITH EDIBLE ROOT** a variety of beet plant with a round dark-red edible root. Latin name: *Beta vulgaris*. **3.** FOOD **BEET PLANT ROOT AS VEGETABLE** the red-colored root of a variety of beet plant, eaten as a vegetable (*usually used in the plural*) [Old English *bēte* < Latin *beta*]

SPELLCHECK See ***beat***.

AKG London

Ludwig van Beethoven

Bee·tho·ven /báy tōvən/, **Ludwig van** (1770–1827) German composer. His symphonies and chamber pieces reached new levels of expressiveness, inspiring the Romantics. He composed 9 symphonies, 32 piano sonatas, and 16 string quartets, among many other works.

> "I used to be able to make all my other circumstances subservient to my art. I admit, however, that by so doing I became a bit crazy."
> [Ludwig van Beethoven, *Letter*; February 1818]

bee·tle[1] /béet'l/ *n* **1. HARD-BACKED INSECT** an insect belonging to a large order characterized by a modified outer pair of wings that forms a hard covering for the inner pair. Order: Coleoptera. **2. INSECT RESEMBLING BEETLE** an insect with an appearance similar to a beetle ■ *vi* (**-tled, -tling, -tles**) *UK* **GO QUICKLY** to go somewhere quickly (*informal*) [Old English *bitula, bitela* < *bītan* "to bite"]

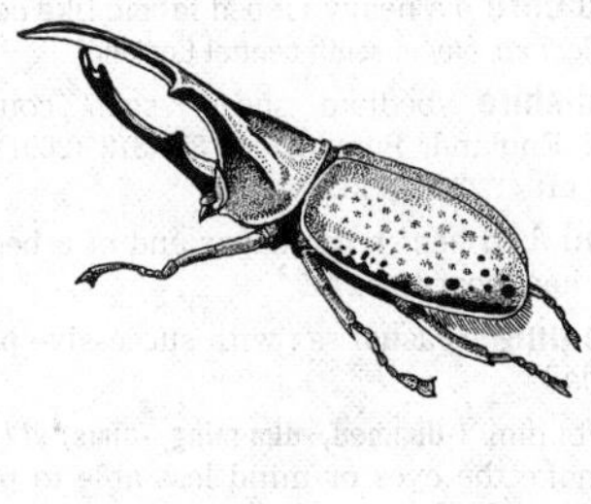

beetle

bee·tle[2] /béet'l/ *n* **1. LARGE MALLET** a large tool with a long handle and a heavy wooden head. Use: driving in stakes, ramming, pounding. **2. TEXTILE-FINISHING MACHINE** a machine that beats cloth to give it a smooth finish ■ *vt* (**-tled, -tling, -tles**) **FINISH CLOTH** to give a finishing treatment to cloth with a beetle [Old English *bētel, bīetel* < Germanic]

bee·tle[3] /béet'l/ (*literary*) *vi* (**-tled, -tling, -tles**) to overhang or jut out ■ *adj* jutting out and bushy ○ *beetle brows* [14C. Origin ?] —**bee·tling** *adj*

bee·tle-browed *adj* having thick, bushy, or jutting eyebrows

bee·tle·weed /béet'l weed/ *n* PLANTS same as **galax**

bee tree *n* any flowering tree that seems particularly attractive to bees, e.g., a basswood

beet·root /béet root/ *n UK* same as **beet** (senses 2–3)

beet sug·ar *n* sugar that has been extracted from sugar beets

beeves plural of **beef** *n* (sense 2)

be·fall /bi fáwl/ (**-fell** /-fél/, **-fall·en** /-fáwlən/, **-fall·ing, -falls**) *vti* to happen, or happen to somebody, especially through the unexpected workings of chance or fate (*literary*)

be·fit /bi fít/ (**-fit·ted, -fit·ting, -fits**) *vt* to be suitable or appropriate for somebody or something —**be·fit·ting** *adj* —**be·fit·ting·ly** *adv*

be·fog /bi fáwg, bi fóg/ (**-fogged, -fog·ging, -fogs**) *vt* (*literary*) **1.** to make somebody or something vague or confused **2.** to cover or hide something from view with fog

be·fore /bi fáwr/ CORE MEANING: a grammatical word indicating that a point in time, event, or situation precedes another in a sequence ○ (prep) *We try all of the products before deciding to stock them.* ○ (conj) *We lost a lot of manufacturing jobs in the 12 years before I became president.* ○ (conj) *She died at the hospital before her parents could reach her side.* ○ (adv) *They had left the subway terminal perhaps twenty minutes before.* ○ (adv) *He has had this nightmare before.*

1. *prep, conj, adv* **EARLIER** earlier than a date, time, or event **2.** *prep, conj* **INDICATES SEQUENCE** used to indicate a sequence of actions, one preceding the other and closely connected with it **3.** *prep* **IN PRESENCE OF** in the presence of a person or body of people ○ *spoke before a huge crowd* **4.** *prep* **WITH MORE IMPORTANCE THAN** indicating that one thing is preferable to or more important than another ○ *Their needs come before yours.* **5.** *prep* **INDICATES LOCATION** located close to something but just ahead of it **6.** *prep* **AHEAD OF** stretching ahead of somebody **7.** *adv* **PREVIOUSLY** on a previous occasion **8.** *conj* **RATHER THAN** used to indicate that somebody would prefer to do one thing rather than what he or she considers to be a worse thing ○ *I'll die before I'll tell you anything about it.* [Old English *beforan* < Germanic]

be·fore·hand /bi fáwr hànd/ *adv* used to indicate that a situation, action, or event happens ahead of time or in advance of something [13C. After Old French *avant main*]

be·foul /bi fówl/ (**-fouled, -foul·ing, -fouls**) *vt* to make something dirty or impure, or diminish somebody or something's moral purity or reputation (*archaic or literary*) —**be·foul·ment** *n*

be·friend /bi frénd/ (**-friend·ed, -friend·ing, -friends**) *vt* to be friendly to somebody, especially to somebody who has no friends and needs help —**be·friend·er** *n*

be·fud·dle /bi fúdd'l/ (**-dled, -dling, -dles**) *vt* **1.** to make somebody confused or perplexed **2.** to make somebody inebriated and unable to think clearly —**be·fud·dled** *adj* —**be·fud·dle·ment** *n*

beg /beg/ (**begged, beg·ging, begs**) *v* **1.** *vti* ASK WITH EMOTION to ask somebody for something such as a favor in a heartfelt, humble, or even humiliating way ○ *begged them for forgiveness* ○ *I beg of you to stop.* **2.** *vti* ASK FOR CHARITY to ask people for gifts of money or food, especially in the street **3.** *vi* SIT UP AND ASK FOR FOOD to ask for food by sitting up and holding out the front legs (*refers to dogs*) **4.** *vt* EVADE MATTER to avoid answering or dealing with a point ○ *beg the question* [Probably < Old English *bedecian* < Germanic]

USAGE See ***question***.

beg off *vi* to ask to be excused from doing something

be·gad /bi gád/ *interj* used to add emphasis to something that is said (*archaic*) [Late 16C. Alteration of *by God*]

be·gan past tense of **begin**

be·get /bi gét/ (**-got** /-gót/, **-got·ten** /-gótt'n/ or **-got, -get·ting, -gets**) *vt* **1.** to be the cause of something **2.** to be the father of a child (*archaic*) [Old English *begietan* "get" < Germanic] —**be·get·ter** *n*

beg·gar /béggər/ *n* **1.** SOMEBODY WHO BEGS somebody who begs for money or food from strangers **2.** POOR PERSON a very poor person ■ *vt* (**-gared, -gar·ing, -gars**) **1.** IMPOVERISH SOMEBODY to make somebody very poor (*literary*) **2.** BE BEYOND BELIEF to be so extraordinary as to be beyond description or belief ○ *a catastrophe that beggars description*

beg·gar·ly /béggərlee/ *adj* insufficient and showing stinginess —**beg·gar·li·ness** *n*

beg·gar's lice (*plural same*), **beg·gar ticks** *n* **1.** a plant with burs that stick to clothes and fur. Genus: *Bidens.* **2.** the burs of a beggar's lice plant

beg·gar-thy-neigh·bor *n* a simple card game for two players in which cards are won and lost until one person holds them all

beg·gar·y /béggəree/ *n* a state of extreme poverty

~~**begger**~~ incorrect spelling of **beggar**

beg·ging bowl *n* a bowl carried by somebody who begs for gifts of food or money

be·gin /bi gín/ (**-gan** /-gán/, **-gun** /-gún/, **-gin·ning, -gins**) *v* **1.** *vti* START to do something that was not being done before ○ *People began to leave.* **2.** *vti* HAVE AS ITS STARTING POINT to have as its starting point, first action, or first part, or be the starting point or first part of something ○ *The story begins with a birthday party.* **3.** *vti* COME OR BRING INTO BEING to come into existence, or cause something to come into existence or take place ○ *The business began as a two-person operation.* **4.** *vt* UNDERTAKE SOMETHING FOR FIRST TIME to undertake, use, or give attention to something for the first time **5.** *vti* START TO SPEAK to start to say something, or start by saying something **6.** *vt* BE CAPABLE OF SOMETHING to be able to succeed in accomplishing a task (*used in negative statements*) ○ *The salary doesn't even begin to meet her expectations.* ○ *I couldn't begin to explain how awful it was.* [Old English *beginnan* < Germanic]

Be·gin /báygin/, **Menachem** (1913–92) Russian-born prime minister of Israel (1977–83). He shared the Nobel Peace Prize with Egyptian president Anwar al-Sadat (1978) and signed the first-ever Israeli treaty with an Arab state (1979). Full name **Begin, Menachem Wolfovitch**

> "The life of every man who fights a just cause is a paradox...We fight, therefore we are."
>
> [Menachem Begin, *The Revolt*; 1948 and 1977]

~~**begining**~~ incorrect spelling of **beginning**

be·gin·ner /bi gínnər/ *n* somebody who has just started to learn or do something

SYNONYMS ***beginner, apprentice, greenhorn, novice, tyro***

CORE MEANING: a person who has not acquired the necessary experience or skills to do something

beginner somebody who has just started to learn or do something ○ *classes for both beginners and advanced students* ○ *a course that teaches even complete beginners to skipper their own yachts* **apprentice** somebody who is being taught the skills of a trade over an agreed period of time by somebody fully trained ○ *became an apprentice joiner* ○ *Local firms wouldn't take him on as an apprentice.* **greenhorn** somebody who lacks experience and may be naive or gullible ○ *You greenhorns don't understand the situation here at all.* **novice** somebody with no previous experience or skill in the activity undertaken ○ *a political novice with no diplomatic experience* ○ *special events for novice horseback riders* **tyro** somebody who has just started to learn or do something ○ *sensible guidelines for the desktop publishing tyro*

be·gin·ner's luck *n* early success that seems inconsistent with somebody's lack of experience

be·gin·ning /bi gínning/ *n* **1.** FIRST PART the first part or early stages of something **2.** START the point in time or space at which something starts, comes into existence, or is first encountered ■ **be·gin·nings** *npl* EARLY CONDITIONS the conditions in which something or somebody starts ■ *adj* NEW new to a job or activity ○ *beginning teachers*

be·gone /bi gáwn, -gón/ *interj* used to tell somebody to go away (*archaic*)

be·go·nia /bi gṓnyə/ *n* a widely grown houseplant and garden plant with ragged-edged leaves. Flowers: round or drooping, brightly colored. Genus: *Begonia.* [Mid-18C. < modern Latin, after Michel *Bégon*, (1638–1710), governor of French Canada]

be·gor·ra /bi gáwrə, -górrə/ *interj Ireland* used as an exclamation or a mild oath (*dated*) [Mid-19C. Alteration of *by God*]

be·got past tense of **beget**

be·got·ten past participle of **beget**

be·grime /bi grī́m/ (**-grimed, -grim·ing, -grimes**) *vt* to cover something with grime

be·grudge /bi grúj/ (**-grudged, -grudg·ing, -grudg·es**) *vt* **1.** to resent the fact that somebody has something ○ *He's always begrudged me my success.* **2.** to be unwilling to give or pay something ○ *She begrudged every dime she paid me.*

be·grudg·ing /bi grújjing/ *adj* showing unwillingness to give somebody something or to let somebody be admired or praised —**be·grudg·ing·ly** *adv*

be·guile /bi gī́l/ (**-guiled, -guil·ing, -guiles**) *vt* **1.** CHARM SOMEBODY to win and hold somebody's attention, interest, or devotion **2.** DECEIVE SOMEBODY to mislead or deceive somebody (*literary*) **3.** CHEAT SOMEBODY to rob somebody of something, or cheat somebody out of something (*literary*) **4.** PASS TIME to pass time in a pleasant way (*literary*) —**be·guile·ment** *n* —**be·guil·er** *n*

be·guil·ing /bi gī́ling/ *adj* having the power to gain people's interest or devotion —**be·guil·ing·ly** *adv*

be·guine /bi geén/ *n* a ballroom dance similar to the rumba, originating in the Caribbean [Early 20C. < French *béguine* < *béguin* "flirtation"]

be·gum /báygəm, beé-/ *n* **1.** a title of respect for a woman in some Muslim communities **2.** a woman of high rank in some Muslim communities [Mid-17C. Via Urdu < East Turkic, "my mistress"]

be·gun past participle of **begin**

be·half /bi háf, -ha̋af/ [14C. Blend of *on his half* + *by half him*, both meaning "on his side"] ◇ **on behalf of** or **on somebody's behalf, in behalf of 1.** as somebody's representative ○ *We chose James to speak on our behalf.* **2.** for somebody's benefit or support, or in somebody's best interests ○ *I thanked everyone on Jane's behalf.*

USAGE on somebody's behalf or **in somebody's behalf?** A distinction frequently overlooked between ***on behalf of*** and ***in behalf of*** is that ***on behalf of*** is preferred in the meaning "as somebody's representative," and ***in behalf of*** in the meaning "in somebody's best interests": *She appeared on behalf of the U.N. Secretary General at a conference held in behalf of the world's children.* Also note that because a person acting ***on somebody's behalf*** is acting *for* another, *on behalf of myself* is illogical and should be avoided.

Be·han /beé ən/, **Brendan** (1923–64) Irish playwright and author. He wrote *The Quare Fellow* (1954), *The Hostage* (1958), and the autobiographical novel *Borstal Boy* (1958). Full name **Behan, Brendan Francis**

> "When I came back to Dublin, I was courtmartialed in my absence and sentenced to death in my absence, so I said they could shoot me in my absence."
>
> [Brendan Behan, *The Hostage*; 1958]

be·have /bi háyv/ (**-haved, -hav·ing, -haves**) *vi* **1.** ACT to act in a particular way that expresses general character, state of mind, or response to a situation or other people ○ *He's been behaving oddly.* **2.** BEHAVE WELL to act in an acceptable way, especially by being polite, good-tempered, and self-controlled ○ *children who won't behave* **3.** PERFORM to perform in or react to particular conditions or circumstances [15C. < BE- + HAVE in the obsolete sense "conduct yourself"]

be·hav·ior /bi háyvyər/ *n* **1.** WAY SOMEBODY BEHAVES the way in which somebody behaves **2.** PSYCHOL RESPONSE the way in which a person, organism, or group responds to a specific set of conditions **3.** WHAT SOMETHING DOES the way that a machine operates or a substance reacts under a specific set of conditions [15C. < BEHAVE, after *haviour* "possession" < Old French *aveir* "have"] —**be·hav·ior·al** *adj* —**be·hav·ior·al·ly** *adv*

be·hav·ior·al con·ta·gion *n* the spread of a type of behavior first exhibited by a few people in a group to the group as a whole

be·hav·ior·al med·i·cine, **be·hav·ior med·i·cine** *n* the interdisciplinary study of behavioral, psychosocial, and biomedical knowledge relevant to the understanding of health and illness

be·hav·ior·al psy·chol·o·gy *n* a branch of psychology based on the observation and modification of the way that people behave

be·hav·ior·al sci·ence *n* a science such as sociology, psychology, or anthropology that is concerned with the ways in which people or animals behave —**be·hav·ior·al sci·en·tist** *n*

be·hav·ior·al ther·a·py *n* PSYCHIAT same as **behavior modification**

be·hav·ior·ism /bi háyvyə rìzzəm/ *n* **1.** an approach to the study of psychology that concentrates exclusively on observing, measuring, and modifying behavior **2.** the theory that statements about the mind and mental states are really about actual or potential behavior —**be·hav·ior·ist** *adj, n* —**be·hav·ior·is·tic** /bi hàyvyə rístik/ *adj*

be·hav·ior med·i·cine *n* PSYCHIAT same as **behavioral medicine**

be·hav·ior mod·i·fi·ca·tion, **be·hav·ior ther·a·py** *n* psychological treatment that attempts to change somebody's behavior by rewarding new and desirable responses and making accustomed undesirable ones less attractive

be·hav·iour *n* Can, UK spelling of **behavior**

be·head /bi héd/ (**-head·ed, -head·ing, -heads**) *vt* to cut the head off somebody or something, especially as a form of execution

be·held past participle, past tense of **behold**

be·he·moth /bi heéməth, beé əməth/ *n* **1.** something that is enormously big or powerful **2.** *also* **Be·he·moth** in the Bible, a huge beast usually thought to be a hippopotamus (Job 40:15) [14C. < Hebrew *bəhēmōṯ* < *bəhēmāh* "beast"]

be·hest /bi hést/ *n* an order or request (*formal*) ○ *arrived at the conference only at her behest* [Alteration of Old English *behǣs* < Germanic, "to bid, call"]

be·hind /bi hī́nd/ CORE MEANING: a grammatical word indicating that somebody or something is in or is going toward a position at the back or rear of something ○ (prep) *From behind the door we heard country music.* ○ (prep) *She was behind the wheel, and I was in the back.* ○ (adv) *Their car was hit from behind.* ○ (adv) *She had to go back because she'd left her money behind.*

1. *prep, adv* AT BACK OF in or toward a position farther back or at the rear of something **2.** *prep, adv* FOLLOWING following somebody or something **3.** *adv* IN DEBT in debt, or in arrears on a payment ○ *months behind on the payments* **4.** *adv* REMAINING used to indicate that somebody or something is left after another's departure ○ *was left behind* **5.** *prep* IN PAST indicates that an achievement or experience happened in the past ○ *My best days are behind me.* **6.** *prep* **LATER THAN** indicates that something is not as far advanced as it should be ○ *seven weeks behind schedule* **7.** *prep* **CAUSING SOMETHING** causing or being responsible for something ○ *the reason behind it* **8.** *prep* **SUPPORTING SOMEBODY** backing or supporting somebody ○ *I'm behind you all the way on this issue.* **9.** *prep* **UNDERNEATH** underneath the external appearance of somebody or something ○ *Behind his calm exterior, he was very confused.* **10.** *n* **BUTTOCKS** somebody's buttocks (*informal*) **11.** *n* **ONE POINT SCORED** in Australian Rules, a single point scored as a result of the ball being kicked between the goal post and the behind post, hit against a goal post, or punched or handled over the goal line [Old English *behindan* < *hindan* "from behind" < Germanic] ◇ **get behind somebody** *or* **something** to give somebody or something strong support ○ *The whole community needs to get behind this airport protest.* ◇ **put something behind you** to ensure that something unpleasant can no longer affect you detrimentally

be·hind·hand /bi hī́nd hànd/ *adj* **1. BEHIND SCHEDULE** not as well advanced as planned or expected **2. LAGGING BEHIND** behind in development or achievement compared to others **3.** FIN **IN ARREARS** in arrears for payment of a debt [Mid-16C. After BEFOREHAND]

be·hind-the-scenes *adj* carried out privately or secretly ○ *a lot of frantic behind-the-scenes negotiation*

Behn /bayn, ben/, **Aphra** (1640–89) English writer. The first professional woman writer in England, she wrote poems, plays, and the early novel *Oroonoko* (1688?). Born **Amis, Aphra**

"Who is't that to women's beauty would submit, / And yet refuse the fetters of their wit?"
[Aphra Behn, *The Forced Marriage*; 1670]

be·hold /bi hṓld/ (**-held** /-héld/, **-hold·ing, -holds**) *vt* to see or observe something or somebody (*formal; often used in commands*) ○ *"Behold her, single in the field, Yon solitary Highland lass!"* (William Wordsworth, *The Solitary Reaper*) [Old English *bihaldan* < Germanic, "watch, guard"] —**be·hold·er** *n*

be·hold·en /bi hṓld'n/ *adj* under an obligation to somebody because of something helpful that person has done [14C. Originally past participle of BEHOLD, in the obsolete sense "hold under obligation"]

be·hoove /bi hóov, bə-/ (**-hooved, -hoov·ing, -hooves**) *vt* to be right and proper or appropriate for somebody (*formal*) ○ *It ill behooves him to complain.* [Old English *behōfian* "to need"]

be·hove /bi hṓv/ (**-hoved, -hov·ing, -hoves**) *vt UK* same as **behoove**

Beh·rens /bérrənz/, **Peter** (1868–1940) German architect and designer. He applied the principles of industrial design to all aspects of his work, and influenced Le Corbusier and Walter Gropius.

Beh·ring /bérring/, **Emil von** (1854–1917) German bacteriologist. He developed serum therapy against tetanus and diphtheria (1890) and won the first Nobel Prize in physiology or medicine (1901). Full name **Behring, Emil Adolph von**

Behr·man /bérmən/, **S. N.** (1893–1973) US playwright. His 21 Broadway plays include sophisticated, witty comedies of manners such as *No Time for Comedy* (1939). Full name **Behrman, Samuel Nathaniel**

Bei·der·becke /bī́dər bèk/, **Bix** (1903–31) US jazz cornetist, pianist, and composer. He was one of the major jazz musicians of his generation. Born **Beiderbecke, Leon Bismarck**

beige /bayzh/ *adj* **VERY PALE BROWN** of a very pale brown color with a tinge of yellow or pink ■ *n* **1. BEIGE COLOR** a very pale brown color with a tinge of yellow or pink **2.** TEXTILES **UNDYED WOOLEN CLOTH** cloth made of undyed or unbleached wool [Mid-19C. < French, perhaps < late Latin *bombax* "cotton"]

bei·gnet /bayn yáy/ *n* **1.** a small piece of seafood, covered in batter and then deep-fried **2.** *Southern US* in southern Louisiana, a square doughnut that has no hole in the center [Mid-19C. < French < *beigne* "bump caused by a blow"; from its shape]

Bei·jing /bày jíng/ national capital of China as well as a cultural, commercial, and educational center. It is situated in the northeastern part of the country, northwest of the Bo Hai Gulf. Population: 11,300,000 (1995). Former name **Peking**

be·ing /bée ing/ present participle of **be**[1] ■ *n* **1. PERSON** a human individual **2. EXISTENCE** the state of existing ○ *the turbulent years during which the new nation came into being* **3. ESSENTIAL NATURE** somebody's essential nature or character ○ *loved the child with all her being* **4. LIVING THING** a living thing, especially one conceived of as supernatural or not living on Earth

Bei·ra /báyrə/ port and capital of Sofala Province, eastern Mozambique, on the Mozambique Channel. Population: 299,300 (1990).

Bei·rut /bay róot/ capital, port, and largest city in Lebanon, situated on the Mediterranean Sea. Population: 1,500,000 (1998 estimate).

Bé·jart /bay zhaár/, **Maurice** (*b.* 1927) French dancer and choreographer known for his expressionist fusion of modern dance, ballet, and acrobatics. Born **Berger, Maurice Jean de**

be·je·sus /bi jéezəss, -jáy-/ *n Ireland* used to emphasize a statement or question [Early 20C. Alteration of *by Jesus*]

be·jew·el /bi jóo əl/ (**-eled, -el·ing, -els**) *vt* to decorate something lavishly with jewels or colorful decorative objects —**be·jew·eled** *adj*

Be·kaa Val·ley /bə kaá/, **Be·káa Val·ley** valley in Lebanon, east of Beirut, running down the center of the country between the Lebanon and Anti-Lebanon mountains. Length: 99 mi./160 km.

bel /bel/ *n* a logarithmic unit for comparing the loudness or strength of signals, equal to 10 decibels [Early 20C. After Alexander Graham BELL]

be·la·bor /bi láybər/ (**-bored, -bor·ing, -bors**) *vt* **1. HARP ON SOMETHING** to repeat or discuss something unnecessarily or at too great a length **2. CRITICIZE SOMEBODY** to subject somebody to a sustained verbal or literary attack (*formal*) **3. BEAT SOMEBODY** to hit somebody hard and repeatedly with something (*literary or humorous*)

be·la·bour (**-boured, -bour·ing, -bours**) *vt* Can, UK spelling of **belabor**

Belarus

Be·la·rus /bèllə róoss/ country in eastern Europe. It became an independent nation after the dissolution of the former Soviet Union in 1991. Language: Belarusian, Russian. Currency: Belarusian ruble. Capital: Minsk. Population: 10,322,151 (2003). Area: 80,153 sq. mi./207,595 sq. km. Official name **Republic of Belarus**

Be·la·ru·sian /bèllə rúsh'n/ *n* **1.** somebody who comes from Belarus **2.** the official language of the Republic of Belarus, belonging to the East Slavic group of Indo-European languages. Native speakers: 11 million. —**Be·la·ru·sian** *adj*

Be·las·co /bə láskō/, **David** (1859–1931) US producer and playwright. The naturalistic productions he staged at his theater in New York City greatly influenced the American stage.

be·lat·ed /bi láytəd/ *adj* occurring after the appropriate or expected time, especially too late to be effective or useful [Early 17C. < *belate* "make late, delay"] —**be·lat·ed·ly** *adv* —**be·lat·ed·ness** *n*

Be·lau ➧ **Palau**

Be·la·un·de Ter·ry /bè laa oon day térree/, **Fernando** (1912–2002) president of Peru (1963–68, 1980–85)

be·lay /bi láy/ *vti* (**-layed, -lay·ing, -lays**) **1.** NAUT **FASTEN LINE ON SHIP** to fasten a rope or line to a securing point on a ship or boat **2.** CLIMBING **SECURE ROPE** to fasten or control the rope to which a climber is attached by wrapping it around a metal device or another person **3.** NAUT **STOP** to stop doing something, or not follow an earlier instruction (*used as a command*) ■ *n* CLIMBING **1. SECURING OF CLIMBER'S ROPE** the fastening or controlling of a climber's rope by wrapping it around a metal device or another person, or the method by which this is done **2. FASTENING POINT** the point to which a climber's rope is fastened [Old English *belecgan* "surround" < Germanic]

be·lay·ing pin *n* a large wooden or metal pin that fits into a hole in a rail on a ship or boat and to which a rope can be fastened

bel can·to /bèl kaántō/ *n* **1.** a style of operatic singing that concentrates on producing a pure and even tone. It was developed in Italy in the 17th and 18th centuries. **2.** a style of expressive melodic instrumental playing that uses the principles of bel canto singing [Late 19C. < Italian, "fine song"]

belch /belch/ (**belched, belch·ing, belch·es**) *vti* **1.** to let gas from the stomach out through the mouth, making a loud noise in the throat **2.** to send out large amounts of steam, smoke, or gas, or come out of something in a thick cloud ○ *chimneys belching smoke* [Old English *bealcettan, bælcan,* perhaps < Germanic] —**belch** *n*

be·lea·guer /bi léegər/ (**-guered, -guer·ing, -guers**) *vt* (*usually passive*) **1.** to make somebody feel harassed, hemmed in, or under severe pressure **2.** to surround somebody or something with an army [Late 16C. < Dutch *belegeren* "camp around, besiege"] —**be·lea·guer·ment** *n*

~~**beleif**~~ incorrect spelling of **belief**

~~**beleive**~~ incorrect spelling of **believe**

Be·lém /bə lém/ port and capital of Pará State on the Pará River in northern Brazil. Population: 1,144,312 (1996).

bel·em·nite /béllәm nīt/ *n* a fossilized cylinder-shaped internal shell of an extinct order of cephalopods common in the Mesozoic era [Early 17C. < modern Latin < Greek *belemon* "a dart"; from its shape]

bel es·prit /bèl es prée, -əs-/ (*plural* **beaux es·prits** /bṑz es prée, -əs-/) *n* a witty, intelligent, and cultured person (*archaic*) [Mid-17C. < French, "fine mind"]

Bel·fast /bél fàst, bel fást/ port and capital of Northern Ireland, located at the head of Belfast Lough on the Lagan River. Population: 277,391 (2001).

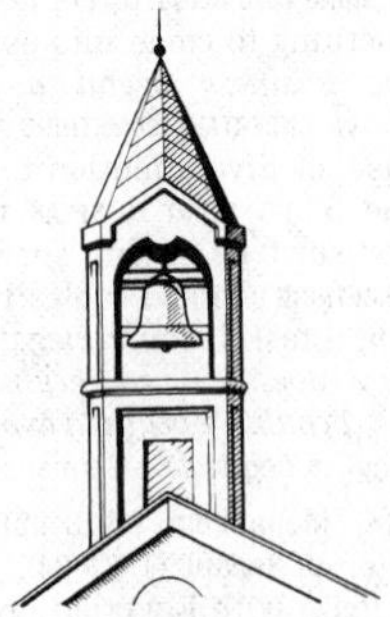

belfry

bel·fry /bélfree/ (*plural* **-fries**) *n* **1.** the part of a church steeple or a tower in which bells are hung **2.** a tower on a building, in which a bell or bells are hung [13C. < Old French *berfrei* "movable siege tower," by association with BELL[1]] —**bel·fried** *adj*

Bel·gae /bél gī̀, -jee/ *npl* an ancient Celtic people who lived in northern Gaul and parts of southern England [Early 17C. < Latin]

Bel·gaum /bel gówm/ city in northern Karnataka State, southwestern India. Population: 506,235 (2001).

Bel·gian /béljʼn/ *n* **SOMEBODY FROM BELGIUM** somebody who comes from Belgium ■ *adj* **1. OF BELGIUM** relating to Belgium, or its people, languages, or cultures **2. OF FLEMISH OR WALLOON** relating to the Flemish or Walloon languages

Bel·gian Con·go former name for **Congo, Democratic Republic of the**

Bel·gian hare *n* a domestic rabbit belonging to a breed with reddish brown fur and long legs and ears

Bel·gian Ma·li·nois /-màllən wáa/ (*plural* **Bel·gian Ma·li·noises** /-wáaz/) *n* a sturdy dog with a short dense coat and black mask, belonging to a breed used for herding animals that is related to the Belgian sheepdog [< French, "of Malines (Mechelen)" in Belgium]

Bel·gian sheep·dog *n* a dog with a long black coat used for herding sheep, belonging to a breed originating in Belgium

Bel·gian Ter·vu·ren /-ter vyŏorən, -tər-/ *n* a sturdy dog with a long brown coat with black tips belonging to a breed related to the Belgian sheepdog [*Tervuren* a commune in Belgium]

Belgium

Bel·gium /béljəm/ country in northwestern Europe, bordering the North Sea. It became independent in 1830. Language: Flemish, French, German. Currency: Euro. Capital: Brussels. Population: 10,289,088 (2003). Area: 11,787 sq. mi./30,528 sq. km. Official name **Kingdom of Belgium**

Bel·grade /bél gràyd/ capital of Yugoslavia and the Republic of Serbia that forms part of Yugoslavia. It is situated at the junction of the Danube and Sava rivers. Population: 1,594,483 (1998).

Bel·gra·no /bel gráanō/, **Manuel** (1770–1820) Argentine general and diplomat. He led Argentine troops in revolt against Spanish rule, winning major battles (1812 and 1813).

be·li /bə lée/ (**-lied, -li·ing, -lies**) *vti Malaysia* same as **buy** *v* (sense 1) (*informal; usually used without inflections*) [< Malay]

Be·li·al /béelee əl/ *n* in the Bible, a personification of evil or worthlessness, often thought of as a devil or demon [13C. < Hebrew *bĕliyya'al* "worthlessness"]

be·lie /bi lī/ (**-lied, -ly·ing, -lies**) *vt* **1.** to disguise the true nature of something **2.** to show that something is not true or real ○ *The evidence belies the testimony of the witness.* [Old English *belēogan* < Germanic]

be·lief /bi léef/ *n* **1.** ACCEPTANCE OF TRUTH OF SOMETHING acceptance by the mind that something is true or real, often underpinned by an emotional or spiritual sense of certainty ○ *belief in an afterlife* **2.** TRUST confidence that somebody or something is good or will be effective ○ *belief in democracy* **3.** SOMETHING THAT SOMEBODY BELIEVES IN a statement, principle, or doctrine that a person or group accepts as true **4.** OPINION an opinion, especially a firm and considered one **5.** RELIGIOUS FAITH faith in God or in a religion's gods [12C. Alteration of Old English *geléafa* after BELIEVE]

be·lief sys·tem *n* **1.** a set of beliefs, especially religious or political beliefs, that form a unified system **2.** a collection and organization of beliefs prevalent in a community or society

be·liev·a·ble /bi léevəb'l/ *adj* seeming to be true or authentic, and capable of being believed or believed in —**be·liev·a·bil·i·ty** /bi léevə bílləteel/ *n* —**be·liev·a·bly** *adv*

be·lieve /bi léev/ (**-lieved, -liev·ing, -lieves**) *v* **1.** *vt* ACCEPT SOMETHING AS TRUE to accept that something is true or real ○ *I don't know which story to believe.* **2.** *vt* ACCEPT SOMEBODY AS TRUTHFUL to accept that somebody is telling the truth ○ *Nobody will believe you!* ○ *I don't believe him.* **3.** *vt* CREDIT SOMEBODY WITH SOMETHING to accept that somebody or something has a particular quality or ability ○ *No one believed her capable of such a malicious remark.* **4.** *vi* THINK THAT SOMETHING EXISTS to be of the opinion that something exists or is a reality, especially when there is no absolute proof of its existence or reality ○ *believe in reincarnation* **5.** *vi* HAVE TRUST to be confident that somebody or something is worthwhile or effective ○ *We all believe in you.* **6.** *vi* THINK SOMETHING IS GOOD to be of the opinion that something is right or beneficial and, usually, to act in accordance with that belief ○ *believed strongly in freedom of expression* **7.** *vi* HAVE RELIGIOUS FAITH to have a belief in God or in a religion's gods [Old English *belyfan*, alteration of *geléfan* < Germanic, "to love, trust"] —**be·liev·er** *n* ◇ **make believe** to pretend, especially in play

~~**beligerent**~~ incorrect spelling of **belligerent**

Bel·in·da /bə líndə/ *n* a small natural satellite of Uranus, discovered in 1986 by the Voyager 2 planetary probe

be·lit·tle /bi lítt'l/ (**-tled, -tling, -tles**) *vt* to reduce or dismiss the importance or quality of somebody or something ○ *I don't want to belittle her achievement.* —**be·lit·tle·ment** *n* —**be·lit·tler** *n* —**be·lit·tling·ly** *adv*

Be·li·veau /bélli vō/, **Jean** (*b.* 1931) Canadian hockey player. A center for the Montreal Canadiens, he was the National Hockey League's most valuable player in 1956 and 1964.

Belize

Be·lize /bə léez/ country in Central America on the Caribbean Sea, bordered to the west by Mexico and Guatemala. It became a British crown colony in 1862 and an independent member of the British Commonwealth in 1981. Language: English, Spanish. Currency: Belizean dollar. Capital: Belmopan. Population: 266,440 (2003). Area: 8,867 sq. mi./22,965 sq. km. Former name **British Honduras** (until 1973) —**Be·li·ze·an** *n, adj*

Be·lize Cit·y city and the main port of Belize on the Caribbean Sea. It was the capital of British Honduras between 1884 and 1972. Population: 53,915 (1997).

Bel·kic /bél kìch/, **Beriz** (*b.* 1946) Bosniac representative of the presidency of Bosnia and Herzegovina (2001–02) which rotates between a Serb, a Bosnian Muslim, and a Croat

bell[1] /bel/ *n* **1.** OBJECT WITH RINGING SOUND a hollow open-ended metal instrument with a rounded top that produces a ringing sound when struck. Bells are traditionally used as summonses and signals. **2.** ELECTRICAL DEVICE PRODUCING SOUND a device activated by electricity that produces a ringing or buzzing signal **3.** SOMETHING BELL-SHAPED something with the curved and open-ended shape of a bell, especially a flower **4.** MUSIC FLARED END OF WIND INSTRUMENT the flared end of a wind instrument, from which the sound emerges **5.** NAUT DURATION OF SHIP'S WATCH the time during a watch on a ship, indicated by rings on a bell, one ring for each half hour that has passed ■ **bells** *npl* MUSIC PERCUSSION INSTRUMENT a percussion instrument consisting of metal tubes or bars hung from a frame that give out a ringing sound when struck ■ *vti* (**belled, bell·ing, bells**) BECOME OR MAKE WIDER to open out, or open something out, into a curved or flared shape similar to that of a bell [Old English *belle* < Germanic] ◇ **ring a bell** to evoke a vague memory of something or somebody (*informal*) ○ *Her name doesn't ring a bell.* ○ *That name doesn't ring a bell with me.*

CULTURAL NOTE *For Whom the Bell Tolls*, a novel (1940) by Ernest Hemingway. Widely viewed as Hemingway's most ambitious work, it is set during the Spanish Civil War and tells the story of Robert Jordan, a US volunteer fighting for the Republicans, who falls in love with a fellow volunteer named Maria. It was made into a movie by Sam Woods in 1943.

bell[2] /bel/ *n* a bellowing sound made by a rutting stag or by a hunting dog during the chase ■ *vi* (**belled, bell·ing, bells**) to make a bellowing sound [Old English *bellan* < Germanic]

Bell /bel/ city in southwestern California, and a southern suburb of Los Angeles. Population: 37,359 (2002 estimate).

Bell, Alexander Graham (1847–1922) Scottish-born US inventor and educator. He made the first intelligible telephonic transmission (1876), patented the telephone (1876), and founded the Bell Telephone Company (1877). Among his numerous other inventions were wax cylinder recordings (1886) and the hydrofoil (1917).

Bell, Sir Francis Henry Dillon (1851–1936) New Zealand lawyer and politician. He was a Reform Party politician and was briefly prime minister of New Zealand (1925). See table at **prime minister**

Bell, Vanessa (1879–1961) British painter and designer. One of the leading British artists to experiment with postimpressionism, she was also a prominent member of the Bloomsbury Group. and the sister of Virginia Woolf. Born **Stephen, Vanessa**

Bel·la ◆ **Ben Bella, Ahmed**

Bel·la Coo·la /bèllə kóolə/ *n* a member of a Native North American people living along the Bella Coola River in British Columbia

bel·la·don·na /bèllə dónnə/ *n* **1.** a drug made from an extremely poisonous plant with small black berries, e.g., atropine **2.** an extremely poisonous plant with small black berries, from which belladonna is obtained. Native to: Europe, Asia. Latin name: *Atropa belladonna*. [Mid-18C. Via modern Latin < Italian, "beautiful lady"; from the use of belladonna to dilate the pupils]

bel·la·don·na lil·y *n* PLANTS same as **amaryllis** (sense 1)

Bel·la·my /bélləmee/, **Edward** (1850–98) US writer. His utopian novel *Looking Backward* (1888) achieved widespread popularity and spread socialist ideas.

bel·lar·mine /bél aar méen, béllər-/ *n* a large earthenware or stoneware jug decorated with a bearded face [Mid-17C. After St. Robert *Bellarmin* (1542–1621), Jesuit cardinal]

bell·bird /bél bùrd/ *n* a bird with a call that sounds like a bell. Native to: tropical America, Australasia. Genera: *Procnias* or *Oreoica* or *Anthornis*.

bell-bot·tom pants, bell-bot·toms *npl* pants that widen below the knees into a bell shape

bell·boy /bél bòy/ *n* same as **bellhop**

bell buoy *n* a floating buoy with a bell on top that is rung by the movement of the waves and gives a warning or positional signal to ships

bell cap·tain *n* somebody in charge of the bellhops in a hotel

bell crank *n* a lever with two arms that share a fulcrum at the point where they join

belle /bel/ *n* **1.** a beautiful woman **2.** a woman considered to be the most conspicuously good-looking of all those living in a place or attending a social event [Early 17C. < French, "beautiful"]

Bel·leek ware /bə léek-/, **Bel·leek** *n* very thin, typically cream-colored porcelain with a lustrous glaze [Mid-19C. After a town in N Ireland]

belle é·poque /bèl ay púk/ *n* an era of cultural refinement, social elegance, and general prosperity and security, especially the last decades of the 19th century and the early years of the 20th prior to World War I [Mid-20C. < French, "fine period"]

Belle Fourche /bèl fóorsh/ river that rises in northeastern Wyoming and flows eastward to join the Cheyenne River in western South Dakota. Length: 350 mi./563 km.

Belle Isle, Strait of /bèl-/ channel separating Newfoundland from Labrador, Canada, connecting the Gulf of St. Lawrence with the Atlantic. Length: 90 mi./100 km.

Bel·ler·o·phon /bə lérrəfən, -fòn/ *n* in Greek mythology, a hero who tamed the winged horse Pegasus and slew the fire-breathing monster Chimera

belles-let·tres /bèl léttrə/ *n* writings that are valued for their elegance and aesthetic qualities rather than for any human interest or moral or instructive content (*takes a singular or plural verb*) [Mid-17C. < French, "fine letters"] —**bel·let·rism** /-lét rìzzəm/ *n* —**bel·let·rist** /-léttrist/ *n*

Belle·ville /bél vìl/ city in southwestern Illinois, an eastern suburb of St. Louis. Population: 41,325 (2002 estimate).

Belle·vue /bél vyoo/ **1.** city in eastern Nebraska, on the western bank of the Missouri River, a southern suburb of Omaha. Population: 46,217 (2002 estimate). **2.** city in west central Washington, beside Lake Washington, a suburb of Seattle. Population: 112,894 (2002 estimate).

bell·flow·er /bél flòw ər/ *n* PLANTS same as **campanula**

bell·found·ry /bél fòwndree/ (*plural* **-ries**) *n* a foundry that specializes in making bells

bell glass *n* CHEM same as **bell jar** (sense 2)

bell·hop /bél hòp/ *n* an employee in a hotel who helps guests by carrying their luggage and running errands

bel·li·cose /bélli kōss/ *adj* ready or inclined to quarrel, fight, or go to war [15C. < Latin *bellicosus* < *bellum* "war"] —**bel·li·cose·ly** *adv* —**bel·li·cose·ness** *n* —**bel·li·cos·i·ty** /bèlli kóssətee/ *n*

bel·lig·er·ence /bə líjjərənss/ *n* the quality of being hostile, ready to start a fight, or ready to go to war

bel·lig·er·en·cy /bə líjjərənssee/ *n* **1.** same as **belligerence 2.** the state of being at war

bel·lig·er·ent /bə líjjərənt/ *adj* **1.** HOSTILE OR AGGRESSIVE hostile, ready to start a fight, or ready to go to war **2.** ENGAGED IN WAR taking part in warfare, especially in a war recognized by international law **3.** OF BELLIGERENT NATION relating to or characteristic of a participant in war or a fight ■ *n* PARTICIPANT IN WAR a participant in a war or fight, especially a nation engaged in a war recognized by international law [Late 16C. < Latin *belligerant-*, present participle of *belligerare* "wage war" < *belliger* "carrying on war" < *bellum* "war" + *gerere* "carry on"] —**bel·lig·er·ent·ly** *adv*

Bel·ling·ham /bélling hàm/ city and port in northwestern Washington, directly south of the Canadian border, at the head of Bellingham Bay. Population: 70,480 (2002 estimate).

Bel·lings·hau·sen /béllingz hòwz'n/, **Fabian Gottlieb von** (1778–1852) Russian explorer. He explored an area of the Antarctic Sea (1819–21) that was later named for him.

Bel·lings·hau·sen Sea predominantly ice-covered sea constituting part of the southern Pacific Ocean, off the coast of Antarctica

Bel·li·ni /be léenee/, **Gentile** (1429?–1507) Italian painter. The son of Jacopo Bellini and brother of Giovanni Bellini, he is best known for his portraits and for his large-scale narrative paintings.

Bel·li·ni /bə léenee/, **Giovanni** (1430?–1516) Italian painter. The son of Jacopo Bellini, he produced calm yet sensuous religious pictures, combining figures and landscape in naturalistic light.

Bel·li·ni, Jacopo (1400?–70?) Italian painter. He produced stylized paintings and drawings with strong architectural elements.

Bel·li·ni /be léenee/, **Vincenzo** (1801–35) Italian composer. His best-known works are the operas *La Sonnambula* (1831) and *Norma* (1831).

bell jar *n* **1.** a glass cover, shaped like a bell, used to protect and display delicate items **2.** a bell-shaped glass cover used to enclose equipment in experiments and prevent gases from escaping or entering

bell·man /bélmən/ (*plural* **-men** /-mən/) *n* **1.** OCCUPATIONS same as **bellhop 2.** a man who rings a bell, especially a town crier

bell met·al *n* an alloy of copper with 20 to 25 percent tin. Use: to cast bells and plain bearings.

Bel·loc /bé lòk, -ək/, **Hilaire** (1870–1953) French-born British writer. He wrote *Cautionary Tales for Children* (1907) and biographies of historical figures including *Napoleon* (1932). Full name **Belloc, Joseph Hilaire Pierre**

> "Lord Finchley tried to mend the Electric Light / Himself. It struck him dead: And serve him right! / It is the business of the wealthy man / To give employment to the artisan."
> [Hilaire Belloc, "Lord Finchley," *More Peers*; 1911]

bel·lo·ta /be lóttə/ *n Hispanic* a sweet acorn, used as fodder for free-range black hogs [Mid-20C. Via Mexican Spanish < Spanish, "acorn"]

bel·low /béllō/ (**-lowed, -low·ing, -lows**) *v* **1.** *vti* to shout something in a loud deep voice **2.** *vi* to give a bull's loud deep roar or a roar like that of a bull [14C. Origin ?] —**bel·low** *n* —**bel·low·er** *n*

Bel·low /béllō/, **Saul** (*b.* 1915) Canadian-born US writer. His novel *Humboldt's Gift* (1975) won the Pulitzer Prize. He won the Nobel Prize in literature (1976).

> "Socially, psychologically, politically, the very essence of human institutions was an extract of what we assumed about death."
> [Saul Bellow, *Humboldt's Gift*; 1975]

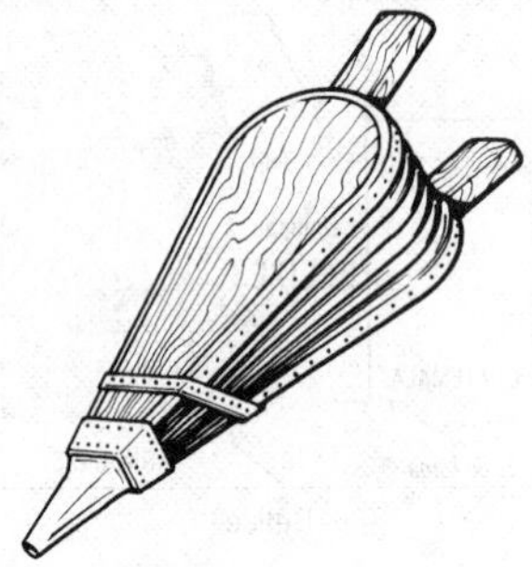

bellows

bel·lows /béllōz/ (*plural same*) *n* **1.** a device or piece of equipment with a chamber that can be expanded to draw air in and compressed to force the air out **2.** something constructed of a pleated material and able to be expanded and contracted, e.g., the part enclosing the lenses on some cameras or photographic enlargers [12C. Probably < Old English *belga*, shortening of *blæstbelig* "blowing bag"]

Bel·lows /béllōz/, **George Wesley** (1882–1925) US artist. He was a realist painter who depicted urban scenes and boxing matches in works such as *Stag at Sharkey's* (1909).

bell pep·per *n* FOOD same as **sweet pepper** [< its shape]

bell·pull /bél pool/ *n* a handle or cord that when pulled makes a bell ring

bell push *n* a button that when pressed causes an electric bell to ring

bell-ring·er *n* **1.** somebody who rings church bells as an ecclesiastical function or a hobby **2.** a musician who plays handbells —**bell-ring·ing** *n*

bells and whis·tles *npl* special features that are not necessary but are incorporated in a product to make it appear more desirable or useful (*informal*)

Bell's pal·sy *n* the inability to move the muscles on one side of the face, so that the expression of the face is distorted. It results from injury to the facial nerve and is usually temporary. [Mid-19C. After Sir Charles *Bell* (1774–1842), Scottish anatomist]

bell tow·er *n* a tower that has a bell or bells housed in it

bell·weth·er /bél we*th*ər/ *n* **1.** INDICATOR OF FUTURE DEVELOPMENTS an indicator of future developments or trends **2.** LEADER somebody who leads others **3.** SHEEP LEADING FLOCK a sheep that leads the rest of the flock, usually wearing a bell around its neck (*archaic*)

Bell·wood /bél wood/ town in northeastern Illinois, a western suburb of Chicago. Population: 20,355 (2002 estimate).

bell·wort /bél wùrt, -wàwrt/ (*plural* **-worts** or *same*) *n* a plant of the lily family. Flowers: yellow, bell-shaped. Native to: North America. Genus: *Uvularia*.

bel·ly /béllee/ *n* (*plural* **-lies**) **1.** MIDDLE PART OF BODY the part of the body of a vertebrate that contains the stomach, intestines, and other organs **2.** FRONT OF BODY AROUND STOMACH the surface of the body of a vertebrate around the stomach **3.** STOMACH the stomach (*informal*) **4.** APPETITE the desire or need for food and drink **5.** BULGING PART a part of something that bulges out, e.g., a sail **6.** INTERIOR CAVITY the interior cavity of a structure, especially a ship **7.** MUSIC UPPER SURFACE OF STRINGED INSTRUMENT the top or front surface of the body of a stringed instrument, over which the strings are stretched ■ *vti* (**-lied, -ly·ing, -lies**) BULGE to bulge or make something bulge ○ *The wind bellied out the sail.* [Old English *belig* "bag" < Indo-European, "to swell"] ◇ **go** *or* **turn belly up** to go bankrupt, fail, or fall through

belly up to *vt* to move close to or stand next to something against which you can lean or press (*informal*)

bel·ly·ache /béllee àyk/ (*informal*) *n* a painful or upset stomach ■ *vi* (**-ached, -ach·ing, -aches**) to complain in an annoying manner —**bel·ly·ach·er** *n*

bel·ly·band /béllee bànd/ *n* a strap passed around the belly of a draft animal and attached to the shafts of the vehicle it is pulling

bel·ly·but·ton /béllee bùtt'n/ *n* the human navel (*informal*)

bel·ly chain *n* a chain designed to be worn around the waist or waist area, especially as an ornament

bel·ly dance *n* a dance of North Africa and southwestern Asia, in which the hips and abdomen are moved rapidly —**bel·ly danc·er** *n* —**bel·ly danc·ing** *n*

bel·ly flop *n* **1.** a shallow dive in which the front of the diver's body hits the water first **2.** AVIAT same as **belly landing** —**bel·ly-flop** *vi*

bel·ly·ful /béllee fool/ *n* (*informal*) **1.** all the food that somebody wants or is able to eat **2.** an undesirable or excessive amount of something ○ *I've had a bellyful of his complaining.*

bel·ly land·ing *n* an emergency landing of an aircraft with the wheels not extended —**bel·ly-land** *vti*

bel·ly laugh *n* a deep and unrestrained laugh

Bel·mon·do /bel món dō/, **Jean-Paul** (*b.* 1933) French actor. His starring role in Jean-Luc Godard's *A Bout de Souffle* (1960) (*Breathless* (1961) established him as a key figure of the French New Wave.

Bel·mont /bél mònt/ **1.** city on the San Mateo Peninsula, south of San Francisco, western California. Population: 26,221 (1998). **2.** town in northeastern Massachusetts. It is a northwestern suburb of Boston and Cambridge. Population: 24,045 (2002 estimate).

Belmont Stakes *n* a race for three-year-old horses that has been run annually since 1867 and, at its present location, Belmont Park in Elmont, New York, since 1905

Bel·mo·pan /bèlmō pán/ capital of Belize, located on the Belize River in the central part of the country. Population: 6,785 (1997).

Be·lo Ho·ri·zon·te /béllō hàwri záwntee/ city and capital of Minas Gerais State in eastern Brazil. Population: 2,091,448 (1996).

Be·loit /bə lóyt/ city in southern Wisconsin, on the Rock River, south of Madison. Population: 35,678 (2002 estimate).

be·long /bi láwng, -lóng/ (**-longed, -long·ing, -longs**) *vi* **1.** BE PROPERTY OF SOMEBODY OR SOMETHING to be the property of a person or organization ○ *Who does this coat belong to?* **2.** BE LINKED TO SOMEBODY OR SOMETHING to be linked to a particular person, group, place, or time by a relationship such as birth, affection, or membership ○ *belongs to a bridge club* **3.** BE CLASSIFIED AS PART OF SOMETHING to be part of a class or group ○ *Tulips belong to the lily family.* **4.** BE PART OF to be a part or component of something else ○ *belonging to the assembly mechanism* **5.** BE IN RIGHT PLACE to be in an appropriate or usual place ○ *Where does this* *chair belong?* **6. BE ACCEPTED SOMEWHERE** to be accepted or made welcome in a place or group ○ *feeling that I didn't belong* [14C. < BE- + obsolete *long* "relate to"]

Be·long·er /bi láwngər, -lóng-/ *n Carib* somebody of African descent who was born and lives on a Caribbean island

be·long·ing /bi láwnging, -lóng-/ *n* the state of being accepted and comfortable in a place or group ■ **be·long·ings** *npl* the things somebody owns or has with him or her

Be·lo·rus·sia /bèllō rúshə/ ➧ **Belarus**

be·lov·ed /bi lúvvəd/; *predicatively* /-lúvd/ *adj* loved very much ■ *n* /bi lúvvid/ somebody who is loved very much ○ *a letter from his beloved*

CULTURAL NOTE ***Beloved***, a novel (1987) by Toni Morrison. It explores the emotional legacy of slavery among Black people in the United States. Set in the years before, during, and after the Civil War, it centers on three generations of Black women, Baby Suggs, a woman freed from slavery, her daughter-in-law Sethe, who escapes to the North from vicious slave owners in Kentucky, and Sethe's daughter Denver, raised in freedom but scarred by her inheritance. They are haunted by the ghost of Beloved, another daughter whom Sethe murdered to save her from being raised in slavery. The novel weaves their memories as they come to terms with their personal and collective past.

be·low /bi lṓ/ CORE MEANING: a grammatical word indicating a position beneath or lower than something ○ (prep) *a river below the town* ○ (adv) *on the shelf below*

1. *prep, adv* **IN LOWER GRADE** at or to a level, standard, or grade that is lower than that specified or understood ○ *animals ranked below humans* ○ *below average* ○ *30 degrees below* **2.** *adv* **FURTHER DOWN** lower down or later on in a text, especially on the same page ○ *see below* ○ *on page 29 below* **3.** *adv* NAUT **LOWER THAN DECK** on or to a level of a ship or boat that is lower than the deck [14C. < earlier form of BY[1] + LOW[1]]

be·low·ground /bi lṓ gròwnd/ *adj* situated under the ground ■ *adv* into or under the ground

be·low-the-fold *adj* relating to the portion of a webpage that is seen only by scrolling down to the middle or bottom of the page and is therefore less commercially valuable

Bel·sen /bélzən/ village in northwestern Germany, about 10 mi./16 km north of Celle. It is the site of the Bergen-Belsen Nazi concentration camp (1943–45).

Bel·shaz·zar /bel sházzər/ *n* in the Bible, a king of Babylon in the sixth century B.C. whose death is foretold in an inscription that mysteriously appears on the wall of his palace during a feast (Daniel 5)

belt /belt/ *n* **STRIP OF MATERIAL AROUND WAIST** a strip of material worn around the waist, used to hold up clothing for the lower body, as decoration, or to carry tools or weapons ■ *v* (**belt·ed, belt·ing, belts**) *vt* **HIT SOMEBODY OR SOMETHING HARD** to strike somebody or something with a hard blow (*informal*) ○ *belted a three-run homer* ■ *n* MECH ENG **BAND AS PART OF MACHINE** a band of strong flexible material used in machinery to transmit motion or power or to move articles ○ *a fan belt* ■ *v* (**belt·ed, belt·ing, belts**) *vi* **MOVE FAST** to move very quickly (*informal*) ○ *belted home as soon as we could* ■ *n* **PARTICULAR AREA** an area or region where a particular item or quality is characteristic ○ *the wheat belt* ■ *v* (**belt·ed, belt·ing, belts**) *vt* **FIX SOMETHING WITH BELT** to fasten or attach something with a belt ■ *n* **STRIP OF SOMETHING DIFFERENT** a band or stripe of a different color, texture, or substance from what it encircles or crosses ■ *v* (**belt·ed, belt·ing, belts**) *vt* **HIT SOMEBODY WITH BELT** to strike somebody with a belt ■ *n* **1.** SPORTS **BELT GIVEN FOR ACHIEVEMENT** a belt awarded to a sports competitor, especially in boxing or the martial arts, as a trophy or a sign of having attained a particular grade **2.** SPORTS **SOMEBODY WITH BELT FOR SPORTING ACHIEVEMENT** somebody awarded a particular belt for a sporting achievement, usually in boxing or one of the martial arts **3.** AUTOMOT same as **seat belt** **4.** ROADS same as **beltway** **5. BLOW** a hard blow (*informal*) **6. DRINK** a drink of liquor (*slang*) **7. EMOTIONAL RESPONSE** a sudden strong emotional reaction (*slang*) [Old English, < Latin *balteus* "girdle"] ◇ **below the belt** unfair and often hurtful ◇ **have something under your belt** to have done or acquired something that will be of benefit to you in the future ○ *has 12 computer science courses under her belt* ◇ **tighten your belt** to reduce your expenditures

belt down *vt* to drink a number of alcoholic drinks in very quick succession (*informal*)

belt out *vt* to sing or play something loudly and enthusiastically (*informal*)

belt up *vti* to fasten a safety belt, or secure somebody with a safety belt

Bel·tane /bél tàyn, -tən/ *n* an ancient Celtic festival marked by the lighting of bonfires. Date: beginning of May. [15C. Via Gaelic *bealltainn* < Old Irish]

belt bomb·er *n* a suicide bomber who conceals explosives around the waist, using a specially designed belt to hold them —**belt bomb** *n*

belt drive *n* a system for transmitting power from one shaft to another by means of an endless flexible belt looped over pulleys mounted on the shafts

belt high·way *n* ROADS same as **beltway**

belt·ing /bélting/ *n* **1.** material used for making belts **2.** belts considered collectively

Bel·ton /bélt'n/ **1.** city in western Missouri, a southern suburb of Kansas City. Population: 23,214 (2002 estimate). **2.** city in central Texas, northeast of Austin and southwest of Waco. Population: 14,621 (2002 estimate).

belt sand·er *n* a sander that uses a continuous belt coated with an abrasive

belt-tight·en·ing *n* a reduction in spending that results in the loss of something previously enjoyed

belt·way /bélt wày/ *n* a highway that surrounds or skirts an urban area ◇ **inside** *or* **outside the Beltway** inside or outside the politically and socially insular community of Washington, D.C.

be·lu·ga /bə lóogə/ (*plural* **-gas** or *same*) *n* **1.** a large white sturgeon. Native to: Black Sea, Caspian Sea. Latin name: *Huso huso* or *Acipenser huso*. **2.** *also* **be·lu·ga cav·i·ar** caviar made from the eggs of the beluga sturgeon **3.** MARINE BIOL same as **white whale** [Late 16C. < Russian, "large white" < *belyĭ* "white"]

bel·ve·dere /bélvi dèer/ *n* a building or part of a building positioned to offer a fine view of the surrounding area [Late 16C. < Italian, "beautiful to see"]

be·ma /béemə/ *n* **1.** *also* **bi·ma** *or* **bi·mah** in a synagogue, the raised platform where the scriptures are read **2.** in a Christian Orthodox church, the raised area where the altar is located [Late 17C. < Greek *bēma* "step, platform"]

Bem·ba /bémbə/ (*plural same* or **-bas**) *n* **1.** a member of an African people who live chiefly in Zambia **2.** a Bantu language spoken in east central Africa and belonging to the Benue-Congo group of languages. Native speakers: 2 million. [Mid-20C. < Bantu] —**Bem·ba** *adj*

Be·mel·mans /béem'lmənz, bémm'l-/, **Ludwig** (1898–1962) Austrian-born US writer and illustrator. He is known for his classic children's book, *Madeleine* (1939).

be·mire /bi mír/ (**-mired, -mir·ing, -mires**) *vt* **1.** to soil somebody or something with mud or dirt (*archaic*) **2.** to cause somebody or something to become stuck in mud (*archaic or literary; usually passive*)

be·moan /bi mṓn/ (**-moaned, -moan·ing, -moans**) *vt* to express grief or disappointment about something

be·muse /bi myóoz/ (**-mused, -mus·ing, -mus·es**) *vt* **1.** to cause somebody to be confused or puzzled **2.** to absorb the attention of somebody —**be·mused** *adj* —**be·mus·ed·ly** /-ədlee/ *adv* —**be·muse·ment** *n*

Be·na·res /bə náarəz, -eez/ former name for **Varanasi**

Ben Bel·la /bèn béllə/, **Ahmed** (*b.* 1918?) Algerian politician. A leading figure in Algeria's war of independence from French rule, he was the country's first prime minister (1962–63) and president (1963–65). Imprisoned from 1965 to 1980, he was exiled in 1980 and returned to Algeria in 1990. Full name **Ben Bella, Mohammed Ahmed**

bench /bench/ *n* **1. LONG BACKLESS SEAT** a long seat for two or more people, usually made without a back or arms **2. WORK TABLE** a long strong work table **3. JUDGE'S SEAT** the seat where a judge sits in a court **4. Bench JUDGE** the judge or magistrate presiding over a court **5. Bench JUDGES** the judges of a court system **6. POST OF JUDGE** the office or position of a judge **7.** SPORTS **SEATS FOR NONPLAYING ATHLETES** in team sports, the seats for players not taking part on the field or court **8. SUBSTITUTE PLAYERS ON SPORTS TEAM** the substitute players of a sports team **9.** NAUT **SEAT IN BOAT** a seat for a rower in a boat **10.** GEOL **LEDGE OF LAND** a narrow flat ledge of land, often the remnant of a former shoreline **11.** MIN EXTRACT **LEDGE IN MINE** a ledge formed by excavation in a mine **12. PLATFORM FOR SHOWING ANIMALS** a platform used for displaying dogs, cats, or other animals at a show ■ *vt* (**benched, bench·ing, bench·es**) **1. EXCLUDE PLAYER** in team sports, to exclude or remove a member of a sports team from play **2. DISPLAY ANIMAL AT SHOW** to display a dog, cat, or other animal on a bench at a show **3. PROVIDE SOMETHING WITH BENCHES** to provide a place with benches [Old English *benc* < Germanic]

Bench /bench/, **Johnny Lee** (*b.* 1947) US baseball player. Regarded as the greatest catcher of his era, he led the Cincinnati Reds to World Series championships (1975, 1976) and was the National League's most valuable player twice (1970, 1972).

Bench·ley /bénchlee/, **Peter** (*b.* 1940) US writer. The son of Robert Benchley, he is the author of *Jaws* (1974) and other thrillers.

Bench·ley, Robert (1889–1945) US humorist, screenwriter, and actor. Known for his wit, he was theater critic of *The New Yorker* and wrote humorous short movies. Full name **Benchley, Robert Charles**

> "If you think that you have caught a cold, call in a good doctor. Call in three good doctors and play bridge."
> [Robert Benchley, "How To Avoid Colds," *From Bed to Worse*; 1934]

bench mark *n* a mark made by a surveyor on a permanent object that shows an established position and elevation and is used as a reference point

bench·mark /bénch maark/ *n* **1. STANDARD** a standard against which something can be measured or assessed **2. TEST OF COMPUTER PERFORMANCE** a standard test to measure the performance of computer hardware or software ■ *adj* **USED AS STANDARD** used as a standard for measuring or assessing something ■ *vt* (**-marked, -mark·ing, -marks**) **1. PROVIDE STANDARD FOR SOMETHING** to provide a standard against which something can be measured or assessed **2. TEST COMPUTER PERFORMANCE** to test the performance of computer hardware or software for comparison with similar products

bench press *n* in weightlifting, a lift where somebody lies on a bench with the feet on the floor and raises a weight from chest level to arm's length —**bench-press** *vti*

bench seat *n* a seat that extends across the full width of a motor vehicle

bench test *n* a trial of a machine or part in the laboratory or workshop to confirm that it works properly before it is installed —**bench-test** *vti*

bench·warm·er /bénch wàwrmər/ *n* a substitute player on a sports team who spends most of the game or match on the bench

bench war·rant *n* a warrant issued by a judge or court ordering the arrest of an offender

bend[1] /bend/ *v* (**bent** /bent/, **bend·ing, bends**) **1.** *vti* **BECOME OR MAKE CURVED** to take on a curved or angled shape, or cause something to do this ○ *The wooden struts bent under pressure.* **2.** *vti* **STOOP** to make a stooping or inclined movement, or cause somebody to do this ○ *I bent to pick up the ball.* **3.** *vti* **CHANGE OR CAUSE TO CHANGE DIRECTION** to change direction or course, or cause something to do this ○ *The path bends to the right.* **4.** *vt* **DISTORT FOR SOMEBODY'S BENEFIT** to adapt or interpret something in a way that was not originally intended, especially for personal benefit or to help somebody else ○ *bend the rules* **5.** *vti* **YIELD OR FORCE TO YIELD** to yield in response to a strong will or force, or force somebody or something to do this **6.** *vti* **CONCENTRATE ON DOING SOMETHING** to concentrate the mind on an activity ○ *bent her mind to the task at hand* **7.** *vt* NAUT **ATTACH** to attach or fasten something, especially a rope ■ *n* **1. CURVE** a curved part of something, especially a curve in a road **2. ACT OF BENDING** an act of bending **3.** NAUT **KNOT JOINING TWO ROPES** a knot that joins one line to another [Old English *bendan* "tie, curve" < Germanic] **—bend·a·ble** *adj* ◇ **around the bend** wild, distracted, or irrational (*slang*)

ORIGIN The prehistoric Germanic word from which ***bend*** is derived is also the ancestor of *band*[2], *bind*, and *bond*, and possibly also of *bundle*.

bend[2] /bend/ *n* a band that crosses a heraldic shield diagonally from top right to bottom left [Old English, < Germanic; later < Old French *bende*]

Bend /bend/ city in central Oregon, east of Eugene, on the eastern bank of the Deschutes River. Population: 57,010 (2002 estimate).

ben·day /bèn dáy/, **Ben Day** *adj* describes a printing process of adding tone to an image by overlaying a transparent sheet patterned with dots before the image is reproduced to make a plate [Early 20C. After *Benjamin Day*, Jr. (1838–1916), US printer]

bend·ed /béndəd/ *adj* in a position so as to be curved or bent (*literary*) ○ *on bended knee*

bend·er /béndər/ *n* a prolonged bout of alcoholic drinking (*slang*)

Ben·di·go /béndigō/ former gold-mining town in central Victoria, Australia, now an important industrial, commercial, and agricultural center. Population: 75,900 (1998).

ben·dro·flu·me·thi·a·zide /bèndrō floo me thī ə zīd/ *n* a diuretic drug that promotes the excretion of salt and water by the kidneys. Use: treatment of edema and hypertension.

bends /bendz/ *n* decompression sickness, especially in divers (*informal; takes a singular or plural verb*)

bend sin·is·ter (*plural* **bends sin·is·ter**) *n* a band that crosses a heraldic shield diagonally from top left to bottom right, used to indicate a line of descent from a birth outside marriage

be·neath /bi neéth/ CORE MEANING: a grammatical word indicating a position underneath or lower than something

1. *prep, adv* **UNDERNEATH** in, at, or to a lower position or less superficial level than that specified or understood ○ *beneath the bed* ○ *Beneath his veneer of politeness lay hostility.* 2. *prep, adv* **LOWER** in, at, or to a lower level, grade, or standard than that specified or understood ○ *beneath the usual standard* 3. *prep* **TOO LOW FOR** too low in status or character for ○ *beneath contempt* ○ *Gossiping is beneath you.* [Old English *binithan, bineothan* "by or from below" < Germanic]

ben·e·dic·i·te /bènni díssətee, bày nay díchi tày/ *n* a blessing or grace used in some Christian religious communities [13C. < Latin, imperative of *benedicere* "bless"]

Ben·e·dict XIV /bénni dìkt/, **Pope** (1675–1758) As pope (1740–58) he encouraged the development of education and science. Born **Lambertini, Prospero**

Ben·e·dict XV, Pope (1854–1922) As pope (1914–22) he was active in organizing war relief during World War I. Born **della Chiesa, Giacomo**

Ben·e·dict, Ruth (1887–1948) US anthropologist. She studied Native American peoples. Her writings include *Patterns of Culture* (1934). Born **Fulton, Ruth**

> "No man ever looks at the world with pristine eyes. He sees it edited by a definite set of customs and institutions and ways of thinking."
> [Ruth Benedict, *Patterns of Culture*; 1934]

Ben·e·dic·tine /bènni díktin, -teen/ *n* a member of a Christian order of monks and nuns founded by St. Benedict of Nursia. ■ *adj* relating to or characteristic of St. Benedict, his rule, or the Christian order that he founded.

ben·e·dic·tion /bènni díksh'n/ *n* 1. **EXPRESSION OF APPROVAL** an expression of approval or good wishes 2. **PRAYER ASKING FOR GOD'S BLESSING** a prayer asking for God's blessing, usually at the end of a Christian service 3. **BLESSEDNESS** in Christianity, the state of being blessed 4. CHR another spelling of **Benediction** [15C. Directly or via French < Latin *benediction-* < *benedicere* "say well to" < *bene* "well" + *dicere* "say"] **—ben·e·dic·tive** *adj* **—ben·e·dic·to·ry** *adj*

Ben·e·dic·tion *n* in the Roman Catholic Church, a devotional service during which the congregation is blessed with the Host

Ben·e·dict of Nur·si·a /-núrssee ə, -núrshə/, **St.** (480–547) Italian monk. He established a Christian monastery at Monte Cassino and is considered the founder of Western monasticism.

Ben·e·dict's so·lu·tion /bénni dìkts-/, **Ben·e·dict's re·a·gent** *n* a chemical solution that turns red in the presence of sugars like glucose that are reducing agents. Use: urine tests for diabetes. [Early 20C. After Stanley Rossiter *Benedict* (1884–1936), US chemist]

Ben·e·dic·tus /bènni díktəss/ *n* 1. a Latin hymn from the Bible beginning "Benedictus qui venit in nomine Domini" ("Blessed is he who comes in the name of the Lord" Luke 1: 68–79) 2. a Latin hymn from the Bible beginning "Benedictus Dominus Deus Israel" ("Blessed be the Lord God of Israel" Matthew 21:9) [Mid-16C. < Latin, past participle of *benedicere* (see BENEDICTION)]

ben·e·fac·tion /bénnə fàkshən, bènnə fákshən/ *n* 1. **DONATION** a donation given to a charity 2. **GOOD DEED** a good deed, especially an act of charity 3. **DOING SOMETHING GOOD** the act of doing good [Mid-17C. < late Latin *benefaction-* < Latin *bene* "well" + *fact-*, past participle of *facere* "do"]

ben·e·fac·tor /bénnə fàktər/ *n* somebody who aids a cause, institution, or person, especially with a gift of money

ben·e·fac·tress /bénnə fàktriss/ *n* a woman who aids a cause, institution, or person, especially with a gift of money

ben·e·fice /bénnəfiss/ *n* 1. CHR **ENDOWED CHURCH LIVING** a church office that provides a living for its holder through an endowment attached to it 2. CHR **REVENUE FOR CHURCH LIVING** the revenue or property that provides the living of the holder of a church benefice 3. HIST **FORM OF FEUDAL TENURE** a form of feudal tenure in which a vassal held land from a superior, especially in return for military service ■ *vt* (**-ficed, -fic·ing, -fic·es**) CHR **PROVIDE SOMEBODY WITH BENEFICE** to provide a member of the clergy with a church office that will yield a living [14C. Via French < Latin *beneficium* "doing well" < *bene* "well" + *fic-*, variant of stem of *facere* "do"]

be·nef·i·cent /bə néffiss'nt/ *adj* 1. doing good or charitable acts 2. producing benefits or advantages [Early 17C. < Latin *beneficent-*, stem of *beneficentior* "more beneficent" < *beneficus* < *bene* "well" + *fic-*, variant of stem of *facere* "do"] **—be·nef·i·cence** *n* **—be·nef·i·cent·ly** *adv*

ben·e·fi·cial /bènnə físh'l/ *adj* 1. producing a good or advantageous effect ○ *The exercise should prove beneficial to his health.* 2. entitling somebody to or entitled to profits or property [15C. Directly or via French < late Latin *beneficialis* < Latin *beneficium* (see BENEFICE)] **—ben·e·fi·cial·ly** *adv*

ben·e·fi·ci·ar·y /bènnə físhee èrree, -físhəree/ *n* (*plural* **-ies**) 1. **SOMEBODY BENEFITING** somebody who receives a benefit from something 2. **LEGAL RECIPIENT OF MONEY** somebody entitled to money or property by a will, trust, or insurance policy 3. **HOLDER OF BENEFICE** a member of the clergy who holds an office that provides a living (**benefice**) ■ *adj* **RELATING TO BENEFICE** relating to a church office that provides a living (**benefice**) or to the member of the clergy who holds it [Early 17C. < Latin *beneficiarius* < *beneficium* (see BENEFICE)]

ben·e·fi·ci·ar·y bank *n* a bank that receives money, especially from another bank

ben·e·fit /bénnəfit/ *n* 1. **ADVANTAGE** something that has a good effect or promotes well-being ○ *They eventually reaped the benefits of all their hard work.* 2. **GOVERNMENT ASSISTANCE** a regular payment made by a government agency such as Social Security to somebody qualified to receive it or in need of financial assistance (*often used in the plural*) 3. BUSINESS **EXTRA EMPLOYEE COMPENSATION** compensation over and above salary given to some employees or partially paid for by the employing company, e.g., health insurance, travel insurance for key people, retirement pay, or stock options 4. **PERFORMANCE FOR CHARITY** a performance by entertainers, athletes, or others to raise money for somebody or something, especially a charity ■ **ben·e·fits** *npl* **MONEY OR COMPENSATION FROM EMPLOYER** extra money or other nonmonetary compensation that an employer gives an employee in addition to salary, e.g., health insurance or vacation days ■ *vti* (**-fit·ed** or **-fit·ted, -fit·ing** or **-fit·ting, -fits**) **GIVE OR RECEIVE BENEFIT** to give somebody or receive help, an advantage, or another benefit ○ *The research would benefit from an injection of new ideas.* [14C. Via Anglo-Norman *benfet*, Old French *bienfait* < Latin *benefactum* "good deed" < *bene* "well" + *facere* "do"] ◇ **give somebody the benefit of the doubt** to assume that somebody is telling the truth about something or is innocent of something because there is not enough evidence that the person is lying or guilty

ben·e·fit of cler·gy *n* 1. the official approval or ministration of a Christian church ○ *married without benefit of clergy* 2. the privilege held by the Christian clergy in the Middle Ages that entitled them to trial by an ecclesiastical court and exemption from trial by secular authorities

Be·ne·lux /bénnə lùks/ *n* Belgium, the Netherlands, and Luxembourg [Mid-20C. Acronym < *Belgium, Netherlands, Luxembourg*]

Be·neš /bé nèsh/, **Eduard** (1884–1948) president of Czechoslovakia (1935–38, 1946–48). He led the Czech government-in-exile during World War II. He resigned after the Communist takeover of his country in 1948.

Be·nét /bi náy/, **Stephen Vincent** (1898–1943) US author and poet. He wrote the long narrative poem *John Brown's Body* (1928), which won a Pulitzer Prize.

> "I have fallen in love with American names, / The sharp names that never get fat, / The snakeskin-titles of mining-claims, / The plumed war-bonnet of Medicine Hat, / Tucson and Deadwood and Lost Mule Flat."
> [Stephen Vincent Benét, *American Names*; 1927]

Be·nét, William Rose (1886–1950) US poet, critic, and editor. The brother of Stephen Vincent Benét, he cofounded *The Saturday Review of Literature* in 1924.

be·nev·o·lent /bə névvələnt/ *adj* 1. showing kindness or goodwill 2. performing good or charitable acts and not seeking to make a profit [15C. Via French < Latin *benevolent-*, present participle of *bene velle* "wish well"] **—be·nev·o·lence** *n* **—be·nev·o·lent·ly** *adv*

Ben·gal /ben gáwl, beng-/ former province of northeastern India. In 1947 it was divided into the Indian state of West Bengal, now Bangla, and East Pakistan, now Bangladesh. **—Ben·ga·lese** /ben gə leéz, bèng gə-/ *n*

Ben·gal, Bay of northeastern section of the Indian Ocean bordered by India, Bangladesh, and Myanmar. Area: 839,000 sq. mi./2,172,000 sq. km.

Ben·ga·li /ben gáwlee, beng-/ *n* 1. somebody who comes from Bangladesh or the state of Bangla in India 2. same as **Bangla**[1] [Late 18C. < Hindi *baṅgālī*] **—Ben·ga·li** *adj*

ben·ga·line /béng gə leén/ *n* a heavyweight ribbed cotton and silk or wool fabric [Late 19C. < French, because of its similarity to cloth made in Bengal]

Ben·gha·zi /ben gaázee, beng-/, **Ben·ga·si, Ban·ghā·zī** city and port in northeastern Libya on the gulf of Sidra. It is near the site of the ancient Greek colony of Euhesperides. Population: 804,000 (1995).

Ben·guel·a /ben gwéllə/ city and capital of Benguela District, on the Atlantic coast of western Angola. Population: 155,000 (1983).

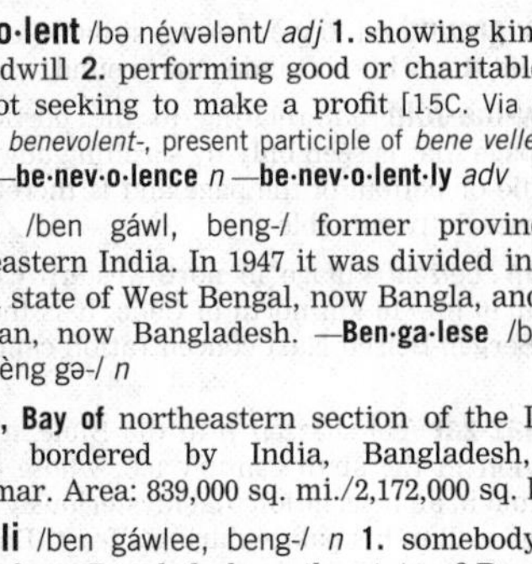
AKG London

David Ben-Gurion

Ben-Gur·i·on /ben go͝oree ən/, **David** (1886–1973) Polish-born prime minister of Israel (1948–53, 1955–63). He was an activist and leader of the movement to establish a Jewish homeland in Palestine, and became Israel's first prime minister. Born **Gruen, David**. See illustration on previous page

~~beneficial~~ incorrect spelling of **beneficial**

~~benifit~~ incorrect spelling of **benefit**

be·night·ed /bi nītəd/ *adj* **1.** unenlightened intellectually, socially, or morally (*formal*) **2.** overtaken by night or the dark (*archaic*) —**be·night·ed·ly** *adv* —**be·night·ed·ness** *n*

be·nign /bi nīn/ *adj* **1. KINDLY** having a kind and gentle disposition or appearance **2. NOT LIFE-THREATENING** not a threat to life or long-term health, especially by being noncancerous ○ *a benign tumor* **3. HARMLESS** neutral or harmless in its effect or influence **4. FAVORABLE** mild or favorable in effect ○ *a benign climate* [14C. Via French < Latin *benignus*] —**be·nign·ly** *adv*

be·nig·nant /bi nígnənt/ *adj* kind and gracious in behavior or appearance —**be·nig·nan·cy** *n*

be·nig·ni·ty /bi nígnətee/ (*plural* **-ties**) *n* **1.** kindness and gentleness of disposition or appearance **2.** a kind or gracious act

Benin

Be·nin /bə nín, be neén/ country in West Africa between Togo and Nigeria, with a short coastline on the Bight of Benin. It became independent from France in 1960. Language: French. Currency: CFA franc. Capital: Porto-Novo. Population: 7,041,490 (2003). Area: 43,484 sq. mi./112,622 sq. km. Official name **Republic of Benin**. Former name **Dahomey** (until 1975) —**Be·nin·ese** /bènnə neéz, -neéss/ *adj, n*

Be·nin, Bight of wide bay in West Africa, the western section of the Gulf of Guinea. It stretches from the mouth of the Volta River to the mouth of the Niger River, with Lagos as one of its principal ports. Length: 450 mi./720 km.

Be·nin Cit·y capital of Edo State in southern Nigeria. It was the capital of the Kingdom of Benin that flourished in the 15th and 16th centuries, producing magnificent brass, bronze, and ivory sculptures. Population: 223,900 (1995 estimate).

ben·i·son /bénnizən, -ssən/ *n* a blessing or benediction (*literary*) [12C. Via Old French *benisson* < Latin *benediction-* (see BENEDICTION)]

ben·ja·min /bénjəmən/ *n* CHEM same as **benzoin** [Mid-16C. Alteration of earlier form of BENZOIN after the name *Benjamin*]

Ben·ja·min /bénjəmən/ *n* in the Bible, the youngest son of Jacob and Rachel and father of the smallest tribe of Israel

Ben·ja·min /bénjəmən/, **Judah** (1811–84) US politician. Secretary of war in Jefferson Davis's Confederate cabinet, he fled to England after the Civil War and made a career as a lawyer. Full name **Benjamin, Judah Philip**

Ben Lo·mond /ben lṓmənd/ mountain in western Scotland, on the eastern side of Loch Lomond. Height: 3,192 ft./973 m.

ben·ne /bénnee/, **ben·e** *n US, Carib* FOOD same as **sesame** (sense 1) [Mid-18C. < Malay *bene*]

Ben·nett /bénnət/, **James Gordon** (1841–1918) US newspaper owner and editor. As editor of the *New York Herald*, he financed H. M. Stanley's African expeditions.

Ben·nett, Richard Bedford, 1st Viscount (1870–1947) Canadian politician and business executive. He was Conservative prime minister of Canada (1930–35). Known as **Iron Heel Bennett**. See table at **prime minister**

Ben Ne·vis /bèn névviss/ highest mountain in the British Isles. It is located in western Scotland, in the Grampian Mountains. Height: 4,406 ft./1,343 m.

Ben·ning·ton /bénningtən/ town and ski resort in southwestern Vermont. It is home to Bennington College. Population: 15,675 (2002 estimate).

ben·ny[1] /bénnee/ (*plural* **-nies**) *n* an amphetamine tablet, especially Benzedrine™ (*slang*) [Mid-20C. Shortening of BENZEDRINE]

ben·ny[2] /bénnee/ *n* BUSINESS, FIN same as **benefit** (sense 3) (*slang*)

Ben·ny /bénnee/, **Jack** (1894–1974) US comedian. He is known for his miserly self-caricature in the *Jack Benny Show* on radio and television (1932–65). Born **Kubelsky, Benjamin**

bensh /bench/ (**benshed, bensh·ing, bensh·es**), **bentsh** (**bentshed, bent·shing, bent·shes**) *vi* to say a Jewish benediction after eating a meal [Via Yiddish *bentshen* < Latin *benedicere* "bless"]

bent[1] /bent/ past participle, past tense of **bend**[1] ■ *adj* **1. CURVED** having a curved, twisted, or angled shape **2. DETERMINED** having a fixed desire to do something ○ *bent on making a name for herself* **3.** *UK* **CORRUPT** dishonest or corrupt in behavior (*slang*) ○ *a bent cop* ■ *n* **1. NATURAL INCLINATION** a strong natural inclination or talent for something **2.** CIV ENG **CROSSWISE SUPPORT** a crosswise framework or member used to strengthen a structure

SYNONYMS See *talent*.

bent[2] /bent/ *n* **1. GRASS OF TEMPERATE REGIONS** a perennial grass. Use: hay, lawns, putting greens. Native to: temperate regions. Genus: *Agrostis*. **2. REEDY GRASS** a stiff reedy grass (*archaic*) **3. GRASS STALK** a flower stalk of a stiff grass (*archaic*) [Old English *beonet* < Germanic]

Ben·tham /bénthəm/, **Jeremy** (1748–1832) British philosopher, jurist, and social reformer. The chief proponent of utilitarianism, he wrote *Introduction to the Principles of Morals and Legislation* (1789).

> "Every law is an evil, for every law is an infraction of liberty."
> [Jeremy Bentham, *An Introduction to the Principles of Morals and Legislation*; 1789]

Ben·tham·ism /bénthə mìzzəm/ *n* the utilitarian philosophy of Jeremy Bentham, which argues that the highest good is the happiness of the greatest number —**Ben·tham·ite** *n, adj*

ben·thic /bénthik/, **ben·thon·ic** /ben thónnik/ *adj* relating to or characteristic of the bottom of a sea, lake, or deep river, or the animals and plants that live there [< BENTHOS]

ben·thos /bén thòss/ *n* the animals and plants that live on or in the sediment at the bottom of a sea, lake, or deep river [Late 19C. < Greek, "depth of the sea"]

ben·to *n* FOOD same as **obento**

Ben·ton /béntən/, **Thomas Hart** (1889–1975) US artist. Known for his naturalistic populist panels and murals, he is credited with founding the regionalist school of painting.

> "The ordinary Missouri mule had more to do with the actual growth of the state than any of its favorite sons."
> [Thomas Hart Benton, defense of a statehouse mural that had been criticized for its focus on the life of ordinary people and things. Quoted in *Smithsonian*; April 1989]

Ben·ton Har·bor city on the southeastern shore of Lake Michigan, in southwestern Michigan. Population: 11,052 (2002 estimate).

ben·ton·ite /béntə nīt/ *n* a light-colored clay that expands in water. Use: oil drilling, paper, pharmaceutical industries. [Late 19C. After Fort Benton, Montana] —**ben·ton·it·ic** /bèntə níttik/ *adj*

bentsh *vi* JUDAISM another spelling of **bensh**

bent·wood /bént wo͝od/ *n* wood that has been bent into a curved shape by being steamed and then put into a mold. Use: furniture.

Be·nue /báyn wày/ the longest tributary of the Niger River in Africa. It rises in northern Cameroon and flows northward and then westward across central Nigeria. Length: 870 mi./1,400 km.

Be·nue-Con·go *n* a large group of Niger-Congo languages spoken across central and southern Africa, of which Bantu languages form the largest subgroup —**Be·nue-Con·go** *adj*

be·numb /bi núm/ (**-numbed, -numb·ing, -numbs**) *vt* **1.** to remove the sense of feeling from a faculty or part of the body, especially by exposure to extreme cold **2.** to make somebody incapable of activity or thought (*usually passive*) —**be·numb·ment** *n*

Benz /benz/, **Karl** (1844–1929) German engineer and automobile manufacturer. He built one of the first gasoline-powered cars. His company merged with Daimler (1926) to form Daimler-Benz and Company. Full name **Benz, Karl Friedrich**

benz- *prefix* same as **benzo-** (*used before vowels*)

benz·al·de·hyde /ben záldə hīd/ *n* a colorless volatile liquid found naturally in and smelling of almonds. Use: manufacture of dyes, flavorings, and perfumes. Formula: C_6H_5CHO.

ben·zal·ko·ni·um chlo·ride /bèn zal kṓnee əm-/ *n* a colorless or pale yellow toxic liquid mixture. Use: biocide in the food industry, preservative in pharmaceutical products. [< *benzylalkylammonium*]

Ben·ze·drine /bénzə dreén/ *tdmk* a trademark for an amphetamine preparation

ben·zene /bén zeén, ben zeén/ *n* a colorless volatile toxic liquid with a distinctive odor. Source: petroleum. Use: manufacture of dyes, polymers, and industrial chemicals. Formula: C_6H_6. Former name **benzol** [Mid-19C. < *benzoic*]

ben·zene ring *n* a molecular structure common to benzene and its derivatives in which six carbon atoms are bonded in a hexagon by alternating single and double bonds

ben·zine /bén zeén, ben zeén/, **ben·zin** /bén zin/ *n* a mixture of liquid hydrocarbons with a carefully selected boiling point range. Source: crude oil. Use: industrial solvent. [Mid-19C. < *benzoic*]

benzo- *prefix* benzene, benzoic acid ○ *benzopyrene* [< BENZOIN]

ben·zo·ate /bénzō àyt/ *n* a salt or ester of benzoic acid. Benzoates contain the group C_6H_5COO- or the ion $C_6H_5COO^-$.

ben·zo·caine /bénzō kàyn/ *n* an anesthetizing drug. Use: in some throat lozenges and skin creams.

ben·zo·di·az·e·pine /bènzō dī ázzə peén, -ázzəpin/ *n* a drug belonging to a group of minor tranquilizers. Use: short-term treatment for sleeping difficulties.

ben·zo·ic ac·id /ben zṓ ik-/ *n* a colorless crystalline solid found in some natural resins. Use: food preservative, manufacture of pharmaceuticals and cosmetics. Formula: C_6H_5COOH.

ben·zo·in /bénzō in, -zòyn/ *n* a toxic white crystalline solid occurring in natural resins or manufactured synthetically. Use: medications, perfumes, incense. Formula: $C_{14}H_{12}O_2$. [Mid-16C. Via French *benjoin* < Arabic *lubānjāwī* "incense from Sumatra"]

ben·zol /bén zàwl, -zōl, -zòl/ *n* CHEM former name for **benzene** [Mid-19C. < *benzoic*]

ben·zo·ni·trile /bènzō nītrəl/ *n* a colorless almond-scented oil with a pungent taste. Use: synthesis of chemicals and resins, solvent.

ben·zo·phe·none /bènzōfi nṓn, bènzō feé nṑn/ *n* a sweet-smelling colorless crystalline solid. Use: manufacture of perfumes, organic compounds. Formula: $(C_6H_5)_2CO$. [Late 19C. < BENZO- + PHENO- + -ONE]

ben·zo·py·rene /bènzō pī́ reén, -pī reén/, **benz·py·rene** /bènz pī́ reén, -pī reén/ *n* a yellow crystalline solid that is highly carcinogenic. Source: tobacco smoke, coal tar. Formula: $C_{20}H_{12}$.

ben·zo·qui·none /bènzōkwi nṓn, bènzō kwí nṑn/ *n* a yellow crystalline solid with an unpleasant odor. Use: photographic developer, dyes, antioxidants. Formula: $C_6H_4O_2$.

ben·zo·yl /bénzō ìl, bén zòyl/ *adj* relating to or containing the group $C_6H_5CO–$ [Mid-19C. < German *Benzoesäure* "benzoic acid" + Greek *hylē* "wood, matter"]

benz·py·rene *n* CHEM same as **benzopyrene**

Ben-Zvi /ben zvée/, **Itzhak** (1884–1963) Russian-born president of Israel (1952–63). A leading Zionist, he moved to Palestine in 1907.

ben·zyl /bénzil, -zeel/ *adj* relating to or containing the group $C_6H_5CH_2–$

ben·zyl al·co·hol *n* a colorless alcohol with a sharp burning taste. Use: synthesis of chemicals, in perfumes and flavorings.

ben·zyl·a·mine /bènzil áy meen, -zeel-/ *n* an amber toxic liquid that is strongly alkaline. Use: synthesis of chemicals and drugs.

Be·o·wulf /báy ə wòolf/ *n* an anonymous Old English epic poem of the eighth century A.D. describing the exploits of the hero Beowulf, in particular his slaying of the monster Grendel and Grendel's mother

be·queath /bi kwée*th*, -kweeth/ (**-queathed, -queath·ing, -queaths**) *vt* **1.** to leave personal or other property to somebody after death by means of a will **2.** to hand down something such as knowledge or a practice to future generations [Old English *becweðan* "speak about" < *cweðan* "speak"] —**be·queath·al** *n* —**be·queath·er** *n* —**be·queath·ment** *n*

be·quest /bi kwést/ *n* **1.** SOMETHING LEFT IN WILL something left to somebody in a will **2.** SOMETHING PASSED DOWN TO POSTERITY something such as knowledge or a practice handed down to future generations **3.** ACT OF BEQUEATHING an act of bequeathing something to somebody [14C. < BEQUEATH]

be·rate /bi ráyt/ (**-rat·ed, -rat·ing, -rates**) *vt* to scold somebody vigorously and at length [Mid-16C. < BE- + *rate* "berate," origin ?]

Ber·ber /búrbər/ (*plural* **-bers** or *same*) *n* **1.** a member of a people living in North Africa **2.** a group of Afro-Asiatic languages spoken across North Africa, especially in Algeria and Morocco, sometimes regarded as a single language with divergent dialects. Native speakers: 12 million. [Mid-18C. < Arabic *barbar*] —**Ber·ber** *adj*

Ber·be·ra /búrbərə/ port on the Gulf of Aden in northwestern Somalia. Population: 65,000 (1987).

ber·be·ris /búrbəriss/ *n* TREES same as **barberry** [Late 16C. Via modern Latin or Old French < medieval Latin *barbaris*]

ber·ceuse /ber sőz/ *n* **1.** a lullaby or cradlesong **2.** an instrumental piece of music, usually in 6/8 time, meant to sound like a lullaby [Late 19C. < French < *bercer* "to rock"]

Berch·tes·ga·den /bérk*h*təss gaád'n/ town in southeastern Bavaria, Germany, a popular ski resort. Adolf Hitler's fortified retreat, the Berghof, was nearby. Population: 7,966 (1997).

Ber·czy /búrkzee/, **William von Moll** (1744–1813) German-born Canadian painter and architect. One of his most famous paintings is *The Woolsey Family* (1809).

ber·dache /bər dásh/ *n* among some Native North American peoples, somebody, usually a man, who takes on the dress, role, and status of the opposite sex [Early 19C. Via French, "catamite" < Arabic *bardaj* "enslaved laborer"]

Be·re·a /bə rée ə/ city in northeastern Ohio, northwest of Akron and southwest of Cleveland. Population: 18,746 (2002 estimate).

be·reave /bi réev/ (**-reaved** or **-reft** /bi réft/, **-reav·ing, -reaves**) *vt* to deprive somebody of a beloved person or a treasured thing, especially through death (*often passive*) [Old English *bereafian* "deprive, rob" < Germanic] —**be·reave·ment** *n* —**be·reav·er** *n*

be·reaved /bi réevd/ *adj* having lost a loved one through death ■ *n* (*plural same*) somebody who has suffered the death of a loved one

be·reft /bi réft/ *adj* **1.** DEPRIVED deprived of somebody or something loved or valued **2.** LACKING lacking in something desirable or necessary ○ *bereft of new ideas* **3.** FEELING SENSE OF LOSS filled with a sense of loss **4.** same as **bereaved**

Ber·e·ni·ce's Hair /bèrrə nĭssiz-/ *n* ASTRON same as **Coma Berenices**

Ber·en·son /bérrənss'n/, **Bernard** (1865–1959) Lithuanian-born US art critic and collector. He wrote extensively about Renaissance painting and was an influential art collector and dealer. Born **Valvrojenski, Bernhard**

> "Between truth and the search for truth, I opt for the second."
> [Bernard Berenson, *Essays in Appreciation*; 1958]

be·ret /bə ráy, bé rày/ *n* a flat round soft hat, usually woolen, with a tight-fitting headband [Early 19C. Via French < late Latin *birrus* "hooded cloak"]

be·ret·ta *n* CHR another spelling of **biretta**

berg[1] /burg/ *n* GEOG same as **iceberg** (sense 1) [Early 19C. Shortening]

berg[2] /burg/ *n S Africa* GEOG same as **mountain** (sense 1) [Early 19C. Via Afrikaans < Dutch *bergh* "mountain"]

Berg /berg/, **Alban** (1885–1935) Austrian composer. He mixed modern and traditional styles in his works, which include the opera *Wozzeck* (1917–22).

Berg /burg/, **Paul** (*b.* 1926) US molecular biologist. He is best known for identifying transfer RNA in 1956, and was awarded the Nobel Prize in chemistry (1980).

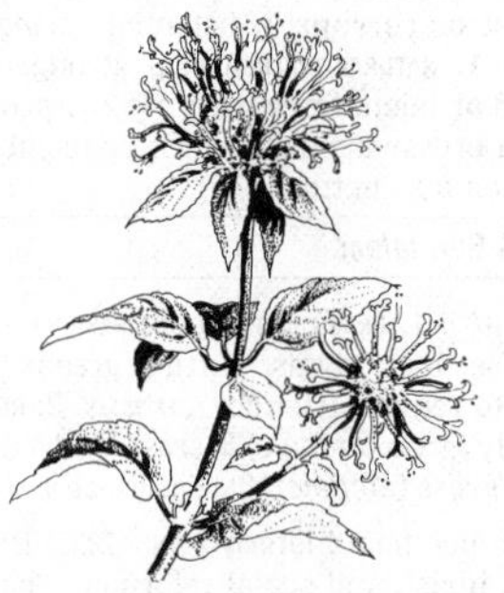

bergamot

ber·ga·mot /búrgə mòt/ (*plural* **-mots** or *same*) *n* **1.** *also* **ber·ga·mot oil** OIL FROM CITRUS FRUIT a fragrant yellow-green essential oil. Source: bergamot fruit rinds. Use: perfumes. **2.** *also* **ber·ga·mot or·ange** SPINY ASIAN CITRUS TREE a spiny citrus tree with sour pear-shaped fruit. Native to: Asia. Latin name: *Citrus bergamia.* **3.** MEDITERRANEAN MINT PLANT a mint plant producing a fragrant oil similar to bergamot oil. Native to: Mediterranean. Latin name: *Mentha citrata.* **4.** *Can, UK* PLANTS N AMERICAN MINT PLANT a wild or garden mint plant. Flowers: scarlet in the wild, white to purple in garden varieties. Native to: North America. Latin name: *Monarda didyma.* US term **bee balm 5.** PLANTS same as **wild bergamot** [Late 17C. After *Bergamo* in N Italy]

Ber·gen /búrgən, bér-/ city and port in southwestern Norway and the administrative capital of Hordaland County. Population: 230,734 (2001).

Ber·gen-Bel·sen ➧ **Belsen**

Ber·gen·field /búrgən féeld/ town in northeastern New Jersey, north of Jersey City and east of Paterson. Population: 26,215 (2002 estimate).

ber·gen·i·a /bùr géenee ə/ (*plural* **-ias** or *same*) *n* a low-growing perennial plant with large leathery leaves. Flowers: early, usually red, purple, or pink on long stalks. Genus: *Bergenia.* [Mid-19C. After Karl August von *Bergen* (1704–60), German botanist and physician]

ber·gère /ber *zh*ér/ (*plural* **-gères** /-*zh*ér/) *n* a chair or sofa with sides and back made of woven cane [Mid-18C. < French, "shepherdess"]

Berg·man /búrgmən/, **Ingmar** (*b.* 1918) Swedish movie director. His many movies include dark brooding classics such as *The Seventh Seal* (1957) and *Persona* (1966). Full name **Bergman, Ernst Ingmar**

> "Eight hours of hard work each day to get three minutes of film. And during those eight hours there are maybe only 10 or 12 minutes if you're lucky, of real creation...Everything and everyone on a movie set must be attuned to finding those minutes of creativity."
> [Ingmar Bergman, *Interview, Playboy*; June 1964]

Berg·man, Ingrid (1915–82) Swedish-born US movie actor. Best known for her role in the movie *Casablanca* (1942), she acted in numerous US and European movies and won three Academy Awards.

> "A kiss is a lovely trick designed by nature to stop speech when words become superfluous."
> [Ingrid Bergman, *Viva*; 1977]

berg·schrund /búrk shròont/ (*plural* **-schrunds** or **-schrund·e** /-shròondə/) *n* a crevasse formed at the head of a glacier [Mid-19C. < German, "mountain cleft"]

Berg·son /bérgss'n/, **Henri** (1859–1941) French philosopher. One of his most influential ideas was that creative energy plays a central role in human development. He won the Nobel Prize in literature (1927). Full name **Bergson, Henri Louis** —**Berg·so·ni·an** /bùrg sṓnee ən/ *n, adj*

> "The present contains nothing more than the past, and what is found in the effect was already in the cause."
> [Henri Bergson, *Creative Evolution*; 1907]

Berg·son·ism /búrgss'n ìzzəm/ *n* the philosophy of Henri Bergson, which posits the existence of a universal life-giving force (**élan vital**)

ber·i·ber·i /bèrree bérree/ *n* a degenerative disease of the nerves caused by a deficiency of the vitamin thiamine and marked by pain, inability to move, and swelling [Early 18C. < Sinhalese, "weakness"]

Ber·ing /béering, bérring/, **Vitus** (1681–1741) Danish-born Russian explorer. He investigated the theory that Asia and North America were once connected. The Bering Sea and Bering Strait are named for him. Full name **Bering, Vitus Jonassen**

Ber·ing land bridge *n* a link between Alaska and Siberia that was above sea level during the Ice Age between 13,000 and 10,000 years ago and provided a route for prehistoric people and animals into the Americas

Ber·ing Sea part of the North Pacific Ocean surrounded by the Aleutian Islands, Siberia, and Alaska. Area: 876,100 sq. mi./2,269,000 sq. km. Depth: 15,659 ft./4,773 m.

Ber·ing Strait narrow stretch of sea connecting the Bering Sea to the Arctic Ocean, and separating Russia from Alaska. At its narrowest point it is 51 mi./82 km wide.

Be·ri·o /bérree ō/, **Luciano** (1925–2003) Italian composer. His experimental compositions combined prerecorded and electronic sounds, and spoken words.

Be·ri·sha /bə réeshə/, **Sali** (*b.* 1944) president of Albania (1992–97). One of the leaders of post-Communist reform in Albania, he was elected as the country's first noncommunist president since World War II.

Berke·le·ian·ism /baárklee ə nìzzəm, búrk-/ *n* the philosophy of George Berkeley, particularly his view that the material world is an idea in God's mind and that an object's existence consists in its being perceived [Early 19C. After George BERKELEY] —**Berke·le·ian** *adj, n*

Berke·ley /búrklee/ city in western California on San Francisco Bay, home to the University of California. Population: 103,640 (2002 estimate).

Berke·ley /búrklee/, **Busby** (1895–1976) US movie director and choreographer. He is famous for his work in Broadway and Hollywood musicals including *42nd Street* (1933). Born **Enos, William Berkeley**

Berke·ley /baárklee, búrk-/, **George** (1685–1753) Irish Anglican bishop and philosopher. He propounded idealist philosophy in *A Treatise Concerning the Principles of Human Knowledge* (1710) and other works.

> "We have first raised a dust and then complain we cannot see."
> [George Berkeley, *A Treatise Concerning the Principles of Human Knowledge*; 1710]

Berke·ley /búrklee, baárk-/, **Sir William** (1606–77)

English-born colonial governor. His policies as governor of Virginia (1641–51, 1660–77) resulted in Bacon's Rebellion (1676).

ber·ke·li·um /bər keélee əm, búrklee-/ *n* a synthetic radioactive element. Source: bombardment of americium-241 with helium ions. Symbol **Bk**. See table at **element** [Mid-20C. After BERKELEY, California]

Berk·shire Hills /bùrk sheer-, -shər-/, **Berk·shires** /búrk sheérz, -shərz/ low forested mountains in western Massachusetts, forming part of the Appalachian Mountains, in a major resort area. The highest peak is Mount Greylock, 3,491 ft./1,064 m.

Berle /burl/, **Milton** (1908–2002) US comedian. After a career in vaudeville, he became a fixture on television in the 1940s and 50s. Born **Berlinger, Milton**. Known as **Mr. Television, Uncle Miltie**

ber·lin /bər lín/, **ber·line** *n* a large and luxurious automobile with a glass partition between the driver and the passengers [Late 17C. After the city of BERLIN; originally a horse-drawn carriage]

Ber·lin /bur lín/ capital and the largest city of Germany. At the end of World War II (1945), the city was divided into East and West Berlin. It was reunified and became the national capital again following the reunification of East and West Germany in 1990. Population: 3,382,200 (2001). —**Ber·lin·er** *n*

Express Newspapers

Irving Berlin

Ber·lin, Irving (1888–1989) Russian-born US songwriter. One of the all-time great writers of American popular songs, including *God Bless America* (1938) and *White Christmas* (1954), he also wrote numerous musicals, including *Annie Get Your Gun* (1946). Born **Baline, Israel**

> "There may be trouble ahead, / But while there's moonlight and music / and love and romance, / Let's face the music / and dance."
> [Irving Berlin, "Let's Face the Music and Dance," *Follow the Fleet*; 1936]

Ber·lin, Sir Isaiah (1909–97) Latvian-born British philosopher and historian. He espoused liberal humanism in works such as *Two Concepts of Liberty* (1959), *Vico and Herder* (1976), and *The Crooked Timber of Humanity* (1990).

> "The goal of philosophy is always the same, to assist men to understand themselves and thus operate in the open, and not wildly, in the dark."
> [Sir Isaiah Berlin, *Concepts and Categories*; 1978]

Ber·lin Wall fortified wall surrounding West Berlin, Germany, built in 1961 to prevent East German citizens traveling to the West. Its demolition in 1989 marked the end of the Cold War.

Ber·lin wool *n* a fine wool yarn. Use: clothes, tapestry.

Ber·lin wool·work *n* needlepoint embroidery stitched with Berlin wools on charts painted by hand, popular especially in the second half of the 19th century

Ber·li·oz /bérlee ōz, -ōss/, **Hector** (1803–69) French composer. He was a seminal figure in 19th-century romanticism. Major works among his symphonies, operas, and masses include the *Symphonie Fantastique* (1831) and the opera *The Trojans* (1856–59). Full name **Berlioz, Louis Hector**

> "Time is a great teacher, but unfortunately it kills all its pupils."
> [Attributed to Hector Berlioz]

Ber·lus·co·ni /bèrloo skónee/, **Silvio** (*b.* 1936) prime minister of Italy (1994, 2001–). His coalition government of 1994 collapsed within a year of election. Despite corruption scandals related to his business empire, he led his center-right party to victory in the 2001 elections.

berm /burm/, **berme** *n* **1.** NARROW PATH a ledge or narrow path along the top or bottom of a slope, at the edge of a road, or along a canal **2.** EARTHEN EMBANKMENT an earthen embankment or wall, usually erected to provide protection from the weather or to act as a landscaping screen **3.** RIDGE ABOVE HIGH-TIDE MARK a natural ridge or flat platform formed at the rear of a beach, above the high-tide mark **4.** MIL LEDGE BETWEEN MOAT AND RAMPART a ledge or narrow path between a moat or ditch and a rampart **5.** MIN EXTRACT ROADWAY IN STRIP MINE a narrow roadway cut in the slope of a strip mine [Early 18C. Via French < Dutch]

Ber·mu·da /bər myóodə/ self-governing British dependency in the western North Atlantic Ocean. It contains more than 150 islands, 20 of which are inhabited. Language: English. Currency: Bermuda dollar. Capital: Hamilton. Population: 64,482 (2001). Area: 20 sq. mi./53 sq. km. —**Ber·mu·dan** *n, adj*

Ber·mu·da bag *n* an oval-shaped handbag with wooden handles and removable covers

Ber·mu·da grass *n* a creeping grass with wiry roots. Use: lawns, pastures, stabilizing sand dunes. Native to: southern Europe. Latin name: *Cynodon dactylon*.

Ber·mu·dan rig *n* SAILING same as **Bermuda rig**

Ber·mu·da on·ion *n* a mild-flavored onion with a round flattened shape

Ber·mu·da rig, Ber·mu·dan rig /bər myóod'n-/, **Ber·mu·dian rig** /bər myóodee ən-/ *n* a fore-and-aft arrangement of a boat's mast and sails consisting of a tall pointed mainsail on a sharply raked mast

Ber·mu·da shorts, Ber·mu·das /bər myóodəz/ *npl* tailored shorts whose legs extend almost to the knee

Ber·mu·da Tri·an·gle *n* an area in the western Atlantic Ocean, between Bermuda, Florida, and Puerto Rico, where many ships and aircraft are believed to have disappeared in mysterious circumstances

Ber·mu·di·an rig *n* SAILING same as **Bermuda rig**

Bern /burn, bern/, **Berne** capital of Switzerland since 1848. Situated on the Aar River in western Switzerland, it is also capital of Bern Canton. Population: 122,500 (2001). —**Ber·nese** *adj*

Ber·na·dette of Lourdes /bùrnə dét-/, **St.** (1844–79) French nun and visionary. She said in 1858 that she had received apparitions of the Virgin Mary near her birthplace, Lourdes, which subsequently became a popular place of Roman Catholic pilgrimage. Born **Soubirous, Marie Bernarde**

Ber·nard /ber naár/, **Claude** (1813–78) French physiologist. He made important discoveries on the role of the pancreas and liver.

> "Man can learn nothing except by going from the known to the unknown."
> [Claude Bernard, *An Introduction to the Study of Experimental Medicine*; 1865]

Ber·nar·dine /búrnə deén/ *n* **1.** CISTERCIAN MONK a Cistercian monk belonging to the branch of the Roman Catholic order reformed by St. Bernard of Clairvaux **2.** NUN a nun belonging to a non-Cistercian Roman Catholic order that follows a rule based on the original Cistercian rule ■ *adj* **1.** OF BERNARDINE relating to or characteristic of a Bernardine **2.** OF ST. BERNARD relating to or characteristic of St. Bernard of Clairvaux or his monastic reforms

Ber·nard of Clair·vaux /bur naárd əv kler vṓ, ber-/, **St.** (1090–1153) French theologian. He became the Cistercian abbot of the influential monastery at Clairvaux (1113) and preached the Second Crusade (1146).

Berne ♦ **Bern**

Ber·ners-Lee /bùrnərz leé/, **Tim** (*b.* 1955) British computer scientist and inventor. He designed and introduced the World Wide Web in 1989 and in 1999 became director of the consortium that manages the World Wide Web. Full name **Berners-Lee, Sir Timothy John**

Ber·nese Alps /bər neéz-/ mountain range in southwestern Switzerland, south of Bern. The highest peaks are the Finsteraarhorn, 14,022 ft./4,274 m, and the Jungfrau, 13,642 ft./4,158 m. The region is a major tourist area.

Barnaby's

Sarah Bernhardt

Bern·hardt /búrn haárt/, **Sarah** (1844–1923) French actor. Known for her passionate performances in tragedy, she founded her own theater company in 1899. Among her most famous roles were Marguerite in *La Dame aux Camélias* by Alexandre Dumas fils and the title role in *Phèdre* by Racine. Born **Bernard, Sarah-Marie-Henriette Rosine**

> "For the theater one needs long arms; it is better to have them too long than too short. An *artiste* with short arms can never, never make a fine gesture."
> [Sarah Bernhardt, *Memories of My Life*; 1907]

Ber·nier /bur nyáy/, **Sylvie** (*b.* 1964) Canadian diver. She was Canada's first diver to win an Olympic gold medal in the 3-meter springboard event.

Ber·ni·ni /bər neénee, ber-/, **Gianlorenzo** (1598–1680) Italian sculptor and architect. The foremost Italian artist of the Baroque period, he produced bronze and marble sculptures and designed many of the most impressive features of St. Peter's Cathedral in Rome. Full name **Bernini, Giovanni Lorenzo**

Ber·noul·li /bər nóolee/, **Daniel** (1700–82) Dutch-born Swiss mathematician and physicist. The son of Johann Bernoulli, he formulated the bernoulli effect governing the conservation of energy in fluid dynamics.

> "It would be better for the true physics if there were no mathematicians on earth."
> [Daniel Bernoulli. Quoted in *The Mathematical Intelligencer*; 1991]

Ber·noul·li, Jakob (1654–1705) Swiss mathematician. The brother of Johann Bernoulli, he wrote *Ars conjectandi* (*The Art of Conjecturing*) (1713) on the theory of probability and made theoretical advances in geometry and calculus.

Ber·noul·li, Johann or **Jean** (1667–1748) Swiss mathematician. He helped write the first textbook on differential calculus. He was the brother of Jakob Bernoulli and the father of Daniel Bernoulli.

Ber·noul·li dis·tri·bu·tion *n* STATS same as **binomial distribution** [After Jakob BERNOULLI]

Ber·noul·li ef·fect *n* the acceleration of the flow of a fluid as its pressure is reduced, as happens when fluid passes through a pipe of changing diameter [After Daniel BERNOULLI]

Ber·noul·li the·o·rem, Ber·noul·li law, Ber·noul·li e·qua·tion *n* **1.** a law in physics whereby the sum of the pressure and the product of one half of the density times the velocity squared is constant along a streamline for steady flow in an incompressible nonviscous fluid at constant height **2.** STATS same as **law of large numbers** [After Jakob BERNOULLI]

Library of Congress

Leonard Bernstein

Bern·stein /búrn stīn, -steen/, **Leonard** (1918–90) US conductor, composer, and pianist. He composed symphonic and choral works and the musicals *Candide* (1956) and *West Side Story* (1957).

> "Einstein said that 'the most beautiful experience we can have is the mysterious.' Then why do so many of us try to explain the beauty of music, thus apparently depriving it of its mystery?"
> [Leonard Bernstein, *The Unanswered Question*; 1976]

Ber·ra /bérrə/, **Yogi** (*b.* 1925) US baseball player and manager. He had an 18-year career as catcher with the New York Yankees, then managed the New York Mets and Yankees. He was celebrated for his humorous malapropisms. Born **Berra, Lawrence Peter**

> "Baseball is ninety percent mental. The other half is physical."
> [Yogi Berra, *Yogi: It Ain't Over...*; 1989]

ber·ried /bérreed/ *adj* **1.** describes a plant bearing berries or small fruits resembling berries **2.** describes a lobster that is carrying eggs

ber·ry /bérree/ *n* (*plural* **-ries**) **1. SMALL JUICY FRUIT** a small juicy or fleshy fruit. Berries are usually round and may be edible or inedible. **2.** BOT **FLESHY SEED-CONTAINING FRUIT** a soft fleshy fruit that contains many seeds. Tomatoes, grapes, and bananas are berries. (*technical*) **3.** BOT **KERNEL** a seed or kernel, e.g., a coffee bean **4.** MARINE BIOL **LOBSTER EGG** an egg of a lobster or other egg-carrying crustacean ■ *vi* (**-ried, -ry·ing, -ries**) **1. SEARCH FOR EDIBLE BERRIES** to gather or hunt for berries to eat **2. BEAR BERRIES** to produce berries (*refers to bushes*) [Old English *beri(g)e* < Germanic]

SPELLCHECK berry or **bury**? Do not confuse the spelling of ***berry*** and ***bury***, which sound similar. A ***berry*** is a small soft fruit, and the word with this spelling is only occasionally used as a verb, meaning "bear or gather berries." The word ***bury*** is always used as a verb, meaning "put in a hole" or "hide by covering": *The dog buried its bone in the yard.*

Ber·ry /bérree/, **Chuck** (*b.* 1926) US singer, songwriter, and guitarist. He was one of the originators of rock and roll, bringing the influence of rhythm and blues to mainstream popular music and recording such classics of the genre as "Roll Over Beethoven" (1956) and "Johnny B. Goode" (1958). Born **Berry, Charles Edward Anderson**

Ber·ry, Halle (*b.* 1968) US actor. She was the first African American woman to win an Academy Award for Best Actress for her role in *Monster's Ball* (2001).

Ber·ry, Martha McChesney (1866–1942) US educator. She founded schools in Appalachia that taught practical skills and became a model for other schools across the South.

Ber·ry·man /bérreemən/, **John** (1914–72) US poet, writer, and critic. He revealed his own emotional struggles in collections such as *77 Dream Songs* (1964), which won a Pulitzer Prize. Full name **Berryman, John McAlpin.** Born **Smith, John**

> "It takes me so long to read the 'paper / said to me one day a novelist hot as a firecracker, / because I have to identify myself with everyone in it, / including the corpses, pal."
> [John Berryman, *77 Dream Songs*; 1964]

ber·seem /bər seém/ *n* a clover grown especially in the southern United States and the Nile Valley. Use: forage, soil improver. Native to: Mediterranean. Latin name: *Trifolium alexandrinum*. [Early 20C. Via Arabic *birsīm* < Coptic *bersīm*]

ber·serk /bər súrk, -zúrk/ *adj* **1.** behaving in an uncontrolled way as a result of anger or irrational feeling ○ *go berserk* **2.** extremely excited or enthusiastic about something (*informal*) ○ *The audience went berserk when she finally appeared.* [Early 19C. < Old Norse *berserk* "wild warrior," probably < the stem of *bjorn* "bear" + *serkr* "shirt"] —**ber·serk·ly** *adv*

ber·serk·er /bər súrkər, -zúr-/ *n* a member of a group of ancient Norse warriors who fought with wild unrestrained aggression

berth /burth/ *n* **1. BED ON SHIP OR TRAIN** a bed, usually built-in, on a ship or a train **2.** NAUT **DOCK FOR SHIP** a place, usually alongside a quay or dock, where a boat ties up or anchors **3.** NAUT **ROOM TO MANEUVER AT SEA** sufficient room between a boat and the shore, another boat, or an object to allow safe maneuvering **4. PARKING PLACE** a place for a motor vehicle to park or be loaded or unloaded **5.** NAUT **JOB ON SHIP** a position as a member of a ship's crew **6. JOB** a job or position of employment (*informal*) ■ *v* (**berthed, berth·ing, berths**) **1.** *vti* NAUT **DOCK SHIP** to dock or moor a vessel, or be docked or moored **2.** *vt* NAUT **ASSIGN MOORING TO VESSEL** to assign a vessel a place to dock or moor **3.** *vt* **ALLOCATE BERTH TO SOMEBODY** to assign somebody a berth on a ship or train [Early 17C. < BEAR² "carry"] ◇ **give somebody** *or* **something a wide berth** to keep well away from somebody or something considered unpleasant or dangerous

ber·tha /búrthə/ *n* a wide long collar around the shoulders of a woman's low-necked dress [Mid-19C. < French *berthe*, after *Bertha* (d. A.D. 783), Carolingian queen]

Ber·thon /ber thóN/, **George Theodore** (1806–92) Austrian-born Canadian portraitist. He is noted for his portraits of the business and judicial elite of Upper Canada.

Ber·til·lon sys·tem /búrt'l òn-, bertee yáwN-/ *n* a former method of identifying people, especially criminals, on the basis of detailed records of their physical measurements and characteristics [Late 19C. After Alphonse *Bertillon* (1853–1914), French criminologist]

Ber·ton /búrt'n/, **Pierre** (*b.* 1920) Canadian journalist, historian, and media personality. His published works of popular history include *Klondike* (1958).

Ber·wyn /búrwin/ city in northeastern Illinois. It is a western suburb of Chicago. Population: 53,309 (2002 estimate).

ber·yl /bérrəl/ *n* a hard, crystalline mineral, composed of beryllium aluminum silicate, that occurs in white, yellow, pink, green, or blue forms. Use: gems. [12C. Via French and Latin *beryllus* < Greek *bērullos*] —**ber·yl·line** /bérrəlin, -līn/ *adj*

be·ryl·li·um /bə ríllee əm/ *n* a gray-white metallic element that is light, hard, brittle, and resists corrosion. Source: beryl. Use: alloys, lightweight construction material, windows in X-ray tubes. Symbol **Be**. See table at **element**

Ber·ze·li·us /bər zeélee əss/, **Jöns Jakob, Baron** (1799–1848) Swedish chemist. He drew up the table of atomic weights and discovered the elements selenium, thorium, and cerium.

bes·an /báy sàn/ *n* FOOD same as **gram flour** [< Hindi]

Be·san·çon /bə zaàN sóN/ city and capital of Doubs Department, in the Franche-Comté Region, eastern France. Population: 117,733 (1999).

Bes·ant /bézz'nt, bə zánt/, **Annie** (1847–1933) British theosophist and politician. She was the first woman elected president of the Indian National Congress (1917). Born **Wood, Annie**

be·seech /bi seéch/ (**-sought** /-sáwt/ or **-seeched, -seech·ing, -seech·es**) *vt* (*literary*) **1.** to ask earnestly or beg somebody to do something ○ *I beseech you to think again.* **2.** to ask urgently for something ○ *beseeching their aid* [12C. < BE- + early form of SEEK] —**be·seech·er** *n* —**be·seech·ing** *adj* —**be·seech·ing·ly** *adv*

~~**beserk**~~ incorrect spelling of **berserk**

be·set /bi sét/ (**-set, -set·ting, -sets**) *vt* (*usually passive*) **1. HARASS SOMEBODY OR SOMETHING** to harass or trouble somebody or something continually ○ *beset by nasty rumors.* **2. SURROUND SOMEBODY OR SOMETHING** to attack somebody or something from all sides (*formal*) **3. SET SOMETHING WITH JEWELS** to surround or set something with jewels or other ornaments (*literary*)

be·set·ting /bi sétting/ *adj* harassing or troubling somebody continually

be·side /bi sīd/ *prep* **1. AT SIDE OF** in a position next to or alongside ○ *Sit beside me.* **2. COMPARED WITH** in comparison with ○ *handsome beside his brother* **3. AS WELL AS** in addition to ○ *in another dictionary beside this one* [Old English *be sīdan* "by the side of"] ◇ **beside yourself** in a very excited or agitated state

USAGE beside or **besides**? ***Beside*** is a preposition referring to physical position: *Come and sit beside me.* It is also used to mean "in addition to," although this can lead to confusion with the meaning "at the side of." ***Besides*** is an adverb meaning "what is more" or "in addition": *It's late, and besides, the weather's too cold.*; *I've money to live on, and plenty more besides.* It is also a preposition meaning "in addition to": *There are other people involved besides us.* Note that ***besides*** is inclusive, whereas *except* is exclusive, so that *Besides Larry, we'll invite John, Jake, and Renée* means that Larry is also invited, whereas *They are all invited except Larry* means that Larry is not invited.

be·sides /bi sīdz/ *adv* **1. MOREOVER** what is more ○ *He's my cousin. Besides, he's good company.* **2. TOO** as well or in addition ○ *I've paid for his education and plenty more besides!* ■ *prep* **AS WELL** in addition to somebody or something specified or understood ○ *Besides fruit, we'll also need cheese and crackers.*

USAGE See ***beside***.

be·siege /bi seéj/ (**-sieged, -sieg·ing, -sieg·es**) *vt* **1. SURROUND PLACE WITH ARMY** to surround a city or stronghold with armed forces in order to bring about its surrender or capture **2. CROWD AROUND SOMEBODY** to crowd around somebody in an oppressive way (*usually passive*) ○ *besieged by reporters outside their hotel* **3. HARASS SOMEBODY OR SOMETHING** to harass a person or organization with insistent demands or complaints (*usually passive*) ○ *The box office was besieged by fans wanting tickets.* [13C. < BE- + obsolete *assiege* < Old French *asegier* < Latin *sedere* "sit"] —**be·sieg·er** *n*

be·smear /bi smeér/ (**-smeared, -smear·ing, -smears**) *vt* **1.** to spread mud, dirt, or a greasy or sticky substance on somebody or something **2.** to bring shame or disgrace on somebody or something

be·smirch /bi smúrch/ (**-smirched, -smirch·ing, -smirch·es**) *vt* **1.** to bring shame or disgrace on somebody's reputation **2.** to make something dirty (*literary*) —**be·smirch·er** *n*

be·som /beézəm/ *n* **1.** a broom, especially one made from a bundle of twigs **2.** in curling, a broom used to sweep the ice in front of a moving stone in order to help it slide [Old English *bes(e)ma* < Germanic] —**be·som** *vt*

be·sot·ted /bi sóttəd/ *adj* **1.** made confused through affection for or attraction to somebody **2.** in a confused mental state, especially through having drunk too much alcohol (*archaic*) [Late 16C. < BE- + obsolete *sot* "stupefy" < Old French, "fool"]

be·sought past participle, past tense of **beseech**

be·span·gle /bi spáng g'l/ (**-gled, -gling, -gles**) *vt* to ornament something with small bright decorations, especially spangles (*literary*)

be·spat·ter /bi spáttər/ (**-tered, -ter·ing, -ters**) *vt* to splash something with mud, paint, or another liquid

be·speak /bi speék/ (**-spoke** /-spṓk/, **-spo·ken** /-spṓkən/, **-speak·ing, -speaks**) *vt* **1. SIGNIFY SOMETHING** to be a sign or indication of something (*formal*) ○ *actions that bespeak complicity* **2. ASK FOR SOMETHING POLITELY** to ask politely for something such as a favor (*formal*) **3. ADDRESS SOMEBODY** to speak to somebody (*literary*)

be·spec·ta·cled /bi spéktək'ld/ *adj* wearing eyeglasses

be·spoke /bi spṓk/ past tense of **bespeak** ■ *adj UK* made to a customer's specifications ○ *a bespoke suit*

be·spo·ken past participle of **bespeak**

be·sprin·kle /bi sprı́ngk'l/ (**-kled, -kling, -kles**) *vt* to sprinkle small quantities of liquid or something light over the surface of something (*literary; often passive*)

Bes·sa·ra·bi·a /bèssə ráybee ə/ historic region in southeastern Europe, between the Prut and Dniester rivers, corresponding roughly to present-day Moldova and part of Ukraine. A much-contested area, it was a province of Romania between 1918 and 1940.

Bes·sel /béss'l/, **Friedrich Wilhelm** (1784–1846) German mathematician and astronomer. He identified and determined the distance of the nearest stars, and predicted the existence of a planet beyond Uranus.

Bes·se·mer /béssəmər/ city south of Birmingham, central Alabama. Population: 29,358 (2001).

Bes·se·mer, Sir Henry (1813–98) British metallurgist. He invented the bessemer process for transforming molten pig iron into steel.

Bes·se·mer proc·ess *n* a largely obsolete method of making steel from impure iron by forcing air through the molten metal in a specialized furnace (**Bessemer converter**) [Late 19C. After Sir Henry BESSEMER]

Bes·sette /be sét/, **Gerard** (*b.* 1920) Canadian novelist and critic. The author of *L'incubation* (1965), he was a leader in Canadian psychoanalytic literary criticism.

best /best/ CORE MEANING: better than anybody or anything else

1. *adj* BETTER THAN ALL OTHERS of the highest quality or standard or the most excellent type ○ *the best days of your life* ○ *wearing her best dress* ○ *the best sprinter of the decade* **2.** *adj* MOST LIKELY TO SUCCEED most likely to have or come near to the desired outcome ○ *the best thing to do in the circumstances* **3.** *adj* MOST INTIMATE liked, trusted, and confided in more than anybody else ○ *my best friend* **4.** *adv* MORE THAN ALL OTHERS in the highest degree or to the greatest extent ○ *likes me best* **5.** *adv* MOST SUCCESSFULLY in a way that is most likely to have or come near to the desired outcome ○ *It works best if you warm it up first.* **6.** *adv* TO HIGHEST STANDARD to a higher standard than anybody or anything else ○ *the best trained horse in the competition* **7.** *n* WHAT IS BEST the best possible things or circumstances ○ *want the best for their family* ○ *will only buy the best* **8.** *n* SOMEBODY OR SOMETHING BETTER THAN OTHERS somebody or something of the highest quality or standard ○ *is the best at hockey* **9.** *n* TOP QUALITY the highest quality or standard that somebody or something is capable of ○ *do your best* ○ *past its best* **10.** *n* TOP ACHIEVEMENT the best time or score that somebody has achieved in a sport or game ○ *trying to beat her personal best in the marathon* **11.** *n* ENDORSEMENT used as an enthusiastic endorsement of something (*slang*) ○ *How is your hotel? – It's the best!* [Old English *betest*, superlative of GOOD and WELL², < Germanic] ◇ **at best** according to the most favorable interpretation ◇ **at somebody's** *or* **its best** performing at the peak of ability or effectiveness ◇ **at the best of times** even when circumstances are at their most favorable ◇ **for the best** likely to have a more favorable outcome ○ *I'm sorry I can't come, but maybe it's for the best.* ◇ **make the best of something** to extract what benefit you can from an unsatisfactory or disadvantageous situation

Best /best/, **Charles H.** (1899–1978) US-born Canadian physiologist. With Frederick Banting, he co-discovered insulin (1922). Full name **Best, Charles Herbert**

best-ball *adj* in golf, using a scoring method in which a golfer competes against a team of two or three other golfers, with the team recording only the best individual score for each hole

best boy *n* the chief assistant to the electrician in charge of lighting (**gaffer**) on a movie or television set

best-ef·forts sale *n* in a securities issue, the sale by an underwriter of as many securities as possible with no obligation to buy those not sold to investors

bes·tial /béschəl, bées-/ *adj* **1.** INHUMAN lacking human feelings of pity or remorse ○ *bestial cruelty* **2.** SEXUALLY DEPRAVED sexual in a depraved or purely physical manner **3.** BRUTISH lacking intellect, reason, or culture **4.** RELATING TO BEAST relating to or characteristic of a beast [14C. Via French < late Latin *bestialis* < Latin *bestia* "beast"] —**bes·tial·ly** *adv*

bes·ti·al·i·ty /bèschee állətee, bèes-/ *n* **1.** sexual activity between a human being and an animal **2.** an act, behavior, or condition more appropriate for an animal than a human being

bes·tial·ize /béschə lı̄z, bées-/ (**-ized, -iz·ing, -iz·es**) *vt* **1.** to make somebody behave or live like an animal **2.** to make somebody inhuman or savage

bes·ti·ar·y /béschee èrree, bées-/ (*plural* **-ies**) *n* a medieval book containing pictures and moralizing stories about real and imaginary animals [Mid-19C. < medieval Latin *bestiarium* < Latin *bestia* "beast"]

be·stir /bi stúr/ (**-stirred, -stir·ring, -stirs**) *vr* **be·stir your·self** to begin to do something after a period of inactivity (*formal*) ○ *After a long afternoon nap, they finally bestirred themselves to start the supper preparations.*

best man *n* a man attending a bridegroom and carrying out important duties during the wedding celebrations

best-of-breed *adj* in marketing, sales, and competitive analysis, used to describe a computer product that is the best available software, hardware, or system in its class

best-off superlative of **well-off**

be·stow /bi stṓ/ (**-stowed, -stow·ing, -stows**) *vt* **1.** to present something, especially something valuable or undeserved, to somebody (*formal*) **2.** to put something somewhere (*archaic*) ○ *"Alonso hence, and bestow your luggage where you found it."* (William Shakespeare, *The Tempest*; 1611) —**be·stow·al** *n* —**be·stow·ment** *n*

SYNONYMS See *give*.

best prac·tice *n* the most effective or efficient method of achieving an objective or completing a task

be·strew /bi stróo/ (**-strewed, -strewed** or **-strewn** /-stróon/, **-strew·ing, -strews**) *vt* (*literary*) **1.** to scatter things over something ○ *a church aisle bestrewn with flowers* **2.** to be scattered over something ○ *the rice that bestrewed the church steps after the wedding*

be·stride /bi strı́d/ (**-strode** /-strṓd/, **-strid·den** /-strı́dd'n/, **-strid·ing, -strides**) *vt* to sit or stand with one foot on or towards each side of something (*formal or literary*) ○ *He bestrode the courtroom entranceway, holding forth on the merits of the case to the assembled press.*

best·sell·er /bèst séllər/ *n* something, especially a book, that is commercially very successful

best·sell·ing /bèst sélling/ *adj* **1.** far more popular and successful than other products on sale at the same time ○ *his bestselling account of life in the wilderness* **2.** writing books that are commercially very successful ○ *a bestselling novelist*

bet /bet/ *n* **1.** ACT OF BETTING an agreement that the person who incorrectly predicts the outcome of a future event will forfeit something, usually money, to another **2.** AMOUNT WAGERED the amount of money that somebody agrees to pay as a bet ○ *She lost her $10 bet.* **3.** WHAT SOMEBODY EXPECTS OR THINKS what somebody expects to happen or thinks is true ○ *My bet is they'll decide to overlook the whole thing.* **4.** SOMEBODY OR SOMETHING LIKELY TO WIN somebody or something likely to be successful ■ *vti* (**bet** or **bet·ted, bet·ting, bets**) **1.** RISK SOMETHING OF VALUE to agree with somebody that something, usually money, will be forfeited by the person who incorrectly predicts the outcome of a future event to the other or fails in some other prearranged challenge ○ *I bet you $10 you can't lift that rock.* **2.** THINK SOMETHING IS TRUE to express certainty that something will happen, has happened, or is true (*informal*) ○ *I bet he's forgotten to bring the keys.* [Late 16C. Origin ?] ◇ **you bet!** used to show emphatic agreement (*informal*) ◇ **your best** *or* **safest bet** the course of action most likely to be productive (*informal*)

be·ta /báytə, béetə/ *n* **1.** 2ND LETTER OF GREEK ALPHABET the second letter of the Greek alphabet, represented in English as "b." See table at **alphabet 2.** FIN MEASURE OF PRICE SENSITIVITY a measure of how volatile the price of a security is, compared to the overall market **3.** PHYS same as **beta particle** ■ *adj* **1.** COMPUT READY FOR TESTING BY CUSTOMERS describes software ready for beta tests ○ *beta version* **2.** PHYS PRODUCED BY RADIOACTIVITY describes electrons formed by the splitting of a neutron into a proton and an electron ○ *beta particles* ○ *beta rays* **3.** CHEM SECOND NEAREST TO DESIGNATED ATOM describes the second nearest atom to a particular atom or group of atoms in an organic molecule **4.** BEING MINOR FORM describes a minor form of a chemical element with more than one form (**allotrope**) **5.** CHEM BEING ONE FORM AMONG OTHERS describes a structural form of a chemical compound having more than one form (**isomer**) [14C. Via Latin and Greek < Canaanite *bet* "house"]

Be·ta *n* the second brightest star in a constellation (*followed by the Latin genitive*) ○ *Beta Centauri*

be·ta am·y·loid *n* a protein that accumulates in clumps in the brain as a result of a gene variation, leading to the memory loss and dementia that are features of Alzheimer's syndrome

be·ta-block·er *n* a drug that regulates the activity of the heart. Use: treatment of high blood pressure.

be·ta-car·o·tene *n* BIOCHEM same as **carotene**

be·ta de·cay *n* the radioactive transformation of an atomic nucleus during which an electron or positron is produced, although the mass number remains unchanged

be·ta e·mis·sion *n* the emission of an electron by a radionuclide —**be·ta e·mit·ter** *n*

be·ta·ine /béetə èen, -in/ *n* a sweet-tasting organic compound. Source: sugar beets. Use: treatment of muscular degeneration. Formula: $C_5H_{11}NO_2$. [Mid-19C. < Latin *beta* "beet"]

be·take /bi táyk/ (**-took** /-tòok/, **-tak·en** /-táykən/, **-tak·ing, -takes**) *vr* **be·take your·self** to go somewhere (*archaic or literary*)

be·ta·me·tha·sone /bàytə méthə sṑn/ *n* a steroid drug. Use: treatment of inflammation, asthma, allergies, and rheumatoid arthritis. [Mid-20C. < BETA + METHYL + HYDROCORTISONE]

Be·tan·court /bétt'n kòor, bé taan kòort/, **Rómulo** (1908–81) president of Venezuela (1959–64). He helped to found the Democratic Action party (1941) and spent periods in exile. As president he instituted reforms that paved the way for democracy.

be·ta-ox·i·da·tion *n* the breakdown of fatty acids during cellular metabolism to produce acetyl coenzyme A

be·ta par·ti·cle *n* a high-speed electron emitted from the nucleus of an atom during radioactive decay and created by the splitting of a neutron into a proton and an electron

be·ta proc·ess *n* PHYS same as **beta decay**

be·ta ray *n* a stream of beta particles

be·ta-re·cep·tor *n* a site on cells in the autonomic nervous system that responds to hormones such as epinephrine and operates to control blood pressure, regulate the heartbeat, and contract muscles

be·ta rhythm *n* a pattern of electrical waves in the brain of somebody who is awake and active, registering on an electroencephalogram at a reading between 18 and 30 hertz

be·ta sheet *n* a flat flexible protein structure consisting of parallel polypeptide chains cross-linked by intermolecular hydrogen bonds

be·ta test *n* a test of a product, especially computer software, by giving it to a few customers to try out, before the final version is put on sale —**be·ta-test** *vt*

be·ta trans·for·ma·tion *n* PHYS same as **beta decay**

be·ta·tron /báytə tròn, béetə-/ *n* a device that accelerates electrons in a circular orbit by means of a rapidly alternating magnetic field. In this way, electrons can reach energies of 340 MeV and may be used to strike a metal target to produce a continuous stream of gamma rays.

be·ta·ware /báytə wèr, béetə-/ *n* a version of computer software that is given to a few customers before the final version is put on sale

be·ta wave *n* a high-frequency electrical wave produced in the human brain and associated with normal wakefulness

bet·cha /béchə/ *contr* a form of "bet you" used mainly in conversation (*nonstandard*) ○ *Betcha he asks me out before the weekend.*

be·tel /beét'l/ (*plural* **-tels** or *same*) *n* an evergreen climbing plant with broad leaves chewed as a mild stimulant and digestive aid. Native to: Asia. Latin name: *Piper betle.* [Mid-16C. Via Portuguese < Malayalam *verrila* < Tamil *vrrilai*]

Be·tel·geuse /beét'l jo͞oz, -jöz/ *n* a bright red variable supergiant star that is the second brightest star in the constellation Orion and the twelfth brightest in the night sky

be·tel nut *n* the dark red seed of the betel palm that is wrapped in betel leaves with lime and chewed as a mild stimulant in some Asian countries

be·tel palm *n* a palm tree that has orange fruit and dark red seeds. Native to: Asia. Latin name: *Areca catechu.*

bete noire /bèt nwaár/ (*plural* **betes noires** /*pronunc. same*/), **bête noire** (*plural* **bêtes noires**) *n* somebody or something that is particularly disliked [Mid-19C. < French, "black beast"]

beth /bet/ *n* the second letter of the Hebrew alphabet, represented in the English alphabet as "b." See table at **alphabet** [Early 19C. < Hebrew *bēt* "house"]

Beth·a·ny /béthənee/ village at the foot of the Mount of Olives near Jerusalem in ancient Palestine. According to the Bible, it was the home of Martha, Mary, and their brother Lazarus who was restored to life by Jesus Christ.

Beth Din /bet deén/ (*plural* **Ba·tei Din** /baá tay-/) *n* a Jewish religious court regulating matters of Jewish law such as dietary laws, divorce, and conversion [Late 18C. < Hebrew *bēt dīn* "house of judgment"]

Be·the /báytə/, **Hans** (*b.* 1906) German-born US physicist. He helped develop the atomic bomb (1943–46). His work on stellar nuclear energy won him the Nobel Prize in physics (1967). Full name **Bethe, Hans Albrecht**

beth·el /béth'l/ *n* (*archaic*) **1.** a place that is regarded as sacred or holy **2.** a chapel for sailors and other seafarers [Early 17C. < Hebrew *bēt- 'ēl* "house of God"]

Beth·el Park /béth'l-/ borough in southwestern Pennsylvania in a former coal-mining region south of Pittsburgh. Population: 33,135 (2002 estimate).

Be·thes·da /bə thézdə/ city northwest of Washington, D.C., in Montgomery County, Maryland. It is home to the National Institutes of Health and to two large army and navy medical centers. Population: 62,936 (1996).

be·think /bi thíngk/ (**-thought** /-tháwt/, **-think·ing**, **-thinks**) *vr* **be·think your·self** to think of or remember something (*archaic*)

Beth·le·hem /béthli hèm, -lee əm/ **1.** town in the West Bank near Jerusalem. Part of Israel since 1967, it has been administered by the Palestinian Authority since 1995. Thought to be the birthplace of King David and Jesus Christ, it is regarded as a holy city by Christians. Population: 21,947 (1997). **2.** city in eastern Pennsylvania on the Lehigh River. It is a major steel-manufacturing center. Population: 71,749 (2002 estimate).

be·thought past participle, past tense of **bethink**

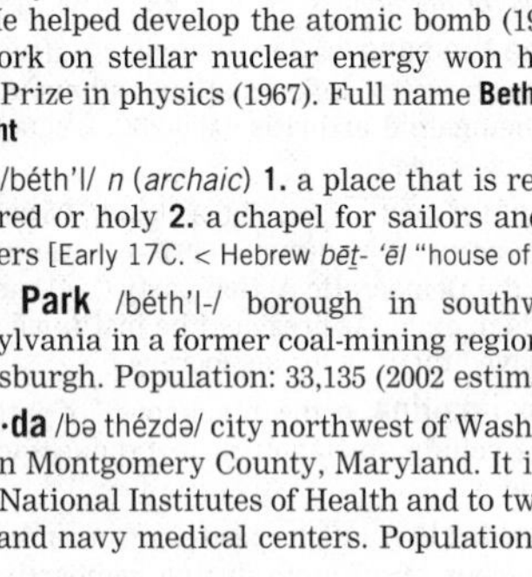

Corbis/Library of Congress

Mary McLeod Bethune

Be·thune /bə tho͞on, -thyo͞on/, **Mary McLeod** (1875–1955) US educator and activist. She founded and was president of what became Bethune-Cookman College, Daytona Beach, Florida. She promoted education for African Americans and founded the National Council of Negro Women (1935).

> "I don't mind being different. I don't want to be Jim-Crowed to a back seat because I'm Black and I don't want to be ushered to a front seat because I'm not white so they can 'palaver' over me."
> [Mary McLeod Bethune. Quoted in *Mary McLeod Bethune*, Emma Gelders Steine; 1957]

be·ti /béttee/ *n Carib* a daughter, or a young girl [Hindi]

be·tide /bi tīd/ (**-tides**) *vti* to happen, or happen to somebody (*literary; usually used in the subjunctive*) ○ *Whether good or ill betide you, trust in yourself.*

be·times /bi tīmz/ *adv* (*archaic*) **1.** early or in good time **2.** in a short time [13C. < form of BY[1]]

Bet·je·man /béchəmən/, **Sir John** (1906–84) British poet. He was poet laureate (1972–84). His books, largely poetic celebrations of rural England, include *A Few Late Chrysanthemums* (1954).

> "Too many people in the modern world view poetry as a luxury, not a necessity like petrol. But to me it's the oil of life."
> [Sir John Betjeman, *Observer (London)*; 1974]

be·to·ken /bi tṓkən/ (**-kened, -ken·ing, -kens**) *vt* to be a sign that something exists or will happen (*literary*)

bet·o·ny /béttənee/ (*plural* **-nies**) *n* **1.** a plant of the mint family. Flowers: purplish. Use: flavorings in herbal teas; herbal medicine. Native to: Europe, Asia. Latin name: *Stachys officinalis.* **2.** a plant resembling true betony **3.** PLANTS same as **lousewort** [14C. < Latin *betonica*]

be·took past tense of **betake**

be·tray /bi tráy/ (**-trayed, -tray·ing, -trays**) *vt* **1.** HELP ENEMY to harm or be disloyal to a country or another person by helping an enemy or giving information that is confidential **2.** SURRENDER SOMEBODY OR SOMETHING TREACHEROUSLY to deliver somebody or something to an enemy ○ *He betrayed his own brother to the secret police.* **3.** GO AGAINST PROMISE to act in a way that is contrary to a promise made ○ *"If an intelligent person is betrayed repeatedly, and humiliated publicly, yet chooses to remain in that situation, one must ask: what are the rewards?"* (Gail Sheehy, *Vanity Fair*; February 1999) **4.** REVEAL SOMETHING to show something, often unintentionally ○ *She said nothing, but her bright eyes betrayed her excitement.* [13C. < BE[1] + Old French *trair* < Latin *tradere* "hand over"] —**be·tray·al** *n* —**be·tray·er** *n*

be·troth /bi trṓth, -tráwth/ (**-trothed, -troth·ing, -troths**) *vt* to promise to marry somebody, or promise that somebody will marry somebody (*archaic*) [14C. < BE- + TRUTH]

be·troth·al /bi trṓth'l, -tráwth'l/ *n* the act of becoming engaged to marry somebody, or the state of being engaged to somebody (*formal*)

be·trothed /bi trṓthd, -tráwtht/ (*plural* **-trotheds** or *same*) *n* the person to whom somebody is engaged to be married (*formal*) —**be·trothed** *adj*

Bet·tel·heim /bétt'l hīm/, **Bruno** (1903–90) Austrian-born US psychologist. A member of the University of Chicago faculty, he was best known for his treatment of autistic children and for his study of the meaning of fairy tales, *The Uses of Enchantment* (1976).

> "No longer can we be satisfied with a life where the heart has its reasons which reason cannot know. Our hearts must know the world of reason, and reason must be guided by an informed heart."
> [Bruno Bettelheim, *Guardian (London)*; March 15, 1990]

Bet·ten·dorf /bétt'n dàwrf/ city in eastern Iowa, on the Mississippi River. Population: 31,547 (2002 estimate).

bet·ter[1] /béttər/ (**-tered, -ter·ing, -ters**) CORE MEANING: indicating that somebody, something, or an action is superior in some way to something or somebody else or is an improvement upon a situation ○ (adj) *Concentrated laundry detergent is better because it requires a smaller box or bottle.* ○ (adj) *She is gradually getting better, albeit slowly.* ○ (adj) *That's hardly going to make things any better.* ○ (adv) *Treatment programs may get the job done better.*

1. *adj* MORE ACCEPTABLE more pleasing or acceptable than something else ○ *That hairstyle is far better than the one you had before.* **2.** *adj* OF GREATER QUALITY of greater quality, usefulness, or suitability than something else ○ *Economic security helps ensure a better future for our children.* ○ *It is better to light a candle than to curse the darkness.* **3.** *adj* IMPROVED IN HEALTH in an improved state of health, after not being well ○ *I'm feeling much better today, thank you.* **4.** *adv* TO HIGHER STANDARD in a more acceptable, appropriate, or effective way ○ *He plays tennis much better than I do.* ○ *I liked her much better after I got to know her.* **5.** *adv* PREFERABLY in a way that is preferable or more advantageous ○ *Such things are better left unsaid.* **6.** *vt* SURPASS SOMETHING to improve on something ○ *She hopes to better the record that she set at last year's championships.* ○ *He summed the whole thing up in a way that I couldn't possibly better.* **7.** *vt* IMPROVE SELF OR THING to improve yourself or something (*formal*) ○ *They tried to better themselves by attaining a good education.* ○ *attempts to better the lot of the refugees* **8.** *n* SUPERIOR PERSON a person who is superior to another in some way (*often used in the plural*) ○ *They think themselves our betters.* [Old English *bettra* < comparative of Germanic, "advantageous"] ◇ **better safe than sorry** it is better to be overcautious than to take unnecessary risks ○ *I think I locked the door, but I'll just go back and check – better safe than sorry!* ◇ **for better or worse** whatever the outcome may be ◇ **get the better of somebody 1.** to defeat or be too strong for somebody **2.** to be too strong for somebody to control ◇ **go one better** to do something that has been done before but in a superior or preferable way ◇ **had better do something** ought to or must do something ○ *You'd better tell them soon.*

bet·ter[2] /béttər/ *n UK* same as **bettor** [Early 17C. < BET]

bet·ter half *n* somebody's wife or husband (*informal humorous*)

bet·ter·ment /béttərmənt/ *n* **1.** a change that improves something, especially somebody's financial or social condition (*formal*) **2.** improvement of a building or land that increases its value

bet·ter-off comparative of **well-off**

bet·ting /bétting/ *n* the activity of placing bets

bet·tor /béttər/ *n* somebody who bets

be·tween /bi tweén/ CORE MEANING: a grammatical word indicating an intermediate point between two places, people, or times ○ (prep) *I was standing between two other women.* ○ (prep) *I intend to pay off my mortgage between now and 2010.* ○ (adv) *He worked two shifts, with an hour off between.*

prep **1.** TO AND FROM from one place to another ○ *She travels between Los Angeles and Santa Monica most days.* **2.** TOGETHER together or in combination with ○ *Between us we should have enough money to pay for the trip.* **3.** INDICATES COMPARISON indicates a comparison, discussion, or relationship involving two people or groups ○ *Reconciliation was hampered by personality conflicts between company executives.* **4.** INDICATES CHOICES indicates two or more possible courses of action ○ *The court offers them a choice between a fine or community service.* [Old English *betwēonum* "by two each" < *twēonum* "two each" < Germanic] ◇ **(just) between you and me, (just) between ourselves** used to indicate that you are about to reveal something confidential

USAGE between or **among**? Although some people insist on using ***among*** and not ***between*** when more than two items are involved, it is established usage to use ***between*** in this meaning as well, especially when ***among*** might sound too formal: *They shared out the money equally between their five children.* ***Among*** is never used when only two items are involved.

be·tween·brain /bi tweén bràyn/ *n* ANAT same as **diencephalon**

be·tween·times /bi tweén tīmz/ *adv* in the intervals between doing other things

be·twixt /bi twíkst/ *adv, prep* same as **between** (*literary*) [Old English *betwēohs* < *tweohs* "for two" < Germanic] ◇ **betwixt and between** between two groups or categories, without belonging to one or the other

~~**beutiful**~~ incorrect spelling of **beautiful**

Beuys /boyz, boyss/, **Joseph** (1921–86) German artist. His avant-garde artworks included assemblages and happenings. He helped to found Germany's Green Party.

BeV PHYS same as **GeV** [< *billion electronvolts*]

bev·el /bévv'l/ *n* **1.** SLANTING EDGE a surface that joins another surface at an angle that is not a right angle **2.** ANGLE the angle at which one surface joins another, when this is not a right angle **3.** TOOL a tool with two legs that can be adjusted to make various angles. Use: measuring or marking angles on something. ■ *vt* (**-eled, -el·ing, -els**) MAKE SLANTING EDGE to shape the edge of something so that it forms an angle other than a right angle with the main surface ○ *a mirror with edges that had been beveled* [Late 17C. < assumed Old French]

bev·el gear *n* either of a pair of gear wheels, one conical and the other flat or conical, connecting and transmitting power between shafts that are not parallel

bev·el square *n* WOODWORK same as **bevel** *n* (sense 3)

bev·er·age /bévvərij, bévrij/ *n* a drink other than water (*used mainly in commercial contexts*) [14C. < Old French *bevrage* < *bevre*, variant of *boire* < Latin *bibere* "to drink"]

Bev·er·ly /bévvərlee/ city on Massachusetts Bay in northeastern Massachusetts. It was home to the first successful cotton mill in the United States. Population: 40,235 (2002 estimate).

Bev·er·ly Hills wealthy residential and commercial city in southwestern California, a western suburb of Los Angeles. Population: 34,857 (2002 estimate).

bev·y /bévvee/ (*plural* **-ies**) *n* **1.** a group of people **2.** a group of animals or birds, especially quail, larks, or roe deer [15C. Origin ?]

be·wail /bi wáyl/ (**-wailed, -wail·ing, -wails**) *vt* to express great sadness about something (*formal*)

be·ware /bi wér/ *vti* to be on guard against somebody or something (*used only as a command and in the infinitive*) [13C. < *be ware* "be careful" < Old English *wær* "watchful" < Germanic]

be·whis·kered /bi wískərd/ *adj* having whiskers ○ *bewhiskered gentlemen in old photographs*

be·wigged /bi wígd/ *adj* wearing a wig

be·wil·der /bi wíldər/ (**-dered, -der·ing, -ders**) *vt* to confuse or puzzle somebody completely [Late 17C. < BE[1] + archaic *wilder*, origin ?] —**be·wil·dered** *adj* —**be·wil·der·ment** *n*

be·wil·der·ing /bi wíldəring/ *adj* extremely confusing —**be·wil·der·ing·ly** *adv*

be·witch /bi wích/ (**-witched, -witch·ing, -witch·es**) *vt* **1.** to fascinate or be very desirable to somebody (*often passive*) ○ *was bewitched by his charm* **2.** to affect somebody or something using a supposed magic spell [13C. < BE- + *witch* "enchant" < WITCH] —**be·witch·er** *n* —**be·witch·ment** *n*

be·witch·ing /bi wíching/ *adj* fascinating, charming, or very desirable —**be·witch·ing·ly** *adv*

bey /bay/ (*plural* **beys**) *n* **1.** a title used for various high-ranking officials in the Ottoman Empire, especially governors of a province **2.** a respectful form of address for men used in Turkey and Egypt [Late 16C. Via Turkish < Old Turkish *beg* "prince"]

be·yond /bee ónd, bi yónd/ CORE MEANING: a grammatical word indicating that something is on the other side of something else, either physically or in the abstract ○ (prep) *They are expanding environmental protection programs beyond the border area.* ○ (prep) *The gift of laughter is beyond price.*

1. *prep, adv* AFTER STATED TIME indicates that something continues after a particular time ○ *will remain the world's leading economy in the next decade and beyond* **2.** *prep* PAST past a stage or situation ○ *Don't attempt to live beyond your income.* **3.** *prep* FARTHER THAN further than a particular state of mind or emotion ○ *The site has proved to be popular beyond anyone's wildest dreams.* **4.** *prep* EXCEPT indicates an exception ○ *He was incapable of any emotion beyond a certain rueful irony.* **5.** *prep* IMPOSSIBLE FOR indicates that something is impossible for somebody to do ○ *It is beyond me to describe the complexities of this problem.* **6.** *n* THE HEREAFTER the form of existence that some people believe the spirit reaches after death ○ *He feels that his late parents watch over him from the beyond.* **7.** *n* WHAT IS OUT THERE an area that lies outside what is known ○ *Humanity stands at the edge of the solar system, contemplating the beyond.* [Old English *begeondan* < *be* form of BY[1] + *geondan* (see YOND)]

bez·el /bézz'l/ *n* **1.** the face of a cutting tool, especially a chisel, that slopes toward the cutting edge **2.** the groove that holds the glass of a watch, light, or instrument dial in position [Late 16C. < Old French]

Bé·ziers /bay zyáy/ city in Hérault Department in the Languedoc-Roussillon Region of southern France. It is situated in an important wine-producing region. Population: 69,153 (1999).

be·zique /bə zeék/ *n* **1.** a card game like pinochle, played with the highest 64 cards from two decks **2.** the combination of the queen of spades and the jack of diamonds, which gains a high score in the game of bezique [Mid-19C. < French *besigue*]

be·zoar /beé zàwr/ *n* a hard mass of material such as fruit or hair found in the intestines of a ruminant animal, formerly believed to be an antidote to poison [15C. Via French *bezourd* < Arabic *badhizahr* < Persian *padzahr* < *pad* "protection (against)" + *zahr* "poison"]

Be·zos /báy zàwss/, **Jeff** (*b.* 1964) US Internet entrepreneur. A graduate in electrical engineering and computer science, he worked in finance and information technology before setting up a retail site on the Internet in 1995.

bf, b.f., B/F, b/f *abbr* **1.** PRINTING boldface **2.** ACCT brought forward

BF *abbr* Belgian franc

bg *abbr* Bulgaria (*used in Internet addresses*) See table at **domain name**

BG, B.G. *abbr* Brigadier General

B-girl[1] *n* a woman employed by a bar to entertain and encourage customers to spend money freely (*slang dated*) [< BAR[1]]

B-girl[2] *n* a young woman who is a devotee of hip-hop and rap music culture (*slang*) [Abbreviation of *break* (see BREAKDANCING)]

bh *abbr* Bahrain (*used in Internet addresses*) See table at **domain name**

Bh *symbol* bohrium

BHA *n* a waxy solid used as a preservative in processed foods. Full form **butylated hydroxyanisol**

Bha·dra·pa·da /baádrə paádə/, **Bha·dra** /baádrə/ *n* in the Hindu calendar, the sixth month of the year, lasting 31 days and falling about the same time as August to September. See table at **calendar**

Bha·ga·vad·gi·ta /baágə vaad geétə/, **Bha·ga·vad-Gi·ta** *n* a Hindu religious text in which the god Krishna teaches the importance of detachment from personal aims, the fulfillment of religious duties, and devotion to God [Late 18C. < Sanskrit *Bhagavadgītā* "song of the blessed one" (Krishna) < *bhagavant-* "blessed" + *gītā* "song"]

Bhag·wan /bug waán/ *n S Asia* **1.** RELIG same as **God 2.** a teacher, especially somebody who is revered [Via Hindi *bhagwān* < Sanskrit *bhagavān* < *bhaj* "adore"]

bhai /bī/ *n S Asia* **1.** same as **brother** *n* (sense 1) **2.** used as a friendly form of address for a man [< Hindi *bhāi*, related to Sanskrit *bhrātr* "brother"]

Bhai /bī/ *n* a title of respect that is used after a Sikh man's name to indicate distinction

bhai·gan /bī́ gan/, **bai·gan** *n Carib* same as **eggplant** (senses 1–2) [< Hindi]

bha·jan /bújən/ *n S Asia* a Sikh or Hindu hymn [Early 20C. < Sanskrit *bhajana*]

bha·ji /baájee/ (*plural* **-jis**), **bha·jee, ba·jee, bha·ji·a** /baájee ə/ (*plural same* or **-as**) *n* in South Asian cuisine, a spicy deep-fried vegetable fritter, or a dish of these fritters [< Hindi *bhāji* "fried vegetables"]

bhak·ti /baáktee/ *n* in Hinduism, the practice of loving devotion to God as the means of salvation [Mid-19C. < Sanskrit, "devotion"]

bhang /bang/, **bang** *n* a drug made from the Indian hemp or cannabis plant [Late 16C. Via Portuguese < Persian and Urdu *bang*, Hindi *bhan* < Sanskrit *bhanga*]

bhang·ra /báng grə/ *n S Asia* an energetic form of folk dance from the Punjab [Mid-20C. < Punjabi]

bhar·al /baárəl/ *n* a wild sheep with a bluish-gray coat and horns that curve backward. Native to: Himalayan region. Latin name: *Pseudois nayaur*. [Mid-19C. < Hindi]

Bhar·a·ti·ya /baárə tee yə/ *adj S Asia* relating to or originating from India [< Hindi *Bharat* "India"]

bhar·ta /baártə/ *n* in South Asian cuisine, a spicy vegetable dish made with broiled vegetables, especially eggplants, and yogurt

Bhat·pa·ra /baat paárə/, **Bhāt·pā·ra** city in Bangla State, north of Kolkata, India. It was an ancient seat of Sanskrit learning. Population: 304,952 (1991).

Bhav·na·gar /bow núggər, baav-/, **Bhāv·na·gar** city on the Gulf of Khambhat in Gujarat State, western India. Founded in 1723, it is a major industrial and commercial center. Population: 517,578 (2001).

bhel·pu·ri /báyl pòoree/ *n* in South Asian cuisine, a spicy snack made with puffed rice and onions [< Hindi *bhel* "mixture" + *pūrī* "fried unleavened bread" (see PURI)]

Bho·pal /bō paál/, **Bhō·pal** city and capital of Madhya Pradesh State, central India. It was the site of the world's worst industrial accident when a gas leak at a chemical plant killed more than 3,300 people in 1984. Population: 1,454,830 (2001).

B ho·ri·zon *n* an intermediate layer of soil beneath the A horizon, containing some organic matter and clay

bhp, b.h.p. *abbr* MECH ENG brake horsepower

BHT *n* a crystalline solid used as an antioxidant for fats and oils, especially in processed foods. Full form **butylated hydroxytoluene**

Bhu·ba·nesh·war /bòobə néshwər/, **Bhu·ba·nes·war** capital city of Orissa state in eastern India. Population: 412,000 (1991).

Bhu·mi·bol A·dul·ya·dej /pòomi pōn aa dòonlə dàyt/ ➧ **Rama IX**

Bhutan

Bhu·tan /boo tán, -taán/ landlocked country in the eastern part of the Himalaya range between India and the Tibet region of China. Language: Dzongkha. Currency: ngultrum. Capital: Thimphu. Population: 2,139,549 (2003). Area: 18,100 sq. mi./47,000 sq. km. Official name **Kingdom of Bhutan** —**Bhu·tan·ese** /bòotə neéz, -neéss/ *n, adj*

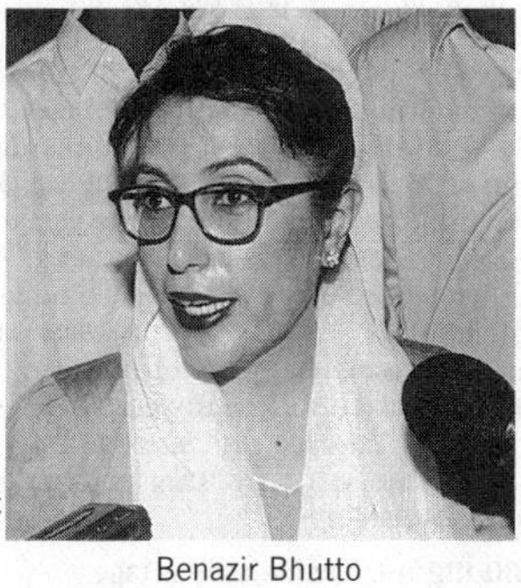

Popperfoto

Benazir Bhutto

Bhut·to /bo͞otō/, **Benazir** (*b.* 1953) prime minister of Pakistan (1988–90, 1993–96). The daughter of Prime Minister Zulfikar Ali Bhutto (1928–79), she led the Pakistan People's Party. See illustration on previous page

"You cannot be fueled by bitterness. It can eat you up but it cannot drive you."
[Attributed to Benazir Bhutto]

bi[1] /bī/ *adj* same as **bisexual** (sense 1) (*slang*) [Mid-20C. Shortening]

bi[2] *abbr* Burundi (*used in Internet addresses*) See table at **domain name**

Bi *symbol* CHEM ELEM bismuth

bi- *prefix* two, twice, both ○ *biaxial* ○ *bimonthly* [< Latin, stem of *bis* "twice," *bini* "two by two" < Indo-European, "two"]

SPELLCHECK bi-, buy, by, or **bye**? Do not confuse the spelling of ***bi-***, ***buy***, ***by***, or ***bye***, which sound similar. ***Bi-*** is a prefix meaning "two" or "both" (as in *biannual*, *bilateral*), whereas the prefix ***by-*** means "secondary" or "past" (as in *byproduct*, *bygone*). Note that the noun ***by-election*** can also be spelled ***bye-election***. ***Buy*** is chiefly used as a verb, meaning "acquire by payment" (as in *buy a house*), and occasionally as a noun: *These boots were a good buy.* ***By*** is an adverb or preposition meaning "beside," "past," "through," etc. (as in *stand by the window, as the years flew by*). ***Bye*** is used as a noun, denoting an automatic advance in a competition, or as a short form of *goodbye*.

BIA *abbr* POL Bureau of Indian Affairs

Bi·a·fra /bee áffrə, -aáfrə/ region of eastern Nigeria that was declared a secessionist state by the majority Ibo people between 1967 and 1970. Official name **Republic of Biafra** —**Bi·a·fran** *n, adj*

bi·a·ly /bee aálee/ (*plural* **-lys**) *n* a flat, round, baked roll with small pieces of baked onion on top [Mid-20C. Shortening of *bialystoker* "of Białystok"]

Bi·a·ly·stok /bee aáwi stàwk/, **Bi·a·ly·stok** /bee aáli-/ capital of Bialystok Province in northeastern Poland. It is an industrial city in a predominantly agricultural region. Population: 282,500 (1997).

Bi·an·ca /bee ángkə, byaángkə/ *n* a small natural satellite of Uranus, discovered in 1986 by the Voyager 2 planetary probe

bi-and-bi *n Can* Canada's French- and English-language cultures (*informal*)

bi·an·nu·al /bī ánnyoo əl/ *adj* happening twice in a year

USAGE biannual or **biennial**? ***Biannual*** means "twice a year" whereas ***biennial*** means "every two years." Because many people are unsure about which is which, it is often advisable to use the more straightforward expressions *twice-yearly* and *two-yearly*: *Interest is paid twice-yearly*, or, *Interest is paid twice a year. They met at a series of two-yearly conferences on the environment*, or, *They met at a series of conferences on the environment held every two years.*

Biar·ritz /beé ə rìts, beè ə ríts/ tourist resort on the Bay of Biscay in the Pyrénées-Atlantiques Department, southwestern France. Population: 30,055 (1999).

bi·as /bī əss/ *n* (*plural* **-as·es** or **-as·ses**) **1.** PREFERENCE an unfair preference for or dislike of something ○ *a bias in favor of internal candidates* **2.** TEXTILES DIAGONAL LINE a line that runs diagonally across the weave of a fabric ○ *a dress cut on the bias* **3.** ELECTRONICS VOLTAGE APPLIED the voltage applied across an electronic device, especially a transistor or valve, to determine the conditions under which it operates **4.** STATS DISTORTION OF RESULTS the distortion of a set of statistical results by a variable not considered in the collection, or the variable itself ■ *vt* (**-ased** or **-assed, -as·ing** or **-as·sing, -as·es** or **-as·ses**) INFLUENCE SOMEBODY to influence somebody or something unfairly ■ *adj* DIAGONAL running diagonally across the weave of a fabric ○ *a bias seam* ■ *adv* DIAGONALLY diagonally across the weave of a fabric ○ *The sleeves are bias-cut.* [Mid-16C. Via French < Old Provençal *biais* "slant" < Greek *epikarsios* "oblique"] —**bi·ased** *adj*

bi·as bind·ing *n UK* same as **bias tape**

bi·as-cut *adj* **1.** part or all of a garment cut on the bias **2.** cut diagonally across the weave of a fabric ○ *a bias-cut skirt*

bi·as-ply *adj* describes tires made with the strands of the fabric crossing each other diagonally

bi·as tape *n* a long narrow strip of material, cut on the bias, and used to form the edge of a hem or to bind the edges of a garment

bi·as volt·age *n* ELEC ENG same as **bias** *n* (sense 3)

bi·ath·lon /bī áthlən, -lòn/ *n* a competition that combines cross-country skiing with rifle shooting at targets along the course [Mid-20C. < BI- + Greek *athlon* "prize from a contest"] —**bi·ath·lete** *n*

bi·ax·i·al /bī áksee əl/ *adj* having two axes —**bi·ax·i·al·ly** *adv*

bib /bib/ *n* **1.** a small piece of material fastened under a child's chin to protect the clothing while eating **2.** the front part of a pinafore, apron, or pair of overalls that covers the chest [Late 16C. Probably < *bib* "drink frequently" < Latin *bibere* "to drink"] ◇ **somebody's best bib and tucker** somebody's finest clothes (*informal*)

Bib. *abbr* CHR **1.** Bible **2.** biblical

bibb /bib/ *n* a part attached to the mast of a sailing ship to support the trestletrees [Late 18C. Variant of BIB]

bibbed /bibd/ *adj* having a bib ○ *a bibbed apron*

bib·ber /bíbbər/ *n* somebody who regularly drinks alcohol (*archaic*) [Mid-16C. < *bib* "drink frequently" (see BIB)]

Bibb let·tuce /bìb-/ *n* a variety of lettuce that forms a small loose head of dark green leaves [Mid-20C. After Major John *Bibb* (1789–1884), US horticulturist]

bib·cock /bíb kòk/ *n* a faucet with a nozzle that is bent downward [Late 18C. Origin ?]

bi·be·lot /beébə lō, bee bló/ *n* a small and attractive ornament or piece of jewelry [Late 19C. < French, doubling of *bel* "beautiful"]

bi·bi /beébee/ *n S Asia* a non-European woman with whom somebody has a sexual or romantic relationship [Early 19C. < Hindi, Urdu]

bibl. *abbr* LITERAT **1.** bibliographical **2.** bibliography

Bi·ble /bīb'l/ *n* **1.** CHRISTIAN HOLY BOOK the sacred book of the Christian religion **2.** JEWISH HOLY BOOK the Hebrew scriptures, the sacred book of the Jewish religion **3.** *also* **bi·ble** HOLY BOOK the holy book of any religion **4.** *also* **bi·ble** COPY OF BIBLE a copy or edition of the Bible **5.** *also* **bi·ble** ESSENTIAL BOOK a book that is considered an authority on a particular subject ○ *a bible for beginning gardeners* ▶ See table on next page [14C. < Latin *biblia (sacra)* "(sacred) books" < Greek, plural of *biblion* (see BIBLIO-)]

Bi·ble Belt *n* the areas of the South and Midwest in the United States that are characterized by strong Protestant beliefs and strict interpretation of the Bible

Bi·ble-thump·er *n* a committed Christian whose outspoken evangelizing is regarded by some as extreme (*slang; offensive*)

bib·li·cal /bíbblik'l/, **Bib·li·cal** *adj* **1.** relating to the Bible, or written about in the Bible **2.** like the Bible, especially in style of language —**bib·li·cal·ly** *adv*

Bib·li·cist /bíbblissist/, **bib·li·cist** *n* **1.** a scholar who studies the Bible **2.** somebody who interprets the Bible strictly or literally —**Bib·li·cism** *n*

biblio- *prefix* book ○ *bibliomania* ○ *bibliography* [< Greek *biblion* "small book" < *biblos* "papyrus, scroll" < *Bublos*, Phoenician city from which papyrus was imported]

bib·li·og·ra·phy /bìbblee óggrəfee/ (*plural* **-phies**) *n* **1.** BOOK SOURCES a list of books and articles consulted, appearing at the end of a book or other text **2.** BOOKS ON SUBJECT a list of books and articles on a subject **3.** LIST OF PUBLICATIONS a list of the books and articles written by a specific author or issued by a specific publisher **4.** BOOK HISTORY the history of books and other publications, and the work of classifying and describing them [Late 17C. Directly or via French < modern Latin *bibliographia* < Greek *biblion* (see BIBLIO-) + Latin *graphia* (see -GRAPHY)] —**bib·li·og·ra·pher** *n* —**bib·li·o·graph·ic** /bìbblee ə gráffik/ *adj* —**bib·li·o·graph·i·cal** *adj* —**bib·li·o·graph·i·cal·ly** *adv*

bib·li·o·man·cy /bíbblee ə mànssee/ *n* an attempt to foretell the future or answer a question by picking a passage at random from a book, especially the Bible

bib·li·o·ma·ni·a /bìbblee ə máynee ə, -máynyə/ *n* an extreme fondness for books, especially the collecting of them —**bib·li·o·ma·ni·ac** *n*

bib·li·o·phile /bíbblee ə fīl/ *n* a collector of books

bib·u·lous /bíbbyələss/ *adj* tending to drink too much alcohol (*formal*) [Late 17C. < Latin *bibulus* < *bibere* "to drink"] —**bib·u·lous·ly** *adv* —**bib·u·lous·ness** *n*

ORIGIN The Latin word *bibere* "to drink," from which ***bibulous*** is derived, is also the source of English *beer*, *beverage*, and *imbibe*.

bi·cam·er·al /bī kámmərəl/ *adj* having two separate and distinct lawmaking assemblies, e.g., the Senate and the House of Representatives in the United States [Mid-19C. < BI- + Latin *camera* "chamber, vault" (see CAMERA)] —**bi·cam·er·al·ism** *n* —**bi·cam·er·al·ist** *n*

bi·carb /bī kaárb/ *n* FOOD same as **bicarbonate of soda** (*informal*) [Early 20C. Shortening]

bi·car·bon·ate /bī kaárbə nàyt, -nit/ *n* CHEM same as **hydrogen carbonate**

bi·car·bon·ate of so·da *n* sodium bicarbonate, especially when used as an antacid or a leavening agent

bice /bīss/ *n* a dull blue color or pigment [14C. < French *bis* "dark gray"] —**bice** *adj*

bice blue *n* a deep sky-blue color —**bice blue** *adj*

bice green *n* a bright leaf-green color —**bice green** *adj*

bi·cen·ten·a·ry /bī sen ténnəree, bī séntənèrree/ *UK n* (*plural* **-ries**) same as **bicentennial** ■ *adj* same as **bicentennial**

bi·cen·ten·ni·al /bī sen ténnee əl/ *n* an anniversary on which something is 200 years old ■ *adj* marking or celebrating a 200th anniversary —**bi·cen·ten·ni·al·ly** *adv*

bi·ceph·a·lous /bī séffələss/ *adj* having two heads, or two parts resembling heads [Early 19C. < BI- + Greek *kephalē* "head"]

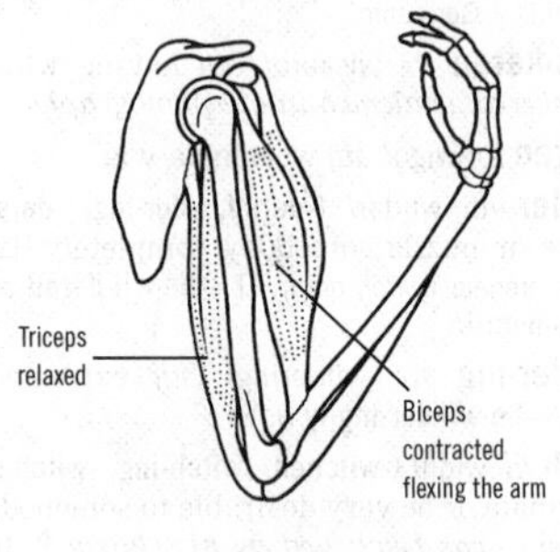

biceps

bi·ceps /bī sèps/ (*plural same* or **-ceps·es**) *n* a muscle that has two points of attachment at one end, especially one (**biceps brachii**) in the upper arm and one (**biceps femoris**) in the back of the thigh [Mid-17C. Via French < Latin, "two-headed" < *caput* "head"] —**bi·cip·i·tal** /bī síppit'l/ *adj*

biche /beesh/ ◇ **break biche** *Carib* to miss attendance at school, deliberately and without legitimate excuse

bick·er /bíkər/ (**-ered, -er·ing, -ers**) *vi* to argue in a bad-tempered way about something unimportant [13C. < Middle Dutch *bicken* "stab, attack" + English *-er* "repeatedly"]

bi·coas·tal /bī kōst'l/ *adj* traveling between two coasts, occurring on each of two coasts, or extending between two coasts, especially the East and West coasts of North America ○ *a bicoastal marriage – he, in Hollywood; she, on Broadway* ■ *n* somebody regularly traveling between the East and West coasts of North America or living at least part of the time on each coast ○ *bicoastals who take the red-eye out of LA every Sunday for New York*

BOOKS OF THE BIBLE

There is no straightforward explanation of the origin of either the Jewish or the Christian canon of scripture. The Jewish scriptures listed represent the Hebrew Bible as it came to be fixed probably at some time in the 2nd century AD. There existed, however, an alternative version in Greek, known as the Septuagint, which contained seven books that are now found in the Roman Catholic and Eastern Orthodox canons. These are usually known collectively as the Apocrypha, though modern biblical scholars prefer the term deuterocanonical books.

The Old Testament canon was formally fixed for western Christians in the 16th century, when Protestant denominations for the most part adopted the shorter Jewish canon. Roman Catholicism formally embraced the Septuagint as the basis for its Bible at the Council of Trent in 1546. The Orthodox churches accepted effectively the same canon as the Roman Catholic one in 1672 at the Synod of Jerusalem, though the Russian Orthodox Church remained ambivalent, and at least down to the mid-20th century tended to omit the deuterocanonical books from its canon.

**indicates deuterocanonical books*

Jewish Scriptures		Old Testament: Roman Catholic and Eastern Orthodox	Old Testament: Protestant
The Law	Genesis	Genesis	Genesis
	Exodus	Exodus	Exodus
	Leviticus	Leviticus	Leviticus
	Numbers	Numbers	Numbers
	Deuteronomy	Deuteronomy	Deuteronomy
The Prophets	Joshua	Joshua	Joshua
	Judges	Judges	Judges
		Ruth	Ruth
	1 Samuel	1 Samuel	1 Samuel
	2 Samuel	2 Samuel	2 Samuel
	1 Kings	1 Kings	1 Kings
	2 Kings	2 Kings	2 Kings
		1 Chronicles	1 Chronicles
		2 Chronicles	2 Chronicles
		Ezra	Ezra
		Nehemiah	Nehemiah
		Tobit*	
		Judith*	
		Esther	Esther
		1 Maccabees*	
		2 Maccabees*	
		Job	Job
		Psalms	Psalms
		Proverbs	Proverbs
		Ecclesiastes	Ecclesiastes
		Wisdom of Solomon*	
		Ecclesiasticus*	
		Song of Songs	Song of Solomon
	Isaiah	Isaiah	Isaiah
	Jeremiah	Jeremiah	Jeremiah

Jewish Scriptures		Old Testament: Roman Catholic and Eastern Orthodox	Old Testament: Protestant
Prophets (continued)		Lamentations	Lamentations
		Baruch*	
	Ezekiel	Ezekiel	Ezekiel
		Daniel	Daniel
	Hosea	Hosea	Hosea
	Joel	Joel	Joel
	Amos	Amos	Amos
	Obadiah	Obadiah	Obadiah
	Jonah	Jonah	Jonah
	Micah	Micah	Micah
	Nahum	Nahum	Nahum
	Habakkuk	Habakkuk	Habakkuk
	Zephaniah	Zephaniah	Zephaniah
	Haggai	Haggai	Haggai
	Zechariah	Zechariah	Zechariah
	Malachi	Malachi	Malachi
The Writings	Psalms		
	Proverbs		
	Job		
	Song of Songs		
	Ruth		
	Lamentations		
	Ecclesiastes		
	Esther		
	Daniel		
	Ezra		
	Nehemiah		
	1 Chronicles		
	2 Chronicles		

New Testament
Matthew
Mark
Luke
John
Acts of the Apostles
Romans
1 Corinthians
2 Corinthians
Galatians
Ephesians
Philippians
Colossians
1 Thessalonians
2 Thessalonians
1 Timothy
2 Timothy
Titus
Philemon
Hebrews
James
1 Peter
2 Peter
1 John
2 John
3 John
Jude
Revelation

bi·col·or /bī kùllər/, **bi·col·ored** /bī kùllərd/ *adj* having two colors

bi·con·cave /bī kon káyv, bī kón kàyv/ *adj* describes a lens with two faces that are concave

bi·con·di·tion·al /bī kən díshən'l/ *n* a proposition in logic involving two statements, one of which is true if, and only if, the other is true

bi·con·vex /bī kon véks, bī kón vèks/ *adj* describes a lens with two faces that are convex

bi·cul·tur·al /bī kúlchərəl/ *adj* relating to or containing two cultures ○ *a bicultural society* —**bi·cul·tur·al·ism** *n*

bi·cus·pid /bī kúspid/ *adj* with two cusps or points ○ *a bicuspid tooth* ■ *n* a tooth with two points, especially one of the eight teeth (**premolars**) that come between the canines and the molars in adult humans [Mid-19C. < BI- + Latin *cuspid-*, stem of *cuspis* "point, spear"]

bi·cus·pid valve *n* ANAT same as **mitral valve**

bicycle

bi·cy·cle /bī sik'l, -sik'l, -sīk'l/ *n* a vehicle with two wheels and a seat that is moved by pushing pedals with the feet, and steered by handlebars at the front wheel ■ *vi* (**-cled, -cling, -cles**) to travel by bicycle —**bi·cy·cler** *n*

bi·cy·cle mo·to·cross *n* full form of **BMX**

bi·cy·clic /bī síklik, -sík-/ *adj* **1.** consisting of or arranged in two circles, rings, or cycles **2.** describes a molecule containing atoms arranged in two rings

bid /bid/ *v* (**bade** /bad, bayd/ or **bid, bid·den** /bídd'n/ or **bid** or **bade, bid·ding, bids**) **1.** (*past and past participle* **bid**) *vti* OFFER MONEY AT AUCTION to offer an amount of money for something at an auction **2.** (*past and past participle* **bid**) *vi* OFFER PRICE FOR WORK to offer to do a piece of work for a specific price ○ *bidding for the contract* **3.** *vt* SAY TO SOMEBODY to say something to somebody as a greeting or farewell ○ *She called in on her way to the airport to bid us goodbye.* **4.** (*past and past participle* **bid**) *vti* CARDS STATE NUMBER OF TRICKS to declare the number of card tricks expected to be taken **5.** (*past and past participle* **bid**) *vi* TRY TO ACHIEVE SOMETHING to make an attempt to achieve a goal ○ *He hasn't decided whether or not he'll bid for the presidency.* **6.** *vt* ORDER SOMEBODY to tell somebody to do something (*archaic*) ○ *We were bidden to sit quietly, and so we did.* **7.** *vt* INVITE SOMEBODY to invite somebody somewhere (*archaic*) ■ *n* **1. OFFER MADE TO PAY** an offer of money for something at an auction **2. OFFER** an offer to do a piece of work for a specific price ○ *bids were invited for the contract* **3. ATTEMPT** an attempt to do something or get something ○ *in a desperate bid to save the situation* **4. CARDS STATEMENT OF TRICKS** a statement of the number of tricks that a player expects to take in a card game [Old English *biddan* "to request," *beodan* "to offer," both < Germanic] — **bid·der** *n*

bid in *vt* to bid at an auction for something already owned, in order to increase its final selling price

bid up *vt* to make bids that are intended to increase the price of something, not to obtain it

b.i.d. *adv* twice a day (*used in prescriptions*) [Latin *bis in die*]

Bi·dault /bee dṓ/, **Georges** (1899–1983) prime minister of France (1949–50). He was a Resistance leader during World War II, and held several ministerial posts after the Allied liberation of France. Full name **Bidault, Georges Augustin**

> "The weak have one weapon: the errors of those who think they are strong."
> [Georges Bidault, *Observer (London)*; July 15, 1962]

bid·da·ble /bíddəb'l/ *adj* likely to do as asked or ordered —**bid·da·bil·i·ty** /biddə bíllətee/ *n*

Bid·de·ford /bíddəfərd/ city in southwestern Maine, on the southern bank of the Saco River, southwest of Portland. Population: 21,685 (2002 estimate).

bid·den past participle of **bid**

bid·ding /bídding/ *n* **1.** the making of bids at an auction or in a card game **2.** somebody's orders or instructions ○ *lots of paperwork to do at the boss's bidding*

Bid·dle /bídd'l/, **Nicholas** (1786–1844) US financier. A lawyer and editor, he was president of the Second Bank of the United States (1823–36).

bid·dy /bíddee/ (*plural* **-dies**) *n* **1.** same as **chicken** *n* (sense 1) **2.** an offensive term for a woman whose behavior is regarded as fussing or interfering (*slang insult*) [Early 17C. Origin ?]

bide /bīd/ (**bode** /bōd/ or **bid·ed, bid·ed, bid·ing, bides**) *vi* to stay, remain, or wait (*archaic*) ○ *Bide here with us a while.* [Old English *biden* < Indo-European]

bi·det /bee dáy/ *n* a low bathroom plumbing fixture resembling a toilet and equipped with a spray or jet of water, used for washing the genital and anal areas [Mid-17C. < French, literally "pony" < *bider* "to trot"]

bid price *n* the price that a dealer on the stock exchange will pay for a security

Bie·der·mei·er /beédər mī ər/ *adj* belonging to or typical of a highly conventional neoclassical style of home decoration and furnishing that was popular among the middle class in 19th-century Germany [Early 20C. < the surname of a fictional poet created by Ludwig Eichrodt (1827–92)]

Bie·le·feld /beélə fèlt/ city in North Rhine-Westphalia State, western Germany, situated at the northern edge of the Teutoberg Forest. Population: 324,067 (1997).

Bien·court /byaaN koór/, **Charles de, Baron de Saint-Just** (1591?–1623) French-born Canadian colonial administrator. He was the original administrator of the French colony of Acadia in present-day Nova Scotia.

Bi·en Ho·a /beè ən hṓ ə/ city in southern Vietnam east of Ho Chi Minh City, on the Dong Nai River. Population: 273,953 (1989).

bi·en·ni·al /bī énnee əl/ *adj* **1.** happening every two years **2.** describes a plant that lives for two years and produces flowers and fruit in the second year [Early 17C. < Latin *biennis* "two-yearly" or *biennium* "two year period"] —**bi·en·ni·al** *n* —**bi·en·ni·al·ly** *adv*

USAGE See ***biannual.***

bier /beer/ *n* **1.** a table on which a casket or a corpse is placed **2.** a wooden frame on which a corpse or a coffin is carried to where it will be buried (*literary*) [Old English *bǣr* < Germanic]

SPELLCHECK See ***beer.***

Bierce /beerss/, **Ambrose** (1842–1914?) US writer. Known for his satirical political articles and short stories, he wrote *The Devil's Dictionary* (1911). He disappeared in Mexico in 1913. Full name **Bierce, Ambrose Gwinett**

> "ACCIDENT, n. An inevitable occurrence due to the action of immutable natural laws."
> [Ambrose Bierce, *The Devil's Dictionary*; 1911]

Bier·stadt /beér stàt, -shtaàt/, **Albert** (1830–1902) German-born US artist. He was associated with the Hudson River School of painters. His romantic landscapes include *Rocky Mountains* (1863).

bi·eth·nic /bī éthnik/ *adj* belonging or relating to two different ethnic groups

bi·fa·cial /bī fáysh'l/ *adj* **1.** describes leaves with upper and lower surfaces that are different from each other **2.** having two sides or surfaces

bi·far·i·ous /bī féree əss/ *adj* describes plant parts that are arranged in two rows, one on each side of an axis [Mid-17C. < Latin *bifarius* "doing twice" < *-farius* "doing"] —**bi·far·i·ous·ly** *adv*

biff /bif/ (**biffed, biff·ing, biffs**) *vt* to hit somebody with the fist (*informal*) [Mid-19C. An imitation of the sound caused] —**biff** *n*

bif·fy /bíffee/ (*plural* **-fies**) *n Can, Midwest* a toilet, especially an outhouse (*informal*) [Probably variant of PRIVY]

bi·fid /bífid/ *adj* divided at one end into two equal parts [Mid-17C. < Latin *bifidus* "twice divided" < *findere* "to divide"] —**bi·fid·i·ty** /bī fíddətee/ *n* —**bi·fid·ly** *adv*

bi·fi·lar /bī fílər/ *adj* describes a part suspended on two parallel wires or threads, especially the moving part of an electrical measuring instrument [Mid-19C. < BI- + Latin *filum* "thread"]

bi·flag·el·late /bī flájjəlit, -làyt/ *adj* describes a cell that has two slender appendages (**flagella**)

bi·fo·cal /bī fṓk'l, bī fṓk'l/ *adj* describes lenses with sections that have different focal lengths, especially in glasses for near and distant vision ■ **bi·fo·cals** *npl* a pair of glasses with bifocal lenses

bi·fur·cate *vti* /bífər kàyt, bī fúr-/ (**-cat·ed, -cat·ing, -cates**) to be split or branched off into two parts, or split something into two parts ■ *adj* /bī fur kàyt, bī fúr kàyt, bī furkət, bī fúrkət/ separating or branching off into two parts [Early 17C. < Latin *bifurcat-*, past participle of *bifurcare* "fork twice" < *furca* "fork" (see FORK)] —**bi·fur·ca·tion** /bìfər káysh'n/ *n*

big /big/ *adj* (**big·ger, big·gest**) **1. OF GREAT SIZE** of great size, number, or amount ○ *a big crowd* **2. OF GREAT POWER** of great power or volume ○ *A big cheer went up.* **3. SIGNIFICANT** significant or important to somebody ○ *your big moment* **4. SIGNIFICANTLY GREAT** significantly or surprisingly great ○ *You're making a big mistake.* **5. IMPORTANT** important and powerful ○ *one of the big fashion houses* **6. MAGNANIMOUS** generous or noble ○ *She's a woman with a big heart.* **7. AMBITIOUS** full of boastful or unrealistic ambition ○ *She's not likely to fall for his big talk.* **8. OLDER** older or grown-up (*usually used by or to children*) ○ *When I'm big, I'll be rich and famous.* **9. ENTHUSIASTIC** enthusiastic about something or somebody (*informal*) ○ *I'm a big baseball fan.* **10. GREAT** used to make a word convey greater dislike or disapproval (*informal*) ○ *It's all a big con, really.* **11. FILLED** filled with or swollen by something (*literary*) ○ *eyes big with tears* **12. PREGNANT** in an obvious state of pregnancy (*archaic*) ○ *She was big with child.* **13. WINE FULL-BODIED** full-bodied and full of flavor ○ *The best accompaniment to this dish would be a big Chianti.* ■ *adv* **1. AMBITIOUSLY** in a way that is ambitious, and often boastful or unrealistic ○ *You have to think big if you want to get anywhere.* **2. SUCCESSFULLY** in a highly successful way (*informal*) ○ *This approach should go over big at the convention.* [14C. Origin ?] — **big·ness** *n* ◇ **big on** enthusiastic about or recognizing the importance of something (*informal*) ◇ **make it big** to be extremely successful (*informal*)

big·a·mous /bíggəməss/ *adj* involved in or constituting an illegal marriage made when an existing marriage is still valid [Late 19C. < Latin *bigamus* (see BIGAMY)] —**big·a·mous·ly** *adv*

big·a·my /bíggəmee/ *n* the crime of marrying somebody while being legally married to somebody else [13C. < Latin *bigamus* "marriage twice" < Greek *gamos* "marriage"]

Big Ap·ple *n* New York City (*informal*) [< APPLE in jazz musicians' sense "job, engagement"]

big band *n* a large jazz or dance band, especially one that was popular in the 1930s and 1940s

big bang *n* the explosion of a single extremely dense mass of matter that started the universe according to a popular theory (**big bang theory**)

big beast *n* (*informal*) **1.** somebody who is regarded as successful or influential in a particular field or activity **2.** a powerful piece of equipment that uses the latest technology

big beat *n* a type of blues with a heavy backbeat, a precursor of rock and roll

Big Ben *n* **1.** the large clock above the Houses of Parliament in London, or the tower in which it stands **2.** the large bell that chimes the hours in the clock tower of the Houses of Parliament in London [After Sir *Benjamin* Hall, Chief Commissioner of Works]

Big Bend Na·tion·al Park /bìg bénd-/ national park in southwestern Texas, known for its scenery and wildlife, and bounded by the Rio Grande. Area: 1,252 sq. mi./3,242 sq. km.

Big Board *n* the New York Stock Exchange (*informal*)

big box store *n* a retail superstore that sells a very wide range of merchandise, from large household appliances to items such as groceries and pharmaceuticals [Perhaps because of the sizes of the cardboard boxes in which some of the merchandise is delivered]

big boys *npl* important or influential people in a particular field or activity (*informal*)

Big Broth·er *n* a person or group who exerts dictatorial control and maintains a constant watch over others, often while presenting a caring image [Used in the English author George Orwell's novel *Nineteen Eighty-Four* (1949)] —**Big Broth·er·ism** *n*

big bucks *npl* a large amount of money (*slang*)

big busi·ness *n* the activity of large commercial organizations, or these organizations considered as a group

big cat *n* any large carnivorous wild mammal related to the domestic cat. Lions, tigers, leopards, lynxes, and mountain lions are types of big cats. Family: Felidae.

big cheese *n* an important person (*informal*)

Big Chill *n* death, a near-death experience, or a state of perilous misery (*slang*) ○ *When the deck crane's cable snapped, that seaman came very close to the Big Chill.* [< the film *The Big Chill* (1983)]

big cit·y *n* the largest city in an area ○ *the lure of the big city*

big-cit·y *adj* typical of life in a large metropolitan area ○ *the fast-paced big-city lifestyle*

big crunch *n* the cosmic implosion that one theory of the universe holds will ultimately result if there is enough mass in the universe for gravity to slow, halt, and eventually reverse the current expansion

big dad·dy *n* (*slang*) **1.** somebody or something that is respected, powerful, or well known ○ *the big daddy of the blues guitar* **2.** the head of an organization, especially one who exerts paternalistic control

big deal (*informal*) *interj* used to counter that something is less impressive or important than somebody thinks it is ○ *So he's head of a department. Big deal.* ■ *n* something that is very important ○ *Let's not make a big deal out of a minor misunderstanding.*

Big Dip·per *n* the seven brightest stars in the constellation Ursa Major

Big Eas·y *n* New Orleans, Louisiana (*informal*) [< *The Big Easy* (1970), novel by James Conaway]

big en·chi·la·da, Big En·chi·la·da *n* (*slang*) **1.** somebody who is in charge **2.** the top prize or award in a competition [First used in the Watergate tapes to describe the US Attorney General]

bi·ge·ner·ic /bī jə nérrik/ *adj* describes a hybrid produced from two different genera

~~biger~~ incorrect spelling of **bigger**

big·eye /bíg ì/ (*plural* **-eyes** or *same*) *n* a small sea fish with rough reddish or silvery scales and very large eyes. Native to: tropical and subtropical waters. Family: Priacanthidae.

big-eye *adj Carib* greedy or covetous

Big·foot /bíg fòot/ *n* **1.** LEGENDARY HUMANOID OF NW AMERICA a large hairy humanoid said to live in the wilderness areas of northwestern North America, and described as standing 7–10 ft./2–3 m tall **2.** *also* **big·foot** ESTABLISHED EXPERT a well-known and highly respected expert in a field **3.** POWERFUL JOURNALIST a powerful journalist employed by a large newspaper, network, or news syndicate (*slang*) ○ *"Along with other media bigfeet, I chatted up [two senior administration officials]..."* (William Safire *New York Times*; December 16, 2003) [Mid-20C. < the size of the footprints it is said to leave]

big game *n* **1.** large wild animals hunted for sport, especially the larger African mammals **2.** the main purpose of a complex or risky set of actions (*informal*)

big·ge·ty *adj* another spelling of **biggity**

big·gie /bíggee/ *n* **1.** something that is big (*informal*) **2.** somebody or something that is very significant, important, powerful, or successful (*slang*) ◇ **no biggie** not particularly important or serious (*informal*)

big·gish /bíggish/ *adj* fairly large, although not extremely large ○ *The house is really nice, and it's got a biggish back yard.*

big·gi·ty /bíggitee/, **big·ge·ty** *adj regional* in a conceitedly impudent or cocky way [Late 19C. Perhaps < BIG after UPPITY]

big gov·ern·ment *n* government perceived as being excessively big-spending and attempting to control too many aspects of people's lives

big gun *n* a powerful or influential person (*informal*)

big guy *n* same as **big shot**

big hair *n* hair that is rather long with a lot of body, often teased or sprayed so that it stands away from the head (*informal*)

big·head /bíg hèd/ *n* **1.** somebody regarded as too proud of his or her abilities, achievements, or appearance (*informal insult*) **2.** too much conceit (*informal*)

big·head·ed /big héddəd/ *adj* too proud of personal abilities, achievements, or appearance (*informal*)

big-heart·ed *adj* showing kindness and willingness to help and support others —**big-heart·ed·ly** *adv* —**big-heart·ed·ness** *n*

big hit·ter *n* a very successful company or product, or a successful or influential person in a particular field (*informal*)

big·horn /bíg hàwrn/ (*plural* **-horns** or *same*) *n* a large wild mountain sheep that has a long coarse brown coat and very large curving horns. Native to: western North America. Genus: *Ovis*.

Big·horn /bíg hàwrn/ river flowing from Wyoming into Montana. It is a major tributary of the Yellowstone. Length: 336 mi./541 km.

Big·horn Moun·tains mountain range in north central Wyoming and southern Montana, forming part of the Rocky Mountains. The highest peak is Cloud Peak, 13,187 ft./4,019 m. Bighorn National Forest lies in the range.

big house *n* a large penitentiary (*slang*)

bight /bīt/ *n* **1.** a wide curving bend in a shoreline, forming a bay **2.** a loop or slack curve in a rope [Old English *byht* < Indo-European, "to bend"]

big league *n* **1.** a major sports league, especially in baseball **2.** the highest level of achievement in a field, or the people who occupy the top positions in it (*informal*)

big-league *adj* among the most successful or influential in a field (*informal*)

big lie, Big Lie *n* a gross misrepresentation of the facts concerning a major issue, especially for political purposes

big ma·mou /-mə mòo/ *n* the most crucial or important thing (*informal*) [After *Mamou*, town in Louisiana called "The Big Mamou" in a popular song]

Big Man *n* in some cultures, a male leader whose leadership is based on influence, not official or formally recognized authority

big man on cam·pus *n* a student whom others respect or who holds an important position in a student organization (*informal*)

big mon·ey *n* large sums of money (*informal*)

big·mouth /bíg mòwth/ (*plural* **-mouths** /-mòwths, -mòwthz/) *n* (*informal*) **1.** somebody regarded as noisy, vulgar, or boastful **2.** somebody who cannot keep a secret

big·mouthed /bíg mòwthd/ *adj* (*informal*) **1.** unable to keep a secret **2.** loud and boastful

big name *n* a well-known and successful person, organization, or product (*informal*) —**big-name** *adj*

big noise *n* an important or influential person (*informal*)

big·no·ni·a /big nṓnee ə/ *n* an evergreen woody climbing bush. Flowers: trumpet-shaped, red, orange, or yellow. Native to: tropical America. Genus: *Bignonia*. [Late 18C. < modern Latin, after Abbé J. P. Bignon (1662–1743), French librarian]

Big One *n* the event or accomplishment that is of supreme import (*slang*)

big·ot /bíggət/ *n* somebody with strong opinions, especially on politics, religion, or ethnicity, who refuses to accept different views [Late 16C. < French] —**big·ot·ed** *adj* —**big·ot·ry** *n*

big phar·ma *n* the pharmaceutical industry seen as influential on political and commercial policies

big sci·ence *n* any area of scientific research that needs major capital investment

big screen *n* the movie industry and films made for the movie industry, as opposed to television or video

big shot *n* a person with or claiming to possess much power or influence (*informal*)

Big Sioux /-sòo/ river that rises in South Dakota and empties into the Missouri River in Iowa. Length: 400 mi./650 km.

Big Spring city and major oil-refining center in western Texas, northeast of Midland and Odessa. Population: 24,798 (2002 estimate).

big stick *n* a threat of force or severe penalties

Big Sur /-súr/ region on the Pacific coast of west central California, south of Monterey. Its rugged coastline and extensive forests have made it a popular tourist destination.

big tent *n* a group or political party whose members represent a diverse range of opinion and background ○ *big-tent politics* —**big-tent** *adj*

big-tick·et *adj* costing a lot of money (*informal*)

big time (*slang*) *n* the highest level of achievement and success in a profession or other activity ○ *Now that you've appeared on Broadway, you've hit the big time.* ■ *adv* on a grand scale, or to a significant degree ○ *He had messed up his life big time.* —**big tim·er** *n*

big toe *n* the largest and innermost digit of the foot

big top *n* **1.** a large round tent, especially the main tent, used for circus performances **2.** the performing of circus entertainments

big tree *n* TREES same as **giant sequoia**

big wheel *n* same as **big cheese** (*informal*)

big·wig /bíg wìg/ *n* an important person with considerable power or influence (*slang*) [Early 18C. Because important people once wore full-length wigs, whereas ordinary people wore short ones]

Bi·hac /bee haák/ city in northwestern Bosnia and Herzegovina, devastated by fighting during the Bosnian-Croatian-Serbian War. Population: 50,000 (1999).

Bi·har /bee haár/, **Bi·hār** state in northeastern India that is crossed by the Ganges River and shares a border with Nepal. Capital: Patna. Population: 82,878,796 (2001). Area: 38,301 sq. mi./99,199 sq. km.

Bi·ha·ri /bi haáree/ (*plural same* or **-ris**) *n* a member of a people who live mostly in the Indian state of Bihar, and also in Bangladesh and Pakistan [Late 19C. < Hindi *bihārī*] —**Bi·ha·ri** *adj*

Bi·ja·pur /bi jaá poor/, **Bi·jā·pur** city in northern Karnataka State, southern India. It is known for its medieval Islamic architecture. Population: 253,307 (2001).

bi·jec·tion /bī jékshən/ *n* a mathematical mapping between two spaces in which every element in each space corresponds to only one element of the other space for mapping in either direction [Mid-20C. < BI- + INJECTION] —**bi·jec·tive** *adj*

bi·jou /beé zhoo/ (*plural* **-jous** /-zhooz/ or **-joux** /-zhoo/) *n* a small delicate jewel or ornamental object [Mid-17C. Via French, "trinket" < Breton *bizoù* "jeweled ring" < *biz* "finger"]

Bi·ka·ner /beékə neér/, **Bī·kā·ner** walled city in Rajasthan State, northwestern India. It was founded in 1488 and was formerly capital of the princely state of Bikaner. Population: 416,289 (1991).

bike /bīk/ (*informal*) *n* VEHICLES **1.** same as **bicycle 2.** same as **motorcycle** ■ *vi* (**biked, bik·ing, bikes**) to ride somewhere on a bicycle or motorcycle [Late 19C. Shortening of BICYCLE]

bik·er /bíkər/ *n* somebody who rides a motorcycle, especially somebody who belongs to a gang of riders

bik·er jack·et *n* a short leather jacket with a front zipper, originally worn by motorcyclists and popular especially during the 1990s

bike·way /bík wày/ *n* a route or traffic lane for bicycles

Bi·ki·la /bi keélə/, **Abebe** (1932–73) Ethiopian athlete. The first Black African Olympic gold medalist, he set a world record running barefoot in the marathon in the Rome Olympics in 1960.

bi·ki·ni /bi keénee/ *n* a woman's or girl's two-piece bathing suit consisting of a bra-style top and panties-style bottoms ■ **bi·ki·nis** *npl* very scanty briefs for women or men [Mid-20C. After BIKINI] —**bi·ki·nied** *adj*

Bi·ki·ni /bə keénee/ atoll consisting of 36 islets in the Marshall Islands, in the western Pacific Ocean. It was used as a nuclear testing site by the United States between 1946 and 1958. Area: 1.93 sq. mi./5 sq. km.

bi·ki·ni line *n* the area where the top of a woman's thighs meets the lower edge of her bikini or underwear

Bi·ko /beékō/, **Steve** (1946–77) South African political activist. A founding member and the first president of the Black Consciousness Movement, he was arrested several times in the early 1970s and died after being beaten in police custody in 1977. Full name **Biko, Stephen Bantu**

> "We have set out on a quest for true humanity, and somewhere on the distant horizon we can see the glittering prize...In time we shall be in a position to bestow upon South Africa the greatest gift possible—a more human face."
> [Steve Biko, "Black Consciousness and the Quest for a True Humanity," *Steve Biko: I Write What I Like*; 1978]

bi·la·bi·al /bī láybee əl/ *adj* describes a consonant pronounced by bringing both lips into contact with each other or by rounding them. In English, the bilabial consonants are "b," "p," "m," and "w." —**bi·la·bi·al** *n* —**bi·la·bi·al·ly** *adv*

bi·lat·er·al /bī láttərəl/ *adj* **1.** involving or carried out by two groups, especially the political representatives of two countries ○ *bilateral talks* **2.** relating to or affecting both of two sides ○ *bilateral kidney failure* —**bi·lat·er·al·ism** *n* —**bi·lat·er·al·ly** *adv*

bi·lat·er·al sym·me·try *n* symmetry in which an imaginary plane divides an object into right and left halves, each side being a mirror image of the other. Most animals exhibit this symmetry.

bi·lay·er /bí lày ər/ *n* a membrane that consists of two layers of molecules

Bil·ba·o /bil baá ō, -bów/ industrial city and Spain's leading port in the Basque Country, northern Spain. It is the site of the Guggenheim Museum, opened in 1997. Population: 353,950 (2002).

bil·ber·ry /bíll bèrree/ (*plural* **-ries**) *n* **1.** an edible blue-black berry **2.** a wild bush that produces bilberries. Native to: northern Europe. Genus: *Vaccinium.* [Late 16C. Origin ?]

bil·by /bílbee/ (*plural* **-bies**) *n* a carnivorous marsupial similar in size to a rat. It has large ears, a pointed nose, a long furry tail and lives in a burrow. Native to: Australasia. Genus: *Macrotis.* [Late 19C. < Yuwaalaraay *bilbi*]

bil·dungs·ro·man /bíl dòongz rō maàn/ *n* a novel about the early years of somebody's life, exploring the development of his or her character and personality [Early 20C. < German, "education-novel"]

bile /bīl/ *n* **1.** PHYSIOL **DIGESTIVE FLUID** a yellowish green fluid produced in the liver, stored in the gallbladder, and passed through ducts to the small intestine, where it plays an essential role in emulsifying fats **2. BITTERNESS** feelings of bitterness and irritability (*literary*) **3.** HIST **BODILY HUMOR** according to medieval medicine, one of the four basic fluids of the body (**humors**), an excess of which was thought to make somebody prone to anger [Mid-16C. Via French < Latin *bilis*]

bi·lec·tion /bō lékshən/ *n* ARCHIT another spelling of **bolection**

bile duct *n* a tube that carries bile from the liver or gallbladder to the small intestine. The hepatic and cystic ducts merge to form the common bile duct.

bi·lev·el *adj* **1. TWO-LEVEL** having or comprising two levels ○ *a bi-level commuter coach* ○ *a bi-level approach to process analysis* **2. HAVING TWO GROUND-FLOOR LEVELS** having two ground-floor levels divided by a vertical partition ■ *n* **BI-LEVEL HOUSE** a bi-level house

bilge /bilj/ *n* **1. LOWER PART OF BOAT** the part of a boat below the water where the sides curve inward to the keel **2. INSIDE OF LOWER PART OF BOAT** the area inside the bottom of a boat, beneath the lowest floorboards **3. DIRTY WATER IN BOAT BOTTOM** dirty water that collects inside the bottom of a boat **4. BARREL'S WIDEST PART** the widest part of a barrel or cask **5. PAP** ridiculous talk or ideas (*informal*) ○ *a load of bilge* ■ *vti* (**bilged, bilg·ing, bilg·es**) **SPRING LEAK** to be, or cause a boat to be, damaged in the lower part of the hull and start leaking [15C. Probably alteration of BULGE]

bilge keel *n* either of two fin-shaped underwater projections on each side of a boat's hull, designed to control rolling

bilge wa·ter *n* NAUT same as **bilge** *n* (sense 3)

bil·har·zi·a /bil haár zee ə/ *n* **1.** ZOOL same as **schistosome 2.** MED same as **schistosomiasis** [Mid-19C. < modern Latin, after Theodor *Bilharz* (1825–62), German physician]

bil·har·zi·a·sis /bìl haar zí əssiss/ *n* MED same as **schistosomiasis**

bil·i·ar·y /bíllee èrree/ *adj* **1.** relating to bile or the transporting of bile **2.** affecting a bile duct or the system of ducts in the liver ○ *biliary cirrhosis* [Mid-18C. < Latin *bilis* "bile"]

bi·lin·e·ar /bī línnee ər/ *adj* relating to or representing a mathematical expression with two variables, e.g., x + y, neither of which is squared, cubed, or raised to another power or exponent

bi·lin·gual /bī líng gwəl, -gyòo əl/ *adj* **1. SPEAKING TWO LANGUAGES** able to speak two languages easily and naturally **2. IN TWO LANGUAGES** written, expressed, or conducted in two languages ○ *a bilingual dictionary* ■ *n* **BILINGUAL SPEAKER** somebody who speaks two languages easily and naturally [Mid-19C. < Latin *bilinguis* < *bi-* "two" + *lingua* "tongue, speech"] —**bi·lin·gual·ly** *adv*

bi·lin·gual·ism /bī líng gwə lìzzəm, -gyòo ə lìzzəm/ *n* **1.** the ability to speak two languages easily and naturally **2.** the regular use of two languages in everyday communication

bil·ious /bíllyəss/ *adj* **1. NAUSEATED** unsettled in the stomach, as if about to vomit **2. NAUSEATINGLY UNPLEASANT** extremely unpleasant to look at ○ *The walls were painted a bilious green.* **3. DISAGREEABLE** bad-tempered and irritable (*literary*) ○ *a bilious stare* [Mid-16C. < Latin *biliosus* < *bilis* "bile"] —**bil·ious·ly** *adv* —**bil·ious·ness** *n*

bil·i·ru·bin /bìlli ròobin/ *n* a reddish yellow bile pigment that is an intermediate product of the breakdown of hemoglobin in the liver. Too much bilirubin in the blood causes jaundice. [Late 19C. < German < Latin *bilis* "bile" + *ruber* "red"]

bil·i·ver·din /bìlli vúrdin/ *n* a greenish bile pigment that is an intermediate product of the breakdown of hemoglobin in the liver and in turn breaks down to produce bilirubin [Mid-19C. < German < Latin *bilis* "bile" + French *vert* "green"]

bilk /bilk/ (**bilked, bilk·ing, bilks**) *vt* **1. CHEAT SOMEBODY** to cheat somebody, especially by swindling him or her out of money (*informal*) **2. AVOID PAYING SOMEBODY OR SOMETHING** to avoid paying a debt or a person to whom money is owed (*informal*) **3. AVOID OR EVADE SOMEBODY** to escape from or elude somebody [Mid-17C. Origin ?] —**bilk·er** *n*

bill^{1} /bil/ *n* **1. STATEMENT OF MONEY OWED** a written statement of how much money is owed for items purchased or services provided ○ *I'll send you the bill.* **2. AMOUNT OWED** the amount of money owed for items or services provided, as shown on a statement ○ *The bill for the meal came to $150!* **3. AMOUNT PAID** the amount that a person, company, or organization has to pay in taxes, salaries, or other charges **4.** POL **LAW PROPOSAL** a written proposal for a new law, discussed and voted upon by the members of a legislative body **5. ADVERTISING NOTICE** a notice, poster, or leaflet advertising something **6. LIST OF ITEMS** a list, especially of entertainment features or acts in a show, or the program of entertainment itself ○ *We've got a brilliant new comedian on the bill tonight.* **7. PIECE OF PAPER MONEY** a piece of paper money **8. $100** one hundred dollars, or a piece of paper money worth one hundred dollars (*slang*) ■ *vt* (**billed, bill·ing, bills**) **1. SEND REQUEST FOR PAYMENT TO SOMEBODY** to send somebody a statement of how much money is owed for items bought or services provided ○ *Bill me for the cost of dry-cleaning.* **2. ADVERTISE SOMETHING** to advertise an event or performance, especially using posters ○ *It's billed as the biggest ice show on the East Coast.* **3. DESCRIBE SOMETHING AS SOMETHING** to describe something that is going to happen or be produced as having a particular quality ○ *billed as the technological advance of the decade* [14C. Via Anglo-Norman *bille* < medieval Latin *bulla* "seal on a document"] —**bill·a·ble** *adj* —**bill·er** *n* ◇ **fill** *or* **fit the bill** to be suitable for a particular purpose

bill^{2} /bil/ *n* **1.** BIRDS, ZOOL same as **beak** (senses 1, 4) **2.** NAUT the point at the very end of one of the arms of an anchor [Old English *bile*, origin ?] ◇ **bill and coo** to kiss and whisper intimately, as young lovers do, in a way thought to be reminiscent of the affectionate behavior of doves

bill·board^{1} /bíl bàwrd/ *n* **1. ADVERTISING BOARD** a very large board erected by the roadside or attached to a building, used for displaying advertisements **2. INTRODUCTORY SELECTION OF HIGHLIGHTS** a selection of the highlights of something such as a television show or a program of sports events, presented as an introduction to it ■ *vt* (**-boarded, -board·ing, -boards**) **PROMOTE SOMETHING** to promote or advertise something (*often passive*) ○ *a political program billboarded as "the people's right to reply"*

bill·board^{2} /bíl bàwrd/ *n* a ledge on the front of a boat or ship to which the anchor is secured

bill·bug /bíl bùg/ *n* a weevil whose larvae feed on the roots of cereal grasses. Genus: *Calendra* or *Sitophilus.* [Mid-19C. < BILL^{2}, because of its pointed snout]

Bille·ric·a /bil ríkə, bèllə-/ town in northeastern Massachusetts, northwest of Boston, on the Concord River. Population: 39,453 (2001).

bil·let^{1} /bíllit/ *n* **1.** MIL **ACCOMMODATIONS FOR SERVICE PEOPLE** a private home or a guest house providing temporary accommodations for people in the armed forces **2.** MIL **ORDER TO PROVIDE ACCOMMODATIONS** an official order to a householder to provide temporary accommodations for a member of the armed forces **3. EMPLOYMENT POSITION** a position of employment together with its tasks (*informal*) ○ *an easy billet* ■ *v* (**-let·ed, -let·ing, -lets**) MIL **1.** *vti* **ASSIGN SOLDIER TO TEMPORARY ACCOMMODATIONS** to arrange for a member of the armed forces to have temporary accommodations in a particular house, or to have such temporary accommodations somewhere **2.** *vt* **PROVIDE TEMPORARY ACCOMMODATIONS FOR SOLDIER** to provide temporary accommodations for a member of the armed forces [15C. < Anglo-Norman *bilette* "written orders" < variant of Old French *bulle* (see BULL^{2})]

bil·let^{2} /bíllit/ *n* **1. CHUNK OF WOOD** a short thick piece of wood, especially firewood **2.** METALL **METAL BAR IN SEMIFINISHED STATE** a metal bar or block with a simple shape that requires further working **3.** ARCHIT **PART OF DECORATIVE MOLDING** one of a series of short, evenly spaced blocks or cylinders forming part of a decorative molding [15C. < Old French *billette* "small log" < *bille* "log"]

bil·let-doux /bì lay dóo/ (*plural* **bil·lets-doux** /-dóo, -dóoz/) *n* a letter expressing affectionate and romantic thoughts [Late 17C. < French, "sweet note"]

bill·fish /bíl fish/ (*plural same* or **-fish·es**) *n* a large fish with jaws resembling spears that lives near the surface and is hunted for sport. Marlin, sailfish, and swordfish are billfish. Native to: tropical and semitropical waters. Family: Xiphiidae. [< BILL^{2}]

bill·fold /bíl fōld/ *n* a pocket-sized folding container for paper money, credit cards, stamps, and photographs, sometimes with a compartment for loose change [< BILL^{1}]

bill·hook /bíl hòok/ *n* a tool with a wooden handle and a large broad curved blade. Use: cutting branches off trees. [< obsolete *bill* "bladed or pointed weapon"]

bil·liard /bíllyərd/ *adj* relating to or used in billiards ○ *a billiard table*

bil·liards /bíllyərdz/ *n* an indoor game in which a felt-tipped stick (**cue**) is used to hit three balls across a cloth-covered table into pockets (*takes a singular verb*) [Late 16C. < French *billard* < *bille* "log"]

bill·ing /bílling/ *n* **1. POSITION IN TERMS OF ADVERTISING** the particular importance or prominence given to a performer or event in advertisements ○ *an exciting young band currently getting top billing* **2. ADVERTISING** the advertising or promoting of a performance, event, or product **3.** BUSINESS **TOTAL BUSINESS TRANSACTED** the total amount of business transacted in a given period, especially in advertising, insurance, or law, or the value of that business (*often used in the plural*) ○ *The law firm's billings are up this month.* ○ *She charged 1,000 billing hours to that case.* [< BILL^{1}]

Bil·lings /bíllingz/ city on the Yellowstone River in southern Montana, northeast of Yellowstone National Park. Population: 92,008 (2002 estimate).

Bil·lings, Josh (1818–85) US humorist. He is known for his deliberately misspelled portrayal of rural life. Pseudonym of **Shaw, Henry Wheeler**

> "Nature never makes blunders; when she makes a fool she means it."
> [Josh Billings, "Affurisms," *Josh Billings: His Sayings*; 1865]

bil·lion /bíllyən/ (*plural* **-lions** or *same*) *n* **1. ONE THOUSAND MILLION** one thousand million, written as 1 followed by nine zeros **2.** *UK* **ONE MILLION MILLION** one million million, written as 1 followed by 12 zeros (*dated*) **3. LARGE NUMBER** an extremely large but unspecified number of people or things (*informal; often pl*) **4. BILLION IN MONEY** a billion dollars [Late 17C. < French, "million million" < *bis* "twice" + *million* (see MILLION)] —**bil·lionth** *n, adj*

bil·lion·aire /bìllyə nér/ *n* **1.** somebody who has money and property worth more than a billion dollars **2.** somebody who is extremely wealthy [Late 19C. After MILLIONAIRE]

bill of en·try *n* a list of goods to be imported or exported presented to officials at a customhouse

bill of ex·change *n* a document setting out an instruction to pay a particular person a fixed sum of money on a particular date or when the person requests payment

bill of fare *n* **1.** a menu of food available in a restaurant or served at a special function **2.** a list of items, especially events in a program of entertainment (*informal*)

bill of goods *n* **1.** a quantity of goods to be delivered **2.** something fake or not worth having (*informal*) ○

We're being sold the same old bill of goods by the present administration.

bill of health *n* a certificate stating that the crew of a ship is healthy and is not affected by infectious diseases ◇ **a clean bill of health 1.** a good report on somebody's state of health **2.** a good report about the state of something such as the efficiency or profitability of an organization

bill of in·dict·ment *n* a document setting out the criminal charges against somebody, presented to a grand jury

bill of lad·ing *n* a list of merchandise being transported, especially by ship, together with the conditions that apply to its transportation

bill of par·tic·u·lars *n* a list of the charges, claims, or counterclaims made in a legal action

bill of rights *n* a list of basic human rights as guaranteed by the laws of a country

Bill of Rights *n* the first ten amendments to the US Constitution, which protect people's basic human rights

bill of sale *n* a document stating that something has been sold or transferred to the ownership of another party

bil·lon /bíllən/ *n* **1.** an alloy consisting of a small amount of silver or gold mixed with a base metal such as copper, used especially for making coins **2.** an alloy of silver with copper in high proportion, used especially for making medals [Early 18C. < French, "ingot, bronze money" < *bille* "log"]

bil·low /bíllō/ *v* (**-lowed, -low·ing, -lows**) **1.** *vti* SWELL WITH AIR to fill with air, or cause something made of fabric to fill with air, and swell outward ○ *the wind billowing their dresses* **2.** *vi* MOVE IN CURLING MASS to move upward or along in a curling or rolling mass ○ *smoke that billowed from the room* ■ *n* MOVING CURLING MASS a curling or rolling mass of something such as waves or clouds of smoke that moves upward or along [Mid-16C. < Old Norse *bylgja* "wave" < Indo-European, "to swell"] —**bil·low·y** *adj*

bill·post·er /bíl pōstər/, **bill·stick·er** /bíl stìkər/ *n* somebody who puts up advertising notices in public places ○ *Billposters will be prosecuted.* [< BILL[1]] —**bill·post·ing** *n*

bil·ly[1] /bíllee/ (*plural* **-lies**) *n* ARMS, POLICE same as **billy club** [Mid-19C. Origin ?]

bil·ly[2] /bíllee/ (*plural* **-lies**) *n UK* a light metal cooking pot with a lid and a semicircular wire handle, used for boiling water or cooking food on a campfire [Mid-19C. Origin ?]

bil·ly[3] /bíllee/ (*plural* **-lies**) *n* same as **billy goat**

bil·ly·can /bíllee kàn/ *n* same as **billy**[2] [< BILLY[2]]

bil·ly club *n* a short stick or club used as a weapon by a police officer [< BILLY[1]]

bil·ly goat *n* a male goat [< *Billy* pet form of *William*]

Bil·ly the Kid /bìllee-/ (1859–81) US outlaw. A notorious robber and cattle rustler on the Western frontier, he claimed to have killed at least 21 people. He used numerous aliases, and the facts of his life are not clearly known. Born **McCarty, Henry.** Known as **Bonney, William H.**

bi·lo·bate /bī lṓ bàyt/, **bi·lobed** /bī lṓbd/ *adj* having or consisting of two lobes ○ *a bilobate leaf*

Bi·lox·i /bə lúksee, -lók-/ city and port in southeastern Mississippi, midway between New Orleans, Louisiana and Mobile, Alabama. Population: 49,809 (2002 estimate).

bil·tong /bíl tòng, -tàwng/ *n S Africa* strips of lean meat cured by salting and drying [Early 19C. < Afrikaans < Dutch *bil* "buttock, rump" + *tong* "tongue"]

Bim /bim/ *n* somebody who comes from Barbados (*informal*) [Mid-19C. Origin ?]

bi·ma, bi·mah *n* JUDAISM another spelling of **bema** (sense 1)

bi·man·u·al /bī mánnyoo əl/ *adj* done with or needing the use of two hands —**bi·man·u·al·ly** *adv*

bim·bo /bímbō/ (*plural* **-bos**) *n* (*slang*) **1.** an offensive term for an attractive woman who is regarded as unintelligent and shallow **2.** an offensive term for a man or woman who is regarded as unintelligent or superficial [Early 20C. Probably < Italian, "baby, small child"]

bi·me·tal·lic /bī mə tállik/ *adj* containing or consisting of two metals

bi·me·tal·lic strip *n* a strip composed of two metals fixed together, each with a different coefficient of expansion and, therefore, bending at different rates when heated. Bimetallic strips are used in thermostats, thermal switches, and some thermometers.

bi·mil·le·nar·y /bī míllə nèrree, bīmə lénnəree/ *adj* relating to or celebrating a 2,000th anniversary ■ *n* (*plural* **-ies**) the 2,000th anniversary of something

bi·mod·al /bī mṓd'l/ *adj* relating to or consisting of a series of observations with two peaks, representing two statistical values that occur with equal frequency and more often than any other value ○ *bimodal distribution* —**bi·mo·dal·i·ty** /bīmō dállətee/ *n*

bi·mo·lec·u·lar /bīmə lékyələr/ *adj* relating to, consisting of, or formed from two molecules

bi·month·ly /bī múnthlee/ *adj, adv* **1.** OCCURRING EVERY TWO MONTHS produced or held every two months **2.** OCCURRING TWICE MONTHLY produced or held twice a month ■ *n* (*plural* **-lies**) BIMONTHLY PUBLICATION a publication such as a magazine or journal that appears every two months or twice a month

USAGE See *biweekly*.

bi·mor·phe·mic /bī mawr féemik/ *adj* consisting of two of the smallest units of meaning in language (**morphemes**). The word "fallen" is bimorphemic, comprising the free morpheme "fall" and the bound past participle morpheme "-en."

bin /bin/ *n* **1.** LARGE STORAGE CONTAINER a large storage container, e.g., an industrial container for grain or coal, or an open container holding merchandise in a store **2.** *UK* TRASH CONTAINER a container for trash or wastepaper (*often used in combination*) ○ *a wastepaper bin* **3.** STORAGE SHELVES FOR WINE a set of shelves with compartments for storing bottles of wine in a cellar ■ *vt* (**binned, bin·ning, bins**) STORE SOMETHING IN BIN to put something in a storage bin [Old English *binn* < Celtic]

bi·na·ry /bīnəree/ *adj* **1.** IN TWO PARTS consisting of two parts **2.** MATH OF NUMBER SYSTEM BASED ON TWO using or belonging to a number system that has 2, not 10, as its base ○ *binary notation* **3.** CHEM HAVING ONLY TWO CHEMICAL ELEMENTS consisting of two different chemical elements only **4.** CHEM HAVING TWO CHEMICALS MIXING TOXICALLY consisting of or using two harmless components that combine to form an extremely toxic product **5.** MUSIC same as **duple** ■ *n* (*plural* **-ries**) **1.** MATH BINARY NUMBER SYSTEM a number system that has 2, not 10, as its base ○ *written in binary* **2.** MATH BINARY DIGIT a binary number or digit **3.** COMPUT DATA ENCODING PROTOCOL a protocol for encoding data in a file either in a sequence of printable characters or human-readable text, or a file encoded in this manner **4.** ASTRON same as **binary star 5.** ARMS same as **binary weapon** [15C. < late Latin *binarius* < Latin *bini* "two together"]

bi·na·ry code *n* a computer code that uses the binary number system. Numbers and letters are translated into signals that a computer reads as sequences of ones and zeros called binary digits (**bits**).

bi·na·ry cod·ed dec·i·mal *n* a numbering system in which each digit of a decimal is converted into a binary number

bi·na·ry dig·it *n* either of the digits 0 and 1, used in the binary system

bi·na·ry file *n* a computer file that contains data in a raw or nontext state made up of characters that only a computer can read. Executable programs are stored and transmitted in binary files, as are most numerical data files.

bi·na·ry fis·sion *n* the reproduction of a cell or a one-celled organism by division into two nearly equal parts

bi·na·ry form *n* a musical form that has two complementary parts, both usually repeated

bi·na·ry no·ta·tion *n* COMPUT same as **binary system**

bi·na·ry star *n* a pair of stars that revolve around their common center of mass under mutual gravitational attraction

bi·na·ry sys·tem *n* a number system with 2 as its base, numbers being expressed as sequences of the digits 0 and 1. For example, the number 5 is written as 101, representing one 1, no 2s, and one 4, read from right to left.

bi·na·ry weap·on *n* a bomb or artillery shell that contains two chemicals that are harmless in isolation but combine to form a toxic compound before reaching the target

bi·na·tion·al /bī náshən'l, -náshnəl/ *adj* relating to or involving two nations

bin·au·ral /bī náwrəl, bi-/ *adj* **1.** relating to both ears or the perception of sound by both ears **2.** recorded onto two separate channels using two microphones, so as to sound realistic when heard through headphones [Mid-19C. < Latin *bini* "two together"]

bind /bīnd/ *v* (**bound** /bownd/, **bind·ing, binds**) **1.** *vt* TIE SOMETHING FIRMLY TO SOMETHING to tie something firmly to something else by winding a cord tightly and repeatedly around both things **2.** *vt* TIE SOMEBODY'S HANDS OR FEET TOGETHER to tie somebody's hands or feet together to make it difficult to escape (*often passive*) ○ *had bound him hand and foot* **3.** *vt* WRAP SOMETHING TIGHTLY to wind a cord, tape, or bandage firmly around something to protect it or hold it together ○ *You have to bind the wound firmly.* **4.** *vt* HANDICRAFT PROTECT EDGE OF FABRIC to protect or decorate the edge of a piece of material by stitching over it or attaching a strip of fabric to it **5.** *vt* PUBL PUT BOOK TOGETHER to attach pages to one another and put them in a cover to form a book, leaflet, or other publication **6.** *vti* LINK PEOPLE EMOTIONALLY to form a link or relationship between people based on loyalty, affection, or a shared experience ○ *the instinct that binds mother and child* **7.** *vti* STICK TOGETHER to stick together, or cause things to stick together, so as to form a solid mass ○ *The water, sand, and cement bind to form workable mortar.* **8.** *vti* CHEM FORM CHEMICAL BOND to form a chemical bond with a substance **9.** *vt* MED MAKE SOMEBODY CONSTIPATED to make somebody's feces firmer and more solid (*refers to food or medicine*) **10.** *vi* ENG BECOME STIFF OR STUCK to become stiff, stuck, or unable to move freely (*refers to mechanical parts*) ○ *The brakes are binding.* **11.** *vt* FORCE SOMEBODY TO DO SOMETHING to oblige or compel somebody to do something, e.g., by invoking a law, contract or promise (*often passive*) ○ *bound by her oath of office* **12.** *vt* EMPLOY SOMEBODY AS APPRENTICE formerly, to employ somebody as an apprentice under the terms of an agreement that obliged the apprentice to work for a fixed period, often several years ■ *n* **1.** FENCING MOVEMENT PUSHING FENCER'S BLADE AWAY in fencing, a movement that pushes an opponent's blade out of line **2.** CHESS DOMINANT POSITION IN CHESS in chess, a position of dominance in the center of the board that restricts an opponent's moves [Old English *bindan* < Indo-European] ◇ **bound up with somebody** *or* **something** closely involved with or connected to somebody or something ◇ **in a bind** in a difficult or unpleasant situation, especially a situation in which every option leads to difficulties

bind off *vti* HANDICRAFT same as **cast off** (sense 3)

bind over *vt* to accept bail from an accused person, obligating the accused to appear at trial ○ *The accused was bound over for trial.*

bind·er /bīndər/ *n* **1.** HARD COVER FOR PAPERS a stiff cover with clips inside for holding loose sheets of paper or magazines **2.** MACHINE FOR BINDING BOOKS OR PAPERS a machine for holding sheets of paper together to form a book or booklet **3.** BOOKBINDER somebody whose job is to make books by assembling the pages and putting on the cover **4.** CORD OR TIE a length of cord, string, or tape that is used to tie things together **5.** SOMETHING THAT STICKS THINGS a substance added to form dry ingredients into a solid mass or to maintain an even consistency throughout a liquid or semiliquid substance **6.** AGRIC DEVICE OR MACHINE FOR MAKING SHEAVES an attachment on a reaping machine for bundling cut grain into sheaves, or a reaping machine with this attachment **7.** COMM STATEMENT BINDING SOMEBODY TO AGREEMENT a formal statement together with the payment of a deposit, showing that somebody has serious intentions of going ahead with an agreement, especially an agreement to purchase insurance

bind·er·y /bī́ndəree/ (*plural* **-ies**) *n* a place where books are made by assembling the pages and putting on the cover

bin·di /bíndee/ (*plural* **-dis**) *n* a small usually red decorative mark worn in the middle of the forehead by women. Traditionally it was worn only by Hindu married women and unmarried girls, but not by widows. [< Hindi *bindī*]

bind·ing /bī́nding/ *n* **1.** PUBL **BOOK COVERING** the cover of a book, or the material used to cover books **2.** PUBL **SOMETHING HOLDING BOOK'S PAGES TOGETHER** the glue, strip of plastic, or other material that holds the pages of a book or booklet together **3. CORD USED FOR TYING** something that is used to tie or protect things, especially a cord or tape that is wound repeatedly around something **4.** HANDICRAFT **FABRIC EDGING** a strip of fabric or tape attached to the edge of a piece of material to prevent it from fraying **5.** SKIING **SKI FASTENING** one of the fastenings on a ski or snowboard that hold the ski to the boot ■ *adj* **OBLIGING SOMEBODY TO DO SOMETHING** creating a legal or moral obligation to do something, with no possibility of withdrawal or avoidance ○ *a binding agreement*

bind·ing en·er·gy *n* **1.** the energy required to remove a particle from a system, e.g., an electron from an atom **2.** the energy required to separate a system into its individual particles or components

bind·ing site *n* a cavity on the surface of a protein that contains a pattern of amino acids arranged so that they can form a chemical bond only with a specific molecule

bin·dle·stiff /bínd'l stìf/ *n* a homeless person who travels from place to place carrying a bundle of possessions (*informal*) [Early 20C. < *bindle* "bundle" (probably < German dialect *bindel*) + STIFF "hobo"]

bind·weed /bī́nd wèed/ *n* a plant with long twining stems, especially a wild plant with large white funnel-shaped flowers, generally regarded as a weed. Genera: *Convolvulus* or *Calystegia*.

bin end *n* one of the last bottles remaining from a single production of wine, often sold at a reduced price

binge /binj/ *n* **1. HEAVY DRINKING OR EATING SESSION** a short period when somebody drinks or eats too much, especially a period of uncontrolled drinking or eating caused by a disorder such as alcoholism or bulimia **2. SPREE** a short period of time when something is done in an unrestrained way ○ *a shopping binge* ■ *vi* (**binged, binge·ing** or **bing·ing, bing·es**) **1. EAT TOO MUCH** to eat far too much food very quickly, sometimes as a symptom of an eating disorder such as bulimia **2. BE SELF-INDULGENT WITH SOMETHING** to do or consume something in an unrestrained self-indulgent way ○ *stay in all day and binge on old movies* [Early 19C. Origin ?] —**bing·er** *n*

binge drink·ing *n* the consumption of an excessive amount of alcohol in a short period of time, usually in order to get drunk

Bing·ham /bíngəm/, **George Caleb** (1811–79) US artist. He is known for his paintings depicting quiet landscapes and American pioneer life.

Bing·ham, Hiram (1789–1869) US cleric. He founded the first Protestant mission in Hawaii and translated the Bible into Hawaiian.

Bing·ham·ton /bíngəmtən/ city in New York where the Susquehanna and Chenango rivers meet, southeast of Ithaca. Population: 46,736 (2002 estimate).

bin·go /bíng gō/ *n* **LOTTERY GAME WITH NUMBERED CARDS** a game played with numbered cards in which numbers are selected at random and the first person to cover all or specific numbered slots on his or her card wins ■ *interj* **1. CALL IN BINGO** a shout of success, called by a player who has won a game of bingo **2. EXCLAMATION OF SUCCESS** used to express satisfaction at sudden success or achievement [Early 20C. Origin ?]

Bin La·den /bin la̍adən/, **Osama** (*b.* 1957) Saudi-born leader of al Qaeda, a militant Islamic organization associated with several terrorist incidents, including the four September 11, 2001, attacks on the United States

bin·na·cle /bínnək'l/ *n* a support or mounting for a ship's compass [15C. Alteration of Spanish *bitácula* < Latin *habitaculum* "housing" < *habitare* "inhabit"]

bin·oc·u·lar /bə nókyələr, bī-/ *adj* involving or using both eyes, or relating to vision using both eyes [Mid-18C. < Latin *bini* "two together" + *oculus* "eye"] —**bin·oc·u·lar·i·ty** /bə nòkyə lárrətee, bī-/ *n*

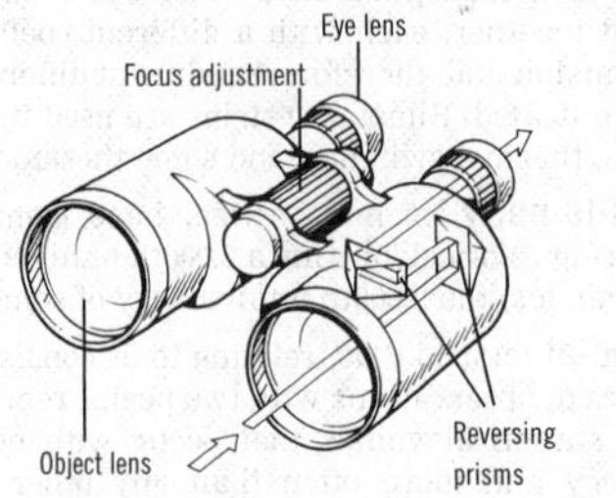

binoculars

bin·oc·u·lars /bə nókyələrz, bī-/ *npl* a device for looking at distant objects that magnifies what is seen using a lens for each eye

bi·no·mi·al /bī nṓmee əl/ *n* **1.** MATH **EXPRESSION WITH TWO TERMS** a mathematical expression made up of two terms linked by a plus or minus sign **2.** BIOL **TWO-PART NAME OF ORGANISM** a pair of Latin or Latinized words forming a scientific name in the classification of plants, animals, and microorganisms. The first word represents the genus and the second the species. ■ *adj* **1.** BIOL **HAVING TWO NAMES** relating to or consisting of the two Latin or Latinized parts of a scientific name in the classification of plants, animals, and microorganisms **2.** MATH **HAVING TWO MATHEMATICAL TERMS** relating to or consisting of the two terms of a mathematical expression linked by a plus or minus sign [Mid-16C. < modern Latin *binomius* < Latin *bi-* "two" + Greek *nomos* "part"] —**bi·no·mi·al·ly** *adv*

bi·no·mi·al co·ef·fi·cient *n* a number that multiplies the variables in a two-part mathematical expression, e.g., the numbers 3 and 4 in the expression 3x-4y

bi·no·mi·al dis·tri·bu·tion *n* a formula that indicates the probability of achieving a given number of successful outcomes in a predetermined number of statistical trials when the probability of success is the same for each trial

bi·no·mi·al no·men·cla·ture *n* the system of assigning two-part Latin or Latinized scientific names to plants, animals, and microorganisms, with the first word denoting the genus and the second the species

bi·no·mi·al the·o·rem *n* a mathematical formula used to calculate the value of a two-part mathematical expression that is squared, cubed, or raised to another power or exponent, e.g., $(x+y)^n$, without explicitly multiplying the parts themselves

bin·tu·rong /bin to͝or àwng, -òng/ *n* a mammal resembling a cat, with a thick black coat, a long tail, and tufts on its ears. The largest of the civet family, it lives in dense forests, uses its tail for grasping branches when climbing, and can swim to catch fish. Native to: Southeast Asia. Latin name: *Arctictis binturong*. [Early 19C. < Malay]

bi·nu·cle·ate /bī no͞oklee ət, -nyo͞o-/, **bi·nu·cle·at·ed** /-àytəd/, **bi·nu·cle·ar** /-ər/ *adj* having two distinct cell nuclei

bi·o /bī́ ō/ (*plural* **-os**) *n* a biographical work (*informal*) ○ *reads mostly fiction and celebrity bios* [Mid-20C. Shortening of BIOGRAPHY]

bio- *prefix* **1.** BIOL life, biology ○ *bioengineering* ○ *biography* ○ *biochemistry* **2.** biological warfare ○ *bioweapon* **3.** involving the use of biological or chemical weapons ○ *bioterrorism* [< Greek *bios* "life, way of living" < Indo-European, "to live"]

bi·o·ac·cu·mu·la·tion /bì ō ə kyo͞omyə láysh'n/ *n* the accumulation of a harmful substance such as a radioactive element, a heavy metal, or an organochlorine in an organism, especially an organism that forms part of the food chain —**bi·o·ac·cu·mu·late** /-kyo͞omyə làyt/ *vi* —**bi·o·ac·cu·mu·la·tive** *adj* /-kyo͞omyə làytiv/

bi·o·ac·tive /bì ō áktiv/ *adj* producing an effect in living tissue or in a living organism

bi·o·ac·tiv·i·ty /bì ō ak tívvətee/ *n* the effect that a substance or agent has on an organism or living tissue

bi·o·as·say /bì ō á sày, -a sáy/ *n* a technique for determining the concentration or potency of a substance such as a drug by measuring its effect on an organism —**bi·o·as·say** *vt*

bi·o·as·tron·o·my /bì ō ə strónnəmee/ *n* the study of the possibility of life in the universe other than on Earth

bi·o·aug·men·ta·tion /bì ō awg men táysh'n/ *n* the addition of microorganisms to human or industrial waste in order to reinforce the natural biological processes that produce nonpolluting products —**bi·o·aug·ment** /-awg mént/ *vt*

bi·o·a·vail·a·bil·i·ty /bì ō ə vàylə bíllətee/ *n* the extent and rate to which a drug is taken up by the body in a physiologically active form

bi·o·break *n* a short break, e.g., during a meeting, when people go to the toilet and generally refresh themselves

bi·o·ca·tal·y·sis /bì ō kə tálləssiss/ *n* the stimulation of a chemical reaction by a biochemical agent such as an enzyme —**bi·o·cat·a·lyze** /bì ō kátt'l ìz/ *vt* —**bi·o·cat·a·lyst** /-kátt'list/ *n* —**bi·o·cat·a·lyt·ic** /-kàt'l íttik/ *adj*

bi·o·ce·no·sis /bì ō si nṓssiss/ (*plural* **-ses** /-sèez/) *n* a diverse group of species or organisms with its own distinct habitat, interacting to form an ecological community [Late 19C. < modern Latin < Greek *bios* "life" + *koinōsis* "sharing" < *koinos* "common"]

bi·o·chem·i·cal /bì ō kémmik'l/ *adj* relating to the chemical substances present in living organisms and the reactions and methods used to identify or characterize them —**bi·o·chem·i·cal·ly** *adv*

bi·o·chem·i·cal ox·y·gen de·mand *n* a measure of the pollution present in water, obtained by measuring the amount of oxygen absorbed from the water by the microorganisms present in it

bi·o·chem·is·try /bì ō kémmistree/ *n* **1.** the scientific study of the chemical substances, processes, and reactions that occur in living organisms **2.** the chemistry or composition of a particular organism or system —**bi·o·chem·ist** *n*

bi·o·chip /bī́ ō chìp/ *n* a semiconductor chip that uses organic molecules to store and process information

bi·o·cide /bī́ ə sīd/ *n* a chemical designed to kill organisms, especially microorganisms —**bi·o·cid·al** /bì ə sī́d'l/ *adj*

bi·o·clas·tic rock /bì ō klastik-/ *n* rock formed from organic remains

bi·o·cli·mat·ic /bì ō klī máttik/ *adj* relating to the relationship between climate and living organisms, or to the study of bioclimatology

bi·o·cli·ma·tol·o·gy /bì ō klīmə tóllәjee/ *n* the study of how climate affects living organisms —**bi·o·cli·ma·tol·o·gist** *n*

bi·o·com·pat·i·bil·i·ty /bì ō kəm patə bíllətee/ *n* the compatibility of a donated organ or an artificial limb with the living tissue into which it is implanted or with which it is brought into contact. Incompatibility leads to toxic reactions or immunological rejection. —**bi·o·com·pat·i·ble** /bì ō kəm páttəb'l/ *adj*

bi·o·com·put·er /bī́ ō kəm pyo͞otər/ *n* a very fast computer whose calculations are performed using biological processes instead of semiconductor technology

bi·o·con·trol /bī́ ō kən trōl/ *n* ECOL same as **biological control**

bio·con·ver·sion /bì ō kən vúrzhən/ *n* the conversion of one organic substance into another or into energy by biological processes or organisms

bi·o·da·ta /bī́ ō dàytə, -dáttə/ *n* **1.** *S Asia* same as **résumé** (sense 1) (*takes a singular or plural noun*) **2.** information relating to a particular person and his or her financial, professional, or educational history, stored in a database and used, e.g., in banking, job recruiting, and marketing (*takes a singular or plural verb*)

bi·o·de·grad·a·ble /bī ō di gráydəb'l/ *adj* made of substances that will decay relatively quickly as a result of the action of bacteria and break down into elements such as carbon that are recycled naturally —**bi·o·de·grad·a·bil·i·ty** /bī ō di gràydə bíllətee/ *n*

bi·o·de·grade /bī ō di gráyd/ (**-grad·ed, -grad·ing, -grades**) *vi* to decay naturally as the result of the action of bacteria —**bi·o·de·gra·da·tion** /bī ō dèggrə dáysh'n/ *n*

bi·o·die·sel /bī ō deéz'l, -ss'l/ *n* a substitute for diesel fuel made wholly or partly from organic products, especially processed vegetable oils such as soybean oil and peanut oil

bi·o·di·ver·si·ty /bī ō dī vúrssətee/ *n* the range of organisms present in a particular ecological community or system. It can be measured by the numbers and types of different species, or the genetic variations within and between species.

bi·o·dy·nam·ics /bī ō dī námmiks/ *n* the study of how energy, motion, and other forces affect living organisms (*takes a singular verb*) —**bi·o·dy·nam·ic** *adj*

bio·e·lec·tric·i·ty /bī ō ilek tríssətee, -eélek-/ *n* electric current generated by living tissue —**bi·o·e·lec·tric** /bī ō i léktrik/ *adj*

bi·o·en·er·get·ics /bī ō enər jéttiks/ *n* **1. STUDY OF ENERGY IN LIVING THINGS** the study of the conversion of energy in organisms and biological systems, e.g., in photosynthesis (*takes a singular verb*) **2. THERAPIES DESIGNED TO RELEASE ENERGY** a combination of therapies, including breathing and body exercise and the free expression of feelings and impulses, designed to relieve tension and release physical and emotional energy (*takes a plural verb*) **3. THERAPY INVOLVING POSTURE AND MOVEMENT** a therapy, devised by Wilhelm Reich in the 1940s, that uses an analysis of somebody's physical posture and movements to enhance emotional well-being (*takes a singular verb*) —**bi·o·en·er·get·ic** *adj*

bi·o·en·gi·neer·ing /bī ō enjə neéring/ *n* the use of engineering principles and techniques to solve medical problems, e.g., in the design of artificial limbs or in organ replacement —**bi·o·en·gi·neer** *n* —**bi·o·en·gi·neered** *adj*

bi·o·eth·a·nol /bī ō éthə nàwl/ *n* a fuel for internal-combustion engines that is made by adding alcohol obtained from biological material to gasoline so that it produces fewer pollutants

bi·o·eth·ics /bī ō éthiks/ *n* the study of the moral and ethical choices faced in medical research and in the treatment of patients, especially when the application of advanced technology is involved (*takes a singular verb*) —**bi·o·eth·i·cal** *adj* —**bi·o·eth·i·cist** *n*

bi·o·fab·ric /bī ō fàbrik/ *n* a fabric impregnated with genetically engineered bacteria that eat odors, absorb sweat, and continually regenerate dirt and dust repellents

bi·o·feed·back /bī ō feéd bàk/ *n* the use of monitoring devices that display information about the operation of a bodily function that is not normally consciously controlled, e.g., heart rate or blood pressure. This helps a patient to learn to control the function consciously.

bi·o·film /bī ō film/ *n* a thin layer of microbial cells, e.g., a bacterium or fungus, held to the surface of something by the material the microbes produce. The plaque that forms on teeth is a biofilm.

bi·o·fil·ter /bī ō filtər/ *n* a filter system using microorganisms to transform or break down the organic compounds of a pollutant into carbon dioxide, water, and salts —**bi·o·fil·tra·tion** /bī ō fil tráysh'n/ *n*

bi·o·fla·vo·noid /bī ō fláyvə nòyd/ *n* a biologically active compound found in citrus and other fruits

bi·o·fu·el /bī ō fyoō əl/ *n* a renewable fuel that is derived from biological matter, e.g., biodiesel, biogas, and methane

biog. *abbr* 1. biographer 2. biographical 3. biography

bi·o·gas /bī ō gàss/ *n* a mixture of carbon dioxide and methane. Source: fermentation of organic waste. Use: fuel.

bi·o·gen·e·sis /bī ō jénnəssiss/ *n* **1.** the generation of living things from other preexisting life forms **2.** the theory that living things can arise only from other living things and cannot be spontaneously created **3.** BIOL same as **recapitulation** (sense 2) —**bi·o·ge·net·ic** /bī ō jə néttik/ *adj*

bio·gen·ic /bī ō jénnik/ *adj* resulting from biological activity or from living things ○ *a biogenic amine*

bi·o·ge·o·chem·is·try /bī ō jeé ō kémmistree/ *n* the study of the distribution of elements between organisms and their surroundings —**bi·o·ge·o·chem·i·cal** *adj*

bi·o·ge·og·ra·phy /bī ō jee óggrəfee/ *n* the study of the geographic distribution of plants and animals —**bi·o·ge·og·ra·pher** *n* —**bi·o·ge·o·graph·ic** /bī ō jee ə gráffik/ *adj* —**bi·o·ge·o·graph·i·cal** *adj*

bi·og·ra·phee /bī òggrə feé/ *n* somebody whose life is described in a biography

bi·og·ra·phy /bī óggrəfee/ (*plural* **-phies**) *n* **1.** an account of somebody's life written or produced by another person, e.g., as a book, movie, or television program **2.** books about people's lives, considered as a whole or as a type of literature [Late 17C. Via French and Latin < medieval Greek *biographia* "writing about lives" < Greek *bios* "life" + *graphein* "write"] —**bi·o·graph·er** *n* —**bi·o·graph·i·cal** /bī ə gráffik'l/ *adj*

bi·o·haz·ard /bī ō hàzzərd/ *n* a risk to human beings or their environment, especially one presented by a toxic or infectious agent —**bi·o·haz·ard·ous** /bī ō házzərdəss/ *adj*

bi·o·in·for·mat·ics /bī ō infər máttiks/ *n* the use of computers to extract and analyze biological data, especially in studying the nucleotide sequences of DNA and other nucleic acids (*takes a singular verb*) —**bi·o·in·for·mat·ic** *adj* —**bi·o·in·for·ma·ti·cian** /-infərmə tísh'n/ *n*

bi·o·in·stru·men·ta·tion /bī ō ìnstrə men táysh'n/ *n* instruments used to record and display information about the body's functions, or the use of such instruments

Bi·o·ko /bee ōkō/ island in the Gulf of Guinea that forms part of Equatorial Guinea. It contains the national capital, Malabo. Population: 57,190 (1983). Area: 779 sq. mi./2,020 sq. km. Former name **Fernando Póo** (until 1973), **Macías Nguema** (1973–79)

biol. *abbr* **1.** biological **2.** biology

bi·o·lis·tics /bī ō lístiks/ *n* a method of genetic modification involving the shooting of small particles of gold coated with DNA or messenger RNA directly into cells or tissues at high velocity (*takes a singular verb*) [Late 20C. Blend of BIOLOGICAL + BALLISTICS] —**bi·o·lis·tic** *adj* —**bi·o·lis·ti·cal·ly** *adv*

bi·o·log·i·cal /bī ə lójjik'l/ *adj* **1. OF LIVING THINGS** relating to living organisms ○ *biological diversity* **2. OF BIOLOGY** relating to the science of biology **3. CONTAINING ENZYMES** containing enzymes that are intended to digest stains caused by natural substances ○ *biological detergent* **4. GENETICALLY RELATED** related by birth, not by adoption ○ *my biological mother* ■ *n* **MEDICATION OR VACCINE FROM LIVING ORGANISMS** a drug or other compound produced by living organisms. It is often a commercially important product of genetic modification. —**bi·o·log·i·cal·ly** *adv*

bi·o·log·i·cal clock *n* the set of mechanisms within living organisms that link physiological processes with daily, monthly, or seasonal cycles or with stages of development and aging

bi·o·log·i·cal con·trol *n* a method of reducing or eliminating plant pests by introducing predators or microorganisms that attack the targeted pests but spare other species in the area

bi·o·log·i·cal ox·y·gen de·mand *n* ENVIRON same as **biochemical oxygen demand**

bi·o·log·i·cal shield *n* a massive structure, usually made of concrete and steel, built around the core of a nuclear reactor to protect operating personnel from radiation

bi·o·log·i·cal war·fare *n* the use of microorganisms to cause disease or death to humans, animals, or plants

bi·o·log·i·cal weap·on *n* a missile, bomb, or other device that delivers harmful biological agents

bi·ol·o·gy /bī óllәjee/ *n* **1. SCIENCE OF LIFE** the science that deals with all forms of life, including their classification, physiology, chemistry, and interactions **2. LIFE IN ONE PLACE** the forms of life in a particular environment and their behavior, development, and history ○ *the biology of desert regions* **3. PARTICULAR ORGANISM'S MAKEUP** the structure and functioning of a particular organism ○ *the biology of the fruit fly* [Early 19C. Via French < German *Biologie* < Greek *bios* "life"] —**bi·ol·o·gist** *n*

bi·o·lu·mi·nes·cence /bī ō loōmə néssənss/ *n* the generation and emission of light by organisms such as fireflies, some bacteria and fungi, and many animals that live in the ocean —**bi·o·lu·mi·nes·cent** *adj*

bi·o·mag·net·ics /bī ō mag néttiks/ *n* the use of magnets and magnetic fields in the treatment of medical conditions, or the study of this subject (*takes a singular verb*)

bi·o·mag·ni·fi·ca·tion /bī ō màgnəfi káysh'n/ *n* BIOL same as **bioaccumulation**

bi·o·mass /bī ō màss/ *n* **1. MASS OF ORGANISMS IN ECOSYSTEM** the mass of living organisms within a particular environment, measured in terms of weight per unit of area **2. PLANT AND ANIMAL WASTE AS FUEL** plant and animal material, especially agricultural waste products, used as a source of fuel **3. ORGANISM'S DRY WEIGHT** the mass of material in a living organism or in a community of organisms, usually measured in terms of dry weight

bi·o·ma·te·ri·al /bī ō mə teéree əl/ *n* **1.** any material that performs, aids, or replaces a natural function, e.g., one used as a medical implant **2.** a biodegradable material of plant origin. Use: packaging, clothing, bedding.

bi·o·math·e·mat·ics /bī ō màthə máttiks/ *n* the application of mathematical methods and formulas to medical or biological phenomena (*takes a singular verb*) —**bi·o·math·e·mat·i·cal** *adj* —**bi·o·math·e·ma·ti·cian** /-màthəmə tísh'n/ *n*

bi·ome /bī ōm/ *n* a division of the world's vegetation that corresponds to a defined climate and is characterized by specific types of plants and animals, e.g., tropical rain forest or desert. The world's lakes and oceans may also be considered biomes, although they are less susceptible to climatic influences than terrestrial biomes.

bi·o·me·chan·ics /bī ō mi kánniks/ *n* the study of body movements and of the forces acting on the musculoskeletal system (*takes a singular verb*) ■ *npl* the mechanical forces at work in a particular body or organ (*takes a plural verb*) —**bi·o·me·chan·i·cal** *adj* —**bi·o·me·chan·i·cal·ly** *adv*

bi·o·med·i·cal en·gi·neer·ing *n* MED same as **bioengineering**

bi·o·med·i·cine /bī ō méddəssin/ *n* **1.** the employing of the principles of biology, biochemistry, physiology, and other basic sciences to solve problems in clinical medicine **2.** the study of the body's ability to withstand the stresses of unusual or extreme environments —**bi·o·med·i·cal** /bī ō méddik'l/ *adj*

bi·o·met·rics /bī ō méttriks/ *n* (*takes a singular verb*) **1.** the application of statistical techniques to biological data **2.** the use of measurable, biological characteristics such as fingerprints or iris patterns to identify a person to an electronic system —**bi·o·met·ric** *adj* —**bi·o·met·ric·al** *adj* —**bi·o·met·ric·al·ly** *adv*

bi·om·e·try /bī ómmətree/ *n* same as **biometrics** —**bi·o·met·rist** *n*

bi·o·mi·met·ic /bī ō mi méttik/ *n* a complex biochemical molecule such as a peptide protein that is synthesized to resemble a substance occurring naturally in the body

bi·o·min·er·al·i·za·tion /bī ō mìnnərəli záysh'n/ *n* a process in which organisms transform organic matter into mineral matter, e.g., in the formation of bone —**bi·o·min·er·al** /bīō mínnərəl/ *n* —**bi·o·min·er·al·ized** *adj*

bi·o·mol·e·cule /bī ō mólli kyoōl/ *n* **1.** one of the molecules from which living organisms are made **2.** a molecule of a compound produced by or important to a biological organism —**bi·o·mo·lec·u·lar** /bī ō mə lékyələr/ *adj*

bi·o·mon·i·tor·ing /bī ō mónnitəring/ *n* the measurement and tracking of a chemical substance in a living organism or biological material such as blood or urine, usually for the purpose of monitoring environmental pollution or chemical exposure

bi·o·mor·phic /bī ō máwrfik/ *adj* relating to a form, pattern, or mechanical system that resembles a living organism in shape, appearance, function, or motion ○ *a biomorphic drug that mimics phosphate* —**bi·o·morph** /bī ō màwrf/ *n* —**bi·o·mor·phism** /bī ō máwrf ìzzəm/ *n* —**bi·o·mor·pho·sis** /bī ō mawr fṓssiss/ *n*

bi·on·ic /bī ónnik/ *adj* **1. HAVING ELECTRONICALLY POWERED ORGANS** in science fiction, used to describe a human being who has had some human organs or functions replaced or enhanced by electronically powered parts that give superhuman capabilities **2. HAVING SUPERHUMAN QUALITIES** having superhuman strength, speed, or intensity (*informal*) ○ *a bionic appetite* **3.** BIOL **INVOLVING BIONICS** relating to or involving bionics [Early 20C. < BIO- + ELECTRONIC]

bi·on·ics /bī ónniks/ *n* (*takes a singular verb*) **1.** the study of biological function and mechanics, and their application to machine design **2.** the use of electronic devices to replace damaged limbs and organs

bi·o·nom·ics /bī ō nómmiks/ *n* a theory suggesting that economics can usefully be thought of as similar to an evolving ecosystem (*takes a singular verb*) [Late 19C. < BIO-, after ECONOMICS]

-biont *suffix* an organism that lives under particular conditions ○ *halobiont* [< SYMBIONT]

bi·o·or·gan·ic /bī ō awr gánnik/ *adj* describes a carbon-based (**organic**) compound produced by an organism or having biological importance

bi·o·phar·ma·ceu·ti·cal /bī ō faarmə sṓotik'l/ *n* a drug produced by biotechnological methods

bi·o·phys·ics /bī ō fízziks/ *n* the science that applies the laws and methods of physics to the study of biological processes (*takes a singular verb*) —**bi·o·phys·i·cal** *adj* —**bi·o·phys·i·cal·ly** *adv* —**bi·o·phys·i·cist** /-issist/ *n*

bi·o·pic /bī ō pìk/ *n* a movie about the life of a well-known or interesting person (*informal*) [Mid-20C. Contraction of *biographical picture*]

bi·o·pir·a·cy /bī ō pírəssee/ *n* the commercial development of genetic resources such as plants with medicinal properties or genes for resistance to disease without compensating the inhabitants or government of the area where the substances or materials were originally discovered —**bi·o·pi·rate** *n*

bi·o·pol·y·mer /bī ō pólləmər/ *n* a polymer produced in living organisms

bi·o·proc·ess /bī ō prò sess, -prō sess/ *n* a method for producing commercially useful biological material

bi·o·pros·pect·ing /bī ō pró spèkting/ *n* the process of searching for and extracting potential pharmaceutical compounds from plants —**bi·o·pros·pect** *vi* —**bi·o·pros·pec·tor** *n*

bi·op·sy /bí òpsee/ (*plural* **-sies**) *n* the removal of a sample of tissue from a living person for laboratory examination [Late 19C. < BIO- + Greek *opsis* "a viewing" < *ōps* "eye"] —**bi·op·sic** /bī ópsik/ *adj* —**bi·op·tic** *adj*

bi·o·psy·chol·o·gy /bī ō sī kólləjee/ *n* BIOL, PSYCHOL same as **psychobiology**

bi·o·re·ac·tor /bí ō ree àktər/ *n* **1.** a microorganism that, through its biochemical reactions, can produce medically or commercially useful materials, e.g. yeast producing beer by fermentation or genetically modified bacteria producing insulin **2.** a large tank for growing microorganisms used in industrial production

bi·o·re·me·di·a·tion /bī ō ri meedee áysh'n/ *n* the use of biological methods to restore contaminated land, especially the addition of bacteria and other organisms that consume or neutralize contaminants in the soil

bi·o·rhythm /bī ō rithəm/ *n* a cyclic change that takes place within living organisms, e.g., sleeping, waking, or the reproductive cycle. Some people believe that biorhythms affect behavior, mood, and sense of well-being. (*often used in the plural*) —**bi·o·rhyth·mic** /bī ō ríthmik/ *adj* —**bi·o·rhyth·mi·cal·ly** *adv*

bi·o·rhyth·mics /bī ō ríthmiks/ *n* the branch of science dealing with biorhythms (*takes a singular verb*)

BIOS /bī òss/ *n* a small unerasable computer program that contains the instructions needed to begin operation and controls the data flow between the operating system and application programs and the hardware devices. Full form **basic input-output system**

bi·o·sat·el·lite /bī ō sàtt'l īt/ *n* a satellite designed for living beings, including humans, to live in

bi·o·sci·ence /bī ō sī ənss/ *n* a science that studies structures, functions, interactions, or other aspects of living organisms, e.g., biology, ecology, physiology, or molecular biology

bi·o·sci·en·tist /bī ō sī əntist/ *n* a specialist in any of the life sciences such as biology, ecology, physiology, or molecular biology

bi·o·scope /bī ə skōp/ *n S Africa* (*archaic*) **1.** a movie theater **2.** a motion picture

bi·o·se·cu·ri·ty /bī ō sə kyóorətee/ *n* the protection of the economy, environment, and health of living things from diseases, pests, and bioterrorism

bi·o·sen·sor /bī ō sènssər, -sawr/ *n* an apparatus that uses a biological agent such as an enzyme or organelle to detect, measure, or analyze chemicals. Biosensors are increasingly used in tests to diagnose medical conditions such as blood pressure.

bi·o·sep·a·ra·tion /bī ō sepə ráysh'n/ *n* the use of biological agents such as plants, enzymes, or biological membranes to separate components, e.g., in the purification of proteins or water or in the manufacture of food and pharmaceuticals

bi·o·sig·na·ture /bī ō sígnəchər, -choor/ *n* a substance such as an element, isotope, or molecule present in a meteorite that is characteristic of life and is used as evidence of past or present life

-biosis *suffix* a particular mode of life ○ *necrobiosis* [< Greek *biōsis* "way of living" < *bioun* "to live" < *bios* "life"] —**-biotic** *suffix*

bi·o·sphere /bī ə sfeer/ *n* the whole area of Earth's surface, atmosphere, and sea that is inhabited by living things —**bi·o·spher·ic** /bī ə sféerik, -sférrik/ *adj*

bi·o·sphere re·serve *n* a nationally or internationally protected area managed primarily to preserve natural ecological processes. Biosphere reserves are often open to tourists.

bi·o·spher·ic cy·cles *npl* the natural recycling processes essential to life on Earth, involving the principal elements that make up the biosphere. They include the oxygen cycle, carbon cycle, nitrogen cycle, and water cycle.

bi·o·stat·ics /bī ō státtiks/ *n* the branch of science dealing with the relationship between the structure and the function of an organism (*takes a singular verb*) —**bi·o·stat·ic** *adj* —**bi·o·stat·i·cal·ly** *adv*

bi·o·sta·tis·tics /bī ō stə tístiks/ *n* the application of statistics to biological systems and organisms (*takes a singular verb*)

bi·o·stim·u·la·tion /bī ō stimmyə láysh'n/ *n* the addition of nutrients to a polluted site in order to encourage the growth of naturally occurring chemical-degrading microorganisms

bi·o·stra·tig·ra·phy /bī ō strə tíggrəfee/ *n* the branch of science that uses animal and plant fossils to date and correlate sequences of sedimentary rocks

bi·o·strome /bī ə strōm/ *n* a thin layer in a rock formation that consists of organic material such as fossils deposited at the site where they lived [Early 20C. < modern Latin *biostroma* < Greek *bios* "life" + *strōma* "bed, covering"]

bi·o·sur·face /bī ō sùrfəss/ *n* the region on the surface of a protein, enzyme, or receptor that acts as a binding site for molecules

bi·o·sur·ger·y /bī ō sùrjəree/ *n* the use of living organisms in surgery and postsurgical treatment, especially the use of maggots or leeches to clean wounds

bi·o·syn·the·sis /bī ō sínthəssiss/ *n* the synthesis of chemical substances as the result of biological activity —**bi·o·syn·thet·ic** /bī ō sin théttik/ *adj* —**bi·o·syn·thet·i·cal·ly** *adv*

bi·o·sys·tem·at·ics /bī ō sistə máttiks/ *n* the study of the relationships among groups of species using criteria such as morphology, biochemistry, and DNA comparisons, especially to determine the history of a species (*takes a singular verb*) —**bi·o·sys·tem·at·ic** *adj*

bi·o·ta /bī ṓtə/ *n* the total complement of animals and plants in a particular area ○ *The biotas of tropical forests are the richest of all.* [Early 20C. Via modern Latin < Greek *biotē* "life" < *bios* "life"]

bi·o·tech /bī ō tèk/ *n* BIOCHEM, INDUST same as **biotechnology** (sense 1) (*informal*) [Late 20C. Shortening]

bi·o·tech·ni·cal /bī ō téknik'l/ *adj* relating to or involving biotechnology

bi·o·tech·nol·o·gy /bī ō tek nólləjee/ *n* **1.** the use of biological processes in industrial production. Early examples of biotechnology include the making of cheese, wine, and beer, while later developments include vaccine and insulin production. **2.** BIOL same as **molecular biology** —**bi·o·tech·no·log·i·cal** /bī ō teknə lójjik'l/ *adj* —**bi·o·tech·no·log·i·cal·ly** *adv* —**bi·o·tech·nol·o·gist** *n*

bi·o·te·lem·e·try /bī ō tə lémmətree/ *n* the remote monitoring of vital processes, e.g., by attaching a signaling device to an animal. The information is transmitted to a central processor, where it is analyzed electronically.

bi·o·ter·ror·ism /bī ō térrə rìzzəm/, **bi·o·ter·ror** /bī ō tèrrər/ *n* terrorist acts involving the use of biological or chemical weapons —**bi·o·ter·ror·ist** *adj, n* —**bi·o·ter·ror·is·tic** /bī ō terə rístik/ *adj*

bi·o·ther·a·py /bī ō thèrrəpee/ *n* the treatment of disease with substances produced through the activity of living organisms such as serums, vaccines, or antibiotics

bio·threat /bī ō thrèt/ *n* a real or perceived threat of the use of biological or chemical weapons

bi·ot·ic /bī óttik/ *adj* relating to life and living organisms, or caused by living organisms [Early 17C. Via late Latin < Greek *biōtikos* "of life, lively" < *bios* "life"]

bi·ot·ic po·ten·tial *n* the optimal ability of an organism or species to survive and reproduce successfully

bi·o·tin /bī ətin/ *n* a B complex vitamin found in egg yolk and liver, used in fat metabolism. Deficiency can lead to dermatitis, loss of appetite, hair loss, and anemia. Formula: $C_{10}H_{16}N_2O_3S$. [Mid-20C. < Greek *biotos* "life, sustenance" < *bios* "life"]

bi·o·tite /bī ə tīt/ *n* a black, dark brown, or green silicate mineral of the mica group. Source: igneous and metamorphic rocks. [Mid-19C. After J.-B. *Biot* (1774–1862), French physicist]

bi·o·tope /bī ə tōp/ *n* a small area with a distinct set of environmental conditions that supports a particular ecological community of plants and animals [Early 20C. < German *Biotop* < Greek *topos* "place"]

bi·o·tron /bī ə tròn/ *n* a place in a laboratory in which temperature and other environmental conditions can be controlled

bi·o·troph /bī ə trōf/ *n* a parasite that feeds on the living tissue of its host

bi·o·type /bī ə tīp/ *n* a naturally occurring group of individuals with the same genetic makeup (**genotype**) —**bi·o·typ·ic** /bī ə típpik/ *adj*

bi·o·war·fare /bī ō wáwr fèr/ *n* warfare involving the use of biological weapons

bio·weap·on /bī ō wèppən/ *n* a biological or chemical weapon —**bi·o·weap·on·ry** /bī ō wéppənree/ *n*

bi·pa·ren·tal /bī pə rént'l/ *adj* descended from two parents, male and female, as opposed to being the product of asexual reproduction

bi·pa·ri·e·tal /bī pə rī ət'l/ *adj* relating to or involving both parietal bones of the skull, particularly with respect to the measurement of the distance between their rounded projections

bip·a·rous /bíppərəss/ *adj* **1.** giving birth to two offspring at one time **2.** producing two branches from a single stem

bi·par·ti·san /bī paartiz'n, -tiss'n/ *adj* relating to, undertaken by, or including two political parties ○ *bipartisan support* —**bi·par·ti·san·ism** *n* —**bi·par·ti·san·ship** *n*

bi·par·tite /bī paar tīt/ *adj* **1.** made or shared by two groups of people ○ *a bipartite agreement* **2.** describes leaves that are almost completely divided into two parts —**bi·par·tite·ly** *adv* —**bi·par·ti·tion** /bī paar tísh'n/ *n*

bi·ped /bī́ pèd/ *n* an animal with only two legs for locomotion, e.g., a human being [Mid-17C. Directly or via French *bipède* < Latin *biped-* "two-footed" < *ped-* "foot"]

bi·ped·al /bī pédd'l/ *adj* describes an animal that has two legs or feet [15C. < Latin *bipedalis* < *biped-* (see BIPED)]

bi·ped·al·ism /bī pédd'l ìzz'm/ *n* the practice of walking upright on two feet, as opposed to moving on all four limbs

bi·pha·sic /bī fáyzik/ *adj* having two phases

bi·phen·yl /bī fénn'l, -fée̅n'l/ *n* a white crystalline substance. Use: fungicide, heat transfer agent, synthesis of organic compounds. Formula: $C_{12}H_{10}$.

bi·pin·nate /bī pínn àyt/ *adj* describes leaves divided into leaflets that are themselves subdivided —**bi·pin·nate·ly** *adv*

bi·plane /bī́ plàyn/ *n* an airplane with two sets of wings, one above the other, of a type built and flown mainly in the early part of the 20th century

bi·pod /bī́ pòd/ *n* a stand or support that has two legs

bi·po·lar /bī pṓlər/ *adj* **1.** WITH TWO POLES having two physical poles or extremities **2.** HAVING TWO DIFFERENT IDEAS having two completely different opinions, attitudes, or natures **3.** GEOG RELATING TO EARTH'S POLES relating to, involving, or found at both the North and South Poles **4.** PSYCHIAT HAVING MANIC AND DEPRESSED PERIODS characterized by shifts between episodes of mania and depression **5.** ELECTRONICS USING NEGATIVE AND POSITIVE CHARGE CARRIERS describes electronic devices, especially transistors, in which both negative and positive charge carriers are utilized —**bi·po·lar·i·ty** /bī pō lárrətee/ *n*

bi·po·lar dis·or·der *n* a psychiatric disorder characterized by extreme mood swings, ranging between episodes of acute euphoria (**mania**) and severe depression

bi·po·ten·ti·al·i·ty /bìpə tenshee állətee/ *n* the potential in early embryological development for a cell or organ to differentiate in one of two ways, especially for a gonad to become either an ovary or a testis

bi·prism /bī́ prizz'm/ *n* a glass prism that produces a double image of a single object

bi·pro·pel·lant /bìprə péllənt/ *n* a substance made up of two elements, usually a fuel and an oxidizer, that is used to propel a rocket

BIPS /bips/ *abbr* E-COMMERCE bank Internet payment system

bi·quad·rat·ic /bī kwo dráttik/ *adj* relating to the fourth power of a number ○ *a biquadratic equation* ■ *n* an equation that involves the fourth power of a number

bi·ra·cial /bī ráysh'l/ *adj* relating to, made up of, or involving people of two different races —**bi·ra·cial·ism** *n* —**bi·ra·cial·ly** *adv*

bi·ra·di·al /bī ráydee əl/ *adj* with both bilateral and radial symmetry, as found in some primitive animals that live in the sea

bi·ra·mous /bī ráyməss/ *adj* divided into or forming two branches ○ *a biramous appendage*

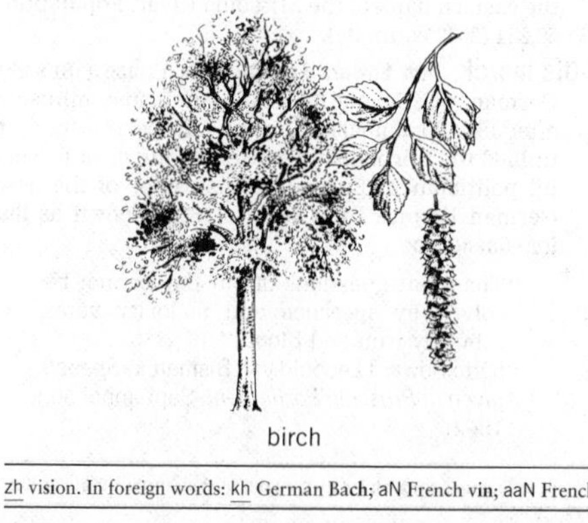

birch

birch /burch/ *n* **1.** TALL TREE WITH PEELING BARK a tall slender tree with papery, peeling bark. Native to: northern hemisphere. Genus: *Betula.* **2.** WOOD OF BIRCH the pale wood of the birch tree **3.** ROD FOR FLOGGING SOMEBODY a birch rod or bundle of twigs, formerly used to beat people as a punishment ■ *vt* (**birched, birch·ing, birch·es**) PUNISH SOMEBODY BY BEATING to beat somebody with a birch rod as a punishment [Old English *birce* < Indo-European]

Birch·er /búrchər/ *n* a member of the John Birch Society, a right-wing political organization in the United States whose main purpose is fighting Communism [Mid-20C. After John *Birch*, US Baptist missionary]

bird /burd/ *n* **1.** TWO-LEGGED WINGED ANIMAL a two-legged, warm-blooded animal with wings, a beak, and a body covered with feathers. Birds lay eggs from which their young hatch, and most species can fly. Class: Aves. **2.** BIRD EATEN AS FOOD a bird such as a turkey, chicken, duck, goose, or game hen cooked and eaten as food **3.** TYPE OF PERSON somebody of a particular type (*slang*) ○ *He's a wise old bird.* **4.** AIRPLANE OR SPACECRAFT an aircraft, satellite, or rocket (*slang*) **5.** RACKET GAMES same as **shuttlecock 6.** SPORTS same as **clay pigeon** (sense 1) [Old English *brid* "young bird," origin ?] —**bird·like** *adj* ◇ **a bird in the hand is worth two in the bush** it is better to keep something that you can be certain of than risk losing it in an attempt to get something better ◇ **birds of a feather (flock together)** people of similar character, tastes, interests, or opinions (tend to associate with one another) ◇ **give** *or* **flip** *or* **shoot somebody the bird** to hold the middle finger erect with the back of the hand toward somebody, as an insult (*slang*) ◇ **kill two birds with one stone** to achieve two goals with one action ◇ **(strictly) for the birds** worthless or unacceptable (*slang*) ◇ **the birds and the bees** the facts about sexual reproduction in humans (*informal humorous*)

Bird /burd/, **Larry** (*b.* 1956) US basketball player. As the Boston Celtics' star forward (1979–92), he led them to three NBA championships and was three times the NBA's most valuable player. Full name **Bird, Larry Joe**

bird·bath /búrd bàth/ (*plural* **-baths** /-bàthz/) *n* a small shallow basin containing water that is placed outside a house for birds to bathe in

bird·brain /búrd bràyn/ *n* an offensive term for somebody who is regarded as silly or mildly unintelligent (*informal insult*) —**bird·brained** *adj*

bird·cage /búrd kàyj/ *n* a cage made of thin bars used to keep birds in captivity

bird·call /búrd kàwl/ *n* **1.** the sound or cry of a bird, especially a warning cry **2.** a device that imitates a bird's call, used especially in trying to hunt or catch birds

bird colo·nel *n* a full colonel in the US Army, Air Force, or Marine Corps (*informal*) [< the insignia of an eagle worn by a US colonel]

bird dog *n* a dog used to bring back game birds after they have been shot

bird-dog (**bird-dog·ged, bird-dog·ging, bird-dogs**) *vti* to watch somebody or something carefully and persistently (*informal*)

bird·er /búrdər/ *n* HOBBIES same as **birdwatcher**

bird flu *n* a type of influenza that affects birds including domestic chickens and is capable of infecting humans

bird·house /búrd hòwss/ (*plural* **-hous·es** /-hòwzəz/) *n* **1.** a small box or shelter built for birds to nest in **2.** BIRDS same as **aviary**

bird·ie /búrdee/ *n* **1.** GOLF in golf, a score in which the ball is hit into the hole using one stroke fewer than the accepted standard number of strokes (**par**) for that hole **2.** RACKET GAMES same as **shuttlecock** ■ *vt* (**-ied, -ie·ing, -ies**) GOLF to score a birdie in playing a hole in golf

bird·ing /búrding/ *n* the hobby of birdwatching

bird·life /búrd līf/ *n* **1.** all the birds that live in an area or region ○ *South African birdlife* **2.** birds in large numbers ○ *The islands are home to a wide variety of birdlife.*

bird·lime /búrd līm/ *n* a sticky substance made from plants that is spread on trees to catch birds ■ *vt* (**-limed, -lim·ing, -limes**) to spread a sticky substance on trees in order to catch birds

bird louse *n* a wingless insect with a flattened body that is not truly parasitic but lives on the feathers and skin debris of birds, often causing skin irritation. Suborder: Mallophaga.

bird of par·a·dise *n* **1.** a bird, the male of which often has unusual feathers used in spectacular mating displays. Native to: New Guinea and adjacent islands, eastern Australia. Family: Paradisaeidae. **2.** an ornamental plant. Flowers: orange and blue petals resembling a bird's head and crest. Native to: southern Africa, South America. Genus: *Strelitzia.*

bird of pas·sage *n* **1.** a bird that migrates from one region or country to another according to the season **2.** somebody who rarely stays in the same place for long

bird of peace *n* a white dove as a symbol of peace

bird of prey *n* a bird that kills for food and has sharp talons and a sharp curved beak. Owls, eagles, and hawks are birds of prey.

bird pep·per *n* **1.** a small pod-shaped hot-tasting fruit eaten cooked or raw as a vegetable **2.** a tropical plant that produces bird peppers. The bird pepper is thought to be the ancestor of the sweet pepper and many hot peppers. Latin name: *Capsicum frutescens.*

bird·seed /búrd sèed/ *n* seed, or a mixture of seeds, usually used for feeding caged or wild birds

Birds·eye /búrdz ī/, **Clarence** (1886–1956) US inventor and business executive. He pioneered the retailing of quick-frozen and dehydrated foods.

bird's-eye *n* **1.** a pattern for fabric composed of diamond shapes with a dot in the middle of each **2.** fabric with a bird's-eye pattern

bird's-eye ma·ple *n* wood from the sugar maple that has a curled pattern in the grain reminiscent of a bird's eye

bird's-eye view *n* **1.** a view that is seen from somewhere very high up **2.** an overall impression or summary of something, without details

bird's-foot tre·foil *n* a creeping wild plant with seedpods in the shape of a bird's foot. Flowers: yellow with red tips. Latin name: *Lotus corniculatus.*

bird·shot /búrd shòt/ *n* small lead shot designed to be fired from a shotgun

bird's nest *n* a food delicacy, usually used in soups, that is obtained from high cliffs in Southeast Asia and is thought to be a swift's nest built with the bird's saliva. It is believed by the Chinese to be good for the skin and lungs. (*hyphenated when used before a noun*) ○ *bird's-nest soup*

bird's-nest fern *n* a fern with long green fronds shaped like a bird's nest that grows on the ground or on trees. Native to: South Asia, parts of Australia, the South Pacific islands. Latin name: *Asplenium nidus.*

bird·song /búrd sàwng/ *n* the sounds made by a bird to attract a mate or defend territory

bird spi·der *n* a large hairy spider from tropical America that eats birds. Family: Aviculariidae.

bird strike *n* a collision between a bird and an aircraft in flight

bird·watch·er /búrd wòchər/ *n* somebody who observes birds in their natural habitats as a hobby —**bird·watch·ing** *n*

bi·re·frin·gence /bī ri frínjənss/ *n* the splitting of one ray of light into two in an anisotropic medium —**bi·re·frin·gent** *adj*

bi·reme /bī́ reem/ *n* an ancient warship with two ranks of oars on each side [Late 16C. < Latin *biremis* "two-oared" < *remus* "oar"]

Bi·ren·dra Bir Bik·ram Shah Dev /bi rènd raa beer bìk ram shaá dèv/, **king of Nepal** (1945–2001) He acceded to the Nepalese throne in 1972 and ruled as an absolute monarch before instituting democratic reforms in 1990. In 2001 he was shot by his son, Crown Prince Dipendra, in a massacre that killed most of the royal family.

bi·ret·ta /bə réttə/, **be·ret·ta** *n* a stiff hat worn by

Roman Catholic clerics that has three upright sections meeting at the center on top. Priests wear black birettas, bishops purple ones, and cardinals red ones. [Late 16C. < Italian *berretta* or Spanish *birreta* < late Latin *birrus, birrum* "hooded cape or cloak"]

bi·ri·a·ni *n* FOOD another spelling of **biryani**

Bir·ken·head /bùrkən héd, búrkən hèd/ city and port in Merseyside, England, opposite Liverpool on the Wirral Peninsula. Population: 93,087 (1991).

birl·ing /búrling/ *n* a game played by lumberjacks in which players have to balance on spinning floating logs [Late 16C. < Gaelic *birlinn, beirlinn*]

Bir·ming·ham /búrming hàm, -əm/ **1.** city in northern Alabama. Just south of the Appalachian Mountains, it is the largest city in the state. Population: 239,416 (2002 estimate). **2.** city in southeastern Michigan, just southeast of Pontiac. It is a northwestern suburb of Detroit. Population: 19,280 (2002 estimate). **3.** second largest city in England and a major industrial center. Located in the West Midlands, it has three universities and two cathedrals. Population: 977,087 (2001).

Bir·ney /búrnee/, **Earle** (1904–95) Canadian poet. He wrote experimental poetry in the 1960s. Full name **Birney, Alfred Earle**

Bir·ney, James (1792–1857) US abolitionist. He advocated the emancipation of slaves and ran twice as the Liberty Party candidate for president (1840, 1844). Full name **Birney, James Gillespie**

birr[1] /bur/ *US, Scotland vti* (**birred, bir·ring, birrs**) to make a whirring sound, or cause something to make a whirring sound ■ *n* a whirring sound [14C. < Old Norse *byrr* "favorable wind"]

birr[2] /beer/ *n* the main unit of Ethiopian currency. See table at **currency** [Late 20C. < Amharic]

birth /burth/ *n* **1.** EVENT OF BEING BORN the emergence of the young of a human or animal from the mother's womb into the outside world ○ *The father was present at the birth.* ○ *articles give birth and death dates* **2.** PROCESS OF HAVING BABY the process of having a baby or young emerge from the womb ○ *the growing number of home births* **3.** CIRCUMSTANCES OF BIRTH the time or place at which a baby or other offspring is born **4.** SOMEBODY'S HERITAGE somebody's social or national origins ○ *a man of noble birth* ○ *Italian by birth* **5.** ORIGIN the origin, beginning, or formation of something ○ *the birth of jazz* ■ *adj* BIOLOGICALLY RELATED AS PARENT biologically related to somebody, especially as a parent, rather than related by adoption ○ *her birth mother* ■ *vt Can, Southern US* HAVE OR DELIVER BABY to have a child emerge from the womb, or deliver a woman's child [13C. < Old Norse *byrð* < Indo-European] ◇ **give birth 1.** to produce a child or young from the womb **2.** to originate or be responsible for creating something ○ *a revolution that gave birth to a free nation*

birth ca·nal *n* the passageway including the cervix and vagina through which a fetus emerges from the womb into the outside world

birth cer·tif·i·cate *n* an official document that states when and where somebody was born and the parents' names

birth con·trol *n* the deliberate limiting, usually by contraceptive means, of the number of children born

birth·day /búrth dày, -dee/ *n* **1.** the day on which somebody is born **2.** the day in each year that is the anniversary of the day somebody was born (*often used before a noun*)

CULTURAL NOTE ***The Birthday Party***, a play (1958) by British dramatist Harold Pinter. It tells of a young man called Stanley whose comfortable life in a seaside boarding house is disrupted by the arrival of two mysterious and intimidating strangers, Goldberg and McCann. Noted for its sinisterly formal dialogue, the play creates a disturbing atmosphere of paranoia and fear.

birth·day suit *n* a state of nakedness (*slang humorous*)

birth de·fect *n* MED same as **congenital anomaly** (*dated informal*)

birth fam·i·ly *n* the family that an adopted child was originally born into ○ *Do you have any idea of the whereabouts of the birth family?*

birth fa·ther, birth·fa·ther /búrth fàathər/ *n* a person's biological father, especially in the case of an adopted child

birth·ing /búrthing/ *n* the process of giving birth, especially when using natural childbirth methods ■ *adj* designed to facilitate childbirth ○ *a birthing pool*

birth·ing cen·ter *n* a clinic or hospital that provides medical care during labor and childbirth in a friendly environment resembling the mother's own home

birth·ing chair *n* a chair designed to support a woman and ease the process of childbirth by enabling gravity to act on the fetus as it moves through the birth canal

birth·ing room *n* an area set up for childbirth in a hospital or other building and intended to provide congenial surroundings that do not suggest a clinical context

birth·mark /búrth maàrk/ *n* a reddish or brown marking seen on the skin of some newborn babies that typically remains visible for life

birth moth·er, birth·moth·er /búrth mùthər/ *n* a person's biological mother, especially in the case of an adopted child

birth pang *n* same as **contraction** ■ **birth pangs** *npl* a difficult or troubled period at the start of something

birth par·ent, birth·pa·rent /búrth pèrrənt/ *n* somebody's biological mother or father, especially in the case of an adopted child

birth·place /búrth plàyss/ *n* a place where a particular person was born or where something first started ○ *Shakespeare's birthplace* ○ *the birthplace of classical philosophy*

birth·rate /búrth ràyt/ *n* the number of live births per 1,000 members of the population in a year ○ *a declining birthrate*

birth·right /búrth rìt/ *n* **1.** a basic right that somebody has or is thought to be entitled to from birth ○ *Freedom of speech is our birthright.* **2.** property or money that somebody feels entitled to because it belongs in the family

birth·root /búrth ròot, -ròot/ (*plural* **-roots** or *same*) *n* a plant whose roots were formerly used by Native Americans to help ease childbirth. Native to: North America. Genus: *Trillium*.

birth·stone /búrth stòn/ *n* a precious or semiprecious stone that is popularly associated with the month in which somebody was born. A birthstone is believed by some people to bring luck.

birth·wort /búrth wùrt, -wàwrt/ *n* a climbing plant with heart-shaped leaves. Native to: Europe. Latin name: *Aristolochia clematitis*. [Because formerly used to help ease pain during childbirth]

bi·ry·a·ni /bìrree aánee/, **bi·ri·a·ni** *n* in South Asian cuisine, a dish containing spicy colored rice mixed with meat, fish, or vegetables ○ *chicken biryani* [Mid-20C. Via Hindi < Persian *biriyān* "fried, grilled"]

bis /biss/ *adv* to be played or sung again (*used as a musical direction*) ■ *interj* used by members of an audience to call for an encore [Early 17C. Via French and Italian < Latin, "twice" < Indo-European, "two"]

Bis·cay, Bay of /bíss kày/ arm of the North Atlantic Ocean between western France and northern Spain. Area: 86,101 sq. mi./223,000 sq. km.

Bis·cayne Bay /biss káyn-, bíss kàyn-/ shallow inlet of the Atlantic Ocean on the East Coast of southern Florida. The city of Miami is on the northern shore, and Biscayne Bay National Park is to the east. Length: 40 mi./60 km.

bis·cot·to /bi skóttō/ (*plural* **-ti** /-tee/) *n* a hard oblong cookie, often containing nuts and usually flavored with anise [< Italian, "biscuit"]

bis·cuit /bískit/ *n* **1.** SMALL ROUND PIECE OF BREAD a small round plain piece of bread that rises with baking powder or soda and is then baked in an oven **2.** *UK* same as **cookie** (sense 1) **3.** COLORS LIGHT BROWN HUE a light brown color **4.** CERAMICS UNGLAZED POTTERY pottery that has been fired but not glazed [14C. < Old French *bescuit* "twice-cooked" < Latin *bis* "twice" + *coctus*, past participle of *coquere* "cook"] —**bis·cuit** *adj*

bis·cuit fir·ing *n* the first firing of something made of clay, at a relatively low temperature

bis·cuit ware *n* pots or pottery that have been through a first firing at a relatively low temperature

bise /beez/ *n* a sharp dry northerly wind that blows in Switzerland and neighboring parts of Italy and France [14C. < French]

bi·sect /bī sèkt, bī sékt/ (**-sect·ed, -sect·ing, -sects**) *vt* **1.** to split something into two parts ○ *The river bisects the town.* **2.** to divide something into two exactly equal parts [Mid-17C. < BI- + Latin *sect-*, past participle of *secare* "cut"] —**bi·sec·tion** /bī séksh'n/ *n* —**bi·sec·tion·al** *adj* —**bi·sec·tion·al·ly** *adv*

bi·sec·tor /bī sèktər, bī séktər/ *n* a straight line or plane that divides an angle or another line into two exactly equal parts

bi·sex·u·al /bī sékshoo əl, -sékshəl/ *adj* **1.** ATTRACTED TO BOTH SEXES sexually attracted to both men and women, or engaging in both heterosexual and homosexual activity **2.** BOTH MALE AND FEMALE IN CHARACTER having both male and female characteristics **3.** HAVING MALE AND FEMALE REPRODUCTIVE ORGANS describes something such as a flower that has both male and female reproductive organs —**bi·sex·u·al** *n* —**bi·sex·u·al·i·ty** /bī sekshoo állətee/ *n* —**bi·sex·u·al·ly** *adv*

Bish·kek /bish kék/ capital of Kyrgyzstan, in the northern part of the country, on the Chu River, just south of the border with Kazakhstan. Population: 585,800 (1996).

Bi·sho /béeshō/ capital of Eastern Cape Province in South Africa. Population: 8,000 (1987).

bish·op /bíshəp/ *n* **1.** a senior Christian cleric, especially in the Roman Catholic, Episcopal, and Orthodox churches, who is in charge of the spiritual life and administration of a particular region (**diocese**) **2.** a chess piece that can be moved diagonally across the board over any number of squares of the same color [Old English *biscop*, via Germanic < variant of Latin *episcopus* "bishop, overseer" < Greek *episkopos* "overseer" < *skopos* "watcher"]

Bish·op /bíshəp/, **Elizabeth** (1911–79) US poet. Known for her personal, reflective poetry, she won the Pulitzer Prize for her collection *North and South: A Cold Spring* (1955).

> "Is it lack of imagination that makes us come / to imagined places, not just stay at home?"
> [Elizabeth Bishop, "Questions of Travel," *Questions of Travel*; 1965]

bish·op·ric /bíshəprik/ *n* **1.** BISHOP'S DIOCESE an area that a bishop is in charge of **2.** BISHOP'S SEE a place where a bishop's cathedral is situated **3.** RANK OF BISHOP the rank or office of a bishop [Pre-12C. < BISHOP + Old English *rīce* "realm, power"]

bish·op sleeve *n* a wide sleeve that is gathered at the wrist

bish·op's weed *n* PLANTS same as **goutweed**

Bis·kra /biss kraá/ city and oasis on the edge of the Sahara Desert in Biskra Province, northeastern Algeria. Population: 128,280 (1987).

Bis·la·ma /biss laámə/ *n* the national language of Vanuatu in the Pacific, a modern form of Beach-la-Mar. Native speakers: 128,000. [Late 20C. Representing the local pronunciation of BEACH-LA-MAR] —**Bis·la·ma** *adj*

Bis·marck /bíz maàrk/ capital of North Dakota, on the eastern bank of the Missouri River. Population: 56,234 (2002 estimate).

Bis·marck, Otto Edward Leopold von, Prince (1815–98) German politician. As Prussian prime minister after 1862, he embarked on the European wars that unified the German states. He was the most powerful politician in Europe as chancellor of the new German Empire from 1871 to 1890. Known as **the Iron Chancellor**

> "The great questions of our day cannot be solved by speeches and majority votes ...but by iron and blood."
> [Otto Edward Leopold von Bismarck, *Speech given in Prussian Parliament*; September 30, 1862]

Bis·marck Ar·chi·pel·a·go group of over 200 islands, forming part of Papua New Guinea, in the western Pacific Ocean, off New Guinea. Area: 19,173 sq. mi./49,658 sq. km.

Bis·marck Sea arm of the southwestern Pacific Ocean northeast of New Guinea and north of New Britain

bis·mil·lah /biss míllə/ *interj* an invocation of the name of Allah, often said by Muslims before beginning to do something [Late 18C. < Arabic *bi-smi-llāh(i)*, first word in the Koran]

bis·muth /bízməth/ *n* a heavy, brittle, reddish white, crystalline metallic element. Source: ores of lead, silver, copper, and gold. Use: alloys, medicines. Symbol **Bi**. See table at **element** [Mid-17C. < obsolete German *Bismut*, modern Latin *bisemutum* < Middle High German *wise* "meadow" + *muth* "claim to a mine"]

bison

bi·son /bíss'n/ (*plural same*) *n* a large hairy animal resembling an ox but with a massive head and shoulders and a humped back. Native to: America, Europe. Genus: *Bison*. [Early 17C. Directly or via French < Latin < Germanic]

bisque[1] /bisk/ *n* a rich soup made from shellfish ○ *lobster bisque* [Mid-17C. < French]

bisque[2] /bisk/ *n* **1.** CERAMICS same as **biscuit** (sense 4) **2.** a pinkish brown color [Mid-17C. Alteration of BISCUIT, perhaps after French] —**bisque** *adj*

bisque[3] /bisk/ *n* in a game of tennis, golf, or croquet, an extra turn, stroke, or point that is given as an advantage to a weaker player [Mid-17C. < French]

Bis·sau /bi sów/ city on the northern shore of the Geba River estuary and capital of Guinea-Bissau since 1941. Population: 233,000 (1995).

bis·sex·tile /bī sékstil, -stīl, bi-/ *adj* having the extra day in a year that makes it a leap year ○ *bissextile month* ■ *n* same as **leap year** [Late 16C. < late Latin *bis(s)extilus* < Latin *bi(s)sextus (dies)* "twice-sixth (day)," February 24, the sixth day before March 1, counted twice in a leap year in the ancient Roman calendar]

bis·tort /bís tàwrt/ *n* a plant with an S-shaped underground stem (**rhizome**). Flowers: bright pink, in spikes. Use: formerly, in medicine. Native to: Europe, Asia. Latin name: *Polygonum bistorta*. [Early 16C. Directly or via French < assumed medieval Latin *bistorta* < Latin *bis* "twice" + *torta*, feminine past participle of *torquere* "twist"]

bis·tou·ry /bístəree/ (*plural* **-ries**) *n* a thin surgical knife designed to cut from the inside outward, formerly used to cut open abscesses or enlarge fistulas [Mid-18C. < French]

bis·tro /beéstrō, bís-/ (*plural* **-tros**) *n* a small restaurant or bar [Early 20C. < French]

bi·sul·fate /bī súl fàyt/ *n* CHEM same as **hydrogen sulfate**

bi·sul·fide /bī súl fīd/ *n* CHEM same as **disulfide**

bi·sul·fite /bī súl fīt/ *n* CHEM same as **hydrogen sulfite**

bit[1] /bit/ *n* **1.** PIECE a small piece of something ○ *There were bits of paper everywhere.* **2.** SHORT AMOUNT OF TIME a very short period of time or distance ○ *I'll do it in a bit.* **3.** EVERYTHING ABOUT ROLE all the aspects of a particular role in life (*informal*) ○ *did the whole two-career marriage bit* **4.** TWELVE-AND-ONE-HALF CENTS an eighth of a dollar (*dated slang; used in the plural*) ○ *two bits* [Old English *bita* < *bītan* "to bite" (see BITE)] ◇ **a bit** somewhat (*informal*) ○ *feels a bit tired* ◇ **bit by bit** gradually ◇ **bits and pieces** miscellaneous small objects (*informal*) ○ *I collected up my bits and pieces and left.* ◇ **do your bit** to contribute your share to work that needs to be done ◇ **every bit** in every way ○ *She is every bit as skilled as he is.* ◇ **to bits** very much, or to the greatest degree possible (*informal*) ○ *I just love the kids to bits!*

bit[2] /bit/ *n* **1.** MOUTHPIECE OF BRIDLE a part of a bridle consisting of a metal mouthpiece held in a horse's mouth by the reins and used to control the horse **2.** DETACHABLE PART OF DRILL a small metal tool that is inserted into a drill or brace and used for boring or drilling **3.** TOOL BLADE the part of a plane that is used for cutting **4.** PART OF KEY the part of a key that moves the tumblers or bolt of a lock **5.** PART OF PINCERS the gripping part of a pair of pincers ■ *vt* (**bit·ted, bit·ting, bits**) **1.** PUT BIT ON HORSE to put a bit into the mouth of a horse **2.** RESTRAIN SOMEBODY to restrain or hold somebody back [Old English *bite* < Indo-European] ◇ **champ** *or* **chafe at the bit** to be impatient for something to happen or because no action is possible ◇ **get** *or* **take** *or* **have the bit between your teeth** to start something and refuse stubbornly to stop

bit[3] /bit/ *n* **1.** in binary notation, either of the digits 0 or 1 used to represent one of only two outcomes, e.g., on or off **2.** the smallest unit of information storable in a computer or peripheral device, expressed as 0 or 1. Eight bits make a byte, the common measure of memory or storage capacity. [Mid-20C. Blend of BINARY + DIGIT]

bit[4] past participle, past tense of **bite**

bit buck·et *n* an imaginary electronic trash can in cyberspace into which all lost e-mail and news messages disappear (*humorous*)

bitch /bich/ *n* **1.** FEMALE DOG a female dog, or the female of another related animal such as a fox, or of another carnivore such as a ferret **2.** TABOO TERM a highly offensive term for a woman that deliberately insults her temperament (*taboo insult*) **3.** SOMETHING DIFFICULT a difficult thing or situation (*slang; often offensive*) ○ *That lock's a real bitch to open.* **4.** COMPLAINT a querulous nagging complaint (*slang; often offensive*) ■ *vi* (**bitched, bitch·ing, bitch·es**) (*often offensive*) **1.** BE NASTY ABOUT SOMEBODY to talk about somebody who is not present in an unpleasant or malicious way (*slang*) **2.** COMPLAIN CONTINUALLY to complain or grumble about something continually [Old English *bicce*, perhaps < Old Norse]

bitch·y /bíchee/ (**-i·er, -i·est**) *adj* malicious or unpleasant in speaking to, talking about, or behaving toward somebody (*slang; often offensive*) —**bitch·i·ly** *adv* —**bitch·i·ness** *n*

bite /bīt/ *v* (**bit** /bit/, **bit·ten** /bítt'n/ *or* **bit, bit·ing, bites**) **1.** *vti* GRIP WITH TEETH to hold something tightly, tear something off, or cut through something using the teeth ○ *I bit into the fruit.* **2.** *vt* PIERCE SKIN to puncture or tear the skin of a person or animal using fangs, teeth, mouthparts, or a stinger ○ *got bitten by a spider* **3.** *vti* GRIP SOMETHING FIRMLY to make firm or secure contact with something ○ *This stripped screw isn't biting.* **4.** *vi* CORRODE SOMETHING to eat into something with a corrosive action ○ *The acid had bitten into the metal surface.* **5.** *vti* PENETRATE SOMETHING WITH SHARP EDGE to cut into something with a sharpened tool or other sharp-edged object ○ *The saw blade bit the wood.* **6.** *vti* CAUSE DISCOMFORT to cause a cold sharp sensation that is quite painful ○ *an icy wind that bites to the bone* **7.** *vi* TAKE BAIT to attempt to take the bait that has been placed on the end of a fishing line (*refers to fish*) ○ *no fish biting today* **8.** *vi* RISE TO SOMEBODY ELSE'S BAIT to respond when somebody else tries to get you involved in a scheme or an argument (*informal*) ○ *Even though baited by the opposing attorney in court, she refused to bite.* **9.** *vi* BE EFFECTIVE to have an effect or influence ○ *The trade sanctions are at last beginning to bite.* ■ *n* **1.** SEIZURE OF SOMETHING WITH TEETH the action of taking something between the teeth and tearing it off **2.** MOUTHFUL a piece of food torn off with the teeth **3.** INJURY FROM TEETH OR INSECT an injury that has been caused by an animal or insect puncturing or tearing the skin with teeth, fangs, mouthparts, or a stinger ○ *a mosquito bite* **4.** ATTEMPT BY FISH TO TAKE BAIT an attempt by a fish to eat the bait that has been put on the end of a fishing line **5.** PIQUANCY a pleasantly sharp taste **6.** WIT AND INTELLIGENCE a penetrating and intelligent quality **7.** COLDNESS a cold sharp sensation that is quite painful ○ *There's a bite in the air today.* **8.** MECH ENG DEPTH OF MACHINE TOOL'S BLADE the depth to which a machine tool can cut **9.** MECH ENG GRIP the grip that something such as a tool has on something else **10.** DENT FIT OF TEETH the way the upper and lower teeth meet and fit together when the jaw is closed **11.** CHEM CORROSIVE EFFECT the corrosive effect of acid on a surface **12.** FISHING PERIOD WHEN FISH EAT a time when fish usually feed and so are more easily caught ○ *The catfish bite is usually the heaviest and best in the evening.* [Old English *bītan* < Indo-European] —**bit·a·ble** *adj* —**bit·er** *n* ◇ **bite off more than you can chew** to take on more than you can deal with (*informal*)

bite back *v* **1.** *vt* to hold back from saying something or openly crying ○ *I bit back my tears.* **2.** *vti* to make a sharp retort

bite·plate /bīt plàyt/ *n* a removable acrylic dental device that sticks to the roof of the mouth and is worn to encourage the back teeth to come through or to correct an overbite

bite-sized, bite-size *adj* small enough to be eaten as a single mouthful ○ *cut the meat into bite-sized pieces*

bit flip *n* the switching of a digital bit from 0 to 1 or from 1 to 0

Bi·thyn·i·a /bi thínnee ə/ ancient country of northwestern Asia Minor, on the Black Sea in present-day Turkey

bit·ing /bīting/ *adj* **1.** cold enough to cause discomfort or pain ○ *a biting north wind* **2.** sarcastic and clever —**bit·ing·ly** *adv*

bit map *n* a representation of a graphic image in computer memory consisting of rows and columns of dots, each corresponding to a pixel. For monochrome images one bit of data is sufficient to represent each dot, while colors and shades of gray require more than one bit per dot.

bit-map (**bit-mapped, bit-map·ping, bit-maps**) *vt* to represent a graphic image in computer memory as a matrix of dots, or recreate the image on a computer screen from such a bit map

bit-mapped font /bìt mapt-/ *n* a screen or printer font with characters formed as a pattern of pixels or dots

BITNET /bít nèt/ *abbr* COMPUT Because It's Time Network

bi·tok /beétok/ *n* fried ground beef patties served with a sour cream sauce [Via Russian < French *bifteck (haché)* "(ground) beef" < English BEEFSTEAK]

bit part *n* a small role in a movie or play

bit stream *n* a simple unstructured sequence of bits transmitting data in the form of binary digits

bitt /bit/ *n* either of a pair of posts on a ship's deck for fastening cables (*often used in the plural*) ■ *vt* (**bitt·ed, bitt·ing, bitts**) to fasten something around a bitt [15C. Origin ?]

bit·ten past participle of **bite**

bit·ter /bíttər/ *adj* **1.** STRONG AND SHARP IN TASTE having a sharp strong unpleasant taste such as the taste of orange peel **2.** RESENTFUL angry and resentful ○ *a bitter smile* **3.** DIFFICULT TO ACCEPT mentally painful, or very hard to accept ○ *a bitter blow* **4.** HOSTILE expressing intense hostility ○ *bitter fighting* **5.** VERY COLD penetratingly and unpleasantly cold ○ *a bitter wind* [Old English *biter* < Indo-European] —**bit·ter·ly** *adv* —**bit·ter·ness** *n*

bit·ter al·mond *n* **1.** an almond containing hydrogen cyanide. Use: food flavoring. **2.** a tree that produces bitter almonds

bit·ter al·oes *n* PHARM same as **aloes** (sense 1)

bit·ter ap·ple *n* PLANTS, PHARM same as **colocynth**

bit·ter·brush /bíttər brùsh/ *n* a bush with yellow flowers. Native to: western North America. Latin name: *Purshia tridentata*.

bit·ter cress *n* a plant belonging to the mustard family that often grows in damp places. Flowers: white, in clusters. Genus: *Cardamine*.

bit·ter end *n* the very end of something, however unpleasant it is ○ *They held out to the bitter end.* [Originally "end of a cable or mooring rope secured on board ship," *bitter* perhaps < BITT, but now interpreted as "painful"]

bit·ter·en·der /bìttər éndər/ *n US, S Africa* a highly

obstinate and inflexible person who takes a stand, refusing to budge until he or she is forced by adverse circumstances to do so ○ *The senior advisors in the administration, bitter-enders refusing to divulge information to the courts, were eventually forced to resign.*

bit·ter·leaf /bíttər leef/ *n W Africa* COOK, BOT same as **ndole**

bit·tern[1] /bíttərn/ *n* a bird of the heron family with mottled brownish feathers and a booming call. It lives among reeds in marshes. Family: Ardeidae. [Early 16C. Alteration of *bitore*, probably < Anglo-Latin *butorius* or Old French *butor* < Latin *butio* "bittern" + *taurus* "bull"]

bit·tern[2] /bíttərn/ *n* the bitter liquid that is left after common salt has crystallized from sea water. Use: source of bromides, magnesium. [Late 17C. < BITTER + *-n*, origin ?]

bit·ter·nut /bíttər nùt/ *n* **1.** a thin-shelled nut with a bitter kernel **2.** a tree that produces bitternuts. Native to: eastern North America. Latin name: *Carya cordiformis.*

bit·ter or·ange *n* **1.** a bitter-tasting citrus fruit. Use: marmalade. **2.** the tree that bears bitter oranges. Native to: tropical and subtropical regions. Latin name: *Citrus aurantium.*

bit·ter pill *n* something unpleasant that nonetheless must be accepted ○ *Not getting the job was a bitter pill for him to swallow.*

bit·ter·root /bíttər ròot, -ròot/ *n* a plant with edible starchy roots that is able to thrive in dry surroundings. Native to: western North America. Latin name: *Lewisia redivia.*

Bit·ter·root Range /bíttər ròot-/ mountain range in the northern Rocky Mountains, extending approximately 435 mi./700 km along the Idaho-Montana border. Its highest peak is Scott Peak, 11,393 ft./3,473 m.

bit·ters /bíttərz/ *n* a slightly alcoholic liquid flavored with plant extracts. Use: mixer in some cocktails. (*takes a singular verb*) ■ *npl* a bitter-tasting liquid used as a digestive aid (*takes a plural verb*)

bit·ter·sweet /bíttər swèet/ *adj* **1.** BOTH BITTER AND SWEET smelling or tasting both bitter and sweet at the same time **2.** BOTH HAPPY AND SAD causing feelings of happiness and sadness at the same time ■ *n* (*plural* **-sweets** or *same*) **1.** PLANT WITH BRIGHT CAPSULES AND SEEDS a poisonous climbing plant that has orange capsules containing bright red seeds. Native to: North America. Genus: *Celastus.* **2.** *US* PLANTS POISONOUS FLOWERING PLANT a sprawling plant with poisonous red fruits resembling berries, and stems that taste bitter then sweet when chewed. Latin name: *Solanum dulcamara.* Can term **woody nightshade**

bit·ter·weed /bíttər wèed/ *n* an American plant such as sneezeweed or some species of ragweed that contains a bitter-tasting substance

bit·ty /bíttee/ (**-ti·er, -ti·est**) *adj* **1.** extremely small in size or physical stature (*informal*) ○ *a little bitty kid riding a tricycle* **2.** *UK* made up of lots of different parts that do not seem to fit together ○ *a very bitty movie*

bi·tu·men /bi tóomən, -tyóomən, bī-/ *n* a sticky mixture of hydrocarbons found in substances such as asphalt and tar. Source: petroleum. [15C. < Latin, "asphalt"] —**bi·tu·mi·noid** *adj* —**bi·tu·mi·nous** *adj*

bi·tu·mi·nize /bi tóomə nìz, -tyóomə-, bī-/ (**-nized, -niz·ing, -niz·es**) *vt* to cover or treat something with bitumen, or convert something into bitumen —**bi·tu·mi·ni·za·tion** /bi tòoməni záysh'n, bi tyòomə-, bī-/ *n*

bi·tu·mi·nous coal *n* soft coal that burns with a smoky flame

~~biulding~~ incorrect spelling of **building**

bi·va·lence /bī váyləns/ *n* in classical systems of logic, the property that a proposition has of being either true or false

bi·va·lent /bī váylənt/ *adj* **1.** GENETICS describes structurally identical (**homologous**) chromosomes that come together during cell division (**meiosis**) **2.** CHEM same as **divalent** ■ *n* GENETICS a pair of bivalent chromosomes

bi·valve /bī vàlv/ *n* a saltwater or freshwater invertebrate animal that has its body contained within two shells joined by a hinge. Oysters, mussels, and clams are bivalves. —**bi·valved** *adj* —**bi·val·vu·lar** /bī válvyələr/ *adj*

bi·var·i·ate /bī vérree ət, -àyt/ *adj* relating to or involving two variables

biv·ou·ac /bívvoo àk, bív wàk/ *n* **1.** MILITARY OR MOUNTAINEERING CAMP a very simple temporary camp that is set up and used by soldiers or mountaineers **2.** BRIEF OVERNIGHT STAY a short stay, usually overnight, often with minimum equipment ■ *vi* (**-acked, -ack·ing, -acs**) MAKE CAMP to set up and stay in a very simple temporary camp [Early 18C. < French, probably < Low German *bīwake* < *bi-* "by" + *wake* "watch, vigil"]

bi·week·ly /bī wéeklee/ *adj* **1.** COMING OUT EVERY TWO WEEKS produced or appearing every two weeks **2.** COMING OUT TWICE PER WEEK produced or appearing twice a week ■ *adv* **1.** ONCE EVERY TWO WEEKS at two-week intervals **2.** TWICE PER WEEK twice during a one-week period ■ *n* (*plural* **-lies**) BIWEEKLY PUBLICATION a publication that appears every two weeks or twice a week

USAGE How many times is **biweekly**? Confusion is caused by the fact that ***biweekly***, *bimonthly*, and *biyearly* can mean either "once every two weeks (or months or years)" or "twice a week (or month or year)." If you want to avoid doubt, it is better to reword the sentence: *The talks are held twice a week at the local school. The talks are held every two weeks at the local school.*

bi·year·ly /bī yéerlee/ *adj* **1.** COMING OUT EVERY TWO YEARS produced or appearing every two years **2.** COMING OUT TWICE PER YEAR produced or appearing twice a year ■ *adv* **1.** ONCE EVERY TWO YEARS at two-year intervals **2.** TWICE PER YEAR twice during a one-year period

USAGE See ***biweekly.***

biz[1] /biz/ *n* a business of a particular type, typically involving fashion, entertainment, or the media (*slang*) [Mid-19C. Shortened < BUSINESS]

biz[2] *abbr* ONLINE business (*used in Internet addresses*) See table at **domain name**

~~bizare~~ incorrect spelling of **bizarre**

bi·zarre /bi záar/ *adj* amusingly or grotesquely strange or unusual [Mid-17C. Via French, "odd," formerly "brave, handsome" <Spanish *bizarro* "brave" < Italian *bizzarro* "angry"] —**bi·zarre·ly** *adv* —**bi·zarre·ness** *n*

bi·zar·re·rie /bi záarəree/ *n* amusing or grotesque strangeness or oddity [Mid-18C. < French < *bizarre* (see BIZARRE)]

Bi·zet /bee záy/, **Georges** (1838–75) French composer. He completed the opera *Carmen* just before his death. Born **Bizet, Alexandre César Léopold**

bi·zil·li·on *n* another spelling of **bazillion** (*slang*)

bi·zon·al /bī zṓn'l/ *adj* made up of two zones

Bjørn·son /byúrnssən/, **Bjørnstjerne** (1832–1910) Norwegian writer and politician. The national poet of Norway, his work includes the Norwegian national anthem and the novel *The Fisher Girl* (1868). He won the Nobel Prize in literature (1903). Full name **Bjørnson, Bjørnstjerne Martinius**

Bk *symbol* CHEM ELEM berkelium

bk. *abbr* **1.** BANKING bank[1] **2.** book

bks. *abbr* **1.** MIL barracks **2.** books

bl. *abbr* barrel

B.L. *abbr* Bachelor of Laws

B/L *abbr* bill of lading

blab /blab/ *vi* (**blabbed, blab·bing, blabs**) (*informal*) **1.** to talk indiscreetly about something that is supposed to be secret **2.** to chatter in a mildly incoherent way ■ *n* same as **blabbermouth** [13C. Probably ultimately < Germanic, an imitation of the sound of vacuous talking]

blab·ber /blábbər/ (*informal*) *vi* (**-bered, -ber·ing, -bers**) to chatter in a mildly incoherent way ■ *n* **1.** same as **blabbermouth 2.** the sound made by people talking loudly and incoherently [14C. Probably < BLAB]

blab·ber·mouth /blábbər mòwth/ (*plural* **-mouths** /-mòwthz/) *n* somebody who is regarded as talking too much and revealing secrets (*informal*)

black /blak/ *adj* **1.** OF DARKEST COLOR being the color of coal or carbon **2.** DEVOID OF LIGHT completely dark, with no light **3.** PEOPLES another spelling of **Black 4.** BEVERAGES CONTAINING NO MILK served without adding milk or cream ○ *black coffee* **5.** FUNNY AND MACABRE dealing with very serious things in a humorous and often macabre way ○ *black humor* **6.** MIL CLANDESTINE carried out in the utmost secrecy **7.** FULL OF ANGER filled with anger or hostility ○ *in a black mood* **8.** HOPELESS so depressing as to end all hope ○ *The future is looking black.* **9.** DIRTY covered with mud, soil, or any other dark substance **10.** SERIOUSLY BAD OR UNFORTUNATE causing or associated with severely bad conditions or misfortune ○ *a black day for the industry* **11.** DISHONORABLE extremely dishonorable and deserving the most serious criticism **12.** EVIL relating to evil ■ *n* **1.** DARKEST COLOR a color value that has no hue as a result of the absorption of nearly all light from all visible wavelengths **2.** COAL-COLORED DYE OR PIGMENT a pigment or dye that is the color of carbon or coal **3.** PEOPLES another spelling of **Black 4.** TEXTILES, CLOTHING VERY DARK-COLORED MATERIAL OR CLOTHES fabric or clothing that is black in color **5.** TOTAL DARKNESS complete darkness **6.** BOARD GAMES BLACK PIECE a black piece in a game such as chess or checkers ■ *vt* (**blacked, black·ing, blacks**) **1.** COLOR SOMETHING BLACK to make something black or cover something in black **2.** USE BLACK POLISH ON SOMETHING to cover something, especially shoes or boots, with black polish **3.** BRUISE EYE to hit somebody's eye so that it becomes very bruised and turns a purplish black color [Old English *blæc*, origin ?] —**black·ish** *adj* —**black·ness** *n* ◇ **in the black** not in debt or overdrawn

USAGE See ***Black.***

black out *v* **1.** *vi* MED LOSE CONSCIOUSNESS to lose consciousness, sight, or memory temporarily **2.** *vt* BROADCAST WITHDRAW PROGRAMS to refuse to broadcast radio or television programs, or a sports event for which tickets are still available **3.** *vt* MAKE SOMETHING UNREADABLE to cover a piece of writing with black color so that it cannot be read **4.** *vt* MIL EXTINGUISH OR HIDE LIGHTS to ensure that all lights in an inhabited area are turned off or covered up at night to prevent it from being seen from enemy aircraft **5.** *vt* ELEC REMOVE ELECTRICAL SUPPLY FROM PLACE to cause a place to undergo a failure of its electrical supply **6.** *vt* COMMUNICATION WITHHOLD INFORMATION to withhold news or information about a subject **7.** *vi* COMMUNICATION LOSE RADIO COMMUNICATION to lose radio communication between an aircraft or ship and headquarters **8.** *vt* ERASE SOMETHING FROM MEMORY to refuse to remember an upsetting fact, event, or experience

Black /blak/ *adj* **1.** ⚠ DARK-SKINNED belonging to an African people or to another ethnic group with dark skin, e.g., Australian Aboriginals **2.** ⚠ PEOPLES RELATING TO AFRICAN AMERICAN PEOPLE relating to a US ethnic group descended from dark-skinned African peoples ■ *n* **1.** ⚠ MEMBER OF DARK-SKINNED PEOPLE a member of an African ethnic group or another ethnic group with dark skin **2.** PEOPLES AFRICAN AMERICAN PERSON a member of a US ethnic group descended from dark-skinned African peoples

USAGE The word ***Black*** is standard in current usage for a dark-skinned person of African origin or descent. However, many Americans of African descent prefer the more formal term *African American*, used both as noun and adjective. The term ***Black*** is sometimes extended to include other peoples who are not white such as those of South Asia, but this use is generally regarded as unacceptable, the preferable use being specific names such as *Indian* or *Malay.*

Black /blak/, **Davidson** (1884–1934) Canadian anthropologist. He identified "Peking Man" *(Sinanthropus pekinensis)*, a prehistoric human species later assigned to *Homo Erectus*, in China in the late 1920s.

Black, Hugo (1886–1971) associate justice of the US Supreme Court (1937–71). He was known for upholding a literal interpretation of the First Amendment of the Constitution. Full name **Black, Hugo LaFayette**

> "No higher duty, or more solemn responsibility rests upon this Court than that of translating into living law and maintaining this constitutional shield ...for the benefit of every human being subject to our Constitution—of whatever

race, creed, or persuasion."
[Hugo Black, *Speech in a lawsuit*; 1940]

Black, Sir James Whyte (*b.* 1924) British pharmacologist. He discovered the first beta-blocking drug, leading to new treatments for heart disease. He shared the Nobel Prize in physiology or medicine (1988).

Black, Samuel (1780–1841) Scottish-born Canadian explorer and fur trader known for the journal he kept of his discoveries

Shirley Temple

Black, Shirley Temple (*b.* 1928) US actor and diplomat. An actor from age 3, she made 25 movies, including *The Little Colonel* (1935), that made her Hollywood's biggest box-office draw. Her later diplomatic service included the US ambassadorship to the United Nations (1969–70).

"I stopped believing in Santa Claus at an early age. Mother took me to see him in a department store and he asked me for my autograph."
[Attributed to Shirley Temple Black]

black al·der *n* TREES same as **winterberry**

black-and-blue *adj* covered with bruises, or feeling very bruised (*not hyphenated when used after a verb*)

Black and Tan *n* a member of the armed force that was sent by the British to Ireland in 1920–21 to fight Sinn Féin. Their uniform was khaki, with a black beret and armband.

black and white *n* **1.** material either handwritten or printed **2.** a visual medium without colors, and in hues of black, white, and shades of gray

black-and-white *adj* **1.** NOT IN COLOR representing an image in which colors have been converted to black, white, and shades of gray ○ *a black-and-white photograph* **2.** REPRODUCING IMAGES NOT IN COLOR reproducing images in which colors have been converted to black, white, and shades of gray (*not hyphenated when used after a verb*) ○ *a black-and-white television* **3.** CLEAR-CUT clear-cut and straightforward, allowing no room for compromise or doubt (*not hyphenated when used after a verb*) ○ *Everything is black and white as far as she's concerned.*

Black An·gus *n* same as **Angus**[1]

black arts *npl* forms of magic attempted for evil purposes, calling upon evil spirits or the devil

black bag job *n* an illegal clandestine entry into somebody's premises by a law enforcement agency or a private detective (*slang*)

black·ball /blák bàwl/ *vt* (**-balled, -ball·ing, -balls**) **1.** KEEP SOMEBODY FROM JOINING to prevent somebody from becoming a member of a club by voting against the person **2.** EXCLUDE SOMEBODY FROM GROUP to exclude somebody from a group or profession ■ *n* **1.** NEGATIVE VOTE a vote against somebody, especially somebody wanting to join a group **2.** VOTING TOKEN a black ball used to show a negative vote (*archaic*)

black bass /-báss/ *n* a large freshwater fish that is popular as a game fish. Native to: North America. Genus: *Micropterus.*

black bean *n* **1.** DRIED BEAN a small black seed dried and used in cooking **2.** BEAN PLANT a soya bean or French bean plant that produces black beans **3.** TROPICAL TREE a tree with smooth bark, dark green leaves, and wood that is used in furniture-making. Native to: rain forests of eastern Australia. Latin name: *Castanospermum australe.* **4.** FERMENTED SOYBEAN a black-seeded soybean used fermented in East Asian cooking ○ *black bean sauce*

black bear *n* **1.** a bear that lives in forests and ranges from brownish yellow to black in color. Native to: North America. Latin name: *Euarctos americanus.* **2.** a bear that has a black coat with a whitish V-shaped mark on its chest. Native to: Central and eastern Asia. Latin name: *Selenarctos thibetanus.*

black belt *n* **1.** BELT SHOWING SKILL IN MARTIAL ARTS a belt worn by somebody who has reached the highest level of skill in a martial art such as judo or karate **2.** SOMEBODY WITH BLACK BELT somebody at the highest level of skill in a martial art, entitled to wear a belt that is black **3.** *also* **Black Belt** FERTILE AGRICULTURAL REGION a region in the southern United States, stretching from Georgia across Alabama and Mississippi, with extremely fertile dark soil

blackberry

black·ber·ry /blák bèrree/ (*plural* **-ries**) *n* **1.** a small sweet dark purple fruit composed of a cluster of small round fruitlets **2.** a large bush with arching, often thorny, stems that produces blackberries. Native to: Europe. Latin name: *Rubus fruticosus.*

black bile *n* one of the four humors that were once believed to be the base of somebody's character. Black bile was associated with a melancholy temperament.

black birch *n* TREES, INDUST same as **sweet birch**

blackbird

black·bird /blák bùrd/ *n* **1.** a bird with black feathers showing a metallic sheen or bold patterns of yellow, orange, or red. Native to: North America. Family: Icteridae. **2.** a common songbird of the thrush family, the male of which has black feathers and a yellow beak and the female, brown feathers. Native to: Europe. Latin name: *Turdus merula.*

black·board /blák bàwrd/ *n* a board of either a dark color or white that is written on with contrasting chalk or erasable markers, used especially in classrooms

black·bod·y /blák bòddee/ (*plural* **-ies**) *n* an ideal object that would absorb all of the radiation incident on it without reflecting any radiation

black·bo·dy ra·di·a·tion *n* the thermal radiation that would be emitted by a blackbody. The distribution of energy in such radiation depends solely on the temperature of the source.

black book *n* **1.** a book in which somebody keeps the names and telephone numbers of private friends, especially boyfriends or girlfriends (*informal*) **2.** a book in which the names of people who are to be punished or blacklisted are kept

black bot·tom pie *n* a dessert with a layer of chocolate on the bottom and vanilla pudding on top

black box *n* **1.** AVIAT same as **flight recorder** **2.** an electronic component whose constituents or circuitry are unknown or irrelevant, but whose function is understood

black bread *n* a very dark rye bread that is particularly popular in Germany and Slavic countries

black·buck /blák bùk/ (*plural* **-bucks** or *same*) *n* a rare, small antelope, the male of which has a black back, white underbelly, and spiral horns. Native to: South Asia. Latin name: *Antilope cervicapra.*

Black·burn /blák bùrn/ industrial city in Lancashire, northwestern England. Population: 139,491 (1996).

black·cap /blák kàp/ *n* **1.** a small brown-gray warbler, the male of which has a black-topped head. Native to: Europe, Asia, Africa. Latin name: *Sylvia atricapilla.* **2.** PLANTS same as **black raspberry**

black cher·ry *n* **1.** DARK-COLORED CHERRY a dark-skinned cherry, especially one of a North American variety **2.** CHERRY WOOD the wood of a North American cherry tree. Use: furniture, musical instruments. **3.** WILD N AMERICAN CHERRY TREE a large wild cherry tree that has dark bark and white flowers and produces black cherries. Native to: North America. Latin name: *Prunus serotina.*

black·cock /blák kòk/ (*plural* **-cocks** or *same*) *n* the male of the black grouse

black co·hosh *n* a plant whose roots are used medicinally in the treatment of many gynecological problems, including menopausal symptoms and painful menstruation. It was used extensively by Native North Americans. Native to: North America. Latin name: *Cimicifuga racemosa.*

black com·e·dy *n* comedy containing bitter jokes about unpleasant aspects of life

black cow *n Midwest* a root beer float made with vanilla ice cream

black crap·pie *n* a medium-sized edible sunfish with black-spotted skin. Native to: lakes and rivers of eastern North America. Latin name: *Pomoxis nigromaculatus.* [*Crappie*, origin ?]

black cur·rant *n* **1.** a small black berry that grows in bunches **2.** a fruit bush that produces black currants. Latin name: *Ribes nigrum.*

black·damp /blák dàmp/ *n* atmospheric conditions in an underground mine that prevent normal breathing because insufficient oxygen remains after an explosion

Black Death *n* the bubonic plague epidemic that killed over 50 million people throughout Asia and Europe in the 14th century [Probably < the color of the buboes]

black di·a·mond *n* **1.** MINERALS same as **carbonado** **2.** the black variety of hematite. Use: source of iron. ■ **black di·a·monds** *npl* lumps of coal (*informal*)

black dwarf *n* a white dwarf star that has cooled over a long period of time and no longer emits significant radiation

black e·con·o·my *n* the part of an economy that consists of unofficial or illegal, and therefore untaxed, earnings

black·en /blákən/ (**-ened, -en·ing, -ens**) *v* **1.** *vti* to become darker or black, or cause something to become darker or black **2.** *vt* to harm or damage somebody's reputation

Black Eng·lish *n* same as **African American Vernacular English**

Black Eng·lish Ver·nac·u·lar *n* same as **African American Vernacular English**

WORLD ENGLISH See ***African American Vernacular English.***

Black·ett /blákət/, **Patrick, Baron** (1897–1974) British physicist. He discovered the positron (1932) and received the Nobel Prize in physics (1948) for his work on cosmic radiation. Full name **Blackett, Patrick Maynard Stuart**

black eye *n* an area of bruising around somebody's eye

black-eyed bean *n UK* same as **black-eyed pea**

black-eyed pea *n* **1.** a small beige bean with a black spot, traditionally eaten on New Year's Day in some parts of the United States **2.** a legume widely cultivated in the southern United States for forage and for its seeds. Latin name: *Vigna unguiculata.*

black-eyed Su·san /-so͝oz'n/ *n* **1.** a plant of the daisy family. Flowers: yellowish orange with a dark conical center. Native to: North America. Latin name: *Rudbeckia hirta.* **2.** a climbing plant. Flowers: yellow with purple centers. Native to: tropical Africa. Latin name: *Thunbergia alata.*

black·face /blák fàyss/ *n* makeup to blacken the face and other exposed areas of skin, used by a non-Black singer or other performer, especially formerly in minstrel shows

black·fel·la /blák fèllə/, **black·fel·low** /-fèllō/ *n* a highly offensive term for an Australian Aboriginal (*informal insult*)

black·fish /blák fìsh/ (*plural same* or **-fish·es**) *n* **1.** a small freshwater fish that is very abundant. Native to: Arctic North America and Siberia. Latin name: *Dallia pectoralis.* **2.** a female salmon that has spawned **3.** same as **pilot whale 4.** same as **tautog**

black flag *n* same as **Jolly Roger**

black-flag (**black-flagged, black-flag·ging, black-flags**) *vt* to signal to a racing driver to pull into the pits by waving a black flag

black fly (*plural* **black flies** or *same*) *n* a small dark biting gnat that causes painful itchy welts in people and animals. Family: Simuliidae.

black·fly /blák flì/ (*plural* **-flies** or *same*) *n* a black aphid that infests many plants. Genus: *Aphis.*

Black·foot /blák fo͝ot/ (*plural* **-feet** /-feet/ or *same*) *n* **1.** a member of a group of Native North American peoples living in Alberta, Saskatchewan, and Montana **2.** an Algonquian language spoken in Alberta and Montana. Native speakers: 8,000. [Late 18C. Translation of Blackfoot *Siksika*, perhaps from walking across burned prairies] —**Black·foot** *adj*

black-foot·ed fer·ret *n* a weasel that has a light-colored coat and blackish patches on its face, tail, and feet. Native to: North America. Latin name: *Mustela nigripes.*

Black For·est wooded highland region in Baden-Württemberg State, southwestern Germany that contains the sources of the Danube and Neckar rivers. Area: 2,000 sq. mi./5,180 sq. km.

Black For·est cake *n* a rich chocolate cake that is topped and filled with cherries and whipped cream [Probably from the cake's dark color]

Black Fri·ar *n* a member of the Dominican order of friars

black gold *n* petroleum, viewed as a source of wealth (*informal*)

black grouse *n* a large grouse with a lyre-shaped tail, the male of which is black with white patches on its wings. Native to: Europe, western Asia. Latin name: *Lyrurus tetrix.*

black·guard /blággərd, blá gaard/ *n* somebody regarded as dishonest or as having few, if any, principles (*dated*) —**black·guard·ism** *n* —**black·guard·ly** *adj*

black gum *n* TREES same as **sour gum**

Black Hand *n* an early 20th-century criminal organization of Sicilian immigrants in the United States that practiced blackmail and violence (*informal*) [Translation of Italian *La Mano Negra*]

Black Hawk /blák hàwk/ (1767–1838) Sauk leader. He fought against the westward displacement of Native North Americans by white settlers in what became known as the Black Hawk War (1832).

> "May the Great Spirit shed light on yours—and that you may never experience the humility that the power of the American government has reduced me to, is the wish of him, who, in his native forests, was once as proud and bold as yourself."
> [Black Hawk, *Remark to General Henry Atkinson*; 1833]

black·head /blák hèd/ *n* **1.** a small plug of dark fatty matter blocking a follicle on the skin, especially on the face **2.** an infectious disease of turkeys and related fowl resulting in darkened head skin. It is caused by a protozoan.

Black Hills mountainous region in western South Dakota and northeastern Wyoming, a mining area famous for the granite sculptures of Mount Rushmore National Memorial. The highest point is Harney Peak. Height: 7,242 ft./2,207 m. Area: 6,000 sq. mi./15,000 sq. km.

Black Hills spruce *n* a slow-growing evergreen tree of the pine family with cylindrical cones. Native to: northern part of North America. Latin name: *Picea glauca* var. densata.

black hole *n* **1.** an area in space with such a strong gravitational pull that no matter or energy can escape from it. Black holes are believed to form when stars collapse in on themselves. **2.** a place or thing into which objects disappear and are not expected to be seen again

Black Hole of Cal·cut·ta *n* **1.** a dungeon in Kolkata (formerly Calcutta) in which, in 1756, 123 out of 146 prisoners were said to have died of suffocation **2.** an uncomfortably overcrowded place (*informal*)

black ice *n* a thin, almost invisible, layer of ice formed when rain falls on a surface that is below freezing

black·ing /bláking/ *n* polish formerly used to make shoes and stoves black

black·jack /blák jàk/ *n* **1.** CARDS **CARD GAME** a card game in which the winner is the player holding cards of a total value closest to, but not more than, 21 points **2.** CARDS **WINNING COMBINATION OF CARDS** a combination of an ace and a face card, which is a winning hand in blackjack **3.** ARMS **SHORT CLUB** a weapon in the form of a short leather-covered club **4.** MINERALS **BLACK MINERAL** a black variety of the mineral sphalerite or zinc blende ■ *interj* CARDS **INDICATING WIN AT BLACKJACK** used to indicate to other players that a blackjack has been dealt ■ *vt* (**-jacked, -jack·ing, -jacks**) **1. HIT SOMEBODY WITH CLUB** to hit somebody with a short club **2. FORCE** to force somebody to do something (*slang*) [Early 20C. < JACK[1] "playing card"]

black·jack oak *n* a small oak tree with blackish bark. Native to: southeastern United States. Latin name: *Quercus marilandica.*

Black Ket·tle /blák kètt'l/ (1803?–68) Cheyenne leader. He led the Southern Cheyenne, many of whom were massacred by US forces in 1864, and was himself killed in a massacre.

black knight *n* a company that makes an unwelcome attempt to take over another company

black lead *n* a commercial form of graphite

black·leg /blák lèg/ *n* **1.** VET **DISEASE OF FARM ANIMALS** an infectious bacterial disease of farm animals that causes swellings on the legs **2.** BOT **POTATO DISEASE** a disease of potato plants caused by the bacterium *Erwinia carotovora* that makes the lower stems rot **3. DISEASE OF OILSEED RAPE** a fungal disease of cabbage, oilseed rape, and similar plants caused by the bacterium *Leptosphaeria maculans* that makes the stems rot **4.** GAMBLING **GAMBLER WHO CHEATS** a cheat at cards or horseracing (*informal*) **5.** *UK* **SOMEBODY WHO WORKS DURING STRIKE** a worker who is criticized and despised by striking colleagues for working during a strike (*disapproving*)

black let·ter *n* PRINTING same as **gothic** *n* (sense 3)

black light *n* **1.** any invisible electromagnetic radiation, e.g., ultraviolet or infrared light **2.** a bulb, tube, or other device that emits black light when stimulated with electrical current

black·list /blák lìst/ *n* **1. LIST OF DISAPPROVED PEOPLE** a list of people or groups who are under suspicion or excluded from something ○ *a credit blacklist* **2. LIST OF UNWANTED E-MAILS** a list of e-mail addresses, e.g., of unknown senders, to which somebody does not want to permit access ■ *vt* (**-list·ed, -list·ing, -lists**) **1. PUT SOMEBODY ON BLACKLIST** to add somebody's name to a blacklist **2. CONDEMN** to shun or condemn somebody for behavior that breaks implicit or explicit rules

black lo·cust *n* **1.** a tall tree with compound leaves and fragrant white flowers in spring. Native to: North America. Latin name: *Robinia pseudoacacia.* **2.** the hard, light-colored wood of a black locust

black lung *n* MED same as **anthracosis**

black·ly /bláklee/ *adv* in an angry or threatening way

black mag·ic *n* magic attempted for evil purposes, calling upon evil spirits or the devil

black·mail /blák màyl/ *n* **1.** the act of forcing somebody to pay money or do something by threatening to reveal shameful or incriminating facts about him or her **2.** unfair threatening or incriminating of somebody, as a way of achieving a result [Mid-16C. < obsolete *mail* "tribute, tax" < Old Norse *mál* "speech, agreement"] —**black·mail** *vt* —**black·mail·er** *n*

black mark *n* a record of something that somebody has done that gives people a bad opinion of him or her ○ *Avoiding the family reunion counted as a black mark against me.*

black mar·ket *n* a system of buying and selling officially controlled goods illegally —**black mar·ket·eer** *n* —**black mar·ket·eer·ing** *n* —**black mar·ket·er** *n*

black mass *n* an imitation of a Christian Mass said to be conducted by worshipers of the devil

black mea·sles *n* a severe form of measles, with bleeding under the skin causing dark spots or patches (*takes a singular or plural verb*)

black mon·ey *n* money earned unofficially or illegally

Black Monk *n* a member of the Benedictine order of monks, who wear black cloaks over their white habits

Black·more /blák màwr/, **R. D.** (1825–1900) British writer. The best known of his novels is *Lorna Doone* (1869). Full name **Blackmore, Richard Doddridge**

> "Here was I, a yeoman's boy, a yeoman every inch of me, even where I was naked; and there was she, a lady born, and thoroughly aware of it, and dressed by people of rank and taste, who took pride in her beauty, and set it to advantage."
> [R. D. Blackmore, *Lorna Doone*; 1869]

Black Moun·tains mountain range in western North Carolina, part of the Blue Ridge and the highest range in the Appalachians. Its highest peak is Mount Mitchell, 6,684 ft./2,037 m, the highest peak in the United States east of the Mississippi River.

Black·mun /blákmən/, **Harry** (1908–99) associate justice of the US Supreme Court (1970–94). He became identified with his decision supporting abortion rights in *Roe* v. *Wade* (1973). Full name **Blackmun, Harry Andrew**

Black Mus·lim *n* a member of the Nation of Islam, an almost exclusively African American Islamic denomination based in the United States

Black na·tion·al·ist *n* a member of a political organization that promotes separate self-governing communities or states for Black people —**Black na·tion·al·ism** *n*

black night·shade *n* a plant of the nightshade family that has poisonous leaves and black berries. Flowers: white, star-shaped. Latin name: *Solanum nigrum.*

black·out /blák òwt/ *n* **1.** ELEC **LOSS OF ELECTRIC LIGHT** a failure of an electrical supply **2.** MED **LOSS OF CONSCIOUSNESS** a temporary loss of consciousness, sight, or memory **3.** BROADCAST **WITHDRAWAL OF BROADCASTING** a refusal to broadcast radio or television programs, or a sports event for which tickets are still available **4.** COMMUNICATION **WITHHOLDING OF INFORMATION** the withholding of news or information about a subject, especially by official sources **5.** MIL **PERIOD OF EXTINGUISHING OR HIDING LIGHTS** a period during wartime in which all lights are to be turned off or covered up at night to prevent inhabited areas from being seen from enemy aircraft **6.** COMMUNICATION **LOSS OF RADIO COMMUNICATION** a loss of radio communication between an aircraft or ship and headquarters **7.** TRAVEL **PERIOD OF FULL-PRICE TRAVEL** a period during which promotional offers and benefits, e.g., those given to frequent fliers, cannot by used for air travel

Black Pan·ther *n* a member of a militant African American political organization opposed to white domination that was active in the United States especially in the late 1960s and early 1970s [*Panther*

< the emblem used by certain Black Power electoral candidates in Alabama in the mid-1960s]

black pep·per *n* dark brown seasoning made by grinding pepper seeds that have not had their black outer covering removed

black·poll /blák pōl/, **black·poll war·bler** *n* a small songbird with streaky plumage found in conifer forests. Native to: North America. Latin name: *Dendroica striata*.

Black·pool /blák pòol/ seaside resort in Lancashire, northwestern England, famous for its tower, built in 1895 and modeled on the Eiffel Tower, Paris. Population: 142,283 (2001).

black pow·der *n* gunpowder containing saltpeter, sulfur, and charcoal. Use: in fireworks and muzzleloading firearms; formerly, in mines and quarries.

Black Pow·er *n* a movement formed by Black people to engender social equality and emphasize pride in their racial identity via Black cultural and political institutions and organizations

black pud·ding *n UK* same as **blood sausage**

black rac·er *n* a dark-colored nonpoisonous snake. Native to: eastern United States. Latin name: *Coluber constrictor*.

black rasp·ber·ry *n* **1.** a small edible dark-colored raspberry **2.** a prickly bush that grows wild and produces black raspberries. Native to: North America. Latin name: *Rubus occidentalis*.

black rat *n* a common dark brown rat that is a household pest and a carrier of plague. It was originally from Asia but spread to coastal cities throughout the world. Latin name: *Rattus rattus*.

black rot *n* a plant disease that causes blackening as well as decay

Blacks·burg /bláks bùrg/ town in southwestern Virginia, southwest of Salem, on the western side of the Allegheny Mountains. Population: 40,108 (2002 estimate).

Black Sea large inland sea linked to the Mediterranean by the Bosporus, the Sea of Marmara, and the Dardanelles. It is bordered by Bulgaria, Romania, Ukraine, Russia, Georgia, and Turkey. Area: 178,000 sq. mi./461,000 sq. km.

black shale *n* a mudstone that contains organic carbon, e.g., an oil-bearing shale

black sheep *n* somebody regarded by the other members of a family or group as not living up to their standards and expectations [Because black wool is less valuable than white]

Black·shirt /blák shùrt/, **black·shirt** *n* a member of any European fascist movement active before and during World War II, especially a member of the Italian Fascist Party [< the party's uniform]

black·smith /blák smìth/ *n* somebody whose job is making and repairing iron and metal objects such as horseshoes [< *black* applied to iron]

black·snake /blák snàyk/ *n* **1.** REPT a dark-colored, chiefly nonvenomous, snake. Genera: *Coluber* or *Elaphe*. **2.** REPT same as **black racer 3.** a long tapering whip made of braided strips of leather or hide

black spot *n* a plant disease that causes black patches to form on leaves, particularly on roses

black spruce *n* a dark green conifer found in marshy areas. Native to: northern North America. Latin name: *Picea mariana*.

Black·stone /blák stōn, -stən/, **Sir William** (1723–80) British jurist. He wrote the classic *Commentaries on the Laws of England* (1765–69).

Black Stone *n* the sacred stone in the Kaaba in the great mosque in Mecca, believed to have been given by God. It is reddish black in color.

Black Stud·ies *n* an academic subject or curriculum that deals with the history, culture, and literature of Black communities worldwide, often with an emphasis on African American culture (*takes a singular verb*)

black swal·low·tail *n* a common North American swallowtail butterfly with black, blue, and white markings and two small red eyespots on the trailing edge of its hind wing. Latin name: *Papilio polyxenes*.

black swan *n* a large swan with black plumage and a red beak. Native to: Australia, New Zealand. Latin name: *Cygnus atratus*.

black-tailed deer *n* a mule deer with a tail that is black on top. Native to: western North America. Latin name: *Odocoileus hemionus columbianus*.

black tea *n* dark-colored tea leaves that have been fermented before being dried

black·thorn /blák thàwrn/ *n* **1.** a thorny black-stemmed bush with small blue-black berries (**sloes**). Native to: Europe, Asia. Latin name: *Prunus spinosa*. **2.** a walking stick made from the hard wood of the blackthorn

black tie *n* **1.** a black bow tie worn on formal occasions **2.** a formal style in men's dress that includes a black bow tie and a tuxedo —**black-tie** *adj*

black·top /blák tòp/ *n* **1.** ROAD-SURFACING MATERIAL a road-surfacing material bound together with a tarry substance such as asphalt **2.** ROAD MADE WITH BLACKTOP a road or other area with a blacktop surface ■ *vti* (**-topped, -top·ping, -tops**) COAT SURFACE WITH BLACKTOP to cover a road or other surface with blacktop

black vine wee·vil *n* INSECTS same as **vine weevil**

black vul·ture *n* **1.** a common vulture with black feathers and a bald black head. Native to: North and South America. Latin name: *Coragyps atratus*. **2.** a large dark vulture. Native to: southern Europe, western Asia. Latin name: *Aegypius monachus*.

black wal·nut *n* **1.** INDUST N AMERICAN WALNUT WOOD the hard black wood of a North American walnut tree. Use: veneers, cabinets. **2.** EDIBLE NUT the hard-shelled nut of a North American walnut tree **3.** N AMERICAN WALNUT TREE a walnut tree that yields hard black wood and bears black edible walnuts. Native to: North America. Latin name: *Juglans nigra*.

black·wa·ter fe·ver /blák wàwtər-/ *n* a serious condition, developing from malaria, that causes a rapid and massive loss of red blood cells and turns the urine dark red or blackish

Black·well /blák wèl, -wəl/, **Antoinette Louisa** (1825–1921) US minister and feminist. She was the first woman formally ordained as a minister of a Protestant church in the United States (1853), and wrote about women's rights.

> "Conventionality has indeed curtailed feminine force by hindering healthful and varied activity."
> [Antoinette Louisa Blackwell, *The Sexes Throughout Nature*; 1875]

Black·well, Elizabeth (1821–1910) British-born US physician. The first woman to earn a medical degree in the United States (1849), she founded a women's medical college in New York (1868) and later practiced in England. Emily Blackwell was her sister.

Black·well, Emily (1826–1910) British-born US physician. She was a pioneering woman physician who with her sister Elizabeth Blackwell developed the New York Infirmary for Women and Children (1853). She was dean of its medical school (1869–99).

black widow

black wid·ow *n* a highly poisonous spider, the female of which has a black body with an hourglass-shaped red marking on the abdomen. Native to: temperate North America and East Asia. Latin name: *Latrodectus mactans*. [< the female's habit of eating her mate]

blad·der /bláddər/ *n* **1.** BODILY SAC FOR LIQUID OR GAS an organ or other body part for storing a liquid or gas, especially the sac that stores urine (**urinary bladder**) or the sac that stores bile (**gallbladder**) **2.** INFLATABLE INNER BAG an inflatable part of something, especially a football, that resembles a bag **3.** BOT SAC IN PLANT a sac found in plants such as bladder wrack that stores air to help the plant to float or, as in bladderwort, traps insects **4.** MED FLUID-FILLED BLISTER a blister or small sac filled with fluid [Old English *blædre, blæddre* < Indo-European] —**blad·der·y** *adj*

blad·der cam·pi·on *n* a wild plant with a swollen calyx. Flowers: white. Native to: Europe. Latin name: *Silene vulgaris*.

blad·der fern *n* a small delicate fern that grows in rocks and walls and has a bulbous seed pod. Latin name: *Cystoperis fragilis*.

blad·der kelp *n* a brown alga with inflated bladders from which streamers that resemble leaves are suspended

blad·der·nose /bláddər nōz/ *n* MARINE BIOL same as **hooded seal**

blad·der·nut /bláddər nùt/ *n* **1.** a small tree or bush with clusters of small white flowers and bulbous seed pods. Genus: *Staphylea*. **2.** the seed pod of a bladdernut tree or bush

blad·der worm *n* the larva of a tapeworm, shaped like a sac and armed with six hooks. Class: Cestoda.

blad·der·wort /bláddər wùrt, -wàwrt/ *n* a water plant with floating leaves bearing small bladders that are used to trap insects. Genus: *Utricularia*.

blad·der wrack *n* a brown seaweed that has bulbous air bladders on its fronds that allow them to float. It grows between the high and low water line. Latin name: *Fucus vesiculosus*.

blade /blayd/ *n* **1.** CUTTING PART the flat sharp-edged cutting part of a tool or weapon **2.** LONG THIN FLAT PART a long thin flat part of some tools or machines, e.g., of a propeller **3.** THIN LEAF a long thin leaf, especially of grass **4.** FLAT STRIKING PART the flat striking part of something such as an oar or a golf club **5.** same as **razor blade 6.** PART OF ICE SKATE the metal part of an ice skate that glides on the ice **7.** PHON PART OF TONGUE the flat upper part of the tongue just behind the tip **8.** ARCHAEOL STONE FRAGMENT a parallel-sided stone flake that is at least twice as long as it is wide **9.** ARMS SWORD a sword (*literary*) **10.** DASHING MAN an energetic fun-loving man (*dated informal*) ■ **blades** *npl* ROLLER-SKATING IN-LINE ROLLER SKATES in-line roller skates (*informal*) ■ *vi* (**blad·ed, blad·ing, blades**) SKATE ON IN-LINE ROLLER SKATES to skate on in-line roller skates (*informal*) [Old English *blæd* < Germanic] —**blad·ed** *adj*

blad·ing /bláyding/ *n* the activity of skating on in-line roller skates (*informal*)

blag /blag/ (**blagged, blag·ging, blags**) *vt UK* to obtain something by deceit, scrounging, or cajoling (*slang*) ○ *He blagged his way into the party.* [Late 19C. Origin ?]

blah /blaa/ *n* NONSENSE talk or writing that is inane or boring (*informal*) ■ **blahs** *npl* MALAISE a condition of feeling bored, restless, and listless ○ *She's got the blahs today.* ■ *vi* (**blahed, blahing, blahs**) TALK NONSENSE to talk in a meaningless way (*informal; often repeated for emphasis*) ■ *adj* DULL dull and uninteresting or uninterested (*informal*) ○ *feeling really blah today* [Early 20C. An imitation of vacuous talk]

Blaine /blayn/ city in southeastern Minnesota. It is a northern suburb of St. Paul, and lies northeast of Minneapolis. Population: 48,535 (2002 estimate).

Blaine, James G. (1830–93) US politician. Speaker of the House of Representatives (1869–75) and secretary of state (1881, 1889–92), he was a presidential candidate (1884). Full name **Blaine, James Gillespie**

Blair /bler/, **Tony** (*b.* 1953) British prime minister. A member of Parliament from 1983, he was elected Labor Party leader in 1994 and became prime minister in 1997. He was re-elected in 2001. Full name **Blair, Anthony Charles Lynton**. See table at **prime minister**. See illustration on next page

> "My vision for the 21st century is of a popular politics reconciling themes which in the past have wrongly been viewed as antagonistic—patriotism and inter-

Popperfoto
Tony Blair

nationalism; rights and responsibilities; the promotion of enterprise and the attack on poverty and discrimination."
[Tony Blair, *Lecture to the Fabian Society, London*; 1998]

Blair·ism /blér ìzzəm/ *n UK* the political policies and style of government of Tony Blair, typified by moderate and gradual social reform, financial prudence, and tight control over policy presentation —**Blair·ite** *n, adj*

Blake /blayk/, **Edward** (1833–1912) Canadian politician. He was the premier of Ontario (1871–72) and leader of the Liberal Party (1880–87).

"The history of the diplomatic service of England, as far as Canada is concerned, has been a history of error, wrong, and concession."
[Edward Blake, *Speech to the Canadian Parliament*; 1882]

Blake, Eubie (1883–1983) US musician. He was a composer of shows including the revue *Shuffle Along* (1921). Born **Blake, James Herbert**

"Down South where I come from you don't go around hitting too many white keys."
[Attributed to Eubie Blake]

Blake, Peter (*b.* 1932) British painter. An important figure in British Pop Art, he designed the album cover for the Beatles' *Sergeant Pepper's Lonely Hearts Club Band* (1967). His work is often described as deliberately naive and is influenced by folk art and popular culture. Full name **Blake, Peter Thomas**

Blake, Robert (1599–1657) English admiral. He blockaded Lisbon and destroyed Prince Rupert's squadron (1650). In 1657 he destroyed the Spanish treasure fleet off Tenerife.

Blake, William (1757–1827) British poet, painter, and engraver. He wrote *Songs of Innocence* (1789), *The Marriage of Heaven and Hell* (1790–93), and *Jerusalem* (1804–20), illustrating his poetry with highly original engravings and watercolors. He championed mystical wisdom and the unfettered imagination in the face of 18th-century rationalism. See Cultural note at **experience** —**Blake·i·an** *adj*

"I care not whether a Man is Good or Evil; all that I care / Is whether he is a Wise Man or a Fool. Go! put off Holiness, / And put on Intellect."
[William Blake, *Jerusalem*; 1804–20]

Bla·key /bláykee/, **Art** (1919–90) US jazz drummer and bandleader. His innovations as a drummer led to the development of bebop and hard bop. His band, the Jazz Messengers (1954), showcased young musicians. Full name **Blakey, Arthur**

blame /blaym/ *vt* (**blamed, blam·ing, blames**) **1. CONSIDER SOMEBODY RESPONSIBLE** to consider somebody to be responsible for something wrong or unfortunate that has happened ○ *She blames me for the failure of the company.* **2. CRITICIZE SOMEBODY** to find fault with somebody (*used in negative statements and questions*) ○ *I don't blame you for wanting to know what happened.* ■ *n* **RESPONSIBILITY** responsibility for something wrong or unfortunate that has happened ○ *It's still not clear where the blame lies.* ○ *I'm not taking the blame for your mistakes.* [12C. Via Old French *bla(s)mer* < Latin *blastemare*, alteration of *blasphemare* "revile" (see BLASPHEME)] —**blam·a·ble** *adj* —**blame·ful** *adj* —**blame·wor·thi·ness** *n* —**blame·wor·thy** *adj* ◇ **be to blame** to be responsible for something wrong or unfortunate that has happened ○ *Who's to blame for the mix-up?*

blame cul·ture *n* a set of attitudes, e.g., within a business organization, that is characterized by an unwillingness to take risks or accept responsibility for mistakes because of a fear of criticism or prosecution

blame·less /bláymləss/ *adj* **1.** not responsible for something wrong or unfortunate that has happened ○ *No one involved is entirely blameless.* **2.** doing nothing bad or wrong ○ *a blameless life* —**blame·less·ly** *adv* —**blame·less·ness** *n*

Blanc, Mont ♦ **Mont Blanc**

blanch /blanch/ (**blanched, blanch·ing, blanch·es**), **blench** /blench/ (**blenched, blench·ing, blench·es**) *v* **1.** *vt* **PUT FOOD BRIEFLY IN BOILING WATER** to put food in boiling water for a few seconds in order to loosen the skin or to kill enzymes **2.** *vi* **TURN PALE** to become pale suddenly ○ *He blanched at the mention of her name.* **3.** *vt* **WHITEN VEGETABLES BY GROWING IN DARK** to grow vegetables, especially celery and endive, in dark conditions in order to whiten the stems and improve their flavor **4.** *vti* **LOSE OR REMOVE COLOR FROM SOMETHING** to lose color, or cause something to lose color [14C. < French *blanchir* "whiten" < *blanche*, feminine of *blanc* "white"] —**blanch·er** *n*

blanc·mange /blə maánj, -maánzh/ *n* a cold dessert similar to pudding made with milk, sugar, flavorings, and cornstarch [14C. < Old French *blanc mangier* < *blanc* "white" + *mangier* "food" < *mangier* "eat" (see MANGER)]

bland /bland/ *adj* **1. INSIPID** lacking flavor, character, or interest ○ *a bland diet* **2. FREE OF STRESS** free from anything annoying or upsetting **3. UNEMOTIONAL** without emotion [Mid-17C. < Latin *blandus* "smooth, flattering"] —**bland·ly** *adv* —**bland·ness** *n*

blan·dish /blándish/ (**-dished, -dish·ing, -dish·es**) *vti* to persuade somebody by flattery (*archaic*) [14C. < Old French *blandiss-* (see BLANDISHMENT)] —**blan·dish·er** *n*

blan·dish·ment /blándishmənt/ *n* **1.** the use of flattery and enticements to persuade somebody to do something **2.** a piece of flattery intended to persuade somebody to do something (*formal*; *often used in the plural*) ○ *impervious to all blandishments* [Late 16C. < archaic *blandish* < Old French *blandiss-*, stem of *blandir* < Latin *blandus* "smooth, flattering"]

blank /blangk/ *adj* **1. NOT MARKED** not written on, drawn on, or printed on ○ *a blank page* **2. UNBROKEN** lacking any features or openings ○ *a sheer, blank rock wall* ○ *a blank corridor* ○ *not a cloud in the blank blue sky* **3. LACKING INTEREST, AWARENESS, OR UNDERSTANDING** having or showing no interest, awareness, or understanding ○ *a blank expression* **4. UNEVENTFUL OR UNPRODUCTIVE** characterized by lack of useful action or result ○ *It was one of those blank periods when nothing particular was happening.* **5. TOTAL** complete or absolute ○ *a blank refusal to cooperate* ■ *n* **1. EMPTINESS OF MIND** a complete absence of awareness or memory ○ *I remember hearing a loud noise: the rest is a blank.* **2. VOID** a period about which nothing is known ○ *There are a lot of blanks in her account of the event.* **3. SPACE IN WHICH TO WRITE** a space left empty in which to write, in a form or document ○ *Fill in the blanks.* **4. MARK INDICATING MISSING WORD** a mark (–) in writing or print indicating that a word or letter is missing ○ *a word meaning solitary, spelled a l – – e* **5. DOCUMENT WITH BLANK SPACES** a form or document with spaces for writing in **6.** *also* **blank cart·ridge** ARMS = **blank cartridge 7.** MANUF **PIECE FROM WHICH ARTICLE IS MADE** a piece of metal or other material that will be shaped to produce a finished item **8. BULL'S EYE** the bull's eye of a target ■ *v* (**blanked, blank·ing, blanks**) **1.** *vt* **OBLITERATE SOMETHING** to delete or black something out ○ *The names had been blanked.* **2.** *vi* **FORGET TEMPORARILY** to forget something suddenly and temporarily ○ *I tried to recall their names, but I just blanked.* **3.** *vt* **PREVENT SOMEBODY FROM SCORING** to prevent an opponent from making any score [13C. < French *blanc* "white"] —**blank·ly** *adv* —**blank·ness** *n* ◇ **draw a blank** to be unsuccessful in a search or inquiry ◇ **fire** *or* **shoot blanks** to be unable to impregnate a woman because of a low sperm count (*slang*; *sometimes considered offensive*) ◇ **go blank** to be unable to think of or remember something ○ *I tried to remember her name but my mind went blank.*

blank out *v* **1.** *vt* **COVER SOMETHING** to cover something completely so that it cannot be seen or read **2.** *vt* **ERASE SOMETHING FROM MIND** to refuse to remember or acknowledge a fact, event, or memory **3.** *vi* **LOSE AWARENESS** to become dazed or unconscious **4.** *vi* **FADE AWAY** to diminish in intensity or loudness

blank car·tridge *n* a gun cartridge that contains explosive but no bullet

blank check *n* **1.** a signed check that has not yet had the amount payable filled in **2.** complete freedom to act or decide (*informal*) ○ *They gave us a blank check in our negotiations.*

blank en·dorse·ment *n* an endorsement on a bill of exchange that does not name a payee and so may benefit the bearer

blan·ket /blángkət/ *n* **1. CLOTH BED COVERING** a piece of cloth used especially as a cover for a bed **2. COVERING LAYER** a layer of something covering an area completely **3.** PHYS **LAYER AROUND CORE OF NUCLEAR REACTOR** in a nuclear reactor, a layer of material surrounding the radioactive core used to reflect neutrons or to create more fissile material **4.** PRINTING **SHEET TRANSFERRING IMAGE** a sheet that is wrapped round the cylinder of a printing press which transfers the impression in ink to the surface being printed on ■ *adj* **APPLYING GENERALLY** applying to all areas or situations ○ *We have blanket approval for our proposals.* ■ *vt* (**-ket·ed, -ket·ing, -kets**) **1. COVER SOMETHING WITH LAYER** to cover something with a thick layer ○ *The streets were blanketed with snow.* **2. APPLY UNIFORMLY** to apply all over something in a uniform manner ○ *The county was blanketed with leaflets.* **3.** SAILING **PREVENT WIND REACHING SAILS OF SHIP** to take the wind from the sails of another boat by sailing to windward of it [14C. < Old N French *blanquet*, Old French *blanchet* < *blanc* "white"]

blan·ket bond *n* an insurance contract providing a financial institution with cover against losses resulting from employee dishonesty or theft

blan·ket stitch *n* looped stitching with wide gaps between stitches, used to reinforce the edge of a piece of fabric

blank verse *n* unrhymed poetry that has a regular rhythm and line length, especially iambic pentameter

blan·quette /blaaN két/ *n* a dish consisting of white meat such as veal cooked in a white sauce ○ *blanquette of veal* [Mid-18C. < French < Old N French *blanquet* (see BLANKET)]

Blan·tyre-Lim·be /blàn tīr lím bày/ largest city in Malawi and the administrative headquarters of the Southern Region. Population: 2,000,000 (1998).

blare /bler/ (**blared, blar·ing, blares**) *v* **1.** *vti* to make a loud harsh noise ○ *speakers blaring rock music* **2.** *vt* to proclaim something loudly or prominently ○ *"Heiress disappears," the headlines blared.* [14C. Probably an imitation of the sound] —**blare** *n*

blar·ney /blaárnee/ (*informal*) *n* **1. PERSUASIVE FLATTERING TALK** flattering talk intended to persuade somebody **2. NONSENSE** unintelligent or insincere talk ■ *vti* (**-neyed, -ney·ing, -neys**) **WHEEDLE** to persuade somebody with flattery [Late 18C. After the BLARNEY STONE]

Blar·ney /blaárnee/ village in County Cork, southern Republic of Ireland. Population: 2,146 (2002).

Blar·ney Stone *n* a stone in Blarney Castle, near Cork in Ireland, that is said to give the power of persuasive talk to people who kiss it

bla·sé /blaa záy/ *adj* not impressed or worried by something, usually because of having experienced it before [Early 19C. < French, "satiated"]

blas·pheme /blass féem, bláss féem/ (**-phemed, -phem·ing, -phemes**) *v* **1.** *vi* to swear in a way that insults religion **2.** *vti* to treat God or sacred things disrespectfully through words or action [14C. Via French < ecclesiastical Latin *blasphemare* "revile" < Greek *blasphēmein* < *blasphēmos* "evil-speaking"] —**blas·phem·er** /blass féemər, blásfəmər/ *n*

blas·phe·mous /blásfəməss/ *adj* expressing or involving disrespect for God or sacred things —**blas·phe·mous·ly** *adv* —**blas·phe·mous·ness** *n*

blas·phe·my /blásfəmee/ (*plural* **-mies**) *n* **1.** disrespect for God or sacred things **2.** something done or said that shows disrespect for God or sacred things

blast /blast/ *n* **1. EXPLOSION** an explosion, or a sudden rush of air caused by an explosion ○ *Several homes were destroyed by the blast.* **2. STRONG AIR OR GAS CURRENT** a sudden strong current of air or wind **3. LOUD EXPLOSIVE SOUND** the sound made by an explosion ○ *We were almost deafened by the blasts.* **4. INSTRUMENT'S LOUD SOUND** a short loud sound made on an instrument, whistle, or car horn **5. OUTBURST** a loud or angry outburst ○ *a blast of criticism* **6. GOOD TIME** an enjoyable occasion of fun and laughter (*slang*) ○ *The party was a real blast!* ■ *v* (**blast·ed, blast·ing, blasts**) **1.** *vt* **BLOW SOMETHING UP WITH EXPLOSIVES** to destroy or break open something using explosives ○ *Rescuers blasted a hole in the rock.* **2.** *vt* **HIT SOMETHING HARD** to strike something with great force (*informal*) ○ *She blasted the ball into the net.* **3.** *vti* **MAKE LOUD NOISE** to come out with great force or volume, or make something do this (*informal*) **4.** *vt* **GIVE SOMEBODY OR SOMETHING STRONG CRITICISM** to criticize somebody or something severely (*informal*) [Old English *blǣst* < Indo-European] —**blast·er** *n* ◇ **(at) full blast** at maximum volume or speed

SYNONYMS See ***criticize***.

blast away *vi* to fire a gun repeatedly (*informal*)

blast off *vti* to launch a rocket, spacecraft, or astronaut into space, or be launched into space

-blast *suffix* embryonic cell ○ *melanoblast* [< Greek *blastos* "bud, germ, sprout"] —**-blastic** *suffix*

blast·ed /blástəd/ *adj, adv* used to express mild annoyance (*informal*) ○ *Then the blasted handle broke.* ■ *adj* affected by a withering disease or a similar destructive force (*literary*) ○ *a blasted heath*

blas·te·ma /bla steemə/ (*plural* **-mas** or **-ma·ta** /-mətə/) *n* a group of unspecialized animal cells from which an organ or new tissue develops [Mid-19C. < Greek *blastēma* "sprout"] —**blas·te·mal** *adj* —**blas·te·mat·ic** /blàstə máttik/ *adj* —**blas·te·mic** *adj*

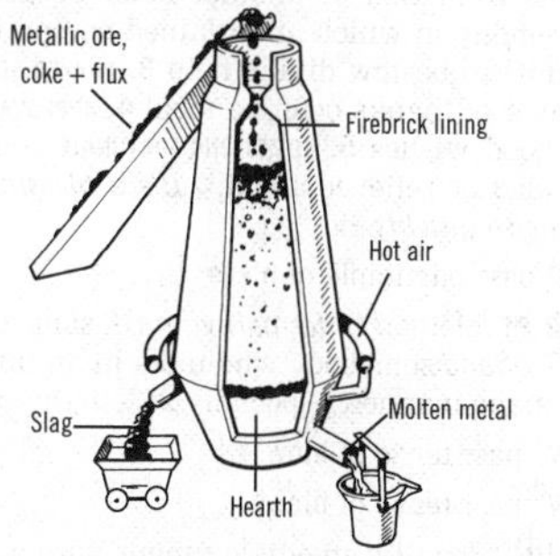

blast furnace

blast fur·nace *n* a vertical shaft furnace for smelting metals. Fuel, ores, and slag-forming rock are loaded from above, and air is blown in from the bottom to raise the temperature. The molten metal is tapped periodically from the base.

blast·ing pow·der *n* a form of gunpowder containing sodium nitrate instead of potassium nitrate that is used in blasting rock and ores

blast in·jec·tion *n UK* a method of fuel injection that uses air pressure to atomize the fuel as it enters the cylinder of an internal-combustion engine

blasto- *prefix* bud, germ ○ *blastomycosis* [< Greek *blastos* "bud, germ, sprout"]

blas·to·coel /blástə seel/, **blas·to·coele** *n* the cavity that forms within the mass of cells (**blastula**) in a developing embryo and fills with fluid [Late 19C. < BLASTO- + Greek *koilos* "hollow"] —**blas·to·coe·lic** /blàstə séelik/ *adj*

blas·to·cyst /blástə sìst/ *n* a mammalian embryo at the stage when it is implanted in the wall of the womb —**blas·to·cys·tic** /blàstə sístik/ *adj*

blas·to·derm /blástə dùrm/ *n* a layer of cells arising from the repeated division of a fertilized mammalian egg that develops into an embryo [Mid-19C. < BLASTO- + Greek *derma* "skin"] —**blas·to·der·mat·ic** /blàstədər máttik/ *adj* —**blas·to·der·mic** /blàstə dúrmik/ *adj*

blast·o·disk /blástō dìsk/, **blast·o·disc** *n* the disk-shaped part on the upper surface of the yolk of a fertilized egg where the embryo begins to form, as in reptiles, birds, and some fish

blast·off /blást àwf, -òf/ *n* the launch of a rocket, spacecraft, or missile

blas·to·gen·e·sis /blàstə jénnəssiss/ *n* asexual reproduction by budding —**blas·to·ge·net·ic** /blàstə jə néttik/ *adj* —**blas·to·gen·ic** *adj*

blas·to·mere /blástə meer/ *n* a cell of an animal embryo (**blastula**) formed by the division of a fertilized egg cell

blas·to·my·co·sis /blàstō mī kṓssiss/ *n* a fungal infection causing lesions on the lungs, skin, or mucous membranes

blas·to·pore /blástə pàwr/ *n* an opening in a young embryo that develops into the anus in some mammals —**blas·to·por·al** /blàstə páwrəl/ *adj* —**blas·to·por·ic** *adj*

blas·to·sphere /blástə sfeer/ *n* BIOL same as **blastula**

blas·to·spore /blástə spàwr/ *n* a fungal spore produced by budding

blas·tu·la /bláschələ/ (*plural* **-las** or **-lae** /-lee/) *n* an embryo at an early stage of development, consisting of a hollow ball of cells [Late 19C. < modern Latin < Greek *blastos* "bud, germ, sprout"] —**blas·tu·lar** *adj* —**blas·tu·la·tion** /blàschə láysh'n/ *n*

blat[1] /blat/ (*informal*) *v* (**blat·ted, blat·ting, blats**) **1.** *vi* to make a bleating sound **2.** *vti* same as **blab** *v* (sense 1) ■ *n* a bleating sound [Mid-19C. An imitation of the sound]

blat[2] /blat/, **blatt** *n* a popular newspaper (*slang*) [Mid-20C. < German *Blatt* "leaf, sheet (of paper)"]

bla·tant /bláyt'nt/ *adj* **1.** obtrusive and conspicuous in an offensive way, often intentionally ○ *blatant falsehoods* **2.** excessively or offensively noisy (*literary*) [Late 16C. Perhaps alteration of Scottish *blatand* "bleating," or < Latin *blatire* "to babble"] —**bla·tan·cy** *n* —**bla·tant·ly** *adv*

USAGE blatant or **flagrant**? Both words describe openly offensive behavior, but there is a difference. ***Blatant*** emphasizes the brazen conspicuousness of the offense, as in *a blatant breach of good faith in the negotiations*, whereas ***flagrant*** emphasizes the shocking seriousness or gravity that the offense has: *flagrant racism*. A ***blatant*** lie is one so bare-faced that no one can miss it, whereas ***flagrant*** disregard for human life is unforgivably shameless or outrageous. Avoid using ***blatant*** to mean merely "obvious": *There seems to be a blatant contradiction....* In sentences like this, substitute *obvious, clear,* or *glaring* for ***blatant***.

blath·er /bláthər/ (**-ered, -er·ing, -ers**) *vi* to talk in an unintelligent or inane manner, especially at length (*informal*) [15C. < Old Norse *blaðra* "to chatter, babble"] —**blath·er** *n* —**blath·er·er** *n*

blath·er·skite /bláthər skìt/, **bleth·er·skite** /bléthər-/ *n* (*dated informal*) **1.** somebody who enjoys silly or unimportant chat **2.** chat about silly or unimportant things [Mid-17C. < Scottish dialect *skate* "contemptible person"]

blatt *n* MEDIA another spelling of **blat**[2]

blax·ploi·ta·tion /blàk sploy táysh'n/ *n* depiction of Black people in movies or other media in a way that appeals to popular and often inaccurate or negative notions of their experiences and qualities (*informal*) [Late 20C. Blend of *Blacks* + EXPLOITATION]

blaze[1] /blayz/ *vi* (**blazed, blaz·ing, blaz·es**) **1. BURN BRIGHTLY** to burn brightly and fiercely **2. SHINE** to shine or appear to shine brightly **3. EXPERIENCE STRONG EMOTION** to be affected by a strong emotion (*informal*) ○ *blazing with indignation* **4. FIRE GUN** to fire a gun repeatedly ■ *n* **1. BRIGHT FIRE** a brightly or intensely burning fire, or a large fire **2. CONSPICUOUS DISPLAY** a display that attracts attention ○ *a blaze of publicity* ■ **blaz·es** *npl* **ADDING EMPHASIS** used to add emphasis (*informal*) ○ *What in blazes did you do that for?* ○ *run like blazes* [Old English *blæse* "torch, bright flame" < Germanic]

SYNONYMS See ***fire***.

blaze[2] /blayz/ *n* **1. WHITE MARK ON ANIMAL'S FACE** a white streak on the face of a horse or other animal **2. MARK SHOWING WAY** a mark indicating a path, originally a cut made in a tree trunk ■ *vt* (**blazed, blaz·ing, blaz·es**) **1. MARK PATH** to indicate a new path by making marks **2. DO SOMETHING NEW** to lead the way in doing something new ○ *He blazed the way to the understanding of DNA's structure.* [Mid-17C. Perhaps < Old Norse *blesi*, Middle High German *blasse*, or Middle Low German *bles* "white mark"]

blaze[3] /blayz/ (**blazed, blaz·ing, blaz·es**) *vt* to spread news or information loudly and clearly ○ *blazed the scandal all over the front page* [14C. < Middle Dutch *blāzen* "swell" < Indo-European]

blaz·er /bláyzər/ *n* a sports jacket for men or women, sometimes in a bright color or pattern [Mid-17C. < the typically bright color]

blaz·ing /bláyzing/ *adj* **1. INTENSE** feeling or showing intense emotions ○ *a blazing row* **2. HOT** very hot ○ *sitting in the blazing sun* ■ *adv* **EXTREMELY** extremely or intensely ○ *blazing hot* —**blaz·ing·ly** *adv*

blaz·ing star *n* **1. WHITE-FLOWERED PLANT** a plant of the lily family. Flowers: white, with long heads. Native to: North America. Latin name: *Chamaelirium luteum*. **2. WHITE- OR PURPLE-FLOWERED PLANT** a plant of the composite family. Flowers: long heads of small white or purplish flowers. Native to: North America. Genus: *Liatris*. **3. PLANT WITH CLINGING LEAVES** a plant with rough leaves that may stick to clothing. Flowers: yellow, orange, or red. Native to: North America. Genus: *Mentzelia*.

bla·zon /bláyz'n/ *vt* (**-zoned, -zon·ing, -zons**) **1. PROCLAIM SOMETHING WIDELY** to announce something widely or ostentatiously **2.** HERALDRY **DEPICT COAT OF ARMS** to create or describe a coat of arms using the traditional symbols ■ *n* HERALDRY **COAT OF ARMS** a coat of arms, or a technical description of one [13C. < French *blason* "shield"] —**bla·zon·er** *n* —**bla·zon·ment** *n*

bla·zon·ry /bláyz'nree/ *n* **1.** HERALDRY **MAKING OR EXPLAINING COATS OF ARMS** the art of creating or explaining coats of arms **2.** HERALDRY **COATS OF ARMS** coats of arms individually or collectively **3. BRILLIANT DISPLAY** a bright or showy display (*literary*)

bleach /bleech/ *n* **1. COLOR-REMOVING SUBSTANCE** a chemical that removes or whitens color or staining and also cleans and disinfects **2. APPLICATION OF BLEACH** an act of using bleach on something ■ *v* (**bleached, bleach·ing, bleach·es**) **1.** *vt* **USE BLEACH ON SOMETHING** to clean or whiten something using bleach **2.** *vti* **LIGHTEN IN COLOR** to make something whiter or lighter, or become lighter or whiter [Old English *blǣcan* "make white" < *blǣc* "pale, shining" < Germanic] —**bleach·er** *n*

bleach·ers /bleechərz/ *npl* (*sometimes used in the singular*) **1.** seats in an uncovered area of a sports stadium **2.** retractable tiered benches for spectators in an indoor sports arena [Late 19C. < the sun's bleaching of the exposed benches]

bleach·ing pow·der *n* a white powder obtained from calcium hydroxide and chlorine. Use: disinfectant, bleaching agent. Formula: CaCl(OCl).

bleak /bleek/ *adj* **1. UNWELCOMING** providing little comfort or shelter ○ *a cabin on a bleak hilltop* **2. DISCOURAGING** without hope or expectation of success or improvement ○ *The company's future looks bleak.* **3. COLD AND CLOUDY** unpleasantly cold, dull, and windy ○ *bleak winter days* [14C. < Old Norse *bleikr* "pale, white, shining" < Germanic] —**bleak·ly** *adv* —**bleak·ness** *n*

CULTURAL NOTE ***Bleak House***, a novel (1852–53) by British writer Charles Dickens. Among the strands of the complex plot are the interminable court case of Jarndyce and Jarndyce; the guilty secret of Lady Dedlock and the tragic consequences of her discovery that her illegitimate daughter, Esther Summerson, is still alive; and Esther's relationship with her kindly and devoted guardian John Jarndyce. The novel combines the excitement of a murder mystery with a bitter satire of the legal system.

blear /bleer/ (**bleared, blear·ing, blears**) *vt* to make eyes misty or eyesight dim, e.g., with tears (*archaic or literary; usually passive*) [14C. Origin ?]

blear·y /bleeree/ (**-i·er, -i·est**) *adj* **1.** not seeing clearly owing to mistiness or blurring, especially that associated with sleepiness ○ *a bleary gaze* **2.** obscured and not easy to see —**blear·i·ly** *adv* —**blear·i·ness** *n*

blear·y-eyed *adj* seeing unclearly, especially because of sleepiness or drunkenness

bleat /bleet/ (**bleat·ed, bleat·ing, bleats**) *vi* **1.** to make the wavering cry of a sheep, goat, or calf **2.** to complain about something in an irritating way (*informal*) [Old English *blǣtan* < Germanic, an imitation of the sound] —**bleat** *n* —**bleat·er** *n*

bleb /bleb/ *n* **1.** a small blister on the skin **2.** a small bubble, e.g., in glass [Early 17C. Alteration of BLOB] —**bleb·by** *adj*

bleed /bleed/ *v* (**bled** /bled/, **bled, bleed·ing, bleeds**) **1.** *vi* LOSE BLOOD to lose blood from the body, through a wound or because of illness ○ *The wound was bleeding heavily.* **2.** *vt* TAKE BLOOD FROM PERSON OR ANIMAL to take blood from a person or animal, especially in order to treat a disease **3.** *vi* FEEL SORROW to feel sadness or pity ○ *My heart bleeds for her in her loss.* **4.** *vi* RELEASE COLOR to release color when wet or being washed (*refers to fabrics*) **5.** *vi* EXUDE SAP to exude sap from a wound (*refers to plants*) **6.** *vt* TAKE MONEY OR RESOURCES FROM SOMEBODY to use up large amounts of money or resources from a person or organization, especially dishonestly (*informal*) **7.** *vt* DRAW LIQUID OR GAS FROM SOMETHING to draw liquid or gas out of a container or pressurized system ○ *bleed a radiator* **8.** *vti* PRINTING OVERRUN PAGE to print something, or be printed, so that part of it is cut off by the edge of the page **9.** *vti* PRINTING MAKE COLORS OF ILLUSTRATION RUN to print something, or be printed, so that colors run into other colors or over the edge of an illustration ■ *n* **1.** INSTANCE OF BLEEDING an instance of losing blood **2.** PRINTING SOMETHING THAT OVERRUNS PRINTED PAGE an illustration or piece of text printed in such a way that part of it is cut off the page [Old English *blēdan* < Germanic]

bleed·er /bleedər/ *n* a blood vessel that bleeds during surgery and requires clamping or other measures to stop it

bleed·ing /bleeding/ *n* loss of blood from the body as a result of illness or injury ■ *adj, adv UK* used for emphasis, as a milder form of "bloody" (*slang*)

bleed·ing edge *adj* relating to innovative technology that has yet to be thoroughly tested for feasibility (*informal*) [Suggested by LEADING EDGE and the risk involved in innovation]

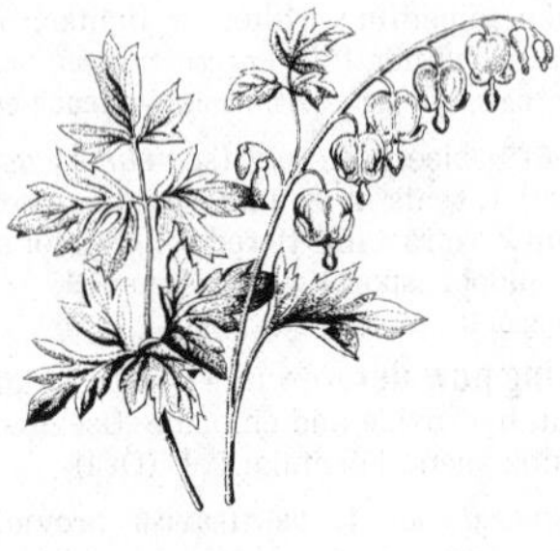

bleeding heart

bleed·ing heart *n* **1.** a garden plant with arching stems. Flowers: pink, red, white, heart-shaped. Genus: *Dicentra.* **2.** somebody regarded as naively kind or sympathetic, especially toward left-wing or liberal causes

bleed·ing-heart lib·er·al *n* a political liberal who is thought too sympathetic or sentimental (*informal; sometimes offensive*)

bleed valve *n* a valve that can be opened to let liquid or gas out of a tank or pressurized system, often used for safety purposes to release small amounts of excess fluid or gas

bleep /bleep/ *n* ELECTRONIC SOUND a short high-pitched electronic noise, intended as a signal and repeated intermittently ■ *v* (**bleeped, bleep·ing, bleeps**) **1.** *vt* BROADCAST REMOVE OFFENSIVE LANGUAGE to remove offensive material from a broadcast, and replace it with a short high-pitched electronic sound ○ *They bleeped most of his comments.* **2.** *vi* MAKE ELECTRONIC SOUND to make a short high-pitched electronic noise [Mid-20C. An imitation of the sound]

bleep out *vt UK* same as **bleep** *v* (sense 1)

bleep·er /bleepər/ *n UK* TELECOM same as **pager**

blem·ish /blémmish/ *n* **1.** SPOILING MARK OR FLAW a mark or imperfection that spoils the appearance of something ○ *a cream that hides skin blemishes* **2.** SPOILING FAULT something that spoils somebody's reputation or good record ■ *vt* (**-ished, -ish·ing, -ish·es**) MAR to spoil the appearance or reputation of something [14C. < Old French *ble(s)miss-* "make pale, injure"] —**blem·ish·er** *n*

SYNONYMS See *flaw*[1].

blench[1] /blench/ (**blenched, blench·ing, blench·es**) *vi* to move back or away in fear [Old English *blencan* "deceive, cheat," origin ?] —**blench·er** *n*

blench[2] /blench/ *vi* COOK, GARDENING same as **blanch**

blend /blend/ *v* (**blend·ed, blend·ing, blends**) **1.** *vti* MIX INGREDIENTS to mix a substance with another substance so that the two do not readily separate ○ *blend the butter and sugar together* **2.** *vt* CREATE PRODUCT BY MIXING DIFFERENT TYPES to create a food or beverage by mixing different types of the same substance (*often passive*) ○ *blended tea* **3.** *vti* INTERMINGLE to mix with other people or things without being conspicuous, or mix something in this way ○ *blend fact and fiction* **4.** *vti* MAKE PLEASING COMBINATION to combine things or qualities to create a pleasing effect, or be combined in this way ○ *instruments blending harmoniously* **5.** *vi* SHADE IMPERCEPTIBLY INTO EACH OTHER to shade from one color to another without obvious transitions or boundaries ■ *n* **1.** MIXTURE a mixture or combination ○ *an interesting blend of traditional styles and modern materials* **2.** FOOD OR DRINK MIXTURE a food or beverage created by mixing different types of the same substance ○ *an expensive coffee blend* **3.** WORD MADE BY JOINING TWO WORDS a new word made by joining parts of other words, as in "telex," formed from "teleprinter" and "exchange" [14C. Probably < Old Norse *blend-* "to mix"]

SYNONYMS See *mixture.*

blend in *vi* **1.** to have personal qualities that suit a situation well ○ *He's a likable boy who blends in well.* **2.** to be difficult to see or distinguish from similar things around

blende /blend/ *n* **1.** MINERALS same as **sphalerite** **2.** a metallic sulfide ore [Late 17C. < German *blenden* "deceive"]

blend·ed whis·key *n* whiskey made by blending two or more whiskeys or whiskey and neutral spirits

blend·er /bléndər/ *n* **1.** an electrical kitchen appliance used to liquidize and blend foods **2.** somebody or something that blends things, especially a person or company that blends foods or drinks

Blen·heim /blénnəm/ **1.** site of the Battle of Blenheim in 1704, where an English army, led by the 1st Duke of Marlborough, defeated French and Bavarian troops in the War of the Spanish Succession. It is near the present-day village of Blindheim, southwestern Germany. **2.** wine-producing borough in the Wairau Valley in the South Island of New Zealand. Population: 26,550 (2001).

blen·ny /blénnee/ (*plural* **-nies** or *same*) *n* a small scaleless long-bodied fish found in rocky coastal areas and coral reefs. Family: Blenniidae. [Mid-18C. < Latin *blennius* < Greek *blennos* "slime," from the fish's covering of mucus]

bleph·a·ri·tis /blèffə rítiss/ *n* inflammation of one or both eyelids [Mid-19C. < Greek *blepharon* "eyelid"]

Blé·ri·ot /bláyree ō/, **Louis** (1872–1936) French aviator. He was the first person to fly across the English Channel (1909).

bles·bok /bléss bòk/ (*plural* **-boks** or *same*) *n* a reddish brown antelope that has a white streak on its nose. Native to: southern Africa. Latin name: *Damaliscus dorcas.* [Early 19C. < Afrikaans < Dutch *bles* "white facial streak" + *bok* "buck"]

bless /bless/ (**blessed, blessed** or **blest** /blest/, **bless·ing, bless·es**) *vt* **1.** MAKE SOMEBODY OR SOMETHING HOLY to bestow holiness on somebody or something in a religious ceremony ○ *The bishop blessed the new chapel.* **2.** PROTECT SOMEBODY OR SOMETHING to watch over somebody or something protectively ○ *We prayed for God to bless our marriage.* **3.** WISH SOMEBODY OR SOMETHING WELL to declare approval and support for somebody or

blesbok

something ○ *The governor has blessed the new plan.* **4.** CONFER DESIRABLE QUALITY ON SOMEBODY to give somebody a desirable quality or talent (*usually passive*) ○ *blessed with brains as well as good looks* **5.** THANK SOMEBODY to express heartfelt thanks to somebody (*often expressing a wish*) ○ *Bless you for speaking up for my child!* [Old English *blētsian* < Germanic] —**bless·er** *n*

bless·ed /bléssəd/ *adj* **1.** HOLY made holy **2.** BEATIFIED declared holy by the pope, usually as the first stage toward being declared a saint **3.** BESTOWING JOY bringing happiness or good luck ○ *The rain has brought farmers blessed relief from the long drought.* ■ *adj, adv* USED FOR EMPHASIS used to add emphasis in an expression of annoyance (*informal*) ○ *She wouldn't say a blessed thing about it.* —**bless·ed·ly** *adv* —**bless·ed·ness** *n*

Bless·ed Sac·ra·ment *n* in various Christian churches, the bread and wine that has been blessed for use in Communion

Bless·ed Vir·gin Mary, Bless·ed Vir·gin *n* a title for Mary, the mother of Jesus Christ, used mainly in Catholic churches

bless·ing /bléssing/ *n* **1.** GOD'S HELP help believed to come from God or another deity **2.** RELIGIOUS ACT a ceremony in which an ordained person invokes or claims to bestow divine help **3.** PRAYER BEFORE MEAL a prayer of thanks before a meal **4.** APPROVAL approval or good wishes **5.** SOMETHING FORTUNATE something to be glad or relieved about ○ *It's a blessing that you came so quickly.*

blest past participle of **bless**

bleth·er /bléthər/ (*informal*) *vi, n UK* same as **blather** ■ *n Scotland* somebody who talks in an unintelligent or inane manner, especially at length

blew[1] past tense of **blow**[1]

blew[2] past tense of **blow**[3]

ble·wit /blóo it/ *n* an edible fungus with a brown cap and a bluish stem. Genus: *Lepista.* [Early 19C. Probably < variant of BLUE, from the color of its stem]

Bligh /blī/, **William** (1754–1817) British naval officer. Cast adrift in the Pacific by mutineers of the HMS *Bounty* (1789), he navigated nearly 4,000 miles in an open boat to reach Timor. He was promoted to rear admiral in 1811 and vice admiral in 1814.

blight /blīt/ *n* **1.** DESTRUCTIVE FORCE something that spoils or damages things severely **2.** RUINED STATE a severely spoiled or ruined state, especially of an urban area ○ *urban blight* **3.** PLANT DISEASE a plant disease, caused by bacteria, fungi, or viruses, in which symptoms range from brownish blotches on the foliage to withering of the entire plant without rotting **4.** *UK* AGRIC same as **potato blight** ■ *vt* (**blight·ed, blight·ing, blights**) **1.** RUIN SOMETHING to spoil or damage something severely ○ *a football career blighted by injury* **2.** PLANTS, BOT AFFECT PLANT WITH BLIGHT to cause a plant to wither without rotting [Mid-16C. Origin ?]

Bligh·ty /blītee/, **bligh·ty** *n UK* England or Great Britain (*slang dated humorous*) [Early 20C. < Hindi *bilāyatī* "foreign, European," originally used by British soldiers in India for "home"]

bli·mey /blīmee/ *interj UK* used to express amazement or shock (*informal*) ○ *Blimey, that's expensive!* [Late 19C. Alteration of *blind me!* or *blame me!*]

blimp[1] /blimp/ *n* a nonrigid airship that nowadays uses helium rather than hydrogen to remain buoyant [Early 20C. Origin ?]

blimp² /blimp/, **Colo·nel Blimp** *n UK* somebody who is stubborn, pompous, or unreasonably conservative (*humorous*) [Mid-20C. After a cartoon character invented by David Low (1891–1963)]

blin FOOD plural of **blini**

blind /blīnd/ *adj* **1.** UNABLE TO SEE unable to see, permanently or temporarily **2.** UNABLE TO RECOGNIZE unwilling or unable to understand something ○ *blind to the consequences* **3.** UNCONTROLLABLE so extreme and uncontrollable as to make somebody behave irrationally ○ *blind rage* ○ *blind fear* **4.** UNQUESTIONING not based on fact and usually total and unquestioning ○ *blind prejudice* **5.** UNAWARE lacking awareness ○ *a blind stupor* **6.** NOT GIVING CLEAR VIEW not providing a clear view and possibly dangerous ○ *a blind corner* **7.** HANDICRAFT MADE ON UNDERSIDE OF FABRIC hidden from sight on the underside of a fabric **8.** WITHOUT DOORS OR WINDOWS without doors, windows, or openings ○ *a blind wall* **9.** CLOSED AT ONE END closed off at one end ○ *a blind unused tunnel* **10.** DONE WITHOUT LOOKING done without looking or while unable to see ○ *blind taste tests* **11.** DONE UNPREPARED done without preparation or the relevant information ○ *a blind presentation* **12.** DESIGNED TO BE BIAS-FREE describes scientific experiments or similar evaluations in which information is withheld in order to obtain an unprejudiced result ○ *a blind trial* **13.** BOT WITHOUT GROWING POINT describes a plant in which growth stops because the growing point has been damaged, perhaps by pests, nutrient deficiency, waterlogging of the soil, or drought ■ *adv* **1.** WITHOUT PRIOR EXAMINATION OR PREPARATION without previously thinking about or preparing for something ○ *You shouldn't buy livestock blind.* **2.** AVIAT USING ONLY INSTRUMENTS using information from aircraft instruments, without being able to see ○ *flying blind* **3.** TOTALLY totally or utterly (*informal*) ○ *an unscrupulous lawyer who robbed his clients blind* ■ *vt* (**blind·ed, blind·ing, blinds**) **1.** MAKE SOMEBODY PERMANENTLY BLIND to make somebody permanently unable to see **2.** MAKE SOMEBODY TEMPORARILY BLIND to make somebody temporarily unable to see ○ *blinded by the light* **3.** MAKE SOMEBODY UNABLE TO JUDGE PROPERLY to make somebody unable to judge or act rationally ○ *blinded by rage* **4.** CONFUSE SOMEBODY to make it difficult for somebody to understand something ○ *Stop trying to blind us with statistics.* ■ *n* **1.** WINDOW COVERING a device that is pulled down to shut out the light from a window **2.** COVER OR SUBTERFUGE something that is intended to conceal the true nature of somebody's activities **3.** PROXY a person or organization whose public activities conceal a secret purpose **4.** OBSTRUCTION anything that blocks the free passage of light, sight, or air ○ *The trees act as a blind to sunlight.* **5.** HUNTING HIDING PLACE FOR HUNTERS bushes, undergrowth, or other shelter in which shooters can hide, especially when hunting fowl [Old English, < Indo-European, "confusion, obscurity"] —**blind·ly** *adv* —**blind·ness** *n*

blind al·ley *n* **1.** a narrow alley or passage that is closed off at one end **2.** something that produces no worthwhile results

blind cer·tif·i·cate *n* in e-commerce, a means of tracking visitors to websites anonymously by identifying the user's system but not his or her name

blind date *n* **1.** a date arranged between people who have not seen or met each other before **2.** somebody whom you meet on a blind date

blind·er /blīndər/ *n* something that prevents clear vision or understanding ■ **blind·ers** *npl* a pair of flaps attached to a horse's bridle, one beside each eye, to keep the horse looking straight ahead

blind·fold /blīnd fōld/ *n* BANDAGE TIED OVER EYES a piece of cloth tied over the eyes to prevent the wearer from seeing ■ *vt* (**-fold·ed, -fold·ing, -folds**) **1.** PUT BANDAGE OVER EYES OF SOMEBODY to prevent somebody from seeing by putting a bandage or other material over the person's eyes **2.** PREVENT SOMEBODY FROM UNDERSTANDING to prevent somebody from understanding clearly [Early 16C. By folk etymology (< FOLD¹) < past tense of obsolete *blindfell* "make unable to see"]

blind gut *n* ANAT same as **cecum**

blind·ing /blīnding/ *adj* causing inability to see, especially temporarily, by being bright ○ *a blinding flash of light* —**blind·ing·ly** *adv*

blind·man's buff /blīnd manz-/ *n* a children's game in which one player is blindfolded and has to catch and identify other players by touch [*Buff* shortening of BUFFET² "stroke with the hand"]

blind pig *n US regional, Can* LEISURE same as **blind tiger**

blind side *n* the area that is out of your field of vision ○ *The cyclist came up on my blind side.*

blind·side /blīnd sīd/ (**blind·sid·ed, blind·sid·ing, blind·sides**) *vt* **1.** to attack somebody suddenly and physically by hitting the person on a side where his or her peripheral vision is obstructed **2.** to take somebody unawares suddenly, with detrimental results to that person

blind snake *n* a small nonvenomous snake with scales over its eyes, adapted for burrowing and eating small soil invertebrates. Native to: tropical regions. Families: Typhlopidae or Leptotyphlopidae or Anomalepididae.

blind spot *n* **1.** ANAT same as **optic disk** **2.** AREA OF IGNORANCE a subject that somebody is ignorant about ○ *have a blind spot for math* **3.** DIRECTION IN WHICH VISION IS OBSCURED an area or direction, especially on a road, in which somebody's vision is obscured **4.** ACOUSTICS ACOUSTICALLY UNSATISFACTORY AREA an area in an auditorium where things cannot be heard clearly **5.** BROADCAST PLACE WITH POOR RADIO RECEPTION an area within the normal range of a radio transmitter where reception is poor

blind stag·gers *n* a disorder of the nervous system in livestock that results in a lurching gait and loss of voluntary movement. It may be caused by a mineral deficiency or ingestion of a poisonous plant. (*takes a singular verb*)

blind ti·ger *n regional* a place where liquor is sold or served illegally [< the custom of exhibiting stuffed animals in speakeasies]

blind trust *n* a legal arrangement in which a trustee manages funds for the benefit of somebody who has no knowledge of the specific management actions taken by the trustee

blind·worm /blīnd wùrm/ *n* REPT same as **slowworm** [15C. < the animal's small eyes]

bling bling /blìng blíng/, **bling** *adj* having or displaying ostentatious material wealth (*slang*) [Probably an imitation of the sound of a cash register]

bli·ni /bleēnee, blínnee/ (*plural* **bli·nis** or **blin** /blin/ or *same*) *n* a small pancake made with yeast and buckwheat flour, traditional in Russia and other parts of Eastern Europe [Late 20C. < Russian *blin*, plural (singular *blin*)]

blink /blingk/ *v* (**blinked, blink·ing, blinks**) **1.** *vti* CLOSE AND REOPEN EYES to close and reopen both eyes rapidly **2.** *vti* LOOK WHILE BLINKING to look at somebody or something while blinking **3.** *vt* REMOVE SOMETHING BY BLINKING to open and shut the eyes rapidly to remove something from them ○ *He blinked away his tears.* **4.** *vi* FLASH to flash on and off, especially as a signal **5.** *vt* TRANSMIT MESSAGE BY BLINKING LIGHT to transmit a message by making a light flash on and off **6.** *vi* WAVER to waver from a course of action ○ *After a ten-week strike, it was management that finally blinked.* ■ *n* **1.** ACT OF BLINKING EYES a rapid closing and reopening of both eyes **2.** METEOROL same as **iceblink, snowblink** [13C. Partly variant of BLENCH¹, partly < Middle Dutch *blinken* "to glitter"] ◇ **on the blink** not working properly (*informal*) ○ *The television's on the blink.*

blink·er /blíngkər/ *n* a light that flashes in order to give a message or warning, especially on a motor vehicle. Blinkers were used to send coded messages, especially between ships, to avoid interception of radio signals during World Wars I and II. ■ **blink·ers** *npl UK* same as **blinders** (*see* **blinder**) ■ *vt* (**-ered, -er·ing, -ers**) *UK* to put blinders on a horse

blink·ered /blíngkərd/ *adj* **1.** unable or unwilling to understand anything outside a very narrow range ○ *took a very blinkered attitude* **2.** *UK* wearing blinkers —**blink·ered·ness** *n*

blink·ing green light *n* a tentative affirmative decision on a matter, contingent upon future developments (*slang*) ○ *When I came on board as screenwriter, the project had a blinking green light.*

blintz /blints/, **blin·tze** /blíntsə/ *n* a pancake folded around a filling and then baked or fried [Early 20C. Via Yiddish *blintse* < Russian *blinets* "little pancake" < *blin* "pancake"]

blip /blip/ *n* **1.** SPOT ON DISPLAY SCREEN a spot of light, often accompanied by a high-pitched sound, indicating the position of something on a screen ○ *The submarine shows up as a series of faint blips on the screen.* **2.** ELECTRONICS same as **bleep** **3.** SUDDEN DEVIATION a sudden temporary problem in the normal progress of something ■ *vi* (**blipped, blip·ping, blips**) MAKE BLIP to produce a blip [Late 19C. An imitation of the sound]

bliss /bliss/ *n* **1.** perfect happiness ○ *It was bliss to have a day at home.* **2.** a state of spiritual joy [Old English, alteration of *blīs* < Germanic, "gentle, kind"]

CULTURAL NOTE ***Bliss***, a novel (1981) by Australian writer Peter Carey. A fable about the battle between good and evil, it tells the story of advertising executive Harry Joy who, after a successful heart bypass operation, becomes convinced that he has woken up in Hell. It was made into a movie by Ray Lawrence in 1985.

bliss out *vi* to go into a state of extreme happiness or euphoria (*slang*) ○ *bliss out on chocolates*

bliss·ful /blísf'l/ *adj* **1.** characterized by perfect happiness ○ *a look of blissful contentment* **2.** serenely happy because of being unaware of something ○ *blissful ignorance* —**bliss·ful·ly** *adv* —**bliss·ful·ness** *n*

B list *n* a list of people who are fairly well-known but not as sought after for social functions and other activities as the very famous (*hypenated before a noun*)

blis·ter /blístər/ *n* **1.** MED PAINFUL SWELLING ON SKIN a painful swelling on the skin containing fluid (**serum**) **2.** PLANTS, BOT SWELLING ON PLANT RESULTING FROM DISEASE a swelling in a leaf or other plant part indicating disease **3.** BUBBLE ON PAINT a bubble containing liquid or air on paintwork or rubber **4.** AVIAT AIRCRAFT DOME a rounded, usually transparent dome on the fuselage of an aircraft, used for observation ■ *vti* (**-tered, -ter·ing, -ters**) FORM BLISTERS to be raised in a blister or blisters, or to cause blisters to form on something [14C. Origin ?] —**blis·ter·y** *adj*

blis·ter bee·tle *n* a soft-bodied beetle that secretes for its own defense a substance that raises burning blisters on the skin of vertebrates. Family: Meloidae.

blis·ter·ing /blístəring/ *adj* **1.** extremely hot **2.** extremely scornful or critical ○ *a blistering attack on the governor's failures* —**blis·ter·ing·ly** *adv*

blis·ter pack *n* a package in which small items such as pills are contained in raised domes of plastic

B.Lit. /beē lít/ *abbr* Bachelor of Literature [Latin *Baccalaureus Litterarum*]

blithe /blīth, blīth/ *adj* **1.** happy, cheerful, and carefree **2.** casually indifferent ○ *with a blithe disregard for anyone's feelings* [Old English *blīþe* < Germanic, "gentle, kind"] —**blithe·ly** *adv* —**blithe·ness** *n*

blith·er /blíthər/ *vi* same as **blather** (*informal*) [Mid-19C. Variant]

blith·er·ing /blíthəring/ *adj UK* used to express annoyance with and contempt for somebody or something (*informal*) ○ *It's a blithering nuisance.*

B.Litt. /beē lít/ *abbr* Bachelor of Literature [Latin *Baccalaureus Litterarum*]

blitz /blits/ *n* **1.** MIL SUSTAINED AERIAL ATTACK a heavy air raid intended to obliterate a target **2.** MIL same as **blitzkrieg** **3.** CONCERTED EFFORT a concentrated effort to get something done (*informal*) ○ *a last-minute blitz to finish the book* **4.** FOOTBALL CHARGE ON PASSER in football, a direct attack on the passer, by one or more players who usually stay behind the line of scrimmage, to try to prevent a pass ■ *v* (**blitzed, blitz·ing, blitz·es**) **1.** *vt* MIL DESTROY SOMETHING BY AERIAL BOMBING to attack or destroy a target by bombardment from the air **2.** *vt* DEFEAT SOMEBODY COMPREHENSIVELY to defeat a person or team overwhelmingly in a competition, especially a sports event **3.** *vt* DEAL WITH SOMETHING ENERGETICALLY to concentrate a lot of effort on something to get it done (*informal*) **4.** *vt* TRY TO OVERWHELM SOMEBODY to subject somebody to an overwhelming amount of something, often in order to force him or her into agreement or submission (*informal*) ○ *blitzed with a stream of facts* **5.** *vti* FOOTBALL CHARGE PASSER in football, to charge the passer in order to prevent a pass [Mid-20C. Shortening of BLITZKRIEG]

blitzed /blitst/ *adj* very drunk (*slang*)

blitz·krieg /blíts krèeg/ *n* a swift military offensive using ground and air forces [Mid-20C. < German, "lightning war"]

bliv·et /blívvət/, **bliv·it** *n* 1. CARRIER FOR LIQUID a collapsible rubberized bladder used to transport and store fuel and water in forward areas of a battlefield 2. SOMETHING POINTLESS OR ANNOYING something useless, pointless, or annoying (*slang*) 3. PROBLEM DIFFICULT TO SOLVE an intractable problem, especially in computing (*slang*) 4. SOMETHING DIFFICULT TO NAME something whose name you do not know or cannot remember (*slang*) [Mid-20C. Origin ?]

Blix·en /blíksən/, **Karen** ➧ **Dinesen, Isak**

bliz·zard /blízzərd/ *n* a severe snowstorm with strong winds and poor visibility. For a snowstorm to be classified as a blizzard, winds must exceed 35 mi./56 km per hour and the temperature must be -7°C/20°F or lower. [Early 19C. Origin ?]

blk. *abbr* 1. block 2. bulk

B.LL. *abbr* Bachelor of Laws [Latin *Baccalaureus Legum*]

BLM *abbr* Bureau of Land Management

bloat /blōt/ *vti* (**bloat·ed, bloat·ing, bloats**) 1. SWELL to become swollen or inflated, or make something do this 2. EXCESSIVELY EXPAND to increase excessively, or make something do this 3. SWELL WITH PRIDE to become or cause to become unpleasantly proud or conceited ■ *n* 1. EXCESSIVE INCREASE an excessive amount, or an excessive increase in something ○ *corporate bloat* 2. VET CATTLE DISEASE a disease affecting cattle and sheep, characterized by excessive gas in the main stomach compartment (**rumen**) [Early 17C. Probably < Old Norse *blautr* "soft, wet"]

bloat·ed /blṓtəd/ *adj* 1. SWOLLEN swollen with liquid, air, or gas 2. OVERFULL AFTER OVEREATING overfull and feeling uncomfortable after eating too much 3. TOO LARGE excessively large ○ *a bloated expense account* —**bloat·ed·ness** *n*

bloat·er /blṓtər/ *n* 1. a large herring that has been soaked in brine and smoked 2. a common freshwater cisco. Native to: Great Lakes. Latin name: *Coregonus hoyi.* [Mid-19C. < obsolete *bloat herring*, origin ?]

bloat·ware /blṓt wèr/ *n* a computer program with many, often superfluous features that take up so much memory that the computer's performance is impaired (*informal*) [Late 20C. After SOFTWARE]

blob /blob/ *n* 1. SOFT MASS a soft lump or drop of something such as paint or glue 2. SMALL SPOT OF COLOR a small rounded spot of color 3. INDISTINCT FORM an indistinct or shapeless form or object ■ *vt* (**blobbed, blob·bing, blobs**) PUT BLOBS ON SOMETHING to apply blobs of color or a soft substance to something [15C. Origin ?]

bloc /blok/ *n* 1. a group of countries or political parties with a shared aim ○ *former Soviet bloc countries* ○ *a 12-nation trading bloc* 2. a usually temporary grouping within a legislature, made up of diverse members acting together for a common interest or purpose ○ *the largest opposition bloc* [Early 20C. < French (see BLOCK)]

SPELLCHECK bloc or **block**? Do not confuse the spelling of ***bloc*** and ***block***, which sound similar. A ***bloc*** is a group of countries or political parties with a common aim. The word ***block*** has a much wider range of meanings and uses: As a noun it may denote a lump, a square object, a large building, or an obstruction (as in *a block of wood, an office block*); as a verb it principally means "obstruct" (as in *roads blocked by snow*).

Bloch /blok/, **Ernest** (1880–1959) Swiss-born US composer. He incorporated themes from Jewish music in such works as his symphony *Israel* (1912–16).

block /blok/ *n* 1. SOLID LUMP a large solid piece of a hard substance, usually with flat sides 2. CONSTR BUILDING UNIT a large flat-sided piece of hard material such as stone or wood, used in building 3. LEISURE same as **building block** (sense 2) 4. CHOPPING BASE a large piece of wood used for chopping things on 5. STREET SECTION the section of a street between two parallel streets ○ *The post office is in the middle of the next block.* 6. GROUP OF BUILDINGS a group of buildings in a town or city bounded on each side by a street ○ *going for a walk around the block* 7. UNBROKEN EXPANSE OR AREA a uniform expanse of something such as color 8. SET OF SIMILAR ITEMS a set of similar items sold as a unit ○ *a block of tickets* 9. COMPUT UNIT OF DATA in computing, a set of contiguous data that performs some action as a unit ○ *a block of text* 10. STRETCH OF TIME an uninterrupted period of time ○ *set aside a 90-minute block* 11. STAMPS GROUP OF POSTAGE STAMPS a group of four or more postage stamps forming a rectangle 12. LARGE BUILDING a building divided into offices or apartments 13. SPECIAL-PURPOSE BUILDING a building or part of a building designed for a particular purpose 14. PRINTING PRINTING DEVICE a piece of wood, metal, or stone with a design engraved on it, used for printing 15. AUCTIONEER'S PLATFORM a stand on which articles in an auction are displayed 16. PLACE FOR BEHEADING PEOPLE a large piece of wood or stone on which people were beheaded in former times 17. POL another spelling of **bloc** 18. OBSTRUCTION something that obstructs or prevents progress 19. SPORTS OBSTRUCTION OF PLAY in some sports, an act of deliberately preventing a ball or another player from moving forward 20. FOOTBALL OBSTRUCTING PLAYERS in football, an act of preventing defensive players from interfering with movement toward the goal 21. SPORTS same as **starting block** 22. MED OBSTRUCTION OF PHYSIOLOGICAL FUNCTION an interruption of the normal functioning of an organ of the body 23. DISRUPTION OF PSYCHOLOGICAL PROCESSES an inability to begin or continue a psychological process, often attributed to emotional stress ○ *I forgot – I must have had a mental block.* 24. MECH ENG same as **engine block** ■ *v* (**blocked, block·ing, blocks**) 1. *vt* OBSTRUCT MOVEMENT to prevent or restrict movement through, into, or out of something ○ *The gutters are blocked with leaves.* ○ *He stood in front of me, blocking my way.* 2. *vt* HINDER PROGRESS OF SOMETHING to prevent something from taking place ○ *Her promotion was blocked by the senior vice president.* 3. *vt* OBSTRUCT SIGHT OF SOMETHING to obstruct somebody's line of sight ○ *blocking my view* 4. *vti* SPORTS OBSTRUCT PLAYER OR BALL in some sports, to prevent a ball or another player from moving forward 5. *vti* FOOTBALL OBSTRUCT PLAYER in football, to prevent a defensive player from interfering with movement toward the goal 6. *vti* MED PREVENT NORMAL PHYSIOLOGICAL FUNCTIONING to prevent the normal functioning of a physiological process ○ *a blocked tear duct* 7. *vt* FAIL TO REMEMBER to fail to remember something, or prevent a memory from being recalled ○ *could not block the memory of the accident* 8. *vt* MAKE SOMETHING INTO BLOCK to shape something into a block 9. *vt* SUPPORT SOMETHING WITH BLOCK to support or strengthen something using a block 10. *vt* SHAPE SOMETHING ON BLOCK to mold something with or on a block 11. *vt* PRINTING STAMP SOMETHING USING BLOCK to stamp a surface with a title or using an engraved block 12. *vt* THEATER REHEARSE BASIC MOVEMENTS FOR SCENE to plan and rehearse the basic movements and positions for the actors in a scene [14C. Via Old French *bloc* < Middle Dutch *blok* "tree trunk"] ◇ **block and level** to level a portable structure by placing blocks of various heights under its corners ◇ **knock somebody's block off** to punch somebody in the head (*slang*) ◇ **on the block** for sale at an auction

SPELLCHECK See ***bloc***.

SYNONYMS See ***hinder***[1].

block in *vt* 1. PREVENT FROM MOVING to prevent somebody or something moving from a place by being in the way or by placing something in the way ○ *Two double-parked cars have blocked us in.* 2. SHADE EMPTY SPACES to fill in the blank spaces on an outline design with color 3. SKETCH SOMETHING IN OUTLINE to make a quick, rough sketch showing the general outlines or idea of a place or plan 4. FILL SOMETHING IN to fill in something hollow so that it becomes solid

block off *vt* 1. to put up or form a barrier in front of something in order to prevent anybody or anything from entering ○ *Police blocked off the street.* 2. to put up or form a barrier that prevents something from being seen

block out *vt* 1. PUT THOUGHT OUT OF MIND to prevent a disturbing thought from entering the mind 2. DESCRIBE SOMETHING WITHOUT DETAIL to describe something in a general fashion, without great detail ○ *block out a proposal* 3. PHOTOGRAPHY COVER PART OF NEGATIVE to cover part of a negative or stencil when printing from it to prevent that part from appearing

block up *vti* to prevent movement through something by filling in all the space, or become completely obstructed

block·ade /blo káyd/ *n* 1. PREVENTION OF ACCESS an organized action to prevent people or goods entering or leaving a place 2. FORCES FORMING BLOCKADE the ships or forces used to maintain a blockade 3. OBSTACLE OR OBSTRUCTION something that prevents access to a place ■ *vt* (**-ad·ed, -ad·ing, -ades**) 1. SUBJECT PLACE TO BLOCKADE to impose a blockade on a place 2. BLOCK ACCESS TO PLACE to obstruct access to a place [Late 17C. Perhaps after AMBUSCADE] —**block·ad·er** *n*

block·age /blókij/ *n* 1. something that obstructs movement through a pipe or channel ○ *a blockage in an artery* 2. the act of blocking something

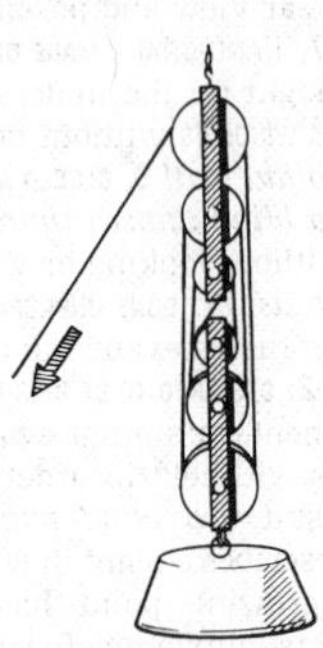

block and tackle

block and tack·le (*plural* **blocks and tack·les**) *n* a system of two pulley blocks, each with at least one pulley with rope or cable threaded through, used for hoisting or hauling. The greater the number of pulleys, the greater the weight that can be raised by the same force on the rope or cable.

block·bust·er /blók bùstər/ *n* 1. POPULAR SUCCESS something such as a book, play, or film that is either very large or achieves enormous commercial success (*informal*) 2. PERSON WHO PRACTICES BLOCKBUSTING somebody who persuades people to sell their houses by instilling fear of declining property values (*informal*) 3. ARMS HUGE DESTRUCTIVE BOMB a large high-explosive bomb designed to demolish buildings over a large area (*dated*)

block·bust·ing /blók bùsting/ *n* the practice of persuading homeowners to sell their homes quickly at low prices for fear of declining property values (*informal*) ■ *adj* sensational and enormously successful commercially ○ *a blockbusting novel*

block cap·i·tal *n* same as **block letter**

block di·a·gram *n* a diagram in which the essential parts of a system or process are represented by labeled rectangles

block·er /blókər/ *n* 1. a drug that prevents a physiological function 2. in football, an offensive player who tries to keep the defense from reaching the ball, kicker, or passer

block grant *n* a grant of money from the federal budget to state or local governments to spend on local services

block·head /blók hèd/ *n* somebody who is regarded as very unintelligent (*insult*)

block·house /blók hòwss/ (*plural* **-hous·es** /-hòwzəz/) *n* 1. a small military building with apertures to fire through, used as part of a defensive system or an observation post 2. a fort constructed from heavy wooden beams

Block Is·land /blók-/ island in the Atlantic Ocean at the northern end of Long Island Sound in southern Rhode Island. A resort and fishing center, it is named for the Dutch sailor Adriaen Block, who landed there in 1614. Population: 836 (1990). Area: 11 sq. mi./28 sq. km.

block let·ter *n* 1. a plain capital letter that is not joined to other letters ○ *Fill out the form in block letters.* 2. a compressed sans serif typeface or individual letter

block par·ty *n* a party for all the people who live on the same block or street

block plane *n* a small carpenter's plane with the

blade at a low pitch. Use: cutting across the grain of wood.

block print·ing *n* printing from hand-carved or engraved blocks

block·y /blókee/ (**-i·er, -i·est**) *adj* three-dimensional, boxy in shape, and seemingly solid

Bloc Qué·bé·cois /blòk kày bay kwaá/ *n* a Canadian federal political party whose members come from Quebec and espouse that province's interests, especially sovereignty or separation from Canada

Bloem·fon·tein /bloóm faan tàyn/ city and judicial capital of South Africa, capital of Free State Province, in central South Africa. Population: 126,867 (1991).

blog /blog/ (*slang*) *n* ONLINE same as **weblog** ■ *vi* (**blogged, blog·ging, blogs**) to create or run a weblog [Contraction] —**blog·ger** *n*

blog·o·sphere /bloggə sfeer/ *n* the World Wide Web environment in which bloggers communicate with each other

blog·ware /blóg wèr/ *n* computer software tools for creating a weblog

Blois /blwaa/ capital of Loir-et-Cher Department in central France, on the Loire River, northeast of Tours. It is famous for its magnificent Renaissance chateau. Population: 49,171 (1999).

bloke /blōk/ *n UK* same as **man** *n* (sense 1) (*informal*) [Mid-19C. < Shelta]

blond /blond/, **blonde** *adj* **1.** FAIR yellowish or golden in color **2.** FAIR-HAIRED AND LIGHT-SKINNED with fair hair and a light-colored skin **3.** LIGHT COLORED light-colored, ranging from yellowish brown to grayish yellow ○ *blond wood* **4.** BLEACHED describes wood that is light-colored, usually through bleaching ○ *blond walnut* ■ *n* FAIR-HAIRED PERSON a person with blond hair [15C. Via French < medieval Latin *blundus* "yellow"] —**blond·ness** *n*

USAGE blond or **blonde**? When describing the color of somebody's hair, ***blond*** is normally used of a person of either sex: *Jane has blond hair.* When used as a noun or adjective to describe somebody directly, ***blond*** is often used of a man or boy and ***blonde*** of a woman or girl: *He is blond. Jane is blonde/is a blonde.*

blood /blud/ *n* **1.** RED FLUID CIRCULATING IN BODY the red fluid that is pumped from the heart and circulates around the bodies of humans and other vertebrates **2.** BODY FLUID OF INVERTEBRATES a liquid found in invertebrates that has functions similar to those of vertebrate blood **3.** BLOODSHED bloodshed or killing **4.** VITAL LIFE FORCE blood considered as a vital life force **5.** FAMILY OR KINSHIP family background or descent from an ancestor, especially when viewed as determining a person's character or appearance **6.** PURE BREEDING pure breeding in animals, especially horses **7.** MEMBERS OF GROUP people considered for their potential to strengthen and improve an organization (*informal*) ○ *bring in new blood* **8.** BLACK MAN a Black man (*slang; used primarily among Black people*) ■ *vt* (**blood·ed, blood·ing, bloods**) **1.** MIL INITIATE TROOPS IN BATTLE to subject troops to their first experience of battle **2.** HUNTING LET DOG TASTE BLOOD to give a dog its first taste of the blood of a freshly killed animal in order to make it eager to hunt [Old English *blōd* < Germanic] ◇ **be out for** *or* **after somebody's blood** to be intending to punish somebody ◇ **blood is thicker than water** family ties and loyalties take precedence over other relationships ◇ **have blood on your hands** to be responsible for somebody's death ◇ **in cold blood** deliberately, and in a way that shows a complete lack of emotion ○ *was murdered in cold blood* ◇ **make somebody's blood boil** to make somebody extremely angry ◇ **make somebody's blood run cold** to frighten or horrify somebody ◇ **spill blood** to wound or kill people ◇ **sweat blood** to make a great effort

blood bank *n* **1.** a place where blood or blood plasma is stored for use in transfusion **2.** the blood or blood plasma stored in a blood bank

blood·bath /blúd bàth/ (*plural* **-baths** /-bàthz/) *n* a battle or fight characterized by mass killing

blood broth·er *n* either of two men or boys who have sworn mutual loyalty and friendship

blood clot *n* a thick mass of coagulated blood

blood count *n* **1.** the number of red and white blood cells and platelets in a given volume of blood **2.** a determination of the number of blood cells and platelets in a blood count

blood·cur·dling /blúd kùrdling/ *adj* arousing extreme fear ○ *bloodcurdling screams*

blood do·nor *n* somebody who gives blood for use in transfusions

blood dop·ing *n* the practice of reinjecting an athlete with his or her own red blood cells shortly before a competition in order to enhance performance. The practice is illegal in most organized competitions.

blood·ed /blúddəd/ *adj* belonging to a superior breed ○ *blooded mares*

blood feud *n* a long-lasting feud between families or clans involving murder

blood·fin /blúd fìn/ *n* a small red-finned freshwater fish, often kept in aquariums. Native to: Argentina. Latin name: *Aphyocharax rubripinnis.*

blood fluke *n* a parasitic flatworm found in human blood that relies on two hosts, humans and some types of snails, to complete its life cycle. Native to: tropical Asia and Africa. Genus: *Schistosoma.*

blood group *n* a class into which human blood is divided for transfusion purposes according to the presence or absence of antigens that determine its immunological compatibility. The ABO system is the most commonly known set of blood groups.

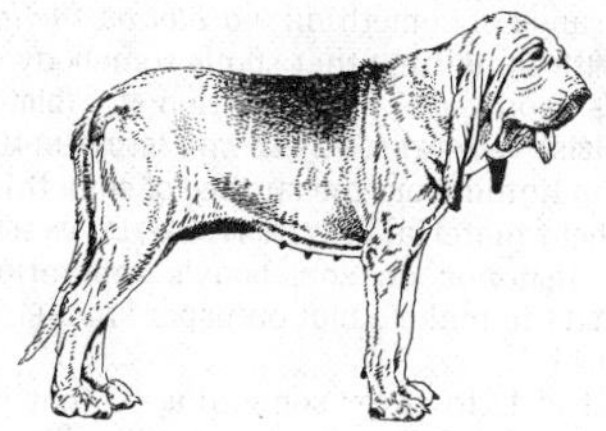

bloodhound

blood·hound /blúd hòwnd/ *n* **1.** a large powerful dog with drooping ears, sagging jowls, and a keen sense of smell, formerly used for tracking **2.** a detective who is relentless in pursuing people or things (*informal*)

blood·less /blúdləss/ *adj* **1.** WITHOUT KILLING OR VIOLENCE conducted without killing or great violence ○ *a bloodless coup* **2.** PALE AND ANEMIC pale and anemic-looking **3.** LACKING LIVELINESS dull and lacking liveliness ○ *a bloodless performance* **4.** LACKING EMOTION cold and lacking in human emotion ○ *bloodless statistics* **5.** LACKING BLOOD lacking blood or the expected amount of blood —**blood·less·ly** *adv* —**blood·less·ness** *n*

blood·let·ting /blúd lètting/ *n* **1.** FIGHTING CAUSING INJURIES OR DEATHS fighting that results in many people being injured or killed **2.** MED REMOVAL OF BLOOD FROM BODY the removal of blood, usually by making an incision in a vein, for therapeutic purposes. Although historically common, bloodletting is used only rarely in modern times to treat specific medical conditions. **3.** HR EJECTION OF PEOPLE the large-scale laying off of employees in a corporation ○ *the latest round of corporate bloodletting* —**blood·let·ter** *n*

blood·line /blúd lìn/ *n* a direct line of descent from a specific human or animal ancestor, especially with respect to the common characteristics shared by that ancestor's descendants

blood lust *n* a strong desire to take part in or witness killing or violence

blood·meal /blúd meel/ *n* dried powdered animal blood. Use: to enrich animal feeds, as fertilizer for plants.

blood mon·ey *n* **1.** FEE FOR HIRED KILLER the fee paid to a hired killer **2.** MONEY GAINED AT ANOTHER'S EXPENSE money that somebody gains at the expense of another person's life or well-being **3.** REWARD FOR FINDING KILLER a reward paid to somebody for giving information about a criminal, especially a murderer **4.** COMPENSATION PAID FOR KILLING in some cultures, compensation paid to the relatives of somebody who has been killed or murdered

blood or·ange *n* an orange that has deep red flesh

blood plas·ma *n* PHYSIOL same as **plasma** (sense 1)

blood poi·son·ing *n* infection of the blood, generally caused either by the presence in the blood of microorganisms (**septicemia**) or of toxins produced by body cells (**toxemia**)

blood pres·sure *n* **1.** the pressure exerted by the blood against the walls of blood vessels. Blood pressure depends on the strength of the heartbeat, thickness and volume of the blood, the elasticity of the artery walls, and general health. **2.** MED same as **hypertension**

blood pro·duct *n* a substance such as plasma extracted from donated blood for use in the treatment of various medical conditions

blood pud·ding *n* FOOD same as **blood sausage**

blood quan·tum *n* the degree of Native American descent that a person has, e.g., one quarter, or the fact of being proven a direct heir of documented Native Americans whose names are listed in tribal rolls

blood quantum card *n* a card that documents and proves one's Native American ancestry by tribe and by degree of blood relationship to documented ancestors

blood red *n* a deep vivid red color —**blood red** *adj*

blood re·la·tion, blood rel·a·tive *n* somebody who is related to another person by birth rather than marriage

blood·root /blúd ròot, -ròot/ (*plural* **-roots** or *same*) *n* a plant that has poisonous deep-red sap in its roots. Native to: eastern North America. Latin name: *Sanguinaria canadensis.*

blood sau·sage *n* a dark-colored sausage whose main ingredient is pig's blood

blood se·rum *n* MED same as **serum** (sense 1)

blood·shed /blúd shèd/ *n* activity resulting in killings or injuries

blood·shot /blúd shòt/ *adj* inflamed and red as a result of the widening of small blood vessels in the white of the eye ○ *bloodshot eyes*

blood sport *n* a sport in which animals are killed. Hunting and bullfighting are blood sports.

blood·stain /blúd stàyn/ *n* a dark stain left by dried blood —**blood·stained** *adj*

blood·stock /blúd stòk/ *n* thoroughbred horses, especially when bred and sold for horseracing

blood·stone /blúd stōn/ *n* a deep green variety of chalcedony with small red spots or streaks of red jasper. Use: gems.

blood·stream /blúd streem/ *n* the flow of blood circulating through the blood vessels of a person or animal

blood·suck·er /blúd sùkər/ *n* **1.** a parasite that sucks blood from its host, e.g., a leech or mosquito **2.** somebody who exploits somebody else, especially by extortion or blackmail —**blood·suck·ing** *n, adj*

blood sug·ar *n* the concentration of glucose in the blood

blood test *n* a scientific analysis of a sample of blood

blood·thirst·y /blúd thùrstee/ (**-i·er, -i·est**) *adj* **1.** eager to take part in or witness violence and bloodshed **2.** full of intentional violence or killing —**blood·thirst·i·ly** *adv* —**blood·thirst·i·ness** *n*

blood type *n* MED same as **blood group**

blood ves·sel *n* an artery, vein, or capillary through which blood flows

blood·worm /blúd wùrm/ *n* **1.** the red larva of a freshwater midge. Genus: *Chironomus.* **2.** a reddish segmented worm often used as fishing bait. Genera: *Tubifex* or *Polycirrus.*

REGIONAL NOTE Although recorded from Canada throughout the Middle Atlantic states, ***bloodworm*** is most frequently used in New Jersey.

blood·y /blúddee/ *adj* (**-i·er, -i·est**) **1. BLOODSTAINED** covered or smeared with blood ○ *Her hands were bloody and shaking.* **2. RELATING TO BLOOD** resembling or containing blood **3. INVOLVING MUCH BLOODSHED** involving a great deal of killing and bloodshed ■ *adv UK* **SWEARWORD** used as a swearword or to add emphasis (*slang; sometimes considered offensive*) ○ *a bloody good job too!* ■ *vt* (**-ied, -y·ing, -ies**) **STAIN SOMETHING WITH BLOOD** to stain or smear something with blood —**blood·i·ly** *adv* —**blood·i·ness** *n*

blood·y mar·y (*plural* **blood·y mar·ys**), **Blood·y Mar·y** *n* a cocktail consisting of vodka, tomato juice, and spices

blood·y-mind·ed *adj UK* intentionally uncooperative and obstructive (*informal*) —**blood·y-mind·ed·ly** *adv* —**blood·y-mind·ed·ness** *n*

bloom[1] /bloom/ *n* **1. FLOWER** a flower, especially on a plant cultivated chiefly for its flowers **2. MASS OF FLOWERS** the mass of flowers on a single plant **3. FLOWERING** the state of being in flower ○ *roses in full bloom* **4. HEALTHY APPEARANCE OR COMPLEXION** a fresh, youthful, healthy complexion **5. PRIME** the condition of greatest freshness or health (*literary*) ○ *in the bloom of youth* **6.** BOT **WHITE COATING ON LEAVES OR FRUIT** a thin white coating on the leaves of some plants and on fruits **7.** ENVIRON same as **algal bloom** ■ *vi* (**bloomed, bloom·ing, blooms**) **1. COME INTO FLOWER** to open into flower ○ *The roses bloomed early this year.* **2. PRODUCE PLANTS** to produce abundant plant life, especially unexpectedly ○ *make the desert bloom* **3. APPEAR HEALTHY** to appear healthy and vigorous **4. PROSPER OR FLOURISH** to reach the fullest stage of development or maturity **5. APPEAR SUDDENLY** to appear suddenly, usually in a cloud ○ *A cloud of smoke bloomed under the rocket.* **6.** ENVIRON **BECOME COVERED WITH ALGAE** to become discolored on the surface because of an excessive growth of algae or phytoplankton (*refers to bodies of water*) [13C. < Old Norse *blóm* < Indo-European] —**bloom·y** *adj*

bloom[2] /bloom/ *n* a bar of steel or wrought iron hammered or rolled from an ingot ■ *vt* (**bloomed, bloom·ing, blooms**) to convert an ingot of iron or steel into a bloom [Old English *blōma*, origin ?]

bloom·er /bloómər/ *n* **1. PLANT THAT FLOWERS** a flowering plant, especially considered with respect to the time of its flowering ○ *an early bloomer* **2. DEVELOPER** somebody who grows up or reaches a level of competence at a particular stage of development ○ *described herself as a late bloomer* **3.** *UK* **EMBARRASSING MISTAKE** a mildly embarrassing mistake (*informal humorous*) [Mid-18C. In sense 3 shortening and alteration of *blooming error*]

Bloom·er /bloómər/, **Amelia** (1818–94) US feminist and reformer. She was founding editor of the feminist journal *The Lily* (1849–55), and advocated less constricting clothing for women. Born **Amelia Jenks**

> "We all felt that the dress was drawing attention from what we thought to be of far greater importance...In the minds of some people the short dress and woman's rights were inseparably connected. With us, the dress was but an incident, and we were not willing to sacrifice greater questions to it."
> [Amelia Bloomer. Quoted in *The Bloomer Girls*, Charles N. Gattey; 1968]

bloom·ers /bloómərz/ *npl* (*dated*) **1. BAGGY UNDERWEAR** baggy underwear for women or girls, especially garments that reach down to just above the knee **2. WOMEN'S LOOSE SPORTS PANTS** loose pants gathered at the knee, worn by women for cycling or swimming in the late 19th century **3. LONG LOOSE WOMEN'S PANTS** long loose pants gathered at the ankle and formerly worn by women and girls under a shorter skirt [Mid-19C. After Amelia BLOOMER]

Bloom·field /bloóm feéld/ town in Essex County, northeastern New Jersey, directly north of Newark. Population: 47,526 (2002 estimate).

bloom·ing /bloóming/ *adj* flourishing and in exceptionally good health or condition ■ *adj, adv UK* used to add emphasis, as a euphemistic alternative for "bloody" (*dated informal*) ○ *a blooming nuisance*

Bloo·ming·ton /bloómingtən/ **1.** city in central Illinois, directly north of Decatur. Population: 67,417 (2002 estimate). **2.** city in southern Indiana, southwest of Indianapolis. It is home to Indiana University. Population: 69,987 (2002 estimate). **3.** city on the Minnesota River in southeastern Minnesota. It is a southern suburb of Minneapolis. Population: 84,092 (2002 estimate).

Blooms·bur·y Group /bloómz bèrree-, bloómzbəree-/ *n* a group of artists and writers who congregated in the Bloomsbury area of London after World War I. They shared political views and an experimental approach to their respective fields.

bloop /bloop/ *vt* (**blooped, bloop·ing, bloops**) in baseball, to hit the ball high and short, so that it lands just beyond the infield ■ *n* BASEBALL same as **blooper** (sense 2) [Early 20C. An imitation of the sound of a missile]

bloop·er /bloópər/ *n* **1. EMBARRASSING MISTAKE** a mildly embarrassing mistake (*informal humorous*) **2.** BASEBALL **HIGH HIT** in baseball, a short, high hit that lands just beyond the infield **3.** BASEBALL **UNDERHAND PITCH** in baseball, a lobbed underhand pitch

Blo·quiste /blo keést/ *n Can* a member or supporter of the Bloc Québécois [Late 20C. < Canadian French < *Bloc (Québécois)*]

blos·som /blóssəm/ *n* **1. MASS OF FLOWERS ON TREE** a mass of flowers appearing on a tree or bush ○ *apple blossom* **2. BLOOM** a single flower **3. FLOWERING** the state of flowering ○ *cherry trees in blossom* ■ *vi* (**-somed, -som·ing, -soms**) **1. COME INTO FLOWER** to open into flower **2. DEVELOP WELL** to develop in a pleasing or promising way **3. STOP BEING SHY** to stop being shy and reserved [Old English *blōstm* < Indo-European] —**blos·som·y** *adj*

blossom out *vi* same as **blossom** *v* (sense 2)

blot[1] /blot/ *n* **1. STAIN** a stain or spot caused by a drop of liquid **2. EYESORE** something ugly that spoils the appearance of something ○ *a blot on the landscape* **3. BLEMISH** something that spoils somebody or something's good name or reputation ■ *v* (**blot·ted, blot·ting, blots**) **1.** *vt* **DRY SOMETHING WITH ABSORBENT MATERIAL** to soak up liquid from the surface of something using absorbent material **2.** *vt* **BRING DISREPUTE ON SOMEBODY** to bring dishonor on somebody's reputation **3.** *vti* **CREATE BLOT** to make a blot on paper [14C. Probably < N Germanic]

blot out *vt* **1.** to cover something so that it can no longer be seen **2.** to remove something painful from the mind

blot[2] /blot/ *n* in backgammon, a piece placed alone on a point and therefore exposed to capture by the opposing player [Late 16C. Probably < Dutch *bloot* "exposed, naked"]

blotch /bloch/ *n* **1. SPOT OR MARK** an irregularly shaped spot or mark **2. BLEMISH ON SKIN** a reddish patch on the skin **3.** PLANTS **PLANT DISEASE** any fungal disease of plants marked by discolored areas on leaves and stems ■ *vti* (**blotched, blotch·ing, blotch·es**) **MARK WITH BLOTCHES** to mark something with blotches, or become marked with blotches [Early 17C. Blend of BLOT[1] + BOTCH] —**blotch·i·ly** *adv* —**blotch·i·ness** *n* —**blotch·y** *adj*

blot·ter /blóttər/ *n* **1.** a sheet of blotting paper that absorbs ink or water **2.** a book used for recording daily events and transactions ○ *a police blotter*

blot·ting pa·per *n* soft paper used for soaking up ink from paper

blot·to /blóttō/ *adj* extremely inebriated (*slang*) [Early 20C. < BLOT[1]]

blouse /blowss, blowz/ *n* **1. WOMAN'S SHIRT** a woman's shirt **2. CADET'S OR SOLDIER'S TUNIC** a tunic, sometimes loose and sometimes very snug, that is a part of some military uniforms **3. ETHNIC SMOCK** a loose-fitting shirt or smock, often part of traditional costume ■ *vti* (**bloused, blous·ing, blous·es**) **HANG IN LOOSE FOLDS** to make an item of clothing hang in loose gathers or folds, or hang in this way [Early 19C. < French]

blou·son /blów sòn, -ss'n, bloó zòn, -z'n/ *n* a woman's garment resembling a shirt that is gathered at the waist [Early 20C. < French]

blo·vi·ate /blṓ vee àyt/ (**-at·ed, -at·ing, -ates**) *vi* to speak at length in a pompous self-aggrandizing way (*slang*) [Mid-19C. Mock Latin alteration of BLOW[1]] —**blo·vi·a·tion** /blṑvee áysh'n/ *n*

blow[1] /blō/ *v* (**blew** /bloo/, **blown** /blōn/, **blow·ing, blows**) **1.** *vi* **BE MOVING AS AIR** to be in motion as an air current ○ *It blew all night.* **2.** *vt* **MOVE WITH AIR CURRENT** to move something with an air current, especially air exhaled through the mouth ○ *I blew the dust off the shelf.* **3.** *vti* **EXHALE** to expel a stream of air from the mouth ○ *She blew on her soup.* **4.** *vt* **FORM SOMETHING BY BLOWING** to make bubbles or smoke rings by expelling a stream of air from the mouth **5.** *vt* **CLEAR NOSE** to clear the nose by forcing air through it **6.** *vti* **SOUND BY BLOWING** to make a sound from a musical instrument by blowing air into it, or emit a sound when blown **7.** *vt* **SEND KISS** to send somebody a symbolic kiss by kissing your hand and then blowing across it **8.** *vi* **EXPEL MOIST AIR** to expel moist air from the lungs up through the blowhole (*refers to whales and other sea mammals*) **9.** *vi* **BREATHE HARD** to breathe hard or pant through exertion **10.** *vt* **EXHAUST HORSE** to cause a horse to breathe hard through overexertion **11.** *vt* **SHAPE HOT GLASS** to give shape to molten glass by forcing air into it **12.** *vti* **DESTROY OR MOVE BY EXPLOSION** to destroy or displace something or somebody violently ○ *The blast blew the roof off.* **13.** *vt* **OPEN SOMETHING BY FORCE** to break open something that is firmly shut using explosives **14.** *vti* AUTOMOT **PUNCTURE** to cause a blowout in a tire, or experience a blowout (*informal*) **15.** *vti* ELEC **BURN OUT** to burn out and break an electrical circuit, or cause a piece of equipment to do this ○ *The toaster blew when I plugged it in.* **16.** *vti* **BREAK BECAUSE OF PRESSURE** to be ruptured, or cause something to rupture, under excess pressure **17.** *vt* **MISS OPPORTUNITY** to fail to take advantage of an opportunity (*slang*) **18.** *vt* **WASTE MONEY** to spend money wastefully (*slang*) ○ *blew a bundle of dough on fast cars* **19.** *vt* **EXPOSE SECRET** to expose something secret (*slang*) ○ *blew his cover* **20.** *vt* **DISREGARD SOMETHING** to disregard something as trivial (*dated informal; usually used as a command*) ○ *Blow the expense!* **21.** *vti* **LEAVE SUDDENLY** to leave a place suddenly (*slang*) ○ *Let's blow this joint.* **22.** *vi US* **BOAST** to brag (*informal*) **23.** *vti* MUSIC **PLAY MUSIC INFORMALLY** to play music, especially informally or with other musicians (*slang*) **24.** *vt* **INHALE DRUG** to take a drug by inhalation (*slang*) **25.** *vt* **OFFENSIVE TERM** an offensive term meaning to fellate (*slang*) ■ *n* **1. ACT OF BLOWING** an act or instance of blowing **2.** MUSIC **SOUND PRODUCED BY BLOWING** the sound produced by blowing on a musical instrument **3. STRONG WIND** a strong wind (*informal*) **4.** DRUGS same as **cocaine** (*slang*) [Old English *blāwan* < Indo-European]

◇ **blow it** to spoil your chances of success (*slang*)

blow away *v* **1.** *vti* **MOVE BY WIND** to move something from its place, or to be moved, by the force of a current of air or the wind **2.** *vt* **KILL SOMEBODY** to shoot somebody dead (*slang*) **3.** *vt* **DEFEAT SOMEBODY DECISIVELY** to subject somebody to an overwhelming defeat (*slang*) **4.** *vt* **OVERWHELM SOMEBODY** to affect somebody emotionally in an overwhelming way (*slang*) ○ *an epic movie that just blew me away*

blow in *vi* **1.** to arrive or enter a place in a casual way (*slang*) ○ *blew in at midnight* **2.** to start producing oil (*refers to oil wells*)

blow off *v* **1.** *vti* **RELEASE GAS** to release a gas or liquid under pressure **2.** *vt* **FAIL TO MEET SOMEBODY** to disregard an obligation to attend something or meet somebody (*slang*) ○ *Lee blew off our lunch date.* **3.** *vt* **SLIGHT SOMEBODY** to treat somebody or something as unimportant (*slang*) ○ *He just blew me off.*

blow out *v* **1.** *vti* **EXTINGUISH** to extinguish a flame with a blast of air or wind **2.** *vr* **DIE DOWN** to return to a state of calm after a storm (*refers to storms and winds*) ○ *blow itself out* **3.** *vi* AUTOMOT **PUNCTURE** to puncture suddenly and at high speed (*refers to tires*) **4.** *vi* INDUST **EMIT UNCONTROLLABLY** to release oil or gas explosively (*refers to gas or oil wells*)

blow over *vi* **1.** to become less violent (*refers to storms*) **2.** to no longer excite strong feelings (*informal*) ○ *It was quite a scandal but it all blew over.*

blow up *v* **1.** *vti* **DESTROY BY EXPLOSION** to destroy something or kill somebody by causing an explosion, or be destroyed in this way **2.** *vti* **EXPLODE OR DETONATE** to detonate an explosive, or explode **3.** *vti* **INFLATE** to blow air into something so that it becomes swollen, or swell as a result of being filled with air **4.** *vt* PHOTOGRAPHY **ENLARGE IMAGE** to enlarge a photograph **5.** *vi* **BECOME ANGRY** to become angry suddenly and unexpectedly (*informal*) **6.** *vi* **BEGIN TO BLOW** to begin to develop or gather force (*refers to winds or storms*) **7.** *vt* **EXAGGERATE SOMETHING** to exaggerate the value or importance of something (*informal*) **8.** *vt* MOVIES, PHOTOGRAPHY **EXPAND IMAGES** to expand the images of a motion picture from a smaller gauge of film to a larger or to expand a small portion of an image so that it becomes the subject of another

blow[2] /blō/ *n* **1.** HARD HIT a hard hit with a fist or weapon ○ *a nasty blow on the head* **2.** ACTION HELPING CAUSE an important action that helps a cause or belief ○ *They struck an important blow for civil rights.* **3.** SETBACK a sudden setback ○ *a blow to his confidence* [15C. Origin ?]

blow[3] /blō/ (**blew** /bloo/, **blown** /blōn/, **blow·ing**, **blows**) *vti* to blossom, or cause something to blossom (*archaic or literary*) [Old English *blōwan* < Germanic]

blow·back /bló bàk/ *n* **1.** MECH ENG REARWARD FLOW OF GASES the reverse flow of gases in a system, e.g., through the carburetor of an internal-combustion engine during the compression cycle **2.** ARMS FIREARM POWDER RESIDUE the powdery residue that is released or ejected upon firing bullets or shells from a weapon **3.** REACTION a reaction or effect resulting from an action or cause, usually a negative reaction (*informal*) ○ *the blowback from the press revelations*

blow-by-blow *adj* describing something in great detail ○ *a blow-by-blow account*

blow-dry *vt* to dry and style hair using a hair dryer ■ *n* a hairstyle produced by blow-drying

blow-dry·er *n* **1.** a handheld hair dryer for blow-drying hair **2.** same as **hair dryer**

blow·er /bló ər/ *n* **1.** BLOWING MACHINE a machine that produces a current of air or gas ○ *a leaf blower* **2.** LOW-PRESSURE COMPRESSOR an air compressor that produces air at low pressure **3.** BRAGGART a boastful person (*informal*)

blow·fish /bló fish/ (*plural same or* **-fish·es**) *n* FISH same as **puffer** (sense 2)

blow·fly /bló flī/ (*plural* **-flies**) *n* a large fly such as a bluebottle or greenbottle that lays its eggs in rotting meat, in dung, or in open wounds. Family: Calliphoridae. [Early 19C. < BLOW[1] "deposit eggs"]

blow·gun /bló gùn/ *n* a long narrow tube through which darts or pellets are shot by blowing

blow·hard /bló haàrd/ *n* somebody who boasts but is considered ineffectual

blow·hole /bló hòl/ *n* **1.** NOSTRIL OF SEA MAMMAL a nostril in the top of the head of a whale, dolphin, or similar sea mammal that allows the exchange of air from the lungs **2.** BREATHING HOLE IN ICE a hole in ice where water mammals come to the surface to breathe **3.** CIV ENG AIR VENT a vent to permit the escape of air or gas from a tunnel or passage **4.** GEOL HOLE IN CAVE ROOF a hole in the roof of a sea cave through which sea water is forced by waves **5.** METALL BUBBLE IN INGOT a gas pocket formed in a metal as it solidifies

blow job *n* an offensive term for an act of fellatio (*slang*)

blow·lamp /bló làmp/ *n UK* CONSTR same as **blowtorch**

blown[1] /blōn/ *adj* **1.** SWOLLEN swollen or inflated **2.** OUT OF BREATH out of breath and panting **3.** MADE BY BLOWING made or shaped by blowing ○ *blown glass* **4.** same as **flyblown**

blown[2] past participle of **blow**[3]

blow·off /bló àwf, -òf/ *n* **1.** a discharge of surplus gas or fluid under pressure **2.** a device through which surplus gas or liquid under pressure is released

blow·out /bló òwt/ *n* **1.** TIRE PUNCTURE a sudden puncture of a tire **2.** GUSH OF OIL OR GAS a sudden rush of oil or gas from an oil well to the surface **3.** CLEAR VICTORY a victory by a wide margin in a game or competition (*informal*) ○ *won in a blowout on Saturday* **4.** BIG PARTY a big party with ample food and drink (*slang*)

blow·pipe /bló pīp/ *n* **1.** *UK* ARMS same as **blowgun** **2.** CHEM a small tube that leads a jet of air into a flame to increase its heat **3.** a long narrow iron tube used in glass blowing to shape molten glass

blow·sy *adj* another spelling of **blowzy**

blow·torch /bló tàwrch/ *n* a small, usually portable, gas burner that intensifies the heat of its flame by a blast of air or oxygen

blow·up /bló ùp/ *n* **1.** PHOTOGRAPHIC ENLARGEMENT an enlargement of a photograph or picture **2.** EXPLOSION an explosion caused by a bomb or similar device **3.** OUTBURST OF TEMPER a sudden outburst of temper (*informal*) **4.** MOVIES, PHOTOGRAPHY EXPANDED FILM a motion picture on a larger gauge of film that has been expanded in size from a smaller gauge, e.g., from 16 mm to 35 mm

blow·y /bló ee/ (**-i·er**, **-i·est**) *adj* windy or breezy (*informal*)

blow·zy /blówzee/ (**-zi·er**, **-zi·est**), **blow·sy** (**-si·er**, **-si·est**) *adj* **1.** with a reddish face and coarse complexion **2.** slovenly and careless in appearance [Early 17C. < obsolete *blowze* "wench"] —**blow·zi·ly** *adv* —**blow·zi·ness** *n*

BLS *abbr* Bureau of Labor Statistics

BLT (*plural* **BLTs** or **BLT's**) *n* a sandwich with a filling of bacon, lettuce, and tomato

blub·ber /blúbbər/ *n* **1.** FAT OF OCEAN MAMMALS the insulating fat of whales and other large ocean mammals. Use: source of oil, food. **2.** UNSIGHTLY FAT unsightly body fat (*informal; sometimes considered offensive*) ■ *v* (**-bered**, **-ber·ing**, **-bers**) (*informal*) **1.** *vi* SOB LOUDLY to sob in a loud and unattractive manner **2.** *vt* SAY SOMETHING WHILE SOBBING to say something while sobbing [14C. Origin ?] —**blub·ber·er** *n* —**blub·ber·y** *adj*

bludg·eon /blújjən/ *vt* (**-eoned**, **-eon·ing**, **-eons**) **1.** HIT SOMEBODY WITH HEAVY OBJECT to hit somebody repeatedly with a heavy object ○ *bludgeoned to death* **2.** COERCE OR BULLY SOMEBODY to coerce or bully somebody into doing something ■ *n* SHORT HEAVY WEAPON a short heavy club used as a weapon [Mid-18C. Origin ?] —**bludg·eon·er** *n*

blue /bloo/ *adj* (**blu·er**, **blu·est**) **1.** OF COLOR OF SKY having or resembling the color of the sky on a cloudless day **2.** SLIGHTLY PURPLE IN SKIN COLOR with the skin appearing slightly purple because of cold, bruising, or exertion **3.** BIOL BLUE-GRAY describes animals and plants that are bluish or blue-gray in color ○ *a blue whale* ○ *a blue spruce* **4.** GLOOMY gloomy or melancholy (*informal*) ○ *feeling blue* ○ *a blue day* **5.** EXPLICIT depicting or referring to sex in an explicit or offensive way (*informal*) ○ *blue jokes* **6.** PURITANICAL rigidly conservative in moral and social views (*dated*) **7.** ASTRON HAVING BLUESHIFT describes an astronomical object that exhibits a blueshift ■ *n* **1.** COLOR OF SKY the color of the sky on a cloudless day. Blue is one of the three primary colors of light and pigment. **2.** BLUE PIGMENT a blue dye or pigment **3.** DISTANCE the far distance (*informal*) ○ *disappeared off into the blue* **4.** ARCHERY BLUE PART OF TARGET the blue ring on the target in archery **5.** *also* **Blue** MEMBER OF UNION ARMY a member of the Union Army in the Civil War **6.** *also* **Blue** UNION ARMY the Union Army in the Civil War **7.** INSECTS BLUE BUTTERFLY a common blue small-winged butterfly. Subfamily: Plebeiinae. ■ *v* (**blued**, **blue·ing** or **blu·ing**, **blues**) **1.** *vti* MAKE OR BECOME BLUE to make something blue, or become blue **2.** *vt* TREAT SOMETHING WITH BLUING to treat white fabrics or clothing with bluing [13C. < Old French *bleu* < Indo-European] —**blue·ness** *n* ◇ **out of the blue** unexpectedly ○ *The offer came out of the blue.*

blue ba·by *n* a baby born with a bluish skin color (**cyanosis**) as a result of a congenital heart condition that causes the mixing of venous and arterial blood

blue·beard /bloŏ beerd/, **Blue·beard** *n* a man who marries and then kills successive wives [Early 19C. After *Blue Beard*, translation of French *Barbe Bleue*, character in a story by Charles Perrault (1628–1703)]

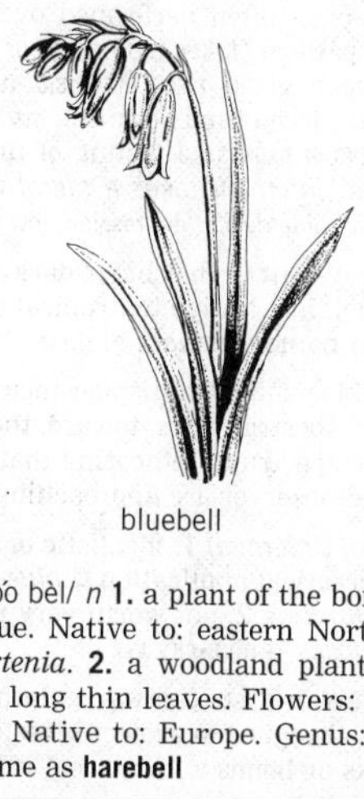

bluebell

blue·bell /bloŏ bèl/ *n* **1.** a plant of the borage family. Flowers: blue. Native to: eastern North America. Genus: *Mertenia*. **2.** a woodland plant of the lily family with long thin leaves. Flowers: small, blue, bell-shaped. Native to: Europe. Genus: *Endymion*. **3.** PLANTS same as **harebell**

blue·ber·ry /bloŏ bèrree/ (*plural* **-ries**) *n* **1.** a bluish black edible berry **2.** a cultivated fruit bush that bears blueberries. Native to: North America. Genus: *Vaccinium*.

blue·bill /bloŏ bìl/ *n* **1.** BIRDS same as **scaup** **2.** a bird of the waxbill family with a heavy metallic blue bill. Native to: Africa. Genus: *Spermophaga*.

blue·bird /bloŏ bùrd/ *n* a thrush that has bright blue feathers and a bluish or reddish-brown breast. Native to: North America. Genus: *Sialia*.

blue-black *adj* black tinged with blue or with a blue sheen when caught by the light —**blue-black** *n*

blue blood, **blue·blood** /bloŏ blùd/ *n* **1.** the quality of being royal or aristocratic by birth **2.** somebody of royal or aristocratic birth, or somebody born into a respectable and very wealthy family —**blue-blood·ed** *adj*

blue·bon·net /bloŏ bònnət/ *n* **1.** a low-growing lupine. Flowers: light blue, in spikes. Native to: Texas. Latin name: *Lupinus texensis* or *Lupinus subcarnosus*. **2.** a wide round flat cap of blue wool, formerly worn in Scotland

blue book *n* **1.** LIST OF ELITE a book listing names and details of socially prominent people (*informal*) **2.** US SCHOOL EXAM BOOK a thin blank notebook with blue covers, used in schools for writing examination answers **3.** LISTING OF STATE EMPLOYEES a book published by a state government listing its elected officials and employees, and often including a brief history of the state **4.** GOVERNMENT REPORT an official government report bound in a blue cover, especially one published by the British or Canadian government

blue·bot·tle /bloŏ bòtt'l/ *n* **1.** a large buzzing fly with an iridescent blue body that lays its eggs in decaying plant and animal material. Genus: *Calliphora*. **2.** a blue-flowered plant, especially a cornflower or grape hyacinth

blue box *n* **1.** an illegal device formerly used to defraud pay telephones by reproducing tones that would permit free calls **2.** *Can* a box made of blue plastic, used in households to hold recyclable waste

blue cat *n* a large bluish freshwater catfish that may grow to over 100 lb./450 kg. Native to: Mississippi valley. Latin name: *Ictalurus furcatus*.

blue cheese *n* a whitish cheese with veins of blue mold

blue chip *n* **1.** FIN VALUABLE STOCK IN RELIABLE COMPANY a stock selling for a high price because it belongs to a company that is considered to be well-established, highly successful, and reliable **2.** BUSINESS VALUABLE ASSET OR COMPANY an extremely valuable asset, especially a well-established, successful, and reliable company **3.** GAMBLING POKER CHIP a blue-colored gambling chip of high value —**blue-chip** *adj*

blue-chip·per *n* **1.** a blue-chip company **2.** a young athlete or sports player that shows great promise (*informal*)

blue·coat /bloŏ kòt/ *n* somebody who wears a blue coat, especially a police officer (*archaic*)

blue cod *n* **1.** an ocean fish related to perches that is a popular food fish. Native to: New Zealand. Latin name: *Parapercis colias*. **2.** the flesh of a blue cod used as food

blue co·hosh *n* a perennial plant of the barberry family with large blue berries, that is used in herbal medicine to induce labor in childbirth. Native to: North America. Latin name: *Caulophyllum thalictroides*.

blue-col·lar *adj* relating to workers who do manual or industrial work that often requires special work clothes or protective clothing —**blue-col·lar** *n*

blue crab *n* an edible bluish crab. Native to: Atlantic and Gulf coasts of northern America. Latin name: *Callinectes sapidus*.

blue·curls /bloŏ kùrlz/ *n* a plant of the mint family. Flowers: blue with curled blue stamens. Native to: North America. Genus: *Trichostema*. (*takes a singular or plural verb*)

blue dev·il *n* a capsule containing the narcotic and sedative barbiturate amobarbital (*slang*)

blue-eyed boy *n UK* same as **fair-haired boy** (*informal*)

blue-eyed Mar·y *n* a plant of the snapdragon family that has blue and white flowers. Native to: North America. Latin name: *Collinsia verna.*

blue-eyed soul *n* soul music written and played by white musicians (*informal*)

blue·fin /bloó fìn/, **blue·fin tu·na** *n* a large tuna that is caught for sport and food. Native to: temperate seas. Latin name: *Thunnus thynnus.*

blue·fish /bloó fìsh/ (*plural same* or **-fish·es**) *n* **1.** a bluish fish with a silver underside, caught for sport and food. Native to: temperate and tropical regions of the Atlantic and Indian oceans. Latin name: *Pomatomus saltatrix.* **2.** a fish with bluish coloring

blue flag *n* an iris with large blue-violet flowers. Native to: North America. Latin name: *Iris versicolor.*

blue fox *n* **1.** an arctic fox with a tawny brown coat that turns pale blue-gray in winter. Latin name: *Alopex lagopus.* **2.** the fur of a blue fox

blue funk *n* a state of melancholy (*dated informal*)

blue·gill /bloó gìl/ (*plural* **-gills** or *same*) *n* a freshwater sunfish. Native to: eastern and central North America. Latin name: *Lepomis macrochirus.*

blue·grass /bloó gràss/ *n* **1.** a style of country music from the southern United States, usually played on fiddle, banjo, guitar, or mandolin and featuring close harmony and instrumental solos (*often used before a noun*) **2.** a blue-green grass. Native to: North America, Europe. Use: fodder, lawns. Genus: *Poa.*

Blue·grass State *n* a nickname for Kentucky

blue-green al·gae *npl* BIOL same as **cyanobacteria**

blue grouse *n* a gray to brown grouse, distinguished by an orange or yellow patch above the eye of the male. Native to: forests of western North America. Latin name: *Dendragapus obscurus.*

blue gum *n* **1.** a tall eucalyptus tree with aromatic leaves and smooth blue-gray bark. Use: medicinal oil, timber. Native to: Australia. Latin name: *Eucalyptus globulus.* **2.** a eucalyptus tree that has smooth blue-gray bark. Native to: Australia. Genus: *Eucalyptus.*

blue heav·en *n* DRUGS same as **blue devil** (*slang*)

blue helmet *n* a member of a United Nations-controlled military unit

blue·ing *n* TEXTILES another spelling of **bluing**

blue·ish *adj* COLORS another spelling of **bluish**

blue·jack·et /bloó jàkət/ *n* an enlisted man in the navy (*slang*)

blue jay *n* a noisy bird with blue feathers, a crested head, and a white underside. Native to: North America. Latin name: *Cyanocitta cristata.*

blue jeans *npl* a pair of jeans made of blue denim

blue law *n* **1.** a law regulating moral conduct, e.g., a law prohibiting the sale of alcohol on Sundays **2.** a law intended to govern moral conduct in colonial New England [*Blue* in the sense of "puritanical"]

blue line *n* either of two blue lines that divide a hockey rink into the defensive, neutral, and offensive zones

blue moon *n* **1.** a long period of time (*informal*) ○ *once in a blue moon* **2.** a second full moon in a calendar month. As there is a full moon every 29.5 days, a blue moon is a comparatively rare event.

Blue Moun·tains /bloó-/ plateau region about 47 mi./65 km west of Sydney, Australia, part of the Great Dividing Range. Its highest point is Bird Rock, 3,871 ft./1,134 m. Area: 540 sq. mi./1,400 sq. km.

Blue Nile river in northeastern Africa that rises in Ethiopia and supplies about 70 percent of the water that reaches Khartoum, where it joins the White Nile to form the Nile proper. Length: 850 mi./ 1,370 km.

blue·nose /bloó nòz/ *n* somebody excessively concerned with morals (*dated informal*)

Blue·nos·er /bloó nòzər/, **Blue·nose** /bloó nòz/ *n Can* a person who was born in and who lives in Nova Scotia (*slang*) [?]

blue note *n* a musical note played or sung slightly lower than usual, especially in blues and jazz

blue on blue *adj* describes a friendly-fire attack or casualty occurring during a combat operation on sea or land, or in the air

blue pag·es *npl* the section of the telephone book that contains listings of government agencies and departments [Because usually printed on blue paper]

blue-pen·cil (**blue-pen·ciled** or **blue-pen·cilled, blue-pen·cil·ing** or **blue-pen·cil·ling, blue-pen·cils**) *vt* to edit a piece of writing by marking it, in order to shorten, censor, or delete it [< the use of a blue pencil in the editing process]

Blue Pe·ter *n* a blue flag with a white square in the middle, used by ships to signal that they are ready to sail [Because the pattern on the flag represents P in the International Code of Symbols]

blue-plate *adj* describes a main course offered by a restaurant at a lower price than usual ○ *We had the blue-plate special.* [Because cheap fixed-price meals used to be served on blue plates divided into compartments]

blue point *n* a domestic cat, especially a Siamese, that has a bluish cream coat and dark gray markings on its extremities (**points**)

blue·point /bloó pòynt/ (*plural same* or **-points**) *n* a small oyster. Native to: northeastern coastal waters of United States. Latin name: *Crassostrea virginica.* [Late 18C. After *Blue Point,* Long Island]

blue·print /bloó prìnt/ *n* **1.** PRINT OF PLAN a photographic print of a technical drawing with white lines printed on a blue background, or a similarly produced print with blue lines on a white background, usually of an architectural or engineering design **2.** PLAN OR GUIDE a plan of action or a guide to doing something ○ *His administration's policies became a blueprint for those that followed.* ■ *vt* (**-print·ed, -print·ing, -prints**) **1.** MAKE PRINT OF SOMETHING to make a blueprint of something, especially a technical drawing **2.** MAKE PLAN FOR SOMETHING to make or be a plan for something

blue rac·er *n* a blue-green subspecies of the blacksnake. Native to: central United States. Latin name: *Coluber constrictor flaviventris.*

blue rib·and *n UK* same as **blue ribbon** (sense 2)

blue rib·bon *n* **1.** an emblem or badge made of blue ribbon and awarded for first prize in a competition **2.** the highest distinction or first prize in a particular field —**blue-rib·bon** *adj*

blue-rib·bon ju·ry *n* a jury of well-educated people chosen by the court for a case involving issues that are difficult to follow

Blue Ridge, Blue Ridge Moun·tains mountain range in the United States, extending from northern Georgia across western North Carolina and western Virginia into West Virginia. It is the easternmost range of the Appalachian Mountains, with its highest peak at Mount Mitchell 6,684 ft./2,037 m.

blues /blooz/ *n* **1.** STYLE OF MUSIC a type of popular music that developed from African American folk songs in the early 20th century, consisting mainly of slow sad songs often performed over a repeating harmonic pattern (*takes a singular or plural verb*) **2.** (*plural same*) MUSIC PIECE OF MUSIC a song or instrumental piece of music in the style of the blues ■ *npl* FEELING OF SADNESS a feeling of unhappiness or low spirits (*informal; takes a plural verb*) [Mid-18C. < dated slang *blue devils* "depression, low spirits"]

blue shark *n* a shark that has a dark blue back and white underside. Native to: tropical and temperate seas. Latin name: *Prionace glauca.*

blue·shift /bloó shìft/ *n* a displacement in the wavelengths of spectral lines toward the blue end of the visible spectrum, indicating that the radiation source and observer are approaching each other

blue-sky *adj* (*informal*) **1.** idealistic or visionary and without practical application ○ *blue-sky research* ○ *blue-sky thinking* **2.** not worth very much money ○ *blue-sky stocks* —**blue-sky** *vi*

blue-sky law *n* a state law regulating the sale of securities, designed to protect investors from being sold stocks or bonds with no real value

blues·man /bloózmən/ (*plural* **-men** /-mən/) *n* a man who plays or sings the blues

Blue Springs city in western Missouri, southeast of Independence and Kansas City. Population: 49,451 (2002 estimate).

blue spruce *n* a common evergreen tree with short sharp blue-gray needles. Native to: Rocky Mountains of North America. Latin name: *Picea pungens.*

blue·stem /bloó stèm/ *n* a grass that has smooth bluish leaf sheaths and slender spikes in pairs or clusters, used for hay in the western United States. Native to: North America. Latin name: *Andropogon gerardii* or *Schizachyrium scoparium.*

blue·stock·ing /bloó stòking/ *n* an offensive term for a woman who has intellectual, scholarly, or literary interests

ORIGIN At the literary gatherings held at the houses of fashionable mid-18th century hostesses, it became the custom to wear casual rather than formal dress. In the case of gentlemen's stockings, this meant gray worsted (called "blue" at that time) rather than black silk. This lack of decorum was disapproved of in some quarters, and one Admiral Boscowan dubbed the participants the "Blue Stocking Society." Women who attended the gatherings thus became known as "Blue Stocking Ladies" (even though it was men who had worn the stockings).

blue·stone /bloó stòn/ *n* a blue-gray sandstone. Use: building, paving.

blue streak *n* a fast-moving person or thing (*informal humorous*) ◇ **talk a blue streak** to talk very quickly and without pausing (*informal*)

blues·wom·an /blooz wòomman/ (*plural* **-wom·en** /-wìmmin/) *n* a woman who plays or sings the blues

blues·y /bloózee/ (**blue·si·er, blue·si·est**) *adj* composed or performed in or like the style of the blues (*informal*) ○ *a bluesy ballad*

blue·tongue /bloó tùng/ *n* a viral disease of sheep, goats, and cattle transmitted by biting insects, especially mosquitoes, that involves fever, inflammation, ulceration, and death of tissue around the mouth and tongue

Blue·tooth /bloó tòoth/ *tdmk* a trademark for a wireless technology that enables devices such as portable computers, cell phones, and portable handheld devices to connect to each other and to the Internet

blu·ets /bloó əts/ (*plural same*), **blu·et** /bloó it/ *n* a plant of the madder family. Flowers: small, pale blue to white, four-petaled, with yellow centers. Native to: North America. Genus: *Hedyotis.* (*+ singular or plural verb*) [Early 18C. Plural of *bluet* < French *bl(e)uet* "small blue" < *bleu* "blue"]

blue vit·ri·ol *n* CHEM same as **copper sulfate** (*archaic*)

blue wa·ter *n* the ocean far away from the shore

blue-wa·ter *adj* operating on or traveling over the oceans ○ *a blue-water sailor*

blue·weed /bloó wèed/ (*plural* **-weeds** or *same*) *n* **1.** PLANTS same as **viper's bugloss** **2.** a weedy sunflower plant with blue-gray leaves. Native to: southwestern United States. Latin name: *Helianthus ciliaris.*

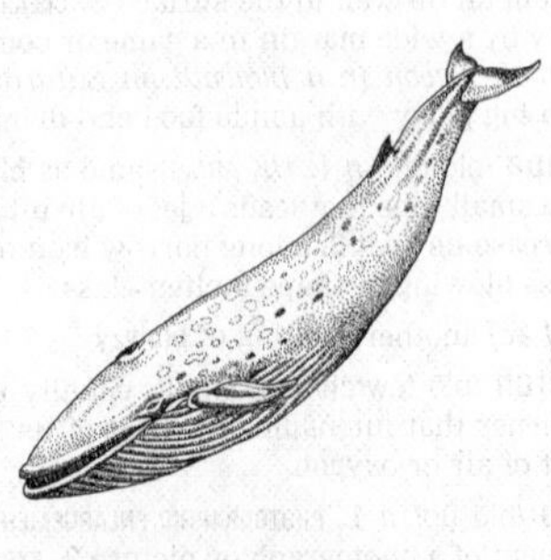

blue whale

blue whale *n* a slate-blue whale, the world's largest living animal, that migrates between polar and equatorial seas. Latin name: *Balaenoptera musculus.*

bluff[1] /bluf/ (**bluffed, bluff·ing, bluffs**) *v* **1.** *vti* **DECEIVE SOMEBODY** to deceive, mislead, or instill fear or doubt in somebody by a false show of strength or confidence **2.** *vti* **DECEIVE PLAYERS ABOUT CARDS** to try to deceive other players in a card game about the true value of the cards you have **3.** *vt Malaysia, Singapore* **MISLEAD SOMEBODY** to try to mislead somebody about something relatively unimportant (*informal*) [Late 17C. < Dutch *bluffen* "brag" or *bluf* "bragging"] —**bluff** *n* —**bluff·a·ble** *adj* —**bluff·er** *n*

bluff[2] /bluf/ *n* **1. CLIFF WITH BROAD FACE** a high steep bank, cliff, or headland, especially one with a broad face **2.** *Can* **GROUP OF TREES ON PRAIRIE** a group of trees surrounded by prairie or grassland ■ *adj* **BLUNT BUT KIND IN MANNER** cheerful and friendly, but outspoken and often insensitive to others' feelings [Early 17C. < Dutch *blaf* "flat"] —**bluff·ly** *adv* —**bluff·ness** *n*

blu·ing /blo͞o ing/, **blue·ing** *n* a substance used in laundering to prevent white materials from turning yellow

blu·ish /blo͞o ish/, **blue·ish** *adj* of a color that is near to blue or contains some blue

Blum /bloom/, **Léon** (1872–1950) French politician. He was France's first socialist prime minister and served three terms (1936–37, 1938, 1946–47).

"A French Jew, of a long line of French ancestors, speaking only the language of my country, mainly nourished by its culture, refusing to leave at a moment when I faced the greatest dangers."
[Léon Blum. Quoted in *Europe Since 1870*, James Joll; 1970]

Blum·berg /blo͞om bùrg/, **Baruch S.** (*b.* 1925) US biochemist. His research led to the development of a vaccine against hepatitis B and won him a shared Nobel Prize in physiology or medicine (1976). Full name **Blumberg, Baruch Samuel**

Blume /bloom/, **Judy** (*b.* 1938) US writer. Her fiction for young people deals openly with contemporary issues such as divorce and has attracted a large readership.

blun·der /blúndər/ *v* (**-dered, -der·ing, -ders**) **1.** *vi* **MAKE SERIOUS MISTAKE** to make a serious or embarrassing mistake as a result of carelessness or ignorance **2.** *vi* **MOVE CLUMSILY** to stumble or move clumsily **3.** *vti* **ACT IN CONFUSED WAY** to act or speak in a manner that is clumsy, ignorant, or thoughtless ■ *n* **SERIOUS MISTAKE** a serious or embarrassing mistake resulting from carelessness or ignorance [14C. < N Germanic < Indo-European] —**blun·der·er** *n* —**blun·der·ing·ly** *adv*

SYNONYMS See *mistake*.

blunderbuss

blun·der·buss /blúndər bùss/ *n* **1.** a short wide-muzzled firearm of the 17th century, used to fire shot with a scattering effect at close range **2.** somebody who is clumsy (*informal*) [Mid-17C. Alteration of Dutch *donderbus* < *donder* "thunder" + *bus* "gun"]

blunge /blunj/ (**blunged, blung·ing, blung·es**) *vt* to mix clay with water and chemicals to create the material for making pottery commercially [Early 19C. Blend of PLUNGE + other *bl-* words such as BLOW[1] and BLEND] —**blung·er** *n*

blunt /blunt/ *adj* **1. NOT SHARP** having a cutting edge or point that is not sharp **2. INSENSITIVELY FRANK OR HONEST** very frank or straightforward and showing no delicacy or consideration ■ *v* (**blunt·ed, blunt·ing, blunts**) **1.** *vti* **MAKE SOMETHING LESS SHARP** to make the cutting edge or point of something less sharp **2.** *vt* **LESSEN OR WEAKEN SOMETHING** to make something such as a sense or an emotion less effective or less intense [13C. Perhaps < Old Norse *blundr* "dozing"] —**blunt·ly** *adv* —**blunt·ness** *n*

Blunt /blunt/, **Anthony** (1907–83) British art historian and Soviet spy. He was Surveyor of the Queen's Pictures (1945–72), but was stripped of his knighthood and disgraced after the public disclosure (1979) of his role as a Soviet spy in the ring that included Guy Burgess and Donald Maclean. Full name **Blunt, Anthony Frederick**

blur /blur/ *n* **1. FUZZY OR UNCLEAR IMAGE** something that cannot be seen clearly, e.g., because it moves too quickly or because it is not distinctly remembered **2. SMEAR OR SMEARED AREA** a mark on something that makes it unclear, or an area of something that is unclear ■ *vti* (**blurred, blur·ring, blurs**) **1. MAKE OR BECOME VAGUE** to become less clear or distinct, or make something such as an idea less clear or distinct ○ *blurred the line between right and wrong* **2. MAKE OR BECOME FUZZY** to become fuzzy or unclear, or make something fuzzy or unclear ■ *adj Malaysia, Singapore* **CONFUSED** confused or uncertain about something (*informal*) ○ *I am very blur about linguistics.* [Mid-16C. Probably variant of BLEAR] —**blurred·ness** *n* —**blur·ri·ly** *adv* —**blur·ri·ness** *n* —**blur·ry** *adj*

blurb /blurb/ *n* a short piece of writing that praises and promotes something, especially a paragraph on the cover of a book (*slang*) [Early 20C. Coined by Gelett Burgess (1866–1951), US humorist] —**blurb** *vt*

blurt /blurt/ (**blurt·ed, blurt·ing, blurts**) *vt* to say something suddenly or impulsively, as if by accident ○ *blurted out an apology* [Late 16C. Probably an imitation of the sound]

blush /blush/ *vi* (**blushed, blush·ing, blush·es**) **1. BECOME RED IN FACE** to turn red in the face because of emotion, especially embarrassment, shame, modesty, or pleasure **2. BECOME EMBARRASSED** to feel embarrassed or ashamed (*formal*) **3. TURN RED OR PINK** to become red or pink (*literary*) ■ *n* **1. REDDENING OF FACE** a reddening of the face caused by emotion, especially embarrassment, shame, modesty, or pleasure **2. RED OR PINK** a red color or rosy glow **3.** COSMETICS **PINK MAKEUP FOR CHEEKS** a pink or reddish powder or cream applied to the face, especially to accent the cheekbones [Old English *blyscan* < Indo-European] —**blush·ful** *adj* —**blush·ing** *adj* —**blush·ing·ly** *adv*

blush·er /blúshər/ *n UK* same as **blush** *n* (sense 3)

blush wine *n* wine with a slight pink tinge

blus·ter /blústər/ *v* (**-tered, -ter·ing, -ters**) **1.** *vti* **SPEAK OR SAY LOUDLY OR ARROGANTLY** to speak loudly, boisterously, or arrogantly, or say something in this way **2.** *vti* **BEHAVE IN BULLYING WAY** to behave or do something in a bullying or threatening way **3.** *vi* **BLOW LOUDLY IN GUSTS** to blow in sudden loud gusts (*refers to winds*) ■ *n* **1. LOUD ARROGANT SPEECH** loud, boisterous, or arrogant speech **2. BULLYING BEHAVIOR** bullying or threatening behavior **3. LOUD GUST** a sudden loud gust of wind **4. LOUD FUSS** a loud or angry commotion [Early 15C. < Middle Low German *blustern* "blow violently"] —**blus·ter·er** *n* —**blus·ter·ing·ly** *adv* —**blus·ter·y** *adj*

Blvd. *abbr* ROADS Boulevard

Bly /blī/, **Nellie** (1867–1922) US journalist. She used her platform as a *New York World* journalist to campaign for social issues, and gained notoriety for her 72-day round-the-world trip (1889–90). Pseudonym of **Seaman, Elizabeth Cochrane**

B lym·pho·cyte *n* IMMUNOL same as **B cell**

Blyth /blīth/ industrial port in Northumberland, northern England. Population: 35,327 (1991).

Blyth, Chay (*b.* 1940) British yachtsman. He was the first person to sail single-handed around the world traveling east to west (1970–71). Born **Blyth, Charles**

Blythe·ville /blīth vìl/ city in northeastern Arkansas, south of the Missouri border and west of the Mississippi River. Population: 17,555 (2002 estimate).

b.m. *abbr* **1.** MEASURE board measure **2.** PHYSIOL bowel movement

BMEWS *abbr* MIL ballistic missile early warning system

BMI *abbr* body mass index

B mov·ie *n* a low-budget movie that was formerly shown in addition to the main feature —**B-mov·ie** *adj*

bmp *abbr* a file extension for a bit map file. Full form **bit map**

B.Mus. *abbr* EDUC Bachelor of Music

BMX *n* the riding or racing of bicycles designed for use on rough terrain or open country. Full form **bicycle motocross**

bn *abbr* Brunei (*used in Internet addresses*) See table at **domain name**

bn. *abbr* **1.** MIL battalion **2.** billion

Bn. *abbr* **1.** baron **2.** MIL battalion

B'nai B'rith /bə này bríth/ *n* an international Jewish social service organization founded in New York in 1843 [< Hebrew, "Sons of the Covenant"]

bo[1] /bō/ *n* used as a friendly form of address to a man or boy (*informal*) ○ *"Hey, bo!"* [Early 19C. Origin ?]

bo[2] *abbr* Bolivia (*used in Internet addresses*) See table at **domain name**

BO *n* an unpleasant smell that comes from somebody because of sweat, lack of hygiene, or a physical disorder (*informal*) Full form **body odor**

b.o. *abbr* **1.** BUSINESS branch office **2.** FIN broker's order **3.** FIN buyer's option

bo·a /bō ə/ *n* **1.** a nonvenomous, often large snake that kills by winding its body around its prey and suffocating it. Native to: tropical America, Africa, Asia. Family: Boidae. **2.** a long fluffy scarf of feathers or fur worn by women around the neck [14C. < Latin, "large water snake"]

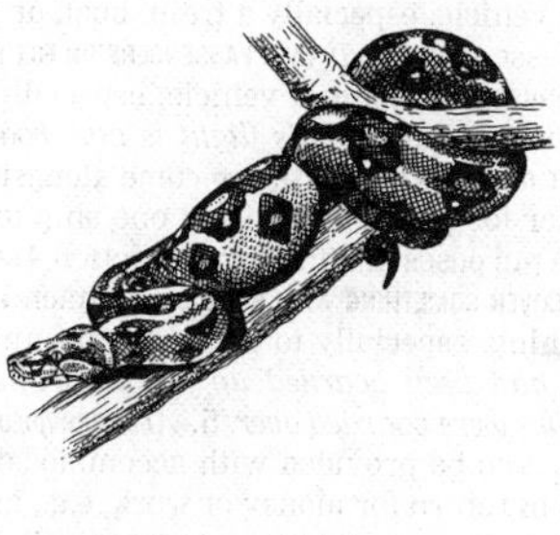

boa constrictor

bo·a con·stric·tor *n* a large snake of the boa family that kills by winding its body around its prey and crushing it. Native to: tropical Central and South America. Latin name: *Boa constrictor*.

boar

boar /bawr/ *n* (*plural* **boars** or *same*) **1. UNCASTRATED PIG** a male pig that has not been castrated **2. MALE MAMMAL** a male mammal, e.g., a male badger, beaver, or raccoon **3.** ZOOL same as **wild boar** ■ *adj Carib* **MALE** indicating a male animal, e.g., a boar-hog [Old English *bār* < W Germanic]

SPELLCHECK boar or **bore**? Do not confuse the spelling of ***boar*** and ***bore***, which sound similar. The word ***boar*** is only used as a noun, denoting an animal. The word ***bore*** is principally used as a verb, meaning "cause to lose interest" or "make a hole": *I won't bore you with the details. The insects bore through the bark.* It is also the past tense of the verb *bear*: *I bore them no ill will.* As a noun, ***bore*** denotes an uninteresting person or thing, the internal diameter of a pipe or gun barrel, or a large powerful wave.

board[1] /bawrd/ *n* **1.** FLAT PIECE OF WOOD a piece of wood cut into a flat rectangular shape, especially a long narrow piece used for building **2.** FLAT SURFACE FOR PARTICULAR PURPOSE a flat piece of wood, plastic, or other rigid material, used for a particular purpose, e.g., for chopping food **3.** BOARD GAMES FLAT SURFACE FOR GAME a flat surface on which a game is played, especially a piece of wood or cardboard marked with colored areas for a game such as chess **4.** COMPOSITE MATERIAL PRESSED INTO SHEET a rigid sheet material such as plywood made by compressing layers of other materials **5.** CONTROL PANEL a panel on which the controls of a piece of electrical equipment are mounted **6.** EDUC same as **blackboard 7.** same as **bulletin board** (sense 1) **8.** ELECTRONICS same as **circuit board 9.** SWIMMING same as **diving board 10.** SURFING same as **surfboard 11.** same as **scoreboard 12.** SPORTS same as **snowboard 13.** BASKETBALL same as **backboard** (sense 1) **14.** PUBL BOOK COVER either of the pair of pieces of stiff cardboard that together form the front and back covers of a book **15.** NAUT BOAT'S SIDE the side of a boat **16.** GROUP CHOSEN TO MAKE DECISIONS a group of people chosen to make executive or managerial decisions for an organization **17.** DAILY MEALS daily meals provided at the place where somebody lives, usually for money or in return for work **18.** TABLE LAID WITH FOOD a table used for meals, especially one with food laid out on it (*archaic*) **19.** SAILING DISTANCE SAILED INTO WIND the distance covered by a sailing vessel in one period of sailing as near as possible into the wind ■ **boards** *npl* **1.** THEATRICAL STAGE the stage in a theater **2.** HOCKEY RINK ENCLOSURE the wooden wall that surrounds a hockey rink ■ *v* (**board·ed, board·ing, boards**) **1.** *vti* GET ONTO VEHICLE AS PASSENGER to get onto a vehicle, especially a train, boat, or airplane, as a passenger **2.** *vti* TAKE PASSENGERS ON FOR JOURNEY to take passengers onto a vehicle, especially a train, boat, or airplane ○ *This flight is now boarding.* **3.** *vt* NAUT ATTACK OR INSPECT SHIP to come alongside a ship in order for people to go from one ship to another for the purposes of attack or inspection **4.** *also* **board up** *vt* COVER SOMETHING WITH BOARDS to attach boards to something, especially to cover any openings ○ *The house had been boarded up for the winter.* ○ *The windows were boarded over.* **5.** *vti* BE PROVIDED WITH ROOM AND MEALS to be provided with accommodations and meals in return for money or work, e.g., in a school or guesthouse, or provide somebody with these [Old English *bord* < Germanic, "board, plank" and "border, ship's side"] ◇ **go by the board** to be neglected, no longer used, cast aside, or destroyed ◇ **on board 1.** into or on a vehicle, especially a train, boat, or airplane **2.** into an existing group or project (*informal*) ○ *As soon as we bring this new analyst on board, the workload should return to normal.* ◇ **take something on board** to understand or realize something fully

SPELLCHECK Do not confuse the spelling of ***board*** and ***bored*** ("tired and impatient"), which sound similar.

board bridge *n* BOARD GAMES same as **duplicate bridge**

board cer·ti·fi·ca·tion *n* official and documented recognition from an official panel of experts in a professional field such as medicine that somebody is highly qualified in that field

board-cer·ti·fied *adj* officially certified as expert in a particular field after passing an exam and meeting strict standards

board·er /báwrdər/ *n* **1.** somebody who pays to sleep and eat in a private home or boarding house **2.** somebody who tries to get onto a ship to capture it

board ex·am *n* **1.** in the United States, an examination taken by somebody in order to qualify for work in a particular field, e.g., medicine or dentistry **2.** in the United States, an examination taken as part of the admission procedure for some colleges and universities

board foot *n* a unit of volume for measuring lumber, equal to the volume of a board that is one foot square and one inch thick

board game *n* a game such as chess or backgammon that involves moving pieces around on a board marked with colored areas

board·ing /báwrding/ *n* a number of wooden boards, especially when used for a particular purpose, e.g., to make a floor or a fence

board·ing house *n* a private home that provides a room and meals to paying guests who are usually long-term residents

board·ing pass *n* an additional ticket or document that a passenger must have in order to be allowed onto an aircraft or ship

board·ing school *n* a school that provides some or all students with accommodations and daily meals

board meas·ure *n* a system for measuring lumber volume based on the board foot

board of ed·u·ca·tion *n* EDUC same as **school board**

board of trade *n* an organization of businesses and banks that has the goal of promoting commercial interest in a state, city, or other area

board·room /báwrd ròom, -rŏŏm/ *n* a room where the members of a board meet

board·sail·ing /báwrd sàyling/ *n* SPORTS same as **windsurfing** —**board·sail·or** *n*

board·walk /báwrd wàwk/ *n* a raised walkway made of boards, often built along beaches at beach resorts

Bo·as /bō àz/, **Franz** (1858–1942) German-born US anthropologist. He helped establish anthropology as an academic discipline. He advocated a scientific approach to anthropological investigation and supported the theory of cultural relativism.

> "Much of what we ascribe to human nature is no more than a reaction to the restraints put upon us by our civilization."
> [Franz Boas. Quoted in *Coming of Age in Samoa*, Margaret Mead; 1928]

boast[1] /bōst/ *v* (**boast·ed, boast·ing, boasts**) **1.** *vti* OVER-EMPHASIZE POSSESSIONS OR ACCOMPLISHMENTS to refer immodestly to possessions or achievements **2.** *vt* POSSESS SOMETHING DESIRABLE to possess or contain something, especially something desirable ○ *Our town boasts the world's biggest roller coaster.* ■ *n* **1.** EXCESSIVELY PROUD STATEMENT an immodest reference to possessions or achievements **2.** DESIRABLE POSSESSION something possessed that is desirable [13C. < Anglo-Norman *bost* "boasting" < N Germanic] —**boast·er** *n* —**boast·ful** *adj* —**boast·ful·ly** *adv* —**boast·ful·ness** *n*

boast[2] /bōst/ (**boast·ed, boast·ing, boasts**) *vt* to shape stone roughly using a chisel [Early 19C. Origin ?]

boat /bōt/ *n* **1.** SMALL VESSEL FOR TRAVELING ON WATER a small, often open vessel for traveling on water **2.** SHIP OR SUBMARINE a watercraft of any size or type **3.** SOMETHING SHAPED LIKE BOAT an open container shaped like a boat, e.g., one for holding gravy or incense ■ *v* (**boat·ed, boat·ing, boats**) **1.** *vi* TRAVEL BY BOAT to travel by boat, or ride in a boat for pleasure **2.** *vt* CARRY SOMETHING BY BOAT to move or transport something by boat **3.** *vt* FISHING PULL FISH TO BOAT to bring a caught fish to a boat [Old English *bāt* < Germanic] ◇ **in the same boat** in the same situation or having the same problems as somebody else (*informal*) ◇ **miss the boat** to fail to take advantage of an opportunity (*informal*) ◇ **rock the boat** to cause trouble, especially by questioning an accepted situation (*informal*)

boat·bill /bṓt bìl/ *n* a bird of the heron family with a large, dark, heavy beak. Native to: tropical America. Latin name: *Cochlearius cochlearius.*

boat deck *n* a deck on a ship where the lifeboats are carried

boa·tel /bō tél/, **bo·tel** *n* **1.** a waterside hotel where people traveling in boats can stay and moor their boats **2.** a ship that functions as a hotel [Mid-20C. Blend of BOAT + HOTEL]

boat·er /bṓtər/ *n* **1.** somebody who rides in a boat **2.** a circular straw hat with a flat brim, a flat crown, and a hatband

boat hook *n* a long pole with a hook on one end, used for pulling or pushing boats, rafts, or logs, or for picking up items from the water

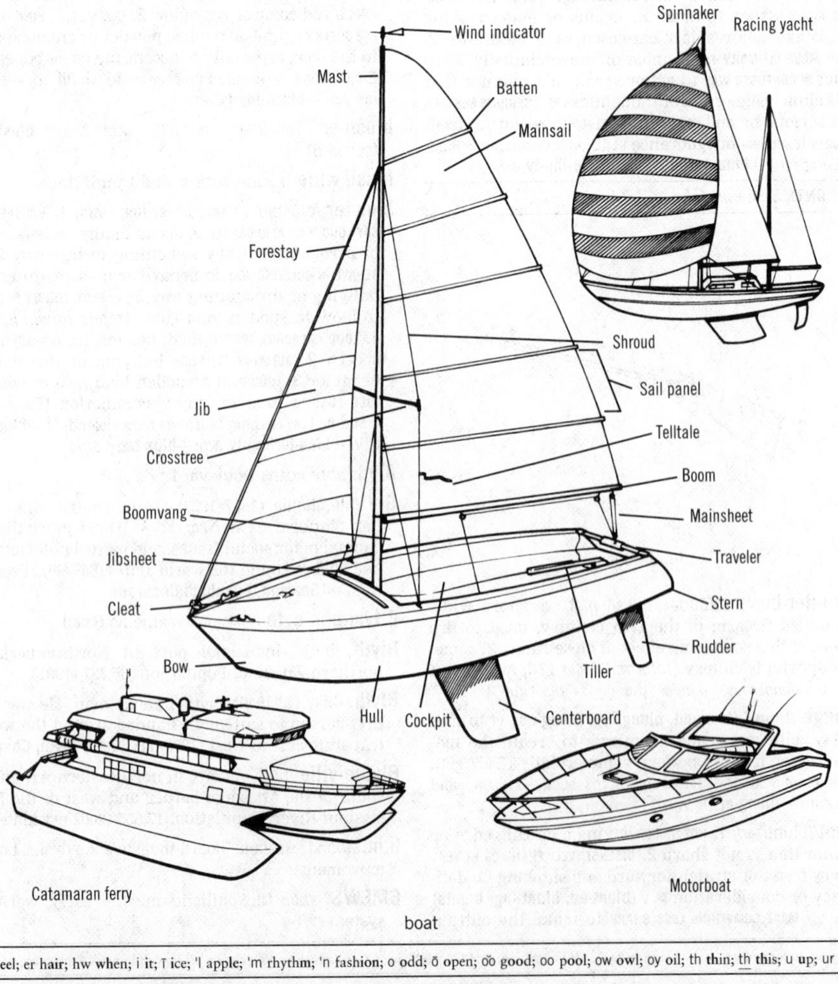

boat

boat·house /bṓt hòwss/ (*plural* **-hous·es** /-hòwzəz/) *n* a small building beside water, in which boats are kept

boat·load /bṓt lṑd/ *n* **1.** an amount of something or a number of people that fills a boat **2.** a large amount of something or a large number of people (*informal*)

boat·man /bṓtmən/ (*plural* **-men** /-mən/) *n* somebody who operates or works on a boat, especially somebody who takes people for rides on a boat or who rents boats out to others —**boat·man·ship** *n*

boat neck *n* a wide shallow neckline that runs from shoulder to shoulder and is equally deep at the front and back, similar to the neckline of a traditional sailor's blouse

boat peo·ple *npl* refugees who leave their country by boat

boat-rock·er *n* somebody who is unafraid to challenge the status quo or stir up controversy

boat·swain /bṓss'n/, **bo's'n, bo·sun** *n* a noncommissioned officer or warrant officer on a ship in charge of the maintenance of the vessel, its boats, and other equipment [Old English *bātswegen* < BOAT + Old Norse *sveinn* "boy" (see SWAIN)]

boat·swain's chair *n* a board supported by ropes, slung over the side of a ship or up in the rigging for somebody to sit on while working

boat train *n* a train that takes people between a dockside and a town, usually timed to coincide with the arrival or departure of a ferry or liner

boat·wo·man /bṓt wòommən/ (*plural* **-wo·men** /-wìmmin/) *n* a woman who operates or works on a boat, especially one who takes people for rides on a boat or who rents boats out to others

boat·yard /bṓt yaàrd/ *n* an area where boats are built or maintained

bob[1] /bob/ *vi* (**bobbed, bob·bing, bobs**) **1.** BOUNCE to bounce up and down quickly and repeatedly, especially in and out of the water while floating **2.** MAKE CURTSY, BOW, OR NOD to make a quick movement, especially a curtsy, bow, or nod ■ *n* **1.** SMALL HANGING OR BOUNCING OBJECT a small hanging or bouncing object, e.g., a weight on a plumb line or a fishing bobber **2.** CURTSY, BOW, OR NOD a quick movement such as a curtsy, bow, or nod [14C. Probably an imitation of the sound]

bob[2] /bob/ *n* **1.** WOMAN'S SHORT HAIRCUT a woman's short haircut, especially a straight cut at chin length **2.** SOMETHING CUT SHORT something that has been shortened, e.g., a horse's tail when docked, a dog's ears when clipped **3.** OPERATION ON NOSE a surgical shortening or reshaping of the nose (*informal*) **4.** SPORTS same as **bobsled** (*informal*) ■ *vt* (**bobbed, bob·bing, bobs**) CUT HAIR SHORT to cut a person's hair or a horse's tail short so that it is all one length [14C. Origin ?]

bob[3] /bob/ (*plural same*) *n UK* a shilling in the former British currency system (*informal*) [Late 18C. Origin ?]

bob[4] /bob/ *n* a small polishing wheel of felt or leather ■ *vt* (**bobbed, bob·bing, bobs**) to polish something using a bob [Probably < BOB[2]]

bob·ber /bóbbər/ *n* a light object attached to a fishing line that floats on the surface of the water to keep the bait at the correct depth

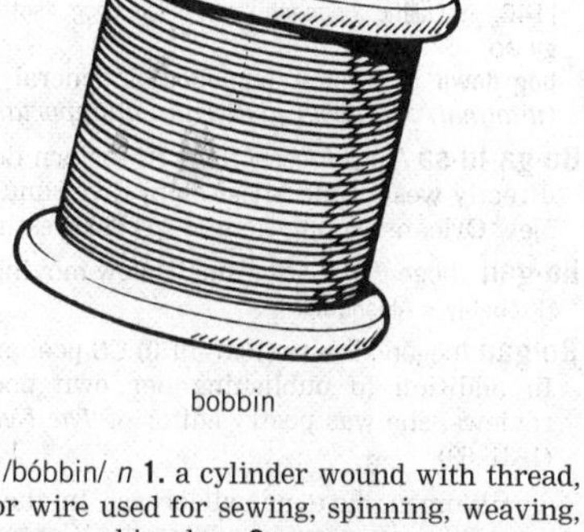

bobbin

bob·bin /bóbbin/ *n* **1.** a cylinder wound with thread, yarn, or wire used for sewing, spinning, weaving, knitting, or making lace **2.** a narrow cotton cord, often braided, formerly used for trimming and binding [Mid-16C. < French *bobine* "sewing instrument" < Old French *balbiner*, probably alteration of *balbier* "to stutter" < Latin *balbus* "stuttering"]

bob·bi·net /bòbbə nét/ *n* a machine-made net fabric with a hexagonal mesh

bob·bin lace *n* a lace made by winding thread on bobbins around pins stuck into a pillow

bob·ble /bóbb'l/ *n* MISTAKE a mistake or blunder (*informal*) ■ *v* (**-bled, -bling, -bles**) **1.** *vti* MOVE UP AND DOWN to move, or cause something to move, quickly and repeatedly up and down **2.** *vt* HANDLE CLUMSILY to handle clumsily something such as a ball when playing a game, or to do something ineptly (*informal*) [Early 19C. Probably < BOB[1]]

bob·by /bóbbee/ (*plural* **-bies**) *n UK* POLICE same as **policeman** (*informal dated*) [Mid-19C. < pet form of *Robert*, after Sir Robert PEEL, who introduced the 1828 Police Act]

bob·by pin *n* a hair clip made of a tightly folded piece of wire that slides into the hair and holds it in place [Probably < BOB[2] "short haircut"]

bob·by socks /-sòks/, **bob·by sox** *npl* ankle socks that fold over at the top, popular among teenage girls in the 1940s and 1950s [Probably < BOB[2]]

bob·by·sox·er /bóbbee sòksər/ *n* a teenage girl of the 1940s and 1950s (*informal*)

bob·cat /bób kàt/ *n* a medium-sized wildcat that is related to the lynx and has reddish brown fur with black markings, tufted ears, and a short tail. Native to: North America. Latin name: *Lynx rufus.* [Late 19C. < BOB[2], from its short tail]

Bob·cat *tdmk* a trademark for hydraulic excavating machinery and loaders

bob·o·link /bóbbə lìngk/ (*plural* **-links** or *same*) *n* a small bird, white and yellow above and black underneath, that nests in meadowland and has a distinctive bubbly song. Native to: North and South America. Latin name: *Dolichonyx oryzivorus.* [Late 18C. An imitation of the bird's call]

Bo·bo·tov Kuk /bàwbə tawf kòok/ mountain in Montenegro, Federal Republic of Yugoslavia. It is the highest peak in the Dinaric range. Height: 8,274 ft./2,522 m.

bob skate *n* an ice skate that has two parallel blades, usually used by children [< BOB[2], from its shortness]

bob·sled /bób slèd/ *n* **1.** RACING SLED a long racing sled with steering, brakes, a seat for two or more people, and two pairs of runners, one in front and one in back **2.** SLED MADE OF TWO SHORT SLEDS a long sled made of two short sleds attached one behind the other, used for recreation or for carrying things over snow ■ *vi* (**-sled·ded, -sled·ding, -sleds**) GO IN BOBSLED to ride or race in a bobsled

bob·sleigh /bób slày/ *n, vi* (**-sleighed, -sleigh·ing, -sleighs**) *UK* SPORTS same as **bobsled**

bob·stay /bób stày/ *n* on a sailing boat, a rope used to hold down a bowsprit [*Bob*, origin ?]

bob·tail /bób tàyl/ *n* **1.** an animal's tail that is naturally short or has been cut short **2.** an animal, especially a horse or dog, that has a short or shortened tail [Mid-16C. < BOB[2], from its shortness] —**bob·tailed** *adj*

bob·white /bób wìt, -hwìt/ (*plural* **-whites** or *same*) *n* a small brown mottled quail with white markings on its head. Native to: central and eastern North America. Latin name: *Colinus virginianus.* [Early 19C. An imitation of the bird's call]

bo·cac·cio /bə kaáchō, -kaáchee ō/ (*plural same* or **-cios**) *n* a large brown rockfish. Native to: Pacific coast of North America. Latin name: *Sebastes paucispinis.* [Late 19C. < Italian *bocaccio* "ugly mouth" < Latin *bucca* "mouth"]

Bo·ca Ra·ton /bṑkə rə tṓn/ city and resort near Palm Beach in southeastern Florida, on the shore of the Atlantic Ocean. Population: 77,411 (2002 estimate).

Boc·cac·cio /bō kaáchee ō, -chō/, **Giovanni** (1313–75) Italian writer and humanist. He wrote the *Decameron* (written 1348–53, published 1353), a collection of 100 tales told by refugees from the Florentine plague of 1348. A classic of world literature, it profoundly influenced English writers such as Shakespeare.

> "Although love dwells in gorgeous palaces, and sumptuous apartments, more willingly than in miserable and desolate cottages, it cannot be denied but that he sometimes causes his power to be felt in the gloomy recesses of forests, among the most bleak and rugged mountains, and in the dreary caves of a desert."
> [Giovanni Boccaccio, *Decameron*; 1353]

boc·ce /bóchee/, **boc·ci** *n* an Italian game similar to lawn bowling, usually played on a long earth-floored court [Early 20C. Via Italian *bocce*, plural of *boccia* "(round) ball" < Vulgar Latin *bottia* "boss"]

Boc·che·ri·ni /bṑkə reénee, bòkə-/, **Luigi** (1743–1805) Italian composer and cellist. A prolific writer of chamber music, he composed for the Spanish and Prussian courts. Full name **Boccherini, Luigi Rodolfo**

boc·ci *n* LAWN BOWLING another spelling of **bocce**

Boche /bosh, bawsh/ (*plural* **Boches** or *same*), **boche** (*plural* **boches** or *same*) *n* an offensive term for Germans considered collectively, especially German soldiers of World War I (*dated*) [Early 20C. Shortening of French *alboche*, blend of *allemand* "German" + *caboche* "cabbage, blockhead"]

Bo·chum /bṓkəm, bṓ k͟hòom/ city in the industrial Ruhr district of North Rhine-Westphalia, Germany. Population: 401,129 (1997).

bock beer /bók-/ *n* a dark rich beer [Mid-19C. < German *Bockbier*, alteration of *Einbecker Bier*, after *Einbeck*, Germany]

bod /bod/ *n* (*slang*) **1.** somebody's body or figure **2.** same as **person** (sense 1) [Late 18C. Shortening of BODY]

B.O.D. *abbr* biochemical oxygen demand

bo·da·cious /bō dáyshəss/, **bow·da·cious** (*informal humorous*) *adj* **1.** *Midwest, Southern US* BOLD outrageously arrogant or uninhibited ○ *a bodacious lie* **2.** *Midwest, Southern US, UK* IMPRESSIVE remarkable or excellent ○ *That's one bodacious boat!* ■ *adv Midwest, Southern US* VERY extremely ○ *I'm bodacious hungry.* [Mid-19C. Perhaps alteration of dialect blend of BOLD + AUDACIOUS] —**bo·da·cious·ly** *adv*

bode[1] /bōd/ (**bod·ed, bod·ing, bodes**) *vti* to be a particular indication of something that is about to happen ○ *This does not bode well for the future of the organization.* [Old English *bodian* "announce, foretell" < *boda* "messenger" < Germanic]

bode[2] past tense of **bide**

bo·de·ga /bō dáygə/ *n Hispanic* **1.** a small grocery store in a Spanish-speaking neighborhood **2.** in a Spanish-speaking country, a wine shop or a warehouse for the storage of wine [Mid-19C. Via Spanish < Latin *apotheca* "storehouse"]

Bod·en·heim /bṓd'n hīm/, **Maxwell** (1893–1954) US writer. He lived a bohemian lifestyle in Greenwich Village, New York City, and published poems and novels including a volume of *Selected Poems* (1946). Born **Bodenheimer, Maxwell**

Bo·dhi·dhar·ma /bṑdi daármə/ (*fl* 6th century) Indian monk. He was the founder of the Zen school of Buddhism.

bo·dhi·satt·va /bṑdi sútvə/ *n* in Buddhism, a deity or being who has attained enlightenment worthy of nirvana but who remains in the human world to help others [Early 19C. < Sanskrit *bodhi* "perfect knowledge" + *sattva* "being, reality"]

bodh·rán /bów raán/ *n* a shallow drum used in Irish and sometimes Scottish folk music, covered on one side with goatskin, held in one hand, and played with the other using a stick [Late 20C. < Irish]

bod·ice /bóddiss/ *n* **1.** the part of a woman's dress or undergarment that covers the upper body **2.** a close-fitting, often laced-up top worn over a blouse in the past or as part of some national costumes [Mid-16C. < plural of BODY]

bod·ice rip·per *n* a popular historical romance in fiction or film that has sexually explicit content and usually involves a melodramatic seduction (*slang*) [< typical scenes where a seducer tears a woman's bodice open]

-bodied *adj, suffix* having a body of a particular kind ○ *a wide-bodied aircraft*

bod·i·less /bóddeeləss/ *adj* having no body or physical substance

bod·i·ly /bódd'lee/ *adj* **PHYSICAL** relating to, involving, or typical of the body ■ *adv* **1. PHYSICALLY** physically or in the flesh **2. USING PHYSICAL FORCE** by taking hold of somebody or something with the hands and using physical strength ○ *bodily removed him from the building*

bod·kin /bódkin/ *n* **1. LARGE BLUNT NEEDLE** a long thick blunt needle with a large eye **2. HOLE-PUNCHING TOOL** a small slender tool with a sharp point used for making holes in cloth or leather **3.** PRINTING **TYPESETTING TOOL** a long sharp typesetting tool [14C. Probably < Celtic, "small dagger"]

bo·dom /bṓdəm/ *n* a highly valued Ghanaian bead with a black center made of powdered glass [< Ashanti]

bod·y /bóddee/ *n* (*plural* **-ies**) **1. PHYSICAL FORM OF HUMAN OR ANIMAL** the complete material structure or physical form of a human being or animal **2. DEAD HUMAN OR ANIMAL REMAINS** the physical remains of a dead person or animal **3. TORSO** the main part of the physical structure of a human being or animal, not including the head, arms, legs, or wings **4. SOMEBODY'S FIGURE** somebody's figure or build, especially with regard to shape and muscle tone ○ *a great body* **5. GROUP** an organized group of people such as lawmakers, students, or soldiers ○ *a legislative body* **6. COLLECTION** a collection or amount of something, considered as a whole ○ *a body of evidence* **7. MASS** an individual mass of something, especially water or land ○ *a large body of water* **8. MAIN PART OF VEHICLE** the main part of a vehicle, e.g., the fuselage of an aircraft or the outer shell of a car **9. MAIN PART OR MAJORITY** the main or central part of something, e.g., the majority of a quantity **10.** BUILDINGS **NAVE** the nave or central part of a church **11.** MUSIC **MAIN PART OF MUSICAL INSTRUMENT** the largest part of a musical instrument, especially the soundbox of a stringed instrument **12. MAIN PART OF SOMETHING WRITTEN** the main part of a piece of writing ○ *in the body of the text* **13. FULLNESS OF FLAVOR IN WINE** the extent to which a wine seems full when tasted. Body increases with alcohol content and density. ○ *a French red with plenty of body* **14. THICKNESS OF LIQUID** the thickness or opacity of a liquid such as paint or soup **15. FULLNESS OF TEXTURE** a fullness and bounciness in texture or appearance ○ *designed to give hair more body* **16. FIRMNESS OF FABRIC** the firmness of a type of cloth **17.** *UK* CLOTHING same as **body suit 18. UPPER PART OF GARMENT** the part of a garment that covers the torso **19. PERSON** used to refer to a person or yourself in an impersonal way (*informal*) ○ *This treatment could make a body feel unwelcome!* **20.** CERAMICS **MATERIAL FOR MAKING CERAMICS** a blend of clay and other raw materials used in making a ceramic piece **21.** PHYS **PHYSICAL OBJECT** a distinguishable physical object **22.** MATH **OBJECT REPRESENTED MATHEMATICALLY** a physical object represented mathematically ■ *vt* (**-ied, -y·ing, -ies**) **GIVE SHAPE TO SOMETHING** to give shape or substance to something (*literary*) [Old English *bodig*, origin ?]

bod·y ar·mor *n* a protective covering for the upper part of the torso

bod·y bag *n* a bag designed to hold a dead body, usually made of plastic and fitted with a zipper

bod·y blow *n* **1.** something that causes great physical, financial, or emotional damage to somebody or something **2.** a punch that lands between the neck and the waist

bod·y board *n* a short polystyrene surfboard on which a surfer lies rather than stands

bod·y·build·ing /bóddee bìlding/ *n* the practice of developing the muscles of the body through weight-lifting and diet —**bod·y·build·er** *n*

bod·y bun·ker *n US* a small shield attached to the arm for fending off stones and other light projectiles. Can term **body shield**

bod·y cav·i·ty *n* **1.** an opening into the body, e.g., the mouth, esophagus, vagina, rectum, or ear **2.** ZOOL same as **coelom**

bod·y-cen·tered *adj* describes crystals that have an atom in the middle of each unit cell as well as at the corners

bod·y·check /bóddee chèk/ *n* in some sports, especially hockey or soccer, an illegal act of using the body to obstruct an opposing player ■ *vt* (**-checked, -check·ing, -checks**) in some sports, especially hockey or soccer, to use the body to obstruct an opposing player illegally

bod·y clock *n* BIOL same as **biological clock**

bod·y cor·po·rate (*plural* **bod·ies cor·po·rate**) *n* a group of people legally recognized as being able to act as one body

bod·y count *n* a count of the number of dead bodies resulting from an incident, especially of soldiers killed after combat

bod·y dou·ble *n* somebody whose body is filmed instead of that of an actor, especially in a scene involving nudity

bod·y Eng·lish *n* natural and unconscious body movements made as if to influence the movement of a thrown ball or other moving object (*informal*)

bod·y flu·id *n* **1.** a liquid produced by the body, e.g., blood, saliva, semen, vaginal secretions, milk, urine, sweat, or tears **2.** the water content of the body

bod·y·guard /bóddee gaàrd/ *n* a person or group of people paid to protect somebody from physical attack

bod·y-hug·ging *adj* fitting tightly on the body

bod·y im·age *n* somebody's own impression of how his or her body looks

bod·y lan·guage *n* bodily mannerisms, postures, and facial expressions that can be interpreted as unconsciously communicating somebody's feelings or psychological state

bod·y mass in·dex *n* an index that expresses adult weight in relation to height. It is calculated as weight in kilograms divided by height in meters squared, or 704.5 times weight in pounds divided by height in inches squared. A body mass index of less than 25 is considered normal, and one of over 30 implies obesity.

bod·y o·dor *n* HEALTH full form of **BO**

bod·y pack·er *n* somebody who swallows illegal narcotics in order to smuggle them (*slang*)

bod·y pol·i·tic *n* the people of a nation or any politically organized state, considered as a group

bod·y pop·ping *n* a type of dancing, popular especially in the 1980s, involving convulsive, sinuous, or robotic movements (*slang*) —**bod·y pop·per** *n*

bod·y search *n* a thorough physical search of somebody suspected of hiding something such as weapons or narcotics on his or her person

bod·y·shap·er /bóddee shàypər/ *n UK* a woman's elasticized undergarment reaching from bust to hips, intended to produce a more streamlined body shape

bod·y shield *n* **1.** a small shield held in front of the body to protect it from blows, e.g., by a police officer during a riot, or by somebody training in a martial art **2.** a small shield attached to the arm for fending off stones and other light projectiles

bod·y shirt *n* a shirt that fits closely to the body, often worn under other clothing and sometimes fastened at the crotch with snaps

bod·y shop *n* a workshop where car bodies are repaired (*informal*)

bod·y snatch·er *n* in the past, somebody who stole corpses from graves, usually to sell for medical study —**bod·y·snatch·ing** *n*

bod·y stock·ing *n* a close-fitting one-piece garment that covers the body and sometimes the arms and legs

bod·y suit *n* a woman's close-fitting, one-piece garment that covers the torso and is fastened at the crotch by snaps

bod·y·surf /bóddee sùrf/ (**-surfed, -surf·ing, -surfs**) *vi* to surf without a board by lying on a wave and using the body as a surfboard —**bod·y·surf·er** *n* —**bod·y·surf·ing** *n*

bod·y wall *n* the part of an animal's body that forms its external surface, encloses the body cavity, and consists of layers of skin and muscle

bod·y warm·er *n* a sleeveless quilted vest, worn outdoors primarily to retain body heat in cold weather

bod·y·work /bóddee wùrk/ *n* **1.** AUTOMOT **AUTO BODY** the outer frame of a car or other motor vehicle **2.** AUTOMOT **REPAIR OF MOTOR VEHICLE BODY** the work of repairing the outer frame of a car or other motor vehicle **3.** HEALTH **MASSAGE OR PHYSICAL MANIPULATION OF BODY** physical manipulation of the human body, including all types of massage, to improve general health or posture, or to treat injuries

boehm·ite /báy mìt, bṓ-/ *n* a light gray to dark red-brown mineral consisting of hydrous aluminum oxide. Source: bauxite. [Early 20C. After Johann *Böhm* (1895–1952), German chemist]

Boe·o·tia /bee ṓshə/ region of ancient Greece, northwest of Athens. Its city-states formed the Boeotian League under the leadership of Thebes.

Boer /bawr, boor/ *n* somebody of Dutch descent who lives in South Africa [Mid-19C. < Dutch *boer* "farmer"] —**Boer** *adj*

Boer War *n* a war fought in South Africa from 1899 to 1902 between the British and the descendants of the Dutch, ending eventually in a British victory

Bo·e·thi·us /bō éethee əss/, **Anicius Manlius Severinus** (480?–524) Roman philosopher. He wrote *The Consolation of Philosophy* (523?), works on logic, and commentaries on Aristotle. His writings influenced scholars in medieval Europe.

> "If chance is defined as an event produced by random motion without any causal nexus, I would say there is no such thing as chance."
> [Anicius Manlius Severinus Boethius, *The Consolation of Philosophy*; 523?]

BOF *abbr* COMPUT beginning of file

boff[1] /bof/ *n* **1. PUNCH OR SLAP** a blow with the fist or open hand (*informal*) **2. OFFENSIVE TERM** an offensive term for sexual intercourse (*slang*) ■ *v* (**boffed, boff·ing, boffs**) **1.** *vt* **PUNCH OR SLAP SOMEBODY** to hit somebody with the fist or open hand (*informal*) **2.** *vti* **OFFENSIVE TERM** an offensive term meaning to have sexual intercourse with somebody (*slang*) [Early 20C. An imitation of the sound of a blow]

boff[2] /bof/ *n* (*dated informal*) **1.** a joke that gets a big laugh **2.** a big hearty laugh **3.** same as **boffo** [Mid-20C. Probably contraction of BOX OFFICE, indicating a box-office success]

bof·fin /bóffin/ *n UK* a scientific expert, especially one involved in research, who is regarded as being unconventional or absent-minded (*informal*) [Mid-20C. Origin ?]

bof·fo /bóffō/ *adj* excellent or extremely successful (*dated informal*) ■ *n* (*plural* **-fos**) a conspicuous success, especially a hit show or stage play

bof·fo·la /bo fṓlə/ *n* same as **boffo** [Mid-20C. Extension of BOFF[2]]

Bo·fors gun /bṓ fàwrz-, bóo-/ *n* a 40 mm antiaircraft gun with one or two barrels, developed in Sweden and used by US and British forces in World War II [After a munitions site in Sweden]

bog /bawg, bog/ *n* an area of wet marshy ground, largely consisting of accumulated decomposing plant material. It supports vegetation such as cranberries and moss and may ultimately turn into peat. [14C. < Gaelic *bognach* "marsh" < *bog* "soft"] —**bog·gy** *adj*

bog down *vt* to slow somebody's general progress (*informal*) ○ *got bogged down in unimportant details*

Bo·ga·lu·sa /bṓgə lóossə/ town in eastern Louisiana, directly west of the Mississippi River and north of New Orleans. Population: 13,064 (2002 estimate).

bo·gan /bṓgən/ *n Can* a small slow-moving stream [Probably < Algonquian]

Bo·gan /bṓgən/, **Louise** (1897–1970) US poet and critic. In addition to publishing her own poetry and reviews, she was poetry editor of *The New Yorker* (1931–69).

> "Women have no wilderness in them, / They are provident instead, / Content in

the tight hot cell of their hearts / To eat dusty bread."
[Louise Bogan, "Women"; 1923]

bo·gart /bṓ gaàrt/ (**-gart·ed, -gart·ing, -garts**) *v* **1.** *vt* to take more than a fair share of something (*slang dated*) **2.** *vti* to behave in a hostile, belligerent, or intimidating way (*slang*) ○ *He's trying to bogart his way in.* [Mid-20C. Probably after Humphrey BOGART]

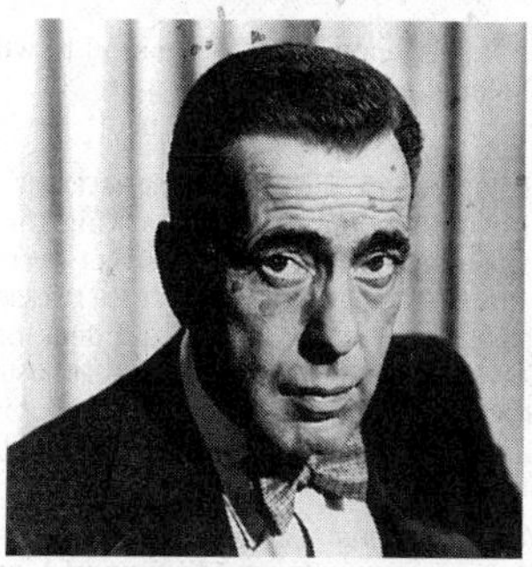

Humphrey Bogart

Bo·gart /bṓ gaàrt/, **Humphrey** (1899–1957) US movie actor. The classic American "tough-but-tender" leading man, his many movies include *Casablanca* (1942) and *The African Queen* (1951). Full name **Bogart, Humphrey DeForest**

"The only thing you owe the public is a good performance."
[Attributed to Humphrey Bogart]

bog as·pho·del *n* a plant of the lily family with grassy leaves that is common in boggy areas. Flowers: small, yellow, in clusters. Native to: Europe. Latin name: *Narthecium ossifragum* or *Narthecium americanum.*

bo·gey /bṓgee/ *n* (*plural* **bogeys**) **1.** CAUSE OF TROUBLE something that troubles, annoys, or frightens somebody (*slang*) **2.** GOLF **ONE OVER PAR** a golf score of one over par for a particular hole **3.** AIR FORCE **UNIDENTIFIED FLYING AIRCRAFT** an aircraft in flight that cannot be identified, especially one assumed to be hostile (*slang*) **4.** PARANORMAL same as **bogeyman** (sense 1) **5.** *UK* same as **booger** (sense 2) (*slang*) ■ *vt* (**bo·geyed, bo·gey·ing, bo·geys**) GOLF **SCORE ONE OVER PAR FOR HOLE** in golf, to score one over par at a hole [Mid-19C. Alteration of BOGLE]

bog·ey·man /bŏŏggee màn, bṓgee-/ (*plural* **-men** /-mèn/), **bo·gy·man, boog·ey·man** /bŏŏgee-/ (*plural* **-men**) *n* **1.** an imaginary person or monster that causes fear or is invoked to cause fear, especially in children **2.** somebody or something regarded as hateful, evil, or frightening ○ *The specter of an election-vote recount is this year's political bogeyman.*

bog·gle /bógg'l/ (**-gled, -gling, -gles**) *v* **1.** *vi* **HESITATE WITH SECOND THOUGHTS** to hesitate before doing something, usually because of being overwhelmed, afraid, or concerned **2.** *vti* **BAFFLE OR BECOME BAFFLED** to astonish or confuse somebody or something, or become astonished or confused (*informal*) ○ *The mind boggles!* **3.** *vti* **MAKE TRIVIAL MISTAKE** to make a trivial mistake, or mismanage something (*informal*) [Late 16C. Probably related to BOGLE] —**bog·gler** *n*

bo·gie /bṓgee/ *n* a framework mounted on a set of wheels on the undercarriage of a vehicle. Railroad vehicles have one at each end and they swivel to allow the vehicle to go around a curve. [Mid-19C. Origin ?]

bo·gle /bṓg'l/ *n* same as **bogeyman** (sense 1) (*archaic or regional*) [Early 16C. Origin ?]

Bo·gor /bṓ gàwr/ city in Indonesia, near Jakarta, on western Java island. It is known for its botanical gardens. Population: 3,696,848 (1997).

Bo·go·tá /bṑgə taá/ capital of Colombia situated on a plateau in the eastern Andes. It is Colombia's largest city and its commercial, cultural, and political center. Population: 6,422,198 (2000).

bog rose·mar·y *n* an evergreen bush of the heath family. Flowers: pink or white, urn-shaped. Latin name: *Andromeda polifolia.*

bog spav·in *n* a chronic puffy inflammation of the soft tissue of the hock joint of horses

bog·trot·ter /báwg tròtter, bóg-/ *n* a highly offensive term for an Irish or Irish-American person (*slang insult*)

bogue /bōg/ *adj* same as **bogus** (sense 2) ■ *n* same as **cigarette** (*slang*) ■ *vti* (**bogued, bogu·ing, bogues**) to smoke a cigarette (*slang*) [Shortening]

bogue out *vi* to become useless (*slang; refers to computer technology*)

bo·gus /bṓgəss/ *adj* **1.** false, dishonest, or fraudulently imitating something **2.** not good, pleasant, or acceptable (*slang*) [Early 19C. < *Bogus*, a machine for producing counterfeit money, origin ?] —**bo·gus·ly** *adv* —**bo·gus·ness** *n*

ORIGIN The word ***bogus*** is first recorded in American usage in the 1820s, referring to a machine for producing counterfeit money; its modern uses seem to have developed from there. Its ultimate origins remain unclear, but one suggestion is that it comes from *tantrabogus*, a word reportedly in use in New England in the early 19th century for "a sinister-looking object" (which itself may have been based on *bogy*, meaning "devil"). Another theory is that it may be related to Hausa *boko*, meaning "deceit, fraud," and may have crossed the Atlantic with transported slaves.

bo·gy·man *n* same as **bogeyman**

Bo Hai /bṑ hí/ large inlet of the Yellow Sea on the northeastern coast of China

bo·hea /bō heé/ *n* a low-quality black Chinese tea [Early 18C. < Chinese dialect *Bu-yi*, variant of *Wu-yi*, after the Wu-Yi hills in SE China]

bo·he·mi·a /bō heémee ə/ *n* **1.** a community of artists and other people whose lifestyles are regarded as unconventional **2.** the lifestyle considered characteristic of bohemians

Bo·he·mi·a /bō heémee ə/ historic region in the western Czech Republic. A former kingdom, it was the westernmost province of Czechoslovakia from 1918 to 1939 and from 1945 to 1949, but it was then divided into several districts. Area: 20,100 sq. mi./52,060 sq. km.

bo·he·mi·an /bō heémee ən/ *n* somebody, often a writer or an artist, who does not live according to the conventions of society —**bo·he·mi·an** *adj* —**bo·he·mi·an·ism** *n*

Bo·he·mi·an /bō heémee ən/ *n* **1.** somebody who comes from Bohemia **2.** LANG same as **Czech** (sense 3) (*dated*) ■ *adj* belonging to Bohemia, or its people or culture

Bo·he·mi·an Breth·ren *npl* a Protestant Christian society, founded by the Hussites in Bohemia in 1467, that became the Moravian Church in 1722

bo·ho /bṓhō/ *n* (*plural* **-hos**), *adj* same as **bohemian** (*slang*)

Bohr /bawr/, **Niels** (1885–1962) Danish physicist. He won the Nobel Prize in physics (1922) for his work on quantum theory. He participated in US atomic bomb development during World War II and later worked for the peaceful application of nuclear technology. Full name **Bohr, Niels Henrik David**

"An expert is a man who has made all the mistakes which can be made in a very narrow field."
[Attributed to Niels Bohr]

Bohr ef·fect *n* the effect of carbon dioxide on the binding of oxygen to hemoglobin [Mid-20C. After Christian *Bohr* (1855–1911), Danish physiologist]

bohr·i·um /báwree əm/ *n* an unstable radioactive chemical element. Source: produced artificially by nuclear fusion. Symbol **Bh**. See table at **element** [Late 20C. After Niels BOHR]

Bohr the·o·ry *n* a theory of atomic structure postulating that electrons move around a nucleus in distinct orbits and that a jump between orbits is accompanied by the absorption or emission of a photon. It was the earliest important attempt to apply quantum theory to atomic structure. [Mid-20C. After Niels BOHR]

bo·hunk /bṓ hùngk/ *n* an offensive term for somebody from central or southeastern Europe (*slang insult*) [Early 20C. Blend of BOHEMIAN + *hunk*, shortening of HUNGARIAN]

boil[1] /boyl/ *v* (**boiled, boil·ing, boils**) **1.** *vti* **HEAT TO OR REACH BOILING POINT** to heat a liquid until it forms bubbles and turns to gas, or to reach this state **2.** *vti* **CONTAIN OR CAUSE TO CONTAIN BOILING LIQUID** to contain liquid that has reached the boiling point, or cause the liquid in a container to boil **3.** *vti* **COOK IN BOILING LIQUID** to cook something by submerging it in boiling liquid for a period of time, or be cooked in this way ○ *Boil the spaghetti for about eight minutes.* **4.** *vti* **PLACE IN BOILING WATER** to put something such as clothing into boiling water, e.g., to clean or sterilize it, or be put into boiling water for these purposes **5.** *vi* **GET VERY HOT** to be or become extremely hot (*informal*) **6.** *vi* **BUBBLE UP ON SURFACE** to be stirred up and have bubbles breaking on the surface **7.** *vi* **GET VERY ANGRY** to be or become very angry ■ *n* **1.** **STATE OF BUBBLING AT HIGH TEMPERATURE** the point at which a liquid bubbles because it has reached the temperature at which it turns to gas, or the state of bubbling at this temperature **2.** *Can, Southern US* **OUTDOOR SEAFOOD PICNIC** an outdoor picnic at which shellfish are boiled and eaten (*informal*) ○ *a Low Country crab boil* [13C. Via Old French *boillir* < Latin *bullire* "to bubble" < *bulla* "a bubble"]

boil away *vti* to turn completely into steam, or turn all of a quantity of liquid into steam by boiling it

boil down *v* **1.** *vti* to make a liquid mixture thicker and reduce its volume by heating it rapidly until much of the liquid turns to steam, or be made thicker in this way **2.** *vt* to condense or summarize something such as information or text (*informal*)

boil down to *vt* to mean or amount to something in essence (*informal*) ○ *It all boils down to the single question: Is he telling the truth?*

boil off *vti* to remove something such as alcohol from a mixture by heating the mixture rapidly until it turns to steam, or be removed in this way

boil over *v* **1.** *vti* to reach or cause a liquid to reach boiling point and be so full of bubbles that some of it spills from the container **2.** *vi* to become too intense or out of control ○ *her anger boiled over*

boil[2] /boyl/ *n* a painful pus-filled abscess on the skin caused by bacterial infection of a hair follicle [Old English *byl* "inflammation" < W Germanic]

Boi·leau /bwaa lṓ/, **Nicolas** (1636–1711) French writer. He was the author of *The Art of Poetry* (1674), a statement of the principles of classical verse. Full name **Boileau-Despréaux, Nicolas**

"A fool always finds a greater fool to admire him."
[Nicolas Boileau, *L'Art poétique (The Art of Poetry)*; 1674]

boil·er /bóylər/ *n* **1.** a large tank in which water is heated and stored, either as hot water or as steam, and used for heating or generating power **2.** a chicken suitable for boiling ○ *boilers, fryers, and roasters on sale today*

boil·er·mak·er /bóylər màykər/ *n* **1.** a drink of whiskey followed by a drink of beer **2.** an industrial worker who makes large metal objects, especially boilers

boil·er·plate /bóylər plàyt/ *n* **1.** **PLATE USED FOR MAKING BOILERS** steel plate used for making boilers **2.** **CLICHÉD WRITING** writing that says nothing new, informative, or interesting **3.** **FORMULAIC LANGUAGE** stock or formulaic language such as that used in legal forms and documents such as powers of attorney and authors' contracts **4.** COMPUT **REUSABLE UNIT OF CODE** a unit of IT code writing that can be reused

boil·er room *n* **1.** an area or room that houses one or more boilers for generating power or hot water **2.** a room from which telemarketers using high-pressure sales tactics, usually by telephone and often illegal, try to sell financial products or real estate of questionable value (*informal*)

boil·er-room *adj* relating to or being political campaign workers who perform administrative support tasks and make polling phone calls for a candidate

boil·ing /bóyling/ *adj* **1.** extremely hot **2.** extremely angry

boil·ing meat *n regional* fatback

REGIONAL NOTE See ***fatback.***

boil·ing point *n* **1.** the temperature at which a heated liquid turns to gas, e.g., 100°C or 212°F for water at sea level **2.** the point at which people lose their tempers or a situation becomes critical

boing /boyng/ *n* the sound made by something that bounces [Mid-20C. An imitation of the sound]

Bois ♦ **Du Bois, W. E. B.**

Boi·se /bóyssee, bóyzee/ **1.** capital and largest city of Idaho, on the Boise River. Population: 189,847 (2002 estimate). **2.** river in southwestern Idaho rising in the Sawtooth Mountains and emptying into the Snake River. Length: 95 mi./150 km.

bois·ter·ous /bóystərəss, -strəss/ *adj* **1.** full of noisy enthusiasm and energy, and often roughness or wildness **2.** wild, rough, or stormy [13C. Alteration of *boistous*, via Old French *boistos* "clumsy, rough" < Latin *buxus* "made from box-tree wood"] —**bois·ter·ous·ly** *adv* —**bois·ter·ous·ness** *n*

~~boistrous~~ incorrect spelling of **boisterous**

Bok /bok/, **Edward** (1863–1930) Dutch-born US editor. He edited *The Ladies' Home Journal* (1889–1919) and won a Pulitzer Prize for *The Americanization of Edward Bok* (1920). Full name **Bok, Edward William**

Bo·kas·sa /bō kássə/, **Jean Bédel** (1921–96) Central African national leader and president (1966–77) and emperor (1977–79) of the Central African Republic. He seized power in the Central African Republic (1966) and ruled until his overthrow in 1979, the last two years as self-declared emperor.

bok choy /bòk chóy/ *n* a Chinese cabbage with long white stalks and narrow green leaves. Latin name: *Brassica chinensis*. [Mid-20C. < Chinese (Guangdang dialect) *baahk-choi* "white vegetable"]

Bok·mål /bŏŏk màwl, bṓk-/ *n* an official form of the Norwegian language, which is closer to Danish than Nynorsk [Mid-20C. < Norwegian < *bok* "book" + *mål* "language"]

Bol. *abbr* **1.** Bolivia **2.** Bolivian

bo·la /bṓlə/, **bo·las** /-ləss/ *n* a strong cord with weights attached to the ends, used for catching cows by South American cowhands (**gauchos**) who throw it to entangle the cows' legs [Early 19C. Via Spanish, "ball" < Latin *bulla* "bubble"]

bo·la tie *n* CLOTHING same as **bolo tie**

bold /bōld/ *adj* **1. FEARLESS AND ADVENTUROUS** willing and eager to face danger or adventure with a sense of confidence and fearlessness **2. REQUIRING OR SHOWING DARING** requiring or showing fearlessness, daring, and often originality **3. IMPUDENT OR PRESUMPTUOUS** lacking in modesty or impolitely assertive **4. CLEAR AND CONSPICUOUS** standing out and therefore easily noticed ○ *bold colors* **5. STEEP** rising abruptly and steeply from the surroundings ○ *a bold cliff* **6.** PRINTING **DARKER THAN STANDARD** having darker thicker lines than standard type, fonts, or lettering ■ *n* PRINTING **TYPE DARKER THAN STANDARD** type, fonts, or lettering with darker thicker lines than is standard ■ *vt* (**bold·ed, bold·ing, bolds**) PRINTING **PUT SOMETHING IN BOLD TYPE** to set, print, or display text in bold type [Old English *bald* < Indo-European] —**bold·ly** *adv* —**bold·ness** *n*

bold·face /bṓld fàyss/ *adj* PRINTING same as **bold** *adj* (sense 6) ■ *n* PRINTING same as **bold** ■ *vt* (**-faced, -fac·ing, -fac·es**) to make letters darker and thicker for emphasis

bold·faced /bṓld fàyst/ *adj* **1.** showing impudence or lack of shame or modesty **2.** PRINTING same as **bold** *adj* (sense 6)

bole[1] /bōl/ *n* the trunk of a tree [14C. < Old Norse *bolr*]

SPELLCHECK bole or **bowl**? Do not confuse the spelling of ***bole*** and ***bowl***, which sound similar. ***Bole*** is used only as a noun, denoting the trunk of a tree or a reddish brown clay. The word ***bowl*** is much more frequent in general usage and can be used as a noun or a verb. As a noun it denotes a round container (as in *a bowl of milk*) or a ball used in bowling; as a verb it means "roll or throw a ball" or "move smoothly and quickly," as in *bowling along the lane.*

bole[2] /bōl/ *n* a reddish brown clay used as a pigment [14C. < late Latin *bolus* "clod of earth" (see BOLUS)]

bo·lec·tion /bō lékshən/ *n* a molding covering an architectural joint and projecting beyond it, usually S-shaped in cross section [Mid-17C. Origin ?]

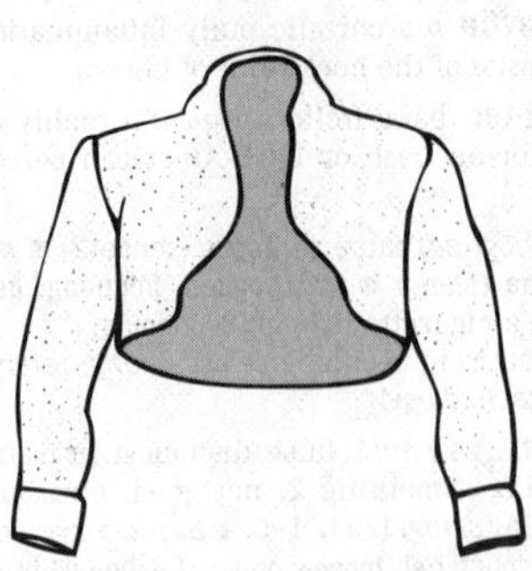

bolero (sense 3)

bo·le·ro /bō lérrō, bə-/ (*plural* **-ros**) *n* **1.** DANCE **SPANISH DANCE** a Spanish dance in triple time that involves much foot-stamping and dramatic posing **2.** MUSIC **SPANISH DANCE MUSIC** the music for a bolero. A famous example was written for full orchestra by Ravel. **3.** CLOTHING **SHORT OPEN JACKET** a short jacket, with or without sleeves, worn open over a blouse or shirt [Late 18C. < Spanish < *bola* "ball" (see BOLA)]

bo·le·tus /bō leétəss/ (*plural* **-tus·es** or **-ti** /-tī/) *n* a fungus that has a rounded cap with pores rather than gills on the underside. Cep mushrooms are an edible species of boletus. Genus: *Boletus*. [Early 16C. < Latin]

Bol·eyn /bŏŏllin, bŏŏ lín/, **Anne** queen of England and Ireland (1507?–36). She was the second wife of Henry VIII (1533–36) and the mother of Elizabeth I. Henry VIII accused her of adultery and had her beheaded.

> "The king has been very good to me. He promoted me from a simple maid to be a marchioness. Then he raised me to be a queen. Now he will raise me to be a martyr."
> [Attributed to Anne Boleyn]

bo·lide /bṓ līd, -lid/ *n* a bright meteor that explodes [Early 19C. < French, < Greek *bolis* "missile"]

Bo·ling·brook /bṓling brŏŏk, bŏŏling-/ city in northeastern Illinois, a southwestern suburb of Chicago. Population: 62,797 (2002 estimate).

bo·li·var /bō leé vaár, bóllәvər/ (*plural* **-li·vars** or **-li·var·es** /bō lee vaá ress/) *n* the main unit of Venezuelan currency. See table at **currency** [Late 19C. After Simón BOLÍVAR]

Bo·lí·var /bólə vaár, bóllə-, bō leé vaar/, **Simón** (1783–1830) South American revolutionary. He was the leader of the independence movement that drove the Spanish from Venezuela, Colombia, Ecuador, Peru, and Bolivia (1812–24). Known as **the Liberator**

> "Do not adopt the best system of government, but the one that is most likely to succeed."
> [Simón Bolívar, *Letter to Jamaica*; September 6, 1815]

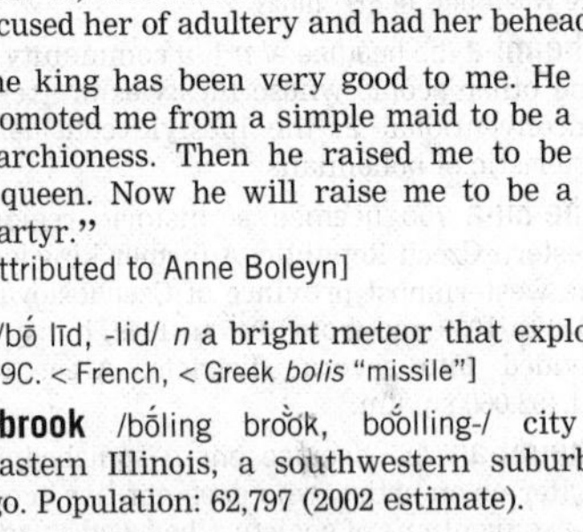

Bolivia

Bo·liv·i·a /bə lívvee ə, bō-/ landlocked country in west central South America. Part of the Inca empire, it was conquered by the Spanish in 1538 and became independent in 1825. Language: Spanish. Currency: boliviano. Capital: La Paz. Population: 8,586,443 (2003). Area: 424,164 sq. mi./1,098,581 sq. km. Official name **Republic of Bolivia** —**Bo·liv·i·an** *n, adj*

bo·li·vi·a·no /bə lìvvee aánō, bō-/ (*plural* **-nos**) *n* the main unit of Bolivian currency. See table at **currency** [Late 19C. < Spanish, "Bolivian"]

boll /bōl/ *n* a rounded seedpod or capsule, especially of cotton [15C. < Middle Dutch *bolle* "round object"]

Böll /böl/, **Heinrich** (1917–85) German novelist. His works include *The Lost Honor of Katharina Blum* (1974). He received the Nobel Prize in literature (1972).

> "Strangely enough I like the kind to which I belong: people."
> [Heinrich Böll, *The Clown*; 1965]

bol·lard /bóllərd/ *n* **1.** *UK* **POST FOR GUIDING TRAFFIC** a strong, heavy, usually concrete post marking the edge of an area such as sidewalks on street corners that traffic must keep off **2.** NAUT **POST FOR MOORING BOATS** a strong post on a wharf, or on the deck of a boat, used for securing ropes **3.** CLIMBING **ROCK SUITABLE FOR SECURING ROPE** in climbing, a spike of rock or a pillar of ice around which a rope can be secured [Mid-19C. Probably < BOLE[1]]

bol·lix /bólliks/ (*slang*) *n* a mess or muddle, especially one caused by bungling ■ *vt* (**-lixed, -lix·ing, -lix·es**) to make a mess or muddle of something ○ *bollix a job* ○ *They got my travel arrangements totally bollixed up.* [Mid-20C. Alteration of BOLLOCKS]

bol·locks /bólləks/ *interj UK* a highly offensive term indicating strong disbelief or disagreement (*taboo*) [Mid-18C. Variant of *ballocks*]

boll wee·vil *n* a weevil whose larvae infest and destroy cotton bolls. Native to: southern United States, Mexico. Latin name: *Anthonomus grandis*.

boll·worm /bṓl wùrm/ *n* a moth larva, especially the corn earworm or pink bollworm, that feeds on and destroys cotton and other crops

Bol·ly·wood /bóllee wŏŏd/ *n* the extravagantly theatrical Indian motion picture industry [Mid-20C. Blend of BOMBAY + HOLLYWOOD[1]]

bo·lo /bṓlō/ (*plural* **-los**) *n* in the Philippines, a machete with a single-edged blade [Early 20C. < Philippine Spanish]

bo·lo·gna /bə lṓnee, -nə, -nyə/ *n* **1.** a large smoked sausage made with a variety of finely ground seasoned meats, usually including beef and pork **2.** a sausage similar to a smoked beef or pork bologna, made with finely ground chicken or turkey [Mid-19C. After BOLOGNA, Italy]

Bo·lo·gna /bə lṓnyə/ capital of Bologna Province and Emilia-Romagna Region, in northern Italy. It was an important cultural center in the Middle Ages and Renaissance. Population: 371,217 (2001).

bo·lo·gnese /bōlə náyz/, **Bo·lo·gnese** *adj* **1.** describes an Italian sauce for pasta, made with ground meat and tomato **2.** describes pasta served with bolognese sauce ○ *spaghetti bolognese* [Early 19C. < Italian, "(in the style) of Bologna"]

bo·lom·e·ter /bō lómmәtər/ *n* an instrument for measuring radiant energy by determining the changes of resistance in an electrical conductor [Late 19C. < Greek *bolē* "ray"] —**bo·lo·met·ric** /bōlə méttrik/ *adj* —**bo·lom·e·try** /bō lómmətree/ *n*

bo·lo punch *n* in boxing, a long powerful swinging uppercut

bo·lo tie /bṓlō-/, **bo·la tie** /bṓlə-/ *n* a thin necktie made of cord and fastened in front by a clasp [Alteration of BOLA]

Bol·she·vik /bṓlshə vìk, ból-/ *n* **1. RUSSIAN COMMUNIST** a member of the radical group within the Russian Social Democratic Labor Party that became the Communist Party in 1918 **2.** *also* **bol·she·vik COMMUNIST OR COMMUNIST SYMPATHIZER** a Communist or somebody who shares the ideals of Communism **3.** *also* **bol·she·vik POLITICAL RADICAL** a revolutionary or radical socialist (*disapproving*) [Early 20C. < Russian *bol'shevik* < *bol'she* "more"; because the radicals were in the majority]

Bol·she·vism /bṓlshə vìzzəm, ból-/, **bol·she·vism** *n* **1.** the ideology and policies of the Bolsheviks, especially advocacy of the forcible overthrow of capitalism **2.** Communism or revolutionary socialism (*dated*)

bol·shie /bṓlshee, ból-/, **bol·shy** *n* (*plural* **-shies**) POL same as **Bolshevik** (*dated informal*) ■ *adj UK* (*informal*) **1.** tending to be argumentative or uncooperative **2.** politically radical or subversive [Early 20C. < BOLSHEVIK] —**bol·shi·ly** *adv*—**bol·shi·ness** *n*

bol·son /bōl són/ *n Southwest US* in the deserts of the southwestern United States and Mexico, a flat-bottomed depression surrounded by mountains, typically containing a saltpan or salt lake [Mid-19C. < American Spanish *bolsón* "big purse" < Spanish *bolsa* "purse, pouch" < medieval Latin *bursa* (see BURSA)]

bol·ster[1] /bṓlstər/ *vt* (**-stered, -ster·ing, -sters**) **1.** ENCOURAGE SOMETHING THROUGH SUPPORT to strengthen something through support or encouragement **2.** KEEP SOMETHING RAISED to prop something up ■ *n* **1.** LONG CYLINDRICAL PILLOW a long firm cylindrical pillow placed under other pillows to support them **2.** MECH ENG PAD PREVENTING FRICTION a pad or cushion affixed to machinery to prevent friction or give support **3.** ARCHIT HORIZONTAL SUPPORTING TIMBER a short horizontal timber positioned between the top of a post and the beam it supports, to spread the load of the post [Old English, "cushion" < Indo-European, "to swell"] —**bol·ster·er** *n*

bol·ster[2] /bṓlstər/ *n* a chisel with a wide cutting edge, used for cutting stone [Early 20C. Alteration of *boaster* < *boast* "cut with a chisel," origin ?]

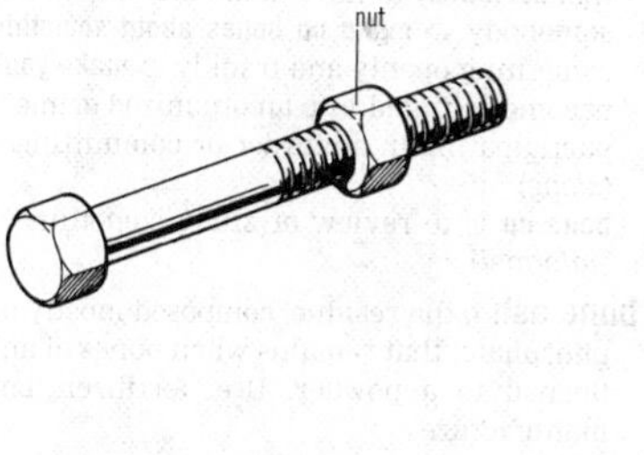

bolt (sense 2)

bolt[1] /bōlt/ *n* **1.** BAR FOR FASTENING DOOR a sliding bar that fits into a socket and secures a door or gate **2.** SHORT SCREW a short cylindrical metal bar with a screw thread, used with a nut **3.** METEOROL LIGHTNING FLASH a flash of lightning appearing briefly as a jagged line of light **4.** TEXTILES ROLL OF FABRIC a rolled length of fabric or wallpaper **5.** ARMS ARROW FOR CROSSBOW a short arrow for use with a crossbow **6.** ARMS PART OF GUN in a breech-loading firearm, a sliding rod, bar, or plate that ejects a used cartridge and closes the breech **7.** POL REFUSAL OF SUPPORT a refusal to support a political party, candidate, or policy **8.** CLIMBING METAL PIN in climbing, a small metal spike used to provide an anchor in rock faces ■ *v* (**bolt·ed, bolt·ing, bolts**) **1.** *vt* LOCK SOMETHING WITH BOLT to fasten a door or gate by sliding a bolt into a socket **2.** *vi* RUSH AWAY to move suddenly and quickly, especially out of fright **3.** *vt* DEVOUR FOOD HURRIEDLY to swallow food hurriedly without chewing **4.** *vt* HUNTING EXPEL ANIMAL FROM HIDING PLACE to flush out a wild animal that is hidden or concealed **5.** *vi* BOT PREMATURELY PRODUCE SEEDS to flower and produce seeds earlier than expected or wanted **6.** *vt* TEXTILES ROLL FABRIC OR PAPER INTO BOLT to roll fabric or wallpaper into a bolt **7.** *vt* POL REFUSE TO SUPPORT SOMEBODY OR SOMETHING to refuse to support a political party, candidate, or policy [Old English, "crossbow bolt," origin ?] ◇ **like a bolt from the blue** very suddenly and unexpectedly ◇ **make a bolt for something** to make a sudden rush toward something ◇ **shoot your bolt** to use all your resources

bolt[2] /bōlt/ (**bolt·ed, bolt·ing, bolts**) *vt* to filter a substance through a cloth or sieve, especially flour (*archaic*) [12C. < Old French *buleter* < Germanic]

bolt-ac·tion *adj* describes a gun with a sliding bolt that replaces the used cartridge and closes the breech

bolt·er /bṓltər/ *n* **1.** SHOW JUMPING HORSE LIKELY TO BOLT a horse that is liable to frighten easily and run **2.** POL SOMEBODY WHO ABANDONS POLITICAL PARTY somebody who abandons a political party or candidate **3.** NAVY FAILED CARRIER LANDING a failed landing on an aircraft carrier that results in the pilot having to fly off and try again ■ *vi* (**-ered, -er·ing, -ers**) NAVY ABORT CARRIER LANDING to be forced to fly off and try again after failing to engage the arresting gear while landing an airplane on an aircraft carrier

bolt·hole /bṓlt hṑl/ *n* a place of escape, especially for an animal fleeing from danger ○ *The rabbit ran down a bolthole.*

Bol·ton /bṓltən/ industrial city in Lancashire, northwestern England. Population: 261,037 (2001).

bol·to·ni·a /bōl tṓnee ə/ (*plural* **-as** or *same*) *n* a perennial flower of the daisy family. Flowers: white, pink, violet. Native to: North America. Genus: *Boltonia.* [Late 18C. < modern Latin, after James *Bolton*, 18C British botanist]

bolt·rope /bṓlt rṑp/ *n* a rope sewn along the lower edge or leading edge of a sail to strengthen it

Boltz·mann con·stant /bòltsmən-/ *n* the ratio of the universal gas constant to Avogadro's number. Symbol **k** [After Ludwig *Boltzmann* (1844–1906), Austrian physicist]

bo·lus /bṓləss/ *n* **1.** INTRAVENOUS INJECTION OF DRUG a rapidly absorbed intravenous injection of a drug **2.** LARGE PILL a very large pill **3.** ROUND MASS a soft rounded ball, especially of chewed food [Mid-16C. Via late Latin < Greek *bōlos* "clod of earth"]

bo·ma /bṓmə/ *n* **1.** in central and eastern Africa, an enclosed camp or an enclosure for animals **2.** in central and eastern Africa, a police post or magistrate's office [Late 19C. < Kiswahili]

bomb /bom/ *n* **1.** EXPLOSIVE PROJECTILE a missile containing explosive or other destructive material **2.** SPECIALIZED EXPLOSIVE DEVICE a device that contains explosive material, especially one designed to explode after some time **3.** *also* **Bomb** ATOMIC BOMB the atomic bomb considered as the absolute weapon of mass destruction (*often used with "the"*) ○ *lived in dread of the Bomb during the Cold War* **4.** ARTS ARTISTIC FAILURE a performance that is a commercial or artistic failure (*informal*) **5.** FOOTBALL LONG FORWARD PASS in football, a long high forward pass, especially one that results in a touchdown (*informal*) **6.** CONTAINER FOR AEROSOL a container holding a compressed gas **7.** *UK* MUCH MONEY a great deal of money (*informal*) ○ *It cost a bomb.* **8.** MED DEVICE FOR DIRECTING RADIATION a device that contains radioactive material and is used to beam therapeutic radiation at a patient **9.** GEOL SOLIDIFIED LAVA a solidified rounded or teardrop-shaped mass of lava from a volcano **10.** SOMETHING OR SOMEBODY GOOD something or somebody extremely good or exciting (*slang*) ○ *Their lead singer is the bomb.* ■ *v* (**bombed, bomb·ing, bombs**) **1.** *vti* ATTACK ENEMY TARGETS WITH BOMBS to drop bombs on people or places, or to attack or destroy them with bombs ○ *bombing enemy territory* **2.** *vi* FAIL MISERABLY to fail badly as a performance (*informal*) ○ *The play bombed on Broadway.* **3.** *vt* DEFEAT OVERWHELMINGLY to defeat somebody or something overwhelmingly (*informal*) **4.** *vi* MOVE VERY FAST to move exceptionally fast, especially in a vehicle (*informal*) **5.** *vi* CRASH SUDDENLY to fail suddenly while in operation (*informal; refers to computers*) [Late 17C. Via French, Italian, and Latin < Greek *bombos* "booming sound"]

bomb out *vt* to destroy a building or structure completely by bombing it (*usually passive*)

bom·bard /bom baárd/ *vt* (**-bard·ed, -bard·ing, -bards**) **1.** ATTACK SOMEBODY OR SOMETHING WITH MISSILES to attack an enemy or enemy territory intensively with sustained artillery fire or bombs **2.** HIT SOMEBODY REPEATEDLY to attack somebody persistently and vigorously **3.** OVERWHELM SOMEBODY to direct toward somebody something such as questions or requests in great quantities **4.** PHYS HIT SOMETHING WITH HIGH-ENERGY PARTICLES to direct high-energy particles against atoms or nuclei ■ *n* HIST, ARMS MEDIEVAL CANNON a cannon used in medieval times to throw large stones [15C. < French *bombarder* < *bombarde* "cannon" < Latin *bombus* < Greek *bombos* "booming sound"] —**bom·bard·er** *n* —**bom·bard·ment** *n*

bom·bar·dier /bòmbər deér/ *n* a member of a military aircraft crew who releases bombs [Mid-16C. < French < *bombarde* "cannon" (see BOMBARD)]

bom·bar·dier bee·tle *n* a beetle that squirts volatile acrid liquid when attacked. Latin name: *Brachinus crepitans.*

bom·bar·don /bómbər dòn, bom baárd'n/ *n* **1.** a brass wind instrument of the tuba family **2.** a bass reed stop on an organ [Mid-19C. < Italian *bombardone* < medieval Latin *bombarda* "bombard" (see BOMBARD)]

bom·ba·sine *n* TEXTILES another spelling of **bombazine**

bom·bast /bóm bàst/ *n* language that is full of long or pretentious words, used to impress others [Late 16C. Alteration of Old French *bombace* "cotton stuffing," via medieval Latin *bombax* "cotton" < Greek *bombux* "silk, silkworm"] —**bom·bas·tic** /bom bástik/ *adj* —**bom·bas·ti·cal·ly** *adv*

Bom·bay /bom báy/ former name for **Mumbai**

Bom·bay duck *n* **1.** in South Asian cuisine, a fish, especially the bummalo, dried, salted, grilled, and served as a pungent relish **2.** FISH same as **bummalo** [Mid-19C. < Marathi *bombīla* "bummalo," by association with BOMBAY, from where the fish were exported]

bom·ba·zine /bómbə zeén/, **bom·ba·sine** *n* a twilled silk or cotton and worsted material, usually dyed black. Use: formerly, mourning clothes. [Late 16C. Via French *bombasin* < medieval Latin *bombycinus* "silken" < Latin *bombyx* "silk, silkworm" < Greek *bombux*]

bomb bay *n* the compartment on board a bomber aircraft in which the bombs are carried

bomb cal·o·rim·e·ter *n* a device for measuring calorific values in which substances are burned inside a sealed vessel

bomb dis·pos·al *n* the task or process of rendering bombs harmless by defusing them, removing them, or detonating them in a controlled explosion (*hyphenated when used before a noun*) ○ *a bomb-disposal expert*

bombe /bom, bawNb/ *n* a dome-shaped frozen or set dessert [Late 19C. < French, "bomb," from the shape of the mold]

bom·bé /bom báy/ *adj* describes furniture with a bulging convex shape, typical of French rococo furniture of the 18th century [Early 20C. < French, "swollen"]

bombed /bomd/ *adj* **1.** severely damaged or destroyed by bombing **2.** intoxicated by alcohol or a drug (*slang*)

bombed out *adj* (*hyphenated when used before a noun*) **1.** driven out by bomb damage **2.** made uninhabitable by bombing

bomb·er /bómmər/ *n* **1.** an aircraft designed for carrying and dropping bombs **2.** somebody who plants bombs

bomb·er jack·et *n* a short jacket, usually leather, with an elastic waist and usually a zipper at the front [< the wearing of such jackets by the crews of US bomber aircraft]

bomb·ing /bómming/ *n* **1.** the act or process of dropping bombs from aircraft **2.** the act of setting and detonating a bomb with the intent to kill victims

bomb·let /bómmlət/ *n* a small bomb or explosive device packed into a larger bomb

bomb·proof /bóm prooff/ *adj* constructed to withstand the impact of bombs

bomb scare *n* a warning or suspicion of a bomb being in a place, resulting in the evacuation of people from the immediate and surrounding area

bomb·shell /bóm shèl/ *n* **1.** ARMS ARTILLERY EXPLOSIVE OR BOMB an artillery shell or a bomb **2.** SURPRISING NEWS an unexpected and shocking piece of news (*informal*) **3.** STUNNING WOMAN a very good-looking and glamorous woman (*dated informal*)

bomb shel·ter *n* a building or underground structure designed to protect people from the impact of a bomb

bomb·sight /bóm sīt/ *n* a device in an aircraft for aiming bombs

bomb site *n* an area devastated by bombs

bom·by·cid /bómbi sid/ *adj* belonging to the family of moths that includes the silkworm moths. Family: Bombycidae. [< modern Latin *Bombycidae* < Latin *bombyc-* "silkworm" < Greek *bombux*] —**bom·by·cid** *n*

Bon, Cape /bawN/ peninsula in northeastern Tunisia

Bo·na, Mount /bṓnə/ highest peak in the Wrangell Mountains, southern Alaska. Height: 16,421 ft./ 5,005 m.

bo·na fide /bṓnə fīd, bṑnə fídee, bónnə fīd, bònnə fídee/ *adj* **1.** authentic and genuine in nature ○ *a bona fide offer* **2.** without any intention to deceive [< Latin, "with good faith"]

bo·na fi·des /-fídeez, -fīdz/ *n* a sincere statement or evidence of good intentions (*takes a singular verb*) ■ *npl* credentials authenticating somebody's true identity, background, intentions, and good faith ○ *a defector whose bona fides could not be established*

Bo·naire Is·land /baw nér-/ island in the Netherlands Antilles off the coast of Venezuela. It is a popular tourist destination. Population: 12,533 (1994). Area: 112 sq. mi./290 sq. km.

bo·nan·za /bə nánzə/ *n* **1.** a source that yields great riches or success **2.** an extremely valuable mineral deposit [Early 19C. Via Spanish < medieval Latin *bonacia* "calm seas," alteration of *malacia* "calm seas" after Latin *bonus* "good"]

Bo·na·parte /bṓnə paart/ ➧ **Napoleon I**

Bo·na·parte, Jérôme (1784–1860) French soldier and politician. He was the youngest brother of Napoleon I, who made him king of Westphalia (1807–13).

Bo·na·parte, Joseph (1768–1844) French soldier and diplomat. He was the older brother of Napoleon I, who made him king of Naples (1806–08) and Spain (1808–13).

Bo·na·parte, Louis (1778–1846) French soldier and politician. He was a younger brother of Napoleon I, who made him king of Holland (1806–10).

Bo·na·parte, Lucien (1775–1840) French diplomat and politician. A younger brother of Napoleon I, he opposed Napoleon's despotic reign and spent much of his life in exile.

Bo·na·part·ism /bṓnə paar tìzzəm/ *n* **1.** government by or on the pattern of Napoleon I **2.** support for Napoleon I or Napoleon III or their dynasty —**Bo·na·part·ist** *n, adj*

Bon·a·ven·ture /bònnə vénchər/, **Bon·a·ven·tu·ra** /bònnə ven chóorə, -tóorə, -tyóorə/, **St.** (1221?–74) Italian monk and theologian. He was minister general of the Franciscan order (1257) and wrote the official biography of St. Francis (1263). Born **Fidanza, Giovanni di**

bon·bon /bón bòn/ *n* **1.** a candy confection **2.** something that is sweet and insubstantial [Late 18C. < French, literally "good-good" < Latin *bonus* "good"]

bon·bon·nière /bònbon yér/ *n* an ornamental bowl or box for candy [Early 19C. < French < *bonbon* (see BONBON)]

bond /bond/ *n* **1.** ADHESION the way in which one surface sticks to another **2.** ADHESIVE SUBSTANCE a substance that makes objects adhere **3.** LINK BETWEEN PEOPLE a link that binds people together in a relationship **4.** RESTRAINT a situation that limits somebody socially, psychologically, or emotionally **5.** LAW SOLEMN PROMISE a solemn agreement promising to do something **6.** FIN CERTIFICATE PROMISING DEBT REPAYMENT a certificate issued by a government or company promising to pay back borrowed money at a fixed rate of interest on a specified date **7.** LAW DOCUMENT PROMISING TO PAY a document that legally obliges one party to pay money to another **8.** LAW PAYMENT SECURING BAIL a sum of money paid to secure the release from prison of somebody awaiting trial, on the condition that the person appears on the date of the trial **9.** SOMETHING THAT BINDS an object such as a rope, band, or chain that binds somebody or something **10.** POLICY PROTECTING AGAINST FINANCIAL LOSS an insurance policy held by an employer or contractor that protects clients' or customers' money against financial loss occasioned by a third party **11.** CHEM FORCE BINDING ATOMS AND IONS a fundamental attractive force that binds atoms and ions in a molecule. There are different types of bonds, e.g., covalent and ionic. **12.** COMM SAFE STORAGE secure storage of goods before payment of duty **13.** CONSTR TECHNIQUE FOR OVERLAPPING BRICKS an overlapping pattern in which bricks or tiles can be laid **14.** INDUST same as **bond paper** **15.** BEVERAGES same as **bonded whiskey** ■ *v* (**bond·ed, bond·ing, bonds**) **1.** *vti* ADHERE OR MAKE SURFACES ADHERE to stick together, or make two surfaces stick together **2.** *vti* PSYCHOL LINK EMOTIONALLY to link together, or cause people to be linked together, emotionally or psychologically **3.** *vt* COMM STORE GOODS SECURELY to store goods securely until duty is paid **4.** *vti* FIN CONVERT INTO DEBT UNDER BOND to convert something, or be converted, into a debt with a bond as security **5.** *vi* CHEM HAVE CHEMICAL BOND to be linked with a chemical bond (*refers to atoms or ions*) **6.** *vt* CONSTR OVERLAP BRICKS OR TILES to lay bricks or tiles so that they overlap in a pattern **7.** *vt* HANDICRAFT FUSE FABRICS TOGETHER to fuse two fabrics together [13C. Variant of BAND[2]] —**bond·a·ble** *adj*—**bond·er** *n*

bond·age /bóndij/ *n* **1.** SLAVERY the condition of being enslaved or forced into serfdom **2.** PHYSICAL RESTRAINT DURING SEX the practice of being tied up or restrained physically during sex acts **3.** RESTRICTION the condition of being controlled by something that limits freedom [14C. < Anglo-Norman < Old Norse *bóndi* "husbandman" < present participle of *búa* "dwell"]

bond·ed /bóndəd/ *adj* **1.** INSUR PROTECTED BY INSURANCE protected by insurance against financial losses caused by a third party **2.** STORED BEFORE TAXATION stored securely until duty or tax is paid **3.** MADE TO ADHERE IN LAYERS chemically attached or fused together in layers

bond·ed ware·house *n* a warehouse that holds goods awaiting duty or tax to be paid on them

bond·ed whis·key, bond *n* a whiskey that has been aged at least four years in a bonded warehouse before use

bond en·er·gy *n* the amount of energy that has to be supplied to break a chemical bond between two atoms in a molecule

bond·hold·er /bónd hṑldər/ *n* an owner of government or company bonds

Bon·di Beach /bón dī-/ coastal suburb of Sydney, Australia. It is a popular surfing and tourist center.

bond·ing /bónding/ *n* **1.** PROCESS OF BINDING THINGS TOGETHER the process by which something is bonded **2.** PSYCHOL FORMATION OF EMOTIONAL BONDS the formation of a close emotional tie between people, e.g., the establishment of a relationship between a mother and her newly born infant **3.** DENT COATING TOOTH the process of coating a tooth with a durable resinous substance

bond·man /bóndmən/ (*plural* **-men** /-mən/) *n US* a man who is enslaved or a serf. Can term **bondsman**

bond pa·per *n* a strong white paper of high quality

bond·ser·vant /bónd sùrvənt/ *n* a serf or enslaved person [15C. < *bond* "bound in servitude"]

bonds·man /bóndzmən/ (*plural* **-men** /-mən/) *n* **1.** somebody responsible for a legal bond **2.** *Can, UK* same as **bondman** [13C. < *bond* "bound in servitude"]

bonds·per·son /bóndz pùrss'n/ (*plural* **-per·sons** or **-peo·ple** /-peep'l/) *n* somebody responsible for a legal bond

bond·stone /bónd stṑn/ *n* building brick or a stone that extends into the interior of a wall in order to strengthen it

bond·wom·an /bónd wòommən/ (*plural* **-wom·en** /-wìmmin/), **bonds·wom·an** /bóndz-/ *n US* a woman who is enslaved or a serf. Can term **bondswoman** [14C. < *bond* "bound in servitude"]

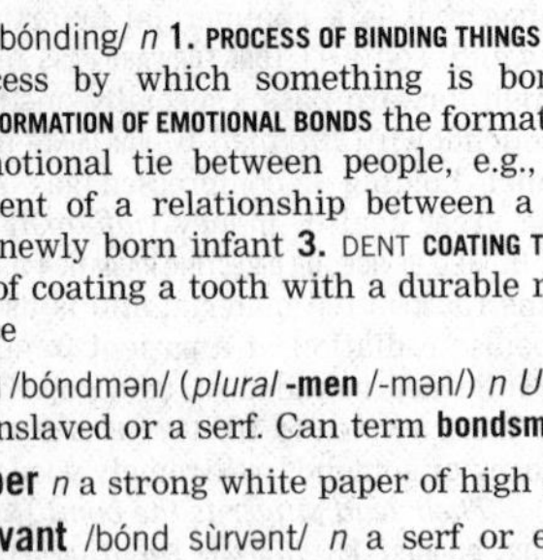

bone

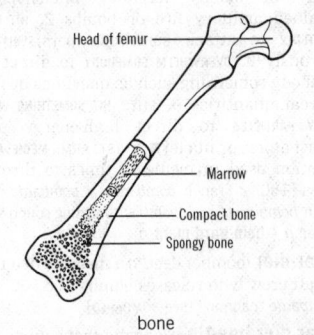

bone /bṓn/ *n* **1.** SECTION OF SKELETON one of the hard parts forming the skeleton in vertebrate animals **2.** MATERIAL MAKING UP BONES the main material that forms a vertebrate skeleton, principally collagen fiber and calcium phosphate **3.** SUBSTANCE RESEMBLING BONE something hard that resembles the bone of a vertebrate skeleton, e.g., whalebone or ivory **4.** SOMETHING GIVEN AS SUBSTITUTE something intended solely to soothe or placate somebody (*slang*) ○ *The press secretary tossed a small bone to the press as they clamored for information.* **5.** COLORS IVORY COLOR the ivory or off-white color of bone **6.** CLOTHING STRIP USED AS STIFFENING a flat strip of hard material such as whalebone or plastic used to stiffen a garment ■ **bones** *npl* **1.** DEAD BODY the skeleton or corpse of a dead person or animal **2.** STRUCTURE the structure or framework of something **3.** LIVING BODY somebody's living body (*humorous*) ○ *I must rest my weary bones.* **4.** MUSIC PAIR OF RHYTHMICALLY CLACKING BARS a pair of bars or strips of wood, metal, or bone that are struck together sharply to make musical rhythms **5.** GAMBLING DICE a pair of dice (*slang*) ■ *vt* (**boned, bon·ing, bones**) **1.** COOK REMOVE BONES FROM FOOD to remove the bones from fish, meat, or poultry when preparing it for cooking or eating **2.** CLOTHING STIFFEN GARMENT to add flat strips to stiffen a garment **3.** OFFENSIVE TERM an offensive term meaning to have sexual intercourse with somebody (*slang*) ■ *adv* VERY extremely or totally ○ *He's bone idle!* ○ *I am bone tired.* [Old English *bān* < Germanic, "long bone"] ◇ **feel** *or* **know it in your bones** to be sure that something is true without having any proof or being able to explain why ◇ **have a bone to pick with somebody** to have cause for disagreement with somebody ◇ **make no bones about something** to say something openly and frankly ◇ **make your bones** to become initiated into an organized crime family by participating in a murder or committing a murder (*slang*)

bone up *vi* to review or study something intensely (*informal*)

bone ash *n* the residue, composed mostly of calcium phosphate, that remains when bones of animals are burned to a powder. Use: fertilizer, bone china manufacture.

bone chi·na *n* **1.** a fine white porcelain made from a mixture of clay and bone ash **2.** articles made of bone china

bone dry *adj* containing no moisture at all

bone·fish /bṓn fish/ (*plural same* or **-fish·es**) *n* a large game fish found in warm shallow waters. Latin name: *Albula vulpes*.

bone·head /bṓn hèd/ *n* an offensive term for somebody regarded as unintelligent (*insult*) —**bone·head·ed** *adj* —**bone·head·ed·ness** *n*

bone·less /bṓnləss/ *adj* having had the bones removed in preparation for cooking or eating

bone mar·row *n* a soft reddish substance inside some bones that is involved in the production of blood cells. New white and red blood cells are formed only in the marrow of the flat bones such as the ribs, breastbone, or pelvis in adults.

bone meal *n* ground animal bones, used as a fertilizer or in animal feed [< MEAL[2]]

bone of con·ten·tion *n* a subject of constant argument or disagreement between people [< dogs fighting over a bone]

bon·er /bṓnər/ *n* **1.** EMBARRASSING MISTAKE an embarrassing mistake (*informal*) **2.** ERECTION an erect penis (*slang*) **3.** COOK DEVICE THAT BONES something that is designed for boning something, or somebody who bones something ○ *a fish boner*

bone·set /bṓn sèt/ (*plural same* or **-sets**) *n* a plant of the daisy family believed to have healing properties. Native to: North America. Genus: *Eupatorium*.

bone spav·in *n* an inflammation of the bones in a horse's hock, resulting in swelling and lameness

bone struc·ture *n* the shape and relative prominence of somebody's facial features as formed by the bones underneath ○ *good bone structure*

Bon·e·var·di /bònə vaardee/, **Marcelo** (1929–94) Argentine artist. He is best known for his geometric figures on relief constructions.

bone·yard /bṓn yaard/ *n* (*informal*) **1.** same as **cemetery** **2.** a place where discarded metal objects are collected before being recycled

bon·fire /bón fīr/ *n* a large fire built outside for

burning garbage, as part of a celebration, or as a signal [14C. < BONE]

CULTURAL NOTE ***Bonfire of the Vanities***, a novel (1988) by Tom Wolfe. Using the story of the trial of wealthy New York bond trader Sherman McCoy for the accidental killing of a young African American man, Wolfe satirizes the US media, legal system, and art world. It was made into a movie by Brian de Palma in 1990.

Bon·fire Night *n* the anniversary of the day on which Guy Fawkes' plot to blow up the British parliament (**the Gunpowder Plot**) was discovered in 1605, marked with fireworks and bonfires in the United Kingdom and other Commonwealth countries. Date: November 5.

bong[1] /bong, bawng/ *n, interj* **REVERBERATING SOUND** a deep resonant sound, especially from a bell ■ *n* CLIMBING **METAL PITON** a wide piton made out of folded sheet metal ■ *vi* (**bonged, bong·ing, bongs**) **MAKE REVERBERATING SOUND** to make a deep resonant sound [Mid-19C. An imitation of the sound]

bong[2] /bong, bawng/ *n* a water pipe for smoking marijuana or other drugs (*slang*) [Late 20C. Probably < Thai *baung*]

bon·go /bóng gō, báwng gō/ (*plural* **-gos** or **-goes** or *same*) *n* a forest-dwelling antelope having a reddish coat with vertical white stripes and distinctive spiraling horns. Native to: central Africa. Latin name: *Boocercus euryceros*. [Mid-19C. < Kikongo]

bon·go drums, bon·gos *npl* a set of two small deep-bodied drums that are held between the knees and beaten with the fingers [< American Spanish *bongó*]

Bon·hoef·fer /bón hőfər/, **Dietrich** (1906–45) German pastor and theologian. He was active in the German Resistance during World War II, and was executed in 1945 for involvement in a plot to assassinate Adolf Hitler.

> "Man has learned to cope with all questions of importance without recourse to God as a working hypothesis."
> [Dietrich Bonhoeffer. Quoted in *Letters and Papers from Prison*, Eberhard Bethge, ed.; 1981]

bon·ho·mie /bònnə mée/ *n* easy good-humored friendliness [Late 18C. < French *bonhomme* "good man"] —**bon·ho·mous** /bónnəməss/ *adj*

Bon·i·face /bónni fàss, -fàyss/, **St.** (680?–754?) Saxon missionary. Commissioned to preach to the German peoples in 718, he became a bishop in 723. He was killed by non-Christians in Friesia. Born **Wynfrid**. Known as **the Apostle of Germany**

Bon·i·face VIII, Pope (1234?–1303) As pope from 1294 to 1303, he proclaimed the supremacy of the papacy over temporal law. Born **Gaetani, Benedetto**

Bo·nin Is·lands /bőnin-/ volcanic island group in Japan in the Pacific Ocean. The islands were held under US control from 1945 to 1968. Population: 2,303 (1985). Area: 40 sq. mi./104 sq. km.

bo·ni·to /bə neétō/ (*plural* **-tos** or *same*) *n* **1. FISH OF MACKEREL FAMILY** a game fish relating to tuna, with dark stripes on its back. Native to: Atlantic and Pacific waters. Genus: *Sarda*. **2. BONITO AS FOOD** the flesh of a bonito eaten as food **3. FISH RESEMBLING BONITO** a fish such as the skipjack that resembles or is related to the bonito [Late 16C. Probably < Spanish, "pretty" < Latin *bonus* "good"]

bonk /bongk/ *v* **1.** *vt* **BANG SOMETHING OR SOMEBODY** to bang or hit something or somebody (*informal*) **2.** *vti* **HIT SOMETHING** in snowboarding, to strike or collide with something while riding a snowboard (*slang*) ■ *n* **SHARP BLOW** a sharp blow, typically on the head [Early 20C. An imitation of the sound]

bon·kers /bóngkərz/ *adj* an offensive term meaning irrational (*slang*) [Mid-20C. Origin ?]

bon mot /bàwN mṓ/ (*plural* **bons mots** /bàwN mṓ, -mṓz/) *n* a witty comment [< French, "good word"]

Bonn /bon, bawn/ city on the Rhine in North Rhine-Westphalia state, west central Germany. It was the capital of the former West Germany from 1949 to 1990. Population: 293,072 (1997).

Bon·nard /bō naár/, **Pierre** (1867–1947) French painter. In his early career he was a conventional painter of decorative scenes. After 1900 his pictures, often of bathing women, were notable for their use of light and color.

bonnet

bon·net /bónnət/ *n* **1. WOMAN'S HAT** a hat framing the face and usually tied under the chin, worn by a woman or girl **2.** *UK* AUTOMOT same as **hood**[1] *n* (sense 3) **3. NATIVE N AMERICAN HEADDRESS** a ceremonial feathered headdress traditionally worn by some Native North Americans **4. CHIMNEY COWL** a wire cover fitted over a chimney pot **5.** MECH ENG **PROTECTIVE COVER** a protective cap or cover fitting over a machine part **6.** SAILING **EXTRA PIECE OF SAIL** an extra strip of canvas laced to the base of a foresail, used to extend it when the wind is light [14C. < Old French *bonet* < medieval Latin *abonnis* "headgear"] —**bon·net·ed** *adj*

Bon·ne·ville Salt Flats /bònnəvil-/ barren salt plain in northwestern Utah, the bed of a prehistoric lake. It has been used for setting world land speed records since the 1930s. Area: 100 sq. mi./260 sq. km.

Bon·nie Prince Char·lie /bònnee prinss chaárlee/ ♦ **Stuart, Charles Edward**

bon·ny /bónnee/ (**-ni·er, -ni·est**), **bon·nie** *adj N England, Scotland* **1. ATTRACTIVE** pleasing to look at **2. SUBSTANTIAL** fairly large **3. EXCELLENT** extremely good [15C. Origin ?] —**bon·ni·ly** *adv* —**bon·ni·ness** *n*

bo·no·bo /bə nṓbō/ (*plural* **-bos**) *n* a rare black arboreal chimpanzee. Native to: West Africa, south of the Congo River. Latin name: *Pan paniscus*. [Mid-20C. < a Central African language]

bonsai

bon·sai /bón sī, bon sí, -zī/ (*plural same* or **-sais**) *n* **1.** the art of growing miniaturized forms of trees and bushes by rigorous pruning of roots and branches **2.** a tree or bush miniaturized using bonsai techniques [Early 20C. < Japanese < *bon* "basin" (< Middle Chinese *bən*) + *sai* "to plant" (< Middle Chinese *tsəj*)]

bon·se·lla /bon séllə/ *n S Africa* a small reward, often of candies, given to a good customer by a trader [Early 20C. < Zulu *bansela* "express thanks in tangible form, give a small present"]

bon·spiel /bón speel, -shpeel/ *n* a curling match or tournament [Mid-16C. Probably < Dutch or Low German]

bon ton /bàwN táwN, bon tón/ *n* (*literary*) **1.** good taste, style, or manners ○ *People thought it bon ton to be seen attending such an occasion.* **2.** fashionable society [< French, "good tone"]

bo·nus /bṓnəss/ *n* **1. UNEXPECTED EXTRA** an extra unexpected advantage **2.** FIN **EXTRA MONEY** an amount of money given in addition to normal pay, especially as a reward **3.** FIN **PREMIUM PAID TO SOMEBODY** an extra dividend or premium paid to the purchaser, holder, promoter, or vendor of a stock or insurance policy **4.** FIN **SPECIAL GOVERNMENT PAYMENT TO INDIVIDUALS** a special payment by a government to a person **5.** FIN **PREMIUM PAID FOR AGREEING TO SOMETHING** a premium paid for signing a contract or taking out a loan [Late 18C. < Latin, "good"]

bon vi·vant /bòN vee vaáN/ (*plural* **bons vi·vants** /*pronunc. same*/), **bon vi·veur** /-vee vúr/ (*plural* **bons vi·veurs** /-vúrz/) *n* somebody who enjoys the luxuries in life, especially good food and wine [*Bon vivant* < French, "somebody who lives well"; *bon viveur* formed in English after *bon vivant* and French *viveur* "living person"]

bon voy·age /bòN vwaa yaázh/ *interj* used to wish somebody an enjoyable and safe trip [< French, "good journey"]

bon·y /bónee/ (**-i·er, -i·est**) *adj* **1. HAVING PROMINENT BONES** extremely thin and with prominent bones **2.** FOOD **CONTAINING MANY BONES** containing many bones, and often difficult to eat **3.** ANAT **OF OR LIKE BONE** consisting of or resembling bone **4.** FISH **WITH BACKBONE** describes fish that have a skeleton of bone, as distinct from cartilaginous fish such as sharks. The great majority of fish are bony. Class: Osteichthyes. —**bon·i·ness** *n*

bonze /bonz/ *n* a Buddhist monk in Southeast Asia, China, or Japan [Late 16C. Via French and Portuguese < Japanese *bonsō* < *bon* "ordinary" + *sō* "monk"]

boo /boo/ *interj* **1. EXPRESSING DISAPPROVAL** used to express dissatisfaction or contempt, especially at a speaker or performer **2. USED TO STARTLE SOMEBODY** used to surprise or startle somebody ■ *n* **SOUND OF DISAPPROVAL OR SURPRISE** an utterance of "boo!" in order to startle somebody or to show dissatisfaction ■ *vti* (**booed, boo·ing, boos**) **EXPRESS DISAPPROVAL** to shout "boo!" in order to express dissatisfaction or contempt of somebody, especially a speaker or performer [Early 19C. Originally an imitation of a cow's lowing] ◇ **not say boo** to be silent or reticent (*informal*)

boob[1] /boob/, **boo·by** /bóobee/ (*plural* **-bies**) *n* a woman's breast (*slang; often considered offensive; usually plural*) [Mid-20C. < *bubby*, origin ?]

boob[2] /boob/ *n* **1. UNINTELLIGENT PERSON** somebody who is regarded as unintelligent or ignorant (*slang*) **2.** *UK* **UNFORTUNATE MISTAKE** an unfortunate and embarrassing mistake (*informal*) ■ *vi* (**boobed, boob·ing, boobs**) *UK* **MAKE UNFORTUNATE MISTAKE** to make an unfortunate and embarrassing mistake (*informal*) [Early 20C. Shortening of BOOBY[1]]

boo-boo *n* **1.** a mistake or tactless remark (*informal*) **2.** a cut, injury, or sore place on the body (*baby talk*) [Mid-20C. Probably < BOOB[2]]

boo·book /bóo bòok/ (*plural* **-books** or *same*) *n* a small owl with grayish brown to dark brown feathers and greenish yellow eyes set in a large facial mask. Native to: Australia, New Zealand. Latin name: *Ninox novaeseelandiae*. [Early 19C. < an Australian Aboriginal language; an imitation of the bird's call]

boob tube[1] *n UK* a short strapless stretchy top for women (*informal*) [< BOOB[1]]

boob tube[2] *n* same as **television** (*informal*) [< BOOB[2]]

boo·by[1] /bóobee/ (*plural* **-bies**) *n* **1.** somebody regarded as silly or unintelligent (*dated informal*) **2.** a large seabird of the gannet family, with brown, black, and/or white feathers, often with a brightly colored beak and feet. Native to: tropical regions. Family: Sulidae. [Early 17C. Probably alteration of Spanish *bobo* < Latin *balbus* "stammering"]

boo·by[2] *n* ANAT same as **boob**[1]

boo·by hatch *n* **1.** an offensive term for a mental health facility (*slang*) **2.** a cover for a small hatchway on a sailing ship [< BOOBY[1] (sense 2), because a favorite haunt for these birds on a ship]

boo·by prize *n* a prize given as a joke to the person or team coming last in a competition

boo·by trap *n* **1.** a bomb that is hidden or disguised and is designed to explode when touched or moved **2.** a trap set as a practical joke

boo·by-trap (**boo·by-trapped, boo·by-trap·ping, boo·by-traps**) *vt* to place a booby trap in a place or attach one to something (*often passive*)

boo·dle /bóod'l/ *n* **1.** a large amount of money that has been acquired or used in a corrupt way (*slang*)

2. same as **caboodle** [Early 17C. < Dutch *boedel* "estate, possessions"]

boog·er /bŏŏggər/ *n* 1. same as **bogeyman** (sense 1) (*informal*) 2. a lump of mucus in or from somebody's nose (*slang*) [Mid-19C. Probably alteration of BUGGER[1]]

boog·ey·man (*plural* **-men**) *n* another spelling of **bogeyman**

boog·ie /bŏŏggee/ *vi* (**-ied, -ie·ing, -ies**) 1. to dance to fast rock music (*informal*) 2. to go somewhere specified, on foot or by vehicle (*slang*) ○ *Let's boogie along to the French Quarter.* ○ *Get your coat; it's time to boogie out of here.* ■ *n* MUSIC same as **boogie-woogie** [Mid-20C. Origin ?]
boogie on down *vi* to go off somewhere (*slang*)

Boog·ie /bŏŏggee/ *tdmk* a trademark for a short flexible surfboard on which a surfer lies prone

boog·ie-woog·ie /bŏŏggee wŏŏggee/ *n* a jazz piano style derived from the blues

boo·hoo /boo hŏŏ/ *n, interj* used to represent the sound of noisy weeping ■ *vi* (**-hooed, -hoo·ing, -hoos**) to weep noisily [Mid-19C. An imitation of the sound]

book /bŏŏk/ *n* 1. **BOUND COLLECTION OF PAGES** a collection of printed or manuscript pages sewn or glued together along one side and bound between rigid boards or flexible covers 2. **PUBLISHED WORK** a published work of literature, science, or reference, or a work intended for publication 3. **BOUND SET OF BLANK SHEETS** a bound set of blank sheets of paper, e.g., for writing in 4. **SET OF THINGS BOUND TOGETHER** a set of objects such as matches or fabric samples that are bound together 5. **DIVISION OF LITERARY WORK** a major division of a literary work or of the Bible 6. **SET OF RULES** the body of rules or procedures relevant to a situation ○ *likes to do things by the book* 7. **BOOKMAKER'S RECORD** a record kept by a bookmaker of the bets made and of the money paid out 8. **SCRIPT OR LIBRETTO** the script of a play or the libretto of an opera 9. CARDS **NUMBER OF TRICKS NEEDED FOR SCORING** in cards, the number of tricks that need to be won by a player or side before a trick can count as a score 10. **IMAGINARY RECORD** an imaginary record, archive, or repository of knowledge 11. **RECORD ABOUT SPORTS OPPONENTS** in sports, a record of facts and information about the strengths and weaknesses of a player or team 12. THEATER same as **promptbook** 13. *also* **Book BIBLE** the Christian Bible or Hebrew scripture ■ **books** *npl* 1. ACCT **FINANCIAL ACCOUNTS** the financial records and accounts of an organization 2. **LEARNING** academic study ■ *v* (**booked, book·ing, books**) 1. *vti* **RESERVE PLACE** to arrange for somebody to keep a place available at a specified time, e.g., at the theater or in a restaurant 2. *vt* **ENGAGE SOMEBODY** to engage somebody in advance to do something or be somewhere, especially as a performer (*often passive*) 3. *vt* LAW **CHARGE SOMEBODY WITH CRIMINAL OFFENSE** to charge somebody with a criminal offense, pending legal proceedings (*often passive*) 4. *vi* **DEPART** to leave a place (*slang*) ○ *Yo man, let's book!* 5. *vt UK* **TAKE NAME OF OFFENDING PLAYER** in sports, to officially record the name of a player who has committed an offense (*often passive*) [Old English *bōc* "written document" < Indo-European, "beech"] —**book·er** *n* ◇ **a closed book** somebody or something about which little, if anything, is known or understood ◇ **an open book** somebody or something that is easy to understand or know about because nothing is concealed ◇ **bring somebody to book** to make somebody account for his or her behavior ◇ **cook the books** to alter records, especially financial accounts, to conceal irregularities or wrongdoing (*slang*) ◇ **in somebody's book** in somebody's opinion ◇ **in somebody's good** *or* **bad books** in or out of favor with somebody ◇ **make book on something** to accept bets on the likelihood of something happening ◇ **throw the book at somebody** to charge somebody with all the offenses that he or she may be guilty of, or punish somebody with the maximum penalty
book up *vi* to sell all that is available of something in advance (*usually passive*)

book·a·ble /bŏŏkəb'l/ *adj* able to be applied for in advance and reserved

book·bind·er /bŏŏk bìndər/ *n* somebody who binds books, especially as a profession —**book·bind·er·y** *n* —**book·bind·ing** *n*

book·case /bŏŏk kàyss/ *n* a set of shelves, either fixed to a wall or free-standing, used for holding books

book club *n* 1. an organization that offers its members books at reduced prices 2. a small informal group that meets to discuss books and related topics

~~**bookeeping**~~ incorrect spelling of **bookkeeping**

book·end /bŏŏk ènd/ *n* 1. **SUPPORT FOR ROW OF BOOKS** either of a pair of supports placed at each end of a row of books 2. **DEFENSIVE PLAYER IN FOOTBALL** in football, a player positioned at one of the ends of the defensive line (*informal*) ■ *vt* **OCCUR EITHER SIDE OF** to occur, or make something occur, on both sides or at the beginning and end of something (*informal*) ○ *bookend a speech with anecdotes*

book-en·try *adj* relating to the recording of ownership of a security on a financial institution's computer systems instead of using certificates

Book·er Prize /bŏŏkər-/ *n* a cash prize awarded annually originally by the company Booker McConnell and now by the Man Group for a recently published work of fiction by a British, Irish, or Commonwealth writer —**Book·er Prize·win·ner** *n*

book·ie /bŏŏkee/ *n* GAMBLING same as **bookmaker** (sense 1) (*informal*) [Late 19C. < BOOKMAKER]

book·ing /bŏŏking/ *n* 1. an arrangement by which something such as a theater seat or hotel room is kept for somebody's use at a specific time 2. a contract or arrangement for an entertainer to perform somewhere

book·ing clerk *n UK* somebody who sells tickets, especially railroad tickets

book·ish /bŏŏkish/ *adj* devoted to reading, especially to the exclusion of other things —**book·ish·ly** *adv* —**book·ish·ness** *n*

book·keep·ing /bŏŏk keeping/ *n* the activity or profession of recording the money received and spent by a person, business, or organization —**book·keep·er** *n*

book learn·ing *n* knowledge obtained from books instead of from experience

book·let /bŏŏklət/ *n* a small book with a paper cover and few pages, usually containing information about a particular subject

book·louse /bŏŏk lòwss/ (*plural* **-lice** /-lìss/) *n* a small wingless insect that destroys books by feeding on the paste used in the binding. Order: Psocoptera.

book lung *n* the breathing organ in spiders and other arachnids, with membranous tissue arranged in folds that resemble the leaves of a book

book·mak·er /bŏŏk màykər/ *n* 1. somebody who takes bets and pays winners 2. a book designer, printer, or binder —**book·mak·ing** *n*

book·man /bŏŏkmən/ (*plural* **-men** /-mən/) *n* a book enthusiast or collector (*dated*)

book·mark /bŏŏk maark/ *n* 1. **MARKER IN BOOK** a strip of material inserted between the pages of a book to mark a place in it 2. ONLINE **MARKER IN ELECTRONIC TEXT** an electronic marker in a word processed document, identifying it for reference or retrieval 3. ONLINE **ADDRESS OF INTERNET SITE** the address of a favorite Internet site electronically listed ■ *vt* (**-marked, -mark·ing, -marks**) ONLINE **LIST INTERNET ADDRESS** to list the address of an Internet site

book·mo·bile /bŏŏk mō beel/ *n* a large motor vehicle equipped as a small lending library, used for taking books to people, especially in rural areas

Book of Chang·es *n* PHILOSOPHY same as **I Ching** (sense 2)

Book of Com·mon Prayer *n* the official book giving the order and content of services in the Episcopal Church. Since 1980 the Alternative Service Book has also been in use.

book of hours *n* a medieval service book, used especially in monasteries, containing the offices, prayers, and services prescribed for the various canonical hours

Book of Kells /-kélz/ *n* an illuminated manuscript of the Christian Gospels, produced at Kells in Ireland in the 8th century and now kept at Trinity College, Dublin

Book of Life *n* CHR same as **Bible**

Book of Mor·mon *n* a book believed by members of the Church of Jesus Christ of Latter-Day Saints to have been revealed by the prophet Mormon to Joseph Smith. It contains the history of an ancient American people to whom Jesus Christ is believed to have appeared, and is said to have been written originally on golden tablets.

book·plate /bŏŏk plàyt/ *n* a label for sticking into the front of a book, bearing the name of the owner and sometimes a coat of arms or personal design

book·rest /bŏŏk rèst/ *n* a support, often angled, for an open book

book·sell·er /bŏŏk sèllər/ *n* somebody who deals in books

book·shelf /bŏŏk shèlf/ (*plural* **-shelves** /-shèlvz/) *n* a shelf designed for holding books

book·shop /bŏŏk shòp/ *n* a store, especially a small one, that specializes in selling books

book·stall /bŏŏk stàwl/ *n* a stall where books are sold

book·stand /bŏŏk stànd/ *n* 1. same as **bookstall** 2. a support for an open book, often adjustable and made of wood, metal, or plastic

book·store /bŏŏk stàwr/ *n* a store that sells books

book val·ue *n* 1. the value of a commodity or asset according to the accounting records of the firm owning it 2. the net value of a business after liabilities have been deducted from assets

book·worm /bŏŏk wùrm/ *n* 1. somebody who loves reading (*informal*) 2. an insect whose larvae eat the paper or binding paste in books

Boole /bool/, **George** (1815–64) British mathematician and logician. His system of Boolean algebra, presented in *An Investigation of the Laws of Thought* (1854), applied symbols to logical propositions. Boolean logic is important in designing and programming computers.

Bool·e·an /boolee ən/ *adj* using a system of symbolic logic that uses combinations of logical operators such as "AND," "OR," and "NOT" (**Boolean operators**) to determine relationships between entities. Boolean operations are extensively used in writing computer programs and in computer searches using keywords. [Mid-19C. After George BOOLE]

Bool·e·an al·ge·bra *n* a form of algebra concerned with the logical functions of variables that are restricted to two values, true or false. Boolean algebra is fundamental to circuit design and to the design, function, and operation of computers.

Bool·e·an op·er·a·tor *n* a connecting word or symbol that allows a computer user to include or exclude items in a text search

boom[1] /boom/ *v* (**boomed, boom·ing, booms**) 1. *vi* **MAKE LOUD DEEP SOUND** to make a loud deep reverberating sound 2. *vt* **UTTER SOMETHING LOUDLY** to say something in a loud deep voice 3. *vi* ECON **EXPERIENCE SIGNIFICANT INCREASE IN TRADE** to experience a significant expansion of business and investment, either across an economy or in a specific market ○ *Business is booming.* 4. *vt* **CAMPAIGN FOR SOMEBODY** to campaign vigorously for somebody ■ *n* 1. **LOUD DEEP SOUND** a loud deep reverberating sound 2. ZOOL **DEEP LOUD BIRD OR ANIMAL NOISE** a deep loud cry made by some birds and animals. Bitterns and grouse boom. 3. **SIGNIFICANT INCREASE IN AMOUNT** a significant increase in the amount of something such as a population level ○ *a population boom* 4. ECON **SIGNIFICANT INCREASE IN BUSINESS** a significant expansion of business and investment, either across an economy or in a specific market ○ *a boom in sales* [15C. Perhaps < Dutch *bommen* "to hum, buzz"; an imitation of the sound] —**boom·y** *adj*

boom[2] /boom/ *n* 1. MOVIES, MEDIA **EXTENDABLE OVERHEAD POLE** an extendable pole carrying overhead equipment such as a camera for positioning over a television or movie set 2. SAILING **BEAM HOLDING SAIL AT ANGLE** a beam to which the bottom edge of a sail is attached in order to hold the sail at an advantageous angle to the wind 3. MIL, INDUST **FLOATING BARRIER** a floating barrier used to confine or restrict something, e.g., a barrier to protect a harbor from attack or to confine an oil spill **4.** FREIGHT **POLE USED TO MOVE CARGO** a long pole extending from the mast of a derrick to lift or lower cargo **5.** AVIAT **CONNECTING SPAR FOR AIRCRAFT** a spar that connects the tail and the fuselage in some aircraft [Mid-16C. < Dutch, "beam, pole"] ◇ **lower the boom** to initiate action to prevent something or punish somebody (*informal*)

boom and bust, boom or bust *n* the alternation in an economy or market between immoderate growth and collapse and recession

boom box *n* a large radio and cassette or CD player with a built-in speaker at each end, carried by a handle at the top (*informal*)

boom·er /bóomər/ *n* **1.** same as **baby boomer** (*informal*) **2.** somebody who moves to a place that is experiencing an economic boom **3.** NAVY a nuclear-powered submarine armed with ballistic missiles (*slang*)

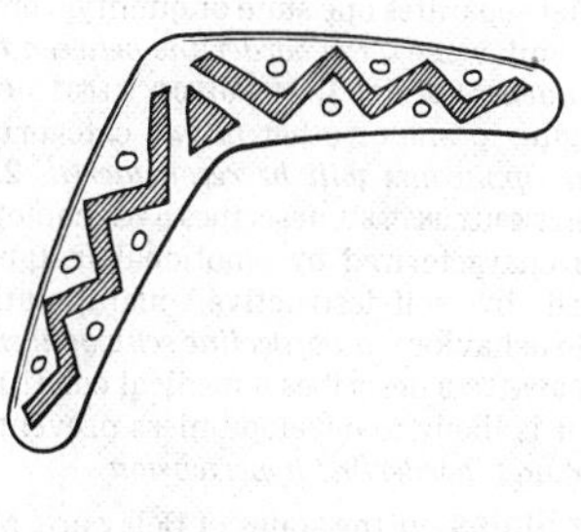

boomerang

boo·mer·ang /bóomə ràng/ *n* **1.** CULTL ANTHROP, ARMS **CURVED MISSILE** a flat curved piece of wood used as a weapon by Australian Aboriginals that is designed to return to the person who throws it **2. SOMETHING HARMFUL TO INITIATOR** something that does inadvertent harm to its initiator ■ *vi* (**-anged, -ang·ing, -angs**) **BACKFIRE ON INITIATOR** to backfire on the initiator of an action, causing that person harm [Late 18C. < an Australian Aboriginal language]

boom·ing /bóoming/ *adj* **1.** increasingly successful economically ○ *the booming futures market* **2.** loud and deep in tone ○ *a booming voice*

boom·let /bóomlət/ *n* a short period of sudden and intense economic growth

boom town *n* a town that significantly increases in size and wealth, often as the result of new and profitable industry

boom vang *n* the pulley that controls the vertical position of the boom

boon /boon/ *n* **1.** something that functions as a blessing or benefit to somebody **2.** a gift or favor from somebody (*archaic or literary*) [12C. < Old Norse *bón* "prayer, petition" < Indo-European, "speak"]

boon com·pan·ion *n* an intimate friend from whom somebody is inseparable [Via French *bon* < Latin *bonus* "good"]

boon·dock /bóon dòk/ *n Philippines* same as **mountain** (sense 1) [Mid-20C. < Tagalog *bundok*]

boon·docks /bóon dòks/ *npl* a place regarded as remote, provincial, and lacking sophistication (*informal*)

boon·dog·gle /bóon dàwg'l, -dògg'l/ *n* (*informal*) **1.** an activity or project that is unnecessary and wasteful of time or money, especially one undertaken for personal or political gain **2.** a government project of little practical value funded to gain political favor [Mid-20C. An invented word: originally a braided leather cord made by Scouts] —**boon·dog·gle** *vi* —**boon·dog·gler** *n*

Boone /boon/, **Daniel** (1734–1820) American frontiersman. He lived on the frontier from an early age and played a major part in the exploration and settlement of Kentucky.

> "I can't say I was ever lost, but I was bewildered once for three days."
> [Attributed to Daniel Boone]

boon·ies /bóoneez/ *npl* same as **boondocks**

boor /boor/ *n* somebody who behaves in a crass, insensitive, or ill-mannered way [Mid-16C. < Dutch *boer* "peasant"] —**boor·ish** *adj* —**boor·ish·ly** *adv* —**boor·ish·ness** *n*

Boor·man /báwrmən/, **John** (*b.* 1933) British movie director. After a successful career making documentaries for the BBC, he directed Hollywood feature films, including *Deliverance* (1972) and *Hope and Glory* (1987).

> "Movie-making is the process of turning money into light. All they have at the end of the day is images flickering on a wall."
> [John Boorman. Quoted in *The Oxford Book of Money*, Kevin Jackson, ed.; 1995]

boost /boost/ *vt* (**boost·ed, boost·ing, boosts**) **1. IMPROVE SOMETHING** to improve, strengthen, or encourage somebody or something **2. INCREASE SOMETHING** to cause something to increase ○ *measures to boost productivity* **3. PUSH SOMEBODY OR SOMETHING UP** to help somebody or something to get up or over something by giving a push from below **4.** ELEC **RAISE VOLTAGE** to increase the voltage in an electrical circuit **5.** COMM **PROMOTE SOMETHING** to promote or advertise something widely and intensively so that people will buy it **6. STEAL SOMETHING** to steal something, especially from a store (*informal*) ■ *n* **1. IMPROVEMENT** something that helps to improve, strengthen, or encourage somebody or something ○ *gave his career a much-needed boost* **2. INCREASE IN SOMETHING** an increase or sudden growth in something ○ *a boost in income* **3. PUSH FROM BELOW** a push from below to help somebody or something to get up or over something **4. PROMOTIONAL CAMPAIGN** a campaign promoting or advertising something [Early 19C. Origin ?]

boost·er /bóostər/ *n* **1. VIGOROUS PROMOTER OF SOMETHING OR SOMEBODY** an enthusiastic promoter or supporter of something or somebody, e.g., of a team **2. SOMEBODY OR SOMETHING THAT CAUSES IMPROVEMENT** somebody or something that improves, strengthens, or encourages somebody or something (*usually used in combination*) ○ *a morale-booster* **3.** ELECTRONICS **RADIO-FREQUENCY AMPLIFIER** a radio-frequency amplifier that amplifies weak television or radio signals and retransmits them so that they can be received by viewers or listeners **4.** AEROSP same as **booster rocket** **5.** TECH **DEVICE THAT MAKES SOMETHING MORE EFFECTIVE** a device used to increase the effectiveness of a piece of equipment **6.** IMMUNOL **SUPPLEMENTARY DOSE OF VACCINE** a repeat dose of a vaccine given some time after the initial course to maintain the level of immunity provided by the previous dose **7. SHOPLIFTER** somebody who engages in shoplifting (*slang*)

boost·er ca·bles *npl* ELEC ENG same as **jumper cables**

boost·er·ism /bóostə rìzzəm/ *n* the practice or habit of publicizing and promoting something, especially a place, product, or enterprise (*informal*)

boost·er rock·et *n* an engine in a space vehicle that is used to give thrust during the launch

boost·er seat *n* a seat that can be placed over another seat in a motor vehicle or at a table to raise a child into a higher position

boot[1] /boot/ *n* **1. STRONG SHOE EXTENDING UP LOWER LEG** a strong item of footwear that covers part of the lower leg (*often used in combination*) ○ *an ankle boot* **2. HARD KICK** the act of kicking somebody or something with great force **3. DISMISSAL FROM JOB** dismissal from employment or from a personal relationship (*informal*) ○ *was given the boot* **4.** MECH ENG **PROTECTIVE COVERING** a protective covering, e.g., a rubber sheath for protecting a coupling between two shafts **5.** AUTOMOT same as **Denver boot** **6.** RIDING **COVERING FOR HORSE'S LEG** a protective covering for the lower part of a horse's leg **7.** MIL **MILITARY RECRUIT** a naval or marine corps recruit (*informal*) **8.** BASEBALL **FUMBLE OF BASEBALL** in baseball, a fumble of a ground ball hit to an infielder **9.** HIST **INSTRUMENT OF TORTURE** an instrument of torture that was used in the past to enclose and crush the victim's foot **10.** *UK* AUTOMOT same as **trunk** (sense 2) ■ *vt* (**boot·ed, boot·ing, boots**) **1. KICK SOMEBODY OR SOMETHING HARD** to kick somebody or something with great force **2.** same as **boot out** (*informal*) **3. KICK HORSE WHILE RIDING** to urge a horse on by kicking or digging in with the heels while riding it **4. MAKE ERROR** to make a fumble or error (*informal*) **5.** AUTOMOT **PUT BOOT ON CAR** to attach a Denver boot to the wheel of an illegally parked car to prevent it being driven away [14C. < Old French *bote*] ◇ **get too big for your boots** to become overconfident (*informal*) ◇ **lick somebody's boots** to be extremely obsequious to somebody

boot out *vt* to force somebody to leave a place, group of people, or job (*informal*)

boot[2] /boot/ *n* the process of starting or restarting a computer and loading the operating system ■ *vi* (**boot·ed, boot·ing, boots**) to start or restart a computer and load the operating system, or be started up in this way [Late 20C. Shortening of BOOTSTRAP in *bootstrap loader*, a simple program that enables a computer to start up and load its full operating system]

boot up *vt* to start or restart a computer and load the operating system

boot[3] /boot/ [Old English *bōt* "remedy" < Indo-European, "good"] ◇ **to boot** in addition or also

boot·black /bóot blàk/ *n* especially formerly, a person who cleans people's shoes in the street

boot camp *n* **1. CAMP FOR MILITARY RECRUITS** a training camp for military recruits (*informal*) **2. CAMP FOR DELINQUENTS** a disciplinary camp to which juvenile offenders are sent **3. TRAINING COURSE** a training session or course (*informal*) ○ *a home computing boot camp* [< BOOT[1] "naval or marine corps recruit"]

boot cut *adj* describes pants with legs that are flared at the bottom to fit over boots

boo·tee /bóotee/, **boo·tie** *n* **1.** a soft woolen boot for a baby **2.** an ankle boot for a woman or child

Bo·ö·tes /bō ṓ teez/ *n* a constellation of the northern hemisphere, dominated by the bright star Arcturus. See illustration at **constellation** [Mid-16C. Via Latin < Greek *boōtēs* "plowman, Boötes" < *bous* "ox" + *ōthein* "to push"]

booth /booth/ (*plural* **booths** /boo<u>th</u>z, booths/) *n* **1. SMALL TENT OR STALL** a tent, stall, or other light structure at a fair or exhibit, offering some form of entertainment or goods for sale **2. SMALL PARTITIONED ENCLOSURE** a partitioned enclosure or small room shaped like a box that offers privacy, e.g., when telephoning, selling tickets, or voting **3. RESTAURANT COMPARTMENT** a small, partly enclosed area in a restaurant with a table and high-backed seats **4. SMALL ROOM USED IN BROADCASTING** a small soundproof room used for recording sound or for broadcasting [12C. < N Germanic]

Booth /booth/, **Edwin** (1833–93) US actor. A leading actor of tragic theatrical roles, he was best known for his portrayal of Hamlet. He was the brother of John Wilkes Booth. Full name **Booth, Edwin Thomas**

Booth, John Wilkes (1838–65) US actor and the assassin of Abraham Lincoln. He was the brother of actor Edwin Booth. A partisan of the Confederacy during the Civil War, he shot Abraham Lincoln at Ford's Theatre in Washington, D.C., on April 14, 1865, and was himself killed soon afterward.

Booth, Shirley (1898–1992) US actor. She won an Academy Award for the movie *Come Back Little Sheba* (1952).

Booth, William (1829–1912) British religious leader. He founded the Christian Mission (1865), later called the Salvation Army (1878), pursuing social reform and setting up charities in city slums.

Boo·thi·a Pen·in·su·la /bóothee ə-/ the northernmost tip of mainland North America, in Northwest Territories, Canada, directly west of Baffin Island. Area: 12,500 sq. mi./32,300 sq. km.

boot hill, Boot Hill *n* a cemetery in a settlement on the US frontier, especially one for gunfighters killed in action

Booth·royd /bóoth ròyd/, **Betty** (*b.* 1929) British politician. She was the first woman speaker of the House of Commons (1992–2000), and became a life peer in 2000. See illustration on next page

> "Good temper and moderation are the characteristics of parliamentary language."
> [Betty Boothroyd, *Independent (London)*; February 9, 1995]

bored /bawrd/ *adj* tired of and slightly annoyed by a person or situation that is not interesting, exciting, or entertaining

SPELLCHECK See ***board***.

bore·dom /báwrdəm/ *n* the feeling of being bored ○ *I nearly died of boredom.*

bore·hole /báwr hōl/ *n* a deep hole drilled into the ground to obtain samples for geologic study or to release or extract water or oil

~~boreing~~ incorrect spelling of **boring**

bor·er /báwrər/ *n* **1.** a machine or hand tool used for boring holes **2.** an organism, especially an insect or a mollusk, that bores into a plant or into wood or rock

Borg /bawrg/, **Björn** (*b.* 1956) Swedish tennis player. He was the Wimbledon men's singles champion from 1976 to 1980 and won the French singles title six times. Full name **Borg, Björn Rune**

"I want to be known as the best player of all time."
[Björn Borg, *New York Times*; July 8, 1979]

Bor·ge /báwrgə/, **Victor** (1909–2000) Danish-born US musician. He is famous for his solo comedy shows performed at the piano.

Bor·ges /báwr hèss/, **Jacobo** (*b.* 1931) Venezuelan artist. He is noted for his paintings portraying social themes.

Bor·ges, Jorge Luis (1899–1986) Argentinean writer. An avant-garde poet and essayist, he is famous for his short stories, of which *Fictions* (1945) and *The Aleph* (1949) are outstanding collections. He was director of Venezuela's National Library from 1955 to 1973.

"To fall in love is to create a religion that has a fallible god."
[Jorge Luis Borges, "The Meeting in a Dream," *Other Inquisitions*; 1952]

Bor·gia /báwrjə, -zhə/, **Cesare, Duke of the Romagna** (1476?–1507) Italian soldier. The illegitimate son of Pope Alexander VI and the brother of Lucrezia Borgia, he conquered several central Italian city-states in an attempt to found his own kingdom.

Bor·gia, Lucrezia (1480–1519) Italian art patron. During her third marriage, to the Duke of Este, she attracted Italy's foremost painters and writers to her court in Ferrara. She was the sister of Cesare Borgia.

Bor·glum /báwrgləm/, **Gutzon** (1867–1941) US sculptor. He spent his last 14 years carving the giant sculptures of four US presidents into the rock face of Mount Rushmore. Full name **Borglum, John Gutzon de la Mothe**

bo·ric /báwrik/ *adj* relating to or containing boron [Mid-19C. < BORON]

bo·ric ac·id *n* a weak acidic white crystalline solid. Use: fire retardant, antiseptic, manufacture of heat-resistant glass and ceramics. Formula: H_3BO_3.

bor·ing[1] /báwring/ *adj* stimulating no interest or enthusiasm —**bor·ing·ly** *adv* —**bor·ing·ness** *n*

SYNONYMS ***boring, dull, monotonous, tedious, uninteresting***

CORE MEANING: without qualities that engage somebody's interest

boring lacking in interest, stimulation, or variety ○ *The public is not that interested in boring details about procedures.* ○ *Living in the mountains is wonderful, but it can get quite boring after a while.* **dull** not interesting because of a lack of liveliness, humor, or variety; **monotonous** not interesting because of too much uniformity and repetition ○ *Rory stood at Janice's side, humming something monotonous.* ○ *If short and simple sentences dominate your writing, it may become monotonous.* **tedious** wearying to the point of physical as well as mental discomfort ○ *forced to take part in long and tedious debates* ○ *The movie's pacing is tedious at times; the dialogue strays.* **uninteresting** failing to engage somebody's interest rather than arousing actual impatience or weariness ○ *a stolid, uninteresting couple* ○ *The town had been largely rebuilt and looked uninteresting.*

bor·ing[2] /báwring/ *adj* describes animals or tools that make holes in things

Bor·laug /báwr làwg/, **Norman** (*b.* 1914) US agronomist. He developed the high-yield wheat that launched the "green revolution" in the developing world. He received the Nobel Peace Prize (1970). Full name **Borlaug, Norman Ernest**

Bor·mann /báwr maan/, **Martin** (1900–45?) German Nazi politician. A close and loyal adviser of Adolf Hitler, he stayed with Hitler to the end of World War II, when he is thought to have been killed by a sniper.

born /bawrn/ *adj* **1.** BROUGHT INTO LIFE brought into existence as a baby or as young from a mother's womb ○ *a child born in Birmingham* **2.** BEGUN developed from a particular source or root cause ○ *a realization born of long experience* **3.** NATURALLY PREDISPOSED having a particular natural talent or innate character trait ○ *a born leader* **4.** BY BIRTH given a particular status or condition by or at birth (*often used in combination*) ○ *a Canadian-born singer-songwriter* ◇ **born and bred** coming from a particular place or background and usually having the qualities or character regarded as representative of it

USAGE See ***borne***.

Born /bawrn/, **Max** (1882–1970) German-born British physicist. He shared the Nobel Prize (1954) for his work in quantum physics.

"Only two possibilities exist: either one must believe in determinism and regard free will as a subjective illusion, or one must become a mystic, and regard the discovery of natural laws as a meaningless illusion."
[Max Born, *Bulletin of Atomic Scientists*; 1957]

Bor·na dis·ease /báwrnə-/ *n* an often fatal infectious viral disease of horses, sheep, and cattle that can be passed on to human beings, in whom it can cause psychiatric disorders [After *Borna*, city in Saxony, Germany]

born-a·gain *adj* **1.** OF SOMEBODY WITH NEW CHRISTIAN FAITH relating to somebody with a new and passionately felt and expressed Christian faith **2.** EVANGELICALLY CHRISTIAN relating to evangelical Christianity **3.** ENTHUSIASTIC with all the enthusiasm of somebody who has been recently converted to a cause or an idea ■ *n* same as **born-again Christian**

born-a·gain Chris·tian *n* somebody with a new and passionately felt and expressed Christian faith [< John 3:3 "Except a man be born again, he cannot see the kingdom of God" (referring to a spiritual rebirth)]

borne past participle of **bear**[2]

USAGE borne or **born**? ***Borne*** is the past participle of the verb *to bear*: *The following points should be borne in mind. His account is simply not borne out by the facts.* In meanings relating to birth, ***borne*** is used when the mother is the subject of the verb, or when the verb is passive followed by the preposition *by*: *Maria had already borne six children. The twins were borne by an Italian mother.* When the subject is the child, ***born***, an old past participle of *bear*, is the form used: *He was not born in a hospital.* ***Born*** is also the adjective used in a combination, to indicate condition, location, or status of birth: *newly born pups* and *a southern-born poet.*

Bor·ne·o /báwrnee ō/ island of the Malay Archipelago in the Pacific Ocean, divided into Sabah and Sarawak, which are states of Malaysia; Brunei, an independent sultanate; and Kalimantan, part of Indonesia. Population: 10,470,800 (1995). Area: 290,000 sq. mi./751,100 sq. km. —**Bor·ne·an** *n, adj*

Born-Ha·ber cy·cle /bàwrn háybər-/ *n* a cycle of chemical reactions used for calculating either the energy required to break down a crystalline solid into its constituent ions (**lattice energy**) or the energy required to break a chemical bond into noncrystalline solids (**bond energy**) [Mid-20C. After Max BORN and Fritz *Haber* (1868–1934), German chemist]

Born·holm /báwrn hōlm, -hŏm/ island and tourist area in southeastern Denmark, in the Baltic Sea. Population: 45,067 (1994). Area: 227 sq. mi./588 sq. km.

Born·holm dis·ease *n* an acute epidemic viral infection whose symptoms include fever and chest pain [Because first identified on BORNHOLM]

born·ite /báwr nīt/ *n* a brown metallic mineral. Use: source of copper. [Early 19C. After Ignatius von *Born* (1742–91), Austrian mineralogist]

boro- *prefix* boron ○ *borosilicate* [< BORON]

Bo·ro·din /báwrə dìn/, **Aleksander** (1833–87) Russian composer and chemist. A professor of chemistry in St. Petersburg, he wrote the opera *Prince Igor* and other orchestral and chamber works. Full name **Borodin, Aleksander Porfiryevich**

Bo·ro·di·no /bàwrə déenō/ village in Russia about 70 mi./110 km west of Moscow. It was the site in 1812 of an important victory by Napoleon.

bo·ron /báw ròn/ *n* a yellow-brown element that is hard and brittle, with properties intermediate between a metal and nonmetal. Source: borax, kernite. Use: alloys, glass, ceramics, in nuclear reactors to absorb radiation. Symbol **B**. See table at **element** [Early 19C. < BORAX, after CARBON]

bo·ro·sil·i·cate /bàwrō síllikət, -sílli kàyt/ *n* a salt of boric and silicic acids. Use: manufacture of heat- and chemical-resistant glass.

bor·ough /búr ō, búrrō/ *n* **1.** DISTRICT OF CITY an administrative division of a large city, responsible for running local services such as housing and education **2.** SELF-GOVERNING TOWN in some states, a town that has formed itself into a legal corporation and governs itself **3.** ENGLISH TOWN in England, a town that once had special privileges granted to it by royal charter [Old English *burg* "fortress, fortified town" < Germanic, "protect"]

Bor·ro·mi·ni /bàwrə méenee/, **Francesco** (1599–1667) Italian architect. He designed the church of San Carlo alle Quattro Fontane in Rome (1638–41). Born **Castelli, Francesco**

bor·row /báwrō, bórrō/ *v* (**-rowed, -row·ing, -rows**) **1.** *vt* USE SOMEBODY ELSE'S PROPERTY to get temporary possession or use of something belonging to somebody else, usually after asking permission ○ *Dad, can I borrow the car?* **2.** *vti* RECEIVE MONEY AS LOAN to arrange to be given money by somebody or by a bank or other financial institution for a fixed period of time. The money is normally paid back in installments, with interest. ○ *We've already borrowed heavily this year.* **3.** *vt* TAKE BOOK FROM LIBRARY to take out a book or other item from a library for an agreed period of time **4.** *vti* COPY SOMETHING FROM SOMEBODY'S WORK to copy something from somebody else's work, especially a work of art of some kind ○ *Some shots were clearly borrowed from Hitchcock.* **5.** *vti* LING TAKE SOMETHING FROM ANOTHER LANGUAGE to adopt a word from another language **6.** *vi* GOLF PUTT TO ALLOW FOR SLOPE in golf, to putt to the left or right of a straight line on a green to allow for the effect of the slope **7.** *vi* GOLF VEER LEFT OR RIGHT to veer to the left or right as a result of the slope of a green (*refers to golf balls*) ■ *n* GOLF EXTENT OF VEERING the degree to which a golf ball veers to the left or right as a result of the slope of a green [Old English *borgian* "borrow against security" < Germanic, "protect"] —**bor·row·er** *n*

USAGE borrow, lend, or **loan**? All these verbs are used in connection with the temporary use or possession of something that belongs to somebody else. When you borrow something from somebody, you get it: *Can I borrow your car for an hour? I borrowed $100 from my brother.* When you ***lend*** or ***loan*** something to somebody, you give it: *My brother lent me $100. Will you loan me your car for an hour?* ***Lend*** can be used figuratively, whereas ***loan*** cannot: *The old silver lends* [not *loans*] *an air of elegance to an otherwise drab room.* ***Borrow*** and ***lend/loan*** are not interchangeable in standard English and should not be confused.

borrow home *vt Malaysia* to borrow something and take it home ○ *Can I borrow this book home?*

bor·row·ing /báwrō ing, bórrō ing/ *n* **1.** ACT OF GETTING SOMETHING ON LOAN an act of gaining the temporary possession of something **2.** PROCESS OF BORROWING the process of agreeing to accept money from a bank and pay it back later ○ *an increase in government borrowing* **3.** AMOUNT BORROWED an amount of money borrowed ○ *substantial borrowings in the region of* *half a million dollars* **4.** LING **ADOPTED WORD** a word that has been adopted from another language **5.** **COPIED IDEA** an idea copied from somebody else's work, especially from a work of art of some kind

bor·row pit *n* a hole left where stones or other materials have been dug up for use in construction work elsewhere

borscht /bawrsht/ *n* a Russian or Polish soup whose main ingredient is beets [Early 19C. < Russian *borshch*]

borscht belt *n* a show business circuit centered on the many hotels in the Catskill Mountains that were formerly the destination of Jewish vacationers (*informal*)

bort /bawrt/ *n* a diamond of inferior quality that is used industrially on grinding wheels and other abrasive devices [Early 17C. Origin ?]

bor·zoi /báwr zòy/ (*plural* **-zois**) *n* a tall graceful domestic dog with a long silky coat, belonging to a breed formerly used in Russia to hunt wolves [Late 19C. < Russian < *borzyĭ* "swift"]

Bosc /bosk/ *n* a variety of pear that has a long neck, a reddish yellow skin, and juicy sweet flesh [After Louis *Bosc*, 19C Belgian horticulturist]

bos·cage /bóskij/ *n* densely growing trees and bushes [14C. < Old French < Germanic]

Hieronymus Bosch

Bosch /bosh, bawsh/, **Hieronymus** (1450?–1516) Dutch painter. His allegorical paintings teeming with demons and monsters include *The Seven Deadly Sins* and *The Garden of Earthly Delights*. Born **Aken, Jerome van**

Bosch, Juan Domingo (1909–2001) writer and president of the Dominican Republic (1962–63). He lived in exile from 1937 to 1961 during the dictatorship of Rafael Trujillo. He was elected president in 1962, but was overthrown by the army after seven months and never regained office.

Bose /bōss, bawss/, **Sir Jagadis Chandra** (1858–1937) Indian physicist and botanist. He invented a means of measuring minute plant movements and growth and founded the Bose Research Institute, Kolkata, India (1917).

Bose-Ein·stein con·den·sa·tion /bōss-/ *n* a process in which the bosons of a particle system enter the lowest-energy ground state at a specific temperature [After S. N. *Bose* (see BOSON) and Albert EINSTEIN] —**Bose-Ein·stein con·den·sate** *n*

bosh /bosh/ *interj* used to dismiss as nonsense what has just been said (*dated informal*) [Mid-19C. < Turkish *boş* "empty, worthless"]

bosk·y /bóskee/ (**-i·er, -i·est**) *adj* densely covered with small trees or bushes (*literary*) [Late 16C. < variant of BUSH[1]]

bo's'n *n* NAUT same as **boatswain**

Bos·ni·a /bóznee ə/ the northern region of Bosnia and Herzegovina

Bos·ni·a and Her·ze·go·vi·na /bòznee ə ənd háirtsəgō veenə/ country in the former Federal People's Republic of Yugoslavia that declared its independence in 1992. In 1995, following civil war between Muslims, Serbs, and Croats, it was divided into two self-governing provinces: a Muslim-Croat Federation and a Serb Republic. Language: Serbo-Croatian. Currency: marka. Capital: Sarajevo. Population: 3,989,018 (2003). Area: 19,741 sq. mi./51,129 sq. km. Official name **Republic of Bosnia and Herzegovina**

Bosnia and Herzegovina

Bos·ni·ac /bóznee ak/ *n* a Muslim inhabitant of Bosnia and Herzegovina —**Bos·ni·ac** *adj*

Bos·ni·an /bóznee ən/ *n* **1.** somebody who comes from a region in the north of Bosnia and Herzegovina **2.** somebody who comes from Bosnia and Herzegovina —**Bos·ni·an** *adj*

bos·om /bŏŏzzəm, bŏŏzəm/ *n* **1.** **SOMEBODY'S CHEST** the chest of a man or woman **2.** **WOMAN'S BREASTS** the breasts of a woman **3.** **WOMAN'S BREAST** either of the breasts of a woman (*dated*) **4.** **CLOTHING COVERING BREASTS** the part of a garment that covers a woman's breasts **5.** **PROTECTIVE PLACE** a familiar source of protection, security, or affection (*literary*) ○ *back in the bosom of her family* **6.** **SEAT OF EMOTION** the place where emotions are felt (*literary*) ■ *adj* **CLOSE IN FRIENDSHIP** describes a friend to whom somebody is very close (*informal*) ○ *a bosom buddy* [Old English *bōsm*, origin ?]

bos·om·y /bŏŏzzəmee/ (**-i·er, -i·est**) *adj* describes a woman with large breasts

bo·son /bōsson/ *n* an elementary particle that has zero or integral spin and obeys statistical rules that place no restriction on the number of identical particles that may be in the same state. Photons and alpha particles are bosons. [Mid-20C. After Satyendra Nuath *Bose* (1894–1974), Indian physicist]

Bos·po·rus /bóspərəss/, **Bos·pho·rus** /bósfərəss/ strait linking the Black Sea and the Sea of Marmara. It separates European and Asian Turkey. Length: 19 mi./31 km.

boss[1] /bawss, boss/ *n* **1.** **SOMEBODY IN CHARGE** somebody who is in charge of others, especially in a work environment ○ *asked the boss for some time off* **2.** **SOMEBODY DOMINANT** the dominant partner in a relationship or the dominant member of a group, who tends to make decisions and give instructions (*informal; often ironic*) **3.** **POWERFUL POLITICIAN** a politician who exerts a controlling influence, e.g., by applying pressure on others to vote in a particular way (*informal*) ■ *vt* (**bossed, boss·ing, boss·es**) *also* **boss a·round** **GIVE SOMEBODY ORDERS** to give somebody orders in an authoritarian way that is often resisted or resented ○ *You find the big kids trying to boss the little kids around.* ○ *The big kids try to boss the little ones.* ■ *adj* **EXCELLENT** so good as to dominate in a group (*dated slang*) ○ *a boss drummer* [Early 19C. < Dutch *baas* "master"] ◇ **be your own boss 1.** to work under your own authority, e.g., with freelance or self-employed status **2.** to make decisions relating to your own life, instead of having them dictated by others

boss[2] /bawss, boss/ *n* **1.** **KNOB** a round raised part that sticks out from a surface, e.g., a stud at the center of a shield **2.** ARCHIT **CEILING DECORATION** a decorative knob on a vaulted ceiling at points where the ribs meet **3.** COMPUT GAMES **HARD-TO-DEFEAT OPPONENT IN COMPUTER GAME** in computer games, an opponent who is hard to defeat but must be defeated in order to complete a game level **4.** BIOL **SWELLING** a round swelling on a plant or on the horn of an animal **5.** MECH ENG **SHAFT PART** a thicker part of a shaft at a point where another part is attached to it **6.** GEOL **VOLCANIC ROCK MASS** a mass of volcanic rock with a roughly circular cross section and vertical sides [14C. < Old French *boce*]

bos·sa no·va /bòssə nŏvə, bàwssə-/ *n* **1.** a lively ballroom dance similar to the samba that originated in Brazil in the early 1960s **2.** the music for a bossa nova [Mid-20C. < Portuguese, "new trend"]

boss bat·tle *n* a battle with a major opponent at the end of a computer game level

Bos·sier Cit·y /bṓzhər-/ city in northwestern Louisiana on the Red River, on the northwestern outskirts of Shreveport. Population: 57,156 (2002 estimate).

boss·ism /báw sìzzəm, bó sìzzəm/ *n* political control, especially the control of a big city's political machine, by one person who is usually not an office holder and whose methods are usually corrupt

boss·y /báwssee, bóssee/ (**-i·er, -i·est**) *adj* fond of or prone to giving orders ○ *The other children don't like it when you're bossy.* —**boss·i·ly** *adv* —**boss·i·ness** *n*

boss·y·boots /báwssee bŏŏts, bóssee-/ (*plural same*) *n UK* somebody who bosses other people around (*informal*)

bos·ton /báwstən, bós-/ *n* a version of whist in which two decks of cards are used and players bid for the right to name trumps [Early 19C. < French, probably after BOSTON]

Bos·ton /báwstən, bós-/ capital and largest city of Massachusetts. Situated at the mouth of the Charles River on Boston Bay, it is home to Boston College, Boston University, and Northeastern University, among other universities. Population: 589,281 (2002 estimate). —**Bos·to·ni·an** /baw stṓnee ən, bo-/ *n, adj*

Bos·ton bull, Bos·ton bull·dog *n* DOGS same as **Boston terrier**

Bos·ton crab *n* a wrestling hold in which a wrestler is grabbed by the legs, turned face down, and sat on

Bos·ton cream pie *n* a round sandwich cake filled with cream or custard and covered with chocolate sauce

Bos·ton fern *n* a fern with delicate, crested fronds, popular as a houseplant. Latin name: *Nephrolepis exaltata* var. bostoniensis.

Bos·ton i·vy *n* a cultivated climbing plant with leaves consisting of three black lobes that turn red in the fall. Latin name: *Parthenocissus tricuspidata*.

Bos·ton let·tuce *n* a variety of lettuce with a round head and tender, yellow and green leaves

Bos·ton rock·er *n* a rocking chair with a seat that curves up to meet a high back

Bos·ton Tea Par·ty *n* a protest against British taxes made by the citizens of Boston in 1773 that led to the American Revolution. The protesters boarded three British ships and threw their cargoes of tea overboard.

Bos·ton ter·ri·er *n* a stocky dog with a smooth brindled or black coat and white markings, belonging to a breed originating in Boston that is a cross between a bulldog and a terrier

bo·sun *n* NAUT same as **boatswain**

Bos·well /bóz wèl, -wəl/, **James** (1740–95) Scottish lawyer and biographer. He met the writer Samuel Johnson in 1763 and after two decades of close association wrote his *Life of Samuel Johnson* (1791), one of the masterpieces of English biography.

> "He who praises everybody, praises nobody."
> [James Boswell, *The Life of Samuel Johnson*; 1791]

Bos·worth Field /bózwərth-/ site of a decisive battle in 1485 when Henry Tudor defeated Richard III and claimed the English throne

bot[1] /bot/ *n* a larva of a botfly [Early 16C. Probably < Low Dutch]

bot[2] /bot/ *n* a computer program performing routine or time-consuming tasks such as searching websites automatically or semi-independently (*usually used in combination*) [Late 20C. Shortening of ROBOT]

BOT *abbr* COMPUT beginning of tape

bot. *abbr* BOT **1.** botanical **2.** botany

bo·tan·i·cal /bə tánnik'l/, **bo·tan·ic** /bə tánnik/ *adj* relating to plants, especially to the scientific study of plants ■ *n* a drug or product made from plants (*often used in the plural*) [Mid-17C. < French *botanique* or late Latin *botanicus* < Greek *botanikos* < *botanē* "plant"] —**bo·tan·i·cal·ly** *adv*

bo·tan·i·cal gar·den, bo·tan·ic gar·den *n* an area, often open to the public, in which exotic, rare, or scientifically interesting plants are grown and studied (*often used in the plural*)

bot·a·nist /bótt'nist/ *n* somebody with an expert scientific knowledge of, or a strong interest in, plants [Mid-17C. < French *botaniste* < *botanique* (see BOTANICAL)]

bot·a·nize /bótt'n ìz/ (**-nized, -niz·ing, -niz·es**) *vti* to collect or study plants (*informal*) [Mid-18C. Via modern Latin *botanizare* < Greek *botanizein* "gather plants" < *botanē* "plant"] —**bot·a·niz·er** *n*

bot·a·ny /bótt'nee/ (*plural* **-nies**) *n* 1. STUDY OF PLANTS the scientific study of plants 2. PLANT LIFE OF AREA the plant life that exists within a particular area 3. BIOLOGICAL CHARACTERISTICS OF PLANT the biological description of a plant or group of plants [Late 17C. < BOTANICAL]

Bot·a·ny Bay /bótt'nee-/ bay south of Sydney, New South Wales, Australia. It was Captain Cook's first landing site on the continent in 1770.

Bot·a·ny wool *n* a fine merino wool. Use: yarns, fabrics. [After BOTANY BAY]

botch /boch/ (*informal*) *vt* (**botched, botch·ing, botch·es**) *also* **botch up** to do something very badly out of clumsiness or lack of care ○ *managed to botch a simple repair job* ○ *botched the piano concerto up* ■ *n* a job or task that has been done very badly [14C. Origin ?] —**botch·er** *n* —**botch·i·ly** *adv* —**botch·i·ness** *n* —**botch·y** *adj*

bo·tel *n* BOATING, TRAVEL another spelling of **boatel**

bot·fly /bót flì/ (*plural* **-flies**) *n* a two-winged hairy parasitic fly that lays its eggs under the skin or in the digestive tract, sometimes causing serious illness. Botflies live as parasites on mammals, especially horses, sheep, cattle, and people. Families: Oestridae or Gasterophilidae.

both /bōth/ *adj, pron* relating to or consisting of two people or things considered together ○ *For once, I like both candidates.* ○ *There are only two licensed outlets, and both are in Asbury Park.* ■ *conj* used with two facts or alternatives joined by "and" to indicate that not just one but also the other one is included ○ *Truancy is now treated as both a law-enforcement and an educational issue.* [13C. < Old Norse *báðir*]

USAGE ***Both*** has several roles, as a pronoun (*I like both*), adjective (*I like both boys*), or conjunction (*They are both pleasant and cheerful*). Its mobility in a sentence is so great that its meaning can become ambiguous. In the last example, it is not immediately clear whether ***both*** belongs with "they" or with the complement of the sentence, "pleasant and cheerful"; in speech, intonation will normally clarify the intention. However, when writing, you need to ensure that you are not leaving the reader in doubt. The principal restriction applying to ***both*** is that it should refer to two people or things and no more; if three or more are meant, it is necessary to use *each*, which behaves grammatically in ways quite similar to ***both***. (However, *each* is regarded as singular while ***both*** is plural, and ***both*** alone allows the construction *I saw them both.*) When pairing ***both*** with *and*, it is important to retain a balance between the two parts of the construction with regard to the position of ***both*** and the types of words linked: *She is both charming and intellectual* [not *She is both charming and an intellectual*] or *He both sings well and likes to paint* [not *He is both a fine singer and likes to paint*]. In terms of possession, *of* + ***both*** is clearer, as in *the parents of both, the responsibility of both*, as opposed to *both their parents* and *both their responsibility* or *both their responsibilities*.

Bo·tha /bṓtə, bṓ taa/, **P. W.** (*b.* 1916) South African politician. He was prime minister (1978–84) and first executive state president (1984–89) of South Africa. Full name **Botha, Pieter Willem**

"South Africa will not allow the double standards and hypocrisy of the Western world, even in the application of legal principles, to stand in the way of our responsibility to protect our country."
[P. W. Botha, *Speech*; 1986]

both·er /bóthər/ *v* (**-ered, -er·ing, -ers**) 1. *vi* MAKE EFFORT to take the time or trouble to do something (*often used in negative statements*) ○ *He didn't even bother to get out of the car.* 2. *vti* BE WORRIED OR WORRY SOMEBODY to feel worried, anxious, or upset, or make somebody feel like this ○ *It bothers me to think of you all on your own.* 3. *vt* DISTURB SOMEBODY to annoy or disturb somebody, e.g., by interrupting or by making unwelcome advances ○ *Is the music bothering you?* 4. *vt* CAUSE PHYSICAL PAIN TO SOMEBODY to make somebody feel physical discomfort or pain ○ *My back is bothering me again.* ■ *n* 1. EFFORT trouble or effort to do something ○ *Don't go to all that bother for me.* 2. SOURCE OF ANNOYANCE somebody or something that causes annoyance, e.g., by making noise [Late 17C. Origin ?]

SYNONYMS ***bother, annoy, bug, disturb, trouble, worry***

CORE MEANING: to interfere with somebody's peace or composure

bother to feel worried, anxious, or upset, or make somebody feel like this ○ *Sorry to bother you.* ○ *He is not bothered in the slightest by these hints of change.* **annoy** to harass somebody repeatedly ○ *The wasps buzzing round them as they ate were beginning to annoy them.* **bug** (*informal*) to cause somebody persistent trouble and annoyance ○ *something that's been bugging me* ○ *He's always bugging my son's friends with questions.* **disturb** to interrupt or distract somebody when he or she is doing something ○ *disturbing her while she was reading* **trouble** to put somebody to the inconvenience of doing something ○ *I'm sorry to trouble you, but I need your help.* **worry** to annoy somebody by making insistent demands or complaints ○ *Reporters and photographers kept worrying the family with requests for interviews.*

---

both·er·a·tion /bòthə ráysh'n/ *interj* used as an expression of mild annoyance (*dated informal*)

both·er·some /bóthərssəm/ *adj* causing annoyance and inconvenience

Both·ni·a, Gulf of /bóthnee ə/ northern part of the Baltic Sea, situated between Finland and Sweden. Area: 45,200 sq. mi./117,000 sq. km.

both·y /bóthee/ (*plural* **-ies**) *n Scotland* a simple house or hut, originally a farmer's or crofter's cottage, now usually a hut providing shelter for hikers or climbers [Late 18C. Probably < variant of BOOTH]

Bo·tox /bṓ tòks/ *tdmk* a trademark for a preparation of botulinum toxin, a protein that relaxes muscle contractions. It is sometimes injected under the skin to erase facial wrinkles.

bo tree /bṓ-/ *n* a tree of the fig family that is regarded as sacred by Hindus and Buddhists. Native to: South Asia. Latin name: *Ficus religiosa*. [Mid-19C. Partial translation of Sinhalese *bōgaha* < *bō* (< Pali, Sanskrit *bodhi* "perfect knowledge") + *gaha* "tree"]

bot·ry·oid·al /bòttree óyd'l/ *adj* describes minerals and plant parts shaped like a bunch of grapes [Late 18C. < Greek *botruoeidēs* < *botrus* "bunch of grapes"]

bots /bots/ *n* an intestinal disease of horses, sheep, and cattle, caused by infection with botfly larvae (*takes a singular or plural verb*)

Bot·swa·na /bot swáanə/ landlocked country in southern Africa that shares borders with Namibia, Zambia, Zimbabwe, and South Africa. It became an independent member of the Commonwealth in 1966. Language: English, Setswana. Currency: pula. Capital: Gaborone. Population: 1,573,267 (2003). Area: 224,607 sq. mi./581,730 sq. km. Official name **Republic of Botswana**. Former name **Bechuanaland** (until 1966) —**Bot·swa·nan** *n, adj*

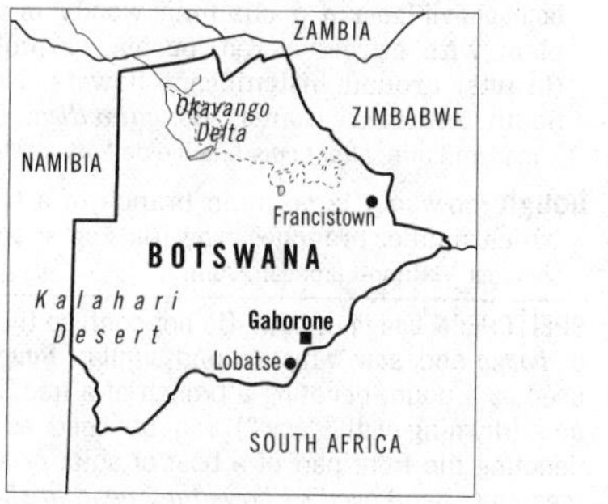

Botswana

botte /bot/ *n* a thrust or hit in fencing [14C. < Old French *bot(te)* "blow, hit"]

Sandro Botticelli: *The Birth of Venus* (after 1482)

Bot·ti·cel·li /bòtti chéllee/, **Sandro** (1445–1510) Italian painter. He specialized in classical themes, exemplified in paintings such as *The Birth of Venus* and *Primavera*. Born **Filipepi, Alessandro di Mariano**

bot·tle /bótt'l/ *n* 1. CONTAINER FOR LIQUIDS a container for liquids, usually made of glass or plastic, with a narrow neck and no handle 2. AMOUNT IN BOTTLE the amount of liquid contained in a bottle 3. CONTAINER FOR BABY'S MILK a plastic or glass container with a rubber nipple used for feeding a baby, or an amount of milk given from such a container ○ *Has he had his bottle yet?* 4. ALCOHOL alcoholic beverages, or the habit of drinking alcohol to excess (*informal*) ○ *fond of the bottle* ■ *vt* (**-tled, -tling, -tles**) 1. PUT LIQUID IN BOTTLE to put a liquid that can be consumed in a bottle for storage or sale 2. *UK* PRESERVE FOOD IN JARS to store fruit or vegetables in a preserving liquid in a glass container [14C. Via Old French *boteille* < medieval Latin *butticula* "little cask" < late Latin *buttis* "cask, barrel"]

bottle up *vt* 1. to contain, hold, or entrap something or somebody, especially a group of people 2. to conceal or repress strong feelings ○ *all the resentment she's been bottling up for years*

bot·tle bank *n UK* a large container or group of containers in which members of the public can deposit used glass bottles and jars for recycling

bot·tle·brush /bótt'l brùsh/ *n* a bush or small tree that has a mass of spiky flowers with large stamens. Native to: Australia. Genus: *Callistemon or Melaleuca*. [< the plant's resemblance to a cylindrical brush for cleaning bottles]

bot·tled /bótt'ld/ *adj* stored or sold in bottles

bot·tle-feed *vt* to feed a baby or a young animal milk from a bottle, as distinct from breast-feeding or suckling it

bot·tle gourd *n* a climbing plant that produces bottle-shaped fruits. Use: containers for liquids, when dried. Native to: Europe. Latin name: *Lagenaria siceraria*.

bot·tle-green *adj* of a dark green color, like some wine bottles —**bot·tle green** *n*

bot·tle·neck /bótt'l nèk/ *n* 1. a junction or a narrow section of a road that slows traffic or causes traffic jams 2. a delay caused when one part of a process or activity is slower than the others and so hinders overall progress

bot·tle-nosed dol·phin, bot·tle·nose dol·phin /bótt'l nōz-/ *n* a dolphin with a long snout. Native to: warm waters. Latin name: *Tursiops truncatus*.

bot·tle o·pen·er *n* a metal tool used to pry the metal tops off bottles

bot·tler /bótt'lər/ *n* a company that bottles beverages as part of a manufacturing process

bot·tle tree *n* a tree with a swollen bottle-shaped trunk and an unpleasant smell. Native to: Australia. Genus: *Brachychiton*.

bot·tom /bóttəm/ *n* **1. LOWEST PART** the lowest or deepest part of something ○ *From the bottom of the hill it seems a long way up.* **2. UNDERSIDE** the underneath side or surface of something ○ *rust on the bottom of the boat* **3. FARTHEST POINT** the part of something that is farthest away ○ *ponies grazing at the bottom of the field* **4. LAND UNDER WATER** the ground underneath a sea, lake, or river ○ *Can you dive down and touch the bottom?* **5. END OF LIST** the end of a list or series, especially the lowest level of excellence or achievement ○ *teams at the bottom of the league* **6. ROOT CAUSE** the fundamental, often hidden, cause or origin of something ○ *get to the bottom of the problem* **7. LOWEST RANK** the lowest level in a hierarchy ○ *worked her way up from the bottom* **8. BUTTOCKS** somebody's buttocks, or, particularly when speaking to children, any body part in this general area (*informal*) **9. PART COVERING LOWER BODY** the part of a two-piece garment such as a tracksuit or bikini that covers the lower body (*often used in the plural*) **10. VALLEY** a dry valley or hollow (*often used in place names*) ○ *Six Mile Bottom* ■ *adj* **1. LOWEST** in the lower or lowest position ○ *Look on the bottom shelf.* **2. LEAST SUCCESSFUL** in the position of least excellence or achievement ○ *the bottom five teams* ■ *v* (**-tomed, -tom·ing, -toms**) **1.** *vi* **HIT SEA FLOOR** to scrape the underside against the floor of the sea or a river, because the water is too shallow (*refers to boats*) **2.** *vt* **OVERLOAD TRANSISTOR** to overload a transistor to the point where additional input produces no additional output [Old English *botm* < Indo-European] ◇ **at bottom** in reality, when external appearances are stripped away ◇ **bottoms up** used as a drinking toast (*informal*) ◇ **from the bottom of your heart** with the utmost sincerity ◇ **hit (rock) bottom** to reach the lowest point in your personal, professional, or emotional life

bottom out *vi* after a decline, to stop falling any lower and stabilize at a low level ○ *After plummeting 200 points, the stock market finally bottomed out.*

bot·tom dead-cen·ter *n* the position of a piston in an engine or pump when it is at the bottom of its stroke

bot·tom drawer *n UK* same as **hope chest** (sense 1) [Because items were traditionally kept in the lowest drawer of a chest of drawers]

bot·tom feed·er *n* **1.** a freshwater or saltwater animal, especially a fish that feeds on material drifting to the bottom of a body of water **2.** somebody who profits by taking advantage of other people (*slang insult*)

bot·tom fish·ing *n* the purchase of securities, real estate, or businesses when prices are unusually low as a result of adverse market conditions —**bot·tom fish·er** *n*

bot·tom·land /bóttəm lànd/ *n* low-lying fertile land bordering a river

bot·tom·less /bóttəmləss/ *adj* **1. VERY DEEP** so deep as to appear to have no bottom **2. PLENTIFUL** with unlimited or seemingly unlimited resources, especially of money ○ *a bottomless fund* **3. UNFATHOMABLE** too well hidden to be discovered or too mysterious to be understood —**bot·tom·less·ness** *n*

bot·tom line *n* **1. UNAVOIDABLE FACTOR** the most important factor that must be accepted, however reluctantly ○ *The bottom line is that the sponsors want a French driver on the team.* **2. PROFIT OR LOSS** the final profit or loss that a company makes at the end of a given period of time **3. LOWEST ACCEPTABLE AMOUNT** the least amount of money regarded as acceptable in a business transaction

bot·tom·most /bóttəm mōst/ *adj* at the very lowest level ○ *the bottommost rung of the ladder*

bot·tom quark *n* a quark with an electric charge of $-\frac{1}{3}$, zero charm, zero isotopic spin, and zero strangeness

bot·tom round *n* a cut of beef from the outer part of a round

bot·tom·set bed /bóttəm set-/ *n* a layer of sediment deposited by a river at the base of an accumulating delta

bot·ty /bóttee/ (*plural* **-ties**) *n* the buttocks (*baby talk*) [Late 19C. Alteration of BOTTOM]

bot·u·lin /bóchəlin/ *n* a toxin produced by the bacterium *Clostridium botulinum* that causes botulism [Early 20C. < modern Latin *botulinus* (see BOTULINUM)]

bot·u·li·num /bòchə línəm/, **bot·u·li·nus** /-línəss/ *n* a bacterium that causes botulism when it is present in food. It is an anaerobic bacterium, requiring the absence of free oxygen. Latin name: *Clostridium botulinum.* [Early 20C. < modern Latin, neuter of *botulinus* < Latin *botulus* "sausage"] —**bot·u·li·nal** *adj*

bot·u·lism /bóchə lìzzəm/ *n* a serious form of food poisoning caused by eating preserved food that has been contaminated with botulinum organisms. The toxin affects the central nervous system and causes progressive muscular paralysis. [Late 19C. < German *Botulismus* "sausage poisoning" < Latin *botulus* "sausage"]

Boua·ké /bwaá kay/ city and capital of Bouaké Department, central Côte d'Ivoire. Population: 329,850 (1988).

bou·bou /bóoboo/ *n* a bird of the shrike family that is black with a white flash on each wing. It is known for singing in pairs. Native to: Africa. Genus: *Laniarius.* [Late 20C. < an African language]

bou·chée /boo sháy/ *n* a small bite-sized pastry case filled with a meat, fish, or vegetable mixture [Mid-19C. < French, "mouthful" < *bouche* "mouth" < Latin *bucca* "cheek"]

Bou·cher /boo sháy/, **François** (1703–70) French painter. He worked at the court of Louis XV, painting mythological and pastoral scenes in the rococo style.

Bou·cher, Pierre (1622?–1717) French-born Canadian soldier and landowner. He is known for his records of his experiences of life in New France.

bou·clé /boo kláy/ *n* a yarn with loops or bumps along its length that produces a bumpy effect when knitted or woven (*often used before a noun*) [Late 19C. < French, past participle of *boucler* "curl" < Latin *buccula* "cheek strap of a helmet" < *bucca* "cheek"]

Bou·dic·ca /bóodikə/, **Bo·ad·i·ce·a** /bṑ ədə sée ə/ (*d.* A.D. 62) English tribal queen. The queen of the Iceni, she raised a rebellion against the Romans, who had invaded her kingdom. She sacked London, Colchester, and St. Albans, and destroyed the Roman Ninth Legion.

bou·din /boo dán, -dáN/ *n* **1.** a French blood sausage **2.** a spicy sausage made of pork, pork liver, and rice that is a popular ingredient in Louisiana Creole cuisine [Mid-19C. < French < Latin *botulus* "sausage"]

bou·doir /bóo dwàawr, -dwàwr/ *n* a woman's bedroom or private sitting room [Late 18C. < French, "place to sulk in" < *bouder* "to pout, sulk"]

bouf·fant /boo faánt/ *adj* describes a woman's hairstyle in which hair is backcombed or teased to give fullness and height [Early 19C. < French, present participle of *bouffer* "swell or puff up"] —**bouf·fant** *n*

bou·gain·vil·lae·a *n* PLANTS another spelling of **bougainvillea**

Bou·gain·ville /bóogən vìl, bóo gaN véel/ largest island of the Solomon Islands group, in eastern Papua New Guinea, in the southwestern Pacific Ocean. Area: 3,880 sq. mi./10,000 sq. km.

Bou·gain·ville, Louis Antoine, comte de (1729–1811) French navigator. He made the first French circumnavigation of the world (1766–69).

bou·gain·vil·le·a /bòogən víllee ə, -víllyə, -vée ə, bṑ-/, **bou·gain·vil·lae·a** *n* a climbing woody ornamental plant with attractive red, purple, or pink leaves (**bracts**) around insignificant flowers. Native to: South America. Genus: *Bougainvillea.* [Mid-19C. < modern Latin, after Louis Antoine de BOUGAINVILLE]

bough /bow/ *n* a large main branch of a tree, from which smaller branches grow [Old English *bōg* "bough, shoulder" < Indo-European, "arm"]

SPELLCHECK bough or **bow**? Do not confuse the spelling of ***bough*** and ***bow***, which sound similar. ***Bough*** is only used as a noun, denoting a branch of a tree. The word ***bow*** (rhyming with "cow") can be used as a noun, denoting the front part of a boat or ship, or as a verb, meaning "bend over": *I bowed my head in shame. The branches were bowed down with fruit.*

CULTURAL NOTE ***The Golden Bough***, a book (1890) by the British anthropologist Sir James George Frazer. It is an encyclopedic, rationalistic survey of mythology and religion that suggests a strong connection between belief in magic and religious faith. Hugely influential in its time, it notably provided T. S. Eliot with several striking images for his poem *The Waste Land* (1922).

bought /bawt/ past participle, past tense of **buy** ■ *adj* commercially made rather than homemade

bought·en /báwt'n/ *adj US regional, Can* commercially made rather than homemade ○ *"Better to go down dignified/ With boughten friendship at your side."* (Robert Frost, *Provide, Provide*) [Late 18C. < BOUGHT after *foughten*, archaic form of FOUGHT]

REGIONAL NOTE The term ***boughten*** endures as a Northern folk term spreading westward out of New England, across the Northern states to the Pacific and virtually unused in the South Midland and Southern states. It is commonly still heard in the compound *store-boughten*, as in *I don't like store-boughten bread.*

bou·gie /bóozhee, -jee/ *n* a medical instrument in the form of a flexible tube, inserted into a body passage such as the rectum to open it to allow medicines or instruments to be introduced [Mid-18C. < French, after the town of *Bougie* (Arabic *Bijāya*) in Algeria, which traded in wax]

bouil·la·baisse /bòoyə báyss, bóolyə bàyss/ *n* a rich soup made with fish and originating from the south of France [Mid-19C. Via French < modern Provençal *bouiabaisso*]

bouil·lon /bóol yòn, -yən, bóo yòn/ *n* a clear liquid that is traditionally made by boiling meat, bones, and vegetables together. It is sometimes served as a soup, but usually used as a stock for soups and stews. [Mid-17C. < French < *bouillir* (see BOIL[1])]

bouil·lon cube *n* a small cube of dried and concentrated food extracts that, when added to hot water, makes a stock for use in soups, stews, and sauces

Boul. *abbr* Boulevard

Bou·lan·ger /bóo laaN zháy/, **Nadia** (1887–1979) French composer and music teacher. She composed vocal and instrumental music until 1918, then concentrated on teaching composition. Her students included Aaron Copland, Philip Glass, Walter Piston, and Virgil Thomson. Full name **Boulanger, Nadia Juliette**

boul·der /bṓldər/ *n* **1.** a large round rock **2.** a large fragment of rock greater than 8 in./200 mm in diameter [15C. Shortening of *boulderstone*, partial translation of a N Germanic word]

Boul·der /bṓldər/ resort city in northern Colorado, northwest of Denver, southeast of Rocky Mountain National Park, original home of the University of Colorado, opened in 1877. Population: 94,167 (2002 estimate).

boul·der clay *n* GEOL same as **till**[4]

bould·er·ing /bṓldəring/ *n* rock climbing that involves undertaking short and extremely difficult slopes —**bould·er·er** *n*

Boul·ding /bṓlding/, **Kenneth** (1910–93) British-born US economist. His *The Meaning of the Twentieth Century* (1964) concerns ethical aspects of socioeconomic issues during peacetime. Full name **Boulding, Kenneth Ewart**

boule /bool/ *n* a pear-shaped imitation gemstone made in a furnace from synthetic aluminum oxide (**corundum**) [Early 20C. < French (see BOWL[2])]

boules /boolz/ *n* an outdoor game of French origin, similar to bowling. It is traditionally played on open dusty ground in public places with heavy metal balls that are tossed backhand. (*takes a singular verb*) [Early 20C. < French, plural of *boule* (see BOWL[2])]

boul·e·vard /bóollə vaàrd, bóolə-/ *n* **1.** a wide street, especially one lined by trees (*often used in place names*) **2.** *Can, Midwest* a median strip, or a strip of planted ground between the lanes of a divided highway [Mid-18C. Via French, "(promenade on the site of) a rampart" < Middle Low German, Middle Dutch *bolwerk* (see BULWARK)]

bou·le·vard·ier /bo͝olə vaard yáy, -eér/ *n* a fashionable sophisticated man who treats life with lighthearted cynicism (*dated*) [Late 19C. < French < *boulevard* (see BOULEVARD)]

boul·e·vard strip *n Can, Midwest* a median strip or a strip of planted ground between the lanes of a divided highway, or a strip of ground between a sidewalk and a street

bou·le·ver·se·ment /bo͝olə vèrssə maáN/ *n* a scene of shouting and anger (*formal*) [Late 17C. < French, "upset, upheaval" < *bouleverser* "turn over like a ball" < *boule* (see BOWL[2])]

Bou·lez /boo léz/, **Pierre** (*b.* 1925) French composer and conductor. He has conducted major orchestras in Europe and the United States and championed new music.

boulle /bool/ *n* elaborate inlay work on furniture, using tortoiseshell, ivory, or brass in scroll shapes. It was popular in France in the 17th century. (*often used before a noun*) [Early 19C. < French, after André Charles *Boulle* (1642–1732), French cabinetmaker]

~~boullion~~ incorrect spelling of **bouillon**

Bou·logne-sur-Mer /boo lōn soor mèr, -láwnyə-/, **Boulogne** city and port on the English Channel in Pas-de-Calais Department, northwestern France. Population: 44,859 (1999).

Bou·mé·di·enne /boo màydee én/, **Houari** (1932–78) Algerian nationalist and president (1965–78). He commanded the liberation forces during Algeria's war of independence from French rule (1960–62). Born **Boukharouba, Muhammad Brahim**

bounce /bownss/ *v* (**bounced, bounc·ing, bounc·es**) **1.** *vti* SPRING AWAY FROM SURFACE to move away quickly after hitting a surface, or throw something so that it hits a surface and moves away ○ *bouncing a tennis ball against a wall* ○ *Onlookers saw the car bounce off a tree.* **2.** *vi* JUMP UP AND DOWN to jump up and down repeatedly on a soft surface ○ *children bouncing on trampolines* **3.** *vt* LIFT CHILD ON KNEE to move a baby or small child gently up and down in your arms or on your knees **4.** *vti* REFLECT FROM SURFACE to strike a surface, or cause something to strike a surface, and be reflected back ○ *the use of a fixed orbiting satellite to bounce the transmission signal back to Earth* **5.** *vi* MOVE UP AND DOWN ON SPOT to move up and down repeatedly in almost the same location ○ *with her long blonde hair bouncing as she walked* **6.** *vi* WALK ENERGETICALLY to walk energetically or cheerfully ○ *She bounced up to the guests and breezily said hello.* **7.** *vti* REFUSE TO PAY to refuse payment of a check, or be refused by a bank, because there is insufficient money in the account on which it is drawn **8.** *vt* WRITE BAD CHECK to write a check that the bank will not honor **9.** *vt* THROW SOMEBODY OUT to eject somebody from a place or expel somebody from a club or other organization (*slang*) ○ *managed to get themselves bounced out of the restaurant* **10.** *vi* COME BACK to be returned undelivered to a sender (*used in e-mails or text messages*) ○ *My last e-mail to you bounced.* ■ *n* **1.** ACT OF REBOUNDING a springing away from a surface after hitting it ○ *hit the ball before the second bounce* **2.** SPRINGINESS the capacity of a ball or other object to bounce, or of a surface to cause objects hitting it to bounce **3.** BOBBING MOVEMENT a swinging or bobbing movement, or the capacity to swing or bob up and down ○ *a conditioner guaranteed to give your hair added bounce* **4.** ENERGY lively energy **5.** same as **convention bounce** (*informal*) ○ *a post-convention bounce* [13C. Origin ?] ◇ **bounce something off somebody** to mention something, especially an idea or suggestion, to somebody in order to get reactions or opinions ○ *She bounced a couple of theories off the students.*

bounce back *vi* to recover quickly and completely after a bad experience

bounc·er /bównssər/ *n* **1.** a security guard who usually stands at the door of a nightclub or other place of entertainment and is responsible for preventing undesirable people from entering and for ejecting troublemakers **2.** in baseball, a ball that bounces along the ground after being hit

bounc·ing /bównssing/ *adj* describes a healthy and active baby ○ *the proud parents of a beautiful bouncing baby boy*

bounc·ing Bet /-bét/ *n US* a low-growing perennial plant. Flowers: pink, white. Use: formerly, as a soap substitute. Latin name: *Saponaria officinalis.* Can term **soapwort** [Nickname for *Elizabeth*]

bounc·y /bównssee/ (**-i·er, -i·est**) *adj* **1.** LIVELY lively and energetic **2.** BOUNCING WELL tending to bounce or capable of bouncing well ○ *bouncy material used in making tennis balls* **3.** SPRINGY tending to bounce objects hitting it or resting on it —**bounc·i·ly** *adv* —**bounc·i·ness** *n*

bound[1] /bownd/ past participle, past tense of **bind** ■ *adj* **1.** CERTAIN TO DO SOMETHING certain to happen or do something because custom, experience, or common sense dictates it ○ *If you play music late at night, people are bound to complain.* **2.** OBLIGATED obliged to do something or behave in a particular way, e.g., for legal or moral reasons ○ *All the member countries are bound by the provisions of the Treaty of Rome.* **3.** DETERMINED firmly resolved ○ *She was bound to become the best in the business.*

bound[2] /bownd/ (**bound·ed, bound·ing, bounds**) *vi* to move quickly and energetically, with large strides or jumps ○ *A puppy came bounding across the lawn.* [Early 16C. Via French *bondir* "resound, rebound" < Latin *bombire* "to buzz" < *bombus* < Greek *bombos* "booming sound"] —**bound** *n*

bound[3] /bownd/ *adj* **1.** traveling toward a particular place (*often used in combination*) ○ *a Spanish trawler bound for the Irish Sea* ○ *homeward bound* **2.** certain to reach or achieve something ○ *young performers bound for international stardom* [Late 16C. Originally *boun* < Old Norse *búinn*, past participle of *búa* "prepare"; probably influenced by BOUND[1]]

bound[4] /bownd/ *vt* (**bound·ed, bound·ing, bounds**) **1.** SURROUND AREA to form the boundary to an area or site ○ *grounds bounded on three sides by the river* **2.** RESTRICT SOMETHING to impose limits on something ○ *political views not bounded by moral convictions* ■ *n* MATH LIMITING NUMBER a number that represents the upper or lower end of a range of possible values ■ *adj* **1.** LING NOT CONSTITUTING WORD describes a unit of meaning (**morpheme**) that cannot be used on its own as a word **2.** GRAM NOT CONSTITUTING SENTENCE describes a grammatical element such as a clause that can only be used with another element [14C. < Anglo-Norman *bounde*, Old French *bodne* < medieval Latin *butina*; originally "boundary marker"]

bound·a·ry /bówndəree, -dree/ (*plural* **-ries**) *n* **1.** the official line that divides one area of land from another ○ *Multinational companies operate across national boundaries.* **2.** the point at which something ends or beyond which it becomes something else ○ *pushing back the boundaries of human knowledge* [Early 17C. Alteration of *bounder* < BOUND[4]]

bound·a·ry con·di·tion *n* the mathematical set of requirements that must be met in order for the solution to a set of differential equations to be found

bound·a·ry lay·er *n* the region of a viscous fluid such as air or water that is closest to the surface of a solid moving relative to the fluid

bound·ed /bówndəd/ *adj* describes a mathematical set that has an upper and lower limiting number (**bound**)

bound·en /bównd'n/ past participle of **bind** (*archaic*) ■ *adj* relating to that which binds somebody morally ○ *It is your bounden duty to consider the honor of the family.*

bound·er /bówndər/ *n* (*dated informal; insult*) **1.** somebody, especially a man, who behaves in a dishonorable or morally unacceptable way **2.** an ill-bred, social-climbing man [Late 19C. < BOUND[2]]

bound·less /bówndləss/ *adj* seeming to have no end or limit —**bound·less·ly** *adv* —**bound·less·ness** *n*

~~boundry~~ incorrect spelling of **boundary**

bounds /bowndz/ *npl* limits, especially restrictions on what can happen or what can be done ○ *a joke that goes beyond the bounds of good taste* ◇ **know no bounds** to be very great, strong, or intense ○ *an ego that knows no bounds* ◇ **out of bounds 1.** outside the area where somebody is allowed to go ○ *The bar is out of bounds to students.* **2.** beyond what is acceptable ○ *Discussion of the candidate's private life is out of bounds.*

boun·te·ous /bówntee əss/ *adj* (*literary*) **1.** giving generously **2.** given in generous measure [14C. Alteration (after PLENTEOUS) of Old French *bontif* < *bonté* (see BOUNTY)] —**boun·te·ous·ly** *adv* —**boun·te·ous·ness** *n*

boun·ti·ful /bówntəf'l/ *adj* (*literary*) **1.** giving generously, particularly to less fortunate people **2.** in plentiful supply —**boun·ti·ful·ly** *adv* —**boun·ti·ful·ness** *n*

SYNONYMS See ***generous.***

Boun·ti·ful /bówntəf'l/ city in northern Utah, north of Salt Lake City. It was founded by a Mormon pioneer in 1847. Population: 41,270 (2002 estimate).

boun·ty /bówntee/ (*plural* **-ties**) *n* **1.** REWARD a reward of money offered for finding a criminal or other wanted person, or for killing a person or a predator **2.** ABUNDANT SUPPLY a plentiful or generous supply (*literary*) ○*"As a grand mansion, "The Broadway Estate" is home to a bounty of rooms, each with a distinct personality."* (Patti Martinhome, *Living Page*; 1997) **3.** GENEROSITY generosity in giving (*literary*) ○*"a trifling additional claim upon your bounty and good nature"* (Sir Walter Scott, *Waverley*; 1814) [14C. Via French *bonté* < Latin *bonitas* "goodness" < *bonus* "good"]

boun·ty hunt·er *n* **1.** somebody who captures criminals for reward money **2.** somebody who hunts animals for reward money

Boun·ty Is·lands /bówntee-/ group of 13 uninhabited islands in the southwestern Pacific Ocean, 415 mi./668 km east of New Zealand. The islands are part of New Zealand. Area: 0.54 sq. mi./1.4 sq. km.

bou·quet /bō káy, boo-/ *n* **1.** BUNCH OF FLOWERS a bunch of cut flowers that have been specially chosen or arranged **2.** SCENT OF WINE the characteristic pleasant smell of wine **3.** PRAISE an expression of congratulation or praise (*literary*) [Early 18C. < French, "thicket" < Old French *bois* "forest" < Germanic]

SYNONYMS See ***smell.***

bou·quet gar·ni /boo kày gaar neé/ (*plural* **bou·quets gar·nis** /*pronunc. same*/) *n* a bunch of mixed herbs, or an equivalent dried herb mixture in a small bag, that is used to add flavor to stews, soups, and sauces [Mid-19C. < French, "garnished bouquet"]

bou·quet·ier /bo͝okə tyér, -teér/ *n* a small trumpet-shaped container used to hold the flowers in a bouquet

Bou·ras·sa /boo raássə/, **Henri** (1868–1952) Canadian politician and journalist. A member of the Canadian House of Commons (1896–99, 1900–07, 1925–35), he was a leading French Canadian nationalist. He was founding editor of the nationalist daily newspaper *Le Devoir* (1910–32).

> "I am a liberal of the British school. I am a disciple of Burke, Fox, Bright, Gladstone, and of the other Little Englanders who made Great Britain and its possessions what they are."
> [Henri Bourassa, *Speech to the Canadian Parliament*; March 13, 1900]

bour·bon /búrbən/ *n* a type of whiskey distilled mainly in the United States from a fermented mixture of hot water and grain (**mash**) containing at least 51% corn [Mid-19C. After *Bourbon* County, Kentucky]

bour·don /bo͝ord'n/ *n* **1.** the bass pipe on a set of bagpipes, or the bass note it produces **2.** the bass stop on an organ, especially on a 16-foot pipe [Mid-19C. < French, "drone"]

Bour·don gauge *n* a pressure gauge with a flattened curved tube that straightens under pressure, allowing the force to be measured [After Eugène *Bourdon* (1808–84), French hydraulic engineer]

bour·geois /boor zhwaá, bo͝or zhwaá/ *adj* **1.** associated with affluent middle-class people, who are often characterized as conventional, conservative, or materialistic in outlook **2.** according to Marxist theory, relating to the social class that owns the means of producing wealth and is regarded as exploiting the working class [Mid-16C. < French, "citizen of a city or borough" < Latin *burgus* "castle, borough" < Germanic] —**bour·geois** *n*

Bour·geois /boor zhwaá/, **Léon Victor** (1851–1925) French politician. He was one of the founders of the League of Nations, and received the Nobel Peace Prize (1920). Full name **Bourgeois, Léon Victor Auguste**

bour·geoi·sie /bòor zhwaa zeé/ *n* **1.** affluent middle-class people materialistic in outlook **2.** the social class that, according to Marxist theory, owns the means of producing wealth and is regarded as exploiting the working class [Early 18C. < French < *bourgeois* (see BOURGEOIS)]

bour·geoi·si·fy /boor zhwaázə fì/ (**-fied, -fy·ing, -fies**) *vt* to impose bourgeois values on somebody or something, or make somebody or something bourgeois in character —**bour·geoi·si·fi·ca·tion** /boor zhwaázəfi káysh'n/ *n*

Bour·geoys /boor zhwaá/, **Marguerite** (1620–1700) French-born Canadian nun. She founded the Congrégation de Nôtre-Dame de Montréal to teach the poor of Montréal.

Bour·gui·ba /boor geébə/, **Habib** (1903–2000) Tunisian politician. He led Tunisia's independence movement against French rule and was the country's first prime minister (1956–57) and president (1957–87). Full name **Bourguiba, Habib ibn Ali**

bour·gui·gnonne /bòor geen yṓn/ *adj* cooked in a red wine sauce with mushrooms and small whole onions, in a style that originated in the Burgundy region of France [Early 20C. < French < *Bourgogne* "Burgundy"]

Bourke-White /bùrk wít, -hwít/, **Margaret** (1906–71) US photographer and writer. She was a leading photojournalist who was closely identified with *Life*. She was the magazine's staff photographer from 1936 to 1969.

> "Nothing attracts me like a closed door. I cannot let my camera rest until I have pried it open, and I wanted to be first."
> [Margaret Bourke-White, *Portrait of Myself*; 1963]

bourn[1] /bawrn/, **bourne** *n* a small stream that flows only in the winter months [14C. S English variant of BURN[2]]

bourn[2] /bawrn/ *n* (*archaic*) **1.** a boundary between one place or one thing and another ○ *"I'll set a bourn how far to be beloved."* (William Shakespeare, *Antony and Cleopatra*; 1606) **2.** something that is aimed for or aspired to [Early 16C. Via French *borne* < Old French *bodne* (see BOUND[4])]

Bourne·mouth /báwrnməth/ seaside resort on the English Channel in Dorset, southern England. Population: 163,444 (2001).

bourse /boorss/, **Bourse** *n* a European stock exchange, especially the one in Paris [Late 16C. Via French < medieval Latin *bursa* "bag, purse" < Greek *bursa* "leather"]

bou·stro·phe·don /bòostrə feéd'n, -feé dòn/ *n* an ancient method of inscribing and writing in which lines are written alternately from right to left and from left to right [Early 17C. < Greek, "as the ox turns in plowing" < *bous* "ox" + *-strophos* "turning" < *strephein* "to turn"] —**bou·stroph·e·don·ic** /bòo stròffi dónnik/ *adj*

bout /bowt/ *n* **1.** ATTACK OF ILLNESS a temporary or short-lived attack of illness, usually a common and not very serious illness ○ *a recent bout of the flu* **2.** SHORT PERIOD OF ACTIVITY a short time spent doing something, often something considered distasteful ○ *periodic bouts of violence* **3.** FIGHT a boxing or wrestling match [Mid-16C. Origin ?]

bou·tique /boo teék/ *n* **1.** SMALL CLOTHES STORE a small store that sells fashionable clothes **2.** SMALL SPECIALIST STORE a small store selling specialized, often luxury, goods or services of any kind ■ *adj* SERVING LUXURY MARKET catering to a specialized, often luxury, market ○ *a boutique travel service* [Mid-18C. Via French < Greek *apothēkē* "storehouse"]

bou·tique brew·er·y *n* FOOD INDUST same as **microbrewery**

bou·tique ho·tel *n* an upmarket, often stylish hotel with an individual character and decor

bou·tique me·di·cine *n* private medical care offering personalized services in return for a retainer fee

bou·ton /boo táwn/ *n* the knob or swelling on a nerve-cell extension (**axon**) at the point where it forms a junction (**synapse**) with a neuron [Mid-19C. < French (see BUTTON)]

bou·ton·niere /bòot'n eér, -yér/, **bou·ton·nière** *n* a small flower worn in a buttonhole [Late 19C. < French < *bouton* (see BUTTON)]

Bou·tros-Gha·li /bòotrōss gaálee/, **Boutros** (*b.* 1922) Egyptian diplomat. He was the sixth secretary-general of the United Nations (1992–96).

> "I survived the Egyptian bureaucracy. If you can do that you can run the UN."
> [Boutros Boutros-Ghali, *New York Times*; October 16, 1993]

bou·var·di·a /boo vaár dee ə/ *n* a bush with thin straight leaves and tubular flowers in various bright colors. Native to: Mexico and Central America. Genus: *Bouvardia*. [Late 18C. < modern Latin, after Charles *Bouvard* (1572–1658), superintendent of the King's Garden, Paris]

bou·vier /boo vyáy/ *n* a large powerful dog with a rough fawn or black coat, belonging to a breed originally developed in Belgium to herd cattle [Early 20C. < French, shortened < *bouvier des Flandres* "cowherd of Flanders"]

~~**bouy**~~ incorrect spelling of **buoy**

~~**bouyant**~~ incorrect spelling of **buoyant**

bouzouki

bou·zou·ki /bòo zóokee, bə-/ (*plural* **-kis**) *n* a long-necked stringed musical instrument of Greek origin similar in appearance and sound to a mandolin [Mid-20C. < modern Greek *mpouzouki*]

bo·vid /bṓvid/ *adj* relating or belonging to the family of hollow-horned, hoofed, ruminant animals that includes cattle, sheep, and antelopes. Family: Bovidae. [Late 19C. < Latin *bov-* (see BOVINE)] —**bo·vid** *n*

bo·vine /bṓ vìn, -veen/ *adj* **1.** OF CATTLE GENUS relating or belonging to the genus of ruminant animals that includes cattle, oxen, and buffalo. Genus: *Bos.* **2.** SLOW displaying the slowness regarded as typical of cattle and related animals (*literary*) ■ *n* ANIMAL RELATED TO CATTLE an animal belonging to the same genus as cattle [Early 19C. < late Latin *bovinus* < Latin *bov-*, stem of *bos* "ox"]

bo·vine so·ma·to·trop·in, **bo·vine growth hor·mone** *n* a hormone in cattle that regulates growth and milk production. It can also be produced artificially by genetic engineering and used to increase milk yields.

bo·vine spon·gi·form en·ceph·a·lop·a·thy *n* MED, VET full form of **BSE**

bow[1] /bō/ *n* **1.** LOOPED KNOT a knot in which the loops remain visible, e.g., in tied shoelaces or in ribbons used for decorating gifts or hair **2.** WEAPON FOR FIRING ARROWS a weapon used to fire arrows, consisting of a curved flexible piece of wood and a taut string fastened to the two ends **3.** ROD FOR PLAYING STRINGED INSTRUMENTS a wooden rod with horsehair tightly stretched between the two ends, used for playing stringed instruments **4.** CURVED SHAPE OR PART something that has a rounded or semicircular shape, e.g., a part of a building or a loop in a river **5.** FRAME

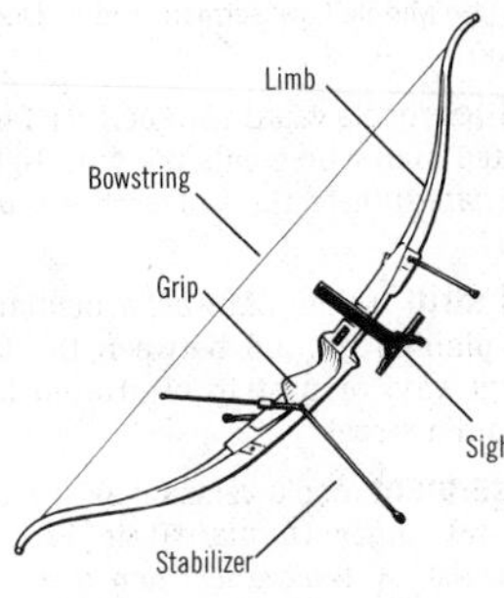

bow (sense 2)

OF GLASSES the frame for a pair of glasses or the part of the frame that curls around the ear **6.** ARCHERY, HIST same as **bowman**[1] (*literary*) **7.** METEOROL same as **rainbow** *n* (sense 1) ■ *v* (**bowed, bow·ing, bows**) **1.** *vti* BEND SOMETHING INTO CURVE to bend, or bend something, into a rounded or bow shape **2.** *vti* USE BOW ON STRINGED INSTRUMENT to draw a bow across the strings of a stringed instrument **3.** *vt* INDICATE BOWING FOR MUSIC to mark a piece of music to indicate which notes are to be played with the bow moving in one direction across the strings and which are to be played with it moving in the opposite direction [Old English *boga* < Germanic, "to bend"]

bow[2] /bow/ *v* (**bowed, bow·ing, bows**) **1.** *vti* BEND HEAD OR BODY FORWARD to bend the head forward, or to bend forward from the waist, as a signal of respect, greeting, consent, submission, or acknowledgment ○ *bowing her head in shame* **2.** *vti* BEND SOMETHING OR DROOP to bend something over so that it droops, or to be bent in this way ○ *branches bowed down with fruit* **3.** *vi* YIELD to accept something and yield to it, often unwillingly ○ *In the end they had to bow to the inevitable and sell their house.* ■ *n* BENDING FORWARD OF UPPER BODY a bending forward of the upper part of the body to show respect, greeting, consent, submission, or acknowledgment [Old English *būgan* < Germanic, "to bend"] ◇ **bow and scrape** to be excessively polite or attentive in an attempt to ingratiate yourself with somebody

bow[3] /bow/ *n* **1.** the front section of a boat or ship **2.** the rower or oar closest to the front of a boat [Early 17C. < Low German *boog* or Middle Dutch *boeg*]

SPELLCHECK See ***bough***.

Bow /bō/, **Clara** (1905–65) US actor. She enjoyed a brief career in the late 1920s as the most popular female movie star in the country, but spent her last three decades in retirement. Known as **the It Girl**

bow·da·cious *adj, adv Midwest, Southern US* another spelling of **bodacious** (*informal humorous*)

Bow·ditch /bówdich/, **Nathaniel** (1773–1838) American mathematician and astronomer. His *New American Practical Navigator* (1802) became the standard sailors' navigation guide.

bowd·ler·ize /bṓdlə rìz, bówd-/ (**-ized, -iz·ing, -iz·es**) *vti* to remove parts of a work of literature that are considered indecent [Mid-19C. < Thomas Bowdler (1754–1825), who published an edition of Shakespeare omitting scenes that he considered unsuitable] —**bowd·ler·ism** *n* —**bowd·ler·i·za·tion** /bōdləri záysh'n, bòwd-/ *n* —**bowd·ler·iz·er** *n*

bow·el /bów əl, bowl/ *n* **1.** ANAT same as **intestine** (*often used in the plural*) **2.** a section or part of the intestine, especially the part of the intestine that connects to the anus ■ **bow·els** *npl* the deepest or innermost part of something ○ *the bowels of the ship* [13C. Via Anglo-Norman *buel*, Old French *boël* < Latin *botellus* "small sausage" < *botulus* "sausage"]

Bow·ell /bṓ əl/, **Sir Mackenzie** (1823–1917) British-born Canadian politician. He was prime minister of Canada (1894–96).

bow·el move·ment *n* **1.** the passing of feces out of the body through the anus **2.** feces passed through the anus

Bow·en ther·a·py /bṓ ən-/ *n* a therapeutic technique that initiates healing and encourages emotional stability using manipulation of muscles and connective tissues [Mid-20C. After Tom *Bowen* (1916–82), its Australian originator]

bow·er[1] /bów ər/ *n* **1. SHADY SHELTER** a shady leafy shelter or recess in a garden or woods **2. WOMAN'S BEDROOM OR APARTMENTS** a woman's bedroom or private apartments, especially in a medieval castle **3. PICTURESQUE COTTAGE** a picturesque country cottage, especially one that is used as a retreat (*literary*) [Old English *būr* "dwelling" < Indo-European, "be, live"] —**bow·er·y** *adj*

bow·er[2] /bów ər/ *n* the anchor positioned at the bow of a boat [15C. < BOW[3]]

bowerbird

bow·er·bird /bów ər bùrd/ *n* a bird that is noted for the elaborate structures that the male builds for courtship. Native to: New Guinea, Australia. Family: Ptilonorynchidae.

Bow·er·y /bów ə ree, bówree/ *n* a street and area in lower Manhattan, New York City, that was a famous theatrical district in the 19th century

bow·fin /bṓ fìn/ (*plural* **-fins** or *same*) *n* a freshwater fish with a mottled greenish brown body and a long dorsal fin. Native to: eastern North America. Latin name: *Amia calva*.

bow·front /bṓ frùnt/ *adj* **1.** describes a piece of furniture with a front that curves outward ○ *a bowfront desk* **2.** designed or constructed with a bow window at the front

bow·head /bṓ hèd/ (*plural* **-heads** or *same*) *n* a baleen whale that lives in the Arctic seas and has an arched upper jaw. Latin name: *Balaena mysticetus*.

Bow·ie /bóo ee/ city in west central Maryland, west of Annapolis and northeast of Washington, D.C. Population: 52,123 (2002 estimate).

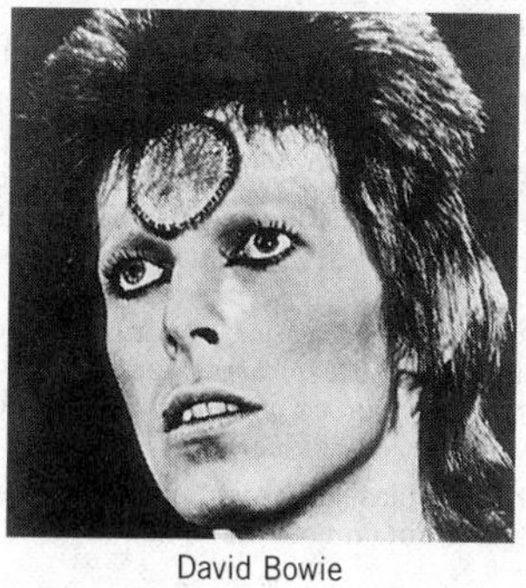

David Bowie

Bow·ie /bṓ ee, bów ee/, **David** (*b.* 1947) British pop singer and actor. He pioneered glam rock in the 1970s. His albums include *The Rise and Fall of Ziggy Stardust* and *The Spiders from Mars* (1972). Born **Jones, David Robert**

> "The 1970s for me was the beginning of the 21st century – it was the beginning of a true pluralism of social attitudes."
> [Attributed to David Bowie]

Bow·ie /bóo ee, bṓ ee/, **Jim** (1796?–1836) US pioneer. A colonel in the Texas army, he died at the Battle of the Alamo. Full name **Bowie, James**

bowie knife

bow·ie knife /bṓ ee-, bóo ee-/ *n* a single-edged hunting knife, about 15 in./38 cm long and curved near the point, with a short hilt and a guard for the hand [Mid-19C. After Jim BOWIE, who popularized it]

bow·knot /bṓ nòt/ *n* a decorative knot in the form of a bow

bowl[1] /bōl/ *n* **1. ROUND CONTAINER** an open container, usually round in shape and wider than it is deep, typically used for holding food and liquids **2. AMOUNT IN BOWL** the contents of a bowl, or the amount a bowl can hold **3. PART LIKE BOWL** a bowl-shaped part of something ○ *a toilet bowl* **4. DEPRESSION IN GROUND** a round depression in the surface of the land **5.** *also* **Bowl STADIUM** a bowl-shaped stadium or amphitheater **6. FOOTBALL GAME** a postseason game played between champion or high-ranking football teams. The Super Bowl™ is the professional championship game, and the Rose Bowl™ is the oldest college postseason game. **7. MILDLY ALCOHOLIC DRINK** a mildly alcoholic beverage, or the type of cup used for drinking it (*literary*) [Old English *bolla* < Indo-European, "swell, be round"] —**bowl·ful** *n*

SPELLCHECK See ***bole***[1].

bowl[2] /bōl/ *v* (**bowled, bowl·ing, bowls**) **1.** *vti* **ROLL BALL** in bowling or lawn bowling, to throw or roll a ball **2.** *vi* **GO BOWLING** to take part in a game of bowling **3.** *vti* **SEND BALL TO PERSON BATTING** in cricket, to send a ball, usually overarm, to a batsman or batswoman **4.** *vt* **SCORE POINTS IN BOWLING** in bowling, to score a given number of points ○ *He bowled 250 last night.* **5.** *vti* **MOVE QUICKLY** to move or roll smoothly and quickly, or make something do this ○ *He bowled down the highway on his motorcycle.* ■ *n* **1. WOODEN BALL USED IN LAWN BOWLING** a wooden ball used in the game of lawn bowling, which has slightly flattened sides in order to make it roll in a curve **2. ROLL OF BALL** in bowling or lawn bowling, one roll of the ball **3. REVOLVING DRUM** a rotating cylinder or drum in a machine [15C. Via French *boule* < Latin *bulla* "bubble"]
bowl over *vt* **1.** to amaze or delight somebody (*often used in the passive*) ○ *I was completely bowled over by their generous offer.* **2.** to knock something or somebody down, especially accidentally during a headlong rush ○ *The dog bowled three chairs over in its excitement.*

bow·leg·ged /bṑ léggəd, -légd/ *adj* having legs that curve outward around or below the knee area [Mid-16C. < BOW[1]]

bow·legs /bṓ lègz/ *n* a condition in which the legs curve outward around or below the knee area (*takes a singular verb*) —**bow·leg** *n*

bowl·er /bṓlər/ *n* **1.** somebody who takes part in a game of bowling or lawn bowling **2.** in cricket, the player who bowls the ball **3.** CLOTHING same as **derby**

bowl·er hat, bowl·er *n UK* same as **derby** (sense 3) [Mid-19C. After William *Bowler*, 19C British hatter]

Bowles /bōlz/, **Paul** (1910–99) US writer and composer. He lived in Tangier, Morocco, after 1952. He composed music for movies and opera and wrote novels such as *The Sheltering Sky* about US expatriates (1949). Full name **Bowles, Paul Frederick**

bow·line /bṓ lin, -līn/ *n* **1. KNOT FORMING TIGHT LOOP** a knot used to form a loop that will not slip at the end of a piece of rope **2. LINE FOR CONTROLLING SAIL** a line for controlling one of the vertical edges of a square sail **3. KNOT IN END OF CLIMBING ROPE** a fixed knot in the end of a climbing rope [14C. < Middle Low German *bōlīne* or Middle Dutch *boechline* "line from the ship's bow"]

bowl·ing /bṓling/ *n* **1.** a game played by rolling a ball so that it knocks down pins **2.** BOWLING same as **lawn bowling 3.** in cricket, the throwing of the ball, usually overarm, to somebody who is batting

bowl·ing al·ley *n* **1.** a building where people go to bowl **2.** the long narrow smooth expanse of floor down which a ball is rolled in bowling

bowl·ing ball *n* the heavy ball used in the game of bowling, with holes in it for the bowler's thumb and two fingers

bowl·ing green *n* a piece of natural grass outdoors or a piece of artificial grass indoors for playing lawn bowling

Bowl·ing Green /bṓling-/ **1.** city in south central Kentucky, on the western bank of the Barren River, southwest of Louisville. Population: 50,226 (2002 estimate). **2.** city in northwestern Ohio, south of Toledo. Bowling Green State University was founded there in 1910. Population: 29,482 (2002 estimate).

bowls /bōlz/ *n UK* same as **lawn bowling** (*takes a singular verb*)

bow·man[1] /bṓmən/ (*plural* **-men** /-mən/) *n* somebody who uses a bow and arrows, or a crossbow —**bow·man·ship** *n*

bow·man[2] /bówmən/ (*plural* **-men** /-mən/) *n* **1.** a man or boy who rows at the bow of a boat **2.** a bowperson on a sailboat, especially a man

Bow·man's cap·sule /bṓmənz-/ *n* a cup-shaped part of the kidney that extracts waste and water from the blood and produces urine [Late 19C. After Sir William *Bowman* (1816–92), British surgeon]

bow·per·son /bów pùrss'n/ (*plural* **-per·sons** or **-peo·ple** /-peèp'l/) *n* **1.** a crew member on a sailboat who is responsible for the deck and sail work at the bow **2.** somebody who rows at the bow of a boat

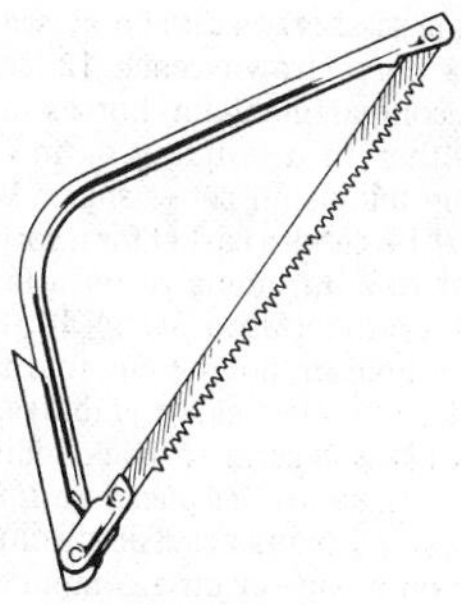

bow saw

bow saw /bṓ-/ *n* a saw with a thin blade held in a bow-shaped frame with a narrow handle, used for cutting curves

Bow·ser /bówzər/ *tdmk* a trademark for a mobile tanker with a pumping apparatus, used to transport fuel for aircraft or military vehicles, or water

bow shock /bów shòk/ *n* a violent wave, about 21 billion miles from the Sun, where the interstellar medium is pushed outward by the heliopause [After the crescent-shaped wave made by a ship as it moves through water]

bow·shot /bṓ shòt/ *n* the distance that an arrow travels when it has been shot from a bow

bow·sprit /bów sprìt, bṓ-/ *n* a beam that projects forward from the bow of a boat, to which the stays of the foremast are fastened [14C. < Low German *bōgsprēt* or Middle Dutch *boechspriet* "pole at a ship's bow"]

bow·string /bṓ strìng/ *n* the taut string on an archer's bow, usually made of strands of hemp

bow·string hemp *n* **1.** fiber from the leaves of a tropical perennial plant. Use: bowstrings, mats, nets. **2.** a tropical plant with thick leaves grouped in rosettes, from which bowstring hemp is obtained. Native to: Africa, Asia. Genus: *Sansevieria*.

bow tie /bṓ- / *n* a short tie, knotted in a bow at the neck

bow weight /bṓ-/ *n* the amount of force needed to pull a bowstring back to its fullest extent

bow win·dow /bṓ-/ *n* a bay window that is curved

bow-wow /bów wòw/ *interj* IMITATION OF BARKING used to imitate the bark of a dog ■ *n* NOISY PUBLIC OUTCRY a public clamor about something or somebody (*slang*) ○ *All the bow-wow over the trial eventually died down.* ■ *vi* (**bow-wowed, bow-wow·ing, bow-wows**) BARK OR IMITATE BARKING to bark, or imitate the sound of barking [Late 16C. An imitation of the sound]

bow·yer /bṓ yər/ *n* somebody who makes bows for archery [13C. < BOW[1] + -IER]

box[1] /boks/ *n* **1.** CONTAINER a container for objects or dry goods, often with a removable or hinged lid, and usually square or rectangular **2.** CAPACITY OF BOX the amount of something a box holds or could hold **3.** RECTANGULAR SHAPE a square or rectangular shape printed on paper, or on a computer screen, usually containing information or requiring information to be entered in it ○ *Check the boxes if the following items apply to you.* **4.** AREA OR STRUCTURE WITH BEST SEATS an enclosed area in a public building or at a sports venue, especially a theater, stadium, or racetrack, that contains the best and most luxurious seats **5.** ENCLOSED AREA IN COURTROOM the enclosed area in a courtroom that is reserved for particular participants in a court case ○ *jury box* **6.** SMALL BUILDING PROVIDING SHELTER a small building that is used as a shelter, especially by military personnel ○ *a sentry box* **7.** EQUIPMENT CONTAINER a container, usually affixed to a wall or on a stand, that houses equipment such as a fire extinguisher, emergency telephone, or first-aid materials **8.** POST OFFICE BOX a post office box or similar private mailbox, used as a mailing address either because it is convenient or in order to protect the privacy of the addressee **9.** BATTER'S BOX in baseball, the rectangular area marked by lines near home plate, in which the batter stands **10.** SPORTS PART OF PLAYING AREA in sports such as baseball and soccer, a marked-off part of the playing area used for a special purpose, or subject to special rules **11.** DRIVER'S SEAT IN HORSE-DRAWN COACH a raised seat for the driver in a horse-drawn coach **12.** COMPARTMENT FOR LIVESTOCK a compartment for horses or other farm animals, either in a building or in a vehicle **13.** TELEVISION the television set (*slang*) ○ *What's on the box tonight?* **14.** COFFIN a casket for a corpse (*informal*) **15.** OFFENSIVE TERM an offensive term for a woman's vulva and vagina (*taboo slang*) **16.** HOLE IN TREE TO COLLECT SAP a hole or hollow cut into the base of a tree in order to collect sap ■ *vt* (**boxed, box·ing, box·es**) **1.** PACK THINGS IN BOXES to pack individual items into boxes ○ *There are 300 pieces waiting to be boxed before shipping.* **2.** OUTLINE SOMETHING WITH BOX to enclose something on a page or on a computer screen in a box ○ *Box the title to make it stand out more.* **3.** CUT HOLE IN TREE FOR SAP to cut a box in the base of a tree to collect the sap [Pre-12C. Via late Latin *buxis* < Greek *puxis* "wooden container" < *puxos* "boxwood, box tree"] —**box·ful** *n*

box in *vt* to surround somebody or something by or with something else, so that it is impossible to move ○ *My car is completely boxed in by those trucks.*

box[2] /boks/ (**boxed, box·ing, box·es**) *vti* to fight using the techniques of boxing, or fight somebody in a boxing match ○ *He boxed in exhibition bouts to entertain the crowds.* [14C. Origin ?]

box on *vi* **1.** to continue with a boxing match. It is usually a command, given by the referee after a fight has been stopped for a count or other interruption. **2.** to continue or persevere with something

box[3] /boks/ (*plural same* or **box·es**) *n* **1.** a dense evergreen tree or bush with shiny dark green oval leaves. Use: hedges. Genus: *Buxus.* **2.** INDUST same as **boxwood** (sense 2) [Pre-12C. Via Latin *buxus* < Greek *puxos*]

box[4] /boks/ *vti* SAILING same as **boxhaul** [Mid-18C. Origin ?]

box beam *n* CONSTR same as **box girder**

box bed *n* an old-fashioned bed, enclosed on three sides and the top by a wooden structure resembling a box

box·board /bóks bàwrd/ *n* a tough cardboard made from wood and wastepaper pulp, used for making boxes

box calf *n* black calfskin leather that has been tanned with chromium salts [Early 20C. After Joseph *Box*, 19C maker of boots in London]

box cam·er·a *n* a camera shaped like a box, with a simple lens that has a fixed focus and a single shutter speed

box can·yon *n* a canyon with steep walls that can be entered readily only from the downstream direction. Box canyons were formerly often used to pen stock such as cattle and horses.

box·car /bóks kaàr/ *n* a fully enclosed railroad car, usually with sliding doors, that is used to transport freight

box coat *n* a coat that hangs loosely from the shoulders

boxed set *n* COMM same as **box set** (sense 2)

box el·der *n* a fast-growing maple tree. Native to: North America. Latin name: *Acer negundo.* [< BOX[3]]

box end wrench *n* a wrench with an angled head to allow access to nuts and bolts located in positions not easily reached

box·er[1] /bóksər/ *n* a fighter in boxing matches [Late 17C. < BOX[2]]

box·er[2] /bóksər/ *n* a person or machine whose task it is to pack things into boxes

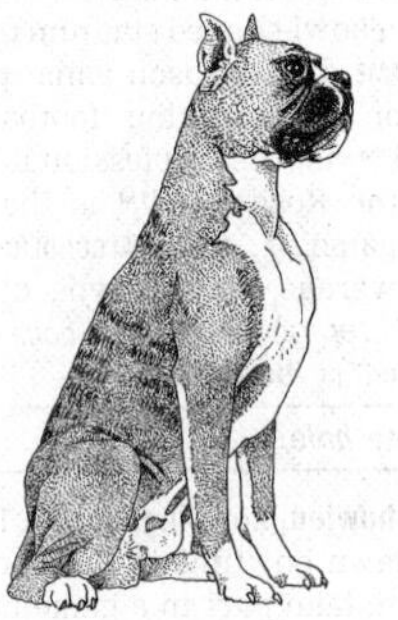

boxer

box·er[3] /bóksər/ *n* a medium-sized dog that has a flat face with a black mask and a short brownish tan coat, belonging to a breed developed in Germany [Early 20C. Via German < English *boxer*; because of its wide flattened nose]

Box·er *n* a member of a secret society in China that launched the Boxer Rebellion [Early 20C. Translation of Chinese *yì hé quán* "righteous harmonious fists"]

Box·er Re·bel·lion *n* an unsuccessful rebellion in China in 1900, the objective of which was to drive out all foreigners, remove all foreign influence, and compel Chinese Christians to give up their religion

box·er shorts, box·ers /bóksərz/ *npl* underpants with a gathered waistband and loose-fitting short legs [Because they resemble trunks worn by boxers]

box·fish /bóks fish/ (*plural same* or **-fish·es**) *n* FISH same as **trunkfish**

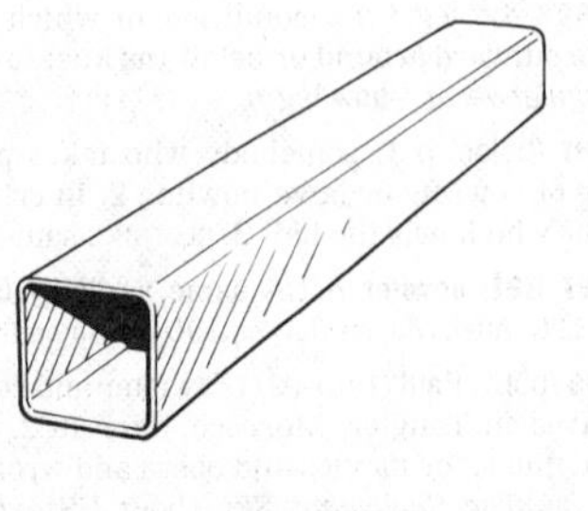

box girder

box gird·er *n* a hollow girder or beam that is square or rectangular in section

box·haul /bóks hàwl/ (**-hauled, -haul·ing, -hauls**) *vti* to turn a square-rigged sailing ship onto a new tack by causing the wind to fill the back side of the foresails and steering hard around [Mid-18C. < BOX[4]]

box·ing /bóksing/ *n* the sport of fighting with the fists, with the objective of knocking out the opposing boxer, or inflicting enough punishment to cause the other boxer to quit or be judged defeated

Box·ing Day *n* a public holiday in England, Wales, and some Commonwealth countries. Date: December 26. [Because traditionally the day on which Christmas gifts, "boxes," were given to service workers]

box·ing glove *n* a thick padded glove tied at the wrist, worn by boxers for fighting

box·ing ring *n* a square raised platform with roped-in sides, used as the fighting arena in boxing matches. Each fighter has a designated corner diagonally opposite the other.

box jel·ly·fish (*plural same* or **box jel·ly·fish·es**) *n* a highly poisonous jellyfish that has a box-shaped body with venomous tentacles. Native to: tropical Australia. Latin name: *Chironex fleckeri.*

box junc·tion *n UK* an intersection with yellow crossed lines painted on the road surface, marking an area that traffic is not permitted to block

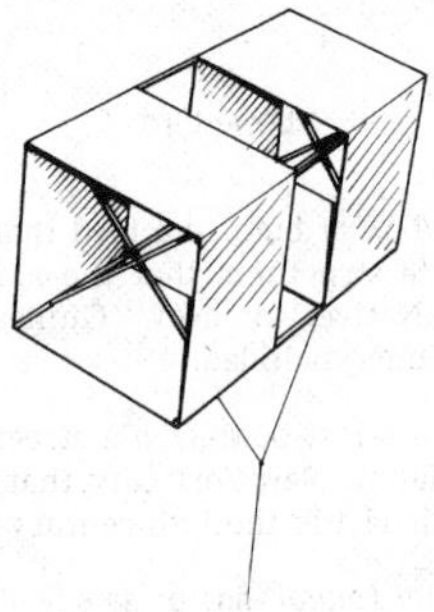

box kite

box kite *n* a kite without a tail, consisting of two open-ended boxes joined by thin sticks

box la·crosse *n Can* a form of lacrosse played inside a closed arena by two teams of six players each

box lunch *n* **1.** a lunch for one person, packed in a small box **2.** FOOD same as **obento**

box lyre *n* a plucked stringed instrument, formed from a hollow wooden box with strings running across the soundboard, which are attached to arms jutting out to form a crossbar. Box lyres were known in ancient Sumer in 2800 B.C. and were widely played in Europe until A.D. 1000.

box num·ber *n* the number assigned to an anonymous address for mail, either at a post office or as a reference for a reply to a newspaper advertisement

box of·fice *n* **1.** PLACE WHERE TICKETS ARE BOUGHT the place where tickets are bought for entertainments such as movies, plays, or concerts **2.** MONEY FROM TICKET SALES ticket sales for a theatrical or cinematic entertainment, or the income from these sales (*informal; often used before a noun*) ○ *box office receipts* **3.** AUDIENCE POPULARITY drawing power to attract an audience to a theater (*informal*) ○ *The show makes great box office.* [Originally where a box in the theater could be reserved]

box pleat *n* a pleat in which fabric is folded under and back again on both sides, and pressed flat

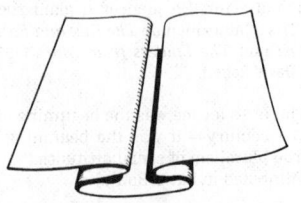

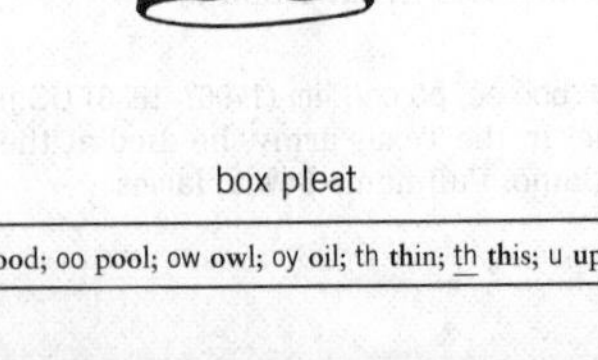

box pleat

box score *n* a printed summary of a game, especially a baseball game, in table form, listing the players and their positions and performance in the game

box seat *n* **1.** a seat in a box in a theater or a sports stadium **2.** TRANSP same as **box**[1] *n* (sense 11)

box set *n* **1.** a stage set with a ceiling and three walls **2.** *also* **boxed set** /bòkst-/ a set of similar items that are packaged together in a box and sold as a single unit, e.g., a set of music recordings ○ *a four-CD box set*

box so·cial *n* an event in which donated box lunches are auctioned off to raise money

box span·ner *n UK* same as **box wrench**

box spring *n* a base for a mattress consisting of a set of coiled springs in a frame, covered with fabric

box stall *n* a large enclosed stall within a building in which a large untethered farm animal such as a bull or stallion may move around freely

box step *n* the basic step in ballroom dancing, in which the feet are moved in a square-shaped pattern

box·thorn /bóks thàwrn/ (*plural* **-thorns** or *same*) *n* TREES same as **matrimony vine** [< BOX[3]]

box tur·tle, **box tor·toise** *n* a land turtle with a hinged shell on the underside of its body that can close up over its head and forelimbs for protection. Native to: North America. Genus: *Terrapene*.

box·wood /bóks wòod/ (*plural same* or **-woods**) *n* **1.** TREES same as **box**[3] (sense 1) **2.** the hard close-grained yellow wood of the evergreen box tree or bush

box wrench *n* a wrench whose ends are closed, rather than open, so that the end completely surrounds the nut or bolt head

box·y /bóksee/ (**-i·er**, **-i·est**) *adj* shaped like a cube or rectangular box, or giving the impression of squareness —**box·i·ness** *n*

boy /boy/ *n* **1.** YOUNG MALE a young male person ○ *I've had this hobby since I was a boy.* **2.** SON somebody's male child ○ *I'm very proud of that boy of mine.* **3.** YOUNG MAN WITH PARTICULAR JOB a male child or teenager described in terms of his job ○ *a delivery boy* **4.** MALE FROM PARTICULAR AREA a youth or man who comes from or was raised in a particular area or has a particular background ○ *He's a local boy.* **5.** WAY OF ADDRESSING MALE ANIMAL a way of addressing a male animal, especially a dog or a horse ○ *Get down, boy!* ■ **boys** *npl* GROUP OF MALE FRIENDS a group of men of any age who often socialize ○ *a night out with the boys* ■ *interj* EXCLAMATION OF SURPRISE used to express surprise, pleasure, or disgust ○ *Oh boy! Would you just take a look at that!* [13C. Origin ?] —**boy·hood** *n*

bo·yar /bō yaár, bóy ər/ *n* between the 12th and early 18th centuries, a member of a class of the higher Russian nobility ranking below a prince. The boyars headed the civil and military administration of the country. [Late 16C. < Russian *boyarin* "grandee"]

boy band *n* a pop group made up of personable young men who sing and dance to synthesized music but do not play instruments

boy·cott /bóy kòt/ (**-cott·ed**, **-cott·ing**, **-cotts**) *vt* to cease or refuse to deal with something such as an organization, a company, or a process, as a protest against it or as an effort to force it to become more acceptable ○ *Some called for the elections to be boycotted, insisting they were rigged.* [Late 19C. After Captain Charles *Boycott* (1832–97), estate manager in Ireland] —**boy·cott** *n* —**boy·cott·er** *n*

Boy·er /bo yáy/, **Charles** (1897–1978) French actor. He appeared in many romantic roles, including *Mayerling* (1936), and received a special Academy Award in 1943 for his work in promoting Franco-American cultural relations.

Boy·er /bóy ər/, **Herbert W.** (*b.* 1936) US biochemist. He codeveloped the recombinant DNA techniques that became the basis of genetic engineering.

Boy·er /bo yáy/, **Jean Pierre** (1776–1850) Haitian politician. He played a major role in gaining independence for Haiti, and served as president of the republic (1818–43).

boy·friend /bóy frènd/ *n* a man with whom somebody has a romantic or sexual relationship

boy·ish /bóy ish/ *adj* resembling a very young man's fresh looks or youthful behavior in a way that is pleasing or attractive —**boy·ish·ly** *adv* —**boy·ish·ness** *n*

Boyle /boyl/, **Robert** (1627–91) Irish-born English scientist. He is considered one of the founders of modern scientific method and of the science of chemistry.

Boyle's law *n* the principle that the volume of a confined gas at constant temperature varies inversely with its pressure [After Robert BOYLE]

boy-meets-girl *adj* based on a developing romance between a young man and a young woman, and treated in a predictable or hackneyed way in film or print ○ *It's a typical boy-meets-girl story where they live happily ever after.*

Boyne /boyn/ river that rises in the Bog of Allen, County Kildare, Republic of Ireland, and empties into the Irish Sea near Drogheda. The Battle of the Boyne was fought on the banks of the river near Drogheda in 1690, when forces led by William III of England defeated the army of James II.

boy next door *n* a type of man or boy who is unaffected, approachable, and perceived as similar to yourself ○ *an actor who has achieved international stardom without losing his image as the boy next door*

Boyn·ton Beach /bòyntən-/ city and vacation spot in southeastern Florida, north of Fort Lauderdale. Population: 63,683 (2002 estimate).

boy·o /bóy ō/ *n* used as a form of address for a boy or man, chiefly among Irish-Americans (*slang; sometimes disapproving*) ○ *Relax, boyo. This job is going to be a snap.*

boy scout *n* a man who is considered to be naive or overzealous (*insult*)

Boy Scout *n* **1.** a member of the Boy Scouts of America, an organization whose objectives are to develop character, physical fitness, and citizenship, often through community and outdoor activities **2.** another spelling of **boy scout**

boy·sen·ber·ry /bóyz'n bèrree/ (*plural* **-ries**) *n* **1.** a large purplish black fruit with a taste similar to a loganberry **2.** a plant that produces boysenberries, a hybrid of the loganberry, blackberry, and raspberry. Genus: *Rubus*. [Mid-20C. After Rudolph *Boysen* (1895–1950), US botanist]

boy toy *n* **1.** FLIRTATIOUS YOUNG WOMAN a young woman who appears deliberately to try to attract and please men (*informal insult; sometimes considered offensive*) **2.** OFFENSIVE TERM an offensive term for a young man who is the lover of an older person **3.** GADGET APPEALING TO MEN an expensive and high-tech device or other piece of equipment regarded as appealing especially to men [Late 20C. Reversal of TOY BOY]

boy won·der *n* a talented and bright young man

Boze·man /bṓzmən/ city in southwestern Montana, on the edge of Gallatin National Forest. It is home to Montana State University. Population: 29,459 (2002 estimate).

bo·zo /bṓzō/ *n* an offensive term for somebody who says or does something unwise (*informal insult*) [Early 20C. Origin ?]

BP, **B.P.** *abbr* MED blood pressure

bp. *abbr* **1.** baptized **2.** CHEM, GENETICS base pair **3.** *also* **B/P** FIN bills payable **4.** birthplace **5.** CHESS bishop

B.Pharm. /bee faárm/ *abbr* Bachelor of Pharmacy

B.Phil. *abbr* EDUC Bachelor of Philosophy

bpi *abbr* COMPUT, MEASURE **1.** bits per inch **2.** bytes per inch

B.P.O.E., **BPOE** *abbr* Benevolent and Protective Order of Elks

bps *n* a measurement of data transfer speed, e.g., in modems and serial ports. Full form **bits per second**

Bq *symbol* MEASURE, PHYS becquerel

b quark *n* PHYS same as **bottom quark**

br *abbr* Brazil (*used in Internet addresses*) See table at **domain name**

Br *symbol* CHEM bromine

BR *abbr* **1.** bathroom **2.** bedroom **3.** *also* **B/R** FIN bills receivable (*used in e-mails or text messages*)

br. *abbr* **1.** branch **2.** METALL brass **3.** brief **4.** METALL bronze **5.** brother **6.** brown

Br. *abbr* **1.** Britain **2.** British **3.** Brother

bra /braa/ *n* an undergarment designed to support and shape a woman's breasts [Mid-20C. Shortening of BRASSIERE]

Bra·bant /brə bánt/ former duchy from 1190 to 1830 in Western Europe, now divided between the Netherlands and Belgium

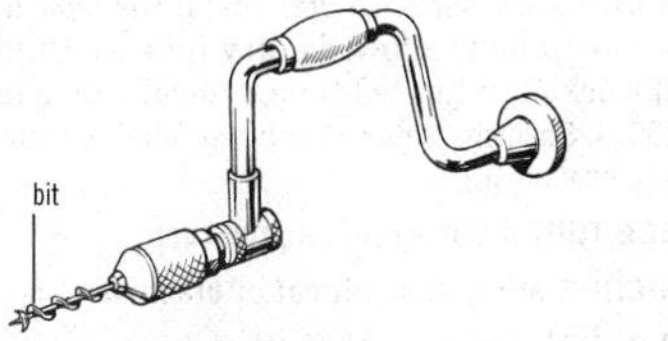

brace (sense 6)

brace[1] /brayss/ *n* **1.** CLAMP a device that keeps something steady or holds two things together **2.** CONSTR SUPPORT FOR SOMETHING CONSTRUCTED a device used to hold a structure or part steady or upright, e.g., a beam or wooden framework **3.** MED SUPPORT FOR PART OF BODY an orthopedic appliance that holds or supports part of the body **4.** DENT APPLIANCE AFFIXED TO TEETH a dental appliance that is wired or otherwise affixed to the teeth and can be tightened in order to straighten them (*usually used in the plural*) **5.** (*plural same*) PAIR a pair of similar things such as wild birds or animals, hunting dogs, or pistols ○ *two brace of pheasants* **6.** WOODWORK TOOL FOR HOLDING DRILL BIT a tool with an adjustable socket at one end for holding a drill bit, and a handle like a crank at the other for turning the bit **7.** PRINTING, MATH EITHER OF SYMBOLS { } either of a pair of symbols, { }, used singly in printing or writing to group items together in a table or list or as a pair in mathematical formulae **8.** MATH SYMBOL OF MATHEMATICAL GROUPING either of a pair of symbols, { }, for additional grouping of mathematical quantities after parentheses and square brackets have been used **9.** MUSIC BRACKET CONNECTING LINES OF MUSIC in music notation, a thick line or bracket connecting a group of staves such as all the choral parts or the accompaniment **10.** MUSIC ADJUSTER FOR DRUM TENSION a sliding loop on the cords of a drum, used to change its tension **11.** MIL STIFF MILITARY POSTURE a very erect stiff posture with the chest thrust out, hands at the sides, feet together, and chin tucked in, taught to military recruits and cadets **12.** ARCHERY, FENCING same as **bracer**[2] ■ **brac·es** *npl Can, UK* SUSPENDERS a pair of suspenders ■ *v* (**braced**, **brac·ing**, **brac·es**) **1.** *vti* PREPARE FOR SOMETHING BAD to prepare for something difficult, dangerous, or unpleasant that is about to happen ○ *Coastal residents are bracing for the hurricane.* ○ *brace yourself* ○ *The financial markets braced themselves for a rise in interest rates.* **2.** *vti* ASSUME POSITION PROVIDING SUPPORT FOR BODY to put your body or a part of it into a position intended to provide support or to reduce the effects of an impact or blow ○ *braced her back against the wall* **3.** *vt* SUPPORT OR STRENGTHEN SOMETHING WITH CLAMP to support or strengthen something, especially part of a building, with a clamping device [14C. Via Old French, "two outstretched arms" < Latin *bracchia*, plural of *brachium* "arm" (see BRACHIUM)]

brace up *vi* to be strong and resolute in facing difficulty ○ *Brace up and face the facts.*

brace[2] /brayss/ *n* on a square-rigged sailing ship, a rope used to control the spar that extends a sail [Early 17C. Perhaps alteration of French *bras de vergue* "yard arm," after BRACE[1]]

brace and bit *n* a hand tool for boring holes, consisting of a crank handle at one end and a drill bit at the other

brace·let /bráysslit/ *n* a piece of jewelry that is worn around the wrist or arm, e.g., a chain or bangle ■ **brace·lets** *npl* a pair of handcuffs (*slang*) [15C. < French < Latin *bracchiale* "armlet" < *brachium* "arm" (see BRACHIUM)]

brace po·si·tion *n* a protective position that somebody adopts before impact in a crash, protecting the head with the arms and bringing the legs up underneath the chest

brac·er[1] /bráyssər/ *n* **1.** somebody or something that braces **2.** an invigorating, often alcoholic drink (*informal*) [Mid-16C. < BRACE[1]]

bra·cer[2] /bráyssər/, **brace** *n* a leather guard worn by fencers and archers to protect the arm [14C. < Old French *bracière* < *bras* "arm" < Latin *brachium* (see BRACHIUM)]

bra·ce·ro /brə sérrō/ (*plural* **-ros**) *n Hispanic* a Mexican worker who is allowed entry into the United States to work for a limited time, typically on a farm [Early 20C. < Spanish, "laborer" < *brazo* "arm" < Latin *brachium* (see BRACHIUM)]

brace root *n* BOT same as **prop root**

bra·chi·a ANAT, ZOOL plural of **brachium**

bra·chi·al /bráykee əl, brákee-/ *adj* relating to or resembling an arm, foreleg, or wing [Late 16C. < Latin *brachialis* < *brachium* (see BRACHIUM)]

bra·chi·ate /bráykee it, -àyt, brákee-/ *adj* having arms or appendages like arms ■ *vi* (**-at·ed, -at·ing, -ates**) to move along by swinging from one hold to the next with the arms (*refers to tree-dwelling animals*) [Mid-18C. < Latin *brachiatus* < *brachium* (see BRACHIUM)] —**bra·chi·a·tion** /bràykee áysh'n, bràkee-/ *n* —**bra·chi·a·tor** *n*

brachio- *prefix* arm ○ *brachiocephalic* [< Latin *brachium* (see BRACHIUM)]

bra·chi·o·ce·phal·ic /bràykee ō sə fállik, bràkee-/ *adj* relating to or supplying blood to the arms and the head

bra·chi·o·ce·phal·ic ar·ter·y *n* ANAT same as **innominate artery**

bra·chi·o·pod /bráykee ə pòd, brákee-/ *n* an invertebrate ocean animal with a hinged shell enclosing tentacles. Phylum: Brachiopoda. [Mid-19C. < modern Latin *Brachiopoda* < Latin *brachium* (see BRACHIUM) + Greek *-pod* (see -POD)] —**bra·chi·o·pod** *adj*

bra·chi·o·sau·rus /bràykee ə sáwrəss, bràkee-/ (*plural* **-rus·es** or **-ri** /-rī/), **bra·chi·o·saur** /bráykee ə sàwr, brákee ə-/ *n* a dinosaur with a massive sloping body up to 100 ft./30 m long. Genus: *Brachiosaurus.* [Early 20C. < modern Latin < Latin *brachium* (see BRACHIUM) (from the unusual length of the animal's humerus bones) + Greek *sauros* "lizard"]

bra·chi·um /bráykee əm/ (*plural* **-chi·a** /-kee ə/) *n* **1.** an arm, especially the upper arm (*technical*) **2.** a structure that corresponds to an arm, e.g., a wing [Mid-18C. Via Latin < Greek *brakhiōn* "upper arm," literally "shorter" < *brakhus* (see BRACHY-)]

brachy- *prefix* short ○ *brachypterous* [< Greek *brakhus* < Indo-European, "short"]

brach·y·ce·phal·ic /bràkee sə fállik/, **brach·y·ceph·a·lous** /-séffələss/ *adj* with a short, broad, and almost spherical head —**brach·y·ceph·a·lism** /bràkee séffə lìzzəm/ *n* —**brach·y·ceph·a·ly** /-séffəlee/ *n*

brach·y·dac·tyl·ic /bràkee dak tíllik/, **brach·y·dac·ty·lous** /-dáktələss/ *adj* with unusually short fingers or toes —**brach·y·dac·tyl·i·a** /-dak tíllee ə/ *n* —**brach·y·dac·ty·ly** /-dáktəlee/ *n*

bra·chyl·o·gy /brə kílləjee/ *n* **1.** brevity in speech or writing, or an instance of this **2.** a shortened form of an expression, used in informal speech [Mid-16C. Via late Latin < Greek *brakhulogia* "shortness of speech"] —**bra·chyl·o·gous** /brə kílləgəss/ *adj*

bra·chyp·ter·ous /brə kíptərəss/ *adj* describes insects and some species of diving birds with short or not fully developed wings —**bra·chyp·ter·ism** *n*

brac·ing /bráyssing/ *adj* making you feel refreshed or invigorated ○ *a bracing cold shower* ■ *n* a system of braces that are used to support or strengthen a structure —**brac·ing·ly** *adv*

bra·ci·o·la /bra̋achee ṓlə, braa chṓlə/ (*plural* **-las** or **-le** /-lay, -lə/) *n* a thin slice of meat that is usually wrapped around a stuffing and cooked in wine [Mid-20C. < Italian, "something cooked over coals" < *brace* "live coals"]

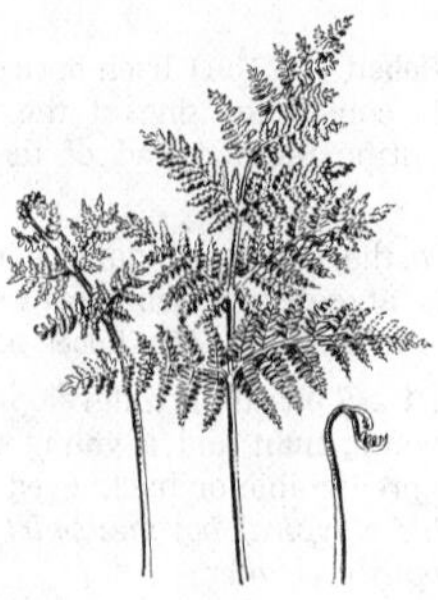

bracken

brack·en /brákən/ (*plural same* or **-ens**) *n* a large fern with extensive underground stems and large triangular fronds that is poisonous to livestock. Native to: most temperate and tropical regions. Latin name: *Pteridium aquilinum.* [14C. < assumed Old Norse *brakni*]

brack·et /brákit/ *n* **1.** L-SHAPED STRUCTURE ON WALL an L-shaped structure that is attached to a wall to hold up something such as a shelf or speaker **2.** TYPE OF SHELF a shelf with an integral part that attaches to the wall as its support and can sometimes be swiveled **3.** PRINTING EITHER OF SYMBOLS [ ] either of a pair of symbols, [ ], used in keying or printing to indicate the insertion of special commentary such as that made by an editor **4.** *UK* PRINTING same as **parenthesis** (sense 1) (*often used in the plural*) **5.** PRINTING PAIRED PUNCTUATION MARK any of the set of signs used in pairs to separate words from surrounding text, including the angle bracket and the brace **6.** GROUP WITHIN SET LIMITS a section of a population or group that falls within particular defined limits ○ *taxpayers in the $50,000 to $70,000 bracket* ■ *vt* (**-et·ed, -et·ing, -ets**) **1.** PUT SOMETHING INSIDE BRACKETS to put something, especially text or a mathematical equation, inside brackets **2.** SUPPORT SOMETHING WITH BRACKETS to attach brackets to something, especially a wall, or support something with brackets **3.** GROUP PEOPLE OR THINGS TOGETHER to group or class people or things together, usually because they are similar in some way ○ *The two shows, both about 30-something women, will inevitably be bracketed together.* [Late 16C. Perhaps < French *braguette* "codpiece" (because of the shape) < Latin *bracae* "breeches"] —**brack·et·ing** *n*

USAGE ***Brackets*** are used around text that is added by somebody other than the original writer or speaker, especially to explain or comment on a word or phrase used in a quotation: *He wrote "As we traveled across Rhodesia (now Zimbabwe) the weather changed for the worse."* They are also used to provide information needed when a quotation is taken out of its original context: *She said "I have never seen him (the accused) before."* The word *sic* (Latin for "thus"), enclosed in brackets, indicates that the preceding word, although wrong, is the one actually used: *The notice read "In case of fire please excite* (*sic*) *the building by the nearest door."*

---

brack·et fun·gus *n* a fungus that forms growths that look somewhat like shelves. The growths generally appear on tree trunks and other wooden structures.

brack·ish /brákish/ *adj* somewhat salty, especially from being a mixture of fresh and salt water [Mid-16C. < Dutch *brak* "salty water"] —**brack·ish·ness** *n*

bract /brakt/ *n* a modified leaf that arises from the stem at the point where the flower or flower cluster develops. Although often green and inconspicuous, bracts may sometimes be large and brightly colored, as in a poinsettia. [Late 18C. < Latin *bractea* "thin metal plate, gold leaf"] —**brac·te·al** /bráktee əl/ *adj*

brac·te·ate /bráktee it, -àyt/ *adj* describes a plant that has bracts ■ *n* a decorated dish or plate made of precious metal [Early 19C. < Latin *bracteatus* < *bractea* "thin metal plate, gold leaf"]

brac·te·ole /bráktee ōl/ *n* an organ resembling a leaf or scale that arises from a branch of a flower cluster where the flowers develop, and where the entire cluster itself develops above a bract [Early 19C. < Latin *bracteola* "small bract" < *bractea* "thin metal plate, gold leaf"] —**brac·te·o·late** /bráktee ə lit, -làyt/ *adj*

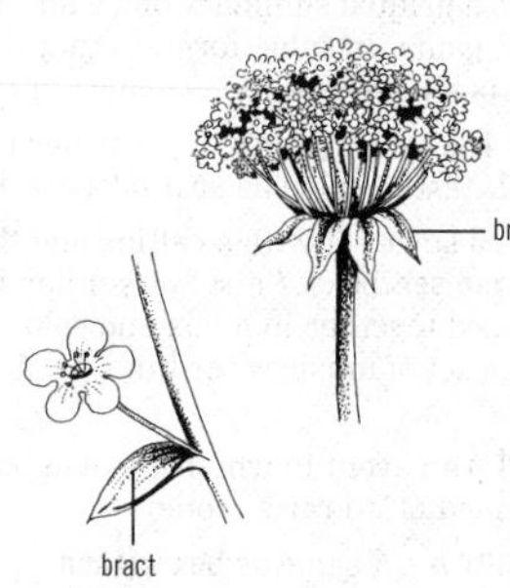

bract

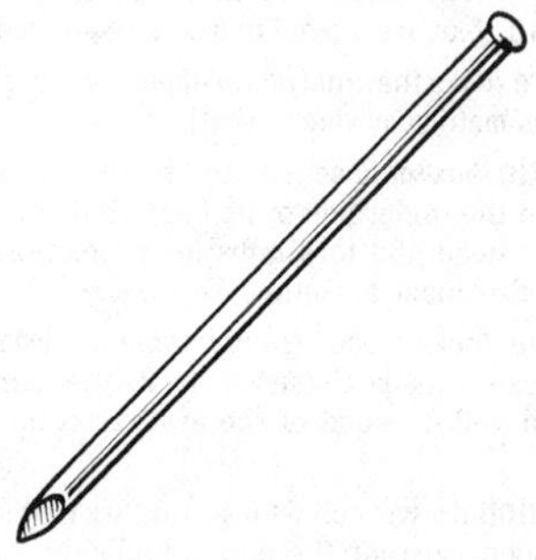

brad

brad /brad/ *n* a thin tapered nail with a head that is small and either circular or flat on one side [13C. < Old Norse *broddr* "spike"]

brad·awl /brád àwl/ *n* a hand tool with a pointed tip, used for making holes in wood, leather, and other materials, to allow screws and nails to be inserted

Brad·bur·y /brádbəree/, **Malcolm** (1932–2000) British novelist, critic, and scholar. Many of his novels such as *The History Man* (1975) deal with academic life. Full name **Bradbury, Malcolm Stanley**

Brad·bur·y, Ray (*b.* 1920) US writer best known for his science fiction novels and stories, including *The Martian Chronicles* (1950) and *Fahrenheit 451* (1953). Full name **Bradbury, Ray Douglas**

> "You have to know how to accept rejection and reject acceptance."
> [Ray Bradbury. Quoted by Richard North Patterson, WAMU NPR affiliate, Washington, D.C.; April 5, 1995]

Brad·dock /bráddək/, **Edward** (1695–1755) British general. He led British forces in North America (1755) during the French and Indian War, and was killed in an ambush at Fort Duquesne, near present-day Pittsburg, from which George Washington escaped.

Bra·den·ton /bráyd'ntən/ city in western Florida, northwest of Sarasota, on the southern side of Tampa Bay. Population: 51,364 (2002 estimate).

Brad·ford /brádfərd/ industrial city in West Yorkshire, northern England. Population: 467,665 (2001).

Brad·ford, William (1590–1657) English-born Puritan leader and New England colonial administrator. He sailed to North America on the *Mayflower* (1620) and was governor of the Plymouth colony almost continuously from 1621 through 1656. His *History of Plimouth Plantation* (1620–47), published in 1856, is still a major historical source.

> "May not and ought not the children of these fathers rightly say: 'Our fathers were Englishmen which came over this great ocean, and were ready to perish in this wilderness.'"
> [William Bradford, *History of Plimouth Plantation, 1620–47*; 1856]

Brad·ford, William (1663–1752) English-born American printer. He printed the first American Book of

Common Prayer (1710) and in 1725 began publishing the New York *Gazette*, New York's first newspaper.

Brad·ley /brádlee/, **Bill** (*b.* 1943) US political leader. He was a long-serving Democrat in the US Senate (1979–97) after a ten-year career as a professional basketball star with the New York Knicks. He made a bid for the Democratic nomination for the US Presidency in 2000, but withdrew after losing many primaries to Al Gore. Full name **Bradley, William Warren**

> "There has never been a great athlete who died not knowing what pain is."
> [Bill Bradley. Quoted in *A Sense of Where You Are*, John McPhee; 1965]

Brad·ley, Francis Herbert (1846–1924) British philosopher. A major figure in the idealist movement, his philosophy drew on the work of Hegel. His works include *Principles of Logic* (1883) and *Appearance and Reality* (1893).

Brad·ley, Omar (1893–1981) US general. During World War II he was responsible for Allied campaigns in Tunisia, Sicily, and France, where he commanded 1.4 million US troops. He was famous for his concern for the ordinary soldier. Full name **Bradley, Omar Nelson**. Known as **the GI General**

> "The way to win an atomic war is to make certain it never starts."
> [Omar Bradley, *Observer (London)*; April 20, 1952]

Brad·ley, Thomas (1917–98) US politician. A former police officer, he was the first Black mayor of Los Angeles (1973–93).

Brad·street /brád street/, **Anne** (1612?–72) English-born American New England poet. An early settler (1630) and the wife of a governor of the Massachusetts Bay Colony, she is regarded as the first English poet in America. Her verse was originally published in England in 1650. Born **Dudley, Ann**

> "I am obnoxious to each carping tongue, / Who sayes my hand a needle better fits, / A Poet's Pen, all scorne, I should thus wrong; / For such despight they cast on female wits: / If what I doe prove well, it won't advance, / They'll say it's stolne, or else, it was by chance."
> [Anne Bradstreet, "The Prologue," *The Tenth Muse Lately Sprung up in America*; 1650]

Bra·dy /bráydee/, **James** (*b.* 1940) US presidential aide. President Ronald Reagan's press secretary, he was wounded in an assassination attempt on the president in 1981 and with his wife Sarah Brady subsequently became a staunch advocate of gun control legislation. The so-called Brady Bill of 1993 mandating waiting periods and license fees for firearms takes its name from his efforts.

Bra·dy, Mathew B. (1823?–96) US photographer. His photographs of prominent personalities, including Abraham Lincoln, and of the Civil War fixed the popular impression of the United States in the mid-19th century.

brady- *prefix* slow ○ *bradycardia* [< Greek *bradus*]

Bra·dy Bill *n* gun control legislation passed in 1993 requiring that anyone wishing to purchase a handgun wait a mandatory period for a background check, that he or she be licensed to own a handgun, and that the handgun be registered

brad·y·car·di·a /bràddi kaárdee ə/ *n* slowness of the heart rate, usually measured as fewer than 60 beats per minute in an adult human [Late 19C. < BRADY- + Greek *kardia* "heart"] —**brad·y·car·dic** *adj*

brad·y·ki·nin /bràddi kínin, -kínnin/ *n* a chemical (**peptide**) produced in the blood when tissues are injured that plays a role in inflammation [Mid-20C. < BRADY- + Greek *kinein* "to move"]

brae /bray/ *n Scotland* a hill or slope (*often used in place names*) [14C. < Old Norse *brá* "eyelash"]

brag /brag/ *vi* (**bragged, brag·ging, brags**) **TALK WITH TOO MUCH PRIDE** to talk with excessive pride about an achievement or possession ○ *The police arrested him after he bragged about the bank robbery to his friends.* ■ *n* **1. BOASTFUL REMARK** a boastful statement or display of arrogant behavior **2. SUBJECT OF BOAST** something bragged or boasted about **3. SOMEBODY WHO BRAGS** a boastful person **4.** CARDS **CARD GAME** a card game similar to poker [14C. Origin ?] —**brag·ger** *n* —**brag·ging** *n, adj* —**brag·ging·ly** *adv*

Bra·ga /braágə/ city and capital of the mountainous district of Braga, northwestern Portugal. Population: 63,033 (1981).

Bra·ge *n* MYTHOL same as **Bragi**

Bragg /brag/, **Braxton** (1817–76) US Confederate general. He was defeated in the Chattanooga Campaign (1863) during the Civil War.

Bragg, Sir Lawrence (1890–1971) Australian-born British physicist. He collaborated with his father, Sir William Bragg, in developing an X-ray technique for examining crystals. They shared the Nobel Prize in physics (1915). Full name **Bragg, Sir William Lawrence**

Bragg, Sir William Henry (1862–1942) British physicist. With his son, Sir Lawrence Bragg, he developed an X-ray technique for examining crystals. They shared the Nobel Prize in physics (1915).

brag·ga·do·ci·o /bràggə dóssee ō, -shee ō, -shō/ (*plural* **-os**) *n* **1.** empty boasting and swaggering self-aggrandizement **2.** somebody who boasts in a swaggering self-aggrandizing way [Late 16C. Alteration of *Braggadocchio*, personification of boastfulness in Spenser's *Faerie Queene*]

brag·gart /brággərt/ *n* somebody who talks immodestly or with excessive pride about himself or herself [Late 16C. < French *bragard* < *braguer* "to brag"]

Bragg's law /brágz-/ *n* a law stating the angle at which X-rays reflected from a crystal are most intense [Early 20C. After Sir William Henry BRAGG and Sir Lawrence BRAGG]

Bra·gi /braágee/, **Bra·ge** /braágə/ *n* in Nordic mythology, the god of poetry, eloquence, and music

Brahe /braa, braáhee, braá ə/, **Tycho** (1546–1601) Danish astronomer. He employed extremely precise observations of stars and planets to correct inaccuracies in existing astronomical tables.

Brah·ma[1] /braámə/ *n* **1.** in Hinduism, the god of knowledge and understanding, regarded as the protector of the world and in later tradition called the creator **2.** HINDUISM same as **Brahman** (sense 1) [< Sanskrit *brāhmaṇa-* < *brahman-* "priest"]

Brah·ma[2] /braámə, bráy-/ *n* a large domestic fowl with heavily feathered legs and feet and a small tail and wings, belonging to a breed that originated in Asia [Mid-19C. Shortening of *Brahmaputra fowl*; because first imported from a town on the Brahmaputra River in India]

Brah·man /braámən/ *n* **1.** in Hinduism, the ultimate impersonal reality underlying everything in the universe, from which everything comes and to which it returns **2.** HINDUISM same as **Brahma**[1] (sense 1) **3.** *also* **brah·man** HINDUISM another spelling of **Brahmin** (senses 1–2) [Late 18C. < Sanskrit *brahman-* "priest"] —**Brah·man·ic** /braa mánnik/ *adj* —**Brah·man·i·cal** *adj*

Brah·ma·na /braámənə/ *n* a sacred Hindu text belonging to a group of commentaries on the Vedas [< Sanskrit *brāhmaṇam* < *brāhmaṇa-* (see BRAHMIN)]

Brah·ma·ni /braámənee/, **brah·ma·ni** *n* a woman of the Brahmin caste [Late 18C. < Sanskrit *brāhmaṇī*, feminine of *brāhmaṇa-* (see BRAHMIN)]

Brah·man·ism, **brah·man·ism** *n* another spelling of **Brahminism** —**Brah·man·ist** *n*

Brah·ma·pu·tra /braámə pootrə/ river in Tibet and northeastern India. It rises in the Himalayan range in Tibet, flows east and southwestward through northeastern India, and empties into the delta of the Ganges in Bangladesh. Length: 1,800 mi./2,900 km.

Barnaby's

Brahmin: a Brahmin priest

Brah·min /braámin/ (*plural* **-mins** or *same*), **brah·min**, **Brah·man** (*plural* **-mans** or *same*), **brah·man** *n* **1. HIGHEST HINDU CASTE** the first of the four Hindu castes, the members of which are priests and scholars of Vedic literature **2. MEMBER OF FIRST CASTE** a member of the Brahmin caste **3. MEMBER OF CULTURAL ELITE** a member of a cultural, social, or intellectual elite, especially in New England in the past [15C. < Sanskrit *brāhmaṇa-* < *brahman-* "priest"] —**Brah·min·ic** /braa mínnik/ *adj* —**Brah·min·i·cal** *adj*

Brah·min·ism /braámə nìzzəm/, **brah·min·ism**, **Brah·man·ism**, **brah·man·ism** *n* the traditional social and religious system of Vedic Hinduism —**Brah·min·ist** *n*

AKG London

Johannes Brahms

Brahms /braamz/, **Johannes** (1833–97) German composer. His works include four symphonies, two piano concertos, and *A German Requiem* (1868).

Bra·hu·i /braa hoó ee/ (*plural* **-is** or *same*) *n* **1.** a Dravidian language spoken in southwestern Pakistan. Native speakers: 2 million. **2.** a member of a Brahui-speaking people who live in southwestern Pakistan [Early 19C. < Brahui] —**Bra·hu·i** *adj*

braid /brayd/ *n* **1.** TEXTILES **DECORATIVE SILKY CORD** a decorative and often silky cord or interwoven thread. Use: trimming, binding, decorating uniforms, edging for soft furnishings. **2. SOMETHING INTERWOVEN** something that is made of three or more interwoven strands, e.g., a loaf of bread baked from woven strands of dough **3.** HAIR **INTERWOVEN STRANDS OF HAIR** a length of hair divided into three or more interwoven strands and worn down the back ○ *She wore her hair in braids.* ■ *vt* (**braid·ed, braid·ing, braids**) **1. INTERWEAVE STRANDS** to interweave three or more strands of something, especially hair **2. MAKE SOMETHING BY BRAIDING** to make something by interweaving strands, strips, or other components ○ *braid a rug* **3. TRIM SOMETHING WITH DECORATIVE CORD** to decorate uniforms or edge furnishings with silky cord [Old English *bregdan* "weave, lay hold of" < Germanic]

braid·ed /bráydəd/ *adj* **1. INTERWOVEN** interwoven from three or more strands **2. EDGED WITH DECORATIVE CORD** decorated or edged with silky cord, especially gold cord **3. CONSISTING OF INTERCONNECTED TRACKS OR CHANNELS** composed of interconnected tracks or channels that divide and reunite ○ *a braided river*

braid·ing /bráyding/ *n* **1.** decorative silky cord. Use: trimming uniforms and furnishings. **2.** embroidery worked in decorative silky thread

Brà·i·la /brə eélə/ city and capital of Brăila County, southeastern Romania. Situated on the Danube, it is Romania's second largest port. Population: 234,648 (1997).

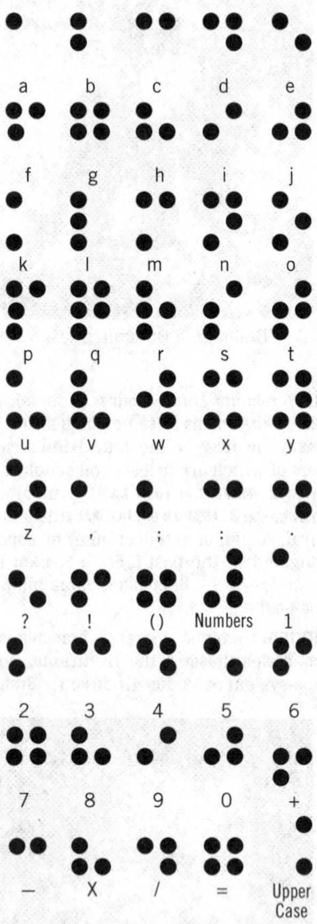

Braille

Braille /brayl/ *n* a writing system for vision-impaired or sightless people, consisting of patterns of raised dots that are read by touch [Mid-19C. After Louis BRAILLE]

Braille /brayl/, **Louis** (1809–52) French educator. He was unable to see from early childhood and in 1829 he invented the Braille system of raised dots to enable vision-impaired or sightless people to read and write.

Braill·er /bráylər/, **Braille·writ·er** /brayl rītər/ *n* a machine similar to a typewriter that prints Braille

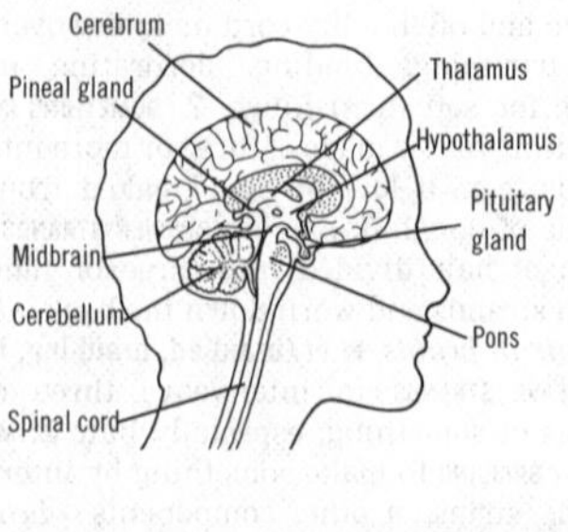

brain: cross section of human brain

brain /brayn/ *n* **1.** ORGAN OF THOUGHT AND FEELING the controlling center of the nervous system in vertebrates, connected to the spinal cord and enclosed in the cranium. It consists of a mass of nerve tissue and nerve-supporting and nourishing tissue (**neuroglia**), is the center of thought and emotions, and regulates bodily activities. **2.** CENTER OF INVERTEBRATE NERVOUS SYSTEM a nervous-system center in some invertebrates that is functionally similar to the brain in vertebrates **3.** MIND somebody's intellectual ability ○ *He's got a good brain.* **4.** INTELLIGENCE somebody's natural intelligence (*usually used in the plural*) ○ *She's got brains as well as beauty.* **5.** SOMEBODY INTELLIGENT somebody very intelligent (*informal*) **6.** MOST INTELLIGENT PERSON IN GROUP the person in a group who is considered the most intelligent and who devises plans or strategies for it (*informal; usually used in the plural*) ○ *Lee's the brains of the family.* ■ **brains** *npl* ANIMAL'S BRAIN AS FOOD the brain of an animal cooked and eaten as food ■ *vt* (**brained, brain·ing, brains**) HIT SOMEBODY ON HEAD to hit somebody violently on the head (*slang*) [Old English *brægen* < W Germanic] ◇ **have something on the brain** to be obsessed with something (*informal*) ◇ **pick somebody's brain** to ask questions of somebody, in order to learn what he or she knows about something ◇ **rack your brains** to try very hard to remember something or solve a problem

brain buck·et *n* a protective helmet worn when engaging in sports such as climbing or motorcycling (*slang*)

brain·case /bráyn kàyss/ *n* the part of the skull enclosing the brain

brain cell *n* one of the millions of cells that make up the brain ◇ **not have a brain cell (between them)** an offensive phrase meaning to be regarded as having very low intellectual ability (*informal*)

brain·child /bráyn chīld/ (*plural* **-chil·dren** /-chìldrən/) *n* an original plan or idea attributed to a person or group (*informal*)

brain cor·al *n* coral that forms rounded colonies resembling the folds of the human brain. Genus: *Meandrina.*

brain dam·age *n* injury to the brain tissue that can impair its ability to function

brain-dead *adj* **1.** lacking functions of the brain and central nervous system as measured by brain wave activity on an electroencephalogram over a specific period of time **2.** an offensive term meaning having extremely low intellectual ability (*slang*)

brain death *n* the end of all functions of the brain and central nervous system as measured by brain wave activity on an electroencephalogram over a specific period of time. There are strict legal criteria for determining brain death, since its occurrence can allow cessation of life support or removal of organs for transplantation.

brain drain *n* the movement of highly skilled people, especially scientists and technical workers, to a country offering better opportunities (*informal*)

Brain·erd /bráynərd/ city in central Minnesota, on the Mississippi River, north of St. Cloud. Population: 13,312 (2002 estimate).

brain fe·ver *n* inflammation of the brain or its covering membranes (*archaic*)

brain·less /bráynləss/ *adj* lacking or not requiring intelligence (*disapproving*) ○ *a brainless activity* —**brain·less·ly** *adv* —**brain·less·ness** *n*

brain·pan /bráyn pàn/ *n* ANAT same as **braincase**

brain·pow·er /bráyn pòwr/ *n* somebody's intellectual capability

brain·stem /bráyn stèm/ *n* the part of the brain between the spinal column and the cerebral hemispheres. It consists of the midbrain, pons, and medulla oblongata.

brain·storm /bráyn stàwrm/ *n* **1.** BRILLIANT IDEA a sudden, exciting idea (*informal*) ○ *I just had a brainstorm! I'll tell you how we can do it.* **2.** BRIEF PSYCHOLOGICAL DISTURBANCE a momentary psychological disturbance ■ *vti* (**-stormed, -storm·ing, -storms**) THINK QUICKLY AND CREATIVELY to generate creative ideas spontaneously, usually for problem-solving, and especially in an intensive group discussion that does not allow time for reflection —**brain·storm·er** *n* —**brain·storm·ing** *n*

brains trust *n* **1.** *UK* same as **brain trust** (sense 1) **2.** *UK* a group of experts who informally discuss issues of public interest, especially on television or radio

brain·teas·er /bráyn teèzər/ *n* a difficult or complex problem that requires careful thought in order to solve it, often done for amusement (*informal*)

Brain·tree /bráyn treè/ town in eastern Massachusetts. It is a southern suburb of Boston, directly south of Quincy. Population: 33,917 (2002 estimate).

brain trust *n* **1.** a group of high-level advisers, usually unofficial, to a government or administration **2.** *also* **Brain Trust** a group of high-level academics who helped President Franklin Delano Roosevelt to formulate the New Deal, especially prior to his taking office —**brain trust·er** *n*

brain·wash /bráyn wòsh, -wàwsh/ (**-washed, -wash·ing, -wash·es**) *vt* **1.** to impose a set of usually political or religious beliefs on somebody by the use of various coercive methods of indoctrination, including destruction of the victim's prior beliefs **2.** to induce somebody to believe or do something, e.g., to buy a new product, especially by means of constant repetition or advertising

brain·wash·ing /bráyn wòshing, -wàwshing/ *n* **1.** the imposition of a set of usually political or religious beliefs on somebody by the use of various coercive methods of indoctrination, including destruction of the victim's prior beliefs **2.** the inducing of somebody to believe or do something, e.g., to buy a new product, especially by means of constant repetition or advertising [Mid-20C. Translation of Chinese *xǐnǎo* < *xǐ* "to wash" + *nǎo* "brain"]

brain wave *n* **1.** one of the rhythmic waves of voltage arising from electrical activity within brain tissue **2.** *UK* same as **brainstorm** *n* (sense 1) (*informal*)

brain·work /bráyn wùrk/ *n* concentrated intellectual activity, especially that required to do a job —**brain·work·er** *n*

brain·y /bráynee/ (**-i·er, -i·est**) *adj* extremely intelligent (*informal*) —**brain·i·ly** *adv* —**brain·i·ness** *n*

braise /brayz/ (**braised, brais·ing, brais·es**) *vt* to cook food, especially meat or vegetables, by browning briefly in hot fat, adding a little liquid, and cooking at a low temperature in a covered pot [Mid-18C. < French *braiser* < *braise* "live coals"]

brake[1] /brayk/ *n* **1.** DEVICE THAT SLOWS OR STOPS MACHINE the part of a machine or vehicle that slows it down or stops it (*often used in the plural*) **2.** RESTRAINT a slowing down or stopping of something such as expenditure or development, or something that causes this ○ *The brake on investment is largely a result of political factors.* ■ *v* (**braked, brak·ing, brakes**) **1.** *vti* SLOW OR STOP MACHINE to slow down or stop, or make something such as a vehicle or a machine slow down or stop ○ *The driver braked hard.* **2.** *vt* SLOW OR HALT DEVELOPMENT to slow down or halt the progress of something or an increase in something [Late 18C. Perhaps < BRAKE[4]]

SPELLCHECK See ***break.***

brake[2] /brayk/ (*plural same* or **brakes**) *n* **1.** a fern with compound leaves resembling feathers, popular as a houseplant. Genus: *Pteris.* **2.** BOT same as **bracken** [14C. Perhaps back-formation < BRACKEN]

SPELLCHECK See ***break.***

brake[3] /brayk/ *n* an area of dense undergrowth, bushes, or brush [Old English *bracu,* origin ?]

brake[4] /brayk/ *n* **1.** a tool or machine for crushing and separating flax or hemp fibers **2.** a machine, frequently hydraulically powered, for precision bending and folding of sheet metal [15C. < Middle Low German or Middle Dutch]

brake[5] /brayk/ *n* a lever or handle on a pump or other machine [Early 17C. Origin ?]

brake chute *n* AUTOMOT same as **brake parachute**

brake drum *n* the metal cylinder attached to the wheel of a vehicle that slows the rotation of the wheel when pressure is applied by the brake shoe

brake fade *n* a decrease in the braking efficiency of a motor vehicle, caused by the overheating of the brakes

brake flu·id *n* an oily liquid used in hydraulic brake systems to transmit pressure from the brake pedal to the brakes

brake horse·pow·er *n* a measure of the work produced by an engine, calibrated in horsepower and determined by the force exerted on a friction brake

brake light *n* a rear light on a motor vehicle that lights up when the driver brakes

brake lin·ing *n* the thin, replaceable strip of material attached to a brake shoe

brake·man /bráykmən/ (*plural* **-men** /-mən/) *n* **1.** a member of a train crew or other railroad employee who operates, inspects, or repairs brakes, usually a man **2.** somebody who operates the brakes on a bobsled, especially in a team of men

brake pad *n* a replaceable block of material that presses against the surface of a disk brake

brake par·a·chute *n* a parachute that is attached to the back of a vehicle and acts as a brake

brake·per·son /bráyk pùrss'n/ *n* **1.** a member of a train crew or other railroad employee who operates, inspects, or repairs brakes **2.** somebody who operates the brakes on a bobsled

brake shoe *n* a curved block that presses a brake lining against a brake drum to slow the turning of a wheel

brake·wom·an /bráyk wŏŏmmən/ (*plural* **-wom·en** /-wìmmin/) *n* **1.** a woman member of a train crew or other railroad employee who operates, inspects, or repairs brakes **2.** a woman who operates the brakes on a bobsled

brak·ing dis·tance /bráyking-/ *n* the distance that a vehicle needs to come to a complete stop when the brakes have been applied

bra·less /braáləss/ *adj, adv* not wearing a bra

Bra·man·te /brə maán tay/, **Donato** (1444–1514) Italian architect and painter. He rebuilt and renovated the Vatican and St. Peter's in Rome (1505–06). Born **d'Antonio, Donato di Pascuccio**

bram·ble /brámb'l/ *n* **1.** BLACKBERRY a blackberry fruit **2.** PRICKLY BUSH WITH EDIBLE FRUIT a prickly bush of the rose family, especially blackberry or raspberry canes. Genus: *Rubus.* **3.** PRICKLY BUSH a prickly bush similar or related to a wild blackberry, e.g., a sweetbriar [Old English *bræmbel* < Germanic, "thorny bush"]

bram·bling /brámbling/ *n* a small bird related to the chaffinch, with black and rusty brown feathers. Native to: northern Europe, Asia. Latin name: *Fringilla montifringilla.* [Mid-16C. Perhaps < BRAMBLE + -LING[1]]

bram·bly /brámblee/ (**-bli·er, -bli·est**) *adj* covered in or containing prickly bushes, especially blackberries or wild roses ○ *a brambly garden*

Bramp·ton /brámptən/ city and industrial center in southeastern Ontario, Canada. Population: 325,428 (2001).

bran /bran/ *n* the husks of cereal grain that are removed during milling. Use: supplementary source of dietary fiber. [13C. < French]

Bran /bran/ *n* in Celtic mythology, a giant god who ruled Britain and installed his son, Gwern, as king of Ireland

Bran·agh /bránnə/, **Kenneth** (*b.* 1960) British actor and director, born in Northern Ireland. His work on stage and in movies includes *Henry V* (1989). Full name **Branagh, Kenneth Charles**

branch /branch/ *n* **1.** PART OF TREE GROWING FROM TRUNK a woody limb of a tree that grows out from a larger limb or from the trunk **2.** BOT PART OF PLANT STEM OR ROOT a subdivision of the stem, root, or flower cluster of a plant **3.** SOMETHING LIKE TREE BRANCH something that resembles a branch of a tree in structure ○ *the branches of the stag's antlers* **4.** LOCAL UNIT IN ORGANIZATION a store, bank, or other organization that is part of a larger group and is located in a different part of a geographic area from the parent organization ○ *The account is held at the bank's Elm Street branch.* **5.** DISTINCT PART OF LARGE ORGANIZATION a subdivision of a large organization, usually with a specialized mission ○ *Each branch of the military has a distinctive history and reputation.* **6.** PART OF SUBJECT AREA a part of a large area of study ○ *Ethics is a branch of philosophy.* **7.** FAMILY LINE a line of a family that is descended from a common ancestor ○ *the Peruvian branch of the family* **8.** GEOG TRIBUTARY STREAM a river or stream flowing into another river ○ *a branch of the Colorado River* **9.** *Southern US* GEOG CREEK a small stream or a creek ○ *A branch runs through our lower pasture.* **10.** *Southern US* BEVERAGES DRINKING WATER drinking water, especially from a clean spring or stream, and used particularly for mixing with bourbon **11.** COMPUT ALTERNATIVE INSTRUCTION SEQUENCE a sequence of computer program instructions in a set of alternative sequences that are activated according to specific conditions **12.** MATH PART OF CURVE a distinctive part of a curve that is separated from the rest of the curve, e.g., by discontinuities or extreme points ■ *v* (**branched, branch·ing, branch·es**) **1.** *vti* DIVIDE to divide into smaller parts, or cause something to do this ○ *Part of the path branches off toward the river.* **2.** *vi* BOT HAVE BRANCHES to grow branches **3.** *vi* EXPAND ACTIVITIES OR INTERESTS to become involved in something new, especially as a way of extending or expanding personal interests or business activities ○ *The company has branched into the multimedia market.* **4.** *vi* COMPUT JUMP TO ALTERNATE PROGRAM PATH to execute an alternative sequence of computer program instructions as a result of the detection of a specific condition [13C. Via French *branche* < late Latin *branca* "paw"] —**branch·let** /bránchlit/ *n*

REGIONAL NOTE See *run.*

branch out *vi* to do something different, often involving an element of risk

-branch *suffix* gills ○ *opisthobranch* [< Latin *branchia* (see BRANCHIA)]

bran·chi·a /brángkee ə/ (*plural* **-ae** /-ee/) *n* a gill in water animals or a similar structure found in the embryos of higher animals, including human beings [Late 17C. Via Latin < Greek *bragkhia* "gills"] —**bran·chi·al** *adj* —**bran·chi·ate** *adj*

bran·chi·al cleft, bran·chi·al groove *n* AMPHIB, FISH same as **gill slit** (*technical*)

bran·chi·o·pod /brángkee ə pòd/ *n* a small, usually freshwater crustacean with a segmented body and flat gill-bearing appendages. Subclass: Branchiopoda. [Early 19C. < modern Latin *Branchiopoda* < Latin *branchia* "gills" + Greek *-pod* (see -POD)] —**bran·chi·o·pod** *adj* —**bran·chi·op·o·dous** /bràngkee óppədəss/ *adj*

branch line *n* a part of a railroad system that is routed to smaller towns and villages that are not served by a main line, particularly in Europe

branch of·fi·cer *n* the person in charge of a branch of an organization, especially a bank

branch plant *n Can* a subsidiary business owned and controlled by a company based in another country

branch wa·ter *n Southern US* BEVERAGES same as **branch** *n* (sense 10)

Bran·cu·si /bran kóozee, braang kóosh/, **Constantin** (1876–1957) Romanian sculptor. He was a pioneer of 20th-century European sculpture and was particularly concerned with the inner form of his subject.

> "Architecture is inhabited sculpture."
> [Constantin Brancusi. Quoted in *Themes and Episodes*, Igor Stravinsky; 1966]

brand /brand/ *n* **1.** COMM PRODUCT OR MANUFACTURER a name, usually a trademark, of a product or manufacturer, or the product identified by this name ○ *What brand of shampoo do you use?* **2.** RECOGNIZABLE TYPE OF SOMETHING a distinctive type of something ○ *an unusual brand of humor* **3.** AGRIC MARK BURNED ON ANIMAL a mark burned into the hide of a range animal to identify it as the property of a particular ranch, farm, or owner ○ *The Triple S is the brand on all our steers.* **4.** HIST MARK ON CRIMINAL OR ENSLAVED PERSON formerly, a mark made on the skin of a criminal or a slave, especially to identify the owner **5.** SIGN OR MARK OF DISGRACE a sign or mark of disgrace, infamy, or notoriety ○ *He bore the brand of disloyalty.* **6.** BURNED OR BURNING PIECE OF WOOD a piece of wood that is burned or smoldering (*archaic*) **7.** TORCH a flaming torch (*literary*) **8.** ARMS same as **sword** (sense 1) (*literary*) **9.** FUNGI FUNGAL DISEASE OF PLANTS a fungal disease that affects garden plants by causing brown spots to appear on leaves ■ *vt* (**brand·ed, brand·ing, brands**) **1.** MARK SKIN OR HIDE OF ANIMAL to mark an animal's skin or hide with a hot iron, especially as a means of identification ○ *All the cattle have been branded.* **2.** DESCRIBE SOMEBODY OR SOMETHING AS BAD to class somebody or something as bad, illegal, or undesirable, often arbitrarily ○ *was branded as a cheat* **3.** MAKE INDELIBLE IMPRESSION ON SOMEBODY to make an indelible mark or impression on somebody or something ○ *The words "Duty, Honor, Country" are branded into the hearts of all West Pointers.* [Old English, "burning stick" < Indo-European, "be hot"] —**brand·er** *n*

brand·ed /brándəd/ *adj* bearing a company name or trademark, usually considered a mark of prestige or quality

Bran·deis /brán dìss/, **Louis** (1856–1941) associate justice of the US Supreme Court. He was an important legal theoretician and a liberal member of the Supreme Court (1916–39). Full name **Brandeis, Louis Dembitz**

> "The federal Constitution is perhaps the greatest of human experiments."
> [Louis Brandeis. Quoted in *The Words of Justice Brandeis*, Solomon Goldman, ed.; 1953]

AKG London

Brandenburg Gate

Bran·den·burg Gate /brándən burg-/ *n* a large neoclassical stone gateway in Berlin, Germany, a symbol of the city and a focal point for public gatherings

bran·died /brándeed/ *adj* cooked or preserved in brandy

brand·ing /bránding/ *n* the use of advertising, distinctive design, and other means to make consumers associate a specific product with a specific manufacturer

brand·ing i·ron *n* an iron tool that is heated and pressed onto a surface, especially an animal's hide, in order to leave a permanent identifying mark

bran·dish /brándish/ (**-dished, -dish·ing, -dish·es**) *vt* to wave something about, especially a weapon, in a menacing, theatrical, or triumphant way [14C. < French *brandiss-*, stem of *brandir* < *brand* "sword"] —**bran·dish·er** *n*

brand lead·er *n* the best-selling product in a particular category

brand·ling /brándling/ *n* a small reddish brown earthworm that is often used as bait by anglers. Latin name: *Eisenia foetida.* [Mid-17C. Because of its coloring, like a burning brand]

brand loy·al·ty *n* the tendency to buy a particular brand of a product

brand name *n* a trade name for a product or service produced by a particular company. It may or may not be a registered trademark. ○ *A computer with a brand name can cost 10 percent more.* —**brand-named** *adj*

brand-new *adj* completely new and unused [As if newly made in a furnace]

Marlon Brando

Bran·do /brándō/, **Marlon** (*b.* 1924) US actor. His numerous Hollywood movies include *A Streetcar Named Desire* (1951) and *The Godfather* (1972). See illustration on previous page

Bran·don /brándən/ second largest city in Manitoba Province, Canada. Population: 39,716 (2001).

Brandt /brant, braant/, **Willy** (1913–92) German politician. He was mayor of West Berlin (1957–66) and was elected Chancellor of the Federal Republic of Germany in 1969. His pursuit of reconciliation between East and West earned him the Nobel Peace Prize (1971). Born **Frahm, Herbert Ernst Karl**

> "A Europe living in peace calls for its members to be willing to listen to the arguments of the others, for the struggle of convictions and interests will continue. Europe needs tolerance. It needs freedom of thought, not moral indifference."
> [Willy Brandt, *Address given on the presentation of a Nobel Peace Prize*; December 11, 1971]

bran·dy /brándee/ *n* a liquor that is distilled from the fermented juice of grapes or other fruit [Early 17C. Shortening of *brandy-wine* < Dutch *brandewijn* "burned (i.e. distilled) wine"]

bran·dy Al·ex·an·der *n* a cocktail with a base of brandy

bran·dy but·ter *n UK* same as **hard sauce**

Bran·dy·wine Creek /brándee wīn-/ the site near Philadelphia, Pennsylvania, of an important defeat of the Continental Army by the British forces in 1777

brane /brayn/ *n* a spatial dimension in space–time arising out of string theory [Late 20C. Shortening of MEMBRANE]

branks /brangks/ *npl* a device consisting of a metal frame for the head and a bit to restrain the tongue, formerly used to restrain and punish women thought to be quarrelsome or nagging [Mid-16C. Origin ?]

bran·ni·gan /bránnigən/ *n* **1.** a loud quarrel or brawl **2.** a drinking binge [Early 20C. Probably < the Irish surname *Brannigan*]

Bran·son /bránssən/, **Richard** (*b.* 1950) British entrepreneur. Under the Virgin corporate umbrella he developed business interests in music retailing, broadcasting, and transportation. Full name **Branson, Richard Charles Nicholas**

> "Develop the business around the people; build it, don't buy it; and, then, be the best."
> [Richard Branson, *Speech to the Institute of Directors, London*; May 1993]

brant /brant/ (*plural* **brants** or *same*) *n* a small, dark-colored wild goose. Native to: Arctic regions. Genus: *Branta.* [14C. Variant of BRENT GOOSE]

Brant /brant/, **Joseph** (1742–1807) Mohawk leader. He allied his people with the British during the Revolutionary War. Born **Thayendanega**

Brant·ford /brántfərd/ city in southeastern Ontario, Canada, on the Grand River directly north of Niagara Falls. Population: 86,417 (2001).

Braque /braak, brak/, **Georges** (1882–1963) French painter. He was one of the founders, with Pablo Picasso, of the cubist movement.

> "There is only one thing in art that has value: that which one cannot explain."
> [Georges Braque. Quoted in "Late Lyrics: Braque," *Art in America*, Jed Perl; 1983]

brash[1] /brash/ *adj* **1.** self-assertive in an aggressive or rude way **2.** acting or made in a hasty or impulsive fashion ○ *The candidates are realistic about their chances on Tuesday and are not making any brash predictions.* [Early 19C. Origin ?] —**brash·ly** *adv* —**brash·ness** *n*

brash[2] /brash/ *adj* describes wood that is easily cracked or broken (*technical*) [Mid-16C. Origin ?]

brash[3] /brash/ *n* a pile of loose trash, e.g., broken rocks or garden refuse [Late 18C. Origin ?]

brash·y /bráshee/ (**-i·er, -i·est**) *adj* **1.** loosely broken or fragmented ○ *soft brashy ice* **2.** easily cracked or broken

Bra·sí·lia /brə zíllyə/ city and capital of Brazil. A relatively new city, laid out on an uninhabited site in 1957, it is in the Federal District, east central Brazil. Population: 2,051,146 (2000).

Bra·şov /brásh ov/ city and capital of Braşov County, central Romania. Population: 319,908 (1997).

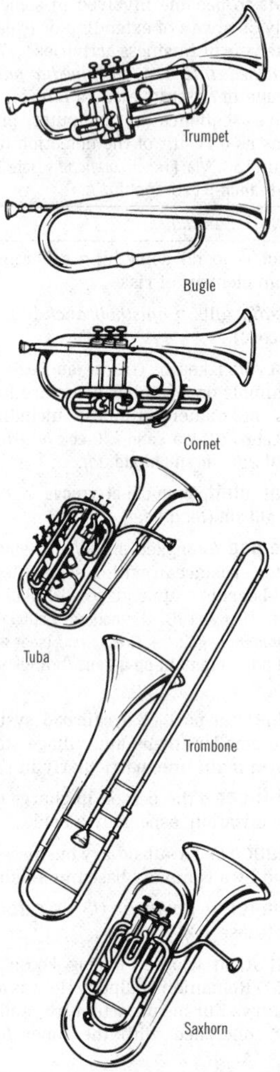

brass: brass musical instruments

brass /brass/ *n* **1.** YELLOW ALLOY a hard yellow shiny metal that is an alloy of zinc and copper, frequently with the addition of other metallic elements to impart specific properties **2.** ITEMS MADE OF BRASS a collection of ornaments or items made of brass ○ *clean the brass* **3.** ITEM MADE OF BRASS an ornament or item made of brass (*usually used in the plural*) ○ *horse brasses* **4.** ENGRAVED PLATE OF BRASS an engraved plaque or tablet made of brass, especially one set into the floor or wall of a church **5.** MUSIC BRASS MUSICAL INSTRUMENTS musical instruments made of brass such as trumpets and trombones, considered as a group (*often used in the plural*) **6.** MUSIC PLAYERS OF BRASS INSTRUMENTS the players of brass instruments, especially when considered as one of the four main sections of an orchestra (*often used in the plural*) **7.** MIL HIGH-RANKING OFFICERS high-ranking officers, especially in the military (*informal*) **8.** EXCESSIVE SELF-ASSURANCE extreme and usually excessive self-confidence (*informal*) ○ *He had the brass to lie about every aspect of his background.* **9.** *N England* MONEY money or cash (*informal*) **10.** MECH ENG REPLACEABLE LINER FOR BEARING a replaceable brass or bronze liner for a bearing [Old English *bræs*, origin ?]

Bras·saï /bra sī/ (1899–1984) Hungarian-born French photographer. His photographs documenting Parisian nightlife in the 1930s were published as *Paris by Night* (1933). Pseudonym of **Halasz, Gyula**

> "...there is only one criterion for a good photograph: that it be unforgettable."
> [Brassaï. Quoted in "Guest Speaker: Brassaï. The Three Faces of Paris," *Architectural Digest*, Avis Berman; July 1984]

brass band *n* a band consisting of brass wind instruments and sometimes percussion instruments

brass·bound /bráss bòwnd/ *adj* **1.** trimmed or banded with brass or a similar metal **2.** unreasonably inflexible in manner or character

brass-col·lar *adj* never abandoning a particular political party and always voting a straight ticket ○ *brass-collar Democrats*

bras·se·rie /bràssə rée, bràss rée/ *n* a type of restaurant that will serve customers drinks with or without food [Mid-19C. < French, "brewery" < Old French *bracier* "brew" < Latin *brace* "malt" < Celtic]

brass hat *n* a high-ranking military officer (*slang*) [< the gold braid on officers' caps]

bras·si·ca /brássikə/ *n* a plant of the mustard family, e.g., cabbage, kale, broccoli, cauliflower, or mustard. Genus: *Brassica.* [Early 19C. Via modern Latin, genus name < Latin, "cabbage"]

brass·ie /brássee/ *n* a golf club, classified as a two wood, that has a brass-plated sole (*informal*)

bras·siere /brə zéer/ *n* CLOTHING same as **bra** [Early 20C. < French, "bodice" < *bras* "arm" < Latin *brachium* (see BRACHIUM)]

brass knuck·les *npl* a metal chain or a set of rings attached to a bar that can be put over the fingers to serve as a weapon

brass ring *n* the opportunity for success, or hard-earned success (*informal*) ○ *to have a shot at the brass ring at last* [< the custom of giving a free ride to any child who grabbed one of the rings hung around a carousel]

brass rub·bing *n* a copy made by putting paper over an engraved plaque or tablet, especially one in a church, and rubbing it with a soft substance such as chalk or graphite

brass tacks *npl* the most basic or fundamental parts of a situation or issue (*informal*) ○ *Let's get down to brass tacks.*

brass·ware /bráss wèr/ *n* items such as plates and ornaments made from brass

brass·y /brássee/ (**-i·er, -i·est**) *adj* **1.** FLASHY AND VULGAR brightly dressed in a cheap and showy way, and behaving too confidently or noisily **2.** SOUNDING LIKE BRASS INSTRUMENTS dominated by or resembling the sounds of brass musical instruments, and therefore typically short, harsh, and high-pitched ○ *a brassy mixture of reggae, funk, calypso, and jazz* **3.** BRAZENLY OVERBEARING brazen or strident in style ○ *a brassy management approach* **4.** OF BRASS made of or containing brass **5.** GOLDEN YELLOW golden yellow in color —**brass·i·ly** *adv* —**brass·i·ness** *n*

brat /brat/ *n* **1.** somebody, especially a child, who is regarded as tiresomely demanding and selfish in a childish way **2.** the son or daughter of a serving member of one of the armed forces (*informal*) ○ *an army brat* [Mid-16C. Origin ?] —**brat·tish** *adj* —**brat·ty** *adj*

Bra·ti·sla·va /bràtti slaávə, braáti-/ capital and largest city of Slovakia. It lies on the Danube River in the southwest of the country, about 35 mi./56 km east of Vienna. Population: 449,547 (1999).

brat pack *n* a group of successful or affluent young people, especially actors (*informal*) [After RAT PACK]

Bratsk /braatsk/ city in Siberia, eastern Russia, developed as a home for employees of the Bratsk Dam hydroelectric plant on the Angara River. Population: 301,742 (1995).

Brat·tain /brátt'n/, **Walter H.** (1902–87) Chinese-born US physicist. He shared a Nobel Prize in physics (1956) for his research on transistors and semiconductors. Full name **Brattain, Walter Houser**

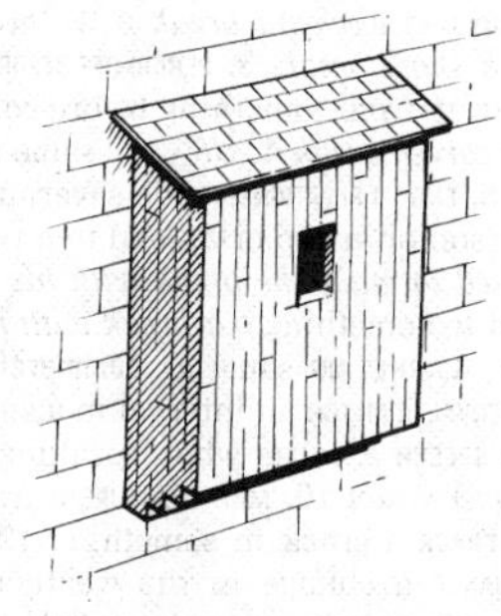

brattice (sense 2)

brat·tice /bráttiss/ *n* **1.** a partition used to assist ventilation in a mine **2.** in medieval times, a temporary wooden parapet or gallery erected on the battlements of a fortress and used during a siege [13C. Via Anglo-Norman, Old French *bretesche* < medieval Latin *bretescha (turris)* "British (tower)"]

Brat·tle·bo·ro /brátt'lbərō/ town in southeastern Vermont, on the western bank of the Connecticut River, east of Bennington. Population: 11,987 (2002 estimate).

brat·wurst /brát wùrst, braát-, brát vòorst, braát-/ *n* a highly seasoned fresh German sausage made of pork or of pork and veal [Early 20C. < German, "frying sausage"]

Braun ♦ von Braun, Wernher

Braun·schwei·ger /brówn shwìgər/ *n* spicy smoked liver sausage [Early 20C. < German, after *Braunschweig* (Brunswick), Germany]

bra·va /braá vaá, braa vaá/ *interj, n* a cry of approval for a woman or girl performer by members of a theater audience [Early 19C. < Italian, "excellent"]

bra·va·do /brə vaádō/ *n* a real or pretended display of courage or boldness ○ *set out to travel the world with more bravado than common sense* [Late 16C. Alteration of Spanish *bravada* < *bravo* (see BRAVE)]

brave /brayv/ *adj* (**brav·er, brav·est**) **HAVING OR SHOWING COURAGE** having or showing courage, especially when facing danger, difficulty, or pain ■ *n* **NATIVE N AMERICAN WARRIOR** a Native North American warrior (*dated*) ■ *npl* **BRAVE PEOPLE** those people who are courageous ■ *vt* (**braved, brav·ing, braves**) **1. FACE ONSLAUGHT OF SOMETHING** to face the onslaught of something unpleasant with courage and resolution **2. CHALLENGE SOMETHING** to defy something despite there being only a small chance of being victorious [15C. Via French < Italian *bravo* "bold" or Spanish *bravo* "brave, savage," < Latin *barbarus* (see BARBAROUS)] —**brave·ly** *adv* —**brave·ness** *n*
brave out *vt* to live through something that is difficult or unpleasant

brave new world *n* the world of the future, usually either a technology-based utopia or a sinister totalitarian world devoid of human values (*often ironic*) [Mid-20C. < *Brave New World* (1932), novel by Aldous HUXLEY]

CULTURAL NOTE ***Brave New World***, a novel (1932) by British writer Aldous Huxley. Written partly as a response to more utopian writers of the day, it depicts a bleak and sterile future civilization in which feelings are stimulated by drugs, and babies are bred in factories.

brav·er·y /bráyvəree, bráyvree/ *n* courage in the face of danger, difficulty, or pain [Mid-16C. < French *braverie* or Italian *braveria*, both < Italian *bravo* "bold"]

SYNONYMS See ***courage***.

bra·vis·si·mo /braa víssə mò/ *interj* used as a cry of great and enthusiastic approval by members of a theater audience [Mid-18C. < Italian, "most excellent"]

bra·vo /braávō, braa vṓ/ *interj* **AUDIENCE'S SHOUT OF APPROVAL** used as a cry of approval by members of a theater audience ■ *n* (*plural* **-vos**) **1. SHOUT OF "BRAVO"** a cry of "bravo" to express approval **2. ASSASSIN** a hired assassin (*archaic*) [Mid-18C. < Italian, "excellent"]

Bra·vo /braávō/ *n* a code word for the letter "B," used in international radio communications

bra·vu·ra /brə vòorə, -vyòorə/ *n* **1. DAZZLING ARTISTIC FLAIR** great skill that is shown when something artistic is done in an exciting or innovative way ○ *a bravura performance* **2. SHOWY DISPLAY** showy style or behavior ■ *adj* **WITH OR REQUIRING FLAIR** displaying or requiring great artistic skill and style ○ *the bravura vividness of her versatile performance* [Mid-18C. < Italian, "courage, spirit" < *bravo* "bold"]

braw /braw/ *adj Scotland* excellent, attractive, or pleasant [Late 16C. Variant of BRAVE]

brawl /brawl/ *n* **1. NOISY FIGHT** a noisy fight, especially in a public place **2. LOUD PARTY** a noisy boisterous party (*slang*) **3. DEEP LOUD SOUND** a deep loud roaring sound, especially the sound of rushing water ■ *vi* (**brawled, brawl·ing, brawls**) **1. FIGHT NOISILY** to fight noisily, especially in a public place **2. MAKE DEEP LOUD SOUND** to make a deep loud roaring sound, especially the sound of rushing water [14C. Origin ?] —**brawl·er** *n* —**brawl·ing** *n*

brawl·y /bráwlee/ (**-i·er, -i·est**) *adj* involved in a fight, or always ready to become involved in one (*informal*)

brawn /brawn/ *n* **1.** very strong muscles, especially on the arms and legs **2.** physical strength, especially as opposed to intellectual power **3.** *UK* FOOD same as **headcheese** [14C. < Anglo-Norman *braun* "fleshy part of the leg" < Germanic]

brawn·y /bráwnee/ (**-i·er, -i·est**) *adj* **1.** muscular and strong-looking **2.** having the skin hardened by calluses —**brawn·i·ly** *adv* —**brawni·ness** *n*

bray[1] /bray/ (**brayed, bray·ing, brays**) *v* **1.** *vi* to make the sound a donkey makes **2.** *vti* to speak, laugh, or say something in a harsh high-pitched rasping voice [13C. < Old French *braire* "to cry"] —**bray** *n* —**bray·er** *n*

bray[2] /bray/ (**brayed, bray·ing, brays**) *vt* **1.** to crush something to a fine powder or consistency **2.** to spread ink in a thin layer on a surface [14C. < Anglo-Norman *braier*, Old French *breier* < Germanic]

Braz. *abbr* **1.** Brazil **2.** Brazilian

braze /brayz/ (**brazed, braz·ing, braz·es**) *vt* to join two pieces of metal together with a solder that has a high melting point [Mid-16C. < Old French *braser* "to burn"] —**braz·er** *n*

bra·zen /bráyz'n/ *adj* **1. BOLD AND UNASHAMED** showing or expressing boldness and a complete lack of shame **2. HARSH-SOUNDING** with an unpleasantly loud and resonant sound **3. OF OR LIKE BRASS** made of brass or resembling it, especially in color or hardness (*literary*) [Old English *bræsen* "made of brass" < BRASS] —**bra·zen·ly** *adv* —**bra·zen·ness** *n*
brazen out, brazen through *vt* to face a difficult situation confidently, without showing shame or embarrassment

bra·zier[1] /bráyzhər/ *n* a metal container used outdoors for burning coal or charcoal, either for cooking or to keep people warm [Late 17C. < French *brasier* < *braise* "hot coals"]

bra·zier[2] /bráyzhər/ *n* somebody who works on brass articles [14C. Probably < BRASS, after GLAZIER]

bra·zil /brə zíl/ *n UK* FOOD same as **Brazil nut** (sense 1) [14C. < medieval Latin *brasilium*]

Brazil

Bra·zil /brə zíl/ largest country in South America. Colonized by the Portuguese from 1500 onward, it became an independent republic in 1889. Language: Portuguese. Currency: real. Capital: Brasília. Population: 182,032,600 (2003). Area: 3,300,171 sq. mi./8,547,404 sq. km. Official name **Federative Republic of Brazil** —**Bra·zil·i·an** *n, adj*

Bra·zil Ba·sin basin of the Atlantic Ocean on the western side of the Mid-Atlantic Ridge. Depth: 16,400 ft./5,000 m.

Bra·zil nut *n* **1.** a long thick edible seed with a hard shell that is nearly triangular in cross section, borne in clusters inside large round capsules **2.** an evergreen tree that bears Brazil nuts. Native to: tropical southern America. Latin name: *Bertholletia excelsa*.

bra·zil·wood /brə zíl wòod/ *n* red wood from various tropical and North American trees, especially a tree native to Brazil. Use: manufacture of red dyes, violin bows.

Braz·os /brázzōss/ river that flows from northern Texas southeastward into the Gulf of Mexico near Freeport. Length: 923 mi./1,490 km.

Braz·za·ville /brázzə vìl/ capital city of the Republic of the Congo and a major port on the Congo River. It was founded in 1880 by the French explorer Pierre Savorgnan de Brazza (1852–1905). Population: 1,187,000 (1999).

B.R.E. *abbr* Bachelor of Religious Education

breach /breech/ *n* **1. FAILURE TO MAINTAIN SOMETHING** a failure to obey, keep, or preserve something such as a law, trust, or promise ○ *a breach of confidentiality* **2. ESTRANGEMENT** a breakdown in friendly relations **3. HOLE** a hole in something that is caused by something else forcing its way through **4. GAP** a gap that results when somebody or something leaves **5. WHALE'S LEAP** a leap out of the water by a whale ■ *v* (**breached, breach·ing, breach·es**) **1.** *vt* **BREAK LAW OR PROMISE** to fail to obey, keep, or preserve something such as a law, trust, or promise **2.** *vt* **MAKE OPENING THROUGH SOMETHING** to break down an obstruction to allow something to pass through it **3.** *vt* **SURPASS LIMIT** to go beyond a target or limit ○ *a proposal to breach the budgetary limit* **4.** *vti* **LEAP OUT** to leap out of the water (*refers to whales*) [13C. < Old French *breche* < Germanic] —**breach·a·ble** *adj*

SPELLCHECK breach or **breech**? Do not confuse the spelling of ***breach*** and ***breech***, which sound similar. ***Breach*** is a noun or verb referring to an opening or the breaking of something, as in *step into the breach, a breach of the peace, to breach their defenses.* ***Breech*** is a noun denoting the rear part of a gun barrel or of the body, as in *a breech birth.*

breach of prom·ise *n* a failure to fulfill a promise, especially formerly the breaking of a promise to marry somebody

breach of the peace *n UK* the criminal offense of behaving in a noisy and violent way in public

bread /bred/ *n* **1. FOOD MADE FROM FLOUR AND WATER** a food typically made by mixing flour, water, and yeast and allowing it to rise before baking it **2. MEANS OF SURVIVAL** food, sustenance, or a means of survival or support **3. MONEY** money to live on (*dated slang*) [Old English *brēad*, origin ?] ◇ **cast your bread upon the waters** to spend time and effort, especially to help others, without expecting any immediate advantage for yourself (*literary*) ◇ **know which side your bread is buttered (on)** to know what is to your advantage (*informal*)

SPELLCHECK bread or **bred**? Do not confuse the spelling of ***bread*** and ***bred*** (past tense and past participle of *breed*), which sound similar.

bread and but·ter *n* **1.** a dependable source of income **2.** something that is the essential or sustaining part of something else

bread-and-but·ter *adj* **1.** concerned with basic but important things **2.** providing the main source of somebody's income or livelihood ○ *a bread-and-butter job*

bread-and-but·ter let·ter, bread-and-but·ter note *n* a letter or note expressing thanks for somebody's hospitality

bread-and-but·ter pud·ding *n UK* FOOD same as **bread pudding**

bread and cir·cus·es *npl* something done or given to keep people happy, especially something provided or encouraged by governments to win popular appeal or avert public unrest [Translation of Latin *panis et circenses*]

bread·bas·ket /bréd bàskit/ *n* **1.** BASKET FOR BREAD a basket in which bread is served **2.** CEREAL-GROWING REGION a region that is an important grower of grain **3.** BELLY the stomach or abdomen (*dated slang*)

bread bin *n UK* HH same as **breadbox**

bread·board /bréd bàwrd/ *n* **1.** BOARD FOR CUTTING BREAD ON a board for cutting or kneading bread on **2.** ELEC ENG TEST VERSION OF ELECTRICAL CIRCUIT a preliminary version of an electrical or electronic circuit put together for test purposes ■ *vt* (**-board·ed, -board·ing, -boards**) ELEC ENG MAKE TEST VERSION OF CIRCUIT to make a preliminary version of an electrical or electronic circuit for test purposes —**bread·board·ing** *n*

bread·box /bréd bòks/ *n* a container in which to store bread to keep it fresh

bread·crumb /bréd krùm/ *n* a tiny piece of bread, either soft or hard (*often used in the plural*)

bread·ed /bréddəd/ *adj* describes food that is coated in breadcrumbs and fried or baked ○ *breaded chicken fillets*

bread·fruit /bréd froot/ (*plural same or* **-fruits**) *n* **1.** a large round seedless tropical fruit **2.** an evergreen tree that bears breadfruit. Native to: Pacific Islands. Latin name: *Artocarpus altilis*. [Late 17C. Because it has a texture like bread when cooked]

bread·line /bréd līn/ *n* **1.** a line of people waiting for handouts of free food **2.** *UK* a very low standard of living, with only just enough food and money to survive [Originally "line of people for unsold bread"]

bread mold *n* a fungus that grows on decaying bread and other foods, forming a dense cottony growth. Latin name: *Rhizopus nigricans*.

bread·nut /bréd nùt/ *n* **1.** the large edible seed of a yellow tropical fruit **2.** a large tree with yellow fruits containing breadnuts. Native to: tropical America. Latin name: *Brosimum alicastrum*.

bread pud·ding *n* a dessert made with buttered bread that is layered in a dish, sometimes with raisins, covered in a mixture of egg, sugar, milk, and spices and then baked

bread·root /bréd ròot, -ròot/ *n* **1.** a starchy tuber, formerly used as food by many Native North American peoples **2.** a perennial plant of the pea family that produces breadroot. Native to: North America. Latin name: *Psoralea esculenta*.

bread·stuff /bréd stùf/ *n* bread in any form, or the flour, meal, or grain used to make it

breadth /bredth/ *n* **1.** DISTANCE FROM SIDE TO SIDE the distance or measurement of something from one side to the other **2.** STANDARD WIDTH OF FABRIC a standardized width that a product, especially fabric, is manufactured in, or a piece of fabric in a standardized width **3.** GREAT EXTENT the extent of something, especially when it is impressively great ○ *the breadth of her knowledge* **4.** BROAD-MINDEDNESS an open and tolerant view of life and the world ○ *breadth of vision* [Early 16C. < obsolete *brede* "breadth" < Germanic, after LENGTH]

breadth·ways /brédth wàyz/, **breadth·wise** /-wīz/ *adv* with the broad side of something facing forward

bread·win·ner /bréd wìnnər/ *n* somebody whose earnings are a family's main income

break /brayk/ *v* (**broke, bro·ken** /brṓkən/ *or* **broke** *regional archaic* /brōk/, **break·ing, breaks**) **1.** *vti* SEPARATE SOMETHING INTO PIECES to become damaged and separate into pieces, or damage something so that it separates into pieces ○ *It broke in two.* **2.** *vti* DAMAGE BODY PART to damage a hard body part such as a bone, or sustain such a break ○ *She broke her leg.* **3.** *vti* DAMAGE PART OF MACHINE to damage a part of a tool or machine so that it stops functioning properly, or become damaged and stop functioning properly ○ *The washing machine is broken.* **4.** *vti* TEAR SURFACE to become torn, or make a tear or hole in a surface or seal, allowing the possibility of a leak or spill ○ *Store the milk in the refrigerator after breaking open the seal on the bottle.* **5.** *vt* DISOBEY RULE to disobey a rule or law ○ *He's broken the law.* **6.** *vt* GO BACK ON WORD to renege on a promise or agreement ○ *broke her word* **7.** *vt* END BAD SITUATION to end, change, or rectify a difficult or disadvantageous situation ○ *break the deadlock between rival factions* **8.** *vt* END SILENCE to end a period of silence **9.** *vti* FINISH RELATIONSHIP to end an involvement with a person or group **10.** *vt* END SOMETHING to finish something, bring it to an end, or stop somebody doing it ○ *break the coffee-drinking habit* **11.** *vt* INTERRUPT SOMETHING to interrupt something temporarily ○ *The distraction broke her train of thought.* **12.** *vt* RUIN SOMEBODY'S LIFE to destroy somebody's career, resolve, courage, or hope of success ○ *The media can make or break her.* **13.** *vti* ESCAPE to escape from a restraint ○ *break free* **14.** *vi* TAKE PERIOD FOR REST to take a rest period from work or an activity ○ *break for lunch* **15.** *vt* STAND BETWEEN PERSON AND SOMETHING to stand in the way of or weaken the force of something such as a fall or blow ○ *He tried to break her fall.* **16.** *vt* BEAT RECORD to beat a previous record **17.** *vt* EXCEED LIMIT to exceed a limit or constraint ○ *break the speed limit* **18.** *vti* REVEAL OR BE REVEALED to reveal something personally, or be revealed, particularly by the media ○ *She broke it to me gently.* ○ *Panic ensued when the news broke.* **19.** *vi* BECOME DEEPER to settle into an adult man's voice register (*refers to a boy's voice*) **20.** *vi* STOP SPEAKING FROM EMOTION to stop speaking and hesitate when overcome with emotion ○ *Her voice broke and tears slid down her face.* **21.** *vi* MUSIC CHANGE TONE WITH REGISTER to change in tone or quality when changing register (*refers to voices or musical instruments*) **22.** *vi* BECOME DAYLIGHT to become light at sunrise **23.** *vi US, Carib* MOVE SUDDENLY to move suddenly or quickly toward somebody or something ○ *broke for the nearest shelter from the storm* **24.** *vi* METEOROL CHANGE WEATHER PATTERN to change after a settled period of weather **25.** *vi* METEOROL SUDDENLY START to begin to rain, snow, or hail suddenly **26.** *vi* OCEANOG TURN TO SURF to start collapsing into surf when close to shore or hitting rocks or similar objects (*refers to waves*) **27.** *vt* INTERPRET CODE to understand a code and be able to translate it accurately **28.** *vt* PROVE SOMETHING UNTRUE to prove that something is untrue or wrong ○ *new evidence that broke the defendant's alibi* **29.** *vt* LAW INVALIDATE WILL to use legal means to declare a will invalid **30.** *vt* CRIME BLOW OPEN SAFE to open a safe using explosives **31.** *vt* RIDING TRAIN HORSE TO ACCEPT HARNESS to train a horse to become accustomed to a saddle, bit, and rider **32.** *vt* MONEY SWAP BILL FOR CHANGE to exchange a bill of money for smaller units of money, either coins or smaller bills and coins ○ *break a $20 bill* **33.** *vi* MED FLOW OUT IN CHILDBIRTH to flow out when the amniotic sac around an unborn baby breaks during the first stage of labor (*refers to amniotic fluid*) ○ *Her water has broken.* **34.** *vi* TURN OUT to happen or turn out in a particular way ○ *Things are breaking well.* **35.** *vt* REDUCE TO POVERTY to cause somebody to be extremely poor or bankrupt **36.** *vti* FISH EMERGE OUT OF WATER to emerge or erupt above the surface of a body of water **37.** *vt* MIL DEMOTE SOMEBODY to demote somebody to a lower rank **38.** *vt* ELEC INTERRUPT FLOW OF ELECTRIC CURRENT to interrupt the flow of electricity in an electrical circuit **39.** *vi* FIN FALL SHARPLY to fall in price (*refers to stock exchange quotations*) **40.** *vti* TENNIS WIN GAME OFF OPPONENT'S SERVICE in tennis, to win a game in which the other player is serving **41.** *vi* BOXING, WRESTLING SEPARATE FROM CLINCH to separate after being in a boxing or wrestling clinch **42.** *vi* SPORTS SPEED UP IN RACE to increase speed suddenly in a race **43.** *vi* BASEBALL CHANGE DIRECTION IN AIR to change direction while moving through the air (*refers to a baseball*) **44.** *vi* CRICKET CHANGE DIRECTION ON BOUNCING to change direction after bouncing (*refers to a cricket ball*) **45.** *vt* CRICKET KNOCK OVER WICKET in cricket, to hit and knock over a bail from the wicket **46.** *vi* HORSERACING START OFF IN HORSERACE in horseracing, to start off at the start of a race **47.** *vi* CUE GAMES TAKE FIRST SHOT in billiards or pool, to take the opening shot in a game or frame **48.** *vi* PHON BECOME DIPHTHONG to change in pronunciation, becoming a diphthong (*refers to vowels*) **49.** *vt Carib* ENTER A PLACE ILLEGALLY to enter a place illegally to steal ○ *They broke two houses last night.* **50.** *vi Carib* HAVE ORGASM to have an orgasm (*slang; usually refers to men*) ■ *n* **1.** PERIOD OFF FROM ACTIVITY a period taken away from an activity for a rest, change, or meal ○ *a lunch break* ○ *Let's take a break now.* **2.** BRIEF VACATION a short vacation away from home ○ *a weekend break* ○ *We needed to get away for a short break.* **3.** PERIOD OFF BEFORE CONTINUING a period away from something before continuing it again ○ *a career break* **4.** *UK* EDUC same as **recess** *n* (sense 1) **5.** END TO RELATIONSHIP the severance of links with a person or group or an end to a relationship ○ *He wanted to make the break with his partner.* **6.** END an end to something ○ *a break with tradition* **7.** BROADCAST, MARKETING same as **commercial break** **8.** SPORTS INTERVAL IN MATCH an interval in a sports match **9.** PAUSE IN SPEECH a pause when speaking ○ *a break in the conversation* **10.** MED FRACTURE a fracture in a bone **11.** CRACK a crack in something **12.** METEOROL WEATHER CHANGE a change in the weather **13.** LUCKY OPPORTUNITY FOR SUCCESS an unexpected opportunity that allows somebody to achieve something or become successful (*informal*) ○ *He got his first break when he was spotted playing college football.* **14.** PIECE OF LUCK a piece of good luck or bad luck ○ *a lucky break* ○ *a bad break* **15.** FIN ADVANTAGEOUS FINANCIAL SITUATION an advantageous financial situation in which somebody is repaid or makes a reduced payment ○ *a tax break* **16.** ESCAPE ATTEMPT a sudden attempt to escape ○ *make a break for it* **17.** DISCONTINUITY a discontinuity in something, by which it changes in quality or level **18.** SUNRISE the time when the sun first rises (*literary*) ○ *at the break of day* **19.** TENNIS WINNING OF GAME OFF OPPONENT'S SERVICE in tennis, the winning of a game in which the other player is serving **20.** HORSERACING START OF RACE the start of a horserace **21.** ELEC INTERRUPTION IN FLOW OF ELECTRICITY an interruption in the flow of electricity in an electrical circuit **22.** MUSIC INSTRUMENTAL PART IN SONG an instrumental part in a piece of pop music **23.** MUSIC IMPROVISED JAZZ SOLO an improvised solo part in a piece of jazz music **24.** MUSIC CHANGE IN REGISTER a change in register in a voice or musical instrument **25.** LITERAT same as **caesura** (senses 1–2) **26.** FIN FALL IN PRICES a sudden fall in prices, particularly in a stock market **27.** CUE GAMES SERIES OF SUCCESSFUL SHOTS in billiards or pool, a sequence of successful shots in one player's turn, or the points scored from them **28.** CUE GAMES FIRST SHOT THAT SCATTERS BALLS in billiards or pool, an opening shot, which in pool scatters the balls **29.** BOWLING FAILURE TO KNOCK DOWN ALL PINS a failure to knock down all the pins in bowling after the second throw **30.** MEDIA ACCESS TO CB RADIO CHANNEL access for a CB radio operator to a radio channel ■ *interj* BOXING, WRESTLING USED TO SEPARATE FIGHTERS used to command boxers or wrestlers to separate from a clinch [Old English *brecan* < Indo-European] ◇ **break even** to make neither a profit nor a loss from a venture ◇ **give somebody a break** to stop nagging or criticizing somebody, or start treating somebody fairly (*informal*) ◇ **if it ain't broke, don't fix it** do not try to improve something that is satisfactory as it is (*informal*) ◇ **make a clean break** to end a relationship or association completely and permanently

SPELLCHECK break or **brake**? Do not confuse the spelling of ***break*** and ***brake***, which sound similar. Both words can be used as nouns or verbs, but ***break*** has a wider range of meaning and is the more frequent of the two, generally referring to separation, destruction, violation, or interruption, as in *to break a window, to break the rules, a break for refreshments*. ***Brake*** means "a device used to slow or stop a vehicle" or "apply a brake" and is sometimes used figuratively, as in *put a brake on expenditure*. ***Brake*** is also another word for bracken or undergrowth and the name of a type of fern.

break away *vi* **1.** LEAVE OR GET AWAY to sever relations with or detach from a person or group **2.** DEPART FROM CUSTOM to change or depart from established customs or procedures **3.** PULL AWAY QUICKLY to depart or pull away from somebody or something, usually at high speed **4.** *Carib* BECOME UNCONTROLLABLE to get out of control

break down *v* **1.** *vt* TEAR DOWN to destroy something, or cause something to fall or collapse **2.** *vti* BECOME OR MAKE EMOTIONAL to become upset emotionally, or cause somebody to become upset emotionally **3.** *vti* EXPERIENCE OR CAUSE HEALTH COLLAPSE to experience, or cause somebody to experience, a physical or psychological collapse **4.** *vti* STOP RESISTING to yield or end any resistance, or cause somebody to yield or somebody's resistance to end **5.** *vi* FAIL TO FUNCTION PROPERLY to stop working, or stop working properly, effectively, or usefully **6.** *vti* **WEAKEN** to become weak and ineffective, or cause somebody or something to become weak and ineffective **7.** *vt* **ANALYZE SOMETHING BY DIVIDING INTO PARTS** to analyze or examine something by reducing it to its simplest terms or component parts **8.** *vi* **BE DIVISIBLE INTO ELEMENTS** to divide into separate parts when analyzed, or be reducible to separate parts **9.** *vti* **DECOMPOSE CHEMICALLY** to decompose chemically, or cause something to undergo chemical decomposition **10.** *vi* ELEC ENG **EXPERIENCE ELECTRICAL INSULATION FAILURE** to experience a sudden failure of an insulating material to halt the current flow

break in *v* **1.** *vi* **ENTER FORCIBLY** to enter a place or building forcibly and usually illegally **2.** *vi* **START TALKING** to interrupt a conversation or discussion **3.** *vt* **BEGIN USING SOMEBODY OR SOMETHING NEW** to begin to employ somebody new, supplying the training needed for good performance, or use something new, providing necessary modifications ○ *breaking the new assistant in gently*

break into *vt* **1. ENTER BUILDING FORCIBLY** to enter a building or place forcibly and usually illegally **2. INTERRUPT CONVERSATION** to interrupt something that is being said or discussed **3. DO SOMETHING SUDDENLY** to begin an act or activity suddenly ○ *broke into song* ○ *broke into a run* **4. START WORK IN NEW FIELD** to begin working in a profession or field, often after having tried to do so for some time without success ○ *break into television*

break off *v* **1.** *vt* **TAKE OFF PIECE OF SOMETHING** to separate a piece from a solid mass or the main part of something **2.** *vti* **END RELATIONSHIP OR JOINT ACTIVITY** to discontinue a relationship or interaction with a person or group **3.** *vi* **STOP SPEAKING** to stop talking, usually abruptly **4.** *vi regional* METEOROL same as **clear up** (sense 1)

break out *v* **1.** *vi* **BEGIN ABRUPTLY** to happen or begin suddenly and strongly **2.** *vi* **HAVE SKIN RASH** to develop a case of acne or a rash, especially suddenly **3.** *vi* **BECOME FREE FROM SOMETHING** to escape or emerge from something such as a prison that confines, restrains, or traps **4.** *vt* **PREPARE SOMETHING FOR USE** to open something or get something ready for use or action ○ *broke out the emergency rations* **5.** *vt* **CLASSIFY DATA ITEMS** to classify, summarize, outline, or separate data items in order to analyze, explain, or identify something

break through *vti* to burst or advance quickly and suddenly through an obstruction or opposition

break up *v* **1.** *vt* **DIVIDE OR INTERRUPT SOMETHING** to divide or separate something into pieces, or interrupt its continuity **2.** *vti* **END** to cause a relationship, interaction, or gathering to end, or come to an end **3.** *vi* **DISPERSE** to separate and go in different directions, or have members separate **4.** *vti* **CAUSE EMOTIONAL RESPONSE** to burst into tears or laughter, or cause somebody to burst into tears or laughter **5.** *vi* TELECOM **LOSE PHONE COMMUNICATION** to start to lose clear communication when using a cellular phone ○ *You're breaking up.*

break with *vt* to separate from somebody or from a tradition, rule, or trend

break·a·ble /bráykəb'l/ *adj* likely to be broken if not handled carefully ■ *n* something that is easily broken if not handled carefully (*usually used in the plural*) —**break·a·ble·ness** *n*

break·age /bráykij/ *n* **1. SOMETHING BROKEN** something that has been broken, usually accidentally (*usually used in the plural*) ○ *All breakages must be paid for.* **2. ACT OF BREAKING** the act of breaking something **3. DAMAGE** damage as a result of breaking something

break·a·way /bráykə wày/ *n* **1. SOMETHING BREAKING OFF** somebody or something that breaks away or has broken away **2. SOMETHING MADE TO BREAK OFF** something that is designed to break away or break apart from the whole **3. ACT OF BREAKING AWAY** the breaking away of somebody or something **4.** SPORTS **QUICK SURGE FORWARD** in sports, a sudden attack or movement away from the rest of a group of players or competitors **5.** *Carib* **DANCE STYLE** a lively style of dancing **6.** *Carib* **DANCE MUSIC** the music for breakaway dancing, usually calypso ■ *adj* **1. MADE TO BREAK OFF** designed to break away or apart, either as a safety mechanism or to create an illusion **2. HAVING SEVERED TIES** having broken ties or connections to somebody or a group ■ *vi Carib* **DANCE WITH INDIVIDUAL STYLE** to dance to a section of music that has heavy rhythm and brass, especially with individually improvised movements

break·beat /bráyk bèet/ *n* a drum pattern with a syncopated beat that is electronically looped, used mostly in jungle, drum and bass, and hard-core music

break·bone fe·ver /bràyk bōn-/ *n* MED same as **dengue**

break·danc·ing /bráyk dànssing/ *n* an acrobatic style of solo dancing to rap music, typically involving spinning of the body on the ground. Breakdancing started in the United States in the 1980s. [Late 20C. Perhaps related to BREAKDOWN "fast dance"] —**break·dance** *n, vi* —**break·danc·er** *n*

break·down /bráyk dòwn/ *n* **1. FAILURE TO OPERATE** a failure to operate, or an interruption of the operation of a machine or vehicle **2. DISRUPTION IN COMMUNICATIONS** a disruption of the understanding and interaction between people or groups ○ *the breakdown in the talks* **3.** MED **PERSONAL HEALTH CRISIS** a sudden physical or psychological collapse **4. DATA SUMMARY OR EXPLANATION** a summary, explanation, or analysis of data items collected **5. DECOMPOSITION INTO PARTS** a breaking down of something into its essential components or parts **6.** ELEC ENG **SUDDEN PASSAGE OF CURRENT THROUGH INSULATOR** the sudden passage of electrical current through an insulator **7.** DANCE **FOLK DANCE** a fast US folk dance

break·down lor·ry, **break·down truck** *n UK* same as **wrecker**

break·down volt·age *n* the voltage at which a sudden and large increase in current through an insulator or semiconductor happens

break·er[1] /bráykər/ *n* **1. LARGE WHITE-CAPPED WAVE** a large, usually white-capped, wave that is cresting or breaking, especially onto a shore **2.** ELEC ENG same as **circuit breaker 3. BREAKDANCER** somebody who does breakdancing (*slang*) **4. BREAKING MACHINE** something that is used to crush or break up rocks, fibers, or other substances **5. HORSE TRAINER** somebody who trains horses to be ridden ■ *interj* **OPENING MESSAGE OF RADIO TRANSMISSION** used by CB radio operators to announce that they are beginning to transmit on a channel [12C. < BREAK]

break·er[2] /bráykər/ *n* a small cask for water, used especially on a lifeboat [Mid-19C. < Spanish *barrica* "cask"]

break-e·ven /bràyk éevən/, **break-e·ven point** *n* the point or level of financial activity at which expenditure equals income or the value of an investment equals its cost, with the result that there is neither a profit nor a loss

break·fast /brékfəst/ *n* the first meal of the day, usually eaten in the morning (*often used before a noun*) [15C. < BREAK + FAST[2]] —**break·fast** *vi* —**break·fast·er** *n* ◇ **eat** *or* **have somebody for breakfast** to defeat or destroy somebody without any difficulty whatsoever (*slang*) ○ *The tabloid media will eat the movie star for breakfast over this revelation.*

break·fast bar *n* **1.** a breakfast served buffet style in a hotel or restaurant with a variety of foods from which to choose **2.** a counter in a kitchen at which informal meals and snacks are served

break·fast pa·per *n* MEDIA the early morning edition of a newspaper ○ *"Reporters from powerful breakfast papers humbled themselves..."* (James Wolcott *Vanity Fair*; June 2003) [Because usually read at breakfast.]

break·fast shed *n Carib* **1.** a building where schools or charities supply meals at very low cost, usually for children **2.** a restaurant that serves creole and local food, where customers choose which food they want from a number of cooks who share the premises

break·front /bráyk frùnt/ *adj* describes a piece of furniture such as a cabinet or bookcase with a central section that juts forward slightly —**break·front** *n*

break-in *n* **1.** an illegal forced entry into a building or enclosed place **2.** a trial run or an initial period of employment or operation during which somebody's or something's performance is evaluated and training or troubleshooting is done

break·ing /bráyking/ *n* **1.** the changing of a simple vowel into a diphthong when some other speech sounds come before or after it. For example, the vowel in "feet" becomes a diphthong in "feel." **2.** DANCE same as **breakdancing** (*slang*)

break·ing and en·ter·ing *n* the crime of forcibly entering property, usually in order to steal from it

break·ing point *n* **1.** the point at which somebody loses the ability to deal physically, psychologically, or emotionally with a stressful situation **2.** the point at which a condition or situation reaches a crisis

break·neck /bráyk nèk/ *adj* so fast or quick as to be hazardous or reckless ○ *at breakneck speed*

break of day *n* the time when the sun rises in the morning

break·off /bráyk àwf, -òf/ *n* a discontinuation of something, especially when this is abrupt ○ *the breakoff of negotiations*

break·out /bráyk òwt/ *n* **1.** a forceful escape or emergence from being confined, restrained, or trapped **2.** a summary or breakdown of data that has been collected

break point *n* in tennis, a point that, if won, results in the player who is not serving winning the game

break·point /bráyk pòynt/ *n* **1.** a point where something stops, pauses, changes, or breaks apart **2.** a pause inserted into a computer program so that the registers and memory locations can be examined to correct a programming logic error

break·through /bráyk thròo/ *n* **1. IMPORTANT DISCOVERY** an important new discovery, especially in science, medicine, or technology, that has a dramatic and far-reaching effect **2. REMOVAL OF BARRIER TO PROGRESS** an event that causes or marks the breaking down of a barrier to progress **3.** MIL **PENETRATION OF ENEMY LINE** an attacking army's advance through and beyond an enemy's line of defense ■ *adj* **BRINGING PUBLIC RECOGNITION** bringing public attention and fame to a performer

break·through bleed·ing *n* bleeding from the womb that occurs between menstrual periods

break·up /bráyk ùp/ *n* **1. BREAKING APART OR UP** the separation of something such as a company or country into separate units ○ *the breakup of the Soviet Union* **2. END OF RELATIONSHIP** the breaking off or discontinuation of a personal relationship **3. SPRING THAW OF LODGED ICE** the melting or breaking apart of lodged ice in rivers and harbors in the spring **4. EMOTIONAL BREAKDOWN** a loss of control over the emotions

break·up val·ue *n* the amount that a company would be worth if it were liquidated for its assets. It is sometimes expressed as an amount per share.

break·wa·ter /bráyk wàwtər/ *n* an offshore barrier that protects a harbor or other coastal area from the full force of the sea

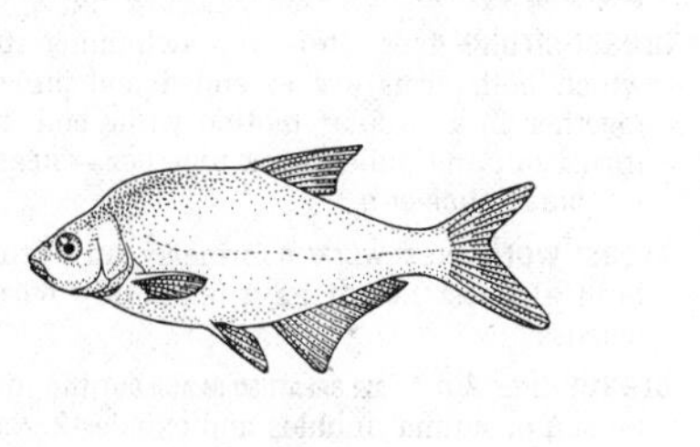

bream

bream[1] /breem, brim/ (*plural same* or **breams**) *n* **1. THIN-BODIED FRESHWATER FISH** a freshwater fish that has a deep thin body and is yellowish in color. Native to: Europe, Asia. Latin name: *Abramis brama.* **2. FRESHWATER FISH LIKE BREAM** a freshwater fish that resembles the bream. Native to: North America, introduced into Europe and Asia. Genus: *Lepomis.* **3.** FISH same as **sea bream** (sense 2) **4. FOOD** the flesh of a bream as food [14C. < Old French *bre(s)me* < Germanic]

bream[2] /breem/ (**breamed, bream·ing, breams**) *vt* to scrape the shells, seaweed, and mud off the bottom of a boat (*archaic*) [Early 17C. Probably < Middle Dutch *bremme* "broom, furze"]

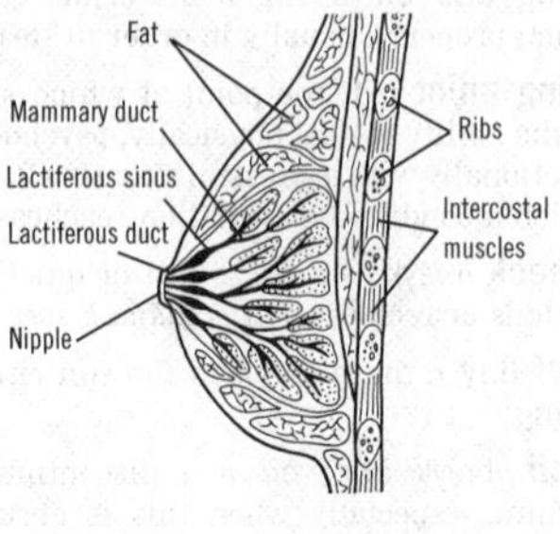

breast: cross section of female breast

breast /brest/ *n* **1. ORGAN ON CHEST** either of two soft rounded organs on each side of the chest in women and men. In women the organs are more prominent and produce milk after childbirth. **2.** ZOOL **MAMMAL'S MILK GLAND** a milk-producing gland in mammals that corresponds to the human breast **3. SOMEBODY'S CHEST** the front of the human chest **4.** CLOTHING **GARMENT SECTION** the part or section of clothing covering the front of the chest **5.** ZOOL **ANIMAL'S CHEST** the chest of an animal, especially a mammal or bird **6.** FOOD **MEAT FROM ANIMAL'S CHEST** meat from the chest of an animal, especially from a chicken or other poultry **7. ROUNDED PART** a part that is rounded or projecting, or in some way resembles a breast ○ *the breast of a hill* **8. SEAT OF EMOTIONS** the chest regarded as the place where human emotions reside (*literary*) ○ *with pride filling my breast* **9. FONT OF NOURISHMENT** a source of sustenance or protection (*literary*) ■ *vt* (**breast·ed, breast·ing, breasts**) **1. PUSH SOMETHING WITH CHEST** to touch or push against something with the chest ○ *She breasted the tape just seconds ahead of the next runner.* **2. REACH HILLTOP** to reach the summit of a hill **3. FACE SOMETHING BOLDLY** to confront a difficulty squarely and boldly and deal with it in a determined way [Old English *brēost* < Germanic, perhaps < Indo-European, "swelling"] ◇ **make a clean breast of something** to confess or admit to something, especially something previously denied or withheld

breast·bone /brést bōn/ *n* a long bone running down the front of the chest, flat in many animals but ridged in most birds. In humans, the top seven pairs of ribs are connected to it.

REGIONAL NOTE See ***pulley bone***.

breast-feed *vti* to feed a baby by holding it so that it can suck milk from the breast (*refers to women*)

breast·plate /brést plàyt/ *n* **1.** a piece of armor that covers the chest **2.** a garment worn over the breast by Jewish high priests in ancient times, set with 12 precious stones representing the 12 tribes of Israel

breast·stroke /brést stròk/ *n* a swimming stroke in which both arms are extended and pulled back together in a circular motion while both legs are thrust out and pulled back together —**breast·stroke** *vi* —**breast·strok·er** *n*

breast·work /brést wùrk/ *n* formerly, an earthen wall built at chest height as a temporary barrier for defense

breath /breth/ *n* **1. AIR BREATHED IN AND OUT** the air that a person or animal inhales and exhales **2. AIR EXHALED** the air that somebody exhales, especially with reference to how it feels or smells to somebody nearby **3. BREATHING OF AIR** an inhaling or exhaling of air, or the entire process of inhaling and exhaling ○ *take a deep breath* **4. HINT** a faint hint of something ○ *a breath of scandal* **5. LIFE** the vital force or spirit of a living person or animal **6. SHORT PAUSE** a momentary pause or respite **7. WAFT** a fleeting or slight fragrance or movement of air ○ *not a breath of wind* **8. SOFT SOUND** a sound or whispering that is soft and almost inaudible [Old English *bræ* "odor, especially of something burning or cooking" < Indo-European, "heat"] ◇ **a breath of fresh air** somebody or something that is refreshingly new and exciting ◇ **catch your breath 1.** to stop breathing for an instant, especially because of shock or physical pain **2.** to regain a normal breathing rhythm after exertion ◇ **don't hold your breath** used to indicate that it is extremely unlikely that something will happen (*informal*) ◇ **in the same breath** at almost the same moment or shortly afterward ◇ **out of breath** breathing heavily because of physical exertion ◇ **take somebody's breath away** to astonish or greatly impress somebody ◇ **under your breath** in a whispering or muttering voice ◇ **with bated breath** full of anxious anticipation

USAGE breath or **breathe**? The noun is ***breath*** (*not a breath of air moving*), and the verb is ***breathe*** (*hard to breathe in the sultry air*). Only the verb has the *-e* at the end.

breath·a·ble /bréethəb'l/ *adj* **1.** suitable or possible for people to breathe **2.** describes fabric that allows air in and body moisture out in order to keep the wearer cool and dry —**breath·a·bil·i·ty** /brèethə bíllətee/ *n*

Breath·a·lyz·er /brétha lìzər/ *tdmk* a trademark for an apparatus that measures a subject's blood alcohol concentration from his or her breath

breathe /breeth/ (**breathed, breath·ing, breathes**) *v* **1.** *vti* **TAKE IN AIR** to repeatedly and alternately take in and blow out air in order to stay alive ○ *breathe in deeply* **2.** *vt* **EXPEL SUBSTANCE WITH BREATH** to expel fire, smoke, or other gas from the mouth or nose along with the breath, or be exhaled in this way ○ *a dragon breathing fire* **3.** *vt* **SMELL SOMETHING** to take in the aroma of something **4.** *vti* **TAKE IN AIR** to take in air, e.g., for combustion or in order to equalize internal and external pressure (*refers to machines*) **5.** *vi* TEXTILES **ALLOW AIR THROUGH** to allow air and moisture to pass through fabric or clothing **6.** *vt* **SAY SOMETHING SECRETIVELY** to say something in a soft voice or secretively **7.** *vt* **GIVE SOMEBODY OR SOMETHING QUALITY** to instill a particular quality in somebody or something ○ *breathed new life into the group* **8.** *vti* **EXUDE QUALITY** to suggest a quality in abundance, or be suggested or displayed noticeably **9.** *vi* **LIVE** to be alive **10.** *vi* **DEVELOP FLAVOR THROUGH EXPOSURE TO AIR** to be exposed to air in order to develop flavor (*refers to wine*) **11.** *vti* **PAUSE TO REST** to give a person or an animal such as a horse time to rest and allow a normal breathing rhythm to be restored **12.** *vi* **WAFT GENTLY** to blow softly or move gently [13C. < BREATH] ◇ **breathe easy** *or* **freely** *or* **easily** to relax and stop worrying about something or things in general

USAGE See ***breath***.

breathed /bretht, breethd/ *adj* **1.** pronounced without vibrating the vocal cords **2.** with a particular type of breathing (*usually used in combination*)

breath·er /bréethər/ *n* **1.** a short rest while in the middle of doing something (*informal*) ○ *In extreme heat you have to make sure you take a breather every hour or so.* **2.** a vent in an area or enclosure that is otherwise sealed

breath·ing /bréething/ *n* **1.** the process of taking air into the lungs and pushing it out again **2.** in ancient Greek, the pronouncing of an initial vowel with an "h" sound before it (**rough breathing**), or without an "h" sound (**smooth breathing**), or either of the symbols indicating these pronunciations

breath·ing room *n US* an opportunity to relax or straighten out problems without pressure, constraints, interruptions, or interference. Can term **breathing space**

breath·less /bréthləss/ *adj* **1. UNABLE TO BREATHE PROPERLY** experiencing difficulty in breathing, or breathing faster than normal, because of physical exertion or illness **2. WITH SHALLOW BREATHING** breathing very shallowly because of intense emotion such as fear or excitement **3. EXCITING OR INTENSE** capable of causing difficulties in breathing because of intense excitement, emotion, or speed ○ *breathless speed* **4. HOT AND WITHOUT BREEZE** lacking any air movement or breeze ○ *a breathless room* **5. NOT ALIVE** dead and no longer breathing (*literary*) —**breath·less·ly** *adv* —**breath·less·ness** *n*

breath·tak·ing /bréth tàyking/ *adj* evoking strong emotions, especially excitement, awe, or shock —**breath·tak·ing·ly** *adv*

breath test *n* a test using a device that a person breathes into to determine the level of alcohol in the breath, especially one conducted by police on the driver of a road vehicle

breath·y /bréthee/ (**-i·er, -i·est**) *adj* **1.** with a discernible sound of breathing accompanying spoken words **2.** without proper control of the breath, which creates an uneven or weak vocal or instrumental sound —**breath·i·ly** *adv* —**breath·i·ness** *n*

Bré·beuf /bráy bōōf/, **Jean de, St.** (1593–1649) French-born Canadian missionary. He worked as a Jesuit missionary among the Huron people in Canada after 1625.

brec·ci·a /bréchee ə, bréchə, bréshee ə, bréshə/ *n* a coarse-grained sedimentary rock made of sharp fragments of rock and stone cemented together by finer material. Breccia is produced by volcanic activity or erosion, including frost shattering. [Late 18C. < Italian, "gravel"] —**brec·ci·al** *adj* —**brec·ci·ate** /-ayt/ *vti* —**brec·ci·a·tion** /brèchee áysh'n/ *n*

Brecht /brekt, brekht/, **Bertolt** (1898–1956) German playwright and director. One of the most influential dramatists of the 20th century, he was the author of *The Threepenny Opera* (1928) in collaboration with Kurt Weill, *Mother Courage* (1941), and *The Caucasian Chalk Circle* (1945). After 1948 he worked with the Berliner Ensemble in East Berlin. Full name **Brecht, Eugene Bertolt Friedrich**

> "Those who have had no share in the good fortunes of the mighty often have a share in their misfortunes."
> [Bertolt Brecht, *The Caucasian Chalk Circle*; 1945; tr. 1948]

Breck·in·ridge /brékən rìj/, **John C.** (1821–75) US soldier and politician. He was James Buchanan's vice president (1857–61). During the Civil War he was a Confederate general and secretary of war. Full name **Breckinridge, John Cabell**

bred /bred/ past participle, past tense of **breed** ■ *adj* raised in a particular manner (*used in combination*) ○ *city-bred*

SPELLCHECK See ***bread***.

Bre·da /bréedə/ city in North Brabant Province, the Netherlands, near Rotterdam. Population: 160,398 (2000).

bred-in-the-bone *adj* **1.** deeply ingrained or firmly established **2.** describes a habit, especially a bad habit, that has become deeply ingrained over time

breech /breech/ *n* **1.** ARMS **BACK OF GUN BARREL** the rear part of the barrel of a rifle or shotgun, near the stock **2.** MECH ENG **PART OF PULLEY** the lower part of a pulley block, to which the rope, cable, or chain is fixed **3.** ANAT **BUTTOCKS** the back lower portion of the trunk of the body [Old English *brēc*, plural of *brōc* "garment covering the thighs and lower trunk" < Germanic]

SPELLCHECK See ***breach***.

breech birth *n* the delivery of a baby with its buttocks or feet, rather than its head, emerging first

breech·block /bréech blòk/ *n* the part of a breech-loading gun that is detached from the barrel to allow cartridges to be loaded into the back of the barrel

breech·cloth /bréech klàwth, -klòth/ (*plural* **-cloths**) *n* CLOTHING same as **loincloth**

breech de·liv·er·y *n* MED same as **breech birth**

breech·es /bríchəz, bree-/, **britch·es** /bríchəz/ *npl* **1.** pants with legs that come down to the knee **2.** trousers of any kind (*informal*) [13C. Plural of BREECH]

breech·es buoy *n* a piece of equipment used for transferring people between moving ships, consisting of a canvas harness suspended from a pulley and line that links the ships

breech·ing /bréeching, brích-/ *n* **1.** RIDING **STRAP ON HORSE'S HARNESS** the strap of a harness that passes behind the hindquarters of a horse or donkey **2.** ZOOL **HAIR ON ANIMAL'S HINDQUARTERS** the short hair or wool on the rump and hind legs of an animal such as a sheep, goat, or dog **3.** ARMS **GUN'S BREECH PARTS** parts of a gun that form or make up the breech **4.** NAVY **ROPE SECURING SHIP'S GUN** in former times, ropes used to secure guns to the side of a ship to control the recoil

breech·load·er /breéch lōdər/ *n* a gun that is loaded by inserting cartridges through the back of the barrel —**breech·load·ing** *adj*

breed /breed/ *n* **1.** BIOL **DISTINCT ANIMAL OR PLANT** a strain of an animal or plant with identifiable characteristics that distinguish it from other members of its species, especially one whose characteristics are preserved by controlled mating or propagation **2. SOMEBODY OR SOMETHING OF PARTICULAR TYPE** a particular type of thing or person, especially one that can be easily distinguished from other similar things or people ○ *a new breed of managers* ■ *v* (**bred** /bred/, **breed·ing, breeds**) **1.** *vti* BIOL **MATE AND PRODUCE YOUNG** to mate and give birth to offspring **2.** *vt* AGRIC **RAISE ANIMALS OR PLANTS** to reproduce and raise animals or plants, especially for commercial purposes or for shows and competitions **3.** *vt* GENETICS **SELECT ANIMALS OR PLANTS** to select animals or plants as part of a process of improving or preserving their special characteristics **4.** *vti* **PRODUCE SOMETHING** to produce or create something, or be produced or created ○ *Experience breeds confidence.* **5.** *vt* INDUST **MAKE NUCLEAR FUEL** to make fissionable substances using a breeder reactor [Old English *brēdan* < Indo-European,"heat"]

breed·er /breédər/ *n* **1. SOMEBODY WHO BREEDS ANIMALS OR PLANTS** somebody who breeds animals or propagates plants **2. ANIMAL OR PLANT USED FOR BREEDING** an animal or plant kept to produce offspring **3. CAUSAL FACTOR** a cause or a source of something **4. OFFENSIVE TERM** an offensive term for somebody who is heterosexual (*slang insult*) **5.** INDUST same as **breeder reactor**

breed·er re·ac·tor *n* a nuclear reactor that produces more fuel than it consumes. This kind of reactor is used mainly to produce plutonium.

breed·ing /breéding/ *n* **1. UPBRINGING** somebody's upbringing, education, and training in manners and other social skills, especially an upbringing that produces polished manners and self-assurance **2. ANCESTRY** somebody's family or ancestry **3. REPRODUCTION** the mating and producing of young (*often used before a noun*) ○ *prime breeding stock* **4.** GENETICS **DEVELOPMENT OF IMPROVED SPECIMENS** the development of new types of plants or animals with improved characteristics **5.** INDUST **REACTOR'S FUEL PRODUCTION EXCEEDING CONSUMPTION** production of fissionable material in a breeder reactor in quantities in excess of the fuel it consumes

breed·ing ground *n* **1.** an area where animals mate and produce young **2.** an environment or situation that is likely to produce or encourage a particular phenomenon ○ *The festival is a breeding ground for new comedy talent.*

breeze /breez/ *n* **1.** METEOROL **LIGHT TO MODERATE WIND** a wind ranging in strength from light to moderate, with a speed of 4 to 31 mph/6 to 50 kph **2. SOMETHING EASY** a task or object that is easily achieved (*informal*) ■ *v* (**breezed, breez·ing, breez·es**) **1.** *vi* **GO SOMEWHERE BRISKLY** to move quickly and confidently or cheerfully into or out of a place **2.** *vti* **ACCOMPLISH SOMETHING EASILY** to progress through something easily and with little difficulty or effort ○ *He breezed through his certification test.* [Mid-16C. Probably < Spanish *brisa*, Portuguese *briza* "northeast wind"] ◇ **shoot the breeze** to spend time chatting (*slang*)

breeze block *n UK* INDUST same as **cinder block** [< French *braise* "hot coals"]

breeze·way /breéz wāy/ *n* a roofed passageway with open sides that connects two buildings such as a house and a garage

breez·i·ly /breézəlee/ *adv* in a lively, cheerful, and relaxed way

breez·y /breézee/ (**-i·er, -i·est**) *adj* **1.** with a light to moderate wind **2.** lively, cheerful, and relaxed —**breez·i·ness** *n*

breg·ma /brégmə/ (*plural* **-ma·ta** /-mətə/) *n* the place on the skull at the top of the forehead where the frontal bone and the two parietal bones meet, used as a reference point when measuring skulls [Late 16C. < Greek, "front of the head"] —**breg·mat·ic** /breg máttik/ *adj*

Brel /brel/, **Jacques** (1929–78) Belgian-born French singer and songwriter. His songs included "Les bourgeois" and "Ne me quitte pas," and were widely recorded by other singers, including Frank Sinatra and Ray Charles.

> "I'm obsessed by those things that are ugly and sordid, that people don't want to talk about."
> [Jacques Brel. Quoted in *Jacques Brel*, Alan Clayson; 1996]

Bre·men /bráymən, brémmən/ city, major port, and capital of the state of Bremen in northwestern Germany. It is situated on the Weser River, about 43 mi./69 km from the North Sea. Population: 539,400 (2000).

Bre·mer·ha·ven /bráymər haávən, brémmər-/ port and city in Bremen State, northwestern Germany, on the Weser River estuary. Population: 130,847 (1997).

Brem·er·ton /brémmərtən/ city on Puget Sound in western Washington. Since 1891 it has been the site of the Puget Sound Naval Shipyard, a major US Navy repair and installation center. Population: 36,306 (2002 estimate).

brems·strah·lung /bréms shtraàləng, brémz-/ *n* the electromagnetic radiation that is produced by an electrically charged subatomic particle such as an electron when it is suddenly slowed down by the electric field of an atomic nucleus [Mid-20C. < German < *bremsen* "brake" + *Strahlung* "radiation"]

Bren·dan /bréndən/, **St.** (486?–578?) Irish saint and traveler. He founded the monastery of Clonfert in County Galway (561). Known as **the Navigator**

Bren·nan /brénnən/, **Walter** (1894–1974) US character actor. A three-time Academy Award winner, he is best remembered as Amos McCoy on television's *The Real McCoys* (1957–62).

Bren·nan, William J., Jr. (1906–97) associate justice of the US Supreme Court (1956–90). During his long tenure he was known for his dedication to maintaining freedom of speech. Full name **Brennan, William Joseph, Jr.**

> "Capital punishment...treats members of the human race...as objects to be toyed with and discarded."
> [William J. Brennan, Jr., *Address, University of California, Hastings College of Law, Los Angeles Times*; November 19, 1985]

Bren·ner Pass /brénnər-/ Alpine mountain pass linking Innsbruck, Austria, and Bolzano, Italy. With a maximum elevation of 4,497 ft./1,371 m, it has been an important route between Austria and Italy since antiquity.

brent goose /brént-/ *n UK* BIRDS same as **brant** [Origin ?]

Brent·wood /brént wòod/ community forming part of Islip, a town situated on Long Island, New York. Population: 49,463 (1991).

Br'er /brur, brer/ *n Southern US* a written representation of the way African Americans in the Southern United States supposedly once pronounced the word "brother" when using it as a form of address

bre·sao·la /bre sṓlə, bri zṓlə/ *n* Italian salt-cured air-dried beef. It is often served with a dressing of olive oil, lemon juice, and black pepper. [Late 20C. < Italian < *brasare* "cook slowly"]

Bre·scia /bréshə/ city and capital of Brescia Province, Lombardy Region, northern Italy. Population: 187,576 (2001).

Bres·son /bre sóN/, **Robert** (1907–99) French movie director. His movies include *Diary of a Country Priest* (1951) and *The Trial of Joan of Arc* (1962).

> "I never use professional actors nowadays...For in my opinion the moment actors assume certain expressions, the result cannot be true cinema, only filmed theater."
> [Robert Bresson, *Interview, Montreal Star*; July 16, 1966]

Brest /brest/ port and largest city in Finistère Department in the Bretagne Region, western France. Population: 149,634 (1999).

breth·ren /bréth̲rən/ plural of **brother** *n* (senses 2, 4, 5) ■ *npl* **1.** members of the same family, group, class, or community (*literary or humorous*) ○ *the weaker brethren among us* **2.** the members, especially men, of a church or other religious group (*archaic or literary*) [12C. Old plural of BROTHER]

Breth·ren *npl* a strict Protestant Christian denomination

Bret·on /brétt'n/ *n* **1.** somebody who comes from Brittany **2.** a Celtic language, related to Cornish, that is spoken in mostly rural areas of Brittany. Native speakers: 500,000. —**Bret·on** *adj*

LANGUAGE HERITAGE See ***Celtic.***

Bre·ton /brə tóN/, **André** (1896–1966) French poet and essayist. He was a Dadaist and a founder of the surrealist movement.

> "Subjectivity and objectivity commit a series of assaults on each other during a human life out of which the first one suffers the worse beating."
> [André Breton, *Nadja*; 1928]

Bret·ton Woods /brétt'n-/ tourist resort in New Hampshire. In 1944, it hosted the United Nations Bretton Woods Conference where the International Monetary Fund and the International Bank for Reconstruction and Development were set up. Area: 16 sq. mi./41 sq. km.

Breu·er /bróy ər/, **Josef** (1842–1925) Austrian physician. He pioneered the use of hypnosis in the treatment of hysteria and collaborated briefly with Sigmund Freud on the development of catharsis in psychoanalysis.

Breu·er, Marcel (1902–81) Hungarian-born US architect. He designed the Whitney Museum of American Art (1966) and other modernist buildings, and is regarded as the designer of the tubular steel-framed chair. Full name **Breuer, Marcel Lajos**

Breu·ghel ▸ **Brueghel, Jan**

breve /brev, breev/ *n* **1.** a mark, ˘, placed over a vowel to show that it has a short sound or used to show a short or unstressed syllable in poetry **2.** a musical note that is equal in length to two whole notes [14C. Variant of BRIEF]

bre·vet /brə vét, brévvit/ *n* (*plural* **-vets**) a temporary promotion of a military officer without an increase in pay ■ *vt* (**-vet·ed, -vet·ing, -vets**) to promote a military officer by brevet [14C. < French, "little letter" < Old French *brief* "letter"] —**bre·vet·cy** *n*

bre·vi·ar·y /breévee èrree/ (*plural* **-ies**) *n* in the Roman Catholic Church, a book that contains the hymns, psalms, and prayers prescribed for each day [15C. < Latin *breviarium* "summary, abridgment" < *breviare* "shorten"]

brev·i·ty /brévvətee/ *n* **1.** shortness in time **2.** the economical use of words in speech or writing [15C. Via French < Latin *brevitas* < *brevis* "short"]

brew /broo/ *vti* (**brewed, brew·ing, brews**) **1. MAKE BEER** to make beer or similar alcoholic drinks by a process of steeping, boiling, and fermenting grain with hops, sugar, and other ingredients **2. MAKE TEA OR COFFEE** to prepare tea or coffee for drinking by infusing it to develop its flavor, or infuse to develop flavor **3. DEVELOP THREATENINGLY** to form or develop ominously or threateningly, or concoct something ominous or threatening ○ *A scandal was brewing.* ■ *n* **1. BEER** beer, or a type of beer such as lager or ale ○ *What's the local brew?* **2. BREWED BEVERAGE** a drink such as coffee or tea made by infusion, or a serving of such a drink (*informal*) **3. MIXTURE** a combination of ingredients or components of any kind [Old English *breowan* < Germanic] —**brew·er** *n* —**brew·ing** *n*

brew·er's yeast *n* the yeast that is used in brewing beer, also used as a dietary source of vitamins, especially vitamin B. Latin name: *Saccharomyces cerevisiae.*

brew·er·y /bróo əree, bróoree/ (*plural* **-ies**) *n* a company that brews beer, or a building where beer or a similar drink is brewed

brew·is /bróo iss, brooz/ *n New England* broth thickened with bread, or a dish of bread soaked in milk, broth, or gravy [13C. < Old French *bro(u)ez* (plural), *bro(u)et* (singular) < *breu* < Germanic]

brew·pub /bro͞o pùb/ *n* a restaurant or bar where the beer is made on the premises

Brew·ster /bro͞ostər/, **Sir David** (1781–1868) British physicist. He studied optics and invented the kaleidoscope (1916). Brewster's Law calculates the refraction index of a glass surface.

Brew·ster, William (1567–1644) English-born American spiritual leader of the Plymouth Colony. He sailed as a colonist to what is now Massachusetts on the *Mayflower*.

Brew·ster's law *n* a law relating a material's index of refraction to the tangent of the material's angle of polarization [After Sir David BREWSTER]

Brey·er /brī́ ər/, **Stephen** (*b.* 1938) associate justice of the US Supreme Court. Known for his carefully reasoned opinions, he was appointed an associate justice in 1994. Full name **Breyer, Stephen Gerald**

Brezh·nev /brézh nef, -nyif/, **Leonid Ilyich** (1906–82) Soviet leader. General secretary of the Soviet Communist Party (1964–82) and president of the U.S.S.R. (1977–82), he exerted strong control over Warsaw Pact countries.

Bri·an Bó·rú /brī ən bə ro͝o/ king of Ireland (941?–1014). He extended his power across Southern Ireland and was acknowledged as ruler of all Ireland in 1002. He was killed after defeating the Vikings at Clontarf. Known as **Brian Boroimhe, Boru "Brian of the Tribute"**

Bri·and /bree aánd, -aáN/, **Aristide** (1862–1932) French politician. He was elected prime minister of France 11 times between 1909 and 1929. He shared the Nobel Peace Prize (1926) and contributed to the Kellogg-Briand Pact (1928), which outlawed war.

> "Draw back the rifles, draw back the machine guns, draw back the cannons—trust in conciliation, in arbitration, in peace!...A country grows in history not only because of the heroism of its troops on the field of battle, it grows also when it turns to justice and to right for the conservation of its interests."
> [Aristide Briand, *Speech, Geneva, Switzerland*; September 10, 1926]

bri·ar[1] /brī́ ər/ (*plural* **-ars** or *same*), **bri·er** (*plural* **-ers** or *same*) *n* **1.** a tobacco pipe made from the wood of a root **2.** a bush of the heather family with hard woody roots from which tobacco pipes are made. Native to: southern Europe. Latin name: *Erica arborea*. [Mid-19C. < French *bruyère* "wild heather"]

ORIGIN English has two words *briar.* Both can also be spelled *brier,* and their meanings are similar, so they tend to get confused. One goes back to Old English, when it was applied to any prickly bush, especially the blackberry; in modern usage it is applied to a type of wild rose. The other is much more recent. It refers to "wild heather," and it was borrowed from French *bruyère.* At first it was spelled *bruyer* in English, but because of its similarity to *briar* in the "wild rose" sense, it too came to be spelled *briar.* It is the root of this type of *briar* that is used to make tobacco pipes.

bri·ar[2] /brī́ ər/ *n* PLANTS another spelling of **brier**[2]

bri·ard /bree aár, bree aárd/ *n* a dog with a stiff and slightly wavy coat of a single color, usually black, belonging to an ancient French breed developed as sheepdogs [Mid-20C. < French, "of Brie," area of NE France]

bri·ar·root /brī́ ər ro͞ot, -ro͝ot/ *n* the root of the European briar. Use: source of briarwood. [Mid-19C. < BRIAR[1]]

bri·ar·wood /brī́ər wo͝od/ *n* wood from the root of the European briar. Use: making tobacco pipes.

bribe /brīb/ *vti* (**bribed, brib·ing, bribes**) to give somebody money or some other incentive to do something, especially something illegal or dishonest ■ *n* money or another incentive given to bribe somebody [14C. < Old French *briber, brimber* "beg" < *bribe* "morsel of food given to a beggar"] —**brib·a·ble** *adj* —**brib·er** *n*

brib·er·y /brībəree/ (*plural* **-ies**) *n* the offering of money or other incentives to persuade somebody to do something, especially something dishonest or illegal

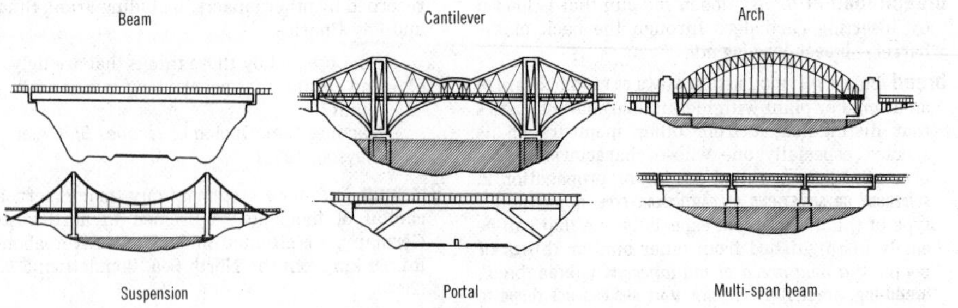

bridge

bric-a-brac /bríkə bràk/ *n* small ornamental objects that are of interest or sentimental value but of little monetary value [Mid-19C. < French < obsolete *à bric et à brac* "at random"]

Brice /brīss/, **Fanny** (1891–1951) US entertainer. She appeared in various revues, movies, and radio programs. Her life inspired the musical *Funny Girl* (1964). Born **Borach, Fannie**

> "Your audience gives you everything you need; there is no director who can direct you like an audience."
> [Fanny Brice. Quoted in *The Fabulous Fanny*, Norman Katlov; 1953]

brick /brik/ *n* **1.** HARD BLOCK USED FOR CONSTRUCTION a rectangular block of clay or a similar material that is baked until it is hard and is used for building houses, walls, and other large permanent structures **2.** BRICKS OR THEIR MATERIAL bricks collectively, or the material they are made of **3.** BLOCK a rectangular block of something, e.g., of ice cream or coffee **4.** *UK* LEISURE same as **building block 5.** RELIABLE SUPPORTIVE PERSON a helpful or supportive person (*dated informal*) ■ *vt* (**bricked, brick·ing, bricks**) **1.** MAKE SOMETHING WITH BRICKS to use bricks to build something or as a liner or paving material for something **2.** CLOSE SOMETHING UP WITH BRICKS to close something up or wall something off with bricks and mortar ○ *the window had been bricked up* [15C. < Middle Dutch *bricke*, later reinforced by French *brique*] ◇ **hit the bricks** (*informal*) **1.** to go out and actively look for something, e.g., a job or housing **2.** to go on strike

brick-and-mor·tar *adj* E-COMMERCE same as **bricks-and-mortar**

brick·bat /brík bàt/ *n* **1.** a harshly unfavorable criticism **2.** a broken fragment of something hard that is used as a missile [Mid-16C. < BAT[1] "piece, lump"]

brick·lay·er /brík lày ər/ *n* somebody trained to construct houses, walls, and other large permanent structures by cementing bricks together with mortar —**brick·lay·ing** *n*

brick-red *adj* of a warm brownish red color similar to that of bricks —**brick red** *n*

bricks-and-mor·tar, brick-and-mor·tar *adj* having and using actual business or retail premises, as opposed to operating solely or mainly via the Internet

brick·work /brík wùrk/ *n* **1.** the brick structure of something such as a wall, building, or walk **2.** the technique or skill of laying bricks

brick·works /brík wùrks/ (*plural same*) *n* a factory where bricks are made

brick·yard /brík yaàrd/ *n* a place where bricks are made, stored, or sold

bri·co·lage /bree kō laázh, brikō-/ *n* something that is made or put together with whatever materials happen to be available [Mid-20C. < French < *bricoler* "do odd jobs" < *bricole* (see BRICOLE)]

bri·cole /bri kṓl, brík'l/ *n* **1.** CUE GAMES TYPE OF BILLIARDS SHOT in billiards, a shot where the cue ball touches the cushion after hitting the target ball and before hitting another ball **2.** ARMS ANCIENT MILITARY CATAPULT a catapult that ancient and medieval soldiers used to launch stones **3.** MIL SOLDIER'S HARNESS FOR HAULING GUNS a harness worn by soldiers in the past for hauling guns [Early 16C. Via French < Provençal *bricola* or Italian *briccola*]

bri·dal /brī́d'l/ *adj* for or associated with brides or weddings ■ *n* a wedding or marriage ceremony [Old English *bryd-ealu* "wedding with much ale" < BRIDE + ALE, altered after -AL[1]]

SPELLCHECK bridal or **bridle**? Do not confuse the spelling of ***bridal*** and ***bridle***, which sound similar. ***Bridal*** is chiefly used as an adjective, meaning "of brides or weddings," as in *the bridal party.* The word ***bridle*** can be used as a noun or verb, referring to part of a horse's harness or, figuratively, a restraint: *He removed the bridle and saddle from his horse. She bridled her rage.* The verb ***bridle*** can also mean "show anger or indignation": *He bridled at the criticism.*

bri·dal par·ty *n* the group of people at a wedding that includes the bride, bridegroom, members of their immediate families, the bridesmaids, and the groomsmen

bri·dal show·er *n* a party given by the woman friends of a woman who is about to get married, at which she is given presents

bri·dal suite *n* a luxurious and expensive room in a hotel, used especially by newlywed couples on their honeymoon

bri·dal wreath *n* a bush with arching branches. Flowers: small, white. Genus: *Spiraea.*

bride /brīd/ *n* a woman who is about to marry or who has just married [Old English *bryd* < Germanic]

bride·groom /brī́d gro͞om, -gro͝om/ *n* a man who is about to marry or who has just married [Old English *brȳdguma* < BRIDE + *guma* "man," altered after GROOM]

bride price *n* in some societies, a payment in the form of money or property made by the groom to the bride or her family

brides·maid /brī́dz màyd/ *n* a girl or woman who helps the bride on her wedding day

bride-to-be (*plural* **brides-to-be**) *n* a woman who is about to get married ○ *Greg returns from Europe with his bride-to-be next week.*

bridge[1] /brij/ *n* **1.** STRUCTURE ALLOWING PASSAGE ACROSS OBSTACLE a structure that is built above and across a river, road, or other obstacle to allow people or vehicles to cross it **2.** LINK OR MEANS OF APPROACH something that provides a link, connection, or means of coming together **3.** NAUT SHIP'S CONTROL ROOM OR PLATFORM the platform or room on a ship or other vessel from which the captain controls its course **4.** DENT PARTIAL FALSE TEETH a set of one or more false teeth that are attached to adjoining teeth. It can be permanently anchored to natural teeth (**fixed bridge**), or set into a metal appliance and temporarily clipped on to natural teeth (**removable bridge**). **5.** ANAT TOP OF NOSE the top bony part of the nose between the eyes **6.** OPHTHALMOL PART OF EYEGLASSES the part of a pair of eyeglasses that connects the two lenses together at the front and rests on the nose **7.** MUSIC PART OF STRINGED INSTRUMENT the part of a stringed instrument that keeps the strings away from its body. It is high and curved on a violin but shallow and straight on a guitar. **8.** MUSIC LINKING PIECE OF MUSIC a transitional or connecting section in a musical work **9.** CUE GAMES CUE REST WITH HIGH END a long-handled support for a player's cue in billiards, with a high arching end **10.** CUE GAMES HAND USED AS REST the player's hand used as a rest for the cue in billiards and snooker **11.** ELEC ENG PART OF ELECTRICAL CIRCUIT a part of an electrical circuit fitted with a device that measures electrical resistance or capacitance **12.** ONLINE TELECOMMUNICATIONS CONNECTION a telecommunications connection between two local area networks ■ *vt* (**bridged, bridg·ing, bridg·es**) **1.** CIV ENG **BUILD BRIDGE ACROSS SOMETHING** to build a bridge across an obstacle to allow people or vehicles to get across it **2. CREATE UNDERSTANDING BETWEEN PEOPLE** to create a means of communication or understanding between people or a means of reconciling their differences [Old English *brycg* < Germanic] —**bridge·a·ble** *adj* —**bridge·less** *adj* ◇ **build bridges** to try to make friends with somebody who has previously been an enemy ◇ **burn your bridges** to do something that makes it difficult or impossible to return to your former position ◇ **cross that bridge when you come to it** to think about or worry about something only when it becomes a reality or a priority

bridge² /brij/ *n* a card game derived from whist and played with one deck of cards divided among four players, who play in two pairs. The term is generally used to refer to contract bridge, which is the most popular form of the game. [Late 19C. Origin ?]

bridge fi·nanc·ing *n* short-term borrowing while longer-term borrowing is arranged

bridge·head /bríj hèd/ *n* **1.** MIL **ARMY'S POSITION SEIZED IN ENEMY TERRITORY** a forward position seized by advancing troops in enemy territory and serving as a basis for further advances **2.** MIL **DEFENSIVE MILITARY POSITION** a fortified position from which troops defend the end of a bridge that is nearest to the enemy **3. PIONEERING FOOTHOLD** a position from which further advancement can be attained **4. END OF BRIDGE** the area immediately surrounding the end of a bridge

bridge loan *n* a sum of money borrowed to finance something until permanent financing can be obtained, especially one to finance the purchase of a new property until an old one is sold

Bridg·end /bri jénd/ county in southern Wales. Capital: Bridgend. Population: 128,654 (2001). Area: 102 sq. mi./264 sq. km.

Bridge of Sighs *n* a 16th-century canal bridge in Venice, Italy, believed to be named for the sighs of prisoners crossing the bridge to be tried or executed

Bridge·port /bríj pàwrt/ coastal city in southwestern Connecticut where the Pequonnock River empties into Long Island Sound. Population: 140,104 (2002 estimate).

Bridg·er /bríjjər/, **James** (1804–81) US pioneer. He guided many expeditions in the American West.

Bridg·es /bríjjəz/, **Robert** (1844–1930) British poet. The author of *Eros and Psyche* (1885), *The Spirit of Man* (1916), and *The Testament of Beauty* (1929), he was appointed British poet laureate in 1913.

Bridg·et, St. /bríjjət/ ♦ **Brigid of Ireland**

bridge town *n* either of a pair of cities or towns on the US–Mexican border separated by the Rio Grande, e.g., Laredo (Texas) and Nuevo Laredo (Mexico)

Bridge·town /bríj tòwn/ capital, main port, and tourist center of Barbados, in the southwest of the island. Population: 136,000 (2001).

bridge·work /bríj wùrk/ *n* **1.** the provision of false teeth to replace missing or removed natural teeth **2.** DENT same as **bridge**¹ *n* (sense 4)

bridg·ing loan /bríjjing/ *n UK* FIN same as **bridge loan**

Bridg·man /bríjmən/, **P. W.** (1882–1961) US physicist. He won the Nobel Prize in physics (1946) in recognition of his work on thermodynamics. Full name **Bridgman, Percy Williams**

bri·dle /brī́d'l/ *n* **1.** RIDING **HARNESS FOR HORSE'S HEAD** a set of leather straps fitted to a horse's head and incorporating the bit and the reins **2. RESTRAINING THING** something that acts as a control or restraint ■ *v* (**-dled, -dling, -dles**) **1.** *vt* RIDING **FIX BRIDLE ON HORSE** to provide a horse with a bridle **2.** *vi* **SHOW ANGER OR INDIGNATION** to react with slight anger or indignation, sometimes by rearing the head **3.** *vt* **EXERCISE CONTROL OR RESTRAINT** to show restraint in expressing a feeling or control in curbing something [Old English *brīdel* < Germanic]

SPELLCHECK See ***bridal.***

bri·dle path *n* a path or trail for horseback riding

Brie /bree/ *n* a soft cow's-milk cheese with a whitish rind, originally made in Brie in northeastern France

brief /breef/ *adj* **1. NOT LASTING LONG** lasting for only a short time ○ *a brief conversation* **2. CONCISE** containing only the necessary information, without any extra details **3. CURT** curt and abrupt in conversation ○ *a brief exchange between adversaries* **4.** CLOTHING **SCANTY** describes clothing that leaves much of the wearer's body exposed ■ *n* **1. SYNOPSIS OF DOCUMENTS** a synopsis of a larger document or group of documents **2. BRIEFING** a briefing, or the information conveyed during one **3.** LAW **ATTORNEY'S CASE SUBMITTED TO COURT BEFOREHAND** an outline of how a legal case will be argued, together with evidence and supporting statements, submitted by an attorney to a court prior to a trial **4.** LAW **OUTLINE OF LEGAL CASE FOR ATTORNEY** an outline of one side of a legal case for an attorney, containing the evidence and points of law pertinent to the argument of the case **5.** CHR **PAPAL LETTER** a letter from the Pope, less formal than a papal bull ■ **briefs** *npl* CLOTHING **SNUG UNDERWEAR** men's or women's close-fitting underwear for the lower body ■ *vt* (**briefed, brief·ing, briefs**) **1. GIVE INFORMATION TO PREPARE SOMEBODY** to give somebody all the necessary information about something in preparation for a discussion or decision **2. SUMMARIZE SOMETHING** to make a summary of something, especially in writing [13C. Via Old French < Latin *brevis* "short"] —**brief·er** *n* —**brief·ly** *adv* —**brief·ness** *n* ◇ **in brief** used to introduce a summary ○ *In brief, then, you think he should resign.*

briefcase

brief·case /breéf kàyss/ *n* a small rectangular case with a handle, used for carrying books and papers

brief·ing /breéfing/ *n* **1.** a meeting held to provide information about the main facts of an issue or situation **2.** the information conveyed at a briefing

bri·er¹ /brī́ ər/ *n* PLANTS another spelling of **briar**¹

bri·er² /brī́ ər/, **bri·ar** *n* a thorny wild plant, especially a trailing rose [Old English *brēr*, origin ?] —**bri·er·y** *adj*

brig /brig/ *n* **1. SAILING SHIP** a two-masted sailing ship with square-rigged sails on both masts **2. SHIP'S PRISON** a secure area in a ship of the US Navy, which can be used as a prison while the ship is at sea **3. MILITARY PRISON** a building or part of a building that is used as a prison in a US military installation [Early 18C. Shortening of BRIGANTINE]

Brig. *abbr* MIL **1.** brigade **2.** brigadier

bri·gade /bri gáyd/ *n* **1. MILITARY UNIT** a military unit consisting of two or more combat battalions or regiments and associated support units. It is smaller than a division and is commanded by a brigadier general or a colonel. **2. GROUP WITH COMMON GOAL OR CHARACTERISTIC** a group of people organized to achieve a particular goal or characterized by a common trait such as attitude, background, appearance, or activities ■ *vt* (**-gad·ed, -gad·ing, -gades**) **ORGANIZE PEOPLE INTO TASK FORCE** to organize a group of people in order to achieve a particular goal [Mid-17C. Via French < Italian *brigata* "military company" < *brigare* "contend, brawl" < *briga* "strife"]

brig·a·dier gen·er·al /briggə dèer-/ (*plural* **brig·a·diers gen·er·al**), **brig·a·dier** *n* an officer in the US or Canadian armies, air forces, or Marines of a rank above colonel

brig·and /bríggənd/ *n* a bandit operating in wild or isolated terrain, usually as a member of a roving band (*literary*) [14C. Via Old French < Italian *brigante* < present participle of *brigare* (see BRIGADE)] —**brig·and·age** *n* —**brig·and·ism** *n* —**brig·and·ry** *n*

brig·an·dine /bríggən deèn/ *n* a coat of chain-mail body armor, worn in medieval times [15C. Directly or via Old French < Italian *brigantina* < *brigante* (see BRIGAND)]

brig·an·tine /bríggən teèn/ *n* a two-masted sailing ship with square-rigged sails on the foremast and fore-and-aft sails on the mainmast [Early 16C. Directly or via Old French *brigandine* < Italian *brigantino* "fighting ship" < *brigante* (see BRIGAND)]

Brig. Gen. *abbr* MIL brigadier general

Briggs /brigz/, **Robert** (1911–83) US embryologist. His research on frog embryos with Thomas J. King at the Institute for Cancer Research in Philadelphia led to the creation of the first amphibian clones in 1951.

bright /brīt/ *adj* **1. SHOWING LIGHT** emitting or reflecting strong light ○ *The moon is bright tonight.* **2. ILLUMINATED** illuminated with strong natural or artificial light ○ *a bright day* **3. INTENSELY COLORED** intense in color, or decorated with intense colors ○ *bright blue* **4. INTELLIGENT** showing an ability to think, learn, or respond quickly ○ *She was brighter than other children her age.* **5. CHEERFUL** cheerful and lively ○ *He seems much brighter this morning.* **6. LIKELY TO BE SUCCESSFUL** likely to be successful ○ *predicted a bright future for the company* **7.** ACOUSTICS **CLEAR-SOUNDING** describes sounds that have a clear crisp quality and little harmonic resonance **8. BEAUTIFUL** remarkably beautiful or handsome (*archaic*) ■ *adv* **WITH LIGHT** with a great deal of light ■ *n* RELIG **SOMEBODY WITHOUT SUPERNATURAL BELIEFS** a person, e.g., an atheist, who has a naturalist, as opposed to a supernaturalist, view of the world, and who therefore considers himself or herself to be more rational than religious believers ■ **brights** *npl* **HEADLIGHTS** the headlights on a motor vehicle when set to high beam [Old English *beorht* < Indo-European, "shine"] —**bright·ish** *adj* —**bright·ly** *adv*

SYNONYMS See ***intelligent.***

Bright /brīt/, **John** (1811–89) British politician. A leading radical, he was associated with the Anti-Corn Law League and the Reform Act of 1867.

"England is the mother of parliaments."
[John Bright, *Times (London)*; January 19, 1865]

bright·en /brī́t'n/ (**-ened, -en·ing, -ens**) *v* **1.** *vi* **LOOK HAPPY** to become enthusiastic, lively, or happy ○ *She brightened visibly at the suggestion.* **2.** *vt* **ADD INTEREST** to add color or interest to something ○ *Their visit brightened the day for us.* **3.** *vi* METEOROL **BECOME LESS OVERCAST** to become less dull or rainy ○ *It's going to brighten this afternoon.* **4.** *vti* **ILLUMINATE OR GET LIGHTER** to increase the amount of light emitted or reflected by something, or be filled with an increasing amount of light **5.** *vti* **MAKE OR BECOME MORE PROMISING** to seem more promising, or make something seem more promising

brighten up *vti* to become brighter, lighter, more colorful, or livelier, or make somebody or something do this

bright·en·er /brī́t'nər/ *n* a compound added to some soaps or laundry detergents to make white or light-colored fabrics look brighter

bright-eyed ◇ **bright-eyed and bushy-tailed** noticeably energetic and lively

bright lights *npl* the entertainment and activities of a big city (*informal*)

bright line *n* a crucially important behavioral boundary or standard not to be crossed ○ *a bright line rule*

bright neb·u·la *n* a cloud of material in space that appears bright because it is illuminated by the stars around it

bright·ness /brī́tnəss/ *n* **1. STRENGTH OF LIGHT** the intensity of light reflected or emitted by something **2. SMARTNESS** the ability to think, learn, or respond quickly **3. CHEERFULNESS** a cheerful and lively manner **4. PROMISE OF SUCCESS** the promise of a successful outcome **5. CLARITY OF SOUND** a clear crisp sound quality with little harmonic resonance **6.** OPTICS **LIGHT EMITTED IN PARTICULAR DIRECTION** the intensity of light (**luminance**) emitted by an object in a particular direction, used by an observer to compare the luminance of other visible objects **7.** PHYS **ATTRIBUTE OF COLOR** the attribute of a color that makes its appearance comparable to a standard neutral such as black, gray, or white

Brigh·ton /brīt'n/ seaside resort on the English Channel in East Sussex, southern England. Population: 257,817 (2001).

Bright's dis·ease /brīts-/ *n* an inflammatory disease of the kidneys, e.g., glomerulonephritis [Mid-19C. After Richard *Bright* (1789–1858), British physician]

bright·work /brīt wùrk/ *n* fittings or trimmings of polished metal or varnished wood, e.g., on a vehicle or boat

bright young thing *n* **1.** a young intelligent person thought likely to succeed **2.** a member of a young and fashionable social set in Great Britain in the 1920s and 1930s who regarded themselves as setting new fashions in dress, music, behavior, and style

Bri·gid of Ire·land /bríjjət-/, **St.** (453?–524?) Irish abbess. She founded four religious communities for women in Ireland.

~~**briliant**~~ incorrect spelling of **brilliant**

brill /bril/ (*plural same* or **brills**) *n* an edible flatfish that is closely related to the turbot. Native to: Europe. Latin name: *Scophthalmus rhombus*. [15C. Origin ?]

Brill /bril/, **Abraham Arden** (1874–1948) Austrian-born US psychiatrist. He practiced Freudian psychology and advocated using psychoanalysis to treat patients with psychiatric disorders.

Bril·lat-Sa·va·rin /bree yaà saa vaa ráN/, **Anthelme** (1755–1826) French politician and writer. His *Physiology of Taste* (1825) is a classic of gastronomic literature. Full name **Brillat-Savarin, Jean Anthelme**

"Tell me what you eat and I will tell you what you are."
[Anthelme Brillat-Savarin, "Aphorismes, pour servir de prolégomènes" ("Aphorisms to serve as prolegomena"), Physiologie du goût (Physiology of Taste); 1825]

bril·liance /bríllyənss/, **bril·lian·cy** /-see/ *n* **1.** **BRIGHTNESS** extreme brightness or radiance **2.** **GREAT INTELLIGENCE OR TALENT** exceptional intelligence, ability, skill, or talent ○ *the technical brilliance of the pianist's performance* **3.** **SPLENDOR** imposing splendor or magnificence

bril·liant /bríllyənt/ *adj* **1.** **EXTREMELY BRIGHT OR RADIANT** extremely bright or radiant ○ *brilliant sunshine* ○ *a brilliant smile* **2.** **VIVID** vividly colored ○ *a brilliant shade of green* **3.** **INTELLIGENT OR TALENTED** showing exceptional intelligence, ability, skill, or talent ○ *a brilliant mathematician* **4.** **EXCELLENT** distinguished by excellence **5.** **SPLENDID** imposingly splendid or magnificent ■ *adj, interj UK* **GREAT** used to express great satisfaction with somebody or something (*informal*) [Late 17C. < French *brillant*, present participle of *briller* "shine" < Italian *brillare*] —**bril·liant·ly** *adv* —**bril·liant·ness** *n*

bril·liant-cut *adj* describes a gemstone that is cut into a multifaceted shape to maximize brilliance. A brilliant-cut gemstone is shaped like two polygonal pyramids joined base to base, with the point of the upper pyramid cut off to form a large flat facet.

bril·lian·tine /bríllyən teen/ *n* **1.** an oily hair cream, used by men to keep hair in place and make it look glossy **2.** a shiny lightweight fabric, often made from cotton woven with mohair or worsted [Late 19C. < French *brillantine* < *brillant* (see BRILLIANT)]

brim /brim/ *n* **1.** **HAT EDGE** the rim around the edge of a hat, shaped to stand out from the head **2.** **TOP EDGE** the top edge of a container such as a cup or bowl ■ *v* (**brimmed, brim·ming, brims**) **1.** *vti* **BE FULL TO TOP** to fill something, or be full, to the top edge ○ *The cup was brimming with hot coffee.* **2.** *vi* **BURST** to have an unusually plentiful supply of something ○ *He was brimming with ideas.* **3.** *vi* **OVERFLOW** to be so full as to be overflowing ○ *eyes brimming with tears* [13C. Origin ?] —**brim·less** *adj*

brim·ful /brím fo͝ol/ *adj* **1.** describes a container that is full to its top edge **2.** having an unusually plentiful supply of something ○ *brimful of energy*

brim·stone /brím stōn/ *n* CHEM same as **sulfur** (*archaic*) [12C. < Old English *byrne* "burning" < *birnan* (see BURN[1])]

Brin·di·si /bríndi zee/ capital of Brindisi Province, Apulia Region, southern Italy. It is a port and important ferry terminal for ships carrying tourist traffic to or from Greece. Population: 89,081 (2001).

brin·dle /brínd'l/ *adj* same as **brindled** ■ *n* brindled coloring [Late 17C. Back-formation < BRINDLED]

brin·dled /brínd'ld/ *adj* tawny brown or gray marked with darker streaks or patches [Late 17C. Alteration of *brinded* (influenced by GRIZZLED or SPECKLED), origin ?]

brine /brīn/ *n* **1.** **SALT WATER FOR PRESERVING** water containing a significant amount of salt, used for curing, preserving, and developing flavor in food **2.** **SEA WATER** the salt water of the sea (*literary*) **3.** **SALT SOLUTION** a strong salt solution ■ *vt* (**brined, brin·ing, brines**) **TREAT SOMETHING WITH SALT WATER** to preserve, can, pickle, or soak something in salt water [Old English *brīne*, origin ?] —**brin·er** *n* —**brin·ish** *adj*

Bri·nell hard·ness /bri nél-/ *n* the hardness of a metal or alloy, determined by pressing a steel ball into its surface under standard pressure and measuring the surface area of the resulting indentation [Early 20C. After Johan A. *Brinell* (1849–1925), Swedish engineer]

Bri·nell hard·ness num·ber, **Bri·nell num·ber** *n* a number expressing the hardness of a metal or alloy. It is the ratio of the pressure applied to a steel ball forced into the surface of the metal to the surface area of the resulting indentation.

brine shrimp *n* a small crustacean that lives in salt lakes and brine pools and is used as food for aquarium fish. Genus: *Artemia*.

bring /bring/ (**brought** /brawt/, **bring·ing, brings**) *v* **1.** *vt* **ACCOMPANY OR CARRY SOMEBODY OR SOMETHING** to come from one place to another with somebody or something ○ *Please bring me a glass of water.* **2.** *vt* **ATTRACT SOMETHING** to draw something to yourself or another person ○ *This charm is supposed to bring luck.* **3.** *vt* **MAKE SOMETHING HAPPEN** to cause something to take place ○ *The heavy rain brought flooding.* **4.** *vt* **PUT SOMETHING IN PARTICULAR STATE** to force somebody or something to arrive at a particular situation or condition ○ *The chairperson brought the meeting to a close.* **5.** *vt* **CAUSE SOMETHING TO ENTER MIND** to cause something to enter somebody's mind ○ *Seeing you brings memories of good times.* **6.** *vr* **MAKE YOURSELF DO SOMETHING** to persuade or force yourself to do something (*usually with negatives or in questions*) ○ *She still can't bring herself to think about the tragedy.* **7.** *vt* **SELL FOR PARTICULAR PRICE** to be sold for a particular price **8.** *vt* LAW **BEGIN ACTION** to begin a legal action **9.** *vt* **PRESENT EVIDENCE** to present evidence before a court **10.** *vt Malaysia, Singapore, UK regional* **TAKE SOMEBODY OR SOMETHING** to take somebody or something somewhere ○ *I brought my friend to the airport when she left.* [Old English *bringan* < Indo-European] —**bring·er** *n*

bring about *vt* to make something happen

bring around *vt* **1.** to revive somebody who has lost consciousness **2.** to make somebody change an opinion and agree with you ○ *We eventually brought him around to our view.*

bring back *vt* **1.** to evoke memories of something forgotten **2.** to restore something that has been discontinued ○ *widespread support for bringing back on-the-spot fines*

bring down *vt* **1.** **TOPPLE SOMEBODY OR SOMETHING** to cause the downfall of a person, group, or institution **2.** **KILL OR WOUND PERSON OR ANIMAL** to make a person or animal fall by wounding or killing it **3.** *Can* POL **PRESENT BILL** to present a bill or other piece of legislation in a parliament

bring forth *vt* **1.** to bear young **2.** to produce fruit or flowers

bring forward *vt* **1.** **BRING SOMETHING CLOSER IN TIME** to move something such as an appointment or an event to an earlier date or time **2.** **SUGGEST SOMETHING FOR CONSIDERATION** to offer something for discussion or consideration **3.** ACCT **CARRY AMOUNT TO NEXT PAGE** to carry a sum from one column or page to the next

bring in *vt* **1.** **INTRODUCE SOMETHING** to introduce something such as a new policy or law **2.** **EARN OR ACQUIRE SOMETHING** to acquire money as profits, pay, or interest ○ *She barely brings in enough to live on.* **3.** LAW **PRESENT SOMETHING IN COURT** to present something in a court of law **4.** **GET OIL WELL TO PRODUCE** to cause an oil well to begin producing oil **5.** **SUGGEST SOMETHING** to introduce something for discussion or consideration

bring off *vt* **1.** to succeed in doing something difficult **2.** an offensive term meaning to cause somebody to have an orgasm (*slang*)

bring on *vt* **1.** **CAUSE** to be the cause of something happening or appearing ○ *exhaustion brought on by overwork* **2.** **ENCOURAGE DEVELOPMENT** to further the development of a quality or of the person who possesses it **3.** **MAKE SOMEBODY OR SOMETHING APPEAR** to cause somebody or something to appear ○ *Does stress bring the headaches on?*

bring out *vt* **1.** **MAKE SOMETHING KNOWN** to cause something to become known **2.** **CALL ATTENTION TO SOMETHING** to emphasize a quality in somebody or something ○ *That outfit brings out the red in your hair.* **3.** **INTRODUCE SOMETHING FOR SALE** to produce or issue something for sale to the public ○ *The company has just brought out a new version of the software.* **4.** **INTRODUCE SOMEBODY TO SOCIETY** to introduce a debutante to society

bring to *vt* **1.** to restore somebody to consciousness **2.** to head a ship into the wind in order to slow it down or stop it

bring up *vt* **1.** **RAISE SUBJECT** to raise a subject for discussion **2.** **REAR CHILD** to provide care, training, and education for a child until maturity **3.** **MAKE SOMEBODY OR SOMETHING STOP SUDDENLY** to cause somebody or something to come to a standstill **4.** **VOMIT SOMETHING** to cough something up, or expel something from the stomach through the mouth

brink /bringk/ *n* **1.** the very edge of something such as a steep drop or riverbank **2.** the crucial point in a situation when something disastrous or momentous is about to happen ○ *teetering on the brink of bankruptcy* [13C. < Old Norse *brekka* "slope"]

brink·man·ship /bríngkmən shìp/, **brinks·man·ship** /bríngksmən-/ *n* the practice, especially in international relations, of taking a dispute to the verge of conflict in the hope of forcing the opposition to make concessions

brin·y /brīnee/ *adj* (**-i·er, -i·est**) relating to, containing, or tasting like sea water ■ *n UK* same as **sea** (sense 1) (*literary*) —**brin·i·ness** *n*

bri·o /breé ō/ *n* lively energy [Mid-18C. < Italian]

bri·oche /bree áwsh/ *n* a sweet French bread roll made from a dough enriched with eggs and butter [Early 19C. < French < Old French *brier* "knead"]

bri·o·lette /breè ə lét/ *n* a gem cut in the shape of a teardrop or oval [Mid-19C. < French]

bri·quette /bri két/, **bri·quet** *n* a small rectangular block of compressed material such charcoal, sawdust, or coal dust. Use: fuel. [Late 19C. < French, "little brick" < *brique* "brick"]

bris /briss/ (*plural* **bris·es**) *n* the religious circumcision ceremony for a Jewish boy [Early 20C. < Hebrew *bərīṯ (mīlāh)* "covenant (of circumcision)"]

Bris·bane /brízbən, bríz bàyn/ city on the Brisbane River and the capital of Queensland, eastern Australia. Population: 1,574,600 (1998). —**Bris·ban·ite** *n, adj*

brisk /brisk/ *adj* **1.** **QUICK** done quickly and energetically ○ *a brisk walk* **2.** **BRUSQUE** speaking or behaving in an abrupt way ○ *a brisk reply* **3.** **BUSY** showing or experiencing much activity ○ *Business was brisk.* **4.** **INVIGORATING** refreshingly cool ○ *brisk autumn days* [Late 16C. Probably < French *brusque* (see BRUSQUE)] —**brisk·ly** *adv* —**brisk·ness** *n*

bris·ket /brískit/ *n* **1.** the breast of a four-legged animal **2.** a cut of meat, especially of beef, taken from an animal's breast [14C. Origin ?]

bris·ling /brízzling, bríss-/ (*plural same* or **-lings**) *n* **1.** a small fish of the herring family. Latin name: *Clupea sprattus*. **2.** the flesh of a brisling used as food [Early 20C. < Norwegian or Danish]

bris·tle /bríss'l/ *n* **1.** **STIFF HAIR** a short stiff hair on an animal or plant, or a mass of short stiff hairs growing, especially on a hog's back or a man's face **2.** **HAIR ON BRUSH** the short stiff natural or synthetic hair on a brush ■ *v* (**-tled, -tling, -tles**) **1.** *vti* **HAVE OR SET HAIR ON END** to make the hair or fur stand upright in response to fear or anger, or to show such a response **2.** *vi* **BECOME OFFENDED** to react somewhat angrily or indignantly to somebody or something ○ *He bristled at the suggestion.* **3.** *vi* **ABOUND** to have an abundance of something ○ *a mighty battleship bristling with guns* **4.** *vt* **GIVE SOMETHING BRISTLES** to provide or cover something with bristles [13C. < Old English *byrst* "bristle"]

bris·tle·cone pine /bríss'l kōn-/ *n* a small pine tree with bristly cones, the longest-living tree in the world. Native to: California. Genus: *Pinus.*

bris·tle·tail /bríss'l tàyl/ (*plural* **-tails** or *same*) *n* a wingless insect that has a long segmented abdomen with two or three long bristles at the end. Order: Thysanura.

bris·tling /bríssling/ *adj* **1.** thick with stiff hairs **2.** reacting with anger or indignation

bris·tly /bríssle̅e̅/ (**-tli·er, -tli·est**) *adj* **1.** prickly and rough with bristles **2.** easily provoked to anger or indignation —**bris·tli·ness** *n*

Bris·tol /bríst'l/ **1.** city in central Connecticut, northeast of Waterbury and southwest of Hartford. Population: 60,541 (2002 estimate). **2.** town and port in eastern Rhode Island, on a peninsula reaching into Narragansett Bay. Population: 22,815 (2002 estimate). **3.** city in northeastern Tennessee, on the Tennessee–Virginia border, northeast of Johnson City. Population: 24,889 (2002 estimate). **4.** city in Virginia, southwest of Abingdon, opposite Bristol, Tennessee. Population: 17,118 (2002 estimate). **5.** university city and seaport on the Avon River in southwestern England. Population: 380,615 (2001).

Bris·tol board *n* fine smooth lightweight cardboard, used in design and drawing [Early 19C. After BRISTOL England]

Bris·tol Chan·nel arm of the Atlantic Ocean between southern Wales and southwestern England, into which the Severn River flows. Length: 85 mi./140 km.

brit /brit/ (*plural* **brits** or *same*) *n* **1.** the young form of some fish including the herring and the sprat **2.** a mass of tiny organisms in the ocean, especially crustaceans, that whalebone whales and some fish feed on [Early 17C. Origin ?]

Brit /brit/ *n* a British person (*informal*) [Early 20C. Shortening]

Brit. *abbr* **1.** Britain **2.** British

Brit·ain /brítt'n/ **1.** island in the Atlantic Ocean off the northwestern coast of Europe, including England, Scotland, and Wales. Area: 88,753 sq. mi./229,870 sq. km. **2.** ◊ **Great Britain**

Bri·tan·nia[1] /bri tánnyə/ *n* **1.** the personification and symbol of Great Britain, shown as a seated woman wearing a helmet and holding a trident **2.** *also* **bri·tan·nia** METALL same as **Britannia metal** [Pre-12C. < Latin *Brit(t)annia*]

Bri·tan·nia[2] /bri tánnyə/ the Roman name for the southern part of Britain

Bri·tan·nia met·al, bri·tan·nia met·al *n* an alloy of tin, antimony, and copper that is similar to pewter and is used for decorative items and for bearings

Bri·tan·nic /bri tánnik/ *adj* belonging to Great Britain (*dated formal*) ○ *Her Britannic Majesty*

~~**Britanny**~~ incorrect spelling of **Brittany**

britch·es /bríchəz/ *npl* CLOTHING same as **breeches** ◇ **too big for your britches** behaving in a self-important manner (*dated informal*)

brith *n* JUDAISM same as **bris**

~~**Britian**~~ incorrect spelling of **Britain**

Brit·i·cism /brítti sìzzəm/ *n* something such as a word or custom that is characteristic of the British or of Great Britain [Mid-19C. < BRITISH, after SCOTTICISM or GALLICISM]

Brit·ish /bríttish/ *npl* the people of the United Kingdom of Great Britain and Northern Ireland ■ *n* **1.** LANG same as **British English 2.** the language spoken by the ancient Celtic people who lived in southern Britain [Old English *Brettisc, Brittisc* < *Bret* "ancient Briton," directly or via Latin *Britto* < Celtic] —**Brit·ish** *adj*

Brit·ish Broad·cast·ing Cor·po·ra·tion *n* full form of **BBC**

WORLD ENGLISH ***British English*** is the English language as used in the United Kingdom of Great Britain (England, Scotland, and Wales) and Northern Ireland. With a population of over 57 million, the United Kingdom is the second largest primary English-speaking country after the United States, and it continues to have prestige as the place of origin of the English language. The term British English is not, however, precise, being variously used to refer to: all varieties of English in the United Kingdom as a whole; all varieties in Great Britain as a whole; all varieties in England alone; the forms of only the standard language in the United Kingdom as a whole; those forms in Great Britain as a whole; those forms in England alone; and, notably, that variety of the standard language based on upper- and middle-class usage (especially at the turn of the 20th century in southeastern England).

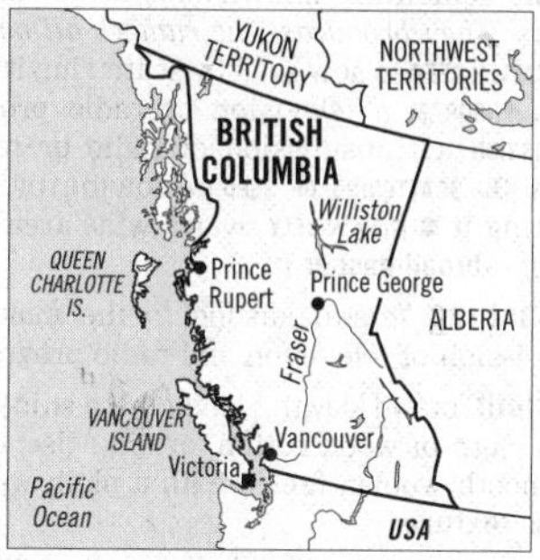

British Columbia

Brit·ish Co·lum·bi·a /brìttish-/ westernmost province of Canada, situated on the Pacific coast, north of the US border, west of Alberta, and south of Yukon Territory and the Northwest Territories. Capital: Victoria. Population: 3,907,738 (2001). Area: 364,764 sq. mi./944,735 sq. km.

Brit·ish Com·mon·wealth of Na·tions *n* POL same as **Commonwealth** (sense 3)

Brit·ish Em·pire *n* a group of colonies, protectorates, and other territories brought under British rule after the late 16th century. Most of Great Britain's former colonies became independent after World War II and, as sovereign states, many joined the Commonwealth.

Brit·ish Eng·lish *n* the form of English used by people in the United Kingdom

Brit·ish·er /bríttishər/ *n* a British subject or a person from Great Britain (*informal*)

Brit·ish Gui·a·na former name for **Guyana**

Brit·ish Hon·du·ras former name for **Belize**

Brit·ish In·di·a *n* the part of South Asia under British administration from 1765 to 1947, when the independent states of India and Pakistan were created

Brit·ish In·di·an O·cean Ter·ri·to·ry British overseas territory in the Indian Ocean, consisting of five uninhabited coral islands, the largest of which is Diego Garcia. Area: 23 sq. mi./60 sq. km.

Brit·ish Isles group of islands in the northeastern Atlantic, separated from mainland Europe by the North Sea and the English Channel. It consists of the large islands of Great Britain and Ireland and almost 5,000 surrounding smaller islands and islets.

Brit·ish Le·gion *n* a charitable organization in the United Kingdom that provides help for former members of the armed forces

Brit·ish So·ma·li·land former British protectorate in East Africa from 1884 until 1960, when it united with Italian Somaliland to form the republic of Somalia

Brit·ish Stan·dard Time *n* the time that was used from 1968 to 1971 in the United Kingdom, one hour ahead of Greenwich Mean Time

Brit·ish Sum·mer Time *n* the time, one hour ahead of Greenwich Mean Time, used in the United Kingdom from the end of March to the end of October. It is intended to make better use of the hours of daylight in this part of the year.

Brit·ish ther·mal u·nit *n* the amount of heat needed to raise the temperature of one pound of water by one degree Fahrenheit, equal to approximately 1055 joules

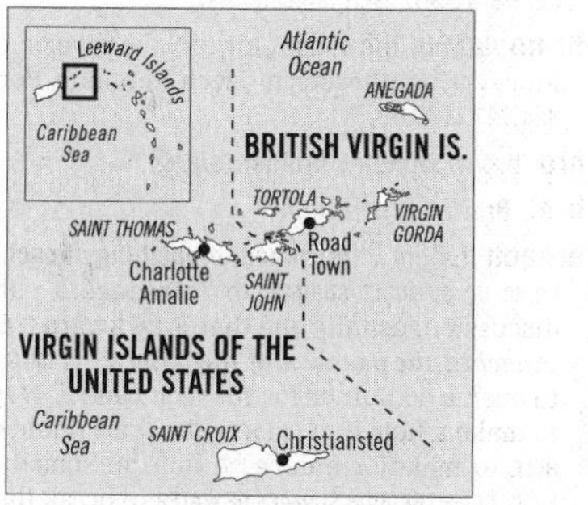

British Virgin Islands and Virgin Islands of the United States

Bri·tish Vir·gin Is·lands /vúrjin-/ dependent territory of the United Kingdom consisting of 36 islands in the eastern Caribbean Sea, east of Puerto Rico. Capital: Road Town. Population: 20,812 (2001). Area: 59 sq. mi./153 sq. km.

Brit·ish West In·dies British dependent territories in the Caribbean, including Anguilla, the British Virgin Islands, the Cayman Islands, Montserrat, and the Turks and Caicos

Brit·on /brítt'n/ *n* **1.** somebody who comes from Great Britain **2.** a member of an ancient Celtic people who once lived in southern Britain [13C. Via French *Breton* < Latin *Britton-* < Celtic]

Brit·pop /brít pòp/ *n* a style of pop music originating in the United Kingdom in the 1990s and reminiscent of the rock and roll style of 1960s bands such as the Beatles

brit·ska *n* VEHICLES another spelling of **britzka**

Brit·tain /brítt'n/, **Vera** (1893–1970) British writer. Her World War I memoir *Testament of Youth* (1933) speaks for a generation of young people whose lives were forever changed by the experience of war. Full name **Brittain, Vera Mary**

> "It is probably true to say that the largest scope for change still lies in men's attitude to women, and in women's attitude to themselves."
> [Vera Brittain, *Lady into Woman*; 1953]

Brit·ta·ny /brítt'nee/ peninsular region in northwestern France, between the Bay of Biscay and the English Channel. Its capital is Rennes. Population: 2,906,197 (1999). Area: 10,505 sq. mi./27,209 sq. km.

Brit·ten /brítt'n/, **Benjamin** (1913–76) British composer. Regarded as one of the finest of British composers of the 20th century, he wrote orchestral works, the operas *Peter Grimes* (1945) and *Billy Budd* (1951), and the *War Requiem* (1961). Full name **Britten, Edward Benjamin, Baron Britten of Aldeburgh**

brit·tle /brítt'l/ *adj* (**-tler, -tlest**) **1. HARD AND BREAKABLE** hard and likely to break or crack ○ *plastic that has become brittle with age* **2. SHARP-SOUNDING** describes a voice that has a sharp, unnerving quality **3. NOT FRIENDLY** tense, irritable, and lacking personal warmth ○ *a brittle quality to her that I didn't like* ■ *n* **TOFFEE NUT CANDY** a crunchy candy made from caramel and nuts [14C. < Old English *gebryttan* "shatter"] —**brit·tle·ly** *adv* —**brit·tle·ness** *n*

brit·tle-bone dis·ease *n UK* MED **1.** same as **osteoporosis 2.** same as **osteogenesis imperfecta**

brit·tle·bush /brítt'l bŏŏsh/ (*plural* **-bush·es** or *same*) *n* a desert bush with brittle gray leaves and yellow flowers. Native to: North America. Latin name: *Encelia farinosa.*

brit·tle star *n* an invertebrate ocean animal similar to a starfish but with thinner, longer, and more flexible arms. Class: Ophiuroidea.

Brit·ton·ic *adj, n* LANG, PEOPLES same as **Brythonic**

brit·zka /brítskə/, **brit·ska** *n* a horse-drawn carriage with a rear-facing front seat and a folding top over the back seat [Early 19C. < Polish *bryczka*]

Brix scale /brĭks-/ *n* a hydrometer scale used for measuring the sugar content of a solution at a particular temperature [Late 19C. After Adolf S. *Brix* (1798–1890), German scientist]

Br·no /búrnō/ industrial city in the former region of Moravia, southeastern Czech Republic. Population: 384,727 (1999).

bro /brō/ *n* same as **brother** (*slang*)

bro., **Bro.** *abbr* brother

broach /brōch/ *v* (**broached, broach·ing, broach·es**) **1.** *vt* BRING UP DIFFICULT SUBJECT to introduce a subject for discussion, usually one that is awkward ○ *He finally broached the question of the loan.* **2.** *vt* OPEN CONTAINER to open a container for the first time **3.** *vt* PIERCE CASK to make a hole in a cask to draw off liquid **4.** *vt* BORE HOLE to make or enlarge a hole in something **5.** *vi* NAVY COME THROUGH SURFACE OF WATER to break the surface of water from below without completely emerging (*refers to submarines*) **6.** *vi* NAUT TURN SIDEWAYS TO WIND to be turned broadside to the wind, e.g., by heavy seas, with a risk of capsizing (*refers to boats*) ■ *n* **1.** TOOL FOR HOLES a tool for enlarging holes **2.** TOOL FOR PIERCING CASKS a tool used for making holes in casks **3.** ROASTING SPIT a spit for roasting meat over a fire **4.** JEWELRY same as **brooch** [14C. < Old French *brocher* "to stitch" < *broche* "skewer, long needle"] —**broach·er** *n*

SPELLCHECK Do not confuse the spelling of ***broach*** and ***brooch*** ("a dress ornament"), which sound similar.

broad /brawd/ *adj* **1.** WIDE large from one side to the other ○ *a broad forehead* ○ *six inches broad* **2.** LARGE AND SPACIOUS extending a great distance in all directions ○ *the broad steppes* **3.** MEASURED ACROSS measured from side to side ○ *as broad as it is long* **4.** FULL AND CLEAR full and clear to see ○ *a broad grin* ○ *broad daylight* **5.** COVERING WIDE RANGE comprehensive in content, knowledge, experience, ability, or application ○ *She has very broad interests.* **6.** NOT DETAILED general and lacking detail ○ *I'll give you a broad outline of the project.* **7.** WIDESPREAD OR GENERALIZED widespread or generalized throughout a large and diverse group of people ○ *a broad feeling of disillusionment in the party* **8.** OBVIOUS meant to be easily understood ○ *dropping broad hints about their plans* **9.** UNOBSTRUCTED with nothing blocking the way ○ *in broad view* **10.** TOLERANT tending to tolerate or accept the ideas and conduct of other people, even when these are very different from your own ○ *I think I have fairly broad views on the whole.* **11.** POTENTIALLY OFFENSIVE potentially offensive to accepted standards of propriety ○ *broad humor* **12.** PHON STRONGLY REGIONAL describes a regional accent that is very strong or pronounced **13.** PHON SHOWING ONLY MAIN DIFFERENCES describes a phonetic transcription that gives only major differences **14.** PHON PRONOUNCED WITH TONGUE DOWN describes a vowel pronounced with the tongue low and flat and the mouth open wide ■ *n* **1.** WIDE PART the wide part of something ○ *He slapped Jack across the broad of his back.* **2.** OFFENSIVE TERM an offensive term for a woman (*slang*) ■ *adv* COMPLETELY to the fullest extent [Old English *brād* < Germanic] —**broad·ness** *n*

broad ar·row *n* an arrow with a wide barbed head

Broad Aus·tra·lian *n* Australian English spoken with a strong Australian accent

WORLD ENGLISH See ***Australian English***.

broad·ax /bráwd àks/ *n* a heavy battleax with a wide blade

broad·band /bráwd bànd/ *adj* **1.** using a wide range of electromagnetic frequencies **2.** able to transfer large amounts of data at high speed

broad bean *n* **1.** a large flat green seed cooked and eaten as a vegetable **2.** a plant of the pea family with long pods that produces broad beans. Native to: Europe. Latin name: *Vicia faba*.

broad·bill /bráwd bìl/ (*plural* **-bills** or *same*) *n* a bird with often brightly colored feathers and a short broad beak. Native to: tropical Africa and Asia. Family: Eurylaimidae.

broad-brush *adj* attempting to cover all situations, conditions, or instances ○ *a broad-brush approach*

broad·cast /bráwd kàst/ *v* (**-cast** or **-cast·ed, -cast·ing, -casts**) **1.** *vti* TRANSMIT RADIO SIGNALS to transmit a program or information on television or radio **2.** *vi* PERFORM ON RADIO OR TV to take part in a radio or television program **3.** *vt* MAKE SOMETHING WIDELY KNOWN to make something known to a large number of people ○ *They broadcast the rumors all over town.* **4.** *vt* SCATTER SEED to sow seed by scattering it by hand ■ *n* **1.** PROGRAM a television or radio program **2.** TRANSMISSION a transmission of radio or television signals **3.** SCATTERING OF SEED a sowing of seed by scattering it ■ *adv* WIDELY over a wide area —**broad·cast** *adj* —**broad·cast·er** *n*

broad·cast·ing /bráwd kàsting/ *n* the making and transmission of television and radio programs

broad·cloth /bráwd klàwth, -klòth/ *n* **1.** a shiny, closely woven cloth of wool, cotton, or silk. Use: clothing. **2.** a smooth woolen fabric with a plain weave and a dense texture

broad·en /bráwd'n/ (**-ened, -en·ing, -ens**) *vti* **1.** to make something wider, or become wider **2.** to enlarge the range or magnitude of something, or become wider in range or magnitude

broad gauge *n* a railroad track that has a distance between the rails that is greater than the standard 56.5 in./143.5 cm. Broad gauge allows greater passenger comfort and carrying capacity, but increases the cost of construction.

broad-gauge *adj* **1.** relating to or designed for a railroad using broad gauge **2.** wide in application or range

broad jump *n* a long jump in track-and-field sports (*dated*)

broad·leaf /bráwd leef/ *n* (*plural* **-leaves** /-leevz/ or *same*) a tobacco plant that has broad leaves suitable for making cigars ■ *adj* same as **broad-leaved**

broad-leaved, **broad·leaf**, **broad-leafed** *adj* describes deciduous or evergreen trees such as holly or maple that have wide rather than needle-shaped leaves

broad·loom /bráwd loom/ *adj* describes carpet that is woven on a wide loom so that it can be laid with few or no seams ■ *n* a carpet woven on a wide loom that can be laid with few or no seams

broad·ly /bráwdlee/ *adv* **1.** GENERALLY in general terms ○ *Broadly speaking, there are two types of tourists.* **2.** MOSTLY for the most part ○ *It is broadly based on the German prototype.* **3.** WITH ENTHUSIASTIC SMILE with a smile that shows enthusiasm or friendliness ○ *smiling broadly*

broad·ly-based *adj* involving or covering a wide range of people or things

broad-mind·ed *adj* willing to tolerate a wide range of ideas and behavior —**broad-mind·ed·ly** *adv*—**broad-mind·ed·ness** *n*

broad mon·ey *n* ECON same as **M2**

Broads /brawdz/ area of over 30 shallow freshwater lakes and lagoons in Norfolk and Suffolk, eastern England. A popular tourist destination, it is managed by the Broads Authority and was made a Special Statutory Authority, with similar status to that of a national park, in 1988.

broad·sheet /bráwd sheet/ *n Can, UK* PRINTING same as **broadside** *n* (sense 3)

broad·side /bráwd sìd/ *vt* (**-sid·ed, -sid·ing, -sides**) HIT SIDE OF SOMETHING to collide with the side of something ○ *The car was broadsided by the train.* ■ *n* **1.** LARGE FLAT SURFACE a large flat and usually vertical surface ○ *the broadside of the barn* **2.** STRONG SPOKEN OR WRITTEN ATTACK a strong spoken or written attack on somebody ○ *a vicious broadside on the President* **3.** *US* PRINTING LARGE PAPER SIZE a large sheet of paper that is printed on one side, or something such as an advertisement that is printed on one side of a large sheet of paper. Can term **broadsheet** **4.** NAUT SHIP'S SIDE the side of a ship above the water line from bow to quarter **5.** NAUT SHIP'S GUNS all the guns on one side of a ship **6.** NAUT FIRING OF SHIP'S GUNS the simultaneous firing of all the guns on one side of a ship ■ *adv* **1.** WITH SIDE with the side facing toward something ○ *The ship hit the rocks broadside.* **2.** WITHOUT OBJECTIVE with no apparent objective ○ *Her proposals were attacked broadside.*

broad-spec·trum *adj* describes antibiotics or other chemicals that destroy a wide range of organisms such as bacteria or agricultural pests

broad·sword /bráwd sàwrd/ *n* a sword with a wide flat blade designed for cutting rather than for thrusting

broad·tail /bráwd tàyl/ *n* **1.** the black wavy fur of a prematurely born karakul lamb **2.** ZOOL same as **karakul** (sense 2)

Broad·way /bráwd wày/ *n* **1.** a long avenue in Manhattan, New York City, part of which is the main thoroughfare of the city's theater district **2.** the commercial theater business in the United States ○ *This is not Broadway material.*

Brob·ding·nag·i·an /bròbding nággee ən/ *adj* extraordinarily large (*literary*) [Early 18C. < *Brobdingnag*, fictitious land of giants in Jonathan Swift's *Gulliver's Travels* (1726)]

bro·cade /brō káyd/ *n* a heavy silk, cotton, or woolen fabric with a raised design, often in metallic threads ■ *vt* (**-cad·ed, -cad·ing, -cades**) to weave a fabric with a raised design [Late 16C. Via Spanish or Portuguese *brocado* < Italian *broccato* < *brocco* "twisted thread, shoot" < Latin *brocchus*] —**bro·cad·ed** *adj*

broccoli

broc·co·li /brókəlee/ *n* **1.** heads of tight green, purple, or white flower buds, cooked and eaten as a vegetable **2.** a plant of the cabbage family that produces broccoli. Heading broccoli has green flower heads like cauliflower, and sprouting broccoli has multiple small purple or white flowering shoots. Latin name: *Brassica oleracea* var. italica. [Mid-17C. < Italian, plural of *broccolo* "cabbage sprout" < *brocco* "shoot" < Latin *brocchus*]

bro·chette /brō shét/ *n* **1.** a small skewer on which chunks of food are broiled or roasted **2.** food, especially meat or fish, that has been cooked on a brochette [15C. < French, "little skewer" < *broche* "skewer, long needle"]

bro·chure /brō shoor/ *n* a booklet or pamphlet that contains descriptive information or advertising [Mid-18C. < French, "something stitched together" < *brocher* (see BROACH)]

bro·chure site *n* a simple, often one-page website advertising a company's products and giving contact details

Brock /brok/, **Sir Isaac** (1769–1812) British-born Canadian soldier. He was a military commander during the War of 1812.

Brock·en /brókən/ the highest point in the Harz Mountains, central Germany. It is associated with folklore and traditional rites, including Walpurgis Night, or the Witches' Sabbath. Height: 3,743 ft./1,141 m.

Brock·ton /bróktən/ city in southeastern Massachusetts, a southern suburb of Boston and northeast of Taunton. Population: 95,437 (2002 estimate).

~~**brocoli**~~ incorrect spelling of **broccoli**

bro·der·ie an·glaise /brōdəree ong gláyz/ *n* embroidery in the form of an ornamental pattern of small holes with stitched edges [Mid-19C. < French, "English embroidery"]

Brod·sky /bródskee/, **Joseph** (1940–96) Soviet-born US poet and essayist. He won the Nobel Prize in literature (1987) and was US poet laureate (1991–92).

> "The greatest thing a society can do to a citizen is to leave him alone."
> [Joseph Brodsky. Remarks at Dartmouth College Commencement, *New York Times*; June 12, 1989]

bro·gan /brṓgən/ *n* a heavy ankle-high work boot [Mid-19C. < Irish or Scottish Gaelic *brōgan* "little shoe" < *brōg* (see BROGUE²)]

Bro·glie /braw glée/, **Louis Victor, Prince de** (1892–1987) French physicist. He was awarded the Nobel Prize in physics (1929) for his work on electron waves and particles. Full name **Broglie, Louis Victor Pierre Raymond**

brogue¹ /brōg/ *n* a regional accent, especially the accent of Irish people speaking English [Early 18C. Origin ?]

brogue² /brōg/ *n* **1.** *UK* CLOTHING same as **wingtip** (sense 1) **2.** a simple heavy untanned shoe formerly worn in Ireland and Scotland [Late 16C. Via Irish and Scottish Gaelic *brōg* < Old Norse *brók* "leg covering"]

broil¹ /broyl/ *v* (**broiled, broil·ing, broils**) **1.** *vt* **COOK USING DIRECT HEAT** to cook food below direct heat, or be cooked in this way **2.** *vti* **BE VERY HOT** to make somebody or something extremely hot, or become extremely hot ○ *We had been broiling in the sun all morning.* **3.** *vi* **BE VERY ANGRY** to be extremely angry ■ *n* **1. USE OF DIRECT HEAT** a use of direct heat to cook something under **2. BROILED FOOD** a food cooked under direct heat [14C. < Old French *bruler*]

broil² /broyl/ *n* a brawl (*archaic*) [15C. < Anglo-Norman *broiller* "mix up, confuse," Old French *brōoillier* < *breu* "broth"] —**broil** *vi*

broil·er /bróylər/ *n* **1. ROASTING CHICKEN** a young chicken for roasting **2. GRATE FOR BROILING FOOD** a pan or grate on or under which to broil food **3. STOVE COMPARTMENT FOR BROILING** a part of a stove or oven in which to broil food **4. HOT DAY** a very hot day (*informal*)

broil·er pan *n* a metal tray used to hold food while broiling under a grill

broke¹ /brōk/ past tense of **break**

broke² /brōk/ *regional* past participle of **break** (*archaic*) ■ *adj* (*informal*) **1.** without any money to spend **2.** totally bankrupt [Early 18C. Alteration of BROKEN] ◇ **go for broke** to risk everything to achieve a goal (*informal*)

bro·ken /brṓkən/ past participle of **break** ■ *adj* **1. NO LONGER WHOLE** in two or more pieces, e.g., after having been dropped or struck with something hard **2. OUT OF ORDER** no longer in working condition ○ *The CD player is broken.* **3. NOT KEPT** not honored or fulfilled ○ *a broken promise* **4. NOT CONTINUOUS** lacking continuity ○ *a broken line* **5. UNEVEN** having an uneven surface ○ *We traveled over broken terrain.* **6. WEAKENED** physically weakened ○ *His health was broken.* **7. DESTROYED BY ADVERSITY** destroyed or badly hurt by grief or misfortune ○ *a broken man* **8. SPLIT APART** split apart by divorce, separation, or desertion ○ *came from a broken home* **9.** LANGUAGE **IMPERFECTLY SPOKEN** spoken in an imperfect or halting manner ○ *in broken English* **10. INCOMPLETE** lacking parts necessary to be complete ○ *a broken set of books* **11. DISORGANIZED** lacking order or harmony ○ *escaping in broken ranks* [Old English *brocen*, past participle of BREAK] —**bro·ken·ly** *adv* —**bro·ken·ness** *n*

Bro·ken Ar·row /brṑkən árrō/ city in northeastern Oklahoma, a southeastern suburb of Tulsa. Population: 83,088 (2002 estimate).

bro·ken chord *n* a chord played as a quick succession of notes (**arpeggio**) instead of simultaneously

bro·ken con·sort *n* a musical ensemble made up of instruments of different types, used especially in music of the Renaissance

bro·ken-down *adj* **1.** damaged or not working ○ *a broken-down old machine* **2.** in very poor condition ○ *a broken-down house*

bro·ken-field *adj* in football, making quick changes in direction while carrying the ball downfield in order to avoid widely scattered opposing players ○ *broken-field running*

bro·ken·heart·ed /brṑkən háartəd/ *adj* extremely sad because of the end of a love affair, great disappointment, or bereavement —**bro·ken·heart·ed·ly** *adv* —**bro·ken·heart·ed·ness** *n*

Bro·ken Hill city in western New South Wales, Australia. It is an important center for silver, lead, and zinc mining. Population: 20,908 (2002 estimate).

bro·ken road *n Carib* especially in Grenada, an unpaved or closed road or one that is under construction and may be impassable

bro·ker /brṓkər/ *n* **1.** somebody who is paid to act as an agent for others, e.g., in negotiating contracts or buying and selling goods and services **2.** FIN same as **stockbroker 3.** POL same as **power broker** ■ *vt* (**-kered, -ker·ing, -kers**) to act as an agent in arranging a deal, sale, or contract [14C. < Anglo-Norman *brocour* "small trader"]

bro·ker·age /brṓkərij/ *n* **1. PAYMENT TO BROKER** a fee paid to somebody who acts as a financial agent for somebody else **2. BROKER'S BUSINESS** the business of being a broker **3. STOCKBROKING COMPANY** a company whose business is buying and selling stocks and bonds for its clients

bro·ker-deal·er *n* in the United Kingdom, somebody employed on the Stock Exchange to buy and sell stocks, shares, goods, or assets on behalf of somebody else

bro·kered CD *n* a certificate of deposit issued by a bank and sold in bulk to a brokerage for selling on to its customers

brom- *prefix* bromine, bromic ○ *bromate* [< BROMINE, BROMIDE]

bro·mate /brṓ màyt/ *n* a salt, ester, or ion of bromic acid ■ *vt* (**-mat·ed, -mat·ing, -mates**) CHEM same as **brominate**

brome·grass /brṓm gràss/, **brome** /brōm/ *n* a tall grass with small drooping flower spikes. Some types of bromegrass are cultivated for hay, while others are weeds. Native to: temperate regions. Genus: *Bromus*. [Mid-18C. Via modern Latin *Bromus* < Greek *bromos, brōmos* "oats"]

bro·me·lain /brṓmə làyn, -lən/, **bro·me·lin** /-lən/ *n* an enzyme extracted from pineapples, used in alternative medicine to help the digestion of proteins, reduce blood clotting, counter inflammation, and boost immunity [Late 19C. < modern Latin *Bromelia*, after O. *Bromel* (see BROMELIAD)]

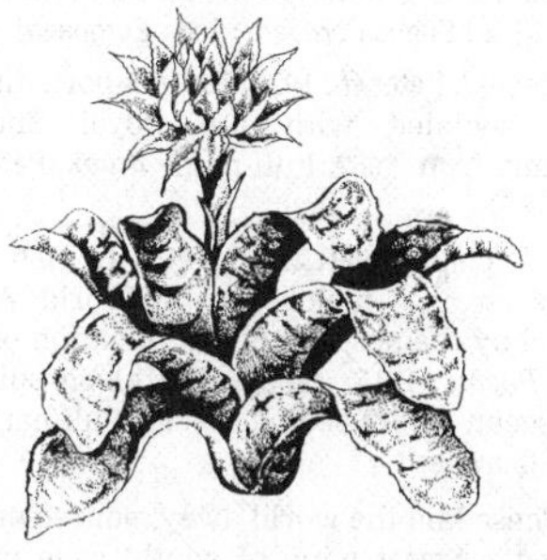

bromeliad

bro·me·li·ad /brō méelee àd/ *n* a tropical plant with fleshy leaves forming a funnel that holds water, often growing on another plant for physical support. Native to: Central and southern America. Family: Bromeliaceae. [Mid-19C. After Olaf *Bromel* (1639–1705), Swedish botanist]

bro·mic /brṓmik/ *adj* relating to or containing bromine with a valence of five

bro·mic ac·id *n* an unstable colorless acid that is a strong oxidizing agent. Use: manufacture of pharmaceuticals and dyes. Formula: $HBrO_3$.

bro·mide /brṓ mīd/ *n* **1.** CHEM **BROMINE COMPOUND** a compound containing bromine and another element or group, e.g., silver bromide **2.** CHEM **POTASSIUM BROMIDE** potassium bromide, especially when used as a sedative **3. UNORIGINAL SAYING** a saying that lacks originality or significance

bro·mide pa·per *n* a light-sensitive photographic paper that is coated with silver bromide emulsion

bro·mid·ic /brō míddik/ *adj* without originality or interest

bro·mi·nate /brṓmi nàyt/ (**-nat·ed, -nat·ing, -nates**) *vt* to treat or combine a substance with bromine or a bromine compound —**bro·mi·na·tion** /brṑmi náysh'n/ *n*

bro·mine /brṓ meen/ *n* a pungent, dark red, volatile, liquid, nonmetallic element of the halogen series. Use: sedatives, photographic materials. Symbol **Br**. See table at **element** [Early 19C. < French *brome* < Greek *brōmos* "stench"]

bro·mo·ben·zene /brṑmō bén zeen/ *n* a heavy colorless liquid with a pungent odor. Use: synthesis of chemicals, solvent.

bro·mo·crip·tine /brṑmō kríp teen/ *n* a drug that functions like dopamine. Use: treatment of excessive lactation, breast pain, some forms of infertility, growth disorder, and Parkinsonism.

bronc /brongk/ *n* same as **bronco** (*informal*) [Late 19C. Shortening]

bronch- *prefix* ANAT same as **broncho-** (*used before vowels*)

bron·chi ANAT plural of **bronchus**

bron·chi·al /bróngkee əl/ *adj* relating to or affecting the tubes (**bronchi**) that carry air from the windpipe into the lungs ○ *a bronchial infection* —**bron·chi·al·ly** *adv*

bron·chi·al pneu·mo·nia *n* MED same as **bronchopneumonia**

bron·chi·al tube *n* a tubular passage forming part of a network of airways to and within the lungs. Two main tubes (**bronchi**) lead from the windpipe to each lung, dividing into smaller bronchi and subsequently bronchioles.

bron·chi·ec·ta·sis /bròngkee éktəssiss/ *n* chronic dilation of the airways to and within the lungs, causing coughing and excessive mucus production [Late 19C. < late Latin *bronchia* (see BRONCHIOLE) + Greek *ektasis* "dilation"]

bron·chi·ole /bróngkee ōl/ *n* a narrow tube inside the lungs that branches off the main air passages (**bronchi**) [Mid-19C. < modern Latin *bronchiolus* < late Latin *bronchia* < Greek *brogkhos* (see BRONCHUS)] —**bron·chi·o·lar** /bròngkee ṓlər/ *adj*

bron·chi·tis /brong kī́tiss/ *n* inflammation of the mucous membrane in the airways (**bronchial tubes**) of the lungs, resulting from infection or irritation and causing breathing problems and severe coughing —**bron·chit·ic** /brong kíttik/ *adj*

broncho- *prefix* bronchus, bronchial ○ *bronchoscope* [Via late Latin < Greek *brogkhos* (see BRONCHUS)]

bron·cho·di·la·tor /bròngkō dī láytər, bròngkō dī́ làytər/ *n* a drug that relaxes the main air passages (**bronchi**) and eases breathing. Use: asthma treatment.

bron·cho·pneu·mo·nia /bròngkō noo mṓnee ə/ *n* inflammation of the lungs caused by an infection in the air passages (**bronchioles**)

bron·cho·scope /bróngkə skṑp/ *n* a thin instrument with a light on the end, used for looking inside the air passages (**bronchi**) leading to the lungs —**bron·cho·scop·ic** /bròngkə skóppik/ *adj* —**bron·cho·scop·i·cal·ly** *adv* —**bron·chos·co·pist** /brong kóskəpist/ *n* —**bron·chos·co·py** /-kóskəpee/ *n*

bron·chus /bróngkəss/ (*plural* **-chi** /-kī, -kee/) *n* a tube leading from the windpipe to a lung, which provides for the passage of air [Late 17C. Via modern Latin < Greek *brogkhos* "windpipe" < Indo-European]

bron·co /bróngkō/ (*plural* **-cos**) *n* a wild or partly broken horse, used in rodeos [Mid-19C. < Spanish, "rough, wild"]

bron·co·bust·er /bróngkō bùstər/ *n* a person who breaks wild horses (*informal*)

Bronf·man /brónfmən/, **Samuel Leonard** (1891?–1971) Canadian business executive. He was the founder and chief operating officer of the distilling company Seagrams.

Bron·të /bróntee/, **Anne** (1820–49) British novelist and poet. Sister of Charlotte Brontë and Emily Brontë, she wrote the novels *Agnes Grey* (published in 1847) and *The Tenant of Wildfell Hall* (published in 1848).

> "What is it that constitutes virtue, Mrs. Graham? Is it the circumstance of being able and willing to resist temptation; or that of having no temptations to resist."
> [Anne Brontë, *The Tenant of Wildfell Hall*; 1848]

Barnaby's

Charlotte Brontë

Bron·të, Charlotte (1816–55) British novelist. Elder sister of Emily Brontë and Anne Brontë, she wrote *Jane Eyre* (1847) and *Villette* (1853).

> "Conventionality is not morality. Self-righteousness is not religion. To attack the first is not to assail the last. To pluck the mask from the face of the Pharisee, is not to lift an impious hand to the Crown of Thorns."
> [Charlotte Brontë, *Jane Eyre*; 1847]

Bron·të, Emily (1818–48) British poet and novelist. Sister of Charlotte Brontë and Anne Brontë, she wrote *Wuthering Heights* (1847). See Cultural note at **height**

> "If all else perished, and he remained, I should still continue to be; and if all else remained, and he were annihilated, the universe would turn to a mighty stranger: I should not seem a part of it."
> [Emily Brontë, *Wuthering Heights*; 1847]

bron·to·sau·rus /bròntə sáwrəss/, **bron·to·saur** /bróntə sàwr/ *n* PALEONT same as **apatosaurus** (*dated*) [Late 19C. < modern Latin *Brontosaurus* < Greek *brontē* "thunder" + *sauros* "lizard"]

Bronx /brongks/ northernmost of the five boroughs of New York City, located on the mainland with the Harlem and Hudson rivers to the west, Westchester County to the north, Long Island Sound to the east, and the East River to the south. Population: 1,354,068 (2002 estimate).

Bronx cheer *n* a loud sound showing disapproval that is made by sticking the tongue out between closed lips and blowing (*informal*)

bronze /bronz/ *n* **1.** COPPER AND TIN ALLOY a hard yellowish brown alloy of copper and tin, sometimes containing small amounts of other metals. Bronze is harder than copper and is often cast to make statues. **2.** COPPER-BASED ALLOY an alloy of copper with a substance other than tin, e.g., aluminum or silicon **3.** SCULPTURE BRONZE WORK OF ART an object that is made from bronze, especially a statue or other piece of cast sculpture **4.** SPORTS same as **bronze medal** (*informal*) **5.** COLORS DEEP YELLOWISH BROWN COLOR a deep yellowish brown color, like that of bronze ■ *v* (**bronzed, bronz·ing, bronz·es**) **1.** *vt* MAKE SOMETHING LOOK LIKE BRONZE to give something the yellowish brown sheen or weathered patina of bronze **2.** *vti* TAN SKIN to make somebody's skin suntanned, or become suntanned (*informal*) [Early 18C. Via French < Italian *bronzo*] —**bronze** *adj* —**bronzed** *adj* —**bronz·er** *n* —**bronz·y** *adj*

Bronze Age *n* a period of cultural history, approximately between 3500 and 1500 B.C., that succeeded the Stone Age and was characterized by the use of tools made of bronze

bronze med·al *n* a medal that is awarded to a person who places third in a competition, especially a sporting event —**bronze med·al·ist** *n*

Bronze Star *n* a US military award given for heroism or meritorious service in nonaerial combat

Bron·zi·no, Il /bron zeénō/ ➧ **il Bronzino**

bron·zite /brón zīt/ *n* an iron-containing variety of enstatite with a metallic sheen

brooch /brōch, brooch/, **broach** /brōch/ *n* a piece of jewelry that is fastened to a garment by a hinged pin and catch. Brooches are usually worn by women on the upper part of a garment. [13C. < Old French *broche* "skewer, long needle"]

SPELLCHECK See *broach*.

brood /brood/ *v* (**brood·ed, brood·ing, broods**) **1.** *vi* WORRY to be preoccupied with a troublesome or unwelcome thought **2.** *vi* THINK UNPLEASANT THOUGHTS to think resentful, dark, or miserable thoughts **3.** *vti* HATCH EGGS to sit on or hatch eggs, or cover nestlings for warmth **4.** *vi* BE HEAVY OR OMINOUS to loom or hang heavily and ominously (*literary*) ○ *dark clouds brooding overhead* ■ *n* **1.** YOUNG OF BIRDS OR ANIMALS the young of an animal, especially young birds, that are born and reared together **2.** FAMILY'S CHILDREN the children of one family (*informal humorous*) **3.** GROUP OF SIMILAR PEOPLE a group whose members share a common origin or background ○ *the latest brood of avant-garde artists* ■ *adj* KEPT FOR BREEDING describes a female farm animal that is kept for the purpose of producing young ○ *a brood mare* [Old English *brōd* < Indo-European, "heat"]

brood·er /bróodər/ *n* **1.** HEATED PLACE FOR YOUNG ANIMAL a heated area or enclosure for raising young fowl. It provides an optimum environment in which heat, light, food, and water can be carefully controlled. **2.** FEMALE BIRD SITTING ON EGGS a female bird that sits on eggs to keep them warm before they hatch **3.** PERSON WHO WORRIES somebody who worries a lot about things

brood·mare /bróod mèr/ *n* a mare that is kept specially for breeding

brood·y /bróodee/ (**-i·er, -i·est**) *adj* **1.** describes a hen that is ready to sit on eggs to keep them warm before they hatch, especially a hen that is no longer able to lay eggs **2.** showing deep thought, anxiety, or resentment ○ *His long broody silences were hard to bear.* —**brood·i·ly** *adv* —**brood·i·ness** *n*

brook[1] /brŏŏk/ *n* a small freshwater stream [Old English *brōc* < Germanic]

brook[2] /brŏŏk/ (**brooked, brook·ing, brooks**) *vt* to put up with something (*literary; used in negative statements*) ○ *I will brook no interference in this matter.* [Old English *brūcan* < Indo-European]

Brook /brŏŏk/, **Peter** (*b.* 1925) British-born director. He was associated with the Royal Shakespeare Company from 1962. Full name **Brook, Peter Stephen Paul**

Brooke /brŏŏk/, **Rupert** (1887–1915) British poet. His reputation as a major poet of World War I was secured by the posthumous publication of *1914 and Other Poems* (1915). He died of blood poisoning in the Aegean before seeing action. Full name **Brooke, Rupert Chawner**

> "These laid the world away; poured out the red / Sweet wine of youth; gave up the years to be / Of work and joy, and that unhoped serene, / That men call age; and those who would have been, / Their sons, they gave, their immortality."
> [Rupert Brooke, "The Dead"; 1914]

Brook·er /brŏŏkər/, **Bertram** (1888–1955) British-born Canadian artist and writer. He painted *Sounds Assembling* (1928) and wrote *Think of the Earth* (1937).

Brook Farm *n* an experimental cooperative community established by a group of writers and scholars on a farm in West Roxbury, Massachusetts. It lasted from 1841 to 1846.

Brook·field /brŏŏk feeld/ **1.** city in southeastern Wisconsin, a northwestern suburb of Milwaukee, near Lake Michigan. Population: 39,510 (2002 estimate). **2.** suburb of Chicago, Illinois, west of the Des Plaines River. The Brookfield Zoo, established in 1934, is a major tourist attraction. Population: 18,899 (2002 estimate).

brook·ite /brŏŏ kīt/ *n* a translucent or reddish brown to black crystalline mineral composed of titanium dioxide [Early 19C. After Henry J. *Brook* (1771–1857), British mineralogist]

Brook·line /brŏŏk līn/ town in eastern Massachusetts, a southwestern suburb of Boston. It was the birthplace of President John F. Kennedy. Population: 57,032 (2002 estimate).

Brook·lyn /brŏŏklin/ one of the five boroughs of New York City, located on the western tip of Long Island with Staten Island and Manhattan to the west and Queens to the north and east. Population: 2,465,326 (2000).

Brook·lyn Cen·ter city in southeastern Minnesota, a northwestern suburb of Minneapolis. Population: 28,753 (2002 estimate).

Brook·lyn Park city in southeastern Minnesota, north of Minneapolis, on the Mississippi River. Population: 68,128 (2002 estimate).

Brook·ner /brŏŏknər/, **Anita** (*b.* 1928) British writer. Her novel *Hotel du Lac* (1984) won Britain's Booker Prize.

> "In real life, of course, it is the hare who wins. Every time. Look around you. And in any case it is my contention that Aesop was writing for the tortoise market...Hares have no time to read. They are too busy winning the game."
> [Anita Brookner, *Hotel du Lac*; 1984]

Brook Park city in northeastern Ohio, a southwestern suburb of Cleveland. Population: 20,940 (2002 estimate).

Brooks /brŏŏks/, **Gwendolyn** (1917–2000) US poet. Her *Annie Allen* (1949) won a Pulitzer Prize. Other works include *Children Coming Home* (1992). Full name **Brooks, Gwendolyn Elizabeth**

> "This is the urgency: Live! / and have your blooming in the noise of the whirlwind."
> [Gwendolyn Brooks, "The Second Sermon on the Warpland," *The Mecca*; 1968]

Brooks, Mel (*b.* 1926) US movie actor and director. His films include *The Producers* (1968) and *Blazing Saddles* (1974). Born **Kaminsky, Melvin**

> "Tragedy is if I cut my finger. Comedy is if I walk into an open sewer and die."
> [Mel Brooks, *New Yorker*; October 30, 1978]

Brooks, Van Wyck (1886–1963) US critic and biographer. He wrote *The Flowering of New England, 1815–65* (1936).

Brooks Range mountain range of northern Alaska, stretching from Kotzebue Sound eastward to the Canadian border, separating the North Slope from the Yukon Basin. Its highest peak is Mount Chamberlin, 9,239 ft./2,816 m.

brook trout *n* **1.** a freshwater fish of the salmon family that is a popular game fish. Native to: eastern North America, introduced elsewhere. Latin name: *Salvelinus fontinalis.* **2.** the flesh of a brook trout as food

broom /broom, brŏŏm/ *n* **1.** BRUSH FOR SWEEPING a brush with a head of twigs or bristles attached to a long thin handle, used for sweeping indoors or outdoors **2.** PLANT WITH BRIGHT YELLOW FLOWERS a wild or cultivated bush. Flowers: bright yellow. Native to: Europe, Asia. Latin name: *Cytisus scoparius.* **3.** PLANT LIKE BROOM a bush resembling broom. Flowers: yellow. Native to: Europe, Asia. Genera: *Genista* or *Spartium.* ■ *vt* (**broomed, broom·ing, brooms**) SWEEP SOMETHING to sweep something with a broom or brush [Old English *brōm* < Germanic]

broom·corn /broom kàwrn, brŏŏm-/ *n* a type of sorghum with long stiff stalks. Use: making brooms. Latin name: *Sorghum bicolor.*

Broom·field /broom feeld/ city in northern Colorado, southeast of Boulder and northwest of Denver. Population: 40,823 (2002 estimate).

broom·rape /broom ràyp, brŏŏm-/ *n* a plant that lives

on the roots of other plants, including crops. Genus: *Orobanche*. [Late 16C. < medieval Latin *rapum* "tuber"]

broom·stick /broom stik, broom-/ *n* **1.** the long handle of a broom **2.** a long-handled broom with a head of twigs

broom·tail group·er /broom tayl-, broom-/ *n* a heavy-bodied large-jawed fish found in Pacific coastal waters of California and Mexico. Latin name: *Mycteroperca xenarcha*.

Broon·zy /broonzee/, **Big Bill** (1893–1958) US musician. He incorporated a wide range of influences as a master composer and performer of blues. Born **Conley, William Lee**

bros., Bros. *abbr* COMM brothers

broth /brawth, broth/ *n* **1.** a liquid made by cooking vegetables, meat, seafood, or poultry in water for a long time, used as a base for soups and sauces **2.** a clear soup made by cooking meat, poultry, fish, seafood, or vegetables in water and then removing them [Old English *broþ* < Indo-European, "heat, boil"]

broth·el /bróth'l/ *n* a place where people pay to have sexual intercourse with prostitutes [14C. < Old English *broen* "ruined." Originally "worthless person, prostitute"; current use a shortening of *brothel-house*]

broth·er /brúthər/ *n* **1.** MALE SIBLING a boy or man who has the same father and mother as another person **2.** (*plural* **broth·ers** or **breth·ren** /bréthrən/) FELLOW MEMBER a man who belongs to the same ethnic group, religion, profession, trade, or organization as another man ○ *fraternity brothers* **3.** CLOSE MALE FRIEND used to address a close male friend **4.** (*plural* **broth·ers** or **breth·ren**) CHR LAY MEMBER a member of a religious order for men **5.** (*plural* **broth·ers** or **breth·ren**) CHR DEVOTED RELIGIOUS WORKER a man who devotes himself to the work of a men's religious order without having been professed ■ *interj* EXPRESSING SURPRISE OR ANNOYANCE used to express surprise, annoyance, or disappointment (*informal*) ○ *Oh, brother! What happened here today?* [Old English *brōþor* < Indo-European]

broth·er·hood /brúthər hood/ *n* **1.** GOODWILL a feeling of fellowship and sympathy for other people **2.** GROUP OF MEN an organization of men who are united for a common purpose, e.g., a labor union **3.** ALL MEMBERS all the members of a particular profession or trade **4.** HAVING SAME PARENTS the relationship of brothers

broth·er-in-law (*plural* **broth·ers-in-law**) *n* **1.** SISTER'S HUSBAND the husband of somebody's sister **2.** SPOUSE'S BROTHER the brother of somebody's husband or wife **3.** SPOUSE'S SISTER'S HUSBAND the husband of the sister of somebody's husband or wife

broth·er·ly /brúthərlee/ *adj* showing feelings that a brother might be expected to have toward his sister or brother —**broth·er·li·ness** *n*

brougham /broom, broo əm, brōm, brō əm/ *n* a one-horse carriage with an open seat at the front for the driver and a closed compartment at the back for passengers, used in the 19th century [Mid-19C. After Lord *Brougham* (1778–1868)]

brought past participle, past tense of **bring**

brought·up·sy /bráw tùpsee/ *n* Carib especially in Tobago, good manners indicating that somebody has been brought up well (*informal*) ○ *She eh have no broughtupsy.*

brou·ha·ha /broo haa haa/ *n* **1.** public criticism or protest ○ *all the brouhaha over the drug's side effects* **2.** a noisy commotion or uproar (*informal*) [Late 19C. < French]

Broun /broon/, **Heywood** (1888–1939) US journalist and novelist. He was a cofounder of the Newspaper Guild and a social campaigner. Full name **Broun, Heywood Campbell**

> "Posterity is as likely to be wrong as anybody else."
> [Heywood Broun, *Sitting on the World*; 1924]

brow /brow/ *n* **1.** the area on somebody's face above the eyes and below the hairline **2.** ANAT same as **eyebrow** (sense 1) **3.** the top edge of a hill or the highest part of a slope [Old English *brū* < Indo-European]

bro·wal·li·a /brə wáalee ə/ (*plural same* or **-as**) *n* an ornamental plant of the nightshade family. Flowers: blue, white, violet. Native to: America. Genus: *Browallia*. [Late 18C. < modern Latin, after Johann *Browall* (1707–55), Swedish botanist]

brow·band /brów bànd/ *n* a strap that is part of a horse's bridle and goes across its forehead

brow·beat /brów beet/ (**-beat, -beat·en** /-beet'n/, **-beat·ing, -beats**) *vt* to bully or intimidate somebody sternly ○ *I will not be browbeaten into making a hasty decision.* —**brow·beat·er** *n*

brown /brown/ *n* **1.** COLOR BETWEEN RED AND YELLOW a color that varies between red and yellow, similar to the color of wood or soil **2.** BROWN CLOTHING fabric or clothing that is brown in color ○ *We had to wear brown for school.* **3.** BROWN PIGMENT OR DYE a pigment or dye that has or is near to the color of wood or soil **4.** BROWN OBJECT an object that is brown in color ○ *She decided to take the brown.* ■ *adj* **1.** BROWN IN COLOR of the color brown ○ *the fruit was brown and rotten* **2.** SUNTANNED deeply suntanned or sunburned **3.** UNPROCESSED describes foodstuffs that are partially or wholly unprocessed so that their natural brown color remains ○ *brown sugar* ■ *vti* (**browned, brown·ing, browns**) MAKE OR BECOME BROWN to make something brown or become brown, e.g., in cooking or sunbathing [Old English *brūn* < Indo-European, "bright, brown"] —**brown·ish** *adj* —**brown·ness** *n*

Brown /brown/, **Sir Arthur Whitten** (1886–1948) British aviator. With John Alcock, he made the first transatlantic flight, from Newfoundland to Ireland, which took 16 hours 12 minutes.

Brown, Capability (?1716–83) British landscape gardener. He landscaped the grounds of many English country houses, including Blenheim Palace in Oxfordshire and Chatsworth in Derbyshire, and created a naturalistic style of landscape design. Born **Brown, Lancelot**

Brown, Charles Brockden (1771–1810) American writer. Considered by many to have been the first American novelist, he wrote the gothic novel *Wieland* (1798).

Brown, George (1818–80) Scottish-born Canadian journalist and politician. He founded the *Toronto Globe* and was prime minister for two days in 1858.

> "Those who seek to change an established government by force of arms assume a fearful responsibility—a responsibility which nothing but the clearest and most intolerable injustice will acquit them for assuming."
> [George Brown, *Speech, Toronto*; 1863]

Brown, James (*b.* 1928) US singer and songwriter. His use of polyrhythmic beats in songs such as "Papa's Got A Brand New Bag" (1965) and "Sex Machine" (1970) were highly influential in the development of funk and many subsequent forms of popular dance music. Known as **the Godfather of Soul**

Brown, Jim (*b.* 1936) US football player. He was an outstanding fullback with the Cleveland Browns (1957–65) and later acted in movies including *The Dirty Dozen* (1967). Full name **Brown, James Nathaniel**

Brown, John (1800–59) US abolitionist leader. Convicted of treason after a failed attempt to launch a slave rebellion, he was hanged in Virginia. The song "John Brown's Body" commemorates his actions.

> "I am fully persuaded that I am worth inconceivably more to hang than for any other purpose."
> [John Brown, *Remark*; November 2, 1859]

Brown, Moses (1738–1836) US philanthropist. He helped eradicate slavery in Rhode Island and started the first US cotton factory (1789).

Brown, Olympia (1835–1926) US suffragist and cleric, the first woman ordained as a cleric in a major US denomination

brown ad·i·pose tis·sue *n* PHYSIOL same as **brown fat**

brown al·ga *n* an alga found in the ocean that has chlorophyll masked by brown pigment. Kelps and wracks are brown algae. Division: *Phaeophyta*.

brown-bag (**brown-bagged, brown-bag·ging, brown-bags**) *vti* **1.** to bring a lunch to work from home, typically in a brown paper bag or similar container **2.** to take your own alcoholic drink into a public establishment such as a restaurant or a club that does not have a license to sell alcohol (*informal*)

brown bear *n* a bear that is mainly brown in color, e.g., a grizzly bear. Native to: western North America, northern Europe, northern Asia. Latin name: *Ursus arctos*.

Brown Bet·ty /-béttee/ *n* a baked apple dessert made from apples, breadcrumbs, sugar, spices, butter, and sometimes raisins

brown bread *n* **1.** bread made using whole-wheat flour **2.** an old-fashioned bread containing molasses, made to rise with baking soda, and either steamed or baked

brown coal *n* a soft brown-black fossil fuel with visible plant remains and a high moisture content

brown dwarf *n* a star that is smaller than a planet and has a mass equivalent to less than one-tenth of the Sun's mass

Browne /brown/, **Sir Thomas** (1605–82) English doctor and essayist. His best-known work, *Religio Medici* (1635?), is a discourse on scientific reasoning and religious faith.

brown earth *n* soil formed in temperate humid regions under deciduous forests and characterized by a dark brown layer rich in organic material

brown fat *n* a dark-colored fatty tissue in many mammals, especially hibernating animals and human babies, that produces heat in order to control body temperature

brown·field /brówn feeld/ *n* an urban development site that has been previously built on or environmentally contaminated and is currently unusable or abandoned [Late 20C. After GREENFIELD]

Brown·i·an move·ment /brównee ən-/, **Brown·i·an mo·tion** *n* the random movement of microscopic particles suspended in a liquid or gas that occurs as a result of collisions with molecules of the surrounding medium [After Robert *Brown* (1773–1858), British botanist]

brown·ie /brównee/ *n* **1.** a piece of flat rich chocolate cake baked in a square or rectangular pan and sometimes containing chopped nuts **2.** in folklore, a small supernatural being believed to do helpful work at night

Brown·ie *n* a member of the Girl Scouts of the United States of America, aged from six to eight years of age [Because of the brown uniform]

brown·ie point, Brown·ie point *n* a notional credit earned for doing something helpful, especially in order to please (*informal*) [< the points used by Brownies for advancement]

Brown·ing /brówning/, **Elizabeth Barrett** (1806–61) British poet. Her works include *Sonnets from the Portuguese* (1850), *Aurora Leigh* (1856), and *Poems Before Congress* (1860). She married Robert Browning in 1846 and lived with him in Italy. Born **Barrett, Elizabeth**

> "'Yes,' I answered you last night; / 'No,' this morning, sir, I say / Colours seen by candle-light / Will not look the same by day."
> [Elizabeth Barrett Browning, "The Lady's Yes"; 1844]

Brown·ing, Robert (1812–89) British poet. His works include *Men and Women* (1855), *Dramatis Personae* (1864), and *The Ring and the Book* (1868–69). He married Elizabeth Barrett Browning in 1846. See Cultural note at **Pied Piper**

> "Ah, but a man's reach should exceed his grasp, / Or what's a heaven for?"
> [Robert Browning, "Andrea del Sarto," *Men and Women*; 1855]

Brown·ing au·to·mat·ic ri·fle *n* an air-cooled, gas-operated, magazine-fed rifle with a .30 caliber barrel, capable of firing between 200 and 350 rounds per minute with an effective range of 2,000 ft./600 m [After John M. *Browning* (1855–1926), US arms designer]

Brown·ing ma·chine gun *n* an air- or water-cooled, belt-fed, automatic machine gun with either a .30 or .50 caliber barrel, capable of firing over 500 rounds per minute [See BROWNING AUTOMATIC RIFLE]

brown lace·wing *n* an insect with brownish wings that often feeds on agricultural pests. Family: Hemerobiidae.

brown·lands /brówn làndz/ *npl* land for development that has been previously developed but is currently unused

brown lung dis·ease, **brown lung** *n* MED same as **byssinosis**

brown mus·tard *n* **1.** the dark reddish brown, oil-rich seeds of a mustard plant. Use: cooking spice. **2.** an annual plant of the mustard family with irregularly lobed leaves that produces brown mustard seeds. Latin name: *Brassica juncea.*

brown·nose /brówn nōz/ (**-nosed, -nos·ing, -nos·es**) *vti* to be unnaturally subservient or obsequious to somebody in authority (*slang; sometimes offensive*) [Implying willingness to undertake stigmatized intimacy as in the offensive phrase *kiss ass*] —**brown·nose** *n* —**brown·nos·er** *n*

brown·out /brówn òwt/ *n* **1.** DIMMING OF LIGHTS a dimming of lights or reduction in the use of electrical appliances in a city or region, especially as an economy measure **2.** POWER REDUCTION a temporary reduction in electrical power caused by high consumer demand or by a technical malfunction **3.** LAPSE OF CONCENTRATION a temporary lapse of concentration or focus [Mid-20C. After BLACKOUT]

brown owl *n* BIRDS same as **tawny owl**

brown pa·per *n* thick strong brown-colored paper used for wrapping packages and for making paper bags

brown patch *n* a soil-borne fungal disease of grass that produces round dead patches

brown rat *n* an extremely destructive rat found in populated areas. Native to: originally Europe and Asia, now worldwide. Latin name: *Rattus norvegicus.*

brown re·cluse spi·der *n* a pale brown poisonous spider with a violin-shaped mark on the head area. Native to: United States, South America. Latin name: *Loxosceles reclusa.*

brown rice *n* unpolished rice in which the yellowish brown outer layer containing the bran remains intact, making it more nutritious than white rice

brown rot *n* a disease of ripe tree fruits such as apples and peaches, caused by fungi. The infected fruit turns brown, and concentric yellow rings appear on the plant. Genus: *Rhizoctonia.*

brown sauce *n* a sauce made from a dark meat stock, thickened with flour that has been browned in fat

Brown Shirt *n* **1.** a member of a Nazi uniformed paramilitary organization that originally formed Adolf Hitler's personal bodyguard and was later used as a militia. Brown Shirts assisted Hitler's rise to power, but lost their influence to the SS following the assassination of their leader Erich Röhm in 1934. **2.** an offensive term for somebody who is regarded as being a violent racist (*insult*) [Translation of German *Braunhemd*, from the brown uniform shirts of the Nazi storm troopers]

brown·stone /brówn stōn/ *n* **1.** a reddish brown sandstone used as a building material **2.** a house or building made from or faced with reddish brown sandstone, especially an apartment building in New York City

brown sug·ar *n* **1.** REFINED SUGAR WITH MOLASSES a soft light or dark brown sugar made from refined white sugar combined with mild refined molasses and used in cooking **2.** UNREFINED SUGAR unrefined or partially refined sugar **3.** HEROIN the drug heroin (*slang*)

Browns·ville /brównz vìl/ city and port in southern Texas, on the Río Grande, opposite Matamoros, Mexico. Population: 150,425 (2002 estimate).

Brown Swiss *n* a large brown dairy cow belonging to a hardy breed originating in Switzerland

brown-tail moth *n* a white and brown moth whose caterpillars destroy the leaves of trees and produce a substance that is toxic to humans. Native to: Europe, eastern United States. Latin name: *Euproctis chrysorrhoea.*

brown thrash·er *n* a bird that is related to the mockingbird and has a long tail, long curving beak, reddish brown back, and white breast with black spots. Native to: eastern and central United States, rain forests of Dominica and the Lesser Antilles. Latin name: *Toxostoma rufum.*

brown trout *n* **1.** a common brownish freshwater fish. Native to: Europe, northern America. Latin name: *Salmo trutta.* **2.** the flesh of a brown trout as food

browse /browz/ *v* (**browsed, brows·ing, brows·es**) **1.** *vi* LOOK THROUGH OR OVER SOMETHING CASUALLY to look through or over something, especially merchandise in a store, in a leisurely manner with the hope of finding something of interest **2.** *vti* READ CASUALLY to read through something quickly or superficially **3.** *vti* COMPUT, ONLINE SCAN COMPUTER FILES to scan and view files in a computer database or on the Internet, especially on the World Wide Web **4.** *vti* ZOOL FEED ON LEAVES AND SHOOTS to feed on tender vegetation such as the shoots, leaves, or twigs above ground level of bushes or trees (*refers to animals*) ■ *n* **1.** SESSION OF BROWSING a superficial read through something such as a newspaper, or a leisurely look over something such as the merchandise in a store **2.** FEEDING PERIOD a session during which an animal feeds on tender shoots or twigs of bushes and trees **3.** TENDER VEGETATION USED AS FOOD the tender shoots, leaves, or twigs above ground level of bushes and trees used as food by animals [Early 16C. Via obsolete French *broust* < Old French *brost* < Germanic]

brows·er /brówzər/ *n* **1.** a piece of computer software used to search for information on the World Wide Web **2.** somebody who looks at something such as a book or merchandise for sale, in a leisurely or superficial manner

Bru·beck /broó bèk/, **Dave** (*b.* 1920) US pianist and composer. He is known for his progressive jazz compositions such as *Take Five* (1959). Full name **Brubeck, David William**

> "Jazz is about the only form of art existing today in which there is freedom of the individual without the loss of group contact."
> [Dave Brubeck. Quoted in *The Jazz Book*, Joachim Berendt; 1982]

bru·cel·lo·sis /broòssə lóssiss/ *n* a chronic infectious disease of some domestic animals that can be transmitted to human beings through contaminated milk [Mid-20C. < modern Latin *Brucella*, genus name of causative bacteria, after Sir David *Bruce* (1855–1931), Scottish physician]

Bruch /broòk, broòkh/, **Max** (1838–1920) German composer. His compositions include a violin concerto and the *Kol Nidrei* variations (1880–81), which draw on Hebrew melodies.

bru·cine /broó seen/ *n* a poisonous white crystalline alkaloid. Source: nux vomica seeds. Use: denaturation of alcohol. Latin name: *Strychnos nux-vomica.* Formula: $C_{23}H_{26}N_2O_4$. [Early 19C. < modern Latin *Brucea*, genus name of a tree formerly thought to bear the bark that the substance is derived from]

bru·cite /broó sìt/ *n* a magnesium hydroxide mineral. Source: hydrothermal deposits, metamorphosed limestone. [Early 19C. After Archibald *Bruce* (1777–1818), US mineralogist]

Bruck·ner /broóknər/, **Anton** (1824–96) Austrian composer. He wrote nine symphonies and four masses. His music was influenced by Wagner and Schubert.

Brue·ghel /bróyg'l, broóg'l/, **Brue·gel, Breu·ghel, Jan** (1568–1625) Flemish painter. The son of Pieter Brueghel he produced still lifes and landscape paintings.

Brue·ghel, Brue·gel, Breu·ghel, Pieter (1520–69) Flemish painter. He produced religious and moral allegories in contemporary landscapes, depicting peasant life in works such as *Peasant Wedding* (1568). Known as **Pieter Brueghel the Elder**

Bruges /broozh/ capital of West Flanders Province, western Belgium. It is famous for its traditional lace industries. Population: 116,559 (2001).

bru·in /broó in/, **Bruin** *n* used as a name for a bear in folklore, fables, and children's stories [15C. < Middle Dutch, "brown"]

bruise /brooz/ *n* **1.** SKIN DISCOLORATION CAUSED BY INJURY a tender area of skin discoloration caused by blood leaking from blood vessels damaged by pressure or impact **2.** DAMAGE TO PLANT TISSUE damage to underlying plant or fruit tissue, visible as a soft discolored area on the unbroken surface and caused by pressure or impact **3.** EMOTIONAL INJURY an injury that is not physical, e.g., hurt feelings or damaged self-esteem ■ *v* (**bruised, bruis·ing, bruis·es**) **1.** *vti* INJURE CAUSING SKIN DISCOLORATION to injure a part of the body, or sustain an injury, resulting in discoloration caused by blood leaking from damaged blood vessels **2.** *vti* DAMAGE PLANT TISSUE to damage plant tissue by pressure or impact, or sustain such damage, leaving a softened and discolored surface area **3.** *vt* UPSET SOMEBODY to injure somebody's feelings or harm somebody's self-esteem ○ *I was bruised by the criticism.* **4.** *vt* COOK CRUSH FOOD to crush or pound food, especially to extract juice from it or bring out its flavor [Partly < Old English *brȳsan* "crush," and partly < Anglo-Norman *bruser* "break" < Germanic]

bruis·er /broózər/ *n* a large strong man or youth, e.g., a boxer, bodyguard, bar bouncer, or football player (*informal*)

bruis·ing /broózing/ *n* bruises or the dark patches left on the surface of bruised skin ■ *adj* causing emotional, psychological, or physical pain

bruit /broot/ *n* **1.** RUMOR OR REPORT a story, true or untrue, that is passed around among people (*archaic*) **2.** MED SIGNIFICANT SOUND INSIDE BODY a medically significant sound heard inside the body, usually with the aid of a stethoscope, and caused by turbulent blood flow within the heart or blood vessels ■ *vt* (**bruit·ed, bruit·ing, bruits**) SPREAD STORY to circulate stories, whether true or untrue [15C. < Old French < past participle of *bruire* "roar"]

Brû·lé /broo láy/, **Étienne** (1592?–1632) French-born Canadian explorer. He lived among Native Americans and was perhaps the first European to see the Great Lakes.

brume /broom/ *n* a weather condition in which fog or mist is present, or the fog or mist itself (*literary*) [Early 18C. Via French, "fog" < Latin *bruma* "winter"] —**bru·mous** *adj*

brum·ma·gem /brúmməjəm/, **Brum·ma·gem** *n* something, especially imitation jewelry, that is cheap and gaudy [Mid-17C. < *Brummagem*, dialectal form of BIRMINGHAM, England, originally referring to counterfeit coins made there]

Brum·mell /brúmm'l/, **Beau** (1778–1840) British dandy. A courtier and friend of George IV, he was a fashion-setter in Regency England. Born **Brummell, George Bryan**

brunch /brunch/ *n* a meal that combines breakfast and lunch, eaten late in the morning [Late 19C. Blend of BREAKFAST + LUNCH]

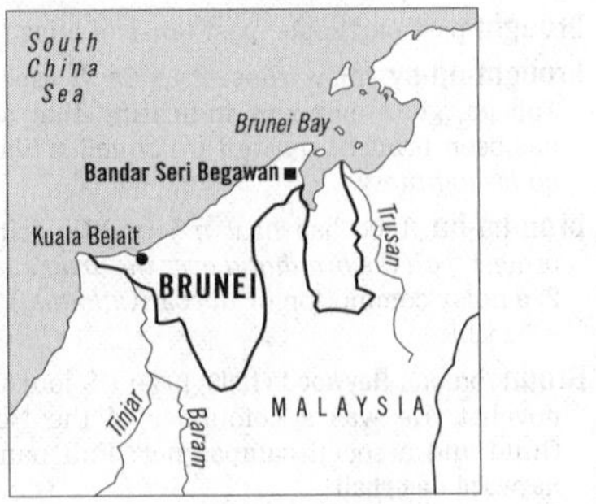

Brunei

Bru·nei /broo nì/ country bisected by the Malaysian state of Sarawak in northwestern Borneo, eastern Asia. It became an independent member of the British Commonwealth in 1984. Language: Malay. Currency: ringgit or Brunei dollar. Capital: Bandar Seri Begawan. Population: 358,098 (2003). Area: 2,226 sq. mi./5,765 sq. km. Official name **Negara Brunei Darussalam**

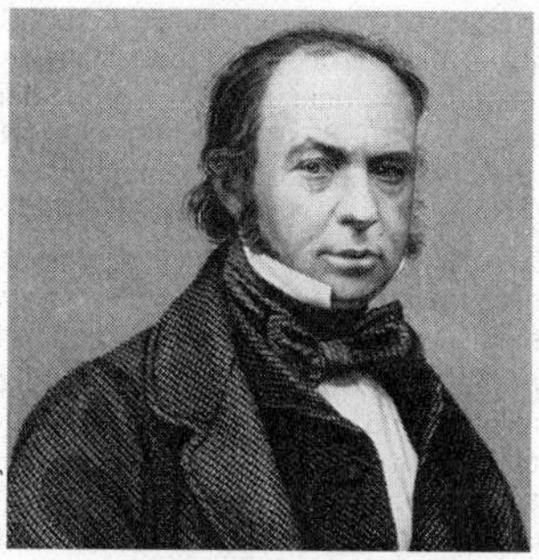

Isambard Kingdom Brunel

Bru·nel /broo nél/, **Isambard Kingdom** (1806–59) British engineer. He designed the Clifton Suspension Bridge and constructed the *Great Western* (1837), the first steamship designed to cross the Atlantic.

Bru·nel·les·chi /bro͝onə léskee/, **Filippo** (1377–1446) Italian architect and sculptor. One of the greatest Renaissance architects, he designed the dome of the cathedral in Florence (1420–61) and built several churches in Florence. Born **di Ser Brunellesco, Filippo**

bru·net /broo nét/ *n* somebody with dark or brown hair [Mid-16C. < French < *brun* "brown" < Germanic] —**bru·net** *adj*

bru·nette /broo nét/ *n* a girl or woman with dark brown hair [Early 17C. < French, feminine form of *brunet* (see BRUNET)] —**bru·nette** *adj*

Brun·hild /bro͝on híld/, **Brun·hil·de** /-híldə/ *n* in medieval Germanic mythology, the queen of Iceland who promises to marry whoever can defeat her in battle. Siegfried does so on behalf of King Gunther.

Bru·no /bro͞onō/, **St.** (1030?–1101) German monk in the French mountains at Chartreuse. He founded a monastery of hermit monks (1084), which later became the Carthusian contemplative order. Known as **Bruno the Carthusian**

Bruns·wick /brúnzwik/ **1.** city in southeastern Georgia, on the northern shore of St. Simons Sound, southwest of Savannah. Population: 15,598 (2002 estimate). **2.** town in southeastern Maine, on the Androscoggin River, southeast of Lewiston and northeast of Portland. Population: 21,364 (2002 estimate). **3.** city in northern Ohio, southwest of Cleveland. Population: 35,200 (2002 estimate).

Bruns·wick stew *n* a stew that contains vegetables and usually wild game meat such as squirrel or rabbit [After *Brunswick* County, Virginia]

brunt /brunt/ *n* **1.** the main force or effect of something such as a blow or criticism ○ *We always had to bear the brunt of her anger.* **2.** the greater part or the main burden [14C. Origin ?]

bru·schet·ta /broo skéttə, -shéttə/ *n* Italian bread toasted and drizzled with olive oil, usually served with added garlic and chopped tomatoes [< Italian < *bruscare* "roast over coals"]

brush[1] /brush/ *n* **1. TOOL WITH BRISTLES ATTACHED TO HANDLE** an implement consisting of bristles, hair, or wire set into a handle, used for grooming the hair, painting, polishing, scrubbing, or sweeping **2. USE OF BRUSH** the use of a brush, e.g., to groom the hair or to sweep a surface **3. LIGHT CONTACT** a light stroke or momentary contact **4. SHORT UNPLEASANT ENCOUNTER** a brief unpleasant encounter ○ *a brush with evil* **5. BUSHY TAIL OF FOX** a bushy tail, especially the tail of a fox as a hunting trophy **6. ELECTRICAL CONDUCTOR** an electrical conductor that makes sliding contact between a stationary and a moving part of a generator or motor while completing a circuit and conveying a current **7.** ELEC same as **brush discharge** ■ *v* **(brushed, brush·ing, brush·es) 1.** *vti* **USE BRUSH ON SOMETHING** to use a brush to clean, groom, or polish something **2.** *vt* **APPLY SOMETHING WITH BRUSH** to apply something such as paint or varnish to a surface using a brush **3.** *vt* **REMOVE SOMETHING WITH BRUSH** to remove something with a brush or a sweeping motion **4.** *vt* **REJECT SOMETHING** to dismiss, ignore, or rebuff something or somebody in an abrupt or curt manner ○ *They brushed aside the suggestion.* **5.** *vti* **GRAZE AGAINST SOMETHING** to touch something lightly and briefly in passing [14C. < Old French *broisse*, probably variant of *broce* (see BRUSH[2])] —**brush·er** *n* —**brush·y** *adj* ◇ **tar somebody with the same brush** to attribute unfairly the faults and failings of somebody to another person

brush off *vt* to dismiss or disregard somebody or something in an abrupt manner

brush up *vt* to refresh or renew knowledge of or skill in something

brush[2] /brush/ *n* **1. THICK UNDERGROWTH** a dense undergrowth of small trees and bushes **2. LAND COVERED WITH THICK UNDERGROWTH** land covered with a dense undergrowth of small trees and bushes **3.** same as **brushwood** (sense 1) **4. BACKWOODS** wild and sparsely populated woodland [14C. < Anglo-Norman *brousse*, variant of Old French *broce* "broken branches"]

brush bor·der *n* a dense layer of tiny protuberances that lines some absorbing cells such as those in the intestine and kidney

brush cut *n* a hairstyle with the hair cropped close to the head so that it stands up like the bristles of a brush

brush dis·charge *n* a luminous electric discharge between two conductors, consisting of a flow of ionized particles with less intensity than a spark [< its appearance]

brushed /brusht/ *adj* **1.** describes a knitted or woven fabric that has a nap produced by brushing it during manufacture **2.** describes a metallic surface with a nonreflective sheen

brush·fire /brúsh fīr/ *n* **1. FIRE IN DRY BRUSH** a fire in dry brush and scrub that usually spreads quickly **2. SMALL CRISIS** a minor crisis, often one of many **3. SMALL WAR** a localized but often intensely fought war ■ *adj* **INVOLVING LOCAL MILITARY** involving only small-scale and local military mobilization

brush·mark /brúsh maark/ *n* a mark or line left by the bristles of a brush on a painted or varnished surface

brush·off /brúsh àwf, -òf/ *n* an abrupt dismissal, rejection, or snub (*informal*)

brush·stroke /brúsh strōk/ *n* a movement of a paintbrush that produces a particular look or mark on a painted surface, or the mark itself

brush·wood /brúsh wo͝od/ *n* **1.** cut or broken branches and twigs **2.** same as **brush**[2] (senses 1–2)

brush·work /brúsh wùrk/ *n* **1.** the characteristic manner in which an artist applies paint with a brush **2.** the product of an artist's use of a brush in painting

brusque /brusk/ *adj* abrupt, blunt, or curt in manner or speech [Early 17C. Via French < late Latin *bruscum* "coarse, rough"] —**brusque·ly** *adv* —**brusque·ness** *n*

Brus·sels /brúss'lz/ largest city and capital of Belgium. It is situated in the center of Belgium and is the headquarters of the European Union and the North Atlantic Treaty Organization (NATO). Population: 954,460 (1999).

Brus·sels car·pet *n* a carpet with a heavy patterned pile of small woolen loops attached to a linen base

Brus·sels grif·fon *n* BREED same as **griffon** (sense 1) [Because the breed originated in Belgium]

Brus·sels lace *n* **1.** a fine lace with a floral design, made with bobbins or with needle and thread, that originated in or near Brussels **2.** a machine-made net lace with an appliqué design

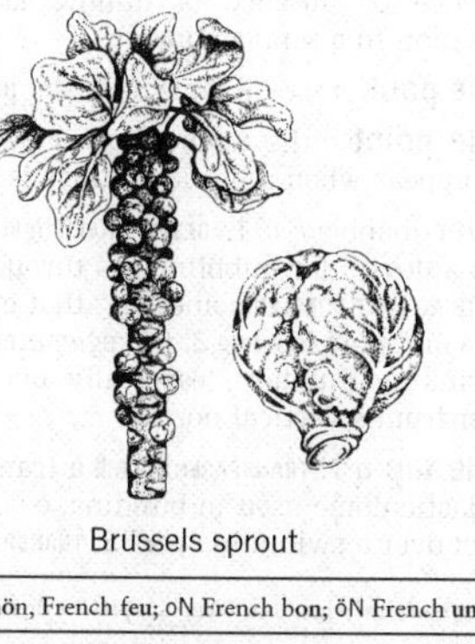
Brussels sprout

Brus·sels sprout *n* **1.** a small green swollen bud like a tiny cabbage that is eaten as a vegetable **2.** a plant related to cabbage that has a thick stalk lined with Brussels sprouts. Latin name: *Brassica oleracea*. [Because first grown near Brussels]

brut /broot/ *adj* describes wine, especially sparkling white wine, that is extremely dry in taste [Late 19C. < French]

bru·tal /bro͞ot'l/ *adj* **1. RUTHLESS AND CRUEL** extremely ruthless or cruel **2. HARSH AND SEVERE** unrelentingly harsh and severe ○ *a brutal regimen* **3. DIRECT IN MANNER** direct or insensitive in manner or speech ○ *with brutal frankness* [15C. Directly or via French < medieval Latin *brutalis* < Latin *brutus* (see BRUTE)] —**bru·tal·ly** *adv* —**bru·tal·ness** *n*

bru·tal·ism /bro͞ot'l ìzzəm/ *n* a style of modern architecture characterized by massiveness, a lack of exterior decoration, harsh lines, and the exposure of structural materials —**bru·tal·ist** *n, adj*

bru·tal·i·ty /broo tállətee/ (*plural* **-ties**) *n* **1.** cruel, harsh, or ruthless behavior or treatment **2.** a cruel, harsh, or ruthless act

bru·tal·ize /bro͞ot'l īz/ (**-ized, -iz·ing, -iz·es**) *vt* **1.** to make somebody brutal or unfeeling **2.** to treat somebody brutally, cruelly, or harshly —**bru·tal·i·za·tion** /bro͞ot'li záysh'n/ *n*

brute /broot/ *n* **1. SOMEBODY BRUTAL** somebody regarded as cruel, ruthless, or insensitive **2. ANIMAL** an animal other than a human being (*literary*) ■ *adj* **1. PURELY PHYSICAL** purely physical or instinctive, rather than intellectual or reasoned **2. CRUEL OR SAVAGE** displaying extreme cruelty and savagery **3. STARK** unremittingly harsh or severe **4. CRUDE OR BARBARIC** describes behavior, actions, or instincts that are considered crude, especially those prompted by physical desire and hunger **5. OF BEASTS** relating or belonging to lower animals, as opposed to human beings [15C. Via French < Latin *brutus* "stupid, like an animal" < Indo-European, "heavy"] —**brut·ism** *n*

brut·ish /bro͞otish/ *adj* **1. SAVAGE** cruel, ruthless, or violent in behavior, actions, or instincts **2. LACKING INTELLIGENCE** coarse or crude in a manner that suggests a lack of intelligence **3. RELATING TO BEASTS** relating to or characteristic of lower animals —**brut·ish·ly** *adv* —**brut·ish·ness** *n*

Bru·tus /bro͞otəss/, **Lucius Junius** (*fl* late 6th century B.C.) Roman consul. He drove the Etruscan royal family, the Tarquins, out of Rome and founded the Roman republic. He was elected one of the first two Roman consuls.

Bru·tus, Marcus Junius (85?–42 B.C.) Roman general. He sided with Pompey against Caesar during the civil war (49 B.C.), and was a principal conspirator in Caesar's assassination (44 B.C.). He was defeated by Mark Antony and Octavian at Philippi (42 B.C.), and committed suicide.

brux·ism /bro͝oks ìzzəm/ *n* the unconscious habit of grinding or gritting the teeth that occurs during sleep or in stressful situations and can lead to excessive wear of the teeth [Mid-20C. < Greek *brukein* "gnash the teeth"]

Bry·an /brī ən/ city in eastern Texas, northeast of Austin and northwest of Houston. Population: 66,669 (2002 estimate).

Bry·an, William Jennings (1860–1925) US reformer, orator, and lawyer. Three times the losing Democratic candidate for president, he advocated unlimited coinage of silver, notably in his famous "Cross of Gold" speech (1896). As the winning prosecutor in the Scopes trial (1925), he upheld the right of the states to ban the teaching of evolution.

> "The humblest citizen of all the land, when clad in the armor of a righteous cause, is stronger than all the hosts of error."
> [William Jennings Bryan, *The First Battle: A Story of the Campaign of 1896*; 1896]

Bry·ant /brī ənt/, **William Cullen** (1794–1878) US poet, critic, and editor. His work included the nature poems "Thanatopsis" (1817) and "To a Waterfowl" (1821).

> "The melancholy days are come, the saddest of the year, / Of wailing winds

and naked woods and meadows brown and sear."
[William Cullen Bryant, "The Death of the Flowers"; 1832]

Bryce Can·yon Na·tion·al Park /brīss-/ national park in southwestern Utah, established in 1928 and noted for its highly colored, unusually eroded rock formations. Area: 56 sq. mi./145 sq. km.

Brym·ner /brímnər/, **William** (1855–1925) Scottish-born Canadian painter. He was an influential art teacher.

Bryn·hild /brín hìld/ *n* in Norse mythology, a Valkyrie who is woken from an enchanted sleep by Sigurd and later tricked into marrying his brother-in-law, Gunnar

bryo- *prefix* moss ○ *bryophyte* [< Greek *bruon*]

bry·ol·o·gy /brī óllajee/ *n* the branch of plant science concerned with the study of hornworts, mosses, and liverworts —**bry·o·log·i·cal** /brī ə lójjik'l/ *adj* —**bry·ol·o·gist** *n*

bry·o·ni·a /brī ṓnee ə/ *n* a homeopathic remedy prepared from bryony. Use: treatment of flu and other conditions. [Pre-12C. < Latin (see BRYONY)]

bry·o·ny /brī́ anee/ *n* a climbing plant with large leaves, tendrils, and red or black berries. Native to: Europe, North Africa. Genus: *Bryonia*. [Pre-12C. Via Latin *bryonia* < Greek *bruonia* < *bruein* "teem"]

bry·o·phyte /brī́ ə fìt/ *n* a nonflowering plant, often growing in damp places, that has separate gamete-bearing and spore-bearing forms, e.g., moss. Division: *Bryophyta*. —**bry·o·phyt·ic** /brī̀ ə fíttik/ *adj*

bry·o·zo·an /brìə zṓ ən/ *n* an invertebrate ocean animal that reproduces by budding. Bryozoans often form colonies on the sea bottom or attached to seaweed. Phylum: Bryozoa. [Late 19C. < modern Latin *Bryozoa* < Greek *bruon* "moss" + *zoion* "animal"] —**bry·o·zo·an** *adj*

Bryth·on /bríth'n, bri thón/ *n* somebody who speaks Breton, Welsh, or Cornish [Late 19C. < Welsh]

Bry·thon·ic /bri thónnik/, **Brit·ton·ic** /-tónnik/ *n* a group of languages that belongs to the Celtic branch of Indo-European languages and includes Breton, Cornish, and Welsh. Native speakers: 1 million. ■ *adj* relating to the Brythons, or their language or culture [Late 19C. < Welsh *Brython* "Briton"]

bs *abbr* Bahamas (*used in Internet addresses*) See table at **domain name**

BS *abbr* **1.** EDUC Bachelor of Surgery **2.** ACCT balance sheet

B.S. *abbr* **1.** EDUC Bachelor of Science **2.** ACCT balance sheet **3.** LAW bill of sale **4.** bullshit (*slang taboo*)

BSA *abbr* Boy Scouts of America

BSc. *abbr* EDUC Bachelor of Science

BSE *n* a disease that affects the nervous system of cattle, believed to be caused by a transmissible protein particle (**prion**) and related to Creutzfeldt-Jakob disease in humans. Full form **bovine spongiform encephalopathy**

B share *n* a mutual fund investment in which the main charges are levied toward the end of the investment period

B-side *n* the side of a vinyl pop-music or jazz single that does not contain the title track and is considered less important

B.S.N. *abbr* EDUC Bachelor of Science in Nursing

BST *abbr* AGRIC bovine somatotropin

bt *abbr* Bhutan (*used in Internet addresses*) See table at **domain name**

Bt. *abbr* baronet

b-to-b *abbr* business-to-business

btry. *abbr* MIL battery

Btu, btu, BTU *abbr* MEASURE British thermal unit

BTW, btw *abbr* by the way (*used in e-mails or text messages*)

bty. *abbr* MIL battery

bu. *abbr* **1.** bureau **2.** MEASURE bushel

bua·ya /bwáa yə/ *n Malaysia, Singapore* a man who tends to flirt (*informal*) [< Malay, "crocodile"]

bub /bub/ *n* used as a term of address to an unnamed male person, especially one encountered and spoken to casually (*slang*) [Mid-19C. Shortening and alteration of BROTHER]

bub·ba /búbbə/ *n* **1.** *Can, Southern US* a typically rural white Southern man with traditional or conservative values and political opinions (*sometimes considered offensive*) **2.** *Southern US* a brother or friend who is close enough to regard as a brother (*often a term of address between man friends or brothers*) [Mid-19C. Alteration of BROTHER]

bub·ble /búbb'l/ *n* **1.** THIN GLOBE-SHAPED AIR-FILLED FILM a thin spherical or dome-shaped film that is filled with air or a gas **2.** SOMETHING LIKE BUBBLE something spherical or dome-shaped like a bubble **3.** GLOBULE WITHIN LIQUID OR SOLID a globule of air or a gas in a liquid such as a soft drink or in a solid such as glass **4.** GURGLING SOUND a gurgling sound made by a boiling or effervescent liquid **5.** SOUND OF MANY BUBBLES BURSTING a sound produced by bubbles forming and bursting **6.** DOME a dome, usually made of transparent glass or plastic **7.** PROTECTED AREA a protected, isolated, or exempted area **8.** FALSE CONFIDENCE a false feeling of confidence or security ○ *The rocketing housing market is a bubble that will surely burst.* **9.** RISKY PLAN a risky or unreliable business enterprise or speculative plan, especially one proving to be fraudulent or unsuccessful ○ *suffered when the dot-com bubble burst* ■ *v* (**-bled, -bling, -bles**) **1.** *vi* EFFERVESCE OR BOIL UP to form or produce spherical or dome-shaped pockets of air or gas in a liquid **2.** *vi* GURGLE to move or flow with a gurgling sound **3.** *vi* EMERGE OR APPEAR to emerge or rise to the surface ○ *the views and attitudes that are now bubbling up* **4.** *vi* BE LIVELY WITH EMOTION to be animated with or display an emotion such as excitement, happiness, or anger ○ *bubbling with mirth* **5.** *vt* EXPRESS SOMETHING ENTHUSIASTICALLY to say something with great animation and friendly enthusiasm **6.** *vt* MAKE SOMETHING BUBBLE to cause something to form bubbles or to move in bubbles through a liquid [14C. Probably an imitation of the sound of bubbling water]

bub·ble and squeak *n UK* a British dish consisting of leftover cooked potatoes and cabbage chopped up and fried together [Because of the sounds during cooking]

bub·ble bath *n* **1.** a usually perfumed and colored preparation in liquid or crystal form that is added to bath water in order to make it foam **2.** a bath to which a preparation has been added to make the water foam

bub·ble cham·ber *n* a chamber containing a liquid, usually liquid hydrogen just above its boiling point, in which the trail of a particle can be observed as a line of bubbles created by the particle

bub·ble·gum /búbb'l gùm/ *n also* **bub·ble gum 1.** CHEWING GUM THAT FORMS BUBBLES chewing gum that can be blown from the mouth into large bubbles **2.** POP MUSIC FOR TEENAGERS commercial pop music aimed at the younger teenage market and usually considered to be lacking originality (*informal*) ■ *adj also* **bub·ble-gum** (*informal*) **1.** APPEALING TO ADOLESCENTS appealing to or characteristic of the style, taste, or behavior of adolescents, especially when considered immature **2.** BLAND, INSIPID, OR VAPID lacking originality, careful mature thought, or seriousness

bub·ble-jet print·er *n* a printer in which heated ink forms bubbles that burst onto the paper

bub·ble mem·o·ry *n* computer memory in which data is stored as binary digits represented by the presence or absence of minute areas of magnetization in a semiconductor

bub·ble pack *n* MANUF same as **blister pack**

bub·ble point *n* the temperature at which bubbles first appear when a liquid mixture is heated

bub·bler /búbblər/ *n* **1.** DEVICE THAT BUBBLES GAS THROUGH LIQUID a device for bubbling gas through a liquid **2.** SOMETHING THAT BUBBLES something that emits bubbles, e.g., a mountain spring **3.** *US regional* DRINKING FOUNTAIN a drinking fountain, especially one that spouts water from a vertical nozzle

bub·ble top *n* **1.** TRANSPARENT DOME a transparent glass or plastic dome used in building, e.g., one forming a roof over a swimming pool **2.** TRANSPARENT DOME USED AS VEHICLE TOP a transparent dome, usually made of bulletproof plastic or glass, that forms the top or roof of a motor vehicle used by a public figure such as a head of state **3.** VEHICLE WITH TRANSPARENT DOME AS ROOF a motor vehicle that has a bubble top —**bub·ble·top** *adj*

bub·ble-wrap /búbb'l ràp/ *n* a sheet of plastic material covered with air-filled bubbles, used for wrapping fragile objects in order to protect them in transit

bub·bly /búbblee/ *adj* (**-bli·er, -bli·est**) **1.** CHEERFULLY EXCITED feeling and exhibiting cheerful excitement **2.** FOAMY OR EFFERVESCENT full of or producing bubbles **3.** LIKE BUBBLES resembling a bubble or bubbles in shape or sound ■ *n* CHAMPAGNE sparkling wine, especially champagne (*informal*) —**bub·bli·ness** *n*

Bu·ber /bóobər/, **Martin** (1878–1965) Austrian-born Israeli theologian and philosopher. He was an intellectual leader of German Jews before World War II and expounded his influential religious philosophy of dialogue in his best-known work, *I and Thou* (1922).

"God does not want to be believed in, to be debated and defended by us, but simply to be realized through us."
[Martin Buber. Quoted in *On Judaism*, N. Glazer (ed.), Eva Jose et al. (trs.); 1967]

bu·bo /byóobō/ (*plural* **-boes**) *n* swelling and inflammation of a lymph node, especially in the area of the armpit or groin [14C. Via Latin < Greek *boubōn* "swelling in the groin"]

bu·bon·ic /boo bónnik/ *adj* describes a swelling (**bubo**) of the lymph nodes

bu·bon·ic plague *n* an infectious fatal epidemic disease, caused by the bacterium *Yersinia pestis* transmitted by fleas that have previously bitten an infected animal or person, and characterized by fever, chills, and the formation of swellings (**buboes**). In the 14th century, an extensive epidemic of it occurred, known as the Black Death. In modern times, infection is limited and sporadic and can be treated successfully with antibiotics. [< Latin *bubon-*, stem of *bubo* (see BUBO)]

bu·bon·o·cele /boo bónnə sèel/ *n* an incomplete hernia of the groin accompanied by swelling [Early 17C. Via modern Latin < Greek *boubōnokēlē* "groin rupture"]

buc·cal /búk'l/ *adj* **1.** relating to or forming part of the cheek ○ *the buccal surface of a tooth* **2.** relating to the mouth [Early 19C. < Latin *bucca* "cheek"]

buc·cal smear *n* a gentle scraping of the inside of the cheek with a spatula in order to obtain DNA samples and cells for chromosomal and other studies

buc·ca·neer /bùkə néer/ *n* **1.** PIRATE a pirate, especially one who preyed on Spanish colonies and shipping in the Caribbean in the 17th century **2.** UNSCRUPULOUS ADVENTURER OR BUSINESSPERSON a ruthless or unscrupulous adventurer, businessperson, or politician ■ *vi* (**-neered, -neer·ing, -neers**) ACT LIKE BUCCANEER to be or behave like a buccaneer [Mid-17C. < French *boucanier* < *boucaner* "cook over an open fire"] —**buc·ca·neer·ing** *adj, n* —**buc·ca·neer·ish** *adj*

buc·ci·na·tor /búksə nàytər/ *n* a flat thin muscle that compresses the cheek and is used in blowing and chewing [Late 17C. < Latin < *buccinare* "blow the trumpet" < *buccina*, a kind of trumpet]

Bu·ceph·a·lus /byoo séffələss/ *n* the favorite war horse of Alexander the Great, which he tamed when still a boy

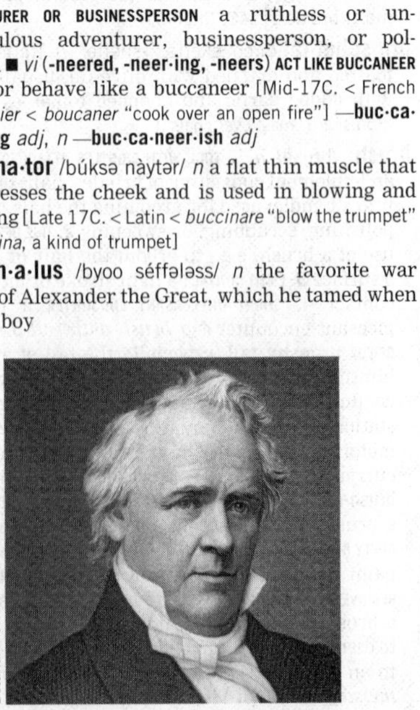

James Buchanan

Bu·chan·an /byoo kánnən, bə-/, **James** (1791–1868) 15th president of the United States. A Federalist turned Democrat, he was a US Representative (1821–31), Senator (1834–45), and secretary of state (1845–49). During his presidency (1857–61) he was unable to avert the Civil War (1861–65). See illustration on previouse page and table at **president**

Bu·cha·rest /bóokə rèst/ largest city and capital of Romania. It is situated on a plain in the southeastern part of the country, north of the Danube River. Population: 2,037,005 (1999).

Bu·chen·wald /bóokən wàwld, bóo<u>kh</u> ən-/ village near Weimar, central Germany, that was the site of a World War II Nazi concentration camp (1937–45)

Buch·ner /bóoknər, bóo<u>kh</u>-/, **Eduard** (1860–1917) German chemist. He attributed the fermentation of yeast to enzyme reaction and won the Nobel Prize in chemistry (1907) for this discovery.

Buch·ner fun·nel, Büch·ner fun·nel *n* a cylindrical filter funnel with a flat perforated base through which liquids are drawn under reduced pressure [After Eduard BUCHNER]

bu·chu /bóo koo/ (*plural* **-chus** or *same*), **bu·cku** (*plural* **-ckus** or *same*) *n* a bush with leaves that are used as a mild diuretic and urinary antiseptic. Native to: southern Africa. Genus: *Agathosma*. [Mid-18C. Via Afrikaans < Nama]

Buch·wald /búk wàwld/, **Art** (*b.* 1925) US journalist. His popular column, first appearing in the *International Herald Tribune* and later widely syndicated in the United States, offered a satirical view of American life and politics. Full name **Buchwald, Arthur**

> "This is not an easy time for humorists because the government is far funnier than we are."
> [Art Buchwald, *New York Times*; June 28, 1987]

buck[1] /buk/ *n* **1. MALE ANIMAL** a male animal of some species, including the antelope, deer, goat, kangaroo, and rabbit **2.** (*plural same* or **bucks**) *S Africa* **ANTELOPE OR DEER** an antelope or deer of either sex **3.** INDUST same as **buckskin** (sense 1) **4. ARTICLE MADE OF BUCKSKIN** an object made of buckskin, e.g., a shoe **5. VIRILE YOUNG MAN** a man, especially a strong, virile, impetuous, or spirited young man (*dated informal*) **6. DANDY OR FOP** a young man who takes elaborate care to be neat and stylish (*archaic*) ■ *adj* **OF LOWEST MILITARY GRADE** of the lowest grade within a particular military category [Old English *buc* "male deer," *bucca* "male goat" < Germanic]

buck up *vti* to become more cheerful, confident, or encouraged, or make somebody do this (*informal*)

buck[2] /buk/ *v* (**bucked, buck·ing, bucks**) **1.** *vi* **JUMP UPWARD** to jump or rear upward with the back arched and the legs stiff (*refers to horses*) **2.** *vt* **THROW RIDER** to throw a rider by rearing or jumping upward on the hind legs or forelegs **3.** *vi* **MAKE JOLTING MOTION** to move in a jerky or erratic manner **4.** *vti* **STAND IN OPPOSITION** to oppose or resist something obstinately ○ *buck the trend* **5.** *vi* **STRIVE WITH DETERMINATION FOR SOMETHING** to use grit and determination in striving for something, typically over the long term (*informal*) ○ *buck for a promotion* **6.** *vt* **GAMBLE AGAINST SOMETHING** to take a risk against something ○ *buck the odds* **7.** *vti* **BUTT WITH LOWERED HEAD** to charge against somebody or something with the head lowered ■ *n* **ACT OF BUCKING** the movement or action of bucking [Mid-19C. < BUCK[1]]

buck[3] /buk/ *n* (*informal*) **1.** a United States, Canadian, Australian, or New Zealand dollar **2.** a specified or unspecified amount of money [Mid-19C. Shortening of BUCKSKIN, used as a unit of exchange on the American frontier] ◇ **make a fast** *or* **quick buck** to make a profit on a quick and often dishonest transaction

buck[4] /buk/ *n* **1.** a covered block used as a vaulting horse **2.** CONSTR same as **sawhorse** [Early 19C. < BUCK[1]]

buck[5] /buk/ *n* a counter or marker formerly used in poker and passed from one player to another to indicate some obligation, especially somebody's turn to deal [Mid-19C. Origin ?] ◇ **pass the buck** to shift responsibility to somebody else (*informal*)

Buck /buk/, **Pearl S.** (1892–1973) US writer. She is best known for novels depicting Chinese life, including *The Good Earth* (1931), which won the Pulitzer Prize. She won the Nobel Prize in literature (1938). Born **Sydenstricker, Pearl**

> "Nothing and no one can destroy the Chinese people. They are relentless survivors. They are the oldest civilized people on earth. Their civilization passes through phases but its basic characteristics remain the same. They yield, they bend to the wind, but they never break."
> [Pearl S. Buck, *China, Past and Present*; 1972]

buck·a·roo /bùkə róo/ (*plural* **-roos**), **buck·er·oo** (*plural* **-oos**) *n* **1.** a cowhand in the southwestern United States (*informal*) **2.** a cowhand who breaks wild horses [Early 19C. Alteration of Spanish *vaquero* "cowboy," after BUCK[2]]

REGIONAL NOTE See ***vaquero***.

buck·bean /búk bēen/ *n* a marsh plant of the gentian family. Flowers: white, pink, purplish. Native to: northern hemisphere. Latin name: *Menyanthes trifoliata*. [Late 16C. Translation of Flemish *boks boonen* "goat's beans"]

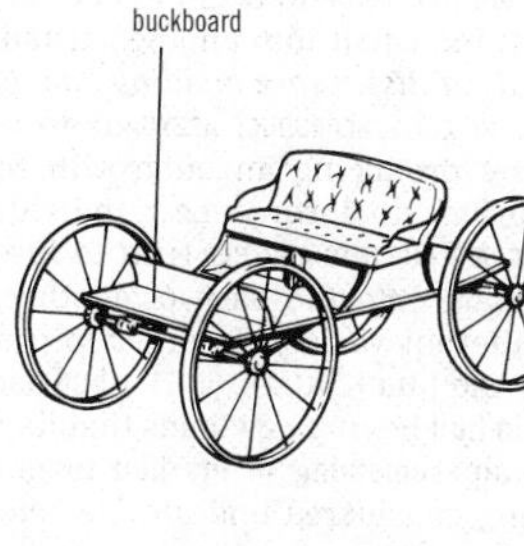

buckboard

buck·board /búk bàwrd/ *n* an open four-wheeled horse-drawn carriage with the seat or seats mounted on a flexible board between the front and rear axles [Late 17C. < obsolete *buck* "belly, body (of a wagon)"]

buck·er·oo *n* AGRIC another spelling of **buckaroo** (*informal*)

buck·et /búkit/ *n* **1. CYLINDRICAL CONTAINER** a container, usually cylindrical in shape with an open top and a semicircular handle, used for catching or holding liquids or solids **2. BUCKETFUL** the contents of a bucket, or the amount that a bucket will hold **3. LARGE QUANTITY** a very large quantity or amount of something (*informal; often used in the plural*) ○ *buckets of money* **4. SOMETHING LIKE BUCKET** something resembling a bucket in shape or function, e.g., a compartment on the outer edge of a water wheel or the scoop on a mechanical shovel **5.** FOOD INDUST **FOOD CONTAINER** a large plastic or paper container for food, e.g., fried chicken or ice cream **6.** TRANSP same as **bucket seat** **7.** BASKETBALL same as **basket** (sense 5) ■ *v* (**-et·ed, -et·ing, -ets**) **1.** *vt* **PUT SOMETHING IN BUCKET** to carry, hold, lift, or put something in a bucket **2.** *vi* **MOVE FAST** to move or drive fast, jerkily, haphazardly, or recklessly (*informal*) ○ *We went bucketing down the freeway.* [13C. < Anglo-Norman *buket* < Germanic] ◇ **kick the bucket** to die (*slang*)

buck·et bri·gade *n* a line of people formed to pass buckets of water from hand to hand, especially to put out a fire

buck·et·ful /búkit fòol/ *n* **1.** the contents of a bucket or the amount that a bucket will hold **2.** a very large quantity or amount of something (*informal; usually used in the plural*)

buck·et lad·der *n* a continuous chain of buckets used for excavating land or dredging riverbeds (*hyphenated when used before a noun*) ○ *a bucket-ladder dredger*

buck·et seat *n* an individual seat with a rounded back in a vehicle or aircraft

buck·et shop *n* a dishonest unregistered stockbrokerage that speculates on stocks and commodities using its clients' capital [Originally a saloon selling liquor from buckets]

buck·eye /búk ī/ *n* **1.** a prickly or smooth fruit of a tree or bush of the horse chestnut family, or the large shiny brown poisonous seed it contains **2.** (*plural* **buck·eyes** or *same*) the tree or bush that produces buckeyes. Native to: North America. Genus: *Aesculus*. [Mid-18C. Because of the seed's resemblance to a deer's eye]

Buck·eye /búk ī/ *n* somebody who comes from Ohio (*informal*) [Because of the abundance of buckeye trees in Ohio]

Buck·eye State *n* a nickname for Ohio

buck fe·ver *n* (*informal*) **1.** nervous excitement felt by an inexperienced hunter at the sight of game **2.** nervous excitement felt by somebody faced with a new situation, experience, or responsibility

buck·horn /búk hàwrn/ *n* **1. MATERIAL FROM BUCK'S HORN** the material from the horn of a male deer or antelope. Use: handles for knives and tools. **2. HORN OF BUCK** the horn of a male deer or antelope **3.** (*plural* **buck·horns** or *same*) **PLANT WITH LEAVES RESEMBLING ANIMAL'S HORN** a plant with leaves shaped like the horns of a deer or antelope. Native to: Europe, Asia. Latin name: *Plantago coronopus*.

buck·hound /búk hòwnd/ *n* a hound used for chasing game, especially deer

Buck·ing·ham /búkingəm, búking hàm/, **George Villiers, 2nd Duke of** (1628–87) English courtier. He was a privy councilor to Charles II and one of the most influential political figures of the Restoration. He is remembered for his satirical comedy *The Rehearsal* (1671).

> "The world is made up for the most part of fools and knaves, both irreconcilable foes to truth."
> [George Villiers Buckingham, "To Mr Clifford On His Humane Reason," *Dramatic Works*; 1715]

Buck·ing·ham Pal·ace /bùkingəm pálləss, -ham-/ *n* the official London residence of the British monarch, built in 1703

Buck·ing·ham·shire /búkingəm shēer, -ham-, -shər/ county in southern England, northwest of London. Its administrative center is Aylesbury. Population: 479,026 (2001). Area: 1,883 sq. mi./727sq. km.

buck·le /búk'l/ *n* **1. METAL FASTENER** a clasp, usually consisting of a metal frame with a hinged prong, for fastening two loose ends, especially the ends of a belt, shoe, or strap **2. ORNAMENT LIKE BUCKLE** an ornament that resembles a buckle, e.g., one on a shoe or a hat **3. BULGING OR BENDING PART** a bend or kink in something such as a rope, or a bulge in something such as a piece of wood ■ *v* (**-led, -ling, -les**) **1.** *vti* **FIX SOMETHING WITH BUCKLE** to fasten something such as a shoe or seat belt with a buckle, or be fastened with such a device **2.** *vti* **BEND OR CAUSE SOMETHING TO BEND** to bend out of shape, warp, or crumple, usually because of heat or pressure, or bend something in this way **3.** *vi* **COLLAPSE** to collapse or lose physical strength completely, sometimes as a result of a structural defect or weakness **4.** *vi* **GIVE IN** to succumb or yield to mental or emotional pressure [14C. Via Anglo-Norman *bucle*, Old French *bocle* < Latin *buccula* "cheek strap of a helmet" < *bucca* "cheek"]

buckle down *vi* to set out to accomplish something with vigor or determination (*informal*)

buckle under *vi* to give in under pressure or stress

buckle up *vti* to fasten the buckle on a belt designed to keep the wearer securely in a seat in a vehicle or an aircraft

buck·ler /búklər/ *n* a small round shield either worn on the forearm or held by a short handle at arm's length [13C. < Old French *bocler* < *bocle* "boss of a shield" (see BUCKLE)]

buck·ler fern *n* a perennial deciduous or semi-evergreen fern that grows to about 3 ft./1 m in height. Native to: Europe. Genus: *Dryopteris*. [Because of the flap of tissue covering the receptacle in which its spores are formed]

Buck·ley /búklee/, **William F., Jr.** (*b.* 1925) US writer and editor. A conservative political commentator, he was founding editor of the *National Review* (1955) and hosted the television program "Firing Line"

(1966). His books include *The Culture of Liberty* (1993). Full name **Buckley, William Frank, Jr.**

> "The most casual student of history knows that, as a matter of fact, truth does *not* necessarily vanquish...The cause of truth must be championed, and it must be championed dynamically."
> [William F. Buckley, Jr., *God and Man at Yale*; 1951]

buck·min·ster·ful·ler·ene /bùkminstər fo͝ollə reen/ *n* a stable form (**allotrope**) of carbon containing 60 atoms [Late 20C. < the molecule's resemblance to the geodesic dome structure invented by R. Buckminster FULLER]

buck·na·ked, **buck na·ked** *adj* wearing no clothes at all

buck·o /búkō/ (*plural* **-os**) *n* **1.** a swaggering bully or bossy person (*slang*) **2.** *N Am, Ireland* a boy or man (*informal*) [Late 19C. < BUCK[1]]

buck-pass·ing *n* the shifting of blame or responsibility to somebody else (*informal*) [< BUCK[5]] —**buck-pass·er** *n*

buck·ram /búkrəm/ *n* a coarse cotton or linen fabric that has been stiffened with starch, gum, or latex. Use: bookbinding, stiffening clothes. ■ *adj* resembling buckram in rigidity [14C. < Old French *boquerant* "cloth from Bukhara"]

bucks /buks/ *npl* buckskin breeches or shoes, especially casual oxford shoes

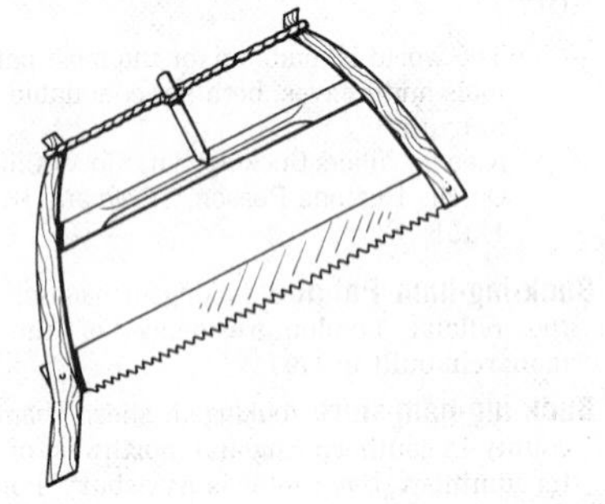

bucksaw

buck·saw /búk sàw/ *n* a saw in which the blade is set in an "H"-shaped frame [Mid-19C. < BUCK[4]]

buck·shot /búk shòt/ *n* a large size of lead shot used in shotgun shells, especially for hunting game

buck·skin /búk skìn/ *n* **1.** DEERSKIN the skin of a male deer **2.** SOFT LEATHER a soft pliable grayish yellow leather, usually with a suede finish, originally made from deerskin and now usually from sheepskin **3.** SOMEBODY WEARING BUCKSKIN somebody wearing clothes made of buckskin, especially an American colonist living in the backwoods or an early frontier soldier (*archaic*) ■ **buck·skins** *npl* BUCKSKIN GARMENTS clothing made from buckskin leather, especially jackets, chaps, hats, and moccasins

buck·thorn /búk thàwrn/ (*plural* **-thorns** or *same*) *n* a thorny bush or small tree with black berries. Genus: *Rhamnus*. [Late 16C. Translation of modern Latin *cervi spina* "stag's thorn"]

buck·tooth /bùk to͞oth/ (*plural* **-teeth** /-teeth/) *n* a protruding upper front tooth (*informal*) —**buck·toothed** *adj*

buck·u *n* TREES another spelling of **buchu**

buck·wheat /búk weet, -hweet/ *n* **1.** a triangular seed that can be ground into flour. Use: cereal foods, animal fodder. **2.** a plant that produces buckwheat. Native to: Asia. Latin name: *Fagopyrum esculentum*. [Mid-16C. Anglicization of Middle Dutch *boecweite* "beech wheat"; because its grains resemble beech nuts]

buck·y·ball /búkee bàwl/ *n* a stable ball-shaped molecule of carbon (**fullerene**), especially the molecule containing 60 atoms (**buckminsterfullerene**) (*informal*) [Late 20C. < *Bucky*, nickname of R. Buckminster FULLER]

buck·y tube /búkee-/ *n* a tube-shaped molecule consisting of carbon atoms, usually 60 (*informal*) [Late 20C. After BUCKYBALL]

bu·cli·zine /byo͞oklə zeen, -zīn/ *n* an antihistamine drug. Use: control of nausea, vomiting, and some types of migraine.

bu·col·ic /byoo kóllik/ *adj* **1.** OF COUNTRYSIDE relating to or characteristic of the countryside or country life ○ *a writer of bucolic poems* **2.** OF SHEPHERDS relating to or characteristic of shepherds, herdsmen, or flocks ■ *n* LITERAT PASTORAL POEM a poem about the countryside or country life [Early 16C. Via Latin < Greek *boukolikos* < *boukolos* "cowherd"] —**bu·col·i·cal·ly** *adv*

bud[1] /bud/ *n* **1.** OUTGROWTH ON PLANT STEM an outgrowth on a stem or branch consisting of a shortened stem and immature leaves or flowers, often enclosed by protective scales **2.** UNOPENED FLOWER a flower that has not yet opened **3.** ZOOL REPRODUCTIVE OUTGROWTH OF SIMPLE ORGANISM an asexually produced outgrowth of a simple organism such as an invertebrate or a yeast that breaks away from the parent and develops into a new individual **4.** SOMETHING LIKE PLANT BUD something shaped like a plant bud **5.** SOMEBODY OR SOMETHING IMMATURE somebody or something that is small, immature, or not yet fully developed ■ *v* (**bud·ded, bud·ding, buds**) **1.** *vi* PRODUCE PLANT BUDS to produce outgrowths that develop into flowers or leaves **2.** *vi* START TO GROW to start to develop or grow from a plant bud **3.** *vi* BEGIN TO DEVELOP to begin to develop or grow from something small into another, usually larger thing ○ *Seeds of dissent are budding among the new recruits.* **4.** *vi* ZOOL REPRODUCE ASEXUALLY to reproduce asexually by producing an outgrowth that eventually separates to form a new individual **5.** *vt* GARDENING GRAFT BUD INTO ANOTHER PLANT to insert a bud from one plant into the bark of another, usually one of a different variety, in order to propagate a plant from the bud [14C. Origin ?] —**bud·der** *n* —**bud·less** *adj* ◇ **in bud** having new buds that have not yet opened ◇ **nip something in the bud** to put an end to something considered undesirable before it can develop (*informal*)

bud[2] /bud/ *n* same as **buddy** *n* (sense 2) (*informal*) [Mid-19C. Shortening]

Bu·da·pest /bo͞odə pèst, -pèsht/ capital and largest city of Hungary. It is situated on the Danube River in northern Hungary near the Slovak border. Population: 1,811,522 (2001).

Buddha: Daibutsu (Great Buddha), Kamakura, Japan

bud·dha /bo͞oddə/, **Bud·dha** *n* **1.** in Buddhism, somebody who has attained perfect enlightenment **2.** a statue, picture, or other representation of the Buddha [Late 17C. < Sanskrit, past participle of *budh-* "wake up, be enlightened"]

Bud·dha /bo͞oddə/ (563?–483? B.C.) Nepalese-born Indian philosopher and founder of Buddhism. About 528, he renounced his life as a prince and began his teaching after having attained enlightenment through meditation. Born **Gautama, Siddharta**. Known as **Sakyamuni**

> "I do not fight with the world but the world fights with me."
> [Buddha. Quoted in *Buddhism*, Edward Conze; 1951]

Bud·dha·hood /bo͞oddə ho͝od/ *n* the state of spiritual enlightenment attained by the Buddha

Bud·dhism /bo͝od ìzzəm, bo͞od-/ *n* a world religion or philosophy based on the teaching of the Buddha and holding that a state of enlightenment can be attained by suppressing worldly desires

Bud·dhist /bo͝oddist, bo͞od-/ *n* somebody who professes Buddhism —**Bud·dhist** *adj* —**Bud·dhis·tic** /boo dístik, bo͞o dístik/ *adj*

bud·dhu /bo͞o do͞o/ *n* *S Asia* an offensive term that deliberately insults somebody's intelligence or capacity to learn (*informal*) [< Hindi]

bud·ding /búdding/ *adj* PROMISING beginning to show a particular talent ○ *a budding actor* ■ *n* **1.** BOT DEVELOPMENT OF BUDS the formation and growth of buds on a plant stem **2.** GARDENING GRAFTING OF BUD artificial propagation, especially of woody plants, by grafting a bud from one variety onto the stem of another **3.** ZOOL ASEXUAL REPRODUCTION a form of asexual reproduction in which an outgrowth of the parent becomes constricted and eventually separates to form a new individual, as occurs in invertebrates and yeasts

bud·dle /búdd'l/ *n* a sloping trough in which crushed ore is separated from waste by washing with water [Mid-16C. Origin ?]

bud·dle·ia /búddlee ə, bud leeə/ (*plural* **-ias** or *same*) *n* a deciduous ornamental bush or small tree with flowers that attract butterflies. Flowers: small, scented, purple, in tapering heads. Native to: South America. Latin name: *Buddleja davidii*. [Late 18C. < modern Latin, after Adam *Buddle* (d. 1715), English botanist]

bud·dy /búddee/ *n* (*plural* **-dies**) **1.** FRIEND a good friend, coworker, companion, or partner (*informal*) **2.** TERM OF ADDRESS FOR MALE a form of address to a man or boy (*informal*) ○ *Hey, buddy!* **3.** HELPER TO AIDS PATIENT a volunteer who gives help and support to somebody who has AIDS ■ *vi* (**-died, -dy·ing, -dies**) HELP SOMEBODY WHO HAS AIDS to act as a helper to somebody with AIDS [Mid-19C. Perhaps alteration of BROTHER]

buddy up *vi* to become friends with or work closely with somebody else (*informal*)

bud·dy-bud·dy *adj* appearing to enjoy a close friendship (*informal*)

bud·dy mov·ie, **bud·dy film** *n* a movie focusing on the adventures and friendship of two central characters of the same gender

bud·dy stores *npl* fuel tanks on a host aircraft from which fuel can be transferred to another plane during flight (*slang*)

bud·dy sys·tem *n* an arrangement by which people are paired for mutual safety, e.g., in mountain climbing

bu·des·o·nide /byoo déssə nīd/ *n* a corticosteroid drug taken by inhalation or in tablets. Use: treatment of hay fever and nasal polyps.

budge[1] /buj/ (**budged, budg·ing, budg·es**) *vti* **1.** to move, or move something, especially with difficulty or effort (*usually used in negative statements*) ○ *I tried moving the machine, but it wouldn't budge.* **2.** to change an attitude, decision, or opinion, or make somebody do this ○ *Once she's made up her mind, she'll refuse to budge.* [Late 16C. Via French *bouger* < assumed Vulgar Latin *bullicare* "keep bubbling up" < Latin *bullire* (see BOIL[1])]

budge[2] /buj/ *n* a fur, usually lambskin, worn with the wool outward [14C. Origin ?]

Budge /buj/, **Don** (1915–2000) US tennis player. One of the greatest players of his generation, he was the first tennis player ever to win a grand slam (1938). Full name **Budge, John Donald**

budg·er·i·gar /bújjəree gaar/ *n* a small bright green parrot with a yellow head that is often kept as a cagebird. Native to: central Australia. Latin name: *Melopsittacus undulatus*. [Mid-19C. < Yuwaalaraay *gijirigaa*]

budg·et /bújjət/ *n* **1.** PLAN FOR ALLOCATING RESOURCES a plan specifying how resources, especially time or money, will be allocated or spent during a particular period **2.** MONEY FOR PARTICULAR PURPOSE the total amount of money allocated or needed for a particular purpose or period of time **3.** QUANTITY OR SUPPLY a quantity, stock, or supply of something **4.** *regional* BAG OR POUCH a bag, pouch, or wallet ■ *adj* CHEAP OR ECONOMICAL suitable for somebody with a limited amount of money to spend ■ *v* (**-et·ed, -et·ing, -ets**) **1.** *vti* PLAN SPENDING to plan the allocation, expenditure, or use of resources, especially money or time ○ *budget $40* *a head* ○ *budget for growth* **2.** *vt* **PUT SOMETHING IN BUDGET** to provide for or enter something in a budget **3.** *vi* **LIVE WITHIN SPENDING LIMITS** to live within a budget ○ *Having budgeted well all their lives, they can afford to retire early.* [15C. < Old French *bougette* "leather pouch, purse" < *bouge* (see BULGE)] —**budg·et·ar·y** *adj* —**budg·et·er** *n*

budg·et def·i·cit *n* the amount by which government expenditure exceeds revenue

budg·ie /bújjee/ *n* a budgerigar, especially one kept as a domestic pet (*informal*) [Early 20C. Shortening]

bud scale *n* a scaly leaf that is part of a protective sheath around a plant bud and is sometimes hairy or resinous

bud·worm /búd wùrm/ *n* a moth larva that feeds on conifer buds and is one of the most destructive pests in North America. Latin name: *Harmolga fumiferana.*

Bue·na Park /bwàynə-/ city in southern California, southeast of Los Angeles. Population: 79,015 (2002 estimate).

Bue·na·ven·tu·ra /bwàynə ven tŏŏrə, -tyŏŏrə/ city and major port on the Pacific Coast of western Colombia. Population: 266,988 (1995).

Bue·na Vis·ta /bwàynə vístə, bwè naa vée staa/ village in Coahuila State, Mexico, the site of a US victory in the Mexican War in 1847

Bue·no /bwáynō/, **Maria** (*b.* 1940) Brazilian tennis player. She won singles titles at the US championships (1959, 1963, 1964, 1966) and at Wimbledon (1959, 1960, and 1964). Full name **Bueno, Marie Ester Audion**

Bue·nos Ai·res /bwàynəss í reez, -áa reez/ capital and largest city of Argentina, situated in the eastern part of the country. It is a port on the Río de la Plata and the nation's commercial and cultural center. Population: 2,776,138 (2001).

buff[1] /buf/ *vt* (**buffed, buff·ing, buffs**) **1. POLISH SOMETHING** to clean or polish something with a piece of soft material **2. MAKE SURFACE SOFT** to make the surface of something, especially of leather, soft and velvety by raising a nap ■ *n* **1.** COLORS **PALE YELLOWISH BEIGE** a dull yellowish beige color **2.** INDUST **SOFT LEATHER** a soft thick undyed leather that is made chiefly from the skins of buffalo, elk, or oxen and has a light yellow color **3.** TEXTILES **POLISHING CLOTH** a cloth of soft material such as leather or velvet, often mounted on a block and used for polishing **4.** ENG **POLISHING DISK** a revolving disk consisting of layers of cloth impregnated with abrasive powders. Use: polishing metal or other hard bright surfaces. **5.** CLOTHING **LEATHER GARMENT** a garment made of buff leather, e.g., a military uniform coat ■ *adj* **1.** COLORS **PALE YELLOWISH BEIGE** of a dull yellowish beige color **2. OF SOFT LEATHER** made of buff leather [Late 16C. Alteration of French *buffle* "buffalo" < late Latin *bufalus* (see BUFFALO)] ◇ **in the buff** naked (*informal*)

buff up *vi* to become or make yourself physically fit and strong through exercise and diet (*informal*)

buff[2] /buf/ *n* somebody who is enthusiastic and knowledgeable about something (*informal*) ○ *an opera buff* [Early 19C. < the buff-leather overcoats formerly worn by volunteer firefighters ("fire buffs") in New York City]

buff[3] /buf/ *adj* **1.** physically fit and strong, especially through exercise and a controlled diet (*informal*) **2.** having a handsome or beautiful face and physique (*slang*) [Late 20C. Probably < BUFF[1]]

buf·fa·lo /búffə lō/ *n* (*plural* **-loes** or **-los** or *same*) **1. TYPE OF HORNED CATTLE** a type of horned cattle belonging to various species, including the African buffalo and domesticated breeds of the Asian water buffalo. Family: Bovidae. **2. BISON** a North American bison **3.** FISH same as **buffalo fish** ■ *vt* (**-loed, -lo·ing, -loes**) (*informal*) **1. BAFFLE SOMEBODY** to throw somebody into a state of confusion and puzzled bewilderment **2. INTIMIDATE SOMEBODY** to coerce or inhibit somebody aggressively [Mid-16C. Via Portuguese or Italian < late Latin *bufalus* < Greek *boubalos* "gazelle"]

Buf·fa·lo /búffə lō/ city and port in western New York State beside Lake Erie and on the Niagara River. Population: 287,698 (2002 estimate).

Buf·fa·lo Bill /-bíl/ ➧ **Cody, William Frederick**

buf·fa·lo bug *n* INSECTS same as **carpet beetle**

buf·fa·lo chips *npl* dried buffalo dung used as fuel (*informal*)

buf·fa·lo fish *n* a large freshwater fish of the sucker family that resembles the carp and has a humped back. Native to: Mississippi Valley. Genus: *Ictiobus.*

buf·fa·lo grass *n* a short gray-green grass. Use: forage, lawns. Native to: plains of central North America. Latin name: *Buchloë dactyloides.*

Buf·fa·lo Grove village in northeastern Illinois, a northwestern suburb of Chicago. Population: 43,307 (2002 estimate).

buf·fa·lo jump *n* a cliff over which buffalo were stampeded by the Native North American peoples of the plains in order to provide a source of food

buf·fa·lo moz·za·rel·la *n* a fresh mozzarella cheese made from a combination of water buffalo milk and cow's milk

buf·fa·lo robe *n* the skin of the North American bison, prepared with the hair left on and used as a blanket, coat, or rug

buf·fa·lo sol·dier, Buf·fa·lo Sol·dier *n* an African American soldier in the US Army during the period between the Civil War and World War I (*informal*)

buf·fa·lo wings *npl* fried chicken wings, usually served in barbecue sauce [Because supposedly first served in a restaurant in or named for the city of BUFFALO]

buff·er[1] /búffər/ *n* **1. PROTECTOR AGAINST IMPACT** somebody or something that reduces shock or impact or protects against other harm, usually by interception **2.** COMPUT **MEMORY AREA** a temporary storage area for data being transmitted between two devices that function at different speeds. A buffer enables a faster device such as a computer to complete sending the data and begin another task without waiting for a slower device such as a printer. **3.** CHEM **SUBSTANCE MAINTAINING PH** a substance that minimizes a change in pH of a solution by neutralizing added acids and bases, or a solution containing such a substance **4.** *UK* RAIL **DEVICE ON TRAIN OR TRACK** a spring-loaded or hydraulic pad attached to the end of rolling stock or at the end of a railroad track. It stops the train running off the end of the track and may also absorb impact. ■ *vt* (**-ered, -er·ing, -ers**) **1. CUSHION SOMETHING AGAINST SHOCK** to protect something against impact, or reduce the shock of an impact **2.** CHEM **ADD BUFFER TO SOLUTION** to add to a solution a substance that will keep its pH constant [Mid-19C. < obsolete *buff* "hit something softly," perhaps < French *bufe* (see BUFFET[2])]

buff·er[2] /búffər/ *n* **1.** an implement or tool for polishing something, especially the fingernails **2.** somebody who polishes something with a buffer **3.** INDUST, TEXTILES same as **buff**[1] *n* (sense 2), *adj* (sense 1) [Mid-19C. < BUFF[1]]

buff·er state *n* a small neutral state that lies between two potentially hostile powers and reduces the risk of conflict between them

buff·er stock *n* a stock of a basic commodity accumulated by a government when supplies are plentiful and prices low, and held for use when supplies are short to stabilize the price

buff·er zone *n* **1.** a neutral area that lies between hostile forces and reduces the risk of conflict between them **2.** an area designed to form a barrier that prevents potential conflict or harmful contact

buf·fet[1] /bə fáy, boo-/ *n* **1. SELF-SERVICE MEAL** a meal at which people serve themselves from various dishes set out on a serving counter or table **2. TABLE WITH REFRESHMENTS** a serving counter or table on which meals or refreshments are displayed **3.** FURNITURE **DINING-ROOM SIDEBOARD** a piece of dining-room furniture with drawers for storing tableware [Early 18C. < French, "footstool, sideboard"]

buf·fet[2] /búffət/ *n* **1. BLOW STRUCK WITH HAND** a blow struck with the fist or hand **2. REPEATED BLOW** a heavy or repeated blow or stroke **3.** AVIAT same as **buffeting** ■ *v* (**-fet·ed, -fet·ing, -fets**) **1.** *vt* **STRIKE AGAINST SOMETHING REPEATEDLY** to knock or strike against something heavily or repeatedly **2.** *vt* **HIT SOMETHING WITH HAND** to hit somebody or something sharply with the fist or hand **3.** *vi* **STRUGGLE TO PROGRESS** to proceed under difficult conditions [Pre-12C. < Old French, "small blow" < *bufe* "blow," an imitation of the sound] —**buf·fet·er** *n*

buf·fet·ing /búffəting/ *n* an irregular shaking of a part or the whole of an aircraft during flight, usually caused by strong winds

Buf·fett /búffət/, **Warren** (*b.* 1930) US financier. He bought a small Massachusetts-based textile company in 1969 and converted it into a billion-dollar investment company with corporate holdings in a variety of major businesses. Full name **Buffett, Warren Edward**

> "At too many companies, the boss shoots the arrow of managerial performance, and then hastily paints the bull's-eye around the spot where it lands."
>
> [Warren Buffett, *Shareholder*; June 1989]

buf·fi plural of **buffo**

buff·ing wheel /búffing-/ *n* a wheel covered with a soft material such as lamb's wool, leather, or velvet and used to shine or polish something, especially metal

buf·fle·head /búff'l hèd/ (*plural* **-heads** or *same*) *n* a small diving duck, the male of which has black and white feathers and a large fluffy head, while the female is dark brown. Native to: North America. Latin name: *Bucephala albeola.* [Mid-17C. < obsolete *buffle* "buffalo" < French (see BUFF[1]); because of its large head]

buf·fo /bŏŏfō/ (*plural* **-fi** /-fee/ or **-fos**) *n* in opera, a male singer of comic roles [Mid-18C. < Italian < *buffare* (see BUFFOON)] —**buf·fo** *adj*

Buf·fon /boo fóN/, **Georges Louis Leclerc, Comte de** (1707–88) French naturalist. His major work was *Histoire naturelle* (1749–89), the first scientific account of the history of the Earth.

buf·foon /bə fóon/ *n* **1.** somebody behaving in a silly way **2.** somebody who amuses others by clowning or joking [Mid-16C. Via French < Italian *buffone* < *buffare* "puff, act the clown," an imitation of the sound]

buf·foon·er·y /bə fóonəree/ *n* silly behavior

buff wheel *n* MANUF same as **buffing wheel**

bug /bug/ *n* **1. INSECT WITH PIERCING AND SUCKING MOUTHPARTS** an insect with thickened forewings and mouthparts adapted for piercing and sucking. Order: Hemiptera. **2. INSECT REGARDED AS PEST** an insect or similar organism, especially one considered to be a pest, e.g., an aphid, bedbug, or cockroach ○ *can't stand having bugs in the house* **3. AILMENT CAUSED BY GERM** a mild illness caused by an unspecified germ or microorganism (*informal*) ○ *got a stomach bug* **4. DEFECT** a defect or flaw in a design, machine, or system (*informal*) ○ *We're working to get the bugs out before the system becomes operational.* **5.** COMPUT **PROGRAMMING ERROR** an error in a computer program (*informal*) **6.** TELECOM **HIDDEN LISTENING DEVICE** a concealed electronic device, usually a small microphone, that is used for listening to or recording private conversations (*informal*) **7. CRAZE OR OBSESSION** a strong and often widespread enthusiasm for or obsession with something (*informal*) ○ *had been bitten by the theater bug* ■ *v* (**bugged, bug·ging, bugs**) **1.** *vt* **PESTER SOMEBODY** to cause somebody persistent trouble and annoyance (*informal*) ○ *Go away and stop bugging me!* **2.** *vt* **HIDE LISTENING DEVICE IN SOMETHING** to conceal an electronic listening device in something ○ *She suspected her office had been bugged.* **3.** *vt* **LISTEN TO SOMETHING SECRETLY** to listen to or eavesdrop on a conversation using an electronic listening device ○ *He thinks someone is bugging his phone conversations.* **4.** *vi* **BULGE OUTWARD** to grow large, especially in bulging outward, as the eyes do when somebody is surprised or scared (*informal; refers to eyes*) [14C. Origin ?]

SYNONYMS See *bother.*

bug off *vi* to go away quickly, usually as a result of being ordered to do so (*slang*) ○ *We just told him to bug off and leave us alone.*

bug out *vi* (*slang*) **1.** to become suddenly very angry or upset, or start behaving in an irrational way **2.** to hurry away, especially from a military post, in fear or panic or to avoid duty ○ *They had contempt for certain soldiers who just wanted to bug out.*

Bug /book, boog/ **1.** river that rises in Ukraine and forms the border between Ukraine and Poland, and between Poland and Belarus before joining the Vistula near Warsaw. Length: 470 mi./756 km. **2.** river in western Ukraine, flowing southeast into the Black Sea. Length: 500 mi./805 km.

bug·a·boo /búggə bòo/ (*plural* **-boos**) *n* something that causes fear, annoyance, or trouble, especially an imagined threat or problem [Mid-18C. Origin ?]

Bu·gan·da /boo gáandə/ former kingdom in the area north of Lake Victoria, southern Uganda. It became part of Uganda in 1962 and the kingdom was dissolved in 1967.

Bu·gat·ti /boo gáatee/, **Ettore** (1881–1947) Italian automobile designer and manufacturer. He is best known for the race cars he produced in the 1930s. Full name **Bugatti, Ettore Arco Isidoro**

bug·bane /búg bàyn/ *n* a perennial plant that has large compound leaves. Flowers: small, white, in spike-shaped clusters. Native to: Europe. Latin name: *Cimicifuga foetida.* [Because its flowers are reputed to repel insects]

bug·bear /búg bèr/ *n* **1. CONTINUING PROBLEM** a continuing source of annoyance or difficulty **2. SOURCE OF FEAR** a source of obsessive or groundless fear **3. MONSTER** a monster invented to frighten children, traditionally in the form of a bear that eats those who misbehave [Late 16C. < obsolete *bug* "hobgoblin" + BEAR[1] (sense 1)]

bug-eyed *adj* (*informal*) **1.** having protruding eyes **2.** wide-eyed with amazement or fear

bug·ger[1] /búggər/ (*taboo*) *n* a highly offensive term for somebody who practices anal intercourse ■ *vti* (**-gered, -ger·ing, -gers**) a highly offensive term meaning to practice anal intercourse with somebody [Mid-16C. Via French *bougre* "heretic" < medieval Latin *Bulgarus* "Bulgarian (belonging to the Orthodox Church)"; from a Western Christian association of heresy with anal intercourse]

bug·ger[2] /búggər/ *n* somebody who plants listening devices in an object or place [Mid-20C. < BUG]

bug·ger·y /búggəree/ *n* a highly offensive term for anal intercourse (*taboo*)

bug·gy[1] /búggee/ (*plural* **-gies**) *n* **1. HORSE-DRAWN VEHICLE** a lightweight horse-drawn carriage **2. BATTERY-POWERED VEHICLE** a small battery-powered vehicle used for a particular purpose ○ *a dune buggy* **3. BABY CARRIAGE** a lightweight baby carriage [Mid-18C. Origin ?]

bug·gy[2] /búggee/ (**-gi·er, -gi·est**) *adj* **1. INSECT-RIDDEN** infested with insects **2. NUTTY** eccentric (*slang*) **3. PRONE TO COMPUTER BUGS** containing or prone to develop computer bugs (*informal*) [Early 18C. < BUG] —**bug·gi·ness** *n*

bug·house /búg hòwss/ *n* an offensive term for a mental health facility (*slang*) [Late 19C. < BUG "obsession, obsessive person"]

bug juice *n* (*slang*) **1.** a sugary brightly colored beverage **2.** a spray, liquid, or lotion used to repel insects

bu·gle[1] /byóog'l/ *n* a brass instrument like a short trumpet without valves, used for military signals [14C. Via Old French < Latin *buculus*, diminutive of *bos* "ox"] —**bu·gle** *vi* —**bu·gler** *n*

bu·gle[2] /byóog'l/ *n UK* BOT same as **bugleweed** (sense 1) [13C. Directly or via Old French < late Latin *bugula*]

bu·gle bead, **bu·gle** *n* a tube-shaped bead made of glass or plastic used in embroidery or bead trimmings [Late 16C. Origin ?]

bu·gle·weed /byóog'l wèed/ *n* **1.** a low-growing plant related to mint, often used as ground cover in temperate gardens. Flowers: blue, pink, white. Genus: *Ajuga.* **2.** an aromatic plant related to mint. Flowers: blue, white. Genus: *Lycopus.*

bu·gloss /byóo glòss/ *n* a hairy plant related to borage. Flowers: blue, drooping in clusters. Genus: *Lycopsis.* [14C. < Latin *buglossus* < Greek *buglōssus* "ox-tongued" (from the shape and roughness of the leaves)]

buhl /bool/ *n* FURNITURE another spelling of **boulle** [Early 19C. Via German < French *boulle* (see BOULLE)]

buhr·stone /búr stòn/, **bur·stone, burr·stone** *n* **1.** a rough hard quartz rock. Use: formerly, millstones, grindstones. **2.** a millstone or grindstone made from buhrstone [Mid-17C. < variant of BURR[1] (because of the stone's roughness)]

build /bild/ *v* (**built** /bilt/, **build·ing, builds**) **1.** *vt* **MAKE SOMETHING BY JOINING PARTS** to make a structure by putting the parts of it together ○ *to build a wall* **2.** *vt* **HAVE SOMETHING BUILT** to have a building or other structure made ○ *The emperor built a number of these pavilions.* **3.** *vti* **FORM OR DEVELOP** to form or develop something such as an enterprise or a relationship, or be formed or developed ○ *building a solid business reputation* **4.** *vi* **INCREASE** to increase or mount steadily ○ *Tension is starting to build.* ■ *n* **1. BODY STRUCTURE** somebody's physical structure, shape, and size ○ *the wrestler's heavy build* **2.** COMPUT **STAGE OF SOFTWARE DEVELOPMENT** a stage in the development of computer software in which two or more independently developed software components are linked so that they can be tested in conjunction with one another ○ *testing the first build of the program* **3. STANDARD OF CONSTRUCTION** the standard of construction of something such as a vehicle [Old English *byldan* "construct a house" < *bold* "dwelling" < Germanic, "dwell"]

build in *vt* **1.** to construct a piece of furniture so that it becomes part of the structure of a room, or add an object so that it becomes part of something else ○ *built in bookshelves over the desk* **2.** to add something to a system or organization ○ *The designers will build in options that buyers can choose from.*

build into *vt* to add something as a permanent feature of something else ○ *These safeguards will be built into the system.*

build on *vt* **1.** to use something as a basis for further development or improvement ○ *hoping to build on the success of their first CD* **2.** to add something as an extra part joined to an existing building ○ *The sun porch was built on about ten years later.*

build up *v* **1.** *vti* **DEVELOP** to increase or develop gradually, or make something do this ○ *Traffic is building up on the interstate.* **2.** *vt* **PRAISE EXCESSIVELY** to emphasize or exaggerate the good qualities of somebody or something ○ *I expected someone more impressive after the way she built him up.* **3.** *vt* **MAKE SOMEBODY STRONGER AND HEALTHIER** to make somebody stronger and healthier, especially by feeding

build up to *vt* to develop toward a point or climax

build·a·ble /bíldəb'l/ *adj* describes land that is suitable for building on

build·er /bíldər/ *n* **1.** a person or company engaged in building or repairing houses or other large structures **2.** a detergent additive that improves cleaning properties

build·ing /bílding/ *n* **1.** a structure with walls and a roof, e.g., a house or factory **2.** the business or task of constructing houses, factories, bridges, and other large structures (*often used before a noun*) ○ *building materials*

build·ing and loan as·so·ci·a·tion *n* BANKING same as **savings and loan association**

build·ing block *n* **1. CHILD'S TOY BLOCK** one of a set of children's wooden or plastic blocks **2. COMPONENT** an element or component regarded as contributing to the growth of an organization, plan, or system ○ *discovered clumps of dark matter that were the building blocks of today's galaxies* **3. BRICK-SHAPED CONSTRUCTION BLOCK** a large block of concrete or similar hard material, used for building houses and other large structures

build·ing line *n* a line on a property beyond which no building is allowed

build·ing pa·per *n* a damp-proofing and insulating material consisting of a bitumen and fiber mix sandwiched between heavy-duty paper

build·ing sick·ness *n* MED same as **sick building syndrome**

build·ing site *n* an area where construction, structural alteration, or repair work is being carried out

build·ing so·ci·e·ty *n* a financial organization in the United Kingdom that pays interest on savings accounts, lends money for buying and improving houses, and provides other banking services

build-up /bíld ùp/ *n* **1. ACCUMULATION** a large amount of something or a large number of things gradually accumulated or developed ○ *prevents the buildup of plaque* **2. RUN-UP TO EVENT** a period of time in which preparations are being made for a particular important event **3. IMPRESSIVE DESCRIPTION** a description that emphasizes or exaggerates the good qualities of somebody or something

built /bilt/ past participle, past tense of **build** ■ *adj* attractively well-proportioned in body shape (*informal*) ○ *Her new boyfriend's really built.*

built-in *adj* **1.** designed or fitted as a fixed or permanent part **2.** forming a natural feature or characteristic ○ *the built-in optimism that she brings to every job*

built-in ob·so·les·cence *n* INDUST same as **planned obsolescence**

built-up *adj* **1.** containing many buildings **2.** having several layers or added thickness ○ *built-up heels*

~~buisness~~ incorrect spelling of **business**

Bu·jold /bóo zhōld/, **Genevieve** (*b.* 1942) French-Canadian-US movie actor. She played Anne Boleyn in the movie *Anne of the Thousand Days* (1969).

Bu·jum·bu·ra /bòojəm bóorə/ capital and largest city of Burundi. It is situated in the western part of the country, on Lake Tanganyika. Population: 634,479 (1991 estimate).

Bu·ka·vu /boo kaá vóo/ capital of Sud-Kivu Region in the eastern Democratic Republic of the Congo. It is situated on Lake Kivu, close to the border with Rwanda. Population: 418,000 (1985).

Bu·kha·ra /boo kaárə, -khaárə/ city in southern Uzbekistan, in the Amu Darya valley, west of Samarkand. Population: 236,000 (1994).

Bu·kha·ri /boo kaáree/ (810–870) Arabian scholar. He traveled throughout the Muslim world and compiled the oral traditions of the Prophet Muhammad into the Sunni foundation text, *al-Sahih* ("The Genuine"). Full name **Bukhari, Muhammad ibn-Ismail al-**

Bu·kha·rin /boo kaárin, -khaárin/, **Nicolay Ivanovich** (1888–1938) Russian revolutionary and political theorist. He was leader of the October Revolution of 1917 and edited the Communist Party newspaper *Pravda* (1917–29). He was arrested in Joseph Stalin's Great Purge (1937) and executed.

Bu·la·wa·yo /bòolə wáy ō/ industrial city on the Matsheumlope River, southwestern Zimbabwe. Population: 620,936 (1992).

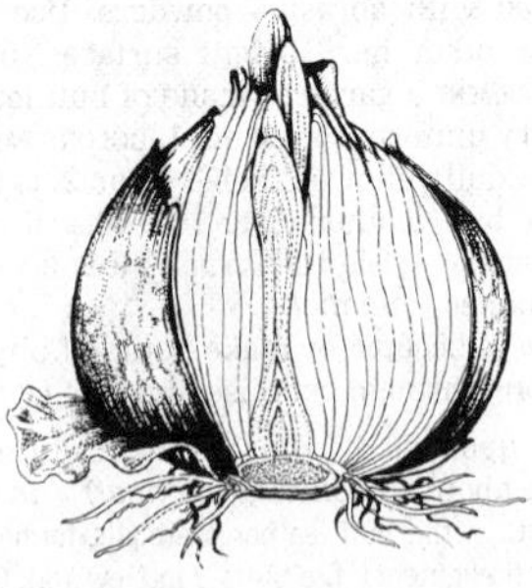

bulb

bulb /bulb/ *n* **1. UNDERGROUND PLANT PART** an underground plant storage organ, e.g., a corm, tuber, or rhizome, from which a new plant grows every year **2. PLANT GROWING FROM BULB** a plant that develops from a bulb or other underground storage organ, e.g., a tulip or crocus **3.** ELEC same as **light bulb** **4. ROUNDED PART** a rounded part of something, e.g., the mercury reservoir of a thermometer or the squeezable rubber ball on a dropper **5.** ANAT **ROUNDED PART OF BODY ORGAN** a rounded or enlarged section of a cylindrical body part [Mid-16C. Via Latin *bulbus* < Greek *bolbos* "bulbous root, onion"]

bul·bil /búlb'l, búl bil/, **bul·bel** /búlb'l, búl bèl/ *n* a new bulb growing like a bud on a plant or leaf stem [Mid-19C. < modern Latin *bulbillus*, diminutive of Latin *bulbus* (see BULB)]

bul·bo·u·re·thral gland /bùlbō yoo reéthrəl-/ *n* ANAT same as **Cowper's gland** [< Latin *bulbus* (see BULB)]

bul·bous /búlbəss/ *adj* **1.** rounded and swollen-looking **2.** growing from a plant bulb —**bul·bous·ly** *adv* —**bul·bous·ness** *n*

bul·bul /bŏŏl bŏŏl/ *n* **1.** a generally grayish or brownish songbird. Native to: tropical Africa and Asia. Family: Pycnonotidae. **2.** a songbird frequently mentioned in Persian poetry, taken to be a nightingale [Mid-17C. < Persian, an imitation of its song]

Bul·finch /bŏŏl finch/, **Charles** (1763–1844) US architect. He developed the federal style of American architecture with buildings such as the State House in Boston (completed 1798) and the completion of the US Capitol (1830).

Bul·finch, Thomas (1796–1867) US writer. He wrote a series of books popularizing mythology, including *The Age of Fables* (1855) and *The Age of Chivalry* (1858).

Bul·ga·nin /bul gánnin/, **Nikolay Aleksandrovich** (1895–1975) premier of the USSR (1955–58). After Joseph Stalin's death, he worked closely with Nikita Khruschev to try to establish détente with the West.

bul·gar *n* FOOD another spelling of **bulgur**

Bul·gar /búl gaar/ *n* a member of an ancient Slavic people who settled in areas of present-day Bulgaria around the 7th century A.D. They abandoned their Finno-Ugric language and adopted the Slavic language and customs of the people they subjugated. [Mid-18C. < medieval Latin *Bulgarus* < Old Church Slavonic *Bulgary* (plural) "Bulgars"]

Bulgaria

Bul·gar·i·a /bul gérree ə/ country in southeastern Europe, on the western shores of the Black Sea. Part of the Ottoman Empire from the 14th to the late 19th centuries, it gained independence in 1908. Language: Bulgarian. Currency: lev. Capital: Sofia. Population: 7,537,929 (2003). Area: 42,855 sq. mi./110,994 sq. km. Official name **Republic of Bulgaria**

Bul·gar·i·an /bul gérree ən/ *n* **1.** somebody who comes from Bulgaria **2.** the official language of Bulgaria, belonging to the South Slavic group of Indo-European languages. Native speakers: 9 million. —**Bul·gar·i·an** *adj*

bulge /bulj/ *vi* (**bulged, bulg·ing, bulg·es**) **1.** SWELL to expand or swell **2.** BE OVERFILLED to contain so much that the sides expand outward (*informal*) ○ *The shoppers carried bags bulging with groceries.* ■ *n* **1.** PART THAT EXPANDS OUTWARD an area or part that curves or has expanded outward **2.** INCREASE a sudden temporary increase ○ *a bulge in the population figures* [12C. Via Old French *boulge* "leather sack, bag" < Latin *bulga* < Gaulish] —**bulg·ing** *adj* —**bulg·y** *adj*

bul·gur /búlgər, bŏŏl-/, **bul·ghur, bul·gar, bul·gur wheat** *n* wheat that has been parboiled, dried, and cracked into small pieces. It is a common ingredient in southwestern Asian and vegetarian cooking. [Mid-20C. Via Turkish < Persian *bulgūr* "bruised grain"]

bu·lim·i·a /boo léemmee ə, -límmee ə/ *n* a condition in which bouts of overeating are followed by undereating, use of laxatives, or self-induced vomiting. It is associated with depression and anxiety about putting on weight. [14C. Via modern Latin < Greek *boulimia* "hunger of an ox" < *bous* "ox" + *limos* "hunger"] —**bu·lim·ic** *adj, n*

bulk /bulk/ *n* **1.** LARGE SIZE large size or mass **2.** LARGE BODY a large or overweight person's body ○ *eased his bulk through the narrow passageway* **3.** FIBER IN FOOD the indigestible fiber that is a constituent of some food **4.** MAJORITY the greater part of something ○ *The bulk of the funding will come from the federal government.* ■ *adj* IN LARGE QUANTITY in or of a large quantity ■ *vi* (**bulked, bulk·ing, bulks**) GAIN WEIGHT to gain weight, especially by deliberately adding additional muscle mass [15C. Partly < Old Norse *búlki* "heap" (< Indo-European, "swell"); partly < Old English *būc* "belly" (< Germanic)] ◇ **in bulk 1.** in large quantities or amounts **2.** loose, instead of being commercially packaged

bulk up *vti* to increase in size or volume, or make somebody or something do this (*informal*)

bulk buy *n* a large amount of something or a number of things bought at one time, usually at a reduced rate —**bulk-buy** *vti* —**bulk buy·ing** *n*

bulk car·ri·er *n* a ship that carries loose unpackaged cargo such as coal or grain

bulk·head /búlk hèd/ *n* **1.** a partition inside a ship, aircraft, or large vehicle **2.** a wall built to hold back something such as water or soil [15C. < Old Norse *bálkr* "partition"]

bulk·ing /búlking/ *n* the increase in the volume of sand, cement, and other building materials when they become damp

bulk mail *n* material, typically advertising, that is sent through the mail in very large quantities at a reduced unit cost

bulk·y /búlkee/ (**-i·er, -i·est**) *adj* **1.** large and awkward to carry or move **2.** heavily built, broad, or muscular —**bulk·i·ly** *adv* —**bulk·i·ness** *n*

bull[1] /bŏŏl/ *n* **1.** MALE OF CATTLE an uncastrated adult male of any breed of domestic cattle or other bovine animal **2.** MALE MAMMAL a sexually mature male of any of various large mammals, including whales, seals, moose, and elephants **3.** FIN BUYER OF RISING SECURITIES an investor who buys securities in anticipation of rising prices, intending to resell them for profit **4.** BIG MAN a hefty or aggressive man ■ *v* (**bulled, bull·ing, bulls**) **1.** *vti* PUSH to push forcefully or energetically ○ *He bulled his way into the reception.* **2.** *vt* FIN RAISE PRICES WITH SPECULATIVE BUYING to attempt to raise prices in a particular commodity or market by buying large quantities and thus reducing availability and increasing demand [Pre-12C. < Old Norse *boli*] ◇ **take the bull by the horns** to deal with a difficult situation forcefully and decisively (*informal*)

bull[2] /bŏŏl/ *n* **1.** a written statement formally issued by the pope and bearing an official seal **2.** CHR same as **bulla** (sense 3) [13C. Via French < Latin *bulla* "bubble, seal, sealed document"]

bull[3] /bŏŏl/ *n* an offensive term for talk or writing dismissed as foolish or inaccurate (*slang*) [Early 17C. Origin ? Now often taken as an abbreviation of BULLSHIT] ◇ **shoot the bull** to chatter idly (*slang*)

Bull /bŏŏl/ *n* ASTRON, ZODIAC same as **Taurus** (sense 2) [Early 16C. Translation of Latin *Taurus*]

bul·la /bŏŏllə/ (*plural* **-lae** /-lee/) *n* **1.** MED same as **blister** *n* (sense 1) (*technical*) **2.** a rounded bony protruding part of the body **3.** the pope's official seal [14C. < Latin, "bubble, seal, sealed document"]

bull·bait·ing /bŏŏl bàyting/ *n* the former entertainment of setting fierce dogs to attack a bull, popular in medieval times

bull bars *npl* a metal framework mounted on the front of a vehicle to protect it against impact

bull·corn /bŏŏl kàwrn/ *n, interj Southwest US* utter nonsense (*informal*) [Mid-20C. After BULLSHIT]

bulldog

bull·dog /bŏŏl dàwg, -dòg/ *n* **1.** MUSCULAR DOG a muscular dog with smooth hair, belonging to a breed developed in England for contests with bulls **2.** PISTOL a short-barreled revolver ■ *vt* (**-dogged, -dog·ging, -dogs**) **1.** ATTACK to attack like an angry bulldog **2.** FORCE STEER TO GROUND to force a steer to the ground by pulling on its horns and twisting its neck —**bull·dog·ger** *n*

bull·doze /bŏŏl dōz/ (**-dozed, -doz·ing, -doz·es**) *v* **1.** *vt* DEMOLISH SOMETHING WITH BULLDOZER to demolish a building or clear debris using a bulldozer **2.** *vt* FORCE SOMEBODY OR SOMETHING to force somebody to do something or something to happen by behaving stubbornly or ruthlessly (*informal*) **3.** *vti* FORCE WAY THROUGH SOMETHING to force a way past or through an obstruction (*informal*) [Late 19C. Origin ?]

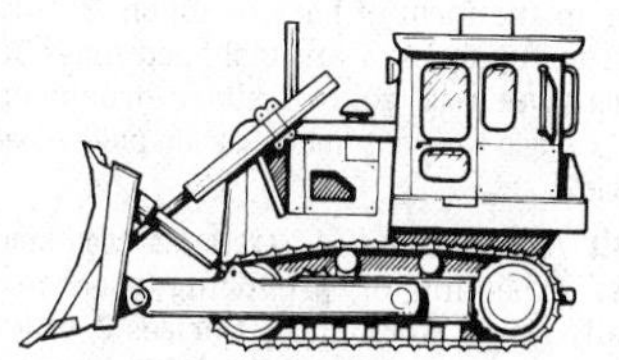

bulldozer

bull·doz·er /bŏŏl dōzər/ *n* a construction vehicle with tracks or large wheels and a wide blade used for moving earth or debris

bull dyke *n* an offensive term for a lesbian whose appearance or behavior is considered unfeminine (*slang*)

bul·let /bŏŏllət/ *n* **1.** AMMUNITION USED IN FIREARM a projectile fired from a handgun, rifle, or other small firearm, usually pointed and cylindrical and made of metal **2.** *also* **bul·let point** DOT a large printed dot used to highlight items in a printed list **3.** FAST BALL a ball thrown or pitched with exceptional force, as in baseball or football **4.** FINAL REPAYMENT OF LOAN a final loan payment, representing the initial sum borrowed excluding interest, which was paid during the term of the loan [Early 16C. < French *boulet* "small ball" < *boule* (see BOWL[2])] ◇ **bite the bullet** to deal with a situation that is unpleasant but unavoidable (*informal*) ◇ **sweat bullets** to make an extraordinary effort, usually because of great anxiety (*slang*)

bul·let·ed /bŏŏllətəd/ *adj* describes a printed item marked by a bullet ○ *a bulleted list*

bul·le·tin /bŏŏllətin, -t'n/ *n* **1.** NEWS BROADCAST a short broadcast containing a single item of news **2.** ANNOUNCEMENT an official announcement **3.** NEWSLETTER a newsletter issued by an organization or institution [Mid-18C. < Italian *bulletino* "small papal bull" < *bulla* < Latin (see BULL[2])]

bul·le·tin board *n* **1.** a board on which notices are pinned **2.** *also* **bul·le·tin board sys·tem** an online forum used to exchange e-mails, chat, and access software

bul·let loan *n* a loan that is repaid in full in a single payment on a set date

bul·let point *n* PRINTING same as **bullet** (sense 2)

bul·let·proof /bŏŏllət pròof/ *adj* **1.** able to resist the penetration of bullets ○ *bulletproof glass* **2.** invulnerable to attack or criticism (*informal*) ○ *Nobody's bulletproof in this company.*

~~**bullettin**~~ incorrect spelling of **bulletin**

bul·let train *n* a high-speed passenger train in Japan

bul·let·wood /bŏŏllət wŏŏd/ *n* **1.** the tough durable wood of a tropical American tree **2.** a tree grown for its tough durable wood. Native to: tropical America. Latin name: *Manilkara bidentata.*

bull fid·dle *n* same as **double bass** (*informal*)

bull·fight /bŏŏl fìt/ *n* a traditional public entertainment, especially in Spain and Mexico, in which a bull is baited and killed —**bull·fight·er** *n* —**bull·fight·ing** *n*

bull·finch /bo͝ol fìnch/ *n* a small bird with a short thick beak, a black head, and a pink to red breast. Native to: Europe, Asia. Latin name: *Pyrrhula pyrrhula.*

bull·frog /bo͝ol fràwg, -fròg/ *n* a large frog with a deep croak. Native to: eastern North America. Genus: *Rana.* [Mid-18C. < its strong croak]

bull·head /bo͝ol hèd/ *n* **1.** a common catfish of rivers and lakes. Native to: North America. Genus: *Ictalurus.* **2.** a large-headed fish such as the freshwater sculpin. Genus: *Cottus.*

bull·head·ed /bo͝ol hèddəd/ *adj* stubborn and uncooperative (*informal*) —**bull·head·ed·ly** *adv* —**bull·head·ed·ness** *n*

bull·horn /bo͝ol hàwrn/ *n* a device that consists of a handheld microphone with a cone-shaped speaker attached, used for amplifying the voice

bul·lion /bo͝ollyən/ *n* **1.** BARS OF GOLD OR SILVER gold or silver in the form of bars or ingots **2.** MASS OF METAL metal in the form of an unshaped mass **3.** TEXTILES GOLD OR SILVER BRAID gold or silver ornamental braid [15C. < Anglo-Norman, "mint" < Latin *bullire* "boil" < *bulla* "bubble"]

bull·ish /bo͝ollish/ *adj* **1.** EXPECTING GOOD STOCK MARKET FIGURES expecting or producing good results, especially rising stock market prices **2.** OPTIMISTIC confident and optimistic (*informal*) **3.** BRAWNY broad and strong —**bull·ish·ly** *adv* —**bull·ish·ness** *n*

bull mar·ket *n* a stock market in which prices are rising and are expected to continue rising

bull mas·tiff *n* a large muscular dog with smooth hair, belonging to a breed developed by crossing the bulldog and the mastiff

bull·necked /bo͝ol nèkt/ *adj* having a short thick neck

bull·nose /bo͝ol nōz/ *n* a disease of hogs that causes the snout to swell

bull·nosed /bo͝ol nōzd/ *adj* having a rounded protruding front part (*technical*) ○ *a stair tread with a bullnosed edge*

bul·lock /bo͝ollək/ *n* **1.** a young domestic bull **2.** a castrated domestic bull [Old English *bulluc* < *bula* "bull"]

bul·lock's heart *n* FOOD same as **custard apple** (sense 1)

bull·pen /bo͝ol pèn/ *n* **1.** BASEBALL WARM-UP AREA in baseball, the part of the field where the relief pitchers warm up **2.** BASEBALL RELIEF PITCHERS a baseball team's relief pitchers **3.** TEMPORARY CELL a cell for prisoners waiting to be brought into court (*informal*) **4.** AREA FOR CLERICAL WORKERS an area containing the desks of many white-collar workers, often separated by movable partitions of limited height

bull·ring /bo͝ol rìng/ *n* an arena where bullfights are held

Bull Run /bo͝ol rùn/ stream in northeastern Virginia, near the city of Manassas, southwest of Washington, D.C. It was the site of two important Confederate victories during the Civil War, on July 21, 1861, and August 29–30, 1862, also called the Battles of Manassas.

bull ses·sion *n* an informal discussion (*informal*)

bull's-eye, **bull's eye** *n* **1.** MIDDLE OF TARGET the center of a target, which usually carries the highest score ○ *She hit the bull's eye perfectly.* **2.** TOP-SCORING SHOT a shot that hits the center of a target **3.** PRECISE ACHIEVEMENT a precise or highly effective achievement (*informal*) **4.** THICK LENS a small thick lens for intensifying light **5.** ROUND WINDOW a small round window, especially a disk of thick glass in a ship's deck for letting in light below deck ■ *interj* RECOGNIZING PRECISE ACHIEVEMENT used to acknowledge and commend a precise or highly effective achievement (*informal*)

bull·shit /bo͝ol shìt/ (*slang*) *n* an offensive term for talk or writing dismissed as foolish or inaccurate ■ *vti* (**-shit·ted, -shit·ting, -shits**) **1.** an offensive term meaning to say things that are completely untrue or very foolish **2.** an offensive term meaning to try to intimidate, deceive, or persuade somebody with deceitful or foolish talk —**bull·shit·ter** *n*

bull snake *n* a large burrowing nonpoisonous snake with yellow and brown markings that feeds mainly on rodents. Native to: North America. Genus: *Pituophis.*

bull ter·ri·er *n* a muscular dog with smooth hair, belonging to a breed developed in England by crossing the bulldog with a breed of terrier

bull this·tle *n* a thistle with a large flowering head. Native to: Europe, naturalized in North America. Latin name: *Cirsium vulgare.*

bull·whip /bo͝ol wìp, -hwìp/ *n* a long heavy whip made of braided strips of hide, knotted at the end ■ *vt* (**-whipped, -whip·ping, -whips**) to beat somebody with a bullwhip

bul·ly[1] /bo͝ollee/ *n* (*plural* **-lies**) an aggressive person who intimidates or mistreats weaker people ■ *vt* (**-lied, -ly·ing, -lies**) to intimidate or mistreat a weaker person [Mid-16C. Probably < Middle Dutch *boele* "lover"] ◇ **bully for you!** used to express approval (*dated; used ironically*)

bul·ly[2] /bo͝ollee/ *n UK* canned corned or pickled beef (*dated*) [Mid-18C. Anglicization of *bouilli* "boiled beef" < French, past particle of *bouillir* "boil" < Latin *bullire*]

bul·ly·boy /bo͝ollee bòy/ *n* an aggressive bully or thug

bul·ly pul·pit *n* a position of prominent authority that gives the holder a wide audience, e.g., a political office

bul·ly·rag /bo͝ollee ràg/ (**-ragged, -rag·ging, -rags**), **bal·ly·rag** /bállee-/ *vt* to persecute somebody with insults or cruel practical jokes (*informal*) [Late 18C. Origin ?]

bul·ly tree *n US* a tropical American tree that yields a sap from which a hard rubber substance (**balata**) is made. Latin name: *Manilkara bidentata.* Can term **balata**

bul·rush /bo͝ol rùsh/ *n* **1.** WATERSIDE PLANT a plant with leaves like grass that grows in wet conditions. Genus: *Scirpus.* **2.** *Can, UK* MARSH PLANT a tall marsh plant. Genus: *Typha.* US term **cattail** **3.** BIBLE PAPYRUS in the Bible, a papyrus plant [15C. Probably blend of BULL[1] + RUSH[2]]

bul·wark /bo͝olwərk, búl-/ *n* **1.** DEFENSIVE WALL a structure such as a wall or fortification built to keep out attackers **2.** PROTECTION somebody or something that gives protection or support ○ *The alliance is regarded as a bulwark of economic stability in the region.* **3.** HARBOR WALL a wall built out into the sea to shelter a harbor ■ **bul·warks** *npl* SHIP'S SIDES the sides of a ship projecting above the deck ■ *vt* (**-warked, -wark·ing, -warks**) **1.** PROTECT PLACE WITH WALLS to fortify or protect a place by building walls around it **2.** SAFEGUARD SOMEBODY OR SOMETHING to defend or support somebody or something strongly [15C. < Middle Dutch, Middle Low German *bolwerk* "rampart made of tree trunks" < *bole* "tree trunk" + *werk* "work"]

bum[1] /bum/ (*informal*) *n* **1.** GOOD-FOR-NOTHING somebody regarded as irresponsible or worthless **2.** HOBO a homeless person living on the street (*sometimes considered offensive*) **3.** DEVOTEE somebody who is excessively devoted to a particular activity or place ○ *a ski bum* ■ *vt* (**bummed, bum·ming, bums**) BEG to get something by asking or begging ■ *adj* USELESS useless, worthless, or of poor quality ○ *gave me some pretty bum advice* [Mid-19C. Shortening of BUMMER] ◇ **give somebody the bum's rush** to order or force somebody abruptly to leave a place (*informal*)

bum out *vt* to annoy or depress somebody (*slang*)

bum[2] /bum/ *n UK* the buttocks (*informal*) [14C. Origin ?]

bum bag *n UK* same as **fanny pack**

bum·ber·shoot /búmbər shoot/ *n* same as **umbrella** (*humorous*) [Late 19C. Alteration of blend of UMBRELLA + PARACHUTE]

bum·ble[1] /búmb'l/ (**-bled, -bling, -bles**) *v* **1.** *vti* to speak in a hesitant or muddled way **2.** *vt* to move or proceed clumsily **3.** *vt* same as **bungle** (*informal*) [Mid-16C. Origin ?] —**bum·bler** *n*

bum·ble[2] /búmb'l/ (**-bled, -bling, -bles**) *vi* to make a humming sound [14C. An imitation of the sound]

bum·ble·bee /búmb'l bèe/ *n* a large hairy bee that nests in burrows and makes a loud droning noise in flight. Native to: North America, Europe, Asia. Genus: *Bombus.*

bum·ble·pup·py *n UK* same as **tetherball** [Early 19C. Origin ?]

bum·bling /búmbling/ *adj* speaking or behaving in a clumsy or confused way (*informal*)

bum·boat /búm bōt/ *n* a small boat that is used for selling goods to ships at anchor [Late 17C. < BUM[1]]

bum·bum /búm bùm/ *n Carib* the buttocks

bumf /bumpf, bumf/, **bumph** *n UK* unwanted or uninteresting printed material, especially official forms and documents (*slang*) [Late 19C. Shortening of *bum fodder* "toilet paper"]

bum·fuz·zle /búm fùzz'l, bùm fúzz'l/ (**-zled, -zling, -zles**) *vt Southern US* to confuse somebody (*informal*) [Early 20C. Alteration of BAMBOOZLE]

bum·ma·lo /búmməlō/ (*plural same*) *n* **1.** a small blunt-nosed fish found in brackish water. Native to: South Asia. Latin name: *Harpadon nehereus.* **2.** the flesh of a bummalo used as food [Late 17C. Probably alteration of Marathi *bombīl*]

bummed /bumd/, **bummed out** *adj* unhappy as a result of an unpleasant experience (*slang*)

bum·mer /búmmər/ *n* (*slang*) **1.** ANNOYING THING something annoying or unpleasant **2.** FLOP a failure **3.** BAD REACTION TO DRUG a bad reaction to a hallucinogenic drug [Mid-19C. Probably < German *Bummler* "idler, layabout" < *bummeln* "stroll or loaf around"]

bump /bump/ *v* (**bumped, bump·ing, bumps**) **1.** *vti* KNOCK SOMETHING to hit or knock something, especially accidentally **2.** *vti* MOVE UNSTEADILY to jolt or bounce along, or move something in a jolting or bouncing way ○ *We bumped along the dirt road.* **3.** *vt* TURN AWAY PASSENGER to turn away an airline passenger with a reserved seat because the flight has been overbooked (*informal*) ■ *n* **1.** LUMP ON SURFACE a raised area on a flat surface ○ *a bump in the road* **2.** SWELLING ON BODY a swelling on the body caused by an impact ○ *a bump on the elbow* **3.** ACCIDENTAL KNOCK a light blow or impact, especially an accidental one ○ *that bump dented the bodywork* **4.** SOUND OF IMPACT the dull sound of one thing hitting another **5.** RAISED AREA ON SKULL a raised area at different points on the skull, formerly thought to indicate intelligence or personality type [Mid-16C. An imitation of the sound of a bump] ◇ **bump and grind** to dance erotically, thrusting and rotating the pelvis (*slang*)

bump into *vt* **1.** to meet somebody by chance **2.** to knock against or hit somebody or something accidentally

bump off *vt* to murder somebody (*slang*)

bump up *vt* to increase prices suddenly and sharply (*informal*)

bump up against *vt* **1.** to come into contact with something, usually making a sound **2.** to come into conflict with somebody

bump·er /búmpər/ *n* **1.** PROTECTING BAR ON VEHICLE a projecting rim or bar on the front or back of a vehicle, designed to protect it from damage **2.** BROADCAST DEVICE SEPARATING SECTIONS OF PROGRAM a device such as a piece of music that separates the content of a radio or television program from a commercial break (*slang*) ■ *adj* LARGE unusually large or successful ○ *a bumper crop* ○ *a bumper year for apples*

bump·er car *n* a small electric car designed to be bumped against other similar cars in a raised enclosure as part of a fairground entertainment

bump·er stick·er *n* a small adhesive sign, typically mounted on a car bumper or window

bump·er-to-bump·er *adj, adv* forming a line of close slow-moving vehicles ○ *bumper-to-bumper traffic* ○ *drive bumper-to-bumper*

bump·kin[1] /búmpkin, búm-/ *n* a country person regarded as unsophisticated (*informal*) [Late 16C. Origin ?]

bump·kin[2] /búmpkin, búm-/, **bum·kin** /búm-/ *n* a pole at the back of a boat to which a sail is attached by a rope [Mid-17C. < Dutch *boomken* < *boom* "tree"]

bump·tious /búmpshəss/ *adj* stating opinions aggressively or self-importantly [Early 19C. Blend of BUMP + FRACTIOUS] —**bump·tious·ly** *adv* —**bump·tious·ness** *n*

bump·y /búmpee/ (**-i·er, -i·est**) *adj* **1.** UNEVEN having a rough or uneven surface ○ *a bumpy road* **2.** BOUNCY uncomfortably bouncy or rough ○ *a bumpy ride* **3.** DIFFICULT with setbacks from time to time (*informal*) ○ *Things seemed to be going well, but it looks like this project's going to be bumpy after all.* —**bump·i·ly** *adv* —**bump·i·ness** *n*

bum rap *n* a false or fraudulent accusation or appraisal (*slang*)

bum steer *n* a piece of misleading information or bad advice (*slang*)

bun /bun/ *n* **1.** ROUND BREAD ROLL a small round bread roll, sometimes sweetened and with added fruit or spice **2.** HAIR COILED AT BACK OF HEAD hair gathered in a tight round coil on the back or top of the head ■ **buns** *npl* BUTTOCKS a person's buttocks (*slang*) [14C. Origin ?]

bunch /bunch/ *n* **1.** COLLECTION OF THINGS a number of people or things grouped or joined together ○ *people in bunches waiting for the doors to open* ○ *a bunch of parsley* **2.** CLUSTER OF FRUITS a cluster of fruits growing on a stem **3.** GROUP OF PEOPLE a group of people, usually with a common characteristic or interest (*informal*) ○ *a fiercely competitive bunch* **4.** A LOT OF PEOPLE OR THINGS a large number of people or things (*informal*) ○ *Expect a whole bunch of new features in the next version.* ■ *vti* (**bunched, bunch·ing, bunch·es**) GATHER to gather things or people into a cluster or close group, or gather in this way [14C. Origin ?] —**bunch·i·ness** *n* —**bunch·y** *adj*

bunch·ber·ry /búnch bèrree/ (*plural* **-ries**) *n* a creeping plant of the dogwood family that bears red berries. Native to: North America, eastern Asia. Latin name: *Cornus canadensis.*

Bunche /bunch/, **Ralph** (1904–71) US diplomat. He worked as a U.N. mediator resolving Arab–Israeli conflicts and received the Nobel Peace Prize (1950). Full name **Bunche, Ralph Johnson**

bunch·flow·er /búnch flòwr/ *n* a perennial plant of the lilac family with leaves like grass. Flowers: pale green, in clusters. Native to: eastern United States. Latin name: *Melanthium virginicum.*

bunch grass *n* any grass that grows in clumps or tufts

Bun·cho Ta·ni /bùnchō taánee/ (1763–1840) Japanese artist. A noted book illustrator, he was responsible for introducing the Western style to Japanese painting.

bun·co /búngkō/ (*plural* **-coes**), **bun·ko** (*plural* **-koes**) *n* a trick or scheme that deceives people into parting with money (*slang*) [Late 19C. Origin ?] —**bun·co** *vt*

bund[1] /bund/ *n S Asia* an embankment or dike that surrounds rice fields or a reservoir and acts as a breakwater to prevent flooding [Early 19C. Via Urdu *band* < Persian]

bund[2] /boǒnd, bund/, **Bund** *n* a political organization, especially a socialist Jewish labor movement in tsarist Russia or a German–American group of Nazi sympathizers in the United States in the 1930s and 1940s [Late 19C. < German, "association"]

bun·dle /búnd'l/ *n* **1.** COLLECTION OF THINGS HELD TOGETHER a number of things tied, wrapped, or held together **2.** A LOT OF MONEY a large sum of money (*slang*) **3.** BIOL BAND OF PARALLEL TISSUES a band of tissue such as muscle or nerve fibers or vascular tissue in plants **4.** COMPUT SET OF COMPUTER EQUIPMENT a package of computer hardware and software supplied at an inclusive price ■ *v* (**-dled, -dling, -dles**) **1.** *vt* TIE THINGS TOGETHER to tie or wrap a number of things together **2.** *vt* COMPUT SUPPLY COMPUTER EQUIPMENT to package computer hardware and software together at an inclusive price **3.** *vt* SHOVE SOMEBODY OR SOMETHING to push somebody or something roughly and hurriedly (*informal*) ○ *bundled the suspect into the police car* **4.** *vi* SLEEP IN SAME BED to sleep in the same bed with somebody while both fully dressed (*dated*) [14C. < Dutch *bundel*] —**bun·dler** *n* ◇ **drop a bundle** to spend a large amount of money (*slang*)

bundle off *vt* to send somebody away hurriedly (*informal*) ○ *We bundled the children off to school.*

bundle up *v* **1.** *vt* to gather things into a bundle **2.** *vti* to dress in warm clothes, or dress somebody in warm clothes (*informal*) ○ *Bundle up, it's cold outside.*

bun·dle sheath cell *n* in some vascular plants, a specialized photosynthetic cell where the initial products of photosynthesis undergo the removal of carbon dioxide

bung /bung/ *n* **1.** STOPPER a stopper or plug, especially one made of cork or rubber **2.** *UK* PAYOFF an illicit fee paid to a soccer player, manager, or agent to facilitate a player transfer (*slang*) ■ *vt* (**bunged, bung·ing, bungs**) **1.** PLUG HOLE to plug or seal a hole with a bung **2.** *UK* PLACE CARELESSLY to put something somewhere roughly or hurriedly (*informal*) [15C. < Middle Dutch *bonghe*, probably < late Latin *puncta* "puncture" < Latin *pungere* "to prick"]

bun·ga·low /búng gəlō/ *n* **1.** ONE-STORY HOUSE a single-story house **2.** LIGHTWEIGHT TROPICAL HOUSE in Southeast Asia and the South Pacific, a simply built one-story house with a veranda and a wide, gently sloping roof **3.** *Malaysia, Singapore* HOUSE a house, usually of two or more stories [Late 17C. < Hindi *banglā* "of Bengal"]

bun·gee /bún jeè/ *n* a cord or rope made from elastic material [Early 20C. Origin ?]

bun·gee jump *n* a dive from a high place using an elastic cord tied to the ankles as a restraint —**bun·gee jump·ing** *n*

bung·hole /búng hōl/ *n* **1.** a hole in a barrel or vat, used for drawing off the contents and closed with a bung **2.** an offensive term for the anus (*slang*)

bun·gle /búng g'l/ (*informal*) *vt* (**-gled, -gling, -gles**) to cause something to fail through carelessness or incompetence ○ *bungled the job* ■ *n* a careless or clumsy action or mistake [Mid-16C. Probably to suggest the action] —**bun·gler** *n* —**bun·gling** *adj* —**bun·gling·ly** *adv*

bun·ion /búnnyən/ *n* an inflammation of the sac (**bursa**) around the first joint of the big toe, accompanied by swelling and sideways displacement of the joint [Early 18C. Directly or via English dialect *bunny* "lump, swelling" < Old French *buigne* "bump on the head"]

bunk[1] /bungk/ *n* **1.** SIMPLE BED a simple narrow bed built on a shelf or in a recess **2.** FURNITURE same as **bunk bed 3.** SLEEPING PLACE any bed or place to sleep (*informal*) **4.** *regional* AGRIC PILE OF VEGETABLES a heap of vegetables, usually potatoes, covered with earth and mulch and sometimes stored in a shed ■ *vi* (**bunked, bunk·ing, bunks**) SLEEP SOMEWHERE to sleep in a place away from home (*informal*) ○ *"You may as well bunk at the YMCA and get in on their recreation programs."* (Garrison Keillor, *We Are Still Married*; 1989) [Mid-18C. Origin ?]

REGIONAL NOTE See ***bank***[2].

bunk[2] /bungk/ *n* talk or writing dismissed as nonsensical or inaccurate (*slang*) [Early 20C. Shortened < BUNKUM]

bunk bed *n* either of a pair of single beds fitted one on top of the other

bun·ker /búngkər/ *n* **1.** UNDERGROUND SHELTER an underground shelter, especially one built for troops, with a fortified gun position above ground **2.** GOLF SAND HAZARD a sand-filled hollow on a golf course, built as a hazard **3.** SHIPPING FUEL-STORAGE CONTAINER a fuel-storage container on a ship **4.** LARGE OUTDOOR CONTAINER a large outdoor bin or chest ■ *vt* (**-kered, -ker·ing, -kers**) **1.** GOLF SEND BALL INTO BUNKER to hit a golf ball into a bunker **2.** PUT SOMETHING IN OUTDOOR BIN to put or store something in a large outdoor bin or chest [Mid-16C. Origin ?]

bun·ker bust·er *n* a powerful laser-guided bomb designed to penetrate a reinforced target and explode

Bun·ker Hill /búngkər-/ hill in Boston, Massachusetts, near the site of the first battle of the American Revolution in 1775. Height: 110 ft./34 m.

bunk·house /búnk hòwss/ (*plural* **-hous·es** /-hòwzəz/) *n* a building providing simple sleeping facilities

bun·kum /búngkəm/ *n* talk or writing dismissed as nonsensical or inaccurate (*informal*) [Mid-19C. Alteration of *Buncombe* County, N Carolina, whose congressman defended a dull and irrelevant speech by saying he made it to impress the people of Buncombe]

bun·ny /búnnee/ (*plural* **-nies**) *n* a child's word for a rabbit (*informal*) [Early 17C. < dialect *bun* "rabbit's tail, rabbit" < Gaelic *bun* "stump, bottom"]

bun·ny hug *n* a lively ballroom dance popular in the United States in the early 20th century

bun·ny slopes *npl* the gentlest slopes in a ski resort or complex, designed for beginners to use [Origin ?]

bu·no·dont /byoónə dònt/ *adj* having molar teeth with separate rounded ridges (**cusps**), typical of omnivores [Late 19C. < Greek *bounos* "mound"]

Bun·ra·ku /boǒn raá koó, boǒn raá-/ *n* traditional Japanese puppetry using large wooden puppets, each worked by several puppeteers who are visible to the audience and with a separate narrator offstage [Early 20C. < Japanese, after the *Bunraku-za* theater]

Bun·sen /búnssən/, **Robert Wilhelm** (1811–99) German chemist and physicist. One of the discoverers of spectrum analysis (1859), he also invented a galvanic battery. He popularized the laboratory gas burner that bears his name.

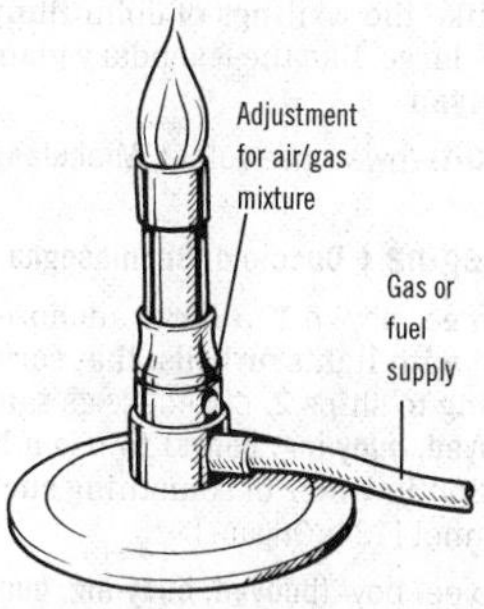

Bunsen burner

Bun·sen burn·er *n* a portable tube-shaped gas burner with an adjustable hole to control air intake and flame type, used in laboratories [Late 19C. After R. W. BUNSEN]

Bun·shaft /bún shàft/, **Gordon** (1909–90) US architect. His innovations in designing public and corporate buildings included the use of sloping façades.

bunt[1] /bunt/ (**bunt·ed, bunt·ing, bunts**) *vt* **1.** in baseball, to hit a pitched ball very gently, holding the bat horizontally with both hands **2.** same as **butt**[1] *v* (sense 1) [Mid-18C. An imitation of the sound of something being hit] —**bunt** *n* —**bunt·er** *n*

bunt[2] /bunt/ *n* the baggy middle part of a sail [Late 16C. Origin ?]

bun·tal /búnt'l/ *n* straw from the large leaves of the talipot palm tree [Early 20C. < Tagalog]

bunt·ing[1] /búnting/ *n* a small seed-eating songbird related to the finch, with a short heavy beak and usually brown or gray feathers. Family: Emberizidae. [13C. Origin ?]

bunt·ing[2] /búnting/ *n* strings of cloth or paper decorations for hanging outdoors [Early 18C. Origin ?]

bunt·line /búnt lìn/ *n* a rope attached to the bottom of a square sail, used to roll up the sail [Early 17C. < BUNT[2]]

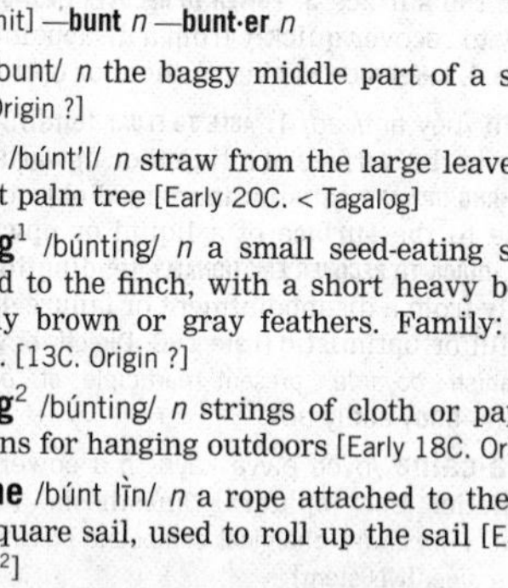

Luis Buñuel

Bu·ñu·el /boōnyoo él/, **Luis** (1900–83) Spanish movie director. One of the greatest masters of filmmaking, he incorporated uncompromising social criticisms in works such as *The Discreet Charm of the Bourgeoisie* (1972).

bun·ya /búnnyə/, **bun·ya-bun·ya**, **bun·ya pine** *n* a tall tree with cones containing edible seeds. Native to: Australia. Latin name: *Araucaria bidwillii.* [Mid-19C. < Yagara *bunya-bunya*]

Bun·yan /búnnyən/, **John** (1628–88) English preacher and writer. A Puritan, he was jailed for 12 years for his religious beliefs. He wrote the autobiographical *Grace Abounding to the Chief of Sinners* (1666) and the great spiritual allegory *The Pilgrim's Progress* (published in two parts 1678, 1684). See Cultural note at **pilgrim**

> "Who would true valor see, / Let him come hither; / One here will constant be, / Come wind, come weather / There's no discouragement / Shall make him once relent / His first avow'd intent / To be a pilgrim."
> [John Bunyan, *The Pilgrim's Progress*; 1684]

Bun·yan·esque /bùnnyə nésk/ *adj* **1.** richly allegorical, like the writings of John Bunyan **2.** supernaturally large, like the legendary giant lumberjack Paul Bunyan

Buo·nar·ro·ti /bwàw naa rṓtee/, **Michelangelo** ♦ **Michelangelo**

Buon·in·seg·na ♦ **Duccio di Buoninsegna**

buoy[1] /bóo ee, boy/ *n* **1.** a large anchored float, often equipped with lights or bells, that serves as a guide or warning to ships **2.** EMERGENCIES same as **life buoy** ■ *vt* (**buoyed, buoy·ing, buoys**) to use a buoy to mark the location in water of something such as a hazard or a channel [13C. Origin ?]

buoy[2] /bóo ee, boy/ (**buoyed, buoy·ing, buoys**) *vt* to keep something from falling or sinking ○ *steps to buoy the country's currency* [Late 16C. < Spanish *boyar* "to float" < *boya* "buoy"]

buoy up *vt* **1.** to keep somebody cheerful or optimistic in spite of difficulties ○ *The arrival of the children has buoyed us all up.* **2.** to give support or encouragement to somebody ○ *Buoyed up by a few wise investments, the company went on to prosper the following year.*

buoy·an·cy /bóy ənssee, bóo yənssee/, **buoy·ance** /-ənss/ *n* **1.** TENDENCY TO FLOAT the tendency of an object to float **2.** FORCE CAUSING FLOATING the tendency of a liquid or gas to cause less dense objects to float or rise to the surface **3.** POWER TO RECOVER EMOTIONALLY the ability to recover quickly from a disappointment or failure **4.** CHEERFULNESS cheerfulness or optimism

buoy·ant /bóy ənt/ *adj* **1.** ABLE TO FLOAT tending to float or rise to the surface of a liquid or upward in a gas **2.** PUSHING UPWARD causing immersed objects to float or rise to the surface of a liquid or upward in a gas **3.** QUICK TO RECOVER EMOTIONALLY tending to recover quickly from a disappointment or failure **4.** CHEERFUL cheerful or optimistic [Late 16C. Directly or via French < Spanish *boyante*, present participle of *boyar* (see BUOY[2])] —**buoy·ant·ly** *adv*

bu·pi·va·caine /byoo pívvə kàyn/ *n* a powerful local anesthetic. Use: epidural anesthesia. [Late 20C. < BUTYL + *piperidyl*, chemical compound (< PIPERIDINE) + *-va-* + *-caine*, INN stem]

bu·pres·tid /byoo préstid/ *n* a metallic-colored beetle that bores into wood during the larval stage. Native to: tropics. Family: Buprestidae. [Mid-19C. < modern Latin *Buprestidae* (plural) < Greek *bouprēstis* "ox-sweller" < *bous* "ox"]

bu·pro·pi·on /byoo prṓpee òn/ *n* an oral antidepressant medication used also in assisting patients to stop tobacco smoking. It works to inhibit neuronal uptake of, e.g., dopamine, in the central nervous system. [Late 20C. < BUTYL + *propiophenone*, a ketone < PROPIONIC ACID + PHENYL]

bur /bur/, **burr** *n* **1.** PRICKLY SEED HUSK a prickly husk covering the seeds of plants such as burdock **2.** TREE GROWTH a lumpy outgrowth of wood on a tree **3.** TOOL FOR REMOVING BURRS a tool used for removing the rough edges from metal that has been cut or drilled **4.** BONE DRILL an instrument for drilling holes in bone, especially into the skull [14C. Probably < N Germanic]

Bur. *abbr* **1.** Burma **2.** Burmese

Bu·ra·ku·min /bŏŏ rákŏŏ mìn/ *npl* members of the lowest Japanese sector of society [Mid-20C. < Japanese, "hamlet people"]

bu·ran /boo ráan/ *n* a strong wind in central Asia, bringing dust storms in summer and blizzards in winter [Mid-19C. Via Russian < Turkic *boran*]

burb /burb/, **'burb** *n* GEOG same as **suburb** (*slang*) [Shortening]

Bur·bank /búr bàngk/ **1.** city in southwestern California, in the San Fernando Valley, a northern suburb of Los Angeles. Population: 102,913 (2002 estimate). **2.** city in northeastern Illinois, a suburb of Chicago. Population: 28,095 (2002 estimate).

Bur·bank, Luther (1849–1926) US horticulturist and botanist. He developed many different varieties of fruits, vegetables, and flowers.

> "The scientist is a lover of truth for the very love of truth itself, wherever it may lead."
> [Luther Burbank, *The Harvest of the Years*; 1927]

bur·ber /búrbər/ *n* US SOC SCI same as **suburbanite** (*slang*)

bur·ble /búrb'l/ *v* (**-bled, -bling, -bles**) **1.** *vi* MAKE BUBBLING SOUND to make a gentle bubbling sound, like the sound of running water **2.** *vti* SPEAK EXCITEDLY to speak or say something in a fast excited way (*informal*) **3.** *vi* AVIAT HAVE EDDYING MOTION to become turbulent (*refers to the airflow around an aircraft's wing*) ■ *n* **1.** GENTLE SOUND a gentle bubbling or gurgling sound **2.** STREAM OF TALK a flow of fast excited talking (*informal*) **3.** AVIAT BREAK IN AIRFLOW a break in the flow of air around an aircraft's wing, which causes turbulence [14C. An imitation of the sound] —**bur·bler** *n* —**bur·bly** *adv*

bur·bot /búrbət/ (*plural same* or **-bots**) *n* **1.** a freshwater fish of the cod family. Native to: North America, northern Europe, Asia. Latin name: *Lota lota.* **2.** the flesh of a burbot used as food [14C. < Old French *borbette*]

Burck·hardt /búrk haart/, **Jakob** (1818–97) Swiss art historian. Professor of history at Basel University, Switzerland (1843–93), he wrote works on the Italian Renaissance and Greek civilization including the classic *The Civilization of the Renaissance in Italy* (1860). Full name **Burckhardt, Jakob Christopher**

bur·den[1] /búrd'n/ *n* **1.** WORRYING RESPONSIBILITY a difficult or worrying responsibility or duty ○ *the burdens of parenthood* **2.** SOMETHING CARRIED a load being carried ○ *carrying a heavy burden on his back* **3.** SHIPPING SHIP'S CAPACITY the maximum weight of cargo that a ship can carry ■ *vt* (**-dened, -den·ing, -dens**) **1.** GIVE RESPONSIBILITY TO SOMEBODY to give somebody a task that is difficult to deal with or something worrying to think about **2.** GIVE SOMEBODY LOAD TO CARRY to cause somebody or something to carry a burden [Old English *byrthen* < Indo-European, "to bear"]

bur·den[2] /búrd'n/ *n* **1.** a chorus in a song **2.** a main or recurring theme in a book, piece of music, speech, or argument (*literary*) [14C. < French *bourdon* "bass, drone," influenced by BURDEN[1]]

SYNONYMS See *subject.*

bur·den of proof *n* the responsibility of proving a case or argument, especially in a court of law

bur·den·some /búrd'nssəm/ *adj* difficult or worrying to bear or deal with

bur·dock /búr dòk/ *n* a tall biennial plant with a long taproot. Flowers: small, prickly, purple. Native to: temperate areas. Genus: *Arctium.* [Late 16C. < BURR[1] + DOCK[1]]

bu·reau /byŏŏrō/ (*plural* **-reaus** or **-reaux** /-rōz/) *n* **1.** GOVERNMENT DEPARTMENT a government department, or a branch of a government department **2.** ORGANIZATION an organization, or a branch of an organization **3.** CHEST OF DRAWERS a chest of drawers, especially a low one **4.** WRITING DESK a narrow desk with a writing surface and drawers [Late 17C. < French, literally "baize" (used for desks)]

bu·reauc·ra·cy /byoo rókrəssee/ (*plural* **-cies**) *n* **1.** ADMINISTRATIVE SYSTEM an administrative system, especially in a government, that divides work into specific categories carried out by special departments of nonelected officials **2.** OFFICIALS COLLECTIVELY the nonelected officials of an organization or department **3.** STATE OR ORGANIZATION a state or organization operated by a hierarchy of paid officials **4.** FRUSTRATING RULES complex rules and regulations applied rigidly [Early 19C. < French *bureaucratie* < *bureau* "office" + *-cratie* "rule"]

bu·reau·crat /byŏŏrə kràt/ *n* **1.** an administrative or government official **2.** an official who applies rules rigidly —**bu·reau·cra·tism** /byoo rókrə tìzzəm/ *n*

bu·reau·crat·ese /byoo ròkrə teéz/ *n* excessively formal, jargon-filled language associated with bureaucrats

bu·reau·crat·ic /byŏŏrə kráttik/ *adj* **1.** relating to the way administrative systems are organized ○ *the bureaucratic structure* **2.** applying rules rigidly within an administrative system or government —**bu·reau·crat·i·cal·ly** *adv*

bu·reau·cra·tize /byoo rókrə tīz/ (**-tized, -tiz·ing, -tiz·es**) *vt* **1.** to change a system into a bureaucracy **2.** to make a system or procedure rigid or complex —**bu·reau·cra·ti·za·tion** /byoo ròkrəti záysh'n/ *n*

bu·reau de change /byŏŏrō də shaaNzh/ (*plural* **bu·reaus de change** /byŏŏrō-/ or **bu·reaux de change** /byŏŏrō-/) *n* UK an office or part of a bank where foreign currency is exchanged [< French, "office of exchange"]

Bu·ren /byŏŏrən/ ♦ **Van Buren, Martin**

Bu·ren /bü ráN/, **Daniel** (*b.* 1938) French artist. He is known for his unconventional conceptual and installation works, often characterized by the use of striped material.

> "In art, banality soon becomes extraordinary."
> [Daniel Buren. Quoted in "Beware!", *Conceptual Art*, Ursula Meyer; 1972]

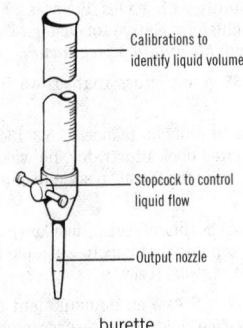

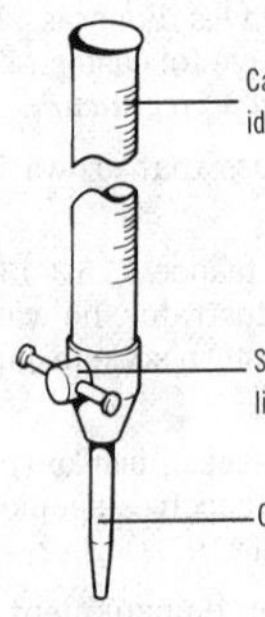

burette

bu·rette /byoo rét/ *n* a glass tube with measurements marked on the side and a stopcock at the bottom. Use: in laboratories to release an accurately measured quantity of liquid. [Mid-19C. < French < *buire* "jug"]

bur·fi /búrfee/, **bar·fi** /báar-/ *n* in South Asian cuisine, confectionery made from milk and sugar, often with nuts or cardamom, and shaped into a square or diamond [Via Hindi < Persian *barfī* "icy, snowy"]

burg[1] /burg/ *n* a city or town (*informal*) [Mid-19C. < German *Burg* < Germanic]

burg[2] /burg/ *n* an ancient fortress or walled town [Mid-18C. < late Latin *burgus* "town"]

Bur·gas /boor gaass/ Black Sea port and capital of Burgas Province, eastern Bulgaria. Population: 199,470 (1996).

bur·gee /bur jeé, búr jeè/ *n* an identification flag flown from the top of a mast, e.g., a sailing club pennant [Mid-18C. Origin ?]

bur·geon /búrjən/ (**-geoned, -geon·ing, -geons**) *vi* (*literary*) **1.** to produce new buds and leaves, or swell and develop into leaves and flowers **2.** to flourish or develop rapidly [14C. < French *bourgeonner* < *bourgeon* "a shoot or bud" < late Latin *burra* "wool"]

bur·geon·ing /búrjəning/ *adj* growing or expanding rapidly ○ *burgeoning wealth*

burg·er /búrgər/ *n* **1.** FOOD same as **hamburger** (sense 2) **2.** a round flat patty made of chicken, fish, vegetables, or nuts, usually cooked and served in a bun [Mid-20C. Shortened < HAMBURGER]

Bur·ger /búrgər/, **Warren** (1907–95) chief justice of the US Supreme Court. Appointed by President Nixon on the strength of his reputation as a judicial conservative, he sat on the US Supreme Court from 1969 to 1986. Full name **Burger, Warren Earl**

> "Free speech carries with it some freedom to listen."
> [Warren E. Burger, majority opinion, prohibiting courtroom closure to the press; July 2, 1980]

-burger *suffix* resembling ground beef or a hamburger ○ *veggieburger*

bur·gess /búrjəss/ *n* a member of the lower legislative house in Maryland or Virginia before the American Revolution

Bur·gess /búrjəss/, **Anthony** (1917–93) British writer and critic. His books include *A Clockwork Orange* (1962) and *A Dead Man in Deptford* (1993). Born **Wilson, John Anthony Burgess**

> "Without class differences, England would cease to be the living theater it is."
> [Anthony Burgess, *Observer (London)*; May 26, 1985]

Bur·gess, Guy (1911–63) British Soviet spy. Recruited as a Soviet agent while a student at Cambridge University in the 1930s, he worked for British intelligence and the Foreign Office. After being charged with serious misconduct, he escaped to the Soviet Union in 1951 with Donald Maclean. Full name **Burgess, Guy Francis de Moncy**

Bur·gess, John William (1844–1931) US political scientist and educator. In addition to scholarly publications and teaching, he established political science as an academic discipline and helped make Columbia a major university by founding the School of Political Science there in 1880.

burgh /burg, búrrō, búrrə/ *n* **1.** in Scotland, a town, especially one incorporated by royal charter **2.** same as **borough** (sense 3) (*archaic*) [Variant of BOROUGH]

burgh·er /búrgər/ *n* **1.** MEDIEVAL MERCHANT a merchant in a medieval European town **2.** CITIZEN a citizen, especially a prosperous or conservative member of the middle class (*humorous*) **3.** PRE-19C PARLIAMENTARY REPRESENTATIVE a parliamentary representative from a corporate town, borough, or university before 19th-century reforms [Late 16C. Partly < BURGH, partly < German or Dutch *burger* < *burg* (see BURG[2])]

Burgh·ley /búrlee/, **Sir William Cecil, 1st Baron** (1520–98) English politician. He was chief secretary of state to Elizabeth I after 1558, and formulated many of the domestic and foreign policies that made the Elizabethan Age a period of power and prosperity in England.

bur·glar /búrglər/ *n* somebody who enters or remains in a building intending to commit a felony, usually theft [Mid-16C. < obsolete legal French *burgier*]

bur·glar a·larm *n* an electronic device designed to make a loud noise when somebody enters a building in any way other than that intended by the resident or owner

bur·glar·ize /búrglə rīz/ (**-ized, -iz·ing, -iz·es**) *vt* to enter a building intending to commit a felony, usually theft (*often passive*)

bur·glar·proof /búrglər proof/ *adj* secured with locks, alarms, or other devices so as to discourage or prevent unauthorized entry

bur·gla·ry /búrgləree/ (*plural* **-ries**) *n* **1.** the crime of entering a building to commit a felony, usually theft **2.** an act of entering a building illegally to commit theft —**bur·glar·i·ous** /bur glérree əss/ *adj* —**bur·glar·i·ous·ly** *adv*

bur·gle /búrg'l/ (**-gled, -gling, -gles**) *vt UK* CRIME same as **burglarize** [Late 19C. Back-formation < BURGLAR]

~~burgler~~ incorrect spelling of **burglar**

bur·go·mas·ter /búrgə màstər/ *n* the mayor or chief magistrate in some northern European towns [Late 16C. < Dutch *burgomeester* "town master"]

Bur·gos /boor gōss/ capital of Burgos Province in Castile-León, northern Spain. Population: 167,962 (2002).

Bur·goyne /bur góyn, búr gòyn/, **John** (1722–92) British army general. His attempt to lead a British invasion into New York from Canada was thwarted at Saratoga (1777). He also wrote plays, including *The Heiress* (1786).

> "After a fatal procrastination...we took a step as decisive as the passage of the Rubicon, and now find ourselves plunged at once in a most serious war without a single requisition, gunpowder excepted, for carrying it on."
> [John Burgoyne, *Letter from Boston*; April 1775]

Bur·gun·di·an /bər gúndee ən/ *n* **1.** PEOPLES SOMEBODY FROM BURGUNDY, FRANCE somebody who comes from the Burgundy region of east-central France **2.** HIST MEMBER OF GERMANIC PEOPLE a member of a Germanic people who established a kingdom in Burgundy in the 5th century A.D. **3.** MUSIC EARLY RENAISSANCE COMPOSER a member of a 15th-century group of European composers noted for their chansons and masses, especially one of those employed by the dukes of Burgundy [Early 17C. < BURGUNDY]

bur·gun·dy /búrgəndee/ *n* **1.** *also* **Bur·gun·dy** red or white wine produced in the Burgundy region of east central France **2.** a deep red color, like that of red burgundy wine —**bur·gun·dy** *adj*

Bur·gun·dy /búrgəndee/ region, formerly a kingdom and duchy, located in east central France. It is an important wine-producing area. French name **Bourgogne**

bur·i·al /bérree əl/ *n* the act or ceremony of putting a dead body into the ground or into the sea (*often used before a noun*) ○ *a burial place* [Old English *byrgels* < *byrgan* (see BURY)]

bur·i·al cham·ber *n* a small room or enclosed space where somebody has been buried

bur·i·al ground *n* an area of land where dead bodies are buried, especially an ancient site

Bur·i·at *n* PEOPLES, LANG another spelling of **Buryat**

Bur·i·dan's ass /byoorəd'nz-/ *n* a situation used to demonstrate the impracticality of making choices according to a formal system of reasoning [After Jean *Buridan* (1300–58), French philosopher]

bur·ied treas·ure *n* valuable items buried or thought to be buried in the ground for safekeeping

bu·rin /byoorin/ *n* **1.** an engraver's chisel for making grooves **2.** a prehistoric flint tool resembling a chisel, used for cutting and engraving during the Upper Paleolithic period [Mid-17C. < French]

burke /burk/ (**burked, burk·ing, burkes**) *vt* **1.** KEEP SOMETHING QUIET to prevent information from becoming known **2.** KEEP SOMEBODY QUIET to prevent somebody from revealing information **3.** EVADE SOMETHING to evade an issue or question **4.** MURDER SOMEBODY DISCREETLY to murder somebody silently and without leaving marks or wounds, especially by suffocation (*dated*) [Early 19C. After William BURKE]

Burke /burk/, **Edmund** (1729–97) Irish-born British writer, political philosopher, and politician. As a Whig member of Parliament (1765–94), he was one of the greatest orators of the age. His *Reflections on the Revolution in France* (1790) condemned the French Revolution and reached a wide European audience.

> "If any ask me what a free government is, I answer, that for any practical purpose, it is what the people think so. Liberty, too, must be limited in order to be possessed."
> [Edmund Burke, *Letter to the Sheriffs of Bristol*; 1777]

Bur·ki·na Fa·so /bər keenə faássō/ landlocked country in West Africa. A former French territory, it became independent in 1960. Language: French. Currency: CFA franc. Capital: Ouagadougou. Population: 13,228,460 (2003). Area: 105,900 sq. mi./274,200 sq. km. Official name **Democratic Republic of Burkina Faso**. Former name **Upper Volta** (until 1984)

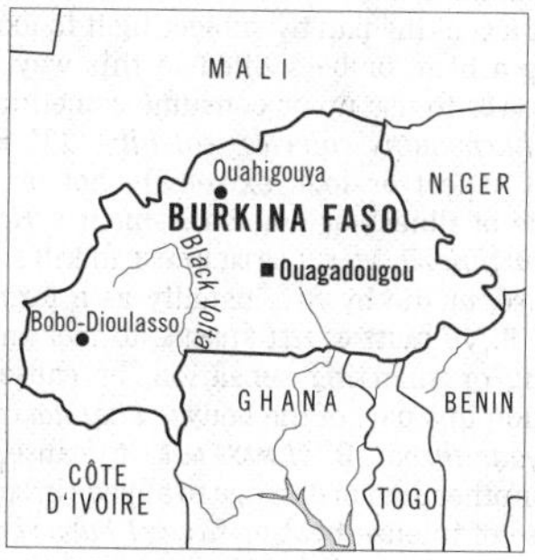

Burkina Faso

Bur·kitt's lym·pho·ma /bùrkits-/ *n* a rare malignant tumor attacking white blood cells, associated with a virus spread by insects. It is found mainly in children in Central Africa. [Mid-20C. After Denis *Burkitt* (1911–93), British surgeon]

burl /burl/ *n* **1.** KNOT ON TREE a knotty growth on a tree trunk **2.** KNOTTY WOOD knotty wood, or a decorative veneer made from a burl of a tree **3.** KNOT IN CLOTH a knot in thread or cloth ■ *vt* (**burled, burl·ing, burls**) REMOVE KNOTS FROM CLOTH to pick knots off newly woven cloth [15C. Via Old French *bourle* "tuft of wool" < late Latin *burra* "wool"] —**burl·er** *n*

bur·lap /búr làp/ *n* coarse cloth woven from jute, hemp, or a similar rough thread [Late 17C. Origin ?]

bur·lesque /bur lésk/ *n* **1.** MOCKERY BY LUDICROUS IMITATION the mocking of a serious matter or style by imitating it in an incongruous way **2.** WORK USING BURLESQUE a literary or dramatic work that uses burlesque **3.** LUDICROUS IMITATION an incongruous imitation of something **4.** VARIETY SHOW a variety show of a type that often includes striptease ■ *vt* (**-lesqued, -lesq·uing, -lesques**) MOCK SOMETHING BY LUDICROUS IMITATION to mock something serious by imitating it in an incongruous way [Mid-17C. Via French < Italian *burlesco* < *burla* "mockery, fun"] —**bur·lesq·uer** *n*

bur·ley /búrlee/ *n* a light-colored, thin-leaved tobacco grown mainly in Kentucky [Late 19C. Origin ?]

Bur·lin·game /búrling gàym/ city in western California, on the San Mateo peninsula, a southern suburb of San Francisco. Population: 27,773 (2002 estimate).

Bur·ling·ton /búrlingtən/ **1.** city and port in the southeastern corner of Iowa, southwest of Davenport, on the western bank of the Mississippi River. Population: 26,048 (2002 estimate). **2.** city on the banks of the Haw River near Lake Townsend in north central North Carolina. It is the site of the battle of Alamance (1771), which saw an army of rebel farmers, known as Regulators, defeated by the royalist governor's militia. Population: 44,900 (2000). **3.** city in northwestern Vermont, on Lake Champlain. It is home to the University of Vermont. Population: 39,466 (2002 estimate).

bur·ly /búrlee/ (**-li·er, -li·est**) *adj* **1.** strong and with a broad sturdy frame ○ *flanked by two burly bodyguards* **2.** rough and robust ○ *a burly laugh* [14C. Probably < assumed Old English *borlic* "excellent" < Indo-European, "carry"] —**bur·li·ness** *n*

Bur·ma /búrmə/ former name for **Myanmar** —**Bur·man** *adj, n*

bur mar·i·gold *n UK* BOT same as **beggar's lice** (sense 1)

Bur·mese /bur meez, -meess/ (*plural same*) *n* **1.** somebody who comes from Myanmar, formerly Burma **2.** the official Tibeto-Burman language of Myanmar. Native speakers: 20–27 million. —**Bur·mese** *adj*

Bur·mese cat *n* a domestic cat belonging to a breed with a chocolate-colored or silvery-brown coat and yellow eyes, similar in build to the Siamese cat

burn[1] /burn/ *v* (**burned** or **burnt** /burnt/, **burn·ing, burns**) **1.** *vti* BE OR SET ON FIRE to be on fire, or cause something to be on fire **2.** *vti* DESTROY SOMETHING BY FIRE to destroy something by fire, or be destroyed by fire ○ *The house was burned to the ground.* **3.** *vt* DAMAGE SOMETHING

BY FIRE to injure, damage, or affect somebody or something with fire or extreme heat ○ *I burned my hand on the iron.* **4.** *vti* **OVERCOOK SOMETHING** to spoil food or a cooking pan by subjecting it to too intense or long a heat, or be spoiled in this way **5.** *vt* **USE SOMETHING UP** to use up or consume something ○ *You won't burn many calories watching TV.* **6.** *vi* **FEEL FEVERISH** to feel or look extremely hot or feverish because of illness or embarrassment ○ *Her cheeks were burning.* **7.** *vti* **KILL OR DIE BY FIRE** to kill somebody with fire, or die by fire, usually as a form of execution **8.** *vti* **CAUSE OR FEEL STINGING** to feel an intense stinging or smarting sensation, or cause such a sensation in a part of the body ○ *That hot coffee will burn your throat.* **9.** *vt* **MAKE MARK** to cause a mark, hole, or other sign of damage to appear in something because of intense heat or fire ○ *I burned a hole in my shirt with the iron.* **10.** *vti* **SUNBURN** to become sunburned, or cause a person or part of the body to become sunburned ○ *My skin burns easily.* **11.** *vt* **CHEAT SOMEBODY** to cheat or swindle somebody (*informal; usually passive*) ○ *We really got burned on that deal.* **12.** *vt* **USE SOMETHING AS FUEL** to use something for heat or energy ○ *burn gas* **13.** *vi* **IMPRESS DEEPLY** to create a deep and lasting impression on somebody or something ○ *His words were burning in my brain.* **14.** *vi* **SUFFER PAIN** to suffer pain through fire **15.** *vi* **EMIT ENERGY** to emit heat or light ○ *A light was burning outside the front porch.* **16.** *vti* **ELECTROCUTE** to electrocute somebody, or be electrocuted (*informal*) **17.** *vi* **CONTAIN FIRE** to contain a fire, or operate by means of fire ○ *a fireplace burning brightly* **18.** *vi* **FEEL STRONG EMOTION** to feel an emotion very intensely ○ *burning with shame* **19.** *vi* **YEARN** to yearn to do or acquire something ○ *burning to succeed* **20.** *vti* CHEM **COMBUST** to undergo combustion, or cause something to undergo combustion **21.** *vt* COMPUT **COPY DATA TO CD** to copy data onto a CD-ROM or DVD-ROM. It can then be used to transport the content or to create multiple copies. ■ *n* **1.** MED **HEAT INJURY** an injury caused by fire, heat, radiation, chemical action, electricity, or friction, resulting in redness and blistering of the skin and often causing damage to underlying tissues **2. FIRE OR HEAT MARK** a mark or hole left on or in something such as fabric, wood, or plastic as a result of burning **3. STINGING** a stinging sensation or feeling of intense heat ○ *the burn of the iodine on my skin* **4. ANGER** a state of anger ○ *He's been in a slow burn all morning.* **5. SKIN BURN** sunburn or windburn **6.** FITNESS **SENSATION OF BURNING** a sensation of burning that occurs during strenuous exercise, and the positive psychological sensation associated with it ○ *You can feel the burn after an hour of aerobics.* **7.** AEROSP **ROCKET ADJUSTMENT** a controlled firing of a rocket's engine for adjusting course and position [Old English *birnan* "be on fire," *bærnan* "cause something to burn" < Germanic] —**burn·a·ble** *adj*

burn down *vti* to catch fire and burn until almost nothing remains, or burn something such as a building in order to destroy it

burn in *vt* **1.** to operate a semiconductor-based device or piece of software continuously to test for defects **2.** to expose a specific part of an image on photographic paper while masking other areas so that they are not exposed any further

burn off *v* **1.** *vt* **GET RID OF EXCESS FAT** to use up energy or get rid of unwanted fat by exercising ○ *burn off a few extra calories* **2.** *vt* AGRIC **REMOVE VEGETATION** to remove vegetation by fire or with chemicals, either to clear the land or in preparation for harvesting a root crop **3.** *vt* INDUST **GET RID OF EXCESS GAS** to get rid of unwanted gas by burning it, e.g., at an oil-well head **4.** *vti* METEOROL **DISSIPATE** to dissipate fog or clouds by the heat of the sun, or be dissipated in this way

burn out *v* **1.** *vi* **FINISH BURNING** to stop burning when reduced to nothing **2.** *vti* **WEAR OUT THROUGH HEAT** to stop working because of too much heat or friction, or cause something to stop working in this way ○ *The motor must have burned out.* **3.** *vti* **BECOME EXHAUSTED** to become exhausted or unwell through too much hard work, stress, or reckless living, or make somebody exhausted or unwell in this way (*informal*) ○ *You'll burn yourself out if you don't slow down.*

burn up *v* **1.** *vti* **DESTROY BY FIRE** to destroy something by intense heat or fire, or be destroyed in this way **2.** *vi* **BE VERY HOT** to be very hot or overheated ○ *burning up with fever* **3.** *vt* **ANNOY** to annoy somebody or make somebody angry (*informal*)

burn² /burn/ *n N England, Scotland* a stream or brook [Old English *burna* < Indo-European, "to boil"]

burn bag *n* a bag for putting secret or politically sensitive documents in before burning them

burned-out /bùrnd-/, **burnt-out** /bùrnt-/ *adj* **1.** exhausted physically or emotionally through too much hard work, stress, or reckless living **2.** destroyed on the inside by fire

Burne-Jones /bùrn jṓnz/, **Sir Edward** (1833–98) British artist and designer. A leading member of the pre-Raphaelite school, he painted classical and mythological subjects in a dreamlike style. His book illustrations and designs for stained glass and tapestries showed the strong influence of medieval art. Born **Jones, Edward Coley**

burn·er /búrnər/ *n* **1. RING ON RANGE** one of the circular rings or plates on a gas or electric range that produces heat or a flame **2. PART OF STOVE OR LAMP** the part of a fuel-burning stove, lamp, or heater that produces a flame when lit **3. FURNACE** an incinerator or furnace that burns fuel, waste products, or trash **4. LARGE GRAFFITI** a large, complex mural or graffiti painted by a graffiti artist, usually on the outside wall of a building (*slang*)

bur·net /bər nét/ (*plural* **-nets** *or* **same**) *n* a perennial herb of the rose family. Genus: *Sanguisorba.* [14C. < Old French *brunet, brunete* < *brun* "brown" < Germanic]

Bur·net /bər nét, búrnit/, **Sir Macfarlane** (1899–1985) Australian biologist. He was joint winner of the Nobel Prize in physiology or medicine (1960) for his work in immunology. Full name **Burnet, Sir Frank Macfarlane**

Bur·nett /bər nét/, **Frances Hodgson** (1849–1924) British-born US writer. She wrote children's books, including the classic novel *The Secret Garden* (1911). Born **Hodgson, Frances Eliza**. See Cultural note at **garden**

Bur·ney /búrnee/, **Fanny** (1752–1840) British novelist and diarist. Her novels include *Evelina* (1778). Her diaries covering 1768–85, published posthumously, are among the classic documents of late-18th-century British social history. Born **Frances Burney**

> "Now I am ashamed of confessing that I have nothing to confess."
> [Fanny Burney, *Evelina*; 1778]

Burn·ham /búrnəm/, **Forbes** (1923–85) Guyanan politician. He was prime minister (1964–80) and president (1980–85) of Guyana. Full name **Burnham, Linden Forbes Sampson**

burn-in *n* a final test for semiconductor-based devices or software in which they are operated for a prescribed period to find defects

burn·ing /búrning/ *adj* **1. ON FIRE** producing flames, or on fire **2. VERY HOT** extremely hot **3. ARDENT** emotionally intense or strong ○ *He spoke with a burning passion.* **4. IMPORTANT** of immediate or urgent importance ○ *one of the burning issues of the day* ■ *adv* **EXTREMELY** so as to produce intense heat ○ *a burning hot day*

burn·ing bush *n* **1.** a bush with bright red berries or foliage. Genus: *Euonymus.* **2.** PLANTS same as **gas plant** **3.** a bushy annual plant with narrow light green leaves that turn red in fall, e.g., the summer cypress [Alluding to Exodus 3]

burn·ing glass *n* a convex lens that can concentrate the sun's rays to produce an intense spot of heat or fire at the focus

bur·nish /búrnish/ *vt* (**-nished, -nish·ing, -nish·es**) **1. POLISH SOMETHING** to polish metal until it shines **2. MAKE SOMETHING SHINY** to make something such as pottery or fabric shine by rubbing it with a smooth instrument ■ *n* **SHINY SURFACE** a smooth shiny finish ○ *a bowl with a bright burnish* [14C. < Old French *burniss-*, stem of variant of *brunir* "make bright or brown" < *brun* (see BURNET)] —**bur·nish·er** *n*

bur·nished /búrnisht/ *adj* **1.** polished until shiny **2.** brown and lustrous or smooth (*literary*) ○ *the burnished coat of the chestnut mare*

Burn·ley /búrnlee/ city in Lancashire, northwestern England, a center of textile production. Population: 89,542 (2001).

bur·noose /bur no͝oss/, **bur·nous**, **burn·ouse** *n* a long hooded cloak worn by some Arabs, or a garment resembling this [Late 16C. Via French *burnous* < Arabic *burnus* < Greek *birros* "hooded cloak"]

burn·out /búrn òwt/ *n* **1. EXHAUSTION** psychological exhaustion and diminished efficiency resulting from overwork or prolonged exposure to stress ○ *reported a high rate of burnout among nurses* **2. EXTREMELY EXHAUSTED PERSON** somebody affected by psychological exhaustion (*informal*) **3.** MECH ENG **MACHINE FAILURE THROUGH HEAT** failure of a machine or part of a machine to work because of overuse or excessive heat or friction **4.** AEROSP **ROCKET FAILURE** failure of a rocket or jet engine to work because the fuel supply has been exhausted or cut off

burn rate *n* the rate at which a company uses up its cash

Burns /burnz/, **George** (1896–1996) US comedian and actor. He conducted one of the longest-running acts in show business, encompassing vaudeville, radio, movies, and television, and won an Academy Award for *The Sunshine Boys* (1975).

> "It's nice to be here. When you're 99 years old, it's nice to be anyplace."
> [George Burns, *USA Today*; June 20, 1995]

Barnaby's

Robert Burns

Burns, Robert (1759–96) Scottish poet. The author of *Poems Chiefly in the Scottish Dialect* (1786) and hundreds of songs, he is regarded as Scotland's national poet. His many works include the songs "Auld Lang Syne" and "Scots Wha Hae," and the narrative poem "Tam O'Shanter."

> "Man's inhumanity to man. / Makes countless thousands mourn!"
> [Robert Burns, "Man Was made to Mourn"; 1786]

Burns, Tommy (1881–1955) Canadian boxer. He was Canada's only world heavyweight boxing champion (1906–08).

Burn·side /búrn sīd/, **Ambrose** (1824–81) US army general. He fought in campaigns against the Native Americans on the frontier and served as a general in the Union Army in the Civil War. His spectacular side whiskers inspired the creation of the term "sideburns." Full name **Burnside, Ambrose Everett**

burn·sides /búrn sīdz/ *npl* heavy side whiskers and a mustache worn with a clean-shaven chin [Late 19C. After Ambrose BURNSIDE]

burnt /burnt/ past participle, past tense of **burn¹** ■ *adj* describes a pigment or dye that has been darkened through a heating process ○ *burnt umber*

burnt al·mond *n* a candy with an almond in the center and a coating of burnt sugar

burnt of·fer·ing *n* **1.** in some religions, an animal or other offering that is burned on an altar as a sacrifice **2.** a dish of burnt or overcooked food that is nevertheless served (*humorous*)

burnt-out *adj* same as **burned-out**

burnt si·en·na *n* **1.** a reddish brown pigment or dye originally obtained by roasting raw sienna **2.** a dark reddish brown color —**burnt si·en·na** *adj*

burnt um·ber *n* **1.** a dark brown pigment or dye originally obtained by roasting raw umber **2.** a deep brown color —**burnt um·ber** *adj*

burp /burp/ *n* **NOISE MADE THROUGH MOUTH** a noise made through the mouth when air is suddenly forced up through the esophagus from the stomach ■ *v* **(burped, burp·ing, burps) 1.** *vi* **BELCH** to make a noise through the mouth when air is suddenly forced up through the esophagus from the stomach **2.** *vt* **MAKE BABY BRING UP GAS** to make a baby expel air from its stomach through its esophagus after feeding by rubbing or patting its back [Mid-20C. An imitation of the sound]

burp gun *n* a lightweight submachine gun (*informal*)

bur·qa /búrkə/, **bur·ka** *n* a garment with veiled eyeholes covering the entire body, worn in public by some Muslim women [Mid-19C. Via Urdu or Persian *burka'* < Arabic *burku'*]

burr[1] /bur/ *n* **1.** ENG **ROUGH EDGE** a rough edge on material such as metal after it has been cut or drilled **2.** ENG, BOT another spelling of **bur** (senses 1–3) ■ *vt* **(burred, burr·ing, burrs) 1. CREATE ROUGH EDGE ON SOMETHING** to create a rough edge on a piece of metal or other piece of work by cutting or drilling **2. REMOVE ROUGH EDGE FROM SOMETHING** to remove a rough edge from a piece of metal or other piece of work [Variant of BUR]

burr[2] /bur/ *n* **1.** a whirring or buzzing sound ○ *the steady burr of the machines downstairs* **2.** a rolled or trilled pronunciation of the "r" sound in some regional accents of English [Mid-18C. Origin ?] —**burr** *vti*

burr[3] /bur/ *n* a washer that fits around the end of a rivet [14C. Shortening of Old English *burg* (see BOROUGH); originally "circle"]

Burr /bur/, **Aaron** (1756–1836) vice president of the United States. He was Thomas Jefferson's first vice president (1801–05). He killed Alexander Hamilton in a duel after a long public feud (1804). He fled and tried to create an independent nation in the US southwest, but was later acquitted of treason.

bur·ra /búrrə/ *adj S Asia* large or important [Early 19C. < Hindi *baṛā* "great"]

Bur·ra Din /-dín/ *n S Asia* same as **Christmas** [< Hindi *din* "day"]

bur·ri·to /bə reétō/ (*plural* **-tos**) *n* in Mexican cooking, a flour tortilla wrapped around a filling of meat, beans, or cheese [Mid-20C. < American Spanish, "small burro" < Spanish *burro* (see BURRO)]

bur·ro /búrō, bóor ō/ (*plural* **-ros**) *n* a small donkey, especially one that is used as a pack animal [Early 19C. < Spanish, back-formation < *borrico* "donkey" < late Latin *burricus* "small horse"]

bur·ro's tail *n* a Mexican plant popular as a houseplant for its hanging stems and thick, succulent leaves that resemble tails. Latin name: *Sedum morganianum.*

Bur·roughs /búrrōz/, **Edgar Rice** (1875–1950) US writer. He created the character Tarzan in a series of popular novels starting in 1914.

Bur·roughs, John (1837–1921) US naturalist, essayist, and poet. He wrote essays on nature and possessed extensive natural history collections.

> "To treat your facts with imagination is one thing, to imagine your facts is another."
> [John Burroughs, *The Heart of Burroughs Journals*; 1928]

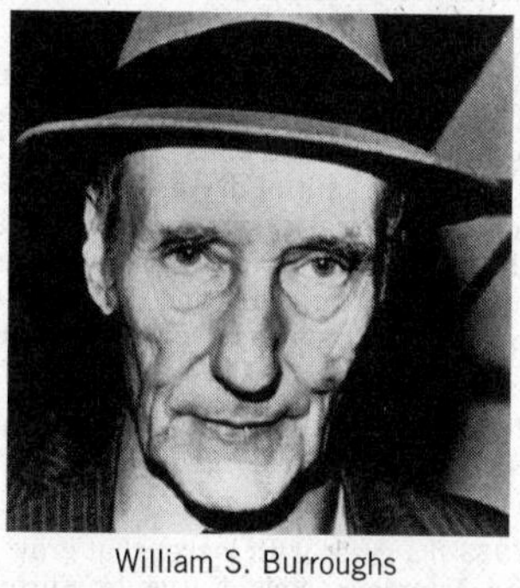

William S. Burroughs

Bur·roughs, William S. (1914–97) US writer. A leading figure of the Beat Generation, he wrote *The Naked Lunch* (1959) and *The Soft Machine* (1961). Full name **Burroughs, William Seward.** See Cultural note at **lunch**

> "Writers live the sad truth just like everyone else. The only difference is, they file reports."
> [William S. Burroughs, *Naked Lunch*; 1959]

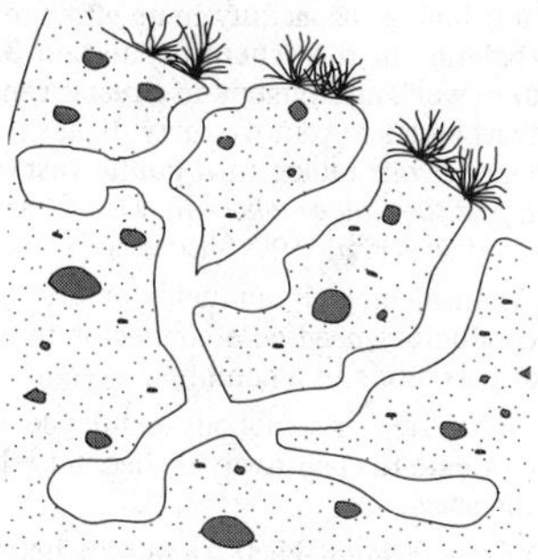

burrow

bur·row /búrrō/ *n* **1. RABBIT'S HOME** a hole or tunnel dug as a living space by a small animal such as a rabbit **2. SNUG PLACE** a small snug place created by digging or hollowing ■ *v* **(-rowed, -row·ing, -rows) 1.** *vti* **DIG HOLE OR TUNNEL** to make a hole or tunnel by digging **2.** *vi* **BE IN BURROW** to hide or live in a burrow **3.** *vi* **PENETRATE BY DIGGING** to move through something solid by digging or by creating a space ○ *He burrowed through the undergrowth.* **4.** *vi* **LOOK INTO SOMETHING THOROUGHLY** to research or investigate something very thoroughly ○ *had spent years burrowing into the history of the era* [13C. Variant of BOROUGH] —**bur·row·er** *n*

burr·stone *n* GEOL another spelling of **buhrstone**

bur·ry[1] /búree/ (**-ri·er, -ri·est**) *adj* **1.** covered in burrs **2.** resembling a burr or burrs [15C. < BURR[1]]

bur·ry[2] /búree/ (**-ri·er, -ri·est**) *adj* characterized by or spoken with a burr [Mid-19C. < BURR[2]]

bur·sa /búrssə/ (*plural* **-sas** or **-sae** /-see/) *n* a fluid-filled body sac that reduces friction around joints or between other parts that rub against one another [Early 19C. Via modern Latin < medieval Latin, "bag, purse" < Greek, "wineskin"] —**bur·sal** *adj*

Bur·sa /búr saà/ city in northwestern Turkey, south of the Sea of Marmara, south of Istanbul, and west of Ankara. It was the capital of the Ottoman Empire from 1326 to 1402. Population: 1,095,842 (1997).

bur·sa of Fa·bri·cius /bùrssə əv fə breéshəss/ *n* an organ in immature birds that produces B lymphocytes. It resembles a sac and is situated in part of the lower pelvic region **(cloaca)**. [After Girolamo *Fabrici* (1533–1619), Italian anatomist (Latinized)]

bur·sar /búrssər/ *n* an official who has charge of funds, particularly in a university, college, school, or monastery [13C. Directly or via French < medieval Latin *bursarius* < *bursa* (see BURSA)] —**bur·sar·ship** *n*

bur·sa·ry /búrssəree/ (*plural* **-ries**) *n* **1.** a grant or scholarship offered to a student at a school, college, or university in some countries such as Canada and Scotland **2.** the office or room where a bursar works [Late 17C. < medieval Latin *bursaria* "bursar's office" < *bursa* (see BURSA)] —**bur·sar·i·al** /bur sérree əl/ *adj*

burse /burss/ *n* in the Roman Catholic Church, a flat case that is used for carrying a special linen cloth **(corporal)** when celebrating Mass [13C. Directly or via French < medieval Latin *bursa* (see BURSA)]

bur·si·tis /bur sítiss/ *n* inflammation of a fluid-filled sac **(bursa)** of the body, particularly at the elbow, knee, or shoulder joint

burst /burst/ *v* **(burst, burst·ing, bursts) 1.** *vi* **SPLIT OR BREAK** to split or break apart suddenly and violently because of excess internal pressure ○ *The suitcase had burst open.* **2.** *vt* **MAKE SOMETHING SPLIT** to cause something to split open suddenly and disgorge its contents, e.g., by piercing it or applying external pressure **3.** *vi* **BE VERY FULL** to be so full as to appear close to splitting open or overflowing ○ *Every hotel in town was bursting with tourists.* **4.** *vt* **RUPTURE SOMETHING** to rupture an internal organ or blood vessel **5.** *vt* **FLOW OVER SOMETHING** to overflow the normal limit of containment ○ *The river burst its banks.* **6.** *vi* **MOVE SUDDENLY** to go, come, or move suddenly and with great energy and speed ○ *Angry protesters burst in on the meeting.* **7.** *vi* **BE OVERWHELMED** to feel an emotion so intensely that it is almost overwhelming ○ *I thought I would burst with excitement.* **8.** *vi* **BECOME SUDDENLY NOTICED** to appear suddenly and become noticed and prominent at a particular time and in a particular situation ○ *an exciting new product about to burst onto the market* **9.** *vt* **DIVIDE PAPER** to separate continuous stationery such as computer printout into individual sheets ■ *n* **1. EXPLOSION OR RUPTURE** a sudden and often noisy splitting or breaking open of something **2. SHORT INTENSE PERIOD** a short, sudden, and intense period of an activity or phenomenon ○ *a burst of publicity* **3. SUSTAINED ACTIVITY** a period of sustained activity ○ *I read it in two bursts.* ○ *a burst of speed* **4. GUNFIRE** a short, sudden, and noisy volley of gunfire **5.** ONLINE, COMPUT **SINGLE AMOUNT OF DATA** an amount of data sent or received in one operation [Old English *berstan* < Germanic] —**burst·er** *n*

burst into *vt* **1.** to start to happen or appear suddenly and often dramatically ○ *The truck crashed and burst into flames.* ○ *Spring saw the landscape burst into life.* **2.** to give sudden and full expression to a strong emotion such as laughter or tears ○ *burst into tears*

burst out *v* **1.** *vi* to start expressing something suddenly and fully ○ *burst out laughing* **2.** *vt* to say something suddenly, as if a suppressed emotion or opinion had been welling up inside

burst·ing /búrsting/ *adj* **1. OVERFLOWING** so full of an emotion or a quality that it is almost impossible to contain it ○ *bursting with energy* **2. ABSOLUTELY FULL** full to the point of overflowing ○ *a city bursting with refugees* **3. EAGER** wanting to do something very much (*informal*) ○ *I was bursting to tell her the news.* **4. WITH FULL BLADDER** needing desperately to urinate (*informal*)

burst·ing disk *n* a safety device in a vessel used in an industrial process consisting of a thin metal disk that is designed to rupture when subjected to unusually high pressure

bur·stone *n* GEOL another spelling of **buhrstone**

burst·y /búrstee/ *adj* moving, transferred, or transmitted in short uneven spurts, as is stellar radiation from a pulsar, traffic at a tollbooth, or data in a computer network

bur·then /búrthən/ (*archaic*) *n* same as **burden**[1] ■ *vt* **(-thened, -then·ing, -thens)** same as **burden**[1] [Variant]

bur·ton /búrt'n/ *n* a light tackle with double or single blocks used for hoisting [Early 18C. Alteration of obsolete *Breton (tackle)*, origin ?]

Bur·ton /búrt'n/ city in eastern Michigan, on the Thread River. It is a suburb of Flint. Population: 30,385 (2002 estimate).

Bur·ton, Harold (1888–1964) associate justice of the US Supreme Court (1945–58). He was appointed by President Truman. Full name **Burton, Harold Hitz**

Bur·ton, Sir Richard (1821–90) British explorer and linguist. He was one of the first Europeans to enter Mecca and Medina. He also traveled extensively in Africa and translated several books, including *The Arabian Nights* (1885–88) and *The Perfumed Garden* (1886). Full name **Burton, Sir Richard Francis**

Bur·ton, Richard (1925–84) Welsh-born British actor. His movies include *Look Back in Anger* (1959) and *Cleopatra* (1963).

> "An actor is something less than a man while an actress is something more than a woman."
> [Richard Burton. Quoted in *Halliwell's Filmgoer's and Video Viewer's Companion (8th ed.)*, Leslie Halliwell; 1990]

Bur·ton, Tim (*b.* 1960) US movie director. He directed *Batman* (1989) and *Edward Scissorhands* (1990).

Bur·ton-up·on-Trent /bùrt'n ə pon trént/ city on the Trent River in Staffordshire, central England. It is a historic brewing center. Population: 60,525 (1991).

Burundi

Bu·run·di /bo͝o ro͝ondee/ landlocked country in east central Africa. It is bordered by Rwanda to the north, Tanzania to the east and south, and the Democratic Republic of the Congo to the west. Language: Kirundi, French. Currency: Burundi franc. Capital: Bujumbura. Population: 6,096,156 (2003). Area: 10,747 sq. mi./27,834 sq. km. Official name **Republic of Burundi**. Former name **Ruanda-Urundi** (until 1962) —**Bu·run·di·an** *n, adj*

bur·y /bérree/ (**-ied, -y·ing, -ies**) *v* **1.** *vt* **PUT SOMETHING IN HOLE** to dig a hole, put something in it, and replace the soil or other material removed ○ *a dog burying its bone* **2.** *vt* **INTER DEAD BODY** to put a dead body in a grave dug in the ground, or sometimes under water, usually as part of a religious ritual ○ *He asked to be buried at sea.* **3.** *vt* **LOSE SOMEBODY THROUGH DEATH** to lose somebody, especially a spouse or a close relative, through death ○ *She has buried four husbands.* **4.** *vt* **HIDE SOMETHING BY COVERING** to hide something by covering it with a lot of things so that it cannot be seen ○ *He buried the letter under a pile of books.* **5.** *vt* **COVER SOMEBODY OR SOMETHING UP** to cover somebody or something completely with something ○ *was buried under the rubble* **6.** *vt* **OBSCURE SOMETHING** to make something difficult to find, notice, or distinguish ○ *The announcement was buried at the end of the program.* **7.** *vt* **SINK SOMETHING DEEPLY** to sink something deeply into something else so that it is difficult to see or retrieve ○ *The splinter had buried itself under his nail.* **8.** *vt* **HIDE HEAD FROM SIGHT** to put the face or head somewhere, usually on or under a soft and yielding surface ○ *She buried her face in her hands.* **9.** *vt* **MOVE CARD** to move a playing card from the top to another location in the deck **10. bur·y your·self** *vr* **CONCENTRATE INTENSELY ON SOMETHING** to concentrate exclusively and intensely on something ○ *She tended to bury herself in her work.* **11.** *vt* **SUPPRESS OR FORGET SOMETHING** to suppress or forget something unpleasant or undesirable ○ *their efforts to bury the past* [Old English *byrgan* < Germanic, "protection, shelter"]

SPELLCHECK See ***berry***.

Bur·y /bérree/ city in Lancashire, northwestern England, on the Irwell River. Population: 180,608 (2001).

Bur·yat /bo͝or yaát/, **Bur·iat** *n* **1.** a member of a people living in southeastern Russia **2.** an Altaic language spoken by the Buryats, considered to be a dialect of Mongolian. Native speakers: 300,000. [Mid-19C. < Mongolian *Buriyad*] —**Bur·yat** *adj*

Bur·y St. Ed·munds /bèrree saynt édməndz/ market town in Suffolk, eastern England. Its name comes from the Saxon king St. Edmund, who is buried there. Population: 31,237 (1991).

bus /buss/ *n* (*plural* **bus·es** or **bus·ses**) **1. LARGE PASSENGER VEHICLE** a long motor vehicle with many seats, usually divided by a central aisle. Buses transport fare-paying passengers along a specific route. **2. CAR OR PLANE** a vehicle, especially a car or plane (*informal*) ○ *I can't get this old bus to start!* **3.** COMPUT **DATA CHANNEL** a channel or path for transferring computer data, especially between the central processing unit and a peripheral device **4. HAND TRUCK** a four-wheeled cart or hand truck used for carrying things such as dishes in restaurants **5.** ARMS **ROCKET WARHEAD** the final stage of a multistage rocket, containing the warhead **6.** AEROSP **SPACECRAFT COMPONENT** the part of a space exploration vehicle that contains the atmospheric reentry probes ■ *v* (**bused** or **bussed, bus·ing** or **bus·sing, bus·es** or **bus·ses**) **1.** *vti* **GO OR CARRY PASSENGERS BY BUS** to travel or transport passengers to a particular destination by bus **2.** *vt* **TRANSPORT SCHOOLCHILDREN** to transport schoolchildren by bus to a school distant from their homes, especially in an effort to achieve ethnic balance in the school population **3.** *vi* **WORK AS BUSBOY** to work as a busboy in a restaurant or café **4.** *vt* **REMOVE DISHES** to remove dirty dishes and other meal debris from tables in a public restaurant or café ○ *a fast food place where they expect you to bus your own dishes* [Early 19C. Shortening of OMNIBUS]

bus bar *n* an electrical conductor or group of electrical conductors used as a connector in a circuit, especially as a bus in a computer system

bus·boy /búss bòy/ *n* somebody employed in a restaurant or café to clear away dishes, set tables, and assist the servers

bus·by /búzbee/ (*plural* **-bies**) *n* a tall fur helmet worn by some soldiers, including some British guards regiments [Mid-18C. Origin ?]

bush[1] /bo͝osh/ *n* **1. WOODY BRANCHED PLANT** a woody plant that is smaller than a tree and has many branches growing up from the lower part of the main stem **2. THICKET** a thick clump of bushes **3. UNCULTIVATED AND UNSETTLED LAND** wild, uncultivated, and sparsely populated areas of land covered with natural vegetation, especially in Africa and Australia ○ *living in the bush* **4. DENSE MASS** a dense large mass of something, especially hair or beard ○ *a bush of black hair* **5. TABOO TERM** a highly offensive term for a woman's pubic hair (*taboo slang*) **6.** *Can* FORESTRY same as **woodlot** **7. BUSHY TAIL** a bushy tail, especially of a fox **8. VINTNER'S SIGN** a bunch of ivy hung outside a tavern to show that wine is sold inside (*archaic*) ■ *vi* (**bushed, bush·ing, bush·es**) **BRANCH OUT** to branch out, spread, or grow thick like a bush ○ *hair bushing out around her head* [< assumed Old English *bysc* and Old Norse *buski* < Germanic] ◇ **beat around the bush** to discuss a subject without coming to the point

bush[2] /bo͝osh/ *n Can, UK* ENG same as **bushing** (sense 1) [Mid-16C. < Middle Dutch *busse*, via Germanic < Latin *pyxis* "box, cap" < late Greek *puxis* "box"]

Bush /bo͝osh/, **Barbara** (*b.* 1925) US first lady (1989–93). She founded the Barbara Bush Foundation for Family Literacy (1989) to promote literacy in the United States.

George Bush

Bush, George (*b.* 1924) 41st president of the United States. A Republican, he was Ronald Reagan's vice president (1981–88) before his election to the presidency. His presidency (1989–93) was notable for the passage of the Americans with Disabilities Act (1990) and, in foreign policy, the Gulf War (1990) against Iraq and the end of the Cold War. Full name **Bush, George Herbert Walker**. See table at **president**

"A line has been drawn in the sand."
[George Bush, on deploying troops to the Persian Gulf after Iraq's invasion of Kuwait; August 8, 1990]

Bush, George W. (*b.* 1946) 43rd president of the United States. The son of former US president George Bush, he was elected Republican governor of Texas in 1994 and 1998 and became president in 2001. Full name **Bush, George Walker**. Known as **Dubya**. See table at **president**

"Terrorist attacks can shake the foundations of our biggest buildings, but they cannot touch the foundation of America. These acts shattered steel, but they cannot dent the steel of American resolve."
[George W. Bush, *Address to the Nation*; September 11, 2001]

George W. Bush

Bush, Jack (1909–77) Canadian painter. He moved from representational to radical abstract art.

Bush, Laura (*b.* 1946) US first lady (2001–). She takes a strong interest in family, literacy, and women's health issues. Full name **Bush, Laura Welch**

Bush, Vannevar (1890–1974) US inventor and engineer. He invented a differential analyzer (1931), the forerunner of the analog computer.

"Science has a simple faith, which transcends utility. Nearly all men of science, all men of learning for that matter, and men of simple ways too, have it in some form and in some degree. It is the faith that it is the privilege of man to understand, and that this is his mission."
[Vannevar Bush, "The Search for Understanding," *Science Is Not Enough*; 1967]

bush ba·by *n* a small nocturnal primate that lives in trees and has big round eyes, large ears, and a long tail. Native to: Africa. Family: Galagidae.

bush-bath *n Carib* a bath containing herbs, taken to avert evil influences especially after illness or childbirth or a run of bad fortune

bush bean *n* a bean that grows in bush form and does not require support for climbing. Latin name: *Phaseolus vulgaris*.

bush·buck /bo͝osh bùk/ (*plural* **-bucks** or *same*) *n* a small antelope that has a reddish brown coat, usually with white stripes, and twisted horns. Native to: sub-Saharan Africa. Latin name: *Tragelaphus scriptus*. [Mid-19C. Translation of Afrikaans *bosbok* < Dutch *bosch* "bush" + *bok* "buck"]

bush clo·ver *n* a plant with three-leafed compound leaves and small flowers. Use: forage, erosion control, and decoration. Genus: *Lespedeza*.

bushed /bo͝osht/ *adj* exhausted from overwork or lack of sleep (*informal*) [Late 19C. The state typical of somebody wandering in the bush]

Bu·shehr /boo sheér/, **Bu·shire** city in southwestern Iran, southwest of Shiraz. It is a major port on the Persian Gulf. Population: 140,615 (1994).

bush·el /bo͝osh'l/ *n* **1. US UNIT OF VOLUME** a unit of measure in the US Customary system used for measuring dry goods, equal to 64 US pints (35.24 liters) **2. FORMER UK UNIT OF VOLUME** a unit of dry or liquid measure in the British Imperial system, equal to 8 imperial gallons (36.37 liters), formerly used for measuring items such as wheat, fruit, and liquids **3. CONTAINER** a container that has a capacity of one bushel [15C. < Old French *boisel*]

bush·fire /bo͝osh fìr/ *n* a fire in the bush or in a forest area that spreads quickly and goes out of control easily

bush grass *n* a grass with leaves that grow tall like reeds in damp clay soils. Native to: Europe, Asia. Latin name: *Calamagrostis epigejos*.

bush·ham·mer /bo͝osh hàmmər/ *n* a powered hammer with small pyramidal points cut into the working surface, used to form a rough surface on stonework

[Late 19C. Probably translation of German *Boszhammer* < *boszen* "to beat"]

bush hon·ey·suck·le *n* a deciduous bush. Flowers: yellow, in small clusters. Native to: eastern North America. Genus: *Diervilla*.

Bu·shi·do /bo͝oshi dō/ *n* the code of honor and behavior of the Japanese warrior class (**samurai**), emphasizing self-discipline, courage, and loyalty [Late 19C. < Japanese *bushidō* < *bushi* "warrior" (< Middle Chinese *wushi* + *dō* "way") (< Middle Chinese *daw*)]

bush·ing /bo͝oshing/ *n* **1.** *US* ENG **METAL SLEEVE** a cylindrical metal sleeve used to prevent abrasion, as a bearing, or as a guide for tool parts such as valve rods. Can term **bush**² **2. INSULATION** a layer of electrical insulation that allows a live conductor to pass through a grounded wall **3. PIPE ADAPTOR** an adaptor or screw-piece for connecting two different sizes of pipe [Mid-19C. < BUSH²]

Bu·shire ▶ **Bushehr**

Bush·ism /bo͝osh izzəm/ *n* a spoken grammatical error or misuse of a word or phrase by President George W. Bush that changes the intended meaning of a statement or is amusing, or a similar mistake in speech made by somebody else. ○ *"misunderestimate" and other Bushisms* [Late 20C. After George W. BUSH]

Bush·i·stan /bo͝oshə stàn/ *n* **1.** the part of Kurdistan that lies within Iraq (*humorous slang; used in 1991–92 during and after the first Gulf War*) **2.** POL the supporters and inner circle of advisers of US President George W. Bush. (*slang disapproving*) [Late 20C. Sense 1 < George BUSH + KURDISTAN; sense 2 < George W. BUSH + AFGHANISTAN]

bush jack·et *n* a lightweight cotton jacket resembling a shirt, with patch pockets and a belt

bush league *n* **1.** a minor league in baseball **2.** a sphere of activity for those who cannot compete with the best ○ *a lawyer in the bush leagues* —**bush-league** *adj* —**bush-leagu·er** *n*

bush line *n Can* a small airline that serves remote settlements, especially in the north of Canada

Bush·man /bo͝oshmən/ (*plural* **-men** /-mən/) *n* an offensive term for a member of the San people

bush·mas·ter /bo͝osh màstər/ *n* a large venomous snake with grayish brown markings, growing up to 12 ft./3.6 m in length. Native to: Central and South America. Latin name: *Lachesis mutus*.

bush meat *n W Africa* the flesh of wild animals killed for food

bush med·i·cine *n Carib* traditional medical remedies, prepared from plants, especially herbs

Bush·nell /bo͝oshnəl/, **David** (1742–1824) US inventor. He is credited with the invention of the *Turtle*, an early submarine (1775).

Bush·nell, Horace (1802–76) US minister. His liberal religious writings included *God in Christ* (1849).

bush pig *n* a black or brown wild pig that has small tusks and long tufts of hair on the face and ears. Native to: southern Africa. Latin name: *Potamochoerus porcus*.

bush pi·lot *n* a pilot who flies a small plane into and out of areas that are difficult to reach with other means of transportation

bush·rang·er /bo͝osh ràynjər/ *n* somebody who lives in or explores the wild parts of the country

bush-shrike (*plural* **bush-shrikes** or *same*) *n* a bird of the shrike family, typically olive-backed with a bright yellow or red breast, that chases its prey on foot. Native to: African forests. Genera: *Malaconotus* or *Chlorophoneus*.

bush tel·e·graph *n* **1.** a method of communicating information or rumors swiftly and unofficially by word of mouth or other means (*informal*) **2.** a method of communicating over distances, e.g., using drumbeats

bush·whack /bo͝osh wàk, -hwàk/ (**-whacked, -whack·ing, -whacks**) *v* **1.** *vi* **CUT THROUGH WOODS** to cut a way through thick woods or forest **2.** *vi* **TRAVEL THROUGH WOODS** to travel through woods, forest, or the bush **3.** *vi* **FIGHT AS GUERRILLA** to fight as a guerrilla **4.** *vt* **AMBUSH SOMEBODY** to attack somebody suddenly from a concealed position (*informal*)

bush·whack·er /bo͝osh wàkər, -hwàkər/ *n* **1. SOMEBODY TRAVELING OR LIVING IN BUSH** somebody who travels or lives in isolated regions **2.** HIST **CONFEDERATE GUERRILLA** a Confederate guerrilla in the Civil War **3. RURAL GUERRILLA** a guerrilla who fights in remote or rural areas **4. CLEARING TOOL** a tool for clearing or cutting a way through bush, trees, or undergrowth

bush·y /bo͝oshee/ (**-i·er, -i·est**) *adj* **1. THICK** very thick and full ○ *bushy eyebrows* **2. DENSE AND WOODY** with many branches growing up together, producing a rounded shape like a bush **3. COVERED WITH BUSHES** covered or overgrown with bushes —**bush·i·ly** *adv* —**bush·i·ness** *n*

bus·i·ly /bízzəlee/ *adv* in an active, energetic, and concentrated way ○ *busily cleaning the house*

~~**busines**~~ incorrect spelling of **business**

busi·ness /bíznəss/ *n* **1. LINE OF WORK** a particular trade or profession ○ *the retail business* **2. COMMERCIAL ORGANIZATION** a company or other organization that buys and sells goods, makes products, or provides services ○ *take over an ailing business* **3. COMMERCIAL ACTIVITY** commercial activity involving the exchange of money for goods or services ○ *a good person to do business with* **4. LEVEL OF COMMERCE** the amount of commercial activity or patronage that exists at a particular time ○ *Business is poor right now.* **5. COMMERCIAL PRACTICE** commercial practice or procedure ○ *It's bad business to neglect smaller clients.* **6. PATRONAGE** the commercial dealings that a person or organization has with another person or organization ○ *If this goes on, I shall take my business elsewhere!* **7. IMPORTANT MATTERS** tasks or important things that somebody has to do or deal with ○ *We have important business to discuss.* **8. PRIVATE MATTERS** personal responsibilities and concerns ○ *What business is it of yours?* **9. AFFAIR** a situation or event that is characterized by difficulty, fuss, or unpleasantness ○ *that business about the tickets* **10. UNSPECIFIED ACTIVITIES** activities or things that are not clearly described or defined ○ *designing, measuring, and all that kind of business* **11. SOMETHING EXCELLENT** something very impressive or excellent (*informal*) ○ *He thinks his new car is really the business.* **12.** THEATER **ACTOR'S SMALL ACTIONS** an action or series of actions performed by an actor for dramatic or comic effect or to fill in a pause when little is happening on stage ■ *adj* **OF COMMERCE** relating to, belonging to, or involving commerce and the world of professional workers ○ *good business practice* [Old English *bisignis* "anxiety, distress" < *bisig* "anxious, busy"] ◇ **do your business** to defecate (*informal; euphemistic*) ◇ **get down to business** to deal with important matters, leaving extraneous ones behind ◇ **have no business doing something** to have no right to do something ◇ **like nobody's business** very hard or strongly (*informal*) ◇ **mean business** to be serious and determined about something ◇ **mind your own business** to attend to your own affairs and not interfere in other people's concerns ◇ **not be in the business of doing something** to consider something inappropriate or outside the usual area of responsibility ◇ **out of business** not or no longer trading or operating as a business ○ *restaurants that go out of business within a few months of opening*

busi·ness ad·min·is·tra·tion *n* a course of study at a university, college, or other institution of higher education that teaches the basic principles of business and business practices

busi·ness card *n* a small card printed with somebody's name, job title, business address, and contact numbers

busi·ness class *n* a superior level of service in air travel that is less expensive than first class and caters to business travelers (*hyphenated when used before a noun*) —**busi·ness class** *adv*

busi·ness col·lege *n* a college of higher education where students learn basic business skills such as accounting and management

busi·ness cy·cle *n* a recurrent cycle of growth, decline, recession, and recovery in the economic activity of a capitalist country

busi·ness day *n* a day on which stock exchanges and banks are open for business

busi·ness dis·trict *n* an area reserved for, or composed mainly of, retail businesses or offices

busi·ness end *n* the part of a tool or device that performs the intended function, as opposed to the body or handle (*informal*) ○ *the business end of a gun*

busi·ness en·ve·lope *n* a standard envelope used for business mail that holds letter-size paper folded in thirds

busi·ness hours *npl* the normal hours that most offices are open, usually between about 9 AM and 5:30 PM

busi·ness·like /bíznəss lìk/ *adj* **1.** showing qualities or attributes that are useful and desirable in a business context, e.g., efficiency, practicality, and methodicalness ○ *a very businesslike operation* **2.** practical and unemotional

busi·ness·man /bíznəss màn/ (*plural* **-men** /-mèn/) *n* a man who works in business, especially at a senior level

busi·ness park *n* an area designed to accommodate businesses and light industry, with large numbers of companies all grouped together, usually on the outskirts of a town or city

busi·ness·per·son /bíznəss pùrss'n/ (*plural* **-peo·ple** /-peep'l/ or **-per·sons**) *n* somebody who works in business, especially at a senior level

busi·ness plan *n* a plan that sets out the future strategy and financial development of a business, usually covering a period of several years

busi·ness school *n* a graduate school that offers M.B.A. courses and related courses of study

busi·ness stud·ies *n* the study of the activities involved in running a business, especially the financial and managerial aspects (*takes a singular verb*)

busi·ness suit *n* a suit consisting of a coat and pants, or a coat and skirt, appropriate for wearing in the office

busi·ness-to-busi·ness *adj* relating to Internet transactions between business organizations, rather than between a business and consumers

busi·ness·wom·an /bíznəss wo͝omman/ (*plural* **-wom·en** /-wimmin/) *n* a woman who works in business, especially at a senior level

bus·ing /bússing/, **bus·sing** *n* the transportation of children by bus to a school distant from their homes in an effort to achieve ethnic balance in the school population

busk /busk/ *n* a strip of wood, steel, or whalebone used to stiffen the front of a corset [Late 16C. Via French *busc* < Italian *busco* "splinter" < Germanic]

bus·kin /búskin/ *n* **1. ATHENIAN ACTOR'S BOOT** a thick-soled laced boot worn by tragic actors in ancient Greece to give them extra height **2. GREEK DRAMA** tragic drama, particularly in the ancient Greek style (*archaic*) **3. MEDIEVAL SANDAL** a calf-length laced boot worn in the Middle Ages [Early 16C. Probably via Old French *bousequin*, variant of *brousequin* < Middle Dutch *broseken*]

bus lane *n* in some cities or towns, a road lane that can only be used by buses during busy hours of the day

bus·load /bús lōd/ *n* the number of passengers that a bus carries or can carry ○ *demonstrators arriving in busloads*

bus·man's hol·i·day /bùssmənz-/ *n* a vacation or leisure activity that is similar to the work somebody normally engages in (*informal*) [Probably < drivers of horse-drawn buses being driven around on their own bus]

bus mouse *n* a mouse attached to a computer bus using a special card or port

bus net·work *n* a computer network in which all nodes are connected to a single bus

Bu·son /bo͞o sàwn/ (1716–84) Japanese poet and artist. He is noted for his haiku and was regarded as one of the finest painters of his time. Known as **Yosa Buson**

buss /buss/ *n regional* a kiss [Late 16C. Probably variant of obsolete *bass* "to kiss," via French *baiser* < Latin *basiare*] —**buss** *vti*

bus·sing *n* EDUC another spelling of **busing**

bus stop *n* a designated place along a specific route where a bus stops to pick up or let off passengers

bust[1] /bust/ *n* **1.** a woman's breasts **2.** a sculpture of somebody's head and shoulders [Mid-17C. Via French *buste* < Italian *busto*]

bust[2] /bust/ *v* (**bust·ed** or **bust, bust·ing, busts**) **1.** *vti* **MAKE OR BECOME USELESS** to stop operating properly, or cause something to stop operating properly (*informal*) ○ *Your brother just busted our TV!* **2.** *vti* **BREAK OR GET BROKEN** to break or damage something by hitting it or by subjecting it to a powerful impact, or be broken in this way (*informal*) ○ *I busted my leg skiing.* **3.** *vti* **BURST** to burst something, or undergo bursting **4.** *vt* **HIT SOMEBODY** to hit somebody hard (*informal*) ○ *He busted the villain over the head.* **5.** *vt* **BREAK UP ORGANIZATION** to break up an organization when it has become too powerful (*informal*) **6.** *vt* CRIME **RAID PLACE** to mount a police raid on a place, especially in connection with illegal drugs (*slang*) **7.** *vt* CRIME **CATCH SOMEBODY DOING SOMETHING ILLEGAL** to catch and punish somebody for doing something illegal or against the rules (*informal*) ○ *got busted for skipping class* **8.** *vti* FIN **MAKE OR BECOME BANKRUPT** to make somebody bankrupt, or become bankrupt (*informal*) **9.** *vt* MIL **DEMOTE SOMEBODY** to demote a member of the armed forces (*informal*) **10.** *vt* RIDING **TAME HORSE FOR RIDING** to break in a horse (*informal*) **11.** *vi* CARDS **GO OVER LIMIT** in blackjack, to accumulate cards totaling more than 21 points **12.** *vi* CARDS **FAIL TO COMPLETE HAND** in poker, to fail to complete a flush or straight ■ *n* **1.** **FAILURE** somebody or something that fails completely (*informal*) ○ *The plan seemed perfect in theory, but it was a bust in reality.* **2.** FIN **BANKRUPTCY** bankruptcy or financial failure ○ *periods of boom and bust* **3.** **PUNCH** a punch or blow (*informal*) **4.** **PARTY** a disorganized party or celebration (*informal*) **5.** CRIME **POLICE RAID** a police raid or arrest, especially in connection with illegal drugs (*slang*) ■ *adj* (*informal*) **1.** **DAMAGED** broken or no longer working **2.** FIN **BANKRUPT** judged legally to be unable to pay off personal debts ○ *go bust* [Mid-18C. Alteration of BURST] —**bust·ed** *adj*

bust up *v* (*informal*) **1.** *vt* **DISRUPT OR STOP** to disrupt or stop something such as a meeting or gathering **2.** *vt* **DAMAGE** to cause damage to something **3.** *vi* **BREAK UP** to end a relationship in a violent quarrel

Bus·ta·man·te /bòostə maán tàyl/, **Sir Alexander** (1884–1977) Jamaican politician. He served as independent Jamaica's first prime minister (1962–67). Born **Clarke, William Alexander**

bus·tard /bústərd/ (*plural* **-tards** or *same*) *n* a bird with long legs, a round body, a long neck, and a fairly short beak. Native to: open grassy land in southern Europe, Asia, Africa, and Australia. Family: Otididae. [15C. Probably < assumed Anglo-Norman *bustarde*, blend of *bistarde* + *oustarde*, both < Latin *avis tarda* "slow bird"]

bust·er /bústər/ *n* **1.** used as a jocular or mildly threatening term of address, usually for a man or boy (*informal*) **2.** RIDING same as **broncobuster** **3.** somebody or something that breaks up or destroys something (*informal; usually in combination*) ○ *a union buster* [Mid-19C. < BUST[2], or alteration of *burster*]

bus·tier /booss tyáy/ *n* a close-fitting sleeveless and usually strapless bodice worn by women as lingerie or clothing [Late 20C. < French < *buste* (see BUST[1])]

bus·tle[1] /búss'l/ *vi* (**-tled, -tling, -tles**) to work or behave in an ostentatiously hurried and energetic way ○ *He bustled around in preparation for their arrival.* ■ *n* hurried and energetic activity ○ *a great bustle surrounding the arriving guests* [14C. Origin ?] —**bus·tler** *n*

bus·tle[2] /búss'l/ *n* a pad or frame worn in the 19th century under the top of a woman's long skirt to fill it out at the back [Late 18C. Origin ?]

bus·tling /búss'ling, bússling/ *adj* full of or characterized by hurried and energetic activity —**bus·tling·ly** *adv*

bust·y /bústee/ (**-i·er, -i·est**) *adj* having large breasts (*informal*)

bu·sul·fan /byoo súlfən/ *n* a drug used in the treatment of some types of chronic leukemia [Mid-20C. Blend of BUTANE, BUTYL + SULFONYL SULFONATE]

bu·sul·phan *n UK* PHARM another spelling of **busulfan** (*dated*)

bus·y /bízzee/ *adj* (**-i·er, -i·est**) **1.** **OCCUPIED** fully occupied in a particular activity, especially work ○ *She seemed too busy even to talk to me.* ○ *He was busy writing letters all morning.* **2.** **FULL OF BUSTLE** full of activity, with a large number of people moving around ○ *the busy city streets* **3.** **NOT FREE** committed to something that has previously been planned or arranged and so unable to undertake another activity ○ *I'm sorry but I'm busy tomorrow night.* **4.** TELECOM **UNAVAILABLE TO USE** describes a telephone line that is in use and so unavailable **5.** **ACTIVE** engaged in or characterized by constant, and usually purposeful, activity ○ *busy people who lead busy lives* **6.** **ELABORATE** characterized by overcomplex detail, colors, or patterns ○ *a very busy painting* ■ *v* (**-ied, -y·ing, -ies**) **1.** **bus·y your·self** *vr* **OCCUPY YOURSELF** to start doing something that will keep you occupied and working for a period of time ○ *busied himself with the wedding arrangements* **2.** *vt* **OCCUPY SOMEBODY** to occupy somebody ○ *The work busied him all afternoon.* [Old English *bisig* "busy, anxious"] —**bus·y·ness** *n*

bus·y bee *n* somebody who is always very busy and active (*informal*)

bus·y·bod·y /bízzee bòddee/ (*plural* **-ies**) *n* somebody who meddles with other people's business (*informal*)

bus·y Liz·zie /-lízzee/ (*plural same* or **bus·y Liz·zies**) *n* BOT same as **impatiens**

bus·y sig·nal *n* a repeating burst of sound on a telephone line that indicates the line is in use

bus·y·work /bízzee wùrk/ *n* activities assigned or undertaken that take up time but do not necessarily yield productive results

but *stressed* /but/; *unstressed* /bət/ CORE MEANING: a grammatical word used in the middle of or at the beginning of a sentence to introduce something that is true in spite of either being or seeming contrary to what has just been said ○ *I thought it was late, but it was only 9 o'clock.* ○ *Not one, but two offers were received.* ○ *Yes, but not now.* ○ *It's true her name is Spanish, but she's actually Greek.* ○ *I'm a blond, but both my mother and father have dark hair.*

1. *conj* **INTRODUCING OPPOSING PROPOSITION** used to introduce a statement that disagrees with something just said, or that expresses an emotion such as surprise or disbelief at what was just said ○ *"I don't think you're qualified for the job." "But I have all the right credentials!"* **2.** *conj* **INTRODUCING FURTHER INFORMATION** used to introduce a clause or a new sentence that adds information such as background or reasoning ○ *Jeff isn't coming with us. But he doesn't like horror movies anyway.* **3.** *conj* **EXCEPT THAT** used to introduce a dependent clause, e.g., a reason for doing or not doing something ○ *I would have called, but I couldn't find a phone.* **4.** *conj* **WITHOUT SOMETHING HAPPENING** used to indicate that something does not happen without something else happening or being the case (*formal; usually used after negatives*) ○ *She never leaves home but she forgets her keys.* **5.** *conj* **THAT** used to introduce a subordinate clause ○ *It's not so difficult but I can't understand it.* **6.** *conj* **WHEN** than or when (*informal*) ○ *I'd no sooner put the phone down but it rang again.* **7.** *conj, prep* **EXCEPT** used to indicate the exception to a statement just made ○ *He could do nothing but stand and watch her leave.* ○ *There was nothing but a lump of moldy bread in the drawer.* **8.** *adv* **ONLY, JUST, OR MERELY** used to indicate that something happens or is true just to the extent mentioned and not more (*formal*) ○ *This is but one of the bread-making techniques used.* ○ *He arrived but a minute ago.* ○ *We can but try.* **9.** *adv* **FOR EMPHASIS** used to emphasize a statement (*slang*) ○ *Man, but he's fast!* **10.** *npl* **buts OBJECTIONS** objections to something (*informal*) ○ *Allow time to consider all the ifs, ands, or buts from the children.* [Old English *būtan* "outside, without, except, but" < Germanic] ◇ **but for** if not for, or if it had not been for ◇ **but that 1.** except that (*archaic or formal*) ○ *Nothing is important but that I see you again.* **2.** used as a subordinating conjunction equivalent to "that" following negative words such as "doubt" and "deny" (*archaic; follows a negative*)

USAGE Can **but** begin a sentence? Some people object to the use of ***but***, like *and*, at the beginning of a sentence, regarding it as a joining word that has to have words on either side of it. This is a mistaken notion with no foundation in English structure and usage. It is, however, advisable to reserve this use for occasions when the special effect that initial position affords is needed; otherwise it can become an awkward affectation.

But is not usually followed by a comma. A comma may precede ***but*** when an independent clause follows, thus: *I wanted to leave early, but* [not *but,*] *the rest of the group did not.*

Avoid unnecessary redundancy in using ***but*** and other terms such as *however* together.

When ***but*** is used to indicate an exception, as in *No one but me has* (or *No one but I have*) *seen the document*, either wording can be used, according to your interpretation of the function of ***but***: is it a preposition, as in the first variation, or is it a conjunction, as in the second variation? Though strong cases have been made for both wordings, the prepositional wording does carry slightly more weight. You can recast the sentence as *No one has seen the document but me*, where its prepositional function is quite clear.

USAGE See ***help***.

but- *prefix* containing a group of four carbon atoms ○ *butene* [< BUTYRIC]

bu·ta·di·ene /byoōtə dī́ een/ *n* a colorless flammable gas. Source: petroleum. Use: manufacture of synthetic rubber, nylon, latex paints. Formula: C_4H_6. [Early 20C. < BUTANE]

bu·ta·nal /byoōt'nəl/ *n* CHEM same as **butyraldehyde** [Late 20C. < BUTANOL]

bu·tane /byoō tàyn/ *n* a colorless, highly flammable gas that has two different molecular structures (**isomers**). Source: natural gas. Use: lighter fluid, fuel. Formula: C_4H_{10}. [Late 19C. < BUTYL]

bu·ta·no·ic ac·id /byoōtənō ik-/ *n* CHEM same as **butyric acid** [< BUTANE]

bu·ta·nol /byoōtə nàwl, byoōt'n àwl/ *n* a colorless toxic liquid with four different molecular structures (**isomers**). Use: solvents, manufacture of organic compounds. Formula: C_4H_9OH.

bu·ta·none /byoōtə nōn/ *n* a colorless flammable liquid with an odor similar to acetone. Use: solvent, paint stripper, in resins. [Early 20C. < BUTANE]

butch /bŏŏch/ *adj* **1.** **MASCULINE AND STRONG** describes a man who is extremely masculine and strong **2.** **OFFENSIVE TERM** an offensive term meaning unfeminine in appearance (*slang*) ■ *n* **1.** **OFFENSIVE TERM** an offensive term for a woman whose appearance is considered unfeminine (*slang*) **2.** HAIR same as **crew cut** [Mid-20C. Probably < the nickname *Butch*]

butch·er /bŏŏchər/ *n* **1.** **MEAT SELLER** somebody who sells meat at retail **2.** **SLAUGHTERER** somebody who slaughters animals for their meat **3.** COMM **PREMISES OF BUTCHER** a store that sells prepared raw meat and meat products **4.** **BRUTAL KILLER** somebody who kills people in a brutal manner **5.** **INEXPERT PROPONENT OF SOMETHING** somebody who does something badly and produces unattractive results ○ *a butcher of the sonnet form* ■ *vt* (**-ered, -er·ing, -ers**) **1.** **KILL ANIMAL FOR FOOD** to slaughter and prepare the meat of an animal for food **2.** **KILL PEOPLE BRUTALLY** to kill people in a brutal way **3.** **BOTCH SOMETHING** to do something badly and produce unattractive results (*informal*) ○ *The original script had been butchered.* [13C. < Anglo-Norman form of Old French *bo(u)chier* "slaughterer of he-goats" < *boc* "he-goat"] —**butch·er·er** *n*

butch·er·bird /bŏŏchər bùrd/ *n* **1.** a bird of the shrike family that impales its prey on thorns and barbed wire. Genus: *Lanius.* **2.** a songbird, usually with black or black-and-white feathers, that impales insects and other prey on thorns. Native to: Australasia. Genus: *Cracticus.*

butch·er knife *n* a large heavy-duty knife for use in the kitchen or for butchering

butch·er's broom *n* an evergreen bush with stiff stems. Use: formerly, making brooms. Native to: Mediterranean. Latin name: *Ruscus aculeatus.*

butch·er's knife *n* HOUSEHOLD UK spelling of **butcher knife**

butch·er·y /bo͝ochəree/ (*plural* **-ies**) *n* **1.** BRUTAL KILLING brutal, senseless, and cruel slaughter of people, usually in large numbers ○ *an act of appalling butchery* **2.** USE OF KNIVES ON CARCASS the use of knives or other tools to remove meat from an animal's carcass ○*"The tools are often found in association with broken animal bones, which sometimes show signs of butchery."* ("*Ape at the Brink*," *Discover Magazine*; 1994) **3.** BUTCHER'S WORK the work of somebody who sells meat at retail or who slaughters animals for their meat **4.** INCOMPETENCE an incompetent attempt at a job, performance, or activity (*informal*) ○ *the singer's butchery of the melody* [14C. < French *boucherie* < Old French *bo(u)chier* (see BUTCHER)]

butch hair·cut *n* HAIR same as **crew cut**

Bute /byoot/ island off the southwestern coast of Scotland, in the Firth of Clyde. It is separated from the mainland by the Kyles of Bute. Area: 46 sq. mi./119 sq. km.

bu·tene /byo͞o tēen/ *n* a colorless, flammable, easily liquefiable gas with three different molecular structures (**isomers**). Use: manufacture of polymers. Formula: C_4H_8. [Late 19C. < BUTYL]

bu·te·o /byo͞otee ō/ (*plural* **-os**) *n* a large, broad-winged, soaring hawk. Native to: North America, Europe, Asia. Genus: *Buteo*. [Mid-20C. Via modern Latin (genus name) < Latin, "(kind of) hawk or falcon"]

Bu·the·le·zi /bo͞otə láyzee/, **Mangosuthu Gatsha** (*b.* 1928) South African politician. He was chief minister of KwaZulu, a Black South African homeland (1976–94), and founded Inkatha, a Zulu nationalist organization. Also known as **Dr Buthelezi**

but·ler /búttlər/ *n* the male head servant in a large or important household, with responsibilities that include overseeing the other staff, taking care of the wine and silverware, and sometimes receiving guests [13C. < Anglo-Norman *buteler*, Old French *boteillier* "cup-bearer" < *boteille* (see BOTTLE)]

But·ler /búttlər/ city and manufacturing center in western Pennsylvania, north of Pittsburgh. Population: 14,841 (2002 estimate).

But·ler, Nicholas Murray (1862–1947) US educator. He was president of Columbia College (1902–12) and the newly formed Columbia University (1912–45), and shared the Nobel Peace Prize (1931) for his role as president of the Carnegie Endowment for International Peace (1925–45).

But·ler, Samuel (1612–80) English satirist. He wrote *Hudibras*, a poetic satire on the Puritans (1663–78).

> "Oaths are but words, and words but wind."
> [Samuel Butler, *Hudibras*; 1664]

but·ler's pan·try, but·ler·y /búttləree/ *n* a room situated between a kitchen and dining room, used for serving food and for storage

butt[1] /but/ *v* (**butt·ed, butt·ing, butts**) **1.** *vt* RAM SOMEBODY OR SOMETHING to hit or push against somebody or something with the head or horns **2.** *vi* STICK OUT to project or jut out ■ *n* PUSH a push with the head or horns [15C. Via Anglo-Norman *buter*, Old French *bo(u)ter* < Germanic] —**but·ter** *n*

butt in *vi* to interrupt and attempt to join in a conversation or activity without being invited ○ *He's always trying to butt in on our conversations.*

butt out *vi* to keep out of other people's business or conversation (*slang*)

butt[2] /but/ *n* **1.** OBJECT OF RIDICULE OR CONTEMPT somebody or something that is an object of ridicule or contempt for other people ○ *He became the butt of their satire.* **2.** HINGE a butt hinge, or either of its two parts **3.** CONSTR same as **butt joint** ■ **butts** *npl* **1.** ARCHERY, RIFLERY MOUND BEHIND TARGET in archery and rifle shooting, a mound of earth behind the target, designed to stop any stray bullets or arrows **2.** ARCHERY TARGET RANGE a target range in archery **3.** ARCHERY, RIFLERY TARGET a target at a shooting or archery range [14C. < French *but* "goal"]

butt[3] /but/ *n* **1.** BUTTOCKS a person's or animal's buttocks (*informal*; *sometimes considered offensive*) **2.** THICK END the thicker or larger end of something, e.g., the part of a rifle held against the shoulder **3.** CIGARETTE END the part of a cigarette that remains after the rest has been smoked ■ *vti* (**butt·ed, butt·ing, butts**) ABUT to lie with one flat end against the flat end of something else, or place something in such a position ○ *The beam butts against the wall.* [15C. Origin ?]

butt[4] /but/ *n* **1.** a large cask for holding wine or ale **2.** a unit for measuring liquid volume equal to 126 US gallons (approximately 477 liters) [15C. Via Anglo-Norman *but*, Old French *bot* < late Latin *buttis*]

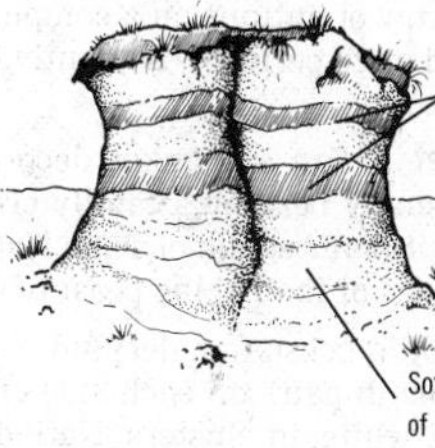

butte

butte /byoot/ *n* *US regional*, *Can* a hill that rises abruptly from a flat area of land, with steep sides and a flat top [Mid-19C. < French, "mound, hillock"]

REGIONAL NOTE See *mesa*.

Butte /byoot/ city in southwestern Montana, situated more than 1 mi./1.7 km above sea level in the Rocky Mountains. It was settled by gold prospectors in the 1860s and is still a mining center. Population: 33,403 (2002 estimate). Full name **Butte-Silver Bow**

but·ter /búttər/ *n* **1.** SOFT CREAMY SPREAD a soft, pale yellow, fatty food made by churning cream and used for cooking and spreading on food ○ *bread and butter* **2.** SUBSTANCE LIKE BUTTER a substance that is similar to butter in consistency or appearance ○ *apple butter* ■ *vt* (**-tered, -ter·ing, -ters**) PUT BUTTER ON SOMETHING to spread butter on something, or add butter to something [Old English *butere*, via Germanic < Latin *butyrum* < Greek *bouturon*] ◇ **look as if butter wouldn't melt in your mouth** to look more innocent than you really are

butter up *vt* to flatter somebody in the hope of winning favor or cooperation (*informal*)

but·ter-and-eggs *n* PLANTS same as **toadflax** (sense 1) (*takes a singular or plural verb*)

but·ter·ball /búttər bàwl/ *n* **1.** an offensive term for somebody regarded as being overweight (*informal*) **2.** BIRDS same as **bufflehead**

but·ter bean *n* **1.** a lima bean (*regional*) **2.** *US regional*, *Can* PLANTS, FOOD same as **wax bean**

but·ter·bur /búttər bùr/ (*plural* **-burs** or *same*) *n* a waterside plant with large soft leaves. Flowers: purple. Native to: Europe, Asia. Genus: *Petasites*. [Because butter was formerly wrapped in its leaves]

but·ter·cup /búttər kùp/ *n* a plant that grows in grassland. Flowers: yellow, cup-shaped. Native to: cold or temperate regions. Genus: *Ranunculus*.

but·ter·cup squash *n* a small winter squash with a flattish top, dark green skin, and yellow-orange flesh. Latin name: *Cucurbita maxima*.

but·ter·fat /búttər fàt/ *n* the natural fats found in dairy products

but·ter·fin·gers /búttər fìng gərz/ (*plural same*) *n* somebody who tends to drop things accidentally (*informal*) —**but·ter·fin·gered** *adj*

but·ter·fish /búttər fish/ (*plural same* or **-fish·es**) *n* **1.** a small inshore fish, found worldwide, that is a popular food because of its high lipid content and fine flavor. Family: Stromateidae. **2.** the flesh of a butterfish as food [Late 17C. < its slippery mucous coating]

butterfly

but·ter·fly /búttər flī/ *n* (*plural* **-flies**) **1.** INSECT WITH BIG COLORFUL WINGS an insect with two pairs of often brightly colored wings and knobbed antennae. It develops from a caterpillar and lives for only a short time. Order: Lepidoptera. **2.** SWIMMING STROKE a swimming stroke in which both arms are lifted simultaneously above and over the head while both feet are kicked up and down **3.** SWIMMING COMPETITION a race in which swimmers do the butterfly stroke **4.** SOMEBODY LACKING CONCENTRATION somebody who is unable to concentrate for long **5.** FIN DEAL ON STOCK MARKET the buying and selling of options on the stock market on the same day but at different prices or with different expiration dates ■ **but·ter·flies** *npl* VAGUE NAUSEA a nervous feeling in the stomach ■ *vt* (**-flied, -fly·ing, -flies**) COOK SPLIT FOOD to split a piece of food such as meat or fish along its length, separating it into halves that remain joined [Old English *buttorflēoge*; reference to "butter" unexplained]

CULTURAL NOTE ***Madame Butterfly***, an opera (1904) by Italian composer Giacomo Puccini. Set in Nagasaki, Japan, it tells of the love of a young Japanese woman, Cio-Cio San, for a US naval officer, Lieutenant Pinkerton, who half-heartedly agrees to an arranged marriage with her. When Pinkerton later returns from a three-year sojourn in the United States with another wife, a heartbroken Cio-Cio San commits suicide.

but·ter·fly bal·lot *n* a ballot paper with the candidates' names printed on one or both sides of a central spine, in which the voter has to punch holes with a stylus to register a vote [< its resemblance to the outspread wings of a butterfly]

but·ter·fly bush *n* PLANTS same as **buddleia** [Because its flowers attract butterflies]

but·ter·fly chair *n* a chair made from a continuous folded metal rod with four upward-pointing corners on which a fitted canvas seat rests

but·ter·fly di·a·gram *n* a graphic representation of the appearance of sunspots over an 11-year cycle [< its shape]

but·ter·fly ef·fect *n* the supposed influence exerted on a dynamic system by a small change in initial conditions [After a 1979 scientific paper "Does the flap of a butterfly's wings in Brazil set off a tornado in Texas?" by Edward N. Lorenz]

but·ter·fly fish *n* a small boldly patterned fish with a flattish body and a tapered snout. Native to: tropics. Family: Chaetodontidae.

but·ter·fly nut *n* CONSTR same as **wing nut**

but·ter·fly stroke *n* SWIMMING same as **butterfly** (sense 2)

but·ter·fly valve *n* **1.** a valve consisting of a disk that turns inside a pipe, especially one used as a throttle valve in a carburetor **2.** a valve consisting of two semicircular plates that are hinged around a central spindle, used to allow flow in one direction only [< its shape]

but·ter·fly weed *n* a wild plant whose roots have medicinal properties. Flowers: bright orange, in clusters. Native to: North America. Latin name: *Asclepias tuberosa*. [Because it attracts butterflies]

but·ter knife *n* a small knife with a broad blunt blade, used for spreading butter

but·ter·milk /búttər mìlk/ *n* **1.** the sour-tasting liquid that is left over after milk or cream has been churned to make butter. Use: in baking. **2.** a sour-tasting drink that is made by adding micro-organisms to milk

but·ter·nut /búttər nùt/ *n* **1.** NUT an edible nut, similar in appearance to a walnut and with a slightly sweet taste **2.** WOOD a hard light-brown walnut wood. Use: furniture. **3.** TREE a walnut tree that produces butternuts and yields butternut wood **4.** *also* **But·ter·nut** CONFEDERATE SOLDIER a Confederate soldier in the Civil War (*informal*) ■ **but·ter·nuts** *npl* CONFEDERATE SOLDIERS' UNIFORMS brown clothes dyed with dye made from the husks of butternuts, especially the uniforms of Confederate soldiers in the Civil War

but·ter·nut squash *n* a beige-colored winter squash shaped like a club with a bulbous end and firm yellow-orange flesh. Latin name: *Cucurbita moschata*.

but·ter·scotch /búttər skòch/ *n* **1.** BRITTLE SUGAR CANDY a brittle brown-colored candy made from butter and brown sugar **2.** BUTTERSCOTCH FLAVORING a flavoring made from the ingredients used in butterscotch **3.** COLORS LIGHT BROWN a light brown color [Mid-19C. Probably because first made in Scotland] —**but·ter·scotch** *adj*

but·ter tart *n Can* a tart filled with butter, sugar or syrup, and usually raisins

but·ter·weed /búttər wèed/ *n* a wild plant with yellow flowers. Family: Compositae.

but·ter·wort /búttər wùrt, -wàwrt/ (*plural* **-worts** or *same*) *n* a carnivorous bog plant with a rosette of sticky fleshy leaves that trap and digest insects. Native to: Europe, Asia, North America. Genus: *Pinguicula*.

but·ter·y[1] /búttəree/ (**-i·er, -i·est**) *adj* **1.** resembling, tasting like, or containing butter ○ *a smooth, buttery taste* **2.** tending or serving to flatter [14C. < BUTTER] —**but·ter·i·ness** *n*

but·ter·y[2] /búttəree/ (*plural* **-ies**) *n* a room in which food or drinks are stored [14C. < Anglo-Norman *boterie*]

butt hinge *n* a hinge consisting of two parts, one of which is attached to a door jamb, the other to the door itself, allowing the door to swing open and shut [< BUTT[2]]

butt·in·sky /but ínskee/ (*plural* **-skies**) *n* somebody who intrudes on other people's affairs or conversations (*informal*) [Early 20C. < *butt in* + *-sky* (common Slavic noun ending)]

butt joint *n* a joint consisting of two parts of wood or other material that are placed squarely together rather than overlapping or interlocking [< BUTT[2]]

but·tock /búttək/ *n* **1.** in humans, either of the two fleshy mounds above the legs and below the hollow of the back (*often used in the plural*) **2.** the rump of an animal [Old English *buttuc* "end ridge of land" < assumed *butt* "ridge"]

but·ton /bútt'n/ *n* **1.** DISK FOR HOLDING CLOTHES TOGETHER a flat and usually round piece of plastic or other material on a piece of clothing that fits into a slit or loop on another part and holds the two parts together **2.** ELECTRICAL SWITCH a small disk fitted in an electrical appliance or attached to a surface that activates an electrical connection when pressed **3.** SMALL ROUND OBJECT a small round object that resembles a button **4.** SMALL BADGE WORN ON CLOTHES a small round flat metal or plastic badge with an image or words printed on it, worn attached to clothes **5.** BIOL ROUNDED PART a rounded knob-shaped part or organ, e.g., the head of an unripe mushroom **6.** COMPUT SMALL ACTIVATING ICON ON COMPUTER SCREEN a small oblong image in a dialog box of a computer-screen display, activated to perform a task by clicking with the mouse or pressing the "Enter" key **7.** COMPUT ACTIVATING PART OF COMPUTER MOUSE the part of a computer mouse that, when pressed, performs a function such as inserting the cursor at a specific point **8.** FENCING PROTECTIVE COVERING ON FOIL a small rounded plastic or rubber covering placed on the tip of a fencing foil to protect participants from injury **9.** REPT END OF RATTLESNAKE'S TAIL the terminal section of a rattlesnake's tail ■ *v* (**-toned, -ton·ing, -tons**) **1.** *vti* FASTEN WITH BUTTONS to fasten something with a button or buttons **2.** *vi* HAVE BUTTONS SOMEWHERE to have buttons that can be fastened on a particular side of a garment opening or in a particular place on the garment ○ *The dress buttons at the back.* **3.** *vt* PUT BUTTON IN HOLE to put a button through a slit or loop designed to receive it ○ *I never button the top button of my shirt.* **4.** *vt* SHUT MOUTH to close the mouth or lips and be quiet (*informal*) ○ *Just button it!* [14C. < French *bouton* "bud, knob" < Germanic] —**but·ton·er** *n* ◇ **on the button** exactly right (*informal*) ◇ **push** *or* **press all the right buttons** to do all the right or appropriate things ◇ **push somebody's buttons** to provoke a reaction in somebody deliberately

button up *v* **1.** *vt* DO UP BUTTONS to fasten something with buttons **2.** *vt* CLOSE SOMETHING TIGHTLY to close or seal something tightly **3.** *vi* STOP TALKING to stop talking or refuse to talk (*informal*)

but·ton bar *n* a row of buttons on a computer screen that are clicked on to perform frequently used functions

but·ton blan·ket *n Can* a blanket decorated with buttons and usually bearing a family crest that is part of the traditional regalia of some Native North American peoples of the Pacific coast of Canada

but·ton·bush /bútt'n bo͝osh/ *n* a deciduous bush with leaves that grow in pairs on each side of the stem. Flowers: small, white, in clusters. Native to: North America. Latin name: *Cephalanthus occidentalis*. [Mid-18C. < its flower heads]

but·ton-down *adj* **1.** describes a collar that has a buttonhole at the end of each flap to fasten it to the front of a shirt **2.** *US* same as **buttoned-down** (*informal*)

but·toned-down /bútt'nd-/ *adj* having a conservative and traditional manner (*informal*) ○ *stuffy, buttoned-down types*

but·ton·hole /bútt'n hōl/ *n* **1.** HOLE FOR BUTTON a slit in a garment through which a button is passed to fasten two pieces of material together **2.** *UK* same as **boutonniere** ■ *vt* (**-holed, -hol·ing, -holes**) **1.** ACCOST SOMEBODY to compel somebody to listen, allowing no avenue of escape (*informal*) ○ *He buttonholed me outside my office.* **2.** GIVE SOMETHING BUTTONHOLES to make buttonholes in something **3.** SEW WITH BUTTONHOLE STITCH to sew something with a buttonhole stitch to reinforce it —**but·ton·hol·er** *n*

but·ton·hole stitch *n* a tightly worked looped stitch used for reinforcing buttonholes

but·ton·hook /bútt'n ho͝ok/ *n* **1.** a small hook formerly used for pulling small buttons through buttonholes on tight boots or gloves **2.** in football, an offensive play in which the pass receiver approaches the goal and then cuts back toward the line of scrimmage

but·ton·mold /bútt'n mōld/ *n* a small piece of plastic, metal, or wood that forms the base of a button covered in fabric or leather

but·ton mush·room *n* **1.** an immature unopened mushroom, typically sold canned or bottled **2.** a small mushroom cultivated for food. Latin name: *Agaricus bisporus*. [< its shape]

but·ton nose *n* a small short flattish nose

but·ton·quail /bútt'n kwàyl/ (*plural same* or **-quails**) *n* a small terrestrial bird related to the crane, with no hind toe. Native to: southern Europe, Asia, Africa, Australia. Family: Turnicidae.

but·ton snake·root *n* **1.** PLANTS same as **blazing star** (sense 2) **2.** a wild plant with whitish flowers, used for treating snakebite. Native to: southeastern United States. Latin name: *Eryngium yuccifolium*. [< its small discoid flower heads]

but·ton tow *n UK* a ski lift in which the occupant straddles a disk attached to a metal pole suspended from a moving cable

but·ton·wood /bútt'n wo͝od/ *n* **1.** *US regional, Can* TREES same as **sycamore** (sense 2) **2.** the wood of a tropical mangrove tree **3.** a mangrove tree that yields buttonwood. Native to: American and African tropics. Latin name: *Conocarpus erectus*.

REGIONAL NOTE ***Buttonwood*** in the sense of "sycamore" is used chiefly in the North, from Massachusetts and Vermont to Pennsylvania and New Jersey, and including parts of Canada. The term is virtually unknown west of the Mississippi River.

but·tress /búttrəss/ *n* **1.** SUPPORT FOR WALL a solid structure, usually made of brick or stone, that is built against a wall to support it **2.** SOMEBODY OR SOMETHING THAT GIVES SUPPORT somebody or something that acts as a source of support, help, or reinforcement ○ *The constitution is a buttress of our civil rights.* **3.** PROJECTING ROCK a large projecting rock mass that appears to support the rock above it **4.** HOOF PART the pointed horny rear part of a horse's hoof ■ *vt* (**-tressed, -tress·ing, -tress·es**) **1.** SUPPORT WALL to support a wall with a buttress **2.** SUPPORT OR REINFORCE SOMETHING to support, help, or reinforce something, especially an argument, analysis, or point of view ○ *He buttressed his views with lengthy quotations from the scriptures.* [14C. < Old French *(ars) bouterez* "thrusting (arch)" < *bouter* (see BUTT[1])]

butt shaft *n* a blunt-headed arrow used for archery practice [< BUTT[3]]

butt-weld (**butt-weld·ed, butt-weld·ing, butt-welds**) *vt* to weld a joint in which the two pieces are placed end to end rather than overlapped —**butt weld** *n*

bu·tut /bo͞o to͞ot/ *n* a subunit of Gambian currency. See table at **currency** [Late 20C. < Wolof]

bu·tyl /byo͞ot'l, byo͞o tìl/ *n, adj* relating to the group of atoms derived from butane after the loss of a hydrogen atom. Formula: C_4H_9-. [Mid-19C. < BUTYRIC]

bu·tyl ac·e·tate *n* CHEM same as **butyl ethanoate**

bu·tyl al·co·hol *n* CHEM same as **butanol**

bu·tyl·ate /byo͞ot'l àyt/ (**-at·ed, -at·ing, -ates**) *vt* to introduce a butyl group or groups into a chemical compound —**bu·tyl·a·tion** /byo͞ot'l áysh'n/ *n*

bu·tyl·at·ed hy·drox·y·an·i·sole /byo͞ot'l aytəd hī dròksee ánnə sōl/ *n* CHEM full form of **BHA**

bu·tyl·at·ed hy·drox·y·tol·u·ene /-hī dròksee tóllyoo èen/ *n* CHEM full form of **BHT**

bu·tyl·ene /byo͞ot'l èen/ *n* CHEM same as **butene**

bu·tyl eth·a·no·ate *n* a colorless flammable toxic liquid with a fruity odor and three different molecular structures (**isomers**). Use: lacquer solvent. Formula: $C_6H_{12}O_2$.

bu·tyl rub·ber *n* a synthetic rubber that is extremely resistant to abrasion, tearing, sunlight, and chemical attack. Use: inner tubes, hose, insulation, seals for food jars.

bu·ty·ra·ceous /byo͞otə ráyshəss/ *adj* containing, resembling, or producing butter (*technical*) [Mid-17C. < BUTYRIC]

bu·tyr·al·de·hyde /byo͞otə ráldə hīd/ *n* a colorless flammable liquid. Use: manufacture of solvents, resins, and plasticizers. Formula: C_4H_8O.

bu·ty·rate /byo͞otə ràyt/ *n* a salt or ester of butyric acid [Mid-19C. < BUTYRIC]

bu·tyr·ic /byoo tèerik/ *adj* **1.** relating to or containing butanoic acid **2.** relating to or containing butter (*technical*) [Early 19C. < Latin *butyrum* (see BUTTER)]

bu·tyr·ic ac·id *n* a thick colorless liquid that causes the smell of rancid butter. Use: in flavorings, scents. Formula: C_3H_7COOH.

bu·ty·rin /byo͞otərin/ *n* a colorless liquid ester or oil with three different molecular structures (**isomers**). Source: formed from butanoic acid and glycerol and found in butter. [Early 19C. Blend of BUTYRIC + GLYCERIN]

bux·om /búksəm/ *adj* describes a woman with a full figure (*humorous*) [Assumed Old English *(ge)būhsum* "pliable" < *(ge)būgan* "to bend" < Germanic] —**bux·om·ly** *adv* —**bux·om·ness** *n*

Bux·te·hude /bo͝okstə ho͞odə/, **Dietrich** (1637?–1707) Danish-born German organist and composer. A prolific composer of sacred music for the organ, he moved to Germany in 1668 and was greatly admired by J. S. Bach and Handel.

buy /bī/ *v* (**bought** /bawt/, **buy·ing, buys**) **1.** *vti* ACQUIRE SOMETHING BY PAYMENT to pay money for something in order to obtain it ○ *They bought me a bike for my birthday.* ○ *People just aren't buying at the moment.* **2.** *vt* OBTAIN SOMETHING FROM SOMEBODY BY BRIBERY to obtain information, help, or loyalty from somebody in exchange for money **3.** *vt* OBTAIN TIME to obtain more time to reach a desired end by taking strategic action ○ *a maneuver that should buy us another* *week* **4.** *vt* OBTAIN SOMETHING BY SACRIFICE to obtain something by sacrificing something else of equivalent value ○ *buy peace with land* **5.** *vi* BE BUYER FOR COMPANY OR PERSON to purchase goods on behalf of a company or another person ○ *She buys for a large New York store.* **6.** *vt* BELIEVE SOMETHING to accept or believe something proposed as true (*informal*) ○ *I don't buy the part about an international conspiracy.* ■ *n* **1.** SOMETHING BOUGHT something that you pay money for, considered relative to its worth ○ *a good buy* **2.** EXCHANGE OF MONEY FOR GOODS an exchange of money for goods or services [Old English *bycgan* < Germanic] — **buy·a·ble** *adj*

SPELLCHECK See *bi-*.

buy back, buy home *vt Malaysia* to buy something and take it home ○ *We bought back pizzas for supper.*

buy in *v* **1.** *vi* PAY TO TAKE PART IN SOMETHING to pay in order to take part in or have a share of something **2.** *vi* PURCHASE STOCK IN COMPANY to purchase stock in a company as the controlling interest **3.** *vt* WITHDRAW ITEM FROM AUCTION to withdraw an item from sale at an auction because it has failed to reach its upset price

buy into *vt* **1.** PURCHASE STOCK IN COMPANY to purchase an amount of stock in a company **2.** PAY TO PARTICIPATE IN SOMETHING to pay money in order to take part in something ○ *buy into a timeshare* **3.** ACCEPT SOMETHING to accept or believe in a proposition or idea (*informal*) ○ *I don't buy into that "greed is good" attitude.*

buy off *vt* to bribe somebody in order to prevent something happening or ensure cooperation ○ *They tried to buy off the entire jury.*

buy out *vt* **1.** PAY SOMEBODY TO RELINQUISH INTEREST to pay somebody to relinquish interest in a property or other enterprise ○ *She was bought out by her partners.* **2.** MIL RELEASE SOMEBODY FROM MILITARY SERVICE to pay money to release somebody from military service **3.** COMM PURCHASE ENTIRE STOCK OF COMPANY to purchase the entire stock of or controlling financial interest in a company or business

buy up *vt* **1.** to purchase all, or all that is available, of a commodity ○ *They've been buying up property in the area.* **2.** to purchase something in great quantity without regard to expense ○ *buying up modern paintings*

buy-back *n* the repurchase of something such as stock, currency, real estate, or goods, according to a previously made contractual agreement

buy·down /bī̆ dòwn/ *n* an advance cash payment on a loan made in order to reduce the interest charge and size of the periodic payment

buy·er /bī̆ ər/ *n* **1.** somebody who buys or intends to buy something **2.** somebody whose job is to choose and buy goods for a company or another person

buy·er's mar·ket *n* a situation in which supply exceeds demand, prices are relatively low, and buyers therefore have an advantage

buy-in *n* commitment to achieving a shared goal ○ *Successful change begins with acquiring employees' buy-in to the change process.*

buy·out /bī̆ òwt/ *n* **1.** the purchase of an entire amount or quantity of something **2.** the purchase of a controlling interest in a company ○ *a management buyout*

buzz /buz/ *n* **1.** STEADY HUMMING SOUND a steady low humming sound like that of a bee ○ *the low buzz of insects flitting over the flowers* **2.** HUM OF TALK a low murmur of conversation made by a group of people, especially when they are excited or interested in something ○ *a buzz of voices emerging from the living room* **3.** ELECTRONIC HUMMING SOUND the sound made by a buzzer **4.** FEELING OF EXCITEMENT a feeling of excitement or satisfaction often linked with a sense of achievement (*informal*) ○ *It gives me a tremendous buzz to hear someone saying the lines that I've written.* **5.** INTOXICATION a feeling of intoxication (*slang*) **6.** TELEPHONE CALL a telephone call to somebody (*informal*) **7.** LATEST GOSSIP the latest gossip or information within an industry or a locale (*informal*) ○ *The buzz at the festival was that he'd pick up an award for best director.* **8.** FAD a short-lived interest or enthusiasm (*informal*) **9.** PUBLICITY publicity, or interest generated by publicity (*informal*) ○ *a new book that is generating lots of buzz* ■ *v* (**buzzed, buzz·ing, buzz·es**) **1.** *vi* MAKE STEADY HUMMING SOUND to make a steady low humming sound like that of a bee **2.** *vi* BE ANIMATED to be animated by the talk or activity of people ○ *The room was buzzing with excitement.* **3.** *vi* MOVE SPEEDILY to move around speedily and busily ○ *buzzing around in small cars that dodged through traffic* **4.** *vti* WORK BUZZER to activate a buzzer **5.** *vt* LET SOMEBODY INTO BUILDING ELECTRONICALLY to admit somebody to a building by activating an electronic system that controls a door ○ *waiting for them to buzz me in* **6.** *vi* MAKE ELECTRONIC HUMMING SOUND to make an electronic humming noise when activated ○ *When the timer buzzes, turn the oven down.* **7.** *vi* BE EXCITED to be filled with anxious or excited thoughts ○ *My head was buzzing with all the things I'd heard that night.* **8.** *vi* BE RINGING to be filled with a continuous ringing sound, e.g., after being exposed to loud noise ○ *My ears were buzzing after the concert.* **9.** *vt* TELEPHONE SOMEBODY to call somebody on the telephone or on an intercom (*informal*) **10.** *vt* AVIAT FLY LOW OVER PEOPLE OR PLACE to fly an aircraft low over people or buildings, or across the path of other aircraft (*informal*) [14C. An imitation of the sound]

buzz off *vi* to go away (*informal*)

buz·zard /búzzərd/ (*plural* **-zards** or *same*) *n* **1.** a North American vulture, e.g., the turkey vulture **2.** *UK* BIRDS same as **buteo 3.** somebody who is regarded as mean, bad-tempered, or unpleasant (*dated*) [14C. < Old French *busard*]

buzz bomb *n* MIL same as **robot bomb**

buzz cut *n* a hairstyle in which the hair is cut very close to the skull with a razor

buzz·er /búzzər/ *n* an electronic device that makes a humming or buzzing sound when activated

buzz saw *n* TOOLS same as **circular saw**

buzz·word /búz wùrd/ *n* a fashionable word or concept, often associated with a specific group of people and not understood by outsiders (*informal*) ○ *the latest media buzzword*

b.v. *abbr* ACCT book value

B vi·ta·min *n* a water-soluble vitamin belonging to a group that is essential to the working of some enzymes. The B vitamins are B1 thiamine, B2 riboflavin, B6 pyridoxine, B12 cobalamin, B5 pantothenic acid, folic acid, and biotin.

BVM *abbr* Blessed Virgin Mary [Latin *Beata Virgo Maria*]

bvt *abbr* MIL **1.** brevet **2.** breveted

bw *abbr* **1.** biological weapons **2.** black-and-white **3.** ONLINE Botswana (*used in Internet addresses*) See table at **domain name**

BW *abbr* **1.** bacteriological warfare **2.** biological warfare **3.** *also* **B/W** black-and-white

bwa·na /bwáanə/ *n E Africa* used as a respectful term of address for a man [Late 19C. < Kiswahili]

B.W.I. *abbr* **1.** Baltimore-Washington International Airport **2.** British West Indies

BWR *abbr* INDUST boiling-water reactor

BWV *abbr* MUSIC Bach Werke-Verzeichnis (*used before numbers identifying the works of J. S. Bach*)

BX *abbr* MIL, COMM Base Exchange

bx. *abbr* box[1]

by[1] /bī/ CORE MEANING: a grammatical word expressing a spatial relationship, indicating that somebody or something is beside or close to somebody or something else ○ (prep) *standing by the window* ○ (adv) *A large crowd of shoppers stood by watching.*

1. *prep, adv* PAST SOMEBODY OR SOMETHING IN SPACE indicates movement past somebody or something, sometimes including a brief stop (*used following a verb expressing movement*) ○ *He drove by his apartment building.* ○ *The server strolled by, pouring us some more coffee.* **2.** *prep* ALONG next to or along something **3.** *prep* THROUGH passing through something ○ *entering by the back door* **4.** *prep* BEFORE THAT TIME happening or required at or before a particular time ○ *reservations required by Sunday* **5.** *prep* DURING happening during a particular time period ○ *By day he worked in a canning factory.* **6.** *prep* IN MEASURES OF at a rate based on a particular measure such as time, weight, or volume ○ *sold by weight* **7.** *prep* MATH INDICATES FACTOR OR DIVISOR used in multiplication and division to indicate a number or quantity being multiplied, or to indicate the number or quantity that divides another ○ *What is 144 divided by 12?* **8.** *prep* MEASURE INDICATES DIMENSIONS used between the measurements of the dimensions of an object, expressing area or volume ○ *2 feet by 3* **9.** *prep* MEASURE DIFFERING IN AMOUNT OF used to indicate an amount, extent, or rate at which something increases, decreases, or differs ○ *Tax rates are to be cut by 0.25%.* **10.** *prep* MEASURE INDICATES DIRECTION used to indicate a direction ○ *north by northwest* **11.** *prep* IN AMOUNTS OF PARTICULAR SIZE in groups or amounts of a particular size ○ *Visitors arrived by the truckload.* **12.** *prep* AFTER SAME THING used to link two identical words to indicate a progression or sequence ○ *One by one we told our stories.* ○ *You can see an improvement day by day.* **13.** *prep* INDICATES CAUSE used to indicate the person or thing performing an action or causing a situation or reaction (*used following a passive verb*) ○ *He was hit by a ball.* **14.** *prep* INDICATES CREATOR, AUTHOR, OR ARTIST used to indicate the person who wrote or created something such as a written piece or work of art ○ *written by A. A. Milne* **15.** *prep* USING METHOD OR MEDIUM used to indicate the particular mode, method, or action through which something occurs or is done ○ *traveling by ocean liner* ○ *She earns a living by playing the harp.* **16.** *prep* INDICATES MEANS used to indicate the action used to achieve something (*followed by a gerund*) ○ *The key to attracting banks to small locales is by attracting more businesses.* **17.** *prep* IN PARTICULAR MANNER with, in, or through a particular manner of doing something ○ *used by permission of the author* **18.** *prep* ACCORDING TO UNCHANGING QUALITY in terms of a particular attribute or function ○ *a teacher by profession and a learner by nature* **19.** *prep* IN COMPLIANCE WITH in order to comply with something, especially the law ○ *By law, patients must have access to their records.* **20.** *prep* AT PARTICULAR PART at a particular part of something, e.g., a hand or corner ○ *held the dancer by the waist* **21.** *adv* IN NAME OF SOMETHING SACRED used to indicate something considered holy when making a solemn oath or promise ○ *By all that is sacred, I ask you to stop.* **22.** *adv* AWAY OR ASIDE into a place for safekeeping for use later ○ *I spent some of the money and put some by for hard times.* [Old English *bī* < Germanic] ◇ **by and by** after a while (*literary*) ◇ **by the by, by the bye** used to introduce a question or piece of information that is not connected with the subject being discussed

SPELLCHECK See *bi-*.

by[2] *abbr* ONLINE Belarus (*used in Internet addresses*) See table at **domain name**

b.y. *abbr* billion years

by-, bye- *prefix* **1.** secondary ○ *byroad* ○ *byproduct* **2.** past ○ *bygone* [< BY[1]]

BYAM *abbr* ONLINE between you and me (*used in e-mails or text messages*)

Byb·los /bíbbləss, bíb lòss/ ancient Phoenician city, near modern-day Beirut, Lebanon, on the Mediterranean Sea. It was the principal city of Phoenicia in the second millennium B.C., and an important source of papyrus.

by-blow *n* a blow that hits somebody or something by chance or in passing

by·catch /bī̆ kàch/ *n* fish that are caught unintentionally in addition to the required species

~~**bycicle**~~ incorrect spelling of **bicycle**

bye[1] /bī/ *n* the right to proceed to the next round of a competition without contesting the present round, often through nonappearance of an opponent [Mid-16C. Variant of BY[1]]

bye[2] /bī/ *interj* same as **goodbye** (*informal*) [Early 18C. Shortening]

SPELLCHECK See *bi-*.

bye- *prefix* another spelling of **by-**

SPELLCHECK See *bi-*.

bye-bye[1] *interj* same as **goodbye** (*informal*)

bye-bye[2] *n* bed or sleep (*baby talk*) [< a refrain used in lullabies]

by·e·lec·tion, **bye-e·lec·tion** *n* an election held between official general or local elections to fill a vacant seat, e.g., to replace a member of a parliament or a city council member who has died or resigned

Bye·lo·rus·sia /byèllō rúshə/ *n* former name for **Belarus** —**Bye·lo·rus·sian** *n, adj*

by-form *n* a slightly changed form of a word that begins to be used at a later date

by·gone /bī́ gàwn, -gòn/ *adj* existing or having happened a long time ago ○ *reminders of a bygone age* ■ *n* something that happened, existed, or was manufactured a long time ago (*often used in the plural*) ◇ **let bygones be bygones** to forgive past offenses or resentments

BYKT *abbr* ONLINE but you know/knew that (*used in e-mails or text messages*)

by·law /bī́ làw/ *n* **1.** a law or regulation that governs the internal affairs of a company or other organization ○ *company bylaws* **2.** a secondary law [13C. Probably < Old Norse *blagu* "town law" < *br* "town" + *lagu* "law"]

by·line /bī́ lìn/ *n* **1.** the name of the author of an article in a newspaper or magazine, printed at the head of the article **2.** SOCCER same as **goal line** ■ *vt* (**-lined, -lin·ing, -lines**) to write an article that will include a byline

by·name /bī́ nàym/ *n* **1.** same as **nickname 2.** same as **surname**

BYOB *abbr* bring your own bottle (*used on party invitations*)

by·pass /bī́ pàss/ *n* **1.** ROAD AROUND PLACE a road built around a town or city to keep through traffic away from the center **2.** SURG **OPERATION TO REROUTE BLOOD** a surgical operation to redirect the blood, usually via a grafted blood vessel, carried out when the existing blood vessel has become blocked ○ *a heart bypass* **3.** MED **NEW ROUTE FOR BLOOD** a new route for the blood, created by a bypass operation **4.** ELEC ENG same as **shunt** *n* (sense 3) **5.** UTIL **EMERGENCY CHANNEL** a channel such as a pipe carrying gas or water that is brought into use when the main channel is blocked ■ *vt* (**-passed, -pass·ing, -pass·es**) **1. GO AROUND PLACE** to avoid a place by traveling around it **2.** ROADS **BUILD ROAD ROUND PLACE** to build a bypass around a town or city **3. AVOID SOMETHING** to avoid an obstacle, obstruction, or problem by using an alternative route or method **4. AVOID STANDARD PROCEDURE** to ignore or avoid a standard procedure for doing something, or ignore somebody who is usually consulted

by·play *n* matters of subsidiary importance or interest that take place while the main action is going on, e.g., in a stage play

by·prod·uct /bī́ pròddəkt/ *n* **1.** something produced as a secondary result of the manufacture or production of something else, often something useful or commercially valuable **2.** something that happens as an incidental result of something else

Byrd /burd/, **Richard** (1888–1957) US naval officer and explorer. He claimed to be the first person to fly over the North Pole (1926) and led five expeditions to Antarctica (1928–56). Full name **Byrd, Richard Evelyn**

Byrd, William (1543–1623) English composer. He was appointed organist for the Chapel Royal in 1572. His work includes three Latin masses (1589–91), madrigals, and instrumental pieces.

Byrnes /burnz/, **James Francis** (1879–1972) US lawyer and secretary of state (1945–47). He was an associate justice of the US Supreme Court (1941–42) but resigned to serve as head of federal agencies for economic stabilization (1942–43) and economic mobilization (1943–45) during World War II. As secretary of state, he represented the United States at the postwar peace talks.

by·road /bī́ rōd/ *n* a side road carrying a small volume of traffic

By·ron, Cape /bī́rən/ cape in northeastern New South Wales, Australia, near the town of Byron Bay. It is the most easterly point on the Australian mainland.

AKG London

Lord Byron

By·ron, George Gordon Noel, 6th Baron Byron (1788–1824) British poet. He was an influential figure of the Romantic movement. His major works include *Childe Harold's Pilgrimage* (1812–18) and the long satirical poem *Don Juan* (1819–24). After scandalizing London with his promiscuity, Lord Byron lived abroad, largely in Italy, and died aiding the Greeks in their revolt against the Turks. Known as **Lord Byron**

> "Roll on, thou deep and dark blue ocean—roll! / Ten thousand fleets sweep over thee in vain; / Man marks the earth with ruin—his control / Stops with the shore."
> [Lord Byron, *Childe Harold's Pilgrimage*; Canto IV; 1818]

By·ron·ic /bī rónnik/ *adj* **1.** relating to or characteristic of Lord Byron or his poetry **2.** describes a brooding and solitary man who seems capable of great passion and suffering

bys·si MARINE BIOL, TEXTILES plural of **byssus**

bys·si·no·sis /bìssi nṓssiss/ *n* a respiratory disease caused by prolonged inhalation of dust from textile fibers, marked by coughing, wheezing, shortness of breath, and permanent lung damage [Late 19C. < Latin *byssinus* "of fine linen" < *byssus* (see BYSSUS)]

bys·sus /bíssəss/ (*plural* **-sus·es** or **-si** /-sī/) *n* **1.** a mass of strong silky threads that mollusks such as mussels use to attach themselves to rocks and other hard surfaces **2.** fine linen used by the ancient Egyptians to wrap mummies [14C. Via Latin, "fine linen" < Greek *bussos* < Semitic]

by·stand·er /bī́ stàndər/ *n* somebody who observes but is not involved in something

by·stand·er ef·fect *n* the reluctance of members of a crowd to intervene in an incident they are witnessing

byte /bīt/ *n* **1.** a group of eight bits of computer information, representing a unit of data such as a number or letter **2.** a unit of computer memory equal to that needed to store a single character [Mid-20C. Probably alteration of BIT³ after BITE "morsel," or acronym < *binary digit eight*]

by·way /bī́ wày/ *n* **1.** a small side road not regularly used by people or traffic **2.** the less important aspects of a particular pursuit or field of knowledge ○ *the byways of numismatics*

by·word /bī́ wùrd/ *n* **1. WELL-KNOWN EXAMPLE** somebody or something that is well known for a particular quality ○ *The magazine became a byword for cutting-edge style.* **2. CATCH PHRASE** a word or phrase that is in common use at a particular time **3. PROVERB** a proverb in common use at a specific place or time or among a group [Old English *bīwyrde* "proverb," translation of Latin *proverbium*]

byz·an·tine /bízz'n tèen, -tīn, bi zántin/ *adj* **1.** extremely complex or intricate **2.** marked by deviousness or scheming [Mid-20C. < BYZANTINE]

Byz·an·tine /bízz'n tèen, -tīn, bi zántin/ *adj* **1.** ANCIENT HIST **OF BYZANTIUM** relating to the ancient city of Byzantium **2.** HIST **OF EASTERN ROMAN EMPIRE** relating to the eastern part of the late Roman Empire (**Byzantine Empire**) **3.** ART, ARCHIT **OF BYZANTINE ART OR ARCHITECTURE** relating to or typical of the colorful religious art or the ornate architecture developed under the Byzantine Empire **4.** CHR **OF EASTERN ORTHODOX CHURCH** relating to the Eastern Orthodox Church and its traditions ■ *n* ANCIENT HIST **SOMEBODY FROM BYZANTIUM** somebody who came from the ancient city of Byzantium or the Byzantine Empire [Late 16C. < Latin *Byzantinus* < *Byzantium* < Greek *Buzantion*]

Byz·an·tine Church *n* CHR same as **Orthodox Church** (sense 1)

Byz·an·tine Em·pire *n* the eastern part of the late Roman Empire, from A.D. 330 to 1453, when its capital Constantinople fell to the Ottoman Turks. It was the center of Orthodox Christianity.

By·zan·ti·um /bi zánshee əm, -zántee-/ ancient Greek city on the site of modern-day Istanbul, conquered by the Romans in A.D. 196, and rebuilt in A.D. 330 by Constantine the Great, who renamed it Constantinople. As the capital of the Byzantine Empire (until 1453), it was the largest city in the Christian world.

bz *abbr* ONLINE Belize (*used in Internet addresses*) See table at **domain name**

Cc

c[1] /see/ (*plural* **c's**), **C** (*plural* **C's** or **Cs**) *n* **1. 3RD LETTER OF ENGLISH ALPHABET** the third letter of the English alphabet, representing a consonant sound **2. LETTER "C" WRITTEN** a written representation of the letter "c" **3. ROMAN 100** the Roman numeral for 100

c[2] *symbol* **1.** CHEM concentration **2.** PHYS the speed of light in a vacuum **3.** CHESS used to refer to the third vertical row of squares from the left on a chessboard

c[3] *abbr* **1.** canceled **2.** PHYS, MEASURE candle **3.** MEASURE carat **4.** MATH constant **5.** MEASURE cubic

C[1] /see/ (*plural* **C's** or **Cs**) *n* **1. "C"-SHAPED OBJECT** something shaped like a letter "C" **2.** MUSIC **1ST NOTE IN C MAJOR** the first note of a scale in C major **3.** MUSIC **SOMETHING THAT PRODUCES C** a string, key, or pipe tuned to produce the note C **4.** MUSIC **SCALE BEGINNING ON C** a scale or key that starts on the note C **5.** MUSIC **WRITTEN SYMBOL OF C** a graphic representation of the tone of C **6.** EDUC **3RD HIGHEST GRADE** the third highest grade in a series, e.g., an average grade for academic work **7.** COMPUT **PROGRAMMING LANGUAGE** a high-level computer programming language **8.** DRUGS same as **cocaine** (*slang*) ◇ **the big C** cancer (*slang*)

C[2] *symbol* **1.** ELEC ENG capacitance **2.** CHEM ELEM carbon **3.** BIOCHEM cytosine **4.** PHYS heat capacity

C[3] *abbr* **1.** MEASURE Celsius **2.** MEASURE centigrade **3.** HIST century **4.** PHYS charm **5.** EDUC College **6.** POL Congress **7.** ELEC coulomb **8.** ONLINE see (*used in e-mails or text messages*)

C++ /see pluss plúss/ *n* an object-oriented version of the programming language C, developed in the 1980s

c., C. *abbr* **1.** MEASURE capacity **2.** MAPS cape **3.** carton **4.** case **5.** BASEBALL catcher **6.** MONEY cent **7.** MONEY centavo **8.** MONEY centime **9.** HIST century **10.** chapter **11.** CHR church **12.** circa (*used before dates*) **13.** POL consul **14.** copy **15.** PUBL copyright **16.** MIL corps **17.** SPORTS cup **18.** MEASURE gallon

C. *abbr* **1.** CHR Catholic **2.** POL Chancellor **3.** chief **4.** city **5.** Companion **6.** POL Congress **7.** POL Conservative **8.** SPORTS court

C2B /see tə bee/ *abbr* E-COMMERCE consumer-to-business

C3I /see three í/ *n* command, control, communications, and intelligence, which are the operational aspects of military science, as opposed to training or logistics

ca *abbr* Canada (*used in Internet addresses*) See table at **domain name**

Ca *symbol* CHEM ELEM calcium

CA *abbr* **1.** MAIL California **2.** ONLINE certificate authority (*used in e-mails*)

ca. *abbr* HIST circa (*used before dates*)

c.a. *abbr* **1.** chartered accountant **2.** chronological age

C.A. *abbr* **1.** Central America **2.** Central American **3.** ACCT chartered accountant **4.** chronological age

C/A *abbr* FIN **1.** capital account **2.** credit account

CAAT *abbr* E-COMMERCE certificate authority administration tool

cab /kab/ *n* **1.** CARS same as **taxi** **2. DRIVER'S COMPARTMENT** the part of a large vehicle such as a truck, a locomotive, or a large crane where the driver or operator sits **3. HORSE-DRAWN VEHICLE FOR HIRE** a lightweight horse-drawn carriage formerly used for public hire ■ *v* (**cabbed, cab·bing, cabs**) **1.** *vi* **RIDE IN TAXI** to go somewhere by taxi **2.** *vt* **TAKE SOMETHING BY TAXI** to transport something or somebody by taxi ○ *cab a package downtown* **3.** *vi* **DRIVE TAXI** to drive a taxi as a job [Early 19C. Shortening of CABRIOLET]

CAB *abbr* Civil Aeronautics Board

ca·bal /kə bál/ *n* **1. GROUP OF PLOTTERS** a group of conspirators or plotters, particularly one formed for political purposes **2. SECRET PLOT** a secret plot or conspiracy, especially a political one **3. CLIQUE** an exclusive group of people ■ *vi* (**-balled, -bal·ling, -bals**) **CONSPIRE AS GROUP** to form a group and plot together against somebody or something [Early 17C. Via French *cabale* < medieval Latin *cab(b)ala* "secret teaching" (see KABBALAH)]

Cab·a·la *n* JUDAISM another spelling of **Kabbalah**

ca·ba·let·ta /kàbbə léttə, kaábə-/ *n* **1.** a short simple aria of 19th-century Italian opera, usually found in conjunction with a preceding cavatina **2.** the final section of an aria or duet, typically with a lively rhythm [Mid-19C. < Italian, "little stanza" < Latin *copula* "link"]

ca·bal·la·do /kàbb'l yaádō, kàbbə laádō/ (*plural* **-dos**) *n Southwest US* AGRIC same as **string** (sense 19) [Mid-20C. < Spanish *caballada* < *caballo* "horse"]

REGIONAL NOTE See *remuda.*

cab·al·le·ro /kàbbə lérrō, kaább'l yérrō/ (*plural* **-ros**) *n* **1.** in Spain or Spanish-speaking countries, a knight, cavalier, or gentleman **2.** *Southwest US* a horseman [Mid-19C. Via Spanish < late Latin *caballarius* < Latin *caballus* "horse"]

ca·ban·a /kə bánnə, kə bánnyə/ *n* a shelter in which swimmers or sunbathers can change their clothes, on a beach or by a swimming pool [Late 19C. Via Spanish < late Latin *capanna* "hut"]

cab·a·ret /kàbbə ráy/ *n* **1.** a floorshow consisting of singing, dancing, and comic acts, performed in a restaurant, club, or bar **2.** a restaurant, club, or bar offering a cabaret [Mid-17C. Via French < Old French dialect *camberet* "little room" < Latin *camera* "room" (see CAMERA)]

cabbage

cab·bage /kábbij/ *n* **1.** FOOD **LEAVES AS FOOD** a roundish head of closely layered green, white, or red leaves, eaten raw or cooked as a vegetable **2.** PLANTS **EDIBLE PLANT WITH CLOSELY LAYERED LEAVES** a short-stemmed plant that produces cabbage. Latin name: *Brassica oleracea* var. capitata. **3.** PLANTS **PLANT LIKE CABBAGE** a plant related to cabbage, e.g., Chinese cabbage **4.** FOOD **EDIBLE PALM BUD** the bud of a number of species of palm, eaten as a vegetable **5.** MONEY **PAPER MONEY** money, especially in the form of banknotes (*dated slang*) [15C. < Old French *caboche*, variant of *caboce* "head"] —**cab·bag·y** *adj*

cab·bage but·ter·fly *n* a light-colored butterfly whose larvae (**cabbageworms**) feed on the leaves of cabbages and related plants. Family: Pieridae.

cab·bage let·tuce *n* a variety of lettuce that has a rounded head like a cabbage

cab·bage palm *n* **1.** a palm tree whose leaf buds resemble cabbages and are eaten as a vegetable. Latin name: *Roystonea oleracea*. **2.** a palm or similar plant resembling a cabbage

cab·bage pal·met·to *n* a palm tree with edible leaf buds and fan-shaped leaves that are used in Christian celebrations on Palm Sunday. Native to: southeastern United States, Bahamas. Latin name: *Sabal palmetto.*

cab·bage rose *n* a hybrid bush rose grown in gardens. Flowers: fragrant, double. Latin name: *Rosa centifolia.*

cab·bage sal·ad *n regional* same as **coleslaw**

REGIONAL NOTE *Cabbage salad* is essentially a Northern term, belonging especially to New York State, Michigan, and Wisconsin. It is rare in the Middle, Southern, Rocky Mountain, and Pacific states.

cab·bage·town /kábbij tòwn/ *n Can* an inner-city slum (*informal*) [Late 20C. After *Cabbagetown*, a contemptuous nickname of a run-down area of Toronto, where the poor population of Anglo-Saxon origin were said to live on cabbage]

cab·bage·worm /kábbij wùrm/ *n* a larva that feeds on cabbage and related plants, especially the larva of the cabbage butterfly

Cab·ba·la *n* JUDAISM another spelling of **Kabbalah**

cab·by /kábbee/ (*plural* **-bies**), **cab·bie** *n* a driver of a taxi (*informal*)

Cab·ell /kább'l/, **James Branch** (1879–1958) US writer and essayist. Known for his satirical and controversial novel *Jurgen, or Comedy of Justice* (1919), which was temporarily suppressed as immoral, he became popular in the 1920s.

> "The optimist proclaims that we live in the best of all possible worlds; and the pessimist fears this is true."
> [James Branch Cabell, *The Silver Stallion*; 1926]

ca·ber /káybər/ *n* a long thick wooden pole thrown end over end in an event (**tossing the caber**) in Scottish Highland Games [Early 16C. < Gaelic *cabar* "pole"]

Cab·er·net Sau·vi·gnon /kàbbər nay sō veen yṓn/ *n* **1.** a dry red wine made from a variety of black grape originally grown in southwestern France **2.** a black grape variety. Use: winemaking. [< French]

Ca·be·za de Va·ca /kə báyzə də vaákə/, **Álvar Núñez** (1490?–1557?) Spanish explorer. He led European expeditions to various regions in the Americas.

cab·in /kábbin/ *n* **1.** BUILDINGS **WOODEN HUT** a small simple house, especially one made of wood in forest or mountain areas **2.** TRAVEL **SMALL ROOM ON SHIP** a small room on a boat or ship, where people live or sleep **3.** NAUT **SHELTER ON BOAT** a covered or enclosed compartment that houses the wheel on a boat or yacht, used for shelter in bad weather and often as a living space **4.** AVIAT **AIRPLANE INTERIOR** the part of a passenger airplane where the passengers sit, or the part of a cargo airplane where the cargo is carried **5.** AEROSP **CREW QUARTERS ON SPACECRAFT** the part of a spacecraft where the crew work, live, or sleep **6.** NAVY **ROOM ON**

SHIP the commanding officer's room on a warship ■ *vti* (**-ined, -in·ing, -ins**) KEEP SOMEBODY CONFINED to confine somebody in a small enclosed space, or live confined in this way (*literary; usually passive*) [14C. Via Old French *cabane* < late Latin *capanna* "hut"]

CULTURAL NOTE ***Uncle Tom's Cabin***, a novel (1852) by Harriet Beecher Stowe. Set in the American South, it is the story of an enslaved African American man, Uncle Tom, who is sold by his kindly owners and eventually dies at the hands of a vicious new master named Simon Legree. Such was this abolitionist novel's influence that it was described as one of the causes of the Civil War.

cab·in boy *n* a boy who acted as a servant on board a sailing ship, waiting on officers and passengers (*dated*)

cab·in class *n* a class of accommodation on some passenger ships that is lower than first class and higher than tourist class ■ *adj, adv* in cabin class on a passenger ship

cab·in crew *n* the staff on a passenger aircraft whose job is to attend to passengers

cab·in cruis·er *n* a large, powerful motorboat with varying amounts of living space

Ca·bin·da /kə bíndə/ Angolan exclave bounded by the Republic of Congo to the north and the Democratic Republic of Congo to the south. Capital: Cabinda. Population: 152,100 (1992). Area: 2,807 sq. mi./7,270 sq. km.

cab·i·net /kábbinət/ *n* **1.** PIECE OF FURNITURE an upright piece of furniture usually made of wood and consisting of drawers, shelves, and compartments for storing or displaying objects **2.** TV OR RADIO COVERING the outer casing of a television or stereo system, especially the wooden casing of an old-fashioned model **3.** *also* **Cab·i·net** GOVERNMENT LEADER'S ADVISERS a group of senior officials appointed by a president, prime minister, or other government leader to advise on policy **4.** PRIVATE ROOM a small private room (*archaic*) ■ *adj* FOR DISPLAY IN CABINET small or decorative enough to be displayed in a cabinet [Mid-16C. < French, "small room" < Old Picard *cabine* "room for gambling"]

cab·i·net·mak·er /kábbinət màykər/ *n* a skilled worker who specializes in making high-quality furniture —**cab·i·net·mak·ing** *n*

cab·i·net min·is·ter *n UK* in Britain, Canada, and some other countries, a senior government minister who is in a cabinet

cab·i·net·work /kábbinət wùrk/, **cab·i·net·ry** /kábbinətree/ *n* wooden furniture made to a high standard by a cabinetmaker

cab·in fe·ver *n* an emotional condition, marked by irritability, distress, or depression, caused by prolonged isolation or confined living quarters (*informal*)

ca·ble /káyb'l/ *n* **1.** STRONG ROPE OR WIRE a strong thick rope or steel wire, used for lifting, pulling, towing, or securing things **2.** ELEC BUNDLE OF ELECTRICAL WIRES a group of wires for transmitting electrical signals that are bound together and usually have shared or common insulation **3.** NAUT MOORING ROPE OR CHAIN a rope or chain attached to an anchor or used for mooring a ship **4.** TELECOM OVERSEAS TELEGRAM a telegram originally sent by underseas cable, now usually by telephone, radio, or satellite **5.** MEDIA same as **cable television 6.** HANDICRAFT same as **cable stitch** ■ *v* (**-bled, -bling, -bles**) **1.** *vti* SEND TELEGRAM to send somebody a telegram **2.** *vt* TELECOM SEND SOMETHING VIA TELEGRAM to send something such as money or information to somebody in a distant place by sending a telegram **3.** *vt* FASTEN OR EQUIP SOMETHING WITH CABLES to fasten something with cables, or attach cables to something **4.** *vt* TELECOM SUPPLY PLACE WITH CABLE TV to connect a building or area to a cable telecommunications network [Pre-12C. Via Anglo-Norman, Old N French < late Latin *capulum* "halter" < Latin *capere* "seize"] —**ca·bler** *n* —**ca·bling** *n*

Ca·ble /káyb'l/, **George Washington** (1844–1925) US writer, known for his novels and short stories set in New Orleans

ca·ble-ac·cess *adj* showing programs that are made locally and often of local interest only, as opposed to commercially produced material ○ *a cable-access channel*

Barnaby's

cable car

ca·ble car *n* **1.** a car suspended from an overhead cable, used to transport passengers up and down steep hills or across valleys **2.** a car on a cable railroad

ca·ble·cast /káyb'l kàst/ *n* a broadcast over a cable television network [Late 20C. < CABLE + *-cast* < BROADCAST] —**ca·ble·cast·er** *n* —**ca·ble·cast·ing** *n*

ca·ble·gram /káyb'l gràm/ *n* TELECOM same as **cable** *n* (sense 4)

ca·ble-laid *adj* describes thick ropes made of three thinner ropes, each with three strands, twisted together counterclockwise

ca·ble mo·dem *n* a high-speed modem enabling a computer to connect to the Internet via a cable television network

ca·ble rail·road, ca·ble rail·way *n* a hillside railroad consisting of a track along which cars are pulled by a moving cable that is operated by a stationary engine

ca·ble re·lease *n* a cable equipped with a control button and attached to a camera in order to take photographs without shaking the camera, e.g., during long exposures

ca·ble-stayed bridge *n* a suspension bridge with the cables that support the deck connected directly to the bridge's piers rather than to suspenders

ca·ble stitch *n* a knitting stitch that produces a pattern resembling twisted rope

ca·blet /káyblət/ *n* a cable-laid rope that has a circumference of less than 10 in./25 cm

ca·ble tel·e·vi·sion, ca·ble·vi·sion /káyb'l vi̲zh'n/, **ca·ble** *n* a television system in which signals are sent to a central antenna and then transmitted by cable to subscribers rather than broadcast

ca·ble·way /káyb'l wày/ *n* a transportation system consisting of an overhead cable from which are suspended cars or containers

cab·o·chon /kábbə shòn/ *n* **1.** a highly polished rounded unfaceted gem **2.** the gem-cutting style that results in a cabochon [Mid-16C. < French, "little head" < Old French *caboche* "head"] —**cab·o·chon** *adj, adv*

Ca·bo·clo /kə bó klòo, -klṓ/, **ca·bo·clo** *n* somebody descended from one or more of the indigenous peoples of Brazil especially a Brazilian [Early 19C. < Brazilian Portuguese]

ca·bom·ba /kə bómbə/ *n* PLANTS same as **fanwort**

ca·boo·dle /kə bóod'l/ [Late 19C. Probably alteration of BOODLE] ◇ **the whole caboodle** all the people or things in question (*slang*)

ca·boose /kə bóoss/ *n* **1.** RAIL LAST TRAIN CAR the last car on a freight train, with eating and sleeping facilities for the train crew. Most freight trains no longer have a caboose. **2.** *Can* BUNKHOUSE a mobile bunkhouse used by lumberjacks **3.** NAUT SHIP'S GALLEY a kitchen on the deck of a boat (*archaic*) **4.** *UK* NAUT GALLEY HOUSING the structure on a boat's deck that houses the galley (*archaic*) [Mid-18C. < Dutch *cabuyse*]

Cab·ot /kábbət/, **George** (1752–1823) US politician. He was a US senator (1791–96) and headed the Hartford Convention (1814).

Cab·ot, John (1450?–99?) Italian explorer. He made the first recorded contact (1497) with North America after the Vikings. Born **Giovanni Caboto**

Cab·ot, Sebastian (1476?–1557) Italian-born English navigator and cartographer. He made expeditions to North and South America (1508–09, 1525–28) for Spain and England and published a world map (1544).

cab·o·tage /kábbə taa̲zh/ *n* **1.** trade, shipping, or navigation that takes place in coastal waters within the boundaries of a single country **2.** the right of a country to operate internal traffic, especially air traffic, using its own carriers and not those of other countries [Mid-19C. < French < *caboter* "coast along" < Spanish *cabo* "cape, headland" < Latin *caput* "head"]

cab·o·teur /kàbbə túr/ *n Can* a coastal trading ship or boat, especially one plying the Gulf of St. Lawrence and the St. Lawrence River. (*dated*) [< French < *caboter* (see CABOTAGE)]

Ca·bral /kə braál/, **Pedro Álvares** (1460?–1526?) Portuguese explorer. He was the first European to visit present-day Bahia, Brazil, and declared it a Portuguese territory.

Ca·bril·lo /kə breélō, kə breé yō/, **Juan Rodríguez** (*d.* 1543) Portuguese-born Spanish explorer. He joined forces with Cortés in Mexico from 1520 and explored the western coast of North America (1542), reaching northern California.

Ca·bri·ni /kə breénee/, **Frances Xavier, St.** (1850–1917) Italian-born US social-welfare worker. She was the first Roman Catholic American saint (1946). Known as **Saint of the Immigrants, Mother Cabrini**

cab·ri·ole /kábbree ōl/ *n* **1.** a curving furniture leg tapering into a decorative foot, popular in the early 18th century **2.** a ballet movement in which the dancer leaps into the air with one leg outstretched sideways and the other beating against it [Late 18C. < French, "leap" < *cabrioler*, variant of *caprioler* "to caper"]

cab·ri·o·let /kàbbree ə láy/ *n* **1.** a two-door convertible automobile **2.** a two-wheeled, two-seater, horse-drawn carriage with a folding roof [Mid-18C. < French < *cabrioler* "to caper"; from the bouncing motion of a horse-drawn vehicle]

cab·stand /káb stànd/ *n* TRANSP same as **taxi stand**

cac- *prefix* same as **caco-** (*used before vowels*)

ca·ca·o /kə kaá ō, -káy ō/ (*plural* **-os** or *same*) *n* **1.** a dried fatty seed. Use: source of cocoa, chocolate, and other foods and products. **2.** a tropical American evergreen tree with fleshy pods containing cacao seeds. Latin name: *Theobroma cacao*. **3.** FOOD same as **cocoa bean 4.** INDUST same as **cocoa butter** [Mid-16C. < Spanish < Nahuatl *cacauatl* "cacao tree"]

ca·ca·o bean *n* FOOD same as **cocoa bean**

ca·ca·o but·ter *n* INDUST same as **cocoa butter**

cac·cia·to·re /kaàchə táwree/ *adj* cooked with mushrooms, tomatoes, and herbs (*usually used after nouns*) ○ *chicken cacciatore* [Mid-20C. < Italian, "hunter"; because originally used of a sauce for game]

Cá·ce·res /kássə ràyss/, **Andres Avelino** (1836–1923?) Peruvian soldier and politician. He was president of Peru (1886–90 and 1894–95).

ca·cha·ca /kə shaássə/ *n* a Brazilian rum made from sugar cane

cach·a·lot /káshə lòt, -lṑ/ *n* MARINE BIOL same as **sperm whale** [Mid-18C. Via French < Spanish or Portuguese *cachalote*]

cache /kash/ *n* **1.** HIDDEN SUPPLY a hidden store of things, especially weapons or valuables **2.** SECRET PLACE FOR HIDING THINGS a secret place where a store of things is kept hidden **3.** COMPUT MEMORY FOR COMPUTER DATA an area of high-speed computer memory used for temporary storage of frequently used data ■ *vt* (**cached, cach·ing, cach·es**) **1.** HIDE SUPPLY OF THINGS to store a hidden supply of things, especially weapons or valuables, in a secret place **2.** COMPUT HOLD DATA IN MEMORY to store data in a cache [Late 18C. < French < *cacher* "press"]

SPELLCHECK cache or **cash**? Do not confuse the spelling of ***cache*** and ***cash***, which sound similar. ***Cache*** can be used as a noun or verb, referring to a secret hidden supply or to an area of computer memory, as in *an arms cache, cached data*. The word ***cash***, which is much more frequent in general usage, can also be used as a noun or verb. As a noun it denotes money in the form of coins and bills (as in *paid in cash*); as a verb it means "exchange for cash" (as in *cash a check*).

ca·chec·tic /kə kéktik/ *adj* affected by or relating to cachexia [Early 17C. < Greek *kakhektikos*, related to *kakhexia* (see CACHEXIA)]

cache mem·o·ry *n* COMPUT same as **cache** (sense 3)

cache·pot /kásh pòt, kásh pō/ *n* a decorative container for a flowerpot [Late 19C. < French, "hide pot"]

ca·chet /ka sháy/ *n* **1.** QUALITY THAT ATTRACTS ADMIRATION a quality of distinction and style that people admire and approve of **2.** OFFICIAL MARK an official seal or stamp on a letter or other document **3.** STAMPS COMMEMORATIVE POSTMARK a commemorative mark stamped on mail to mark an event **4.** STAMPS COLLECTOR'S MARK a small mark made on the back of a postage stamp by a stamp collector **5.** PHARM EDIBLE MEDICINE CAPSULE an edible capsule formerly used for containing unpleasant-tasting medicine [Early 17C. < French, "stamp" < Old French *cacher* "press"]

ca·chex·i·a /kə kéksee ə/ *n* a condition marked by loss of appetite, weight loss, muscular wasting, and general mental and physical debilitation. It is associated with the advanced stage of diseases such as cancer. [Mid-16C. Via French or late Latin < Greek *kakhexia* < *kakos* "bad" + *hexis* "habit"]

cach·in·nate /kákə nàyt/ (**-nat·ed, -nat·ing, -nates**) *vi* to laugh convulsively and loudly (*literary*) [Early 19C. < Latin *cachinnat-*, past participle of *cachinnare*, an imitation of the sound] —**cach·in·na·tion** /kàkə náysh'n/ *n* —**cach·in·na·tor** *n*

ca·chou /ka shóo, ká shoo/ *n* **1.** a perfumed pastille that sweetens the breath **2.** CHEM same as **catechu** [Late 16C. Via French < Malayalam *kaccu*]

ca·chu·cha /kə chóochə/ *n* **1.** a lively Andalusian dance in 3/4 time for a solo dancer with castanets **2.** the music for a cachucha [Mid-19C. < Spanish]

ca·cique /kə séek/ *n* **1.** NATIVE AMERICAN CHIEF in South America during colonial times, a Native American chief **2.** *Hispanic* POLITICAL LEADER especially in Latin America or Spain, a local political boss **3.** TROPICAL AMERICAN SONGBIRD a boldly colored blackbird that feeds on fruit and insects, and nests in colonies. Native to: tropical Central and South America. Genus: *Cacicus*. [Mid-16C. Via Spanish or French < Taino]

cack·le /kák'l/ *v* (**-led, -ling, -les**) **1.** *vi* LAUGH HARSHLY AND SHRILLY to laugh a harsh high-pitched malicious laugh, often suggesting pleasure at others' misfortune **2.** *vt* SAY SOMETHING WITH HARSH SHRILL LAUGH to say something with a malicious high-pitched laugh **3.** *vi* MAKE SQUAWKING NOISE to squawk shrilly, especially after laying an egg (*refers to hens*) ■ *n* MALICIOUS LAUGH a high-pitched malicious laugh or tone of voice [12C. < Middle Low German or Middle Dutch *kākel(e)n*, an imitation of the sound] —**cack·ler** *n*

caco- *prefix* bad ○ *cacology* [< Greek *kakos*]

cac·o·de·mon /kàkə déemən/, **cac·o·dae·mon** *n* a supposed evil spirit [Late 16C. < Greek *kakodaimōn*]

cac·o·dyl /kákə dìl/ *n* a poisonous oily flammable liquid that contains arsenic and has an unpleasant garlicky smell. Formula: $C_4H_{12}As_2$. [Mid-19C. < Greek *kakōdēs* "bad-smelling"] —**cac·o·dyl·ic** /kàkə díllik/ *adj*

ca·cog·ra·phy /kə kóggrəfee/ *n* (*formal*) **1.** poor handwriting **2.** incorrect spelling —**ca·co·graph·ic** /kàkə gráffik/ *adj* —**ca·co·graph·i·cal** *adj*

cac·o·mis·tle /kákə mìss'l/, **cac·o·mix·le** /-mìks'l/ *n* a carnivorous mammal resembling a cat with brown fur and a long black-banded tail. Native to: southwestern United States and Mexico. Latin name: *Bassariscus astutus*. [Mid-19C. Via American Spanish *cacomixtle* < Nahuatl *tlacomiztli* "half mountain lion"]

ca·coph·o·ny /kə kóffənee/ (*plural* **-nies**) *n* **1.** an unpleasant combination of loud, often jarring, sounds **2.** the use of harsh unpleasant sounds in language, e.g., for literary effect [Mid-17C. Via French < Greek *kakophōnia* < *kakophōnos* "bad-sounding"] —**ca·coph·o·nous** *adj*

cactus

cac·tus /káktəss/ (*plural* **-ti** /-tì/ or **-tus·es** or *same*) *n* a spiny leafless plant with fleshy stems and branches and often with brilliantly colored flowers. Native to: dry desert regions of the Americas. Family: Cactaceae. [Mid-18C. Via Latin, "cardoon" < Greek *kaktos*]

cac·tus wren *n* BIRDS a wren, the largest in North America, that makes its nest in the dense part of the cholla cactus. Native to: southwestern United States and northern Mexico. Family: Troglodytidae.

ca·cu·mi·nal /kə kyóomən'l/ *adj* PHON same as **retroflex** (sense 2) [Mid-19C. < Latin *cacuminare* "make pointed" < *cacumen* "point"]

cad /kad/ *n* a man whose conduct, especially toward women, is considered unscrupulous or dishonorable (*dated*) [Mid-19C. Shortening of CADDIE] —**cad·dish** *adj* —**cad·dish·ly** *adv* —**cad·dish·ness** *n*

CAD /kad/ *abbr* computer-aided design

ca·das·tre /kə dástər/, **ca·das·ter** *n* an official register containing information on the value, extent, and ownership of land for the purposes of taxation [Late 18C. Via French < Italian *catastico* < Greek *katastikhon* "list" < *kata stikhon* "line by line"] —**ca·das·tral** *adj*

ca·dav·er /kə dávvər/ *n* a dead body, especially one that is to be dissected [14C. < Latin < *cadere* "to fall"] —**ca·dav·er·ic** *adj*

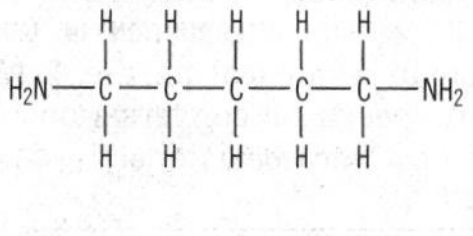

cadaverine

ca·dav·er·ine /kə dávvə rèen/ *n* a thick toxic colorless liquid with an extremely unpleasant smell, produced when flesh rots. Formula: $C_5H_{14}N_2$.

ca·dav·er·ous /kə dávvərəss/ *adj* **1.** EXTREMELY THIN thin to the point of resembling a skeleton or corpse **2.** PALE deathly pale (*literary*) **3.** OF CORPSES suggesting death or corpses (*formal or literary*) —**ca·dav·er·ous·ly** *adv* —**ca·dav·er·ous·ness** *n*

CAD/CAM /kád kàm/ *abbr* computer-aided design and manufacturing

cad·dice *n* TEXTILES another spelling of **caddis**

cad·dice fly *n* INSECTS another spelling of **caddis fly**

cad·dice worm *n* INSECTS another spelling of **caddis worm**

cad·die /káddee/, **cad·dy** *n* (*plural* **-dies**) a golfer's assistant who carries a bag of clubs and performs other duties ■ *vi* (**-died, -dy·ing, -dies**) to act as a caddie for a golfer [Late 18C. Scots form of CADET]

cad·dis /káddiss/, **cad·dice** *n* a coarse woolen fabric, braid, or yarn [Mid-16C. Via French < Provençal]

cad·dis fly, cad·dice fly *n* an insect with four membranous wings, multijointed antennae, and larvae (**caddis worms**) that live in water. Order: Trichoptera.

cad·dis worm, cad·dice worm *n* a larva of a caddis fly. Caddis worms live in water inside a protective silken case that is covered with sand and debris.

Cad·do /káddō/ (*plural same* or **-dos**) *n* a member of a confederacy of Native North Americans in central Oklahoma who formerly lived in the Red River area of Arkansas, Louisiana, and east Texas [Via American French < Caddoan *kaduhdáčču'* in the language of the Caddo people] —**Cad·do** *adj*

Cad·do·an /káddō ən/ *n* a family of Native North American languages spoken by members of the Caddo confederacy, including Pawnee

cad·dy[1] *n, vi* GOLF another spelling of **caddie**

cad·dy[2] /káddee/ (*plural* **-dies**) *n* **1.** a small box or tin used for storing something, especially tea **2.** a plastic or metal case for a CD-ROM [Late 18C. Alteration of *catty* < Malay *kati*, a standard measure for tea]

-cade *suffix* procession ○ *motorcade* [< CAVALCADE]

ca·delle /kə dél/ *n* a small black beetle that feeds on grain and other stored foods. Native to: found worldwide. Latin name: *Tenebroides mauritanicus*. [Mid-19C. Via French < Latin *cadellus* "little dog"]

ca·dence /káyd'nss/, **ca·den·cy** (*plural* **-cies**) *n* **1.** RHYTHM the beat or measure of something such as a dance or a march that follows a set rhythm **2.** FALLING TONE a drop in the pitch of the voice, e.g., at the end of a sentence **3.** INTONATION the rise and fall of the voice during speech **4.** RHYTHM IN LANGUAGE the rhythmic flow of poetry or prose **5.** MUSIC MUSICAL SEQUENCE a short sequence of notes that marks the end of a piece or passage of music. In tonal music, a cadence brings about a harmonic resolution. [14C. Via Old French, "rhythm" < Italian *cadenza* "falling away" < Latin *cadere* "to fall"] —**ca·denced** *adj*

ORIGIN The Latin word *cadere* "to fall," from which **cadence** is derived, is also the source of English *accident, cadaver, cascade, case*[1]*, chance, cheat, coincide, decay, deciduous, incident, occasion*, and *Occident*.

ca·den·tial /kə dénsh'l/ *adj* **1.** relating to rhythm or a rhythmic cadence **2.** relating to cadenzas or a musical cadence

ca·den·za /kə dénzə/ *n* an elaborate solo passage of virtuoso playing or singing near the end of a section or piece of music, sometimes improvised by the soloist [Mid-18C. < Italian (see CADENCE)]

cade oil *n* PHARM same as **juniper tar**

ca·det /kə dét/ *n* **1.** MILITARY TRAINEE a young man or woman who is training to become a full member of the armed forces or the police force, especially a student at a military or naval academy **2.** YOUNG PERSON IN UNIFORMED ORGANIZATION somebody of school age who attends a military school or is a member of a uniformed organization with a military theme **3.** YOUNGER SON a younger son or brother (*dated*) **4.** same as **pimp** (*slang*) [Early 17C. < French, originally Gascon dialect *capdet* "younger son" (because noble Gascon families traditionally sent younger sons into the army) < Latin *caput* "head"] —**ca·det·ship** *n*

Ca·dette /kə dét/ *n* a member of a division of the Girl Scouts of America for girls between 11 and 14 years [Mid-20C. < CADET]

cadge /kaj/ (**cadged, cadg·ing, cadg·es**) *vti* to scrounge or beg something from somebody (*informal*) [Early 17C. Back-formation < CADGER]

cadg·er /kájjər/ *n* somebody who habitually borrows things or requests favors (*informal*) [15C. Origin ?]

ca·di /káadee/, **qa·di** *n* in a Muslim community where Islamic law is followed, a minor judge [Late 16C. < Arabic *ḳāḍī*]

Cad·il·lac /kádd'l àk/ city in Michigan, southeast of Traverse City, situated on Lake Cadillac in a forested region. Population: 10,034 (2002 estimate).

Cad·il·lac, Antoine Laumet de la Mothe, Sieur de (1658–1730) French-born Canadian colonial administrator. He founded present-day Detroit (1701) and served as the governor of Louisiana (1710–17).

Ca·diz /kə díz, káydiz/, **Cá·diz** capital of Cádiz Province and a major port in the autonomous region of Andalusia in southwestern Spain. Population: 136,239 (2002).

cad·mi·um /kádmee əm/ *n* a soft malleable toxic bluish white metallic element. Source: ores of copper and lead. Use: alloys, electroplating, nuclear reactors, dental amalgams, pigments, electronics. Symbol **Cd**. See table at **element** [Early 19C. < Latin *cadmia* "zinc ore" < Greek *kadm(e)ia gē* "earth of Cadmus," because the substance came originally from Thebes]

cad·mi·um sul·fide *n* an orange or yellowish brown poisonous salt. Use: in paints as a pigment, in medicine, in electronic parts. Formula: CdS.

cad·mi·um yel·low *n* a bright yellow pigment that contains cadmium sulfide, or a paint prepared with this pigment

Cad·mus /kádməss/ *n* in Greek mythology, a prince who slew a dragon and planted its teeth in the ground, from which armed men sprouted and began fighting each other. With the five survivors Cadmus founded Thebes.

cad·re /káddree, káa dràỳ/ *n* **1.** MIL MILITARY UNIT a group of experienced professionals at the core of a military organization who are able to train new recruits and expand the operations of the unit **2.** POL **CORE OF ACTIVISTS** a core group of political activists or revolutionaries **3. CORE GROUP** a controlling or representative group at the center of an organization **4. SMALL GROUP OF TEAM-SPIRITED PEOPLE** a tightly knit, highly trained group of people **5. MEMBER OF UNIT** a member of a cadre [Mid-19C. Via French, "frame" < Italian *quadro* "framework" < Latin *quadrum* "square"]

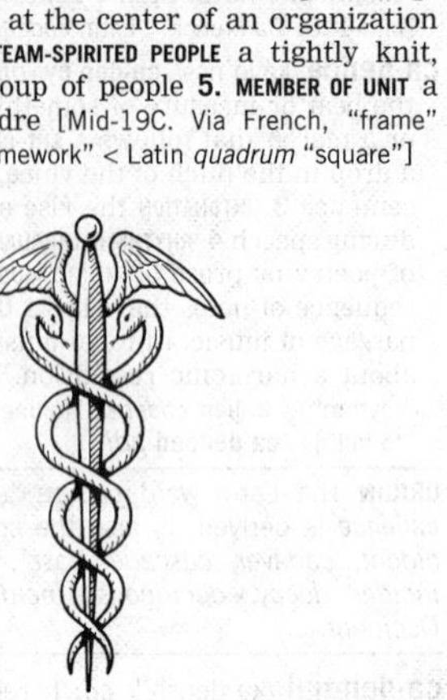

caduceus

ca·du·ce·us /kə do͝ossee əss, kə do͝oshəss/ (*plural* **-i** /kə do͝ossee ī/) *n* **1.** in classical mythology, a winged staff entwined with two serpents, the symbol of Hermes or Mercury and associated with the Greek god of healing, Asclepius **2.** a symbol of the US Army Medical Corps and various other medical organizations that is modeled on Hermes' caduceus [Late 16C. Via Latin < Doric Greek *karuk(e)ion* < *kērux* "herald"] —**ca·du·ce·an** *adj*

ca·du·ci·ty /kə do͝ossətee/ *n* (*literary*) **1.** the weakening or loss of physical or mental powers that sometimes occurs in later life **2.** the quality of being perishable or impermanent [Mid-18C. < French *caducité* < *caduc* "transitory" < Latin *caducus* (see CADUCOUS)]

ca·du·cous /kə do͝okəss/ *adj* describes a plant or animal part that drops off or is shed in the early stages of development, as are some leaves or flower parts [Late 18C. < Latin *caducus* "liable to fall" < *cadere* "to fall"]

CAE *abbr* computer-aided engineering

cae·cil·ian /sə síllyən, sə séllee ən/ *n* a limbless tropical amphibian that looks like an earthworm, has small or no eyes, and burrows in the soil. Order: Gymnophiona. [Late 19C. < modern Latin *Caecilia* < Latin *caecilia* "slowworm"]

cae·cum *n* ANAT another spelling of **cecum**

Caed·mon /kádmən/ (650?–680?) English monk and poet. The hymn on the Creation that he composed and that was written down by Bede is the earliest Christian poem in Old English.

Cae·lum /seéləm/ *n* a constellation of the southern hemisphere [< Latin, "chisel"; from its shape]

Caen /kaaN/ capital of the Calvados Department in the Basse-Normandie Region, in northwestern France. It was the scene of heavy fighting in World War II. Population: 113,987 (1999).

cae·no·gen·e·sis *n* another spelling of **cenogenesis**

Caer·nar·von /kaar naárvən/ walled town on the Menai Strait, in Ceredigion, Wales. Edward II, the first Prince of Wales, was born in Caernarvon Castle. Population: 9,695 (1991). Welsh name **Caernarfon**

caer·phil·ly /kaar fíllee/ *n* a pale crumbly cheese made in Wales [Early 20C. After *Caerphilly*, Wales]

Caer·phil·ly /kaar fíllee/ town in south Wales, best known for the cheese that bears its name. Population: 28,481 (1991).

cae·ru·lo·plas·min *n* PHYSIOL another spelling of **ceruloplasmin**

Cae·sar /seézər/ *n* **1.** the title given to a Roman emperor, especially from the reign of Augustus to that of Hadrian **2.** *also* **cae·sar** somebody, e.g., a ruler or leader, who acts like a dictator [Old English *casere* < Latin *Caesar*, family name of Julius CAESAR]

Cae·sar /seézər/, **Julius** (100–44 B.C.) Roman general who emerged from civil war as dictator of Rome and was assassinated by republican conspirators. Full name **Caesar, Gaius Julius**

> "I came, I saw, I conquered."
> [Julius Caesar. Quoted in *The Twelve Caesars*, Suetonius; A.D. 121?]

Cae·sa·re·a /seèzə reé ə/ ancient seaport on the coast of Samaria, and the Roman capital of Palestine, situated approximately 22 mi./35 km south of present-day Haifa, Israel

cae·sar·e·an *n, adj US* MED another spelling of **cesarean**

Cae·sar·e·an /si záiree ən/, **Cae·sar·i·an** *n Can, UK* an operation to deliver a baby by cutting through the mother's abdominal wall and womb. US term **cesarean**

Cae·sar·e·an sec·tion *n Can, UK* MED same as **Caesarean**

Cae·sar·i·an *n* MED another spelling of **Caesarean**

cae·sar sal·ad *n* a salad made with lettuce, croutons, Parmesan cheese, and anchovies, with an egg-based dressing [After *Caesar* Gardini, Mexican restaurant proprietor]

cae·si·um *n* CHEM another spelling of **cesium**

caes·pi·tose *adj* BOT another spelling of **cespitose**

cae·su·ra /si zo͝orə, si zho͝orə/ (*plural* **-ras** or **-rae** /-ree/), **ce·su·ra** (*plural* **-ras** or **-rae**) *n* **1.** LITERAT **PAUSE IN LINE OF VERSE** a pause in a line of poetry, especially to allow its sense to be made clear or to follow the rhythms of natural speech, often near the middle of the line **2.** LITERAT **BREAK IN LINE OF VERSE** in classical poetry, a break between two words that are part of the same unit of rhythm (**foot**), usually near the middle of the line **3.** MUSIC **INTERRUPTION IN MUSIC** a brief interruption in a musical phrase **4. PAUSE** a pause or break in speech or conversation (*formal*) [Mid-16C. < Latin, "cut" < *caedere* "to cut"] —**cae·su·ral** *adj* —**cae·su·ric** *adj*

ORIGIN The Latin word *caedere*, "to cut," from which ***caesura*** is derived, is also the source of English *chisel, concise, decide, excise*[2], *incise, precise*, and *scissors*.

ca·fé /ka fáy, kə fáy/ *n* a small informal restaurant serving drinks, snacks, and often light meals [Early 19C. Via French, "(place serving) coffee" < Turkish *kahveh* "coffee" or Arabic *qahwah* "coffee, wine"]

CAFE /ká fày/ *n* a federally mandated average fuel-consumption rate for the vehicles produced by a manufacturer. Full form **corporate average fuel economy**

ca·fé au lait /ka fày ō láy/ (*plural* **ca·fé au laits** /-ō láyz/ or **ca·fés au lait** /ka fày-/) *n* **1.** coffee with hot milk **2.** a pale brown color, like that of milky coffee [Mid-18C. < French, "coffee with milk"] —**ca·fé au lait** *adj*

ca·fé lat·te *n* BEVERAGES same as **latte**

ca·fé noir /ka fày nwaár/ (*plural* **ca·fés noirs** /*pronunc. same*/) *n* coffee without milk or cream [< French, "black coffee"]

ca·fé so·ci·e·ty *n* celebrities and media people who attend fashionable events and visit fashionable restaurants, clubs, and resorts

caf·e·te·ri·a /kàffə teéree ə/ *n* a self-service restaurant or coffee shop, especially one in a workplace or school [Mid-19C. < American Spanish < *café* "coffee"]

caf·e·te·ri·a ben·e·fit *n* an employee benefit, e.g., health insurance coverage, that is selected from a range of choices designed to meet different needs

caf·e·te·ri·a-style *adj* allowing people to choose from a variety of different things

ca·fe·tière /kàffə tyáir, -teér/ *n UK* same as **French press** [Mid-19C. < French < *café* (see CAFÉ)]

caf·e·to·ri·um /kàffə táwree əm/ (*plural* **-ri·ums** or **-ri·a** /-ree ə/) *n* a large room, usually in school, that doubles as a cafeteria and an auditorium [Mid-20C. Blend of CAFETERIA + AUDITORIUM]

caf·fein FOOD INDUST, PHARM another spelling of **caffeine**

caf·fein·at·ed /káffə nàytəd/ *adj* containing caffeine

caf·feine /ka feén, ká feèn/, **caf·fein** *n* a stimulant found in coffee, tea, and cola nuts. Use: in soft drinks, medicine, and painkillers. [Mid-19C. < French, < *café* "coffee"]

caf·fein·ism /káffi nìzzəm, káffee ə nìzzəm/ *n* a condition caused by an excessive amount of caffeine in the body, resulting in symptoms of high blood pressure, diarrhea, palpitations, accelerated breathing, and insomnia

caf·fe lat·te /ka fày laá tay/, **caf·fè lat·te** *n* BEVERAGES same as **latte**

~~**caffiene**~~ incorrect spelling of **caffeine**

caf·tan /káf tàn, káftən, kaf tán/, **kaf·tan** *n* **1.** a full-length tunic or robe for men, usually made of rich fabric, worn chiefly in eastern Mediterranean countries **2.** a western imitation of the caftan, often brightly colored and worn by men and women. It was popular in the 1970s and is still associated with hippy culture. [Late 16C. Via Turkish < Persian *kaftān*]

cage /kayj/ *n* **1. METAL ENCLOSURE FOR ANIMAL** an enclosure, usually made from bars or wire, in which to keep animals or birds **2. ENCLOSING OR PROTECTING WIRE-MESH STRUCTURE** a wire-mesh structure used to protect or enclose something **3. ELEVATOR PLATFORM** the part of an elevator that people stand in, particularly an elevator in a mine shaft **4.** BASEBALL **SCREEN TO STOP BALLS** in baseball, a screen behind home plate that stops thrown or fouled balls **5.** BASKETBALL **BASKET** in basketball, the basket (*informal*) **6.** HOCKEY **HOCKEY GOAL** the goal in ice hockey (*informal*) **7. TEMPORARY PRISON CELL** a barred room or strong mesh enclosure for confining prisoners temporarily, e.g., in a police station ■ *vt* (**caged, cag·ing, cag·es**) **1. PUT PERSON OR ANIMAL IN CAGE** to place or keep a person or animal in a cage **2. PUT IN CONFINING CONDITIONS** to confine a person or animal in conditions resembling those of a cage [12C. Via Old French < Latin *cavea* "enclosure, dungeon"] —**caged** *adj* ◇ **rattle somebody's cage** to annoy or upset somebody deliberately ○ *"We kept after him and kept after him and finally rattled his cage a little bit, he said." (Cincinnati Post; 1997)*

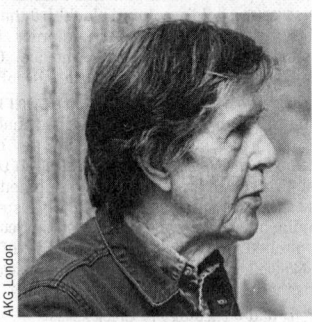

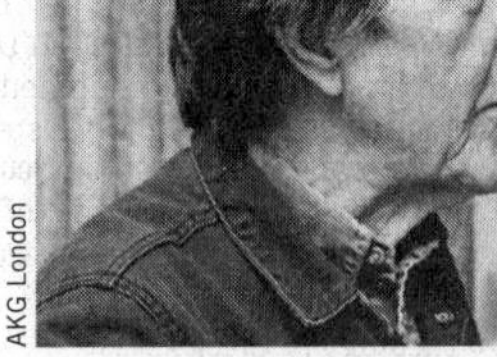

AKG London

John Cage

Cage /kayj/, **John** (1912–92) US composer. His avant-garde music includes *4'33"* (1952), in which musicians sit silently with their instruments. Full name **Cage, John Milton, Jr**

> "Composing's one thing, performing's another, listening's a third. What can they have to do with one another?"
> [John Cage, *Silence*; 1961]

Cage, Nicholas (*b.* 1964) US actor. He frequently plays offbeat movie characters, as in his Academy Award-winning performance in *Leaving Las Vegas* (1995).

cage·bird /káyj bùrd/ *n* a bird that is often kept as a pet in a cage, e.g., a parakeet or parrot

cage·ling /káyjling/ *n* a bird that is being kept as a pet in a cage (*archaic or literary*)

ca·gey /káyjee/ (**-gi·er, -gi·est**), **ca·gy** *adj* secretive and refusing to be open, frank, or direct (*informal*) [Late 19C. Origin ?] —**ca·gi·ly** *adv* —**ca·gi·ness** *n*

SYNONYMS See ***cautious***.

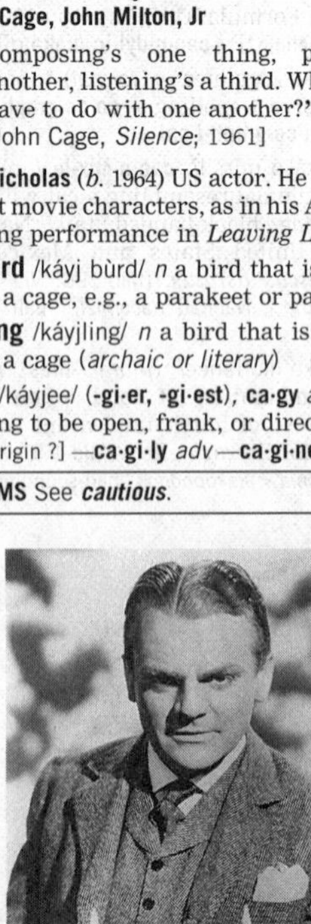

James Cagney

Cag·ney /kágnee/, **James** (1899–1986) US movie actor, known for both comic and tough gangster roles. Full name **Cagney, James Francis**. See illustration on previous page

> "I went into show business strictly from hunger. Starvation helps to turn you into a good actor, I guess."
> [James Cagney. Quoted in *Film-makers Speak*, Jay Leyda (ed.); 1977]

Ca·guas /kaá gwaáss/ city in eastern Puerto Rico, south of San Juan and southeast of Bayamon. Population: 92,429 (1990).

ca·gy *adj* another spelling of **cagey**

ca·hier /kaa yáy/ *n* a written report of a meeting, e.g., of a parliamentary group (*formal*) [Late 18C. Via French < Latin *quaternis* "set of four" < *quattuor* "four"; because originally a pamphlet made from four folded sheets of paper]

Ca·ho·ki·a Mounds /kə hṑkee ə-/ group of prehistoric Native American mounds, including the largest prehistoric earthwork in the United States, situated 8 mi./13 km northeast of East Saint Louis, Illinois

ca·hoots /kə hoóts/ [Early 19C. Origin ?] ◇ **in cahoots (with somebody)** collaborating with somebody, especially with the intention of conspiring against somebody else (*informal*)

ca·how /kə hów/ *n* a brown-and-white endangered petrel that burrows into the ground. Native to: Bermuda. Latin name: *Pterodroma cahow*. [Early 17C. An imitation of its call]

Ca·huil·la /kə weé ə/ (*plural same* or **-las**) *n* **1.** a member of a Native North American people who live in the Sonoran and Mojave desert regions of southern California **2.** the language of the Cahuilla, belonging to the Shoshone group of Uto-Aztecan languages, now spoken by very few people [Mid-19C. < Cahuilla, "masters"]

CAI *abbr* computer-aided instruction

Cai·a·phas /káy əfəss, kī́-/ (*fl* A.D. 18–37) Jewish high priest. According to the Bible, he presided over the trial of Jesus Christ.

Cai·cos Is·lands ➧ **Turks and Caicos Islands**

cai·man /káymən/ (*plural* **-mans** or *same*), **cay·man** *n* a reptile related to the alligator but smaller and slimmer and with a proportionally longer tail. Native to: tropical America. Genus: *Caiman*. [Late 16C. Via Spanish < Carib *caymán*]

Cain /kayn/ *n* in the Bible, the elder son of Adam and Eve, who killed his brother Abel (Genesis 4) ◇ **raise Cain** to cause a noisy disturbance (*informal*)

Caine /kayn/, **Michael** (*b.* 1933) British actor. His films include *Zulu* (1963) and *Hannah and her Sisters* (1986), for which he won an Academy Award. Born **Micklewhite, Maurice Joseph**

-caine *suffix* a synthetic alkaloid anesthetic ○ *phenacaine* [< COCAINE]

cai·pi·rin·ha /kī pi reényə/ *n* a Brazilian cocktail consisting of cachaca, sugar, crushed lime, and ice

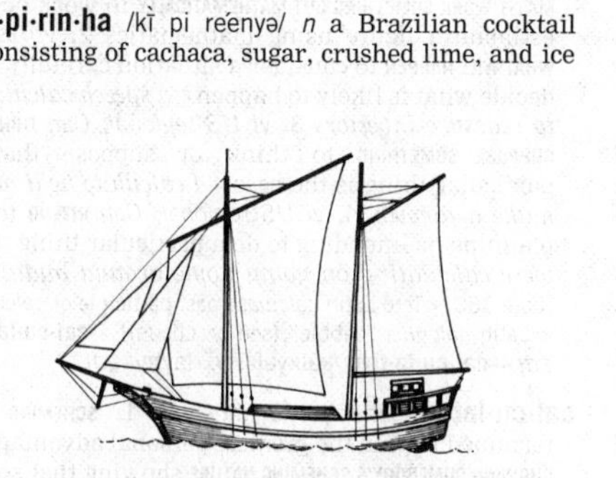

caïque

ca·ïque /kaa eék, kīk/ *n* **1.** a small sailboat or motorboat used in the Greek Islands and the eastern Mediterranean **2.** a long narrow rowboat used in the waters around Turkey [Early 17C. Via French < Turkish *kayik*]

cairn /kern/ *n* **1.** a pile of stones set on a hill or mountain to mark a spot for walkers and climbers, or as a memorial to somebody who died there **2.** BREED same as **Cairn** [Mid-16C. < Gaelic *carn* "heap of stones"] —**cairned** *adj*

Cairn /kern/, **Cairn ter·ri·er** *n* a small terrier with a shaggy coat of rough hair, belonging to a breed originally developed in Scotland

cairn·gorm /kérn gàwrm/, **cairn·gorm stone** *n* a smoky yellow, gray, or brown form of quartz, found in Scotland. Use: jewelry. [Late 18C. After the CAIRNGORM MOUNTAINS]

Cairn·gorm Moun·tains /kérn gawrm-/, **Cairn·gorms** /kérn gàwrmz/ range of the Grampian Mountains in northeastern Scotland. Its highest peak is Ben Macdhui, 4,296 ft./1,309 m.

Cairn·gorm stone *n* MINERALS same as **cairngorm**

Cairns /kernz/ coastal city in northeastern Queensland, Australia. It is the main gateway to the northern Great Barrier Reef and a major tourist resort. Population: 119,256 (2002 estimate).

Cairn ter·ri·er *n* BREED same as **Cairn**

Cai·ro /kīrō/ capital of Egypt and Africa's largest city. It is situated on the Nile River, at the southern end of the Nile delta. Population: 6,789,000 (1998).

cais·son /káy sòn, kάyss'n/ *n* **1.** CONSTR **UNDERWATER WORK CHAMBER** a bottomless watertight chamber filled with compressed air, used as a base from which construction work is carried out underwater **2.** NAUT **FLOAT TO RAISE SHIPS** a hollow structure attached to a sunken object such as a wrecked ship, then pumped full of air until it acts as a float, raising the object to the surface **3.** CIV ENG, NAUT **WATER BLOCK** a floating watertight structure used to keep water from entering a dry dock, canal lock, or basin **4.** ARMS **AMMUNITION BOX** a large container for ammunition **5.** MIL **HORSE-DRAWN VEHICLE** a two-wheeled horse-drawn vehicle, formerly used to carry ammunition but now often used to carry coffins at state or military funerals **6.** ARCHIT same as **coffer** (sense 2) [Late 17C. Via French < Italian *cassone* "large box" < *cassa* "box" < Latin *capsa*]

cais·son dis·ease *n* MED same as **decompression sickness**

cai·tiff /káytif/ *n* same as **coward** (*archaic*) [13C. Via Old French *caitif* "captive, wretched person" < Latin *captivus* < *capere* "take"] —**cai·tiff** *adj*

Cait·ra /káytrə/ *n* in the Hindu calendar, the first month of the year, lasting 30 or 31 days and falling about the same time as March to April. See table at **calendar**

ca·je·put /kájjə poót/ *n* **1.** a pungent medicinal oil **2.** a small flowering tree or bush naturalized in Florida that yields cajeput. Native to: South and Southeast Asia, Australia. Latin name: *Melaleuca leucadendron*. [Late 18C. < Malay *kayuputih* "white tree"]

ca·jole /kə jṓl/ (**-joled, -jol·ing, -joles**) *vti* to persuade somebody to do something by flattery or gentle but persistent argument [Mid-17C. < French *cajoler*] —**ca·jol·er** *n* —**ca·jol·er·y** *n*

Ca·jun /káyjən/ *n* **1.** somebody from Louisiana who is descended from French colonists exiled in the 18th century from Acadia in present-day Canada **2.** a dialect of French spoken in Louisiana that developed from the French spoken by 18th-century settlers who were expelled from Acadia, Canada [Mid-19C. Alteration of *Acadian* "(inhabitant) of Acadia"] —**Ca·jun** *adj*

cake /kayk/ *n* **1.** **BAKED SWEET FLOUR-BASED FOOD** a baked sweet food usually made from flour, fat, sugar, eggs, and other ingredients **2.** **SHAPED PORTION OF GROUND OR CHOPPED FOOD** an individual portion of ground or chopped food, shaped into a flat round piece and cooked, often by frying or broiling ○ *potato cakes* **3.** **BLOCK OF SOMETHING** a solid block of something, e.g., soap, ice, or chocolate **4.** **THICK LAYER** a thick layer of something that has collected over a period of time **5.** **SOMETHING DIVIDED UP** something that is to be shared or divided up, e.g., an amount of money ○ *Everyone wants a slice of the cake.* ■ *v* (**caked, cak·ing, cakes**) **1.** *vti* **FORM CRUST ON SOMETHING** to form, or cover something with, a thick layer of a substance such as dirt, grease, or grime ○ *My boots were caked with mud after I walked through the field.* **2.** *vi* **FORM INTO CAKE** to form into a solid mass ■ *n* **TABOO TERM** a highly offensive term for a woman's genitals (*taboo*) [12C. < Old Norse *kaka* "flat round loaf"] —**cak·ey** *adj* ◇ **have your cake and eat it (too)** to try to enjoy the advantages of two things, each of which tends to make the other impossible ◇ **take the cake** (*informal*) **1.** to be even worse than all the other bad or annoying things that went before **2.** to be outstandingly good or successful

cake mix *n* dried ingredients that can be used to make a cake, sold in a box or package

cake slice *n* a kitchen utensil with a flat triangular blade, used for serving slices of cake

cake·walk /káyk wàwk/ *n* **1.** **SOMETHING VERY EASY** something that is very easy to do (*informal*) **2.** **COMPETITION BASED ON WALKING** an informal contest to music, with a cake as a prize for executing the most elaborate or amusing walking steps, popular among African Americans in the 19th century **3.** DANCE **STRUTTING DANCE** a popular dance with elaborate or strutting steps **4.** MUSIC **MUSIC** the music for a cakewalk —**cake·walk** *vi* —**cake·walk·er** *n*

CAL[1] *abbr* **1.** CALENDAR calendar **2.** MEASURE caliber

CAL[2] /kal/ *abbr* COMPUT computer-assisted learning

Cal. *abbr* California

Cal·a·bar bean /kállə baar-/ *n* the dark brown poisonous seed of a tropical climbing plant. Use: source of drug physostigmine. Native to: Africa. Latin name: *Physostigma venenosum*. [After *Calabar*, Nigeria]

cal·a·bash /kállə bàsh/ *n* **1.** **FRUIT OR GOURD** a large ball-shaped fruit of a tropical American tree, or of the bottle gourd or some other gourd **2.** **CONTAINER** the hollowed-out dried shell of a calabash, bottle gourd, or other gourd **3.** **TROPICAL AMERICAN EVERGREEN TREE** a tropical evergreen tree that bears calabashes. Flowers: bell-shaped. Native to: tropical America. Latin name: *Crescentia cujete*. **4.** PLANTS same as **bottle gourd** [Mid-17C. Via French *calabasse* < Persian *karbuz* "melon"]

Cal·a·bash /kállə bàsh/ *n* a way of preparing food in the southeastern United States that involves deep-frying seafood and piling it up on serving plates [After a town in N Carolina]

cal·a·boose /kállə boóss/ *n* *Southwest US* same as **jail** *n* (sense 1) (*archaic or humorous*) [Late 18C. Via Louisiana French *calabouse* < Spanish *calabozo* "dungeon" < assumed Vulgar Latin *cala* "protected place" + Latin *fodere* "dig"]

REGIONAL NOTE ***Calaboose*** in the sense of "jail" was commonly used across the South and West of the United States, with a few instances in the Northeast.

cal·a·bre·se /kàllə bráyzee/ *n* a variety of green broccoli [Mid-20C. < Italian, "of Calabria"]

Ca·la·bri·a /kə láybree ə, kə laábree ə/ region in southern Italy forming the "toe" of the Italian peninsula. It includes the provinces of Cataranzo, Cosenza, and Reggio di Calabria. Capital: Catanzaro. Population: 2,050,478 (2000). Area: 5,822 sq. mi./15,080 sq. km.

ca·la·di·um /kə láydee əm/ *n* a tropical plant with white, green, red, or pink variegated leaves, widely grown as a houseplant. Native to: Americas. Genus: *Caladium*. [Mid-19C. < modern Latin, < Malay *keladi*]

Ca·lais /ka láy, kállay/ seaport on the English Channel in the Pas-de-Calais Department, Nord-Pas-de-Calais Region, in northwestern France. The Calais-Dover route is the shortest crossing between France and the United Kingdom. Population: 77,333 (1999).

cal·a·lu /kállə loó/ (*plural* **-lus**), **ca·la·loo** (*plural* **-loos**), **cal·la·loo** *n Carib* **1.** **CARIBBEAN GREENS** the leaves of various plants when used as salad, in soups, or cooked as greens **2.** **SOUP** a thick soup made of calalu with okra, green bell peppers, coconut milk, onions, herbs, and crab **3.** **MIXTURE** a complex mixture or confusion [Mid-18C. < American Spanish *calalú*]

cal·a·man·co /kàllə mángkō/ *n* a glossy woolen fabric with a checked pattern on one side [Late 16C. Origin ?]

cal·a·man·der /kállə màndər/ *n* the hard black-and-brown striped wood of a number of Asian trees. Use: furniture-making. [Early 19C < Sinhalese *kalumādirriya*]

ca·la·ma·ri /kaàlə maáree, kàllə-/ *npl* squid served as food, especially in Mediterranean cuisine [Late 20C. < Italian, plural of *calamaro* "squid" < medieval Latin *calamarium* "pen-case" (from the shape of the squid's internal shell) < Latin *calamus* (see CALAMUS)]

cal·a·mi BIOL plural of **calamus**

cal·a·mine /kállə mīn, -min/ *n* **1.** a pink zinc oxide and ferric oxide powder. Use: in lotions and creams to soothe irritated skin. **2.** MINERALS same as

smithsonite [Late 16C. Via Old French < medieval Latin *calamina*, alteration of Latin *cadmia* "zinc ore" (see CADMIUM)]

cal·a·mint /kállə mìnt/ (*plural* **-mints** or *same*) *n* a plant of the mint family. Flowers: drooping, white, pink, or purple. Genera: *Satureja* or *Calamintha*. [14C. Via Old French *calament* < Greek *kalaminthē*]

cal·a·mite /kállə mīt/ *n* a plant that grew in the Paleozoic era, related to the horsetail. Genus: *Calamites*. [Mid-19C. < modern Latin *calamites* < Latin *calamus* (see CALAMUS)]

ca·lam·i·tous /kə lámmitəss/ *adj* causing great trouble, tragedy, or disaster [Mid-16C. Directly or via French < Latin *calamitosus* < *calamitas* "disaster"] —**ca·lam·i·tous·ly** *adv*

ca·lam·i·ty /kə lámmətee/ (*plural* **-ties**) *n* **1.** a disastrous situation or event **2.** misery or distress resulting from a disastrous event (*archaic*) [14C. Via French < Latin *calamitas* "disaster"]

Library of Congress

Calamity Jane

Ca·lam·i·ty Jane /kə làmmətee jáyn/ (1852?–1903) US frontierswoman. She worked as a scout in the American West. Born **Canary, Martha Jane**. Real name **Burke** or **Burk, Martha Jane**

cal·a·mon·din /kàllə móndin/ *n* **1.** the small tart orange-yellow fruit of a hybrid citrus tree **2.** a hybrid citrus tree that bears calamondins. Native to: Philippines. Latin name: *Citrofortunella mitis*. [Early 20C. < Tagalog *kalamundíng*]

cal·a·mus /kálləməss/ (*plural* **-mi** /-mī/) *n* **1.** ASIAN PALM a tropical Asian palm tree. Use: rattan. Genus: *Calamus*. **2.** ROOT OF SWEET FLAG the aromatic root of the sweet flag plant. Use: source of an oil used in perfumery. **3.** PLANTS same as **sweet flag 4.** FEATHER SHAFT the hollow shaft of a feather [14C. Via Latin < Greek *kalamos* "reed, pen"]

ca·lan·do /kə laándō/ *adv, adj* played with gradually decreasing volume and slowing tempo (*used as a musical direction*) [Early 19C. < Italian, "slackening"]

ca·lan·dri·a /kə lándree ə/ *n* the cylindrical core of a nuclear reactor with vertical holes [Early 20C. < Spanish < Greek *kulindros* "cylinder"]

cal·a·the·a /kàllə theé ə/ *n* a tropical evergreen plant with showy variegated leaves, widely grown as a greenhouse plant and houseplant. Native to: South America. Genus: *Calathea*. [< modern Latin, < Greek *kalathos* "basket"]

cal·a·ver·ite /kàllə vér īt/ *n* a silvery white or yellowish mineral that contains gold [Mid-19C. After *Calaveras* County, California]

calc. *abbr* MATH **1.** calculation **2.** calculus

calc- *prefix* same as **calci-**

cal·ca·ne·us /kal káynee əss/ (*plural* **-i** /-ī/) *n* ANAT same as **heel bone** (*technical*) [Mid-18C. < late Latin, "heel" < Latin *calc-*] —**cal·ca·ne·al** *adj*

cal·car[1] /kál kaàr/ (*plural* **-car·i·a** /-kérree ə/) *n* a spur on a plant or animal part, e.g., on a bird's leg or at the base of a petal [Early 19C. < Latin, "spur" < *calc-* "heel"]

cal·car[2] /kál kaàr/ *n* a furnace formerly used in glass-making for burning materials to make (**frit**), the viscous substance from which glass is subsequently made [Mid-17C. < Italian *calcara*]

cal·car·e·ous /kal kérree əss/ *adj* **1.** containing or characteristic of calcium carbonate **2.** growing on limestone or in earth containing limestone ○ *calcareous algae* [Late 17C. < Latin *calcarius* "of lime" < *calc-* "lime"] —**cal·car·e·ous·ly** *adv*

cal·car·i·a BIOL plural of **calcar**[1]

cal·car·if·er·ous /kàlkə ríffərəss/ *adj* describes a plant or animal part that has a spur on it [Mid-19C. < Latin *calcar* (see CALCAR[1])]

cal·ce·o·lar·i·a /kàlssee ə lérree ə/ *n* a small plant, often grown as a houseplant. Flowers: speckled, slipper-shaped. Native to: tropical America. Genus: *Calceolaria*. [Late 18C. < modern Latin, < Latin *calceolus* "little shoe"]

cal·ces ANAT plural of **calx**

Cal·chas /kál kàss/ *n* in Greek mythology, a soothsayer who accompanied the Greeks during the Trojan War, advising them, among other things, to build the Trojan Horse

calci- *prefix* calcium, calcium salt, lime ○ *calcific* [< Latin *calc-*, stem of *calx* (see CALX)]

cal·cic /kálssik/ *adj* relating to, containing, or derived from calcium or lime

cal·cif·er·ol /kal síffə rōl, -ròl/ *n* BIOCHEM same as **vitamin** D_2 [Mid-20C. < CALCIFEROUS]

cal·cif·er·ous /kal síffərəss/ *adj* producing or containing calcium carbonate or other calcium salts

cal·cif·ic /kal síffik/ *adj* producing lime salts, or involved in their production

cal·ci·fuge /kálssə fyoōj/ *n* a plant that is best suited for growth in an acidic soil —**cal·cif·u·gal** /kal síffyəg'l/ *adj* —**cal·cif·u·gous** *adj*

cal·ci·fy /kálssə fī/ (**-fied, -fy·ing, -fies**) *vti* **1.** CHEM TURN INTO LIME to convert a substance into lime, or be converted into lime **2.** MED TURN HARD WITH CALCIUM to become, or cause a body part to become, hard or stiff as a result of the deposit of calcium salts **3.** BECOME OR MAKE RIGID AND UNCHANGING to become, or cause something to become, rigid and unchanging (*formal*) —**cal·ci·fi·ca·tion** /kàlssəfi káysh'n/ *n*

cal·ci·mine /kálssə mīn/ *n* a mixture of zinc oxide, water, and glue, sometimes with a coloring added, brushed onto interior walls as a decorative and sealing finish ■ *vt* (**-mined, -min·ing, -mines**) to cover a wall with calcimine [Mid-19C. Origin ?]

cal·cine /kal sīn, kál sīn/ (**-cined, -cin·ing, -cines**) *vti* to heat a solid to a high temperature, converting it to a powdery residue by drying, decomposing, or oxidizing it, or to undergo this process [14C. < medieval Latin *calcinare* "burn until like lime" < Latin *calc-* (see CALCIUM)] —**cal·ci·na·tion** /kàlssə náysh'n/ *n*

cal·ci·no·sis /kàlssə nṓssiss/ *n* a medical condition in which nodules of calcium are deposited in soft body tissues

cal·cite /kál sīt/ *n* a colorless or white crystalline mineral that is a form of calcium carbonate. Source: limestone, marble, chalk. Use: cement, plaster, glass, paints. Formula: $CaCO_3$. —**cal·cit·ic** /kal síttik/ *adj*

cal·ci·to·nin /kàlssi tṓnin/ *n* a hormone, produced by the thyroid and parathyroid glands, that increases the deposition of calcium in bones

cal·cit·ri·ol /kálsə treé òl/ *n* a form of Vitamin D. Use: to control or reverse bone loss. [Late 20C. Probably < CALCIUM + TRIOL]

cal·ci·um /kálssee əm/ *n* a soft silvery white element that is an alkaline earth metal constituting about three percent of the Earth's crust. It is essential to the formation of bones and teeth. Symbol **Ca**. See table at **element** [Early 19C. < Latin *calc-*, stem of *calx* (see CALX)]

cal·ci·um a·cet·y·lide *n* CHEM same as **calcium carbide**

cal·ci·um an·tag·o·nist *n* a drug that dilates the arteries and slows the heart. Use: treatment of angina.

cal·ci·um car·bide *n* a colorless or grayish black powdery compound. Use: generation of acetylene gas. Formula: CaC_2.

cal·ci·um car·bon·ate *n* a white crystalline solid that is one of the most common natural substances. Source: chalk, limestone, marble, animal shells, bones. Use: antacids, paint, cement, toothpaste. Formula: $CaCO_3$.

cal·ci·um chlo·ride *n* a white salt that absorbs moisture easily and quickly. Use: drying gases, deicing roads, in pulp and paper treatment. Formula: $CaCl_2$.

cal·ci·um cy·an·am·ide *n* a white or grayish black crystalline compound that releases ammonia slowly in the presence of water. Use: fertilizers. Formula: $CaCN_2$.

cal·ci·um cy·a·nide *n* a white or grayish black powder that decomposes in humid conditions to produce hydrogen cyanide. Use: formerly, insecticide, rodent poison, in fumigation. Formula: $Ca(CN)_2$.

cal·ci·um cy·cla·mate *n* a sweet-tasting salt of cyclamic acid. Use: formerly, sugar substitute. Formula: $Ca(C_6H_{11}NHSO_3)_2.2H_2O$.

cal·ci·um fluo·ride *n* a colorless or white substance occurring naturally as fluorite. Formula: CaF_2.

cal·ci·um glu·co·nate *n* a calcium salt. Use: mineral supplement, treatment of calcium deficiency and osteoporosis. Formula: $CaC_{12}H_{22}O_{14}$.

cal·ci·um hy·drox·ide *n* a white alkaline powder. Source: action of water on calcium oxide. Use: manufacture of cement, plaster, and glass. Formula: $Ca(OH)_2$.

cal·ci·um hy·po·chlo·rite *n* a white crystalline solid, soluble in water, that is a stable chlorine carrier. Use: bleaching agent, disinfectant, bactericide. Formula: $Ca(OCl)_2$.

cal·ci·um ni·trate *n* a white solid that absorbs moisture very quickly and is a strong oxidizer. Use: fertilizer, explosives. Formula: $Ca(NO_3)_2.4H_2O$.

cal·ci·um ox·ide *n* a white crystalline powder. Use: manufacture of steel and glass, refining of aluminum, copper, and zinc, treatment of sewage. Formula: CaO.

cal·ci·um phos·phate *n* a phosphate of calcium, existing in different forms. Source: rocks, animal bones. Use: as fertilizer in the form of bone ash.

cal·ci·um sul·fate *n* a white odorless crystal or powder. Source: anhydrite, gypsum. Use: drying agent, building material. Formula: $CaSO_4$.

cal·crete /kál kreet/ *n* an accumulation in the soil of a layer of calcium carbonate and other alkaline minerals just below the surface [Early 20C. Blend of CALC- + CONCRETE]

calc·spar /kálk spaàr/ *n* MINERALS same as **calcite** [Early 19C. <CALC- + SPAR[3]]

calc-tu·fa /kálk toōfə, kálk tyoōfə/ *n* MINERALS same as **tufa**

cal·cu·la·ble /kálkyələb'l/ *adj* **1.** able to be worked out or estimated using mathematics **2.** likely to behave in the way that is expected —**cal·cu·la·bil·i·ty** /kàlkyələ bíllətee/ *n*

cal·cu·late /kálkyə làyt/ (**-lat·ed, -lat·ing, -lates**) *v* **1.** *vti* MATH WORK SOMETHING OUT MATHEMATICALLY to work out or estimate a figure using mathematics **2.** *vti* DECIDE WHAT WILL HAPPEN to consider a situation carefully and decide what is likely to happen ○ *a speech calculated to reassure investors* **3.** *vt US regional, Can* THINK OR SUPPOSE SOMETHING to think or suppose that a particular thing is the case ○ *I calculate he'll never make a farmer.* **4.** *vi US regional, Can* INTEND to be planning or intending to do a particular thing ○ *We were calculating on going home around midnight.* [Late 16C. < late Latin *calculat-*, past participle of *calculare* < Latin *calculus* "pebble" (see CALCULUS)] —**cal·cu·lat·ed** *adj* —**cal·cu·la·tive** /kálkyələtiv, -làytiv/ *adj*

cal·cu·lat·ing /kálkyə làyting/ *adj* **1.** SCHEMING determined to gain the greatest personal advantage **2.** SHOWING SOMEBODY'S SCHEMING NATURE showing that somebody is determined to gain the greatest personal advantage **3.** PLANNING CAREFULLY making careful assessments before acting ○ *a calculating candidate who carefully preplanned all statements to the media* —**cal·cu·lat·ing·ly** *adv*

cal·cu·la·tion /kàlkyə láysh'n/ *n* **1.** MATH PROCESS OF CALCULATING SOMETHING the process of working out the answer to a mathematical problem, or a step in this process **2.** ESTIMATE an estimate or answer obtained by calculating **3.** SCHEMING consideration of something, especially when thinking of personal advantage —**cal·cu·la·tion·al** *adj*

calculator

cal·cu·la·tor /kálkyə làytər/ *n* a device used to compute arithmetic operations, especially a small hand-held electronic device

cal·cu·lous /kálkyələss/ *adj* relating to hard formations of minerals (**calculi**) in the body

cal·cu·lus /kálkyələss/ (*plural* **-li** /-lī/ or **-lus·es**) *n* **1.** MATH **BRANCH OF MATHEMATICS** a branch of mathematics dealing with the way that relations between some sets (**functions**) are affected by very small changes in one of their variables (**independent variables**) as they approach zero. It is used to find slopes of curves, rates of change, and volumes of curved figures. **2.** MATH, LOGIC **METHOD OF CALCULATION** a method or system of calculation using symbols or symbolic logic **3.** MED **STONE** a stone or concretion, especially one in the kidney, gallbladder, or urinary bladder (*technical*) **4.** DENT same as **tartar** (sense 1) **5. NONMATHEMATICAL DECISION-MAKING CRITERIA** a nonmathematical evaluation, estimation, or computation, e.g., in short- or long-term decision making or strategy formulation ○ *"Democrats win points in this calculus."* (*US News World Report*; 1998) [Mid-17C. < Latin, "pebble," diminutive of *calx* (see CALX)]

Cal·cut·ta /kal kúttə/ former name for **Kolkata**

cal·da·ri·um /kal dérree əm/ (*plural* **-ri·a** /-ree ə/) *n* the hot room in an ancient Roman bathhouse [Mid-18C. < Latin, < *calere* "be warm"]

AKG London

Alexander Young Calder

Cal·der /káwldər/, **Alexander** (1898–1976) US painter and sculptor, known for his abstract sculptures, especially mobiles and stabiles

> "The sense of motion in painting has long been considered one of the primary elements of composition...Just as one can compose colors, or forms, so I can compose motions."
> [Alexander Calder, "Alexander Calder: Cosmic Imagery and the use of Scientific Instruments," *October Arts*, Joan M. Marter; 1978]

cal·de·ra /kal dérrə/ (*plural* **-ras**) *n* a large crater in a volcano, caused by a major eruption followed by the collapse of the volcanic pipe walls that form the volcano's cone. It may later contain a lake. [Late 17C. Via Spanish < late Latin *caldaria* "cooking pot" < Latin *caldus* "warm"]

Cal·de·rón de la Bar·ca /kaaldə rōn della baárkə/, **Pedro** (1600–81) Spanish dramatist and poet. He wrote comedies and religious allegories including *Life is a Dream* (1635). Full name **Calderón de la Barca y Henao, Pedro**

> "He dreams who thrives and prospers in this life. / He dreams who toils and strives. He dreams who injures, / Offends, and insults. So that in this world/Everyone dreams the thing he is, though no one / Can understand it."
> [Pedro Calderón de la Barca, *Life is a Dream*; 1635]

Cal·dey Is·land /káwldee-/ small island off the coast of Pembrokeshire, Wales, and location of a Cistercian monastery. Population: 50. Area: 1 sq. mi./2.6 sq. km. Welsh name **Ynys Pyr**

cal·dron /káwldrən/, **caul·dron** *n* **1.** a large metal pot in which liquids are boiled **2.** a situation of great tension, unrest, and stressfulness ○ *"He is heading into a caldron in the House of Representatives."* (*US News & World Report*; 1998) [13C. < Anglo-Norman, Old N French *caudron* < late Latin *caldaria* "cooking pot" < Latin *calidus* "hot"]

Cald·well /káwld wèl, -wəl/ city in southwestern Idaho, on the southern bank of the Boise River, west of Boise. Population: 29,466 (2002 estimate).

Cald·well, Erskine (1903–87) US writer. His novels about rural poverty include *Tobacco Road* (1932). Full name **Caldwell, Erskine Preston**

> "Here is hard-core unemployment, widespread and chronic; here is a region of shacks...In this region of steep mountains, a person is exceptionally fortunate if he is able to hack out two or three ten-foot rows of land for potatoes or beans."
> [Erskine Caldwell, *Around About America*; 1964]

Cald·well, Janet Taylor (1900–85) British-born US writer. She is known for her novels about family dynasties, including *Dynasty of Death* (1938).

Cald·well, Sarah (*b.* 1928) US conductor and opera producer, associated with the Boston Opera Company, and known for unusual opera productions

> "If you approach an opera as though it were something that always went the same way, that's what you get. I approach an opera as if I didn't know it."
> [Sarah Caldwell. Quoted in "Sarah Caldwell: The Flamboyant of the Opera," *MS*, Jane Scovell Appleton; May 1975]

Cal·e·do·ni·a /kàllə dṓnee ə/ **1.** Roman name for the northern part of Britain **2.** poetic name for Scotland

Cal·e·do·ni·an /kàllə dṓnee ən/ *n* **1. SCOT** a Scottish person (*literary*) **2. GEOLOGIC ERA** the era of geologic time in northwestern Europe, 500 million to 395 million years ago, during which many mountains were formed ■ *adj* **1. OF SCOTLAND** relating to Scotland or its people, language, or culture (*literary*) **2. OF GEOLOGIC ERA** relating to the Caledonian era of geologic time

Cal·e·do·ni·an Ca·nal /kàllə dṓnee ən-/ major waterway of Scotland. It consists of canals linking Loch Linnhe in the southwest with Loch Lochy, Loch Ness, and the Moray Firth in the northeast. Length: 97 mi./60 km.

cal·en·dar /kálləndər/ *n* **1. CHART OF YEAR** a chart showing the days and months of the year, especially a particular year **2. SYSTEM OF CALCULATING YEAR** a system of calculating the days and months of the year and when the year begins and ends **3. SCHEDULE** a schedule of events, usually covering a period of a year **4. LIST** an official list of things to be done or considered ■ *vt* (**-dared, -dar·ing, -dars**) **SCHEDULE SOMETHING** to enter something in a calendar or diary ▶ See table on next page [12C. Via Anglo-Norman < Latin *calendarium* "moneylender's account book" < *calendae* "first day of the month"]

cal·en·dar day *n* the period of 24 hours from midnight to midnight

ca·len·dar·ize /kálləndə rīz/ *vt* same as **calendar**

cal·en·dar month *n* CALENDAR same as **month** (senses 1, 3)

cal·en·dar year *n* **1.** the period of 365 or 366 days from January 1 to December 31 **2.** the period of time between a date in one year and the same date in the next

cal·en·der /kálləndər/ *n* a machine with rollers, used to form thin sheets from paper, plastic, or other material, or to impart a desired surface finish [Early 16C. Via French *calendre* < assumed Vulgar Latin *colondra*, alteration (influenced by Latin *columna* "column") of Latin *cylindrus* "roller"] —**cal·en·der** *vt* —**cal·en·der·er** *n*

cal·ends /kálləndz, káy-/, **kal·ends** *n* in the ancient Roman calendar, the first day of the month (*takes a singular or plural verb*) [14C Via French *calendes* < Latin *calendae* "first day of the month"]

ca·len·du·la /kə lénjələ/ (*plural* **-las** or *same*) *n* a garden plant of the daisy family. Flowers: bright orange or yellow. Use: in cooking, for medical purposes. Latin name: *Calendula officinalis*. [Late 16C. < modern Latin < Latin *calendae* "first day of the month"; from its use in treating menstrual disorders]

cal·en·ture /kállən chŏŏr/ *n* a fever occurring in tropical regions, formerly believed to be caused by heat [Late 16C. Via French < Spanish *calentura* < Latin *calere* "be warm"]

calf[1] /kaf/ (*plural* **calves** /kavz/) *n* **1. YOUNG COW OR BULL** a young cow or bull of a domestic breed of cattle **2. YOUNG ANIMAL** the young of some animals such as elephants, whales, giraffes, and buffalos **3.** INDUST same as **calfskin** (sense 1) **4. PIECE OF ICEBERG** a large piece of ice that has broken away from an iceberg [Old English *cælf* < Germanic] ◇ **kill the fatted calf** to have a great celebration in honor of somebody, usually a family member who has been absent for some time

calf[2] /kaf/ (*plural* **calves** /kavz/) *n* the fleshy part at the back of the leg below the knee [14C. < Old Norse *kálfi*]

calf·skin /káf skìn/ *n* **1.** fine leather made from the skin of calves **2.** the skin of a calf

Cal·ga·ry /kálgəree/ city in southern Alberta, Canada. It is an important center for transportation, finance, and the petroleum industry. Population: 879,277 (2001).

Cal·houn /kal hṓōn/, **John Caldwell** (1782–1850) vice president of the United States. He served as vice president (1825–32) under John Quincy Adams and Andrew Jackson.

> "The government of the absolute majority instead of the government of the people is but the government of the strongest interests; and when not efficiently checked, it is the most tyrannical and oppressive that can be devised."
> [John Caldwell Calhoun, *Speech to the Senate*; February 15, 1833]

Ca·li /kaálee/ capital of Valle de Cauca Department and second largest city in Colombia. It is situated on the Cali River in western Colombia. Population: 2,111,000 (1999).

cal·i·ber /kállibər/ *n* **1. ABILITY** somebody's ability, intelligence, or character ○ *We don't often get candidates of her caliber.* **2.** ARMS **BORE OF FIREARM** the internal diameter of a pipe, cylinder, or the barrel of a firearm **3.** ARMS **SIZE OF BULLET** the external diameter of a projectile such as a bullet or a shell [Mid-16C. Via French < Italian *calibro* or Spanish *calibre*, probably < Arabic *kālib* "mold"]

cal·i·brate /kálli bràyt/ (**-brat·ed, -brat·ing, -brates**) *vt* **1.** MEASURE **MARK SCALE ON SOMETHING** to establish and mark the units on a measuring instrument **2.** MEASURE **ENSURE ACCURACY OF SOMETHING** to test and adjust the accuracy of a measuring instrument or process **3.** ARMS **MEASURE BORE OF SOMETHING** to measure the internal diameter of a pipe, cylinder, or the barrel of a firearm —**cal·i·bra·tor** *n*

cal·i·bra·tion /kàlli bráysh'n/ *n* **1.** the checking of a measuring instrument against an accurate standard to determine any deviation and correct for errors **2.** a mark showing one of the units of measurement on a measuring instrument

cal·i·bre *n* ARMS Can, UK spelling of **caliber**

ca·li·ces RELIG, ANAT plural of **calix**

ca·li·che /kə leéchee/ *n* **1.** a layer of clay or sand containing minerals such as sodium nitrate and sodium chloride, found in dry regions of South America **2.** GEOL same as **calcrete** [Mid-19C. < American Spanish]

cal·i·cle *n* ZOOL same as **calyculus**

cal·i·co /kállikō/ (*plural* **-coes**) *n* **1. BRIGHT COTTON CLOTH** a coarse cotton cloth with a bright printed pattern **2.** *UK* **WHITE COTTON CLOTH** a white or unbleached cotton cloth **3. ANIMAL WITH BLOTCHED COAT** an animal with a

CALENDARS AND FESTIVALS

The Gregorian calendar was introduced in 1582 by Pope Gregory XIII, replacing the Julian calendar, and is based on a solar year of 365 days plus an extra day every four years (the leap year) and in centenary years evenly divisible by 400. The other calendars shown are based on lunar months. Each Hindu month is divided in two equal parts: krsna-paksa and sukla-paksa. Both the Hindu and the Jewish calendars are adjusted at intervals to the solar year. The Islamic calendar is not adjusted to the solar year so advances through the solar year on a 32.5 year cycle. The first month of each calendar is marked with a 1. Note, in the Jewish calendar, although Tishri is considered the first month of the civil year, Nisan is the first month of the religious year.

Gregorian calendar	Jewish calendar	Hindu calendar	Islamic calendar
1 January *31 days*	Tevet *29 days*	Pausa *30 days*	1 Muharram *30 days*
February *28 days*[1]	Shevat *30 days*	Magha *30 days*	Safar *29 days*
March *31 days*	Adar *29 days*[2]	Phalguna *30 days*	Rabi I *30 days*
April *30 days*	Nisan *30 days*	1 Caitra *30 days*[5]	Rabi II *29 days*
May *31 days*	Iyar *29 days*	Vaisakha *31 days*	Jumada I *30 days*
June *30 days*	Sivan *30 days*	Jyaistha *31 days*	Jumada II *29 days*
July *31 days*	Tammuz *29 days*	Asadha *31 days*	Rajab *30 days*
August *31 days*	Av *30 days*	Sravana *31 days*	Sha'ban *29 days*
September *30 days*	Elul *29 days*	Bhadrapada *31 days*	Ramadan *30 days*
October *31 days*	1 Tishri *30 days*	Asvina *30 days*	Shawwal *29 days*
November *30 days*	Heshvan *29 days*[3]	Kartika *30 days*	Dhu al-Qa'dah *30 days*
December *31 days*	Kislev *29 days*[4]	Margasirsa *30 days*	Dhu al-Hijjah *30 days*[6]
	Tevet	Pausa	

Notes

1 February has 29 days in a leap year.
2 The intercalary month Adar Sheni (29 days) is added every 3 years to adjust the Jewish calendar to the solar year.
3 The month Heshvan has 30 days in some years.
4 The month Kislev has 30 days in some years.
5 Caitra has 31 days in a leap year.
6 The month Dhu al-Hijjah has 30 days in some years.

Christian festivals

Annunciation *March 25*
Ascension *40 days after Easter*
Christmas *December 25: Roman Catholic and Protestant churches; January 6: Eastern Orthodox churches*
Easter *First Sunday after the full moon of the vernal equinox*
Epiphany *January 6*
Pentecost *Seventh Sunday after Easter*
Transfiguration *August 6: Roman Catholic and Protestant churches; August 19: Eastern Orthodox churches*
Trinity *First Sunday after Pentecost*

Jewish festivals

Hanukkah *25 Kislev for eight days*
Passover *14 Nisan for seven days*
Purim *14 Adar*
Rosh Hashanah *1 and 2 Tishri*
Shavuoth *6 Sivan*
Sukkoth *15 Tishri for eight or nine days*
Yom Kippur *10 Tishri*

Hindu festivals

Dussehra *First half of Asvina*
Diwali *Second half of Asvina*
Ganesh Chaturthi *Early Bhadrapada*
Holi *Early Phalguna*
Krishna Jayanti *Late Sravana*
Rakhi Bandham *Full moon of Sravana*
Shiva Ratri *Middle of Magha*

Islamic festivals

Ashora *10 Muharram*
Eid al-Adha *10 Dhu al-Qa'dah to 1 Dhu al-Hijjah*
Eid al-Fitr *1 Shawwal*
Lailat al-Miraj *27 Rajab*
Lailat al-Baraah *15 Sha'ban*
Lailat al-Qadr *27 Ramadan*
Mawlid al-Nabi *12 Rabi I*
Ras al-Am *1 Muharram*
Ramadan

blotched coat, usually white with black and reddish patches [Mid-16C. Alteration of *Calicut* (now KOZHIKODE), India, from which such cloth was exported]

cal·i·co bass *n* FISH same as **black crappie**

cal·i·co bush *n* same as **mountain laurel**

cal·i·co moth *n* a moth with orange-and-white markings, sometimes seen migrating in large swarms. Native to: United States. Genus: *Utetheisa*.

ca·lif *n* ISLAM another spelling of **caliph**

Calif. *abbr* California

ca·lif·ate *n* ISLAM another spelling of **caliphate**

Cal·i·for·nia /kàlli fáwrnyə/ the most populous state in the United States, bordered by the Pacific Ocean, Oregon, Nevada, Arizona, and Mexico. Capital: Sacramento. Population: 35,116,033 (2002 estimate). Area: 158,869 sq. mi./411,469 sq. km. —**Cal·i·for·nian** *n, adj*

Cal·i·for·nia, Gulf of arm of the Pacific Ocean that extends northward between mainland Mexico and

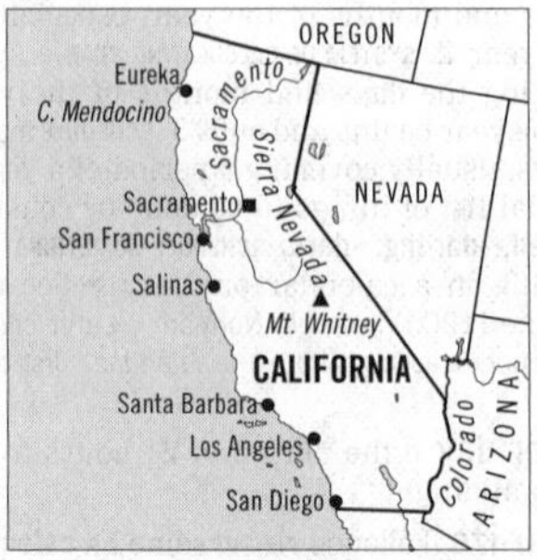

California

Baja California. Area: 59,000 sq. mi./152,810 sq. km. Former name **Cortés, Sea of**

Cal·i·for·nia bay *n* TREES same as **California laurel**

Cal·i·for·nia con·dor *n* a large, dark gray or brown vulture with a wingspan of about 10 ft./3 m and a naked head and neck. It is being rescued from extinction by a captive breeding program. Native to: southeastern United States. Latin name: *Gymnogyps californianus*.

Cal·i·for·nia Cur·rent current in the northern Pacific Ocean. It flows from north to south along the western coast of North America before turning west.

Cal·i·for·nia lau·rel *n* an evergreen tree of the laurel family with small green or purple fruits. Flowers: small, green, in clusters. Native to: coast of western United States. Latin name: *Umbellularia californica*.

Cal·i·for·nia pop·py, Cal·i·for·nian pop·py *n* an annual plant with bluish divided leaves. Flowers: bright red to yellow. Latin name: *Eschscholzia californica*.

Cal·i·for·ni·a quail (*plural* **Cal·i·for·ni·a quails** or *same*) *n* a quail with a rounded black plume on top of its head, that moves on the ground in flocks, flying only when compelled to. Native to: Western northern America. Latin name: *Calipepla californica*.

Cal·i·for·ni·a val·ley quail *n* same as **California quail**

cal·i·for·nite /kàlli fáwr nīt/ *n* a compact form of green vesuvianite found in California, resembling jade. Use: ornamental stone.

cal·i·for·ni·um /kàlli fáwrnee əm/ *n* a synthetic radioactive metallic element. Source: bombardment of curium or americium with neutrons. Use: neutron source. Symbol **Cf**. See table at **element** [Mid-20C. Because first synthesized at the University of California]

Ca·lig·u·la /kə líggyələ/ (A.D. 12–41) Roman emperor. A despotic ruler (A.D. 37–41), he bankrupted the state with his extravagance and was assassinated. Full name **Gaius Julius Caesar Germanicus**

> "Would that the Roman people had but one neck!"
> [Attributed to Caligula, *Life of Caligula*, Suetonius; 121?]

cal·i·per /kállipər/ *n* **1. MEASURING INSTRUMENT** an instrument used to measure the internal or external dimensions of objects and consisting of two curved hinged legs joined at one end (*usually used in the plural*) **2. MEASURING INSTRUMENT FOR LARGE OBJECTS** a measuring instrument with a fixed arm and an arm that moves along a graduated scale, used for measuring the diameter of large cylindrical objects such as logs **3.** *UK* **LEG BRACE** a leg splint consisting of metal rods and straps that enables the hip bone, rather than the foot, to support weight when walking ■ *vt* (**-pered, -per·ing, -pers**) **MEASURE SOMETHING WITH CALIPER** to measure something using a caliper [Late 16C. Origin ?]

ca·liph /káylif, kállif/, **ca·lif, ka·lif, kha·lif** *n* a title taken by Islamic rulers such as the Turkish sultans that asserts religious authority to rule, derived from that of Muhammad [14C. Via French *caliphe* < Arabic *kalīfa* "successor, deputy" < *kalafa* "succeed"]

ca·liph·ate /káyli fàyt, kálli-/, **ca·lif·ate, ka·lif·ate, kha·lif·ate** *n* the territory over which a caliph's rule extends, or the time for which it lasts

cal·is·then·ics /kàlliss thénniks/ *npl* vigorous physical exercises for improving fitness and muscle tone, including pushups, sit-ups, and jumping jacks (*takes a plural verb*) ■ *n* the practice of performing calisthenics (*takes a singular verb*) [Early 19C. < Greek *kallos* "beauty" + *sthenos* "strength"] —**cal·is·then·ic** *adj*

ca·lix /káyliks, káll-/ (*plural* **-li·ces** /-li seez/) *n* **1.** a chalice or cup **2.** ANAT same as **calyx** (sense 2) [Early 18C. < Latin (see CHALICE)]

calk[1] /kawk/ *n* **1. HORSESHOE SPIKE** a metal spike on a horseshoe to prevent slipping **2. SPIKED PLATE PROTECTING SOLES** a spiked plate attached to the bottom of a boot or shoe to prevent slipping and preserve the sole ■ *vt* (**calked, calk·ing, calks**) **FIT CALK ON SOMETHING** to put a calk on a horseshoe, boot, or shoe [Late 16C. Origin ?]

calk[2] *vt* CONSTR another spelling of **caulk**

call /kawl/ *v* (**called, call·ing, calls**) **1.** *vti* **SAY SOMETHING OR SPEAK LOUDLY** to say something or speak in a loud voice ○ *"Supper's ready," he called from the kitchen.* **2.** *vt* **DESCRIBE SOMEBODY OR SOMETHING AS SOMETHING** to describe or think of somebody or something in a particular way ○ *I'd call him a fool.* **3.** *vt* **REFER TO SOMEBODY** to use a particular term to address or refer to somebody ○ *He always called his father "Sir."* **4.** *vt* **SUMMON SOMEBODY OR SOMETHING** to summon or alert somebody or something by means of a formal request ○ *I'll call a cab.* **5.** *vt* **READ SOMETHING OUT** to read names or numbers from a list **6.** *vti* **TELEPHONE SOMEBODY** to contact somebody by telephone or radio **7.** *vt* **NAME SOMEBODY OR SOMETHING** to give somebody or something a name ○ *What are you going to call the baby?* **8.** *vi* **CRY** to give a characteristic cry (*refers to birds or animals*) **9.** *vi* **VISIT SOMEBODY** to visit somebody or the place where somebody lives or works ○ *I called to see her yesterday.* **10.** *vti* **MAKE REQUEST FOR SOMETHING TO HAPPEN** to make an official order or request for something such as a meeting ○ *An emergency meeting has been called for July 15th.* **11.** *vt* **PREDICT SOMETHING** to predict what is going to happen, especially in politics ○ *It's a very hard result to call.* **12.** *vti* DANCE **INSTRUCT DANCERS** to direct people who are dancing, e.g., in a square dance **13.** *vt* FIN **DEMAND REPAYMENT OF SOMETHING** to demand repayment of a loan or bond issue ○ *call a loan* **14.** *vt* **CHALLENGE SOMEBODY** to challenge somebody to prove something, especially to demand to see somebody's hand in a game of poker ○ *call her on the facts* **15.** *vti* **DECLARE CHOICE IN GAME** to make a declaration in a game, e.g., to choose heads or tails, or choose trumps in a card game ○ *I'll toss, you call.* **16.** *vt* SPORTS **OFFICIALLY DECIDE SOMETHING IN GAME** to make an official decision in a sports event or a game ○ *called a foul* **17.** *vt* SPORTS **POSTPONE GAME** to postpone or stop a sports event because of bad weather or other unsuitable conditions ○ *The game was called when it got too dark to play anymore.* ■ *n* **1. SHOUT** a shout or cry **2. BIRD OR ANIMAL CRY** the characteristic sound made by a bird or animal **3.** HUNTING **HUNTER'S DEVICE TO ATTRACT GAME** a device that imitates the cry of a bird or other animal, used as a lure in hunting **4. SIGNAL** a signal given by a sound, e.g., on a horn or whistle **5. TELEPHONE COMMUNICATION** a telephone conversation, or an attempt to get in touch with somebody by telephone **6. REQUEST TO COME** a request for somebody to come ○ *The rescue squads answer thousands of calls a year.* **7. EXPRESSED WISH** a demand or request for something to be done ○ *There have been calls for him to resign.* **8. FEELING OF DUTY** a feeling that a particular job or way of life is a personal duty **9. VISIT** a short visit to somebody at his or her house or place of work ○ *made a few calls on the way home* **10.** SPORTS, LEISURE **REFEREE'S DECISION** a decision made by a referee **11. DECISION** a decision or choice to be made by somebody ○ *It's your call.* **12.** LEISURE **DECLARATION IN GAME** a declaration made during a game, e.g., the choice of heads or tails when a coin is tossed **13. PREDICTION** a prediction of what is about to happen, especially in politics ○ *In terms of changing policy at election time, it's a difficult call to make.* **14. DEMAND OR OBLIGATION** a demand or obligation that somebody has to fulfill ○ *I'd like to help, but I have many calls on my time.* **15.** FIN same as **call option** **16. REMINDER** a reminder, given electronically, by telephone, or in person, that somebody should wake up or that something is about to happen **17. STRONG APPEAL OF PLACE OR LIFESTYLE** the feeling of strong attraction exerted by a particular place or way of life ○ *the call of the wild* [12C. < Old Norse *kalla*] ◇ **be on call** to be on duty away from the workplace, available to be summoned ◇ **there's no call for something** *or* **to do something 1.** used to say that a particular remark or action is not welcome or necessary ○ *There's no call to get angry.* **2.** people do not want something, especially a particular commercial product ○ *There's no call for bathing suits at this time of year.*

CULTURAL NOTE ***The Call of the Wild***, a novel (1903) by Jack London. Noted for its unsentimental portrayal of pioneer life, it is the tale of a dog, "Buck," who is sent to the Yukon to work as a sled dog. After demonstrating his strength and courage in the service of humans, he takes to the wild with a pack of wolves.

call back *v* **1.** *vti* **TELEPHONE SOMEBODY AGAIN** to contact somebody by telephone again ○ *If she's busy, I'll call back later.* **2.** *vti* **RETURN TELEPHONE CALL TO SOMEBODY** to telephone somebody in order to return that person's telephone call ○ *My money's running out – can you call me back?* **3.** *vt* **ASK TO RETURN** to recall somebody, e.g., for a second audition or interview, or to return to a job **4.** *vi UK* **VISIT SOMEBODY AGAIN** to visit somebody again

call down *vt* **1.** to pray or appeal for good or bad things to happen to somebody **2.** to rebuke somebody who has done something wrong ○ *The judge called the lawyers down for their unseemly courtroom antics.*

call for *vt* **1. MAKE REQUEST FOR SOMETHING TO HAPPEN** to make a demand or request for something to be done **2. NEED** to need or require a particular thing or quality **3. ARRIVE AND PICK UP** to arrive and pick up somebody **4. SUGGEST AS LIKELY** to suggest that something is likely to happen (*refers to weather forecasts*) ○ *The weathercasters are calling for thunderstorms in the late afternoon.*

call forth *vt* to inspire an emotion, energy, or courage

call in *v* **1.** *vt* **ASK HELP FROM SOMEBODY** to ask somebody to come and give advice or help **2.** *vi* **TELEPHONE PLACE OF WORK** to telephone a place of work in order to get or leave a message **3.** *vt* **ASK FOR SOMETHING TO BE REPAID** to ask for a debt or loan to be repaid **4.** *vt* **ARRANGE RETURN OF SOMETHING** to arrange for or request that something be returned, e.g., outdated currency or defective goods

call off *vt* **1.** to cancel or stop an event **2.** to order a dog or a person to stop attacking somebody

call on *vt* **1.** to ask or tell somebody to do something **2.** to visit somebody, often in a formal manner

call out *vt* **1. SUMMON SOMEBODY TO HELP** to summon a person or an organization to give help **2. ORDER WORKERS TO STRIKE** to tell workers to stop work and go on strike **3. CHALLENGE SOMEBODY TO FIGHT** to challenge somebody to a duel or fight (*archaic*)

call up *vt* **1.** *UK* same as **draft** *v* (sense 1) **2. SUMMON SOMEBODY OR SOMETHING IN RESERVE** to summon somebody or something that is available in reserve ○ *The governor called up the National Guard.* **3.** COMPUT **DISPLAY SOMETHING ON COMPUTER SCREEN** to instruct a computer to find and display a particular piece of information ○ *call up last month's sales figures* **4. EVOKE SOMETHING** to bring back memories of something

call upon *vt* **1.** to ask somebody in a formal way to do something **2.** to make demands on somebody or on somebody's abilities

cal·la /kállə/ *n* PLANTS same as **calla lily**

call·a·ble /káwləb'l/ *adj* **1.** describes a loan that is repayable on demand **2.** describes a stock or bond that is convertible before reaching maturity

Cal·la·ghan /kálləhən, -hàn/, **James, Baron Callaghan of Cardiff** (*b.* 1912) British politician. He was home secretary (1967–70), foreign secretary (1974–76), and Labor prime minister (1976–79). He became a Life Peer in 1987. Full name **Callaghan, Leonard James**. See table at **prime minister**

> "Britain has lived for too long on borrowed time, borrowed money and even borrowed ideas."
> [James Callaghan, *Observer (London)*; October 3, 1976]

Cal·la·ghan, Morley Edward (1903–90) Canadian writer. His novels, known for their hard-hitting realism, include *They Shall Inherit the Earth* (1935) and *The Loved and the Lost* (1955).

cal·la lil·y, **cal·la** *n* **1.** an ornamental lily, originally from southern Africa, that has a white funnel-shaped cone around a long yellow spike bearing the flowers themselves. Latin name: *Zantedeschia aethiopica*. **2.** an ornamental lily of the arum type, with a large, brightly colored, funnel-shaped cone around a long flower spike. Genus: *Zantedeschia*.

cal·la·loo *n Carib* same as **calalu**

Ca·llao /kaa yów/ city and chief seaport of Peru, situated on Callao Bay 8 mi./13 km west of Lima. Population: 424,294 (1998).

AKG London

Maria Callas

Cal·las /kálləss, kaáləss/, **Maria** (1923–77) US-born operatic soprano. One of the leading opera singers of the mid-20th century, she was known for her incisive portrayals of such characters as Norma and Tosca. Born **Kalogeropoulos, Maria Anna Sofia Cecilia**

call·back /káwl bàk/ *n* **1. RETURN CALL** a telephone call made back to somebody who has recently phoned **2. RECALLING OF SOMEBODY** an act of asking somebody to return, especially for a second audition **3. PRODUCT RECALL** the recalling of a faulty product by a manufacturer

call·board /káwl bàwrd/ *n* a board backstage in a theater, giving information to actors and other people involved in a production

call box *n* **1.** a telephone alongside a highway, used for reporting emergencies **2.** *UK* TELECOM same as **telephone booth**

call·boy /káwl bòy/ *n* **1.** somebody in a theater who tells the actors when the time for them to go on stage is approaching **2.** TRAVEL same as **bellhop 3.** a man prostitute

call cen·ter *n* a place that handles high-volume incoming telephone calls on behalf of a large organization

call·er /káwlər/ *n* **1.** somebody who makes a telephone call or a visit **2.** an announcer, e.g., of moves in a square dance or of numbers in a game of bingo

call·er ID *n* an electronic device attached to a telephone that, on a small screen, shows the name and telephone number of somebody who is calling or has called

Cal·les /kaá yèss/, **Plutarco Elías** (1877–1945) Mexican politician. He was secretary of the interior (1920–23) and president of Mexico (1924–28).

call girl *n* a prostitute who makes appointments with clients by telephone

cal·lig·ra·phy /kə líggrəfee/ *n* **1.** the art or skill of producing beautiful or artistic handwriting **2.** beautiful or artistic handwriting [Early 17C. < Greek *kalligraphia* "beautiful writing" < *kallos* "beauty" + *graphein* "write"] —**cal·lig·ra·pher** *n* —**cal·li·graph·ic** /kàlli gráffik/ *adj* —**cal·li·graph·i·cal·ly** *adv* —**cal·lig·ra·phist** *n*

call-in *n* **1.** a radio or television show in which the listeners or viewers phone and express their opinions **2.** a telephone call from a radio listener or a television viewer to a talk show ○ *You will be interviewed live for 30 minutes on a show with call-ins.*

call·ing /káwling/ *n* **1.** a strong urge to follow a particular career or do a particular type of work **2.** a job or profession

call·ing card *n* **1.** a small card bearing the name and sometimes the address of a visitor **2.** TELECOM same as **phonecard 3.** something that serves to identify somebody or something ○ *a drop of blood containing the DNA calling card of an unknown person*

cal·li·o·pe /kə lī́ əpee, kállee ōp/ *n* an organ that generates sound by the release of steam or compressed air through pipes, with tunes often played mechanically, as on a player piano. Calliopes are usually found in fairgrounds or circuses. [Mid-19C. < Latin *Calliope* "Calliope"]

Cal·li·o·pe /kə lī́ əpee/ *n* in Greek mythology, the Muse of epic poetry, one of the nine Muses believed to inspire and nurture the arts [Via Latin < Greek *Kalliopē*, literally "beautiful-voiced"]

cal·li·per *n, vt* MED, MEASURE Can, UK spelling of **caliper**

cal·li·pyg·i·an /kàllə píjjee ən/, **cal·li·py·gous** /kàllə pīgəss/ *adj* having well-shaped buttocks (*literary*) [Late 18C. < Greek *kallipūgos* "beautiful buttocks" (applied to a statue of Aphrodite) < *kallos* "beauty" + *pugē* "buttocks"]

Cal·lis·to /kə líst ō/ *n* **1.** in Greek mythology, a nymph who was changed into a bear by Hera and later became the constellation Ursa Major **2.** a large satellite of Jupiter that was discovered in 1610 [Via Latin < Greek *Kallistō* < *kalos* "beautiful"]

call let·ters *npl* a group of letters used for identification by a radio transmitting station

call loan *n* a loan that must be repaid on demand

call mon·ey *n* money that has been borrowed and is repayable on demand

call num·ber *n* LIBRARIES same as **shelf mark**

call of na·ture *n* a need to urinate or defecate (*humorous*)

call op·tion *n* a financial document that gives somebody the right, but not the obligation, to buy an asset at a particular striking price on or before a particular date

cal·lose /ká lòss/ *n* a polysaccharide found in plant cell walls and formed in flowering plants in response to injury. It consists of chains of linked glucose units. [Mid-19C. < Latin *callosus* (see CALLOUS)]

cal·los·i·ty /kə lóssətee/ (*plural* **-ties**) *n* a local thickening of the outer layer of the skin caused by repeated friction or pressure

cal·lous /kálləss/ *adj* showing no concern that other people are or might be hurt or upset [14C. Directly or via French < Latin *callosus* "hardened by friction" < *callus* "hard skin"] —**cal·lous·ly** *adv* —**cal·lous·ness** *n*

SPELLCHECK callous or **callus**? Do not confuse the spelling of ***callous*** and ***callus***, which sound similar. ***Callous*** is an adjective meaning "insensitive or unfeeling," as in *a callous remark*. ***Callus*** is a noun that usually denotes a patch of thickened skin on the hand or foot.

---

cal·loused /kálləst/, **cal·lused** *adj* having an area of hard thickened skin

cal·low /kállō/ *adj* young or immature, and lacking the experience of life that comes with adulthood [Old English *calu* < Germanic] —**cal·low·ness** *n*

Cal·lo·way /kállə wày/, **Cab** (1907–94) US jazz musician, known for his exuberant performances, catch phrase "hi-de-ho," and scat singing. Full name **Calloway, Cabell**

call sign *n* a signal used for identification by a radio transmitting station or a unit or operator in radio communication with others

call slip *n* a form for requesting a library book that is not kept on the shelves used by the public

call to quar·ters *n* **1.** a signal requiring army personnel to return to barracks **2.** a period of time during which army personnel must remain in barracks

call-up *n UK* MIL same as **draft** *n* (sense 4)

cal·lus /kálləss/ *n* **1.** PATCH OF THICKENED SKIN a hard thickened area of skin, especially on the palm of the hand or the sole of the foot, caused by repeated pressure or friction **2.** MED MASS FORMED IN HEALING BONE a mass of fibrous tissue, calcium, cartilage, and bone that forms progressively during the healing of a bone fracture **3.** BOT PLANT TISSUE plant tissue that forms at the site of a wound, or that develops during tissue culture of plant parts, giving rise to new plantlets ■ *vti* (**-lused, -lus·ing, -lus·es**) DEVELOP CALLUS to develop a callus or calluses, or cause something to do so [Mid-16C. < Latin]

SPELLCHECK See ***callous***.

---

cal·lused *adj* another spelling of **calloused**

call wait·ing *n* **1.** a facility for taking a telephone call while another is in progress on the same line, usually putting the first on hold **2.** a service offered by a telephone company that allows somebody to answer an additional incoming call without disconnecting from the current call

calm /kaam/ *adj* **1.** NOT ANXIOUS without anxiety or strong emotion **2.** NOT STORMY smooth and without any large waves ○ *smooth sailing on calm seas* **3.** NOT WINDY without wind or storms ○ *forecasting a calm evening after heavy rain* **4.** NOT VIOLENT free from civil disturbance or violence ○ *The city was reported calm after a curfew was imposed.* ■ *n* **1.** PEACE AND QUIET a situation of complete peace and quiet, with no noise, trouble, or anxiety **2.** ABSENCE OF WIND still weather, without wind or waves caused by wind **3.** METEOROL LOWEST POINT OF BEAUFORT SCALE a wind of no more than 1 mi./1.6 km per hour, classified as the lowest force on the Beaufort scale ■ *vt* (**calmed, calm·ing, calms**) MAKE SOMEBODY LESS TENSE to make somebody less anxious or upset [14C. Probably directly or via French *calme* < late Latin *cauma* "heat of the day" < Greek *kauma*] —**calm·ly** *adv* —**calm·ness** *n*

calm down *vti* to become or make somebody become less excited, anxious, or upset

calm·a·tive /kaámətiv, kálmətiv/ *adj* having a calming or quieting effect

cal·mod·u·lin /kal mójjəlin/ *n* a calcium-binding protein found in the cells of most living organisms that controls many enzyme processes [Late 20C. Contraction of CALCIUM + MODULATE + -IN]

cal·o·mel /kállə mèl, -məl/ *n* a mercury compound. Use: fungicide, insecticide, formerly, as a purgative. [Late 17C. < modern Latin]

ca·lor·ic /kə láwrik/ *adj* same as **calorific** (sense 1) —**ca·lor·i·cal·ly** *adv*

cal·o·rie /kálləree/ *n* **1.** UNIT OF ENERGY a unit of energy equal to 4.1855 joules, originally defined as the quantity of heat required to raise the temperature of 1 g of pure water by 1° C. It has now been superseded by the joule in scientific usage. **2.** LARGER UNIT OF ENERGY a unit of energy equal to the heat required to raise the temperature of 1 kg of pure water by 1° C **3.** UNIT OF FOOD ENERGY a unit of energy-producing potential in food, equal to one large calorie. This energy, if not used, is converted to fat and stored. [Mid-19C. < French < Latin *calor* "heat" < *calere* "be warm"]

cal·o·rif·ic /kàllə ríffik/ *adj* **1.** relating to heat or calories, especially the number of calories contained in food **2.** containing many calories, and so likely to be fattening

cal·o·rif·ic val·ue *n* the amount of heat released by the combustion of a mass of fuel

cal·o·rim·e·ter /kàllə rímmətər/ *n* an apparatus for measuring the amount of heat given out or taken in during a process such as combustion or change of state. The measurements are often made by observing the amount of solid liquefied, or liquid vaporized, under set conditions. —**ca·lor·i·met·ric** /kàlləri méttrik, kə làwrə méttrik/ *adj* —**ca·lor·i·met·ri·cal·ly** *adv* —**cal·o·rim·e·try** *n*

cal·o·rize /kállə rīz/ (**-rized, -riz·ing, -riz·es**) *v* to treat the surface of steel or iron with aluminum powder and heat to 800–1,000° C to prevent or reduce rusting [Mid-20C. < Latin *calor* (see CALORIE)]

cal·o·type /kállə tīp/ *n* **1.** a 19th-century photographic process producing a negative on a plate wetted with silver iodide **2.** a photograph produced by the calotype process [Mid-19C. < Greek *kalos* "beautiful"]

Ca·loun·dra /kə lówndrə/ city and beach resort in Queensland, Australia, situated north of Brisbane. Population: 78,798 (2002 estimate).

cal·pac /kál pak, kal pák/, **cal·pack, kal·pak** *n* a high-peaked felt or sheepskin hat worn by men in Turkey and parts of eastern Central Asia [Late 16C. < Turkish *kalpak*]

calque /kalk/ *n* LANGUAGE same as **loan translation** [Mid-20C. < French, "copy" < Latin *calcare* (see CAULK)]

cal·trop /káltrəp, káwltrəp/ *n* **1.** (*plural* **cal·trops** or *same*) a spiny plant harmful to livestock. Native to: Europe, naturalized in California. Latin name: *Tribulus terrestris*. **2.** PLANTS same as **star thistle 3.** PLANTS same as **water chestnut** (sense 3) **4.** MIL a military device with four spikes arranged so that one will always point upward, scattered on the ground to lame horses or puncture tires [Pre-12C. Variant of obsolete *calcatrippe* "thistle" < medieval Latin *calcatrippa*]

cal·u·met /kállyə mèt, -mət/ *n* a long-stemmed ceremonial pipe used by some Native American peoples [Late 17C. < French, "pipe," dialect variant of *chalumeau* < Latin *calamus* "reed"]

Cal·u·met Cit·y /kállyə met-/ city in northeastern Illinois, situated 20 mi./32 km south of Chicago, on the Illinois-Indiana border. Population: 38,849 (2002).

ca·lum·ni·ate /kə lúmnee àyt/ (**-at·ed, -at·ing, -ates**) *vt* to accuse somebody falsely, or slander somebody (*formal*) [Mid-16C. < Latin *calumniat-*, past participle of *calumniare* < *calumnia* (see CALUMNY)] —**ca·lum·ni·a·tion** /kə lùmnee áysh'n/ *n* —**ca·lum·ni·a·tor** *n*

cal·um·ny /kálləmnee/ (*plural* **-nies**) *n* (*formal*) **1.** the making of false statements about somebody with malicious intent **2.** a slanderous statement or false accusation [15C. < Latin *calumnia* "false accusation" < *calvi* "deceive"] —**ca·lum·ni·ous** /kə lúmnee əss/ *adj* —**ca·lum·ni·ous·ly** *adv*

cal·va·dos /kálvə dṓss, kálvə dṓss/ *n* apple brandy distilled from cider, made in the Normandy region of France [Early 20C. After *Calvados*, Normandy]

cal·var·i·um /kal vérree əm/ (*plural* **-i·a** /-ee ə/) *n* the upper domed portion of the skull (*technical*) [Late 19C. Alteration of Latin *calvaria* "skull" < *calvus* "bald"]

cal·va·ry /kálvəree, kálvree/ (*plural* **-ries**) *n* **1.** a time of great suffering (*literary*) **2.** a sculpture representing Jesus Christ's crucifixion [Early 18C. < CALVARY]

Cal·va·ry /kálvəree/ *n* a hill just outside the city walls of ancient Jerusalem where the Crucifixion of Jesus Christ took place, according to the Bible [< Latin *calvaria* "skull," translating Greek *golgotha* (see GOLGOTHA)]

Cal·va·ry cross *n* a Christian cross mounted on three symmetrical steps

calve /kav, kaav/ (**calved, calv·ing, calves**) *vti* **1.** to give birth to a calf **2.** to release a mass of ice that breaks away (*refers to a glacier or iceberg*) [Old English *calfian* < *cælf* "calf"]

Cal·vert /kálvərt/, **Cecelius, 2nd Baron Baltimore** (1605–75) English-born American colonial administrator. He inherited Maryland (1632), settled the colony, and implemented the policies written into its charter.

Cal·vert, Charles, 3rd Baron Baltimore (1637–1715) English-born American colonial administrator. He governed the Maryland colony (1661–89).

Cal·vert, George, 1st Baron Baltimore (1580?–1632) English-born American absentee colonial administrator. He established the colony of Maryland (1632) and advocated religious tolerance.

Cal·vert, Leonard (1606–47) English-born American colonial administrator. He was the first governor of Maryland (1633–47).

calves[1] ZOOL plural of **calf**[1]

calves[2] ANAT plural of **calf**[2]

Cal·vin /kálvin/, **John** (1509–64) French-born Swiss Protestant reformer. He founded a Presbyterian government in Switzerland and developed the doctrine of the Protestant Reformation in *Institutes of the Christian Religion* (1536).

Cal·vin cy·cle *n* a series of reactions that take place in photosynthesis by which carbon dioxide is converted to glucose [After Melvin *Calvin* (1911–97), US biochemist]

Cal·vin·ism /kálvi nìzzəm/ *n* the religious doctrine of John Calvin, which maintains that salvation comes through faith in God, and also that God has already chosen those who will believe and be saved —**Cal·vin·ist** *n, adj* —**Cal·vin·is·tic** /kàlvi nístik/ *adj* —**Cal·vin·is·ti·cal·ly** *adv*

Cal·vi·no /kal véenō/, **Italo** (1923–85) Cuban-born Italian novelist. His works, including *If on a Winter's Night a Traveler* (1979), contain a unique blend of realism and fantasy.

> "I have tried to remove weight, sometimes from people, sometimes from heavenly bodies, sometimes from cities; above all I have tried to remove weight from the structure of stories and from language."
> [Italo Calvino, *Six Memos for the Next Millennium*; 1988]

Cal·vo /kálvō, kaálvō/, **Carlos** (1824–1906) Argentine diplomat, historian, and lawyer. He formulated the Calvo Doctrine (1869), which set new guidelines regarding national debt.

calx /kalks/ (*plural* **calx·es** or **cal·ces** /kál sèez/) *n* **1.** the powdery oxide of a metal that is formed when an ore or a mineral is roasted **2.** the rounded part at the back of the heel [15C. < Latin, "lime, limestone" < Greek *khalix* "pebble"]

ca·ly·ces BOT plural of **calyx**

ca·lyc·u·lus /kə líkyələss/ (*plural* **-li** /-lī/), **ca·ly·cle** /káylik'l, kállik'l/, **ca·li·cle** *n* a small cup-shaped structure, e.g., the depression at the top of a coral skeleton [Late 19C. < Latin, "calyx of a flower," diminutive of *calyx* "husk" (see CALYX)] —**ca·lyc·u·lar** *adj* —**ca·lyc·u·late** /kə líkyə làyt, -lət/ *adj*

ca·lyp·so /kə lípsō/ (*plural* **-sos**) *n* **1.** a Caribbean, especially Trinidadian, ballad with a lively dance rhythm, that deals satirically with social and political topics **2.** Caribbean dance music that has syncopated rhythms, is usually improvised, and is often played by a steel band [Early 20C. Origin ?]

Ca·lyp·so /kə lípsō/ *n* **1.** in Greek mythology, a nymph who kept Odysseus on her island for seven years **2.** a small irregularly-shaped natural satellite of Saturn, discovered in 1980

ca·lyx /káyliks, kálliks/ (*plural* **ca·lyx·es** or **cal·y·ces** /-li sèez/) *n* **1.** the group of sepals, usually green, around the outside of a flower that encloses and protects the flower bud **2.** one of the funnel-shaped hollows in the pelvis of the kidney, through which urine passes to the ureter [Late 17C. Via Latin < Greek *kalux* "husk, shell" < *kaluptein* "conceal"]

cal·zo·ne /kal zṓnee, -zṓn/ (*plural* **-nes** or **-ni** /-nee/) *n* a semicircular Italian turnover made from pizza dough with a tasty filling [Late 20C. < Italian, literally "trouser leg" < Latin *calceus* "shoe" < *calx* "heel"]

cam /kam/ *n* an irregularly shaped projection on a rotating shaft that changes rotary motion into a reciprocating up-and-down motion in another machine part (**cam follower**) that touches it [Late 18C. < Dutch *kam* "comb"]

CAM /kam/ *abbr* COMPUT, MANUF computer-aided manufacturing

Ca·ma·güey Ar·chi·pel·a·go /kàmmə gwày-/ group of coral islands situated off east central Cuba, including the islands of Romano, Sabinal, and Coco, and extending approximately 150 mi./241 km from northwest to southeast

ca·ma·ra·der·ie /kaàmə raàdəree, kàmmə ráddəree/ *n* a feeling of close friendship and trust among a group of people [Mid-19C. < French < *camarade* (see COMRADE)]

Ca·margue /kə maárg/ delta region of marshes, lagoons, and farmland in southern France. The sparsely populated region is known for its wild bulls, white horses, and flamingos.

cam·a·ril·la /kàmmə rílla, -réeyə/ *n* a group of advisers, especially a secretive group advising an important person [Mid-19C. < Spanish, "small room" < *camara* "room"]

Cam·a·ril·lo /kàmmə rée ō/ city in southwestern California, east of Santa Barbara and northwest of Los Angeles. Population: 59,444 (2002 estimate).

cam·as /kámməss/ (*plural* **ca·mass·es** or *same*), **cam·ass** (*plural* **ca·mass·es** or *same*) *n* **1.** a plant with grassy leaves and an edible bulb. Flowers: blue and white, in clusters. Native to: North America. Latin name: *Camassia quamash*. **2.** PLANTS same as **death camas** [Early 19C. < Chinook Jargon *qamaš*]

cam·ber /kámbər/ *n* **1.** CONVEX CURVE IN ROAD a slight convex curve in a structure, especially the curve in the surface of a road **2.** SLANT OF VEHICLE'S WHEELS a slant in the steerable wheels on a vehicle that makes them slightly closer together at the bottom than at the top ■ *vti* (**-bered, -ber·ing, -bers**) MAKE CURVED SHAPE to form something with a camber, or be formed in this way [Early 17C. Via French *cambre* "arched" < Latin *camur* "curved inward"] —**cam·bered** *adj*

cam·bist /kámbist/ *n* a dealer in foreign exchange [Early 19C. Via French < Italian *cambista* < medieval Latin *cambium* (see CAMBIUM)]

cam·bi·um /kámbee əm/ (*plural* **-bi·ums** or **-bi·a** /-bee ə/) *n* a cylindrical layer of cells in plant roots and stems that produces the new tissue responsible for increased girth, particularly sap-conducting tissues, xylem and phloem, and bark [Late 17C. < medieval Latin *cambium* "exchange" < Latin *cambire* "to exchange"] —**cam·bi·al** *adj*

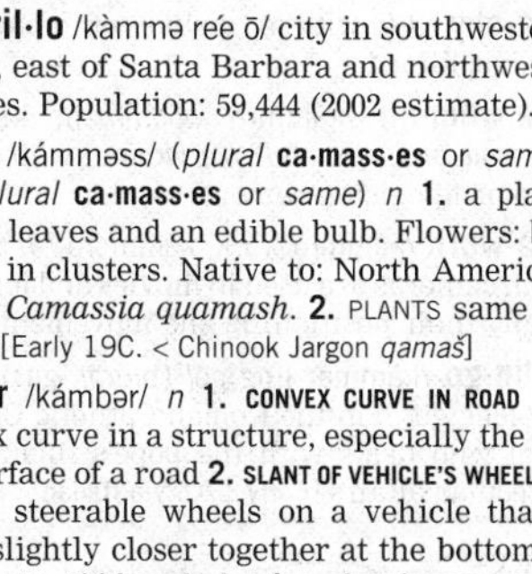

Cambodia

Cam·bo·di·a /kam bṓdee ə/ country in Southeast Asia, in the southern part of Indochina, bordered by Thailand, Laos, Vietnam, and the Gulf of Thailand. Language: Khmer, French. Currency: riel. Capital: Phnom Penh. Population: 13,124,764 (2003). Area: 69,898 sq. mi./181,035 sq. km. Official name **Kingdom of Cambodia**. Former name **Kampuchea** (1976–89), **Khmer Republic** (1970–75)

Cam·bo·di·an /kam bṓdee ən/ *n* **1.** somebody who comes from Cambodia **2.** LANG same as **Khmer**[1] (sense 3) (*dated*) —**Cam·bo·di·an** *adj*

cam·bo·gia /kam bṓjə/ TREES same as **gamboge** (sense 2)

Cam·bri·an /kámbree ən/ *n* PREHISTORIC PERIOD the period of geologic time, 570 million to 500 million years ago, during which invertebrate animal life, including trilobites, appeared, and marine algae developed. See table at **geologic time** ■ *adj* **1.** GEOL OF CAMBRIAN relating to the period of geologic time known as the Cambrian **2.** WELSH relating to or from Wales [Mid-17C. < medieval Latin *Cambria* "Wales" < Welsh *Cymry*]

Cam·bri·an Moun·tains /kámbree ən-/ mountain system of Wales, running from north to south and covering about two-thirds of the country. It includes Snowdon, the Brecon Beacons, and the Black Mountains. The highest peak is Aran Fawddwy 2,970 ft./905 m.

cam·bric /káymbrik/ *n* a thin white linen or cotton fabric [14C. After *Kamerijk* "Cambrai"]

Cam·bridge /káym brij/ **1.** university city in eastern England. It lies on the Cam River, and is the administrative headquarters of Cambridgeshire and a local government district. Population: 108,863 (2001). **2.** city in Massachusetts. It is home to Harvard University, founded in 1636, Radcliffe College, founded in 1879, and the Massachusetts Institute of Technology, founded in 1865. Population: 101,807 (2002 estimate).

Cam·bridge·shire /káymbrij shèer, -shər/ county of eastern England. Population: 552,658 (2001). Area: 1,316 sq. mi./3,409 sq. km.

Cam·by·ses I /kam bī seez/ (*fl* 6th century B.C.) Persian king. He reigned over a dynasty in present-day Iraq around 600–559 B.C. His son, Cyrus the Great, founded the Persian Empire.

Cam·by·ses II (*d.* 522 B.C.) Persian king. He reigned from 529 B.C. to 522 B.C., and conquered Egypt (525 B.C.) to expand the Persian Empire.

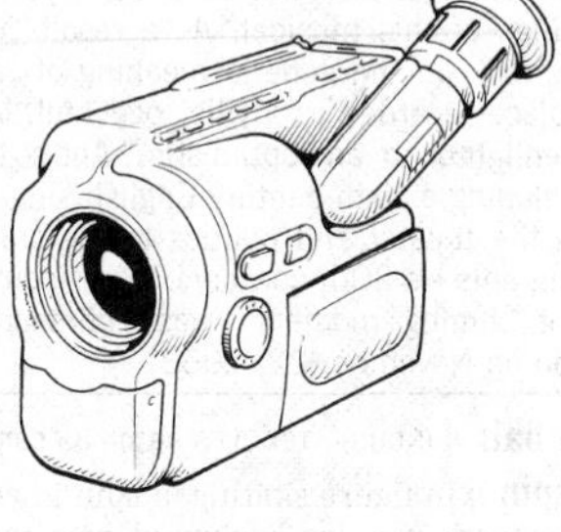

camcorder

cam·cord·er /kám kàwrdər/ *n* a portable video camera and recorder [Late 20C. Blend of CAMERA + RECORDER]

Cam·den /kámdən/ city and port in southwestern New Jersey, on the eastern bank of the Delaware River. Population: 79,685 (2002 estimate).

Cam·den, William (1551–1623) English antiquary and historian. He compiled a topographical account of the British Isles, *Britannia* (1586).

came past tense of **come**

cam·el /kámm'l/ *n* **1.** (*plural* **cam·els** or *same*) DESERT ANIMAL a ruminant animal that has either one or two humps on its back and is adapted to a dry climate. Genus: *Camelus*. **2.** COLORS LIGHT BROWN COLOR a light sandy brown color **3.** NAUT same as **caisson** (sense 2) **4.** PASSENGER VEHICLE a tractor-trailer with a long trailer that has two humps, designed to carry many passengers and used as a means of public transportation in Cuba [Pre-12C. Via Latin < Greek *kamēlos* < Semitic] —**cam·el** *adj*

cam·el·back /kámm'l bàk/ *adj* shaped like an arch or a camel's hump

cam·el·eer /kàmm'l éer/ *n* a rider or controller of a camel

cam·el hair, cam·el's hair *n* **1.** HAIR OF CAMEL hair from the camel. Use: clothing, rugs. **2.** TEXTILES FABRIC soft fabric containing camel hair or a similar fiber. Use: coats. **3.** ART PAINTBRUSH an artist's paintbrush, normally made of squirrel hair and used primarily for watercolors

~~camelia~~ incorrect spelling of **camellia**

cam·e·lid /kámm'lid, kə méllid/ *n* a member of the family that includes camels, llamas, and their relatives, all of which have feet with two toes and thick leathery soles. Family: Camelidae.

ca·mel·lia /kə meélyə, kə meélee ə/ (*plural* **-lias** or *same*) *n* **1.** an ornamental bush of the tea family with glossy evergreen leaves and rose-shaped flowers. Latin name: *Camellia japonica.* **2.** a tree or bush of the tea family that resembles a camellia. Genus: *Camellia.* [Mid-18C. < modern Latin < *Camellus*, Latinized name of Joseph *Kamel* (1661–1706), Moravian Jesuit missionary and botanist]

Ca·mel·lia State *n* a nickname for Alabama

ca·mel·o·pard /kə méllə paàrd/ *n* ZOOL same as **giraffe** (*archaic*) [14C. < Latin *camelopardus* < Greek *kamēlopardalis* < *kamēlos* "camel" + *pardalis* "pard" (because the animal has a head like a camel and spots like a leopard)]

Ca·mel·o·par·da·lis /kə mèllə paàrd'liss, kə mèllō-/, **Ca·mel·o·par·dus** /-paàrdəss/, **Ca·mel·o·pard** /kə méllə paàrd/ *n* a large faint constellation of the northern hemisphere. See illustration at **constellation** [Via Latin < Greek *kamēlopardalis* (see CAMELOPARD)]

Cam·e·lot /kámmə lòt/ *n* **1.** in Arthurian legend, the city of King Arthur **2.** a place or situation regarded as very enlightened, cultured, beautiful, and peaceful

CULTURAL NOTE ***Camelot***, the 1960 musical by Alan Jay Lerner and Frederick Loewe, takes its title from the site of King Arthur's legendary sixth-century English court, and its tragic yet lavishly produced story centers on Arthur, his queen, Guinevere, and Lancelot. The word "Camelot" soon came to be associated in the US public mind with the youthful stylishness, sophistication, and optimism of President John F. Kennedy's administration (1961–63), chiefly because the musical's popularity coincided in time with the period of John and Jacqueline Kennedy's occupation of the White House. Further, the media reported that the First Couple enjoyed listening to recordings of this musical. As a result "Camelot" eventually took on the generic meaning of "a period, time, or place regarded as idyllic, peaceful, idealistic, youthful, enlightened, and optimistic." And so the mythology enveloping a sixth-century English king was conferred via the theater and politics to the grandson of Irish immigrants – a 20th-century US president – whose "one brief shining moment" was cut short by assassination on November 22, 1963.

cam·el's hair *n* INDUST, TEXTILES same as **camel hair**

cam·el spin *n* in figure skating, a spin in which the skater extends one leg backward in a raised and horizontal position

Cam·em·bert /kámməm bèr/ *n* a small round soft French cheese with an edible white rind that becomes more intense in flavor and softer in the center as it ripens [Late 19C. After a town in Normandy, France]

cam·e·o /kámmee ō/ *n* **1.** a semiprecious stone carved to give a raised design in one color against a background of another, especially a pale head against a darker background **2.** a single brief appearance by a famous actor in a movie or play [15C. < Italian]

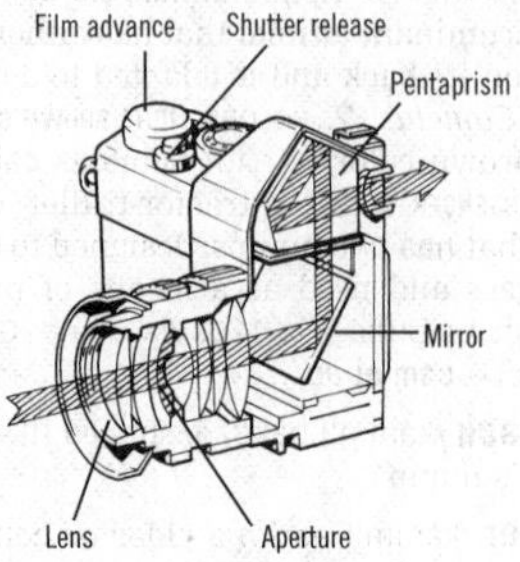

Camera

cam·er·a /kámmərə, kámmrə/ *n* **1.** DEVICE FOR TAKING PHOTOGRAPHS a device for taking photographs by letting light from an image fall briefly onto sensitized film, usually by means of a lens-and-shutter mechanism **2.** DEVICE FOR MAKING PICTURES a device that converts images into electrical signals for television transmission, video recording, or digital storage **3.** COMPUT GAMES COMPUTER GAME VIEWPOINT in a computer game, an imaginary camera located at the point that would produce the image shown on a computer screen [Early 18C. Via Latin, "vault, chamber" < Greek *kamara*]

~~cameraderie~~ incorrect spelling of **camaraderie**

cam·er·a lu·ci·da /-lóossidə/ (*plural* **cam·er·a lu·ci·das**) *n* a box or chamber that allows images to be projected onto a surface so they can be traced [Early 18C. < Latin, "bright chamber"]

cam·er·a·man /kámmrə màn, kámmərə-, -mən/ (*plural* **-men** /-mèn, -mən/) *n* a man who operates a movie or television camera

cam·er·a ob·scu·ra /-əb skyóorə, -ob-/ *n* a box or small darkened room into which an image of what is outside is projected using a small hole, and sometimes a simple lens, in one of the sides of the box or room [Early 18C. < Latin, "dark chamber"]

cam·er·a·per·son /kámmrə pùrss'n, kámmərə-/ *n* an operator of a movie or television camera

cam·er·a-read·y *adj* describes material in its final publishable format, ready to be photographed or electronically scanned for the purpose of preparing printing plates

cam·er·a-shy *adj* with a dislike of being photographed or filmed

cam·er·a·wom·an /kámmrə wòommən, kámmərə-/ (*plural* **-wom·en** /-wìmmin/) *n* a woman who operates a movie or television camera

cam·er·a·work /kámmrə wùrk, kámmərə-/ *n* the ways in which cameras are used in movies and television, especially their positioning and movement

cam·er·lin·go /kàmmər líng gō/ (*plural* **-gos**), **cam·er·len·go** /-léng gō/ *n* in the Roman Catholic Church, a cardinal who deals with the pope's financial and other secular affairs [Early 17C. Via Italian < Frankish]

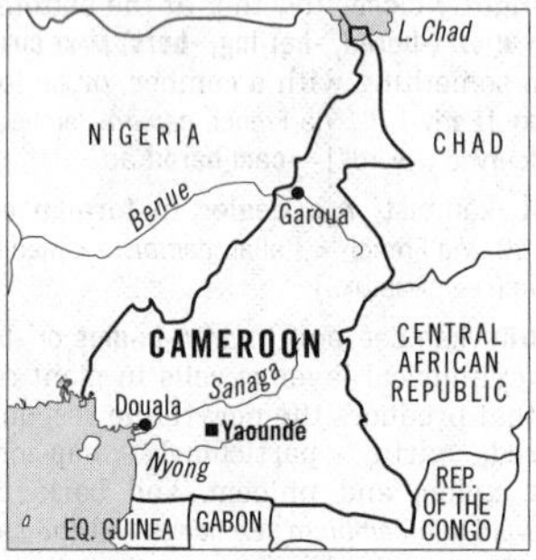

Cameroon

Cam·e·roon /kàmmə róon/ **1.** country in west central Africa. It became a German protectorate in 1884. After World War I it was divided into French and British Cameroon. French Cameroon became independent in 1960. In 1961, part of British Cameroon joined Nigeria, while the rest joined French Cameroon in a federal republic. Cameroon became a unitary state in 1972 and became an independent member of the British Commonwealth in 1995. Language: French, English. Currency: CFA franc. Capital: Yaoundé. Population: 15,746,179 (2003). Area: 183,569 sq. mi./475,442 sq. km. Official name **Republic of Cameroon** **2.** active volcano in southwestern Cameroon that had a major eruption in 1982. It is the highest mountain in West Africa. Height: 13,435 ft./4,095 m.

cam fol·low·er *n* a machine part that moves up and down in contact with a cam on a rotating shaft

cam·i /kámmee/ (*plural* **-is**) *n* CLOTHING same as **camisole** (*informal*) [Early 20C. Shortening]

cam·i·sa·do /kàmmə sáydō, -saádō/ (*plural* **-does**) *n* a surprise attack at night (*archaic*) [Mid-16C. < Spanish *camisada* "attack in your shirt" (because attackers wore shirts over their armor in order to recognize each other) < *camisa* "shirt"]

ca·mise /kə meéz, -meéss/ *n* a style of loose shirt or tunic worn in former times [Early 19C. < Arabic *kamīṣ*]

cam·i·sole /kámmi sòl/ *n* **1.** a woman's sleeveless undergarment covering the upper torso **2.** a woman's sleeveless top with thin shoulder straps and a straight neckline ○ *a camisole top* [Early 19C. < French < late Latin *camisia* "linen shirt, nightgown"]

Cam·lan /kámmlən/ *n* in Arthurian legend, the battlefield in southwestern England where King Arthur was mortally wounded by his traitorous nephew Mordred before being carried away to Avalon

cam·o /kámmō/ *n* camouflage clothes or material used by military personnel (*slang*) [Shortening of CAMOUFLAGE]

Ca·mões /kə móynsh/, **Ca·mo·ëns** /kámmō ənss/, **Luís (Vaz) de** (1524?–80) Portuguese poet. His best-known work, *Os Lusíadas* (*The Lusiads*) (1572), is considered Portugal's national epic.

~~camoflage~~ incorrect spelling of **camouflage**

ca·mo·gie /kə mṓgee/ *n* an Irish stick-and-ball game that is a form of hurling played by women [Early 20C. < Irish Gaelic *camógaíocht* < *camóg* "crooked stick"]

cam·o·mile *n* PLANTS another spelling of **chamomile**

ca·moo·di /kə móodee/ (*plural* **-dis**) *n* REPT same as **anaconda** [Early 19C. < Arawak *kamudu*]

Ca·mor·ra /kə máwrə/ *n* a secret society formed in Italy in the early 1800s that was involved in criminal and terrorist activities. The Camorra allied itself with Garibaldi and helped to eject the ruling Bourbons, then declined in the early 20th century and was suppressed in 1922 by Mussolini's Fascist government. [Mid-19C. < Italian]

cam·ou·flage /kámmə flaàzh, -flaàj/ *n* **1.** CONCEALMENT OF THINGS concealment of things, especially troops and military equipment, by disguising them to look like their surroundings, e.g., by covering them with branches or leaf-clad netting **2.** CONCEALING DEVICES devices designed to conceal by imitating the colors of the surrounding environment ○ *a camouflage jacket* **3.** PROTECTIVE COLORATION IN ANIMALS the devices that animals use to blend into their environment in order to avoid being seen by predators or prey, especially coloration **4.** DISGUISE something that is intended to hide, disguise, or mislead ■ *vt* (**-flaged, -flag·ing, -flag·es**) **1.** HIDE SOMETHING to conceal something by making it match its surroundings, especially in appearance **2.** DISGUISE SOMETHING to disguise something in order to mislead somebody, often somebody perceived as a threat ○ *camouflaged his true intentions* [Early 20C. < French < *camoufler* "to disguise" < Italian *camuffare*] —**cam·ou·flag·er** *n*

camp[1] /kamp/ *n* **1.** PLACE WITH REMOVABLE ACCOMMODATIONS a place where short-term accommodations such as tents or camper vehicles for vacationers have been temporarily erected or sited **2.** PLACE OF SUMMER RECREATION FOR CHILDREN a place, usually residential, offering recreational activities and skill development for children during the summer ○ *music camp* **3.** PLACE FOR TEMPORARY STAY a set of buildings where people are housed temporarily, e.g., as prisoners, refugees, or troops ○ *a prison camp* **4.** *regional* RUSTIC SHACK a small, very rustic house in an isolated place, used for weekend fishing or hunting trips ○ *a fishing camp on one of the Great Lakes* **5.** GROUP a group of people who share the same ideas, beliefs, or aims, or who form one of the sides in a debate ○ *members of the environmentalist camp* ■ *vi* (**camped, camping, camps**) **1.** STAY TEMPORARILY to stay in temporary accommodations, especially in a tent ○ *We camped by a stream.* **2.** TAKE TEMPORARY POSITION to take up a temporary position somewhere, e.g., as a protester or in alternative accommodations ○ *We'll camp on his doorstep until we get some action.* [Early 16C. Via French < Latin *campus* "field, site for military exercises"]

camp out *vi* **1.** to live or sleep outdoors, with or without a tent ○ *camping out under the stars for a few nights.* **2.** to take up a temporary position somewhere, e.g., as a protester or in alternative accommodations ○ *camping out at a friend's house*

camp[2] /kamp/ *adj* **1.** AFFECTING CONVENTIONAL FEMININITY exaggeratedly or affectedly feminine, especially in a man **2.** AMUSINGLY BRASH deliberately and exaggeratedly brash or vulgar in an amusing, often self-parodying way ■ *n* **1.** EXAGGERATED FEMININITY exaggeratedly or affectedly feminine behavior, especially in men **2.** DELIBERATE OUTRAGEOUSNESS deliberate outrageousness for humorous effect ○ *The performance is high camp.* [Early 20C. Origin ?] —**camp** *vi* —**camp·y** *adj* ◇ **camp it up** (*informal*) **1.** to behave in a deliberately outrageous way for humorous effect **2.** to behave in an exaggeratedly or affectedly feminine way, especially to emphasize the fact of being gay (*usually refers to men*) **3.** to overact in a stage or musical production

Camp /kamp/, **Walter Chauncey** (1859–1925) US football coach. He invented many of the current rules of the game at Yale University (1888–92).

cam·paign /kam páyn/ *n* **1.** POL **VOTE-SEEKING ACTIVITIES** a series of events, e.g., rallies and speeches, that are intended to persuade voters to vote for a specific politician or party ○ *ran an expensive national campaign* **2. PLANNED ACTIONS** a planned and organized series of actions intended to achieve a specific goal, especially fighting for or against something or raising people's awareness of something ○ *an advertising campaign* **3.** MIL **MILITARY OPERATIONS** a series of military or terrorist operations taking place in one area over a period, intended to achieve a specific objective ■ *vi* (**-paigned, -paign·ing, -paigns**) **1. WORK TOWARD GOAL** to take part in a campaign to achieve a specific goal ○ *campaigned tirelessly for the lifting of the embargo* **2. SEEK VOTES** to take part in a political campaign ○ *campaigned with incumbents in Southern states* [Early 17C. < French *campagne* "open country" < Latin *campus* "field"] —**cam·paign·er** *n*

~~**campain**~~ incorrect spelling of **campaign**

campanile

cam·pa·ni·le /kàmpə neélee/ (*plural* **-les** or **-li** /-lee/) *n* a bell tower, especially a freestanding bell tower of the kind found in Italy [Mid-17C. < Italian < *campana* "bell" < late Latin *campana* (see CAMPANOLOGY)]

cam·pa·nol·o·gy /kàmpə nóllәjee/ *n* the study or practice of bell ringing [Mid-19C. < modern Latin *campanologia* < late Latin *campana* "bell" < Latin *campanus* "of Campania" (S Italy), former source of bronze for making bells] —**cam·pa·nol·o·gist** *n*

cam·pan·u·la /kam pánnyələ/ *n* an annual or perennial plant, widely grown as a garden plant. Flowers: bell-shaped, blue, white, or pink. Native to: northern temperate regions. Genus: *Campanula.* [Early 17C. < modern Latin, "little bell" < late Latin *campana* (see CAMPANOLOGY)]

camp bed *n UK* CAMPING, FURNITURE same as **cot**[1] (sense 1)

Camp·bell /kámb'l/ city in western California, southeast of San Francisco and southwest of San Jose. Population: 37,474 (2002 estimate).

Camp·bell /kámbəl/, **Keith** (*b.* 1954) British microbiologist. With Ian Wilmut he was responsible for the first successful cloning of a mammal from adult cells.

Corbis

Kim Campbell

Camp·bell, Kim (*b.* 1947) Canadian politician. She held several positions in Brian Mulroney's cabinet (1989–93) before becoming Canada's first woman prime minister (1993). Born **Campbell, Avril Phaedra.** See table at **prime minister**

> "In a democracy, government isn't something that a small group of people do to everybody else, it's not even something they do for everybody else, it should be something they do with everybody else."
> [Kim Campbell, *Press conference*; March 25, 1993]

Camp·bell, Wilfred (1858?–1918) Canadian writer. His works include the poetry collection *Lake Lyrics* (1889) and the novel *Ian of the Orcades* (1906).

Camp·bell, William Wallace (1862–1938) US astronomer. He was a pioneer in using spectroscopy to determine the velocity of stars. His published works include *Stellar Motions* (1913).

Camp·bell-Ban·ner·man /-bánnərmən/, **Sir Henry** (1836–1908) British politician. He was leader of the Liberal Party (1899–1908). As British prime minister (1905–08) he granted self-government to the Transvaal and the Orange Free State in South Africa. See table at **prime minister**

Camp Da·vid /-dáyvid/ presidential retreat in Catoctin Mountain Park, central Maryland, established by President Franklin D. Roosevelt in 1942. President Jimmy Carter hosted talks there in 1978 between Menachem Begin and Anwar al-Sadat, the presidents of Israel and Egypt, that led to the Camp David Accords, offering a framework for peace in the Middle East.

Cam·pe·che /kam peéchee/ **1.** state in southeastern Mexico on the Yucatán Peninsula. Capital: Campeche. Population: 690,689 (2000). Area: 21,930 sq. mi./56,800 sq. km. **2.** capital of Campeche State in southeastern Mexico. It is located on the coast in the northwestern part of the state. Population: 229,144 (2000).

camp·er /kámpər/ *n* **1. SOMEBODY WHO CAMPS** somebody who goes camping ○ *accessories for campers and hikers* **2. RECREATIONAL VEHICLE** a motor vehicle equipped as a self-contained traveling home, smaller than a motor home. It has basic facilities for cooking, washing, and sleeping. **3. TRAILER FOR LIVING IN** a trailer equipped as a self-contained traveling home, hauled by a car

cam·pe·si·no /kàmpə seénō, kaàmpə-/ (*plural* **-nos**) *n Hispanic* in Latin American countries, a farmer or agricultural worker [Mid-20C. < Spanish < Latin *campus* "field"]

camp·fire /kámp fīr/ *n* a wood fire built outside by campers, for cooking on or for warmth

Camp Fire *n* an organization for boys and girls that aims to teach them personal skills, leadership, and social responsibility

camp fol·low·er *n* **1.** a civilian who follows a military unit from place to place in order to earn money by supplying products or services, especially services as a prostitute **2.** a supporter of a group or an organization who does not belong to it

camp·ground /kámp grownd/ *n* an outdoor area designed for camping, usually providing campers with some facilities such as showers, toilets, and a store

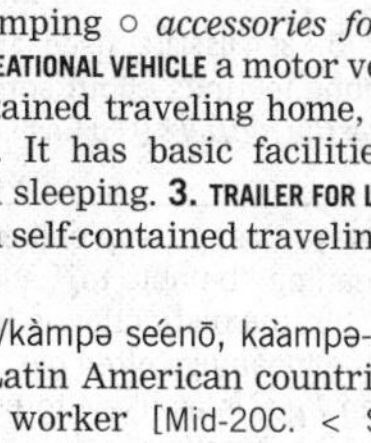

camphor

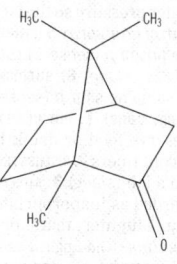

cam·phor /kámfər/ *n* a strong-smelling compound. Use: in medicinal creams, manufacture of celluloid, plastics, and explosives. Formula: $C_{10}H_{16}$. [14C. Directly or via French < medieval Latin *camphora*, via Arabic and Malay < Sanskrit *karpūra*] —**cam·phor·ic** /kam fáwrik/ *adj*

cam·phor·ate /kámfə ràyt/ (**-at·ed, -at·ing, -ates**) *vt* to treat or impregnate something with camphor

cam·phor ice *n* an ointment used to relieve minor skin ailments, made of camphor mixed with white wax and castor oil

cam·phor oil *n* the oil that is distilled from the steamed bark and wood of the camphor tree

cam·phor tree *n* an evergreen tree, sometimes cultivated as an ornamental, with aromatic wood and bark that are a source of camphor. Native to: East Asia. Latin name: *Cinnamomum camphora.*

cam·phor·weed /kámfər weèd/ *n* either of two flowering plants of the composite family that have small clusters of flowers. Native to: North America. Latin name: *Heterotheca subaxillaris* or *Pluchea camphorata.*

cam·pim·e·try /kam pímmətree/ *n* the measuring of the field of vision or the sensitivity of the retina to color and space [Early 20C. < Latin *campus* "field"]

Cam·pi·nas /kam peénəss/ city in eastern São Paulo State, southeastern Brazil, northwest of São Paulo. Population: 908,906 (1996).

camp·ing /kámping/ *n* living outdoors in a tent or trailer while on vacation or as a recreational activity ○ *camping equipment*

cam·pi·on /kámpee ən/ *n* a flowering plant of the pink family. Flowers: pink, red, white. Native to: northern hemisphere. Genera: *Lychnis* or *Silene.* [Mid-16C. Origin ?]

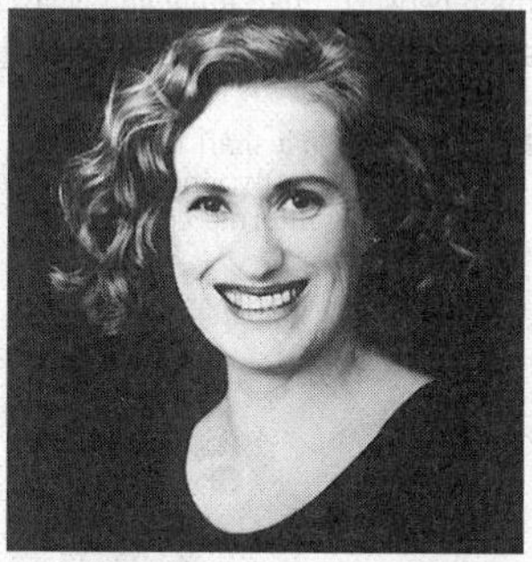

Jane Campion

Cam·pi·on /kámpee ən/, **Jane** (*b.* 1954) New Zealand movie director. She directed the Academy Award-winning *The Piano* (1993).

camp meet·ing *n* a religious rally held outdoors, especially one lasting several days with participants camping nearby

cam·po /kámpō, kaámpō/ (*plural* **-pos**) *n* **1.** in South America, a large grassy plain with scattered bushes and small stunted trees **2.** *Hispanic* the countryside or a rural area [Mid-19C. Via American Spanish or Portuguese, "field" < Latin *campus*]

Cam·po·bel·lo /kàmpə béllō/ island off the southwestern coast of New Brunswick, Canada, a favorite summer vacation spot of Franklin D. Roosevelt. Area: 27 sq. mi./70 sq. km. Population: 1,317 (1991).

Cam·po Gran·de /kàmpō graándə, kaàmpō graándee/ city and capital of Mato Grosso do Sul State, southwestern Brazil. Population: 565,943 (1993).

camp·o·ree /kàmpə reé/ *n* a gathering of Boy Scouts or Girl Scouts from a particular area [Early 20C. Probably blend of CAMP[1] + JAMBOREE]

Cam·pos /kámpəss, kaám pōss/ city in Rio de Janeiro State, southeastern Brazil, situated on the Paraíba River. Population: 389,547 (1996).

camp rob·ber *n US regional, Can* a bird, especially the gray jay, that visits campgrounds to steal food

REGIONAL NOTE ***Camp robber*** is common in the Upper Rocky Mountain states and the Pacific Northwest. The bird is also called *camp robin, camp thief, Rocky Mountain magpie,* and *Canadian camp robber.*

camp rob·in *n regional* BIRDS same as **gray jay**

camp·site /kámp sìt/ *n* **1.** a single unit of land within a campground, for a camper to pitch a tent on or park a trailer or camper on **2.** *UK* same as **campground**

camp·stool /kámp sto͞ol/ *n* a stool that folds up for easy storage and carriage, designed for use when camping

camp thief *n regional* same as **gray jay**

REGIONAL NOTE See *camp robber.*

cam·pus /kámpəss/ *n* **1.** COLLEGE OR UNIVERSITY SITE an area of land that contains the main buildings and grounds of a university, college, or school ○ *accommodations on campus* **2.** EDUCATIONAL INSTITUTION a university or college ○ *a campus newspaper* **3.** SITE a site on which the buildings of an organization or institution are located ○ *a dormitory for nursing students on the hospital campus* [Late 18C. < Latin, "field"]

cam·pus nov·el *n* a novel that satirizes university life. The genre appeared in Britain in the late 1970s and early 1980s.

cam·py·lo·bac·ter /kámpəlō bàktər/ *n* a rod- or spiral-shaped bacterium that is a common cause of food poisoning in humans and of spontaneous abortion in farm animals [Late 20C. < modern Latin < Greek *kampulos* "bent" + *baktērion* (see BACTERIUM)]

cam·py·lo·bac·ter en·ter·i·tis *n* an intestinal infection by the organism *Campylobacter jejuni* that is usually acquired from contaminated water, milk, or poultry. It is a common cause of travelers' diarrhea.

Cam Ranh Bay /kàm ran-, kaàm raan-/ inlet of the South China Sea, situated on the southeastern coast of Vietnam between Phan Rang and Nha Trang

Cam·rose /kám rōz/ city in east central Alberta, Canada. Population: 14,854 (2001).

cam·shaft /kám shàft/ *n* a shaft that has one or more cams attached, especially one that operates the valves in a vehicle's internal combustion engine

Canada

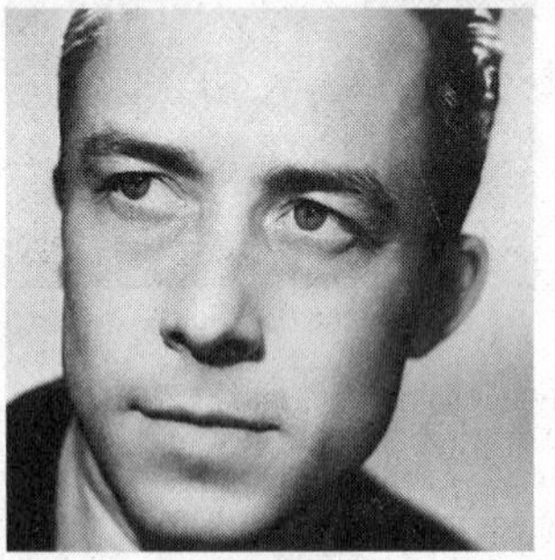

Albert Camus

Ca·mus /kaa mo͞o/, **Albert** (1913–60) Algerian-born French novelist, essayist, and dramatist. He wrote *The Stranger* (1942) and *The Plague* (1947), and was awarded the Nobel Prize in literature (1957). See Cultural note at **stranger**

> "I am not made for politics because I am incapable of wishing for, or accepting the death of my adversary."
> [Albert Camus, *The Rebel*; 1951]

cam wheel *n* a wheel that functions as a cam

cam·wood /kám wo͝od/ *n* **1.** the hard red wood of a West African tree. Use: formerly, cabinet making, red dye. **2.** a tree that produces camwood. Native to: West Africa. Latin name: *Baphia nitida.* [Late 17C. Probably < Temne *k'am*]

can[1] *stressed* /kan/; *unstressed* /kən/ CORE MEANING: a modal verb used to indicate that it is possible for something to be done or made use of in a particular way ○ *Loans can be made over the phone.*
modal v **1.** BE ABLE TO to have the ability, knowledge, or opportunity to do something ○ *Can you swim?* **2.** BE LIKELY to be likely to be true or to be the case ○ *It can be dangerous.* **3.** BE ALLOWED TO to be allowed to do something, either by legal or moral right or by permission ○ *Can I go?* **4.** BE ACCEPTABLE used to make polite requests, suggestions, or offers ○ *Can I make a suggestion?* **5.** BE POSSIBLE used in questions to emphasize strong feelings about something ○ *What on earth can be the matter?* [Old English *cunnan* < Indo-European]

USAGE can or **may**? Many people draw a distinction between ***can***, meaning "be able to," and ***may***, meaning "be allowed to," but the distinction is hard to maintain in practice and the meanings often overlap. In everyday conversation, *Can I go?* is as likely to be used as *May I go?*, and the context, together with intonation, usually makes it clear what is meant. In more formal situations it is wise to maintain the distinction, if only because many people expect it. Note that ***may*** has ambiguities of its own. *He may go* can mean either "he is allowed to go" or "it is possible that he will go"; again, intonation and context clarify the matter. The negative contraction ***mayn't*** is awkward, and ***can't*** is usually used instead: *Can't we come too?*

can[2] /kan/ *n* **1.** FOOD CONTAINER a sealed metal container, usually cylindrical, in which food or drink is preserved or packaged and sold **2.** METAL CONTAINER WITH REPLACEABLE LID a metal container with a removable lid or cap, especially one for storing or packaging liquids such as chemicals or paint **3.** CONTENTS OF CAN the contents of a metal container ○ *We used up three cans of paint.* **4.** PRESSURIZED CONTAINER a metal container that holds liquid under pressure so that it can be released as a spray ○ *a can of hair spray* **5.** SHIPPING same as **can buoy 6.** same as **prison** *n* (sense 1) (*slang*) **7.** same as **toilet** (senses 1–2) (*slang*) **8.** BUTTOCKS the buttocks (*slang*) **9.** NAVY same as **ship** *n* (sense 1) (*slang*) ■ *vt* (**canned, can·ning, cans**) **1.** PUT IN METAL CONTAINERS to package or preserve food or drink by putting it in sealed airtight containers **2.** DISMISS FROM JOB to dismiss somebody from a job (*slang*) **3.** STOP SOMETHING to stop something regarded as inappropriate under the circumstances, e.g., laughter, tears, or jokes (*slang*) ○ *Just can the giggling.* [Old English *canne* < Germanic or late Latin *canna*] —**can·ful** *n* —**can·ner** *n* ◇ **in the can** (*informal*) **1.** in the final edited form ready for broadcasting or distribution ○ *as soon as the movie is in the can* **2.** successfully completed or negotiated

can. *abbr* **1.** canceled **2.** cancellation **3.** MIL cannon **4.** MUSIC canon[1] (sense 7) **5.** LITERAT canto

Can. *abbr* **1.** Canada **2.** Canadian

Ca·naan /káynən/ *n* in the Bible, the part of ancient Palestine west of the Jordan River

Ca·naan·ite /káynə nìt/ *n* **1.** a member of a Semitic people who lived in Canaan from around 3000 B.C. until 1000 B.C. **2.** an extinct Semitic language once spoken in the region between the Jordan River and the Mediterranean Sea —**Ca·naan·ite** *adj*

Canad. *abbr* Canadian[1]

Can·a·da /kánnədə/ federation occupying the northern half of North America and the second largest country in the world. It became an independent member of the British Commonwealth in 1931. Language: English, French. Currency: Canadian dollar. Capital: Ottawa. Population: 32,207,113 (2003). Area: 3,849,674 sq. mi./9,970,610 sq. km.

Can·a·da bal·sam *n* a thick resin secreted from the bark of the balsam fir

Can·a·da Day *n* a Canadian annual holiday marking the day in 1867 when Canada became the first British colony to become a dominion. Date: July 1. Former name **Dominion Day**

Can·a·da De·pos·it In·su·rance Cor·po·ra·tion *n* GOV full form of **CDIC**

Ca·na·da East former name for **Quebec**[1] (sense 2) (1841–67)

Can·a·da goose *n* a large goose with a brownish body, a black head and neck, and a white patch on its throat. Native to: North America, introduced into Europe. Latin name: *Branta canadensis.*

Can·a·da jay *n* BIRDS same as **gray jay**

Can·a·da lil·y *n* a lily with small orange funnel-shaped flowers. Native to: North America. Latin name: *Lilium canadense.* See illustration on next page

Can·a·da lynx *n* a dark gray lynx. Native to: Canada, northern United States. Latin name: *Lynx canadensis.*

Can·a·da Rev·e·nue A·gen·cy *n* the Canadian government department responsible for the collection

WORLD ENGLISH ***Canadian English*** is the variety of English as it is used in the federation of Canada, which is geographically the largest English-speaking country in the world. However, in demographic terms (with a population of over 31 million, of whom over 7 million are French-speaking, mainly in the province of Quebec), it is the third largest. Canadian English has coexisted for about 230 years with Canadian French, which predates it by a century, as the French were Canada's first main European settlers. English and French are co-official languages in a nation whose linguistic mosaic includes indigenous languages (including Cree, Inuktitut, Iroquois, and Ojibwa) and immigrant languages (including Cantonese, Italian, and Ukrainian).

There are at least three regional varieties of spoken Canadian English: (1) that of the Atlantic provinces, in which the Newfoundland dialect is the most distinctive; (2) that of Quebec, whose English-speakers are influenced by French, and whose French-speakers, when using English, range from native-speaker fluency to varying mixtures of the two languages; (3) that of the rest of Canada, whose educated variety (focused on Ontario) is generally taken as the national norm. Written and printed Canadian English blends the conventions of the United Kingdom (decreasingly influential) and, increasingly, those of the United States. US spelling tends to predominate. Official federal bilingualism often leads to hybrid formulas such as *Jeux Canada Games* (blending French *Jeux Canada* and English *Canada Games*). In Canadian English *r* is pronounced in such words as *art, door,* and *worker.* Another feature is the use of the particle *eh* with a rising tone at the end of a sentence, as in *It's nice, eh?*

Distinctively Canadian English vocabulary includes: (1) adoptions from indigenous languages, as in *anorak* and *kayak* (both international), *mackinaw* (a bush jacket), *muskeg* (mossy, swampy land); (2) adoptions from French, as in *anglophone* and *francophone* (both in the French style, without a capital letter), *caboteur* (a coastal trading vessel); (3) British English usages adapted for local purposes, including *riding* (originally one of three divisions of Yorkshire, England, which in Canada means a political constituency), and *prime minister* (the federal first minister), contrasted with *premier* (the first minister of a provincial government).

of income and other taxes and the enforcement of the tax laws

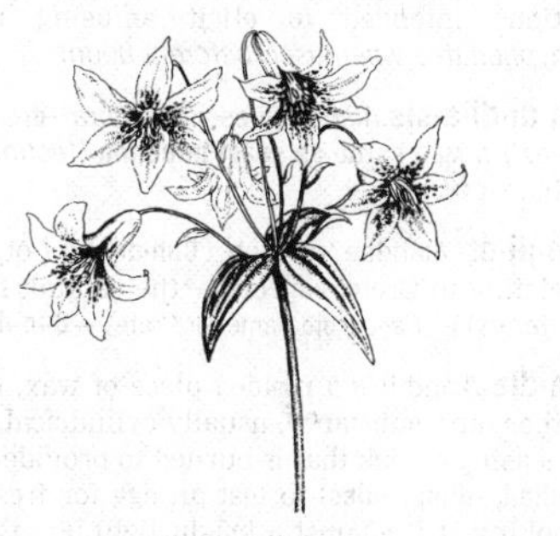

Canada lily

Can·a·da this·tle *n* a variety of creeping thistle, sometimes regarded as a serious weed. Native to: Europe and Asia, introduced into North America. Latin name: *Cirsium arvense.*

Ca·na·da West former name for **Ontario** (1841–67)

Ca·na·di·an[1] /kə náydee ən/ *adj* relating to Canada, or its people, languages, or cultures ■ *n* somebody who comes from Canada

Ca·na·di·an[2] /kə náydee ən/ river in the southwestern United States that flows from southern Colorado across New Mexico and Texas into Oklahoma. Length: 906 mi./1,460 km.

Ca·na·di·an Al·li·ance *n* a Canadian conservative political party dissolved in 2003 when it joined with the Progressive Conservative Party to form the Conservative Party of Canada

Ca·na·di·an ba·con *n* relatively fat-free bacon from the loin or rib end of a hog

Ca·na·di·an Broad·cast·ing Cor·po·ra·tion *n* full form of **CBC**

Ca·na·di·an camp rob·ber *n regional* BIRDS same as **gray jay**

REGIONAL NOTE See ***camp robber.***

Ca·na·di·an Eng·lish *n* the variety of English spoken in Canada

Ca·na·di·an foot·ball *n* a form of football that is similar to US football but takes place on a larger field, has 12 players on each team, and uses three rather than four plays to advance at least ten yards or score

Ca·na·di·an French *n* the variety of French that is spoken in parts of Canada, especially Quebec

Ca·na·di·an hem·lock *n* a coniferous evergreen tree that produces lumber and pulpwood. Native to: Canada. Latin name: *Tsuga canadensis.*

Can·a·di·an·ism /kə náydee ə nìzzəm/ *n* a word or other expression originating in or restricted in use to Canada

Ca·na·di·an·ize /kə náydee ə nīz/ (**-ized, -iz·ing, -iz·es**) *vti* to make something Canadian in form, content, or status, or become Canadian —**Ca·na·di·an·i·za·tion** /kə nàydee əni záysh'n/ *n*

Ca·na·di·an lynx *n* VERTEB same as **Canada lynx**

Ca·na·di·an Shield /kə nàydee ən sheéld/ plateau region of eastern Canada extending southward and eastward from Hudson Bay. Area: 1,776,070 sq. mi./4,600,000 sq. km.

Ca·na·di·an whis·key *n Can* blended whiskey made mainly from rye

Ca·na·di·en /kə nàydee én/ *n Can* a French Canadian man [Mid-19C. < French]

Ca·na·di·enne /kə nàydee én/ *n Can* a French Canadian woman [Mid-19C. < French]

ca·naille /kə nī, -náyl/ *n* the lowest class of people (*disapproving*) [Late 16C. Via French < Italian *canaglia* "pack of dogs" < Latin *canis* "dog"]

ca·nal /kə nál/ *n* **1.** TRANSP **WATERWAY** an artificial waterway constructed for use by shipping, for irrigation, or for recreational use. A canal may take in parts of natural rivers along its course. **2.** ANAT **TUBE IN BODY** a tube-shaped passage in the body, carrying air, liquids, or semisolid material **3.** ASTRON **FEATURE ON MARS** an apparent surface marking on Mars, formerly thought to be part of a system of water channels, a view discredited by more recent data [15C. < French, alteration (based on Italian *canale* or Latin *canalis*) of *chanel* < Latin *canalis* "pipe, canal" < *canna* (see CANE)]

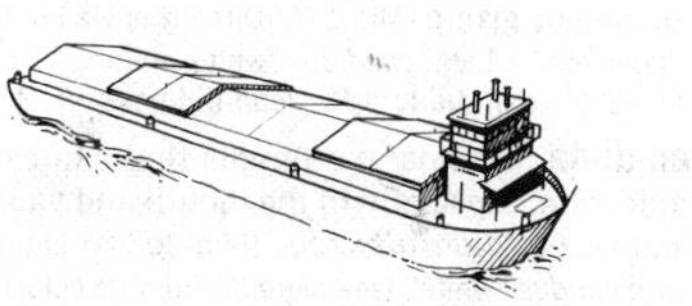

canal boat

ca·nal boat *n* a long boat used on canals to carry freight or for recreational boating

Ca·nal du Mi·di /kə nàl dōō mee deé/ canal in southern France that links the Bay of Biscay to the Mediterranean Sea

Ca·na·let·to /kànnə léttō/, **Antonio** (1697–1768) Italian artist, known especially for his views of Venice and London. Born **Canal, Giovanni Antonio**

can·a·lic·u·lus /kànnə líkyələss/ (*plural* **-li** /-lī/) *n* a minute canal or duct in the body, especially one of the four narrow tubes that carry tears from behind the eyelids to the lacrimal sac [Mid-16C. < Latin, "little pipe" < *canalis* (see CANAL)] —**can·a·lic·u·lar** *adj* —**can·a·lic·u·late** /-lət, -làyt/ *adj*

can·a·lize /kánn'l īz/ (**-lized, -liz·ing, -liz·es**) *v* **1.** *vt* **BUILD CANALS IN AREA** to provide an area with canals, or convert existing waterways into canals **2.** *vi* **FLOW INTO CHANNEL** to flow into or form a new channel **3.** *vt* **DIRECT SOMETHING** to direct or focus something such as energy or enthusiasm in a particular direction (*formal*) —**can·a·li·za·tion** /kànn'li záysh'n/ *n*

Can-Am *adj Can* relating to or involving both Canada and the United States [< Shortenings]

Can·an·dai·gua /kànnən dáygwə/ city in northwestern New York, at the northern end of Lake Canandaigua. Population: 11,256 (2002 estimate).

can·a·pé /kánnə pày, kánnəpee/ *n* a bite-sized base of bread, cracker, or pastry with a topping, served as an appetizer or to accompany drinks [Late 19C. Via French, literally "sofa" < medieval Latin *canopeum* (see CANOPY)]

ca·nard /kə naárd/ *n* **1.** **HOAX** a deliberately false report or rumor, especially something silly intended as a joke (*literary*) **2.** **AIRCRAFT PART LIKE WING** a small projection like a wing near the nose of an aircraft, attached in order to create extra horizontal stability **3.** **AIRCRAFT** an aircraft fitted with a canard [Mid-19C. < French, literally "duck," an imitation of the sound]

Ca·nar·ies /kə nérreez/ ♦ **Canary Islands**

Ca·nar·ies Cur·rent cold current of the North Atlantic Ocean, flowing south from the Canary Islands down the western coast of northern Africa, joining the westward-flowing equatorial current west of Mauritania and Senegal

ca·nar·y /kə nérree/ (*plural* **-ies**) *n* **1.** BIRDS a small yellow songbird of the finch family that has been domesticated as a pet and as a show bird. Native to: Canary Islands and adjacent islands. Latin name: *Serinus canarius.* **2.** WINE a sweet wine from the Canary Islands, similar to Madeira **3.** COLORS same as **canary yellow** [Late 16C. < French *Canarie*, chief island of the Canary Islands < Latin *Canaria Insula* "Isle of Dogs," from the large dogs that inhabited it in Roman times] —**ca·nar·y** *adj*

ca·nar·y creep·er *n* a climbing plant with small yellow flowers. Native to: Peru. Latin name: *Tropaeolum peregrinum.*

ca·nar·y grass *n* an annual grass plant cultivated for its seeds that are sold as birdseed. Native to: northwestern Africa, Canary Islands. Latin name: *Phalaris canariensis.*

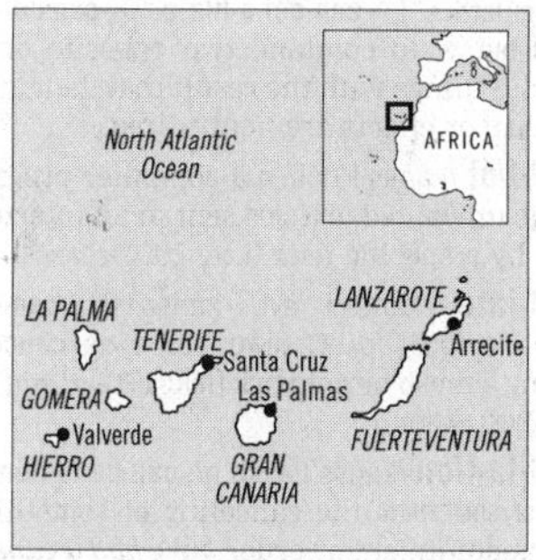

Canary Islands

Ca·nar·y Is·lands /kə nérree-/, **Ca·nar·ies** /kə nérreez/ autonomous region of Spain consisting of a group of islands off the northwestern coast of Africa, comprising the provinces of Las Palmas and Santa Cruz de Tenerife. They consist of seven large islands and various islets. The climate is subtropical and tourism is important, especially on the islands of Gran Canaria and Tenerife. Population: 1,631,498 (1995). Area: 2,808 sq. mi./7,273 sq. km. Spanish name **Islas Canarias**

ca·nar·y yel·low *n* a bright yellow color —**ca·nar·y yel·low** *adj*

ca·nas·ta /kə nástə/ *n* **1.** a variant of the card game rummy played with two 52-card decks. Players are dealt 15 cards, the goal being to collect groups of seven similar cards. **2.** a point-scoring set of cards in canasta [Mid-20C. Via Spanish, "basket" < Latin *canistrum*, because two decks of cards (a "basketful") are used]

Ca·nav·er·al, Cape /kə návvərəl/ cape in Brevard County, Florida, situated on the eastern coast of the Canaveral peninsula. It is the home of the John F. Kennedy Space Center and has been the launching site of US crewed space flights since 1961. Former name **Kennedy, Cape** (1963–73)

Can·ber·ra /kánbərə, -bèrrə/ capital city of Australia, located in the Australian Capital Territory in southeastern Australia. Construction of this new capital began in 1913 and the national parliament moved here from its temporary seat in Melbourne in 1927. Population: 321,819 (2002 estimate). —**Can·ber·ran** *n, adj*

can buoy *n* an unlighted marker buoy for shipping, cylindrical or cone-shaped above the water

canc. *abbr* **1.** canceled **2.** cancellation

can·can /kán kàn/ *n* a dance of French origin in which a chorus line of women perform high kicks to reveal their underwear. It originated in the 1840s in the music halls in Paris. [Mid-19C. < French]

can·can skirt *n* a skirt with layers of ruffles and attached underwear that is shown by cancan dancers when the skirt is lifted during the dance

can·cel /kánss'l/ *v* (**-celed, -cel·ing, -cels**) **1.** *vti* **STOP SOMETHING FROM HAPPENING** to stop a previously arranged event from happening ○ *We had to cancel five classes because nobody showed up.* ○ *The guest speaker is sick and has had to cancel.* **2.** *vti* **END CONTRACT** to withdraw officially or legally from a contract ○ *Members are free to cancel at any time.* **3.** *vt* **MARK DOCUMENT AS USED** to invalidate a legal or official document to show that it has been used and cannot be reused ○ *machines that cancel postage stamps* **4.** *vt* **REVERSE INSTRUCTION** to reverse an instruction to a machine, especially a computer, or bring a machine's operation to an end ○ *Cancel the download from the Internet.* **5.** *vt* **DELETE SOMETHING** to mark something for deletion, usually by drawing a line through it **6.** *vti* **NEGATE IDENTICAL FACTOR** to neutralize the effect of another factor or circumstance **7.** *vt* MATH **REMOVE COMMON FACTOR** to remove a common factor from the numerator and denominator of a fraction or the common terms from the two sides of an equation ○ *The twelves cancel and you end up with 8 times 6 again.* ■ *n* **1.** PRINTING **INSERTED PAGE** a new page or section of a book inserted to replace a missing original or an original that contained errors **2.** PRINTING **PAGE TO BE REPLACED** a faulty page or section of a book replaced by another **3.** same as **cancellation** (sense 3) [14C. Via French < Latin *cancellare* "cross out" < *cancelli* "lattice" < *cancer* "grating, lattice"] —**can·cel·a·ble** *adj* —**can·cel·er** *n*

cancel out *vt* to combine two opposite or equally powerful things with the result that their strengths, qualities, or effects are neutralized

can·cel·bot /kánss'l bòt/ *n* a computer program that cancels unwanted articles sent to an Internet newsgroup by a specific user [Late 20C. < CANCEL + ROBOT]

can·cel·late /kánss'l àyt, kánss'lət/, **can·cel·lat·ed** /kánss'l àytəd/ *adj* **1.** ANAT same as **cancellous 2.** forming a mesh or network [Mid-17C. < Latin *cancellat-* (see CANCELLATION)]

can·cel·la·tion /kànss'l áysh'n/, **can·ce·la·tion** *n* **1. CANCELING OF SOMETHING** the canceling of something such as an appointment or order ○ *We had a cancellation, so we can fit you in at two o'clock.* ○ *There is a cancellation charge if you withdraw your order.* **2. THING MADE AVAILABLE** something that has become available because the person who reserved it has canceled, e.g., a seat in a theater **3. CANCELING MARK** a mark that officially or legally invalidates something, especially a postage stamp [Mid-16C. < Latin *cancellat-*, past participle of *cancellare* (see CANCEL)]

can·cel·lous /kánss'ləss, kan sélləss/ *adj* describes bone that has a mesh of hollows on the inside, as opposed to being compact or dense [Mid-19C. < Latin *cancelli* (see CANCEL)]

can·cer /kánssər/ *n* **1. MALIGNANT TUMOR** a malignant tumor or growth caused when cells multiply uncontrollably, destroying healthy tissue. The different forms are sarcomas, carcinomas, leukemias, and lymphomas. **2. ILLNESS CAUSED BY TUMOR** the illness or condition that is caused by the presence of a malignant tumor **3. FAST-SPREADING BAD PHENOMENON** something, usually something negative, that develops or spreads quickly and usually destructively **4.** CONSTR **GRADUAL DESTRUCTION OF BUILDING MATERIAL** gradual erosion or damage occurring in building materials, believed to be caused by inherent manufacturing faults ○ *concrete cancer* [Pre-12C. < Latin, literally "crab"] —**can·cer·ous** *adj*

Can·cer /kánssər/ *n* **1.** ASTRON **CONSTELLATION IN NORTHERN HEMISPHERE** a zodiacal constellation of the northern hemisphere between Gemini and Leo. See illustration at **constellation 2.** ZODIAC **4TH SIGN OF ZODIAC** the fourth sign of the zodiac, represented by a crab and lasting from approximately June 21 to July 22. Cancer is classified as a water sign, and its ruling planet is the Moon. **3.** ZODIAC **SOMEBODY BORN UNDER CANCER SIGN** somebody whose birthday falls between June 21 and July 22 [Pre-12C. < Latin (see CANCER); from the constellation's sideways movement across the sky] —**Can·cer** *adj* —**Can·cer·i·an** /kan sérree ən/ *n, adj*

can·cer·o·pho·bi·a /kànssərə fṓbee ə/ *n* an obsessive fear of developing cancer

can·cer stick *n* same as **cigarette** (*slang*)

can·croid /káng kròyd/ *adj* like a crab in shape, structure, or movement ■ *n* MED same as **squamous cell carcinoma** [Early 19C. < Latin *cancr-*, stem of *cancer* "crab, cancer"]

Can·cún /kàn kṓōn/ island resort on the northeastern coast of Quintana Roo state, Mexico. Population: 319,632 (2000).

can·del·a /kan déllə/ *n* the basic SI unit of luminous intensity. Symbol **cd** [Mid-20C. < Latin (see CANDLE)]

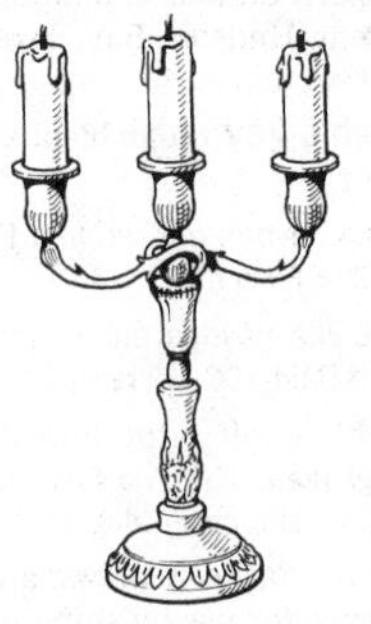

candelabrum

can·de·la·brum /kànd'l aábrəm, -ábbrəm/ (*plural* **-bra** /-brə/ or **-brums**) *n* a large decorative candleholder with several arms or branches, or a similarly shaped electric light fixture [Early 19C. < Latin < *candela* (see CANDLE)]

can·did /kándid/ *adj* **1. HONEST** honest or direct in a way that people find either refreshing or distasteful ○ *a surprisingly candid admission* **2. PHOTOGRAPHED INFORMALLY** photographed or filmed without the subject knowing or having the opportunity to prepare or pose ○ *a candid documentary* ■ *n* **UNPOSED PHOTOGRAPH** an unposed and informal photograph of a person or group [Mid-17C. Directly or via French *candide* "guileless" < Latin *candidus* "white, shining" < *candere* "be white"] —**can·did·ly** *adv* —**can·did·ness** *n*

can·di·da /kándidə/ *n* a fungus that can cause yeast infection, especially in the mouth and vagina. Latin name: *Candida albicans.* [Mid-20C. < Latin, feminine of *candidus* "white" (see CANDID); from its color]

can·di·date /kándi dàyt, -dət/ *n* **1. APPLICANT FOR OFFICE** somebody who is being considered for a political office or an official position ○ *names of candidates for mayor* **2. APPLICANT FOR JOB** an applicant or suitable person for a job ○ *Candidates should have experience in market research.* **3. PERSON SUSCEPTIBLE TO DISEASE OR TREATMENT** a patient who seems suitable for a particular treatment, or is likely to be affected by a particular disease ○ *a prime candidate for a heart attack* **4. EXAM TAKER** somebody who takes an exam, especially somebody who is scheduled to receive a degree upon passing exams ○ *a candidate for a Master's degree.* **5. COMPETITOR** somebody competing with others for a prize, grant, or award ○ *the candidates for best director* [Early 17C. Directly or via French *candidat* < Latin *candidatus* "(candidate) clothed in white"; from the white togas worn by candidates for election in ancient Rome] —**can·di·da·cy** /-dəssee/ *n* —**can·di·da·ture** /-dəchər, -də chōōr/ *n*

SYNONYMS ***candidate, contender, contestant, aspirant, applicant, entrant***

CORE MEANING: somebody who is seeking to be chosen for something or to win something

candidate somebody who is being considered for a job, grant, or prize, running for office, or taking part in an examination ○ *the liberal Democratic candidate* ○ *candidates for the newly created posts* **contender** a competitor, especially somebody who has a good chance of winning ○ *a contender for the best supporting actor award* ○ *He is emerging as a strong contender for the presidency.* **contestant** somebody who takes part in a contest or competitive event ○ *a contestant on a popular TV quiz show* ○ *To win, the contestant must score eleven points.* **aspirant** somebody who is hoping to achieve distinction or advancement ○ *another senatorial aspirant* ○ *a challenge from a rival aspirant to the throne* **applicant** somebody who has formally applied to be a candidate for something ○ *the starting salary of the successful applicant* ○ *It's claimed that the company is turning away hundreds of job applicants.* **entrant** somebody who enters a competition or examination ○ *I was the only entrant, so the event was canceled.*

can·did cam·er·a *n* the use of hidden cameras to film subjects unawares, often in stage-managed situations intended to elicit amusing responses (*hyphenated when used before a noun*)

can·di·di·a·sis /kàndə dī́ əssiss/ (*plural* **-di·a·ses** /-dī́ ə sèez/) *n* MED same as **yeast infection** (*technical*) [Mid-20C. < CANDIDA]

Can·di·ot /kándee ət, -òt/, **Can·di·ote** /-ōt, -ət/ *adj* relating to Crete, especially the capital, Heraklion (*literary*) [< *Candy*, old name for Crete] —**Can·di·ot** *n*

can·dle /kánd'l/ *n* a molded piece of wax, tallow, or other fatty substance, usually cylindrical in shape, encasing a wick that is burned to provide light ■ *vt* (**-dled, -dling, -dles**) to test an egg for freshness by looking at it against a bright light [Pre-12C. < Latin *candella*, earlier *candela* < *candere* "be white, glow"] ◇ **burn the candle at both ends** to get up very early and go to bed very late ◇ **not hold a candle to somebody** to be not nearly as good at something as somebody ○ *As a writer, he doesn't hold a candle to his mother.*

can·dle·ber·ry /kánd'l bèrree/ (*plural* **-ries**) *n* a bush or tree that has berries that can be used for making candles

can·dle·fish /kánd'l fish/ (*plural* **-fish·es** or *same*) *n* an oily saltwater fish. Native to: northern Pacific Ocean. Latin name: *Thaleichthys pacificus.* [< the former use of the dried fish as a lamp by pushing a piece of bark through it as a wick]

can·dle·hold·er /kánd'l hṑldər/ *n* a holder for a candle, often a decorative one

can·dle·light /kánd'l lìt/ *n* **1.** the light that a burning candle provides ○ *reading by candlelight* **2.** twilight, the time when candles would have been lit (*literary*)

can·dle·lit /kánd'l lìt/ *adj* lit by candles, or done by candlelight ○ *a silent candlelit march through the streets*

Can·dle·mas /kánd'lməss/ *n* a Christian feast marking the purification of the Virgin Mary and the presentation of the infant Jesus Christ in the Temple. Date: February 2. [Pre-12C. < CANDLE + MASS]

can·dle·nut /kánd'l nùt/ *n* **1.** an oil-rich seed of a tropical tree that is sometimes threaded with a wick to serve as a candle in Asia and Polynesia **2.** a tropical tree of the spurge family that bears candlenuts. Native to: Asia, Polynesia. Latin name: *Aleurites moluccana.*

can·dle·pin /kánd'l pìn/ *n* a slim pin used in the bowling game candlepins [< its shape]

can·dle·pins /kánd'l pìnz/ *n* a bowling game using slender pins and a ball smaller than that used in tenpins (*takes a singular verb*)

can·dle·pow·er /kánd'l pòwr/ *n* luminous intensity measured in candelas

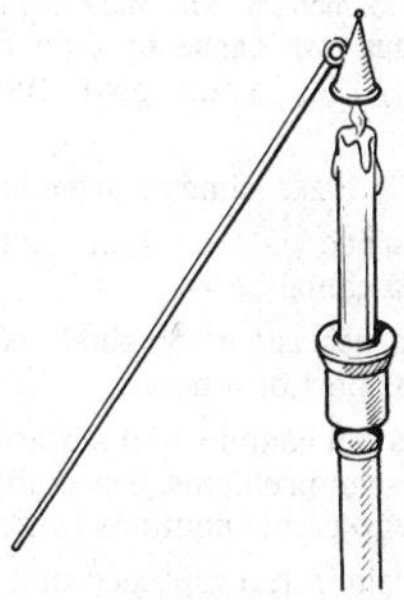

candlesnuffer

can·dle·snuff·er /kánd'l snùffər/ *n* a device, usually made of metal, consisting of a small cone on the end of a long thin handle, placed over the flame of a candle to put it out

can·dle·stick /kánd'l stìk/ *n* a tall thin holder for a single candle

can·dle·wick /kánd'l wìk/ *n* **1. THICK STRING** thick string used for candle wicks **2. COTTON FABRIC** tufted cotton fabric. Use: bedcovers, bathrobes. **3. EMBROIDERY YARN** soft cotton yarn used for embroidery

can·dle·wood /kánd'l wòod/ *n* **1.** resinous wood burned for light and fuel **2.** a tree or bush that produces candlewood

can-do *adj* eager to take on a job or challenge and confident of success (*informal*) ○ *We're only looking at can-do executives with proven track records.*

Can·dolle /kan dṓl, kaaN dáwl/, **Augustin Pyrame de** (1778–1841) Swiss botanist. He was the originator of taxonomy, the science of classification of plants still in general use.

can·dor /kándər/ *n* honesty or directness, whether refreshing or distasteful ○ *He spoke of their conspicuous candor and bravery.* [14C. < Latin, "glossy whiteness" < *cand-*, base of *candidus* (see CANDID)]

can·dour *n* Can, UK spelling of **candor**

CAN·DU re·ac·tor /kán doo-, kan dóo-/ *n* a form of nuclear reactor designed and built in Canada that uses replaceable fuel bundles and heavy water to moderate fission and cool the reactor core [Acronym < CANADA + DEUTERIUM + URANIUM]

C&W *abbr* MUSIC country and western

can·dy /kándee/ *n* (*plural* **-dies**) **1. SMALL CONFECTIONS** small sweet food items usually eaten for pleasure and not as part of a meal, e.g., chocolate bars, mints, and toffee ○ *Our store sells the finest chocolate candy in the country.* **2. PIECE OF CONFECTIONERY** a small hard, chewy, or soft piece of food made from sugar and other ingredients or flavorings such as chocolate, nuts, fruit, or peppermint **3. HARD DRUGS** heroin, cocaine, or another hard drug (*slang*) ■ *v* (**-died, -dy·ing, -dies**) **1.** *vt* **COAT WITH SUGAR SYRUP** to coat food with sugar or sugar syrup, or be coated with sugar or sugar syrup **2.** *vt* **STEEP IN SUGAR** to dress a food by impregnating it with sugar, in order either to preserve it or to make it more pleasant to eat **3.** *vti* **TURN SUGAR SOLUTION INTO CRYSTALS** to turn a sugar solution into crystals, especially by boiling it, or be converted into sugar crystals [13C. Via Old French *candi* < Arabic *qandī* "crystalized into sugar" < *qand* "cane sugar"]

can·dy ap·ple *n* an apple on a stick coated with a mixture of caramel or melted cinnamon candy

can·dy-ass *n* an offensive term for somebody regarded as weak or cowardly, especially a man (*slang*) —**can·dy-ass** *adj*

can·dy bar *n* a chocolate bar or a piece of confectionery, often one containing chocolate, made in a block, not as separate bite-sized pieces

can·dy cane *n* a long slender red-and-white striped hard candy that is bent into a curve at one end

can·dy·floss /kándi flòss/ *n UK* same as **cotton candy**

can·dy man *n* **1.** a drug trafficker (*slang*) **2.** formerly, a roving seller of candy

can·dy store *n* a store where candy is sold

can·dy-striped *adj* with a pattern of narrow stripes in a single color on a white background

can·dy strip·er *n* a volunteer worker in a hospital, especially a young person [< the volunteers' red-and-white striped uniform]

can·dy·tuft /kándee tùft/ *n* a flowering plant with thin leaves. Flowers: white, red, or purple, in clusters. Native to: Europe, Mediterranean. Genus: *Iberis.* [Early 17C. < *Candy*, old name for Crete]

cane /kayn/ *n* **1. WALKING STICK** a stick that people use to help them walk **2. BAMBOO STEM** a hollow lightweight stem of a tropical plant, especially bamboo, used in various ways in the house and garden, e.g., as a growing support for plants **3. WOVEN STEMS** the stems of various palms and grass plants, e.g., rattan, woven together to make furniture, baskets, and other household items **4. STEM OF FRUIT PLANT** the long woody stem of various fruit-bearing plants, e.g., the raspberry or blackberry **5. LONG-STEMMED PLANT** a coarse grass or reed with long stiff stems, e.g., sugar cane or sorghum **6. STICK FOR PUNISHMENT BEATINGS** a long flexible stick for administering beatings, especially one formerly used to punish schoolchildren ■ *vt* (**caned, can·ing, canes**) **BEAT SOMEBODY** to beat somebody with a cane, especially, formerly, to punish a schoolchild [14C. Via Old French *cane* < Latin *canna* "reed" < Greek *kanna* < Semitic]

cane·brake /káyn bràyk/ *n* an area of land planted or overgrown with cane

ca·nelle knife /kə nél-/ *n* a small kitchen implement, similar to a vegetable peeler or zester, with a slot and a V-shaped blade for cutting strips from the skins of citrus fruits [< French *canneler* "to groove, flute" < *cane* (see CANE)]

cane piece *n* in the Caribbean, a field of sugar cane, especially one that is isolated and belongs to a small farmer

can·er /káynər/ *n* a maker or repairer of furniture and other items made of cane

ca·nes·cent /kə néss'nt/ *adj* **1.** describes plant parts that have a white or whitish gray covering of fine hairs **2.** becoming white or grayish (*literary*) [Mid-19C. < Latin *canescent-*, present participle of *canescere* "grow white" < *canus* "white, hoary"] —**ca·nes·cence** *n*

cane sug·ar *n* sucrose obtained from sugar cane or sugar beets

Ca·nes Ve·nat·i·ci /káyneez və náttə sèe/ *n* a constellation of the northern hemisphere. See illustration at **constellation** [< Latin, "hunting dogs"]

cane toad *n* a large toad introduced into Australia to control pests in sugar cane but now a pest in its own right. Native to: South America. Latin name: *Bufo marinus.*

Ca·net·ti /kə néttee/, **Elias** (1905–94) Bulgarian-born British writer. His broad output includes literary criticism, history, memoirs, and his only novel, *Der Blendung* (1936), translated into English (1946) as *The Tower of Babel.* He won the Nobel Prize in literature (1981).

can·field /kán fèeld/ *n* a gambling game developed from the card game solitaire [Early 20C. After Richard Albert *Canfield* (1855–1914), US gambler]

cangue /kang/, **cang** *n* a heavy wooden yoke worn on the shoulders and enclosing the neck and arms, formerly used in China for punishing petty criminals [Late 17C. Via French < Portuguese *canga* "yoke" < Vietnamese *gong*]

Ca·nic·u·la /kə níkyələ/ *n* ASTRON same as **Sirius** [12C. < Latin (see CANICULAR)]

ca·nic·u·lar /kə níkyələr/ *adj* relating to the star Sirius [14C. < late Latin *canicularis* < Latin *canicula* "little dog" < *canis* "dog"]

ca·nid /kánnid, káy-/ *n* a carnivorous mammal of the dog family, which includes foxes, wolves, jackals, dingoes, coyotes, and domestic breeds [Late 19C. < modern Latin *Canidae* < Latin *canis* "dog"]

ca·nine /káy nīn/ *adj* relating to dogs ○ *a canine trainer* ○ *members of the canine family* ■ *n* **1.** a pointed tooth between the incisors and the first bicuspids. Most mammals have two in each jaw. **2.** same as **dog** *n* (sense 1) (*often humorous*) [15C. Directly or via French < Latin *caninus* < *canis* "dog"]

ca·nine dis·tem·per *n* a viral disease of dogs that causes high fever and is often fatal

ca·nine tooth *n* DENT same as **canine** *n* (sense 1)

can·ing /káyning/ *n* a punishment beating with a cane, especially a beating of a kind formerly administered to schoolchildren

Ca·nis Ma·jor /kàyniss-, kànniss-/ *n* a constellation of the southern hemisphere containing the star Sirius. Canis Major and Canis Minor represent dogs following at the heels of Orion the Hunter. See illustration at **constellation** [< Latin, "greater dog"]

Ca·nis Mi·nor /kàyniss-, kànniss-/ *n* a constellation near the celestial equator containing the star Procyon. See illustration at **constellation** [< Latin, "lesser dog"]

can·is·tel /kánni stèl, kànni stél/ *n* **1.** a sweet egg-shaped fruit with a strong musky smell **2.** a tree that bears canistels. Native to: Mexico, Central America, Caribbean. Latin name: *Pouteria campechiana.* [< American Spanish]

can·is·ter /kánnistər/ *n* **1. FOOD CONTAINER** a metal container with a lid, for storing tea, coffee, or other dry foods **2. PRESSURIZED CONTAINER** a pressurized metal container holding a substance released as a spray **3. SEALED CONTAINER** a strong sealed metal container for hazardous chemicals **4.** ARMS **EXPLOSIVE** a weapon used in former times consisting of a metal shell filled with gas and shot or shrapnel, designed to explode when thrown or fired from a cannon [Late 15C. Via Latin < Greek *kanastron* "wicker basket" < *kanna* "reed"]

can·ker /kángkər/ *n* **1.** VET **ANIMAL DISEASE** a disease of animals, e.g., a disease of horses that makes their hooves spongy, a disease that can cause ulcers in the outer ears of some animals, or a throat infection of some birds **2.** BOT **PLANT DISEASE** a disease that creates open wounds on the trunks and branches of woody plants. Cankers can be caused by bacteria, fungi, or pests. **3. EVIL** an evil or corrupting influence that spreads and is difficult to wipe out ○ *"This canker that eats up Love's tender spring"* (William Shakespeare, *Venus and Adonis*; 1593) ■ *vti* (**-kered, -ker·ing, -kers**) **1.** BOT **DEVELOP PLANT DISEASE** to develop canker, or cause the trunks and branches of woody plants to develop canker **2. MAKE OR BECOME CORRUPT** to become a source of spreading corruption or evil, or cause something to decay as a result of spreading corruption or evil [14C. Via Old N French *cancre* < Latin *cancr-* "crab"] —**can·ker·ous** *adj*

can·ker brake *n* PLANTS same as **Christmas fern** [*Brake* perhaps shortening of BRACKEN]

can·ker·root /kángkər ròot, -ròot/ *n* PLANTS same as **goldthread**

can·ker sore *n* an ulcer on the lips or inside the mouth

can·ker·worm /kángkər wòrm/ *n* the larva of either of two types of moth that destroys the leaves and fruit of trees in North America. Latin name: *Paleacrita vernata* or *Alsophila pometaria.*

can·na /kánnə/ *n* a perennial tropical plant with luxuriant foliage. Flowers: red or yellow, in clusters. Native to: Caribbean, Central America. Genus: *Canna.* [Mid-18C. Via modern Latin *Canna* < Latin *canna* (see CANE)]

can·na·bi·di·ol /kànnəbi dée àwl, -dī àwl/ *n* one of the chemical constituents of cannabis. Formula: $C_{21}H_{28}(OH)_2$. [Mid-20C. < CANNABIS + DI-[1] + -OL[1]]

can·na·bi·noid /kə nábbi nòyd/ *n* an organic chemical substance belonging to a group that comprises the active constituents of cannabis [Mid-20C. < CANNABIS]

can·na·bis /kánnəbiss/ *n* **1.** a drug produced in various forms from the dried leaves and flowers of the hemp plant, smoked or chewed. Its recreational use is illegal in many countries. **2.** the hemp plant, especially when grown as a source of the drug cannabis. Latin name: *Cannabis sativa.* [Early 18C. Via Latin < Greek *kannabis*]

can·na·bis res·in *n* the drug cannabis in the form of a greenish black resin

Can·nae /kánnee/ battlefield situated near present-day Barletta, southeastern Italy. It was the site of Hannibal's major defeat of the Roman army during the Second Punic War in 216 B.C.

canned /kand/ *adj* **1.** PRESERVED IN CAN preserved by being sealed into an airtight metal container **2.** PRERECORDED prerecorded in a standardized form for general use, rather than recorded for a specific broadcast or performance ○ *canned laughter* **3.** UNVARYING used repeatedly with little or no variation, and therefore lacking freshness or originality ○ *The interpreter gave us a canned history of the site.* **4.** DRUNK extremely drunk (*slang*) **5.** ONLINE HAVING STANDARD DESIGN describes a website or its features that are designed according to a standard template rather than to somebody's personal specifications ○ *canned questions*

can·nel /kánn'l/, **can·nel coal** *n* a bituminous coal that burns brightly and creates a lot of smoke [Mid-16C. Dialect variant of CANDLE; from its bright flame]

can·nel·lo·ni /kànn'l ōnee/ *n* wide tubes or rolls of pasta that are stuffed with a filling, topped with sauce, then baked [Mid-20C. < Italian, plural of *cannellone* "tubular noodle" < Latin *canna* (see CANE)]

can·ne·lure /kánn'l o͝or/ *n* a groove around the cylindrical part of a bullet [Mid-18C. < French < *canneler* "make a groove in" < *canne* "reed" < Old French *cane* (see CANE)]

can·ner·y /kánnəree/ (*plural* **-ies**) *n* a factory where food is packaged into cans

Cannes /kan, kaan/ resort and seaport on the French Riviera that is the site of an annual international film festival. It is situated in the Alpes-Maritimes Department in the Provence-Alpes-Côtes-d'Azur administrative region of southern France. Population: 67,304 (1999).

can·ni·bal /kánnib'l/ *n* **1.** somebody who eats human flesh **2.** an animal that eats the flesh of other animals of the same species [Mid-16C. < Spanish *Canibales*, variant of *Caribes* < Arawak *carib*, the Carib people] —**can·ni·bal·ism** *n*

can·ni·bal·is·tic /kànnib'l ístik/ *adj* relating to, involving, or practicing cannibalism —**can·ni·bal·is·ti·cal·ly** *adv*

can·ni·bal·ize /kánnib'l īz/ (**-ized, -iz·ing, -iz·es**) *vt* **1.** to take parts from something, especially a machine, in order to use them elsewhere ○ *cannibalized the other vehicles for spare parts when their supply line failed* **2.** to eat the flesh of another human being or of an animal of the same species —**can·ni·bal·i·za·tion** /kànnib'li zāysh'n/ *n*

can·ni·kin /kánnikin/ *n* a small can, especially one used for drinking from [Late 16C. < Dutch *kanneken* "little can" < Middle Dutch *canne* "can"]

Can·ning /kánning/, **Charles John, 1st Earl Canning** (1812–62) British colonial administrator. He was governor-general (1856–58) and first viceroy (1858–62) of British India.

Can·ning, George (1770–1827) British politician. As foreign secretary of Britain (1807–10, 1822–27) he encouraged independence movements in Latin America. He was briefly British prime minister (1827).

> "Give me the avowed, erect and manly foe; / Firm I can meet, perhaps return the blow; / But of all plagues, good Heaven, thy wrath can send, / Save me, oh, save me, from the candid friend."
> [George Canning, "New Morality," *The Anti-Jacobin*; 1821]

Can·niz·za·ro re·ac·tion /kànni tsaàrō-/ *n* a chemical process in which some aldehydes are broken down into alcohols and acid salts in the presence of a strong alkali [After Stanislao *Cannizzaro* (1826–1910), Italian chemist]

Can·nock /kánnək/ former mining city in Staffordshire, central England, situated northwest of Birmingham. Population: 92,126 (2001).

can·no·li /kə nōlee/ (*plural same*) *n* a deep-fried sweet Italian pastry with a soft cheese and candied fruit filling [Mid-20C. < Italian, plural of *cannolo* "little tube" < Latin *canna* (see CANE)]

can·non /kánnən/ *n* **1.** (*plural* **can·nons** or *same*) HISTORICAL WEAPON in former times, a weapon that fired heavy iron balls or other projectiles through a simple iron tube **2.** MODERN WEAPON a modern heavy artillery weapon large enough to need to be mounted for firing, e.g., on a warship or on a tracked vehicle **3.** AIRCRAFT GUN a rapid-firing gun mounted on an aircraft **4.** *UK* CUE GAMES same as **carom** *n* (sense 1) **5.** BELL LOOP the loop at the top of a bell from which it is suspended ■ *v* (**-noned, -non·ing, -nons**) **1.** *vi* COLLIDE to collide with something or bounce off it at great speed and with a lot of force ○ *a 35-yard field goal that cannoned off the post* **2.** *vt* MIL same as **cannonade** *v* (sense 1) **3.** *vi UK* CUE GAMES same as **carom** *v* (sense 1) [14C. Via French < Italian *cannone* "large tube" < Latin *canna* (see CANE)]

SPELLCHECK cannon or **canon**? Do not confuse the spelling of ***cannon*** and ***canon***, which sound similar. ***Cannon*** is chiefly used as a noun denoting a weapon, especially one formerly used to fire heavy iron balls. It is also used as a verb, meaning "collide" or "rebound": *The car cannoned into the bridge.* The word ***canon*** is a noun with numerous meanings, including "a rule or decree," "a list of saints," "a collection of religious writings or artistic works," and "a member of the clergy of a cathedral."

Can·non /kánnən/, **Joseph Gurney** (1836–1926) US political leader. He was a powerful Republican Speaker of the House of Representatives (1903–11) during a long congressional career (1873–1923). Known as **Uncle Joe**

can·non·ade /kànnə náyd/ *n* **1.** BOMBARDMENT a sustained bombardment with heavy artillery **2.** SOMETHING RESEMBLING BOMBARDMENT something that sounds or feels like an artillery bombardment ○ *"The deep cannonade of roaring thunder belched forth its fearsome challenge."* (Edgar Rice Burroughs, *Tarzan of the Apes*; 1914) ■ *v* (**-ad·ed, -ad·ing, -ades**) **1.** *vti* BOMBARD SOMEBODY OR BE BOMBARDED to subject an enemy to, or be subjected to, a cannonade **2.** *vt* ATTACK SOMEBODY to subject somebody to a sustained attack, e.g., with words of criticism or reproach [Mid-16C. Via French < Italian *cannonata* < *cannone* (see CANNON)]

can·non·ball /kánnən bawl/ *n* **1.** BALL FIRED FROM CANNON a heavy metal or stone ball fired from a cannon **2.** JUMP INTO WATER a jump into water with the body tucked into a ball, usually with the head down and the knees drawn up to the chest ■ *vi* (**-balled, -ball·ing, -balls**) TRAVEL QUICKLY to travel at great speed (*informal*) ○ *The train cannonballed through the dark tunnel.*

can·non·ball tree *n* a tree that produces round fruits with woody husks that are used to make containers and utensils. Native to: South America. Latin name: *Couroupita guianensis.*

can·non bone *n* a bone in the lower limbs of some hoofed animals, resulting from the fusing of the metatarsals or metacarpals [< its tubular shape]

can·non·eer /kànnə néer/ *n* formerly, a soldier who fired a cannon [Mid-16C. Via French < Italian *cannoniere* < *cannone* (see CANNON)]

can·non fod·der *n* (*informal*) **1.** members of the lowest ranks of the military, regarded as an expendable resource in wartime **2.** a person or group regarded as a resource to be exploited or sacrificed

can·not /ká nòt, kə nót/ *contr* the usual way of writing "can not"

USAGE See ***help***.

can·nu·la /kánnyələ/ (*plural* **-las** or **-lae** /-lee/), **can·u·la** *n* a flexible tube with a sharp-pointed part at one end that is inserted into a duct, vein, or cavity in order to drain away fluid or to administer drugs [Late 17C. < Latin, "little tube" < *canna* (see CANE)]

can·nu·late /kánnyə làyt/, **can·u·late** *vt* (**-lat·ed, -lat·ing, -lates**) to insert a tube (**cannula**) into a duct, vein, or cavity in order to drain away fluid or to administer drugs ■ *adj* having a tubular shape (*technical*) —**can·nu·la·tion** /kànnyə láysh'n/ *n*

can·ny /kánnee/ (**-ni·er, -ni·est**) *adj* shrewd enough not to be easily deceived ○ *a canny negotiator* [Late 16C. < CAN[1] "know"] —**can·ni·ly** *adv* —**can·ni·ness** *n*

ca·noe /kə no͞o/ *n* a lightweight boat, pointed at each end, that can be paddled by one or two people and can carry passengers. Canoes were originally made from natural materials, but modern canoes are made of aluminum or of molded plastic and fiberglass. ■ *vi* (**-noed, -noe·ing, -noes**) to paddle a canoe, often as a sport or hobby [Mid-16C. Via Spanish *canoa* < Carib *canaoua*; modern form influenced by French *canoë*] ◇ **paddle your own canoe** to take control of and responsibility for your own life and affairs (*informal*)

ca·noe birch *n* TREES same as **paper birch**

ca·noe·ing /kə no͞o ing/ *n* the sport, hobby, or activity of paddling a canoe

ca·noe·ist /kə no͞o ist/ *n* somebody who canoes, especially as a sport or a hobby

can of worms *n* a complicated situation that results from unforeseen problems, especially an issue that seems likely to create conflicts (*informal*)

ca·no·la /kə nōlə/ *n* **1.** a rapeseed that yields oil with high nutritional quality **2.** FOOD same as **canola oil** [Late 20C. < CANADA]

ca·no·la oil *n* a rapeseed oil that has a high level of monounsaturated fatty acids. Use: cooking oil.

can·on[1] /kánnən/ *n* **1.** GENERAL RULE a general rule, principle, or standard ○ *one of the fundamental canons of free-market economics* **2.** RELIG RELIGIOUS DECREE a decree issued by a religious authority, especially one ruling on religious practices **3.** RELIG BODY OF RELIGIOUS WRITINGS a set of religious writings regarded as authentic and definitive and forming a religion's body of scripture **4.** CHR LIST OF SAINTS in the Roman Catholic Church, the complete list of all the saints **5.** CHR PART OF MASS in the Roman Catholic Mass, the prayer during which the bread and wine are consecrated **6.** ARTS SET OF ARTISTIC WORKS a set of artistic works established as genuine and complete, e.g., the works of a particular writer, painter, or moviemaker ○ *one of the best-known pictures in the Welles canon* **7.** MUSIC STAGGERED SINGING OR PLAYING a musical technique in which different instruments or voices enter one after the other, each playing or singing exactly the same sequence of notes, resulting in often complex counterpoint [Pre-12C. Via Latin < Greek *kanōn* "rule"]

SPELLCHECK See ***cannon***.

can·on[2] /kánnən/ *n* **1.** a member of the Christian clergy who is on the permanent staff of a cathedral and has specific duties in relation to the running of it **2.** CHR same as **canon regular** [12C. Via Old French *canonie* < ecclesiastical Latin *canonicus* "(somebody living) according to a rule" < Latin *canon* (see CANON[1]); altered after CANON[1]]

cañ·on *n* GEOG another spelling of **canyon**

can·on·ess /kánnənəss/ *n* in the Roman Catholic Church, a woman who belongs to a religious order in which members live under a rule, not a vow

ca·non·i·cal /kə nónnik'l/, **ca·non·i·c** /kə nónnik/ *adj* **1.** ARTS OF CANON OF WORKS relating to or belonging to the biblical canon or a canon of artistic works established as genuine and complete **2.** RELIG FOLLOWING CANON LAW conforming to or authorized by canon law **3.** CONFORMING TO GENERAL PRINCIPLES conforming to accepted principles or standard practice **4.** CHR OF CATHEDRAL OR REGULAR CANONS relating to members of the clergy who are canons **5.** MUSIC OF MUSICAL CANON relating to a musical canon, or sung or played in a canon [15C. < medieval Latin *canonicalis* < Latin *canon* (see CANON[1])] —**ca·non·i·cal·ly** *adv*

ca·non·i·cal hour *n* **1.** in the Roman Catholic Church, one of the daily prayer times when specific prayers are said. These times are the matins with lauds, prime, terce, sext, nones, vespers, and compline. **2.** in the Church of England, any time between 8 a.m. and 6 p.m. when marriages can officially be celebrated

ca·non·i·cals /kə nónnik'lz/ *npl* ceremonial robes worn by members of the clergy during a religious ceremony

can·on·ic·i·ty /kànnə níssətee/ *n* inclusion in a religious or secular canon, or status as an included item

can·on·ize /kánnə nīz/ (**-ized, -iz·ing, -iz·es**) *vt* **1.** DECLARE SOMEBODY AS SAINT in the Roman Catholic Church, to declare a deceased person to be a saint **2.** GIVE RELIGIOUS APPROVAL TO SOMETHING to declare something to be acceptable or valid according to canon law **3.** GLORIFY SOMETHING to idolize somebody or glorify something ○ *"And fame in time to come canonize us"* (William Shakespeare, *Troilus and Cressida*; 1601) [14C.

< medieval Latin *canonizare* < Latin *canon* (see CANON[1])] —**can·on·i·za·tion** /kànnəni záysh'n/ *n* —**can·on·iz·er** *n*

can·on law *n* the body of laws that governs the affairs of the Christian church or a particular branch of it

can·on reg·u·lar (*plural* **can·ons reg·u·lar**) *n* a member of any of several Roman Catholic orders of monks living in communities that follow Augustinian rules

can·on·ry /kánnənree/ (*plural* **-ries**) *n* **1.** the status or position of a religious canon **2.** the salary that a religious canon receives

ca·noo·dle /kə nóod'l/ (**-noo·dled, -nood·ling, -noo·dles**) *vti* to kiss and cuddle somebody in a mildly romantic or sexual way (*informal*) ○ *couples canoodling in the dark* [Mid-19C. Origin ?]

can o·pen·er *n* a device, either electric-powered or operated by hand, used for opening cans, especially cans of food

canopic jar

ca·no·pic jar /kə nòppik-/, **Ca·no·pic jar** *n* a jar used in ancient Egypt to hold the embalmed entrails of a mummy [Late 19C. < Latin *Canopicus* < *Canopus*, port in ancient Egypt]

Ca·no·pus /kə nṓpəss, kə nóppəss/ *n* the brightest star in the constellation Argo and the second brightest star in the sky after Sirius. Because it is so bright, spacecraft often take Canopus as a reference point for orientation.

can·o·py /kánnəpee/ (*plural* **-pies**) *n* **1.** COVERING FOR SHELTER a covering put above something to provide shelter or for decoration, especially a fabric covering that can be removed or folded away **2.** BOT TREETOPS the uppermost layer of vegetation in a forest, consisting of the tops of trees forming a kind of ceiling **3.** SKY the sky regarded as a covering or ceiling (*literary*) ○ *the vast canopy of stars* **4.** BUILDINGS ROOFED STRUCTURE a roofed structure that covers an area, especially one that shelters a passageway between two buildings **5.** SPORTS PART OF PARACHUTE the part of a parachute that opens and fills with air **6.** AVIAT COCKPIT COVER the transparent cover of an aircraft's cockpit [14C. Via medieval Latin *canopeum* "canopy above an altar" < Greek *kōnōpeion* "bed with a mosquito net" < *kōnōps* "mosquito"] —**can·o·pied** *adj*

~~**canot**~~ incorrect spelling of **cannot**

Ca·no·va /kə nṓvə/, **Antonio, Marquis of Ischia** (1757–1822) Italian sculptor. His neoclassical works include figures of Napoleon I and George Washington.

canst *stressed* /kanst/; *unstressed* /kənst/ *v* an archaic form of the verb "can" used with "thou"

cant[1] /kant/ *n* **1.** CLICHÉD TALK boring talk filled with clichés and platitudes **2.** HYPOCRITICAL TALK insincere talk, especially regarding morals or religion **3.** JARGON the special language or vocabulary of a particular group, especially a group whom some people look down on ■ *vi* (**cant·ed, cant·ing, cants**) SPEAK CANT to use cant, especially to speak or lecture others hypocritically on matters of religion or morals [Mid-16C. Probably < Latin *cantare* "sing"] —**cant·ing** *adj* —**cant·ing·ly** *adv*

ORIGIN The Latin word *cantare*, "to sing," from which ***cant*** is probably derived, and the related noun *cantus* "singing" are also sources of English *accent, cantabile, cantata, canto, chant* and *incantation.*

cant[2] /kant/ *n* **1.** SLOPE slope, degree of slope, or a sloping surface **2.** JOLT a jolt that knocks something out of its straight or level position ■ *v* (**cant·ed, cant·ing, cants**) **1.** *vt* JOLT SOMETHING to knock something out of its straight or level position **2.** *vti* PUT AT ANGLE to lie, or set something, at an angle [14C. Via Middle Low German *kante* or Middle Dutch *cant* "edge" < Latin *cantus* "tire"]

can't /kant/ *contr* cannot

Cant. *abbr* Canticle of Canticles

can·ta·bi·le /kaan taábi lày/ *adj, adv* in a smooth, flowing, and melodious style (*used as a musical direction*) ■ *n* a cantabile passage or piece of music [Early 18C. < Italian, "that can be sung"]

Can·ta·bri·an Moun·tains /kan tàybree ən-/ mountain range extending about 300 mi./480 km west from the Pyrenees across northern Spain. The highest peak is Torre Cerredo. Height: 8,688 ft./2,648 m.

Can·ta·brig·i·an /kàntə bríjjee ən/ *n* **1.** a student or graduate of the University of Cambridge, England **2.** somebody who comes from Cambridge, England, or Cambridge, Massachusetts [Mid-16C. < Latin *Cantabrigia* "Cambridge (England)"] —**Can·ta·brig·i·an** *adj*

can·ta·la /kan taálə/ *n* **1.** a coarse strong fiber from the leaves of an agave. Use: nets, rope, twine. **2.** the tropical plant that produces cantala. Native to: America. Latin name: *Agave cantala.* [Early 20C. Origin ?]

can·ta·loupe /kánt'l ṑp/, **can·ta·loup** *n* a round melon with a netted, often ridged rind and aromatic orange flesh. Latin name: *Cucumis melo reticulatus.* [Late 18C. Via French < Italian *Cantaluppi*, papal villa near Rome where a similar melon was introduced from Armenia]

can·tan·ker·ous /kan tángkərəss/ *adj* **1.** easily angered and difficult to get along with **2.** difficult to work with or use (*informal*) [Mid-18C. Probably alteration of rancorous] —**can·tan·ker·ous·ly** *adv* —**can·tan·ker·ous·ness** *n*

can·ta·ta /kən taátə/ *n* a musical composition for voices and instruments, usually on a religious theme, containing arias, choruses, and recitatives [Early 18C. Via Italian < Latin, feminine past participle of *cantare* "sing" < *canere*]

cant dog *n* FORESTRY same as **cant hook** [< CANT[2] + DOG "mechanical device"]

can·teen /kan téen/ *n* **1.** PORTABLE DRINKING FLASK a small container used by campers or soldiers for carrying liquids such as drinking water **2.** CAFETERIA a place where food is served, especially at a military base or workplace **3.** TEMPORARY FOOD STAND a mobile or temporary food stand **4.** *UK* SOLDIERS' STORE a store selling food, toiletries, and other items on a military base **5.** *UK* FLATWARE BOX a box or chest with compartments for storing flatware [Mid-18C. Via French *cantine* < Italian *cantina* "cellar"]

~~**canteloupe**~~ incorrect spelling of **cantaloupe**

can·ter[1] /kántər/ *n* **1.** HORSE'S MEDIUM PACE a smooth easy gait of a horse or donkey, slower than a gallop but faster than a trot **2.** HORSE RIDE a horse ride at a canter ■ *v* (**-tered, -ter·ing, -ters**) **1.** *vi* GO AT CANTER to move or ride at a canter **2.** *vt* MAKE HORSE CANTER to make a horse go at a canter [Early 18C. Shortening of *Canterbury gallop*; from the pace of medieval pilgrims who rode to the shrine of St. Thomas à Becket in Canterbury, England]

can·ter[2] /kántər/ *n* somebody who talks cant or who uses cant [Early 17C. < CANT[1]]

Can·ter·bur·y /kántər bèrree/ city in Kent, England. Its cathedral is the mother church of the Church of England. Population: 135,278 (2001).

Can·ter·bur·y bells (*plural same*) *n* an ornamental garden plant with blue, bell-shaped flowers. Native to: Europe. Latin name: *Campanula medium.* [Origin ?]

can·tha·ris /kánthəriss/ (*plural* **-thar·i·des** /kan thárri deez/) *n* INSECTS same as **Spanish fly** (sense 1) [14C. Via Latin < Greek *kantharis*]

can·thi ANAT plural of **canthus**

cant hook *n* a wooden pole with a pivoting metal hook at one end, used in forestry for handling logs [< CANT[2]]

can·thus /kánthəss/ (*plural* **-thi** /-thī/) *n* the corner or angle at each side of the eye [Mid-17C. Via Latin < Greek *kanthos*]

can·ti·cle /kántik'l/ *n* a song or chant, especially a hymn containing words derived from the Bible, used in the Christian liturgy [13C. < Latin *canticulum* "little song" < *canticum* "song" < *cantus* (see CANTO)]

Can·ti·cle of Can·ti·cles *n* BIBLE same as **Song of Solomon**

can·ti·le·na /kànt'l éenə/ *n* a smooth-flowing melodious line in vocal or instrumental music [Mid-18C. Directly or via Italian < Latin, "song" < *cantus* (see CANTO)]

can·ti·le·ver /kánt'l eevər/ *n* **1.** BUILDINGS PROJECTION SUPPORTED AT ONE END a projecting structure that is attached or supported at only one end **2.** BUILDINGS SUPPORTING BRACKET a bracket that supports a balcony or a cornice **3.** AEROSP WING WITH NO EXTERNAL BRACE an aircraft wing constructed without external braces ■ *v* (**-vered, -ver·ing, -vers**) **1.** *vt* BUILDINGS ATTACH SOMETHING AT ONE END to construct something in such a way that it is attached or supported at only one end **2.** *vi* EXTEND OUTWARD to project outward with an unsupported end [Mid-17C. Origin ?] —**can·ti·le·vered** *adj*

can·ti·le·ver bridge *n* a bridge consisting of arms projecting outward from supporting piers and joined together by a simple span where the two arms meet

can·til·late /kánt'l àyt/ (**-lat·ed, -lat·ing, -lates**) *vti* to chant or intone something, especially passages of the Hebrew scriptures [Mid-19C. < Latin *cantillat-*, past participle of *cantillare* "sing low" < *cantare* (see CANTATA)] —**can·til·la·tion** /kànt'l áysh'n/ *n*

can·ti·na /kan téenə/ *n Southwest US* a bar or wine shop, especially in a Spanish-speaking country or region [Late 19C. Via Spanish, "bar, wine cellar" < Italian, "cellar"]

Can·tin·flas /kántin flàss/ (1911–93) Mexican movie actor. He was known for his comic characters and, off-screen, for his campaigning for social justice. Born **Moreno Reyes, Mario**

can·tle /kánt'l/ *n* the raised back part of a saddle for a horse [14C. Via Anglo-Norman < medieval Latin *cantellus* "small corner" < Latin *cant(h)us* (see CANT[2])]

can·to /kántō/ (*plural* **-tos**) *n* a section out of several into which a long poem may be divided [Late 16C. Via Italian < Latin *cantus* "song" < *cantare* (see CANTATA)]

can·ton /kántən, kán tòn/ *n* **1.** PART OF COUNTRY a division of a country, especially one of the states into which Switzerland is divided **2.** PART OF FRENCH ARRONDISSEMENT a division of a French arrondissement **3.** PART OF FLAG a rectangular division in the top corner of a flag, next to the staff **4.** HERALDRY PART OF SHIELD a small square or oblong division of a heraldic shield, usually in the top left corner [Early 16C. Via French < Provençal < Latin *cant(h)us* (see CANT[2])] —**can·ton·al** /kántən'l, kan tónn'l/ *adj*

Can·ton /kántən, kán tòn/ **1.** ➧ **Guangzhou 2.** city in Mississippi, northeast of Jackson, between the Big Black River and the Pearl River. Population: 12,955 (2002 estimate). **3.** city in northeastern Ohio, southeast of Akron; home of the Football Hall of Fame. Population: 79,772 (2002 estimate).

Can·ton·ese /kàntə néez, -néess/ (*plural same*) *n* **1.** the Chinese language of Guangzhou (Canton) and the province of Guangdong, China, also widely spoken elsewhere in the world. Native speakers: 70 million. **2.** somebody who comes from Guangzhou or the surrounding province of Guangdong —**Can·ton·ese** *adj*

can·ton·ment /kan tṓnmənt, kan tónmənt/ *n* **1.** TEMPORARY TROOP ACCOMMODATIONS temporary accommodations for troops, especially the winter quarters of an army **2.** ASSIGNMENT OF TROOPS TO QUARTERS the assignment of troops to temporary quarters **3.** MILITARY CAMP IN BRITISH INDIA a permanent military station in India during the time of British imperial rule **4.** *UK* MILITARY TRAINING CAMP a large military training camp, especially formerly [Mid-18C. < French *cantonnement* < *cantonner* "quarter, billet" < *canton* (see CANTON)]

Can·ton ware *n* Chinese porcelain and other ceramic ware of types exported from China during the 18th and 19th centuries [Early 20C. Because exported from China by way of CANTON (Guangzhou)]

Can·to·pop /kántō pòp/ *n SE Asia* pop music of Southeast Asia, originally sung in Hong Kong's Cantonese but now also in Mandarin, English, and Japanese. It is characterized by a decorous balladic style sung by musicians who are neatly dressed.

can·tor /kántər/ *n* **1.** a Jewish religious official who is the chief singer of the liturgy in a synagogue **2.** somebody who leads the singing in a synagogue or congregation [Mid-16C. < Latin, "singer" < *cantare* (see CANTATA)] —**can·to·ri·al** /kan táwree əl/ *adj*

Can·tor /kántər/, **Eddie** (1892–1964) US stage performer. He was known for his song "Banjo Eyes" and energetic performances in vaudeville and on Broadway. Born **Iskowitz, Israel**

> "It takes 20 years to be an overnight success."
> [Eddie Cantor, *New York Times*; October 20, 1963]

can·tor·is /kan táwriss/ *adj* sung by the part of the choir on the north side of a cathedral or church [Mid-17C. < Latin, "of the singer," form of *cantor* (see CANTOR)]

can·tus /kántəss/ (*plural same*) *n* **1.** MUSIC same as **cantus firmus 2.** a melody or style of singing used in the medieval Christian church [Late 16C. < Latin (see CANTO)]

can·tus fir·mus /-fúrməss/ (*plural* **can·tus fir·mi** /-fúr mī/) *n* a melody, often derived from chant, that forms the basis of a composition to which other melodic lines are added [< Latin, "firm song"]

can·ty /kántee/ (**-ti·er, -ti·est**) *adj N England, Scotland* cheerful, lively, or sprightly [Early 18C. < Scottish and English dialect *cant* "bold"] —**can·ti·ly** *adv* —**can·ti·ness** *n*

Ca·nuck /kə núk/ *n* (*slang*) **1.** somebody from Canada **2.** an offensive term for a French-Canadian person [Mid-19C. Probably < (a Native American pronunciation of) CANADA]

can·u·la MED another spelling of **cannula**

can·u·late MED another spelling of **cannulate**

Ca·nute /kə nóot, -nyóot/, **Cnut, Knut** (994?–1035) king of England (1016–35), Denmark (1018–35), and Norway (1028–35). Known for his wise and effective rule, he is said to have ordered the tide to turn back in order to demonstrate his inability to control nature. Popularly, and wrongly, it is thought that he actually expected to turn back the tide.

can·vas /kánvəss/ *n* **1.** TEXTILES **HEAVY FABRIC** a strong heavy cotton, hemp, or jute fabric. Use: sails, tents, furnishings. **2.** ART **FABRIC FOR PAINTING ON** a piece of canvas on which a painting is done, especially in oils **3.** ART **PAINTING** a painting that has been done on a canvas **4. BACKGROUND** the background against which events happen **5.** HANDICRAFT **CLOTH FOR NEEDLEWORK** a fabric with a coarse loose weave. Use: embroidery, tapestry. **6.** SAILING **SAIL** a vessel's sail or sails **7. TENT** a tent or group of tents **8.** BOXING, WRESTLING **FLOOR OF BOXING OR WRESTLING RING** the floor of a boxing or wrestling ring when covered with canvas ■ *vt* (**-vased, -vas·ing, -vas·es**) **PUT CANVAS ON SOMETHING** to cover or line something with canvas [14C. Via Old French *canevas* < Latin *cannabis* "hemp" (from which the cloth was made)] ◇ **under canvas** living in a tent

SPELLCHECK canvas or **canvass**? Do not confuse the spelling of ***canvas*** and ***canvass***, which sound similar. The word ***canvas*** is chiefly used as a noun, denoting a heavy fabric, a piece of canvas used for painting, or something made from canvas such as a tent or sail, as in *spend the night under canvas.* The word ***canvass*** is chiefly used as a verb, meaning "solicit orders, opinions, or votes," "debate," or "inspect."

can·vas·back /kánvəss bàk/ *n* a wild duck, the male of which has a white back and a reddish brown head and neck. Native to: North America. Latin name: *Aythya valisineria*.

can·vass /kánvəss/ *v* (**-vassed, -vass·ing, -vass·es**) **1.** *vti* **VISIT SOMEBODY TO SOLICIT SOMETHING** to travel around an area asking people for something such as sale orders, opinions, or votes **2.** *vt* **DEBATE SOMETHING** to debate or discuss something thoroughly **3.** *vt* **LOOK AT**

canvasback

SOMETHING CAREFULLY to examine something in detail ○ *The ballots were thoroughly canvassed to confirm their authenticity.* ■ *n also* **can·vas 1. OPINION POLL** a survey of public opinion, especially before an election **2. SALE OFFER TO MEMBERS OF GROUP** an offer of something, especially something for sale, to people in a particular area or group **3. CAREFUL INSPECTION** a detailed examination of something [Early 16C. < CANVAS] —**can·vass·er** *n*

SPELLCHECK See *canvas*.

can·yon /kánnyən/, **ca·ñon** *n* a deep narrow valley with steep sides, often with a stream running through it [Mid-19C. Via Mexican Spanish *cañón* < Spanish, "large tube" < *caña* "pipe" < Latin *canna* (see CANE)]

REGIONAL NOTE ***Canyon*** in the names of geographic features is a Western term, originally from Texas and extending through the Rocky Mountain states to the Pacific coast. It is rare in the East and Midwest, and absent from the Midlands and the South.

can·yon·eer·ing /kànnyə néering/, **can·yon·ing** /kánnyəning/ *n* **1.** the sport or activity of descending fast-flowing mountain streams in gorges by jumping in while wearing a wet suit and being carried down by the current **2.** the activity of traveling through canyons using skills such as rappelling, climbing, traversing, or swimming

Can·yon·lands Na·tion·al Park /kànyən làndz-/ national park in southeastern Utah, established in 1964 and noted for its rock formations. Area: 528 sq. mi./1,366 sq. km.

can·zo·na /kan zṓnə, kaant sṓnə/ *n* **1.** MUSIC a song resembling a madrigal but simpler and less serious in form and content **2.** MUSIC an instrumental piece in the style of a canzona **3.** LITERAT same as **canzone** (sense 1) [Late 19C. < Italian < *canzone* "song" (see CANZONE)]

can·zo·ne /kan zṓnee, kaant sṓ nāy/ (*plural* **-nes** or **-ni** /-zṓnee, -sṓnee/) *n* **1.** a love poem written by a troubadour in medieval Italy or Provence **2.** MUSIC same as **canzona** (senses 1–2) [Late 16C. Via Italian < Latin *cantion-* "singing" < *cant-*, past participle of *canere* "sing"]

can·zo·net /kànzə nét/, **can·zo·net·ta** /-néttə/ *n* **1.** a short light English song of the 17th or 18th century, originally intended for a group of singers or for a soloist with accompaniment **2.** a Renaissance song with different parts for different singers, similar to the madrigal [Late 16C. < Italian *canzonetta* "small canzone" < *canzone* (see CANZONE)]

can·zo·ni LITERAT, MUSIC plural of **canzone**

Cao Dai /kòw dī/ *n* a religious movement originating in Vietnam that combines features of both eastern and western religions [Mid-20C. < Vietnamese, "great palace"]

cap /kap/ *n* **1. HAT** a covering for the head, usually soft and close fitting and often with a visor and no brim **2. UNIFORM HAT** a head covering, usually part of a uniform, worn to identify the wearer's occupation or rank **3. PROTECTIVE COVERING FOR HAIR** a head covering worn to protect the hair, usually close-fitting or elasticized around the edge **4. HAT WORN AT ACADEMIC CEREMONY** an academic mortarboard, worn with a gown on a ceremonial occasion **5. COVER** a removable cover or lid that closes the end of something when it is not in use ○ *a lens cap* **6. COVERING AT TIP** something that covers the top or tip of something, especially as protection **7. TOP PART** the top part of something such as a hill or mountain **8. UPPER LIMIT** an upper limit on something, e.g., the amount that may be spent on an item **9. EXPLOSIVE FOR TOY GUN** a small quantity of explosive enclosed in paper for use in a toy gun **10.** ARMS same as **percussion cap 11.** DENT **COVERING FOR TOOTH** a covering to preserve or replace the crown of a tooth **12.** FUNGI **TOP OF MUSHROOM** the dome-shaped upper part of some fungi such as mushrooms **13.** BOT **SPORE-CAPSULE COVERING** the hood that covers the spore-bearing capsule of mosses and liverworts **14.** BIRDS **PATCH OF COLOR ON BIRD'S HEAD** a patch of feathers of a distinct color on the top of a bird's head, extending to the level of the eyes **15.** ARCHIT **TOP OF COLUMN** the upper part of a column or pedestal **16.** AUTOMOT **NEW SURFACE FOR TIRE** a new layer of rubber applied to the surface of a worn tire **17.** BIOL **MOLECULE CLUSTER** an aggregation of molecules at one end of something such as a cell or virus **18.** GEOL same as **cap rock 19.** MATH **SET INTERSECTION SYMBOL** a mathematical symbol (∩) representing the intersection of two sets ■ *vt* (**capped, cap·ping, caps**) **1. COVER SOMETHING WITH CAP** to put a cap over something **2. LIE ON TOP OF SOMETHING** to cover the top or tip of something **3. SURPASS SOMETHING** to improve on something that has already happened or been done **4. COMPLETE SOMETHING** to add the finishing touch to something such as an effort or a process **5. IMPOSE LIMIT ON SOMETHING** to put an upper limit on something such as the amount of money to be charged or spent **6. AWARD SPECIAL HAT** to give somebody a special cap as a symbol of achievement or as an honor **7.** *Scotland* EDUC **GIVE SOMEBODY DEGREE** to award an academic degree to somebody **8.** CHEM **FORM CLUSTER OF MOLECULES** to form a cluster of molecules on something [Pre-12C. < late Latin *cappa* "hood, hooded cloak"] —**cap·ful** *n* ◇ **cap in hand** with a humble or apologetic attitude ◇ **set your cap at** *or* **for somebody** to try to attract somebody, especially with a view to marriage (*dated*)

CAP[1] *abbr* AVIAT Civil Air Patrol

CAP[2] /kap/ *abbr* COMPUT computer-aided production

cap. *abbr* **1.** MEASURE capacity **2.** capital **3.** FIN capitalize **4.** capital letter **5.** ANAT caput

Ca·pa /káppə/, **Robert** (1913–54) Hungarian-born US photographer. He covered combat from the Spanish Civil War to the Vietnam War, where he was killed by a landmine.

ca·pa·bil·i·ty /kàypə bíllətee/ (*plural* **-ties**) *n* **1. NATURAL ABILITY** the power or practical ability necessary for doing something ○ *Her capability to increase sales by endorsement is valuable to us.* **2. RANGE OF ABILITY** the potential ability of somebody or something to do something ○ *There is some doubt about the company's technological capabilities.* **3.** COMPUT **FUNCTION** a facility to carry out a particular set of operations ○ *a graphics capability*

SYNONYMS See *ability*.

ca·pa·ble /káypəb'l/ *adj* **1. DOING SOMETHING WELL** good at a particular task or job or at a number of different things ○ *a very capable hotel manager* **2. ABLE TO DO PARTICULAR THING** possessing the qualities needed to do a particular thing ○ *not capable of murder* **3. LIABLE TO SOMETHING** permitting or susceptible to something ○ *an action capable of being misinterpreted* **4.** LAW **LEGALLY COMPETENT** considered legally competent to do something [Mid-16C. Via French < late Latin *capabilis* < Latin *capere* "take"] —**ca·pa·ble·ness** *n*

ca·pa·bly /káypəblee/ *adv* in a competent or efficient way

ca·pa·cious /kə páyshəss/ *adj* big enough to contain a large quantity [Early 17C. < Latin *capac-* "able to hold" < *capere* "take"] —**ca·pa·cious·ly** *adv* —**ca·pa·cious·ness** *n*

ca·pac·i·tance /kə pássitənss/ *n* ELEC **1. ABILITY TO STORE ELECTRIC CHARGE** the ability of a substance to store an electric charge **2. ABILITY OF COMPONENT TO STORE CHARGE** the ability of an electronic component to store an electric charge **3. MEASURE OF ELECTRIC CHARGE STORAGE** a measure of the capacitance of a substance, equal to the surface charge divided by the electric potential. Symbol **C 4. PART OF ELECTRIC CIRCUIT** the part of an electric circuit that has capacitance

ca·pac·i·tate /kə pássi tàyt/ (**-tat·ed, -tat·ing, -tates**) *vt* **1. MAKE SOMEBODY CAPABLE** to make somebody able, fit, or qualified to do something (*formal*) **2.** LAW **GIVE SOMEBODY LEGAL POWER** to make somebody legally able to do something **3.** PHYSIOL **CAUSE CHANGE IN SPERM COATING** to cause the coatings on a sperm to be able to interact with proteins on the ovum —**ca·pac·i·ta·tion** /kə pàssi táysh'n/ *n*

ca·pac·i·tive /kə pássitiv/ *adj* relating to electrical capacitance —**ca·pac·i·tive·ly** *adv*

ca·pac·i·tor /kə pássitər/ *n* an electrical component, used to store a charge temporarily, consisting of two conducting surfaces separated by a nonconductor (**dielectric**)

ca·pac·i·ty /kə pássətee/ (*plural* **-ties**) *n* **1. VOLUME** a measure of the amount that can be held or contained by something **2. MAXIMUM VOLUME** the maximum amount that can be held or taken in ○ *The theater was filled to capacity.* **3. MAXIMUM PRODUCTIVITY** the maximum amount of output or productivity ○ *a factory operating at less than full capacity* **4. MENTAL OR PHYSICAL ABILITY** mental or physical ability for something or to do something **5. OFFICIAL ROLE** an official function or position that somebody has ○ *in my capacity as team captain* **6.** ELEC **MEASURE OF ELECTRIC OUTPUT** a measure of the electric output of a battery or generator **7.** COMPUT **COMPUTER STORAGE SPACE** the amount of data that can be stored by a computer device **8.** LAW **LEGAL COMPETENCE** the legal ability or qualification to do something such as make an arrest or a will [15C. Via French < Latin *capacitas* < *capac-* (see CAPACIOUS)]

SYNONYMS See ***ability***.

cap and bells *npl* a cap with bells attached to it, traditionally worn by a court jester, or the complete outfit of a court jester

ca·par·i·son /kə párriss'n/ *n* **1. DECORATIVE COVERING FOR HORSE** an ornamental covering for a horse, especially for a warhorse in former times **2. HARNESS OR SADDLE DECORATIONS** a decorative harness for a horse or decorations for its saddle or other fittings **3. ELABORATE CLOTHING** elaborate or rich clothing and ornaments [Early 16C. < obsolete French *caparasson*] —**ca·par·i·son** *vt*

cape[1] /kayp/ *n* **1. LOOSE OUTER GARMENT** a sleeveless outer garment that is fastened at the neck and hangs loosely from the shoulders **2. COAT PART LIKE CAPE** a piece of material like a cape that forms part of a coat or other garment **3.** BIRDS **FEATHERS ON BIRD'S SHOULDER** a covering of short feathers on the shoulders of some birds, especially fowl [Mid-16C. Via French < late Latin *cappa* "hood, hooded cloak"]

cape[2] /kayp/ *n* a point of land that juts out into water, especially a headland significant for navigation [14C. Via French *cap* < Latin *caput* "head"]

Cape Bret·on High·lands Na·tion·al Park /kayp brètt'n-/ national park situated on northern Cape Breton Island, Nova Scotia, and established in 1936. Area: 367 sq. mi./951 sq. km.

Cape Bret·on Is·land island in northern Nova Scotia, Canada, separated from the mainland by the Strait of Canso. Area: 3,981 sq. mi./10,311 sq. km.

Cape Cod, Cape Cod cot·tage *n* a colonial style of house usually one-and-a-half stories high, with clapboard siding, a compact rectangular floor plan, and a steep gable roof [Early 20C. After *Cape* CAPE COD]

Cape Cod Na·tion·al Sea·shore /-kòd-/ national park on Cape Cod, Massachusetts, established in 1961 and noted for its beaches, sand dunes, and marshes. Area: 68 sq. mi./177 sq. km.

Cape Col·oured *n* in South Africa, somebody of mixed ethnic descent in the Western Cape Province, speaking Afrikaans or English [After the CAPE OF GOOD HOPE]

Cape Cor·al /-káwrəl/ city in southwestern Florida, on the Caloosahatchee River near the Gulf of Mexico. Population: 112,899 (2002 estimate).

Cape Dutch *n* the form of Dutch that developed into Afrikaans [*Cape* after the CAPE OF GOOD HOPE; *Dutch* refers to the early settlers or the language] —**Cape Dutch** *adj*

ca·peesh /kə peésh/ *interj* do you understand? [Mid-20C. < Italian *capisce* "he or she understands," form of *capire* "understand"]

Cape Fear /-feér/ river in North Carolina flowing southeastward from the confluence of the Haw and Deep rivers to the Atlantic Ocean below Wilmington. Length: 202 mi./325 km.

Cape Gi·rar·deau /-jə raárdō/ city in southeastern Missouri, on the Mississippi River, southeast of St. Louis. Population: 35,665 (2002 estimate).

Cape goose·ber·ry *n* a tropical plant of the nightshade family that bears edible yellow berries. Native to: Americas. Latin name: *Physalis peruviana*. [< its cultivation in the CAPE OF GOOD HOPE]

Cape Hat·ter·as Na·tion·al Sea·shore /-hàttərəss-/ national park in eastern North Carolina, established in 1937 and noted for its beaches and wildlife. It includes Pea Island National Wildlife Refuge. Area: 47 sq. mi./123 sq. km.

Cape jas·mine *n* PLANTS same as **gardenia**

Ča·pek /chaá pèk/, **Karel** (1890–1938) Czech writer. His drama *R.U.R.* (short for "Rossum's Universal Robots") (1921), satirizes mechanization.

cap·e·lin /káppəlin, kápplin/, **cap·lin** /kápplin/ *n* a small edible sea fish of the smelt family. Native to: northern and Arctic seas. Latin name: *Mallotus villosus*. [Early 17C. Via French < medieval Latin *cappellanus* "custodian of St. Martin's cloak" < late Latin *cappa* "hood, hooded cloak"]

Ca·pel·la /kə péllə/ *n* a double star that is the brightest star in the constellation Auriga

cap·el·li·ni /kàppə leénee/ *n* long fine noodles, resembling thin spaghetti (*takes a singular or plural verb*) [< Italian, "little hairs"]

Cape Look·out Na·tion·al Sea·shore /-lòok owt-/ national park on the Outer Banks, in eastern North Carolina. Established in 1966, it was designated a Biosphere Reserve in 1986. Area: 44 sq. mi./114 sq. km.

Cape Pe·nin·su·la peninsula that extends south of Cape Town, South Africa, ending in the Cape of Good Hope

Cape prim·rose *n* BOT same as **streptocarpus** [Probably after the CAPE OF GOOD HOPE or CAPE PROVINCE]

Cape Prov·ince former province of South Africa, successor to the British-ruled Cape Colony. In 1994 the region was divided into the three provinces of Eastern Cape, Northern Cape, and Western Cape.

ca·per[1] /káypər/ *n* **1. PLAYFUL JUMP** a playful leap or dancing step **2. PLAYFUL ACT OR TRICK** a lighthearted adventurous act or prank **3. QUESTIONABLE ACTIVITY** a dangerous or illegal activity, especially one involving robbery (*informal*) ■ *vi* (**-pered, -per·ing, -pers**) **PRANCE HAPPILY** to leap or dance around in a happy playful manner [Late 16C. Shortening of CAPRIOLE]

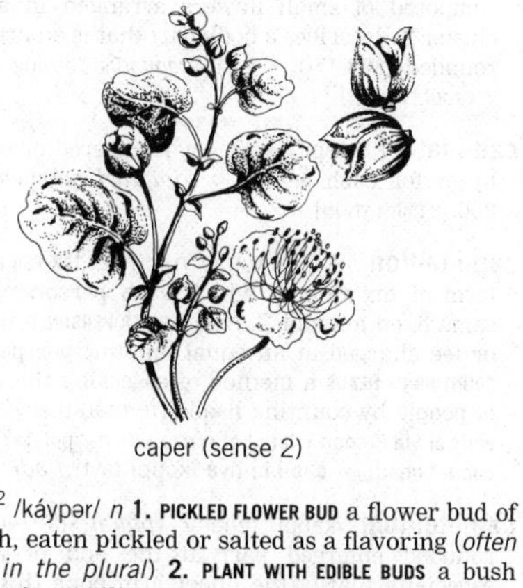

caper (sense 2)

ca·per[2] /káypər/ *n* **1. PICKLED FLOWER BUD** a flower bud of a bush, eaten pickled or salted as a flavoring (*often used in the plural*) **2. PLANT WITH EDIBLE BUDS** a bush with spiny trailing stems, cultivated for its capers. Native to: Mediterranean. Latin name: *Capparis spinosa*. **3. PLANT RELATED TO CAPER** a plant in the same family as the caper. Family: Capparidaceae. [14C. Directly or via French *câpres* < Latin *capparis* < Greek *kapparis*; modern form from misunderstanding *-s* as the plural suffix]

cap·er·cail·lie /kàppər káylee, -káylyee/ (*plural same* or **-lies**), **cap·er·cail·zie** /-káylzee/ (*plural same* or **-zies**) *n* a large woodland bird of the grouse family, with dark gray feathers. Native to: Europe, Asia. Latin name: *Tetrao urogallus*. [Mid-16C. < Gaelic *capull coille* "horse of the wood"]

Ca·per·na·um /kə púrnee əm/ city of ancient Palestine, situated on the northwestern shore of the Sea of Galilee

cap·er spurge *n* an annual plant that produces a milky fluid (**latex**) and has seeds with a high oil content, of potential interest as biodiesel. It is reputed to repel moles. Native to: Europe, naturalized in North America. Latin name: *Euphorbia lathyris*. [< CAPER[2]]

cape·skin /káyp skìn/ *n* a soft light leather made from South African sheepskin [After the CAPE OF GOOD HOPE]

Cape spar·row *n* a common sparrow. Native to: South Africa. Latin name: *Passer melanurus*.

Ca·pe·tian /kə peésh'n/ *n* a member of the royal dynasty founded by Hugh Capet that ruled France from A.D. 987 to 1328 ■ *adj* relating to the Capetians or the period of their rule [Mid-19C. < Franch *Capetien*]

Cape Town legislative capital of South Africa and capital of Western Cape Province. It is situated at the northern end of the Cape Peninsula at the foot of Table Mountain. Population: 2,893,256 (2001). Afrikaans name **Kaapstad**

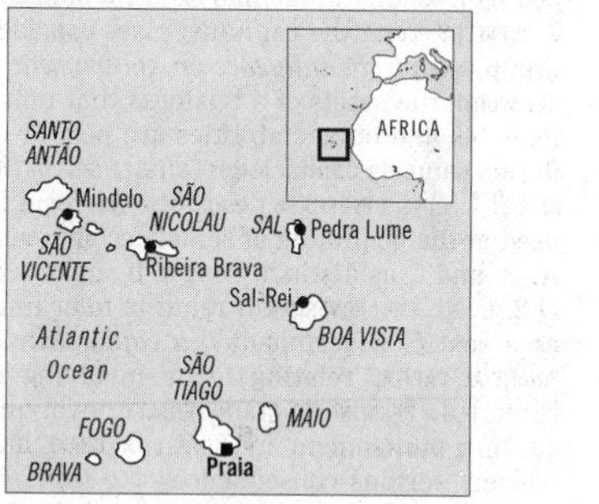

Cape Verde

Cape Verde /-vúrd/ **1.** island country lying about 400 mi./644 km off the coast of Senegal in West Africa. A former Portuguese colony, it became independent in 1975. Language: Portuguese. Currency: escudo. Capital: Praia. Population: 412,137 (2003). Area: 1,557 sq. mi./4,033 sq. km. Official name **Republic of Cape Verde.** Portuguese name **Cabo Verde 2.** same as **Cape Vert**

Cape Vert /kàp vér/ peninsula in western central Senegal. Its tip is the westernmost point of the African mainland. Length: 20 mi./32 km.

cape·work /káyp wùrk/ *n* the skill of a bullfighter in using a cape to control the movements of a bull [Early 20C. < CAPE[1]]

Cape York Pe·nin·su·la peninsula in northern Queensland, Australia, the most northerly point on the Australian mainland. Area: 49,100 sq. mi./127,200 sq. km.

cap gun *n* a toy gun that can be loaded with a small quantity of explosive enclosed in paper (**cap**)

Cap-Hai·tien /kàp háysh'n/ seaport in northern Haiti. Population: 92,122 (1995).

ca·pi·as /káypee əss/ *n* a warrant authorizing an officer of the law to arrest the person named on the warrant (*dated*) [< Latin, "you are to seize" < *capere* "take"]

cap·il·la·ceous /kàppə láyshəss/ *adj* **1.** resembling a hair **2.** having many filaments that resemble hair or thread [Early 18C. < Latin *capillaceus* < *capillus* "hair"]

cap·il·lar·i·ty /kàppə lárrətee/ *n* **1.** PHYS same as **capillary action 2.** the state of being capillary [Mid-19C. < French *capillarité* < Latin *capillus* "hair"]

cap·il·lar·y /káppə lèrree/ *n* (*plural* **-ies**) **1.** ANAT **THIN BLOOD VESSEL** an extremely narrow thin-walled blood vessel that connects small arteries (**arterioles**) with small veins (**venules**) to form a network throughout the body **2.** SCI same as **capillary tube** ■ *adj* **1.** PHYS **OF CAPILLARY ACTION** relating to or involving capillary action ○ *capillary attraction* **2.** ANAT **OF BLOOD CAPILLARIES** relating to the capillaries of the blood system **3. RESEMBLING HAIR** as fine and slender as a hair **4. SMALL**

IN DIAMETER having a very small internal diameter [Mid-17C. < Latin *capillaris* < *capillus* "hair"]

cap·il·lar·y ac·tion *n* a phenomenon in which a liquid's surface rises, falls, or becomes distorted in shape where it is in contact with a solid. It is caused by the difference between the relative attraction of the molecules of the liquid for each other and for those of the solid.

cap·il·lar·y bed *n* the collective mass of capillaries in the body or in a particular part of it

cap·il·lar·y tube *n* a tube with a very small internal diameter, especially a glass tube with a fine bore and thick walls used in thermometers and similar pieces of equipment

cap·i·ta ANAT plural of **caput**

cap·i·tal[1] /káppit'l/ *n* **1.** SEAT OF GOVERNMENT a city that is the seat of government of a country, state, or province **2.** CENTER OF ACTIVITY a city that is the center of a particular activity **3.** MATERIAL WEALTH material wealth in the form of money or property **4.** CASH FOR INVESTMENT money that can be used to produce further wealth **5.** ECONOMIC RESOURCE a resource or resources that can be used to generate economic wealth ○ *a waste of human capital* **6.** ADVANTAGE advantage derived from or useful in a particular situation ○ *a powerful senator's seemingly endless political capital* **7.** WEALTHY PEOPLE the capitalist class considered as a group ○ *capital's influence on government policy* **8.** NET WORTH the assets of a business that remain after its debts and other liabilities are paid or deducted **9.** LING same as **capital letter** (*often used in the plural*) ■ *adj* **1.** LING UPPERCASE describes the form of letters used at the beginning of sentences and names, e.g., A, B, and C as distinct from a, b, and c ○ *a capital D* **2.** GEOG, POL GOVERNMENT relating to or functioning as a seat of government ○ *a capital city* **3.** FIN OF FINANCIAL CAPITAL relating to or involving financial capital **4.** RELATING TO DEATH PENALTY involving or incurring punishment by death **5.** GRAVE having extremely serious consequences ○ *a capital blunder that sealed their fate* **6.** PRINCIPAL constituting or belonging to the highest category ○ *a national issue of capital importance* **7.** *UK* same as **excellent** (*dated*) [12C. Via French < Latin *capitalis* "of the head" < *caput* "head"]

USAGE Do not confuse ***capital*** with ***capitol***, which has a similar pronunciation. The noun ***capital*** means, among other things, "a city that is a nation's or state's seat of government" (*Washington, D.C., is our nation's capital*). The noun ***capitol***, in lowercase, denotes the building or complex of buildings in which a state legislature sits (*visited the Missouri capitol*); when capitalized, ***Capitol*** refers to the buildings in which the US Congress sits (*toured the Capitol on Capitol Hill*). ***Capital*** can be a noun or an adjective, while ***capitol*** is a noun only.

cap·i·tal[2] /káppit'l/ *n* the upper part of an architectural pillar or column, on top of the shaft and supporting the entablature [13C. Via French < late Latin *capitellum* (see CAPITELLUM)]

USAGE See ***capital***[1].

cap·i·tal ac·count *n* **1.** a business account that records how much the owners or stockholders have invested in a company **2.** a statement of a company's or individual person's net worth at a particular time

cap·i·tal al·low·ance *n* money spent by a company on fixed assets and deducted from its profits before taxes are calculated

cap·i·tal as·set *n* FIN same as **fixed asset**

cap·i·tal ex·pen·di·ture *n* expenditure on long-term business assets (**fixed assets**) such as buildings

cap·i·tal gain *n* a profit made from the sale of a financial asset such as stock or a house (*often used in the plural*)

cap·i·tal gains tax *n* a tax on profit above a fixed level made from the sale of financial assets

cap·i·tal goods *npl* goods that are used in the production of other goods, as opposed to being sold to consumers

cap·i·tal-in·ten·sive *adj* using or requiring a proportionately large financial expenditure relative to the amount of labor involved

cap·i·tal·ism /káppit'l ìzzəm/ *n* an economic system based on the private ownership of the means of production and distribution of goods, characterized by a free competitive market and motivation by profit

cap·i·tal·ist /káppit'list/ *n* **1.** INVESTOR an investor of money in business for profit **2.** BELIEVER IN CAPITALISM a supporter of capitalism, or a participant in a capitalist economy **3.** SOMEBODY RICH somebody who is wealthy, especially somebody made rich by capitalism and considered to be greedy (*informal*) ■ *adj* **1.** OF CAPITALISM relating to or involving capitalism or capitalists **2.** *also* **cap·i·tal·is·tic** /kàppit'l ístik/ FAVORING CAPITALISM practicing or supporting capitalism —**cap·i·tal·is·ti·cal·ly** *adv*

cap·i·tal·ize /káppit'l ìz/ (**-ized, -iz·ing, -iz·es**) *v* **1.** *vti* LING USE CAPITAL LETTERS FOR SOMETHING to write or print something with capital letters or an initial capital letter **2.** *vi* BENEFIT FROM SOMETHING to profit by or take advantage of something ○ *to capitalize on an opponent's mistake* **3.** *vt* FIN USE SOMETHING AS CAPITAL to use debt or budgeted expenditure as capital for development **4.** *vt* FINANCE SOMETHING to supply capital for a business enterprise **5.** *vt* FIN AUTHORIZE ISSUE OF CAPITAL STOCK to authorize a business enterprise to issue a particular amount of capital stock **6.** *vt* FIN EXCHANGE DEBT FOR STOCK to convert a corporation's debt into shares of stock **7.** *vt* ACCT TREAT EXPENSES AS ASSETS to treat an expenditure as an asset in a business account instead of as an expense **8.** *vt* FIN VALUE FUTURE INCOME to determine the current value of a future cash flow, earnings, or other income —**cap·i·tal·iz·a·ble** *adj* —**cap·i·tal·i·za·tion** /kàppit'li záysh'n/ *n*

cap·i·tal let·ter *n* an alphabetical letter in the larger form used to begin sentences and names, e.g., A, B, and C as distinct from a, b, and c

cap·i·tal lev·y *n* a tax on fixed assets or property

cap·i·tal·ly /káppitəlee/ *adv* in a way that arouses admiration (*dated*)

cap·i·tal mar·ket *n* a financial market involving institutions that deal with securities with a life of more than one year

cap·i·tal pun·ish·ment *n* execution as a punishment for a person convicted of committing a crime

cap·i·tal ship *n* a ship that belongs to the largest and most heavily armed class of warships

cap·i·tal stock *n* the amount of stock that a company issues or the value of that stock

cap·i·tate /káppi tàyt/ *adj* **1.** describes a flower head composed of small flowers arranged in a dense cluster **2.** describes a body part that is enlarged and rounded [Mid-17C. < Latin *capitatus* "having a head" < *caput* "head"]

cap·i·tat·ed /káppi tàytəd/ *adj* numbered or assessed by or for each person ○ *capitated payments* [Late 20C. < CAPITATION]

cap·i·ta·tion /kàppi táysh'n/ *n* **1.** FIXED TAX PER PERSON a form of taxation in which each person pays the same fixed amount **2.** FIXED FEE PER PERSON a payment or fee charged at an equal amount per person **3.** COUNTING OF HEADS a method of assessing the number of people by counting heads (*formal*) [Early 17C. Directly or via French < late Latin *capitation-* "poll tax" < Latin *capit-* "head"] —**cap·i·ta·tive** /káppi tàytiv/ *adj*

cap·i·tel·lum /kàppi téllәm/ (*plural* **-la** /-lə/) *n* a rounded enlarged part at the end of a bone, especially that of the upper arm bone (**humerus**) that forms the elbow joint with one of the lower bones (**radius**) [Early 18C. < Latin, "little head" < *caput* "head"]

cap·i·tol /káppit'l/ *n* a building or group of buildings in which a state legislature meets and where other state government offices may be housed [14C. Via French < Latin *Capitolium*, temple of Jupiter in Rome < *caput* "head"]

USAGE See ***capital***[1].

CORBIS

Capitol, Washington, D.C.

Cap·i·tol *n* the white marble domed building in Washington, D.C., where the US Congress meets

Cap·i·tol Hill *n* the US Congress (*informal*)

Cap·i·to·line Hill /káppitə lìn-/ *n* a hill in ancient Rome on which the temple of Jupiter stood, site also of the Tarpeian Rock [Early 17C. < Latin *Capitolinus* < *Capitolium* (see CAPITOL)]

Cap·i·tol Reef Na·tion·al Park /kàppit'l-/ national park in south central Utah. Established as a national monument in 1937, it became a national park in 1971. Area: 378 sq. mi./979 sq. km.

ca·pit·u·la BIOL plural of **capitulum**

ca·pit·u·lar /kə píchələr/ *adj* **1.** CHR OF ECCLESIASTICAL CHAPTER relating to or belonging to a cathedral or other ecclesiastical chapter **2.** BOT DENSELY CLUSTERED describes a flower head (**capitulum**) consisting of many small flowers **3.** ANAT ROUNDED describes the rounded end (**capitulum**) of a bone [Early 16C. < late Latin *capitularis* < Latin *capitulum* (see CAPITULUM)] —**ca·pit·u·lar·ly** *adv*

ca·pit·u·lar·y /kə píchə lèrree/ (*plural* **-ies**) *n* **1.** a member of an ecclesiastical chapter **2.** a civil or ecclesiastical decree or set of decrees [Mid-17C. < late Latin *capitularius* < Latin *capitulum* (see CAPITULUM)]

ca·pit·u·late /kə píchə làyt/ (**-lat·ed, -lat·ing, -lates**) *vi* **1.** to surrender, especially under agreed conditions **2.** to give in to an argument, request, pressure, or something unavoidable [Late 17C. < French *capituler* "come to terms" < Latin *capitulare* "draw up under distinct heads" < *capitulum* (see CAPITULUM)] —**ca·pit·u·lant** *n* —**ca·pit·u·la·tor** *n* —**ca·pit·u·la·to·ry** /-ə tàwree/ *adj*

SYNONYMS See ***yield***.

ca·pit·u·la·tion /kə pìchə láysh'n/ *n* (*formal*) **1.** GIVING UP surrender or a giving up of resistance **2.** TERMS OF SURRENDER a document that sets out the agreed terms of surrender **3.** SUMMARY an outline or summary in document form

ca·pit·u·lum /kə píchələm/ (*plural* **-la** /-lə/) *n* **1.** a flower head that looks like a large single flower but consists of numerous tiny flowers clustered together on a disk. Daisies and sunflowers have this type of flower head. **2.** a rounded enlarged body part, e.g., at the end of a bone or at the tips of an insect's antennae [Early 18C. < Latin, "little head" < *caput* "head"]

ca·piz /kə píz, káppiz/ *n* **1.** a small mollusk with a hinged shell. Native to: Philippines. Latin name: *Placuna placenta*. **2.** *also* **ca·piz shell** the shell of the capiz. Use: jewelry, lampshades, ornaments. [< a language in the Philippines]

cap·let /kápplət/ *n* a small oval tablet of medicine taken orally

cap·lin *n* FISH another spelling of **capelin**

cap'n *n* used in writing to represent the pronunciation of "captain" when addressing or referring to the captain of a ship

ca·po[1] /káypō/ (*plural* **-pos**) *n* a small movable bar fitted across all the strings of a guitar or similar instrument to raise the pitch [Mid-20C. Shortening of *capo tasto* < Italian, "head stop"]

ca·po[2] /kaápō, káppō/ (*plural* **-pos**) *n* a leader in the Mafia or a similar criminal organization [Mid-20C. Via Italian < Latin *caput* "head"]

ca·po·ei·ra /kàppoo áyrə/ *n* a martial art and dance form, originally from Brazil, that is used to promote physical fitness and grace of movement [Late 20C. < Portuguese]

ca·pon /káy pòn, -pən/ *n* a male chicken castrated to improve its growth and the quality of its flesh for eating [Pre-12C. Via Anglo-Norman < Latin]

ca·po·na·ta /kaàpə naátə/ *n* a dish made from chopped eggplant and other vegetables [Mid-20C. < Italian < Latin *capon-* "capon"]

Library of Congress

Al Capone

Ca·pone /kə pṓn/, **Al** (1899–1947) Italian-born US gangster and racketeer. Active in Chicago during the Prohibition era, he was imprisoned in 1931 for tax evasion. Full name **Capone, Alphonse**. Known as **Scarface**

> "I've been accused of every death except the casualty list of the World War."
> [Al Capone, *The Bootleggers*, Kenneth Allsop; 1961]

cap·o·ral /káppərəl, kàppə rál/ *n* a strong dark coarse tobacco [Mid-19C. < French *tabac du caporal* "corporal's tobacco" (being superior to *tabac du soldat* "soldier's tobacco")]

ca·pote /kə pṓt/ *n* a long coat or cloak, usually with a hood [Early 19C. < French, "little cape" < *cape* "cape" < late Latin *cappa* "hood, hooded cloak"]

AKG London

Truman Capote

Ca·po·te /kə pṓtee/, **Truman** (1924–84) US writer. His best-known works are the novel *Breakfast at Tiffany's* (1958) and the widely acclaimed "nonfiction novel" *In Cold Blood* (1966).

> "I sat looking at Manhattan and wondering what sort of ruin it would make."
> [Truman Capote, "On Brooklyn Heights," *A Capote Reader*; 1987]

Capp /kap/, **Al** (1909–79) US cartoonist, known for his comic strip *L'il Abner* (1934–77). Born **Alfred Gerald Caplin**

cap·pel·let·ti /kàppə léttee/ *n* small pieces of pasta shaped like pointed hats, filled with a seasoned mixture of cheese or meat (*takes a singular or plural verb*) [Mid-20C. < Italian, "little hats" < *capella* "hat" < medieval Latin *capellus* "little hat" < late Latin *cappa* "hood, hooded cloak"]

cap·per /káppər/ *n* **1. CAP-FITTING MACHINE** a machine that fits caps on bottles **2. FINISHING TOUCH OR FINAL STRAW** something good or bad that is the last in a string of such events (*informal*) **3. DECOY FOR CRIME** a decoy or lure, especially somebody who acts as a shill in a con game (*archaic slang*)

cap pis·tol *n* LEISURE, ARMS same as **cap gun**

cap·puc·ci·no /kàppə cheé nō, kaàpə-/ (*plural* **-nos**) *n* a drink made with espresso coffee and frothed hot milk, sometimes topped with powdered chocolate or cinnamon [Mid-20C. < Italian, "Capuchin (friar)" < *cappuccio* "hood" < late Latin *cappa* "hood, hooded cloak"; from the color of the habit]

~~**cappucino**~~ incorrect spelling of **cappuccino**

Cap·ra /káppra/, **Frank** (1897–1991) US movie director and producer. He is best known for his comic "little guy" movies of the 1930s and 40s. *It Happened One Night* (1934) was the first movie to win all five major Academy Awards.

> "I made mistakes in drama. I thought drama was when actors cried. But drama is when the audience cries."
> [Frank Capra, *Cinemas No. 12, Antenne 2 (French television)*; February 1983]

Ca·pri /kə preé, káppree, kaápree/ island resort in Napoli Province, Campania Region, southern Italy. It is situated near the southern entrance to the Bay of Naples. Population: 7,064 (2001). Area: 4.02 sq. mi./10 sq. km.

cap·ric ac·id /kàpprik-/ *n* a white crystalline acid. Source: animal fats, oils. Use: manufacture of artificial fruit flavors, perfumes, plasticizers, and resins. Formula: $C_{10}H_{20}O_2$. [< Latin *capr-* "goat"; from its smell]

ca·pric·cio /kə preéchō, kə preéchee ō/ (*plural* **-cios**) *n* **1. LIVELY INSTRUMENTAL WORK** a piece of instrumental music with a free form, an improvisatory style, and usually a lively tempo **2. PRANK** a lighthearted act or prank **3. WHIM** a sudden idea, impulsive decision, or change of mind [Early 17C. < Italian (see CAPRICE)]

ca·pric·cio·so /kə preèchee ṓssō, kaàpree chṓssō/ *adj, adv* in a lively and fanciful manner (*used as a musical direction*) [Mid-18C. < Italian < *capriccio* (see CAPRICE)]

ca·price /kə preéss/ *n* **1.** a tendency to sudden impulsive decisions or changes of mind **2.** a sudden unexpected action or change of mind **3.** MUSIC same as **capriccio** (sense 1) [Mid-17C. Via French < Italian *capriccio* "head with hair standing on end" < *capo* "head" (< Latin *caput*) + *riccio* "hedgehog" (< Latin *(h)ericius*)]

ca·pri·cious /kə príshəss, kə preéshəss/ *adj* tending to make sudden unexpected changes —**ca·pri·cious·ly** *adv* —**ca·pri·cious·ness** *n*

Cap·ri·corn /káppri kawrn/ *n* **1.** ZODIAC **10TH SIGN OF ZODIAC** the tenth sign of the zodiac, represented by a goat with a fish's tail and extending from December 22 to January 19. Capricorn is classified as an earth sign, and its ruling planet is Saturn. **2.** *also* **Cap·ri·corn·i·an** *or* **Cap·ri·corn·e·an** /kàppri káwrniən/ ZODIAC **SOMEBODY BORN UNDER CAPRICORN** somebody whose birthday falls between December 22 and January 19 **3.** ASTRON **CONSTELLATION IN SOUTHERN HEMISPHERE** a zodiacal constellation of the southern hemisphere. See illustration at **constellation 4.** GEOG same as **tropic of Capricorn** [Pre-12C. < Latin *capricornus* "goat's horn" < *caper* "goat" + *cornu* "horn"] —**Cap·ri·corn** *adj*

Cap·ri·cor·nus /kàppri káwrnəss/ *n UK* same as **Capricorn** (sense 3)

cap·ri·fig /káppra fig/ *n* a fig produced by a wild fig tree [15C. Partial translation of Latin *caprificus*]

cap·rine /ká prīn/ *adj* relating to or resembling a goat [15C. < Latin *caprinus* < *caper* "goat"]

cap·ri·ole /káppree ōl/ *n* **1.** in dressage, a vertical leap in which all four of the horse's feet leave the ground and then its hind legs are kicked out **2.** a playful leap or jump performed in ballet [Late 16C. Via French < Latin *capreolus* "little goat" < *caper* "goat"] —**cap·ri·ole** *vi*

ca·pri pants /kə preé-/, **Ca·pri pants**, **ca·pris** /kə preéz/, **Ca·pris** *npl* close-fitting women's pants that end just below the knee [Mid-20C. After the island of CAPRI]

Ca·pri·vi Strip /kə preévee-/ narrow extension of Namibia, running eastward about 280 mi./450 km from northeastern Namibia to the Zambezi River. It is bordered by Angola and Zambia to the north and Botswana to the south.

cap rock *n* **1.** a layer of rock that lies above a salt dome and consists of anhydrite, gypsum, or limestone **2.** an impermeable layer of rock that lies above a deposit of gas or oil and prevents it from percolating upward

ca·pro·ic ac·id /kə prṓ ik-/ *n* a liquid fatty acid. Source: fats, oils, made synthetically. Use: flavorings, medicine. Formula: $C_6H_{12}O_2$. [< Latin *capr-* "goat"; from its smell]

ca·pryl·ic ac·id /kə prillik-/ *n* an oily fatty acid with an unpleasant taste and smell. Source: animal fats. Use: in dyes, perfumes. Formula: $C_8H_{16}O_2$. [< Latin *capr-* "goat"; from its smell]

caps. *abbr* **1.** capital letters **2.** PHARM capsule

cap·sa·i·cin /kap sáy əssin/ *n* a colorless compound. Source: hot peppers. Use: medicine, flavoring. Formula: $C_{18}H_{27}NO_3$. [Late 19C. Alteration of *capsicine* < CAPSICUM]

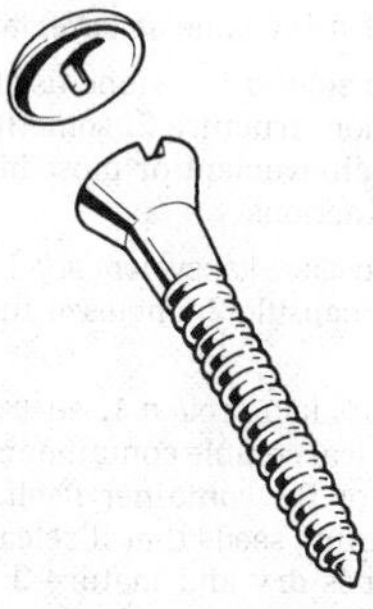

cap screw

cap screw *n* a long-threaded bolt with a head that may be square, hexagonal, slotted, or socketed

Cap·si·an /kápsee ən/ *adj* belonging to a late Paleolithic culture of northern Africa and southern Europe, characterized by the use of geometrically shaped tools and distinctive art forms such as engraved limestone slabs [Early 20C. < French *capsien* < Latin *Capsa* "Gafsa," town in Tunisia] —**Cap·si·an** *n*

cap·si·cum /kápsikəm/ *n* **1.** a hot red pepper fruit, eaten raw or cooked as a vegetable, and often dried **2.** FOOD same as **pepper** *n* (sense 4) [Late 16C. < modern Latin]

cap·sid /kápsid/ *n* the outer coat of protein that surrounds a virus particle [Mid-20C. < Latin *capsa* "box"]

cap·size /káp sīz, kap sīz/ (**-sized, -siz·ing, -siz·es**) *vti* to overturn on the surface of water, or cause a boat to overturn (*refers to boats*) [Late 18C. Origin ?]

cap sleeve

cap sleeve *n* a very short sleeve that hangs over the shoulder but does not extend beyond the armhole on the underside

caps lock *n* a key on a computer keyboard or typewriter that, if pressed once, causes all subsequent letters to be typed as capital letters

cap·so·mere /kápsə meer/ *n* one of the individual protein units that make up the outer coat (**capsid**) of a virus [Mid-20C. < CAPSID]

cap·stan /kápstən/ *n* **1.** a device consisting of a vertical rotatable drum around which a cable is wound. Use: moving heavy weights, hauling in ropes on a ship. See illustration on next page **2.** a rotating shaft in a tape recorder that pulls the magnetic tape past the head [14C. Via Provençal *cabestan* < Latin *capistrum* "halter" < *capere* "seize"]

cap·stan bar *n* a long lever used to turn a capstan by hand

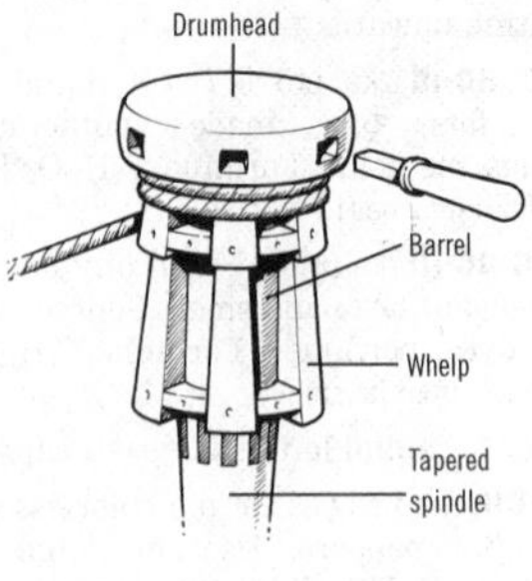

capstan

cap·stan lathe *n UK* same as **turret lathe**

cap·stone /káp stōn/ *n* **1.** a stone used at the top of a wall or another structure **2.** something considered the highest achievement or most important action in a series of actions

cap·su·lar /kápsələr, kápsyələr/ *adj* **1.** relating to or resembling a capsule **2.** enclosed in or in the form of a capsule

cap·sule /káps'l, káp sool/ *n* **1.** PHARM **PILL OR CASING** a small cylindrical soluble container enclosing a dose of medicine, or the container itself **2.** BOT **SEED CASE** a fruit containing seeds that it releases by splitting open when it is dry and mature **3.** BOT **SPORE SAC** a sac containing the spores of a moss or a liverwort **4.** MICROBIOL **GELATINOUS COVERING OF MICROORGANISM** a gelatinous covering that surrounds some microorganisms **5.** ANAT **MEMBRANE SURROUNDING BODY PART** a membrane or sac enclosing an organ or body part **6.** ANAT **WHITE MATTER IN BRAIN** a layer of white fibers in the forebrain **7.** AEROSP same as **space capsule 8.** AVIAT **EJECTABLE COCKPIT** a sealed cockpit in an aircraft that can be ejected in an emergency **9. SHORT SUMMARY** a very brief summary **10.** MANUF **SEAL ON BOTTLE** a protective seal, e.g., the metal, plastic, or wax covering that protects the cork of a wine bottle ■ *adj* **1. VERY BRIEF** expressed in an extremely brief or highly condensed way **2. COMPACT** very small or compact ■ *vt* (**-suled, -sul·ing, -sules**) same as **capsulize** [Mid-17C. Via French < Latin *capsula* "little box" < *capsa* "box" < *capere* "take"] —**cap·su·late** /kápsə làyt, kápsyə-/ *adj*

cap·sule col·lec·tion *n* a set, e.g., of fashion garments and accessories or furniture, comprising all the basic or key items

cap·sule ho·tel *n* in Japan, a hotel in which the rooms are lockable cubicles

cap·sule ward·robe *n* a person's basic collection of coordinating clothes that can be used to form the basis of outfits for all occasions

cap·sul·ize /kápsə līz, kápsyə līz/ (**-ized, -iz·ing, -iz·es**) *vt* **1.** to express something in a very brief or condensed way **2.** to put something into a capsule or into the form of a capsule

cap·su·lot·o·my /kàpsə lóttəmee/ (*plural* **-mies**) *n* a surgical procedure involving cutting into the capsule surrounding a body part, e.g., cutting into the lens of the eye during the removal of a cataract

Capt. *abbr* Captain

cap·tain /káptən/ *n* **1.** NAUT **SAILOR IN COMMAND** the commander of a ship **2.** AEROSP **PILOT IN COMMAND** the pilot in command of a civil aircraft **3.** NAVY **NAVY OR COAST GUARD OFFICER** an officer in the US or Canadian navies or the US Coast Guard of a rank above commander **4.** MIL **US COMPANY GRADE OFFICER** an officer in the US Army, Air Force, or Marine Corps of a rank above first lieutenant **5.** MIL **OFFICER IN CANADIAN FORCES** an officer in the Royal Canadian Army or Air Force of a rank above lieutenant **6. SENIOR POLICE OR FIRE OFFICER** a police officer in charge of a precinct, or a fire department officer, usually ranking above a lieutenant and below a chief **7. OFFICER OF OTHER ARMY** an officer of corresponding rank in the army of any other country **8. TEAM LEADER** a leader of a team in a sport or game **9. IMPORTANT PERSON** an influential leader in a field or organization ○ *captains of industry* **10. SUPERVISOR** a title sometimes given to a supervisor such as the person in charge of bellhops or restaurant servers ■ *vt* (**-tained, -tain·ing, -tains**) **COMMAND SOMETHING** to be the captain of something [14C. Via Old French *capitain* < late Latin *capitaneus* "chief" < Latin *caput* "head"] —**cap·tain·cy** *n*

cap·tain's chair *n* a wooden chair with a saddle seat and a low curved back and arms supported on vertical spindles

cap·tain's mast *n* a disciplinary hearing at which a captain or commanding officer of a navy ship or force hears and acts on cases against enlisted personnel

cap·tan /káptən, káp tàn/ *n* an agricultural fungicide in the form of a white powder, used on fruits, flowers, and vegetables. Formula: $C_9H_8Cl_3NO_2S$. [Mid-20C. Shortening of MERCAPTAN]

cap·tion /kápshən/ *n* **1. DESCRIPTION OF ILLUSTRATION** a short description or title accompanying an illustration in a printed text **2.** MOVIES **MOVIE OR TELEVISION SUBTITLE** a printed explanation in a motion picture or on television, especially a translation of dialogue accompanying a scene or an explanation preceding a scene **3.** PRINTING, PUBL **HEADING OR SUBHEADING** a heading or subheading in a document or article **4.** LAW **HEADING OF LEGAL DOCUMENT** an attachment to or heading of a legal document that identifies the circumstances of its production and the sources of its authority [14C. < Latin *caption-* "act of taking" < *capt-* (see CAPTIVE)] —**cap·tion** *vt* —**cap·tion·less** *adj*

cap·tious /kápshəss/ *adj* **1.** tending to find fault and make trivial and excessive criticisms **2.** intended to confuse or entrap an opponent in an argument [14C. Directly or via French < Latin *captiosus* < *caption-* (see CAPTION)] —**cap·tious·ly** *adv* —**cap·tious·ness** *n*

cap·ti·vate /káptə vàyt/ (**-vat·ed, -vat·ing, -vates**) *vt* to attract and hold somebody's attention by charm or other pleasing or irresistible features [Early 16C. < late Latin *captivat-*, past participle of *captivare* "capture" < Latin *captivus* (see CAPTIVE)] —**cap·ti·va·tion** /kàptə váysh'n/ *n* —**cap·ti·va·tor** *n*

cap·ti·vat·ing /káptə vàyting/ *adj* attracting and holding somebody's attention by charm or other pleasing or irresistible features —**cap·ti·vat·ing·ly** *adv*

cap·tive /káptiv/ *n* **1. PRISONER** a person or animal that is forcibly confined or restrained, especially somebody held prisoner **2. SOMEBODY DOMINATED BY EMOTION** somebody gripped by a strong emotion such as love or anger ■ *adj* **1. UNABLE TO ESCAPE** prevented from escaping **2. FORCED TO USE OR ACCEPT SOMETHING** forced by circumstances to buy, accept, or pay attention to something, usually because there is no other option or no means of escape ○ *a captive audience* **3. VERY ATTRACTED** irresistibly attracted to somebody or something [15C. < Latin *captivus* < *capt-*, past participle of *capere* "take"]

cap·tiv·i·ty /kap tívvətee/ *n* the state of being a prisoner, or a period of time that somebody is held prisoner

cap·to·pril /káptə prìl/ *n* a drug that blocks the action of a vasoconstrictor (**angiotensin**). Use: control of high blood pressure. [Late 20C. < MERCAPTAN + -O- + *-pril*, INN stem]

cap·tor /káptər, káp tàwr/ *n* a person or animal that takes or holds another person or animal prisoner [Mid-16C. < Latin < *capt-* (see CAPTIVE)]

cap·ture /kápchər/ *vt* (**-tured, -tur·ing, -tures**) **1. TAKE SOMEBODY PRISONER** to catch and then forcibly lock up or restrain a person or animal **2. SEIZE PLACE** to seize or gain control over a place **3. TAKE SOMETHING IN GAME** to win control or gain possession of something in a game or contest **4. DOMINATE SOMEBODY'S THOUGHTS** to enchant or dominate somebody's mind, especially somebody's imagination, or hold somebody's attention ○ *The stories about travel captured their imaginations most.* **5. WIN SOMEBODY'S LOVE** to win the love or affection of somebody, especially by being charming or attractive **6. REPRESENT SOMETHING ACCURATELY** to describe or represent something, especially something fleeting or intangible, in a lasting medium such as painting, writing, filmmaking, or sculpture ○ *a picture capturing the innocence of childhood* **7.** COMPUT **RECORD DATA ON COMPUTER** to record and store data in the memory of a computer or as a computer file **8.** PHYS **GAIN PARTICLE** to gain an additional elementary particle ■ *n* **1. BEING TAKEN OR TAKING PRISONER** the act of being captured or of capturing somebody or something **2. SOMEBODY OR SOMETHING CAPTURED** somebody or something that has been captured and held in captivity **3.** COMPUT **RECORDING OF DATA** the recording and storage of data in the memory of a computer or as a computer file **4.** PHYS **GAIN OF PARTICLE** a process in which an atom, ion, molecule, or nucleus gains an additional elementary particle, often followed by an emission of radiation **5.** GEOG **DIVERSION OF RIVER OVER TIME** the diversion of the headwaters of one river into the channel of another, brought about by erosion over a long period of time [Mid-16C. Via French < Latin *captura* "seizure" < *capt-* (see CAPTIVE)] —**cap·tur·er** *n*

Cap·u·a /káppyoo ə/ town in Caserta Province, Campania Region, southern Italy. Population: 19,041 (2001).

~~**capuccino**~~ incorrect spelling of **cappuccino**

ca·puche /kə poōch, -poōsh/ *n* a large hood on a cloak, especially the cowl worn by a Capuchin monk [Late 16C. Via French < Italian *cappuccio* (see CAPPUCCINO)]

capuchin

cap·u·chin /káppyəchin, kə pyoōchin, káppyəshin, kə pyoōshin/ *n* **1.** *also* **cap·u·chin mon·key** an agile and intelligent long-tailed monkey with a tuft of hair on its head that resembles a monk's cowl. Native to: forests of Central and South America. Latin name: *Cebus capucinus*. **2.** a hooded cloak formerly worn by women [Mid-18C. < CAPUCHIN]

Cap·u·chin /káppyəchin, kə pyoōchin, káppyəshin, kə pyoōshin/ *n* a member of an independent order of Franciscan friars founded in 1525 in Italy [Late 16C. Via French < Italian *cappuccino* (see CAPPUCCINO)]

cap·u·chin mon·key *n* VERTEB same as **capuchin** (sense 1)

ca·put /káypət, káppət/ (*plural* **-pi·ta** /káppitə/) *n* **1.** the most prominent part of something such as a bodily organ **2.** the head (*technical*) [Mid-17C. < Latin]

capybara

cap·y·ba·ra /kàppi baárə, -bárrə/ (*plural* **-ras** or *same*) *n* the largest living rodent, resembling a large guinea pig, which can grow to a length of more than 4 ft./1.2 m. Native to: Central and South America. Latin name: *Hydrochoerus hydrochaeris*. [Early 17C. Via Spanish *capibara* or Portuguese *capivara* < Tupi *capiuára* < *capī* "grass" + *uára* "eater"]

car /kaar/ *n* **1.** CARS **PASSENGER-CARRYING ROAD VEHICLE** a road vehicle, usually with four wheels and powered by an internal-combustion engine, designed to carry a small number of passengers **2.** RAIL **VEHICLE ON RAILS** a vehicle designed to run on rails, e.g., a streetcar or a railroad car **3.** TRANSP **TRAVELING COMPARTMENT FOR PEOPLE OR THINGS** the part of an airship, balloon, or cable car for carrying passengers and cargo **4. ELEVATOR** the box-shaped container of an elevator in which people or goods are carried up or down **5.** VEHICLES same as **chariot** (*archaic or literary*) [14C. Via Anglo-Norman, Old French *carre* < Latin *carrum, carrus* < Celtic] —**car·ful** *n*

car. *abbr* MEASURE carat

car·a·bao /kárrə bòw, kaárə-/ (*plural same* or **-baos**) *n* ZOOL same as **water buffalo** [Early 20C. Via Spanish < Visayan *karabáw* < Malay *kêrbau*]

car·a·bid /kárrəbid, kə rábbid/ *n* a beetle that lives in the soil. Many species feed on other insects. Family: Carabidae. [Late 19C. < modern Latin *Carabidae* < Latin *carabus* "sea crab" < Greek *karabos* "horned beetle"]

car·a·bi·neer /kàrrəbi neér/, **car·a·bi·nier** *n* a soldier armed with a lightweight short-barreled rifle (**carbine**) [Mid-17C. < French *carabinier* < *carabine* (see CARBINE)]

car·a·bi·ner /kárrə beénər/, **kar·a·bi·ner** *n* an oblong metal ring with a spring-hinged fastening, used in rock and mountain climbing for such purposes as clipping a freely running rope to a piton [Mid-20C. < German *Karabiner-haken* "spring-hook"; because it attaches a carbine rifle to a belt]

car·a·bi·ne·ro /kàrrəbi nérrō/ (*plural* **-ros**) *n* **1.** in Spain, a member of the national police force **2.** in the Philippines, a customs officer, coast guard, or revenue officer [Mid-19C. < Spanish < *carabina* "carbine" < French *carabine* (see CARBINE)]

car·a·bi·nier *n* MIL another spelling of **carabineer**

ca·ra·bi·nie·re /kàrrəbi nyérree, kaárəbi nyérr ay/ (*plural* **-ri** /-ree/) *n* in Italy, a member of the national police force [Mid-19C. Via Italian < French *carabinier* (see CARABINEER)]

caracal

car·a·cal /kárrə kàl/ (*plural* **-cals** or *same*) *n* **1.** a medium-sized wildcat with long legs, a smooth reddish brown coat, a short tail, and long tufted ears. Native to: dry savannas of Africa and southern Asia. Latin name: *Lynx caracal.* **2.** the fur of the caracal [Mid-18C. Via French or Spanish < Turkish *karakulak* < *kara* "black" + *kulak* "ear"]

car·a·car·a /kàrrə kárrə, -kə raá/ *n* a large long-legged carrion-eating or predatory bird of the falcon family. Native to: Central and South America. Genus: *Polyborus.* [Mid-19C. Via Spanish or Portuguese *caracará* < Tupi-Guarani, an imitation of its cry]

Ca·ra·cas /kə rákəss/ city and capital of Venezuela, situated at an altitude of approximately 3,000 ft./900 m. Population: 1,975,787 (2000).

car·ack *n* NAUT another spelling of **carrack**

car·a·cole /kárrə kōl/, **car·a·col** *n* in dressage, a half turn to the left or right performed by a horse and rider ■ *vti* (**-coled, -col·ing, -coles; -coled, -col·ing, -cols**) to perform a caracole, or cause a horse to perform a caracole [Early 17C. < French *caracoler* < *caracol(e)* "snail's shell, spiral"]

Ca·ract·a·cus ♦ **Caratacus**

car·a·cul *n* INDUST another spelling of **karakul**

ca·rafe /kə ráf/ *n* **1.** CONTAINER FOR SERVING DRINKS a container with a wide cylindrical base, a narrow neck, and a flared open top, usually made of glass and used to serve liquids, especially wine or water at the table **2.** CONTAINER FOR COFFEE a glass pot with a lip for pouring and a handle, used especially with a drip coffeemaker to brew and serve coffee **3.** QUANTITY IN CARAFE the contents or capacity of a carafe [Late 18C. Via French < Italian *caraffa*]

ca·ram·ba /kə raámbə/ *interj* used to express surprise, amazement, or dismay (*slang*) [Mid-19C. < Spanish]

car·am·bo·la /kàrrəm bṓlə/ *n* **1.** a smooth-skinned yellow fruit with lengthwise ridges that give it a star-shaped cross section. The thin skin is edible, and the juicy, slightly crisp fruit has a delicate flavor. **2.** a tropical evergreen tree that bears carambolas. Latin name: *Averrhoa carambolas.* [Late 16C. < Portuguese, probably < Marathi *karambal*]

car·a·mel /kárrəməl, -mèl, kaármәl/ *n* **1.** CHEWY CANDY a chewy candy that can be soft or firm, made with butter, milk, and sugar **2.** BURNED SUGAR sugar melted or dissolved in a small amount of water and heated until it turns golden or dark brown. Use: a flavoring and coloring. **3.** YELLOWISH BROWN COLOR a yellowish brown color [Early 18C. Via French < Spanish *caramelo*, alteration of Provençal *canamel* "sugar cane" < Latin *canna* "cane" + *mel* "honey"] —**car·a·mel** *adj*

car·a·mel·ize /kárrəmə līz, kaármə-/ (**-ized, -iz·ing, -iz·es**) *vti* to heat sugar or boil dissolved sugar until it turns dark brown, or undergo this process [Mid-19C. < French *caraméliser* < *caramel* (see CARAMEL)] —**car·a·mel·i·za·tion** /kàrrəməli záysh'n, kaármәli-/ *n*

ca·ran·gid /kə ránjid, -ráng gid/ *n* a spiny-finned sea fish of the family that includes the jack and pompano. Family: Carangidae. [Late 19C. < modern Latin *Carangidae* < *Caranx* < Spanish *caranga* "shad, horse mackerel"]

car·a·pace /kárrə pàyss/ *n* **1.** a thick hard case or shell made of bone or chitin that covers part of the body, especially the back, of an animal such as a crab or turtle **2.** a method of self-protection, e.g., shy or arrogant behavior [Mid-19C. Via French < Spanish *carapacho*]

car·at /kárrət/ *n* a standard unit of mass used for precious stones, especially diamonds, equal to 200 milligrams [15C. Via French < Greek *keration* "fruit of the carob" < *keras* "horn"; because carob beans were used as standard weights for small quantities]

SPELLCHECK carat or **carrot**? Do not confuse the spelling of ***carat*** and ***carrot***, which sound similar. The noun denoting a measure of precious stones or gold is spelled ***carat***, as in *24-carat gold.* The noun denoting the orange root vegetable, or the plant that produces it, is spelled ***carrot.***

Ca·ra·ta·cus /kə ráttəkəss/, **Ca·rac·ta·cus** /-ráktəkəss/ (*fl* A.D. 50) British tribal ruler. He was defeated by the Romans.

Ca·ra·vag·gi·o /kàrrə vaájō/, **Michelangelo Merisi da** (1573–1610) Italian painter. He was an exponent of the baroque style, and his tempestuous life is reflected in his realistic and dramatically lit works.

car·a·van /kárrə vàn/ *n* **1.** GROUP OF DESERT MERCHANTS WITH CAMELS a group of traders, especially in northern Africa and Asia, crossing the desert together for safety, usually with a train of camels **2.** GROUP OF TRAVELERS a group of people, vehicles, or supervised animals that are traveling together for security **3.** VEHICLE FOR LIVING IN a large covered vehicle or van used as a traveling home, particularly by Roma people or circus performers **4.** *UK* same as **trailer** ■ *vi* (**-vanned** or **-vaned, -van·ning** or **-van·ing, -vans**) **1.** TRAVEL TOGETHER to travel in a group **2.** *UK* SPEND TIME IN CAMPER to vacation or travel around in a camper [Late 16C. Via French *caravane* < Persian *kārwān* "group of desert travelers"] —**car·a·van·ner** *n*

car·a·van·se·rai /kàrrə vánssə rī/ (*plural* **-rais**), **car·a·van·sa·ry** /-səree/ (*plural* **-ries**) *n* **1.** a large inn with a central courtyard, found in some eastern countries and used by caravans crossing the desert **2.** TRANSP same as **caravan** *n* (senses 1–2) [Late 16C. < Persian *kārwānsarāī* < *kārwān* "group of desert travelers" + *sarāī* "inn"]

car·a·van site *n UK* same as **trailer park**

car·a·vel /kárrə vèl/, **car·a·velle, car·vel** /kaárv'l, kaár vèl/ *n* a light sailing ship with two or three masts, used in the Mediterranean from the 14th to the 17th centuries [Early 16C. < French *caravelle*, Portuguese *caravela* "small ship" < Greek *karabos* "crayfish"]

car·a·way /kárrə wày/ *n* **1.** a plant with finely divided leaves that bears caraway seeds. Flowers: small, white or pinkish, in clusters. Native to: Europe, Asia. Latin name: *Carum carvi.* **2.** FOOD same as **caraway seed** [13C. Directly or via Old French *carvi* < medieval Latin *carui*]

car·a·way seed *n* the aromatic dried ripe fruit of the caraway plant. Use: spice.

carb[1] /kaarb/ *n* ENG same as **carburetor** (*informal*) [Mid-20C. Shortening]

carb[2] /kaarb/ *n* a carbohydrate, or a high-carbohydrate food (*slang*) [Mid-20C. Shortening of CARBOHYDRATE]

carb- *prefix* CHEM same as **carbo-** (*used before vowels*)

car·ba·mate /kaárbə màyt, kaar bá màyt/ *n* a salt or ester of carbamic acid. Use: pesticides. [Mid-19C. < CARBAMIC ACID]

car·ba·maz·e·pine /kaárbə mázzə peén/ *n* an analgesic anticonvulsant drug. Use: treatment of epilepsy, pain, bipolar disorder. [Late 20C. Rearrangement of *dibenzazepinecarboxamide*]

car·bam·ic ac·id /kaar bàmmik-/ *n* an acid that exists only in the form of its salt or ester. Formula: NH_2COOH. [< CARBO- + AMIDE]

car·ba·mide /kaárbə mīd, kaar bámmid/ *n* CHEM same as **urea** [Mid-19C. < CARBO- + AMIDE]

car·ban·i·on /kaar bán ī ən, -bánn ī òn/ *n* an organic ion that has a carbon atom with a negative charge [Mid-20C. < CARBO- + ANION]

car·barn /kaár baarn/ *n* a building where buses or streetcars are stored

car·ba·ryl /kaárbə rìl/ *n* an insecticide used as a substitute for DDT in a broad range of applications [Mid-20C. Blend of CARBAMATE + ARYL]

car·ba·zole /kaárbə zōl, kaar bá zōl/ *n* a compound derived from coal tar and used in the production of some dyes. Formula: $C_{12}H_9N$.

car·bene /kaár been/ *n* a highly reactive, short-lived molecule containing a carbon atom with only three bonds

car·ben·i·cil·lin /kaar bènni síllin/ *n* an antibiotic derived from penicillin [Mid-20C. < *carb(boxy)-ben(zylpen)i-* + *-cillin*, INN stem]

car·bide /kaár bīd/ *n* **1.** a compound containing carbon and one other element, especially a metal **2.** CHEM same as **calcium carbide** [Mid-19C. < CARBON]

car·bim·a·zole /kaar bímmə zōl/ *n* a drug that inhibits the formation of thyroid hormones. Use: management of hyperthyroidism.

car·bine /kaár been, -bīn/ *n* a lightweight rifle with a short barrel [Early 17C. < French *carabine* < *carabin* "mounted musketeer"]

car·bi·neer /kaárbi neér/ *n* MIL same as **carabineer**

car·bi·nol /kaárbə nàwl, -nòl/ *n* CHEM same as **methanol** [Mid-19C. < CARBON + -INE]

car·bo /kaárbō/ (*plural* **-bos**) *n* carbohydrate, or a carbohydrate (*slang*) ○ *Pasta is a good source of carbo.* [Shortening]

carbo- *prefix* carbon, carbonic ○ *carbocyclic* [< French < *carbone* (see CARBON)]

car·bo·cy·clic /kaárbō síklik, -síklik/ *adj* describes a chemical compound containing a closed ring of carbon atoms

car·bo·hy·drase /kaárbō hī dràyss, -dràyz/ *n* an enzyme that aids the breakdown of a carbohydrate [Early 20C. < CARBOHYDRATE]

car·bo·hy·drate /kaárbō hī dràyt/ *n* **1.** a biological compound containing carbon, hydrogen, and oxygen that is an important source of food and energy **2.** food containing carbohydrates

car·bo·hy·drate load·ing *n* a controversial practice of first starving the body of carbohydrates, then following a high-carbohydrate diet just before an athletic event in an attempt to increase performance

car·bol·ic ac·id *n* CHEM same as **phenol** (sense 1) [Mid-19C. < CARBO- + -OL[1]]

car·bo-load·ing *n* TRACK AND FIELD same as **carbohydrate loading** (*slang*)

car bomb *n* an explosive device concealed inside or under a vehicle and detonated by remote control or when the engine is started

car-bomb *vt* to place a car bomb in or under a vehicle, or use such an explosive-laden vehicle against a target

car·bon /kaárbən/ *n* **1.** CHEM ELEM a nonmetallic element that exists in two main forms, diamond and graphite, and has the ability to form large numbers of organic compounds. Source: coal, petroleum. See table at **element 2.** COMM same as **carbon copy** (sense 1) (*informal*) **3.** PAPER same as **carbon paper** (*informal*) **4.** something made of carbon, especially an electrode or a lamp filament [Late 18C. Via French *carbone* < Latin *carbon-* "coal"] —**car·bon·ous** *adj*

car·bon 12 /-twélv/ *n* an isotope of carbon with relative atomic mass of 12. Use: baseline in determining atomic mass.

car·bon 14 /-fawr teén/ *n* a naturally radioactive isotope of carbon with atomic mass of 14 and a half-life of 5,780 years. Use: as tracer, in carbon dating.

car·bon-14 dat·ing, **car·bon-14 meth·od** *n* ARCHAEOL same as **carbon dating**

car·bo·na·ceous /kaàrbə náyshəss/ *adj* relating to, containing, or resembling carbon

car·bon·ade *n* FOOD another spelling of **carbonnade**

car·bo·na·do /kaàrbə náydō, -naádō/ (*plural* **-dos** or **-does**) *n* a dark diamond or cluster of diamonds. Use: drilling, polishing. [Mid-19C. < Portuguese]

car·bo·na·ra /kaàrbə naárə/ *n* a hot pasta dish prepared with eggs, chopped ham or bacon, and cheese ○ *spaghetti carbonara* [Mid-20C. < Italian *(alla) carbonara* "on the charcoal grill" < *carbone* "charcoal" < Latin *carbon-* "coal"]

car·bon arc *n* an electric discharge between two carbon electrodes or between an electrode and a metal to be welded, characterized by bright light and intense heat

Car·bo·na·ri /kaàbə naáree/ *npl* in early 19th-century Italy, members of a secret society that sought to establish a unified liberal republican government [Early 19C. < Italian, plural of *carbonaro* "charcoal burner" < Latin *carbon-* "coal"; from their use of symbols from the charcoal-burning trade]

car·bon·ate *n* /kaárbə nàyt, -nət/ **1.** CHEM **SALT OR ESTER** a salt or ester of carbonic acid **2.** MINERALS **MINERAL** a mineral composed of carbonates ■ *vt* /kaárbə nàyt/ (**-at·ed, -at·ing, -ates**) **1.** CHEM **CHANGE SUBSTANCE INTO CARBONATE** to convert a chemical compound into a carbonate **2.** FOOD INDUST **MAKE LIQUID BUBBLY AND GASEOUS** to make a liquid bubbly and gaseous by introducing carbon dioxide into it **3.** CHEM same as **carbonize** (sense 1) —**car·bon·a·tion** /kaàrbə náysh'n/ *n* —**car·bon·a·tor** *n*

car·bon·ate plat·form *n* a broad extensive belt-shaped deposit of carbonate materials created in shallow warm oceanic waters during the Cambrian period

car·bon·a·tite /kaar bónnə tīt/ *n* an unusual alkaline igneous rock high in carbonate materials, found in eastern Africa and thought to derive from the Earth's mantle [Early 20C. < CARBONATE]

car·bon bi·sul·fide *n* CHEM same as **carbon disulfide**

car·bon black *n* a form of finely divided carbon. Source: partial combustion of petroleum or natural gas. Use: manufacture of pigment, ink, rubber.

car·bon brush *n* a block of carbon in an engine or generator that conveys current between the moving and the stationary parts

car·bon cop·y *n* **1.** a duplicate of written or drawn material that is made by using carbon paper **2.** somebody or something that is identical to or very much like somebody or something else (*informal*) ○ *This situation is a carbon copy of last year's crisis.*

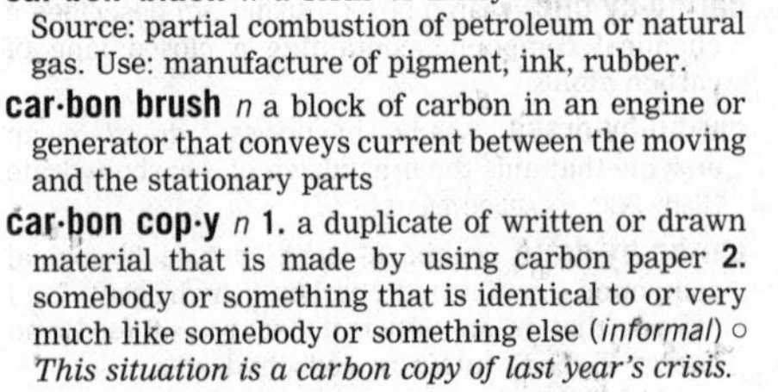

carbon cycle

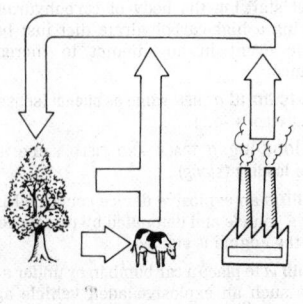

car·bon cy·cle *n* **1.** the exchange of carbon between living organisms and the environment. Carbon dioxide is taken from the atmosphere by photosynthesizing plants and returned by the respiration of plants and animals and by the combustion of fossil fuels. **2.** a chain reaction believed to generate significant energy in some stars, in which carbon is used as a catalyst to fuse four hydrogen nuclei into one helium nucleus

Car·bon·dale /kaárbən dàyl/ **1.** town in southwestern Illinois, southeast of Belleville. Population: 25,168 (2002 estimate). **2.** town in northeastern Pennsylvania, northeast of Scranton. It was formerly an important coal-mining center. Population: 9,559 (2002 estimate).

car·bon dat·ing *n* a method of dating organic remains based on their content of carbon 14

car·bon di·ox·ide *n* a heavy colorless odorless atmospheric gas. Source: respiration, combustion. Use: during photosynthesis, in refrigeration, carbonated drinks, fire extinguishers. Formula: CO_2.

car·bon di·sul·fide *n* a colorless poisonous flammable liquid containing impurities that give it a rotten-egg smell. Use: solvents, fumigants, manufacture of cellophane and rayon. Formula: CS_2.

car·bon e·mis·sions *npl* carbon dioxide and carbon monoxide produced by motor vehicles and industrial processes and forming pollutants in the atmosphere

car·bon fi·ber *n* a very strong light carbonized acrylic thread. Use: reinforcing resins, metals, and ceramics, making turbine blades.

car·bon fix·a·tion *n* the process by which plants synthesize carbon dioxide into organic compounds

car·bon·ic /kaar bónnik/ *adj* containing carbon

car·bon·ic ac·id *n* a weak acid. Source: dissolving of carbon dioxide in water. Formula: H_2CO_3.

car·bon·ic an·hy·drase /-an hī dràyss, -dràyz/ *n* an enzyme in living tissue such as blood cells, that contains zinc and aids the transfer of carbon dioxide from the tissues to the lungs

car·bon·if·er·ous /kaàrbə nífərəss/ *adj* containing or yielding coal or carbon

Car·bon·if·er·ous /kaàrbə nífərəss/ *n* the period of geologic time, 360 million to 290 million years ago, during which true reptiles first appeared and vast swamps created coal-forming sediments. See table at **geologic time** [Because numerous coal deposits were formed] —**Car·bon·if·er·ous** *adj*

car·bo·ni·um i·on /kaar bṓnee əm-/ *n* an organic ion that has a carbon atom bearing a positive charge [Early 20C. < CARBO-, after AMMONIUM]

car·bon·i·za·tion /kaàrbəni záysh'n/ *n* **1.** the burning, fossilization, or chemical treatment of something that turns it into carbon **2.** the process of covering or coating something with carbon **3.** CHEM same as **destructive distillation**

car·bon·ize /kaárbə nīz/ (**-ized, -iz·ing, -iz·es**) *v* **1.** *vti* to turn into carbon by partial burning, by fossilization, or through chemical treatment, or turn something into carbon in this way **2.** *vt* to cover or coat the surface of something with carbon —**car·bon·iz·er** *n*

car·bon·less /kaárbənləss/ *adj* chemically treated to make duplicate copies without the use of carbon paper

car·bon mi·cro·phone *n* a microphone containing carbon granules that change resistance according to the vibrating pressure of sound waves, thereby modulating the frequency of the sound waves

car·bon mon·ox·ide *n* a colorless odorless toxic gas. Source: burning of carbon-containing compounds or fuels with insufficient air. Formula: CO.

car·bon·nade /kaárbə nàyd/, **car·bon·ade** *n* a stew made with beef and onions cooked in beer [Mid-17C. < French < *carbone* (see CARBON)]

car·bon-neu·tral *adj* relating to activities that compensate for the effects of carbon-dioxide emissions, e.g., the planting of trees in urban areas to offset the effects of vehicle emissions

car·bon-ni·tro·gen cy·cle *n* PHYS, ASTRON, CHEM same as **carbon cycle** (sense 2)

car·bon pa·per *n* paper used for making copies, coated on one side with a waxy pigment that often contains carbon

car·bon proc·ess, **car·bon print·ing** *n* a printing process that uses sensitized carbon tissue to produce positive prints

car·bon sink *n* a forest or other area of vegetation that absorbs large quantities of carbon dioxide from the atmosphere, especially one planted specifically for this purpose

car·bon star *n* a star that has a lower temperature and proportionately more carbon in relation to nitrogen than other stars

car·bon steel *n* steel containing carbon with properties that vary according to the carbon content

car·bon tax *n* a proposed tax on fossil fuels such as coal, oil, and natural gas that would be proportionately based on their respective carbon content. The purpose of a carbon tax would be to help reduce the emission of greenhouse gases into the atmosphere.

car·bon tet·ra·chlo·ride *n* a colorless nonflammable toxic liquid. Use: as a solvent, refrigerant, dry cleaning agent, in fire extinguishers. Formula: CCl_4.

car·bon trad·ing *n* a system of credits that allows a company or country that reduces its carbon-dioxide emissions below a target level to sell the extra reduction as a credit to a company or country that has not met the target level

car·bon val·ue *n* a measurement of the extent to which a lubricant forms carbon when in use

car·bon·yl /kaárbənil, kaárbə neél/, **car·bon·yl·ic** /kaàrbə níllik/ *adj* relating to or containing the group of atoms =C=O found in some organic and inorganic compounds

car·bon·yl chlo·ride *n* CHEM same as **phosgene**

car·bon·yl·ic *adj* CHEM same as **carbonyl**

car boot sale *n UK* a sale of second-hand and new merchandise from the trunks of people's cars, usually taking place on an open-air site rented for the purpose

car·borne /kaár bàwrn/ *adj* in a car or traveling by automobile ○ *roads jammed with carborne commuters*

Car·bo·run·dum /kaàrbə rúndəm/ *tdmk* a trademark for abrasives composed of silicon carbide

carboxy- *prefix* carboxyl ○ *carboxypeptidase* [< CARBOXYL]

car·box·y·he·mo·glo·bin /kaar bòksee heemə glṓbin/ *n* a compound formed when inhaled carbon monoxide binds to hemoglobin

car·box·yl /kaar bóksəl/ *adj* containing the organic acid group of atoms **COOH**

car·box·yl·ase /kaar bóksə làyss, -làyz/ *n* an enzyme that aids the transfer of carbon dioxide

car·box·y·late *n* /kaar bóksə làyt, -lət/ any salt or ester of a carboxylic acid ■ *vt* /kaar bóksə làyt/ (**-lat·ed, -lat·ing, -lates**) to form a carboxylic acid by introducing a carboxyl group or carbon dioxide into a compound —**car·box·yl·a·tion** /kaar bòksə láysh'n/ *n*

car·box·yl·ic ac·id /kaàr bok síllik-/ *n* an organic acid that contains the carboxyl group

car·box·y·meth·yl·cel·lu·lose /kaar bòksee meth'l séllyə lōss/ *n* a derivative of cellulose. Use: paper production, food processing, medicines.

car·box·y·pep·ti·dase /kaar bòksee pépti dàyss, -dàyz/ *n* a protein-digesting enzyme secreted from the pancreas

car·boy /kaár bòy/ *n* a large container made of plastic or glass, usually protected by a wooden casing and used to hold corrosive liquids such as acids [Mid-18C. Ultimately < Persian *karāba* "large glass flagon"]

car bra *n* a cover fastened around the front of an automobile to protect the grille

car·bun·cle /kaár bùngk'l/ *n* **1.** a multiple-headed boil **2.** a red gemstone, especially a garnet, that is smoothly rounded and polished [13C. Via Old French *charbu(n)cle* < Latin *carbunculus* "small coal" < *carbon-* "coal"] —**car·bun·cled** *adj* —**car·bun·cu·lar** /kaar búngkyələr/ *adj*

car·bu·ra·tion /kaárbə ráysh'n/ *n* the process of mixing the correct proportions of liquid fuel with air to achieve combustion [Late 19C. < CARBURET]

car·bu·ret /kaárbə ràyt, -rèt/ (**-ret·ed, -ret·ing, -rets**) *vt* to mix a gas with hydrocarbons in order to increase fuel energy [Early 19C. < obsolete *carburet* "carbide" < CARBO- + *-uret*, chemical suffix < modern Latin *-uretum*]

car·bu·ret·ed /kaárbə ràytəd, kaárbə rèttəd/ *adj* equipped with a carburetor

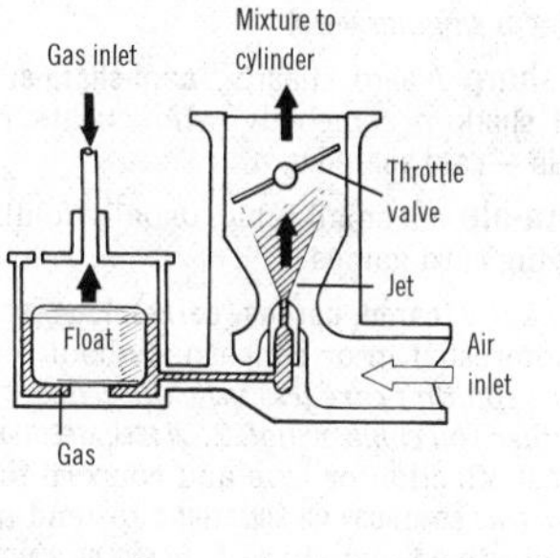

carburetor

car·bu·re·tor /kaárbə ràytər/ *n* a device in an internal combustion engine that mixes liquid fuel and air in the correct proportions, vaporizes them, and transfers the mixture to the cylinders [Mid-19C. < CARBURET]

car·bu·ret·tor *n* ENG Can, UK spelling of **carburetor**

car·bu·rize /kaárbə rīz/ (**-rized, -riz·ing, -riz·es**) *vt* CHEM same as **carbonize** (sense 2) [Mid-19C. < CARBURET] —**car·bu·ri·za·tion** /kaárbəri záysh'n/ *n*

car·ca·jou /kaárkə jòo, -zhòo/ (*plural* **-jous** or *same*) *n* ZOOL same as **wolverine** [Early 18C. Via Canadian French < Montagnais *kwa:hkwa:če:w*]

car·cass /kaárkəss/ *n* **1. DEAD BODY OF ANIMAL** the dead body of an animal, especially one slaughtered and prepared for use as meat **2. PERSON** a living person's body (*humorous*) ○ *Move your carcass!* **3. REMAINS OF SOMETHING** the remains of something decayed or almost totally destroyed **4. BASIC STRUCTURE** the basic structure or framework of something [14C. < Anglo-Norman *carcois*, French *carcasse*]

Car·cas·sonne /kaárkə sáwn, -sṓn/ city and capital of Aude Department, southern France, situated on the Aude River 57 mi./92 km southeast of Toulouse. Population: 43,950 (1999).

Car·che·mish /kaárkə mìsh/ ancient city on the Euphrates River, northeast of Aleppo in present-day northern Syria

carcin- *prefix* MED same as **carcino-** (*used before vowels*)

carcino- *prefix* cancer ○ *carcinogenic* [< Greek *karkinos* "crab, cancer"]

car·cin·o·gen /kaar sínnəjən, kaárss'nə jèn/ *n* a substance or agent that can cause cancer. Radiation and some chemicals and viruses are carcinogens.

car·ci·no·gen·e·sis /kaárss'nə jénnəssiss/ *n* the production of cancerous cells

car·cin·o·gen·ic /kaárss'nə jénnik/ *adj* capable of causing cancer —**car·ci·no·ge·nic·i·ty** /kaárss'nōjə níssətee/ *n*

car·ci·noid /kaárss'n òyd/ *n* a small benign or malignant tumor on the walls of the small intestine that sometimes produces physiologically active compounds such as serotonin or prostaglandins that are normally deactivated by the liver [Early 20C. < CARCINOMA]

car·ci·noid syn·drome *n* a condition in which small tumors (**carcinoids**) on the walls of the small intestine release excessive amounts of serotonin or prostaglandins. Symptoms include flushing, headaches, diarrhea, and asthma.

car·ci·no·ma /kaárss'n ṓmə/ *n* a malignant tumor that starts in the surface layer (**epithelium**) of an organ or body part and may spread to other parts of the body [Early 18C. Via Latin < Greek *karkinōma* < *karkinos* "crab"; from the pattern of the surrounding blood vessels] —**car·ci·no·ma·toid** *adj* —**car·ci·nom·a·tous** /-ómmətəss/ *adj*

car·ci·no·ma·to·sis /kaárss'n ōmə tṓssiss/ *n* a condition in which cancer has spread widely throughout the body

car·ci·no·sar·co·ma /kaárss'nō saar kṓmə/ (*plural* **-mas** or **-ma·ta** /-mətə/) *n* a malignant tumor containing features of both a carcinoma and a sarcoma

car·ci·no·sis /kaárss'n ṓssiss/ *n* MED same as **carcinomatosis**

car coat *n* an overcoat that ends at mid-thigh

card: playing cards

card[1] /kaard/ *n* **1. PAPER WITH PICTURES AND GREETINGS** a folded piece of stiff paper with illustrations, used to send greetings for birthdays, anniversaries, or other special occasions **2.** CARDS **PRINTED STIFF PAPER FOR GAMES** a small piece of stiff paper, part of a set, that is printed with symbols or figures and used to play games or tell fortunes **3. STIFF PAPER SHOWING IDENTITY** a small piece of stiff paper or plastic that shows somebody's identity, business position, or membership in a club or organization **4. PLASTIC CARD STORING INFORMATION** a small piece of plastic that holds information in a magnetic strip or microprocessor, used in financial activities such as getting cash from ATMs or making phone calls **5.** COMMUNICATION same as **postcard 6.** COLLECTING **COLLECTABLE STIFF PAPER WITH PICTURE** a piece of stiff paper with a picture on one side, collected as part of a set of such items **7.** SOCCER **COLORED CARD SHOWN TO SOCCER PLAYER** in soccer, a small piece of red or yellow stiff paper that is shown to a player who has violated the rules during a match **8. AMUSING PERSON** an amusing or eccentric person (*dated informal*) **9.** COMPUT same as **punch card 10.** COMPUT **CIRCUIT BOARD** a printed circuit board **11.** NAVIG same as **compass card 12.** COMPUT same as **expansion card 13.** WINE **WINE LIST** a wine list in a restaurant **14. MENU** a restaurant menu ○ *We ate our way through the entire card.* **15.** DRUGS **PORTION OF DRUGS** a portion of a narcotic, especially heroin (*slang*) ■ *vt* (**card·ed, card·ing, cards**) (*informal*) **1. ASK SOMEBODY FOR IDENTIFICATION** to ask somebody to show identification, usually to check that the person is of legal age to drink alcohol or be admitted somewhere **2.** GOLF **RECORD GOLF SCORE** to record a score after playing a hole or round of golf [15C. Via French *carte* < Latin *c(h)arta* "papyrus leaf" < Greek *khartēs*] ◇ **have** *or* **keep a card up your sleeve** to have a secret plan or tactic ready to be used if necessary (*informal*) ◇ **have the cards stacked against you** to be in a situation that is extremely disadvantageous to you and that may prevent you from achieving your goals (*informal*) ◇ **hold all the cards** to be in complete control of a situation (*informal*) ◇ **in the cards** likely to happen (*informal*) ○ *The collapse of the banking giant had been in the cards for some time.* ◇ **play your cards close to your chest** *or* **vest** to be secretive about plans, thoughts, or feelings (*informal*) ◇ **play your cards right** to take the fullest possible advantage of your chances of success (*informal*) ◇ **put** *or* **lay your cards on the table** to reveal openly what your intentions and plans are (*informal*)

card in *vi* to sign into a place, usually a place of work, by using a magnetic card

card out *vi* to sign out of a place, usually a place of work, by using a magnetic card

card[2] /kaard/ *vt* (**card·ed, card·ing, cards**) **COMB AND CLEAN WOOL OR COTTON** to comb out and clean wool, cotton, or other fibers before spinning ■ *n* **1. TOOL OR MACHINE FOR CARDING** a tool or machine with wire teeth used to comb out or clean wool, cotton, or other fibers before spinning **2. DEVICE TO MAKE CLOTH NAPPED** a device for raising the nap on cloth [14C. Via French < late Latin *cardus* "thistle" < Latin *carduus*] —**card·er** *n*

card- *prefix* MED same as **cardio-**

car·da·mom /kaárdəməm/, **car·da·mon** /-mən/, **car·da·mum** /-məm/ *n* **1.** the aromatic pods and seeds of a tropical plant, used whole or crushed as a spice or flavoring **2.** a perennial tropical plant with large hairy leaves that bears cardamom pods. Flowers: small, white, in clusters. Latin name: *Elettaria cardamomum.* [14C. Directly or via French < Latin *cardamomum* < Greek *kardamōmon* < *kardamon* "cress" + *amōmon* "amomum"]

car·dan joint /kaárd'n-/ *n* a universal joint that can rotate when out of alignment [Early 20C. After Gerolamo *Cardano* (1501–76), Italian mathematician]

car·dan shaft *n* part of the transmission system in some vehicles [See CARDAN JOINT]

card·board /kaárd bàwrd/ *n* a stiff light material made from wastepaper pulp. Use: especially for making containers or packaging for goods. ■ *adj* two-dimensional or lacking in depth ○ *gave a cardboard rendition of the sonata*

card-car·ry·ing *adj* **1.** officially listed as belonging to an organization and subscribing to its beliefs (*often disapproving*) **2.** deeply committed to a cause or movement (*informal*)

card cat·a·log *n* an alphabetical listing of items such as names and addresses or books in a library, with each item on a separate card

card·ed /kaárdəd/ *adj* **1.** in soccer, shown a red or yellow card as a warning that a player has violated a rule **2.** *Can* describes an amateur athlete who is being funded by a government grant to enable him or her to pursue training

Cár·de·nas /kaárd'n aàss/, **Lázaro** (1895–1970) Mexican politician and soldier. He served in various Mexican military and government posts before serving as president (1934–40).

card·hold·er /kaárd hōldər/ *n* an owner of a card that carries information, especially a credit, debit, bank, or phone card

cardi- *prefix* MED same as **cardio-**

car·di·a /kaárdee ə/ (*plural* **-ae** /-èe/ or **-as**) *n* the opening of the esophagus into the stomach, or the upper part of the stomach where it is connected to the esophagus [Late 18C. < Greek *kardia* "heart"]

car·di·ac /kaárdee àk/ *adj* **1.** relating to or affecting the heart **2.** relating to the upper part of the stomach, where it is connected to the esophagus [Early 17C. Via French < Latin *cardiacus* < Greek *kardia* "heart"]

car·di·ac ar·rest *n* the sudden stopping of the heartbeat and therefore of the pumping action of the heart. Cardiac arrest requires immediate treatment to prevent brain damage and death.

car·di·ac com·pres·sion, **car·di·ac mas·sage** *n* rhythmic compression of somebody's heart in order to restore or maintain blood circulation after the person has had a heart attack

car·di·ac out·put *n* the amount of blood pumped by the heart over a given time period

car·di·al·gia /kaardee áljə, -áljee ə/ *n* 1. MED same as **heartburn** (*technical*) 2. pain in or near the heart [Mid-17C. Via modern Latin < Greek *kardialgia* < *kardia* "heart"]

Car·diff /kaardif/ capital and largest city of Wales. It is the home of the Welsh Assembly and is an important industrial center. Population: 305,353 (2001). Welsh name **Caerdydd**

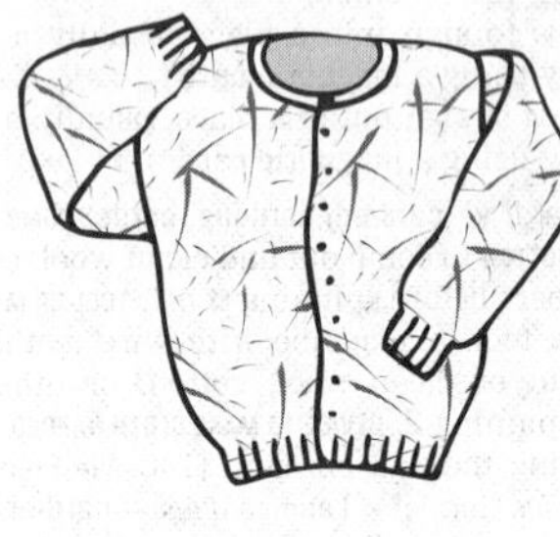

cardigan

car·di·gan /kaardigən/ *n* a long-sleeved sweater that fastens up the front [Mid-19C. After James Thomas Brudenell, 7th Earl of *Cardigan* (1797–1868), British soldier and politician]

Car·di·gan Bay /kaardigən-/ large semicircular bay on the western coast of Wales. Tremadoc Bay forms its northern portion. Length: 65 mi./105 km.

Car·di·gan Welsh cor·gi *n* a dog with a long tail belonging to the larger of two breeds of corgi [After *Cardiganshire*, former county in Wales]

Car·din /kaar dán/, **Pierre** (*b.* 1922) Italian-born French fashion designer. He designed costumes for Jeanne Moreau in the movie *La Baie des Anges* (1963).

"The jean! The jean is the destructor...a dictator! It is destroying creativity."
[Pierre Cardin, *Parade*; June 1976]

cardinal (sense 3)

car·di·nal /kaard'nəl/ *n* 1. CHR **ROMAN CATHOLIC DIGNITARY** in the Roman Catholic Church, one of the group of clergy, next in rank to the pope, who elect the pope from their own number and act as his advisers 2. COLORS **DEEP RED** a deep strong red color, like that of the robes of a cardinal 3. BIRDS **BRIGHT RED BIRD** a crested finch, the male of which has bright red plumage with a black face. Native to: North America. Latin name: *Cardinalis cardinalis*. 4. MATH same as **cardinal number** 5. CLOTHING **WOMAN'S HOODED CAPE** a woman's short cape with a hood, originally scarlet in color, that was worn in the 17th and 18th centuries ■ *adj* 1. **IMPORTANT** fundamentally important 2. COLORS **BRIGHT RED** of a deep strong red color [12C. Via French < Latin *cardinalis* < *cardin-* "hinge"] —**car·di·nal·ly** *adv*

car·di·nal·ate /kaard'nələt, -làyt/, **car·di·nal·ship** /kaard'nəl ship/ *n* CHR 1. **ALL CARDINALS** the cardinals of the Roman Catholic Church regarded collectively 2. **TERM OF OFFICE OF CARDINAL** the term of office of a Roman Catholic cardinal 3. **OFFICE OF CARDINAL** the rank or office of a Roman Catholic cardinal

car·di·nal flow·er *n* a perennial lobelia. Flowers: brilliantly colored, usually red, in clusters. Native to: central and eastern North America. Latin name: *Lobelia cardinalis*.

car·di·nal num·ber *n* a number used to denote quantity but not order, e.g., 4 or 42

car·di·nal point *n* any of the four principal points of the compass, North, South, East, or West

car·di·nal·ship *n* CHR same as **cardinalate**

car·di·nal vir·tue *n* one of the principal virtues in the classical or Christian traditions. In the classical tradition they are justice, prudence, temperance, and fortitude, and in the Christian tradition they are justice, prudence, temperance, fortitude, faith, hope, and charity.

car·di·nal vow·el *n* a member of a fixed set of vowel sounds, based on the position of the tongue and the shape of the mouth cavity, and spaced at approximately equal acoustic intervals

card in·dex *n UK* COMM, LIBRARIES same as **card catalog**

cardio- *prefix* heart ○ *cardiopulmonary* [< Greek *kardia*]

car·di·o·ac·cel·er·a·tor /kaardee ō ək séllə ràytər/ *n* a drug or other agent that increases the heart rate —**car·di·o·ac·cel·er·a·tion** /-sèllə ráysh'n/ *n*

car·di·o·gen·ic /kaardee ō jénnik/ *adj* resulting from activity or disease of the heart

car·di·o·gram /kaardee ə gràm/ *n* a graphic record made by a cardiograph, especially an electrocardiogram

car·di·o·graph /kaardee ə gràf/ *n* an instrument for recording heart activity, used in the diagnosis of heart disorders —**car·di·og·raph·er** /kaardee óggrəfər/ *n* —**car·di·o·graph·ic** /kaardee ə gráffik/ *adj* —**car·di·o·graph·i·cal** *adj* —**car·di·o·graph·i·cal·ly** *adv* —**car·di·og·ra·phy** /kaardee óggrəfee/ *n*

car·di·ol·o·gy /kaardee óllajee/ *n* a branch of medicine dealing with the diagnosis and treatment of heart disorders and related conditions —**car·di·o·log·i·cal** /kaardee ə lójjik'l/ *adj* —**car·di·ol·o·gist** *n*

car·di·o·meg·a·ly /kaardee ō méggəlee/ *n* pathological enlargement of the heart

car·di·o·my·o·cyte /kaardee ō mī ō sīt/ *n* a cell of muscular tissue in the heart —**car·di·o·my·o·cy·tic** /-mī ō síttik/ *adj*

car·di·o·my·op·a·thy /kaardee ō mī óppəthee/ *n* a disease of the heart muscle, usually chronic and with an unknown or obscure cause

car·di·op·a·thy /kaardee óppəthee/ (*plural* **-thies**) *n* a heart disease or disorder

car·di·o·pul·mo·nar·y /kaardee ō pŏŏlmə nèrree, -púlmə-/ *adj* relating to both the heart and the lungs

car·di·o·pul·mo·nar·y by·pass *n* a procedure by which the blood is artificially circulated and oxygenated by a heart-lung machine so that surgery may be carried out on the heart

car·di·o·pul·mo·nar·y re·sus·ci·ta·tion *n* an emergency technique to revive somebody whose heart has stopped beating that involves clearing the person's airways and then alternating heart compression with mouth-to-mouth respiration

car·di·o·res·pi·ra·to·ry /kaardee ō réspərə tàwree, -ri spírə-/ *adj* relating to both the heart and the respiratory system

car·di·o·tho·rac·ic /kaardee ō thə rássik/ *adj* relating to both the heart and the chest

car·di·o·vas·cu·lar /kaardee ō váskyələr/ *adj* relating to both the heart and the blood vessels

car·di·tis /kaar dítiss/ *n* inflammation of the heart [Late 18C. < Greek *kardia* "heart"]

-cardium *suffix* part of the heart ○ *endocardium* [< modern Latin < Greek *kardia* "heart"]

car·doon /kaar dóon/ (*plural same or* **-doons**) *n* a large perennial plant related to the artichoke with spiny leaves and edible roots and leafstalks. Native to: southern Europe. Latin name: *Cynara cardunculus*. [Early 17C. < French *cardon* < Latin *carduus* "thistle"]

Car·do·zo /kaar dózō/, **Benjamin Nathan** (1870–1938) associate justice of the US Supreme Court. He served from 1932 until his death.

"History, in illuminating the past, illuminates the present, and in illuminating the present, illuminates the future."
[Benjamin Nathan Cardozo, *The Nature of the Judicial Process*; 1921]

card·phone /kaard fōn/ *n UK* a pay phone operated by a phonecard

cards /kaardz/ *n* a game played using playing cards (*takes a singular verb*)

card·sharp /kaard shaarp/, **card·sharp·er** /-shaarpər/, **card shark** *n* somebody who cheats regularly at cards —**card·sharp·ing** *n*

card ta·ble *n* a small table, usually folding, used for playing card games

care /ker/ *v* (**cared, car·ing, cares**) 1. *vti* **BE CONCERNED** to be interested in or concerned about something ○ *I said I couldn't care less if he did leave.* ○ *I don't care whether you come or not.* 2. *vi* **FEEL AFFECTION AND CONCERN** to feel affection or love and concern for somebody 3. *vi* **TEND SOMEBODY OR SOMETHING** to tend or supervise somebody or something 4. *vi* **LIKE OR WANT SOMETHING** to like or be in favor of something (*formal*) ○ *Would you care for dessert?* ■ *n* 1. **UPKEEP** the process of maintaining something in good condition ○ *a skin care treatment* 2. **CAREFUL ATTENTION** careful attention to avoid damage or error 3. **WORRY** a worry or cause for anxiety ○ *without a care in the world* 4. **WORRIED STATE OF MIND** a troubled state of mind arising from worry or grief 5. SOC WELFARE **ATTENTIVE TREATMENT OF SOMEBODY** the providing of whatever is needed for the well-being of somebody who is dependent or physically or mentally challenged ○ *responsible for the 20 children in her care* ○ *residential care* 6. **LEGAL OVERSIGHT OF SOMEBODY** legal oversight of and responsibility for somebody such as a minor ○ *was put into the care of temporary foster parents* [Old English *caru* "sorrow" < Indo-European] ◇ **in care of** into the temporary possession of an addressee who will ensure that the item will be delivered to the intended recipient ○ *sent the letter to her in care of her parents* ◇ **take care** 1. to behave prudently, with regard for your own safety 2. used as an affectionate farewell to somebody (*informal*) ◇ **take care of somebody** *or* **something** 1. to provide for the needs of somebody or something 2. to deal with somebody or something effectively

USAGE could care less or **couldn't care less**? In informal English *I could care less* is all but synonymous with *I couldn't care less*, except that it carries overtones of irony. However, it is best avoided in writing.

SYNONYMS See *worry*.

CARE /ker/ *abbr* Cooperative for American Relief Everywhere

care as·sis·tant *n* HEALTH SERVICES same as **care worker**

ca·reen /kə réen/ (**-reened, -reen·ing, -reens**) *v* 1. *vi* **SWAY OR SWERVE WHILE MOVING** to move forward at high speed, swaying, lurching, or swerving from one side to the other ○ *a motorcycle careening around sharp curves* 2. *vi* **MOVE RAPIDLY** to rush or move carelessly ○ *He seemed to careen from one job to the next.* 3. *vti* NAUT **TURN BOAT ON SIDE** to turn a boat over on its side, especially for repairs or cleaning, or turn over onto the side 4. *vi* SAILING **HEEL IN WIND** to heel over to one side while sailing [Early 17C. < *careen* "act of careening a boat," via French *carène* < Latin *carina* "keel, nutshell"; in senses 1 and 2 influenced by CAREER] —**ca·reen·er** *n*

ca·reer /kə réer/ *n* 1. **LONG-TERM OR LIFELONG JOB** a job or occupation regarded as a long-term or lifelong activity 2. **PROFESSIONAL PROGRESS** somebody's progress in a chosen profession or during that person's working life 3. **GENERAL PROGRESS** the general path or progress taken by somebody or something ○ *a piece of legislation whose career is rich with conflicting amendments* 4. **RAPID FORWARD LURCHING MOTION** a rushing onward while lurching or swaying ■ *adj* 1. **PROFESSIONAL FOR LIFE** trained for and expecting to work in a particular occupation for an entire working life rather than briefly ○ *a career diplomat* 2. **PERFORMING ILLEGAL ACTS THROUGH LIFETIME** committing illegal acts throughout a lifetime, without apparent remorse or desire for self-improvement ○ *a career criminal, who* *was imprisoned after 25 years of armed robbery* ■ *vi* (**-reered, -reer·ing, -reers**) LURCH RAPIDLY ONWARD to rush forward while lurching or swaying [Mid-16C. < French *carrière* < Latin *carrus* (see CAR)]

CULTURAL NOTE ***My Brilliant Career***, a novel (1901) by Australian writer Miles Franklin. It is an account of a young girl's struggle to choose between an independent career and a comfortable life as the wife of a wealthy landowner. It was made into a movie directed by Gillian Armstrong in 1979.

ca·reer coach *n* somebody who offers another person professional guidance and advice on career change or improvement

ca·reer coun·sel·or *n* somebody whose job is to advise high-school students on possible careers and jobs as they approach graduation

ca·reer gap·per *n* somebody who takes a prolonged leave from a job to travel or do alternative, especially charitable work, usually abroad

ca·reer·ism /kə re̍er ìzzəm/ *n* the behavior of somebody whose principal motivation is career advancement —**ca·reer·ist** *n*

ca·reers of·fi·cer *n* *UK* same as **career counselor**

ca·reer wom·an *n* a woman who has a career or who takes her working life seriously

care·free /kér frée/ *adj* having no worries or responsibilities —**care·free·ness** *n*

care·ful /kérf'l/ *adj* **1.** PAINSTAKING showing close attention to accuracy and detail **2.** CAUTIOUS taking reasonable care to avoid risks **3.** WATCHFUL watchful and protective about something **4.** *UK* NOT OVERSPENDING OR BEING WASTEFUL making sure that money or resources are not spent or used wastefully or without thought —**care·ful·ly** *adv* —**care·ful·ness** *n*

SYNONYMS ***careful, conscientious, scrupulous, thorough, meticulous, painstaking, assiduous, punctilious, finicky, fussy***

CORE MEANING: exercising care and attention in doing something

careful showing close attention to accuracy and detail ○ *The project was given approval after careful consideration.* ○ *the result of some very careful planning* **conscientious** showing great care, attention, and industriousness in carrying out a task or role ○ *a very conscientious secretary* ○ *Are you always so conscientious about keeping promises?* **scrupulous** having or showing careful regard for what is morally right, or for correct procedure ○ *draw up the contract with scrupulous care* ○ *I will be absolutely scrupulous in not favoring one candidate.* **thorough** extremely careful to include everything that is needed ○ *a thorough investigation* ○ *a thorough understanding of programming principles* **meticulous** extremely careful and precise ○ *meticulous attention to detail* ○ *pasted the reviews with meticulous care into her scrapbook* **painstaking** involving or showing great care and attention to detail ○ *years of painstaking research* ○ *a thorough and painstaking investigation* **assiduous** showing persistent and hard-working effort in doing something ○ *paid assiduous attention to the layout of new streets* ○ *He is assiduous in ensuring compliance with the law.* **punctilious** very careful about the conventions of correct behavior and etiquette ○ *She was usually punctilious about telling her mother if she was going to be late.* ○ *He always has been punctilious in the exercise of his duties.* **finicky** difficult to please, and tending to concentrate on small or unimportant details ○ *Some advocacy groups are finicky about these issues.* ○ *finicky car buyers* **fussy** tending to worry over details or trivial things ○ *She's got every right to be fussy about the seating plan for the wedding.* ○ *This bird isn't all that fussy about its nesting site.*

~~**carefull**~~ incorrect spelling of **careful**

care·giv·er /kér gìvvər/ *n* **1.** somebody who has the principal responsibility for caring for a child or dependent adult, especially in the home **2.** a medical worker or allied health professional who assists in the management of an illness or disability —**care·giv·ing** *n*

~~**careing**~~ incorrect spelling of **caring**

care la·bel *n* a label, sewn onto a piece of clothing or other item, that gives cleaning instructions for the item

care·less /kérləss/ *adj* **1.** NOT GIVING CAREFUL ATTENTION not giving enough careful attention to the details of something **2.** SHOWING NO CONCERN disregarding or showing no concern about something **3.** NOT CAREFULLY WORKED ON not carefully nurtured or practiced, but done or assumed easily and naturally ○ *a careless charm* **4.** HAVING NO ANXIETIES having no cares or worries **5.** OFFERING OR GETTING NO CARE giving or receiving no care or attention —**care·less·ly** *adv*

care·less·ness /kérləssnəss/ *n* **1.** LACK OF ATTENTION lack of careful attention to the details of something **2.** EXAMPLE OF NEGLIGENCE an example of negligence or of a failure to take enough trouble with something **3.** LACK OF CONCERN lack of concern about something

care pack·age *n* a package of food or personal items for somebody far from home such as a member of the armed forces or a student boarding at a school (*informal*)

car·er /káirər/ *n* **1.** *UK* same as **caregiver** (sense 1) **2.** same as **home health aide**

ca·ress /kə réss/ *vt* (**-ressed, -ress·ing, -ress·es**) **1.** TOUCH SOMEBODY AFFECTIONATELY to touch or stroke somebody or something affectionately **2.** AFFECT SOMEBODY IN SOOTHING WAY to touch, pass over, or affect somebody in a soothing or pleasant way ■ *n* GENTLE TOUCH a gentle affectionate touch or embrace [Mid-17C. Via French *caresse* < Italian *carezza* < Latin *carus* "dear"] —**ca·ress·er** *n* —**ca·res·sive** *adj* —**ca·res·sive·ly** *adv*

ca·ress·ing /kə réssing/ *adj* gentle and soothing —**ca·ress·ing·ly** *adv*

car·et /kárrət/ *n* a mark (‸) made on printed or manuscript material to show where something such as a letter or word should be inserted [Late 17C. < Latin *caret* "there is lacking," form of *carere* "to lack"]

care·tak·er /kér tàykər/ *n* **1.** TEMPORARY OFFICE HOLDER a temporary holder of a post **2.** SOC WELFARE same as **caregiver** (sense 1) **3.** SOMEBODY OFFERING EMOTIONAL SUPPORT somebody giving care or emotional support to another **4.** *UK* SOMEBODY WHO TAKES CARE OF BUILDING somebody who supervises the care of a property such as an office building or a school

care·tak·er gov·ern·ment *n* a government that is in power temporarily, e.g., until an election is held

Ca·rew /kə ro͞o, kérroo/, **Thomas** (1595?–1645?) English poet, diplomat and author. He wrote witty lyrics in the Cavalier tradition, as well as the masque *Coelum Britannicum* (1634).

> "He that loves a rosy cheek, / Or a coral lip admires, / Or, from star-like eyes, doth seek / Fuel to maintain his fires; / As old Time makes these decay, / So his flames must waste away."
> [Thomas Carew, "Disdain Returned"; 1640]

care·ware /káir wàir/ *n* COMPUT software that is made available to users in exchange for a donation to charity

care work·er *n* somebody employed to look after people who are physically or mentally challenged and who live in residential accommodations

care·worn /kér wàwrn/ *adj* exhausted or otherwise badly affected by anxiety or worry

Car·ey /kérree/, **George** (*b.* 1935) British Anglican archbishop. He was bishop of Bath and Wells (1987–91) before being appointed archbishop of Canterbury. He retired in 2002.

> "My fear will be that in 15 years time, Jerusalem, Bethlehem, once centers of strong Christian presence, might become a kind of Walt Disney Theme Park."
> [George Carey, *Observer (London)*; January 12, 1992]

Car·ey /káiree/, **Peter Philip** (*b.* 1943) Australian writer. His novels include *Illywhacker* (1985), and he has twice won Britain's Booker Prize, with *Oscar and Lucinda* (1988) and *True History of the Kelly Gang* (2001). See Cultural note at **bliss**

car·fare /kaar fèr/ *n* the amount charged for a ride on a bus or streetcar or in a taxicab

car·go /kaárgō/ (*plural* **-goes** or **-gos**) *n* **1.** goods carried as freight by sea, road, or air **2.** a load of something [Mid-17C. < Spanish < late Latin *car(ri)care* "to load" < Latin *carrus* (see CAR)]

car·go cult *n* in some southwestern Pacific islands, a religion whose devotees believe that ancestral spirits will return to the island bringing modern consumer goods and wealth

car·go dress *n* a casual dress with cargo pockets on the skirt

car·go pants *npl* pants with cargo pockets, often on the legs

car·go pock·et *n* a large pocket with a pleat and a flap, sewn onto the outside of a garment

car·go skirt *n* a skirt with cargo pockets

car·hop /kaár hòp/ *n* somebody who serves food to people in cars at a drive-in restaurant [Mid-20C. < CAR + BELLHOP]

car·i·ad /kárree əd/ *n* *Wales* used as an affectionate form of address (*informal*) [< Welsh]

~~**cariage**~~ incorrect spelling of **carriage**

Car·ib /kárrib/ (*plural* **-ibs** or *same*) *n* **1.** a member of a group of Native American people who live in Central America, northeastern South America, and the Lesser Antilles **2.** a language of the Cariban family spoken in Venezuela and neighboring countries. Native speakers: 20,000. [Mid-16C. Via Spanish *caribe* < Arawak *carib*] —**Car·ib** *adj*

Carib. *abbr* Caribbean

Car·i·ban /kárrəbən, kə reébən/ (*plural* **-bans** or *same*) *n* **1.** PEOPLES, LANG same as **Carib** (sense 1) **2.** a group of about 30 languages spoken in northern South America. Native speakers: 40,000. —**Car·i·ban** *adj*

Car·ib·be·an[1] /kàrrə beé ən, kə ríbbee ən/ *adj* **1.** OF CARIBBEAN relating to the Caribbean or its peoples, languages, or cultures **2.** OF CARIBS relating to the Caribs or their language or culture ■ *n* SOMEBODY FROM CARIBBEAN somebody who comes from a Caribbean island

Car·ib·be·an[2] /kàrrə beé ən, kə ríbbee ən/ region comprising three main island groups, the Greater Antilles, the Lesser Antilles, and the Bahamas, extending from the southeastern tip of Florida to the coast of Venezuela and separating the Caribbean Sea from the Atlantic Ocean

Car·ib·be·an Eng·lish *n* the variety of English spoken in the Caribbean islands. See panel on next page

Ca·rib·be·an Sea arm of the Atlantic Ocean, surrounded by the Greater and Lesser Antilles, northern South America, and eastern Central America. Area: 1,049,000 sq. mi./2,718,000 sq. km. Depth: Cayman Trench 24,720 ft./7,535 m.

ca·ri·be /kə reébee/ *n* FISH same as **piranha** [Mid-19C. < Spanish (see CARIB)]

Car·i·boo Moun·tains /kárrə boo-/ mountain range in E British Columbia, Canada. The highest peak is Mount Sir Wilfrid Laurier, 11,499 ft./3,505 m.

caribou

car·i·bou /kárrə bo͞o/ (*plural same* or **-bous**) *n* a large deer that lives in large herds and has large branched antlers on both sexes. Native to: northern regions. Genus: *Rangifer*. [Mid-17C. Via Canadian French < Mi'kmaq *ğalipu* "snow shoveler"; because it removes snow to find grass]

Car·i·bou In·u·it *n* a member of an Inuit people living in the Barren Grounds in northern Canada. They depend upon caribou for survival.

WORLD ENGLISH ***Caribbean English***, also called *West Indian English*, is the variety of English as used in the Caribbean region. Since their European discovery by Columbus in 1492, the islands and coasts of the Caribbean have been claimed, disputed, settled, and governed by the Spanish, Portuguese, French, British, Dutch, Danish, and Americans with obvious long-term varied effects on the languages spoken there. Most of the territories are now independent, but colonization has created a complex inheritance. In such mainland areas as Belize and Guyana, indigenous languages survive; in all territories there is a complex "continuum" between standard American and British English, Dutch, French, and Spanish on the one hand and their related creoles on the other.

In general terms, the creoles have a majority of European vocabulary items, as well as words from other languages, with varying degrees of African and other structural features. In most Anglo-Caribbean territories, although school-based standard English is the official language, it is a minority form. Apart from Barbados and Guyana, *r* is usually not pronounced in such words as *art, door,* and *worker* in Caribbean English. The most salient differences between the Creole-like varieties of Caribbean English and standard English include the absence of inflected endings in *-ing* and *-ed*, e.g. *name* for *named*; the absence of some past verb forms; the absence of *-s* in third-person singular present verb and plural nouns; the pronunciation of /th/ as /t/ or /d/; and the different usage of parts of speech, e.g. *tired* as both adjective and verb, *hungry* as both adjective and noun.

car·i·ca·ture /kárrəkə cho͝or, -chər/ *n* **1. COMIC EXAGGERATION** a drawing, description, or performance that exaggerates somebody's or something's characteristics for humorous or satirical effect **2. TRAVESTY** a ridiculously inappropriate or unsuccessful version of or attempt at something **3. ART OF CARICATURES** the art of creating caricatures [Mid-18C. < Italian *caricatura* < *caricare* "exaggerate, load" < late Latin *carricare* (see CARGO)] —**car·i·ca·ture** *vt* —**car·i·ca·tur·ist** *n*

CARICOM /kárrə kòm/ *abbr* Caribbean Community and Common Market

car·ies /kérreez/ *n* progressive decay of a tooth or, less commonly, a bone [Late 16C. < Latin] —**car·i·ous** *adj*

CARIFTA /ka ríftə/ *abbr* Caribbean Free Trade Association

car·il·lon /kárrə lòn, -lən/ *n* **1. SET OF STATIONARY BELLS** a set of chromatically tuned stationary bells, usually hung in a tower and played from a keyboard **2. TUNE PLAYED ON SET OF BELLS** a tune played on a keyboard connected to a set of stationary bells **3. ORGAN STOP IMITATING BELLS** an organ stop that imitates the sound of a carillon [Late 18C. < French] —**car·il·lon** *vi*

car·il·lon·neur /kàrrələ núr/ *n* somebody who plays a carillon [Late 18C. < French < *carillon* "carillon"]

ca·ri·na /kə rī́nə, -réenə/ *n* **1. BIRDS** same as **keel** *n* (sense 3) (*technical*) **2.** the boat-shaped part of a pea flower, formed by the two fused lower petals **3.** a keel-shaped body part, e.g., the ridge at the base of the windpipe where it divides to form the bronchi [Early 18C. < Latin, "keel"] —**ca·ri·nate** /kárrə nàyt/ *adj*

Ca·ri·na *n* a constellation of the southern hemisphere containing the star Canopus. See illustration at **constellation**

car·ing /kérring/ *adj* **1. SHOWING CONCERN** compassionate or showing concern for others **2. RELATING TO PROFESSION LOOKING AFTER PEOPLE** belonging or relating to a profession that involves looking after people's physical, medical, or general welfare, e.g., nursing or social work ■ *n* **PROVISION OF MEDICAL OR SIMILAR CARE** provision of medical or other types of care, either professionally or in general —**car·ing·ly** *adv*

car·i·o·ca /kàrree ṓkə/ *n* **1.** a Brazilian dance similar to the samba **2.** the music for a carioca [Mid-20C. < Portuguese < a Tupian language]

Car·i·o·can /kàrree ṓkən/, **Car·i·o·ca** /kèrree ṓkə/ *n* somebody who comes from Rio de Janeiro, Brazil —**Car·i·o·can** *adj*

car·i·o·gen·ic /kàrree ō jénnik, kàrree ə-/ *adj* causing tooth decay [Mid-20C. < CARIES]

car·i·ole /kárree ōl/, **car·ri·ole** *n* a small open carriage or covered cart, the former drawn by one horse [Mid-18C. Via French < Italian *carriuola* "little car" < *carro* "car" < Latin *carrus* (see CAR)]

car·jack·ing /kaár jàking/ *n* the crime of holding up a car and either stealing it, robbing the driver, or forcing the driver to drive somewhere for criminal purposes [Late 20C. Blend of CAR + HIJACKING] —**car·jack** *vti* —**car·jack·er** *n*

Carle·ton /kaárltən/, **Guy, 1st Baron Dorchester** (1724–1808) Irish-born Canadian soldier and governor of Quebec. He advocated French-Canadian culture and opposed elected assemblies.

car·ling /kaárling, -lin/ *n* a fore-and-aft wooden beam that supports a boat's deck, especially around an opening in the deck such as a hatchway [14C. < Old Norse]

Car·lisle /kaar lī́l, kaár lī̀l/ **1.** town in Cumbria, northwestern England. It is a local government district and the administrative center of Cumbria. Population: 18,036 (2002). **2.** borough in southern Pennsylvania, southwest of Harrisburg. Population: 18,036 (2002 estimate).

Car·list /kaárlist/ *n* a supporter of Don Carlos or his descendants as rightful monarchs of Spain during the 19th century [Mid-19C. < Spanish *carlista* < Don Carlos]

car·load /kaár lṑd/ *n* **1.** a full complement of people able to ride in an automobile **2.** the minimum weight at which freight qualifies for a reduced rate

car·load rate *n* a reduced rate for shipping freight

Car·los /kaárləss, kaárlōss/, **Don** (1788–1855) Spanish pretender to the throne. His claim to the Spanish throne (1833), reasserted by his descendants, led to the Carlist Wars (1833–39, 1872–76). Full name **Carlos Maria Isidro**

Car·lo·vin·gi·an *n, adj* HIST same as **Carolingian**

Car·low /kaárlō/ county in Leinster Province, in the southeastern part of the Republic of Ireland. Area: 346 sq. mi./896 sq. km.

Carls·bad /kaárlz bàd/ **1.** city in southeastern New Mexico on the Pecos River, southeast of Roswell and southwest of Hobbs. Population: 25,196 (2002 estimate). **2.** city and resort in southwestern California, north of San Diego, on the Pacific Ocean. Population: 86,639 (2002 estimate).

Carls·bad Cav·erns Na·tion·al Park national park in southeastern New Mexico, established in 1930 and noted for its chain of caverns that have unusual geologic formations. Area: 73 sq. mi./189 sq. km.

Carl·son /kaárlss'n/, **Chester Floyd** (1906–68) US inventor. He invented xerography (1938) that led to the introduction of the first photocopying machine (1958).

Carl XVI Gus·taf /kaarl gús taáf/, **king of Sweden** (*b.* 1946) He succeeded his grandfather, Gustaf VI, in 1973

Car·lyle /kaar lī́l, kaár lī̀l/, **Thomas** (1795–1881) Scottish historian, essayist, and author of *Sartor Resartus* (1833–34), *The French Revolution* (1837), and *Oliver Cromwell's Letters and Speeches, with Elucidations* (1845)

> "The great law of culture is: Let each become all that he was created capable of becoming."
> [Thomas Carlyle, "Jean Paul Friedrich Richter," *Critical and Miscellaneous Essays*; 1838]

> "A well-written Life is almost as rare as a well-spent one."
> [Thomas Carlyle, "Richter," *Critical and Miscellaneous Essays*; 1838]

car·mak·er /kaár màykər/ *n* a manufacturer of motor vehicles, specifically automobiles

car·man /kaármən/ (*plural* **-men** /-mən/) *n* the driver of a streetcar or subway train (*dated*)

Car·man /kaármən/, **Bliss** (1861–1929) Canadian poet. His best known poems appear in the three-volume *Vagabondia* (1894–1901), many of which in praise of the beauty of nature. Full name **Carman, William Bliss**

> "The scarlet of the maples can shake me like a cry / Of bugles going by. / And my lonely spirit thrills / To see the frosty asters like a smoke upon the hills."
> [Bliss Carman, "A Vagabond Song," *Songs from Vagabondia*; 1894]

Car·mar·then /kər maárthən, kaar-/ seaport and administrative city of Carmarthenshire. Population: 13,524 (1991). Welsh name **Caerfyrddin**

Car·mar·then·shire /kər maárthən shèer, kaar-, -shər/ county in southern Wales, with its headquarters in Carmarthen. Population: 172,842 (2001). Area: 926 sq. mi./2398 sq. km.

Car·me /kaármee/ *n* a small satellite of Jupiter that was discovered in 1938

Car·mel /kaármәl, kaar mél/ city and artists' colony in western California, southwest of San Jose, on the Pacific Ocean. Population: 4,133 (2002 estimate).

Car·mel, Mount /kaármәl/ mountain in northern Israel, near the Mediterranean Sea, with many biblical associations. Height: 1,789 ft./545 m.

Car·mel·ite /kaármə lī̀t/ *n* **1.** a member of an order of mendicant friars, founded around 1155 and called Our Lady of Mount Carmel **2.** a member of the order of nuns of Our Lady of Mount Carmel, founded in 1452 and noted for the strictness of its rule [15C. Directly or via French < medieval Latin *Carmelita*, after CARMEL, MOUNT] —**Car·mel·ite** *adj*

Car·mi·chael /kaár mī̀k'l/ unincorporated settlement in Sacramento County, central California, near Sacramento. Population: 49,742 (2000).

Car·mi·chael, Hoagy (1899–1981) US singer and songwriter. He wrote the music for the song "Stardust" (1929). Full name **Carmichael, Hoagland Howard**

car·min·a·tive /kaar mínnətiv, kaármə nàytiv/ *adj* relieving flatulence or colic by expelling gas [15C. < medieval Latin *carminat-*, past participle of *carminare* "heal by incantation" < Latin *carmin-* "song"] —**car·min·a·tive** *n*

car·mine /kaármin, -mīn/ *n* **1.** a deep purplish red color **2.** a bright red pigment made from cochineal [Early 18C. < French *carmin* < Arabic *ḳirmiz* "kermes"] —**car·mine** *adj*

Car·na·by Street /kaárnəbee-/ *n* a street in Soho, central London, notable in the 1960s as the heart of the new youth-centered fashion trade

prehistoric stone monuments at Carnac, France

Car·nac /kaár nàk/ village in Morbihan Department, Bretagne Region, in western France. It is famous for its prehistoric stone monuments, which number more than 3,000.

car·nage /kaárnij/ *n* **1.** widespread and indiscriminate slaughter or massacre, especially of human beings **2.** serious injury to a great many people, e.g., in a major accident [Early 17C. Via French < Italian *carnaggio* < medieval Latin *carnaticum* "flesh (especially as tribute)" < Latin *carn-* "flesh"]

car·nal /kaárn'l/ *adj* **1. RELATING TO PHYSICAL NEEDS** relating to somebody's physical needs or appetites, especially as contrasted with spiritual or intellectual qualities (*formal*) **2. SENSUAL** sensual or sexual **3. RELATING TO BODY** relating to or consisting of the body (*formal*) [15C. < ecclesiastical Latin *carnalis* < Latin *carn-* "flesh"] —**car·nal·ist** *n* —**car·nal·i·ty** /kaar nállətee/ *n* —**car·nal·ly** *adv*

car·nal knowl·edge *n* same as **sexual intercourse** (*formal*)

car·nall·ite /kaárn'l ìt/ *n* a white or pale hydrous chloride mineral containing magnesium and potassium. Use: source of potassium, fertilizers. [Mid-19C. After Rudolf von *Carnall* (1804–74), German mining engineer]

car·nap /kaár nàp/ (**-napped, -nap·ping, -naps**) *vi Philippines* to steal a car (*informal*) —**car·nap·per** *n*

Car·nap /kaár nàp/, **Rudolf** (1891–1970) German-born US philosopher and logician. He used mathematics and probability statistics to arrive at a system of inductive logic.

> "Logic is the last scientific ingredient of Philosophy; its extraction leaves behind only a confusion of nonscientific, pseudo-problems."
> [Rudolf Carnap, *The Unity of Science*; 1934]

car·nas·si·al /kaar nássee əl/ *adj* describes the larger sharp cheek teeth in the upper and lower jaw of a carnivore that are adapted for cutting flesh [Mid-19C. < French *carnassier* "carnivorous" < Latin *carn-* "flesh"]

Car·na·tic /kaar náttik/ *adj* GEOG same as **Karnatak** [Early 19C. After *Carnatic*, linguistic region in south central India between the Eastern Ghats and the Coromandel coast, now part of Madras state < KARNATAKA]

Car·na·tic mu·sic *n* MUSIC same as **Karnatak music**

carnation

car·na·tion /kaar náysh'n/ *n* **1.** a perennial plant of the pink family. Flowers: fragrant white, pink, or red with fringed petals, often smelling of cloves. Latin name: *Dianthus caryophyllus*. **2.** a pale reddish pink color [Mid-16C. Via French < late Latin *carnation-* "fleshiness" < Latin *carn-* "flesh"] —**car·na·tion** *adj*

car·nau·ba /kaar náwbə, -nówbə/ (*plural same* or **-bas**) *n* **1.** a fan palm with an edible root and leaves that yield carnauba wax. Native to: Brazil. Latin name: *Copernica prunifera*. **2.** INDUST same as **carnauba wax** [Mid-19C. Via Portuguese < Tupi]

car·nau·ba wax *n* wax obtained from the young leaves of the carnauba tree. Use: polish, candles.

Car·né /kaar náy/, **Marcel** (1909–96) French movie director. His "poetic realism" is seen at its height in *Les Enfants du Paradis* (1945) (*Children of Paradise*, 1946).

car·ne a·sa·da /kaárnay ə saádə/ *n Hispanic* **1.** beefsteak marinated in lemon or lime juice, hot pepper, and spices, cooked on a grill and served with tortillas **2.** a mass execution, followed by the burning of the victims' bodies, perpetrated by some Mexican drug lords [Late 20C. < Spanish, "roast meat"]

Car·ne·gie /kaárnəgee, kaar náygee, -néggee/, **Andrew** (1835–1919) Scottish-born US industrialist and philanthropist who made a fortune in the steel industry. His philanthropic gifts endowed numerous public libraries in the United States.

> "Concentrate your energy, thought and capital exclusively upon the business in which you are engaged…'Don't put all your eggs in one basket' is all wrong. I tell you 'put all your eggs in one basket, and then watch that basket.'"
> [Andrew Carnegie, *Speech, Curry Commercial College, Pittsburgh*; June 23, 1885]

Car·ne·gie /kaárnəgee/, **Dale** (1888–1955) US writer. His works on public speaking and self-esteem include *How to Win Friends and Influence People* (1936). Born **Carnegey, Dale**

> "There is only one way under high heaven to get the best of an argument—and that is to avoid it."
> [Dale Carnegie, *Dale Carnegie's Scrapbook*; 1959]

car·nel·ian /kaar neélyən/, **cor·nel·ian** /kawr-/ *n* a hard reddish translucent semiprecious stone that is a variety of chalcedony. Use: gems. [Late 17C. Alteration (influenced by Latin *carn-* "flesh") of *cornelian* < obsolete French *corneline*]

car·net /kaar náy/ *n* **1.** a set of travel tickets or coupons costing less than the individual tickets purchased separately **2.** a customs document for a car that allows it to be taken across national borders without payment of duty [Early 19C. < French]

car·ney, **car·nie** *n* another spelling of **carny**[1]

car·nit·as /kaar neétəss/ *npl Hispanic* a Mexican dish of seasoned fried meat, usually pork, served with tortillas (*takes a singular or plural verb*) [Late 20C. < Mexican Spanish, "small pieces of meat" < *carne* "meat"]

car·ni·tine /kaárni teèn/ *n* an amino acid that transports fatty acids into muscle cells for energy production [Early 20C. < Latin *carn-* "flesh"]

car·ni·val /kaárnəvəl/ *n* **1.** PUBLIC CELEBRATION a public festive occasion or period, often with street processions, costumes, music, and dancing **2.** OUTDOOR SHOW a traveling outdoor amusement show with rides and sideshows **3.** ENTERTAINMENT WITH GAMES AND PRIZES an organized event with a program of games, competitions, and prizes **4.** PERIOD BEFORE LENT the period just before Lent begins. It is celebrated in some Roman Catholic areas with a public festival such as Mardi Gras in New Orleans. [Mid-16C. Via Italian *carnevale* < medieval Latin *carnelevamen* "cessation of meat eating" < Latin *carn-* "flesh"]

car·ni·vore /kaárnə vàwr/ *n* **1.** FLESH-EATING ANIMAL an animal that eats other animals **2.** CARNIVOROUS PLANT a carnivorous plant **3.** SOMEBODY WHO EATS MEAT somebody who is not a vegetarian and likes to eat meat (*humorous*) [Mid-19C. Via French < Latin *carnivorus* (see CARNIVOROUS)]

car·niv·o·rous /kaar nívvərəss/ *adj* **1.** feeding mainly on the flesh of other animals **2.** able to catch and digest animals such as insects and small invertebrates ○ *a carnivorous plant* [Late 16C. < Latin *carnivorus* "meat-eating" < *carn-* "flesh"] —**car·niv·o·rous·ly** *adv* —**car·niv·o·rous·ness** *n*

Car·not cy·cle /kaar nṓ-/ *n* a theoretical reversible heat-engine cycle that gives maximum efficiency [After Nicholas Léonard Sadi *Carnot* (1796–1832), French physicist]

car·no·tite /kaárnə tìt/ *n* a yellow radioactive mineral. Use: source of radium and uranium. [Late 19C. After Marie Adolphe *Carnot* (1839–1920), French inspector of mines]

Car·not prin·ci·ple *n* the principle that the efficiency of a reversible heat engine depends on the maximum and minimum temperatures of the working fluid during the operating cycle [See CARNOT CYCLE]

car·ny[1] /kaárnee/ (*plural* **-nies**), **car·nie**, **car·ney** (*plural* **-neys**) *n* (*informal*) **1.** LEISURE same as **carnival** (sense 2) **2.** a worker in a fairground or carnival [Mid-20C. Shortening of CARNIVAL]

car·ny[2] /kaárnee/ (**-nied, -ny·ing, -nies**) *vt UK* to try to persuade somebody to do something (*informal*) [Early 19C. Origin ?]

Ca·ro /kaárō/, **Qa·ro, Joseph ben Ephraim** (1488–1575) Spanish-born Palestinian Talmudic scholar. His *Shulhan Arukh* (1564–65), codifying religious law, is a major text of Orthodox Judaism.

Car·o /kaárō/, **Miguel Antonio** (1843–1909) Colombian politician, writer, and poet. President of Colombia (1894–98), he was also a noted writer.

car·ob /kárrəb/ (*plural* **-obs** or *same*) *n* **1.** EDIBLE POWDER LIKE CHOCOLATE an edible powder with a taste similar to that of chocolate, made from the seeds and pods of an evergreen tree **2.** EDIBLE POD a long dark-colored edible pod that contains a sweet-tasting pulp **3.** EVERGREEN TREE WITH EDIBLE PODS an evergreen tree with edible pods from which carob powder is made. Flowers: red. Native to: Mediterranean. Latin name: *Ceratonia siliqua*. [Mid-16C. Via obsolete French *car(r)obe* < Arabic *karrūb(a)*]

ca·roche /kə rṓch, -rṓsh/ *n* a grand horse-drawn carriage used on ceremonial occasions [Late 16C. Via obsolete French *carroche* < Italian *carraccio* "large chariot" < Latin *carrum* (see CAR)]

car·ol /kárrəl/ *n* JOYFUL HYMN a joyful religious song or hymn, especially a Christian song celebrating Christmas ■ *v* (**-oled, -ol·ing, -ols**) **1.** *vi* SING CHRISTMAS SONGS to sing hymns that celebrate Christmas, especially as a group going from house to house **2.** *vti* SING SOMETHING JOYOUSLY to sing or call out something in a joyful and lively way (*literary*) ○ *The sun shone, and the birds were caroling.* [13C. < Old French *carole*] —**car·ol·er** *n*

CULTURAL NOTE ***A Christmas Carol***, a novella (1843) by Charles Dickens. It recounts the story of an avaricious merchant, Ebenezer Scrooge, who is visited by the ghosts of Christmas Past, Christmas Present, and Christmas Yet to Come. Confronted by the effects of his miserly behavior on others, Scrooge resolves to become a more generous and charitable person. Over time, the name *Scrooge* has come to mean a petty malicious miser.

Car·o·le·an *adj* HIST same as **Caroline**

ca·ro·li COINS plural of **carolus**

Ca·ro·li·na /kàrrə lī́nə/ **1.** city in northeastern Puerto Rico. It is a southeastern suburb of San Juan. Population: 188,427 (1996). **2.** ♦ **North Carolina, South Carolina**

Ca·ro·li·na all·spice *n* a deciduous bush. Flowers: large, fragrant. Native to: southeastern United States. Latin name: *Calycanthus floridus*. [After the former British colony of *Carolina* (now NORTH CAROLINA and SOUTH CAROLINA)]

Ca·ro·li·na jas·mine, **Ca·ro·li·na yel·low jas·mine** *n* PLANTS a poisonous evergreen climbing plant. Flowers: fragrant, yellow, trumpet-shaped. Native to: southeastern United States. Latin name: *Gelsemium sempervirens*. [See CAROLINA ALLSPICE]

Ca·ro·li·nas /kàrrə lī́nəz/ *n* the former colonies or present-day states of North Carolina and South Carolina

Ca·ro·li·na wren *n* a relatively large wren with a white throat, rusty brown back, and a short upright tail. Native to: mainly southeastern United States. Family: Troglodytidae.

Car·o·line /kárrə līn, -lin/, **Car·o·le·an** /kàrrə leé ən/ *adj* **1.** relating to the English kings Charles I and Charles II or their reigns **2.** relating to any king or emperor called Charles [Early 17C. < medieval Latin *Carolinus* < *Carolus* "Charles"]

Car·o·line Is·lands /kárrə līn-/ archipelago consisting of more than 600 islands, north of New Guinea in the western Pacific Ocean. Area: 450 sq. mi./1,165 sq. km.

Car·o·lin·gi·an /kàrrə línjee ən, -línjən/, **Car·lo·vin·gi·an** /kaárlə vínjən, kaárlə vínjee ən/, **Car·o·lin·i·an** /-línnee ən/ *adj* relating to the dynasty of Frankish kings descended from the Emperor Charlemagne that ruled France and Germany from the 8th to the 10th centuries ■ *n* a king of the Frankish dynasty descended from Charlemagne

Car·o·lin·i·an /kàrrə línnee ən/ *adj* **1.** relating to North or South Carolina, or their people or culture **2.** HIST another spelling of **Carolingian**

car·o·lus /kárrələss/ (*plural* **-lus·es** or **-li** /-lī/) *n* a gold coin named for any king or emperor called Charles, especially Charles I of England [Early 16C. < medieval Latin *Carolus* "Charles"]

car·om /kárrəm/ *n* **1.** BILLIARDS SHOT a shot in billiards in which the cue ball hits one object ball and rebounds to hit another ball **2.** POOL SHOT a shot in pool in which the object ball is rebounded off another ball and into a pocket **3.** REBOUND FOLLOWING COLLISION a collision that is followed by one of the objects rebounding off at an angle ■ *v* (**-omed, -om·ing, -oms**)

1. *vi* REBOUND OFF BALL to rebound off another ball in pool or billiards 2. *vti* REBOUND OR CAUSE TO REBOUND OFF SOMETHING to rebound off another object or series of objects, or cause this to happen ○ *The car swerved and caromed off the railing.* [Late 18C. Shortening of *carambole* < Spanish *carambola*, probably < *bola* "ball"]

car·om bil·liards *n* billiards played on a table with no pockets

car·o·tene /kárrə teen/, **car·o·tin** /kárrət'n/ *n* an orange or red plant pigment that occurs in several forms (**isomers**), one of which is important in nutrition [Mid-19C. < Latin *carota* (see CARROT)]

ca·rot·e·noid /kə rótt'n òyd/, **ca·rot·i·noid** *n* one of a group of orange or red plant pigments that includes the carotenes —**ca·rot·e·noid** *adj*

Ca·roth·ers /kə rúthərz/, **Wallace Hume** (1896–1937) US chemist. He invented the synthetic fibers neoprene and nylon while working for the Du Pont Company.

ca·rot·id /kə róttid/, **ca·rot·id ar·ter·y** (*plural* **ca·rot·id ar·ter·ies**) *n* a large artery on each side of the neck that supplies blood to the head [Early 17C. Via French *carotide* or modern Latin *carotides* < Greek *karōtides* < *karoun* "stupefy"]

ca·rot·id bod·y *n* a cluster of cells and nerve fibers in each carotid that is sensitive to oxygen and acidity levels in the blood and is part of the system that regulates them

ca·rot·id si·nus *n* a slight bulge in each carotid that contains pressure-sensitive nerve endings and forms part of the system that monitors and controls blood pressure

car·o·tin *n* BIOCHEM another spelling of **carotene**

ca·rot·i·noid *n* BIOCHEM another spelling of **carotenoid**

ca·rous·al /kə rówz'l/ *n* a noisy and boisterous drinking party (*literary*)

ca·rouse /kə rówz/ (**-roused, -rous·ing, -rous·es**) *vi* to drink and become noisy, especially in a group (*literary*) [Mid-16C. < German *gar aus (trinken)* "(drink) right up"] —**ca·rouse** *n* —**ca·rous·er** *n*

car·ou·sel /kàrrə sél, kárrə sèl/ *n* 1. LEISURE same as **merry-go-round** (sense 1) 2. a circular conveyor belt, especially one at an airport displaying baggage for arriving passengers to pick up 3. a circular rotating holder that loads photographic slides into a projector one at a time [Mid-17C. Via French *carrousel* < Italian *carosello* "tilting match"]

ca·rou·sel re·tal·i·a·tion *n US* POL, INTERNAT REL retaliation in a trade dispute, especially one between the United States and the European Union, involving the imposition of punitive import tariffs on a list of imports that is changed at regular intervals to spread the effect more widely

carp[1] /kaarp/ (**carped, carp·ing, carps**) *vi* to keep complaining or finding fault, especially about unimportant things ○ *I wish you'd stop carping, I'm doing my best.* [13C. < Old Norse *karpa* "brag"] —**carp·er** *n*

SYNONYMS See ***complain***.

carp[2] /kaarp/ (*plural same or* **carps**) *n* 1. a large fish with a single fin on its back, found worldwide in lakes and slow-moving rivers. Latin name: *Cyprinus carpio.* 2. any fish of the carp family, which includes goldfish and koi. Family: Cyprinidae. [14C. Via French < late Latin *carpa*]

-carp *suffix* part of a fruit ○ *pericarp* [< modern Latin *-carpium* < Greek *karpos* (see CARPO-)] —**-carpous** *suffix*

car·pac·cio /kaar paáchō, -chee ō/ *n* a dish of raw beef or tuna sliced thinly, moistened with olive oil and lemon juice, and seasoned [Mid-20C. After Vittore *Carpaccio* (circa 1460–1525), Italian painter who favored red pigments]

car·pal /kaárp'l/ *adj* relating to the bones in the wrist ■ *n* a bone in the wrist [Mid-18C. < CARPUS]

car·pal tun·nel syn·drome *n* a condition of pain and weakness in the hand caused by repetitive compression of a nerve that passes through the wrist into the hand

car park *n UK* same as **parking lot**

Car·pa·thi·an Moun·tains /kaar pàythee ən-/, **Car·pa·thi·ans** mountain system in eastern Europe, situated along the border between Slovakia and Poland and extending southward through Ukraine and eastern Romania. Its highest peak is Gerlachovka 8,711 ft./2,655 m.

car·pe di·em /kaàr pay deè èm/ *interj* used as an invocation to enjoy the present and not worry about the future ■ *n* the act of living for the moment and enjoying the present [< Latin, "seize the day"]

car·pel /kaárp'l/ *n* a female reproductive organ in a flower, enclosing the fertilized ovules that are developing into seeds. It consists of the stigma and usually a style. [Mid-19C. < French *carpelle* or modern Latin *carpellum* "little fruit" < Greek *karpos* "fruit"] —**car·pel·lar·y** /kaárp'l èrree/ *adj* —**car·pel·late** *adj*

Car·pen·tar·i·a, Gulf of /kaàrpən térree ə/ large gulf on the northern coast of Australia, lying between Arnhem Land in the west and the Cape York Peninsula in the east. Area: 120,000 sq. mi./310,000 sq. km.

car·pen·ter /kaárpəntər/ *n* BUILDER OF WOODEN STRUCTURES a builder or repairer of wooden objects or structures ■ *v* (**-tered, -ter·ing, -ters**) 1. *vi* BUILD WOODEN STRUCTURES to build and repair wooden structures, or the wooden parts of them (*technical*) 2. *vt* MAKE SOMETHING WOODEN to make something by cutting and joining pieces of wood ○ *He had carpentered a series of perfectly fitting dovetail joints.* 3. *vt* MAKE SOMETHING IN EFFICIENT WAY to make or devise something efficiently and systematically ○ *They met every day, in the vain attempt to carpenter an agreement that would be acceptable to both sides.* [12C. < Anglo-Norman, Old French *carpentier* < late Latin *carpentarius (artifex)* "carriage(maker)" < *carpentum* "two-wheeled carriage"]

car·pen·ter ant *n* a large black or brown ant that bores into wood to make its nest. It usually bores into old or rotten wood, but it can also attack lumber in homes and cause much damage. Genus: *Camponotus.*

car·pen·ter bee *n* a bee that bores tunnels into wood to lay its eggs. Families: Xylocopidae or Ceratinidae.

car·pen·ter jeans *npl* jeans or dungarees with loops large enough to carry tools high up on the sides or back of the legs, originally worn by carpenters and others working with tools

Car·pen·ters·ville /kaárpəntərz vìl/ village in northeastern Illinois, southeast of Rockford, on the western bank of the Fox River. Population: 34,235 (2002 estimate).

Car·pen·ti·er /kaàr pen tyér/, **Alejo** (1904–80) Cuban writer and musicologist. His novel *Los pasos perdidos* (1953) (*The Lost Steps* (1956) is a fictional diary of a Cuban musician traveling up the Amazon. His blend of realism and surrealism influenced other Central and South American writers.

car·pen·try /kaárpəntree/ *n* 1. the work or occupation of building and repairing things made of wood such as houses and boats, or the wooden parts of them ○ *a career in carpentry* 2. the work or objects produced by a carpenter ○ *fine carpentry for sale*

car·pet /kaárpət/ *n* 1. FLOOR COVERING thick fabric for covering a floor 2. PIECE OF FLOOR COVERING a piece of thick heavy fabric covering the floor of a room or area 3. LAYER OR COVERING a layer or covering (*literary*) ○ *a carpet of leaves* ■ *vt* (**-pet·ed, -pet·ing, -pets**) 1. COVER FLOOR WITH CARPET to cover a floor, or the floor of a room, with a carpet ○ *We could carpet every room in the house with the money she spent on that rug.* 2. COVER SOMETHING to cover something in a layer (*literary*) ○ *The valley was carpeted with flowers.* [14C. < Old French *carpite* or medieval Latin *carpita* < Latin *carpere* "to pluck"] ◇ **roll out the red carpet** to give a special welcome to a distinguished visitor ◇ **sweep something under the carpet** to conceal or ignore something that needs attention

car·pet·bag /kaárpət bàg/ *n* TRAVELING BAG a traveling bag made of a thick fabric such as carpet, commonly used in the 19th century ■ *adj* OF CARPETBAGGERS relating to or involving carpetbaggers or carpetbagging ■ *vi* (**-bagged, -bag·ging, -bags**) BE CARPETBAGGER to act as a carpetbagger

car·pet·bag·ger /kaárpət bàggər/ *n* 1. a Northerner who moved to the southern United States after the Civil War, especially one seeking political or commercial advantage 2. an outsider whose only interest in coming to a place is to win it as a political seat —**car·pet·bag·ger·y** *n* —**car·pet·bag·ging** *adj*

car·pet bee·tle *n* a small beetle whose larvae feed on fabric, furs, or animal remains. Genera: *Anthrenus* or *Attagenus.*

car·pet-bomb (**car·pet-bombed, car·pet-bomb·ing, car·pet-bombs**) *vt* 1. to bomb an area intensively 2. to conduct an intensive campaign, especially in the media, to sway public opinion or to destroy somebody's reputation —**car·pet-bomb·ing** *n*

car·pet fit·ter *n UK* same as **carpetlayer**

car·pet grass *n* a coarse grass that forms a tight matted growth and is widely used in warm humid areas for turf and pasture. Genus: *Axonopus.*

car·pet·ing /kaárpəting/ *n* 1. thick fabric used for covering floors 2. carpets regarded collectively ○ *How much do you want to spend on carpeting?*

car·pet·lay·er /kaárpət lày ər/ *n* somebody who cuts and fits wall-to-wall carpet

car·pet slip·per *n* a slipper with the upper section made of thick fabric

car·pet snake *n* a large python with a pattern of scales on its back resembling a traditional carpet. Native to: southern Australia. Latin name: *Morelia variegata.*

car·pet·sweep·er /kaárpət sweèpər/ *n* a device for lifting dirt off carpets, with a long handle and revolving brushes in a wheeled casing

car·pet·weed /kaárpət weèd/ *n* a low close-growing weed. Flowers: tiny, greenish white. Native to: North America. Latin name: *Mollugo verticillata.*

car phone *n* a mobile phone designed for use in a car

car·pi ANAT plural of **carpus**

carp·ing /kaárping/ *adj* complaining or finding fault, or tending to ○ *his usual carping comments* —**carp·ing·ly** *adv*

carpo- *prefix* fruit ○ *carpophagous* [< Greek *karpos* < Indo-European, "gather"]

car·pol·o·gy /kaar póllәjee/ *n* the branch of botany that deals with the study of fruits and seeds —**car·po·log·i·cal** /kaárpə lójjik'l/ *adj* —**car·pol·o·gist** *n*

car·pool /kaár poòl/ *n* 1. GROUP USING OWN CARS IN TURN a group of associated people sharing the use of their cars, each in turn driving the others 2. SHARED DRIVING ARRANGEMENTS the actual arrangement made by a group of people such as coworkers or parents to share the duty of driving to and from somewhere 3. *UK* BUSINESS, CARS same as **motor pool** ■ *vi* (**-pooled, -pool·ing, -pools**) SHARE DRIVING RESPONSIBILITIES WITH GROUP to drive or be driven regularly from one place to another as a small group, with each member sharing driving responsibilities

car·pool lane *n* a lane in an expressway designated for use only by vehicles with two or more occupants

car·poph·a·gous /kaar póffəgəss/ *adj* ZOOL same as **frugivorous**

car·po·phore /kaárpə fàwr/ *n* 1. the part of a flower that bears the carpels and stamens 2. the part of some fungi that contains the spores or supports the part that contains them

car·port /kaár pàwrt/ *n* an open-sided shelter for a parked car, attached to a house or other building

car·po·spore /kaárpə spàwr/ *n* a spore that forms in some red algae after fertilization

car·pus /kaárpəss/ (*plural* **-pi** /-pī/) *n* 1. any bone in the set of eight that form the wrist joint 2. any bone in the set of bones that form the joint between the forelimb of a vertebrate animal and its foot or paw, corresponding to the wrist [Late 17C. Via modern Latin < Greek *karpos*]

Carr /kaar/, **Emily** (1871–1945) Canadian painter and writer. She was noted for her landscape paintings of British Columbia and her interest in Native American folk art. Her first book, *Klee Wyck* (1941), is a collection of short stories.

Car·rà /kə rá/, **Carlo** (1881–1966) Italian painter. A prominent member of the Futurist movement in his early career, he later adopted Giorgio de Chirico's metaphysical style of painting.

car·rack /kárrək/, **car·ack** *n* a large trading ship common in the Mediterranean between the 14th and 16th centuries [14C. < French *caraque*]

car·ra·geen /kàrrə geén, kárrə geén/, **car·ra·gheen** *n* **1.** PLANTS same as **Irish moss 2.** FOOD INDUST another spelling of **carrageenan** [Early 19C. < Irish *carraigín*]

car·ra·geen·an /kàrrə geénən, kárrə geénən/, **car·ra·geen·in** *n* a complex carbohydrate obtained from edible red seaweeds, especially the seaweed Irish moss. Use: commercial preparation of food and drink. [Late 19C. < CARRAGEEN]

car·ra·gheen /kárrə geèn, kárrə geén/ *n* PLANTS, FOOD INDUST another spelling of **carrageen**

~~carraige~~ incorrect spelling of **carriage**

Car·ran·tuo·hill /kàrrən tóo əl/, **Car·raun·tuo·hill, Car·ran·tu·al** highest mountain in Ireland, in the Macgillicuddy's Reeks range in the southwest of the country. Height: 3,414 ft./1,041 m.

Car·ran·za /kə ránzə, -raánzə/, **Venustiano** (1859–1920) Mexican revolutionary and politician. He was the first president of the Mexican Republic (1914–20).

Car·ra·ra /kə raárə/ city in Massa-Carrara Province, Tuscany Region, in north central Italy. It is famous for its quarry, which produces some of the world's finest marble. Population: 65,034 (2001).

Car·raun·tuo·hill another spelling of **Carrantuohill**

Car·ré ▸ **Le Carré, John**

~~carreer~~ incorrect spelling of **career**

car·re·four /kárrə fàwr/ *n* (*archaic*) **1.** ROADS same as **crossroads** (sense 1) **2.** a public square at a place where several roads meet [15C. Via French < Latin *quadrifurcus* "four-forked"]

car·rel /kárrəl/, **car·rell** *n* a bay, cubicle, or small room where one person can study in private, e.g., in a library [Late 16C. Alteration of CAROL "circle"]

Car·rel /kə rél, kárrəl/, **Alexis** (1873–1944) French biologist and surgeon. He developed the vascular surgical technique that led to organ transplants. He won the Nobel Prize in physiology or medicine (1912).

> "Intelligence is almost useless to the person whose only quality it is."
> [Alexis Carrel, *Man, the Unknown*; 1935]

car·rell *n* LIBRARIES another spelling of **carrel**

Car·re·ra /kə rérrə/, **Andrade Jorge** (1903–78) Ecuadorian poet. Often considered one of the greatest Spanish-language poets of the 20th century, he was also a diplomat.

Car·re·ra /kə ráirə/, **Rafael** (1814–65) Guatemalan revolutionary and politician. He served as elected president of Guatemala (1844–48) and was declared president for life (1851). Full name **Carrera, José Rafael**

Car·re·as /kə rérrəss/, **José** (*b.* 1946) Spanish singer. An operatic tenor, he became an international star in the 1970s.

~~carress~~ incorrect spelling of **caress**

car·riage /kárrij/ *n* **1.** HORSE-DRAWN VEHICLE a four-wheeled horse-drawn private passenger vehicle, especially one that is large and comfortable **2.** WHEELED PLATFORM a wheeled platform on which something is carried or supported **3.** WAY OF HOLDING BODY the way somebody holds his or her head and body when walking (*formal*) ○ *She was a tall woman with a beautiful upright carriage.* **4.** TAKING AND DELIVERING GOODS the transporting and delivering of goods **5.** CHARGE FOR TAKING AND DELIVERING GOODS a charge made for transporting and delivering goods **6.** MOVING PART OF MACHINE a part of a machine that holds and moves another part, e.g., the rotating and sliding paper holder on a typewriter **7.** same as **baby carriage 8.** *UK* RAILROAD COACH a railroad passenger coach

car·riage bolt *n* a large square-necked threaded bolt that has a snap head and is used in building

car·riage clock *n* a small clock set in a case with a handle on top, originally used as a travel clock but now ornamental

car·riage dog *n* VERTEB same as **Dalmatian** (sense 1) [Because the dogs were kept to run in attendance on a carriage]

car·riage horse *n* a horse used to pull carriages

car·riage re·turn *n* the key or lever on a typewriter that sends the paper-holding carriage back and rotates it to move the paper upward, ready to begin a new line

car·riage trade *n* the most wealthy and prestigious of possible customers ○ *They carry only the highest quality goods, catering to the carriage trade.*

car·riage·way /kárrij wày/ *n UK* the part of a main road used for vehicles, especially one side of a major two-way road, carrying traffic in one direction only

~~Carribean~~ incorrect spelling of **Caribbean**

car·rick bend /kàrrik-/ *n* an intertwining knot similar to a granny knot, used for tying ropes together [Probably alteration of CARRACK]

car·rick bitt *n* one of the two posts that support a ship's windlass [See CARRICK BEND]

car·ri·er /kárree ər/ *n* **1.** TRANSPORTER OF PEOPLE OR GOODS a person or company whose function or business is to transport things or people from one place to another ○ *These airlines are among the world's most popular carriers.* **2.** TRANSMITTER OF DISEASE a person or animal that is infected with a disease without displaying any of the symptoms and can pass it to others **3.** SYMPTOMLESS TRANSMITTER OF GENE an individual possessing a gene for a particular genetic trait or disorder without being affected by it, because two copies of the gene, one from each parent, are usually necessary for the characteristic to show itself **4.** PART OF MACHINE CONVEYING MOTION a part of a machine that carries and moves something or transmits motion to another part **5.** LUGGAGE RACK a metal frame on which luggage can be tied to a road vehicle or bicycle **6.** NAVY same as **aircraft carrier 7.** MEANS OF TRANSMITTING ACTIVE SUBSTANCE a neutral substance to which an active ingredient or agent is added as a way of applying or transferring the ingredient or agent ○ *Mix the dye and the carrier in equal proportions.* **8.** BEARER OF ELECTRIC CHARGE something that carries electric current, e.g., an electron or ion **9.** RADIO WAVE CARRYING INFORMATION an electromagnetic wave that is modulated to carry a signal in radio or television transmission **10.** SOMEBODY WHO DELIVERS MAIL a Postal Service employee who delivers and picks up mail **11.** COMMUNICATIONS COMPANY a telephone, television, or radio company **12.** INSURANCE COMPANY a company that provides insurance

car·ri·er air wing *n* a squadron of aircraft operating from an aircraft carrier

car·ri·er bag *n UK* a large plastic or paper shopping bag with handles, especially one supplied by a store

car·ri·er pi·geon *n* a domestic pigeon trained to deliver messages and return home

car·ri·er wave *n* TELECOM same as **carrier** (sense 9)

car·ri·ole *n* VEHICLES another spelling of **cariole**

car·ri·on /kárree ən/ *n* **1.** ROTTING ANIMAL FLESH the rotting flesh of a dead animal **2.** SOMETHING DECAYING something that is decaying or disgusting (*literary*) ■ *adj* OF DECOMPOSING FLESH relating to rotting flesh or the eating of such flesh [13C. < Anglo-Norman, Old French *caroi(g)ne* < Latin *caro* "flesh"]

car·ri·on crow *n* a medium-sized crow similar to a rook but with a heavier beak and black face. Native to: Europe. Latin name: *Corvus corone.*

car·ri·on flow·er *n* **1.** a climbing plant with small greenish flowers that smell like rotting flesh. Native to: North America. Genus: *Smilax.* **2.** a succulent plant with foul-smelling star-shaped flowers. Native to: tropics. Genus: *Stapelia.*

Car·roll /kárrəl/, **Charles** (1737–1832) US political leader. A leader of the American Revolution, he signed the Declaration of Independence (1776) and was a US senator (1789–92) from South Carolina. Known as **Carroll of Carrollton, Charles**

Car·roll, Lewis (1832–98) British writer. He wrote the children's classics *Alice's Adventures in Wonderland* (1865) and *Through the Looking Glass and What Alice Found There* (1871). Under his real name, he was also a distinguished geometrician and photographer. Pseudonym of **Dodgson, Charles Lutwidge.** See Cultural note at **wonderland**

> "Sentence first—verdict afterwards"
> [Lewis Carroll, *Alice's Adventures in Wonderland*; 1865]

> "'The time has come,' the Walrus said, / 'To talk of many things: / Of shoes and ships – and sealing wax – / Of cabbages – and kings / And why the sea is boiling hot – / And whether pigs have wings.'"
> [Lewis Carroll, *Through the Looking Glass and What Alice Found There*; 1871]

Car·roll·ton /kárrəltən/ city in northeastern Texas. Population: 115,107 (2002 estimate).

car·ron·ade /kárrə nàyd, kàrrə náyd/ *n* a lightweight iron cannon formerly used on ships [Late 18C. After *Carron*, a district of Falkirk, central Scotland, site of an ironworks]

car·rot /kárrət/ *n* **1.** THIN ORANGE ROOT VEGETABLE a thin tapering orange-colored root eaten raw or cooked as a vegetable **2.** PLANT WITH EDIBLE ORANGE-COLORED ROOT a biennial plant that produces carrots. Latin name: *Daucus carota.* **3.** PLANTS same as **Queen Anne's lace 4.** INCENTIVE something tempting, offered in order to persuade somebody to do something ○ *They offer you the carrot of a year's free gasoline if you buy the car there and then.* [15C. Via French < Latin *carota* < Greek *karōton*]

SPELLCHECK See *carat.*

car·rot-and-stick *adj* relating to or characterized by the use of persuasion involving a combination of rewards and punishments ○ *During the fast-paced negotiations, the diplomats employed a carrot-and-stick strategy.*

car·rot cake *n* a cake made with finely grated carrots that give it a moist texture and delicate flavor

car·rot·y /kárrətee/ *adj* **1.** TASTING LIKE CARROTS like carrots in taste **2.** RED describes hair that is red or auburn **3.** OF BRIGHT ORANGE COLOR of a bright reddish orange color

car·ry /kárree/ *v* **(-ried, -ry·ing, -ries) 1.** *vt* HOLD AND TRANSPORT SOMEBODY OR SOMETHING to take somebody or something that you are holding or supporting to another place ○ *The suitcase was too heavy for her to carry.* **2.** *vt* TAKE SOMEBODY OR SOMETHING TO ANOTHER PLACE to take somebody or something to another place ○ *a truck carrying farm produce* **3.** *vt* MOVE SOMEBODY OR SOMETHING ALONG to take and move somebody or something by a flow or impetus ○ *The current carried them swiftly downstream.* ○ *She could hear children's voices, carried on the light breeze.* **4.** *vt* BE CHANNEL OR ROUTE FOR SOMETHING to be the means by which something passes or is transmitted from one place to another ○ *The pipeline will carry oil to the coast.* **5.** *vt* TELL SOMETHING to communicate or convey information, an idea, or a feeling by way of content or in an indirect manner ○ *The article carries wider implications than you may think.* **6.** *vt* HAVE SOMETHING WITH YOU to have something with you, e.g., in your pocket or in a purse ○ *Staff should carry identification at all times.* **7.** *vt* HAVE TRANSMISSIBLE DISEASE to be infected with a disease and capable of infecting others ○ *You may be carrying a virus without knowing it.* **8.** *vt* HOLD OR CONTAIN to hold, contain, or support something ○ *How much does the tanker carry?* ○ *a high roof carried on slender pillars* **9.** *vt* PUBLISH, BROADCAST, OR DISPLAY SOMETHING to feature or include an article, picture, item of news, or piece of information ○ *That evening, all the major networks carried the story.* ○ *Every pack carries a government health warning.* **10.** *vt* KEEP SOMETHING FOR SALE to keep something as stock in a store ○ *We don't carry household goods.* **11.** *vi* BE HEARD AT DISTANCE to be audible at a distance ○ *Sound carries a long way over water.* **12.** *vt* SUPPORT WEAKER ELEMENT to support or compensate for a weaker element or participant ○ *The rest of the department has to carry him.* **13.** *vt* MAKE SOMEBODY SUCCEED OR ENDURE to give somebody the incentive, impetus, or encouragement to achieve or deal with something ○ *Their exhilaration at this success may carry them further up in the league standings.* ○ *The audience cheered, carried along on a wave of enthusiasm.* **14.** *vt* INCLUDE OR RESULT IN SOMETHING to have something as a quality, feature, or consequence ○ *Reckless driving carries a heavy penalty.* **15.** *vti* BE PREGNANT to be pregnant with a child ○ *She carried the child to term.* **16.** *vt* DEVELOP IDEA to develop an idea in discussion or action ○ *If you carry that argument to its logical conclusion, no one should get married at all.* **17.** *vt* MOVE OR BEHAVE to move or behave in a particular way, especially with confidence or dignity ○ *He was a handsome man who carried himself with dignity.* ○ *She carried her head high, and looked her accusers in the eye.* **18.** *vt* BE RESPONSIBLE FOR SOMETHING to bear the responsibility for something ○ *The president carries heavy duties.* **19.** *vti* ACCEPT OR BE ACCEPTED BY VOTING to accept a proposal by voting for it, or be so accepted ○ *The nomination was carried, 40–29.* **20.** *vt* GAIN SOMEBODY'S SUPPORT to win the support or sympathy of a person or group, especially by making a speech or appeal ○ *It looked for a moment as if he would carry the crowd.* **21.** *vt* STAY IN TUNE WHEN SINGING to be able to sing and stay in tune ○ *Can you carry a tune?* **22.** *vt* TRANSFER ITEM IN ACCOUNT OR CALCULATION to transfer a figure from one group or column to another in accounts or in a calculation **23.** *vi* BE HIT PARTICULAR DISTANCE to reach a particular distance after being struck ○ *Her approach shot didn't carry to the green.* **24.** *vt* CAPTURE PLACE to capture a place in battle ○ *Their charge carried the hill.* **25.** *vi* HAVE FIREPOWER RANGE to have a particular range of fire ○ *an artillery shell that carried for miles* **26.** *vt* PALM BALL IN BASKETBALL in basketball, to keep a hand in illegal contact with the ball **27.** *vt* PROVIDE FORAGE FOR ANIMALS to yield enough forage or grazing crops for animals to survive ○ *fields that can carry llamas as well as cattle* **28.** *vt* WIN VOTES OF AREA to win a majority of the votes in an area or in an election ○ *The incumbent carried all the cities in her district, and won.* **29.** *vt* TRANSP ACCOMMODATE VEHICULAR TRAFFIC to be able to withstand a particular degree or amount of vehicular traffic ○ *a freeway that can carry hundreds of thousands of vehicles a day* **30.** *vt* MOVE WITH BALL IN SPORT in a sport such as football, to bring a ball forward a particular distance ○ *Their first rush carried the ball well into the defenders' half.* **31.** *vt* LIST SOMEBODY AS DEBTOR to continue to keep somebody as a debtor in the financial accounts ○ *We've carried him for two quarters; enough is enough.* **32.** *vi* HAVE WEAPON to be in possession of a weapon, especially a gun (*slang*) ○ *We knew his goons would be carrying too.* **33.** *vt Southern US* DRIVE SOMEBODY IN VEHICLE to transport somebody in a motor vehicle from one location to another ○ *Call me when you arrive; I'll carry you home from the airport.* ■ *n* (*plural* **-ries**) **1.** DISTANCE COVERED the distance covered by something struck, thrown, launched, or fired, or the reach of something such as a voice **2.** ACT OF RUNNING WITH BALL in football, a sprint with the ball ○ *a 50-yard carry that won the game* **3.** PLACE WHERE BOAT IS CARRIED the land over which a canoe must be carried at a portage [14C. Directly or via Anglo-Norman < Old French *carier* < *car* (see CAR)]

carry away *vt* to make somebody become less controlled, reasonable, or attentive by arousing his or her emotion or interest (*usually passive*) ○ *I was completely carried away by the beauty of it.*

carry back *vt* to transfer something such as a tax credit so that it is calculated against the previous year's income

carry forward *vt* **1.** to transfer an item to the next section or column in accounts or in a calculation **2.** to transfer something such as a tax credit or liability so that it is calculated against the next year's income

carry off *vt* **1.** REMOVE SOMEBODY OR SOMETHING to take something or somebody away purposefully or by force ○ *carried him off, kicking and screaming, to his crib* **2.** WIN SOMETHING to win a prize (*informal*) ○ *She carried off the award for best newcomer.* **3.** DO SOMETHING WELL to succeed in doing something well or producing a good effect ○ *He was nervous about chairing the meeting, but carried it off in style.* ○ *It's a very sophisticated outfit, but she can't quite carry it off.* **4.** CAUSE DEATH OF SOMEBODY to kill somebody (*usually passive*) ○ *Half the settlers were carried off by smallpox.*

carry on *v* **1.** *vti* KEEP DOING SOMETHING to continue to do something ○ *Please just carry on with your work and pretend we're not here.* ○ *She carried on the business after her father retired.* **2.** *vt* BE INVOLVED IN SOMETHING to be engaged in something ○ *They were carrying on an intense conversation in a corner of the bar.* **3.** *vi* BEHAVE FOOLISHLY OR IMPROPERLY to behave or talk in a way that is socially awkward or improper (*informal*) ○ *I'm ashamed of the way he's been carrying on in public.* **4.** *vi* HAVE AFFAIR to have a casual affair with somebody (*informal disapproving*)

carry out *vt* **1.** to complete a task or activity ○ *carry out research* **2.** to do something that has been ordered, planned, or stated as a goal ○ *We will carry out your instructions to the letter.*

SYNONYMS See ***perform.***

carry over *v* **1.** *vti* LEAVE SOMETHING TO BE FINISHED LATER to leave the last part of something to be done at a later date ○ *There were so many candidates that the ceremonies were carried over to the next morning.* **2.** *vt* TRANSFER ITEM IN ACCOUNT OR CALCULATION to transfer an item to the next group or column in accounts or in a calculation **3.** *vt* TRANSFER SOMETHING TO NEXT YEAR to transfer an allowance or entitlement from one year to the next **4.** *vi* CONTINUE TO EXIST to continue to exist or produce an effect in changed circumstances ○ *The dislike he always felt for me has obviously carried over into our relationship at work.*

carry through *v* **1.** *vt* DO WHAT WAS PLANNED to complete or accomplish something planned ○ *We outlined our policy before the election, and we are determined to carry it through.* **2.** *vt* HELP SOMEBODY SURVIVE to give somebody the support or strength needed to overcome a difficulty ○ *It was my family's support that carried me through.* ○ *Only his determination not to be humiliated carried him through the next five hours.* **3.** *vi* SURVIVE to continue to exist ○ *It is an old tradition that has carried through into the information age.*

car·ry·all /kárree àwl/ *n* **1.** LARGE SOFT TRAVEL BAG a container or soft-sided bag for carrying belongings **2.** PASSENGER VEHICLE WITH FACING BENCHES a large passenger vehicle with two facing benches **3.** HORSE-DRAWN CARRIAGE a covered horse-drawn carriage for four people [Early 18C. Alteration of CARIOLE; partly < CARRY + ALL]

car·ry·back /kárree bàk/ *n* an amount of money such as a tax credit that is transferred to the accounts for the previous year

car·ry·case /kárree kàyss/ *n* a small case with a handle, used for carrying a laptop computer, documents, or other things

car·ry·cot /kárree kòt/ *n UK* a lightweight portable bed for a baby, often detachable from a wheeled base

car·ry·ing /kárree ing/ *adj* **1.** describes a voice or a sound that can be heard clearly from a distance ○ *speaking in a carrying voice that could be heard in the next office* **2.** *S Asia* expecting a baby ○ *My wife is carrying.*

-carrying *suffix* **1.** bearing or transporting a particular thing ○ *passenger-carrying* ○ *disease-carrying* ○ *knife-carrying* **2.** reaching a particular distance ○ *far-carrying*

car·ry·ing ca·pac·i·ty *n* **1.** NUMBER OF THINGS OR PEOPLE ALLOWED the number of things or people a vehicle or container can hold **2.** NUMBER OF ANIMALS LAND SUPPORTS the number of animals a region can support **3.** NUMBER OF PEOPLE REGION SUPPORTS the number of individuals a region can support in terms of its resources

car·ry·ing charge *n* **1.** COST OF HOLDING ASSETS the cost to a business of holding or storing assets from which it currently earns no income **2.** INTEREST ON UNPAID BALANCE interest charged on the unpaid balance of a sum of borrowed money, especially the price of something that is being paid for in installments **3.** *UK* DELIVERY OR STORAGE CHARGE a charge for storing or delivering a customer's goods

car·ry·ing-on (*plural* **car·ry·ings-on**) *n* behavior regarded as immature or improper (*informal*) ○ *I won't have that kind of carrying-on in my house.*

car·ry·on /kárree òn/ *n* a piece of luggage suitable for taking in the cabin of an aircraft ■ *adj* describes or relating to luggage small enough to be carried and stowed in the cabin of an aircraft

car·ry·out /kárree òwt/ *n US, Scotland* an item of ready-to-eat food bought in a store or restaurant and taken elsewhere to be eaten (*often used before a noun*) ○ *a carryout pizza*

car·ry·o·ver /kárree òvər/ *n* **1.** something left over that is continued on, extended, or transferred to the next period ○ *This policy is a carryover from the previous administration.* **2.** an item transferred to the next group or column in accounts or in a calculation

car seat *n* **1.** a small seat for children, strapped inside a car **2.** a driver's or passenger's seat in a car

car·sick /kaár sìk/ *adj* made nauseated from the motion of a vehicle you are traveling in —**car·sick·ness** *n*

Car·son /kaárss'n/, **Johnny** (*b.* 1925) US entertainer. He hosted *The Tonight Show* (1962–92).

Car·son, Kit (1809–68) US hunter and scout. He accompanied the western expeditions of John Charles Frémont (1842–46) and helped Union forces in the Civil War. Full name **Carson, Christopher**

UPI/Corbis-Bettmann

Rachel Carson

Car·son, Rachel (1907–64) US ecologist. In *Silent Spring* (1962) she argued that agricultural pesticides damage the food chain. See Cultural note at **silent**

> "No witchcraft, no enemy action had silenced the rebirth of new life in this stricken world. The people had done it themselves."
> [Rachel Carson, *Silent Spring*; 1962]

Car·son Cit·y capital of Nevada, in the western part of the state, directly east of Lake Tahoe and south of Reno. Population: 54,311 (2002 estimate).

cart /kaart/ *n* **1.** HORSE-DRAWN VEHICLE CARRYING GOODS an open horse-drawn vehicle, especially one with only two wheels, used for carrying goods or as a farm vehicle **2.** VEHICLE PUSHED BY HAND a light vehicle or barrow pushed by hand **3.** WHEELED CARRIER FOR MERCHANDISE OR BAGGAGE a container or platform on small wheels on which things are pushed along, e.g., supermarket items or airport baggage **4.** HORSE-DRAWN CARRIAGE a light horse-drawn carriage with two wheels **5.** SMALL MOTORIZED VEHICLE a lightweight motorized vehicle, e.g., one used by golfers on a course **6.** WHEELED TABLE a small table on wheels, used for taking food and drinks to the table ■ *vt* (**cart·ed, cart·ing, carts**) **1.** CARRY SOMEBODY OR SOMETHING ROUGHLY to take or pull somebody or something roughly or with difficulty (*informal*) ○ *I had to cart the Christmas tree home myself.* ○ *Do you have to cart all those books around?* **2.** TRANSPORT SOMETHING OR SOMEBODY to carry or transport something or somebody, especially in a cart ○ *carting the produce to market* ○ *We seem to spend half of Saturday carting the kids everywhere.* [12C. < Old Norse *kartr*] —**cart·a·ble** *adj* ◇ **put the cart before the horse** to do or say things in the wrong order

cart·age /kaártij/ *n* the cost of transporting or delivering goods by cart

Car·ta·ge·na /kaartə gáynə, -jéenə, -háynə/ **1.** capital of Bolívar Department in northwestern Colombia, a port on the Caribbean Sea's Bay of Cartagena. Population: 877,000 (1999). **2.** city, port, and naval base in the province and autonomous region of Murcia, southeastern Spain. Population: 188,003 (2002).

carte blanche /kaart blaánch, -blaáNsh/ *n* permission or authority given to somebody to act with freedom or discretion ○ *She's been given carte blanche to make whatever changes she thinks necessary.* [< French, "white card"]

carte du jour /kaárt də zhoór/ (*plural* **cartes du jour** /kaárt-/) *n* a restaurant menu showing what is available on a particular day [< French, "card of the day"]

car·tel /kaar tél/ *n* **1.** an alliance of business companies formed to control production, competition, and prices **2.** a political alliance among parties or groups having common goals [Mid-16C. Via German *Kartell* < French *cartel* < Italian *cartello* "placard" < Latin *c(h)arta* (see CARD[1])]

car·tel·ize /kaárt'l ìz/ (**-ized, -iz·ing, -iz·es**) *vti* to form a cartel of business companies or political groups ○ *The market leaders had every incentive to cartelize.*

car·ter /kaártər/ *n* somebody who uses a cart for transporting goods or for farm work

Car·ter /kaártər/, **Angela** (1940–92) British writer. Her novels include *The Magic Toyshop* (1967), *Nights at the Circus* (1984), and *Wise Children* (1991).

> "Myth deals in false universals, to dull the pain of particular circumstances."
> [Angela Carter, "Polemical Preface," *The Sadeian Woman*; 1979]

Car·ter, Howard (1873–1939) British archaeologist and draftsman. An Egyptologist, he was largely responsible for discovering the tomb of Tutankhamen in 1922.

Jimmy Carter

Car·ter, Jimmy (*b.* 1924) 39th president of the United States. As Democratic president (1977–81) he negotiated the Panama Canal Treaty (1978) and the Camp David Accords between Israel and Egypt (1978–79). He was awarded the Nobel Peace Price in 2002. Full name **Carter, Jr., James Earl**. See table at **president**

> "A simple and proper function of government is just to make it easy for us to do good and difficult for us to do wrong."
> [Jimmy Carter, *Acceptance speech, Democratic National Convention, New York City*; July 15, 1976]

Car·ter, Rosalynn (*b.* 1927) US first lady (1977–81). She took a strong interest in the performing arts, and in programs to aid mental health, the community, and the elderly. Born **Smith, Rosalynn**

> "I knew it was a man's world, but I needed to know. I'd be damned if I'd leave."
> [Rosalynn Carter, on sitting in on Cabinet meetings, *New York Times*; June 14, 1983]

Car·ter·et /kaártərət/, **Sir George** (1610?–80) English-born American absentee colonial administrator. He was granted part of present-day New Jersey (1664) by King Charles II.

Car·te·sian /kaar teézh'n/ *adj* relating to René Descartes or his writings or theories [Mid-17C. < modern Latin *Cartesianus* < *Cartesius*, Latinized form of DESCARTES] —**Car·te·sian** *n*

Car·te·sian co·or·di·nate *n* **1.** one of a pair of coordinates giving the location of a point on a plane, relative to an origin and two perpendicular axes **2.** one of three coordinates giving the location of a point in space, relative to an origin and three mutually perpendicular planes

Car·te·sian·ism /kaar teézh'n ìzzəm/ *n* the philosophy of René Descartes, especially his belief in a distinction between the observing mind and the observed world

Car·te·sian plane *n* a plane having all points defined by Cartesian coordinates

Car·te·sian prod·uct *n* a set of all the pairs of elements from two sets that have their first element from the first set and the second from the second set

Car·thage /kaárthij/ site of an ancient city, founded by the Phoenicians on the northern coast of Africa in 814 B.C. The site is now in a suburb of Tunis, capital of Tunisia. —**Car·tha·gin·i·an** /kaárthə jínnee ən/ *n, adj*

Car·thu·sian /kaar thoózh'n/ *n* a member of a contemplative Roman Catholic order of monks and nuns founded in France in the 11th century [Mid-16C. < medieval Latin *Carthusianus* < *Carthusia* "Chartreuse," France, where the order's first monastery was built] —**Car·thu·sian** *adj*

Car·tier /kaar tyáy, kaártee ày/, **Sir George-Étienne** (1814–73) Canadian politician and railroad magnate. He was prime minister of Canada (1858–62).

> "If today Canada is a portion of the British Empire, it is due to the conservatism of the French-Canadian clergy."
> [Sir George-Étienne Cartier, *Confederation Debates*; February 7, 1865]

Car·tier, Jacques (1491–1557) French navigator. He was the first European to explore and chart the St Lawrence River in eastern North America (1534).

Car·tier-Bres·son /kaar tyày brə sőN, -brə sáwN/, **Henri** (*b.* 1908) French photographer. He is known for his black-and-white photographs of French life.

> "In a portrait, I'm looking for the silence in somebody."
> [Henri Cartier-Bresson, *Observer (London)*; May 15, 1994]

Car·tier Is·land /kaártee áy-/ small uninhabited island off the northern coast of Western Australia

car·ti·lage /kaárt'lij/ *n* the tough elastic tissue that is found in the nose, throat, and ear and in other parts of the body and forms most of the skeleton in infancy, changing to bone during growth [15C. Via French < Latin *cartilago*]

car·ti·lag·i·nous /kaárt'l ájjinəss/ *adj* **1.** resembling, made of, or relating to cartilage **2.** having a skeleton composed mostly of cartilage

car·ti·lag·i·nous fish *n* a fish with a skeleton made entirely of cartilage. Shark, rays, and ratfish are cartilaginous fish. Class: Chondrichthyes.

Cart·land /kaártlənd/, **Dame Barbara** (1901–2000) British novelist. She wrote more than 400 books, mostly popular romances. Born **Hamilton, Mary Barbara**

> "I'm the only author with 200 virgins in print"
> [Dame Barbara Cartland, *Town & Country*; December 1977]

cart·load /kaárt lòd/ *n* **1.** a very large amount (*informal*) **2.** the amount that a cart can carry

car·to·gram /kaártə gràm/ *n* a diagrammatic map showing the population and other statistics of a region [Late 19C. < French *cartogramme* < *carte* "map"]

car·to·graph·ic /kaártə gráffik/, **car·to·graph·i·cal** /-gráffik'l/ *adj* **1.** relating to maps ○ *cartographic design* **2.** in the form of a map ○ *cartographic representation* —**car·to·graph·i·cal·ly** *adv*

car·tog·ra·phy /kaar tóggrəfee/ *n* the science, skill, or work of making maps [Mid-19C. < French *cartographie* < *carte* "map"] —**car·tog·ra·pher** *n*

car·to·man·cy /kaártə mànssee/ *n* fortune-telling by using playing cards [Late 19C. < French *cartomancie* < *carte* (see CARD[1])]

car·ton /kaárt'n/ *n* **1.** CARDBOARD BOX a cardboard box in which something such as merchandise, movable property, or mail is packaged **2.** PLASTIC OR CARDBOARD CONTAINER a container made of plastic or waxed cardboard in which food or drink is sold **3.** CONTENTS OF CONTAINER the contents of a carton ○ *drank a whole carton of orange juice* ■ *vt* (**-toned, -ton·ing, -tons**) PUT SOMETHING IN CARTON to put something in a carton ○ *Most of our milk is sold cartoned.* [Early 19C. Via French < Italian *cartone* (see CARTOON)]

car·toon /kaar toón/ *n* **1.** ANIMATED MOVIE a movie made using animation instead of live actors, especially a humorous film intended primarily for children **2.** SEQUENCE OF DRAWINGS a sequence of drawings that tell a short story, published in a newspaper or magazine **3.** SATIRICAL DRAWING a humorous drawing published in a newspaper or magazine and commenting on a topical event or theme **4.** HUMOROUS DRAWING a humorous drawing published in a newspaper or magazine, intended to entertain and often accompanied by a caption **5.** PREPARATORY DRAWING a drawing done, often in great detail, as a preliminary version of a painting or other work of art [Late 16C. Via Italian *cartone* "pasteboard" (on which artists' preparatory drawings were made) < Latin *c(h)arta* (see CARD[1])] —**car·toon·ist** *n* —**car·toon·y** *adj*

car·toon·ish /kaar toónish/, **car·toon·y** /kaar toónee/ *adj* resembling a humorous or animated cartoon —**car·toon·ish·ly** *adv*

car·top /kaár tòp/ *adj* attached to or designed to be carried on a car's roof

car·toph·i·ly /kaar tóffəlee/ *n* the collecting of cigarette cards as a hobby [Mid-20C. < French *carte* "card" or Italian *carta*] —**car·toph·i·list** *n*

cartouche: gold signet ring with cartouche of Tutankhamen

car·touche /kaar toósh/ *n* **1.** CASING FOR GUNPOWDER the paper casing of a firework or cartridge **2.** DECORATIVE PANEL a decorative panel in the form of a frame or unrolled scroll, sometimes containing writing, forming an artistic or architectural feature **3.** FRAME FOR NAME an oval or oblong shape containing writing, especially one containing a king's name in Egyptian hieroglyphics [Early 17C. Via French < Italian *cartoccio* "paper cornet" < *carta* "paper"]

car·tridge /kaártrij/ *n* **1.** CASING OF BULLET a cylindrical case holding an explosive charge and a bullet or shot, which is put into a gun **2.** CONTAINER WITH HIGH EXPLOSIVES a container used in blasting that contains high explosives **3.** CONTAINER FOR LIQUID OR POWDER a container for liquid or powder that is loaded into a device, e.g., a removable ink container for a pen or printer ○ *toner cartridges* **4.** CASE FOR LOADING SOMETHING INTO MACHINE a sealed plastic case containing something such as photographic film, a cassette, or a set of computer disks that can be loaded into an appropriate device **5.** PART OF HI-FI TONE ARM the part of the arm of a record player that holds the needle [Late 16C. Anglicization of French *cartouche* (see CARTOUCHE)]

car·tridge belt *n* a belt that holds gun cartridges or cartridge clips

car·tridge case *n* the casing of a gun cartridge

car·tridge clip *n* a container for bullets, loaded directly into an automatic weapon

car·tridge pen *n* a pen that holds a replaceable ink cartridge

cart track *n UK* a rough track or narrow unsurfaced road used by farm vehicles

car·tu·lar·y /kaárchə lèrree/ (*plural* **-ies**) *n* **1.** a collection of official records, especially those relating to a large estate or a religious community **2.** a room or building where official records are kept [Mid-16C. < medieval Latin *c(h)artularium* < Latin *c(h)artula* "document" < *c(h)arta* (see CARD[1])]

cart·wheel /kaárt weél, -hweél/ *n* **1.** ACROBATIC MOVEMENT an acrobatic movement in which the body is turned sideways onto the hands, then over onto the feet again **2.** *UK* WOODEN WHEEL OF CART a large wooden spoked wheel for a cart **3.** LARGE COIN a large coin, especially a silver dollar (*dated*) ■ *vi* (**-wheeled, -wheel·ing, -wheels**) DO CARTWHEEL to perform a cartwheel

cart·wright /kaárt rīt/ *n* somebody who makes carts

Cart·wright /kaárt rīt/, **Edmund** (1743–1823) British inventor and cleric. He is credited with the invention of the power loom for cotton-spinning (1785).

Cart·wright, John (1740–1824) British politician and reformer. He campaigned for the abolition of slavery and against British taxation in North America.

> "One man shall have one vote."
> [John Cartwright, *People's Barrier Against Undue Influence*; 1780]

Cart·wright, Peter (1785–1872) US Methodist Episcopal cleric. He delivered lively sermons throughout the Midwest.

ca·run·cle /kə rúngk'l/ *n* **1.** a fleshy growth on the head or body, e.g., a rooster's comb **2.** a colored outgrowth of tissue in some types of seeds near the point of attachment to the plant [Late 16C. Via obsolete French < Latin *caruncula* "small piece of flesh" < *caro* "flesh"] —**ca·run·cu·lar** /kə rúngkyələr/ *adj* —**ca·run·cu·late** /-lət, -làyt/ *adj* —**ca·run·cu·lat·ed** *adj* —**ca·run·cu·lous** *adj*

Ca·ru·so /kə roōssō/, **Enrico** (1873–1921) Italian operatic tenor. A powerful singer and actor, he specialized in the operas of Verdi and Puccini.

car·va·crol /kaárvə kròl/ *n* an oily liquid with the smell of mint. Source: savory, oregano, thyme. Use: in flavorings, perfumes, as a disinfectant. [Mid-19C. < modern Latin *(Carum) carvi* "caraway" + Latin *acris* "sharp"]

carve /kaarv/ (**carved, carv·ing, carves**) *v* **1.** *vti* MAKE SOMETHING BY CUTTING AND SHAPING to make an object or design by cutting and shaping a hard material such as wood or stone ○ *statues carved from marble* ○ *I remembered carving her name on a tree, years ago.* **2.** *vt* CUT SUBSTANCE TO MAKE SOMETHING to cut and shape a material such as wood or stone in order to make an object or design **3.** *vti* CUT MEAT to cut cooked meat into slices **4.** *vt* MAKE SHAPE BY NATURAL FORCE to make a shape by an eroding action ○ *dunes carved into strange shapes by the wind* [Old English *ceorfan* < Germanic, "to scratch"]
carve out *vt* to make or achieve something through sustained hard work ○ *She carved out a niche for herself in the world of investigative journalism.*
carve up *vt* **1.** to divide something, or ownership of something, into rough or crude parts (*informal*) ○ *Their intention was to invade and carve up the kingdom among themselves.* **2.** to wound somebody with a blade (*slang*)

car·vel *n* NAUT same as **caravel**

car·vel-built /kaárv'l-, -vel-/ *adj* describes a boat or ship made of planks of wood with their edges flush, not overlapping

carv·en /kaárvən/ *adj* carved (*archaic or literary*) ○ *thrones of carven onyx* ○ *Let the decree be carven in stone.* [14C. Old past participle of CARVE]

carv·er /kaárvər/ *n* **1.** COOK same as **carving knife 2.** SOMEBODY WHO CARVES somebody who carves meat **3.** DINING CHAIR WITH ARMS a dining chair with arms, designed to stand at the head of the table ■ **carv·ers** *npl* CARVING KNIFE AND FORK a large knife and fork for carving meat

Car·ver /kaárvər/, **George Washington** (1864–1943) US botanist. He was noted for his research into the industrial uses of the peanut, soybean, and sweet potato. He invented "Carver's hybrid" cotton.

> "When you can do the common things of life in an uncommon way you'll command the attention of the world."
> [George Washington Carver. Quoted in *World's Great Men of Color*, Joel Augustus Rogers; 1947]

carv·ing /kaárving/ *n* **1.** an object or design formed by cutting and shaping a material such as wood or stone ○ *The walls were covered with carvings depicting gods and heroes.* **2.** the work or act of carving something ○ *The carving of the panels was exquisite.*

carv·ing knife *n* a large knife for slicing meat

car wash *n* **1.** a business establishment where motor vehicles are washed automatically by machine or can be washed manually **2.** a shed or structure for washing motor vehicles automatically with revolving brushes and jets of water

Car·y /kérree, kárree/, **Joyce** (1888–1957) Irish-born British novelist. His bittersweet humor characterizes such works as *The Horse's Mouth* (1944). Full name **Cary, Arthur Joyce Lunel**

> "It is the misfortune of an old man that though he can put things out of his head he can't put them out of his feelings."
> [Joyce Cary, *To be a Pilgrim*; 1942]

caryatid

car·y·at·id /kàrree áttid, kárree ə tìd/ (*plural* **-ids** or **-i·des** /-i deèz/) *n* a column in the shape of a draped female figure supporting a structure such as the frieze or porch of a classical Greek temple [Mid-16C. Via Latin < Greek *karuatides* "maidens of Karuai" (Caryae, Greece), priestesses of Artemis] —**car·y·at·i·dal** *adj* —**car·y·at·i·de·an** /kàrree ati deè ən, -ə tíddee ən/ *adj* —**car·y·a·tid·ic** /kàrree ə tíddik/ *adj*

car·y·op·sis /kàrree ópsiss/ (*plural* **-op·ses** /-óp seèz/ or **-op·si·des** /-si deèz/) *n* a dry fruit that looks like a seed, borne by grasses and cereal crops such as wheat [Early 19C. < modern Latin < Greek *karuon* "nut" + *opsis* "appearance"]

CAS *abbr* EDUC Certificate of Advanced Study

CASA *abbr* LAW Court-Appointed Special Advocate

ca·sa·ba /kə saábə/ *n* a winter melon, similar to the honeydew and cantaloupe, with whitish flesh. Latin name: *Cucumis melo* var. inodorus. [Late 19C. After *Kasaba* (now Turgutlu), Turkey]

Cas·a·blan·ca /kàssə blángkə, kaàssə blaángkə/ largest city and chief port in Morocco. It is situated on the Atlantic coast, about 50 mi./80 km southwest of Rabat. Population: 2,940,623 (1994). Arabic name **Dar el-Beida**

Ca·sa Gran·de /kaàssə graándee, -graán day, kàssə grándee/ city in southern Arizona, south of Mesa, near the Santa Cruz River. Population: 28,697 (2002 estimate).

Ca·sals /kə sálz/, **Pablo** (1876–1973) Spanish cellist and composer. He was widely regarded as the greatest cellist of his generation.

> "The most perfect technique is that which is not noticed at all."
> [Pablo Casals. Quoted in *The Song of the Birds*, Julian Lloyd Webber (ed.); 1985]

Cas·a·no·va /kàssə nṓvə/ *n* a charming seducer of women who moves quickly from one casual relationship to another or who constantly pesters women in his pursuits [Early 20C. After Giovanni Jacopo CASANOVA]

Ca·sa·no·va /kàssə nṓvə/, **Giovanni Giacomo, Chevalier de Seingalt** (1725–98) Italian adventurer and author. He was a soldier, diplomat, and spy whose amorous reputation rests on his posthumously published 12-volume *History of My Life* (1826–38).

Ca·sas ♦ **Las Casas, Bartolomé de**

cas·bah /káz baà/, **kas·bah** *n* **1.** in North Africa, a fortress or palace **2.** in North Africa, the older part of a city or town, often the market area [Mid-18C. Via French < Arabic *qaṣbah* "fortress"]

cas·cade /ka skáyd/ *n* **1.** WATERFALL a small waterfall or series of waterfalls **2.** DOWNWARD FLOW OF SOMETHING a fast downward flow of liquid or small objects **3.** HANGING MASS a flowing mass of something that hangs down or lies along a surface ○ *The bride carried a cascade of roses and baby's breath.* **4.** SCI SUCCESSION a succession of things such as chemical reactions or components in an electrical circuit, each of which activates, affects, or determines the next ■ *v* (**-cad·ed, -cad·ing, -cades**) **1.** *vti* FLOW to flow fast and in large amounts, or cause something to flow in this way **2.** *vi* HANG OR LIE to hang or lie in a flowing mass ○ *Flowering plants cascaded down the fronts of the buildings.* **3.** *vt* COMPUT OVERLAP WINDOWS ON COMPUTER SCREEN to arrange the windows on a computer screen so that they overlap, with the title bar of each visible **4.** *vi* MOVE ON TO NEXT THING to move on to others in succession ○ *If it is not claimed, the jackpot will cascade down to the holder of the next numbers drawn.* **5.** *vt* PASS INFORMATION ON TO OTHERS to pass on something, especially something that has been learned, to other people in succession ○ *Trained helpers can then cascade their knowledge to larger groups.* [Mid-17C. Via French < Italian *cascata* < Latin *cadere* "to fall"]

Cas·cade Range /ka skáyd-/ range of mountains in the western United States, forming the northern continuation of the Sierra Nevada range. Its highest peak is Mount Rainier, 14,410 ft./4,392 m. Length: 700 mi./1,127 km.

cas·cad·ing men·u *n* a menu in a computer program that opens when a choice is selected from another menu

cas·car·a /ka skárrə/ *n* **1.** *also* **cas·car·a buck·thorn** a bush or small tree from whose dried bark a strong laxative was formerly made. Native to: northwestern United States. Latin name: *Rhamnus purshiana.* **2.** formerly, a strong laxative made from the dried bark of a North American bush or small tree [Late 19C. Shortening of CASCARA SAGRADA]

cas·car·a sa·gra·da /-sə graádə/ *n* the dried bark of the cascara tree. Use: formerly, as a strong laxative. [< Spanish *cáscara sagrada* "sacred bark"]

case[1] /kayss/ *n* **1.** SITUATION a situation or set of circumstances ○ *I don't think the usual rules apply in this case.* ○ *Sometimes anxiety causes weight loss, but that's not the case here.* **2.** INSTANCE an instance or example of something ○ *This seems to be a case of mistaken identity.* **3.** SOMETHING EXAMINED OR INVESTIGATED a subject of investigation or scrutiny by a professional person such as a doctor or police officer **4.** ACTUAL FACT the reality or truth of a particular situation ○ *The case is that the witness has lied under oath.* **5.** ISSUE a matter in question or a problem ○ *The case here is simply a matter of excessive expenditures, isn't it?* **6.** LAW SOMETHING EXAMINED IN LAW COURT a matter examined or judged in a court of law ○ *It'll be some weeks before your case comes to trial.* **7.** LAW ARGUMENTS a set of arguments and evidence supporting a legal claim in court ○ *He presented his case calmly and with skill.* **8.** ARGUMENT FOR OR AGAINST an argument for or against something ○ *You can make a good case for holding a referendum.* **9.** GRAM GRAMMATICAL FORM OF WORD a form of a noun, pronoun, or adjective that indicates its syntactic relation to surrounding words **10.** TYPE OF PERSON somebody of a particular type or in a particular condition, especially an unfortunate one (*informal*) ○ *He's a hopeless case.* **11.** ODD PERSON an odd or eccentric person (*informal*) ■ *vt* (**cased, cas·ing, cas·es**) INSPECT PLACE to assess or survey a place with a view to robbing it (*slang*) [13C. Via Old French *cas* "event" < Latin *casus* < *cadere* "to fall"] ◇ **a case in point** a relevant example ○ *A case in point is the steady drop in unit sales.* ◇ **be on somebody's case** to persist in pestering somebody to do something (*slang*) ◇ **get off somebody's case** to stop pestering somebody to do something (*slang*) ○ *Get off my case! I'll finish mowing the lawn later.* ◇ **in any case 1.** no matter what may happen ○ *Come over if you want, I'll be home in any case.* **2.** used to support a point that has just been mentioned ○ *Maybe he just got bored. In any case, he left rather early.* ◇ **in case of something** if something happens ○ *In case of fire, leave by the nearest exit.* ◇ **(just) in case 1.** in preparation for an event that may possibly happen ○ *Take your umbrella, just in case.* **2.** used to introduce a piece of information and explain the reason for giving it ○ *In case you're unaware of the fact, this is a nonsmoking area.*

case² /kayss/ *n* **1. HOLDER OR OUTER COVERING** something that serves as a container or covering **2. CONTAINER** a container with its contents ○ *bought a case of soft drinks* **3. PIECE OF BAGGAGE** an item of baggage, especially a suitcase **4.** PRINTING **KIND OF PRINTED CHARACTER** one of the two kinds of printed character, either a capital or small letter **5.** PRINTING **TRAY HOLDING PRINTING TYPE** in hot-metal printing, a tray with compartments in which individual printing blocks are kept **6. PAIR** a pair, especially of pistols **7.** CIV ENG same as **casing** (sense 3) ■ *vt* (**cased, cas·ing, cas·es**) **PUT COVERING AROUND SOMETHING** to enclose something in a covering [13C. Via Old French dialect *casse* < Latin *capsa* "box" < *capere* "to hold"]

CASE /kayss/ *abbr* COMPUT **1.** computer-aided software engineering **2.** computer-aided systems engineering

ca·se·ase /káyssee àyss, -àyz/ *n* a bacterial enzyme that aids the breakdown of casein [20C. < CASEIN]

ca·se·ate /káyssee àyt/ (**-at·ed, -at·ing, -ates**) *vi* to undergo caseation [Late 19C. Back-formation < CASEATION] —**ca·se·ous** *adj*

ca·se·a·tion /kàyssee áysh'n/ *n* the process by which dead tissue decays into a firm and dry mass, characteristic of tuberculosis [Mid-19C. < medieval Latin *caseation-* < Latin *caseus* "cheese"]

case·book /káyss bòòk/ *n* **1.** a record of legal or medical cases and their conduct **2.** a collection of academic writings on a subject

cased glass /káyst-/, **case glass** *n* decorative glass consisting of several colored layers with some areas cut away in different patterns

case goods *npl* **1. MERCHANDISE SOLD IN BULK** merchandise often sold in multiple packs, e.g., beer or fruit juice **2. BOX-SHAPED FURNITURE** types of furniture that have a box-shaped structure and provide storage space, e.g., bureaus **3. FURNITURE SOLD AS SETS** bedroom or dining-room furniture that is sold as sets

case gram·mar *n* a system of grammar that analyzes sentences in terms of the semantic relation of the noun or noun phrase and other sentence components to the main verb

case·hard·en /káyss haàrd'n/ (**-ened, -en·ing, -ens**) *vt* **1.** to harden the surface of an iron alloy by heating and then cooling in water **2.** to make somebody unsympathetic or unfeeling as a result of extended involvement in dealing with difficult and distressing problems

case his·to·ry *n* **1.** a record of somebody's medical or social history kept by a doctor or social worker **2.** a record of how an issue or problem has been dealt with, consulted as a guide to how to handle it or similar events in the future ○ *He researched the case histories of earlier attempts at farming on that river.*

ca·sein /káy seen, káyssee in/ *n* one of a group of proteins found in milk. Use: in plastics, adhesives, and paints. [Mid-19C. < Latin *caseus* "cheese"]

ca·sein·ate /kay seé nàyt, káyssee ə-/ *n* a compound of casein and calcium or sodium

ca·sein·o·gen /kay seenəjən, kàyssee ínnəjən/ *n* the main protein in milk, from which casein is formed

case knife *n* **1.** same as **table knife 2.** same as **sheath knife** (*archaic*)

case law *n* law established on the basis of previous verdicts

case·load /káyss lōd/ *n* the number of cases to be dealt with during a specific period by a professional such as a doctor or a lawyer

case·mate /káyss màyt/ *n* a fortified compartment on an old sailing ship, or a rampart where a cannon was mounted [Mid-16C. Directly or via French < Italian *casamatta*]

case·ment /káyssmənt/ *n* a window that opens on hinges located at one side, as distinct from one that slides up and down [15C. Via Anglo-Latin *cassimentum* < Latin *capsa* (see CASE²)]

ca·se·ose /káyssee ōss/ *n* a chemical produced in the digestion of cheese [20C. < Latin *caseus* "cheese"]

ca·sern /kə zúrn/, **ca·serne** *n* a barracks, especially a temporary one [Late 17C. Via French *caserne* < Latin *quaterna* "hut for four"]

casement

case shot *n* formerly, a type of cannon shell containing shrapnel

case stat·ed *n* an outline of the circumstances of a legal case prepared by one court for another court to use in making its decision, e.g., in an appeal hearing or a retrial

case stud·y *n* **1.** an analysis of a particular case or situation used as a basis for drawing conclusions in similar situations **2.** a record of somebody's problems and how they were dealt with, especially by a doctor or social worker

case sys·tem *n* the teaching of law through the study of important and representative cases rather than by studying theory

cas·e·vac /kázzə vàk/, **CASEVAC** *n* the removal, by motor vehicle or aircraft, of wounded or otherwise injured military personnel from a theater of operations or from a training site, and their transport to a hospital for treatment ■ *vt* (**-vacked, -vack·ing, -vacs**) MIL, MED to transport wounded or injured military personnel from a theater of operations or from a training site to a hospital for treatment [Late 20C. Blend of CASUALTY + EVACUATION]

case·work /káyss wùrk/ *n* a system in which a social worker is made responsible for particular clients on a long-term basis —**case·work·er** *n*

case·worm /káyss wùrm/ *n* INSECTS same as **caddis worm** [Early 17C. < the protective case it builds around itself]

cash¹ /kash/ *n* **1. COINS AND BILLS** money in the form of coins or bills as distinct from money orders or credit **2. CURRENCY OR CHECKS** money used as immediate payment in any form, e.g., currency or checks (*informal*) ○ *earn some cash* ■ *vt* (**cashed, cash·ing, cash·es**) **EXCHANGE SOMETHING FOR CURRENCY** to exchange a check or money order for coins or bills ○ *You can cash your paycheck at the bank.* [Late 16C. Directly or via obsolete French *casse* < Italian *cassa* "money box" < Latin *capsa* (see CASE²)] —**cash·a·ble** *adj* ◇ **cash on the barrelhead** *or* **barrel** money paid at the time something is purchased ○ *I paid $14, cash on the barrelhead, for the whole lot.*

SPELLCHECK See *cache.*

cash in *v* **1.** *vt* to withdraw from a business investment such as an insurance policy and take the money that is due **2.** *vi* to make large amounts of money (*slang*) ○ *When the stock was sold, she really cashed in.*

cash in on *vt* to exploit a situation in order to get personal benefit, especially money ○ *Everyone who knew him wanted to cash in on his rise to fame.*

cash out *v* **1.** *vti* **SELL ASSET TO PROFIT** to sell off an asset such as land that has been held for a long time in order to make a profit **2.** *vi* COMM **ADD UP DAY'S TAKINGS** to add up the day's takings of a store or similar business **3.** *vi* **COMMIT SUICIDE** to commit suicide (*slang*)

cash up *vi UK* same as **cash out**

cash² /kash/ (*plural same*) *n* formerly, a coin of low value in China and some South Asian countries [Late 16C. Via Portuguese *caixa* < Tamil *kāču*]

Cash /kash/, **Pat** (*b.* 1965) Australian tennis player. He won the Wimbledon men's singles championship in 1987. Full name **Cash, Patrick Hart**

"If the ball is there, hit it."
[Pat Cash, *The Sunday Times (London)*; July 5, 1987]

CASH /kash/ *n* a military field hospital (*informal*) Full form **Combat Support Hospital**

cash-and-car·ry *n* (*plural* **cash-and-car·ries**) **1. INEXPENSIVE STORE** a store selling inexpensive goods that are paid for in cash and taken away by the buyer **2. POLICY OF SELLING WITHOUT DELIVERY SERVICE** a policy of selling items for cash with no delivery service to customers ■ *adj* **CASH-ONLY AND WITHOUT DELIVERY** sold or operating on a basis of cash-only payments by buyers who take their goods away at the time of purchase

cash bar *n* a bar at a large party or reception at which drinks have to be paid for individually

cash·book /kásh bòòk/ *n* a book for keeping a record of money spent and received

cash box *n* a lockable box for cash, especially one holding the daily takings of a small business

cash card *n* a coded plastic card that a bank customer uses to access an account by means of an ATM

cash cow *n* a profitable business or product with low overhead, often used to fund other businesses or investments (*slang*)

cash crop *n* a crop grown for direct sale, and not for personal consumption

cash dis·pens·er *n UK* BANKING same as **ATM**

cash·ew /ká shòò, kə shóò/ *n* **1.** *also* **cash·ew nut** a kidney-shaped nut that is edible when roasted **2.** an evergreen tree that produces cashew nuts and oil. Native to: South America. Latin name: *Anacardium occidentale.* [Late 16C. Via Portuguese < Tupi *acajú*]

cash·ew ap·ple *n* the edible swollen stalk by which a cashew nut is attached to its stem. Use: preserves.

cash flow *n* **1.** the pattern of income and expenses, and its consequences for how much money is available at a given time **2.** the prediction or assessment of a company's income and expenditure over a period of time

cash·ier¹ /ka sheér/ *n* **1. WORKER TAKING AND PAYING MONEY** somebody who works in a store or bank and handles customers' money transactions **2. SOMEBODY RESPONSIBLE FOR FINANCIAL TRANSACTIONS** an official in an organization who is responsible for receiving and paying out money and keeping financial records ■ *vi* (**-iered, -ier·ing, -iers**) **BE CASHIER** to work as a cashier, especially in a place of business such as a restaurant or bar [Late 16C. Directly or via Dutch *cassier* < French *caissier* < *casse* (see CASH¹)]

ca·shier² /ka sheér/ (**-shiered, -shier·ing, -shiers**) *vt* to dismiss somebody from the armed forces because of misconduct [Early 16C. Via Dutch *kasseren* "disband (soldiers)" < French *casser* "to break" < Latin *quassare* (see QUASH²)]

cash·ier's check *n* a guaranteed check issued by a bank against money taken from a customer's account or against cash provided for this purpose

cash·less /káshləss/ *adj* using an electronic means of exchanging money instead of dealing in cash

cash ma·chine *n* BANKING same as **ATM**

cash·mere /kázh meer, kásh-/ *n* **1.** the soft wool from a Himalayan goat **2.** a woolen fabric made from cashmere [Late 17C. Early spelling of KASHMIR]

cash meth·od *n* a method of accounting that counts income or expenses at the time they are actually received or paid out, irrespective of when they are earned or incurred

cash on de·liv·er·y *adv* with full payment for ordered merchandise to be made by the buyer to the person delivering the goods ○ *bought the coat cash on delivery*

cash·point /kásh pòynt/ *n UK* same as **ATM**

cash-poor *adj* financially sound but having little readily available cash

cash ra·tio *n* the ratio that a bank must maintain between available cash and total deposits

cash reg·is·ter *n* a machine in a store that records sales, calculates totals, and has a drawer for money

cash-starved *adj* having very little money or financial support

cash-strapped *adj* having insufficient money (*informal*)

Cas·i·mir III /kázzi meer/, **King of Poland** (1309–70) His reign (1333–70) as the "Peasants' King" saw the introduction of fairer laws and peace through diplomacy. He founded Kraków University (1364). Known as **Casimir the Great**

Cas·i·mir force, Cas·i·mir ef·fect *n* a small electrostatic force between a pair of conductors in a vacuum [After Hendrick *Casimir* (1909–2000), Dutch physicist]

cas·ing /káyssing/ *n* **1.** OUTER COVERING an outer covering, e.g., the sheath of an electrical cable or the skin of a sausage **2.** FRAME FOR DOOR OR WINDOW a frame containing a door, window, or stairway **3.** LINER PIPE IN WELL a liner pipe or tube in a water, oil, or gas well

ca·si·no /kə seénō/ (*plural* **-nos**) *n* **1.** a private club, or a room in a club, hotel, or other establishment, where gambling takes place **2.** *also* **cas·si·no** a point-scoring card game in which players combine cards exposed on the table with cards in their hands, with the 10 of diamonds being the highest-valued card [Mid-18C. < Italian, "small house" < Latin *casa* "house"]

ca·si·no so·ci·e·ty *n* a society in which large amounts of money are used and gained in business ventures by a small number of people and organizations while the broad public interest is neglected

cask /kask/ *n* **1.** BARREL CONTAINING ALCOHOL a wooden barrel containing alcoholic drink **2.** CONTAINER LIKE BARREL a container resembling a barrel, whether or not of wood **3.** CONTENTS OF BARREL the contents of a barrel or similar container **4.** INDUST same as **flask** (sense 6) [Early 16C. Directly or via French *casque* < Spanish *casco* "helmet, skull" < Latin *quassare* (see QUASH[2])]

cas·ket /káskət/ *n* **1.** same as **coffin** **2.** a decorative box for valuables [15C. Origin ?]

Cas·par·ian strip /ka spérree ən strìp/ *n* a thin impervious band of material in the cell walls of some plants resembling suberin or lignin [After Robert *Caspary*, 19C German botanist]

Cas·per /káspər/ city in east central Wyoming, on the northern bank of the North Platte river. Population: 50,024 (2002 estimate).

Cas·pi·an Sea /kàspee ən-/ large landlocked salt lake lying between southeastern Europe and Asia. It is the world's largest inland body of water. Area: 143,000 sq. mi./371,000 sq. km.

casque /kask/ *n* **1.** a helmet from a suit of armor **2.** a horny growth on the head of a bird, fish, or reptile, resembling a helmet [Late 17C. < French (see CASK)] —**casqued** *adj*

Cass /kass/, **Lewis** (1782–1866) US politician. He was secretary of war (1831–36) during the Seminole and Black Hawk wars and ran unsuccessfully for US president (1848).

Cas·san·dra /kə sándrə/ *n* somebody whose warnings of impending disaster are ignored [Early 17C. After *Cassandra*, daughter of Priam, king of Troy, who was granted the gift of prophecy but was condemned never to be believed]

cas·sa·ta /kə saátə/ *n* **1.** a brightly colored Italian ice cream containing nuts, candied fruit and layers or streaks of different flavors **2.** a Sicilian sponge cake, layered and coated with sweetened ricotta, flavored with candied fruit and chopped chocolate, and eaten as a celebration cake or dessert [Early 20C. < Italian]

cas·sa·tion /kə sáysh'n, ka-/ *n* **1.** a court of appeal in countries that follow the Napoleonic code of civil law **2.** an 18th-century instrumental work similar in form to a divertimento [15C. < Latin *cassat-*, past participle of *cassare* "annul"]

Cas·satt /kə sát/, **Mary** (1845–1926) US artist. She is known for intimate impressionist portraits of mothers with their children, e.g., *The Bath* (1891).

cas·sa·va /kə saávə/ *n* **1.** a large thick-skinned tuber that is poisonous when raw and untreated but like the potato when boiled. Use: as a vegetable in many tropical countries, as a source of tapioca. **2.** a tropical plant that produces cassava. Latin name: *Manihot esculenta*. [Mid-16C. < Taino *casávi*]

Cas·se·grain·ian tel·e·scope /kassə gràynee ən-/ *n* an astronomical telescope that uses a large concave mirror and a small convex mirror to form an image [Late 19C. After Giovanni *Cassegrain* (1625–1712), French astronomer]

Cas·sel ♦ **Kassel**

cas·se·role /kássə rōl/ *n* **1.** COOKING POT a deep heavy cooking pot suitable for use in an oven **2.** COOKED DISH a stew or other moist food dish, cooked slowly at a low heat in a covered pot or dish **3.** LABORATORY CONTAINER a porcelain container used for heating substances in a laboratory ■ *vt* (**-roled, -rol·ing, -roles**) COOK FOOD IN LIQUID to cook food slowly at a low heat with liquid in a covered pot [Early 18C. < French, "small pan" < *casse* "pan" < Greek *kuathos* "cup"]

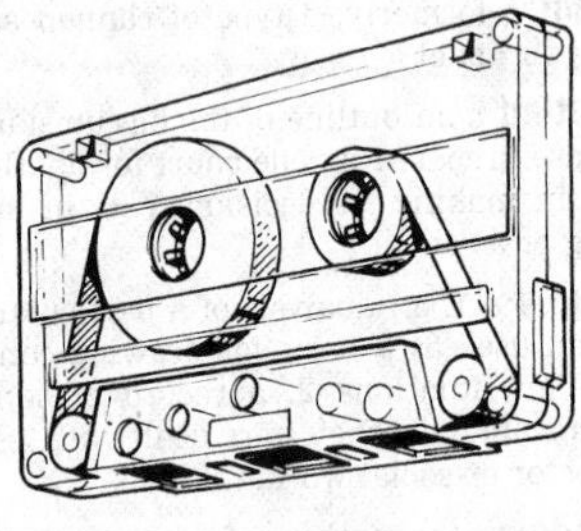

cassette

cas·sette /kə sét/ *n* **1.** a sealed plastic case containing a length of audiotape or videotape wound around spools ready for use **2.** a sealed plastic case containing a supply of something such as ink for insertion into a machine such as a printer [Late 18C. < French, "small box" < *casse* (see CASH[1])]

cas·sette deck *n* a tape deck that plays or records audio cassettes

cas·sette play·er *n* a machine that plays cassettes, but does not record audio

cas·sette re·cord·er *n* a machine, especially a portable one, that plays and records audio cassettes

cas·sia /káshə/ *n* **1.** an evergreen Asian tree with an aromatic bark. Latin name: *Cinnamomum aromaticum*. **2.** the bark of the cassia tree [Pre-12C. Via Latin < Hebrew *qĕṣī'āh*]

Cas·si·ni di·vi·sion /kə seénee-, kaa-/, **Cas·si·ni's di·vi·sion** *n* the dark area between the two brightest rings, the middle and outermost, of Saturn [Early 20C. After Giovanni Domenico *Cassini* (1625–1712), Italian-born French astronomer]

cas·si·no *n* CARDS another spelling of **casino** (sense 2)

Cas·si·o·pe·ia /kàssee ə peé ə/ *n* a constellation of the northern hemisphere. See illustration at **constellation**

cas·sis /kə seéss, ka-/ *n* a syrupy, usually alcoholic, cordial made in France from black currants, often mixed with white wine to make kir [Late 19C. < French, "black currant," probably < Latin *cassia* (see CASSIA)]

cas·sit·er·ite /kə síttə rìt/ *n* a dark-colored mineral consisting of tin oxide. Use: source of tin. [Mid-19C. < Greek *kassiteros* "tin"]

Cas·sius /káshəss, kássee əss/ (*fl* 53–42 B.C.) Roman general and conspirator. A leader in the assassination of Julius Caesar (44 B.C.), he committed suicide when defeated by Mark Antony. Full name **Gaius Cassius Longinus**

cas·sock /kássək/ *n* a full-length, usually black robe worn by priests, their assistants, and singers in church choirs [Mid-16C. Via French *casaque* "long coat" < Italian *casacca* "riding coat"] —**cas·socked** *adj*

cas·so·ne /kə sōnee/ *n* a highly decorated Italian chest of the Middle Ages and the Renaissance period [Late 19C. < Italian < *cassa* (see CASH[1])]

cas·sou·let /kàssə láy/ *n* a French stew of white beans cooked in a casserole with meat [Mid-20C. < French, "small stew pan" < Greek *kuathos* "cup"]

cas·so·war·y /kássə wèrree/ (*plural* **-ies**) *n* a large black flightless bird, with colorful wattles and a large bony head shield, that resembles an ostrich or emu. Native to: northeastern Australia, New Guinea. Genus: *Casuarius*. [Early 17C. < Malay *kesuari*]

cast /kast/ *v* (**cast, cast·ing, casts**) **1.** *vt* THROW SOMEBODY OR SOMETHING to throw somebody or something, especially somebody or something that is light in weight ○ *casting pebbles into a river* **2.** *vt* CARRY SOMEBODY OR SOMETHING ASHORE to carry somebody or something to the seashore (*refers to the sea*) ○ *pieces of driftwood cast up by the incoming tide* **3.** *vt* FLING SOMETHING DOWN OR AWAY to throw something away from yourself, usually with force ○ *We cast pieces of bread onto the lake to attract fish.* **4.** *vt* FISHING THROW FISHING LINE INTO WATER to throw a line, baited hook, or fishing net into the water **5.** *vt* POL REGISTER VOTE to register or deposit a vote **6.** *vt* CAUSE SOMETHING TO APPEAR SOMEWHERE to make something such as light or shadow appear in a place ○ *The bulb cast an eerie green glow over everything.* **7.** *vt* HAVE DISPIRITING EFFECT to produce a dispiriting, sobering, or saddening effect on somebody or something ○ *Her mother's absence cast a shadow over the wedding plans.* **8.** *vt* CREATE MISTRUST to generate a sense of uncertainty, distrust, or suspicion about somebody or something ○ *an accident that has cast doubt over the project's future* **9.** *vt* DIRECT LOOK AT SOMEBODY OR SOMETHING to direct the eyes or a look toward somebody or something, often in a surreptitious, disapproving, or anxious manner ○ *casting a discreet glance at his watch* **10.** *vt* DISMISS SOMETHING FROM MIND to remove or banish something from the mind deliberately, decisively, and often with difficulty (*formal*) **11.** *vt* PUT SOMEBODY SOMEWHERE ROUGHLY to put or throw somebody or something somewhere, especially in a rough or brutal way (*formal*) ○ *cast into the dungeon* **12.** *vti* ARTS SELECT PARTICIPANTS FOR PERFORMANCE to choose somebody for a particular role in a drama, dance, or other performance, or choose people for all the roles in a production ○ *He was badly cast as Othello.* **13.** *vt* DESCRIBE SOMEBODY AS SOMETHING to classify or describe somebody in a particular way ○ *I seem to have been cast as the villain in this affair.* **14.** *vt* MANUF FORM SOMETHING USING MOLD to pour something such as molten metal or plaster into a mold and allow it to solidify in order to create an object **15.** *vt* SHED SOMETHING to shed something such as the skin ○ *a snake that had cast its skin* **16.** *vt* DROP SOMETHING to drop or lose something ○ *a horse that had cast a shoe* **17.** *vt* ACCT CALCULATE SOMETHING to add something up or calculate something **18.** *vt* ASTROL PREDICT SOMEBODY'S FUTURE to predict somebody's future ■ *n* **1.** ACT OF THROWING the flinging, hurling, or throwing of something, or an instance of this **2.** LENGTH OF THROW the distance that something is thrown ○ *a 20-yard cast of a harpoon* **3.** ARTS PERFORMERS the actors or other performers in a drama, dance, or other production **4.** MANUF MOLDED OBJECT an object that is made by pouring a molten substance, especially metal, into a mold and leaving it to solidify so that it takes on the shape of the mold **5.** MANUF MOLD a container of a particular shape into which a molten substance, especially metal, is poured and left to solidify **6.** MED SUPPORT FOR BROKEN BONE a stiff plaster of Paris or fiberglass casing that holds a broken bone in place while it is healing ○ *He came back with his leg in a cast.* **7.** MANUF, ARTS MOLTEN IMPRESSION an impression formed by pressing soft or molten material over or inside something and letting it harden or dry ○ *a cast of the pianist's hands* **8.** GEOL, PALEONT PRESERVED SEDIMENT preserved sediment that results from an impression such as a footprint being filled in **9.** EMOTIONAL OR PSYCHOLOGICAL TYPE the nature or quality of somebody's character or mind ○ *a sly cast to his face* **10.** OPHTHALMOL same as **squint** **11.** OVERSPREADING OF ONE THING ONTO ANOTHER the overspreading of something, especially an added color, that results in modification of the hue or general appearance of something else **12.** TINGE a general suggestion of something such as a color ○ *The mud gave a brown cast to the water.* **13.** FISHING THROW OF LINE OR NET a throw of a fishing line or net into the water **14.** FISHING THROWN LINE OR NET a fishing line or net that is thrown into the water **15.** GAMBLING, LEISURE DICE THROW a throw of dice, or the number that has been thrown **16.** BIOL SOMETHING SHED BY ORGANISM a part of an organism that has been shed in a natural recurring process, e.g., an insect casing, a snake skin, or worm feces [12C. < Old Norse *kasta* "to throw"] —**cas·ta·bil·i·ty** /kàstə bíllətee/ *n* —**cast·a·ble** *adj*

SYNONYMS See ***throw***.

cast around *or* **about** *vi* to search for something or try to devise a solution to a problem
cast aside *vt* **1.** to reject and abandon somebody or something regarded as no longer interesting or useful ○ *You can't just cast him aside like that!* **2.** to abandon something such as a feeling or belief (*formal*) ○ *You must cast your doubts aside and trust in me.*
cast away *vt* to shipwreck somebody, especially on a desert island
cast off *v* **1.** *vt* **GET RID OF SOMEBODY OR SOMETHING** to reject or abandon somebody or something regarded as no longer useful or attractive ○ *I cast off that old coat years ago.* **2.** *vti* NAUT **UNTIE MOORING LINES** to untie the ropes securing a boat to its mooring so that it can move away **3.** *vti* HANDICRAFT **FINISH KNITTING** to make the last row of stitches in a piece of knitting by looping each stitch over the next and removing it from the needle **4.** *vti* PUBL **FIT TEXT** to calculate the amount of space a piece of text will take up when it has been typeset
cast on *vti* to make the first row of stitches in a piece of knitting
cast out *vt* to reject, abandon, or eject somebody or something (*formal*)

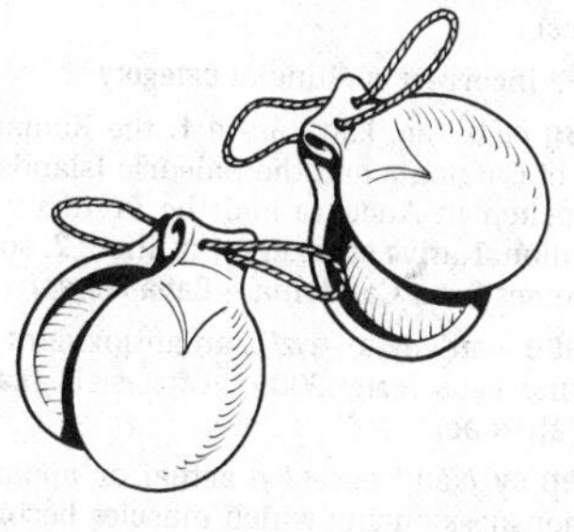
castanets

cas·ta·net /kàstə nét/ *n* either of a pair of small curved pieces of hard wood or plastic that are joined at the top and used to make a rhythmic clicking sound. They are held in the palm of the hand and tapped together, traditionally by Spanish flamenco dancers and musicians. [Early 17C. < Spanish *castañeta*, literally "small chestnut" < *castaña* "chestnut" < Latin *castanea*]

cast·a·way /kástə wày/ *n* the survivor of a shipwreck —**cast·a·way** *adj*

cast down *adj* experiencing feelings of dejection, depression, or sadness

caste /kast/ *n* **1. HINDU SOCIAL CLASS** one of the four main hereditary classes into which Hindu society is divided, dictating the social position and status of people according to their professions. Though discrimination based on caste has been illegal since 1947, it still occurs in some areas. **2. HINDU CLASS SYSTEM** the Hindu system of organizing society into hereditary classes **3. SOCIAL CLASS** the class and rank or position of somebody in a society, according to birth, occupation, or some other criterion **4.** INSECTS **RANK IN INSECT COLONY** a group of insects that has a specialized role in a colony or hive of social insects such as ants or bees [Mid-16C. < Spanish, Portuguese *casta* "pure race" < Latin *castus* "pure"]

Cas·tel Gan·dol·fo /kaas tel gaan dáwlfō, kàs tel gan-/ village in Rome province, Lazio Region, just south of Rome, Italy. It contains a palace that is the summer residence of the pope. Population: 7,930 (2001).

cas·tel·lan /kástələn/ *n* formerly, the governor or manager of a castle [14C. Via Old N French < medieval Latin *castellanus* < Latin *castellum* (see CASTLE)]

cas·tel·lat·ed /kástə làytəd/ *adj* **1.** ARCHIT **HAVING SERRATIONS ALONG TOP** having battlements or a serrated top edge like the walls of a castle **2. INDENTED OR SERRATED** having indented or serrated edges ○ *an ornate tablecloth with a castellated edge* **3. HAVING CASTLE NEARBY** having a castle as part of the surroundings or landscape (*literary*) ○ *the castellated French countryside* [Late 17C. < medieval Latin *castellatus* "having a castle" < Latin *castellum* (see CASTLE)]

Cas·tel·o Bran·co /kə stèllō bráŋgkō/, **Humberto** (1900–67) Brazilian soldier and national leader. He established a dictatorship and ruled Brazil from 1964 until his death.

caste mark *n* a mark, usually a painted dot on the forehead, that shows a Hindu person's caste

cast·er /kástər/ *n* **1. SOMEBODY WHO CASTS** somebody or something that casts something else **2.** *also* **cas·tor SMALL WHEEL UNDER FURNITURE** a small wheel on a mount that allows it to turn in all directions, attached under the corners of furniture and other heavy objects to make them easier to move **3.** *also* **cas·tor SMALL CONDIMENT CONTAINER** a small container with a perforated top or open mouth for sprinkling sugar, salt, or other condiments **4.** *also* **cas·tor CONDIMENT STAND** a small stand that holds condiment containers

cas·ter steer·ing *n* a type of steering found in horse-drawn vehicles, steam wagons, traction engines, and trailers, in which the whole front axle swivels around a central point

cas·ti·gate /kásti gàyt/ (**-gat·ed, -gat·ing, -gates**) *vt* to criticize or rebuke somebody or somebody's behavior severely (*formal; often passive*) ○ *They were strongly castigated for their refusal to act.* [Early 17C. < Latin *castigat-*, past participle of *castigare* "chastise" < *castus* "chaste"] —**cas·ti·ga·tion** /kàsti gáysh'n/ *n* —**cas·ti·ga·tor** *n* —**cas·ti·ga·tor·y** /kástigə tàwree/ *adj*

SYNONYMS See ***criticize.***

Cas·tile /kas teel/ central region of Spain that formed the core of the Kingdom of Castile, under which Spain was united in the 15th and 16th centuries

Cas·tile soap *n* hard white unperfumed soap made from olive oil and lye

Cas·til·ian /ka stíllyən/, **Cas·til·lian** *n* **1.** the standard form of Spanish, based on the dialect spoken in Castile, Spain **2.** somebody who comes from Castile, Spain —**Cas·til·ian** *adj*

Cas·til·la /kə stíllə/, **Ramón** (1797–1867) Peruvian army officer and politician. He was the president of Peru (1845–51 and 1855–62) and abolished slavery in his country.

cast·ing /kásting/ *n* **1. MAKING OF OBJECTS USING MOLDS** the making of a solid object by pouring molten metal, glass, or plastic into a mold and allowing it to cool **2.** MANUF, ARTS **OBJECT MADE WITH MOLD** an object made using a mold **3.** FISHING **THROW OF FISHING LINE** the throwing out of a fishing line or net **4. SOMETHING THROWN** something that is thrown out or thrown off **5.** ARTS **SELECTION PROCESS FOR PERFORMERS** the choosing of actors or other performers for a drama, dance, or other production, usually by audition, interview, or screen test **6.** ARTS **CHOICE OF PERFORMERS** the choice of actors or other performers for roles in a drama, dance, or other production, especially as seen as a feature of a particular production ○ *The script was very sharp but the casting was terrible.*

cast·ing couch *n* the granting of usually sexual favors in return for work in a film, television, or other production (*informal*)

cast·ing vote *n* the deciding vote in a ballot or debate, cast by the chairperson or presiding officer when votes for and against something are equally divided

cast i·ron *n* iron with a high carbon content, so that it is hard but brittle, and must be shaped by casting, rather than by hammering or beating

cast-i·ron *adj* **1.** METALL **OF CAST IRON** made from cast iron **2. VERY STRONG** extremely strong or resistant ○ *a politician with a cast-iron will* **3. ALLOWING NO CHANGE** not permitting any alteration of its terms ○ *a cast-iron agreement*

cas·tle /káss'l/ *n* **1. FORTRESS** a large fortified building or complex of buildings, usually with tall solid walls, battlements, and a permanent garrison, built especially during the Middle Ages **2. FORTIFIED HOUSE** especially in the 18th and 19th centuries, a large magnificent house built to resemble a fortified castle of the past **3. PRIVATE REFUGE** the building, property, or place to which somebody, especially the owner, turns for privacy or refuge **4.** CHESS same as **rook**[2] ■ *vti* (**-tled, -tling, -tles**) CHESS **MOVE KING AND ROOK** in chess, to move the king two squares to the left or right and move the nearest rook over the king to the adjacent square on the opposite side [Pre-12C. < Latin *castellum* "fortified village" < *castrum* "fortified place"] ◇ **build castles in the air** *or* **in Spain** to have dreams or plans that are extremely unlikely to be realized

Cas·tle /káss'l/, **Irene Foote** (1893–1969) US dancer. She and her husband, Vernon Castle, were innovators in ballroom dance.

> "The one big target for the crusaders was the tango. I suppose its opponents objected to the man bending the woman over backwards and peering into her eyes with a smoldering passionate look."
> [Irene Foote Castle, *Castles in the Air*, 1958]

cas·tled /káss'ld/ *adj* ARCHIT same as **castellated** (sense 1)

Cast·le Peak /kàss'l-/ **1.** mountain in the Sierra Nevada range, eastern Fresno County, central California. Height: 10,668 ft./3,252 m. **2.** mountain in Gunnison and Pitkin counties, central Colorado. Height: 14,265 ft./4,348 m. **3.** mountain in southwestern Custer County, central Idaho. Height: 14,265 ft./4,348 m.

Cas·tle·reagh /káss'l rày/ river in northern New South Wales, Australia, that rises in the Warrumbungle Range and joins the Macquarie River west of Walgett. Length: 342 mi./550 km.

Cas·tle·reagh, Robert Stewart, 2nd Marquis of Londonderry (1769–1822) Irish-born British government official and diplomat. As British foreign secretary (1812–22), he secured long-lasting European peace at the Congress of Vienna (1814–15).

cast net *n* a round or cone-shaped net thrown by anglers and withdrawn by means of lines attached to its opening

cast·off /kást àwf, -òf/ *n* **1.** somebody or something that has been rejected or abandoned because no longer considered useful or attractive (*often used in the plural*) ○ *I don't want your old castoffs!* **2.** a calculation of the length of a piece of text made before fitting copy into available space

cas·tor[1] /kástər/ *n* HOUSEHOLD, FURNITURE another spelling of **caster** (senses 2–4) [Late 17C. Alteration of CASTER; probably associated with CASTOR[2]]

cas·tor[2] /kástər/ *n* **1. BEAVER OIL** a brown oily aromatic substance secreted from glands in a beaver's groin. Use: in medicine and perfumes. **2. BEAVER FUR** the fur of a beaver **3. FUR HAT** a hat made of beaver fur or imitation beaver fur **4.** TEXTILES **HEAVY FABRIC** a heavy woolen cloth [14C. Via French or Latin < Greek *kastōr* "beaver"]

Cas·tor /kástər/ *n* the second brightest star in the constellation Gemini

Cas·tor and Pol·lux /-póllәks/ *npl* in Greek and Roman mythology, the twin sons of Leda and the brothers of Helen of Troy and Clytemnestra

cas·tor bean *n* **1.** PLANTS same as **castor-oil plant 2.** the poisonous seed of the castor-oil plant. Use: source of castor oil.

cas·tor oil *n* a thin yellowish oil obtained from the seeds of the castor-oil plant. Use: laxative, lubricant. [Origin ?]

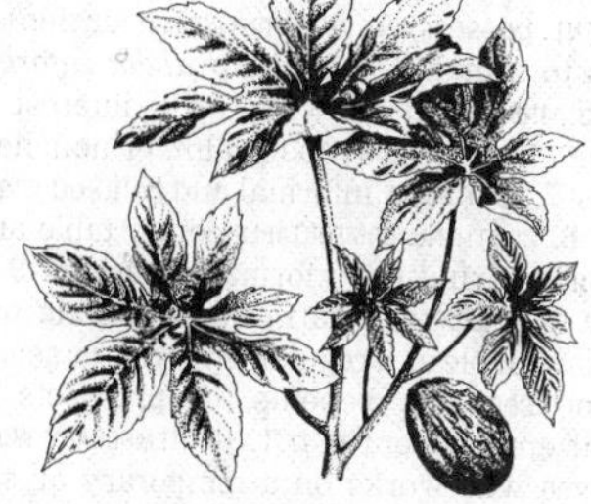
castor-oil plant

cas·tor-oil plant *n* a tall tropical plant with large lobed leaves that is cultivated for ornament and for its seeds, from which castor oil is produced. Native to: Africa. Latin name: *Ricinus communis.*

cas·tra·me·ta·tion /kàstrəmə táysh'n/ *n* the creation and laying out of a military encampment [Late 17C. < French *castramétation* < Latin *castra metari* "measure or mark out a camp"]

cas·trate /ká stràyt/ (**-trat·ed, -trat·ing, -trates**) *vt* **1.** to remove the testicles of a man or male animal, making reproduction impossible. Animals are sometimes castrated to make them more docile and to prevent disease. **2.** to take away the strength, power, force, or vigor of somebody or something ○ *The department was castrated through heavy budget cuts.* [15C. < Latin *castrat-*, past participle of *castrare* "cut off"] —**cas·trat·er** *n* —**cas·tra·tion** /ka stráysh'n/ *n*

cas·tra·tion com·plex *n* according to Freudian psychology, a subconscious fear in men of having their genitals removed as a punishment for wanting to have sexual intercourse with their mother

ca·stra·to /ka straátō, kə-/ (*plural* **-ti** /-tee/ or **-tos**) *n* in the past, a male singer who was castrated before puberty in order to retain a soprano or alto voice [Mid-18C. < Italian, "castrated one" < Latin *castrat-* (see CASTRATE)]

Cas·tries /kaás treéz, -treéss/ capital city of St. Lucia. Population: 60,934 (1998).

Cas·tro /kástrō/, **Cipriano** (1858–1924) Venezuelan national leader. He served as president after a coup until he himself was deposed (1899–1908).

Popperfoto

Fidel Castro

Cas·tro, Fidel (*b.* 1927) Cuban politician. He led the revolution that overthrew Fulgencio Batista and headed a Communist government as prime minister (1959–76), becoming president in 1976.

> "A revolution is not a bed of roses. A revolution is a struggle to the death between the future and the past."
> [Fidel Castro, *Speech, Havana*; January 1961]

Cas·tro·ism /kástrō ìzzəm/ *n* the Communist political, social, and economic policies of Fidel Castro and his supporters —**Cas·tro·ist** *n, adj* —**Cas·tro·ite** *n, adj*

Cas·tro Val·ley town in Alameda County, western California, situated north of Hayward. Population: 57,292 (2000).

ca·su·al /kázhoo əl/ *adj* **1. CHANCE OR UNPREMEDITATED** happening or done by chance or without prior thought or planning **2. KNOWN ONLY SLIGHTLY** known only slightly or involving only slight knowledge of somebody or something ○ *a casual acquaintance at work* **3. SUPERFICIAL** not involving emotional commitment or loyalty, or lacking in thoroughness or seriousness **4. LENIENT** possessing a permissive or lenient approach to things ○ *very casual about enforcing the rules* **5. INDIFFERENT** showing little interest or enthusiasm **6. NONCHALANT** cool, calm, or nonchalant in manner **7. NOT FORMAL** informal and relaxed ○ *a casual dinner* **8.** CLOTHING **COMFORTABLE** comfortable and suitable for wearing on informal occasions **9.** HR **OCCASIONAL OR TEMPORARY** relating to or taking on work that is available at irregular intervals or seasonally, with no security, benefits, or prospects of permanent employment ■ *n* **1.** HR **TEMPORARY WORKER** an employee who works on a temporary or seasonal basis **2.** MIL **SOLDIER ON TEMPORARY ASSIGNMENT** a soldier who is temporarily attached to a unit while waiting to be assigned to a permanent unit [14C. Directly or via French < Latin *casualis* < *casus* "event"] —**ca·su·al·ly** *adv* —**ca·su·al·ness** *n*

ca·su·al·ty /kázhoo altee/ (*plural* **-ties**) *n* **1. ACCIDENT VICTIM** somebody who has a fatal accident or receives a serious injury **2.** MIL **INJURED OR DEAD SOLDIER** a member of the armed forces who is killed or injured during combat **3. VICTIM** somebody or something destroyed or suffering as an indirect result of a particular event or circumstances [15C. Alteration of medieval Latin *casualitas* "chance" < *casualis* (see CASUAL)]

ca·su·al·wear /kázhoo əl wèr/ *n* comfortable clothes suitable for wearing on informal occasions

ca·su·a·ri·na /kàzhoo ə reénə, -rínə/ (*plural* **-nas** or *same*) *n* a tree with hard, durable wood and needle-shaped leaves that form whorls at the end of short branches. Native to: Australia, parts of Asia. Genus: *Casuarina*. [Late 18C. < modern Latin < *casuarius* "cassowary"; from the similarity of its branches to the bird's feathers]

ca·su·ist /kázhoo ist/ *n* **1.** somebody, especially a theologian, who tries to settle questions of ethics or morals by applying general rules and principles to them **2.** a subtle, sophisticated, and sometimes deceptive reasoner, especially on moral issues (*disapproving*) [Early 17C. Via French < modern Latin *casuista* < Latin *casus* "event"] —**ca·su·is·tic** /kàzhoo ístik/ *adj* —**ca·su·is·ti·cal** *adj* —**ca·su·is·ti·cal·ly** *adv*

ca·su·ist·ry /kázhoo istree/ *n* **1.** the application of general rules and principles to questions of ethics or morals in order to resolve them **2.** the use of subtle, sophisticated, and sometimes deceptive argument and reasoning, especially on moral issues, in order to justify something or mislead somebody (*disapproving*)

ca·sus bel·li /kàyssəss bélli, kaássəss bé lee/ (*plural same*) *n* a situation or event that causes, or is the pretext for starting, a war or other conflict (*formal*) [< modern Latin, "occasion of war"]

cat /kat/ *n* **1. FURRY ANIMAL THAT PURRS AND MEOWS** a small domesticated mammal that has soft fur, sharp claws, pointed ears, and, usually, a long furry tail, and makes characteristic purring or meowing sounds. Cats are widely kept as pets or to catch mice. Latin name: *Felis catus*. **2.** same as **big cat 3. OFFENSIVE TERM** an offensive term for a woman who is regarded as spiteful or malicious (*informal insult*) **4. MAN** a man (*dated slang*) ○ *He's a real cool cat.* **5.** NAUT **ANCHOR TACKLE OR CATHEAD** a set of heavy tackle used for raising an anchor to the cathead, or the cathead itself **6.** NAVY same as **cat-o'-nine-tails 7.** FISH same as **catfish 8.** same as **catamaran** (*informal*) **9.** same as **catboat** (*informal*) **10.** AUTOMOT same as **catalytic converter** (*informal*) **11.** same as **prostitute** *n* (sense 1) (*archaic*) ■ *v* (**cat·ted, cat·ting, cats**) **1.** *vt* NAUT **RAISE ANCHOR** to raise the anchor to the cathead **2.** *vi* **SEARCH FOR PARTNER** to travel around in search of a sexual partner (*slang*) [Old English *catt(e)* < Germanic] ◇ **has the cat got your tongue?** used to prompt somebody to speak or to ask the reason for his or her silence ◇ **let the cat out of the bag** to disclose secret or confidential information, usually accidentally ◇ **like a cat on a hot tin roof** *or* **hot bricks** extremely nervous or agitated ◇ **play cat and mouse with somebody** to treat somebody who is in your power in such a way that he or she does not know what you are going to do next ◇ **rain cats and dogs** to rain very heavily (*informal*) ◇ **when the cat's away the mice will play** when somebody in authority is absent, those he or she is in charge of will misbehave

CAT *abbr* **1.** AVIAT clear-air turbulence **2.** /kat/ FIN computer-aided trading **3.** /kat/ MED computerized axial tomography

cata- *prefix* **1.** down, apart ○ *catabolism* ○ *catalysis* **2.** against [< Greek *kata*]

ca·tab·o·lism /kə tábbə lìzzəm/, **ka·tab·o·lism** *n* the production of energy through the conversion of complex molecules into simpler ones [Late 19C. < Greek *katabolē* "throwing down" < *ballein* "to throw"] —**cat·a·bol·ic** /kàttə bóllik/ *adj* —**cat·a·bol·i·cal·ly** *adv*

ca·tab·o·lite /kə tábbə lìt/ *n* a product of catabolism, especially a waste product

cat·a·chre·sis /kàttə kreéssiss/ *n* the incorrect use of words, e.g., by mixing metaphors or applying terminology wrongly [Mid-16C. Via Latin < Greek *katakhrēsis* < *katakhrēsthai* "to misuse"] —**cat·a·chres·tic** /-kréstik/ *adj* —**cat·a·chres·ti·cal** *adj* —**cat·a·chres·ti·cal·ly** *adv*

cat·a·clysm /káttə klìzzəm/ *n* **1.** a sudden and violent upheaval or disaster that causes great changes in society **2.** a terrible and devastating natural disaster such as a flood [Early 17C. Via French < Greek *kataklusmos* "deluge" < *kluzein* "wash"] —**cat·a·clys·mal** /kàttə klízməl/ *adj* —**cat·a·clys·mic** *adj* —**cat·a·clys·mi·cal·ly** *adv*

cat·a·comb /káttə kōm/ *n* (*often used in the plural*) **1.** an underground cemetery consisting of passages or tunnels with rooms and recesses used as burial chambers leading off them. In ancient Rome, Christians used catacombs for burial. **2.** an underground network of passages or tunnels [Pre-12C. Via French < late Latin *catacumbas*, subterranean cemetery of St. Sebastian in Rome]

ca·tad·ro·mous /kə táddrəməss/ *adj* describes fish such as eels that spend most of their lives in fresh water but migrate to salt water to breed [Late 19C. <CATA- after ANADROMOUS]

cat·a·falque /káttə fàlk, -fàwlk/ *n* **1.** a raised and decorated platform on which the coffin of a distinguished person lies in state before or during a funeral **2.** in the Roman Catholic Church, a structure resembling a coffin that is used to represent a dead person at a requiem mass given after the person's funeral [Mid-17C. Via French < Italian *catafalco*]

~~catagory~~ incorrect spelling of **category**

Cat·a·lan /kátt'l àn, kàtt'l án/ *n* **1.** the Romance language of Catalonia and the Balearic Islands, Spain, also spoken in Andorra and the French region of Roussillon. Native speakers: 7 million. **2.** somebody who comes from Catalonia —**Cat·a·lan** *adj*

cat·a·lase /kátt'l àyss, -àyz/ *n* an antioxidant enzyme in living cells [Early 20C. < CATALYSIS] —**cat·a·lat·ic** /kàtt'l áttik/ *adj*

cat·a·lep·sy /kátt'l èpsee/ *n* actual or apparent unconsciousness during which muscles become rigid and remain in any position in which they are placed. The condition occurs naturally in diseases such as schizophrenia or epilepsy and can be induced by hypnosis or drugs. [14C. Directly or via French < late Latin *catalepsia* < Greek *katalēpsis* "seizure" < *katalambanein* "seize upon" < *lambanein* "seize"] —**cat·a·lep·tic** /kàtt'l éptik/ *adj* —**cat·a·lep·ti·cal·ly** *adv*

cat·a·lex·is /kàtt'l éksiss/ *n* the lack of one syllable in the final foot of a line of verse [Mid-19C. < Greek *katalēxis* "termination" < *katalēgein* "leave off" < *lēgein* "cease"] —**cat·a·lec·tic** /-éktik/ *adj*

cat·a·log /kátt'l òg/, **cat·a·logue** *n* **1.** COMM **LIST OF GOODS FOR SALE** a list of priced and illustrated items for sale, presented in book form or in other formats including CD-ROM or video **2. EXHIBITION GUIDE** a booklet that lists and often illustrates the objects on show at an exhibition **3.** LIBRARIES **LIST OF BOOKS** a list of the holdings in a library, usually arranged according to subject, title, or author **4. SERIES OF THINGS** a list of things or events that relate to an issue or person, especially those that are unpleasant or undesirable ○ *a catalog of disasters* **5. A-Z CARD FILE** an alphabetical card file **6.** *US* **COURSE LIST** a list of courses offered at an academic institution. Can term **prospectus** ■ *v* (**-loged, -log·ing, -logs; -logued, -logu·ing, -logues**) **1.** *vti* **MAKE CATALOG OF ITEMS** to classify and list items to form a catalog **2.** *vt* **PUT SOMETHING IN CATALOG** to enter something in a catalog ○ *I have cataloged all the new additions to the collection.* **3.** *vi* **BE LISTED** to be listed in a catalog, especially with a specific price or value ○ *a diamond ring that catalogs at a vastly inflated price* **4.** *vt* **LIST SERIES OF THINGS OR EVENTS** to list or describe a series of related events, items, or qualities ○ *a history of the twentieth century that catalogs many examples of human ingenuity* [15C. Via French < Greek *katalogos* "list" < *katalegein* "pick out" < *legein* "choose"] —**cat·a·log·er** *n*

Cat·a·log·ing in Pub·li·ca·tion *n* material in the front of a book detailing the name of the author, the subject, date of copyright, publisher's name and address, and related information

cat·a·logue rai·son·né /kàtt'l og rayzə náy, -rezə-/ (*plural* **cat·a·logues rai·son·nés** /kàtt'l ogz rayzə náy, -rezə náy/) *n* a detailed list of works by a particular artist, especially one produced to accompany an exhibition or collection [Late 18C. < French, "reasoned catalog"]

Cat·a·lo·nia /kàtt'l ṓnyə/ autonomous region in northeastern Spain. It contains the provinces of Barcelona, Girona, Lléida, and Tarragona. Capital: Barcelona. Population: 6,343,110 (2002). Area: 12,399 sq. mi./32,113 sq. km. Catalan name **Catalunya**. Spanish name **Cataluña** —**Cat·al·o·nian** *adj, n*

ca·tal·pa /kə tálpə/ *n* a tree with large heart-shaped leaves and long thin pods. Flowers: creamy, bell-shaped, in clusters. Native to: North America, Asia. Genus: *Catalpa*. [Mid-18C. < Creek *katalpa* < *ka* "head" + *talpa* "wing," from the shape of the flower]

Cat·a·lun·ya /kàa taa lóon yaa/, **Cat·a·lu·ña** ➧ **Catalonia**

cat·a·lyse *vt* CHEM UK spelling of **catalyze**

ca·tal·y·sis /kə tálləssiss/ (*plural* **-y·ses** /-ə seèz/) *n* an increase in the rate of a chemical reaction as a result of the action or use of a catalyst [Mid-17C. Via modern Latin, "dissolution" < Greek *katalusis* < *kataluein* "dissolve" < *luein* "set free"]

cat·a·lyst /kátt'list/ *n* **1.** a substance that increases the rate of a chemical reaction without itself undergoing any change **2.** somebody or something that makes a change happen or brings about an event ○ *The quarrel acted as a catalyst for the breakup of their partnership.* [Early 20C. < CATALYSIS]

cat·a·lyt·ic /kàtt'l íttik/ *adj* involving or causing an increase in the rate of a chemical reaction by the action or use of a catalyst [Mid-19C. < Greek *katalutikos* "able to dissolve" < *katalusis* (see CATALYSIS)] —**cat·a·lyt·i·cal·ly** *adv*

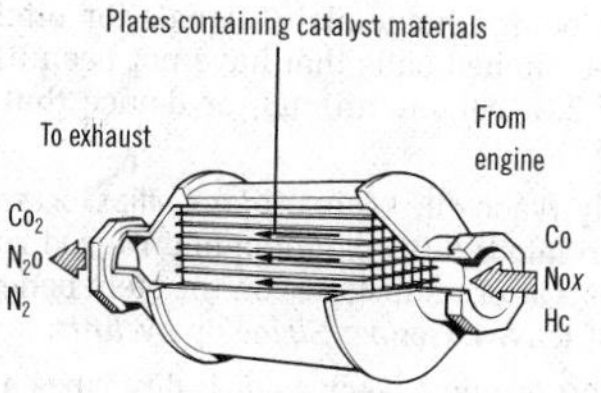

catalytic converter

cat·a·lyt·ic con·vert·er *n* in the exhaust system of a motor vehicle, a chamber in which gases mix with air so that pollutants such as carbon monoxide can be oxidized. The chamber contains a platinum-iridium catalyst.

cat·a·lyt·ic crack·er *n* an oil-refinery device that breaks down large molecules from crude oil into smaller ones that are useful as fuel, using heat and a catalyst to lower the required temperature

cat·a·lyze /kátt'l ìz/ (**-lyzed, -lyz·ing, -lyz·es**) *vt* **1.** INCREASE CHEMICAL REACTION RATE to increase the rate of a chemical reaction by the action or use of a catalyst **2.** BRING SOMETHING ABOUT to cause a particular thing to happen, or bring about a particular state of affairs ○ *The hearings have catalyzed the passage of financial reforms.* **3.** TRANSFORM SOMETHING to cause something to undergo basic change [Late 19C. < CATALYSIS]

cat·a·lyz·er *n* AUTOMOT ➧ **catalytic converter**

cat·a·ma·ran /kàttəmə rán/ *n* **1.** a sailboat or engine-powered boat that has two identical hulls fixed together by a rigid framework **2.** a simple raft made from logs or floats tied together [Early 17C. < Tamil *kaṭṭumaram* "tied wood"]

cat·a·mite /káttə mìt/ *n* a boy kept by a man for sexual intercourse (*literary*) [Late 16C. Via Latin *catamitus* < Greek *Ganumēdēs* "Ganymede"]

cat·a·mount /káttə mòwnt/, **cat·a·moun·tain** /kàttə mównt'n/ *n* VERTEB same as **mountain lion** [Mid-17C. < *cat of the mountain*]

cat and mouse *n regional* the game of tick-tack-toe [< German *Katz und Maus*]

REGIONAL NOTE As a name for tick-tack-toe, ***cat and mouse*** is used mainly in the Upper Midwest, but also as far south as Arkansas, Oklahoma, and Texas.

cat-and-mouse *adj* cruel or sadistic, especially in exploiting, compounding, and enjoying somebody else's suffering or fear

ca·taph·o·ra /kə táffərə/ *n* the use of a word or phrase, usually a pronoun, that refers to something mentioned later, as does "it" in "It's easy to make mistakes" [Late 20C. Blend of CATA- + ANAPHORA] —**cat·a·phor·ic** /kàttə fáwrik/ *adj*

cat·a·pho·re·sis /kàttəfə reéssiss/ (*plural* **-re·ses** /-reé seèz/) *n* SCI same as **electrophoresis** [Late 19C. < CATA- + Greek *phorēsis* "being carried"] —**cat·a·pho·ret·ic** /-fə réttik/ *adj* —**cat·a·pho·ret·i·cal·ly** *adv*

cat·a·pla·sia /kàttə pláyzhə, -zhee ə/ *n* the degeneration of cells or tissue to a more primitive or embryonic form —**cat·a·plas·tic** /-plástik/ *adj*

cat·a·plex·y /káttə plèksee/ *n* the sudden temporary inability to move, caused by shock, fear, or ecstasy [Late 19C. < Greek *kataplēxis* "stupefaction" < *kataplēssein* "strike down" < *plēssein* "strike"] —**cat·a·plec·tic** /kàttə pléktik/ *adj*

cat·a·pult /káttə pùlt, -pòolt/ *n* **1.** ARMS, HIST MEDIEVAL WEAPON a large heavy war machine used in medieval times to hurl large stones at an enemy **2.** ARMS PLANE OR MISSILE LAUNCHER a mechanism on an aircraft carrier or warship, used to launch planes or missiles **3.** *UK* ARMS same as **slingshot** ■ *v* (**-pult·ed, -pult·ing, -pults**) **1.** *vti* HURL SOMETHING to throw something with great force from a catapult (*often passive*) ○ *The fighters were catapulted from the carrier at 30-second intervals.* **2.** *vti* FLING OR BE FLUNG to throw somebody or something violently into the air by collision, impact, or a force that has an effect like a catapult, or be thrown in this way ○ *They were catapulted out of their seats by the force of the impact.* **3.** *vt* CHANGE CIRCUMSTANCES FOR SOMEBODY to thrust somebody unexpectedly and suddenly into a particular situation ○ *the hit that catapulted her to fame at the tender age of fifteen* [Late 16C. Directly or via French < Latin *catapulta* < Greek *katapeltēs* < *pallein* "hurl"]

cat·a·ract /káttə ràkt/ *n* **1.** OPHTHALMOL EYE DISEASE an eye disease in which the lens becomes covered in an opaque film that affects sight, eventually causing total loss of sight. The condition usually affects older people and is generally found in both eyes to varying degrees. It can be treated surgically by replacing the lens with an artificial implant. **2.** OPHTHALMOL FILM OVER EYE LENS the lens of the eye or the membrane surrounding it (**capsule**) that has become opaque as a result of disease **3.** GEOG WATERFALL a series of river rapids and small waterfalls with only moderate vertical drop (*literary*) **4.** FLOOD a heavy downpour of rain or a great flood (*literary*) [15C. < Latin *cataracta* "portcullis" < Greek *kataraktēs* "down-dashing" < *katarassein* "dash down" < *arassein* "to strike"]

ca·tarrh /kə taár/ *n* inflammation of a mucous membrane, especially in the nose or throat, causing an increase in the production of mucus, as happens in the common cold [15C. Via French *catarrhe* < Greek *katarrhous* < *katarrhein* "flow down" < *rhein* "flow"] —**ca·tarrh·al** *adj* —**ca·tarrh·ous** *adj*

cat·arrh·ine /káttə rìn/ *adj* describes primates that have nostrils set close together and facing downward ■ *n* an animal with nostrils set close together and facing downward, e.g., a human or an ape. Suborder: Catarrhini. [Mid-19C. < CATA- + Greek *rhinos* "nose"]

ca·tas·tro·phe /kə tástrəfee/ *n* **1.** DISASTER a terrible disaster or accident, especially one that leads to great loss of life **2.** TOTAL FAILURE an absolute failure, often in humiliating or embarrassing circumstances **3.** THEATER RESOLUTION OF PLOT the concluding part of the action in a drama, especially a classical tragedy, when the plot is resolved **4.** GEOL VIOLENT SEISMIC CHANGE a sudden and violent change in the Earth's crust caused by an earthquake, flood, or any other natural process **5.** INSUR EVENT CAUSING HUGE INSURANCE CLAIM an event causing losses of insured property above a specific monetary limit and affecting a substantial number of policyholders and insurers [Mid-16C. Via Latin *catastropha* < Greek *katastrophē* "overturning" < *katastrephein* "overturn" < *strephein* "turn"]

cat·a·stroph·ic /kàttə stróffik/ *adj* **1.** DISASTROUS causing or liable to cause widespread damage or death ○ *The rapid spread of the infection had a catastrophic effect on livestock.* **2.** AWFUL completely unsuccessful or very bad ○ *The party was a catastrophic affair.* **3.** HEALTH SERVICES LIFE-THREATENING AND REQUIRING EXPENSIVE TREATMENT so serious in nature as to require extensive, long-term, and expensive medical treatment ○ *catastrophic illnesses* **4.** INSUR PROVIDING EXTENSIVE COVERAGE FOR HIGH EXPENSES describes insurance plans, policies, or coverage appropriate to protect the insured party against expenses incurred in the event of a life-threatening condition requiring extensive medical intervention —**cat·a·stroph·i·cal·ly** *adv*

ca·tas·tro·phism /kə tástrə fìzzəm/ *n* **1.** a theory, now discredited, that the geologic features of Earth were formed by a series of sudden violent catastrophes rather than a gradual evolutionary process. A more recent version of this theory holds that the evolutionary process of geologic development has on occasions been supplemented by such catastrophes. **2.** an outlook or attitude that foresees disaster as the only possible outcome of any action or situation —**ca·tas·tro·phist** *n*

cat·a·to·ni·a /kàttə tṓnee ə/ *n* a condition, often associated with schizophrenia, characterized by periods of inertia or apparent stupor and rigidity of the muscles [Late 19C. < CATA- + Greek *tonos* "tone"]

cat·a·ton·ic /kàttə tónnik/ *adj* **1.** in a state of inertia or apparent stupor often associated with schizophrenia, characterized by rigidity of the muscles **2.** in a stupefied or unconscious state, especially one caused by drunkenness (*informal*) —**cat·a·ton·i·cal·ly** *adv*

cat·a·wam·pus /kàttə wómpəss/ *US regional, Can adj* in a diagonal position or arrangement ■ *adv* diagonally [Mid-19C. Origin ?]

REGIONAL NOTE See ***antigoglin***.

ca·taw·ba /kə táwbə/ *n* **1.** a fruity red wine made from a variety of black grape grown in the eastern United States **2.** a reddish-colored variety of the fox grape. Native to: North America. Use: wine production. [Early 19C. After the *Catawba* River in the Carolinas]

Ca·taw·ba /kə táwbə/ (*plural* same or **-bas**) *n* **1.** a member of a Native North American people who once lived along the Carolinian Catawba and Wateree rivers and whose surviving members now live mainly in South Carolina **2.** the Siouan language of the Catawba people, now nearly extinct [Early 18C. After the *Catawba* River in the Carolinas] —**Ca·taw·ba** *adj*

cat·bird /kát bùrd/ *n* a songbird with dark gray feathers and a black cap whose call sounds like the cry of a cat. Native to: North America. Latin name: *Dumetella carolinensis*.

cat·bird seat *n* a position or situation that gives somebody power and an edge over others, especially competitors or opponents (*informal*) [Origin ?]

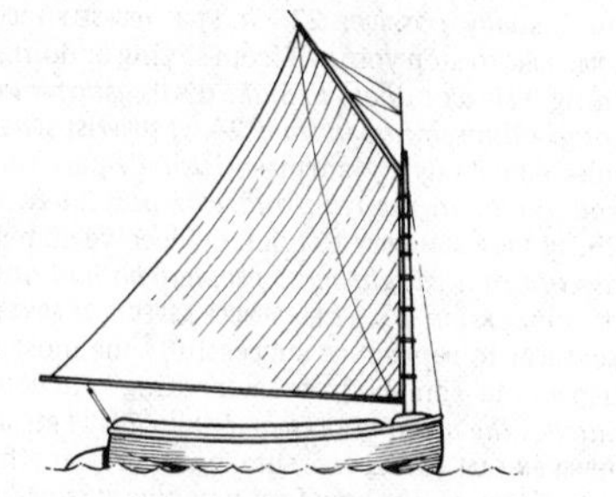

catboat

cat·boat /kát bṓt/ *n* a sailboat that is broad across the beam and has a single sail on a mast positioned near the front [Late 19C. Origin ?]

cat bur·glar *n* a burglar who, using stealth and agility, breaks into properties, especially through high windows or small openings [< the burglar's agility, likened to that of a cat]

cat·call /kát kàwl/ *n* a whistle or shout expressing disapproval or dislike, especially at a sporting event or live performance [Mid-17C. < the resemblance to cats' nocturnal cries] —**cat·call** *vti*

catch /kach, kech/ *v* (**caught** /kawt/, **catch·ing, catch·es**) **1.** *vti* STOP SOMETHING WITH HANDS to take hold of or stop something that is traveling through the air **2.** *vt* COLLECT FALLING OBJECTS FROM BELOW to collect from below something such as rain that is falling **3.** *vt* GRASP SOMEBODY OR SOMETHING to take tight hold of somebody or something suddenly ○ *He caught me by the shoulder.* **4.** *vt* CAPTURE ANIMAL to capture or trap an animal **5.** *vt* CAPTURE CRIMINAL to capture somebody, especially a criminal or somebody suspected of wrongdoing, after a search or chase ○ *Have they caught the culprit?* **6.** *vt* REACH SOMEBODY OR SOMETHING to reach or get alongside a person or vehicle moving ahead, usually while moving quickly ○ *trying to catch the car in front* **7.** *vt* GET ON BOARD PUBLIC TRANSPORTATION to arrive in time to board a bus, train, or other form of public transportation ○ *I have a plane to catch.* **8.** *vti* GET DISEASE to become infected with a disease **9.** *vt* SURPRISE SOMEBODY DOING WRONG to surprise or stop somebody who is in the act of doing something illegal or forbidden ○ *He caught her taking money from the register.* ○ *caught me reading her diary* **10.** *vt* SURPRISE SOMEBODY DOING SOMETHING EMBARRASSING to surprise or observe somebody who is doing something considered embarrassing, impolite, or private ○ *I caught him gazing at himself in the mirror.* **11.** *vt* ATTRACT SOMEBODY'S ATTENTION to attract the interest or attention of others ○ *a campaign that had caught the nation's imagination* **12.** *vti* MANAGE TO HEAR SOMETHING to manage to hear what is being said ○ *I'm sorry, I didn't quite catch that.* **13.** *vt* UNDERSTAND SOMETHING to understand the right meaning of something ○ *He didn't seem to catch the drift of what was being said.* **14.** *vt* NOTICE SOMETHING SUBTLE OR FLEETING to notice something subtle in the way somebody is speaking or behaving that tells you how that person really feels ○ *I caught a note of sarcasm in his voice.* **15.** *vt* SEE PERFORMER OR PRODUCTION to see a particular television program, movie, or play, or see a particular person performing in something (*informal*) ○ *If you get the chance, try and catch the new production of "Hamlet."* **16.** *vt* MANAGE TO MEET SOMEBODY to manage to meet or talk to somebody, especially somebody who is very busy (*informal*) ○ *I was hoping to catch the doctor before she left.* **17.** *vt* GET SOMETHING YOU NEED to get food, drink, or rest only hurriedly or in small amounts (*informal*) ○ *We can stop and catch a bite to eat.* **18.** *vt* STRIKE SOMEBODY to strike somebody with a blow ○ *a blow that caught him on the side of the head* **19.** *vt* TAKE IMPACT OF SOMETHING to receive the impact or force from something such as a blow or the force of somebody's anger or emotions ○ *He caught the full impact of the blast.* **20.** *vti* ENTANGLE SOMETHING to entangle or hook something such as clothing on something sharp, or become entangled or hooked, sometimes resulting in damage ○ *She caught her blouse on a nail.* **21.** *vti* TRAP SOMETHING to trap something in an opening or door, or become trapped ○ *I caught my fingers in the mailbox.* **22.** *vt* DELAY SOMEBODY to delay somebody or hold somebody up (*usually passive*) **23.** *vr* STOP YOURSELF FROM DOING SOMETHING to stop yourself from saying or doing something ○ *He was about to make a sarcastic remark but caught himself just in time.* **24.** *vt* SURPRISE SOMEBODY to take somebody by surprise (*usually passive*) ○ *She got caught in the rain and was absolutely soaked.* **25.** *vt* TRICK SOMEBODY to trick or deceive somebody ○ *a scam that caught most people who had any sense of compassion* **26.** *vt* REPRODUCE ASPECTS OF SOMETHING OR SOMEBODY to reproduce successfully the most typical aspects of somebody or something ○ *a novel that catches the mood of prewar Berlin* **27.** *vt* RECORD SOMETHING ON FILM to record somebody or something on film or tape ○ *the very first time this elusive bird has been caught on film* **28.** *vi* BE CARRIED BY EMOTION to be eager to do something, or reach for something eagerly ○ *She caught at the opportunity of making some extra cash.* **29.** *vi* BEGIN TO BURN to ignite, become alight, or begin to burn ○ *catch fire* **30.** *vi* PLAY BASEBALL AS CATCHER to act as catcher on a baseball team ○ *Clevenger will be catching again in the second game of the season.* **31.** *vt* PLACE SOMETHING ON OR AGAINST SOMETHING to put or rest something on or lean something against something else (*slang; used in Black English*) ■ *n* **1.** ACT OF CATCHING SOMETHING the catching of something such as a ball **2.** SOMEBODY WHO CAN CATCH a skilled catcher of something ○ *He missed the ball again! He's such a lousy catch!* **3.** BALL GAME a game in which people throw a ball to each other and catch it **4.** MOVE IN BALL GAMES a move in which a player in baseball, basketball, or football catches the ball **5.** NUMBER OF THINGS CAUGHT the amount or number of things caught, e.g., when fishing ○ *Not much of a catch today, I'm afraid.* **6.** DEVICE THAT CLOSES OR FASTENS a device for fastening something such as a door, window, or piece of jewelry **7.** SNAG a hidden or unexpected problem, especially one suspected to exist because everything seems too good to be true (*informal*) ○ *Okay, it sounds great: where's the catch?* **8.** BREAK IN VOICE a brief moment when somebody's voice becomes husky or unclear because of intense emotion ○ *There was a slight catch in his voice as he read the letter out loud.* **9.** IDEAL OR DESIRABLE PERSON somebody or something regarded as ideal or particularly desirable, especially as a marriage partner (*informal*) ○ *Her friends regarded Tom as quite a catch.* **10.** HUMOROUS SONG a round or canon with humorous, often risqué, words, popular in the 17th and 18th centuries [12C. < Anglo-Norman or Old French *cachier* "chase" < Latin *captare* "try to catch" < *capere* "take"] —**catch·a·ble** *adj* ◇ **be caught short** to be taken by surprise and therefore put at a disadvantage ◇ **catch it** to get into trouble (*informal*)

catch on *vi* (*informal*) **1.** to become popular or widely used **2.** to understand a new idea, task, or process ○ *pretty slow to catch on*

catch out *vt* **1.** DEVISE WAY TO SHOW SOMEBODY'S MISTAKES to find ways of exposing errors or ignorance in order to embarrass somebody or show superiority (*informal*) ○ *He would try to catch me out by asking awkward questions during safety inspections.* **2.** EXPOSE WRONGDOER to catch somebody doing something wrong or illegal, especially when deliberately setting out to do so (*informal*) **3.** CATCH BALL HIT BY SOMEBODY in baseball, to catch a ball hit by a player while it is still in the air, forcing the player or the player's team to retire

catch up *v* **1.** *vti* REACH SOMEBODY OR SOMETHING TRAVELING AHEAD to get alongside a person or vehicle that was moving ahead **2.** *vt* PICK SOMETHING OR SOMEBODY UP to quickly pick something or somebody up in the hands or arms ○ *He caught up all the papers and strode off.* **3.** *vti* GET OR BRING UP TO DATE to make up for lost time by working harder, bring something closer to completion, or bring somebody up to date on current conditions ○ *I must catch up on my reading.* ○ *He offered to catch me up on recent developments.* **4.** *vt* ENGROSS SOMEBODY to absorb somebody's attention completely (*usually passive*) ○ *I was so caught up in my work that I didn't have time for lunch.* **5.** *vt* INVOLVE SOMEBODY UNHAPPILY to involve somebody in something undesirable (*usually passive*) ○ *They were caught up in the whole messy affair even though they tried to stay out of it.* **6.** *vi Malaysia, Singapore* STAY EVEN WITH to progress at the same rate as somebody else **7.** *vi* HEAR SOMEBODY'S NEWS to speak to somebody in order to hear what he or she has been doing since the last meeting ○ *We spent an hour catching up with old friends.* ○ *enjoyed catching up on all their news*

catch up on *vt* to have a delayed effect on somebody ○ *Three nights without sleep is beginning to catch up on me.*

catch up with *vt* **1.** to find somebody who has committed a crime or done something wrong, especially after a search or chase ○ *By the time the police caught up with him, he had changed his name and moved to Brazil.* **2.** to finally have an effect on somebody who has, until now, seemed to be free from the usual consequences ○ *All those late nights will catch up with you eventually.*

Catch-22 /-twentee tóo/ (*plural* **Catch-22's** or **Catch-22s**), **catch-22** *n* a situation or predicament from which it is impossible to extricate yourself because of built-in illogical rules and regulations [After the novel *Catch-22* by Joseph Heller]

CULTURAL NOTE ***Catch-22***, a novel (1961) by Joseph Heller. The title of this dark satire relates to the skewed military logic that entraps the protagonist, Yossarian, a pilot serving in Italy during World War II. He tries to get himself grounded by being pronounced insane, but is told that only an insane person would want to fly, and his desire not to fly proves that he is, in fact, sane, and so must continue to fly. The term ***Catch-22*** eventually came to have a more general meaning of a situation in which somebody is trapped by illogical conditions and restrictions.

catch·all /kách àwl, kéch-/ *n* **1.** something that covers a wide range of possibilities, meanings, ideas, or situations (*often used before a noun*) ○ *one of those catchall phrases that doesn't really mean very much at all* **2.** a container or storage area for holding a wide variety of miscellaneous items

catch and re·lease *n* a conservation policy adopted by some anglers whereby they release some or all of the fish they catch in order to sustain fish populations

catch-as-catch-can *n* NO-HOLDS-BARRED WRESTLING a style of wrestling in which most holds are permitted, including many that are not allowed in other wrestling styles ■ *adj* MAKING DO making do with whatever is available ○ *We took a catch-as-catch-can approach to our summer vacation.* ■ *adv* USING WHAT COMES TO HAND using whatever happens to be available ○ *The press conference was arranged catch-as-catch-can at very short notice.*

catch ba·sin *n* **1.** a device or receptacle at the entrance of a sewer designed to prevent obstructive material from entering and blocking the sewer **2.** an area or reservoir for catching drainage water or runoff

catch crop *n* a fast-growing crop grown between the harvest and planting of two main crops, between the rows of a main crop, or as a substitute after a crop failure [< catching an opportunity to grow it]

catch·er /káchər, kéchər/ *n* **1.** the baseball player who stands behind home plate, signals for pitches, and catches pitched balls that have not been hit by the batter **2.** a person, animal, or device that catches things

catch·fly /kách flī, kéch-/ (*plural* **-flies** or *same*) *n* a plant related to the campion and ragged robin that exudes a sticky substance on the stem beneath each pair of leaves. Genus: *Silene* or *Lychnis.*

catch·ing /káching, kéch-/ *adj* **1.** describes an illness that can be transmitted to other people ○ *Don't worry: it's not catching!* **2.** passed from one person to another like an infection ○ *a pessimism that seemed to be catching* **3.** same as **catchy** (sense 2)

catch·ment /káchmənt, kéch-/ *n* **1.** RAINWATER RECEPTACLE a structure, reservoir, or container for collecting rainwater **2.** COLLECTED RAINWATER the rainwater that collects in a specific container or area **3.** COLLECTING OF RAINWATER the collecting or catching of rainwater especially over an area of land surrounding a river or lake

catch·ment ar·e·a *n* **1.** the area from which a particular school or hospital will accept pupils or patients **2.** the area of land that drains rainfall into a river or lake

catch·pen·ny /kách pènnee, kéch-/ *adj* cheap and made to be sold quickly and easily without much regard for quality (*dated*)

catch phrase *n* a phrase used so frequently by a particular person that it becomes identified with him or her

catch pit *n UK* same as **catch basin** (sense 1)

catch-up /kách ùp, kéch-/ *n* FOOD same as **ketchup**

catch-up *n* an increase in the amount or quality of something to bring it up to a desired or established standard ○ *a budgetary catch-up that managed at the last minute to fund the agency through the fourth quarter* ◇ **play catch-up** in a sport or game, to try to match the performance of another competitor

catch·wa·ter drain /kách wwawtər-, kéch-/ *n* a drain cut along the edge of high ground to catch water from it and divert it so that it does not run onto low-lying ground

catch·weight /kách wàyt, kéch-/ *adj* describes a contest in a sport such as wrestling or horseracing that has no weight restrictions [Early 19C. Origin ?]

catch·word /kách wùrd, kéch-/ *n* **1.** POPULAR WORD a word or phrase that is so frequently used, often over a short period of time, that it comes to be identified with a particular feeling, quality, or idea ○ *catchwords of the 1980s such as "upwardly mobile" and "yuppie"* **2.** *Can, UK* WORD MARKING RANGE OF MATERIAL

COVERED a word printed at the top of a page in a dictionary or other reference book, usually the first or last entry for that page. US term **guide word 3. BINDER'S CUE** the first word of a page of printed text repeated at the bottom right-hand corner of the previous page, originally placed there to draw the binder's attention to it **4.** THEATER **ACTOR'S CUE** a cue for an actor to come on stage or to speak

catch·y /káchee, kéchee/ (**-i·er, -i·est**) *adj* **1. MEMORABLE** easy to remember because of having a simple and effective melody or wording **2. ATTRACTING ATTENTION** tending to attract interest or attention because of a notable, unique, or pleasing character or quality ○ *an attempt to come up with a catchy name for a new soft drink* **3. TRICKY** designed to catch people out or trip them up ○ *There were some catchy questions on the English test.* **4. FITFUL** coming in spasmodic or irregular bursts ○ *light rain with catchy squalls of wind* —**catch·i·ness** *n*

cat crack·er *n* INDUST same as **catalytic cracker**

cat·e·che·sis /kàttə keéssiss/ *n* religious instruction given in advance of baptism or confirmation [Early 17C. Via ecclesiastical Latin < Greek *katēkhēsis* "instruction by word of mouth" < *katēkhein* (see CATECHIZE)] —**cat·e·chet·i·cal** /-kéttik'l/ *adj*

cat·e·chin /káttə kìn/ *n* a yellow crystalline substance. Use: in tanning and dyeing. Formula: $C_{15}H_{14}O_6$. [Mid-19C. < CATECHU]

cat·e·chism /káttə kìzzəm/ *n* **1. QUESTION-AND-ANSWER TEACHING** instruction in the principles of Christianity using set questions and answers **2. RELIGIOUS QUESTIONS AND ANSWERS** the series of questions and answers that are used to test somebody's religious knowledge in advance of Christian baptism or confirmation **3. QUESTION-AND-ANSWER BOOK** a book containing questions and answers used to test the religious knowledge of somebody preparing for Christian baptism or confirmation **4. BOOK FOR ROTE LEARNING** a handbook that teaches the basic principles of a subject, especially by repetition **5. BODY OF PRINCIPLES FOLLOWED UNTHINKINGLY** a body of basic beliefs and principles followed unthinkingly **6. INTERROGATION** a close and intense session of questioning on a particular subject, especially forming part of an examination or an interrogation [Early 16C. < ecclesiastical Latin *catechismus* < ecclesiastical Greek *katēkhizein* (see CATECHIZE)] —**cat·e·chis·mal** /kàttə kízm'l/ *adj*

cat·e·chist /káttəkist/ *n* an instructor in the basic principles of Christianity, especially one who teaches somebody preparing for baptism or confirmation —**cat·e·chis·tic** /kàttə kístik/ *adj*—**cat·e·chis·ti·cal** *adj*

cat·e·chize /káttə kìz/ (**-chized, -chiz·ing, -chiz·es**) *vt* **1.** to instruct somebody in the basic principles of the Christian religion using questions and answers **2.** to question somebody closely, e.g., in an examination or interrogation [15C. Via ecclesiastical Latin *catechizare* < ecclesiastical Greek *katēkhizein* < *katēkhein* "sound through" < *ēkhē* "sound"] —**cat·e·chi·za·tion** /kàttəki záysh'n/ *n* —**cat·e·chiz·er** *n*

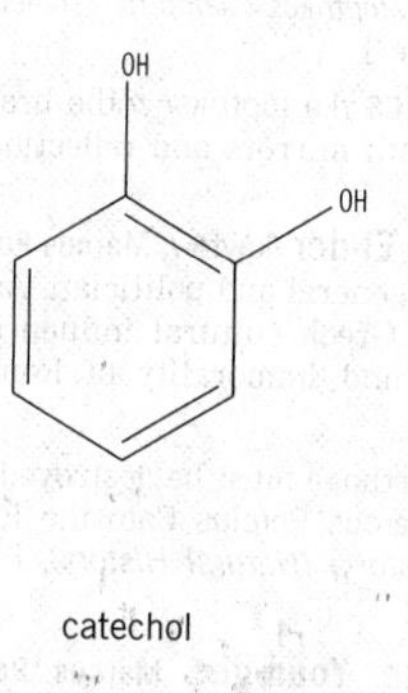

catechol

cat·e·chol /káttə kàwl, -kòl/ *n* a colorless crystalline solid. Use: photographic developer, antioxidant, manufacture of dyes and pharmaceuticals. Formula: $C_6H_6O_2$. [Late 19C. < CATECHU]

cat·e·cho·la·mine /kàttə kólə meen, -káwlə-/ *n* a compound that acts as a neurotransmitter or hormone

cat·e·chu /káttə choo/ *n* an astringent water-soluble substance extracted from an Asian acacia tree. Use: in medicine, dyeing. [Late 17C. < modern Latin, alteration of Malay *kacu*]

cat·e·chu·men /kàttə kyóomən/ *n* somebody who receives instruction in preparation for Christian baptism or confirmation [14C. Directly or via French < ecclesiastical Latin *catechumenus* < Greek *katēkhoumenos* "being instructed," form of *katēkhein* (see CATECHIZE)] —**cat·e·chu·men·ism** *n*

cat·e·gor·i·cal /kàttə gáwrik'l/, **cat·e·gor·ic** /kàttə gáwrik/ *adj* **1.** leaving no room for doubt, question, or contradiction ○ *The press office has issued a categorical denial of these allegations.* **2.** involving or relating to the use of categories or categorization —**cat·e·gor·i·cal·ly** *adv* —**cat·e·gor·i·cal·ness** *n*

cat·e·gor·i·cal im·per·a·tive *n* according to the moral philosophy of Immanuel Kant, an unconditional moral law applying to all rational beings and independent of all personal desires and motives

cat·e·go·rize /káttəgə rìz/ (**-rized, -riz·ing, -riz·es**) *vt* to place somebody or something in a particular category and define or judge the person or thing accordingly ○ *It was originally categorized as a cactus, but it's actually a succulent.* —**cat·e·go·riz·a·ble** *adj* —**cat·e·go·ri·za·tion** /kàttəgəri záysh'n/ *n*

cat·e·go·ry /káttə gàwree/ (*plural* **-ries**) *n* a group or set of things, people, or actions that are classified together because of common characteristics ○ *There are choices available in the following categories: leisure, fitness, health.* [15C. Via late Latin < Greek *katēgoria* "statement" < *katēgorein* "speak against" < *agora* "marketplace"]

SYNONYMS See ***type.***

ca·te·na /kə teénə/ (*plural* **-nae** /-neè/ or **-nas**) *n* a series of connected commentaries on or excerpts of writings, especially comments on the Bible written by early Christian theologians [Mid-17C. < Latin, "chain"]

cat·e·nac·cio /kàttə náchee ō/ *n* in soccer, a strongly defensive formation involving one free defender positioned behind his or her teammates [Late 20C. < Italian, literally "door bolt" < Latin *catena* "chain"]

cat·e·nar·y /kátt'n èrree, kə teénəree/ (*plural* **-ies**) *n* the curve adopted by a length of heavy cable, rope, or chain of uniform density, hanging between two points, or something with this shape [Mid-18C. < modern Latin *catenaria* < Latin *catena* "chain"] —**cat·e·nar·y** *adj*

cat·e·nate /kátt'n àyt/ (**-nat·ed, -nat·ing, -nates**) *vt* **1.** to form something into a chain or a series of chains **2.** to form atoms of the same chemical element into a chain held together by chemical bonds [Early 17C. < Latin *catenat-*, past participle of *catenare* "to chain" < *catena* "chain"]

ca·ter /káytər/ (**-tered, -ter·ing, -ters**) *vti* **1.** to provide what is wanted or needed in a particular situation or by a particular group of people ○ *We try to cater to all tastes in our bookstore.* **2.** to provide food and drink for a social or business function ○ *They've been asked to cater the wedding.* [Late 16C. Shortening of obsolete *acater* "caterer" < Anglo-Norman *acateor* < *ac(h)ater* "buy" < Latin *capere* "take"] —**ca·ter·er** *n*

cat·er-cor·nered /káttər kawrnərd/, **cat·er-cor·ner, cat·ty-cor·nered** /káttee-/, **cat·ty-cor·ner** *adj* **DIAGONAL** positioned or arranged diagonally ■ *adv* **1. DIAGONALLY** in a diagonal position or arrangement ○ *They sit cater-cornered in history class.* **2. OPPOSITE** diagonally opposite something or somebody else ○ *Their office is cater-cornered from the bank.* [*Cater* < dialect, "diagonally" < French *quatre* "four"]

cat·er·pil·lar /káttər pìllər/ *n* the larva of a butterfly or moth, with a long soft body, many short legs, and often brightly colored or spiny skin [15C. Alteration of assumed Old French *catepelose* < assumed late Latin *catta pilosa* "hairy cat"]

Cat·er·pil·lar /káttər pillər/ *tdmk* a trademark for tractors that have continuous treads composed of chain

~~**caterpiller**~~ incorrect spelling of **caterpillar**

cat·er·waul /káttər wàwl/ *vi* (**-wauled, -waul·ing, -wauls**) **1. YOWL** to make a loud howling noise **2. MAKE LOUD HARSH NOISE** to make a loud noise that offends the ears ○ *a street musician caterwauling in the background while we tried to talk* ■ *n* **YOWL** a loud howl or cry [14C. Origin ?]

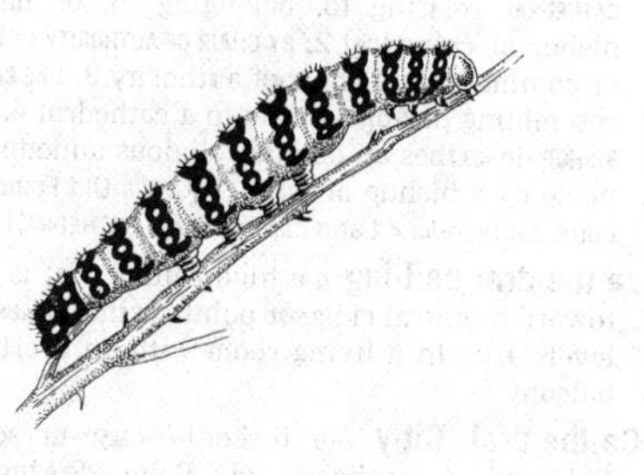

caterpillar

cat·fight /kát fìt/ *n* **1.** a fight that takes place among cats **2.** a vicious argument or fight, especially between women (*informal*)

cat·fish /kát fish/ (*plural same* or **-fish·es**) *n* a scaleless, usually freshwater fish with long whiskers (**barbels**) around its mouth that are sensitive to touch, taste, and smell. Order: Siluriformes. [< its barbels, likened to a cat's whiskers]

cat·gut /kát gùt/ *n* a tough thin cord made from the dried intestines of animals. Use: stringing musical instruments, surgical thread. [Late 16C. Probably < CAT (for unknown reasons)]

cath. *abbr* ELECTRONICS cathode

Cath. *abbr* **1.** cathedral **2.** Catholic

Cath·ar /ká thaar/ *n* a member of a medieval European heretical Christian sect who believed that salvation lay in the adoption of a spiritual way of life [Late 16C. Via medieval Latin *Cathari* "Cathars" < Greek *katharoi* "the pure" < *katharos* "pure"] —**Cath·a·rism** *n* —**Cath·a·rist** *n* —**Cath·a·rist·ic** /kàthə rístik/ *adj*

ca·thar·sis /kə thaárssiss/ (*plural* **-thar·ses** /-thaar seez/) *n* **1. EMOTIONAL RELEASE** an experience or feeling of spiritual release and purification brought about by an intense emotional experience **2. EMOTIONAL PURIFICATION THROUGH GREEK TRAGEDY** according to Aristotle, a purifying of the emotions that is brought about in the audience of a tragic drama through the evocation of intense fear and pity **3. PSYCHOLOGICAL PURGING OF COMPLEXES** in psychology, the process of bringing to the surface repressed emotions, complexes, and feelings in an effort to identify and relieve them, or the result of this process **4. PURGING OF BOWELS** cleansing or purging of the bowels [Early 19C. Via modern Latin < Greek *katharsis* < *kathairein* "to purge" < *katharos* "pure"]

ca·thar·tic /kə thaártik/ *adj* **1. PURIFYING** producing a feeling of being purified emotionally, spiritually, or psychologically as a result of an intense emotional experience or therapeutic technique ○ *a film that had a truly cathartic effect on me* **2. HAVING PURGATIVE EFFECT ON BOWELS** describes a medicine that causes emptying of the bowels ■ *n* **PURGATIVE MEDICINE** a medicine that causes emptying of the bowels —**ca·thar·ti·cal·ly** *adv*

Ca·thay /ka tháy/ medieval name for China

cat·head /kát hèd/ *n* a horizontal wooden or iron beam projecting from a ship's bow, where the anchor is carried and hoisted [< CAT "raise the anchor"]

ca·thect /kə thékt, ka-/ (**-thect·ed, -thect·ing, -thects**) *vt* to concentrate emotional or psychic energy on something such as an object, a person, or an idea [Mid-20C. Back-formation < *cathectic* < CATHEXIS] —**ca·thec·tic** *adj*

ca·the·dra /kə theédrə/ (*plural* **-dras** or **-drae** /-dree/) *n* **1. BISHOP'S THRONE** a bishop's official seat or throne **2. BISHOP'S RANK OR OFFICE** the official rank, office, or jurisdiction of a bishop **3. OFFICIAL CHAIR** an official chair of an office or position, used by an authority figure [15C. Via Latin < Greek *kathedra* < *kata* "down" + *hedra* "seat"]

ca·the·dral /kə theédr'l/ *n* **1. BISHOP'S CHURCH** a church that contains a bishop's throne and is the most important church in the bishop's diocese **2. LARGE**

CHURCH a large, important church ■ *adj* 1. **OF BISHOP OR CATHEDRAL** relating to, belonging to, or having a bishop or cathedral 2. **BY CHAIR OF AUTHORITY** related to or coming from a chair of authority 3. **LIKE CATHEDRAL** resembling or appropriate to a cathedral 4. **MADE BY BISHOP** describes an official religious announcement made by a bishop or pope [13C. Via Old French < late Latin *cathedralis* < Latin *cathedra* (see CATHEDRA)]

ca·the·dral ceil·ing *n* a high ceiling that is slanted toward a central ridge or point, or that takes in two levels, e.g., in a living room with an overhanging balcony

Ca·the·dral Cit·y /kə thēedr'l-/ city in southern California, southeast of Palm Springs and southwest of Joshua Tree National Park. Population: 46,295 (2002 estimate).

ca·thep·sin /kə thépsən/ *n* an enzyme that digests proteins after cell death [Early 20C. < German *Kathepsin* < Greek *kathepsein* "to digest," literally "boil down" < *hepsein* "to boil"]

Willa Cather

Cath·er /káthər/, **Willa** (1873–1947) US writer. Her novels include the Pulitzer Prize-winning *One of Ours* (1922). Full name **Cather, Willa Sibert**

> "One cannot divine nor forecast the conditions that will make happiness; one only stumbles upon them by chance, in a lucky hour, at the world's end somewhere."
> [Willa Cather, "Le Lavandou," *Virago Book of Women Travellers*; 1996]

Cath·er·ine I /káthrin/ (1684–1727) empress of Russia (1725–27). An influential adviser to her husband, Peter the Great, she was proclaimed empress after his death. Born **Marta Skavronskaya**

Cath·er·ine (of Ar·a·gon) /kàthrin əv árrə gòn/ (1485–1536) Spanish-born queen of England (1509–33) as the first wife of Henry VIII. The annulment of their marriage in 1533 precipitated the English Reformation.

> "I came not into this realm as merchandise, nor yet to be married to any merchant."
> [Catherine (of Aragon), *Letter*; 1533]

Catherine the Great

Cath·er·ine (the Great) (1729–96) German-born empress of Russia (1762–96). After deposing her husband, Tsar Peter III (1762) she extended and consolidated Russian power and culture.

> "I shall be an autocrat: that's my trade. And the good Lord will forgive me: that's his."
> [Attributed to Catherine (the Great)]

Cath·er·ine de Méd·i·cis /-də méddi chēe, kaa trēen də màydee sēess/, **Cath·er·ine de Med·i·ci** (1519–89) Italian-born queen of France (1547–59). As the widow of the French king Henry II she was regent of France (1560–63) and may have instigated the St. Bartholomew's Day Massacre (1572).

Cath·er·ine wheel *n UK* same as **pinwheel** (sense 2) [Late 16C. After St. *Catherine* of Alexandria, executed on a spiked wheel]

cath·e·ter /káthətər/ *n* a thin flexible tube that is inserted into a part of the body to inject or drain away fluid or to keep a passage open [Early 17C. Via late Latin < Greek *kathetēr* < *kathienai* "send down" < *hienai* "send"]

cath·e·ter·ize /káthətə rīz/ (**-ized, -iz·ing, -iz·es**) *vt* to insert a catheter into a patient or a part of the body —**cath·e·ter·i·za·tion** /kàthətəri záysh'n/ *n*

ca·thex·is /kə théksiss, ka-/ (*plural* **-thex·es** /-thék sēez/) *n* the concentration of a great deal of psychological and emotional energy on one particular person, thing, or idea [Early 20C. < Greek *kathexis* "holding" < *katekhein* "hold fast" < *ekhein* "to hold"]

ca·thi·o·der·mie /kàthee ō dúrmee/ *n* a beauty treatment in which an electric current is passed over the skin, through a special gel with which the skin is covered [Late 20C. < French]

cath·ode /ká thōd/ *n* 1. **NEGATIVE ELECTRODE** the negative electrode of an electrolytic cell 2. **ELECTRON SOURCE** the negatively charged source of electrons in an electron tube 3. **POSITIVE TERMINAL** the positive terminal of a cell that is producing electrical energy by a chemical process that cannot be reversed [Mid-19C. < Greek *kathodos* "way down" < *hodos* "way"] —**ca·tho·dal** /ka thōd'l/ *adj* —**ca·tho·dal·ly** *adv*

cath·ode ray *n* a stream of electrons that is emitted from a cathode in a vacuum tube

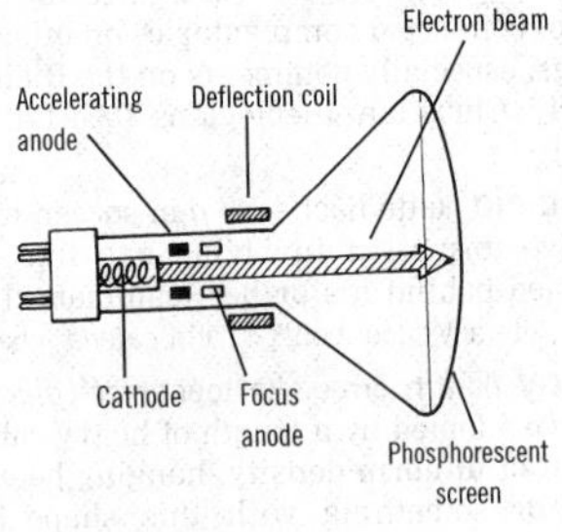

cathode-ray tube

cath·ode-ray tube *n* a vacuum tube in which a stream of electrons is produced and directed onto a fluorescent screen, e.g., in a television or visual display unit, creating images and text

ca·thod·ic /ka thóddik/ *adj* relating to or involving a cathode —**ca·thod·i·cal·ly** *adv*

ca·thod·ic pro·tec·tion *n* the prevention of electrolytic corrosion in something metallic such as an underground pipe or a ship by making it the cathode in an electrolytic cell

cat hole *n* either of two holes at the stern of a ship through which large ropes are passed

cath·o·lic /káthlik, káthəlik/ *adj* 1. **ALL-INCLUSIVE** including or concerned with all people 2. **USEFUL TO ALL** useful or interesting to a wide range of people 3. **ALL-EMBRACING** interested in or sympathetic to a wide range of things [14C. Via Latin < Greek *katholikos* "universal" < *katholou* "in general" < *kata* "in regard to" + *holos* "whole"] —**ca·thol·i·cal·ly** /kə thóllikəlee/ *adv*

Cath·o·lic /káthlik, káthəlik/ *adj* 1. **ROMAN CATHOLIC** belonging to or characteristic of the Roman Catholic Church 2. **CHRISTIAN** belonging to the community of all Christian churches 3. **OF HISTORICAL UNITED CHURCH** belonging to the united Christian church that existed before its separation into different churches, or to any church that regards itself as continuing the traditions of that united church ■ *n* **CHURCH MEMBER** a member of the Roman Catholic Church [14C. Via ecclesiastical Latin < Greek *katholikē (ekklēsia)* "universal (church)" < *katholikos* (see CATHOLIC)]

Cath·o·lic Church *n* 1. CHR same as **Roman Catholic Church** 2. any church that regards itself as continuing the traditions of the Christian church before it was divided into separate churches

Cath·o·lic E·pis·tles *npl* the books of the Bible that were originally letters attributed to James, Peter, John, and Jude, and were addressed to the Christian churches as a whole rather than to a local church [< CATHOLIC *adj* (sense 2)]

Ca·thol·i·cism /kə thóllə sizzəm/ *n* 1. the beliefs, doctrines, and rituals of a Catholic church, especially those of the Roman Catholic Church 2. membership of a Catholic church, especially of the Roman Catholic Church

cath·o·lic·i·ty /kàthə lissətee/ *n* 1. wideness of range of tastes or interests 2. the quality of including or applying to everyone or everything

Cath·o·lic·i·ty *n* CHR same as **Catholicism**

ca·thol·i·cize /kə thóllə sīz/ (**-cized, -ciz·ing, -ciz·es**) *vti* to broaden something such as an idea, classification, or range of things, or become broader

Ca·thol·i·cize (**-cized, -ciz·ing, -ciz·es**) *vti* to convert somebody to Catholicism, or be converted to Catholicism

cat·house /kát hòwss/ *n* same as **brothel** (*slang*) [Mid-20C. < CAT "prostitute"]

Cat·i·line /kátt'l īn/ (108?–62 B.C.) Roman conspirator. His plan to foment revolution by assassinating Marcus Cicero failed, and he was killed in battle with republican forces. Full name **Lucius Sergius Catilina**

cat·i·on /kát ī ən/ *n* an ion that has a positive electric charge and is attracted toward the cathode in electrolysis [Mid-19C. < Greek *kata* "down" + ION] —**cat·i·on·ic** /kàt ī ónnik/ *adj*

cat·kin /kátkin/ *n* a long hanging furry cluster of tiny leaves and flowers without petals, produced by trees such as willows, birches, alders, and poplars [Late 16C. < obsolete Dutch *katteken* "kitten"]

Cat·lin /káttlin/, **George** (1796–1872) US artist and writer. His paintings are records of Native American life. His books include *My Life Among the Indians* (1867).

cat lit·ter *n* absorbent material that is used to fill a box in which a cat can urinate and defecate indoors

cat·mint /kátmint/ *n UK* same as **catnip**

cat·nap /kát nàp/ *n* a short light sleep —**cat·nap** *vi* —**cat·nap·per** *n*

cat·nip /kátnip/ *n* a plant of the mint family with grayish leaves and a strong smell that attracts cats. Flowers: blue or white. Genus: *Nepeta*. [Early 18C. < variant of obsolete *nep* "catmint" < Latin *nepeta*]

cat-o'-nine-tails (*plural same*) *n* a whip with several, usually nine, strands of knotted rope, formerly used for flogging in the navy

Ca·tons·ville /káyt'nz vil/ village in Baltimore County, Maryland, situated southwest of the city of Baltimore. Population: 39,820 (2000).

ca·top·tric /kə tóptrik/, **ca·top·tri·cal** /-trik'l/ *adj* relating to or involving a mirror or reflection [Mid-16C. < Greek *katoptrikos* < *katoptron* "something that looks back" < *op-* "see"]

ca·top·trics /kə tóptriks/ *n* the branch of optics that deals with mirrors and reflection (*takes a singular verb*)

Ca·to the El·der /káytō-/, **Marcus Porcius** (234–149 B.C.) Roman general and politician. As censor he fought against Greek cultural influence and against the luxury and immorality of Rome. Known as **the Censor**

> "Carthage must be destroyed."
> [Marcus Porcius Cato the Elder, *Naturalis Historia (Natural History)*, Pliny the Elder; 77]

Ca·to the Youn·ger, **Marcus Porcius** (95–46 B.C.) Roman politician. Known as a defender of republican Roman values, he opposed the rise of Julius Caesar and committed suicide after his defeat by Caesar in Utica.

cat rig *n* the rig of a catboat, usually with a gaff

CAT scan /kát skàn/ *n* 1. a diagnostic radiological scan in which cross-sectional images of a part of the body are formed through computerized axial tomography and shown on a computer screen **2.** MED same as **CAT scanner**

CAT scan·ner *n* a diagnostic radiological scanning machine used to make a CAT scan

cat's cra·dle *n* a children's game in which a loop of string is threaded between the fingers of both hands in variable complex patterns [Origin ?]

cat scratch dis·ease, **cat scratch fe·ver** *n* an illness marked by fever and swollen lymph glands, thought to be caused by a bacterium transmitted to humans by the scratch of a cat

cat's-eye *n* **1.** **SEMIPRECIOUS STONE** a gemstone, especially chrysoberyl or chalcedony, cut so as to reflect a narrow silvery band of light that seems to come from within **2.** **REFLECTIVE ROAD MARKER** a small reflecting device that is set into a road surface, curb, or post to assist drivers at night in staying on the road or within lanes **3.** **GLASS MARBLE** a clear glass marble with a core or swirl of color at the center

Cats·kill Moun·tains /kátskil-/ group of mountains in the Appalachian system, in southeastern New York, situated along the western bank of the Hudson River. Its highest peak is Slide Mountain, 4,204 ft./1,281 m.

cat's pa·ja·mas, **cat's me·ow** *n* an excellent or special person or thing (*dated slang*)

cat's-paw *n* **1.** a victim of trickery who is manipulated into doing something for another person **2.** a knot with two loops, used for attaching a rope to a hook

cat·suit /kát so͞ot/ *n* a close-fitting one-piece pantsuit [Because it gives a sleek outline]

cat·sup /kátsəp/ *n* FOOD same as **ketchup**

cat's whisk·ers *n* *UK* same as **cat's pajamas**

Catt /kat/, **Carrie Chapman** (1859–1947) US suffragist. She was president of the International Woman Suffrage Alliance (1904–23). Born **Lane, Carrie**

> "When a just cause reaches its flood-tide, as ours has done in that country, whatever stands in the way must fall before its overwhelming power."
> [Carrie Chapman Catt, *Speech, Stockholm, Sweden*; 1911]

cat·tail /kát tàyl/ *n* *US* a tall, slender marsh plant. Flowers: brown, tube-shaped, in furry spikes. Genus: *Typha*. Can term **bulrush**

cat·ta·lo /kátt'lō/ (*plural* **-loes** or **-los**) *n* BREED same as **beefalo** [Late 19C. Blend of CATTLE + BUFFALO]

cat·ter·y /káttəree/ (*plural* **-ies**) *n* a place where cats are bred or cared for

cat·tish /káttish/ *adj* same as **catty** —**cat·tish·ly** *adv* —**cat·tish·ness** *n*

cat·tle /kátt'l/ *npl* **1.** large domesticated mammals kept for the production of milk, meat, and hides, and also as draft animals. Cows and oxen are common types of cattle. Genus: *Bos*. **2.** people who are regarded as lacking individuality, especially a crowd of people regarded as an undifferentiated mass [13C. Via Anglo-Norman *catel* < Latin *capitale* "funds"]

cat·tle call *n* an audition in which large numbers of often inexperienced actors try for various minor parts

cat·tle grid *n* *UK* same as **cattle guard**

cat·tle grub *n* a parasitic larva of the warble fly, which causes a swelling under the skin of cattle and horses

cat·tle guard *n* a grid of metal bars over a shallow pit in a road, designed to stop animals, but not people or vehicles, from leaving an enclosed area

cat·tle·man /kátt'lmən, -màn/ (*plural* **-men** /-mən, -mèn/) *n* a man who owns, raises, or works with cattle

cat·tle·per·son /kátt'l pùrss'n/ (*plural* **-per·sons** or **-peo·ple** /-peèp'l/) *n* somebody who owns, raises, or works with cattle

cat·tle plague *n* AGRIC, MED same as **rinderpest**

cat·tle prod *n* an electrified rod designed for driving and controlling cattle by giving them mild shocks

cat·tle tick *n* a tick that feeds chiefly on the blood of cattle and transmits the parasites responsible for Texas fever and other cattle diseases. Native to: tropical regions. Genus: *Boophilus*.

cat·tle truck *n* *UK* same as **stock car** (sense 2)

cat·tle·wom·an /kátt'l wo͝omən/ (*plural* **-wom·en** /-wimmin/) *n* a woman who owns, raises, or works with cattle

cat·tle·ya /káttlee ə, kat láy ə, kat leé ə/ (*plural* **-yas**) *n* an orchid that is a popular greenhouse plant. Flowers: purple, pink, or white. Native to: tropical America. Genus: *Cattleya*. [Early 19C. < modern Latin, after William *Cattley* (died 1832), British patron of botany]

Cat·ton /kátt'n/, **Bruce** (1899–1978) US historian. He wrote many volumes on the Civil War. Full name **Catton, Charles Bruce**

cat train *n* a series of linked sleds mounted on runners that is pulled over snow by a tractor with Caterpillar™ treads

cat·ty /káttee/ (**-ti·er**, **-ti·est**) *adj* **1.** saying spiteful or malicious things about somebody, especially in a subtle way **2.** resembling a cat, especially in being cautious or secretive —**cat·ti·ly** *adv* —**cat·ti·ness** *n*

cat·ty-corn·ered, **cat·ty-corn·er** *adj* same as **cater-cornered**

Ca·tul·lus /kə túlləss/, **Gaius Valerius** (84?–54? B.C.) Roman poet. He wrote love poems addressed to "Lesbia" and satirical attacks on Julius Caesar. —**Ca·tul·lan** *adj*

> "I hate and love."
> [Gaius Valerius Catullus, *Carmina*; 60? B.C.]

CATV *abbr* MEDIA community antenna television

cat·walk /kát wàwk/ *n* **1.** a long narrow raised platform along which the models walk in a fashion show **2.** a narrow walkway high above the ground, e.g., along the side of a building or behind the stage in a theater [Because cats can walk safely on narrow surfaces]

Cau·ca·sia /kaw káyzhə/ region of southeastern Europe and southwestern Asia, divided by the Caucasian Mountains and containing Georgia, Armenia, Azerbaijan, and southern Russia. Area: 154,441 sq. mi./400,000 sq. km.

Cau·ca·sian /kaw káyzh'n/ *adj* **1.** **WHITE-SKINNED** relating to people who are light-skinned or of European origin **2.** **OF FORMER ETHNIC GROUP** belonging to the light-skinned peoples of Europe, northern Africa, and western and southern Asia, formerly considered a distinct ethnic group (*not in technical use*) **3.** **OF CAUCASIA** relating to Caucasia, or its peoples, languages, or cultures **4.** **OF LANGUAGES OF CAUCASIA** belonging to two unrelated language families spoken in the area around the Caucasus Mountains ■ *n* **1.** **WHITE PERSON** somebody light-skinned or of European origin **2.** **MEMBER OF FORMER ETHNIC GROUP** a member of the people formerly termed Caucasian (*not in technical use*) **3.** **SOMEBODY FROM CAUCASIA** somebody who comes from Caucasia **4.** **LANGUAGES OF CAUCASIA** either of two unrelated language families spoken in the area around the Caucasus Mountains, Kartvelian or South Caucasian, and North Caucasian

Cau·ca·soid /káwkə zòyd, -sòyd/ (*not in technical use*) *adj* same as **Caucasian** *adj* (sense 2) ■ *n* same as **Caucasian** *n* (sense 2)

Cau·ca·sus Moun·tains /káwkəssəss-/ mountain range that is considered a boundary between Europe and Asia, extending through Georgia, Armenia, Azerbaijan, and southwestern Russia. Its highest peak is El'brus 18,510 ft./5,642 m.

cau·cus /káwkəss/ *n* **1.** **POLITICAL MEETING** a closed meeting of people from one political party, especially a local meeting to select delegates or candidates **2.** **SPECIAL-INTEREST GROUP** a group of people, often within a larger group such as a legislative assembly, who unite to promote a particular policy or particular interests ○ *the Congressional Black Caucus* ■ *vi* (**-cused**, **-cus·ing**, **-cus·es**) **FORM CAUCUS** to hold or meet in a caucus [Mid-18C. Origin ?]

cau·dal /káwd'l/ *adj* **1.** like or relating to a tail **2.** situated in or extending toward the hind part of the body [Mid-17C. < modern Latin *caudalis* < Latin *cauda* "tail"] —**cau·dal·ly** *adv*

cau·date /káw dàyt/, **cau·dat·ed** /-dàytəd/ *adj* with a tail or an appendage like a tail [Early 17C. < medieval Latin *caudatus* < Latin *cauda* "tail"] —**cau·da·tion** /kaw dáysh'n/ *n*

cau·dex /káw dèks/ (*plural* **-di·ces** /-di seez/ or **-dex·es**) *n* **1.** a trunk of a tree that bears leaves only at its apex, as in a palm or tree fern **2.** the swollen stem base of some nonwoody perennial plants that survives over the winter and from which new growth is produced [Late 18C. < Latin, "tree trunk," variant of *codex* "block of wood"]

cau·dil·lis·mo /kòw deel yeézmō, kòwdee-/ *n* government by a dictator or caudillo [Mid-19C. < Spanish < *caudillo* (see CAUDILLO)]

cau·dil·lo /kow deé yō, -deél yō/ (*plural* **-los**) *n* *Hispanic* in a Spanish-speaking country, a military or political leader, especially a dictator [Mid-19C. Via Spanish, "leader" < late Latin *capitellum* "little head" < *caput* "head"]

caught past participle, past tense of **catch**

caul /kawl/ *n* **1.** the membrane surrounding the amniotic fluid, a part of which sometimes covers a baby's head when it is born **2.** same as **omentum** [14C. Origin ?]

caul·dron *n* another spelling of **caldron**

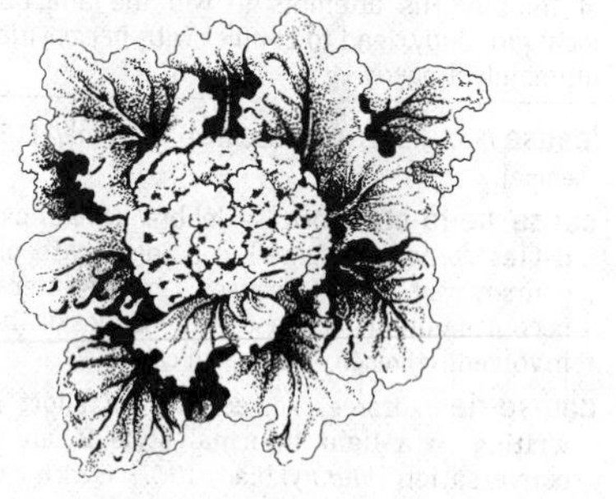

cauliflower

cau·li·flow·er /káwli flòwr/ *n* **1.** a large solid head of tight white or light-green florets, eaten raw or cooked as a vegetable **2.** a plant related to the cabbage that produces cauliflowers. Latin name: *Brassica oleracea* var. botrytis. [Late 16C. Alteration of modern Latin *cauliflora* < Latin *caulis* "stem" + *flor-* "flower"]

cau·li·flow·er ear *n* an ear that is permanently swollen and misshapen as a result of bleeding into the ear tissues after being repeatedly struck, usually in boxing

caulk /kawk/, **calk** *vt* (**caulked**, **caulk·ing**, **caulks**; **calked**, **calk·ing**, **calks**) **1.** to make a boat or the seams between its planks watertight by filling the seams with waterproof material such as pitch **2.** to fill in the cracks or gaps in something such as a pipe or a window frame using a waterproof material ■ *n* same as **caulking** [15C. < Old French *cauquer* "to tread" < Latin *calcare* < *calc-* "heel"] —**caulk·er** *n*

caulk·ing /káwking/ *n* material used to make a boat watertight by filling in its seams or to stop up the cracks or gaps in something

caus·al /káwz'l/ *adj* **1.** **BEING OR INVOLVING CAUSE** involving or being the cause of something else or the relationship of cause and effect **2.** GRAM **EXPRESSING CAUSE** expressing or indicating a cause or the relationship of cause and effect ■ *n* GRAM **WORD EXPRESSING CAUSE** a word or other grammatical element that expresses the reason or cause of something, or a relationship of cause and effect —**caus·al·ly** *adv*

cau·sal·gia /kaw záljə, -záljee ə/ *n* a persistent burning sensation of the skin, caused usually by injury to a peripheral nerve [Mid-19C. < Greek *kausos* "burning"] —**cau·sal·gic** *adj*

cau·sal·i·ty /kaw zállətee/ *n* **1.** the principle that everything that happens must have a cause **2.** the action that causes an effect, or the ability to cause an effect

cau·sa·tion /kaw záysh'n/ *n* **1.** the fact that something causes an effect, or the action of causing an effect **2.** the relationship between a cause and its effect

caus·a·tive /káwzətiv/ *adj* **1.** INVOLVING CAUSE AND EFFECT involving or being the cause of something or the relationship of cause and effect **2.** EXPRESSING CAUSE describes verbs that express the action of something causing something else ■ *n* VERB EXPRESSING CAUSE a causative verb, or a form or class of causative verbs —**caus·a·tive·ly** *adv* —**caus·a·tive·ness** *n*

cause /kawz/ *n* **1.** WHAT MAKES SOMETHING HAPPEN a person or thing that makes something happen or exist or is responsible for something that happens ○ *the cause of all the uproar* **2.** REASON a reason or grounds for doing or feeling something ○ *no cause for complaint* **3.** PRINCIPLE a principle or idea that people believe in or work for **4.** INTEREST the interests and goals of a group of people **5.** LEGAL CASE a lawsuit, or the reason that a suit is brought in a court of law **6.** DISCUSSION SUBJECT something under discussion or to be decided ■ *vt* (**caused, caus·ing, caus·es**) BE REASON FOR SOMETHING to make something happen or exist, or be the reason for somebody doing something or for something happening [13C. Via Old French < Latin *causa* "reason, motive"] —**caus·a·bil·i·ty** /kàwzə bíllətee/ *n* —**caus·a·ble** *adj* —**cause·less** *adj* —**caus·er** *n*

CULTURAL NOTE ***Rebel Without a Cause***, a movie (1955) by US director Nicholas Ray. The movie that made actor James Dean a symbol of an alienated generation, it is the story of Jim, a youth who seems unable to stay out of trouble. His attempts to win the affections of a local girl, Judy, lead to conflict with her boyfriend and, ultimately, tragedy.

'cause /kəz, kawz/ *conj* because (*informal*) [15C. Shortening]

cause cé·lè·bre /kàwz sə lébbrə/ (*plural* **causes cé·lè·bres** /*pronunc. same*/) *n* a legal case or public controversy that arouses great interest and becomes famous because of the issues or the people involved [< French, "celebrated case"]

cau·se·rie /kṓzəree, kṓzree/ *n* **1.** a short piece of writing in a light informal style **2.** an informal conversation (*literary*) [Early 19C. < French < *causer* "to chat" < Latin *causari* "discuss" < *causa* "case, subject"]

cause·way /káwz wày/ *n* **1.** a raised path or road over a marsh or water or across land that is sometimes covered by water **2.** a road or path with a paved or cobbled surface [15C. < archaic *causey* "causeway" (via Anglo-Norman *caucie* < medieval Latin *calciata (via)* "paved (road)" < Latin *calx* "limestone") + WAY]

caus·tic /káwstik/ *adj* **1.** SARCASTIC very sarcastic and intended to mock, offend, or belittle somebody **2.** CORROSIVE corrosive or burning by chemical action ■ *n* **1.** SUBSTANCE THAT CORRODES a substance that can corrode or burn away other substances by chemical action, especially a strong alkali **2.** CURVE FORMED BY REFLECTIONS a peaked curve formed on a plane by parallel light rays reflected or refracted from a cylindrical or spherical surface. Caustics can sometimes be seen on the surface of drinks in glazed mugs or cups, or on the base of the mug or cup when empty. [14C. Via Latin < Greek *kaustikos* < *kaustos* "combustible" < *kaiein* "to burn"] —**caus·ti·cal** *adj* —**caus·ti·cal·ly** *adv* —**caus·tic·i·ty** /kaw stíssətee/ *n*

SYNONYMS See *sarcastic*.

caus·tic pot·ash *n* CHEM same as **potassium hydroxide**

caus·tic so·da *n* CHEM same as **sodium hydroxide**

cau·ter·ize /káwtə rìz/ (**-ized, -iz·ing, -iz·es**) *vt* to seal a wound, or destroy damaged or infected tissue, with a heated instrument, a laser, an electric current, or a caustic substance [14C. < French *cautériser* < Latin *cauterium* (see CAUTERY)] —**cau·ter·i·za·tion** /kàwtəri záysh'n/ *n*

cau·ter·y /káwtəree/ (*plural* **-ies**) *n* **1.** an instrument or substance used to seal a wound or to destroy damaged or infected tissue by burning **2.** the process or action of sealing a wound or destroying damaged or infected tissue by burning [14C. Via Latin *cauterium* < Greek *kautērion* "branding iron" < *kaiein* "to burn"]

cau·tion /káwsh'n/ *n* **1.** CAREFULNESS care, thoughtfulness, lack of haste, and close attention that enable somebody to avoid the risks involved in a task or procedure **2.** WARNING a warning to somebody to be careful about something **3.** UNUSUAL PERSON a surprising or amusing person or thing (*dated*) ■ *vt* (**-tioned, -tion·ing, -tions**) **1.** WARN SOMEBODY to warn or advise somebody that something is risky or dangerous **2.** LAW GIVE SOMEBODY WARNING ABOUT EVIDENCE to give a formal warning to somebody who has been arrested that anything he or she says may be used in evidence [Late 16C. Via French < Latin *caution-* < *caut-*, past participle of *cavere* "take heed"] —**cau·tion·er** *n* ◇ **throw caution to the wind(s)** to be reckless

cau·tion·ar·y /káwsh'n èrree/ *adj* involving, giving, or being a warning

cau·tious /káwshəss/ *adj* having or showing care, thoughtfulness, restraint, and lack of haste [Mid-17C. < CAUTION] —**cau·tious·ly** *adv* —**cau·tious·ness** *n*

SYNONYMS ***cautious, careful, chary, circumspect, prudent, vigilant, wary, guarded, cagey***

CORE MEANING: showing care or restraint

cautious having or showing care, thoughtfulness, restraint, and lack of haste ○ *his cautious approach to economic reform* ○ *Years of army training had taught him to be cautious when faced with an unknown situation.* **careful** taking reasonable care to avoid risks ○ *Be very careful when you withdraw money from an ATM.* ○ *I was extra careful not to make any mistakes.* **chary** cautiously reluctant to act ○ *Why had Janet been so chary of telling the simple truth?* **circumspect** taking into consideration all possible circumstances and consequences before acting ○ *Both men offered only circumspect answers to my question.* ○ *Officials were understandably circumspect about the incident.* **prudent** using good judgment to consider likely consequences and act accordingly ○ *prudent financial planning for foreseeable expenses* ○ *It's certainly prudent to use sunscreen if you are out in the midday sun.* **vigilant** watchful and alert, especially to guard against danger, difficulties, or errors ○ *Doctors are urging the public to be vigilant about the killer virus.* ○ *A vigilant neighbor foiled the attempted burglary.* **wary** showing watchfulness or suspicion ○ *She was always wary of dogs.* ○ *People were becoming more wary about voicing their opinions in public.* **guarded** reluctant to share information with others ○ *Her responses to the questions were heavily guarded.* ○ *His voice was guarded, with a deliberate note of skepticism.* **cagey** (*informal*) secretive and refusing to be open, frank, or direct ○ *She was cagey about why she had rejected the offer.* ○ *Asked about his recent career, he remained cagey.*

Cau·ve·ry /káwvəree/, **Kā·ve·ri** river in southern India. It rises in the Western Ghats, Karnataka State, and flows through Tamil Nadu to the Bay of Bengal. Length: 470 mi./760 km.

cav., Cav. *abbr* MIL cavalry

cav·al·cade /kàvv'l káyd, kávv'l kàyd/ *n* **1.** a procession, especially one of people on horses, in carriages, or in cars **2.** a series or procession of things or people, especially a spectacular or dramatic one [Late 16C. Via French < Italian *cavalcata* < *cavalcare* "ride on horseback" < medieval Latin *caballicare* < Latin *caballus* "horse"]

cav·a·lier /kàvv'l éer/ *adj* CARELESS showing an arrogant or jaunty disregard or lack of respect for something or somebody ■ *n* **1.** GENTLEMAN a gallant or chivalrous man, especially one escorting a lady (*formal*) **2.** MOUNTED SOLDIER a knight or soldier in former times who fought on horseback (*archaic*) [Mid-16C. Via French < Italian *cavaliere* "knight" < medieval Latin *caballarius* "horseman" < Latin *caballus* "horse"] —**cav·a·lier·ly** *adv*

Cav·a·lier *n* a supporter of King Charles I in the English Civil War

cav·a·lier King Charles span·iel *n* BREED same as **King Charles spaniel** (sense 2)

ca·val·la /kə vállə/ (*plural same* or **-las**) *n* **1.** an ocean fish with a flat body and forked tail. Native to: tropics. Family: Carangidae. **2.** FISH same as **king mackerel** [Early 17C. Via Spanish *caballa* "horse mackerel" < Latin *caballus* "horse"]

cav·al·ry /kávv'lree/ (*plural* **-ries**) *n* **1.** formerly, the part of an army made up of soldiers trained to fight on horseback **2.** the more mobile part of a modern army, using armored vehicles and helicopters [Mid-16C. Via French < Italian *cavalleria* "mounted militia" < *cavallo* "horse" < Latin *caballus*] —**cav·al·ry·man** *n*

Cav·an /kávvən/ county in the Republic of Ireland. It was one of the nine counties that formed the historic province of Ulster. Population: 52,944 (2002). Area: 730 sq. mi./1,891 sq. km.

ca·va·ti·na /kàvvə téenə, kaàə-/ (*plural* **-nas** or **-ne** /-nee/) *n* a short and simple operatic song, especially a slow aria of Italian opera of the 18th and 19th centuries, usually followed by a livelier cabaletta [Early 19C. < Italian]

cave /kayv/ *n* a large, naturally hollowed-out place in the ground, or in rock above ground, that can be reached from the surface or from water ■ *vt* (**caved, cav·ing, caves**) to hollow out or undermine something [13C. < Old French < Latin *cavus* "hollow"]

cave in *v* **1.** *vti* to collapse or cause something to collapse because of pressure or because of being undermined **2.** *vi* to yield to persuasion or threats, after trying to resist

ca·ve·at /kávvee àt, kaávee-, káyvee-/ *n* **1.** something said as a warning, caution, or qualification **2.** an official request to a court not to proceed with a case without notice to the person making the request [Mid-16C. < Latin, "let him or her beware" < *cavere* "to heed"]

ca·ve·at emp·tor /-émp tawr/ *n* the commercial principle that the buyer is responsible for making sure that goods bought are of a reasonable quality, unless the seller is offering a guarantee of their quality [Early 16C. < Latin, "let the buyer beware"]

cave·fish /káyv fìsh/ (*plural same* or **-fish·es**) *n* a small fish with underdeveloped eyes that lives in subterranean waters. Native to: North America. Family: Amblyopsidae.

cave-in *n* **1.** COLLAPSE a collapse of something caused by pressure or undermining **2.** FALLEN STRUCTURE a place where a structure such as a roof or floor has collapsed because of pressure or being undermined **3.** YIELDING a giving in to persuasion or threats, after trying to resist

Cav·ell /kávv'l, kə vél/, **Edith** (1865–1915) British nurse. She was executed by the Germans during World War I for helping Allied soldiers escape from occupied Belgium.

> "Standing, as I do, in view of God and eternity, I realize that patriotism is not enough. I must have no hatred or bitterness toward anyone."
> [Edith Cavell, *Times (London)*; October 23, 1915]

cave·man /káyv màn/ (*plural* **-men** /-mèn/) *n* **1.** somebody living in a cave, especially a prehistoric human of the Paleolithic period **2.** a man who behaves in a brutish or uncivilized way (*informal*)

cave paint·ing *n* a painting made on the wall of a cave by Paleolithic people

cav·ern /kávvərn/ *n* LARGE CAVE a large underground cave or a large chamber in a series of caves ■ *vt* (**-erned, -ern·ing, -erns**) **1.** MAKE SOMETHING HOLLOW to make a mountain, cliff, or area of ground hollow **2.** PUT SOMETHING IN CAVE to enclose something in a cave or cavern (*literary*) [14C. Directly or via French < Latin *caverna* < *cavus* "hollow"]

cav·ern·ous /kávvərnəss/ *adj* **1.** like or suggestive of a cavern, especially in being large, dark, deep, and hollow **2.** having a hollow, resonating sound —**cav·ern·ous·ly** *adv* —**cav·ern·ous·ness** *n*

cav·es·son /kávvəss'n/ *n* a stiff noseband used in breaking horses [Late 16C. Via French *caveçon* < medieval Latin *capitium* "head covering" < Latin *capit-* "head"]

ca·vet·to /kə véttō/ (*plural* **-ti** /-tee/) *n* a concave architectural molding with a curve that is roughly a quarter circle [Mid-17C. < Italian, diminutive of *cavo* "hollow" < Latin *cavus*]

cave·wom·an /káyv wŏŏmmən/ (*plural* **-wom·en** /-wìmmin/) *n* a woman living in a cave, especially a prehistoric woman of the Paleolithic period

cav·i·ar /kávvee aàr, kaávee-/, **cav·i·are** *n* the salted roe of a large fish, particularly the sturgeon, eaten as a delicacy [Mid-16C. Via French < Italian *caviaro* < Turkish *havyar* < Persian dialect *khāvyār*]

cav·i·ard /kávvee aàrd/ *n* *Southwest US* AGRIC same as

string (sense 19) [Early 19C. Anglicization of Spanish *caballada* (see CABALLADO)]

REGIONAL NOTE See *remuda.*

cav·i·are *n* FOOD another spelling of **caviar**

cav·il /kávvəl/ *vi* (**-iled** or **-illed, -il·ing** or **-il·ling, -ils**) to make objections about something on small and unimportant points ■ *n* a trivial and unreasonable objection [Mid-16C. Via French *caviller* < Latin *cavillari* < *cavilla* "mockery"] —**cav·il·er** *n*

cav·ing /káyving/ *n* the activity or sport of exploring and climbing in underground caves and passages —**cav·er** *n*

ca·vi·tand /kávvitənd/ *n* a molecule, especially a synthetic receptor, that is hollow and has one open end [Late 20C. < CAVITY]

cav·i·tate /kávvi tàyt/ (**-tat·ed, -tat·ing, -tates**) *vt* to form bubbles or cavities in a substance [Early 20C. Back-formation < CAVITATION]

cav·i·ta·tion /kàvvi táysh'n/ *n* **1.** DISTURBANCE OF LIQUID the rapid formation and collapse of bubbles in a liquid, caused by the movement of something in the liquid such as a propeller, or by waves of high-frequency sound **2.** PITTING OF SURFACE the pitting of a solid surface as a result of the forces of repeated cavitation in a surrounding liquid **3.** FORMATION OF CAVITIES IN TISSUE the formation of cavities in body tissue, caused by a disease, e.g., as an effect of tuberculosis on the lungs [Late 19C. < CAVITY]

cav·i·ty /kávvətee/ (*plural* **-ties**) *n* **1.** HOLLOW PLACE a hole or hollow space in something **2.** DENT HOLE IN TOOTH a hole in a tooth, caused by decay **3.** ANAT HOLLOW WITHIN BODY a hollow area inside the body [Mid-16C. Via French < late Latin *cavitas* < Latin *cavus* "hollow"]

ca·vo-re·lie·vo /kaàvō ri léevō, kày-/ (*plural* **ca·vo-re·lie·vos** or **ca·vo-re·lie·vi** /-vee/) *n* a relief sculpture in which even the highest part lies below the level of the original surface, or this style of relief sculpture [Late 19C. < Italian, "hollow relief"]

ca·vort /kə váwrt/ (**-vort·ed, -vort·ing, -vorts**) *vi* to behave in a physically lively and uninhibited way [Late 18C. Origin ?]

Ca·vour /kə vóor/, **Camillo Benso, Conte di** (1810–61) Italian politician. He was prime minister of Piedmont (1852–59, 1860–61) and chief architect of the unification of Italy (1861).

cav·vy /kávvee/ (*plural* **-vies**) *n Southwest US* AGRIC same as **string** (sense 19) [Shortening of CAVIARD]

REGIONAL NOTE See *remuda.*

ca·vy /káyvee/ (*plural* **-vies**) *n* a short-tailed rodent of the family that includes the guinea pig, many of which dig burrows. Native to: South America. Family: Caviidae. [Late 18C. Via modern Latin *Cavia* < Galibi *cabiai*]

caw /kaw/ (**cawed, caw·ing, caws**) *vi* to make the loud harsh cry of a crow or a related bird, or make a sound like this [Late 16C. An imitation of the sound] —**caw** *n*

Cax·ton /kákstən/, **William** (1422?–91) English printer. He established the first printing press in England (1476?) and printed over 100 books, including *The Canterbury Tales.*

> "I, according to my copy, have done set it in imprint, to the intent that noble men may see and learn the noble acts of chivalry, the gentle and virtuous deeds that some knights used in those days."
> [William Caxton. Quoted in *Le Morte D'Arthur,* Thomas Malory; 1485]

cay /kee, kay/ *n* a small low island or reef in the ocean, made of coral or sand, especially in the Caribbean [Late 17C. < Spanish *cayo* "shoal"]

Cay·enne /kī én, kay én/ city and capital of French Guiana, situated in the northern coast of Cayenne Island. Population: 41,000 (1990).

cay·enne pep·per, cay·enne *n* a very hot-tasting red powder made from the dried and ground fruit and seeds of several kinds of chili. Use: in cooking and as a gastric astringent. [Early 18C. < Tupi *kyynha,* altered after CAYENNE]

cay·man *n* ZOOL another spelling of **caiman**

Cay·man Is·lands /káymən-/ group of three islands, situated in the northwestern Caribbean Sea, approximately 200 mi./320 km northwest of Jamaica. Capital: George Town. Population: 35,527 (2001). Area: 100 sq. mi./259 sq. km.

Ca·yu·ga /kay yóogə, kī yóogə/ (*plural same* or **-gas**) *n* a member of an Iroquois people who once lived along Cayuga Lake, and who now live mainly in western New York, Wisconsin, Ontario, and Oklahoma. The Cayuga were one of the five peoples who formed the Iroquois Confederacy, later known as the Six Nations. [Mid-18C. < Iroquoian, "the place where locusts were taken out"] —**Ca·yu·ga** *adj*

Ca·yu·ga Lake /kay yóogə-, kī-/ one of the Finger Lakes, situated in Cayuga and Seneca counties, central New York State. Area: 66 sq. mi./170 sq. km.

cay·use /kī yóoss, kī yóoss/ *n Can, Northwest US* a small pony belonging to a western North American breed [Mid-19C. Shortening of *Cayuse pony,* after the *Cayuse,* a Native American people]

CB *abbr* **1.** ONLINE call back (*used in e-mails or text messages*) **2.** MEDIA citizens band

CBA *abbr* BUSINESS cost-benefit analysis

CBC *n* in Canada, the crown corporation that provides radio and television services to the public. Full form **Canadian Broadcasting Corporation**

cbd *abbr* FREIGHT cash before delivery

C.B.D. *abbr* **1.** FREIGHT cash before delivery **2.** BUSINESS central business district

CBE *abbr UK* Commander of the (Order of the) British Empire (*used as a title*)

CB·er /see bée ər/ *n* a user of a radio on the Citizens Band

CBI *abbr* computer-based instruction

CBS *abbr* Columbia Broadcasting System

CBT *abbr* COMPUT, EDUC computer-based training

CBW *abbr* MIL **1.** chemical and biological warfare **2.** chemical and biological weapon

cc *abbr* **1.** Cocos Islands (*used in Internet addresses*) See table at **domain name 2.** cubic centimeter

CC *abbr* **1.** PUBLIC ADMIN City Council **2.** closed caption (*used in television guides to indicate that a program is available with captions for hearing-impaired people*)

cc. *abbr* LITERAT chapters

c.c. *abbr* **1.** BUSINESS (carbon) copy **2.** cubic centimeter ■ *n* E-MAIL OR PAPER DOCUMENT COPY a copy of an e-mail or other document sent to a recipient or recipients ○ *sent cc's to all concerned committee members* ■ *v* SEND COPY TO SOMEBODY to use the cc line in an e-mail in order to send a copy of the message to another recipient or to others, or to photocopy a document and send it to another recipient or to others

CCA *abbr* **1.** E-COMMERCE cardholder certificate authority **2.** ACCT current-cost accounting

CCC *abbr* Civilian Conservation Corps

CCD *abbr* **1.** COMPUT charge-coupled device **2.** Confraternity of Christian Doctrine

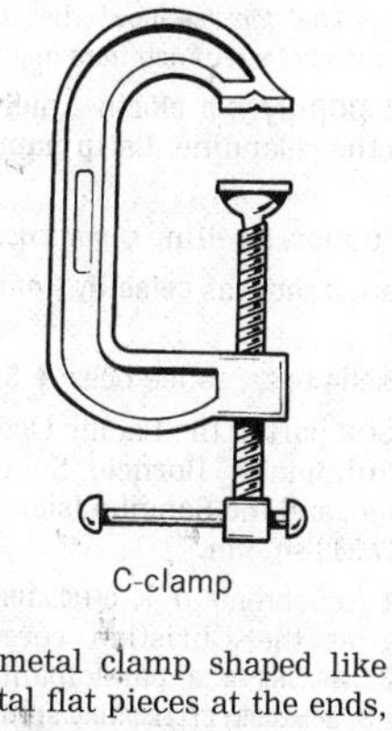

C-clamp

C-clamp *n* a metal clamp shaped like a letter C, with horizontal flat pieces at the ends, that can be adjusted by a screw

C clef *n* a symbol on a musical staff that shows the position of middle C. The alto and tenor clefs are the only commonly used C clefs today, and are found mostly in viola, cello, and bassoon music.

CCTV *abbr* BROADCAST closed-circuit television

CCU *abbr* HEALTH SERVICES coronary care unit

cd[1] *symbol* MEASURE, PHYS candela

cd[2] *abbr* Democratic Republic of the Congo (*used in Internet addresses*)

Cd *symbol* CHEM ELEM cadmium

CD *abbr* **1.** BANKING certificate of deposit **2.** MIL Civil Defense **3.** RECORDING, COMPUT compact disk **4.** Corps Diplomatique (*often displayed on the backs of cars that belong to embassies*)

cd. *abbr* MEASURE cord

c/d *abbr* **1.** ACCT carried down **2.** FIN cum dividend

C/D *abbr* BANKING certificate of deposit

CD burn·er *n* COMPUT same as **CD writer**

CDC *abbr* HEALTH SERVICES Centers for Disease Control and Prevention

CDD *abbr* MIL certificate of disability for discharge

CDE *n* a compact disk that can have its contents erased and something else recorded onto it. Full form **compact disk erasable**

CDIC *n* in Canada, a crown corporation that insures deposits in Canadian banks. Full form **Canada Deposit Insurance Corporation**

cDNA *abbr* GENETICS complementary DNA

CDR[1] *n* a compact disk that can be used to record something but cannot be erased. Full form **compact disk recordable**

CDR[2] *abbr* MIL Commander

Cdr. *abbr* MIL Commander

CD re·writer *n* a piece of equipment used to record data onto a CD-RW

CD-ROM /see dee róm/ *n* a compact disk containing a large amount of data, including text and images, that can be viewed using a computer but cannot be altered or erased. Full form **compact disk read-only memory**

CD-RW *n* a compact disk that can have its contents erased and something else recorded onto it many times. Full form **compact disk rewritable**

CDT *abbr* TIME Central Daylight Time

CDV *abbr* MEDIA **1.** CD-video **2.** compact video disk

CD-vid·e·o *n* **1.** a compact disk used to store and play back video images **2.** a player for compact disks that store and play back video images

CDW *abbr* INSUR collision damage waiver

CD writ·er *n* a piece of equipment used to record data permanently onto a compact disc

Ce *symbol* CHEM ELEM cerium

CE *abbr* **1.** OCCUPATIONS, CHEM chemical engineer **2.** OCCUPATIONS, CIV ENG civil engineer **3.** CALENDAR Common Era **4.** ONLINE creative editing (*used in e-mails*)

USAGE See *A.D.*

C.E. *abbr* **1.** OCCUPATIONS, CHEM chemical engineer **2.** OCCUPATIONS, ENG chief engineer **3.** OCCUPATIONS, CIV ENG civil engineer **4.** CALENDAR Common Era

USAGE See *A.D.*

CEA *abbr* GOV Council of Economic Advisors

ce·a·no·thus /see ə nṓthəss/ *n* a bush with small dark green leaves. Flowers: blue, white, or pink, in clusters. Native to: North America. Genus: *Ceanothus.* [Late 18C. Via modern Latin < Greek *keanōthos* "thistle"]

~~**Ceasar**~~ incorrect spelling of **Caesar**

cease /seess/ (**ceased, ceas·ing, ceas·es**) *v* **1.** *vt* to put an end or stop to something ○ *The magazine will cease free distribution to nonmembers.* **2.** *vi* to come to an end or stop ○ *The rain ceased as if a faucet had been turned off.* [14C. Via French < Latin *cessare* < *cedere* "give way"] ◇ **without cease** without stopping, or without a break

cease·fire /seess fìr/ *n* **1.** an agreement between opposing sides in a conflict that they will stop fighting, usually for a limited time during which they will try to reach a more permanent peace agreement **2.** a military order to stop firing

cease·less /seéssləss/ *adj* without pause or end —**cease·less·ly** *adv* —**cease·less·ness** *n*

Ceau·şes·cu /chow shéskoo/, **Nicolae** (1918–89) Romanian politician. The Communist president of Romania (1967–89), he was overthrown and executed in a popular revolution.

Ce·bu /say boó/ island of the Philippines, in the Pacific Ocean, near the islands of Negros and Mindanao. Population: 2,646,000 (1990). Area: 1,707 sq. mi./4,422 sq. km.

Cec·chet·ti /chay kéttee/, **Enrico** (1850–1928) Italian ballet dancer, choreographer, and teacher. Dancers trained by his technique included Anna Pavlova, Alicia Markova, and Leonide Massine.

Cec·il /séss'l/, **Robert** ➧ **Salisbury, Robert Arthur Talbot Gascoyne-Cecil**

Cec·il, William ➧ **Burghley, Sir William Cecil**

Ce·cil·ia /sə seélyə/, **St.** (*fl*230) Roman Christian martyr. She is regarded as the patron saint of music.

ce·cro·pi·a moth /si krṓpee ə-/ *n* a large silkworm moth with red, white, and black wings. Native to: North America. Latin name: *Hyalophora cecropia.* [Mid-19C. < modern Latin *Cecropia,* after *Cecrops,* mythological first king of Attica and founder of Athens]

ce·cum /seékəm/ (*plural* **-ca** /-kə/), **cae·cum** *n* the pouch, open at one end, in which the large intestine begins [Early 18C. < Latin *(intestinum) caecum* "blind (gut)" < *caecus* "blind"] —**ce·cal** /seékəl/ *adj* —**ce·cal·ly** *adv*

ce·dar /seédər/ *n* **1.** TALL EVERGREEN TREE a tall evergreen tree with spreading branches, needles, and large rounded upright cones. Native to: Europe, Asia, Africa. Genus: *Cedrus.* **2.** TREE LIKE TRUE CEDAR an evergreen tree that resembles a cedar **3.** WOOD FROM CEDAR the wood of a cedar tree [Pre-12C. Via Old French *cedre* < Greek *kedros*]

Ce·dar /seédər/ river that flows southeastward from southeastern Minnesota to southeastern Iowa, where it joins the Iowa River. Length: 300 mi./480 km.

ce·dar-ap·ple rust *n* a disease that develops first on red cedars and then on apple trees in its progress through its life cycle and is caused by a rust fungus, *Gymnosporangium juniperi-virginianae*

Ce·dar Cit·y city in southwestern Utah, north of Zion National Park and northeast of Saint George. Population: 21,427 (2002 estimate).

Ce·dar Falls city in northeastern Iowa, on the Cedar River, northwest of Waterloo and Cedar Rapids. Population: 36,660 (2002 estimate).

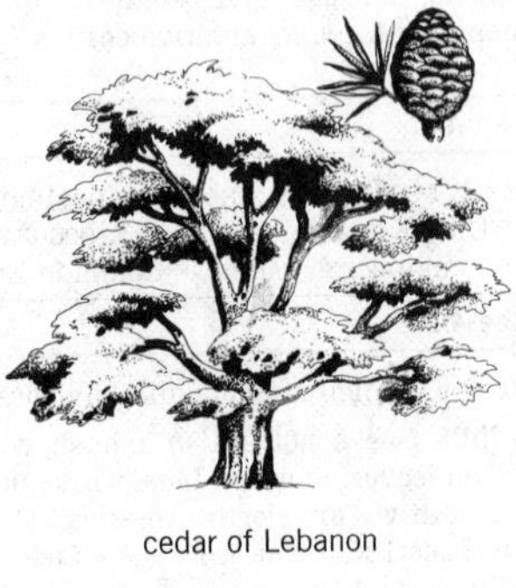

cedar of Lebanon

ce·dar of Leb·a·non *n* a tall long-lived cedar with horizontally spreading branches. Native to: Lebanon, Turkey. Latin name: *Cedrus libari.*

Ce·dar Rap·ids city in eastern Iowa, on the Cedar River, northwest of Davenport. Population: 122,514 (2002 estimate).

cede /seed/ (**ced·ed, ced·ing, cedes**) *vt* to surrender or give up something such as land, rights, or power, to another country, group, or person [Early 16C. Via French < Latin *cedere* "give way"]

SPELLCHECK cede or **seed**? Do not confuse the spelling of *cede* and *seed*, which sound similar. ***Cede***, the less frequent of the two words, is a verb meaning "surrender or give up," as in *to cede territory.* ***Seed*** is chiefly used as a noun, meaning "a part or parts of a plant" (as in *grass seed, grapes with no seeds*) or "a graded competitor in some sports" (as in *the number one seed*); it is also used as a verb, meaning "sow, shed, or remove seeds."

ORIGIN The Latin word *cedere* "to give way," from which *cede* is derived, is also the source of English *abscess, accede, ancestor, cease, concede, decease, exceed, precede, predecessor, proceed, procession, recede,* and *succeed.*

ce·di /sáydee/ (*plural same*) *n* the main unit of Ghanaian currency. See table at **currency** [Mid-20C. < Fanti *sedi* "small shell"]

ce·dil·la /sə díllə/ (*plural* **-las**) *n* in some languages, a mark placed beneath the letters c (ç) and s (ş) that signals a change in the pronunciation of the letter. In French and Portuguese, it shows that c is pronounced like s, not k. In modern Turkish it shows that c and s are voiceless rather then voiced. See table at **diacritic** [Late 16C. < obsolete Spanish, "little z" < Latin *zeta*]

CEGEP /sáy zhèp/, **cegep** *n* in Quebec, an institution above secondary level offering two-year programs leading to university and three-year programs qualifying students in a variety of professions and trades. Full form **Collège d'Enseignement Général et Professionnel**

cei·ba /sáybə/ (*plural* **-bas**) *n UK* same as **silk-cotton tree** [Early 17C. Via Spanish < Arawak, "giant tree"]

ceil /seel/ (**ceiled, ceil·ing, ceils**) *vt* **1.** to construct a ceiling for a room **2.** to line a ceiling with a material such as plaster or wood [Early 16C. Origin ?]

cei·lidh /káylee/ *n* a party with singing and dancing to Scottish or Irish traditional music and storytelling [Late 19C. Via Irish *céilidhe,* Scottish Gaelic *ceilidh* < Old Irish *célide* "visit" < *céle* "companion"]

ceil·ing /seéling/ *n* **1.** INSIDE TOP OF ROOM the overhead surface of a room, or the material used to line this surface **2.** UPPER LIMIT a level above which something such as a price, rent, or wage is not allowed to rise **3.** AVIAT FLYING HEIGHT the maximum height at which an aircraft can fly **4.** METEOROL CLOUD LEVEL the highest point, usually the base of a layer of clouds, from which the surface of Earth can be seen [Mid-16C. < CEIL] —**ceil·inged** *adj* ◇ **go through the ceiling** to rise to a very high level ◇ **go through** *or* **hit the ceiling** to become very angry

ceil·om·e·ter /see lómmətər/ *n* an instrument for measuring the height of a cloud ceiling [Mid-20C. < CEILING]

cel·a·don /séllə dòn, séllәd'n/ *n* **1.** a pale grayish green color **2.** Chinese porcelain with a grayish green glaze [Mid-18C. < French *céladon,* after a character in D'Urfé's romance *L'Astrée*] —**cel·a·don** *adj*

cel·an·dine /séllən dīn, -deen/ *n* **1.** a tall plant of the poppy family that has yellow flowers in summer and bright orange, poisonous sap. Latin name: *Cheladonium majus.* **2.** PLANTS same as **lesser celandine** [Pre-12C. Via Old French *celidoine* < Greek *khelidonion* < *khelidōn* "swallow"; because it flowered in spring, when swallows returned from migration]

cel·an·dine pop·py *n* a North American plant that resembles the celandine. Latin name: *Stylophorum diphyllum.*

-cele *suffix* tumor, swelling ○ *varicocele* [< Greek *kēlē*]

ce·leb /sə léb/ *n* same as **celebrity** (*informal*) [Early 20C. Shortening]

Cel·e·bes /séllə beez, sə leé beez/ ➧ **Sulawesi**

Cel·e·bes Sea part of the Pacific Ocean, surrounded by the Philippines, Borneo, Sulawesi, the Sulu Archipelago, and the Sangihe Islands. Area: 165,000 sq. mi./427,348 sq. km.

cel·e·brant /sélləbrənt/ *n* **1.** OFFICIATING PRIEST a priest officiating at the Christian ceremony of Communion **2.** WORSHIPER a participant in a religious ceremony **3.** SOMEBODY CELEBRATING somebody who celebrates something [Mid-19C. < Latin *celebrant-,* present participle of *celebrare* (see CELEBRATE)]

cel·e·brate /séllə bràyt/ (**-brat·ed, -brat·ing, -brates**) *v* **1.** *vti* SHOW HAPPINESS AT SOMETHING to show happiness that something good or special has happened by doing such things as eating and drinking together or playing music ○ *I told them about my promotion, and we went out to celebrate.* ○ *a noisy crowd of fans celebrating the victory* **2.** *vt* MARK OCCASION to mark a special occasion or day by ceremonies or festivities **3.** *vti* PERFORM RELIGIOUS CEREMONY to perform a religious ceremony according to the prescribed forms **4.** *vt* PRAISE SOMETHING to praise something publicly or make it famous ○ *a popular song celebrating his greatest victory* [Mid-16C. < Latin *celebrat-,* past participle of *celebrare* "attend a festival" < *celeber* "frequented, famous"] —**cel·e·bra·tion** /sèllə bráysh'n/ *n* —**cel·e·bra·tor** *n* —**cel·e·bra·to·ry** /séllәbrə tàwree, sə lébbrə-/ *adj*

cel·e·brat·ed /séllə bràytəd/ *adj* famous and admired

ce·leb·ri·ty /sə lébbrətee/ (*plural* **-ties**) *n* **1.** somebody who is famous during his or her own lifetime **2.** the state of being famous [14C. Directly or via French < Latin *celebritas* < *celeber* "famous"]

ce·leb·ri·ty nov·el *n* a full-length work of fiction written by a celebrity not previously associated with writing

cel·e·cox·ib /sèlli kóksib/ *n* an anti-inflammatory drug that is an oxygenase inhibitor. Use: treatment of osteoarthritis and rheumatoid arthritis. [Late 20C. Contraction and alteration of *selective COX-2 inhibitor*]

ce·le·ri·ac /sə lérree àk/ *n* a type of celery that forms a root like an irregularly shaped turnip, eaten cooked or raw as a vegetable. Latin name: *Apium graveolens* var. rapaceum. [Mid-18C. Alteration of CELERY]

ce·ler·i·ty /sə lérrətee/ *n* quickness in movement or in doing something (*literary*) [15C. Via French < Latin *celeritas* < *celer* "swift"]

celery

cel·er·y /sélləree/ *n* **1.** LONG-STEMMED VEGETABLE the long crisp flattish leaf stalks of a cultivated plant, eaten raw or cooked as a vegetable **2.** CELERY PLANT the plant that produces celery. Latin name: *Apium graveolens* var. dulce. **3.** SEASONING the seeds of the celery plant. Use: seasoning. [Mid-17C. < French *céleri* < Greek *selinon* "parsley"]

cel·er·y cab·bage *n* PLANTS, FOOD same as **Chinese cabbage** (sense 1) [Because the long stalks topped with leaves resemble celery]

cel·er·y root *n* PLANTS, FOOD same as **celeriac**

ce·les·ta /sə léstə/, **ce·leste** /sə lést/ *n* a musical instrument with keys that make hammers strike metal plates to create a soft tinkling sound [Late 19C. Alteration of French *céleste* "celestial" < Latin *caelestis* (see CELESTIAL)]

ce·les·tial /sə léschəl/ *adj* **1.** relating to, suitable for, in, or typical of heaven **2.** relating to, involving, or observed in the sky or outer space [14C. < French < Latin *caelestis* < *caelum* "sky, heaven"] —**ce·les·tial·ly** *adv*

ce·les·tial bod·y *n* an object that is permanently present in the sky, e.g., a star or a planet

ce·les·tial e·qua·tor *n* the great circle in which the plane of the Earth's equator intersects the celestial sphere

ce·les·tial globe *n* a globe showing the positions of astronomical objects in the sky

ce·les·tial ho·ri·zon *n* ASTRON same as **horizon** (sense 3)

ce·les·tial me·chan·ics *n* the branch of astronomy concerned with the motions and positions of astronomical objects in gravitational fields (*takes a singular verb*)

ce·les·tial nav·i·ga·tion *n* navigation in which the positions of astronomical objects are used to triangulate the position of a ship or aircraft

ce·les·tial pole *n* either of the two points where a line in continuation of the Earth's axis intersects thecelestial sphere

ce·les·tial sphere *n* the imaginary sphere around the Earth on which the Sun, Moon, stars, and planets appear to be placed

cel·es·tite /séllə stīt, sə lé stīt/, **cel·es·tine** /séllə steen, -stīn/ *n* a white or colored mineral consisting of strontium sulfate. Use: source of strontium. [Early 19C. < Latin *caelestis* (see CELESTIAL)]

ce·li·ac /seelee àk/, **coe·li·ac** *adj* relating to, involving, or contained in the abdomen [Mid-17C. Via Latin < Greek *koiliakos* < *koilia* "abdomen" < *koilos* "hollow"]

ce·li·ac dis·ease *n* a disorder caused by a sensitivity to gluten that makes the digestive system unable to deal with fat. Symptoms include diarrhea and anemia.

cel·i·bate /sélləbət/ *adj* **1.** abstaining from sex **2.** unmarried, especially because of a religious vow [Early 19C. < Latin *caelibatus* < *caelebs* "unmarried"] —**cel·i·ba·cy** *n* —**cel·i·bate** *n* —**cel·i·bate·ly** *adv*

Cé·line /say leén/, **Louis-Ferdinand** (1894–1961) French novelist and doctor. Misogyny and anti-Semitism characterize such works as his *Journey to the End of the Night* (1932). Born **Destouches, Louis-Ferdinand**

> "Truth is a never-ending agony. The truth of this world is death. One must choose—die or lie. I've never been able to kill myself."
> [Louis-Ferdinand Céline, *Voyage au bout de la nuit (Journey to the End of the Night)*; 1932]

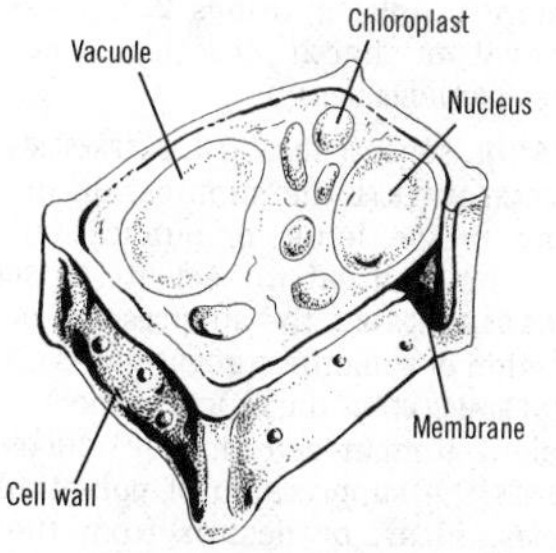

cell: structure of a plant cell

cell /sel/ *n* **1.** BIOL **BASIC UNIT OF LIVING THING** the smallest independently functioning unit in the structure of an organism, usually consisting of one or more nuclei surrounded by cytoplasm and enclosed by a membrane. Cells also contain organelles such as mitochondria, lysosomes, and ribosomes. **2. ROOM FOR HOLDING PRISONER** a room in a prison, in which one or more prisoners are confined, or a small room in a police station, used to confine somebody who has been arrested **3. SMALL ROOM** a very small and simple room, especially in a monastery or convent **4. SMALL ENCLOSED STRUCTURE** a small contained or hollow unit in a structure, e.g., a compartment in a honeycomb or the reproductive organs of a plant, or an area on an insect's wing **5.** ELEC, ENG **SOMETHING THAT PRODUCES ELECTRICITY** a device that produces electrical energy by the chemical action of electrodes in an electrolyte **6.** ELEC same as **solar cell 7.** POL **ACTIVIST GROUP** a small group of people who work together and are part of a larger organization, especially members of a political organization who work in secret **8.** TELECOM **RANGE OF MOBILE PHONE TRANSMITTER** the area covered by one of the transmitters in a mobile telephone system that automatically switches a traveling user between short-range radio stations **9.** COMPUT **SPACE IN TABLE** a space for information in a table such as a computer spreadsheet, formed where a row and a column intersect **10.** CHR **DEPENDENT RELIGIOUS COMMUNITY** a small religious house that is dependent on a larger religious community [Pre-12C. Via French < Latin *cella* "small chamber"] —**celled** *adj* —**-celled** *suffix*

cel·la /séllə/ (*plural* **-lae** /-lee/) *n* the inner room of a classical Greek or Roman temple, containing the shrine or statue of the god [Late 17C. < Latin, "small chamber"]

cel·lar /séllər/ *n* **1. UNDERGROUND ROOM** a room wholly or partly underground that is not suitable as living space and is usually used for storage **2.** BUILDINGS same as **basement 3.** BUILDINGS same as **storm cellar 4.** same as **wine cellar 5. LOWEST STANDING** the lowest standing, grade, or rank, e.g., for an athlete (*slang*) ■ *vt* (**-lared, -lar·ing, -lars**) **STORE WINE** to store something, especially wine, in a cellar [13C. Via Anglo-Norman < late Latin *cellarium* "group of storage chambers" < Latin *cella* "small chamber"]

cel·lar·age /séllərij/ *n* **1.** a fee charged for storing something in a cellar **2.** a cellar or cellars, or the amount of space in a cellar

cel·lar dwel·ler *n* a team habitually at the bottom of its league (*slang*)

cel·lar·er /séllərər/ *n* a supervisor of food and drink supplies, especially in a monastery

cel·lar·ette /sèllə rét/, **cel·lar·et** *n* a cabinet or sideboard for storing bottles of wine and glasses

cel·lar·man /séllərmən/ (*plural* **-men** /-mən/) *n* a man who is in charge of the cellar in a bar or restaurant and is responsible for maintaining good storage conditions

cell·block /sél blòk/ *n* a group of cells forming a unit in a prison

cell di·vi·sion *n* the process by which a cell divides to form two new cells, either to produce identical cells (**mitosis**) or to produce cells with half the number of chromosomes (**meiosis**)

Cel·li·ni /che léenee/, **Benvenuto** (1500–71) Italian sculptor and goldsmith. His autobiography is considered a classic work of Renaissance literature.

cel·list /chéllist/ *n* a musician who plays the cello

cell·mate /sél màyt/ *n* somebody who shares a cell with another prisoner

cell mem·brane *n* the membrane that surrounds the cytoplasm, through which substances pass in and out of the cell

cel·lo /chéllō/ (*plural* **-los**) *n* a large stringed instrument of the violin family that is held upright between a seated player's knees and played with a bow. The cello has a full deep sound. [Late 19C. Shortening of VIOLONCELLO]

ORIGIN ***Cello*** is shortened from *violoncello*, an Italian diminutive of *violone* "double-bass viol."

cel·lo·bi·ose /sèllə bī ōss, -ōz/ *n* a sugar obtained by the breakdown of cellulose. Formula: $C_{12}H_{22}O_{11}$. [Early 20C. < CELLULOSE + BI- + -OSE[2]]

cel·lo·phane /séllə fàyn/ *n* a thin transparent waterproof material. Source: wood pulp. Use: wrapping, covering. [Early 20C. < CELLULOSE]

cell phone /sél fōn/ *n* a portable telephone operated through a cellular radio network [Late 20C. Contraction of *cellular telephone*]

cel·lu·lar /séllyələr/ *adj* **1. CONTAINING SMALL PARTS OR GROUPS** relating to small parts or groups that make up a whole **2.** BIOL **OF LIVING CELLS** relating to or consisting of living cells **3.** TELECOM **ORGANIZED INTO CELLS** organized as a system of cells, especially for radio communication **4.** GEOL, INDUST **POROUS** porous in texture and containing many small cavities **5.** TEXTILES **OPEN-TEXTURED** woven or knitted to produce thick open-textured cloth [Mid-18C. Via French < modern Latin *cellularis* < Latin *cellula* (see CELLULE)] —**cel·lu·lar·i·ty** /sèllyə lárrətee/ *n* —**cel·lu·lar·ly** *adv*

cel·lu·lar phone *n* TELECOM same as **cell phone**

cel·lu·lar ra·di·o *n* a type of radio communication used for mobile phones that consists of a network of transmitters, each covering a small area. The traveling user is automatically switched between radio stations.

cel·lu·lar tel·e·phone *n* TELECOM same as **cell phone**

cel·lu·lase /séllyə làyss, -làyz/ *n* an enzyme that converts cellulose into sugars [Early 20C. < CELLULOSE]

cel·lule /sél yoōl/ *n* a small cell in a living organism [Mid-19C. Via French < Latin *cellula* "small cell" < *cella* "small chamber"]

cel·lu·lite /séllyə līt/ *n* fatty deposits beneath the skin that give a lumpy or grainy appearance to the skin surface, especially on the thighs or buttocks [Mid-20C. < French < *cellule* (see CELLULE)]

cel·lu·li·tis /sèllyə lītiss/ *n* infection and inflammation of the tissues beneath the skin

cel·lu·loid /séllyə lòyd/ *n* **1. COLORLESS PLASTIC** a flammable transparent plastic made from nitrocellulose and a plasticizer such as camphor **2.** MOVIES **FILM** the photographic film used for making movies **3.** MOVIES **MOVIES** the movies as a medium or art form [Mid-19C. < CELLULOSE] —**cel·lu·loid** *adj*

cel·lu·lo·lyt·ic /sèllyəlō líttik/ *adj* describes a process or an organism that can degrade cellulose [Mid-20C. < CELLULOSE]

cel·lu·lose /séllyə lōss, -lōz/ *n* the main constituent of the cell walls of plants and algae. Use: plastics, lacquers, explosives, synthetic fibers. [Mid-19C. < French < Latin *cellula* (see CELLULE)] —**cel·lu·lo·sic** /sèllyə lóssik/ *adj*

cel·lu·lose ac·e·tate *n* a chemical compound produced by the reaction of acetic or sulfuric acid on cellulose. Use: photographic film, plastics, textile fibers, varnishes.

cel·lu·lose ni·trate *n* CHEM same as **nitrocellulose**

cell wall *n* the outermost layer of a cell in plants and some fungi, algae, and bacteria, that provides a supporting framework

cell yell *n* loud conversation on a cellular telephone in a public place or on public transportation, irritating to others

ce·lo·sia /si lōzhə/ (*plural* **-sias** or *same*) *n* a plant belonging to a genus that includes cockscomb. Flowers: feathery, yellow to purplish red. Genus: *Celosia*. [Early 19C. < modern Latin < Greek *kēlos* "burnt"]

Cel·si·us /sélssee əss, sélshəss/ *adj* using or measured on an international metric temperature scale on which water freezes at 0° and boils at 100° under normal atmospheric conditions. The term "Celsius" is usually preferred to "centigrade," especially in technical contexts. ◊ **Fahrenheit** [Mid-19C. After Anders *Celsius* (1701–44), Swedish astronomer]

celt /selt/ *n* a prehistoric chisel or ax that has a metal or stone head with a beveled edge [Early 18C. < medieval Latin *celtis* "chisel"]

Celt /kelt, selt/, **Kelt** /kelt/ *n* **1.** a member of an ancient Indo-European people who lived in central and western Europe. They were driven to the western fringes of the continent by the Romans and some Germanic peoples, especially the Angles and Saxons. **2.** somebody who speaks or whose ancestors spoke a Celtic language [Mid-16C. Via Latin *Celtae* "Celts" < Greek *Keltoi*]

Celt·i·ber·i·an /sèlti bérree ən, kèlt-/ *n* a member of an ancient Celtic people who lived in the Iberian peninsula [Early 17C. < Latin *Celtiberia*, ancient province of Iberia < *Celtae* (see CELT) + *Iberia*] —**Celt·i·ber·i·an** *adj*

Celt·ic /kéltik, séltik/ *adj* **OF CELTS** relating to the Celts, or their languages or cultures ■ *n* **1. INDO-EUROPEAN LANGUAGE GROUP** an Indo-European group of languages that includes Irish, Scottish Gaelic, Welsh, and Breton and has Brythonic and Goidelic subgroups. Native speakers: 1.5 million. **2. ANCESTOR OF MODERN CELTIC LANGUAGES** the reconstructed language that is the ancestor of modern Celtic languages ▶ See panel on next page

Celt·ic cross *n* a cross that has a broad ring around the intersection of the upright and crossbar

Celt·i·cism /sélti sìzzəm, kélt-/ *n* **1.** a word or idiom of Celtic origin that has become naturalized in another language. In English, examples include "plaid" from Scottish Gaelic, "leprechaun" from Irish Gaelic. **2.** a custom or belief of Celtic origin

Celt·ic Sea /kèltik-, sèl-/ extension of the Atlantic Ocean between the Republic of Ireland to the north and southwestern England to the south

cem·ba·lo /chémbə lō/ (*plural* **-li** /-lee/ or **-los**) *n* MUSIC same as **harpsichord** [Mid-19C. < Italian, contraction of

LANGUAGE HERITAGE ***Celtic*** Much of English is made up of words from other languages, and it might be expected that Celtic, the group of languages spoken by the inhabitants of the British Isles before both the Roman and Anglo-Saxon invasions, would be an important early contributor. In fact the Celtic legacy in Old English is slight: ***lough***, the Irish word for a lake that has the same ancestor as Scottish ***loch***, is the only significant survivor. The majority of the words of Celtic origin are of later date, and relate primarily to Scottish, Irish, and Welsh culture, history, or landscape. In the cultural sphere Scottish Gaelic has contributed, for example, ***caber***, ***cairn*** (a pile of stones), ***claymore*** (from Gaelic *claidheamh mor* "great sword"), and ***pibroch*** (from Gaelic *piobaireachd* "art of piping," the first element of which derives from English *pipe*); and especially items of clothing such as ***trews*** and ***plaid***. Some of these migrants have both Scottish and Irish origins, for example, ***brogue*** (via Irish and Scottish Gaelic *brōg* from Old Norse *brók* "leg covering"), ***ceilidh*** (via Irish *céilidhe* and Scottish Gaelic *ceilidh* from Old Irish *célide* "visit"), ***clan*** (via Gaelic *clan* "offspring" from Old Irish *cland*, ultimately from Latin *planta* "sprout"), and ***sporran*** (via Scottish Gaelic from Middle Irish). Scottish Gaelic has given the world ***whiskey*** (from *usquebea*, *usque beatha* "water of life"). Irish culture is reflected both in terms of folklore, for example, ***banshee*** and ***leprechaun***, and in 20th-century terms relating to the modern Irish state, for example, ***Dáil Éireann*** "Irish assembly," ***Garda***, the police force of the Republic of Ireland, and ***Taoiseach***, the title of its prime minister. The best-known Welsh cultural migrant is probably ***eisteddfod***, "traditional music and poetry festival."

The three main Celtic languages are well represented in terms of local geography, geology, and archaeology, but the lesser Breton and Cornish languages also make an appearance in these categories with ***menhir*** (Breton), "large single upright prehistoric stone" and ***vug*** (Cornish), "small hole in a rock or vein." Scottish Gaelic and Irish are represented by, for example, ***esker*** "long narrow ridge of sand or gravel," ***glen*** "long narrow valley," and ***inch*** "small island," as well as by ***loch*** or ***lough***; ***crag*** is also from a Celtic language, probably Welsh *craig* or Gaelic *creagh*. From Welsh come ***cist*** "Stone Age coffin," ***cromlech*** "circle of prehistoric standing stones" and "ancient stone burial chamber," and ***cwm*** "cirque." In zoology Cornish makes its contribution with the shark, ***porbeagle***, and fish, ***wrasse***, Scottish Gaelic with the birds ***capercaillie*** and ***ptarmigan***, and Welsh with the ***corgi*** dog. In botany the ***shamrock***, of course, comes from Ireland.

Less obvious migrants of Celtic origin include ***bijou*** (immediately from French, but the French word was adopted from Breton *bizoù* "jeweled ring," from *biz* "finger"); ***bunny***, the child's word for "rabbit," which goes back to Gaelic *bun* "stump, bottom"; ***galore***, from Irish *go leor* "sufficiency"; ***pillion***, an early migrant to English (15th century), from Gaelic *pillean*, Irish *pillin* "little couch"; ***slew***, an informal word for "large quantity or number," which came in the mid-19th century from Irish *sluagh* "multitude"; ***slogan***, originally the battle cry of a Scottish Highland clan; and ***trousers*** (from Gaelic *triubhas* "close-fitting shorts," from which ***trews*** also derives).

clavicembalo < medieval Latin *clavicymbalum* < Latin *clavis* "key" + *cymbalum* (see CYMBAL)] —**cem·ba·list** *n*

ce·ment /sə mént/ *n* **1.** POWDER FOR CONCRETE a fine gray powder of calcined limestone and clay. Use: mixed with water and sand to make mortar, or with water, sand, and aggregate to make concrete. **2.** CONCRETE a building material that sets hard to form concrete, made by mixing cement with water, sand, and aggregate **3.** GLUE a glue or similar bonding substance **4.** BOND UNITING PEOPLE something that unites people or groups **5.** DENT SUBSTANCE USED IN DENTISTRY a substance used in dentistry for filling cavities and anchoring bridgework or crowns **6.** ANAT same as **cementum** **7.** GEOL MATERIAL BINDING ROCK a substance that binds together the particles in sedimentary rocks and fills the spaces ■ *v* (**-ment·ed, -ment·ing, -ments**) **1.** *vti* FIX OR BECOME FIXED WITH CEMENT to fix something in place with cement or a similar substance, or become fixed in this way **2.** *vt* APPLY CEMENT TO SOMETHING to cover or fill something with cement or a similar substance **3.** *vti* STRENGTHEN RELATIONSHIP to make a relationship between people strong or permanent, or become strong or permanent [14C. Via French *ciment* < Latin *caementum* "quarry stone," (plural) "stone chips" < *caedere* "hew"] —**ce·ment·er** *n* ◇ **set in cement** firmly established and without any likelihood of change

ce·men·ta·tion /sèe men táysh'n/ *n* **1.** APPLYING OF CEMENT the application of cement or a similar substance to something, or the result of this **2.** METALL HEATING OF METAL WITH POWDER the modification of a solid, especially a metal, by heating it with one or more other substances that will diffuse into the surface, e.g., the production of steel by heating it with charcoal **3.** GEOL SEDIMENTARY ROCK FORMATION the process in which percolating ground water deposits a cementing material to form a sedimentary rock **4.** CIV ENG CEMENTING OF ROCKS the injecting of cement into holes or fissures in rocks to make them watertight or strong

ce·ment·ite /sə mén tīt/ *n* a hard brittle compound of iron and carbon that forms in some types of cast iron, in carbon steels, and in alloys of carbon and iron. Formula: Fe_3C.

ce·ment mix·er *n* **1.** a transportable machine with a revolving drum in which cement powder, water, sand, and other materials can be mixed to make concrete, mortar, or stucco **2.** a truck with a large revolving drum for mixing, transporting, and pouring concrete

ce·men·tum /sə méntəm/ *n* the thin layer of bony tissue that covers the dentine of the roots and neck of a tooth [Mid-19C. < Latin *caementum* (see CEMENT)]

~~**cemetary**, **cemetry**~~ incorrect spelling of **cemetery**

cem·e·ter·y /sémmə tèrree/ (*plural* **-ies**) *n* an area of ground in which the dead are buried [14C. Via late Latin *coemeterium* < Greek *koimētērion* "dormitory" < *koiman* "put to sleep"]

CEMF *abbr* PHYS counter-electromotive force

cen. *abbr* **1.** central **2.** TIME century

-cene *suffix* recent ○ *Pliocene* [< Greek *kainos* "new"]

ceno- *prefix* another spelling of **coeno-**

cen·o·bite /sénnə bīt/, **coen·o·bite** *n* a member of a religious community [15C. Via French *cénobite* or ecclesiastical Latin *coenobita* < Greek *koinobion* "common life"] —**cen·o·bit·i·cal** /sènnə bíttik'l/ *adj*

ce·no·gen·e·sis /sèenə jénnəsiss, sènnə-/, **coen·o·gen·e·sis, caen·o·gen·e·sis** *n* the development by an embryo, fetus, or larva of organs or body parts that are lost in adult life

cen·o·taph /sénnə tàf/ *n* a monument erected as a memorial to a dead person or dead people buried elsewhere, especially people killed fighting a war [Early 17C. < Greek *kenotaphion* "empty tomb" < *kenos* "empty" + *taphos* "tomb"] —**cen·o·taph·ic** /sènnə táffik/ *adj*

ce·no·te /si nṓtee/ *n* a deep natural hole found in limestone, especially in Yucatán, Mexico. Cenotes were holy for the Maya, who used them as places of sacrifice. [Mid-19C. Via Yucatán Spanish < Maya *tzonot*]

Ce·no·zo·ic /sèenə zṓ ik, sènnə-/ *n* the most recent era of geologic time, beginning about 65 million years ago, during which modern plants and animals evolved. See table at [Mid-19C. < Greek *kainos* "new"] —**Ce·no·zo·ic** *adj*

cense /senss/ (**censed, cens·ing, cens·es**) *vt* **1.** to perfume a place or worshipers with incense **2.** to burn incense to a deity at an altar or shrine [14C. Shortening of French *encenser* < Latin *incendere* "set fire to" (see INCENSE[1])]

cen·ser /sénssər/ *n* a container used for burning incense, especially one that is swung in a religious procession or ceremony [13C. < Old French *censier*, shortening of *encensier* < *encens* (see INCENSE[1])]

cen·sor /sénssər/ *n* **1.** OFFICIAL REMOVING OBJECTIONABLE MATERIAL an official who examines plays, movies, letters, or publications with a view to removing or banning content considered to be offensive or a threat to security **2.** SOMEBODY WHO SUPPRESSES SOMETHING somebody or something that suppresses or controls something that may offend or harm others **3.** ANCIENT ROMAN OFFICIAL in ancient Rome, either of two elected

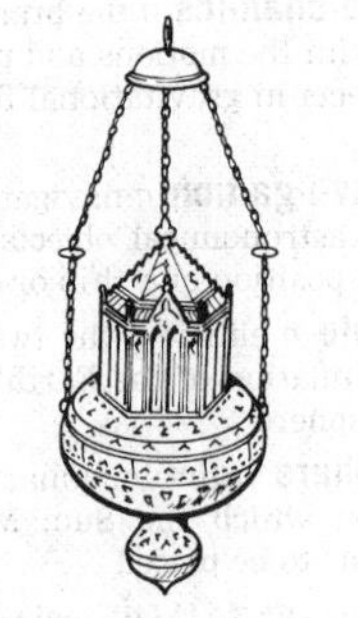

censer

magistrates who were responsible for holding censuses, overseeing public morals, and controlling aspects of finance and taxation **4.** PSYCHIAT INHIBITING FORCE IN MIND in psychology, a mechanism believed to be responsible for what can and cannot emerge from the subconscious to the conscious mind. It is thought to prevent harmful memories, ideas, and desires from reaching the conscious level. ■ *vt* (**-sored, -sor·ing, -sors**) **1.** REMOVE OFFENSIVE PARTS FROM SOMETHING to remove or change any part of a play, movie, letter, or publication considered offensive or a threat to security **2.** EXERCISE CONTROL OVER SOMETHING to suppress or control something that may offend or harm others [Mid-16C. < Latin < *censere* "appraise"] —**cen·sor·a·ble** *adj* —**cen·so·ri·al** /sen sáwree əl/ *adj*

USAGE censor or **censure**? Though spelled similarly these two words are pronounced differently and have different meanings. A ***censor*** is a person who suppresses or removes information (*Military censors have excised some of the target photos for security reasons*), while ***censure*** is severe criticism or condemnation (*the object of a strongly worded censure*). Both words can be verbs, and as such they preserve their distinct meanings.

cen·so·ri·ous /sen sáwree əss/ *adj* **1.** inclined or eager to criticize people or things **2.** expressing strong disapproval or harsh criticism —**cen·so·ri·ous·ly** *adv* —**cen·so·ri·ous·ness** *n*

cen·sor·ship /sénssər shìp/ *n* **1.** SUPPRESSION OF PUBLISHED OR BROADCAST MATERIAL the suppression of all or part of a play, movie, letter, or publication considered offensive or a threat to security **2.** SUPPRESSION OF SOMETHING OBJECTIONABLE the suppression or attempted suppression of something regarded as objectionable **3.** ANCIENT ROMAN OFFICE the office, authority, or term of an ancient Roman censor **4.** PSYCHIAT SUPPRESSION OF MEMORIES the suppression of potentially harmful memories, ideas, or desires from the conscious mind

cen·sure /sénshər/ *n* **1.** DISAPPROVAL severe criticism **2.** OFFICIAL CONDEMNATION official expression of disapproval or condemnation, e.g., of a legislator by the legislature ■ *vt* (**-sured, -sur·ing, -sures**) **1.** CRITICIZE SOMEBODY OR SOMETHING to make a formal, often public statement of disapproval of somebody or something **2.** CONDEMN SOMEBODY OR SOMETHING OFFICIALLY to express official disapproval or condemnation of somebody or something, e.g., by a vote of a legislature [14C. < Latin *censura* "judgment" < *censere* "appraise"] —**cen·sur·a·ble** *adj* —**cen·sur·er** *n*

USAGE See *censor*.

SYNONYMS See ***criticize*** and ***disapprove***.

cen·sus /sénssəss/ (*plural* **-sus·es**) *n* **1.** COUNT OF POPULATION an official count of a population carried out at set intervals **2.** SYSTEMATIC COUNT a systematic count or survey **3.** REGISTRATION FOR TAXATION IN ANCIENT ROME in ancient Rome, a registration of the population and their property that was used for assessing taxes [Early 17C. < Latin < *censere* "appraise"]

cent /sent/ *n* a subunit of currency in the United States, Canada, Australia, New Zealand, South Africa, the European Union, and several other countries. See table at **currency** [14C. Directly or via French, "hundred," or Italian *cento* < Latin *centum*] ◇ **not worth a red cent** worthless

cent. *abbr* **1.** MEASURE centigrade **2.** central **3.** TIME century

cent- *prefix* same as **centi-**

cen·tal /sént'l/ *n UK* same as **hundredweight** (sense 1) [Late 19C. < Latin *centum* "hundred"]

cen·tas /sén ta̋ass/ (*plural same*) *n* a subunit of Lithuanian currency. See table at **currency**

centaur

cen·taur /sén tàwr/ *n* in Greek mythology, a creature with the head, arms, and torso of a man joined to the body of a horse at its neck [14C. Via Latin *centaurus* < Greek *kentauros*]

Cen·tau·rus /sen táwrəss/ *n* a prominent constellation of the southern hemisphere containing the stars Alpha Centauri and Beta Centauri. See illustration at **constellation**

cen·tau·ry /sén tàwree/ (*plural* **-ries**) *n* a plant of the gentian family. Flowers: pink or purple. Use: in herbal medicine. Latin name: *Centaurium erythaea*. [14C. < late Latin *centaurea* < Latin *centaurus* (see CENTAUR); because supposedly discovered by the centaur Chiron]

cen·ta·vo /sen ta̋avō/ (*plural* **-vos**) *n* a subunit of currency in several Spanish- and Portuguese-speaking countries. See table at **currency** [Late 19C. < Spanish, Portuguese, "hundredth" < Latin *centum* "hundred"]

Cent·com /sént kòm/, **CENT·COM** *n* the US military headquarters and its combined service-branch staff responsible for operations in the Arabian Peninsula, Iraq, the northern Red Sea region, the Gulf States, and parts of South and Central Asia and eastern Africa [Late 20C. Acronym of *Central Command*]

cen·te·nar·i·an /sènt'n éree ən/ *n* **100-YEAR-OLD PERSON** somebody who is a hundred years of age or more ■ *adj* **1. 100 YEARS OLD** at least a hundred years of age **2. OF CENTENARIANS** relating to or characteristic of people who are a hundred years of age or more

cen·ten·a·ry /sen ténnəree, sént'n èree/ *adj* **1. OF CENTURY** relating to or involving a period of one hundred years **2. ONCE-A-CENTURY** occurring every hundred years **3.** *UK* same as **centennial** *adj* (sense 3) ■ *n* (*plural* **-ries**) **1. CENTURY** a period of one hundred years **2.** *UK* same as **centennial** [Early 17C. < Latin *centenarius* "containing a hundred" < *centeni* "hundred each" < *centum* "hundred"]

cen·ten·ni·al /sen ténnee əl/ *adj* **1. OF CENTURY** relating to or involving a period of a hundred years **2. ONCE CENTURY** occurring every hundred years **3. OF 100TH ANNIVERSARY** marking an anniversary of one hundred years ■ *n* **100TH ANNIVERSARY** the hundredth anniversary of something, or a celebration held to mark the anniversary [Late 18C. < Latin *centum* "hundred," after BIENNIAL] —**cen·ten·ni·al·ly** *adv*

Cen·ten·ni·al State *n* a nickname for Colorado

cen·ter /séntər/ *n* **1. MIDDLE POINT OR PART** the middle point, area, or part of something that is the same distance from all edges, ends, or opposite sides **2.** MATH **MIDDLE OF CIRCLE OR SPHERE** the interior point that is the same distance from all points on the circumference of a circle, the surface of a sphere, or the vertices of a polygon **3.** MATH **MIDDLE OF LINE** the point on a line that is the same distance from both ends **4. FOOD FILLING** the filling of a chocolate, doughnut, or other food **5. MAIN PART OF TOWN** the part of a town or city where the main stores, offices, and other facilities are situated **6. PLACE FOR PARTICULAR ACTIVITY** a place where a particular activity is carried on ○ *a sports center* **7. FOCUS OF ATTENTION** the point that is the focus of attention or interest ○ *the issue at the center of the controversy* **8. INFLUENTIAL PLACE OR ORGANIZATION** a place, area, or group of people exerting control or influence over somebody or something else ○ *a center of design innovation* **9. CLUSTER OR CONCENTRATION** a place or part where something is concentrated or focused ○ *a population center* **10.** *also* **Center** POL **POLITICAL MODERATES** those political parties or the section of a party holding views that are neither left-wing nor right-wing **11. PIVOTAL POINT OR AXIS** the point or line around which something rotates **12.** PHYS **POINT WHERE FORCE ACTS** in physics, the point at or through which a force is considered to act **13.** SPORTS **MIDDLE PLAYER OR POSITION** in some sports, a player or position in the middle of the field or court, usually responsible for initiating play **14.** BASEBALL same as **center field** **15.** ANAT **GROUP OF NERVE CELLS REGULATING FUNCTION** a group of nerve cells, especially within the central nervous system, that controls a particular function of the body **16.** MECH ENG **CONICAL PART OF LATHE** the part of a lathe that supports the work to be turned **17.** MECH ENG **MARK TO GUIDE DRILL** a dimple made in metal with a pointed tool (**center punch**) to mark the center of a larger hole to be drilled ■ *v* (**-tered, -ter·ing, -ters**) **1.** *vt* **PUT SOMETHING IN MIDDLE** to position something in the middle of something **2.** *vti* **FOCUS ON THEME** to focus on a theme or topic, or cause something to do this ○ *The debate centers on the possible health risks involved.* **3.** *vti* **CONCENTRATE SOMEWHERE** to be concentrated, or cause something to be concentrated, in a particular place **4.** *vt* SPORTS **PASS BALL TOWARD MIDDLE** in some sports, to pass, hit, or kick a ball or puck from the edge of the playing area toward the middle **5.** *vt* FOOTBALL **PASS FOOTBALL BACK BETWEEN LEGS** in football, to pass the ball back between the legs at the beginning of a down [14C. Directly or via French < Latin *centrum* < Greek *kentron* "point" < *kentein* "to prick"]

cen·ter back *n* in various sports, a player or position in the middle of the back line

cen·ter bit *n* a drill attachment or tool for boring or cutting that has a pointed projection in the middle and cutters at the sides

cen·ter·board /séntər bàwrd/ *n* a keel in a sailboat that can be retracted upward in shallow water

Cen·ter·each /séntər reech/ town in Suffolk County, New York, situated on Long Island southeast of Stony Brook. Population: 26,720 (1996).

cen·tered /séntərd/ *adj* **1.** positioned at the same distance from all edges, ends, or opposite sides **2.** exhibiting confidence, self-awareness, and often a sense of determination —**cen·tered·ness** *n*

cen·ter field *n* **1.** in baseball, the part of the outfield behind second base **2.** the position of the baseball player who plays center field —**cen·ter field·er** *n*

cen·ter·fold /séntər fòld/ *n* **1.** a single illustration, advertisement, or feature that covers the two facing pages in the middle of a magazine or newspaper, especially a photograph of a naked or nearly naked model **2.** the subject of a centerfold photograph, especially a naked or nearly naked model **3.** MEDIA same as **center spread** (sense 1)

cen·ter for·ward *n* in sports such as soccer and hockey, the player or position in the middle of the forward attacking line

~~centergrade~~ incorrect spelling of **centigrade**

cen·ter half·back *n* in soccer and field hockey, the player or position in the middle of the halfback-line

cen·ter·line /séntər lìn/ *n* **1.** a solid or dashed line on a road that marks where traffic should flow, either separating lanes going in opposite directions or multiple lanes going in the same direction **2.** a real or imaginary line through or along the middle of something

cen·ter of cur·va·ture *n* the center of a circle whose radius is perpendicular to a line tangent to any point on the concave side of a smooth curve

cen·ter of ex·cel·lence *n* a place where the highest standards of achievement are aimed for in a particular sphere of activity

cen·ter of grav·i·ty *n* **1.** the point through which the sum of gravitational forces on a body can be considered to act **2.** PHYS same as **center of mass**

cen·ter of mass *n* the point at which the total mass of a body or system is assumed to be centered and upon which the sum of external forces can be considered to act

cen·ter·piece /séntər peess/ *n* **1.** an object placed in the middle of something as decoration or to attract attention **2.** the most important part or feature of something

cen·ter punch *n* in metalworking, a pointed tool used for making a dimple to guide a drill bit prior to drilling a hole

Cen·ters for Dis·ease Con·trol and Pre·ven·tion *n* an agency of the federal government concerned mainly with protecting the health and safety of the people of the United States (*takes a singular verb*)

cen·ter spread *n* **1.** the two pages that face each other in the middle of a magazine or newspaper **2.** a magazine or newspaper article featured in the middle to give it prominence

cen·ter stage *n* **1. MIDDLE OF STAGE** the middle area of a theater stage **2. FOCUS OF INTEREST** the center of people's attention or interest ■ *adv* **1. IN MIDDLE OF STAGE** in or to the middle area of a theater stage **2. TO CENTER OF ATTENTION** at or to the center of people's attention or interest

Cen·ter·ville /séntər vìl/ **1.** city in southwestern Ohio, a southeastern suburb of Dayton. Population: 23,072 (2002 estimate). **2.** city in northern Utah, east of the Great Salt Lake and north of Salt Lake City. Population: 23,072 (2002 estimate).

cen·tes·i·mal /sen téssəməl/ *adj* **1. IN 100THS** divided into hundredths **2. 1/100TH** constituting one one-hundredth of something **3. USING BASE OF 100** describes a number system that uses a base of 100 ■ *n* **100TH PART** one hundredth of something [Late 17C. < Latin *centesimus* "hundredth" < *centum* "hundred"] —**cen·tes·i·mal·ly** *adv*

cen·tes·i·mo /sen téssəmō/ (*plural* **-mos** or **-mi** /-mee/) *n* a subunit of currency in Uruguay and Panama. See table at **currency** [Mid-19C. < Italian < Latin *centesimus* (see CENTESIMAL)]

centi- *prefix* **1.** hundred ○ *centipede* **2.** hundredth ○ *centipoise* [Via French < Latin *centum* "hundred"]

cen·ti·grade /sénti gràyd/ *adj* a temperature scale, especially Celsius, based on a range of one hundred

cen·ti·gram /sénti gràm/ *n* a metric unit of mass equal to one hundredth of a gram. Symbol **cg**

cen·ti·li·ter /sénti leetər/ *n* a metric unit of volume equal to one hundredth of a liter. Symbol **cl**

cen·til·lion /sen tíllyən/ (*plural* **-lions** or *same*) *n* **1.** in the United States, Canada, and France, the number represented by the figure 1 followed by 303 zeros **2.** in the United Kingdom and Germany, the number represented by the figure 1 followed by 600 zeros [Mid-19C. < CENTI-, after MILLION and similar words]

cen·time /sa̋an teem, saan téem/ *n* a subunit of currency in some French-speaking countries. See table at **currency** [Early 19C. < French < Latin *centesimus* (see CENTESIMAL)]

cen·ti·me·ter /sénti meetər/ *n* a metric unit of length equal to one hundredth of a meter. Symbol **cm**

cen·ti·me·ter-gram-sec·ond *adj* relating to or using a measurement system that has the centimeter as the basic unit for length, the gram for mass, and the second for time. In scientific contexts the centimeter-gram-second system has been largely replaced by the SI system.

cen·ti·mo /séntəmō/ (*plural* **-mos**) *n* a subunit of currency in several Spanish-speaking countries. See table at **currency** [Late 19C. Via Spanish < French *centime* (see CENTIME)]

cen·ti·mor·gan /sénti màwrgən/ *n* a unit of measurement used to indicate how closely genes are linked together on the same chromosome [Mid-20C. After Thomas Hunt MORGAN]

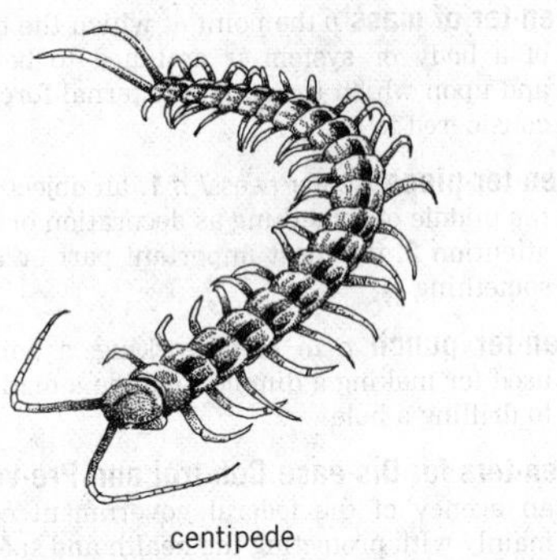

centipede

cen·ti·pede /séntə pèed/ *n* a small fast-moving invertebrate with a long slender body divided into many segments, most of which bear one pair of legs. Class: Chilopoda.

cen·ti·pede grass *n* a low-growing grass that grows in dense mats. Native to: Asia. Latin name: *Eremochloa ophiuroides*.

cen·ti·poise /sénti pòyz/ *n* a unit of measurement for viscosity in the centimeter-gram-second system that is equal to one hundredth of a poise

cent·ner /séntnər/ *n* **1.** BRITISH UNIT OF MASS in the United Kingdom, a unit of mass equal to 100 lb./45.3 kg **2.** EUROPEAN UNIT OF MASS in some European countries, a unit of mass equal to 110.23 lb./50 kg **3.** SOVIET UNIT OF MASS in countries of the former Soviet Union, a unit of mass equal to 220.46 lb./100 kg [Mid-16C. < German *Zentner* < Latin *centenarius* "of a hundred"]

centr- *prefix* same as **centro-** (*used before a vowel*)

cen·tra ANAT plural of **centrum**

cen·tral /séntrəl/ *adj* **1.** IN MIDDLE in, near, or forming the middle of something **2.** EQUIDISTANT FROM OTHER POINTS at approximately the same distance from a number of different points or places **3.** IN MAIN PART OF TOWN in the part of a town or city where the main stores, offices, and other facilities are situated **4.** HAVING CONTROL OVER PARTS controlling the activities of connected, subordinate, or subsidiary parts ○ *a central authority* **5.** HAVING LINKED COMPONENTS describes a system of linked devices controlled by a single unit or at a single point **6.** CRUCIAL of critical importance or great influence ○ *The notion is central to their thinking on the subject.* **7.** DOMINANT with a major or the principal role **8.** ANAT RELATING TO CENTRUM relating to the centrum of a vertebra **9.** PHON SAID WITH TONGUE IN MIDDLE POSITION describes a vowel articulated with the tongue at or near the middle of the hard palate, as is the final vowel in "cola" ■ *n* **1.** SUPERVISORY OFFICE a main office or location that coordinates the work of several branches or a group of people ○ *fund-raising central for the pledge drive* **2.** CENTER OF ACTIVITY a focal point for a particular activity or type of person (*informal*) ○ *Come on over, there are lots of people here – it's party central!* [Mid-17C. < Latin *centralis* < *centrum* (see CENTER)] —**cen·tral·ly** *adv*

Cen·tral Af·ri·can Fed·er·a·tion /sèntrəl-/ federation from 1953 to 1963 of Nyasaland, Northern Rhodesia, and Southern Rhodesia, equivalent to present-day Malawi, Zambia, and Zimbabwe

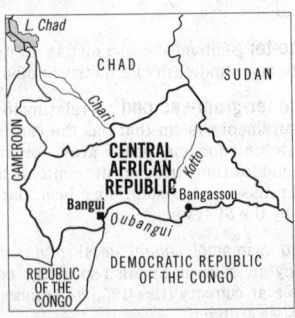

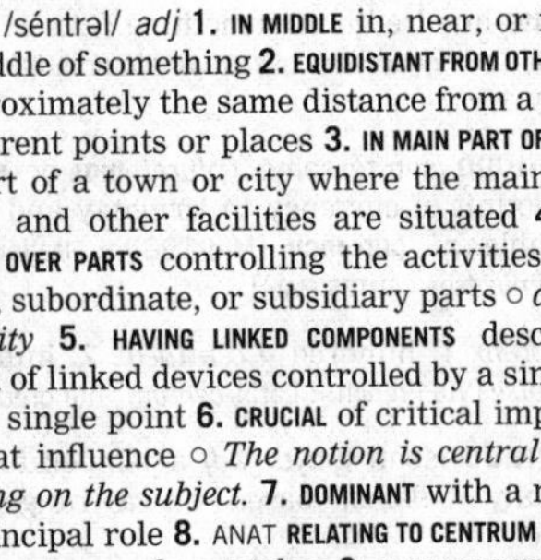

Central African Republic

Cen·tral Af·ri·can Re·pub·lic landlocked country in central Africa. Formerly part of French Equatorial Africa, it became independent in 1960. It is bordered by Chad, Sudan, the Democratic Republic of the Congo, the Republic of the Congo, and Cameroon. Language: French. Currency: CFA franc. Capital: Bangui. Population: 3,683,538 (2003). Area: 240,324 sq. mi./622,436 sq. km. Former name **Ubangi-Shari** (until 1958)

Cen·tral A·mer·i·ca the southern part of North America, extending from the southern border of Mexico to northwestern Colombia, South America. It includes the countries of Guatemala, Belize, Honduras, El Salvador, Nicaragua, Costa Rica, and Panama. Population: 31,300,000 (1993). Area: 202,000 sq. mi./523,000 sq. km. —**Cen·tral A·mer·i·can** *n, adj*

cen·tral an·gle *n* an angle formed in the center of a circle by the meeting of two radii

Cen·tral A·sia region comprising the countries of Kazakhstan, Kyrgyzstan, Tajikistan, Turkmenistan, and Uzbekistan

cen·tral bank *n* a financial institution whose function is to regulate state fiscal and monetary activities, e.g., the US Federal Reserve Bank. It is responsible for the issue of bills and for controlling the flow of currency. —**cen·tral bank·er** *n*

cen·tral cast·ing *n* the department in a film production company whose function is to select appropriate actors to audition for parts

cen·tral city *n* a densely populated city at the heart of a metropolitan area

Cen·tral Com·mit·tee *n* in a Communist party, the part of the bureaucracy responsible for party policy

Cen·tral Day·light Time *n* a variation of Central Standard Time, in the zone that includes the central states of the United States and the central provinces of Canada, from early April to late October, when clocks are set an hour ahead

Cen·tral Eur·o·pe·an Time *n* the standard time adopted by most Western European countries, one hour ahead of Universal Time

cen·tral gov·ern·ment *n* the area of government that is concerned with national issues such as taxation, defense, international relations, and trade

cen·tral heat·ing *n* a system designed to heat a whole building from a single source of heat by pumping hot water or air to room radiators or vents —**cen·tral·ly heat·ed** *adj*

Cen·tral·ia /sen tráylyə/ city in southwestern Washington, south of Olympia, in a major lumbering area. Population: 14,912 (2002 estimate).

Cen·tral In·tel·li·gence Agency *n* full form of **CIA**

Cen·tral Is·lip town in Suffolk County, New York, situated on Long Island, directly east of Brentwood. Population: 26,028 (1996).

cen·tral·ism /séntrə lìzzəm/ *n* the concentration of control, especially political control, in a single authority —**cen·tral·ist** *n, adj* —**cen·tral·is·tic** /sèntrə lístik/ *adj*

cen·tral·i·ty /sen trállətee/ *n* **1.** CRITICAL ROLE the crucial importance of somebody or something **2.** POSITION IN MIDDLE the location of somebody or something in or near the middle of something **3.** LOCATION IN MAIN PART OF TOWN the location of something in the part of a town or city where the main shops, offices, and other facilities are situated

cen·tral·ize /séntrə lìz/ (**-ized, -iz·ing, -iz·es**) *vti* **1.** to remove political or administrative power from local or subordinate levels and concentrate it in a central authority **2.** to concentrate or collect something at a single point —**cen·tral·i·za·tion** /sèntrəli záysh'n/ *n* —**cen·tral·iz·er** *n*

Cen·tral Mount Stu·art mountain in central Australia, considered the geographic center of the continent. Height: 2,772 ft./845 m.

cen·tral nerv·ous sys·tem *n* the part of the nervous system, consisting of the brain and spinal cord, that controls and coordinates most functions of the body and mind. Impulses from sense organs travel to the central nervous system and impulses to muscles and glands travel from it.

Cen·tral Park large park in Manhattan in New York City. It was the first urban park to be developed in the United States and served as a model for subsequent city parks.

cen·tral pro·cess·ing u·nit *n* the part of a computer that performs operations and executes software commands

cen·tral res·er·va·tion *n UK* same as **median strip**

Cen·tral Stan·dard Time, Cen·tral Time *n* **1.** the standard time in the time zone centered on 90° W longitude, which includes the central states of the United States and the central provinces of Canada. It is six hours behind Universal Time. **2.** the standard time in the time zone centered on longitude 135° E, which includes the central part of Australia. It is nine-and-a-half hours ahead of Universal Time.

cen·tral sul·cus *n* a deep groove in each of the hemispheres of the brain, separating the frontal and parietal lobes

Cen·tral Time *n* TIME same as **Central Standard Time**

Cen·tral Val·ley irrigated valley situated between the Sacramento and San Joaquin rivers in California, and between the Sierra Nevada and Coastal mountain ranges

cen·tre *n, vti* (**-tred, -tring, -tres**) Can, UK spelling of **center**

centri- *prefix* same as **centro-**

cen·tric /séntrik/, **cen·tri·cal** /-trik'l/ *adj* **1.** AT OR AS MIDDLE located at or constituting the middle of something **2.** ANAT OF OR FROM NERVE CENTER relating to or issuing from a nerve center **3.** BOT WITH CONCENTRIC LAYERS OF TISSUE describes a plant's vascular bundles in which one type of sap-conducting tissue is surrounded by another **4.** BOT TAPERING AND CYLINDRICAL describes leaves that are tapering and cylindrical **5.** MICROBIOL OF RADICALLY SYMMETRICAL DIATOMS describes diatoms which are radially symmetrical. Class: Centrales. [Late 16C. < Greek *kentrikos* < *kentron* (see CENTER)] —**cen·tri·cal·ly** *adv* —**cen·tric·i·ty** /sen tríssətee/ *n*

-centric *suffix* **1.** having a particular number or type of centers ○ *hexcentric* ○ *acentric* **2.** having as its focus of attention, interest, or activity ○ *egocentric* ○ *teen-centric* [< medieval Latin *-centricus* < Latin *centrum* (see CENTER)]

cen·trif·u·gal /sen tríffyəg'l, -tríffəg'l/ *adj* **1.** PHYS AWAY FROM CENTER acting, moving, or pulling away from a center or axis **2.** TECH EMPLOYING CENTRIFUGAL FORCE using or operated by centrifugal force **3.** PHYSIOL same as **efferent** **4.** BOT DEVELOPING OUTWARD describes a plant part or tissue that develops from the center outward **5.** POL DECENTRALIZING POWER tending to disperse political or administrative power away from a central authority ■ *n* TECH SOMETHING USING CENTRIFUGAL FORCE an apparatus that uses centrifugal force, or a rotating drum in such an apparatus —**cen·trif·u·gal·ism** *n* —**cen·trif·u·gal·ly** *adv*

cen·trif·u·gal force *n* an apparent force that seems to pull a rotating or spinning object away from a center

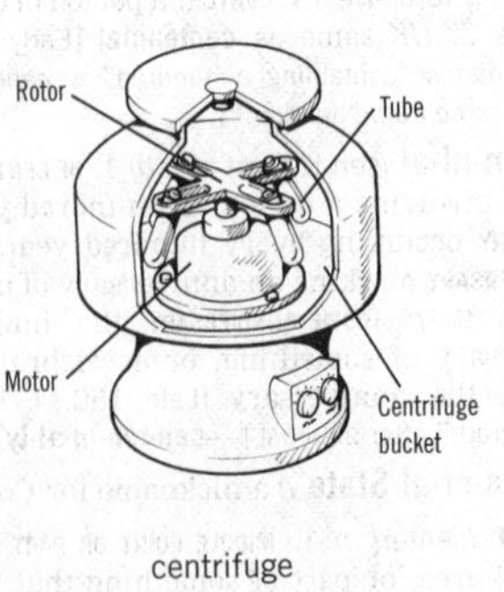

centrifuge

cen·tri·fuge /séntrə fyoòj/ *n* **1.** a device that rotates rapidly and uses centrifugal force to separate substances of different densities **2.** a rotating apparatus used to simulate the effects of gravity or acceleration on humans or animals [Early 18C. < Latin *centrifugus* "fleeing the center" < *fugere* "flee"] —**cen·trif·u·ga·tion** /sèntrəfyə gáysh'n/ *n* —**cen·tri·fuge** *vt*

cen·tri·ole /séntree òl/ *n* in an animal cell, a two-part rod-shaped structure with the parts lying at right angles to each other, located in pairs near the nucleus. During cell division, centrioles move to opposite ends of the cell and form the poles of the spindle fibers that pull the chromosomes apart. [Late 19C. < modern Latin *centriolum* "small center" < Latin *centrum* (see CENTER)]

cen·trip·e·tal /sen tríppət'l/ *adj* **1.** PHYS **TOWARD CENTER** acting, moving, or pulling toward a center or axis **2.** TECH **EMPLOYING CENTRIPETAL FORCE** using or operated by centripetal force **3.** PHYSIOL same as **afferent** **4.** BOT **DEVELOPING INWARD** describes a plant part or tissue that develops from the perimeter inward **5.** POL **CENTRALIZING POWER** tending to concentrate political or administrative power in a central authority [Early 18C. < modern Latin *centripetus* "seeking the center" < Latin *petere* (see PETITION)] —**cen·trip·e·tal·ly** *adv*

cen·trip·e·tal force *n* a force that pulls a rotating or spinning object toward a center or axis

cen·trism /sén trìzzəm/ *n* the holding or advocating of moderate political or other views —**cen·trist** *n, adj*

centro- *prefix* center ○ *centrosome* [< Latin *centrum* (see CENTER)]

cen·tro·bar·ic /sèntrə bárrik/ *adj* relating to a center of gravity [Early 18C. < Greek *kentrobarikē* "center-weight" < *baros* "weight"]

cen·troid /sén tròyd/ *n* PHYS same as **center of mass** [Late 19C. < CENTRO-]

cen·tro·lec·i·thal /sèntrə léssəthəl/ *adj* used to describe an egg with the yolk in the middle [Late 19C. < CENTRO- + LECITHIN + -AL[1]]

cen·tro·mere /séntrə meer/ *n* the point at which two parts **(chromatids)** of a chromosome join and at which the spindle fibers are attached during cell division **(mitosis)** —**cen·tro·mer·ic** /sèntrə mérrik, -meérik/ *adj*

cen·tro·some /séntrə sōm/ *n* a small region of cytoplasm near the nucleus of a cell. In animal cells, it contains rod-shaped structures from which the spindle fibers **(centrioles)** develop in cell division. —**cen·tro·so·mic** /sèntrə sómik/ *adj*

cen·trum /séntrəm/ (*plural* **-trums** or **-tra** /-trə/) *n* a thick mass of bone in a vertebra that is the point of attachment to the vertebrae above and below [Mid-19C. < Latin (see CENTER)]

~~**centry**~~ incorrect spelling of **century**

cen·tum /kéntəm/ *adj* describes ancient Indo-European language groups in which the /k/ sound did not palatalize when preceding a front vowel [Early 20C. < Latin, "hundred"]

cen·tu·ri·on /sen tóoree ən, -chóoree-/ *n* in ancient Rome, an officer in charge of a unit of foot soldiers **(century)** [14C. < Latin *centurion-* < *centuria* (see CENTURY)] —**cen·tu·ri·al** *adj*

cen·tu·ry /sénchəree/ (*plural* **-ries**) *n* **1. 100-YEAR PERIOD IN DATING SYSTEM** a period of a hundred years in a dating system, from a year numbered 1 or 00, e.g., 1901 or 2000, to one ending in 00 or 99, e.g., 2000 or 2099. Centuries are counted forward or backward from a significant event, e.g., the birth of Jesus Christ. **2. 100 YEARS** a period of a hundred years **3. LONG TIME** a very long time (*informal; usually used in the plural*) **4. UNIT OF ROMAN SOLDIERS** in ancient Rome, a group of foot soldiers, originally comprising a hundred men but later between sixty and eighty **5. GROUP OF ROMAN VOTERS** in ancient Rome, a division of citizens designated for voting purposes [14C. < Latin *centuria* "group of a hundred" < *centum* "hundred"]

cen·tu·ry plant *n* a plant with grayish green leaves that takes ten to thirty years to mature and flowers just once before dying. Native to: Mexico, southern United States. Latin name: *Agave americana.* [< the length of its maturation]

CEO, C.E.O. *abbr* BUSINESS chief executive officer

cep /sep/, **cèpe** /sep, seep/ *n* an edible woodland mushroom with a shiny brown cap and a creamy-colored underside. It has a rich nutty flavor. Latin name: *Boletus edulis.* [Mid-19C. Via French *cèpe* < Gascon *cep* "tree trunk, mushroom" < Latin *cippus* "stake"]

cephal- *prefix* same as **cephalo-** (*used before vowels*)

ceph·a·lad /séffə làd/ *adv* in or into a position nearer the head or front

ce·phal·ic /sə fállik/ *adj* relating to the head, or in the region of the head [15C. Via French and Latin < Greek *kephalikos* < *kephalē* (see CEPHALO-)] —**ce·phal·i·cal·ly** *adv*

-cephalic *suffix* having a particular number of heads or a particular kind of head ○ *monocephalic* ○ *brachycephalic* [< Latin *cephalicus* < Greek *kephalē* (see CEPHALO-)]

ce·phal·ic in·dex *n* the ratio of the width to the length of a human skull, measured at the widest and longest points, and multiplied by 100

ceph·a·lin /séffəlin/, **keph·a·lin** /kéffəlin/ *n* one of a group of chemicals found in all tissues, especially the brain

ceph·a·li·za·tion /sèffəli záysh'n/ *n* the tendency for sensory, neural, and feeding organs to be concentrated at the front end of the body, leading to the development of a head during both evolution and embryological development

cephalo- *prefix* head, skull ○ *cephalometry* [Via modern Latin < Greek *kephalē* < Indo-European]

ceph·a·lom·e·try /sèffə lómmətree/ *n* the measurement of human heads, especially using X-rays or ultrasound. It is practiced in dentistry to determine if the mouth can accommodate new teeth and in obstetrics to gauge if a fetal head can pass through the birth canal. —**ceph·a·lo·me·ter** *n* —**ceph·a·lo·met·ric** /sèffəlō méttrik/ *adj*

Ceph·a·lo·ni·a /sèffə lṓnee ə, -lṓnyə/ the largest of the Ionian Islands in western Greece. Population: 39,579 (2001). Area: 290 sq. mi./750 sq. km.

ceph·a·lo·pod /séffələ pòd/ *n* an invertebrate ocean animal with a large head and tentacles, e.g., an octopus, squid, or cuttlefish. Class: Cephalopoda. —**ceph·a·lo·pod** *adj* —**ceph·a·lop·o·dan** /sèffə lóppəd'n/ *adj, n* —**ceph·a·lo·pod·ic** /-lə póddik/ *adj* —**ceph·a·lo·po·dous** /-lóppədəss/ *adj*

ceph·a·lo·spo·rin /sèffələ spáwrin/ *n* an antibiotic belonging to a group of semisynthetic antibiotics with a broad range of effectiveness [Mid-20C. < modern Latin *Cephalosporium*, genus name of the fungus from which originally isolated < *cephalo-* (see CEPHALO-) + *spora* (see SPORE)]

ceph·a·lo·tho·rax /sèffələ tháw ràks/ (*plural* **-rax·es** or **-rac·es** /-rə seez/) *n* the fused head and thorax typical of spiders and other arachnids and many crustaceans

-cephalous *suffix* having a particular number of heads or a particular kind of head ○ *dicephalous* ○ *autocephalous* [< Greek *-kephalos* < *kephalē* (see CEPHALO-)]

-cephaly *suffix* a particular condition of the head or skull ○ *microcephaly* [< Greek *kephalē* (see CEPHALO-)]

Ce·phe·id /séefee id, séffee id/, **Ce·phe·id var·i·a·ble** *n* a star that has regular periods of varying brightness, usually lasting from one to fifty days [Early 20C. < CEPHEUS + -ID]

Ce·pheus /séefyəss/ *n* a constellation of the northern hemisphere. See illustration at **constellation**

ce·ra·ceous /sə ráyshəss/ *adj* like wax in appearance or texture (*technical*) [Mid-18C. < Latin *cera* "wax"]

ce·ram·al /sə rámm'l/ *n* INDUST same as **cermet** [Mid-20C. Blend of CERAMIC + ALLOY]

ce·ram·ic /sə rámmik/ *n* **1.** a hard brittle heat-resistant material made by firing a mixture of clay and chemicals at high temperature **2.** an object made from ceramic [Early 19C. < Greek *keramikos* "of pottery" < *keramos* "pottery"] —**ce·ram·ic** *adj*

ce·ram·ic foam *n* a very light porous solid insulator, made from a ceramic powder and a foaming agent, that can withstand sudden extreme temperature changes

ce·ram·i·cist *n* ARTS same as **ceramist**

ce·ram·ics /sə rámmiks/ *n* the art, technology, or process of making ceramic objects (*takes a singular verb*)

cer·am·ist /sə rámmist/, **ce·ram·i·cist** /sə rámməssist/ *n* somebody who makes ceramic objects

Ce·ram Sea /sáy raam-/ sea in the western Pacific Ocean, in central Moluccas, Indonesia, west of New Guinea. Area: 20,000 sq. mi./51,800 sq. km.

ce·ras·tes /sə ráss teez/ (*plural same*) *n* a poisonous snake that has a projection like a horn above each eye. Native to: North Africa, southwestern Asia. Genus: *Cerastes.* [14C. < Greek *kerastēs* "horned" < *keras* "horn"]

cer·a·toid /sérrə tòyd/ *adj* resembling the horn of an animal in appearance or substance

Cer·ber·us /súrbərəss/ *n* in Greek mythology, the fierce dog that guards the entrance to Hades, usually represented as having three heads —**Cer·ber·e·an** /sùrbə reé ən/ *adj*

-cercal *suffix* having a particular kind of tail ○ *diphycercal* [< French *-cerque* < Greek *kerkos* "tail"]

cer·car·i·a /sər kérree ə/ (*plural* **-ae** /-ee/ or **-as**) *n* the tadpole-shaped larva of various parasitic worms **(flukes)** [Mid-19C. < modern Latin < Greek *kerkos* "tail"] —**cer·car·i·al** *adj*

CERCLA /súrklə/ *abbr* Comprehensive Environmental Response, Compensation, and Liability Act

cer·cus /súrkəss/ (*plural* **-ci** /-see/) *n* either of two sensory appendages at the end of the abdomen of the female mosquito and other insects [Early 19C. Via modern Latin < Greek *kerkos* "tail"] —**cer·cal** *adj*

cere /seer/ *n* the thick skin at the base of the upper beak of some birds such as parrots, which contains the bird's nostrils [15C. < Latin *cera* "wax"]

ce·re·al /séeree əl/ *n* **1. GRAIN** the nutritious grain produced by a cultivated plant belonging to the grass family, e.g., oats, barley, rye, wheat, rice, and corn **2. CROP PLANT** a plant that is cultivated for cereal **3. BREAKFAST FOOD** food made from cereal and eaten especially at breakfast, usually with milk [Early 19C. Directly or via French *céréale* < Latin *cerealis* "of grain cultivation," after CERES[1]]

SPELLCHECK cereal or **serial**? Do not confuse the spelling of ***cereal*** and ***serial***, which sound similar. A ***cereal*** is a type of plant, its grain, or food made from it, as in *cereal crops, breakfast cereal.* The word ***serial*** can be used a noun, denoting a story in episodes, or as an adjective, meaning "forming a series or doing things in a series," as in *a serial killer.*

---

ce·re·al leaf bee·tle *n* a small reddish brown beetle that feeds on the leaves of cereal plants, causing a significant problem for farmers. Latin name: *Oulema melanopus.*

cer·e·bel·lum /sèrrə béləm/ (*plural* **-lums** or **-la** /-lə/) *n* the part of the brain located directly behind the front part **(cerebrum)**, typically consisting of two hemispheres connected by a thin central region, and serving to control and coordinate muscular activity and maintain balance. In humans, it lies between the back of the medulla oblongata and the underside of the posterior part of the cerebral hemispheres. [Mid-16C. < Latin, "small brain" < *cerebrum* "brain"] —**cer·e·bel·lar** *adj*

cer·e·bra *n* ANAT plural of **cerebrum**

cer·e·bral /sə reébrəl, sérrə-/ *adj* **1. OF FRONT OF BRAIN** relating to or located in the front part of the brain **(cerebrum)** **2. OF THE BRAIN** relating to or involving the brain or any part of it **3. INTELLECTUAL** involving the psychological processes of thinking and reasoning rather than the emotions —**cer·e·bral·ly** *adv*

cer·e·bral cor·tex *n* the wrinkled gray outer layer of the front parts of the brain **(cerebral hemispheres)**. Its functions include the perception of sensations, learning, reasoning, and memory. Technical name **pallium** (sense 3)

cer·e·bral dom·i·nance *n* the normal tendency for one of the two sides of the brain **(cerebral hemispheres)** to have stronger control over some functions of the mind and body. When the left hemisphere is dominant, somebody is likely to be right-handed, and vice versa.

cer·e·bral hem·i·sphere *n* either of the two symmetrical halves of the front part of the brain **(cerebrum)**

cer·e·bral pal·sy *n* a condition caused by brain damage around the time of birth and marked by lack of muscle control, especially in the limbs —**cer·e·bral-pal·sied** *adj*

cer·e·bral vas·cu·lar ac·ci·dent *n* MED same as **cerebrovascular accident**

cerebro- *prefix* brain, cerebrum ○ *cerebrovascular* [< Latin *cerebrum* (see CEREBRUM)]

cer·e·bro·side /sérrəbrō sīd/ *n* a fatty chemical (**lipid**) found in the brain and the covering (**myelin sheath**) of some nerves [Late 19C. < CEREBRO- + -OSE[2]]

cer·e·bro·spi·nal /sèrrəbrō spīn'l, sə reébrə-/ *adj* relating to or involving the brain and spinal cord

cer·e·bro·spi·nal flu·id *n* the colorless fluid in and around the brain and spinal cord that absorbs shocks and maintains uniform pressure

cer·e·bro·spi·nal men·in·gi·tis *n* inflammation of the membranes (**meninges**) surrounding the brain and spinal cord, causing high fever and sometimes unconsciousness

cer·e·bro·vas·cu·lar /sèrrəbrō váskyələr, sə reébrə-/ *adj* relating to or involving the blood vessels that supply the brain

cer·e·bro·vas·cu·lar ac·ci·dent, cer·e·bral vas·cu·lar ac·ci·dent *n* any physical event, e.g., a cerebral hemorrhage, that may lead to a stroke (*technical*)

cer·e·brum /sə reébrəm, sérrə-/ (*plural* **-brums** or **-bra** /-brə/) *n* the front part of the brain, divided into two symmetrical halves (**cerebral hemispheres**). In humans, it is where activities including reasoning, learning, sensory perception, and emotional responses take place. [Early 17C. < Latin, "brain" < Indo-European, "head"]

cere·cloth /seér klàwth/ *n* fabric coated with melted wax to make it waterproof [Mid-16C. Alteration of *cered cloth* "waxed cloth," < past participle of *cere* "to wax" < Latin *cerare* < *cera* "wax"]

Cer·e·di·gi·on /kèrrə díggee òn/ county and local council in Wales, occupying the area of the historic county of Cardiganshire. Population: 74,941 (2001). Area: 692 sq. mi./1,793 sq. km.

cer·e·ment /sérrəmənt, seérmənt/ *n* TEXTILES same as **cerecloth** ■ **cer·e·ments** *npl* a burial shroud or clothes [Early 17C. < *cere* (see CERECLOTH)]

cer·e·mo·ni·al /sèrrə mṓnee əl/ *adj* **1. RELATING TO FORMAL OCCASIONS** used on a formal occasion or at a ceremony **2. INVOLVING CEREMONY** involving or done as part of a ceremony ○ *the ceremonial presentation of the awards* **3. NOMINAL** without real power or authority ○ *a largely ceremonial role* ■ *n* **1. FORMAL ETIQUETTE** the correct way to behave on formal occasions **2. RITUAL** a ceremony or set of ceremonies for an occasion **3. ORDER OF SERVICE** the set order of rites or ceremonies in a Christian church, or a book containing this — **cer·e·mo·ni·al·ism** *n* —**cer·e·mo·ni·al·ist** *n* —**cer·e·mo·ni·al·ly** *adv*

USAGE ceremonial or **ceremonious**? ***Ceremonial*** is the more neutral word, describing things that involve ceremony or are a part of it, e.g., *ceremonial occasions.* It is not now used of people. ***Ceremonious*** is used of people or their behavior: a *ceremonious person*, or a person with a *ceremonious manner*, is one who likes and adheres to formalities. Avoid using ***ceremonious*** where ***ceremonial*** is appropriate.

cer·e·mo·ni·ous /sèrrə mṓnee əss/ *adj* **1.** excessively polite or formal, being careful to observe formalities and behave correctly ○ *He replied with ceremonious dignity.* **2.** involving ceremony or consisting of ceremony ○ *ceremonious gestures* —**cer·e·mo·ni·ous·ly** *adv* —**cer·e·mo·ni·ous·ness** *n*

USAGE See ***ceremonial.***

cer·e·mo·ny /sérrə mṓnee/ (*plural* **-nies**) *n* **1. RITUAL FOR FORMAL OCCASION** a formal event to celebrate or solemnize something, e.g., a wedding, an official opening, or an anniversary **2. FORMAL ETIQUETTE** the forms of behavior that are expected or observed on a formal occasion **3. SOCIAL GESTURE** a polite social gesture or ritual performed for the sake of convention [14C. < Latin *caerimonia*] ◇ **stand on ceremony** to behave in a formal manner or insist on formality

Ce·ren·kov ef·fect /chə réng kof-, -kawv-/, **Che·ren·kov ef·fect** *n* the emission of light by a charged particle as it passes through a transparent medium at a speed greater than that of light in the same medium [Mid-20C. After Pavel A. *Cherenkov* (1904–90), Soviet physicist]

Ce·ren·kov ra·di·a·tion /chə réng kof-, -kawv-/, **Che·ren·kov ra·di·a·tion** *n* light emitted by a charged particle as it passes through a transparent medium at a speed greater than that of light in the same medium [Mid-20C. See CERENKOV EFFECT]

Ce·res[1] /seéreez/ *n* **1.** in Roman mythology, the goddess of agriculture. Greek equivalent **Demeter 2.** the largest asteroid and the first to be discovered, in 1801, orbiting between Mars and Jupiter [< Latin]

Ce·res[2] /seéreez/ city in central California, south of Stockton and northeast of San Jose. Population: 36,707 (2002 estimate).

ce·re·us /seéree əss/ *n* **1.** a cactus with spiny ribbed stems, especially a Brazilian species that can reach a height of 40 ft./13 m. Genus: *Cereus.* **2.** any cactus related to the true cereus, e.g., the night-blooming cereus [Late 17C. < modern Latin *Cereus* < Latin *cereus* "candle" < *cera* "wax"]

ce·ri·a /seéree ə/ *n* CHEM same as **ceric oxide** [< modern Latin, plural of *cerium* (see CERIUM)]

ce·ric /seérik, sérrik/ *adj* relating to or containing cerium with a valence of four [Mid-19C. < CERIUM]

ce·ric ox·ide *n* a white crystalline powder. Use: manufacture of ceramics, polishing glass. Formula: CeO_2.

ce·rise /sə reéss, -reéz/ *n* a deep vivid pinkish red color [Mid-19C. < French, "cherry" < Greek *kerasos* "cherry tree"] —**ce·rise** *adj*

ce·ri·um /seéree əm/ *n* a gray malleable metallic element, the most abundant of the rare-earth group. Source: bastnaesite, monazite. Use: metallurgy, glassmaking, ceramics, cigarette-lighter flints. Symbol **Ce**. See table at **element** [Early 19C. < modern Latin < CERES[1]; because the asteroid was discovered just before this element]

cer·met /súr mèt/ *n* a durable substance able to withstand high temperatures, formed by bonding ceramic particles with metal [Mid-20C. Blend of CERAMIC + METAL]

cer·nu·ous /súrnyoo əss/ *adj* describes flowers and buds that droop naturally [Mid-17C. < Latin *cernuus* "inclined forward"]

ce·ro /seérō, sérrō/ (*plural same* or **-ros**) *n* a large edible ocean fish that has silvery sides and large spiny fins. Native to: warm western Atlantic waters. Latin name: *Scomberomorus regalis.* [Late 19C. Alteration of Spanish *sierra* "saw" < Latin *serra*]

ce·ro·tic ac·id /sə rṓtik-, -ròttik-/ *n* a white fatty acid. Source: natural waxes such as beeswax and carnauba wax. Formula: $CH_3(CH_2)_{24}COOH$. [Mid-19C. < Latin *cerotum* "wax salve" < Greek *kērōton* "waxed"]

ce·rous /seérəss/ *adj* relating to or containing cerium with a valence of three [Mid-19C. < CERIUM]

Cer·ri·tos /sə reétəss/ city in southwestern California, a southeastern suburb of Los Angeles. Population: 52,620 (2002 estimate).

CERT /surt/ *abbr* ONLINE computer emergency response team (*used in e-mails*)

cert. *abbr* **1.** certificate **2.** certification **3.** certified

cer·tain /súrt'n/ *adj* **1. WITHOUT DOUBT** having no doubts about something ○ *I'm certain he's the man I saw.* **2. KNOWN OR SET** definitely known, fixed, or settled **3. INEVITABLE** guaranteed to happen or to do something ○ *It's certain they'll lose.* **4. RELIABLE** able to be relied on **5. NOT DEFINED** undeniable but difficult to define, quantify, or express ○ *a certain hesitation in his voice* **6. NOT NAMED** able to be identified but not named ○ *A certain selfish person has used up all the milk.* **7. UNKNOWN OR UNFAMILIAR** used to indicate that only the name of the person, thing, or place mentioned is known ○ *A certain Mr. Esposito was involved.* ■ **SOME** of an imprecise but limited number [13C. Via French < assumed Vulgar Latin *certanus* < Latin *certus* "determined," past participle of *cernere* "decide"] ◇ **certain of** some but not all of (*formal*) ◇ **for certain** without any doubt ◇ **make certain 1.** to check that something has been done or is the case **2.** to take action to achieve something

ORIGIN The Latin word *cernere*, "to separate" or "to decide," from which "certain" is derived, is also the source of English *crime, decree, discern, discreet, discriminate, excrement, excrete, secret,* and *secretary.*

cer·tain·ly /súrt'nlee/ *adv* **1. DEFINITELY** without any doubt or qualification on the part of the speaker ○ *It's certainly a big problem.* **2. USED TO CONCEDE POINT** used to concede a point that has been made ○ *That's certainly an area we could improve upon.* **3. YES** used to indicate unreserved assent ◇ **certainly not** used to indicate emphatic denial or refusal

cer·tain·ty /súrt'ntee/ (*plural* **-ties**) *n* **1. SOMETHING INEVITABLE** a conclusion or outcome that is beyond doubt **2. SOMEBODY OR SOMETHING CERTAIN OF SUCCESS** something that is certain to happen, or somebody assured of a result **3. CONVICTION** complete confidence in the truth of something or an expected outcome ◇ **for a certainty** without any doubt

cer·ti·fi·a·ble /súrtə fī əb'l/ *adj* **1.** capable of being certified as authentic, valid, or qualified **2.** legally or medically declared to be affected by a psychiatric disorder (*dated*) —**cer·ti·fi·a·bly** *adv*

cer·tif·i·cate *n* /sər tíffikət/ **1. DOCUMENT PROVIDING OFFICIAL EVIDENCE** an official document that gives proof and details of something such as personal status, educational achievements, ownership, or authenticity **2. ELECTRONIC IDENTIFICATION** an electronic document verifying somebody's relationship, identity, and responsibilities in financial transactions (*used in e-commerce*) ■ *vt* /sər tíffi kàyt/ (**-cat·ed, -cat·ing, -cates**) **1. GIVE CERTIFICATE TO SOMEBODY OR SOMETHING** to award a certificate to somebody or something **2. PROVE SOMETHING WITH CERTIFICATE** to authorize or provide evidence of something with a certificate [15C. < medieval Latin *certificatum* < past participle of late Latin *certificare* (see CERTIFY)] —**cer·ti·fi·ca·tion** /sùrtəfi káysh'n, sər tìffi-/ *n* —**cer·tif·i·ca·to·ry** /sər tíffikə tàwree/ *adj*

cer·tif·i·cate au·thor·i·ty *n* an organization that issues digital certificates that identify senders of electronic messages

cer·tif·i·cate da·ta·base *n* E-COMMERCE a database storing all certificates issued and used by a certificate authority (*used in e-commerce*)

cer·tif·i·cate of or·i·gin *n* an official document stating what country a consignment of goods has come from

cer·tif·i·cate walk·er *n* E-COMMERCE a computer software program that reads digital certificates and displays their contents (*used in e-commerce*)

cer·ti·fied check *n* a check that the issuing bank guarantees to honor because sufficient funds have been set aside to cover the check

cer·ti·fied mail *n* mail that must be signed for on delivery but that carries no insurance to cover the value of the contents

cer·ti·fied pub·lic ac·count·ant *n* a public accountant who has met the requirements of a particular US state and is therefore allowed to practice there

cer·ti·fy /súrtə fī/ (**-fied, -fy·ing, -fies**) *v* **1.** *vti* **CONFIRM TRUTH OR ACCURACY OF SOMETHING** to state or confirm that something is true or correct **2.** *vt* **GUARANTEE PAYMENT OF CHECK** to indicate on a check that there are sufficient funds to guarantee payment **3.** *vt* **PROVE QUALITY OF SOMEBODY OR SOMETHING** to declare that somebody or something has passed a test or achieved an expected standard **4.** *vt* **ISSUE SOMEBODY OR SOMETHING CERTIFICATE** to award a certificate to somebody or something **5.** *vt* **DECLARE SOMEBODY TO HAVE PSYCHIATRIC DISORDER** to declare somebody officially or legally to have a psychiatric disorder and require confinement in a mental health facility (*dated*) [14C. Via French *certifier* < late Latin *certificare* "make certain" < Latin *certus* (see CERTAIN)] —**cer·ti·fi·er** *n*

~~**certin**~~ incorrect spelling of **certain**

cer·ti·o·rar·i /sùrshee ə rérree, -raáree/ *n* a writ issued by a higher court to obtain records on a case from a lower court so that the case can be reviewed [15C. < late Latin, "be informed," passive of Latin *certiorare* "inform" < *certus* (see CERTAIN); because the word occurs in the writ]

cer·ti·tude /súrti tood/ *n* **1.** the feeling of conviction about something, especially an opinion or religious faith **2.** something that is certain to happen or about which somebody can feel sure [15C. < late Latin *certitudo* < Latin *certus* (see CERTAIN)]

ce·ru·le·an /sə roólee ən/ *adj* of a deep blue color, like the sky on a clear day (*literary*) [Mid-17C. < Latin *caeruleus* < *caelum* "sky"] —**ce·ru·le·an** *n*

ce·ru·lo·plas·min /sə roòlō plázmin/ *n* a copper-transporting protein present in the blood [Mid-20C. < Latin *caeruleus* (see CERULEAN) + PLASMA]

ce·ru·men /sə ro͞omən/ *n* the waxy secretion of glands lining the canal of the external ear (*technical*) [Late 17C. < modern Latin < Latin *cera* "wax"] —**ce·ru·mi·nous** *adj*

ce·ruse /sə ro͞oss, seér o͞oss/ *n* **1.** a cosmetic used in the past that contained white lead. Lead is now known to damage the skin and is no longer used in cosmetics. **2.** white lead used as a pigment and formerly in cosmetics [14C. Via French < Latin *cerussa*]

ce·rus·site /sə rú sìt/ *n* a lead carbonate mineral forming crystals or aggregates of various colors. Use: source of lead. [Mid-19C. < Latin *cerussa* "ceruse"]

Cer·van·tes /sər ván teez/, **Miguel de** (1547–1616) Spanish novelist and dramatist. His *Don Quixote* (1605–15) greatly influenced the development of the novel. Full name **Cervantes Saavedra, Miguel de**

> "Too much sanity may be madness. And maddest of all, to see life as it is and not as it should be!"
> [Miguel de Cervantes, *Don Quixote*; 1605–15]

> "Every man is as Heaven made him, and sometimes a great deal worse."
> [Miguel de Cervantes, *Don Quixote*; 1605–15]

cer·ve·lat /súrvə làt, -làa/ *n* a German cured sausage made from pork and beef, usually smoked, with a mild flavor and a fine texture [Early 17C. Via French < Italian *cervellata* < *cervello* "brain" < Latin *cerebellum* (see CEREBELLUM); because it was made from brains]

cer·vi·cal /súrvik'l/ *adj* **1.** relating or belonging to the cervix of the womb **2.** relating or belonging to the neck, or to any body part that resembles a neck [Mid-19C. < French < Latin *cervic-* "neck"]

cer·vi·cal cap *n* a small, dome-shaped rubber or plastic contraceptive device for women, placed inside the vagina and fitted tightly over the entrance to the cervix

cer·vi·cal smear *n UK* same as **Pap smear**

cer·vi·ces ANAT plural of **cervix**

cer·vi·ci·tis /sùrvi sítiss/ *n* inflammation of the cervix of the womb [Late 19C. < Latin *cervic-* "neck"]

cer·vine /súr vìn/ *adj* relating to, resembling, or typical of a deer [Mid-19C. < Latin *cervinus* < *cervus* "deer"]

cer·vix /súrviks/ (*plural* **-vix·es** or **-vi·ces** /-vi seèz/) *n* **1.** NECK OF WOMB the neck of the womb, consisting of a narrow passage leading to the vagina. The cervix widens greatly during childbirth to permit delivery of the baby. **2.** NECK the neck (*technical*) **3.** PART RESEMBLING NECK any part of the body that resembles a neck in shape or function [15C. < Latin, "neck"]

ce·sar·e·an /si zérree ən/ *n US* an operation to deliver a baby by cutting through the mother's abdomen and womb. Can term **Caesarean** [< the belief that Julius CAESAR was born this way] —**ce·sar·e·an** *adj*

ce·sar·e·an sec·tion *n US* MED same as **cesarean**

ce·si·um /seézee əm/ *n* a rare ductile silver-white element of the alkali metals group that is the most reactive of the elements. Use: photoelectric cells. Symbol **Cs**. See table at **element** [Mid-19C. < modern Latin < Latin *caesius* "bluish gray"; from its blue spectral lines]

ce·si·um clock *n* a clock in which cesium atoms are stimulated by an alternating magnetic field and a precise time is determined when the frequencies of the atoms and the field match

Čes·ké Bu·dě·jo·vi·ce /chèskə bo͝oddə yàwvitsə/ city in southern Bohemia, Czech Republic. It is situated on the Vlatva River, south of Prague. Population: 99,347 (1999).

ces·pi·tose /séspi tòss/, **caes·pi·tose** *adj* describes a plant that grows in tufts or clumps [Late 18C. < Latin *caespit-* "turf"]

ces·sa·tion /se sáysh'n/ *n* a stop, pause, or interruption, especially a permanent discontinuation [15C. < Latin *cessation-* < *cessat-*, past participle of *cessare* "stop"]

ces·sion /sésh'n/ *n* (*formal*) **1.** the ceding or giving up of something, or something ceded in this way, especially land, property, or a right **2.** something ceded or given up, especially land, property, or a right [14C. Directly or via French < Latin *cession-* < *cess-*, past participle of *cedere* "yield"]

cess·pit /séss pìt/ *n* **1.** a pit for the collection of waste matter and water, especially sewage **2.** *UK* same as **cesspool** (sense 2) [Mid-19C. *Cess* < CESSPOOL]

cess·pool /séss po͞ol/ *n* **1.** a covered underground tank or well for the collection of waste matter and water, especially sewage **2.** a foul and putrid place or situation, especially one linked with moral depravity [Late 17C. Probably alteration of *suspiral* "drainpipe" < Old French *suspirail* "breathing hole" < *souspirer* "breathe"]

ces·ta /séstə/ *n* a curved wicker basket for catching and throwing the ball in the sport of jai alai [Early 20C. Via Spanish, "basket" < Latin *cista* (see CHEST)]

ces·ti ANCIENT HIST, CLOTHING plural of **cestus**

c'est la vie /sè laa veé/ *interj* used to express philosophical acceptance of the way things are [Mid-20C. < French, "that's life"]

ces·tode /séss tòd/ *n* ZOOL same as **tapeworm** (*technical*) [Mid-19C. < modern Latin *Cestoda* (plural) < Latin *cestus* (see CESTUS)]

ces·tus /séstəss/ (*plural* **-ti** /-tì/) *n* a girdle or belt, especially one worn by women in ancient Greece [Mid-16C. Via Latin < Greek *kestos* "belt"]

ce·su·ra *n* LITERAT another spelling of **caesura**

CET *abbr* Central European Time

ce·ta·cean /si táysh'n/ *n* a large ocean mammal that has a streamlined body with forelimbs modified as flippers, no hind limbs, and a blowhole on the back, e.g., a whale or a dolphin. Order: Cetacea. [Mid-19C. < modern Latin *Cetacea* (plural) < Latin *cetus* "whale" < Greek *kētos*] —**ce·ta·ceous** /si táyshəss/ *adj*

ce·tane /seé tàyn/ *n* a colorless oily hydrocarbon. Source: petroleum. Use: measuring the ignition quality of diesel fuels, as a solvent. Formula: $C_{16}H_{34}$. [Late 19C. < *cetyl* (see CETYL ALCOHOL)]

ce·tane num·ber, **ce·tane rat·ing** *n* the performance rating of a diesel fuel, expressed as the percentage of cetane in a mixture with 1-methylnaphthalene that shows the same ignition properties. The higher the cetane number, the better the performance.

cete /seet/ *n* a group or company of badgers [15C. Origin ?]

ce·ter·is pa·ri·bus /kàytəriss paárəbəss, sèttəriss párrəbəss/ *adv* used to indicate that something would be the case if everything else under consideration remains the same (*formal*) [Early 17C. < modern Latin, "other things being equal"]

ce·tol·o·gy /si tóllajee/ *n* the branch of zoology concerned with the study of whales, dolphins, and related mammals [Mid-19C. < Latin *cetus* "whale"] —**ce·to·log·i·cal** /seèt'l ójjik'l/ *adj*—**ce·tol·o·gist** *n*

ce·trim·ide /séttrə mìd/ *n* a mixture of ammonium compounds with detergent properties. Use: disinfectant, antiseptic. [Mid-20C. < *ce(tyl)trim(ethyl-ammonium) (brom)ide*]

Ce·tus /seétəss/ *n* a constellation of the celestial equator containing the bright star Mira. See illustration at **constellation**

ce·tyl al·co·hol /seét'l-/ *n* a white waxy solid. Use: manufacture of cosmetics, pharmaceuticals, detergents. [< Latin *cetus* "whale"; because originally isolated from spermaceti]

Cé·vennes /say vén/ mountain range in France extending from the northern Ardèche Department to the southwestern Hérault Department. The highest peak is Mont Mézenc 5,755 ft./1,754 m.

ce·vi·che /se veé chày/, **se·vi·che** *n Hispanic* a Latin American dish of raw fish or shrimp marinated in lemon or lime juice and served as a type of salad with chopped onions and tomatoes [Mid-20C. < American Spanish *seviche*, probably < Spanish *cebo* "fish pieces used for bait" < Latin *cibus* "food"]

Cey·lon /si lón, say-/ former name for **Sri Lanka** —**Cey·lo·nese** /sə lòn eéz, sày lon-/ *adj, n*

Cey·lon moss *n* a red seaweed that is a source of the gelatinous material agar. Native to: eastern Indian Ocean. Latin name: *Gracilaria lichenoides*.

Ce·yx /seé iks/ *n* in Greek mythology, a king of Trachis in Thessaly who died in a shipwreck and whose wife, Alcyone, drowned herself in grief

AKG London

Paul Cézanne: self-portrait

Cé·zanne /say zán, -zaán/, **Paul** (1839–1906) French painter. His postimpressionist representation of nature in such paintings as *Rocky Landscape in Aix* (1887?) inspired cubism.

> "The day is coming when a single carrot, freshly observed, will set off a revolution."
> [Attributed to Paul Cézanne]

cf *abbr* Central African Republic (*used in Internet addresses*) See table at **domain name**

Cf *symbol* CHEM ELEM californium

CF *abbr* **1.** BASEBALL center field **2.** BASEBALL center fielder **3.** cystic fibrosis

cf. *abbr* compare

c.f., **C.F.** *abbr* FREIGHT cost and freight

CFA franc *n* a unit of currency used in several francophone African countries. See table at **currency** [Abbreviation of French *Communauté financière africaine* "African financial community"]

CFB *abbr Can* Canadian Forces Base

CFC *n* a gas containing carbon, hydrogen, chlorine, and fluorine, some forms of which damage the ozone layer in the Earth's atmosphere. Use: refrigerant, aerosol propellant. Full form **chlorofluorocarbon**

CFE *abbr* Conventional Forces in Europe

c.f.i., **C.F.I.** *abbr* SHIPPING cost, freight, and insurance

CFL *abbr Can* Canadian Football League

cfm, **c.f.m.** *abbr* cubic feet per minute

CFO, **C.F.O.** *abbr* chief financial officer

CFP franc *n* the main unit of currency in several French overseas territories in the South Pacific. See table at **currency** [Abbreviation of French *Communauté Française du Pacifique* "French Pacific community"]

cfs, **c.f.s.** *abbr* cubic feet per second

CFTC *abbr* FIN Commodity Futures Trading Commission

cg[1] *symbol* MEASURE centigram

cg[2] *abbr* Congo (*used in Internet addresses*) See table at **domain name**

CG *abbr* captain general

c.g. *abbr* PHYS center of gravity

C.G. *abbr* **1.** MIL Coast Guard **2.** MIL commanding general **3.** INTERNAT REL consul general

cge. *abbr* **1.** FREIGHT carriage **2.** BANKING charge

CGI *abbr* COMPUT **1.** common gateway interface **2.** computer-generated image **3.** computer-generated imagery

cgm *abbr* MEASURE centigram

CGS *abbr* MEASURE centimeter-gram-second system

ch *abbr* Switzerland (*used in Internet addresses*) See table at **domain name**

ch. *abbr* **1.** CHR chaplain **2.** LITERAT chapter **3.** BANKING check **4.** chief **5.** child **6.** children **7.** CHR church

Ch. *abbr* **1.** BROADCAST channel **2.** CHR chaplain **3.** chief **4.** China

C.H., **c.h.** *abbr* **1.** BANKING clearinghouse **2.** courthouse **3.** COMM customhouse

chaat /chaat/, **chat** *n* raw fruits and vegetables in a spicy sauce, eaten as a snack or an accompaniment and originating in northern India [< Hindi]

cha·ba·zite /kábbə zìt/ *n* a pink, yellow, white, or colorless aluminosilicate mineral of the zeolite group. Source: cavities in igneous rocks, hot spring deposits. [Early 19C. < French *chabazie* < Greek *khabazie*, misspelling of *khalazie* < *khalaza* "hail"; from its form and color]

Cha·blis /sha blée, shə-, shábblee/, **cha·blis** *n* **1.** a very dry white wine from the Burgundy region of central France **2.** a semidry white wine, similar to French Chablis, that is made in California or elsewhere

Cha·bri·er /shábbree ày/, **Alexis Emmanuel** (1841–94) French composer. His light operas are rarely performed, but his orchestral rhapsody *España* (1883) remains popular.

Cha·brol /shaa brṓl/, **Claude** (*b.* 1930) French movie director. He was a leader of the French new wave in the 1950s. His films include *Story of Women* (1988).

> "What I like is what people are at the beginning of a scene and what they are at the end of a scene. I'm primarily interested in their relationships, and the plot is just a means to get at the behavior of the characters."
> [Claude Chabrol, *Interview, Times (London)*; May 13, 1972]

cha-cha /chaá chaá/, **cha-cha-cha** /chaá chaa chaá/ *n* **1.** a fast ballroom dance of Latin American origin consisting of three steps and a hip-swaying shuffle **2.** the music for a cha-cha [< American Spanish (Cuban) *cha-cha-cha*, probably an imitation of the musical accompaniment] —**cha-cha** *vi*

chach·ka /chaáchkə/ *n* a inexpensive trinket or souvenir [Mid-20C. Via Yiddish *tshatshke* < Polish *czaczko*]

chac·ma /chákmə/ (*plural* **-mas**) *n* a ground-dwelling baboon with a dark-gray coat and naked face with a long muzzle. Native to: southern Africa. Latin name: *Papio ursinus*. [Mid-19C. < Khoikhoi]

Cha·co /chaákō/ province of northern Argentina. Capital: Resistencia. Population: 931,073 (1999). Area: 38,469 sq. mi./99,633 sq. km.

cha·co·ni·a /chə kṓnee ə/ (*plural* **-as** or *same*) *n* a red flower with large, conspicuous sepals that is the national flower of Trinidad and Tobago. Latin name: *Warszewiczia coccinea*.

cha·conne /shaa káwn, -kón/ *n* **1.** an ancient, moderately slow dance, probably of Spanish origin **2.** a musical composition consisting of variations on a fixed bass line continually repeated (**ground bass**) [Late 17C. Via French < Spanish *chacona*, probably < Basque *chucun* "pretty"]

cha·cun à son goût /shaa kōn aa son gōō/ used to express the individuality or peculiarity of somebody's taste or choice [< French, "each to his or her own taste"]

chad /chad/ *n* **1.** PIECES PUNCHED OUT the mass of waste paper produced by hole-punching machines, formerly from computer punch cards or tapes **2.** PIECE PUNCHED OUT a small piece of waste paper, card, or tape removed from a sheet by a hole-punching machine or tool **3.** PIECE REMOVED TO REGISTER VOTE a piece removed from a ballot paper by a voter or voting machine in order to register a vote against the name of a candidate [Mid-20C. < ?]

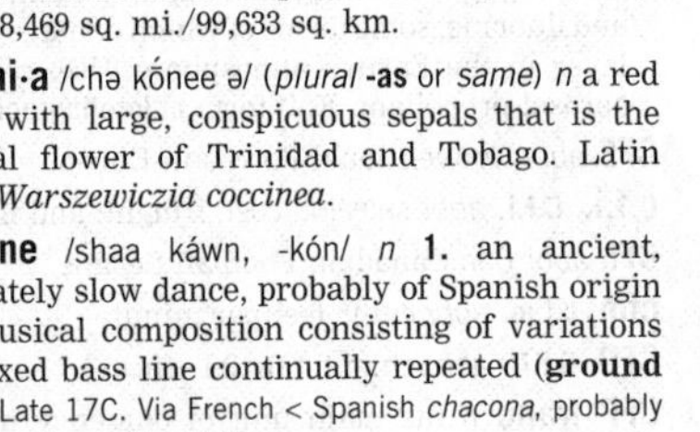

Chad

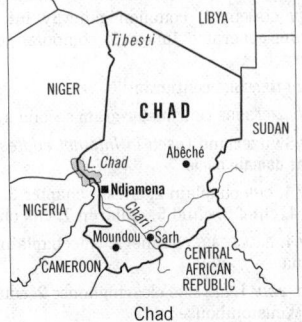

Chad /chad/ landlocked country in north central Africa, bordered on the north by Libya, on the east by Sudan, on the south by the Central African Republic, and on the west by Cameroon, Nigeria, and Niger. A former French territory, it became independent in 1960. Language: French. Currency: CFA franc. Capital: Ndjamena. Population: 9,253,493 (2003). Area: 495,755 sq. mi./1,284,000 sq. km. Official name **Republic of Chad** —**Chad·i·an** *adj, n*

Chad, Lake lake in central Africa, situated at the junction of Nigeria, Niger, and Chad. Area: 6,870 sq. mi./17,800 sq. km.

cha·dar *n* ISLAM another spelling of **chador**

Chad·ic /cháddik/ *n* a large group of languages, spoken in west central Africa, that is a branch of the Afro-Asiatic family of languages. Native speakers: 25 million. —**Cha·dic** *adj*

cha·dor /chúddər/, **cha·dar**, **chud·dar** *n* **1.** a dark traditional garment worn in public by Muslim and sometimes by Hindu women that covers almost all of the head and body **2.** a cloth that is used to cover a Muslim tomb [Early 17C. Directly or via Urdu < Persian *čādar* "sheet, veil"]

chae·ta /keétə/ (*plural* **-tae** /-tee/) *n* a bristle that occurs singly or in clusters in worms such as earthworms and clamworms and helps them to move [Mid-19C. Via modern Latin < Greek *khaitē* "long hair"]

chae·tog·nath /keé tog nàth, keétəg-/ *n* a torpedo-shaped invertebrate ocean animal with an almost transparent body and fins running horizontally down both sides of the trunk and tail. Phylum: Chaetognatha. [Late 19C. < modern Latin *Chaetognatha* < Greek *khaitē* "long hair" + *gnathos* "jaw"] —**chae·tog·na·thous** /kee tógnəthəss/ *adj*

chafe /chayf/ *v* (**chafed, chaf·ing, chafes**) **1.** *vti* BECOME OR MAKE WORN to become sore or worn by rubbing, or make something sore or worn in this way **2.** *vi* CAUSE FRICTION to rub something, causing friction **3.** *vt* RUB SOMETHING TO WARM IT to warm something, especially the hands or other parts of the body, by rubbing **4.** *vti* BECOME ANNOYED, OR ANNOY SOMEBODY to be or make somebody irritated, annoyed, or impatient ■ *n* **1.** SORENESS OR WEAR soreness or wear caused by rubbing **2.** FEELING OF IRRITATION a feeling of irritation, annoyance, or impatience [13C. Via Old French *chaufer* < Latin *calefacere* "make warm" < *calere* "be warm"]

cha·fer /cháyfər/ *n* a large slow-moving scarab beetle, e.g., the cockchafer [Old English *ceafor*, probably < Indo-European, "jaw, mouth"]

chaff[1] /chaf/ *n* **1.** SEED COVERINGS REMOVED BY THRESHING the dry coverings (**bracts**) of grains and other grass seeds that are separated by the process of threshing. When cereal crops are harvested mechanically, chaff is removed by the combine harvester and deposited with the straw in the field. **2.** STRIPS OF METAL TO OBSTRUCT RADAR glass fibers or silvered nylon filaments dispersed into the air as an antiradar measure **3.** WORTHLESS THING something that is worthless or irrelevant [Old English *ceaf* < Germanic] —**chaf·fy** *adj*

chaff[2] /chaf/ *v* (**chaffed, chaff·ing, chaffs**) **1.** *vt* TEASE SOMEBODY LIGHTHEARTEDLY to tease somebody in fun **2.** *vi* BANTER to exchange light-hearted teasing or joking remarks ■ *n* JOKING light-hearted joking or teasing [Early 19C. Origin ?] —**chaff·er** *n*

chaf·fer /cháffər/ *vi* (**-fered, -fer·ing, -fers**) **1.** HAGGLE to haggle or bargain about something **2.** BANDY WORDS to chatter idly ■ *n* BARGAINING bargaining or haggling about something [12C. < Old English *ceap* "bargain" + *faru* "faring"] —**chaf·fer·er** *n*

chaf·finch /chá finch/ *n* a finch with white bars on its wings and a bluish head. Native to: gardens and farmland of Europe and western Asia. Latin name: *Fringilla coelebs*. [Old English *ceaffinc* < *ceaf* "chaff"; because it pecks among farmyard chaff]

chaf·ing dish /cháyfing-/ *n* a shallow pan with a source of heat beneath it, used for cooking food or keeping food warm at the table

Cha·gall /shə gaál, -gál/, **Marc** (1887–1985) Russian-born French painter and designer. His colorful fantasies, anticipating surrealism, stem largely from eastern European Jewish folklore.

> "People have reproached me for putting poetry into my pictures. It is true that there are other things to be required of the art of painting. But show me a single great work that does not have its portion of poetry."
> [Marc Chagall. Quoted in *The World of Marc Chagall*, Roy McMullen; 1968]

Cha·gas' dis·ease /shaágəss-/, **Cha·gas's dis·ease** *n* an often fatal disease, occurring in South and Central America, that affects the heart and nervous system and is caused by a protozoan parasite transmitted by blood-sucking insects [Early 20C. After Carlos *Chagas* (1879–1934), Brazilian physician]

Cha·gos Ar·chi·pe·la·go /chaágəss-/ disputed territory of 52 islands, constituting the British Indian Ocean Territory (a dependency of Great Britain), in the Indian Ocean, south of India. In 1968 the British government forcibly removed the islanders to make way for US military installations but in 2000 a British High Court ruled that this removal was illegal. Area: 23 sq. mi./60 sq. km.

cha·grin /shə grín/ *n* a feeling of vexation or humiliation due to disappointment about something [Mid-17C. < French] —**cha·grin** *vt* —**cha·grined** *adj*

~~**chagrinned**~~ incorrect spelling of **chagrined**

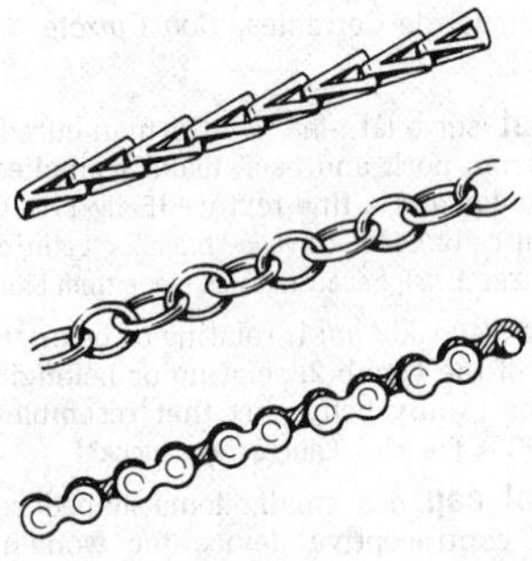

chain

chain /chayn/ *n* **1.** SERIES OF JOINED METAL RINGS a flexible interconnected series of usually metal links that may be used to support, restrain, drive or move something or that may serve as an ornament or decoration **2.** SERIES OF LINKS USED AS ACCESSORY a series of rings, links, or disks used as a necklace, bracelet, or other piece of jewelry **3.** COMM BUSINESSES UNDER ONE MANAGEMENT OR OWNERSHIP a number of stores, hotels, restaurants, or other businesses that are owned by the same company and offer similar goods or services but are found in different locations **4.** GEOG SERIES OF GEOGRAPHIC FORMATIONS a series of associated geographic features or formations such as mountains, lakes, or islands **5.** SOMETHING RESEMBLING CHAIN a series of things or people linked or joined together for some purpose ○ *They stood hand in hand to form a human chain round the perimeter.* **6.** SEQUENCE OF RELATED EVENTS OR FACTS a sequence of facts or events that happen one after the other and are connected in some way **7.** PHYS SERIES OF ATOMS a series of atoms, usually of a single element such as carbon, that are joined in a line or ring within a molecule **8.** BADGE OF OFFICE a chain worn around the neck as a badge of office **9.** MEASURE UNIT OF LENGTH EQUAL TO 66 FT. a unit of length that is now rarely used, equal to 66 ft./20 m. ■ **chains** *npl* RESTRAINING CIRCUMSTANCES feelings or circumstances that restrain or confine somebody (*literary*) ■ *vt* (**chained, chain·ing, chains**) **1.** FASTEN SOMETHING OR SOMEBODY WITH CHAIN to fasten, tie, or restrain something or somebody with a chain or chains **2.** RESTRICT SOMEBODY'S MOBILITY to restrict or confine somebody's freedom of movement or action ○ *She was chained to the computer all day.* [13C. Via Old French *chaeine* < Latin *catena*] —**chained** *adj* —**chain·less** *adj* ◇ **yank somebody's chain** to say something that is untrue in order to tease or annoy somebody (*informal*)

Chain /chayn/, **Sir Ernst Boris** (1906–79) German-born British biochemist. Together with his colleagues Alexander Fleming and Howard Walter Florey, he developed penicillin. They shared the Nobel Prize in medicine (1945).

chain drive *n* an endless linked chain that meshes with the teeth of two sprocket wheels to transfer energy and motion from one wheel to the other —**chain-driv·en** *adj*

chaî·né /shə náy/ (*plural* **-nés** /-náy/) *n* a series of short, usually fast turns made by a ballet dancer moving in a straight line across a floor or stage [Mid-20C. < French, past participle of *chaîner* "to chain" < Old French *chaeine* (see CHAIN)]

chain gang *n* a group of prisoners who work away from the prison and are shackled together, usually with leg irons and a series of chains

chain let·ter *n* a letter sent to a number of people, each of whom is asked to send copies to the same number of new people, sometimes requesting and promising money

chain light·ning *n US* lightning that appears as a jagged line of light splitting into two or more branches near the ground. Can term **forked lightning**

chain-link fence /chàyn lingk-/ *n* a fence formed from lengths of strong wire that are interwoven in a diamond pattern —**chain-link fenc·ing** *n*

chain mail *n* interlinked rings of metal forming a flexible piece of armor, worn by knights in medieval times

chain of com·mand *n* a hierarchy of officials in the armed forces or in business, each reporting to and taking orders from the next most senior person

chain pick·er·el *n* a large slender greenish black freshwater fish of that resembles a young pike and has chain-shaped markings along each flank. Native to: eastern North America. Latin name: *Esox niger*.

chain re·ac·tion *n* **1.** CONNECTED SEQUENCE OF EVENTS a series of events following on quickly from each other, each of which causes the next one **2.** PHYS SELF-SUSTAINING NUCLEAR FISSION a self-sustaining nuclear reaction in which each fission of an atomic nucleus causes neutrons and energy to be emitted, each collision of neutrons with other nuclei causing a further fission **3.** CHEM SERIES OF CHEMICAL REACTIONS a series of chemical reactions in which the product from one reaction helps to create the next one —**chain-re·act** *vi*

chain saw *n* a portable motor-driven saw with cutting teeth made of links that form a continuous chain, used for cutting wood

chain shot *n* two cannonballs or half-balls connected by a chain, formerly used to destroy a ship's rigging

chain-smoke (**chain-smoked, chain-smok·ing, chain-smokes**) *vti* to smoke cigarettes continuously, often lighting the next from the previous one as it is finished —**chain-smok·er** *n*

chain stitch *n* a hand, machine, or crochet stitch in which each stitch forms a loop through the forward end of the previous one to resemble the links of a chain —**chain-stitch** *vti*

chain store *n* one of a series of retail stores, especially department stores or supermarkets, owned by the same company

chair /cher/ *n* **1.** SEAT WITH BACK a seat with a back support, usually for one person. Most chairs have four legs or feet and some have rests for the arms. **2.** same as **electric chair** (*informal*) **3.** CHAIRPERSON somebody presiding over something such as a committee, board, or meeting, or the position of such a person **4.** EDUC SOMEBODY WHO HOLDS ENDOWED PROFESSORSHIP somebody who holds an endowed professorship at a university **5.** MUSIC RANKED POSITION OF ORCHESTRAL MUSICIAN the ranked position of a musician in an orchestra **6.** CONSTR SUPPORTING DEVICE DURING POURING OF CONCRETE a device to keep reinforcing rods in place during the pouring of concrete ■ *vt* (**chaired, chair·ing, chairs**) **1.** PRESIDE OVER SOMETHING to preside over something such as a committee, board, or meeting **2.** *UK* CARRY WINNER ON SHOULDERS to carry a victor or champion on the shoulders in triumph [13C. Via Old French *chaiere* < Latin *cathedra* "seat"]

USAGE ***Chair*** has long been used to mean "the authority or position of chairman," and has been extended to mean "the presiding officer of a committee or meeting," in order to avoid having to use the gender-specific terms *chairman* or *chairwoman*. An alternative is *chairperson*, though it is disliked by some people.

chair·borne /chér bàwrn/ *adj* working at a desk in an office job in the armed forces, rather than having combat or field duties (*informal*)

chair car *n* RAIL same as **parlor car**

chair class *n S Asia* a class of travel on railroad trains in which passengers are provided with reclinable seats similar to those in aircraft

Barnaby's

chair lift

chair lift *n* a series of seats suspended from a moving cable, used to carry passengers up or down a mountain or other slope

chair·man /chérmən/ (*plural* **-men** /-mən/) *n* **1.** the officer who presides over something such as a committee or meeting **2.** *also* **chair·man of the board** the chief officer of a business corporation, elected by its board of directors and responsible for corporate policy and supervision of upper management —**chair·man·ship** *n*

USAGE See *chair*.

chair·per·son /chér pùrss'n/ (*plural* **-sons**) *n* the officer who presides over something such as a committee, board, or meeting

USAGE See *chair*.

chair·wom·an /chér wòommən/ (*plural* **-wom·en** /-wìmmin/) *n* a woman who is the presiding officer of something such as a committee, board, or meeting

USAGE See *chair*.

chaise /shayz/ (*plural* **chaises** /*pronunc. same*/) *n* **1.** FURNITURE same as **chaise longue 2.** a light open two-wheeled carriage for one or more people, usually hooded and drawn by one horse **3.** TRANSP same as **post chaise** [Mid-17C. < French]

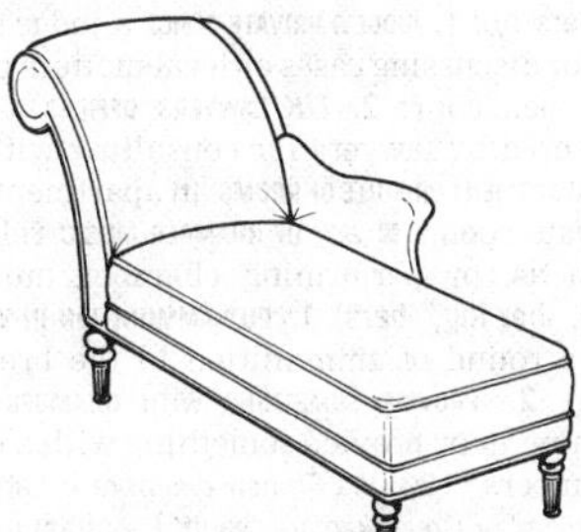

chaise longue (sense 2)

chaise longue /shàyz láwng/ (*plural* **chaise longues** or **chaises longues** /*pronunc. same*/) *n* **1.** a long low foldable chair with an adjustable back, used on a patio or beach **2.** a chair with an elongated seat, one armrest, and sometimes an adjustable back, designed for lying on [< French, "long chair"]

~~**chaise lounge**~~ incorrect spelling of **chaise longue**

chak·ra /cha͡akrə, chúkrə/ *n* in yoga, any of the centers of spiritual power in the body [Late 18C. < Sanskrit *cakra* "wheel"]

cha·la·za /kə láyzə, -lázzə/ (*plural* **-zas** or **-zae** /-zee/) *n* **1.** a spiral chord of albumen that is attached at each end of the yolk to the lining membrane inside a bird's egg, holding it in position **2.** the base of the immature seed of a plant [Early 18C. Via modern Latin < Greek *khalaza* "hail"] —**cha·la·zal** *adj*

cha·la·zi·on /kə láyzee ən/ *n* MED same as **meibomian cyst** [Early 18C. < Greek *khalazion* "small lump" < *khalaza* "hail"]

Chal·ce·don /kálssi dòn, kal sédd'n/ ancient Greek city on the Bosporus near modern-day Istanbul, founded in 685 B.C. —**Chal·ce·do·ni·an** /kàlssə dṓnyən, -dṓnee ən/ *adj, n*

chal·ced·o·ny /kal sédd'nee/ *n* a translucent or grayish semiprecious stone that is a variety of banded quartz. Use: gems, ornaments. [13C. < Latin *c(h)alcedonius* < Greek *khalkēdōn*, mystical stone] —**chal·ce·don·ic** /kàlssə dónnik/ *adj*

chal·cid /kálssid/ *n* a small wasp with bright metallic coloration whose larvae are often parasites of other insects in various stages of life. Superfamily: Chalcidoidea. [Late 19C. < modern Latin *Chalcid-* < Greek *khalkos* "copper"; from its metallic color]

chalco- *prefix* copper ○ *chalcopyrite* [< Greek *khalkos*]

chal·co·cite /kálkə sìt/ *n* a gray to black brittle copper sulfide mineral. Use: source of copper.

chal·cog·ra·phy /kal kóggrəfee/ *n* engraving on copper or brass —**chal·cog·ra·pher** *n* —**chal·co·graph·ic** /kàlkə gráffik/ *adj* —**chal·co·graph·i·cal** *adj* —**chal·cog·ra·phist** *n*

chal·co·lith·ic /kàlkə líthik/ *adj* belonging or relating to the transitional period between the Neolithic and Bronze ages, beginning around 400 B.C., when the use of copper became more prevalent

chal·co·py·rite /kàlkə pí rìt/ *n* a brassy sulfide mineral containing copper and iron. Use: source of copper.

Chal·dae·an *n* PEOPLES, LANG another spelling of **Chaldean**

Chal·de·a /kal dée ə/ ancient region of Mesopotamia, between the Euphrates and the Persian Gulf, in modern-day southern Iraq

Chal·de·an /kal dée ən/, **Chal·dae·an** *n* **1.** a member of an ancient Semitic people who lived in Chaldea in southern Babylonia, where they were the dominant ethnic group during the 8th and 7th centuries B.C. **2.** a dialect of the modern Aramaic language, spoken in Iraq and in the United States [Late 16C. < Latin *Chaldaeus* < Assyrian *kaldū*] —**Chal·da·ic** /kal dáy ik/ *n, adj* —**Chal·de·an** *adj*

Chal·dee /káldee, kal dée/ *n* **1.** the Aramaic language (*dated*) **2.** PEOPLES same as **Chaldean** (sense 1) [14C. Via Old French < Latin *Chaldaeus* (see CHALDEAN)]

~~**chalenge**~~ incorrect spelling of **challenge**

cha·let /sha láy, shá lày/ *n* a house or cottage traditionally made of wood with wide overhanging eaves, in a style originally built in Switzerland [Late 18C. < Swiss French]

Chal·grin /shál gràN/, **Jean-François-Thérèse** (1739–1811) French architect. He was commissioned by Napoleon in 1806 to design the Arc de Triomphe in Paris, although it was not completed until after his death.

chal·ice /chálliss/ *n* **1.** a metal drinking cup or goblet (*literary*) **2.** in the Christian church, a gold or silver cup used for serving the wine at Communion [14C. Directly or via French < Latin *calic-* "cup"]

chal·i·co·there /kállikə thèer/ *n* an extinct mammal resembling a horse with clawed feet and forelimbs slightly longer than the hind limbs. It lived from about 55 million to about 10,000 years ago. Suborder: Chalicotheriidae. [Early 20C. < modern Latin *Chalicotherium* "animal found in gravel" < Greek *khalik-* "pebble" + *thērion* "small animal" < *thēr* "animal"]

chalk /chawk/ *n* **1.** POWDERY WHITE ROCK a soft white or gray fine-grained sedimentary rock consisting of nearly pure calcium carbonate originally formed under the sea and containing minute fossil fragments of marine organisms **2.** SOFT MARKER MADE FROM CHALK a piece of chalk or a similar substance, sometimes colored, used for writing or drawing, e.g., on a blackboard **3.** PIECE OF CHALK FOR BILLIARD CUE a small cube of chalk or similar substance used for rubbing the tip of a pool or billiard cue to increase friction between the cue and the ball ■ *v* (**chalked, chalk·ing, chalks**) **1.** *vti* MAKE CHALK MARK ON SOMETHING to draw, write, or mark something with chalk **2.** *vi* BECOME POWDER to become powdery **3.** *vt* RUB CHALK ON CUE to treat the tip of a pool or billiard cue with chalk [Old English *cealc* "lime(stone), chalk," via Germanic < Latin *calc-* "lime(stone)" < Greek *khalix* "pebble"] ◇ **not by a long chalk** *UK* not by any means

chalk up *vt* **1.** SCORE OR KEEP SCORE OF SOMETHING to score or achieve something, or record a score or victory (*informal*) **2.** ATTRIBUTE SOMETHING to credit or ascribe something to something or somebody (*informal*) **3.** *UK* CHARGE SOMETHING TO SOMEBODY to record the cost of something and charge it to somebody or somebody's account [< the British custom at pubs or bars of writing up with chalk an account of credit given]

chalk·board /cháwk bàwrd/ *n* EDUC same as **blackboard**

chalk·stone /cháwk stōn/ *n* a piece of chalk taken straight from the ground

chalk talk *n* an informal lecture during which illustrations or examples are given on a blackboard

chalk·y /cháwkee/ (**-i·er, -i·est**) *adj* containing or resembling chalk in color or texture —**chalk·i·ness** *n*

chal·lah /kh̲aálə, haálə/, **hal·lah** *n* white bread enriched with eggs, usually in a braided loaf, traditionally eaten by Jews on Friday evening at the Sabbath meal [Early 20C. < Hebrew *ḥallāh*, probably < *ḥll* "pierce"; from its original shape]

chal·lenge /chállənj/ *vt* (**-lenged, -leng·ing, -leng·es**) **1.** INVITE SOMEBODY TO COMPETE to invite somebody to participate in a fight, contest, or competition **2.** DARE SOMEBODY to dare somebody to do something **3.** CALL SOMETHING INTO QUESTION to call something into question by demanding an explanation, justification, or proof **4.** STIMULATE INTELLECT to stimulate somebody by making demands on the intellect **5.** ORDER SOMEBODY TO PRODUCE IDENTIFICATION to order somebody to stop and produce identification or a password **6.** LAW OBJECT TO INCLUSION OF JUROR to make a formal objection against the inclusion of a prospective juror on a jury **7.** MED TEST WHETHER SOMETHING PRODUCES ALLERGY to expose a person or animal to a substance in order to determine whether an allergy or other adverse reaction will occur ■ *n* **1.** INVITATION TO TAKE PART IN CONTEST an invitation to somebody to compete in a fight, contest, or competition **2.** STIMULATING TEST OF ABILITIES a test of somebody's abilities, or a situation that tests somebody's abilities in a stimulating way **3.** QUESTIONING OF SOMETHING a questioning of something by demanding an explanation, justification, or proof **4.** DEMAND FOR IDENTIFICATION an order to somebody to stop and produce identification or a password **5.** LAW OBJECTION AGAINST JUROR an objection against the inclusion of somebody on a jury **6.** CLAIM AGAINST VOTING ELIGIBILITY a claim that somebody is not entitled to a vote or that a vote is invalid **7.** MED TESTING FOR ALLERGY exposure of a person or animal to a substance in order to determine whether an allergy or other adverse reaction will occur [13C. Via Old French *c(h)alengier* "accuse" < Latin *calumniare* "accuse falsely" < *calumnia* "false accusation"] —**chal·lenge·a·ble** *adj*

chal·lenged /chállənjd/ *adj* **1.** having a particular impairment ○ *physically challenged* **2.** lacking in a particular quality (*humorous; sometimes considered offensive*) ○ *judgmentally challenged*

USAGE See *disabled*.

chal·leng·er /chállənjər/ *n* **1.** the issuer of an invitation to a fight, contest, or competition **2.** an opponent of a champion, especially in a boxing match

chal·leng·ing /chállənjing/ *adj* demanding physical or psychological effort of a stimulating kind —**chal·leng·ing·ly** *adv*

chal·lis /shállee/, **chal·lie** *n* a soft lightweight woolen, cotton, or synthetic fabric, often patterned with a small print. Use: clothes. [Mid-19C. Origin ?]

Chal·mette /shal mét/ unincorporated settlement and county seat of St. Bernard parish in southeastern Louisiana, situated on the Mississippi River downstream from New Orleans. Population: 31,860 (1996).

cha·lone /káy lōn, ká-/ *n* a substance produced by cells that inhibits cell division (**mitosis**). Chalones are usually glycoproteins. [Early 20C. < Greek *khalōn*, present participle of *khalan* "slacken"] —**cha·lon·ic** /ka lónik, kay-/ *adj*

chal·ta hai /chùltə hī́/ *adj S Asia* tolerant and easygoing (*informal*) [< Hindi]

chal·u·meau /shàllə mṓ/ (*plural* **-meaux** /-mṓ/) *n* **1.** a woodwind instrument of the 17th and 18th centuries that developed into the clarinet **2.** the lowest register of a clarinet, or its warm tone quality [Early 18C. Via French < late Latin *calamellus* "small reed" < *calamus* "reed" < Greek *kalamos*]

cha·lutz /kh̲aa lŏŏts/ (*plural* **-lutz·im** /-lŏŏtsim/), **ha·lutz** (*plural* **-lutz·im**) *n* a member of a group of Jewish immigrants to Palestine after 1917 who began or worked in agricultural or forestry projects [Early 20C. < Hebrew *ḥaluṣ* "pioneer"]

cha·lyb·e·ate /kə líbbee ət, kə leébee àyt/ *adj* **1.** containing iron salts **2.** having a taste like iron [Mid-17C. < modern Latin *chalybeatus* < Latin *chalybs* "steel" < Greek *khalups*]

cha·ly·bite /kálli bīt/ *n* MINERALS same as **siderite** (sense 1) [Mid-19C. < Greek *khalub-* "steel"]

Cham /kam/ (*plural* **Chams** or *same*) *n* **1.** a member of an indigenous people who formed a kingdom in present-day Vietnam between the 2nd and 17th centuries A.D. and who now live mainly in Cambodia **2.** an Austronesian language spoken in Vietnam and Cambodia. Native speakers: 230,000. —**Cham** *adj*

Cha·mae·leon /kə meélee ən, -lyən/, **Cha·me·leon** *n* a faint constellation near the south celestial pole. See illustration at **constellation**

cham·ae·phyte /kámmi fīt/ *n* a perennial plant that produces dormant winter buds on or close to the ground [Early 20C. < Greek *khamai* "on the ground"]

cham·be·lane /shámbə làyn/ *n Hispanic* a boy who is a young girl's formal escort in a court of honor during her rite of passage welcoming her into adulthood [< Mexican Spanish, probably < English CHAMBERLAIN]

cham·ber /cháymbər/ *n* **1.** MEETING PLACE OF LEGISLATURE OR COURT the place where a legislative or judicial assembly meets ○ *the Senate chamber* **2.** ROOM WITH PARTICULAR FUNCTION a room used for a particular purpose ○ *in the council chamber* **3.** COMPARTMENT OR CAVITY an enclosed space, compartment, or cavity, e.g., one inside a machine, the body, or a plant ○ *the chambers of the heart* **4.** PLACE IN GUN FOR AMMUNITION the compartment for a cartridge in a revolver or rifle or for a shell in a cannon **5.** OFFICIAL ASSEMBLY a legislative or judicial assembly ○ *The upper chamber is expected to pass the bill.* **6.** ORGANIZED BODY OF PEOPLE a body of people organized into a group for a specific purpose ○ *the local chamber of commerce* **7.** OFFICIAL RECEPTION ROOM a reception room in an official residence or a palace **8.** BEDROOM a bedroom or other room in somebody's home (*archaic or literary*) ■ **cham·bers** *npl* **1.** JUDGE'S PRIVATE OFFICE a judge's private office for discussing cases or legal matters not taken up in open court **2.** *UK* LAWYERS' OFFICES a suite of rooms used by lawyers for consulting with clients **3.** *UK* APARTMENT OR SUITE OF ROOMS an apartment or suite of private rooms ■ *adj* OF CHAMBER MUSIC relating to, written as, or performing chamber music ■ *vt* (**-bered, -ber·ing, -bers**) **1.** PUT AMMUNITION IN WEAPON to insert a round of ammunition in the breech of a weapon **2.** PROVIDE SOMETHING WITH CHAMBER to put something in or provide something with a chamber or chambers [12C. Via French *chambre* < Latin *camera* "vault, room" < Greek *kamara* "vault"] —**cham·bered** *adj*

cham·bered nau·ti·lus *n* MARINE BIOL same as **pearly nautilus**

cham·ber·lain /cháymbərlən/ *n* **1.** MANAGER OF ROYAL OR NOBLE HOUSEHOLD an official who manages the household of a monarch or member of the nobility **2.** TREASURER OF MUNICIPALITY the treasurer of a municipality **3.** PRIEST WHO IS PAPAL ATTENDANT a Roman Catholic priest who is an attendant to the pope, often an honorary position [12C. Via Old French < assumed Frankish *kamarling* "little room" < Greek *kamara* "vault"]

Cham·ber·lain /cháymbərlən/, **Neville** (1869–1940) British politician. He resigned as Britain's prime minister (1937–40) after diplomatic and military failures, most notably his advocacy of appeasement toward Nazi Germany. Full name **Chamberlain, Arthur Neville**. See table at **prime minister**

"This is the second time in our history that there has come back from Germany to Downing Street peace with honor. I believe it is peace for our time."
[Neville Chamberlain, *Times (London)*; October 1, 1938]

Cham·ber·lain, Owen (*b.* 1920) US physicist. He shared the Nobel Prize in physics (1959) for his research into atomic nuclei, and discovered the antiproton.

Cham·ber·lain, Wilt (1936–99) US basketball player. He dominated the National Basketball Association during his career (1960–73), winning seven scoring titles. Full name **Chamberlain, Wilton Norman**

cham·ber·maid /cháymbər màyd/ *n* a woman employed to tidy and clean bedrooms in hotels

cham·ber mu·sic *n* classical instrumental music written for a small group such as a quartet or trio and often originally intended for performance in a large room or a small concert hall

cham·ber of com·merce *n* an organization of local businesspeople who work together to promote and protect common interests in trade

cham·ber of hor·rors *n* an exhibition depicting macabre or gruesome objects and incidents [< a room in Madame Tussaud's waxwork exhibition in London, England]

cham·ber or·ches·tra *n* a small orchestra, usually of fewer than 40 players, that performs classical music

cham·ber pot *n* a large bowl used in a bedroom for urination and defecation

Cham·bers·burg /cháymbərz bùrg/ borough in Pennsylvania, southwest of Harrisburg. It was burned down by Confederate troops during the Civil War. Population: 17,839 (2002 estimate).

cham·bray /shám bràỳ/ *n* a fine lightweight cotton or linen fabric with colored fibers interlaced with white [Early 19C. Alteration of *Cambrai*, France]

cham·cha /chúmchə/ *n S Asia* somebody who agrees enthusiastically with the ideas and views of a superior without offering any criticism [< Hindi *camcā* "spoon"; from the use of cutlery in imitation of Westerners]

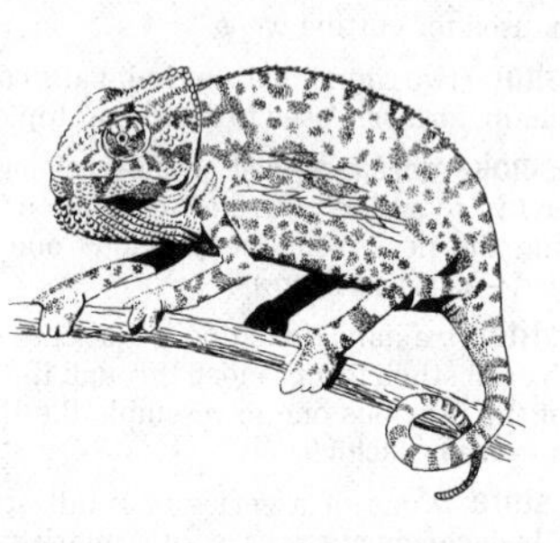

chameleon

cha·me·leon /kə meélyən, -lee ən/ *n* **1.** a tree-dwelling lizard with long thin legs, a strong curled tail, a long sticky tongue, and the ability to change color. Native to: Africa, Madagascar. Family: Chamaeleonidae. **2.** same as **anole** **3.** somebody who frequently and rapidly changes personality or appearance [14C. Via Latin < Greek *khamaileōn* < *khamai* "on the ground" + *leōn* "lion"] —**cha·me·le·on·ic** /kə meélee ónnik/ *adj*

Cha·me·leon *n* ASTRON another spelling of **Chamaeleon**

cha·metz /kh̲aa méts, kh̲áwməts/, **cho·metz, ha·metz, ho·metz** *n* leavened bread or other food that may not be eaten by Jews during Passover [Mid-19C. < Hebrew *ḥāmēṣ*]

cham·fer /chámfər/ *n* a shallow cut, edge, or groove made in wood, usually at an angle of 45 degrees to a corner [Mid-16C. Back-formation < *chamfering* "grooving" < French *chanfrein* "beveled edge" < *chanfraindre* "bevel" < *chant* "edge" + *fraindre* "break"] —**cham·fer** *vt* —**cham·fered** *adj*

cham·fron /chámfrən/ *n* a piece of armor used in medieval times to protect a horse's head in battle [15C. < French *chanfrain*]

cha·mi·so /chə meéssō/, **cha·mise** /chə meéz/ *n* an

evergreen bush with small needle-shaped leaves. Flowers: small, white. Native to: southern California. Latin name: *Adenostoma fasciculatum.* [Mid-19C. Via Mexican Spanish < Spanish *chamizo* "burned stick" < Latin *flamma* "flame"; from its dry appearance]

chamois

cham·ois /shámmee/ (*plural* **-ois** /-eez/ or **-oix** /-eez/) *n* **1. GOAT ANTELOPE** an agile goat antelope that has slender backward-curving horns and a tawny coat that darkens in winter. Native to: mountains of Europe and southwestern Asia. Latin name: *Rupicapra rupicapra.* **2.** *also* **cham·ois leath·er SOFT PLIABLE LEATHER** soft pliable leather, originally made from the hide of the chamois **3.** /shámmee/ **CLOTH FOR POLISHING** a piece of chamois leather, or a natural or synthetic substitute. Use: cleaning, polishing. **4.** COLORS **GRAYISH YELLOW** a grayish yellow color, like that of chamois leather [Mid-16C. Via French < late Latin *camox*] —**cham·ois** *adj*

cham·o·mile /kámmə mīl, -meel/, **cam·o·mile** *n* **1.** the leaves and flowers of an aromatic plant. Use: medicine, herbal teas. **2.** an aromatic perennial plant with delicate leaves. Flowers: yellow and white, similar to daisies. Native to: Europe, Asia. Genera: *Anthemis* or *Matricaria.* [14C. Via Old French *camomille* < medieval Latin *chamomilla* < Greek *khamaimēlon* "earth-apple"; because the flowers smell like apples]

Cha·mor·ro /chaa máwrō/, **Violeta Barrios de** (*b.* 1929) Nicaraguan politician. The manager of the opposition newspaper *La Prensa,* she became president of Nicaragua (1990–96).

champ[1] /champ/ *n* same as **champion** *n* (sense 1) (*informal*) [Mid-19C. Shortening]

champ[2] /champ/ *vti* (**champed, champ·ing, champs**) to bite, chew, or grind something vigorously, noisily, or impatiently ■ *n* the process of biting, chewing, or grinding something vigorously, noisily, or impatiently, or the sound that this makes [Mid-16C. Probably an imitation of the sound] —**champ·er** *n*

cham·pagne /sham páyn/ *n* **1. FRENCH WHITE SPARKLING WINE** a white sparkling wine from northeastern France, often drunk at special occasions **2. WHITE WINE LIKE CHAMPAGNE** a dry or semisweet white wine resembling champagne and made by a similar process **3.** COLORS **PALE BROWNISH GOLD** a very pale brownish gold color ■ *adj* **1. EXTRAVAGANT** involving luxury and indulgence ○ *a champagne lifestyle* **2.** COLORS **PALE BROWNISH GOLD** of the color champagne

Cham·paign /sham páyn/ city in eastern Illinois, west of Urbana, with which it shares the University of Illinois. Population: 69,443 (2002 estimate).

Cham·paigne /sham páyn/, **Philippe de** (1602–74) Flemish-born French painter. Baroque portraiture, notably of his patron Cardinal Armand Richelieu, gives way to classicism in his later religious subjects.

cham·pak /chám pàk, chúm pùk/ (*plural* **-paks** or *same*), **cham·pac** (*plural* **-pacs** or *same*) *n* an evergreen tree sacred to Hindus and Buddhists. Flowers: fragrant, orange-yellow. Native to: Asia. Latin name: *Michelia champaca.* [Late 18C. Via Hindi < Sanskrit *campākā* < Dravidian]

cham·per·ty /chámpərtee/ (*plural* **-ties**) *n* an illegal agreement between a litigant and somebody who aids or finances litigation in return for a share of the proceeds following a successful outcome [15C. < Anglo-Norman *champartie* < Old French *champart* "field rent (a portion of produce received by a feudal lord)" < *champ* "field" + *part* "portion"] —**cham·per·tous** *adj*

cham·pi·gnon /shaaNpin yáwN, sham pínnyən/ *n* a mushroom, especially one cultivated for eating [Late 16C. < French, literally "little country" < *champagne,* via late Latin *campania* < Latin *Campania,* province in Italy]

cham·pi·on /chámpee ən/ *n* **1. SUPREME VICTOR IN CONTEST** somebody who competes in and wins a contest, competition, or tournament, either alone or as a member of a team **2. WINNER OF SHOW** something, e.g., an animal or plant, that wins first place in a show **3. DEFENDER** a defender, supporter, or promoter of somebody or something ○ *a champion of human rights* **4. REMARKABLE PERSON** a personal example of excellence or achievement **5. HERO OR WARRIOR** a hero or warrior, especially a knight who fought in behalf of a monarch in former times ■ *vt* (**-oned, -on·ing, -ons**) **DEFEND** to defend, support, or promote a cause or person [12C. Via Old French, "combatant" < late Latin *campion-* "combatant in the arena" < Latin *campus* "field"]

cham·pi·on·ship /chámpee ən shìp/ *n* **1. CONTEST TO DECIDE CHAMPION** a contest, competition, or tournament that is held to decide who will be the overall winner **2. TITLE OR TIME OF BEING CHAMPION** the designation or period of being a champion **3. DEFENDING OR SUPPORTING SOMEBODY OR SOMETHING** the defense, support, or promotion of a person or cause

Cham·plain, Lake /sham pláyn/ lake situated between Vermont and New York, extending approximately 6 mi./10 km into Canada. Area: 430 sq. mi./1,100 sq. km. Depth: 399 ft./122 m.

Cham·plain /sham pláyn, shaaN pláN/, **Samuel de** (1567?–1635) French explorer. His North American expeditions (1603–08) led to the establishment of New France (Canada). He was later governor of the colony (1633–35).

champ·le·vé /shaaNlə váy/ *n* enamel work in which colored enamels are used to fill channels cut into a metal base [Mid-19C. < French < *champ* "field" + *levé* "raised"] —**champ·le·vé** *adj*

cham·pur·ra·do /chàmpə ráadō/ *n Hispanic* a hot sweet drink thickened with a powder made from corn dough and flavored with chocolate and sometimes spices or fruits [< American Spanish < past participle of *champurrar* "mix a drink"]

chan·a /chúnnə/, **chan·na** *n S Asia* **1.** home-made cheese used in South Asian cooking **2.** FOOD another spelling of **channa** (sense 1) [< Hindi]

chance /chanss/ *n* **1. LIKELIHOOD THAT SOMETHING WILL HAPPEN** the degree of probability that something will happen (*often used in the plural*) ○ *There's a strong chance we'll win.* **2. OPPORTUNITY OR OPPORTUNE TIME** an opportunity or a set of circumstances that makes it possible for something to happen ○ *I was given no chance to explain.* **3. GAMBLE OR RISK** a gamble or other act involving uncertainty or risk ○ *You're taking a chance by not wearing a seat belt.* **4. SUPPOSED FORCE THAT MAKES THINGS HAPPEN** the supposed force that makes things happen in a particular way without any apparent cause ○ *It was pure chance that we met.* ○ *a chance encounter* **5. RAFFLE OR LOTTERY TICKET** a ticket in a raffle or lottery **6.** BASEBALL **OPPORTUNITY TO MAKE PUTOUT IN BASEBALL** in baseball, an opportunity to field a ball and make a putout or assist **7. UNEXPECTED HAPPENING** an unexpected event **8. SOMETHING CAUSED BY LUCK** something caused by luck or fortune ■ *v* (**chanced, chanc·ing, chanc·es**) **1.** *vt* **DO SOMETHING RISKY** to do something knowing that it is risky **2.** *vi* **DO SOMETHING UNPLANNED** to do something or happen without a cause or plan [13C. Via Anglo-Norman < late Latin *cadentia* "falling" < present participle of Latin *cadere* "to fall"] ◇ **by any chance** used to inquire if there is any possibility of something ○ *Could you lend me your copy, by any chance?* ◇ **by chance** unexpectedly or without plan ◇ **fat chance** something that is highly unlikely (*slang*) ◇ **given half a chance** if the slightest opportunity should present itself ○ *He did what most of us would do, given half a chance.* ○ *Given half a chance, he'll talk for hours about his kids.*

chance on *or* **upon** *vt* to find or encounter somebody or something unexpectedly

Chance /chanss/, **Frank** (1877–1924) US baseball player. Playing for the Chicago Cubs, he formed a double-play combination with Joseph Tinker and John Evers.

chan·cel /chánss'l/ *n* an area of a church near the altar for the use of clergy and choir, often separated from the nave by a screen or steps [14C. Via Old French < Latin *cancelli* "little lattices" < *cancer* "lattice"]

chan·cel·ler·y /chánssəlaree, chánsslaree/ (*plural* **-ies**), **chan·cel·lor·y** *n* **1. CHANCELLOR'S RESIDENCE** the official residence of a chancellor **2. CHANCELLOR'S RANK** the position or rank of a chancellor **3.** *US* INTERNAT REL **OFFICES OF EMBASSY OR CONSULATE** the offices of an embassy or a consulate. Can term **chancery** [14C. < French *chancellerie* < *chancelier* (see CHANCELLOR)]

chan·cel·lor /chánssələr, chánsslər/ *n* **1.** POL **HEAD OF PARLIAMENTARY GOVERNMENT** the chief minister of government in some parliamentary democracies **2.** EDUC **CHIEF ADMINISTRATIVE OFFICER OF UNIVERSITY** the chief administrative officer of some universities **3.** LAW **PRESIDING JUDGE** in some states, the presiding judge of a court of equity or chancery **4.** *Can, UK* EDUC **HONORARY HEAD OF UNIVERSITY** the honorary head of a university **5.** *UK* INTERNAT REL **EMBASSY SECRETARY** the main secretary of an embassy [Pre-12C. Via Anglo-Norman *c(h)anceler,* Old French *chancelier* < Latin *cancellarius* "court secretary, attendant at the grating" < *cancelli* (see CHANCEL)] —**chan·cel·lor·ship** *n*

Chan·cel·lor of the Ex·che·quer *n* a member of the British government who is the chief minister of finance

Chan·cel·lors·ville /chánssələrz vìl, chánsslərz-/ crossroads in northeastern Virginia, west of Fredericksburg. It was the site of a major battle of the Civil War on May 1–4, 1863, when Robert E. Lee outmaneuvered Joseph Hooker to win a major Confederate victory.

chan·cel·lor·y *n* another spelling of **chancellery**

chance-med·ley *n* **1.** the killing of an assailant in self-defense during an unexpected brawl **2.** a haphazard event or action, or the randomness of chance [15C. < Anglo-Norman *chance medlee* "mixed chance"; from the idea of being only partly accidental]

chan·cer·y /chánsseree/ (*plural* **-ies**) *n* **1.** *Can, UK* INTERNAT REL same as **chancellery** (sense 3) **2.** POL same as **chancellery** (sense 2) **3.** LAW same as **court of chancery** **4.** LAW in England, the Lord Chancellor's court, one of the five divisions of the High Court of Justice [14C. Contraction of CHANCELLERY]

chan·cre /shángkər/ *n* **1.** a small painless highly infectious ulcer or sore that is the first sign of syphilis and some other infectious diseases **2.** a sore or ulcer at the point where a disease-causing organism (**pathogen**) enters the body [Late 16C. Via French < Latin *cancer* "ulcer"] —**chan·crous** *adj*

chan·croid /sháng kròyd/ *n* **1.** a sexually transmitted disease that produces a painful ragged ulcer at the site of infection, caused by the bacterium *Haemophilus ducreyi* **2.** a painful ragged ulcer that is characteristic of chancroid —**chan·croid·al** /shang króyd'l/ *adj*

chanc·y /chánssee/ (**-i·er, -i·est**) *adj* **1.** involving risks or danger **2.** occurring in a random or haphazard way —**chanc·i·ly** *adv*—**chanc·i·ness** *n*

chandelier

chan·de·lier /shànd'l éer/ *n* a decorative hanging light with several branched parts on which are holders for candles or light bulbs [Mid-18C. < French < *chandelle* "candle" < Latin *candela*] —**chan·de·liered** *adj*

chan·delle /shan dél, shaaN-/ *n* a steep climbing turn in which an aircraft almost stalls as it uses momentum to increase the rate of climb ■ *vi* (**-delled,**

-del·ling, -delles) to climb steeply in an aircraft, turning at the same time and almost stalling [Early 20C. < French (see CHANDELIER)]

Chan·di·garh /chúndigər/, **Chan·dī·garh** city and union territory in northern India, north of Delhi. It is the joint capital of Punjab and Haryana states. Population: 900,914 (2001).

chan·dler /chándlər/ *n* **1.** a seller of particular supplies and goods ○ *a ship's chandler* **2.** a seller or maker of candles [14C. < Anglo-Norman *chaundeler,* Old French *chandelier* < *c(h)andelle* (see CHANDELIER)]

AKG London

Raymond Chandler

Chan·dler /chándlər/, **Raymond** (1888–1959) US writer. He wrote gritty mystery and crime novels such as *The Big Sleep* (1939) and *The Long Goodbye* (1953). Full name **Chandler, Raymond Thornton**

> "Crime isn't a disease, it's a symptom. Cops are like a doctor who gives you aspirin for a brain tumor, except that the cop would rather cure it with a blackjack."
> [Raymond Chandler. Quoted in *New York Times*; November 1, 1987]

chan·dler·y /chándləree/ (*plural* **-ies**) *n* **1.** the place where a chandler's goods are sold or stored **2.** the goods that a chandler deals in

Chan·dra·sek·har lim·it /shaándrə say kaar-/ *n* the upper limit for the mass of a white dwarf star beyond which the star collapses to a neutron star or a black hole [After Subrahmanyan *Chandrasekhar* (1910–95), US astrophysicist]

AKG London

Coco Chanel

Cha·nel /shə nél/, **Coco** (1883–1971) French couturier. Her name became synonymous with a distinctively elegant style of women's suit. Full name **Chanel, Gabrielle Bonheur**

> "There is nothing more comfortable than a caterpillar and nothing more made for love than a butterfly. We need dresses that crawl and dresses that fly."
> [Coco Chanel. Quoted in *Chanel,* Jean Leymarie; 1987]

Cha·ney /cháynee/, **Lon** (1883–1930) US silent movie actor. He specialized in horror roles, especially in *The Hunchback of Notre Dame* (1923) and *The Phantom of the Opera* (1925). Full name **Chaney, Alonso**

~~**changable**~~ incorrect spelling of **changeable**

Chang·chun /chaáng choŏn/ transportation center and capital city of Jilin province in northeastern China. Population: 4,150,000 (1995).

change /chaynj/ *v* (**changed, chang·ing, chang·es**) **1.** *vti* BECOME OR MAKE DIFFERENT to become different, or make something or somebody different ○ *This liquid crystal changes color when you tilt it.* ○ *The town hasn't changed much since I left.* **2.** *vt* SUBSTITUTE OR REPLACE SOMETHING to exchange, substitute, or replace something ○ *We changed the batteries regularly.* **3.** *vti* PASS FROM ONE STATE TO ANOTHER to pass or make something pass from one state or stage to another ○ *Water changes to ice on freezing.* **4.** *vti* REMOVE CLOTHES AND PUT ON OTHERS to remove one or more articles of clothing and replace them with something else ○ *Are you going to change for dinner?* **5.** *vt* REMOVE AND REPLACE SOMETHING to remove something dirty or used and replace it with another that is clean or unused ○ *changing the sheets* **6.** *vti* MOVE FROM ONE VEHICLE TO ANOTHER to get out of one vehicle or means of transportation and continue the journey in another ○ *changed planes in Atlanta* **7.** *vt* FIN EXCHANGE MONEY FOR SMALLER UNITS to exchange a unit of money for an equal amount of money in lower denominations ○ *Can you change a $10 bill for two fives?* **8.** *vt* FIN CONVERT ONE CURRENCY INTO ANOTHER to replace money of one currency with an equivalent amount in another currency, calculated according to an exchange rate **9.** *vi* DEEPEN to become deeper in register (*refers to a boy's voice*) **10.** *vti UK* AUTOMOT same as **shift** *v* (sense 3) ■ *n* **1.** MAKING OR BECOMING DIFFERENT alteration, variation, or modification, or the result of this ○ *There's been a change of plan.* **2.** EXCHANGE OR REPLACEMENT an exchange, substitution, or replacement of something or somebody **3.** VARIANCE FROM ROUTINE a variance from a routine or pattern, especially a welcome one ○ *I could use a change.* **4.** COINS coins collectively, especially coins of a small denomination **5.** MONEY GIVEN BACK the balance of money given back to a customer who has handed over a larger sum than the cost of the goods or services purchased **6.** MONEY EXCHANGED FOR HIGHER DENOMINATION a sum of money given or received for a coin or bill of a higher denomination **7.** FRESH SET OF SOMETHING a different, clean, or fresh set of something, especially clothes **8.** TRANSITION FROM SOMETHING a shift from one state, stage, or phase to another ○ *a change in our thinking* **9.** MUSIC PROCEDURE FOR RINGING BELLS the order in which tuned bells are rung **10.** MED same as **menopause** (*dated informal*) [12C. Via Old French *changer* < late Latin *cambiare* < Latin *cambire* "exchange"] —**chang·er** *n*

SYNONYMS ***change, alter, modify, convert, vary, shift, transform, transmute***

CORE MEANING: to make or become different

change to become different, or make something or somebody different ○ *The society we live in is changing rapidly.* ○ *pressure to change public attitudes toward health* **alter** to make changes to something, especially to an aspect of something, or be changed or become different ○ *trying to alter the widely held perception of the west side as an industrial area* ○ *From March the situation altered rapidly.* **modify** to make minor changes or alterations, especially in order to improve something ○ *Even extroverts are capable of modifying their behavior.* ○ *modifying the curriculum so that it better meets the needs of real children* **convert** to change something from one character, form, or function to another, or be changed in character, form, or function ○ *the process by which you take in food and convert it into energy and heat* ○ *plans to convert the buildings into luxury apartments* **vary** to change within a range of possibilities, or in connection with something else, or make something undergo such a change ○ *Opening times may vary with the season.* ○ *You can vary the menu according to your taste.* **shift** to change from one position or direction to another ○ *The focus of your paper may shift as you write.* ○ *For most of us our native language is alive and constantly shifting.* **transform** to change somebody or something completely, especially improving their appearance or usefulness, or to change in this way ○ *The playground is being transformed into a community garden.* ○ *A good teacher can still transform the life of a student.* **transmute** to change something from one form, nature, or state to another, or be changed in this way ○ *The Old Norse word "borg" meaning "citadel" was later transmuted into "borough"* ○ *His anger swiftly transmuted into grief.* ○ *The ancient alchemists tried to transmute base metals into gold.*

change down *vi UK* same as **downshift** (sense 1)

change off *vi* to alternate tasks, or tasks and work breaks, especially with somebody else

change over *vi* **1.** SUBSTITUTE SOMETHING FOR SOMETHING ELSE to replace one system, method, or product with another **2.** *UK* EXCHANGE OR REVERSE PLACES OR POSITIONS to exchange or reverse places, positions, or roles **3.** *UK* SPORTS EXCHANGE ENDS OF PLAYING FIELD in team sports, to switch to opposite ends of a playing field, usually halfway through a game

change·a·ble /cháynjəb'l/ *adj* capable of changing, or liable to change or vary —**change·a·bil·i·ty** /chàynjə bíllətee/ *n* —**change·a·ble·ness** *n* —**change·a·bly** *adv*

change·ful /cháynjfəl/ *adj* changing frequently —**change·ful·ness** *n*

~~**changeing**~~ incorrect spelling of **changing**

change·less /cháynjləss/ *adj* not liable to change —**change·less·ly** *adv* —**change·less·ness** *n*

change·ling /cháynjling/ *n* in folklore, a child who is secretly substituted for another one by fairies

change of heart *n* a profound change of attitude or opinion

change of life *n* MED same as **menopause** (*informal*)

change of pace *n* **1.** a temporary change in pattern or routine **2.** BASEBALL same as **changeup**

change·o·ver /cháynj ōvər/ *n* **1.** in team sports, the switch of teams to opposite ends of a playing field **2.** a conversion, reversal, or complete change from one position, situation, or system to another

change purse *n* a small receptacle for coins, often carried inside a larger purse

change ring·ing *n* the ordered ringing of a peal of bells in various combinations so that none of the combinations is repeated and all possible permutations are rung

change·up /cháynj ùp/, **change-up** *n* **1.** in baseball, a ball thrown by a pitcher that resembles a fastball but moves more slowly, adversely affecting the batter's timing **2.** an unexpected shift in pace, rhythm, or feeling (*informal*)

Chang Ji·ang /chaáng jee aáng/ ➧ **Yangtze**

Chang·sha /chaáng shaá/ capital of Hunan Province, situated north of Guangzhou, in southeastern China. Population: 1,520,000 (1995).

Chang·zhou /chaáng jṓ/ city situated in the center of the Yangtze River Delta, 100 mi./162 km west of Shanghai. Population: 800,000 (1996).

chan·na /chúnnə/, **cha·na** *n S Asia* **1.** chickpeas, often stewed or served roasted or fried as a snack **2.** FOOD another spelling of **chana** (sense 1)

chan·nel[1] /chánn'l/ *n* **1.** BROADCAST TV OR RADIO STATION a television or radio station broadcasting on a specific band of the frequency spectrum ○ *watching one of the news channels* **2.** BROADCAST FREQUENCY SPECTRUM USED IN TRANSMISSION the portion of a frequency spectrum that is set aside for a specific purpose such as the broadcasting of a television or radio signal **3.** MEANS OF COMMUNICATION a course or means of communication or expression (*often used in the plural*) ○ *information coming through diplomatic channels* ○ *found a channel for his talent in graphic design* **4.** TUBULAR PASSAGE FOR LIQUID a long narrow passage or tube along which a liquid can flow ○ *a drainage channel* **5.** GEOG STRIP OF WATER SEPARATING LAND a wide passage of water between an island and a larger body of land **6.** NAUT NAVIGABLE PASSAGE a navigable route through a river or harbor, especially one that has been deepened by dredging **7.** GEOG ROUTE OF WATERWAY the course of a stream, river, canal, or other waterway **8.** ELECTRONICS PATH FOR ELECTRICAL CURRENT a path for an electrical current or signal **9.** COMPUT PATH FOR COMPUTER SIGNALS a path for electronic signals within a computer or between a computer and a peripheral device **10.** ONLINE WEBSITE SENDING UPDATED INFORMATION a preselected website that can automatically send updated information for immediate display or viewing on request **11.** PARAPSYCHOL SUPPOSED SPIRIT MEDIUM in spiritualism, somebody who supposedly acts as a medium for receiving messages from the spirit world **12.** GROOVE OR TRENCH a long narrow groove or furrow, e.g., in architecture or sculpture ■ *v* (**-neled, -nel·ing, -nels**) **1.** *vt* DIRECT SOMETHING ALONG SPECIFIC ROUTE to direct, guide, or convey something through or along a specific route or toward a specific goal ○ *Channel any suggestions through your manager.* ○ *channeled their* *energy into volunteer work* **2.** *vi* **MAKE CHANNEL** to make a channel in land or water ○ *channeling through bedrock* **3.** *vt* **MAKE GROOVE OR FURROW IN SOMETHING** to cut a long narrow groove or furrow in a surface **4.** *vti* PARAPSYCHOL **SPEAK FOR SUPPOSED SPIRIT** in spiritualism, to act as a medium for a supposed spirit [14C. Via Old French *chanel* < Latin *canalis* "groove" (see CANAL)] —**chan·nel·er** *n*

chan·nel[2] /chánn'l/ *n* a flat piece of wood or metal projecting horizontally from the side of a ship to increase the spread of the ropes or cables (**shrouds**) supporting the mast [Mid-18C. Alteration of *chainwale* < CHAIN + WALE]

chan·nel bass *n* a large reddish edible fish of the drum family. Native to: Atlantic coast of United States. Latin name: *Sciaenops ocellata*.

chan·nel de·pos·it *n* a body of sand deposited by a river, often showing an erratic sinuous pattern

chan·nel-hop (**chan·nel-hopped, chan·nel-hop·ping, chan·nel-hops**) *vi UK* same as **channel-surf** (*informal*) —**chan·nel-hop·per** *n*

chan·nel·ing /chánn'ling/ *n* **1.** **SUPPOSED SPIRITUAL COMMUNICATION THROUGH MEDIUM** in spiritualism, the practice of acting as a medium for receiving messages believed to come from the spirit world **2.** **CREATION OF CHANNEL** the making of a channel in or on something **3.** **TUBING THAT PROTECTS WIRES** a protective casing or container that carries one or more cables or wires inside or outside a building

chan·nel i·ron *n* an iron or steel bar with a U-shaped cross section

Chan·nel Is·lands /chànn'l-/ group of islands in the English Channel, near the French coast. The islands Jersey, Guernsey, Alderney, and Sark are self-governing Crown dependencies. Language: English; Norman French. Population: 143,534 (1991). Area: 75 sq. mi./190 sq. km.

Chan·nel Is·lands Na·tion·al Park national park made up of five islands off the coast of southern California. It has been a national park since 1980. Area: 390 sq. mi./1,009 sq. km.

chan·nel·ize /chánn'l ìz/ (**-ized, -iz·ing, -iz·es**) *vt* **1.** to make a channel for something **2.** to direct something through a channel —**chan·nel·i·za·tion** /chànn'li záysh'n/ *n*

chan·nel·ling *n* Can, UK spelling of **channeling**

chan·nel-surf (**chan·nel-surfed, chan·nel-surf·ing, chan·nel-surfs**) *vi* to use a remote control device to move rapidly through many different television channels (*informal*) —**chan·nel-surf·er** *n*

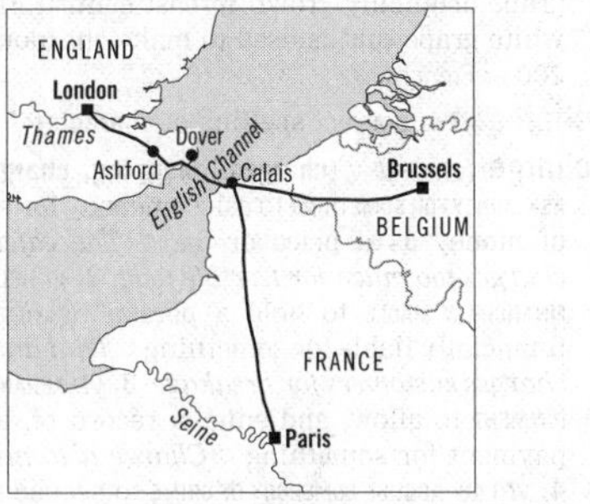

Channel Tunnel: map showing railroad routes using the Channel Tunnel

Chan·nel Tun·nel *n* a railroad tunnel, opened in 1994, that runs underneath the English Channel and links Folkestone in England with Coquelles near Calais in France

Chan·ning /chánning/, **Edward** (1856–1931) US historian. A professor of history at Harvard (1897–1929), he wrote the six-volume *History of the United States* (1905–25).

Chan·ning, William Ellery (1780–1842) US Unitarian cleric. His writings, sermons, and influence on transcendentalism helped to spread Unitarianism throughout New England.

> "I call that mind free which jealously guards its intellectual rights and powers, which calls no man master, which does not content itself with a passive or hereditary faith, which opens itself to light whensoever it may come, which receives new truth as an angel from heaven."
> [William Ellery Channing, "Spiritual Freedom"; 1830]

cha·no·yu /chàa naw yóo/ *n* a Japanese ceremony in which tea is ritually prepared, served, and consumed [Late 20C. < Japanese, "hot water for tea"]

chan·son /shaaN sáwN/ *n* a French song, e.g., a satirical cabaret song of the 20th century or a Renaissance song similar to the madrigal [15C. Via French, "song" < Latin *cantion-* < *cantare* "sing"]

chan·son de geste /shaaN sàwN də zhést/ (*plural* **chan·sons de geste** /*pronunc. same*/) *n* a French epic poem written between the 11th and 14th centuries, usually celebrating legendary events and figures [< French, "song of heroic deeds"]

chant /chant/ *n* **1.** **PHRASE SPOKEN REPEATEDLY BY CROWD** a phrase or slogan repeatedly and rhythmically spoken, often with a simple singsong intonation, especially in unison by a crowd or group **2.** **SOMETHING SPOKEN MONOTONOUSLY OR REPETITIOUSLY** a monotonous or repetitive song or intonation of the voice **3.** **MUSIC FOR RELIGIOUS TEXT** a set of words or syllables sung on the same note, or a single word or syllable sung on a series of notes. Chants are used in psalms, canticles, and other parts of some religious services. **4.** **HYMN OR PRAYER SUNG AS CHANT** a psalm, prayer, or other religious text sung as a chant ■ *vti* (**chant·ed, chant·ing, chants**) **1.** **REPEAT SLOGAN CONTINUALLY** to speak a slogan repeatedly and rhythmically with a simple singsong intonation **2.** **UTTER MONOTONOUSLY** to speak or sing something monotonously **3.** **SING HYMN OR PRAYER AS CHANT** to sing or intone a religious text or part of a religious service as a chant [14C. Via French, "song" < Latin *cantus* < past participle of *canere* "sing"] —**chant·ing·ly** *adv*

chant·er /chántər/ *n* **1.** **SOMEBODY CHANTING SLOGAN** somebody who chants a slogan **2.** **SOMEBODY CHANTING PSALM OR HYMN** somebody who chants a religious musical passage, e.g., a priest or chorister **3.** **PIPE WITH FINGER HOLES ON BAGPIPES** on bagpipes, a pipe with finger holes on which the melody is played **4.** **PIPE FOR PRACTICING BAGPIPES** a pipe used to learn or practice fingering for bagpipes

chan·te·relle /shàntə rél, shaàntə-/ *n* an edible mushroom found in temperate woodlands that has a yellow-to-orange trumpet-shaped cap. Latin name: *Cantharellus cibarius*. [Late 18C. Via French < modern Latin *cantharellus* "little cup" < Latin *cantharus* "drinking vessel" < Greek *kantharos*]

chan·teuse /shaan tő̄z/ (*plural* **-teuses** /-tő̄z/) *n* a woman singer, especially in a nightclub or cabaret [Mid-19C. < French]

chan·tey /chántee, shántee/ (*plural* **-teys**), **chan·ty** (*plural* **-ties**), **shan·ty** /shántee/, **shan·tey** (*plural* **-teys**) *n* a song chanted by sailors as they work [Mid-19C. Origin ?]

chan·ti·cleer /chánti kleèr, shánti-/ *n* a rooster, especially in fairy tales (*literary*) [13C. < Old French *Chantecler* < *chanter* "sing" + *cler* "clear"]

Chan·til·ly[1] /shàn tíllee, shaàNtee yeé/ *n* **1.** *also* **Chan·til·ly lace** a delicate black or white ornamental lace with an outlined design. Use: bridal and evening gowns. **2.** *also* **Chan·til·ly cream** whipped cream, sweetened and often flavored with vanilla

Chan·til·ly[2] /shàn tíllee, shaàNtee yeé/ a town and resort in Oise Department, Picardie region, northern France. Situated about 26 mi./42 km north of Paris, it became famous for its lace and porcelain. Population: 10,902 (1999).

chan·try /chántree/ (*plural* **-tries**) *n* **1.** an endowment to pay for the saying of masses for the soul of the founder or somebody named by the founder **2.** *also* **chan·try chap·el** a chapel or altar endowed for the performance of chantries [14C. < Anglo-Norman *chaunterie*, Old French *chanterie* < *chanter* "sing"]

chan·ty *n* MUSIC another spelling of **chantey**

Cha·nu·kah, Cha·nuk·kah *n* JUDAISM another spelling of **Hanukkah**

cha·ol·o·gy /kay óllәjee/ *n* the study of chaos theory and chaotic systems —**cha·ol·o·gist** *n*

Chao Phra·ya /chòw praa yaá/ river in west central Thailand. Length: 227 mi./365 km.

cha·os /káy òss/ *n* **1.** **DISORDER** a state of complete disorder and confusion **2.** *also* **Cha·os** ASTRON **EARLIEST CONDITION OF UNIVERSE** the unbounded space and formless matter supposed to have existed before the creation of the universe **3.** PHYS **APPARENT DISORDER** the unpredictability inherent in a system such as the weather, in which apparently random changes occur as a result of the system's extreme sensitivity to small differences in initial conditions [15C. Directly or via French < Latin < Greek *khaos* "void, abyss"]

cha·os the·o·ry *n* a theory that complex natural systems obey rules but are so sensitive that small initial changes can cause unexpected final results, thus giving an impression of randomness

cha·ot·ic /kay óttik/ *adj* **1.** completely disordered and out of control **2.** describes the state of a system according to chaos theory [Early 18C. < CHAOS] —**cha·ot·i·cal·ly** *adv*

chap[1] /chap/ *vti* (**chapped, chap·ping, chaps**) **BECOME SORE AND ROUGHENED** to become sore and cracked by exposure to wind or cold, or make skin sore and cracked in this way (*refers to skin*) ■ *n* **1.** **AREA OF SORE SKIN** a sore cracked area of skin, caused by exposure to wind or cold **2.** GEOL **CRACK IN GROUND** a crack or fissure in dry ground [14C. Origin ?] —**chapped** *adj*

chap[2] /chap/ *n UK* a man or youth, especially somebody whose name is not known or not relevant (*informal*) [Late 16C. Shortening of *chapman* "wandering peddler" < *cēap* (see CHEAP)]

chap[3] /chap/ *n* the lower exterior half of the jaw, especially the cheek [Mid-16C. Origin ?]

chap. *abbr* **1.** CHR chaplain **2.** LITERAT chapter

chap·ar·ral /shàppə rál/ *n Southwest US* a dense thicket of bushes or small trees, especially of evergreen oaks in southern California [Mid-19C. < Spanish < *chaparra* "dwarf evergreen oak"]

REGIONAL NOTE See ***mesquite***.

chap·ar·ral bird, chap·ar·ral cock *n* BIRDS same as **roadrunner**

cha·pa·ti /chə paátee/ (*plural* **-tis** or **-ties**), **cha·pat·ti** *n* a thin round unleavened bread used in South Asian cooking [Early 19C. < Hindi *capātī* < *capānā* "flatten"]

chap·book /cháp bòok/ *n* a small booklet of poems, ballads, or stories, originally sold by traveling peddlers [Early 19C. Blend of *chapman* (see CHAP[2]) + BOOK]

chape /chayp, chap/ *n* **1.** the metal tip of a scabbard **2.** the tongue of a buckle [14C. Via French, "cape, hood" < late Latin *cappa* (see CAP)]

cha·peau /sha pṓ/ (*plural* **-peaux** /-pṓ, -pṓz/ or **-peaus**) *n* a hat as an item of high fashion or ceremonial dress (*formal*) [15C. Via French < late Latin *cappellum* "small hooded cloak" < *cappa* (see CAP)]

chap·el /chápp'l/ *n* **1.** **SEPARATE AREA OF CHURCH** a separate area in a Christian church, having its own altar and intended for private prayer **2.** **ROOM FOR CHRISTIAN WORSHIP** a place in a hospital, prison, or other institution, or in a large house, consecrated for Christian worship **3.** *UK* **PROTESTANT CHURCH** a place of worship used by a nonestablished Protestant denomination such as the Methodists or Baptists **4.** **SERVICE IN CHAPEL** a service held in a chapel, especially in a nonestablished Christian church **5.** **SMALL CHURCH** a small Christian church, especially one that is affiliated with a larger church **6.** **PLACE FOR FUNERALS** a funeral home, or a room in a funeral home where funeral services are held **7.** PUBL, MEDIA **LABOR UNION BRANCH** a branch of a labor union in printing and journalism **8.** PUBL, MEDIA **UNION MEETING** a meeting of a printers' or journalists' chapel [12C. Via Old French *chapele* < medieval Latin *cappella* "small hooded cloak" < late Latin *cappa* (see CAP)]

Chap·el Hill /chàpp'l-/ town in north central North Carolina, home to the main campus of the University of North Carolina. Population: 51,636 (2002 estimate).

chap·er·on /sháppə ròn/, **chap·er·one** *n* **1.** somebody who accompanies and supervises a group of young people **2.** somebody, especially an older or married woman, who accompanies and supervises a young single woman at social events [12C. < French, < late

Latin *cappa* (see CAP)] —**chap·er·on** *vti* —**chap·er·on·age** *n*

chap·er·on·in /shàppə rṓnin/ *n* a protein belonging to a large group of protein families involved in the stabilization, translocation, and unfolding of developing proteins

chap·i·ter /cháppitər/ *n* ARCHIT same as **capital**[2] [13C. < French *chapitre* (see CHAPTER)]

chap·lain /cháplin/ *n* a member of the clergy employed to give religious guidance, e.g., to members of the armed forces, schoolchildren, or prisoners [12C. Via Anglo-Norman, Old French *chapelain* < medieval Latin *cappellanus* "guardian of the cloak of St. Martin of Tours" < *cappella* (see CHAPEL)] —**chap·lain·cy** *n* —**chap·lain·ship** *n*

chap·let /cháplət/ *n* **1. WREATH WORN ON HEAD** a decorative circle of beads or flowers worn on the head **2.** CHR **ROMAN CATHOLIC PRAYER BEADS** a string of beads used by Roman Catholics for counting prayers. A chaplet has 55 beads, one third of the number on a rosary. **3.** ARCHIT **BEADED MOLDING** a small molding resembling a string of beads [14C. < French *chapelet* < late Latin *cappa* (see CAP)] —**chap·let·ed** *adj*

Charlie Chaplin

Chap·lin /cháplin/, **Charlie** (1889–1977) British-born US movie actor, director, and producer who is best known for the tramp character that he played in over 70 films. Full name **Chaplin, Sir Charles Spencer**

> "Life is a tragedy when seen in close-up, but a comedy in long-shot."
> [Charlie Chaplin, *Guardian (London)*; December 28, 1977]

chap·man /chápmən/ (*plural* **-men** /-mən/) *n UK* a wandering peddler (*archaic*) [Old English *cēapman* < *cēap* (see CHEAP)]

Chap·man /chápmən/, **John** (1774?–1845) US pioneer who traveled extensively throughout the Ohio River valley planting apple seeds and tending his orchards. Known as **Johnny Appleseed**

chap·pal /chúpp'l/ *n S Asia* a leather sandal with a single strap attached at the sides and passing between the first two toes [Late 19C. < Hindi *cappal*]

chaps /chaps, shaps/ *npl* protective leather leggings, like a pair of pants with no seat or crotch, worn on horseback over ordinary pants by ranch workers, rodeo contestants, and cowboys [Late 19C. Shortening of *chaparejos*, alteration of *chaparreras* < *chaparra* (see CHAPARRAL); because worn when riding through chaparral]

chap·tal·ize /cháptə līz/ (**-ized, -iz·ing, -iz·es**) *vt* to increase the alcohol content of wine by adding sugar before or during fermentation [Late 19C. After J. A. *Chaptal* (1756–1832), French chemist] —**chap·tal·i·za·tion** /chàptəli záysh'n/ *n*

chap·ter /cháptər/ *n* **1. SECTION OF BOOK** one of the main sections of a text, usually having a title or number as a heading **2. PERIOD OF DEVELOPMENT** an identifiable period in the history or development of something ○ *The treaty opened a new chapter in pan-American relations.* **3. BRANCH OF GROUP** a branch of a society or organization **4.** CHR **GROUP OF CANONS** the body of canons of a cathedral or collegiate church **5.** CHR **ASSEMBLY OF CHAPTER** a meeting of a cathedral or church chapter [12C. Via French *chapitre* < Latin *capitulum* "small head" < *caput* "head"] ◇ **give** *or* **quote chapter and verse** to give exact information and detailed references on a topic

Chap·ter 7 *n* a section of the US Federal Bankruptcy Code that deals with the liquidation of an insolvent company and the distribution of any remaining assets

Chap·ter 11 /-i lévvən/ *n* a section of the US Federal Bankruptcy Code that allows an insolvent company to be reorganized, sometimes providing for repayment of debts or the creation of a new corporate entity

chap·ter book *n* a book for young school-age children that is divided into chapters and tells a story in writing rather than through its illustrations

chap·ter house *n* **1.** a building used by a fraternity or sorority **2.** a building used for meetings by a religious chapter

Cha·pul·te·pec /chə pŏŏltə pèk/ rocky hill in Mexico, fortified by Aztec rulers, situated 3 mi./5 km southwest of Mexico City

char[1] /chaar/ (**charred, char·ring, chars**) *v* **1.** *vti* to blacken something or become blackened by burning or scorching **2.** *vt* to turn wood into charcoal by partial burning [Late 17C. Back-formation < CHARCOAL]

char[2] /chaar/ (*plural same* or **chars**), **charr** (*plural same* or **charrs**) *n UK* same as **brook trout** [Mid-17C. Origin ?]

char·a·cin /kárrəssin/ (*plural same* or **-cins**), **char·a·cid** /kárrəssid/ (*plural same* or **-cids**) *n* a small brightly colored freshwater fish often kept in aquariums. Native to: Africa, South America. Family: Characidae. [Late 19C. < modern Latin *Characinus* < Greek *kharax* "pointed stake," also used for a fish]

char·ac·ter /kárrəktər/ *n* **1. DISTINCTIVE QUALITIES** the set of qualities that make somebody or something distinctive, especially somebody's qualities of mind and feeling ○ *It's just not in my character to behave that way.* **2. POSITIVE QUALITIES** qualities that make somebody or something interesting or attractive ○ *an old house full of character* **3. REPUTATION** somebody's public reputation ○ *an attack on his good character that ended in court* **4. SOMEBODY IN BOOK OR MOVIE** one of the people portrayed in a book, play, or movie ○ *None of the central characters is particularly likable.* **5. UNUSUAL PERSON** somebody with an unusual or eccentric personality **6. INDIVIDUAL** somebody considered in terms of personality, behavior, or appearance ○ *a flamboyant character* **7. LETTER OR SYMBOL** any written or printed letter, number, or other symbol **8.** COMPUT **COMPUTER UNIT OF DATA** a single letter, number, or symbol that can be displayed on a computer screen or printer and represents one byte of data [14C. Via French *caractère* < Greek *kharaktēr* "tool for marking" < *kharassein* "engrave" < *kharax* "pointed stake"] ◇ **in** *or* **out of character 1.** typical or untypical of the behavior of a particular person or thing **2.** involved or not involved in the psychological preparations for acting out a particular role in a play, movie, or other dramatic work

char·ac·ter ac·tor *n* an actor who specializes in playing the roles of unusual or distinctive characters

char·ac·ter as·sas·si·na·tion *n* a deliberate and sustained attack on somebody's reputation

char·ac·ter·ful /kárrəktərf'l/ *adj* having many qualities that are interesting or pleasantly unusual

char·ac·ter·is·tic /kàrrəktə rístik/ *n* **1. DEFINING FEATURE** a feature or quality that makes somebody or something recognizable **2.** MATH **WHOLE NUMBER IN LOGARITHM** the whole number (**integer**) found to the left of the decimal point in a common logarithm, e.g., the characteristic of 5.4321 is 5 ■ *adj* **TYPICAL** distinguishing or representative of a particular person or thing —**char·ac·ter·is·ti·cal·ly** *adv*

char·ac·ter·i·za·tion /kàrrəktəri záysh'n/ *n* **1.** the way in which the writer portrays the characters in a book, play, or movie **2.** a description of the character or nature of somebody or something

char·ac·ter·ize /kárrəktə rīz/ (**-ized, -iz·ing, -iz·es**) *vt* **1.** to describe the character or characteristics of somebody or something **2.** to be representative of the way a particular person or thing behaves or looks —**char·ac·ter·iz·a·ble** *adj* —**char·ac·ter·iz·er** *n*

char·ac·ter·less /kárrəktərləss/ *adj* without any interesting or distinctive features ○ *a characterless view*

char·ac·ter rec·og·ni·tion *n* a magnetic or optical process by which letters, numbers, or symbols are recognized and digitized by a computer

char·ac·ter set *n* a complete set of letters, numbers, symbols, and control codes that can be used by a computer

char·ac·ter wit·ness *n* a witness who gives evidence of somebody's good character in a court of law

cha·rade /shə ráyd/ *n* **1.** an absurdly false or pointless act or situation **2.** a clue in the game of charades [Late 18C. < French < modern Provençal *charra* "to chatter"]

cha·rades /shə ráydz/ *n* a game in which somebody provides a visual or acted clue for a word or phrase, often the title of a book, play, or movie, for others to guess (*takes a singular verb*)

cha·ran·ga /chə ráang gə/ *n Hispanic* **1.** a Cuban music ensemble consisting of a flute, piano, violins, a double bass, percussion instruments, and vocalists **2.** the style of dance music played by a charanga [Via American Spanish < Spanish, "light orchestra"]

cha·ran·go /chə ráang gō/ (*plural* **-gos**) *n Hispanic* a small guitar from the Andes, traditionally made from the shell of an armadillo [Early 20C. < American Spanish < *charanga* (see CHARANGA)]

char·broil /chaár bròyl/ (**-broiled, -broil·ing, -broils**) *vt* to broil food over charcoal on a barbecue or on a ridged pan that produces a similar visual effect [Mid-20C. Blend of CHARCOAL + BROIL[1]] —**char·broil·er** *n*

char·coal /chaár kōl/ *n* **1. CARBON** a black or dark gray form of carbon, produced by heating wood or another organic substance in an enclosed space without air. Use: fuel, absorbent, in smelting, in explosives, for drawing. **2.** ART **DRAWING IMPLEMENT** sticks of charcoal used for drawing pictures **3.** ART **DRAWING DONE WITH CHARCOAL** a drawing made using a stick of charcoal **4.** *also* **char·coal-gray** COLORS **DARK GREY COLOR** a dark gray color [14C. Origin ?] —**char·coal** *adj*

char·cu·ter·ie /shaar kŏŏtə reé, -kŏŏtəree/ *n* **1.** cold cooked, cured, or processed meat and meat products **2.** a store that specializes in charcuterie [Mid-19C. < French < obsolete *char cuite* "cooked flesh"]

chard /chaard/ *n* PLANTS same as **Swiss chard** [Mid-17C. Via French *carde* < Latin *cardu(u)s* "thistle"]

Char·din /shaar dáN/, **Jean Baptiste Siméon** (1699–1779) French painter. He was a master of lower-middle-class domestic and genre scenes such as *The Benediction* (1740).

char·don·nay /shaárd'n áy, shaárd'n ày/, **Char·don·nay** *n* **1.** a dry white wine made from a variety of white grape originally grown in east central France **2.** a white grape that is used to make chardonnay [Early 20C. < French]

~~**charecter**~~ incorrect spelling of **character**

charge /chaarj/ *v* (**charged, charg·ing, charg·es**) **1.** *vti* **ASK MONEY FOR SOMETHING** to ask somebody for an amount of money as a price or fee ○ *The cafeteria here charges too much for terrible food.* **2.** *vt* **HOLD SOMEBODY FINANCIALLY LIABLE** to hold a person or organization financially liable for something ○ *That antique store charges customers for breakage.* **3.** *vti* **ARRANGE DEFERRED PAYMENT** to allow, and enter a record of, a deferred payment for something ○ *Charge it to my account.* **4.** *vt* LAW **ACCUSE SOMEBODY OF CRIME** to accuse somebody formally of having committed a crime **5.** *vt* **CRITICIZE SOMEBODY** to criticize somebody for doing something wrong ○ *Her parents unfairly charged her with laziness.* **6.** *vt* **ORDER SOMEBODY TO DO SOMETHING** to order or instruct somebody formally to do something ○ *The judge charged the jury to consider all the facts.* **7.** *vti* **ATTACK IN RUSH** to attack somebody or something by rushing forward, especially in a battle ○ *Police in riot gear charged the lines of demonstrators.* **8.** *vti* ELEC **RESTORE POWER IN BATTERY** to restore the power in a battery by connecting it to a supply of electricity **9.** *vt* **PERVADE SOMETHING** to give an atmosphere of intense interest, excitement, or other strong emotion to a place (*usually passive*) ○ *The concert hall was charged with anticipation.* **10.** *vt* **LOAD OR FILL SOMETHING** to load or fill something, e.g., a gun with explosive (*formal*) **11.** *vt* HERALDRY **PUT HERALDIC DEVICE ON SOMETHING** to put a heraldic device on something such as a shield or banner ■ *n* **1. PRICE OR FEE ASKED** the amount of money asked for something that is for sale or available as a result of payment ○ *an admission charge* ○ *extra charges for tax and insurance* **2.** RESPONSIBILITY the responsibility or duty of looking after somebody or something ○ *He took on the children's welfare as an extra charge.* **3.** SOMEBODY BEING TAKEN CARE OF somebody, especially a child or a member of a minister's congregation, for whom somebody else is responsible ○ *The nanny was keeping a close watch on her little charges.* **4.** LAW ACCUSATION an accusation of wrongdoing, especially an official statement accusing somebody of committing a crime **5.** MIL RUSH TO ATTACK a rush forward to attack, especially in a battle, or the signal for this **6.** ELEC POWER IN BATTERY the power stored in a battery **7.** PHYS ELECTRIC PROPERTY OF MATTER a fundamental characteristic of matter, responsible for all electric and electromotive forces, expressed in two forms known as positive and negative **8.** PHYS EXCESS OR LACK OF ELECTRONS a quantity of electricity caused by an excess or lack of electrons **9.** ARMS EXPLOSIVE FOR DETONATION the amount of explosive used to detonate a shell or cartridge **10.** ENOUGH TO FILL CONTAINER the amount required to fill a container or to make a mechanism work **11.** INSTRUCTION a formal order or instruction to do something, e.g., a judge's instructions to a jury **12.** SUDDEN BURST OF EXCITEMENT a sudden burst of excitement or interest **13.** HERALDRY HERALDIC DESIGN a design or image used as part of a coat of arms [12C. Via French *charger* "load, charge" < late Latin *car(ri)care* < Latin *carrus* "carriage"] ◇ **take charge (of)** to take over control or responsibility for somebody or something

charge·a·ble /chaárjəb'l/ *adj* **1.** liable or able to be charged to a person, organization, or account **2.** describes property or land capable of being subject to a charge or tax —**charge·a·bil·i·ty** /chaàrjə bíllə tee/ *n*

charge ac·count *n* an account that allows a customer to buy goods or services and pay at a later date

charge card *n Can, UK* a card issued to customers by a store, bank, or other organization, used to charge purchases to an account for later payment. US term **credit card**

charge-coup·led de·vice *n* a semiconductor device that converts light patterns into digital signals for a computer, especially in digital cameras and optical scanners

charged /chaarjd/ *adj* tense and causing anxiety, excitement, or anger ○ *a highly charged situation*

char·gé d'af·faires /shaàr zhay də fér/ (*plural* **char·gés d'af·faires** /*pronunc. same*/) *n* **1.** a diplomat ranking immediately below an ambassador who deputizes in the ambassador's absence **2.** a diplomat who heads a minor diplomatic mission [Mid-18C. < French, "somebody in charge of affairs"]

charge den·si·ty *n* the amount of electric charge per unit of area or volume. Symbol ρ

charge nurse *n* a nurse in charge of a hospital ward

charge of quar·ters *n* an enlisted person who administers a military unit, especially at night or during holidays

charg·er[1] /chaárjər/ *n* **1.** ELEC same as **battery charger** **2.** a large strong cavalry horse [15C. < CHARGE]

charg·er[2] /chaárjər/ *n* a large flat serving dish of a kind now mainly collected for display [14C. < Anglo-Norman *chargeour* "something that loads" < Old French *charger* (see CHARGE)]

char·grill /chaár gril/ (**-grilled, -grill·ing, -grills**) *vt UK* same as **charbroil** [Blend of CHARCOAL + GRILL[1]]

Cha·ri /shaáree/ the main tributary feeding Lake Chad in north central Africa. It rises in the Central African Republic. Length: 590 mi./950 km.

~~**charicature**~~ incorrect spelling of **caricature**

Cha·ri-Nile *n* a Nilo-Saharan group of languages spoken in northern Chad, Sudan, Uganda, Kenya, and northeastern Republic of Congo

char·i·ot /chárree ət/ *n* **1.** a two-wheeled horse-drawn vehicle without seats, used in ancient times in races, warfare, or processions **2.** a four-wheeled horse-drawn carriage with rear seats only, used especially on ceremonial occasions [14C. < French < Latin *carrus* "carriage"] —**char·i·o·teer** /chàrree ə teér/ *n*

char·ism /kárrizəm/ *n* RELIG same as **charisma** (sense 2) [15C. < ecclesiastical Latin *charisma* (see CHARISMA)]

cha·ris·ma /kə rízmə/ *n* **1.** the ability to inspire enthusiasm, interest, or affection in others by means of personal charm or influence **2.** (*plural* **cha·ris·ma·ta** /-mətə/) a gift or power believed to be divinely bestowed [Mid-17C. Via ecclesiastical Latin < Greek *kharisma* < *kharis* "favor, grace"]

USAGE Charisma meaning "personal magnetism": In their generalized meanings, ***charisma*** and ***charismatic*** have moved a long way from their original meanings in theology, where they referred to supernatural gifts of speaking, healing, and so on. The modern meanings have developed from a use in sociology, in which the sense is "power of leadership or authority," first used in translations of the German sociologist Max Weber (1864–1920).

char·is·mat·ic /kàrriz máttik/ *adj* **1.** possessing great powers of charm or influence **2.** describes Christian groups or worship characterized by a quest for inspired and ecstatic experiences such as healing, prophecy, and speaking in tongues —**char·is·mat·ic** *n* —**char·is·mat·ic·al·ly** *adv*

USAGE See ***charisma***.

char·i·ta·ble /chárritəb'l/ *adj* **1.** GENEROUS generous to people in need **2.** SYMPATHETIC sympathetic, favorable, or tolerant in judging **3.** COLLECTIVELY DISPENSING HELP dispensing assistance to needy people by means of a group or organization —**char·i·ta·ble·ness** *n* —**char·i·ta·bly** *adv*

char·i·ty /chárrətee/ (*plural* **-ties**) *n* **1.** ORGANIZATION PROVIDING CHARITY an organization that collects money and other voluntary contributions of help for people in need **2.** PROVISION OF HELP the voluntary provision of money, materials, or help to people in need **3.** MATERIAL HELP money, materials, or help voluntarily given to people in need **4.** TOLERANT ATTITUDE the willingness to judge people in a tolerant or favorable way **5.** IMPARTIAL LOVE the impartial love of other people, especially as a Christian virtue [12C. Via French *charité* < Latin *caritas* < *carus* "dear"]

cha·ri·va·ri /shìvvə reé, shívvə reè/ *n UK* same as **shivaree** [Mid-17C. < French]

char·kha /chúrkə, chaárkə/, **char·ka** *n* a spinning wheel, especially for cotton, used in South Asia [Late 19C. Via Urdu *charkạ* < Persian *carḳ(a)*]

char·la·tan /shaárlət'n/ *n* somebody who falsely claims to have special skill or expertise [Early 17C. Via French < Italian *ciarlatano* < *ciarlare* "to babble," an imitation of empty talk] —**char·la·tan·ism** *n* —**char·la·tan·ry** *n*

Char·le·magne /shaárlə màyn/ (742–814) Frankish king and emperor. As emperor of the West (800–814), he inspired the Carolingian Renaissance of European culture.

> "Our task is, with the aid of divine piety, to defend the Holy Church of Christ with arms...Your task, most holy father, is to lift up your hands to God, like Moses, so as to aid our troops."
> [Charlemagne, *Letter to Pope Leo III*; 796]

Char·le·roi /shaárlə ròy, shaàrlə rwaá/ industrial city in Hainault Province, Belgium, south of Brussels. Population: 202,020 (1999).

Charles /chaarlz/ river in eastern Massachusetts that rises near the Rhode Island state border. It flows northeastward and empties into Boston harbor, forming a natural boundary between Cambridge and Boston. Length: 47 mi./76 km.

Charles, Prince of Wales (*b.* 1948) British heir apparent and son of Elizabeth II. He was married to Diana, Princess of Wales, from 1981 to 1996. Full name **Prince Charles Philip Arthur George**

> "I personally would much rather see my title as Defender of Faith, not the Faith, because it means just one interpretation of the faith, which I think is sometimes something that causes a great deal of a problem."
> [Charles, "Charles: The Private Man, the Public Role," *ITV television program*; June 29, 1994]

Charles I (1600–49) king of England, Scotland, and Ireland (1625–49). He succeeded James I in 1625. His determination to rule without Parliament's authority led to the English Civil War (1642–48), which culminated in his execution.

> "For the people; and truly I desire their liberty and freedom, as much as any body: but I must tell you, that their liberty and freedom consists in having the government of those laws by which their life and their goods may be most their own."
> [Charles I, *Speech on the scaffold*; January 30, 1649]

Charles II (1630–85) king of England, Scotland, and Ireland (1660–85). He was exiled during Oliver Cromwell's Protectorate (1653–58), but returned to England and formally ascended the throne after the restoration of the monarchy in 1660.

> "A merry monarch, scandalous and poor."
> [2nd Earl of Rochester, *A Satire on King Charles II*; 1697]

> "My words are my own, and my actions are my ministers'."
> [Charles II. Reply to Lord Rochester.]

Charles V (1500–58) Holy Roman Emperor and, as Charles I, king of Spain. During his reign as Holy Roman Emperor (1519–58), he struggled to keep his Roman Catholic empire together and was finally forced to recognize Protestantism.

> "I speak Spanish to God, Italian to women, French to men, and German to my horse."
> [Attributed to Charles V]

Charles VII (1403–61) king of France (1422–61). During his reign the Hundred Years' War ended with the English losing most of their possessions in France.

Charles IX (1550–74) king of France (1560–74). His reign was marked by religious wars and dominated by his mother, Catherine de Médicis.

Charles X (1757–1836) king of France (1824–30). He lived in England during the French Revolution. When he returned to France his repressive rule led to the revolution of 1830 and his enforced abdication and exile.

Charles, Pierre (1954–2004) prime minister of Dominica (2000–04). He entered parliament in 1986 as a member of the Dominican Labor Party and served as minister for communications and works (2000) before becoming prime minister.

Charles, Ray (*b.* 1932) US singer and pianist whose rhythm-and-blues style took its roots from country and western and gospel music. Born **Robinson, Ray Charles**

> "I believe talent will finally win out in this business. But Jesus could be coming tomorrow, and if no one knew, it wouldn't mean anything. Not even God can afford to ignore promotion."
> [Ray Charles, "Back to the Country," *Brother Ray*; 1978]

Charles Mar·tel /-maar tél/ (688?–741) Frankish king (715–741) of Austrasia (in present northeastern France and southwestern Germany). His forces turned back the Moorish invasion of France (732).

Charles's law /chaárlzəz-/ *n* a law holding that there is a direct relationship between the volume of a gas and its temperature, where its pressure is constant [Late 19C. After J. A. C. *Charles* (1746–1823), French physicist]

Charles·ton[1] /chaárlstən/ *n* a dance, popular in the 1920s, in which the feet are kicked out sideways with the knees kept together [Early 20C. After CHARLESTON[2], S Carolina]

Charles·ton[2] /chaárlstən/ **1.** city and port in southeastern South Carolina where the Ashley, Cooper, and Wando rivers meet. Population: 98,795 (2002 estimate). **2.** capital of West Virginia and the largest city in the state. Population: 51,702 (2002 estimate).

Char·ley *n* MIL another spelling of **Charlie** (sense 3)

char·ley horse /chaárlee-/ *n* a severe muscular cramp, especially in the upper leg (*informal*) [Origin ?]

Char·lie /chaárlee/ *n* 1. CODE WORD FOR LETTER "C" a code word for the letter "C," used in international radio communications 2. COCAINE cocaine used as an illicit drug (*slang*) 3. *also* **Char·ley** *US* VIET CONG used to refer to a member of the Viet Cong during the Vietnam War or to the Viet Cong collectively (*dated slang*) [Early 19C. Pet form of the name *Charles*]

char·lock /chaár lòk/ (*plural same* or **-locks**) *n* a mustard plant that has hairy stems and leaves and is a common weed. Flowers: yellow. Native to: Europe, Asia. Latin name: *Brassica kaber*. [Old English *cerlic*, origin ?]

char·lotte /shaárlət/ *n* a sweet, cold or baked dish prepared in a deep straight-sided container and containing fruit surrounded by sponge cake, cookies, or bread [Late 18C. < French, probably < the name *Charlotte*]

Char·lotte /shaárlət/ city in southern North Carolina, southwest of Winston-Salem and east of the Catawba River. Population: 580,597 (2002 estimate).

Char·lotte A·ma·lie /-ə maályə/ seaport and capital of St. Thomas Island and of the US Virgin Islands. Population: 12,000 (1990).

char·lotte russe /shaárlət róoss/ (*plural* **char·lottes russes** /*pronunc. same*/) *n* a cold set dessert made with cream or custard surrounded by ladyfingers [< French, "Russian charlotte"]

Char·lottes·ville /shaárləts vìl/ city in central Virginia on the western bank of the Rivanna River, northwest of Richmond. Thomas Jefferson's house (**Monticello**) is located nearby, and it is the home of the University of Virginia. Population: 43,833 (2002 estimate).

Char·lotte·town /shaárlət tòwn/ capital city of Prince Edward Island, Canada, situated in the center of the island, on Hillsborough Bay. Population: 38,114 (2001).

charm /chaarm/ *n* 1. ATTRACTIVENESS the power to delight or attract people 2. ATTRACTIVE FEATURE a feature or quality that delights or attracts (*often used in the plural*) 3. SOMETHING SUPPOSED TO BRING LUCK something carried or worn because it is believed to bring good luck or ward off evil 4. TRINKET a miniature metal animal, musical instrument, or similar trinket worn on a bracelet or around the neck 5. MAGIC SPELL a special phrase or rhyme believed to have magical powers 6. PHYS CHARACTERISTIC OF ELEMENTARY PARTICLES a quantum characteristic of elementary particles that accounts for the long lifetime of the J/psi particle, lack of symmetry in hadron interactions, and the failure of some particles to react. Symbol **C** ■ *v* (**charmed, charm·ing, charms**) 1. *vti* DELIGHT PEOPLE to delight or attract people 2. *vt* INFLUENCE PEOPLE to influence somebody or obtain something from somebody by using powers of persuasion and attraction 3. *vti* CAST A SPELL to affect somebody or something by, or as if by, the use of a supposed magic spell [13C. Via French *charme* < Latin *carmen* "song, incantation" < *canere* "sing"] —**charm·er** *n* —**charm·less** *adj*

charmed /chaarmd/ *adj* 1. so pleasant or lucky as to suggest protection by a magic spell 2. PHYS describes an elementary particle that has the property of charm

charmed cir·cle *n* a privileged group or elite

charm·ing /chaárming/ *adj* having the power to delight or attract people ○ *a charming village* ○ *a charming young man* ■ *interj* used ironically to express disapproval or distaste at something just done or said (*informal*) —**charm·ing·ly** *adv*

charm of·fen·sive *n* a campaign to appear more pleasant, attractive, or reasonable in order to gain popularity, e.g., a campaign undertaken by a politician (*informal disapproving*)

charm quark *n* a quark with an electric charge of $+\frac{2}{3}$ and charm of 1

charm school *n* a school for young women that charges tuition and teaches social skills and beauty techniques (*dated*)

char·nel /chaárn'l/ *n* BUILDINGS same as **charnel house** ■ *adj* suggestive of death or a tomb [14C. Via Old French < medieval Latin *carnale* < Latin *carn-* "flesh"]

char·nel house *n* a building or vault in which bones or dead bodies are placed

Cha·ro·lais /shàrrə láy/ (*plural same*), **Cha·rol·lais** *n* a large white cow belonging to a breed originating in France. Raised for: beef. [Late 19C. After Monts du *Charollais*, E France]

Char·on /kérrən/ *n* 1. in Greek mythology, a ferryman who took the souls of the dead across the River Styx to Hades 2. the only known satellite of Pluto, discovered in 1978

cha·ro·seth, **cha·ro·set** *n* JUDAISM another spelling of **haroseth**

char·poy /chaár pòy/ *n* a light bedstead of webbing stretched across a frame, commonly used in South Asia [Mid-17C. Via Urdu *chārpāī* < Persian]

char·qui /chaárkee/ *n* *Southwest US* FOOD same as **jerky**[2] [Early 17C. Via American Spanish < Quechua *cc'arki:*]

charr *n* FISH another spelling of **char**[2]

char·ro /chaárō/ (*plural* **-ros**) *n* *Hispanic* in the southwestern United States, a cowhand, especially an ostentatiously dressed one [Early 20C. < Mexican Spanish, "cowboy," also "gaudy"]

REGIONAL NOTE See ***vaquero***.

chart /chaart/ *n* 1. DIAGRAM OR TABLE a diagram or table displaying detailed information 2. NAVIG MAP TO NAVIGATE BY a map for navigation by sea or air 3. METEOROL WEATHER MAP an outline map that shows weather patterns 4. ASTROL BASIS FOR HOROSCOPE a map that shows the relative positions of the planets at the time of somebody's birth, on which his or her horoscope is based 5. HANDICRAFT STITCHING PLAN a squared grid marked with symbols indicating the placement of stitches in embroidery 6. MUSIC MUSICAL SCORE the score of a musical composition (*technical*) ■ **charts** *npl* LIST OF POPULAR RECORDS a list of the musical recordings that have sold the most copies during a specific period ■ *v* (**chart·ed, chart·ing, charts**) 1. *vt* MAKE CHART OF SOMETHING to make a map, graph, or diagram of something 2. *vt* DESCRIBE PROGRESS to record or describe how something progresses or develops 3. *vi* BE IN MUSIC CHARTS to appear in the music charts ○ *The band's second album charted the day it was released.* [Late 16C. Via French < Latin *charta* "paper, papyrus leaf"] —**chart·a·ble** *adj*

char·ter /chaártər/ *n* 1. STATEMENT OF RIGHTS AND RESPONSIBILITIES a formal written statement describing the rights and responsibilities of a state and its citizens 2. FORMAL DOCUMENT OF INCORPORATION a formal document incorporating an organization, company, or educational institution 3. CONSTITUTION a formal written statement of the aims, principles, and procedures of an organization 4. DOCUMENT OF AUTHORIZATION a document from an organization or society that authorizes the setting up of a new branch 5. SPECIAL PRIVILEGE a special privilege, immunity, or exemption granted to a particular person or group 6. TRANSP RENT OR LEASE OF TRANSPORT the renting or leasing of transport vehicles for personal or special use, or a contract for this purpose 7. TRANSP RENTED OR LEASED TRANSPORT a vehicle chartered for personal or special use 8. SHIPPING same as **charter party** ■ *vt* (**-tered, -ter·ing, -ters**) 1. TRANSP RENT OR LEASE TRANSPORT to rent or lease a vehicle for a personal or special purpose 2. GIVE ORGANIZATION A CHARTER to grant a charter of incorporation to a group or organization [12C. Via French *chartre* < Latin *chartula* < *charta* (see CHART)] —**char·ter·er** *n*

char·tered /chaártərd/ *adj* 1. having been granted a charter 2. *UK* registered with an official body as having satisfied its professional and technical requirements, originally with one granted a royal charter

char·tered ac·count·ant *n* *UK* an accountant who has passed the examinations of a governing professional body that has been granted a royal charter

char·ter flight *n* a flight that has been chartered for a specific trip, especially as part of a vacation package

Char·ter·house /chaártər hòwss/ (*plural* **-hous·es** /-hòwzəz/) *n* a Carthusian monastery [14C. Alteration of Anglo-Norman *Chartrous* or French *Chartreuse* < medieval Latin *Cart(h)usia* (see CARTHUSIAN)]

Char·ter·is /chaártəriss/, **Leslie** (1907–93) British-born US novelist who created the gentleman-crook, Simon Templar ("The Saint"). Born **Yin, Leslie Charles Bowyer**

char·ter mem·ber *n* a founding or original member of a society or organization

Char·ter of Rights *n* a section of the Canadian Constitution stating the rights conferred by Canadian citizenship

char·ter par·ty *n* a contractual arrangement by which the owner of a ship permits another person to use it to carry goods [Via French < medieval Latin *charta partita* "divided charter"]

Char·ter School *n* a publicly financed school run by parents, educators, and companies

Chart·ism /chaár tìzzəm/ *n* the principles and practices of a movement advocating political and social reform in England between 1838 and 1848 [Mid-19C. After the *People's Charter*] —**Chart·ist** *n, adj*

Char·tres /shaart, shaártrə/ capital of the Eure-et-Loire Department in northwestern France. It is situated about 50 mi./80 km southwest of Paris and is famous for its large Gothic cathedral. Population: 40,361 (1999).

char·treuse /shaar tróoz/ *n* a bright yellowish green color [Early 19C. < French (see CHARTERHOUSE)] —**char·treuse** *adj*

Char·treuse /shaar tróoz/ *tdmk* a trademark for a yellow or green aromatic liqueur

chart-top·ping *adj* at the top of the list of musical recordings that have sold the most copies during a specific period —**chart-top·per** *n*

char·wom·an /chaár wòommən/ (*plural* **-wom·en** /-wìmmin/) *n* a woman employed to clean a house or office (*dated*) [Late 16C. < Old English *c(i)err* "turn (of work)"]

char·y /chérree/ (**-i·er, -i·est**) *adj* 1. WARY cautiously reluctant to do something 2. SPARING reluctant to share, give, or use something 3. CONCERNED fussily concerned 4. SHY showing or characterized by shyness or modesty [Old English *cearig* "sorrowful" < Germanic] —**char·i·ly** *adv* —**char·i·ness** *n*

SYNONYMS See ***cautious***.

Cha·ryb·dis /kə ríbdiss/ *n* in Greek mythology, a monster in the form of a dangerous whirlpool at the mouth of the cave of the sea monster Scylla

chase[1] /chayss/ *v* (**chased, chas·ing, chas·es**) 1. *vti* PURSUE SOMEBODY to follow somebody quickly in order to catch him or her 2. *vt* MAKE SOMEBODY RUN AWAY to force a person or animal to run away ○ *The kids chased a black cat out of the garden.* 3. *vi* RUSH AROUND to rush around ○ *I chased around all day.* 4. *vti* PAY PERSISTENT ATTENTION TO SOMEBODY to seek the company of somebody for romantic or sexual purposes, especially in an obvious or unsubtle way ■ *n* 1. PURSUIT an act or situation in which something or somebody is being pursued 2. HORSERACING same as **steeplechase** *n* (sense 1) 3. SOMETHING PURSUED the target of a pursuit, especially an animal 4. MUSIC JAZZ DUET a jazz duet in which the players play alternate phrases and try to outdo each other in virtuosity and invention [13C. Via Old French *chacier* "seize" < Latin *captare* "try to seize" < *capere* "take"] ◇ **cut to the chase** to stop wasting time and get on with what needs to be dealt with (*informal*) ◇ **give chase** to pursue something or somebody forcefully (*formal*)

SYNONYMS See ***follow***.

chase[2] /chayss/ *n* 1. PART OF GUN BARREL the external part of a gun barrel just behind the muzzle 2. GROOVE a channel, groove, or trench for something such as a pipe to lie in or fit into ■ *vt* (**chased, chas·ing, chas·es**) 1. CUT GROOVE IN SOMETHING to cut or grind a channel, groove, or trench in something 2. CUT THREAD IN SCREW to cut a metal screw thread with a machine tool (**chaser**) [Late 16C. Via French *châsse* < Latin *capsa* "box"]

chase[3] /chayss/ (**chased, chas·ing, chas·es**) *vt* to decorate metal or glass by engraving or embossing [15C. Shortening of ENCHASE]

chase[4] /chayss/ *n* a rectangular frame into which metal type or blocks are fitted so that a page or plate can be printed or made [Early 17C. Via French *chas* "enclosed space" < Latin *capsum* "thorax, church nave"]

Chase /chayss/, **Salmon Portland** (1808–73) chief justice of the US Supreme Court (1864–73). He held various government posts, opposed slavery as a senator, and proposed the national bank system as Lincoln's secretary of the treasury.

> "The Constitution, in all its provisions, looks to an indestructible Union composed of indestructible States."
> [Salmon Portland Chase, *Decision on a law case*; 1868]

Chase, Samuel (1741–1811) associate justice of the US Supreme Court (1796–1811). A political leader in the American Revolution, he was appointed to the Supreme Court by George Washington.

chase plane *n* an airplane that follows another aircraft either as an escort or to photograph it

chas·er[1] /cháyssər/ *n* **1. SOMEBODY OR SOMETHING THAT CHASES** somebody or something that forcefully pursues another person or thing **2. DIFFERENT DRINK** a second drink, taken with or after one of a different kind, e.g., beer taken after whiskey (*informal*) **3.** ARMS **NAVAL CANNON** a cannon located at the bow or stern of a vessel and used in pursuing an enemy

chas·er[2] /cháyssər/ *n* **1.** an engraver or embosser of metal or glass **2.** a machine tool for cutting screw threads

Cha·sid *n* JUDAISM another spelling of **Hasid**

chasm /kázzəm/ *n* **1. DEEP HOLE IN EARTH** a deep crack or hole in the ground **2. WIDE DIFFERENCE** a wide difference in feelings, ideas, or interests **3. GAP OR BREAK** a large gap or break in the progress or continuity of something [Late 16C. Via Latin *chasma* < Greek *khasma* "gulf"]

chas·sé /sha sáy/ *n* a gliding step, especially in ballet or square dancing [Early 19C. < French, "chased"] —**chas·sé** *vi*

chas·seur /sha súr/ *adj* cooked in a rich white-wine and mushroom sauce ■ *n* a soldier in a French special unit equipped and trained for rapid deployment [Mid-18C. < French, "hunter"]

Chas·sid *n* JUDAISM another spelling of **Hasid**

chas·sis /shássee, chássee/ (*plural* **chas·sis** /shásseez, chá-/) *n* **1. MAIN FRAME OF VEHICLE** the frame and wheels that support the engine and body of a motor vehicle, or the frame and wheels of a carriage or wagon **2. MOUNTING FOR ELECTRONIC DEVICE** the mounting or supporting structure for the components of an electronic device such as a television **3. AIRCRAFT LANDING GEAR** the landing gear of an aircraft **4. MOUNTING FOR GUN CARRIAGE** a frame on which a gun carriage can move back and forth [Mid-17C. < French *châssis* < Latin *capsa* "box"]

Chas·tain /chass táyn/, **Brandi** (*b.* 1968) US soccer player. She played forward on the US women's national soccer team that won a gold medal in the 1996 Olympics and kicked the winning penalty in the World Cup championship in 1999. Full name **Chastain, Brandi Denise**

chaste /chayst/ (**chast·er, chast·est**) *adj* **1. ABSTAINING FROM SEX** abstaining from sex on moral grounds **2. SEXUALLY FAITHFUL** not having extramarital sexual relations **3. PURE IN THOUGHT AND DEED** behaving in a pure way, with no immoral thoughts **4. PLAIN** plain, simple, and unadorned in style [13C. Via French < Latin *castus* "pure"] —**chaste·ly** *adv* —**chaste·ness** *n*

chas·ten /cháyss'n/ (**-tened, -ten·ing, -tens**) *vt* **1. MAKE SOMEBODY SUBDUED** to make somebody less self-satisfied or self-assertive and more subdued **2. DISCIPLINE SOMEBODY** to subject somebody to discipline **3. MODERATE INTENSITY OF SOMETHING** to moderate the intensity of something [Early 16C. < obsolete *chaste* (see CHASTISE)] —**chas·tened** *adj* —**chas·ten·er** *n* —**chas·ten·ing** *adj*

chaste tree *n* a small tree with aromatic hairy leaves and fragrant clusters of light purplish flowers. Native to: Europe, Asia. Latin name: *Vitex agnus-castus.* [Translation of Latin *agnus castus* < *agnus* "chaste tree" < Greek *agnos*, confused with *hagnos* "chaste"]

chas·tise /chá stīz/ (**-tised, -tis·ing, -tis·es**) *vt* to punish or scold somebody [14C. < obsolete *chaste* "rebuke," via Old French *chastier* < Latin *castigare* (see CASTIGATE)] —**chas·tis·a·ble** *adj* —**chas·tise·ment** *n* —**chas·tis·er** *n*

chas·ti·ty /chástətee/ *n* **1.** the condition or practice of abstaining from sex on moral grounds **2.** plainness or simplicity of style

chas·ti·ty belt *n* a locking device passing around the waist and between the legs, used in medieval times to prevent a woman from having sexual intercourse

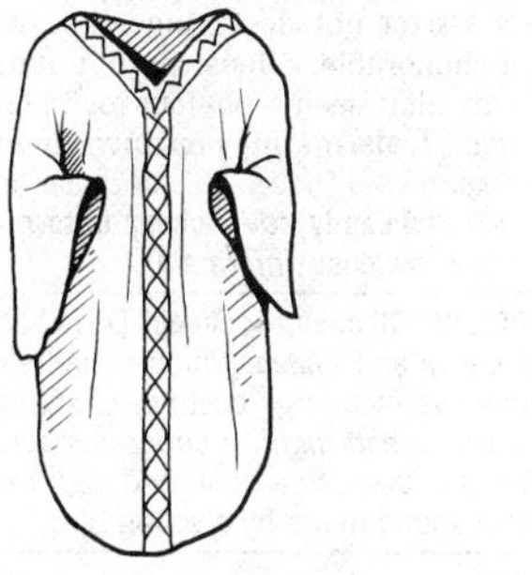

chasuble

chas·u·ble /cházzəb'l, chássəb'l/ *n* a loose, sometimes sleeveless outer garment worn by a Christian priest when celebrating Mass or Communion [13C. Via French < late Latin *casubla*, alteration of Latin *casula* "hooded cloak" < *casa* "house"]

chat /chat/ *vi* (**chat·ted, chat·ting, chats**) **1. TALK INFORMALLY** to talk with somebody in a relaxed informal way **2. EXCHANGE MESSAGES BY COMPUTER** to exchange messages in real time with other computer users ■ *n* **1. INFORMAL TALK** a relaxed informal conversation with somebody **2. EXCHANGE OF MESSAGES BY COMPUTER** an informal exchange of messages in real time with other computer users **3. SONGBIRD WITH CHATTERING CRY** a small songbird related to the thrush with a harsh chattering cry. Subfamily: Turdinae. **4. AUSTRALIAN CHAT** a bird belonging to any of the five species of Australian chat. Native to: Australia. Genus: *Epthianuridae*. [15C. Shortening of CHATTER]

chat up *vt UK* to talk to somebody flirtatiously or flatteringly (*informal*)

Barnaby's

chateau: Chenonceaux, France

cha·teau /sha tṓ/ (*plural* **-teaux** /-tṓ, -tṓz/ or **-teaus** /-tṓ, -tṓz/), **châ·teau** (*plural* **-teaux** /-tṓ, -tṓz/) *n* a castle or large house in France, often one that has a vineyard attached and gives its name to wine produced there [Mid-18C. Via French < Latin *castellum* (see CASTLE)]

Cha·teau·bri·and /shàttō bree aáN/ *n* a thick beefsteak cut from the widest middle part of the filet [Late 19C. After François René, Vicomte de CHATEAUBRIAND]

Cha·teau·bri·and /shàttō bree aáN/, **François Auguste René, Vicomte de** (1768–1848) French writer and diplomat. A founder of the Romantic school of French literature, his best-known work is his biography *Memoires d'Outre-Tombe* (*Memoir from Beyond the Tomb*) (1849–50).

chat·e·lain /shátt'l àyn/ *n* formerly, a man who owned or controlled a castle or other large house [15C. Via French *châtelain* < medieval Latin *castellanus* (see CASTELLAN)]

chat·e·laine /shátt'l àyn/ *n* **1.** *US* **WOMAN WITH LARGE HOUSEHOLD** a woman who is the head of a large fashionable household **2. MISTRESS OF LARGE HOUSE** formerly, a woman who owned or controlled a castle or other large house **3. WOMAN'S CHAIN KEY** a chain and clasp formerly worn at the waist by a woman to hold keys and other small items [Mid-19C. < French *châtelaine*, feminine of *châtelain* (see CHATELAIN)]

chat group *n* a group of people who exchange messages online, especially people who share a common interest

Chat·ham /cháttəm/ city and former naval dockyard on the estuary of the Medway River in Kent, southeastern England. Population: 71,691 (1991).

Chat·ham Is·lands group of islands in the southwestern Pacific Ocean forming part of New Zealand. They are situated 500 mi./800 km east of the South Island. Population: 717 (2001). Area: 372 sq. mi./963 sq. km.

cha·toy·ant /shə tóy ənt/ *adj* having a changeable iridescent luster ■ *n* a chatoyant gemstone, e.g., a cat's eye [Late 18C. < French, "shining like a cat's eyes"] —**cha·toy·an·cy** *n*

chat room *n* a facility in a computer network where participants exchange messages in real time

chat show *n UK* same as **talk show**

Chat·ta·hoo·chee /chàttə hóochee/ river that rises in northeastern Georgia and flows southwest and then southward to the Flint River. Length: 436 mi./702 km.

Chat·ta·noo·ga /chàttə nóogə/ city and port in southeastern Tennessee, on the Tennessee River, near the Tennessee-Georgia border. Population: 155,404 (2002 estimate).

chat·tel /chátt'l/ *n* an item of personal property that is not freehold land and is not intangible. Chattels are typically movable property (**chattels personal**), e.g., furniture or cars, but may also be interests in property (**chattels real**), e.g., leases. [13C. Via Old French *chatel* "property" < Latin *capitalis* (see CAPITAL[1])]

chat·tel mort·gage *n* a mortgage on personal possessions

chat·ter /cháttər/ *vi* (**-tered, -ter·ing, -ters**) **1. TALK RAPIDLY** to talk or converse rapidly and informally about unimportant things **2. MAKE HIGH-PITCHED SOUNDS** to make a rapid series of short high-pitched sounds that seem to resemble speech (*refers to animals or machinery*) **3. CLICK TOGETHER** to click together rapidly because of movement of the jaw caused by fear or cold (*refers to teeth*) **4. VIBRATE DURING CUTTING** to vibrate while cutting or being cut by a tool or machine, causing surface flaws (*refers to a saw blade or surface*) ■ *n* **1. TRIVIAL CONVERSATION** rapid and informal talk or conversation, especially about unimportant things **2. HIGH-PITCHED ANIMAL SOUNDS** rapid short high-pitched sounds made by a bird, animal, or machine that resemble human speech **3. SURFACE FLAWS PRODUCED IN MACHINING** imperfections in a surface, caused by vibration while the surface is being cut by a tool or machine [13C An imitation of the sound]

chat·ter·a·ti /chàttə raátee/ *npl S Asia* educated middle-class people who are interested in current affairs and culture and like to make their views known to each other (*disapproving*)

chat·ter·box /cháttər bòks/ *n* somebody who talks a lot, especially about unimportant things (*informal*)

chat·ter·er /cháttərər/ *n* a talkative person, especially somebody who talks on trivial subjects

chat·ter mark *n* **1.** a crack or groove on the surface of rock, caused by the abrasive action of a glacier on bedrock or by the collision of fragments in water **2.** a mark left on something that has been machined, caused by vibration during the machining process

chat·ty /cháttee/ (**-ti·er, -ti·est**) *adj* **1.** fond of chatting about unimportant things **2.** friendly and informal in tone —**chat·ti·ly** *adv* —**chat·ti·ness** *n*

SYNONYMS See ***talkative.***

Chau·cer /cháwssər/, **Geoffrey** (1343?–1400) English poet and author of *The Canterbury Tales* (1387–1400), one of the finest early works in English. See Cultural note at **tale** —**Chau·cer·i·an** /chaw seéree ən/ *n, adj*

> "This world nys but a thurghfare ful of wo, / And we ben pilgrymes, passynge to and fro; / Death is an ende of every worldly sore."
> [Geoffrey Chaucer, "The Knight's Tale," *The Canterbury Tales*; 1390?]

chaud·froid /shō frwaá/ *n* a hot béchamel sauce with aspic that sets when cold and is used to coat cold cooked foods [Late 19C. < French, "hot-cold"]

chauf·feur /shṓfər, shō fúr/ *n* somebody employed to drive a car ■ *vti* **(-feured, -feur·ing, -feurs)** to drive somebody from place to place in a car, or be employed to drive a car for somebody [Late 19C. < French, "stoker (of a steam car)" < *chauffer* "to heat"]

chaul·moo·gra /chawl móogrə/ *n* a tree with seeds that yield an oil formerly used to treat leprosy. Native to: Southeast Asia. Latin name: *Hydnocarpus kurzii.* [Early 19C. < Bangla *cāul-mugrā*]

chau·tau·qua /shə táwkwə/ *n* an annual summer school or educational gathering, often held outdoors and offering lectures, concerts, and theatrical performances [Late 19C. After *Chautauqua*, New York]

Chau·tau·qua, Lake /shə táwkwə/ lake in southwestern New York, near Lake Erie. Length: 18 mi./29 km.

chau·vin·ism /shṓvə nìzzəm/ *n* **1.** unreasoning, overenthusiastic, or aggressive patriotism **2.** an excessive or prejudiced loyalty to a particular gender, group, or cause [Late 19C. < French *chauvinisme*, after Nicolas *Chauvin*, character in the play *La cocarde tricolore* (1831) by the brothers Cogniard]

chau·vin·ist /shṓvənist/ *n* **1.** somebody with an excessive or prejudiced loyalty to a particular gender, group, or cause **2.** an unreasoning, overenthusiastic, and aggressive patriot —**chau·vin·is·tic** /shṑvə nístik/ *adj* —**chau·vin·is·ti·cal·ly** *adv*

Popperfoto

César Chàvez

Chá·vez /chaá vèz, shaá-/, **César Estrada** (1927–93) US labor leader. He founded the National Farm Workers Association (1962) to help migrant farm workers.

Chá·vez, Hugo (*b.* 1954) president of Venezuela (1999–). He gained considerable popular support for leading a failed coup (1992) and, after serving a two-year prison sentence, launched a new political party, the Fifth Republican Movement, in 1997. Amid a climate of political unrest, he was forced to resign the presidency briefly in April 2002. Full name **Chávez Frías, Hugo Rafael**

chaw /chaw/ *regional vti* **(chawed, chaw·ing, chaws)** to chew tobacco ■ *n* a wad of chewing tobacco [Early 16C. Variant of CHEW]

Cha·yef·sky /chī éfskee/, **Paddy** (1923–81) US playwright and screenwriter. He is known for his realist dramas such as the movie *Marty* (1955). Born **Chayefsky, Sidney**

> "I'm mad as hell, and I'm not going to take it any more."
> [Paddy Chayefsky. Words of lines for a main character, *Network*; 1976]

cha·yo·te /chaa yṓ tày/ *n* **1.** a pear-shaped, furrowed green or white gourd, cooked and eaten as a vegetable **2.** a climbing plant of the gourd family that bears chayotes. Native to: tropical America. Latin name: *Sechium edule.* [Late 19C. Via Spanish < Nahuatl *chayotli*]

cha·zan /khaázən/ (*plural* **-zan·im** /khaa zaánim/ or **-zans**), **ha·zan** (*plural* **-zan·im** or **-zans**), **haz·zan, chaz·zen** (*plural* **-zen·im** or **-zens**) *n* a Jewish religious official who is the chief singer of the liturgy in a synagogue [Mid-17C. < Hebrew *ḥazzān* "cantor"]

cha·ze·rai /haázə rī/ *n* unattractive or unappetizing food or articles

chaz·zen *n* JUDAISM another spelling of **chazan**

cheap /cheep/ *adj* **1.** COSTING LITTLE low in price or cost, or lower in price than might reasonably be expected **2.** CHARGING LITTLE charging low prices but offering good value **3.** POOR QUALITY inexpensive and of poor quality **4.** WORTH LITTLE worth little or accorded little value ○ *In times of war, life is cheap.* **5.** UNDESERVING OF RESPECT not deserving to be respected **6.** UNFAIR dishonorable, offensive, or unfair, especially in a way that seems obvious or calculated ○ *a cheap trick* **7.** STINGY stingy or unwilling to give freely [Old English *cēap* "trade" < Latin *caupo* "innkeeper"] —**cheap** *adv* —**cheap·ly** *adv* —**cheap·ness** *n* ◇ **on the cheap** at very low cost (*informal*)

SPELLCHECK cheap or **cheep**? Do not confuse the spelling of ***cheap*** and ***cheep***, which sound similar. ***Cheap*** is an adjective meaning "costing, charging, or worth little," as in *a cheap flight, a cheap restaurant, a cheap trick.* ***Cheep*** is used as a noun and verb referring to the high shrill sound made by a young bird.

cheap·en /cheépən/ **(-ened, -en·ing, -ens)** *vti* **1.** to make something less expensive, or become less expensive, especially in order to save money or increase profits, rather than to give better value **2.** to lower the quality or reputation of somebody or something, or become lower in quality or reputation

cheap·ie /cheépee/, **cheap·y** (*plural* **-ies**) *n* (*informal*) **1.** something that is cheap **2.** somebody regarded as stingy or ungenerous

cheap·jack /cheép jàk/ *n* a seller of inferior goods ■ *adj* inferior in value or quality [< the name *Jack*]

cheap·o /cheépō/ *adj* cheap in price or cost (*slang*)

cheap shot *n* an unfair or malicious attack on somebody or something, either in print or in speech (*informal*)

cheap·skate /cheép skàyt/ *n* somebody regarded as ungenerous (*informal*) [Late 19C. < US slang *skate* "worn-out horse, contemptible person" < ?]

cheap thrill *n* something providing only short-lived enjoyment or satisfaction

cheap·y *n* another spelling of **cheapie**

cheat /cheet/ *v* **(cheat·ed, cheat·ing, cheats) 1.** *vt* DECEIVE SOMEBODY to deceive or mislead somebody, especially for personal advantage **2.** *vi* BREAK RULES TO GAIN ADVANTAGE to break the rules in a game, examination, or contest, in an attempt to gain an unfair advantage **3.** *vi* BE UNFAITHFUL to have a sexual relationship with somebody other than a spouse or regular sexual partner **4.** *vt* ESCAPE SOMETHING to avoid harm or injury by luck or cunning ■ *n* **1.** DECEITFUL PERSON a deceiver who uses trickery to gain an unfair advantage **2.** DISHONEST TRICK a dishonest or unfair trick **3.** LAW DISHONESTLY OBTAINING PROPERTY the obtaining of somebody else's property by dishonest means **4.** ANNUAL GRASS an annual bromegrass. Native to: Europe, naturalized in North America. Latin name: *Bromus secalinus.* [14C. Shortening of ESCHEAT] —**cheat·er** *n*

cheat code *n* in a computer game, a method of accessing hidden functionality that allows players to cheat, e.g., by becoming invulnerable in a shoot-'em-up or by accessing hidden areas in an adventure game

Che·chen /chéchən/ *n* **1.** somebody who comes from Chechnya **2.** the main language in Chechnya, belonging to the Nakh group of North Caucasian languages. Native speakers: 1 million. —**Che·chen** *adj*

Chech·nya /chéchnee ə, chech nyaá/ autonomous republic in southwestern Russia that formally separated from Ingushetia in 1992. In 1994, Russia refused to recognize Chechnya's independence, resulting in a conflict that ended formally in 1997. Capital: Grozny. Population: 862,000 (1997). Area: 5,790 sq. mi./15,000 sq. km.

check /chek/ *v* **(checked, check·ing, checks) 1.** *vti* EXAMINE SOMETHING to examine something in order to establish its state or condition ○ *Check the doors and windows to make sure they're locked.* **2.** *vti* CONFIRM TRUTH OR ACCURACY OF SOMETHING to confirm or establish that something is true or accurate ○ *We need to check with the insurance company to find out whether we're covered.* **3.** *vi* BE CONSISTENT to be the same as or consistent with something else ○ *What you're telling me now doesn't check with what you told me last week.* **4.** *vt* HALT OR SLOW SOMETHING to stop or slow the progress of some unwelcome process ○ *efforts to check inflation* **5.** *vti* STOP SUDDENLY to stop or pause suddenly, or make somebody or something stop suddenly ○ *In mid-sentence, he checked himself abruptly, looking terribly embarrassed.* **6.** *vt* PREVENT SOMETHING BEING EXPRESSED to prevent or inhibit something from being expressed ○ *Checking the urge to laugh out loud, I buried my head in the newspaper.* **7.** *vt* MARK SOMETHING WITH CHECK MARK to mark something with a check mark ○ *Check here if the billing address is different from the shipping address.* **8.** *vt* REPRIMAND SOMEBODY to criticize somebody for a fault or bad behavior **9.** *vt* SPORTS BLOCK OPPONENT in sports such as ice hockey, to move directly into the path of an opponent, usually making physical contact, in order to block his or her progress **10.** *vt* HAND OVER BAGGAGE to hand over something, especially baggage, so that it can be transported separately from passengers, usually in the same aircraft or vehicle ○ *You must check your luggage before boarding.* **11.** *vt* HAND SOMETHING OVER FOR TEMPORARY KEEPING to hand over something such as a coat in a restaurant, store, or museum, for temporary safekeeping ○ *Do you want to check your coat?* **12.** *vt* CHESS PUT OPPONENT'S KING IN JEOPARDY in chess, to put an opponent's king in a situation in which one of your pieces directly threatens it **13.** *vt* LOOK AT SOMEBODY OR SOMETHING to look at or see somebody or something (*informal*) ■ *n* **1.** EXAMINATION an examination or investigation of something, especially to verify its state or condition ○ *Routine checks should have revealed the cracks in the engine housing.* **2.** SOMETHING THAT TESTS ACCURACY something that can be used or referred to in order to test the accuracy, truth, or safety of something else ○ *Keep this list as a check for the things you have to do.* **3.** MEANS OF RESTRAINING SOMEBODY OR SOMETHING a means of controlling or restraining somebody or something ○ *a check on the dog's aggressive tendencies* **4.** PAPER MONEY SUBSTITUTE a small printed form that, when filled out and signed, instructs a bank to pay a specific sum of money to the person named on it. Can, UK spelling **cheque** **5.** RESTAURANT BILL the bill in a restaurant or bar **6.** NUMBERED TICKET FOR DEPOSITED ITEM a numbered ticket or token given out when an item is left at a checkroom **7.** same as **checkroom** **8.** SYMBOL SHAPED LIKE "V" a symbol shaped like a "V" with a short left side and a long right side, used to indicate approval or preference ○ *A check will appear next to the category you have selected.* **9.** DESIGN PATTERN OF SQUARES a pattern made up entirely of squares in at least two different colors that are arranged alternately **10.** DESIGN SQUARE IN CHECK PATTERN a square in a pattern, in which at least two different colors are arranged alternately ○ *Every third check is red.* **11.** CHESS MOVE ATTACKING KING in chess, a move by which a piece directly threatens the opposing king, or the position resulting from this move. The king must escape from this position to avoid checkmate. ○ *If you move your king there, you'll be in check.* **12.** SPORTS BLOCKING MOVE in sports, a move directly into the path of an attacking opponent ■ *adj* same as **checked** ■ *interj* CHESS WARNING THAT KING IS IN CHECK in chess, used to announce that an opponent's king is in check [14C. < Old French *eschec* "check in chess" < Persian *šāh* "king" (see SHAH)] —**check·a·ble** *adj* ◇ **checks and balances** features in the way a system operates that prevent any one person or group from having too much power or influence ◇ **in check** restrained and under control ○ *managing to keep her anger in check*

check in *v* **1.** *vti* REGISTER AT HOTEL to register as a guest, or register a guest, on arrival at a hotel ○ *Has my colleague checked in yet?* **2.** *vti* ARRIVE FOR TRIP to register and go through the necessary formalities before beginning a trip, especially by air ○ *All passengers should check in at least one hour before departure.* **3.** *vi* MAKE CONTACT to make routine contact with a person or organization to exchange information ○ *The patrols are supposed to check in by radio at half-hourly intervals.*

check into *vt* to investigate something in order to get more information about it or to establish its truth or accuracy ○ *When we checked into his background, we found that he had several convictions for fraud.*

check off *vt* to mark items on a list to show that they have been dealt with

check out *v* **1.** *vi* **LEAVE HOTEL** to pay the bill and leave a hotel or other place ○ *We'll be checking out later this morning.* **2.** *vi* **LEAVE** to leave a particular place or person (*informal*) **3.** *vi* **DIE** to die (*slang*) **4.** *vt* **INVESTIGATE SOMETHING** to establish that something is correct or valid (*informal*) ○ *The date is probably 1961. Check it out, will you?* **5.** *vt* **EVALUATE AND QUALIFY PILOT** to instruct, evaluate the performance of, and then qualify a pilot to fly a specific type of aircraft ○ *She's been checked out to fly helicopters.* **6.** *vt* **TAKE A LOOK AT SOMETHING** to visit a place briefly to get information about it (*informal*) ○ *Let's check out the new pizza place on 44th Street.* **7.** *vi* **BE PROVED TRUE** to prove after investigation to be correct or valid ○ *If the DNA checks out, he's our man.* **8.** *vt* **WITHDRAW** to withdraw an item from a place and register its withdrawal, especially to take a book or other item out of a library on loan ○ *A maximum of three books may be checked out.* **9.** *vti* **PAY IN SUPERMARKET** to pay for something in a supermarket ○ *When I went to check out, I realized I'd left my purse in the car.* **10.** *vt* **TAKE MONEY FOR GOODS AT SUPERMARKET** to calculate and take payment from a customer in a supermarket ○ *This person's in a hurry, so do you mind if I check her out first?*

check over *vt* **1.** to examine something to make sure that it is correct or satisfactory ○ *Could you check over my essay to make sure there are no errors, please?* **2.** to examine somebody carefully to establish his or her state of health ○ *I've checked her over, and there are no broken bones.*

check through *vt* **1.** to examine or review systematically all the parts of something to make sure that it is satisfactory **2.** to arrange for your baggage to be transferred automatically at interim stops on a trip or flight so that you do not get it back until you reach your destination ○ *Our bags are checked through to New Delhi.*

check up *vi* to make inquiries to establish a point ○ *I checked up: no one by that name lives at that address.*

check up on *vt* to make inquiries or obtain information about somebody or something, often secretly and usually because of suspicion or worry

check·book /chék bòòk/ *n* a book of detachable checks

check·book jour·nal·ism *n* the payment of large sums of money to secure exclusive rights to a newspaper story

check box *n* a small square on a computer screen that, when clicked on with a mouse, displays a small cross or check to show that an item has been selected

check dam *n* a dam, usually a small one, that interrupts the flow of a stream and builds up a store of water behind itself

check dig·it *n* in computing, a digit derived from and added to the other digits in a sequence, used to ensure that the sequence is correct

checked /chekt/ *adj* with a pattern of small squares ○ *a red-and-white checked tablecloth*

check·er[1] /chékər/ *n* **1.** somebody who checks something **2.** a cashier in a supermarket or large store

check·er[2] /chékər/ *n* **1.** DESIGN same as **check** *n* (senses 9–10) **2.** **PIECE USED IN CHECKERS** a round flat piece used in the game of checkers ■ *vt* (**-ered, -er·ing, -ers**) **1.** DESIGN **MARK SOMETHING WITH CHECKS** to mark something with a pattern of checks or with alternating areas of light and shade **2.** **DISRUPT CONTINUOUS SUCCESS OF SOMETHING** to affect something adversely from time to time ○ *regrettable incidents that checkered his career* ▶ UK spelling **chequer** [12C. Shortening of EXCHEQUER, which originally denoted the checked chessboard]

check·er·ber·ry /chékər bèrree/ (*plural* **-ries**) *n* **1.** an edible, red, spicy-flavored fruit **2.** a low-growing evergreen bush that bears checkerberries and has fragrant leathery leaves from which an oil (**oil of wintergreen**) is distilled. Native to: eastern North America. Latin name: *Gaultheria procumbens.*

check·er·bloom /chékər blòòm/ *n* a wild perennial mallow. Flowers: reddish pink or purple. Native to: California. Latin name: *Sidalcea malvaeflora.*

check·er·board /chékər bàwrd/ *n* a game board patterned with two colors of squares, usually black and red, arranged alternately, that can be used for playing a variety of games, including checkers

check·ered /chékərd/ *adj* **1.** DESIGN same as **checked** **2.** uneven or inconsistent, and characterized by periods of trouble or controversy as well as periods of success ○ *her checkered past*

check·ered flag *n* a flag patterned with black and white squares that is waved as each participant in a car race crosses the finish line

check·ers /chékərz/ *n* a board game played by two people, each using 12 pieces (**checkers**). The object is to jump over the opponent's pieces and remove them from the board. (*takes a singular verb*)

Check·ers speech /chékərz-/ *n* a political speech dedicated to saving a politician's career by diverting attention from criticism rather than refuting it [After *Checkers*, family dog that vice-presidential candidate Richard M. Nixon referred to in a speech in 1952]

check-in *n* **1.** **REGISTRATION AT HOTEL OR AIRPORT** the process of registering on arrival at a hotel or airport **2.** **REGISTRATION DESK** a place where people check in at a hotel or airport **3.** **SOMEBODY CHECKING IN** a traveler who checks in at a hotel or airport ○ *Since the flight was overbooked, the five late check-ins had to wait.*

check·ing ac·count *n* US a bank account that enables you to make withdrawals or payments to other people using checks. Can term **current account**

check·list /chék lìst/ *n* a list of names, items, or points for consideration or action

check mark *n* same as **check** *n* (sense 8)

check·mate /chék màyt/ *n* **1.** **WINNING CHESS POSITION** in chess, a condition or position in which a player's king cannot escape check and the other player wins the game **2.** **CHESS MOVE THAT ENDS GAME** in chess, a move that produces checkmate, or a game that ends in checkmate ○ *The series was declared a draw with three checkmates apiece.* **3.** **COMPLETE DEFEAT** a situation of defeat or deadlock ■ *vt* (**-mat·ed, -mat·ing, -mates**) **1.** **TRAP KING IN CHESS** in chess, to put an opponent's king in checkmate **2.** **THWART SOMEBODY** to make it impossible for somebody to succeed or proceed further ■ *interj* **ANNOUNCEMENT OF CHECKMATE** in chess, used to announce that an opponent's king is in checkmate [15C. Via Old French *eschec mat* < Persian *šāh māt* "the king is dead"]

check·off /chék àwf, -òf/ *n* direct authorized deduction of union dues from the wages of employees

check·out /chék òwt/ *n* **1.** **DEPARTURE FROM HOTEL** the procedure that involves paying a hotel bill and leaving ○ *We'd like to arrange for a later checkout.* **2.** **SUPERMARKET PAY POINT** a point in a supermarket at which shoppers pay for their purchases and have them bagged ○ *Only three checkouts were open.* **3.** **SOMEBODY CHECKING OUT** a traveler checking out at an airport or a hotel ○ *Apart from a couple of late checkouts, everyone seemed to be ready.* **4.** **INSPECTION OR TEST** an inspection or test carried out to make sure that something is working properly or is suitable for its purpose ○ *a preflight checkout of the plane*

check·point /chék pòynt/ *n* a place where police or other officials stop and check vehicles

Check·point Char·lie *n* a border crossing between East and West Berlin during the Cold War. Once situated on the Friedrichstrasse, it has now been demolished.

check·rail /chék ràyl/ *n* UK RAIL same as **guardrail** (sense 2)

check·rein /chék ràyn/ *n* **1.** US a short rein designed to prevent a horse from lowering its head. Can term **bearing rein** **2.** a rein used when driving a pair of horses, connecting the driving rein of one horse to the mouthpiece of the other

check·room /chék ròòm, -ròòm/ *n* a room in a public building such as a theater, restaurant, train, or bus station where customers can leave belongings

check·sheet /chék shèet/ *n* **1.** same as **checklist** **2.** a data collection form on which data are entered in categories in order to make analysis easier

check·sum /chék sùm/ *n* a value transmitted with a data stream, derived from the other elements in the data stream and used to check for transmission errors in the data. If the transmitted checksum differs from the one derived by the receiving computer, a transmission error has probably occurred and the transmission is repeated.

check·up /chék ùp/ *n* a routine examination or inspection, especially one carried out by a doctor or dentist ○ *Regular checkups are required for all pilots.*

check valve *n* a valve designed to allow liquids to flow in one direction only

ched·ar·im EDUC plural of **cheder**

ched·dar /chéddər/ *n* a hard pale yellow or orange-red cheese with a flavor that ranges from mild to very sharp, depending on its maturity [Mid-17C. After *Cheddar*, England]

ched·er /káydər, khaydər/ (*plural* **-ar·im** /kay daarim, khay-/ or **-ers**) *n* classes in Hebrew language and religious knowledge for younger Jewish children [Late 19C. < Hebrew *ḥeder* "room"]

cheek /cheek/ *n* **1.** **SOFT PART OF FACE** the soft side area of the face between the nose and ear **2.** **BUTTOCK** either side of the buttocks (*informal*) **3.** **BAD MANNERS** impertinent or precocious words or behavior showing, or appearing to show, disregard for good manners or the feelings of others (*informal*) ○ *He had the cheek to ask me for a ride!* [Old English *cēoce* < W Germanic] —**cheeked** *suffix* ◇ **cheek by jowl** side by side or very close together ○ *Antique dolls were crammed cheek by jowl onto the shelves.* ◇ **turn the other cheek** to accept injury or insults without resisting or retaliating

cheek·bone /cheek bōn/ *n* an arch of bone in the face, below the eyes and above the cheeks

cheek·piece /cheek peess/ *n* either of the two straps on a bridle that lie along the cheeks of a horse and join the bit to the crownpiece

cheek pouch *n* a fold of skin in the mouth of some rodents, mammals, and monkeys that acts as a pouch for storing food

cheek tooth *n* a premolar or molar of a mammal, or any one of the teeth behind the canines

Cheek·to·wa·ga /cheektə waagə/ city in northwestern New York; an eastern suburb of Buffalo. Population: 92,949 (2002 estimate).

cheek·y /cheekee/ (**-i·er, -i·est**) *adj* (*informal*) **1.** insolently or playfully rude or disrespectful **2.** UK amusing or endearing despite offending good manners, especially by being mildly sexually improper ○ *The stories are performed by a raconteur with warmth and a cheeky charm.* —**cheek·i·ly** *adv* —**cheek·i·ness** *n*

cheep /cheep/ *n* the high shrill sound made by a young bird ■ *vi* (**cheeped, cheep·ing, cheeps**) to make a high shrill sound characteristic of young birds [Early 16C. An imitation of the sound]

SPELLCHECK See *cheap.*

cheer /cheer/ *n* **1.** **SHOUT OF APPROVAL** a shout that expresses happiness, excitement, encouragement, or praise ○ *A huge cheer went up as the band walked onto the stage.* **2.** **WELL-BEING AND OPTIMISM** a sense of general well-being and optimism ○ *The latest sales figures will bring little cheer.* ■ *v* (**cheered, cheer·ing, cheers**) **1.** *vti* **SHOUT ENCOURAGEMENT OR SUPPORT** to shout encouragement, support, or appreciation, especially to people who are performing or competing ○ *The audience clapped and cheered and demanded three encores.* **2.** *vt* **MAKE SOMEBODY FEEL CHEERFUL** to make somebody feel more cheerful, confident, or optimistic (*often passive*) ○ *They were cheered by the news.* **3.** *vt* **APPROVE OF SOMETHING** to express or feel enthusiasm for something ○ *Business will cheer this decision.* [13C. Via Anglo-Norman *chere* "face" < Latin *cara* < Greek *kara* "head"] —**cheer·er** *n* —**cheer·ing·ly** *adv*

cheer on *vt* to give active or vocal support, especially at a sports event ○ *We went to cheer our team on.*

cheer up *vti* **1.** to become, or make somebody feel, less sad ○ *She cheered up a little when I suggested lunch.* **2.** to become, or make something, brighter or more attractive and welcoming in appearance ○ *A coat of bright yellow paint will cheer up the dingiest of kitchens.*

cheer·ful /chéerf'l/ *adj* **1.** HAPPY AND OPTIMISTIC in a happy and optimistic mood, or happy and optimistic by nature ○ *She remained her usual cheerful self despite recent setbacks.* **2.** BRIGHT AND PLEASANT causing people to feel cheerful ○ *a cheerful light blue* **3.** WILLING AND UNRESENTFUL showing willingness or good humor in complying ○ *They set to work cleaning up the mess with cheerful determination.* —**cheer·ful·ly** *adv* —**cheer·ful·ness** *n*

cheer·i·o /chéeree ṓ/ *interj UK* used to say goodbye (*informal*) [Early 20C. Alteration of CHEER]

cheer·lead·er /chéer lèedər/ *n* **1.** a member of a group of uniformed performers who encourage the crowd to support a team at sports events **2.** an uncritically enthusiastic supporter (*informal disapproving*)

cheer·lead·ing /chéer lèeding/ *n* **1.** the activity of performing as a cheerleader at a sports event **2.** uncritical enthusiastic support for somebody or something (*disapproving*)

cheer·less /chéerləss/ *adj* lacking anything bright, pleasant, or encouraging ○ *a gloomy cheerless day* —**cheer·less·ly** *adv* —**cheer·less·ness** *n*

cheers /cheerz/ *interj* **1.** GOOD HEALTH used to express good wishes just before drinking an alcoholic drink (*informal*) **2.** *UK* THANKS thank you ○ *Cheers, you've been a big help!* **3.** *UK* GOODBYE goodbye or farewell

cheer·y /chéeree/ (**-i·er, -i·est**) *adj* happy or in good spirits —**cheer·i·ly** *adv* —**cheer·i·ness** *n*

cheese /cheez/ *n* **1.** a food made from the pressed curds of the milk of cows, sheep, goats, and some other animals. It can range from hard to semisoft, and from mildly acidic to sharp. Bacteria and acid are added to separate the milk into lumps (**curds**) and a watery liquid (**whey**). The curds are then drained and used to make cheese. **2.** an individual block of cheese [Old English *cēse*, via Germanic < Latin *caseus*]

cheese·board /chéez bàwrd/ *n* **1.** a piece of wood, plastic, or other material used for serving or cutting cheese **2.** a selection of cheeses offered as an alternative or additional course to the dessert course of a meal

cheese·burg·er /chéez bùrgər/ *n* a hamburger covered with melted cheese, served on a bun

cheese·cake /chéez kàyk/ *n* **1.** a dessert consisting of a layer of sweetened soft cheese mixed with cream and eggs on a cracker-crumb or pastry base **2.** photographs of women that highlight their physical appearance, especially in a stereotypical way (*slang*)

cheese·cloth /chéez klàwth, -klòth/ *n* a light woven cotton material. Use: lightweight clothes, originally, to wrap or strain cheese.

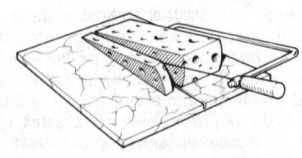

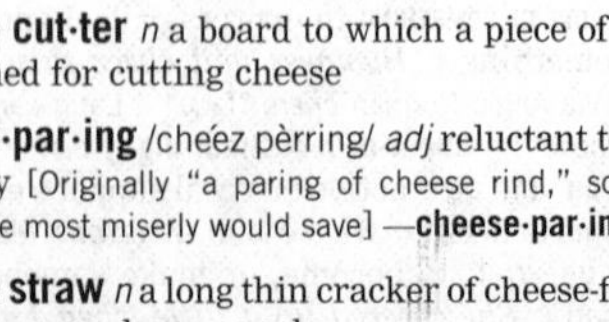

cheese cutter

cheese cut·ter *n* a board to which a piece of wire is attached for cutting cheese

cheese·par·ing /chéez pèrring/ *adj* reluctant to spend money [Originally "a paring of cheese rind," something only the most miserly would save] —**cheese·par·ing** *n*

cheese straw *n* a long thin cracker of cheese-flavored pastry, served as a snack

chees·y /chéezee/ (**-i·er, -i·est**) *adj* **1.** having the flavor or smell of cheese **2.** cheap and tawdry (*informal*) —**chees·i·ness** *n*

cheetah

chee·tah /chéetə/ (*plural* **-tahs** or *same*) *n* a large member of the cat family with a yellowish brown, black-spotted coat, small head, slender body, and long legs that is the fastest land mammal. Native to: Africa, southwestern Asia. Latin name: *Acinonyx jubatus.* [Late 18C. Via Hindi *cītā* < Sanskrit *citraka* "leopard, tiger," literally "spotted" < *citra* "spot"]

Chee·ver /chéevər/, **John** (1912–82) US writer. Many of his novels and short stories are comedies of manners satirizing suburban life.

> "Fear tastes like a rusty knife and do not let her into your home. Courage tastes of blood. Stand up straight. Admire the world. Relish the love of a gentle woman. Trust in the Lord."
> [John Cheever, *The Wapshot Chronicle*; 1957]

chef /shef/ *n* a professional cook, especially the principal cook in a hotel or restaurant [Early 19C. < French, shortening of *chef de cuisine* "head of the kitchen"]

chef-d'oeu·vre /shày dṓvrə, shay dúrv/ (*plural* **chefs-d'oeu·vre** /*pronunc. same*/) *n* a masterpiece, especially one produced by a musician, writer, or artist ○ *He regarded that particular speech as his chef-d'oeuvre.* [< French, "chief piece of work"]

chef's sal·ad *n* a tossed green salad with added tomatoes, sliced hard-boiled eggs, and thin strips of meat and cheese

~~**cheif**~~ incorrect spelling of **chief**

Che·khov /ché kawf, -kawv/, **Anton Pavlovich** (1860–1904) Russian writer. His plays and short stories reveal the emotional depth of ordinary lives and include *The Seagull* (1896) and *The Cherry Orchard* (1904). See Cultural note at **orchard, seagull, sister** —**Chek·ho·vi·an** /che kṓvee ən/ *n, adj*

> "An artist must pass judgment only on what her understands; his range is limited as that of any other specialist."
> [Anton Pavlovich Chekhov, *Letter to A.S. Suvorin*; October 27, 1888]

Che·kiang /chù kyáang, jə gyáang/ ♦ **Zhejiang**

che·la[1] /kéelə/ (*plural* **-lae** /-lee/) *n* the end joint that forms a claw on a limb of a lobster, crab, scorpion, or similar animal (**arthropod**) [Mid-17C. Via modern Latin < Greek *khēlē* "claw"]

che·la[2] /cháy laa/ *n* a pupil or disciple of a Hindu religious teacher [Mid-19C. < Hindi *celā*]

che·late[1] /kée làyt/ *n* COMPOUND OF METAL AND NONMETAL a chemical compound in which metallic and nonmetallic, usually organic, atoms are combined. These compounds are characterized by a ring structure in which a metal ion is attached to two nonmetal ions by covalent bonds. ■ *v* (**-lat·ed, -lat·ing, -lates**) **1.** *vti* COMBINE TO FORM CHELATE to combine, or combine something, with a metal to form a chelate **2.** *vt* MED TREAT SOMEBODY WITH CHELATING AGENT to treat somebody with a chelating agent in order to remove a heavy metal such as lead from the bloodstream —**che·lat·a·ble** /kée làytəb'l/ *adj* —**che·late** *adj* —**che·la·tion** /kee láysh'n/ *n* —**che·la·tor** /kée làytər/ *n*

che·late[2] /kée làyt/ *adj* having chelae, or shaped like a chela

che·lat·ed min·er·al *n* an essential mineral that has been treated to make it more absorbable by the body when used as a dietary supplement

che·lat·ing a·gent *n* a chemical that combines with a metal to form a chelate. Use: treatment of metal poisoning.

che·lic·er·a /kə líssərə/ (*plural* **-ae** /-ee/) *n* either of the first pair of mouthparts of horseshoe crabs and spiders, resembling fangs or pincers and used to grab or poison prey [Mid-19C. < modern Latin < *chela* (see CHELA[1]) + Greek *keras* "horn"]

che·lic·er·ate /kə líssərət, -ràyt/ *n* an invertebrate with feeding appendages shaped like pincers, e.g., a spider or crab. Phylum: Chelicerata. [Early 20C. < modern Latin *chelicerata* < *chelicera* (see CHELICERA)] —**che·lic·er·ate** *adj*

che·li·form /kéelə fàwrm/ *adj* used to describe an appendage shaped like a pincer or chela [Late 18C. < modern Latin *chela* (see CHELA[1])]

Chelms·ford /chélmzfərd/ **1.** cathedral city in Essex, England. Population: 157,072 (2001). **2.** town in northeastern Massachusetts, southwest of Lowell and west of Billerica. Population: 33,996 (2002 estimate).

che·lo·ni·an /ki lṓnee ən/ *n* a reptile, e.g., a turtle or tortoise, that has most of its body enclosed in a hard bony shell. Order: Chelonia. [Early 19C. < modern Latin *Chelonia* < Greek *khelōnē* "tortoise"] —**che·lo·ni·an** *adj*

Chel·sea /chélssee/ **1.** former borough of west central London, now part of the Royal Borough of Kensington and Chelsea. A popular residential area for artists, writers, and musicians in the 18th century, it is also the site of the Chelsea Royal Hospital. **2.** city in eastern Massachusetts, directly northeast of Boston, on the Mystic River. Population: 34,913 (2002 estimate).

Chel·ten·ham /chéltnəm, chéltənəm/ spa and residential city in Gloucestershire, west central England, situated on the western edge of the Cotswold Hills. Population: 110,025 (2001).

Che·lya·binsk /chel yaábinsk/ city and capital of Chelyabinsk Oblast, in western Russia, situated 125 mi./201 km south of Yekaterinburg. Population: 1,393,608 (1995).

chem. *abbr* **1.** chemical **2.** chemist **3.** chemistry

chem-, chemi- *prefix* same as **chemo-**

chem·i·cal /kémmik'l/ *adj* **1.** RELATING TO CHEMISTRY produced by or involved in the processes of chemistry **2.** COMPOSED OF CHEMICAL SUBSTANCES composed of or involving the use of substances produced by the process of chemistry ■ *n* SUBSTANCE USED OR MADE BY CHEMISTRY a substance used in or produced by the processes of chemistry. A chemical has a defined atomic or molecular structure that results from, or takes part in, reactions involving changes in its structure, composition, and properties. [Late 16C. < modern Latin *chimicus* "alchemist," shortening of medieval Latin *alchimicus* < *alchimia* (see ALCHEMY)] —**chem·i·cal·ly** *adv*

chem·i·cal a·buse *n* DRUGS same as **substance abuse**

chem·i·cal bond *n* a force resulting from the redistribution of energy contained by orbiting electrons, which tends to bind atoms together to form molecules

chem·i·cal de·pend·en·cy *n* addiction to a chemical substance or drug

chem·i·cal el·e·ment CHEM same as **element** (sense 6)

chem·i·cal en·er·gy *n* the energy released or absorbed in a chemical reaction during the decomposition or formation of compounds

chem·i·cal en·gi·neer·ing *n* a branch of engineering that deals with the industrial applications of chemistry and chemical processes —**chem·i·cal en·gi·neer** *n*

chem·i·cal e·qua·tion *n* a representation, using chemical symbols in a form resembling a mathematical equation, of the process involved in a chemical reaction

chem·i·cal-free *adj* not addicted to drugs or refraining from the use of drugs (*informal*)

Chem·i·cal Mace *tdmk* a trademark for an aerosol used to immobilize an attacker for a brief time

chem·i·cal peel *n* a beauty treatment that uses a chemical solution to remove the outer layers of skin on the face to reveal smooth new skin without lines or wrinkles

chem·i·cal re·ac·tion *n* a process that changes the molecular composition of a substance by redistributing atoms or groups of atoms without altering the structure of the nuclei of the atoms

chem·i·cal toi·let *n* a portable toilet containing chemicals to neutralize human waste

chem·i·cal war·fare *n* military operations involving the use of weapons containing substances such as nerve gas or poison

chem·i·cal weap·on *n* a weapon containing a substance such as nerve gas or poison

chem·i·cal weath·er·ing *n* the weathering of a rock surface through chemical processes such as oxidation, solution, and hydrolysis

chem·i·lu·mi·nes·cence /kèmmi loomi néss'nss/ *n* emission of light as a result of a chemical reaction, without producing heat —**chem·i·lu·mi·nes·cent** *adj*

che·min de fer /shə màN də fér/ *n* a gambling card game, similar to and derived from baccarat [< French, "railroad"; from the speed at which it is played]

chem·i·ne·a *n* COOK another spelling of **chiminea**

che·mise /shə méez/ *n* **1.** a long loose dress, sometimes loosely belted at the waist or hip **2.** a long loose undergarment shaped like a dress [13C. Via Old French < late Latin *camisia* "shirt"]

chem·i·sette /shèmmi zét/ *n* a decorative undergarment made of lace or other fine material, worn to fill space left at the neckline of a low-cut dress [Early 19C. < French, "small chemise" < *chemise* (see CHEMISE)]

chem·i·sorb /kémmi sàwrb/ (**-sorbed, -sorb·ing, -sorbs**), **chem·o·sorb** /kémmə-/ *vt* to take up a substance by chemisorption [Mid-20C. Back-formation < CHEMISORPTION]

chem·i·sorp·tion /kèmmi sáwrpsh'n/ *n* the process of coating the surface of a substance rather than being absorbed by it, accompanied by chemical bonding between the surface of the material and the adsorbed substance [Mid-20C. Blend of CHEMICAL + ADSORPTION] —**chem·i·sorp·tive** *adj*

chem·ist /kémmist/ *n* **1.** a scientist who works in the field of chemistry **2.** *UK* same as **drugstore** [Mid-16C. Via French < modern Latin *chimista*, shortening of medieval Latin *alchimista* "alchemist" < *alchimia* (see ALCHEMY)]

chem·is·try /kémmistree/ (*plural* **-tries**) *n* **1.** STUDY OF TRANSFORMATION OF MATTER a branch of science dealing with the structure, composition, properties, and reactive characteristics of substances, especially at the atomic and molecular levels **2.** CHEMICAL PROPERTIES OF SOMETHING the chemical composition, structure, and properties of a substance, or the chemical aspects of an activity ○ *the chemistry of wine-making* **3.** REACTION BETWEEN TWO PEOPLE the spontaneous reaction of two people to each other, especially a mutual sense of attraction or understanding

Chem·nitz /kémnits/ city in Saxony, east central Germany. It is a major industrial city. Population: 274,201 (1997). Former name **Karl-Marx-Stadt** (1953–90)

che·mo /kéemō/ *n* MED same as **chemotherapy** (*informal*) [Mid-20C. Shortening]

chemo- *prefix* chemical, chemistry ○ *chemoreceptor* [< CHEMICAL]

che·mo·kine /kéemō kīn/ *n* a protein secreted by lymph cells (**cytokines**) that activates white blood cells during the development of inflammation [Mid-20C. < CHEMOKINESIS]

che·mo·ki·ne·sis /kèemō ki néessiss, -kī-/ *n* increased activity of cells or organisms caused by the presence of a chemical agent

che·mo·lith·o·troph /kèemō líthə tròf/ *n* a bacterium that obtains its energy from inorganic compounds containing iron, nitrogen, or sulfur, and not from living on decaying organisms —**chem·o·lith·o·troph·ic** /kèemō lithə tróffik/ *adj*

che·mo·pro·phy·lax·is /kèemō prōfə láksiss/ *n* the use of chemical agents to prevent disease —**che·mo·pro·phy·lac·tic** *adj*

che·mo·pro·tec·tive /kèemō prə téktiv/ *adj* protecting the body from the effects of chemicals and diseases such as cancer through the antioxidant or immunity-boosting properties of a specific diet or supplement —**che·mo·pro·tec·tion** *n*

che·mo·re·cep·tion /kèemō ri sépsh'n/ *n* the physiological response of an organism or sense organ to a chemical stimulus —**che·mo·re·cep·tive** *adj* —**che·mo·re·cep·tiv·i·ty** /kèemō ri sep tívvətee/ *n*

che·mo·re·cep·tor /kèemō ri séptər/ *n* a sense organ that responds to a chemical stimulus, e.g., a taste bud

che·mo·sen·so·ry /kèemō sénssəree/ *adj* involved in or relating to the perception of chemical agents, especially in the sense of smell

chem·o·sorb *vt* CHEM another spelling of **chemisorb**

che·mo·sphere /kéemə sfeer/ *n* a variable region of the atmosphere, approximately 20 to 120 mi./30 to 190 km above the Earth's surface, where photochemical reactions take place —**che·mo·spher·ic** /kèemə sférrik/ *adj*

che·mo·stat /kéemō stàt/ *n* an apparatus designed to permit the growth of bacterial cultures at controlled rates

che·mo·sur·ger·y /kèemō súrjəree/ *n* surgical removal of dead or diseased tissue by chemical means —**che·mo·sur·gi·cal** *adj*

che·mo·syn·the·sis /kèemō sínthəssiss/ *n* the synthesis of organic molecules by microorganisms using energy derived from chemical reactions —**che·mo·syn·thet·ic** /kèemō sin théttik/ *adj* —**che·mo·syn·thet·i·cal·ly** *adv*

che·mo·tax·is /kèemō táksiss/ *n* movement or change in the position of a cell or organism in response to the presence of a chemical agent —**che·mo·tac·tic** /-táktik/ *adj* —**che·mo·tac·ti·cal·ly** *adv*

che·mo·tax·on·o·my /kèemō tak sónnəmee/ *n* the classification of plants and microorganisms based on their biochemistry —**che·mo·tax·o·nom·ic** /kèemō taksə nómmik/ *adj* —**che·mo·tax·o·nom·i·cal·ly** *adv* —**che·mo·tax·on·o·mist** *n*

che·mo·ther·a·py /kèemō thérrəpee/ (*plural* **-pies**) *n* the use of chemical agents to treat diseases, infections, or other disorders, especially cancer —**che·mo·ther·a·peu·tic** /-therrə pyóotik/ *adj* —**che·mo·ther·a·peu·ti·cal·ly** *adv* —**che·mo·ther·a·pist** *n*

che·mot·ro·pism /ki móttrə pìzzəm/ *n* the movement or growth of an organism or part of an organism in response to a chemical stimulus —**che·mo·trop·ic** /kèemō tróppik/ *adj* —**che·mo·trop·i·cal·ly** *adv*

Chem·ul·po /chèmool páw/ former name for **Inchon**

chem·ur·gy /kémmərjee/ *n* a branch of applied chemistry dealing with the industrial application of organic substances, especially of agricultural origin [Mid-20C. < CHEMICAL] —**che·mur·gic** /kə múrjik/ *adj* —**che·mur·gi·cal** *adj*

chem·zyme /kém zīm/ *n* a substance that acts like an enzyme to increase the effectiveness of a drug [Late 20C. Blend of CHEMO- + ENZYME]

Chen /chen/ *n* a Chinese dynasty that ruled from A.D. 557 to 589

Che·nab /chə náab/, **Che·nāb** river in northwestern India and eastern Pakistan. It flows into the Sutlej, a tributary of the Indus. Length: 600 mi./960 km.

chenette /chénnət/ *n Carib* same as **guinep** (sense 1)

Che·ney /cháynee/, **Dick** (*b.* 1941) vice president of the United States. He was a member of the US House of Representatives (1978–89) and US secretary of state (1989–93) before becoming the vice president (2001–). Full name **Cheney, Richard Bruce**

Cheng·de /chùng dú/, **Ch'eng-te** city and capital of the former Jehol Province, now Hebei Province, in northeastern China, situated on the Luan River, approximately 110 mi./177 km northeast of Beijing. Population: 246,799 (1991).

Cheng·du /chùng dóo/ provincial capital, situated northwest of Chongqing, in Sichuan, China. Population: 4,320,000 (1995).

Ch'eng-te another spelling of **Chengde**

che·nille /shə néel/ *n* **1.** a soft thick cotton or silk fabric with a raised pile. Use: furnishings, clothes. **2.** a thick silk, cotton, or worsted cord or yarn. Use: embroidery, fringes, trimmings. [Mid-18C. Via French, "hairy caterpillar" < Latin *canicula* "little dog" < *canis* "dog"]

Che·nin Blanc /shènnin blaáNgk/ *n* **1.** a white wine originally from the Loire region of west central France but now widely made elsewhere **2.** a variety of white grape used to make Chenin Blanc [< French]

Chen·nai /chə nī/ capital of Tamil Nadu State, on the southeastern coast of India. It is a major port and commercial city. Population: 6,424,624 (2001). Former name **Madras**

Chen·nault /shə náwlt/, **Claire Lee** (1890–1958) US air force general. He retired from the US Air Force in 1937 and formed the Flying Tigers.

Chen Shui-bi·an /chən shwày bee án/ (*b.* 1951) president of Taiwan (2000–). A member of the pro-independence Democratic Progressive Party, he served four years as mayor of Taipei (1994–98) before his election to the presidency.

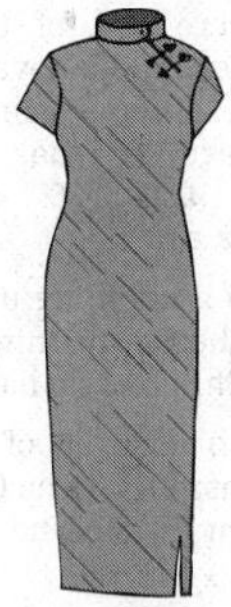

cheongsam

cheong·sam /chòng saám/ *n* a straight dress with a small stand-up collar and a slit in the skirt, worn by Chinese women [Mid-20C. < Cantonese Chinese, "long gown"]

Che·ops /kée ops/ (2549?–2526 B.C.) Egyptian pharaoh. He commissioned the construction of the Great Pyramid at Giza, near Cairo. Born **Khufu**

cheque /chek/ *n* BANKING Can, UK spelling of **check** *n* (sense 4) [Early 18C. Variant of CHECK]

cheq·uer *v* UK spelling of **checker**[2]

Cheq·uers /chékərz/ *n* a country house in Buckinghamshire, in central southern England, that is the official country residence of the British prime minister

Cher /sher/ (*b.* 1946) US entertainer. She turned to acting after a successful singing career and won an Academy Award for *Moonstruck* (1987). Born **La Piere, Cherilyn Sarkisian**

Cher·bourg /shér boorg/ city and port on the English Channel in the Manche Department of the Basse-Normandie Region, in northwestern France. Population: 25,370 (1999).

che·rem /khérrəm, kháyrəm/, **he·rem** *n* formerly, a form of Jewish excommunication involving the separation of a person from the rest of the Jewish community [Early 19C. < Hebrew *ḥerem* < *ḥāram* "to curse"]

Che·ren·kov ef·fect *n* PHYS another spelling of **Cerenkov effect**

cher·i·moy·a /chèrri móy ə/ (*plural* **-as** or *same*) *n* **1.** an edible heart-shaped fruit with creamy white scented flesh and green skin that turns purple-black when ripe **2.** the tree that bears cherimoyas. Native to: South America. Latin name: *Annona cherimola*. [Mid-18C. Via Spanish < Quechua *chirimuya* < *chiri* "cold" + *muya* "circle"]

cher·ish /chérrish/ (**-ished, -ish·ing, -ish·es**) *vt* **1.** LOVE AND CARE FOR SOMEBODY to feel or show great love or care for somebody ○ *He cherishes that girl.* **2.** VALUE SOMETHING HIGHLY to value something such as a right, freedom, or privilege highly ○ *I cherish my independence.* **3.** RETAIN SOMETHING IN MIND to retain a memory or wish in the mind as a source of pleasure or as an ambition ○ *his long-cherished dream* [14C.

< French *chériss-*, stem of *chérir* "hold dear" < *cher* "dear" < Latin *carus*] —**cher·ish·a·ble** *adj* —**cher·ish·er** *n* —**cher·ish·ing·ly** *adv*

Cher·nen·ko /chər nyéngkō/, **Konstantin** (1911–85) Soviet politician. A long-time political ally of Leonid Brezhnev, he became general secretary of the Communist Party of the Soviet Union (1984–85). Full name **Chernenko, Konstantin Ustinovich**

Cher·no·byl /chər nōb'l/ site of a nuclear power plant near Kiev, in Ukraine, where there was a catastrophic accident in 1986

cher·no·zem /chúrnə zĕm/ *n* a fertile black or brown topsoil that is rich in humus and can support crops for long periods of time without the addition of fertilizers. It covers a large proportion of the European and Asian steppe, as well as a belt of land stretching from Saskatchewan in Canada through North Dakota into Texas. [Mid-19C. < Russian, "black earth"] —**cher·no·zem·ic** /chùrnə zémmik/ *adj*

Cher·o·kee /chérrəkee/ (*plural same* or **-kees**) *n* **1.** a member of a Native North American people who once lived in the southeastern United States and now live mainly in Oklahoma and North Carolina. The Cherokee were one of the Five Civilized Nations who, under the Removal Act of 1830, were sent to live on reservations in Oklahoma. **2.** the Iroquoian language of the Cherokee. Native speakers: 10,000. [Late 17C. < obsolete Cherokee *tsaraki*] —**Cher·o·kee** *adj*

Cher·o·kee rose *n* a climbing evergreen rose that grows in the southeastern United States. Flowers: white. Native to: China. Latin name: *Rosa laevigata*.

Cher·o·kee Strip *n* an area of land in northern Oklahoma, purchased from the Cherokee people by the US government in 1891 and made available for settlement in 1893

che·root /shə ro͞ot/ *n* a cigar with two square-cut ends [Late 17C. Via French *cheroute* < Tamil *curuṭṭu* "roll of tobacco"]

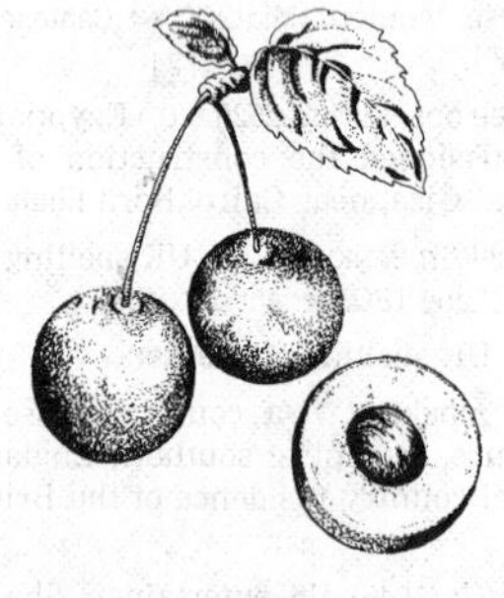

cherry

cher·ry /chérree/ *n* (*plural* **-ries**) **1.** FOOD **SMALL ROUND FRUIT** a small round fruit that has a single hard pit and varies in color from bright red or yellow to dark purplish black **2.** TREES **FRUIT TREE** a tree that bears cherries. Varieties include the sweet cherry, sour cherry, and chokecherry. Genus: *Prunus*. **3.** INDUST **CHERRY WOOD** the wood of the cherry tree. Use: furniture-making, musical instruments. **4.** COLORS same as **cherry red 5. TABOO TERM** a highly offensive term for somebody's virginity, or the hymen as a symbol of a woman's virginity (*taboo*) ■ *adj* **1.** COLORS same as **cherry red 2.** *Midwest* **EXCELLENT** excellent of its kind (*dated slang*) ○ *a totally cherry motorcycle* [14C. Via Old French *cherise* (taken as plural) < medieval Latin *ceresia* < Greek *kerasos* "cherry tree"]

cher·ry birch *n* TREES same as **sweet birch**

cher·ry bomb *n* a powerful round red firecracker that explodes with a loud bang

Cher·ry Hill /chèrree-/ township in southwestern New Jersey, east of Camden and Philadelphia, Pennsylvania. Population: 70,308 (2002 estimate).

cher·ry lau·rel *n* an evergreen bush with shiny leaves. Flowers: white. Native to: Europe, Asia. Latin name: *Prunus laurocerasus*.

cher·ry-pick *vti* **1.** to select only the most lucrative or profitable opportunities, especially in business **2.** to sift through, e.g., evidence or options, selecting only what you like or what supports your strategy, plans, or preconceived notions (*disapproving*)

cherry picker

cher·ry pick·er *n* a mobile crane with an enclosed platform that can be raised to allow somebody to work off the ground, e.g., on an overhead streetlight or wire

cher·ry plum *n* a plum tree that produces red or yellow fruit resembling cherries. Latin name: *Prunus cerasifera*.

cher·ry red *adj* of a deep vivid red color ■ *n* a deep vivid red color

cher·ry·stone /chérree stōn/ *n* a half-grown quahog clam

cher·ry to·ma·to *n* a small tomato with a strong sweet flavor. Latin name: *Lycopersicon esculentum*.

cher·ry·wood /chérree wo͝od/ *n* INDUST same as **cherry** *n* (sense 3)

cher·so·nese /kúrssə neéz, -neéss/ *n* GEOG same as **peninsula** (*archaic*) [Early 17C. Via Latin < Greek *khersonēsos* < *khersos* "dry land" + *nēsos* "island"]

chert /churt/ *n* a brittle microcrystalline quartz. Source: sedimentary rocks. [Late 17C. Origin ?] —**chert·y** *adj*

cherub: garden sculptures at Wendens Ambo, Essex, England

cher·ub /chérrəb/ *n* **1.** an angel depicted as a chubby-faced child with wings, sometimes simply as a child's head above a pair of wings **2.** (*plural* **cher·u·bim** /chérrəbim/ or **cher·ubs**) in Christianity, a member of the eighth of the nine orders in the medieval hierarchy of angels [Pre-12C. Via Latin *cherub*, Greek *kheroub* < Hebrew *kĕrūḇ*, probably < Akkadian; confused with Aramaic *kĕ-rabyā* "like a child"]

che·ru·bic /chə ro͞obik/ *adj* like a cherub in appearance or demeanor —**che·ru·bi·cal·ly** *adv*

Che·ru·bi·ni /kèrroo beénee/, **Luigi** (1760–1842) Italian composer. A prolific composer of operas and sacred music, he was influential as director of the Paris Conservatoire (1821–41). Full name **Cherubini, Maria Luigi Carlo Zenobio Salvatore**

cher·vil /chúrvəl/ *n* **1.** an herb with a mild flavor of aniseed. Use: food seasoning. Latin name: *Anthriscus cerefolium*. **2.** a plant related or similar to the chervil. Genera: *Anthriscus* or *Chaerophyllum*. [Pre-12C. Via Latin *chaerephyllum* < Greek *khairephullon*]

Ches·a·peake /chéssə peek/ city in Virginia, south of Norfolk and Hampton, and east of the Great Dismal Swamp. Population: 206,665 (2002 estimate).

Ches·a·peake Bay largest inlet of the Atlantic Ocean on the East Coast of the United States, bounded by Virginia and Maryland. Area: 3,320 sq. mi./8,365 sq. km.

Ches·a·peake Bay re·triev·er *n* a hunting dog belonging to a breed developed in the United States that has a thick short wavy coat from dark brown to tan in color. It is trained to retrieve game from water.

Chesh·ire[1] /chéshər/ *n* a mild crumbly cheese that is usually white but sometimes red, originally made in Cheshire, England

Chesh·ire[2] /chéshər/ **1.** county in northwestern England, between Manchester and the Welsh border. Population: 673,788 (2001). Area: 900 sq. mi./2,328 sq. km. **2.** town in southern Connecticut, southeast of Waterbury. Population: 29,096 (2002 estimate).

Chesh·ire cat *n* a cat in Lewis Carroll's *Alice's Adventures in Wonderland* whose broad grin remained suspended in the air after the cat itself had disappeared

Chesh·van *n* CALENDAR another spelling of **Heshvan**

chess

chess[1] /chess/ *n* a game played on a checkered board by two players, each with 16 pieces, whose object is to capture (**checkmate**) the opponent's king. Each player begins with a king, a queen, two bishops, two knights, two rooks or castles, and eight pawns. [12C. Shortening of Old French *esches*, plural of *eschec* (see CHECK)]

chess[2] /chess/ *n* a deck board or floorboard of a pontoon bridge [Early 19C. Origin ?]

chess[3] /chess/ *n* **1.** PLANTS same as **cheat** *n* (sense 4) **2.** a weedy bromegrass. Genus: *Bromus*. [Mid-18C. Origin ?]

chess·board /chéss bàwrd/ *n* a square board divided into 64 alternate light and dark squares, used for playing chess. The eight vertical rows of squares are called files, the eight horizontal rows are called ranks, and the squares that stretch diagonally across the board are called diagonals.

chess·man /chéss màn/ (*plural* **-men** /-mèn/) *n* a piece from a set of 32 used in the game of chess

chess pie *n* a pie filled with a rich mixture of eggs, butter, and sugar, often with additional flavorings [Origin ?]

chess·piece /chéss peess/ *n* CHESS same as **chessman**

ches·sy·lite /chéssi līt/ *n* MINERALS same as **azurite** [Mid-19C. After *Chessy*, near Lyons in France]

chest /chest/ *n* **1. UPPER BODY** the part of the body between the neck and the stomach, covering the ribs and the organs that the ribs enclose **2. FRONT PART OF BODY** the outside of the chest ○ *a hairy chest* **3. STRONG RECTANGULAR BOX** a strong rectangular box, usually with a lid and sometimes a lock, used for storage or shipping [Old English *cest*, via W Germanic < Latin *cista* < Greek *kistē* "basket"] —**-chested** *suffix* —**chest·ful** *n* ◇ **get something off your chest** to talk openly about something that has been upsetting, annoying, or worrying you, especially in order to reduce or remove those feelings ◇ **keep your cards** *or* **play something close to your chest** to be discreet or secretive about something

Ches·ter /chéstər/ **1.** ancient walled cathedral city that is the county town of Cheshire, England. Population: 118,210 (2001). **2.** city and port in southeastern Pennsylvania, south of Philadelphia, on the Delaware River. Population: 37,058 (2002 estimate).

ches·ter·field /chéstər fèeld/ *n* **1.** *Can, Northwest US* **SOFA** a large sofa with upright armrests at the same height as the back, usually upholstered in leather and with a rolled-over outward curve along the top **2.** *Can, UK* **COUCH** an upholstered couch or sofa with back and arms of the same height **3. OVERCOAT** an overcoat, usually with concealed buttons and a velvet collar [Mid-19C. After a 19C earl of *Chesterfield*]

Ches·ter·field /chéstər fèeld/ **1.** town in Derbyshire, England, noted for the twisted spire of All Saints' Church. Population: 98,845 (2002). **2.** city in eastern Missouri, on the Missouri River, a western suburb of St. Louis. Population: 47,126 (2002 estimate).

Ches·ter·field, Philip Dormer Stanhope, 4th Earl of Chesterfield (1694–1773) British politician and writer. Secretary of state to George III and a literary wit, he wrote *Letters to his Son* (1774).

> "This man I thought had been a Lord among wits; but, I find, he is only a wit among Lords."
> [Samuel Johnson. Quoted in *Life of Samuel Johnson*, James Boswell; 1791]

Ches·ter·ton /chéstərtən/, **G. K.** (1874–1936) British writer. His books include the Father Brown detective stories and volumes of literary criticism. Full name **Chesterton, Gilbert Keith**

> "If a thing is worth doing, it is worth doing badly."
> [G. K. Chesterton, "Folly and Female Education," *What's Wrong with the World*; 1910]

> "A good novel tells us the truth about its hero; but a bad novel tells us the truth about its author."
> [G. K. Chesterton, *Heretics*; 1905]

Ches·ter White *n* a large white hog with drooping ears belonging to a breed developed in Pennsylvania [Mid-19C. After *Chester* County, Pennsylvania]

chest·nut /chés nùt/ *n* **1. EDIBLE NUT** an edible nut that grows inside a prickly husk and has a glossy brown skin **2.** (*plural* **chest·nuts** or *same*) TREES **TREE THAT PRODUCES CHESTNUTS** a deciduous tree that has long toothed leaves and produces chestnuts. Native to: North America, Europe, Japan, China. Genus: *Castanea.* ◊ **horse chestnut 3.** INDUST **WOOD OF CHESTNUT TREE** the coarse-grained durable wood of the chestnut tree **4. REDDISH BROWN HORSE** a horse with a reddish brown color **5.** ANAT **CALLUS ON HORSE'S LEG** a small hard callus found in several places on the inner surface of a horse's leg and thought to be a vestigial toe **6. REDDISH BROWN COLOR** a deep reddish brown color **7. STALE JOKE OR STORY** a joke or story that has lost its impact through overuse (*informal*) [Early 16C. < obsolete *chesten*, via Old French *chastaine* < Latin *castanea* < Greek *kastanea*] —**chest·nut** *adj*

chest·nut blight *n* a disease that kills chestnut trees and is especially destructive to North American chestnuts. It is caused by the fungus *Cryphonectria parasitica* and was probably imported from Asia into the United States in the early 20th century.

chest·nut oak *n* **1.** a deciduous oak tree with shiny yellow leaves resembling those of a chestnut. Native to: eastern North America. Latin name: *Quercus prinus.* **2.** TREES same as **chinquapin oak**

chest of draw·ers *n* a piece of furniture consisting of a set of drawers in a wooden frame with a flat top, used for storing clothes

chest voice *n* the lowest register of somebody's speaking or singing voice

chest·y /chéstee/ (-i·er, -i·est) *adj* **1. WITH LARGE CHEST** having a well-developed chest (*informal*) **2. CONCEITED** extremely arrogant and conceited (*informal*) **3.** *UK* **HAVING PHLEGM IN LUNGS** showing the effects of a chest complaint, e.g., by having phlegm in the lungs —**chest·i·ness** *n*

Chet·nik /chétnik/ *n* a Serbian nationalist who was part of a group who fought the Turks before World War I, and was involved in guerrilla warfare in World War I and World War II [Early 20C. < Serbo-Croatian *četnik* < *četa* "band, troop"]

chet·rum /chét ro͝om/ (*plural same* or **-rums**) *n* a subunit of currency in Bhutan. See table at **currency** [Late 20C. < Tibetan]

che·val-de-frise /shə vàl də frèez/ (*plural* **che·vaux-de-frise** /shə vō-/) *n* **1.** an obstacle consisting of barbed wire or spikes attached to a wooden frame, used to block an advancing enemy force **2.** a line of jagged glass, nails, or spikes set into masonry on top of a wall to deter intruders [< French, "horse of Friesland"; from its use by the Frisians, who lacked cavalry, during the siege of Groningen (1594)]

che·val·et /shə vá lày, shèvvə láy/ *n* the bridge of a stringed musical instrument [Late 19C. < French, "small horse" < *cheval* "horse" < Latin *caballus*]

che·val glass /shə vál-/ *n* a long mirror that is mounted in a frame so that it can be tilted [< French *cheval* "frame," literally "horse"]

chev·a·lier /shèvvə léer, shə vállee ày/ *n* **1.** used as the title of members of the French Legion of Honor and of other orders **2.** a French knight or nobleman of the lowest rank [14C. Via French < medieval Latin *caballarius* < Latin *caballus* "horse"]

che·vet /chə váy/ *n* a complex of elaborate architectural structures at the eastern end of a church, especially a French Gothic church, usually consisting of a semicircular or polygonal apse with radiating chapels and many buttresses [Early 19C. < French, "pillow"]

Chev·i·ot /shévvee ət/ *n* **1.** a hornless sheep belonging to a breed with short thick wool originating in the Cheviot Hills on the border between Scotland and England **2.** *also* **chev·i·ot** a woolen fabric with a coarse twill weave, originally made from the wool of Cheviot sheep

Chev·i·ot Hills /shévvee ət-/ range of hills along the border of England and Scotland. The highest peak is the Cheviot, 2,676 ft./816 m.

chèv·re /shévvrə/ *n* a soft cheese made from goat's milk [Mid-20C. Via French, "goat" < Latin *capra*, feminine of *caper*]

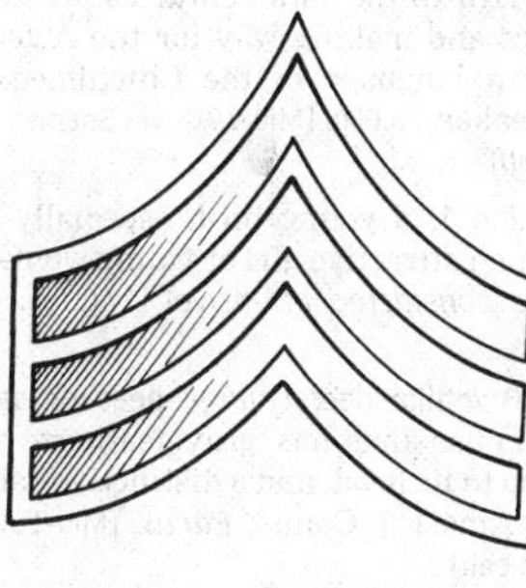

chevron

chev·ron /shévvrən/ *n* **1.** a V-shaped symbol, especially one used as a sign of rank on military or police uniforms **2.** a heraldic ornament in the form of a wide inverted V-shape [14C. < French, "rafter" < Latin *caper* "goat"]

chev·ro·tain /shévvrə tàyn/ (*plural* **-tains** or *same*) *n* a small hornless cud-chewing animal similar to a deer, the male of which has projecting canine teeth. Native to: rain forests of west central Africa and Southeast Asia. Family: Tragulidae. [Late 18C. < French, "small goat" < *chèvre* (see CHÈVRE)]

Chev·y Chase /chèvvee cháyss/ town in Maryland, west of Washington, D.C., on the eastern bank of the Potomac River. Population: 2,760 (2002 estimate).

chew /choo/ *v* (**chewed, chew·ing, chews**) **1.** *vti* **GRIND UP FOOD BEFORE SWALLOWING** to grind up food or other material with the action of the teeth and jaws **2.** *vti* **DAMAGE SOMETHING BY BITING** to gnaw at something repeatedly, usually causing damage ○ *chewing her nails* **3.** *vi* **CHEW TOBACCO** to chew a piece of tobacco ■ *n* **1. CANDY** a candy with a firm texture, which must be chewed before being swallowed ○ *chocolate chews* **2. PIECE OF TOBACCO FOR CHEWING** a piece of tobacco used for chewing [Old English *cēowan* < Germanic] —**chew·a·ble** *adj* —**chew·er** *n*

chew out *vt* to tell somebody off for doing something wrong (*informal*) ○ *Dad chewed me out because I forgot to take out the garbage.*

chew over *vt* to think about or discuss something over a period of time ○ *We chewed the problem over for a couple of days before coming to a decision.*

chew up *vt* **1.** to damage or destroy something, especially something passing through machinery (*informal*) ○ *I'm afraid the machine chewed up your tape.* **2.** to destroy something by biting or chewing it

Che·wa /cháy waà/ *n* a language spoken in Malawi, Zambia, and Mozambique, and belonging to the Bantu group of Niger-Congo languages. Native speakers: 8 million. [< Bantu] —**Che·wa** *adj*

chew·ing gum /cho͞o ing-/ *n* a sweet flavored substance that is chewed but not swallowed. The elastic ingredient in chewing gum used to be chicle from the sapodilla tree, but synthetic equivalents are now commonly used. ○ *a stick of chewing gum*

chew·y /cho͞o ee/ (**-i·er, -i·est**) *adj* having a consistency or texture that requires a good deal of chewing —**chew·i·ness** *n*

Chey·enne[1] /shī én, -án/ (*plural same* or **-ennes**) *n* **1.** a member of a Native North American people who once lived in the western Great Plains. The Cheyenne, along with the Sioux, were instrumental in the defeat of Custer and his forces at the Battle of Little Bighorn. **2.** the Algonquian language of the Cheyenne people. Native speakers: 2,000. [Late 18C. Via Canadian French < Dakota *šahíyena*] —**Chey·enne** *adj*

Chey·enne[2] /shī én, -án/ **1.** river that rises in eastern Wyoming and flows eastward into South Dakota, where it joins the Missouri River. Length: 527 mi./848 km. **2.** city, capital of Wyoming, and county seat of Laramie County, situated in southeastern Wyoming 10 mi./16 km north of the border with Colorado. Population: 53,658 (2002 estimate).

Cheyne-Stokes res·pi·ra·tion /chàyn stṓks-/ *n* a breathing pattern marked by shallow breathing alternating with periods of rapid heavy breathing found in some medical conditions and also occurring at high altitude [Late 19C. After John *Cheyne* (1777–1836), Scottish physician, and William *Stokes* (1804–78), Irish physician]

chez /shay/ *prep* at somebody's home or business premises, especially a restaurant [Mid-18C. Via French < Latin *casa* "cottage"]

chg. *abbr* **1.** FIN change **2.** BANKING charge

Chhat·tis·garh /cháttiss gaàr/ state in eastern India. Capital: Raipur. Population: 20,795,956 (2001). Area: 52,185 sq. mi./135,194 sq. km.

chi[1] /kī/ (*plural* **chis**), **khi** (*plural* **khis**) *n* the 22nd letter of the Greek alphabet, represented in English as "ch" or "kh." See table at **alphabet** [15C. < Greek *khi*]

chi[2] /chee/, **ch'i, Chi, Ch'i, qi, Qi** *n* in Chinese medicine and philosophy, the energy or life force of the universe, believed to flow round the body and to be present in all living things. The manipulation of chi is the basis of acupuncture and Chinese martial arts. [< Chinese *qì* "air, breath"]

Chi·ang Ch'ing another spelling of **Jiang Qing**

Chiang Ching-kuo /chàng chìng kwṓ/ (1910–88) Taiwanese politician. He was president of Taiwan (1978–88) and initiated many economic, social, and political reforms.

Library of Congress

Chiang Kai-shek

Chiang Kai-shek /chàng kī shék/ (1887–1975) Chinese military leader and politician. He helped to overthrow the imperial government (1912) and developed Taiwan's economy as its president (1949–75).

Chi·an·ti /kee áantee/, **chi·an·ti** *n* a light red wine from northwestern Italy [Mid-19C. After the *Chianti* Mountains, Tuscany]

Chi·a·pas /chee áapəss/ state in southeastern Mexico. Capital: Tuxtla Gutiérrez. Population: 3,920,892 (2000). Area: 28,465 sq. mi./73,724 sq. km.

chi·a·ro·scu·ro /kee àarə skóorō/ *n* the use of light and shade in paintings and drawings, or the effect produced by this [Mid-17C. < Italian < *chiaro* "bright" + *oscuro* "dark"] —**chi·a·ro·scu·rism** *n* —**chi·a·ro·scu·rist** *n*

chi·as·ma /kī ázmə/ (*plural* **-mas** or **-ma·ta** /-mətə/) *n* **1.** a crossing over of biological tissue, e.g., the intersection of the optic nerves **2.** the point at which two chromatids join during the fusion and exchange of genetic material (**crossing over**) in cell division [Mid-19C. Via modern Latin < Greek *khiasma* "crosspiece" < *khiazein* "mark with an X" < *khi* "the letter chi"] —**chi·as·mal** *adj* —**chi·as·mic** *adj*

chi·as·mus /kī ázməss/ (*plural* **-mi** /-mī/) *n* a rhetorical construction in which the order of the words in the second of two paired phrases is the reverse of the order in the first. An example is "gray was the morn, all things were gray." [Mid-17C. Via modern Latin < Greek *khiasmos* < *khiazein* (see CHIASMA)]

chi·as·to·lite /kī ástə līt/ *n* a variety of the mineral andalusite that contains carbon impurities in an X-shape [Early 19C. < Greek *khiastos*, past participle of *khiazein* (see CHIASMA)]

Chi·ba /cheé baá/ capital city of Chiba Prefecture, situated on the eastern shore of Tokyo Bay in Honshu, Japan. Population: 880,164 (2002).

Chib·cha /chíbchə/ (*plural same* or **-chas**) *n* **1.** a member of an extinct Native South American people who lived in the Andes Mountains in central Colombia. The Chibcha died out following their defeat by the Spanish conquistador Gonzalo Jeménez de Quesada in the 1530s. **2.** the extinct Chibchan language of the Chibcha people [Early 19C. Via American Spanish < Chibcha *zipa* "chief"]

Chib·chan /chíbchən/ (*plural same* or **-chans**) *n* **1.** a group of Native Central American languages spoken in Colombia and Panama. Native speakers: 100,000. **2.** a member of any of the peoples who speak a language belonging to the Chibchan group —**Chib·chan** *adj*

Chi·bem·ba /chi bémbə/ *n* LANG same as **Bemba** (sense 2) [< Bantu] —**Chi·bem·ba** *adj*

Chi·bou·ga·mau /shee bóogə mō, shi bóogə mō/ town in southwestern Quebec, Canada, situated 150 mi./241 km northwest of Roberval. Population: 7,488 (2001).

chic /sheek/ *adj* stylish and elegant ■ *n* fashionable style and elegance [Mid-19C. < French] —**chic·ness** *n*

Chi·ca·go /shi káagō/ **1.** city and port in northeastern Illinois, situated on Lake Michigan. It is the third largest city in the United States, home to the University of Chicago. Population: 2,886,102 (2002 estimate). **2.** short river in Chicago, Illinois, formed in the city by the confluence of the South Branch and the North Branch. Length: 10 mi./16 km. —**Chi·ca·go·an** *n, adj*

Chi·ca·go Board of Trade *n* a major commodities exchange in Chicago that deals in grain and metal futures

Chi·ca·go Heights city in northeastern Illinois; a southern suburb of Chicago. Population: 32,610 (2002 estimate).

Chi·ca·go School *n* a school of conservative economic thought, associated with the University of Chicago, promoting free markets and capitalism and relying heavily on mathematical analysis

Chi·ca·na /chi káanə/ *n Hispanic* a North American woman or girl of Mexican descent (*sometimes offensive*) [Mid-20C. < Spanish, feminine of *Chicano* (see CHICANO)]

USAGE See *Chicano*.

chi·cane[1] /shi káyn/ *n* **1.** in car racing, a sharp double bend created by placing barriers on the circuit **2.** a bridge or whist hand without trumps or without cards of one suit [Late 19C. < French < *chicaner* "to quibble"]

chi·cane[2] /shi káyn/ (**-caned, -can·ing, -canes**) *vi* to practice chicanery [Late 17C. < French *chicaner* "to quibble"] —**chi·can·er** *n*

chi·can·er·y /shi káynəree/ (*plural* **-ies**) *n* deception or trickery, especially by the clever manipulation of language

Chi·ca·no /chi káanō/ (*plural* **-nos**) *n Hispanic* a North American man or boy of Mexican descent (*sometimes offensive*) [Mid-20C. < American Spanish, variant of Spanish *mexicano* "Mexican" < *México* "Mexico"]

USAGE ***Chicano*** and ***Chicana*** refer only to Mexican Americans. They do not refer to Mexican residents of Mexico. Historically, Chicano is a dialectal variant of the Mexican Spanish word *mexicano*, "a Mexican," and ***Chicana*** is its feminine form. Since opinions about these words can and do differ among the various US Mexican American communities, *Mexican American* is a preferred substitute.

chi·char·ron /cheè char rón/ (*plural* **-ron·es** /-rónnəss/) *n Hispanic* fried pork rinds or cracklings usually seasoned with chili [Mid-19C. < American Spanish]

Chich·es·ter /chíchəstər/ cathedral city in West Sussex, southern England, founded by the Romans. Population: 106,450 (2001).

Chich·es·ter, Sir Francis (1901–72) British aviator and sailor. His feats included a solo Britain-to-Australia flight in 1929 and a solo around-the-world voyage in 1966–67, in *Gipsy Moth IV*. Full name **Chichester, Sir Francis Charles**

Chi·che·wa /chi cháywə/ *n* LANG same as **Chewa** —**Chi·che·wa** *adj*

chi·chi /sheéshee/ *adj* trying too hard or too obviously to be chic or modish ○ *All this designer furniture – isn't it just a bit chichi?* [Mid-20C. < French]

Chi·chi·mec /cheéchee mèk/ (*plural* **-mecs** or *same*) *n* **1.** a member of a group of Native Central American peoples whose ancestors dominated central Mexico from the 11th to the 15th centuries, overthrowing the Toltecs and making way for the Aztecs **2.** the Uto-Aztecan language of the Chichimec peoples. Native speakers: 5,000. [Mid-17C. Via Spanish < Nahuatl *chichimecatl*]

chick /chik/ *n* **1.** a young bird, especially a young chicken **2.** an attractive girl or young woman (*slang; sometimes considered offensive*) [14C. Shortening of CHICKEN]

chick·a·dee /chíkə deè/ (*plural* **-dees** or *same*) *n* a small titmouse that has gray feathers, a darker colored top to its head, and a distinctive call. Native to: North America. Genus: *Parus*. [Mid-19C. An imitation of its call]

Chick·a·hom·i·ny /chìkə hómmənee/ river in east central Virginia, rising northwest of Richmond. Length: 90 mi./145 km.

chick·a·ree /chíkə reè/ (*plural* **-rees** or *same*) *n* a squirrel with red fur that is related to the red squirrel. Native to: western North America. Latin name: *Tamiascurus douglasi*. [Early 19C. An imitation of its cry]

Chick·a·saw /chíkə sàw/ (*plural same* or **-saws**) *n* **1.** a member of a Native North American people who originally lived in northeastern Mississippi and northwestern Alabama, and now live mainly in central and southern Oklahoma. The Chickasaw were one of the Five Civilized Nations who were sent to live on reservations in Oklahoma under the Removal Act of 1830. **2.** the Muskogean language of the Chickasaw. Native speakers: 10,000. [Late 17C. < Chickasaw *čikaša*] —**Chick·a·saw** *adj*

chick·en /chíkən/ *n* **1.** COMMON DOMESTIC FOWL a domestic fowl, usually with brown or black feathers and a fleshy crest on its head. Raised for: meat, eggs. Latin name: *Gallus domesticus*. **2.** MEAT FROM FOWL the meat from a chicken as food **3.** COWARD somebody regarded as cowardly or excessively timid (*informal*) ○ *You'll never do it – you're a chicken!* ■ *adj* COWARDLY showing a lack of courage, or too scared to do a particular thing (*informal; often used by children or young people*) ○ *Are you too chicken to do a high dive?* [Old English *cīcen* < Germanic] ◇ **be running around like a headless chicken** to act in a frantic manner

SYNONYMS See *cowardly*.

chicken out *vi* to fail in or withdraw from something because of a lack of nerve (*slang*) ○ *She chickened out of the climb when she saw how high the cliff was.*

chick·en-and-egg sit·u·a·tion *n* a situation in which it is impossible to know which of two related circumstances occurred first and caused the other

chick·en breast *n* MED same as **pigeon breast** —**chick·en-breasted** *adj*

chick·en feed *n* **1.** food for poultry **2.** an insignificant amount of something, especially money (*slang*)

chick·en-fried steak *n* a cut of beef, usually round steak, that has been tenderized, dredged in flour, and then pan-fried

chick·en hawk *n* **1.** a hawk that preys or is believed to prey on poultry **2.** an offensive term for an older man who seeks young men as sexual partners (*slang*)

chick·en·head /chíkən hèd/ *n* a projection on a rock face that provides a secure handhold for rock climbing [< its shape]

chick·en-heart·ed, chick·en-liv·ered *adj* easily frightened or lacking sufficient courage, boldness, or confidence —**chick·en-heart·ed·ness** *n*

Chick·en Lit·tle *n* an alarmist who warns of imaginary dangers ○ *We won't get anywhere if we listen to the Chicken Littles among us.* [After a fictional hen that was hit on the head by an acorn and said the sky was falling]

chick·en-liv·ered *adj* same as **chicken-hearted**

chick·en louse *n* a biting louse that lives as a parasite on poultry. Latin name: *Menopon pallidum*.

chick·en·pox /chíkən pòks/ *n* a highly infectious viral disease, especially affecting children, characterized by a rash of small itching blisters on the skin and mild fever. Technical name **varicella** [Mid-18C. Origin ?]

chick·en sal·ad air *n* in snowboarding, a trick in which the boarder reaches the trailing hand back between the legs and grabs the heel edge of the board, while holding the leading leg rigidly straight

chick·en·shit /chíkən shìt/ *n* (*slang*) **1.** an offensive term for petty or tedious details or tasks **2.** an offensive term for somebody who is regarded as cowardly or timid —**chick·en·shit** *adj*

chick·en snake *n* REPT same as **rat snake**

chick·en soup *n* in skysurfing, a move or jump that does not go as planned (*slang*)

chick·en wire *n* lightweight flexible galvanized wire fencing, usually made with a hexagonal mesh [< its use as a fence for enclosing chickens]

chick flick *n* a movie that is supposedly of interest primarily to women, because of either its content or cast of characters (*slang; sometimes considered offensive*)

chick lit *n* a genre of fiction targeted to, and written by or about, young and sophisticated urban women (*slang*) [Late 20C. Blend of CHICK (sense 2) and LITERATURE]

chick·pea /chík peè/ *n* **1.** a pale yellow seed about the size of a large pea, cooked as a vegetable **2.** an annual plant that produces chickpeas. Native to: Asia, Mediterranean. Latin name: *Cicer arietinum*. [Early 18C. Alteration of *chich pease* < *chich* "chickpea" (< French *chiche* < Latin *cicer*) + *pease* (see PEA)]

chick·weed /chík weèd/ *n* a common low-growing weed, found on cultivated land. Native to: Europe. Latin name: *Stellaria media*. [Because chickens eat the plant]

Chi·cla·yo /chi klaá yō/ city in northwestern Peru, situated on the Pacific coast. Population: 375,058 (1998).

chic·le /chík'l/ *n* a gummy substance from the latex of the sapodilla tree. Use: main ingredient of chewing gum. [Late 19C. Via American Spanish < Nahuatl *tzictli*] —**chic·ly** *adj*

chi·co /cheékō/ *n* PLANTS same as **greasewood** (sense 1) [Shortening of Spanish *chicalote*]

Chi·co /cheékō/ city in northern California, northwest of Sacramento, in the valley of the Sacramento River. Population: 65,904 (2002 estimate).

Chi·co·pee /chíkə pee/ city in southwestern Massachusetts, at the junction of the Chicopee and Connecticut rivers. Population: 54,833 (2002 estimate).

chic·o·ry /chíkəree/ *n* 1. a dried, roasted, and ground root. Use: coffee additive or substitute. 2. *Can, UK* a plant grown for its pale, slightly bitter, succulent leaves. Use: cooked or raw in salads. Latin name: *Cichorium intybus*. US term **endive** [15C. Via obsolete French *cicoré* "endive" < medieval Latin *cichorea* < Greek *kikhorion*]

Chi·cou·ti·mi /shə kóotə mée/ river in Quebec, Canada, flowing from Laurentides Provincial Park to Lake Kenogami and the Saguenay. Length: 99 mi./160 km.

chide /chīd/ (**chid** /chid/ or **chid·ed**, **chid** or **chid·den** /chídd'n/ or **chid·ed**, **chid·ing**, **chides**) *vti* to reproach somebody gently [Old English *cīdan* < ?] —**chid·er** *n* —**chid·ing** *adj* —**chid·ing·ly** *adv*

chief /cheef/ *adj* 1. MOST IMPORTANT most important, basic, or common 2. HIGHEST IN AUTHORITY highest in authority, position, or rank ■ *n* 1. LEADER the person with the most authority or highest rank in a group or organization 2. CULT ANTHROP same as **chieftain** 3. BOSS a supervisor, manager, or other person in authority, especially in the workplace (*informal*) 4. NAUT SHIP'S PRINCIPAL ENGINEER the principal engineer on a ship 5. NAUT same as **chief petty officer** (*informal*) 6. HERALDRY TOP SECTION OF HERALDIC SHIELD the upper third of the surface area of a heraldic shield [13C. Via French *chef* < Latin *caput* "head"] —**chief·ship** *n*

chief ex·ec·u·tive *n* 1. the highest-ranking member of an executive body, e.g., the head of a government or the governor of a US state 2. BUSINESS, MANAGEMT same as **chief executive officer** 3. the president of the United States

chief ex·ec·u·tive of·fi·cer *n* the highest-ranking executive officer within a company or corporation, who has responsibility for overall management of its day-to-day affairs under the supervision of a board of directors

chief jus·tice *n* 1. a judge who presides over a court that has several judges 2. the presiding justice of the US Supreme Court

chief·ly /chéeflee/ *adv* 1. ABOVE ALL more or more importantly than anyone or anything else ○ *We moved to this area of the city chiefly because it's convenient for getting to work.* 2. IN MAIN for the most part ○ *The human body consists chiefly of water.* ■ *adj* RELATING TO CHIEF relating to or characteristic of a chief

chief mas·ter ser·geant *n* a noncommissioned officer in the US Air Force of a rank above senior master sergeant

chief of na·val op·er·a·tions *n* a senior US naval officer who serves as the Navy's representative to the Joint Chiefs of Staff

chief of staff *n* 1. a general officer in the US Army, Air Force, or Marine Corps who is a member of the Joint Chiefs of Staff 2. the senior officer serving on a military staff, who has responsibility for managing it and for advising the commander

chief of state *n* the formal head of a nation, e.g., a monarch or appointed president

chief op·er·at·ing of·fi·cer *n* the executive responsible to the board for day-to-day running of the company

chief pet·ty of·fi·cer *n* 1. a noncommissioned officer in the US Navy or Coast Guard of a rank above petty officer first class 2. a noncommissioned officer in the Royal Canadian Navy of the highest rank

chief rab·bi *n* the senior religious leader of the Jewish community in the United Kingdom and some other countries

chief·tain /chéeftən/ *n* the leader or titular head of a people or similar ethnic group [13C. < Old French *chevetaine*, alteration of late Latin *capitaneus* (see CAPTAIN)] —**chief·tain·cy** *n* —**chief·tain·ship** *n*

chief war·rant of·fi·cer *n* 1. an officer in the US Army, Navy, Marine Corps, or Coast Guard of a rank above warrant officer and below that of second lieutenant or ensign 2. the highest-ranking noncommissioned officer in the Royal Canadian Army or Air Force

chiff·chaff /chíf chàf/ *n* a small brownish yellow bird with a characteristic repetitive song. Native to: Europe, Asia. Latin name: *Phylloscopus collybita*. [Late 18C. An imitation of its song]

chif·fe·robe *n* FURNITURE another spelling of **chifforobe**

chif·fon /shi fón, shí fòn/ *n* LIGHTWEIGHT FABRIC a very light sheer nylon, rayon, or silk fabric ■ *adj* 1. OF CHIFFON made or consisting of chiffon 2. LIGHT AND FINE resembling chiffon in lightness and fineness 3. COOK FLUFFY describes food with a light fluffy texture, usually created by adding whipped egg whites or gelatin [Mid-18C. < French < *chiffe* "rag, flimsy stuff"]

chif·fon·ade /shìffə náyd, -náad/ *n* vegetables that have been shredded or finely chopped, often used as a garnish for other foods [Late 19C. < French]

chif·fo·nier /shìffə néer/ *n* a tall narrow chest of drawers that often has a mirror attached to the back [Mid-18C. < French]

chifforobe

chif·fo·robe /shíffə rōb/, **chif·fe·robe** /shíff rōb/, **chiff·robe** *n* a tall piece of furniture with drawers and a space for hanging clothes [Early 20C. Blend of CHIFFONIER + WARDROBE]

Chif·ley /chífflee/, **Ben** (1885–1951) Australian politician. He was a trade union activist, Labor Party politician, and prime minister of Australia (1945–49). Full name **Chifley, Joseph Benedict**. See table at **prime minister**

chi·ge·tai /chíggə tī/ (*plural same* or **-tais**), **dzig·ge·tai** /zíggə-/ *n* a wild ass related to the onager. Native to: Mongolia. Latin name: *Equus hemionus*. [Late 18C. < Mongolian *chikitei* "having ears" < *chiki* "ear"]

chig·ger /chíggər/ *n* 1. the bright red parasitic larva of a free-living mite that feeds on the skin and other tissues of mammals, including humans, causing irritation and swelling. Some species transmit diseases such as scrub typhus. Genera: *Trombicula* or *Neotrombicula*. 2. INSECTS same as **chigoe** (sense 1) [Mid-18C. < CHIGOE]

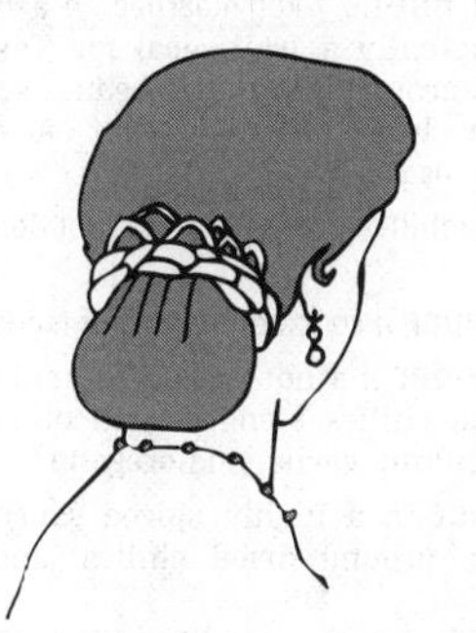
chignon

chi·gnon /shéen yòn, sheen yón/ *n* a woman's hairstyle consisting of a roll of hair worn at the nape of the neck [Late 18C. < French, "nape of the neck, chain" < Latin *catena* "chain"]

chig·oe /chíggō, chéegō/ *n* 1. a small tropical flea, the fertilized female of which burrows under the skin causing painful itching sores that easily become infected. Latin name: *Tunga penetrans*. 2. INSECTS same as **chigger** (sense 1) [Mid-17C. < French *chique* < a W African language]

chi·hua·hua /chə wáa waa, -wáawə, shə-/ *n* a very small dog belonging to a breed originally from Mexico that has pointed ears, protruding eyes, and a disproportionately large head [Early 19C. After CHIHUAHUA]

Chi·hua·hua /chə wáa waa, chee-/ 1. state in northern Mexico. Capital: Chihuahua. Population: 3,0522,907 (2000). Area: 94,960 sq. mi./245,945 sq. km. 2. city and capital of Chihuahua State, northern Mexico. It is located in the central part of the state. Population: 671,790 (2000).

Chi·hua·huan Des·ert /chə wáawən-, chee-/ the largest desert in North America, extending into parts of New Mexico, Texas, and sections of southeastern Arizona. Area: 140,000 sq. mi./360,000 sq. km.

Chi·ka·ma·tsu /chèe kaa máatsoo/, **Monzaemon** (1653–1724) Japanese playwright. He is known for his historical romances and domestic tragedies written for the kabuki theater and Bunraku puppet theater. Born **Sugimori Nobumori**

chik·an /chíkən/ *n* traditional South Asian embroidery with some parts cut out and the edges oversewn or filled, while other parts have crisscross stitches that create a shadowy effect. It is especially associated with Lucknow. [Late 19C. Via Urdu < Persian *čikin*]

Chi·lan·go /chee láng gō/ (*plural* **-gos**) *n Hispanic* a resident of Mexico City [< Mexican Spanish]

chil·a·quil·es /chèela kéeleez/ *n Hispanic* a Mexican dish of shredded corn tortillas cooked with eggs and salsa [< Mexican Spanish]

chil·blain /chíl blàyn/ *n* a red itchy swelling on the fingers, toes, or ears caused by exposure to cold and damp (*often used in the plural*) [Mid-16C. < CHILL + *blain* "inflamed swelling" < Old English *blegen* < W Germanic] —**chil·blained** *adj*

child /chīld/ (*plural* **chil·dren** /chíldrən/) *n* 1. YOUNG HUMAN BEING a young human being between birth and puberty 2. HUMAN OFFSPRING a son or daughter of human parents 3. SOMEBODY NOT YET OF AGE somebody under a legally specified age who is considered not to be legally responsible for his or her actions 4. BABY a baby or infant 5. UNBORN BABY a baby that has not yet been born 6. IMMATURE ADULT an adult who is regarded as behaving in a childish or inappropriately childlike way 7. PRODUCT OR RESULT somebody or something considered to be either produced or strongly influenced by a particular environment, period, or historical figure ○ *a child of nature* ○ *a child of the 1960s* 8. DESCENDANT OR MEMBER OF PEOPLE a descendant of somebody, or a member of a people with a common ancestor or geographic origin (*often used in the plural*) ○ *children of Abraham* [Old English *cild*] ◇ **with child** pregnant (*archaic or literary*)

SYNONYMS See *youth*.

Child /chīld/, **Julia** (*b.* 1912) US cooking expert and author. Since her first television appearance in 1963, she has written several cookbooks and hosted a number of popular cooking series. Full name **Child, Julia McWilliams**

> "Too many cooks spoil the broth, but it only takes one to burn it."
> [Julia Child, *Julia Child's Kitchen*; 1975]

Child, Lydia Maria (1802–80) US abolitionist, suffrage campaigner, and writer. She wrote *The History of the Condition of Women in Various Ages and Nations* (1835) and edited the *National Anti-Slavery Standard* (1840–49).

> "But men never violate the laws of God without suffering the consequences, sooner or later."
> [Lydia Maria Child, "Toussaint L'Ouverture," *The Freedmen's Book*; 1865]

child a·buse *n* severe mistreatment of a child by a parent, guardian, or other adult responsible for his or her welfare, e.g., physical violence, neglect, sexual assault, or emotional cruelty —**child a·bus·er** *n*

child·bear·ing /chíld bèrring/ *n* the process of carrying a child in the womb and giving birth to it (*often used before a noun*) ○ *women of childbearing age*

child·bed /chīld bèd/ *n* the state of a woman in the process of giving birth to a child (*archaic*)

child·birth /chīld bùrth/ *n* the act or process of giving birth to a child ○ *natural childbirth methods*

child·care /chīld kèr/ *n* the care and supervision of a child by an adult, inside the home or elsewhere and usually for pay, during times when the parents or guardians are at work

child-cen·tered *adj* adapted to the needs and concerns of children as opposed to those of adults

childe /chīld/ (*plural* **childes**) *n* a young person of noble birth (*archaic*) [Variant of CHILD]

Chil·ders /chíldərz/, **Erskine** (1870–1922) British-born Irish nationalist and writer. Author of *The Riddle of the Sands* (1903), he joined the IRA and was executed during the Irish Civil War (1922–23).

child·free /chīld frēe/ *adj* **1.** not allowing children in a specific place ○ *This restaurant is a childfree environment.* **2.** having decided not to have children ○ *a childfree couple*

child·hood /chīld hood/ *n* **1.** the state of being a child, or the period of somebody's life when he or she is a child ○ *a happy childhood* **2.** an early period or stage in the development or existence of something ○ *Interplanetary travel is still in its childhood.*

child·ish /chīldish/ *adj* **1.** characteristic of or suitable for a child ○ *a childish voice* **2.** regarded as showing a lack of adult qualities such as emotional restraint, seriousness, or good sense ○ *childish behavior* —**child·ish·ly** *adv* —**child·ish·ness** *n*

USAGE childish or **childlike**? Both words describe people or behavior having qualities associated with children. The difference is that ***childlike*** is complimentary and even affectionate (*childlike innocence*), whereas ***childish*** is a dismissive and disapproving term (*a childish tantrum*).

child la·bor *n* the full-time employment of children, especially of those who are legally too young to work

child·less /chīldləss/ *adj* not having had children —**child·less·ness** *n*

child-lift·ing *n S Asia* the kidnapping of a child

child·like /chīld līk/ *adj* like a child, especially in having a sweet, innocent, unspoiled quality

USAGE See ***childish***.

child mind·er *n UK* somebody who takes care of other people's children in his or her own home, especially when the parents or guardians are working —**child mind·ing** *n*

child prod·i·gy *n* a child who possesses extraordinary abilities or talents, often equal to those of adults

child·proof /chīld proof/ *adj* **1. HARD FOR CHILD TO OPEN** designed to be difficult for a child to open, tamper with, or damage ○ *a bottle with a childproof cap* **2. MADE SAFE FOR CHILDREN** made safe for young children to use or be in, e.g., through the removal of potential dangers and the addition of safety devices ○ *a childproof room* ■ *vt* (**-proofed, -proof·ing, -proofs**) **MAKE SOMETHING SAFE FOR CHILDREN** to make something safe for children to use, or safe against damage or tampering by children

child pro·tec·tive serv·ic·es *npl* a government agency charged with the supervision and protection of children at risk from abuse and neglect, or the supervision and protection administered by it

chil·dren plural of **child**

child re·straint *n* a seat belt or detachable seat designed to protect a child traveling in a vehicle or a plane

child seat *n* a legally mandated detachable seat with a harness, attached to a car seat, used to protect a child too small to wear an adult seat belt

child's play *n* something that is very easy for somebody to do ○ *Skiing these slopes will be child's play for her.*

child sup·port *n* a sum of money paid regularly or in a lump sum by a divorced person to maintain the normal standard of living of his or her children

child tax ben·e·fit *n* in Canada, an allowance or tax-free benefit given by the federal government or the province of Quebec to assist parents in the expense of rearing children below a specific age

chil·e /chíllee/ *n US regional, Can* FOOD another spelling of **chili**

Chile

Chil·e /chíllee/ country in southwestern South America bordered by Peru, Bolivia, Argentina, the Drake Passage, and the Pacific Ocean. Language: Spanish. Currency: peso. Capital: Santiago. Population: 15,665,216 (2003). Area: 292,135 sq. mi./756,626 sq. km. Official name **Republic of Chile** —**Chil·e·an** *n, adj*

Chil·e ni·ter *n* CHEM same as **Chile saltpeter**

Chil·e pine *n* TREES same as **monkey-puzzle**

Chil·e salt·pe·ter *n* a form of sodium nitrate that occurs naturally in dry regions, especially in Chile and Peru. Formula: $NaNO_3$.

chil·es rel·len·os /chèelayz rel láynōs/ *n Hispanic* hot peppers filled with cheese and fried in an egg batter (*takes a singular or plural verb*) [Early 20C. < American Spanish, "stuffed chilies"]

chil·i /chíllee/ (*plural* **-ies**) *n* **1.** a narrow red or green hot-tasting pod produced by various types of capsicum pepper plant. Use: flavoring sauces and relishes. **2.** FOOD same as **chili powder** **3.** FOOD same as **chili sauce** **4.** FOOD same as **chili con carne** [Early 17C. Via Spanish *chile* < Nahuatl *chilli*]

SPELLCHECK chili or **chilly**? Do not confuse the spelling of ***chili*** and ***chilly***, which sound similar. ***Chili*** is a noun denoting a hot pepper, as in *chili con carne, chili powder*. ***Chilly*** is an adjective meaning "cold," as in *chilly weather, a chilly reception*.

chil·i·asm /kíllee àzzəm/ *n* CHR same as **millenarianism** (sense 1) [Early 17C. < Greek *khiliasmos* < *khilias* < *khilioi* "one thousand"] —**chil·i·ast** *n* —**chil·i·as·tic** /kìllee ástik/ *adj*

chil·i·bur·ger /chíllee bùrgər/ *n* a hamburger served topped with chili con carne

chil·i con car·ne /-kon kaárnee/ *n* a highly spiced dish, originally a trail meal for Texas cowboys, made of ground meat and beans, seasoned with chilies or chili powder [Mid-19C. < American Spanish, "chili with meat"]

chil·i·dog /chíllee dàwg, -dòg/ *n* a hot dog topped with chili

chil·i pep·per *n* FOOD same as **chili** (sense 1)

chil·i pow·der *n* a hot-tasting seasoning consisting of ground chilies blended with other seasonings such as cumin, garlic, and oregano

chil·i sauce *n* a highly spiced sauce made with tomatoes, ground dried chilies, and other seasonings

Chil·kat blan·ket /chíl kat-/ *n Can, Northwest US* among Native American peoples of the Pacific Northwest coast of North America, a blanket woven from mountain goat hair with a warp of shredded cedar bark, worn on ceremonial occasions [After the *Chilkat* people of Alaska]

Chil·koot Pass /chìlkoot-/ pass in the coastal range of the northern Rocky Mountains, Canada. Height: 3,501 ft./1,067 m.

chill /chil/ *n* **1. MODERATE COLDNESS** a moderate but often unpleasant degree of coldness ○ *a chill in the air* **2. SUDDEN SHORT FEVER** a sudden short fever with shivering and a sensation of coldness **3. COLDNESS CAUSED BY FEAR** a sudden shuddering feeling of coldness caused by fear, anxiety, or excitement ○ *felt a chill run down my spine* **4. DEPRESSING EFFECT** a depressing or dampening effect on people or on an occasion ○ *The news cast a chill over the party.* **5. LACK OF EMOTIONAL WARMTH** an emotional coldness or unfriendliness in the atmosphere or in somebody's manner **6.** METALL **MOLD USED IN CASTING METAL** a mold made of a highly conductive material such as iron, used to achieve a rapid even cooling when casting metal. The chill may be water-cooled to accelerate the process. ■ **chills** *npl* **FEELING OF ATTRACTION** a feeling of attraction to somebody ○ *That movie star just gives me chills!* ■ *adj* **1. MODERATELY COLD** moderately cold, but usually cold enough to be unpleasant **2. EMOTIONALLY COLD** showing no friendliness or emotional warmth ■ *v* (**chilled, chill·ing, chills**) **1.** *vt* **MAKE SOMEBODY OR SOMETHING COLD** to make somebody or something cold, usually unpleasantly so ○ *a freezing draft that chilled me to the bone* **2.** *vti* **COOL FOOD** to cool food or drink in a refrigerator, or be left to cool there **3.** *vt* **BE DISCOURAGING TO SOMEBODY OR SOMETHING** to have a discouraging or dampening effect on somebody or something **4.** *vi* same as **chill out** (*informal*) **5.** *vti* METALL **HARDEN METAL, OR BECOME HARD** to harden a metal surface, or become hard, by rapid cooling [Old English *ciele* < Germanic] —**chill·ness** *n*

chill out *vi* (*informal*) **1.** to stop being inappropriately anxious or angry **2.** to spend time relaxing

Chil·lán /chee yaán/ city in central Chile, situated 56 mi./90 km northeast of Concepción. Population: 187,557 (1998).

chilled mar·gin /child-/ *n* the edges of an igneous intrusion as it is cooled by contact with the surrounding colder rocks. The margin is marked by a zone of finer-grained crystals.

chill·er /chíllər/ *n* **1.** a refrigerated cooling or storage compartment **2.** a frightening and suspenseful movie or story (*slang*)

chill fac·tor *n* METEOROL same as **windchill factor**

chil·li *n* FOOD Can, UK spelling of **chili**

Chil·li·cothe /chìllə kóthee, -káw-/ city in southern Ohio, directly south of Columbus, on the banks of the Scioto River. Population: 22,145 (2002 estimate).

chill·ing /chílling/ *adj* causing a feeling of dread or horror ○ *a chilling account of his capture* —**chill·ing·ly** *adv*

chill·out /chílowt/ *n UK* same as **downtempo**

chill-out area *n* an area set aside for quieter or more relaxed or restful activities, e.g., in a public place or club

chill-out zone *n* an area of a dance club where people can relax and where relatively quiet music is played (*slang*)

chil·lum /chílləm/ *n* a short straight pipe, usually made of clay, for smoking hashish, marijuana, or tobacco [Late 18C. < Hindi *chilam*]

chill·y /chíllee/ (**-i·er, -i·est**) *adj* **1. MODERATELY COLD** moderately or noticeably cold, usually enough to cause discomfort ○ *Bring a sweater to the park: it'll be chilly later.* **2. FEELING COLD** feeling cold enough to be uncomfortable **3. UNFRIENDLY** characterized by a lack of friendliness or by hostility ○ *a chilly reception* —**chill·i·ly** *adv* —**chill·i·ness** *n*

SPELLCHECK See ***chili***.

chi·lo·pod /kīlə pòd/ *n* an arthropod of the group that includes the centipedes (*technical*) [Mid-19C. < modern Latin *Chilopoda* < Greek *kheilos* "lip"]

Chil·tern Hills /chíltərn-/ range of chalk hills in south central England, running from Oxfordshire to Bedfordshire. The highest peak is Combe Hill, 852 ft./260 m.

Chi·lung /jée lóong/ seaport in northern Taiwan, one of the two ports of Taipei, the major city in Taiwan. Population: 382,118 (1999).

chi·mae·ra /kī méerə, ki-/ *n* **1.** (*plural* **chi·mae·ras** or *same*) a deep-sea fish with a skeleton of cartilage, a smooth-skinned tapering body, and a tail that resembles a whip. Family: Chimaeridae. **2.** GENETICS, BIOCHEM another spelling of **chimera** [Early 19C. < Latin (see CHIMERA)]

Chi·mae·ra *n* MYTHOL another spelling of **Chimera**

Chim·bo·ra·zo /chìmbə ra̍azō/ mountain peak in central Ecuador, and the highest point in the Cordillera Real. Height: 20,702 ft./6,310 m.

Chim·bo·te /chim bṓtee/ seaport in western Peru, situated at the mouth of the Santa River. Population: 314,700 (1991).

chime[1] /chīm/ *n* **1. SOUND OF BELL** the musical ringing sound made by a bell or a set of bells, or a similar sound made by an object such as a doorbell **2. DEVICE FOR STRIKING BELL** a device for striking a bell or a set of bells in order to make a musical sound or play a tune (*often used in the plural*) **3. NOTES SOUNDED BY CLOCK** a series of musical notes sounded by a clock before striking ■ **chimes** *npl* MUSIC **PERCUSSION INSTRUMENT** a set of hanging bells, metal bars, or tubes tuned to a scale, used to produce a musical sound when struck ■ *v* **(chimed, chim·ing, chimes) 1.** *vi* **RING MELODIOUSLY** to make a melodious ringing sound ○ *Did you hear the bells chiming?* **2.** *vt* **INDICATE SOMETHING BY CHIMING** to indicate something, especially the time, by chiming ○ *The clock chimed three o'clock.* **3.** *vt* **PRODUCE MUSICAL SOUND** to strike a bell or bells so as to produce a musical sound **4.** *vi* **HARMONIZE** to harmonize or be in agreement with something else ○ *Her opinion chimed perfectly with my own.* **5.** *vti* **SPEAK IN MUSICAL WAY** to say something or speak in a rhythmic or musical way [13C. Origin ?] —**chim·er** *n*

chime in *vi* **1.** to interrupt or join in a conversation between other people, especially in order to voice an opinion **2.** to agree or combine harmoniously with something else

chime[2] /chīm/ *n* an edge or lip around the rim of a barrel or cask [14C. Probably < assumed Old English *cim*]

chi·me·ra /kī méerə, ki-/, **chi·mae·ra** *n* **1. SOMETHING TOTALLY UNREALISTIC OR IMPRACTICAL** a wildly unrealistic idea or hope or a completely impractical plan **2.** GENETICS **ORGANISM WITH GENETICALLY DIFFERENT TISSUES** an organism, or part of one, with at least two genetically different tissues resulting from mutation, the grafting of plants, or the insertion of foreign cells into an embryo **3.** BIOL, BIOTECH **ORGANISM WITH DNA FROM DIFFERENT SOURCES** an organism that has genetic material from a variety of sources as a result of the insertion of unspecialized cells **(stem cells)** from other species into an embryo [See CHIMERA] —**chi·mer·ism** /kī méer ìzzəm, kímə rìzzəm/ *n*

Chi·me·ra /kī méerə, ki-/ *n* **1.** in Greek mythology, a female fire-breathing monster, typically represented as a combination of a lion's head, goat's body, and serpent's tail **2.** an imaginary monster whose body is a grotesque combination of mismatched animal parts [14C. Via Latin *chimaera* < Greek *khimaira* "she-goat"]

chi·me·ra·plast /kī méerə plàst/ *n* a hybrid molecule of DNA combined with RNA that is used to repair or modify genes during chimeraplasty

chi·me·ra·plas·ty /kī méerə plàstee/ *n* a method of repair or modification of DNA in which a hybrid molecule of DNA combined with RNA is injected into an organism in order to target, bind with, and modify a specific gene —**chi·me·ra·plas·tic** /kī méerə plástik/ *adj*

chi·mer·ic /kī mérrik, ki-/ *adj* describes an organism that is composed of genetically different tissues, either naturally or as a result of a laboratory procedure

chi·mer·i·cal /kī méerik'l, ki-/ *adj* **1.** having no existence in reality or no likelihood of existing or happening **2.** tending to indulge in unrealistic fantasies (*literary*) —**chi·mer·i·cal·ly** *adv*

chim·i·chan·ga /chìmmee cha̍ang gə/ *n Hispanic* a dish that consists of a deep-fried burrito with a spicy meat filling [Late 20C. < Mexican Spanish, "trinket"]

chim·i·ne·a /chìmmə née ə, -náy ə/, **chim·e·ne·a** *n* a large rounded pot with a chimney and an opening in its side, used as a charcoal-burning stove for outdoor heating on patios and at barbecues [< Spanish, "fireplace"]

chim·ney /chímnee/ (*plural* **-neys**) *n* **1. STRUCTURE FOR VENTING GAS OR SMOKE** a hollow vertical structure, usually made of brick or steel, that allows gas, smoke, or steam from a fire or furnace to escape into the atmosphere **2. PART OF STRUCTURE RISING ABOVE ROOF** the part of a chimney that rises above a roof **3. SMOKE-VENTING PASSAGE INSIDE CHIMNEY** a passage or pipe inside a chimney through which smoke or steam escapes **4. GLASS TUBE PROTECTING LANTERN FLAME** a tube, usually made of glass, used to enclose the flame of a lantern in order to promote burning and exclude drafts **5. VOLCANIC VENT** a part of a volcano or an oceanic ridge through which magma percolates, adding to the precipitated mineral matter that has accumulated **6.** CLIMBING **CLEFT IN ROCK FACE** a narrow vertical cleft in a rock face that is large enough for a climber to get inside and use as a means of ascending **7.** *UK* ENG same as **smokestack** (sense 1) [13C. Via Old French *cheminée* < late Latin *caminata* < Latin *camera caminata* "room with a fireplace" < Greek *kaminos* "oven"]

chim·ney pot *n* a short earthenware or metal pipe placed on the top of a chimney in order to increase the draft

chim·ney stack *n UK* a tall, often cylindrical, chimney attached to a factory or other large industrial building

chim·ney sweep *n* somebody whose job is removing soot from chimneys

chim·ney swift *n* a small dark swift that nests in chimneys. Native to: North America. Latin name: *Chaetura pelagica.*

chimp /chimp/ *n* VERTEB same as **chimpanzee** (*informal*) [Late 19C. Shortening]

chimpanzee

chim·pan·zee /chìmpan zée, chim pánzee/ *n* a medium-sized ape with long dark-brown hair covering its body except for its naked face and ears. Native to: equatorial Africa. Latin name: *Pan troglodytes* or *Pan paniscus.* [Mid-18C. Via French < Kikongo]

chin /chin/ *n* **PART OF FACE** the part of the face below the lips, including the usually protruding front portion of the lower jaw ■ *v* **(chinned, chin·ning, chins) 1.** *vi* **MAKE CONVERSATION** to talk casually with somebody about unimportant matters (*slang*) **2.** *vt* **PUT VIOLIN UNDER CHIN** to hold or place a violin under the chin **3.** *vti* **RAISE CHIN TO HIGH BAR** to perform an exercise that involves hanging from a horizontal bar and pulling the body up by the arms until the chin is level with the bar [Old English *cin* < Germanic] ◇ **keep your chin up** to remain cheerful and hopeful in spite of difficulties or hardships (*informal*) ◇ **take it on the chin** to accept misfortune staunchly, without flinching (*informal*)

Ch'in *n* HIST another spelling of **Qin**

chi·na /chīnə/ *n* **1.** porcelain or a similar high-quality translucent or white ceramic material **2.** articles made of china, especially dishes and decorative objects [Late 16C. < Persian *čīnī* "porcelain from China"]

Chi·na /chīnə/ country in East Asia, the largest in the world by population and the third largest by area. Language: Modern Standard Chinese. Currency: yuan. Capital: Beijing. Population: 1,286,975,500 (2003). Area: 3,695,500 sq. mi./9,571,300 sq. km. Official name **People's Republic of China**

chi·na·ber·ry /chīnə bèrree/ (*plural* **-ries**) *n* **1.** a deciduous tree of the mahogany family. Flowers: white or purple, in clusters. Use: shade tree. Native to: Asia. Latin name: *Melia azedarach.* **2.** TREES same as **soapberry** (sense 2) **3.** a fruit produced by either the chinaberry or soapberry tree

China

chi·na clay *n* MINERALS same as **kaolin**

chi·na clos·et *n* a cabinet or cupboard used for storing or displaying china

Chi·na·man /chīnəmən/ (*plural* **-men** /-mən/) *n* an offensive term for a man of Chinese origin (*dated*)

Chi·nan /jée na̍an/ ➧ **Jinan**

Chi·na rose *n* a rose that is the ancestor of many cultivated varieties. Flowers: fragrant, pink, red, or white. Native to: China. Latin name: *Rosa chinensis.*

Chi·na Sea part of the Pacific Ocean extending from Japan to the southern end of the Malay Peninsula, and divided by Taiwan into the East China Sea and the South China Sea

Chi·na syn·drome *n* a hypothetical accident in which the core of a nuclear reactor melts, allowing the radioactive fuel to burn through the floor of its container and straight down into the ground [< the idea of the molten core sinking through the earth and reaching China]

Chi·na·town /chīnə tòwn/ *n* an area of a city inhabited mainly by Chinese people and containing businesses owned by them or selling Chinese products

Chi·na tree *n* TREES same as **chinaberry** (sense 1)

chi·na·ware /chīnə wèr/ *n* plates, dishes, and other tableware made of china

Chi·na·wom·an /chīnə wòòmən/ (*plural* **-wo·men** /-wìmmin/) *n* an offensive term for a woman of Chinese origin (*dated*)

chinch /chinch/, **chinch bug, cinch bug** /sínch-/ *n* **1.** a small black-and-white insect with short wings that causes serious damage to grain crops and grasses by sucking juices from them. Latin name: *Blissus leucopterus.* **2.** *Southern US* INSECTS same as **bedbug** [Early 17C. Via Spanish *chinche* < Latin *cimic-*]

chin·che·rin·chee /chìnchə rínchee/ *n* a plant of the lily family. Flowers: large, fragrant. Native to: southern Africa. Latin name: *Ornithogalum thyrsoides.* [Early 20C. An imitation of the sound created when stalks are rubbed together]

chinchilla

chin·chil·la /chin chíllə/ (*plural* **-las** or *same*) *n* **1. BUSHY-TAILED RODENT** a squirrel-sized rodent with a bushy tail and large round ears. Raised for: fur. Native to: South America. Latin name: *Chinchilla laniger.* **2. CHINCHILLA FUR** the soft silvery-gray fur of a chinchilla **3. WOOLEN CLOTH** a thick woolen fabric. Use: overcoats. [Early 17C. Via Spanish < Aymara or Quechua]

chinch·y /chínchee/ (**-i·er, -i·est**) *adj Southern US* **1.** cheap **2.** miserly [Early 20C. < obsolete *chinch* "miser" < Old French *chiche* "miserly"]

LANGUAGE HERITAGE ***Chinese*** Much of English is made up of words from other languages, and Chinese is an important contributor in this respect. Scholars estimate that there are about 1,000 émigrés from Chinese into English. Two of them, ***spring roll*** and ***brainwashing***, are loan translations. ***Spring roll***, first recorded in English in 1943, is a translation of Chinese *chūn* "spring" and *juǎn* "roll." ***Brainwashing***, first recorded in a September 1950 Florida newspaper article about forcible indoctrination of US prisoners of war captured during the Korean conflict, is a translation of *xǐnǎo*, with *xǐ* meaning "to wash" and *nǎo* "brain." But most of the words are direct borrowings from Cantonese and Modern Standard Chinese. For example, from Cantonese, English has naturalized ***chop suey***, ***kumquat***, ***moo goo gai pan***, ***sampan***, ***taipan***, and ***tong*** (an organized crime gang). From Modern Standard Chinese, English has naturalized ***chow mein***, ***feng shui***, ***ginseng***, ***kowtow***, ***mahjongg***, and ***pongee***.

Modern Standard Chinese and Cantonese have separately given English two homographs (words spelled alike but with different meanings, origins, and sometimes different pronunciations): ***yen***, the Japanese currency unit, and ***yen***, a noun and a verb meaning "wish, desire." ***Yen***, the currency unit, arrived in English in the late 19th century via Japanese from Modern Standard Chinese *yuán*, literally "round." The second ***yen***, whose origin is somewhat murky, was originally associated in English with the argot of opium smokers. It is thought that this ***yen***, which arrived in the early 20th century in the form *yen-yen* ("strong craving for opium"), came from Cantonese *yán* "wish, hope, desire." Occasionally words derive from other forms of Chinese, for example, ***bok choy***, which is from Guangdang dialect.

Most of the words associated with the martial arts are ultimately of Chinese origin, but came into English via Japanese. Examples are ***aikido***, ***dan***, ***judo***, ***jujitsu***, and ***sensei***. An exception is ***kung fu***, a direct late 19th-century borrowing from Chinese *gōngfu*, literally "merit-master."

At least two Chinese words have migrated into English as generic terms: ***gung ho*** and ***kaolin***. First recorded in 1942, ***gung ho*** was the motto of some US Marines operating in Asia during World War II. It comes from Chinese *honghé*, literally "work together," a shortening of *gōngyèhézuòshè* "Chinese Industrial Cooperative Society." ***Kaolin***, which is first recorded in the early 18th century, comes from Chinese *gāoling* "high hill," an area of Jiangxi province where this fine white clay is found.

Chinese has also been the transport medium of some very well-traveled words, one of them ***typhoon***. First recorded in English in the late 16th century, it probably arrived first via Arabic *ṭūfān* "deluge," through English people who experienced heavy storms in South Asia, where Arabic was a language used in Islamic circles. The English respelled the word *touffon* or *tufan*, pronouncing the "ou" as in "you." Thereafter, English ships encountered violent storms while operating in the China Sea. Their crews heard the Cantonese word *taaî fung*, literally "big wind," and picked it up as well, changing the pronunciation of the first syllable from the "ou" sound to an "i" sound, resulting in a further respelling of the word. Thus Cantonese is the most immediate influence on the spelling and pronunciation of the word we use today. But all in all, ***tea*** is perhaps the most internationalized of these word travelers in the sense that it has distanced itself from obvious Chinese cultural and semantic associations. Somewhat of a mysterious émigré, ***tea*** is thought to have come into English in the 17th century via Dutch *tee*. That word was derived from a Malay term traceable to Amoy Chinese dialect *te*, the equivalent of Modern Standard Chinese *chá*. See also ***Japanese***.

Chin·co·teague Is·land /shíngkə teeg-, chíngkə-/ small island in Chincoteague Bay between the eastern coast of Virginia and Assateague Island. It is known for the small wild ponies that live there and for its annual seafood festival.

Chin·co·teague po·ny *n* a small wild horse of North America. Native to: Chincoteague and Assateague islands, off the coast of Virginia.

Chin·dwin /chìn dwín/ tributary of the Irrawaddy River, in Myanmar (Burma). Length: 720 mi./1,200 km.

chine[1] /chīn/ *n* **1.** FOOD **JOINT OF MEAT** a cut of meat that includes part of the backbone **2.** NAUT **BOTTOM CORNER OF A BOAT** the join between the bottom and sides of some boats, especially those with a flat or V-shaped bottom ■ *vt* (**chined, chin·ing, chines**) **CUT MEAT FROM BACKBONE** to cut meat along or across the backbone of a carcass [14C. < Old French *eschine* < Germanic ancestor of SHIN[1] + Latin *spina* "spine"]

chine[2] /chīn/ *n* same as **chime**[2] [15C. Alteration]

Chi·nese /chī néez, -néess/ (*plural same*) *n* **1.** PEOPLES **SOMEBODY FROM CHINA** somebody who comes from China or whose family came from China **2.** LANG **GROUP OF LANGUAGES SPOKEN IN CHINA** a group of related Sino-Tibetan languages spoken across most of China and Taiwan, and by large communities elsewhere. Cantonese, Hokkien, and Modern Standard Chinese are the best-known members of the group. **3.** LANG **OFFICIAL LANGUAGE OF CHINA** the standard language of China and Taiwan and an official language of Singapore, also spoken by large communities elsewhere, that belongs to the Chinese group of Sino-Tibetan languages. Native speakers: 800 million. **4.** **RESTAURANT SELLING CHINESE FOOD** a restaurant or takeout run by Chinese people and cooking food in styles from China (*informal*) **5.** **CHINESE MEAL** food or a meal from a Chinese restaurant (*informal*) —**Chi·nese** *adj*

Chi·nese an·ise *n* PLANTS, FOOD same as **star anise** (sense 2)

Chi·nese box·es *npl* a set of matching boxes graduated in size so that each fits inside the next larger one, and as each opens it reveals another waiting to be opened

Chi·nese cab·bage *n* **1.** a plant with a long head of overlapping wrinkled leaves and broad stalks, popular as a vegetable in Asian cooking. Latin name: *Brassica pekinensis*. **2.** PLANTS same as **bok choy**

Chi·nese cal·en·dar *n* the traditional calendar used in China that divides the year into 24 fifteen-day periods and is based on both the lunar and solar cycles. It has five months containing 29 days, six months of 30 days, and one month of 20 or 30 days.

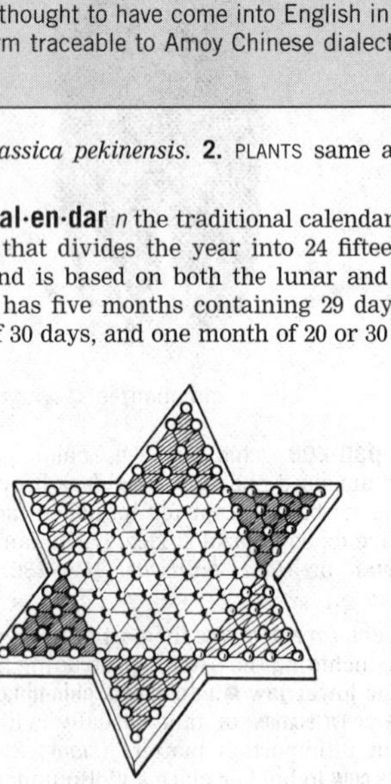

Chinese checkers

Chi·nese check·ers *n* a game played on a board marked with a six-pointed star studded with small holes. Players move or jump marbles hole by hole toward an opposite point of the star. (*takes a singular verb*)

Chi·nese chest·nut *n* a chestnut that is resistant to a blight that affects other chestnuts. Native to: China, Korea. Latin name: *Castanea mollissima*.

Chi·nese Em·pire *n* China during the rule of the emperors, beginning with the Qin dynasty in the 5th century B.C. and ending when the republic was established in 1911–12

Chi·nese goose·ber·ry *n* PLANTS, FOOD same as **kiwi fruit**

Chi·nese lan·tern *n* **1.** a collapsible covering for a light, made of thin brightly colored paper supported by thin wires **2.** *Can, UK* a plant with papery orange-red seed cases. Latin name: *Physalis alkekengi*. US term **winter cherry**

Chi·nese New Year *n* a festival day that falls between 21 January and 19 February and introduces two weeks of celebrations marking the new year

Chinese lantern

Chi·nese pheas·ant *n* BIRDS same as **ring-necked pheasant**

Chi·nese puz·zle *n* a puzzle, either in the form of a game or a problem, that is extremely intricate, ingenious, and difficult to solve

Chi·nese rad·ish *n* PLANTS same as **daikon**

Chi·nese red *n* a vivid red color tinged with orange —**Chi·nese red** *adj*

Chi·nese res·tau·rant syn·drome *n* a group of symptoms, including dizziness, headache, palpitations, and sweating, experienced by some people after eating food containing monosodium glutamate, an ingredient often used in preparing Chinese dishes

Chi·nese shar-pei *n* BREED same as **shar-pei**

Chi·nese wall *n* **1.** a strong or insurmountable barrier, especially one that obstructs the exchange of information **2.** a set of strict rules intended to prevent the exchange of confidential information that might be used illegally for gain between different departments of a stock-exchange business

Chi·nese wa·ter tor·ture *n* a method of psychological torture in which water is persistently dripped onto the victim's forehead

Chi·nese wood block *n* a hollow slotted wooden block that, when struck, makes a sound similar to that of horses' hooves striking the ground

Chi·nese wood oil *n* INDUST same as **tung oil**

Ch'ing *n* HIST another spelling of **Qing**

chink[1] /chingk/ *n* **NARROW OPENING** a small narrow crack or slit ○ *Sunlight was coming in through a chink in the curtains.* ■ *vt* (**chinked, chink·ing, chinks**) **1.** **FILL CRACKS IN SOMETHING** to fill up cracks or holes in something **2.** **FILL SOMETHING WITH CAULK** to fill a gap or hole with caulk **3.** **MAKE CRACKS IN SOMETHING** to make small cracks in something ○ *A flying pebble chinked my car's windshield.* [Early 16C. Origin ?] ◇ **a chink in somebody's armor** a slight weakness that makes somebody vulnerable to attack or exploitation, e.g., an aspect of their character or a point in their argument

chink[2] /chingk/ *n* a short sharp ringing sound, e.g., that of coins or glasses knocking against each other ■ *vti* (**chinked, chink·ing, chinks**) to make, or cause glass or metallic objects to make, a short sharp ringing sound ○ *We chinked glasses and said a toast.* [Late 16C. An imitation of the sound]

Chink /chingk/, **Chink·y** /-kee/ (*plural* **-ies**) *n* a highly offensive term for a Chinese person (*taboo*) [Late 19C. < CHINA]

chin·ka·pin *n* TREES another spelling of **chinquapin**

chinks /chingks/ *vi Carib* to be ungenerous ○ *Doh chinks wid de rum!* [< chink "small piece"]

chin·ky /chínkee/ *adj* characterized by small narrow slits or cracks

Chink·y *n* same as **Chink** (*taboo*)

chin·less /chínləss/ *adj* **1.** having a lower jaw that recedes under the mouth instead of projecting in front of it **2.** lacking strength of character

chin mu·sic *n* **1.** in baseball, a fast pitch intentionally delivered near the chin of a batter who is crowding home plate **2.** foolish or insignificant talk [< the supposed sound of a ball passing close by somebody's face at speed]

chi·no /cheénō/ *n* a durable coarse cotton twill fabric, often khaki-colored. Use: military uniforms, casual pants. ■ **chi·nos** *npl* men's or women's pants made of chino [Mid-20C. < American Spanish, "toasted"; from its original color]

Chi·no /chéenō/ city in southwestern California, a suburb of Los Angeles. Population: 69,961 (2002 estimate).

Chi·no Hills city in southwestern California, an eastern suburb of Los Angeles, southwest of Chino. Population: 72,295 (2002 estimate).

chi·noi·se·rie /shéen waazə rée, sheen wáazəree/ *n* **1.** a style of art and interior design that reflects Chinese influence **2.** an object or decoration in a style reflecting Chinese influence, or such objects and decorations collectively [Late 19C. < French < *chinois* "Chinese"]

Chi·no-La·ti·no /chéenō-/ *adj* combining features of both Chinese and Latin culture, e.g., in cooking

chi·nook /shi nóok, chi-/ *n* **1.** a moist warm wind that blows from the sea and affects weather along the coast of the northwestern United States **2.** a dry warm wind that blows down the eastern slopes of the Rocky Mountains [Mid-19C. < CHINOOK]

Chi·nook /shi nóok, chi-/ (*plural same* or **-nooks**) *n* **1.** a member of a Native North American people who once lived in northwestern Oregon, and who now live in western Washington **2.** the extinct Penutian language of the Chinook people [Early 19C. < Salish *tsinúk*] —**Chi·nook** *adj*

Chi·nook·an /shi nóokən, chi-/ *n* same as **Chinook** (sense 2)

Chi·nook Jar·gon *n* a pidgin language, once used for trading along the western coast of North America, made up of words borrowed from Chinook, Nootka, various Salishan languages, French, and English

Chi·nook salm·on *n* **1.** a large salmon found in the northern Pacific Ocean that spawns in the rivers of North America and northern Asia. Latin name: *Oncorhyncus tshawytscha*. **2.** FOOD the reddish flesh of a chinook salmon used as food

chin·qua·pin /chíngkəpin/, **chin·ka·pin** *n* **1.** EDIBLE NUT an edible chestnut from a North American tree **2.** SMALL DECIDUOUS TREE a small deciduous tree that produces chinquapins. Native to: eastern United States. Latin name: *Castanea pumila*. **3.** LARGE EVERGREEN TREE a large evergreen tree that produces chinquapins. Native to: western North America. Latin name: *Castanopsis chrysophylla*. [Early 17C. < Virginian Algonquian *chechinquamin*]

chin·qua·pin oak *n* an oak tree with toothed leaves. Native to: central and eastern United States. Latin name: *Quercus prinoides* or *Quercus muhlenbergii*.

chin·strap /chín stràp/ *n* a strap attached to a helmet or hat that passes under the chin and is intended to keep the helmet or hat from falling off

chintz /chints/ *n* **1.** a glazed cotton fabric usually printed with a brightly colored pattern **2.** a printed or stained calico fabric made in South Asia [Early 17C. Alteration of *chints*, plural of *chint* "calico cloth" < Hindi *chīṭ* "stain" < Sanskrit *citra* "variegated"]

chintz·y /chíntsee/ (**-i·er, -i·est**) *adj* **1.** PENNY-PINCHING unwilling to spend or share money ○ *He's so chintzy about money.* **2.** TRASHY cheap and gaudy ○ *Don't buy that chintzy suit; it'll fall apart the first time you have it cleaned.* **3.** *UK* FUSSY OR QUAINT describes a fussy, quaint, or would-be genteel style of decor (*informal*)

chin-up *n* an exercise performed by hanging from a horizontal bar and pulling the body up until the chin has been raised above the bar

chin·wag /chín wàg/ (**-wagged, -wag·ging, -wags**) *vi* to engage in casual conversation about events or other people's lives —**chin·wag·ger** *n* —**chin·wag·ging** *n*

chi·on·o·dox·a /kī ənō dóksə, kī ònnə-/ (*plural* **-as** or *same*) *n* a hardy plant that grows from a bulb and flowers in early spring. Native to: Europe, Asia. Genus: *Chionodoxa*. [Late 19C. < modern Latin < Greek *khiōn* "snow" + *doxa* "glory"]

~~**chior**~~ incorrect spelling of **choir**

chip /chip/ *n* **1.** SMALL PIECE BROKEN OR CUT OFF a small piece that has been broken, chopped, or cut off something hard or brittle **2.** CRACK a space or crack left in something hard or brittle after a small piece has been broken off or out of it ○ *This cup has a chip in it.* **3.** PIECE OF THIN CRISP SNACK FOOD a very thin crunchy slice of a starchy food, usually potato or corn, that has been fried until it is crisp ○ *corn chips* **4.** WAFER OF SEMICONDUCTOR MATERIAL a small wafer of semiconductor material, usually silicon, forming the base on which an integrated circuit is laid out, or such a wafer together with its integrated circuit **5.** TOKEN USED AS MONEY a token, often a small round plastic disk, used to represent money in poker and other gambling games **6.** DRIED DUNG a piece of dried animal dung, sometimes used for fuel **7.** *UK* LONG PIECE OF FRIED POTATO a long finger-shaped wedge of potato traditionally fried in deep fat (*usually used in the plural*) ○ *fish and chips* **8.** WOOD CUT AS A WEAVING MATERIAL wood, straw, or other material that has been dried and cut for use in weaving ■ *v* (**chipped, chip·ping, chips**) **1.** *vt* BREAK SMALL PIECE OFF SOMETHING to break one or more small pieces from something hard or brittle **2.** *vi* LOSE SMALL PIECES to become damaged by having a small piece or small pieces break off ○ *paint that will not chip easily* **3.** *vt* HIT SOMETHING IN A HIGH ARC to hit or kick a ball or puck so that it travels a short distance in a high arc ○ *The batter chipped the ball over the first baseman's head into right field.* **4.** *vi* MAKE CHIP SHOT in golf, to play a chip shot **5.** *vt* CARVE SOMETHING BY REMOVING SMALL PIECES to carve or shape something by cutting small pieces off or out of it **6.** *vt* CHOP SOMETHING INTO CHIPS to cut something up into chips ○ *Will you chip the ice for drinks?* [Pre-12C. < Latin *cippus* "stake"] ◇ **cash in your chips 1.** to exit a gambling game **2.** to die (*slang*) ◇ **a chip off the old block** somebody resembling his or her parents (*informal*) ◇ **have a chip on your shoulder** to feel inferior or badly treated and so act in an oversensitive and resentful manner (*informal*) ◇ **let the chips fall where they may** used to say that you are ready for whatever may be about to happen (*informal*) ○ *He's letting the chips fall where they may insofar as the negotiations are concerned.* ◇ **when the chips are down** at a time of crisis or when vital matters are at stake (*informal*)

chip away *v* **1.** *vti* to destroy, reduce, or make something weaker by gradually and persistently attacking it ○ *comments designed to chip away at my self-esteem* **2.** *vi* to break small pieces off something solid persistently and over a period of time

chip in *v* **1.** *vti* CONTRIBUTE to contribute something to a common fund or resource (*informal*) **2.** *vi* INTERRUPT to interrupt a conversation in order to make a comment (*informal*) **3.** *vi* PUT MONEY INTO POKER POOL in poker and other games, to put chips or money into the pool in order to play

chip·board /chíp bàwrd/ *n* a construction material made from compressed wood chips held together by a synthetic resin and produced in the form of hard flat boards

Chip·e·wy·an /chìppə wī ən/ (*plural same* or **-ans**) *n* **1.** a member of a Native North American people who live in northern Saskatchewan, Manitoba, and the Northwest Territories. In the 18th century, they abandoned their nomadic life to settle and become fur traders. **2.** the Athabaskan language of the Chipewyan people. Native speakers: 8,000. [Late 18C. < Cree *cīpwayān* "parka wearer" literally "pointed-skin (wearer)"] —**Chip·e·wy·an** *adj*

chip·head /chíp hèd/ *n* a skilled and enthusiastic user of computers (*slang*)

chipmunk

chip·munk /chíp mùngk/ (*plural* **-munks** or *same*) *n* a striped rodent of the squirrel family that lives on the ground, collects nuts and fruit, and stores food in cheek pouches. Native to: North America, Asia. Genera: *Tamias* or *Eutamias*. [Mid-19C. < Ojibwa *ajidamoonʔ* "squirrel," literally "one that comes down trees headlong"]

chipped beef /chìpt-/ *n* thin slices of dried smoked beef, often served in a cream sauce over rice or toast

Chip·pen·dale /chíppən dàyl/ *adj* describes furniture in an 18th-century English style characterized by graceful flowing lines, cabriole legs, and elaborate ornamentation [After Thomas CHIPPENDALE] —**Chip·pen·dale** *n*

Chip·pen·dale /chíppən dàyl/, **Thomas** (1718–79) British furniture designer. The influence of his neoclassical, increasingly eclectic style was spread through *The Gentleman and Cabinet Maker's Director* (1754).

chip·per[1] /chíppər/ *adj* cheerful and full of vitality (*informal*) [Mid-19C. Origin ?]

chip·per[2] /chíppər/ *n* a person or thing that chips or cuts [Early 16C. < CHIP]

chip·per[3] /chíppər/ (**-pered, -per·ing, -pers**) *vi* **1.** to chirp or twitter like a bird **2.** to talk rapidly or incoherently [Early 18C. Probably an imitation of the sound, influenced by CHIRRUP]

Chip·pe·wa /chíppə wàw, -wàa/ *n* (*plural* **-was** or *same*), *adj* PEOPLES, LANG same as **Ojibwa** [Mid-18C. Alteration]

Chip·pe·wa Falls /chíppə wàw-, -wàa-/ city in western Wisconsin on the western bank of the Chippewa River, northeast of Eau Claire. Population: 12,734 (2002 estimate).

chip·pie *n* **1.** COMM, CONSTR another spelling of **chippy**[1] (*informal*) **2.** BIRDS another spelling of **chippy**[2] (*informal*) **3.** another spelling of **chippy**[3] (*dated slang; sometimes considered offensive*)

chip·ping /chípping/ *n* same as **chip** *n* (sense 1)

chip·ping spar·row *n* a small sparrow with a gray breast, reddish brown crown, and black-and-white stripes near its eyes. Native to: North America. Latin name: *Spizella passerina*. [< CHIPPER[3]]

chip·py[1] /chíppee/ (*plural* **-pies**), **chip·pie** *n UK* a fish and chip shop (*informal*) [Early 20C. < CHIP]

chip·py[2] /chíppee/ (*plural* **-pies**), **chip·pie** *n* a chipping sparrow (*informal*) [Mid-19C. Shortening and alteration]

chip·py[3] /chíppee/ (*plural* **-pies**), **chip·pie** *n* a promiscuous woman or prostitute (*dated slang; sometimes considered offensive*) [Late 19C. < *chip* "cheep like a bird," an imitation of the sound]

chip·py[4] /chíppee/ (**-pier, -pi·est**) *adj Can* behaving in an aggressive or belligerent way [Late 19C < *have a chip on your shoulder*]

CHIPS /chips/ *abbr* E-COMMERCE Clearing House Interbank Payments System

chip·set /chíp sèt/, **chip set** *n* a group of microchips designed to perform one or more related functions as a unit, e.g., to update a computer screen display

chip shot *n* **1.** in sports, a short-range kick or shot in which the ball or puck rises sharply into the air **2.** in golf, a short approach shot, used to loft the ball onto the green

Chi·rac /shee ràak/, **Jacques** (*b.* 1932) French politician. He was prime minister (1974–76 and 1986–88) and, after two unsuccessful attempts, was elected president in 1995 and again in 2002. Full name **Chirac, Jacques René**

chi·ral /kīrəl/ *adj* describes a molecule whose arrangement of atoms is such that it cannot be superimposed on its mirror image [Late 19C. < Greek *kheir* "hand"] —**chi·ral·i·ty** /kī rállətee/ *n*

Chi-Rho /kī rṓ/ *n* a monogram and symbol for Jesus Christ, formed by superimposing the Greek letters *chi* (X) and *rho* (P). See illustration on next page [< CHI[1] + RHO, the first two letters of Jesus Christ's name in Greek]

Chir·i·ca·hua /chèeri kàawə/ (*plural same* or **-huas**) *n* a member of an Apache people who formerly moved from place to place in the southern parts of New Mexico and Arizona and the northern region of Mexico, and now primarily live in Oklahoma and New Mexico —**Chir·i·ca·hua** *adj*

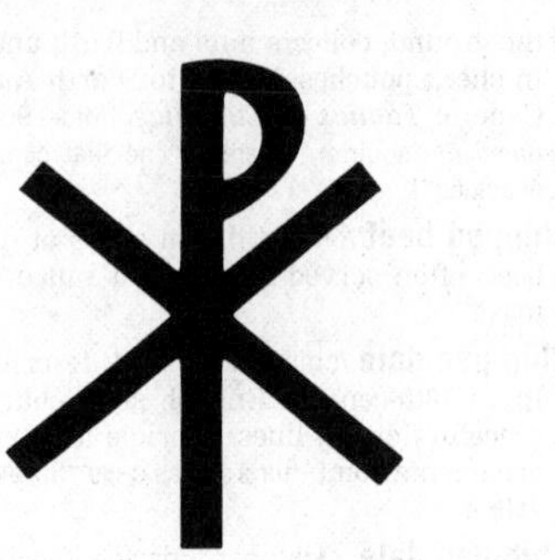

Chi-Rho

Chir·i·ca·hua Na·tion·al Mon·u·ment /chèeri kaáwə-/ national park in southeastern Arizona, established in 1924 and noted for its unusual rock formations. Area: 19 sq. mi./49 sq. km.

Chi·ri·co /kírri kō/, **Giorgio de** (1888–1978) Greek-born Italian painter. His metaphysical dreamscapes of 1910 onward anticipated surrealism.

chiro-, **cheiro-** *prefix* hand ○ *chiromancy* [Via Latin < Greek *kheir*]

chi·rog·ra·phy /kī róggrəfee/ *n* **1.** the art of handwriting (*technical*) **2.** ART same as **calligraphy** (sense 1)

chi·ro·man·cy /kīrə mànsee/ *n* PARANORMAL same as **palmistry** —**chi·ro·man·cer** *n*

Chi·ron /kī ròn/ *n* in Greek mythology, the centaur, known for his great wisdom, who was the tutor of Greek heroes such as Heracles, Achilles, and Jason

chi·ron·o·mid /kī rónnəmid/ *n* a small nonbiting midge that gathers in large breeding swarms, especially near water. Family: Chironomidae. [Late 19C. < modern Latin *Chironomidae* < Greek *kheironomos* "pantomime dancer"]

chi·rop·o·dy /ki róppədee/ *n Can, UK* the branch of medicine concerned with the care and treatment of the feet. US term **podiatry** —**chi·rop·o·dist** *n*

chi·ro·prac·tic /kīrə práktik, kīrə pràktik/ *n* a medical system based on the theory that disease and disorders are caused by a misalignment of the bones, especially in the spine, that obstructs proper nerve functions [Late 19C. < CHIRO- + Greek *praktikos* "effective"] —**chi·ro·prac·tor** *n*

chi·rop·ter·an /kī róptərən/, **chi·rop·ter** /kī róptər/ *n* a flying mammal with forelimbs that have evolved as membranous wings, e.g., a bat (*technical*) [Mid-19C. < modern Latin *Chiroptera* < CHIRO- + Greek *pteron* "wing"]

chi·rop·ti·cal /kī róptik'l/, **chi·rop·tic** /kī róptik/ *adj* relating to the use of refraction, absorption, and emission of radiation in the study of chiral molecules [Late 20C. < CHIRAL + OPTICAL] —**chi·rop·tic·al·ly** *adv*

chirp /churp/ *n* **SHORT HIGH-PITCHED SOUND** a short high-pitched sound, especially as made by a bird ■ *v* (**chirped, chirp·ing, chirps**) **1.** *vi* **MAKE CHIRP** to make a short high-pitched sound **2.** *vti* **SPEAK IN CHEERFUL MANNER** to speak, or say something, in a cheerful, lively, or pert voice [15C. An imitation of the sound]

chirp·y /chúrpee/ (**-i·er, -i·est**) *adj* cheerful and lively (*informal*) —**chirp·i·ly** *adv* —**chirp·i·ness** *n*

chirr /chur/ *n* a shrill harsh trilled sound made by insects such as grasshoppers ■ *vi* (**chirred, chirr·ing, chirrs**) to make a harsh trilled sound [Early 17C. An imitation of the sound]

chir·rup /chúrr əp, chírrəp/ *v* (**-ruped, -rup·ing, -rups**) **1.** *vi* **TWITTER** to utter a series of chirps **2.** *vti* **SPEAK IN A HIGH CHEERFUL VOICE** to speak or say something in a high-pitched voice, and in a cheerful and lively fashion **3.** *vi* **MAKE ENCOURAGING CLUCKING SOUND** to make a clucking sound with the lips, e.g., when encouraging a horse to move faster ■ *n* **CHIRP** a repeated series of chirping or clucking sounds [Late 16C. Alteration of CHIRP] —**chir·rup·y** *adj*

chisel

chis·el /chízz'l/ *n* **TOOL WITH FLAT BEVELED BLADE** a tool for cutting and shaping wood or stone, consisting of a straight flat beveled blade with a sharp square-cut bottom edge inserted in a handle. The chisel is often held in one hand and struck with a hammer or mallet, but is also used freehand. ■ *vti* (**-eled, -el·ing, -els**) **1. CARVE SOMETHING WITH CHISEL** to carve, cut, or work wood or stone using a chisel **2. CHEAT SOMEBODY** to cheat or swindle somebody (*informal*) ○ *was caught chiseling customers* [14C. < Old French < Latin *caes-*, stem of *caedere* "to cut"]

chis·eled /chízz'ld/ *adj* clear-cut or sharply defined in shape or profile ○ *a finely chiseled face*

chis·el·er /chízzlər/ *n* a cheat or swindler (*informal*) [Early 20C. Origin ?]

Chis·holm /chízzəm/, **Shirley Anita** (*b.* 1924) US politician. She was the first African American woman to serve in the US House of Representatives (1969–83).

> "Of my two "handicaps," being female put many more obstacles in my path than being black."
> [Shirley Anita Chisholm, *Unbought and Unbossed*; 1970]

Chis·holm Trail *n* a historic trail used in the 19th century for driving cattle to market, running from San Antonio, Texas, northward to Abilene, Kansas [Mid-19C. After Jesse *Chisholm*, Cherokee Native American]

Chi·şi·nău /kíshə nòw/ city and capital of Moldova, situated on a tributary of the Dniester River, 90 mi./145 km northwest of Odessa, Ukraine. Population: 770,000 (1995). Former name **Kishinev** (1940–91)

chi-square /kī skwèr/ *n* a statistical calculation used to test how well the distribution of a set of observed data matches a theoretical probability distribution. The calculated value is equal to the sum of the squares of the differences divided by the expected values.

chi-square dis·tri·bu·tion *n* a probability function widely used in testing a statistical hypothesis such as the likelihood that a given statistical distribution of results might be reached in an experiment

chit[1] /chit/ *n* a note, bill, or any small slip of paper with writing on it, especially a statement of money owed for food or drink [Late 18C. Shortening of *chitty*, via Hindi *ciṭṭhī* < Sanskrit *citra* "spot," referring to the writing]

chit[2] /chit/ *n* a child, girl, or young woman, especially one whose physical slightness seems to be at odds with an impertinent, forceful, or self-confident manner (*dated*) [14C. Origin ?]

chit·chat /chít chàt/ *n* casual conversation or small talk, or a casual conversation with somebody (*informal*) [Late 17C. Elaboration of CHAT] —**chit·chat** *vi*

chi·tin /kītin/ *n* a tough semitransparent substance that forms part of the protective outer casing (**cuticle**) of some insects and other arthropods, and the cell walls of some fungi [Mid-19C. Via French *chitine* < Greek *khitōn* "tunic"] —**chi·tin·oid** *adj* —**chi·tin·ous** *adj*

chit·lins /chíttlinz/, **chit·lings** *npl Southern US* FOOD same as **chitterlings** [Mid-19C. Contraction]

chi·ton /kīt'n, -tòn/ *n* **1.** a small invertebrate ocean animal that lives on rocks and has a long body protected by a shell consisting of eight overlapping plates. Class: Polyplacophora. **2.** a loose knee-length woolen tunic worn by women and men in ancient Greece [Early 19C. < Greek *khitōn* "tunic"]

chi·to·san /kītə sàn/ *n* a substance derived from the chitin of crab, lobster, and other crustaceans. Use: in medicine, to stop bleeding and speed healing, in cosmetics as a moisturizer, and as a dietary supplement. [Late 19C. < CHITIN + -OSE[2] + -AN[2]]

Chit·ta·gong /chíttə gàwng, -gòng/ chief port of Bangladesh and an important industrial city, situated on the southeastern coast of the country. Population: 1,566,070 (1991).

chit·ter /chíttər/ (**-tered, -ter·ing, -ters**) *vi* to make chirping or twittering sounds [12C. An imitation of the sound]

chit·ter·lings /chíttlinz/ *npl* the small intestines of pigs, especially when prepared as food [13C. Origin ?]

chi·val·ric /shi vállrik, shívvəlrik/ *adj* relating to knights, knighthood, and the knightly code of honor

chiv·al·rous /shívvəlrəss/ *adj* **1.** relating to or reflecting the values of the medieval code of knighthood, especially courtesy, self-sacrifice, and a sense of fair play **2.** describes men, or men's behavior, characterized by consideration and courtesy, especially toward women —**chiv·al·rous·ly** *adv* —**chiv·al·rous·ness** *n*

chiv·al·ry /shívvəlree/ *n* **1. QUALITIES OF IDEAL KNIGHT** the combination of qualities expected of the ideal medieval knight, especially courage, honor, loyalty, and consideration for others, especially women **2. CHIVALROUS BEHAVIOR** considerate and courteous behavior, especially shown by a man toward women **3. MEDIEVAL KNIGHTHOOD** the medieval concept of knighthood, and the customs, practices, social system, and religious and personal ideals associated with knights and their way of life **4. GROUP OF KNIGHTS** knights, noblemen, or armed mounted soldiers, collectively or in a group (*archaic*) [13C. Via Old French *chevalerie* < medieval Latin *caballerius* < Latin *caballus* "horse"]

chive[1] /chīv/ *n* **1.** a long fine hollow leaf with a strong onion flavor. Use: for seasoning food. (*usually used in the plural*) **2.** a plant that produces chives. Flowers: purple, ball-shaped. Latin name: *Allium schoenoprasum*. [14C. Via French < Latin *cepa* "onion"]

chive[2] /chīv/ *n, vt* ARMS same as **shiv** (*slang*)

chiv·vy /chívvee/ (**-vied, -vy·ing, -vies**), **chiv·y** (**-ied, -y·ing, -ies**), **chev·y** /chévvee/ *vt* to urge, pester, or harass somebody, usually in order to make him or her do something or do something more quickly [Late 18C. Probably after *Chevy Chase*, site of a battle (1388) in the Anglo-Scottish border wars]

chla·myd·es CLOTHING plural of **chlamys**

chla·myd·i·a /klə míddee ə/ (*plural* **-as** or *same* or **-ae** /-ee/) *n* **1.** a sexually transmitted disease, the most common in developed countries, caused by the bacterium *Chlamydia trachomatis*. Often producing no symptoms, it can cause infertility, chronic pain, or a tubal pregnancy if left untreated. **2.** a spherical bacterium that causes several eye and urogenital diseases in humans and other animals, and psittacosis in pet birds. Genus: *Chlamydia*. [Mid-20C. < modern Latin < Greek *khlamud-* "mantle"]

chla·myd·i·al /klə míddee əl/ *adj* describes infections that are caused by a bacterium of the genus *Chlamydia*, e.g., trachoma and sexually transmitted infections such as urethritis

chla·myd·o·spore /klə míddə spàwr/ *n* an asexual thick-walled spore produced by some fungi. It is capable of remaining dormant for long periods and surviving adverse conditions. [Late 19C. < Greek *khlamud-*, stem of *khlamus* "mantle"]

chlam·ys /klámmiss, kláy-/ (*plural* **-ys·es** or **-y·des** /-i deez/) *n* a short cloak gathered and fastened at the shoulder, worn by men in ancient Greece [Late 17C. < Greek *khlamus* "mantle"]

chlo·as·ma /klō ázmə/ *n* dark coloration on the skin of the face caused by hormonal changes related to pregnancy, liver disease, or the use of birth control pills. It is made worse by sunlight. [Mid-19C. < Greek *khloazein* "become green"]

chlor- *prefix* same as **chloro-** (*used before vowels*)

chlor·ac·ne /klawr áknee/ *n* a skin eruption resembling acne caused by repeated contact with something containing chlorinated hydrocarbons

chlo·ral /kláwrəl/ *n* a colorless oily toxic liquid with a strong odor. Use: manufacture of chloral hydrate and DDT. Formula: CCl_3CHO.

chlo·ral hy·drate *n* a colorless crystalline solid that is soluble in water. Use: sedative, hypnotic. Formula: $C_2H_3Cl_3O_2$.

chlo·ram·bu·cil /klawr ámbyəssil/ *n* a drug that is toxic to cells. Use: cancer treatment. [Mid-20C. Shortening of its chemical name *4-p-di-(2-chloroethyl)aminophenylbutyric acid*]

chlo·ra·mine /kláwrə meen/ *n* an unstable colorless liquid with a pungent odor. Use: manufacture of hydrazine. Formula: NH_2Cl.

chlo·ram·phen·i·col /klàw ram fénni kòl/ *n* a powerful antibiotic derived from a soil bacterium. It sometimes has the side effect of causing the failure of blood cell production. [Mid-20C. < CHLOR- + AMIDE + PHEN- + NITRO- + GLYCOL]

chlo·rate /kláw ràyt/ *n* any salt of chloric acid [Early 19C. < CHLORIC]

chlor·dane /kláwr dàyn/, **chlor·dan** /-dàn/ *n* a thick toxic colorless to amber-colored liquid that can exist with several different molecular structures (**isomers**). Use: insecticide, fumigant. Formula: $C_{10}H_6Cl_8$. [Mid-20C. < CHLOR- + INDENE + -ANE]

chlor·di·az·e·pox·ide /klàwr dī azə pók sīd/ *n* a yellow crystalline powder. Use: tranquilizer, treatment for alcoholism. Formula: $C_{16}H_{14}ClN_3O$. [Mid-20C. < CHLOR- + DI-[1] + AZO- + EPI- + OXIDE]

chlo·rel·la /klə réllə/ *n* a single-celled green alga that is often used in research. Genus: *Chlorella*. [Early 20C. < modern Latin, "little green (thing)" < Greek *khlōros* "green"]

chlo·ren·chy·ma /klə réngkəmə/ *n* plant tissue that contains chloroplasts, found mainly in leaves [Late 19C. < CHLOROPHYLL]

chlo·ric /kláwrik/ *adj* containing chlorine, especially with a valence of five [Early 19C. < CHLORINE]

chlo·ric ac·id *n* a toxic unstable acid, known only in solution and as chlorate salts. Formula: $HClO_3$.

chlo·ride /kláw rīd/ *n* a compound containing chlorine and one other element [Early 19C. < CHLORINE] —**chlo·rid·ic** /klə ríddik/ *adj*

chlo·ride of lime *n* a powder used as a bleach

chlo·ride shift *n* the reversible exchange of bicarbonate and chloride ions from blood serum to red cells during the transport of carbon dioxide

chlo·ri·nate /kláwri nàyt/ (**-nat·ed, -nat·ing, -nates**) *vt* to combine or treat something with chlorine, especially in order to kill harmful organisms —**chlo·ri·nat·ed** *adj* —**chlo·ri·na·tion** /klàwri náysh'n/ *n* —**chlo·ri·na·tor** *n*

chlo·rine /kláw reen/ *n* a gaseous poisonous corrosive greenish yellow element of the halogen group that is highly reactive and is a product of the electrolysis of sodium chloride. Use: water purification, disinfectant. See table at **element** [Early 19C. < Greek *khlōros* "green"]

chlo·rite[1] /kláw rīt/ *n* a soft green or black aluminosilicate mineral. Source: metamorphic rocks. [Late 18C. Via Latin < Greek *khlōritis*, green precious stone]

chlo·rite[2] /kláw rīt/ *n* any salt of chlorous acid [Mid-19C. < CHLORINE]

chloro- *prefix* **1.** green ○ *chlorophyll* **2.** chlorine ○ *chlorobenzene* [< Greek *khlōros* "green"]

chlo·ro·ben·zene /klàwrō bén zeen/ *n* a combination of chlorine and benzene that produces a colorless flammable liquid smelling of almonds. Use: production of solvents and DDT. Formula: C_6H_5Cl.

chlo·ro·fluor·o·car·bon /klàwrō floorō kaarbən, -flawrō-/ full form of **CFC**

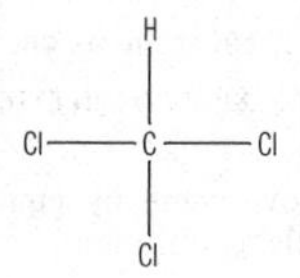

chloroform

chlo·ro·form /kláwrə fàwrm/ *n* a colorless sweet-smelling toxic liquid that rapidly changes to a vapor and causes unconsciousness if inhaled. It is now known to have damaging effects on the ozone layer. Use: formerly, solvent, cleaning agent, anesthetic. Formula: $CHCl_3$. ■ *vt* to make a person or animal breathe in chloroform in order to cause unconsciousness [Mid-19C. < CHLORO- + FORMIC]

chlo·ro·meth·ane /klàwrō mé thàyn/ *n* CHEM same as **methyl chloride**

chlo·ro·phyll /kláwrəfil/, **chlo·ro·phyl** *n* the pigment in plants that captures the light energy required for photosynthesis. In plants and algae, chlorophyll is contained within numerous minute membranous sacs (**chloroplasts**) within cells of the stems and leaves. —**chlo·ro·phyl·lous** /kláwrəfi lōss, klàwrə fí lōss/ *adj*

chlo·ro·pic·rin /klàwrə píkrin/ *n* a colorless toxic liquid that causes tears and vomiting. Use: tear gas, insecticide, disinfectant, in dyes. Formula: CCl_3NO_2. [Mid-19C. < CHLORO- + PICRO-]

chlo·ro·plast /kláwrə plàst/ *n* a membranous sac (**plastid**) that contains chlorophyll and other pigments and is the place where photosynthesis occurs within the cells of plants and algae. While plant cells contain numerous chloroplasts, algal cells often have just one. Each consists of interconnected stacks of disk-shaped membranes in fluid, surrounded by a double membrane. —**chlo·ro·plas·tic** /klàwrə plástik/ *adj*

chlo·ro·prene /kláwrə preen/ *n* a colorless liquid. Use: manufacture of neoprene. Formula: C_4H_5Cl. [Mid-20C. < CHLORO- + ISOPRENE]

chlo·ro·quine /kláwrə kwīn, -kween/ *n* a bitter-tasting crystalline substance. Use: treatment of malaria and amebiasis. [Mid-20C. < CHLORO- + QUINOLINE, from which it is derived]

chlo·ro·sis /klə rōssiss/ *n* **1.** a yellowing or whitening of a plant's leaves and stems caused by a lack of chlorophyll **2.** severe iron-deficiency anemia that produces a greenish tint in the skin —**chlo·rot·ic** /-róttik/ *adj* —**chlo·rot·i·cal·ly** *adv*

chlo·ro·thi·a·zide /klàw rō thī ə zīd/ *n* a drug that relieves fluid retention. Use: treatment of high blood pressure, swelling, and heart failure.

chlor·ous /kláwrəss/ *adj* relating to or containing chlorine with a valence of three [Mid-19C. < CHLORINE]

chlor·prom·a·zine /klawr prómmə zeen, -prōmə-/ *n* a drug. Use: sedative and tranquilizing treatment of psychiatric disorders. [Mid-20C. < CHLOR- + PROMETHAZINE]

chlor·prop·a·mide /klawr próppə mīd/ *n* a drug that lowers blood sugar. Use: treatment of diabetes. [Mid-20C. < CHLOR- + PROPANE + AMIDE]

chlor·tet·ra·cy·cline /klawr tèttrə sīklin, -sī kleen/ *n* an antibiotic drug. Source: soil bacterium. Use: treatment of infections, stimulation of growth in livestock.

ChM *abbr* Master of Surgery

chm., **Chm.** *abbr* **1.** chairman **2.** CHESS checkmate

choc·a·hol·ic *n* another spelling of **chocoholic**

~~**chocalate**~~ incorrect spelling of **chocolate**

chock /chok/ *n* **1.** BLOCK TO STOP SOMETHING MOVING a block of wood or metal used to prevent a wheel from turning, an object from moving, or to support something when it is raised off the ground **2.** SHIP'S FITTING FOR SECURING CABLES a heavy metal fitting attached to the deck of a ship that has two inward-curving horn-shaped projections around which a cable can be secured **3.** METAL ANCHOR FOR CLIMBING a metal device used to provide anchoring systems for climbing or caving ■ *vt* USE CHOCK FOR BRACE to keep something from turning, moving, or falling by using a chock to block or brace it ○ *chock the plane's wheels* [14C. Probably < Old French *ço(u)che* "log"]

chock-a-block *adj* **1.** so crammed with things or crowded with people as to make it almost impossible to get anything or anybody else in or to move around (*informal*) **2.** having the two blocks in a block and tackle tight up against each other [Mid-19C. Alteration of *chock and block* (nautical) "with pulleys drawn close together"]

chock-full *adj* crammed with something (*informal*)

choc·o·hol·ic /chòkə hóllik/, **choc·a·hol·ic** *n* a lover of chocolate who is apparently addicted to it (*humorous*) [Late 20C. < CHOCOLATE + -AHOLIC]

choc·o·late /chókələt, chóklət/ *n* **1.** SMOOTH SWEET BROWN FOOD a food or flavoring, typically a smooth sweet brown solid, made from roasted and ground cacao seeds usually sweetened and mixed with cocoa butter and dried milk. Chocolate is made into bars or candy, or used to flavor other foods, especially cakes, desserts, sauces, and cookies. (*often used before a noun*) ○ *a bar of chocolate* ○ *chocolate cake* **2.** CANDY COVERED IN CHOCOLATE a small piece of candy coated in chocolate, with a hard or soft center **3.** CHOCOLATE DRINK a drink, usually served hot or warm, made from sweetened powdered chocolate mixed with water or milk **4.** BROWN COLOR a deep warm brown color [Early 17C. Directly or via French < Spanish < Nahuatl *chocolatl* "bitter water"] —**choc·o·late** *adj* —**choc·o·lat·ey** *adj*

choc·o·late-box *adj* depicting pretty scenes or pretty people in a stereotypical and usually sentimental or romanticized way ○ *chocolate-box portraits*

choc·o·late chip *n* a small piece of chocolate, used especially in making cookies and desserts ○ *chocolate chip cookies*

choc·o·late phos·phate *n regional* a carbonated drink made by mixing chocolate syrup and seltzer

choc·o·late tree *n* TREES same as **cacao** (sense 2)

choc·o·la·tier /chòkələ teer/ *n* a maker or seller of chocolates [Late 19C. < French < *chocolate* (see CHOCOLATE)]

Choc·taw /chók tàw/ (*plural same* or **-taws**) *n* **1.** a member of a Native North American people who once lived in central and southern Mississippi, and who now live mainly in Oklahoma and southern Mississippi. The Choctaw were one of the Five Civilized Nations who, under the Removal Act of 1830, were sent to live on reservations in Oklahoma. **2.** the Muskogean language of the Choctaw. Native speakers: 10,000. [Early 18C. < Choctaw *čahta*] —**Choc·taw** *adj*

choice /choyss/ *n* **1.** ACT OF CHOOSING SOMETHING OR SOMEBODY a decision to choose one thing, person, or course of action in preference to others ○ *Think very carefully before you make a choice.* **2.** POWER TO CHOOSE the chance or ability to choose between different things ○ *They gave us no choice.* **3.** SELECTION OF THINGS a variety of things, people, or possibilities from which to choose ○ *a wide choice of styles and colors* **4.** CHOSEN OBJECT a person, thing, or course of action chosen by somebody from among a range of possibilities ○ *Red would not have been my choice.* **5.** BEST PART the best or most desirable part ■ *adj* (**choic·er, choic·est**) **1.** HIGH-QUALITY of particularly good quality **2.** RUDE OR EMPHATIC carefully chosen for effectiveness and usually expressing displeasure or dislike in a sufficiently emphatic way (*used euphemistically*) ○ *a few choice words* [13C. < Old French *chois* < *choisir* "choose" < Germanic] —**choice·ness** *n* ◇ **of choice** chosen from among several as being the best or most appropriate ○ *the newspaper of choice*

choice·board /chóyss bàwrd/ *n* a program used on the Internet that allows consumers and online companies to communicate in real time

choir /kwīr/ *n* **1.** GROUP OF SINGERS an organized group of singers who perform together, especially in church, typically combining smaller groups of singers who sing different parts at different pitches **2.** AREA FOR CHURCH CHOIR the part of a church where the choir performs **3.** INSTRUMENT GROUP a group of instruments of the same type **4.** MUSIC same as **choir organ** [13C. Via Old French *quer* < Latin *chorus* (see CHORUS)]

choir·boy /kwīr bòy/ *n* a boy who sings in a church choir

choir·girl /kwīr gùrl/ *n* a girl who sings in a church choir

choir loft *n* a raised gallery or part of the upper story in a church where the choir performs during services

choir·mas·ter /kwīr màstər/ *n* a trainer and conductor of a choir

choir or·gan *n* a manual organ or section of a large organ with sets of soft-toned pipes suitable for accompanying a choir

choir school *n* a school where the members of a cathedral or church choir are educated and attend regular lessons as well as receiving special musical training

choir stalls *npl UK* enclosed seats or pews in the chancel of a church, reserved for the members of the choir

choke[1] /chōk/ *v* (**choked, chok·ing, chokes**) **1.** *vi* STOP BREATHING THROUGH BLOCKAGE OF THROAT to stop breathing, or breathe with great difficulty, because of a blockage in or restriction of the throat **2.** *vt* CONSTRICT THROAT OF SOMEBODY to prevent somebody from breathing by blocking or squeezing the throat **3.** *vt* BLOCK PASSAGE OR CHANNEL to form an obstruction in a passage, channel, pipe, or roadway and prevent anything from passing along it **4.** *vt* PREVENT PLANTS FROM GROWING to prevent plants from developing by growing over them and depriving them of light and air ○ *The bed was choked with weeds.* **5.** *vti* BECOME TOO MOVED TO SPEAK to be overcome with emotion and unable to speak, or make somebody feel so much emotion that he or she cannot speak (*informal*) **6.** *vi* LOSE NERVE AND FALTER to lose nerve or confidence and falter in the middle of saying or doing something (*informal*) ○ *He gets ahead, two sets to one, and then he chokes!* **7.** *vi* REFUSE TO COOPERATE to refuse to cooperate when presented with something unacceptable (*informal*) ○ *We choked on their last demand.* ■ *n* **1.** NOISE OF CHOKING a sound or movement made by somebody choking **2.** FUEL MIXTURE REGULATOR FOR ENGINE a device that controls the ratio of air to fuel in the mixture supplied to an internal-combustion engine ○ *pull the choke out* [Old English *āceocian* < *cēoce* "cheek"] —**chok·ing** *adj* —**chok·ing·ly** *adv*

choke back *vt* to stop the expression of an emotional response to something by a deliberate effort of self-control ○ *I couldn't choke back my tears any longer.*

choke off *vt* to stop the flow, supply, or development of something, usually abruptly

choke up *vti* same as **choke**[1] *v* (sense 5) ○ *I should have said thank-you, but I choked up completely when I saw everyone there.*

choke[2] /chōk/ *n* **1.** the bristly inner inedible part of an artichoke **2.** FOOD same as **artichoke** (*informal*) [Shortening]

choke·ber·ry /chōk bèrree/ *n* **1.** (*plural* **choke·ber·ries**) a small bitter red or purplish fruit **2.** (*plural* **choke·ber·ries** or *same*) a bush that bears chokeberries. Flowers: small, white or pink. Native to: North America. Genus: *Aronia.* [Late 18C. < the bitterness of the fruit]

choke·bore /chōk bàwr/ *n* **1.** a shotgun bore that tapers toward the muzzle to prevent wide scattering of the shot **2.** a shotgun with a bore that tapers toward the muzzle

choke chain *n* a chain serving as a collar and short leash that fits in a sliding loop around an animal's neck, so that when the animal pulls away the chain gets tighter. Choke chains are used in obedience training for dogs and to restrain powerful animals.

choke·cher·ry /chōk chèrree/ *n* **1.** (*plural* **choke·cher·ries**) a dark red or black bitter fruit of a wild cherry **2.** (*plural* **choke·cher·ries** or *same*) a wild cherry tree that bears chokecherries. Flowers: small, white, in clusters. Native to: North America. Latin name: *Prunus virginiana.*

choke coil *n* an induction coil used to limit or suppress the flow of alternating current without stopping the flow of direct current

choke col·lar *n* VET same as **choke chain**

choked /chōkt/ *adj UK* same as **choked up** (*informal*)

choke·damp /chōk dàmp/ *n* MIN EXTRACT same as **black-damp**

choked up *adj* overcome by emotion, usually unhappiness, disappointment, or resentment (*informal*)

choke·hold /chōk hōld/ *n* a tight hold in which one person restrains another by placing an arm around his or her neck, usually from behind

choke·point /chōk pòynt/, **choke point** *n* **1.** AREA OF BLOCKAGE a congested or narrow part where a blockage can occur **2.** NARROW SHALLOW SEA CORRIDOR a place at sea where geography and water depth combine to create a narrow shallow corridor for submarines and surface ships **3.** STICKING POINT a point or situation that is an obstacle to an agreement or results in an impasse ○ *amnesty being the choke point in the political settlement*

chok·er /chōkər/ *n* **1.** a short length of cloth or ribbon, or a short necklace, that fastens closely around the neck and is worn as an ornament **2.** a high close-fitting collar, e.g., a clerical collar

choke route *n* COMPUT a computer firewall that isolates an internal network from the Internet

cho·lan·gi·og·ra·phy /kō lànjee óggrəfee/ *n* X-ray examination of the bile ducts to check for obstructions, carried out after the patient has swallowed a substance that shows up on an X-ray [Mid-20C. < CHOLE-] —**cho·lan·gi·o·gram** /kō lánjee ə gràm/ *n* —**cho·lan·gi·o·graph·ic** /kō lànjee ə gráffik/ *adj*

chole- *prefix* bile, bile ducts, gallbladder ○ *cholelithiasis* [< Greek *kholē* < Indo-European, "yellow-colored"]

cho·le·cal·cif·er·ol /kòləkal síffə ròl, -ràwl/ *n Can, UK* a form of vitamin D found naturally in fish-liver oils and egg yolks. US term **vitamin** D_3

cho·le·cyst /kōlə sìst/ *n* ANAT same as **gallbladder** (*technical*)

cho·le·cys·tec·to·my /kòlə sis téktəmee/ (*plural* **-mies**) *n* a surgical operation to remove the gallbladder —**cho·le·cys·tec·to·mize** *vt*

cho·le·cys·ti·tis /kòlə si stī tiss/ *n* inflammation of the gallbladder, usually caused by a bacterial infection or gallstones

cho·le·cys·tog·ra·phy /kòlə sis tóggrəfee/ (*plural* **-phies**) *n* X-ray examination of the gallbladder after the patient has swallowed a substance that shows up on an X-ray

cho·le·cys·to·ki·nin /kòlə sistə kīnin/ *n* a hormone secreted by cells at the top of the small intestine that stimulates the gallbladder, making it contract and release bile [Early 20C. < CHOLECYST + KININ]

cho·le·li·thi·a·sis /kòlə li thī əssiss/ *n* the formation or presence of gallstones in the gallbladder or bile ducts

chol·er /kóllər/ *n* **1.** anger or bad temper (*literary or archaic*) **2.** one of the four basic fluids (**humors**) of the body according to medieval medicine, thought to make somebody whose body contained too much of it prone to anger and irritability [14C. Via French *colère* < Latin *cholera* "bile" (see CHOLERA)]

chol·er·a /kóllərə/ *n* an acute and often fatal intestinal disease that produces severe gastrointestinal symptoms and is usually caused by the bacterium *Vibrio cholerae* [14C. Via Latin, "illness caused by bile" < Greek *kholera* < *kholē* "bile"] —**chol·e·ra·ic** /kòllə ráy ik/ *adj* —**chol·e·roid** *adj*

chol·er·ic /kóllərik, kə lérrik/ *adj* showing or tending to show anger or irritation (*literary*) [14C. Directly and via French < Latin *cholericus* "bilious" < Greek *kholera* (see CHOLERA)] —**chol·er·i·cal·ly** *adv*

cho·le·sta·sis /kòli stáyssiss, -stássiss/ *n* a stoppage or slowing of the flow of bile —**cho·le·stat·ic** /kòli státtik/ *adj*

cho·les·te·a·to·ma /kə lèstee ə tṓmə, kòlestee-/ *n* a potentially dangerous condition of the middle ear in which a mass of cholesterol and skin scales forms, grows, and invades the local structures, including bone

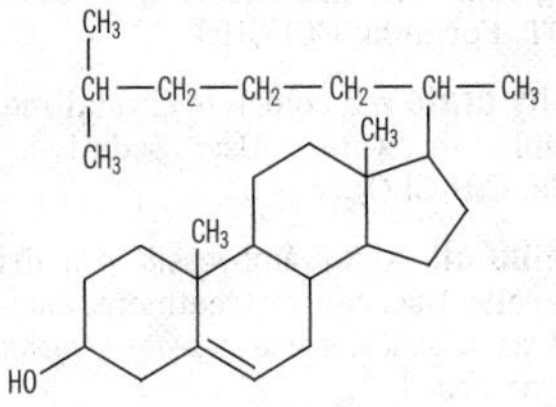

cholesterol

cho·les·ter·ol /kə léstə ràwl/ *n* a steroid alcohol (**sterol**) made by the liver and present in all animal cells. Cholesterol is important to the body as a constituent of cell membranes, and is involved in the formation of bile acid and some hormones. Formula: $C_{27}H_{45}OH$. [Late 19C. < CHOLE- + Greek *stereos* "stiff"]

cho·le·styr·a·mine /kòli stéerə meen, kō léstər a meen/ *n* a synthetic resin that binds cholesterol with bile acids. Use: to lower blood cholesterol. [Mid-20C. < CHOLE- + STYRENE + -AMINE]

cho·li /chōlee/ (*plural* **-lis**) *n S Asia* a short fitted top with short sleeves, worn underneath a sari [Early 20C. < Hindi *colī*]

cho·line /kō leen/ *n* a soluble compound (**amine**) found in animal and plant tissue that is involved in fat transportation and the formation of acetylcholine. Formula: $C_5H_{15}NO_2$. [Mid-19C. < CHOLE-]

cho·lin·er·gic /kòlə núrjik/ *adj* **1.** describes nerves that are activated by acetylcholine or that release it **2.** describes drugs that act like acetylcholine [Mid-20C. < CHOLINE + Greek *ergon* "work"] —**cho·lin·er·gi·cal·ly** *adv*

cho·lin·es·ter·ase /kòli néstə ràyss, -ràyz/ *n* BIOCHEM same as **acetylcholinesterase** [Mid-20C. < CHOLINE + ESTERASE]

chol·la /chóy ə/ (*plural* **-las** or *same*) *n* a cactus that has cylindrical stem segments and yellow spines. Flowers: vividly colored in some cultivated types. Native to: southwestern United States, Mexico. Genus: *Opuntia.* [Mid-19C. Via Mexican Spanish < obsolete Spanish, "top of the head"]

cho·lo /chōlō/ (*plural* **-los**) *n Hispanic* **1.** CULTL ANTHROP same as **mestizo** **2.** a Mexican American gangster or thug [Mid-19C. < American Spanish, after Chollollán (now Cholula) in Mexico]

Cho·lu·la /chə lóolə/ town in Puebla State, central Mexico, situated 8 mi./13 km west of the city of Puebla. Population: 99,794 (2000).

cho·metz *n* JUDAISM another spelling of **chametz**

chomp /chomp/, **chump** /chump/ (*informal*) *vti* (**chomped, chomp·ing, chomps; chumped, chump·ing, chumps**) CHEW NOISILY to take big bites of food and chew steadily, noisily, and with obvious satisfaction ■ *n* **1.** NOISY BITE a big noisy bite into something **2.** SOUND OF BITE the sound made by noisy energetic biting or chewing [Mid-17C. Variant of CHAMP[2]]

Chom·sky /chómskee/, **Noam** (*b.* 1928) US linguist. He is known for his transformational-generative grammar, which revolutionized linguistics, and for his political writings. Full name **Chomsky, Avram Noam**

> "As soon as questions of will or decision or reason or choice of action arise, human science is at a loss."
> [Noam Chomsky, *Listener (London)*; March 30, 1978]

chon /chon/ (*plural same*) *n* a subunit of currency in North and South Korea. See table at **currency** [Mid-20C. < Korean]

chondr- *prefix* same as **chondro-** (*used before vowels*)

chon·dral /kóndrəl/ *adj* relating to or consisting of cartilage

chondri- *prefix* same as **chondro-**

chon·dri·fy /kóndrə fì/ (**-fied, -fy·ing, -fies**) *vti* to change tissue into cartilage, or be changed into cartilage [Late 19C. < Greek *khondros* "cartilage"] —**chon·dri·fi·ca·tion** /kòndrəfi káysh'n/ *n*

chon·drite /kón drìt/ *n* a stony meteorite that contains spherical masses (**chondrules**) of mainly silicate minerals [Mid-19C. < Greek *khondros* "granule"] —**chon·drit·ic** /kon dríttik/ *adj*

chondro- *prefix* **1.** cartilage ○ *chondrocranium* **2.** granule ○ *chondrule* [< Greek *khondros*]

chon·dro·cra·ni·um /kòndrō kráynee əm/ (*plural* **-ni·ums** or **-ni·a** /-nee ə/) *n* the part of an embryo's skull that consists of cartilage that later hardens into bone

chon·dro·ma /kon drṓmə/ (*plural* **-mas** or **-ma·ta** /-mətə/) *n* a benign growth of cartilage

chon·drule /kón drool/ *n* a small spherical mass of mineral matter from outer space, sometimes found in meteorites. Chondrules usually consist of olivine or pyroxene. [Late 19C. < CHONDRITE]

Chong /chong/, **Son** (1676–1759) Korean artist. He was the first Korean to paint in a non-Chinese style, and was noted for his landscapes.

Chong·qing /chàwng chíng, chŏong-/, **Chung·king, Ch'ung-ch'ing** city on the Yangtze River in southern Sichuan Province, southwestern China. It was China's capital from 1937 to 1946. Population: 3,470,000 (1995).

Chon·ju /chàwn jóo/, **Chŏn·ju** capital of North Cholla Province, South Korea, situated 120 mi./193 km south of Seoul. Population: 563,406 (1995).

choo-choo /chóo chòo/, **choo-choo train** *n* a railroad train or locomotive (*baby talk*) [Early 20C. An imitation of the sound of a steam train]

choose /chooz/ (**chose** /chōz/, **cho·sen** /chṓz'n/, **choos·ing, choos·es**) *vti* **1.** to decide which of a number of different things or people is best or most appropriate ○ *chose a partner* **2.** to make a deliberate decision to do something [Old English *cēosan* < Indo-European] —**choos·er** *n*

USAGE ***choose*** or ***chose***? Do not confuse ***choose*** with ***chose***. ***Choose***, rhyming with *blues*, is the infinitive and present tense of the verb, whereas ***chose***, rhyming with *blows*, is the past tense: *I chose the wrong one last time, so I'll let you choose this time.*

choose up *vti* to pick the players wanted on a team for a game

choos·y /chóozee/ (**-i·er, -i·est**), **choos·ey** *adj* very precise or discriminating in preferences (*informal*) —**choos·i·ly** *adv* —**choos·i·ness** *n*

Cho O·yu /chṑ ō yóo/ mountain in the Himalayan range, one of the world's highest peaks. Height: 26,906 ft./8,201 m.

chop[1] /chop/ *v* (**chopped, chop·ping, chops**) **1.** *vt* CUT SOMETHING UP WITH SHARP TOOL to cut something into pieces with downward strokes of an ax, knife, or other sharp-bladed tool ○ *chopped a few carrots* **2.** *vt* CUT SOMETHING OFF to use a quick sharp blow or blows to sever or fell something ○ *chopped down the tree* **3.** *vi* MAKE CHOPPING MOVEMENTS to make downward cutting movements with a tool or with the hand **4.** *vt* FORM SOMETHING BY CHOPPING to make something such as a hole or path by chopping with an ax or other tool ○ *He chopped his way through the undergrowth.* **5.** *vt* HIT BALL WITH SHARP DOWNWARD MOVEMENT to hit a ball with a quick sharp downward movement of a racket or bat, often in order to give the ball backspin **6.** *vt* HIT SHARPLY DOWNWARD to hit somebody or something with a sharp downward motion ■ *n* **1.** SLICE OF MEAT WITH BONE a small piece of red meat cut from the ribs, loin, or shoulder, usually with the bone still attached ○ *pork chops* **2.** SHARP STROKE DOWNWARD a sudden strong downward blow with the hand or a cutting tool ○ *a karate chop* **3.** *UK* DISMISSAL dismissal from a job (*informal*) ○ *was given the chop* **4.** IRREGULAR WAVE MOTION turbulent irregular motion in waves or water ○ *a lot of chop on the bay this morning* **5.** DISTURBED SEA a stretch of choppy water, especially on the sea ○ *hit a bad chop at the inlet* [14C. Variant of CHAP[1]]

chop[2] /chop/ (**chopped, chop·ping, chops**) *vi* to change direction or have a change of mind, especially suddenly or frequently [15C. Variant of CHAP[3]]

chop[3] /chop/ *n* **1.** *Malaysia, Singapore* a wooden, metal, or rubber stamp used to frank documents or seal envelopes **2.** especially in East Asia, a trademark, official stamp, or mark of quality [Early 17C. < Hindi *chāp*] —**chop** *vt*

chop-chop *interj* used to indicate, often in a bossy or arrogant way, that somebody should hurry or do something quickly or right away (*informal*) [Mid-19C. Repetition of pidgin English *chop*, alteration of Cantonese Chinese *gap* "urgent"] —**chop-chop** *adv*

chop·house /chóp hòwss/ (*plural* **chop·hous·es** /-hòwzəz/) *n* a restaurant serving grilled meat, e.g., chops and steaks, as its specialty, especially formerly

cho·pin *n* CLOTHING another spelling of **chopine**

Frédéric François Chopin

Cho·pin /shṓ pàn, shō páN/, **Frédéric François** (1810–49) Polish composer and pianist. His piano compositions include mazurkas, études, preludes, nocturnes, waltzes, polonaises, sonatas, and two concertos.

Cho·pin /shṓ pàn/, **Kate** (1850–1904) US novelist, short-story writer, and poet. She wrote *The Awakening* (1899), a pioneering novel of female sexual discovery.

> "The past was nothing to her; offered no lesson which she was willing to heed. The future was a mystery which she never attempted to penetrate. The present alone was significant."
> [Kate Chopin, *The Awakening*; 1899]

cho·pine /chō péen, chóppin/, **cho·pin** *n* a type of high shoe with a very thick sole worn by European women in the 16th and 17th centuries [Late 16C. < Spanish *chapín*]

chop·log·ic /chóp lòjjik/ *n* the presentation of an argument in a way that is either illogical or pedantic and overcomplicated (*archaic or literary*) [Early 16C. < *chop* "exchange"]

chop·per /chóppər/ *n* **1.** AVIAT same as **helicopter** (*informal*) **2.** BIKE WITH HIGH HANDLEBARS a motorcycle or bicycle with a lowered seat, raised handlebars, and lengthened forks holding the front wheel **3.** CLEAVER a cutting tool with a handle and a sharp broad blade, used especially for chopping up meat or wood **4.** INTERRUPTING DEVICE a device that regularly interrupts an electric current, a beam of light, or some other stream of radiation in order to produce a pulsing flow or beam ■ **chop·pers** *npl* TEETH teeth, especially large or false ones (*slang*) ■ *vti* GO BY HELICOPTER to travel or to transport something or somebody by helicopter (*informal*)

chop·ping block /chópping-/ *n* a heavy block of wood, sometimes mounted on legs, for chopping food or wood on ■ ◇ **somebody's head is on the chopping block** somebody deserves or is likely to be dismissed from his or her job

chop·ping board *n UK* same as **cutting board**

chop·py /chóppee/ (**-pi·er, -pi·est**) *adj* rough, with the surface of the water broken up into many small waves made by strong winds —**chop·pi·ly** *adv* —**chop·pi·ness** *n*

chops /chops/ *npl* **1.** the jaws, or the skin covering the jaws (*informal*) **2.** technique or virtuosity in playing an instrument, especially a wind instrument (*slang*)

chop shop *n* a workshop or garage where stolen vehicles are disguised or broken up for spare parts (*slang*)

chop·sock·y /chóp sòkee/ *n* the genre of movies in which martial arts such as kung fu feature prominently ○ *his latest chopsocky extravaganza* [< CHOP[1] + SOCK[2]]

chop·stick /chóp stìk/ *n* either of a pair of narrow sticks that are held together in one hand and used when eating or preparing East Asian food [Late 17C. < pidgin English (see CHOP-CHOP)]

chop su·ey /chòp sóo ee/ *n* a dish of Chinese-American origin made typically of shredded meat and mixed vegetables [Late 19C. < Cantonese Chinese *tsaâp suì* "mixed bits"]

cho·ra·gus /kə ráygəss/ (*plural* **-gi** /-jì/ or **-gus·es**) *n* the leader of the chorus in ancient Greek drama [Early 17C. Via Latin < Greek *khoragos* "somebody who leads the chorus"] —**cho·rag·ic** /-rájjik/ *adj*

cho·ral /káwrəl/ *adj* **1.** arranged for or performed by a chorus or choir ○ *choral singing* **2.** concerned with choral singing, choruses, or choirs ○ *a choral society* [Late 16C. < medieval Latin *choralis* < Latin *chorus* (see CHORUS)] —**cho·ral·ly** *adv*

cho·rale /kə rál, kaw ráal/ *n* **1.** LUTHERAN HYMN TUNE a hymn tune, especially a slow and stately one, originally intended for congregational singing in the Lutheran Church **2.** PIECE OF MUSIC BASED ON CHORALE a piece of music, especially a choral work, based on a chorale tune or in a style reminiscent of traditional Lutheran church music **3.** GROUP OF SINGERS a group of singers specializing in a particular style of music, especially church music [Mid-19C. < German *Choral(gesang)* "choral (song)"]

cho·rale prel·ude *n* an organ prelude based on a chorale tune, used to introduce congregational singing of the chorale on which it is based or performed as a separate piece

chord[1] /kawrd/ *n* two or more musical notes played or sung simultaneously ○ *an F minor chord* ■ *vt* (**chord·ed, chord·ing, chords**) to play or produce chords to harmonize and embellish a melody [15C. Shortening and alteration of ACCORD after Latin *chorda*] —**chord·al** *adj* ◇ **strike** *or* **touch a chord** to produce an emotional, especially a sympathetic, response in somebody, or jog somebody's memory

USAGE chord or **cord**? In musical contexts the spelling is ***chord***, and this form is also used in figurative expressions that have to do with feelings: *The speech struck the right chord.* In anatomical contexts (*spinal cord, umbilical cord, vocal cords*), ***cord*** is more usual. ***Cord*** is used when referring to a thick, strong string, a belt or cable, and as a measurement of cut wood.

chord[2] /kawrd/ *n* **1.** MATH LINE THROUGH ARC a straight line connecting two points on an arc or circle **2.** CONSTR HORIZONTAL CONNECTING PART the horizontal part of a truss designed to absorb tension, e.g., in a roof **3.** AVIAT AIRFOIL MEASURE the shortest distance between the leading and trailing edges of an airfoil **4.** ANAT another spelling of **cord** (sense 3) [Mid-16C. Alteration of CORD, after Latin *chorda*]

chor·date /káwr dàyt/ *n* an animal that at some stage in its development has a main dorsal nerve cord, a skeletal rod (**notochord**), and gill slits, including all vertebrates and some primitive invertebrate ocean animals. Phylum: Chordata. [Late 19C. < modern Latin *chordata* < Latin *chorda* "cord"] —**chor·date** *adj*

chor·do·phone /káwrdə fōn/ *n* MUSIC same as **stringed instrument** (*technical*) [Mid-20C. < CHORD[1]]

chord or·gan *n* a small electronic organ with special keys to produce chords for accompanying a melody [< CHORD[1]]

chore /chawr/ *n* **1.** a task, especially an ordinary household task, that has to be done regularly (*often used in the plural*) **2.** something that is unpleasant, difficult, awkward, or boring to do [Mid-18C. < alteration of *char* "do some work" < Old English *cierran* "to turn" < Germanic]

SYNONYMS See ***job***.

-chore *suffix* a plant distributed by a particular means ○ *anemochore* [< Greek *khōrein* "to spread"]

cho·re·a /kaw rée ə/ *n* jerky spasmodic movements of the limbs, trunk, and facial muscles, common to various diseases of the central nervous system [Late 17C. Via Latin < Greek *khoreia* "dance"] —**cho·re·al** *adj* —**cho·re·ic** *adj*

cho·re·o·graph /káwree ə gràf/ (**-graphed, -graph·ing, -graphs**) *v* **1.** *vti* to plan out dance movements to a piece of music **2.** *vt* to plan, coordinate, and supervise an event or activity ○ *His job is to choreograph royal weddings and other state occasions.* [Mid-20C. Back-formation < CHOREOGRAPHY] —**cho·re·og·ra·pher** /kàwree óggrəfər/ *n*

cho·re·og·ra·phy /kàwree óggrəfee/ (*plural* **-phies**) *n* **1.** COMPOSING DANCES the planning of movements for dancing **2.** DANCE MOVEMENTS FOR PIECE the steps and movements planned for a dance, or a written record of them **3.** PLANNED MOVEMENT the carefully planned or executed organization of people, things, or an event [Late 18C. < French *chorégraphie* "dance writing" < Greek *khoreia* "dance"] —**cho·re·o·graph·ic** /kàwree ə gráffik/ *adj* —**cho·re·o·graph·i·cal·ly** *adv*

cho·ri·amb /káwree àmb, -àm/ *n* a poetic foot consisting of two short syllables between two long ones or two unstressed syllables between two stressed ones [Early 17C. Via late Latin < Greek *khoriambos* "iamb of a chorus"] —**cho·ri·am·bic** /kàwree ámbik/ *adj*

cho·ric /káwrik/ *adj* performed by or written for a chorus, especially a chorus in classical Greek theater [Early 19C. < late Latin *choricus* < Greek *khoros* "chorus"]

cho·ri·o·al·lan·to·is /kàwree ō ə lántō iss/ *n* a membrane surrounding an embryo. In a bird's or reptile's egg, it lies next to the shell. In mammals, it forms a major part of the placenta. [Mid-20C. < CHORION] —**cho·ri·o·al·lan·to·ic** /kàwree ō àllən tṓ ik/ *adj*

cho·ri·on /káwree òn/ *n* the outer membrane enclosing the embryo of mammals, reptiles, and birds. It has a dense concentration of blood vessels and aids in the formation of the placenta in mammals. [Mid-16C. < Greek *khorion*] —**cho·ri·on·ic** /kàwree ónnik/ *adj*

cho·ri·on·ic go·nad·o·tro·pin *n* a hormone that helps maintain a pregnancy

cho·ri·on·ic vil·lus *n* a tiny outgrowth from the outer membrane (**chorion**) surrounding an embryo that moves into the womb wall with others to form the placenta (*often used in the plural*)

cho·ri·on·ic vil·lus sam·pling *n* a prenatal screening test carried out by examining cells from the tiny hairy outgrowths (**villi**) of the outer membrane (**chorion**) surrounding an embryo, which have the same DNA as the fetus

cho·ris·ter /káwristər/ *n* a member of a chorus, choir, or other group of singers [14C. < Anglo-Norman < Old French *cueriste* < Latin *chorus* (see CHORUS)]

cho·ri·zo /chə réezō/ (*plural* **-zos**) *n Hispanic* a very spicy Mexican or Spanish pork sausage [Mid-19C. < Spanish]

C-ho·ri·zon, C ho·ri·zon *n* the lowermost layer of earth immediately above bedrock

cho·rog·ra·phy /kə róggrəfee/ *n* the preparation of maps in which specific areas or regions are delineated and often highlighted in some way, e.g., by color-coding [Mid-16C. Directly or via French < Latin *chorographia* < Greek *khōrographia* "place writing"] —**cho·rog·ra·pher** *n* —**cho·ro·graph·ic** /kàwrə gráffik/ *adj* —**cho·ro·graph·i·cal·ly** *adv*

cho·roid /káw ròyd/ *n also* **cho·roid coat** a brownish membrane between the retina and the white of the eye in vertebrates that contains blood vessels and large pigmented cells ■ *adj* resembling the chorion in being vascular or membranous [Mid-17C. < Greek *khoroeidēs* < *khorion* "chorion"]

cho·roid plex·us *n* a membrane with many small blood vessels in the fluid spaces of the brain that secretes cerebrospinal fluid

chor·tle /cháwrt'l/ *n* a noisy gleeful laugh [Late 19C. Blend of CHUCKLE + SNORT] —**chor·tle** *vi* —**chor·tler** *n*

cho·rus /káwrəss/ *n* **1.** REPEATED PART OF SONG a set of lines that are sung at least twice in the course of a song, usually being repeated after each verse **2.** LARGE GROUP OF SINGERS a large group of singers who perform choral music or opera together **3.** GROUP OF PERFORMERS a group of people who appear, sing, and sometimes dance together as a unit in a performance, usually providing backing for the principal performers **4.** MUSIC FOR GROUP a musical composition written for a large group of singers, usually with different parts for the different voice types ○ *the Hallelujah Chorus* **5.** MANY VOICES TOGETHER the words spoken or feelings expressed by a group of people at the same time ○ *a chorus of complaints* **6.** GROUP SPEAKING OR MAKING NOISE TOGETHER a group of people or animals all speaking or making a noise together **7.** GROUP OF ACTORS IN GREEK DRAMA a group of actors in ancient Greek drama who sing or speak in unison, generally commenting on the significance of the events that take place in the play **8.** VERSE PASSAGE FOR GREEK DRAMA CHORUS a verse passage in an ancient Greek drama intended to be sung or spoken by the chorus **9.** DRAMA ROLE a role in some Elizabethan and historical dramas for a solo actor, who speaks the introductory prologue, comments on the action, and delivers the epilogue ■ *vt* (**-rused, -rus·ing, -rus·es**) SAY SOMETHING TOGETHER to speak at the same time, saying the same thing or expressing the same feeling or opinion [Mid-16C. Via Latin < Greek *khoros*] ◇ **in chorus** all speaking or making a noise together

cho·rus boy *n* a man or boy who sings and dances as one of the supporting group of performers in a stage or movie production

cho·rus girl *n* a woman or girl who sings and dances as one of the supporting group of performers in a stage or movie production

cho·rus line *n* the chorus of supporting singers and dancers in a musical or variety show

-chory *suffix* same as **-chore**

chose past tense of **choose**

USAGE See ***choose***.

---

cho·sen /chṓz'n/ past participle of **choose** ■ *adj* picked out from or preferred to the rest ○ *one of the chosen few* ■ *npl* RELIG same as **elect** *npl* (sense 2)

cho·sen peo·ple *npl* the Jews, who, according to the Bible and their own belief, were selected by God to play a unique role in world history

chott /shot/ *n* a basin in the deserts of North Africa that periodically fills with water but dries out and becomes a salt flat when the weather is warmer [Late 19C. < Arabic *šaṭṭ* "shore, strand, salt lake"]

chou·ette /shoo ét/ *n* a variation of backgammon in which one player plays against two or more opponents in one game [Late 19C. < French, "barn owl"]

chough /chuf/ *n* a bird of the crow family with glossy black feathers, red legs and feet, and a red or yellow beak. Native to: Europe, Asia. Genus: *Pyrrhocorax*. [12C. Probably an imitation of its call]

chouse /chowss/ (**choused, chous·ing, chous·es**) *vt regional* to herd livestock roughly [Early 20C. Origin ?]

Chou·teau /shoo tṓ/, **René Auguste** (1749–1829) American pioneer. He founded St. Louis, Missouri (1764), and was an important figure in the local fur trade.

choux pas·try /shoō-/ *n* a soft glossy egg-rich pastry that puffs up into a hollow case when baked. It is used in making filled pastries such as cream puffs and éclairs. [< French, literally "cabbage"]

chow[1] /chow/ *n* **1.** same as **food** (sense 2) (*slang*) **2.** FOOD same as **chow-chow** [Late 18C. Shortening of Chinese pidgin English *chow-chow* "food, mixture"]
chow down *vi* to eat food enthusiastically (*informal*)

chow[2] /chow/, **chow chow** *n* a stocky dog with a thick coat, a tail that curls over its back, and a large dark purplish tongue, belonging to a breed originally from China [Late 19C. < pidgin English]

chow-chow *n* **1.** a Chinese mixed vegetable pickle in a yellow sauce, similar to piccalilli **2.** a Chinese mixture of fruit and candied peel in syrup, with stem ginger [see CHOW[1]]

chow·der /chówdər/ *n* a thick soup, especially one made with seafood or fish [Mid-18C. Probably via French *chaudière* "stew pot" < Latin *calidarium* "hot bath"]

chow·der·head /chówdər hèd/ *n* an offensive term for somebody regarded as unintelligent or irrational (*informal insult*) [Mid-19C. Alteration of English dialect *jolter-head*] —**chow·der·head·ed** *adj*

chow line *n* a line of people waiting for a meal (*informal*)

chow mein /chòw máyn/ *n* a dish of soft fried noodles, usually cooked with chopped meat and vegetables, originally from China [< Chinese *chǎo miàn* "fried noodles"]

Chr. *abbr* **1.** CHR Christ **2.** CHR Christian **3.** BIBLE Chronicles

chres·tom·a·thy /kre stómməthee/ (*plural* **-thies**) *n* a collection of literary passages, especially one assembled for language study [Mid-19C. Directly or via French < Greek *khrēstomatheia* "useful learning"] —**chres·to·math·ic** /krèstə máthik/ *adj*

Bettmann/Corbis

Jean Chrétien

Chré·tien /kray tyáN/, **Jean** (*b.* 1934) Canadian prime minister (1993–2003). He became leader of the Liberal Party (1990), leading them to victory in 1993, 1997, and 2000. His premiership was marked by economic restraint and reduced unemployment. Full name **Chrétien, Joseph Jacques Jean**. See table at **prime minister**

> "You end up looking like the fish."
> [Jean Chrétien, on why he disliked fishing with US presidents, *New York Times*; February 25, 1995]

Chré·ti·en de Troyes /kray tyàN də trwáa/ (*fl* 1170) French poet. His epics were the first to incorporate Arthurian legends and the quest for the Holy Grail.

chrism /krízzəm/ *n* **1.** consecrated oil, or a consecrated mixture of balsam and oil, used for anointing people at some ceremonies in the Roman Catholic, Anglican, and Orthodox churches **2.** a ceremonial anointing of somebody with holy oil, especially at confirmation in the Eastern Orthodox churches [Pre-12C. Via medieval Latin *crisma* < Greek *khrisma* "an anointing" < *khriein* "anoint"] —**chris·mal** *adj*

chris·ma·tion /kriz máysh'n/ *n* in the Eastern Orthodox tradition, the act of anointing somebody, or of being anointed, with holy oil in a religious ceremony such as confirmation [Mid-16C. < medieval Latin *chrismation-* < *crisma* (see CHRISM)]

chris·om /krízzəm/ *n* a white robe or shawl worn by an infant for his or her baptism [13C. Alteration of CHRISM]

chris·om child *n* a baby that dies within a month of its baptism (*archaic*)

Christ /krīst/ *n* **1.** CHR same as **Jesus Christ** *n* (sense 1) **2.** BIBLE THE MESSIAH according to the Bible, a savior who will come to deliver God's chosen people **3.** CHR PAINTING OF JESUS CHRIST an artistic representation of Jesus Christ ■ *interj* TABOO TERM a highly offensive term used to express surprise, annoyance, exasperation, or alarm (*taboo*) [Pre-12C. Via Latin *Christus* < Greek *Khristos* "anointed" < *khriein* "anoint"] —**Christ·hood** *n* —**Christ·ly** *adj*

Chris·ta·del·phi·an /krìstə délfee ən/ *n* a member of a Christian group founded by John Thomas in the United States around 1848. Christadelphians reject the doctrine of the Trinity as not in the Bible and believe in the dead being resurrected with the Second Coming of Jesus Christ. [Mid-19C. < late Greek *Khristadelphos* "in brotherhood with Christ"] —**Chris·ta·del·phi·an** *adj*

Christ child *n* Jesus Christ as an infant, especially as depicted in art

Christ·church /kríst chùrch/ city situated near the eastern coast of the South Island, New Zealand, 8

a at; aa father; aw all; ay day; ə about, item, edible, common, circus; e egg; ee eel; er hair; hw when; i it; ī ice; 'l apple; 'm rhythm; 'n fashion; o odd; ō open; oo good; oo pool; ow owl; oy oil; th thin; th this; u up; ur urge;

mi./13 km northwest of Lyttelton. Population: 334,107 (2001).

chris·ten /kríss'n/ *vt* **1. BAPTIZE AND NAME SOMEBODY** to make somebody, especially a baby, a member of the Christian Church in a ceremony that includes a form of baptism and, usually, the giving of a Christian name or names **2. GIVE NAME TO SOMETHING OR SOMEBODY** to give a name to something or somebody, with or without an accompanying ceremony ○ *christen a ship* **3. USE SOMETHING FOR FIRST TIME** to use or wear something for the first time (*informal*) ○ *Shall we christen our new coffeepot?* [Pre-12C. < Old English *cristnian* < *cristen* "Christian" < Latin *christianus*] —**chris·ten·er** *n*

Chris·ten·dom /kríss'ndəm/ *n* **1.** all the areas of the world where Christianity is accepted as the main religion **2.** all Christian people considered as a group (*formal*) [Old English *cristendom* "condition of being Christian" < *cristen* (see CHRISTEN)]

chris·ten·ing /kríss'ning/ *n* a ceremony in a Christian church in which somebody, especially a baby, is baptized and usually given a Christian name or names

Chris·tian /kríschən/ *n* **1. BELIEVER IN JESUS CHRIST AS SAVIOR** somebody whose religion is Christianity **2.** *Malaysia* CHR same as **Protestant** (sense 1) ■ *adj* **1.** CHR **FROM TEACHINGS OF JESUS CHRIST** based on or relating to a belief in Jesus Christ as the Son of God and the Messiah, and acceptance of his teachings, contained in the Gospels **2. RELATING TO CHRISTIANITY** relating to Christianity, or belonging to or maintained by a Christian organization, especially a church ○ *Christian theology* ○ *a Christian school* **3. KIND AND UNSELFISH** showing qualities such as kindness, helpfulness, and concern for others [13C. < Latin *Christianus* < *Christus* (see CHRIST)] —**Chris·tian·ly** *adv*

Chris·tian Dem·o·crat·ic Par·ty *n* a political party of the moderate right, especially in continental Europe —**Chris·tian Dem·o·crat** *n*

Chris·tian E·ra *n* the period of history dating from the year in which Jesus Christ is believed to have been born. Dates in the early Christian Era are often indicated by A.D., and dates before the Christian Era by B.C.

Chris·ti·an·i·ty /krìschee ánnətee, krìstee-/ *n* **1. RELIGION THAT FOLLOWS JESUS CHRIST'S TEACHINGS** the religion based on the life, teachings, and example of Jesus Christ **2. HOLDING OF CHRISTIAN BELIEFS** the fact of holding Christian beliefs or of being a Christian **3. CHRISTIANS AS GROUP** all Christian people considered as a group

Chris·tian·ize /kríschə nīz/ (**-ized, -iz·ing, -iz·es**) *vt* **1.** to change the religious beliefs and practices of a person or group of people from another religion to Christianity **2.** to make somebody or something Christian by imbuing him, her, or it with Christian principles or a Christian spirit —**Chris·tian·i·za·tion** /krìschəni záysh'n/ *n* —**Chris·tian·iz·er** *n*

Chris·tian name *n* a given name, especially one given at a christening

Chris·tian Sci·ence *n* the beliefs and practices of the Church of Christ, Scientist, a religious group founded by Mary Baker Eddy. Its members believe that illness should be overcome or managed through religious faith and observances alone. —**Chris·tian Sci·en·tist** *n*

Chris·tian Scrip·tures *npl* the New Testament of the Bible as distinct from the Hebrew Scriptures

Chris·tian·sted /kríschən stèd/ town situated on the northeastern coast of St. Croix Island, US Virgin Islands. Population: 2,555 (1990).

chris·tie /krístee/, **chris·ty** (*plural* **-ties**) *n* in skiing, a type of turn used for stopping or rapidly changing direction, in which the skier twists sharply aside while keeping the skis parallel to each other [Early 20C. Shortening of *Christiania*, former name of Oslo]

Chris·tie /krístee/, **Dame Agatha** (1890–1976) British novelist and playwright. She wrote over 70 detective novels featuring the sleuths Hercule Poirot and Miss Marple. Full name **Christie, Dame Agatha Mary Clarissa**

> "I don't think necessity is the mother of invention—invention, in my opinion, arises directly from idleness, possibly also from laziness. To save oneself trouble."
> [Dame Agatha Christie, *An Autobiography*; 1977]

AKG London
Dame Agatha Christie

Chris·ti·na /kri steénə/, **queen of Sweden** (1626–89) In 1644 she negotiated the Peace of Westphalia, bringing to an end the Thirty Years' War

> "We grow old more through indolence, than through age."
> [Christina, "Maxims (1660–80)," *The Works of Christina of Sweden*; 1753]

Christ·mas /kríssməss/ *n* **1. FESTIVAL CELEBRATING BIRTH OF JESUS CHRIST** a Christian festival marking the birth of Jesus Christ. Date: December 25. **2. CHRISTMAS PERIOD** the period around December 25, or the Christian church season extending from December 24 to January 6 **3. QUARTER DAY** in England, Wales, and Ireland, one of the four quarter days, falling on December 25 [Old English *Cristes mæsse* "mass of Christ"]

Christ·mas cac·tus *n* a branching cactus cultivated as an ornamental plant. Flowers: red, pink, white, or purplish red. Native to: Brazil. Latin name: *Schlumbergera truncata*. [Because it flowers around December]

Christ·mas card *n* an illustrated greeting card sent at Christmas

Christ·mas car·ol *n* a Christian song celebrating Christmas

Christ·mas club *n* a savings account in which money is deposited regularly throughout the year in order to buy gifts and additional food and drink for Christmas

Christ·mas crack·er *n* same as **cracker** (sense 7)

Christ·mas Day *n* same as **Christmas** (sense 1)

Christ·mas dis·ease *n* a form of hemophilia caused by lack of a protein needed for blood clotting [Mid-20C. After Stephen *Christmas*, who had the disease]

Christ·mas Eve *n* the day or evening of December 24

Christ·mas fern *n* an evergreen fern with dense clusters of thin fronds. Native to: North America. Latin name: *Polystichum acrostichoides*.

Christ·mas Is·land /kríssməss-/ dependency of Australia in the Indian Ocean, 224 mi./360 km south of Java. Population: 1,906 (1996). Area: 150 sq. mi./388 sq. km. ■ former name for **Kiritimati** (until 1981)

Christ·mas rose *n* an evergreen winter-flowering plant, sometimes grown as a pot plant. Flowers: drooping, white. Native to: Europe, Asia. Latin name: *Helleborus niger*. [Because it flowers in winter]

Christ·mas stock·ing *n* a stocking or large sock hung up on Christmas Eve by children and supposed to be filled with presents by Santa Claus during the night

Christ·mas·sy /kríssməssee/ *adj* suggesting the Christmas period, or suitable for Christmas (*informal*) ○ *The decorations look really Christmassy.*

Christ·mas·time /kríssməss tīm/ *n* same as **Christmas** (sense 2)

Christ·mas tree *n* an evergreen tree, especially a conifer or an artificial version of one, that is decorated with lights and ornaments at Christmas

Chris·to /krístō/ (*b.* 1935) Bulgarian-born US artist. He is known for his modern conceptual art, in particular for his "wrapping" of monuments and buildings. Full name **Javacheff, Christo**

Chris·to·cen·tric /krìstə séntrik/ *adj* **1.** assuming, implying, or based on Christian values and beliefs **2.** concentrating or based strongly on Jesus Christ and his teachings

Chris·tol·o·gy /kri stóllәjee/ *n* the branch of theology concerned with the study of the nature, character, and actions of Jesus Christ —**Chris·to·log·i·cal** /krìstə lójjik'l/ *adj* —**Chris·tol·o·gist** *n*

Chris·tophe /kree stáwf/, **Henri** (1767–1820) Haitian leader. He was president of Haiti from 1807 to 1811, when he became self-declared king (1811–20).

Chris·toph·er /krístəfər/, **St.** (*fl* 3rd century) According to legend, he carried Jesus Christ as a child across a river. He is the patron saint of travelers.

Chris·toph·er, Warren (*b.* 1925) US secretary of state (1993–97). He came from a legal background to serve as deputy secretary of state under President Jimmy Carter, and secretary of state under President Bill Clinton.

Christ's thorn, Christ thorn *n* a thorny Asian bush or tree, especially a jujube, a Jerusalem thorn, or a thorny spurge. Branches of such a plant are popularly believed to have been used for Jesus Christ's crown of thorns.

chris·ty *n* SKIING another spelling of **christie**

Chris·ty /krístee/, **Edwin Pearce** (1815–72) US entertainer. He is known for his minstrel troupe *The Christy Minstrels*, whose members were white singers performing in blackface makeup (1840s-50s).

chrom- *prefix* same as **chromo-** (*used before vowels*)

chro·ma /krṓmə/ *n* PHYS same as **saturation** *n* (sense 8) [Late 19C. < Greek *khrōma* "color"]

chro·maf·fin /krṓməfin/ *adj* describes cells in the adrenal medulla that make norepinephrine [Early 20C. < CHROMO- + Latin *affinis* "related"]

chromat- *prefix* same as **chromato-** (*used before vowels*)

chro·mate /krṓ màyt/ *n* any salt or ester of chromic acid [Early 20C. < CHROMIC]

chro·mat·ic /krō máttik/ *adj* **1. USING ALL SEMITONES IN OCTAVE** describes a musical scale that runs through all the semitones in an octave, e.g., using all the keys, black and white, on a keyboard **2. BASED ON CHROMATIC SCALE** describes music that is based on the chromatic scale or that makes frequent use of notes that are outside the key in which it is written **3. RELATING TO COLOR** relating to color and phenomena connected with it [15C. Directly or via French < Greek *khrōmatikos* < *khrōma* "color"] —**chro·mat·i·cal·ly** *adv*

chro·mat·ic ab·er·ra·tion *n* an optical aberration in a lens, caused by a defect, leading to colored light of different colors being refracted differently

chro·mat·i·cism /krō mátti sìzzəm/ *n* the use in music of the chromatic scale or of many notes and harmonies that are foreign to the basic key

chro·ma·tic·i·ty /krṓmə tíssətee/ *n* the color quality of light precisely and uniquely defined in terms of three factors (**chromaticity coordinates**)

chro·mat·ics /krō máttiks/ *n* the science or study of color (*takes a singular verb*) —**chro·ma·tist** /krṓmətist/ *n*

chro·ma·tid /krṓmətid/ *n* either of the two strands into which a chromosome divides in the process of duplicating itself in cell division [Early 20C. < Greek *khrōmat-* "color"]

chro·ma·tin /krṓmətin/ *n* the substance that forms chromosomes and contains DNA, RNA, and various proteins [Late 19C. < Greek *khrōmat-* "color"] —**chro·ma·tin·ic** /krṓmə tínnik/ *adj*

chromato- *prefix* **1.** color ○ *chromatography* **2.** chromatin ○ *chromatolysis* [< Greek *khrōmat-* "color"]

chro·mat·o·gram /krō máttə gràm/ *n* a pattern formed by substances that have been separated by chromatography

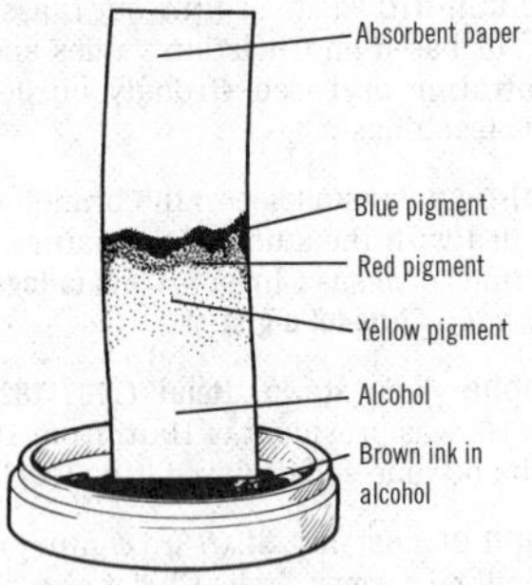

chromatography

chro·ma·tog·ra·phy /krōmə tóggrəfee/ *n* a method of finding out which components a gaseous or liquid mixture contains that involves passing it through or over something that absorbs the different components at different rates —**chro·mat·o·graph** /krō máttə gràf/ *n* —**chro·ma·tog·ra·pher** *n* —**chro·mat·o·graph·ic** /krō màttə gráffik/ *adj* —**chro·mat·o·graph·i·cal·ly** *adv*

chro·ma·tol·y·sis /krōmə tólləssiss/ *n* the breakdown of the substance that forms chromosomes (**chromatin**) within an injured cell nucleus

chro·mat·o·phore /krō máttə fàwr/ *n* **1.** a pigment-containing cell in many animals that, when it expands or contracts, causes a change in the animal's skin coloring. Octopus, squid, and some frogs and lizards contain these cells. **2.** BOT same as **chromoplast** —**chro·mat·o·phor·ic** /krō màttə fáwrik/ *adj*

chrome /krōm/ *n* **1.** CHROMIUM-PLATED METAL shiny chromium-plated metal. Use: to trim cars. **2.** COMPOUND CONTAINING CHROMIUM an alloy, dye, or pigment containing chromium **3.** CHEM same as **chromium** ■ *vt* (**chromed, chrom·ing, chromes**) **1.** COAT METAL WITH CHROMIUM to electroplate a metal with chromium in order to make it shiny and protect it against corrosion **2.** TREAT SOMETHING WITH CHROMIUM COMPOUND to treat a substance with a chromium compound, usually when dyeing or tanning it [Early 19C. Via French < Greek *khrōma* "color"; because compounds containing it are often brightly colored]

-chrome *suffix* color, pigment ○ *phytochrome* [< Greek *khrōma* "color"]

chrome al·um *n* a red-violet crystalline solid. Use: fixing agent in dyeing, tanning, and photography. Formula: $CrK(SO_4)_2.12H_2O$.

chrome green *n* a brilliant green pigment containing chrome yellow and iron blue. Use: fabric dye.

chrome red *n* a bright red-orange pigment containing lead chromate and lead oxide. Use: in paints and dyes.

chrome tape *n* magnetic recording tape that is coated with chromium dioxide

chrome yel·low *n* a yellow pigment containing lead chromate and lead sulfate

chro·mic /krṓmik/ *adj* relating to or containing chromium with a valence of three

chro·mic ac·id *n* an unstable oxidizing acid existing only in solution or in the form of a salt. Formula: H_2CrO_4.

chro·mite /krṓ mìt/ *n* a brownish black mineral ore consisting of an oxide of iron and chromium. Use: source of chromium.

chro·mi·um /krṓmee əm/ *n* a hard bluish white metallic element. Source: chromite. Use: alloys and electroplating to increase hardness and corrosion resistance. Symbol **Cr**. See table at **element**

chro·mi·um di·ox·ide *n* a black crystalline solid. Use: to coat recording tape with magnetic properties. Formula: CrO_2.

chro·mo /krṓmō/ (*plural* **-mos**) *n* PRINTING same as **chromolithograph** [Mid-19C Shortening]

chromo- *prefix* **1.** color, pigment ○ *chromolithograph* ○ *chromogen* **2.** chromium ○ *chromite* [< Greek *khrōma* "color"]

chro·mo·dy·nam·ics /krō mō dī námmiks/ *n* PHYS same as **quantum chromodynamics**

chro·mo·gen /krṓmәjәn/ *n* **1.** any substance that is capable of being converted into a biological pigment or a dye, e.g., through oxidation **2.** any microorganism that produces a pigment —**chro·mo·gen·ic** /krōmə jénnik/ *adj*

chro·mo·lith·o·graph /krōmə líthə gràf/ *n* a colored picture produced by making and superimposing multiple lithographs, each of which adds a different color —**chro·mo·li·thog·ra·pher** /krōməli thóggrəfər/ *n* —**chro·mo·lith·o·graph·ic** /krōmə lithə gráffik/ *adj* —**chro·mo·li·thog·ra·phy** /krōməli thóggrəfee/ *n*

chro·mo·mere /krṓmə meer/ *n* a small dense bead-shaped granule of chromatin, found at intervals along a chromosome during cell division —**chro·mo·mer·ic** /krōmə meérik, -mérrik/ *adj*

chro·mo·ne·ma /krōmə neémə/ (*plural* **-ma·ta** /-mətə/) *n* the coiled central filament that forms the core of a chromosome strand (**chromatid**) [Early 20C. < CHROMO- + Greek *nēma* "thread"] —**chro·mo·ne·mal** *adj*

chro·mo·phore /krṓmə fàwr/ *n* a group of atoms in a molecule that produces color in dyes and other compounds through selective absorption of light, e.g., the azo group —**chro·mo·phor·ic** /krōmə fáwrik/ *adj*

chro·mo·plast /krṓmə plàst/ *n* a membrane-surrounded structure (**plastid**) in a plant cell that contains pigment. Red, yellow, or orange chromoplasts contain carotenoid pigments, and green chromoplasts (**chloroplasts**) contain chlorophyll.

chro·mo·pro·tein /krōmə prṓ teen/ *n* a protein combined with a pigment

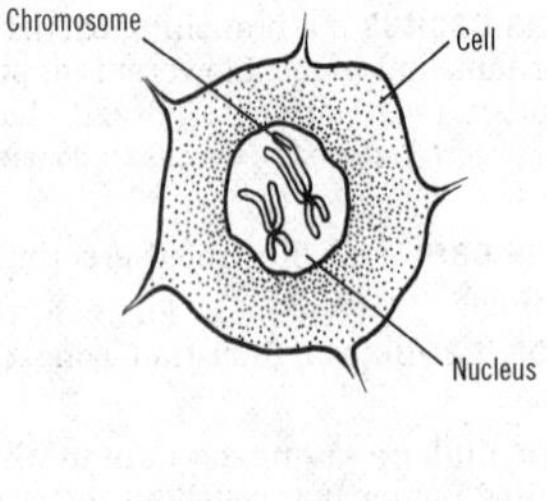

chromosome

chro·mo·some /krṓmə sōm/ *n* a rod-shaped structure, usually found in pairs in a cell nucleus, that carries the genes that determine sex and the characteristics an organism inherits from its parents. A human body cell usually contains 46 chromosomes arranged in 23 pairs. [Late 19C. < German *Chromosom* < Greek *khrōma* "color" + *sōma* "body"; because chromosomes readily take up dye] —**chro·mo·so·mal** /krōmə sṓm'l/ *adj*

chro·mo·some band *n* a pattern produced in a chromosome by using a stain, making the chromosome identifiable from other chromosomes

chro·mo·some map *n* same as **genetic map**

chro·mo·some num·ber *n* the number of chromosomes present in the cell nucleus of a species of plant or animal. A human body usually has a chromosome number of 46.

chro·mo·sphere /krṓmə sfeer/ *n* **1.** the lower region of the Sun's atmosphere, between the photosphere and the corona **2.** the lower region of the atmosphere of any star —**chro·mo·spher·ic** /krōmə sfeérik, -sférrik/ *adj*

chro·mous /krṓməss/ *adj* relating to or containing chromium, especially chromium in its divalent state [Mid-19C. < CHROMIUM]

chron. *abbr* **1.** LITERAT chronicle **2.** TIME chronological **3.** TIME chronology

Chron. *abbr* BIBLE Chronicles

chron- *prefix* TIME same as **chrono-** (*used before vowels*)

chron·ic /krónnik/ *adj* **1.** LONG-LASTING describes an illness or medical condition that lasts over a long period and sometimes causes a long-term change in the body **2.** WITH LONG-TERM ILLNESS having a particular long-term illness or condition ○ *a chronic asthmatic* **3.** ALWAYS PRESENT always present or recurring **4.** HABITUAL repeatedly doing something or behaving compulsively ○ *a chronic liar* [15C. Via French < Greek *khronikos* "of time" < *khronos* "time"] —**chron·i·cal·ly** *adv* —**chro·nic·i·ty** /krə níssətee/ *n*

chron·ic dai·ly head·aches *npl* a condition in which the patient is affected by a series of extremely painful, recurring migraine and tension headaches that are present for 15 or more days a month [Early 21C.]

chron·ic fa·tigue syn·drome *n* an illness without a known cause that is characterized by long-term exhaustion, muscle weakness, depression, and sleep disturbances. It may be a reaction to a viral infection in somebody already debilitated.

chron·i·cle /krónnik'l/ *n* **1.** HISTORICAL ACCOUNT an account of events presented in chronological order **2.** NARRATIVE a narrative or fictional account ■ *vt* (**-cled, -cling, -cles**) MAKE RECORD OF HAPPENINGS to record an event or series of events in chronological order [14C. < Anglo-Norman *cronicle*, alteration of Old French *cronique* < Greek *khronika* (plural) "annals" < *khronos* "time"] —**chron·i·cler** *n*

Chron·i·cles /krónnik'lz/ *n* either of two books of the Bible that tell the story of the Israelites from the creation of Adam to the middle of the 6th century B.C. (*takes a singular verb*) See table at **Bible**

chron·ic wast·ing dis·ease *n* a highly contagious brain disease in deer and elk that has no early overt symptoms but results in the brain deteriorating and taking on a spongy appearance. It is believed to be caused by an abnormal transmissible protein (**prion**) and related to BSE in cattle.

chrono- *prefix* time ○ *chronograph* [< Greek *khronos* "time"]

chron·o·bi·ol·o·gy /krònnə bī óllәjee/ *n* the study of recurring cycles of events in the natural world —**chron·o·bi·o·log·ic** /-bī ə lójjik/ *adj* —**chron·o·bi·ol·o·gist** *n*

chron·o·gram /krónnə gràm, krṓnə-/ *n* a phrase or inscription containing letters indicating a date. Roman numerals are often used in this way. —**chron·o·gram·mat·ic** /krònnə grə máttik, krṓnə-/ *adj* —**chron·o·gram·mat·i·cal·ly** *adv*

chron·o·graph /krónnə gràf, krṓnə-/ *n* an instrument such as a stopwatch that records time with great accuracy —**chron·o·graph·ic** /krònnə gráffik, krṓnə-/ *adj* —**chron·o·graph·i·cal·ly** *adv*

chronol. *abbr* TIME **1.** chronological **2.** chronology

chron·o·log·i·cal /krònnə lójjik'l, krṓnə-/, **chron·o·log·ic** /-lójjik/ *adj* **1.** presented or arranged in the order in which events occur or occurred **2.** relating to chronology —**chron·o·log·i·cal·ly** *adv*

chron·o·log·i·cal age *n* somebody's real age, as opposed to the age suggested by his or her mental or physical development

chro·nol·o·gy /krə nóllәjee/ (*plural* **-gies**) *n* **1.** ORDER OF EVENTS the order in which events occur, or their arrangement according to this order **2.** LIST OF EVENTS a list or table of events arranged in order of occurrence **3.** STUDY OF ORDER IN TIME the study of the order in which things occur, or the science of determining this [Late 16C. < modern Latin *chronologia* "discourse of time" < Greek *khronos* "time"] —**chro·nol·o·gist** *n*

chron·o·met·ric /krònnə méttrik, krṓnə-/, **chron·o·met·ri·cal** /-méttrik'l/ *adj* relating to or designed for the accurate measurement of time —**chron·o·met·ri·cal·ly** *adv*

chro·nom·e·try /krə nómmətree/ *n* the study of the accurate measurement of time —**chro·nom·e·ter** *n*

chron·on /krṓ nòn/ *n* a unit of time equal to the time that it would take for a photon to cross the diameter of an electron, taken as approximately 10^{-24} seconds [< CHRONO- + -ON[1]]

chron·o·scope /krónnə skōp, krṓnə-/ *n* an electronic instrument that is designed to measure very small intervals of time with extreme precision —**chron·o·scop·ic** /krònnə skóppik, krṓnə-/ *adj*

chrys·a·lid /krísssəlid/ *adj* describes the stage between larva and adult in an insect and the protective covering formed at this time ■ *n* (*plural* **chrys·a·lids** or **chry·sal·i·des** /kri sállə deez/) INSECTS same as

chrysalis [Late 18C. < Latin *chrysa(l)lid-*, stem of *chrysa(l)lis* (see CHRYSALIS)]

chrys·a·lis /kríss'liss/ (*plural* **-lis·es**) *n* **1. INSECT BETWEEN LARVA AND ADULT** an insect at the stage of changing from larva to adult, during which it is inactive and encased in a hard cocoon **2. INSECT COCOON** the hard cocoon that protects a butterfly, moth, or other pupa during its change from larva to adult **3. THING DEVELOPING** anything in an early or intermediate stage of development (*literary*) [Early 17C. Via Latin *chrysal(l)is* < Greek *khrūsalis* < *khrūsos* "gold"; from the color or sheen of some pupae]

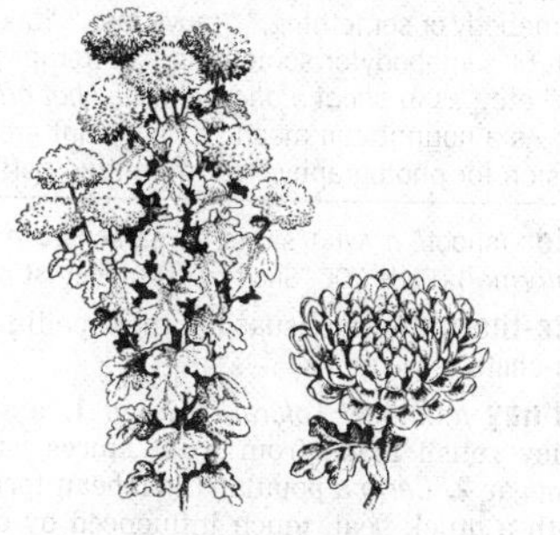

chrysanthemum

chry·san·the·mum /kri sánthəməm, -zán-/ *n* a perennial garden plant with many cultivated varieties. Flowers: brightly colored, many varied shapes, small densely clustered petals. Genus: *Chrysanthemum.* [Mid-16C. < Greek *khrūsanthemon* "gold flower"; from the color of the corn marigold]

Chry·se /krīssee/ lowland plain in the northern equatorial region of Mars where Viking 1 landed in 1976

chrys·el·e·phan·tine /kriss elə fán tīn, -teen/ *adj* describes classical Greek sculptures that are made of or overlaid with gold and ivory [Early 19C. < Greek *khrūselephantinos* < *khrūsos* "gold" + *elephas* "elephant, ivory"]

Chrys·ler /krísslər/, **Walter Percy** (1875–1940) US automobile manufacturer. He introduced the Chrysler automobile (1924) and founded the Chrysler Corporation (1925).

chryso- *prefix* gold, golden ○ *chrysotile* [< Greek *khrūsos* "gold" < Semitic]

chrys·o·ber·yl /krísso bèrrəl/ *n* a green, yellow, or brown variety of beryl. Use: gems. [Mid-17C. < Latin *chrysoberyllus* < Greek *khrūsos* "gold" + *bērullos* "beryl"]

chrys·o·mel·id /krísso méllid, -meélid/ *n* a small brightly colored leaf-eating beetle. Colorado potato beetles are chrysomelids. Family: Chrysomelidae. [Late 19C. < modern Latin *Chrysomelidae* (plural) < *Chrysomela* < Greek *khrūsomēlon* "golden apple"]

chrys·o·prase /krísso pràyz/ *n* a bright green semiprecious stone that is a variety of chalcedony. Use: gems. [13C. Via French < Greek *khrūsoprasos* "golden leek"]

Chry·sos·tom /kríssəstəm/, **John, St.** (349?–407) Syrian theologian and orator. He was bishop of Constantinople and a church father of both the Roman Catholic and the Eastern Orthodox traditions.

chrys·o·tile /krísso tīl/ *n* a green, gray, or white fibrous variety of the mineral serpentine. Use: formerly in heat-resistant materials. [Mid-19C. < CHRYSO- + Greek *tilos* "fiber" < *tillein* "to pluck"]

chthon·ic /thónnik/, **chtho·ni·an** /thónee ən/ *adj* relating to the underworld as described in Greek mythology [Late 19C. < Greek *khthōn* "earth"]

chub /chub/ (*plural* **chubs** or *same*) *n* a fish with a thick rounded body found in fresh water. Family: Cyprinidae. [15C. Origin ?]

chub·by /chúbbee/ (**-bi·er, -bi·est**) *adj* pleasantly or charmingly plump, especially in the way that healthy babies and toddlers often are —**chub·bi·ly** *adv* —**chub·bi·ness** *n*

chuck[1] /chuk/ *vt* (**chucked, chuck·ing, chucks**) **1. THROW SOMETHING CARELESSLY** to throw something, especially in a careless or casual way (*informal*) **2. DISCARD SOMETHING** to get rid of something unwanted (*informal*) **3. EJECT SOMEBODY** to remove somebody from a place or a position (*informal*) **4. ABANDON SOMETHING** to give something up, especially a job (*informal*) **5. TICKLE SOMEBODY UNDER CHIN** to give somebody an affectionate pat or tickle under the chin ■ *n* **1. CARELESS THROW** a throw, especially a careless or casual one (*informal*) **2. AFFECTIONATE TICKLE UNDER CHIN** an affectionate pat or tickle under somebody's chin [Early 16C. Origin ?]

SYNONYMS See *throw.*

chuck[2] /chuk/ *n* **1.** a clamping device with three or four adjustable jaws. Use: to hold a piece of woodwork or metalwork in a lathe or a bit in a drill. **2.** a cut of beef that extends from the neck to the shoulder blade **3.** *US regional, Can* same as **food** (sense 2) (*informal*) [Late 17C Variant of CHOCK]

chuck[3] /chuk/ *vi* (**chucked, chuck·ing, chucks**), *n* same as **cluck** *v* (sense 1) [14C. An imitation of the sound] —**chuck** *n*

chuck-a-luck *n* a game in which players bet on the possible combinations of three dice when thrown

chuck·hole /chúk hōl/ *n* *Midwest* ROADS same as **pothole** (sense 1) [Mid-19C. < CHUCK[1]]

chuck·le /chúk'l/ *vti* (**-led, -ling, -les**) to laugh quietly or to yourself, or say something with a quiet laugh ■ *n* a quiet or inward laugh [Late 16C. < CHUCK[3]] —**chuck·ler** *n* —**chuck·ling·ly** *adv*

chuck wag·on *n* a vehicle carrying food and cooking supplies, originally a horse-drawn wagon for transients such as cowboys (*informal*) [Origin ?]

chuck·wal·la /chúk wòllə/ (*plural* **-las** or *same*) *n* a large lizard with a dark body and a blunt yellow tail. Native to: deserts of southwestern United States and Mexico. Latin name: *Sauromalus obesus.* [Late 19C. Via Mexican Spanish *chachuala* < Cahuilla *tcáxxwal*]

chuck-will's-wid·ow *n* a large bird of the nightjar family with mottled brown markings. Native to: central and southern United States. Latin name: *Caprimulgus carolinensis.* [Late 18C. An imitation of its call]

chud·dar *n* ISLAM another spelling of **chador**

chu·fa /choófə/ *n* a plant of the sedge family with an edible tuber that looks like a nut. Native to: Africa. Latin name: *Cyperus esculentus.* [Mid-19C. < Spanish, "fluff, nonsense"]

chuffed /chuft/ *adj* *UK* very pleased or satisfied (*informal*) [Mid-20C. < English dialect *chuff* "plump, chubby, happy," origin ?]

chug[1] /chug/ *vi* (**chugged, chug·ging, chugs**) **1. MAKE REPEATED THUDDING SOUND** to make a repetitive thudding sound like that of a small engine **2. MOVE WITH CHUGGING SOUND** to move along slowly with a chugging sound under the power of an engine **3. CONTINUE IN STEADY FASHION** to continue steadily doing the usual things (*informal*) ■ *n* **CHUGGING NOISE** the chugging noise that an engine makes [Mid-19C. An imitation of the sound]

chug[2] /chug/ (**chugged, chug·ging, chugs**) *vt* to drink something, especially beer, quickly and without pausing (*slang*) [Late 20C. An imitation of the sound of gulping]

Chu·gach Moun·tains /choó gach-/ mountain range in southern Alaska, stretching 300 mi./480 km from St. Elias Mountains in the east to Cook Inlet in the west. The highest peak is Mount Marcus Baker, 13,176 ft./4,016 m.

chug·a·lug /chúggə lùg/ (*slang*) *vt* (**-lugged, -lug·ging, -lugs**) same as **chug[2]** ■ *adv* gulping, without pause [Mid-20C. An imitation of the sound of somebody swallowing]

chu·kar /chúkər/ *n* a grayish brown partridge with red legs and beak, introduced into the western United States as a game bird. Native to: South Asia. Latin name: *Alectoris chukar.* [Early 19C. < Hindi *cakor,* probably an imitation of its cry]

Chuk·chi /choókchee/ (*plural same* or **-chis**), **Chuk·chee** (*plural same* or **-chees**) *n* **1.** a member of an indigenous people of northeastern Siberia. The Chukchi were the first to breed huskies as working dogs. **2.** a language spoken in northeastern Siberia, belonging to a small isolated language family. Native speakers: 12,000. [Early 18C. < Russian] —**Chuk·chi** *adj*

Chuk·chi Sea /choókchee-/ part of the Arctic Ocean, situated north of the Bering Strait between Asia and North America

chuk·ka /chúkə/, **chuk·ka boot** *n* a casual ankle-high lace-up boot, typically made of suede [Variant of CHUKKER]

chuk·ker /chúkər/, **chuk·kar** *n* any of the six periods of continuous play in a polo match, each lasting approximately 7.5 minutes [Late 19C. < Hindi *cak(k)ar* "circular course" < Indo-European]

Chu·la·long·korn /choòlə láwng kàwrn/, **Rama V** (1853–1910) Siamese monarch who ruled from 1868 until 1910, and was noted for his modernization programs

Chu·la Vis·ta /choòlə vístə/ city in southwestern California, a southern suburb of San Diego, close to the US-Mexico border. Population: 193,919 (2002 estimate).

chum[1] /chum/ *n* **1. FRIEND** a close friend (*informal*) **2. WAY OF ADDRESSING MAN** used as a term of address for a man (*dated informal*) ■ *v* (**chummed, chum·ming, chums**) **1.** *vi* **BE FRIENDS** to be friends with somebody, or behave in a friendly way toward somebody **2.** *vi* **SHARE ROOM WITH SOMEBODY** to share a room with somebody, e.g., in a school dormitory (*dated*) **3.** *vt regional, Scotland* **GO WITH SOMEBODY** to accompany somebody somewhere [Late 17C. Probably shortening of *chamber-fellow*]

chum[2] /chum/ *n* **1. FISH BAIT** an angler's bait, especially chopped fish, scattered on the water **2. CHEAP TRINKETS** inexpensive trinkets such as cuff links and pins bearing the US presidential seal (*slang*) ■ *vti* (**chummed, chum·ming, chums**) **USE FISH CHUM** to fish using chum on the water [Mid-19C. Origin ?]

chum[3] /chum/ (*plural* **chums** or *same*) *n* FISH same as **chum salmon** [Early 20C. < Chinook Jargon *tzum (samun)* "spotted (salmon)"]

Chu·mash /choó màsh/ (*plural same* or **-mash·es**) *n* a member of a Native North American people who once lived in coastal southwestern California, and who now live in the Santa Barbara area —**Chu·mash** *adj*

chum·my /chúmmee/ (**-mi·er, -mi·est**) *adj* friendly or on close terms (*informal*) [Late 19C. < CHUM[1]] —**chum·mi·ly** *adv* —**chum·mi·ness** *n*

chump[1] /chump/ *n* somebody who is unwise or easily deceived (*informal*) [Early 18C. Origin ?]

chump[2] /chump/ *vti, n* same as **chomp**

chump change *n* an insignificant amount of money (*slang*)

chum salm·on *n* a salmon with wavy vertical green streaks and blotches. Native to: northern Pacific waters. Latin name: *Oncorhynchus keta.* [< CHUM[3]]

Chung·king, Ch'ung-ch'ing ➧ Chongqing

chunk[1] /chungk/ *n* **1.** a thick squarish piece of something, e.g., bread, wood, or meat **2.** a large amount or part of something [Late 17C. Alteration of CHUCK[2]]

chunk[2] /chungk/ *vi* (**chun·ked, chunk·ing, chunks**), *n* same as **clunk** *n* (sense 1) ■ *vti* (**chun·ked, chunk·ing, chunks**) same as **clunk** *v* [Late 19C. An imitation of the sound]

chunk·float·er /chúngk flōtər/ *n* *regional* a storm whose violent winds or heavy rains spread debris

REGIONAL NOTE See *trashmover.*

chunk·y /chúngkee/ (**-i·er, -i·est**) *adj* **1. WITH LUMPS** containing lumps or small pieces **2. SQUARE AND SOLID** solid and square-shaped ○ *a chunky table* **3. SHORT AND BROAD** short, broad, and sometimes overweight (*informal*) —**chunk·i·ly** *adv* —**chunk·i·ness** *n*

Chun·nel /chúnn'l/ *n* same as **Channel Tunnel** (*informal*) [Early 20C. Blend of CHANNEL[1] + TUNNEL]

chun·ni /chúnnee/ (*plural* **-nis**) *n S Asia* CLOTHING same as **dupatta** [< Punjabi]

chup /chup/ *interj S Asia* used to tell somebody to be quiet [< Hindi *cuprao*]

chup·pah *n* JUDAISM another spelling of **huppah**

church /church/ *n* **1. RELIGIOUS BUILDING** a building for public worship, especially in the Christian religion **2.** *also* **Church RELIGION'S FOLLOWERS AS GROUP** all the followers of a religion, especially the Christian religion, considered collectively **3. RELIGIOUS SERVICE** a religious service that takes place in a church ○ *go to church* **4. CLERGY** the clergy as distinct from lay people **5.** *also* **Church RELIGIOUS AUTHORITY** religious authority as opposed to the authority of the state **6.** *also* **Church BRANCH OF CHRISTIAN RELIGION** a denomination or branch of the Christian religion ■ *vt* **(churched, church·ing, church·es)** CHR **GIVE SOMEBODY CHURCH BLESSING** to give a blessing in church to somebody, especially a woman who has recently given birth (*often passive*) [Old English *cir(i)ce*, via Germanic < Greek *kuriakon dōma* "house of the lord" < *kurios* "lord"] ◇ **right church, wrong pew** used to indicate that somebody is correct in a general way, but wrong in a particular way

Church /church/, **Frederick Edwin** (1826–1900) US painter. A leader of the Hudson River school, he painted landscapes such as *Niagara Falls* (1857).

church fa·ther *n* a Christian writer of the pre-8th century group of scholars who established the doctrines and practices of Christianity in their work (*usually used in the plural*)

church·go·er /chúrch gṑ ər/ *n* an attender of a church service or church services —**church·go·ing** *n, adj*

Chur·chill /chúrchil/ **1.** seaport in northeastern Manitoba, Canada, situated on Hudson Bay at the mouth of the Churchill River. Population: 1,089 (1996). **2.** river that flows across south-central Labrador, Newfoundland, Canada, from Ashuanipi Lake, emptying into Lake Melville. The river provides hydroelectric power. Length: 208 mi./335 km. **3.** river that flows through numerous lakes from Lac la Loche in Saskatchewan through Manitoba, into Hudson Bay. Length: 1,000 mi./1,600 km.

Chur·chill, Charles (1731–64) British poet. His satirical verse includes *The Rosciad* (1761).

> "Fashion—a word which knaves and fools may use,/Their knavery and folly to excuse."
> [Charles Churchill, *The Rosciad*; 1761]

Sir Winston Churchill

Chur·chill, Sir Winston (1874–1965) British politician and writer. As prime minister (1940–45, 1951–55) he led Britain through World War II. He wrote *The Second World War* (1948–53) and won the Nobel Prize in literature (1953). Full name **Churchill, Sir Winston Leonard Spencer**. See table at **prime minister** —**Chur·chil·lian** /chur chílyən/ *adj*

> "We shall fight in France, we shall fight on the seas and oceans, we shall fight…in the air, we shall defend our island, whatever the cost may be, we shall fight on the beaches, we shall fight on the landing grounds, we shall fight in the fields and in the streets, we shall fight in the hills; we shall never surrender."
> [Sir Winston Churchill, *Speech to the British Parliament*; June 4, 1940]

Chur·chill Falls falls on the Churchill River, western Labrador, Newfoundland, Canada, situated 225 mi./362 km from Lake Melville. Height: 300 ft./90 m.

church key *n* a metal tool with a bottle opener at one end and a sharp-pointed triangular head for opening cans at the other end

church·ly /chúrchlee/ *adj* similar to, suitable for, or typical of a church —**church·li·ness** *n*

church·man /chúrchmən/ (*plural* **-men** /-mən/) *n* **1.** a man who is a member of the clergy **2.** a man who is a practicing member of a church —**church·man·ship** *n*

church mode *n* any of a group of eight scales used for church music in the Middle Ages, e.g., the Dorian, Phrygian, or Lydian mode

Church of Christ, Sci·en·tist *n* the official name of the Christian Science Church

Church of Eng·land *n* the church that is the established church in England, governed by bishops and with the reigning monarch as its titular head

Church of Je·sus Christ of Lat·ter-Day Saints *n* a church founded by Joseph Smith in 1830, based on teachings in the Book of Mormon, and centered in Salt Lake City, Utah

Church of Rome *n* CHR same as **Roman Catholic Church**

Church of the Breth·ren *n* a conservative Protestant church in the United States that is active mainly in the Midwest and the Middle Atlantic states

church·per·son /chúrch pùrss'n/ (*plural* **-peo·ple** /-peèp'l/ *or* **-per·sons**) *n* **1.** somebody who is a member of the clergy **2.** somebody who is a practicing member of a church

church school *n* a private school affiliated with a church that provides children with a general education as well as religious instruction

Church Sla·von·ic *n, adj* LANG same as **Old Church Slavonic**

church·war·den /chúrch wàwrd'n/ *n* **1.** a lay person who manages secular matters in an Anglican church **2.** a long-stemmed clay tobacco pipe

church·wom·an /chúrch wŏŏmən/ (*plural* **-wom·en** /-wìmmin/) *n* **1.** a woman who is a member of the clergy **2.** a woman who is a practicing member of a church

church·y /chúrchee/ (**-i·er, -i·est**) *adj* **1.** zealously, even intolerantly, religious **2.** resembling or suggesting a church

church·yard /chúrch yaàrd/ *n* an area surrounding a church that is sometimes used as a graveyard

chur·i·dars /chŏŏrə daàrz/ *npl* long close-fitting pants worn by both men and women in or from northern parts of South Asia [< Hindi]

churl /churl/ *n* somebody regarded as having bad manners [Old English *ceorl* "man, freeman of the lowest rank" < Germanic]

churl·ish /chúrlish/ *adj* **1.** characteristic of somebody with bad manners **2.** surly, sullen, or miserly —**churl·ish·ly** *adv* —**churl·ish·ness** *n*

churn /churn/ *n* **BUTTER MAKER** a container or device in which milk or cream is stirred vigorously to produce butter ■ *v* **(churned, churn·ing, churns) 1.** *vt* **STIR MILK OR CREAM** to stir or beat milk or cream vigorously to make butter **2.** *vt* **MAKE BUTTER** to make butter by beating milk or cream **3.** *vti* **SPLASH VIOLENTLY** to move violently, or cause a liquid or soft solid to move violently **4.** *vi* **FEEL UNSETTLED** to move unpleasantly, as if in a churn ○ *My stomach was churning.* **5.** *vt* FIN **TRADE STOCKS FREQUENTLY FOR COMMISSION** to buy and sell stocks and bonds on a frequent basis in order to earn brokerage commissions [Old English *cyrin* < Germanic] —**churn·er** *n*

churn out *vt* to produce or issue something quickly or regularly and in large quantities

churr /chur/ **(churred, churr·ing, churrs), chirr (chirred, chirr·ing, chirrs)** *vi* to make the high-pitched vibrating sound typical of some birds such as the nightjar, and some insects such as the cicada [Mid-16C. An imitation of the sound] —**churr** *n*

Chur·ri·gue·ra /chŏŏrri gáyrə/, **José Benito** (1665–1725) Spanish architect. His high baroque style is characterized by spiral pillars and elaborate ornamentation. —**Chur·ri·gue·resque** /chŏŏrrigə résk/ *adj*

chur·ro /chŏŏrō/ (*plural* **-ros**) *n Hispanic* a thick fritter made from a coil of dough [Mid-20C. < Spanish]

chute[1] /shoot/ *n* **1. SLOPE TO DROP THINGS DOWN** an inclined channel or passage that something can slide down **2.** LEISURE **CHILDREN'S SLIDE** a children's slide in a park or swimming pool **3. SNOW-COVERED SLOPE** a snow- or ice-covered slope or channel for sports such as tobogganing or bobsledding **4. SLOPE OR DROP ON WATERCOURSE** a waterfall, rapids, or steep descent in a river or stream **5.** AGRIC **SLOPING PASSAGE FOR ANIMALS** a narrow passageway through which animals are driven to be branded, sheared, loaded, dipped, or sprayed ■ *vt* **(chuted, chut·ing, chutes) DROP SOMETHING DOWN CHUTE** to convey something such as coal or dirty laundry down a chute [Early 19C. < French, "fall" < Latin *cadere* "to fall"]

SPELLCHECK chute or **shoot**? Do not confuse the spelling of ***chute*** and ***shoot***, which sound similar. ***Chute*** is chiefly used as a noun, denoting a slope to slide or drop things down; it is occasionally used as a verb, meaning "send down a chute." ***Chute*** is also a short form of *parachute*. The word ***shoot*** is a verb or noun with a wide range of meanings and uses. As a verb it can mean "fire a weapon at somebody or something," "move fast," "take a photograph of somebody or something," "attempt to score a goal," etc., as in *shoot a pheasant, he shot off down the road*. As a noun it can mean "a new plant growth," "an occasion for photography," or "a hunting party."

---

chute[2] /shoot/ *n* AVIAT same as **parachute** *n* (sense 1) (*informal*) [Early 20C. Shortening] —**chut·ist** *n*

chute-the-chute *n* LEISURE another spelling of **shoot-the-chute**

chut·ney /chútnee/ (*plural* **-neys**) *n* **1.** a sweet and spicy relish made from fruit, spices, sugar, and vinegar **2.** *Carib* a popular Caribbean form of song with a quick beat, much influenced by calypso in rhythm and choice of subjects [Early 19C. < Hindi *caṭnī*]

chutz·pah /hŏŏtspə, k̲h̲ŏŏts-/, **hutz·pah, chutz·pa** *n* (*informal*) **1.** boldness coupled with supreme self-confidence **2.** impudent rudeness or lack of respect [Late 19C. Via Yiddish < Aramaic *ḥuṣpā*]

Chu·vash /chŏŏ vaàsh, choo vaàsh/ *n* a Turkic language spoken west of the Urals in central Russia. Native speakers: 2 million. [Via Russian < Chuvash *čăvaš*] —**Chu·vash** *adj*

chyle /kīl/ *n* a milky fluid consisting of lymph and emulsified fat that forms in the small intestine during digestion [15C. Via late Latin < Greek *khūlos* "animal or plant juice"] —**chy·la·ceous** /kī láyshəss/ *adj* —**chy·lous** *adj*

chy·lo·mi·cron /kīlə mī́ kròn/ *n* a microscopic particle, containing fats, cholesterol, phospholipids, and protein, formed in the small intestine and absorbed into the blood during digestion

chyme /kīm/ *n* a thick fluid mass of partially digested food and gastric secretions passed from the stomach to the small intestine [Early 17C. Via late Latin < Greek *khūmos* "animal or plant juice" < Indo-European] —**chy·mous** *adj*

chy·mo·pa·pa·in /kīmō pə páy in, -pī̀ in/ *n* an enzyme found in papayas that helps digest proteins. Use: medicines, meat tenderizer.

chy·mo·sin /kīməssin/ *n* BIOCHEM same as **rennin** [< CHYME + -OSE[2]]

chy·mo·tryp·sin /kīmō trípsin/ *n* a protein-digesting enzyme in pancreatic juice [Mid-20C. < CHYME] —**chy·mo·tryp·tic** *adj*

chy·mo·tryp·sin·o·gen /kīmō trip sínnəjən/ *n* the inactive form of chymotrypsin that is converted into chymotrypsin by the enzyme trypsin

chy·pre /sheéprə/ *n* perfume made from sandalwood [Late 19C. < French, "Cyprus"]

ci *abbr* **1.** ONLINE Côte d'Ivoire (*used in Internet addresses*) See table at **domain name 2.** MEASURE cubic inch

Ci[1] *abbr* METEOROL cirrus

Ci[2] *symbol* MEASURE, PHYS curie

CI *abbr* **1.** Cayman Islands **2.** INSUR certificate of insurance **3.** FREIGHT cost and insurance

CIA *n* a federal bureau responsible for gathering foreign intelligence and conducting counter-intelligence activities. Full form **Central Intelligence Agency**

CIAA *abbr* Central Intercollegiate Athletic Association

cia·bat·ta /chə báttə/ *n* a flat white Italian bread made with olive oil [Late 20C. < Italian, "slipper"; from the shape of the loaf]

ciao /chow/ *interj* used to say hello or goodbye (*informal*) [Early 20C. < Italian, literally "(I am your) slave"]

Ciar·di /chaárdee/, **John** (1916–86) US poet and critic. In addition to poems and translations, he wrote accessible critical works such as *How Does a Poem Mean?* (1950).

"Modern art is what happens when painters stop looking at girls and persuade themselves that they have a better idea."
[Attributed to John Ciardi]

CIB *abbr UK* **1.** BANKING Chartered Institute of Bankers **2.** POLICE Criminal Investigation Branch

ci·bo·ri·um /si báwree əm/ (*plural* **-ri·a** /-ree ə/) *n* **1.** a canopy that stands on four pillars over the altar in some Christian churches **2.** a small container with a lid, used to hold the consecrated wafers for Communion [Mid-16C. Via medieval Latin < Greek *kibōrion* "seed vessel of a water lily"]

CIC *abbr* MIL Counterintelligence Corps

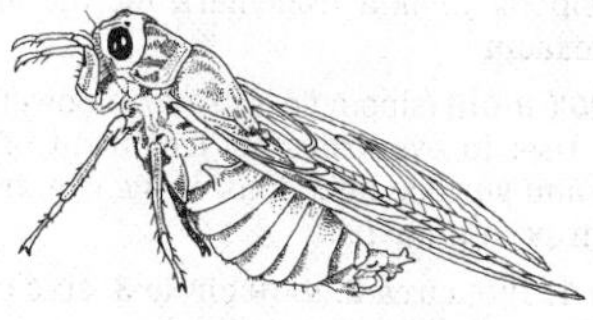

cicada

ci·ca·da /si káydə, -kaádə/ (*plural* **-das** or **-dae** /-deé/) *n* a large winged insect that lives in trees and tall grass, the male of which makes a shrill sound. Family: Cicadidae. [15C. < Latin]

ci·ca·da kill·er *n* a large hunting wasp that feeds on adult cicadas. Latin name: *Sphecius speciosus*.

ci·ca·la /si kaálə/ (*plural* **-las** or **-le** /-lay/) *n* INSECTS another spelling of **cicada** [Late 18C. Directly or via Italian < Latin]

cic·a·trix /síkətriks/ (*plural* **cic·a·tri·ces** /sìkə trī́ seez/) *n* **1.** MED same as **scar**[1] *n* (sense 1) (*technical*) **2.** a scar left on a stem where a leaf used to be attached [Mid-17C. < Latin, "scar"] —**cic·a·tri·cial** /sìkə trísh'l/ *adj* —**ci·cat·ri·cose** /si káttri kòss/ *adj*

cic·a·trize /síkə trīz/ (**-trized, -triz·ing, -triz·es**) *vti* to heal and form a scar, or cause a wound to heal and form a scar (*technical*) [15C. < French *cicatriser* < *cicatrice* "scar"] —**cic·a·tri·za·tion** /sìkətri záysh'n/ *n*

cic·e·ly /síssəlee/ *n* PLANTS same as **sweet cicely** [Late 16C. < Latin *seselis*, assimilated to the woman's name *Cicely*]

cic·e·ro /síssə rō/ *n* a size of printed character slightly larger than the pica [< its first use (1458) for an edition of the works of CICERO]

Cic·e·ro /síssə rō/ town in northeastern Illinois; a southwestern suburb of Chicago. Population: 84,254 (2002 estimate).

Cic·e·ro, Marcus Tullius (106–43 B.C.) Roman philosopher, writer, and politician. He was Rome's greatest orator during a long political career. His letters and essays are known for their rich prose style. —**Cic·e·ro·ni·an** /sìssə rṓnee ən/ *adj*

"When you have no basis for an argument, abuse the plaintiff."
[Marcus Tullius Cicero, *Pro Flacco*; 1st century B.C.]

cic·e·ro·ne /sìssə rṓnee, chìchə-/ (*plural* **-nes** or **-ni** /-nee/) *n* a guide for tourists [Early 18C. < Italian, after CICERO; from a guide's knowledge and eloquence]

cich·lid /síklid/ *n* a tropical freshwater fish with spiny fins, popular as an aquarium fish. Family: Cichlidae. [Late 19C. < modern Latin *Cichlidae* < Greek *kikhlē*, a kind of fish]

Cid /sid/, **El** (1040?–99) Spanish military leader. Legend obscures the true nature of "The Lord Champion" who fought both for and against Spain's Moorish rulers, and was virtual dictator of Valencia from 1094 to 1099. Born **Vivar, Rodriguez Díaz de**

CID[1] *n* the detective branch of the UK police force. Full form **Criminal Investigation Department**

CID[2] *abbr* ONLINE (*used in e-mails or text messages*) consider it done

-cide *suffix* **1.** killer ○ *fungicide* **2.** killing ○ *tyrannicide* [Via French < Latin *-cida* "killer," *-cidium* "killing" < *caedere* "to kill"] —**-cidal** *suffix*

ci·der /sídər/ *n* **1.** a nonalcoholic drink made from freshly pressed apples **2.** *UK* same as **hard cider** [13C. Via Old French *sidre* < Hebrew *šēkār* "alcoholic drink"]

ci·der vin·e·gar *n* a light vinegar made from cider

ci-de·vant /see də vaáN/ *adj, adv* used to indicate that what follows was somebody's former name, office, or title (*formal*) [Early 18C. < French, "before this"]

~~**cieling**~~ incorrect spelling of **ceiling**

Cien·fue·gos /syen fwáy gōss/ city and capital of Cienfuegos Province, central Cuba, situated on Cienfuegos Bay. Population: 132,000 (1996).

C.I.F., c.i.f. *abbr* **1.** central information file **2.** cost, insurance, and freight

c.i.f.c.i. *abbr* FREIGHT cost, insurance, freight, commission, and interest (*used in quotes to indicate what is included in the price*)

cig /sig/ *n* same as **cigarette** (*informal*) [Late 19C. Shortening]

ci·gar /si gaár/ *n* a cylindrical roll of tobacco leaves for smoking, with thin brown paper or a single tobacco leaf as an outer covering [Early 18C. Directly or via French *cigare* < Spanish *cigarro*, probably < Mayan *sik'ar* "smoking"] ◇ **close but no cigar** the answer, response, or result is not good enough (*informal*)

~~**cigaret**~~ incorrect spelling of **cigarette**

cig·a·rette /síggə rèt, sìggə rét/, **cig·a·ret** *n* **1.** a cylindrical roll of shredded tobacco leaves for smoking, with an outer covering of thin, usually white, paper **2.** a roll of shredded leaves of any kind for smoking, e.g., marijuana leaves or leaves of herbs ○ *a marijuana cigarette* [Mid-19C. < French, "small cigar" < *cigare* (see CIGAR)]

cig·a·rette light·er *n* same as **lighter**[1] (sense 1)

cig·a·rette pants *npl* women's pants with straight close-fitting legs

cig·a·rette pa·per *n* a sheet of thin paper with gum on one edge, used with loose tobacco to roll cigarettes

cig·a·ril·lo /sìggə rílló/ (*plural* **-los**) *n* a slender cigar about the same size as a cigarette [Mid-19C. < Spanish, "small cigar" < *cigarro* (see CIGAR)]

ci·gar-store In·di·an *n* a wooden figure of a Native North American man holding a bunch of cigars in his hands, formerly used as a sign indicating that a store sold tobacco products

~~**cigerette**~~ incorrect spelling of **cigarette**

~~**ciggarette**~~ incorrect spelling of **cigarette**

cig·gy /síggee/ (*plural* **-gies**) *n* same as **cigarette** (*informal*) [Mid-20C. Shortening and alteration]

ci·lan·tro /si laántrō, -lántrō/ *n* coriander leaves. Use: spice in cooking. [Early 20C. Via Spanish < Latin *coriandrum* "coriander"]

cil·i·a MICROBIOL plural of **cilium**

cil·i·ar·y /síllee èrree/ *adj* **1.** describes the short threads (**cilia**) projecting from some cells and the beating movement they make **2.** describes the tissue and muscle that surrounds the lens of the eye [Late 17C. < CILIUM]

cil·i·ar·y bod·y *n* the ring-shaped part at the front of the eye that connects the pigmented layer (**choroid**) of the eyeball with the iris diaphragm. It also contains the ciliary muscle, which alters the curvature of the lens.

cil·i·ate /síllee àyt, -ət/ *n* a simple microscopic organism with projecting threads that thrash to help it to move along. Phylum: Ciliophora. [Mid-18C. < CILIUM] —**cil·i·ate** *adj* —**cil·i·a·ted** /-àytəd/ *adj*

cil·ice /sílliss/ *n* **1.** TEXTILES same as **haircloth** **2.** a garment made of haircloth [Late 16C. Via French < Greek *Kilikia* "Cilicia," district of Anatolia; because made of goats' hair from Cilicia]

~~**cilinder**~~ incorrect spelling of **cylinder**

cil·i·um /síllee əm/ (*plural* **-i·a** /-ee ə/) *n* **1.** a tiny projecting thread, found with many others on a cell or microscopic organism, that beats rhythmically to aid the movement of a fluid past the cell or movement of the organism through liquid **2.** MED same as **eyelash** (*technical*) [Early 18C. < Latin, "eyelash"]

Cim·ar·ron /símmə rṑn/ river rising in northeastern New Mexico and flowing across Kansas and Oklahoma to the Arkansas River near Tulsa. Length: 600 mi./970 km.

cim·bal·om /símbələm, tsímb-/ *n* a musical instrument resembling a hammered dulcimer, used especially in Hungarian folk music [Late 19C. Via Hungarian < Italian *cimbalo* "dulcimer"]

Cim·bri /sím brī, kímbree/ *npl* a Germanic people who lived in parts of Jutland and the Rhine valley during the second century B.C. They began to spread southward, but were routed by the Romans in 101 B.C. [< Latin]

ci·met·i·dine /sī méttə deen/ *n* a drug that decreases production of stomach acid. Use: peptic ulcer treatment. [Late 20C. < CYANO- + METHYL + -IDINE]

ci·mex /sí mèks/ (*plural* **cim·i·ces** /sími seez/) *n* a bedbug or related insect that feeds on birds, humans, and other mammals. Genus: *Cimex*. [Late 16C. < Latin, "bedbug"]

Cim·me·ri·an /sə meéree ən/ *adj* dark and gloomy (*literary*) ■ *n* in Greek mythology, a member of a people who lived in a land of perpetual darkness [Late 16C. < Latin *Cimmerius* < Greek *Kimmerios*]

~~**cinamon**~~ incorrect spelling of **cinnamon**

CINC, C in C *abbr* MIL Commander in Chief

cinch /sinch/ *n* **1.** SOMETHING EASILY DONE something that can be done or achieved with very little effort (*informal*) **2.** SOMETHING CERTAIN something that is absolutely certain to happen (*informal*) **3.** RIDING STRONG GIRTH a girth for a saddle, consisting of a thick strap secured by passing the end through two metal rings **4.** FIRM GRIP a firm grip (*archaic*) ■ *vt* (**cinched, cinch·ing, cinch·es**) **1.** TIGHTEN to tighten something by constricting it **2.** RIDING PUT GIRTH ON HORSE to put a cinch on a horse **3.** GRASP SOMETHING AROUND MIDDLE to grasp something around the middle, as a belt does (*informal*) **4.** ASSURE SOMETHING to make certain of something (*informal*) [Mid-19C. < Spanish *cinche* "girth" < Latin *cingere* "gird"]

cinch belt *n* a waist belt fashionable for women in the 1950s that was worn tight to make the waist appear smaller

cinch bug *n* INSECTS same as **chinch**

cin·cho·na /sing kṓnə, sin chṓnə/ *n* **1.** *also* **cin·cho·na bark** the dried bark of a South American tree. Use: source of quinine and some other drugs. **2.** an evergreen tree or bush that produces cinchona. Native to: South America. Genus: *Cinchona*. [Mid-18C. < modern Latin, after the Countess of *Chinchón* (1576–1641), vicereine of Peru] —**cin·chon·ic** /sing kónnik, sin chónnik/ *adj*

cin·cho·nine /síngkə neen, sínchə-/ *n* a colorless crystalline solid. Source: cinchona bark. Use: treatment of malaria. Formula: $C_{19}H_{22}N_{20}$.

cin·cho·nism /síngkə nìzzəm, sínchə-/ *n* a condition resulting from the excessive use of quinine and other drugs derived from cinchona bark. The symptoms are headache, ringing in the ears, temporary deafness, and dizziness.

Cin·cin·na·ti /sìnssə náttee, -náttə/ city in southwestern Ohio on the Ohio-Kentucky border, on the Ohio River, southwest of Dayton. Population: 323,885 (2002 estimate).

Cin·cin·na·tus /sìnssə náttəss/, **Lucius Quinctius** (519?–430 B.C.) Roman general and politician. Considered a model of republican Roman values, he was twice appointed dictator when Rome was under attack. After defeating the enemy, he refused all honors and retired to his farm.

Cin·co de May·o /seéngkō də maáyō/ *n Hispanic* a celebration among Mexican communities in Mexico and North America marking the Mexican defeat of French troops at the Battle of Puebla in 1862. Date: May 5. [< Spanish, "5th of May"]

cinc·ture /síngkchər/ *n* a girdle or belt, especially a cord or sash tied around a priest's, monk's, or nun's habit [Late 16C. < Latin *cinctura* "girdle" < *cingere* "gird"]

cin·der /síndər/ *n* **BURNED WOOD OR FUEL** a small piece of charred wood or coal, especially one that continues to glow ■ **cin·ders** *npl* **1. ASHES** the ashes that remain after a fire has burned out **2.** INDUST **SLAG** waste material produced by smelting **3.** GEOL **FRAGMENTS OF SOLIDIFIED LAVA** loose fragments of porous solidified lava that is ejected from a volcano and builds up around the crater [Old English *sinder* "slag" < Germanic] —**cin·der·y** *adj*

cin·der block *n* a light, usually hollow, block made from coal ashes mixed with cement that is used in building and construction work

Cin·der·el·la /síndə réllə/ *n* an object of undeserved neglect ■ *adj* achieving sudden recognition or success, or relating to somebody or something achieving this [Mid-19C. After the fairy-tale character *Cinderella*, who is neglected by her stepmother and sisters but enabled by her fairy godmother to attend a ball and meet a prince]

cine- *prefix* film, motion picture ○ *cinephile* [< CINEMA]

cin·e·aste /sínnee àst/ *n* **1.** a fan of movies and moviemaking **2.** a maker of movies [Early 20C. < French < *ciné*, shortening of *cinématographe* (see CINEMA)]

cin·e cam·er·a /sínnee-/ *n UK* same as **movie camera** [Shortening of *cinematographic*]

cin·e film *n UK* same as **movie film** [Shortening of *cinematographic*]

cin·e·ma /sínnəmə/ *n* **1. MOVIES COLLECTIVELY** movies considered collectively (*formal*) **2.** *UK* **MOVIE INDUSTRY** the movie industry, or the business of making movies **3. MOVIE THEATER** a movie theater [Early 20C. < French *cinéma*, shortening of *cinématographe*, literally "movement writing" < Greek *kinēma* "movement"]

cin·e·ma·go·er /sínnəmə gṑ ər/ *n UK* same as **moviegoer**

cin·e·mat·ic /sìnnə máttik/ *adj* **1.** typical of the style in which movies are made **2.** relating to movies or moviemaking —**cin·e·mat·i·cal·ly** *adv*

cin·e·ma·tize /sínnəmə tīz/ (**-tized, -tiz·ing, -tiz·es**) *vt* to adapt a play, novel, or other work for the cinema

cin·e·ma·tog·ra·phy /sìnnəmə tóggrəfee/ *n* the art or technique of photographing and lighting motion pictures —**cin·e·ma·tog·ra·pher** *n* —**cin·e·mat·o·graph·ic** /sìnnə matə gráffik/ *adj* —**cin·e·mat·o·graph·i·cal·ly** *adv*

ci·né·ma vé·ri·té /sìnnəmə verri táy, see nay maà verree táy/ *n* a style of filmmaking characterized by a search for an authentic documentary feel. The term was first applied to a series of French documentary films in the 1960s. [Mid-20C. < French, "cinema of truth"]

cin·e·ole /sínnee ṑl/, **cin·e·ol** *n* CHEM same as **eucalyptol** [Late 19C. Reversal of modern Latin *oleum cinae* "wormseed oil"]

cin·e·phile /sínnə fīl/ *n* MOVIES same as **cineaste** (sense 1)

cin·e·rar·i·a /sìnnə rérree ə/ *n* a plant cultivated for its mass of blue, purple, or red flowers resembling daisies. Native to: Canary Islands. Latin name: *Senecio hybridus*. [Late 16C. < modern Latin < Latin *ciner-* "ashes"; from the fluffy gray leaves of the plant originally called this]

cin·e·rar·i·um /sìnnə rérree əm/ (*plural* **-i·a** /-ee ə/) *n* a place where the ashes of a corpse are stored [Mid-18C. < late Latin < Latin *ciner-* "ashes"]

cin·er·ar·y /sínnə rèrree/ *adj* relating to ashes, especially human ashes [Mid-18C. < Latin *cinerarius* < *ciner-* "ashes"]

ci·ne·re·ous /sə neéree əss/ (*literary*) *adj* **1. LIKE OR OF ASHES** resembling or consisting of ashes **2. OF GRAY COLOR** of an ash-gray color ■ *n* **GRAY COLOR** an ash-gray color [15C. < Latin *cinereus* < *ciner-* "ashes"]

cin·er·in /sínnərən/ *n* an oily liquid compound. Source: pyrethrum. Use: insecticides. [Mid-20C. < Latin *ciner-* "ashes"]

cin·gu·lum /síng gyələm/ (*plural* **-la** /-lə/) *n* **1.** a part of the body that surrounds or encircles another part **2.** a band or stripe that encircles a plant or animal [Early 19C. < Latin, "girdle" < *cingere* "gird"] —**cin·gu·late** /síng gyələt/ *adj*

cin·na·bar /sínnə baàr/ *n* **1.** MINERALS **MINERAL SOURCE OF MERCURY** a reddish brown mineral consisting of mercuric sulfide. Use: source of mercury. **2.** CHEM **RED PIGMENT** red mercuric sulfide. Use: pigment. **3.** COLORS **BRIGHT RED** a bright red color tinged with orange [14C. Via Latin < Greek *kinnabari*] —**cin·na·bar** *adj* —**cin·na·bar·ine** /sínnəbə reèn, -bərin/ *adj*

cin·na·bar moth *n* a large European moth that has orange-red wings. It was introduced into the western United States in an attempt to control ragwort, the main food of its orange- and black-striped caterpillars. Latin name: *Hypocrita jacobaeae*.

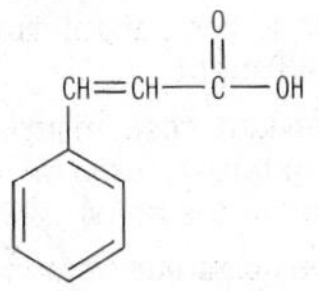

cinnamic acid

cin·nam·ic ac·id /sə nàmmik-/ *n* a white odorless acid that is insoluble in water. Use: perfume manufacture. Formula: $C_9H_8O_2$. [< its presence in cinnamon oil]

cin·na·mon /sínnəmən/ *n* **1.** FOOD **SPICE OBTAINED FROM BARK** a spice that is dried aromatic tree bark, used as strips or ground into powder **2.** TREES **ASIAN TREE** a tropical evergreen tree that produces cinnamon. Native to: Asia. Genus: *Cinnamomum*. **3.** COLORS **REDDISH BROWN COLOR** a warm reddish brown color [14C. < French *cinnamome*] —**cin·nam·ic** /sə námmik/ *adj* —**cin·na·mon** *adj*

cin·na·mon bear *n* a North American black bear that has reddish brown fur

cin·na·mon stone *n* MINERALS same as **essonite** [< its color]

cin·que·cen·to /chìngkwə chéntō/ *n* the 16th century, especially with reference to Italian art and architecture [Mid-18C. < Italian, "500," shortening of *milcinquecento* "1500"]

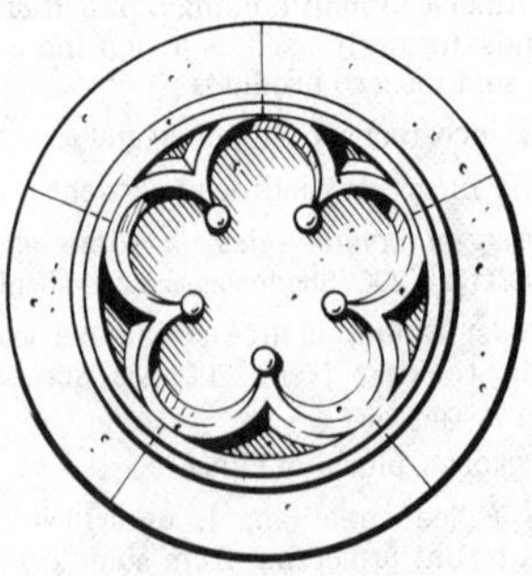

cinquefoil (sense 2)

cinque·foil /síngk fòyl, sángk-/ (*plural* **-foils** or *same*) *n* **1.** PLANTS same as **potentilla** **2.** an architectural design in the form of five arcs joined together [13C. < Latin *quinquefolium* "five leaves"]

Cinque Ports /sìngk-/ group of seaports on the southeastern coast of England: Sandwich, Dover, Hythe, Romney and Hastings. They historically supplied the monarch with ships in return for special privileges.

CIO *abbr* **1.** ONLINE check it out (*used in e-mails or text messages*) **2.** *also* **C.I.O.** Congress of Industrial Organizations **3.** ONLINE cut it out (*used in e-mails or text messages*)

ciop·pi·no /chə peénō/ *n* a thick seafood soup or stew with tomatoes, spices, and herbs [Mid-20C. Origin ?]

Ci·pan·go /si páng gō/ *n* in medieval mythology, an island off the eastern coast of Asia, perhaps modern-day Japan

ci·pher /sīfər/, **cy·pher** *n* **1. WRITTEN CODE** a written code in which the letters of a text are replaced with others according to a system **2. CODE KEY** the key to a cipher **3. TEXT IN CODE** a text written in cipher **4.** DESIGN **DESIGN OF INTERLACING INITIALS** a decorative design consisting of a set of interlaced initials **5.** MUSIC **FAULT IN ORGAN VALVE** a fault in an organ valve that causes a pipe to sound continuously without the key having been pressed ■ *v* (**-phered, -pher·ing, -phers**) **1.** *vt* **WRITE IN CODE** to write a text or message in cipher **2.** *vi* MUSIC **SOUND OWING TO FAULT** to sound continuously because of a faulty valve (*refers to organs or organ pipes*) [14C. Via Old French *cif(f)re* < Arabic *ṣifr* "zero"]

ci·pol·in /síppəlin/ *n* Italian marble with green and white streaks [Late 18C. Directly or via French < Italian *cipollino* "small onion" < *cipolla* "onion"; because its pattern resembles the layers of an onion]

Cip·ro /sípprō/ *tdmk* a trademark for the antibiotic ciprofloxacin

cip·ro·flox·a·cin /sìpprō flóksə sin/ *n* a powerful antibiotic. Use: in eye drops for treatment of corneal ulcers and surface infections of the eye, treatment of anthrax in humans.

cir. *abbr* **1.** TIME circa **2.** MATH circle **3.** ELEC circuit **4.** PUBL circulation **5.** MATH circumference

cir·ca /súrkə/ *prep* used before a date to indicate that it is approximate or estimated [Mid-19C. < Latin < *circus* "circle"]

cir·ca·di·an /sər káydee ən/ *adj* describes a pattern repeated approximately every 24 hours [Mid-20C. < Latin *circa* "about" + *dies* "day"]

Cir·cas·sian /sər kásh'n, -káshee ən/ *n* a group of languages spoken in southern Russia, northern Georgia, and Turkey, belonging to the Abkhaz-Adyghean branch of North Caucasian languages. Native speakers: 1.5 million. [Mid-16C. < *Circassia*, Latinized form of Russian *Cherkes*] —**Cir·cas·sian** *adj*

Cir·ce /súrssee/ *n* in Greek mythology, the daughter of Hecate and the Sun, who lured sailors to her island where she made love to them and then turned them into pigs [12C. Via Latin < Greek *Kirkē*] —**Cir·ce·an** /súrsee ən, sur seé ən/ *adj*

cir·ci·nate /súrssə nàyt/ *adj* describes leaves or fronds that are coiled with the tip in the center, as in most ferns [Early 19C. < Latin *circinatus*, past participle of *circinare* "make round" < *circinus* "pair of compasses" < *circus* "circle"] —**cir·ci·nate·ly** *adv*

Cir·ci·nus /súrssinəss/ *n* a small inconspicuous constellation in the southern hemisphere near Centaurus [Early 19C. < Latin *circinus* (see CIRCINATE)]

~~**circiut**~~ incorrect spelling of **circuit**

cir·cle /súrk'l/ *n* **1. SHAPE OF PERFECT HOLLOW RING** a two-dimensional geometric figure formed of a curved line surrounding a center point, every point of the line being an equal distance from the center point **2. AREA INSIDE CIRCLE** the area enclosed by a circle **3. CIRCLE-SHAPED THING** an area or object in the shape of a circle **4. CIRCLE-SHAPED PATTERN** an arrangement or pattern in the shape of a circle **5. GROUP OF PEOPLE** a group of people who share a common interest, profession, activity, or social background **6. CURVED ROUTE** a course or route that follows a curved path **7. CYCLE** a process or series of events that ends at the point at which it began or that repeats itself continuously **8.** THEATER **RAISED THEATER SEATING** a section of tiered seating in a theater that is above ground level ■ *v* (**-cled, -cling, -cles**) **1.** *vti* **MOVE ALONG CURVING ROUTE** to move, or move around something, following a curving route or path that ends where it began and usually repeats its cycle **2.** *vt* **MAKE MARK AROUND SOMETHING** to draw a ring around something in order to mark it or draw attention to it **3.** *vt* **SURROUND PLACE OR AREA** to surround a place or an area with people [Pre-12C. Via French < Latin *circulus* "small circle" < *circus* "circle"] —**cir·cler** *n* ◇ **come full circle** to return to an earlier or first position or situation after leaving it ◇ **go** *or* **run around in circles** to be very busy without actually achieving anything

cir·cle graph *n* STATS same as **piechart**

cir·clet /súrklət/ *n* **1.** a circular decoration, especially a decorative band worn on the head **2.** a small circle (*literary*)

cir·cuit /súrkit/ *n* **1.** CIRCULAR PATH a route or path that follows a curved course and finishes at the point at which it began **2.** AREA BOUNDED BY CIRCULAR PATH an area that lies inside a circular route or path **3.** SINGLE TRIP AROUND CIRCULAR PATH a single complete trip around a circular route or path **4.** REGULAR TRIP a trip that somebody such as a salesperson or circuit court judge regularly makes around an area **5.** LAW STOPS DURING TRIP the places visited by somebody on a regular circuit, especially those where a circuit court judge sits periodically **6.** ROUND OF EVENTS a series of events or places regularly attended or visited by the same group of people **7.** ONGOING SERIES OF COMPETITIONS an ongoing series of competitions or tournaments in which the same group of players regularly participate **8.** ELEC ROUTE FOR ELECTRICITY a route around which an electrical current can flow, beginning and ending at the same point **9.** SPORTS SET OF EXERCISES a complete round of exercises in circuit training **10.** ARTS CHAIN OF ARTS LOCATIONS a group of theaters, movie theaters, or clubs under the same management or showing the same performances or movies in rotation **11.** CHR LOCAL GROUP OF METHODIST CHURCHES a group of Methodist churches that form a local division of the Church's national administration ■ *vti* (**-cuit·ed, -cuit·ing, -cuits**) MOVE AROUND ALONG CIRCULAR PATH to follow a circuit around something (*formal*) [14C. Via French < Latin *circuitus* < *circuire* "go around" < *ire* "go"]

cir·cuit board *n* a thin insulating board on which electronic components and connections are mounted or etched

cir·cuit break·er *n* a device that can automatically stop the flow of electricity in a circuit if there is too much current to operate safely

cir·cuit court *n* a court that moves from place to place within a particular judicial district

cir·cu·i·tous /sər kyōō ətəss/ *adj* lengthy because very indirect [Mid-17C. < medieval Latin *circuitosus* < Latin *circuire* (see CIRCUIT)] —**cir·cu·i·tous·ly** *adv* —**cir·cu·i·tous·ness** *n*

cir·cuit rid·er *n* formerly, a cleric who traveled from church to church preaching, especially in rural areas

cir·cuit·ry /súrkətree/ (*plural* **-ries**) *n* **1.** CIRCUIT COMPONENTS the components of an electric circuit **2.** ELECTRICAL SYSTEM the system of circuits in an electrical or electronic device **3.** LAYOUT OF CIRCUIT the design or layout of an electric circuit

cir·cuit train·ing *n* a form of sports training that involves performing different exercises in rotation

cir·cu·i·ty /sər kyōō ətee/ (*plural* **-ties**) *n* the indirect and lengthy nature of something, especially the way somebody speaks, argues, or reasons [Mid-16C. < French *circuité* < Latin *circuire* (see CIRCUIT)]

cir·cu·lar /súrkyələr/ *adj* **1.** SHAPED LIKE CIRCLE having the shape of a perfect circle, or resembling a circle in shape **2.** ENDING WHERE BEGINNING following a curved route or path that ends at the point where it began **3.** CIRCUITOUS indirect and complicated **4.** WIDELY DISTRIBUTED intended for distribution to a large number of people **5.** LOGIC NOT LOGICAL describes an argument that does not move logically to a satisfactory conclusion because it assumes as true something that needs to be proved or demonstrated ■ *n* WIDELY DISTRIBUTED NOTICE a letter, advertisement, or other notice distributed to a large number of people [14C. Via Anglo-Norman < late Latin *circularis* < Latin *circulus* (see CIRCLE)] —**cir·cu·lar·ly** *adv*

cir·cu·lar breath·ing *n* the technique of using the cheeks to force air out of the mouth while breathing in through the nose, used by woodwind and brass players to hold long notes

cir·cu·lar func·tion *n* MATH same as **trigonometric function**

cir·cu·lar·i·ty /sùrkyə lárrətee/ *n* **1.** CIRCULAR SHAPE the quality or fact of being circular in shape **2.** COMPLEXITY AND INDIRECTNESS the indirect and complicated nature of something such as a method or route **3.** LOGIC ILLOGICAL NATURE the illogical nature of something such as an argument or piece of reasoning [Late 16C. < medieval Latin *circularitas* < *circularis* (see CIRCULAR)]

cir·cu·lar·ize /súrkyələ rīz/ (**-ized, -iz·ing, -iz·es**) *vt* **1.** to publicize something by distributing leaflets or notices widely **2.** to ask people for support or survey public opinion by sending out questionnaires, letters, or leaflets —**cir·cu·lar·i·za·tion** /sùrkyələri záysh'n/ *n*

cir·cu·lar meas·ure *n* the measurement of an angle in units (**radians**) that relate it to the angle formed in the center of a circle by a sector

cir·cu·lar saw *n* an electrically powered saw with a circular toothed blade that rotates at high speed

cir·cu·late /súrkyə làyt/ (**-lat·ed, -lat·ing, -lates**) *v* **1.** *vi* MOVE AROUND CIRCULAR SYSTEM to move freely through a circuit or follow a circular route **2.** *vti* PASS AROUND to distribute or pass something from person to person or from place to place, or be passed in this way **3.** *vi* FLOW FREELY to move or flow freely in an enclosed space or defined area **4.** *vi* MINGLE to move from person to person or group to group at a social gathering in order to talk with different people (*informal*) [15C. < Latin *circulat-*, past participle of *circulare* < *circulus* (see CIRCLE)] —**cir·cu·lat·a·ble** *adj* —**cir·cu·la·tor** *n*

cir·cu·lat·ing dec·i·mal /sùrkyə layting-/ *n* MATH same as **repeating decimal**

cir·cu·lat·ing li·brar·y *n* LIBRARIES same as **lending library**

cir·cu·lat·ing me·di·um *n* anything used as money, e.g., a valuable commodity, paper money, or illegal drugs

cir·cu·la·tion /sùrkyə láysh'n/ *n* **1.** MOVEMENT OF BLOOD AROUND BODY the continuous movement of blood through all parts of the body **2.** FLOW the free movement of something such as air or water in an enclosed space **3.** DISTRIBUTION OR COMMUNICATION the passing or communication of something such as news, information, or money, from place to place or from person to person **4.** PUBL NUMBER DISTRIBUTED OF PUBLICATION the number of copies of a publication that are sold or distributed to readers in a given period **5.** FIN USE AS MONEY valid use as currency **6.** LIBRARIES LIBRARY DEPARTMENT the department of a lending library that oversees the lending and retrieval of books and other items

cir·cu·la·to·ry /súrkyələ tàwree/ *adj* relating to the circulation of the blood

cir·cu·la·to·ry sys·tem *n* the system consisting of the heart, blood vessels, and lymph vessels that pumps blood and lymph around the body

circum- *prefix* around ○ *circumlunar* [< Latin *circus* "circle"]

cir·cum·am·bi·ent /sùrkəm ámbee ənt/ *adj* surrounding (*literary*) —**cir·cum·am·bi·ent·ly** *adv*

cir·cum·am·bu·late /sùrkəm ámbyə làyt/ (**-lated, -lat·ing, -lates**) *vi* to avoid the point of a subject or discussion (*formal*) —**cir·cum·am·bu·la·tion** /sùrkəm ambyə láysh'n/ *n*

cir·cum·cise /súrkəm sīz/ (**-cised, -cis·ing, -cis·es**) *vt* **1.** to remove all or part of the foreskin from the penis of a boy or man, either for hygiene reasons or as part of a religious ritual **2.** to cut away the skin (**prepuce**) covering the clitoris, or remove the clitoris of a girl or woman, usually as part of a religious ritual [13C. < Old French *circonciser* < Latin *circumcis-*, past participle of *circumcidere* "cut around" < *caedere* "to cut"] —**cir·cum·cis·er** *n*

cir·cum·ci·sion /sùrkəm sízh'n/ *n* **1.** REMOVAL OF MALE'S FORESKIN the removal of all or part of the foreskin from the penis **2.** REMOVAL OF CLITORIS OR PREPUCE the cutting away of the skin (**prepuce**) covering the clitoris, or the removal of the clitoris **3.** RELIGIOUS CEREMONY WITH CIRCUMCISION especially in Judaism or Islam, a religious ceremony during which a circumcision is performed on boys

Cir·cum·ci·sion *n* a Roman Catholic festival held until 1970 marking the circumcision of Jesus Christ. Date: January 1.

cir·cum·fer·ence /sər kúmfərənss, -kúmfrənss/ *n* **1.** DISTANCE AROUND CIRCLE the distance around the edge of a circle **2.** DISTANCE AROUND SOMETHING the distance around the edge of an object or a place that is roughly circular **3.** EDGE OF SOMETHING the edge of a round object or area [14C. < Latin *circumferentia* < *circumferent-*, present participle of *circumferre* "carry around" < *ferre* "carry"] —**cir·cum·fer·en·tial** /sər kùmfə rénsh'l/ *adj* —**cir·cum·fer·en·tial·ly** *adv*

cir·cum·flex /súrkəm flèks/, **cir·cum·flex ac·cent** *n* in some languages, a mark (ˆ) placed above a letter to indicate a specific pronunciation, usually different from that of the unaccented letter, or a contraction. Circumflexes may be written over vowels as in French or over consonants as in Esperanto. See table at **diacritic** [Late 16C. < Latin *circumflexus*, past participle of *circumflectere* "bend around" < *flectere* "bend"]

cir·cum·flu·ent /sər kúmfloo ənt/, **cir·cum·flu·ous** /-əss/ *adj* flowing all around a thing or place (*formal*)

cir·cum·lo·cu·tion /sùrkəm lō kyōōsh'n/ *n* **1.** the use of more words than necessary to express something, especially to avoid saying it directly **2.** something said using more words than necessary, especially to avoid expressing it directly [15C. Directly or via French < Latin *circumlocution-* "speaking around" < *locution-* (see LOCUTION)] —**cir·cum·loc·u·to·ry** /-lókyə tàwree/ *adj*

cir·cum·lu·nar /sùrkəm lōōnər/ *adj* around or surrounding the Moon

cir·cum·nav·i·gate /sùrkəm návvi gàyt/ (**-gat·ed, -gat·ing, -gates**) *vt* to sail or fly around something such as the world or an island —**cir·cum·nav·i·ga·ble** *adj* —**cir·cum·nav·i·ga·tion** /-navi gáysh'n/ *n* —**cir·cum·nav·i·ga·tor** *n*

cir·cum·po·lar /sùrkəm pṓlər/ *adj* located or living near one or both poles of Earth or another planet

cir·cum·po·lar star *n* a star that is always visible above the horizon at a given latitude

cir·cum·scribe /súrkəm skrīb/ (**-scribed, -scrib·ing, -scribes**) *v* **1.** to limit the power of something or somebody to act independently (*formal; often passive*) **2.** to draw one geometric figure around another so that they touch at every corner (**vertex**) of the enclosed figure or at every side of the enclosing figure without cutting across each other [14C. < Latin *circumscribere* "write around" < *scribere* "write"] —**cir·cum·scrib·a·ble** *adj* —**cir·cum·scrib·er** *n*

cir·cum·scrip·tion /sùrkəm skrípshən/ *n* **1.** RESTRICTION OF POWER the limiting of the power of something or somebody to act independently (*formal*) **2.** MATH ENCLOSING OF SOMETHING WITHIN GEOMETRIC SHAPE the act of drawing one geometric figure around another so that they touch at every corner (**vertex**) of the enclosed figure or at every side of the enclosing figure without cutting across each other **3.** MATH DRAWN SHAPE a shape drawn or enclosed by circumscription **4.** COINS INSCRIPTION ROUND CIRCULAR EDGE a circular inscription around the edge of a coin or medal —**cir·cum·scrip·tive** *adj* —**cir·cum·scrip·tive·ly** *adv*

cir·cum·so·lar /sùrkəm sṓlər/ *adj* around or surrounding the Sun

cir·cum·spect /súrkəm spèkt/ *adj* taking into consideration all possible circumstances and consequences before acting [15C. < Latin *circumspect-*, past participle of *circumspicere* "look around" < *specere* "look"] —**cir·cum·spec·tion** /sùrkəm spéksh'n/ *n* —**cir·cum·spec·tive** *adj* —**cir·cum·spect·ly** *adv*

SYNONYMS See ***cautious***.

cir·cum·stance /súrkəm stànss/ *n* **1.** CONDITION AFFECTING SITUATION a condition that affects what happens or how somebody reacts in a particular situation (*usually used in the plural*) ○ *Circumstances have arisen that make it impossible to continue.* **2.** UNCONTROLLABLE CONDITIONS the conditions that affect somebody's life and that are beyond his or her control ○ *a victim of circumstance* **3.** WAY SOMETHING HAPPENS the way an event happens or develops ○ *Mystery still surrounds the exact circumstances of the accident.* **4.** EVENT an event or occurrence (*formal*) ■ **cir·cum·stanc·es** *npl* CONDITIONS the social, financial, material, or spiritual conditions that somebody lives in ○ *Please report any change in your circumstances.* [12C. Directly or via French < Latin *circumstantia* < *circumstant-*, present participle of *circumstare* "stand around" < *stare* "stand"] ◇ **under** *or* **in no circumstances** no matter what the situation might be ○ *You must under no* *circumstances reveal your password.* ◇ **under** *or* **in the circumstances** taking everything into account ○ *She performed very well under the circumstances.*

cir·cum·stanced /súrkəm stànst/ *adj* living in a particular state or set of conditions (*formal*) ○ *She came from a family that was happily circumstanced.*

cir·cum·stan·tial /sùrkəm stánsh'l/ *adj* **1. BASED ON INFERENCE** containing or based on facts that allow a court to deduce that somebody is guilty without conclusive proof ○ *circumstantial evidence* **2. SPECIAL** related to particular circumstances **3. FORMAL** with a great deal of formality and ceremony **4. DETAILED** thorough and very detailed (*formal*) —**cir·cum·stan·ti·al·i·ty** /sùrkəm stanshee állətee/ *n* —**cir·cum·stan·tial·ly** *adv*

cir·cum·stan·ti·ate /sùrkəm stánshee àyt/ (**-at·ed, -at·ing, -ates**) *vt* to provide evidence to support an argument or allegation (*formal*) —**cir·cum·stan·ti·a·tion** /sùrkəm stanshee áysh'n/ *n*

cir·cum·stel·lar /sùrkəm stéllər/ *adj* around or surrounding a star

cir·cum·ter·res·tri·al /sùrkəm tə réstree əl/ *adj* around or surrounding Earth

cir·cum·val·late /sùrkəm vá làyt/ (**-lat·ed, -lat·ing, -lates**) *vt* to protect a town or camp by surrounding it with a rampart or a defensive wall (*archaic or formal*) [Mid-17C. < Latin *circumvallat-*, past participle of *circumvallare* "fortify with a rampart around" < *vallum* "rampart" < *vallus* "stake"] —**cir·cum·val·la·tion** /-va láysh'n/ *n*

cir·cum·vent /sùrkəm vént, súrkəm vènt/ (**-vent·ed, -vent·ing, -vents**) *vt* **1.** to find a way of avoiding restrictions imposed by a rule or law without actually breaking it ○ *an attempt to circumvent the ban* **2.** to anticipate and counter somebody's plans [15C. < Latin *circumvent-*, present participle of *circumvenire* "come around" < *venire* "come"] —**cir·cum·vent·er** *n* —**cir·cum·ven·tion** /sùrkəm vénsh'n/ *n* —**cir·cum·ven·tive** *adj*

cir·cum·vo·lu·tion /sùrkəm və lóosh'n/ *n* a turning or winding movement around a central axis [15C. < Latin *circumvolut-*, past participle of *circumvolvere* "turn around" < *volvere* "turn"] —**cir·cum·vo·lu·to·ry** /-vóllyə tàwree/ *adj*

cir·cus /súrkəss/ *n* **1. TRAVELING ENTERTAINERS** a group of traveling entertainers, including clowns, acrobats, and sometimes animal trainers and their animals **2. TRAVELING SHOW** a performance given by circus entertainers, or the place where they perform **3. ROMAN STADIUM** an open stadium built by the ancient Romans to stage chariot races or fights between gladiators **4. ROMAN SHOW** a performance staged in a Roman stadium **5.** *UK* **PLACE WHERE STREETS MEET** an open space, approximately circular in shape, where several streets meet ○ *Piccadilly Circus* **6. SELF-IMPORTANT EVENT** a confused, noisy, or overwhelming event or situation, especially one that seems full of self-importance (*informal*) ○ *a media circus* [14C. < Latin, "ring, circle"] —**cir·cus·y** *adj*

ORIGIN The Latin word *circus*, "ring," "circle," from which ***circus*** is derived, is also the source of English *circle, circular, circulate,* and *search*.

cir·cus catch *n* in baseball or football, a catch involving a leap, a dive, or a roll (*informal*)

Cir·cus Max·i·mus /-máksiməss/ *n* a stadium in Rome that was used in ancient times to stage chariot races and fights between gladiators [< Latin, "biggest racetrack"]

ci·ré /sə ráy/ *adj* **SHINY** describes fabric with a shiny highly glazed finish ■ *n* **1. SHINY FINISH** a very shiny highly glazed finish achieved by treating a fabric with wax or heat **2. SHINY FABRIC** a fabric with a shiny finish [Early 20C. < French, past participle of *cirer* "to wax" < *cire* "wax" < Latin *cera*]

cire per·due /seer pur dóo/ *n* same as **lost wax** (*technical*) [Late 19C. < French, "lost wax"]

cirque /surk/ *n* a semicircular hollow with steep walls formed by glacial erosion on mountains. It often forms the head of a valley. [Mid-19C. Via French < Latin *circus* "ring"]

cir·rho·sis /si róssiss/ *n* a chronic progressive disease of the liver characterized by the replacement of healthy cells with scar tissue [Early 19C. < modern Latin < Greek *kirrhos* "orange-colored"] —**cir·rhot·ic** /si róttik/ *adj*

cir·ri METEOROL, ZOOL plural of **cirrus**

cir·ri·form /seerə fàwrm/ *adj* shaped like a long slender tendril or tentacle [Early 19C. < Latin *cirrus* "curl"]

cir·ri·ped /seerə pèd/, **cir·ri·pede** /-peed/ *n* a sea crustacean that lives fixed in one spot and draws food by means of slender hairs (**cirri**). Subclass: Cirripedia. [Mid-19C < modern Latin *Cirripedia* "with curly legs" < Latin *cirrus* "curl"]

cir·ro·cu·mu·lus /seerō kyóomyələss/ (*plural* **-li** /-lī/) *n* a high-altitude cloud formed of icy particles. It occurs in lines of small rounded clouds often resembling fish scales and sometimes called a mackerel sky.

cir·ro·stra·tus /seerō stráttəss, -stráytəss/ (*plural* **-ti** /-tī/) *n* a cirrus cloud resembling a transparent white veil high in the sky. It indicates wet weather.

cir·rus /seerəss/ (*plural* **-ri** /-rī/) *n* **1.** a thin wispy cloud, occurring as narrow bands of tiny ice particles, that forms at the highest and coldest point of the cloud region **2.** a slender tentacle with sensory or locomotive function, or a part resembling one [Early 18C. < Latin, "curl, fringe"] —**cir·rate** /seer àyt, seerət/ *adj*

cis /siss/ *adj* having two atoms or groups on the same side of a double bond between carbon atoms [Late 18C. < Latin (see CIS-)]

CIS *abbr* Commonwealth of Independent States

cis- *prefix* on the near side of ○ *cisatlantic* [< Latin *cis* < Indo-European, "this"]

cis·al·pine /siss ál pīn/ *adj* **1.** situated south of the Alps **2.** relating to a movement in the Roman Catholic Church to limit papal power and encourage the independence of local churches [Mid-16C. < Latin *cisalpinus* "on this side of the Alps" (as viewed from Rome) < *alpinus* "alpine"]

cis·at·lan·tic /siss ət lántik/ *adj* situated on the same side of the Atlantic Ocean as the writer or speaker

CISC *abbr* complex instruction set computer

cis·co /sískō/ (*plural* **-coes** *or* **-cos**) *n* a silvery freshwater whitefish found in deep lakes. Native to: North America. Genus: *Coregonus*. [Mid-19C. Back-formation < Canadian French *ciscoette*, alteration (influenced by *-ette* "small") of Ojibwa *bemidewiskawed* "that which has oily skin"]

Cis·kei /sís kī/ former homeland of South Africa, now part of Eastern Cape Province

cis·lu·nar /siss lóonər/ *adj* situated between the Earth and the Moon

cis·mon·tane /siss món tàyn/ *adj* on the same side of the mountains as the writer or speaker

cis·pa·dane /sìspə dáyn/ *adj* situated on the southern side of the Po River in northern Italy [Late 18C. < CIS- + Latin *Padus* "the Po"]

cis·plat·in /siss pláttin/, **cis·plat·i·num** /-pláttinəm/ *n* a drug that adds an alkyl group to DNA. Use: treatment of ovarian and testicular cancer. [Late 20C. < CIS- + *-platin*, INN stem]

ciss·ing /síssing/ *n* the appearance of marks such as bubbles or pits in paintwork. It is a result of failure of the paint to adhere properly to the surface. [Late 20C. Origin ?]

cis·sy *n, adj* another spelling of **sissy** (*informal offensive insult*)

cist /sist/, **kist** /kist/ *n* a wood or stone coffin, dating from the latter part of the Stone Age [Early 19C. < Welsh, "chest"]

Cis·ter·cian /si stúrsh'n/ *adj* relating to an austere contemplative Christian order of monks and nuns founded by reformist Benedictines in 1098 ■ *n* a member of the Cistercian order of monks and nuns [15C. < French *cistercien* < Latin *Cistercium* "Cîteaux," near Dijon, France]

cis·tern /sístərn/ *n* **1.** a tank for storing water, especially one connected to a toilet **2.** an underground tank for storing rainwater **3.** ANAT same as **cisterna** [13C. Via French < Latin *cisterna* < *cista* "chest" < Greek *kistē*]

cis·ter·na /si stúrnə/ (*plural* **-nae** /-nee/) *n* a pouch or cavity that contains a body fluid [Late 19C. < Latin *cisterna* (see CISTERN)] —**cis·ter·nal** *adj*

cis·tron /sís tròn/ *n* a section of DNA containing the genetic code for a short chain of amino acids (**polypeptide**) that is the smallest functional unit carrying genetic information [Mid-20C. < CIS- + TRANS- + -ON[1]] —**cis·tron·ic** /sis trónnik/ *adj*

cit. *abbr* **1.** cited **2.** citizen **3.** COMPUT, TELECOM computer-integrated telephony

cit·a·del /síttəd'l, síttə dèl/ *n* **1.** a fortress or strongly fortified building in or near a city, used as a place of refuge **2.** an organization or institution that strongly defends a particular way of life or principle [Mid-16C. Directly or via French < Italian *cittadella* "little city" < obsolete *cittade* "city" < Latin *civitat-* (see CITY)]

Cit·a·del *n* the Military College of South Carolina, in Marion Square, Charleston, South Carolina, named for the building in which it was first housed, a 19th-century fortress

ci·ta·tion /sī táysh'n/ *n* **1. OFFICIAL ACKNOWLEDGMENT OF MERIT** an official document or speech that praises somebody's actions, accomplishments, or character **2. EXTRACT FROM WORK** a quotation from an authoritative source that is used to support an idea or argument **3. ACT OF CITING SOMETHING** the act or process of citing something **4.** LAW **ORDER TO APPEAR IN COURT** a writ for somebody to appear in a court of law **5.** LAW **REFERENCE TO PREVIOUS DECISION** a reference to a previous decision by a court or legal authority, specifying precisely where it is documented **6.** LAW **USE OF PRECEDENT** the legal practice or process of referring to precedent —**ci·ta·tion·al** *adj* —**ci·ta·to·ry** /sītə tàwree/ *adj*

cite /sīt/ *vt* (**cit·ed, cit·ing, cites**) **1. QUOTE SOMETHING OR SOMEBODY** to mention something or somebody as an example to support an argument or help explain what is being said (*formal*) **2.** LAW **NAME SOMEBODY** to name somebody officially in a court case **3.** LAW **ORDER TO APPEAR IN COURT** to order somebody officially to appear in court **4.** MIL **OFFICIALLY PRAISE SOMEBODY** to praise the actions of a member of the armed services in an official document (*often passive*) ■ *n* same as **citation** (sense 2) (*informal*) [15C. < Latin *citare* "summon repeatedly" < *citus*, past participle of *ciere* "summon"]

SPELLCHECK Do not confuse the spelling of ***cite***, ***site*** ("a place," "locate something"), and ***sight*** ("seeing," "see something"), which sound similar.

cith·a·ra /síthərə, síthrə/, **kith·a·ra** /kíthərə, kíthrə/ *n* a stringed musical instrument played in ancient Greece, resembling a lyre [Late 18C. Via Latin < Greek *kithara*]

cit·ied /sítteed/ *adj* having a city or cities

cit·i·fy /sítti fī/ (**-fied, -fy·ing, -fies**) *vt* (*disapproving*) **1.** to develop an area and make it more urban **2.** to make somebody adopt the customs, behavior, or dress of those who live in cities —**cit·i·fi·ca·tion** /sìttifi káysh'n/ *n* —**cit·i·fied** *adj*

cit·i·zen /síttiz'n/ *n* **1. LEGAL RESIDENT OF COUNTRY** somebody who has the right to live in a country because he or she was born there or has been legally accepted as a permanent resident **2. COUNTY, TOWN, OR CITY DWELLER** a permanent resident of a county, town, or city **3. CIVILIAN** somebody who is not a member of the armed forces, a police officer, or a public official [13C. < Anglo-Norman *citezein* < Old French *citeain* < Latin *civitat-* (see CITY)] —**cit·i·zen·ly** *adj*

CULTURAL NOTE ***Citizen Kane***, a movie (1941) by US director Orson Welles. Repeatedly nominated as one of the greatest movies of all time, it is the story of the rise and the tormented private life of a fictional media baron, Charles Foster Kane (supposedly based on the life of the billionaire publisher William Randolph Hearst). The film's many stylistic innovations include the use of mock-newsreel footage and striking deep-focus photography.

cit·i·zen·ry /síttiz'nree/ (*plural* **-ries**) *n* the citizens of a place or area collectively

cit·i·zen's ar·rest *n* an arrest made by an ordinary citizen rather than by a police officer

cit·i·zens band *n* radio frequencies used by the

general public to talk to one another over short distances

cit·i·zen·ship /sĭttiz'n shĭp/ *n* **1.** the legal status of being a citizen of a country **2.** the duties and responsibilities that come with being a member of a community

Ci·tlal·té·petl /seē tlaal táy pètt'l/ volcanic peak in central Veracruz State, eastern Mexico, and the highest peak in Mexico. Height: 18,406 ft./5,610 m.

ci·tole /sĭttōl/ *n* MUSIC same as **cittern** [14C. < French, probably diminutive of Latin *cithara* (see CITHARA)]

cit·ral /sĭttrəl/ *n* a volatile pale yellow liquid with a pleasant odor. Source: lemon grass oil. Use: in perfumes, flavorings. Formula: $C_{10}H_{16}O$.

cit·rate /sĭt ràyt/ *n* a salt or ester of citric acid

cit·ric /sĭttrik/ *adj* relating to citrus fruit

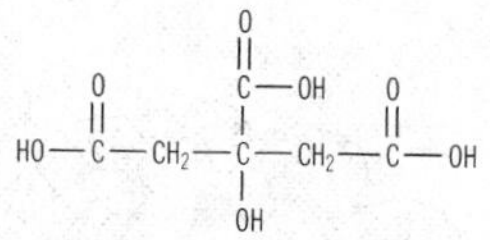

citric acid

cit·ric ac·id *n* a weak colorless acid. Source: lemon, lime, and pineapple juice, fermentation of sugars. Use: flavorings. Formula: $C_6H_8O_7$.

cit·ric ac·id cy·cle *n* CHEM same as **Krebs cycle**

cit·ri·cul·ture /sĭttri kùlchər/ *n* the cultivation of citrus fruits [Early 20C. < CITRUS] —**cit·ri·cul·tur·ist** *n*

ci·trine *n* /si treēn, sĭ treēn/ **1.** MINERALS **YELLOW QUARTZ** a brownish yellow semiprecious stone that is a variety of quartz. Use: gems. **2.** COLORS **GREENISH YELLOW COLOR** a greenish yellow color, like that of a lemon ■ *adj* /si treēn/ COLORS **GREENISH-YELLOW** of the color citrine [Late 16C. Via French *citrin(e)* "lemon colored" < medieval Latin *citrinus* < Latin *citrus* "citrus tree"]

cit·ron /sĭttrən/ *n* **1.** FOOD **CITRUS FRUIT LIKE LARGE LEMON** the fruit of an evergreen citrus tree, resembling a large lemon in shape and color and having a thick aromatic rind **2.** FOOD **CANDIED RIND** the candied rind of a citron. Use: food decoration and flavoring. **3.** TREES **THORNY CITRUS TREE** a small thorny evergreen citrus tree that bears citrons. Latin name: *Citrus medica*. **4.** PLANTS **WATERMELON** a small watermelon that has inedible white flesh and a hard rind. Latin name: *Citrullus lanatus* var. citroides. **5.** COLORS same as **citrine** *n* (sense 2) [Early 16C. < French, alteration (influenced by *limon* "lemon") of Latin *citrus* "citrus tree"] —**cit·ron** *adj*

cit·ro·nel·la /sĭttrə néllə/ *n* **1.** a pale yellow aromatic oil. Source: a tropical grass. Use: in perfumes and soaps, as insect repellent. **2.** *also* **cit·ro·nel·la grass** a tropical grass that has bluish green lemon-scented leaves and contains oil. Native to: Asia. Latin name: *Cymbopogon nardus*. [Mid-19C. Via modern Latin < French *citronnelle* "lemon oil" < *citron* (see CITRON)]

cit·ro·nel·lal /sĭttrə néllal/ *n* a colorless liquid that smells like lemons. Source: citronella oil. Use: perfumes, flavorings. Formula: $C_{10}H_{18}O$.

cit·ro·nel·la oil *n* CHEM same as **citronella** (sense 1)

cit·ro·nel·lol /sĭttrə né làwl, -lòl/ *n* an alcohol. Source: citronellal. Formula: $C_{10}H_{20}O$.

cit·ron wood *n* the wood of the citron tree or of the sandarac tree

cit·rul·line /sĭttrə leēn, sĭttrəlin/ *n* an amino acid formed in the liver during the production of urea [Mid-20C. < medieval Latin *citrullus* "watermelon" < Latin *citrus* "citrus tree"]

cit·rus /sĭttrəss/ *n* oranges, lemons, limes, grapefruit, pomelos, and related fruit collectively (*often used before a noun*) ○ *citrus fruits* [Early 19C. < Latin, "citron tree, citrus tree"]

Cit·rus Heights /sĭttrəss-/ city in Sacramento County, central California, situated northeast of Sacramento. Population: 88,567 (2002 estimate).

cit·tern /sĭ turn/ *n* a medieval stringed instrument similar to a lute but with wire strings and a flat back [Mid-16C. Probably blend of Latin *cithara* (see CITHARA) + GITTERN]

cit·y /sĭttee/ (*plural* **-ies**) *n* **1.** **VERY LARGE URBAN AREA** an urban area where a large number of people live and work **2.** **US URBAN CENTER OF GOVERNMENT** in the United States, an incorporated urban center that has self-government, boundaries, and legal rights established by state charter **3.** **PEOPLE IN CITY** the inhabitants of a city collectively **4.** **CANADIAN URBAN AREA** in Canada, a town or urban area that has been incorporated and given the title of city by a provincial government **5.** *UK* **LARGE UK TOWN** in the United Kingdom, a large town that has received the title of city from the Crown. It is usually the seat of a bishop, and so often has a cathedral. **6.** **EXTREME THING** a thing, place, or situation that is a good or extreme example of its type (*slang; used in combination*) ○ *It was panic city outside.* [12C. Via Old French *cité* < Latin *civitat-* "citizenship, community" < *civis* "citizen"]

Cit·y *n UK* same as **City of London**

cit·y coun·cil *n* a group of elected officials responsible for the government of a city or other municipality

cit·y desk *n* a newspaper department that deals with local news

cit·y ed·i·tor *n* the newspaper editor in charge of local news

cit·y fa·ther *n* a member of a city or town council or a civil officer who has limited judicial authority

cit·y hall *n* **1.** **CITY ADMINISTRATORS** the administrators and elected officials who run a city **2.** **BUREAUCRACY** the bureaucracy that runs a city, especially when regarded as insensitive or inflexible (*disapproving*) **3.** *also* **Cit·y Hall** **CITY COUNCIL BUILDING** the building where a city council has its main administrative offices

cit·y man·ag·er *n* an administrator appointed by a municipal council to run its affairs

Cit·y of Lon·don /sĭttee-/ the oldest part of London, England, and its business and financial heart. Population: 7,185 (2001). Area: 1 sq. mi./2.6 sq. km.

cit·y room *n* the department of a newspaper that deals with local news

cit·y·scape /sĭttee skàyp/ *n* **1.** a view of a city or town landscape **2.** a photograph or painting of part of a city or town

cit·y slick·er *n* a worldly resident of a city (*informal disapproving*)

cit·y-state *n* a independent state consisting of a sovereign city and its surrounding territory

cit·y·wide /sĭttee wīd/ *adj* involving the whole of a particular city ■ *adv* so as to involve the whole of a particular city

Ci·u·dad Bo·lí·var /seē oō daad bō leē vaar/, **Ci·u·dad Bo·lí·var** river port and capital of Bolívar State, eastern Venezuela, situated on the Orinoco River. Population: 258,112 (1992).

Ci·u·dad de Nau·cal·pan de Juá·rez /-də nō kaal paan də hwaa rèss/ suburban city in south central Mexico, west of Mexico City. Population: 851,500 (2000).

Ci·u·dad Juá·rez /-hwaa rèss, -waa-/ city in Chihuahua State, northern Mexico, across the Rio Grande from El Paso, Texas. Population: 1,218,818 (2000).

Ci·u·dad Ma·de·ro /-mə dérrō/ suburban city on the Gulf of Mexico in Tamaulipas State, eastern Mexico north of Tampico. Population: 187,300 (2000).

Ci·u·dad O·bre·gón /-ōbrə gón/ city in Sonora State, northwestern Mexico, southeast of Hermosillo. Population: 165,572 (1980). Former name **Cajeme**

Ci·u·dad Re·al /-ray aál/ capital of Ciudad Real Province, in the Castile-La Mancha Region, south central Spain. Population: 65,084 (2002).

Ci·u·dad Vic·to·ri·a /-vik táwree ə/ capital of Tamaulipas State, northeastern Mexico, situated 150 mi./241 km southeast of Monterrey. Population: 256,900 (2002).

civ·et /sĭvvət/ *n* **1.** *also* **civ·et cat** **WILD ANIMAL LIKE CAT** a small carnivorous mammal that resembles a cat in appearance. Native to: Africa, Asia. Family: Viverridae. **2.** COSMETICS **MUSKY SUBSTANCE** a yellow or brown greasy substance smelling strongly of musk, secreted by the anal glands of a civet. Use: perfume manufacture. **3.** **FUR** the fur of a civet [Mid-16C. Via French *civette* < Italian *zivetto* < medieval Latin *zibethum* < Arabic *zabād* "civet perfume"]

civ·ic /sĭvvik/ *adj* **1.** relating to the government of a town or city ○ *civic reception* **2.** connected with the duties and obligations of belonging to a community ○ *civic pride* [Mid-17C. < Latin *civicus* < *civis* "citizen"] —**civ·i·cal·ly** *adv*

civ·ic cen·ter *n* a municipal entertainment complex containing an indoor arena that can be used for sports, concerts, and trade shows

civ·ic hol·i·day *n Can* in most Canadian provinces, a public holiday. Date: first Monday in August.

civ·ic-mind·ed *adj* taking an active interest in the community needs and affairs of a town or city —**civ·ic-mind·ed·ness** *n*

civ·ics /sĭvviks/ *n* the study of the rights and duties of citizens (*takes a singular verb*)

civ·ies *n* CLOTHING another spelling of **civvies**

civ·il /sĭvv'l/ *adj* **1.** **POLITE** polite, but in a way that is cold and formal **2.** **RELATING TO CITIZENS** relating to what happens within a state or between different citizens or groups of citizens ○ *civil war* **3.** **NOT MILITARY** connected with ordinary citizens and organizations as opposed to the armed forces ○ *the civil authorities* **4.** **NOT RELIGIOUS** performed by a state official such as a registrar rather than a member of the clergy ○ *civil marriage* **5.** same as **civic** (sense 2) **6.** LAW **HAPPENING BETWEEN INDIVIDUALS** involving individual people or groups in legal action other than criminal proceedings ○ *a civil action* [14C. < Latin *civilis* < *civis* "citizen"]

civ·il code *n* the codified body of statutes in Quebec that derives from Roman and Napoleonic civil law

civ·il de·fense *n* **1.** the organization and training of civilian volunteers to help the armed forces, police, and emergency services in the event of a war, a national emergency, or a natural disaster **2.** civilian volunteers who take part in civil defense (*takes a singular or plural verb*)

civ·il dis·o·be·di·ence *n* the deliberate breaking of a law by ordinary citizens, carried out as nonviolent protest or passive resistance

civ·il en·gi·neer·ing *n* the branch of engineering concerned with the planning, design, and construction of such things as roads, bridges, and dams —**civ·il en·gi·neer** *n*

ci·vil·ian /si vĭllyən/ *n* a citizen who is not a member of the armed forces [Early 14C. < Old French *civilien* "of civil law" < *civil* "civil" < Latin *civilis* (see CIVIL)] —**ci·vil·ian** *adj*

ci·vil·ian·ize /si vĭllyə nīz/ (**-ized, -iz·ing, -iz·es**) *vt* to change something from military to civilian use —**ci·vil·ian·i·za·tion** /si vìllyəni záysh'n/ *n*

ci·vil·i·ty /si vĭllətee/ (*plural* **-ties**) *n* **1.** the formal politeness that results from observing social conventions **2.** something said or done in a formally polite way

civ·i·li·za·tion /sĭvv'li záysh'n/ *n* **1.** **HIGHLY DEVELOPED SOCIETY** a society that has a high level of culture and social organization **2.** **ADVANCED DEVELOPMENT OF SOCIETY** an advanced level of development in society that is marked by complex social and political organization, and material, scientific, and artistic progress **3.** **ADVANCED SOCIETY IN GENERAL** all the societies at an advanced level of development considered collectively **4.** **POPULATED AREAS** places where people live, rather than uninhabited areas **5.** **CIVILIZING PROCESS** the process of creating a high level of culture in a particular society or region **6.** **COMFORT** the level of material comfort that somebody is used to (*humorous*)

civ·i·lize /sĭvv'l īz/ (**-lized, -liz·ing, -liz·es**) *vt* **1.** to create a high level of culture and social organization in a society **2.** to teach somebody to behave in a more socially and culturally acceptable way —**civ·i·liz·a·ble** *adj* —**civ·i·liz·er** *n*

civ·i·lized /sívv'l ìzd/ *adj* **1.** having advanced cultural and social development **2.** refined in tastes

civ·il law *n* **1.** LAW OF CITIZENS' RIGHTS the law of a state dealing with the rights of private citizens **2.** ANCIENT ROMAN LAW the law of ancient Rome, especially the part concerned with private citizens **3.** LAW BASED ON ROMAN LAW a system of law based on Roman law rather than common law or canon law

civ·il lib·er·ties *npl* the basic rights guaranteed to individual citizens by law, e.g., freedom of speech and action —**civ·il lib·er·tar·i·an** *n*

civ·il list *n* in the United Kingdom, the money paid each year by the state to support the royal family [Originally for the civil government of the state]

civ·il·ly /sívv'lee/ *adv* in a polite but not particularly warm or enthusiastic way

civ·il rights *npl* rights that all citizens of a society are supposed to have, e.g., the right to vote or to receive fair treatment from the law. These rights as conceived in US law are set forth in the 13th and 14th Amendments to the US Constitution and in some congressional acts.

civ·il ser·vant *n* an employee in a government department

civ·il serv·ice *n* all the government departments of a state and the people who work in them

civ·il un·ion *n* a ceremony celebrating the affirmation of a partnership shared by a same-sex couple or a couple who choose not to marry

civ·il war *n* a war between opposing groups within a country

Civ·il War *n* **1.** the civil war fought in the United States from 1861 to 1865 between the North and the slave-owning states of the South **2.** the civil war fought in England between the Royalist supporters of Charles I and the Parliamentarians led by Oliver Cromwell, between 1642 and 1648

civ·il year *n* CALENDAR same as **calendar year** [*Civil* "legally recognized"]

civ·vies /sívviz/, **civ·ies** *npl* ordinary clothes as opposed to a military uniform (*informal*) [Late 19C. Shortening and alteration of CIVILIAN, probably after CLOTHES]

civ·vy /sívvee/ (*plural* **-vies**) *n* MIL same as **civilian** (*informal*) [Early 20C Shortening and alteration]

CIX /kiks/ *abbr* commercial Internet exchange (*used in e-commerce*)

C.J. *abbr* **1.** Chief Judge **2.** Chief Justice

CJD *abbr* Creutzfeldt-Jakob disease

ck *abbr* Cook Islands (*used in Internet addresses*) See table at **domain name**

ck. *abbr* **1.** MEASURE cask **2.** BANKING check

CKD *abbr* COMM completely knocked down (*used of goods that are sold in parts to be assembled later*)

CKO *abbr* BUSINESS chief knowledge officer

cl *abbr* **1.** TRANSP carload **2.** MEASURE centiliter **3.** Chile (*used in Internet addresses*) See table at **domain name** **4.** class **5.** classification **6.** RELIG clergy **7.** FURNITURE closet **8.** CLOTHING cloth

Cl *symbol* CHEM ELEM chlorine

clab·ber /klábbər/, **clab·ber milk** *n regional* sour milk that has curdled [Early 19C. Shortening of *bonnyclabber* < Irish *bainne clabair* "thick milk for churning"]

clack /klak/ (**clacked, clack·ing, clacks**) *v* **1.** *vti* to make a short hard loud noise, or cause something to make such a noise **2.** *vi* to chatter constantly or rapidly (*informal*) **3.** *vi* same as **cluck** *v* (sense 1) [13C. An imitation of the sound] —**clack** *n* —**clack·er** *n*

clack valve *n* a valve with a hinged flap that swings open

Clac·to·ni·an /klak tốnee ən/ *n* a Lower Paleolithic culture of northwestern Europe that made stone chopping tools [After CLACTON-ON-SEA] —**Clac·to·ni·an** *adj*

Clac·ton-on-Sea /kláktən on seé/ seaside resort on the North Sea coast of Essex, England. Population: 45,065 (1991).

clad[1] /klad/ past participle, past tense of **clothe** ■ *adj* **1.** wearing particular clothes ○ *clad in blue* **2.** covered in a particular thing (*literary; often used in combination*) ○ *iron-clad* [13C. < Old English *clāðed*, past participle of *clāðian* (see CLOTHE)]

clad[2] /klad/ (**clad, clad·ding, clads**) *vt* **1.** to cover a wall or building with cladding **2.** to cover or plate a metal with a layer of another metal, especially to make armor plating [Mid-16C. Probably < CLAD[1]]

clad- *prefix* same as **clado-** (*used before vowels*)

Clad·dagh ring /klá dàk-/ *n* a ring usually in the form of two hands clasping a heart surmounted by a crown, originally given in Ireland as a token of affection [Late 20C. After a village near Galway city, Ireland]

clad·ding /kládding/ *n* **1.** OUTER LAYER ON BUILDING a layer of stone, tiles, or wood added to the outside of a building to protect it or improve its insulation or appearance **2.** METAL COATING a protective metal coating bonded onto another metal **3.** COMPUT COVERING FOR OPTICAL FIBER a covering for optical fiber that reflects light back to the core and strengthens the cable

clade /klayd/ *n* a group of organisms, e.g., a species, that are considered to share a common ancestor [Mid-20C. < Greek *klados* "branch"]

clad·ist /kláydist/ *n* a biologist who classifies organisms according to the principles of cladistics —**clad·ism** *n*

cla·dis·tics /klə dístiks/ *n* a system of biological classification that groups organisms on the basis of their observed shared characteristics in order to deduce the common ancestors (*takes a singular verb*) —**cla·dis·tic** *adj* —**cla·dis·ti·cal·ly** *adv*

clado- *prefix* branch, shoot ○ *cladogram* [< Greek *klados* < Indo-European, "to strike"]

cla·doc·er·an /klə dóssərən/ *n* a tiny freshwater crustacean such as a water flea. Order: Cladocera. [Early 20C. < modern Latin *Cladocera* < Greek *klados* "branch" + *keras* "horn"] —**cla·doc·er·an** *adj*

clad·ode /klá dōd/ *n* BOT same as **cladophyll** —**cla·do·di·al** /klə dṓdee əl/ *adj*

clad·o·gen·e·sis /klàddō jénnəsiss, klàydō-/ *n* evolutionary change regarded as taking place by the splitting of an ancestral species into two or more different descendant species —**clad·o·ge·net·ic** /klàddō jə néttik, klàydō-/ *adj* —**clad·o·ge·net·i·cal·ly** *adv*

clad·o·gram /kláddə gràm, kláydə-/ *n* a tree-shaped diagram showing evolutionary relationships and the points where species appear to have diverged from common ancestors

clad·o·phyll /kláddəfil/ *n* a flattened stem similar to a leaf

cla·fou·ti /klaà foo teé/ *n* a fruit and batter pastry, typically made with cherries [Late 20C. < French < dialect *clafir* "to stuff" + standard French *foutre* "to stuff"]

claim /klaym/ *vt* (**claimed, claim·ing, claims**) **1.** MAINTAIN SOMETHING IS TRUE to say, without proof or evidence, that something is true ○ *He claims we've already met.* **2.** DEMAND SOMETHING AS ENTITLEMENT to demand officially something that somebody has a right to or owns **3.** END SOMEBODY'S LIFE to cause the loss of somebody's life **4.** WIN TITLE to take a title, prize, or record **5.** DEMAND ATTENTION to force somebody to give attention ■ *n* **1.** SOMETHING THAT MAY BE TRUE an assertion that something is true, unsupported by evidence or proof **2.** BASIS FOR GETTING SOMETHING the basis for demanding or getting something **3.** DEMAND FOR SOMETHING a demand for something somebody has a right to or owns **4.** INSUR, SOC WELFARE OFFICIAL REQUEST FOR MONEY an official request for money or other benefits from the state or an organization **5.** INSUR, SOC WELFARE MONEY REQUESTED the amount of money requested in a claim **6.** LAW LEGAL RIGHT TO LAND the legal right to own a piece of land and to mine it for minerals **7.** LAW PIECE OF LAND the piece of land to which somebody claims a legal right [14C. < Old French *clamer* "to call" < Latin *clamare*] —**claim·a·ble** *adj* —**claim·er** *n* ◇ **lay claim to something** to say that you have a right to something, or take what you think you have a right to

ORIGIN The Latin word *clamare*, "to call," from which *claim* is derived, is also the source of English *acclaim*, *clamor*, *exclaim*, and *proclaim*.

claim·ant /kláymənt/ *n* somebody who claims something such as benefits or an inheritance

claims ad·just·er *n* INSUR same as **adjuster**

Clair /kler/, **René** (1898–1981) French movie director and scriptwriter. *The Italian Straw Hat* (1927) established him as a master of light comedy. Born **Chomette, René-Lucien**

clair de lune /klèr də lóon/ *n* **1.** a pale blue or grayish blue glaze used on porcelain **2.** a pale bluish gray color [Late 19C < French, "light of the moon"] —**clair de lune** *adj*

clair·voy·ance /kler vóy ənss/, **clair·voy·an·cy** /-ənssee/ *n* the supposed ability to perceive things that are usually beyond the range of human senses [Mid-19C. < French < *clairvoyant* "clear-sighted" < *voyant* present participle of *voir* "see"]

clair·voy·ant /kler vóy ənt/ *n* somebody who is supposedly able to perceive things that are usually beyond the range of human senses [Late 17C. < French (see CLAIRVOYANCE)] —**clair·voy·ant** *adj* —**clair·voy·ant·ly** *adv*

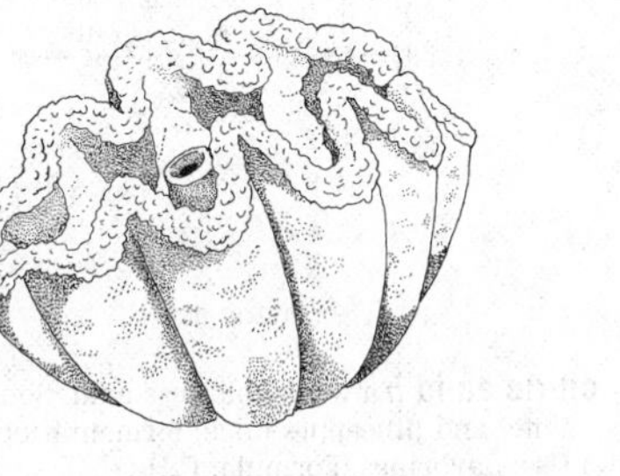

clam

clam /klam/ *n* **1.** BURROWING SHELLFISH an invertebrate animal with a shell in two parts and a muscular foot used to burrow into sand. Many are edible and the largest is nearly 5 ft./1.5 m long. Native to: oceans, rivers, lakes. Class: Pelecypoda. **2.** CLAM FLESH the soft edible flesh of a clam **3.** SECRETIVE PERSON a shy or secretive person (*informal*) **4.** MONEY same as **dollar** (sense 1) (*slang*) ■ *vi* (**clammed, clam·ming, clams**) COLLECT CLAMS to gather clams as food [Early 16C. < obsolete *clam-shell* "clamp-shell" < Old English *clamm* "bond, grip" < Indo-European, "form into a ball"]

clam up *vi* to become suddenly secretive or unwilling to talk (*informal*)

cla·mant /kláymənt/ *adj* demanding attention (*literary*) [Mid-17C. < Latin *clamant-*, present participle of *clamare* "call"] —**cla·mant·ly** *adv*

clam·bake /klám bàyk/ *n* **1.** a picnic in which seafood such as clams and other foods are cooked and eaten **2.** a relaxed party or other gathering (*informal*)

clam·ber /klámbər/ *vi* (**-bered, -ber·ing, -bers**) to climb quickly but awkwardly, using hands and feet ■ *n* a climb that involves clambering [14C. Probably < *clamb*, former past tense of CLIMB + suffix denoting repetition] —**clam·ber·er** *n*

clam chow·der *n* a thick soup made from clams and potatoes

clam·dig·gers /klám dìggərz/ *npl* casual pants reaching to the middle of the wearer's calf [Because worn for digging clams]

clam-flat *n regional* a bank of mud left exposed by the tide where clams are plentiful

clam·mer /klámmər/ *n* a digger or dredger for clams

clam·my /klámmee/ (**-mi·er, -mi·est**) *adj* **1.** slightly damp and unpleasantly cold **2.** warm and damp [14C. Probably < *clam* "to smear," back-formation < *clamde*, past tense of Old English *clǣman* < Germanic, "clay"] —**clam·mi·ly** *adv* —**clam·mi·ness** *n*

clam·or /klámmər/ *vi* (**-ored, -or·ing, -ors**) **1.** DEMAND NOISILY to demand something noisily or desperately **2.** SHOUT LOUDLY to shout at the same time as other people, and make a lot of noise ■ *n* **1.** PERSISTENT DEMAND a persistent demand for something, made in an excited or angry way **2.** LOUD NOISE a loud noise, especially one made by people shouting together

[14C. Via French < Latin *clamor-* < *clamare* "to call"] —**clam·or·er** *n*

clam·or·ous /klámmərəss/ *adj* **1. DEMANDING ATTENTION** demanding attention loudly and insistently **2. LOUD** loud and excited or angry **3. NOISY** making a loud noise —**clam·or·ous·ly** *adv* —**clam·or·ous·ness** *n*

clam·our *vi, n* Can, UK spelling of **clamor**

clamp /klamp/ *n* **1. HOLDING DEVICE** a mechanical device with movable jaws. Use: to hold two things firmly together or one object firmly in position. **2.** *UK* same as **Denver boot** ■ *vt* **(clamped, clamp·ing, clamps) 1. FASTEN THINGS TOGETHER** to fasten two or more things firmly together using a clamp **2. HOLD SOMETHING FIRMLY** to hold something firmly and tightly in position **3.** *UK* same as **boot**[1] *v* (sense 5) [15C. Probably < assumed Middle Dutch or Middle Low German *klampe*]

clamp down *vi* to take firm action to limit something bad or control somebody doing something bad (*informal*) ○ *Police have clamped down on illegal parking in the area.*

clamp·down /klámp dòwn/ *n* firm official action taken to limit something bad or control somebody doing something bad (*informal*)

clamp·er /klámpər/ *n* a spiked metal frame fastened under a shoe to provide extra grip on ice or snow

clam·shell /klám shèl/ *n* **1.** the shell of a clam **2.** a dredging bucket that has two hinged jaws (*informal*)

clam·worm /klám wùrm/ *n US* a segmented marine worm that burrows into sand or mud and is used by fishermen as bait. Genus: *Nereis.* Can term **ragworm** [Because it buries itself in sand or mud like a clam]

clan /klan/ *n* **1. GROUP OF FAMILIES** a group of families related through a common ancestor or marriage **2. LARGE FAMILY** a group of people who are all members of a particular family (*informal*) **3. RELATED SCOTTISH FAMILIES** a group of Scottish families with common ancestors, a common surname, and a single chief **4. GROUP WITH SHARED AIM** a group of people who act together because they have the same interests or aims (*informal*) [15C. < Gaelic *clann* "offspring" < Old Irish *cland* < Latin *planta* "sprout"]

Clan·cy /klánssee/, **Tom** (*b.* 1947) US writer. His thriller novels include *The Hunt for Red October* (1984). Full name **Clancy, Thomas L., Jr.**

clan·des·tine /klan déstin/ *adj* needing to be concealed, usually because it is illegal or unauthorized [Mid-16C. < Latin *clandestinus* < *clam* "secretly"] —**clan·des·tine·ly** *adv* —**clan·des·tine·ness** *n* —**clan·des·tin·i·ty** /klàndə stínnətee/ *n*

SYNONYMS See *secret.*

clang /klang/ *vti* **(clanged, clang·ing, clangs) 1. MAKE LOUD RINGING NOISE** to make the ringing sound of two metal objects hitting each other **2. MOVE MAKING CLANGING SOUND** to move or operate with a clanging sound ■ *n* **LOUD RINGING NOISE** a ringing sound made by two metal objects hitting each other [Late 16C. < Latin *clangere* "emit a ringing sound"]

clang·er /klángər/ *n UK* an unwise or embarrassing mistake (*informal*) ○ *drop a clanger*

clan·gor /klángər, kláng gər/ *n* **1.** a clang or repeated loud clanging **2.** a din or uproar —**clan·gor·ous** *adj* —**clan·gor·ous·ly** *adv*

clank /klangk/ *vti* **(clanked, clank·ing, clanks) 1. MAKE METALLIC NOISE** to make the short loud sound of two heavy metal objects hitting each other **2. MOVE MAKING CLANKING SOUND** to move or operate with a clanking sound ■ *n* **METALLIC NOISE** a short loud sound made by two heavy metal objects hitting each other [Mid-17C. Probably an imitation of the sound] —**clank·ing·ly** *adv* —**clank·y** *adj*

clan·nish /klánnish/ *adj* inclined to stick together as a group and exclude outsiders —**clan·nish·ly** *adv* —**clan·nish·ness** *n*

clans·man /klánzmən/ (*plural* **-men** /-mən/) *n* a man who is a member of a Scottish clan

clans·per·son /klánz pùrss'n/ (*plural* **-peo·ple** /-peèp'l/) *n* a member of a Scottish clan (*usually used in the plural*)

clans·wom·an /klánz wòommən/ (*plural* **-wom·en** /-wìmmin/) *n* a woman who is a member of a Scottish clan

clap[1] /klap/ *v* **(clapped, clap·ping, claps) 1.** *vti* **APPLAUD** to hit the hands together repeatedly to express approval **2.** *vti* **HIT HANDS TOGETHER** to hit the hands together quickly and loudly **3.** *vti* **HIT HANDS IN RHYTHM** to hit the hands together repeatedly in time with a beat **4.** *vt* **PUT SOMETHING SOMEWHERE QUICKLY** to move something or somebody to or against something quickly ○ *clapped him into jail* ■ *n* **1. SUDDEN LOUD SOUND** the sound made by striking the palms together once, or a sound resembling this **2. EXPRESSION OF APPROVAL THROUGH APPLAUSE** an expression of approval by loud continuous clapping **3. CLAPPING RHYTHMICALLY** a session of rhythmic clapping [Old English *clæppan* < Germanic, an imitation of the sound]

clap[2] /klap/ *n* MED same as **gonorrhea** (*slang*) [Late 16C. Origin ?]

clap·board /klábbərd, kláp bàwrd/ *n* a long narrow wooden board that has one edge thicker than the other. Use: to clad buildings. [Mid-17C. Alteration, by partial translation, of obsolete *clapholt* < Low German *klappholt* < *klappen* "clap, split" + *holt* "wood"]

clapped-out /klàpt-/ *adj UK* worn out and in very poor condition (*informal; not hyphenated when used after a verb*)

clap·per /kláppər/ *n* **1. PART MAKING BELL RING** a piece of metal inside a bell that strikes its sides, making it ring **2. SOMEBODY WHO CLAPS** somebody who claps his or her hands ■ **clap·pers** *npl* **MUSICAL INSTRUMENT** a musical instrument consisting of two flat pieces of wood that are held between the thumb and forefinger and clapped together

clapperboard

clap·per·board /kláppər bàwrd/ *n* a pair of hinged boards filmed at the start of each take in a movie and clapped together to help to synchronize the soundtrack with the movie

clap·trap /kláp tràp/ *n* nonsense, especially pompous or important-sounding nonsense (*informal*) [Late 18C. Originally, in the theater, a device or line to elicit clapping]

claque /klak/ *n* **1.** a group of people hired to applaud a performance **2.** a group of people around a rich or famous person whom they praise and support uncritically (*disapproving*) [Mid-19C. < French < *claquer* "to clap," an imitation of the sound]

cla·queur /klákər/ *n* a member of a rich or famous person's entourage who gives uncritical praise or support [Mid-19C. < French, "clapper" < *claquer* (see CLAQUE)]

cla·ra·bel·la /klàrrə béllə/, **cla·ri·bel·la** *n* an eight-foot flute stop on an organ [Mid-19C. < Latin *clara bella* "clear and beautiful"]

Clare /kler/ coastal county in Munster Province, southwestern Republic of Ireland. Population: 94,006 (2002). Area: 1,231 sq. mi./3,188 sq. km.

Clare (of As·si·si) /klèr əv ə seéssee/, **St.** (1194–1253) Italian nun. She was a follower of St. Francis of Assisi, alongside her sister St. Agnes. The three founded the order of the Poor Ladies of Damiano, or Poor Clares. Born **Offreducio, Chiara**

Clare /kler/, **John** (1793–1864) British poet and naturalist. He wrote *Poems Descriptive of Rural Life* (1820) and *The Shepherd's Calendar* (1827).

> "I love at eventide to walk alone / Down narrow lanes oerhung with dewy thorn / Where from the long grass underneath the snail / Jet black creeps out and sprouts his timid horn."
> [John Clare, "Summer Moods," *Selected Poems and Prose of John Clare*; 1966]

Clare·mont /klér mònt/ city in southwestern California; an eastern suburb of Los Angeles. Population: 34,831 (2002 estimate).

clar·ence /klárrənss/ *n* an enclosed four-wheeled carriage that seats four and has a glass front [Mid-19C. After the Duke of *Clarence*, later WILLIAM IV]

Clar·en·don /klárrəndən/ *n* a style of boldface roman type [Mid-19C. Probably after the *Clarendon* Press in Oxford, England]

clar·et /klárrət/ *n* **1.** red wine from the Bordeaux area of southwestern France **2.** a deep purplish red color, like that of claret [Early 18C. < Old French *(vin) claret* "light-colored (wine)" < Latin *vinum claratum* "clarified wine," *claratum* form of *clarare* "clarify" < *clarus* "clear"] —**clar·et** *adj*

clar·et cup *n* an iced summer drink made from claret, brandy, lemon, and sugar, sometimes with sherry or curaçao added

cla·ri·bel·la *n* MUSIC another spelling of **clarabella**

clar·i·fy /klárrə fī/ **(-fied, -fy·ing, -fies)** *v* **1.** *vt* **MAKE SOMETHING CLEARER** to make something clearer by explaining it in greater detail **2.** *vti* **MAKE BUTTER CLEAR** to make butter or fat clear by gently heating it and removing any impurities, or become clear through this process **3.** *vti* **MAKE LIQUID CLEAR** to make a liquid clear and pure, or become clear and pure, usually by filtering [14C. Via Old French < late Latin *clarificare* "make clear" < Latin *clarus* "clear"] —**clar·i·fi·ca·tion** /klàrrəfi káysh'n/ *n* —**clar·i·fi·er** *n*

clar·i·net /klàrrə nèt/ *n* a musical instrument of the woodwind family, with a straight body and a single reed [Mid-18C. < French *clarinette* "little clarion" < *clarine* "clarion" < Latin *clarus* "clear"]

clar·i·net·tist /klàrrə néttist/, **clar·i·net·ist** *n* somebody who plays the clarinet

clar·i·on /klárree ən/ *n* **1.** a four-foot organ stop that sounds like a trumpet **2.** a medieval trumpet with a clear high-pitched tone [14C. < medieval Latin *clarion-* < Latin *clarus* "clear"]

clar·i·on call *n* an urgent or inspiring appeal to people to do something [< the use of the clarion as a signal in war]

clar·i·ty /klárrətee/ *n* **1. CLEARNESS OF EXPRESSION** the quality of being clearly expressed **2. CLEARNESS OF THOUGHT** clearness in what somebody is thinking **3. CLEARNESS OF REPRODUCTION** the quality of being clear in sound or image **4. TRANSPARENT QUALITY** the quality of being clear, pure, or transparent ○ *wine of great clarity* [Early 17C. < Latin *claritat-* < *clarus* "clear"]

Clark /klaark/, **George Rogers** (1752–1818) American soldier. He led troops against British forces in the American Revolution (1775–83).

Bettmann/Corbis

Helen Clark

Clark, Helen Elizabeth (*b.* 1950) New Zealand politician. She became leader of the New Zealand Labor Party in 1993 and prime minister in 1999. See table at **prime minister**

Clark, Joe (*b.* 1939) Canadian politician. He became the leader of the Conservative Party in 1976 and served as prime minister from 1979 to 1980. Full name **Clark, Charles Joseph**. See table at **prime minister**

> "Political freedom is rare enough in the world, but the kind of social and cultural freedom which is the hallmark of Canada is even less common."
> [Joe Clark, *Speech to the Canadian Parliament*; February 18, 1977]

Clark, Mark Wayne (1896–1984) US army general. He led the Allied armies in Italy during World War II and commanded UN forces in Korea (1952–53).

> "I was the first American commander to put his signature to a paper ending a war when we did not win it."
> [Mark Wayne Clark. Quoted in *Speaking Freely*, Stuart Berg Flexner and Anne H. Soukhanov; 1997]

Clark, Tom Campbell (1899–1977) associate justice of the US Supreme Court (1949–67). He was appointed in 1949 by President Truman after serving as his attorney general (1945–49).

Clark, William (1770–1838) US explorer. He was coleader of the Lewis and Clark Expedition that explored the Far West (1804–06).

Clark cell *n* a standard battery cell with a mercury anode surrounded by a paste of mercury sulfate, and a zinc cathode immersed in saturated zinc sulfate solution [Late 19C. After Josiah Latimer *Clark* (1822–98), British engineer]

Clarks·burg /klaárks bùrg/ city in northern West Virginia, on the West Fork River, northeast of Charleston. Population: 16,498 (2002 estimate).

Clarks·dale /klaárks dàyl/ city in northwestern Mississippi on the Sunflower River, southwest of Oxford. Population: 20,290 (2002 estimate).

Clarks·ville /klaárks vìl/ city in northwestern Tennessee, northwest of Nashville, where the Red and Cumberland rivers meet. Population: 105,898 (2002 estimate).

cla·ro /klaárō/ (*plural* **-ros**) *n* a mild light-colored cigar [Late 19C. Via Spanish, "light" < Latin *clarus* "clear"]

clar·sach /klaár sàkh, -səkh/ *n* a small harp of ancient Scotland and Ireland [15C. < Irish *cláirseach*, Gaelic *clársach*]

clar·y /klérree/ (*plural* **-ies**) *n* a perennial plant of the mint family. Native to: southern Europe. Genus: *Salvia*. [14C. Via obsolete French *clarie* < medieval Latin *sclarea*]

clash /klash/ *v* (**clashed, clash·ing, clash·es**) **1.** *vi* FIGHT OR ARGUE to come into verbal or physical conflict with somebody **2.** *vi* BE AT ODDS WITH SOMETHING to be incompatible ○ *The conclusions clash with the evidence.* **3.** *vti* MAKE LOUD NOISE to make a loud harsh metallic noise, or hit things together to make such a noise **4.** *vi* NOT HARMONIZE to look unpleasant or inharmonious when together ○ *The orange of the upholstery clashes with the pink of the paintwork.* ■ *n* **1.** FIGHT OR ARGUMENT a short fierce encounter, verbal or physical, with another person or group **2.** LOUD METALLIC SOUND a loud harsh metallic noise **3.** LACK OF HARMONY a jarring or unpleasant juxtaposition of incompatible colors **4.** CONFLICT CAUSED BY DIFFERENCE a difference of opinions or qualities that causes conflict ○ *a clash of personalities* [Early 16C. An imitation of the sound]

SYNONYMS See ***fight.***

clasp /klasp/ *vt* (**clasped, clasp·ing, clasps**) **1.** HOLD SOMEBODY OR SOMETHING TIGHTLY to hold somebody or something tightly with the hands or arms ○ *She clasped the baby tightly to herself in the surging crowd.* ○ *I clasped the handrail as the boat lurched.* **2.** FASTEN THINGS to fasten or hold two things together with a device designed for this purpose ■ *n* **1.** SMALL BUCKLE OR FASTENING a small fastening for holding things such as bags or jewelry closed or together **2.** TIGHT HOLD a firm tight hold with the arms, a hand, or a device for fastening or holding things together **3.** IDENTIFYING ATTACHMENT ON MILITARY MEDAL a small metal bar on the ribbon of a medal that identifies the military action or service for which the honor was awarded [14C. Origin ?]

clasp·er /klásper/ *n* **1.** either of a pair of structures located in the anal region of some male insects and crustaceans and used to grasp a female during copulation **2.** either of a pair of long reproductive organs on the pelvic fins of male sharks and rays

clasp knife *n* a pocket knife with one or more blades and sometimes other devices that can be folded back into the handle

class /klass/ *n* **1.** GROUP TAUGHT TOGETHER a group of students or pupils who are taught or study together **2.** PERIOD OF TEACHING a period when students meet to be taught a particular subject ○ *When's our next biology class?* **3.** SPECIFIC SUBJECT TAUGHT a particular course of instruction **4.** STUDENTS WHO GRADUATE TOGETHER the group of students who graduate from an institution in the same year **5.** GROUP WITHIN SOCIETY a group of people within a society who share the same social and economic status **6.** SOCIAL GROUP WITH SIMILAR OPPORTUNITIES a category of people who have a similar level of opportunity to obtain economic resources and prestige **7.** STRUCTURE OF SOCIETY the structure of divisions in a society determined by the social or economic grouping of its members **8.** ELEGANCE IN STYLE elegance in appearance, behavior, or lifestyle (*informal*) ○ *a First Lady with real class* **9.** EXCELLENCE admirable skill or excellence in performance (*informal*) ○ *a player who lacks class* **10.** DIVISION ACCORDING TO QUALITY a categorization of services or goods according to quality ○ *This airline has several classes of seating.* **11.** GROUP OF SIMILAR ITEMS a group of things with at least one common characteristic **12.** SET OF RELATED ORGANISMS a major category in the taxonomic classification of related organisms, comprising a group of orders ○ *Elephants and dolphins both belong to the class Mammalia.* **13.** MATH, LOGIC same as **set**[2] *n* (sense 7) **14.** *UK* UNIVERSITY HONORS DEGREE GRADE a grade assigned to university honors degrees in the United Kingdom ■ *vt* (**classed, class·ing, clas·ses**) ASSIGN SOMEBODY OR SOMETHING TO GROUP to assign somebody or something to a particular category or group ○ *if you're classed as eligible to vote* [Mid-16C. < Latin *classis* "political class"]

SYNONYMS See ***type.***

class. *abbr* **1.** ARTS classic **2.** ARTS classical **3.** BIOL, GOV classification **4.** BIOL, GOV classified

class act *n* a person or thing regarded as an example of excellence (*informal*)

class ac·tion *n* an action brought by one or a number of litigants representing others sharing the same legal problem and seeking remedy or relief for all

class-con·scious *adj* **1.** overly concerned about people's relative social status **2.** describes a person or political party that believes in class struggle —**class-con·scious·ness** *n*

clas·ses CHR plural of **classis**

clas·sic /klássik/ *adj* **1.** TOP QUALITY generally considered to be of the highest quality or lasting value, especially in the arts **2.** DEFINITIVE authoritative and perfect as a standard of its kind ○ *a classic example of a mixed metaphor* **3.** ALWAYS FASHIONABLE always fashionable and elegant, usually because of simplicity and restraint in style ○ *the classic "little black dress"* **4.** GENERALLY ACCEPTED conforming to generally accepted principles or methods **5.** EXTREMELY AND USUALLY COMICALLY APROPOS apropos to an extreme degree, usually with a comical or ironic twist (*informal*) ○ *It was classic – the way she tripped while she was telling us all to be careful!* ■ *n* **1.** WORK OF HIGHEST QUALITY something created or made, especially a work of art, music, or literature, that is generally considered to be of the highest quality and of enduring value ○ *The novel has become a 20th-century classic.* ○ *a design classic* **2.** SIMPLE ELEGANT GARMENT a piece of clothing of a simple and enduring style **3.** OUTSTANDING OR TYPICAL EXAMPLE something that is an outstanding or typical example of its kind ○ *Last night's show was a classic.* **4.** MAJOR SPORTING EVENT a major sporting event, e.g., a horserace or golf tournament **5.** SOMETHING COMICALLY APROPOS something that is comically or ironically apropos (*informal*)

USAGE classic or **classical**? There is some overlap in the meanings of these words, but essentially ***classic*** describes the value or status of something (*a classic example of Art Deco*), whereas ***classical***, though often implying a judgment of value or worth, is a more factual reference to the literature, art, and culture of the ancient world or to the high period of an art form (*a classical education, classical music, classical ballet*). A ***classic*** is something created or made that is of the highest quality, whereas ***classics*** is the study of the languages and cultures of ancient Greece and Rome.

clas·si·cal /klássik'l/ *adj* **1.** RELATING TO ANCIENT GREECE OR ROME relating or belonging to the ancient Greeks or Romans or their cultures ○ *classical literature* ○ *a classical scholar* **2.** IN ANCIENT GREEK OR ROMAN STYLE in the style of ancient Greece or Rome, especially in architecture **3.** OF MUSIC CONSIDERED TO BE SERIOUS describes music that is considered serious or intellectual and is usually written in a traditional or formal style, as opposed to such genres as pop, rock, and folk music **4.** OF 18C AND 19C MUSIC describes the style of music composed in Europe in the 18th and 19th centuries **5.** STUDYING LATIN AND GREEK consisting of or involving the study of the ancient Greek and Latin languages and literature ○ *a classical education* **6.** ORTHODOX OR CONSERVATIVE considered as the traditional or authoritative form of something ○ *classical Freudianism* **7.** same as **classic** *adj* (sense 2) **8.** PHYS EXCLUDING QUANTUM THEORY AND RELATIVITY not taking into account quantum theoretical or relativistic effects [Late 16C. < Latin *classicus* "of the first class" < *classis* "political class"] —**clas·si·cal·i·ty** /klàssi kállətee/ *n* —**clas·si·cal·ness** *n*

USAGE See ***classic.***

clas·si·cal con·di·tion·ing *n* the teaching of a response to a new stimulus by pairing it repeatedly with a stimulus for which there is a biological reflex. The best-known example is Pavlov's experiment in which dogs heard a bell ring every time food appeared and eventually started salivating at the sound of the bell alone. ◊ **operant conditioning**

clas·si·cal·ism *n* ARTS same as **classicism**

clas·si·cal Lat·in *n* the form of the Latin language used between the end of the 1st century B.C. and the 3rd century A.D., when the standard authors of classical literature wrote

clas·si·cal·ly /klássik'lee/ *adv* **1.** SIMPLY STYLED in a simple and elegant style **2.** AS TRADITIONALLY ACCEPTED OR DONE in a manner that is traditionally accepted and belongs in the mainstream of the relevant art **3.** IN MANNER OF GRECO-ROMAN CULTURE in the style of ancient Greece or Rome **4.** AS USUALLY OCCURS used to indicate what usually or typically happens ○ *Classically, cases like this are solved through painstaking investigation.* **5.** AS TYPICAL EXAMPLE as a classic example of something **6.** IN CLASSIC WAY in a classic or classical manner

clas·si·cal school *n* the economic theory of wealth creation, derived from the principles of Adam Smith and others, that advocates free trade

clas·si·cism /klássi sìzzəm/, **clas·si·cal·ism** /klássik'l ìzzəm/ *n* **1.** RESTRAINED STYLE IN ARTS a style of art and architecture based on Greek and Roman models or principles, characterized by regularity of form and restraint of expression **2.** GREEK OR LATIN IDIOM a Greek or Latin phrase or expression **3.** STUDY OF GRECO-ROMAN CULTURE the study or knowledge of ancient Greece and Rome

clas·si·cist /klássissist/ *n* **1.** a scholar of ancient Greek and Latin **2.** a supporter of classicism in the arts

clas·si·cize /klássi sīz/ (**-cized, -ciz·ing, -ciz·es**) *vt* to imbue something with classical qualities or characteristics ○ *classicized the design of the windows*

clas·sics /klássiks/ *n also* **Clas·sics** the academic study of the languages, literature, and history of ancient Greece and Rome (*takes a singular verb*) ■ *npl* a body of ancient Greek and Roman literature (*takes a plural verb*)

USAGE See ***classic.***

clas·si·fi·ca·tion /klàssifi káysh'n/ *n* **1.** ORGANIZATION INTO GROUPS the allocation of items to groups according to type ○ *classification of members according to abilities and interests* **2.** CATEGORY a group or category within an organized system ○ *The classification "history" can be further subdivided.* **3.** CATEGORIZATION OF LIVING THINGS the categorization of organisms into defined groups on the basis of identified characteristics. The Linnaean classification groups organisms into species, genera, families, and higher taxonomic groups on the basis of visible resemblances, while other systems may use other determining factors, e.g., the molecular relationships among the groups. **4.** DESIGNATION AS SENSITIVE INFORMATION the restriction of sensitive government or military information to authorized people [Late 18C. < French < *classe* "class" < Latin *classis* "political class"] —**clas·si·fi·ca·to·ry** /klássifikə tàwree, kla síffikə-/ *adj*

clas·si·fi·ca·tion sched·ule *n* the complete plan and content of a library's cataloging system

clas·si·fied /klássi fìd/ *adj* **1. SECRET OR SENSITIVE** available only to authorized people for reasons of national security. The basic categories of classified information are confidential, secret, and top secret. **2. GROUPED BY TYPE** arranged in groups according to a classification system ■ **clas·si·fieds** *npl* **GROUP OF ADVERTISEMENTS** classified advertisements printed together in a newspaper or magazine (*informal*)

clas·si·fied ad·ver·tise·ment, clas·si·fied ad *n* a small advertisement positioned with others of similar content in a newspaper or magazine

clas·si·fy /klássi fì/ (**-fied, -fy·ing, -fies**) *vt* **1.** to assign things or people to categories **2.** to designate information as being available only to authorized people for reasons of security [Late 18C. Back-formation < CLASSIFICATION] —**clas·si·fi·a·ble** *adj* —**clas·si·fi·er** *n*

class in·ter·val *n* any of the intervals into which adjacent discrete values of a variable are divided

clas·sis /klássiss/ (*plural* **clas·ses** /klá seez/) *n* **1.** in some Reformed churches, a governing body composed of elders and pastors **2.** a district or group of churches governed by a classis [Late 16C. < Latin, "political class"]

class·ism /klá sìzzəm/ *n* discrimination or prejudice based on social or economic class —**class·ist** *adj, n*

class·less /klásslǝss/ *adj* **1.** not having social or economic classes **2.** not belonging to or associated with a particular social or economic class —**class·less·ness** *n*

class·mate /kláss màyt/ *n* a member of the same school class as another person

class num·ber *n* a series of letters and/or numbers on a book or other publication in a library identifying it, the category of its subject matter, and usually its shelf location

class·room /kláss ròom, -ròom/ *n* a room, especially in a school or college, where classes are held

class strug·gle *n* the Marxist principle of a continuous struggle for political and economic power between the ruling and working classes

class·work /kláss wùrk/ *n* school work that students do in lessons at school, as opposed to at home or after school

class·y /klássee/ (**-i·er, -i·est**) *adj* very stylish and elegant (*informal*) —**class·i·ly** *adv* —**class·i·ness** *n*

clast /klast/ *n* a fragment of rock produced by the breaking down of larger rocks [Mid-20C. Back-formation < CLASTIC]

clas·tic /klástik/ *adj* **1.** able to be separated into parts or have parts removed to enable better study ○ *Clastic models are often used to teach anatomy.* **2.** describes rock that is composed of fragments of other rocks [Late 19C. < French *clastique* < Greek *klastos* "broken in pieces"]

clath·rate /kláth ràyt/ *n* **CRYSTAL WITH EMBEDDED SUBSTANCE** a solid compound with a physical structure in which molecules of one substance are fully enclosed within the crystal structure of another ■ *adj* **1. WITH CRYSTAL-EMBEDDED SUBSTANCE** having molecules of one substance enclosed fully within the crystal structure of another substance **2. LIKE LATTICE** resembling a lattice in structure or appearance [Mid-19C. < Latin *clathrat-*, past participle of *clathrare* "fit with bars" < *clathri* "lattice" < Greek *klēthra* "bars"]

clat·ter /kláttər/ *v* (**-tered, -ter·ing, -ters**) **1.** *vti* **MAKE RATTLING NOISE** to make, or cause something to make, a loud rattling noise ○ *We heard the horses' hooves clattering down the cobbled road.* **2.** *vi* **CHATTER NOISILY** to chatter or prattle, especially noisily ■ *n* **1. BANGING METALLIC SOUND** a loud metallic banging or rattling noise ○ *the clatter of pots and pans in the kitchen* **2. NOISY CHATTER** noisy chatter and prattling talk **3. LOUD COMMOTION** a noisy disturbance [Assumed Old English *clatrian* < Germanic, probably an imitation of the sound] —**clat·ter·er** *n* —**clat·ter·ing·ly** *adv*

Clau·del /klō dél/, **Paul Louis Charles Marie** (1868–1955) French writer and diplomat. His symbolism and devout Catholicism inform such dramas as *The Satin Slipper* (1928–29).

clau·di·ca·tion /klàwdi káysh'n/ *n* **1.** limping or impaired gait, especially as a result of reduced blood supply to the leg muscles **2.** MED same as **intermittent claudication** [15C. < Latin *claudication-* < *claudicare* "to limp" < *claudus* "gait-impaired"]

clause /klawz/ *n* **1.** a group of words consisting of a subject and its predicate **2.** a distinct section of a document, especially a legal document, that is usually separately numbered [13C. < French < assumed Latin *clausa* "close of a rhetorical period" < *claudere* "to close"] —**claus·al** *adj*

claus·tro·phobe /kláwstrə fòb/ *n* PSYCHIAT same as **claustrophobic** [Mid-20C. Back-formation < CLAUSTROPHOBIA]

claus·tro·pho·bi·a /klàwstrə fóbee ə/ *n* an irrational fear of being in a confined or enclosed space [Late 19C. < modern Latin < *claustrum* (see CLOISTER)]

claus·tro·pho·bic /klàwstrə fóbik/ *adj* **1. CONFINED OR CRAMPED** unpleasantly or uncomfortably confined ○ *The room is claustrophobic but painting the walls a light color might help.* **2. OF OR HAVING CLAUSTROPHOBIA** relating to or having claustrophobia ■ *n* **SOMEBODY WHO FEARS ENCLOSED SPACES** somebody who is affected by claustrophobia —**claus·tro·pho·bi·cal·ly** *adv*

cla·vate /kláy vàyt/ *adj* with one end thicker than the other ○ *Some protozoa have clavate cilia.* [Early 19C. < modern Latin *clavatus* < Latin *clava* "club (for striking)"] —**cla·vate·ly** *adv*

cla·ve[1] /klaá vày/ *n* either of a pair of hardwood sticks that are hit together to make a clicking sound [Early 20C. Via American Spanish < Spanish, "keystone" < Latin *clavis* "key"]

clave[2] /klayv/ past tense of **cleave**[2]

clav·i·cem·ba·lo /klàvvi chémbəlō/ (*plural* **-los**) *n* MUSIC same as **harpsichord** [Mid-18C. Via Italian < medieval Latin *clavicymbalum*, literally "key cymbal"]

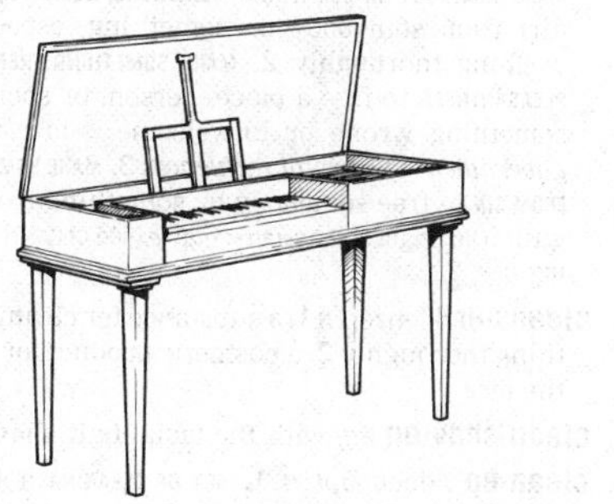

clavichord

clav·i·chord /klávvi kàwrd/ *n* a keyboard instrument of the 15th to 19th centuries, a precursor of the modern piano, in which small wedges strike horizontal strings to produce a soft sound [15C. < medieval Latin *clavichordium* < Latin *clavis* "key" + *chorda* "string"] —**clav·i·chord·ist** *n*

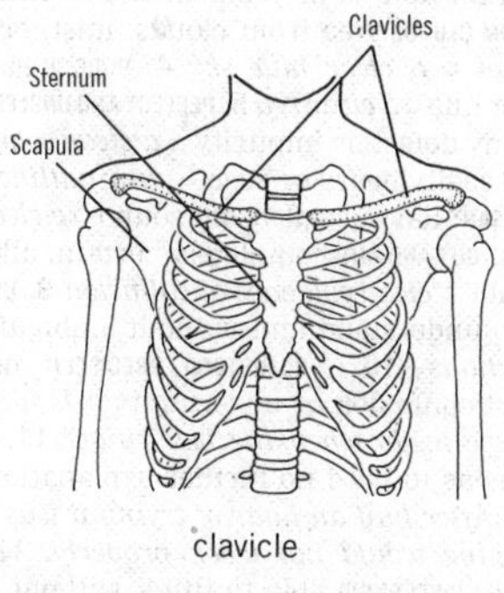

clavicle

clav·i·cle /klávvik'l/ *n* **1.** the long curved bone that connects the upper part of the breastbone with the shoulder blade at the top of each shoulder in humans **2.** a bone or structure with a function similar to that of the human clavicle in some other animals. It is reduced or absent in many mammals. [Early 17C. < Latin *clavicula* "small key" < *clavis* "key"] —**cla·vic·u·lar** /klə víkyələr, kla-/ *adj*

cla·vier /klə veér, klávvee ər/ *n* **1.** a stringed keyboard musical instrument **2.** the keyboard of a musical instrument [Early 18C. Directly or via German *Klavier* < French < medieval Latin *claviarius* "key-bearer" < Latin *clavis* "key"]

Cla·vi·us /kláyvee əss/ large walled plain on the Moon near the south pole, approximately 140 mi./225 km in diameter

claw /klaw/ *n* **1. ANIMAL'S SHARP NAIL** a pointed curved nail on the end of each toe in birds, some reptiles, and some mammals **2. PINCER** an appendage used for grasping in crabs and other invertebrates **3. APPENDAGE RESEMBLING CLAW** something resembling a claw in shape or function, e.g., a mechanical grabbing device ■ *v* (**clawed, claw·ing, claws**) **1.** *vti* **ATTACK WITH CLAWS** to scratch or dig at something or somebody with claws, fingernails, or something similar ○ *The dogs had clawed at the door.* **2.** *vt* **FORM SOMETHING BY SCRATCHING** to form something by digging or scratching with claws or something similar ○ *Using our bare hands we clawed a hole in the sand.* [Old English *clawu* < Germanic] —**clawed** *adj* —**claw·less** *adj*

claw off *vi* to avoid the dangers of a lee shore or other hazard by sailing as close to the wind as possible on alternate tacks

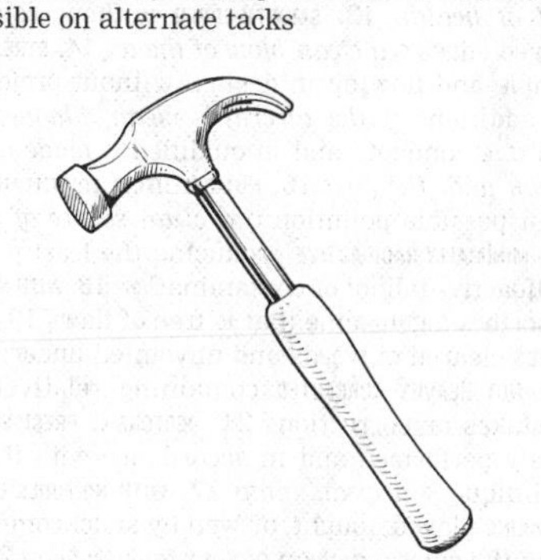

claw hammer

claw ham·mer *n* **1.** a hammer with a tapered fork at one end of its head for removing nails **2.** CLOTHING same as **swallow-tailed coat** (*informal*)

clay /klay/ *n* **1. TYPE OF FINE SOIL OR ROCK** a fine-grained material consisting mainly of hydrated aluminum silicates that occurs naturally in soil and sedimentary rock. Use: in making bricks, ceramics, and cement. **2. MODELING SUBSTANCE** a substance like clay used for modeling **3. HEAVY STICKY EARTH** earth, especially heavy sticky wet earth **4. HUMAN BODY** the physical body of a human being, particularly the matter of which it is composed (*literary*) ○ *From clay we are made.* **5.** TENNIS same as **clay court 6.** SPORTS same as **clay pigeon** (sense 1) ■ *vt* (**clayed, clay·ing, clays**) **COVER SOMETHING WITH CLAY** to cover or fill something with clay [Old English *clæg* < Indo-European] —**clay·ey** *adj*

Clay /klay/, **Cassius** ➧ **Ali, Muhammad**

Clay, Henry (1777–1852) US politician. He long served in Congress and was the architect of the Missouri Compromise (1820–21) and the Compromise of 1850 that temporarily averted civil war.

"I had rather be right than be President."
[Henry Clay, *Speech in the Senate*; 1850]

clay court *n* a tennis court with a hard surface made of crushed clay or shale

Clay·ma·tion /klay máysh'n/ *tdmk* a service mark for an animated motion-picture process using clay figurines that are moved and filmed so as to create lifelike imagery and motion

clay min·er·al *n* hydrated aluminum silicate. Source: clay.

clay·more /kláy màwr/ *n* **1.** a large double-edged broadsword formerly used by Scottish Highlanders **2.** ARMS same as **claymore mine** [Early 18C. < Gaelic *claidheamh mor* "great sword"]

clay·more mine *n* a landmine in the shape of a convex disk that is placed above ground and detonates horizontally. It is designed to kill or maim approaching personnel.

clay·pan /kláy pàn/ *n* hardpan that is composed mainly of clay

clay pig·eon *n* **1.** a clay disk hurled into the air from a machine and used as a target for shooting **2.** somebody who is vulnerable to attack (*slang*)

clay·stone /kláy stṑn/ *n* a compact fine-grained rock containing primarily clay particles

clean /kleen/ *adj* **1.** NOT DIRTY free from dirt or impurities ○ *clean hands* **2.** UNADULTERATED containing no foreign matter or pollutants ○ *a clean water supply* **3.** FREE OF INFECTION not infected or diseased ○ *a clean wound* **4.** WASHED freshly laundered or washed after use ○ *fetched some clean shirts* **5.** PARTICULAR ABOUT PERSONAL HYGIENE taking pains over personal hygiene or grooming ○ *He is very clean in his habits.* **6.** EMPTY containing nothing at all (*informal*) ○ *The apartment was stripped clean by the previous tenants.* **7.** MORALLY UPRIGHT morally pure and upright **8.** FAIR not corrupt or dishonest ○ *a clean verdict* **9.** NOT RUDE not rude or obscene **10.** BLANK without anything on it, especially anything written ○ *a clean sheet of paper* **11.** WITH NO POLICE RECORD having or showing no record of convictions or penalties, e.g., for driving offenses ○ *Don's record is clean.* **12.** FREE OF PROBLEMS without problems or difficulties ○ *The doctor gave me a clean bill of health.* **13.** SMOOTH-EDGED without rough or jagged edges ○ *a clean blow of the ax* **14.** STREAMLINED simple and flowing in design, without projections or additions ○ *the aircraft's clean silhouette* **15.** COMPLETE complete and unqualified ○ *made a clean break with the past* **16.** NOT POLLUTING producing the least possible pollution ○ *a clean source of energy* **17.** MINIMALLY RADIOACTIVE producing the least possible radioactive fallout or contamination **18.** WITH NO FLAWS describes a gemstone that is free of flaws **19.** FREE OF WEEDS cleared of weeds and unwanted undergrowth **20.** NOT HEAVILY CORRECTED containing relatively few mistakes or corrections **21.** PERFORMED PRECISELY precisely performed and in accordance with the best technique ○ *a clean jump* **22.** WITH NO FOULS OR RULE-BREAKING played, fought, or won by strict compliance with the rules ○ *a clean victory for our team* **23.** WITH NO ILLEGAL DRUGS not containing or possessing illegal drugs (*slang*) **24.** UNADDICTED free from addiction to narcotic drugs or other substances (*slang*) **25.** WITH NO CONCEALED ARMS not carrying concealed weapons (*slang*) ○ *A body search revealed that the suspect was clean.* **26.** INNOCENT not guilty of a specific crime (*slang*) **27.** JUDAISM RITUALLY UNDEFILED describes somebody who is ritually undefiled according to Jewish law **28.** JUDAISM ABLE TO BE LAWFULLY EATEN describes food that may be eaten according to Jewish law **29.** CHR PURE IN SPIRIT spiritually pure or purified ■ *v* (**cleaned, clean·ing, cleans**) **1.** *vti* MAKE SOMETHING FREE OF DIRT to rid something of dirt or impurities ○ *Have you finished cleaning your room?* **2.** *vt* REMOVE DIRT to get rid of unwanted dirt, stains, or marks ○ *cleaned the mud from her boots* **3.** *vi* GET FREE OF DIRT to become free of dirt, chiefly because of a content or structure that easily repels it ○ *This acrylic rug cleans easily.* **4.** *vt* RID SOMETHING OF CORRUPTION to free something of dishonest practices ○ *bent on cleaning the system of corruption.* **5.** *vt* PREPARE DEAD ANIMAL FOR COOKING to prepare a dead animal for cooking by removing its entrails **6.** *vt* REMOVE CONTENTS OF SOMETHING to use up the contents of something ○ *The children cleaned their plates and asked for more.* ■ *n* SESSION OF CLEANING a spell of removing unwanted dirt or marks ■ *adv* **1.** IN ORDER TO REMOVE DIRT so as to make something free from dirt **2.** IN ORDER TO REMOVE EVIDENCE so as to rid something of incriminating evidence **3.** WITH NO OBSTRUCTION directly, especially without having any obstruction **4.** CLEANLY in a clean way ○ *Does this type of gas burn clean?* ○ *We wanted to play the game clean.* **5.** ENTIRELY completely or utterly (*informal*) ○ *I clean forgot to call.* [Old English *clǣne* < Germanic, "pure"] —**clean·a·ble** *adj* —**clean·ness** *n* ◇ **come clean** to confess or tell the truth about something (*informal*)

clean out *vt* to use up or steal all of somebody's money or belongings (*slang*) ○ *Buying the new bike cleaned me out.*

clean up *v* **1.** *vti* MAKE SOMETHING CLEAN OR NEAT to make somebody or something clean or neat ○ *Can you just give me a minute to clean up in here?* **2.** *vt* ERADICATE SOMETHING UNPLEASANT to rid a place of something unpleasant such as pollution or crime **3.** *vi* MAKE MONEY to acquire a large amount of money (*slang*) ○ *They really cleaned up in the stock market last year.*

clean and jerk *n* in weightlifting, a movement in which the weight is lifted to shoulder height, held there briefly, and then quickly pushed above the head

clean-cut *adj* **1.** neat in dress or appearance ○ *a clean-cut young officer in a spotless uniform* **2.** distinctly outlined or designed **3.** same as **clear-cut** *adj* (sense 1)

clean·er /kléenər/ *n* **1.** somebody whose job is to clean the interior of a building **2.** a chemical or machine used for cleaning

clean·ers /kléenərz/ *n* a business establishment where clothes and other items are taken to be dry-cleaned ○ *My best suit is at the cleaners.* ◇ **take somebody to the cleaners** to deprive somebody of his or her money or possessions by dishonest means (*slang*)

clean-limbed *adj* having a well-proportioned and youthful-looking body

clean·li·ness /klénlinəss/ *n* the degree to which somebody keeps clean or a place is kept clean ○ *a small hotel noted for its cleanliness*

clean-liv·ing *adj* never doing anything that might be considered immoral or unhealthy

clean·ly /kléenlee/ *adv* **1.** EASILY OR EFFICIENTLY with ease or efficiency ○ *a cleanly executed triple jump on the ice* **2.** WITHOUT JAGGED EDGES in a manner that does not leave rough edges ○ *The saw cut cleanly.* **3.** FAIRLY in a fair manner **4.** IN CLEAN WAY in a way that is clean ○ *Work cleanly in the kitchen, avoiding spills.*

clean room *n* a room maintained with minimal contamination from dust or bacteria. Such rooms are used in the aerospace and electronics industries and in various kinds of scientific research.

cleanse /klenz/ (**cleansed, cleans·ing, cleans·es**) *vt* **1.** MAKE SOMEBODY OR SOMETHING THOROUGHLY CLEAN to remove dirt from somebody or something, especially by washing thoroughly **2.** MAKE SOMETHING FREE FROM UNPLEASANTNESS to free a place, person, or society from something wrong or unwelcome ○ *to cleanse the government of corrupt influences* **3.** MAKE SOMEBODY FREE FROM SIN to free somebody or something from sin or guilt [Old English *clǣnsian* < *clǣne* (see CLEAN)] —**cleans·ing** *n*

cleans·er /klénzər/ *n* **1.** a substance for cleaning something thoroughly **2.** a cosmetic product for cleaning the face

clean-shav·en *adj* with the facial hair shaved off

clean·up /kléen ùp/ *n* **1.** ACT OF CLEANING a thorough cleaning ○ *This garage needs a good cleanup.* **2.** ELIMINATION OF SOMETHING BAD an elimination of something unpleasant or unwanted **3.** LARGE GAIN a large and often illicit acquisition of assets (*slang*) **4.** BATTING POSITION IN BASEBALL in baseball, the fourth position in the batting order, usually held for a known heavy hitter who can drive in runs

clear /kleer/ *adj* **1.** FREE FROM WHAT DIMS free from anything that darkens or obscures ○ *a clear stream* **2.** TRANSPARENT able to be seen through ○ *clear glass* **3.** FREE FROM CLOUDS free from clouds, mist, or airborne particles ○ *a clear blue sky* **4.** PURE IN HUE pure in color or hue ○ *a clear red* **5.** PERFECT AND UNBLEMISHED free from any defect or impurity ○ *a clear complexion* **6.** DISTINCT easily heard or seen ○ *clear outlines* **7.** SOUNDING PLEASANT having a pleasant sound ○ *a clear singing voice* **8.** OUT-AND-OUT completely certain, allowing for no doubt ○ *clear evidence of collusion* **9.** UNAMBIGUOUS easy to understand and without ambiguity ○ *clear instructions* **10.** UNDERSTOOD PRECISELY understood without confusion or uncertainty ○ *Is it clear what you have to do when the bell rings?* **11.** EVIDENT so obvious as to need no further explanation or guidance ○ *After half an hour of trying it was clear that the engine would not work properly.* **12.** MENTALLY SHARP AND DISCERNING able to think without confusion ○ *You'll do better in the exam if you keep your mind clear.* **13.** WITHOUT GUILT free from feelings of guilt or blame ○ *a clear conscience* **14.** UNOBSTRUCTED free from obstructions or hindrances ○ *Keep the aisles clear.* **15.** EMPTY empty, with all movable items removed **16.** NOT ATTACHED TO OR TOUCHING SOMETHING free of, or freed from, connection or contact ○ *must be clear of any moving parts* **17.** NET net of deductions or charges ○ *I earn a clear $500 a week.* **18.** NOT FINANCIALLY OBLIGATED not having any debt or financial obligation **19.** SHOW JUMPING UNPENALIZED without any penalties being incurred ○ *jumped a clear round* ■ *adv* **1.** OUT OF THE WAY completely away from something ○ *Please stand clear of the doors until the vehicle has stopped.* **2.** ALL THE WAY totally or completely (*informal*) ○ *They moved clear across the country.* ■ *v* (**cleared, clear·ing, clears**) **1.** *vi* DISSIPATE AND DISPERSE to undergo the process of dissolving or dispersing, thereby disappearing ○ *By noon the fog had finally cleared.* **2.** *vi* NO LONGER BE FOGGY OR DULL to brighten and become free of adverse conditions ○ *There will be rain in the morning, but the skies will clear by the early afternoon.* **3.** *vti* MAKE OR BECOME TRANSPARENT to become or make something transparent or translucent ○ *The water cleared as the particles sank to the bottom.* **4.** *vt* RID SOMETHING OF EXTRANEOUS MATTER to free something of impurities or unwanted matter ○ *clear a drain of blockages* **5.** *vt* RID THROAT OF OBSTRUCTIONS to rid the throat of phlegm or other obstructions by coughing **6.** *vt* CLARIFY THOUGHTS to remove confusion or misunderstanding from the mind ○ *I'd like a few minutes to clear my head before going into the meeting.* **7.** *vi* RETURN TO SENSES to become or make the mind free from the dulling effects of alcohol, drugs, illness, or a blow to the head ○ *After my head had cleared I was able to stand up again.* **8.** *vt* PROVE SOMEBODY INNOCENT to free somebody from suspicion or blame ○ *anxious to clear her name* **9.** *vt* REMOVE OBJECTS OR OBSTRUCTIONS FROM SOMETHING to empty a space of objects or obstructions ○ *The room had been cleared.* **10.** *vt* FORM SPACE FOR SOMEBODY OR SOMETHING to make a route for somebody or something by removing obstructions **11.** *vt* REMOVE PEOPLE FROM PLACE to empty a building or place of people, e.g., for security reasons ○ *Police had to clear the area.* **12.** *vt* DISENTANGLE SOMETHING to straighten out something that is snarled or otherwise in disarray or disorder ○ *Hurry up and clear that anchor line!* **13.** *vt* MOVE PAST SOMETHING WITHOUT TOUCHING to move past or over something without touching it ○ *If we stay on this course we should clear the buoy.* **14.** *vti* ALLOW TO UNLOAD OR DEPART to be allowed to unload or depart, or allow a vehicle or cargo to unload or passengers to depart, after customs and other formalities have been dealt with ○ *The plane has been cleared for landing.* **15.** *vt* GIVE SOMEBODY AUTHORIZATION to authorize somebody to do something or go somewhere ○ *You are now cleared to enter the restricted area.* **16.** *vt* GAIN MONEY AS PROFIT to earn or acquire something as profit (*informal*) ○ *We cleared $5,000 on the deal.* **17.** *vt* PAY OFF DEBT to settle a debt **18.** *vi* MOVE BETWEEN ACCOUNTS to be authorized and credited to the account of the payee ○ *Checks take three days to clear.* **19.** *vti* SETTLE BANKING ACCOUNTS to settle the accounts of a banking transaction through a clearinghouse **20.** *vt* GET BALL OUT OF DEFENSE AREA to get the ball or puck out of the defense area **21.** *vt* DELETE DATA to delete data from a computer display or storage device ■ *n* OPEN SPACE an empty or open area or space ○ *The deer were standing in the clear.* [13C. Via Old French *cler* < Latin *clarus* "clear, bright"] —**clear·a·ble** *adj* —**clear·er** *n* —**clear·ness** *n* ◇ **in the clear** free from suspicion or blame

ORIGIN The Latin word *clarus*, "clear," "bright," from which ***clear*** is derived, is also the source of English *chiaroscuro, claret, clarify, clarion,* and *declare.*

clear away *vt* to tidy somewhere by removing objects and other materials

clear out *v* **1.** *vi* to leave a place quickly or urgently (*informal*) ○ *We cleared out as fast as we could.* **2.** *vt* to remove the contents of something such as a room or closet, or to neaten something by removing some of its contents ○ *clearing out the attic*

clear up *v* **1.** *vi* BECOME BRIGHTER to become brighter, e.g., after rain **2.** *vti* MAKE OR GET BETTER to alleviate or cure something, or be alleviated or cured **3.** *vti* PUT SOMETHING IN ORDER to straighten up something by removing or arranging disorganized contents ○ *Please clear up all this mess before you leave.* **4.** *vt* SOLVE OR EXPLAIN SOMETHING to solve a mystery or explain a misunderstanding ○ *Here is a big problem that has never been fully cleared up.*

clear·ance /kleéranss/ *n* **1.** REMOVING UNWANTED OBJECTS the removal of obstructions or unwanted objects such as dilapidated buildings or overgrown bushes before building or cultivating **2.** PERMISSION FOR SOMETHING TO HAPPEN permission to do something or for something to take place ○ *several aircraft awaiting clearance to take off* **3.** WIDTH OR HEIGHT OF OPENING the width or height of an opening or passage ○ *Clearance on these freeway overpasses is limited, so big trucks must detour.* **4.** CHEAP SALE OF MERCHANDISE a sale of goods at reduced prices in order to clear stock **5.** PASSAGE OF COMMERCIAL DOCUMENTS the passage of commercial documents through a clearinghouse **6.** REMOVAL OF PEOPLE FROM LAND the forcible removal from an area of land of the people who have traditionally lived there **7.** GETTING BALL OUT OF DEFENSE AREA in games, the process of clearing the ball or puck from the defense area **8.** MIL same as **security clearance** **9.** FORESTRY same as **clearing** (sense 1)

clear-cut *adj* **1.** UNAMBIGUOUS so definite as to leave no possibility of ambiguity **2.** DISTINCTLY OUTLINED with a distinct outline or form ○ *a clear-cut silhouette of a naval frigate on the horizon* ■ *vt* REMOVE ALL TREES FROM AREA to cut down and remove all of the trees from a forest or other area of land ■ *n* LAND WITH ALL TREES REMOVED land from which all the trees and undergrowth have been cut and removed

clear-eyed *adj* **1.** DISCERNINGLY PERCEPTIVE able to discern things clearly **2.** SHARP-EYED having sharp sight **3.** BRIGHT-EYED having bright eyes

clear-fell *vt UK* same as **clear-cut**

Clear·field /kleér feéld/ city in northern Utah, east of the Great Salt Lake and northwest of Salt Lake City. Population: 26,309 (2002 estimate).

clear-head·ed *adj* able to think clearly and decisively, especially in difficult circumstances —**clear-head·ed·ly** *adv* —**clear-head·ed·ness** *n*

clear·ing /kleéring/ *n* **1.** a space without trees in an area of land that is wooded or overgrown **2.** exchange between banks of checks, drafts, and notes, and the settlement of consequent differences

clear·ing bank *n UK* any bank that uses a central clearinghouse for transferring credits and checks between itself and other banks

clear·ing·house /kleéring hòwss/ (*plural* **-hous·es** /-hòwzəz/) *n* **1.** an institution where financial transactions between member banks are canceled against each other, leaving only balances to be paid **2.** an agency that collects and distributes information

clear·ing house in·ter·bank pay·ment sys·tem *n* an electronic system for international dollar payments and currency exchanges (*used in e-commerce*)

Clear Lake /kleér-/ lake in northwestern California, popular for leisure activities. It is the largest freshwater lake in the state. Length: 25 mi./40 km.

clear·ly /kleérlee/ *adv* **1.** WITH NO PROBLEM IN HEARING in a way that is easy to hear **2.** WITH NO PROBLEM IN SEEING in a way that is easy to see **3.** WITH NO PROBLEM IN UNDERSTANDING in a way that is easy to understand ○ *a clearly phrased piece of legislation* **4.** LOGICALLY in a logical and unconfused manner ○ *a clearly written legal brief* **5.** OBVIOUSLY used to acknowledge that a statement is undeniably true ○ *Clearly, we must take immediate action.*

clear-out *n UK* a session of removing the contents of something such as a room, or of straightening it by removing some of its contents ○ *We had a great clear-out at the weekend and now we've got room for the new table.*

clear-sight·ed *adj* **1.** having or showing good perception or judgment **2.** having sharp vision —**clear-sight·ed·ly** *adv* —**clear-sight·ed·ness** *n*

clear·sto·ry *n* ARCHIT same as **clerestory**

Clear·wa·ter /kleér wàwtər/ city in western Florida on the Gulf of Mexico, directly west of Tampa. Population: 108,313 (2002 estimate).

clear·way /kleér wày/ *n UK* a section of road where drivers may not normally stop

clear·wing /kleér wìng/ *n* a moth with scaleless transparent wings that is active during the daytime. Family: Sesiidae.

cleat /kleet/ *n* **1.** HARD PIECE ATTACHED UNDER SHOE a small piece of metal or hard plastic attached to the sole of a shoe to improve its grip **2.** NAUT DEVICE FOR SECURING BOAT a device with two projections pointing in opposite directions to which a rope can be tied to secure a boat **3.** DEVICE ON BOOT FOR CLIMBING TREES a device with a blade or set of sharp projections that is attached to a boot to assist in climbing trees or poles **4.** WEDGE-SHAPED SUPPORT a wooden or other wedge attached to a structure in order to support it ■ **cleats** *npl* PAIR OF SPORTS SHOES a pair of shoes with small projections on the soles used for playing sports on soft surfaces ■ *vt* (**cleat·ed, cleat·ing, cleats**) **1.** PROVIDE SOMETHING WITH CLEATS to fix a cleat or cleats to something, or support something using a cleat **2.** SECURE ROPE TO CLEAT to tie a rope to a cleat [14C. Ultimately < W Germanic, "firm lump"]

cleav·age /kleévij/ *n* **1.** CREASE VISIBLE BETWEEN BREASTS the hollow visible between a woman's breasts when a low-cut garment is worn **2.** SPLIT IN SOMETHING a split, division, or separation of something **3.** ACT OF SPLITTING division or splitting **4.** GEOL, MINERALS ROCK OR MINERAL FRACTURE the splitting of minerals or rocks along natural planes of weakness determined by their internal crystal lattice. The angle of cleavage is one of the features used to identify minerals. **5.** BIOL REPEATED DIVISION OF FERTILIZED EGG the repeated division of a fertilized ovum (**zygote**) before formation of the early embryo (**blastula**). The zygote does not increase in size during this process because the cells become progressively smaller after each division. **6.** CHEM SPLITTING OF MOLECULE the splitting of a molecule into simpler molecules through the breaking of a chemical bond

cleave[1] /kleev/ (**cleaved** or **cleft** /kleft/ or **clove** /klōv/, **cleaved** or **cleft** or **clo·ven** /klṓvən/, **cleav·ing, cleaves**) *vti* **1.** SPLIT to split, or make something split, especially along a plane of natural weakness **2.** CUT PATH THROUGH SOMETHING to make a way through something (*literary*) **3.** PENETRATE SOMETHING to penetrate or pierce something deep or dense such as water or heavy undergrowth (*literary*) [Old English *clēofan* < Indo-European] —**cleav·a·ble** *adj*

cleave[2] /kleev/ (**cleaved** or **clove** /klōv/ or **clave** /klayv/, **cleaved, cleav·ing, cleaves**) *vi* to cling closely, steadfastly, or faithfully to somebody or something (*formal*) ○ *Is it wrong to cleave to such fond memories?* [Old English *cleofian* < Indo-European]

cleav·er /kleévər/ *n* a heavy knife with a broad blade, used by butchers

Clea·ver /kleévər/, **Eldridge** (1935–98) US political activist. He became minister of information of the Black Panther Party (1967) but left the United States to avoid arrest (1968). He advocated armed revolution, but later became a born-again Christian.

cleav·ers /kleévərz/ *n* an annual plant with slender sprawling stems, narrow leaves, and spiny round fruits that cling to animals and clothing. Native to: Europe, Asia. Latin name: *Galium aparine*. (*takes a singular verb*) [Alteration of Old English *clife*, related to CLEAVE[2]; because its bristles stick to whatever they come in contact with]

Cle·burne /kleé bùrn/ city in northern Texas, south of Fort Worth and north of Waco. Population: 27,492 (2002 estimate).

clef /klef/ *n* in written or printed music, a symbol placed at the beginning of each staff to indicate the pitch [Late 16C. Via French < Latin *clavis* "key"]

cleft[1] /kleft/ *n* **1.** a small indentation in a surface such as skin or land ○ *The river descends through a cleft in the cliffs.* **2.** a substantial gap or division separating two things (*formal*) ○ *the cleft between the party members and the leadership* [Old English *geclyft* < Germanic]

cleft[2] /kleft/ past participle, past tense of **cleave**[1] ■ *adj* having been separated into two or more sections by division

cleft lip *n* an upper lip congenitally divided into two parts that have been only partially reunited by surgery

cleft pal·ate *n* a congenital fissure along the midline of the roof of the mouth. It is caused by a failure of the two sides of the hard palate to meet and fuse during fetal development and is often associated with a cleft lip.

cleis·tog·a·mous /klī stóggəməss/ *adj* relating to or bearing small flowers that do not open, are self-pollinated in the bud, and appear in addition to brighter flowers on the same plant [Late 19C. < Greek *kleistos* "closed" < *kleiein* "to close"] —**cleis·tog·a·mous·ly** *adv* —**cleis·tog·a·my** *n*

Clel·and /klélland/, **John** (1709–89) British government official and writer, author of the bawdy *Fanny Hill, the Memoirs of a Woman of Pleasure* (1748–49)

clem·a·tis /klémmətiss, klə máttiss/ (*plural* **-tis·es** or *same*) *n* a climbing plant with fluffy seed heads. Flowers: large, flat, typically blue, purple, pink, or white. Native to: northern temperate regions. Genus: *Clematis*. [Mid-16C. Via Latin, "clematis, periwinkle" < Greek *klēmatis* < *klēma* "vine branch"]

Cle·men·ceau /klèmmən sṓ, kle maaN-/, **Georges** (1841–1929) French journalist and politician. He was prime minister of France (1906–09, 1917–20) and helped to formulate the Treaty of Versailles, which formally ended World War I.

> "We have won the war: now we have to win the peace, and it may be more difficult."
> [Georges Clemenceau. Quoted in *Clemenceau*, D. R. Watson; 1974]

clem·en·cy /klémmənssee/ (*plural* **-cies**) *n* **1.** SHOWING MERCY the tendency to show mercy or leniency ○ *appealed for clemency for the imprisoned activists* **2.** ACT OF MERCY an act that bestows or shows mercy toward another person ○ *the judge's clemency toward the youth* **3.** MILDNESS IN WEATHER mildness or temperateness, especially in the weather ○ *the clemency of areas affected by the Gulf Stream*

Clem·ens /klémmənz/, **Roger** (*b.* 1962) US baseball player. Renowned for his fastball, he won the Cy Young Award as the American League's best pitcher a record six times in his career with the Boston Red Sox, the Toronto Blue Jays, and the New York Yankees.

Clem·ens, Samuel Langhorne ➧ **Twain, Mark**

clem·ent /klémmənt/ *adj* **1.** showing or experiencing no extremes in weather conditions **2.** showing mercy or leniency [15C. < Latin *clement-* "mild, gentle"] —**clem·ent·ly** *adv*

Clem·ent I /klémmənt/, **St.** (*d.* A.D. 101?) Roman pope (A.D. 92?–101?). The third or fourth successor to St. Peter, he probably wrote the *Epistle to the Corinthians* (A.D. 95?), a vital document on papal authority. Known as **Clement of Rome**

Clem·ent VII (1478–1534) pope. During his papacy (1523–34), Rome was sacked (1527) by troops of the Holy Roman Emperor and the English church broke with Rome (1533). Born **Giulio de' Medici**

Cle·men·te /klə mén tay/, **Roberto** (1934–72) Puerto Rican-born US baseball player. Playing for the Pittsburgh Pirates (1955–72), he won 12 Gold Gloves for fielding and was also an outstanding batter. Full name **Clemente, Roberto Walker**

cle·men·tine /klémmən tīn, -teen/ *n* an orange-colored citrus fruit, bred by crossing a tangerine with a Seville orange [Early 20C. < French *clémentine*]

Clem·son /klémss'n/ city in northwestern South Carolina, on the northeastern shore of Hartwell Lake, northwest of Anderson. Population: 11,967 (2002 estimate).

clench /klench/ *v* (**clenched, clench·ing, clench·es**) **1.** *vt* HOLD TEETH OR FIST TIGHTLY TOGETHER to close your teeth or fist tightly, e.g., when angry **2.** *vt* CLUTCH SOMETHING to hold or grip something tightly ○ *He clenched the rope in his teeth.* **3.** *vti* CONTRACT to contract, or cause a muscle to contract, suddenly, often as a result of sudden tension or emotion ○ *His jaw clenched as he waited.* **4.** *vt* NAUT another spelling of **clinch** *v* (sense 4) ■ *n* **1.** TIGHT HOLD a tight hold or grip ○ *She held the steering wheel in a tight clench.* **2.** DEVICE THAT GRIPS TIGHTLY a mechanical device that holds or grips something firmly [Old English *beclencan* < Germanic, "to stick"] —**clenched** *adj*

Cle·o·pat·ra /kleé ə páttrə/ (69–30 B.C.) Egyptian monarch. A queen (51–30 B.C.) of legendary beauty, she and her lover Mark Antony were defeated by Octavian's forces at Actium (31 B.C.).

CLEP /klep/ *tdmk* a trademark for a standardized test for gaining college credit by examination in the

United States. Full form **College-Level Examination Program**

clep·sy·dra /klépsədrə/ (*plural* **-dras** or **-drae** /-drèe/) *n* an ancient device used for measuring time by noting the amount of water or mercury that passes through a small aperture during a particular period [Mid-17C. Via Latin < Greek *klepsudra* < *kleptein* "steal" + *hudor* "water"]

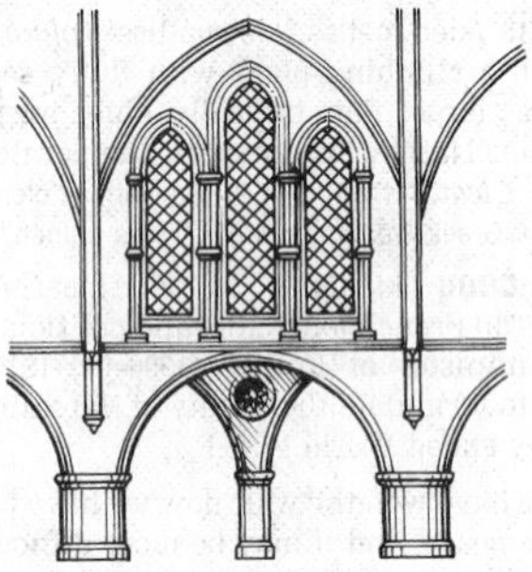

clerestory

clere·sto·ry /kleér stàwree/ (*plural* **-ries**), **clear·sto·ry** *n* the upper part of the wall of a building, especially of a church nave, that contains windows [< earlier spelling of CLEAR]

cler·gy /klúrjee/ (*plural* **-gies**) *n* the body of people ordained for religious service, especially in the Christian church (*takes a singular or plural verb*) [13C. Partly < Old French *clergie* (< *clerc* "cleric"); partly < *clergé* "body of clerks"; both < ecclesiastical Latin *clericus* (see CLERK)]

cler·gy·man /klúrjeemən/ (*plural* **-men** /-mən/) *n* a man who is a member of the clergy

cler·gy·wom·an /klúrjee wòommən/ (*plural* **-wom·en** /-wìmmin/) *n* a woman who is a member of the clergy

cler·ic /klérrik/ *n* a member of the clergy [Early 17C. < ecclesiastical Latin *clericus* (see CLERK)]

cler·i·cal /klérrik'l/ *adj* **1.** OF OFFICE WORK relating to office work, especially of a routine administrative kind **2.** OF CLERGY relating or belonging to the clergy **3.** PROMOTING CLERICALISM advocating or supporting clericalism —**cler·i·cal·ly** *adv*

cler·i·cal col·lar *n* a stiff white collar, continuous at the front, worn by some members of the Christian clergy

cler·i·cal·ism /klérrik'l ìzzəm/ *n* **1.** a policy of supporting the power or views of the clergy **2.** the power or influence of the clergy —**cler·i·cal·ist** *n*

cler·i·hew /klérrə hyoò/ *n* a humorous or satirical verse consisting of two rhyming couplets in lines of irregular meter about somebody who is named in the verse [Early 20C. After Edmund *Clerihew* Bentley (1875–1956), British writer]

clerk /klurk/ *n* **1.** OCCUPATIONS, COMM same as **salesclerk 2.** SERVICE DESK WORKER somebody at a service desk who helps and advises other people **3.** GENERAL OFFICE WORKER a worker who performs general office duties such as keeping records or sending out correspondence **4.** GOVERNMENT WORKER WHO KEEPS RECORDS an official who keeps transcripts and other records of a legislative or other body **5.** LAW ADMINISTRATOR IN COURT OF LAW an administrator of the business of a court **6.** LAW LAWYER WHO WORKS FOR JUDGE a lawyer, typically one just recently graduated from law school, who is employed as an assistant to a sitting judge **7.** CHR CLERIC a member of the clergy (*formal*) [Pre-12C. Via ecclesiastical Latin *clericus* "of the clergy" < Greek *klērikos* < *klēros* "heritage"] —**clerk** *vi* —**clerk·dom** *n* —**clerk·ship** *n*

clerk·ly /klúrklee/ *adj* **1.** relating to or characteristic of a clerk ○ *a clerkly attention to detail in the midst of a crisis* **2.** same as **scholarly** (*archaic*) —**clerk·li·ness** *n*

Cler·mont-Fer·rand /kler mòN fə raàN/ capital of Puy-de-Dôme Department, Auvergne Region, south central France. It is an industrial city. Population: 137,140 (1999).

cle·veite /kleè vìt/ *n* a crystalline form of uraninite [Late 19C. After Per T. *Cleve* (1840–1905), Swedish chemist]

Cleve·land /kleévlənd/ **1.** city and port in northeastern Ohio on the southeastern shore of Lake Erie. Population: 467,851 (2002 estimate). **2.** city in southeastern Tennessee, northeast of Chattanooga and southwest of Athens. Population: 37,380 (2002 estimate).

Grover Cleveland

Cleve·land, Grover (1837–1908) 22nd and 24th president of the United States. A Democrat with a reputation for scrupulous honesty, he spent both his terms as president (1885–89, 1893–97) opposing special interests and the political spoils system. Full name **Cleveland, Stephen Grover**. See table at **president**

Cleve·land Heights city in northeastern Ohio, an eastern suburb of Cleveland. Population: 49,734 (2002 estimate).

clev·er /klévvər/ *adj* **1.** SHOWING INTELLIGENCE demonstrating mental agility and creativity ○ *It's a clever idea, but will it work?* **2.** INTELLIGENT having sharp mental abilities **3.** GLIBLY FACILE showing highly capable mental abilities in a showy or superficial way ○ *Don't give me one of your clever answers.* **4.** DEXTEROUS highly skilled in using the hands **5.** *New England* EASILY MANAGED describes an animal that is easily managed and controlled **6.** *New England* EASYGOING BUT NOT BRIGHT friendly, easygoing, and affable in manner and personality but not particularly smart **7.** *Southern US* HAVING PLEASANT DISPOSITION having a pleasant disposition and personality [13C. Origin ?] —**clev·er·ly** *adv* —**clev·er·ness** *n*

SYNONYMS See ***intelligent***.

clev·is /klévviss/ *n* a U-shaped device with a hole at the end of each prong through which a pin or bolt can be pushed to secure another part in place [Late 16C. Origin ?]

clew /kloo/ *n* **1.** BALL OF THREAD a wound ball of thread or yarn **2.** SAILING CORNER OF FORE-AND-AFT SAIL the rear lower corner of a triangular or four-sided sail set along the length of a boat **3.** SAILING CORNER OF SAIL SET ACROSS BOAT either of the two lower corners of a sail such as a square sail or a spinnaker set parallel to the width of a boat ■ **clews** *npl* NAUT HAMMOCK CORDS the cords by which a hammock is suspended ■ *vt* (**clewed, clew·ing, clews**) ROLL THREAD INTO BALL to roll thread or yarn into a ball [Old English *cliwen*, probably related to CLAW]

clew up *vt* to furl a square sail by pulling on lines attached to its lower corners

CLI *abbr* ECON cost-of-living index

cli·an·thus /klī ánthəss/ (*plural* **-thus·es** or *same*) *n* a plant of the pea family. Flowers: scarlet in drooping clusters. Native to: Australia, New Zealand. Genus: *Clianthus*. [Mid-19C. < modern Latin < Greek *kleos* "glory" + *anthus* "flower"]

cli·ché /klee sháy/ *n* **1.** a phrase or word that has lost its original effectiveness or power from overuse **2.** an overused activity or notion [Mid-19C. < French, past participle of *clicher* "stereotype"]

cli·chéd /klee sháyd/ *adj* having lost all original effectiveness or power as a result of overuse

Cli·chy /klee sheé/ northern industrial suburb of Paris, France. Population: 50,179 (1999).

click /klik/ *n* **1.** SHORT SHARP SOUND a short sharp sound, often metallic but not resonant **2.** COMPUT PRESS OF COMPUTER MOUSE BUTTON a single action of pressing and releasing a button on a computer mouse **3.** MECH ENG MECHANICAL COMPONENT FOR LOCKING POSITION a component of a mechanical device that holds a part in a locking position **4.** PHON SOUND PRODUCED BY SUCKING IN AIR a consonant sound produced by sucking in air and moving the tongue against the soft palate. It is part of the phonemic system of some African languages such as Xhosa, but in English is used only for the sound represented by "tut-tut." Technical name **suction stop** ■ *v* (**clicked, click·ing, clicks**) **1.** *vti* MAKE SHORT SHARP SOUND to make, or cause something to make, a short sharp sound **2.** *vti* COMPUT PRESS COMPUTER MOUSE BUTTON to press and release a button of a computer mouse ○ *Click on "yes."* **3.** *vi* BECOME CLEARLY UNDERSTOOD to be understood suddenly (*informal*) ○ *It finally clicked where I'd seen him before.* **4.** *vi* EASILY COMMUNICATE OR WORK TOGETHER to communicate or work together easily and readily (*informal*) ○ *The partners never clicked.* **5.** *vi* BE SUCCESS to be successful or popular (*informal*) ○ *The new show clicked from the very first performance.* [Late 16C. An imitation of the sound]

click·able /klíkəb'l/ *adj* describes an item on a computer screen that may be activated by clicking on it with the mouse

click-and-mor·tar *adj* BUSINESS same as **clicks-and-mortar**

click art *n* computer clip art for use in illustrating electronic documents

click bee·tle *n* a beetle that can right itself when inverted by springing into the air with a clicking sound. Family: Elateridae.

click·er /klíkər/ *n* somebody or something that clicks, especially a remote control or a counting device

click rate *n* the number of times that a site in an Internet advertisement is visited, as a percentage of the number of times the advertisement is viewed (*used in e-commerce*)

clicks-and-mor·tar, **click-and-mor·tar** *adj* describes a hybrid business involved in e-commerce that also markets its products through a traditional store or uses other physical structures such as warehouses (*used in e-commerce*) [After *bricks-and-mortar*]

click·stream /klík streèm/ *n* the path of mouse clicks that somebody makes in navigating the Internet, sometimes used in marketing research (*used in e-commerce*)

click·through /klík thròo/ *n* a measure of the effectiveness of an Internet advertisement, based on the number of times the viewer accesses the advertisement (*used in e-commerce*)

cli·ent /klī ənt/ *n* **1.** SOMEBODY USING PROFESSIONAL SERVICE a person or organization taking advice from an attorney, accountant, or other professional person **2.** CUSTOMER a person or organization to whom goods or services are provided and sold **3.** USER OF SOCIAL SERVICES AGENCY a user of the services offered by a social services agency **4.** PERSON OR ENTITY HELPED BY ANOTHER a person or entity dependent on the protection or patronage of another person or entity ○ *the former Soviet Union and its clients in the Middle East* **5.** COMPUT COMPUTER PROGRAM THAT REQUESTS DATA a computer program that obtains data from a program on another computer, often one linked on a network. An Internet browser is a specific kind of client. [14C. < Latin *client-* "dependent" < *cluere* "obey"] —**cli·en·tal** *adj* —**cli·ent·less** *adj*

cli·ent·age /klī əntij/ *n* a social system in which free commoners receive the patronage of wealthy or influential aristocrats. It was common in ancient Rome and has become a feature of some modern societies.

cli·ent-cen·tered ther·a·py *n* a form of psychotherapy in which the therapist seeks to elicit solutions to problems by gaining the trust of the patient through careful questioning. It was founded by Carl Rogers in the 1940s and is still used widely as a counseling method.

cli·en·tele /klī ən tél, kleè-/ *n* the clients or customers of a professional organization or business, considered as a group ○ *bars that have a youthful clientele* [Mid-16C. Directly and via French < Latin *clientela* < *client-* (see CLIENT)]

cli·ent-serv·er, **cli·ent/serv·er** *adj* describes a computer network in which processing is divided between a client program running on a user's machine and a network server program. One server can provide data to, or perform storage-intensive processing tasks in conjunction with, one or more clients.

cli·ent state *n* a country that depends on another for economic, political, or military support

cliff /klif/ *n* a high steep rock or ice face, especially a rock face extending along a coastline [Old English *clif* < Germanic] —**cliff·y** *adj*

cliff brake *n* a fern often found on dry rocky areas or on cliffs that has compound, often leathery, leaves. Genus: *Pellaea.* [Back-formation < BRACKEN (taken as plural)]

cliff dwell·er *n* a member of an Anasazi people who constructed dwellings on ledges of cliffs in what is now the southwestern United States

Barnaby's
cliff dwelling: Mesa Verde, Colorado

cliff dwell·ing *n* a building or group of buildings lived in by cliff dwellers

cliff·hang·er /klíf hàngər/ *n* **1.** an unresolved ending in a part of a serialized drama or book that leaves the audience or reader eager to know what will happen next **2.** a situation full of tension or suspense because it is not clear what will happen next [< early serial films in which characters were left hanging off the edge of a cliff at the end of an episode] —**cliff·hang·ing** *adj*

Cliff·side Park /klífsīd-/ borough in northeastern New Jersey, northeast of Jersey City and opposite New York City. Population: 22,954 (2002 estimate).

Clif·ton /klíftən/ city in northeastern New Jersey, northwest of Newark and Jersey City, near the Passaic River. Population: 79,626 (2002 estimate).

Clif·ton Park town in eastern New York, northeast of Schenectady. Population: 34,383 (2002 estimate).

cli·mac·ter·ic /klī máktərik, klī mak térrik/ *n* **1.** a period in which critically important changes take place **2.** PHYSIOL same as **menopause** (*technical*) **3.** BOT a stage in the ripening of some fruits such as apples when the rate of respiration increases [Mid-16C. < French < Greek *klimaktēr* "rung of a ladder" < *klimax* "ladder"] —**cli·mac·ter·ic** *adj* —**cli·mac·ter·i·cal·ly** *adv*

cli·mac·tic /klī máktik/ *adj* **1.** extremely exciting or decisive **2.** relating to or forming a climax [Late 19C. < CLIMAX] —**cli·mac·ti·cal·ly** *adv*

USAGE climactic or **climatic**? ***Climactic***, coming from *climax*, means "exciting or decisive" and "forming a climax," as in *The hard-fought election was climactic* [not *climatic*]. *In a climactic* [not *climatic*] *passage, the author kills off the heroine.* ***Climatic***, coming from *climate*, means "relating to weather," as in *severe climatic* [not *climactic*] *changes caused by global warming.*

cli·mate /klīmət/ *n* **1.** METEOROL **TYPICAL WEATHER IN REGION** the average weather or the regular variations in weather in a region over a period of years **2. PLACE WITH PARTICULAR WEATHER** a place with a particular type of weather ○ *I prefer a warm climate.* **3. INDOOR ENVIRONMENT** the prevailing conditions or environment in an indoor setting such as an office ○ *a climate-controlled building* **4. SITUATION** the situation or atmosphere that prevails at a particular time or place ○ *the exciting intellectual climate on campus* [14C. Via late Latin < Greek *klimat-* "slope, region of the earth"]

cli·mate change *n* long-term alteration in global weather patterns, especially increases in temperature and storm activity, regarded as a potential consequence of the greenhouse effect

cli·mat·ic /klī máttik/ *adj* relating to, causing, or caused by weather changes —**cli·mat·i·cal·ly** *adv*

USAGE See ***climactic.***

cli·mat·ic zone *n* an area of the Earth's surface that possesses a distinct type of climate. There are eight major climatic zones, roughly demarcated by lines of latitude. These consist of the tropical zone near the equator, two subtropical and two temperate zones, one boreal zone in the northern hemisphere, and the two polar ice caps.

cli·ma·tol·o·gy /klīmə tólləjee/ *n* the scientific study of climates —**cli·ma·to·log·ic** /klīmətə lójjik/ *adj* —**cli·ma·to·log·i·cal** *adj* —**cli·ma·to·log·i·cal·ly** *adv* —**cli·ma·tol·o·gist** *n*

cli·max /klī màks/ *n* **1. KEY MOMENT** the most important or exciting point in something such as an event or a story **2.** PHYSIOL **ORGASM** a sexual orgasm **3.** LITERAT **EVER-INTENSIFYING SEQUENCE OF PHRASES** a sequence of phrases or sentences, each more forceful or intense than the last, or the conclusion of such a sequence **4.** ECOL **FINAL STAGE IN ECOLOGICAL COMMUNITY'S DEVELOPMENT** a late or final stage in the development of an ecological community in which the composition of plants and animals is relatively stable and well matched to environmental conditions ■ *v* (**-maxed, -max·ing, -max·es**) **1.** *vti* **REACH KEY POINT** to reach the most important or exciting point in something such as an event or a story, or bring something to its most important or exciting point **2.** *vi* PHYSIOL **HAVE ORGASM** to have a sexual orgasm [Mid-16C. Via late Latin < Greek *klimax* "ladder, progression"]

climb /klīm/ *v* (**climbed, climb·ing, climbs**) **1.** *vti* **ASCEND USING HANDS AND FEET** to move toward the top of something, especially using the hands and feet ○ *climb a ladder* **2.** *vti* **MOVE UPWARD** to move upward, or move toward the top of something, by any means, and typically through continual or gradual effort ○ *climb the stairs* ○ *The plane climbed through a low cloud layer.* **3.** *vi* CLIMBING **BE MOUNTAINEER** to go up mountains or rocks on foot or using hands and feet as a sport **4.** *vi* **MOVE WITH EFFORT** to maneuver the body somewhere with effort or difficulty ○ *I managed to climb out of bed.* **5.** *vi* **RISE IN AMOUNT** to rise in value or amount ○ *temperature climbing into the nineties* **6.** *vti* **MOVE HIGHER SOCIALLY OR PROFESSIONALLY** to move to a higher social or professional position **7.** *vti* BOT **GROW UPWARD ON SOMETHING** to grow upward by using plants or objects as a support, e.g., by producing shoots or tendrils that cling to them ■ *n* **1. ACT OF CLIMBING** the process of moving to the top of something ○ *It was a steep climb to the top.* **2.** CLIMBING **HILL OR MOUNTAIN** a route used to go up a hill, mountain, or rock, or the hill, mountain, or rock itself **3. RISE IN VALUE OR AMOUNT** a rise in the value or amount of something [Old English *climban*, via W Germanic, "adhere" < Indo-European, "form into a ball"] —**climb·a·ble** *adj*

SPELLCHECK Do not confuse the spelling of ***climb*** and ***clime*** ("place with a particular climate"), which sound similar.

climb into *vt* to put on clothes, usually easy-to-wear ones (*informal*)

climb out of *vt* to take off clothes, usually easy-to-wear ones (*informal*)

climb·er /klīmər/ *n* **1. SOMEBODY WHO CLIMBS MOUNTAINS** somebody who climbs rocks or mountains as a sport **2.** BOT **PLANT THAT CLINGS** a plant that attaches itself to other plants or objects such as posts and walls as it grows **3. SOMEBODY ADVANCING SOCIALLY** somebody who steadily gains in rank or status, especially somebody who is unscrupulous and ambitious (*disapproving; usually used in combination*) ○ *derided the newcomers as social climbers*

climb·ing /klīming/ *n* the sport of climbing mountains or rocks

climb·ing fern *n* a fern that climbs and grows as pairs of twining fronds. E.g., Use: baskets, fish traps, mats. Native to: tropical and warm-temperate regions. Genus: *Lygodium.*

climb·ing frame *n UK* same as **jungle gym**

climb·ing iron *n* same as **crampon**

climb·ing wall *n* a wall with handholds and footholds, often located indoors, that is designed to provide practice at rock-climbing

clime /klīm/ *n* a place with a particular type of climate (*formal; often used in the plural*) ○ *off to sunnier climes* [Late 16C. Via Latin < Greek *klima* "slope"]

SPELLCHECK See ***climb.***

~~**climing**~~ incorrect spelling of **climbing**

-clinal *suffix* sloping, slanting ○ *isoclinal* [< Greek *klinein* "to lean"]

cli·nan·dri·um /kli nándree əm/ (*plural* **-dri·a** /-dree ə/) *n* a hollow in the upper column of the flower of an orchid, containing the anther [Mid-19C. < modern Latin, "stamen bed" < Greek *klinē* "couch"]

clinch /klinch/ *v* (**clinched, clinch·ing, clinch·es**) **1.** *vt* **RESOLVE SOMETHING DECISIVELY** to settle in a positive way the outcome of something such as a business deal or an argument **2.** *vi* **PUT ARMS AROUND OPPONENT** in boxing or wrestling, to put your arms around an opponent's body so as to pin the opponent's arms and prevent an exchange of blows **3.** *vt* CONSTR **FLATTEN END OF NAIL** to bend or flatten the protruding end of a nail or rivet, or attach two or more things together using nails or rivets in this way **4.** *vt* NAUT **FASTEN SOMETHING WITH KNOT** to fasten or secure something with a knot in a rope that is created by making a half hitch ■ *n* **1. PASSIONATE EMBRACE** a tight passionate embrace between lovers **2. TACTIC OF PINNING OPPONENT'S ARMS** in boxing or wrestling, a tactic designed to prevent an exchange of blows in which you put your arms around an opponent's body, pinning the opponent's arms to his or her sides **3.** CONSTR **NAIL WITH END BENT OVER** a nail or rivet with its protruding end bent over, or a fastening made in this way **4.** NAUT **KNOT IN ROPE** a knot in a rope that is created by making a half hitch [Mid-16C. Origin ?]

clinch·er /klínchər/ *n* **1. DECIDING FACTOR** the factor that decides the outcome of something such as an argument or a contest (*informal*) **2.** CONSTR **NAIL WITH END BENT OVER** a nail or rivet that has its protruding end bent over **3.** CONSTR **TOOL FOR BENDING NAIL** a tool for bending the ends of nails or rivets

cline /klīn/ *n* **1.** a continuum between two extremes **2.** a gradual variation in the characteristics of a plant or animal species that occurs when it is distributed over an area with differing environmental or geographic conditions [Mid-20C. < Greek *klinein* "to lean"] —**clin·al** *adj* —**cli·nal·ly** *adv*

ORIGIN The Indo-European word from which ***cline*** is ultimately derived, is also the ancestor of English *clinic, decline, enclitic, incline, ladder, lean*[1], and *recline.*

Cline /klīn/, **Patsy** (1932–63) US singer. Her slick, sentimental country songs such as "Crazy" (1961) attracted huge popular audiences. She died in a plane crash at the peak of her career. Born **Hensley, Virginia Patterson**

-cline *suffix* slope ○ *syncline* [Back-formation < -CLINAL]

cling /kling/ *vi* (**clung** /klung/, **cling·ing, clings**) **1. HOLD ONTO SOMEBODY OR SOMETHING TIGHTLY** to hold onto somebody or something tightly with the hands or arms **2. ADHERE TO SOMETHING** to adhere to something by sticking to it or staying very close to it **3. RETAIN IDEAS OR CUSTOMS** to refuse to give up something such as a belief or tradition that you have grown fond of or used to **4. HAVE EMOTIONAL NEED FOR SOMEBODY** to have a strong emotional attachment to somebody **5. LINGER** to linger, usually in the air, resisting dispersion or dissipation ■ *n* **1. STICKING QUALITY** the tendency of something to stick to surfaces **2.** BOT same as **clingstone** [Old English *clingan* "adhere" < Germanic] —**cling·er** *n* —**cling·ing·ly** *adv*

cling·fish /klíng fish/ (*plural same* or **-fish·es**) *n* a small fish whose pelvic fins have been modified into a sucking disk that it uses to attach itself to rocks or other objects. Family: Gobiesocidae.

Cling·mans Dome /klíngmənz-/ mountain on the boundary of North Carolina and Tennessee, and the highest peak in the Great Smoky Mountains. Height: 6,643 ft./2,025 m.

cling·stone /klíng stōn/ *n* a fruit with flesh that sticks to the pit. Some varieties of peach, nectarine, and plum have fruit of this type.

cling·y /klíngee/ (**-i·er, -i·est**) *adj* (*informal*) **1.** too dependent on the company or emotional support of other people **2.** sticking closely to the body ○ *a clingy fabric* —**cling·i·ness** *n*

clin·ic /klínnik/ *n* **1.** HEALTH SERVICES **MEDICAL CENTER** a medical center for outpatients, attached to a hospital or forming part of it **2.** HEALTH SERVICES **SPECIALIZED MEDICAL CENTER** a medical center that specializes in a particular condition or area of medicine **3.** HEALTH SERVICES **GROUP MEDICAL PRACTICE** an office or suite of offices where a number of doctors practice general medicine as a partnership **4.** EDUC **BEDSIDE TEACHING SESSION FOR MEDICAL STUDENTS** a teaching session during which student doctors are allowed to examine patients in hospital wards, or the teaching of medicine by this method **5. GROUP INSTRUCTION SESSION** a teaching session in which an expert in a particular field gives practical instruction and advice to a group ○ *a tennis clinic* [Mid-19C. Via French *clinique* < Greek *klinikē* (*tekhnē*) "(method of treating) the bedridden" < *klinikos* "of a bed" < *klinē* "bed" < *klinein* "to lean"]

-clinic *suffix* having a particular number of obliquely intersecting axes ○ ***triclinic*** [< Greek *klinein* "to lean"]

clin·i·cal /klínnik'l/ *adj* **1.** MED **BASED ON MEDICAL TREATMENT OR OBSERVATION** based on or involving medical treatment, practice, observation, or diagnosis **2. UNEMOTIONAL** practical and unemotional **3. SEVERE IN DECOR OR DESIGN** plain and severe in design, especially so as to seem uncomfortable —**clin·i·cal·ly** *adv*

clin·i·cal e·col·o·gy *n* the branch of medicine dealing with the supposed effects of the modern technological environment on human health, especially the relationship of allergies to the increase in chemicals in the environment

clin·i·cal end·point *n* a medical development that demonstrates that a definable stage in an illness has been reached

clin·i·cal nurse man·ag·er *n* the administrative manager of the nursing staff in a hospital

clin·i·cal psy·chol·o·gy *n* the branch of psychology that deals with the diagnosis and treatment of psychological and behavioral problems —**clin·i·cal psy·chol·o·gist** *n*

clin·i·cal ther·mom·e·ter *n* a thermometer used for measuring the temperature of somebody's body, which continues to register the observed temperature until reset

cli·ni·cian /kli nísh'n/ *n* **1.** a medical professional who works directly with patients, as distinct from one working in research **2.** a medical professional who practices or teaches in a clinic

clink[1] /klingk/ (**clinked, clink·ing, clinks**) *vti* to make, or cause something to make, the short, high-pitched, slightly ringing sound that metal or glass objects make when they knock against each other [14C. Ultimately an imitation of the sound] —**clink** *n*

clink[2] /klingk/ *n* a correctional institution, especially a prison (*dated slang*) [Early 16C. < the *Clink*, former prison in Southwark, borough of London]

clink·er[1] /klíngkər/ *n* **1. BALL OF COAL RESIDUE** a hard mass of ash and partially fused coal that remains after coal is burned in a fire or furnace **2. HARD BRICK** an overhard brick that has been fired in a kiln for too long ■ *vi* (**-ered, -er·ing, -ers**) **FORM LUMPY BURNED RESIDUE** to form hard lumps of ash and partially fused coal after burning [Mid-17C. Alteration of obsolete *clincard* < obsolete Dutch *klinckaerd* "brick" < *klinken* "to ring"; from the sound made by a brick when struck]

clink·er[2] /klíngkər/ *n* (*informal*) **1.** a failure, or something of very poor quality **2.** a wrong note in a piece of music [Mid-20C. < CLINK[1]]

clink·er-built *adj* describes a boat that has a hull made of overlapping planks [< *clinker* "clinched nail" < *clink* "secure a nail," variant of CLENCH]

clink·stone /klínk stōn/ *n* MINERALS same as **phonolite** [Translation of German *Klingstein* "ringing stone"; from its metallic resonance when struck]

clino- *prefix* slope, slant ○ *clinometer* [< Greek *klinein* "to lean"]

cli·nom·e·ter /klī nómmətər/ *n* an instrument used in surveying or geology to measure the angle of a slope or incline —**cli·no·met·ric** /klīnə méttrik/ *adj* —**cli·no·met·ri·cal** *adj* —**cli·nom·e·try** *n*

clin·o·py·rox·ene /klīnō pī rók seen/ *n* a silicate mineral of the pyroxene group, containing calcium, iron, and magnesium, and forming monoclinic crystals, e.g., augite

cli·no·stat /klīnə stàt/ *n* a piece of laboratory equipment with a turntable that allows a plant placed on it to be exposed to a stimulus such as light equally on all sides

-clinous *suffix* **1.** having stamens and pistils in a particular number of flowers ○ *diclinous* **2.** descending from a particular line ○ *matriclinous* [< Greek *klinein* "to lean"]

Clin·ton /klíntən/ **1.** city in Iowa, on the western bank of the Mississippi River, southeast of Cedar Rapids. Population: 27,443 (2002 estimate). **2.** city in central Mississippi, west of Jackson and east of Vicksburg. Population: 24,082 (2002 estimate).

Hillary Rodham Clinton and Bill Clinton

Clin·ton, Bill (*b.* 1946) 42nd president of the United States (1993–2001). Before his election to the White House he was Democratic governor of Arkansas (1978–80, 1982–92). In 1999 he was impeached and acquitted by the Senate for perjury and obstruction of justice. Full name **Clinton, William Jefferson**. See table at **president**

> "There is nothing wrong with America that cannot be cured by what is right with America."
> [Attributed to Bill Clinton]

Clin·ton, de Witt (1769–1828) US politician. He was governor of New York (1817–23), and ran for the US presidency in 1812.

Clin·ton, George (1739–1812) vice president of the United States. He was governor of New York (1777–95 and 1801–04) before becoming the 4th US vice president (1805–12).

Clin·ton, Hillary Rodham (*b.* 1947) US lawyer, first lady (1993–2001), and senator. After eight years as first lady, she was elected to the US Senate in 2000.

> "'It takes a village to raise a child'…a timeless reminder that children will only thrive if their families thrive and if the whole of society cares enough to provide for them."
> [Hillary Rodham Clinton, *New York Times*; February 5, 1996]

clin·to·ni·a /klin tṓnee ə/ *n* a broad-leafed perennial plant of the lily family with blue or purple berries. Flowers: white, yellow, or purplish. Genus: *Clintonia.* [Mid-19C. < modern Latin, after De Witt CLINTON]

Cli·o /klī ō/ (*plural* **-os**) *n* **1.** in Greek mythology, the Muse of history, one of the nine Muses believed to inspire and nurture the arts **2.** an annual award for excellence in television or radio advertising

cli·o·met·rics /klī ō méttriks/ *n* the study of economic history using statistics, advanced methods of data processing, analysis of mathematical data, and economic modeling (*takes a singular verb*) [Mid-20C. < CLIO] —**cli·o·met·ric** *adj* —**cli·o·me·tri·cian** /klī ō me trísh'n/ *n*

clip[1] /klip/ *v* (**clipped, clip·ping, clips**) **1.** *vt* **CUT OR TRIM SOMETHING** to cut or trim something, or cut it off, e.g., with scissors or shears ○ *clipped the dog's hair* **2.** *vt* **CUT SOMETHING OUT** to remove something from something else by cutting ○ *clipping a coupon from the newspaper* **3.** *vt* **SHORTEN TIME TAKEN FOR SOMETHING** to reduce the time taken to complete something ○ *clipped two minutes off the world record* **4.** *vt* **SIDESWIPE SOMEBODY OR SOMETHING** to make physical contact with somebody or something with a light glancing slapping blow (*informal*) ○ *clipped the other car with my fender* **5.** *vt* PHON **TRUNCATE SPEECH SOUND** to shorten a speech sound **6.** *vt* LING **ABBREVIATE WORD** to shorten a word or other expression by abbreviating it or dropping a syllable **7.** *vi* **GO FAST** to move at a brisk pace (*informal*) **8.** *vt* **SWINDLE SOMEBODY** to cheat or swindle somebody, especially by overcharging (*slang*) ■ *n* **1.** MOVIES, MEDIA **FILM OR TV EXTRACT** an extract, especially a short piece, from movie or television footage **2.** MEDIA **EXTRACT FROM PRINT MEDIA** a news story or other article cut out of a print publication **3. GLANCING BLOW** a sideswiping blow **4. RATE OF MOTION** the speed at which somebody or something moves (*informal*) ○ *Food prices shot up at their fastest clip in years.* **5. SINGLE OCCASION** a single time or occasion (*informal*) ○ *Drinks here cost $10 a clip.* [13C. Probably < Old Norse *klippa* "cut short"]

clip[2] /klip/ *n* **1. GRIPPING DEVICE** a device that grips or clasps loose things together or that holds things firmly (*often used in combination*) **2.** ARMS **BULLET HOLDER** a container for bullets, slotted directly into an automatic firearm **3.** JEWELRY **PIECE OF JEWELRY** a piece of jewelry with a gripping device that attaches to clothing **4.** FOOTBALL **ILLEGAL BLOCKING** in football, the act or an instance of illegally blocking a player on an opposing team by hitting that player with the body from behind ■ *v* (**clipped, clip·ping, clips**) **1.** *vti* **HOLD SOMETHING WITH GRIPPING DEVICE** to hold loose things together, or attach one thing to another, using a clip, or be attached in this way **2.** *vt* FOOTBALL **BLOCK PLAYER ILLEGALLY** in football, to block an opposing player illegally by hitting that person from behind [Old English *clyppan* "embrace, fasten" < W Germanic]

clip art *n* prepackaged artwork, available on software for use in documents produced on a computer [Because originally in the form of *clip sheets*, pages of drawings that graphic designers could cut out]

clip·board /klíp bàwrd/ *n* **1.** a small portable board with a clip attached at the top, used for securing papers and providing a hard writing surface **2.** a part of computer memory where cut or copied data are stored temporarily

clip-clop /klìp klóp/ *n* the rhythmic sound made by a walking horse's hooves as they strike hard ground ■ *vi* (**clip-clopped, clip-clop·ping, clip-clops**) to make the sound of hooves striking hard ground [Early 20C. An imitation of the sound]

clip joint *n* a shop or club that habitually overcharges its customers (*slang*) [< CLIP[1] "swindle"]

clip-on *adj* describes something, especially an item of clothing, that is attached by means of a clip ■ *n* an accessory that is attached with a clip, e.g., an earring or a tie

clipped /klipt/ *adj* **1.** trimmed or cut back neatly **2.** spoken with each word pronounced separately and distinctly

clipper

clip·per /klíppər/ *n* **1. FAST SAILING SHIP** a mid-19th-century tall ship with a sharp bow, designed for traveling at fast speeds **2.** METEOROL **WEATHER FRONT** a fast-moving weather front, usually one bringing cold air into a region **3. USER OF CUTTING TOOL** a cutter or shearer of something **4.** ELECTRONICS same as **limiter** (sense 1) ■ **clip·pers** *npl* **TOOL FOR CLIPPING SOMETHING** a hand tool for cutting or clipping something

clip·ping /klípping/ *n* **1.** an article cut out of a newspaper or magazine **2.** FOOTBALL same as **clip**[2] *n* (sense 4) ■ **clip·pings** *npl* pieces of grass or hair that have been cut or clipped off

clip·sheet /klíp shèet/ *n* an item or items from a newspaper or magazine reprinted on one side of the paper only, used for distribution to interested parties

clique /kleek, klik/ *n* a close group of friends or coworkers with similar interests and goals, whom outsiders regard as excluding them [Early 18C. < French *cliquer* "to click, clap," an imitation of the sound] —**cliqu·ey** *adj* —**cliqu·ish** *adj* —**cliqu·ish·ly** *adv* —**cliqu·ish·ness** *n*

cli·tel·lum /klī téllәm/ (*plural* **-la** /-lә/) *n* a glandular section, similar in shape to a saddle, in the body wall of some worms such as earthworms and leeches, that secretes a sticky substance during copulation. The substance is later used to form a sac in which the eggs are deposited. [Mid-19C. Via modern Latin < Latin *clitellae* "packsaddle" (from its shape), literally "little litters"]

clit·ic /klíttik/ *adj* describes a word that cannot be stressed and is pronounced as part of the word that follows or precedes it, e.g., "ve" in "I've" [Mid-20C. Back-formation < ENCLITIC, PROCLITIC] —**clit·ic** *n*

clit·o·ri·dec·to·my /klìttәri déktәmee/ (*plural* **-mies**) *n* the cutting off of all or part of a woman's or girl's clitoris, practiced in some societies as a social or cultural rite of passage

clit·o·ris /klíttәriss/ (*plural* **clit·o·ris·es** or **cli·tor·i·des** /kli táwri dèez/) *n* a sensitive erectile female sex organ at the front junction of the labia minora in the vulva [Early 17C. Via modern Latin < Greek *kleitoris* "little hill"] —**clit·o·ral** *adj*

Clive /klīv/, **Robert, Baron Clive of Plassey** (1725–74) British soldier and colonial administrator who was instrumental in establishing British rule in India. He served as governor of Bengal (1765–67) but later became embroiled in scandal and committed suicide. Known as **Clive of India**

clm. *abbr* column

clo·a·ca /klō áykә/ (*plural* **-cae** /-sèe/) *n* the terminal region of the gut in reptiles, amphibians, birds, and many fish, as well as in some invertebrates. The intestinal, urinary, and genital canals open into it. [Late 16C. < Latin, "sewer, canal"] —**clo·a·cal** *adj*

cloak /klōk/ *n* **1.** OUTER GARMENT a loose sleeveless outer garment that fastens at the neck **2.** ENSHROUDING OBJECT OR FORCE something that covers or conceals things (*formal*) ○ *left under a cloak of secrecy* ■ *vt* (**cloaked, cloak·ing, cloaks**) ENSHROUD SOMETHING to cover or conceal something (*often passive*) [13C. Via Old French *cloque* "bell, cloak" < medieval Latin *clocca*]

cloak-and-dag·ger *adj* involving secrecy or intrigue, often as part of an espionage operation [Translation of French *de cape et d'épée* "of cape and sword," symbols of the rank of characters in dramas of intrigue]

cloak fern *n* a fern that is adapted to dry conditions and is often used as an ornamental plant. Native to: tropical and temperate America. Genus: *Notholaena*.

cloak·room /klṓk ròom, -ròom/ *n* **1.** *UK* same as **coat check 2.** a lounge for members of a legislature, near or connected to the legislative chamber **3.** *UK* same as **restroom**

clob·ber /klóbbәr/ (**-bered, -ber·ing, -bers**) *vt* (*informal*) **1.** HIT SOMEBODY OR SOMETHING to hit somebody or something with great force **2.** DEFEAT SOMEBODY to defeat somebody decisively **3.** TREAT SOMEBODY OR SOMETHING HARSHLY to deal with somebody or something in a harsh or critical way ○ *The movie got clobbered by the critics.* [Mid-20C. Origin ?]

cloche /klōsh/ *n* **1.** a woman's or girl's close-fitting hat with a very narrow brim **2.** a small structure made of glass or clear plastic, placed over cold-sensitive garden plants in cold weather [Late 19C. Via French, "bell" < medieval Latin *clocca*; from the shape]

clock[1] /klok/ *n* **1.** DEVICE DISPLAYING TIME a freestanding device that measures and records time, which it displays by a pointer on a dial or by a digital readout **2.** MEASURING INSTRUMENT WITH DISPLAY a measuring instrument with a dial or a digital display, e.g., any of a vehicle's control gauges, especially the odometer **3.** BUSINESS same as **time clock 4.** ELECTRONIC CIRCUIT THAT SYNCHRONIZES COMPUTER PROCESSES an electronic circuit that generates pulses at a constant rate in order to synchronize the internal operations in a computer **5.** SEED HEAD OF DANDELION the fluffy white seed head of a dandelion **6.** same as **biological clock** (*informal*) ■ *vt* (**clocked, clock·ing, clocks**) **1.** MEASURE TIME SOMEBODY OR SOMETHING TAKES to measure or record the time somebody or something takes, using a stopwatch or an electronic timing device (*informal*) ○ *a car that was clocked at 95 mph* **2.** PUNCH SOMEBODY to punch somebody (*slang*) [14C. Via Middle Dutch, Middle Low German *klocke* < medieval Latin *clocca* "bell"] ◇ **against the clock** with limited time to finish something ◇ **around** *or* **round the clock** day and night, without stopping ◇ **turn** *or* **put the clock(s) back** to return to the conditions of an earlier time

clock in *vi* to arrive for work, or record arrival for work, by inserting a personalized card into a time clock

clock out *vi* to leave work, or record departure from work, by inserting a personalized card into a time clock

clock up *vt* to reach a particular total (*informal*) ○ *clocked up 1,500 miles on this trip*

clock[2] /klok/ *n* a design on the ankle or side of a stocking or sock [Mid-16C. Origin ?]

clock ra·di·o *n* an electronic device that incorporates a digital clock, an alarm clock, and a radio

clock speed *n* the speed of a microprocessor's internal clock that controls how fast a computer makes calculations, usually measured in megahertz (MHz) or gigahertz (GHz)

clock-watch·er *n* an employee who is eager to leave work as soon as possible —**clock-watch·ing** *n*

clock·wise /klók wīz/ *adv, adj* in the same direction that the hands of a clock move around a clock face

clock·work /klók wùrk/ *n* a mechanism consisting of cogs and a wound spring, used to drive a traditional clock or a moving toy ◇ **like clockwork** with unvarying regularity and predictability ○ *Thanks to the volunteers, the event ran like clockwork.*

clod /klod/ *n* **1.** a large lump of soil **2.** somebody regarded as unintelligent and slow-witted (*insult*) [14C. Variant of CLOT] —**clod·dish** *adj* —**clod·dish·ly** *adv* —**clod·dish·ness** *n* —**clod·dy** *adj*

clod·hop·per /klód hòppәr/ *n* somebody regarded as awkward and unsophisticated (*dated informal insult*) ■ **clod·hop·pers** *npl* a pair of large heavy shoes or boots (*informal*) [Early 18C. Originally "plowman"; from walking over plowed land with clods of earth]

clo·fi·brate /klō fī́ bràyt, klō fí bràyt/ *n* a drug used to reduce blood cholesterol, triglycerides, and uric acid [Mid-20C. < *clofibric acid*, probably < CHLORO- + *fibrate*, INN stem]

clog /klog/ *v* (**clogged, clog·ging, clogs**) **1.** *vti* BLOCK GRADUALLY to block a tube or opening gradually with dirt or dust, or become gradually blocked with dirt or dust **2.** *vt* TRANSP HINDER MOVEMENT IN SOMETHING to block something such as a road or tunnel, making movement difficult ■ *n* **1.** CLOTHING HEAVY SHOE a heavy shoe traditionally made of wood, or a shoe with a heavy, traditionally wooden, sole **2.** OBSTRUCTION something that works against somebody as an obstacle or hindrance **3.** WEIGHT RESTRICTING ANIMAL'S MOVEMENT a wooden block fastened to an animal's leg to restrict its movement [14C. Origin ?]

clog up *vti* same as **clog** *v* (sense 1)

clog dance *n* a dance performed by dancers wearing clogs, who tap or stamp in time to music

cloi·son·né /klòyz'n áy/ *adj* decorated with a pattern formed by pieces of enamel in various colors separated by strips of flattened wire [Mid-19C. < French, "partitioned," past participle of *cloisonner* < Old French *cloison* "partition" < Latin *claudere* "to close"] —**cloi·son·né** *n*

clois·ter /klóystәr/ *n* **1.** ARCHIT COVERED WALKWAY AROUND COURTYARD a continuous covered outdoor walkway built against buildings surrounding a central courtyard or quadrangle **2.** RELIG MONASTERY OR CONVENT a place where people live a life of religious seclusion and contemplation, e.g., a monastery or convent **3.** RELIG LIFE OF RELIGIOUS SECLUSION the life of religious seclusion lived by a monk or nun ○ *He chose the cloister rather than the secular world.* **4.** PLACE OF SECLUSION a place where people can be private or secluded ■ *vr* (**-tered, -ter·ing, -ters**) FIND PRIVATE PLACE to find a quiet private place where you can remain undisturbed [13C. Via Old French *cloistre* < medieval Latin *claustrum* < Latin, "bar, bolt" < *claudere* "to close"] —**clois·tral** *adj*

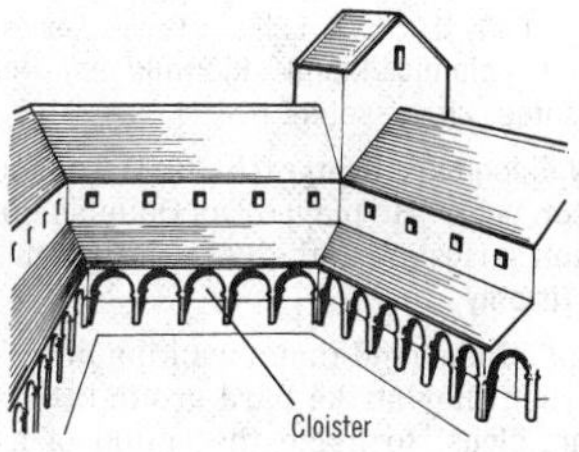

cloister

clois·tered /klóystәrd/ *adj* **1.** SECLUDED secluded from the ordinary life of the world ○ *had led a cloistered life* **2.** RELIG IN MONASTERY living or occurring in a monastery or convent **3.** ARCHIT WITH CLOISTER having a cloister for walking in

clom·i·phene /klómmә fèen, klṓmә-/ *n* a drug that induces ovulation. Use: infertility treatment. [Mid-20C. < CHLORO- + AMINE + PHENYL]

clo·mi·pra·mine /klō míppra mèen/ *n* a tricyclic drug. Use: to treat depression, phobias, and obsessional conditions.

clomp /klomp/ *n, vti* same as **clump**[2]

clone: first clone of an adult animal ("Dolly"), Roslin Institute, Edinburgh (1997)

clone /klōn/ *n* **1.** GENETICS GENETICALLY IDENTICAL ORGANISM a plant, animal, or other organism that is genetically identical to its parent, having developed by vegetative reproduction from a bulb, cutting, or other part, or, in experimental conditions, from a single cell **2.** GENETICS GROUP OF GENETICALLY IDENTICAL PROGENY a collection of organisms, cells, or molecular segments that are genetically identical direct descendants of a single parent by asexual reproduction, e.g., plant cuttings or grafts **3.** COMPUT NEAR COPY OF HARDWARE OR SOFTWARE a hardware device, e.g., a PC, or a piece of software, that is a functional copy of another, more expensive product developed by another manufacturer ■ *v* (**cloned, clon·ing, clones**) **1.** *vti* GENETICS PRODUCE GENETICALLY IDENTICAL ORGANISM to produce an organism that is genetically identical to its parent by vegetative reproduction or a laboratory technique, or be produced in this way **2.** *vt* MAKE COPY OF SOMETHING to produce an exact or near copy of an object or product [Early 20C. < Greek *klōn* "twig"] —**clon·al** *adj* —**clon·al·ly** *adv* —**clon·er** *n*

SYNONYMS See *copy*.

clon·i·dine /klónni dèen, klṓni-/ *n* a drug that relaxes and widens the arteries. Use: treatment of hypertension, migraine headaches, and heart failure. [Late 20C. < CHLORO- + *-onidine*, INN stem]

clo·no·typ·ic /klōnō típpik/ *adj* relating to or characteristic of a clone [Late 20C. < CLONE]

clo·nus /klṓnәss/ *n* a series of rapid repetitive contractions and relaxations in a muscle during movement, which is characteristic of grand-mal epilepsy seizures [Early 19C. Via Latin < Greek *klonos* "turmoil, agitation"] —**clo·nic** /klónik, klónnik/ *adj* —**clo·nic·i·ty** /klō níssətee, klo níssətee/ *n*

Cloo·ney /klo͞onee/, **George** (*b.* 1961) US movie and television actor. He played Dr. Douglas Ross in the television series *ER* in the 1990s. Full name **Clooney, George Timothy**

clop /klop/ *n* the sound that a walking horse's hooves make when they strike hard ground ■ *vi* (**clopped, clop·ping, clops**) to make the sound of a walking horse's hooves striking hard ground [Mid-19C. An imitation of the sound]

clo·que /klō káy/, **clo·qué** *n* a fabric with a raised woven or embossed pattern that makes it look quilted [Early 20C. < French *cloqué* "blistered" < dialect *cloque* "bell, bubble" < medieval Latin *clocca* "bell"]

close[1] /klōss/ *adj* (**clos·er, clos·est**) **1. NEAR** near in space or time ○ *The deadline is getting closer all the time.* **2. ABOUT TO HAPPEN** about to happen, or about to do something ○ *close to collapse* **3. IN FRIENDLY RELATIONSHIP** involved in a very friendly or affectionate relationship ○ *a close friend* **4. CLOSELY RELATED** being a member of somebody's immediate family ○ *invited her parents and other close relatives* **5. INVOLVING REGULAR CONTACT** involving or having regular contact because of a shared interest in something ○ *enjoyed close cooperation* **6. THOROUGH** involving great care and thoroughness ○ *a close inspection* **7. DECIDED BY SMALL MARGIN** decided by, or likely to be decided by, a small margin ○ *a close contest* **8. VERY SIMILAR** very similar to an original ○ *a close copy* **9. NEARLY CORRECT** almost correct, but not exact ○ *You're not quite right, but you're pretty close.* **10. NEARLY PARTICULAR NUMBER OR QUANTITY** approximately the same as a particular number or quantity ○ *There were close to 300 people at the rally.* **11.** TEXTILES **ALLOWING LITTLE SPACE BETWEEN** densely packed or woven with only little spaces between ○ *a close weave* **12. CUT VERY SHORT** cut so as to be very short **13. CLOSELY GUARDED** kept closely guarded **14. NOT GENEROUS WITH MONEY** unwilling to spend or give money **15. STUFFY** oppressively hot and airless **16. SECRETIVELY SILENT** unwilling to talk about something or to reveal feelings ○ *She's very close about the details of her childhood.* **17. DEFENSIVE, WITH SHORT PASSES** in team ball and similar games, involving short passes only, so as to retain possession **18.** PHON **PRODUCED WITH TONGUE NEAR PALATE** describes a vowel sound that is produced with the tongue near the palate, e.g., the "ee" in "tee" ■ *adv* (**clos·er, clos·est**) **1. NEAR TO SOMETHING** near in space or time **2. TIGHTLY** in a snug tight way [13C. Via French *clos* < Latin *clausus*, past participle of *claudere* "close"] —**close·ness** *n*

close[2] /klōz/ *v* (**closed, clos·ing, clos·es**) **1.** *vti* **COVER OPENING** to move, or move something, so that an opening or hole is covered or blocked ○ *closing the door* **2.** *vti* **COME OR BRING TOGETHER** to bring the edges or ends of something together, or be brought together ○ *Close your eyes.* **3.** *vti* **SHUT DOWN BUSINESS FOR SHORT TIME** to stop working or operating, or shut a store or business, for a short period of time or overnight **4.** *vti* COMM same as **close down** **5.** *vt* same as **close off** **6.** *vti* **TERMINATE** to come to an end, or end something such as an activity, period of time, or spoken or written text **7.** *vti* **REDUCE DISTANCE** to reduce the distance between two people or things, especially in a race or chase **8.** *vt* COMM **BRING DEAL TO CLOSURE** to complete a transaction successfully, e.g., a business deal or a house purchase **9.** *vi* FIN **HAVE PARTICULAR END-OF-DAY VALUE** to have a particular value at the end of a day's trading on a stock exchange ○ *Share prices closed higher in heavy trading.* **10.** *vt* COMPUT **DEACTIVATE AND STORE FILE OR PROGRAM** to perform the series of operations necessary to deactivate a computer file or program and store it for later use **11.** *vt* ELEC ENG **COMPLETE ELECTRICAL CIRCUIT** to complete an electric circuit **12.** *vt Malaysia* **SWITCH SOMETHING OFF** to turn or switch something off ■ *n* **1. END** the end of an activity, period of time, or spoken or written text ○ *The applause brought the recital to a close.* **2.** MUSIC same as **cadence** (sense 5) [13C. < French *clos-*, stem of *clore* "to close" < Latin *claudere*] —**clos·a·ble** *adj*

ORIGIN The Latin word *claudere*, "to close," from which ***close*** is derived, is also the source of English *clause, cloister, conclude, conclusive, include, preclude, recluse,* and *seclude*.

close down *vti* to stop operating or trading permanently, or make a factory, business, or school do this

close in *vi* **1.** to move closer and eventually surround somebody or something **2.** to become progressively shorter, with fewer hours of daylight

close off *vt* to prevent people from reaching a place or using a route by blocking access to it (*often passive*)

close out *vt* **1.** to get rid of old merchandise by selling it at reduced prices **2.** BUSINESS, COMM to terminate business operations by selling the business to somebody else

close up *v* **1.** *vti* **LOCK BUILDING** to lock the doors of a building at the end of a working or trading session **2.** *vti* **MOVE CLOSER TOGETHER** to move closer together, or make people or things move closer together **3.** *vti* **BRING TOGETHER** to bring the ends or edges of something together, or be brought together ○ *The surgeon closed up the incision.* **4.** *vi* **HIDE EMOTIONS** to hide your true emotions because you do not want somebody to know or understand you

close with *vt* to enter into physical conflict or a fight with somebody ○ *The two boxers closed with one another.*

close call /klōss-/ *n* a dangerous or unpleasant situation from which somebody just manages to escape

close cor·po·ra·tion /klōss-/, **closed cor·po·ra·tion** *n* a company, the stock of which is closely held by a limited number of shareholders, usually directors or managers, and not publicly traded

close-cropped /klōss-/ *adj* cut very short

closed /klōzd/ *adj* **1. NOT OPEN FOR BUSINESS** describes a business or institution where work, operation, or trading has temporarily or permanently stopped **2. DENYING ACCESS** describes a place to which access is denied or through which passage is not permitted ○ *The road is closed for repairs.* **3. NO LONGER TO BE DISCUSSED** no longer to be discussed or investigated ○ *The subject is closed.* **4. RIGIDLY EXCLUDING OTHERS' IDEAS** rejecting the ideas, beliefs, opinions, or influence of others ○ *His mind is closed against all arguments.* **5. NOT ADMITTING OUTSIDERS** allowing no outsiders in, or tending not to meet with outsiders **6. CONFIDENTIAL AND PRIVATE** carried on or conducted in the strictest confidentiality or secrecy ○ *The bill is being considered by the committee in closed session.* **7.** MATH **FULLY ENCLOSING AREA OR VOLUME** describes a curve, especially a circle, that fully encloses an area, or to describe a solid every surface of which is such a curve **8.** GRAM **HAVING LIMITED NUMBER OF MEMBERS** describes a word class that has a limited number of members, e.g., pronouns or conjunctions **9.** PHON **ENDING IN CONSONANT** describes a syllable that ends in a consonant

closed-cap·tioned *adj* broadcast with captions that can be received on an adapted television set, e.g., with subtitles for people who are hard of hearing

closed cir·cuit *n* an electrical circuit in which there is an uninterrupted endless path for current to flow when voltage is applied —**closed-cir·cuit** *adj*

closed-cir·cuit tel·e·vi·sion, **closed-cir·cuit TV** *n* a television transmission system in which cameras transmit pictures by cable to connected monitors. Surveillance systems are based on this type of transmission.

closed cor·po·ra·tion *n* BUSINESS same as **close corporation**

closed cou·plet *n* a pair of rhymed lines that form a complete sentence or unit of meaning

closed-door *adj* restricted to members or those directly involved, and not open to the general public or the news media

closed-end fund *n* an investment company with a fixed number of shares trading on the stock exchange

closed-end in·vest·ment com·pa·ny *n* a corporation whose capitalization is fixed, whose capital is invested in other companies, and whose own shares are traded by outside investors

closed frac·ture *n* a broken bone that does not protrude through the skin

closed in·ter·val *n* a mathematical set consisting of all the numbers between two given numbers (**endpoints**), including the given numbers. All the whole numbers greater than or equal to 5 and less than or equal to 10 constitute a closed interval.

closed loop *n* a system, usually computer-controlled, that adjusts itself to varying conditions by feeding output information back as input

closed-mind·ed *adj* rigidly and obstinately averse to the consideration of new ideas or other people's arguments —**closed-mind·ed·ly** *adv* —**closed-mind·ed·ness** *n*

close·down /klōz dòwn/ *n* a temporary or permanent stopping of work or operations

closed sea·son *n* the time of the year when it is illegal to hunt and kill some animals, birds, or fish

closed set *n* a mathematical set that includes the limits by which the set is defined, e.g., all the points within and on a circle

closed shop *n* a place of work in which the employer has agreed to employ only members of a particular labor union

closed stance *n* in sports such as baseball or golf, a stance in which the front foot is closer to the line of play than the rear foot

close-fist·ed /klòss fístəd/ *adj* reluctant to spend money —**close-fist·ed·ness** *n*

close-fit·ting /klòss-/ *adj* fitting tightly on the body

close-grained /klòss-/ *adj* describes wood that has dense fibers and a smooth texture

close har·mo·ny /klóss-/ *n* the arrangement of chord tones so that they are as close together as possible, used especially in music for vocal ensembles

close-hauled /klòss-/ *adj, adv* having the sails set for sailing toward the direction from which the wind is blowing

close-in /klóss-/ *adj* **1.** very near to a center of action or activity **2.** taking place at close range

close-knit /klóss-/ *adj* describes a community or group whose members are supportive of and loyal to one another

close·ly /klósslee/ *adv* **1. IN VERY SIMILAR WAY** in a way that is very similar or strongly linked to something ○ *She closely resembles you.* **2. CAREFULLY AND THOROUGHLY** in a careful and thorough way ○ *listening closely* **3. SO AS TO BE NEAR** in a way that is near something in space or time ○ *We heard a bang, closely followed by another.* **4. INTIMATELY** in an intimate manner ○ *worked closely with her* **5. SECRETLY** in a secret or clandestine manner

close-mind·ed /klōss-, klōz-/ *adj* same as **closed-minded**

close·mouthed /klōss mówthd, -mówtht/ *adj* unwilling to talk or to reveal anything

close-or·der drill /klòss-/ *n* a military formation or movement that is conducted with soldiers at close intervals

close·out /klōz òwt/ *n* a sale of all remaining merchandise, at very low prices

close pro·tec·tion of·fi·cer /klòss-/ *n* somebody who is hired to protect somebody, especially a celebrity or public figure, from physical attack

close punc·tu·a·tion /klōss-/ *n* punctuation in which a large number of commas, semicolons, and colons are used

clos·er /klózər/ *n* **1.** in baseball, a relief pitcher who is called in near the end of a game to protect a lead **2.** somebody or something that closes something [14C. < CLOSE[2]]

close-run /klòss-/ *adj* having a very close result

close sea·son /klóss-/ *n UK* SPORTS same as **closed season**

close shave /klòss-/ *n* same as **close call**

close·stool /klóss sto͞ol/ *n UK* formerly, a stool or chair containing a chamber pot [15C. Literally "enclosed stool"]

clos·et /klózzət/ *n* **1. STORAGE PLACE** a large cabinet or recessed area with a door, in which clothes or linens are stored **2. SMALL PRIVATE ROOM** a small private room (*archaic*) **3.** same as **water closet** (*archaic*) ■ *adj* **1. SECRET** having beliefs or behaviors that are not openly acknowledged but kept secret **2. IN THEORY ONLY**

existing in theory or in your imagination but not in reality ○ *This game appeals to closet baseball managers.* ■ *vt* (**-et·ed, -et·ing, -ets**) **PUT SOMEBODY IN PRIVATE PLACE** to put somebody in a small room in order to provide privacy (*often passive*) ○ *He closeted himself in the study all morning.* [14C. < Old French, "small enclosure" < *clos* < Latin *clausum* "enclosure," neuter of *clausus* (see CLOSE[1])] —**clos·et·ful** *n* ◇ **come out of the closet** to acknowledge openly something previously kept secret, especially the fact of being gay or lesbian

clos·et dra·ma *n* a play or plays written to be read rather than performed

close thing /klṓss-/ *n* same as **close call**

close-up /klṓss up/ *n* **1.** PHOTOGRAPHY, MOVIES, MEDIA **CLOSE-RANGE PHOTO OR SHOT** a photograph, or a movie or television shot, taken from a position very close to the subject **2. DETAILED LOOK AT SOMETHING** a detailed view or examination of something ■ *adj, adv* /klṑss úp/ **AT CLOSE RANGE** from a position very near somebody or something else

clos·ing /klṓzing/ *adj* **FINAL** forming or connected with the final part of an activity or period of time ○ *in the closing stages of the game* ■ *n* **1. SOMETHING THAT CLOSES** something that closes, e.g., a fastening on clothes **2. TRANSFER OF PROPERTY OWNERSHIP** a meeting among principals in a real estate transaction, during which legal papers related to the sale and purchase are signed and financial arrangements are made final and binding **3.** LAW same as **closing argument**

clos·ing ar·gu·ment *n* an attorney's final summing up of a case before a judge or jury or both, during which he or she advocates the position of the state or of the individual client

clos·ing date *n* **1.** the final date on which something such as an application for a job can be submitted and be eligible for consideration **2.** a date on which a transaction is concluded, especially when a seller delivers a deed and a buyer pays for it

clos·ing-down sale *n UK* same as **closeout**

clos·ing price *n* the price of a share or bond on a stock exchange recorded at the official close of trading

clos·ing state·ment *n* LAW same as **closing argument**

clos·ing time *n* the time that an establishment such as a store, library, or bar closes and people have to leave

clos·trid·i·um /klo stríddee əm/ (*plural* **-i·ums** or **-i·a** /-ee ə/) *n* a rod-shaped, usually motile, Gram-positive bacterium that can cause serious illnesses including botulism, tetanus, and gas gangrene. Genus: *Clostridium.* [Late 19C. < modern Latin, "little spindle" < Greek *klōstēr* "spindle"] —**clos·trid·i·al** *adj*

clo·sure /klṓzhər/ *n* **1. PERMANENT END OF BUSINESS** the permanent ending of a business or activity **2. BARRING OF ACCESS** blocking the access to a place or blocking a route **3. SOMETHING THAT CLOSES OPENING** a device for closing an opening, e.g., a zipper or a cap on a bottle, or the place where the opening closes **4. CLOSING SOMETHING** an act or process of closing something, e.g., closing an opening or terminating an activity **5.** PSYCHOL **SENSE OF FINALITY** the sense of finality and coming to terms with an experience, felt or experienced over time **6.** *Can, UK* POL same as **cloture** **7.** GEOL **VERTICAL DISTANCE OF ROCK FORMATION** the distance measured vertically between the top of a rock formation (**anticline**) and the lowest contour **8.** MATH **BEING CLOSED SET IN MATHEMATICS** the characteristic of a set in which the application of a given mathematical operation to any member of the set always has another member of the set as its result **9.** PHON **CONTACT BETWEEN VOCAL ORGANS PRODUCING SOUND** a contact made between vocal organs such as the tongue and the soft palate that produces a speech sound ■ *vt* (**-sured, -sur·ing, -sures**) *Can, UK* POL same as **cloture**

clot /klot/ *n* **1. STICKY LUMP** a mass of thickened liquid, especially blood **2. ANY STICKY MASS** a sticky mass of any substance **3. CLUSTER** a cluster of people or things ■ *v* (**clot·ted, clot·ting, clots**) **1.** *vti* **THICKEN AND FORM LUMPS** to thicken, or make a liquid thicken, and form lumps **2.** *vt* **IMPEDE** to hinder the free movement or accessibility of something ○ *The flow of the film is clotted by obscure arguments.* ○ *streets clotted by traffic jams* [Old English *clott* < Indo-European, "form into a ball"] —**clot·tish** *adj*

cloth /klawth, kloth/ *n* **1. FABRIC** fabric made by weaving, knitting, or felting thread or fibers **2. PIECE OF FABRIC** a piece of fabric used for a particular purpose, e.g., a dishcloth (*often used in combination*) **3. CLERGY** the clergy, or the clothes worn by its members **4. SAIL** a sail of a boat **5. PIECE OF FABRIC SCENERY** a painted piece of fabric used as scenery in a theater [Old English *clā* < Germanic]

cloth·bound /kláwth bòwnd, klóth-/ *adj* describes a book that has a cloth-covered hardback cover

clothe /klōth/ (**clothed** or **clad** /klad/, **clothed** or **clad, cloth·ing, clothes**) *vt* **1. DRESS SOMEBODY** to put clothes on somebody (*often passive*) **2. PROVIDE CLOTHING FOR SOMEBODY** to provide somebody with clothes **3. COVER SOMETHING** to completely cover an area ○ *The hills were clothed in mist.* **4. COVER SOMETHING UP** to obscure or conceal something as if wrapping something around it **5. ENDOW SOMEBODY OR SOMETHING** to endow or invest somebody or something with some quality (*usually passive*) [Old English *clāian* < *clā* (see CLOTH)]

clothes /klōthz, klōz/ *npl* **1.** garments that cover the body **2.** all the garments, bed linen, and other articles that are washed when doing the laundry [Old English *clāas*, plural of *clā* (see CLOTH)]

clothes bas·ket *n UK* **1.** same as **clothes hamper 2.** same as **laundry basket**

clothes ham·per *n* a deep container made of wicker, fabric, or other material, used for storing dirty clothes before they are washed

clothes hang·er *n* HOUSEHOLD same as **hanger** (sense 1)

clothes·horse /klṓthz hàwrss, klṓz-/ *n* **1.** somebody who wears the latest fashions (*informal*) **2.** a frame on which clothes are hung to dry indoors

clothes·line /klṓthz lìn, klṓz-/ *n* a cord on which clean laundry is hung to dry, usually outdoors ■ *vt* (**-lined, -lin·ing, -lines**) in football, to knock down an opposing player by catching the player around the neck with an outstretched arm (*informal*)

clothes moth *n* any small moth whose larvae feed on wool and fur. Family: Tineidae.

clothes·pin /klṓthz pìn, klṓz-/ *n* a small clip of plastic or wood, used to secure laundry to a clothesline

clothes press *n* a piece of furniture for storing clothes, with hanging space and sometimes drawers or shelves

cloth·ier /klṓthyər/ *n* a retail seller of clothes or cloth [14C. Alteration of obsolete *clother* < CLOTH]

cloth·ing /klṓthing/ *n* **1.** clothes collectively **2.** a covering for something

Clo·tho /klṓthō/ *n* in Greek mythology, one of the three Fates who influenced human destiny. She held the distaff and spun the thread of life. [< Greek *Klōthō*, literally "I spin"]

cloth of gold *n* a luxury fabric of the Middle Ages woven from silk, or sometimes wool, intermixed with gold thread

clo·trim·a·zole /klō trímə zòl/ *n* an antifungal drug used to treat yeast and fungal infections

clot·ted cream /klòttəd-/ *n UK* a thick cream made by removing the cream from the top of heated milk

clot·ting fac·tor /klótting-/ *n* any substance in the blood that is essential for blood to coagulate

clo·ture /klṓchər/ *US n* the process of closing a debate in the Senate by calling for a vote ■ *vt* (**-tured, -tur·ing, -tures**) to close a debate in the Senate by calling for a vote ▶ Can term (all senses) **closure** [Late 19C. < French *clôture* "closing"]

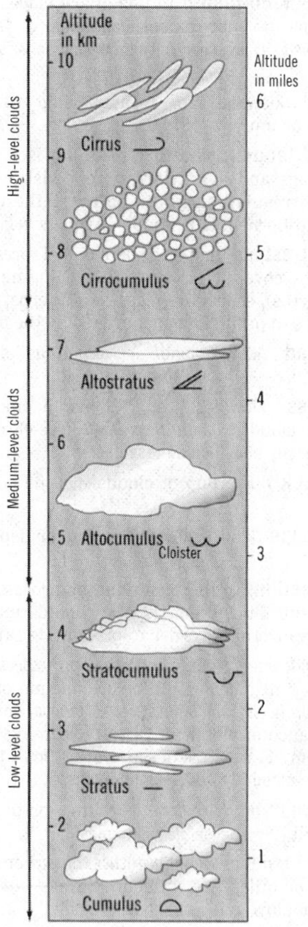

cloud

cloud /klowd/ *n* **1. MASS OF WATER IN SKY** a visible mass of water or ice particles in the atmosphere from which rain and other forms of precipitation fall **2. MASS OF PARTICLES IN AIR** a mass of particles in the air, e.g., dust or smoke ○ *a cloud of smoke* **3. FLYING MASS** an airborne mass of insects or birds **4. DARKER PART** a dark or dim area on something such as jewelry **5. SOMETHING WORRYING** something that causes anxiety or fear ○ *Lack of financial independence was a cloud hanging over our future.* **6. GLOOMY CONDITION** a condition of gloom or despondency ○ *a cloud of despair* **7.** COMPUT **UNPREDICTABLE PART OF COMPUTER NETWORK** an unpredictable or unidentifiable part of a network through which data passes ■ *v* (**cloud·ed, cloud·ing, clouds**) **1.** *vti* **BECOME CLOUDY** to become covered with clouds or mist, or make something cloudy **2.** *vt* **CONFUSE SOMETHING** to make something more confusing ○ *cloud the issue* **3.** *vt* **DETRACT FROM SOMETHING** to make something appear less good ○ *It will cloud her reputation.* **4.** *vt* **IMPAIR SOMETHING** to diminish a mental faculty ○ *Depression had clouded his judgment.* **5.** *vti* **LOOK TROUBLED** to become or cause something to become troubled or gloomy ○ *His face clouded with disappointment.* **6.** *vti* **BECOME OR MAKE SOMETHING OPAQUE** to become or cause something to become opaque or murky ○ *The water was clouded with particles.* [Old English *clūd* "mass of rock, hill"] ◇ **on cloud nine** extremely happy (*informal*) ◇ **under a cloud** in disgrace
cloud over, cloud up *vi* **1.** to become covered with clouds or mist **2.** to become troubled

cloud·ber·ry /klówd bèrree/ (*plural* **-ries**) *n* a creeping perennial plant with yellowish edible berries. Flowers: white. Native to: Europe, North America, Asia. Latin name: *Rubus chamaemorus.*

cloud·burst /klówd bùrst/ *n* a sudden heavy rain shower

cloud cham·ber *n* a device in which the movement of high-energy particles is detected as they pass through a chamber of supersaturated vapor. Observable tracks are formed when droplets condense on the ionized molecules left by the high-energy particles.

cloud-cuck·oo-land *n* an imaginary place in which problems do not exist [Translation of Greek *Nephelokokkugia,* imaginary city in the air in Aristophanes' *Birds*]

cloud·ed /klówdəd/ *adj* **1.** appearing troubled **2.** opaque or murky

cloud·ed leop·ard *n* a rare medium-sized cat with short legs and a grayish to yellowish coat with darker irregular markings. Native to: the area from Nepal to Borneo. Latin name: *Neofelis nebulosa.*

cloud for·est *n* a high-altitude tropical forest that is usually covered by cloud. Clinging plants (**epiphytes**), especially mosses and ferns, grow on the trees in profusion, encouraged by the moisture.

cloud·land /klówd lànd/ *n* same as **dreamland** (sense 2)

cloud·less /klówdləss/ *adj* **1.** bright and sunny without clouds ○ *a cloudless sky* **2.** free of trouble —**cloud·less·ly** *adv* —**cloud·less·ness** *n*

cloud rack *n* a group of clouds moving across the sky

cloud·scape /klówd skàyp/ *n* a view or depiction of clouds

cloud seed·ing *n* the technique or process of scattering substances such as silver iodide into clouds from an aircraft in order to precipitate rain

cloud·y /klówdee/ (**-i·er, -i·est**) *adj* **1. WITH CLOUDS** covered with or full of clouds **2. OPAQUE** opaque or murky ○ *a cloudy liquid* **3. RESEMBLING CLOUDS** having the appearance of clouds **4. TROUBLED** seeming troubled or gloomy **5. NOT CLEAR** obscure or difficult to understand —**cloud·i·ly** *adv* —**cloud·i·ness** *n*

clough /kluf/ *n UK regional* a ravine, or the sloping side of it [Old English *clōh* < Germanic]

clout /klowt/ *n* **1. POWER AND INFLUENCE** the power to direct, shape, or otherwise influence things (*informal*) **2. PUNCH** a blow with the hand or fist (*informal*) **3. ARCHERY TARGET** in archery, a mark or target, especially at a long distance ■ *vt* (**clout·ed, clout·ing, clouts**) **HIT SOMEBODY WITH HAND** to hit somebody or something hard with the hand [Old English *clūt* "patch made of cloth"]

REGIONAL NOTE The use of *clout* to mean "power" and "influence" originated in Chicago, and has spread throughout Illinois and the United States since the 1960s and the administration of Chicago mayor Richard J. Daley.

clove[1] /klōv/ *n* **1.** a dried aromatic flower bud. Use: as a spice. **2.** an evergreen tree with flower buds that are used dried as a spice and other parts that yield aromatic oil of cloves. Native to: the Moluccas. Latin name: *Syzgium aromaticum.* [12C. < Old French *clou (de girofle)* "nail (of the clove tree)" < Latin *clavus* "nail"; from the resemblance of a clove-tree bud to a nail]

clove[2] /klōv/ *n* one of the segments of a compound bulb ○ *a clove of garlic* [Old English *clufu* < Germanic]

clove[3] /klōv/ past tense of **cleave**[1]

clove[4] /klōv/ past tense of **cleave**[2]

clove hitch *n* a knot made of two half-hitches. Use: to attach a rope to a post or to another, thicker, rope. [< former past participle of CLEAVE[1]]

clo·ven /klṓvən/ past participle of **cleave**[1] ■ *adj* split or divided into two parts (*archaic or literary*)

clo·ven hoof, clo·ven foot *n* **1.** the divided hoof of such animals as cattle, sheep, and pigs. Order: Artiodactyla. **2.** an indication of the presence of the devil, traditionally represented in Christianity with a cloven hoof —**clo·ven-hoofed** *adj*

clove oil *n* PHARM same as **oil of cloves**

clove pink *n* PLANTS same as **carnation** (sense 1) [< CLOVE[1]; from its smell]

clo·ver /klṓvər/ *n* **1.** a plant with three-lobed leaves often cultivated as a forage plant, for erosion control, and to provide nectar for bees. Genus: *Trifolium.* **2.** a forage plant similar to clover. Genera: *Meliotus* or *Lespedeza* or *Medicago.* [Old English *clāfre* < Germanic] ◇ **in clover** financially well off (*informal*)

clo·ver·leaf /klṓvər leef/ (*plural* **clover·leaves** /-leevz/) *n* **1.** the three-lobed leaf of a clover plant (*often used before a noun*) ○ *a cloverleaf motif* **2.** an arrangement of highways resembling a four-leaf clover, with entrance and exit ramps enabling traffic to change direction rapidly without intersections

Clo·vis[1] /klṓviss/ *adj* describes a prehistoric North American culture characterized by leaf-shaped flint points that were used as parts of weapons to hunt game [Mid-20C. After CLOVIS[2], New Mexico]

Clo·vis[2] /klṓviss/ **1.** city in central California; an eastern suburb of Fresno. Population: 74,503 (2002 estimate). **2.** city in eastern New Mexico, near New Mexico's border with Texas, southeast of Santa Fe. Population: 32,511 (2002 estimate).

Clo·vis (466?–511) Frankish king (481–511). The first important ruler of the Merovingian dynasty, he enlarged his kingdom until it included most of present-day France and part of Germany.

clown /klown/ *n* **1. COMIC CIRCUS PERFORMER** a comic performer, usually in a circus, who does not speak and wears an outlandish costume and heavy makeup **2. SOMEBODY FUNNY** somebody who behaves comically **3. PRANKSTER** a practical joker **4. ILL-MANNERED PERSON** an ill-mannered or ineffectual person (*informal*) ■ *vi* (**clowned, clown·ing, clowns**) **1. BEHAVE COMICALLY** to behave in a silly or funny way **2. PLAY PRANKS** to play practical jokes **3. PERFORM AS CLOWN** to perform as a circus clown [Mid-16C. Origin ?] —**clown·er·y** *n* —**clown·ing** *n*

clown a·nem·o·ne *n* ZOOL same as **anemone fish**

clown·ish /klównish/ *adj* resembling or characteristic of a clown —**clown·ish·ly** *adv* —**clown·ish·ness** *n*

cloy /kloy/ (**cloyed, cloy·ing, cloys**) *vti* to sicken somebody or become sickened with too much sweetness from something initially pleasing [Mid-16C. Shortening of obsolete *accloy,* via French *encloer* "drive in a nail" < medieval Latin *inclavare* < Latin *clavus* "nail"] —**cloy·ing·ly** *adv* —**cloy·ing·ness** *n*

clo·za·pine /klṓzə peen/ *n* an antipsychotic drug. Use: to treat schizophrenia. [Mid-20C. Contraction of CHLORO- + BENZODIAZEPINE]

cloze test /klōz-/ *n* a test of comprehension and grammar in which a language student supplies appropriate missing words omitted from a text [Alteration of CLOSURE]

CLU *abbr* Chartered Life Underwriter

club /klub/ *n* **1. THICK STICK USED AS WEAPON** a thick heavy stick used as a weapon **2. STICK FOR HITTING BALL** a stick or bat used in some sports, especially golf, to hit a ball ○ *a golf club* **3. ASSOCIATION FOR PURSUING COMMON INTEREST** an association of people with a common interest ○ *a gardening club* **4. NATIONS SHARING SOMETHING** a group of nations or people who have a particular thing in common ○ *the nuclear club* **5. ORGANIZATION FOR A SPORT** an organization formed for the pursuit of a sport on an amateur or a professional basis ○ *a football club* **6. PREMISES OF CLUB** the premises where the activities of a club are pursued ○ *See you at the club tonight!* **7. PLACE FOR DANCING** a place where people dance to recorded music, usually with bars and other leisure facilities **8.** LEISURE same as **nightclub** **9. BUILDING PROVIDING FACILITIES TO MEMBERS** a building that offers facilities and refreshments to members of the organization that owns or occupies it ○ *a gentlemen's club* **10.** CARDS **CARD WITH CLOVERLEAF SYMBOL** a playing card of the suit of clubs **11. BLACK SYMBOL ON PLAYING CARD** a black symbol shaped like a cloverleaf on a playing card **12. ORGANIZATION GIVING DISCOUNTS** a plan or organization in which members receive price reductions in return for regular purchases ○ *a book club* **13.** ARTS same as **Indian club** ■ *v* (**clubbed, club·bing, clubs**) **1.** *vt* **HIT SOMEBODY OR SOMETHING WITH CLUB** to hit somebody or something with a club ○ *She clubbed the ball over the fence.* **2.** *vi* **FORM CLUB** to join or form a club for social purposes or to pursue a common interest **3.** *vi* **DRIFT WITH ANCHOR LOWERED** to drift with an anchor that drags to reduce the speed of the vessel [12C. < Old Norse *klubba* "heavy stick"] ◇ **join the club!** used to tell somebody that you are in the same position as he or she is (*informal*)

club together *vi* **1.** to contribute money collectively for some purpose **2.** to collaborate as a group

club·ba·ble /klúbbəb'l/, **club·a·ble** *adj* sociable, or inclined to join groups or organizations —**club·ba·bil·i·ty** /klùbbə bíllətee/ *n*

clubbed /klubd/ *adj* describes an appendage with a swelling at one end, like a club ○ *clubbed antennae*

club·ber /klúbbər/ *n* **1.** a member of a private club **2.** the wielder of a club

club·bing /klúbbing/ *n* **1.** the activity of going to nightclubs **2.** a medical condition in which the tips of the fingers and toes become thickened, especially at the base of the nail. It may be associated with some lung or heart diseases.

club·by /klúbbee/ (**-bi·er, -bi·est**) *adj* **1. SOCIABLE** enjoying the friendliness associated with clubs **2. TYPICAL OF CLUB** typical of a social club **3. SNOBBISH** socially exclusive and snobbish —**club·bi·ly** *adv* —**club·bi·ness** *n*

club car *n* a railroad car with tables and comfortable chairs where passengers can relax and be served food and drinks

club chair *n* a heavily upholstered chair with a low back and thick arms [< its use in gentlemen's clubs]

club class *n UK* a class of travel on an aircraft between first class and economy class

club·face /klúb fàyss/ *n* the surface of the head of a golf club with which the player strikes the ball

club·foot /klúb fòot/ *n* **1.** a congenital condition of the foot, especially one in which the foot is twisted and turned inward **2.** a foot that is affected by clubfoot —**club·foot·ed** *adj*

club·hand /klúb hànd/ *n* **1.** a congenital condition in which the hand is twisted and turned inward or outward **2.** a hand affected by clubhand —**club·handed** *adj*

club·haul /klúb hàwl/ (**-hauled, -haul·ing, -hauls**) *vti* to force a sailing vessel to change tack by dropping the lee-anchor and hauling in the anchor cable to swing the stern to windward

club·house /klúb hòwss/ *n* **1.** the premises of a club, especially a sports club **2.** a sports team's locker room

club·man /klúbmən/ (*plural* **-men** /-mən/) *n* a man who belongs to one or more exclusive social clubs

club moss *n* a nonflowering plant that typically has creeping stems with small overlapping leaves and reproduces by spores, often borne in club-shaped organs (**strobili**). Order: Lycopodiales.

club·per·son /klúb pùrss'n/ (*plural* **-peo·ple** /-peep'l/ or **-per·sons**) *n* **1.** somebody who belongs to many clubs, especially social or civic organizations **2.** somebody who enjoys going to nightclubs

club·room /klúb ròom, -ròom/ *n* a room in which members of a club meet

club·root /klúb ròot/ *n* a disease affecting plants of the cabbage family, in which the roots become swollen and distorted. Latin name: *Plasmodiophora brassicae.*

clubs /klubz/ *n* one of the four suits used in cards, with a black shape similar to a cloverleaf as its symbol (*takes a singular or plural verb*)

club sand·wich *n* a sandwich consisting of two layers of fillings between three slices of bread [Origin ?]

club so·da *n* BEVERAGES same as **soda water** (sense 1) [< a proprietary name]

club steak *n* FOOD same as **Delmonico steak**

club·wom·an /klúb wòommən/ (*plural* **-wom·en** /-wìmmin/) *n* a woman who belongs to many clubs, especially social or civic organizations

cluck /kluk/ *interj* **USED TO REPRESENT HEN'S CALL** used to imitate the short low clicking sound made by a hen ■ *v* (**clucked, cluck·ing, clucks**) **1.** *vi* **MAKE HEN'S SOUND** to make natural short low clicking sounds (*refers to hens*) **2.** *vti* **EXPRESS SOMETHING WITH CLICKING SOUND** to show disapproval or concern by making short clicking sounds ■ *n* **1. HEN'S CALL** a hen's short low clicking call **2. UNINTELLIGENT PERSON** somebody who is considered mildly unintelligent (*slang*) [15C. An imitation of the sound]

clue /kloo/ *n* **1. AID IN SOLVING MYSTERY** something that helps to solve a mystery or crime **2. AID IN SOLVING CROSSWORD** one of the numbered items of information used to solve a crossword puzzle **3. EXPLANATION FOR BEHAVIOR** an explanation or reason for something that is difficult to understand [Late 16C. Alteration of CLEW] ◇ **not have a clue about something** (*informal*) **1.** to know nothing about something **2.** to be very bad at something

clue in *vt* to provide somebody with useful information ○ *She clued me in about office politics.*

clue·less /klo͞oləss/ *adj* incompetent or ignorant (*slang*) —**clue·less·ness** *n*

Cluj-Na·po·ca /klo͝ozh nə pάwkə/ industrial city and capital of Cluj County in Transylvania, northwestern Romania. Population: 332,297 (1997).

clum·ber span·iel /klúmbər-/, **clum·ber** *n* a thickset short-legged spaniel with a dense silky coat, belonging to an English breed [After *Clumber* Park, Nottinghamshire, England]

clump[1] /klump/ *n* **1. CLUSTER OF THINGS** a compact cluster or group of growing things ○ *a clump of moss* **2. MASS OF SIMILAR THINGS** an undifferentiated mass of something **3. CLUSTER OF CELLS** a cluster of cells such as bacteria or red blood cells, especially one formed during an immune response or when blood of incompatible blood groups is mixed ■ *v* (**clumped, clump·ing, clumps**) **1.** *vti* **COMBINE THINGS INTO MASS** to be gathered or gather things into a mass **2.** *vt* **CAUSE MASSING OF CELLS** to cause cells such as bacteria or red blood cells to combine into a mass, especially as part of an immune response [13C. Probably < Low German *klump*]

clump[2] /klump/, **clomp** /klomp/ *n* a heavy thumping sound ■ *vi* (**clumped, clump·ing, clumps; clomped, clomp·ing, clomps**) to walk or move with a heavy thumping sound [Mid-17C. An imitation of the sound]

clump·y /klúmpee/ (**-i·er, -i·est**) *adj* **1.** large, heavy, and ungainly **2.** composed of or growing in clumps —**clump·i·ly** *adv* —**clump·i·ness** *n*

clum·sy /klúmzee/ (**-si·er, -si·est**) *adj* **1.** poorly coordinated physically **2.** said or done in an awkward or insensitive way ○ *a clumsy remark* [Late 16C. Origin ?] —**clum·si·ly** *adv* —**clum·si·ness** *n*

clung past participle, past tense of **cling**

clunk /klungk/ *n* **1. DULL SOUND** a dull sound like that of a heavy piece of metal hitting something **2. BLOW OR SOUND IT MAKES** a blow, or the sound made by a blow (*informal*) ■ *vti* (**clunked, clunk·ing, clunks**) **MAKE DULL SOUND** to make, or cause something to make, a dull heavy sound [Late 18C. An imitation of the sound]

clunk·er /klúngkər/ *n* (*slang*) **1.** a dilapidated old motor vehicle or piece of machinery **2.** something that is worthless, inferior, or unsuccessful

clunk·y /klúngkee/ (**-i·er, -i·est**) *adj* awkwardly designed or made (*informal*)

Clu·ny lace /klo͞onee-/ *n* a strong white lace made of silk, linen, or cotton [Late 19C. After a town in east-central France]

clu·pe·id /klo͞opee id/ *n* a soft-finned bony fish that has oily flesh, a narrow body, and a forked tail. Herrings, sardines, menhadens, and shad are clupeids. Family: Clupeidae. [Late 19C. < modern Latin *Clupeidae* < Latin *clupea*, a small river fish]

clus·ter /klústər/ *n* **1. DENSE BUNCH** a small group of people or things that are closely packed together ○ *a cluster of diamonds* ○ *a little cluster of onlookers* **2. STARS THAT APPEAR NEAR EACH OTHER** a group of galaxies or stars that are gravitationally interacting in space and appear to an observer on Earth to be close together **3. GROUP OF CONSONANTS** a group of consecutive consonants in the same syllable **4. SUBSET IN STATISTICAL SAMPLE** a statistically significant subset within a population, used in sampling **5. CHORD OF THREE OR MORE NOTES** a chord consisting of three or more notes spaced a semitone apart **6. DESIGN INDICATING MILITARY AWARDS** in the US Army, a small metal design indicating that a medal has been awarded before to the same person **7. GROUP OF BOMBS** a group of bombs dropped together **8. SET OF MINES** a basic unit of mines used in laying a minefield **9. NETWORK OF SMALL COMPUTERS** a network of computers under the control of a larger, more powerful computer ■ *vti* (**-tered, -ter·ing, -ters**) **FORM INTO CLUSTER** to gather something into or form a small group [Old English *clyster* < Germanic] —**clus·tered** *adj* —**clus·ter·y** *adj*

clus·ter a·nal·y·sis *n* a statistical technique that compares multiple characteristics of a population to determine whether individuals fall into different groups

clus·ter bal·loon·ing *n* the sport of piloting a cluster of large helium-filled balloons while sitting in a harness suspended from the balloons —**clus·ter bal·loon·ist** *n*

clus·ter bomb *n* a canister dropped from an aircraft to release a number of small bombs over a wide area

clus·ter con·trol·ler *n* a computer that sorts and files data from smaller computers in a network

clus·ter head·ache *n* a severe recurring headache associated with the release of histamine in the bloodstream, and marked by sudden sharp pain behind one eye or nostril

clutch[1] /kluch/ *v* (**clutched, clutch·ing, clutch·es**) **1.** *vt* **HOLD SOMETHING TIGHTLY** to grip something tightly **2.** *vi* **MAKE GRABBING MOVEMENT** to try to grab hold of something **3.** *vi* **OPERATE CLUTCH** to engage the clutch of a motor vehicle ■ *n* **1. MECHANISM THAT CONNECTS SHAFTS** a device that enables two rotating shafts to be connected and disconnected smoothly, especially one in a motor vehicle that transmits power from the engine to the transmission **2. PEDAL ACTIVATING CLUTCH** the pedal that activates the clutch in a motor vehicle **3. CONTROLLING POWER** control and influence (*often used in the plural*) ○ *We were plainly in his clutches.* **4. CRUCIAL MOMENT** a crucial moment in a critical situation (*informal*) ○ *The clutch came in the seventh inning.* **5. GRIP ON SOMETHING** a tight grip on something ■ *adj* **DEPENDABLE** dependable, or accomplished at precisely the right moment [14C. Variant of obsolete *clitch* "to bend, grasp" < Old English *clyccan* "to grasp"]

clutch[2] /kluch/ *n* **1. GROUP OF EGGS LAID TOGETHER** the number of eggs laid by a bird at one time **2. GROUP OF CHICKENS HATCHED TOGETHER** all the chickens hatched together from one clutch of eggs **3. GROUP OF SIMILAR THINGS** a number of similar people or things (*informal*) [Early 18C. Probably variant of dialectal *cletch* < *cleck* "hatch" < Old Norse *klekja*]

clutch purse *n* a purse that has no strap or handle and is carried under the arm or in the hand

clut·ter /klúttər/ *n* **1. UNTIDY STUFF** a messy collection of objects **2. DISORGANIZED MESS** a condition of disorderliness or overcrowding **3. CONFUSING RADAR IMAGES** images on a radar screen that hinder observation ■ *vt* (**-tered, -ter·ing, -ters**) **FILL SOMETHING WITH CLUTTER** to make a place untidy or overfilled with objects [Mid-16C. Probably variant of obsolete *clotter* "clot repeatedly" < CLOT]

Clyde /klīd/ most important river of Scotland. It flows westward through Glasgow to the Firth of Clyde, where it joins the Atlantic Ocean. Length: 106 mi./171 km.

Clyde·bank /klīd bàngk/ town in western Scotland, on the north bank of the Clyde River. Population: 29,171 (1991).

Clydes·dale /klīdz dàyl/ *n* a strong heavy horse belonging to a breed originally developed in Scotland as draft animals [Late 18C. After an area of the River CLYDE]

clys·ter /klístər/ *n* MED same as **enema** (*archaic*) [14C. Directly or via French < Latin < Greek *klustēr* "syringe" < *kluzein* "wash out"]

Cly·tem·nes·tra /klītəm néstrə/ *n* in Greek mythology, Agamemnon's wife and the queen of Mycenae. Clytemnestra and her lover, Aegisthus, killed Agamemnon on his return from Troy. She was later killed by her son Orestes.

cm[1] *symbol* MEASURE centimeter

cm[2] *abbr* Cameroon (*used in Internet addresses*) See table at **domain name**

Cm *symbol* CHEM ELEM curium

c.m. *abbr* **1.** PHYS center of mass **2.** MIL court-martial

CMA, C.M.A. *abbr* **1.** Canadian Medical Association **2.** certified medical assistant

CMC *abbr* certified management consultant

Cmd. *abbr* MIL Commander

Cmdr. *abbr* MIL Commander

cml. *abbr* **1.** COMM commercial **2.** MED chronic myelogenous leukemia

CMO *abbr* FIN collateralized mortgage obligation

c'mon /kə món/ *contr* come on (*nonstandard*)

CMOS /seē mòss/ *abbr* COMPUT complementary metal oxide semi-conductor

CMSGT *abbr* AIR FORCE chief master sergeant

CMV *abbr* cytomegalovirus

CMYK *n* the standard model for printing in which all colors are described in terms of the quantity of cyan, magenta, yellow, and black they contain

cn *abbr* China (*used in Internet addresses*) See table at **domain name**

cni·dar·i·an /ni dérree ən/ *n* any invertebrate ocean animal that has tentacles surrounding the mouth, e.g., sea anemones, corals, and jellyfish. Phylum: Cnidaria. [Early 20C. < modern Latin *Cnidaria* < Greek *knidē* "nettle" < *knizein* "cause to itch"] —**cni·dar·i·an** *adj*

CNN *abbr* BROADCAST Cable News Network

C-note *n* a one-hundred-dollar bill (*informal*)

CNS *abbr* ANAT central nervous system

CN Tower, Toronto, Canada

CN Tower *n* a tall tower in downtown Toronto, Canada. It is more than 1800 ft./553 m high and was the world's tallest free-standing structure when it was built in 1976.

Cnut another spelling of **Canute**

co *abbr* Colombia (*used in Internet addresses*) See table at **domain name**

Co *symbol* CHEM ELEM cobalt

CO *abbr* **1.** Colorado **2.** *also* **C.O.** commanding officer **3.** *also* **C.O.** conscientious objector

Co. *abbr* **1.** Colorado **2.** Company (*used in names of businesses*) **3.** County (*used in place names*)

c.o. *abbr* **1.** care of **2.** ACCT carried over **3.** cash order

co- *prefix* **1.** together, jointly ○ *coauthor* **2.** associate, alternate ○ *copilot* **3.** to the same degree ○ *coeternal* **4.** complement of an angle ○ *cotangent* [< Latin, variant of *com-* COM-]

co·act *vi*
co·ac·tion *n*
co·ac·tive *adj*
co·ac·tive·ly *adv*
co·ac·tiv·i·ty *n*
co·act·or *n*
co·ad·min·is·ter *vt*
co·ad·min·is·tra·tion *n*
co·an·chor *n, vti*
co·au·thor *n, vt*
co·au·thor·ship *n*
co·cap·tain *vt, n*
co·chair *n, vt*
co·chair·man *n*
co·chair·per·son *n*
co·chair·wom·an *n*
co·cham·pion *n*
co·cre·ate *vt*
co·de·sign *vt*
co·de·sign·er *n*
co·de·vel·op *vt*
co·de·vel·op·er *n*
co·di·rect *v*
co·di·rec·tor *n*
co·dis·cov·er *vt*
co·dis·cov·er·er *n*
co·drive *vt*
co·driv·er *n*
co·ed·it *vt*
co·ed·it·or *n*
co·em·per·or *n*
co·ex·ec·u·tor *n*
co·fi·nance *vt*
co·found *vt*
co·found·er *n*
co·fund *vt*
co·hold·er *n*
co·host *vt, n*
co·host·ess *n*
co·in·vent *vt*
co·in·vent·or *n*
co·in·vest *vt*
co·in·ves·ti·ga·tor *n*
co·in·vest·or *n*
co·mak·er *n*
co·man·age *vt*
co·man·age·ment *n*
co·man·ag·er *n*
co·mem·ber *n*
co·nom·i·nee *n*
co·of·fi·cial *adj*
co·or·gan·ize *vt*
co·or·gan·iz·er *n*
co·own *vt*
co·own·er *n*
co·own·er·ship *n*
co·pre·sent *vt*
co·pre·sent·er *n*

co·pres·i·dent *n*
co·prin·ci·pal *n*
co·pris·on·er *n*
co·pro·duce *vt*
co·pro·duc·er *n*
co·pro·duc·tion *n*
co·pub·lish *vt*
co·pub·lish·er *n*
co·re·cip·i·ent *n*
co·re·gent *n*
co·re·pres·sor *n*
co·re·search·er *n*
co·rul·er *n*
co·script *vt*
co·spon·sor *n, vt*
co·spon·sor·ship *n*
co·ten·ant *n*
co·trust·ee *n*
co·win·ner *n*
co·work·er *n*
co·write *vt*
co·writ·er *n*

c/o *abbr* **1.** MAIL care of **2.** ACCT carried over

CoA *abbr* BIOL coenzyme A

co·ac·er·vate /kō ássər vàyt/ *n* an aggregate of colloidal droplets bound together by electrostatic forces

coach /kōch/ *n* **1. HORSE-DRAWN CARRIAGE** a large enclosed horse-drawn carriage **2. INEXPENSIVE TRAVEL CATEGORY** an inexpensive class of passenger accommodations on a bus, train, or aircraft **3. SOMEBODY WHO TRAINS SPORTS PLAYERS** a trainer of sports players and athletes **4. RAILROAD CAR** a railroad car **5. LONG-DISTANCE BUS** a bus designed for long-distance travel or sightseeing **6. CHEAP SMALL AUTOMOBILE** any inexpensive automobile, especially one with two doors **7. SOMEBODY WHO TRAINS PERFORMERS** a trainer of actors or singers **8. TUTOR** somebody who instructs a person in a particular subject ■ *v* (**coached, coach·ing, coach·es**) **1.** *vt* **TRAIN ATHLETE** to train somebody in a sport **2.** *vt* **TRAIN PERFORMER** to train somebody in acting or singing **3.** *vt* **TRAIN STUDENT** to give somebody private instruction in a particular subject or prepare somebody for an examination **4.** *vti* **TRANSPORT PEOPLE IN COACH** to carry passengers in a horse-drawn coach, or travel by coach [Mid-16C. Via French *coche* < German *Kutsche* < Hungarian *kocsi (szekér)* "(wagon) of Kocs" (village in Hungary)] —**coach·a·ble** *adj*

SYNONYMS See *teach*.

coach bolt *n UK* same as **carriage bolt**

coach·ing /kóching/ *n* **1.** the profession of training and guiding sports teams **2.** training in how to deal with emotional problems and interpersonal relationships

coach·load /kóch lòd/ *n* the total number of people who are traveling in or who fill a coach ○ *coachloads of tourists*

coach·man /kóchmən/ (*plural* **-men** /-mən/) *n* the driver of a horse-drawn coach or carriage

coach·work /kóch wùrk/ *n* the painted bodywork of a road vehicle or railroad car

co·ad·ap·ta·tion /kò a dap táysh'n, -adəp-/ *n* the mutually advantageous development of characteristics in two or more species of organisms —**co·a·dapt·ed** *adj*

co·ad·ju·tant /kō ájjətənt/ *n* a helper or assistant (*formal*) —**co·ad·ju·tant** *adj*

co·ad·ju·tor /kō ájjətər/ *n* **1.** a helper (*formal*) **2.** a bishop who assists a diocesan bishop [15C. Via French < late Latin, literally "helper with" < Latin *adjutor* "helper" < *adjuvare* "to help"]

co·ag·u·la MED plural of **coagulum**

co·ag·u·lant /kō ággyələnt/ *n* a substance that coagulates blood —**co·ag·u·lant** *adj*

co·ag·u·lase /kō ággyə làyss, -làyz/ *n* an enzyme produced by some bacteria that causes coagulation of the blood [Early 20C. < COAGULATE]

co·ag·u·late /kō ággyə làyt/ *vti* (**-lat·ed, -lat·ing, -lates**) **1. MAKE OR BECOME SEMISOLID** to thicken, or cause liquid to thicken, into a soft semisolid mass **2. GROUP TOGETHER IN LARGER MASS** to group together as a mass, or cause the particles in a colloid to group together, as egg white does when heated ■ *n* **COAGULATED MASS** a soft semisolid mass produced by the grouping together of the particles of a colloid [15C. < Latin *coagulat-*, past participle of *coagulare* < *coagere* "drive together"] —**co·ag·u·la·bil·i·ty** /kō àggyələ bíllətee/ *n* —**co·ag·u·la·ble** *adj* —**co·ag·u·la·tion** /kō àggyə láysh'n/ *n* —**co·ag·u·la·tor** *n*

co·ag·u·lat·ing ban·dage *n* a clot-stimulating dressing used to stop arterial bleeding. It contains chitosan, whose positive electrostatic charge offsets negatively charged red blood cells, or the blood-clotting factors fibrinogen and thrombin. These bandages can be placed whole into large wounds or in pieces into smaller wounds. [Late 20C]

co·ag·u·la·tion fac·tor *n* MED same as **clotting factor**

co·ag·u·lum /kō ággyələm/ (*plural* **-la** /-lə/) *n* a clot or coagulated mass of something, especially blood [Mid-16C. < Latin < *coagulare* (see COAGULATE)]

Co·a·hui·la /kò ə wéelə/ state in north central Mexico on the border with Texas. Capital: Saltillo. Population: 2,298,070 (2000). Area: 57,725 sq. mi./149,510 sq. km. Full name **Coahuila de Zaragoza**

coal /kōl/ *n* **1. BLACK ROCK USED AS FUEL** a hard black or dark brown sedimentary rock formed by the decomposition of plant material, widely used as a fuel **2. COAL LUMP** a piece of coal ○ *hot coals* **3. SMALL PIECE OF COMBUSTIBLE MATERIAL** any small piece of combustible material **4.** CHEM same as **charcoal** (sense 1) ■ *v* (**coaled, coal·ing, coals**) **1.** *vt* **CONVERT SOMETHING INTO CHARCOAL** to burn something combustible and convert it into charcoal **2.** *vti* **PROVIDE OR TAKE ON COAL** to supply something with coal, or take on coal [Old English *col* < Indo-European, "glowing ember"] —**coal·y** *adj* ◇ **carry** *or* **take coals to Newcastle** to do something superfluous or supply something that is already plentiful ◇ **rake somebody over the coals** *UK* to reprimand somebody severely

coal black *adj* **1.** completely black **2.** very dark black in color —**coal black** *n*

coal·er /kólər/ *n* a ship or train that transports coal

co·a·lesce /kò ə léss/ (**-lesced, -lesc·ing, -lesc·es**) *vti* to merge or cause things to merge into a single body or group [Mid-16C. < Latin *coalescere* "grow up together" < *alescere* "grow up" < *alere* "nourish"] —**co·a·les·cence** *n* —**co·a·les·cent** *adj*

coal·face /kól fàyss/ *n* the newly exposed rock surface in a mine, from which coal is being cut

coal·field /kól feéld/ *n* an area with coal deposits

coal·fish /kól fìsh/ (*plural* **coal·fish** or **coal·fish·es**) *n* a black-backed or dark-colored edible fish, e.g., a sablefish or pollack

coal gas *n* **1.** a flammable mixture of gases obtained by distilling coal, consisting mainly of methane and hydrogen. Use: fuel. **2.** the gas produced when coal is burned

coal·i·fi·ca·tion /kòləfi káysh'n/ *n* the process in which coal is formed by the action of pressure and heat on buried plant material. The moisture content of the plants is progressively removed and the material remaining is solidified.

co·a·li·tion /kò ə lísh'n/ *n* **1.** a temporary union between two or more groups, especially political parties **2.** the merging of things into one body or mass [Early 17C. < medieval Latin *coalition-* < Latin *coalit-*, past participle of *coalescere* (see COALESCE)] —**co·a·li·tion·ist** *n*

coal meas·ures *npl* a series of strata containing economically workable coal deposits, e.g., the upper Carboniferous rocks of northwestern Europe

coal·mine /kól mìn/ *n* a mine where coal is dug from the ground —**coal·min·er** *n* —**coal·min·ing** *n*

coalmin·er's lung *n* MED same as **anthracosis**

coal oil *n* INDUST same as **kerosene** (*archaic*)

coal pit *n* MIN EXTRACT same as **coalmine**

Coal·port /kól pàwrt/ *n* a variety of white, strongly patterned bone china made in Coalport, near Shrewsbury, England, in the 19th century

Coal·sack /kól sàk/ *n* **1.** a dark cloud of interstellar dust (**nebula**), part of the Crux constellation and visible in the southern hemisphere in front of the Milky Way **2.** a dark interstellar cloud (**nebula**) of the northern hemisphere near the constellation Cygnus

coal scut·tle *n* a metal container for holding and pouring coal for a domestic fire

coal tar *n* a thick black liquid. Source: byproduct in the production of coke. Use: making dyes, drugs, and soap.

coam·ing /kóming/ *n* a raised edging around the cockpit or hatchway of a boat for keeping out water [Early 17C. Origin ?]

co·apt /kō ápt/ (**-apt·ed, -apt·ing, -apts**) *v* to join or bring displaced parts close together in their correct alignment, e.g., the edges of a wound or broken bone [Late 16C. < late Latin *coaptare* "fit together" < Latin *aptus* "fastened, suitable"] —**co·ap·ta·tion** /kō ap táysh'n/ *n*

co·arc·tate /kō áark tàyt/ *adj* **1.** MED **CONSTRICTED** describes any vessel or canal in the body that has become constricted, narrowed, or pressed together **2.** ZOOL **IN HARD SHELL** describes a pupa that is enclosed in a horny oval case ■ *vi* (**-tat·ed, -tat·ing, -tates**) **CONSTRICT** to become narrow, constricted, or pressed together (*refers to blood vessels or other body passages*) [15C. < Latin *coar(c)tat-*, past participle of *coar(c)tare* "press close together" < *artare* "press close" < *artus* "confined, narrow"] —**co·arc·ta·tion** /kō aark táysh'n/ *n*

coarse /kawrss/ (**coars·er, coars·est**) *adj* **1. ROUGH** harsh or rough to the touch **2. WITH THICK GRAINS OR STRANDS** consisting of large grains or thick strands **3. INDELICATE OR TASTELESS** lacking taste or refinement **4. VULGAR** vulgar or obscene **5. UNREFINED** not refined ○ *coarse metal* **6. INFERIOR** of inferior quality [14C. Origin ?] —**coarse·ly** *adv* —**coarse·ness** *n*

SPELLCHECK coarse or **course**? Do not confuse the spelling of ***coarse*** and ***course***, which sound similar. ***Coarse*** is an adjective meaning "rough" or "vulgar," as in *coarse fabric, coarse language*. The word ***course*** is chiefly used as a noun, meaning "a sequence of events," "a route," "a program of study," "part of a meal," etc. (as in *a course of action, the course of the river*). It can also be used as a verb, meaning "run swiftly" or "hunt with dogs": *Tears coursed down his cheeks.*

coarse-grained *adj* **1.** having a large or rough grain **2.** vulgar in speech or manner

coars·en /káwrss'n/ (**-ened, -en·ing, -ens**) *vti* to become or make something coarse or coarser

coast /kōst/ *n* **1. LAND NEXT TO SEA** land beside the sea ○ *sailed along the coast* **2. SLOPE FOR SLEDDING** a slope suitable for sledding **3. SLEDDING DOWN SLOPE** the action of sliding down a slope on a sled ■ *v* (**coast·ed, coast·ing, coasts**) **1.** *vi* **MOVE BY MOMENTUM** to move forward by momentum, without applying power **2.** *vi* **SUCCEED EFFORTLESSLY** to progress with very little effort **3.** *vti* **TRAVEL ALONG SHORE** to sail along a shore [14C. Via French < Latin *costa* "rib, side"] —**coast·al** *adj*

Coast *n* the North American coast bordering the Pacific Ocean

coast·er /kóstər/ *n* **1. MAT FOR GLASS** a mat placed under a glass in order to protect a surface **2. SHIP TRADING ALONG COAST** a ship that sails along a coast to trade **3. SOMETHING THAT COASTS** something that coasts of its own momentum **4.** LEISURE same as **roller coaster** (sense 1) **5. TRAY FOR PASSING BOTTLE** a small tray, sometimes on wheels, for passing a bottle or decanter around a table

coast·er brake *n* a bicycle brake operated by back-pedaling

coast guard *n* **1.** an emergency service that rescues people in difficulties at sea and acts against smuggling **2.** a member of the coast guard

Coast Guard *n* a US military service that enforces maritime laws, acts in emergencies at sea, and maintains navigational aids, in wartime supplementing the navy

coast·land /kóst lànd/ *n* the land along a coast (*often used in the plural*)

coast·line /kóst lìn/ *n* the outline of a coast as viewed from the sea or on a map

Coast Moun·tains /kóst-/ Canadian range following the Pacific coast from Vancouver into Yukon Territory. The highest peak is Mount Waddington, 13,104 ft./3,994 m. Length: 750 mi./1,200 km.

Coast Rang·es long narrow mountain ranges on the western coast of North America, along the Pacific coast from southern Alaska to northwestern Mexico. Highest peak: Mount Logan 19,551 ft./5,959 m.

coast rho·do·den·dron *n* PLANTS same as **Western rhododendron**

Coast Sa·lish *npl* a Salish-speaking Native North American people who live on the northwestern

Pacific coast from southwestern British Columbia to southwestern Washington state

coast-to-coast *adj* from one coast to another of a continent or a nation ○ *The debate had coast-to-coast coverage on the news media.*

coat /kōt/ *n* **1. WARM OUTER GARMENT** an item of clothing with long sleeves that is usually at least knee-length and is worn outdoors over other clothes **2.** *US* **SUIT JACKET** a jacket worn as part of a suit, with a skirt or trousers **3. COVERING ON ANIMAL** the fur, wool, or hair that covers an animal **4. THIN COVERING** any thin layer that covers something ■ *vt* (**coat·ed, coat·ing, coats**) **1. COVER SURFACE** to cover a surface with a thin layer of something (*often passive*) **2. GIVE COAT TO SOMEBODY** to provide somebody with a coat (*usually used in the passive*) [14C. < Old French *cote* < Germanic] —**coat·er** *n*

coat check *n* a room in a public building such as a theater, club, or restaurant where customers can leave coats, umbrellas, and other belongings during their stay

coat·dress /kṓt drèss/ *n* a tailored dress that is shaped like a coat and fastened in front from the neck to the hem, usually with buttons

coat·ed /kṓtəd/ *adj* **1. WITH OUTER LAYER** covered with a layer of something **2. PREPARED FOR WRITING OR PRINTING ON** describes paper that is treated with a fine layer of a mineral to make it suitable for writing or printing on **3. TREATED AGAINST MOISTURE** describes fabric with a treated surface or plastic coating that resists moisture

coa·tee /kō tée/ *n* a military cutaway coat with shortened coat-tails

Coates·ville /kṓts vìl/ city in southeastern Pennsylvania, west of Philadelphia and east of Lancaster. Population: 11,115 (2002 estimate).

coat hang·er *n* a curved frame with a hook, used to drape and hang clothes

co·a·ti /kō aátee/ (*plural* **-tis** or *same*), **co·a·ti·mun·di** /kō aátee múndee/ (*plural* **-dis** or *same*) *n* a South or Central American omnivorous mammal, related to the raccoon, that has a narrow flexible snout and a striped tail. Genus: *Nasua.* [Early 17C. Via Portuguese < Tupi *kua'ti*]

coat·ing /kṓting/ *n* **1.** a thin layer that covers something ○ *a coating of dust* **2.** cloth used to make coats

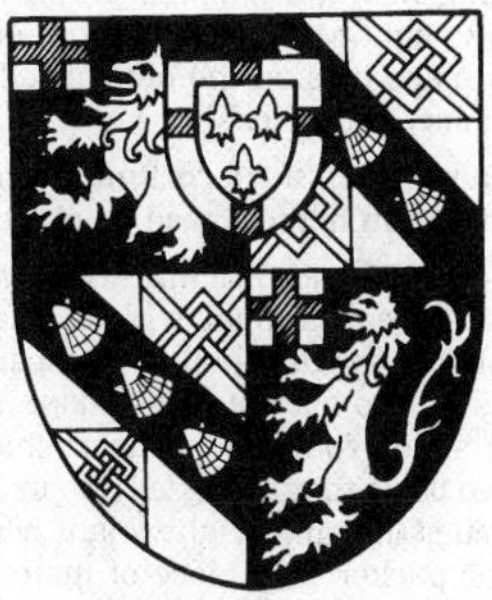

coat of arms

coat of arms *n* **1.** a design on a shield that signifies a particular family, university, or city **2.** a garment that is decorated with a coat of arms [Translation of French *cote d'armes*]

coat of mail *n* a protective garment of armor worn in medieval times, consisting of linked metal rings

coat·rack /kṓt ràk/ *n* a stand or rack fitted with hooks, used for hanging clothes on

coat·room /kṓt ròom, -ròom/ *n* same as **coat check**

coat·tail /kṓt tàyl/ *n* the part below the waist at the back of a coat, especially one of the parts when it is divided into two (*usually used in the plural*) ◇ **on somebody's coattails** helped by somebody else rather than succeeding alone

coax /kōks/ (**coaxed, coax·ing, coax·es**) *v* **1.** *vti* **PERSUADE GENTLY** to persuade somebody gently to do something **2.** *vt* **OBTAIN SOMETHING BY GENTLE PERSUASION** to get something from somebody by gentle persuasion **3.** *vt* **GENTLY MAKE SOMETHING WORK** to manipulate something patiently until it moves or works ○ *I finally coaxed the sticky drawers open.* [Late 16C. < obsolete *cokes* "simpleton," origin ?] —**coax·ing·ly** *adv*

co·ax ca·ble /kṑ aks-/ *n* ELEC same as **coaxial cable** [Shortening]

co·ax·i·al /kō áksee əl/ *adj* **1.** having a common axis **2.** belonging or relating to a coaxial cable —**co·ax·i·al·ly** *adv*

co·ax·i·al ca·ble *n* a cable consisting of an inner core and an outer flexible braided tube, both of conductive material separated by an insulator, used to transmit high-frequency signals at high speeds

cob[1] /kob/ *n* **1. CORE OF CORN EAR** the hard core to which individual kernels of corn are attached **2. SHORT-LEGGED RIDING HORSE** a sturdy short-legged riding horse **3. MALE SWAN** a male swan [15C. Origin ?]

cob[2] /kob/ *n* a crude often irregularly shaped gold or silver coin that circulated in Spanish colonies in the Americas between the 16th and 18th centuries [Late 17C. < Spanish *cabo de barra* "end of bar"; from the coin-sized planchets sliced from cast bars]

co·bal·a·min /kō bálləmin/ *n* PHARM same as **vitamin B_{12}** [Mid-20C. Blend of COBALT + VITAMIN]

co·balt /kṓ bàwlt/ *n* a tough brittle silvery white metallic element. Source: iron, nickel, copper ores. Use: coloring ceramics, alloys. Symbol **Co**. See table at **element** [Late 17C. < German *Kobalt*, variant of *Kobold* "harmful goblin"; from miners' belief that cobalt ore was harmful to neighboring silver ores; originally a trademark]

co·balt 60 /-síkstee/ *n* a naturally radioactive isotope of cobalt with a mass number of 60 that spontaneously emits strong gamma radiation. Use: in radiotherapy and industry.

co·balt bloom *n* MINERALS same as **erythrite** [Translation of German *Kobaltblüte*]

co·balt blue *adj* deep greenish blue in color —**co·balt blue** *n*

co·balt bomb *n* a device containing cobalt 60, used in radiotherapy

co·balt·ic /kō báwltik/ *adj* relating to or containing cobalt, especially with a valence of three

co·balt·ite /kō báwl tīt/ *n* a rare silvery white or grayish mineral consisting of cobalt sulfide and arsenide. Use: ceramics.

co·balt·ous /kō báwltəss/ *adj* relating to or containing cobalt, especially with a valence of two

Cobb /kob/, **Irvin Shrewsbury** (1876–1944) US humorist. He was known for his unpretentious Judge Priest stories.

> "A good storyteller is a person who has a good memory and hopes other people haven't."
> [Attributed to Irvin Shrewsbury Cobb]

Cobb, Ty (1886–1961) US baseball player. Considered one of the game's most outstanding players of all time, he retired from the Detroit Tigers (1905–26) with a career batting average of 0.367. Full name **Cobb, Tyrus Raymond**. Known as **Georgia Peach**

> "Speed is a great asset; but it's greater when it's combined with quickness—and there's a big difference."
> [Ty Cobb. Quoted in *The Tumult and Shouting*, Grantland Rice; 1954]

Cob·bett /kóbbət/, **William** (1763–1835) British writer, journalist, and reformer. He wrote *History of the Protestant Reformation* (1824–27) and *Rural Rides* (1830).

> "To be poor and independent is very nearly an impossibility."
> [William Cobbett, *Advice to Young Men*; 1829]

cob·ble[1] /kóbb'l/ *n* **1.** ROADS same as **cobblestone 2.** a naturally rounded rock fragment between 2.5 and 10 in./64 and 256 mm in diameter ■ *vt* (**-bled, -bling, -bles**) to pave a road with cobblestones [Early 17C. Shortening of COBBLESTONE] —**cob·bled** *adj*

cobble together *vt* to assemble or make something roughly and quickly (*informal*)

cob·ble[2] /kóbb'l/ (**-bled, -bling, -bles**) *vt* to make, repair, or patch footwear [15C. Back-formation < COBBLER[1]]

cob·bler[1] /kóbblər/ *n* a maker or repairer of footwear [13C. Origin ?]

cob·bler[2] /kóbblər/ *n* **1.** a baked fruit dessert with a soft thick crust **2.** an iced drink made of wine, rum or whiskey, and sugar, often garnished with fruit and mint [Early 19C. Probably < COBBLER[1]]

cob·bler's wax *n* a resin used to wax thread

cob·ble·stone /kóbb'l stōn/ *n* a small rounded stone used for paving streets [15C. < COB[1]] —**cob·ble·stoned** *adj*

co·bel·lig·er·ent /kṑ bə líjjərənt/ *n* a person or country that is an ally in a fight or war

co·bi·a /kóbee ə/ (*plural same* or **-as**) *n* a large bony dark-striped fish that is related to the perch and sea bass. Native to: tropical and subtropical seas. Latin name: *Rachycentron canadum.* [Mid-19C. Origin ?]

co·bo /kṓbō/ *n Carib* BIRDS same as **black vulture** (sense 1)

COBOL /kṓ bawl/, **Co·bol** *n* a high-level computer programming language widely adopted for corporate business applications [Mid-20C. Acronym < *common business-oriented language*]

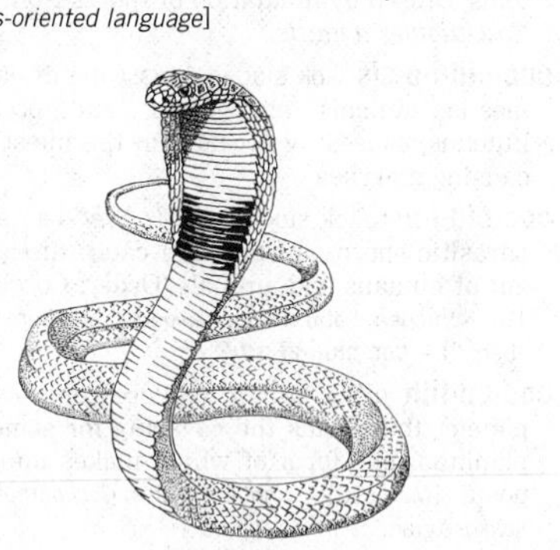

cobra

co·bra /kóbrə/ *n* a venomous snake that, when excited, rears up and spreads the skin behind its head to form a hood. Native to: tropical Asia and Africa. Genera: *Naja* or *Ophiophagus.* [Early 19C. Shortening of *cobra de capello* "snake with a hood" < Portuguese; *cobra* < Latin *cubra* "snake"]

co·brand·ing /kō bránding/ *n* the display of two or more corporate logos on a product or website in order to give the impression that the product or site is a joint enterprise

co·burg /kṓ bùrg/ *n* a thin fabric made of wool and cotton or silk, twilled on one side. Use: dress fabric, lining cloth. [Early 19C. After Prince ALBERT of Saxe-Coburg]

Co·burg /kṓ bùrg/ city in Bavaria, southeastern Germany, near the Czech border. It was the seat of the Dukes of Saxe-Coburg-Gotha, whose line supplied many of Europe's monarchs. Population: 43,928 (1997).

cob·web /kób wèb/ *n* **1. DUSTY SPIDER'S WEB** a fine thread or a web of fine threads spun by a spider, especially when covered with dust **2. SOMETHING LIKE COBWEB** something that resembles a cobweb in being flimsy and insubstantial or in acting as a trap or snare ■ **cob·webs** *npl* **SLUGGISH MENTAL STATE** mental sluggishness and tiredness ○ *I need to blow the cobwebs away.* [14C. < obsolete *cop* "spider" < Old English *ātorcoppe*, probably literally "poison-head"] —**cob·webbed** *adj*—**cob·web·by** *adj*

cob·web site *n* a website that has not been updated for a long period of time

co·ca /kṓkə/ (*plural same*) *n* **1.** the dried leaves of an Andean bush. Use: chewed as a stimulant, processed for cocaine and other alkaloids. **2.** a bush whose leaves yield coca. Native to: Andes. Latin name: *Erythroxylum coca.* [Late 16C. Via Spanish < Aymara *kuka* or Quechua *koka*]

Co·ca·col·o·ni·za·tion /kṓkə koləni záysh'n/ *n* the spread of western, specifically US, popular culture and commercialism to indigenous societies throughout the world, creating a bland uniformity (*disapproving*) [Mid-20C. < *Coca-Cola*, trademark for a cola-flavored drink + colonization]

co·caine /kō káyn, kṓ kàyn/ *n* an addictive narcotic drug obtained from the leaves of the coca plant, taken illegally as a stimulant. Formula: $C_{17}H_{21}NO_4$. [Mid-19C. < COCA]

co·cain·ize /kō káy nīz/ (**-ized, -iz·ing, -iz·es**) *vt* to anesthetize somebody with a topical application of cocaine in paste form in the nose —**co·cain·i·za·tion** /kō kàyni záysh'n, kō kayni-/ *n*

co·car·cin·o·gen /kō ka̋arss'nə jèn, kō kaar sínnəjən/ *n* a substance that does not cause cancer on its own but can increase the effect of carcinogenic factors or substances when acting together with them —**co·car·cin·o·gen·ic** /kō ka̋arss'nə jénnik/ *adj*

coc·ci BIOL plural of **coccus**

coc·cid /kóksid/ *n* an insect that folds its wings over its back when not flying. Scale insects and mealy bugs are coccids. Family: Coccidae. [Late 19C. < modern Latin *coccus* (see COCCUS)] —**coc·cid** *adj*

coc·cid·i·a ZOOL plural of **coccidium**

coc·cid·i·oi·do·my·co·sis /kok sìddə òydō mī kṓssiss/ *n* a respiratory disease of humans and domestic animals in North America, marked by flulike symptoms, caused by inhalation of spores from a fungus *Coccidioides immitis*

coc·cid·i·o·sis /kok sìddee ṓssiss/ *n* a disease of domestic animals and birds, and occasionally humans, caused by coccidia in the intestines, and causing diarrhea

coc·cid·i·um /kok síddee əm/ (*plural* **-i·a** /-ee ə/) *n* a parasitic sporozoan that can cause disease in the gut of humans and animals. Order: Coccidia. [Mid-19C. < modern Latin < Greek *kokkid-* "little berry" < *kokkos* "berry"] —**coc·cid·i·al** *adj*

coc·co·lith /kókə lìth/ *n* a microscopic calcareous platelet that forms the covering for some marine plankton, one form of which makes up chalk deposits [Mid-19C. < modern Latin *Coccolithus* < Greek *kokkos* "grain" + *lithos* "stone"]

coc·cus /kókəss/ (*plural* **coc·ci** /kók sī, kó kī/) *n* **1.** a spherical or nearly spherical microorganism, especially a bacterium **2.** a subdivision of a fruit that contains a single seed and resembles a berry [Early 19C. Via modern Latin < Greek *kokkos* "grain, berry"] —**coc·cal** *adj* —**coc·coid** *adj* —**coc·cous** *adj*

-coccus *suffix* a spherical microorganism ○ *pneumococcus* [< COCCUS]

coc·cyx /kóksiks/ (*plural* **-cy·ges** /-si jeéz/ or **-cy·xes**) *n* a small triangular bone at the base of the spinal column [Late 16C. Via Latin < Greek *kokkux* "cuckoo"; from its resemblance to a cuckoo's beak] —**coc·cyg·e·al** /kok síjjee əl/ *adj*

Co·cha·bam·ba /kṑchə ba̋ambə/ city and capital of Cochabamba Department, central Bolivia, situated northeast of Oruro. Population: 560,284 (1997).

co·chan·nel /kō chánn'l, kó chànn'l/ *adj* relating to a transmission occupying the same frequency band as another

Co·chin /kṓ chin/ major port in Kerala State, southwestern India. Population: 1,355,406 (2001).

coch·i·neal /kòchə neél, kóchə neél/ *n* a red dye obtained from the crushed dried bodies of female cochineal insects. Use: food coloring, fabric dye. [Late 16C. < French *cochenille* or Spanish *cochinilla* < Latin *coccinus* "scarlet" < Greek *kokkos* "berry," because the dried body of the insect was believed to be a berry]

coch·i·neal in·sect *n* a small red scale insect that feeds on cacti. Native to: Mexico, Caribbean. Latin name: *Coccus cacti*.

co·chi·no /ko cheé nō/ *adj Hispanic* dirty or disgusting [< Spanish, "pig"]

Co·chise /kō cheéss, -cheéz/ (1815?–74) Chiricahua Apache leader. He led fighting against white settlers in Arizona Territory (1862–71).

coch·le·a /kóklee ə, kṓklee ə/ (*plural* **-ae** /-ee, -ī/ or **-as**) *n* a spiral structure in the inner ear that looks like a snail shell and contains tiny hair cells whose movement is interpreted by the brain as sound [Mid-16C. Via Latin *coc(h)lea* "snail shell, screw" < Greek *kokhlias*] —**coch·le·ar** *adj* —**coch·le·ate** /kóklee ət, -àyt, kṓklee-/ *adj*

coch·le·ar im·plant *n* a device implanted under the skin that picks up sounds and converts them to impulses transmitted to electrodes placed in the cochlea, restoring some hearing to people with a hearing impairment

Coch·ran /kókrən/, **Jacqueline** (1910–80) US aviator. She was the first woman pilot to break the sound barrier (1953).

cock /kok/ *n* **1.** ADULT MALE CHICKEN an adult male of a domestic fowl, usually only kept for breeding. Cocks have a distinctive crowing call. **2.** MALE BIRD the adult male of a bird **3.** ARMS PART OF GUN the hammer of a gun that, when released by the action of the trigger, makes the gun fire **4.** ARMS RAISED POSITION OF HAMMER OF GUN the raised position of the hammer of a gun when it is ready to fire **5.** TABOO TERM a highly offensive term for a man's penis (*taboo*) **6.** CONSTR same as **stopcock 7.** TILTED POSITION the tilt or angle in the position of somebody's head or hat, often suggesting that he or she is in a good mood ■ *vt* (**cocked, cock·ing, cocks**) **1.** ARMS PREPARE GUN FOR FIRING to pull back the hammer of a gun so that it is ready to be fired when the trigger is pulled **2.** TURN EAR OR EYES to turn an ear or one or both eyes in a particular direction in order to listen for or look out for somebody or something **3.** TILT OR ANGLE SOMETHING to tilt or raise something to one side **4.** SET SOMETHING TO OPERATE to set a device or mechanism so that it will release something such as a camera shutter [Pre-12C. Probably < medieval Latin *coccus*, an imitation of a rooster's crow]

cock·ade /ko káyd/ *n* a rosette, ribbon, or other ornament worn, usually on a hat, as an identifying badge or as part of a livery [Mid-17C. < French *bonnet à la coquarde* "bonnet worn proudly" < obsolete *coquard* "proud" < *coq* "cock"] —**cock·ad·ed** *adj*

cock-a-doo·dle-doo /-dóo/ *n* used as a description or imitation of the sound a rooster makes when it crows —**cock-a-doo·dle-doo** *vi*

cock-a-hoop *adj* **1.** boastful about something that has been achieved **2.** in an unbalanced or twisted position [< *set the cock on the hoop* "celebrate"]

cock-a-leek·ie /-leékee/ *n* a Scottish soup made from a whole chicken and leeks

cock·a·ma·mie /kòkə máymee/, **cock·a·ma·my** *adj* (*informal*) **1.** having very little importance or meaning **2.** not making any sense or lacking plausibility ○ *a cockamamie excuse* [Mid-20C. Probably alteration of DECALCOMANIA]

cock-and-bull sto·ry, **cock-and-bull** *n* a ridiculous and scarcely credible story that somebody tries to convince people is true [Origin ?]

cock·a·poo /kókə pòo/ (*plural* **-poos**) *n* a small dog that is a cross between a cocker spaniel and a poodle [Late 20C. Blend of COCKER SPANIEL + POODLE]

cock·a·tiel /kòkə teél/, **cock·a·teel** *n* a small gray parrot with a white patch on its wing and a prominent crest that is yellow in males. Native to: Australia. Latin name: *Nymphicus hollandicus*. [Late 19C. < Dutch *kaktielje*, probably diminutive of *kaketoe* (see COCKATOO)]

cockatoo

cock·a·too /kókə tòo/ (*plural* **-toos**) *n* a parrot with a prominent crest, often with white or light-colored feathers. Native to: Australia, New Guinea, South and Southeast Asia. Family: Cacatuidae. [Mid-17C. Via Dutch *kaketoe* < Malay *kakatua*; influenced by COCK]

cock·a·trice /kókətriss/ *n* a mythological serpent that was supposed to have hatched from a cock's egg and to be able to kill with its stare [14C. Via Old French *cocatris* < medieval Latin *calcatrix* "tracker" < Latin *calcare* "to track" < *calx* "heel"]

cock·boat /kók bṑt/ *n* a small rowboat, especially one that belongs to a larger ship. Cockboats are often used to ferry stores and provisions between ship and shore. [15C. *Cock* via Old French *coque* < Latin *codex* "block of wood"]

cock·chaf·er /kók chàyfər/ *n* a large European beetle with larvae that destroy trees and other plants. Family: Scarabaeidae.

cock·crow /kók krṑ/ *n* the time of day when the sun begins to show above the horizon (*archaic or literary*)

cocked hat /kòkt-/ *n* a two- or three-cornered hat with a wide turned-up brim that was popular in the 18th century, especially as part of a uniform or livery

cock·er[1] /kókər/ *n* **1.** BREED same as **cocker spaniel 2.** somebody involved in cockfighting either as a breeder or trainer of cocks, or as a regular spectator [Late 17C. < COCK]

cock·er[2] /kókər/ *n UK* used to refer to a close friend (*informal*) [15C. Origin ?]

cock·er·el /kókərəl/ *n* a young male chicken, usually one that is less than a year old [15C. < COCK + diminutive suffix]

cock·er span·iel *n* a small dog with long floppy ears and a soft wavy coat, belonging to a breed of spaniels originally developed for flushing out game [< WOODCOCK]

cock·eye /kók ī/ *n* an offensive term for an eye that is turned inward or outward from the nose so that parallel vision is impossible

cock·eyed /kók īd/ *adj* **1.** FOOLISH not sensible or properly thought out (*informal*) **2.** NOT ALIGNED positioned at an awkward or crooked angle **3.** VERY DRUNK so drunk that it is impossible to see straight (*informal*) **4.** OFFENSIVE TERM an offensive term meaning having one eye that turns inward or outward from the nose

cock feath·er *n* the feather on an arrow positioned at right angles to the notch into which the bow string fits [< COCK "stick up"]

cock·fight /kók fīt/ *n* an organized fight between two roosters, each of which is equipped with sharp metal spurs, in front of spectators who often make bets on the outcome

cock·fight·ing /kók fīting/ *n* the practice of setting two cocks to fight each other in front of spectators who often make bets on the outcome. The sport is illegal in many countries.

cock·horse /kók hàwrss/ *n* a rocking horse, or a stick with an imitation horse's head on one end

cock·le[1] /kók'l/ *n* **1.** SHELLFISH WITH HEART-SHAPED SHELL an invertebrate ocean animal with a small rounded or heart-shaped ridged shell in two parts. Family: Cardiidae. **2.** *also* **cock·le·shell** MARINE BIOL SHELL OF COCKLE the small rounded or heart-shaped ridged shell in two parts that a cockle lives in **3.** *also* **cock·le·shell** SMALL BOAT a small lightweight boat **4.** WRINKLE a crease or pucker in a piece of material such as paper or cloth ■ *vti* (**-led, -ling, -les**) BECOME OR MAKE WRINKLED to become wrinkled or puckered, or make something such as a piece of material wrinkled or puckered [14C. Via French *coquille* "shell" < medieval Greek *kokhulion* < Greek *kogkhē* "conch"] ◇ **warm the cockles of your heart** to give you a feeling of well-being or sentimental contentment

cock·le[2] /kók'l/ *n* a weedy plant that belongs to the pink family, especially the corn cockle, which grows in cornfields [Pre-12C. Origin ?]

cock·le·boat /kók'l bṑt/ *n* same as **cockboat** [Early 17C. < COCKLE[1]]

cock·le·bur /kók'l bùr/ *n* a coarse annual plant with prickly seed husks that attach easily to people's clothes or animals' fur. Genus: *Xanthium*. [Mid-19C. < COCKLE[2]]

cock·le·shell /kók'l shèl/ *n* MARINE BIOL same as **cockle**[1] *n* (senses 2–3)

cock·ney /kóknee/ (*plural* **-neys**), **Cock·ney** *n* **1.** somebody born in London, traditionally within a two-mile radius of the bells of St. Mary-le-Bow church in London's East End. Cockneys are considered to be the "true" Londoners. **2.** the accent or dialect of native Londoners from the East End [14C. < *coken*, obsolete genitive plural of COCK + obsolete *ey* "egg" < Old English *ǣg* < Germanic] —**cock·ney·ism** *n*

cock-of-the-rock (*plural* **cocks-of-the-rock**) *n* a bird, the male of which has bright orange or red feathers and a crest that extend over the beak. Native to: tropical South America. Genus: *Rupicola*. [Because it nests on rocks]

cock·pit /kók pìt/ *n* **1.** AVIAT **PILOT'S PART OF AIRCRAFT** the compartment in an aircraft or spacecraft where the pilot and other crew members sit **2.** MOTOR SPORTS **AREA FOR DRIVER IN RACING CAR** a space for the driver in a racing car **3.** NAUT **ENCLOSURE FOR WHEEL OR TILLER** an enclosure at the stern of a boat for the wheel or tiller **4.** SPORTS **PLACE FOR COCKFIGHTING** an enclosed place where cockfights are held **5.** MIL **FREQUENT BATTLEGROUND** a place where many battles have been fought

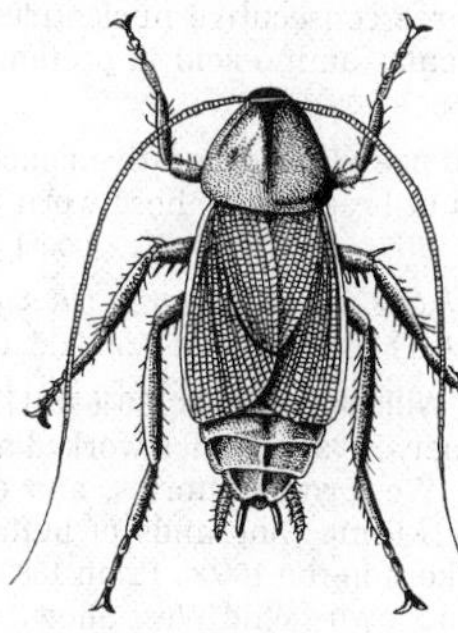

cockroach

cock·roach /kók rōch/ *n* a nocturnal insect with a flat oval body, long antennae, and chewing mouthparts, some species of which are household pests. Order: Blattodea. [Early 17C. By folk etymology < Spanish *cucaracha*]

cocks·comb /kóks kōm/ *n* **1.** the red fleshy crest that grows on the top of a rooster's head **2.** a tropical plant often grown as a houseplant. Flowers: orange or red, appearing as a broad crest or plume resembling a cockscomb. Latin name: *Celosia cristata*. **3.** FASHION another spelling of **coxcomb** (sense 1)

cock·spur /kók spùr/ *n* a spur on the foot of some male birds

cock·suck·er /kók sùkər/ *n* (*taboo offensive insult*) **1.** a highly offensive term of abuse for a man **2.** a highly offensive term for somebody who performs fellatio

cock·sure /kok shòor, kók shòor/ *adj* **1.** absolutely sure of being correct about something or succeeding in some effort **2.** arrogantly confident and self-assured [Early 16C. < *cock*, euphemism for "God"] —**cock·sure·ness** *n*

cock·swain /kók swàyn/ *n* ROWING another spelling of **coxswain**

cock·tail /kók tàyl/ *n* **1.** **MIXED BEVERAGE** a drink that is made up of a mixture of different beverages such as fruit juice or soda and usually alcohol, and served iced or chilled **2.** **LIGHT SNACK** a light appetizer before a main meal, consisting usually of seafood or fruit served with a sauce (*usually used in combination*) ○ *a shrimp cocktail* **3.** **MIXTURE OF THINGS** a mixture of different features or things ○ *a malicious cocktail of lies and gossip* **4.** MED **COMBINATION TREATMENT** a combination of two or more drugs or therapeutic agents given as a single treatment ■ **cock·tails** *npl* **GATHERING TO CONSUME ALCOHOLIC BEVERAGES** a gathering where alcoholic beverages are consumed, sometimes with light snacks, often early in the evening before another social event ■ *adj* **SMALL** small and designed to be eaten as a snack with the fingers or on a cocktail stick ○ *cocktail sausage* [Early 17C. < COCK]

cock·tail cab·i·net game, cock·tail game *n* a type of early computer arcade game housed in a table with the graphics on a screen in the table-top, and played sitting down

cock·tail dress *n* a short dress, often of expensive fabric and semiformal design, worn for an early-evening social occasion such as a cocktail party

cock·tail lounge *n* a bar, sometimes a room in a hotel or restaurant, where cocktails and other drinks are served

cock·tail party *n* a party where cocktails and light snacks are served, often taking place early in the evening before another social event

cock·tail shaker *n* a metal container used for mixing different, usually alcoholic, drinks with ice

cock·tail stick *n* a small pointed wooden or plastic stick on which olives or cherries are placed in cocktails, or on which small items of food such as sausages or cubes of cheese are served

cock·tail ta·ble *n* FURNITURE same as **coffee table**

cock-teas·er, cock-tease *n* a highly offensive term for somebody who makes sexual advances toward a man without intending to have sex with him (*taboo*)

cock·y /kókee/ (**-i·er, -i·est**) *adj* arrogantly confident and sure of yourself (*informal*) —**cock·i·ly** *adv* —**cock·i·ness** *n*

co·co /kṓkō/ (*plural* **-cos**) *n* **1.** PLANTS, FOOD same as **coconut** **2.** *Hispanic* in Cuba, a government-owned, three-wheeled motorcycle housed in a yellow egg-shaped fiberglass body, reserved for paying tourists as taxi transportation (*informal*) [Mid-16C. < Spanish *coco*, Portuguese *côco*, literally "grinning face"; from the appearance of the base of the shell]

co·coa /kṓkō/ *n* **1.** **BROWN POWDER FOR MAKING CHOCOLATE** an unsweetened brown powder made from roasted and ground cocoa beans. Use: making chocolate, cooking, hot drink. **2.** **HOT DRINK MADE WITH COCOA POWDER** a hot drink made with milk or water, cocoa powder, and often sugar **3.** **BROWN COLOR** a light to medium brown color [Early 18C. Alteration of CACAO]

Co·coa Beach /kṑkō-/ city in eastern Florida, southeast of Orlando and directly south of Cape Canaveral. Population: 12,509 (2002 estimate).

co·coa bean *n* the bean-shaped seed of the cacao tree. Use: making cocoa powder and chocolate.

co·coa but·ter *n* a thick oily solid obtained from cocoa beans. Use: making chocolate, in cosmetics and suntan oils.

co·coa·nut *n* FOOD another spelling of **coconut**

co·coa-pay·ol /kṓkō pay òl/ *n Carib* somebody of Spanish, usually Venezuelan, ancestry (*informal*) [Early 19C. *Payol* < Spanish *español* "Spanish"]

co·co-de-mer /kṑkō də mér/ (*plural* **co·cos-de-mer**) *n* **1.** a fan palm, now found only in nature reserves in the Seychelles, that produces the largest seed in the world. Latin name: *Lodoicea maldivica*. **2.** the edible two-lobed fruit of a coco-de-mer palm [Early 19C. < French, "coco from the sea"; because first known from nuts found floating in the sea]

coconut

co·co·nut /kṓkə nùt/ (*plural same* or **-nuts**), **co·coa·nut** *n* **1.** the fruit of the coconut palm, consisting of a hard fibrous husk around a single-seeded nut with firm white flesh that is eaten raw or dried to make copra and a hollow core containing sweet-tasting liquid (**coconut milk**). Use: husk: matting, compost. **2.** the sweet white flesh of the coconut fruit, used widely in cooking and confectionery in the form of small dried flakes **3.** TREES same as **coconut palm**

co·co·nut but·ter *n* solidified coconut oil used in the manufacture of soap and candles

co·co·nut crab *n* a large hermit crab that burrows in the ground and can climb trees. Native to: islands of Pacific and Indian Oceans. Latin name: *Birgus latro*.

co·co·nut mat·ting *n* coarse floor matting made from the fibers that grow on coconut shells

co·co·nut milk *n* the sweet watery juice that is contained within a coconut and is used in drinks and cooking

co·co·nut oil *n* a thick sweet-smelling oil extracted from the flesh of the coconut and used widely in food and cosmetics

co·co·nut palm *n* a tall tropical palm tree with large fruits (**coconuts**). Use: beverages, oil, fiber, utensils, thatch. Latin name: *Cocos nucifera*.

co·coon /kə kòon/ *n* **1.** ZOOL **SHEATH FOR CATERPILLAR** the silky covering with which a caterpillar or other insect larva encloses itself during its transition to an adult state **2.** **SOMETHING SIMILAR TO COCOON** something that resembles a cocoon in the way that it provides protection or a sense of safety **3.** INDUST **COVERING THAT PROTECTS SOMETHING FROM WATER** a cover or protective spray used to seal machinery and make it waterproof, especially military equipment when in storage or transport ■ *v* (**-cooned, -coon·ing, -coons**) **1.** *vt* **WRAP SOMEBODY OR SOMETHING SAFELY** to cover or envelop somebody or something in order to provide warmth or protection ○ *cocooned in a pile of bedclothes* **2.** *vt* **KEEP SOMEBODY SAFE FROM SOMETHING** to protect somebody from unpleasantness or danger **3.** *vi* **WITHDRAW INTO PRIVACY** to withdraw into a state of personal privacy in order to escape stressful everyday life (*informal*) [Late 17C. < French *cocon* < Latin *coccus* "berry" (see COCCUS)] —**co·cooned** *adj*

co·co plum *n* a tropical tree, cultivated for its edible fruit that is usually eaten preserved and, in West Africa, for an oil obtained from its seeds. Native to: tropical America and Africa. Latin name: *Chrysobalanus icaco*.

Co·cos Is·lands /kṓkōss-/ group of 27 small islands in the Indian Ocean that belong to Australia, situated approximately 580 mi./930 km southwest of Java. Population: 595 (1993). Area: 5.5 sq. mi./14 sq. km.

co·cotte /kō kót, kə-/ *n* **1.** a promiscuous woman or prostitute (*literary*) **2.** a heatproof dish in which food can be cooked and served in small portions [Early 20C. Alteration of French *cocasse* < Latin *cucuma* "cooking pot"]

co·coun·sel·ing /kō kównss'ling/ *n* a form of counseling in which participants receive training as counselors and work alternately as counselor and client

AKG London

Jean Cocteau

Coc·teau /kok tṓ, kawk-/, **Jean** (1889–1963) French writer and movie director. His works include the novel *Children of the Game* (1929) and the film *Beauty and the Beast* (1945).

> "Mirrors would do well to reflect a bit more before throwing back images."
> [Jean Cocteau, "Des beaux-arts considérés comme un assassinat" ("On the arts considered as an act of murder"), *Essai de critique indirecte (Essay of Indirect Criticism)*; 1932]

co·cur·ric·u·lar /kō kə ríkyələr/ *adj* not forming part of the official curriculum but complementing it

co·cus·wood /kṓkəss wòod/ (*plural same*) *n* **1.** a hard wood that turns black with age. Use: musical instruments, backs of brushes, inlays. **2.** a tree that yields cocuswood. Native to: Caribbean. Latin name: *Brya ebenus.* [Mid-17C. Origin ?]

Co·cy·tus /kō kítəss, -sítəss/ *n* in Greek mythology, one of the tributaries of the River Styx that flowed through the underworld [< Greek *Kōkutos,* literally "wailing"]

cod[1] /kod/ (*plural same* or **cods**) *n* **1.** a saltwater fish that has three dorsal fins and slender feelers like whiskers (**barbels**) on its jaw, and lives close to the seabed. Family: Gadidae. **2.** the flesh of a cod used as food [14C. Origin ?]

cod[2] /kod/ *n* (*archaic*) **1.** a bag **2.** the sac of skin that contains the testes of a male mammal [Old English *cod(d)* < Germanic]

Cod, Cape /kod/ peninsula in southeastern Massachusetts. One of the prime tourist destinations of New England, it is between 1 mi./2 km and 20 mi./32 km wide and about 65 mi./105 km long.

COD, C.O.D. *abbr* MAIL **1.** cash on delivery **2.** collect on delivery

Cod., cod. *abbr* COMMUNICATION codex

co·da /kódə/ *n* **1.** in some pieces of music, a final section that adds dramatic energy to the work as a whole, usually through intensified rhythmic activity **2.** an additional section at the end of a text such as a literary work or speech that is not necessary to its structure but gives additional information [Mid-18C. Via Italian < Latin *cauda* "tail"]

cod·dle /kódd'l/ (**-dled, -dling, -dles**) *vt* **1.** to treat somebody in an excessively protective and indulgent way **2.** to cook an egg in water just below the boiling point [Late 16C. Origin ?] —**cod·dler** *n*

code /kōd/ *n* **1. SYSTEM OF LETTERS, NUMBERS, OR SYMBOLS** a system of letters, numbers, or symbols into which normal language is converted to allow information to be communicated secretly, briefly, or electronically **2. INFORMATION SYSTEM OF LETTERS OR NUMBERS** a system of letters or numbers that gives information about something such as postal or telephone areas **3.** COMPUT **COMPUTER INFORMATION** a system of symbols, numbers, or signals that conveys information to a computer **4.** LAW, PUBLIC ADMIN **RULES AND REGULATIONS** a system of accepted laws and regulations that govern procedure or behavior in particular circumstances or within a particular profession ○ *the penal code* **5. WAY OF BEHAVING** a set of unwritten rules concerning acceptable standards of behavior ○ *her moral code* **6.** MED **PATIENT WITH NO HEARTBEAT OR BREATHING** a patient whose heart has stopped beating or who has stopped breathing (*slang*) ■ *v* (**cod·ed, cod·ing, codes**) **1.** *vt* **PUT SOMETHING IN CODE** to put a message or text into code **2.** *vt* COMPUT **WRITE COMPUTER PROGRAM** to write a computer program that provides instructions to a computer **3.** *vi* GENETICS **PROVIDE GENETIC INFORMATION** to act as or provide the genetic information that enables a polypeptide, RNA molecule, or one of their constituent groups to be produced (*refers to codons or genes*) **4.** *vi* MED **UNDERGO HEART OR BREATHING STOPPAGE** to go into a state in which the heart has stopped beating or the lungs have ceased to function (*slang*) [Late 16C. < Latin *codex* "block of wood, book, set of statutes"] —**cod·er** *n*

code blue, Code Blue *n* a medical emergency, especially in a hospital, when a patient's heart stops beating or his or her lungs stop functioning

code·book /kōd bo͝ok/ *n* a book containing a key to a code or codes

co·dec /kō dèk/ *n* a piece of equipment that codes and decodes electronic signals [Late 20C. < shortenings of CODE, DECODE]

co·de·fen·dant /kō di féndənt/ *n* one of two or more people who are defending a legal charge or claim in a court of law

co·deine /kō deen/ *n* an opiate drug. Use: to relieve pain and coughing. Formula: $C_{18}H_{21}NO_3$. [Mid-19C. < Greek *kōdeia* "poppy head"]

code name *n* a name used to disguise the identity or nature of somebody or something such as a military operation —**code-name** *vt*

Code Na·po·lé·on /kōd napō lay áwN/ *n* the codification of French laws drawn up under Napoleon between 1804 and 1810 and forming the basis of modern French civil law

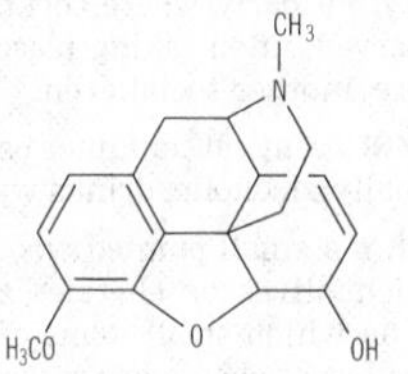

codeine

cod end *n* the narrow end of a purse seine or other trawl net for commercial fishing [< COD[2]]

code of con·duct *n* a set of unwritten rules according to which people in a particular group, class, or situation are supposed to behave

code of prac·tice *n* a set of rules according to which people in a particular profession are expected to behave

co·de·pen·den·cy /kō di péndənssee/, **co·de·pen·dence** /-dənss/ *n* **1.** the dependence of two people, groups, or organisms on each other, especially when this reinforces mutually harmful behavior patterns **2.** a situation in which a person such as the partner of an alcoholic or a parent of a drug-addicted child needs to feel needed by the other person —**co·de·pen·dent** *n, adj*

code red *interj, n* used to indicate that a difficult or dangerous situation has deteriorated drastically so as to constitute an emergency

code-shar·ing *n* an arrangement between two airlines in which they both sell seats on a flight using their own flight numbers

co·de·ter·mi·na·tion /kō di turmi náysh'n/ *n* cooperation between management and employees in making decisions

code word *n* **1. SECRET WORD IDENTIFYING SOMEBODY OR SOMETHING** a secret word or phrase that is used to identify a person, operation, or organization whose true identity is to be kept hidden **2. SECRET PASSWORD** a secret word or phrase that is used as a password in a secret operation **3. EUPHEMISM** a word or phrase used to describe something in a euphemistic way ○ *corporate re-engineering is often just a code word for layoffs*

co·dex /kō dèks/ (*plural* **-di·ces** /-di seez/) *n* a collection of ancient manuscript texts, especially of the Biblical Scriptures, in book form [Late 16C. < Latin, "block of wood, book, set of statutes"]

Co·dex Ju·ris Ca·non·i·ci /kō deks jooriss kə nónni sī/ *n* the official code of canon law of the Roman Catholic Church since 1918, when it replaced the Corpus Juris Canonici. It was revised in 1983. [< ecclesiastical Latin, "code of canon law"]

cod·fish /kód fish/ (*plural same* or **-fish·es**) *n* FISH same as **cod**[1] (sense 1)

codg·er /kójjər/ *n* a man, especially a man of advanced years who is seen as slightly eccentric or amusing (*informal insult*) [Mid-18C. Origin ?]

co·di·ces LITERAT, ANCIENT HIST plural of **codex**

cod·i·cil /kóddəssil/ *n* **1.** an additional part of a will that either modifies it or revokes part of it **2.** an appendix or supplement to a text (*formal*) [15C. < Latin *codicillus*, diminutive of *codex* "block of wood, book, set of statutes"] —**cod·i·cil·la·ry** /kòddə sílləree/ *adj*

cod·i·col·o·gy /kòddə kólləjee/ *n* the study of manuscripts [Mid-20C. < French *codicologie* < Latin *codic-* "book"] —**cod·i·co·log·i·cal** /kòddəkə lójjik'l/ *adj*

cod·i·fy /kóddi fī/ (**-fied, -fy·ing, -fies**) *vt* to arrange things, especially laws, rules, or principles, into an organized system or code —**cod·i·fi·ca·tion** /kòddifi káysh'n/ *n* —**cod·i·fi·er** *n*

cod·ing the·o·ry /kōding-/ *n* the branch of mathematics that applies algebra and number theory to the development of ways of representing information in computer systems and data transmission networks

cod·ling /kóddling/ (*plural* **-lings** or *same*) *n* a small or young cod

cod·ling moth /kóddlin-/, **cod·lin moth** *n* a small moth with a thick body whose larvae feed on apples, pears, and other fruit. Latin name: *Laspeyresia pomonella.*

cod-liv·er oil *n* an oil rich in vitamins A and D that is extracted from the liver of the cod and is often used as a food supplement

co·dom·i·nant /kō dómminənt/ *adj* **1.** describes genes that each have equal effect in making the character they control appear in offspring. The genes for A and B blood groups are codominant and give rise to the AB blood group if they are both inherited. **2.** determining the kinds of species that exist in an ecological community —**co·dom·i·nance** *n*

co·don /kō dòn/ *n* a unit in messenger RNA consisting of a set of three consecutive nucleotides that specifies a particular amino acid in protein synthesis [Mid-20C. < CODE + -ON[1]]

cod·piece /kód peess/ *n* a decorative pouch attached to the crotch of breeches or hose worn by men in the 15th and 16th centuries [15C. < COD[2]]

cods·wal·lop /kódz wòlləp/ *n, interj UK* same as **nonsense** *n* (sense 1) (*dated slang*) [Mid-20C. Origin ?]

Co·dy /kōdee/, **William Frederick** (1846–1917) US scout and entertainer. He sometimes worked as an army scout in the Western territories, and earned his nickname by killing thousands of buffalo to feed railroad workers in the 1860s. From 1883 to 1913 he toured with his own "Wild West Show." Known as **Buffalo Bill**

Coe /kō/, **Sebastian, Lord** (*b.* 1956) British athlete and politician. He broke eight world middle-distance track records and was a Conservative member of parliament (1992–97).

co·ed /kō èd/, **co-ed** *adj* with both male and female students (*informal*) ■ *n* a woman student who attends a college or university where men and women are educated together (*dated informal*) [Late 19C. Shortening of *coeducational*]

co·e·di·tion /kō i dísh'n/ *n* a book published by two or more publishers jointly

co·ed·u·ca·tion /kō ejə káysh'n/ *n* the education of both sexes together —**co·ed·u·ca·tion·al** *adj* —**co·ed·u·ca·tion·al·ly** *adv*

coef. *abbr* coefficient

co·ef·fi·cient /kō i físh'nt/ *n* **1.** the number placed before a letter that represents a variable in algebra, e.g., the "3" of "3x" in the equation "3x = 6" **2.** a numerical constant that is a measure of a property of a substance [Mid-17C. < modern Latin *coefficient-* "combining to produce a result" < Latin *efficient-* (see EFFICIENT)]

co·ef·fi·cient of cor·re·la·tion *n* MATH same as **correlation coefficient**

co·ef·fi·cient of ex·pan·sion *n* the change in length or area of a material per unit length or unit area that accompanies a change in temperature of one degree

co·ef·fi·cient of fric·tion *n* the ratio of the force needed to make two surfaces slide over each other to the force that holds them together. Symbol μ

-coel *suffix* cavity, chamber ○ *pseudocoel* [Via modern Latin *-coela* < Greek *koilos* "hollow" < Indo-European]

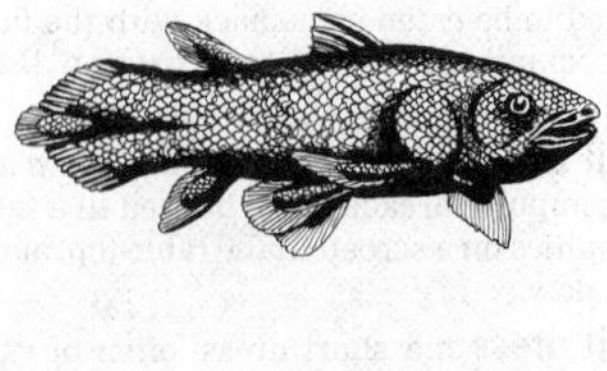

coelacanth

coe·la·canth /séelə kànth/ *n* a large fish that varies from bright blue to brownish and has fleshy lobes at the base of its fins and a three-lobed tail. Coelacanths were thought to have been extinct for 70 million years until a living species was discovered in 1938 off the east coast of Africa. Native to: Indian Ocean. Latin name: *Latimeria chalumnae.* See illustration on previous page [Mid-19C. < modern Latin *Coelacanthus* < Greek *koilos* "hollow" + *akantha* "spine"; because its fins have hollow spines] —**coe·la·can·thine** /séelə kán thìn, séelə kánthin/ *adj* —**coe·la·can·thous** *adj*

-coele *suffix* same as **-coel**

coe·len·te·ra ZOOL plural of **coelenteron**

coe·len·ter·ate /si léntə ràyt, -rət/ *n* ZOOL same as **cnidarian** [Late 19C. < modern Latin *Coelenterata* < Greek *koilos* "hollow" + *enteron* "intestine"] —**coe·len·ter·ic** /séelən térrik/ *adj*

coe·len·ter·on /si léntə ròn/ (*plural* **-te·ra** /-tərə/) *n* the internal body cavity of an invertebrate sea animal (**coelenterate**)

coe·li·ac *adj* ANAT another spelling of **celiac**

coe·lom /séeləm/ (*plural* **-loms** or **-lo·ma·ta** /-lṓmətə, -lómmətə/), **ce·lom** (*plural* **-loms** or **-lo·ma·ta**), **coe·lome** *n* the cavity between the body wall and the gut of many animals, formed when the embryonic mesoderm is divided into two layers [Late 19C. Via German *Koelom* < Greek *koilōma* "a hollow"] —**coe·lom·ic** /si lómmik, -lṓmik/ *adj*

coe·lo·mate /séelə màyt/ *adj* having a cavity between the body wall and the digestive tract —**coe·lo·mate** *n*

coe·lo·stat /séelə stàt/ *n* an instrument with a mirror that rotates parallel to the Earth's axis in order to reflect light from an astronomical object onto a second mirror aimed at a fixed telescope [Late 19C. < Latin *caelum* "sky"]

co·emp·tion /kō émpsh'n/ *n* the purchase of all available supplies of a particular commodity [14C. < Latin *coemption-* "buying up" < *emere* "take, buy"]

Coen /koon/, **Jan Pieterszoon** (1587–1629) Dutch colonial administrator. He secured the East Indies for Holland and founded its capital in Batavia, present-day Jakarta (1619).

coen- *prefix* same as **coeno-** (*used before vowels*)

coeno- *prefix* general, common ○ *coenocyte* [< Greek *koinos* < Indo-European, "together"]

coen·o·bite *n* RELIG another spelling of **cenobite**

coe·no·cyte /séennə sìt/ *n* a cell, part, or organism that contains many nuclei not separated by cell walls, e.g., the threads (**hyphae**) of many fungi or the bodies of some algae —**coe·no·cyt·ic** /séenə síttik/ *adj*

coen·o·gen·e·sis *n* BIOL another spelling of **cenogenesis**

coe·no·sarc /séenə saark/ *n* material linking the stems of individuals within a colony of polyps and containing a highly branched canal system with digestive and circulatory functions [Mid-19C. < COENO- + Greek *sark-* "flesh"]

co·en·zyme /kō én zìm/ *n* a nonprotein compound that combines with a specific protein (**apoenzyme**) to form an active enzyme

co·en·zyme A *n* a complex compound that acts with specific enzymes in energy-producing biochemical reactions

co·en·zyme Q *n* BIOCHEM same as **ubiquinone**

co·e·qual /kō éekwəl/ *adj* equal in size, rank, or status to another [14C. < Latin *coaequalis* "of the same age" < *aequalis* (see EQUAL)] —**co·e·qual** *n* —**co·e·qual·i·ty** /kō i kwóllətee/ *n* —**co·e·qual·ly** *adv*

co·erce /kō úrss/ (**-erced, -erc·ing, -erc·es**) *vt* to make somebody do something against his or her will by using force or threats [15C. < Latin *coercere* "shut in together" < *arcere* "shut in"] —**co·erc·er** *n* —**co·erc·i·ble** *adj*

co·er·cion /kō úrzh'n/ *n* **1.** the use of force or threats to make somebody do something against his or her will **2.** force or threats used to make somebody do something against his or her will —**co·er·cion·ar·y** *adj* —**co·er·cion·ist** *n, adj*

co·er·cive /kō úrssiv/ *adj* using force or threats to make somebody do something against his or her will —**co·er·cive·ly** *adv* —**co·er·cive·ness** *n*

co·er·cive force *n* the magnetic force necessary to demagnetize a substance

co·er·civ·i·ty /kō ur sívvətee/ *n* PHYS same as **coercive force**

co·es·sen·tial /kō i sénsh'l/ *adj* having the same essence or nature [Late 15C. < ecclesiastical Latin *coessentialis* "of the same substance" < late Latin *essentialis* (see ESSENTIAL)] —**co·es·sen·ti·al·i·ty** /kō i senshee állətee/ *n* —**co·es·sen·tial·ly** *adv* —**co·es·sen·tial·ness** *n*

co·e·ter·nal /kō i túrn'l/ *adj* existing together throughout eternity (*formal*) [14C. < ecclesiastical Latin *coaeternus* < Latin *aeternus* (see ETERNAL)] —**co·e·ter·nal·ly** *adv*

co·e·ter·ni·ty /kō i túrnətee/ *n* eternal existence with somebody or something else [Late 16C. < late Latin *coaeternitas* < Latin *aeternitas* (see ETERNITY)]

Coet·zee /kŏt zée/, **J. M.** (*b.* 1940) South African novelist. His works, reflecting turmoil in South Africa, include *The Life and Times of Michael K* (1983) and *Disgrace* (1999), both of which won the Booker Prize. He was awarded the Nobel Prize in Literature in 2003. Full name **Coetzee, John Maxwell**

Coeur d'A·lene /kàwrdə láyn, kàwrd'l áyn/ city and resort in northeastern Idaho, on the northern shore of Coeur d'Alene Lake. Population: 36,259 (2002 estimate).

co·e·val /kō éev'l/ *adj* having the same age, duration, or date of origin (*formal*) [Early 17C. < late Latin *coaevus* < Latin *aevum* "age" < Greek *aiōn*] —**co·e·val·i·ty** /kō i vállətee/ *n* —**co·e·val·ly** *adv*

co·ev·o·lu·tion /kō evə lóosh'n/ *n* the joint development and adaptation to external changes of two or more interdependent species, e.g., parasites and the animals they live on —**co·ev·o·lu·tion·ar·y** *adj*

co·e·volve /kō i vólv/ (**-volved, -volv·ing, -volves**) *vi* to evolve and adapt together, e.g., in the way that parasites and the animals they live on do

co·ex·ist /kō ig zíst/ (**-ist·ed, -ist·ing, -ists**) *vi* **1.** to exist together at the same time and in the same place **2.** to occupy the same place in a peaceful way —**co·ex·is·tence** *n* —**co·ex·is·tent** *adj*

co·ex·tend /kō ik sténd/ (**-tend·ed, -tend·ing, -tends**) *vti* to extend, or make things extend, in or through the same space or length of time —**co·ex·ten·sion** *n*

co·ex·ten·sive /kō ik sténssiv/ *adj* sharing the same limits, boundaries, or scope —**co·ex·ten·sive·ly** *adv*

co·fac·tor /kō fáktər/ *n* a substance that acts with and is essential to the activity of an enzyme, e.g., a coenzyme or metal ion

C. of C. *abbr* COMM chamber of commerce

C. of E. *abbr* CHR Church of England

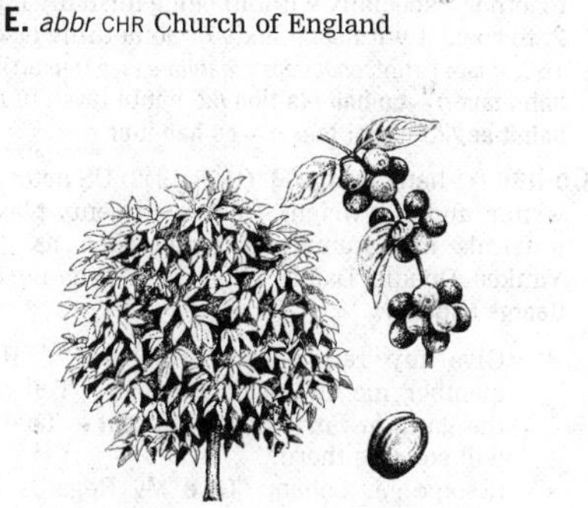

coffee

cof·fee /káwfee, kóffee/ *n* **1.** STRONG CAFFEINE-RICH DRINK a drink containing caffeine and with a mildly stimulating effect that is made from the ground or processed seeds of a tropical tree **2.** SEEDS FOR MAKING COFFEE the roasted seeds (**coffee beans**) of a tropical tree used to make coffee. They are ground, or made into powder or granules that dissolve in hot water. **3.** BUSH YIELDING COFFEE BEANS a bush cultivated for its seeds (**coffee beans**) that are used to make coffee. Genus: *Coffea.* **4.** RICH BROWN COLOR a medium to dark rich brown color [Late 16C. Via Turkish *kahve* < Arabic *kahwa*] —**cof·fee** *adj* ◇ **wake up and smell the coffee** used to tell somebody that he or she is wrong about a particular situation and that it is time to acknowledge reality (*informal*)

cof·fee bean *n* a seed of the coffee tree that is roasted and ground, or processed in other ways, to make coffee

cof·fee break *n* a short break for coffee or other refreshment

cof·fee·cake /káwfee kàyk, kóffee-/ *n* a sweet cake or roll, often containing nuts and raisins, that is eaten with coffee

cof·fee grind·er *n* an electric or hand-operated device for grinding roasted coffee beans

cof·fee·house /káwfee hòwss, kóffee-/ (*plural* **-hous·es** /-hòwzəz/) *n* a place where coffee and other refreshments are served

cof·fee klatch /-klàch/, **cof·fee klatsch** *n* a small social gathering where people drink coffee and engage in casual conversation [Late 19C. Anglicization of KAFFEEKLATSCH]

cof·fee ma·chine *n* **1.** a vending machine that dispenses hot drinks such as coffee, tea, and hot chocolate **2.** a machine in which coffee is made by filtering or forcing heated water at high pressure through coffee grounds into a jug or cup

cof·fee·mak·er /káwfee màykər, kóffee-/ *n* a device, usually an electric appliance, for brewing coffee

cof·fee mill *n* HOUSEHOLD same as **coffee grinder**

cof·fee·pot /káwfee pòt, kóffee-/ *n* a pot with a spout and lid designed for brewing or serving coffee

cof·fee shop *n* **1.** an informal restaurant serving snacks and light meals **2.** a place where coffee and snacks are served and coffee beans are sold

cof·fee ta·ble *n* a low table for use in a living room

cof·fee-ta·ble book *n* a large, usually expensive book with lavish illustrations, especially one used for display or casual perusal rather than reading

cof·fer /káwffər, kóffər/ *n* **1.** STRONGBOX a strong chest or box used for keeping money or valuables safe **2.** ARCHIT CEILING PANEL an ornamental sunken panel in a ceiling or dome **3.** CONSTR same as **cofferdam** (sense 1) ■ **cof·fers** *npl* FUNDS a supply or store of money, often belonging to an organization ■ *vt* (**-fered, -fer·ing, -fers**) **1.** STORE SOMETHING VALUABLE IN STRONGBOX to put money or valuables in a coffer **2.** DECORATE CEILING WITH COFFERS to decorate something, especially a ceiling, with coffers [13C. < French *coffre* < Latin *cophinus* (see COFFIN)]

cof·fer·dam /káwfər dàm, kóffər-/ *n* **1.** a temporary watertight structure that is pumped dry to enclose an area underwater and allow construction work on a ship, bridge, or rig to be carried out **2.** an empty space that acts as a protective barrier between two floors or bulkheads on a ship

cof·fin /káwfin, kóffin/ *n* **1.** BOX FOR CORPSE a long oblong container, usually made of wood, in which a dead body is placed for burial or cremation **2.** PRINTING PRINTING FRAME a frame that holds electrotype or stereotype printing plates ■ *vt* (**-fined, -fin·ing, -fins**) PUT SOMEBODY OR SOMETHING IN COFFIN to place somebody or something in a coffin or in something resembling a coffin [14C. Via Old French *cof(f)in* "little basket" < Latin *cophinus* "basket" < Greek *kophinos*]

cof·fin birth *n* expulsion of a dead fetus during postmortem decomposition of the mother's body, caused, e.g., by pressure of expanding body gases

cof·fin bone *n* the main bone in a horse's hoof

cof·fin cor·ner *n* in football, a corner of the field within ten yards of the goal line of the defending team. Kickers try to kick the ball so that it will bounce out of bounds from this area, forcing the defending team to start their downs close to their own goal.

cof·fin nail *n* same as **cigarette** (*dated slang*)

C. of S. *abbr* MIL chief of staff

cog[1] /kog/ *n* **1.** a projection on the edge of a gearwheel that engages with corresponding parts on another wheel to transfer motion from one wheel to the other. See illustration on next page **2.** somebody regarded as a small and unimportant part of a large organization or system **3.** MECH ENG same as **cogwheel** [13C. Probably < N Germanic] —**cogged** *adj*

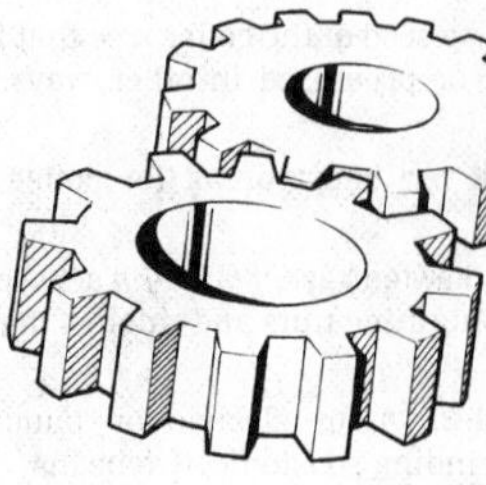

cog

cog² /kog/ *n* a piece that projects from the end of a timber beam and is designed to fit into an opening in another beam to form a joint ■ *vt* (**cogged, cog·ging, cogs**) to join two timber beams with a cog [Early 19C. Probably variant of *cock* "pamper," shortening of COCKER²]

co·gen·er·a·tion /kō jènnə ráysh'n/ *n* the production of two types of energy such as heat or electricity from one source in such a way that both are usable, instead of one being treated as waste energy —**co·gen·er·a·tor** /kō jénnə ràytər/ *n*

co·gent /kṓjənt/ *adj* forceful and convincing to the intellect and reason ○ *a cogent argument* [Mid-17C. < Latin *cogent-*, present participle of *cogere* "drive together" < *agere* "drive"] —**co·gen·cy** *n* —**co·gent·ly** *adv*

SYNONYMS See ***valid***.

cog·i·tate /kójji tàyt/ (**-tat·ed, -tat·ing, -tates**) *vti* to think deeply and carefully about something (*formal*) [Late 16C. < Latin *cogitat-*, past participle of *cogitare*, literally "disturb together" < *agitare* (see AGITATE)] —**cog·i·ta·tion** /kòjji táysh'n/ *n* —**cog·i·ta·tive** *adj*

co·gnac /kōn yàk/ *n* a high-quality brandy distilled from white grapes in Cognac, western France

Co·gnac /káwn yàk, kón-/ town in Charente Department, western France, north of Bordeaux. It is known for the brandy distilled there. Population: 19,534 (1999).

cog·nate /kóg nàyt/ *adj* **1.** LING having the same linguistic root or origin **2.** related by blood or having an ancestor in common (*formal*) [14C. < Latin *cognatus*, literally "born together" < *gnatus*, past participle of *(g)nasci* "be born"] —**cog·nate** *n* —**cog·na·tion** /kog náysh'n/ *n*

cog·nate ob·ject *n* a noun that functions as the object of a verb that is from the same etymological root, as in "to dream a dream" or "to think a thought"

~~**cognative**~~ incorrect spelling of **cognitive**

cog·ni·tion /kog nísh'n/ *n* **1.** the mental faculty or process of acquiring knowledge by the use of reasoning, intuition, or perception **2.** knowledge acquired through reasoning, intuition, or perception [15C. < Latin *cognition-* < *cognoscere* "get to know" < *(g)noscere* "know"] —**cog·ni·tion·al** *adj*

cog·ni·tive /kógnitiv/ *adj* **1.** relating to the process of acquiring knowledge by the use of reasoning, intuition, or perception **2.** relating to thought processes [Late 16C. < medieval Latin *cognitivus* < Latin *cognoscere* (see COGNITION)] —**cog·ni·tive·ly** *adv*

cog·ni·tive dis·so·nance *n* a state of psychological conflict or anxiety resulting from a contradiction between a person's simultaneously held beliefs or attitudes

cog·ni·tive map *n* a map of three-dimensional space maintained in the brain

cog·ni·tive psy·chol·o·gy *n* the branch of psychology concerned with the study of mental states

cog·ni·tive sci·ence *n* the scientific study of knowledge and how it is acquired, combining aspects of philosophy, psychology, linguistics, anthropology, and artificial intelligence

cog·ni·tive ther·a·py *n* a treatment of psychiatric disorders such as anxiety or depression that encourages patients to confront and challenge the distorted way of thinking that characterizes their disorder

cog·ni·tiv·ism /kógniti vìzzəm/ *n* the theory that moral judgments are statements of fact and can therefore be classed as true or false

cog·ni·za·ble /kógnizəb'l, kog nīzəb'l/ *adj* **1.** able to be known or perceived by the human mind (*formal*) **2.** LAW falling within the jurisdiction of a particular court of law and therefore able to be tried by that court —**cog·ni·za·bly** *adv*

cog·ni·zance /kógnizənss/ *n* **1.** KNOWLEDGE knowledge or awareness of something (*formal*) **2.** SCOPE OF SOMEBODY'S KNOWLEDGE the extent or range of what somebody can know and understand (*formal*) **3.** LAW COURT'S RIGHT TO DEAL WITH SOMETHING the right of a court of law to deal with a particular matter **4.** LAW TAKING NOTICE OF FACT notice of a fact or facts taken by a court of law **5.** HERALDRY DISTINGUISHING SIGN a badge or other sign that is worn to distinguish the wearer [14C. < Old French *conis(s)aunce* < Latin *cognoscere* (see COGNITION)]

cog·ni·zant /kógnizənt/ *adj* having knowledge of something (*formal*)

SYNONYMS See ***aware***.

cog·no·men /kog nṓmən/ (*plural* **-no·mens** or **-nom·i·na** /-nómmənə/) *n* **1.** a nickname or name that describes somebody, e.g., "Billy the Kid" (*formal*) **2.** a surname or family name, especially the third name given to a citizen of ancient Rome, e.g., "Cicero" in "Marcus Tullius Cicero" [Early 17C. < Latin, "added name" < *(g)nomen* "name"] —**cog·nom·i·nal** /kog nómmin'l/ *adj*

cog·no·scen·ti /kògnə shéntee, kònnyə-/ (*singular* **-te** /-tay/) *npl* people who have a refined and superior knowledge of a subject, especially the arts [Mid-18C. < obsolete Italian, "people who know," < Latin *cognoscent-*, present participle of *cognoscere* (see COGNITION)]

co·gon /kō gṓn/ *n* a coarse tall grass used, especially in the Philippines, as thatching. Genus: *Imperata*. [Late 19C. Via Spanish < Tagalog *kúgon*]

cog rail·way *n US* a railroad designed for use on steep slopes that has a central cogwheel beneath the engine that engages with a toothed track to pull the train upward. Can term **rack railway**

Cogs·well chair /kógz wel-/ *n* an upholstered armchair with an open part under the armrests and cabriole legs [Origin ?]

cog·wheel /kóg weel, -hweel/ *n* a wheel with a series of projections around the rim that enable it to engage with projections on another wheel or rack to create traction and so produce motion

co·hab·it /kō hábbit/ (**-it·ed, -it·ing, -its**) *vi* **1.** to live together, especially without being formally married **2.** to coexist with somebody or something else [Mid-16C. < late Latin *cohabitare* < *habitare* (see INHABIT)] —**co·hab·i·tant** *n* —**co·hab·i·ta·tion** /kō hàbbi táysh'n/ *n* —**co·hab·it·ee** /kō hàbbi tee/ *n* —**co·hab·it·er** *n*

Co·han /kṓ hàn/, **George M.** (1878–1942) US actor, songwriter, and playwright. He wrote twenty plays and musicals and numerous songs such as "I'm a Yankee Doodle Dandy" (1904). Full name **Cohan, George Michael**

> "Give my regards to Broadway, / Remember me to Herald Square, / Tell all the gang at Forty-Second Street / That I will soon be there."
> [George M. Cohan, "Give My Regards to Broadway," *Little Johnny Jones*; 1904]

co·hen /kṓ ən/ (*plural* **-hens** or **-han·im** /-ənim/), **ko·hen** (*plural* **-han·im**) *n* in Judaism, a person recognized as a descendant of Aaron. The cohanim were priests in the Temple in ancient Jerusalem, and a man identified as a cohen still retains specific obligations in Orthodox Judaism today. [< Hebrew *kohein* "priest"]

Co·hen /kṓ ən/, **Leonard** (*b.* 1934) Canadian poet, novelist, singer, and songwriter. His albums include *Songs of Leonard Cohen* (1968) and *I'm Your Man* (1988).

Co·hen, Morris Raphael (1880–1947) Russian-born US philosopher. His philosophy was a combination of logic, pragmatism, and linguistic analysis.

Co·hen, Stanley (*b.* 1922) US biochemist. He codeveloped the recombinant DNA techniques that became the basis of genetic engineering and shared the 1986 Nobel Prize in Physiology or Medicine.

co·here /kō heer/ (**-hered, -her·ing, -heres**) *vi* **1.** STICK TOGETHER to stick or hold together in a mass that is not easily separated (*formal*) **2.** BE LOGICALLY CONSISTENT to be logically or aesthetically consistent so that all the separate parts fit together and add up to a harmonious or credible whole (*formal*) **3.** PHYS BE HELD TOGETHER BY MOLECULAR FORCES to be held together by the molecular forces of cohesion [Mid-16C. < Latin *cohaerere* < *haerere* "to stick"]

co·her·ent /kō heerənt/ *adj* **1.** LOGICALLY OR AESTHETICALLY CONSISTENT logically or aesthetically consistent and holding together as a harmonious or credible whole **2.** SPEAKING LOGICALLY able to speak clearly and logically ○ *He was so confused and dazed he was barely coherent.* **3.** PHYS STICKING TOGETHER able to hold together to form an inseparable mass **4.** PHYS WITH SAME WAVELENGTH describes electromagnetic waves that have the same wavelength and a fixed phase relationship. Coherent light is produced by lasers. **5.** MEASURE FORMING UNITS WITHOUT INTRODUCING CONSTANTS forming a system of units such as the International System in which the product or quotient of two units gives the unit of the derived quantity —**co·her·ence** *n* —**co·her·ent·ly** *adv*

co·he·sion /kō heezh'n/ *n* **1.** the state or condition of joining or working together to form a united whole, or the tendency to do this **2.** the force of attraction by which the molecules of a solid or liquid tend to remain together [Mid-17C. < Latin *cohaes-*, past participle of *cohaerere* (see COHERE)] —**co·he·sion·less** *adj*

co·he·sive /kō heessiv/ *adj* sticking, holding, or working together as a united whole ○ *welded the team into a cohesive unit* [Early 18C. < Latin *cohaes-* (see COHESION)] —**co·he·sive·ly** *adv* —**co·he·sive·ness** *n*

co·ho /kṓhō/ (*plural* **-hos** or *same*) *n* FISH same as **coho salmon** [Mid-19C. Origin ?]

co·hog /kṓ hàwg, -hòg/ *n regional* MARINE BIOL same as **quahog** [Late 18C. Variant]

co·hort /kṓ hàwrt/ *n* **1.** GROUP OF PEOPLE a united group of people **2.** SUPPORTER a supporter, accomplice, or associate of a leader, especially one to whom special treatment and preference is given (*disapproving*) **3.** STATS GROUP WITH STATISTICAL SIMILARITIES a group of people sharing a common factor such as the same age or the same income bracket, especially in a statistical survey **4.** ANCIENT HIST UNIT OF ROMAN ARMY an ancient Roman military unit equal to one-tenth of a legion and consisting of 300 to 600 men **5.** SOLDIERS a group of soldiers or warriors [15C. < Latin *cohort-* "enclosure"]

co·ho salm·on *n* a small salmon with light-colored flesh. Native to: Pacific, now introduced into inland waters. Latin name: *Oncorhynchus kisutch*.

co·hosh /kṓ hòsh/ *n* PLANTS **1.** same as **black cohosh** **2.** same as **blue cohosh** [Late 18C. < Algonquian *kkwàhas*]

co·hous·ing /kṓ hòwzing/ *n* an arrangement by which people living in communities where tasks such as crop raising and childcare are shared own their private living spaces but share common spaces such as dining areas

co·hune /kō hoon/ *n* a palm with feathery leaves that produces a nut that yields an oil similar to coconut oil. Use: soaps and cosmetics. Native to: Central America. Latin name: *Orbignya cohune*. [Mid-18C. < Miskito]

Co·i·ba Is·land /ko eebə-/ island in the Pacific Ocean off the coast of Panama, site of a national park and penal colony. Population: 850. Area: 191 sq. mi./494 sq. km.

coif /koyf/ *n* **1.** *also* /kwaaf/ SOMEBODY'S HAIRSTYLE the way somebody wears his or her hair (*informal*) **2.** TYPE OF SKULLCAP FOR WOMEN a close-fitting linen cap worn by women in the Middle Ages, now worn by some nuns under their veils **3.** LEATHER SKULLCAP a thick, close-fitting leather cap formerly worn under a hood of chain mail ■ *vt* (**coiffed, coif·fing, coifs**) **1.** *also* /kwaaf/ ARRANGE HAIR to arrange or style somebody's hair (*formal*) **2.** COVER HEAD WITH COIF to cover somebody's head with a coif or with something like a coif [14C. Via Old French *coife* "headdress" < late Latin *cofia* "helmet" < Germanic]

coif·feur /kwaa fúr/ (*plural* **-feurs** /-fúr/) *n* a man who is a hairdresser (*formal*) [Mid-19C. < French < Old French *coife* (see COIF)]

coif·feuse /kwaa fyóōz, -ōz/ (*plural* **-feus·es**) *n* a woman who is a hairdresser (*formal*) [Late 18C. < French, feminine of COIFFEUR]

coif·fure /kwaa fyóōr/ *n* the way somebody wears his or her hair (*formal*) [Mid-17C. < French < *coiffer* "arrange the hair" < Old French *coife* (see COIF)] —**coif·fure** *vt* —**coif·fured** *adj*

coign /koyn/ *n* BUILDINGS same as **quoin**

coign of van·tage *n* a good position from which to observe somebody or something or to take action

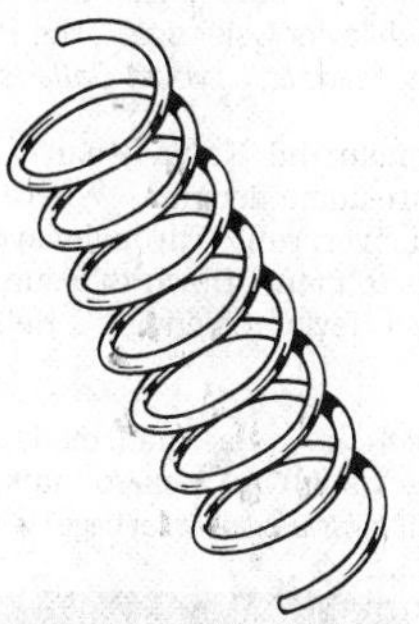

coil

coil /koyl/ *n* **1.** SERIES OF LOOPS a series of connected loops into which something has been wound or gathered **2.** LOOP one of a series of loops into which something has been wound or gathered **3.** SPIRAL something that curls or is curled into a spiral shape **4.** PIPES ARRANGED IN ROWS OR SPIRAL a series of pipes arranged in rows or in a spiral, e.g., in a radiator or condenser **5.** WIRE SPIRAL FOR ELECTRIC CURRENT a spiral of wire through which an electric current is passed to create a magnetic field or to function as an inductor **6.** DEVICE SUPPLYING ELECTRICITY TO SPARK PLUGS a device that supplies a high voltage to the spark plugs in an internal-combustion engine **7.** CONTRACEPTIVE DEVICE a coil-shaped device made of plastic or metal that is placed inside the womb to prevent a woman from becoming pregnant **8.** ROLL OF STAMPS a roll of postage stamps dispensed by a vending machine ■ *v* (**coiled, coil·ing, coils**) **1.** *vti* WIND SOMETHING INTO LOOPS to wind something into a series of connected loops, or form a series of connected loops ○ *The rope had coiled itself around the propeller.* **2.** *vi* CURVE OR BEND to move in a curving, sinuous way [Early 16C. Via Old French *coillir* "gather" < Latin *colligere* (see COLLECT[1])] —**coil·er** *n*

coil pot *n* a pot formed from a structure of coils or ropes of clay laid one on top of the other in a spiral

coil spring *n* a helical spring made from wire

Coim·ba·tore /kòymbə táwr/ industrial city and administrative headquarters of Coimbatore District, Tamil Nadu State, southeastern India. Population: 1,446,034 (2001).

Co·im·bra /kō ímbrə/ historic city and capital of Coimbra District in west central Portugal. Population: 74,616 (1981).

coin /koyn/ *n* **1.** PIECE OF METAL MONEY a usually circular flat piece of metal stamped with its value as money **2.** METAL MONEY money in the form of coins rather than bills or checks **3.** PAPER OR METAL MONEY money in whatever form, as opposed to such things as checks **4.** ALTERNATE BUT EQUIVALENT FORM OF EXPRESSION something considered acceptable as an alternative form of expression ○ *Honesty is her coin of choice.* ■ *vt* (**coined, coin·ing, coins**) **1.** MINT COINS to make a coin or coins **2.** MAKE METAL INTO COINS to make a metal such as gold or silver into coins **3.** CREATE EXPRESSION to invent or devise a word or phrase ■ *adj* COIN-OPERATED requiring a coin or coins to be inserted to make it operate (*usually used in combination*) [14C. < Old French *coin(g)* "wedge, (wedge-shaped) die for stamping coins" < Latin *cuneus* "wedge"] —**coin·a·ble** *adj* —**coin·er** *n*

coin·age /kóynij/ *n* **1.** COINS currency in the form of coins **2.** CURRENCY the system or type of coins in use as currency ○ *decimal coinage* **3.** MAKING OF METAL MONEY the act or process of minting coins **4.** INVENTION OF NEW WORD OR PHRASE the invention of a new word or phrase **5.** NEW WORD OR PHRASE a newly used word or phrase ○ *"Cyberspace" was a popular coinage of the 1980s.*

coin box *n* a box into which coins are inserted to get something from a coin-operated machine

co·in·cide /kò in síd/ (**-cid·ed, -cid·ing, -cides**) *vi* **1.** HAPPEN AT SAME TIME to happen at or around the same time **2.** BE SAME IN POSITION OR FORM to occupy the same place, or be exactly alike in position or form **3.** AGREE to agree exactly [Early 18C. < medieval Latin *coincidere* "fall upon together" < Latin *incidere* "fall upon" < *cadere* "to fall"]

co·in·ci·dence /kō ínssidənss/ *n* **1.** CHANCE HAPPENING something that happens by chance in a surprising or remarkable way **2.** HAPPENING WITHOUT PLANNING the fact of happening by chance ○ *By sheer coincidence, we both ended up at the same restaurant.* **3.** HAVING IDENTICAL FEATURES the fact or condition of happening at the same time or place or being identical

co·in·ci·dent /kō ínssidənt/ *adj* (*formal*) **1.** happening at the same time, or occupying the same position in space **2.** in exact agreement, or matching exactly —**co·in·ci·dent·ly** *adv*

co·in·ci·den·tal /kō inssi dént'l/ *adj* **1.** happening by chance rather than intentionally **2.** happening or existing at the same time —**co·in·ci·den·tal·ly** *adv*

co·in·fec·tion /kò in féksh'n/ *n* infection with two or more diseases or viruses at the same time ○ *TB-HIV coinfection*

coin-op·er·at·ed *adj* describes a device that functions only after the insertion of one or more coins of a specific value

coir /koyr/ *n* a coarse fiber that comes from the husk of the coconut. Use: matting, rope. [Late 16C. < Malayalam *kayaru* "cord, coir"]

co·i·tion /kō ísh'n/ *n* MED same as **sexual intercourse** [Mid-16C. < Latin *coition-* < *coire* (see COITUS)]

co·i·tus /kó itəss/ *n* same as **sexual intercourse** (*formal or technical*) [Mid-19C. < Latin, past participle of *coire* "go together" < *ire* "go"] —**co·i·tal** *adj* —**co·i·tal·ly** *adv*

co·i·tus in·ter·rup·tus /-intə rúptəss/ *n* during sexual intercourse, the deliberate withdrawal of the penis from the vagina before semen is ejaculated, as an attempted method of contraception [< modern Latin, "interrupted coitus"]

co·jones /kə hōneez/ *npl* (*slang*) **1.** an offensive term for the testicles **2.** courage or nerve [Mid-20C. < Spanish, plural of *cojón* "testicle"]

coke[1] /kōk/ *n* a solid residue consisting mainly of carbon, left after the volatile elements have been driven from bituminous coal or other petroleum material. Use: fuel. ■ *vti* (**coked, cok·ing, cokes**) to change something such as bituminous coal into coke, or to become coke or like coke [Mid-17C. Origin ?]

coke[2] /kōk/ *n* cocaine used as an illegal drug (*slang*) [Early 20C. Contraction]

coke·head /kōk hèd/ *n* a frequent user or addict of cocaine (*slang*)

col /kol/ *n* **1.** a low point in a ridge of mountains, often forming a pass between two peaks **2.** a pattern of atmospheric pressure distribution that develops between two anticyclones and two depressions arranged alternately, characterized by light variable winds and often thundery weather in summer or foggy conditions in winter [Mid-19C. Via French < Latin *collum* "neck"]

COL /kol/ *abbr* **1.** COMPUT computer-oriented language **2.** ECON cost of living

col. *abbr* **1.** MAIL collect **2.** EDUC college **3.** SOC SCI colony **4.** color **5.** PRINTING column

Col., Col *abbr* **1.** MIL Colonel **2.** Colorado **3.** BIBLE Colossians **4.** Columbia **5.** Columbian

col- *prefix* same as **com-** (*used before l*)

co·la[1] /kólə/, **ko·la** *n* **1.** a sweet carbonated drink flavored with cola nuts **2.** a tropical evergreen tree cultivated for its reddish seeds (**cola nuts**). Genus: *Cola.* [Early 17C. < Temne *k'ola* "cola nut"]

co·la[2] /kólə/ ANAT plural of **colon**[2]

co·la[3] /kólə/ LITERAT plural of **colon**[1] (sense 3)

~~colaborate~~ incorrect spelling of **collaborate**

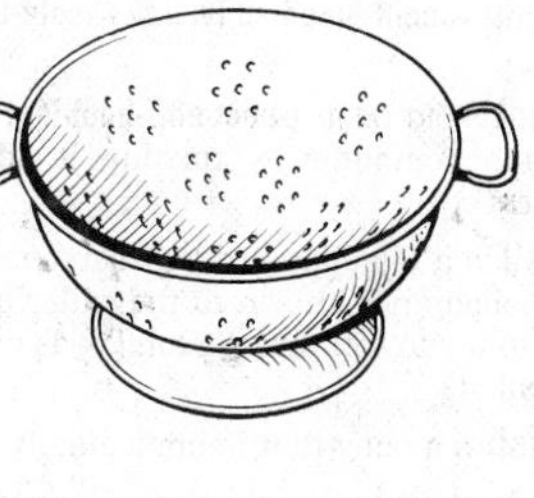

colander

col·an·der /kúlləndər, kóllən-/ *n* a bowl-shaped dish with holes in it. Use: draining food cooked in water and washing vegetables or fruit. [14C. Origin ?]

co·la nut *n* the small hard seed of the cola tree, which contains caffeine and theobromine. Use: carbonated drinks, medicines.

~~colateral~~ incorrect spelling of **collateral**

co·lat·i·tude /kō láttə tood/ *n* the difference between a latitude and 90°

Col·bert /kawl bér/, **Claudette** (1903–96) French-born US movie actor. She acted in Hollywood movies and won an Academy Award for *It Happened One Night* (1934). Born **Chauchoin, Lily Claudette**

Col·bert /kawl báir/, **Jean-Baptiste** (1619–83) French politician. He reformed the French economy as Louis XIV's comptroller general of finance from 1665.

col·can·non /kol kánnən/ *n* an Irish dish made of cabbage and potatoes boiled and mashed together and served with butter or cream [Late 18C. Origin ?]

Col·ches·ter /kól chèstər/ city in northwestern Vermont, east of Lake Champlain and northeast of Burlington. Population: 17,167 (2002 estimate).

col·chi·cine /kólchi seen, kólk-/ *n* a poisonous extract of autumn crocus plants. Use: to inhibit cell division and cause chromosome doubling in plants, to treat gout.

cold /kōld/ *adj* **1.** AT LOW TEMPERATURE at or with a relatively low, uncomfortably low, or unusually low temperature ○ *The weather turned colder.* ○ *a cold drink* **2.** MAKING PLACE SEEM COOLER giving a place a feeling of coolness rather than warmth ○ *Blue is a cold color.* **3.** COOKED HOT THEN COOLED cooked or prepared as a hot food and then cooled ○ *Serve the pie cold, with ice cream.* **4.** TACITURN AND EMOTIONLESS showing no emotion, sympathy, or kindness **5.** UNFRIENDLY AND UNCARING feeling or exhibiting no friendship or sense of caring **6.** STRONG BUT CONTROLLED intense but expressed or shown in a controlled way ○ *cold fury* **7.** SEXUALLY FRIGID giving or feeling no sexual response **8.** HARD TO FOLLOW no longer recent or fresh and so difficult to track or follow ○ *The trail had gone cold.* **9.** NOT NEAR OBJECT OF SEARCH not close to the correct answer or to something being searched for (*informal*) **10.** DEAD dead, especially from a long time before **11.** METALL PROCESSED AT LOW TEMPERATURE processed at a temperature below that at which recrystallization takes place ○ *cold working of steel* ■ *n* **1.** VIRAL INFECTION OF NOSE AND THROAT a viral infection of the nose, throat, and bronchial tubes, characterized by sneezing, nasal congestion, coughing, and headaches **2.** COLD WEATHER low-temperature weather or conditions ○ *The cold made me shiver.* **3.** CONDITION CAUSED BY LOW TEMPERATURE the state or condition of being subjected to low temperatures ■ *adv* **1.** EXTEMPORANEOUSLY without any preparation ○ *sang the part cold* **2.** COMPLETELY completely and without any possibility of a change of mind ○ *turned the proposal down cold* [Old English *c(e)ald* < Indo-European] —**cold·ish** *adj* —**cold·ness** *n* ◇ **blow hot and cold** to display wide extremes of attitude or mood ◇ **come** *or* **be brought in from the cold** to be allowed to take part in something after being previously excluded ◇ **leave somebody cold** to fail to impress or excite somebody ◇ **out in the cold** ignored or denied benefits that other people are getting ○ *The new funding proposals would leave us out in the cold.* ◇ **out cold** unconscious or in a deep sleep (*informal*)

cold-blood·ed *adj* **1.** describes an animal with an internal body temperature that varies according to the temperature of the surroundings **2.** showing a total lack of kindness, pity, or care for somebody's suffering —**cold-blood·ed·ly** *adv* —**cold-blood·ed·ness** *n*

cold·boot /kṓld bo͝ot/ (**-boot·ed, -boot·ing, -boots**) *vt* to restart a computer by turning it off and on. ◊ **warmboot**

cold call *n* a telephone call or personal visit made to somebody not known to the caller or visitor, in order to try to sell that person goods or services —**cold-call** *vt*

cold cash *n* money that is immediately available

cold chis·el *n* a tool consisting of a solid metal shaft with a sharply beveled point or edge that is struck with a hammer or mallet. Use: to break up or shape hard materials such as metal or stone. [Because it can cut cold metal]

cold·cock /kṓld kòk/ (**-cocked, -cock·ing, -cocks**) *vt* to knock somebody unconscious, especially with a blunt instrument (*slang*) [Early 20C. Probably < the idea of knocking somebody cold with a COCK "faucet"]

cold com·fort *n* something intended to be encouraging or reassuring that does not help in practice

cold cream *n* a thick cream used for cleaning and softening the skin, especially on the face

cold cuts *npl* slices of cooked meat that are served cold

cold drink *n* **1.** a chilled drink of water, juice, or something similar **2.** *Southern US, S Africa* a nonalcoholic drink

REGIONAL NOTE See *tonic*.

cold duck *n* a cocktail made with sparkling burgundy and champagne [Translation of German *kalte Ente*, by folk etymology < *kaltes Ende* "cold end," supposedly because leftover champagne and burgundy were poured into a single bottle]

cold feet *npl* a loss of nerve about something planned, causing a person not to go ahead as originally intended [Because a soldier with cold or frozen feet is prevented from fighting]

cold fish *n* somebody regarded as unfeeling or unfriendly (*informal*)

cold frame *n* a box with glass or clear plastic sides and an opening roof, used in gardens for protecting seedlings and other plants from cold weather

cold front *n* the boundary zone of an advancing cold-air mass as it replaces warmer air

cold fu·sion *n* a hypothetical form of nuclear fusion held to take place at room temperature

cold-heart·ed *adj* showing no sympathy or warmth to other people —**cold-heart·ed·ly** *adv* —**cold-heart·ed·ness** *n*

Col·ditz /kṓldits/ site of Colditz Castle, a German prisoner-of-war camp during World War II, from which many prisoners made daring escapes. It is situated about 30 mi./48 km southwest of Leipzig.

cold light *n* light produced from a low-temperature source such as phosphorescence containing no infrared wavelengths and therefore having no heating effects

cold·ly /kṓldlee/ *adv* without emotion, affection, friendliness, or sympathy

cold pack *n* **1.** a bag, cloth, or sheet that is soaked with water or filled with something cold and applied to the body to relieve pain or inflammation **2.** the packing and sterilization of uncooked food in jars or cans

cold-pressed *adj* describes high-grade olive oil produced from the first pressing of the raw olives. The pressed olives are subsequently heated to extract further amounts of oil.

cold-rolled *adj* describes metal that is rolled into sheets under pressure at room temperature in order to retain the crystalline structure of the metal and produce a smooth surface —**cold-rol·ling** *n*

cold rub·ber *n* a durable synthetic rubber made through polymerization at low temperature and used for retreading tires

cold shoul·der *n* a refusal to behave in a friendly or pleasant way toward somebody ○ *He gave me the cold shoulder.* [Because unwelcome guests were formerly given only a cold shoulder of mutton] —**cold·shoul·der** /kṓld shṓldər/ *vt*

cold snap *n* a sudden short period of very cold weather

cold sore *n* a small painful blister on or near the lips, or sometimes the nose, caused by the virus *Herpes simplex* [Because the sores often accompany colds]

cold stor·age *n* chilled or refrigerated conditions in which perishable items, especially food, are kept to preserve them ◇ **in cold storage** ready to be put into action at some later date, but not currently being used

cold store *n* a refrigerated building or area for keeping goods, especially food or furs, in cold conditions to preserve them

cold sweat *n* a very nervous, anxious, or frightened state, often with sweating and cold clammy skin

cold turk·ey *n* **1. ABRUPT WITHDRAWAL OF ADDICTIVE DRUGS** a method of stopping drug addiction by not taking any further drugs and not having any other treatment to protect the addict from the withdrawal symptoms **2. WITHDRAWAL SYMPTOMS** the unpleasant symptoms, usually including nausea and shivering, that accompany a sudden withdrawal from an addictive drug ■ *adv* (*slang*) **1. BLUNTLY AND UNDIPLOMATICALLY** so as to convey the meaning to somebody in a way that cannot be misunderstood **2. DRUGS ABRUPTLY AND COMPLETELY** without a period of gradual withdrawal ○ *quit cold turkey* [Origin ?]

cold type *n* typesetting that is done without casting metal

cold war *n* a relationship between two people or groups that is unfriendly or hostile but does not involve actual fighting or military combat —**cold war·ri·or** *n*

Cold War *n* the hostile yet nonviolent relations between the former Soviet Union and the United States, and their respective allies, from around 1946 to 1989

cold-wa·ter *adj* with cold running water provided but no heating

cold wave *n* **1.** a sudden fall in temperature associated with the passage of air of continental polar origin **2.** a permanent wave in hair that is produced using chemicals rather than heat (*dated*)

cold-weld (**cold-weld·ed, cold-weld·ing, cold-welds**) *vt* to join two metal surfaces using pressure rather than heat —**cold-weld·ing** *n*

cole /kōl/ *n* PLANTS, FOOD same as **kale** (sense 1) [Pre-12C. < Latin *caulis* "stem, cabbage"]

Cole /kōl/, **Thomas** (1801–48) British-born US artist. He painted North American landscapes and is often considered the forerunner of the Hudson River School.

> "It is generally thought that the liberal arts tend to soften our manners; but they do more—they carry with them the power to mend our hearts."
> [Thomas Cole, "Essay on American Scenery 2," *The American Monthly Magazine*; January 1836]

co·lec·to·my /kə léktəmee/ (*plural* **-mies**) *n* a surgical operation in which part or all of the colon is removed [Late 19C. < COLON[2]]

cole·man·ite /kṓlmə nīt/ *n* a white or colorless crystalline mineral consisting of hydrous calcium borate. Use: source of borax. [Late 19C. After William T. *Coleman* (1824–93), US mine owner]

co·le·op·ter·an /kòlee óptərən, kòll-/ *n* an insect with modified forewings that function as tough covers for the membranous hind wings, e.g., beetles. Order: Coleoptera. [Mid-19C. < modern Latin *coleoptera* < Greek *koleopteros* < *koleos* "sheath" + *pteron* "wing"] —**co·le·op·ter·ous** *adj*

co·le·op·tile /kòlee ópt'l, kòllee-/ *n* the first leaf in some grasses that forms a protective sheath around the stem tip (**plumule**) [Mid-19C. < Greek *koleos* "sheath" + *ptilon* "feather"]

co·le·o·rhi·za /kòlee ō rī́zə, kòllee-/ (*plural* **-zae** /-zee/) *n* a protective sheath surrounding the young root of a germinating grass seed [Mid-19C. < Greek *koleos* "sheath" + *rhiza* "root"]

Col·e·ridge /kṓlrij, kṓlərij/, **Samuel Taylor** (1772–1834) British poet. His collection *Lyrical Ballads* (1798), published with William Wordsworth, launched romanticism in English poetry. See Cultural note at **mariner**

> "The fair breeze blew, the white foam flew, / The furrow followed free; / We were the first that ever burst / Into that silent sea."
> [Samuel Taylor Coleridge, "The Rime of the Ancient Mariner," *Lyrical Ballads*; 1798]

> "In Xanadu did Kubla Khan / A stately pleasure-dome decree: / Where Alph, the sacred river, ran / Through caverns measureless to man / Down to a sunless sea."
> [Samuel Taylor Coleridge, "Kubla Khan"; 1797]

cole·slaw /kṓl slàw/ *n* a salad made with shredded raw cabbage usually in a mayonnaise dressing [Late 18C. < Dutch *koolsla* < *kool* "cabbage" + *sla* "salad"]

AKG London

Colette

Co·lette /ko lét, kaw lét/ (1873–1954) French novelist. Among the best known of her many novels are *Chéri* (1920) and *Gigi* (1945). Full name **Colette, Sidonie Gabrielle Claudine**

> "It's nothing to be born ugly. Sensibly, the ugly woman comes to terms with her ugliness and exploits it as a grace of nature."
> [Colette, *Journey for Myself*; 1971]

co·le·us /kṓlee əss/ *n* a plant grown for its brightly colored variegated leaves. Genus: *Coleus*. [Mid-19C. Via modern Latin < Greek *koleos* "sheath"; from the way the plant's filaments are joined]

cole·wort /kṓl wùrt, -wàwrt/ *n* PLANTS, FOOD same as **kale** (sense 1)

Col·fax /kṓl fàks/, **Schuyler** (1823–85) vice president of the United States. He was a Republican US representative (1855–69), and vice president under President Ulysses S. Grant (1869–73).

coli- *prefix* same as **colo-** (*used before vowels*)

col·ic /kóllik/ *n* **1. PAIN IN ABDOMEN** a sudden attack of abdominal pain, often caused by spasm, inflammation, or obstruction **2. CRYING IN BABIES** excessive crying and irritability in infants from a variety of causes, especially stomach or intestinal discomfort **3. SERIOUS DIGESTIVE DISEASE IN HORSES** a serious disease of the digestive system in horses, sometimes leading to fatal intestinal blockage [15C. Via French < Latin *colicus* < Greek *kolikos* "suffering in the large intestine" < *kolon* "large intestine"] —**col·ic** *adj*

col·ick·y /kóllikee/ *adj* experiencing bouts of abdominal pain (**colic**)

co·li·form /kṓlə fàwrm, kóllə-/ *adj* describes rod-shaped bacteria that are normally found in the colons of humans and animals and become a serious contaminant when found in the food or water supply [Early 20C. < modern Latin *coli* "of the large intestine," form of Latin *colon* "large intestine"]

co·lin·e·ar /kō línnee ər/ *adj* **1.** with corresponding parts arranged in a regular linear order **2.** MATH another spelling of **collinear** [Early 20C. < CO- + LINEAR] —**co·lin·e·ar·i·ty** /kōlinnee árrətee/ *n*

col·i·se·um /kòllə seé əm/, **col·os·seum** *n* a large building used as a theater or for sports events [Early 16C. < medieval Latin, "something colossal" < Latin *colosseus* "colossal" < *colossus* "colossus"]

co·lis·tin /kə lístin/ *n* an antibiotic effective against a wide range of organisms. Source: a soil bacterium. Use: to treat gastrointestinal infections. [Mid-20C. < modern Latin *(Bacillus) colistinus* < *coli* (see COLIFORM)]

co·li·tis /kə lítiss/ *n* inflammation of the colon, characterized by lower-bowel spasms and upper abdominal cramps [Mid-19C. < COLON[2]] —**co·lit·ic** /kə líttik/ *adj*

coll. *abbr* **1.** COMM collateral **2.** colleague **3.** MAIL collect **4.** MAIL collection **5.** MAIL collector **6.** EDUC college **7.** EDUC collegiate **8.** LANGUAGE colloquial

coll- *prefix* same as **collo-** (*used before vowels*)

col·lab·o·rate /kə lábbə ràyt/ (**-rat·ed, -rat·ing, -rates**) *vi* **1.** to work with another person or group in order to achieve something **2.** to betray others by working with an enemy, especially an occupying force [Late 19C. < late Latin *collaborat-*, past participle of *collaborare* "work together" < Latin *labor* "toil"] —**col·lab·o·ra·tive** /-ràytiv, -rətiv/ *adj* —**col·lab·o·ra·tive·ly** *adv* —**col·lab·o·ra·tor** *n*

USAGE ***collaborate*** or ***corroborate***? ***Collaborate*** means "to work with others in order to achieve something": *Two authors collaborated on the biography.* ***Corroborate*** means "to present evidence in support of the truth of something": *As any language teacher can corroborate, spelling and grammar are important.* The two words are not interchangeable.

col·lab·o·ra·tion /kə làbbə ráysh'n/ *n* **1.** the act of working together with one or more people in order to achieve something **2.** the betrayal of others by working with an enemy, especially an occupying force —**col·lab·o·ra·tion·ism** *n* —**col·lab·o·ra·tion·ist** *n, adj*

col·lab·o·ra·tive di·vorce *n* a divorce in which the terms are agreed upon by both spouses and their attorneys prior to presenting the final agreement to a judge without a trial

col·lage /kə laázh/ *n* **1.** PICTURE WITH PIECES STUCK ON SURFACE a picture made by sticking cloth, pieces of paper, photographs, and other objects onto a surface **2.** ART OF MAKING COLLAGES the art of making pictures by sticking cloth, pieces of paper, photographs, and other objects onto a surface **3.** COMBINATION OF DIFFERENT THINGS a combination of different things [Early 20C. < French *coller* "to glue" < *colle* "glue" < Greek *kolla*] —**col·lage** *vti* —**col·lag·ist** *n*

col·la·gen /kólləjən/ *n* a fibrous protein found in skin, bone, and other connective tissues [Mid-19C. < French *collagène* < Greek *kolla* "glue"] —**col·la·gen·ic** /kòllə jénnik/ *adj* —**col·lag·e·nous** /kə lájjənəss/ *adj*

col·lag·e·nase /kólləjə nàyss, -nàyz/ *n* any enzyme that breaks down collagen

col·lap·sar /kə láp saàr/ *n* ASTRON same as **black hole** (sense 1) [Late 20C. < COLLAPSE]

col·lapse /kə láps/ *v* (**-lapsed, -laps·ing, -laps·es**) **1.** *vi* FALL DOWN to fall down suddenly, generally as a result of damage, structural weakness, or lack of support ○ *A section of cliff had collapsed into the sea.* **2.** *vi* FAIL ABRUPTLY to fail or come to an end suddenly ○ *Their partnership nearly collapsed under the strain.* **3.** *vi* FALL SUDDENLY to fall or faint because of illness, exhaustion, or weakness ○ *He collapsed from overwork.* **4.** *vi* SUDDENLY SIT OR LIE DOWN to sit or lie down suddenly and relax completely, or give way to emotion ○ *I collapsed into an armchair.* **5.** *vi* BEND DOUBLE WITH EMOTION to bend over double or otherwise contort the body, typically in the throes of emotion such as laughter or crying **6.** *vti* DEFLATE to fold up or become flat from lack of pressure or loss of air, or cause something such as a parachute to do this ○ *The left lung had collapsed.* **7.** *vti* FOLD SOMETHING TO MAKE IT SMALLER to fold something up so that it is smaller or takes up less space, or fold up in this way ■ *n* **1.** FAILURE OR END a failure or sudden end to something ○ *the abrupt collapse of the campaign* **2.** FALLING DOWN the act of falling down suddenly, generally as a result of damage, structural weakness, or lack of support ○ *The roof was in danger of collapse.* **3.** DECREASE IN VALUE a sudden reduction or decrease in value ○ *the threatened collapse of the yen* **4.** SUDDEN ILLNESS a sudden onset of severe illness, resulting in hospitalization or bed rest ○ *in a state of nervous collapse* [Mid-18C. Back-formation < *collapsed* < Latin *collapsus*, past participle of *collabi* "fall together" < *labi* "to fall"] —**col·laps·i·ble** *adj*

col·lar /kóllər/ *n* **1.** GARMENT'S NECKBAND the upright or turned-over neckband of a coat, jacket, dress, shirt, or blouse **2.** BAND AROUND NECK OF ANIMAL a leather, plastic, fabric, or metal band placed around the neck of an animal to identify it or attach it to a lead or leash **3.** AREA RESEMBLING COLLAR an area around the neck of a bird or animal that has a color or marking different from the rest **4.** AGRIC PART OF HARNESS the cushioned ring or other part of a harness that presses against a draft animal's shoulders **5.** RING-SHAPED DEVICE OR PART a ring-shaped device or part on a shaft that guides, seats, or restricts another mechanical part **6.** NECKLACE a close-fitting necklace or one that lies flat over the shoulders **7.** MEAT FROM NECK a cut of meat, especially bacon, taken from an animal's neck **8.** POLICE ARREST an arrest made by a police officer (*slang*) ■ *vt* (**-lared, -lar·ing, -lars**) **1.** FIND OR STOP SOMEBODY to find or stop somebody you want to talk to (*informal*) **2.** CATCH SOMEBODY to catch somebody and hold him or her to prevent escape (*slang*) **3.** MAKE POLICE ARREST to arrest a criminal suspect (*slang*) **4.** PUT COLLAR ON SOMETHING to put a collar on something such as an animal, a garment, or a machine part [14C. Via Old French *colier* < Latin *collare* < *collum* "neck"] —**col·lared** *adj* —**col·lar·less** *adj* ◇ **hot under the collar** angry, irritated, or generally agitated (*informal*)

col·lar·bone /kóllər bōn/ *n* ANAT same as **clavicle** (sense 1)

col·lard /kóllərd/ *n* a variety of kale with a crown of smooth edible leaves ■ **col·lards, col·lard greens** *npl* the leaves of a kale plant, cooked and eaten as a vegetable [Mid-18C. Alteration of *colewort*]

col·lared dove /kòllərd-/ *n* a fawn-colored bird of the pigeon family that has a black collar round its neck. Native to: Near East, central and northern Europe. Latin name: *Streptopelia decaocto.*

col·lared pec·ca·ry *n* ZOOL same as **peccary**

col·late /kō làyt, kə láyt/ (**-lat·ed, -lat·ing, -lates**) *vt* **1.** PUT PAGES IN ORDER to assemble pages in the correct order **2.** COMPARE INFORMATION to bring together pieces of information and compare them in detail **3.** VERIFY PAGE SEQUENCING to verify the correct sequencing and completeness of the pages in a book **4.** ADMIT CLERIC TO BENEFICE to admit a member of the clergy to a benefice [Mid-16C. < Latin *collat-*, past participle of *conferre* "bring together" < *ferre* "bring"] —**col·la·tor** *n*

col·lat·er·al /kə láttərəl/ *n* **1.** PROPERTY AS SECURITY AGAINST LOAN property or goods used as security against a loan and forfeited if the loan is not repaid **2.** DESCENDANT FROM DIFFERENT LINE a relative descended from the same ancestor as another person but through a different set of parents, grandparents, and other forebears ■ *adj* **1.** ACCOMPANYING accompanying but secondary ○ *collateral issues* **2.** ADDITIONAL additional to and in support of something ○ *collateral evidence* **3.** WITH PROPERTY AS SECURITY obtained by putting up property or goods as security, to be forfeited if the loan cannot be paid **4.** DESCENDED FROM SAME ANCESTOR having the same ancestor but descended through a different set of parents, grandparents, and other forebears **5.** PARALLEL running side by side in parallel or corresponding in some way, e.g., in size [14C. < medieval Latin *collateralis*, literally "side by side with" < Latin *lateralis* "on the side" (see LATERAL)] —**col·lat·er·al·i·ty** /kə làttə rállətee/ *n* —**col·lat·er·al·ly** *adv*

col·lat·er·al dam·age *n* unintended damage to civilian life or property during a military operation

col·lat·er·al·ize /kə láttərə lìz/ (**-ized, -iz·ing, -izes**) *vt* to pledge property or goods as security for a loan —**col·lat·er·al·i·za·tion** /kə làttərəli záysh'n/ *n*

col·la·tion /kə láysh'n, kō-/ *n* **1.** COMPARISON OF INFORMATION a detailed comparison between different items or forms of information **2.** ASSEMBLY OF PAGES IN ORDER the assembling of pieces of paper in the right order, particularly the sections of a book prior to binding **3.** TECHNICAL DESCRIPTION OF BOOK the technical description of a book, including its bibliographical details and information about its physical construction, or the act of compiling such a description **4.** LIGHT MEAL a light meal or refreshment ○ *a cold collation* **5.** APPOINTMENT OF CLERGY the appointment of clergy to a benefice **6.** READING OF RELIGIOUS TEXT the reading of a religious text to a gathering of monks [14C. < Latin *collation-* "a bringing together" < *collat-* (see COLLATE)]

col·la·tive /kə láytiv, kō-/ *adj* describes an ecclesiastical benefice to which a member of the clergy is appointed

col·league /kó leèg/ *n* a person somebody works with, especially in a professional or skilled job [Early 16C. Via French < Latin *collega* "person somebody commissions with" < *legare* "commission, entrust" < *lex* "law"] —**col·league·ship** *n*

USAGE colleague or **compatriot**? Students often confuse ***colleague***, which means "a fellow worker," with ***compatriot***, which means "a fellow citizen of a nation" and "a fellow member of a group, especially a military or political group." In formal writing use: *The Chief Justice and her colleagues* [not *compatriots*] *handed down a unanimous ruling.*

col·lect[1] /kə lékt/ *v* (**-lect·ed, -lect·ing, -lects**) **1.** *vt* GATHER THINGS IN ONE PLACE to bring things together ○ *I collected my belongings and left.* **2.** *vt* KEEP THINGS OF SAME TYPE to obtain and keep objects of a similar type because of their interest, value, or beauty **3.** *vt* FETCH SOMEBODY OR SOMETHING to go to get people or objects and bring them somewhere ○ *They collected me from the airport.* **4.** *vt* TAKE MONEY OR PRIZE to take the money or prize to which a person is entitled **5.** *vti* ASK FOR DONATIONS to ask for money from people for a particular purpose **6.** *vti* ACCUMULATE to gather and gradually accumulate in a place **7.** *vi* GRADUALLY ASSEMBLE to come together gradually in a place and form a group or crowd of people ○ *By now an angry crowd had collected.* **8. col·lect your·self** *vr* GET CONTROL OF YOURSELF to gain or regain control of yourself and deliberately calm yourself or prepare yourself psychologically **9.** *vi* GET MONEY to obtain money that is due, e.g., from an insurance policy ■ *adv* SO THAT CALL RECIPIENT PAYS so as to be charged to the receiver of a phone call that is placed ■ *adj* PAYABLE BY RECEIVER charged by the caller to the receiver ○ *He placed two collect calls from his hotel room.* [Mid-16C. Directly or via French < medieval Latin *collectare* < Latin *collect-*, past participle of *colligere* "gather together" < *legere* "gather"]

SYNONYMS ***collect, accumulate, gather, amass, assemble, stockpile, hoard***

CORE MEANING: to bring dispersed things together

collect to bring things together, or to make a collection of similar things as a hobby ○ *Our eyes, ears, and noses collect information about distant objects.* ○ *He started collecting stamps at the age of nine.* **accumulate** to obtain a large amount of something over a period of time ○ *Merchants began to accumulate wealth in the form of gold bullion.* ○ *An enormous amount of material about such families has been accumulated over the past century.* **gather** to bring together people or things to form a group, or compile something such as information or ideas from various sources ○ *We gathered the children at the entrance to the exhibition.* ○ *She was gathering flowers as we strolled round the garden.* ○ *They are gathering together more information on the subject.* **amass** to bring a large quantity of things together over time ○ *the growing evidence that is being amassed by investigators* ○ *He is thought to have amassed a fortune of hundreds of millions of dollars.* **assemble** to bring people or things together, or gather together in one place ○ *one of the greatest orchestras ever assembled* ○ *Assemble all the ingredients before starting to cook.* ○ *All the guests will be assembling in the hall at 12.* **stockpile** to collect and store large amounts of things such as equipment or weapons for future use ○ *U.N. resolutions that banned the country from stockpiling, developing, or using weapons of mass destruction* **hoard** to collect and store, often secretly, large amounts of things such as food or money for future use ○ *She carefully hoarded the extra money she made.* ○ *At the first hint of a supply problem, people start hoarding dry goods.*

col·lect[2] /kóllikt, kó lèkt/ *n* a short formal prayer that can vary according to the day, said before the reading of the epistle in some Christian church services [13C. Via Old French < late Latin *collecta* "assembly" < Latin *collect-* (see COLLECT[1])]

col·lect·a·ble *n, adj* another spelling of **collectible**

col·lec·ta·ne·a /kò lek táynee ə/ *npl* a selection of pieces of writing by an author or by several authors [Mid-17C. < Latin, "things collected" < form of *collectaneus* "collected" < *collect-* (see COLLECT[1])]

col·lect·ed /kə léktəd/ *adj* **1.** CALM AND COMPOSED calm and in control of yourself **2.** BROUGHT TOGETHER AS WHOLE gathered together in one book or set of volumes as the whole of an author's work or work of a particular type **3.** RIDING CONTROLLED IN GAIT moving with a controlled gait —**col·lect·ed·ly** *adv* —**col·lect·ed·ness** *n*

col·lect·i·ble /kə léktəb'l/, **col·lect·a·ble** *n* an object of a type that is valued or sought after by collectors ■ *adj* good for collecting or popular with collectors and much sought after

col·lec·tion /kə léksh'n/ *n* **1.** GROUP OF THINGS OR PEOPLE a group of things or people together in one place **2.** SEVERAL DIFFERENT WORKS TOGETHER a number of different pieces of writing or music together in one book, CD, or record **3.** OBJECTS HELD BY COLLECTOR a set of objects collected for their interest, value, or beauty **4.** PAINTINGS OR OBJECTS IN MUSEUM all the paintings or objects of one kind held by an art gallery or museum **5.** TAKING OF DONATIONS the act of taking money due or given ○ *They took up a collection for him when he was in the hospital.* **6.** TAKING OF MONEY IN CHRISTIAN CHURCH the act of accepting money from worshipers in a Christian church service, or the money so collected **7.** TAKING the taking of something on a regular basis, e.g., letters from mailboxes by the Postal Service, or garbage from buildings **8.** GATHERING TOGETHER the act of gathering things together (*formal*) **9.** RANGE OF NEW CLOTHES a range of newly designed clothes for a particular season ○ *the spring collection* [14C. Via French < Latin *collection-* < *collect-* (see COLLECT[1])]

col·lec·tion a·gen·cy *n* a business that collects payments on unpaid loans or on bills

col·lec·tive /kə léktiv/ *adj* **1.** SHARED BY ALL made or shared by everyone in a group **2.** COLLECTED TO FORM WHOLE collected together to form a whole or added up to form a total from different sources or groups **3.** APPLYING TO MANY applying to a number of individuals taken together ○ *Staff training was the collective responsibility of the three personnel officers.* **4.** WORKER-RUN UNDER STATE SUPERVISION describes a business or other enterprise run by the people who work in it but under the jurisdiction of the state ■ *n* **1.** WORKER-RUN ENTERPRISE an enterprise that is run by its workers under state control, e.g., a farm or factory **2.** MEMBERS OF COLLECTIVE the members of a collective who work in and run the business **3.** GRAM same as **collective noun** —**col·lec·tive·ly** *adv* —**col·lec·tive·ness** *n*

col·lec·tive a·gree·ment *n* a contract of employment negotiated between management and a union

col·lec·tive bar·gain·ing *n* negotiations between management and a union about pay and conditions of employment on behalf of all the workers in the union

col·lec·tive farm *n* a farm that is state-supervised but operated by its laborers

col·lec·tive noun *n* a noun that refers to a group of people or things considered as a single unit. "Committee" and "government" are collective nouns.

USAGE Collective nouns: Examples of collective nouns are *audience, committee, crowd, flock, government, jury,* and *orchestra*, all of which are singular in form but plural in that they refer to groups that are made up of a number of individuals or individual things. Such nouns take singular verbs when they are regarded as units: *The jury has handed down a unanimous verdict.* They take plural verbs when emphasis is placed on the individuals making up the unit: *The jury have been arguing among themselves for 12 hours, and no verdict is expected.* Nouns that denote a class of objects, for example, *furniture* and *luggage*, are always singular: *My luggage is missing.* It is important to avoid inconsistency in your choice of verb and pronoun number when using collective nouns. For instance, this example contains inconsistencies: *The committee has* [singular] *decided to reject the proposal and will give their* [plural: use *its*] *reasons in writing tomorrow.* It is more common for a collective noun to take a plural verb in British English.

---

col·lec·tive se·cu·ri·ty *n* the maintenance of peace and security through the united action of nations

col·lec·tive un·con·scious *n* the inherited part of unconscious thought, memories, and instinct, which, according to Jungian principles, is common to members of a people and is observable through dreams and behavior

col·lec·tiv·ism /kə léktə vìzzəm/ *n* the system of control and ownership of factories and farms and of the means of production and distribution of products by a nation's people —**col·lec·tiv·ist** *n* —**col·lec·tiv·is·tic** /kə lèktə vístik/ *adj* —**col·lec·tiv·is·ti·cal·ly** *adv*

col·lec·tiv·i·ty /kò lek tívvətee/ (*plural* **-ties**) *n* **1.** a state or situation in which people or things are together or work together to form a whole **2.** a group regarded as an aggregate, especially a people

col·lec·tiv·ize /kə léktə vìz/ (**-ized, -iz·ing, -iz·es**) *vt* to run or organize something such as a farm according to principles of collective control —**col·lec·tiv·i·za·tion** /kə lèktəvi záysh'n/ *n*

col·lec·tor /kə léktər/ *n* **1.** SOMEBODY WHO COLLECTS OBJECTS somebody who accumulates objects for their interest, value, or beauty ○ *a stamp collector* **2.** SOMEBODY WHO MAKES COLLECTION somebody whose job is to collect something such as money owed, tickets, or garbage **3.** CONTAINER WHERE THINGS COLLECT something in which things are collected intentionally or where unwanted things collect **4.** TRANSISTOR REGION the region of a transistor toward or through which charge carriers flow —**col·lec·tor·ship** *n*

col·lec·tor's i·tem *n* an object that is sought after or valued highly by collectors

col·leen /kə leén, kólleen/ *n* **1.** *Ireland* a girl, especially a young girl **2.** a girl living or born in Ireland or a girl of Irish descent [Early 19C. < Irish *cailín* "little girl" < *caile* "girl"]

col·lege /kóllij/ *n* **1.** INSTITUTION OF HIGHER LEARNING an institution of higher learning that provides education to undergraduates and awards bachelor's and sometimes master's degrees **2.** UNIVERSITY SCHOOL OR DIVISION a school or a division of a university that usually has its own dean and other administrators and whose faculty teaches and confers degrees in specific academic fields **3.** MEMBERS OF COLLEGE the faculty and students of a college **4.** *UK* PART OF BRITISH UNIVERSITY a division of some of the larger British universities, e.g., Oxford and Cambridge **5.** PROFESSIONAL BODY a group of people, usually of the same profession, who have agreed duties and rights **6.** COLLEGE BUILDINGS the building or buildings of a college **7.** *UK* BRITISH SCHOOL used as part of the name of some British private schools ○ *Eton College* **8.** BODY OF CLERGY a group or body of clergy who live together [14C. Directly or via French < Latin *collegium* "association, corporation" < *collega* (see COLLEAGUE)]

Col·lege Board *tdmk* a service mark for the administration of nationwide aptitude and achievement tests, used by most US colleges and universities in their admission and placement of prospective students

col·lege cred·it *n US* **1.** points earned from study or work that can be used toward a college degree **2.** a reduction in income tax to help compensate for education expenses beyond the secondary level

Col·lege of Arms *n* an institution with jurisdiction in England, Wales, and Northern Ireland that specializes in matters relating to heraldry, the granting of arms, and tracing genealogies

Col·lege of Car·di·nals *n* the body of Roman Catholic cardinals who elect popes, assist the pope in church governance, and manage the Holy See in the absence of a living or elected pope

Col·lege of Her·alds *n* HERALDRY same as **College of Arms**

Col·lege Park /kòllij-/ city in central Maryland, a suburb of the Washington, D.C. metropolitan area and home to the University of Maryland. Population: 25,320 (2002 estimate).

Col·lege Sta·tion city in eastern Texas, southwest of Huntsville. It is home to Texas A&M University. Population: 70,550 (2002 estimate).

col·lege try *n* an all-out effort to achieve something (*informal*) ○ *I'll give it the old college try.*

col·le·gi·a POL plural of **collegium**

col·le·gi·al /kə leéjee əl, -leéjəl/ *adj* **1.** POWER-SHARING with power shared equally between colleagues **2.** OF POWER-SHARING BY BISHOPS relating to a situation or system in the Roman Catholic Church in which the bishops share equal power **3.** OF COLLEGE OR UNIVERSITY involving, typical of, or belonging to a college or university [14C. Directly or via French < late Latin *collegialis* < Latin *collegium* (see COLLEGE)] —**col·le·gi·al·i·ty** /kə leéjee állətee/ *n* —**col·le·gi·al·ly** *adv*

col·le·gian /kə leéjən, kə leéjee ən/ *n* a college undergraduate, graduate student, or recent graduate [15C. < medieval Latin *collegianus* < Latin *collegium* (see COLLEGE)]

col·le·giate /kə leéjət, kə leéjee ət/ *adj* **1.** involving, belonging to, appropriate to, or being a college, including its students and their pursuits **2.** consisting of separate university colleges ■ *n Can* EDUC same as **collegiate institute** [15C. < medieval Latin *collegiatus* "(member) of a college" < Latin *collegium* (see COLLEGE)] —**col·le·giate·ly** *adv*

col·le·giate church *n* **1.** a Roman Catholic or Anglican church that has a chapter of canons but is not a cathedral **2.** a group or association of churches that have pastors in common

col·le·giate in·sti·tute *n Can* in some Canadian provinces, a high school that offers a high level of courses and facilities

col·le·gi·um /kə leéjee əm, -jəm/ (*plural* **-gi·ums** or **-gi·a** /-jee ə, -jə/) *n* **1.** CHR same as **College of Cardinals** **2.** in the former Soviet Union, a committee of equally empowered members in charge of a department or industry [< Latin (see COLLEGE)]

col leg·no /kōl láy nyō/ *adv* to be played by tapping the strings of a stringed instrument with the back of the bow (*used as a musical direction*) [< Italian, "with the wood"]

~~**collegue**~~ incorrect spelling of **colleague**

col·lem·bo·lan /kə lémbələn/ *n* INSECTS same as **springtail** [Late 19C. < modern Latin *Collembola* < Greek *kolla* "glue" + *embolon* "peg"] —**collem·bo·lous** *adj*

col·len·chy·ma /kə léngkimə/ *n* a layer of supportive plant tissue that consists of elongated living cells that have walls unevenly thickened with cellulose and pectin [Mid-19C. < COLLO-] —**col·len·chym·a·tous** /kòllən kímmətəss/ *adj*

Colles' frac·ture /kólliz-/ *n* a fracture of the radius bone in which a piece broken off at the end is displaced toward the back of the wrist. The fracture is commonly caused by falling on the palm of the hand. [Late 19C. After Abraham *Colles* (1773–1843), Irish surgeon]

col·let /kóllət/ *n* **1.** CONE-SHAPED MECHANICAL PIECE a slotted cone-shaped piece that encloses and grips a rod or shaft when inserted into the sleeve of a lathe or other machine **2.** SETTING FOR GEMSTONE a band or claw that holds a gemstone **3.** BAND ATTACHED TO SPRING IN WATCH a ring that holds the hairspring in a watch [15C. < French, "little collar" < *col* "collar" < Latin *collum* "neck"]

col·lide /kə líd/ (**-lid·ed, -lid·ing, -lides**) *vi* **1.** to hit a person or object moving toward you or a person or object you are moving toward ○ *I collided with her in the corridor.* **2.** to come into conflict with somebody else or another group [Early 17C. < Latin *collidere* "shatter," literally "strike together" < *laedere* "strike"]

col·lid·er /kə lídər/, **col·lid·ing-beam ma·chine** *n* a particle accelerator in which two oppositely moving particle beams are made to collide. This allows the particles to use more of their energy to create new particles than when they collide with a fixed target.

collie: a rough collie

col·lie /kóllee/ *n* a dog with a long narrow muzzle, belonging to a breed originally developed to herd sheep. There are shorthaired (smooth) and longhaired (rough) collies. [Mid-17C Origin ?]

~~**colliefour**~~, ~~**collieflower**~~ incorrect spelling of **cauliflower**

col·lier /kóllyər/ *n* **1.** somebody who mines coal (*dated*) **2.** a boat designed to transport coal [13C. < COAL]

col·lier·y /kóllyəree/ (*plural* **-ies**) *n* a coal mine and the buildings associated with it

col·lin·e·ar /kō línnee ər/, **co·lin·e·ar** *adj* lying on or passing through a single straight line [Mid-19C. < COL- + LINEAR] —**col·lin·e·ar·i·ty** /kō lìnnee árrətee/ *n*

col·lins /kóllinz/ *n* an iced drink made with spirits such as gin or vodka and fruit juice such as lemon or lime [Mid-19C. Origin ?]

Col·lins /kóllinz/, **Jackie** (*b.* 1939) British novelist. Her popular novels include *The Bitch* (1978).

Michael Collins

Col·lins, Michael (1890–1922) Irish politician. A creator of the Irish Free State (1922), he was shot by Republicans who opposed the Anglo-Irish Treaty.

> "Think—what have I got for Ireland? Something which she has wanted these past 700 years...I tell you this—early this morning I signed my death warrant."
> [Michael Collins, *Letter to John O'Kane*; December 6, 1921]

Col·lins, Wilkie (1824–89) British novelist. His *The Woman in White* (1860) and *The Moonstone* (1868) were pioneering mystery novels. Full name **Collins, William Wilkie**. See Cultural note at **moonstone**

> "There, in the middle of the broad, bright high road...stood the figure of a solitary Woman, dressed from head to foot in white garments, her face bent in grave inquiry on mine, her hand pointing to the dark cloud over London, as I faced her."
> [Wilkie Collins, *The Woman in White*; 1860]

col·lin·si·a /kə línzee ə, -línssee ə/ *n* a plant with blue, white, or purple flowers. Native to: North America. Genus: *Collinsia.* [Early 19C. After Zaccheus *Collins* (1764–1831), US botanist]

Col·lins·ville /kóllinz vìl/ city in southwestern Illinois, northeast of East Saint Louis. Population: 33,462 (2002 estimate).

Col·lip /kóllip/, **James Bertram** (1892–1965) Canadian biochemist. He perfected a technique for producing pure insulin (1921) and researched other endocrine glands and hormones.

col·li·sion /kə lízh'n/ *n* **1.** CRASH the action of two moving vehicles, ships, aircraft, or other objects hitting each other **2.** AUTOMOBILE INSURANCE COVERAGE automobile insurance that covers damages done to the insured's motor vehicle in the event that it collides with another vehicle or with some other object **3.** CONFLICT BETWEEN IDEAS a conflict between people or their ideas or beliefs **4.** PHYS EXCHANGE OF ENERGY BETWEEN PARTICLES an encounter between two or more particles that come together or close to each other, and exchange or transfer energy [15C. < late Latin *collision-* < Latin *collis-*, past participle of *collidere* (see COLLIDE)] —**col·li·sion·al** *adj* —**col·li·sion·al·ly** *adv*

col·li·sion course *n* a path or course of action that inevitably leads to conflict ○ *The two of them were clearly on a collision course.*

col·li·sion dam·age waiv·er *n* an insurance option available to somebody renting a car that waives the renter's liability for damage to the vehicle as a result of a collision

col·li·sion zone *n* an extensive linear feature marking the collision of two continental plates, characterized by young fold mountains and earthquakes

collo- *prefix* glutinous, gelatinous ○ *collotype* [Via modern Latin < Greek *kolla* "glue"]

col·lo·cate /kóllə kàyt/ *v* (**-cat·ed, -cat·ing, -cates**) **1.** *vi* OCCUR FREQUENTLY WITH ANOTHER WORD to occur frequently in conjunction with another word **2.** *vt* PUT SOMETHING NEXT TO SOMETHING to arrange something so that it is next to or close to something else (*formal*) ■ *n* WORD THAT OCCURS WITH ANOTHER a word that is frequently or typically used with another word [Early 16C. < Latin *collocat-*, past participle of *collocare* "place together" < *locare* "to place"]

col·lo·ca·tion /kòllə káysh'n/ *n* **1.** the association between two words that are typically or frequently used together **2.** an arrangement in which things are placed next to each other or close together —**col·lo·ca·tion·al** *adj*

col·lo·di·on /kə lṓdee ən/ *n* a thick colorless solution of pyroxylin, ether, and alcohol. Use: to treat wounds and hold surgical dressings, formerly, to make photographic plates. [Mid-19C. < Greek *kollōdēs* "gluelike" < *kolla* "glue"]

col·loid /kó lòyd/ *n* **1.** CHEM SUSPENSION OF SMALL PARTICLES a suspension of small particles dispersed in another substance **2.** CHEM PARTICLES IN COLLOID the particles that are suspended in a colloid solution **3.** PHYSIOL SUBSTANCE IN THYROID GLAND a thick gelatinous substance that is produced in the thyroid gland and stores hormones [Mid-19C. < Greek *kolla* "glue"] —**col·loid** *adj* —**col·loid·al** /kə lóyd'l, ko-/ *adj*

col·lop /kólləp/ *n* **1.** SLICE OF MEAT a slice of meat, especially fried bacon **2.** *US, Scotland* FAT FLESH a small roll of fat on the body **3.** PIECE a small piece of something [14C. < N Germanic]

colloq. *abbr* LANGUAGE colloquial

~~**colloquail**~~ incorrect spelling of **colloquial**

col·lo·qui·a plural of **colloquium**

col·lo·qui·al /kə lṓkwee əl/ *adj* appropriate to, used in, or characteristic of spoken language or of writing that is used to create the effect of conversation [Mid-18C. < Latin *colloquium* (see COLLOQUIUM)] —**col·lo·qui·al·i·ty** /kə lṑkwee állətee/ *n* —**col·lo·qui·al·ly** *adv* —**col·lo·qui·al·ness** *n*

col·lo·qui·al·ism /kə lṓkwee ə lìzzəm/ *n* an informal word or phrase that is more common in conversation than in formal speech or writing

col·lo·qui·um /kə lṓkwee əm/ (*plural* **-qui·ums** or **-qui·a** /-kwee ə/) *n* **1.** an academic conference or seminar in which a particular topic is discussed, often with guest speakers **2.** an informal meeting to discuss something [Late 16C. < Latin, "conversation" < *colloqui* "speak with" < *loqui* "speak"]

col·lo·quy /kólləkwee/ (*plural* **-quies**) *n* **1.** a formal conversation or discussion (*formal*) **2.** a literary or other written work in the form of a dialogue [15C. < Latin *colloquium* (see COLLOQUIUM)]

~~**collosal**~~ incorrect spelling of **colossal**

col·lo·type /kóllə tīp/ *n* **1.** a process for making lithographic prints **2.** a print that is made by use of the collotype process

col·lude /kə lóod/ (**-lud·ed, -lud·ing, -ludes**) *vi* to cooperate with somebody secretly in order to do something illegal or undesirable [Early 16C. < Latin *colludere* "play with" < *ludere* "play" < *ludus* "game"] —**col·lud·er** *n*

col·lu·sion /kə lóozh'n/ *n* secret cooperation between people in order to do something illegal or underhanded [14C. Directly or via French < Latin *collusion-* < *collus-*, past participle of *colludere* (see COLLUDE)]

col·lu·sive /kə lóossiv/ *adj* secretly cooperating or involving secret cooperation in order to do something illegal or underhanded [Late 17C. < Latin *collus-* (see COLLUSION)] —**col·lu·sive·ly** *adv* —**col·lu·sive·ness** *n*

col·lu·vi·um /kə lóovee əm/ *n* loose rock and soil at the base of a cliff or steep slope [Mid-20C. < Latin < *colluvies* < *colluere* "wash thoroughly" < *lavere* "to wash"] —**col·lu·vi·al** *adj*

col·ly·wob·bles /kóllee wòbb'lz/ (*informal*) *n* pains or cramps, or both, in the stomach or bowels (*takes a singular or plural verb*) ■ *npl UK* a feeling of nervousness about something (*takes a plural verb*) [Early 19C. Probably < COLIC + WOBBLE]

Colo. *abbr* Colorado

colo- *prefix* intestine ○ *colorectal* [< COLON[2]]

col·o·bi VERTEB plural of **colobus**

col·o·bo·ma /kòllə bṓmə/ *n* a malformation of the retina, iris, or other tissue of the eye, usually present at birth [Mid-19C. Via modern Latin < Greek *koloboma* "part removed in mutilation" < *kolobos* "docked"] —**col·o·bo·ma·tous** *adj*

col·o·bus /kólləbəss/ (*plural* **-bus·es** or **-bi** /-bī/), **col·o·bus mon·key** *n* a large slender monkey that has a long tail and long silky fur but lacks developed thumbs. Native to: Africa. Genus: *Colobus*. [Late 19C. Via modern Latin < Greek *kolobos* "docked, maimed"]

co·lo·ca·tion /kō lō káysh'n/ *n* the sharing of facilities of a hosting center with other Internet clients

col·o·cynth /kóllə sìnth/ *n* **1.** a spongy bitter yellow fruit about the size of a lemon but speckled with green. Use: laxative. **2.** a vine related to the pumpkin and squash that bears colocynths. Native to: Europe. Latin name: *Citrulus colocynthis.* [Mid-17C. Via Latin *colocynthis* < Greek *kolokunthis* < *kolokunthē* "pumpkin, round gourd"]

co·logne /kə lṓn/ *n* a scented liquid with a lighter scent than perfume [Early 19C. After COLOGNE]

Co·logne /kə lṓn/ river port and largest city in the North Rhine-Westphalia state of Germany. Population: 963,817 (1997).

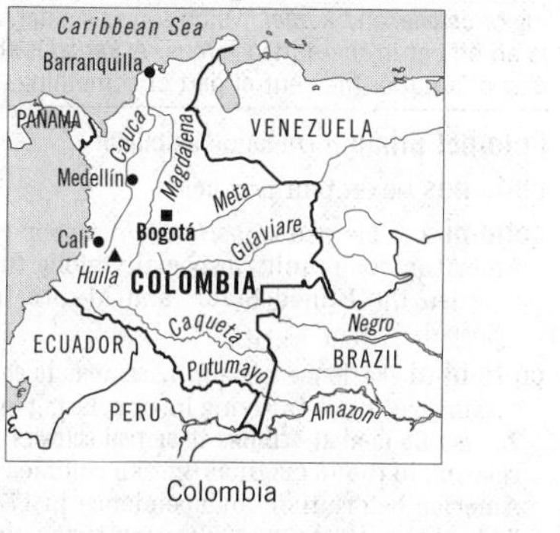

Colombia

Co·lom·bi·a /kə lúmbee ə/ country in northwestern South America surrounded by the Caribbean Sea, Venezuela, Brazil, Peru, Ecuador, Panama, and the Pacific Ocean. Language: Spanish. Currency: peso. Capital: Bogotá. Population: 41,662,073 (2003). Area: 440,831 sq. mi./1,141,748 sq. km. Official name **Republic of Colombia** —**Co·lom·bi·an** *n, adj*

Co·lom·bo /kə lúmbō/ port and commercial capital of Sri Lanka, situated on the western coast. Population: 615,000 (1995).

co·lon[1] /kṓlən/ *n* **1.** PUNCTUATION MARK the punctuation mark (:) used to divide distinct but related sentence components such as clauses in which the second elaborates on the first, or to introduce a list, quotation, or speech. A colon is sometimes used in US business letters after the salutation. Colons are also used between numbers in statements of proportion or time and Biblical or literary references. **2.** MARK USED IN PHONETICS a mark (:) after a vowel in a system of phonetic writing that shows that the vowel is lengthened **3.** (*plural* **co·la** /kṓlə/) UNIT OF CLASSICAL POETRY in Greek or Roman verse, a rhythmic unit consisting of two to six metrical feet with one main accent [Mid-16C. Via Latin < Greek *kōlon* "clause, limb"]

USAGE A ***colon*** is used to divide a sentence when the second part explains or elaborates on what has gone before: *They have put forward a different theory: the phenomenon may be caused by movements within the earth's crust.* It is also used to introduce a list or sometimes a quotation: *You will need the following equipment: a rucksack, waterproof clothing, strong walking boots, and a map. Martin Luther King wrote in* Chaos or Community *(1967): "A riot is at bottom the language of the unheard."* A colon sometimes separates numbers, e.g., in Biblical references, ratios, and clock times: *Genesis 13:8; a ratio of 6:4; the train that departs at 17:42.* When a colon is followed by a full sentence, the first word is often capitalized.

co·lon[2] /kṓlən/ (*plural* **-lons** or **-la** /-lə/) *n* the section of the large intestine that runs from the cecum to the rectum [14C. Via Latin < Greek *kolon* "large intestine"]

co·lón /kə lón/ (*plural* **-lóns** or **-lo·nes** /-lṓ nàyss/) *n* the main unit of currency in Costa Rica and El Salvador. See table at **currency** [Late 19C. After Cristóbal *Colón*, Spanish name of Christopher COLUMBUS]

Co·lón /kə lón/ city and capital of Colón Province, central Panama, situated on Limón Bay at the entrance to the Panama Canal. Population: 158,935 (1996).

co·lon ba·cil·lus *n* a bacterium found in the colon of humans and animals that becomes a serious contaminant when found in the food or water supply. Latin name: *Escherichia coli.*

colo·nel /kúrn'l/ *n* **1.** MILITARY RANK IN UNITED STATES an officer in the US Army, Marine Corps, or Air Force of a rank above lieutenant colonel **2.** MILITARY RANK IN CANADA an officer in the Canadian Army or Air Force of a rank above lieutenant colonel **3.** MILITARY RANK IN UK an officer in the British Army or Royal Marines of a rank above lieutenant colonel **4.** HONORARY TITLE an honorary title in a state militia, bestowed by the governor in some states. This practice is most closely associated with Kentucky, but also occurs in the states of Louisiana and Tennessee. [Mid-16C. Via obsolete French *coronel* < Italian *colonnella*, literally "little column" < *colonna* "column" < Latin *columna* (see COLUMN)] —**colo·nel·cy** *n* —**colo·nel·ship** *n*

SPELLCHECK colonel or **kernel**? Do not confuse the spelling of ***colonel*** and ***kernel***, which sound similar. A ***colonel*** is an officer in the armed forces. A ***kernel*** is the edible part of a nut or the central part of something.

Colo·nel Blimp *n UK* same as **blimp**[2]

co·lo·nes MONEY plural of **colón**

col·o·ni·a /kòllə nee ə/ *n Hispanic* a poor Hispanic-American community, especially along the border between the United States and Mexico [Late 20C. < Spanish, "colony"]

co·lo·ni·al /kə lṓnee əl/ *adj* **1.** RELATING TO COLONY possessing, ruling over, living in, or relating to a colony **2.** *also* **Co·lo·ni·al** RELATING TO BRITISH COLONIES IN AMERICA relating to the 13 original British colonies in North America before their independence in 1776 **3.** *also* **Co·lo·ni·al** OF BRITISH EMPIRE relating to the colonies of the former British Empire, or to the Empire as a whole **4.** IN STYLE OF AMERICAN COLONIES dating from or in a style typical of British North America in the late 17th to the early 19th century **5.** LIVING IN COLONIES describes animals that live in groups or colonies and are dependent on each other. Some, e.g. corals, are physically joined, while others such as insects show social organization and specialized functions. ■ *n* **1.** SOMEBODY WHO LIVES IN COLONY a resident of a colony who comes from the colonizing country **2.** SOMEBODY FROM COLONY somebody whose native country is a colony **3.** COLONIAL-STYLE HOUSE a house built in the neoclassical style popular in the 17th and 18th centuries in the British colonies in America [Late 18C. < COLONY] —**co·lo·ni·al·ly** *adv* —**co·lo·ni·al·ness** *n*

co·lo·ni·al·ism /kə lṓnee ə lìzzəm/ *n* a policy in which a country rules other nations and develops trade for its own benefit —**co·lo·ni·al·ist** *n* —**co·lo·ni·al·is·tic** /kə lṓnee ə lístik/ *adj*

co·lo·ni·al·ize /kə lṓnee ə līz/ (**-ized, -iz·ing, -iz·es**) *vt* to enter a nation or other landmass and try to restructure it into a colony —**co·lo·ni·al·i·za·tion** /kə lṓnee əli záysh'n/ *n*

co·lon·ic /kō lónnik, kə-/ *adj* relating to or situated in the colon ■ *n* same as **colonic irrigation**

co·lon·ic ir·ri·ga·tion, **co·lon·ic hy·dro·ther·a·py** *n* the injection of fluids through the anus into the colon to clean it out

col·o·nist /kóllənist/ *n* **1.** SOMEBODY LIVING IN NEW COLONY an immigrant to a new colony, or one of the founders of it **2.** *also* **Col·o·nist** EUROPEAN SETTLER OF AMERICA one of the early European settlers of North America before it became the United States **3.** ORGANISM MOVING INTO NEW ECOSYSTEM an organism, e.g., a plant such as a weed, that moves into and establishes itself in a new ecosystem

co·lon·i·tis /kōlə nītiss/ *n* MED same as **colitis**

col·o·nize /kóllə nīz/ (**-nized, -niz·ing, -niz·es**) *v* **1.** *vti* ESTABLISH COLONY to establish a colony in another country or place **2.** *vt* GO TO LIVE IN NEW LAND to go to and live permanently as part of a settlement in a foreign land that was previously sparsely inhabited **3.** *vti* BECOME ESTABLISHED IN NEW ECOSYSTEM to establish plants or animals, or become established, in a biological colony in a new ecosystem **4.** *vt* BECOME DOMINANT to become the most important or influential person or thing in a field of activity ○ *Japan's chefs colonize World Cuisine.* —**col·o·niz·a·ble** *adj* —**col·o·ni·za·tion** /kòlləni záysh'n/ *n* —**col·o·niz·er** *n*

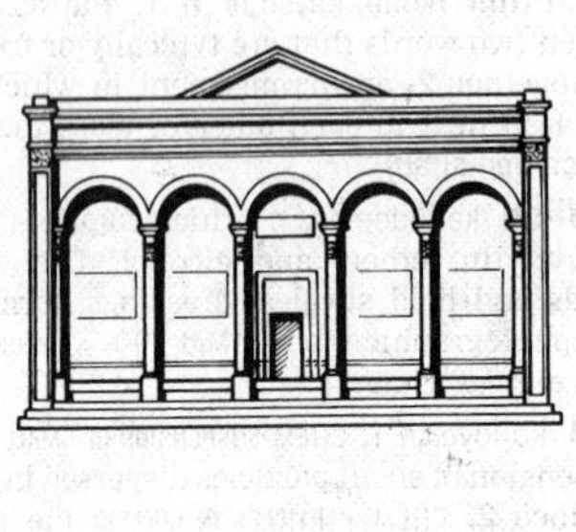

colonnade

col·on·nade /kòllə náyd, kóllə nàyd/ *n* **1.** a row of columns, usually supporting a roof or arches **2.** a row of evenly spaced trees [Early 18C. < French < *colonne* "column" < Latin *columna* (see COLUMN)] —**col·on·nad·ed** *adj*

co·lon·o·scope /kə lónnə skōp/ *n* a long flexible instrument (**endoscope**) used by a physician for viewing the interior of the colon, and often equipped with a device that can remove tissue for biopsy

co·lon·os·co·py /kōlə nóskəpee/ (*plural* **-pies**) *n* a medical examination of the colon by a physician using a colonoscope [< COLON[2]] —**co·lon·o·scop·ic** /kə̀lənə skóppik/ *adj*

col·o·ny /kóllənee/ (*plural* **-nies**) *n* **1.** COUNTRY RULED BY ANOTHER a country or area that is ruled by another country **2.** SETTLEMENT IN AMERICA one of the early settlements in North America that formed the 13 founding states of the United States after independence (*often used in the plural*) **3.** GROUP OF COLONISTS the group of people who have gone to live in a colony **4.** GROUP OF SIMILAR PEOPLE a group of people of the same nationality or ethnic group, doing the same work, or living in the same circumstances, who reside together or near one another ○ *a colony of artists* **5.** AREA WHERE GROUP LIVES the area where a group of people with shared ethnicity, interests, or occupations lives, e.g., in a city **6.** GROUP OF ANIMALS OR PLANTS a group of animals, insects, or organisms of the same kind that are living together and dependent on each other, or a group of plants growing in the same place **7.** MASS OF ORGANISMS a localized mass or growth of organisms such as bacteria in or on a nutrient medium [14C. < Latin *colonia* "farm, settlement" < *colonus* "tiller" < *colere* "cultivate"]

col·o·phon /kóllə fòn/ *n* **1.** the symbol or emblem that is printed on a book and represents a publisher or publisher's imprint **2.** the details of the title, printer, publisher, and publication date given at the end of a book. Colophons are commonly found in early printed books and in modern private press editions. [Early 17C. Via late Latin < Greek *kolophōn* "summit, finishing touch"]

col·or /kúllər/ *n* **1.** PROPERTY CAUSING VISUAL SENSATION the property of objects that depends on the light that they reflect and is perceived as red, blue, green, or other shades **2.** NOT BLACK OR WHITE a manifestation of color, e.g., red or green, as opposed to black, white, or gray ○ *printed in color* **3.** ART PIGMENT a pigment used in painting **4.** SOMETHING THAT ADDS COLOR something that is used to add color to something, e.g., paint, cosmetics, or dye ○ *She chose an auburn color to dye her hair.* **5.** NATURAL SHADE OF COMPLEXION the natural shade or color of somebody's skin as characteristic of race, especially of somebody who is not white ○ *We do not discriminate against people on the basis of color.* **6.** NONWHITE SKIN COLORATION a skin color other than that conventionally described as white ○ *people of color* **7.** HEALTHY LOOK TO SKIN the normal look of somebody's skin, especially in the face, when healthy **8.** EXTRA FACIAL REDNESS an extra redness in somebody's face, e.g., caused by embarrassment or exposure to cold wind **9.** VARIETY OF COLORS brightness and variety in the colors that something such as a room or picture has **10.** INTEREST OR VIVIDNESS a quality in something that gives it interest or immediacy ○ *The story lacks color.* **11.** ART USE OF COLOR IN PAINTING the use of color in painting, as distinct from line, form, or composition ○ *liked her handling of color* **12.** MUSIC SOUND QUALITY the quality of a particular sound **13.** LAW CLAIM OF LEGALITY a claim or appearance of legal right ○ *by color of law* **14.** PHYS HYPOTHETICAL QUANTUM CHARACTERISTIC a hypothetical property of quarks that takes three forms designated red, blue, and green **15.** PHYS HUE AND SATURATION the property or aspect of something that involves hue, lightness, and saturation or, in the case of light, hue, brightness, and saturation **16.** OPTICS ABILITY TO SEE COLORS the aspect of visual perception by which an observer recognizes colors **17.** PRINTING TYPE OF PRINTING INK the type and amount of inks used in a printing job ○ *a four-color brochure* **18.** MIN EXTRACT GOLD FOUND IN GRAVEL a particle of gold found in gravel or sand ■ **col·ors** *npl* **1.** SOMEBODY'S REAL SELF somebody's real beliefs, opinions, ethics, and principles ○ *It showed her up in her true colors.* **2.** NATIONAL, STATE, OR MILITARY FLAG the flag of a nation, state, or military unit, or all of these combined, especially when on parade **3.** COLORS REPRESENTING TEAM OR GROUP the colors that are used to represent a team, school, or other group **4.** CLOTHING WORN IN SPORT the clothing worn by a jockey or an athlete that indicates the horse's owner or the team to which the athlete belongs **5.** *UK* SPORTS TEAM MEMBERS' BADGE a badge or other symbol given to members of a sports team ○ *In her second year she got her rowing colors.* **6.** HERALDRY HERALDIC COLOR the main heraldic colors (**tinctures**) of azure, vert, sable, gules, and purpure ■ *v* (**-ored, -or·ing, -ors**) **1.** *vt* CHANGE COLOR OF SOMETHING to change or add to the color of something using paint, dye, cosmetics, or a similar agent **2.** *vi* TAKE ON COLOR to take on a particular color or change color **3.** *vi* BLUSH to get more red in the cheeks or face than usual, generally because of embarrassment **4.** *vt* SKEW OPINION OR JUDGMENT to influence an opinion or judgment, especially so as to make it less objective [13C. Via Old French < Latin *color*] —**col·or·er** *n* ◇ **nail your colors to the mast** to make your opinions or intentions obvious ○ *They've nailed their colors to the mast and announced that they will not sell their property for redevelopment.* ◇ **with flying colors** to an excellent standard

USAGE See ***African American.***

col·or·a·ble /kúllərəb'l/ *adj* **1.** appearing to be reasonable or true, but in fact being neither ○ *a colorable explanation* **2.** feigned or intended to deceive —**col·or·a·bil·i·ty** /kùllərə bíllətee/ *n* —**col·or·a·ble·ness** *n* —**col·or·a·bly** *adv*

Col·o·ra·do /kòllə ráddō, -raádō/ **1.** state in the western United States bordered by Wyoming, Nebraska, Kansas, Oklahoma, New Mexico, Arizona, and Utah. Capital: Denver. Population: 4,506,542 (2002 estimate). Area: 104,100 sq. mi./269,618 sq. km. **2.**

Colorado

major North American river, rising in northern Colorado and flowing southwest through the Grand Canyon. Length: 1,450 mi./2,330 km. **3.** river in Texas, the longest entirely within the state. It rises in northwestern Texas and flows southeastward into the Gulf of Mexico. Length: 862 mi./1,390 km.

Col·o·ra·do bee·tle *n UK* same as **Colorado potato beetle**

Col·o·ra·do blue spruce *n* TREES same as **blue spruce**

Col·o·ra·do Des·ert desert area of southeastern California west of the Colorado River. It includes the Salton Sea and the Imperial Valley.

Col·o·ra·do pike·min·now /-pīk mìnnō/ *n* a large slender freshwater fish with soft fins. Native to: western North America. Latin name: *Ptychocheilus lucius.*

Col·o·ra·do Pla·teau high dry region covering parts of southeastern Utah, southwestern Colorado, northwestern New Mexico, and northern Arizona. Area: 50,000 sq. mi./129,499 sq. km.

Col·o·ra·do po·ta·to bee·tle *n* a small black-and-yellow striped beetle that feeds on the leaves of potato plants and is a serious agricultural pest. Latin name: *Leptinotarsa decemlineata.*

Col·o·ra·do ru·by *n* a type of red garnet crystal found in the state of Colorado

Col·o·ra·do Springs city in central Colorado, south of Denver and east of Pikes Peak, home to the United States Air Force Academy. Population: 371,182 (2002 estimate).

Col·o·ra·do to·paz *n* **1.** a brownish yellow topaz found in the state of Colorado **2.** a type of brownish yellow quartz that resembles true Colorado topaz

col·or·ant /kúllərənt/ *n* a dye, pigment, ink, or similar agent that is used to add or change color

col·or·a·tion /kùllə ráysh'n/ *n* **1.** the appearance or pattern of color on an object **2.** the pattern of colors naturally occurring on a plant or an insect, bird, or other animal

col·or·a·tu·ra /kùllərə tóorə, kòllər-/ *n* a passage or piece of vocal music characterized by florid and demanding ornamentation, usually consisting of a rapid succession of notes. Coloratura passages are frequent in 18th- and 19th-century arias. [Mid-18C. < obsolete Italian, "coloring"]

col·or·a·tu·ra so·pran·o *n* a soprano with a light versatile voice capable of performing coloratura roles

color bar *n* LAW same as **color line**

col·or·blind /kúllər blīnd/ *adj* **1.** partially or completely unable to distinguish between some colors because of a medical condition **2.** not discriminating between people on the grounds of their ethnic group or the color of their skin —**col·or·blind·ness** *n*

col·or·breed /kúllər brēed/ (**-bred** /-brèd/, **-breed·ing, -breeds**) *vt* to breed plants or animals selectively so that the offspring are of the desired color

col·or·cast /kúllər kàst/ *n* a television program broadcast in color [Mid-20C. After BROADCAST] —**col·or·cast·er** *n*

col·or-code *vt* to classify different types of things by different colors

col·or con·trast *n* the perceived difference in a color that occurs when it is surrounded by another color

col·o·rec·tal /kòlō rékt'l/ *adj* relating to both the colon and rectum

col·ored /kúllərd/ *adj* **1.** HAVING COLOR having a particular color or colors (*often used in combination*) ○ *dark colored* ○ *honey colored* **2.** OFFENSIVE TERM an offensive term meaning belonging to an ethnic group whose members are predominantly dark-skinned (*dated*) **3.** DISTORTED OR BIASED biased or sensationalized ○ *a highly colored account of the incident* ■ *n* OFFENSIVE TERM an offensive term for somebody who belongs to an ethnic group that is predominantly dark-skinned (*dated*)

col·or·fast /kúllər fàst/ *adj* containing a dye that will not fade or wash out [Early 20C. < FAST[1]] —**col·or·fast·ness** *n*

col·or fil·ter *n* a filter made of colored glass or gelatin that absorbs light of a particular color before it reaches the camera lens. It is used to achieve artistic effects or to compensate for weather conditions.

col·or·ful /kúllərf'l/ *adj* **1.** WITH BRIGHT COLORS having bright or varied colors **2.** INTERESTING interesting or exciting and sometimes amusing ○ *a colorful period of history* ○ *the colorful characters of "Alice in Wonderland"* **3.** NOT ORDINARY OR PREDICTABLE characterized by unusual, unconventional, and sometimes illegal behavior ○ *no attempt to hide his colorful past* **4.** FULL OF SWEARWORDS characterized by coarse words or obscenities (*informal; used euphemistically*) —**col·or·ful·ly** *adv* —**col·or·ful·ness** *n*

col·or guard *n* a small group that escorts the flag or colors of a military unit at a military ceremony or in a parade

col·or·if·ic /kùllə ríffik/ *adj* producing or giving color to something

col·or·im·e·ter /kùllə rímmətər/ *n* **1.** an instrument for measuring and specifying colors by comparison with an established set of standard colors **2.** an instrument that determines the concentration of a solution of a colored substance by reference to standard solutions or standard color slides [Mid-19C. < Latin *color* (see COLOR)] —**col·or·i·met·ric** /kùlləri méttrik/ *adj* —**col·or·i·met·ri·cal·ly** *adv* —**col·or·im·e·try** *n*

col·or·ing /kúlləring/ *n* **1.** ACT OF GIVING COLOR the act of giving color to something **2.** COLORING SUBSTANCE a substance that gives color to something, e.g., a food dye **3.** COLOR OF COMPLEXION OR HAIR the shade of somebody's skin or hair color **4.** CHARACTERISTIC COLORS OF BIRD OR ANIMAL the characteristic colors of a bird's plumage or an animal's coat

col·or·ing book *n* a book with drawings for a child to color

col·or·ist /kúllərist/ *n* **1.** ARTIST KNOWN FOR USE OF COLORS a painter whose technique involves special use of color **2.** COLORER somebody whose work involves coloring things **3.** HAIR STYLIST a hair stylist who is professionally qualified to dye hair —**col·or·is·tic** /kùllə rístik/ *adj* —**col·or·is·ti·cal·ly** *adv*

col·or·ize /kúllə rīz/ (**-ized, -iz·ing, -izes**) *vt* to add color to a black-and-white movie, e.g., by using computer techniques

col·or·less /kúllərləss/ *adj* **1.** WITHOUT COLOR lacking color **2.** CHARACTERLESS not interesting or exciting ○ *a colorless personality* **3.** PALE pale or lacking distinctive color —**col·or·less·ly** *adv* —**col·or·less·ness** *n*

col·or line *n* a separation of ethnic groups, physically or socially, either in law or as the result of discrimination

col·or phase *n* **1.** a seasonal variation in the colors of a bird's plumage or an animal's coat **2.** a distinct and permanent color variation shown by a group of animals within a species

col·or·point short·hair /kúller poynt sháwrt hèr/ *n* a domestic cat belonging to a breed with a light-colored coat and darker markings on the face, ears, feet, and tail

col·or scheme *n* a combination of colors used in interior decoration

col·or sub·car·ri·er *n* the component of a television signal that transmits color information to the receiver

col·or·way /kúller wày/ *n* one of a range of possible colors available ○ *The shirt comes in three exciting colorways, taupe, red, and navy.*

col·or wheel *n* the spectrum represented as a circular diagram that shows how colors are related to one another

co·los·sal /kə lóss'l/ *adj* **1.** VERY LARGE unusually or impressively large ○ *a colossal high-rise office building* **2.** VERY GREAT very great or impressive ○ *Our opponents made a colossal blunder.* **3.** SCULPTURE TWICE LIFE SIZE describes sculptures that are twice life size —**co·los·sal·ly** *adv*

col·os·se·um *n* ANCIENT HIST another spelling of **coliseum**

Colosseum, Rome, Italy

Col·os·se·um /kòllə sée əm/ *n* a large amphitheater in Rome, Italy, built in the 1st century A.D. for sports and entertainment

Co·los·sians /kə lósh'nz/ *n* a book of the Bible, originally a letter addressed to the church in the Phrygian city of Colossae, written between A.D. 55 and 63 and traditionally attributed to St. Paul (*takes a singular verb*) See table at **Bible**

co·los·sus /kə lóssəss/ (*plural* **-si** /-ī/) *n* **1.** a statue that is several times larger than life size **2.** an enormously large or powerful person or thing ○ *a colossus among contemporary fashion designers* [14C. Via Latin < Greek *kolossos*]

co·los·to·my /kə lóstəmee/ (*plural* **-mies**) *n* **1.** a surgical operation that creates an artificial anus through an opening made in the abdomen from the colon **2.** an opening surgically created in the abdomen that functions as an anus

co·los·trum /kə lóstrəm/ *n* a yellowish fluid rich in antibodies and minerals that a mother's breasts produce after giving birth and before the production of true milk. It provides newborns with immunity to infections. [Late 16C. < Latin]

col·our *n, vti* Can, UK spelling of **color**

Col·oured /kúllərd/ *S Africa adj* belonging to a group of mixed ethnic origin, formerly a racial classification in the apartheid era ■ *n* somebody whose ancestors were of both African and non-African descent, formerly a racial classification in the apartheid era

col·our sup·ple·ment *n UK* a magazine printed in color and forming a section of a newspaper

col·pi·tis /kol pītiss/ *n* MED same as **vaginitis** (*technical*)

colpo- *prefix* vagina ○ *colposcope* [< Greek *kolpos*]

col·po·scope /kólpə skōp/ *n* a magnifying and photographic instrument used to examine the vagina —**col·po·scop·ic** /kòlpə skóppik/ *adj* —**col·pos·co·py** /kol póskəpee/ *n*

colt /kōlt/ *n* **1.** a young uncastrated male horse, usually under four years of age **2.** a young and inexperienced person (*literary*) [Old English, Origin ?]

Colt /kōlt/, **Samuel** (1814–62) US inventor and manufacturer. He patented a pistol with a revolving cylinder (1836) that was used in the Mexican War (1846–48) and founded a major firearms company.

col·tan /kól tàn/ *n* a metallic ore in the form of black sand that occurs mainly in eastern Democratic Republic of the Congo. Use: source of tantalum for the capacitors used in electronic devices such as cell phones and laptop computers. [Late 20C. < COLUMBITE + TANTALITE]

col·ter *n* AGRIC another spelling of **coulter**

colt·ish /kṓltish/ *adj* energetic and playful in nature —**colt·ish·ly** *adv* —**colt·ish·ness** *n*

Col·ton /kṓlt'n/ city in southern California, a southern suburb of San Bernardino. Population: 49,833 (2002 estimate).

Col·trane /kōl trayn/, **John** (1926–67) US saxophonist and composer. He was a leading proponent of free-form jazz in the 1960s. His compositions include "Giant Steps."

> "If the music doesn't say it, how can words say it *for* the music?"
> [John Coltrane, *Jazz Is*, Nat Hentoff; 1976]

colts·foot /kṓlts fŏŏt/ (*plural* **-foots** or *same*) *n* a plant with large hoof-shaped leaves. Flowers: yellow. Use: in herbal medicine to treat coughs. Native to: Europe, Asia, North America. Latin name: *Tussilago farfara.*

col·u·brid /kólləbrid/ (*plural same* or **-brids**) *n* a snake belonging to a family of mostly nonvenomous snakes. King snakes, garter snakes, and water snakes are colubrids. Family: Colubridae. [Late 19C. < modern Latin *Colubridae* < Latin *colubrid-*, stem of *coluber* "snake"]

col·u·brine /kóllə brīn, -brin/ *adj* **1.** resembling a snake **2.** relating to or belonging to the colubrid snakes [Early 16C. < Latin *colubrinus* < *coluber* "snake"]

co·lu·go /kə lóogō/ (*plural* **-gos** or *same*) *n* VERTEB same as **flying lemur** [Early 18C. < Malay]

Col·um /kólləm/, **Padraic** (1881–1972) Irish poet and dramatist. He was an early supporter of Dublin's Abbey Theatre, where his plays, including *The Land* (1905), were presented.

Co·lum·ba /kə lúmbə/ *n* a small faint constellation of the southern hemisphere between Canis Major and Pictor. See illustration at **constellation**

col·um·bar·i·um /kòlləm bérree əm/ (*plural* **-i·a** /-ee ə/), **col·um·bar·y** /kólləm bèrree/ (*plural* **-ies**) *n* **1.** a chamber or wall in which urns containing the ashes of the dead are stored **2.** a niche in which an urn containing funeral ashes is placed in a columbarium [Mid-18C. < Latin *columba* "dove"]

Co·lum·bi·a /kə lúmbee ə/ **1.** river that flows through southwestern Canada and the northwestern United States and empties into the Pacific Ocean below Portland, Oregon. Length: 1,240 mi./2,000 km. **2.** city in central Missouri, northwest of Jefferson City. It is home to the University of Missouri. Population: 86,981 (2002 estimate). **3.** city in central Tennessee, on the southern bank of the Duck River, south of Nashville. Population: 33,067 (2002 estimate). **4.** capital of South Carolina, on the eastern bank of the Congaree River, northwest of Charleston. Population: 117,394 (2002 estimate).

Co·lum·bi·a Heights city in southeastern Minnesota, on the Mississippi River, a northern suburb of Minneapolis. Population: 18,572 (2002 estimate).

Co·lum·bi·an /kə lúmbee ən/ *adj* relating to the United States, or its peoples or cultures

Co·lum·bi·a Pla·teau region of the western United States incorporating parts of Washington, Oregon, and Idaho. Area: 200,000 sq. mi./517,998 sq. km.

col·um·bine[1] /kólləm bīn/ (*plural* **-bines** or *same*) *n* a perennial plant grown for its flowers. Flowers: various colors with five petals and long spurs. Native to: northern temperate zones. Genus: *Aquilegia.* [14C. Via French < medieval Latin *columbina (herba)* "(plant) like a dove" < Latin *columbinus* (see COLUMBINE[2]); from its resemblance to a cluster of doves]

col·um·bine[2] /kólləm bīn/ *adj* resembling or relating to doves (*literary*) [14C. Via French < Latin *columbinus* "like a dove" < *columba* "dove"]

co·lum·bite /kə lúm bīt/ *n* a black, reddish brown, or transparent mixed oxide mineral containing niobium, iron, and manganese. Use: source of niobium. [Early 19C. < COLUMBIUM]

co·lum·bi·um /kə lúmbee əm/ *n* the element niobium (*not in technical use*) Symbol **Cb** [Early 19C. < modern Latin *Columbia* "America"; because discovered in ore from Massachusetts] —**co·lum·bic** *adj* —**co·lum·bous** *adj*

Co·lum·bus /kə lúmbəss/ **1.** capital and largest city of Ohio. It is home to Ohio State University. Population: 725,228 (2002 estimate). **2.** city in western Georgia, on the Chattahoochee River, east of Phoenix City, Alabama. Population: 185,948 (2002 estimate). **3.** city in Indiana, southwest of Indianapolis, where the Big Blue River and Flatrock Creek meet. Population: 40,927 (2002 estimate).

Co·lum·bus, Christopher (1451–1506) Italian explorer. He reached the Caribbean in 1492, thereby opening the Americas to European trade and colonization.

> "I believe that the earthly Paradise lies here, which no one can enter except by God's leave. I believe that this land which your Highnesses have commanded me to discover is very great, and that there are many other lands in the south of which there have never been reports."
> [Christopher Columbus, *Narrative of his third voyage*; 1498]

Co·lum·bus Day *n* in the United States, a day marking Christopher Columbus's arrival in the New World in 1492. Date: second Monday in October.

col·u·mel·la /kòllə méllə/ (*plural* **-lae** /-lee/) *n* a tiny bone in the middle ear of all land vertebrates that transmits sound waves from the eardrum to the inner ear and corresponds to the stapes in mammals [Late 16C. < Latin, "little column" < *columna* (see COLUMN)] —**col·u·mel·lar** *adj* —**col·u·mel·late** *adj*

col·umn /kólləm/ *n* **1.** ROUND PILLAR an upright support shaped like a long cylinder ○ *a Corinthian column* ○ *the white columns of Mount Vernon* **2.** SOMETHING SHAPED LIKE COLUMN something resembling a column in form ○ *a column of smoke* **3.** REGULAR ARTICLE an item in a newspaper or magazine that is always written by the same person or is always about the same subject **4.** VERTICAL ARRANGEMENT OF NUMBERS a vertical arrangement of figures or mathematical terms **5.** SECTION OF PAGE one of two or more vertical sections of printed material on a page **6.** LINE OF PEOPLE OR THINGS a long line of people or vehicles **7.** ANAT, BOT PART SHAPED LIKE COLUMN a long part of a plant or animal ○ *spinal column* [15C. Directly or via French < Latin *columna*, probably < *columen* "top"] —**col·um·nar** /kə lúmnər/ *adj* —**col·umned** *adj*

co·lum·nar joint·ing *n* the development of parallel prismatic columns in contracting intrusive or extrusive rock undergoing cooling

col·um·ne·a /kə lúmnee ə/ (*plural* **-as** or *same*) *n* a tropical bushy or trailing plant grown as a houseplant. Flowers: colorful, tubular. Native to: America. Genus: *Columnea.* [Late 18C. < modern Latin *Columna*, Latinization of Fabio *Colonna* (1567–1640), Italian writer on plants]

col·umn inch *n* an area on a page one column wide and one inch deep, used to measure the amount of type that would fill that space

col·um·nist /kólləmnist/ *n* a journalist who writes a regular column for a newspaper or magazine ○ *a gossip columnist*

col·ure /kə lóor/ *n* either of two great circles on the celestial sphere that intersect at the celestial poles, one of which connects the equinoctial points on the ecliptic, while the other connects the solstitial points [14C. Via late Latin *coluri* < Greek *kolourai (grammai)* "truncated (lines)" < *kolouros* "truncated" < *kolos* "docked" + *oura* "tail"]

Col·wyn Bay /kólwən-/ coastal resort in Conwy, North Wales. Population: 29,883 (1991).

col·za /kólzə/ *n* PLANTS same as **rape**[2] [Early 18C. Via French (Walloon) < Low German *kōlsāt*, Dutch *koolzaad* < *kool* "cabbage" + *zaad* "seed"]

col·za oil *n* INDUST same as **rape oil**

com *abbr* commercial organization (*used in Internet addresses*) See table at **domain name**

COM /kom/ *n* the process of converting computer output directly to microfilm. Full form **computer output microfilm**

com. *abbr* **1.** ARTS comedy **2.** comic **3.** COMM commerce **4.** COMM commercial **5.** committee **6.** SOC SCI commune[1]

Com. *abbr* **1.** MIL Commander **2.** NAVY Commodore **3.** POL Communist

com- *prefix* together, with, jointly (*used before b, m, n, or p*) ○ *commingle* [< Latin < Indo-European, "together"]

co·ma[1] /kṓmə/ *n* a prolonged state of deep unconsciousness [Mid-17C. Via modern Latin < Greek *kōma* "deep sleep"]

co·ma[2] /kṓmə/ (*plural* **-mae** /-mee/) *n* **1.** a luminous cloud of gas and dust surrounding the head of a comet **2.** a defect in a lens that produces a blurred, comet-shaped image of a point, or the image produced [Early 17C. Via Latin < Greek *komē* "hair of the head"] —**co·mal** *adj*

Co·ma Ber·e·ni·ces /kṓmə bèrrə nī́ seez/ *n* a faint constellation of the northern hemisphere. See illustration at **constellation** [Mid-16C. < Latin, "Berenice's hair," after a 3C B.C. Egyptian queen whose hair, cut off and dedicated as an offering for her husband's safe return from war, is said to have been placed in the stars]

co·ma·dre /ko maa dray/ *n Hispanic* a godmother or close female friend [< Spanish]

co·mal /kō maal/ *n Hispanic* HOUSEHOLD same as **griddle**

Co·man·che /kə mánchee/ (*plural same* or **-ches**) *n* **1.** a member of a Native American people who formerly led a nomadic life in areas of Kansas, Oklahoma, and Texas, and who now live mainly in Oklahoma **2.** the Shoshonean language of the Comanche. Native speakers: 500. [Early 19C. Via Spanish < Southern Paiute or a related language] —**Co·man·che** *adj*

~~**comand**~~ incorrect spelling of **command**

Co·ma·neci /kò maa neech/, **Nadia** (*b.* 1961) Romanian-born US gymnast. At the age of 14, competing for Romania, she was the youngest person to win an Olympic gold medal in gymnastics and the first to attain a perfect 10 mark (1976).

co·ma·tose /kṓmə tòss/ *adj* **1.** in a coma **2.** in a very tired or drunken state (*informal*) ○ *After driving 14 hours in a snowstorm, I was comatose the entire next day.* [Late 17C. < Greek *kōmat-* "deep sleep"] —**co·ma·tose·ly** *adv*

co·mat·u·lid /kə máchəlid/ (*plural* **-lids** or *same*), **co·mat·u·la** /kə máchələ/ (*plural* **-lae** /-lee/ or *same*) *n* an invertebrate sea animal that is free-swimming when it reaches maturity, e.g., a feather star. Order: Comatulida. [Late 19C. < modern Latin *Comatulidae* < late Latin *comatulus* "with neatly curled hair" < Latin *comatus* "having hair"]

comb /kōm/ *n* **1.** INSTRUMENT FOR ARRANGING HAIR an instrument with a row of long thin teeth, used to arrange hair **2.** FASTENING FOR HAIR a piece of plastic or wood with long thin teeth, used to fasten back the hair **3.** TEXTILES TOOL FOR CLEANING WOOL a tool or machine part with long slender teeth, used for cleaning wool or other materials **4.** RIDING same as **currycomb** **5.** CREST OF ROOSTER the fleshy red growth on the head of a rooster or other bird **6.** FOOD same as **honeycomb** *n* (senses 1–2) ■ *vt* (**combed, comb·ing, combs**) **1.** RUN COMB THROUGH HAIR to arrange hair or fur with a comb **2.** TEXTILES CLEAN OR ARRANGE FIBERS to clean or arrange the fibers of wool or other materials using a comb **3.** SEARCH PLACE THOROUGHLY to search an area thoroughly ○ *We combed the house for his keys.* [Old English *camb* < Indo-European, "tooth"] ◇ **go over** *or* **through something with a fine-tooth(ed) comb** to study or search something extremely carefully

comb. *abbr* **1.** combination **2.** combining **3.** CHEM combustion

com·bat *n* /kóm bàt/ **1.** FIGHTING fighting between two people or groups, especially between armies (*often used before a noun*) ○ *He had never seen combat.* ○ *combat troops* **2.** FIGHT OR STRUGGLE a struggle between opposing individuals or forces ○ *combat between good and evil* ■ **com·bats** /kóm bats/ *npl* CASUAL CLOTHES WITH MILITARY LOOK loose-fitting casual clothes, especially pants, with a military style and often in camouflage colors ■ *vt* /kəm bát, kóm bàt/ (**-bat·ed** or **-bat·ted, -bat·ing** or **-bat·ting, -bats**) **1.** TRY TO DESTROY SOMETHING DANGEROUS to attempt to destroy or control something harmful ○ *measures to combat pollution* **2.** RESIST SOMEBODY OR SOMETHING to resist or oppose somebody or something actively [Mid-16C. < French *combattre* "to fight" (literally "fight with") < Latin *battuere* "to beat"] —**com·bat·a·ble** /kəm báttəb'l/ *adj* —**com·bat·er** /kəm báttər/ *n*

com·bat·ant /kəm bátt'nt/ *n* **1.** a person or group taking part in a war **2.** a participant in a struggle or argument

Com·bat Arms *npl* in the US Army, the units that actually engage the enemy in combat, e.g., the infantry, armored vehicle units, or field artillery

com·bat fa·tigue *n US* a psychological disorder resulting from the stress of being involved in a battle and characterized by acute anxiety, depression, and loss of motivation. Can term **battle fatigue**

com·bat game *n* a game in which people take part in simulated combat, e.g., paintball

com·bat·ive /kəm báttiv/ *adj* eager to fight or argue —**com·bat·ive·ly** *adv* —**com·bat·ive·ness** *n*

com·bat pants *npl* loose-fitting casual pants with one or more large pockets on each thigh [Because worn by soldiers]

com·bat pay *n* extra tax-free pay that members of the United States armed forces are awarded while on duty in combat zones

combe /koom/, **coomb**, **coombe** *n UK* primarily in southern England, a small valley with steep sides that seldom has running water in it [Pre-12C. < Celtic]

comb·er /kṓmər/ *n* **1.** a person or machine that combs wool or other materials **2.** a long high wave that crashes onto a beach

com·bi·na·tion /kòmbi náysh'n/ *n* **1. MIXTURE** a mixture of different things or factors, or the act of mixing them ○ *We were saved by a combination of skill and good luck.* **2. COMBINED SET** two or more people or things that are combined to form a set ○ *The red shirt and navy vest make a striking color combination.* **3. NUMBERS THAT OPEN LOCK** a series of numbers or letters needed to open a combination lock **4.** BOXING **SERIES OF PUNCHES** in boxing, two or more punches quickly delivered one after the other **5. ALLIANCE** an association between people or groups established in order to accomplish something **6.** MATH **ARRANGEMENT OF NUMBERS IN SUBSETS** an arrangement of the numbers or symbols in a mathematical set into smaller subsets without regard to the order in which those numbers or symbols appear **7.** MATH **SUBSET** a subset containing a specific number of the elements of a particular set, selected without regard to the order in which they were chosen **8.** CHESS **SEQUENCE OF MOVES INVOLVING MULTIPLE PIECES** in chess, a series of tactical moves involving two or more pieces **9.** CHEM **FORMATION OF COMPOUND** the union of substances in the formation of a chemical compound —**com·bi·na·tion·al** *adj*

SYNONYMS See *mixture*.

com·bi·na·tion lock *n* a lock that opens only when a set of wheels, each with a sequence of numbers from 0 to 9, are aligned to give a specific sequence of numbers

com·bi·na·to·ri·al a·nal·y·sis /kòmbi nə tàwree əl-/ *n* the branch of mathematics dealing with combinations and permutations, especially those relating to probability and statistics

com·bine *v* /kəm bī́n/ (**-bined, -bin·ing, -bines**) **1.** *vti* **JOIN OR MIX TOGETHER** to be joined or mixed together, or join or mix people or things together ○ *Combine the ingredients in a large mixing bowl.* ○ *All these factors combine to make for a truly successful product.* **2.** *vt* **DO THINGS SIMULTANEOUSLY** to undertake two or more activities at the same time ○ *She has successfully combined a career as an attorney and a state senator.* **3.** *vti* CHEM **UNITE CHEMICALLY** to join together, or make substances join together, to form a chemical compound **4.** *vti* AGRIC **HARVEST CROPS WITH MACHINE** to harvest crops using a combine harvester ■ *n* /kóm bīn/ **1. ASSOCIATION** an illegal association of business organizations **2.** AGRIC same as **combine harvester** [15C. < late Latin *combinare* "put two things together" < Latin *bini* "two at a time" < *bi-* (see BI-)] —**com·bin·a·ble** *adj* —**com·bi·na·tive** /kómbi nàytiv/ *adj* —**com·bin·er** *n*

com·bined /kəm bī́nd/ *n* a skiing event consisting of a downhill run and a slalom run that are slightly less arduous than either run as a single event

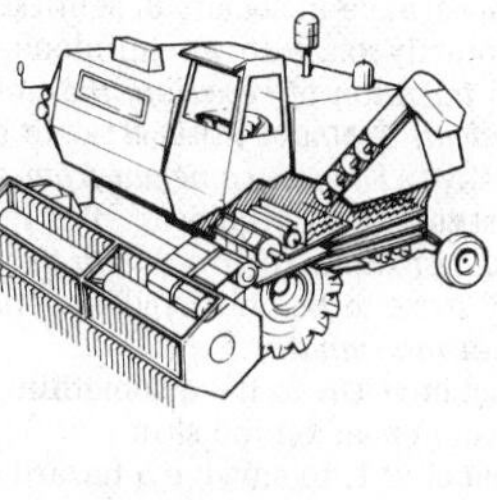

combine harvester

com·bine har·vest·er /kòm bīn-/ *n* a large farm machine that is used to harvest crops

comb·ings /kṓmingz/ *npl* small loose pieces of hair, wool, or other fiber that are collected during combing

com·bin·ing form /kəm bī́ning-/ *n* a form of a word in English or another language that is used only in combination with other words to make compound words, e.g.,"Franco-" in "Franco-British," "bio-" as in "biodegradable"

com·bo /kómbō/ (*plural* **-bos**) *n* **1.** a small jazz or dance band **2.** a combination of several people or components (*informal*) ○ *a burger, fries, and shake combo* [Early 20C. < COMBINATION]

comb·o·ver /kṓm ōvər/ *n* a man's hairstyle designed to conceal baldness by allowing the hair to grow long on one side of the head and combing it over the top (*informal*)

com·bust /kəm búst/ (**-bust·ed, -bust·ing, -busts**) *vti* to react vigorously with oxygen to produce heat and light, seen as a flame, or make something do this [15C. Partly < obsolete *combust* "burned" < Latin *combustus* (see COMBUSTION); partly back-formation < COMBUSTION]

com·bus·ti·ble /kəm bústəb'l/ *adj* **1.** able or likely to catch fire and burn **2.** able to react vigorously with oxygen to produce heat and light, seen as a flame —**com·bus·ti·bil·i·ty** /kəm bùstə bíllətee/ *n* —**com·bus·ti·ble** *n* —**com·bus·ti·bly** *adv*

com·bus·tion /kəm búschən/ *n* **1. IGNITION** the burning of fuel in an engine to provide power **2. CHEMICAL REACTION** a chemical process in which a substance reacts vigorously with oxygen to produce heat and light, seen as a flame **3. EXTREME AGITATION** a state of extreme discontent and agitation [15C. < Latin *combustus*, past participle of *comburere* "burn up" < *urere* "to burn"] —**com·bus·tive** *adj*

com·bus·tion cham·ber *n* an enclosed space in which combustion takes place, e.g., in a jet engine or internal-combustion engine

com·bus·tor /kəm búster/ *n* a combustion system in a jet engine or gas turbine, consisting of the fuel injection system, the igniter, and the combustion chamber

Comdr. *abbr* MIL Commander

Comdt. *abbr* MIL Commandant

come /kum/ (**came** /kaym/, **come, com·ing, comes**) CORE MEANING: a basic intransitive verb expressing movement toward a specified place or person. This verb often expresses the concept of movement coupled with the arrival at a place where an activity will take place. ○ *Come and sit by me.* ○ *Come to my house tomorrow.*

1. *vi* **OCCUR IN MIND** to occur as a thought in the mind ○ *An afterthought came to me while I was shaving.* **2.** *vi* **ORIGINATE** to originate from a place or thing ○ *The meat came from Canadian herds.* **3.** *vi* **HAPPEN** to happen or exist at a particular point or time ○ *I never thought this day would come.* **4.** *vi* **RESULT** to be the result or consequence of something ○ *comes from eating too much chocolate* **5.** *vi* **BE PRODUCED** to be produced in a particular size, color, or style ○ *This model also comes in red.* **6.** *vi* **REACH PLACE** to reach or extend to a particular point or place ○ *Her hair came down to her waist.* **7.** *vi* **REACH STATE** to reach or be brought into a particular state or situation ○ *It just came apart in my hands.* **8.** *vi* **HAVE ORGASM** to reach sexual climax (*slang; sometimes considered offensive*) **9.** *prep* **PRIOR TO** by a particular time in the future ○ *Come July there will be an extra fifty cases to deal with.* **10.** *n* **OFFENSIVE TERM** an offensive term for a man's semen (*slang*) ◇ **come again?** used to ask someone to repeat or explain something (*informal*) ◇ **come off it!** used to express contemptuous disbelief (*informal*) ◇ **come to pass** to happen (*archaic or literary*) ◇ **come to think of** *or* **about it** used to introduce a thought that has just occurred to you or something that you have just remembered (*informal*) ◇ **come what may** whatever happens ○ *He swore that, come what may, he would never let her out of his sight again.* ◇ **have it coming (to you)** to be about to receive the punishment or retribution that you deserve ◇ **how come?** used to ask the reason for something (*informal*) ○ *How come you never told me?*

come about *vi* to take place or occur

come across *v* **1.** *vt* **FIND SOMEBODY OR SOMETHING** to find something or meet somebody by chance ○ *I came across a reference to her in the newspaper.* **2.** *vi* **BE COMMUNICATED** to be clearly communicated ○ *The point came across loud and clear: cutbacks are inevitable.* **3.** *vi* **PRODUCE IMPRESSION** to give a particular impression ○ *She came across as very positive.*

come along *vi* **1. HAPPEN** to happen or appear ○ *We'll deal with whatever comes along.* **2. PROGRESS** to progress or develop (*only used in continuous tenses, usually in questions or with an adverb*) ○ *How's the new recruit coming along?* **3. ACCOMPANY SOMEBODY** to go somewhere with somebody **4.** *UK* **HURRY UP** to move or act more quickly ○ *Come along or we'll be late for dinner.*

come apart *vi* to tear or disintegrate ○ *The dress just came apart when I washed it.*

come around *vi* **1. CHANGE YOUR OPINION** to change your opinion to that of somebody else ○ *They soon came around to our way of thinking.* **2. REGAIN CONSCIOUSNESS** to regain consciousness, e.g., after being knocked out ○ *He finally came around after being unconscious for nearly three hours.* **3. RECUR** to happen again at the expected time ○ *There's excitement in the air when the first football game comes around every year.* **4. VISIT** to visit somebody ○ *Why don't you all come around to my place and have some coffee?*

come at *vt* **1.** to set upon and attack somebody ○ *came at him from behind* **2.** to reach or discover something with difficulty ○ *The only way to come at the facts is to ask pertinent questions.*

come away *vi* to become detached from something ○ *The handle came away in my hand.*

come back *vi* **1. REGAIN POPULARITY** to become popular again ○ *Seventies fashions came back briefly during the mid-nineties.* **2. RETURN TO MIND** to appear or become clear again from somebody's memory ○ *I can't remember the address, but give me a moment and it'll come back to me.* **3. RETORT** to reply energetically or aggressively to somebody ○ *She came back at him immediately with a counterblast.*

come back to *vt* **1.** to reconsider or refer to something again (*informal*) ○ *I'll come back to that question in a moment.* **2.** to speak to somebody again about something at a later time ○ *Do you mind if I come back to you on that one?*

come before *vt* to be submitted for consideration or judgment before a person or group of people with authority ○ *The report is due to come before the committee.*

come between *vt* **1.** to disrupt a relationship ○ *I won't let anything come between us.* **2.** to prevent somebody from having or doing something ○ *He won't let anything come between him and his Saturday football.*

come by *vt* to manage to acquire something ○ *Jobs are not so easy to come by nowadays.*

come down *vi* **1. DECREASE** to decrease in value or amount ○ *Prices are coming down.* **2. REACH DECISION** to make a decision or judgment ○ *The judge came down in favor of the plaintiff's motion.* **3. BE HANDED DOWN** to be passed down from one generation to another ○ *written records that have come down to us from that period* **4. RETURN TO NORMAL CONSCIOUSNESS** to return to a normal state of consciousness after being affected by drugs (*informal*) **5. HAPPEN** to be happening in the present (*slang*) ○ *Hey, dude! What's coming down?*

come down on *vt* to punish or criticize somebody

come down to *vt* to mean or represent something fundamentally, when all nonessential detail has been disregarded

come down with *vt* to catch a cold, the flu, or another minor illness

come for *vt* to arrive at a place to pick somebody or something up

come forward *vi* to show a willingness to offer help or give information

come from *vt* **1.** to have a particular place of origin or source ○ *She came from Ohio.* **2.** be descended from a particular line, family, or stock

come in *vi* **1.** FINISH IN PARTICULAR POSITION to finish a race in a particular position ○ *The American yacht came in fifth.* **2.** ARRIVE to arrive or be received and become available for use, sale, or communication ○ *The spring fashions will be coming in next month.* **3.** BECOME FASHIONABLE to become fashionable or popular ○ *Long hair for men came in during the 1960s.* **4.** PARTICIPATE to become involved in something ○ *There are three other venture capitalists interested in coming in on the deal.* **5.** BEGIN SPEAKING to begin speaking during a discussion or in reply to a radio signal ○ *Senator, do you want to come in on that point? We've only 60 seconds left.* **6.** PROVE to turn out to have a particular level of usefulness ○ *That little knife came in very handy when we went camping.* **7.** TRANSP APPROACH DESTINATION to approach or arrive at a destination ○ *Her flight is coming in at 4:00.* **8.** BECOME HIGHER to become higher, driving water up over the shore (*refers to the tide*) **9.** SUBSTITUTE to enter a game as a substitute for somebody else ○ *It looks like a new defensive lineman has just come in.*

come in for *vt* to be the object of criticism or scrutiny ○ *The policy has come in for scathing attacks by the media.*

come into *vt* to inherit money or property ○ *When her uncle died, she came into a great deal of money.*

come of *vt* to be the result of something ○ *Did anything ever come of your lawsuit?*

come off *v* **1.** *vt* COME LOOSE to become detached or be detachable from something ○ *The top comes off easily.* **2.** *vt* STOP TAKING MEDICINE to stop taking a drug or a medicine ○ *When I came off the prescription painkillers, the doctor put me on aspirin.* **3.** *vt* BE DEDUCTED FROM SOMETHING to be deducted from something **4.** *vi* HAPPEN to take place as planned or predicted (*informal*) ○ *Let's hope the trip comes off.*

come on *v* **1.** *vi* START TO OPERATE to become available for use or begin to function (*refers to a power source or machine*) ○ *The street lights come on at dusk.* **2.** *vi* HURRY to hurry up (*usually used in the imperative*) ○ *Come on, I haven't got all day!* **3.** *vi* USED TO ENCOURAGE SOMEBODY used to encourage somebody who is tired or unwilling (*usually used in the imperative*) ○ *Come on, you can do it if you try.* **4.** *vi* USED TO SHOW DISBELIEF used to tell somebody to stop exaggerating or lying (*usually used in the imperative*) ○ *Come on! You don't expect me to believe that, do you?* **5.** *vi* TO TELL SOMEBODY TO STOP PRETENDING used to tell somebody to drop a pretense or stop behaving in a superior way (*usually used in the imperative*) ○ *Come on! You know you can't afford that car.* **6.** *vt* APPEAR OR SPEAK ON BROADCAST MEDIUM to appear or speak on television or radio ○ *I noticed her voice when she came on the phone.* **7.** *vi* BEGIN AT SCHEDULED TIME to begin at a particular time (*refers to radio or television programs or a stage performer*) ○ *Her favorite show is coming on in an hour, and she never misses it.* **8.** *vi* DEVELOP GRADUALLY to develop gradually ○ *It grew chilly as night came on.* **9.** *vi* ADVANCE to move forward, especially in battle ○ *Our cannon fire tore huge holes in their ranks, but still they came on.* **10.** *vt* THEATER ENTER DURING PLAY to go onto the stage as part of the action ○ *The villain doesn't come on until Act 2.*

come on to *vt* to make sexual advances to somebody (*slang*)

come out *vi* **1.** BECOME KNOWN to be revealed ○ *The facts only came out when journalists began to dig a little deeper.* **2.** PUBL BE PUBLISHED to be published ○ *Her new novel is coming out next month.* **3.** DECLARE OPINION to state an opinion or judgment openly ○ *The majority came out in favor of raising the age limit.* **4.** REVEAL SECRET ABOUT YOURSELF to reveal to other people something about yourself that you have kept secret **5.** ACKNOWLEDGE SEXUALITY to declare openly that you are gay or lesbian **6.** HAVE FIRST SAME-SEX RELATIONSHIP to have your first sexual relationship with somebody of the same sex ○ *I think she came out when she was 17, with her best friend.* **7.** MAKE DEBUT IN SOCIETY to make a first appearance in society **8.** BE UTTERED to be uttered involuntarily or with an unintended effect ○ *We had no intention of revealing the story; it came out by accident.* **9.** BECOME VISIBLE IN SKY to become visible in the sky ○ *The sun came out from behind a cloud.* **10.** BE REMOVABLE to disappear after cleaning ○ *Even the toughest stains come out with this new detergent.* **11.** *UK* STRIKE to begin a strike ○ *The train drivers came out in sympathy.*

come out in *vt UK* to have something such as spots or a rash appear on the skin

come out of *vt* **1.** to survive a hazard or illness ○ *I'd say she came out of the ordeal in pretty good shape.* **2.** to be deducted from an amount of money ○ *The new window will have to come out of your allowance.*

come out with *vt* to say something surprising ○ *never know what children will come out with*

come over *v* **1.** *vi* to change an opinion or allegiance ○ *She says she'll come over if we guarantee her a seat on the board.* **2.** *vt* to affect or overcome somebody

come round *vi Can, UK* same as **come around**

come through *v* **1.** *vi* PERFORM WELL WHEN MOST NEEDED to supply something desperately needed at a critical moment (*informal*) ○ *They could always count on him to come through for them in difficult times.* **2.** *vt* SURVIVE to survive a dangerous or unpleasant experience **3.** *vi* BE RECEIVED to be received or heard, usually through a telecommunications medium **4.** *vt* MOVE THROUGH PLACE to move between one place and another ○ *The porch was so crowded, we had to come through the kitchen.* ○ *Coming through! Coming through! These plates are hot!*

come to *v* **1.** *vi* REGAIN CONSCIOUSNESS to regain consciousness or wake up ○ *The patient came to in the recovery room.* **2.** *vt* TOTAL to amount to a particular total **3.** *vi* NAUT SLOW DOWN OR STOP to slow down or stop (*refers to boats*)

come together *vi* **1.** to meet or gather together in one place **2.** to coalesce successfully from disparate parts ○ *It's all finally starting to come together.*

come under *vt* **1.** to be subjected to something ○ *She came under attack from members of her own party.* **2.** to be classified under a particular heading ○ *Hawthorne comes under American authors.*

come up *vi* **1.** EMERGE FROM WATER to rise to the surface of water ○ *She'll have to come up for air in a minute.* **2.** APPEAR ABOVE HORIZON to appear above the horizon ○ *I enjoy watching the sun come up.* **3.** BE MENTIONED to be mentioned or discussed ○ *a topic that came up in conversation* **4.** OCCUR UNEXPECTEDLY to happen unexpectedly ○ *I won't be able to make lunch; something's come up at work.* **5.** BE HAPPENING SOON to be going to happen in the near future ○ *Coming up next, the news.* **6.** APPEAR IN COURT to be tried in a court of law ○ *Her case comes up next week.* **7.** BE SELECTED AS WINNER to win a prize in a game involving luck ○ *if my numbers come up*

come up against *vt* to meet with something that has to be faced or dealt with ○ *He has come up against fierce criticism.*

come up for *vt* to become due for something ○ *The case is coming up for review.*

come upon *vt* to meet somebody or find something by chance

come up to *vt* to be as good as a particular standard or level ○ *His performance more than came up to expectations.*

come up with *vt* to produce or discover something, in response to a need or challenge ○ *She's come up with a brilliant solution.*

come·back /kúm bàk/ *n* **1.** a return to a successful position or activity ○ *Rumor has it that she's planning a comeback.* **2.** a sharp or witty reply ○ *He's always been one for the quick comeback.*

Com·e·con /kómmə kòn/, **COMECON** *n* an organization of the former Soviet Union and satellite Communist countries aimed at encouraging economic development. It existed between 1949 and 1991. Full form **Council for Mutual Economic Assistance**

co·me·di·an /kə meédee ən/ *n* **1.** COMIC ENTERTAINER an entertainer who amuses an audience with comedy **2.** COMIC ACTOR an actor who plays comic roles **3.** AMUSING PERSON somebody who is or tries to be amusing (*often ironic*) ○ *Some comedian put salt in the sugar bowl.* [Late 16C. < French *comédien* < *comédie* (see COMEDY)]

co·me·di·enne /kə meèdee én/ *n* **1.** WOMAN COMIC ENTERTAINER a woman entertainer who tells jokes **2.** COMIC ACTRESS a woman actor who takes comic roles **3.** AMUSING WOMAN a woman who is or tries to be amusing (*often ironic*) [Mid-19C. < French, form of *comédien* (see COMEDIAN)]

com·e·do /kòmmə dō/ (*plural* **com·e·do·nes** /-kòmmə dṓ neèz/) *n* MED same as **blackhead** (sense 1) (*technical*) [Mid-19C. < Latin, "glutton, worm" < *comedere* "devour" (see COMESTIBLE)]

com·e·do·gen·ic /kòmmədō jénnik/ *adj* tending to cause or aggravate blackheads

come·down /kúm dòwn/ *n* a decline in status or position (*informal*)

com·e·dy /kómmədee/ (*plural* **-dies**) *n* **1.** FUNNY PLAY, MOVIE, OR BOOK a play, movie, or book depicting amusing events **2.** COMIC GENRE comic works, especially plays, considered as a literary genre **3.** COMIC ENTERTAINMENT entertainment that is amusing **4.** COMIC ELEMENTS the humorous aspects of a situation or work of art [14C. Via French *comédie* < Greek *kōmōidia* < *kōmōidos* "comic actor" < *kōmos* "revel" + *aoidos* "singer" < *aeidein* "sing"] —**co·me·dic** /kə meédik/ *adj* —**co·med·i·cal·ly** *adv*

com·e·dy of er·rors *n* a ludicrous situation in which many mistakes are made and things go wrong

com·e·dy of man·ners *n* a comedy that satirizes the manners and customs of a section of society, especially fashionable society

come from a·way *n Can* a newcomer to the Atlantic region of Canada (*informal*)

come-hith·er *adj* sexually inviting or provocative (*humorous*) ○ *a come-hither look*

~~**comeing**~~ incorrect spelling of **coming**

come·ly /kúmmlee/ (**-li·er, -li·est**) *adj* describes a woman who is good-looking (*literary*) [13C. Probably shortening of obsolete *becomely* "becoming" < BECOME] —**come·li·ness** *n*

come-on *n* **1.** something that arouses interest or desire, e.g., a free gift intended to encourage purchasers (*informal*) **2.** a comment or action intended to indicate sexual interest in somebody

com·er /kúmmər/ *n* somebody or something that is likely to succeed (*informal*) ○ *In party power circles he's regarded as a real comer.*

co·mes·ti·ble /kə méstəb'l/ (*formal*) *n* something edible, usually a cooked food ■ *adj* fit for eating [15C. Via French < medieval Latin *comestibilis* < Latin *comestus*, past participle of *comedere* "eat completely" < *edere* "eat"]

comet: Hale-Bopp comet, photographed over Bulgaria (1997)

com·et /kómmət/ *n* an astronomical object that is composed of a mass of ice and dust and has a long luminous tail produced by vaporization when its orbit passes close to the Sun [12C. Directly or via French < Latin *(stella) cometa* "long-haired (star)" < Greek *(astēr) komētēs* < *komē* "hair of the head"] —**com·et·ar·y** *adj* —**co·met·ic** /kə méttik/ *adj*

come·up·pance /kum úppənss/ *n* something unpleasant, regarded as a just punishment for somebody (*informal*) ○ *He got his comeuppance in the end.* [Mid-19C. < *come up*, probably "be tried before a court"]

~~**comfertable**~~ incorrect spelling of **comfortable**

com·fit /kúmfit, kóm-/ *n* a candy consisting of a piece of fruit, a seed, or a nut in a sugar coating [14C.

Via French < Latin *confectum, confecta* < *confectus* (see CONFECT)]

com·fort /kúmfərt/ *n* 1. STATE OF BEING COMFORTABLE conditions in which somebody feels physically relaxed ○ *Enjoy the comfort of your own home.* 2. COMFORTABLE THING something that makes you feel physically relaxed (*often used in the plural*) ○ *the comforts of home* 3. RELIEF FROM PAIN relief from pain or anxiety ○ *They brought comfort to the wounded.* 4. SOMEBODY OR SOMETHING PROVIDING RELIEF somebody or something that provides relief from pain or anxiety ○ *The family has been such a comfort to me since my wife died.* ■ *vt* (**-fort·ed, -fort·ing, -forts**) 1. CHEER SOMEBODY to bring somebody relief from distress or anxiety ○ *The victim's parents were being comforted at home by relatives.* 2. MAKE SOMEBODY COMFORTABLE to make somebody feel pleasantly relaxed ○ *She was comforted by the warmth.* [12C. < Old French *confort* < late Latin *confortare* "strengthen completely" < Latin *fortis* "strong"]

com·fort·a·ble /kúmftəb'l, -fərtəb'l/ *adj* 1. RELAXED feeling comfort or ease ○ *Sit down and make yourselves comfortable.* 2. MAKING SOMEBODY RELAXED making somebody feel physically relaxed ○ *I changed into something more comfortable.* 3. NOT ANXIOUS free from stress or anxiety ○ *I don't feel comfortable with that idea.* 4. WITH ADEQUATE INCOME having enough income ○ *They're not what you'd call well-off, but they're certainly comfortable.* 5. ADEQUATE OR LARGE large enough to prevent anxiety or risk ○ *The candidate won by a comfortable majority.* 6. *UK* MED STABLE PHYSICALLY in a stable physical condition —**com·fort·a·ble·ness** *n*

com·fort·a·bly /kúmftəblee, kúmfərtəblee/ *adv* 1. AT EASE with a feeling of comfort or ease ○ *Are you sitting comfortably?* 2. WITHOUT PROBLEMS with enough of something to stave off worry, especially enough money to live on without worrying about providing essentials ○ *We can manage comfortably on what we earn together.* 3. *UK* EASILY by a large margin ○ *The home team won comfortably.*

com·fort·a·bly off *adj* having an adequate or more than adequate income ○ *They often complain that they can't afford luxuries, but in fact they're quite comfortably off.*

com·fort·er /kúmfərtər/ *n* 1. a warm quilt used as a bed covering 2. somebody who helps to relieve other people's grief or anxieties

Com·fort·er *n* CHR same as **Holy Spirit**

com·fort food *n* easily prepared unsophisticated food that is psychologically comforting, especially food that is high in carbohydrates (*informal*)

com·fort·ing /kúmfərting/ *adj* relieving anxiety or pain —**com·fort·ing·ly** *adv*

com·fort·less /kúmfərtləss/ *adj* affording no comfort ○ *a sterile, comfortless room* —**com·fort·less·ly** *adv* —**com·fort·less·ness** *n*

com·fort lev·el *n* the set of physical or psychological circumstances in which somebody feels most at ease and free from physical discomfort or stress (*informal*) ○ *the comfort level of knowing you have enough savings to meet emergencies*

com·fort sta·tion *n* a public toilet (*used euphemistically*)

com·fort zone *n* same as **comfort level**

com·frey /kúmfree/ *n* a plant with hairy leaves and stems. Flowers: pink, white, or blue, in clusters. Native to: Europe, Asia. Genus: *Symphytum*. [13C. Via Anglo-Norman, Old French < Latin *conferva* < *confervere* "heal," literally "boil together" < *fervere* (see FERVENT)]

com·fy /kúmfee/ (**-fi·er, -fi·est**) *adj* same as **comfortable** (senses 1–2) (*informal*) [Early 19C. Shortening]

com·ic /kómmik/ *adj* 1. FUNNY capable of inducing amusement, smiles or laughter 2. THEATER RELATING TO COMEDY relating to, characteristic of, or appearing in comedy ○ *a great comic routine* ■ *n* 1. ARTS COMEDIAN a comedian or comedienne ○ *worked as a nightclub comic* 2. *UK* PUBL same as **comic book** ■ **com·ics** *npl* COMIC STRIP SECTION the part of a newspaper that consists of comic strips [Late 16C. Via Latin < Greek *kōmikos* < *kōmos* "revel"]

SYNONYMS See *funny*.

com·i·cal /kómmik'l/ *adj* funny to the extent of being absurd, especially if unintentional ○ *comical facial expressions* —**com·i·cal·i·ty** /kòmmi kálləteе/ *n* —**com·i·cal·ly** *adv* —**com·i·cal·ness** *n*

SYNONYMS See *funny*.

com·ic book *n* a magazine that consists almost entirely of stories told in a series of colored panels in which balloons over the characters' heads provide dialogue and the thoughts of the characters

com·ic o·pe·ra *n* 1. an opera with a humorous plot and a happy ending 2. comic operas considered as a musical genre

com·ic re·lief *n* 1. LITERAT, THEATER FUNNY SECTION INSERTED IN SERIOUS WORK relief from tension, or a further heightening of tension by contrast, provided by a comic scene or passage inserted into a serious work 2. LITERAT, THEATER CHARACTERS PROVIDING COMIC INTERVALS a character or set of characters whose function is to provide intervals of comedy in a serious work 3. FUNNY INCIDENT WITHIN SERIOUS SITUATION occasion for laughter in the midst of a tense or serious situation

com·ic strip *n* a series of cartoons that tell a story or a joke

com·ing /kúmming/ *adj* 1. HAPPENING SOON about to happen or start ○ *In the coming election campaign you can expect a media barrage on TV.* 2. PROBABLY SUCCESSFUL likely to be successful in the near future ○ *She's the coming power in this company.* ■ *n* ARRIVAL the arrival of a person or an event

com·ing of age *n* 1. the reaching of the official age of adulthood and legal responsibility 2. the reaching of an advanced stage of development ○ *the coming of age of the computer*

com·ings and go·ings *npl* busy activity in which people arrive and depart frequently

Com·in·tern /kómmin tùrn/ *n* an international organization of Communist parties set up by Lenin in 1919 and abolished in 1943 [Early 20C. < Russian *Komintern* < *kommunisticheskii internatsional'nyi* "communist international"]

~~comission~~ incorrect spelling of **commission**

~~comitee~~ incorrect spelling of **committee**

com·i·ty of na·tions /kómmətee-/ *n* the mutual recognition among nations of one another's laws, customs, and institutions [< Latin *comitas* < *comis* "courteous"]

com·ix /kómmiks/ *npl* comic books and comic strips for an adult readership, especially those containing nudity and obscenity [Late 20C. Alteration of *comics*]

comm. *abbr* 1. COMM commerce 2. COMM commercial 3. commission 4. committee 5. POL commonwealth

com·ma /kómmə/ *n* 1. GRAM a punctuation mark (,) that represents a slight pause in a sentence or is used to separate words and figures in a list 2. MUSIC a short pause or interval in a piece of music 3. INSECTS same as **comma butterfly** [Late 16C. Via Latin < Greek *komma* "piece cut off" < *koptein* "to cut"]

USAGE *Commas* are used in pairs around text that adds extra information and that can be omitted without affecting the structure of the sentence: *He was staying with his sister, a piano teacher, in Paris. The plant, which thrives in acid soils, is grown for its scented foliage.* A comma may also follow a subordinate clause placed at the beginning of a sentence: *If I miss the train, I will be late for the meeting. Born in 1950, he spent his early childhood in Europe.* When commas are used to separate items in lists, the final comma (before and, or, or etc.) is optional: *We invited Sarah, Jack, Kate, and Tom. You can have coffee, tea, cold milk or hot chocolate. They sell books, paper, envelopes, stamps, etc.* Similarly, a series of adjectives used before a noun may or may not be separated by commas: *It was a long, slow, difficult process. She was wearing a long blue knitted scarf.* Commas may also be inserted at appropriate points to break up a lengthy complicated sentence, but it is often better and clearer to split the sentence up into smaller units. A comma should not, however, be used to separate a long subject from a verb: *The girl I used to know many years ago at school was now unrecognizable* (no comma between *school* and *was*). Never use a comma between sentences; this fault is known as a "comma splice."

com·ma but·ter·fly *n* an orange and brown butterfly that has a comma-shaped white mark on the underside of each hind wing. Latin name: *Polygonia calbum*.

Com·mack /kō mak, kó mak/ town in Suffolk County, New York, situated on central Long Island southeast of Huntington. Population: 36,124 (1996).

com·mand /kə mánd/ *n* 1. ORDER an order or instruction given by somebody in authority 2. CONTROL control over somebody or something that is gained by personal power or authority ○ *She sized up the situation and took command.* 3. THOROUGH KNOWLEDGE thorough knowledge of something, especially a language ○ *a fluent command of French* 4. COMPUT OPERATING INSTRUCTION TO COMPUTER an instruction to a computer to carry out an operation 5. MIL MILITARY CONTROL the ability to control an area militarily ○ *Our primary objective is to gain command of the high ground.* 6. MIL GROUP OF OFFICERS IN CONTROL a group of officers who control part of an army ○ *the enemy command* 7. MIL MILITARY GROUP WITH PARTICULAR FUNCTION a unit or units, an organization, or an entire area under the control of one person ■ *v* (**-mand·ed, -mand·ing, -mands**) 1. *vt* ORDER SOMEBODY to give somebody an order or instruction ○ *I command you to let these men go.* 2. *vt* BE ABLE TO OBTAIN SOMETHING to deserve or be entitled to something ○ *With your qualifications you can command a high salary.* 3. *vt* LOOK OVER SOMETHING to be in a position that has a wide view over something ○ *The observation deck commands a breathtaking view of San Francisco Bay.* 4. *vti* MIL HAVE AUTHORITY OVER SOMETHING to control a military unit or a specific area ○ *an officer who commands a special operations battalion* 5. *vt* MIL CONTROL OR DOMINATE AREA to control an area using military force ○ *a fort that commanded the single pass through steep mountains* [13C. Via Anglo-Norman *comaunder*, Old French *comander* < assumed late Latin *commandare* "enjoin strongly" < Latin *mandare* (see MANDATE)] —**com·mand·a·ble** *adj*

com·mand and con·trol *n* 1. a system that directs the course of a missile 2. a military commander's exercise of authority and direction of operations

com·man·dant /kòmmən dánt, -daánt/ *n* an officer in command of a military organization

Com·man·dant of the Ma·rine Corps *n* the highest-ranking officer in the US Marine Corps and its representative on the Joint Chiefs of Staff

com·mand e·con·o·my *n* an economy in which resources and business activity are controlled by the government

com·man·deer /kòmmən deér/ (**-deered, -deer·ing, -deers**) *vt* 1. SEIZE SOMETHING FOR MILITARY PURPOSES to take something from its owner for official or military purposes 2. TAKE SOMETHING OVER to take or use something, often by force 3. MIL FORCE SOMEBODY INTO MILITARY SERVICE to force somebody to serve in the armed forces [Early 19C. Via Afrikaans *kommandeer* < Dutch *kommanderen* "to command" < French *commander* (see COMMAND)]

com·mand·er /kə mándər/ *n* 1. MIL MILITARY OFFICER an officer commanding a military unit 2. NAVY NAVAL OR COAST GUARD RANK an officer in the US, Canadian, or British navies or the US Coast Guard of a rank above lieutenant commander 3. POLICE POLICE OFFICER IN CHARGE a police officer who leads a shift, precinct, or unit 4. MEMBER WITH HIGH RANK a high-ranking member of a knightly and fraternal order

com·mand·er in chief (*plural* **com·mand·ers in chief**) *n* an officer who has supreme command of military forces, in the United States, the president

Com·mand·er in Chief *n* used as an honorific title to denote the president of the United States, as commander of the nation's armed forces

com·mand·ing /kə mánding/ *adj* 1. IMPRESSIVE able to control or dominate ○ *a commanding presence* 2. OVERLOOKING looking out or over something from a high position ○ *a commanding view* 3. DOMINANT demonstrating clear superiority ○ *a commanding lead* —**com·mand·ing·ly** *adv*

com·mand·ing of·fi·cer *n* an officer in command of a military unit or establishment

com·mand key *n* 1. a computer key that gives commands to the computer, expanding the keyboard options 2. a key on a keyboard that causes a device to initiate a predefined action

com·mand-line *adj* using letters or words instead of codes to give instructions to a computer [Because such instructions are entered on one line after a particular character called the *command prompt*]

com·mand·ment /kə mándmənt/ *n* a command from God, especially one of the Ten Commandments

com·mand mod·ule *n* the part of a spacecraft that houses the controls and the crew's living quarters

com·man·do /kə mándō/ (*plural* **-dos** or **-does**) *n* 1. MIL **SPECIALLY TRAINED SOLDIER** a member of a military force specially trained to make dangerous raids 2. MIL **SPECIALLY TRAINED UNIT** a military unit made up of commandos 3. HIST, MIL **BOER FIGHTING UNIT** a force of Boer troops during the Boer War [Late 18C. < Portuguese, "raiding party" < *commandar* "to command"]

com·mand per·form·ance *n* a performance of a play or film given by command of a ruler or state

com·mand post *n* 1. a military headquarters for a command group and its officers during an operation 2. a temporary headquarters for a team of people involved in an operation

com·mand ser·geant ma·jor *n* a noncommissioned officer in the US Army of a rank above first sergeant and master sergeant

com·ma splice *n* the incorrect use of a comma instead of a conjunction to link two independent clauses

com·me·dia dell'arte /kə màydee ə də laártee/ *n* an Italian form of popular comedy developed during the 16th and 17th centuries, characterized by the use of stock characters and familiar plots [Late 19C. < Italian, literally "comedy of art"]

com·mem·o·rate /kə mémmə ràyt/ (**-rat·ed, -rat·ing, -rates**) *vt* 1. to honor the memory of somebody or something in a ceremony ○ *a service held to commemorate the dead* 2. to serve as a memorial to something [Mid-17C. < Latin *commemorat-*, past participle of *commemorare* "call to mind clearly" < *memorare* "remind" < *memor* "mindful"] —**com·mem·o·ra·tive** /-rətiv, -ràytiv/ *adj, n* —**com·mem·o·ra·tor** *n* —**com·mem·o·ra·to·ry** *adj*

com·mem·o·ra·tion /kə mèmmə ráysh'n/ *n* 1. a ceremony or religious service to commemorate a person or an event 2. the act of honoring the memory of a person or an event —**com·mem·o·ra·tion·al** *adj*

com·mence /kə ménss/ (**-menced, -menc·ing, -menc·es**) *vti* to begin happening, or begin something [14C. < Old French *com(m)encier* < Latin *initiare* (see INITIATE)] —**com·menc·er** *n*

com·mence·ment /kə ménssmənt/ *n* 1. the beginning of something (*formal*) ○ *the commencement of open hostilities* 2. a ceremony during which degrees and diplomas are conferred at high schools, colleges, and universities, or the day on which this ceremony takes place

com·mend /kəménd/ (**-mend·ed, -mend·ing, -mends**) *vt* 1. **PRAISE SOMEBODY OR SOMETHING** to praise somebody or something in a formal way ○ *She was commended for her bravery.* 2. **CAUSE SOMETHING TO BE ACCEPTABLE** to show something to possess worthwhile qualities ○ *The plan has much to commend it.* 3. **ENDORSE SOMEBODY OR SOMETHING** to endorse somebody or something as being worthy of approval ○ *I had no hesitation in commending her to them.* 4. **SURRENDER SOMEBODY OR SOMETHING FOR SAFEKEEPING** to entrust somebody, yourself, or your soul to somebody's safekeeping (*formal*) [14C. < Latin *commendare* "entrust completely" < *mandare* (see MANDATE)] —**com·mend·er** *n*

com·mend·a·ble /kə méndəb'l/ *adj* worthy of praise —**com·mend·a·ble·ness** *n* —**com·mend·a·bly** *adv*

com·men·da·tion /kòmmən dáysh'n/ *n* 1. praise of somebody's abilities 2. an award or citation given to somebody in recognition of an outstanding achievement —**com·men·da·to·ry** /kə méndə tàwree/ *adj*

com·men·sal /kə ménss'l/ *adj* describes a relationship between organisms of two different species in which one derives food or other benefits from the association while the other remains unharmed and unaffected [Late 19C. Directly or via French < medieval Latin *commensalis* "at table together" < Latin *mensa* "table"] —**com·men·sal** *n* —**com·men·sal·i·ty** /kò men sállətee/ *n* —**com·men·sal·ly** *adv*

com·men·sal·ism /kə ménsə lìzzəm/ *n* the relationship between organisms of two different species in which one derives food or other benefits from the association while the other remains unharmed and unaffected

com·men·su·ra·ble /kə ménssərəb'l, -ménshər-/ *adj* 1. **RELATED BY MEASUREMENT** related by virtue of sharing the same system of measurement or by being measurable using the same units 2. **COMMENSURATE** proportionate to something else (*formal*) ○ *His salary is commensurable to his ability.* 3. MATH **WITH COMMON FACTOR** divisible by the same unit an even number of times [Mid-16C. < late Latin *commensurabilis* "completely measurable" < *mensurabilis* (see MENSURABLE)] —**com·men·su·ra·bil·i·ty** /kə mènssərə bíllətee, -mènshərə-/ *n* —**com·men·su·ra·bly** *adv*

com·men·su·rate /kə ménssərət, -ménshərət/ *adj* 1. **EQUAL IN SIZE** of the same size or extent 2. **IN PROPORTION** appropriately proportionate ○ *The rewards will be commensurate with the efforts made.* 3. **MEASURED USING COMPATIBLE UNITS** describes units of measurement that belong to the same system such as feet and inches or centimeters and meters [Mid-17C. < late Latin *commensuratus*, literally "measured with" < Latin *mensura* "measure"] —**com·men·su·rate·ly** *adv* —**com·men·su·ra·tion** /kə mènssə ráysh'n, -mènshə-/ *n*

com·ment /kó mènt/ *n* 1. **REMARK** a remark that states a fact or expresses an opinion ○ *Comments are invited from all participants.* 2. **CRITICAL OBSERVATION** an implied or indirect judgment ○ *The film is a comment on the materialism of modern society.* 3. **DISCUSSION** written or spoken discussion, analysis, or criticism ○ *The incident attracted a great deal of press comment.* 4. **EXPLANATORY NOTE** a note that explains a passage in a text 5. COMPUT **NOTE EXPLAINING PROGRAM CODE** a note embedded in a computer program that describes how the following programming code works ■ *vti* (**-ment·ed, -ment·ing, -ments**) **MAKE COMMENT** to state a fact or give an opinion [14C. < Latin *commentum* "invention" < *comment-*, past participle of *comminisci* "invent," literally "think together"]

com·men·tar·i·at /kòmmən térree ət/ *n* print and broadcast media pundits regarded as a group [Late 20C. < COMMENTATOR after words such as PROLETARIAT, SECRETARIAT]

com·men·tar·y /kómmən tèrree/ *n* (*plural* **-ies**) 1. **SERIES OF EXPLANATORY NOTES** a series of notes explaining or interpreting a written text 2. **EXPLANATORY ESSAY** an essay or book that explains a text 3. **CLARIFICATION OF SITUATION** an example illustrating a situation 4. *UK* same as **play-by-play** ■ **com·men·tar·ies** *npl* **RECORD OF EVENTS** a record of events, usually written by somebody who participated in them —**com·men·tar·i·al** /kòmmən térree əl/ *adj*

com·men·tate /kómmən tàyt/ (**-tat·ed, -tat·ing, -tates**) *vi* 1. to provide a commentary, either in radio or television broadcasting or on texts 2. to comment on something in a way that explains or interprets it

com·men·ta·tor /kómmən tàyter/ *n* a reporter and analyst of the news for radio, television, or a newspaper

com·merce /kómmərss/ *n* 1. the large-scale buying and selling of goods and services 2. the study of the principles and practices of commerce [Direct or via French < Latin *commercium* "mutual trade"]

com·mer·cial /kə múrsh'l/ *adj* 1. **RELATING TO COMMERCE** relating to the buying and selling of goods or services 2. COMM **SUITABLE FOR TRADING** appropriate or sufficient for the purposes of trade 3. COMM **FOR INDUSTRIAL USE** produced in bulk for industrial use and often unrefined 4. COMM **DONE FOR PROFIT** done with the primary objective of making money ○ *a commercial venture* 5. COMM **PAID FOR WITH ADVERTISING** supported by revenue from advertising ○ *commercial radio* ■ *n* BROADCAST, COMM **ADVERTISEMENT ON RADIO OR TELEVISION** an advertisement broadcast on radio or television —**com·mer·ci·al·i·ty** /kə mùrshee állətee/ *n*

com·mer·cial art *n* graphic art produced for purposes such as advertising and packaging —**com·mer·cial art·ist** *n*

com·mer·cial bank *n* a bank whose primary business is providing financial services to companies

com·mer·cial break *n* an interval during a radio or television program for the purpose of broadcasting commercials

com·mer·cial col·lege *n* a college that teaches primarily business-related subjects

com·mer·cial·ese /kə mùrsh'l éez, -éess/ *n UK* the language or jargon used by people who work in business

com·mer·cial In·ter·net ex·change *n* E-COMMERCE a connection point between commercial Internet service providers (*used in e-commerce*)

com·mer·cial·ism /kə múrsh'l ìzzəm/ *n* 1. the principles and methods of commerce 2. excessive emphasis on profit-making —**com·mer·cial·ist** *n* —**com·mer·cial·is·tic** /kə mùrsh'l ístik/ *adj*

com·mer·cial·ize /kə múrsh'l ìz/ (**-ized, -iz·ing, -iz·es**) *vt* 1. to apply business principles to something or run it as a business 2. to exploit something for financial gain —**com·mer·cial·i·za·tion** /kə mùrsh'li záysh'n/ *n*

com·mer·cial·ly /kə múrsh'lee/ *adv* in commercial terms, or from a profit-making point of view

com·mer·cial pa·per *n* short-term debt obligations backed only by the good name of the company

com·mer·cial trav·e·ler *n* a traveling company sales representative (*dated*)

com·mer·cial ve·hi·cle *n* a road vehicle designed to transport goods or passengers

com·mess /kómmess/ *n Carib* 1. a commotion or confused situation 2. in Trinidad, any kind of scandal, conflict, or illegal behavior [Late 20C. Via French Creole < French *commerce* "business"]

com·mie /kómmee/, **com·my** (*plural* **-mies**) *n* POL same as **Communist** (*informal disapproving*) [Mid-20C. < COMMUNIST] —**com·mie** *adj*

com·mi·na·tion /kòmmi náysh'n/ *n* (*formal*) 1. a formal denunciation of somebody or something 2. a warning of punishment or vengeance, especially punishment by God [15C. < Latin *comminat-*, past participle of *comminari*, literally "threaten with" < *minari* (see MENACE)] —**com·min·a·to·ry** /kə mínnə tàwree/ *adj*

com·min·gle /kə míng g'l/ (**-gled, -gling, -gles**) *vti* to mix two or more things, or become mixed (*literary*)

com·mi·nute /kómmə nòot/ (**-nut·ed, -nut·ing, -nutes**) *v* 1. *vti* to break, or cause a bone to break, into small parts 2. *vt* to crush or grind something into a powder [Late 16C. < Latin *comminut-*, past participle of *comminuere* "lessen greatly" < *minuere* "lessen"] —**com·mi·nut·ed** *adj* —**com·mi·nu·tion** /kòmmə nóosh'n/ *n*

com·mi·nut·ed frac·ture /kómmə nootəd-/ *n* a fracture in which the bone is broken into fragments

com·mis·er·ate /kə mízzə ràyt/ (**-at·ed, -at·ing, -ates**) *vi* to express sympathy or sorrow [Late 16C. < Latin *commiserat-*, past participle of *commiserari*, literally "lament with" < *miser* "miserable"] —**com·mis·er·a·tive** *adj* —**com·mis·er·a·tive·ly** *adv*

com·mis·er·a·tion /kə mìzzə ráysh'n/ *n* a feeling of sympathy for and understanding of the troubles of somebody else ■ **com·mis·er·a·tions** *npl* expressions of sympathy or sorrow

com·mis·sar /kómmi saàr/ *n* 1. in the former Soviet Union, the chief minister in a government department 2. in the former Soviet Union, a Communist Party official, often attached to a military unit, responsible for providing political education [Early 20C. Via Russian *komissar* < medieval Latin *commissarius* "officer in charge" < Latin *commiss-*, past participle of *committere* (see COMMIT)] —**com·mis·sar·i·al** /kòmmi sérree əl/ *adj*

com·mis·sar·i·at /kòmmi sérree ət/ *n* 1. ARMY **ARMY SUPPLY DEPARTMENT** an army department responsible for organizing food and supplies 2. ARMY **ARMY SUPPLIES** food and other supplies given to soldiers 3. HIST, GOV **FORMER SOVIET GOVERNMENT DEPARTMENT** a government department in the former Soviet Union before 1946 [Late 16C. < assumed medieval Latin *commissariatus* < *commissarius* (see COMMISSAR)]

com·mis·sar·y /kómmi sèrree/ (*plural* **-ies**) *n* 1. **SUPERMARKET ON MILITARY BASE** a store that sells groceries and household supplies, especially one located on a military base **2.** RESTAURANT a cafeteria or restaurant, especially in a motion-picture or television studio **3.** REPRESENTATIVE a deputy or representative

com·mis·sion /kə mísh'n/ *n* **1.** FEE PAID TO AGENT a fee paid to an agent for providing a service, especially a percentage of the total amount of business transacted **2.** TASK a job or task given to a person or a group, especially an order to produce a particular product or piece of work **3.** GROUP WITH TASK a group of people authorized to carry out a duty **4.** AUTHORITY TO ACT AS AGENT the authority granted to a person or organization to act as an agent for another **5.** ACT OF COMMITTING SOMETHING the committing of something, especially a crime or other offense ○ *the commission of a crime* **6.** AUTHORITY OR INSTRUCTION the authority or an instruction to do something (*formal*) **7.** GOV GOVERNMENT GROUP a government agency that has judicial, administrative, or legislative powers **8.** MIL APPOINTMENT AS MILITARY OFFICER an appointment to the rank of officer in the armed forces, or a document conferring such a rank ■ *vt* (**-sioned, -sion·ing, -sions**) **1.** ASSIGN TASK TO SOMEBODY to assign a duty or task to somebody **2.** ORDER SOMETHING SPECIAL to place an order for something that must be specially made or created ○ *have commissioned a new architectural firm to design the building* **3.** START UP PROJECT to bring a new project or facility into operation **4.** MIL MAKE SOMEBODY OFFICER to confer the rank of officer on somebody in the armed forces **5.** NAUT EQUIP SHIP to bring a boat into active service [14C. Directly or via French < Latin *commission-* < *commiss-* (see COMMISSAR)] —**com·mis·sion·al** *adj* —**com·mis·sion·ar·y** *adj* ◇ **in commission 1.** in operational use or working order **2.** in active service, especially as a ship ◇ **on commission** with a percentage of the value of sales being full or partial payment for the work of selling ◇ **out of commission 1.** not in operational use or working order **2.** not in active service, especially as a ship

com·mis·sion·aire /kə mìshə nér/ *n* **1.** in the United Kingdom, a uniformed attendant or usher at a hotel or theater **2.** in Canada, a veteran of the armed forces who belongs to the Corps of Commissionaires, an organization whose uniformed members can be hired to protect buildings and property [Mid-17C. < medieval Latin *commissionarius* < Latin *commission-* (see COMMISSION)]

com·mis·sioned of·fi·cer /kə mìsh'nd-/ *n* an officer in the armed forces or in the US Coast Guard who is appointed by commission, of the rank of second lieutenant or ensign or above

com·mis·sion·er /kə mísh'nər/ *n* **1.** COMMISSION MEMBER a member of a commission **2.** SOMEBODY WORKING FOR COMMISSION somebody authorized by a commission to carry out prescribed duties or tasks **3.** GOV GOVERNMENT OFFICIAL a government representative in an administrative area **4.** PUBLIC ADMIN DEPARTMENT HEAD the head of a public service such as the police or fire department in a town or city **5.** SPORT EXECUTIVE the administrative head of a sport —**com·mis·sion·er·ship** *n*

com·mis·sion mer·chant *n* an agent who buys and sells goods for others and is paid on a commission-only basis

com·mis·sion plan *n* a system of local government in which an elected commission supervises the workings of a municipality's departments instead of the more common mayor or city council

com·mis·sure /kómmi shoǒr/ *n* **1.** ANAT PLACE WHERE CELLS OR ORGANS MEET a line or point where two cells, organs, or body parts meet or connect **2.** ANAT LINKING BAND OF NERVE TISSUE a band of nerve tissue that connects opposite sides of the central nervous system, e.g., the tissue connecting the left and right sides of the brain **3.** BOT PLACE WHERE PLANT PARTS JOIN a junction or seam between two organs or parts, e.g., that between the carpels of a flower [15C. < Latin *commissura* "juncture" < *commiss-* (see COMMISSAR)] —**com·mis·su·ral** /kə mísharəl/ *adj*

com·mit /kə mít/ (**-mit·ted, -mit·ting, -mits**) *v* **1.** *vi* PROMISE DEVOTION to pledge devotion or dedication to somebody or something ○ *He wasn't yet ready to commit to the relationship.* **2.** *vt* PROMISE RESOURCES to devote or pledge something such as time or money to an undertaking **3.** *vt* DO WRONG to do something wrong or illegal ○ *commit a felony* **4.** *vt* ENTRUST SOMETHING TO SOMEBODY to entrust something or somebody to somebody else for protection **5.** *vt* RECORD SOMETHING FOR FUTURE to consign or record something in order to preserve it ○ *committed the numbers to memory* **6.** *vt* ASSIGN SOMETHING FOR DESTRUCTION to give something over for destruction or disposal **7.** *vt* LAW, PSYCHIAT INSTITUTIONALIZE SOMEBODY to confine somebody legally to an institution, e.g., a prison or mental health facility **8.** *vt* POL REFER PROPOSED LAW FOR REVIEW to refer a bill to a legislative committee for review [14C. < Latin *committere* "put together" < *mittere* "put, send"] —**com·mit·ta·ble** *adj* —**com·mit·ter** *n*

~~**commitee**~~ incorrect spelling of **committee**

com·mit·ment /kə mítmənt/ *n* **1.** RESPONSIBILITY something that takes up time or energy, especially an obligation ○ *family commitments* **2.** LOYALTY devotion or dedication, e.g., to a cause, person, or relationship **3.** PREVIOUSLY PLANNED ENGAGEMENT a planned arrangement or activity that cannot be avoided **4.** POL REFERRAL OF BILL FOR REVIEW a referral of a bill to a legislative committee for review **5.** LAW, PSYCHIAT INSTITUTIONALIZING SOMEBODY an act of legally confining somebody to prison or a mental health facility **6.** LAW, CRIME COURT ORDER a written court order confining somebody to prison

com·mit·ment cer·e·mo·ny *n* a formal ceremony, officiated by a cleric or by a chosen friend, that affirms the partnership of a couple who cannot marry or who have chosen not to marry [Late 20C]

com·mit·tal /kə mítt'l/ *n* LAW same as **commitment** (sense 5)

com·mit·ted /kə míttəd/ *adj* devoted to somebody or something such as a cause or relationship —**com·mit·ted·ly** *adv*

com·mit·tee *n* **1.** /kə míttee/ a group of people appointed or chosen to perform a function on behalf of a larger group **2.** /kòmmi teé/ a person to whom something, e.g., the charge of somebody deemed incapable of looking after himself or herself, is committed (*archaic*)

com·mit·tee·man /kə mítteemən/ (*plural* **-men** /-mən/) *n* a man who is a member of one or more committees

com·mit·tee of the whole *n* the entire membership of a legislative body gathering as a whole to consider a matter informally

com·mit·tee per·son *n* somebody who is a member of one or more committees

com·mit·tee·wom·an /kə míttee wòǒmmən/ (*plural* **-wom·en** /-wìmmin/) *n* a woman who is a member of one or more committees

~~**committment**~~ incorrect spelling of **commitment**

com·mo /kómmō/ *n* COMMUNICATION same as **communication** (sense 1) (*informal; often used before a noun*)

com·mode /kə mṓd/ *n* **1.** CHAIR WITH CHAMBER POT a chair or box-shaped piece of furniture holding a chamber pot covered by a lid **2.** PORTABLE WASHSTAND a movable washstand with a cupboard underneath containing a chamber pot or washbasin **3.** DECORATED CABINET a low cabinet or chest of drawers, usually elaborately decorated **4.** CONSTR, HOUSEHOLD same as **toilet** (sense 1) [Late 17C. < French, originally "suitable" < Latin *commodus* "conforming with due measure" < *modus* (see MODE)]

com·mo·di·ous /kə mṓdee əss/ *adj* pleasantly spacious (*formal*) —**com·mo·di·ous·ly** *adv* —**com·mo·di·ous·ness** *n*

com·mod·i·ti·za·tion /kə mòddəti záysh'n/ *n* the process by which a product reaches a point in its development where one brand has no features that differentiate it from other brands, and consumers buy on price alone

com·mod·i·ty /kə móddətee/ (*plural* **-ties**) *n* **1.** an item that is bought and sold, especially an unprocessed material **2.** something that people value or find useful [15C. < Latin *commodus* (see COMMODE)]

com·mod·i·ty art *n* art that is not purely an expression of the artist's ideas, but is tailored in its subject matter and style to appeal to a specific commercial market

com·mo·dore /kómmə dàwr/ *n* **1.** NAVY NAVAL OFFICER a title for a very senior captain in the US Navy who is assigned command responsibilities generally lesser than those of a rear admiral but generally greater than those of a captain **2.** NAVY MERCHANT NAVY CAPTAIN a captain in command of a merchant fleet **3.** SAILING PRESIDENT OF YACHT CLUB the head of a yacht or boat club [Late 17C. Probably alteration of Dutch *komandeur* "commander" < French *commandeur* < Old French *comander* (see COMMAND)]

Com·mo·dus /kómmədəss/, **Lucius Aelius Aurelius** (161–192) Roman emperor (180–192). His reign of violence and despotism led to his eventual assassination.

com·mon /kómmən/ *adj* **1.** SHARED belonging to or shared by two or more people or groups ○ *working toward a common goal* ○ *a doctrine common to several religions* **2.** OF OR FOR ALL relating or belonging to the community as a whole ○ *an area of common land* **3.** EVERYDAY often occurring or frequently seen ○ *a common sight in cities* **4.** WIDELY FOUND describes a widely found species of plant or animal **5.** NON-SPECIALIST used by people who have no specialist knowledge ○ *The common name for "Viscum album" is "mistletoe."* **6.** GENERAL done, used, or held by most people ○ *common practice* **7.** ORDINARY without special privilege, rank, or status ○ *the common man* **8.** OF EXPECTED STANDARD of the standard that most people expect ○ *common courtesy* **9.** VULGAR considered to be ill-bred, or vulgar ○ *common behavior* **10.** MATH WITH EQUAL MATHEMATICAL RELATIONSHIP having an equal relationship to two or more mathematical entities **11.** LITERAT OF VARYING STRESS OR LENGTH describes a syllable that, in a line of poetry, can be either long or short, or stressed or unstressed **12.** CHR USEFUL FOR SEVERAL RELIGIOUS FESTIVALS capable of being used as a service for any of a number of similar religious festivals ■ *n* **1.** PIECE OF PUBLIC LAND an area of land available for anybody to use, e.g., as a public recreation area or, formerly, as pasture for cattle **2.** LAW RIGHT TO USE SOMEBODY'S LAND the legal right to use somebody else's land or waters in a particular way, usually for grazing or fishing **3.** CHR SERVICE FOR SEVERAL RELIGIOUS FESTIVALS a religious service that can be used for any of a number of similar festivals **4.** FIN same as **common stock** [13C. Via French < Latin *communis*] —**com·mon·ness** *n*

com·mon·age /kómmənij/ *n* **1.** RIGHT TO USE JOINTLY the legal right to use something, especially a pasture, in common with other people, or the use that is made of it **2.** PUBLIC OWNERSHIP OF LAND the status of something, usually land, that is publicly owned and available **3.** LAND FOR ALL TO USE land that is publicly owned and available **4.** POL same as **commonalty** (sense 1)

com·mon·al·i·ty /kòmmə nállətee/ (*plural* **-ties**) *n* **1.** the sharing of characteristics or qualities with other individuals **2.** a shared characteristic or quality **3.** POL same as **commonalty** (sense 1) [Late 16C. Alteration of COMMONALTY]

com·mon·al·ty /kómmən'ltee/ *n* **1.** the ordinary people as distinct from the upper classes, especially when considered as a political class **2.** a group or society or its membership (*takes a singular or plural verb*) [13C. Via French < medieval Latin *communalitas* < Latin *communis* "common"]

com·mon bile duct *n* the duct formed by the joining of the duct from the liver and that from the gall bladder

com·mon blue *n* a common butterfly, the male of which is blue and the female usually brown with orange markings. Native to: Europe. Latin name: *Polyommatus icarus.*

com·mon car·ri·er *n* **1.** a company in the business of transporting goods or passengers **2.** a company that provides telecommunications services to the general public, e.g., a telephone company

com·mon chord *n* a major or minor musical chord of three notes (**triad**) that contains a perfect fifth

com·mon cold *n* MED same as **cold** *n* (sense 1)

com·mon de·nom·i·na·tor *n* **1.** a whole number that can be divided exactly by the lower numbers (**denominators**) of two or more fractions. For example, 8 is a common denominator of $\frac{1}{4}$ and $\frac{1}{2}$. **2.** a shared belief or characteristic

com·mon dif·fer·ence *n* the difference between successive terms in an arithmetic series. For example, 3 is the common difference in the series 2, 5, 8, 11.

com·mon di·vi·sor *n* a number that two or more

other numbers can be divided by exactly. For example, 4 is a common divisor of 8, 12, and 20.

com·mon·er /kómmənər/ *n* an ordinary member of society who does not belong to the nobility

Com·mon E·ra *n* the period after the birth of Jesus Christ (*used in dates*)

USAGE See ***A.D.***

com·mon fac·tor *n UK* same as **common divisor**

com·mon frac·tion *n* MATH same as **simple fraction**

com·mon gen·der *n* **1.** in English, the gender of a noun that can refer to a person or animal of either sex, e.g., "leader" and "fox" **2.** in some languages, the gender of those nouns that can be either masculine or feminine but not neuter

com·mon good *n* the advantage or benefit of everyone

com·mon ground *n* something mutually agreed upon, especially as a basis for negotiation

com·mon knowl·edge *n* something that is generally known

com·mon law *n* the body of law developed as a result of custom and judicial decisions, as distinct from the law laid down by legislative assemblies. Common law forms the basis of all law that is applied in England and most of the United States.

com·mon-law *adj* **1.** LAW **WITHOUT OFFICIAL CEREMONY** describes a partner in a marriage that is recognized in some jurisdictions when both parties declare themselves married without an official ceremony **2. OF UNMARRIED COUPLE LIVING TOGETHER** describes a partner in a marriage so called because of the length of time the two unmarried people have lived together as husband and wife **3. OF COMMON LAW** based on or relating to common law

com·mon log·a·rithm *n* a logarithm with ten as its base number

com·mon loon *n* a large black-and-white diving bird. Native to: North America. Latin name: *Gavia immer*.

com·mon·ly /kómmənlee/ *adv* by most people or in most circumstances ○ *The measure was commonly held to be a success.*

com·mon mar·ket *n* an economic association established, typically between nations, with the objective of removing or reducing trade barriers

Com·mon Mar·ket *n* a term used in the 1960s and 1970s to refer to both the European Community and the European Economic Community (*dated*)

com·mon meas·ure *n* **1.** MUSIC same as **common time** **2.** LITERAT the stanza form used for ballads, with four iambic lines rhymed "abab" or "abac" **3.** MATH same as **common divisor**

com·mon me·ter *n* **1.** LITERAT same as **common measure** (sense 2) **2.** the verse form used in many hymns, consisting of four-line verses that alternate lines of eight and six syllables

com·mon mul·ti·ple *n* a number that can be divided exactly by two or more other numbers. For example, 12 is a common multiple of 2, 3, and 4.

com·mon noun *n* a noun that refers to any of a class of people or things, e.g., "singer" and "place," as distinct from a proper noun, e.g., "Lennon" or "Washington." Common nouns can be preceded by words that modify their meaning, e.g., "some" and "any."

com·mon·place /kómmən plàyss/ *adj* **1. EVERYDAY** encountered or happening often **2. DULL** uninteresting as a result of being unoriginal ■ *n* **1. DULL REMARK** an unoriginal remark **2. SOMETHING ORDINARY** something that occurs or is encountered often [Mid-16C. Ultimately translation of Greek *koinos topos* "general theme"] —**com·mon·place·ness** *n*

com·mon·place book *n* a personal notebook used for copying down quotations and memorable passages from other books

com·mon pleas *n* LAW same as **court of common pleas** (*takes a singular verb*)

com·mon pray·er, **Com·mon Pray·er** *n* standard prayers for public worship, especially in the Church of England, as recorded in the Book of Common Prayer

com·mon room *n* **1.** a lounge available to everyone living in a residential community or institution **2.** a sitting room in a college or university where staff or students can relax

com·mons /kómmənz/ *n* **1. COLLEGE DINING HALL** a dining hall in a college or university (*takes a singular verb*) **2.** *also* **Com·mons COMMON PEOPLE** the common people as distinct from the ruling classes (*takes a singular or plural verb*) ■ *npl* COMPUT **SHARED DATA STORE** data stored in the memory of one computer that is available to all computers linked to it by a network (*takes a plural verb*)

Com·mons *n* (*takes a singular or plural verb*) **1.** the politicians who are elected to the lower houses of the UK and Canadian parliaments and represent all the people **2.** GOV same as **House of Commons**

com·mon salt *n* FOOD same as **salt** (sense 1)

com·mon school *n* a public elementary school

com·mon sense *n* sound practical judgment derived from experience rather than study

com·mon·sense /kòmmən sénss/ *adj* based on common sense —**com·mon·sen·si·cal** *adj* —**com·mon·sen·si·cal·ly** *adv*

com·mon stock *n* stock that entitles the holder to a dividend in line with the company's profits, as distinct from preferred stock that gives the holder priority when dividends are paid

com·mon time *n* a musical meter with four quarter notes to the measure, commonly referred to as four-four time

com·mon touch *n* the ability of a celebrity or somebody in public life to behave toward members of the general public in a naturally friendly, informal, and uncondescending way

com·mon·wealth /kómmən wèlth/ *n* **1. NATION OR ITS PEOPLE** a nation or its people considered as a political entity **2. REPUBLIC** a nation or state in which the people govern **3. ASSOCIATION OF STATES** a group of states that have formed an association for the political and economic benefit of all members **4. PEOPLE WITH COMMON INTEREST** a group of people linked by something that they all have in common

Com·mon·wealth *n* **1. TERRITORY ASSOCIATED WITH UNITED STATES** a self-governing territory voluntarily associated with the United States. Puerto Rico and the Northern Mariana Islands are Commonwealths. **2. TITLE FOR SOME STATES** an official title used by the states of Kentucky, Massachusetts, Pennsylvania, and Virginia **3. ASSOCIATION OF BRITAIN AND SOVEREIGN STATES** a political, educational, and development association of sovereign states, most of which are former British colonies, with the British monarch as its head **4.** POL **FEDERATED STATES OF AUSTRALIA** the official designation of the federated states of Australia, often used to refer to the federal government as opposed to the state governments **5.** HIST **REPUBLIC IN 17C ENGLAND** the state and republican government in England from the death of Charles I in 1649 until the restoration of the monarchy in 1660

Com·mon·wealth Day *n* a holiday in some countries of the British Commonwealth. Date: second Monday in March.

Com·mon·wealth Games *npl* a sports contest held every four years involving participants from countries of the British Commonwealth

Com·mon·wealth of In·de·pen·dent States *n* an association formed in 1991 by most of the republics of the former Soviet Union, with ceremonial headquarters in Minsk, Belarus

Com·mon·wealth of Na·tions *n* POL same as **Commonwealth** (sense 3)

com·mon year *n* an ordinary year of 365 days, as distinct from a leap year

com·mo·tion /kə mṓsh'n/ *n* a scene of noisy confusion or activity [14C. < Latin *commotion-* "intensive motion" < *motion-* (see MOTION)] —**com·mo·tion·al** *adj*

comms /komz/ *npl UK* communications, especially for moving troops and supplies (*informal*) [Shortening]

com·mu·nal /kə myo͞on'l, kómmyən'l/ *adj* **1. SHARED** used or owned by all members of a group or community **2. OF COMMUNITIES** relating to communities or to living in communities **3. OF COMMUNE** belonging or relating to a commune **4. RELATING TO DIFFERENT SOCIAL GROUPS** relating to or involving different groups within a society [Early 19C. < late Latin *communalis* < Latin *communis* "common"] —**com·mu·nal·ly** *adv*

com·mu·nal be·reave·ment *n* the phenomenon of widespread distress, e.g., insomnia, depression, and greater susceptibility to heart attacks, seen following a high-profile tragedy among people who have never met those who have died in it

com·mu·nal·ism /kə myo͞on'l ìzzəm/ *n* **1.** the principles and practices of communal living or ownership, or support for a communal society **2.** a greater loyalty to an ethnic or religious group than to society in general —**com·mu·nal·ist** *n* —**com·mu·nal·is·tic** /kə myo͞on'l ístik/ *adj*

com·mu·nal·i·ty /kòmmyə nálləteе/ *n* **1.** shared use or ownership **2.** the spirit of cooperation and solidarity that exists among members of a community or commune

com·mu·nal·ize /kə myo͞on'l ìz, kómmyən'l ìz/ (**-ized, -iz·ing, -iz·es**) *vt* to put something into joint ownership among the members of a community

com·mu·nard /kómmyə naárd/ *n* somebody living in a commune [Late 19C. < French < *commune* (see COMMUNE[1])]

Com·mu·nard *n* a member or supporter of the Paris Commune of 1871

com·mune[1] /kóm yo͞on/ *n* **1. COMMUNAL GROUP** a mutually supportive community in which possessions and responsibilities are shared **2. PEOPLE LIVING IN COMMUNE** a group of families or individual people living in a commune **3. SMALL ADMINISTRATIVE DISTRICT** the smallest administrative district of some countries such as France, Italy, and Switzerland, governed by a mayor and a council [Late 17C. Via French < medieval Latin *communia* < Latin *communis* "common"]

com·mune[2] /kə myo͞on/ (**-muned, -mun·ing, -munes**) *vi* to experience a deep emotional or spiritual relationship with something ○ *communing with nature* [14C. < Old French *comuner* "to share" < *comun* "common" < Latin *communis*]

Com·mune /kóm yo͞on/ *n* the insurrectionary committee that governed Paris at the height of the French Revolution in 1792, originally the driving force behind the executions of members of the previous ruling classes. More moderate forces gradually gained control and by 1795 it had been suppressed.

com·mu·ni·ca·ble /kə myo͞onikəb'l/ *adj* **1.** able to be passed from one person, animal, or organism to another ○ *a communicable disease* **2.** easily communicated, or capable of being communicated [14C. < late Latin *communicabilis* < Latin *communicare* (see COMMUNICATE)] —**com·mu·ni·ca·bil·i·ty** /kə myo͞onikə bíllәteе/ *n* —**com·mu·ni·ca·bly** *adv*

com·mu·ni·cant /kə myo͞onikənt/ *n* **1.** somebody who receives the Christian sacrament of Communion **2.** somebody or something that provides information [15C. < Latin *communicant-*, present participle of *communicare* (see COMMUNICATE)]

com·mu·ni·cate /kə myo͞oni kàyt/ (**-cat·ed, -cat·ing, -cates**) *v* **1.** *vti* **EXCHANGE INFORMATION** to give or exchange information, e.g., by speech or writing ○ *We communicate by e-mail.* **2.** *vt* **CONVEY FEELING OR THOUGHT** to transmit or reveal a feeling or thought by speech, writing, or gesture so that it is clearly understood **3.** *vi* **UNDERSTAND ONE ANOTHER** to share a good personal understanding ○ *siblings who never really communicate* **4.** *vi* **HAVE COMMON ACCESS** to be connected or provide access to each other **5.** *vt* MED **TRANSMIT DISEASE** to pass a disease or infection on to somebody **6.** *vi* CHR **GIVE OR RECEIVE COMMUNION** to give or receive the Christian sacrament of Communion [Early 16C. < Latin *communicat-*, past participle of *communicare* "share" < *communis* "common"] —**com·mu·ni·ca·tor** *n* —**com·mu·ni·ca·tor·y** /-kə tàwree/ *adj*

com·mu·ni·ca·tion /kə myo͞oni káysh'n/ *n* **1. EXCHANGE OF INFORMATION** the exchange of information between people, e.g., by means of speaking, writing, or using a common system of signs or behavior **2. MESSAGE** a spoken or written message **3. ACT OF COMMUNICATING** the communicating of information **4. RAPPORT** a sense of mutual understanding and sympathy **5. ACCESS** a means of access or communication, e.g., a connecting door —**com·mu·ni·ca·tion·al** *adj*

com·mu·ni·ca·tion cord *n UK* same as **emergency cord**

com·mu·ni·ca·tions /kə myōōni káysh'nz/ *n* **STUDY OF HUMAN COMMUNICATION** the study of the different means people use to communicate with each other, e.g., by gesture, speech, telecommunications, and writing (*takes a singular or plural verb*) ■ *npl* **1. SYSTEMS FOR COMMUNICATING** the technology and systems used for sending and receiving messages, e.g., postal and telephone networks **2.** MIL **TRANSPORTATION OF TROOPS** a system of routes and transportation for moving troops and supplies

com·mu·ni·ca·tions sat·el·lite *n* an artificial satellite used to relay data such as radio, telephone, and television signals around the world. Signals may be reflected, but more often they are strengthened using a solar-powered transponder. Satellites often follow a geostationary orbit, remaining in the same position relative to Earth.

com·mu·ni·ca·tion the·o·ry, com·mu·ni·ca·tions the·o·ry *n* the study of all forms of human communication, including branches of linguistics such as semantics as well as telecommunications and other nonlinguistic forms

com·mu·ni·ca·tive /kə myōōni kàytiv/ *adj* **1. TALKATIVE** inclined or ready to talk **2. OF COMMUNICATION** relating to communication or to systems for communication **3.** EDUC **STRESSING PRACTICAL COMMUNICATION** in foreign language teaching, stressing the importance of language as a tool for communicating information and ideas —**com·mu·ni·ca·tive·ly** *adv* —**com·mu·ni·ca·tive·ness** *n*

com·mun·ion /kə myōōnyən/ *n* **1. INTIMACY** a feeling of emotional or spiritual closeness **2. CONNECTION** a relationship, especially one in which something is communicated or shared ○ *What communion can there be between Good and Evil?* ○ *continues to work in communion with the Church to help the needy* **3.** CHR **RELIGIOUS GROUP WITH COMMON FAITH** a religious group with its own set of beliefs and practices, especially a Christian denomination **4.** CHR **FELLOWSHIP BETWEEN RELIGIOUS GROUPS** a sense of shared religious identity and fellowship, especially between members of different Christian denominations [14C. < Latin *communion-* < *communis* "common"] —**com·mu·nion·al** *adj*—**com·mu·nion·al·ly** *adv*

Com·mu·nion *n* **1. CHRISTIAN SACRAMENT** a Christian sacrament that commemorates Jesus Christ's Last Supper, with the priest or minister consecrating bread and wine that is consumed by the congregation **2. COMMUNION SERVICE** the service containing the sacrament of Communion **3. CONSECRATED BREAD AND WINE** the consecrated bread and wine received by worshipers at a Communion service

com·mu·ni·qué /kə myōōni káy, kə myōōni kày/ *n* an official announcement, especially to the press or public [Mid-19C. < French past participle of *communiquer* "communicate" < Latin *communicare* (see COMMUNICATE)]

com·mu·nism /kómmyə nìzzəm/ *n* the political theory or system in which all property and wealth is owned in a classless society by all the members of that society [Mid-19C. < French *communisme* < *commun* "common" < Latin *communis*]

Com·mu·nism *n* **1.** the Marxist-Leninist version of a classless society in which capitalism is overthrown by a working-class revolution that gives ownership and control of wealth and property to the state **2.** any system of government in which a single, usually totalitarian, party holds power, and the state controls the economy

Com·mu·nism Peak /kómmyə nizzəm-/ former name for **Ismail Samani Peak**

com·mu·nist /kómmyənist/ *n* **1.** an advocate or supporter of any type of communism **2.** a participant in communal living [Mid-19C. < French *communiste* < *commun* (see COMMUNISM)] —**com·mu·nist** *adj* —**com·mu·nist·ic** /kòmmyə nístik/ *adj*

Com·mu·nist *n* a supporter of Communism or a member of an organization that supports or practices Communism —**Com·mu·nist** *adj*

com·mu·ni·tar·i·an /kə myōōni térree ən/ *n* a member or supporter of a collectivist or cooperative community or system [Mid-19C. < COMMUNITY] —**com·mu·ni·tar·i·an** *adj* —**com·mu·ni·tar·i·an·ism** *n*

com·mu·ni·ty /kə myōōnətee/ (*plural* **-ties**) *n* **1. PEOPLE IN AREA** a group of people who live in the same area, or the area in which they live ○ *a close-knit fishing community* **2. PEOPLE WITH COMMON BACKGROUND** a group of people with a common background or with shared interests within society ○ *the financial community* **3. NATIONS WITH COMMON HISTORY** a group of nations with a common history or common economic or political interests ○ *the international community* **4. SOCIETY** the public or society in general ○ *a useful member of the community* **5. INTERACTING PLANTS AND ANIMALS** all the plants and animals that live in the same area and interact with one another **6.** ONLINE same as **virtual community** [14C. Via Old French *communeté* < Latin *communitat-* < *communis* "common"]

com·mu·ni·ty an·ten·na tel·e·vi·sion *n* MEDIA same as **cable television**

com·mu·ni·ty cen·ter *n* a building used for a range of community activities

com·mu·ni·ty chest *n* a fund raised by voluntary contributions for local charities and social welfare activities (*dated*)

com·mu·ni·ty col·lege *n* in Canada or the United States, a nonresidential college usually supported by the government offering two-year or three-year courses and awarding diplomas or associate degrees

com·mu·ni·ty home *n* a home provided by a local government or voluntary organization for children who cannot live with relatives or foster parents

com·mu·ni·ty med·i·cine *n* the branch of medicine devoted to the provision of public health care

com·mu·ni·ty nurse *n UK* an experienced nurse with extra training who visits patients in their homes

com·mu·ni·ty of in·ter·est *n* a group of diverse people or organizations with a shared concern who have united to campaign for a common cause

com·mu·ni·ty po·lic·ing *n* policing that seeks to integrate officers into the local community in order to reduce crime and foster good community relations

com·mu·ni·ty prop·er·ty *n* property regarded by law as being jointly owned by husband and wife

com·mu·ni·ty reef *n* a cement undersea burial vault containing cremated remains, used as an alternative to traditional burial at sea

com·mu·ni·ty re·la·tions *npl* **1.** the relationships between different cultural, ethnic, political, or religious groups who live in an area and may come into conflict **2.** mediation between different cultural, ethnic, political, or religious groups living in an area

com·mu·ni·ty ser·vice *n* a penalty requiring that an offender convicted of a relatively minor crime do unpaid work that is beneficial to the community as an alternative to imprisonment

com·mu·nize /kómmyə nīz/ (**-nized, -niz·ing, -niz·es**) *vt* **1.** to transfer something such as land or property from private to public ownership **2.** to apply communist principles of organization to a government or people [Late 19C. < Latin *communis* "common"] —**com·mu·ni·za·tion** /kòmmyəni záysh'n/ *n*

com·mu·tate /kómmyə tàyt/ (**-tat·ed, -tat·ing, -tates**) *vt* to convert alternating electric current to direct current or vice versa

com·mu·ta·tion /kòmmyə táysh'n/ *n* **1.** LAW **REDUCTION IN SEVERITY OF LEGAL PENALTY** the reduction of a prison sentence or other legal penalty to a less severe one **2.** TRANSP **COMMUTER'S TRAVEL** the traveling undertaken by a commuter **3.** ELEC **CONVERSION OF ELECTRIC CURRENT** the converting of an electric current from alternating to direct current or vice versa **4. CONVERSION** an exchange or substitution, e.g., the substitution of one kind of payment for another (*formal*)

com·mu·ta·tion tick·et *n* a passenger ticket valid for multiple trips over a given route during a limited period, sold for less than the total cost of tickets purchased separately for each trip

com·mu·ta·tive /kómmyə tàytiv, kə myōōtətiv/ *adj* **1.** involving or relating to exchanges or substitutions **2.** in mathematics or logic, giving the same result irrespective of the order in which two or more terms or quantities are placed. Addition and multiplication are commutative processes, while subtraction and division are not. —**com·mu·ta·tive·ly** *adv* —**com·mu·ta·tiv·i·ty** /kə myōōtə tívvətee/ *n*

com·mu·ta·tor /kómmyə tàytər/ *n* a device that maintains the direction of flow of electric current in a generator or reverses it in an electric motor

com·mute /kə myōōt/ (**-mut·ed, -mut·ing, -mutes**) *v* **1.** *vi* **TRAVEL REGULARLY BETWEEN PLACES** to travel regularly from one place to another, especially between home and work **2.** *vti* **REPLACE WITH SOMETHING ELSE** to be changed or substituted, or change or substitute one thing for another, e.g., one form of payment for another **3.** *vi* **BE REPLACEMENT** to compensate or act as a substitute **4.** *vt* LAW **REDUCE SEVERITY OF PENALTY** to reduce a legal sentence to a less severe one **5.** *vt* ELEC same as **commutate 6.** *vi* MATH **GIVE SAME RESULT WITH DIFFERENT ORDER** to give the same mathematical result irrespective of the order in which two or more quantities are placed, as in addition but not subtraction [15C. < Latin *commutare* "change altogether" < *mutare* "to change"] —**com·mut·a·ble** *adj*

com·mut·er /kə myōōtər/ *n* **1.** somebody who travels regularly between places, especially between home and work **2.** an airline that provides short flights between major cities

com·my *n* POL another spelling of **commie** (*informal disapproving*)

Co·mo /kṓmō/ resort city and capital of Como Province, Lombardy, northern Italy, on the southwestern shore of Lake Como. Population: 78,680 (2001).

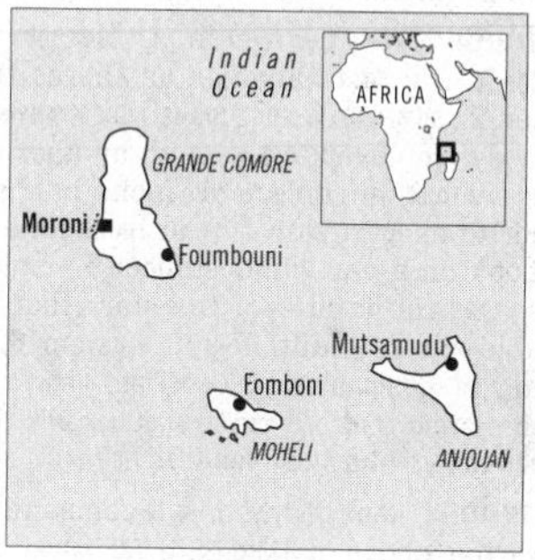

Comoros

Com·o·ros /kómmə rṑz, kə máw rṑz/ an independent state consisting of a group of islands in the Indian Ocean, 180 mi./290 km from Mozambique and 200 mi./320 km from Madagascar. Language: French, Arabic. Currency: Comorian Franc. Capital: Moroni. Population: 632,948 (2003). Area: 719 sq. mi./1,862 sq. km. Official name **Federal Islamic Republic of the Comoros** —**Com·o·ri·an** /kə máwree ən/ *n, adj*

comp[1] /komp/ (*informal*) *n* **SOMETHING FREE** something supplied free of charge e.g., a complimentary theater ticket ■ *adj* **FREE** complimentary or free of charge ○ *a comp copy of the new book* ■ *vt* (**comped, comp·ing, comps**) **GIVE SOMEBODY COMP** to supply somebody with something that is complimentary or free [Late 19C. Shortening of COMPLIMENTARY]

comp[2] /komp/ (*informal*) *n* an accompaniment, especially a jazz accompaniment played on piano or guitar ■ *vti* (**comped, comp·ing, comps**) to play a musical accompaniment, especially in jazz, on piano or guitar [Mid-20C. Shortening of ACCOMPANIMENT]

comp[3] /komp/ *n* HR same as **compensation** (*informal*) [Late 20C. Shortening]

comp. *abbr* **1.** companion **2.** GRAM comparative **3.** compare **4.** HR compensation **5.** COMPUT compilation **6.** COMPUT compiled **7.** complete **8.** MUSIC composer **9.** MATH, BOT composite **10.** composition **11.** CHEM, LING compound **12.** comprehensive **13.** comprising

com·pact[1] *adj* /kəm pákt, kóm pàkt/ **1. SMALL AND EFFICIENTLY ARRANGED** small, with efficient use of available space **2. PACKED TIGHTLY** closely clustered or packed together ○ *a compact bundle of papers* **3. SHORT AND STURDY** short and stocky **4. CONCISE** brief and concise

■ *vti* /kəm pákt/ (**-pact·ed, -pact·ed** or **-pact, -pact·ing, -pacts**) **PACK SOMETHING TIGHTLY** to become, or make something, more dense or firmly packed ■ *n* /kóm pàkt/ **1.** COSMETICS **CASE FOR MAKEUP** a small flat case containing makeup, usually face powder, with a mirror inside the lid **2. SMALLISH CAR** a medium-sized car that is economical to run [14C. < Latin *compactus*, past participle of *compingere* "fasten together" < *pangere* "fasten"] —**com·pact·i·ble** *adj* —**com·pact·ly** *adv* —**com·pact·ness** *n*

com·pact[2] /kóm pàkt/ *n* an agreement between two or more individuals or entities [Late 16C. < Latin *compactum* < past participle of *compacisci* "make an agreement together" < *pacisci* (see PACT)]

com·pact disk, **com·pact disc** *n* a hard plastic disk approximately 4 in./12 cm in diameter on which information such as music or computer data is digitally encoded in a format readable by laser beam

com·pact disk play·er *n* a machine for playing compact disks

com·pact·er *n* HOUSEHOLD another spelling of **compactor**

com·pac·tion /kəm páksh'n/ *n* **1.** the compression of particles to make a dense mass, or the compressed state of the resulting mass **2.** a process in the formation of sedimentary rock in which pressure from overlying sediment forces water from unconsolidated sediment, reducing its volume and yielding solid rock

com·pac·tor /kəm páktər, kóm pàktər/, **com·pact·er** *n* a machine used in the home to compress garbage into small bundles for easy disposal

com·pad·re /kom paá dray/ *n Hispanic* a godfather or close male friend [Mid-19C. < Spanish]

com·pan·ion[1] /kəm pánnyən/ *n* **1. SOMEBODY TO BE WITH** somebody who accompanies or shares time with another **2. SOMEBODY WHOSE JOB IS ACCOMPANYING ANOTHER** somebody employed to live with another person **3. MATCHING ARTICLE** an object or item that goes with another to make a pair **4.** PUBL **HANDBOOK** a guide or handbook on a particular subject **5.** ASTRON **FAINTER OF TWO STARS** the fainter of the stars that make up a double-star or multiple-star system **6.** another spelling of **Companion** [13C. < late Latin *companion-* "somebody who shares bread" < Latin *panis* "bread"] —**com·pan·ion** *vt* —**com·pan·ion·less** *adj*

com·pan·ion[2] /kəm pánnyən/ *n* a companionway, or a covering above it [Mid-18C. Alteration of obsolete Dutch *kompanje* "quarterdeck" < Italian *compagna* "(storeroom for) provisions," < Latin *panis* "bread"]

Com·pan·ion *n* the lowest-ranking member in a British order of knighthood

com·pan·ion·a·ble /kəm pánnyənəb'l/ *adj* friendly, sociable, and good company ○ *They sat in a companionable silence.* —**com·pan·ion·a·ble·ness** *n* —**com·pan·ion·a·bly** *adv*

com·pan·ion a·ni·mal *n* an animal kept for companionship and enjoyment

com·pan·ion·ate /kəm pánnyənət/ *adj* **1.** appropriate for a companion **2.** right for each other

com·pan·ion·ate mar·riage *n* marriage based on mutual affection and shared interests as opposed to purely economic or dynastic considerations

com·pan·ion cell *n* in flowering plants, a cell that lies alongside a sap-conducting sieve-tube element, whose function it is thought to influence. Companion cells have a prominent nucleus and dense cytoplasm, and form fine cytoplasmic connections (**plasmodesmata**) with the adjacent sieve-tube element.

com·pan·ion piece *n* a work, especially of music or literature, that is closely related to another, often by the same composer or author

com·pan·ion·ship /kəm pánnyən shìp/ *n* **1.** the company of friends and the relationship that exists between them **2.** an organized group of people

com·pan·ion·way /kəm pánnyən wày/ *n* a stairway or ladder between decks on a ship

com·pa·ny /kúmpənee/ (*plural* **-nies**) *n* **1.** BUSINESS **BUSINESS** a business enterprise **2. STATE OF BEING TOGETHER** the state of being with other people ○ *He didn't feel at ease in company.* **3. GROUP** a gathering of people **4. COMPANIONS** the people that somebody associates with **5. PARTICULAR TYPE OF COMPANION** somebody seen as providing a particular type of companionship ○ *He can be very good company.* **6. GUEST** a guest or visitor, especially for a meal or overnight stay ○ *We're having company this weekend.* **7.** BUSINESS **BUSINESS PARTNERS** the partners of a business enterprise whose names are not included in the firm's title **8.** ARTS **TROUPE** a group of performing artists such as actors **9.** MIL **GROUP OF TROOPS** a unit of soldiers, usually consisting of two or more platoons **10.** NAVY, NAUT **SHIP'S CREW** the crew and officers of a ship **11. FIREFIGHTERS** a unit of firefighters **12.** BUSINESS, HIST **TRADE GUILD** a medieval trade guild [13C. < Anglo-Norman *compainie* < late Latin *companion-* (see COMPANION[1])]

com·pa·ny car *n* a car owned or leased by a business for use by an employee, often as a fringe benefit

com·pa·ny-grade of·fi·cer *n* MIL same as **company officer**

com·pa·ny man *n* an employee who puts loyalty to an employer before friendship or personal beliefs (*disapproving*)

com·pa·ny of·fi·cer *n* a commissioned officer who holds the rank of captain or below

com·pa·ny town *n* a town whose residents depend on a single business for employment, housing, and shops

com·pa·ny un·ion *n* a labor union established within a company, not affiliated with any national union, and often dominated by the company's management rather than by its membership

compar. *abbr* GRAM comparative

com·pa·ra·ble /kómpərəb'l, kəm párrəb'l/ *adj* **1.** similar enough for a fair comparison to be made ○ *We ate a meal comparable with that of the finest restaurant.* **2.** as good as another or each other ○ *They both have comparable skills.* —**com·pa·ra·bil·i·ty** /kòmpərə bíllətee/ *n* —**com·pa·ra·ble·ness** *n* —**com·pa·ra·bly** *adv*

USAGE comparable to or **comparable with**? ***Comparable*** mimics the verb *compare* in being followed either by *to* or *with*, depending in careful usage on whether unlike or like things are being considered: *The agency provides a service comparable to that of a good library. The hurricane was comparable with the ones that recently hit Florida and Louisiana.*

USAGE See also ***compare***.

com·par·a·tist /kəm párrətist/ *n* somebody who uses a comparative method, e.g., in the study of linguistics [Mid-20C. < French *comparatiste*, < *comparatif* "comparative"]

com·par·a·tive /kəm párrətiv/ *adj* **1. COMPARED WITH OTHERS** considered relative to something known, mentioned, or expected ○ *He passed the test with comparative ease.* **2. INVOLVING COMPARISONS** based on or using comparisons of different things in the investigation of something ○ *comparative linguistics* **3.** GRAM **IN FORM EXPRESSING INCREASE** describes the form of an adjective or adverb that expresses an increase in quality, quantity, or degree, e.g., "quicker" or "more importantly" ■ *n* GRAM **COMPARATIVE FORM OF WORD** a comparative form of an adjective or adverb [15C. < Latin *comparat-*, past participle of *comparare* (see COMPARE)] —**com·par·a·tive·ness** *n*

com·par·a·tive·ly /kəm párrətivlee/ *adv* in comparison with something else ○ *The costs were comparatively high.*

com·pa·ra·tor /kómpə ràytər, kəm párrətər/ *n* **1.** an instrument used for comparing properties such as color or shape of a system or object with those of a standard **2.** a circuit used for comparing the difference between two electronic signals

com·pare /kəm páir/ *v* (**-pared, -par·ing, -pares**) **1.** *vt* **EXAMINE PEOPLE OR THINGS FOR SIMILARITIES** to examine two or more people or things in order to discover similarities and differences between them **2.** *vt* **LIKEN SOMEBODY OR SOMETHING TO ANOTHER** to consider or represent somebody or something as similar to another ○ *"Shall I compare thee to a summer's day?"* (William Shakespeare, *Sonnet*; 1564–1616) **3.** *vi* **BE AS GOOD** to be equal or similar in quality or standing, especially to be as good as another ○ *As an athlete she can compare with the best in the sport.* **4.** *vi* **RELATE IN PARTICULAR WAY** to have a particular relationship with something or somebody else ○ *Its performance compares badly with that of rival engines.* **5.** *vi* **MAKE COMPARISON** to make a comparison between two or more people or things **6.** *vt* GRAM **GIVE FORMS OF ADJECTIVE OR ADVERB** to give the positive, comparative, and superlative forms of an adjective or adverb ■ *n* **COMPARISON** comparison (*literary*) ○ *a painting beautiful beyond compare* [15C. < Latin *comparare* < *compar* "equal with" < *par* "equal"] —**com·par·er** *n*

USAGE Compare to or **compare with**? In careful usage, ***compare to*** is preferred when two unlike things are being likened: *He compared her skin to ivory.* ***Compare with*** is used when the comparison is between similar things and implies differences as well as similarities: *Tourists find our hotels good compared with those of European capitals.* When ***compare*** is used intransitively (i.e., without an object), *with* should always be used: *The new model compares well with others in the same price range.* See also ***comparable***.

com·par·i·son /kəm párriss'n/ *n* **1.** the act or process of examining two or more people or things in order to discover similarities and differences between them ○ *Journalists continue to draw comparisons between the two systems.* ○ *The initial outlay seems insignificant in comparison with the potential profits.* **2.** the quality of being similar ○ *There's no comparison between them.* [14C. Via Old French *comparesoun* < Latin *comparation-*, < *comparat-*, past participle of *comparare* (see COMPARE)]

com·par·i·son-shop *vi* to compare the prices and features of the same or similar items, especially in different stores, in order to find the best deal —**com·par·i·son shop·per** *n*

~~**comparitive**~~ incorrect spelling of **comparative**

com·part·ment /kəm paártmənt/ *n* **1. PARTITIONED SPACE** one of the areas into which an enclosed space is divided **2. TRAIN CAR SECTION** a walled area within a railroad passenger car, with a door and features such as two facing rows of seats or sleeping accommodations **3. SMALLER PART** a separate part of something larger ○ *He liked to divide his life into different compartments.* ○ *a glove compartment* [Mid-16C. < French *compartiment* < late Latin *compartiri* "divide up" < Latin *partiri* "divide" < *pars* "part"] —**com·part·ment·al** /kəm paàrt mént'l/ *adj* —**com·part·men·tal·ly** *adv*

com·part·men·tal·ize /kəm paàrt mént'l ìz/ (**-ized, -iz·ing, -iz·es**) *vt* to divide something into separate areas, categories, or compartments ○ *She had to compartmentalize her home life and work.* —**com·part·men·tal·i·za·tion** /kəm paàrt ment'li záysh'n/ *n*

com·pass /kúmpəss, kómpəss/ *n* **1. DIRECTION FINDER** a device for finding directions, usually with a magnetized needle that automatically swings to magnetic north **2. PERSONAL DIRECTION** a sense of personal direction ○ *a leader who was devoid of moral compass* **3. SCOPE** the scope of something such as a subject or area of study ○ *beyond the compass of the inquiry* **4. HINGED DEVICE FOR DRAWING CIRCLES** a device for drawing circles or measuring distances, e.g., on a map, that consists of two rods, one pointed, the other often holding a pencil, joined by an adjustable hinge (*often used in the plural*) ■ *vt* (**-passed, -pass·ing, -pass·es**) **1.** same as **encompass** (sense 2) **2. UNDERSTAND SOMETHING** to understand something fully and completely (*formal*) ○ *far more than the average mind can compass* **3. ACHIEVE SOMETHING** to achieve or attain something (*literary*) [14C. < French *compas* "circle," *compasser* "to measure" < assumed Vulgar Latin *compassare*, literally "step off" < Latin *passus* "step"] —**com·pass·a·ble** *adj*

com·pass card *n* the circular diagram in a direction-finding compass over which the needle rotates

com·pas·sion /kəm pásh'n/ *n* sympathy for the suffering of others, often including a desire to help [14C. Via French < ecclesiastical Latin *compassion-* < Latin *compass-*, past participle of *compati* (see COMPATIBLE)] —**com·pas·sion·less** *adj*

com·pas·sion·ate /kəm pásh'nət/ *adj* showing feelings of sympathy for the suffering of others, often with a desire to help —**com·pas·sion·ate·ly** *adv* —**com·pas·sion·ate·ness** *n*

com·pas·sion·ate leave *n* emergency leave in exceptional circumstances granted to somebody for personal reasons such as the death of a close relative

com·pas·sion fa·tigue *n* a loss of sympathy for the suffering of others experienced by donors or caregivers as a result of the demands made of them

com·pass plant *n* a plant with leaves that tend to point north and south. Flowers: yellow, similar to a daisy's. Native to: prairie regions of central United States. Latin name: *Silphium laciniatum.*

com·pass rose *n* a circular diagram printed on a chart or map to show the direction of north and other main points of the compass [Because its design was thought to resemble a rose]

com·pass saw *n* a handsaw with a tapering blade, used for cutting curved shapes

com·pass sense *n* the ability of some birds, fish, and insects to use the Earth's magnetic field to guide them across long distances

~~compatable~~ incorrect spelling of **compatible**

com·pat·i·bil·ist /kəm páttəb'list/ *n* a person who believes that you can be wholly free and responsible for your actions, even though every one of those actions has already been predetermined by events occurring well before your birth and thereby out of your control (*formal*)

com·pat·i·ble /kəm páttəb'l/ *adj* **1.** HARMONIOUS able to exist, live, or work together without conflict ○ *a highly compatible couple* **2.** CONSISTENT consistent or in keeping with something else ○ *an observation not compatible with the facts* **3.** COMPUT ABLE TO BE USED TOGETHER in computing, able to be used together with or substituted for another piece of hardware or software ○ *The software isn't PC-compatible.* **4.** MED ACCEPTABLE TO BODY describes blood, organs, or tissue that can be transplanted or transfused into somebody's body without being rejected **5.** BOT ABLE TO POLLINATE EACH OTHER describes plant varieties that are able to pollinate each other successfully **6.** BOT ABLE TO BE GRAFTED describes plants that are able to be grafted onto each other successfully **7.** FUNGI ABLE TO MATE describes fungal strains that are able to mate successfully [Mid-16C. < French < Latin *compati* "suffer together" < *pati* (see PATIENT)] —**com·pat·i·bil·i·ty** /kəm pàttə bílləteè/ *n* —**com·pat·i·ble·ness** *n* —**com·pat·i·bly** *adv*

com·pa·tri·ot /kəm páytree ət/ *n* **1.** somebody from the same country as another person **2.** a fellow member of a group or organization, especially a military or political one [Late 16C. Via French < late Latin *compatriota* "fellow countryman" < *patriota* (see PATRIOT)]

USAGE See ***colleague.***

compd. *abbr* CHEM compound

com·peer /kóm peer, kəm peér/ *n* (*formal*) **1.** the equal or peer of somebody else **2.** somebody who is a close companion or associate of somebody else [14C Via Old French *comper* < Latin *compar* (see COMPARE)]

com·pel /kəm pél/ (**-pelled, -pel·ling, -pels**) *vt* **1.** to force somebody to do something ○ *I felt compelled to listen.* **2.** to make something happen by force [14C. < Latin *compellere*, literally "drive together" < *pellere* "to beat"] —**com·pel·la·ble** *adj* —**com·pel·la·bly** *adv* —**com·pel·ler** *n*

com·pel·ling /kəm pélling/ *adj* **1.** attracting strong interest and attention ○ *a compelling movie about human relationships* **2.** necessitating action or belief ○ *I felt a compelling need to explain my actions.* ○ *some very compelling arguments* —**com·pel·ling·ly** *adv*

com·pend /kóm pènd/ *n* same as **compendium** (sense 1) [Late 16C. Anglicization of Latin *compendium* (see COMPENDIUM)]

com·pen·di·ous /kəm péndee əss/ *adj* containing a wide range of information in a concise form (*formal*) —**com·pen·di·ous·ly** *adv*

com·pen·di·um /kəm péndee əm/ (*plural* **-di·ums** or **-di·a** /-dee ə/) *n* **1.** a comprehensive but brief account of a subject, especially in book form **2.** a list or compilation of various items ○ *Her letter was a compendium of complaints.* [Late 16C. < Latin < *compendere* "weigh together" < *pendere* (see PENSIVE)]

com·pen·sate /kómpən sàyt/ (**-sat·ed, -sat·ing, -sates**) *v* **1.** *vi* MAKE AMENDS to make amends or make up for something ○ *Nothing can compensate for the loss of one's home.* **2.** *vt* PAY SOMEBODY FOR WORK OR LOSS to pay somebody for work done or for something lost ○ *adequately compensated for their efforts* **3.** *vti* COUNTERBALANCE to counterbalance a force or quality **4.** *vi* PSYCHOL OFFSET PERSONALITY WEAKNESS to behave in a way that emphasizes a particular ability or personality trait in order to make up for a deficiency in another [Mid-17C. < Latin *compensat-*, past participle of *compensare*, literally "weigh together" < *pensare* (see PENSIVE)] —**com·pen·sa·ble** /kəm pénssəb'l/ *adj* —**com·pen·sa·tive** /kómpən sàytiv, kəm pénssətiv/ *adj* —**com·pen·sa·tor** *n*

com·pen·sa·tion /kòmpən sáysh'n/ *n* **1.** MONEY IN PAYMENT FOR LOSS an amount of money or something else given to pay for loss, damage, or work done **2.** GIVING OF COMPENSATION the act of giving money or something else to pay for loss, damage, or work done **3.** AMENDS something that makes amends or makes up for something else ○ *one of the compensations of living abroad* **4.** PSYCHOL BEHAVIOR THAT OFFSETS WEAKNESS behavior that emphasizes a particular ability or personality trait in order to make up for a deficiency in another —**com·pen·sa·tion·al** *adj*

com·pen·sa·tion cul·ture *n UK* the tendency to seek financial compensation for any injustice or wrong done by another, or for any physical or mental suffering caused by the action or negligence of another

com·pen·sa·to·ry /kəm pénssə tàwree/ *adj* serving to offset the negative effects or results of something else

com·pen·sa·to·ry dam·ag·es *npl* damages that are awarded in order to compensate a plaintiff for personal injury or injury to property caused by the defendant's wrongful act

com·pen·sa·to·ry growth *n* the growth in size of one part or organ of the body to make up for the failure or loss of another

com·pen·sa·to·ry time *n* additional time off work offered by an employer for additional hours worked by an employee

com·pere /kóm pèr/ *UK n* the host of an entertainment show, especially on television ■ *vti* (**-pered, -per·ing, -peres**) to act as the compere of an entertainment show [Mid-18C. Via French *compère* "godfather" < medieval Latin *compater* < Latin *pater* "father"]

~~competant~~ incorrect spelling of **competent**

com·pete /kəm peét/ (**-pet·ed, -pet·ing, -petes**) *vi* **1.** to try to win or do better than others **2.** to be able to do as well as or better than others ○ *able to compete on the world market* [Early 17C. < late Latin *competere* "strive together" < Latin *petere* "seek"]

com·pe·tence /kómpət'nss/ *n* **1.** ABILITY the ability to do something well, measured against a standard, especially ability acquired through experience or training ○ *People began to question her competence as a teacher.* ○ *I don't doubt his scientific competence for a moment.* **2.** SUFFICIENT INCOME income that is enough to live on (*formal*) **3.** LAW STATE OF BEING LEGALLY QUALIFIED acceptance by a court as legally qualified to be a party or witness **4.** LING LANGUAGE KNOWLEDGE knowledge of a language that enables somebody to speak and understand it **5.** BIOL ABILITY OF CELL TO SPECIALIZE the ability of embryonic cells to respond to an outside stimulus in a way that affects their development into specialized tissue

SYNONYMS See ***ability.***

com·pe·ten·cy /kómpət'nsee/ (*plural* **-cies**) *n* an ability to do something, especially measured against a standard ○ *core competencies*

com·pe·tent /kómpət'nt/ *adj* **1.** ABLE having enough skill or ability to do something well **2.** ADEQUATE good enough or suitable for something ○ *The graphics test showed the printer to be competent, but no more.* **3.** LAW LEGALLY CAPABLE accepted by a court as legally qualified to be a party or witness **4.** MED, BIOL FUNCTIONING NORMALLY able to function normally, especially in response to an antigen [14C. Via French < Latin *competent-*, present participle of *competere* (see COMPETE)] —**com·pe·tent·ly** *adv*

com·pe·ti·tion /kòmpə tísh'n/ *n* **1.** PROCESS OF TRYING TO BEAT OTHERS the process of trying to win or do better than others ○ *Several firms are in competition for the contract.* **2.** CONTEST an activity in which people try to win something or do better than others **3.** OPPOSITION the opposition in a competitive situation, or the level of opposition ○ *keep one step ahead of the competition* ○ *fierce competition* **4.** ECOL STRUGGLE FOR RESOURCES the struggle between organisms of the same or different species for limited resources such as food or light ○ *competition between weeds and flowers* [Early 17C. < late Latin *competition-* < Latin *competere* (see COMPETE)]

com·pet·i·tive /kəm péttətiv/ *adj* **1.** INVOLVING ATTEMPT TO WIN involving or decided by competition ○ *a highly competitive sport* **2.** WANTING TO BEAT OTHERS inclined toward wanting to achieve more than others **3.** BETTER THAN COMPETITION as good as or slightly better than others because of being good value or worth more ○ *competitive prices* —**com·pet·i·tive·ness** *n*

com·pet·i·tive ex·clu·sion *n* the concept that two or more species with identical requirements cannot coexist on the same limited resources because one will compete more successfully than the other

com·pet·i·tive lo·cal ex·change car·ri·er *n* a company that offers an alternate service to the established telephone service provider in a particular area

com·pet·i·tive·ly /kəm péttətivlee/ *adv* **1.** in a way that involves trying to win or do better than others **2.** in a way that is as good as or slightly better than others because of being good value or worth more ○ *competitively priced*

com·pet·i·tor /kəm péttitər/ *n* **1.** an opponent, especially in a commercial market **2.** a person, animal, or group taking part in a competition [Early 16C. < Latin *competere* (see COMPETE)]

com·pi·la·tion /kòmpə láysh'n/ *n* **1.** something created by putting together things that have been gathered from various places ○ *a compilation of new poems* **2.** the process of bringing things together from various places to form a whole

com·pile /kəm pīl/ (**-piled, -pil·ing, -piles**) *vt* **1.** GATHER THINGS TOGETHER to bring things together from various places to form a whole **2.** CREATE SOMETHING BY COMPILING THINGS to create something by putting together things that have been gathered from various places ○ *compile statistical data* **3.** COMPUT TRANSLATE COMPUTER LANGUAGE to convert a computer program written in a high-level language into an intermediate language (**machine language**) using a special program (**compiler**) [14C. < French *compiler*, probably < Latin *compilare* "to plunder"] —**com·pil·er** *n*

com·pil·er /kəm pīlər/ *n* **1.** a person or group that brings things together, especially to create a whole **2.** a computer program that converts another program from a high-level language into an intermediate language (**machine language**)

com·pla·cent /kəm pláyss'nt/ *adj* **1.** self-satisfied and unaware of possible dangers **2.** eager to please [Mid-17C. < Latin *complacent-*, present participle of *complacere* "please very much" < *placere* "to please"] —**com·pla·cen·cy** *n* —**com·pla·cent·ly** *adv*

com·plain /kəm pláyn/ (**-plained, -plain·ing, -plains**) *vi* **1.** EXPRESS UNHAPPINESS to express discontent or unhappiness about a situation **2.** DESCRIBE SYMPTOMS to describe symptoms that are being experienced, e.g., of an illness ○ *complaining of chest pains* **3.** PROTEST to formally make an accusation of wrongdoing or a crime, or register a protest ○ *The neighbors complained to the police about the noise.* [14C. < French *complaign-*, stem of *complaindre* < Latin *plangere* "to beat"] —**com·plain·er** *n* —**com·plain·ing·ly** *adv*

SYNONYMS ***complain, object, protest, grumble, grouse, carp, gripe, whine, nag***

CORE MEANING: to indicate dissatisfaction with something

complain to express discontent or unhappiness about a situation ○ *Nearby neighbors had complained about the noise and the mess.* ○ *He complains bitterly that tests were not done years ago.* **object** to be opposed to something, or express opposition to it ○ *We object strongly to the two proposals.* ○ *Sports bodies have objected on the grounds that the plan would take away space that could be used as a playing field.* **protest** to express strong disapproval or disagreement ○ *a day* *of action to protest the government's health policies* ○ *From eight months onwards, babies are likely to protest loudly at being passed around.* **grumble** to complain or mutter in a discontented way, possibly repeatedly or continually ○ *He picked up his brush and, grumbling, got down to work.* ○ *Investors were grumbling about not being told the whole story.* **grouse** to complain regularly and continually, often in a way that is not constructive ○ *grousing about the commercialism of art* ○ *"These talks are leading nowhere," one of the negotiators groused.* **carp** to keep complaining or finding fault, especially about unimportant things ○ *He was a mean employer, carping all the time.* ○ *We've had a lot of injuries which we haven't carped on too much.* **gripe** (*informal*) to complain continually and irritatingly ○ *griping about the fact that I had not presented him with an advance copy of the book* ○ *You griped when I was in the house all day, and now that I've got a job you are griping at that!* **whine** to complain in an unreasonable, repeated, or irritating way ○ *so-called experts whining about the state of the nation's schools* ○ *whining to me about his problems.* **nag** to find fault with somebody regularly and repeatedly ○ *I was always being nagged about the length of my hair or the untidiness of my room.*

com·plain·ant /kəm pláynənt/ *n* a person or organization that takes legal action against another

com·plaint /kəm pláynt/ *n* **1. STATEMENT OF UNHAPPINESS** a statement expressing discontent or unhappiness about a situation ○ *If you have any complaints, talk to the manager.* **2. SOMETHING MAKING SOMEBODY UNHAPPY** something that makes somebody discontented or unhappy **3. EXPRESSING OF UNHAPPINESS** the act of expressing discontent or unhappiness about a situation ○ *has cause for complaint* **4. AILMENT** a physical disorder, usually something minor **5.** LAW **STATEMENT** a statement setting out the reasons for a legal action **6.** LAW **FORMAL CHARGE** a formal charge that somebody has committed a crime ○ *swore out a complaint against him* [14C. < French *complainte*, feminine past participle of *complaindre* (see COMPLAIN)]

com·plai·sant /kəm pláyss'nt, -pláyz'nt/ *adj* showing a willingness to please others by carrying out, or allowing them to carry out, their wishes [Mid-17C. < French, present participle of *complaire* "agree in order to please" < Latin *complacere* (see COMPLACENT)] —**com·plai·sance** *n* —**com·plai·sant·ly** *adv*

com·pleat /kəm pleét/ *adj* having or exhibiting full knowledge of a particular field or skill (*archaic*) [14C. Variant of COMPLETE]

com·plect·ed /kəm pléktəd/ *adj* having a particular kind of complexion (*informal; usually used in combination*) [Early 19C. Back-formation < COMPLEXION]

com·ple·ment *n* /kómpləmənt/ **1. COMPLETING PART** something that completes or perfects something else **2. ONE OF TWO** either of two things that form a unit **3. FULL QUANTITY** a quantity of people or things that is considered complete ○ *the full complement of warships and replenishing vessels* **4.** GRAM **SENTENCE PART** a word or group of words, excluding the verb, that complete the predicate of a sentence or clause **5.** MATH, LOGIC **ITEMS EXCLUDED FROM SUBSET** the elements of a set that are not included in a particular subset of that set **6.** MATH same as **complementary angle 7.** IMMUNOL **GROUP OF BLOOD PROTEINS** a set of proteins in the bloodstream that, together with antibodies, recognize and attack foreign cells such as bacteria **8.** MUSIC **NOTE INTERVAL** an interval that, when added to a given interval, equals an octave ■ *vt* /kómplə mènt/ (**-ment·ed, -ment·ing, -ments**) **COMPLETE SOMETHING** to complete, perfect, or go well with something else ○ *a light dessert that complements a rich meal* [14C. < Latin *complementum* "something that fills up" < *complere* (see COMPLETE)] —**com·ple·men·tal** /kòmplə mént'l/ *adj* —**com·ple·men·tal·ly** *adv*

USAGE complement or **compliment**? The two words are close in spelling but their meanings are quite different. A ***complement*** is something added to perfect a thing and make it complete, whereas a ***compliment*** is an expression of praise: *A fine wine is the perfect complement to good cooking. The cook received many compliments from the guests that evening.* Both words are also used as verbs, and both have adjectival forms: ***complementary*** and ***complimentary***. ***Complimentary*** has the special meaning "given free"; and so a ***complimentary*** copy of a book is one given without charge, whereas a ***complementary*** copy is one that completes a set of books.

com·ple·men·tar·i·ty /kòmplə men tárrətee/ (*plural* **-ties**) *n* **1.** the condition of things that complement one another **2.** the concept that two different models may be necessary to describe an atomic or subatomic system, e.g., electrons may be regarded as particles or waves in different circumstances

com·ple·men·ta·ry /kòmplə méntəree, -méntree/ *adj* **1. COMPLETING** completing something else **2. MAKING WHOLE** making a pair or whole ○ *At this camp, we regard indoor and outdoor activities as complementary.* **3.** GENETICS **INTERDEPENDENT** describes genes that are interdependent and produce their effect only when present together **4.** MATH **NOT IN SUBSET** describes the elements of a mathematical set that are not included in a particular subset of that set **5.** MATH **FORMING PART OF RIGHT ANGLE** describes either of two angles that together make a right angle **6.** ALTERN MED **OF COMPLEMENTARY MEDICINE** used in or using complementary medicine —**com·ple·men·ta·ri·ly** *adv* —**com·ple·men·ta·ri·ness** *n*

USAGE See ***complement***.

com·ple·men·ta·ry an·gle *n* either of two angles that together make up a right angle

com·ple·men·ta·ry col·or *n* colored light or a color that, when combined with another, produces white or gray

com·ple·men·ta·ry DNA *n* single-stranded DNA made in a laboratory so that its base sequence is complementary to a messenger RNA template. It is assembled by the enzyme reverse transcriptase and may be used in gene cloning or as a gene probe.

com·ple·men·ta·ry gene *n* a gene that produces an observable effect in an organism only in conjunction with another gene

com·ple·men·ta·ry med·i·cine *n* a range of therapies based on the holistic treatment of physical disorders, generally addressing the causes of diseases rather than their symptoms and also taking steps in the prevention of disease. The term embraces therapies such as acupuncture, herbal medicine, and homeopathy.

com·ple·men·ta·tion /kòmplə men táysh'n/ *n* **1.** the act or fact of completing, perfecting, or going well with something else **2.** the effect produced when two separate mutations occur together in an organism and partly or wholly cancel out each other's action

com·ple·ment fix·a·tion *n* the process in which a group of blood proteins (**complement**) is bound to a specific combined antibody-antigen pair as part of the immune reaction to foreign cells

com·ple·men·tiz·er /kómpləmən tìzər/ *n* a word introducing a clause that acts as a complement ○ *"For" in "for Sam to be late is unusual" is a complementizer.*

com·plete /kəm pleét/ *adj* **1. WHOLE** having every necessary part or everything that is wanted ○ *a complete set of Dickens* **2. FINISHED** having reached the normal or expected end ○ *The washer stops when the last spin cycle is complete.* **3. ABSOLUTE** being the greatest degree of something ○ *a complete waste of time* **4. PERFECT** having all the necessary qualities or abilities for a particular role ○ *She is the complete diplomat.* **5.** FOOTBALL **SUCCESSFULLY CAUGHT** in football, used to describe a forward pass that has been successfully caught **6.** BOT **HAVING ALL PRINCIPAL FLOWER PARTS** describes flowers that have all the principal flower parts, which are carpels, petals, sepals, and stamens ■ *v* (**-plet·ed, -plet·ing, -pletes**) **1.** *vt* **MAKE SOMETHING WHOLE** to make something whole by including every necessary part or everything that is wanted ○ *one more goblet to complete the set* **2.** *vt* **FINISH SOMETHING** to finish something or bring it to an end ○ *You have 20 minutes to complete the quiz.* **3.** *vt* **ACCOMPLISH SOMETHING** to carry out or accomplish something ○ *The terms of the sale have been completed.* **4.** *vti* FOOTBALL **THROW PASS THAT IS CAUGHT** in football, to throw a successfully caught forward pass [14C. Directly or via French < Latin *completus*, past participle of *complere* "fill up" < *plere* "fill"] —**com·plete·ness** *n* —**com·ple·tive** *adj* ◇ **complete with** including a particular thing as a feature

ORIGIN The Latin word *plere*, "to fill," from which ***complete*** is derived, is also the source of English *accomplish, complement, compliment, comply, deplete, expletive, implement, replete, supplement*, and *supply*. Its Indo-European ancestor is in turn the source of English *full*[1].

com·plete blood count *n* a diagnostic test used to identify the levels of all blood-cell types in a quantity of blood

com·plete·ly /kəm pleétlee/ *adv* used to emphasize the extent of something ○ *completely wrong* ○ *I completely forgot about it.*

com·plete met·a·mor·pho·sis *n* a metamorphosis that involves the four stages of egg, larva, pupa, and adult in insects such as butterflies, beetles, flies, and bees

com·plet·er /kəm pleétər/ *n* an item that makes a set or another item complete ○ *an eight-piece completer set of china*

com·ple·tion /kəm pleésh'n/ *n* **1. FINISHING OF SOMETHING** the act of finishing something or of bringing it to an end **2. STATE OF BEING FINISHED** the state of being finished or brought to an end ○ *the building is nearing completion* **3.** *UK* LAW **FINAL STAGE OF SALE** the final stage of the sale of real estate, when ownership changes hands **4.** FOOTBALL **CAUGHT PASS** in football, a forward pass that has been successfully caught

com·plex *adj* /kəm pléks, kóm plèks/ **1. COMPLICATED** difficult to analyze, understand, or solve **2. HAVING MANY PARTS** made up of many interrelated parts ■ *n* /kóm plèks/ **1. INTERCONNECTED WHOLE** a whole composed of various interrelated parts ○ *a building complex* **2. INFLUENCE ON BEHAVIOR** a set of related feelings, ideas, or impulses that may be repressed but continues to influence thoughts and behavior ○ *a guilt complex* **3. EXAGGERATED FEELINGS** an exaggerated or obsessive set of feelings about something (*informal*) ○ *He has a complex about eating in restaurants.* **4.** CHEM **COMPOUND OF NONMETAL AND METAL ATOMS** a compound in which nonmetal molecules or ions form weak bonds (**coordinate bonds**) with a central metal atom [Mid-17C. Directly or via French < Latin *complexus*, past participle of *complecti* "weave together" < *plectere* "to plait"] —**com·plex·ly** *adv* —**com·plex·ness** *n*

com·plex con·ju·gate *n* a complex number in a pair of numbers that have the same real components but opposite imaginary components. The complex conjugate of $a + ib$ is $a - ib$.

com·plex frac·tion *n* a fraction with a mixed number or fraction in its numerator or denominator or in both

com·plex·ion /kəm plékshən/ *n* **1.** the quality and color of the skin, especially of the face **2.** the character of something or the way it appears ○ *This development puts an entirely new complexion on the matter.* [14C. < French, "bodily constitution" < Latin *complecti* (see COMPLEX)] —**com·plex·ion·al** *adj* —**com·plex·ioned** *adj*

com·plex·i·ty /kəm pléksətee/ (*plural* **-ties**) *n* **1. COMPLICATED NATURE** the condition of being difficult to analyze, understand, or solve **2. CONDITION OF HAVING MANY PARTS** the condition of being made up of many interrelated parts **3. COMPLICATED THING** one of the interrelated problems or difficulties involved in a complicated matter (*often used in the plural*)

com·plex num·ber *n* a number in the form $a + ib$, where $i = \sqrt{-1}$, that may be either real or imaginary

com·plex plane *n* a plane whose coordinates are expressed as single complex numbers

com·plex sen·tence *n* a sentence containing one or more subordinate clauses

com·pli·ance /kəm plí ənss/, **com·pli·an·cy** /-ənssee/ *n* **1.** the state or act of conforming with or agreeing to do something ○ *in compliance with the court order* **2.** readiness to conform or agree to do something

com·pli·ant /kəm plí ənt/ *adj* **1.** ready to conform or agree to do something **2.** made or done according to requirements or instructions (*often used in combination*) ○ *compliant with the general statutes* ○ *Y2K-compliant* —**com·pli·ant·ly** *adv*

com·pli·cate /kómpli kàyt/ *vt* (**-cat·ed, -cat·ing, -cates**) to make something complex or difficult ○ *Further delay will only complicate matters.* ○ *a complicating* *factor* ■ *adj* describes leaves or insect wings that are folded lengthwise [Early 17C. < Latin *complicat-*, past participle of *complicare* "fold together" < *plicare* "to fold"]

com·pli·cat·ed /kómpli kàytəd/ *adj* **1.** composed of many interrelated parts or features ○ *a complicated diagram* **2.** difficult to understand, deal with, or explain ○ *Life is complicated enough as it is.* —**com·pli·cat·ed·ly** *adv* —**com·pli·cat·ed·ness** *n*

com·pli·ca·tion /kòmpli káysh'n/ *n* **1.** DIFFICULT STATE a difficult or confused state caused by many interrelated factors **2.** DIFFICULTY something that makes something else more difficult or complex ○ *Far from being helpful, this is just a further complication.* **3.** INTRODUCTION OF DIFFICULTY the act of making something complex or difficult **4.** PLOT DEVICE an event or character whose introduction into a story causes difficulty **5.** MEDICAL PROBLEM a disease or problem that arises in addition to the initial condition or during a surgical operation

com·plic·it /kəm plíssit/ *adj* involved in something illegal or wrong ○ *It was clear that some of the staff were complicit in the attempt to cover up the scandal.* [Late 20C. Back-formation < COMPLICITY]

com·plic·i·ty /kəm plíssətee/ *n* involvement with another in doing something illegal or wrong [Mid-17C. < archaic *complice* (see ACCOMPLICE)]

com·pli·ment *n* /kómpləmənt/ **1.** STATEMENT OF PRAISE something said to express praise or approval **2.** GESTURE OF RESPECT OR HONOR something done to show respect or honor ■ **com·pli·ments** *npl* RESPECT expressions of respect and good wishes ○ *My compliments to the chef.* ■ *vt* /kómplə mènt/ (**-ment·ed, -ment·ing, -ments**) **1.** PRAISE SOMEBODY to express praise or approval of somebody **2.** GIVE SOMETHING TO SOMEBODY to give somebody a gift as a sign of respect or honor **3.** CONGRATULATE SOMEBODY to express congratulations to somebody [Mid-17C. Via French < Italian *complimento* < Latin *complementum* (see COMPLEMENT)] ◇ **return the compliment** to respond to a gesture that somebody has made with a similar gesture

USAGE See *complement.*

com·pli·men·ta·ry /kòmplə méntəree, -méntree/ *adj* **1.** expressing praise or approval ○ *a complimentary glance* **2.** given free as a courtesy or favor ○ *complimentary seats* —**com·pli·men·ta·ri·ly** *adv*

USAGE See *complement.*

com·pli·men·ta·ry close *n* the part of a letter, e-mail, or similar communication immediately before the signature, expressing the sender's sentiments, e.g., "Sincerely yours"

com·pline /kómplin, -līn/, **com·plin** /kómplin/ *n* in the Roman Catholic church, the last of the seven separate hours (**canonical hours**) that are set aside for prayer each day [12C. Alteration of Old French *complie* < medieval Latin *(hora) completa* "final (hour)" < Latin *completus* (see COMPLETE)]

com·ply /kəm plí/ (**-plied, -ply·ing, -plies**) *vi* to obey or conform to something such as a rule, law, regulation, or wish [Late 16C. Via obsolete French *complire* < Latin *complere* (see COMPLETE)] —**com·pli·er** *n*

com·po /kómpō/ *n* a substance that is a mix of various ingredients, e.g., cement or mortar (*slang*) [Early 19C. Shortening of COMPOSITION]

com·po·nent /kəm pṓnənt/ *n* **1.** PART a part of something, usually of something bigger ○ *a manufacturer of vehicle components* ○ *one of several major components of our research* **2.** ELEC ELECTRIC PART a device such as a resistor or transistor that is part of an electronic circuit **3.** MATH VECTOR one of a set of vectors whose combination (**resultant**) is another vector **4.** CHEM CONSTITUENT SUBSTANCE one of the substances necessary to describe each phase of a chemical system ■ *adj* FORMING PART forming part of a whole [Mid-16C. < Latin *component-*, present participle of *componere* "put together" < *ponere* "to place"] —**com·po·nen·tial** /kòmpə nénsh'l/ *adj*

com·pon·ent·ize /kəm pṓnən tīz/ (**-ized, -iz·ing, -izes**) *vt* **1.** to divide something into smaller, more manageable, or more flexible parts **2.** to divide a large software application into smaller independently functioning parts

com·port /kəm páwrt/ (**-port·ed, -port·ing, -ports**) *v* (*formal*) **1. com·port your·self** *vr* to behave in a particular way **2.** *vi* to agree or be consistent with something ○ *This does not comport with the established facts.* [14C. < Latin *comportare* "bring together" < *portare* "to carry"]

com·port·ment /kəm páwrtmənt/ *n* the way in which somebody behaves (*formal*)

com·pose /kəm pṓz/ (**-posed, -pos·ing, -pos·es**) *v* **1.** *vt* BE PARTS OF SOMETHING to be the components or parts that make up something ○ *fertilizer composed of organic compounds* ○ *the nations that compose the alliance* **2.** *vt* PUT ELEMENTS TOGETHER to put things together to form a whole ○ *composed a light lunch, using cold cuts and salads* **3.** *vt* ARRANGE ITEMS to arrange things in order to achieve an effect ○ *composing objects for a still life in oils* **4.** *vti* CREATE to create something, especially a piece of music or writing ○ *She is trying to compose a rather difficult letter to her client.* **5.** *vt* CALM SOMEBODY to make somebody become calm ○ *Please compose yourself.* **6.** *vti* SET TYPE to set type in preparation for printing [14C. < French *composer*, alteration (influenced by *poser* "to place") of Latin *componere* (see COMPONENT)]

USAGE See *comprise.*

com·posed /kəm pṓzd/ *adj* not agitated or distracted —**com·pos·ed·ly** /-pṓzədlee/ *adv* —**com·pos·ed·ness** /-ədnəss/ *n*

com·pos·er /kəm pṓzər/ *n* a creator of something, especially of music

com·pos·ite /kəm pózzit/ *adj* **1.** COMPOUND made up of different parts **2.** BOT WITH COMPLEX FLOWER HEADS describes any plant belonging to a large family that has flower heads resembling a single flower but composed of many smaller flowers. Dandelions and daisies are composite plants. Family: Compositae. ■ *n* **1.** SOMETHING MADE OF PARTS something made from different parts ○ *The new law is a composite of previous suggested legislation.* **2.** CRIME IMAGE OF SUSPECT an image of a suspect's face that is created by a police artist or photographer, based on input from witnesses (*informal*) **3.** BOT COMPOSITE PLANT a composite plant **4.** INDUST BUILDING MATERIAL a building material made up of different ingredients [14C. Directly or via French < Latin *compositus*, past participle of *componere* (see COMPONENT)] —**com·pos·ite·ly** *adv* —**com·pos·ite·ness** *n*

Com·pos·ite *adj* belonging to a classical order of architecture that combines features of the Ionic and Corinthian orders

com·pos·ite con·struc·tion *n* a building technique that combines the use of steel and concrete to make supporting columns, resulting in stronger, lighter, and less costly supports

com·pos·ite pho·to·graph *n* an image or scene made up of two or more original images placed side by side, overlapped, or superimposed

com·pos·ite school *n* in some Canadian provinces, a secondary school in which academic, business, and vocational programs are offered

com·pos·ite vol·ca·no *n* GEOL same as **stratovolcano**

com·po·si·tion /kòmpə zísh'n/ *n* **1.** CONSTITUENTS the way in which something is made, especially in terms of its different parts **2.** ARRANGEMENT the way in which the parts of something are arranged, especially the parts of a visual image ○ *the artist's masterly composition of a group portrait* **3.** PUTTING TOGETHER OF THINGS the act or process of combining things to form a whole **4.** CREATION OF MUSICAL OR LITERARY WORK the act or process of creating something such as a piece of music or writing **5.** ARTS ARTISTIC CREATION something created as a work of art, especially a piece of music **6.** PIECE OF WRITING a short piece of writing, especially a school exercise **7.** PRODUCT something created by combining separate parts **8.** LAW SETTLEMENT a settlement whereby creditors agree to accept partial payment of debts by a bankrupt party, usually in return for a consideration such as immediate payment of a lesser amount **9.** LING WORD FORMATION the formation of compound words from separate words **10.** PRINTING TYPESETTING the setting of type in preparation for printing [14C. Via French < Latin *composition-* < *composit-*, past participle of *componere* (see COMPONENT)] —**com·po·si·tion·al** *adj* —**com·po·si·tion·al·ly** *adv*

com·pos·i·tor /kəm pózzitər/ *n* somebody who sets text in type [Mid-16C. < Latin, "compiler" < *composit-* (see COMPOSITION)]

com·pos men·tis /kòmpəss méntiss/ *adj* sane or of sound mind [< Latin, "in control of your mind"]

com·post /kóm pōst/ *n* **1.** DECAYED PLANT MATTER a mixture of decayed plants and other organic matter used by gardeners for enriching soil **2.** COMPOUND a compound or composition of several parts ■ *v* (**-post·ed, -post·ing, -posts**) **1.** *vti* DECAY to convert organic matter to compost, or to be converted to compost **2.** *vt* PUT COMPOST ON SOIL to treat soil or an area of ground by adding compost [14C. Via Old French *composte* "mixture" < Latin *composita* < *composit-* (see COMPOSITION)] —**com·post·a·ble** *adj*

com·post·er /kóm pōstər/ *n* a device, often shaped like a box or barrel, used to collect organic materials to be used later in composting

com·po·sure /kəm pṓzhər/ *n* calm and steady control over the emotions

com·pote /kóm pōt/ *n* **1.** fruit cooked in sugar or syrup, served as a hot or cold dessert **2.** a glass dish with a long stem, used for serving fruit, nuts, or candy [Late 17C. Via French, "mixture" < Old French *composte* (see COMPOST)]

com·pound[1] *n* /kóm pòwnd/ **1.** MIXTURE something made by combining two or more things **2.** CHEM CHEMICAL SUBSTANCE a substance formed by the chemical combination of elements in fixed proportions **3.** GRAM WORD MADE UP OF OTHER WORDS a word that is formed from two or more identifiable words, e.g., "blackbird," "cookbook," or "bullheaded," or, in some analyses, "mother-in-law" or "fire drill" ■ *adj* /kóm pòwnd, kom pównd, kəm-/ **1.** HAVING PARTS made up of two or more parts **2.** GRAM MADE FROM TWO OR MORE WORDS describes a word that is made up of two or more words or word parts **3.** BOT DIVIDED INTO PARTS describes a leaf that is divided into two or more parts (**leaflets**) attached to a single stalk ■ *v* /kom pównd, kəm-/ (**-pound·ed, -pound·ing, -pounds**) **1.** *vti* COMBINE THINGS to add together, or add one thing to another, to form a whole ○ *hatred that was compounded with fear and revulsion* **2.** *vt* MAKE SOMETHING FROM PARTS to make something by combining parts ○ *a medication compounded from several constituent elements* **3.** *vt* INTENSIFY SOMETHING to make something more extreme or intense by adding something to it ○ *Further financial reverses compounded his despair.* **4.** *vt* LAW TAKE BRIBE TO IGNORE CRIME to accept a bribe in return for not prosecuting or informing about a crime **5.** *vti* SETTLE DEBT to settle a debt by paying a lesser amount owed, usually immediately and in a lump sum **6.** *vt* FIN, BANKING ADD INTEREST to calculate or pay interest based on both the principal and the previously accrued interest ○ *6% interest, compounded monthly* [14C. < Old French *compoun-*, stem of *compondre* < Latin *componere* (see COMPONENT)] —**com·pound·a·ble** *adj* —**com·pound·er** *n*

SYNONYMS See *mixture.*

com·pound[2] /kóm pòwnd/ *n* **1.** an enclosed group of buildings for the segregation or restraint of a particular group of people **2.** *Malaysia, Singapore* a garden with a fence or wall around it [Late 17C. < Malay *kampong* "enclosure, village"]

com·pound en·gine *n* an engine in which potential generated in one stage is augmented in another

com·pound eye *n* the eye that most insects and some crustaceans have, made up of several separate light-sensitive parts. See illustration on next page

com·pound fault *n* a series of geologic faults that lie close together, following the same general direction

com·pound frac·tion *n* MATH same as **complex fraction**

com·pound frac·ture *n* MED same as **open fracture**

com·pound in·ter·est *n* interest that is calculated on the combined total of the original sum borrowed (**principal**) and the interest it has already accrued

com·pound me·ter *n* a meter in which the beats of the measure are grouped in threes

com·pound mi·cro·scope *n* a microscope consisting

compound eye

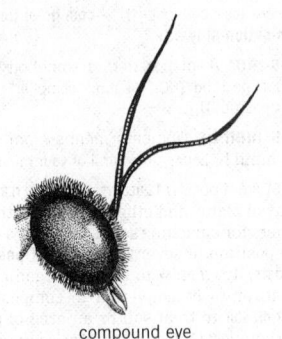

of two lenses or lens systems and an eyepiece, mounted in a tube

com·pound sen·tence *n* a sentence containing two or more clauses that can stand independently. The clauses are often linked by a conjunction, which is sometimes preceded by a comma, as in "We waited for over an hour, but she didn't show up."

com·pound time *n UK* LITERAT same as **compound meter**

com·pre·hend /kòmprə hénd/ (**-hend·ed, -hend·ing, -hends**) *v* **1.** *vti* to grasp the meaning or nature of something ○ *It was hard to comprehend the sheer scale of the problem.* **2.** *vt* to include something as a part of a larger whole (*formal*) [14C. < Latin *comprehendere* "grasp fully" < *prehendere* "seize"] —**com·pre·hend·i·ble** *adj*

com·pre·hen·si·ble /kòmprə hénssəb'l/ *adj* capable of being understood [15C. Directly or via French < Latin *comprehensibilis* < *comprehens-*, past participle of *comprehendere* (see COMPREHEND)] —**com·pre·hen·si·bil·i·ty** /kòmprə henssə bíllətee/ *n* —**com·pre·hen·si·ble·ness** *n* —**com·pre·hen·si·bly** *adv*

com·pre·hen·sion /kòmprə hénsh'n/ *n* **1.** UNDERSTANDING the grasping of the meaning of something **2.** INTELLECTUAL ABILITY the ability to grasp the meaning of something ○ *It's beyond my comprehension.* **3.** EDUC SET OF QUESTIONS ON TEXT an exercise consisting of a set of questions on a short text, designed to test students' understanding of it [15C. Directly or via French < Latin *comprehension-* < *comprehens-* (see COMPREHENSIBLE)]

com·pre·hen·sive /kòmprə hénssiv/ *adj* **1.** INCLUSIVE covering many things or a wide area ○ *a comprehensive survey of public opinion* **2.** INCLUDING ALL including everything, so as to be complete ○ *comprehensive knowledge of the subject* **3.** COVERING MANY EVENTUALITIES describes insurance policies that provide coverage or benefit in most areas ■ *n* EDUC EXAMINATION a final graduate or undergraduate examination in a major field of study (*often used in the plural*) [Early 17C. Directly or via French < Latin *comprehensivus* < *comprehens-* (see COMPREHENSIBLE)] —**com·pre·hen·sive·ly** *adv* —**com·pre·hen·sive·ness** *n*

com·pre·hen·sive ex·am·i·na·tion *n* EDUC same as **comprehensive**

com·press *v* /kəm préss/ (**-pressed, -press·ing, -press·es**) **1.** *vti* SHRINK to make something smaller by applying pressure or a similar process, or become smaller in this way **2.** *vt* PRESS THINGS TOGETHER to press things such as the lips together **3.** *vt* COMPUT MAKE COMPUTER FILES SHORTER to reduce the number of bits required to represent computer text, data, or images so as to save storage space or reduce transmission time ■ *n* /kóm prèss/ **1.** MED TREATMENT PAD a cloth pad, often moistened or medicated, pressed firmly against a part of the body as a treatment, e.g., to stop bleeding **2.** MACHINE a machine for compressing material, especially cotton that is being packed [14C. Via Old French < late Latin *compressare* "keep pressing together" < Latin *comprimere* "press together" < *premere* "to press"] —**com·pressed** *adj* —**com·press·i·bil·i·ty** /kəm prèssə bíllətee/ *n* —**com·press·i·ble** *adj* —**com·press·i·ble·ness** *n* —**com·press·i·bly** *adv*

com·pressed air *n* /kəm prést-/ air that is kept in a container under pressure, often used to power machines

com·pres·sion /kəm présh'n/ *n* **1.** REDUCTION IN SIZE the reduction of the volume or mass of something by applying pressure, or the state of having been treated in this way **2.** PHASE IN ENGINE the phase in the working of an internal-combustion engine in which a combination of fuel and air is compressed in a cylinder before being ignited **3.** COMPUT REDUCTION OF COMPUTER DATA a technique for reducing the number of bits required to represent text, data, or images so as to save storage space or reduce transmission time [14C. Via French < Latin *compression-* < *compress-*, past participle of *comprimere* (see COMPRESS)] —**com·pres·sion·al** *adj*

com·pres·sion ra·tio *n* the ratio between the largest and smallest possible volumes in the cylinder of an internal-combustion engine that contains a combination of fuel and air being compressed

com·pres·sion sack *n* a tubular bag made of synthetic fabric with special straps to compress the bulk of its contents and make it easier for hikers and mountaineers to carry

com·pres·sion wave *n* a longitudinal wave created in a fluid by a compressing force, e.g., a sound wave in air

com·pres·sive /kəm préssiv/ *adj* having the power or tendency to compress [14C. Via French < medieval Latin *compressivus* < Latin *compress-* (see COMPRESSION)] —**com·pres·sive·ly** *adv*

com·pres·sor /kəm préssər/ *n* **1.** a machine that compresses gas so that the power produced when the gas is released can be used to power another machine such as a pneumatic drill **2.** a muscle that compresses or flattens a part of the body

com·pri·mar·i·o /kòmpri mérree ō, -maáree ō/ *n* a secondary role in an opera or ballet, or somebody who performs such a role [< Italian, "jointly primary"]

~~**comprimise**~~ incorrect spelling of **compromise**

com·prise /kəm príz/ (**-prised, -pris·ing, -pris·es**) *vt* **1.** INCLUDE SOMETHING to incorporate or contain something **2.** CONSIST OF SOMETHING to be made up of something **3.** ⚠ CONSTITUTE SOMETHING to make up the whole of something [15C. < French *compris*, past participle of *comprendre* "include" < Latin *comprehendere* (see COMPREHEND)] —**com·pris·a·ble** *adj*

USAGE comprise, consist of, include, compose, or **constitute**? ***Comprise*** and ***consist of*** are concerned with a whole having a number of parts. They are used in the active voice, with the whole as their subject and the parts as their object: *The house comprises three bedrooms, a bathroom, a kitchen, and a living room. The meal consisted of several small dishes that everybody dipped into and shared.* Use of ***comprise*** in the sense "to constitute" is controversial. Avoid constructions like this if you wish to steer clear of criticism: *The house is comprised of three bedrooms, a bathroom, a kitchen, and a living room. Three bedrooms, a bathroom, a kitchen, and a living room comprise the house.* If some rather than all the parts are mentioned, ***include*** may be used instead: *The house includes a kitchen and a living room on the first floor.* ***Compose*** and ***constitute*** are concerned with parts making up a whole. ***Compose*** is normally used in the passive, and ***constitute*** in the active: *The team is composed of several experts in the field. The following commodities constitute the average household diet.*

---

com·pro·mise /kómprə mìz/ *n* **1.** AGREEMENT a settlement of a dispute in which two or more sides agree to accept less than they originally wanted ○ *After hours of negotiations a compromise was reached.* **2.** SOMETHING ACCEPTED RATHER THAN WANTED something that somebody accepts because what was wanted is unattainable **3.** POTENTIAL DANGER OR DISGRACE exposure to danger or disgrace ■ *v* (**-mised, -mis·ing, -mis·es**) **1.** *vi* AGREE BY CONCEDING to settle a dispute by agreeing to accept less than what was originally wanted **2.** *vt* LESSEN VALUE OF SOMEBODY OR SOMETHING to undermine or devalue somebody or something by making concessions ○ *Don't compromise your integrity by telling half-truths.* **3.** *vt* EXPOSE SOMEBODY OR SOMETHING TO DANGER to expose somebody or something to danger or disgrace ○ *This scandal could compromise his chances for reelection.* ○ *drugs that can compromise the immune system* [15C. Via French *compromis* < Latin *compromissum* "mutual agreement" < past participle of *compromittere* "make mutual promises" < *promittere* (see PROMISE)] —**com·pro·mis·er** *n*

com·pro·mis·ing /kómprə mìzing/ *adj* likely to expose somebody to danger or disgrace —**com·pro·mis·ing·ly** *adv*

comp time *n* HR same as **compensatory time** (*informal*)

Comp·ton /kómptən/ city in southwestern California, a southern suburb of Los Angeles situated northeast of Torrance. Population: 95,559 (2002 estimate).

Comp·ton, Arthur Holly (1892–1962) US physicist. He discovered the Compton effect (1922), for which he received the Nobel Prize in physics (1927).

Comp·ton ef·fect *n* the decrease in energy and increase in wavelength experienced by a photon after colliding or interacting with an electron [Early 20C. After A. H. COMPTON]

comp·trol·ler /kən trólər/ *n* FIN same as **controller** (sense 2) [15C. Variant influenced by *compt*, older spelling of COUNT[1]]

com·pul·sion /kəm púlshən/ *n* **1.** FORCE a force that makes somebody do something **2.** COMPELLING an act of compelling or the state of being compelled ○ *You are under no compulsion to leave.* **3.** PSYCHOL PSYCHOLOGICAL FORCE a psychological and usually irrational force that makes somebody do something, often unwillingly ○ *felt an irresistible compulsion* [14C. Via French < late Latin *compulsion-* < Latin *compuls-*, past participle of *compellere* (see COMPEL)]

com·pul·sive /kəm púlssiv/ *adj* **1.** DRIVEN TO DO SOMETHING driven by an irresistible inner force to do something ○ *a compulsive liar* **2.** POWERFULLY INTERESTING exerting a powerful attraction or interest ○ *The TV series was compulsive viewing.* ■ *n* SOMEBODY UNDER PSYCHOLOGICAL COMPULSION somebody whose actions are driven by a usually irrational psychological force —**com·pul·sive·ly** *adv* —**com·pul·sive·ness** *n* —**com·pul·siv·i·ty** /kòm pul sívvətee/ *n*

com·pul·so·ry /kəm púlssəree/ *adj* **1.** NECESSARY required by law or an authority ○ *Attendance at the lecture is compulsory.* **2.** FORCED caused by force, or using force to make somebody do something ■ *n* (*plural* **-ries**) REQUIRED ROUTINE an exercise or routine that participants in a sport such as gymnastics or figure skating must perform as part of a competition (*often used in the plural*) [Early 16C. < medieval Latin *compulsorius* < Latin *compuls-* (see COMPULSION)] —**com·pul·so·ri·ly** *adv* —**com·pul·so·ri·ness** *n*

com·punc·tion /kəm púngkshən/ *n* feelings of shame and regret about doing something wrong [14C. Via French < ecclesiastical Latin *compunction-* < Latin *compunct-*, past participle of *compungere* "sting strongly" < *pungere* "to prick, sting"] —**com·punc·tious** *adj* —**com·punc·tious·ly** *adv*

com·pu·ta·tion /kòmpyə táysh'n/ *n* **1.** the calculating of something, or the result of a calculation **2.** the use of a computer, especially for calculation, or something calculated using a computer —**com·pu·ta·tion·al** *adj* —**com·pu·ta·tion·al·ly** *adv*

com·pute /kəm pyoót/ (**-put·ed, -put·ing, -putes**) *v* **1.** *vt* CALCULATE SOMETHING to calculate an answer or result, especially using a computer **2.** *vi* YIELD RESULT to yield a result, especially a correct result, from calculation ○ *These numbers just don't compute.* **3.** *vi* USE COMPUTER to use a computer or calculator [Early 17C. < Latin *computare* "reckon together" < *putare* "reckon"] —**com·put·a·ble** *adj*

com·put·ed to·mog·ra·phy /kəm pyoótəd-/ *n* a technique for producing images of cross-sections of the body. A computer processes data from X-rays penetrating the body from many directions and projects the results on a screen. This is the technology used when conducting a CT scan.

com·put·er /kəm pyoótər/ *n* **1.** an electronic device that accepts, processes, stores, and outputs data at high speeds according to programmed instructions **2.** somebody who calculates numbers or amounts using a machine —**com·put·er·less** *adj*

com·put·er-aid·ed de·sign *n* the use of a computer and sophisticated graphics software to design products or systems

com·put·er-aid·ed en·gi·neer·ing *n* the use of computers and specialized programs in engineering to automate analysis and testing through simulation of such factors as stress and loads

com·put·er a·ni·ma·tion *n* COMPUT same as **animation** (sense 3)

com·put·er·ate /kəm pyóotərət/ *adj* COMPUT same as **computer-literate** [Late 20C. < COMPUTER, after LITERATE]

com·put·er con·fer·enc·ing *n* the use of computers to allow people at distant sites to exchange text and graphic messages as they would at a meeting

com·put·er crime *n* illegal activities carried out on or by means of a computer. Computer crime includes criminal trespass into another computer system, theft of computerized data, and the use of an on-line system to commit or aid in the commission of fraud.

com·put·er dat·ing *n* the business or practice of putting people's personal information and preferences into a computer that then matches apparently compatible couples

com·put·er·ese /kəm pyóotə réez, -réess/ *n* the technical language used by people involved with computers (*humorous*)

com·put·er game *n* a game in the form of computer software, run on a personal computer or games machine and played by one or more people using a keyboard, mouse, control pad, or joystick. Computer games usually combine sound and graphics and range from traditional games such as chess to fast-moving action games or complex puzzles.

com·put·er graph·ics *n* the use of a computer and specialized software to produce and manipulate pictorial images for purposes of animation, business presentations, and scientific research (*takes a singular verb*) ■ *npl* the images produced by computer graphics (*takes a plural verb*)

com·put·er-in·te·grat·ed te·leph·o·ny *n* COMPUT, TELECOM same as **computer-telephone integration**

com·put·er·ize /kəm pyóotə rīz/ (**-ized, -iz·ing, -iz·es**) *vt* **1.** to install or start using a computer system to organize, control, or automate something, e.g., a mechanical process **2.** to store information in a computer system or process it by computer —**com·put·er·iz·a·ble** *adj* —**com·put·er·i·za·tion** /kəm pyòotəri záysh'n/ *n* —**com·put·er·ized** *adj*

com·put·er·ized ax·i·al to·mog·ra·phy, com·put·er·ized to·mog·ra·phy *n* MED same as **computed tomography**

com·put·er lan·guage *n* COMPUT same as **programming language**

com·put·er-lit·er·ate *adj* having a good understanding and experience of working with a computer or computer system —**com·put·er lit·er·a·cy** *n*

com·pu·ter model·ing *n* the use of computer graphics and other techniques to create a simplified version of something so as to predict and analyze potential technical problems

com·put·er sci·ence *n* the study of the mathematics and technology of computers and their applications

com·put·er-tel·e·phone in·te·gra·tion *n* a system that allows telephonic resources to be made accessible to and controlled by computers so that the same networks can be shared by voice and data traffic

com·put·er vi·rus *n* COMPUT same as **virus** (sense 3)

com·put·ing /kəm pyóoting/ *n* the activity of using computers or computer software

Comr. *abbr* Commissioner

com·rade /kóm ràd, -rəd/ *n* **1.** a close friend or a companion **2.** *also* **Com·rade** a fellow member of a group, especially a fellow soldier or a fellow supporter of a communist or socialist party [Mid-16C. Via French *camerade, camarade* < Spanish *camarada* "barracks mate" < *camara* "room" < Latin *camera* (see CAMERA)] —**com·rade·ly** *adj* —**com·rade·ship** *n*

com·rade-in-arms (*plural* **com·rades-in-arms**) *n* somebody who is fighting on the same side in a war, battle, or other armed struggle

Com·stock·er·y /kóm stòkəree, kúm-/ *n* the removal of, or strong opposition to, anything that could be seen as immoral or obscene in literary, artistic, or broadcast material [Early 20C. After Anthony Comstock (1844–1915), US reformer]

Com·stock Lode /kòm stok-/ *n* a rich vein of gold and silver in western Nevada. It was the site of a prospecting rush after its discovery in 1859 and yielded hundreds of millions of dollars' worth of precious metals before excessive exploitation led to its abandonment in 1898.

con[1] /kon/ *vt* (**conned, con·ning, cons**) **1.** TRICK SOMEBODY to cheat somebody dishonestly, usually out of money or property, by first convincing the victim of something that is untrue **2.** LIE TO SOMEBODY to tell somebody something untrue or misleading **3.** PERSUADE SOMEBODY to persuade or inveigle somebody to agree to something (*informal*) ○ *See if you can con him into a game of basketball!* ■ *n* DISHONEST TRICK a dishonest trick or business ploy that takes advantage of somebody's trust, e.g., telling lies in order to get money or property unfairly [Late 19C. Shortening of CONFIDENCE GAME]

con[2] /kon/ *n* **1.** an argument against doing something, or evidence supporting the view that something should not be done ○ *the pros and cons* **2.** an opponent of something, or somebody who votes against something [Late 16C. Shortening of Latin *contra* "against"]

con[3] /kon/ *n* CRIME same as **convict** (*slang*) [Late 19C. Shortening]

con[4] /kon/ (**conned, con·ning, cons**) *vt* (*archaic*) **1.** to study something with great care and attention **2.** to learn or memorize something [< Old English *cunnan* "know how," *cunnian* "explore" < Indo-European]

con[5] /kon/, **conn** *vt* (**conned, con·ning, cons; conns**) to direct the course of a ship ■ *n* control of the course of a ship, or the controls used [Early 17C. Alteration of obsolete *cond* < French *conduire* < Latin *conducere* (see CONDUCE)]

con[6] /kon/ *prep* used to mean "with" in a musical direction [< Italian, "with"]

con. *abbr* **1.** MUSIC concerto **2.** LAW conclusion **3.** TELECOM, TRANSP connection **4.** COMM consolidated **5.** continued **6.** contra

Con. *abbr* **1.** POL Conservative **2.** Consul

Con·a·kry /kónnəkree/ capital, largest city, and chief Atlantic port of Guinea, in Western Africa. Population: 705,280 (1983 estimate).

con a·mo·re /kòn ə máw rày, -ree, kòn aa máw rày/ *adv* with tender feeling (*used as a musical direction*) [< Italian, "with love"]

Co·nant /kónənt/, **James Bryant** (1893–1978) US educator and chemist. He campaigned for national educational reform and was president of Harvard University (1933–53).

> "There is only one proved method of assisting the advancement of pure science—that of picking men of genius, backing them heavily, and leaving them to direct themselves."
> [James Bryant Conant, *Letter to the editor, New York Times*; August 13, 1945]

con ar·tist *n* a swindler who uses a confidence game to cheat or defraud people

co·na·tion /kō náysh'n/ *n* in psychology, a mental process involving the will, e.g., impulse, desire, or resolve [Mid-19C. < Latin *conation-* < *conat-*, past participle of *conari* "try"] —**co·na·tion·al** *adj* —**co·na·tive** /kónətiv, kónnə-/ *adj*

con bri·o /kon brée ō, kōn-/ *adv* with spirit or vigor (*used as a musical direction*) [< Italian, "with vigor"]

conc. *abbr* **1.** CHEM concentrated **2.** CHEM concentration **3.** concerning **4.** MUSIC concerto **5.** INDUST concrete

con·cat·e·nate *vt* /kon kátt'n àyt, kən-/ (**-nat·ed, -nat·ing, -nates**) **1.** BRING THINGS TOGETHER to connect separate units or items into a linked system **2.** COMPUT LINK UNITS TOGETHER in computing, to link two or more information units, e.g., character strings or computer files, so that they form a single unit ■ *adj* /kon kátt'nət, -kátt'n àyt, kən-/ COMPUT LINKED TOGETHER linked together in a sequence or chain [15C. < late Latin *concatenat-*, past participle of *concatenare* "chain together" < Latin *catena* "chain"]

con·cat·e·na·tion /kon kàtt'n áysh'n, kən-/ *n* **1.** the linking of things together, or the state of being interconnected **2.** the linking of computer characters, strings, or files in a specific order to form a single entity equal to the sum of the lengths of the original entities

con·cave /kon káyv, kón kayv/ *adj* **1.** curved inward like the inner surface of a bowl or sphere **2.** describes a polygon with an interior angle greater than 180° [< Latin *concavus* "hollowed out" < *cavus* "hollow"] —**con·cave·ly** *adv* —**con·cave·ness** *n*

con·cav·i·ty /kon kávvətee/ (*plural* **-ties**) *n* **1.** the state of being concave **2.** a concave part or surface

con·cav·o-con·cave /kon kàyvō-/ *adj* describes a lens that is concave on both surfaces

con·cav·o-con·vex /kon kàyvō-/ *adj* describes a lens that is concave on one surface and convex on the other

con·ceal /kən séel/ (**-cealed, -ceal·ing, -ceals**) *vt* **1.** to put or keep something or somebody out of sight, or prevent the person or thing from being found ○ *The evidence was carefully concealed.* **2.** to keep something secret, or prevent it from being known [13C. Via French < Latin *concelare* "hide well" < *celare* "hide"] —**con·ceal·a·ble** *adj* —**con·ceal·ment** *n*

con·ceal·er /kən séelər/ *n* **1.** flesh-colored makeup that can be applied to the skin to hide blemishes **2.** somebody or something that conceals something

con·cede /kən séed/ (**-ced·ed, -ced·ing, -cedes**) *v* **1.** *vt* RELUCTANTLY ACCEPT SOMETHING TO BE TRUE to admit or acknowledge something, often grudgingly or with reluctance **2.** *vt* GRANT RIGHTS TO SOMEBODY to allow or yield something such as a right or privilege to another person or country **3.** *vti* ADMIT FAILURE BEFORE END to accept and acknowledge defeat in a contest, debate, election, or fight, often without waiting for the final result **4.** *vt UK* GIVE SOMETHING AWAY to allow an opponent or opposing team to gain something valuable, usually a goal or points [15C. Via French < Latin *concedere* "yield completely" < *cedere* "yield"] —**con·ced·er** *n*

~~conceed~~ incorrect spelling of **concede**

con·ceit /kən séet/ *n* **1.** EXCESSIVE SELF-PRIDE a high opinion of your own qualities or abilities, especially one that is not justified **2.** LITERAT EXAGGERATED COMPARISON IN LITERATURE an imaginative poetic image, or writing that contains such an image, especially a comparison that is extreme or far-fetched **3.** WHIMSICAL OBJECT an object created from the imagination **4.** IMAGINATIVE IDEA an idea, opinion, or theme, especially one that is fanciful or unusual in some way **5.** WITTY EXPRESSION a witty, inventive, or amusing expression (*archaic*) ■ *vt* (**-ceit·ed, -ceit·ing, -ceits**) *N England* LIKE SOMETHING to like or tolerate something [14C. < CONCEIVE]

con·ceit·ed /kən séetəd/ *adj* **1.** having or showing an excessively high opinion of your own qualities or abilities **2.** imaginative, fanciful, witty, or ingenious (*archaic*) —**con·ceit·ed·ly** *adv* —**con·ceit·ed·ness** *n*

SYNONYMS See ***proud***.

con·ceiv·a·ble /kən séevəb'l/ *adj* possible to imagine, understand, or believe ○ *We tried every means conceivable to contact her.* —**con·ceiv·a·bil·i·ty** /kən sèevə bíllətee/ *n* —**con·ceiv·a·ble·ness** *n*

con·ceiv·a·bly /kən séevəblee/ *adv* possibly, even if only a remote possibility ○ *You could just conceivably be wrong.*

con·ceive /kən séev/ (**-ceived, -ceiv·ing, -ceives**) *v* **1.** *vti* THINK OF OR IMAGINE SOMETHING to form an idea or concept of something in your mind **2.** *vt* INVENT OR DEVISE SOMETHING to think up something such as a plan or an invention that could be put into action ○ *conceived and written by John Sander* **3.** *vt* START TO EXPERIENCE SOMETHING to produce something from the mind such as an emotion **4.** *vti* BECOME PREGNANT to become pregnant with a child or with young **5.** *vt* UNDERSTAND to understand something [13C. < Old French *conceiv-*, stem of *concevoir* < Latin *concipere* "take in" < *capere* "seize, take"] —**con·ceiv·er** *n*

con·cel·e·brate /kən séllə bràyt/ (**-brat·ed, -brat·ing, -brates**) *vti* to celebrate the Christian Mass or Communion jointly with one or more other priests [Late 16C. < Latin *concelebrat-*, past participle of *concelebrare* "celebrate together" < *celebrare* (see CELEBRATE)] —**con·cel·e·brant** *n* —**con·cel·e·bra·tion** /kən sèllə bráysh'n/ *n*

con·cen·ter /kən séntər, kon-/ (**-tered, -ter·ing, -ters**) *vti* to direct things to a common center, or converge at a common center [Late 16C. < French *concentrer* < *con-* "together" + *centre* "center"]

con·cen·trate /kónss'n tràyt/ *v* (**-trat·ed, -trat·ing, -trates**) **1.** *vti* **THINK INTENSELY ABOUT SOMETHING** to focus all of your thoughts or mental activity on one subject or activity, usually in silence ○ *I found myself unable to concentrate on my work.* **2.** *vti* **DEVOTE EFFORTS TO ONE THING** to direct attention, time, and resources to one particular area or activity, usually over a period of time **3.** *vti* **CLUSTER TOGETHER** to bring things together in the same place or area, or to come together in the same place **4.** *vt* **MAKE SUBSTANCE PURER** to make a substance purer by the removal of another substance, especially by removing a liquid **5.** *vi* EDUC same as **major 6.** *vti* **MAKE SOMETHING THICKER OR STRONGER** to remove water from a substance, usually a liquid, leaving a smaller quantity that is thicker in consistency and stronger in flavor, or become thicker and stronger in this way **7.** *vti* **ACCUMULATE IN TISSUE** to accumulate, or cause a substance to accumulate, in biological tissue over a period of time **8.** *vt* MINERALS **PURIFY ORE** to remove rock and other material from ore to purify it ■ *n* **1. PURE SUBSTANCE** a substance made purer by the removal of another, especially a liquid **2. THICK FOOD SUBSTANCE** a food substance, especially a liquid, made thicker or stronger in flavor by the removal of liquid [Mid-17C. < CONCENTER] —**con·cen·trat·ed** *adj* —**con·cen·trat·ed·ly** *adv* —**con·cen·tra·tive** *adj* —**con·cen·tra·tive·ly** *adv*

con·cen·tra·tion /kònss'n tráysh'n/ *n* **1. FOCUS OF MIND OR RESOURCES** the direction of all thought or effort toward one particular task, idea, or subject **2. CLUSTER OR NUMBER** a large number of things or amount of something collected together in one area ○ *the concentration of computing talent in one part of the country* **3.** EDUC same as **major** (sense 3) **4.** EDUC **FOCUS OF MAJOR IN COLLEGE** the main area of study within a college or university student's major field of study ○ *majored in education with a concentration in theater* **5. STRENGTH OF SOLUTION** the amount of a substance dissolved in another. Symbol *c* **6. MAKING LIQUID THICKER OR STRONGER** the removal of water from something, usually a liquid, to make it thicker or stronger

con·cen·tra·tion camp *n* **1.** any of the prison camps used for exterminating prisoners under the rule of Hitler in Nazi Germany. Conditions were inhuman, and prisoners, mostly Jewish people, were generally starved or worked to death, or killed immediately, resulting in the extermination of more than six million people. **2.** a prison camp used in war for the incarceration of political prisoners or civilians

con·cen·tra·tor /kónss'n tràytər/ *n* **1.** EDUC same as **major** (sense 4) **2.** COMPUT **TELECOMMUNICATIONS DEVICE** a telecommunications device that combines outgoing messages into one message or extracts individual messages from one transmission into which they have been combined **3.** MINERALS **FACTORY THAT PROCESSES MINERAL ORE** an industrial plant that produces purified or concentrated mineral ore **4.** INDUST **MIRROR SYSTEM FOR PRODUCING SOLAR ENERGY** a set of mirrors used to concentrate sunlight in the collection of energy from the sun

con·cen·tric /kən séntrik, kon-/ *adj* **1.** describes circles and spheres of different sizes with the same middle point **2.** with a common axis or center line [14C. < medieval Latin *concentricus* "having the same center" < Latin *centrum* "center"] —**con·cen·tri·cal·ly** *adv* —**con·cen·tric·i·ty** /kònss'n tríssətee/ *n*

Con·cep·ción /kən sèpsi ṓn/ **1.** capital city of Bío-Bío Region, central Chile, situated on the Bío-Bío River, 260 mi./418 km southwest of Santiago. Population: 372,252 (1998). **2.** capital city of Concepción Department, central Paraguay, situated on the Paraguay River. It is the commercial centre of northern Paraguay and serves as a free port for southwestern Brazil. Population: 35,276 (1992).

con·cept /kón sèpt/ *n* **1. SOMETHING THOUGHT OR IMAGINED** something that somebody has thought up, or that somebody might be able to imagine **2. BROAD PRINCIPLE AFFECTING PERCEPTION AND BEHAVIOR** a broad abstract idea or a guiding general principle, e.g., one that determines how a person or culture behaves, or how nature, reality, or events are perceived ○ *the concept of time* **3. UNDERSTANDING OR GRASP** the most basic understanding of something ○ *has little concept of what is involved* **4. WAY OF DOING OR PERCEIVING SOMETHING** a method, plan, or type of product or design [Mid-16C. < late Latin *conceptus* < past participle of Latin *concipere* (see CONCEIVE)] —**con·cep·tu·al** /kən sépchoo əl/ *adj*

con·cept art *n* ARTS same as **conceptual art**

con·cep·tion /kən sépshən/ *n* **1. BROAD UNDERSTANDING** a general understanding of something **2. SOMETHING CONCEIVED IN MIND** a result of thought, e.g., an idea, invention, or plan **3.** BIOL **CONCEIVING OF YOUNG** the fertilization of an egg by a sperm at the beginning of pregnancy **4.** BIOL **FETUS** an embryo or fetus (*technical*) **5. ORIGIN OR BEGINNINGS** the beginnings or origin of something **6. FORMULATION OF IDEA** the process of arriving at an abstract idea or belief or the moment at which such an idea starts to take shape or emerge **7.** same as **concept** (sense 1) [14C. Via French < Latin *conception-* < *concipere* (see CONCEIVE)] —**con·cep·tion·al** *adj* —**con·cep·tive** *adj* —**con·cep·tive·ly** *adv*

con·cept prod·uct *n* a highly advanced and innovative product that is not yet in commercial production

con·cept state·ment *n* an explanation or summary of the overall goals or nature of a project

con·cep·tu·al art *n* art designed to present an idea rather than to be appreciated for its creative skill or beauty, often making use of unconventional media instead of painting or sculpture —**con·cep·tu·al artist** *n*

con·cep·tu·al·ism /kən sépchoo ə lìzzəm/ *n* **1.** the philosophical theory that the existence of something is dependent on our having a mental concept of it **2.** a school of art concerned primarily with the ideas behind a work of art rather than the artwork itself —**con·cep·tu·al·is·tic** /-sèpchoo ə lístik/ *adj* —**con·cep·tu·al·is·ti·cal·ly** *adv*

con·cep·tu·al·ist /kən sépchoo əlist/ *n* **1.** somebody who believes in conceptualism **2.** somebody who creates conceptual art

con·cep·tu·al·ize /kən sépchoo ə līz/ (**-ized, -iz·ing, -iz·es**) *vti* **1.** to arrive at a concept or generalization as a result of things seen, experienced, or believed **2.** to picture, imagine, or perceive something —**con·cep·tu·al·i·za·tion** /kən sèpchoo əli záysh'n/ *n* —**con·cep·tu·al·iz·er** *n*

con·cep·tus /kən séptəss/ (*plural* **-tus·es**) *n* an embryo or fetus along with all the tissues that surround it throughout pregnancy, including the placenta, amniotic sac and fluid, and the umbilical cord (*technical*) [Mid-18C. < Latin, "something conceived" < past participle of *concipere* (see CONCEIVE)]

con·cern /kən súrn/ *n* **1. WORRY** worry, or a cause of worry ○ *His condition is giving rise to concern.* **2. CARING FEELINGS** a feeling of worry, compassion, sympathy, or regard for somebody or something **3. RELEVANT AFFAIR** a matter that affects somebody or that somebody has the right to be involved with ○ *It's no concern of yours.* **4. BUSINESS** a commercial enterprise **5. OBJECT** a gadget or trivial object (*dated*) ■ *vt* (**-cerned, -cern·ing, -cerns**) **1. MAKE SOMEBODY WORRIED** to give somebody an uneasy or anxious feeling **2. BE INTERESTING OR IMPORTANT TO SOMEBODY** to have a direct effect on, or be a matter of significance to, somebody or something **3. INVOLVE SOMEBODY** to require somebody to be involved with something, or get involved with or interested in something **4. BE ON SUBJECT OF SOMETHING** to be about a particular topic [Late 14C. Via French < late Latin *concernere*, literally "sift together" < Latin *cernere* "sift"]

con·cerned /kən súrnd/ *adj* **1. ANXIOUS OR WORRIED** worried or apprehensive, particularly about something such as a situation that is developing or that has newly arisen **2. INTERESTED** attentive to and interested in something **3. INVOLVED** having an active role in or related to something ○ *A message was conveyed to the families concerned.* —**con·cer·ned·ly** /-nədlee/ *adv*

con·cern·ing /kən súrning/ *prep* relating to or involving something or somebody ○ *information concerning her disappearance*

con·cert *n* /kón sùrt, kónssərt/ **1. PUBLIC MUSICAL PERFORMANCE** an event where an individual musician or a group of musicians, e.g., a choir, band, or orchestra, performs in front of an audience **2. AGREEMENT** harmony or accord, e.g., in purpose or action (*formal*) ○ *a concert of criticism* **3. UNIFIED PAIR OR GROUP** a combination of people or things in agreement or harmony (*formal*) ■ *v* /kən súrt/ (**-cert·ed, -cert·ing, -certs**) **1.** *vti* **ACT IN AGREEMENT OR UNITY** to do or plan something in cooperation with another person or group (*formal*) **2.** *vt* **REACH CONSENSUS** to settle or adjust something such as a contract or disagreement by discussion and mutual consent [Late 16C. Via French < Italian *concerto* (see CONCERTO)] ◇ **in concert 1.** playing music or singing at a live concert **2.** working or acting together, especially in a united or harmonious way (*formal*)

con·cer·tan·te /kònchər taántày, -tee/ *adj* **1.** relating to or resembling a concerto, especially one in the baroque style **2.** relating to a symphonic work that highlights individual instruments within the orchestra [Early 18C. < Italian, present participle of *concertare* "bring into harmony"]

con·cert·ed /kən súrtəd/ *adj* **1.** planned or carried out by two or more people working together or with the same goal **2.** written for several soloists to perform together in an ensemble or within the context of a larger-scale work —**con·cert·ed·ly** *adv* —**con·cert·ed·ness** *n*

con·cert·go·er /kónssərt gṑ ər/ *n* somebody who is attending a concert, or somebody who often goes to concerts —**con·cert·go·ing** *adj*

con·cert grand *n* the largest size of grand piano, between 9 ft./2.74 m and 12 ft./3.66 m long, designed for use in a concert hall

con·cert hall *n* a public building designed for performances of music

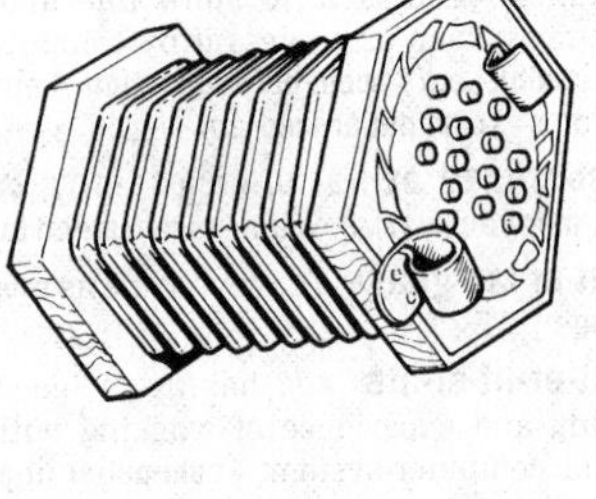

concertina

con·cer·ti·na /kònssər téenə/ *n* a small accordion with button keys [Mid-19C. < CONCERT + Italian suffix *-ina*] —**con·cer·tin·ist** *n*

con·cer·ti·no /kònchər téenō/ (*plural* **-nos** or **-ni** /-nee/) *n* **1.** the solo instrumental group in a piece of music played by a small group of soloists and a larger ensemble (**concerto grosso**) **2.** a small-scale concerto for a single solo instrument [Late 18C. < Italian, "little concerto" < *concerto* (see CONCERTO)]

con·cer·tize /kónssər tīz/ (**-tized, -tiz·ing, -tiz·es**) *vi* to perform in concerts (*refers to soloists or conductors*)

con·cert·mas·ter /kónssərt màstər/ *n* the leader of the first violin section of an orchestra, usually next in rank below the conductor

con·cert·mis·tress /kónssərt mìstrəss/ *n* a woman who is the leader of the first violin section of an orchestra, usually next in rank below the conductor

con·cer·to /kən chértō/ (*plural* **-tos** or **-ti** /-tee/) *n* **1.** an instrumental work for orchestra that highlights a soloist or group of soloists **2.** in music before 1650, a work for voices with organ or continuo [Early 18C. < Italian < *concertare* "bring into harmony"]

con·cer·to gros·so /kən chèrtō grṓssō/ (*plural* **con·cer·ti gros·si** /-chèrtee grṓssee/ or **con·cer·to gros·sos**) *n* a genre of orchestral composition, popular in the 17th century, that contrasts a small group of soloists (**concertino**) with a larger ensemble (**ripieno**) [< Italian, "big concerto"]

con·cert o·ver·ture *n* a short orchestral composition similar to an opera overture but intended for concert performance on its own

con·cert pitch *n* **1.** MUSIC **STANDARD PITCH TO WHICH INSTRUMENTS TUNED** the internationally agreed standard pitch to which orchestral instruments are tuned, typically using the A above middle C as a reference. In an instrument tuned to concert pitch, the A above middle C is at a pitch of 440 cycles per second. **2.** MUSIC **PITCH OF NOTE IN TRANSPOSED MUSIC** the sounding pitch of a note played by an instrument when transposing a piece of written music to a different key, as opposed to the written pitch **3. READINESS** a state of readiness for action (*informal*)

con·ces·sion /kən sésh'n/ *n* **1. RELUCTANT YIELDING** an act or an example of conceding, yielding, or compromising in some way, often grudgingly or unwillingly **2. SPECIAL PRIVILEGE** something, e.g., a privilege, right, or kindness, that is granted to a person or group, usually in view of special circumstances **3. SOMETHING UNWILLINGLY ADMITTED** something acknowledged or admitted, even if unwillingly or grudgingly **4.** COMM **SMALL BUSINESS OUTLET INSIDE ANOTHER ESTABLISHMENT** a branch of a business set up and operating in a place belonging to another commercial enterprise, or a business agreement that grants the right to do this **5. RIGHT TO USE LAND** an official license granted by a landowner or government that allows work such as drilling for oil to be carried out in a specific area of land **6.** *Can* **LAND SUBDIVISION** a subdivision of land in a township survey, mainly in Ontario and Quebec, that was formerly one of the rows of 32 200-acre lots into which each new township was divided **7.** *Can* ROADS same as **concession road 8.** *UK* **CHEAP TICKET** a special reduced price at which tickets for travel or entertainment are sold to some groups of people, e.g., senior citizens, students, or the unemployed [Early 17C. Directly or via French < Latin *concession-* < *concess-*, past participle of *concedere* (see CONCEDE)] —**con·ces·si·ble** /kən séssəb'l/ *adj* —**con·ces·sion·al** *adj*

con·ces·sion·aire /kən sèsh'n ér/, **con·ces·sion·er** /kən sésh'nər/ *n* somebody who holds or operates a concession in a place of business owned by somebody else [Mid-19C. < French *concession* (see CONCESSION)]

con·ces·sion·ar·y /kən sésh'n èrree/ *adj* created or executed as a compromise or goodwill gesture, especially within a negotiating process

con·ces·sion·er *n* COMM same as **concessionaire**

con·ces·sion road, con·ces·sion line *n* in Canada, especially in Ontario and Quebec, a rural road running along the line of the survey of Canada that divided farmland into concessions

con·ces·sion stand *n* a stall selling food and drinks run by somebody who is not employed by the owners of the place in which the stall is located

con·ces·sive /kən séssiv/ *adj* **1.** describes a word or part of a sentence that expresses concession, e.g., the word "although" **2.** relating to or containing a concession [Early 18C. < late Latin *concessivus* < Latin *concess-* (see CONCESSION)] —**con·ces·sive·ly** *adv*

conch /kongk, konch/ (*plural* **conchs** /kongks/ or **conch·es** /kónchiz/) *n* **1.** a tropical invertebrate ocean animal with a large, often brightly colored, spiral shell **2.** the large spiral shell of a conch. Use: horn or trumpet, ornament, jewelry. **3.** ANAT same as **concha**[1] (sense 1) [14C. Via Latin *concha* < Greek *kogkhē* "shell, shellfish"]

conch- *prefix* same as **concho-** (*used before vowels*)

con·cha[1] /kóngkə/ (*plural* **-chae** /-kee/) *n* **1.** a part of the body shaped like a conch shell, e.g., the external ear or the central cavity of the ear **2.** an apse, or the plain partial dome of one [Late 16C. < Latin (see CONCH)] —**con·chal** *adj*

con·cha[2] /kónchə/, **con·cho** (*plural* **-chos**) *n* *Southwest US* a usually silver, shell-shaped ornament that is attached to a cowboy's hatband, chaps, belt, or saddle [Late 19C. Via American Spanish < Spanish, "shell"]

conchi- *prefix* same as **concho-**

con·chi·glie /kən keelee/ *n* pasta formed into small shell shapes [< Italian, "little shells" < Latin *concha* (see CONCH)]

con·chi·o·lin /kong kí əlin, kon kí-/ *n* a fibrous protein in mollusk shells [Late 19C. < modern Latin *conchiola* "little shell" < Latin *concha* (see CONCH)]

concho- *prefix* shell ○ *conchology* [< Latin *concha* (see CONCH)]

con·choi·dal /kong kóyd'l/ *adj* having or being a surface shaped like a bivalve shell with smooth ridges and depressions ○ *conchoidal fracture*

con·chol·o·gy /kong kólləjee/ *n* a branch of zoology dealing with sea shells and the animals that inhabit them —**con·cho·log·i·cal** /kòngkə lójjik'l/ *adj* —**con·chol·o·gist** *n*

con·cierge /kōn syérzh/ (*plural* **-cierges** /*pronunc. same*/) *n* **1.** somebody who is employed at a hotel or apartment building to help the guests or residents, e.g., by dealing with luggage, making travel arrangements, or delivering messages **2.** especially in France, somebody whose job is to staff or watch the entrance to a large residential building, and who usually also lives on the premises [Mid-16C. Via French < Latin *conservus* "fellow slave" < *servus* "slave"]

con·ci·erge me·di·cine *n* MED same as **boutique medicine**

~~**concieve**~~ incorrect spelling of **conceive**

con·cil·i·ar /kən síllee ər/ *adj* belonging to, issued by, or relating to a council [Late 17C. < Latin *concilium* "council, meeting"] —**con·cil·i·ar·ly** *adv*

con·cil·i·ate /kən síllee àyt/ (**-at·ed, -at·ing, -ates**) *vti* **1. BRING DISPUTING SIDES TOGETHER** to work with opposing parties with the goal of bringing them to an agreement or reconciliation **2. GET SOMEBODY'S SUPPORT OR FRIENDSHIP BACK** to bring a disagreement with somebody to an end, or overcome somebody's anger, suspicion, or hostility **3. BE CHARMING** to gain something, especially somebody's friendship, goodwill, or respect, by behaving pleasantly [Mid-16C. < Latin *conciliat-*, past participle of *conciliare* < *concilium* "council, meeting"] —**con·cil·i·a·ble** *adj* —**con·cil·i·a·tion** /kən sìllee áysh'n/ *n* —**con·cil·i·a·tive** *adj* —**con·cil·i·a·tor** *n* —**con·cil·i·a·to·ry** /-ə tàwree/ *adj*

con·cin·ni·ty /kən sínnətee/ (*plural* **-ties**) *n* **1.** a balanced, graceful, polished quality, especially in a literary work **2.** a harmonious structuring of all the parts of something [Mid-16C. < Latin *concinnitas* < *concinnus* "skillfully put together"] —**con·cin·nous** *adj*

con·cise /kən síss/ *adj* using as few words as possible to give the necessary information, or compressed in order to be brief [Late 16C. Directly or via French < Latin *concisus*, past participle of *concidere* "cut down" < *caedere* "to cut"] —**con·cise·ly** *adv* —**con·cise·ness** *n* —**con·ci·sion** /kən sízh'n/ *n*

con·clave /kón klàyv, kóng klàyv/ *n* **1. SECRET MEETING** a private gathering of a select group of people, where discussions are kept secret **2.** CHR **MEETING TO SELECT POPE** the secret meeting at which Roman Catholic cardinals elect a new pope **3.** CHR **ROOMS WHERE POPE IS ELECTED** the private rooms in which the college of Roman Catholic cardinals assembles to elect a new pope [14C. Via French < Latin, "locked room" < *clavis* "key"] —**con·clav·ist** *n*

con·clude /kən klóod/ (**-clud·ed, -clud·ing, -cludes**) *v* **1.** *vt* **COME TO CONCLUSION ABOUT SOMETHING** to form an opinion or make a logical judgment about something after considering everything known about it **2.** *vti* **DECIDE SOMETHING** to reach a decision about something (*dated*) **3.** *vt* **SETTLE SOMETHING** to make a formal agreement complete and fixed, especially after detailed or prolonged discussions or arrangements **4.** *vti* **FINISH** to come to an end, or bring something to an end ○ *concluded the discussion* [13C. < Latin *concludere* "close completely" < *claudere* "to close"] —**con·clud·er** *n*

SYNONYMS See ***deduce***.

con·clu·sion /kən klóozh'n/ *n* **1. DECISION BASED ON FACTS** a decision made or an opinion formed after considering the relevant facts or evidence **2. FINAL PART OF SOMETHING** the part that brings something to a close (*formal*) **3. FINAL SETTLEMENT OF SOMETHING** the completion of a formal agreement or deal, especially after long or detailed discussions and arrangements **4. CLOSING ARGUMENT IN TRIAL** the summation or closing argument at the end of the case being tried **5.** LOGIC **PART OF ARGUMENT DEDUCED FROM EVIDENCE** the portion of an argument for which evidence is presented [14C. Directly or via French < Latin *conclusion-* < *conclus-*, past participle of *concludere* (see CONCLUDE)]

con·clu·sive /kən klóossiv/ *adj* proving a matter beyond all doubt [Late 16C. < late Latin *conclusivus* < Latin *conclus-* (see CONCLUSION)] —**con·clu·sive·ly** *adv* —**con·clu·sive·ness** *n*

con·clu·so·ry /kən klóossəree/ *adj* **1.** convincing, but not to the extent that it cannot be contradicted **2.** same as **conclusive**

con·coct /kən kókt/ (**-coct·ed, -coct·ing, -cocts**) *vt* **1.** to create something by mixing or combining various ingredients in a new way, especially in cooking **2.** to think up a story or plan, especially something imaginative, that is intended to be deceitful or misleading [Mid-16C. < Latin *concoct-*, past participle of *concoquere* "cook together" < *coquere* "to cook"] —**con·coc·ter** *n* —**con·coc·tive** *adj*

con·coc·tion /kən kókshən/ *n* **1. NEW AND UNUSUAL MIXTURE** a new and unusual mixture, especially a drink or dish created by mixing together ingredients **2. CONCOCTING OF MIXTURE** the act or process of combining ingredients to create something new and unusual **3. LIE OR TRICK** a story or plan devised to be deceitful

con·com·i·tance /kən kómmitənss/ *n* **1. EXISTENCE OR OCCURRENCE TOGETHER** the existence or occurrence of something at the same time as, or in connection with, something else **2. SOMETHING CONNECTED WITH SOMETHING ELSE** something that exists at the same time, or in connection with, something else **3.** CHR **CHRISTIAN BELIEF REGARDING COMMUNION** the belief of some Christians that the body and blood of Jesus Christ are embodied in the bread and wine taken at Communion

con·com·i·tant /kən kómmitənt/ *adj* happening or existing along with or at the same time as something else (*formal*) ○ *parenthood and all its concomitant responsibilities* [Early 17C. < late Latin *concomitant-*, present participle of *concomitari* "accompany" < Latin *comit-* "companion"] —**con·com·i·tant** *n* —**con·com·i·tant·ly** *adv*

con·cord /kón kàwrd, kóng kàwrd/ *n* **1. PEACEFUL CO-EXISTENCE** agreement, friendly relations, or peace **2. TREATY** a peace treaty **3.** MUSIC **PLEASING COMBINATION OF SOUNDS** a pleasing sound made when two or more notes are played together (*formal*) **4.** GRAM same as **agreement** (sense 4) [13C. Via French < Latin *concord-* "of one heart" < *cor* "heart"]

Con·cord /kóngkərd/ **1.** city in western California, a northern suburb of the Oakland-San Francisco area, northeast of Berkeley. Population: 125,225 (2002 estimate). **2.** town in northeastern Massachusetts, west of Boston, on the Concord River. On April 19, 1775, it was the site of the first military encounter of the Revolution. Population: 17,028 (2002 estimate). **3.** capital of New Hampshire, in the south of the state, on the Merrimack River. Population: 41,404 (2002 estimate). **4.** city in southwestern North Carolina, northeast of Charlotte. It was a gold-mining town in the 18th century. Population: 58,490 (2002 estimate).

con·cor·dance /kən káwrd'nss/ *n* **1.** similarity or agreement between two or more things **2.** an index of words arranged in alphabetical order, e.g., of all the words in a body or bank of text. A concordance often gives information about the meaning and context of a listed word. [14C. Via French < medieval Latin *concordantia* < Latin *concordant-* (see CONCORDANT)]

con·cor·dant /kən káwrd'nt/ *adj* showing harmony, unity, or agreement (*formal*) [15C. Via French < Latin *concordant-*, present participle of *concordare* "bring into harmony" < *concord-* (see CONCORD)] —**con·cor·dant·ly** *adv*

con·cor·dat /kən káwr dàt/ *n* an official agreement, especially a formal contract between the pope and a national government concerning the religious affairs of a country [Early 17C. Via French < Latin *concordatum* < past participle of *concordare* (see CONCORDANT)]

Con·cord grape *n* a blue-black sweet grape variety from the eastern United States. Use: sparkling and dessert wines, jellies and jams, grape juice. Latin name: *Vitis labrusca*. [Mid-19C. After CONCORD, Massachusetts]

con·cours /kóN kóor/, **con·cours d'é·lé·gance** *n* a meeting at which classic or vintage cars are exhibited and prizes awarded

con·course /kón kàwrss, kóng-/ *n* **1. LARGE OPEN SPACE** a large space where people can gather in a public place or building, e.g., at an airport or train station **2. CROWD** a large number of people who have gathered for a special event (*formal*) 3. GATHERING TOGETHER the action of coming or moving together, or an example of this (*formal*) [14C. Via French < Latin *concursus* "assembly" < *concurs-*, past participle of *concurrere* (see CONCUR)]

con·cres·cence /kən kréss'nss/ *n* 1. the growing or coming together of body parts or organs, especially in the normal early formation of an embryo 2. MED same as **concretion** (sense 3) [Early 17C. < Latin *concrescent-*, present participle of *concrescere* (see CONCRETE)] —**con·cres·cent** *adj*

con·crete *n* /kón kreet, kóng-, kon kreet, kong-/ 1. HARD CONSTRUCTION MATERIAL a mixture of cement, sand, aggregate, and water in specific proportions that hardens to a strong stony consistency over varying lengths of time 2. PHYS MASS OF COALESCED PARTICLES a mass formed when particles coalesce ■ *adj* /kon kreet, kong-/ 1. SOLID AND REAL able to be seen or touched because it exists in reality, not just as an idea 2. DEFINITE certain and specific rather than vague or general ○ *concrete proposals for reform* 3. PHYS SOLIDIFIED made solid by coalescence ■ *vt* /kón kreet, kóng-, kon kreet, kong-/ (**-cret·ed, -cret·ing, -cretes**) PUT CONCRETE SOMEWHERE to cover an area with concrete [14C. Via French < Latin *concretus*, past participle of *concrescere* "grow together" < *crescere* "grow"] —**con·crete·ly** *adv* —**con·crete·ness** *n*

con·crete jun·gle *n* an urban area completely covered with walkways, roads, and buildings, and perceived as a hostile environment

con·crete mu·sic *n* electronic music assembled from recordings of live sounds, usually including natural and mechanical sources, manipulated for effect [Translation of French *musique concrète* "real music"]

con·crete noun *n* a noun that refers to a physical, and usually visible or touchable, object or substance, e.g., "clock" or "elephant"

con·crete po·et·ry *n* verse that uses physical arrangement of the words on the page to add to its meaning and effect

con·cre·tion /kən kreesh'n/ *n* 1. FORMATION OF WHOLE FROM PARTS the process in which separate parts or particles come together into a solid mass 2. SOLID FORMED BY UNIFICATION OF PARTS a hard solid mass formed by parts uniting into a whole 3. MED INORGANIC MASS IN BODY a mass of inorganic material in a body organ or tissue, usually caused by disease 4. GEOL ROUNDED MASS a rounded mass of compact concentric layers within a sediment, built up around a nucleus such as a fossil [Mid-16C. Directly or via French < Latin *concretion-* < *concret-*, past participle of *concrescere* (see CONCRETE)] —**con·cre·tion·ar·y** *adj*

con·cret·ism /kon kreet ìzzəm/ *n* the creation of physical things to represent abstract ideas, especially by the use of concrete poetry —**con·cret·ist** *n*

con·cre·tize /kóngkrə tìz/ (**-tized, -tiz·ing, -tiz·es**) *vt* to make something solid, real, or specific —**con·cre·ti·za·tion** /kòngkrəti záysh'n/ *n*

con·cu·bi·nage /kon kyóobinij, kən-/ *n* the state of being or keeping a concubine

con·cu·bine /kóngkyə bìn, kónkyə-/ *n* 1. a woman who is the lover of a wealthy married man but with the social status of a subordinate form of wife, often kept in a separate home, especially in imperial China 2. a woman who lives with a man and has a sexual relationship with him but is not married to him (*dated*) [13C. Via French < Latin *concubina* "sharer of somebody's bed" < *cubare* "lie down"] —**con·cu·bi·na·ry** /kon kyóobi nèrree/ *adj*

con·cu·pis·cence /kon kyóopiss'nss/ *n* powerful feelings of physical desire (*formal*) [14C. Via French < late Latin *concupiscentia* < *concupiscere* "start longing for" < *cupere* "to desire"] —**con·cu·pis·cent** *adj*

con·cur /kən kúr/ (**-curred, -cur·ring, -curs**) *v* 1. *vti* to have the same opinion as somebody else, or reach agreement independently on a specific point 2. *vi* to happen at the same time [14C. < Latin *concurrere*, literally "run together" < *currere* "run"] —**con·cur·ring·ly** *adv*

SYNONYMS See ***agree***.

con·cur·rent /kən kúr ənt/ *adj* taking place, existing, or running parallel at the same time [14C. < Latin *concurrent-*, present participle of *concurrere* (see CONCUR)] —**con·cur·rence** *n* —**con·cur·rent·ly** *adv*

con·cuss /kən kúss/ (**-cussed, -cuss·ing, -cuss·es**) *vt* to cause somebody concussion, usually by a blow to the head or a jarring fall or jolt [Late 16C. < Latin *concuss-*, past participle of *concutere* "strike together" < *quatere* "to strike"]

con·cus·sion /kən kúsh'n/ *n* 1. MED MILD BRAIN INJURY an injury to the brain, often resulting from a blow to the head, that can cause temporary disorientation, memory loss, or unconsciousness 2. MED INJURY TO BODILY ORGAN an injury to an organ of the body, usually caused by a violent blow or shaking 3. SUDDEN JOLT OR SHOCK any sudden violent jolting or shaking —**con·cus·sive** /-kússiv/ *adj*

~~condem~~ incorrect spelling of **condemn**

con·demn /kən dém/ (**-demned, -demn·ing, -demns**) *vt* 1. GIVE SOMEBODY LEGAL SENTENCE to make a judicial pronouncement stating what punishment has been imposed on a person found guilty of a crime, especially in the case of a heavy penalty or a death sentence 2. CONSIDER SOMEBODY OR SOMETHING GUILTY to judge that somebody or something is to blame for something 3. SAY SOMEBODY OR SOMETHING IS BAD to state that somebody or something is in some way wrong or unacceptable 4. MAKE SOMEBODY EXPERIENCE SOMETHING to force somebody to experience something very unpleasant, especially something permanent or long-lasting 5. BAN USE OR CONSUMPTION OF SOMETHING to issue an official order saying that something such as a building is unfit to be used 6. PROVE SOMEBODY GUILTY to serve as proof of the guilt of somebody 7. LAW APPROPRIATE PROPERTY to take property under eminent domain for public use [14C. Via French < Latin *condemnare* "pass final sentence" < *damnare* (see DAMN)] —**con·dem·na·ble** /-démnəb'l/ *adj* —**con·dem·na·tion** /kòn dem náysh'n, -dəm-/ *n* —**con·dem·na·to·ry** /-démnə tàwree/ *adj*

SYNONYMS See ***criticize***.

con·den·sate /kóndən sàyt, kən dén sàyt/ *n* a substance resulting from condensation, especially a liquid from a vapor

con·den·sa·tion /kòn den sáysh'n, kòndən-/ *n* 1. FILM OF WATER DROPLETS tiny drops of water that form on a cold surface such as a window when warmer air comes into contact with it 2. MAKING SOMETHING SHORTER the state of being compressed or made briefer, or the act or result of summarizing or compressing something 3. PHYS CONVERSION OF GAS TO LIQUID the process by which a vapor loses heat and changes into a liquid 4. CHEM FORMATION OF DENSER MOLECULES the bonding of molecules of a substance to form a larger denser molecule, usually with the release of simpler substances such as water —**con·den·sa·tion·al** *adj*

con·den·sa·tion trail *n* AVIAT same as **vapor trail**

con·dense /kən dénss/ (**-densed, -dens·ing, -dens·es**) *v* 1. *vti* CHANGE FROM GAS TO LIQUID to lose heat and change from a vapor into a liquid, or make a vapor change to a liquid 2. *vti* COOK THICKEN BY REMOVING WATER to make something, especially a food, denser by removing water, or become denser in this way 3. *vt* MAKE TEXT SHORTER to reduce the length of a text by removing unnecessary words or passages or by expressing the content more concisely 4. *vti* CHEM FORM DENSER MOLECULES to bond together to form a larger denser molecule, or make molecules undergo this process [15C. Via French < Latin *condensare* "thicken" < *condensus* "very dense" < *densus* "thick"] —**con·dens·a·bil·i·ty** /kən dènsə bíllətee/ *n* —**con·dens·a·ble** *adj*

con·densed milk /kən dénst-/ *n* milk that is thickened by evaporating most of the water content and then sweetened

con·dens·er /kən dénssər/ *n* 1. PHYS a device that converts a gas to a liquid to obtain either the substance or the released heat 2. OPTICS a lens or mirror used to concentrate light, e.g., onto a transparency or specimen 3. ELEC same as **capacitor**

Con·der /kóndər/, **Charles Edward** (1868–1909) British painter. He was trained in Australia, where he was part of the impressionist Heidelberg School. Among his best-known works is *A Holiday at Mentone* (1888).

con·de·scend /kòndə sénd/ (**-scend·ed, -scend·ing, -scends**) *vi* 1. to behave toward other people as though they are socially or intellectually inferior 2. to do something regarded as unimportant or demeaning in order to impress or appear generous toward others ○ *She condescended to travel with us.* [14C. Via French < ecclesiastical Latin *condescendere* "lower yourself" < Latin *descendere* (see DESCEND)] —**con·de·scend·er** *n*

con·de·scend·ing /kòndə sénding/ *adj* behaving toward other people in a way that shows you consider yourself socially or intellectually superior to them —**con·de·scend·ing·ly** *adv*

con·de·scen·sion /kòndə sénshən/ *n* behavior that implies that somebody is graciously lowering himself or herself to the level of people less important or intelligent [Mid-17C. Via French < ecclesiastical Latin *condescension-* < *condescendere* (see CONDESCEND)]

~~condesending~~ incorrect spelling of **condescending**

con·dign /kən dín/ *adj* well deserved and completely appropriate (*formal*) [14C. Via French < Latin *condignus* "wholly worthy" < *dignus* "worthy"] —**con·dign·ly** *adv*

con·di·ment /kóndimənt/ *n* salt, pepper, mustard, relish, or a similar substance added in small amounts to food, usually at the table, to improve or adjust its flavor [15C. Via French < Latin *condimentum* < *condire* "to preserve"]

con·di·tion /kən dísh'n/ *n* 1. STATE OF REPAIR the particular state of repair or ability to function of an object or piece of equipment ○ *The car is still in good condition.* 2. STATE OF HEALTH a state of physical fitness or general health ○ *out of condition* 3. DISORDER a physical disorder 4. WAY OF BEING a general state or mode of existence, especially one characterized by hardship or suffering 5. SOMETHING NECESSARY something that must exist for something else to happen, e.g., to bring a situation about or make a contract valid ○ *a condition of the agreement* 6. STATUS position, rank, or social status (*formal*) ■ **con·di·tions** *npl* FACTORS AFFECTING PEOPLE the factors or circumstances that affect the situation somebody is living or working in ○ *poor working conditions* ■ *vt* (**-tioned, -tion·ing, -tions**) 1. TRAIN SOMEBODY to make people or animals act or react in a particular way by gradually getting them used to a specific pattern of events 2. MAKE SOMEBODY STRONG OR SOMETHING READY to give somebody or something a treatment to improve general health, soundness, readiness for use, appearance, or performance 3. IMPROVE CONDITION OF HAIR to put conditioner or a similar substance on the hair in order to improve its appearance and texture 4. SPECIFY REQUIREMENT to state a requirement that must be fulfilled, or to make something dependent on a requirement, especially in a legal contract (*formal*) 5. ADAPT SOMETHING to adapt something to specific conditions or activities 6. COOL AIR to make air cooler ○ *Heat pumps condition the air on the first floor.* [13C. Via French < Latin *condition-* "agreement, stipulation" < *condicere* "talk together" < *dicere* "say"] —**con·di·tion·a·ble** *adj*

con·di·tion·al /kən díshən'l, -díshnəl/ *adj* 1. DEPENDENT ON SOMETHING ELSE BEING DONE describes something that will be done or will happen only if and when another thing is done or happens 2. GRAM STATING CONDITION OR LIMITATION describes a clause, conjunction, verb form, or sentence that expresses a condition or limitation 3. MATH TRUE ONLY FOR CERTAIN MATHEMATICAL VALUES true only for some values of one or more variables in a mathematical equation 4. MATH DESCRIBES SERIES OF NUMBERS describes a convergent series of numbers that becomes a divergent series when its terms are converted to their absolute values ■ *n* GRAM CONDITIONAL FORM a conditional clause, conjunction, verb form, or sentence —**con·di·tion·al·i·ty** /kən dìsh'n állətee/ *n* —**con·di·tion·al·ly** *adv*

con·di·tion·al·i·za·tion /kən dìshən'li záysh'n, -dìshnəli-/ *n* the process of turning a statement into a conditional statement, e.g., changing "It will rain" into "If it is cloudy, then it will rain"

con·di·tion·al·ly /kən díshən'lee, -díshnəlee/ *adv* with the proviso that all valid conditions be met

con·di·tion·al prob·a·bil·i·ty *n* the probability that one event will occur, given that another event has occurred or is certain to occur

con·di·tion code *n* a signal, usually in the form of a

number, that indicates the status of a previous arithmetic, logic, or input/output operation

con·di·tioned /kən dísh'nd/ *adj* **1.** having reached a particular or high level of fitness, quality, or performance **2.** brought on unconsciously by a stimulus that triggers a reaction because of a learned association with something else

con·di·tioned re·sponse, **con·di·tioned re·flex** *n* a response to a new second stimulus as a result of association with a prior stimulus. The classic example is Pavlov's experiment in which dogs began to salivate at the sound of a bell, having previously been fed when the bell was rung.

con·di·tioned stim·u·lus *n* in classical psychological conditioning, an otherwise ineffective stimulus that, when paired with an unconditioned stimulus, is able to evoke a conditioned response

con·di·tion·er /kən dísh'nər/ *n* **1.** a liquid or cream applied to hair, either after or with shampoo and usually while the hair is still wet, to make it more manageable or healthier **2.** a substance that makes something such as bread dough or soil easier to manage

con·di·tion·ing /kən dísh'ning/ *n* a method of controlling or influencing the way people or animals behave or think by using a gradual training process

con·do /kóndō/ (*plural* **-dos**) *n* same as **condominium** (senses 1–2) (*informal*) [Mid-20C. Shortening]

con·dole /kən dṓl/ (**-doled, -dol·ing, -doles**) *vi* to express sympathy to somebody who is experiencing grief, loss, or pain, especially over a death (*formal*) [Late 16C. < ecclesiastical Latin *condolere* "grieve together" < *dolere* "suffer"] —**con·do·la·to·ry** *adj* —**con·dol·er** *n* —**con·dol·ing·ly** *adv*

USAGE condole or **console**? These words are easy to confuse because they are both connected with reassuring people in distress. The more common word is ***console***, which takes an object and means "to provide comfort to somebody": *She tried to console her father when his mother died.* ***Condole*** is more formal and means "to express sympathy"; it does not take an object but uses *with*: *She condoled with her father over the death of his mother.*

con·do·lence /kən dṓlənss/ *n* an expression of sorrow and sympathy, usually to somebody who is grieving over a death (*often used in the plural*) —**con·do·lent** *adj* —**con·do·lent·ly** *adv*

con do·lo·re /kòn də láw rày, -ree, kàwn də láw rày/ *adv* in a sad or sorrowful way (*used as a musical direction*) [< Italian, "with sorrow"] —**con do·lo·re** *adj*

con·dom /kóndəm, kúndəm/ *n* a close-fitting rubber covering worn by a man over the penis during sexual intercourse to prevent pregnancy or the spread of sexually transmitted disease [Early 18C. Origin ?]

con·do·min·i·um /kòndə mínnee əm/ *n* **1.** INDIVIDUALLY OWNED APARTMENT an individually owned unit of real estate, especially an apartment or town house, in a building or on land that is owned in common by the owners of the units **2.** BUILDING CONTAINING CONDOMINIUMS a building or complex containing condominium apartments or town houses **3.** STATE RULED BY FOREIGN COUNTRIES a country governed by two or more different countries with joint responsibility **4.** JOINT GOVERNMENT OF TERRITORY the system under which a country or state is ruled by two or more other nations [Early 18C. < modern Latin, "joint right of ownership" < Latin *dominium* (see DOMINION)] —**con·do·min·i·al** *adj*

con·done /kən dṓn/ (**-doned, -don·ing, -dones**) *vt* to regard something that is considered immoral or wrong in a tolerant way, without criticizing it or feeling strongly about it ○ *condoning violence* [Mid-19C. < Latin *condonare* "give up" < *donare* (see DONATION)] —**con·don·a·ble** *adj* —**con·do·na·tion** /kòndə náysh'n, -dō-/ *n* —**con·don·er** *n*

con·dor /kón dàwr, kóndər/ *n* a large vulture with dull black feathers and white around the neck. Native to: Andes. Latin name: *Vultur gryphus.* [Early 17C. Via Spanish *cóndor* < Quechua *kuntur*]

Con·dor·cet /kawn dawr sáy/, **Marie Jean Antoine Nicholas de Caritat, Marquis de** (1743–94) French philosopher, political leader, and mathematician. Among his contributions to French thought are his study of the theory of probability (1785) and his reform of the education system. His best-known work, *Esquisse d'un Tableau Historique des Progrès de l'Esprit Humain (Sketch of the Intellectual Progress of Mankind)* (1795), outlines his belief in human progress.

condor

con·dot·tie·re /kon dòttee é rày, -érree, kòndə tyé rày/ (*plural* **-ri** /-ree/) *n* **1.** a man who led a group of hired soldiers, especially during the period of the Italian Renaissance, between the 13th and 16th centuries **2.** a hired soldier [Late 18C. < Italian, "contractor"]

con·duce /kən dóoss/ (**-duced, -duc·ing, -duc·es**) *vi* to help, contribute, or lead to bringing about an action or event (*formal*) [14C. < Latin *conducere* "bring together" < *ducere* "to lead"] —**con·duc·er** *n* —**con·duc·i·ble** *adj* —**con·duc·ing·ly** *adv*

con·du·cive /kən dóossiv/ *adj* tending to bring about an intended result ○ *tensions not conducive to a good working relationship*

con·duct *v* /kən dúkt/ (**-duct·ed, -duct·ing, -ducts**) **1.** *vt* DO OR RUN SOMETHING to carry out, manage, or control something ○ *Negotiations were conducted in great secrecy.* **2.** *vr* BEHAVE to behave in a particular way ○ *She conducted herself with great dignity.* **3.** *vt* GUIDE SOMEBODY ALONG to lead a person or group of people somewhere by going along with them **4.** *vti* LEAD INSTRUMENTAL OR VOCAL GROUP to lead a group of musicians or a musical performance by signaling the beat with a baton or hand gestures, giving cues, and offering suggestions for interpretation or expression **5.** *vti* TRANSMIT ENERGY to transmit energy such as heat, light, sound, or electricity ■ *n* /kón dùkt/ **1.** BEHAVIOR the way a person behaves, especially in public ○ *language or conduct likely to offend* **2.** HOW SOMEBODY MANAGES SOMETHING the management or execution of matters such as work or official affairs ○ *criticized for his conduct of the campaign* [15C. Directly or via Old French *conduit* < Latin *conduct-*, past participle of *conducere* (see CONDUCE)] —**con·duct·i·bil·i·ty** /kən dùktə bíllətee/ *n* —**con·duct·i·ble** *adj*

SYNONYMS See ***guide.***

con·duc·tance /kən dúktənss/ *n* a measure of the ability of an object or substance to transmit electricity, expressed as the reciprocal of resistance. Symbol *G*

con·duct·ed tour /kən dùktəd-/ *n* a tour of a place of cultural interest, led by a guide who explains the significance of the various sights

con·duc·tion /kən dúksh'n/ *n* **1.** TRANSMISSION OF ENERGY the passage of energy, particularly heat or electricity, through something **2.** TRANSMISSION THROUGH NERVE FIBER the transmission of biochemical or electrical energy through a nerve fiber **3.** CONVEYANCE THROUGH PASSAGE the passage of something through or along something, e.g., water through a pipe

con·duc·tive /kən dúktiv/ *adj* **1.** transmitting or able to transmit energy, particularly heat or electricity **2.** describes a cell that allows a physiological disturbance such as a nerve impulse to pass through it

con·duc·tive ker·a·to·plas·ty *n* a surgical treatment to correct farsightedness that involves the use of heat, delivered via a needle, to shrink tissue and reshape the eyeball

con·duc·tiv·i·ty /kòn duk tívvətee/ (*plural* **-ties**) *n* **1.** the ability of an object or substance to transmit heat, electricity, or sound **2.** ELEC same as **conductance 3.** the ability of tissue to transmit nerve impulses

con·duc·tor /kən dúktər/ *n* **1.** MUSIC DIRECTOR OF ORCHESTRA OR CHOIR somebody in charge of an orchestra or choir who marks time and signals musicians or singers when and how to play or sing **2.** TRANSP SOMEBODY WHO COLLECTS FARES an employee who takes money for tickets on a bus or streetcar **3.** RAIL RAILROAD EMPLOYEE IN CHARGE OF PASSENGERS a railroad employee who is in charge of a train and whose job is to check tickets, announce stops, and attend to passengers' needs and safety **4.** PHYS SOMETHING THAT CONVEYS HEAT OR ELECTRICITY a substance, body, or medium that allows heat, electricity, light, or sound to pass along it or through it. Metals are good conductors of heat because of the high concentration of free electrons they contain. —**con·duc·to·ri·al** /kòn duk táwree əl/ *adj* —**con·duc·tor·ship** *n*

con·duit /kón dōo it, kóndwit/ *n* **1.** CHANNEL FOR LIQUID a pipe or channel that carries liquid to or from a place **2.** PROTECTIVE COVER FOR CABLE a pipe or tube that covers and protects electrical cables **3.** CONVEYER OF INFORMATION somebody or something that conveys information, especially in secret [14C. Original form of CONDUCT]

con·dyle /kón dìl, kónd'l/ *n* a rounded part at the end of a bone that forms a moving joint with a cup-shaped cavity in another bone. The ball part of a ball-and-socket joint such as the hip or shoulder joint is a condyle. [Mid-17C. Via French < Greek *kondulos* "knuckle"] —**con·dy·lar** /kónd'lər/ *adj* —**con·dy·loid** /kónd'l òyd/ *adj*

con·dy·lo·ma /kònd'l ṓmə/ (*plural* **-mas** or **-ma·ta** /-mətə/) *n* a growth resembling a wart on the skin or a mucous membrane, usually of the genitals or anus [14C. Via Latin < Greek *kondulōma* "callous knob or lump" < *kondulos* "knuckle"]

cone /kōn/ *n* **1.** POINTED OBJECT WITH ROUND BASE an object or shape that has a circular base and tapers to a point at the top, or has a circular top and tapers to a point at the bottom **2.** POINTED FIGURE WITH CURVED FLAT BASE a three-dimensional geometric figure formed by straight lines through a fixed point (**vertex**) to the points of a fixed curve (**directrix**). A circular cone has a directrix that is a circle. **3.** CONE-SHAPED WAFER FOR ICE CREAM a cone-shaped or cup-shaped wafer used for serving ice cream, or such a wafer with ice cream in it **4.** PLASTIC CONE-SHAPED ROAD MARKER a plastic cone-shaped object used as a temporary road marker or barrier, e.g., to close off part or all of a road during repairs or after an accident **5.** CONE-SHAPED PAPER FOR MARIJUANA a small cone-shaped paper container from which marijuana is smoked **6.** BOT SEED-BEARING STRUCTURE OF TREE a tightly packed cluster of scales that bears the reproductive organs of coniferous plants such as pines and firs. Male cones produce pollen, and female cones bear seeds. Technical name **strobilus** (sense 1) **7.** BOT REPRODUCTIVE PART OF NONFLOWERING PLANTS a club-shaped, umbrella-shaped, or poker-shaped cluster of fertile leaves that bears the spore-producing organs of a club moss or horsetail **8.** ANAT LIGHT RECEPTOR CELL IN EYE a cone-shaped cell sensitive to light and color in the retina of the eye of a human being or any other vertebrate animal. There are three different types of cone cells, responding to blue, green, or red light. **9.** MARINE BIOL SEA SNAIL WITH CONE-SHAPED SHELL a sea snail with a cone-shaped, vividly marked shell and a poisonous, sometimes fatal, sting. Native to: South Pacific and Indian oceans. Family: Conidae. **10.** GEOG VOLCANO a cone-shaped mountain, especially a volcano ■ *vt* (**coned, con·ing, cones**) MAKE SOMETHING INTO CONE SHAPE to shape something into the form of a cone [15C. Via French < Greek *kōnos* "pine cone, cone"]

~~**conection**~~ incorrect spelling of **connection**

cone·flow·er /kṓn flòwr/ *n* a plant of the daisy family with variously colored flowers with a brown or black cone-shaped center. Native to: North America. Genera: *Echinacea* or *Rudbeckia* or *Ratibida.*

cone·nose /kṓn nòz/, **cone-nosed bug** *n* a bloodsucking insect that feeds on other insects, inflicts painful bites on humans, and transmits diseases. Native to: Mexico, southern and western United States. Family: Reduviidae.

cone shell *n* MARINE BIOL same as **cone** *n* (sense 9)

con es·pres·si·o·ne /kòn ə spressee ṓ này, kàwn-/ *adv* with feeling and expression (*used as a musical direction*) [< Italian, "with expression"] —**con es·pres·si·o·ne** *adj*

Con·es·to·ga wag·on /kònnə stṓgə-/ *n* a large heavy wagon with a high rounded canvas covering, usually drawn by six horses and used for long-distance freight transportation in North America during the 18th and 19th centuries [Early 18C. After a village in SE Pennsylvania]

co·ney /kṓnee/ (*plural* **-neys**), **co·ny** (*plural* **-nies**) *n* **1.** ZOOL **EUROPEAN RABBIT** a rabbit, especially the common domesticated European rabbit **2. RABBIT FUR** rabbit fur used for coats and other articles of clothing **3.** ZOOL same as **hyrax 4.** ZOOL same as **pika 5.** *Southeast US, Carib* FISH **CARIBBEAN FISH** a fish with varying color phases that lives along reefs of the Caribbean Sea [14C. Via Anglo-Norman < Latin *cuniculus* "rabbit, burrow"]

Co·ney Is·land /kṓnee-/ amusement area, formerly a resort, in southern Brooklyn, New York City. It was an island, but has become part of Long Island since the silting up of Coney Island Creek.

conf. *abbr* **1.** confer **2.** conference **3.** CHR confessor **4.** confidential

con·fab /kón fàb/ (*informal*) *n* **1. TALK** a chat or casual discussion **2. GATHERING OF PEOPLE** a gathering of people for discussion or decision-making ■ *vi* (**-fabbed, -fab·bing, -fabs**) **TALK ABOUT SOMETHING** to have a chat or discussion about something [Early 18C. Shortening of *confabulation*]

con·fab·u·late /kən fábbyə làyt/ (**-lat·ed, -lat·ing, -lates**) *vi* **1.** to discuss or have a chat about something (*formal*) **2.** to give fictitious accounts of past events, believing they are true, in order to cover a gap in the memory caused by a medical condition such as dementia or Korsakoff's syndrome [Early 17C. < Latin *confabulat-*, past participle of *confabulari* "talk together" < *fabula* (see FABLE)] —**con·fab·u·la·tion** /-fàbbyə láysh'n/ *n* —**con·fab·u·la·tor** *n* —**con·fab·u·la·to·ry** *adj*

con·fect /kən fékt/ *vt* (**-fect·ed, -fect·ing, -fects**) **1. PUT TOGETHER** to create something by combining different materials or items ○ *the authority to set up rules and confect and enforce a program* **2. MAKE CANDY OR PRESERVES** to make candy by combining ingredients such as sugar, fruit, and nuts, or make preserves (*formal*) ■ *n* /kón fekt/ **SWEET CONFECTION** something such as chocolate that is a sweet confection (*formal*) [14C. < Latin *confect-*, past participle of *conficere* "put or make together" < *facere* "make"]

con·fec·tion /kən fékshən/ *n* **1.** FOOD **SOMETHING SWEET** a sweet food made by combining ingredients such as fruit, nuts, and sugar **2. COMBINATION** the process of combining things, or the result of such combination ○ *a confection of lies and half-truths* **3. ELABORATE CREATION** an often elaborate piece of craftsmanship and skill, e.g., an ornate piece of women's clothing ○ *Her gown was a marvelous confection of lace and tulle.*

con·fec·tion·er /kən fékshənər/ *n* somebody who makes or sells candies

con·fec·tion·ers' sug·ar *n US* finely powdered sugar with cornstarch added, used for making cake icing or for dusting pastries and some types of bread. Can term **icing sugar**

con·fec·tion·er·y /kən fékshə nèrree/ (*plural* **-ies**) *n* **1.** FOOD **CONFECTIONS** candies considered collectively **2.** COOK **CANDY-MAKING** the skill, technique, or practice of making candy **3.** COMM **CONFECTIONER'S STORE** a store where candy is sold

confed. *abbr* POL **1.** confederate **2.** confederation

Confed. *abbr* POL **1.** Confederate **2.** Confederation

con·fed·er·a·cy /kən féddərəssee/ *n* **1.** an alliance of people, states, or parties for a common purpose, or the people, states, or parties in an alliance **2.** a group of people who have joined together to do something unlawful

Con·fed·er·a·cy *n* HIST same as **Confederate States of America**

con·fed·er·al /kən féddərəl/ *adj* **1.** relating to a confederation **2.** relating to the activities of two or more nations —**con·fed·er·al·ist** *n*

con·fed·er·ate *n* /kən féddərət/ **1. ALLY** one of two or more people, groups, or nations that have formed an alliance for a common purpose **2. ACCOMPLICE** a plotter or conspirator ■ *adj* /kən féddərət/ **ASSOCIATED** joined in common purpose ■ *vti* /kən féddə ràyt/ (**-at·ed, -at·ing, -ates**) **UNITE** to form people, groups, or nations into a confederacy, or become part of a confederacy [14C. < late Latin *confoederat-*, past participle of *confoederare* "league together" < *foeder-* (see FEDERAL)] —**con·fed·er·a·tive** /-ràytiv/ *adj*

Con·fed·er·ate /kən féddərət/ *n* a supporter or soldier of the Confederate States of America during the Civil War —**Con·fed·er·ate** *adj*

Con·fed·er·ate Me·mo·ri·al Day *n* a holiday remembering Civil War dead, observed by descendants of Confederate soldiers. Date: spring.

Con·fed·er·ate States of A·mer·i·ca *n* the confederation of the 11 southern states that seceded from the United States in 1861, an act that started the Civil War. Alabama, Arkansas, Florida, Georgia, Louisiana, Mississippi, North Carolina, South Carolina, Tennessee, Texas, and Virginia were the states that seceded.

con·fed·er·a·tion /kən fèddə ráysh'n/ *n* **1. GROUP OF LOOSELY ALLIED STATES** a group of states that are allied together to form a political unit in which they keep most of their independence but act together for purposes such as defense **2. BODY REPRESENTING INDEPENDENT ORGANIZATIONS** a body comprising representatives of independent organizations that wish to cooperate for a common beneficial purpose **3. CONFEDERATING** the formation of a confederation, or the state of being a confederation —**con·fed·er·a·tion·ism** *n* —**con·fed·er·a·tion·ist** *n*

Con·fed·er·a·tion *n* **1.** the original union of Ontario, Quebec, New Brunswick, and Nova Scotia in 1867 into the federation of Canada, afterward joined by the six other provinces **2.** the union of the original 13 states of the United States under the Articles of Confederation from 1781 to 1789

con·fer /kən fúr/ (**-ferred, -fer·ring, -fers**) *v* **1.** *vi* **DISCUSS SOMETHING WITH SOMEBODY** to talk with somebody in order to compare opinions or make a decision **2.** *vt* **GIVE HONOR OR TITLE** to give something such as a title, honor, or favor to somebody (*formal*) ○ *The university conferred an honorary Doctor of Law degree on the president.* **3.** *vt* **GIVE CHARACTERISTIC** to give somebody or something a status or characteristic ○ *His demeanor conferred a sense of dignity on the whole affair.* ○ *genes that confer resistance to certain infections* [15C. < Latin *conferre* "bring together" < *ferre* "bring"] —**con·fer·ment** *n* —**con·fer·ra·ble** *adj* —**con·fer·ral** *n* —**con·fer·rer** *n*

SYNONYMS See ***give***.

~~**confered**~~ incorrect spelling of **conferred**

con·fer·ee /kònfə rée/, **con·fer·ree** *n* **1.** a participant in a conference **2.** the recipient of a title, honor, or favor

con·fer·ence /kónfərənss/ *n* **1. MEETING FOR LECTURES AND DISCUSSION** a meeting, sometimes lasting for several days, in which people with a common interest participate in discussions or listen to lectures to obtain information **2. MEETING FOR SERIOUS DISCUSSION** a meeting to discuss serious matters such as policy or business **3. MEETING OF REPRESENTATIVES OF ORGANIZATION** a usually annual gathering of local representatives of an organization, e.g., a political party, labor union, or church, at which policy matters and other issues are discussed or decided ○ *the Democratic Party Conference* **4.** POL **MEETING OF TWO LEGISLATIVE COMMITTEES** a meeting of select members or committees from two legislative bodies, for the purpose of settling differences between bills they have passed **5.** CHR **AREA ORGANIZATION OF CHURCHES** in some Protestant churches, a regional or national body to which a number of local churches belong ○ *the Friends General Conference* **6. SPORTS LEAGUE** an association or league of sports teams that compete with each other

con·fer·ence call *n* a conversation involving three or more people linked together by telephone

con·fer·enc·ing /kónfərənssing/ *n* the holding of a conference, meeting, or discussion in which the participants are linked by telephone (**audioconferencing**), by telephone and video equipment (**videoconferencing**), or by computer (**computer conferencing**)

con·fer·ree *n* another spelling of **conferee**

con·fess /kən féss/ (**-fessed, -fess·ing, -fess·es**) *v* **1.** *vti* **ADMIT HAVING DONE SOMETHING WRONG** to admit a wrongdoing, crime, or error openly ○ *She confessed to having taken the watch.* ○ *interrupted to confess that I had left the door unlocked* **2.** *vt* **ACKNOWLEDGE SOMETHING TO BE TRUE** to admit the truth of something reluctantly ○ *I must confess I didn't really want to come here tonight.* ○ *asked me about ley lines but I had to confess my ignorance* **3.** *vti* CHR **ADMIT SINS** to reveal sins to a priest or to God and ask for forgiveness ○ *It had been some months since I had confessed.* **4.** *vt* CHR **HEAR SOMEBODY'S CONFESSION** to listen to a confession of sins by somebody ○ *A priest visited her to confess her every day.* **5.** *vt* **ACKNOWLEDGE FAITH IN SOMETHING** to declare faith or belief in something or somebody (*archaic*) [14C. Via French *confesser* < Latin *confess-*, past participle of *confiteri* "acknowledge," literally "declare utterly" < *fateri* "declare"] —**con·fess·a·ble** *adj*

con·fess·ed·ly /kən féssədlee/ *adv* used to indicate that something is admitted to be the case

con·fes·sion /kən fésh'n/ *n* **1. ADMISSION OF WRONGDOING** an admission of having done something wrong or embarrassing ○ *a confession of weakness on her part* **2.** LAW **ADMISSION OF GUILT** a voluntary written or verbal statement admitting the commission of a crime ○ *made a full written confession* **3. OPEN ACKNOWLEDGMENT OF FEELINGS** a profession of emotions or beliefs such as love, loyalty, or faith **4.** CHR **DECLARATION OF SINS** a formal declaration of sins confidentially to a priest or to God **5. SOMETHING ADMITTED** something that is confessed or disclosed **6.** RELIG **DECLARATION OF BELIEFS OR DOCTRINES** a declaration of the beliefs or doctrines of a religious body **7.** CHR **RELIGIOUS GROUP SHARING BELIEFS** a religious group that has a specific set of beliefs and practices

con·fes·sion·al /kən féshən'l, -féshnəl/ *adj* **1. RESEMBLING CONFESSION** suited to, typical of, or resembling an act of confession **2. BEING OF INTIMATE NATURE** relating to or being something intimately autobiographical in nature or content ■ *n* **PLACE FOR CONFESSION IN CHURCH** in the Roman Catholic church, a small wooden stall with a partition behind which a priest sits to hear confession

con·fes·sor /kən féssər/ *n* **1.** CHR **PRIEST** a priest who hears confessions and sometimes acts as a spiritual adviser **2.** CHR **CHRISTIAN NOT DETERRED BY PERSECUTION** a Christian who demonstrates his or her faith despite persecution for it, but without becoming a martyr (*archaic*) **3. SOMEBODY WHO CONFESSES** somebody who makes a confession

con·fet·ti /kən féttee/ *n* small pieces of colored paper or dried flowers thrown over people at festive occasions, especially over the bride and groom at a wedding ■ *adj* similar to confetti in shape or color [Early 19C. < Italian, plural of *confetto* "small sweet thrown at carnivals" < Latin *conficere* (see CONFECT)]

con·fi·dant /kónfi dànt, kònfi daánt/ *n* a person somebody trusts and discusses personal matters and problems with [Mid-17C. Alteration of CONFIDENT]

con·fi·dante /kónfi dànt, kònfi daánt/ *n* a woman somebody trusts and discusses personal matters and problems with [Early 18C. Alteration of CONFIDENT]

con·fide /kən fíd/ (**-fid·ed, -fid·ing, -fides**) *v* **1.** *vti* to tell somebody something that is to remain secret or private ○ *He later confided to me that he had not wanted the position at all.* ○ *He'd been foolish enough to confide in her.* **2.** *vt* to entrust somebody with something such as a valuable object or an important task (*archaic*) [15C. < Latin *confidere* "put your trust in" < *fidere* "to trust" < *fides* "trust"] —**con·fid·er** *n*

con·fi·dence /kónfidənss/ *n* **1. BELIEF IN OWN ABILITIES** self assurance or a belief in your ability to succeed ○ *lacked the confidence needed to reach the top* **2. FAITH IN SOMEBODY TO DO RIGHT** belief or trust in somebody or something, or in the ability of somebody or something to act in a proper, trustworthy, or reliable manner ○ *I have total confidence in her judgment.* **3. SECRET** something told to somebody that is to be kept private **4. TRUSTING RELATIONSHIP** a relationship based on trust and intimacy ○ *She took me into her confidence.* ○ *But I told you it in confidence!*

con·fi·dence game *n* a fraud in which somebody obtains something of value by first gaining the trust of the victim, then betraying that person

con·fi·dence in·ter·val *n* a range of statistical values within which a result is expected to fall with a specific probability

con·fi·dence lim·it *n* in statistics, the highest and lowest values of a confidence interval

con·fi·dence trick *n UK* same as **confidence game** —**con·fi·dence trick·ster** *n*

con·fi·dent /kónfidənt/ *adj* **1.** SELF-ASSURED certain of having the ability, judgment, and resources needed to succeed **2.** CONVINCED sure about the nature or facts of something ○ *We are confident that the market for our products is expanding.* **3.** EXCESSIVELY FORWARD bold and presumptuous in manner [Late 16C. Via French < Latin *confident-*, present participle of *confidere* (see CONFIDE)] —**con·fi·dent·ly** *adv*

con·fi·den·tial /kònfi dénsh'l/ *adj* **1.** PRIVATE AND SECRET carried out or revealed in the expectation that anything done or revealed will be kept private **2.** FOR SELECT GROUP not available to the public, e.g., because it is commercially or industrially sensitive or concerns matters of national security **3.** DEALING WITH PRIVATE AFFAIRS entrusted with somebody's personal or private matters **4.** SUGGESTING CLOSE RELATIONSHIP suggesting familiarity or intimacy that may or may not exist ○ *a confidential whisper* —**con·fi·den·ti·al·i·ty** /-denshee állətee/ *n* —**con·fi·den·tial·ly** *adv*

con·fi·den·tial com·mu·ni·ca·tion *n* a privileged communication with somebody such as a doctor, priest, lawyer, or spouse that a court cannot legally order to be disclosed

con·fid·ing /kən fíding/ *adj* willing to trust others with the knowledge of private or personal matters —**con·fid·ing·ly** *adv*

con·fig·u·ra·tion /kən fìggyə ráysh'n/ *n* **1.** ARRANGEMENT OF PARTS the way the parts of something are arranged and fit together ○ *In terms of boat configuration, deck layouts are all the same.* **2.** SHAPE OR OUTLINE the shape or outline of something, determined by the way its parts are arranged ○ *Geese fly in a V-shaped configuration.* **3.** COMPUT COMPUTER SYSTEM'S SETUP the way in which the software and hardware components of a computer system are arranged and interconnected **4.** PSYCHOL same as **gestalt** **5.** CHEM, PHYS ARRANGEMENT OF ATOMS IN MOLECULE the fixed stable spatial arrangement of atoms within a molecule —**con·fig·u·ra·tion·al** *adj* —**con·fig·u·ra·tion·al·ly** *adv* —**con·fig·u·ra·tive** /kən fíggyə ràytiv/ *adj*

con·fig·ure /kən fíggyər/ (**-ured, -ur·ing, -ures**) *vt* to set up, design, or arrange the parts of something for a specific purpose [14C. < Latin *configurare* "fashion after a pattern," literally "form together" < *figura* "shape"]

con·fine /kən fín/ *vt* (**-fined, -fin·ing, -fines**) **1.** KEEP WITHIN LIMITS to keep somebody or something within particular limits or boundaries ○ *Please confine your comments to the matters at hand.* **2.** KEEP IN SOME PLACE to prevent somebody or something from leaving an enclosed or limited space such as a prison, room, or bed ○ *confined to quarters for insubordination* ■ **con·fines** /kón fìnz/ *npl* BOUNDARIES the boundaries, limits, or scope restricting somebody or something ○ *seeking emotional fulfillment within the confines of a long-term relationship* [15C. < French *confiner* < *confins* (plural) "boundaries" < Latin *confinis* "ending with" < *finis* "end"] —**con·fin·a·ble** *adj* —**con·fin·er** *n*

con·fined /kən fínd/ *adj* small, cramped, and completely enclosed ○ *a confined space*

con·fined aq·ui·fer *n* GEOL same as **artesian aquifer**

con·fine·ment /kən fínmənt/ *n* **1.** restriction or limitation within the boundaries or scope of something **2.** the period of time or the process of giving birth, beginning when a woman goes into labor and ending when a child is born (*dated*)

con·firm /kən fúrm/ (**-firmed, -firm·ing, -firms**) *v* **1.** *vt* PROVE SOMETHING TO BE TRUE to verify the truth or validity of something thought to be true or valid ○ *Similar findings have been confirmed in recent clinical experiments.* **2.** *vti* MAKE SOMETHING DEFINITE to make certain that a tentative arrangement or one made earlier is firm ○ *call to confirm the reservation* **3.** *vt* LEGALLY APPROVE SOMETHING to ratify or make something valid with a formal or legal act ○ *confirmed his appointment to the post with a unanimous vote* **4.** *vt* JUD-CHR ADMIT SOMEBODY INTO RELIGIOUS BODY in Judaism and Christianity, to admit somebody into full membership of a religious body or community **5.** *vt* STRENGTHEN SOMETHING to make something stronger (*formal*) [13C. Via French < Latin *confirmare*, literally "strengthen together" < *firmare* "strengthen"] —**con·firm·a·bil·i·ty** /kən fùrmə bíllətee/ *n* —**con·firm·a·ble** *adj* —**con·firm·a·to·ry** *adj* —**con·firm·er** *n*

con·fir·ma·tion /kònfər máysh'n/ *n* **1.** CONFIRMING SOMETHING the act of verifying or ratifying something ○ *sought confirmation of his suspicions* ○ *the appointment is subject to confirmation by the Senate* **2.** SOMETHING THAT CONFIRMS SOMETHING ELSE something that supports, validates, or verifies something else ○ *a confirmation of my worst fears* ○ *Send written confirmation of the date of delivery.* **3.** CHR ACCEPTANCE INTO CHURCH in Christianity, a religious ceremony that marks somebody's formal acceptance into a church **4.** JUDAISM CEREMONY MARKING BEGINNING OF RESPONSIBLE ADULTHOOD in Reform Judaism, a ceremony that marks the completion of somebody's religious training and entry into full adult membership of the community —**con·fir·ma·tion·al** *adj*

con·firmed /kən fúrmd/ *adj* **1.** SETTLED AND UNLIKELY TO CHANGE firmly settled in a particular habit and unlikely to change ○ *a confirmed teetotaler* **2.** ESTABLISHED AS TRUE having been found or shown to be true or definite ○ *confirmed cases of infection* **3.** CHR MADE MEMBER OF CHURCH received into a Christian church as a full member

con·firm·ed·ly /kənfúrmədlee/ *adv* to an extent or in a way that is unlikely to change

con·fis·cate *vt* /kónfi skàyt/ (**-cat·ed, -cat·ing, -cates**) **1.** TAKE SOMETHING AWAY to take somebody's property with authority, or appropriate property for personal use as if with authority ○ *I'll confiscate that ruler if you don't stop playing with it.* **2.** TAKE SOMETHING AS LEGAL PENALTY to seize property legally forfeited to the public treasury as a penalty ○ *The goods were confiscated by customs.* ■ *adj* /kónfi skàyt, kónfiskət/ (*formal*) **1.** TAKEN BY AUTHORITY taken legally, or forfeited **2.** HAVING FORFEITED PROPERTY having had property taken away legally or by forfeiture [Mid-16C. < Latin *confiscat-*, past participle of *confiscare* "appropriate for the public treasury" < *fiscus* "purse, treasury"] —**con·fis·ca·ble** /kən fískəb'l/ *adj* —**con·fis·ca·tion** /kònfi skáysh'n/ *n* —**con·fis·ca·tor** *n* —**con·fis·ca·to·ry** /kən fískə tàwree/ *adj*

con·fit /kon fée, kawN-/ *n* meat such as goose, duck, or pork that has been cooked and preserved in its own fat [Mid-20C. < French < Latin *conficere* (see CONFECT)]

Con·fi·te·or /kən féetee ər, -àwr/ *n* a Roman Catholic prayer of confession and plea for forgiveness [13C. < Latin, "I confess" < the opening words *Confiteor Deo Omnipotenti* "I confess to Almighty God"]

con·fi·ture /kónfi chòor/ *n* fruit jam or preserve

con·fla·gra·tion /kònflə gráysh'n/ *n* a large fire that causes a great deal of damage [15C. < Latin *conflagration-* < *conflagrare* "burn up" < *flagrare* "to blaze"]

SYNONYMS See ***fire***.

con·flate /kən fláyt/ (**-flat·ed, -flat·ing, -flates**) *v* **1.** *vti* to join or merge two or more things into a unified whole **2.** *vt* to fuse or bring things together ○ *I'm afraid you've mistakenly conflated two separate sets of facts.* [15C. < Latin *conflat-*, past participle of *conflare* "melt together" < *flare* "to blow"] —**con·fla·tion** *n*

con·flict *n* /kón flìkt/ **1.** MIL WAR warfare between opposing forces, especially a prolonged and bitter but sporadic struggle ○ *news that the conflict had reached the outskirts of the capital* **2.** DIFFERENCE a disagreement or clash between ideas, principles, or people ○ *The two sides came into conflict over the proposed contract.* **3.** PSYCHOL MENTAL STRUGGLE a psychological state resulting from the often unconscious opposition between simultaneous but incompatible desires, needs, drives, or impulses **4.** LITERAT PLOT TENSION opposition between or among characters or forces in a literary work that shapes or motivates the action of the plot ■ *vi* /kən flíkt/ (**-flict·ed, -flict·ing, -flicts**) DIFFER to be incompatible, in opposition, or in disagreement ○ *The latest findings conflict with those of the original report.* [15C. < Latin *conflictus*, past participle of *confligere* "strike together, fight" < *fligere* "strike"] —**con·flic·tion** /kən flíksh'n/ *n* —**con·flic·tive** /kən flíktiv/ *adj* —**con·flic·tu·al** /kən flíkchoo əl/ *adj*

SYNONYMS See ***fight***.

con·flict di·a·monds *npl* diamonds mined illegally and traded on the black market to finance a military campaign

con·flict·ed /kən flíktəd/ *adj* ⚠ confused or ambivalent because of competing desires, possibilities, or impulses (*informal*) ○ *I haven't known him when he wasn't conflicted about his relationship with his family.*

USAGE Since many people dislike ***conflicted***, meaning "confused or ambivalent because of competing desires, possibilities, or impulses," it is wise to avoid using the word in formal college writing. It is closely associated with the jargon of psychobabble.

con·flict·ing /kən flíkting/ *adj* **1.** inconsistent or contradictory and unable to be reconciled ○ *We've been receiving conflicting reports about the whereabouts of the kidnappers.* **2.** requiring different and incompatible actions ○ *In the confusion, the men were given conflicting instructions.* —**con·flict·ing·ly** *adv*

con·flict of in·ter·est *n* a conflict between the public and private interests of somebody in an official position, or conflicts between a number of public positions

con·flu·ence /kón floo ənss/ *n* **1.** GEOG MEETING OF STREAMS a flowing together of two or more streams, or a point at which streams combine **2.** GEOG STREAM a stream formed by others combining **3.** MEETING OF TWO OR MORE THINGS a meeting or joining of two or more things, or the place where two or more things meet or join [15C. < late Latin *confluentia* < Latin *confluent-*, present participle of *confluere* "flow together" < *fluere* "flow"] —**con·flu·ent** *adj, n*

con·flux /kón flùks/ *n* GEOG same as **confluence** (senses 1–2) [Early 17C. < Latin *confluxus* "flowed together" < *confluere* (see CONFLUENCE)]

con·fo·cal /kon fók'l/ *adj* having the same focus or foci [Mid-19C. < Latin *con-* "with" + FOCAL] —**con·fo·cal·ly** *adv*

con·form /kən fáwrm/ (**-formed, -form·ing, -forms**) *v* **1.** *vi* BEHAVE ACCEPTABLY to behave or think in a socially acceptable or expected way ○ *the constant pressure to conform* **2.** *vi* FOLLOW STANDARD to comply with a fixed standard, regulation, or requirement ○ *does not conform to current building codes* **3.** *vti* BE OR MAKE SIMILAR to be the same as or very similar to something or somebody, or make something similar ○ *The Assyrian account of the great flood conforms closely with the Biblical account.* [14C. Via French < Latin *conformare*, literally "shape after" < *forma* "shape"] —**con·form·er** *n*

con·form·a·ble /kən fáwrməb'l/ *adj* **1.** IN AGREEMENT consistent or compatible with something ○ *This gradual increase is conformable with the theory.* **2.** SIMILAR similar in form or shape ○ *I think this software is conformable with what you already have on your system.* **3.** COMPLIANT eager to obey or comply with the wishes of others (*literary*) **4.** GEOL ABOVE PREVIOUS LAYER describes a layer of rock that lies on the stratum that was deposited immediately before it, so there is no break in stratigraphic sequence or intervening erosion —**con·form·a·bil·i·ty** /kən fàwrmə bíllətee/ *n* —**con·form·a·ble·ness** *n* —**con·form·a·bly** *adv*

con·for·mal /kən fáwrm'l/ *adj* **1.** describes a mathematical transformation that leaves the angles between intersecting curves unchanged **2.** describes a map that shows the correct shape and scale of a small area

con·for·mance /kən fáwrmənss/ *n* the act of conforming or of bringing about accord or compliance

con·for·ma·tion /kòn fawr máysh'n/ *n* **1.** SOMETHING'S STRUCTURE the shape, outline, or form of something, especially an animal, determined by the way in which its parts are arranged ○ *the ideal conformation of a young horse suitable as a family mount* **2.** SYMMETRY symmetrical arrangement of parts ○ *That sculpture shows excellent conformation.* **3.** CHEM MOLECULAR ARRANGEMENT a spatial arrangement of the atoms of a molecule, especially one that results from rotation around a single bond **4.** CRE-

ATION OF CONFORMITY bringing the process of one thing into accord with another —**con·for·ma·tion·al** *adj* —**con·for·ma·tion·al·ly** *adv*

con·form·ist /kən fáwrmist/ *n* somebody who behaves or thinks in a socially acceptable or expected way ■ *adj* characterized by adherence to accepted norms of behavior or thought —**con·form·ism** *n*

con·form·i·ty /kən fáwrmətee/ *n* **1.** DOING AND THINKING AS OTHERS behavior or thought that is socially acceptable or expected ○ *a certain lack of conformity in his attitudes* **2.** FOLLOWING OF STANDARD compliance with a fixed standard, regulation, or requirement **3.** AGREEMENT IN FORM agreement, correspondence, or similarity in structure, manner, or character

con·found /kən fównd/ (**-found·ed, -found·ing, -founds**) *vt* **1.** BEWILDER SOMEBODY to puzzle or confuse somebody **2.** MAKE THINGS WORSE to cause a confused situation to become even more confused ○ *Shouting at her like that only confounded the problem.* **3.** REFUTE SOMETHING to prove somebody or something to be wrong ○ *confounded the critics and went on to become an international success* **4.** PUT SOMEBODY TO SHAME to cause somebody to feel ashamed or embarrassed ○ *Her presentation confounded everyone who had criticized her.* **5.** FRUSTRATE to prevent somebody or something from succeeding ○ *The lack of progress confounded him and he left in disgust.* **6.** MIX THINGS UP to fail to distinguish between two or more things ○ *I am not confounding modesty with bashfulness.* ○ *He often confounds fact and opinion.* **7.** EXPRESSING ANGER used to express anger at something or somebody (*dated*) ○ *Confound his insolence!* **8.** RUIN SOMETHING to ruin or destroy somebody or something (*archaic*) [13C. Via Anglo-Norman *conf(o)undre* < Latin *confundere* "pour together" < *fundere* "melt, pour"] —**con·found·er** *n* —**con·found·ing·ly** *adv*

con·found·ed /kən fówndəd/ *adj* **1.** puzzled or confused by something ○ *"I don't know what's happened," he sputtered, completely confounded.* **2.** used to express annoyance or irritation (*dated informal*) ○ *Where's that confounded dog?* —**con·found·ed·ly** *adv* —**con·found·ed·ness** *n*

con·fra·ter·ni·ty /kònfrə túrnətee/ (*plural* **-ties**) *n* a group of people united in a common profession or for a purpose, often a group of Christians who have joined together to perform charitable acts [15C. < French *confraternité* < Latin *confrater*, literally "brother with somebody" < *frater* "brother"]

con·frère /kón frèr/ *n* a fellow member of a professional, charitable, or other group (*formal*) [15C. Via French < Latin *confrater* (see CONFRATERNITY)]

con·front /kən frúnt/ (**-front·ed, -front·ing, -fronts**) *vt* **1.** CHALLENGE SOMEBODY FACE TO FACE to come face to face with somebody, especially in a challenge, and usually with hostility, criticism, or defiance **2.** MAKE SOMEBODY AWARE OF SOMETHING to bring something such as contradictory facts or evidence to the attention of somebody, often in a challenging way ○ *confronted her with the evidence* **3.** ENCOUNTER DIFFICULTY to be forced to deal with something, especially an obstacle that must be overcome ○ *This is just one of the difficulties students confront these days.* **4.** BE PROBLEM FOR SOMEBODY to cause difficulty to or present an obstacle for somebody ○ *The hardships that would confront the settlers were blissfully unknown when they started out.* [Mid-16C. Via French < medieval Latin *confrontare* < Latin *front-* "forehead"] —**con·front·er** *n*

con·fron·ta·tion /kònfrən táysh'n/ *n* **1.** ENCOUNTER a face-to-face meeting or encounter, especially a challenging or hostile one **2.** INTERNAT REL HOSTILITY WITHOUT WARFARE hostility between nations stopping short of actual warfare, though probably involving armed forces **3.** CONFLICT BETWEEN IDEAS OR PEOPLE conflict between ideas, beliefs, or opinions, or between the people who hold them ○ *This country is headed for a confrontation over the exploitation of natural resources.* **4.** COMPARISON OR OPPOSITION a comparison or contrast between parts that have been brought together into a whole ○ *Her sculpture is a superb confrontation of traditional and modern elements.* —**con·fron·ta·tion·al** *adj* —**con·fron·ta·tion·ist** *n, adj*

Con·fu·cian /kən fyóosh'n/ *adj* relating to the teachings of Confucius or his followers, emphasizing self-control, adherence to a social hierarchy, and social and political order —**Con·fu·cian** *n* —**Con·fu·cian·ism** *n* —**Con·fu·cian·ist** *n*

Con·fu·cius /kən fyóoshəss/ (551?–479? B.C.) Chinese philosopher, administrator, and moralist. His social and moral teachings, collected in the *Analects*, tried to replace former religious observances.

> "When you meet someone better than yourself, turn your thoughts to becoming his equal. When you meet someone not as good as you are, look within and examine your own self."
> [Confucius, *Analects*; 5th century B.C.]

con fuo·co /kòn foo ókō, kōn-/ *adv* with energy, passion, and fire (*used as a musical direction*) [< Italian, "with fire"] —**con fuo·co** *adj*

con·fuse /kən fyóoz/ (**-fused, -fus·ing, -fus·es**) *vt* **1.** MAKE SOMEBODY UNABLE TO THINK INTELLIGENTLY to make somebody unable to think or reason clearly or act sensibly **2.** MAKE SOMETHING PUZZLING to make something hard or harder to understand ○ *received additional information that only served to confuse the issue* **3.** MIX THINGS UP to mistake one person or thing for another **4.** EMBARRASS SOMEBODY to make somebody feel embarrassed or ill at ease **5.** THROW SOMETHING INTO DISARRAY to cause disorder in something ○ *The dense fog utterly confused traffic on the highway.* [14C. Via French *confus* "perplexed" < Latin *confusus* "mixed up" < *confundere* (see CONFOUND)] —**con·fus·a·bil·i·ty** /kən fyòozə bíllətee/ *n* —**con·fus·a·ble** *adj*

con·fused /kən fyóozd/ *adj* **1.** UNABLE TO THINK INTELLIGENTLY unable to think or reason clearly or to act sensibly **2.** DISORDERED in no logical or sensible order ○ *got his grammar hopelessly confused* **3.** EMBARRASSED embarrassed and not knowing what to say or how to act **4.** NOT DIFFERENTIATED mistaken for each other **5.** PSYCHIAT DISORIENTED having impaired psychological capacity to the extent of being forgetful and no longer able to carry out simple everyday tasks —**con·fus·ed·ly** /-fyóozədlee/ *adv* —**con·fus·ed·ness** /-zədnəss/ *n*

con·fus·ing /kən fyóozing/ *adj* unclear and difficult to understand —**con·fus·ing·ly** *adv*

con·fu·sion /kən fyóozh'n/ *n* **1.** BEWILDERMENT the act of confusing somebody or something, or the state of being confused or perplexed ○ *tried to hide his confusion* **2.** LACK OF CLARITY misunderstanding of a situation or the facts **3.** MISTAKING ONE FOR ANOTHER a failure to distinguish between people or things **4.** DISORDER a chaotic or disordered state **5.** EMBARRASSMENT self-consciousness or embarrassment **6.** PSYCHIAT DISORIENTED STATE OF MIND a psychological state in which somebody is disoriented and no longer able to carry out simple everyday tasks —**con·fu·sion·al** *adj*

con·fu·ta·tion /kònfyə táysh'n/ *n* (*formal*) **1.** the act of proving conclusively that somebody is wrong or that something is false, invalid, or faulty ○ *The lawyer's confutation of the witness's testimony was decisive.* **2.** a fact, observation, or piece of evidence proving that somebody is wrong or that something is false, invalid, or faulty (*often used in the plural*) —**con·fu·ta·tive** /kən fyóotətiv/ *adj*

con·fute /kən fyóot/ (**-fut·ed, -fut·ing, -futes**) *vt* to prove conclusively that somebody is wrong or that something is false, invalid, or faulty (*formal*) [Early 16C. < Latin *confutare* "restrain, answer conclusively"] —**con·fut·a·ble** *adj* —**con·fut·er** *n*

cong. *abbr* **1.** RELIG congregational **2.** POL congress **3.** POL congressional

Cong. *abbr* **1.** RELIG Congregational **2.** POL Congress **3.** POL Congressional

con·ga /kóng gə/ *n* **1.** DANCE DONE IN LINE a Latin American dance in which people form a line and, holding the waist of the person ahead, move three steps forward, then kick out a leg **2.** MUSIC the music for a conga **3.** MUSIC same as **conga drum** ■ *vi* (**-gaed, -ga·ing, -gas**) DANCE to dance the conga [Mid-20C. < American Spanish *(danza) Conga* "dance from the Congo" < Spanish *Congo*]

con·ga drum *n* a tall tapering drum, played with both hands and used in Latin American and African music

con game *n* CRIME same as **confidence game** (*informal*)

con·gé /kón jày, kawN zháy/ (*plural* **-gés**), **con·gee** /kónjee, kən jée/ *n* **1.** PERMISSION formal permission for somebody to leave (*formal*) **2.** DISMISSAL a dismissal, especially an abrupt one (*formal*) **3.** LEAVE-TAKING a departure (*formal*) **4.** BOW a formal bow (*formal*) **5.** ARCHIT CONCAVE MOLDING an architectural molding that is concave in shape [14C. < Old French *congié* < Latin *commeare* "come and go"]

con·geal /kən jéel/ (**-gealed, -geal·ing, -geals**) *vti* **1.** to become thick and solid, or cause a liquid to thicken and solidify **2.** to become firm and strong, or make something firm and strong ○ *Let's act before opposition to our plan congeals.* [14C. Via French < Latin *congelare* "freeze together" < *gelu* "frost"] —**con·geal·er** *n* —**con·geal·ment** *n*

con·gealed sal·ad /kən jéeld-/ *n Southern US* a dish made of flavored gelatin and chopped fruit or vegetables and sometimes nuts, cottage cheese, or marshmallows that is set in a mold and served cold

con·gee *n* another spelling of **congé**

con·ge·la·tion /kònjə láysh'n/ *n* (*technical*) **1.** the process of turning from a liquid into a solid, or the state of being solid as a result of congealing **2.** a liquid that has solidified [15C. Directly or via French < Latin *congelation-* < *congelare* (see CONGEAL)]

con·ge·ner /kónjənər, kən jéenər/ *n* **1.** somebody or something that belongs to the same class, group, or type, e.g., a plant of the same genus as another, or two chemical elements of the same group **2.** a complex organic molecule that develops in wine and spirits during the fermentation and aging processes, thought to be implicated in causing hangovers [Mid-18C. < Latin < *con-* "with" + *gener-* "race, kind"]

con·ge·ner·ic /kònjə nérrik/, **con·gen·er·ous** /kən jénnərəss, kon-/ *adj* describes organisms belonging to the same class, group, or type

con·gen·ial /kən jéenyəl, -nee əl/ *adj* **1.** AGREEABLE pleasant and suited to somebody's character or tastes ○ *found it a very congenial atmosphere* **2.** SIMILAR compatible in tastes, interests, attitudes, or backgrounds ○ *carefree travel with congenial companions* **3.** FRIENDLY having an outgoing pleasant character ○ *Her congenial nature makes her well-loved in the town.* [Early 17C. < Latin *con-* "with" + GENIAL] —**con·ge·ni·al·i·ty** /kən jèenee állətee/ *n* —**con·gen·ial·ly** *adv* —**con·gen·ial·ness** *n*

con·gen·ic /kən jénnik/ *adj* describes animal cells that are genetically identical except for the arrangement of genes in a single restricted chromosome region (**locus**)

con·gen·i·tal /kən jénnit'l/ *adj* **1.** describes an unusual condition present at birth ○ *a congenital disorder* **2.** firmly established as part of somebody's character or beliefs [Late 18C. < Latin *congenitus* "born with" < *genitus*, past participle of *gignere* "beget"] —**con·gen·i·tal·ly** *adv* —**con·gen·i·tal·ness** *n*

con·gen·i·tal a·nom·a·ly *n* a medically significant condition present at birth and resulting from developmental processes

con·ger eel /kóng gər-/, **con·ger** *n* a large scaleless eel. Native to: temperate and tropical coastal waters of the Atlantic Ocean. Latin name: *Conger oceanicus*. [Via French *congre* < Greek *goggros*]

con·ge·ries /kən jéer èez, kónjə rèez/ (*plural same*) *n* a collection or assortment of things ○ *made a nation of what had been a far-flung congeries of states* [Mid-16C. < Latin, "heap, pile" < *congerere* (see CONGEST)]

con·gest /kən jést/ (**-gest·ed, -gest·ing, -gests**) *v* **1.** *vti* to overcrowd a street or area so that movement is slow or difficult, or become overcrowded **2.** *vt* to accumulate as excessive fluid in an organ or body part, as a result of disease or infection [15C. < Latin *congest-*, past participle of *congerere* "collect" < *gerere* "carry"] —**con·gest·ed** *adj* —**con·gest·i·ble** *adj* —**con·ges·tive** *adj*

con·ges·tion /kən jéschən/ *n* **1.** EXCESSIVE TRAFFIC OR PEOPLE a state of overcrowding in a street or other area, making movement slow or difficult **2.** MED EXCESSIVE ACCUMULATION OF FLUID the condition of having an excessive amount of blood or fluid accumulate in an organ or body part, as a result of disease or infection **3.** COMPUT HAVING TOO MUCH INFORMATION TO TRANSFER in computing, a situation in which the amount of information to be transferred is greater than the amount that the data communication path can carry

con·ges·tive heart fail·ure *n* a form of heart failure in which the heart is unable to pump away the blood returning to it fast enough, causing congestion in the veins

con·glom·er·ate *n* /kən glómmərət/ **1. BUSINESS ORGANIZATION INVOLVED IN MANY AREAS** a large business organization that consists of a number of companies that deal with a variety of different business, manufacturing, or commercial activities **2. MIX OF THINGS** a mass formed by gathering a number of dissimilar materials or parts **3.** GEOL **ROCK COMPRISING PIECES OF OTHER ROCKS** coarse-grained sedimentary rock containing fragments of other rock larger than 0.08 in./2 mm in diameter, held together with another material such as clay ■ *adj* /kən glómmərət/ **FORMED BY COMBINING DIFFERENT THINGS** consisting of a mass or accumulation of dissimilar materials or parts ■ *vti* /kən glómmə ràyt/ (**-at·ed, -at·ing, -ates**) **MIX TOGETHER TO FORM MASS** to gather materials or parts into a mass, or be gathered into a mass [Late 16C. < Latin *conglomeratus* "wound into a ball" < *glomer-* "ball"] —**con·glom·er·at·ic** /kən glòmmə ráttik/ *adj* —**con·glom·er·a·tion** /kən glòmmə ráysh'n/ *n* —**con·glom·er·a·tor** /-ràytər/ *n* —**con·glom·er·it·ic** /-ríttik/ *adj*

con·glom·er·at·ed /kən glómmə ràytəd/ *adj* made up of and controlling many parts of an industry ○ *a conglomerated corporation*

Con·go /kóng gō/ Africa's second longest river, which provides a major transportation network. It rises in the south of the Democratic Republic of the Congo and empties into the Atlantic Ocean. Length: 2,718 mi./4,374 km. Former name **Zaire**

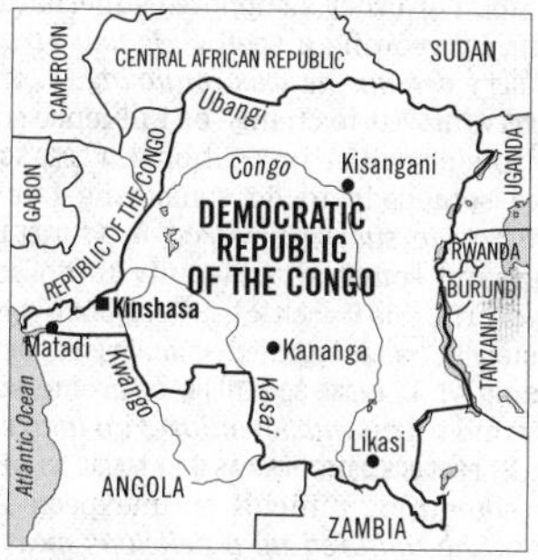

Democratic Republic of the Congo

Con·go, Dem·o·crat·ic Re·pub·lic of the large equatorial country of Central Africa with a coastline on the Atlantic Ocean. Language: French. Currency: Congo franc. Capital: Kinshasa. Population: 56,625,039 (2003). Area: 905,365 sq. mi./2,344,885 sq. km. Former name **Zaire** (1971–97), **Belgian Congo** (1908–60), **Congo Free State** (1885–1908)

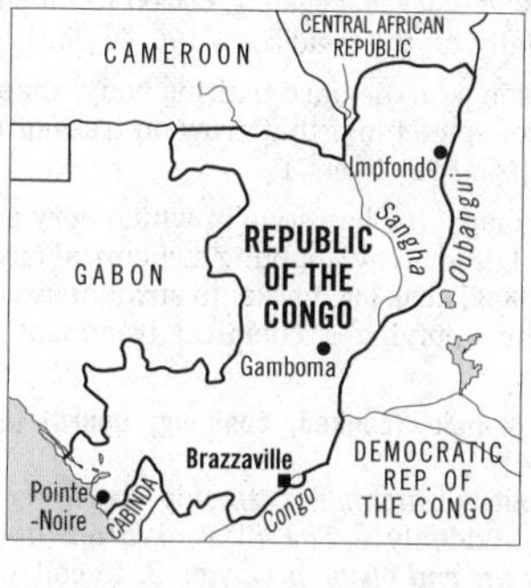

Republic of the Congo

Con·go, Re·pub·lic of the country in west central Africa, on the coast of the Atlantic Ocean. Language: French. Currency: CFA franc. Capital: Brazzaville. Population: 2,954,258 (2003). Area: 132,000 sq. mi./342,000 sq. km. Former name **People's Republic of the Congo** (1970–92)

con·go dye /kóng gō-/ *n* a dye containing nitrogen [Because associated with the Congo region or African Americans from there]

Con·go eel *n* an amphibian that has a long body with gill slits and two pairs of rudimentary limbs that enable it to travel on land. Native to: southeastern United States. Latin name: *Amphiuma means*. [See CONGO DYE]

Con·go franc *n* the main unit of currency in the Democratic Republic of the Congo. See table at **currency**

Con·go Free State former name for **Congo, Democratic Republic of the** (1885–1908)

Con·go·lese /kòng gə léez, -léess/ *n* **1.** somebody who comes from the Democratic Republic of the Congo, the Republic of the Congo, or any of the former countries that they represent **2.** LANG same as **Kongo**[1] (sense 2) [Early 20C. < French *Congolais* < *Congo* "the Congo River"] —**Con·go·lese** *adj*

Con·go red *n* a dye that is red in alkaline solutions and blue in acid solutions. Use: chemical indicator, biological stain, dye. [See CONGO DYE]

Con·go snake *n* AMPHIB same as **Congo eel**

con·gou /kóng gō, -gōō/ *n* a fine grade of Chinese black tea, made from the largest leaf gathered from the tip of a shoot on a tea plant [Early 18C. Shortening of Cantonese *kungfúch'a*, Modern Standard Chinese *gōngfu chá* "tea made for refined tastes," literally "effort tea"]

con·grats /kən gráts/ *npl, interj* an expression of congratulations (*slang*) [Early 20C. Shortening]

con·grat·u·late /kən grácha làyt/ (**-lat·ed, -lat·ing, -lates**) *v* **1.** *vt* to express pleasure or approval to somebody for an achievement or good fortune or on a special occasion **2.** *vr* to feel self-satisfied in having success or good fortune ○ *I was congratulating myself on my driving skills, when I skidded into a snow bank.* [Mid-16C. < Latin *congratulat-*, past participle of *congratulari* "rejoice with" < *gratus* "thankful"] —**con·grat·u·la·tor** *n* —**con·grat·u·la·to·ry** *adj*

con·grat·u·la·tion /kən gràchə láysh'n/ *n* the act of expressing pleasure to somebody for an achievement or good fortune or on a special occasion ○ *made a short speech of congratulation* ■ *npl, interj* **con·grat·u·la·tions** an expression of pleasure or acknowledgment of somebody's success or good fortune or on a special occasion

con·gre·gant /kóng grəgənt/ *n* a member of a religious congregation [Late 19C. < Latin *congregant-*, present participle of *congregare* (see CONGREGATE)]

con·gre·gate *vti* /kóng grə gàyt/ (**-gat·ed, -gat·ing, -gates**) **ASSEMBLE PEOPLE OR ANIMALS** to come together in a group, or gather people or animals into a group ■ *adj* /kóng grəgət/ (*formal*) **1. HAVING COME TOGETHER** gathered or assembled in a group **2. RELATING TO GATHERING** relating to an assembled group [15C. < Latin *congregat-*, past participle of *congregare* "collect together" < *greg-* "flock"] —**con·gre·ga·tive** *adj* —**con·gre·ga·tor** *n*

con·gre·ga·tion /kòng grə gáysh'n/ *n* **1.** RELIG **GROUP OF WORSHIPERS** a group of people who have gathered for a religious service **2.** RELIG **MEMBERS OF SAME CHURCH** the members of a specific church **3.** CHR **ROMAN CATHOLIC RELIGIOUS BODY** a Roman Catholic religious body whose members follow a common rule of life and are bound by simple vows (*formal*) **4.** CHR **DIVISION OF ROMAN CATHOLIC CENTRAL ADMINISTRATION** a section of the central administrative organization (**curia**) of the Roman Catholic Church **5.** CHR **COMMITTEE OF ROMAN CATHOLIC BISHOPS** a committee of Roman Catholic bishops responsible for handling the business of a general council (*formal*) **6. GATHERING** a group of people or things ○ *A congregation of reporters waited outside the courthouse.* **7. COMING TOGETHER** the act of gathering or assembling (*formal*) ○ *Congregation in the halls is not allowed.*

con·gre·ga·tion·al /kòng grə gáyshən'l, -gáyshnəl/ *adj* relating to a congregation

Con·gre·ga·tion·al *adj* relating to Congregationalism or its followers

Con·gre·ga·tion·al Church *n* a Protestant denomination in which each church is self-governing

con·gre·ga·tion·al·ism /kòng grə gáyshən'l ìzzəm, -gáyshnə-/ *n* a system of church organization in which each church is self-governing —**con·gre·ga·tion·al·ist** *n, adj*

Con·gre·ga·tion·al·ism *n* the beliefs and practices of the Congregational Church —**Con·gre·ga·tion·al·ist** *n, adj*

con·gress /kóng grəss/ *n* **1.** a conference or formal meeting of delegates or representatives, e.g., the representatives of a group of nations, to discuss matters of interest or concern **2.** a society or organization of people with common interests and concerns **3.** same as **sexual intercourse** (*dated formal*) [15C. < Latin *congressus*, past participle of *congredi* "go together" < *gradi* "proceed"] —**con·gres·sion·al** /kən gréshən'l, -gréshnəl/ *adj*

Con·gress *n* **1. US LEGISLATURE** the national legislative body of the United States, consisting of the House of Representatives and the Senate **2. SESSION OF CONGRESS** a two-year term of Congress, or the members of Congress during such a term ○ *the 22nd Congress* **3. GOVERNING AND LAW-MAKING BODY** the governing body in some countries ○ *the National People's Congress* **4. NAME OF POLITICAL PARTY** the shortened name of a number of political parties whose name includes the word "Congress," e.g., the African National Congress —**Con·gres·sion·al** *adj*

con·gres·sion·al dis·trict *n* a district within a US state that is entitled to elect one representative to the House of Representatives

Con·gres·sion·al Med·al of Hon·or *n* the highest military decoration in the United States, awarded by Congress for outstanding bravery in action

Con·gres·sion·al Rec·ord *n* a government journal in the United States that records and publishes the proceedings of Congress

con·gress·man /kóng grəssmən/ (*plural* **-men** /-mən/) *n* a man who is a member of the US Congress, especially of the House of Representatives

Con·gress of In·dus·tri·al Or·gan·i·za·tions *n* a federation of industrial labor unions formed in the United States in 1935 and merged with the American Federation of Labor in 1955 to form the AFL-CIO

Con·gress of Vi·en·na *n* a congress held in Vienna between 1814 and 1815 to deal with the territorial and jurisdictional problems remaining after the defeat of Napoleon in the Napoleonic Wars

con·gress·per·son /kóng grəss pùrss'n/ (*plural* **-peo·ple** /-peep'l/) *n* a member of the US Congress, especially of the House of Representatives

con·gress·wom·an /kóng grəss wòomman/ (*plural* **-wom·en** /-wìmmin/) *n* a woman who is a member of the US Congress, especially of the House of Representatives

con·gru·ent /kóng groo ənt, kən gróo-/ *adj* **1. IN AGREEMENT** corresponding to or consistent with each other or with something else (*formal*) ○ *culturally congruent education* **2.** MATH **WITH SAME SHAPE** with identical geometric shapes **3.** MATH **DIFFERING BY EXACTLY DIVISIBLE AMOUNT** describes two numbers whose difference is exactly divisible by a third number (**modulus**) [15C. < Latin *congruent-*, present participle of *congruere* "meet together" < *ruere* "to fall"] —**con·gru·ence** *n* —**con·gru·en·cy** *n* —**con·gru·ent·ly** *adv*

con·gru·i·ty /kən gróo ətee/ *n* (*formal*) **1. AGREEMENT OR CONSISTENCY** the state or fact of agreeing or being consistent with each other or with something else **2. APPROPRIATENESS** the quality or fact of being suitable or appropriate for something **3. SOMETHING AGREED UPON** a point on which there is agreement

con·gru·ous /kóng groo əss/ *adj* **1.** appropriate to or suitable for a purpose or situation (*formal*) **2.** corresponding to or consistent with each other or something else [Late 16C. < Latin *congruus* "suitable" < *congruere* (see CONGRUENT)] —**con·gru·ous·ly** *adv* —**con·gru·ous·ness** *n*

con·ic /kónnik/ MATH *adj* same as **conical** ■ *n* same as **conic section** [Late 16C. Via modern Latin < Greek *kōnikos* < *kōnos* "cone"]

con·i·cal /kónnik'l/ *adj* **1.** shaped like a cone **2.** relating to or having the form of a geometric cone

con·ic pro·jec·tion *n* **1.** a method of making a map by projecting the globe onto a surrounding cone whose point is above one of the poles and then flattening the cone **2.** a map made by conic projection. On a conic projection, the parallels of latitude appear as concentric circles, and the lines of longitude radiate from the center as equal radii.

con·ics /kónniks/ *n* the branch of geometry involving the study of conic sections (*takes a singular verb*)

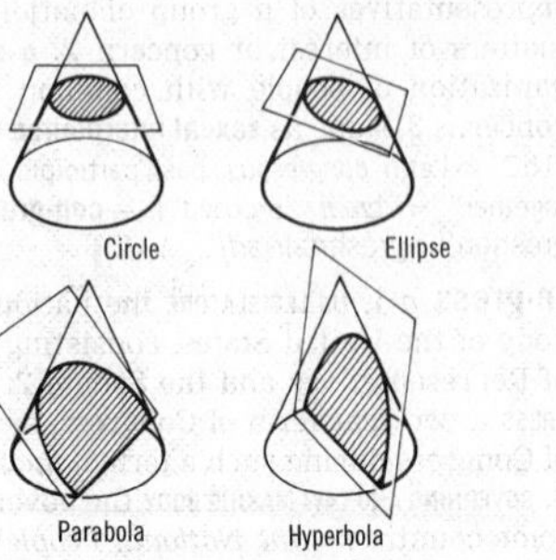

conic section

con·ic sec·tion *n* a curve produced by the intersection of a plane with a circular cone, e.g., a circle, ellipse, hyperbola, or parabola

co·nid·i·a FUNGI plural of **conidium**

co·nid·i·o·phore /kə níddee ə fàwr/ *n* a simple or branched part (**hypha**) of a fungus that produces spores asexually [Late 19C. < CONIDIUM] —**co·nid·i·oph·or·ous** /kə nìddee óffərəss/ *adj*

co·nid·i·um /kə níddee əm/ (*plural* **-i·a** /-ee ə/) *n* an asexually produced spore of some types of fungi [Late 19C. < modern Latin < Greek *konis* "dust"] —**co·nid·i·al** *adj*

co·ni·fer /kónnəfər/ *n* any tree that has thin leaves (**needles**) and produces cones. Many types are evergreen. Pines, firs, junipers, larches, spruces, and yews are conifers. Order: Coniferales. [Mid-19C. < Latin, "cone-bearing" < Greek *kōnos* "cone"] —**co·nif·er·ous** /kə níffərəss/ *adj*

co·ni·ine /kónee èen/ *n* a colorless substance with poisonous properties. Source: poison hemlock. Formula: $C_8H_{17}N$. [Mid-19C. < *conium* "hemlock" < Latin]

conj, **conj.** *abbr* **1.** GRAM conjugation **2.** ASTRON, GRAM conjunction **3.** GRAM conjunctive

con·jec·ture /kən jékchər/ *n* **1.** GUESSWORK the formation of judgments or opinions on the basis of incomplete or inconclusive information ○ *The origin of this ritual is a matter of conjecture.* **2.** SOMETHING GUESSED a conclusion, judgment, or statement based on incomplete or inconclusive information **3.** MATH, SCI UNPROVED THEOREM a theorem in science or mathematics that has still to be proved [14C. Directly or via French < Latin *conjectura* < *conjicere* "throw together" < *jacere* "throw"] —**con·jec·tur·a·ble** *adj* —**con·jec·tur·a·bly** *adv* —**con·jec·tur·al** *adj* —**con·jec·ture** *vti* —**con·jec·tur·er** *n*

con·join /kən jóyn/ (**-joined, -join·ing, -joins**) *vti* to join two or more things, or become joined (*formal*) ○ *conjoined in holy matrimony* [14C. Via French *conjoindre* < Latin *conjungere* "join together" < *jungere* "join"] —**con·join·er** *n*

con·joined twin /kən jóynd-/ *n* either of twins born physically joined together

con·joint /kən jóynt/ *adj* **1.** done by, involving, or relating to two or more combined entities ○ *a conjoint project* **2.** joined or combined —**con·joint·ly** *adv*

con·ju·gal /kónjəg'l/ *adj* relating to marriage or to husbands and wives [Early 16C. < Latin *conjugalis* < *conjugare* (see CONJUGATE)] —**con·ju·gal·i·ty** /kònjə gállətee/ *n* —**con·ju·gal·ly** *adv*

con·ju·gal rights *npl* the rights that a husband or wife is entitled to in a marriage, especially the right to have sexual relations with his or her spouse

con·ju·gal vis·it *n* a visit to a jail by the husband or wife of a prisoner, during which the couple is allowed some privacy, e.g., to allow them to have sexual relations

con·ju·gant /kónjəgənt/ *n* either of a pair of organisms, cells, or gametes in the process of reproducing [Early 20C. < Latin *conjugant-*, present participle of *conjugare* (see CONJUGATE)]

con·ju·gate *v* /kónjə gàyt/ (**-gat·ed, -gat·ing, -gates**) **1.** *vt* GRAM STATE FORMS OF VERB to state systematically the different forms a verb has according to tense, mood, person, and number **2.** *vi* GRAM HAVE DIFFERENT GRAMMATICAL FORMS to have different grammatical forms according to tense, mood, number, or person (*refers to verbs*) **3.** *vt* CHEM JOIN SUBSTANCES to combine two substances in such a way that they can easily be separated again, especially in chemical reactions **4.** *vi* BIOL REPRODUCE to reproduce by physically joining in order to transfer genetic information (*refers to organisms that normally reproduce by division*) ■ *adj* /kónjəgət, -gàyt/ **1.** PAIRED joined in pairs (*formal*) **2.** MATH ADDING UP TO 360 DEGREES describes a pair of angles that together add up to 360 degrees **3.** CHEM DIFFERING BY ONE PROTON describes substances that have such similar molecular structures that one becomes the other through the gain or loss of a proton **4.** CHEM EXISTING TOGETHER IN EQUILIBRIUM describes a state of chemical equilibrium in which two liquids coexist in separate forms, one being the solute and the other the solvent ■ *n* /kónjəgət, -gàyt/ **1.** GRAM VERB FORM one of the different forms of a verb according to tense, mood, person, or number **2.** RESULT OF JOINING a product of joining or union **3.** MATH same as **conjugate complex number** [15C. < Latin *conjugatus*, past participle of *conjugare* "yoke together" < *jugum* "yoke"] —**con·ju·ga·ble** *adj*—**con·ju·gate·ly** *adv*—**con·ju·gate·ness** *n* —**con·ju·ga·tive** *adj* —**con·ju·ga·tor** *n*

con·ju·gate com·plex num·ber *n* either of a pair of complex numbers that are symmetrically located on either side of an x-axis, differing only in the sign of the imaginary component

con·ju·gat·ed /kónjə gàytəd/ *adj* **1.** containing two or more double or triple chemical bonds in alternation with single bonds **2.** describes a double chemical bond separated by a single bond

con·ju·gat·ed pro·tein *n* a protein attached to a nonprotein

con·ju·ga·tion /kònjə gáysh'n/ *n* **1.** GRAM INFLECTION OF VERB the different patterns of inflection of a given verb **2.** GRAM GROUP OF VERBS WITH SAME INFLECTIONS a group of verbs that use the same patterns of inflection **3.** GRAM SET OF VERB INFLECTIONS the complete set of inflections for a verb **4.** ACT OF JOINING TOGETHER the act of joining or uniting, or the state of being joined **5.** BIOL REPRODUCTION IN SIMPLE ORGANISMS the simplest form of reproduction, in which two single-celled organisms such as bacteria or protozoans link together, exchange genetic information, and then separate **6.** BIOL FUSION OF NUCLEI the fusion of the nuclei of a male and a female gamete in algae and fungi **7.** GENETICS PAIRING OF CHROMOSOMES the distribution of pairs of chromosomes into the four nuclei produced by the division of a parent nucleus **8.** CHEM ALTERNATION OF NUMBER OF BONDS the occurrence of two or more double or triple bonds in alternation with single bonds in a molecule —**con·ju·ga·tion·al** *adj* —**con·ju·ga·tion·al·ly** *adv*

con·junct *adj* /kən júngkt, kón jùngkt/ **1.** UNITED attached or joined **2.** LING ADJACENT TO CONSONANT describes consonants that are next to each other within a word without a vowel or vowels between **3.** MUSIC CONSISTING OF SINGLE STEPS IN SCALE relating to or consisting of adjacent notes in a musical scale ■ *n* /kón jùngkt/ LOGIC EITHER PROPOSITION IN CONJUNCTION in logic, either of the two propositions or formulas in a conjunction [15C. < Latin *conjunctus*, past participle of *conjungere* (see CONJOIN)] —**con·junct·ly** *adv*

con·junc·tion /kən júngkshən/ *n* **1.** GRAM CONNECTING WORD a word that is used to link sentences, clauses, phrases, or words, e.g., "and," "but," or "if" **2.** COMBINING OF SEVERAL THINGS the act of joining or combining two or more things **3.** SIMULTANEOUS OCCURRENCE a simultaneous occurrence of events or circumstances **4.** ASTRON ALIGNMENT WITH SUN the position of a planet or the Moon when aligned with the Sun, as seen from Earth **5.** ASTRON CLOSE PROXIMITY OF PLANETS the appearance of two planets very close to each other or in the same place on the celestial sphere **6.** ASTROL ASTROLOGICAL ASPECT in astrology, an aspect of 0° between two planets **7.** LOGIC TYPE OF COMPOUND STATEMENT in logic, a proposition of the form "A and B" that is true only if both A and B are true [14C. < Latin *conjunction-* < *conjunct-*, past participle of *conjungere* (see CONJOIN)] —**con·junc·tion·al** *adj* —**con·junc·tion·al·ly** *adv* ◇ **in conjunction with** together with or combined with something

con·junc·ti·va /kòn jungk tívə/ (*plural* **-vas** or **-vae** /-vee/) *n* a delicate mucous membrane that covers the internal part of the eyelid and is attached to the cornea [14C. < medieval Latin *(tunica) conjunctiva* "connective (membrane)" < Latin *conjunct-* (see CONJUNCTION)] —**con·junc·ti·val** *adj*

con·junc·tive /kən júngktiv/ *adj* **1.** CONNECTIVE serving to join things **2.** COMBINED joined or combined with something else **3.** GRAM OF GRAMMATICAL CONJUNCTIONS relating to conjunctions or their grammatical function, or consisting of conjunctions [15C. < late Latin *conjunctivus* < Latin *conjunct-* (see CONJUNCTION)] —**con·junc·tive·ly** *adv*

con·junc·tive ad·verb *n* an adverb or adverbial phrase that is used to connect parts or clauses of a sentence

con·junc·tive eye move·ment *n* a simultaneous movement of both eyes in the same direction

con·junc·ti·vi·tis /kən jùngkti vítiss/ *n* inflammation of the conjunctiva caused by infection, injury, or allergy

con·ju·ra·tion /kònjə ráysh'n/ *n* **1.** SUPPOSED MAGIC TRICK a supposed magic or supernatural occurrence achieved by pronouncing a spell or chanting **2.** MAGIC SPELL a word or phrase that a magician says when casting a spell (*literary*) **3.** INVOCATION OF SUPPOSED SUPERNATURAL FORCE a summoning or invoking, usually of a supposed supernatural force, by pronouncing a sacred name (*literary*) **4.** PERFORMANCE OF TRICKS the performance of illusions or tricks (*archaic*)

con·jure /kónjər/ (**-jured, -jur·ing, -jures**) *v* **1.** *vi* PERFORM MAGIC TRICKS to perform illusions and magic tricks that require agile hand movements, usually for entertainment **2.** *vti* INVOKE SUPPOSED SUPERNATURAL FORCES to call upon or order a supposed supernatural force or being by reciting a spell ○ *He was struck dumb by the very demons he was conjuring.* **3.** *vt* INFLUENCE SOMETHING WITH SPELL to change or influence something by reciting a spell or invocation **4.** *vt* BEG SOMEBODY to implore somebody to do something (*archaic*) ○ *I conjure you to show me mercy.* **5.** *vt* ORDER SOMEBODY to command somebody solemnly to do something (*archaic*) [13C. Via French < Latin *conjurare* "bind with an oath," literally "swear together" < *jurare* (see JURY)]

conjure up *vt* **1.** EVOKE SOMETHING to create something in the mind ○ *This music conjures up images of rural scenes.* **2.** PRODUCE SOMETHING AS IF BY MAGIC to produce or create something difficult or unexpected as if by magic ○ *She conjured up a delicious meal from the most basic ingredients.* **3.** SUMMON SUPPOSED SUPERNATURAL BEING to call upon a supposed supernatural force or being by reciting a spell or chanting magic words

con·jur·er /kónjərər/, **con·jur·or** *n* **1.** an entertainer who performs tricks involving manual agility and the illusion of magic **2.** a magician, or somebody who summons supposed supernatural forces or beings

conk[1] /kongk/ (*slang*) *n* a blow, especially on the head ■ *vt* (**conked, conk·ing, conks**) to hit somebody, especially on the head [Early 19C. Origin ?]

conk[2] /kongk/ *n* the hard fruiting body, shaped like a shelf, of some fungi that grow on trees or decaying wood [Mid-19C. Origin ?]

conk[3] /kongk/ *n* a hairstyle in which very curly hair is straightened by applying a chemical treatment ■ *vt* (**conked, conk·ing, conks**) to straighten very curly hair by applying a chemical treatment [Mid-20C. Origin ?]

conk[4] /kongk/ (**conked, conk·ing, conks**) [Early 20C. Origin ?]

conk out *vi* (*informal*) **1.** to stop operating or break down suddenly ○ *The TV conked out five minutes before the end of the program.* **2.** to collapse or fall asleep, usually through exhaustion ○ *I conked out the minute I got home.*

conk·er /kóngkər/ *n UK* a horse chestnut without its spiny outer casing, used in the game of conkers [Mid-19C. Probably blend of CONCH, CONK[1] + CONQUER]

conk·ers /kóngkərz/ *n UK* a children's game, usually for two people, in which each player has a conker threaded onto a string and uses it to try to smash the opponent's conker. The game used to be played with snail shells instead of horse chestnuts. (*takes a singular verb*)

Conk·ling /kóngkling/, **Roscoe** (1829–88) US politician. He was a Republican and served in the US House of Representatives (1859–63 and 1865–67) and Senate (1867–81).

con man *n* a swindler who uses a confidence game to cheat or defraud people (*informal*) [Shortening of CONFIDENCE]

con mo·to /kon mṓtō/ *adv* in a lively or brisk way (*used as a musical direction*) [Early 19C. < Italian, "with movement"]

conn *vt, n* NAUT another spelling of **con**⁵

Con·nacht /kónnət, -əkht/, **Con·naught** /kó nawt/ province comprising the counties of Galway, Leitrim, Mayo, Roscommon, and Sligo on the western coast of the Republic of Ireland. Population: 464,296 (2002). Area: 6,611 sq. mi./17,122 sq. km.

con·nate /kó nàyt, kə náyt/ *adj* **1.** describes parts that have grown closely joined to a single structure in a plant or animal **2.** describes water, usually very saline, that has been trapped in sedimentary rock since the original deposits were laid down [Mid-17C. < late Latin *connatus*, past participle of *connasci* "be born with" < Latin *nasci* "be born"] —**con·nate·ly** *adv* —**con·nate·ness** *n*

Con·naught another spelling of **Connacht**

con·nect /kə nékt/ (**-nect·ed, -nect·ing, -nects**) *v* **1.** *vti* **LINK TWO THINGS** to join two or more people, things, or parts ○ *Connect these two wires and it should work.* ○ *A flagstone walk connected the main house with the tool shed.* **2.** *vt* **ASSOCIATE SOMEBODY OR SOMETHING WITH ANOTHER** to make a psychological or emotional association between people, things, or events ○ *She always connected that house with family celebrations.* **3.** *vi* **GET ALONG WELL** to develop a good rapport with somebody ○ *The interview was a disaster – we never really connected.* **4.** *vi* **HIT FIRMLY** to strike, punch, or kick firmly, with good contact between the striking surface and the object struck (*informal*) ○ *The punch connected, and he sank to the ground.* **5.** *vt* TELECOM **ESTABLISH TELECOMMUNICATION LINK FOR SOMEBODY** to set up a communication link between people, organizations, or places ○ *connected to the Internet* **6.** *vt* UTIL **LINK SOMEBODY OR SOMETHING TO UTILITY** to link people or equipment to a source of electricity, water, or gas ○ *Have they connected your cable yet?* **7.** *vi* TRANSP **ALLOW TIME FOR PASSENGERS TO TRANSFER** to arrive shortly before another vehicle or vessel departs, or shortly after another arrives, so as to allow passengers to change from one to the other ○ *The local train connects with the express twice a day.* **8.** *vi* TRANSP **MAKE TRANSPORTATION CONNECTION** to change from one vehicle or vessel to another ○ *those wishing to connect with the overseas flight* [15C. < Latin *connectere* "tie together" < *nectere* "bind"] —**con·nect·a·ble** *adj* —**con·nect·er** *n* —**con·nect·i·ble** *adj* —**con·nect·or** *n*

connect up *vti* same as **connect** (senses 1, 8)

con·nect·ed /kə néktəd/ *adj* **1. JOINED TOGETHER** joined or linked firmly together **2. RELATED** having something in common ○ *The two incidents are probably connected.* **3. WITH BENEFICIAL SOCIAL CONNECTIONS** having useful business or social connections (*often used in combination*) **4.** *UK* **WITH WEALTHY RELATIVES** having upper-class or wealthy relatives (*often used in combination*) ○ *Her husband is well connected.* **5. LOGICAL AND INTELLIGIBLE** ordered in a logical and intelligible way **6.** MATH **DESCRIBING MATHEMATICAL RELATION** describes a mathematical relation for which either the relation or its converse is true for any two members in a set —**con·nect·ed·ly** *adv* —**con·nect·ed·ness** *n*

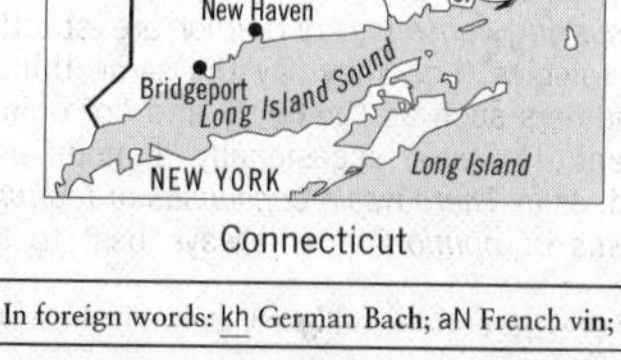

Connecticut

Con·nect·i·cut /kə néttikət/ **1.** southernmost state in New England. It is bordered on the north by Massachusetts, on the east by Rhode Island, on the south by the Long Island Sound, and on the west by New York State. Population: 3,460,503 (2002 estimate). Area: 5,544 sq. mi./14,359 sq. km. **2.** longest river of New England, flowing southward from Massachusetts to enter Long Island Sound. Length: 407 mi./655 km.

Con·nect·i·cut Wits *npl* LITERAT same as **Hartford Wits**

con·nect·ing rod /kə nékting-/ *n* a rod that transmits motion, especially the rod that connects the crankshaft to the piston in an internal-combustion engine

con·nec·tion /kə nékshən/ *n* **1. LINKING OF PEOPLE OR THINGS** the joining together of two or more people, things, or parts **2. PHYSICAL LINK** something that links two or more things ○ *check for a loose connection* **3. LOGICAL LINK** a linking association between people, things, or events ○ *denied any connection with terrorist organizations* **4. TRANSPORTATION LINK** an occasion when passengers change from one vehicle or vessel to another ○ *If we don't hurry, we'll miss our connection in Boston.* **5. VEHICLE SCHEDULED TO PERMIT TRANSFER** a particular bus, train, ferry, or plane that is scheduled to arrive at such a time as to allow passengers to transfer onto it from another scheduled form of transport ○ *Your connection will arrive on platform ten at 9:15.* **6. COMMUNICATION LINK** a communication link, especially between telephones **7. CONTEXT** the relationship of something with its context ○ *In this connection, we need to tighten up all the safety procedures.* **8. INFLUENTIAL CONTACT** a friend, relative, or associate who either has, or has access to, influence or power (*often used in the plural*) ○ *She used her connections to get an interview with the lead singer.* **9. RELATION** a relative, usually a distant relative or a relative by marriage (*often used in the plural*) **10. SUPPLIER OF ILLEGAL SUBSTANCES** a supplier of illegal substances, usually drugs (*slang*) [14C. < Latin *connexion-* < *connex-*, past participle of *connectere* (see CONNECT)] —**con·nec·tion·al** *adj*

con·nec·tion·ism /kə nékshən ìzzəm/ *n* the theory that thoughts and behavior are based on patterns of stimulus and response that have been either inherited or learned

con·nec·tive /kə néktiv/ *adj* **LINKING** joining two or more people, things, or parts ■ *n* **1. LINK** something that joins two or more people, things, or parts **2.** GRAM **LINKING WORD** a word that links sentences, phrases, clauses, or words **3.** BOT **STAMEN TISSUE** the tissue that joins the two lobes of an anther in the stamen of a plant —**con·nec·tive·ly** *adv*

con·nec·tive tis·sue *n* animal tissue that supports, connects, and surrounds organs and other body parts and consists mainly of collagen, elastic and reticular fibers, fatty tissue, cartilage, or bone

con·nec·tiv·i·ty /kò nek tívvətee/ *n* the ability to communicate with another system or piece of hardware or software, or with an Internet site

con·nect-the-dots *adj* (*slang*) **1.** gathering information or facts from different sources to make a coherent whole ○ *The article was a model of connect-the-dots journalism.* **2.** straightforward or obvious ○ *It's a connect-the-dots problem, easily solvable.* [< producing a picture by connecting printed dots]

con·nect time *n* the period of time a user is logged on to a remote computer, e.g., when browsing the Internet

Con·nel·ly /kónn'lee/, **Marc** (1890–1980) US playwright, screenwriter, director, and actor. His play *The Green Pastures* (1930) won a Pulitzer Prize. Full name **Cook Connelly, Marcus**

Con·ne·ma·ra /kònnə maárə/ mountainous coastal area of Galway, in the western part of the Republic of Ireland

Con·ne·ry /kónnəree/, **Sean** (*b.* 1930) Scottish movie actor. He played the starring role in several James Bond movies and won an Academy Award for best supporting actor for *The Untouchables* (1987). Full name **Connery, Thomas Sean**

> "My only grumble about the Bond films is that they don't tax one as an actor. All one really needs is the constitution of a rugby player to get through those 19 weeks of swimming, slugging, and necking."
> [Sean Connery, *Interview, The Sunday Express (London)*; February 14, 1965]

con·nex·ion *n UK* another spelling of **connection**

con·ning tow·er /kónning-/ *n* **1.** a structure on the top of a submarine that is used as the navigation bridge and main point of entrance **2.** the armored pilothouse in the shape of a low dome found on the deck of a warship [< CON⁵]

con·nip·tion /kə nípshən/ *n* a hysterical fit caused by extreme excitement or anger (*informal; often used in the plural*) [Mid-19C. Origin ?]

con·niv·ance /kə nívənss/, **con·niv·ence** *n* **1.** secret joint conspiracy or plotting **2.** unspoken encouragement of or consent to wrongdoing by somebody else

con·nive /kə nív/ (**-nived, -niv·ing, -nives**) *vi* **1.** to plan secretly to do something, usually something wrong or illegal **2.** to pretend not to know about or do nothing to stop a wrongful or illegal act, thus showing encouragement of or consent to the act ○ *He connived at his brother's shoplifting with the understanding that he would share the loot.* [Early 17C. Via French < Latin *connivere* "close your eyes"] —**con·niv·er** *n* —**con·niv·er·y** *n*

con·niv·ence *n* another spelling of **connivance**

con·ni·vent /kə nívənt/ *adj* describes insect wings and flower petals or stamens that converge and touch but remain separate and not fused

con·niv·ing /kə níving/ *adj* devious and scheming —**con·niv·ing·ly** *adv*

~~**connoiseur**~~ incorrect spelling of **connoisseur**

con·nois·seur /kònnə súr/ *n* an expert in an area of the fine or domestic arts, or somebody with discriminating taste in such a specialty [Early 18C. < French < *connoistre* "know" < Latin *cognoscere* (see COGNITION)] —**con·nois·seur·ship** *n*

Con·nol·ly /kónn'lee/, **Maureen** (1934–69) US tennis player. She was the first woman to win all four grand slam tournaments in one year (1953). Full name **Connolly, Maureen Catherine**. Known as **Little Mo**

Con·nors /kónnərz/, **Jimmy** (*b.* 1952) US tennis player. He won 109 professional singles titles, including eight grand slam tournaments, during the 1970s and 1980s. Full name **Connors, James Scott**. Known as **Jimbo**

> "They can give all the coaching they want. But once a guy gets down there on court, he's got to hit the ball himself."
> [Jimmy Connors, *The Times (London)*; June 5, 1984]

con·no·ta·tion /kònnə táysh'n/ *n* **1. IMPLIED ADDITIONAL MEANING** an additional sense or senses associated with or suggested by a word or phrase. Connotations are sometimes, but not always, fixed, and are often subjective. ○ *Patriotism can have some negative connotations for people.* **2. SUGGESTING OF ADDITIONAL MEANING FOR WORD** the implying or suggesting of an additional meaning for a word or phrase apart from the literal or main meaning **3. DEFINING CHARACTERISTIC** in logic, the characteristic or set of characteristics that makes up the meaning of a term and thus defines the objects to which a term can be applied —**con·no·ta·tive** /kónnə tàytiv/ *adj* —**con·no·ta·tive·ly** *adv*

con·note /kə nṓt/ (**-not·ed, -not·ing, -notes**) *vt* **1.** to imply or suggest something in addition to the literal or main meaning ○ *The word "hearth" often connotes coziness and warmth.* **2.** to imply something else as a condition or a consequence ○ *His reluctance to act connotes cowardice.* [Mid-17C. < medieval Latin *connotare* "mark along with" < Latin *notare* "to mark" < *nota* "sign"]

USAGE ***connote*** **or** ***denote?*** ***Denote*** refers to the literal or main meaning of a word, whereas ***connote*** refers to its implications or associations. The word *family*, for example, *denotes* a group of people related by blood or marriage but *connotes* the bonds of affection, trust, and loyalty that unite them.

con·nu·bi·al /kə nóobee əl/ *adj* relating to marriage (*literary*) [Mid-17C. < Latin *connubialis* "relating to marriage" < *connubium* "marriage" < *nubere* "marry"] —**con·nu·bi·al·ly** *adv*

co·no·dont /kṓnə dònt, kónnə-/ *n* a very small tooth-shaped fossil thought to be the remains of a marine organism. Conodonts are commonly found in marine limestone beds from the Paleozoic era and are used by geologists to date rock layers. [Mid-19C. < Greek *kōnos* "cone"]

con·quer /kóngkər/ (**-quered, -quer·ing, -quers**) *v* **1.** *vt* SEIZE AREA BY MILITARY FORCE to take control of a place by force of arms **2.** *vt* DEFEAT PEOPLE IN WAR to win a victory over a people in war **3.** *vt* MASTER SOMETHING DIFFICULT to overcome a difficulty, problem, or illness ○ *conquered his fear of heights* ○ *hoping to show that a zero tolerance policy can conquer street crime* **4.** *vt* CLIMB MOUNTAIN to make a difficult or dangerous mountain ascent ○ *the first woman to conquer Everest* **5.** *vt* WIN SOMEBODY'S ADMIRATION to win somebody's love, affection, or admiration, often through strength of character or seduction, and sometimes somewhat against the person's will ○ *By the end of the last song, she had conquered their hearts.* **6.** *vi* WIN to be victorious [13C. Via Old French *conquerre* < Latin *conquirere* "seek for, procure" < *quaerere* "seek"] —**con·quer·a·ble** *adj*

SYNONYMS See *defeat.*

con·quer·or /kóngkərər/ *n* **1.** a victor in a war **2.** a victor in a competitive event

con·quest /kón kwèst, kóng-/ *n* **1.** SUBJUGATION OF ENEMY the process of taking control of a place or people by force of arms **2.** SOMETHING ACQUIRED BY CONQUERING something that has been acquired through force of arms, e.g., land, people, or goods **3.** SOMEBODY WON OVER somebody whose love, affection, or admiration has been won, often through strength of character or seduction, and sometimes somewhat against the person's will ○ *was another of his many conquests* [13C. Via Old French < Vulgar Latin *conquaesita*, literally "sought diligently" < Latin *quaerere* "seek"]

con·quis·ta·dor /kon keéstə dàwr, kəng-, -kweéstə-/ (*plural* **-quis·ta·dors** or **-quis·ta·dor·es** /-keéstə dáw ràyz/) *n* a Spanish conqueror or adventurer, especially one of those who conquered Mexico, Peru, and Central America in the 16th century [Mid-19C. < Spanish < Latin *conquirere* (see CONQUER)]

AKG London

Joseph Conrad

Con·rad /kón ràd/, **Joseph** (1857–1924) Polish-born British writer. His novels and stories include *Nostromo* (1904), *Lord Jim* (1900), and *Heart of Darkness* (1902). See Cultural note at **heart**

> "You shall judge of a man by his foes as well as by his friends."
> [Joseph Conrad, *Lord Jim*; 1900]

Con·roe /kónrō/ city in eastern Texas, northwest of Houston. Population: 39,065 (2002 estimate).

cons. *abbr* **1.** RELIG consecrated **2.** MAIL consigned **3.** MAIL consignment **4.** LING consonant **5.** *also* **cons** POL constitution **6.** POL constitutional **7.** CONSTR construction

Cons. *abbr* **1.** POL Conservative **2.** POLICE Constable **3.** *also* **Cons.** POL Constitution **4.** INTERNAT REL Consul

con·san·guin·i·ty /kòn san gwínnətee/ *n* **1.** relationship by descent from the same ancestor, and not by marriage or affinity **2.** a close relationship or connection —**con·san·guin·e·ous** *adj*

con·science /kónshənss/ *n* **1.** SENSE OF RIGHT AND WRONG the sense of what is right and wrong that governs somebody's thoughts and actions, urging him or her to do right rather than wrong ○ *Let your conscience be your guide.* **2.** OBEDIENCE TO CONSCIENCE behavior according to what your sense of right and wrong tells you is right ○ *campaigning on behalf of prisoners of conscience* **3.** SHARED MORAL VIEWPOINT a shared concern for moral issues ○ *a social conscience* **4.** PSYCHOANAL PART OF SUPEREGO the part of the superego that passes judgment on thought and behavior to the ego for further consideration [13C. Via Old French < Latin *conscientia* "consciousness" < *conscire* "be conscious," literally "know thoroughly" < *scire* "know"] —**con·science·less** *adj* ◇ **in all** *or* **good conscience 1.** while being fair and reasonable **2.** used to emphasize that what you are saying is truly the case ◇ **on somebody's conscience** causing somebody to feel guilty or anxious about something

USAGE See *conscientious.*

con·science clause *n* a clause in an act, law, or contract that exempts those who have moral or religious objections to complying

con·science mon·ey *n* money paid voluntarily in compensation for a previous act of wrongdoing by which somebody has been harmed

con·science-strick·en, **con·science-smit·ten** *adj* feeling guilty or anxious about having done something wrong

~~consciencious~~ incorrect spelling of **conscientious**

con·sci·en·tious /kònshee énshəss/ *adj* **1.** showing great care, attention, and industriousness in carrying out a task or role ○ *a conscientious parent* **2.** governed by or done according to somebody's sense of right and wrong ○ *a conscientious decision to dedicate an hour a week to volunteer work* [Early 17C. Via French < medieval Latin *conscientiosus* < Latin *conscientia* (see CONSCIENCE)] —**con·sci·en·tious·ly** *adv* —**con·sci·en·tious·ness** *n*

USAGE conscientious or **conscious**? If you are ***conscious*** you are awake or aware: *The patient is conscious; We are conscious of the danger.* ***Conscious*** can also mean "deliberate, intentional," as in *We made a conscious* [not *conscientious*] *move to win the championship.* If you are ***conscientious*** you are diligent and thorough, or governed by your own sense of ethics: *Conscientious students study diligently. I made a conscientious* [not *conscious*] *effort to represent indigent clients pro bono in court.* Both these adjectives can modify nouns such as *decision* and *effort*, but the writer must ensure that the context is clear. A *conscious decision/effort* is one made intentionally and deliberately (*a conscious decision/effort to disregard all risks*); a *conscientious decision/effort* is one involving an ethical judgment (*a conscientious decision/effort to right wrongs when we see them*).

SYNONYMS See *careful.*

con·sci·en·tious ob·jec·tor *n* somebody who, for moral or religious reasons, believes it is wrong to wage war and therefore refuses to join or serve in any branch of the armed services

con·scious /kónshəss/ *adj* **1.** AWAKE awake and responsive to stimuli ○ *He's been seriously injured but he's still conscious.* **2.** KEENLY AWARE fully appreciating the importance of something ○ *I'm conscious of all you've done for us.* **3.** INTENTIONAL considered and deliberate, or done with critical awareness ○ *a conscious effort not to lose her temper* **4.** WELL-INFORMED well-informed on issues relating to a particular topic of serious significance (*often used in combination with adverbs*) ○ *environmentally conscious* **5.** CONCERNED WITH SOMETHING aware of and interested in a particular topic (*often used hyphenated in combination*) ○ *fashion-conscious* ○ *health-conscious* **6.** PSYCHOL FUNCTIONING WITH INDIVIDUAL'S KNOWLEDGE relating to or concerned with a part of the mind that is capable of thinking, choosing, or perceiving ■ *n* PSYCHOL AREA OF MIND AWARE OF SURROUNDINGS the part of the human mind that is aware of the feelings, thoughts, and surroundings [Late 16C. < Latin *conscius* "knowing" < *scire* "know"] —**con·scious·ly** *adv*

USAGE See *conscientious.*

SYNONYMS See *aware.*

con·scious·ness /kónshəssnəss/ *n* **1.** AWARENESS OF SURROUNDINGS the state of being awake and aware of what is going on around you ○ *feelings of dizziness followed by loss of consciousness* **2.** SOMEBODY'S MIND somebody's mind and thoughts ○ *In time, this experience will fade from your consciousness.* **3.** SHARED FEELINGS AND BELIEFS the set of opinions, feelings, and beliefs of a group ○ *national consciousness* **4.** AWARENESS OF PARTICULAR ISSUE awareness of or sensitivity to a particular issue ○ *health consciousness* **5.** PSYCHOL same as **conscious** *n*

USAGE See *conscientious.*

con·scious·ness-rais·ing *n* **1.** the process of increasing people's awareness of a moral or social issue with a view to encouraging them to take action **2.** the increasing of self-awareness, usually through group therapy —**con·scious·ness-rais·er** *n*

con·script *vt* /kən skrípt/ (**-script·ed, -script·ing, -scripts**) to enroll somebody compulsorily in the armed forces ■ *n* /kón skrìpt/ a recruit who has been compulsorily enrolled, especially in the armed forces [15C. < Latin *conscript-*, past participle of *conscribere* "enroll" < *scribere* "write"]

con·scrip·tion /kən skrípsh'n/ *n* the obligatory enrollment of citizens in the armed forces

con·se·crate /kónssə kràyt/ (**-crat·ed, -crat·ing, -crates**) *vt* **1.** RELIG DECLARE PLACE HOLY to declare or set apart a building, area of ground, or specific spot as holy ○ *The cathedral was consecrated in the 12th century.* **2.** DEDICATE SOMETHING TO PARTICULAR PURPOSE to dedicate somebody or something to a particular purpose **3.** MAKE CUSTOM REVERED to cause a custom to be revered **4.** CHR BLESS COMMUNION BREAD AND WINE to sanctify the bread and wine for use in the Communion service as symbols of the body and blood of Jesus Christ **5.** RELIG ORDAIN BISHOP to ordain a priest as a bishop [14C. < Latin *consecrat-*, past participle of *consecrare* "make sacred" < *sacer* "sacred"] —**con·se·cra·tive** *adj* —**con·se·cra·tor** *n* —**con·se·cra·to·ry** /-krə tàwree/ *adj*

con·se·cra·tion /kònssə kráysh'n/ *n* the ceremony in which somebody or something is consecrated

Con·se·cra·tion *n* the process or ceremony of sanctifying the bread and wine during Communion

con·sec·u·tive /kən sékyətiv/ *adj* **1.** following one after another without interruption or break ○ *He hasn't shown up for work for three consecutive days.* **2.** following a logical or chronological sequence [Early 17C. Via French < medieval Latin *consecutivus* < Latin *consecut-*, past participle of *consequi* (see CONSEQUENT)] —**con·sec·u·tive·ly** *adv* —**con·sec·u·tive·ness** *n*

con·sen·su·al /kən sénshoo əl/ *adj* **1.** BY MUTUAL CONSENT involving the agreement of all involved **2.** LAW REQUIRING CONSENT ONLY describes an agreement requiring only the consent of the parties involved to make it binding **3.** PHYSIOL RESPONDING INVOLUNTARILY TO INDIRECT STIMULUS describes an involuntary response by one body part to a stimulus to another, e.g., the pupil of one eye constricting when the other eye is exposed to light [Mid-18C. < Latin *consens-*, past participle of *consentire* (see CONSENT)] —**con·sen·su·al·ly** *adv*

con·sen·sus /kən sénsəss/ *n* **1.** general or widespread agreement among all the members of a group ○ *After hours of deliberation, they finally reached a consensus.* **2.** a concept of society in which the absence of conflict is seen as the equilibrium state of society [Mid-17C. < Latin < past participle of *consentire* (see CONSENT)]

USAGE The word ***consensus*** is often misspelled *concensus*, probably from the erroneous influence of the word *census*.

USAGE Since ***consensus*** already means "a view or opinion that is generally shared," expressions such as *general consensus* and *consensus of opinion* are, strictly speaking, tautologies (i.e., they say the same thing twice), and modifiers such as "general" and "of opinion" are redundant. However, occasionally a modifier can be justified, as in *There was a consensus of feeling, but no consensus of opinion.* It is always best to begin by considering whether or not the word without modifiers expresses what you mean.

con·sent /kən sént/ *vi* (**-sent·ed, -sent·ing, -sents**) **1.** GIVE PERMISSION to give formal permission for something to happen ○ *As soon as they met Robert, her parents consented to the marriage.* **2.** AGREE to agree to do something ○ *She consented to appear as a witness.* ■ *n* **1.** PERMISSION FOR SOMETHING acceptance of or agreement to something proposed or desired by another **2.** CONSENSUS agreement on an opinion or course of action ○ *It was by common consent the best.* [13C. Via Old French < Latin *consentire* "feel with" < *sentire* "feel"] —**con·sent·er** *n*

SYNONYMS See ***agree***.

con·sent de·cree *n* a judicial decree expressing voluntary agreement between parties to a dispute

con·sent·ing a·dult /kən sènting-/ *n* somebody who is old enough to be allowed to participate legally in something and is willing to do so, especially in a sexual activity

~~consentrate~~ incorrect spelling of **concentrate**

con·se·quence /kónssəkwənss/ *n* **1.** RESULT something that follows as a result ○ *This is a direct consequence of your negligence.* **2.** RELATION BETWEEN CAUSE AND EFFECT the relation between a result and its cause **3.** IMPORTANCE importance or significance (*formal; often used in negative statements*) ○ *Your opinion is of no consequence whatsoever to me.* **4.** LOGICAL CONCLUSION a conclusion reached through valid deductive reasoning ■ **con·se·quen·ces** *npl* NEGATIVE RESULTS the unpleasant or difficult results of a previous action [14C. Via French < Latin *consequentia* < *consequi* (see CONSEQUENT)] ◇ **in consequence** as a result of something (*formal*)

con·se·quent /kónssəkwənt/ *adj* **1.** FOLLOWING AS RESULT following as a result or effect ○ *weeks of rain and the consequent flooding* **2.** LOGIC AS LOGICAL CONCLUSION following as a logical conclusion ■ *n* **1.** LOGIC RESULT OF SOMETHING something that follows as a result **2.** LOGIC SECOND HALF OF CONDITIONAL SENTENCE the part of a conditional sentence that expresses the result and is the q clause in a proposition of the form "if p then q" **3.** MATH SECOND TERM OF RATIO the second term in a mathematical ratio [15C. Via French < Latin *consequent-*, present participle of *consequi* "follow along with" < *sequi* "follow"]

con·se·quen·tial /kònssə kwénsh'l/ *adj* **1.** RESULTANT following as a consequence or result of something **2.** IMPORTANT of considerable importance, significance, or value ○ *a consequential figure on the classical music circuit* **3.** TOO SELF-IMPORTANT having an exaggerated opinion of personal qualities or abilities **4.** INSUR ARISING AS INDIRECT COST describes costs, loss, or damage beyond the market value of the object lost or damaged, including other indirect costs arising —**con·se·quen·ti·al·i·ty** /kònsə kwenshee állətee/ *n* —**con·se·quen·tial·ly** *adv* —**con·se·quen·tial·ness** *n*

con·se·quen·tial·ism /kònssə kwénshə lìzzəm/ *n* the tenet by which an action is considered right or wrong depending on whether its outcome is good or bad

con·se·quent·ly /kónssəkwəntlee/ *adv* as a result or in view of something ○ *The joke backfired and the relationship consequently deteriorated.*

~~consern~~ incorrect spelling of **concern**

con·ser·van·cy /kən súrvənssee/ (*plural* **-cies**) *n* an area designated for the protection both of the land and of its wildlife and their habitat

con·ser·va·tion /kònssər váysh'n/ *n* **1.** the preservation, management, and care of natural and cultural resources **2.** the keeping or protecting of something from change, loss, or damage —**con·ser·va·tion·al** *adj*

con·ser·va·tion a·re·a *n* an area of special environmental or historical importance that is protected from casual changes by law

con·ser·va·tion·ist /kònssər váysh'nist/ *n* a supporter of or advocate for the preservation of the environment, especially the natural world

con·ser·va·tion of charge *n* the principle that the total electric charge of an isolated system remains constant, no matter what internal changes take place

con·ser·va·tion of en·er·gy *n* the principle that the amount of energy in an isolated system remains the same, even though the form of energy may change

con·ser·va·tion of mass, con·ser·va·tion of mat·ter *n* the principle that the total mass of an isolated system remains constant, in spite of any physical or chemical changes that may take place

con·ser·va·tion of mo·men·tum *n* the principle that the total linear or angular momentum of an isolated system remains the same

con·ser·va·tism /kən súrvə tìzzəm/ *n* **1.** RELUCTANCE TO ACCEPT CHANGE unwillingness or slowness to accept change or new ideas **2.** RIGHT-WING POLITICAL VIEWPOINT a right-of-center political philosophy based on a tendency to support gradual rather than abrupt change and to preserve the status quo **3.** DESIRE TO PRESERVE CURRENT SOCIETAL STRUCTURE an ideology that views the existing form of society as worthy of preservation

Con·ser·va·tism *n* the principles and practice of Conservative politicians or supporters

con·ser·va·tive /kən súrvətiv/ *adj* **1.** RELUCTANT TO ACCEPT CHANGE in favor of preserving the status quo and traditional values and customs, and against abrupt change **2.** OF CONSERVATISM relating to, characteristic of, or displaying conservatism **3.** CAUTIOUS AND ON LOW SIDE cautiously moderate and therefore often less than the final outcome ○ *Several hundred dollars is probably a very conservative estimate.* **4.** CONVENTIONAL IN APPEARANCE conventional or restrained in style and avoiding showiness ○ *a conservative suit* **5.** USING MINIMUM MEDICAL INTERVENTION designed to help relieve symptoms or preserve health with a minimum of medical intervention ■ *n* **1.** TRADITIONALIST a supporter or advocate of traditional ideas and behavior **2.** SUPPORTER OF CONSERVATISM somebody who believes in or supports conservatism —**con·ser·va·tive·ly** *adv* —**con·ser·va·tive·ness** *n*

Con·ser·va·tive *adj* **1.** OF CONSERVATIVE PARTY relating to, belonging to, or supporting a Conservative Party **2.** OF CONSERVATIVE JUDAISM relating to, associated with, or characteristic of Conservative Judaism ■ *n* SUPPORTER OF CONSERVATIVE PARTY a member or supporter of a Conservative Party

Con·ser·va·tive Ju·da·ism *n* a form of Judaism that accepts most of the principles and practices of traditional Judaism but supports the modification and relaxing of some laws. The movement arose around the turn of the 20th century as a reaction against the more liberal Reform Judaism.

Con·ser·va·tive Par·ty *n* **1.** MAIN UK RIGHT-WING POLITICAL PARTY in the United Kingdom, the principal right-of-center political party. It supports low personal taxation, home ownership, and free-market principles. It was founded in the early 1830s as a successor to the Tory Party. **2.** CANADIAN RIGHT-WING POLITICAL PARTY in Canada, the Conservative Party of Canada, or, formerly, the Progressive Conservative Party **3.** POLITICAL PARTY OPPOSED TO CHANGE in countries other than the United Kingdom and Canada, a political party that is opposed to change (*takes a singular or plural verb*)

Con·ser·va·tive Par·ty of Can·a·da *n* a Canadian political party established in 2003 when members of the Progressive Conservative Party and the Canadian Alliance voted for union. It believes in a united Canada under the British monarchy, free trade, and emphasis on the rights and responsibilities of individuals.

con·ser·va·tize /kən súrvə tìz/ (**-tized, -tiz·ing, -tiz·es**) *vti* to become, or make an organization or person become, conservative or increasingly conservative

con·ser·va·toire /kən sùrvə twáar/ *n* MUSIC same as **conservatory** (sense 1) [Late 18C. Via French < Italian *conservatorio* < late Latin *conservatorium* (see CONSERVATORY)]

con·ser·va·tor /kən súrvətər/ *n* **1.** somebody who preserves or restores works of art or other valued objects in a museum or collection **2.** a person or institution responsible for protecting the interests of a legal incompetent —**con·ser·va·to·ri·al** /kən sùrvə táwree əl/ *adj* —**con·ser·va·tor·ship** *n*

con·ser·va·to·ry /kən súrvə tàwree/ (*plural* **-ries**) *n* **1.** an institution or school where students are taught one of the arts, most commonly music or drama, to a professional standard **2.** a room with glass walls and roof where plants are grown or displayed, often built onto the side of a house [Mid-16C. < late Latin *conservatorium* < Latin *conservare* (see CONSERVE)]

con·serve *vt* /kən súrv/ (**-served, -serv·ing, -serves**) **1.** PROTECT SOMETHING FROM HARM OR DECAY to keep something, especially an important environmental or cultural resource, from harm, loss, change, or decay ○ *the importance of conserving our national heritage* **2.** USE SOMETHING SPARINGLY to use something sparingly so as not to exhaust supplies ○ *some drastic measures to conserve water* **3.** PRESERVE FOOD IN SUGAR to preserve food, especially fruit, in sugar **4.** KEEP MATTER OR ENERGY CONSTANT to keep something such as matter or energy constant through physical changes or chemical reactions ■ *n* /kón sùrv, kən súrv/ FRUIT IN SYRUP a food consisting of fruit in a thick sugar syrup, like jam but less firmly set and usually containing larger pieces of fruit [14C. Via French < Latin *conservare* "preserve well" < *servare* "keep"] —**con·serv·a·ble** *adj* —**con·serv·er** *n*

~~consession~~ incorrect spelling of **concession**

con·sid·er /kən síddər/ (**-ered, -er·ing, -ers**) *v* **1.** *vti* REFLECT ON SOMETHING to think carefully about something ○ *You should consider your next move carefully.* ○ *time to consider whether this is what you really want* **2.** *vt* JUDGE SOMETHING to have something as an opinion or point of view ○ *He considers himself lucky to be alive.* ○ *I consider it unlikely that they'll accept our proposal.* **3.** *vt* RESPECT SOMEBODY OR SOMETHING to show respect for or be thoughtful of somebody's feelings or position ○ *They never seem to consider the feelings of others.* **4.** *vt* WEIGH POSSIBILITIES BEFORE DECIDING to weigh the pros and cons of a situation before making a decision on a course of action ○ *I'm considering my options.* ○ *They're considering buying a new house.* **5.** *vt* EXAMINE AND DISCUSS PROBLEM to examine a problem and discuss it in detail ○ *On this week's show, we're going to consider the following question.* **6.** *vt* TAKE SOMETHING INTO ACCOUNT to take something into account, often in a sympathetic way ○ *We've done very well, all things considered.* **7.** *vt* LOOK CAREFULLY AT SOMETHING to look at something carefully and with concentration (*formal*) [14C. Via French < Latin *considerare*] —**con·sid·ered** *adj* —**con·sid·er·er** *n*

con·sid·er·a·ble /kən síddərəb'l/ *adj* **1.** LARGE large enough in amount or extent to be important ○ *needs a considerable income to afford this apartment* **2.** SIGNIFICANT worthy of consideration or respect ○ *a considerable figure in the art world* ■ *n* GREAT AMOUNT a great deal or amount (*informal*)

con·sid·er·a·bly /kən síddərəblee/ *adv* to a significant degree ○ *He's considerably older than I am.*

con·sid·er·ate /kən síddərət/ *adj* mindful of the needs, wishes, and feelings of others —**con·sid·er·ate·ly** *adv* —**con·sid·er·ate·ness** *n*

con·sid·er·a·tion /kən sìddə ráysh'n/ *n* **1.** CAREFUL THOUGHT careful thought or deliberation ○ *Your application will be given the fullest consideration.* ○ *The proposal is currently under consideration.* **2.** MINDFULNESS OF OTHERS thoughtful concern for or sensitivity toward the feelings of others **3.** RELEVANT FACTOR IN ASSESSING SOMETHING something to be taken into account when weighing the pros and cons of a situation before making a decision ○ *Value for money is one of the most important considerations for our customers.* **4.** DETAILED EXAMINATION detailed discussion or scrutiny ○ *The issue for consideration on today's show is cosmetic surgery.* **5.** PAYMENT a payment or fee in return for a service (*formal*) **6.** RESPECT high regard (*formal*) ○ *She has always been held in great consideration by this congregation.* **7.** SOMETHING MAKING CONTRACT BINDING something done by one of the parties as part of a contractual arrangement that makes it binding, e.g., the payment of the price in a sales agreement ◇ **in consideration of** (*formal*) **1.** because of **2.** as payment for ◇ **of little** *or* **no consideration** not important or significant (*formal*) ◇ **take something into con-**

sideration to take account of special circumstances, often in a sympathetic way

con·sid·er·ing /kən síddəring/ *prep, conj* taking something into account ○ *It's a tremendous bargain, considering the price and how much we need one.* ■ *adv* taking everything into account, often in a sympathetic way (*usually used at the end of a phrase or sentence*) ○ *We've done a really good job, considering.*

~~consience~~ incorrect spelling of **conscience**

con·si·glie·re /kòn seel yé ray/ (*plural* **-si·glie·ri** /-seel yérree/) *n* an adviser to the leader of a crime syndicate [Early 17C. < Italian < Latin *consilium* (see COUNSEL)]

con·sign /kən sín/ (**-signed, -sign·ing, -signs**) *vt* **1.** ENTRUST SOMEBODY OR SOMETHING to hand somebody or something over to the care of another ○ *The children were consigned to the care of the nanny.* **2.** GET RID OF SOMEBODY OR SOMETHING to dispose of somebody or something, usually for a long time, if not permanently ○ *Before fleeing, they consigned the documents to the flames.* **3.** DELIVER SOMETHING to address, deliver, or hand over for later delivery something for sale, safekeeping, or disposal [15C. Via French < Latin *consignare* "certify with a seal" < *signum* "mark"] —**con·sign·a·ble** *adj* —**con·sign·ee** /kòn sī neé/ *n* —**con·sign·er** *n* —**con·sign·or** *n*

con·sign·ment /kən sínmənt/ *n* **1.** DELIVERY a quantity or package of goods delivered or to be delivered **2.** DISPOSAL OF SOMEBODY OR SOMETHING the disposal of somebody or something, usually for a long time, if not permanently **3.** ENTRUSTING OF SOMEBODY OR SOMETHING the handing over of somebody or something to the care of another ◇ **on consignment** on the understanding that payment will be made only when the goods have been sold and that any remaining unsold articles can be returned

con·sign·ment store *n* a retail outlet that stocks and sells goods on a sale-or-return basis, or as an agent selling on behalf of others and receiving a percentage

~~consious~~ incorrect spelling of **conscious**

con·sist /kən síst/ (**-sist·ed, -sist·ing, -sists**) *vi* **1.** to be made up of diverse parts ○ *This dressing consists of oil, lemon juice, and mustard.* **2.** to be based on or defined by something ○ *Her talent consists in her superb musicianship.* [Early 16C. < Latin *consistere* < *sistere* "make stand" < *stare* "to stand"]

USAGE See ***comprise***.

~~consistant~~ incorrect spelling of **consistent**

con·sis·ten·cy /kən sístənssee/, **con·sis·tence** /-tənss/ *n* **1.** CONSTANCY the ability to maintain a particular standard or repeat a particular task with minimal variation ○ *Consistency is important in performing this job.* ○ *"A foolish consistency is the hobgoblin of small minds."* (Ralph Waldo Emerson *Self-Reliance*; 1841) **2.** COHERENCE reasonable or logical harmony between parts ○ *The plot lacked consistency.* **3.** DEGREE OF THICKNESS OR SMOOTHNESS the degree of thickness or smoothness of a mixture ○ *Blend the mixture until it reaches the consistency of thick cream.*

con·sis·tent /kən sístənt/ *adj* **1.** COHERENT reasonably or logically harmonious ○ *The evidence is consistent with the defendant's statement.* ○ *Their accounts of the incident just aren't consistent.* **2.** RELIABLE able to maintain a particular standard or repeat a particular task with minimal variation ○ *He's one of the most consistent hitters in the league.* **3.** MATH WITH COMMON SOLUTIONS having a set of solutions in common, especially for two or more equations or inequalities **4.** LOGIC FREE OF CONTRADICTION containing no provable contradiction [Late 16C. < Latin *consistent-*, present participle of *consistere* (see CONSIST)] —**con·sis·tent·ly** *adv*

con·sis·to·ry /kən sístəree/ (*plural* **-ries**) *n* **1.** CHR ASSEMBLY OF CARDINALS AND POPE in the Roman Catholic Church, an assembly of cardinals convoked and led by the pope **2.** *UK* CHR ANGLICAN DIOCESAN COURT in the Anglican Church, the court of any diocese except Canterbury **3.** CHR CONGREGATIONAL GOVERNING BODY in some Reformed churches, the governing body of a congregation **4.** CHR REGULATORY COURT IN LUTHERAN CHURCHES in Lutheran state churches, a court appointed to regulate ecclesiastical affairs **5.** COUNCIL a council or assembly (*archaic*) [13C. Via Anglo-Norman < late Latin *consistorium* "place of assembly" < Latin *consistere* (see CONSIST)] —**con·sis·to·ri·al** /kònssi stáwree əl/ *adj*

con·so·ci·ate (*formal*) *vti* /kən sṓshee àyt/ (**-at·ed, -at·ing, -ates**) JOIN ASSOCIATION to enter or welcome somebody into a friendly association or alliance ■ *adj* /kən sṓshee ət/ ASSOCIATED associated or united ■ *n* /kən sṓshee ət/ PARTNER an associate or partner [15C. < Latin *consociat-*, past participle of *consociare* "associate" < *socius* "companion"]

con·so·ci·a·tion /kən sòshee áysh'n/ *n* **1.** FRIENDLY ASSOCIATION a friendly association or alliance (*formal*) **2.** ECOL ECOLOGICAL COMMUNITY WITH ONE MAIN SPECIES an ecological community that has one dominant species, e.g., a forest consisting predominantly of beech trees **3.** POL POLITICAL COALITION a grouping of political parties or pressure groups within a region or country that work together to share power **4.** CHR ASSOCIATION OF REFORMED CHURCHES an association of churches or religious societies, especially Congregational churches in New England and Presbyterian churches —**con·so·ci·a·tion·al** *adj*

con·so·la·tion /kònssə láysh'n/ *n* **1.** SOURCE OF COMFORT a source of comfort to somebody who is upset or disappointed ○ *The fortune she left was little consolation for him.* **2.** COMFORT TO SOMEBODY IN DISTRESS comfort to somebody who is distressed or disappointed ○ *Most of those at the funeral murmured some words of consolation as they left.* **3.** SPORTS, LEISURE GAME FOR EARLIER LOSERS a game or contest held for people or teams who have lost earlier in a tournament

con·so·la·tion prize *n* a prize given to comfort the loser or losers in a game or competition

con·sole[1] /kən sṓl/ (**-soled, -sol·ing, -soles**) *vt* to provide a source of comfort to somebody who is distressed or disappointed [Mid-17C. Via French < Latin *consolare* < *solari* "to comfort"] —**con·sol·a·ble** *adj* —**con·so·la·to·ry** *adj* —**con·sol·er** *n* —**con·sol·ing·ly** *adv*

USAGE See ***condole***.

con·sole[2] /kón sòl/ *n* **1.** ELECTRONICS CONTROL PANEL a desk, table, display, or keyboard onto which the controls of an electronic system or some other machine are fixed **2.** FURNITURE CABINET FOR TELEVISION OR STEREO a free-standing cabinet, especially one used to house a television or stereo system **3.** AUTOMOT STORAGE COMPARTMENT IN AUTOMOBILE a small storage compartment in an automobile, fixed between individual seats **4.** FURNITURE same as **console table** **5.** MUSIC ORGAN CONTROLS the part of an organ that houses the keyboards or manuals, pedals, and stops **6.** ARCHIT ORNAMENTAL BRACKET an ornamental bracket, often in the shape of a scroll, used for decoration and for supporting wall fixtures **7.** PLAYER FOR COMPUTER GAME an electronic device that connects to a television set on which computer games and DVDs can be played [Mid-17C. < French]

con·sole ta·ble *n* a small table with curved legs designed to stand against a wall

con·sol·i·date /kən sólli dàyt/ (**-dat·ed, -dat·ing, -dates**) *v* **1.** *vti* UNITE BUSINESS ACTIVITIES to bring businesses or business activities together, or come together, into a single unit **2.** *vti* STRENGTHEN POSITION to increase the strength, stability, or depth of your success or position ○ *This excellent performance has enabled her to consolidate her lead.* **3.** *vti* COMBINE SOMETHING INTO SINGLE MASS to combine separate items or scattered material into a single whole or mass **4.** *vt* FIN COMBINE ACCOUNTS to combine several sets of financial accounts in a single set of accounts [Early 16C. < Latin *consolidat-*, past participle of *consolidare* "make solid" < *solidus* "firm, whole"] —**con·sol·i·da·tor** *n*

con·sol·i·dat·ed school /kən sòlli daytəd-/ *n* a public school for students from several neighboring, often rural, districts

con·sol·i·da·tion /kən sòlli dáysh'n/ *n* **1.** COMBINING OF BUSINESS ACTIVITIES the bringing together of businesses or business activities into a single unit **2.** STRENGTHENING OF POSITION the increasing of the strength, stability, or depth of a person's or group's success or position ○ *The final six weeks saw a consolidation of their position at the top of the league.* **3.** COMBINATION INTO SINGLE MASS the combination of separate items or scattered material into a single whole or mass **4.** GEOL COMPACTING OF LOOSE DEPOSIT INTO ROCK a process by which a loose deposit is compacted into hard rock **5.** PSYCHOL PSYCHOLOGICAL PROCESS THAT FIXES MEMORY the process in the brain that enables somebody to have a lasting memory of a particular event

con·sols /kón sòlz/ *npl* in the United Kingdom, government bonds with a fixed interest rate and no date of maturity [Late 18C. Contraction of *consolidated annuities*]

con·som·mé /kònssə máy/ *n* a thin clear soup made from meat stock. It can be eaten hot, or cold in jellied form. [Early 19C. < French < past participle of *consommer* "use up" < Latin *consummare* (see CONSUMMATE)]

con·so·nance /kónssənənss/, **con·so·nan·cy** /kónssənənssee/ (*plural* **-cies**) *n* **1.** AGREEMENT agreement or harmony (*formal*) **2.** LING SIMILARITY BETWEEN CONSONANTS a close similarity between consonants or groups of consonants, especially at the ends of words, e.g., between "strong" and "ring" **3.** MUSIC PLEASANT COMBINATION OF MUSICAL NOTES a combination of notes that sound pleasing when played simultaneously

con·so·nant /kónssənənt/ *n* **1.** LING SPEECH SOUND OTHER THAN VOWEL a speech sound produced by partly or totally blocking the path of air through the mouth **2.** LETTER REPRESENTING CONSONANT a letter of the alphabet that represents a consonant ■ *adj* **1.** IN AGREEMENT WITH SOMETHING in agreement or harmony with something (*formal*) ○ *delighted to learn that their views were consonant with our own* **2.** MUSIC PLEASING IN HARMONY containing chords or harmonies that are pleasing to hear **3.** LING HAVING SIMILAR SOUNDS having similar sounds, or showing consonance [14C. Via French < Latin *consonant-* "sounding together" < *sonare* "to sound"] —**con·so·nan·tal** /kònssə nánt'l/ *adj* —**con·so·nant·ly** *adv*

con sor·di·no /kòn sawr deénō/ *adv* using a mute or the mute pedal (*used as a musical direction*) [Early 19C. < Italian, "with a mute"]

con·sort *vi* /kən sáwrt/ (**-sort·ed, -sort·ing, -sorts**) ASSOCIATE WITH UNDESIRABLE to associate with or spend time in the company of somebody undesirable (*formal*) ○ *consorting with known criminals* ■ *n* /kón sàwrt/ **1.** *also* **Con·sort** SPOUSE OF MONARCH the husband or wife of a reigning monarch **2.** PARTNER a partner or companion (*formal*) **3.** SHIP THAT ESCORTS ANOTHER a ship that accompanies another on a journey **4.** GROUP SPECIALIZING IN EARLY MUSIC a small group of musicians specializing in works of the baroque or an earlier period [15C. Via French < Latin *consort-* "having the same fate" < *sors* "fortune"] ◇ **in consort with** in association or together with others (*archaic or formal*)

con·sor·ti·um /kən sáwrtee əm, -sáwrshəm, -sáwrshee əm/ (*plural* **-ti·a** /-tee ə/) *n* **1.** an association or grouping of institutions, businesses, or financial organizations, usually set up for a common purpose that would be beyond the capabilities of a single member of the group **2.** LAW the right of a husband or wife to the company, affection, and help of, and sexual relations with, his or her spouse (*archaic*) [Early 19C. < Latin, "fellowship" < *consort-* (see CONSORT)] —**con·sor·ti·al** *adj*

con·spe·cif·ic /kònspə síffik/ *adj* belonging to the same species as another organism —**con·spe·cif·ic** *n*

con·spec·tus /kən spéktəss/ *n* **1.** a general survey or overview of something **2.** an outline or synopsis of something [Mid-19C. < Latin < *conspect-*, past participle of *conspicere* (see CONSPICUOUS)]

con·spic·u·ous /kən spíkyoo əss/ *adj* **1.** easily or clearly visible ○ *The building's most conspicuous feature is its dome-shaped roof.* **2.** attracting attention through being unusual or remarkable ○ *He felt uncomfortably conspicuous, since he was the only man in evening dress.* [Mid-16C. < Latin *conspicuus* < *conspicere* "observe carefully" < *specere* "look at"] —**con·spic·u·ous·ly** *adv* —**con·spic·u·ous·ness** *n*

con·spic·u·ous con·sump·tion *n* the practice of spending large quantities of money, often extravagantly, to impress others

con·spir·a·cist /kən spírrəssist/ *n* somebody who believes that a conspiracy caused an event

con·spir·a·cy /kən spírrəssee/ (*plural* **-cies**) *n* CRIME **1.** PLAN TO COMMIT ILLEGAL ACT TOGETHER a secret plan or agreement between two or more people to commit an illegal or subversive act **2. MAKING OF AGREEMENT BY CONSPIRATORS** the making of a secret plan or agreement to commit an illegal or subversive act **3. GROUP OF CONSPIRATORS** a group of people planning or agreeing in secret to commit an illegal or subversive act [14C. < Anglo-Norman *conspiracie*, alteration of Old French *conspiration* < Latin *conspirat-*, past participle of *conspirare* (see CONSPIRE)]

con·spir·a·cy of si·lence *n* an agreement among a group of people to say nothing in public about a matter of public interest or importance, in order to protect or promote selfish interests

con·spir·a·cy the·o·ry *n* a belief that a particular event is the result of a secret plot rather than the actions of an individual person or chance —**con·spir·a·cy the·o·rist** *n*

con·spir·a·tor /kən spírrətər/ *n* a member of a group of people planning or agreeing in secret to commit an illegal or subversive act

con·spir·a·to·ri·al /kən spìrrə táwree əl/ *adj* indicating or betraying knowledge of or involvement in a conspiracy ○ *a conspiratorial whisper* —**con·spir·a·to·ri·al·ly** *adv*

con·spir·a·to·ri·al·ist /kən spìrrə táwree əlist/ *n* CRIME same as **conspiracist**

con·spire /kən spír/ (**-spired, -spir·ing, -spires**) *vi* **1.** to plan or agree in secret with others to commit an illegal or subversive act ○ *In court, the three defendants admitted to conspiring against the government.* **2.** to combine so as to cause a particular result, often one involving harm, inconvenience, or difficulty ○ *Rain and tears conspired to smudge her carefully applied mascara.* [14C. Via French < Latin *conspirare*, literally "breathe together" < *spirare* "breathe"] —**con·spir·ing·ly** *adv*

con·spi·ri·ol·o·gist /kən spìrree óllәjist/ *n* somebody who believes in conspiracy theories

con spi·ri·to /kon spírritō/ *adv* in a lively or spirited way (*used as a musical direction*) [Late 19C. < Italian, "with spirit"]

const. *abbr* **1.** *also* **const, Const., Const** POLICE Constable **2.** MATH, PHYS constant **3.** *also* **const, Const., Const** POL constitution **4.** POL constitutional

con·sta·ble /kónstəb'l, kún-/ *n* **1. OFFICER BELOW SHERIFF** in some towns or townships, a low-ranking law officer **2. POLICE OFFICER** in the United Kingdom, Canada, Australia, and New Zealand, a police officer of the lowest rank **3. CASTLE WARDEN** the warden of a royal castle or fortress **4. ROYAL HOUSEHOLD OFFICIAL IN MIDDLE AGES** the chief administrative and military officer in a royal household, especially in medieval France and England [12C. Via Old French *conestable* < late Latin *comes stabilis* "count of the stable"] —**con·sta·ble·ship** *n*

Con·sta·ble /kúnstəb'l, kón-/, **John** (1776–1837) British landscape painter. His paintings such as *The Haywain* (1821) came to symbolize rural England.

> "There is nothing ugly; I never saw an ugly thing in my life: for let the form of an object be what it may, light, shade, and perspective will always make it beautiful."
> [John Constable, *Memoirs of the Life of John Constable*, C. R. Leslie; 1843]

con·stab·u·lar·y /kən stábbyə lèrree/ (*plural* **-ies**) *n* **1.** an armed police force that has been organized according to a military model but is separate from the army **2.** in the United Kingdom, a police force for a city or a district —**con·stab·u·lar** *adj*

Con·stance, Lake /kónstənss/ lake in central Europe, in the Alps, on the borders of Austria, Germany, and Switzerland. Area: 210 sq. mi./540 sq. km. Depth: 827 ft./252 m. Length: 46 mi./74 km. German name **Bodensee**

con·stant /kónstənt/ *adj* **1. EVER PRESENT** always present or available ○ *constant whining* ○ *a constant supply of fresh water* **2. HAPPENING OR DONE REPEATEDLY** occurring or made again and again ○ *constant visits to the doctor* **3. NOT CHANGING OR VARYING** remaining the same and not varying with change in other things ○ *kept at a constant pressure* **4. FAITHFUL** faithful and loyal, especially to a husband, wife, or other loved one ■

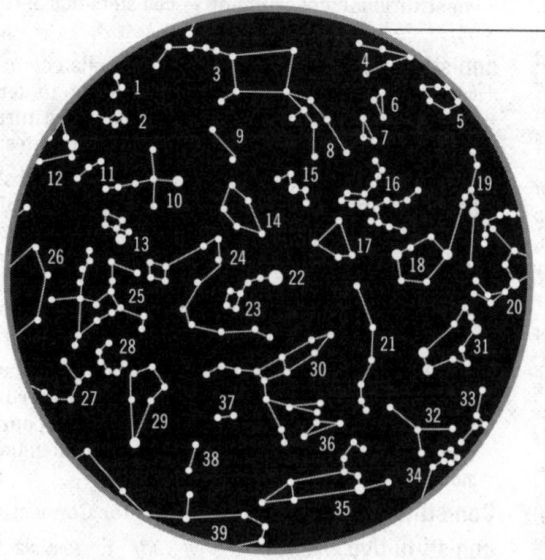

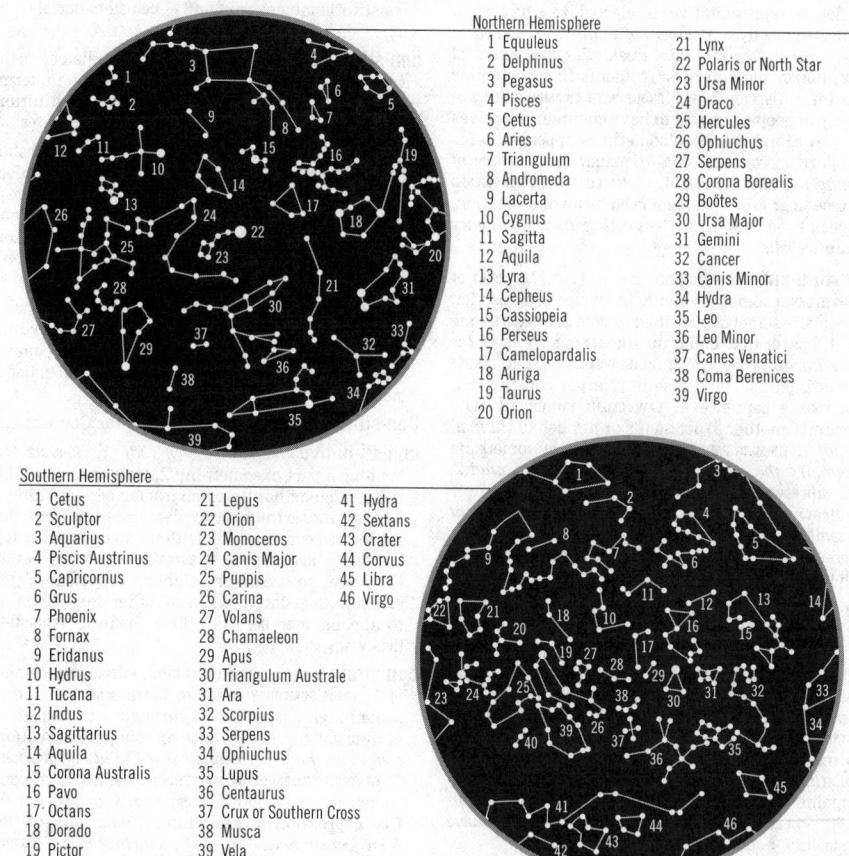

Northern Hemisphere

1 Equuleus	21 Lynx
2 Delphinus	22 Polaris or North Star
3 Pegasus	23 Ursa Minor
4 Pisces	24 Draco
5 Cetus	25 Hercules
6 Aries	26 Ophiuchus
7 Triangulum	27 Serpens
8 Andromeda	28 Corona Borealis
9 Lacerta	29 Boötes
10 Cygnus	30 Ursa Major
11 Sagitta	31 Gemini
12 Aquila	32 Cancer
13 Lyra	33 Canis Minor
14 Cepheus	34 Hydra
15 Cassiopeia	35 Leo
16 Perseus	36 Leo Minor
17 Camelopardalis	37 Canes Venatici
18 Auriga	38 Coma Berenices
19 Taurus	39 Virgo
20 Orion	

Southern Hemisphere

1 Cetus	21 Lepus	41 Hydra
2 Sculptor	22 Orion	42 Sextans
3 Aquarius	23 Monoceros	43 Crater
4 Piscis Austrinus	24 Canis Major	44 Corvus
5 Capricornus	25 Puppis	45 Libra
6 Grus	26 Carina	46 Virgo
7 Phoenix	27 Volans	
8 Fornax	28 Chamaeleon	
9 Eridanus	29 Apus	
10 Hydrus	30 Triangulum Australe	
11 Tucana	31 Ara	
12 Indus	32 Scorpius	
13 Sagittarius	33 Serpens	
14 Aquila	34 Ophiuchus	
15 Corona Australis	35 Lupus	
16 Pavo	36 Centaurus	
17 Octans	37 Crux or Southern Cross	
18 Dorado	38 Musca	
19 Pictor	39 Vela	
20 Columba	40 Pyxis	

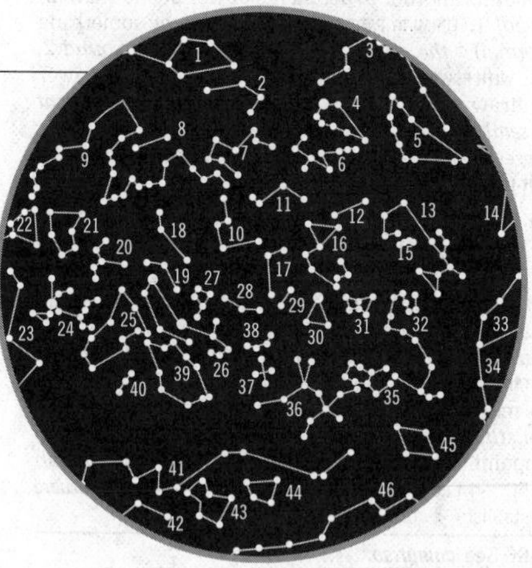

n **1. SOMETHING UNCHANGING** an object, quality, or fact that is invariable or ever present ○ *This preoccupation has become a constant in our daily lives.* **2.** MATH **QUANTITY WITH FIXED VALUE** a mathematical quantity that retains a fixed value in any circumstances or throughout a particular set of calculations. Pi, the ratio of the circumference to the radius of any circle, is a constant. **3.** PHYS **UNVARYING PROPERTY** a property, condition, or quantity that is assumed not to vary for the purposes of a theory or experiment, e.g., the speed of light [14C. Via French < Latin *constant-*, present participle of *constare* "stand together" < *stare* "to stand"] —**con·stan·cy** *n* —**con·stant·ly** *adv*

con·stan·tan /kónstən tàn/ *n* an alloy of copper and nickel whose electrical resistance is unaffected by changes in temperature. Use: resistors, thermocouples. [Early 20C. < CONSTANT]

con·stant dol·lars *npl* dollars valued at a rate that applied on a particular date in the past

Con·stan·tine II /kónstən teen, -tīn/ (*b.* 1940) ex-king of Greece. Succeeding to the throne in 1964, he was exiled in 1967 by a military junta and deposed in 1973. A referendum abolished the Greek monarchy in 1974.

Con·stan·tine (the Great) (274–337) Roman emperor (306–37). He supported Christianity from 312 and was baptized shortly before his death. He moved his capital to Byzantium, renamed Constantinople in 330. Born **Flavius Valerius Aurelius Constantinus**

Con·stan·ti·no·ple /kòn stant'n ṓp'l/ former name for **Istanbul**

con·sta·tive /kónstətiv/ *adj* **1.** relating to a statement that conveys information and is capable of being considered as true or false **2.** relating to verb forms indicating that something has been completed in the past [Early 20C. < Latin *constat-*, past participle of *constare* (see CONSTANT)]

con·stel·late /kónstə làyt/ (**-lat·ed, -lat·ing, -lates**) *vti* to form clusters, e.g., in a constellation, or cause something to do this (*literary*) [Late 16C. < late Latin *constellatus* "with stars together" < Latin *stella* "star"]

con·stel·la·tion /kònstə láysh'n/ *n* **1.** ASTRON **GROUP OF STARS FORMING SHAPE** a group of stars visible from Earth that forms a distinctive pattern and has a name, often derived from Greek mythology, linked to its shape. There are 88 constellations and the groupings are historical rather than scientific. **2.** ASTRON **AREA OF SKY CONTAINING CONSTELLATION** the area of the sky within and around a constellation **3. GATHERING OF CELEBRITIES** a gathering of famous or important people ○ *a glittering constellation of Hollywood stars* **4. GROUP OF RELATED THINGS** a group of things felt to be related to each other in some way ○ *Problems tend to occur not singly, but in constellations.* **5.** ASTROL **ASTROLOGICAL ARRANGEMENT OF PLANETS** the arrangement of the planets in the zodiac at a particular time, believed by astrologers to influence human character or events on Earth —**con·stel·la·tion·al** *adj* —**con·stel·la·to·ry** /kən stéllə tàwree/ *adj*

con·ster·nate /kónstər nàyt/ (**-nat·ed, -nat·ing, -nates**) *vt* to fill somebody with alarm, confusion, or dismay [Mid-17C. < Latin *consternat-*, past participle of *consternare* "make prostrate with fear" < *sternare* "lay low"]

con·ster·na·tion /kònstər náysh'n/ *n* a feeling of alarm, confusion, or dismay, often caused by something unexpected ○ *The news caused worldwide consternation and a panic on the stock exchange.*

con·sti·pate /kónsti pàyt/ (**-pat·ed, -pat·ing, -pates**) *vt* to cause somebody or something to become constipated [Mid-16C. < Latin *constipat-*, past participle of *constipare* "cram together" < *stipare* "to press"]

con·sti·pat·ed /kónsti pàytəd/ *adj* **1.** having difficulty in eliminating solid waste from the body, with feces being hard and dry **2.** unable to flow at the usual rate because of blockage or obstruction

con·sti·pa·tion /kònsti páysh'n/ *n* **1.** a condition in which a person or animal has difficulty in eliminating solid waste from the body and the feces are hard and dry **2.** a state in which the usual flow of something is blocked or obstructed

con·stit·u·en·cy /kən stíchoo ənsee/ (*plural* **-cies**) *n* **1.** GOV **ELECTORAL DISTRICT** one of the areas into which a country is divided for election purposes, and from which a representative is elected to serve in a legislative body ○ *Members of Congress returned to their constituencies this week.* **2.** POL **VOTERS IN CONSTITUENCY** the voters or residents in a particular electoral district **3.** POL **GROUP WITH COMMON OUTLOOK** a group of people thought to have common objectives or views, and therefore sometimes appealed to for support ○ *people outside his usual constituency of young married couples* **4.** COMM **CUSTOMERS CONSIDERED AS GROUP** a group of people served by an organization, especially a business ○ *enlarging its constituency via a website*

con·stit·u·ent /kən stíchoo ənt/ *n* **1.** POL **RESIDENT OF CONSTITUENCY** somebody living in an electoral district, especially somebody entitled to vote **2. INGREDIENT** one of the parts that make up something ○ *one of the constituents of cement* **3.** GRAM **WORD, PHRASE, OR CLAUSE** a word, phrase, or clause in a larger construction such as a sentence **4.** LAW **CLIENT** somebody who appoints another to act on his or her behalf (*formal*) ■ *adj* **1. FORMING PART** forming a part of something (*formal*) ○ *the constituent elements of a compound* **2.** POL **WITH POWER TO DRAW UP CONSTITUTION** having the power to draw up or alter a constitution ○ *a constituent assembly* [15C. Directly or via French < Latin *constituent-*, present participle of *constituere* (see CONSTITUTE)] —**con·stit·u·ent·ly** *adv*

con·sti·tute /kónstə toot/ (**-tut·ed, -tut·ing, -tutes**) *vt* **1. BE SOMETHING** to be, amount to, or have the status of a particular thing ○ *This letter does not constitute an offer of employment.* **2. BE INGREDIENT OF SOMETHING** to make up the whole or a particular part of something ○ *a panel constituted of four individuals* **3. FORMALLY ESTABLISH SOMETHING** to create and establish something formally, especially an official body (*formal*) ○ *constitute an assembly* **4. FORMALLY APPOINT SOMEBODY** to appoint somebody formally to a position (*formal*) [15C. < Latin *constitut-*, past participle of *constituere* "establish" < *statuere* "set up"] —**con·sti·tut·er** *n*

USAGE See ***comprise***.

con·sti·tu·tion /kónstə tóosh'n/ *n* **1.** POL **STATEMENT OF FUNDAMENTAL LAWS** a written statement outlining the basic laws or principles by which a country or organization is governed **2.** POL **DOCUMENT CONTAINING FUNDAMENTAL LAWS** a document or statute outlining the basic laws or principles by which a country or organization is governed **3. SOMEBODY'S GENERAL HEALTH** somebody's general physical and sometimes psychological makeup, especially the body's ability to remain healthy and withstand disease or hardship ○ *has the constitution of an ox* **4. COMPOSITION OF SOMETHING** the parts or members of something, or the way in which they combine to form it ○ *challenge the constitution of the jury* **5. ACT OR PROCESS OF ESTABLISHING SOMETHING** the formal creation or establishment of something

Con·sti·tu·tion *n* the Constitution of the United States, containing seven articles and 26 amendments, that has been in effect since its adoption in 1789

Con·sti·tu·tion Act *n* the 1982 act embodying the constitution of Canada and including the Canadian Charter of Rights and Freedoms as well as provisions of the British North America Act

con·sti·tu·tion·al /kònstə tóoshən'l, -tóoshnəl/ *adj* **1.** POL **IN ACCORDANCE WITH CONSTITUTION** authorized by a constitution, especially the Constitution of the United States ○ *The Supreme Court has to decide whether such punishments are constitutional.* **2.** POL **OF COUNTRY'S OR ORGANIZATION'S CONSTITUTION** relating to the constitution of a country or an organization ○ *constitutional reform* **3.** POL **GOVERNED BY CONSTITUTION** governed or regulated by a constitution **4. RELATING TO SOMEBODY'S HEALTH** relating to, or being part of or a consequence of somebody's general physical and sometimes psychological makeup **5. RELATING TO SOMETHING'S STRUCTURE AND MAKEUP** describes or relating to the way something is composed ○ *a constitutional analysis of the substance* ■ *n* **WALK** a short walk, taken regularly for health reasons —**con·sti·tu·tion·al·ly** *adv*

con·sti·tu·tion·al·ism /kònstə tóoshən'l ìzzəm, -tóoshnə lìzzəm/ *n* **1.** the principles or practice of government regulated by a constitution **2.** belief in constitutional government —**con·sti·tu·tion·al·ist** *n, adj*

con·sti·tu·tion·al·i·ty /kònstə toosh'n állətee/ *n* the validity or permissibility of something in terms of the provisions or principles of a constitution, especially the Constitution of the United States

con·sti·tu·tion·al·ize /kònstə tóoshən'l ìz, -tóoshnə lìz/ (**-ized, -iz·ing, -iz·es**) *vt* **1.** to incorporate a piece of legislation into a constitution, or authorize a practice through it **2.** to make a form of government, a country, or an organization subject to a constitution —**con·sti·tu·tion·al·i·za·tion** /kònstə tóoshən'li záysh'n, -tóoshnəli-/ *n*

con·sti·tu·tion·al mon·ar·chy *n* **1.** a political system in which the head of state is a king or queen ruling to the extent allowed by a constitution **2.** a country with a constitutional monarchy —**con·sti·tu·tion·al mon·arch** *n*

Con·sti·tu·tion State *n* a nickname for Connecticut

con·sti·tu·tive /kónstə tootiv/ *adj* **1. FORMING PART** forming a part of something **2. ESSENTIAL** essential to the particular nature or character of something **3.** BIOCHEM **FORMED CONTINUOUSLY** describes enzymes that are formed continuously without an external stimulus **4.** POL **HAVING POWER TO ESTABLISH INSTITUTION** having the power to create or establish a system of government, legislative body, or other institution, or to appoint members of official bodies —**con·sti·tu·tive·ly** *adv*

con·strain /kən stráyn/ (**-strained, -strain·ing, -strains**) *vt* **1. FORCE SOMEBODY TO ACT** to force somebody to do something, especially through pressure of circumstances or a sense of obligation ○ *Many companies have been constrained to lay off workers.* **2. RESTRICT SOMEBODY OR SOMETHING** to limit or restrict somebody or something, especially to prevent the free expression of something ○ *The industry has been constrained by skill shortages.* **3. RESTRAIN SOMEBODY OR SOMETHING** to hold somebody or something back from an action (*literary*) ○ *We felt constrained by the presence of the others.* [14C. Via Old French *constraindre* < Latin *constringere* "bind tightly together" < *stringere* "draw tight"] —**con·strain·a·ble** *adj* —**con·strain·er** *n*

con·strained /kən stráynd/ *adj* lacking naturalness or spontaneity because of self-consciousness, reserve, or inhibiting circumstances —**con·strain·ed·ly** /kən stráynədlee/ *adv*

con·straint /kən stráynt/ *n* **1. LIMITING FACTOR** something that limits freedom of action ○ *Even in a free society individual liberty must be subject to certain constraints.* ○ *budgetary constraints* **2. STATE OF RESTRICTION** a state in which freedom of action is severely restricted **3. LACK OF SPONTANEITY** a lack of warmth and spontaneity in somebody's manner or in the atmosphere on a particular occasion [14C. < French *constreinte*, feminine past participle of *constraindre* (see CONSTRAIN)]

con·strict /kən stríkt/ (**-strict·ed, -strict·ing, -stricts**) *v* **1.** *vti* **NARROW** to make something, especially a blood vessel, narrower, or become narrower **2.** *vt* **LIMIT OR RESTRICT SOMEBODY OR SOMETHING** to limit the movement of a person or part of the body in an uncomfortable way **3.** *vt* **RESTRICT FLOW OF SOMETHING** to stop or slow down the flow of something such as air, liquid, or blood **4.** *vt* **SQUEEZE** to squeeze something with great force ○ *"For a moment I felt my chest constricted as with a band of iron."* (George van Schaick, *A Top-Floor Idyl*; 1917) **5.** *vt* ZOOL **SUFFOCATE PREY BY SQUEEZING** to squeeze animals caught as prey until they suffocate, as many snakes do to their prey [Mid-18C. < Latin *constrict-*, past participle of *constringere* (see CONSTRAIN)] —**con·stric·tive** *adj* —**con·stric·tive·ly** *adv* —**con·stric·tive·ness** *n*

con·stric·tion /kən stríkshən/ *n* **1. PROCESS OF NARROWING** the process of becoming narrower, or of making something narrower **2. NARROW PLACE** a narrow place or part ○ *A constriction in the tube prevents the mercury from returning to the bulb.* **3.** MED **FEELING OF TIGHTNESS** a feeling of tightness or pressure, especially in the chest or throat **4. RESTRICTION** something that severely restricts somebody's freedom of movement, action, or expression **5.** ZOOL **SUFFOCATION BY SQUEEZING** the process of squeezing animals caught as prey until they suffocate, as many snakes do

con·stric·tor /kən stríktər/ *n* **1.** REPT **SNAKE THAT SQUEEZES PREY TO DEATH** a large nonvenomous snake that coils itself around its prey and suffocates it, e.g., an anaconda, boa, or python **2.** ANAT **MUSCLE** a muscle that tightens to make a part of the body narrower **3. SOMEBODY OR SOMETHING CONSTRICTING** somebody or something that constricts somebody or something else

con·struct *vt* /kən strúkt/ (**-struct·ed, -struct·ing, -structs**) **1. BUILD SOMETHING** to build or assemble something by putting together separate parts in an ordered way **2. CREATE SOMETHING IN MIND** to create something such as a theory as a result of systematic thought **3.** MATH **DRAW SOMETHING ACCURATELY** to draw something accurately using given measurements ■ *n* /kón strùkt/ **CONSTRUCTED THING OR CONCEPT** something that has been systematically put together, usually in the mind, especially a complex theory or subjective notion ○ *sexual identity viewed as a social construct* [15C. < Latin *construct-*, past participle of *construere* "pile together" < *struere* "pile, build"] —**con·struct·i·ble** *adj*

con·struc·tion /kən strúkshən/ *n* **1. ACT OR PROCESS OF CONSTRUCTING** the building of something, especially a large structure such as a house, road, or bridge **2.** BUILDINGS **BUILT STRUCTURE** a structure that has been built **3.** CONSTR **WORKMANSHIP AND MATERIALS** the way in which something has been built, especially with regard to the type and quality of the structure, materials, and workmanship **4.** CONSTR **BUILDING INDUSTRY** the building industry regarded as a whole **5. CREATION OF SOMETHING** the creation of something such as a system or concept from a number of different parts **6. INTERPRETATION** the way in which something is interpreted or explained (*formal*) ○ *put the worst possible construction on the news* **7.** GRAM **COMBINATION OF WORDS** a group of words governed by particular grammatical rules **8.** MATH **GEOMETRIC SHAPE** a geometric figure drawn accurately in accordance with given measurements **9.** ART **WORK OF ART** a visual work of art that is put together from a variety of different materials, abstract in design, and usually three-dimensional —**con·struc·tion·al** *adj* —**con·struc·tion·al·ly** *adv*

con·struc·tion·ist /kən strúkshənist/ *n* an interpreter of a legal text or document

con·struc·tion pa·per *n* thick paper produced in a variety of colors and used especially for school artwork

con·struc·tion site *n* an area where a building or group of buildings is being constructed or repaired, often fenced off to prevent access by those not working there

con·strúc·tive /kən strúktiv/ *adj* **1. USEFUL** carefully considered and meant to be helpful ○ *constructive criticism* **2.** LAW **BASED ON INFERENCE** based on what somebody infers from other statements or circumstances **3.** CONSTR **STRUCTURAL** relating to or involved in construction, especially forming part of the basic structure of a building —**con·struc·tive·ly** *adv* —**con·struc·tive·ness** *n*

con·struc·tive en·gage·ment *n* the policy of maintaining limited political and business links with a country while continuing to demand political or social reform in that country

con·struc·tive mar·gin *n* a boundary between two tectonic plates at which new crust is formed, e.g., the mid-ocean ridges

con·struc·tiv·ism /kən strúkti vìzzəm/ *n* a modern art movement associated with Moscow in the 1920s that produced large nonrepresentational structures made of industrial materials such as plastic, glass, and sheet metal. Its leading figures were Naum Gabo and Antoine Pevsner. —**con·struc·tiv·ist** *n*

con·strue /kən stróo/ (**-strued, -stru·ing, -strues**) *v* **1.** *vt* **INTERPRET SOMETHING IN PARTICULAR WAY** to interpret or understand the meaning of a word, gesture, or action in a particular way ○ *His silence could be construed as an admission of guilt.* **2.** *vti* GRAM **ANALYZE SYNTAX OF TEXT** to analyze the syntax of a piece of text, especially text that is to be translated **3.** *vt* GRAM **USE WORD IN PARTICULAR WAY** to use a word in a grammatical structure, e.g., by making it singular or plural ○ *"Folk" is construed as plural, except when it means "folk music."* [14C. < Latin *construere* (see CONSTRUCT)] —

con·stru·a·bil·i·ty /kən stro͞o ə bíllətee/ n —con·stru·a·ble adj —con·stru·al n —con·stru·er n

con·sub·stan·tial /kòn səb stánsh'l/ adj having the same substance as something else, especially another member of the Holy Trinity [14C. < ecclesiastical Latin *consubstantialis,* literally "substance together" < Latin *substantia* "substance"] —con·sub·stan·ti·al·i·ty /kòn səb stanshee állətee/ n

con·sub·stan·ti·ate /kòn səb stánshee àyt/ (-at·ed, -at·ing, -ates) vti to become united, or unite two things, in one single substance, as the body and blood of Jesus Christ are believed to become one with bread and wine in the Christian doctrine of transubstantiation [Late 16C. < late Latin *consubstantiatus* "united in one substance" < *substantiat-,* past participle of *substantiare* (see SUBSTANTIATE)]

con·sub·stan·ti·a·tion /kòn səb stanshee áysh'n/ n 1. the belief of some Christians that the body and blood of Jesus Christ coexist in the bread and wine consecrated at Communion with the natural elements of which the bread and wine are made. This belief is held mainly by High-Church Anglicans. 2. the process by which the body and blood of Jesus Christ are believed by some Christians to become present in the bread and wine consecrated at Communion

con·sue·tude /kónsswi to͞od/ n established custom or usage (*archaic*) [14C. Directly or via French < Latin *consuetudo* "the state of being completely accustomed" < *suescere* "become accustomed"]

con·sul /kónss'l/ n 1. GOV, INTERNAT REL GOVERNMENT OFFICIAL WORKING ABROAD a government official living in a foreign city to promote the commercial interests of the official's own state and protect its citizens 2. ANCIENT HIST ANCIENT ROMAN MAGISTRATE in ancient Rome, one of the two chief magistrates who were elected to govern annually 3. HIST FORMER FRENCH OFFICIAL one of the three chief magistrates of the first French Republic between 1799 and 1804 [14C. < Latin] —con·su·lar adj —con·sul·ship n

con·su·late /kónssələt/ n 1. INTERNAT REL CONSUL'S OFFICE a consul's office or official residence 2. INTERNAT REL SCOPE OF CONSUL'S RESPONSIBILITIES the political office or period of office of a consul, or the jurisdiction of a consul 3. ANCIENT HIST ANCIENT ROMAN GOVERNMENT the ancient Roman system of government administered by consuls

Con·su·late n 1. the government, consisting of three consuls, that ruled France from 1799 to 1804 2. the period from 1799 to 1804 during which France was ruled by three consuls

con·su·late gen·er·al (*plural* con·su·late gen·er·als or con·su·lates gen·er·al) n the building where a consul general lives or works

con·sul gen·er·al (*plural* con·sul gen·er·als or con·suls gen·er·al) n a consul of the highest rank, usually based in a major foreign city that is important for trade

con·sult /kən súlt/ v (-sult·ed, -sult·ing, -sults) 1. vti ASK FOR SPECIALIST ADVICE to ask for specialist advice or information, especially from a professional ○ *If symptoms persist, consult a doctor.* 2. vti ASK PERMISSION to ask for somebody's opinion or permission before taking action ○ *You'd be wise to consult the boss before you make any major changes.* 3. vt REFER TO SOURCE OF INFORMATION to look at something such as a reference book in order to get information 4. vi GIVE PROFESSIONAL ADVICE to provide specialist advice for a fee ○ *After 15 years in computer programming, I now consult from home.* ■ n /kən súlt, kón sùlt/ CONSULTATION a consultation or discussion about something (*informal*) [Early 16C. Via French < Latin *consultare* "confer" < *consulere* "seek advice"] —con·sult·a·ble adj —con·sult·er n

con·sult·ant /kən súltənt/ n 1. an expert who charges a fee for providing advice or services in a particular field 2. *UK* a senior doctor who is fully qualified in a particular branch of medicine —con·sul·tan·cy n —con·sult·ant·ship n

con·sul·ta·tion /kònss'l táysh'n/ n 1. EXCHANGE OF OPINIONS a discussion aimed at ascertaining opinions or reaching an agreement ○ *After a quick consultation with his wife, he signed the paper.* 2. MEETING WITH EXPERT a meeting with an expert in a particular field to obtain advice ○ *an appointment for a consultation with the heart surgeon* 3. REFERENCE TO SOURCE OF INFORMATION the act of referring to a book or person for information or advice ○ *Consultation of the manual confirmed the problem was the transmission.* 4. WORK OF A CONSULTANT the work or business of providing expert advice or services in a particular field

con·sul·ta·tive /kən súltətiv/ adj available for consultation, or involved in consultation —con·sul·ta·tive·ly adv

con·sult·ing /kən súlting/ adj 1. PROVIDING SPECIALIST ADVICE providing specialist advice to other people who work in the same field 2. OF CONSULTANTS OR CONSULTATION relating to a consultant or consultation ○ *a consulting fee* ■ n BUSINESS OF CONSULTATION the business of being a consultant

con·sult·ing room n *UK* the room in which a doctor sees patients, mainly in a hospital

con·sum·a·ble /kən so͞oməb'l/ adj able or intended to be discarded after use, rather than reused

con·sum·a·bles /kən so͞oməb'lz/ npl goods that have to be bought regularly because they wear out or are used up, e.g., food and clothing

~~consumate~~ incorrect spelling of **consummate**

con·sume /kən so͞om/ (-sumed, -sum·ing, -sumes) v 1. vt EAT OR DRINK SOMETHING to eat or drink something, especially in large amounts 2. vt USE SOMETHING UP to use something in such a way that it cannot be reused or recovered afterward ○ *The newer models consume less gasoline.* 3. vt ENGROSS SOMEBODY to fill somebody's mind or attention fully (*usually passive*) ○ *consumed by a desire for new experiences* 4. vt DESTROY SOMETHING OR SOMEBODY to destroy something or somebody completely ○ *was consumed by fire* 5. vti BUY FROM OTHERS to buy goods or services produced by other people [14C. Directly or via French < Latin *consumere* "take up completely" < *sumere* "take"]

con·sum·er /kən so͞omər/ n 1. BUYER a buyer of goods or services 2. SOMEBODY OR SOMETHING THAT CONSUMES SOMETHING somebody or something that consumes something by eating it, drinking it, or using it up ○ *The country is one of the largest consumers of paper products.* 3. ECOL ORGANISM THAT FEEDS ON OTHERS in an ecological community or food chain, an organism that feeds on other organisms, or on material derived from them. Consumers include herbivorous and carnivorous animals, which feed on plants and other animals respectively, and also organisms such as worms, fungi, and bacteria, which feed on nonliving organic material. —con·sum·er·ship n

con·sum·er con·fi·dence n a measure of how people feel about the future of the economy and their own financial situation, obtained through polling

con·sum·er cred·it n money lent by financial institutions to enable members of the public to buy consumer goods or services. Buying items with monthly payments, credit cards, and charge accounts are all forms of consumer credit.

con·sum·er du·ra·bles npl items that last a relatively long time and are purchased infrequently, e.g., computers and washing machines

con·sum·er-fac·ing adj involving direct contact with, or able to be directly accessed by, consumers ○ *a consumer-facing website*

con·sum·er goods npl goods that are bought by consumers and are not used to produce other goods

con·sum·er·ism /kən so͞omə rìzzəm/ n 1. PROTECTION OF CONSUMERS' RIGHTS the protection of the rights and interests of consumers, especially with regard to price, quality, and safety 2. MATERIALISTIC ATTITUDE an attitude that values the acquisition of material goods (*disapproving*) 3. BELIEF IN BENEFITS OF CONSUMPTION the belief that the buying and selling of large quantities of consumer goods is beneficial to an economy or a sign of economic strength —con·sum·er·ist n, adj

con·sum·er price in·dex n a government-issued index of the retail prices of basic household goods and services

con·sum·er so·ci·e·ty n a society in which the consumption of mass-produced goods is encouraged through mass communication

con·sum·er-to-busi·ness adj relating to Internet transactions between an individual consumer and a business organization, rather than between businesses

con·sum·ing /kən so͞oming/ adj so intense as to take up all of somebody's attention, time, and energy ○ *a consuming interest in horses* —con·sum·ing·ly adv

con·sum·mate vt /kónssə màyt/ (-mat·ed, -mat·ing, -mates) 1. COMPLETE MARRIAGE to make a marriage legally complete and fully valid by having sexual intercourse 2. FULFILL RELATIONSHIP THROUGH SEX to bring a relationship to completion, or gratify a desire, especially by having sexual intercourse (*often passive*) 3. CONCLUDE SOMETHING to bring something such as a business deal to a conclusion (*formal*) ○ *Leaving her business partner to consummate the deal, she boarded a flight for New York.* 4. ACHIEVE SOMETHING to achieve or fulfill something, especially something long sought (*formal; often passive*) ○ *Twelve years of effort and struggle were consummated when the foundation stone for the new theater was laid.* ■ adj /kən súmmət, kónssəmət/ 1. SUPREME OR PERFECT excellent, skillful, or accomplished ○ *with consummate ease* 2. UTTER OR TOTAL possessing or showing a bad quality to an extreme degree ○ *consummate arrogance* [15C. < Latin *consummat-,* past participle of *consummare* "accomplish" < *summa* "the highest thing"] —con·sum·mate·ly adv —con·sum·ma·tive /kónssə màytiv/ adj —con·sum·ma·tor n —con·sum·ma·to·ry /kən súmmə tàwree/ adj

con·sum·ma·tion /kònssə máysh'n/ n 1. PERFECT ENDING the bringing of something to a satisfying conclusion, or the final satisfying completion or achievement of something ○ *The publication of her book was a consummation of her whole life's work.* 2. LEGAL COMPLETION OF MARRIAGE BY SEX the legal completion of a marriage by an act of sexual intercourse between the spouses 3. COMPLETION OF DEAL the finalization of something such as a business deal

con·sump·tion /kən súmpsh'n/ n 1. ACT OF EATING OR DRINKING the eating or drinking of something, or the amount that somebody eats or drinks ○ *unfit for human consumption* 2. ACT OF USING SOMETHING UP the use of natural resources or fuels, or the amount of resources or fuels used ○ *consumption of fossil fuels* 3. CONSUMER EXPENDITURE the purchase and use of goods and services by consumers, or the quantity of goods and services purchased 4. WASTING DISEASE any condition that causes progressive wasting of the tissues, especially tuberculosis of the lungs (*dated*) [14C. Via French < Latin *consumption-* < *consumere* (see CONSUME)]

con·sump·tive /kən súmptiv/ adj 1. ENGAGED IN OR CAUSING CONSUMPTION engaged in, causing, or encouraging the consumption of food, materials, or goods, especially in a wasteful or destructive way 2. AFFECTED BY TUBERCULOSIS affected by a wasting disease, especially tuberculosis of the lungs, or connected with such a disease (*dated*) ■ n SOMEBODY WITH TUBERCULOSIS somebody affected by a wasting disease, particularly tuberculosis of the lungs (*dated*) ○ *a chronic consumptive* [Mid-17C. < medieval Latin *consumptivus* < Latin *consumere* (see CONSUME)] —con·sump·tive·ly adv —con·sump·tive·ness n

cont. abbr 1. containing 2. PUBL contents 3. GEOG continent 4. GEOG continental 5. continued 6. GRAM continuous 7. MED, GRAM contraction 8. control

con·tact /kón tàkt/ n 1. STATE OF COMMUNICATION a state or relationship in which communication happens or is possible ○ *Our only means of contact with the base was a small radio receiver.* ○ *He made contact with his counterpart in the Tokyo office.* 2. ACT OF COMMUNICATING an act of communicating with somebody ○ *All my contacts with her to date have been about business.* 3. PHYSICAL CONNECTION a situation in which two or more things or people actually touch or strike against one another ○ *White phosphorus ignites on contact with the air.* 4. INTERACTION a state in which somebody has access to and can be affected or influenced by people, situations, ideas, or information ○ *You'll come into contact with a variety of people.* 5. ACCESS ARRANGEMENT the right of a child and a separated or divorced parent to meet regularly 6. SOMEBODY WHO CAN HELP an acquaintance who may be socially or professionally helpful ○ *I made some very useful contacts at the trade fair.* 7. DISEASE CARRIER a person or animal seen as a possible carrier of an infectious disease 8. DEVICE MAKING ELECTRICAL CONNECTION a movable part that can be made to touch another conductive part in order to enable an electrical current to pass, e.g., a component of a switch **9.** ELECTRICAL CONNECTION a connection between or the connection of two or more electrical conductors so that current flows between them ■ **con·tacts** *npl* CONTACT LENSES a set of contact lenses (*informal*) ■ *v* (**-tact·ed, -tact·ing, -tacts**) **1.** *vt* REACH SOMEBODY FOR COMMUNICATION to send a message to somebody, or reach somebody, e.g., by telephone or letter, in order to communicate ○ *You can contact me at this number.* **2.** *vti* TOUCH to touch or strike against something ■ *adj* **1.** USED FOR COMMUNICATING WITH SOMEBODY used as a means to contact somebody ○ *a contact address* **2.** WORKING BY TOUCHING working or happening by touching or being touched by something or somebody **3.** CAUSED BY TOUCH caused by touching something that irritates ○ *contact dermatitis* [Early 17C. < Latin *contactus*, past participle of *contingere*, literally "touch with" < *tangere* "to touch"] —**con·tact·a·ble** /kən táktəb'l/ *adj* —**con·tac·tu·al** /kən tákchoo əl/ *adj* —**con·tac·tu·al·ly** *adv*

con·tact bi·na·ry *n* a binary star system in which one of the components is transferring matter to its companion star

con·tact card *n* a smart card with a chip that can be read when touched by a reader

con·tact flight, **con·tact fly·ing** *n* navigation of an aircraft by observing landmarks and other visible guides, without the use of navigational aids

con·tact group *n* a group of people who are neutral in a dispute and meet both sides to try to resolve disagreements through discussion

con·tact in·hi·bi·tion *n* the normal cessation of cell division and growth caused by physical contact with other cells. This normal end to cell division does not function when cancer is present, resulting in uncontrolled reproduction of cells.

con·tact lan·guage *n* a simplified language variety that retains features of other languages contributing to it, used for communication in places where most speakers do not share a common language

con·tact lens *n* a small plastic or glass lens placed directly onto the front of the eye to correct vision or make the iris appear a different color

con·tact·less card /kón tàktləss-/ *n* a smart card with a chip that can be read via radio transmission, e.g., for the collection of road tolls

con·tact print *n* a photographic print made by placing a negative directly on top of photosensitive paper and exposing it to light. This is usually done to check the images on a roll of film before making enlargements from individual negatives.

con·tact sport *n* a sport in which physical contact between players is an integral part of the game, e.g., boxing or ice hockey

con·ta·gion /kən táyjən/ *n* **1.** SPREAD OF DISEASE BY PHYSICAL CONTACT the transmission of disease, especially by physical contact between people or contact with infected objects such as bedding or clothing **2.** DISEASE SPREAD BY PHYSICAL CONTACT an illness that spreads from one person to another, especially by physical contact between persons or contact with infected objects **3.** HARMFUL INFLUENCE a harmful or corrupting influence with a tendency to spread **4.** SPREAD OF FEELING the spreading of an attitude or emotion from person to person among a number of people (*literary*) ○ *the contagion of happiness* [14C. < Latin *contagion-* < *contingere* (see CONTACT)]

con·ta·gious /kən táyjəss/ *adj* **1.** ABLE TO BE PASSED BY CONTACT transmitted from one person to another either by direct contact with the person or by indirect contact, e.g., contact with his or her clothes **2.** CAPABLE OF TRANSMITTING DISEASE affected by or carrying a disease that can be transmitted by direct or indirect contact **3.** LIKELY TO AFFECT OTHERS quickly spread from one person to another ○ *Laughter is contagious.* [14C. < late Latin *contagiosus* < Latin *contingere* (see CONTACT)] —**con·ta·gious·ly** *adv* —**con·ta·gious·ness** *n*

con·ta·gious a·bor·tion *n* a contagious or infectious disease of farm animals that is characterized by spontaneous abortion, e.g., brucellosis

con·tain /kən táyn/ (**-tained, -tain·ing, -tains**) *vt* **1.** HAVE SOMETHING WITHIN to have or hold something inside ○ *This pack contains a training video and set of instructions.* **2.** INCLUDE SOMETHING to include something as part of the contents or makeup ○ *The report contains several inaccuracies.* ○ *drinks that contain caffeine* **3.** CONTROL EMOTION to keep an emotion under control ○ *I couldn't contain myself any longer.* **4.** STOP SOMETHING SPREADING to restrict the movement, spread, or influence of a strong enemy, force, disease, or idea **5.** MATH BE DIVISIBLE BY NUMBER to be divisible by a number, leaving no remainder **6.** MATH FORM SIDES OF ANGLE to form the boundaries that define an angle [13C. Via French *contenir* < Latin *continere* "hold together" < *tenere* "to hold"] —**con·tain·a·ble** *adj*

con·tain·er /kən táynər/ *n* **1.** an object such as a box, jar, or bottle that is used to hold something, especially when it is being stored or transported **2.** a large box of a standard size into which goods are packed so that they can be transported securely and efficiently from departure point to destination by road, sea, or rail, without having to be repacked

con·tain·er·board /kən táynər bàwrd/ *n* heavy corrugated or solid cardboard used to make containers

con·tain·er·ize /kən táynə rìz/ (**-ized, -iz·ing, -iz·es**) *vt* **1.** to pack something in freight containers for transportation by road, sea, or rail, especially commercially **2.** to convert a port, transport system, or industry so that it can handle standard-sized freight containers —**con·tain·er·i·za·tion** /kən tàynəri záysh'n/ *n*

con·tain·er·port /kən táynər pàwrt/ *n* a port capable of handling containerized cargo

con·tain·er ship *n* a ship especially designed to carry cargo that is packed in freight containers

con·tain·ment /kən táynmənt/ *n* **1.** ATTEMPT TO STOP SPREAD OF SOMETHING action taken to restrict the spread of a hostile element such as an enemy or something undesirable such as a disease **2.** CONTROL MEASURE IN NUCLEAR REACTIONS the use of magnetic fields to prevent the reacting particles from touching the containing vessel's walls in a reactor **3.** ACT OR PROCESS OF CONTAINING SOMETHING the act or process of being contained or of containing something

con·tam·i·nate /kən támmi nàyt/ (**-nat·ed, -nat·ing, -nates**) *vt* **1.** to make something impure, unclean, or polluted, especially by mixing harmful impurities into it or by putting it into contact with something harmful ○ *contaminate blood products* **2.** to make something such as soil unfit for use or exploitation as a result of contact with polluting or harmful substances ○ *land contaminated by heavy industry* [15C. < Latin *contaminat-*, past participle of *contaminare* < *contamen*, literally "touching with" < *tangere* "to touch"] —**con·tam·i·na·ble** /kən támminəb'l/ *adj* —**con·tam·i·nant** *n* —**con·tam·i·na·tive** *adj* —**con·tam·i·na·tor** *n*

con·tam·i·na·tion /kən tàmmi náysh'n/ *n* **1.** ACT OF CONTAMINATING SOMETHING the act or process of contaminating something or becoming contaminated, or the unclean or impure state that results from this **2.** SOMETHING THAT CONTAMINATES something that physically contaminates a substance or that corrupts a person morally ○ *The investigators found considerable contamination in the rivers.* **3.** ALTERATION OF WORD OR PHRASE the process by which a word or phrase changes as a result of mistaken association with another word or phrase

con·tan·go /kən táng gō/ *n* (*plural* **-gos**) **1.** BASIC PRICING SYSTEM IN FUTURES TRADING in futures and options trading, a system of pricing whereby longer-term contracts are priced higher than near-term contracts. The higher price on the longer-term contracts is a result of the cost of carrying those commodities for future delivery. **2.** *UK* INTEREST PAYABLE WHEN DELIVERY DELAYED interest payable by a broker when the delivery of and payment for stock is postponed **3.** *UK* POSTPONEMENT OF STOCK DELIVERY formerly, on the London Stock Exchange, the postponement of the delivery of stock to a broker and payment for it, from one account day to the next ■ *vt UK* ARRANGE CONTANGO to arrange for delivery and payment to be postponed when transferring stock in a stock exchange [Mid-19C. Origin ?]

contd. *abbr* continued

conte /kawNt/ *n* **1.** LITERAT same as **short story** (*literary*) **2.** a narrative tale from the Middle Ages [Late 19C. < French < Old French *co(u)nter* (see COUNT[1])]

con·temn /kən tém/ (**-temned, -temn·ing, -temns**) *vt* to view or treat somebody with contempt (*archaic*) [15C. Directly or via French < Latin *contemnere* (see CONTEMPT)] —**con·temn·er** /-témnər/ *n* —**con·tem·ni·ble** /-témnəb'l/ *adj* —**con·tem·ni·bly** /-témnəblee/ *adv*

con·tem·plate /kóntəm plàyt/ (**-plat·ed, -plat·ing, -plates**) *v* **1.** *vt* HAVE SOMETHING AS POSSIBLE INTENTION to think about something as a possible course of action ○ *contemplating a move to a new location* **2.** *vt* CONSIDER SOMETHING to think about something seriously and at length, especially in order to understand it more fully ○ *I sat there, contemplating what she'd said.* **3.** *vi* THINK ABOUT SPIRITUAL MATTERS to think calmly and at length, especially as a religious or spiritual exercise **4.** *vt* LOOK AT SOMETHING THOUGHTFULLY to look at something thoughtfully and steadily ○ *tourists contemplating the restored frescoes* [Late 16C. < Latin *contemplat-*, past participle of *contemplari* "observe carefully" < *templum* "space for observing omens"] —**con·tem·pla·tion** /kòntəm pláysh'n/ *n* —**con·tem·pla·tor** *n*

con·tem·pla·tive /kən témplətiv/ *adj* calm and thoughtful, or inclined to be this way ■ *n* somebody who practices spiritual contemplation, e.g., a monk or nun —**con·tem·pla·tive·ly** *adv* —**con·tem·pla·tive·ness** *n*

con·tem·po·ra·ne·ous /kən tèmpə ráynee əss/ *adj* existing, occurring, or beginning at the same time or during the same period of time as something else [Mid-17C. < Latin *contemporaneus*, literally "time together" < *tempor-* "time"] —**con·tem·po·ra·ne·i·ty** /kən tèmpərə née ətee, -náy ətee/ *n* —**con·tem·po·ra·ne·ous·ly** *adv* —**con·tem·po·ra·ne·ous·ness** *n*

con·tem·po·rar·y /kən témpə rèrree/ *adj* **1.** OF SAME TIME existing or occurring at or dating from the same period of time as something or somebody else ○ *The Celts were dismissed by contemporary chroniclers as barbarians.* **2.** EXISTING in existence now ○ *problems of contemporary urban society* **3.** MODERN IN STYLE distinctively modern in style ○ *contemporary dance* **4.** OF SAME AGE of the same or approximately the same age as somebody else ○ *She and I are more or less contemporary.* ■ *n* (*plural* **-ies**) **1.** SOMEBODY OR SOMETHING OF SAME TIME somebody or something living or existing during the same period of time as another ○ *This 18th-century table is a contemporary of the Shaker furniture in the other room.* **2.** SOMEBODY OF SAME AGE somebody of about the same age as somebody else ○ *It was nice to spend time with my Dad's contemporaries.* **3.** MODERN PERSON OR THING somebody or something in existence at the present time [Mid-17C. < medieval Latin *contemporarius* < Latin *tempor-* "time"] —**con·tem·po·rar·i·ly** *adv* —**con·tem·po·rar·i·ness** *n*

con·tem·po·rize /kən témpə rìz/ (**-rized, -riz·ing, -riz·es**) *vt* **1.** to make something modern or fashionable **2.** to place somebody or something in the same period as somebody or something else [Mid-17C. < late Latin *contemporare* "make contemporary" < Latin *tempor-* "time"] —**con·tem·po·ri·za·tion** /kən tèmpəri záysh'n/ *n*

~~contempory~~ incorrect spelling of **contemporary**

con·tempt /kən témpt/ *n* **1.** a powerful feeling of dislike toward somebody or something considered to be worthless, inferior, or undeserving of respect **2.** LAW same as **contempt of court** [14C. < Latin *contemptus* "scorn" < *contemnere* "despise utterly" < *temnere* "to scorn"]

con·tempt·i·ble /kən témptəb'l/ *adj* deserving to be treated with contempt —**con·tempt·i·bil·i·ty** /kən tèmptə bíllətee/ *n* —**con·tempt·i·ble·ness** *n* —**con·tempt·i·bly** *adv*

con·tempt of court *n* the crime of deliberately failing to obey or respect the authority of a court of law or legislative body

con·temp·tu·ous /kən témpchoo əss/ *adj* feeling, expressing, or demonstrating a strong dislike or utter lack of respect for somebody or something [Early 16C. < medieval Latin *contemptuosus* < Latin *contemnere* (see CONTEMPT)] —**con·temp·tu·ous·ly** *adv* —**con·temp·tu·ous·ness** *n*

con·tend /kən ténd/ (**-tend·ed, -tend·ing, -tends**) *v* **1.** *vt* STATE SOMETHING to argue or claim that something is true **2.** *vi* COMPETE to compete for something, especially a prize or trophy ○ *the teams contending for the cup* **3.** *vi* STRUGGLE OR DEAL WITH SOMETHING to fight with, struggle against, or deal with somebody or something ○ *Their lawyers have a number of awkward issues to contend with.* **4.** *vi* DEBATE WITH SOMEBODY to debate or dispute with somebody (*literary*) [15C. Directly or via French < Latin *contendere* "strive together" < *tendere* "strive"]

con·tend·er /kən téndər/ *n* **1.** a competitor, especially somebody who has a good chance of winning **2.** any competitor in a contest for a prize or title

SYNONYMS See ***candidate.***

con·tent[1] /kón tènt/ *n* **1.** AMOUNT OF SOMETHING IN CONTAINER the amount of something contained in something else ○ *fruit with a high vitamin C content* **2.** SUBJECT MATTER the various issues, topics, or questions dealt with in speech, discussion, or a piece of writing ○ *a speech that was highly emotive in both tone and content* **3.** MEANING OR MESSAGE the meaning or message contained in a creative work, as distinct from its appearance, form, or style **4.** INFORMATION AVAILABLE ELECTRONICALLY information made available by an electronic medium or product **5.** INTELLECTUALLY INTERESTING MATERIAL material or ideas that are considered to be interesting, challenging, or worthwhile **6.** CAPACITY the capacity of a container ■ **con·tents** *npl* **1.** SOMETHING CONTAINED everything that is inside a particular container ○ *picked up the file and emptied its contents onto the desk* **2.** SUBJECT OF TEXT the subject matter of a document or publication ○ *revealed the contents of the letter* **3.** LIST OF SUBJECT OR CHAPTER HEADINGS a list at the front of a publication that gives the title and number of the first page of each new chapter, article, or part [15C. < medieval Latin *contentum* "something contained," form of Latin *contentus*, past participle of *continere* (see CONTAIN)]

con·tent[2] /kən tént/ *adj* **1.** QUIETLY SATISFIED AND HAPPY reasonably happy and satisfied with the way things are **2.** READY TO ACCEPT SOMETHING willing to accept a situation or comply with a proposed course of action ○ *He had to be content with third place in the race.* ■ *v* (**-tent·ed, -tent·ing, -tents**) **1.** *vt* CAUSE SOMEBODY TO FEEL CONTENT to make somebody feel happy or satisfied with something **2.** *vr* ACCEPT OR MAKE DO WITH SOMETHING to accept or make do with something, rather than taking further action or making more demands ○ *He contented himself with a few cutting remarks about lack of discipline and did not take the matter further.* ■ *n* same as **contentment** (sense 1) [15C. Via French < Latin *contentus* (see CONTENT[1])] —**con·tent·ly** *adv*

con·tent·ed /kən téntəd/ *adj* peacefully happy and satisfied with the way things are or with what has been done —**con·tent·ed·ly** *adv* —**con·tent·ed·ness** *n*

con·ten·tion /kən ténshən/ *n* **1.** ASSERTION IN ARGUMENT an opinion or claim stated in the course of an argument ○ *It is my contention that the plan was bound to fail.* **2.** DISAGREEMENT angry disagreement between people ○ *a lot of contention over the quality of the goods* **3.** RIVALRY competition between rivals or opponents ○ *fierce contention for the title* [14C. Directly or via French < Latin *contention-* < *contendere* (see CONTEND)]

con·ten·tious /kən ténshəss/ *adj* **1.** CREATING DISAGREEMENT causing or likely to cause disagreement and disputes between people with differing views ○ *It should have been possible to word the statement in a less contentious way.* **2.** ARGUMENTATIVE frequently engaging in and seeming to enjoy arguments and disputes **3.** LAW SUBJECT TO LITIGATION contested by another interested party ○ *a contentious will* [15C. Via French < Latin *contentiosus* < *contendere* (see CONTEND)] —**con·ten·tious·ly** *adv* —**con·ten·tious·ness** *n*

con·tent·ment /kən téntmənt/ *n* **1.** a feeling of calm satisfaction **2.** a circumstance, or a feature or characteristic of something, that gives rise to satisfaction (*formal or literary*)

con·tent pro·vi·der /kón tent-/ *n* a website containing mainly news or information rather than commercial facilities such as shopping or banking, or a business supplying the information for such a website

con·tent word /kón tent-/ *n* a word that primarily conveys meaning rather than grammatical function, e.g., a noun, verb, or adjective

con·ter·mi·nous /kən túrminəss/, **co·ter·mi·nous** /kō-/ *adj* **1.** INSIDE SAME BOUNDARY enclosed inside a common boundary **2.** ADJACENT next to and sharing a common boundary with something **3.** MEETING IN TIME OR PLACE meeting end to end, so that where or when one finishes the next begins **4.** OF EQUAL EXTENT OR SCOPE equal in length or extent, either in space or time, or having the same range of meaning as another term (*formal*) [Mid-17C. < Latin *conterminus*, literally "boundary with" < *terminus* "boundary"] —**con·ter·mi·nous·ly** *adv* —**con·ter·mi·nous·ness** *n*

con·tes·sa /kən téssə, kon-/ *n* an Italian countess [Early 19C. Via Italian < medieval Latin *comitissa*, feminine of *comit-* "companion"]

con·test *n* /kón tèst/ **1.** COMPETITION TO FIND BEST an organized competition for a prize or title, especially one in which the entrants appear or demonstrate their skills individually and the winner is chosen by a group of judges **2.** STRUGGLE FOR CONTROL a struggle between opposing individuals, organizations, or forces for victory or control ■ *vt* /kən tést/ (**-test·ed, -test·ing, -tests**) **1.** CHALLENGE SOMETHING to challenge or question something **2.** TAKE PART IN CONTEST to take part in a contest or competition [Late 16C. Directly or via French < Latin *contestari* "begin a lawsuit by calling witnesses together" < *testari* "be a witness"] —**con·test·a·ble** /kən téstəb'l/ *adj* —**con·test·a·bly** *adv* —**con·test·er** *n*

con·tes·tant /kən téstənt/ *n* **1.** a competitor in a contest or competition **2.** somebody who challenges something such as a will, verdict, or decision

SYNONYMS See ***candidate.***

con·text /kón tèkst/ *n* **1.** TEXT SURROUNDING WORD OR PASSAGE the words, phrases, or passages that come before and after a particular word or passage in a speech or piece of writing and help to explain its full meaning **2.** SURROUNDING CONDITIONS the circumstances or events that form the environment within which something exists or takes place ○ *The dispute needs to be viewed in its historical context.* **3.** E-COMMERCE DATA TRANSFER STRUCTURE a data structure used to transfer electronic data to and from a business management system [15C. < Latin *contextus* "connected" < *contexere* "weave together" < *texere* "weave"] —**con·tex·tu·al** /kən tékschoo əl/ *adj* —**con·tex·tu·al·ly** *adv*

con·tex·tu·al·ize /kən tékschoo ə lìz/ (**-ized, -iz·ing, -iz·es**) *vt* to place a word, phrase, or idea within a suitable context —**con·tex·tu·al·i·za·tion** /kən tèkschoo əli záysh'n/ *n*

Con·ti /kóntee/, **Tom** (*b.* 1941) Scottish-born British stage and movie actor. He is a versatile character actor whose success dates from his Tony award for the Broadway production of *Whose Life Is It Anyway?* (1979).

con·tig /kón tìg/ *n* a continuous series of overlapping cloned DNA segments derived from the genetic material of a chromosome and used in mapping the physical order of bases along the chromosome [Late 20C. Shortening of CONTIGUOUS]

con·ti·gu·i·ty /kòntə gyóo ətee/ (*plural* **-ties**) *n* (*formal*) **1.** closeness in space or time to something, or actual contact with it along one side **2.** a continuous line, mass, or series ○ *a contiguity of roofs*

con·tig·u·ous /kən tíggyoo əss/ *adj* (*formal*) **1.** ADJOINING sharing a boundary or touching each other physically **2.** NEIGHBORING situated next to something else or to each other **3.** CONTINUOUS connected together so as to form an unbroken sequence in time or an uninterrupted expanse in space [Early 16C. < Latin *contiguus* "touching together" < *contingere* (see CONTACT)] —**con·tig·u·ous·ly** *adv* —**con·tig·u·ous·ness** *n*

con·ti·nent[1] /kóntinənt/ *n* **1.** any of the seven large continuous land masses that constitute most of the dry land on the surface of the Earth. They are Africa, Antarctica, Asia, Australia, Europe, North America, and South America. **2.** the part of the Earth's crust that rises above the oceans [Mid-16C. < Latin *terra continens* "continuous land" < the present participle of *continere* (see CONTAIN)]

con·ti·nent[2] /kóntinənt/ *adj* **1.** able to exercise control over urination and bowel movements **2.** restrained, especially abstaining from sexual activity (*formal*) [14C. < Latin *continent-*, present participle of *continere* (see CONTAIN)] —**con·ti·nence** *n*

Con·ti·nent *n* the mainland of Europe, not including the British Isles

con·ti·nen·tal /kònti nént'l/ *adj* **1.** RELATING TO EARTH'S CONTINENTS relating to, typical of, or belonging to the continents of the Earth **2.** another spelling of **Continental** *adj* (sense 1) **3.** OF CLASSIC EUROPEAN CUISINE relating to the traditional food and dishes of western European countries, especially France ■ *n* **1.** another spelling of **Continental** *n* (sense 1) **2.** WHIT something small and worthless ○ *I wouldn't give a dime for that cheap merchandise, and I don't care a continental what the manufacturer thinks.* —**con·ti·nen·tal·ism** *n* —**con·ti·nen·tal·ist** *n* —**con·ti·nen·tal·ly** *adv*

Con·ti·nen·tal *adj* **1.** OF MAINLAND EUROPE from or relating to mainland Europe **2.** OF ORIGINAL 13 AMERICAN COLONIES from or relating to the 13 colonies that later became the United States ■ *n* **1.** MAINLAND EUROPEAN somebody from mainland Europe (*informal*) **2.** AMERICAN SOLDIER DURING REVOLUTION a soldier in the American army during the Revolution

con·ti·nen·tal break·fast *n* a light breakfast usually consisting of fruit juice, a roll, croissant, or pastry with jam and butter, and coffee or tea [Because it is common on the Continent]

con·ti·nen·tal code *n* COMMUNICATION same as **International Morse code**

Con·ti·nen·tal Con·gress *n* the congress of delegates from the American colonies held before, during, and after the American Revolution. It issued the Declaration of Independence (1776) and drafted the Articles of Confederation (1777).

con·ti·nen·tal crust *n* the part of the outer shell of Earth that constitutes the continents and the rocks beneath them down to the level of the mantle. It is approximately 22 mi./35 km thick in most areas and is composed of sedimentary rocks near the surface and metamorphic rocks at a lower depth.

con·ti·nen·tal di·vide *n* a massive area of high ground in the interior of a continent, from either side of which a continent's river systems flow in different directions

Con·ti·nen·tal Di·vide /kònti nènt'l di vìd/ series of mountain ridges running from Alaska to Mexico and including the Rocky Mountains that forms the main watershed of North America

con·ti·nen·tal drift *n* a theory that explains the formation, alteration, and extremely slow movement of the continents across the Earth's crust. The continents are thought to have been formed from one large landmass that split, drifted apart, and in places collided again.

con·ti·nen·tal mar·gin *n* the region of ocean between the deep sea and shore, consisting of the continental rise, slope, and shelf

con·ti·nen·tal rise *n* the transitional area of the continental margin between the continental slope and abyssal plain

con·ti·nen·tal shelf *n* the gently sloping undersea area surrounding a continent at depths of up to 656 ft./200 m, at the edge of which the continental slope drops steeply to the ocean floor

con·ti·nen·tal slope *n* the steep slope from the continental shelf down to the ocean floor

con·ti·nen·tal U·nit·ed States *n* the United States excluding its island possessions and the state of Hawaii

con·tin·gence /kən tínjənss/ *n* **1.** physical contact between objects **2.** same as **contingency** (sense 1)

con·tin·gen·cy /kən tínjənssee/ (*plural* **-cies**) *n* **1.** SOMETHING THAT MAY HAPPEN an event that might occur in the future, especially a problem, emergency, or expense that might arise unexpectedly and therefore must be prepared for **2.** SOMETHING SET ASIDE FOR UNFORESEEN EMERGENCY provision made against future unforeseen events, e.g., an allocation of funds in a budget **3.** DEPENDENCE UPON CHANCE dependence upon chance or factors and circumstances that are presently unknown **4.** PRECONDITION IN CONTRACT a condition in a contract that has to be fulfilled before the contract is binding **5.** CHANGE IN MEANING PRODUCED BY CLAUSE in systemic grammar, a change in the meaning of the main clause brought about by the addition of a dependent clause introduced by "if," "when," "though," or "since"

con·tin·gen·cy fee *n* a payment for professional services such as those of a lawyer that is made only if the client receives a satisfactory result

con·tin·gen·cy plan *n* a plan designed to deal with a particular problem, emergency, or state of affairs if it should occur

con·tin·gent /kən tínjənt/ *adj* **1.** DEPENDENT ON WHAT MAY HAPPEN dependent on or resulting from a future and as yet unknown event or circumstance ○ *Payment is contingent upon winning the case.* **2.** POSSIBLE BUT NOT CERTAIN possible, but not certain to happen ○ *"...all the advantages of a long slow ramble with Elfride, without the contingent possibility of the enjoyment being spoilt by her becoming weary."* (Thomas Hardy, *A Pair of Blue Eyes*; 1889) **3.** CHANCE happening by chance **4.** LOGIC TRUE ONLY UNDER CERTAIN CONDITIONS true only under some conditions or under existing conditions, and therefore not universally true or valid ■ *n* **1.** GROUP OF PEOPLE a group of people representing a particular organization or belief, or from a particular region or country, and forming part of a larger group **2.** GROUP OF MILITARY PERSONNEL a group of soldiers forming part of a larger force **3.** same as **contingency** (sense 1) [14C. < Latin *contingent-*, present participle of *contingere* (see CONTACT)] —**con·tin·gent·ly** *adv*

con·tin·gent fee *n* COMM same as **contingency fee**

con·tin·gent work·er *n* a temporary employee, often employed for a specific task

~~**continous**~~ incorrect spelling of **continuous**

con·tin·u·al /kən tínnyoo əl/ *adj* **1.** happening again and again, especially regularly **2.** ⚠ continuing almost without interruption or ending [14C. < French *continuel* < *continuer* (see CONTINUE)] —**con·tin·u·al·ness** *n*

USAGE continual or **continuous**? Something ***continual*** continues, with breaks, over a period of time, whereas something ***continuous*** goes on without stopping. So a ***continual*** noise is one that is constantly repeated, like a dog's barking, and a ***continuous*** noise is one that continues without stopping, like the roar of a waterfall. The same distinction applies to the adverbs ***continually*** and ***continuously***: *Hecklers continually interrupted the speaker. She drove continuously for two hours.* In popular usage, however, ***continual*** and ***continually*** are now frequently used to mean "without stopping."

con·tin·u·al·ly /kən tínnyoo əlee/ *adv* **1.** with great frequency or regularity **2.** ⚠ all the time, always without interruption or ending ○ *hard to think with the kids continually screaming*

USAGE See ***continual***.

con·tin·u·ance /kən tínnyoo ənss/ *n* **1.** CONTINUATION OF SOMETHING the fact or quality of continuing into the future **2.** LENGTH OF TIME SOMETHING LASTS the period of time that something lasts or continues **3.** ADJOURNMENT a postponement of legal proceedings until a later date

con·tin·u·ant /kən tínnyoo ənt/ *n* a speech consonant made with the vocal passage partly open for breath to pass through, thus enabling the sound to be prolonged at will, e.g., "l," "f," or "s"

con·tin·u·a·tion /kən tìnnyoo áysh'n/ *n* **1.** PROCESS OF CONTINUING the process of continuing something without interruption **2.** ADDITION OR EXTENSION an additional part that extends something that already exists or has already begun **3.** STARTING AGAIN AFTER INTERRUPTION the renewal of an action, event, or process after it has been interrupted

con·tin·u·a·tive /kən tínnyoo ətiv, -àytiv/ *adj* **1.** AIDING CONTINUITY causing or helping something to continue (*formal*) **2.** GRAM EXPRESSING CONTINUATION expressing the continuation of an action, or indicating that a discourse is moving on to another point ■ *n* GRAM WORD EXPRESSING CONTINUATION a continuative clause, phrase, or word —**con·tin·u·a·tive·ly** *adv*

con·tin·u·a·tor /kən tínnyoo àytər/ *n* somebody who continues something, especially work started by somebody else, or somebody or something that maintains continuity

con·tin·ue /kən tínnyoo/ (**-ued, -u·ing, -ues**) *v* **1.** *vti* KEEP GOING to last, or make something last, beyond the present or throughout a period of time ○ *pledge to continue campaigning against the ban* ○ *Talks between the two sides continued during May.* **2.** *vti* NOT STOP to keep up an activity or state already begun ○ *were able to continue broadcasting without interruption* **3.** *vti* START SOMETHING AGAIN to start doing something again after an interruption or pause ○ *We'll continue this discussion later.* **4.** *vti* BEGIN SPEAKING AGAIN to begin speaking again, or say something, after an interruption or pause **5.** *vti* MAKE SOMETHING LONGER to extend, or extend something, beyond a particular point or beyond its original length **6.** *vi* MOVE FARTHER to move or travel farther in a particular direction ○ *Continue east along the coast path.* **7.** *vt N Am, Scotland* POSTPONE CASE to postpone legal proceedings [14C. Via French < Latin *continuare* "make continuous" < *continere* (see CONTAIN)] —**con·tin·u·a·ble** *adj* —**con·tin·ued** *adj* —**con·tin·u·er** *n*

con·tin·ued frac·tion *n* a fraction with a whole number as numerator, and a number plus a fraction as denominator, the denominator in turn having a number plus a fraction as its denominator. If there is a finite number of terms, it is said to be terminating, otherwise it is nonterminating.

con·tin·u·ing /kən tínnyoo ing/ *adj* having existed for some time, currently in existence, and likely to remain so in the future —**con·tin·u·ing·ly** *adv*

con·tin·u·ing ed·u·ca·tion *n* **1.** adult education, usually in the form of short or part-time courses, continuing throughout a person's life **2.** regular courses or training designed to bring professionals up to date with the latest developments in their particular field

con·ti·nu·i·ty /kònti nóo ətee/ (*plural* **-ties**) *n* **1.** UNCHANGING QUALITY the fact of staying the same, of being consistent throughout, or of not stopping or being interrupted ○ *measures to ensure continuity of supply* ○ *the stability and continuity of traditional rural life* **2.** CONSISTENT WHOLE something that remains consistent or uninterrupted throughout ○ *This program has benefited from two important continuities, in staffing and leadership.* ○ *stressed the continuities with the past* **3.** CONSISTENCY BETWEEN MOVIE OR BROADCAST PARTS consistency in the details from one part of a movie or broadcast to another ○ *discrepancies in continuity* **4.** SEAMLESSNESS OF NARRATIVE smoothness in the narrative flow in a movie or broadcast **5.** DETAILED SCRIPT a comprehensive script that includes full details of the contents of each shot or scene, including such items as camera positions and costume features **6.** SPOKEN LINK IN BROADCASTING commentary by a television or radio broadcaster that fills the time between the end of one program or program segment and the beginning of the next

con·tin·u·o /kən tínnyoo ō/ (*plural* **-os**) *n* an instrumental bass accompaniment, usually played on a keyboard, with numbers written beneath the notes so that musicians can improvise and provide harmony [Early 18C. < Italian, "continuous" < Latin *continuus* (see CONTINUOUS)]

con·tin·u·ous /kən tínnyoo əss/ *adj* **1.** UNCHANGED OR UNINTERRUPTED continuing without changing, stopping, or being interrupted in space or time ○ *three days of continuous rain* **2.** UNBROKEN having no gaps, holes, or breaks ○ *a continuous line* **3.** GRAM same as **progressive** *adj* (sense 6) **4.** MATH RELATING TO DIFFERENCE OF FUNCTION VALUES relating to a line or curve along which the difference between function values at any two points within a given interval will approach zero if the interval is decreased sufficiently **5.** RELATING TO UNINTERRUPTED CHEMICAL MANUFACTURING relating to chemical manufacturing in which material is processed in an uninterrupted stream. Continuous processes are usually advantageous for large-scale chemical production. [Mid-17C. < Latin *continuus* "uninterrupted" < *continere* (see CONTAIN)] —**con·tin·u·ous·ly** *adv* —**con·tin·u·ous·ness** *n*

USAGE See ***continual***.

con·tin·u·ous as·sess·ment *n* assessment of students' progress based on work they do or tests they take throughout the term or year, rather than on a single examination

con·tin·u·ous cre·a·tion the·o·ry *n* ASTRON same as **steady-state theory**

con·tin·u·ous spec·trum *n* a sequence of frequencies that is without breaks over a relatively wide range of wavelengths

con·tin·u·ous wave *n* an electromagnetic wave generated as an unbroken train of constant frequency and amplitude, rather than in pulses

con·tin·u·um /kən tínnyoo əm/ (*plural* **-a** /-yoo ə/ or **-ums**) *n* **1.** a link between two things, or a continuous series of things, that blend into each other so gradually and seamlessly that it is impossible to say where one becomes the next ○ *A rainbow forms a continuum of color.* **2.** a set of real numbers between any two of which a third can always be found, and in which there are no gaps [Mid-17C. < Latin, form of *continuus* (see CONTINUOUS)]

con·tort /kən táwrt/ (**-tort·ed, -tort·ing, -torts**) *v* **1.** *vti* to become so twisted as to take on an unnatural or grotesque shape, or to twist something, especially a part of the body, in this way ○ *Fear had contorted their faces.* **2.** *vt* to change something so greatly that it becomes unrecognizable ○ *to contort the truth* [15C. < Latin *contort-*, past participle of *contorquere* "twist violently" < *torquere* "to twist"] —**con·tor·tive** *adj*

con·tort·ed /kən táwrtəd/ *adj* **1.** greatly or violently twisted out of shape **2.** describes plant parts such as sepals or leaves whose margins overlap in the bud like playing cards in a hand, so that they appear to be twisted —**con·tort·ed·ly** *adv* —**con·tort·ed·ness** *n*

con·tor·tion /kən táwrsh'n/ *n* **1.** a twisting of something, especially a part of the body, out of its natural shape **2.** a bewilderingly complex maneuvering or manipulation of something ○ *verbal contortions*

con·tor·tion·ist /kən táwrsh'nist/ *n* **1.** somebody who bends his or her own body into unusual shapes, especially as entertainment ○ *You'd have to be a contortionist to get into those jeans.* **2.** somebody who twists or distorts something such as a statement ○ *a debater skilled as a logical contortionist* —**con·tor·tion·is·tic** /kən tàwrshə nístik/ *adj*

con·tour /kón toor/ *n* **1.** OUTLINE an outline, especially of something curved or irregular (*often used in the plural*) ○ *The contours of the hills were characteristically rounded.* **2.** GENERAL NATURE the general character or nature of something ○ *scenes that establish the contour of the play* **3.** GEOG same as **contour line** ■ *adj* **1.** SHAPED OR FITTED shaped to fit something, especially the shape of somebody's body ○ *contour furniture* **2.** FOLLOWING LAND'S SHAPE following the lay of the land, rather than cutting through or across it ○ *contour farming* ■ *vt* (**-toured, -tour·ing, -tours**) **1.** SHAPE SOMETHING TO FIT to shape one thing so that it fits the outlines of another ○ *furniture that is contoured to the human body* **2.** PUT CONTOUR LINES ON MAP to mark contour lines on something such as a map **3.** MAKE SOMETHING FOLLOW SHAPE OF LAND to build or operate something so that it follows the natural shape of the land ○ *roads that are sensitively contoured* [Mid-17C. < French < Italian *contornare* "draw in outline," literally "turn with" < Latin *tornare* (see TURN)]

con·tour feath·er *n* a medium-sized feather of a bird that forms part of its external body covering and determines its shape, excluding the wings and tail

con·tour in·ter·val *n* the interval between contour lines on a map, or the altitude the interval represents ○ *at contour intervals of 50 to 100 feet*

con·tour line *n* a line on a map connecting points on a land surface that are the same elevation above sea level ○ *On this map, contour lines show you where the mountains are.*

con·tour map *n* a map that uses contour lines to show the shapes and elevations of land surfaces

contr. *abbr* **1.** GRAM contraction **2.** MUSIC contralto **3.** control

Con·tra /kóntrə/ *n* a member of the United States-backed counterrevolutionary force that tried to overthrow the Nicaraguan government in the 1980s [Late 20C. < Spanish *contrarevolucionario* "counter-revolutionary"]

contra- *prefix* **1.** against, opposite, contrasting ○ *contraindicate* **2.** lower in pitch ○ *contrabass* [< Latin *contra* "against" < Indo-European, "together"]

con·tra·band /kóntrə bànd/ *n* **1.** ILLEGAL IMPORTS AND EXPORTS goods that are illegally imported or exported, e.g., goods that evade duty or are prohibited by law from being taken into or out of a country ○ *dealers in contraband* **2.** ILLEGAL TRADE illegal trade, especially the illegal importing or exporting of goods **3.** SUPPLIES FORBIDDEN TO WARRING SIDES goods that a neutral country must not supply to either side in a war **4.** SLAVE ENTERING UNION TERRITORY a slave who escaped to, or was taken behind, Union lines during the Civil War ■ *adj* **1.** ILLEGALLY TRADED bought or sold, especially imported or exported, illegally ○ *truckloads of contraband cigarettes* **2.** FORBIDDEN FROM BEING IMPORTED OR EXPORTED forbidden by law from being traded, especially as an import or export [Late 16C. Via Spanish *contrabanda* < Italian *contrabbando*, literally "against proclamation" < *bando* "proclamation" < Germanic] —**con·tra·band·age** *n* —**con·tra·band·ist** *n*

con·tra·bass /kóntrə bàyss/ *n* **1.** MUSIC same as **double bass 2.** INSTRUMENT PITCHED LOWEST OF ITS FAMILY an instrument pitched an octave below the usual range for that family of instruments **3.** CONTRABASSIST an instrumentalist in an orchestra or band who plays the contrabass ■ *adj* PITCHED OCTAVE BELOW pitched an octave below the usual range of that instrument ○ *contrabass clarinet* [Early 19C. < Italian *contrabbasso* < *basso* "bass"] —**con·tra·bass·ist** /kòntrə báyssist/ *n*

con·tra·bas·soon /kòntrə bə so͞on/ *n* **1.** a U-shaped woodwind instrument that is the largest in the oboe family and has a pitch an octave below the bassoon **2.** an instrumentalist in an orchestra or chamber group who plays the contrabassoon —**con·tra·bas·soon·ist** *n*

con·tra·cep·tion /kòntrə sépsh'n/ *n* **1.** the prevention of pregnancy using artificial methods such as condoms and birth-control pills or natural methods such as avoiding sex during the woman's known fertile periods **2.** a method or device used to prevent pregnancy [Late 19C. < CONTRA- + CONCEPTION]

con·tra·cep·tive /kòntrə séptiv/ *n* DEVICE PREVENTING FERTILIZATION a device used to prevent fertilization of an egg, e.g., a condom worn by a man during intercourse, or a pill taken regularly by a woman ■ *adj* **1.** OF CONTRACEPTION relating to contraception ○ *contraceptive advice* **2.** PREVENTING INSEMINATION designed to prevent sperm from fertilizing an egg ○ *various contraceptive methods and devices*

con·tra·cep·tive ring *n* a plastic ring inserted into the vagina that releases a constant flow of a contraceptive drug

con·tract *n* /kón tràkt/ **1.** FORMAL AGREEMENT a formal or legally binding agreement, e.g., one for the sale of property, or one setting out terms of employment ○ *Such actions would be in breach of contract.* **2.** DOCUMENT RECORDING AGREEMENT a document that records a formal or legally binding agreement ○ *sign a contract* **3.** AGREEMENT TO MARRY a formal agreement to marry (*dated*) **4.** PAID ASSASSIN'S ASSIGNMENT a hiring of an assassin to kill somebody (*informal*) ○ *a contract killing* **5.** HIGHEST BRIDGE BID IN ONE HAND in bridge, a winning bid in a single hand, in which partners agree regarding the number of tricks they can take **6.** NUMBER AND SUIT OF CONTRACT in bridge, the number and suit of the tricks agreed on by the highest bidders **7.** CARDS same as **contract bridge** ■ *v* /kən trákt, kón tràkt/ (**-tract·ed, -tract·ing, -tracts**) **1.** *vti* SHRINK OR LESSEN to shrink or become smaller, or make something shrink or become smaller ○ *metals expanding and contracting as temperatures change* **2.** *vti* TIGHTEN OR DRAW TOGETHER to become tighter or draw together, or make something tighter or draw something together ○ *see the muscles contracting under the skin* **3.** *vt* FORMALLY OR LEGALLY AGREE TO DO SOMETHING to make a formal or legally binding agreement with somebody to do something, especially work (*often passive*) ○ *I'm not contracted to work on Sundays.* **4.** *vt* GET ILLNESS to catch or develop an illness or disease **5.** *vt* SHORTEN WORD OR PHRASE to shorten a word by leaving out letters or syllables, or a phrase by leaving out words **6.** *vt* ARRANGE MARRIAGE to arrange a marriage formally (*dated*) [14C. Directly or via French < Latin *contractus*, past participle of *contrahere* "draw together" < *trahere* "to draw"] —**con·tract·i·bil·i·ty** /kən tràktə bíllətee/ *n* —**con·tract·i·ble** /kən tráktəb'l/ *adj* —**con·tract·i·ble·ness** *n*

contract out *v* **1.** *vt* to offer work to other companies or workers outside the organization that is commissioning the work **2.** *vi UK* to withdraw from something by making a formal or legally binding declaration ○ *employees contracting out of the state pension scheme*

con·tract bridge *n* the most common variety of bridge, in which points are awarded only for tricks bid and won

con·trac·tile /kən trákt'l/ *adj* able or tending to shrink, tighten, or become narrower —**con·trac·til·i·ty** /kòn trak tíllətee/ *n*

con·trac·tile vac·u·ole *n* a membrane-surrounded cavity within a cell that regulates the water content of the cell by absorbing water and then contracting to expel it

con·trac·tion /kən tráksh'n/ *n* **1.** REDUCTION IN SIZE a shrinking or reducing ○ *alternate expansion and contraction* **2.** CONTRACTING OF BODY PART a tightening or narrowing of a muscle, organ, or other body part **3.** TIGHTENING OF WOMB MUSCLES EFFECTING CHILDBIRTH a tightening of the muscles of the womb that occurs at increasingly frequent intervals immediately before childbirth and eventually pushes the baby out of the womb **4.** SHORTENED WORD a shortened form or shortening of a word or phrase, e.g., "he'll" for "he will." In English, the omitted letter or letters are usually marked with an apostrophe or a period, depending on the type of contraction. —**con·trac·tion·al** *adj* —**con·trac·tion·ar·y** *adj* —**con·trac·tive** *adj*

con·trac·tor /kón tràktər/ *n* **1.** COMPANY OR PERSON UNDER CONTRACT a company or person with a formal contract to do a specific job, supplying labor and materials and providing and overseeing staff if needed ○ *a building contractor* ○ *The contractors are handling the electrical wiring.* **2.** THING THAT CONTRACTS something that contracts, e.g., a muscle **3.** SOMEBODY WHO MAKES CONTRACT one of the parties to a contract

con·tracts /kón tràkts/ *n* the branch of law that deals with contracts (*takes a singular verb*) ○ *She made a career in contracts.*

con·trac·tu·al /kən trákchoo əl/ *adj* contained in, arising from, or in the form of a formal or legally binding agreement ○ *fulfilling your contractual obligations* —**con·trac·tu·al·ly** *adv*

con·trac·ture /kən trákchər/ *n* a permanent tightening or shortening of a body part such as a muscle, tendon, or the skin, often affecting its shape

con·tra·dance, con·tra·danse *n* DANCE another spelling of **contredanse**

con·tra·dict /kòntrə díkt/ (**-dict·ed, -dict·ing, -dicts**) *vt* **1.** to argue against the truth or correctness of somebody's statement or claim **2.** to show that something is not true or that the opposite is true ○ *The results contradicted all previously held theories.* [Late 16C. < Latin *contradict-*, past participle of *contradicere* "speak against" < *dicere* "speak"] —**con·tra·dict·a·ble** *adj* —**con·tra·dict·er** *n* —**con·tra·dic·tive** *adj* —**con·tra·dic·tive·ly** *adv*

SYNONYMS See *disagree*.

---

con·tra·dic·tion /kòntrə díksh'n/ *n* **1.** something that has aspects that are illogical or inconsistent with each other ○ *a contradiction in terms* **2.** a statement, or the making of a statement, that opposes or disagrees with somebody or something ○ *I can say without fear of contradiction that she is our best worker.*

con·tra·dic·to·ry /kòntrə díktəree/ *adj* **1.** INCONSISTENT inconsistent either within itself or in relation to others **2.** OPPOSING holding or consisting of an opposite view **3.** ARGUMENTATIVE tending to take opposite views —**con·tra·dic·to·ri·ly** *adv* —**con·tra·dic·to·ri·ness** *n*

con·tra·dis·tinc·tion /kòntrə di stíngkshən/ *n* differentiation between two things by identifying their contrasting qualities —**con·tra·dis·tinc·tive** *adj* —**con·tra·dis·tinc·tive·ly** *adv*

con·trail /kón trày l/ *n* AVIAT same as **vapor trail** [Mid-20C. Contraction of *condensation trail*]

con·tra·in·di·cate /kòntrə índi kàyt/ (**-cat·ed, -cat·ing, -cates**) *vt* to state something to be inadvisable while taking particular medication because of a likely adverse reaction ○ *Taking aspirin with this drug is contraindicated.* —**con·tra·in·di·cant** *n* —**con·tra·in·di·ca·tion** /kòntrə indi káysh'n/ *n* —**con·tra·in·dic·a·tive** /kòntrə in díkətiv/ *adj*

con·tra·lat·er·al /kòntrə láttərəl/ *adj* describes a body part that is on the opposite side of the body, or that acts in conjunction with such a part

con·tral·to /kən tráltō/ (*plural* **-tos**) *n* **1.** LOWEST FEMALE VOCAL RANGE the lowest vocal range for women's voices, below soprano and mezzo-soprano **2.** SOMEBODY WITH CONTRALTO SINGING VOICE a singer, usually a woman, with a contralto voice **3.** PART FOR CONTRALTO a singing part for a contralto **4.** LOW SPEAKING VOICE a naturally low speaking voice in a woman ○ *warm contralto tones* [Mid-18C. < Italian, "below alto"]

con·tra·po·si·tion /kòntrəpə zísh'n/ *n* **1.** a position opposite to or against something ○ *took up a stand in contraposition to government policy* **2.** in logic, the relation of a proposition to its contrapositive [Mid-16C. < late Latin *contraposition-* < Latin *contraponere* "place opposite" < *ponere* "to place"]

con·tra·pos·i·tive /kòntrə pózzətiv/ *n* in logic, a conditional proposition that negates another conditional proposition and also reverses its clauses. The proposition "if not q then not p" is the contrapositive of the proposition "if p then q."

con·trap·pos·to /kòntrə pó stō/ (*plural* **-tos**) *n* a relaxed asymmetric pose of the human body in art, especially sculpture, in which the shoulders and hips are turned in different planes [Early 20C. < Italian, past participle of *contrapporre* < Latin *contraponere* (see CONTRAPOSITION)]

con·trap·tion /kən trápshən/ *n* a device or machine, especially one that appears strange or improvised ○ *They'd rigged up a contraption for opening the door.* [Early 19C. Origin ?]

con·tra·pun·tal /kòntrə púnt'l/ *adj* describes polyphonic music with very active and strongly differentiated parts [Mid-19C. < Italian *contrapunto* "counterpoint" < *punto* "point" < Latin *punctum* (see POINT)] —**con·tra·pun·tal·ly** *adv*

con·tra·pun·tist /kòntrə púntist/ *n* a composer of music in counterpoint or in a contrapuntal style [Late 18C. < Italian *contrapuntista* < *contrapunto* (see COUNTERPOINT)]

con·trar·i·an /kən trérree ən/ *n* **1.** a habitual opponent of accepted policies, opinions, or practices ○ *a thoroughgoing contrarian, accepting nothing anyone says* **2.** an investor who goes against current market trends, e.g., by buying stocks that most other investors are selling

con·tra·ri·e·ty /kòntrə rī́ ətee/ (*plural* **-ties**) *n* **1.** the state or quality of opposing or being contrary **2.** a point of difference or inconsistency

con·trar·i·wise /kón treree wīz, kən trérree wīz/ *adv* **1.** IN OPPOSITE WAY in the opposite way or direction or on the opposite side **2.** ON OTHER HAND used to introduce a statement in direct opposition to what has already been said **3.** UNHELPFULLY in a way that obstructs or hinders progress ○ *Unfortunately, things turned out contrariwise, and we had to give up the idea.*

con·trar·y /kon trèrree/ *adj* **1.** CONFLICTING not at all in agreement with something ○ *Such arrangements were contrary to his moral code.* **2.** OPPOSITE opposite in direction ○ *flew in a direction contrary to the rest of the airplanes* **3.** OBSTRUCTING OR HINDERING PROGRESS making forward motion extremely hard ○ *slowed by contrary winds* **4.** /kón trèrree, kən tréree/ DELIBERATELY DISOBEDIENT willfully disobedient or uncooperative ○ *a contrary child* **5.** LOGIC UNABLE TO BE TRUE AT ONCE describes a pair of propositions that cannot both be true, though they may both be false ■ *n* THE OPPOSITE the opposite of something ○ *Actually, the contrary is true.* [13C. Via Anglo-Norman < Latin *contrarius* < *contra* "against"] —**con·trar·i·ly** *adv* —**con·trar·i·ness** *n* ◇ **contrary to** differently from ◇ **on** *or* **to the contrary** quite the reverse is true

con·trast *n* /kón tràst/ **1.** MARKED DIFFERENCE a difference, or something that is different ○ *in stark contrast to the luxury they formerly enjoyed* **2.** JUXTAPOSITION OF DIFFERENT THINGS an effect created by placing or arranging very different things such as colors, shades, or textures next to each other **3.** DEGREE OF LIGHTNESS AND DARKNESS the difference, or the use of differences, between the lightest and the darkest parts of something, e.g., to create a special effect in a painting, photograph, or television image ■ *vti* /kən trást, kón tràst/ (**-trast·ed, -trast·ing, -trasts**) SEEM OR MAKE THINGS SEEM DIFFERENT to compare different things or arrange them in a way that highlights their differences, or be markedly different when compared with something ○ *These poems have a mature voice when contrasted with her earlier work.* [15C. Via French < Italian *contrastare* "stand against" < Latin *stare* "to stand"] —**con·trast·a·ble** /kən trástəb'l/ *adj* —**con·trast·a·bly** *adv* —**con·trast·ing** /kən trásting/ *adj* —**con·trast·ing·ly** *adv*

con·trast·ive /kən trástiv/ *adj* forming a contrast, or using contrasting colors, tones, or textures —**con·trast·ive·ly** *adv* —**con·trast·ive·ness** *n*

con·trast me·di·um *n* a substance opaque to X-rays that is used to fill a body cavity, making the outline of the body part easier to see on an X-ray photograph. Barium is frequently used as a contrast medium.

con·trast·y /kón tràstee/ *adj* showing sharp contrast between the lightest and darkest areas in a photograph or television or motion picture image

con·tra·vene /kòntrə véen/ (**-vened, -ven·ing, -venes**) *vt* **1.** to break a rule or law ○ *outdated equipment that contravenes the safety regulations* **2.** to disagree with or oppose a statement or decision ○ *There was no question of contravening the committee's findings.* [Mid-16C. < late Latin *contravenire* "come against" < Latin *venire* "come"] —**con·tra·ven·er** *n* —**con·tra·ven·tion** /-vénsh'n/ *n*

~~contraversial~~ incorrect spelling of **controversial**

con·tre·coup /kóntrə ko͞o/ *n* an injury to one side of an organ, especially the brain, as a result of a blow that causes it to swing inside the retaining cavity [Mid-18C. < French, "a blow opposite" < *coup* (see COUP)]

con·tre·danse /kóntrə dànss, -dàanss/, **con·tra·dance, con·tra·danse** *n* **1.** a folk dance in which two pairs of partners face each other **2.** the music for a contredanse [Early 19C. < French, by folk etymology (influenced by *contre* "against") < English *country dance*]

con·tre·temps /kóntrə taaN, kàwntrə taaN/ *n* an unfortunate occurrence, especially an awkward or embarrassing one (*formal*) [Late 17C. < French, literally "against the time"]

contrib. *abbr* **1.** contribution **2.** contributor

con·trib·ute /kən tríbbyoot/ (**-ut·ed, -ut·ing, -utes**) *v* **1.** *vti* DONATE MONEY OR TIME to give something such as money or time, especially to a common fund or for a specific purpose ○ *contributed generously to environmental causes* **2.** *vi* BE PARTIAL CAUSE OF SOMETHING to be one of the factors that causes something ○ *a heart condition that contributed to his early death* **3.** *vti* OFFER OPINION to offer opinions or advice in a meeting or discussion ○ *I felt I had nothing new to contribute to the debate.* **4.** *vti* PROVIDE WORKS FOR PUBLICATION to supply material for a publication or broadcast [Mid-16C. < Latin *contribut-*, past participle of *contribuere* "bring in together" < *tribuere* "to grant"] —**con·trib·u·tive** *adj* —**con·trib·u·tive·ly** *adv* —**con·trib·u·tive·ness** *n* —**con·trib·u·tor** *n*

con·tri·bu·tion /kòntri byo͞osh'n/ *n* **1.** DONATION something such as money or time that is given, especially to a common fund or for a specific purpose ○ *a contribution toward my college education.* **2.** REGULAR PAYMENT a regular fixed amount paid, e.g., to a retirement fund, often deducted from somebody's wages **3.** ROLE PLAYED IN ACHIEVING SOMETHING the part played by somebody or something in causing a result ○ *She recognized the contribution of her parents to her success.* **4.** MATERIAL SUPPLIED FOR PUBLICATION OR BROADCAST a piece of material that forms part of a publication or broadcast **5.** TIP OR GRATUITY a gift of extra money for a service

con·trib·u·to·ry /kən tríbbyə tàwree/ *adj* **1.** HELPING SOMETHING HAPPEN partly responsible for something ○ *Poor diet is often a contributory factor.* **2.** GIVEN IN COMMON WITH OTHERS given along with others to a common fund or project **3.** REQUIRING EMPLOYEE TO PAY IN PART describes an insurance or retirement plan in which the employee shares the cost of the premiums with the employer ■ *n* (*plural* **-ries**) SOMEBODY WHO MAKES CONTRIBUTION somebody who donates money or time

con·trib·u·to·ry neg·li·gence *n* a victim's share in the responsibility for an accident, when care to prevent it could have been taken by the victim as well as the other party

con·trite /kən trít/ *adj* **1.** deeply sorry for having behaved wrongly **2.** done or said out of a sense of guilt or remorse ○ *full of contrite promises* [13C. Via French < Latin *contritus*, past participle of *conterere* "rub together" < *terere* "rub"] —**con·trite·ly** *adv* —**con·trite·ness** *n*

con·tri·tion /kən trísh'n/ *n* **1.** deep and genuine feelings of guilt and remorse **2.** in the Roman Catholic Church, repentance for past sins and a firm resolve not to sin in the future ○ *acts of contrition*

con·tri·vance /kən trívənss/ *n* **1.** DEVIOUS PLOT a plan intended to deceive **2.** SCHEMING the making of cunning or deceitful plans **3.** CREATIVE SOLUTION something clever done to accomplish something ○ *a contrivance to fool the enemy* **4.** GADGET a cleverly made device or machine to fulfill a need ○ *a contrivance for keeping your back straight*

con·trive /kən trív/ (**-trived, -triv·ing, -trives**) *v* **1.** *vti* DO SOMETHING CREATIVELY to accomplish something by being clever and creative ○ *She contrived a meeting between the warring factions.* **2.** *vt* MAKE SOMETHING INGENIOUS to make something in a skillful or ingenious way ○ *A tree house had been contrived from bits of scrap.* **3.** *vt* MANAGE TO DO SOMETHING to accomplish something difficult or unexpected ○ *She somehow contrived to be both an effective and a well-liked teacher.* **4.** *vti* PLOT to formulate clever or deceitful schemes ○ *The gang contrived a way to hack into the main computer system.* [13C. Via Old French *contro(u)ver* "invent" < medieval Latin *contropare* "compare" < Latin *tropus* "turn, manner" < Greek *tropos*] —**con·triv·a·ble** *adj* —**con·triv·er** *n*

con·trived /kən trívd/ *adj* **1.** not natural and spontaneous ○ *Her apology was very contrived.* **2.** unrealistic and unconvincing ○ *a movie with a contrived ending* —**con·triv·ed·ly** /kən trívədlee/ *adv*

con·trol /kən tról/ *vt* (**-trolled, -trol·ling, -trols**) **1.** MANAGE to exercise power or authority over something such as a business or nation ○ *The company is controlled largely by foreign interests.* **2.** OPERATE MACHINE to work or operate something such as a vehicle or machine ○ *Computers control many of the safety features on board.* **3.** RESTRAIN OR LIMIT SOMETHING to limit or restrict somebody or something, e.g., in expression, occurrence, or rate of increase ○ *The administration set out to control inflation.* ○ *her inability to control her temper* **4.** FIN OVERSEE FINANCIAL AFFAIRS to regulate the financial affairs of a business or other large organization **5.** ACCT VERIFY ACCOUNTS to examine financial accounts and verify them as correct ■ *n* **1.** ABILITY TO MANAGE SOMETHING ability or authority to manage or direct something ○ *circumstances beyond our control* **2.** OPERATING SWITCH a mechanical or electronic device used to operate a vehicle or machine ○ *Turn down the heat control.* **3.** SKILL skill in using something or in performing (*often used in combination*) ○ *players with excellent ball control* **4.** LIMITS AND RESTRICTIONS the process of limiting or restricting somebody or something, or the methods used in this ○ *an era of wage and price control* **5.** PLACE OF INSPECTION OR DIRECTION a place at which something is checked or inspected or from which something is directed (*usually used in combination*) ○ *passengers filing through passport control* **6.** COMPARATIVE STANDARD IN EXPERIMENT a subject taking part in an experiment or survey but not involved in the procedures affecting the rest of the experiment, thus acting as the standard against which the results are compared ○ *We have sixteen mice, of which the eight controls have been matched for age and weight.* **7.** SUPERVISING PERSON OR GROUP a person or group that supervises or monitors operations or operatives ○ *Their intelligence agents report to control twice a week.* **8.** COMPUT same as **control key** **9.** PARANORMAL SPIRIT THAT SUPPOSEDLY GUIDES SEANCE a spirit that is believed to help a medium gain access to other spirits being called up in a seance **10.** BASEBALL PITCHER'S PRECISION the ability of a pitcher to place a pitch precisely, especially in the strike zone ○ *The pitcher had great control in the top of the seventh.* ■ **con·trols** *npl* **1.** MEANS OF CONTROLLING the means by which a machine is operated ○ *nobody at the controls* **2.** RULES the regulations governing a system ○ *import controls* [15C. Via Anglo-Norman *contreroller* < medieval Latin *contrarotulare* "check against a duplicate register" < *rotul-* "little roll" (see ROLL)] —**con·trol·la·bil·i·ty** /kən trōlə bíllətee/ *n* —**con·trol·la·ble** *adj* —**con·trol·la·bly** *adv*

con·trol freak *n* somebody who exerts an excessive control over others and his or her own life (*slang*)

con·trol gene *n* a gene that regulates the development and specialization of cells

con·trol grid *n* ELECTRONICS same as **grid** (sense 5)

con·trol group *n* in an experiment, the group of test subjects left untreated or unexposed to some procedure and then compared with treated subjects in order to validate the results of the test

con·trol key *n* a computer key pressed together with other keys to perform specific functions

~~controll~~ incorrect spelling of **control**

con·trolled /kən tróld/ *adj* **1.** KEPT UNDER CONTROL kept in check and not expressed fully or at all ○ *She spoke with scarcely controlled fury.* **2.** CAREFULLY REGULATED carefully measured and regulated, especially in relation to medical treatments or scientific experiments ○ *They tested the effectiveness of controlled doses of the drug.* **3.** DONE WITH SKILL AND DISCIPLINE showing the skill, judgment, and discipline needed in order to achieve a desired result, without doing too little or too much ○ *His controlled performance as Lear was masterful.*

con·trolled sub·stance *n* a substance subject to statutory control, especially a drug that can be obtained legally only with a doctor's prescription

con·trolled us·er *n* a drug addict who is able to maintain an otherwise normal way of life

con·trol·ler /kən trólər/ *n* **1.** SOMEBODY WHO CONTROLS OR ORGANIZES SOMETHING somebody in a managing, supervising, or monitoring position **2.** FIN FINANCIAL SUPERVISOR somebody whose job is to oversee financial matters in a business or government department **3.** CONTROLLING DEVICE a device or mechanism that controls something —**con·trol·ler·ship** *n*

con·trol·ling in·ter·est *n* ownership of enough of a company's stock to allow the holder to control the business

con·trol pan·el *n* the collection of lights, digital displays, and switches used to monitor and control the operation of a vehicle, device, or machine

con·trol rod *n* a rod or cylinder made of or containing neutron-absorbing material such as graphite, used to control the rate of fission in a nuclear reactor

con·trol room *n* a room from which an organization coordinates the activities of a large group of people or the operation of a number of machines

con·trol sur·face *n* a movable surface that controls the direction of an aircraft, rocket, or missile, e.g., a rudder or elevator

con·trol tow·er *n* a high building at an airport, from which air-traffic controllers organize the movements of incoming and outgoing aircraft by radioing their pilots

con·tro·ver·sial /kòntrə vúrsh'l/ *adj* **1.** provoking strong disagreement or disapproval, e.g., in public debate ○ *controversial policies* **2.** enjoying or habitually engaging in controversy —**con·tro·ver·sial·ist** *n* —**con·tro·ver·si·al·i·ty** /kòntrə vurshee állətee/ *n* —**con·tro·ver·sial·ly** *adv*

con·tro·ver·sy /kóntrə vùrssee/ (*plural* **-sies**) *n* disagreement on a contentious topic, strongly felt or expressed by all those concerned, or an instance of this [14C. < Latin *controversia* < *controversus* "disputed," literally "turned against" < *vertere* "to turn"]

con·tro·vert /kóntrə vùrt/ (**-vert·ed, -vert·ing, -verts**) *vt* to argue strongly against something [Mid-16C. < Latin *contro-*, form of *contra-* "against" + *vertere* "to turn"] —**con·tro·vert·er** *n* —**con·tro·vert·i·ble** *adj* —**con·tro·vert·i·bly** *adv*

con·tu·ma·cious /kòntoo máyshəss/ *adj* **1.** flagrantly disobedient or rebellious **2.** persistently refusing to appear in court or to obey a court order without good reason —**con·tu·ma·cious·ly** *adv* —**con·tu·ma·cious·ness** *n*

con·tu·ma·cy /kən to͞oməssee/ *n* **1.** flagrant disobedience or rebelliousness **2.** persistent refusal to appear in court or to obey a court order without good reason [13C. < Latin *contumacia* < *contumac-* "insolent"]

con·tu·me·li·ous /kòntə meélee əss/ *adj* having or showing an insulting, scornful, or contemptuous attitude (*archaic or literary*) —**con·tu·me·li·ous·ly** *adv*

con·tu·me·ly /kən tóoməlee, kón tòoməlee, kóntəmlee/ (*plural* **-lies**) *n* (*archaic or literary*) **1.** insulting, scornful, or contemptuous language or treatment **2.** an openly insulting, scornful, or contemptuous remark [14C. Via French < Latin *contumelia*]

con·tuse /kən tóoz/ (**-tused, -tus·ing, -tus·es**) *vt* to bruise a body part (*technical*) [14C. < Latin *contus-*, past participle of *contundere* "beat small" < *tundere* "to beat"]

con·tu·sion /kən tóozh'n/ *n* an injury to the body in which skin and bone are not broken but damage is done to tissues under the skin, causing a bruise (*technical*)

co·nun·drum /kə núndrəm/ *n* **1.** something puzzling, confusing, or mysterious **2.** a riddle, especially one with an answer in the form of a play on words [Early 17C. Origin ?]

SYNONYMS See ***problem.***

con·ur·ba·tion /kònnər báysh'n/ *n* a large urban area created when neighboring towns spread into and merge with each other [Early 20C. < *con-*, variant of COM- + Latin *urb-* "city"]

conv. *abbr* **1.** conversation **2.** FIN, AUTOMOT convertible **3.** RELIG convocation

Conv. *abbr* Conventual

con·va·lesce /kònvə léss/ (**-lesced, -lesc·ing, -lesc·es**) *vi* to spend time recovering from an illness or the effects of medical treatment, especially by resting [15C. < Latin *convalescere* < *valescere* "grow strong" < *valere* "be strong"]

con·va·les·cent /kònvə léss'nt/ *n* a patient who is recovering from an illness or the effects of medical treatment —**con·va·les·cence** *n* —**con·val·es·cent** *adj*

con·vec·tion /kən véksh'n/ *n* **1.** circulatory movement in a liquid or gas, resulting from regions of different temperatures and different densities rising and falling in response to gravity **2.** heat transfer within the atmosphere involving the upward movement of huge volumes of warm air, leading to subsequent condensation and cloud formation [Mid-19C. < late Latin *convection-* < Latin *convehere* "bring together" < *vehere* "carry"] —**con·vec·tion·al** *adj* —**con·vec·tive** *adj* —**con·vec·tive·ly** *adv*

con·vec·tion ov·en *n* an oven with a fan that circulates heat throughout the oven, so that food on all levels cooks uniformly

con·vec·tor /kən véktər/ *n* a heater that depends on convection of air to transfer heat from the heating element [Early 20C. < CONVECTION]

con·vene /kən veén/ (**-vened, -ven·ing, -venes**) *v* **1.** *vt* **ARRANGE MEETING** to call people together for a formal meeting ○ *A meeting of the working group has been convened for tomorrow.* **2.** *vi* **GATHER FOR MEETING** to come together for a formal meeting **3.** *vt* **CALL BEFORE COURT** to order somebody to appear before a court, tribunal, or other decision-making body [15C. < Latin *convenire* "come together" < *venire* "come"] —**con·ven·a·ble** *adj* —**con·ven·er** *n* —**con·ven·or** *n*

~~**conveniant**~~ incorrect spelling of **convenient**

con·ven·ience /kən veényənss/ *n* **1.** **QUALITY OF BEING CONVENIENT** the quality of being or making things easy, useful, or of increasing comfort ○ *have the convenience of working at home* **2.** **SOMEBODY'S PERSONAL COMFORT** personal comfort, or circumstances that promote somebody's personal comfort ○ *All rooms have cooking facilities, for our guests' convenience.* **3.** **SOMETHING PROVIDING EASE OR COMFORT** something that makes life easier or more comfortable, especially a labor-saving device ○ *apartments supplied with every modern convenience* **4.** *UK* **LAVATORY** a lavatory, especially in a public place

con·ven·ience food *n* packaged food that can be prepared quickly and easily, e.g., in a microwave or by adding boiling water

con·ven·ience store *n* a small store near a residential area that stocks food and general goods and is open long hours

con·ven·ient /kən veényənt/ *adj* useful or suitable, because it makes things easier, is close by, or does not involve much effort or trouble ○ *Choose a time convenient for you.* [14C. < Latin *convenient-*, present participle of *convenire* (see CONVENE)] —**con·ven·ient·ly** *adv*

con·vent /kónvənt, kón vènt/ *n* **1.** a community of women who live a life devoted largely to religious worship **2.** the building occupied by a community of religious women [13C. Via Anglo-Norman *covent* < Latin *conventus* "assembly" < *convenire* (see CONVENE)]

con·ven·ti·cle /kən véntik'l/ *n* **1.** an unlawful or secret religious gathering **2.** a building where a conventicle is held [14C. < Latin *conventiculum* "small assembly" < *convenire* (see CONVENE)] —**con·ven·ti·cler** *n*

con·ven·tion /kən vénshən/ *n* **1.** **GATHERING** a gathering of people who have a common interest or profession ○ *He's attending an optometrists' convention in Iowa.* **2.** **PEOPLE ATTENDING FORMAL MEETING** the people present at a convention **3.** **MEETING TO SELECT CANDIDATES** a meeting of delegates of a political party for the purpose of selecting candidates, or the delegates attending such a meeting ○ *the Democratic and Republican conventions* ○ *The convention roared as the president stepped to the podium.* **4.** **FORMAL AGREEMENT** an agreement between groups, especially an international agreement slightly less formal than a treaty ○ *under the terms of the Geneva Convention* **5.** **USUAL WAY OF DOING THINGS** the customary way in which things are done within a group ○ *designs that flout convention* **6.** **FAMILIAR DEVICE** a standard technique or well-used device, especially in the arts ○ *Her style does not follow the usual literary conventions.* **7.** CARDS **CODED BID** in bridge, a bid intended for a partner to understand differently from its face value, because of a prearranged bidding system [15C. Via French < Latin *convention-* < *convenire* (see CONVENE)]

con·ven·tion·al /kən vénshən'l, -vénshnəl/ *adj* **1.** **SOCIALLY ACCEPTED** conforming to socially accepted customs of behavior or style, especially in a way that lacks imagination ○ *They didn't want a conventional wedding.* **2.** **USUAL OR ESTABLISHED** using well-established methods or styles ○ *conventional cooking on a stove rather than in a microwave* **3.** **OF GATHERING OF PEOPLE** relating to a large gathering of people with a common interest or purpose **4.** ARMS **WITHOUT NUCLEAR ENERGY** not involving the use of nuclear weapons or energy **5.** LAW **BASED ON CONSENT** in law, based or dependent on the consent of the various parties —**con·ven·tion·al·ism** *n* —**con·ven·tion·al·ist** *n* —**con·ven·tion·al·ly** *adv*

con·ven·tion·al·i·ty /kən vènshə nállətee/ (*plural* **-ties**) *n* **1.** adherence to social conventions in behavior, tastes, or methods **2.** a socially accepted way of behaving or of doing something ○ *the conventionalities of a formal occasion*

con·ven·tion·al·ize /kən vénshən'l ìz, -vénshnə lìz/ (**-ized, -iz·ing, -iz·es**) *vt* to make something conventional, especially in style or taste ○ *His flights of fancy had become conventionalized as the Gothic style.* —**con·ven·tion·al·i·za·tion** /kən vènshən'li záysh'n, -vènshnəli-/ *n*

con·ven·tion·al wis·dom *n* general or widespread belief ○ *Conventional wisdom dictates that such skills merit high rewards.*

con·ven·tion bounce *n* an increase in the support for a presidential candidate following nomination at a party convention (*informal*)

con·ven·tion·eer /kən vènshə neér/ *n* a participant in a convention

con·vent school *n* a school for girls in which some or all of the teachers are nuns

con·ven·tu·al /kən vénchoo əl/ *adj* relating to or resembling a convent in quietness, simplicity, or discipline ○ *living a quiet conventual life* ■ *n* a woman who lives in a convent —**con·ven·tu·al·ly** *adv*

Con·ven·tu·al *n* a member of a branch of a Franciscan order of friars who live a less austere life than in other branches

con·verge /kən vúrj/ (**-verged, -verg·ing, -verg·es**) *vi* **1.** **MEET** to reach the same point coming from different directions ○ *the place where the roads converge* **2.** **BECOME SAME** to become gradually less different and eventually the same ○ *political beliefs that were rapidly converging* **3.** **ARRIVE AT SAME DESTINATION** to gather or meet at the same destination ○ *Delegates from all over the world are converging on the city of New York.* **4.** MATH **APPROACH FINITE LIMIT** to approach a finite limit as the number of terms in an infinite series increases **5.** BIOL **DEVELOP SIMILAR CHARACTERISTICS** to develop, independently of other species, superficially similar characteristics in response to a set of environmental conditions, e.g., the development of wings in birds and insects [Late 17C. < late Latin *convergere* "lean together" < Latin *vergere* "to bend"]

con·ver·gence /kən vúrjənss/, **con·ver·gen·cy** /kən vúrjənsee/ (*plural* **-cies**) *n* **1.** **COMING TOGETHER** a coming together from different directions, especially a uniting or merging of groups or tendencies that were originally opposed or very different **2.** MATH **CONDITION OF CONSTANT OR INCREASING DIFFERENCES** the characteristic of a series or sequence of numbers in which the difference between each term and the following term remains constant or increases **3.** BIOL **SIMILAR DEVELOPMENT** the tendency of different species to develop similar characteristics in response to a set of environmental conditions **4.** METEOROL **MEETING OF AIR MASSES** the meeting of different air masses, often resulting in vertical air currents **5.** OPHTHALMOL **TURNING OF EYES INWARD** the turning inward of both eyes in order to look at something nearer than the previous object viewed **6.** COMPUT **INTEGRATION OF IT SERVICES** automated mapping and integration of information technology environments available to a user —**con·ver·gent** *adj*

con·ver·gent ev·o·lu·tion *n* BIOL same as **convergence** (sense 3)

con·ver·gent mar·gin *n* a boundary between two tectonic plates that are moving together, one dipping under the other

con·ver·sant /kən vúrss'nt/ *adj* knowing about or familiar with something from experience or study ○ *not conversant with local customs* [14C. < French, present participle of *converser* (see CONVERSE[1])] —**con·ver·sance** *n* —**con·ver·sant·ly** *adv*

con·ver·sa·tion /kònvər sáysh'n/ *n* **1.** **CASUAL TALK** an informal talk with somebody, especially about opinions, ideas, feelings, or everyday matters ○ *a telephone conversation* **2.** **TALKING** the activity of talking to somebody informally ○ *in conversation with one of the cleaners* **3.** **INFORMAL TALK ABOUT ISSUE** an informal talk about something involving representatives from various interested groups **4.** COMPUT **REAL-TIME INTERACTION WITH COMPUTER** an interaction with a computer carried on in real time **5.** **NONVERBAL EXCHANGE** a nonverbal exchange or interaction **6.** LAW same as **criminal conversation** [14C. Via French < Latin *conversation-* < *conversari* "turn yourself around" < *conversare* (see CONVERSE[1])]

con·ver·sa·tion·al /kònvər sáyshən'l, -sáyshnəl/ *adj* **1.** relating to informal talking, especially to the ability to say interesting things ○ *got stuck with a seatmate who was a conversational dud* **2.** informal in language and style, and usually dealing with or suitable for simple subjects ○ *She writes in an easy conversational style.* ○ *conversational German* —**con·ver·sa·tion·al·ly** *adv*

con·ver·sa·tion·al·ist /kònvər sáyshən'list, -sáyshnəlist/, **con·ver·sa·tion·ist** /-sáysh'nist/ *n* somebody who enjoys engaging in conversation and can converse in an enjoyable way ○ *Her husband's not much of a conversationalist.*

con·ver·sa·tion piece *n* **1.** something that attracts people's interest and leads to conversation ○ *I don't think much of the sculpture in their front yard, but I guess it makes a good conversation piece.* **2.** a portrait painting of a group of stylish people in a domestic or landscape setting

con·ver·sa·zi·o·ne /kònvər saatsee ónee/ (*plural* **-ni** /-ónee/ or **-nes**) *n* a social gathering to hear a talk on or discuss a topic related to the arts (*formal*) [Mid-18C. < Italian, "conversation" < Latin *conversare* (see CONVERSE[1])]

con·verse[1] *vi* /kən vúrss/ (**-versed, -vers·ing, -vers·es**) **1.** to have a conversation ○ *a place where they can converse uninterrupted* **2.** COMPUT to interact with a computer in real time, as if engaged in a dialogue ■ *n* /kón vùrss/ same as **conversation** (sense 2) (*archaic*) ○ *They were deep in converse with one* *another.* [14C. Via French *converser* < Latin *conversare* "live with" < *versari* "occupy yourself" < *vertere* "to turn"] —**con·vers·er** *n*

con·verse[2] /kón vùrss, kən vúrss/ *n* **1.** OPPOSITE the opposite of something ○ *Actually, the converse is true.* **2.** LOGIC REVERSED CATEGORICAL SENTENCE a categorical sentence in which the subject and predicate have been reversed, e.g., "all dogs are collies" from "all collies are dogs" ■ *adj* OPPOSITE opposite or reverse [14C. < Latin *conversus*, past participle of *convertere* (see CONVERT)] —**con·verse·ly** *adv*

con·ver·sion /kən vúrzh'n/ *n* **1.** ALTERATION a change in the nature, form, or function of something ○ *a conversion of waste land into a sports field* **2.** SOMETHING ALTERED something that has been changed in nature, form, or function, especially a building or room ○ *These apartments are conversions.* **3.** CHANGE OF MEASURING SYSTEM a change from one measuring or calculating system to another, or a calculation done to bring about the change ○ *the conversion from miles to kilometers* **4.** CHANGING OF SOMEBODY'S BELIEFS an adoption of new opinions or beliefs, especially in religion ○ *his conversion to Islam* **5.** FOOTBALL CONVERTING FOLLOWING TOUCHDOWN in football, a successful kick between the goal posts or a run or pass into the end zone following a touchdown **6.** LOGIC REVERSING TERMS IN CATEGORICAL SENTENCE the reversing of the subject and predicate in a categorical sentence, forming a new sentence, e.g., "all dogs are collies" from "all collies are dogs" **7.** LAW UNLAWFUL HOLDING OF ANOTHER'S PROPERTY unlawful treating of somebody else's property as your own **8.** LAW CHANGING OF PROPERTY CLASSIFICATION the changing of one type of property to another, e.g., from joint to separate property [14C. Via French < Latin *conversion-* < *convers-*, past participle of *convertere* (see CONVERT)] —**con·ver·sion·al** *adj*—**con·ver·sion·ar·y** *adj*

con·ver·sion dis·or·der *n* a neurosis marked by the appearance of physical symptoms such as partial loss of muscle function without physical cause but in the presence of psychological conflict

con·vert *v* /kən vúrt/ (**-vert·ed, -vert·ing, -verts**) **1.** *vti* CHANGE SOMETHING'S CHARACTER to change something from one character, form, or function to another, or be changed in character, form, or function ○ *a process for converting waste into usable fuel* **2.** *vti* CHANGE SOMETHING'S FUNCTION to change the function or use of something, or be able to change in function or use ○ *sofas that convert into beds* **3.** *vt* CHANGE MEASURING OR CALCULATING UNITS to change units of one measuring or calculating system into units of another ○ *the formula for converting liters into gallons* **4.** *vti* CHANGE SOMEBODY'S BELIEFS to adopt new opinions or beliefs, especially religious beliefs, or change the opinions or beliefs of somebody ○ *His wife converted to Judaism.* **5.** *vi* FOOTBALL SCORE AFTER TOUCHDOWN in football, to score following a touchdown by kicking a football between the goal posts, which earns one point, or running or passing the ball into the end zone, which earns two **6.** *vt* LOGIC REVERSE TERMS IN CATEGORICAL SENTENCE to reverse the subject and predicate in a categorical sentence, forming a new sentence, e.g., "all dogs are collies" from "all collies are dogs" **7.** *vt* LAW UNLAWFULLY HOLD ANOTHER'S PROPERTY to treat somebody else's property as your own unlawfully **8.** *vt* LAW CHANGE CLASSIFICATION OF PROPERTY to change the classification of property, e.g., from joint to separate property, in the course of a transaction ■ *n* /kón vùrt/ SOMEBODY WITH CHANGED BELIEFS somebody who has chosen a new way of life or a new set of beliefs ○ *a convert to Christianity* ○ *a convert to health food* [13C. Via French < Latin *convertere* "turn around" < *vertere* "to turn"] ◇ **preach to the converted** to advocate a viewpoint to people who already have it

SYNONYMS See ***change.***

con·vert·er /kən vúrtər/, **con·ver·tor** *n* **1.** TECH DEVICE THAT CONVERTS a device that converts something, e.g., an electrical device that converts alternating current into direct current **2.** PHYS FREQUENCY CHANGER an electronic component for changing one frequency to another **3.** METALL FURNACE a furnace for refining molten metal **4.** COMPUT DATA CODE CHANGER in computing, a device for changing data from one form to another, e.g., from analog to digital **5.** INDUST same as **converter reactor**

con·vert·er re·ac·tor *n* a nuclear reactor that converts one nuclear fuel into another, especially fertile into fissile material

con·vert·i·ble /kən vúrtəb'l/ *adj* **1.** CAPABLE OF BEING CONVERTED capable of being changed from one form, function, or use to another ○ *Nationalism, as history demonstrates, is too easily convertible into bitterness and selfishness.* **2.** FIN EXCHANGEABLE FOR GOLD OR ANOTHER CURRENCY able to be legally exchanged for gold or for another currency **3.** FIN EXCHANGEABLE FOR STOCK exchangeable for other assets, especially a fixed number of shares in ordinary stock ■ *n* **1.** CAR WITH REMOVABLE ROOF a car with a roof that can be folded back or taken off ○ *a flashy red convertible* **2.** FIN same as **convertible security** —**con·vert·i·bil·i·ty** /kən vùrtə bíllətee/ *n* —**con·vert·i·bly** *adv*

con·vert·i·ble se·cu·ri·ty *n* a security that may be exchanged for other assets, especially a fixed number of shares in ordinary stock

con·ver·tor *n* TECH, SCI another spelling of **converter**

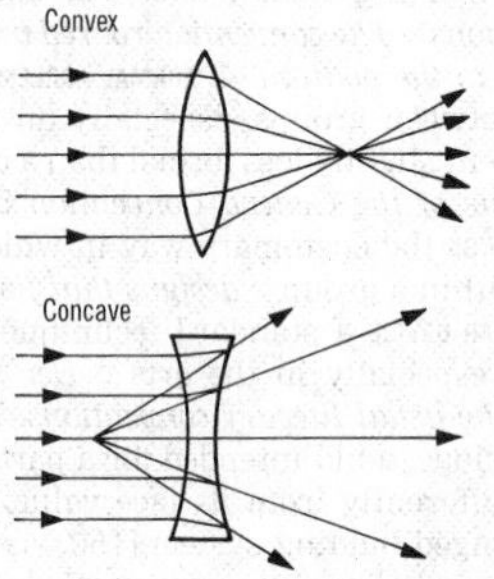

convex: convex and concave lenses

con·vex *adj* /kón vèks/ **1.** OUTWARDLY CURVING having a surface that curves outward rather than inward **2.** OPTICS SHAPED LIKE SPHERE'S EXTERIOR shaped like the exterior of a sphere, paraboloid, ellipsoid, or other outwardly curved surface ○ *a convex lens* **3.** MATH CONTAINING NO ANGLE ABOVE 180° describes a polygon with no interior angle greater than 180° ■ *vti* /kón vèks, kən véks/ (**-vexed, -vex·ing, -vex·es**) CURVE OUTWARD to curve outward, or make something curve outward [Late 16C. < Latin *convexus* "vaulted, arched"] —**con·vex·ly** /kon vékslee/ *adv*

con·vex·i·ty /kon véksətee/ (*plural* **-ties**) *n* **1.** the quality of curving outward **2.** an outwardly curving surface or part

con·vex·o-con·cave /kon vèksō-/ *adj* describes a lens that is convex on one side and concave on the other

con·vex·o-con·vex /kon vèksō-/ *adj* describes a lens that is convex on both sides

con·vey /kən váy/ (**-veyed, -vey·ing, -veys**) *vt* **1.** COMMUNICATE SOMETHING to communicate or express something ○ *a look that conveyed all the tenderness he felt for her* **2.** MEAN SOMETHING to have something as a meaning or connotation ○ *"Majesty" conveys grandeur.* **3.** TRANSFER SOMETHING THROUGH CARRIER to transfer or transmit something along a wire, pipe, tube, or other carrier **4.** TAKE SOMEBODY SOMEWHERE to take somebody or something somewhere (*formal*) **5.** LAW CHANGE OWNERSHIP OF SOMETHING to transfer ownership of something ○ *The title to the property was conveyed last June.* [14C. Via Old French *conveier* < medieval Latin *conviare* "go together on the road" < Latin *via* "road"] —**con·vey·a·ble** *adj*

con·vey·ance /kən váy ənss/ *n* **1.** MOVING OF SOMETHING the conveying of something, especially the transportation or transmission of something from one place to another ○ *the conveyance of information from the mainland to the islands* **2.** VEHICLE a vehicle or other means of transportation (*formal*) ○ *public conveyances* **3.** LAW TRANSFER OF OWNERSHIP a document that legally transfers ownership, or the transfer itself —**con·vey·anc·er** *n* —**con·vey·anc·ing** *n*

con·vey·or /kən váy ər/, **con·vey·er** *n* **1.** a device that transports or transmits something, especially a conveyor belt **2.** a person or thing that transmits something, especially news ○ *a conveyor of good tidings*

con·vey·or belt *n* a device that consists typically of a continuous wide flat rubber loop moved by electrically operated rollers, used to move objects from one place to another nearby

con·vict *v* /kən víkt/ (**-vict·ed, -vict·ing, -victs**) **1.** *vt* DECLARE SOMEBODY GUILTY to declare somebody guilty of a crime in a court of law (*often passive*) ○ *had been previously convicted of fraud* **2.** *vi* ARRIVE AT GUILTY VERDICT to reach a verdict of guilty ○ *juries who will convict on the slimmest evidence* **3.** *vt* SHOW SOMEBODY TO BE AT FAULT to show that somebody is in the wrong in some respect ○ *actions that convicted her of selfishness* ■ *n* /kón vìkt/ SOMEBODY IN PRISON somebody serving a prison sentence ○ *an escaped convict* [14C. < Latin *convict-*, past participle of *convincere* (see CONVINCE)] —**con·vict·a·ble** *adj*

con·vic·tion /kən víksh'n/ *n* **1.** FIRMLY HELD BELIEF a belief or opinion that is held firmly ○ *It's my conviction that they are lying.* **2.** FIRMNESS OF BELIEF firmness of belief or opinion ○ *said with complete conviction* **3.** GUILTY VERDICT an act of finding somebody guilty of a crime, or an instance of being found guilty ○ *The accused has no previous convictions.* —**con·vic·tion·al** *adj*

USAGE conviction or **persuasion**? ***Conviction*** is "a firmly held belief" and "firmness of belief": *It is my conviction* [not *persuasion*] *that the defendant newspaper's First Amendment rights have been violated. I say this with total conviction* [not *persuasion*]: *we are headed for a recession.* ***Persuasion*** is "the act or ability to get someone else to accept your opinion, belief, or viewpoint," "a set of beliefs," and "a group of people with particular beliefs," as in *She used great persuasion in conveying her position to the voters; a politician of the conservative persuasion.*

con·vince /kən víns/ (**-vinced, -vinc·ing, -vinc·es**) *vt* **1.** to make somebody sure or certain of something ○ *We are convinced of his guilt.* **2.** to persuade somebody to believe or do something ○ *Nothing would convince them to invest in such a scheme.* [Mid-16C. < Latin *convincere* "prove wrong" < *vincere* "overcome"] —**con·vinc·er** *n* —**con·vinc·i·ble** *adj*

USAGE convince or **persuade**? Traditionally, to ***convince*** somebody is to make him or her certain of something, and to ***persuade*** somebody is to induce him or her to act: *She convinced him that he had talent and persuaded him to study music.* Because of this distinction, some people still object to the use of an infinitive after ***convince***, pointing out that *She convinced him to...* involves inducing someone to act. Nonetheless, the distinction is quickly disappearing by force of widespread usage, and constructions like this one are increasingly seen in the work of reputable writers: *After a long series of tests I was convinced to go ahead with the surgery despite the risks.*

con·vinc·ing /kən vínssing/ *adj* **1.** PERSUASIVE able to persuade somebody to believe that something is true or to act ○ *convincing arguments* **2.** ABLE TO PERSUADE PEOPLE skilled at making people believe something ○ *a convincing impostor* **3.** BEYOND DOUBT impressively clear or definite ○ *a convincing victory* —**con·vinc·ing·ly** *adv* —**con·vinc·ing·ness** *n*

SYNONYMS See ***valid.***

con·viv·i·al /kən vívvee əl/ *adj* **1.** enjoyable because of its friendliness ○ *spent many a convivial evening at the club* **2.** fond of the company of others ○ *He was famously convivial.* [Mid-17C. < Latin *convivialis* < *convivium* "feast" < *vivere* "to live"] —**con·viv·i·al·ist** *n* —**con·viv·i·al·i·ty** /kən vìvvee állətee/ *n* —**con·viv·i·al·ly** *adv*

con·vo·ca·tion /kònvə káysh'n/ *n* **1.** a large formal assembly, e.g., of a college or university community, or the senior members of a church **2.** the arranging or calling of a formal meeting [14C. < Latin *convocation-* < *convocare* (see CONVOKE)] —**con·vo·ca·tor** /kónvə kàytər/ *n*

con·voke /kən vṓk/ (**-voked, -vok·ing, -vokes**) *vt* to call a formal meeting, or call people together for a meeting [Late 16C. < Latin *convocare* "call together" < *vocare* "to call"] —**con·voc·a·tive** /-vókətiv/ *adj* —**con·vok·er** *n*

con·vo·lute /kónvə lo͞ot/ *vti* (**-lut·ed, -lut·ing, -lutes**) to twist or coil something in folds ○ *The snake's coils were tightly convoluted.* ■ *adj* describes petals or leaves that are rolled from the sides so that one side is wrapped around the other [Late 17C. < Latin *convolut-*, past participle of *convolvere* "twist around" < *volvere* "to roll"] —**con·vo·lute·ly** *adv*

con·vo·lut·ed /kónvə lòotəd/ *adj* **1.** too complex or intricate to understand easily ○ *convoluted sentences* **2.** having many twists, coils, or whorls ○ *the brain's convoluted surface* —**con·vo·lut·ed·ly** *adv* —**con·vo·lut·ed·ness** *n*

con·vo·lu·tion /kònvə lóosh'n/ *n* **1.** TWISTED SHAPE a curve, coil, or twist **2.** TWISTED RIDGE ON BRAIN SURFACE a ridged fold on the surface of the brain **3.** INTRICACY a complexity or intricacy, especially one of many ○ *The plot had so many convolutions it was difficult to follow.* —**con·vo·lu·tion·al** *adj* —**con·vo·lu·tion·ar·y** *adj*

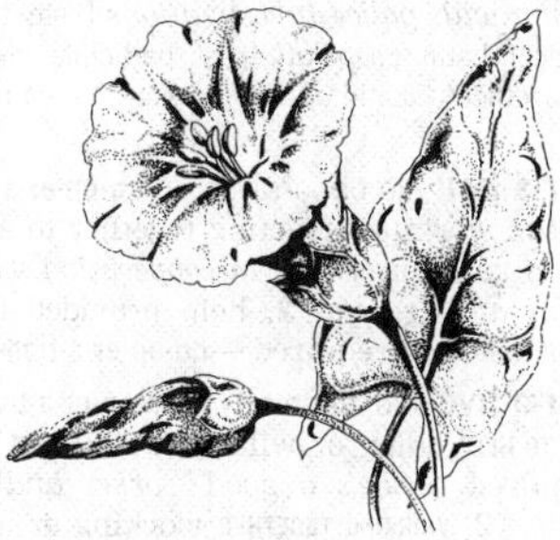

convolvulus

con·vol·vu·lus /kən vólvyələss/ (*plural* **-lus·es** or **-li** /-lī/) *n* a plant of the morning-glory family, many of which have a twining growth habit, including bindweed. Flowers: trumpet-shaped. Genus: *Convolvulus.* [Mid-16C. < Latin < *convolvere* (see CONVOLUTE)]

con·voy /kón vòy/ *n* **1.** VEHICLES OR SHIPS TRAVELING TOGETHER a group of vehicles or ships traveling together, often with an escort for protection ○ *convoys of trucks on the highway* ○ *traveling in convoy* **2.** VEHICLES' OR SHIPS' ESCORT a protective escort for a group of vehicles or ships ■ *vt* (**-voyed, -voy·ing, -voys**) ESCORT VEHICLES OR SHIPS to travel as an escort to protect a group of vehicles or ships [14C. < French *convoi* < Old French *conveier* (see CONVEY)]

con·vul·sant /kən vúlssənt/ *adj* causing convulsions ■ *n* a drug that causes convulsions

con·vulse /kən vúlss/ (**-vulsed, -vuls·ing, -vuls·es**) *v* **1.** *vti* SHAKE UNCONTROLLABLY to jerk or shake violently and uncontrollably, or make a muscle or body part go into a repetitive spasm **2.** *vt* CAUSE TO SHAKE to make somebody shake with laughter or a strong emotion (*often passive*) ○ *convulsed with panic* **3.** *vt* DISRUPT SOMETHING to cause extreme disruption or disturbance in something ○ *Problems in the Asian economies convulsed the New York markets.* [Mid-17C. < Latin *convuls-*, past participle of *convellere* "pull violently" < *vellere* "pull"]

con·vul·sion /kən vúlshən/ *n* (*often used in the plural*) **1.** UNCONTROLLABLE SHAKING a violent shaking of the body or limbs caused by uncontrollable muscle contractions, which can be a symptom of brain disorders and other conditions **2.** DISTURBANCE an extreme disruption or disturbance (*literary*) ■ **con·vul·sions** *npl* LAUGHTER fits of laughter —**con·vul·sion·ar·y** *adj*

con·vul·sive /kən vúlssiv/ *adj* **1.** sudden, jerky, or uncontrollable **2.** undergoing or producing uncontrollable jerking of the body or limbs —**con·vul·sive·ly** *adv* —**con·vul·sive·ness** *n*

Con·way /kón wày/ city in central Arkansas, north of Little Rock and directly east of the Arkansas River. Population: 45,915 (2002 estimate).

Con·way, Jill Ker (*b.* 1934) Australian-born US historian and writer. She is noted for her autobiography *The Road from Coorain* (1989).

con wo·man *n* a woman swindler who uses a confidence game to cheat or defraud people (*informal*)

co·ny *n* ZOOL another spelling of **coney**

coo /koo/ *v* (**cooed, coo·ing, coos**) **1.** *vi* MAKE SOUND OF PIGEON to make the deep hooting sound that is characteristic of pigeons **2.** *vti* SPEAK VERY TENDERLY to speak with affected or exaggerated admiration, or say something in this way ○ *young lovers cooing to each other* ■ *n* BIRD'S SOUND the deep hooting sound that pigeons make [Mid-17C. An imitation of the sound]

COO *abbr* BUSINESS chief operating officer

co·oc·cur *vi* **1.** to happen at the same time and place **2.** to appear together in the same contexts (*refers to speech sounds and other linguistic elements*) —**co·oc·cur·rence** *n*

cook /kòok/ *v* (**cooked, cook·ing, cooks**) **1.** *vti* PREPARE FOOD to prepare food for a meal **2.** *vi* MAKE OR BECOME HOT to make food safe and appetizing by heating it, or undergo heating in order to become ready to eat ○ *The onions have been cooking for a while.* ○ *Cook the beef until it is tender.* **3.** *vi* HAPPEN to be happening or developing (*informal*) ○ *I had the feeling that something was cooking.* **4.** *vi* BE UNCOMFORTABLE IN HEAT to feel extreme discomfort in hot conditions (*informal*) ○ *cooking in an overcrowded bus* **5.** *vt* CHANGE SOMETHING IN ORDER TO DECEIVE to alter or tamper with information or evidence fraudulently (*slang*) ○ *accountants who had cooked the books* **6.** *vi* WORK WELL to be working or performing superbly (*slang*) ○ *It only took a couple of songs before the band was really cooking.* **7.** *vt* HEAT ILLEGAL DRUG to heat an illegal drug such as heroin (*slang*) **8.** *vt* SHOW TO BE WRONG to show that a presented problem is wrong, especially because it has more than one solution ■ *n* SOMEBODY WHO PREPARES FOOD somebody who prepares and cooks food, usually as a job or in a particular way ○ *an excellent cook* [Pre-12C. Via assumed Vulgar Latin *cocus* "cook" < Latin *coquus* < *coquere* "to cook"] —**cook·a·ble** *adj* ◇ **too many cooks (in the kitchen) spoil the broth** the help or involvement of too many people can do more harm than good

cook up *vt* **1.** to prepare or improvise a meal quickly **2.** to invent something untrue or dishonest such as an excuse (*informal*) **3.** DRUGS same as **cook** *v* (sense 7) (*slang*)

Cook, Mount /kòok/ peak of the St. Elias Range in southwestern Yukon Territory. Height: 13,760 ft./4,194 m.

Cook, James, Captain (1728–79) British explorer and cartographer. During three great voyages (1768–71, 1772–75, 1776–79) he charted New Zealand and Australia and explored the Antarctic and the northwestern coast of North America.

> "At daylight in the morning we discovered a bay which appeared to be tolerably well sheltered from all winds, into which I resolved to go with the ship."
> [Attributed to James Cook. Recording his arrival at Botany Bay; April 20, 1770]

Cook, Thomas (1808–92) British travel agent. In 1841 he organized a railroad excursion for a temperance group which began tourism in its modern form.

cook·book /kòok bòok/ *n* a book containing recipes for preparing food or, more generally, detailed directions for a process of any kind

Cooke /kòok/, **Jay** (1821–1905) US banker. He helped to finance the federal government during the Civil War. His failed attempt to finance the building of the Northern Pacific Railroad caused the financial panic of 1873.

cook·er /kòokər/ *n* **1.** a device that cooks food, especially in a particular way ○ *a slow cooker* **2.** *UK* same as **stove**[1] *n* (sense 1)

cook·er·y /kòokəree/ (*plural* **-ies**) *n* **1.** COOK same as **cooking** *n* (sense 1) **2.** a type or style of cooking ○ *Mediterranean cookery* ○ *vegetarian cookery* **3.** a place where food is prepared and cooked

cook·er·y book *n UK* same as **cookbook**

Cooke·ville /kòok vìl/ city in north central Tennessee, southeast of Nashville and north of Chattanooga. Population: 25,901 (2002 estimate).

cook·ie /kòokee/, **cook·y** (*plural* **-ies**) *n* **1.** SMALL FLAT SWEET CAKE a small flat crisp baked cake, especially one made from sweetened dough ○ *a box of cookies* **2.** TYPE OF PERSON somebody who is regarded as being of a particular type or disposition (*informal*) ○ *She's one smart cookie.* **3.** ONLINE COMPUTER FILE CONTAINING USER INFORMATION a computer file containing information about a user that is sent to the central computer with each request. The server uses this information to customize data sent back to the user and to log the user's requests. [Early 18C. < Dutch *koekje* "little cake" < *koek* "cake"] ◇ **that's the way the cookie crumbles** that is the way things tend to happen (*informal*) ◇ **toss your cookies** to vomit (*slang*)

cook·ie cut·ter *n* a shaped template with a sharp edge. Use: pressing into a sheet of dough to make cookie shapes.

cook·ie-cut·ter *adj* seemingly mass-produced without distinctive features ○ *cookie-cutter houses*

cook·ing /kòoking/ *n* **1.** PREPARATION OF FOOD the process or activity of preparing food for eating **2.** PREPARED FOOD food that has been prepared for eating ○ *She doesn't like my cooking.* ■ *adj* USED IN COOKING intended for use in cooking rather than for consumption raw or on its own ○ *a bottle of cooking sherry*

Cook Is·lands group of predominantly volcanic islands in the South Pacific, lying approximately 2,800 mi./4,500 km south of Hawaii and 1,600 mi./2,600 km northeast of New Zealand. They are self-governing in free association with New Zealand. Population: 20,611 (2001). Area: 92 sq. mi./237 sq. km.

cook-off *n* the final round of a cooking competition, in which only the top contestants compete

cook·out /kòok òwt/ *n* a party at which food is cooked and eaten outdoors

Cook's tour *n* a quick tour or survey, with attention only to the main features (*informal*) ○ *The book doesn't try to give anything more than a Cook's tour of European history.* [After Thomas COOK]

cook·stove /kòok stòv/ *n* **1.** a stove used for cooking, as distinct from one designed to heat a room **2.** a portable stove used for cooking on camping trips

Cook Strait area of ocean separating the North Island and the South Island of New Zealand, noted for its treacherous currents. At its narrowest it is 14 mi./22 km wide.

cook·top /kòok tòp/ *n* a flat area on a stove that includes heating units and a surface that can be used for food preparation

cook-up *n* a Caribbean dish of mixed meats, seafood, and rice

cook·ware /kòok wèr/ *n* utensils used in cooking, e.g., pots, pans, and dishes

cook·y /kòokee/ *n* **1.** COOK same as **cook** (*informal*) **2.** another spelling of **cookie**

cool /kool/ *adj* **1.** FAIRLY COLD somewhat cold, usually pleasantly so **2.** STAYING CALM staying calm or not showing emotions, especially nervousness or fear **3.** FASHIONABLE fashionable and sophisticated (*informal*) ○ *looking cool* **4.** UNFRIENDLY unfriendly or unenthusiastic ○ *They gave us a somewhat cool reception.* **5.** EMPHASIZING SUM OF MONEY used to emphasize how large a sum of money is (*slang*) ○ *a cool $3.2 million* **6.** EXCELLENT used to indicate approval or admiration (*slang*) ○ *a cool idea* **7.** OK used to indicate agreement or acceptance (*slang*) ○ *That's cool, no problem.* **8.** SEEMING COLD giving an impression of coldness ○ *a cool mint green* **9.** KEEPING TEMPERATURE LOW made of fabric that keeps the body at a pleasant temperature when it is hot ■ *vti* (**cooled, cool·ing, cools**) **1.** MAKE OR BECOME LESS WARM to become less warm, or cause somebody or something to become less warm ○ *Wait until the mixture cools.* ○ *The room was cooled by a large fan.* **2.** MAKE OR BECOME LESS INTENSE to make somebody or something less intense, or become less intense ○ *anything that might cool his anger* ■ *n* **1.** SLIGHT CHILL moderate coldness, especially in relation to greater heat or coldness ○ *the cool of the evening* **2.** CALMNESS the ability to remain calm in difficult circumstances (*informal*) **3.** STYLISHNESS stylishness that is attractive without being ostentatious (*informal*) ■ *adv* CALMLY in a calm self-controlled way (*informal*) ○ *Just act cool.* ■ *interj* EXPRESSING PLEASURE used to express pleasure, or excitement at a prospect or event (*slang*) ○ *You're coming too? Cool!* [Old English *cōl* < Indo-European, "cold"] —**cool·ness** *n* ◇ **be cool with** to agree with or be willing to accept something ○ *I'm cool with that.* ◇ **cool it** used to tell somebody to calm down (*slang*) ◇ **keep your cool** to remain calm (*informal*) ◇ **lose your cool** to become angry and excitable (*informal*)

cool down *vti* **1.** to make somebody or something less warm, or become less warm ○ *Wait till the* *engine cools down before you lift the hood.* **2.** to make somebody or something calm or calmer after strong feeling or excitement, or become calm or calmer ○ *Only when studio officials had cooled the two men down was the show able to continue.*

cool off *v* **1.** *vi* to become comfortably cool again ○ *I went for a swim to cool off.* **2.** *vti* to become calm or unemotional again after being angry or passionate, or make somebody regain calmness (*informal*) ○ *After a few months, their relationship cooled off.*

cool out *vi Carib* to relax and enjoy yourself (*informal*)

cool·ant /kóolənt/ *n* a substance, usually a liquid, used to prevent overheating in an engine or other mechanism

cool bag, **cool box** *n UK* same as **cooler** (sense 1)

cool·er /kóolər/ *n* **1.** **INSULATED FOOD CONTAINER** a portable insulated container used to keep food cool outdoors **2.** **COOL PLACE OR CONTAINER** a compartment or container in which something is cooled or kept cool **3.** **COLD DRINK** a refreshing drink, e.g., an iced mixture of wine, fruit juice, and soda water or a chilled nonalcoholic drink such as an iced coffee **4.** **PRISON** a prison or prison cell (*slang*)

Cool·gar·die /kool gáardee/ gold-mining town in southern Western Australia. It was once the third largest town in the state. Population: 4,176 (2001).

cool head *n* **1.** an ability to remain calm and sensible in dangerous or difficult situations **2.** somebody who has a cool head

cool-head·ed *adj* staying calm in tense situations

Bettmann/Corbis

Calvin Coolidge

Coo·lidge /kóolij/, **Calvin** (1872–1933) 30th president of the United States. A pro-business Republican president (1923–29), he presided over a period of prosperity, but refused renomination in 1928 following the economic collapse that led to the Great Depression. Full name **Coolidge, John Calvin**. See table at **president**

> "Patriotism is easy to understand in America; it means looking out for yourself while looking out for your country."
> [Attributed to Calvin Coolidge]

Coo·lidge, Grace (1879–1957) US first lady (1923–29), formerly a teacher of children with hearing disabilities. Her natural good humor made her one of the most popular first ladies. Full name **Coolidge, Grace Anna Goodhue**

coo·lie /kóolee/ *n* **1.** in South Asia, China, and parts of East and Southeast Asia, an offensive term for a local man hired cheaply to do manual labor **2.** an offensive term for somebody brought to the United States from China during the 19th century to construct railroads **3.** an offensive term for an employee who is treated as merely one of many unworthy of concern [Mid-17C. < Hindi *kūlī*]

cool·ing /kóoling/ *adj* making you feel cooler in a pleasant way —**cool·ing·ly** *adv*

cool·ing-off pe·ri·od *n* **1.** an agreed pause in a dispute to allow tempers to cool and peaceful solutions to be examined **2.** a period of reflection allowed before making a legally binding commitment

cool·ing tow·er *n* a tall open-topped structure in which the steam produced by an industrial process is condensed

cool jazz *n* jazz with a light tone and relaxed character, popular in the mid-20th century, especially on the West Coast of the United States

cool·ly /kóol lee/ *adv* **1.** in a calm or relaxed way ○ *She coolly marched up to the desk and demanded to see the manager.* **2.** without friendliness or enthusiasm ○ *He greeted her coolly.*

coolth /koolth/ *n* **1.** pleasant coolness or coldness relative to greater heat or cold (*informal or humorous*) **2.** the quality of being very self-confident and informed about current trends (*slang*) ○ *Don't you admire her coolth?* [Mid-16C. < COOL]

Coo·mas·sie /koo máassee, -mássee/ former name for **Kumasi**

coomb /koom/, **coombe** *n* GEOG another spelling of **combe**

coon /koon/ *n* **1.** ZOOL same as **raccoon** (*informal*) **2.** a highly offensive term for a Black person (*taboo*) [Mid-18C. < RACCOON] ◇ **in a coon's age** in a long time (*informal*)

coon-ass /kóon àss/, **coon·ass** *n Southern US* **1.** a term for a person of French Acadian ancestry, used chiefly in Louisiana, northeastern and southeastern Texas, and parts of Mississippi and southern Tennessee (*sometimes offensive*) ○ "... *she was (he'd said) 'the prettiest little coon-ass gal you ever saw.'*" (Donna Tartt, *The Little Friend*; 2003) **2.** a highly offensive term for a person regarded by the speaker as inferior (*taboo*) [Mid-20C. Folk etymology of French *conasse*, "female genitals"]

coon·can /kóon kàn/ *n* a card game from Mexico that is similar to rummy and played with one or two packs [Late 19C. By folk etymology < American Spanish *conquián* < Spanish *con quién?* "with whom?"]

coon·hound /kóon hòwnd/ *n* a dog with smooth hair, belonging to a breed developed in the United States for hunting raccoons

Coon Rap·ids /kóon-/ city in southeastern Minnesota, on the Mississippi River, a northwestern suburb of Minneapolis. Population: 62,329 (2002 estimate).

coon·skin /kóon skìn/ *n* **1.** the pelt of a raccoon **2.** an item of clothing made from coonskin

coon·tie /kóontee/ (*plural* **-ties** or *same*) *n* **1.** edible starch, similar to arrowroot, obtained from the underground stem of a plant **2.** an evergreen plant that resembles a palm and has compound leaves, cones, and thick underground stems that yield coontie. Native to: southern Florida, Mexico. Genus: *Zamia*. [Late 18C. < Seminole *kunti*]

coop[1] /koop/ *n* **1.** **ENCLOSURE FOR POULTRY** an enclosure or hut in which poultry is kept **2.** **FISHING BASKET** a wicker basket used for catching fish **3.** **PRISON** a prison or prison cell (*slang*) [13C. Origin ?] ◇ **fly the coop** to escape or leave a place (*informal*)

coop up *vt* to keep somebody in a confined space

coop[2] *abbr* **1.** business cooperative (*used in e-mails*) **2.** nonprofit cooperative (*used in Internet addresses*) See table at **domain name**

co-op /kó òp, kō óp/, **coop** *n* **1.** a cooperative organization or venture, especially an apartment building or a marketing enterprise (*informal*) **2.** a program of study that allows students to combine liberal-arts and technical courses by using the resources of two different colleges or universities (*informal*) **3.** same as **babysitting co-op** [Mid-19C. Shortening of COOPERATIVE]

coop·er /kóopər/ *n* somebody skilled in making and repairing wooden barrels ■ *vti* (**-ered**, **-er·ing**, **-ers**) to make or repair wooden barrels [15C. < Middle Dutch *kūper* < *kūpe* "cask"]

Coo·per /kóopər/, **Gary** (1901–61) US movie actor. He starred in Westerns, winning Academy Awards for *Sergeant York* (1941) and *High Noon* (1952).

Coo·per, James Fenimore (1789–1851) US writer. Among his *Leather-Stocking Tales* about frontier life is the novel *The Last of the Mohicans* (1826). See Cultural note at **last**[1]

> "History, like love, is apt to surround her heroes with an atmosphere of imaginary brightness."
> [James Fenimore Cooper, *The Last of the Mohicans*; 1826]

Coo·per, Peter (1791–1883) US industrialist and philanthropist. He manufactured the first US steam locomotive (1830) and promoted public education.

Coo·per, Samuel (1609–72) English miniaturist. His portraits in oils, including those of Oliver Cromwell and John Milton, brought new vivacity and realism to the miniature style.

coop·er·age /kóopərij/ *n* **1.** **COOPER'S CRAFT** the craft of making and repairing wooden barrels **2.** **COOPER'S WORKPLACE** a place where wooden barrels are made and repaired **3.** **COOPER'S FEE** the fee charged by a cooper for making or repairing barrels

co·op·er·ate /kō óppə ràyt/ (**-at·ed**, **-at·ing**, **-ates**), **co-op·er·ate** *vi* **1.** to work or act together to achieve a common goal **2.** to do what is asked or required ○ *cooperate with police investigations* [Late 16C. < ecclesiastical Latin *cooperat-*, past participle of *cooperari* "work together" < Latin *operari* "to work"] —**co·op·er·a·tor** *n*

co·op·er·a·tion /kō òppə ráysh'n/, **co-op·er·a·tion** *n* **1.** the act of working or acting together to achieve a common goal ○ *working in cooperation with international aid agencies* **2.** help provided by doing what is asked or required —**co·op·er·a·tion·ist** *n*

co·op·er·a·tive /kō óppərətiv/, **co-op·er·a·tive** *adj* **1.** **WILLING TO HELP** doing or willing to do what is asked or required ○ *She's a good worker and very cooperative.* **2.** **WORKING TOGETHER** working or acting together with others, or done by people working or acting together ○ *a cooperative effort* **3.** BUSINESS **OF JOINTLY OWNED APARTMENT BUILDING** relating to a building with apartments owned by a corporation of tenants in which shares of expenses are calculated on the basis of the value of the tenant's apartment **4.** BUSINESS **OPERATED COLLECTIVELY** owned jointly by all its members or workers, who share all profits equally ○ *a cooperative farm* ■ *n* **1.** **JOINTLY OWNED APARTMENT BUILDING** an apartment building that is jointly owned by the residents, or an apartment in such a building **2.** **BUSINESS OWNED BY WORKERS** a business that is jointly owned by the people who run it, with all profits shared equally ○ *a workers' cooperative* —**co·op·er·a·tive·ly** *adv* —**co·op·er·a·tive·ness** *n*

Coo·pers·town /kóopərz tòwn/ village in central New York on Otsego Lake, home to the Baseball Hall of Fame. Population: 1,969 (2002 estimate).

co-opt /kō ópt/ (**co-opt·ed**, **co-opt·ing**, **co-opts**) *vt* **1.** **ADOPT SOMETHING** to adopt or appropriate something such as a political issue or idea as your own **2.** **INVOLVE OPPONENT IN LARGER GROUP** to absorb an opponent or opposing group into a larger group or society by making promises and concessions **3.** **APPOINT SOMEBODY BY AGREEMENT** to appoint somebody to a body by agreement with the other members [Mid-17C. < Latin *cooptare* "choose mutually" < *optare* "choose"] —**co-op·ta·tion** /kō op táysh'n/ *n* —**co-op·ta·tive** /-óptətiv/ *adj* —**co-op·tion** *n* —**co-op·tive** *adj*

co·or·di·nate, **co-or·di·nate** *v* /kō áwrdə nàyt/ (**-nat·ed**, **-nat·ing**, **-nates**) **1.** *vt* **ORGANIZE SOMETHING COMPLEX** to organize a complex enterprise in which numerous people are involved and bring their contributions together to form a coherent or efficient whole ○ *responsible for coordinating the campaign* **2.** *vti* **MAKE PARTS MOVE TOGETHER** to make moving parts such as parts of the body work together in sequence or in time with one another, or work together in this way ○ *hand and eye coordinating perfectly for the overhead shot* **3.** *vt* **PUT THINGS TOGETHER** to place or class things together ○ *Before we can proceed, all our files have to be coordinated.* **4.** *vi* **WORK TOGETHER** to work together as a unit ○ *members of the team coordinating brilliantly* **5.** *vti* **GO WELL TOGETHER** to make a pleasing combination or match ○ *outfit and accessories that coordinate stylishly* ■ *n* /kō áwrd'nət/ **1.** MATH, MAPS **NUMBER SPECIFYING POSITION** each of a set of numbers that together describe the exact position of something such as a place on a map with reference to a set of axes ○ *Did you receive the coordinates for your target?* **2.** **SOMEBODY OR SOMETHING EQUAL** somebody or something that is equal in rank or importance **3.** CHEM, PHYS **VARIABLE** a variable used with others to describe the state of a physical or chemical system ■ **co·or·di·nates** *npl* **MATCHING CLOTHES** clothes that are designed to be worn together ■ *adj* /kō áwrd'nət/ **1.** **EQUAL** equal in rank or importance **2.** GRAM **HAVING SAME GRAMMATICAL FUNCTION** having the same grammatical function in a syntactic structure ○ *Both "got up" and "ate" are coordinate verbs in the sentence "I got up and ate breakfast."* **3.** CHEM, PHYS **INVOLVING SET OF VARIABLES** involving the use of coordinates [Mid-17C. < CO- + Latin *ordinat-*, past participle of *ordinare* "set in order"] —**co·or·di·nat·ed** *adj*—**co·or·di·nate·ly** *adv*—**co·or·di·nate·ness** *n*—**co·or·di·na·tive** *adj*

co·or·di·nate bond *n* a chemical bond between two atoms created by the sharing of a pair of electrons, both supplied by one atom. A coordinate bond is a type of covalent bond.

co·or·di·nate clause *n* a clause in a sentence that has the same grammatical function or status as another clause and is usually joined to it by a coordinating conjunction such as "and" or "but"

Co·or·di·nat·ed U·ni·ver·sal Time *n* TIME same as **Universal Time**

co·or·di·nate ge·om·e·try *n* MATH same as **analytic geometry**

co·or·di·nat·ing con·junc·tion /kō àwrdə nayting-/ *n* a word that joins two words or clauses with the same grammatical function or status, e.g., "and" or "but"

co·or·di·na·tion /kō àwrdə náysh'n/, **co·or·di·na·tion** *n* **1.** the skillful and balanced movement of different parts, especially parts of the body, at the same time **2.** the combining of diverse parts or groups to make a unit, or the way these parts work together

co·or·di·na·tion com·plex, co·or·di·na·tion com·pound *n* a chemical compound containing one or more ions, atoms, or molecules bound by coordinate bonds to a central metallic atom

co·or·di·na·tion num·ber *n* the number of ions, atoms, or molecules attached by coordinate bonds to the metallic atom in a complex

co·or·di·na·tor /kō áwrdə nàytər/, **co·or·di·na·tor** *n* **1.** somebody responsible for organizing diverse parts of an enterprise or groups into a coherent or efficient whole **2.** GRAM same as **coordinating conjunction**

Coo·sa /kóossə/ river in the southern United States, formed in northern Georgia by the confluence of the Etowah and Oostanaula rivers. Length: 286 mi./460 km.

Coos Bay /kóoss-/ city in southwestern Oregon, on an inlet of Coos Bay on the Pacific Ocean. Population: 15,281 (2002 estimate).

Coot

coot /koot/ (*plural* **coots** or *same*) *n* **1.** a water bird with long lobed toes, black feathers, and a white beak and forehead. Native to: Europe, Asia, North America. Genus: *Fulica.* **2.** somebody regarded as odd, eccentric, or unreasonably stubborn (*informal insult*) [13C. Origin ?]

coot·er /kóotər/ *n* a large freshwater turtle. Native to: eastern United States. Genus: *Chrysemys.* [Early 19C. < Gullah]

coo·tie /kóotee/ *n* a louse of the kind that infests people (*informal*) [Early 20C. Probably < Malay *kutu*]

cop[1] /kop/ *n* same as **police officer** (*informal*) ■ *vt* (**copped, cop·ping, cops**) (*slang*) **1. STEAL** to steal something, especially by snatching it hurriedly ○ *Those kids copped candy bars from the store.* **2. TOUCH OR GLIMPSE SOMEBODY OR SOMETHING** to touch or look at somebody or something quickly and furtively ○ *copped a look at the answers to the quiz* **3. OBTAIN DRUGS** to obtain illegal drugs **4. GET SOMETHING DESIRABLE** to come into possession of something considered desirable ○ *managed to cop two tickets to the Super Bowl* [Early 18C. Probably variant of *cap* "to catch," via French *caper* < Latin *capere* "seize"; noun partly < the verb, partly shortening of COPPER[2]] ◇ **cop a plea** to negotiate with a prosecutor in order to avoid prosecution for a serious crime by agreeing to plead guilty to a lesser crime (*slang*)

cop out *vi* to withdraw from an activity because of lack of nerve or inclination (*slang*)

cop[2] /kop/ *n* a cone-shaped roll of thread on a spindle [Old English *coppe* "summit," origin ?]

Co·pa·ca·ba·na /kōpə kə bánnə/ beach resort and residential area in southern Rio de Janeiro, Brazil

co·pa·cet·ic /kōpə séttik/, **co·pa·set·ic** *adj* excellent or very good (*slang*) [Early 20C. Origin ?]

co·pal /kóp'l, kō pàl/ *n* a hard resin obtained from various tropical trees. Use: making varnish. [Late 16C. Via Spanish < Nahuatl *copalli*]

Co·pán /kō paán/ ancient city of the Maya people, in northwestern Honduras. It is an important archaeological site.

co·par·ent·ing /kō pérrənting/ *n* **1.** the care and raising of children by two people who have divorced or separated **2.** shared responsibility for raising children between two people who are not legally married, especially a same-sex couple —**co·par·ent** *n*

co·part·ner /kō paártnər/ *n* a close partner or associate, especially one who has an equal stake in a company —**co·part·ner·ship** *n*

co·pa·set·ic *adj* another spelling of **copacetic** (*slang*)

co·pay /kō páy/ *n* same as **copayment** (*informal*)

co·pay·ment /kō páymənt/ *n* an arrangement by which two or more parties make complementary payments on a loan or other financial obligation, or a payment made in this way, especially a patient's payment for a medical expense partially covered by insurance

cope[1] /kōp/ (**coped, cop·ing, copes**) *vi* to deal successfully with a difficult problem or situation [14C. < Old French *co(l)per* "to strike" < Greek *kolaphos* "blow"] —**cop·er** *n*

cope[2] /kōp/ *n* **1.** a long sleeveless ceremonial cape worn by priests in some Christian churches **2.** ARCHIT same as **coping** ■ *vt* (**coped, cop·ing, copes**) to lay a protective top course of brick or stone (**coping**) on a wall [13C. Via medieval Latin *capa* "cloak, hood" < late Latin *cappa*] —**coped** *adj*

co·peck *n* MONEY another spelling of **kopek**

Co·pen·ha·gen /kōpən hàygən, -haágən/ capital and largest city of Denmark, situated on the eastern coast of Sjælland Island and the northern coast of Amager Island. Population: 491,148 (2001). Danish name **København**

Co·pen·ha·gen blue *adj* of a grayish blue color —**Co·pen·ha·gen blue** *n*

co·pe·pod /kōpə pòd/ (*plural* **-pods** or *same*) *n* a tiny crustacean that lives among plankton and is an important food source for many fish. Native to: oceans, lakes. Subclass: Copepoda. [Late 19C. < modern Latin *Copepoda* < Greek *kōpē* "oar" + *-pod* "foot"; from its paddle-shaped feet]

Co·per·ni·can /kō púrnikən, kə-/ *adj* **1.** relating to Nicolaus Copernicus or the Copernican system **2.** profoundly important or far-reaching (*literary*) ○ *a Copernican change in attitudes*

Co·per·ni·can sys·tem *n* the theory of Nicolaus Copernicus regarding the mechanics of the solar system, which postulates that the Earth and other planets revolve around the Sun. This theory challenged the Ptolemaic system of astronomy that had prevailed since the 2nd century.

Co·per·ni·cus /kō púrnikəss, kə-/ large crater on the Moon in the northwestern quadrant, 58 mi./93 km in diameter. It is the center of a major system of rays on the lunar surface.

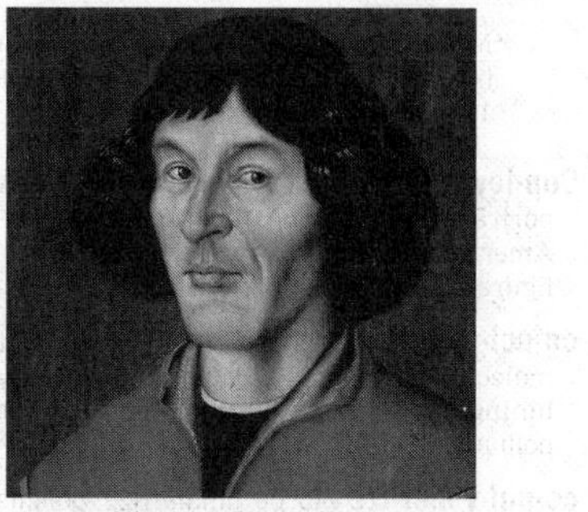

AKG London

Nicolaus Copernicus

Co·per·ni·cus, Nicolaus (1473–1543) Polish astronomer. His major work, *On the Revolutions of the Celestial Spheres* (1543), postulated that the Earth and other planets revolve around the Sun, and laid the foundations of modern astronomy. Born **Kopernik, Mikołaj**

cope·stone /kōp stōn/ *n* any of the stones that form the top edge of a wall [Mid-16C. < COPE[2]]

cop·i·er /kóppee ər/ *n* a device that makes copies of something such as software or recordings

co·pi·lot /kō pìlət/ *n* a second pilot in an aircraft, who shares the flying but is not in command

cop·ing /kōping/ *n* the top, often sloping, course of brick or stone on top of a wall that forms a protective cap against the weather [Mid-16C. < COPE[2] *v*]

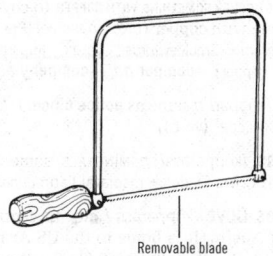

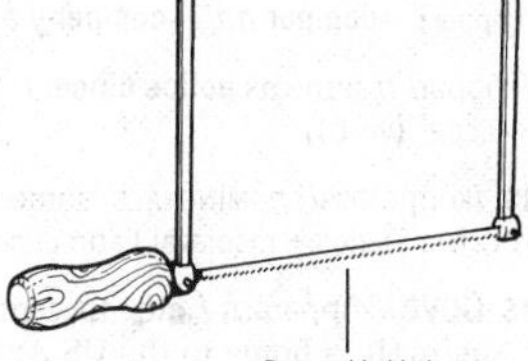

coping saw

cop·ing saw *n* a saw with a thin flexible blade held tight in a U-shaped frame. Use: cutting curves in wood.

co·pi·ous /kōpee əss/ *adj* produced or existing in large quantities [14C. < French *copieux* or Latin *copiosus* < *copia* "abundance"] —**co·pi·ous·ly** *adv*—**co·pi·ous·ness** *n*

co·pi·ta /kō péetə/ *n* **1.** a traditional Spanish tulip-shaped sherry glass, or a drink of sherry served in one **2.** *Hispanic* an alcoholic drink [Mid-19C. < Spanish, "little cup"]

co·pla·nar /kō pláynər/ *adj* lying in the same plane —**co·pla·nar·i·ty** /kōplə nárrətee/ *n*

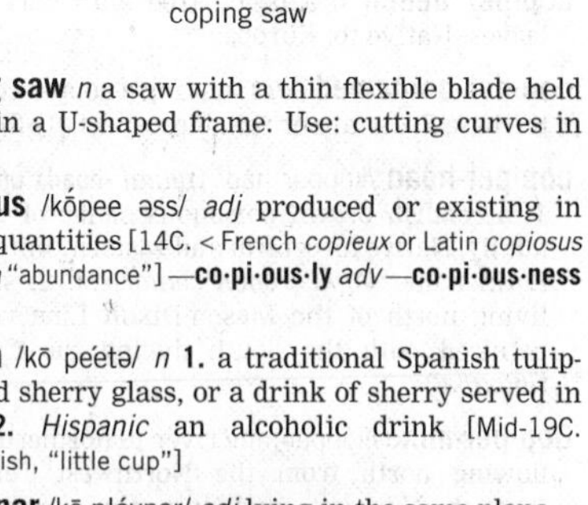

AKG London

Aaron Copland

Cop·land /kōplənd/, **Aaron** (1900–90) US composer whose music was often based on folk themes. He won the Pulitzer Prize in music for *Appalachian Spring* (1944).

"Music is in a continual state of becoming."
[Aaron Copland, *Music and Imagination*; 1952]

Cop·ley /kópplee/, **John Singleton** (1738–1815) American portrait painter. The foremost artist of colonial America, he painted many portraits of political figures.

co·pol·y·mer /kō póllimər/ *n* a substance with a high molecular weight that results from chemically combining two or more monomers —**co·pol·y·mer·ic** /kō pòlli mérrik/ *adj*

co·pol·y·mer·ize /kō pə límmə rīz, -póllimə-/ (**-ized, -iz·ing, -iz·es**) *vt* to unite two or more monomers chemically to form a copolymer —**co·pol·y·mer·i·za·tion** /kō pə lìmməri záysh'n, kō pòllimərì-/ *n*

cop-out *n* (*slang*) **1.** EXCUSE FOR NOT TAKING ACTION a feebly transparent excuse or explanation for refusing to face up to something **2.** EVASION OF RESPONSIBILITY a feeble avoidance of a responsibility or commitment **3.** SOMEBODY WHO BACKS OUT OF SOMETHING somebody who avoids an obligation or a commitment ○ *What a bunch of cop-outs!*

cop·per[1] /kóppər/ *n* **1.** REDDISH BROWN METAL a malleable, reddish brown metallic element that is a good conductor of electricity and heat. Source: ores such as chalcopyrite. Use: wiring, coatings, alloys. Symbol **Cu**. See table at **element** **2.** REDDISH BROWN COLOR a reddish brown color, like that of polished copper **3.** *UK* SMALL COIN a low-value coin made of copper or brass (*informal*) ○ *a pocketful of coppers* **4.** INSECTS REDDISH BROWN BUTTERFLY a small reddish brown butterfly. Genera: *Lycaena* or *Heodes*. ■ *vt* (**-pered, -per·ing, -pers**) COVER SOMETHING WITH COPPER to cover or coat something with copper (*often passive*) [Pre-12C. < late Latin *cuprum* < Greek *Kupros* "Cyprus," important ancient source of copper] —**cop·per** *adj* —**cop·per·y** *adj*

cop·per[2] /kóppər/ *n* same as **police officer** (*slang insult*) [Mid-19C. < COP[1] (verb)]

cop·per·as /kóppərəss/ *n* MINERALS same as **ferrous sulfate** [15C. Via French < medieval Latin *cuperosa*]

Cop·per·as Cove /kóppərəss-/ city in central Texas, north of Austin. It is home to the US Army base at Fort Hood. Population: 29,599 (2002 estimate).

cop·per beech *n* a beech tree with dark reddish leaves. Native to: Europe.

cop·per-bot·tomed *adj* **1.** having a copper coating on the base **2.** certain or reliable, especially financially

cop·per·head /kóppər hèd/ (*plural* **-heads** or *same*) *n* **1.** a reddish brown poisonous snake of the viper family. Native to: central and eastern United States. Latin name: *Agkistrodon contortrix*. **2.** somebody living north of the Mason-Dixon Line who sympathized with the South during the Civil War (*informal*)

Cop·per·mine /kópper mīn/ river in northern Canada, flowing north from the Northwest Territories, through Nunavut, and into the Arctic Ocean. Length: 525 mi./845 km.

cop·per·plate /kóppər plàyt/ *n* **1.** PRINTING PLATE a polished copper printing plate with a design etched or engraved on it **2.** PRINT a print made from a copperplate **3.** NEAT HANDWRITING neat handwriting, especially in the style of copybooks produced from copperplates

cop·per py·rites *n* MINERALS same as **chalcopyrite**

cop·per·smith /kóppər smìth/ *n* somebody who makes or repairs copper objects

cop·per sul·fate *n* a poisonous blue compound containing copper and sulfur. Use: textile dyeing, electroplating, fungicides, wood preservatives. Formula: $CuSO_4$.

cop·pice /kóppiss/ *n* an area of densely growing small trees, especially one in which the trees are regularly cut back to encourage more growth ■ *vt* (**-piced, -pic·ing, -pic·es**) to cut back trees periodically to encourage young growth [Mid-14C. < Old French *copeïz* < *coper* (see COPE[1])]

Express Newspapers

Francis Ford Coppola

Cop·po·la /kóppələ/, **Francis Ford** (*b.* 1939) US movie director. He directed the *Godfather* trilogy (1972, 1974, 1990).

"*Apocalypse Now* is not about Vietnam, it is Vietnam. We were in the jungle; there were too many of us; we had access to too much money, too much equipment; and, little by little, we went insane."
[Francis Ford Coppola. Quoted in *Films Illustrated*; October 1979]

co·pra /kṓprə, kóp-/ *n* the dried flesh of a coconut, from which coconut oil is obtained [Late 16C. Via Portuguese < Malayalam *koppara*]

Cop·ra·tes /kópprə teez/ giant canyon on Mars running east–west to the equatorial region. It is over 500 mi./800 km long and 60 mi./95 km wide in places.

copro- *prefix* dung, excrement ○ *coprophilous* [< Greek *kopros*]

co·pro·ces·sor /kō pró sèssər/ *n* a second processor in a computer, improving performance by handling specialized tasks

cop·ro·la·li·a /kòpprə láylee ə/ *n* the uncontrolled use of violent and obscene language, especially as a result of an illness such as Tourette's syndrome

cop·ro·lite /kópprə līt/ *n* a piece of fossilized dung from which information about eating patterns in prehistoric times can be discovered —**cop·ro·lit·ic** /kòpprə líttik/ *adj*

cop·rol·o·gy /kə próllәjee/ *n* an obsession with defecation, especially as expressed in art and literature

cop·roph·a·gy /kə próffəjee/ *n* the eating of dung by some species of insects or animals —**cop·roph·a·gous** /kə próffəgəss/ *adj*

cop·ro·phil·i·a /kòpprə físllee ə/ *n* an obsessive and often sexual interest in feces and defecation —**cop·ro·phil·i·ac** *n* —**cop·ro·phil·ic** *adj*

cop·roph·i·lous /kə próffiləss/ *adj* describes organisms that live on or in dung, as some insects or fungi do

copse /kops/ *n* TREES same as **coppice** [Late 16C. Contraction]

cop shop *n* a police station (*informal*)

Copt /kopt/ *n* **1.** a member of the Coptic Church **2.** an Egyptian of non-Arab descent [Early 17C. Via French or modern Latin < Arabic *al-ḳibṭ* "the Copts" < Coptic *Gyptios* "Egyptian" < Greek *Aiguptios*]

cop·ter /kóptər/ *n* AVIAT same as **helicopter** (*informal*) [Mid-20C. Shortening]

Cop·tic /kóptik/ *n* a language formerly spoken in Egypt, a later form of ancient Egyptian and one of the Afro-Asiatic languages. Coptic survives as the liturgical language of Egyptian Monophysite Christians. ■ *adj* relating or belonging to the Copts, Coptic, or the Egyptian Monophysite Christian Church

Cop·tic Church *n* the Egyptian Christian Church, established in the 6th century and adhering to the doctrine of the Monophysites

cop·u·la /kóppyələ/ (*plural* **-las** or **-lae** /-lee/) *n* **1.** GRAM LINKING VERB a verb that links the subject of a sentence with an adjective or noun phrase **(complement)** relating to it, e.g., "be" or "seem" **2.** LOGIC LINK BETWEEN SUBJECT AND PREDICATE a form of the verb "to be" linking the subject and the predicate in some propositions, e.g., "are" in "Some dogs are poodles" **3.** LINK BETWEEN TWO THINGS anything that provides a link between two things (*formal*) [Early 17C. < Latin, "link"] —**cop·u·lar** *adj*

cop·u·late /kóppyə làyt/ (**-lat·ed, -lat·ing, -lates**) *vi* to have sexual intercourse [Early 17C. < Latin *copulat-*, past participle of *copulare* "join together" < *copula* "link"] —**cop·u·la·tion** /kòppyə láysh'n/ *n* —**cop·u·la·to·ry** /-lə tàwree/ *adj*

cop·u·la·tive /kóppyə làytiv, -lə-/ *adj* **1.** linking or joining (*formal*) **2.** relating to a verb that links the subject with its complement or to the function of such a verb (*technical*) —**cop·u·la·tive·ly** *adv*

cop·y /kóppee/ *n* (*plural* **-ies**) **1.** REPRODUCTION something that is made exactly like something else in appearance or function **2.** ONE OF MANY one of many identical specimens of something produced in large numbers, especially something printed or published **3.** WRITTEN TEXT the written text to be published in a book, newspaper, or magazine, as distinct from visual material or graphics ■ *v* (**-ied, -y·ing, -ies**) **1.** *vt* MAKE IDENTICAL VERSION OF SOMETHING to make another example or specimen that is exactly the same as something else **2.** *vt* DO SAME AS SOMEBODY to do exactly what somebody else does **3.** *vti* CHEAT BY DOING SAME to reproduce the work of another person fraudulently **4.** *vt* SEND COPY TO SOMEBODY to send a copy to somebody, especially a copy of a letter or other document ○ *All heads of departments should have been copied.* [14C. Via French < Latin *copia* "abundance"] —**cop·y·a·ble** *adj*

SYNONYMS *copy, reproduce, duplicate, clone, replicate, re-create*

CORE MEANING: to make something that resembles something else to a greater or lesser degree

copy to make another example or specimen that is exactly the same as something else ○ *Please complete this form or carefully copy all the information on to a plain sheet of paper.* **reproduce** to make a copy of something by technical means ○ *an attempt to reproduce human speech digitally* ○ *No part of this publication may be reproduced without the prior permission of the publisher.* **duplicate** to make an identical version of something one or more times ○ *Give the notes to my assistant so they can be duplicated.* ○ *She had duplicated in adult life the pattern of behavior she had learned as a child.* **clone** to make a near or exact copy, especially of a piece of equipment or biological material. ○ *the scientist who first cloned sheep* ○ *The gene has been cloned and sequenced.* **replicate** to make an identical version of something repeatedly and exactly, or do something again in exactly the same way ○ *anecdotal evidence which cannot be replicated in the laboratory* ○ *The original findings have been replicated by other investigators.* **re-create** to make something that appears to be the same as something that no longer exists, or that exists in a different place ○ *The company has gone all-out to re-create the play's 1970s atmosphere.* ○ *At their best, gardens can re-create a corner of paradise.*

---

copy down *vt* to make a written copy of something ○ *Reporters copied down his every word.*
copy in *vt* same as **copy** *v* (sense 4)

cop·y·book /kóppee bòòk/ *n* a book containing models of handwriting for young students to copy ■ *adj* following guidelines slavishly and showing no originality

cop·y·boy /kóppee bòy/ *n* somebody who runs errands in a newspaper office

cop·y·cat /kóppee kàt/ (*informal*) *n* somebody, especially a child, who slavishly imitates another ■ *adj* done in close imitation of somebody or something else

cop·y cloth·ing *n Hong Kong* clothes that are copies of designer garments, usually passed off as genuine

cop·y desk *n* a desk at which written material is edited for publication

cop·y·ed·it /kóppee èddət/ (**-it·ed, -it·ing, -its**) *vti* to read written material and correct it for publication

cop·y·ed·i·tor /kóppee èddətər/ *n* a reader and corrector of written texts for publication

cop·y·hold·er /kóppee hōldər/ *n* **1.** a stand that holds documents upright while they are being read or keyed **2.** somebody who reads written material aloud to a proofreader

cop·y·ist /kóppee ist/ *n* **1.** somebody who makes copies of handwritten documents or music **2.** a mere imitator of others

cop·y ma·chine *n* same as **photocopier**

cop·y pro·tec·tion *n* a means of preventing unauthorized duplication of computer software —**cop·y-pro·tect·ed** *adj*

cop·y·read·er /kóppee reèdər/ *n* somebody who reads and edits newspaper articles to prepare them for publication

cop·y·right /kóppee rīt/ *n* **CREATIVE ARTIST'S CONTROL OF ORIGINAL WORK** the legal right of creative artists or publishers to control the use and reproduction of their original works ■ *adj* **PROTECTED BY COPYRIGHT** controlled or restricted by a copyright ■ *vt* (**-right·ed, -right·ing, -rights**) **GET COPYRIGHT OF SOMETHING** to secure the copyright on a creative work —**cop·y·right·a·ble** *adj*—**cop·y·right·er** *n*

cop·y·right de·pos·it li·brar·y *n* a library that receives a free copy of every book published in the United States

~~copywright, copywrite~~ incorrect spelling of **copyright**

cop·y·writ·er /kóppee rītər/ *n* somebody who writes advertisements or promotional material —**cop·y·writ·ing** *n*

coq au vin /kòk ō váN, -ván/ (*plural* **coqs au vin** /kòk-/ or **coq au vins** /-váNz, -vánz/) *n* a dish of chicken cooked in red wine with other ingredients [< French, "cock in wine"]

co·quet /kō két/ (*literary*) *vi* (**-quet·ted, -quet·ting, -quets**) **1. FLIRT** to act coyly and flirtatiously **2. ACT FRIVOLOUSLY** to act casually or frivolously ■ *n* **MAN WHO FLIRTS** a flirtatious man [Late 17C. < French, "little cock" < *coq* "cock"] —**co·quet·ry** /kṓkətree/ *n*

co·quette /kō két/ *n* a flirtatious woman [Mid-17C. < French, feminine of *coquet* (see COQUET)] —**co·quet·tish** *adj*—**co·quet·tish·ly** *adv*—**co·quet·tish·ness** *n*

co·quille /kō keél/ *n* **1. SEAFOOD DISH** a dish of seafood baked and served in a scallop shell or a scallop-shaped dish **2. SHELL OR SHELL-SHAPED DISH** a scallop shell or a scallop-shaped dish **3.** FENCING **GUARD ON FOIL** a bell-shaped guard on a fencing foil [< French (see COCKLE[1])]

co·qui·na /kō keénə/ *n* **1.** a soft limestone formed largely from crushed shells and coral. Use: building material in the Caribbean and the southeastern United States. **2.** a small clam common off the coasts of the eastern and southern United States. Genus: *Donax*. [Mid-19C. < Spanish, "cockle shell"]

co·qui·to /kō keétō/ (*plural* **-tos** or *same*) *n* a palm tree with edible nuts and sweet sap that is used to make wine. Native to: Chile. Latin name: *Jubaea chilensis*. [Mid-19C. < Spanish, "little coco shell" < Portuguese *côco* (see COCO)]

cor. *abbr* **1.** corner **2.** MUSIC cornet **3.** correction **4.** COMMUNICATION correspondence **5.** MEDIA correspondent

Cor. *abbr* BIBLE Corinthians

cor·a·cle /káwrək'l/ *n* a small round boat made from animal skins stretched over a wicker frame [Mid-16C. < Welsh *corwgl* < Middle Irish *curach*]

cor·a·coid /káwrə kòyd/ *n* a bony projection on the shoulder blade in most mammals [Mid-18C. Via modern Latin < Greek *korakoeidēs* "like a crow" (from its resemblance to a crow's beak) < *korax* "crow, raven"]

coral

cor·al /káwrəl/ *n* **1. MARINE ORGANISM** a marine organism that lives in colonies and has an external skeleton. Class: Anthozoa. **2. HARD MARINE DEPOSIT** a hard deposit consisting of the skeletons of coral, often forming ocean reefs **3. SOMETHING MADE OF CORAL** a piece of coral, especially red coral or an object made from one **4. DEEP PINKISH ORANGE COLOR** a deep pinkish orange color **5. LOBSTER'S OR CRAB'S EGGS** the unfertilized eggs of a lobster or crab that turn pinkish orange when cooked [14C. Via French < Greek *korallion*] —**cor·al** *adj*—**cor·al·loid** *adj*

cor·al bean *n* TREES same as **coral tree**

cor·al·bells *npl* a perennial plant that produces clusters of tiny pinkish orange or white bell-shaped flowers. Native to: southwestern United States, Mexico. Latin name: *Heuchera sanguinea*.

cor·al·ber·ry /káwrəl bèrree/ (*plural* **-ries** or *same*) *n* **1.** a bush that produces dark red berries that persist into winter. Native to: North America. Latin name: *Symphoricarpos orbiculatus*. **2.** an evergreen bush. Native to: eastern Asia. Genus: *Ardisia*.

Cor·al Ga·bles /kàwrəl gáyb'lz/ city on Biscayne Bay in Florida, west of Miami. It is home to the University of Miami. Population: 42,631 (2002 estimate).

cor·al·line /káwrə lìn, -lin/ *adj* **1. OF OR LIKE CORAL** relating to or resembling coral **2. PINKISH** of a pinkish red or pinkish orange color ■ *n* **1. CALCIUM-COVERED RED ALGA** a red alga whose fronds are covered or impregnated with calcium deposits. Genus: *Corallina*. **2. ORGANISM THAT RESEMBLES CORAL** a sponge or other organism that resembles coral

cor·al reef *n* an ocean reef composed of the skeletons of living coral, together with minerals and organic matter

cor·al·root /káwrəl ròot/ (*plural* **-roots** or *same*) *n* a leafless orchid with small insignificant flowers that feeds through roots that resemble coral. Genus: *Corallorhiza*.

Cor·al Sea sea in the southwestern Pacific Ocean bounded by Australia, New Guinea, the Solomon Islands, and Vanuatu

cor·al snake *n* **1.** a poisonous and mainly nocturnal snake that is strikingly marked with red, black, and yellow or white bands. Native to: North and South America. Genera: *Micrurus* or *Micruroides*. **2.** a poisonous snake that is red with yellow and black bands. Native to: eastern Australia. Latin name: *Brachyurophis australis*.

Cor·al Springs city in southeastern Florida, northwest of Fort Lauderdale and southwest of Boca Raton. Population: 125,674 (2002 estimate).

cor·al tree *n* a thorny bush or small tree with brightly colored seeds growing in long pods and flowers that are pollinated by birds. Flowers: large, red or orange. Native to: tropical and subtropical regions. Genus: *Erythrina*.

cor an·glais /kàwr awng gláy/ (*plural same* or **cors an·glais** /*pronunc. same*/) *n Can, UK* a woodwind instrument like an oboe but larger and lower-pitched. US term **English horn** [< French, "English horn"]

co·ran·to /kə rántō, -raán-/ (*plural* **-tos**) *n* DANCE same as **courante** (sense 2) [Mid-16C. Alteration of French *courante* "running"]

cor·ban /káwr bàn, -baàn, kawr bán, -baán/ *n* **1.** an offering to God made by the ancient Hebrew people **2.** an offering made to the Temple of Jerusalem [14C. Via Greek < Hebrew *qorbān* "offering" < *qārab* "approach"]

cor·beau /kàwr bṓ/ *n Carib* BIRDS same as **black vulture** (sense 1)

cor·beil /káwrb'l, kawr báy/, **cor·beille** *n* a stone carving of a basket of fruit or flowers as a feature on a building [Mid-18C. Via French *corbeille* < late Latin *corbicula* "small basket" < Latin *corbis* "basket"]

corbel

cor·bel /káwrb'l, -bèl/ *n* **SUPPORTING STONE BRACKET** a bracket of brick or stone that juts out of a wall to support a structure above it ■ *vt* (**-beled, -bel·ing, -bels**) **1. LAY MASONRY UNITS TO FORM PROJECTION** to lay stones or bricks in layers so that each juts out above the one below to form a supporting bracket **2. SUPPORT SOMETHING WITH CORBELS** to support a cornice or other structure on corbels [14C. < Old French, "little raven" < *corp* "raven" < Latin *corvus*; from its original profile resembling a beak from being cut slantwise]

cor·bel·ing /káwrbəling, -bèlling/ *n* a structural system using corbels as supports

Cor·bett /káwrbət/, **James John** (1866–1933) US boxer. He was the world heavyweight boxing champion from 1892 to 1897. Known as **Gentleman Jim**

cor·bie-step, **cor·bie·step** /káwrbee stèp/ *n* each of a series of decorative steps going up the side of a gable [< the idea that only crows can reach them]

cor·bi·na /kawr beénə/ (*plural* **-nas** or *same*), **cor·vi·na** /kawr veénə/ *n* a food and game fish that is popular with anglers along the coast of California. Native to: Pacific. Latin name: *Menticirrhus undulatus*. [Early 20C. Via American Spanish < Spanish *corvino* "like a raven" (from its color) < Latin *corvinus* (see CORVINE)]

Cor·bu·sier ♦ **Le Corbusier**

cord /kawrd/ *n* **1. STRING OR ROPE** thick strong string or thin rope ○ *cords of Venetian blinds* **2. ELECTRIC CABLE** flexible insulated electric cable **3. BODY PART RESEMBLING ROPE** a part of the body resembling cord, e.g., the spinal cord or the umbilical cord **4. FASTENING OR BELT** a length of material used as a fastening or belt **5. RIBBED FABRIC** any fabric with a ribbed surface, especially corduroy **6. UNIT OF VOLUME FOR CUT TIMBER** a unit of volume for cut timber, equal to 128 cu. ft. (approximately 3.6 cu. m) ■ **cords** *npl* **PANTS** corduroy pants (*informal*) ○ *a pair of cords* ■ *vt* (**cord·ed, cord·ing, cords**) **1. TIE SOMETHING WITH CORD** to fasten or tie something with cord or rope ○ *Are the packages corded and ready to ship?* **2. STACK WOOD IN CORDS** to stack wood in units with a volume of one cord [13C. Via Old French *corde* < Latin *chorda* < Greek *khordē* "string"] —**cord·er** *n*

USAGE See *chord*[1].

cord·age /káwrdij/ *n* **1.** the amount of wood in a stack, measured in cords **2.** ropes or cords collectively, especially the lines and rigging of a ship

cor·date /káwr dàyt/ *adj* describes a leaf that is heart-shaped [Mid-18C. < modern Latin *cordatus* < Latin *cord-* "heart"] —**cor·date·ly** *adv*

Cor·day /kawr dáy/, **Charlotte** (1768–93) French assassin. She supported the moderate Girondins during the French Revolution, and was guillotined after murdering the Jacobin extremist Jean Paul Marat. Full name **Corday d'Armont, Marie Anne Charlotte**

cord·ed /káwrdəd/ *adj* **1. RIBBED** describes a fabric with a ribbed surface **2. TIED UP** securely tied up with string or rope **3. WITH TIGHT MUSCLES** having tensed or well-developed muscles visible as ridges or ripples

Cor·de·li·a /kawr deélee ə/ *n* a small natural satellite of Uranus, discovered in 1986 by the Voyager 2 planetary probe. Its gravitational influence appears to help stabilize the outer ring of Uranus.

cord grass *n* a coarse grass found on coastal salt marshes or mudflats. Genus: *Spartina*.

cor·dial /káwrjəl/ *adj* **1.** HOSPITABLY WARM friendly and affectionate **2.** DEEPLY FELT sincere or profound (*literary*) ○ *has a cordial dislike for dogs* **3.** REFRESHING stimulating or invigorating (*literary*) ■ *n* **1.** BEVERAGES same as **liqueur** **2.** TONIC a stimulating or medicinal drink [14C. < medieval Latin *cordialis* "of the heart" < Latin *cord-* "heart"] —**cor·dial·ly** *adv* —**cor·dial·ness** *n*

cor·dial·i·ty /kàwr jállətee, -jee állətee/ *n* friendliness and affection ○ *We were surprised by the cordiality of their response.*

cor·di·er·ite /káwrdee ə rìt/ *n* a purplish blue or gray aluminosilicate mineral containing magnesium and iron. Source: metamorphic rocks. [Early 19C. After Pierre L. *Cordier* (1777–1861), French geologist]

cor·dil·le·ra /kàwrd'l yérrə/ (*plural* **-ras**) *n* a system of mountain ranges consisting of approximately parallel ridges [Early 18C. < Spanish < *cordilla* "small cord" < *cuerda* "cord" < Latin *chorda* (see CORD)]

Cor·dil·le·ras /kàwrd'l yérrəz/, **Cor·dil·le·ra** system of mountain ranges in western North America, including the Sierra Nevada, the Coast and Cascade ranges, and the Rocky Mountains. Highest peak: Mount McKinley 20,320 ft./6,194 m.

cord·ite /káwr dìt/ *n* a smokeless explosive, usually made of gunpowder and nitroglycerin [Late 19C. < CORD; from its stringy appearance]

cord·less /káwrdləss/ *adj* powered by an internal battery and not needing to be continuously attached by a cable to an external electricity supply

cord·less tel·e·phone *n* a telephone, powered by a recharging battery, with a portable handset that can be removed from its base unit and has a short-range radio link to it

cór·do·ba /káwrdəbə/ *n* the main unit of Nicaraguan currency. See table at **currency** [Early 20C. After Francisco Fernández de *Córdoba* (1475–1526), Spanish explorer]

Cor·do·ba /káwrdəbə/, **Cór·do·ba** **1.** city and capital of Cordoba Province in central Argentina. It is the site of the National University of Cordoba, founded in 1613. Population: 1,157,507 (1991). **2.** *also* **Cor·do·va** /káwrdō vaà/ city in Andalusia, southern Spain. It is the capital of Córdoba Province. Population: 314,805 (2002). **3.** resort and trading city in east central Mexico. Population: 170,652 (2000).

cor·don /káwrd'n, -dòn/ *n* **1.** PEOPLE OR VEHICLES ENCIRCLING AREA a line of police officers or soldiers, or their vehicles, surrounding an area to control access to it **2.** RIBBON a piece of ribbon worn for decoration or as a sign of rank or a mark of honor **3.** GARDENING FRUIT TREE WITH SHORT SIDE SHOOTS a fruit tree grown as a single stem at an angle against a support, with its side branches pruned back close to the stem **4.** ARCHIT same as **stringcourse** [Late 16C. < Old French, "small cord" < *corde* (see CORD)]
cordon off (**cordoned off, cordoning off, cordons off**) *vt* to surround an area with a line of police officers, soldiers, or their vehicles, to control access to it

cor·don bleu /kàwr dawn blő, -doN-/ *adj* **1.** OF HIGHEST CLASS describes a cook or cooking of the highest class **2.** WITH CHEESE AND HAM describes a way of preparing meat, especially veal, by rolling a thin slice around cheese and ham and then coating in breadcrumbs ■ *n* (*plural* **cor·don bleus**) **1.** MASTER CHEF a cook of the very highest class, especially a master chef **2.** KNIGHT'S RIBBON a blue ribbon worn by knights of the highest order in Bourbon France [Early 18C. < French, "blue ribbon"]

cor·don sa·ni·taire /kawr dàwN saanee tér/ *n* **1.** a barrier erected to control the spread of a disease by restricting movement to and from the infected area **2.** a neutral state, or a string of neutral states, lying between two states that are hostile to each other [Mid-19C. < French, "sanitary line"]

Cor·do·va /kawr dővə/ **1.** city in southeastern Alaska, on the northern shore of Prince William Sound, southeast of Anchorage. Population: 2,395 (2002 estimate). **2.** ♦ **Cordoba**

cor·do·van /káwrdəvən/ *n* a fine soft leather originally made from goatskin and now usually made from horsehide [Late 16C. < Spanish *cordován*, after CORDOBA, Spain]

cor·du·roy /káwrdə ròy/ *n* a heavy cotton fabric with a ribbed nap running lengthwise ■ **cor·du·roys** *npl* pants made of corduroy [Late 18C. Probably < CORD + *duroy*, a coarse woolen fabric]

cor·du·roy road *n* a road made of logs across muddy or swampy ground [Because its surface resembles corduroy]

cord·wood /káwrd wòod/ *n* wood in stacks with a volume of one cord, or cut into lengths of 4 ft./1.2 m for stacking in cords

core /kawr/ *n* **1.** ESSENTIAL PART the central or most important part of something ○ *the core of the argument* **2.** CENTRAL PART OF FRUIT the fibrous central part of some fruit, containing the seeds **3.** GEOL CENTER OF EARTH the central part of Earth, or the corresponding part of another astronomical object. Earth's core is molten in parts and is composed of an alloy of iron and nickel. **4.** COMPUT COMPUTER MEMORY the main memory of a computer, which was composed of arrays of ring-shaped magnets before the introduction of semiconductor memories **5.** COMPUT PIECE OF COMPUTER MEMORY formerly, a ring-shaped piece of magnetic material used to store digital data in a computer, each core representing one binary digit (**bit**) **6.** GEOL SAMPLE OBTAINED BY DRILLING a tubular segment of rock, ice, or other material obtained as a study sample by drilling **7.** INDUST CENTRAL PART OF NUCLEAR REACTOR the central part of a nuclear reactor in which fission takes place **8.** ELEC IRON IN TRANSFORMER a block of iron in a coil or transformer, used to intensify and direct the magnetic field produced by a current in surrounding coils **9.** PREHIST STONE USED TO MAKE TOOLS a block of stone from which tools or flakes are chipped ■ *adj* ESSENTIAL of central or fundamental importance ○ *The company's core business is steel manufacturing.* ○ *core competencies* ■ *vt* (**cored, cor·ing, cores**) TAKE CORE OUT OF FRUIT to remove the core from a piece of fruit [13C. Origin ?] —**cor·er** *n*

CORE /kawr/ *abbr* Congress of Racial Equality

core cit·y *n* GEOG same as **inner city**

core com·pe·ten·cy *n* an area of expertise that is fundamental to a particular job or function

core cur·ric·u·lum *n* the subjects that all students are required to study at school

core dump *n* **1.** a transfer of data from the main memory of a computer, usually to external storage **2.** a long-winded response to a simple question (*informal humorous*)

co·ref·er·en·tial /kō refə rénshəl/ *adj* referring to the same person or thing ○ *In the sentence "Mary lost her purse," "Mary" and "her" are coreferential.*

~~**corelate**~~ incorrect spelling of **correlate**

co·re·lig·ion·ist /kō ri líjjənist/ *n* an offensive term for somebody of the same religion as another person whose beliefs are disapproved of

Co·rel·li /kə réllee/, **Arcangelo** (1653–1713) Italian composer and violinist. He was a virtuoso violinist. His chamber music set a baroque style that influenced Johann Sebastian Bach.

core mem·o·ry *n* COMPUT same as **core** *n* (sense 4)

co·req /kō rék/ *n* EDUC same as **corequisite** (*informal*)

co·req·ui·site /kō rékwizit/ *n* a course of study that must be taken along with another

~~**corespondence**~~ incorrect spelling of **correspondence**

co·re·spon·dent, **co·re·spon·dent** /kō ri spóndənt/ *n* somebody named in a divorce suit as the alleged adulterous sexual partner of the respondent —**co·re·spon·den·cy** *n*

core sub·ject *n* a subject that all students are required to study at school, e.g., English or mathematics

core time *n* the part of the working day during which workers on flextime must be present at work

corf /kawrf/ (*plural* **corves** /kawrvz/) *n* a wagon used inside a mine for transporting mined coal or ore [15C. Via Middle Dutch or Middle Low German *korf* "basket" < Latin *corbis*]

Cor·fu /kawr fóo, káwr fòo/ most northerly island in the Ionian Islands, west of Greece. It is a major tourist center. Population: 107,592 (1991). Area: 247 sq. mi./641 sq. km.

cor·gi /káwrgee/ (*plural* **-gis**) *n* a small dog with short legs and smooth hair, belonging to one of two breeds, the Cardigan Welsh corgi and the Pembroke Welsh corgi [Early 20C. < Welsh < *cor* "dwarf" + *ci* "dog"]

cor·i·a·ceous /kàwree áyshəss/ *adj* like leather in texture or appearance (*technical*) [Late 17C. < late Latin *coriaceus* < Latin *corium* "leather"]

co·ri·an·der /kàwree ándər/ *n* **1.** the leaves or seeds of an aromatic plant, or a powder made from the crushed seeds. Use: food seasoning. **2.** the annual aromatic plant from which coriander is taken. Native to: Asia, Mediterranean. Latin name: *Coriandrum sativum*. [13C. Via French < Greek *koriandron*]

Cor·inth /káwrinth/ **1.** ancient Greek city and modern town 3 mi./5 km to its northeast. The ruins of the ancient city are about 50 mi./80 km west of Athens. Population: 27,412 (1991). Greek name **Kórinthos** **2.** city in the northeastern corner of Mississippi, the site of a major Civil War battle. Population: 14,019 (2002 estimate).

Co·rin·thi·an /kə rínthee ən/ *adj* **1.** OF CORINTH relating to the ancient Greek city or modern Greek town of Corinth **2.** ARCHIT SLENDER AND ORNATE AT TOP describes a slender architectural column with an ornate capital **3.** DEBAUCHED debauched or ostentatiously luxurious (*literary*) **4.** SPORTS OF SPORTS CLUB used in the name of sports clubs and competitions ■ *n* **1.** SOMEBODY FROM CORINTH somebody from Corinth in Greece **2.** SPORTS WEALTHY SPORTSPERSON a wealthy amateur sportsperson, especially somebody fond of yachting (*humorous*)

Co·rin·thi·an or·der *n* an ancient Greek order of architecture characterized by a slender column with an ornate capital [< its origin in CORINTH]

Co·rin·thi·ans /kə rínthee ənz/ *n* either of two books of the Bible, originally letters addressed to the church at Corinth and traditionally attributed to St. Paul. (*takes a singular verb*) See table at **Bible**

Co·ri·o·la·nus /kàwree ə láynəss, kə rì ə lánnəss/ *n* in Roman legend, the defeater of the Volsci in the 5th century B.C.

Co·ri·o·lis ef·fect /kàwree őliss-/ *n* the observed deflection of something such as a missile in flight relative to the surface of Earth, caused by Earth's rotation beneath the object. The deflection is to the right in the northern hemisphere and to the left in the southern hemisphere. [After Gaspard de *Coriolis* (1792–1843), French mathematician]

Co·ri·o·lis force /kàwri őliss-/ *n* an apparent but nonexistent force used to describe the effect of Earth's rotation on the motion of moving objects [See CORIOLIS EFFECT]

co·ri·um /káwree əm/ (*plural* **-ri·a** /-ree ə/) *n* **1.** MED same as **dermis** **2.** the leathery middle part of the forewing of some insects [Early 19C. < Latin, "hide, leather"]

cork /kawrk/ *n* **1.** BOTTLE STOPPER a usually cylindrical piece of material used as a bottle stopper **2.** OUTER BARK OF CORK OAK the light flexible outer bark of the cork oak tree. Use: for bottle stoppers, as an insulator. **3.** FISHING FLOAT USED IN FISHING a small float used in fishing to maintain a hook or net suspended in the water **4.** BOT LAYER OF PLANT TISSUE dead tissue that forms a protective outer layer on plants and is part of the bark in woody plants ■ *vt* (**corked, cork·ing, corks**) **1.** SEAL CONTAINER WITH CORK to stop or seal something, especially a bottle, with a cork **2.** RESTRAIN FEELINGS to restrain feelings, especially strong negative ones such as anger or grief (*informal*) **3.** BLACKEN FACE AND HANDS to blacken something, especially somebody's face and hands, with charred cork [13C. Probably via Middle Dutch < Arabic dialect *kurk* "cork-soled sandal"] ◇ **blow** *or* **pop your cork** to lose your temper (*slang*)

Cork /kawrk/ **1.** county town of County Cork, southern Ireland. It is a port on the Lee River and the second largest city in the Republic of Ireland. Population: 123,062 (2002). **2.** coastal county in Munster Province, southwestern Republic of Ireland. Population: 420,510 (2002). Area: 1,231 sq. mi./3,188 sq. km.

cork·age /káwrkij/ *n* a fee charged at some restaurants for serving wine and other alcoholic drinks that customers bring in from elsewhere

cork·board /káwrk bàwrd/ *n* **1.** a thin sheet made from compressed cork granules, typically used as a floor covering and as wall insulation before plastic was available **2.** a bulletin board made with compressed cork granules

cork cam·bi·um *n* a zone of actively dividing tissue near the outer surface of a woody plant that produces cork

corked /kawrkt/ *adj* **1.** SEALED sealed or stopped with a cork or other object **2.** TAINTED BY CORK given an unpleasant flavor by substances from a tainted cork ○ *Waiter, this wine's corked!* **3.** BLACKENED blackened with burnt cork

cork·er /káwrkər/ *n* **1.** a person or machine that fits corks, especially into bottles **2.** *UK* somebody or something particularly striking or special (*informal*) ○ *It was a corker of a day.*

cork oak *n* an evergreen oak whose thick bark is a source of cork. Native to: Mediterranean. Latin name: *Quercus suber*.

cork·screw /káwrk skrōō/ *n* DEVICE FOR REMOVING CORKS FROM BOTTLES a device for taking corks out of bottles, usually a pointed spiral of metal attached to a handle or simple lever ■ *v* (**-screwed, -screw·ing, -screws**) **1.** *vi* MOVE IN SPIRAL PATH to move in a spiral path ○ *watched anxiously as the plane corkscrewed toward the ground* **2.** *vt* WIND SOMETHING IN SPIRAL to wind or twist something in a spiral ■ *adj* SPIRAL-SHAPED shaped like a spiral ○ *corkscrew curls*

cork tree *n* TREES same as **cork oak**

cork·wood /káwrk wòod/ (*plural* **-woods** or *same*) *n* **1.** a deciduous bush or small tree that grows in wetlands and has light porous wood. Native to: southeastern United States. Latin name: *Leitneria floridana*. **2.** the light, porous wood of the corkwood or any similar wood, e.g., balsa

cork·y /káwrkee/ (**-i·er, -i·est**) *adj* **1.** made from or resembling cork **2.** having the taste or smell of cork —**cork·i·ness** *n*

corm /kawrm/ *n* a short swollen underground stem base in some plants such as crocuses and gladioli that stores food over the winter and produces new foliage in the spring. New corms often form on top of old ones and are used as a means of propagating new plants. [Mid-19C. Via modern Latin < Greek *kormos* "lopped-off tree trunk"] —**cor·mous** *adj*

cormorant

cor·mo·rant /káwrmərənt/ *n* **1.** a large diving bird with webbed feet, a hooked beak, and a long neck that can expand to swallow fish. Native to: coastal waters. Family: Phalacrocoracidae. **2.** somebody considered greedy or rapacious (*informal*) [13C. Alteration of Old French *cormaran* "sea raven" < *corp* "raven" + *marenc* "of the sea" (< Latin *marinus*)]

corn[1] /kawrn/ *n* **1.** GRAIN OF CEREAL PLANT the grain of a tall annual cereal plant that produces densely packed ears of grains attached to a central core. Use: as a vegetable, ground for flour, to produce oil, or for livestock feed. **2.** CEREAL PLANT PRODUCING CORN the cereal crop that yields corn. It has been cultivated as a food crop since ancient times. Native to: Central, South America. Latin name: *Zea mays*. **3.** *UK, Ireland* WHEAT, BARLEY, OR OATS any cereal crop, especially wheat, barley, or oats **4.** METEOROL, SKIING same as **corn snow** **5.** BEVERAGES same as **corn whiskey** **6.** CORNY ITEM OR MATERIAL something trite or overly sentimental (*informal*) ■ *vt* FOOD INDUST PRESERVE FOOD WITH SALT to preserve food using grains of salt or brine [Old English < Indo-European, "grain"]

corn[2] /kawrn/ *n* a hardened or thickened, often painful, area of skin, usually on a toe, caused by friction or pressure [14C. Via French < Latin *cornu* "horn"]

corn·ball /káwrn bàwl/ (*informal*) *n* somebody regarded as naively sentimental ■ *adj* trite or overly sentimental ○ *a cornball movie* [Mid-20C. Originally "sweet ball of popcorn," often sold at carnivals and regarded as unsophisticated]

Corn Belt *n* the area of the Great Plains and the Midwest where corn and soybeans are the principal crops

corn bor·er *n* a moth whose larvae bore into and feed on corn. There are different species, including the European corn borer and the southern corn borer. Family: Pyralidae.

corn·braid /káwrn bràyd/ HAIR *n* same as **cornrow** ■ *vt* (**-braid·ed, -braid·ing, -braids**) same as **cornrow**

corn bread, corn·bread /káwrn brèd/ *n* bread made from cornmeal

corn broom *n US regional, Can* a push broom that is strong enough to use outdoors

REGIONAL NOTE See *yard broom*.

corn cake *n Southern US* FOOD same as **johnnycake**

corn chip *n* a crisp thin piece of fried cornmeal batter, eaten as a snack food

corn·cob /káwrn kòb/ *n* the hard core of an ear of corn, on which the kernels grow

corn·cob pipe *n* a pipe for smoking tobacco with a bowl made from part of a dried corncob

corn·cock·le /káwrn kòk'l/ (*plural* **-les** or *same*) *n* an annual plant with poisonous seeds, once common as a weed in grain fields. Flowers: reddish purple. Native to: Mediterranean. Latin name: *Agrostemma githago*. [Early 18C. < CORN[1] + COCKLE[2]]

corn·crake /káwrn kràyk/ *n* a speckled bird with a harsh call, a short beak, and reddish wings. Native to: fields and meadows of Europe and Asia. Latin name: *Crex crex*.

corn·crib /káwrn krìb/ *n* a ventilated building used for the storage and drying of corn

corn·dodg·er /káwrn dòjjər/ *n Southern US* a ball of cornmeal batter that is deep-fried, baked, or boiled

corn dog *n* a hot dog on a stick, coated in cornmeal batter and deep-fried, typically sold at fairs and carnivals

corn·dog·ging /káwrn dàwging, -dògging/ *n* a surfing initiation ritual in which a surfer is rolled in sand after surfing by his or her fellow surfers (*slang*)

cor·ne·a /káwrnee ə/ (*plural* **-as** or **-ae** /-nee èe/) *n* the transparent convex membrane that covers the pupil and iris of the eye [14C. < medieval Latin *cornea tela* "horny tissue" < Latin *cornu* "horn"; from its fibrous consistency] —**cor·ne·al** *adj*

corn ear·worm *n* a large striped American moth larva that feeds destructively on corn, tomatoes, cotton bolls, and many other plants. Latin name: *Heliothis zea*.

corned /kawrnd/ *adj* cooked and then preserved in salt or brine ○ *corned mutton* [Early 17C. < CORN[1] "preserve with salt"]

corned beef *n* beef that has been cooked, preserved in salt or brine, and often canned

Cor·neille /kawr náy/, **Pierre** (1606–84) French playwright. His plays include the tragedies *Le Cid* (1637), *Horace* (1640), and *Polyeucte* (1643).

> "Who is all-powerful should fear all things."
> [Pierre Corneille, *Cinna*; 1641]

cor·nel /káwrn'l/ (*plural* **-nels** or *same*) *n* any plant related to dogwood. Genus: *Cornus*. [15C. < Old French *corneille* < Latin *cornus*]

cor·nel·ian /kawr néelyən/ *n* MINERALS same as **carnelian**

cor·nel·ian cher·ry *n* a small deciduous tree cultivated for its clusters of bright yellow spring flowers and small red sour fruits. Native to: southern Europe. Latin name: *Cornus mas*.

Cor·nell /kawr nél/, **Joseph** (1903–72) US sculptor. He is best known for his assemblages of surreal objects enclosed in small glass-fronted wooden boxes.

Cor·nell, Katharine (1898–1974) US stage actor who achieved international recognition from the 1920s until 1960

cor·ner /káwrnər/ *n* **1.** MEETING OF LINES OR SURFACES the angle formed where two or more lines or surfaces meet ○ *the four corners of a square* **2.** AREA ENCLOSED BY CONVERGING LINES the area enclosed where two lines or surfaces meet ○ *the corner of the room* **3.** PROJECTING PART OF SOMETHING a projecting angular part of something ○ *She bumped her knee on the corner of the table.* **4.** PLACE WHERE TWO ROADS MEET the place where two roads or streets meet ○ *the store on the corner* **5.** DIFFICULT SITUATION a difficult or embarrassing position, especially one from which there is no easy way of escape ○ *got himself into a corner about his previous statements* **6.** QUIET PLACE a secluded, peaceful, or secret place ○ *Let's find a quiet corner where we can sit and talk.* **7.** REMOTE PLACE an area or place, especially one that is remote ○ *Explorers then voyaged to every corner of the world.* **8.** OBJECT PUT OVER CORNER an object made to fit over a corner of something, especially to protect it ○ *a diary with metal corners* **9.** COMM CONTROL OF MARKET a monopoly of a particular commodity acquired in order to control its market price **10.** BASEBALL PART OF BASEBALL STRIKE ZONE in baseball, a location on either edge of home plate, forming part of the strike zone **11.** SPORTS PART OF PLAYING FIELD OR SURFACE in various sports, part of the playing field or surface where two boundaries meet **12.** HOCKEY, FOOTBALL KICK OR SHOT FROM CORNER in some sports, a free kick or shot from a corner of the field given to the attacking team when a defending player knocks the ball over the goal line **13.** BOXING, WRESTLING PART OF RING in boxing and wrestling, any of the four parts of a ring where the ropes are attached to the posts, especially the two where the competitors rest between rounds ■ *adj* **1.** LOCATED ON CORNER situated on a street corner ○ *a corner store* **2.** INTENDED FOR CORNER intended to be put in a corner ○ *a corner cabinet* **3.** SITUATED AT CORNER at or in a corner of something ○ *sat at a corner table* ■ *v* (**-nered, -ner·ing, -ners**) **1.** *vt* FORCE SOMEBODY INTO DIFFICULT POSITION to force a person or an animal into a position from which escape is difficult **2.** *vt* PUT SOMEBODY OR SOMETHING IN CORNER to place somebody or something in a corner **3.** *vt* PROVIDE SOMETHING WITH CORNERS to give corners to something **4.** *vt* COMM ACQUIRE MONOPOLY WITHIN COMMERCIAL MARKET to acquire a monopoly of a particular commodity and so be able to control its market price ○ *an attempt to corner the soybean market* **5.** *vi* TURN CORNER to drive around a corner (*refers to vehicles or their drivers*) **6.** *vti* HOCKEY, FOOTBALL TAKE CORNER in some sports, to take a free kick or hit from a corner of the field on the opponents' goal line [13C. < Anglo-Norman < Latin *cornua*, plural of *cornu* "horn, point"] ◇ **cut corners** to do something in a quicker, cheaper, or less careful way than is desirable or wise ◇ **in somebody's corner** providing somebody with support ○ *You can't lose with him in your corner.* ◇ **turn the corner** to get past the worst part of a difficult or dangerous situation

cor·ner·back /káwrnər bàk/ *n* in football, either of two defensive halfbacks placed behind the linebackers and near the sidelines

Cor·ner Brook /káwrnər-/ city on the western coast of the province of Newfoundland, Canada, on the Humber River. Population: 20,009 (2001).

cor·nered /káwrnərd/ *adj* **1.** IN DIFFICULT POSITION in a difficult or embarrassing position, especially when there is no easy way of escape **2.** WITH CORNERS with a particular number or type of corners (*usually used in combination*) **3.** WITH NUMBER OF CONTENDERS with a particular number of contenders ○ *a three-cornered struggle for the championship*

cor·ner·man /káwrnər màn/ (*plural* **-men** /-mèn/) *n* **1.** PLAYER IN CORNERS in various sports, a team member assigned to play, or adept at playing, in the corners, e.g., a basketball forward or a football cornerback **2.** BOXER'S ASSISTANT a supporter in a boxer's corner who gives advice, refreshment, and encouragement between rounds **3.** **POLITICAL AIDE** an adviser, especially to a political candidate (*slang*)

cor·ner·stone /káwrnər stòn/ *n* **1.** **VITAL PERSON OR THING** somebody or something fundamentally important **2.** **STONE AT CORNER OF TWO WALLS** a stone joining two walls where they meet at a corner **3.** **FIRST STONE OF NEW BUILDING** the first stone laid at a corner where two walls begin and form the first part of a new building

cor·ner store *n* a small store, especially one at the corner of two streets, where a limited range of groceries and general goods is sold

cor·ner·wise /káwrnər wìz/, **cor·ner·ways** /-wàyz/ *adv, adj* diagonal or diagonally, or with a corner at the front

cor·net /kawr nét/ *n* **1.** MUSIC **BRASS INSTRUMENT LIKE TRUMPET** a three-valved brass instrument shaped like a compressed trumpet. Its tubing is more conical than a trumpet and it has a softer warmer sound. **2.** MUSIC same as **cornetist** **3.** /kawr nét, káwr nit/ FOOD INDUST **PAPER CONE FOR HOLDING CANDY** a piece of paper folded into a cone shape and used to hold small edible things, especially candy **4.** /kawr nét, káwr nit/ CLOTHING **WOMAN'S HEADDRESS** a headdress of starched cloth worn by women in the 12th to 15th centuries **5.** /kawr nét, káwr nit/ CLOTHING, CHR **NUN'S HEADDRESS** a large white headdress worn by some Christian nuns in the 12th and 13th centuries [14C. < French, "small horn" < *corne* "horn" < Latin *cornu*]

cor·net·fish /kawr nét fish/ (*plural same* or **-fishes**) *n* an ocean fish that has a long tubular snout ending in a small mouth and a forked tail with a long trailing extension from its center. Native to: tropical or subtropical waters. Family: Fistularidae.

cor·net·ist /kawr néttist/, **cor·net·tist** *n* somebody who plays a cornet

cor·nett /kawr nét/ *n* a Renaissance and baroque wooden horn with six keys and a cup mouthpiece [Late 19C. Variant of CORNET]

cor·net·tist *n* MUSIC another spelling of **cornetist**

corn-fed *adj* **1.** fed or fattened on corn **2.** robust but unsophisticated (*informal*)

corn·field /káwrn fèeld/ *n* a field in which corn is growing

corn·flakes /káwrn flàyks/ *npl* a breakfast cereal consisting of small pieces of toasted corn, usually eaten with cold milk

corn·flour /káwrn flòwr/ *n UK* FOOD same as **cornstarch**

corn·flow·er /káwrn flòwr/ *n* an annual plant. Flowers: blue, pink, white, or purple when cultivated. Native to: Europe, Asia, naturalized in North America. Latin name: *Centaurea cyanus*.

corn·flow·er blue *n* a deep brilliant purplish blue color —**corn·flow·er-blue** *adj*

corn·husk /káwrn hùsk/ *n* the leafy outer covering of an ear of corn

corn·husk·er /káwrn hùskər/ *n* **1.** somebody or something that removes the husks from corn **2.** *also* **Corn·husk·er** somebody who comes from Nebraska

Corn·husk·er State *n* a nickname for Nebraska

corn·husk·ing /káwrn hùsking/ *n* **1.** a social event in which participants husk corn and later eat, dance, and sing **2.** the removal of the husks from ears of corn

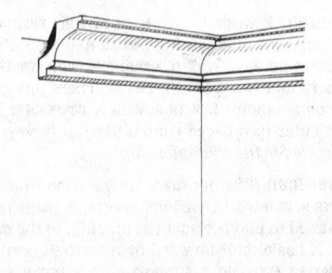

cor·nice /káwrniss/ *n* **1.** **PROJECTING MOLDING ALONG WALL** a projecting horizontal molding along the top of a wall or building **2.** **DECORATIVE PLASTER MOLDING** a decorative plaster molding around a room where the walls and ceiling meet **3.** ARCHIT **PART OF CLASSICAL BUILDING** the top projecting section of the part of a classical building that is supported by the columns (**entablature**) **4.** CLIMBING **OVERHANG OF SNOW** an overhanging mass of snow or ice formed by wind action ■ *vt* (**-niced, -nic·ing, -nic·es**) ARCHIT **PUT CORNICE ON WALL** to decorate or finish a wall or building with a cornice [Mid-16C. Via obsolete French < Italian]

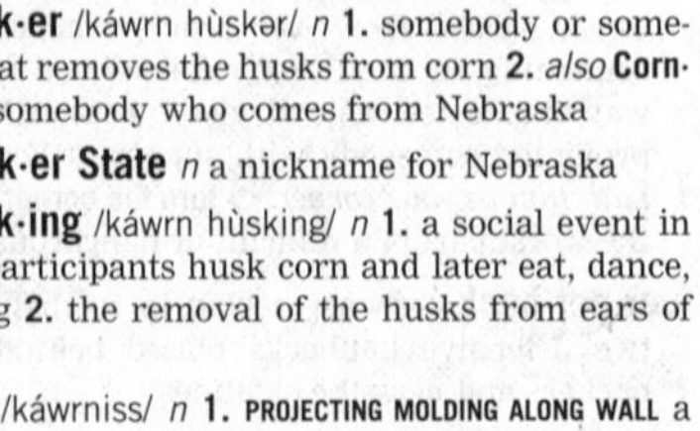

cornice

cor·niche /káwrnish, kawr néesh/ *n* a coast road, especially one cut into a cliff [Mid-19C. < French, modern form of *cornice* (see CORNICE)]

cor·ni·fi·ca·tion /kàwrnəfi káysh'n/ *n* the conversion of skin cells into keratin or other horny material such as nails or scales [Mid-19C. < Latin *cornu* "horn"]

Corn·ing /káwrning/ city in southern New York, northwest of Elmira, on the Cohocton River. Population: 10,716 (2002 estimate).

Cor·nish /káwrnish/ *adj* **OF CORNWALL** relating to Cornwall in southwestern England or its extinct Celtic language ■ *npl* **PEOPLE OF CORNWALL** the people of Cornwall in southwestern England ■ *n* **EXTINCT CELTIC LANGUAGE** an extinct Celtic language spoken in Cornwall until the late 18th century. Breton is the living language most closely related to Cornish.

LANGUAGE HERITAGE See ***Celtic***.

Corn Laws *npl* a group of laws introduced in Great Britain in 1804 and repealed in 1846 that were designed to restrict the importation of foreign grain by imposing duty on it. This caused bread prices to rise and led to riots.

corn lil·y *n* a plant of the iris family. Flowers: various colors, resembling lilies, on tall, wiry stems. Native to: southern Africa. Genus: *Ixia*.

corn·meal /káwrn mèel/ *n* flour made from corn

corn oil *n* oil extracted from corn. Use: cooking, margarine, salad oil, soaps.

corn on the cob *n* an ear of corn that is cooked and served whole

Corn·plant·er /káwrn plàntər/ (1735?–1836) Seneca leader. He made treaties with settlers, and was rejected by his people.

corn·pone /káwrn pòn/ *n Southern US* fried or baked bread made with cornmeal ■ *adj* relating to country life and people in being simple, unpretentious, and homely (*informal*)

corn pop·py *n* a common wild plant that often grows in cultivated fields. Flowers: large, scarlet. Native to: Europe, Asia. Latin name: *Papaver rhoeas*.

corn·row /káwrn rò/ *n* a narrow parallel braid of hair in a set of braids covering the head and made close against the scalp ■ *vt* (**-rowed, -row·ing, -rows**) to style hair in cornrows [Late 20C. Because the braids resemble kernels of corn]

corn sal·ad *n* a plant of the valerian family that often grows in grain fields and has edible leaves. Latin name: *Valerianella locusta*.

corn silk *n* the tuft of silky fibers growing at the tip of an ear of corn. Use: diuretic in herbal medicine.

corn smut *n* a fungal disease of corn that produces dark swellings on the grain

corn snow *n* fallen snow that has a grainy surface because it has thawed and refrozen

corn·starch /káwrn staàrch/ *n* fine-grained, starchy flour made from corn, especially used as a thickener in cooking

corn sug·ar *n* a type of sugar (**dextrose**) extracted from cornstarch

corn syr·up *n* syrup made from cornstarch. Use: sweetener in many foods.

cor·nu /káwr nòo/ (*plural* **-nu·a** /-nòo ə/) *n* a part that resembles a horn or has a horn-shaped pattern [Late 17C. < Latin, "horn"] —**cor·nu·al** *adj*

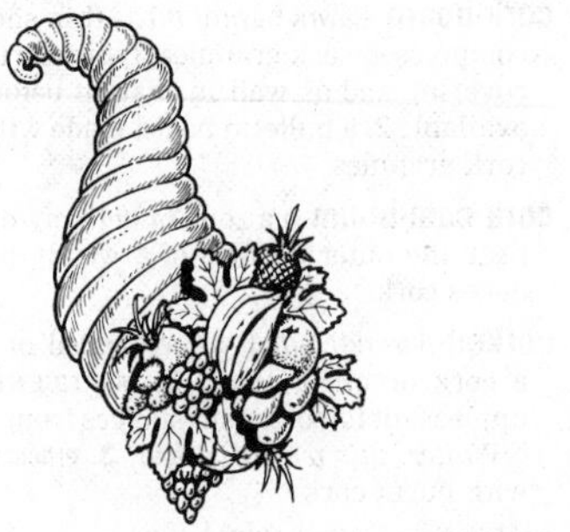

cornucopia

cor·nu·co·pi·a /kàwrnə kòpee ə/ *n* **1.** **ABUNDANCE** a great abundance of something **2.** ARTS **GOAT'S HORN OVERFLOWING WITH PRODUCE** a painting or other representation of a goat's horn overflowing with fruits, flowers, and vegetables, used to symbolize plenty or prosperity **3.** **HORN-SHAPED CONTAINER** an ornament or container shaped like a goat's horn **4.** MYTHOL **HORN OF GOAT THAT SUCKLED ZEUS** in Greek mythology, the horn of the goat that suckled Zeus [Early 16C. Via late Latin < Latin *cornu copiae* "horn of plenty"] —**cor·nu·co·pi·an** *adj*

cor·nute /kawr nòot/, **cor·nut·ed** /-nòotəd/ *adj* relating to a horn or horns [Early 17C. < Latin *cornutus* "horned" < *cornu* "horn"]

Corn·wall /káwrn wàwl, -wəl/ **1.** county in the extreme southwest of England, bordered on three sides by the ocean. Population: 499,114 (2001). Area: 1,357 sq. mi./3,515 sq. km. **2.** city on the St. Lawrence River in southeastern Ontario, Canada, 68 mi./110 km southwest of Montreal. Population: 48,287 (2001).

Corn·wal·lis /kawrn wólliss/, **Charles, 1st Marquis and 2nd Earl Cornwallis** (1738–1805) British army general and politician. He commanded forces in North Carolina during the American Revolution and was defeated at Yorktown.

corn whis·key *n* whiskey distilled from mash made mostly of corn

corn·y /káwrnee/ (**-i·er, -i·est**) *adj* unsophisticated and trite ○ *a corny love scene* [Late 16C. < CORN[1]] —**corn·i·ly** *adv* —**corn·i·ness** *n*

co·rol·la /kə rólla, -rólə/ *n* the petals of a flower collectively, forming a ring around the reproductive organs and surrounded by an outer ring of sepals [Mid-18C. < Latin, "garland," literally "little crown" < *corona* "crown"]

cor·ol·lar·y /káwrə lèrree/ *n* (*plural* **-ies**) **1.** **NATURAL CONSEQUENCE** something that is a natural consequence of or accompaniment to something else **2.** LOGIC **STATEMENT EASILY PROVED FROM ANOTHER** a proposition that follows, with little or no further reasoning, from the proof of another **3.** LOGIC **OBVIOUS DEDUCTION** something that is very obviously or easily deduced from something already proven **4.** **SOMETHING ADDED** something added to something else, e.g., something appended to a document ■ *adj* **FOLLOWING** following as a consequence or result [14C. < Latin *corollarium* "money paid for a garland" < *corolla* (see COROLLA)]

cor·o·man·del /káwrə mánd'l/ *n* INDUST same as **calamander** [Mid-19C. After the COROMANDEL COAST]

Cor·o·man·del Coast /kàwrə mánd'l-/ southern part of the eastern Indian coastline in the states of Tamil Nadu and Andhra Pradesh, on the Bay of Bengal

co·ro·na /kə rónə/ (*plural* **-nas** or **-nae** /-nèe/) *n* **1.** ASTRON **RING OF LIGHT AROUND MOON** a ring of light visible around a luminous body, especially the Moon, typically as a result of optical effects caused by thin cloud, water droplets, or ice in the Earth's atmosphere **2.** ASTRON **PART OF SUN'S ATMOSPHERE** the outermost part of the Sun's atmosphere **3.** BOT **LIP OF FLOWER TRUMPET** the prominent, sometimes frilly lip of the petal tube or trumpet corolla of some flowers such as daffodils and narcissi **4.** ANAT **TOP OF BODY PART** the top of a part of the body, e.g., the crown of the head or a tooth **5.** PHYS same as **corona discharge** **6.** ARCHIT **PART OF CORNICE** the flat vertical surface of a cornice just above the bottom surface (**soffit**) **7.** **LONG CIGAR** a long cigar with a blunt rounded mouth end **8.** **CIRCULAR**

CHANDELIER a circular hanging chandelier, especially in a church [Mid-16C. < Latin, "crown"] —**cor·o·nal** /káwrən'l, kə rṓn'l/ *adj*

Co·ro·na /kə rṓnə/ city in southern California, southwest of Riverside. Population: 138,326 (2002 estimate).

Co·ro·na Aus·tra·lis /-aw stráyliss, -strálliss/ *n* a constellation of the southern hemisphere. See illustration at **constellation**

Co·ro·na Bo·re·al·is /-bàwree áyliss, -álliss/ *n* a constellation of the northern hemisphere. See illustration at **constellation**

co·ro·na dis·charge *n* a luminous discharge from the surface of an object that is highly charged electrically, caused by ionization of the surrounding gas

Co·ro·na·do /kàwrə naádō/ city in southwestern California, across the bay from San Diego. Population: 23,862 (2002 estimate).

Co·ro·na·do, Francisco Vásquez de (1510–54) Spanish explorer. He led the first European expeditions to what is now the southwestern United States.

co·ro·na·graph /kə rṓnə gràf/, **co·ro·no·graph** *n* a telescope that masks the bright disk of the Sun so that the Sun's corona can be studied

cor·o·nal su·ture *n* a junction extending side-to-side across the crown of the skull between the two parietal bones and the frontal bone

cor·o·nar·y /káwrə nèrree/ *n* (*plural* **-ies**) MED **1.** same as **coronary thrombosis 2.** same as **heart attack** (sense 1) (*informal*) ■ *adj* **1.** describes the arteries that supply blood to the muscle tissue of the heart, or the veins that take blood away from it **2.** relating to disease of the coronary arteries and veins, and conditions associated with it ○ *coronary care* [Early 17C. < Latin *coronarius* "crown shaped" < *corona* "crown"]

cor·o·nar·y ar·ter·y *n* an artery supplying blood to the muscles of the heart, either of a pair arising from the aorta. The left artery divides into two almost immediately, giving rise to the common assumption that there are three coronary arteries.

cor·o·nar·y by·pass *n* an operation in which a new blood vessel is grafted onto the heart to replace a blocked coronary artery

cor·o·nar·y throm·bo·sis *n* the blocking of a coronary artery by a blood clot, which obstructs the blood supply to the heart muscle, resulting in death of the muscle and, often, a heart attack

cor·o·nar·y vein *n* a vein of the group that drains blood from the muscles of the heart

cor·o·na·tion /kàwrə náysh'n/ *n* the ceremony or act of crowning a monarch [14C. Via French < medieval Latin *coronation-* < Latin *corona* "crown"]

co·ro·na·vi·rus /kə rṓnə vīrəss/ *n* a single-stranded RNA virus that causes major illnesses in animals and humans and is a cause of the common cold. Family: Coronaviridae.

cor·o·ner /káwrənər/ *n* a public official formerly responsible for investigating deaths that appear not to have natural causes. Coroners are now largely replaced by medical examiners. [13C. < Anglo-Norman *coruner* "officer of the crown" < *corune* (see CROWN)] —**cor·o·ner·ship** *n*

cor·o·net /kàwrə nét, kórrə-/ *n* **1. SMALL CROWN** a small crown, especially one worn by a prince or a peer rather than a reigning monarch **2. WOMAN'S HEAD DECORATION** a circular ornamental band worn by women on the head **3.** VET **TOP OF HORSE'S HOOF** the upper part of a horse's hoof, where the horn of the hoof meets the skin of the pastern [14C. < French, "little crown" < *corone* (see CROWN)]

co·ro·no·graph *n* ASTRON same as **coronagraph**

Co·rot /kaw rṓ/, **Jean-Baptiste Camille** (1796–1875) French landscape and portrait painter. His freely handled landscapes influenced the Barbizon School and impressionism. Postimpressionists admired the tonal contrasts of his earlier, classical work.

corp. *abbr* BUSINESS corporation

Corp. *abbr* MIL corporal²

~~**corperation**~~ incorrect spelling of **corporation**

cor·po·ra plural of **corpus**

cor·po·ral¹ /káwrpərəl, -prəl/ *adj* relating to or affecting the body [14C. Via French < Latin *corporalis* < *corpus* "body"] —**cor·po·ral·ly** *adv*

USAGE corporal or **corporeal**? ***Corporal*** means "relating to the body" and is mainly used in *corporal punishment*, in reference to the infliction of physical hurt. ***Corporeal*** means "material or physical" rather than "spiritual": *The gods of antiquity were regarded not just as spirits but were thought to enjoy a corporeal existence.*

cor·po·ral² /káwrpərəl, -prəl/ *n* a noncommissioned officer in various armed forces, of a rank immediately below sergeant, or, in Canada, a master corporal [Mid-16C. Via French < Italian *caporale* "of the head" < *capo* (see CAPO²)]

cor·po·ral³ /káwrpərəl, -prəl/ *n* a white, usually linen, cloth on which the consecrated bread and wine are placed in the Christian sacrament of Communion [14C. Directly or via French < medieval Latin *(pallium) corporale* "(cloth) for the body"]

cor·po·ral·i·ty /kàwrpə rállətee/ *n* the state of being in physical or bodily form rather than spiritual form

cor·po·ral pun·ish·ment *n* the striking of a somebody's body as punishment

cor·po·rate /káwrpərət, -prət/ *adj* **1. INVOLVING CORPORATION** relating or belonging to a corporation **2. OF CORPORATION'S EMPLOYEES** designed for, suitable for, or associated with people who work for large corporations ○ *corporate fashions* **3. INCORPORATED** legally united to form a body that can act as a unit **4. OF GROUP AS WHOLE** relating to or involving a group as a whole (*formal*) ■ *n* BUSINESS same as **corporation** (sense 1) (*informal*) [16C. < Latin *corporatus*, past participle of *corporare* "form a body" < *corpus* "body"] —**cor·po·rate·ly** *adv*

cor·po·rate bond *n* a bond issued by a corporation rather than by a national or local government

cor·po·rate hos·pi·tal·i·ty *n* free entertainment offered by a company to customers or trading partners, e.g., at major sporting events, as a way of winning their favor

cor·po·rate kill·ing *n UK* a proposed criminal offense under which companies and similar organizations, and their directors, would be held responsible for the deaths of employees, clients, or passengers occurring as a result of the company's negligence

cor·po·rate-owned life in·sur·ance *n* life insurance taken out on an employee by the employer with the corporation as beneficiary, often without the knowledge of the family of the insured

cor·po·rate tax *n* tax paid on the profits of a corporation

cor·po·rate wel·fare *n* laws and government subsidies that, in the opinion of some people, favor corporations unfairly at the expense of ordinary taxpayers (*disapproving*)

cor·po·ra·tion /kàwrpə ráysh'n/ *n* **1. GROUP REGARDED AS INDIVIDUAL BY LAW** a company recognized by law as a single body with its own powers and liabilities, separate from those of the individual members. Corporations perform many of the functions of private business, governments, educational bodies, and the professions. **2. LOCAL GOVERNING AUTHORITY** the governing authority of an incorporated municipality such as a city or town **3. GROUP ACTING AS SINGLE ENTITY** a group of people acting as a single entity [15C. < late Latin *corporation-* < Latin *corporatus* (see CORPORATE)]

cor·po·ra·tion tax *n UK* same as **corporate tax**

cor·po·rat·ism /káwrpərə tìzzəm, káwrprə-/, **cor·po·ra·tiv·ism** /káwrpərətiv ìzzəm, káwrprə-/ *n* a system of running a state using the power of organizations such as businesses and labor unions that act, or claim to act, for large numbers of people —**cor·po·ra·tist** *adj, n*

cor·po·re·al /kawr páwree əl/ *adj* **1.** relating to or involving the physical body rather than the mind or spirit **2.** material or physical rather than spiritual [Early 17C. < late Latin *corporealis* < Latin *corpus* "body"] —**cor·po·re·al·i·ty** /kawr pàwree állətee/ *n* —**cor·po·re·al·ly** *adv*

USAGE See ***corporal***¹.

cor·po·re·i·ty /kàwrpə rée ətee/ *n* the condition of existing as something material or physical [Early 17C. < French *corporéité* < Latin *corpus* "body"]

corps /kawr/ (*plural* **corps** /kawrz/) *n* **1.** MIL **SPECIALIZED MILITARY FORCE** a military force that carries out specialized duties **2.** MIL **TACTICAL UNIT** a tactical military unit that is made up of two or more divisions with additional supporting services **3. GROUP OF ASSOCIATED PEOPLE** a group of people who work together or are associated ○ *the press corps* [Late 16C. Via French < Latin *corpus* "body"]

corps de bal·let /kàwr də ba láy/ (*plural* **corps de bal·let** /*pronunc. same*/) *n* the dancers of a ballet company who perform as a group rather than individually [< French, "dance company"]

corpse /kawrps/ *n* a dead body, especially of a human being [14C. Directly or via French < Latin *corpus* "body"]

corps·man /káwrmən, káwrz-/ (*plural* **-men** /káwrmən, káwrz-/) *n* in the US armed forces, an enlisted person with training in giving first aid and basic medical treatment

cor·pu·lent /káwrpyələnt/ *adj* somewhat overweight [15C. < Latin *corpulentus* < *corpus* "body"] —**cor·pu·lence** *n* —**cor·pu·lent·ly** *adv*

cor pul·mo·na·le /kàwr pŏolmə naálee, -pùlmə-, -pŏolmə náilee, -pùlmə-/ *n* enlargement and failure of the right ventricle of the heart, caused by disease of the lungs or pulmonary blood vessels [< modern Latin, "pulmonary heart"]

cor·pus /káwrpəss/ (*plural* **-po·ra** /-pərə/) *n* **1. BODY OF WRITINGS** a body of writings by a particular person, on a particular subject, or of a particular type ○ *one of the most popular works in the Shakespearean corpus* **2. MAIN PART** the main part of something **3.** ANAT **PART OF ORGAN** the main portion of something such as an organ or other body part, or a mass of tissue with a distinct function ○ *the corpus of the uterus* **4.** FIN **CAPITAL** the capital or principal of a sum of money **5.** LING **COLLECTION OF LANGUAGE EXAMPLES** a large collection of written, and sometimes spoken, examples of the usage of a language, employed in linguistic analysis [Early 18C. < Latin, "body"]

cor·pus al·bi·cans /kàwrpəss álbə kanz/ (*plural* **cor·po·ra al·bi·can·ti·a** /-albə kántee ə/) *n* an area of white scar tissue formed in an ovary by the decay of the corpus luteum when implantation of a fertilized egg fails to occur [< modern Latin, "whitening body"]

cor·pus cal·lo·sum /kàwrpəss kə lṓssəm/ (*plural* **cor·po·ra cal·lo·sa** /kàwrpərə kə lṓssə/) *n* the thick band of nerve fibers that connects the two hemispheres of the brain in higher mammals and allows the hemispheres to communicate [< modern Latin, "callous body"]

Cor·pus Chris·ti¹ /kàwrpəss krístee/ *n* a mainly Roman Catholic festival honoring the institution of Communion. Date: Thursday after Trinity Sunday. [< medieval Latin, "body of Christ"]

Cor·pus Chris·ti² /kàwrpəss krístee/ city and port in southeastern Texas, on the southern shore of Corpus Christi Bay. Population: 278,520 (2002 estimate).

cor·pus·cle /káwrpəss'l, -pùss'l/ *n* **1.** a small independent body, especially a cell in blood or lymph **2.** a discrete particle, especially a photon [Mid-17C. < Latin *corpusculum* "small body" < *corpus* "body"] —**cor·pus·cu·lar** /kawr púskyələr/ *adj*

cor·pus·cu·lar the·o·ry *n* the theory that light consists of a stream of particles. It was originally introduced by Isaac Newton, and has applications in quantum physics. The theory cannot be used to explain all the properties of light.

cor·pus de·lic·ti /kàwrpəss di lík tī/ *n* the body of facts that show that a crime has been committed, including physical evidence such as a corpse [< modern Latin, "body of the crime"]

cor·pus lu·te·um /kàwrpəss lŏotee əm/ (*plural* **cor·po·ra lu·te·a** /kàwrpərə lŏotee ə/) *n* a yellow mass of tissue that forms in a part of the ovary (**Graafian**

follicle) after ovulation in mammals and secretes the hormone progesterone. If no pregnancy is established, the corpus luteum degenerates, but it continues to secrete the hormone if pregnancy occurs. [< modern Latin, "yellow body"]

cor·pus stri·a·tum /kàwrpəss strī áytəm/ (*plural* **cor·po·ra stri·a·ta** /kàwrpərə strī áytə/) *n* a mass of striped gray and white nervous tissue, in each hemisphere of the brain [< modern Latin, "striated body"]

corr. *abbr* 1. correct 2. corrected 3. correction 4. COMMUNICATION correspondence 5. MEDIA correspondent

cor·ral /kə rál/ *n* 1. AGRIC **PLACE FOR LIVESTOCK** a fenced area in which livestock or horses are kept 2. HIST **CIRCLE OF WAGONS** a temporary defensive enclosure formed by wagons arranged in a circle ■ *vt* (**-ralled, -ral·ling, -rals**) 1. AGRIC **PUT ANIMALS IN CORRAL** to gather animals together and drive them into a corral 2. HIST **PUT WAGONS IN CIRCLE** to form wagons into a temporary defensive circle 3. **ACQUIRE THINGS** to gather together and take control of people or things (*informal*) ○ *hopes to corral sufficient funding for the project* [Late 16C. < Spanish]

cor·ra·sion /kə ráyzh'n/ *n* the mechanical erosion of a surface by fragments of rock carried by water, wind, or ice [Late 19C. < Latin *corras-*, past participle of *corradere* "scrape together" < *radere* "to scrape"] —**cor·ra·sive** /kə ráyssiv, -ziv/ *adj*

cor·rect /kə rékt/ *vt* (**-rect·ed, -rect·ing, -rects**) 1. **REMOVE ERRORS FROM SOMETHING** to take the errors out of something 2. **INDICATE ERRORS IN SOMETHING** to point out or mark the errors in something 3. **RECTIFY IMPERFECTION** to rectify an imperfection in something, or counteract something wrong or undesirable ○ *wears glasses to correct his astigmatism* 4. **MODIFY SOMETHING** to modify something such as behavior in order to make it acceptable or bring it up to a standard 5. **PUNISH SOMEBODY TO GAIN IMPROVEMENT** to punish or scold somebody, especially a child, to bring about improvement or reform ■ *adj* 1. **ACCURATE** accurate or without errors ○ *the correct time* 2. **ACCEPTABLE** acceptable, or meeting a required standard ○ *correct dress* [14C. < Latin *correct-*, past participle of *corrigere* "rule completely" < *regere* "to rule"] —**cor·rect·a·ble** *adj* —**cor·rect·ly** *adv* —**cor·rect·ness** *n* —**cor·rec·tor** *n*

cor·rec·tion /kə rékshən/ *n* 1. **ALTERATION THAT CORRECTS SOMETHING** an alteration that removes an error 2. **WRITTEN COMMENT ON ERROR** something written beside an error in a text to point out what should be there instead 3. **REMOVAL OF ERRORS** the removal of errors from something, or the indication of errors in something 4. **MODIFICATION TO CALCULATION** an adjustment made to a calculation or measurement to compensate for an observed deviation from ideal conditions 5. **PUNISHMENT TO REFORM SOMEBODY** punishment, especially when meant to improve or reform the person punished 6. FIN **FALL IN PRICES** a fall in prices or activity in a stock market following a rise or busy period ■ **cor·rec·tions** *npl* **TREATMENT OF OFFENDERS** a governmental system of dealing with criminals by imprisonment, rehabilitation, parole, and probation

cor·rec·tion·al /kə rékshən'l/ *adj* 1. about, involving, or intended as correction 2. of or involved in the system of dealing with criminals by imprisonment, rehabilitation, parole, and probation

cor·rec·tion·al fa·cil·i·ty *n* a prison or other institution where criminals are confined

cor·rec·tion flu·id *n* an opaque liquid used to paint over a written or printed error and provide a surface for adding a correction

cor·rec·tions of·fi·cer *n* somebody employed in a prison to guard and supervise the inmates

cor·rec·ti·tude /kə réktə to͞od/ *n* the fact of being correct, especially in behavior and manners [Late 19C. Blend of CORRECT + RECTITUDE]

cor·rec·tive /kə réktiv/ *adj* acting or intended to correct something ○ *corrective action* ■ *n* something that corrects or is meant to correct something —**cor·rec·tive·ly** *adv*

cor·rec·tive shoe *n* a specially fitted shoe that compensates for physical malformation in the foot

Cor·reg·gio /kə réjjō/ (1489–1534) Italian painter. His work is characterized by sensuous nude figures, skillful use of light and shadow, and luminous colors. Born **Antonio Allegri**

Cor·reg·i·dor /kə réggi dàwr/ island at the entrance to Manila Bay in the Philippines. During World War II, it was the scene of intense fighting by US and Filipino forces against Japanese troops until its capture by the Japanese in May 1942. It was recaptured by US forces in 1945. Area: 1.93 sq. mi./5 sq. km.

cor·re·late *v* /káwrə làyt/ (**-lat·ed, -lat·ing, -lates**) 1. *vti* **HAVE OR SHOW MUTUAL RELATIONSHIP** to have a mutual or complementary relationship, or show that two or more things such as a cause and an effect have a mutual or complementary relationship ○ *How do these results correlate with your findings?* 2. *vt* **GATHER AND COMPARE THINGS** to gather together and compare related things such as results or reports ○ *Her job is to correlate the statistics from a range of sources and prepare a report.* ■ *adj* /káwrələt, -làyt/ **HAVING SHARED PROPERTIES** having mutual or complementary properties ■ *n* /káwrələt, -làyt/ 1. **COMPLEMENTARY THING** something that shares mutual or complementary properties with something else 2. STATS **VARIABLE RELATED TO ANOTHER VARIABLE** either of two variables that are related with the result that a variation in one is accompanied by a linear variation of the other [Mid-18C. Back-formation < CORRELATION] —**cor·re·lat·a·ble** *adj* —**cor·re·la·tor** *n*

cor·re·la·tion /kàwrə láysh'n/ *n* 1. **MUTUAL OR COMPLEMENTARY RELATIONSHIP** a relationship in which two or more things are mutual or complementary, or one thing is caused by another ○ *the close correlation between the two factors* 2. **ACT OF CORRELATING** the act of correlating, or the condition of being correlated 3. STATS **RELATEDNESS OF VARIABLES** the degree to which two or more variables are related and change together [Mid-16C. < medieval Latin *correlation-* "mutual relationship" < Latin *relation-* (see RELATION)] —**cor·re·la·tion·al** *adj*

cor·re·la·tion co·ef·fi·cient *n* a number or function indicating the degree of correlation between two variables. It ranges between 1 for high positive correlation to –1 for high negative correlation, with 0 indicating a purely random relationship.

cor·rel·a·tive /kə rélləti v/ *adj* 1. **BEING CORRELATES** in a mutual or complementary relationship 2. GRAM **TOGETHER BUT NOT ADJACENT** functioning together but not usually adjacent, as the conjunctions "either" and "or" ■ *n* 1. same as **correlate** *n* (sense 1) 2. GRAM **CORRELATIVE WORD** a word, especially a conjunction, that functions with another but is not usually adjacent to it —**cor·rel·a·tive·ly** *adv* —**cor·rel·a·tive·ness** *n* —**cor·rel·a·tiv·i·ty** /kə rèllə tívvətee/ *n*

cor·re·spond /kàwrə spónd/ (**-spond·ed, -spond·ing, -sponds**) *vi* 1. **CONFORM OR BE CONSISTENT** to conform, be consistent, or be in agreement with something else 2. **BE SIMILAR** to be similar or equivalent 3. **WRITE TO ONE ANOTHER** to communicate with somebody by exchanging written messages [Early 16C. Via French < medieval Latin *correspondere* "respond to each other" < Latin *respondere* (see RESPOND)]

cor·re·spon·dence /kàwrə spóndənss/ *n* 1. **WRITTEN COMMUNICATION** communication by means of exchanged written messages such as letters or e-mail 2. **WRITTEN MESSAGES** written messages, especially letters 3. **CONFORMITY** conformity, consistency, or agreement between two or more things 4. **SIMILARITY** similarity or equivalence between two or more things

cor·re·spon·dence course *n* an educational course in which the teaching organization sends lessons and tests to students by mail or e-mail and students return completed work in the same way

cor·re·spon·dence school *n* an educational organization that teaches through correspondence courses

cor·re·spon·dent /kàwrə spóndənt/ *n* 1. **SOMEBODY COMMUNICATING IN WRITING** somebody who communicates in writing, e.g., by letter or e-mail ○ *Most of my correspondents have e-mail now.* 2. **SOMEBODY PROVIDING SPECIAL REPORTS** somebody employed by a news organization, especially a newspaper or broadcasting company, to provide reports from a particular place or on a particular subject ○ *our Paris correspondent* 3. BUSINESS **SOMEBODY DEALING WITH DISTANT BUSINESS** a person or company that regularly does business with another, especially one that is distant 4. **SOMETHING THAT CORRESPONDS** something that conforms or agrees with, or is similar to, something else (*formal*) ■ *adj* same as **corresponding** (sense 2)

cor·re·spond·ing /kàwrə spónding/ *adj* 1. **CONSISTENT** consistent, conforming, or in agreement with something else ○ *Line up the prongs on one half with the corresponding sockets on the other.* 2. **ANALOGOUS** similar or equivalent to something else in one or more important respects ○ *the corresponding word in her own language* 3. **WORKING FROM DISTANCE** interacting or contributing from a distance, e.g., by mail ○ *a corresponding member based in China* 4. **DEALING WITH CORRESPONDENCE** handling or assigned to handle correspondence

cor·re·spond·ing an·gles *npl* the angles formed on the same side of two lines and a third line (**transversal**) that intersects them, each of the four angles at each intersection corresponding to the four angles at the other

cor·re·spond·ing·ly /kàwrə spóndinglee/ *adv* in a way that is consistent, equivalent, or similar ○ *A large company has correspondingly large problems.*

cor·ri·da /kaw re͞edə/ *n* a program of bullfights [Late 19C. < Spanish, "running" (of bulls) < Latin *currere* "to run"]

cor·ri·dor /káwridər/ *n* 1. **PASSAGE INSIDE BUILDING** a passage between parts of a building, often with a series of rooms opening onto it 2. RAIL, NAUT **PASSAGEWAY IN RAILROAD CAR OR SHIP** a passageway in a railroad car or ship giving access to cabins or compartments 3. INTERNAT REL **STRIP OF LAND** a narrow strip of land belonging to one country and projecting through another, e.g., to give a landlocked country access to a port 4. GEOG **POPULATED STRIP BETWEEN URBAN AREAS** a densely populated strip of land connecting two or more urban areas ○ *the northeastern corridor* 5. AVIAT **REGION OF AIRSPACE FOR AIR TRAFFIC** a region of airspace designated for use by air traffic 6. AEROSP **SPACECRAFT FLIGHT PATH** a predetermined flight path that a spacecraft follows upon reentry into the Earth's atmosphere [Late 16C. Via French < Italian *corridore* < Latin *currere* "to run"]

Cor·rie·dale /káwree dàyl/ (*plural* **-dales** or *same*) *n* a sheep belonging to a breed without horns developed in New Zealand. Raised for: wool, meat. [Early 20C. After an estate in New Zealand]

cor·ri·gen·da /kàwri jéndə/ *n* PUBL same as **errata** (*see* **erratum**) (*takes a singular or plural verb*) ■ plural of **corrigendum**

cor·ri·gen·dum /kàwri jéndəm/ (*plural* **-da** /-də/) *n* an error to be corrected [Early 19C. < Latin, "thing to be corrected"]

cor·rob·o·rate /kə róbbə ràyt/ (**-rat·ed, -rat·ing, -rates**) *vt* to give or represent evidence of the truth of something ○ *The photographs corroborate the verbal account.* [Mid-16C. < Latin *corroborat-*, past participle of *corroborare* "strengthen together" < *roborare* "strengthen"] —**cor·rob·o·ra·tion** /kə ròbbə ráysh'n/ *n* —**cor·rob·o·ra·tive** *adj* —**cor·rob·o·ra·tive·ly** *adv* —**cor·rob·o·ra·tor** *n* —**cor·rob·o·ra·to·ry** *adj*

USAGE See *collaborate.*

cor·rode /kə rṓd/ (**-rod·ed, -rod·ing, -rodes**) *v* 1. *vti* to destroy something progressively by chemical action, or be destroyed in this way 2. *vt* to undermine or destroy something gradually ○ *The constant criticism has corroded the candidate's public image.* [14C. < Latin *corrodere* "gnaw away" < *rodere* "gnaw"] —**cor·ro·dant** *n* —**cor·rod·er** *n* —**cor·ro·di·bil·i·ty** /kə rṓdə bíllətee/ *n* —**cor·rod·i·ble** *adj*

~~corrolary~~ incorrect spelling of **corollary**

cor·ro·sion /kə rṓzh'n/ *n* 1. CHEM **DESTRUCTION BY CHEMICAL ACTION** a process by which something, especially a metal, is destroyed progressively by chemical action, as iron is when it rusts 2. **CORRODED MATERIAL** material produced by corrosion, e.g., rust 3. **GRADUAL DESTRUCTION** the gradual destruction or undermining of something ○ *a steady corrosion of the public trust* 4. **RESULT OF CORROSION** the condition produced by corrosion [14C. < late Latin *corrosion-* < Latin *corros-*, past participle of *corrodere* (see CORRODE)] —**cor·ro·si·ble** /kə rɔ́ssəb'l/ *adj*

cor·ro·sive /kə rɔ́ssiv/ *adj* **1.** CHEM **CHEMICALLY DESTRUCTIVE** able to destroy something progressively by chemical action **2. GRADUALLY DESTRUCTIVE** destroying or undermining something gradually **3. VERY SARCASTIC** very strongly sarcastic or bitter ○ *a corrosive review* ■ *n* CHEM **DESTRUCTIVE SUBSTANCE** a substance that is able to destroy something progressively by chemical action, e.g., an acid [14C. Via French < medieval Latin *corrosivus* < Latin *corros-* (see CORROSION)] —**cor·ro·sive·ly** *adv* —**cor·ro·sive·ness** *n*

cor·ro·sive sub·li·mate *n* CHEM same as **mercuric chloride**

cor·ru·gate /káwrə gàyt/ *vti* (**-gat·ed, -gat·ing, -gates**) to fold into parallel ridges and troughs, or fold something such as a sheet of cardboard into parallel ridges and troughs ■ *adj* same as **corrugated** [Early 17C. < Latin *corrugat-*, past participle of *corrugare* "wrinkle completely" < *rugare* "to wrinkle"] —**cor·ru·ga·tion** /kàwrə gáysh'n/ *n*

cor·ru·gat·ed /káwrə gàytəd/ *adj* **1.** folded into parallel ridges and troughs **2.** made from a corrugated material ○ *a shed with a corrugated roof*

cor·ru·ga·tor /káwrə gàytər/ *n* a muscle that wrinkles the skin when it contracts

cor·rupt /kə rúpt/ *adj* **1. IMMORAL OR DISHONEST** immoral or dishonest, especially as shown by the exploitation of a position of power or trust for personal gain **2. DEPRAVED** extremely immoral or depraved **3.** COMPUT **CONTAINING ERRORS** describes computer data or software that is unusable or unreliable because of the presence of errors that have been introduced unintentionally ○ *a corrupt computer file* **4. CONTAINING COPYING ERRORS** containing undesirable changes in meaning or errors made in copying ○ *a corrupt transcription of the manuscript* **5. CONTAMINATED** contaminated or tainted by something else (*archaic*) **6. ROTTEN** putrid or decomposing (*archaic*) ■ *v* (**-rupt·ed, -rupt·ing, -rupts**) **1.** *vti* **BECOME OR MAKE SOMEBODY DISHONEST** to become dishonest, or destroy or compromise somebody's morality or honesty **2.** *vti* **BECOME OR MAKE SOMEBODY DEPRAVED** to become immoral or depraved, or cause somebody to become immoral or depraved **3.** *vt* COMPUT **INTRODUCE ERRORS INTO COMPUTER DATA** to introduce unintentional errors into computer data or software, making it unusable or unreliable **4.** *vt* **SPOIL TEXT WITH COPYING ERRORS** to make undesirable changes in meaning or introduce other errors into a text during copying **5.** *vt* **CONTAMINATE SOMETHING** to contaminate something or taint somebody (*archaic*) **6.** *vt* **ROT SOMETHING** to make something rot or become putrid (*archaic*) [14C. < Latin *corruptus*, past participle of *corrumpere* "break completely" < *rumpere* "to break"] —**cor·rup·ter** *n* —**cor·rupt·i·ble** *adj* —**cor·rupt·ly** *adv* —**cor·rupt·ness** *n*

cor·rup·tion /kə rúpsh'n/ *n* **1. DISHONESTY FOR PERSONAL GAIN** dishonest exploitation of power for personal gain **2. DEPRAVITY** extreme immorality or depravity **3. UNDESIRABLE CHANGE** an undesirable change in meaning or another error introduced into a text during copying **4. CORRUPTING OF SOMETHING** the corrupting of something or somebody, or the state of being corrupt **5.** LING **ALTERED WORD OR PHRASE** a word or phrase that has been altered from its original form **6. ROTTING** rotting or putrefaction, or the state of being rotten or putrid (*archaic*) [14C. Via French < Latin *corruption-* < *corruptus* (see CORRUPT)]

cor·rup·tive /kə rúptiv/ *adj* having a bad effect on somebody's character or behavior —**cor·rup·tive·ly** *adv*

cor·sage /kawr saázh/ *n* a small bouquet worn on the bodice of a dress or the lapel of a jacket [Early 19C. < French < Old French *cors* "body"]

cor·sair /káwr sèr/ *n* **1.** NAUT, HIST **PIRATE** a pirate, especially one based on the North African coast between the 16th and 19th centuries **2.** HIST **PRIVATE SHIP COMMISSIONED BY GOVERNMENT** a privately owned ship commissioned by a government to attack foreign ships, especially one based on the coast of North Africa **3.** HIST **OWNER OF PRIVATEER** the owner of a ship commissioned by a government to attack ships of other countries [Mid-16C. Via French < medieval Latin *cursarius* < Latin *cursus* "hostile incursion" < past participle of *currere* "to run"]

corse·let /káwrsslət/ *n* **1.** *also* **cor·se·lette** /kàwrssə lét/ a garment combining a corset and a bra **2.** *also* **cors·let** armor covering the upper body [15C. < French < Old French *cors* "body"]

cor·set /káwrssət/ *n* **1. STIFF GARMENT** a stiffened garment worn by women to shape the waist and breasts **2. STIFF UNDERGARMENT** a stiff undergarment with laces to fasten it tightly, formerly worn to shape and support the body **3.** MED **INJURY SUPPORT** a stiffened garment worn by men or women for back support when injured [13C. < French < Old French *cors* "body"] —**cor·set·ed** *adj*

Cor·si·ca /káwrssikə/ mountainous island in the Mediterranean Sea, an administrative region of France. Population: 249,737 (1990). Area: 3,350 sq. mi./8,680 sq. km. —**Cor·si·can** *adj, n*

Cor·si·ca·na /kàwrsi kánnə/ town in Texas, south of Dallas, noted as a center for the oil industry since 1896. Population: 25,187 (2002 estimate).

cors·let *n* ARMS another spelling of **corselet** (sense 2)

Cor·tá·zar /káwrtə zaàr, kawr tà zaàr/, **Julio** (1914–84) Belgian-born Argentinean writer, known for his surrealist works, including the novel *Hopscotch* (1963)

> "The unusual is only found in a very small percentage, except in literary creations, and that is exactly what makes literature."
>
> [Julio Cortázar, *The Winners*; 1960]

corte de hon·or /kàwr tay day on áwr/ (*plural* **cor·tes de hon·or**) *n Hispanic* the group of formal escorts of a young girl at her rite of passage party (**quinceañera**) welcoming her into adulthood [< Spanish, "court of honor"]

cor·tege /kawr tézh/, **cor·tège** *n* **1.** a procession, especially a funeral procession **2.** a retinue of servants or attendants [Mid-17C. Via French < Italian *corteggio* < *corteggiare* "attend court" < *corte* "court" < Latin *cohort-* "enclosed space"]

Cor·tés, Sea of /kawr téz/ former name for **California, Gulf of**

Cor·tés /kawr téz/, **Hernán** (1485–1547) Spanish explorer. He conquered Mexico in 1521 for Spain, and served as its governor (1523–28).

cor·tex /káwr tèks/ (*plural* **-ti·ces** /-ti seèz/ or **-tex·es**) *n* **1.** the outer layer of a solid organ or part of the body, e.g., the outer covering of the kidney or brain (**cerebral cortex**) **2.** the tissue in plant stems and roots between the outer layer (**epidermis**) and the central core (**stele**) [Mid-17C. < Latin, "bark"] —**cor·ti·cal** /káwrtik'l/ *adj*

cortic- *prefix* same as **cortico-** (*used before vowels*)

cortico- *prefix* cortex, cortical ○ *corticospinal* [< Latin *cortic-* "bark"]

cor·ti·coid /káwrti kòyd/ *n* a drug that acts in a similar way to the hormone produced by the outer layer of the adrenal gland

cor·ti·co·spi·nal /kàwrtikō spín'l/ *adj* relating to or connecting the outer covering of the brain (**cerebral cortex**) and the spinal cord

cor·ti·co·ste·roid /kàwrtikō sté ròyd, -steér-/ *n* **1.** an adrenal steroid hormone involved in metabolism and immune response **2.** a synthetic drug similar to a natural corticosteroid. Use: reduction of inflammation and allergic reactions, prevention of graft rejection.

cor·ti·co·tro·pin /kàwrtikō trṓpin/, **cor·ti·co·tro·phin** /-fin/ *n* BIOCHEM same as **ACTH** [Mid-20C. Contraction of *adrenocorticotrophic hormone*]

cor·ti·sol /káwrti sàwl, -zàwl, -sòl, -zòl/ *n* BIOCHEM same as **hydrocortisone** (sense 1) [Mid-20C. < CORTISONE]

cor·ti·sone /káwrti zṑn/ *n* a steroid hormone secreted by the adrenal cortex [Mid-20C. Contraction of *corticosterone*, a type of corticosteroid]

Cort·land /káwrtlənd/ town in New York, on the Tioughnioga River, northwest of Binghamton. Population: 18,799 (2002 estimate).

Cor·to·na ♦ **Pietro da Cortona**

co·run·dum /kə rúndəm/ *n* a hard mineral form of alumina that crystallizes in a range of colors. Use: gems, abrasives. [Early 18C. < Tamil *kuruntam*]

cor·us·cate /káwrə skàyt/ (**-cat·ed, -cat·ing, -cates**) *vi* (*literary*) **1.** to give off flashes of bright light **2.** to show brilliance or virtuosity [Early 18C. < Latin *coruscat-*, past participle of *coruscare* "to glitter"] —**co·rus·cant** /kə rúskənt/ *adj* —**cor·us·cat·ing** *adj* —**cor·us·ca·tion** /kàwrə skáysh'n/ *n*

Cor·val·lis /kawr válliss/ city in western Oregon, southwest of Salem, on the Willamette River. Population: 49,781 (2002 estimate).

cor·vée /kawr váy, káwr vày/ *n* **1.** in feudal times, a day of unpaid labor required of a serf for a manorial lord **2.** a period of labor formerly sometimes required by a state in lieu of taxes, especially in pre-Revolutionary France [14C. Via French < Latin *corrogata*, past participle of *corrogare* "summon together" < *rogare* "ask"]

corves MIN EXTRACT plural of **corf**

cor·vette /kawr vét/ *n* **1.** an armed naval escort vessel, smaller than a destroyer **2.** formerly, a small wooden sailing ship with one tier of guns [Mid-17C. < French < Dutch *korf* "small ship," literally "basket" < Latin *corbis*]

cor·vid /káwrvid/ *n* a bird of the family that includes crows, jays, and magpies. Family: Corvidae. [Mid-20C. < modern Latin *Corvidae* < Latin *corvus* "raven"]

cor·vi·na[1] *n* FISH same as **corbina**

cor·vi·na[2] /kawr veénə/ *n* a red grape variety from northeastern Italy. Use: making light red wine.

cor·vine /káwr vīn/ *adj* relating to crows or the crow family (*literary*) [Mid-17C. < Latin *corvinus* < *corvus* "raven"]

Cor·vus /káwrvəss/ *n* a small constellation of the southern hemisphere. See illustration at **constellation**

Cor·y·bant /káwri bànt/ (*plural* **-bants** or **-ban·tes** /kàwri bán teèz/) *n* in the religion of ancient Phrygia, a priest of the goddess Cybele who performed wild ecstatic dances [15C. < Latin *Corybant-* < Greek *Korubas*] —**Cor·y·ban·tic** /kàwri bántik/ *adj*

cor·ymb /káw rìmb, -rim/ *n* a flat flower head consisting of flowers whose stalks grow from different points on the flower stem but reach approximately the same height [Early 18C. Via French < Greek *korumbos* "summit"] —**cor·ymbed** *adj* —**cor·ym·bose** /káwrim bṓss/ *adj* —**co·rym·bous** /kə rímbəss/ *adj*

cor·y·phée /kàwri fáy/ *n* a leading ballet dancer who usually performs with a small group of other dancers [Early 19C. Via French < Greek *koruphaios* "chorus leader" < *koruphē* "head"]

co·ry·za /kə rízə/ *n* **1.** MED **NASAL CONGESTION** severe nasal congestion **2.** MED **COLD** a common cold (*technical*) **3.** VET **BIRD DISEASE** a respiratory disease of chickens and turkeys, caused by bacteria [Early 16C. Via Latin < Greek *koruza* "nasal mucus, catarrh"] —**co·ry·zal** *adj*

cos[1] /koss/ (*plural* **cos·es** or *same*) *n UK* PLANTS same as **romaine** [Late 17C. After COS]

cos[2] /kōz/ *abbr* MATH cosine

'cos /kəz, kawz/ *conj* same as **because** (*informal*) [Early 19C. Shortening and alteration]

Cos /koss, kawss/ second largest of the Greek Dodecanese Islands, lying off the coast of Turkey in the Aegean Sea. Population: 20,350 (1981). Area: 111 sq. mi./287 sq. km. Greek name **Kos**

COS *abbr* **1.** *also* **c.o.s.** FREIGHT cash on shipment **2.** MIL chief of staff

Co·sa Nos·tra /kṑssə nṓstrə/ *n* in the United States, an organized crime organization linked with the Mafia of Sicily [Mid-20C. < Italian, "our concern"]

Cos·by /kózbee/, **Bill** (*b.* 1937) US comedian, actor, producer, educator, and writer best known for his work in television, in particular his role in *The Cosby Show* (1984–92). Full name **Cosby, Jr., William Henry**

> "It isn't a matter of Black is beautiful as much as it is white is not *all* that's beautiful."
>
> [Bill Cosby, *Interview, Playboy*; May 1969]

"The seven ages of man have become preschooler, Pepsi generation, baby boomer, mid-lifer, empty nester, senior citizen, and organ donor."
[Bill Cosby, *Time Flies*; 1987]

co·sec /kṓ sèk/ *abbr* MATH cosecant

co·se·cant /kō seékənt/ *n* for a given angle in a right triangle, a trigonometric function equal to the length of the hypotenuse divided by that of the side opposite the angle

co·seis·mal /kō sízməl/ *n* a line on a map that connects places where the effects of an earthquake were felt at the same time

Co·sen·za /kō zénssə, -zéntsə/ capital of Cosenza Province, Calabria Region, southern Italy. Population: 72,998 (2001).

Cos·grave /kóz gràyv/, **Liam** (*b.* 1920) Irish politician and lawyer. The son of William Thomas Cosgrave, he led the Fine Gael party from 1965 to 1977 and was prime minister of Ireland from 1973 to 1977.

co·sign /kṓ sìn, kō sín/ (**-signed, -sign·ing, -signs**) *vt* **1.** to sign something jointly with one or more other people or representatives of other bodies **2.** to guarantee a loan, lease, or other contractual agreement undertaken by another person by signing the contract along with that person —**co·sign·er** *n*

co·sig·na·to·ry /kō sígnə tàwree/ (*plural* **-ries**) *n* a person, government, or organization that signs a document or treaty jointly with others

co·sine /kṓ sìn/ *n* for a given angle in a right triangle, a trigonometric function equal to the length of the side adjacent to the angle divided by the hypotenuse

cos·me·ceut·i·cal /kòzmə sóotik'l/ *n* a product that falls between the categories designated as pharmaceuticals and cosmetics, especially in terms of marketing [Late 20C. Blend of COSMETIC + PHARMACEUTICAL]

cos·met·ic /koz méttik/ *n* **1.** BEAUTIFYING SUBSTANCE a preparation that is applied to the face or the body to make it more attractive, e.g., lipstick (*often used in the plural*) **2.** SUPERFICIALLY ATTRACTIVE ASPECT something added or done to something else to cover up defects ■ *adj* **1.** INTENDED TO BEAUTIFY intended to improve somebody's physical appearance ○ *cosmetic surgery* **2.** DONE ONLY FOR APPEARANCES done to make something seem better but having no real value ○ *The changes to the code of conduct were purely cosmetic, since attitudes remained fundamentally the same.* **3.** DECORATIVE designed or added for decorative purposes rather than to have any real function [Early 17C. Via French *cosmétique* < Greek *kosmētikos* "skilled in ornamenting" < *kosmein* "arrange" < *kosmos* "order"] —**cos·met·i·cal·ly** *adv*

cos·me·ti·cian /kòzmə tísh'n/ *n* somebody who makes or sells cosmetics, or who applies them professionally

cos·met·ic sur·ger·y *n* plastic surgery that is intended to improve the appearance of a part of the body, e.g., the shape of the nose or the size of the breasts

cos·me·tol·o·gy /kòzmə tóllǝjee/ *n* the study of cosmetics, or the art or profession of using cosmetics [Mid-19C. < French *cosmétologie* < *cosmétique* (see COSMETIC)] —**cos·me·tol·o·gist** *n*

cos·mic /kózmik/ *adj* **1.** OF WHOLE UNIVERSE relating to the whole universe **2.** ASTRON OF UNIVERSE APART FROM EARTH describes outer space or a part of the universe other than the Earth **3.** ENORMOUS very great in size or significance ■ *interj* EXPRESSING AMAZEMENT used to express amazement or wonder (*slang*) [Mid-17C. < Greek *kosmikos* < *kosmos* "universe"] —**cos·mi·cal·ly** *adv*

cos·mic dust *n* small particles of solid matter found in outer space, often collected in clouds

cos·mic ra·di·a·tion *n* radiation consisting of cosmic rays

cos·mic ray *n* a stream of high-energy radiation that reaches Earth from outer space

cos·mic string *n* an extremely long and thin astronomical object thought to be a space–time defect formed when the universe began

cosmo- *prefix* the universe, space ○ *cosmology* [< Greek *kosmos* "universe"]

cos·mo·chem·is·try /kòzmō kémmistree/ *n* the scientific study of the chemical composition of the universe —**cos·mo·chem·i·cal** *adj*

cos·mog·o·ny /koz móggənee/ (*plural* **-nies**) *n* **1.** the study of the origin of the universe or of a part of it **2.** a theory that seeks to explain the origin of the universe [Late 17C. < Greek *kosmogonia* "creation of the world" < *kosmos* "universe"] —**cos·mo·gon·ic** /kòzmə gónnik/ *adj* —**cos·mo·gon·i·cal** *adj* —**cos·mo·gon·i·cal·ly** *adv* —**cos·mog·o·nist** *n*

cos·mog·ra·phy /koz móggrəfee/ (*plural* **-phies**) *n* the study and description or mapping of the entire world or of the universe [14C. Via late Latin < Greek *kosmographia* < *kosmos* "universe"] —**cos·mog·ra·pher** *n* —**cos·mo·graph·ic** /kòzmə gráffik/ *adj* —**cos·mo·graph·i·cal** *adj* —**cos·mo·graph·i·cal·ly** *adv*

cos·mo·log·i·cal ar·gu·ment *n* a logical argument that tries to prove the existence of God from empirical information about the universe

cos·mo·log·i·cal prin·ci·ple *n* the principle that the universe would look the same to observers at any point in it as it does to us

cos·mol·o·gy /koz móllǝjee/ *n* **1.** the philosophical study of the nature of the universe **2.** the scientific study of the origin and structure of the universe [Mid-17C. < modern Latin *cosmologia* < Greek *kosmos* "universe"] —**cos·mo·log·ic** /kòzmə lójjik/ *adj* —**cos·mo·log·i·cal** *adj* —**cos·mo·log·i·cal·ly** *adv* —**cos·mol·o·gist** *n*

cos·mo·naut /kózmə nàwt/ *n* an astronaut in the space programs of Russia and the former Soviet Union [Mid-20C. Blend of COSMOS[1] + ASTRONAUT, after Russian *kosmonavt*]

cos·mop·o·lis /koz móppəliss/ *n* a large city where people from many different countries and cultures live [Mid-19C. < Greek *kosmos* "universe" + *polis* "city"]

cos·mo·pol·i·tan /kòzmə póllit'n/ *adj* **1.** MADE UP OF DIVERSE PEOPLES composed of or containing people from different countries and cultures **2.** SHOWING CULTURAL DIVERSITY showing the influence of many countries and cultures ○ *the city's cosmopolitan atmosphere* **3.** INTERNATIONAL IN SCOPE having worldwide relevance or scope ○ *events of national and cosmopolitan importance* **4.** KNOWLEDGEABLE AND REFINED showing a breadth of knowledge and refinement from having traveled widely ○ *his wide-ranging and cosmopolitan interests* **5.** ECOL OCCURRING WORLDWIDE describes plants or animals growing or occurring in many different parts of the world ■ *n* **1.** WELL-TRAVELED PERSON a sophisticated traveler to many different countries **2.** COCKTAIL a cocktail consisting of vodka, orange-flavoured liqueur, cranberry juice, and lime juice [Mid-17C. < COSMOPOLITE]

cos·mop·o·lite /koz móppə lìt/ *n* TRAVEL same as **cosmopolitan** *n* (sense 1) [Early 17C. Via French < Greek *kosmopolitēs* "citizen of the world" < *kosmos* "universe" + *polis* "city"] —**cos·mop·o·lit·ism** *n*

cos·mos[1] /kóz mòss, -məss/ *n* **1.** the universe considered as an ordered and integrated whole **2.** an ordered system or harmonious whole [13C. < Greek *kosmos* "order, universe"]

cos·mos[2] /kóz mòss, -məss/ (*plural* **-mos·es** or *same*) *n* a tall plant with flowers of various colors that resemble large daisies. Native to: tropical America. Genus: *Cosmos.* [Early 19C. Via modern Latin < Greek *kosmos* "order, universe, ornament"]

Cos·sack /kó sàk/ *n* **1.** a peasant of Polish or Russian descent living in southeastern Russia or in Siberia or Ukraine. Cossacks are noted for their skill in horsemanship. **2.** a member of a Russian army unit whose soldiers are or were Cossacks [Late 16C. Via Russian *kazak* < Turkic, "nomad, adventurer"]

cos·set /kóssət/ (**-set·ed, -set·ing, -sets**) *vt* to give somebody or something excessive care and protection (*disapproving*) [Mid-16C. Origin ?]

cost /kawst/ *v* (**cost, cost·ing, costs**) **1.** *vt* HAVE PARTICULAR PRICE to require the payment of a particular sum **2.** *vti* BE EXPENSIVE to require payment of a large sum of money by somebody (*informal*) **3.** *vt* CAUSE LOSS OF SOMETHING to cause somebody or something to lose, sacrifice, or suffer something **4.** (*past and past participle* **cost·ed**) *vt* CALCULATE MONEY REQUIRED FOR SOMETHING to calculate the price or expense of something ■ *n* **1.** AMOUNT PAID FOR SOMETHING the amount of money required to be paid for something **2.** MONEY SPENT DOING SOMETHING the amount of money spent in producing or doing something **3.** LOSS OR EFFORT the loss, sacrifice, suffering, or effort involved in doing something **4.** same as **cost price** ■ **costs** *npl* **1.** LEGAL EXPENSES the amount of money that is spent pursuing a legal action, especially those expenses that a losing party may be required to pay **2.** TOTAL SUM OF MONEY the calculated amount of money needed for something ○ *housing costs* [14C. Via Old French *co(u)ster* < Latin *constare* "stand firm" < *stare* "to stand"] —**cost·less** *adj*

cos·ta /kóstə/ (*plural* **-tae** /-tee/) *n* **1.** ANAT same as **rib** (sense 1) (*technical*) **2.** a part of something such as a leaf or a wing that resembles a rib [Mid-19C. < Latin, "rib"] —**cos·tal** *adj*

Cos·ta Bra·va /kòstə braávə, kàwstə-/ resort region on the Mediterranean coast of northeastern Spain, north of Barcelona

cost ac·count·ant *n* an accountant who calculates and provides detailed information on the cost of producing something or carrying out an operation in a business, and compares actual costs with expected costs

cost ac·count·ing *n* accounting that is concerned with providing detailed information on the cost of producing something or carrying out an operation in a business

Cos·ta del Sol /-del sáwl/ resort region on the Mediterranean coast of southern Spain

cos·tae plural of **costa**

Cos·ta Me·sa /-máyssə/ city in southwestern California, south of Long Beach, on the Pacific coast. Population: 110,126 (2002 estimate).

co·star /kṓ staar/, **co-star** *n* JOINT LEAD ACTOR an actor who shares prominence with another actor in a production ■ *v* (**-starred, -star·ring, -stars**) **1.** *vi* TOP THE BILL WITH OTHERS to share prominence with another actor or actors in a production **2.** *vt* FEATURE SOMEBODY AS LEAD ACTOR to include or feature somebody as one of the lead actors

cos·tard /kóstərd/ *n* a large English cooking apple [13C. < Anglo-Norman < *coste* "rib" < Latin *costa*]

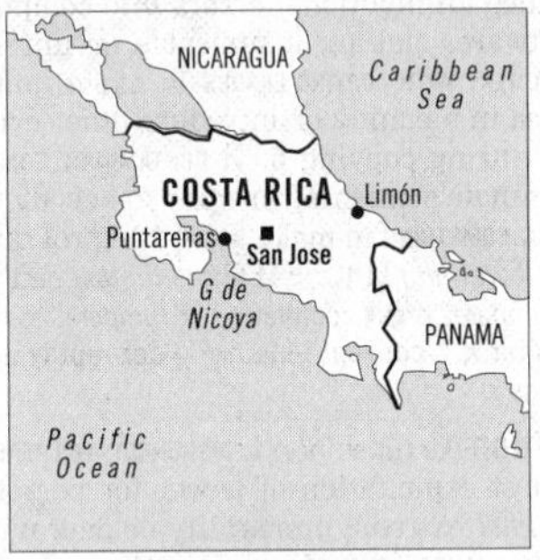

Costa Rica

Cos·ta Ri·ca /-reékə/ country in southern Central America between the Caribbean Sea and the Pacific Ocean. Language: Spanish. Currency: colón. Capital: San José. Population: 3,896,092 (2003). Area: 19,714 sq. mi./51,060 sq. km. Official name **Republic of Costa Rica** —**Cos·ta Ri·can** *n, adj*

cos·tate /kóstət, káw stàyt/ *adj* describes a leaf that has ridges or is ribbed [Early 19C. < Latin *costatus* < *costa* "rib"]

cost-ben·e·fit a·nal·y·sis *n* a method of project evaluation that compares the potential benefits with the anticipated costs

cost cen·ter *n* a section of a business to which costs can be assigned in an analysis of the relationship of costs and the value of benefits arising from them

cost-cut·ting *n* the taking of action to reduce costs, especially in a business, or the actions taken (*often used before a noun*) ○ *a cost-cutting exercise*

cost-ef·fec·tive *adj* economically worthwhile in terms of what is achieved for the amount of money spent —**cost-ef·fec·tive·ly** *adv* —**cost-ef·fec·tive·ness** *n*

cost·ing /káwsting/ *n* the cost that has been calculated for undertaking a project (*often used in the plural*)

cos·tive /kóstiv/ *adj* **1.** constipated, or causing constipation (*technical*) **2.** slow to act or speak (*literary*) [14C. Via French < Latin *constipatus*, past participle of *constipare* (see CONSTIPATE)] —**cos·tive·ly** *adv* —**cos·tive·ness** *n*

cost·ly /káwstlee/ (**-li·er, -li·est**) *adj* **1. EXPENSIVE** costing large sums of money to buy **2. LUXURIOUS** using expensive and luxurious materials **3. INVOLVING EFFORT OR TIME** involving a great deal of effort, time, or sacrifice **4. DAMAGING** causing great loss, damage, or suffering —**cost·li·ness** *n*

cost of liv·ing *n* the amount of money spent on food, clothing, housing, and other basic necessities (*hyphenated when used before a noun*)

cost-of-liv·ing in·dex *n* ECON same as **consumer price index**

cost-plus *n* a pricing system that calculates the price of a product by adding a fixed percentage as profit to the production cost

cost price *n* the price that somebody selling something paid for it

cost-push, cost-push in·fla·tion *n* inflation in which price rises result from increased production costs or similar factors rather than from customer demand

cos·tume /kós to͞om/ *n* **1. THEATRICAL CLOTHES** clothes worn to make a person look like somebody or something else, especially in a theatrical performance **2. REGIONAL OR HISTORICAL DRESS** the clothes traditionally worn in a particular place or during a particular period in the past ○ *national costume* ○ *18th-century costume* **3. CLOTHES FOR PARTICULAR ACTIVITY** the clothing appropriate for a particular activity (*dated*) ■ *vt* (**-tumed, -tum·ing, -tumes**) **1. PUT SOMEBODY IN COSTUME** to provide somebody with a costume **2. PROVIDE COSTUMES FOR SHOW** to provide clothes for a theatrical production [Early 18C. Via French < Italian *costume*, literally "custom, fashion" < Latin *consuetudin-* (see CUSTOM)]

cos·tume jew·el·ry *n* decorative jewelry that does not contain precious stones or metals

cos·tume par·ty *n* a party at which guests wear clothing suggestive of a historical period, a character from a film, or some other theme

cos·tum·i·er /ko sto͞omee ər, kàwss toom yáy/, **cos·tum·er** /kóss to͞omər, ko sto͞omər/ *n* a maker or supplier of costumes for a play, show, or festivity [Mid-19C. < French < *costumer* "provide with a costume" < *costume* (see COSTUME)]

co-sur·vi·vor *n* a close relative or friend of somebody who has experienced a traumatizing event, e.g., a rape victim, AIDS patient, or victim of a disaster

co·sy *adj, n* UK spelling of **cozy**

cot[1] /kot/ *n* **1.** a narrow collapsible bed for occasional or camping use, usually consisting of a lightweight metal or wood frame and a canvas surface or thin mattress **2.** *UK* BABYWARE same as **crib** *n* (sense 1) [Mid-17C. < Hindi *khāṭ* "framework strung with rope and used as a bed," via Sanskrit *khaṭvā* < Tamil *kaṭṭu* "tie"]

cot[2] /kot/ *n* **1.** a cover for an injured finger, shaped like the finger of a glove **2.** a small cottage (*archaic or literary*) [Old English < Germanic]

cot[3] /kot/ *abbr* MATH cotangent

cot[4] *n* AGRIC another spelling of **cote**

co·tan /kṓ tàn/ *abbr* MATH cotangent

co·tan·gent /kō tánjənt/ *n* for a given angle in a right triangle, a trigonometric function equal to the length of the side adjacent to the angle divided by that of the side opposite the angle —**co·tan·gen·tial** /kō tan jénsh'l/ *adj*

cot death *n UK* MED same as **crib death**

cote /kōt/, **cot** /kot/ *n* a small shelter, especially one for birds or animals (*usually used in combination*) [Old English < Germanic]

cot·eau /kə tṓ/ (*plural* **-eaus**) *n Can, Midwest* a hilly upland or divide between valleys [Mid-19C. < French, "hillside"]

Côte d'A·zur /kṑt də zo͝or/ part of the French Riviera near the Italian border, including Cannes, Nice, and Monaco

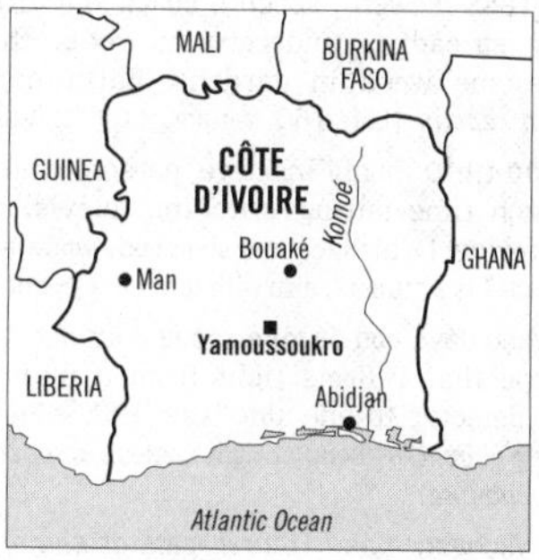

Côte d'Ivoire

Côte d'I·voire /-dee vwaár/ country in West Africa, situated north of the Gulf of Guinea and east of Liberia. Language: French. Currency: CFA franc. Capital: Yamoussoukro. Population: 16,962,491 (2003). Area: 124,503 sq. mi./322,462 sq. km. Official name **Republic of Côte d'Ivoire**. Former name **Ivory Coast**

Côte d'Or /-dáwr/ administrative region and major wine-producing area in Burgundy, east-central France. The main city in the region is Dijon. Population: 506,755 (1999). Area: 3,383 sq. mi./8,763 sq. km.

co·ter·ie /kṓtəree, kōtə rée/ *n* a small exclusive group of people who share the same interests [Early 18C. < French < Middle Low German *kote* "cottage"]

co·ter·mi·nous *adj* same as **conterminous**

coth /kawth/ *abbr* hyperbolic cotangent [Late 19C. < *cot*, shortening of COTANGENT + *h* for HYPERBOLIC]

co·tid·al /kō tī́d'l/ *adj* describes a line that joins together locations on a coastal map where tides occur simultaneously

co·til·lion /kə tíllyən, kō-/ (*plural* **-lions** or **-lons**) *n* **1. FORMAL DANCE** a formal evening ball or semiformal afternoon dance **2. FRENCH DANCE** a complex French dance popular in the 18th century **3. DANCE LIKE QUADRILLE** a dance similar to a quadrille **4. MUSIC** the music for a cotillion [Early 18C. < French *cotillon*, literally "petticoat" < Old French *cote* (see COAT)]

co·tin·ga /kō tíng gə, kə-/ *n* a bird with a broad beak and rounded wings, the male of some species having brightly colored plumage and unusual modified wing and head feathers. Native to: Central and South America. Family: Cotingidae. [Late 18C. Via French < Tupi *cutinga*]

co·to·ne·as·ter /kə tṓnee àstər/ *n* a bush with small oval leaves, cultivated for its red or orange berries that often remain throughout the winter. Native to: Europe, South Asia. Genus: *Cotoneaster*. [Mid-18C. < modern Latin < Latin *cotoneum* (see QUINCE)]

Co·to·nou /kṓtō no͞o, kōtə-/ port and capital of Atlantique Province, southern Benin. Population: 750,000 (1994).

Co·to·pa·xi /kōtə páksee/ volcano in central Ecuador, in the Andes. It is the highest active volcano in the world. Height: 19,347 ft./5,897 m.

co-tri·mox·a·zole /kō trī móksə zōl/ *n* a compound antibacterial agent. Use: treatment of urinary-tract infections. [Late 20C. < CO- + blend of *trimethoprim* + *sulfamethoxazole*]

Cots·wold /kóts wṑld/ *n* a sheep with fine long wool belonging to a breed originating in the Cotswolds, England ■ *adj* relating to the Cotswolds, in southern England [Mid-19C. < COTSWOLDS]

Cots·wolds /kóts wṑldz/ range of limestone hills in southwestern England, extending 50 mi./80 km from near Bath to northern Oxfordshire

cot·ta /kóttə/ *n* in the Roman Catholic Church and in some Anglican and Lutheran churches, a short surplice reaching to just above the waist, worn by clergy, acolytes, and choristers [Mid-19C. < Italian < Germanic]

cot·tage /kóttij/ *n* **1. SMALL RURAL HOUSE** a small house, usually situated in the countryside **2. VACATION HOME** a small vacation home in the country or beside the ocean **3. SMALL RESIDENTIAL UNIT** a small residential unit, e.g., at a camp, in which residents can be housed in groups **4.** *UK* **PUBLIC BATHROOM** a public restroom, especially one used by gay men for sexual encounters (*slang*) [14C. < Anglo-Norman *cotage* or Anglo-Latin *cotagium* < Germanic] —**cot·tag·ey** *adj*

cot·tage cheese *n* a soft white low-fat cheese with a distinctive lumpy texture and mild flavor

cot·tage coun·try *n Can* an area that has many summer cottages and is extensively used for outdoor recreation

cot·tage cur·tains *npl* a double set of curtains hanging one above the other, with the top pair usually overlapping the bottom pair and able to be tied back to let in light

Cot·tage Grove /kòttij-/ town in southeastern Minnesota, on the Mississippi River, a southeastern suburb of St. Paul. Population: 31,090 (2002 estimate).

cot·tage hos·pi·tal *n UK* a small rural hospital that does not have any resident medical staff

cot·tage in·dus·try *n* a small-scale business involving people who mostly work at home

cot·tag·er /kóttijər/ *n* **1.** a vacationer staying at a cottage **2.** *Can* a summer resident in a resort

cot·tag·ing /kóttijing/ *n UK* gay sex or a search for gay partners in public restrooms, a practice that was especially prevalent in the years when gay sex was a criminal offense (*slang*)

Cott·bus /kótbəss, -bo͝oss/ city in Cottbus District, Brandenburg, Germany, near the Polish border. Population: 125,643 (1997).

cot·ter /kóttər/ *n* **1.** a wedge, key, or bolt used to keep two parts of something such as machinery together **2.** MECH ENG same as **cotter pin** [14C. Origin ?] —**cot·tered** *adj* —**cot·ter·less** *adj*

cot·ter pin *n* a split pin inserted through corresponding holes in machine parts such as a nut and a shaft, and then bent so that it holds the parts in place

cot·ton[1] /kótt'n/ *n* **1. SOFT FIBER** a soft white downy fiber that grows in seed pods. Use: textiles. **2. FABRIC MADE FROM COTTON** fabric woven or knitted from spun cotton fiber **3. YARN OR THREAD** yarn or thread made from cotton or a synthetic substitute **4. SOMETHING MADE OF COTTON** something made of cotton fabric (*often used in the plural*) **5.** PLANTS **BUSH PRODUCING DOWNY FIBER** the tropical or subtropical bush that produces cotton. Genus: *Gossypium*. **6. SUBSTANCE LIKE COTTON** a substance that resembles cotton fiber but is produced by another plant such as the cottonwood [14C. Via French *coton* < Arabic *kuṭun*]

cot·ton[2] /kótt'n/ (**-toned, -ton·ing, -tons**) [< obsolete *cotton* "prosper," probably < COTTON[1], from the realization that raising a nap increased its value]

cotton on *vi* to grasp the meaning of what is being said or done (*informal*)

cotton to *vt* **1.** to take a liking to somebody **2.** to grasp the meaning of what has been said or done

Cot·ton /kótt'n/, **John** (1584–1652) English Puritan cleric. He preached Puritanism in England, and after emigrating to the Massachusetts Bay Colony in 1633 became an influential religious figure in New England. Known as **The Patriarch of New England**

cot·ton ball *n* a small ball of cotton wool, used for removing makeup or cleansing the skin or a wound

Cot·ton Belt *n* an extensive agricultural area in the southeastern United States where cotton is the main crop

cot·ton can·dy *n* a very sweet, usually pink, candy consisting of a mass of fluffy threads of spun sugar, often sold wrapped around a paper tube

cot·ton gin *n* a machine for separating seeds, husks, and other unwanted material from cotton fiber

cot·ton grass *n* a reedy marsh plant that has white tufted cottony flower heads. Native to: northern temperate areas. Genus: *Eriophorum*.

cot·ton moth *n* a migratory owlet moth that is a pest in cotton fields. Native to: North America. Latin name: *Alabama argillacea*.

cot·ton·mouth /kótt'n mòwth/ (*plural* **-mouths** /-mòwt͟hz, -mòwths/) *n* REPT same as **water moccasin** (sense 1) [Mid-19C. < the whitish color inside its mouth]

cot·ton-pick·ing *adj* used to indicate disapproval, annoyance, or emphasis (*slang*) [Because cotton-picking was done by only the poorest laborers]

cot·ton·seed /kótt'n seed/ *n* the seed of the cotton plant. Use: source of oil, meal.

cot·ton·seed cake *n* compressed cottonseed produced from the residue remaining after the extraction of oil. Use: livestock feed.

cot·ton stain·er *n* an insect that pierces cottonseed pods (**bolls**) and stains the fibers. Genus: *Dysdercus*.

Cot·ton State *n* the state of Alabama (*informal*)

cot·ton swab *n* a short stick with a small amount of absorbent cotton wound tightly onto one or both ends, used, e.g., in cleaning ears or applying makeup

cot·ton·tail /kótt'n tàyl/ *n* a small rabbit with brown or gray fur and a tail with a white cottony underside. Native to: North America. Genus: *Sylvilagus*.

cot·ton waste *n* waste cotton yarn. Use: cleaning material.

cot·ton·wood /kótt'n wòod/ (*plural* **-woods** or *same*) *n* a poplar tree that has seeds with cottony tufts. Native to: North America. Latin name: *Populus deltoides*.

cot·ton wool *n* **1.** raw unprocessed cotton **2.** *UK* same as **absorbent cotton** (*hyphenated when used before a noun*)

cot·ton·y /kótt'nee/ *adj* looking or feeling like cotton

cot·ton·y-cush·ion scale *n* a small sap-sucking insect that damages citrus crops in California and elsewhere. Native to: Australia. Latin name: *Icerya purchasi*.

COTW *n* the countries that opposed Saddam Hussein in the Iraq War of 2003. Full form **Coalition of the Willing**

-cotyl *suffix* cotyledon ○ *hypocotyl* [< COTYLEDON]

cot·y·le·don /kòtt'l eéd'n/ *n* **1.** the first leaf, or one of the first pair of leaves, produced by the seed of a flowering plant. They may serve as food stores, remaining in the seed at germination, or produce food by photosynthesis. **2.** a tuft of projections (**villi**) on the placenta of a mammal [Mid-16C. Via Latin, "navelwort" < Greek *kotulēdōn* "cup-shaped cavity" < *kotulē* "cup"] —**cot·y·le·don·al** *adj*—**cot·y·le·don·ar·y** *adj*—**cot·y·le·don·ous** *adj*

cot·y·lo·saur /kótt'lə sàwr/ *n* an extinct reptile with a heavy body and short legs, probably the first land vertebrate. Order: Cotylosauria. [Early 20C. < Greek *kotulē* "cup" + *sauros* "lizard"]

couch[1] /kowch/ *n* **1.** LONG SEAT a piece of upholstered furniture on which two or more people can sit side by side **2.** DOCTOR'S LONG SEAT a long seat with a headrest that a patient lies on when visiting a doctor, especially a psychiatrist **3.** BARLEY MALTING FRAME a frame on which barley grain is spread during malting **4.** FIRST COAT OF PAINT a layer of paint or varnish applied to a canvas as a first coat ■ *v* (**couched, couch·ing, couch·es**) **1.** *vt* PHRASE SOMETHING IN PARTICULAR WAY to express something using a particular style or choice of words **2.** *vti* LIE OR LAY DOWN to lie down, or lay somebody or something down (*archaic or literary; often passive*) **3.** *vt* FOOD INDUST SPREAD BARLEY FOR MALTING to spread barley on a frame for malting **4.** *vt* ARMS LOWER LANCE to lower a lance into position for an attack **5.** *vt* SURG REMOVE CATARACT to remove a cataract by pushing down the lens of the eye **6.** *vt* HANDICRAFT EMBROIDER BY HOLDING DOWN THREAD to embroider a pattern by holding down threads with other threads passed through the material [14C. < French *couche* (noun), *coucher* "lie down" < Latin *collocare* (see COLLOCATE)] —**couch·er** *n*

couch[2] /kowch, kooch/ *n* PLANTS same as **couch grass**

couch·ant /kówchənt/ *adj* in heraldry, used to describe an animal lying down with its head raised [15C. < French, present participle of *coucher* (see COUCH[1])]

cou·chette /koo shét/ *n* **1.** a seat in a compartment on a continental European train that can be converted into a sleeping berth **2.** a compartment of a train containing couchettes [Early 20C. < French, "small bed" < *couche* (see COUCH[1])]

couch grass /kówch-, kóoch-/, **couch** *n* a grass with rapidly spreading underground roots that is a troublesome weed in gardens. Latin name: *Agropyron repens*. [Late 16C. Variant of QUITCH GRASS]

couch po·ta·to *n* an inactive person who spends too much time sitting watching television (*slang disapproving*) [< the idea that somebody who watches the "boob tube" is a "tuber"; also with reference to potato chips]

cou·dé /koo dáy/, **cou·dé tel·e·scope** *n* an astronomical telescope that reflects light from a main mirror onto a detector to one side [Late 19C. < French, past participle of *couder* "bend at right angles" < *coude* "elbow" < Latin *cubitum*]

cou·gar /kóogər, -gaar/ (*plural* **-gars** or *same*) *n* same as **mountain lion** [Late 18C. Via French *couguar* < Guarani *cuguaçuarana*]

cough /kawf/ *v* (**coughed, cough·ing, coughs**) **1.** *vi* EXPEL AIR FROM LUNGS NOISILY to release air through the windpipe and mouth sharply and noisily **2.** *vt* EXPEL SOMETHING BY COUGHING to expel something from the lungs or windpipe by coughing **3.** *vi* MAKE SHARP NOISE to make a noise that is similar to the sound of somebody coughing ■ *n* **1.** ACT OR SOUND OF COUGHING a sudden noisy release of air through the windpipe and mouth, often expelling an obstruction **2.** ILLNESS CAUSING COUGHING an illness causing coughing because of an infection in the lungs [14C. Ultimately < Germanic, an imitation of the sound] —**cough·er** *n*
cough up *vti* to give something reluctantly, e.g., money or information (*slang*)

cough drop *n* a medicated candy for soothing a cough or sore throat

cough syr·up *n* a medicated syrup that soothes or suppresses a cough

~~**cought**~~ incorrect spelling of **caught**

co.uk *abbr* UK commercial organization (*used in Internet addresses*) See table at **domain name**

could /kòod, kəd/ CORE MEANING: a modal auxiliary verb used as the past tense of "can" ○ *My mother did the best she could for my brother and me.* ○ *She could perform on the trapeze.* ○ *His feet were so swollen that he could hardly walk.* ○ *We were so tired we couldn't stay awake.*
1. *modal v* EXPRESSING POSSIBILITY used to indicate that something is possibly true or happening in the future ○ *She thinks that medical technology could be the field for her.* **2.** *modal v* EXPRESSING REQUEST used when making polite requests ○ *Could you close the window please?* **3.** *modal v* INDICATING POSSIBLE PAST SITUATION used to indicate a possible situation in the past that did not happen ○ *We could have gone.* **4.** *modal v* EXPRESSING POLITE OFFER used to make polite offers and suggestions ○ *You could stay at my place.* **5.** *vi* FOR EMPHASIS used in questions to emphasize strong feelings about something ○ *How could you do that?* [Old English *cūe*, past tense of *cunnan* "know" (see CAN[1]); altered after SHOULD, WOULD]

could·n't /kóodd'nt/ *contr* could not

couldst /kòodst/ 2nd person singular past of **could** (*archaic*)

could've /kóoddəv/ *contr* could have (*informal*)

USAGE See *of*.

---

cou·lee /kóolee/ *n* **1.** LAVA FLOW a thick short flow of viscous molten lava **2.** *Can, Northwest US* DEEP GULLY DRY IN SUMMER a deep gully formed by rain or melting snow and usually dry in the summer **3.** *Southern US* SMALL STREAM a small stream, canal, or bayou **4.** *Southern US* STREAMBED a streambed, sometimes dry **5.** *Midwest* SHALLOW VALLEY a broad shallow valley [Early 19C. < French, "flow" < feminine past participle of *couler* "to flow" < Latin *colare* "to strain"]

cou·lis /kóolee/ *n* a thin purée of fruit or vegetables used as a garnish [Late 20C. Via French < Old French *coleïs* "flowing"]

cou·lisse /koo leéss/ *n* in a theater, a piece of side scenery on a stage or the space between two of these pieces (*often used in the plural*) [Early 19C. < French < *(porte) coulisse* "sliding (door)" < Old French *(porte) coleïce* (see PORTCULLIS)]

cou·loir /kool waár/ *n* a broad mountain gully, especially one prone to avalanches [Early 19C. < French, "channel" < *couler* (see COULEE)]

cou·lomb /kóo lòm/ *n* the SI unit of electric charge equal to the amount of charge transported by a current of one ampere in one second. Symbol **C** [Late 19C. After Charles Augustin de *Coulomb* (1736–1806), French physicist]

Cou·lomb's law /kóo lomz-/ *n* a law of electricity stating that the force of attraction or repulsion between two electric charges is proportional to their product and inversely proportional to the square of the distance between them [See COULOMB]

cou·lom·e·try /koo lómmətree/ *n* a means of analyzing the results of a process of electrolysis by measuring the amount of electricity used in the process to determine the amount of the substance produced [Mid-20C. < COULOMB] —**cou·lo·met·ric** /kòolə méttrik/ *adj* —**cou·lo·met·ri·cal·ly** *adv*

coul·ter /kóltər/, **col·ter** *n* a vertical blade attached to a plow that cuts into the soil in front of a plowshare [Pre-12C. < Latin *culter* "knife"]

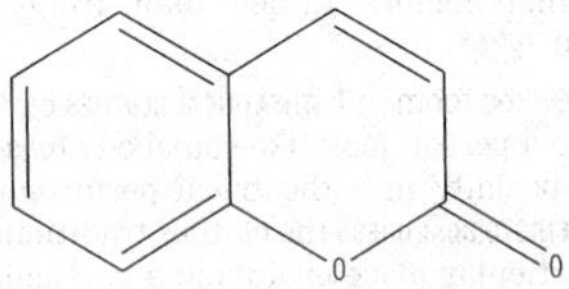

coumarin

cou·ma·rin /kóomərin/ *n* a fragrant compound. Source: plants or made synthetically. Use: in perfumes and medicine. Formula: $C_9H_6O_2$. [Mid-19C. < French *coumarine* < Tupi *cumarú* "tonka bean tree," a source of coumarin] —**cou·ma·ric** *adj*

cou·mes·tan /kóomi stàn/ *n* a phytoestrogen found especially in red clover and bean sprouts [Late 20C. < COUMARIN]

cou·mes·trol /koo mé stràwl/ *n* a phytoestrogen found especially in alfalfa [Mid-20C. < COUMARIN]

~~**councelor**~~ incorrect spelling of **counselor**

coun·cil /kównss'l/ *n* **1.** PEOPLE RUNNING LOCAL AFFAIRS a group of people elected to govern a local district **2.** COMMITTEE an appointed or elected body of people with an administrative, advisory, or representative function **3.** CHURCH ASSEMBLY an assembly of church representatives who meet to decide matters of discipline and doctrine **4.** COUNCIL MEETING a meeting of a council **5.** MEETING FOR DISCUSSION a meeting to discuss or decide something [Pre-12C. Via Anglo-Norman *cuncile* < Latin *concilium* "calling together"]

USAGE council or **counsel**? ***Council*** is a noun only, meaning a body of people, especially in an advisory or administrative context. ***Counsel*** is both a noun and a verb, and has to do with advice, particularly of a professional nature, and the giving of it. The noun ***counsel*** most often means a lawyer or lawyers, whereas a *counselor* gives some other kind of professional advice, as in a *debt counselor* or *marriage counselor*. The verb describes the activity of such advisers: *The company psychologist counsels employees experiencing stress. International financial analysts counseled caution.*

---

coun·cil ar·e·a *n UK* the geographic or administrative area under the control of a local council

Coun·cil Bluffs /kòwnss'l blúffs/ city in southwestern Iowa, on the Missouri River, directly east of Omaha, Nebraska. Population: 58,640 (2002 estimate).

coun·cil cham·ber *n* a room where a council gathers for discussion

coun·cil·lor *n* PUBLIC ADMIN another spelling of **councilor**

coun·cil·man /kównss'lmən/ (*plural* **-men** /-mən/) *n* a man who is a member of a council, especially of a local government

coun·cil-man·ag·er plan *n* a type of local government in the United States in which an elected city council hires a professional administrator to run the public services and other operations of the city

Coun·cil of Eu·rope *n* an organization of European states founded in 1949 to further political unity

Coun·cil of the Eu·ro·pe·an Un·ion *n* the main decision-making body of the European Union, attended by one minister from each of its constituent national governments who has the power to commit his or her government to a decision

Coun·cil of Trent *n* a Roman Catholic Church council held in Trento, Italy, from 1545 to 1563 to respond to the threat of Protestantism. The council reaffirmed and defined Roman Catholic beliefs and laid the foundation for the Counter-Reformation.

coun·cil of war *n* **1.** a wartime meeting of military officers to discuss a plan of action **2.** a meeting called to formulate a plan of action in an emergency

coun·cil·or /kówns'lər/, **coun·cil·lor** *n* **1.** an elected or appointed member of an advisory council **2.** a member of a council elected to govern a local district —**coun·cil·or·ship** *n*

coun·cil·per·son /kównss'l pùrss'n/ (*plural* **-per·sons** or **-peo·ple** /-pèep'l/) *n* a member of a council, especially of a local government

coun·cil·wom·an /kównss'l wòomman/ (*plural* **-wom·en** /-wìmmin/) *n* a woman member of a council, especially of a local government

coun·sel /kównss'l/ *n* **1.** COURT LAWYER a lawyer or group of lawyers who conduct cases in court or give legal advice (*takes a singular or plural verb*) **2.** SOMEBODY WHO GIVES ADVICE somebody whose advice is sought or who acts as an official adviser **3.** ADVICE advice sought from or given by somebody, especially somebody who is wise or knowledgeable (*formal; often used in the plural*) **4.** CONSULTATION consultation with others (*archaic or literary*) ■ *vt* (**-seled, -sel·ing, -sels**) **1.** ADVISE SOMEBODY TO DO SOMETHING to advise somebody on a particular course of action (*formal*) **2.** ADVISE SOMEBODY ON PERSONAL PROBLEMS to give somebody advice and support on personal or psychological matters, usually in a professional context [12C. Via Old French *conseil* < Latin *consilium* "consultation" < *consulere* "seek advice"] ◇ **keep your own counsel** to keep your thoughts and intentions secret

USAGE See ***council.***

PRONUNCIATION The word *counsel* ("lawyer, adviser") is correctly pronounced /kównss'l/, not /kónss'l/, which is the pronunciation of *consul* ("government official working abroad").

SYNONYMS See ***recommend.***

coun·se·lee /kòwnssə lée/ *n* somebody who receives counseling

coun·sel·ing /kównss'ling/, **coun·sel·ling** *n* **1.** help with personal or psychological matters usually given by a professional **2.** meetings with a counselor to receive help with personal or psychological problems

coun·sel·or /kównss'lər/, **coun·sel·lor** *n* **1.** ADVISER ON PERSONAL PROBLEMS somebody, usually a professional, who helps others with personal, social, or psychological problems **2.** ADVISER ON SPECIAL SUBJECT a professional who gives advice on such matters as careers, education, or health **3.** SOMEBODY WHO GIVES ADVICE somebody such as a friend who gives advice **4.** *also* **coun·sel·or-at-law** (*plural* **coun·sel·ors-at-law**) *or* **coun·sel·lor-at-law** (*plural* **coun·sel·lors-at-law**) ATTORNEY an attorney, especially one who acts for a client in a trial **5.** HIGH-RANKING DIPLOMAT a diplomat ranking below an ambassador or minister **6.** CHILDREN'S SUPERVISOR a supervisor of young people at a summer camp —**coun·se·lor·ship** *n*

count[1] /kownt/ *v* (**count·ed, count·ing, counts**) **1.** *vti* SAY NUMBERS to say numbers in order, usually starting at one **2.** *vti* ADD UP to add things up to see how many there are or to find the value of an amount of money **3.** *vt* INCLUDE SOMEBODY OR SOMETHING to include somebody or something in a calculation ○ *If you count me and Jodie, there will be 15 people.* **4.** *vti* CONSIDER OR BE CONSIDERED to consider somebody or something, or be considered, in a particular way or as a particular thing **5.** *vi* BE OF IMPORTANCE to be of importance or value **6.** *vi* HAVE VALUE to have a specific value **7.** *vti* KEEP TIME to keep musical time by counting beats ■ *n* **1.** SAYING OF NUMBERS an act of saying numbers in order **2.** FINDING OF TOTAL an addition of people or things to find a total **3.** TOTAL OF SOMETHING a total that is reached by adding things up **4.** ONE OF MANY POINTS any one of a number of points, e.g., in a discussion **5.** CHARGE AGAINST SOMEBODY a charge against somebody who is on trial **6.** BALLS AND STRIKES ON BASEBALL BATTER in baseball, the number of balls and strikes that a batter has accumulated during a turn at bat **7.** BOXING REFEREE'S COUNT in boxing, a count to ten by the referee during which a boxer who has been knocked down must stand up or lose the match [14C. < Old French *conte* (noun), *co(u)nter* "reckon" < Latin *computare* "reckon together"] ◇ **keep count** to count and remember the number of people or things counted ◇ **lose count** to fail to count accurately or remember the number of people or things counted ◇ **out** *or* **down for the count 1.** unconscious or deeply asleep and unlikely to wake again for some time (*slang*) **2.** BOXING unable to stand up, after being knocked down, within the ten-second count given by the referee in a boxing match, and therefore losing the match

count against *vt* to be damaging to somebody's interests or prospects

count down *vi* to count backward from a number to zero or from a given time to something such as the launch of a rocket

count in *vt* to include somebody in a plan

count on, count up·on *vt* **1.** to rely on somebody to do something **2.** to be sure that something will happen

count out *vt* **1.** COUNT THINGS ONE BY ONE to count something such as money one item at a time **2.** NOT INCLUDE SOMEBODY to exclude somebody from a plan **3.** DECLARE BOXER DEFEATED BY COUNTING TEN to disqualify a boxer who has been knocked down and fails to get up within ten seconds

count toward *or* **towards** *vt* to be included as part of something

count upon *vt* same as **count on**

count[2] /kownt/ *n* a nobleman in some European countries, of a rank equal to that of a British earl [14C. Via Old French *conte* < Latin *comit-* "companion," literally "somebody who goes with"]

count·a·ble /kówntəb'l/ *adj* **1.** able to be counted **2.** describes a noun that can be preceded by "a" or "an" followed by a plural verb, and usually has a distinct plural form —**count·a·bil·i·ty** /kòwntə bíllətee/ *n* —**count·a·bly** *adv*

count·down /kównt dòwn/ *n* **1.** BACKWARD COUNT a count in descending order before an event such as a rocket launch **2.** ACTIVITIES BEFORE EVENT the activities carried on during the period of time before something such as a rocket launch **3.** PREPARATORY PERIOD the period immediately preceding an important event

coun·te·nance /kówntənənss/ (*formal*) *n* **1.** FACE OR EXPRESSION somebody's face, or the expression on it **2.** COMPOSURE composure or self-control ■ *vt* (**-nanced, -nanc·ing, -nanc·es**) TOLERATE OR APPROVE SOMETHING to tolerate, accept, or give approval to something [13C. < Old French *contenance* "demeanor," literally "contents" < *contenir* (see CONTAIN)] —**coun·te·nanc·er** *n*

count·er[1] /kówntər/ *n* **1.** FLAT SURFACE a flat surface on which food or drink is served, merchandise is displayed, or business is transacted **2.** FLAT SURFACE IN KITCHEN a flat surface in a kitchen on which food can be prepared or dishes laid out **3.** SMALL MARKER in board games a small object, often a flat disk, used to mark a player's position or to keep score **4.** IMITATION COIN an object, usually a flat disk, used as a substitute for a coin [14C. Via Anglo-Norman *counteor* < medieval Latin *computatorium* "place for counting" < Latin *computare* "reckon together"] ◇ **under the counter** secretly and unofficially, usually because there is something illegal about what is being done

coun·ter[2] /kówntər/ *vti* (**-tered, -ter·ing, -ters**) **1.** CONTRADICT OR OPPOSE SOMETHING to say something that contradicts or opposes what somebody has said **2.** DO SOMETHING IN OPPOSITION to do something in opposition to what somebody else is doing, so as to make it less effective **3.** PUNCH OPPONENT IN RETURN in boxing, to defend yourself against a punch from an opponent, and deliver a punch in return ■ *adv* **1.** OPPOSITE in the opposite direction **2.** CONTRARILY in a contrary manner ■ *adj* CONTRADICTING contradicting or opposing something ○ *a counter blow* ■ *n* **1.** RESPONSE a response made in retaliation to something that has been said **2.** OPPOSITE OF SOMETHING something that is the opposite of something else or that is done in opposition to something else **3.** BOXING RETURNING PUNCH in boxing, a punch that counters a punch aimed by an opponent **4.** FENCING PARRY in fencing, a parry in which the foils make a circular movement **5.** NAUT END OF SHIP'S STERN the part of the stern of a ship or boat that juts out above the water line **6.** PRINTING HOLLOW PART OF TYPEFACE a hollow part of a piece of type, e.g., the inner parts of the letters "p" and "d" **7.** MOVING AWAY FROM ATTACKING LINEMEN in football, a move in which the player carrying the football runs to the side of the field away from the attacking linemen [14C. < COUNTER-] ◇ **run counter to something** to be in direct contrast or opposition to something

count·er[3] /kówntər/ *n* **1.** a device that counts automatically **2.** somebody whose job is to count something such as votes [14C. Partly via Anglo-Norman *count(e)our*, Old French *conteor* < Latin *computator* < *computare* "reckon together"; partly < COUNT[1]]

counter- *prefix* **1.** contrary, opposing ○ *counterattack* **2.** complementary, corresponding ○ *counterpart* [Via Anglo-Norman *countre-* < Latin *contra* (see CONTRA-)]

coun·ter·ac·cu·sa·tion *n*	**coun·ter·plot** *n, vi*
coun·ter·a·gent *n*	**coun·ter·ploy** *n*
coun·ter·ag·gres·sion *n*	**coun·ter·pro·pos·al** *n*
coun·ter·ar·gue *vi*	**coun·ter·pro·test** *n*
coun·ter·as·sault *n*	**coun·ter·ques·tion** *n*
coun·ter·bid *n*	**coun·ter·raid** *n*
coun·ter·block·ade *n*	**coun·ter·ral·ly** *n*
coun·ter·blow *n*	**coun·ter·re·ac·tion** *n*
coun·ter·brace *vt*	**coun·ter·re·form** *n*
coun·ter·cam·paign *n*	**coun·ter·re·sponse** *n*
coun·ter·com·plaint *n*	**coun·ter·re·tal·i·a·tion** *n*
coun·ter·con·spir·a·cy *n*	**coun·ter·shot** *n*
coun·ter·coup *n*	**coun·ter·spy** *n*
coun·ter·crit·i·cism *n*	**coun·ter·state·ment** *n*
coun·ter·de·mand *n*	**coun·ter·step** *n*
coun·ter·de·ploy·ment *n*	**coun·ter·strat·e·gy** *n*
coun·ter·ef·fort *n*	**coun·ter·strike** *n*
coun·ter·ev·i·dence *n*	**coun·ter·stroke** *n*
coun·ter·fire *n*	**coun·ter·sug·ges·tion** *n*
coun·ter·force *n*	**coun·ter·suit** *n*
coun·ter·hy·poth·e·sis *n*	**coun·ter·sur·veil·lance** *n*
coun·ter·in·fla·tion *n*	**coun·ter·tac·tics** *npl*
coun·ter·in·fla·tion·ar·y *adj*	**coun·ter·threat** *n*
coun·ter·in·flu·ence *n*	**coun·ter·thrust** *n*
coun·ter·or·der *n*	**coun·ter·trend** *n*
coun·ter·play *n*	**coun·ter·view** *n*

coun·ter·act /kòwntər ákt/ (**-act·ed, -act·ing, -acts**) *vt* to prevent something from having an effect, or lessen its effect —**coun·ter·ac·tion** *n* —**coun·ter·ac·tive** *adj* —**coun·ter·ac·tive·ly** *adv*

coun·ter·ar·gu·ment /kówntər àargyəmənt/ *n* a fact or opinion that challenges the reasoning behind somebody's proposal and shows that there are grounds for taking an opposite view

coun·ter·at·tack /kówntər ə tàk/ *n* an attack made in response to an attack by an enemy or opponent

coun·ter·at·trac·tion /kòwntər ə tráksh'n/ *n* something set up to draw people away from another attraction

coun·ter·bal·ance /kówntər bàllənss/ *vt* (**-anced, -anc·ing, -anc·es**) **1.** HAVE OPPOSING EFFECT ON SOMETHING to be or have an equal and opposing force or effect on something **2.** BALANCE SOMETHING WITH EQUAL WEIGHT to make something balance by putting equal weight on the opposite side ■ *n* **1.** COUNTERBALANCING PERSON OR THING somebody or something that has an equal and opposing force or effect on somebody or something else **2.** BALANCED STATE a state of balance with an equal and opposing force or effect **3.** WEIGHT THAT BALANCES ANOTHER a weight that exactly balances another weight

coun·ter·bat·te·ry fire /kówntər bàttəri-/ *n* firing

weapons with the objective of destroying enemy artillery

coun·ter·blast /kówntər blàst/ *n* an attack on somebody in speech or writing, made in response to an attack by that person

coun·ter·change /kówntər chàynj/ (**-changed, -chang·ing, -chang·es**) *v* **1.** *vti* to interchange the parts or positions of two things **2.** *vt* to checker or dapple something with colors

coun·ter·charge /kówntər chaàrj/ *n* **1.** ACCUSATION AGAINST ACCUSER an accusation made against the person or group who has accused another of something **2.** MIL CHARGE AGAINST AGGRESSORS a charge made by police or military forces against a group of aggressors ■ *vt* (**-charged, -charg·ing, -charg·es**) CHARGE ACCUSER WITH SOMETHING to bring a charge against an accuser

coun·ter·check /kówntər chèk/ *n* **1.** SECOND CHECK a check made to ensure that a previous check was correct **2.** RESTRAINT ON SOMETHING something that acts to block or restrain something else ■ *v* (**-checked, -check·ing, -checks**) **1.** *vti* CHECK AGAIN to carry out a second check on something, in order to ensure that the first was accurate **2.** *vt* RESTRAIN SOMETHING to act in order to block the force or action of something

coun·ter·claim *n* /kówntər klàym/ a claim entered by the defendant in a court of civil law, as a response to the original claim that was entered against the defendant by the plaintiff ■ *vi* /kòwntər kláym/ (**-claimed, -claim·ing, -claims**) to make a claim in response to, or as a defense against, an earlier claim —**coun·ter·claim·ant** /kòwntər kláymənt/ *n*

coun·ter·clock·wise /kòwntər klók wīz/ *adv, adj* in the direction opposite to the one that the hands of a clock move

coun·ter·con·di·tion·ing /kòwntər kən dísh'ning/ *n* a process of psychological conditioning that attempts to replace somebody's undesired habitual response to a particular situation with a desired learned response

coun·ter·cul·ture /kówntər kùlchər/ *n* a culture that has ideas and ways of behaving that are consciously and deliberately very different from the cultural values of the larger society that it is part of —**coun·ter·cul·tur·al** /kòwntər kúlchərəl/ *adj* —**coun·ter·cul·tur·ist** *n*

coun·ter·cur·rent /kówntər kùr ənt/ *n* **1.** CURRENT FLOWING OPPOSITE WAY a current that flows in the opposite direction to another current **2.** CONTRARY TREND a trend that is contrary to the prevailing one ■ *adj* **1.** FLOWING IN OPPOSITE DIRECTION flowing in the opposite direction to another current **2.** USING OPPOSING CURRENTS involving the flow of two currents in opposite directions —**coun·ter·cur·rent·ly** *adv*

coun·ter·cy·cli·cal /kòwntər síklik'l, -sīk-/ *adj* designed to compensate for the undesirable effects of business cycles

coun·ter·dem·on·stra·tion /kòwntər demmən stráysh'n/ *n* a public demonstration that is held to oppose the purpose of another demonstration that was recently held or is currently being held —**coun·ter·dem·on·stra·tor** /kòwntər démmən stràytər/ *n*

coun·ter·es·pi·o·nage /kòwntər éspee ə naàzh/ *n* government activity designed to detect and prevent spying by an enemy

coun·ter·ex·am·ple /kówntər ig zàmp'l/ *n* a fact or argument that indicates that a theory, scientific hypothesis, or mathematical theorem is not true

coun·ter·fac·tu·al /kòwntər fákchoo əl/ *adj* not reflecting or considering the facts

coun·ter·feit /kówntərfit/ *adj* **1.** FORGED made as a copy of something, especially money, in order to defraud or deceive people **2.** FALSE pretended in order to deceive somebody ○ *counterfeit geniality* ■ *v* (**-feit·ed, -feit·ing, -feits**) **1.** *vti* FORGE to make realistic copies of something, especially money, in order to defraud or deceive people **2.** *vt* PRETEND TO FEEL SOMETHING to pretend to have an emotion in order to deceive somebody ■ *n* FORGERY a copy of something, especially money, made in order to defraud or deceive people [14C. < Anglo-Norman *countrefet,* past participle of *countrefaire* "counterfeit" < medieval Latin *contrafacere* < Latin *contra-* "against" + *facere* "make, do"] —**coun·ter·feit·er** *n*

~~counterfit~~ incorrect spelling of **counterfeit**

coun·ter·foil /kówntər fòyl/ *n* the part of a check, ticket, or other paper used in a financial transaction that is detached and kept by the issuer as a record

coun·ter·fort /kówntər fàwrt/ *n* a buttress that sticks out at right angles from a wall [Late 16C. < French *contrefort* < Old French *contreforcier* "buttress"]

coun·ter·glow /kówntər glō/ *n* ASTRON same as **gegenschein** [Mid-19C. Translation of German *Gegenschein*]

coun·ter·heg·e·mon·ic /kòwntər hejə mónnik/ *adj* contrary to the prevailing fashion, especially in intellectual matters

coun·ter·in·sur·gen·cy /kòwntər in súrjənssee/ *n* military and political activities undertaken by a government to defeat a rebellion or guerrilla movement —**coun·ter·in·sur·gent** *n*

coun·ter·in·tel·li·gence /kòwntər in téllijənss/ *n* government and military activities designed to gather information about enemy spies, thwart their activities, and supply them with false information

coun·ter·in·tu·i·tive /kòwntər in tóo itiv/ *adj* not in accordance with what would naturally be assumed or expected ○ *I know it's counterintuitive, but the highest grade in this system is D and the lowest is A.* —**coun·ter·in·tu·i·tive·ly** *adv*

coun·ter·ir·ri·tant /kòwntər írrit'nt/ *n* **1.** a worry or annoyance that distracts somebody from attending to another worry or annoyance **2.** a skin cream that produces an irritation to reduce underlying tissue inflammation —**coun·ter·ir·ri·ta·tion** /kòwntər írri táysh'n/ *n*

coun·ter·leak /kówntər leèk/ *n* exposure to a reporter, by an anonymous source, of somebody else's leaking of information, with the result that the reporter may then suspect a conspiracy

coun·ter·man /kówntər màn, -mən/ (*plural* **-men** /-mèn, -mən/) *n* a man who serves food at a counter, e.g., in a diner, delicatessen, or luncheonette

coun·ter·mand /kówntər mànd, kòwntər mánd/ *vt* (**-mand·ed, -mand·ing, -mands**) **1.** CANCEL COMMAND to give an order or instruction that a previous order or instruction should not be followed **2.** CALL SOMEBODY OR SOMETHING BACK to recall somebody or something sent somewhere by a previous order ■ *n* ORDER CANCELING ANOTHER an order canceling a previous order [15C. < French *contremander* < Latin *mandare* (see MANDATE)]

coun·ter·march /kówntər maàrch/ *n* **1.** RETURN MARCH a march, especially one undertaken by soldiers, back from a position following the same route as that taken on the outward march **2.** CHANGE IN MARCHING DIRECTION a marching maneuver in which soldiers change the direction they are marching in while retaining their positions within a formation **3.** COMPLETE CHANGE OF APPROACH a complete change in somebody's behavior or way of doing things ■ *v* (**-marched, -march·ing, -march·es**) **1.** *vti* MARCH BACK to return from a position by marching back along the same route, or make soldiers do this **2.** *vi* CHANGE DIRECTION OF MARCHING to change the direction of a formation of marching soldiers without altering the positions of the individual soldiers

coun·ter·mea·sure /kówntər mèzhər/ *n* something that is done in reaction to and as a defense against a hostile action by somebody else, or something that is done in order to deal with a threat

coun·ter·mine /kówntər mīn/ *v* (**-mined, -min·ing, -mines**) **1.** *vti* EXPLODE ENEMY'S MINES IN AREA to place explosive mines in an area in order to explode mines placed there by an enemy **2.** *vti* DIG TUNNELS AGAINST ENEMY'S TUNNELS to dig underground tunnels in order to intercept or destroy tunnels dug by an enemy **3.** *vt* SECRETLY FOIL PLOT to take secret action against somebody's plans ■ *n* **1.** TUNNEL DUG AGAINST ENEMY'S TUNNELS a tunnel dug to intercept or destroy tunnels dug by an enemy **2.** SECRET ACTION TO FOIL PLOT a secret action designed to undermine or destroy a plot or scheme

coun·ter·move /kówntər moòv/ *n* a move made in response to an opponent's move, e.g., in a game ■ *vi* (**-moved, -mov·ing, -moves**) to act in response to an opponent's action, e.g., in a game —**coun·ter·move·ment** *n*

coun·ter·of·fen·sive /kówntər ə fénssiv/ *n* a major attack or series of attacks made by a military force in response to the attacks made by an enemy

coun·ter·of·fer /kówntər àwffər, -òffər/ *n* a revised offer from somebody who rejects another person's offer as unsatisfactory, made in part to continue their negotiations toward a purchase or agreement

coun·ter·pane /kówntər pàyn/ *n* a cover for a bed and its bedding (*dated*) [15C. Alteration of *counterpoint,* via French < medieval Latin *culcita puncta* "stitched quilt"]

coun·ter·part /kówntər paàrt/ *n* **1.** SOMEBODY OR SOMETHING CORRESPONDING TO ANOTHER somebody or something that resembles another or functions similarly in a different system or group **2.** MATCHING PART OR THING either of two parts that fit together or are complementary ○ *I identified bolt A but could not find its counterpart, socket B.* **3.** ACTOR PLAYING OPPOSITE ANOTHER an actor who plays opposite somebody else in a play or movie **4.** COPY OF LEGAL DOCUMENT a copy of a lease, contract, or other legal document that is held by one party to a transaction and that duplicates the copy held by the other party

coun·ter·par·ty /kówntər paàrtee/ (*plural* **-ties**) *n* one of the two people, companies, or organizations involved in a business transaction, as referred to by the other participant in the transaction

coun·ter·per·son /kówntər pùrss'n/ *n* somebody who serves food at a counter, e.g., in a diner, delicatessen, or luncheonette

coun·ter·plan /kówntər plàn/ *n* **1.** a plan made to defeat or respond to another plan **2.** a plan prepared as an alternative or substitute for the primary plan

coun·ter·plea /kówntər pleè/ *n* a plea made by the plaintiff in a court of law in response to the plea made by the defendant

coun·ter·point /kówntər pòynt/ *n* **1.** SOUNDING TOGETHER OF MELODIES in a piece of music, the sounding together of two or more melodic lines each of which displays an individual and differentiated melodic contour and rhythmic profile **2.** MELODY COMBINED WITH ANOTHER in a piece of music, a melodic line or part that is sung or played at the same time as another **3.** CONTRASTING ELEMENT in a work of art, a theme or element that forms a contrast with another ■ *vt* (**-point·ed, -point·ing, -points**) **1.** CONTRAST WITH SOMETHING to make an effective contrast with something, especially in a work of art ○ *Richard's social ease counterpoints his sister's awkwardness.* **2.** ARRANGE MUSIC IN COUNTERPOINT to add one or more melodic lines in counterpoint in a piece of music [15C. Via French < medieval Latin *(cantus) contrapunctus* "(song) with notes marked opposite (the melody)"]

coun·ter·poise /kówntər pòyz/ *n* **1.** COUNTERACTING WEIGHT a weight that balances another weight **2.** COMPENSATING FACTOR something that has the effect of diminishing or compensating for the effect of something else ○ *The government had covertly encouraged the fascists as a counterpoise to the reformers.* **3.** BALANCED STATE a state of equilibrium ■ *vt* (**-poised, -pois·ing, -pois·es**) **1.** OPPOSE AND BALANCE SOMETHING to counteract or compensate for something by providing an equal force, influence, or weight **2.** MAKE SOMETHING BALANCED to bring something into a state of balance [15C. Alteration of French *contrepeis* "counterweight"]

coun·ter·pro·duc·tive /kòwntər prə dúktiv/ *adj* producing problems or difficulties instead of helping to achieve a goal ○ *A direct challenge to her authority is likely to be counterproductive.* —**coun·ter·pro·duc·tive·ly** *adv* —**coun·ter·pro·duc·tiv·i·ty** /kòwntər produk tívvətee/ *n*

coun·ter·punch /kówntər pùnch/ *n* a punch made by a boxer in response to an opponent's punch —**coun·ter·punch** *vi* —**coun·ter·punch·er** *n*

coun·ter·ref·or·ma·tion /kòwntər refər máysh'n/ *n* a reform or reform movement that seeks to reverse the effects of earlier reforms

Coun·ter Ref·or·ma·tion, Coun·ter-Ref·or·ma·tion *n* the movement of reform and regeneration instituted by the Roman Catholic Church in 1545 to counter the increasing strength of Protestantism in Europe as a result of the Reformation

coun·ter·rev·o·lu·tion /kòwntər revə lóosh'n/ *n* subversive activity with the objective of undoing the effects of a previous revolution and overthrowing the government or social system that it produced —**coun·ter·rev·o·lu·tion·ist** *n*

coun·ter·rev·o·lu·tion·ar·y /kòwntər revə lóosh'n èrree/ *n* (*plural* **-ies**) **1.** SOMEBODY FIGHTING REVOLUTIONARY GOVERNMENT somebody, especially a member of a military force, who seeks to overthrow a national government or social system established by a revolution **2.** SOMEBODY OPPOSED TO REVOLUTION an opponent of a revolution as a means of political and social change ■ *adj* OPPOSED TO REVOLUTION opposed to a specific revolution or to revolution as a means of political and social change

coun·ter·sank past tense of **countersink**

coun·ter·scarp /kówntər skaarp/ *n* the slope or bank on the outer side of the ditch outside a fort [Late 16C. Via French *contrescarpe* < Italian *controscarpa* < *scarpa* "scarp"]

coun·ter·shad·ing /kówntər shàyding/ *n* a pattern of coloring on an animal's skin or coat where the upper parts are darker than the lower, counteracting the effects of sun and shade and camouflaging the animal

coun·ter·shaft /kówntər shàft/ *n* an intermediate shaft that transmits power from the main shaft to a working part but rotates in the opposite direction, especially in a belt drive or gear drive

coun·ter·sign /kówntər sīn/ *vt* (**-signed, -sign·ing, -signs**) to sign a document that somebody else has signed, e.g., as a witness to the signature or to confirm an authorization ■ *n* **1.** an agreed and secret sign, word, or signal given as a password to a military sentry in order to pass **2.** LAW same as **countersignature**

coun·ter·sig·na·ture /kòwntər sígnachər, -chòor/ *n* a signature added to a document that has already been signed, e.g., to witness the first signature or to confirm an authorization

coun·ter·sink /kówntər singk/ *vt* (**-sank** /-sàngk/ or **-sunk** /-sùngk/, **-sunk, -sink·ing, -sinks**) **1.** MAKE HOLE TO INCLUDE SCREW HEAD to widen the top of the hole for a screw or bolt so that the head will fit into the hole and be level with or below the surface **2.** MAKE SCREW HEADS LEVEL WITH SURFACE to place screws, bolts, or nails in wood or another material so that their heads are level with or below the surface of the material ■ *n* **1.** HOLE THAT ACCEPTS SCREW HEAD a hole for a screw or bolt that is wider at the top so that the head will fit into the hole and be level with or below the surface **2.** COUNTERSINKING TOOL a special drill bit or other tool for countersinking holes for screws or bolts

coun·ter·stain /kówntər stàyn/ *n* an additional stain applied to a specimen to be examined under a microscope, in order to bring out features not revealed by the primary stain ■ *vt* (**-stained, -stain·ing, -stains**) to use a counterstain on a microscope specimen

coun·ter·sub·ject /kówntər sùb jekt/ *n* a second theme or melodic line that contrasts with the main one in a fugue or other piece of music employing counterpoint

coun·ter·sue /kówntər sòo/ (**-sued, -su·ing, -sues**) *vti* to bring a lawsuit against somebody who is suing you

coun·ter·sunk past participle, past tense of **countersink**

coun·ter·ten·or /kówntər tènnər/ *n* **1.** an adult male singing voice that is higher than tenor and covers the alto range, produced by singing in falsetto **2.** a man whose singing voice is a countertenor [14C. Via French *contrateneur* < obsolete Italian *contratenore* "against the tenor"]

coun·ter·ter·ror /kówntər tèrrər/ *adj* intended or used to combat terrorism

coun·ter·ter·ror·ism /kòwntər térrə rìzzəm/ *n* military or political activities intended to combat or prevent terrorism —**coun·ter·ter·ror·ist** *adj, n*

coun·ter·top /kówntər tòp/ *n* the surface of a counter, especially a kitchen counter, or of the top of a display or storage case in a store

coun·ter·trade /kówntər tràyd/ *n* a system of international trade in which countries exchange goods or services, rather than pay for imports with currency —**coun·ter·trad·er** *n*

coun·ter·trans·fer·ence /kòwntər transs fúr ənss, -trànssfərənss/ *n* a process that sometimes occurs in psychoanalytic therapy where repressed emotions in the therapist are awakened by identification with the experiences and feelings of the patient

coun·ter·type /kówntər tīp/ *n* **1.** a type that is the complete opposite of another type **2.** a type that corresponds with or is equivalent to another type

coun·ter·vail /kòwntər váyl, kówntər vàyl/ (**-vailed, -vail·ing, -vails**) *v* **1.** *vti* to exert a counteracting power or influence against something, especially against a harmful force, idea, or influence **2.** *vt* to offset or compensate for something [14C. < Anglo-Norman *contrevaloir*, literally "be worth against"]

coun·ter·weigh /kòwntər wáy/ (**-weighed, -weigh·ing, -weighs**) *vt* to counterbalance something

coun·ter·weight /kówntər wàyt/ *n* **1.** a weight that balances another weight **2.** something such as a force, idea, or influence that counteracts or compensates for something else —**coun·ter·weight·ed** *adj*

coun·ter·wom·an /kówntər wòomman/ (*plural* **-wom·en** /-wìmmin/) *n* a woman who serves food at a counter, e.g., in a diner, delicatessen, or luncheonette

coun·ter·work /kówntər wùrk/ *n* **1.** work or action undertaken to counteract other work or another action **2.** fortifications against an attack

count·ess /kówntəss/ *n* **1.** the wife or widow of a count or earl **2.** a woman who holds the rank of count or earl [12C. Via Old French *contesse* < medieval Latin *comitissa* < Latin *comit-* "companion"]

count·ing /kównting/ *prep* taking a particular person or thing into consideration in a total ○ *We were thirteen in all, not counting the children in the party.*

count·ing·house /kównting hòwss/ *n* the place where the financial work of a business is done or where its accounts are kept (*archaic*)

count·less /kówntləss/ *adj* many more than it is possible or convenient to count ○ *I've told him countless times to be more careful.* —**count·less·ly** *adv*

count noun *n* a noun that refers to one thing rather than a mass of something and that can be used with "a" or "an," with a number, and in the plural. Examples of English count nouns are "cat," "sheep," and "child."

count pa·la·tine (*plural* **counts pa·la·tine**) *n* **1.** LOCAL RULER IN HOLY ROMAN EMPIRE a count who ruled over his own domain (**county palatine**) in the Holy Roman Empire, or an official who ruled an area of the empire as the emperor's representative **2.** SOMEBODY WITH JUDICIAL POWER OVER COUNTY in former times, an earl or other nobleman in England or Ireland who held the highest judicial authority and other supreme powers within his own domain (**county palatine**) **3.** ROMAN PALACE OFFICIAL in the late Roman Empire, a palace official with judicial authority

coun·tri·fied /kúntri fīd/, **coun·try·fied** *adj* **1.** having a style or quality appropriate to the country ○ *a pretty, countrified row of houses* **2.** not fashionable or sophisticated and of a style or quality considered typical of rural areas

coun·try /kúntree/ *n* (*plural* **-tries**) **1.** SEPARATE NATION a nation or state that is politically independent, or a land that was formerly independent and remains separate in some respects **2.** HOMELAND the nation or state where somebody was born or is a citizen **3.** GEOGRAPHICALLY DISTINCT AREA a large area of land regarded as distinct from other areas, e.g., because of its natural boundaries or because it is inhabited by a specific group of people **4.** FARMED AND UNDEVELOPED AREA an area that is farmed or remains in a relatively undeveloped state, as distinct from cities, towns, and other built-up areas ○ *a house in the country* **5.** REGION WITH SPECIAL CHARACTER a region that is distinguished by particular characteristics or is associated with a particular activity, person, or group of people ○ *Since this was rebel country, checkpoints were set up along the road.* **6.** NATION'S PEOPLE the people of a nation or state, especially when affected as a group by political or other events ○ *a scandal that rocked the country* **7.** MUSIC same as **country music** ■ *adj* **1.** CHARACTERISTIC OF RURAL AREAS characteristic of rural areas or the people living there **2.** OF COUNTRY MUSIC characteristic of, similar to, or performing country music [13C. < Old French *cuntrée* < assumed Vulgar Latin *(terra) contrata* "(land) lying opposite" < Latin *contra* "against"] —**coun·try·ish** *adj*

coun·try and west·ern *n* MUSIC same as **country music** (*hyphenated when used before a noun*)

coun·try bump·kin *n* same as **bumpkin**[1]

coun·try club *n* a club for social and leisure activities with facilities for golf, tennis, or other outdoor sports, usually located in the suburbs or the country

coun·try cous·in *n* somebody from a rural area whose unsophisticated reactions to city life are considered amusing (*dated*)

coun·try-dance *n* a folk dance in which several couples move within a square, a circle, or two lines —**coun·try-danc·ing** *n*

coun·try·fied *adj* another spelling of **countrified**

coun·try gen·tle·man *n* a man who owns an estate in the country

coun·try house *n* a house in the country, usually a large residence or a second home

coun·try·man /kúntreemən/ (*plural* **-men** /-mən/) *n* **1.** a citizen by birth or adoption of the same nation as somebody else **2.** a rural resident, especially a man raised in the country who is familiar with rural life

coun·try mar·riage *n Can* formerly in Canada, a common-law marriage between a fur trader of European origin and a Native North American woman

coun·try mile *n* a long distance (*informal*)

coun·try mu·sic *n* popular music, based on the traditional music of the rural South and the cowboy music of the West, whose songs express strong personal emotions. Country musicians typically play such instruments as the guitar and fiddle. —**coun·try mu·si·cian** *n*

coun·try·per·son /kúntree pùrss'n/ (*plural* **-peo·ple** /-peep'l/ or **-per·sons**) *n* **1.** a citizen by birth or adoption of the same nation as somebody else **2.** a rural resident, especially somebody raised in the country who is familiar with rural life

coun·try risk *n* the likelihood that a country will be unable or unwilling to repay its debts

coun·try rock[1] *n* rock music that is strongly influenced by country music

coun·try rock[2] *n* rock that has been intruded by magma or that surrounds veins of mineral ore

coun·try·seat /kùntree seet/ *n* an estate or a large house in the country that is a family's hereditary property

coun·try·side /kúntree sīd/ *n* **1.** an area of land that is farmed or in a relatively undeveloped state ○ *a village set in the wooded countryside* **2.** the people who live in a rural area ○ *The entire countryside was up in arms against the proposed development.*

coun·try·wide /kúntree wīd/ *adj, adv* throughout an entire nation ○ *a countrywide organization for professional women* ○ *rates that were increased countrywide*

coun·try·wom·an /kúntree wòommən/ (*plural* **-wom·en** /-wìmmin/) *n* **1.** a woman who is a citizen by birth or adoption of the same nation as somebody else **2.** a woman who lives in the country, especially one raised there who is familiar with rural life

coun·ty /kówntee/ (*plural* **-ties**) *n* **1.** a unit of local government and one of the administrative subdivisions that the states of the United States and, excepting major cities, all of England and Wales are divided into **2.** the people who live in a county [13C. Via Anglo-Norman *counté* < Latin *comitatus* "group of companions" < *comit-* "companion"]

coun·ty a·gent *n* a government employee who provides advice to the residents of a rural county on subjects such as agriculture and home economics

coun·ty clerk *n* a local government official who keeps records and maintains documents for a county and its residents

coun·ty coun·cil *n* a local government body administering a county in the United Kingdom and some parts of the United States

coun·ty court *n* a local court of a state having jurisdiction in civil and criminal matters in one or more counties

coun·ty fair *n* a local fair featuring the sale of farm produce and the presentation of livestock in competitions and displays

coun·ty pa·la·tine (*plural* **coun·ties pa·la·tine**) *n* **1.** the lands governed by a nobleman or imperial official with the rank of count palatine in the Holy Roman Empire **2.** formerly in England and Ireland, the lands administered by an earl or other nobleman who exercised judicial authority

coun·ty seat *n* a town or city that is the seat of local government for a county

coun·ty town *n UK* same as **county seat**

coun·ty·wide /kówntee wīd/ *adj, adv* throughout an entire county

coup /koo/ *n* **1.** SEIZURE OF POLITICAL POWER the sudden violent overthrow of a government and seizure of political power, especially by the military **2.** SUCCESSFUL ACTION a success that is unexpected and achieved with exceptional skill ○ *Getting the author to come and speak was quite a coup.* **3.** FEAT OF BRAVERY among some Native American peoples, a feat of bravery during battle, especially touching an enemy warrior without harming him [Late 18C. Via French, "blow" < medieval Latin *colpus* < Greek *kolophos* "blow with the fist"]

coup de fou·dre /ko͝o də fo͞odrə/ (*plural* **coups de fou·dre** /*pronunc. same*/) *n* a sudden overwhelming feeling of love for somebody [< French, "stroke of lightning"]

coup de grâce /ko͝o də graáss/ (*plural* **coups de grâce** /*pronunc. same*/), **coup de grace** (*plural* **coups de grace**) *n* **1.** a final blow or shot that kills a person or animal, especially one intended to end suffering **2.** the final action that assures victory or success, especially in a sporting event [< French, "blow of mercy"]

USAGE When foreign words and expressions enter our language, how much adaptation does their pronunciation undergo? At first a borrowed word is generally recognized as foreign, and is pronounced much as it would be in its original language. As time goes on, pronunciation and even spelling are likely to be modified so as to be more typical of English, until the word's foreign origins are invisible except to etymologists (word historians). *Discotheque, laissez-faire, mayonnaise,* and *uncle,* for example, are at various points along this continuum of assimilation. Curiously, ***coup de grâce*** is often mistakenly pronounced *ko͝o də graá,* as people, perhaps having heard, for example, *bourgeois, esprit de corps,* and *foie gras* pronounced without their final consonants, imagine the expression should be pronounced in French. But the correct French pronunciation is more like the correct English pronunciation: *ko͝o də gráss.*

coup de main /ko͝o də máN/ (*plural* **coups de main** /*pronunc. same*/) *n* a sudden, fierce, and successful surprise attack against an enemy [< French, "blow of the hand"]

coup d'é·tat /ko͝o day taá/ (*plural* **coups d'é·tat** or **coup d'é·tats** /*pronunc. same*/) *n* POL same as **coup** (sense 1) [< French, "stroke of state"]

coup de thé·â·tre /ko͝o də tay aátrə/ (*plural* **coups de thé·â·tre** /*pronunc. same*/) *n* **1.** SURPRISING TURN OF EVENTS something that occurs in a very dramatic way, especially a sensational and unexpected turn of events **2.** EFFECTIVE PIECE OF THEATER a strongly dramatic moment in a play or other theatrical production, produced by an exceptional piece of writing, performance, or staging **3.** SUCCESSFUL PLAY a play or other theatrical performance that is very successful [< French, "stroke of theatre"]

coup d'oeil /ko͝o dőyə/ (*plural* **coups d'oeil** /*pronunc. same*/) *n* a quick look at something, especially one that provides an overall general impression [< French, "stroke of the eye"]

coupe[1] /koop/ *n* **1.** a dessert of ice cream and fruit **2.** a small shallow glass bowl, often with a stem, for fruit and ice cream [Late 19C. Via French, "goblet" < late Latin *cuppa* (see CUP)]

coupe[2] /koop/ *n* a car with two doors and a hard, fixed roof that seats two people or has a small rear seat [Early 20C. Variant of COUPÉ]

cou·pé /koo páy, koop/ *n* a closed four-wheeled carriage that has two inside seats for passengers and a driver's seat outside in the front [Mid-19C. < French *(carrosse) coupé* "cut-down (carriage)" (because smaller than earlier models), past participle of *couper* "cut" (see COPE[1])]

Cou·pe·rin /ko͞opə ráN/, **François** (1668–1733) French composer and organist. The best-known member of a musical family, his baroque keyboard compositions greatly influenced Johann Sebastian Bach. Known as **Le Grand**

cou·ple /kúpp'l/ *n* **1.** TWO SIMILAR THINGS two things of the same kind that are together or are considered as a pair ○ *found a couple of mugs in the cupboard* **2.** SEVERAL a few things of the same kind ○ *There are a couple of questions I'm not sure about.* **3.** TWO PEOPLE SHARING LIVES two people who are married, are living together, or have an intimate relationship **4.** TWO PEOPLE DOING SOMETHING TOGETHER two people, especially a man and a woman, who are sitting, walking, dancing, or working together ○ *There were only a few couples on the dance floor.* **5.** SOMETHING THAT JOINS something that links or joins two similar things **6.** MECH ENG SYSTEM OF OPPOSING FORCES in mechanics, a system of two equal forces that are parallel and operate in opposite directions **7.** HUNTING PAIR OF DOGS a pair of hunting dogs attached to each other by a leash, or the double collar and leash on which they are held **8.** PHYS, ELEC ELECTRICAL CONTACT a connection of two dissimilar metals that develops an electric current in the presence of an electrical conductor (**electrolyte**) ■ *v* (**-pled, -pling, -ples**) **1.** *vt* ASSOCIATE TWO THINGS to associate or combine one person or thing with another ○ *High prices coupled with poor living conditions made their lives difficult.* **2.** *vt* JOIN TWO THINGS to join or link two things or people ○ *to couple freight cars* **3.** *vi* HAVE SEX to have sexual intercourse (*formal*) ■ *adj* A FEW two or a few (*informal*) ○ *a couple days ago* [13C. Via French < Latin *copula* "link"] —**cou·ple·dom** *n*

USAGE When ***couple*** refers to two partners or married people, it may be treated as singular or plural, depending on whether the couple acts as a single unit or as two separate people within the relationship: *The couple wants to be married before the end of the year. The couple have not reconciled, and continue to live apart.* However, if a pronoun refers to ***couple***, it is almost always plural (*they, them, their*), and so the verb should be plural as well: *The couple have* [not *has*] *repeatedly asked that their privacy be respected.* In other uses, ***couple*** is often followed by *of* and a plural noun, in which case it is treated as plural: *A couple of books were on the table.* In informal uses the strict sense of "two" may be expanded to "several." The use of ***couple*** without *of* in such contexts (*I bought a couple CDs.*) is increasingly heard but should be avoided in formal writing.

cou·pler /kúpplər/ *n* **1.** *US* CONNECTOR FOR RAILROAD CARS a device on a railroad car that enables the cars to be connected to form a train. Can term **coupling 2.** ENG same as **coupling** (sense 4) **3.** MEANS OF COUPLING THINGS something or somebody that joins or combines two things **4.** DEVICE CONNECTING KEYBOARDS on an organ or harpsichord, a mechanical or electronic device that connects two keyboards so that all the keys can be played from one keyboard

cou·plet /kúpplət/ *n* two lines of verse that form a unit alone or as part of a poem, especially two that rhyme and have the same meter [Late 16C. < French, "little couple" < *couple* (see COUPLE)]

cou·pling /kúppling/ *n* **1.** SOMETHING THAT JOINS TWO THINGS something that joins two things, especially a device for connecting two pieces of pipe, hose, or tube **2.** JOINING TWO THINGS TOGETHER a joining together or linking of two persons or things ○ *a disastrous coupling of two very different singers* **3.** SEX ACT an act of sexual intercourse **4.** MECH ENG LINK THAT TRANSFERS POWER a part of a mechanical system by which power is transmitted from one rotating part to another part **5.** *Can, UK* RAIL same as **coupler** (sense 1) **6.** ZOOL TRUNK OF ANIMAL'S BODY the part of the body of a four-legged animal between the forequarters and hindquarters **7.** ELEC CONNECTION OF ELECTRICAL CIRCUITS a means of connecting two electrical circuits so that power can be passed between them, or the process of connecting electrical circuits in this way

cou·pon /ko͞o pòn, kyo͞o-/ *n* **1.** VOUCHER REDEEMED BY STORE OR COMPANY a voucher that entitles somebody to a discount, refund, or gift, typically issued as a sales promotion **2.** ORDER FORM a printed form, e.g., in an advertisement, that may be filled in and returned to order a product or request information **3.** FORM FOR PAYMENT BY INSTALLMENTS a form or card showing the payment due on a specific date for something that is paid for on an installment plan. The card is returned with the payment. **4.** CERTIFICATE OF INTEREST ON BOND a detachable part of a bond that indicates a date and the amount of interest paid on that date. The holder must present it in order to receive payment of the interest. **5.** TICKET IN RATIONING SYSTEM a ticket issued under a rationing system that entitles somebody to an amount of a rationed item and that must be handed in in exchange for that item [Early 19C. < French, "piece cut off" < *couper* (see COPE[1])]

cou·pon·ing /ko͞o pònning, kyo͞o-/ *n* the use of coupons as a means of promoting a product's sales or of saving money on purchases

cour·age /kúr ij/ *n* the ability to face danger, difficulty, uncertainty, or pain without being overcome by fear or being deflected from a chosen course of action ○ *She showed great courage throughout this difficult time.* [13C. < Old French *corage* < Latin *cor* "heart"] —**cou·ra·geous** /kə ráyjəss/ *adj* —**cou·ra·geous·ly** *adv* —**cou·ra·geous·ness** *n*

CULTURAL NOTE ***The Red Badge of Courage***, a novel by Stephen Crane (1895). Set during the Civil War, it tells the story of an idealistic soldier, Henry Fleming, who panics in battle and temporarily deserts. During a scuffle with another deserter, he receives a minor wound. Returning to battle bearing this "badge of courage," he performs with heroism but is wracked by guilt.

SYNONYMS ***courage, bravery, valor, fearlessness, nerve, guts, pluck, mettle***

CORE MEANING: personal resoluteness in the face of danger or difficulties

courage the ability to face danger, difficulty, uncertainty, or pain without being overcome by fear or being deflected from a chosen course of action ○ *a supreme act of courage under fire* ○ *She must pluck up courage and tell him the truth.* **bravery** courage in the face of danger, difficulty, or pain ○ *A friend paid tribute to his bravery throughout his long illness.* **valor** courage, especially that shown in war or battle ○ *He was awarded the Congressional Medal of Honor for his valor.* ○ *He praised the valor and determination of our troops.* **fearlessness** resoluteness in the face of dangers or challenges ○ *a police officer displaying determination, fearlessness, and devotion to duty* ○ *We walked across the viaduct with the fearlessness of the young.* **nerve** coolness, steadiness, and self-assurance ○ *He didn't have the nerve to upset his boss's plans.* ○ *She almost lost her nerve and backed out.* **guts** (*slang*) strength of character and boldness ○ *It takes a lot of guts to get back to normal activities after such a terrible injury.* ○ *Why don't they have the guts to tackle the government?* **pluck** courage and determination in meeting danger or difficulty ○ *Very few people have had the pluck to stand up to their mother.* ○ *It took pluck to face up to her critics.* **mettle** spirited determination ○ *Only time will tell if she has the mettle to rise to the challenge.* ○ *He showed his mettle in putting on the show against the odds.*

~~**courageous**~~ incorrect spelling of **courageous**

cou·rante /koo raánt/ *n* **1.** a musical composition in quick triple time, often part of a baroque suite **2.** a dance of French and Italian origin in triple time with short quick steps [Late 16C. < French, "running"]

Cour·bet /koor báy/, **Gustave** (1819–77) French painter. He was a leading French realist with such controversial works as *Burial at Ornans* (1850). A supporter of the Paris Commune (1871), he died in exile.

"To record the manners, ideas, and aspect of the age as I myself saw them—to be a man as well as a painter—in short to create a living art—that is my aim."
[Gustave Courbet, *Realism*; 1855]

cou·reur de bois /kòo rör də bwaá/ (*plural* **cou·reurs de bois** /*pronunc. same*/) *n* somebody of French or French and Native American descent who trapped and traded furs in the 18th and 19th centuries in the north and northwest of what is now Canada [Early 18C. < French, "woods runner"]

cour·gette /koor zhét/ *n UK* PLANTS, FOOD same as **zucchini** [Mid-20C. < French, "small gourd," via Old French *cohourde* < Latin *cucurbita*]

cou·ri·er /kóoree ər, kúree-/ *n* **1.** OFFICIAL MESSENGER a diplomat, soldier, or other person with the responsibility of carrying and delivering official documents **2.** SECRET MESSENGER a smuggler or illicit carrier of something such as illegal drugs **3.** SOMEBODY PROVIDING DELIVERY SERVICE a person or company that delivers documents or small and valuable packages by hand **4.** *UK* TRAVELERS' GUIDE a paid guide and helper who accompanies a group of travelers and makes arrangements for them, especially somebody employed by a travel agency to do this ■ *vt* (**-ered, -er·ing, -ers**) SEND SOMETHING BY COURIER to send a document or package by a commercial courier service [14C. < French, "runner" < Latin *currere* "to run"]

course /kawrss/ *n* **1.** PROGRAM OF STUDY a program of study or training, especially one that leads to a degree or certificate from an educational institution **2.** CLASS TAUGHT AT EDUCATIONAL INSTITUTION a session or series of sessions that students attend to learn a subject, often as part of a school curriculum that leads to a degree or certificate ○ *a short course in comparative literature* **3.** ACTION CHOSEN an action or series of actions that somebody decides to take ○ *The simplest course of action would be to say nothing.* **4.** SEQUENCE OF EVENTS the progression or development of a sequence of events, especially a development that is normal or expected ○ *events that changed the course of history* **5.** PERIOD OF TIME the progression or development of a period of time ○ *in the course of the afternoon* **6.** DIRECTION TRAVELED the direction or route along which something travels **7.** PATH OF RIVER the route followed by a river or stream or by something very long such as a road or boundary **8.** PART OF MEAL one of two or more different dishes or types of food that are served in sequence during a meal **9.** PLACE FOR RACE OR SPORT an area where a race is run or where a sport in which players progress over the area is played ○ *a golf course* **10.** ESTABLISHED SEQUENCE OF TREATMENT a sequence of medical treatment, exercise, or medication that is followed over a period of time ○ *on a course of antidepressants* **11.** ONWARD MOVEMENT swift onward movement ○ *Nothing could interrupt his headlong course.* **12.** GREYHOUND CHASE a chase or race by dogs such as greyhounds **13.** LAYER OF BRICKS one of the layers of bricks that make up a wall **14.** LOWEST SAIL ON SHIP the lowest sail or row of sails on a square-rigged ship ■ *v* (**coursed, cours·ing, cours·es**) **1.** *vi* RUN FAST to flow or run swiftly **2.** *vti* HUNT ANIMALS WITH GREYHOUNDS to hunt animals, especially hares, with greyhounds or other dogs that hunt by sight **3.** *vt* USE GREYHOUNDS FOR HUNTING to use greyhounds or other dogs that hunt by sight [13C. Via French *cours* < Latin *cursus*, past participle of *currere* "to run"] ◇ **in due course** after the lapse of an appropriate period of time ◇ **of course 1.** without any question or doubt ○ *Of course you must go!* **2.** used to show that the speaker has just understood something or agrees with something ○ *"We must tell nobody about this." "Of course."* **3.** used to point out a possibility that somebody may not have considered **4.** as may be expected ○ *Of course, we were hoping it would never happen to us.* ◇ **off course** away from the direction that you were going in ○ *The boat was blown off course.* ◇ **on course** in the right direction, or in a favorable position to achieve what you want to do ○ *We were on course to complete the project on time.*

SPELLCHECK See *coarse.*

cours·er[1] /káwrssər/ *n* **1.** a dog that is trained to hunt its quarry by sight instead of by scent **2.** a hunter who uses coursers [Early 17C. < COURSE]

cours·er[2] /káwrssər/ *n* a strong swift horse (*literary*) [13C. < Old French *corsier* < Latin *cursus* (see COURSE)]

cours·er[3] /káwrssər/ *n* a bird related to plovers that is a swift runner. Native to: dry regions of Africa and Asia. Subfamily: Glariolidae. [Mid-18C. Anglicization of modern Latin *Cursorius* < Latin *cursor* (see CURSORY)]

course·ware /káwrss wèr/ *n* software and data used in computer-based training [Late 20C. < COURSE + SOFTWARE]

course·work /káwrss wùrk/ *n* work that is assigned to students as part of an educational course and counts toward the grade given for the course

cours·ing /káwrssing/ *n* the sport of hunting with dogs such as greyhounds that follow their quarry using sight instead of scent

court[1] /kawrt/ *n* **1.** MEETING WHERE LEGAL JUDGMENTS ARE MADE a session of an official body that has authority to try cases, resolve disputes, or make other legal decisions ○ *She's threatening to take us to court over this.* **2.** *also* **Court** JUDGE the constituted authority presiding over a court of law ○ *The court heard opening arguments on Tuesday.* **3.** COURTROOM OR COURTHOUSE a place where a court of law is held **4.** OPEN SPACE WITHIN WALLS an open space partly or completely surrounded by buildings and walls **5.** OPEN AREA INSIDE BUILDING a large open or roofless area within a building **6.** AREA FOR BALL GAME an area marked off for playing a sport such as tennis or basketball **7.** MONARCH'S ATTENDANTS the ministers, courtiers, and officials of the royal household who attend a king or queen **8.** MEETING OF MONARCH AND ATTENDANTS an occasion when a king or queen and the ministers, courtiers, and officials of the royal household are assembled **9.** MONARCH'S RESIDENCE the place where a king or queen and the court are usually in residence **10.** IMPORTANT PERSON'S FOLLOWERS a group of people who devote their time to the service and flattery of a noble, rich, or important person **11.** SHORT STREET a short street of houses that is closed at one end **12.** GOVERNING BODY the governing body or council of an organization such as a corporation or academic institution [13C. Via Anglo-Norman < Old French *cort* < Latin *cohort-* "enclosed space"] ◇ **be laughed out of court** to be ridiculed so severely that what you have to say is not considered seriously (*informal*) ◇ **pay court to somebody 1.** to try to win influence with somebody or to win somebody's approval or favor through flattery or attentiveness **2.** to try to win somebody's love (*dated*) ◇ **rule something out of court** to refuse absolutely to allow something to take place

court[2] /kawrt/ (**court·ed, court·ing, courts**) *v* **1.** *vt* BE ATTENTIVE TO SOMEBODY to try to win influence with somebody or to win somebody's approval or favor through flattery or attentiveness **2.** *vt* TRY TO GAIN SOMETHING to try to gain something such as somebody's attention or admiration by behaving in ways that are intended to attract or encourage it **3.** *vt* RISK EXPERIENCING SOMETHING BAD to behave in a way that increases the likelihood of failure, injury, or other misfortune ○ *courted disaster* **4.** *vt* WOO SOMEBODY to try to win somebody's love (*dated*) **5.** *vi* BE SWEETHEARTS to spend time together in a romantic relationship as a prelude to getting married (*dated*) ○ *We used to come here when we were courting.* **6.** *vt* ZOOL TRY TO ATTRACT MATE to engage in behavior that is designed to attract another animal or bird as a mate [Early 16C. < Old Italian *corteare* < Latin *cohort-* "enclosed space"]

court bouil·lon /koor bóol yòn, kawr bóol yòn/ *n* a liquid used for poaching fish, made with water flavored with vegetables, herbs, and wine or vinegar. The liquid is discarded after the fish has been poached. [< French, "short broth"]

court card *n UK* same as **face card**

court case *n* LAW same as **case**[1] *n* (sense 6)

cour·te·ous /kúrtee əss/ *adj* polite in a way that shows consideration of others or good manners [13C. < Old French *corteis* "courtly" < *cort* (see COURT[1])] —**cour·te·ous·ly** *adv* —**cour·te·ous·ness** *n*

cour·te·san /káwrtəzən/ *n* a prostitute or mistress, especially one associated with a rich, powerful, or upper-class man who provides her with luxuries and status [Mid-16C. Via French *courtisane* < Italian *cortigiana* "female courtier" < *corte* "court" < Latin *cohort-* "enclosed space"]

cour·te·sy /kúrtəssee/ *n* (*plural* **-sies**) **1.** POLITE OR CONSIDERATE BEHAVIOR consideration for other people, or good manners ○ *He didn't even have the courtesy to offer me a seat.* **2.** POLITE OR CONSIDERATE ACTION something done out of politeness or consideration for another person ○ *We should certainly go, if only as a courtesy to Helen.* ■ *adj* **1.** FOR SAKE OF POLITENESS given or done as a courtesy ○ *a courtesy call* **2.** PROVIDED FREE provided free of charge ○ *A courtesy limousine will take you to the airport.* [13C. < Old French *curtesie* < *corteis* "courtly" < Latin *cohort-* "enclosed space"] ◇ **(by) courtesy of somebody** through somebody's generosity or help

cour·te·sy card *n* a card given to customers of a supermarket or other business that entitles them to special benefits or privileges

cour·te·sy light *n* a light inside the passenger compartment of a vehicle that turns on automatically when the door is opened

cour·te·sy ti·tle *n* a personal title that is used to address somebody out of politeness or as a social convention even though the person is not professionally or socially entitled to it

court·house /káwrt hòwss/ (*plural* **-hous·es** /-hòwzəz/) *n* **1.** a building where a court of law is held **2.** a building where the offices of a county government are located

court·i·er /káwrtee ər, -tyər/ *n* **1.** an aristocrat who frequents a royal court or attends a king or queen **2.** somebody who flatters a more important person [13C. < Anglo-Norman *courteour* < Old French *courtoyer* "be at court" < *cort* (see COURT[1])]

~~courtious~~ incorrect spelling of **courteous**

court·ly /káwrtlee/ (**-li·er, -li·est**) *adj* **1.** WITH REFINED MANNERS showing great delicacy and refinement in behavior **2.** INSINCERELY POLITE insincerely polite or deferential in order to win somebody's favor **3.** OF HIGHEST QUALITY rich or fine and suitable for a royal court —**court·li·ness** *n*

court·ly love *n* a medieval European code of behavior that idealized the love of a knight for a usually married noblewoman and prescribed how they should act toward each other

court-mar·tial *n* (*plural* **courts-mar·tial** or **court-mar·tials**) **1.** MILITARY COURT a military court that tries members of the military and others for offenses under military law **2.** MILITARY TRIAL a trial by court-martial ■ *vt* (**court-mar·tialed, court-mar·tial·ing, court-mar·tials**) TRY BY MILITARY COURT to try somebody by a military court for an offense under military law

court of ap·peals *n* a court that has authority to hear appeals of the judgments of lower courts

court of chan·cer·y *n* a court of equity, ruling on matters not covered by common law

court of claims *n* a federal court that has jurisdiction over claims brought against the government

court of com·mon pleas *n* a court in some states that has general jurisdiction

court of do·mes·tic re·la·tions *n* LAW same as **family court**

court of hon·or *n* a military court that investigates questions involving personal honor

court of in·quir·y *n* a military tribunal that investigates a matter of concern, especially in order to determine whether official charges should be brought

court of law *n* a court that hears legal cases and issues rulings based on legal statutes or common law

court of rec·ord *n* a court that has its proceedings placed on an official permanent record and has the power to give penalties for contempt of court

Court of Saint James's *n* the court of the monarch of the United Kingdom, to which ambassadors are accredited

court or·der *n* an official order issued by the judge of a court, requiring or forbidding somebody to do something

Cour·trai /koor tráy/ city in West Flanders, western

Belgium. It is known for its textile industries. Population: 75,099 (1999).

court re·cord·er *n UK* same as **court reporter**

court re·port·er *n* a stenographer who records the proceedings of a law court and prepares a verbatim report of them

court·room /káwrt ro͞om, -ro͝om/ *n* a room used for holding a session of a court of law

court·ship /káwrt ship/ *n* **1. PRELUDE TO MARRIAGE** the period of a romantic relationship before marriage **2. TRYING TO GAIN SOMEBODY'S LOVE** the act of paying attention to somebody with a view to developing a more intimate relationship **3. INGRATIATING BEHAVIOR** friendly and often ingratiating attention for the purpose of winning a favor or establishing an alliance or other relationship **4.** ZOOL **MATING BEHAVIOR** behavior designed to attract another animal or bird as a mate, or the time during which an animal or bird engages in this

court·side /káwrt sīd/ *adj, adv* at the side of an athletic court where a match or game such as tennis or basketball is being played

court ten·nis *n* the original form of tennis, played on an indoor court whose sides have walls off which the ball may be played

court watch *n* a community program set up to allow concerned citizens to observe trial proceedings in order to ensure the effectiveness of the legal system and the competency and fairness of judges

court·yard /káwrt yaard/ *n* an area of ground that is surrounded by buildings, lies inside a large building, or is adjacent to a building and enclosed by walls

cous·cous /ko͞oss ko͞oss/ *n* **1.** a food resembling tiny grains, made from semolina and cooked by steaming or soaking in boiling water **2.** a North African dish consisting of a spicy stew of meat and vegetables served with couscous [Late 16C. Via French < Arabic *kuskus* < *kaskasa* "pulverize"]

cous·in /kúzz'n/ *n* **1. UNCLE'S OR AUNT'S CHILD** a child of somebody's uncle or aunt **2. DISTANT RELATIVE** somebody to whom somebody else is related through the brother or sister of a grandparent, great-grandparent, or an even older ancestor **3. SOMEBODY WITH MUCH IN COMMON** somebody with whom another feels connected because of similar ancestry, ethnic background, or interests ○ *our Canadian cousins* **4. RELATED THING** something that is similar to or connected with something else ○ *The new idea is a cousin of chaos theory.* **5. TERM OF ADDRESS BETWEEN SOVEREIGNS** used by European sovereigns as a term of address for another sovereign or a member of a royal family [13C. Via French < Latin *consobrinus* "mother's sister's child" < *sobrinus* "maternal cousin"]

Cou·sin /koo záN/, **Victor** (1792–1867) French philosopher. He wrote studies of Blaise Pascal and Immanuel Kant. His original works include *Philosophical Fragments* (1826).

> "Art for art's sake."
> [Victor Cousin, "Cours de philosophie," *Du Vrai, du beau et du bien (Lectures on the True, the Beautiful, and the Good)*; 1853]

cous·in-ger·man (*plural* **cous·ins-ger·man**) *n* FAMILY same as **cousin** (sense 1) (*dated*) [14C. < French *cousin germain*; *germain* < Latin *germanus* (see GERMAN)]

Cou·sy /ko͞ozee/, **Bob** (*b.* 1928) US basketball player. He led the Boston Celtics to six championships between 1950 and 1963. Full name **Cousy, Robert**

couth /kooth/ (*humorous*) *adj* showing very good manners or great social sophistication ■ *n* very good manners or great social sophistication [Late 19C. Back-formation < UNCOUTH]

cou·ture /koo to͝or/ *n* **1.** the design and production of fashionable high-quality custom-made clothes **2.** high-quality clothing made to order by a fashion designer [Early 20C. Via French < late Latin *consutura* "sewing together" < Latin *suere* "sew"]

cou·tu·rier /koo to͝oree ər, -ee ày/ *n* a designer of fashionable high-quality custom-made clothes [Late 19C. < French, "dressmaker" < *couture* (see COUTURE)]

cou·tu·rière /koo to͝oree ər, -èr/ *n* a woman designer of fashionable high-quality custom-made clothes [Early 19C. < French, feminine of *couturier* (see COUTURIER)]

cou·tur·i·fy /koo to͝orə fī/ (**-fied, -fy·ing, -fies**) *vt* to make a garment stylish by using fine fabrics, unusual colors, or other features of designer clothing (*informal*) [Late 20C. < COUTURE]

cou·vade /koo vaád/ *n* the mimicking of childbirth by the father while it is taking place, a custom in some Native South American societies [Mid-19C. < French, "hatching" < *couver* "to hatch" < Latin *cubare* "lie down"]

co·va·lence /kō váyləns/, **co·va·len·cy** /kō váylənsee/ *n* chemical valence involving the sharing of electrons

co·va·lent /kō váylənt/ *adj* describes a chemical bond in which the attractive force between atoms is created by the sharing of electrons —**co·va·lent·ly** *adv*

co·var·i·ance /kō vérree ənss/ *n* a statistical measure of the tendency of two variables to change in conjunction with each other. It is equal to the product of their standard deviations and correlation coefficients.

co·var·i·ant /kō vérree ənt/ *adj* exhibiting a tendency to change in conjunction with another statistical variable

Co·var·ru·bi·as /kòvə ro͞obee əss/, **Miguel** (1904–57) Mexican artist, author, and ethnologist. He was known for his book and magazine illustrations, and his ethnographic studies of Native Americans.

cove /kōv/ *n* **1. BAY IN SHORELINE** a small bay on the shore of the sea or a lake, especially one that is enclosed by high cliffs **2. NOOK IN CLIFF** a small semicircular recessed valley in the side of a hill or cliff **3.** *also* **cov·ing** /kóving/ **CURVE AT TOP OF WALL** an inwardly curved surface at the point where a wall meets a ceiling **4. CURVED MOLDING** a molding that curves inward ■ *vti* (**coved, cov·ing, coves**) **HAVE OR GIVE INWARD CURVE** to have a cove, or design or build a wall with a cove [Old English *cofa* "bedchamber, alcove" < Germanic, "hollow place providing shelter"]

co·vel·lite /kō vé līt, kóvə-/ *n* a purple mineral consisting of thin sheets of copper sulfide [Mid-19C. After Niccolò *Covelli* (1790–1829), Italian mineralogist]

cov·en /kúvvən, kóvən/ *n* a meeting or group of witches, usually 13 in number [Mid-17C. Variant of obsolete *covin* "company, agreement," via French < medieval Latin *convenium* < Latin *convenire* (see CONVENE)]

cov·e·nant /kúvvənənt/ *n* **1. SOLEMN AGREEMENT** a solemn agreement that is binding on all parties **2.** LAW **LEGALLY BINDING AGREEMENT** a formal and legally binding agreement or contract such as a lease, or one of the clauses in an agreement of this kind. A covenant is often used to require an owner or user of a parcel of land to do or refrain from doing something. **3.** LAW **LAWSUIT FOR BREACH OF AGREEMENT** a lawsuit for damages that is brought because of the breaking of a legal covenant **4.** BIBLE **MUTUAL PROMISES OF GOD AND ISRAELITES** in the Bible, the promises that were made between God and the Israelites, who agreed to worship no other gods ■ *vt* (**-nant·ed, -nant·ing, -nants**) **PROMISE LEGALLY TO DO SOMETHING** to promise something in a covenant [13C. < Old French, present participle of *convenir* "agree" (see CONVENE)] —**cov·e·nant·al** /kùvvə nánt'l/ *adj* —**cov·e·nant·al·ly** *adv*

cov·e·nan·tee /kùvvənən tée/ *n* somebody to whom something is promised in a covenant

cov·e·nant·er /kúvvənəntər/, **cov·e·nan·tor** *n* somebody who undertakes a covenant

Cov·e·nant·er *n* a defender of the Scottish Presbyterian Church in the 17th century

cov·e·nant mar·riage *n* a form of marriage contract whose statute imposes stricter than usual conditions for couples wishing to marry or get divorced, e.g., premarital counseling and a two-year separation prior to divorce

cov·e·nan·tor *n* LAW another spelling of **covenanter**

Cov·en·try /kúvvəntree/ **1.** town in western Rhode Island, on the northern bank of the Pawtuxet River. Population: 34,664 (2002 estimate). **2.** historic cathedral city in Warwickshire, England, and the home of Warwick University. It has also been a car manufacturing center. Population: 301,900 (2000). ◇ **send somebody to Coventry** *UK* to refuse to speak to or associate with somebody as a punishment or mark of disapproval

co·ven·ture /kō vénchər/, **co·ven·ture** *vti* (**-tured, -tur·ing, -tures**) to undertake a business venture in partnership with another person or company ■ *n* a business agreement, deal, or partnership involving two or more companies

cov·er /kúvvər/ *v* (**-ered, -er·ing, -ers**) **1.** *vt* **PUT SOMETHING OVER SOMETHING ELSE** to put something over the whole of or the upper surface of something, e.g., in order to hide, protect, or decorate it **2.** *vt* **BE ALL OVER SOMETHING** to lie across or in a layer over the whole of or the upper surface of something ○ *rocks covered with seaweed* **3.** *vt* **KEEP SOMEBODY WARM** to put something such as a blanket over or around somebody for warmth ○ *She covered him with the quilt.* **4.** *vt* **BE WRAPPED AROUND SOMETHING** to be lying over or wrapped around somebody to provide warmth ○ *She was covered only by a thin blanket.* **5.** *vt* **PUT CLOTHING ON** to put a piece of clothing on part of your own or somebody else's body ○ *Keep your head covered if you're going out.* **6.** *vt* **BE WORN ON BODY** to be worn on part of the body **7.** *vt* **PUT LID ON SOMETHING** to put a lid or protective covering over something **8.** *vt* **TALK OR WRITE ABOUT SOMETHING** to deal with a subject in a discussion, speech, book, or article ○ *His talk covered several aspects of corporate law.* **9.** *vt* **PROVIDE NEWS OF SOMETHING** to be responsible for reporting, videotaping, or photographing an event or a particular class of events for a newspaper or a broadcasting company ○ *covers foreign affairs for a cable channel* **10.** *vt* **INCLUDE INSTANCE** to take something into account and provide an adequate treatment of it ○ *The law only covers commercial vehicles.* **11.** *vt* **EXTEND OVER AREA** to include the whole of an area, either physically or as a field of operations or responsibility ○ *an office complex covering three blocks* ○ *a long-term development blueprint covering the whole city* **12.** *vt* **TRAVEL DISTANCE** to travel a particular distance **13.** *vt* **HIDE SOMETHING** to conceal a feeling, action, or situation by presenting a different appearance or directing attention elsewhere ○ *covered my mistake by changing the subject* **14.** *vt* INSUR **INSURE SOMEBODY** to provide insurance protection to somebody **15.** *vt* INSUR **INSURE AGAINST SOMETHING** to provide insurance protection against a type of hazard or risk **16.** *vt* **PAY FOR SOMETHING** to be sufficient to pay for something ○ *$20 should cover it.* **17.** *vt* **PROTECT SOMEBODY OR SOMETHING FROM ATTACK** to protect somebody, a part of an army, or a piece in chess or another game from attack by occupying a position nearby **18.** *vt* **AIM GUN AT SOMEBODY OR SOMETHING** to have a person or place in the aim or range of a gun, especially in order to provide protection against a possible attack **19.** *vt* **WATCH SOMEBODY OR SOMETHING** to maintain a watch on or a patrol of something, e.g., to track somebody's movements ○ *covered the rear exit to block their escape* **20.** *vi* **DO SOMEBODY'S JOB** to do the work of somebody who is absent for a time ○ *He's covering for me while I'm away.* **21.** *vi* **TELL LIES FOR SOMEBODY** to keep people from learning the real truth about somebody ○ *covered for him by lying* **22.** *vt* MUSIC **RECORD NEW VERSION OF SONG** to record a new version of a song that was first sung or made popular by another performer **23.** *vt* SPORTS **DEFEND AREA AGAINST OPPONENT** to play defense against a particular opponent or in a particular position or area on a playing surface **24.** *vt* CARDS **PLAY HIGHER CARD** to play a card that has a higher value than one already played by somebody else **25.** *vt* GAMBLING **MATCH ANOTHER GAMBLER'S BET** to match the amount of money bet by another gambler **26.** *vti* FIN **BUY REPLACEMENT STOCK** to buy shares of stock or commodities in order to replace others that have been borrowed from a broker and sold with the expectation that the price will fall **27.** *vt* ZOOL **COPULATE WITH FEMALE** to copulate with a female animal, especially a mare (*refers especially to stallions*) ■ *n* **1. SOMETHING THAT COVERS SOMETHING** one thing that hides, protects, or covers something else, or is used to cover something **2. LID** something that covers the top of a container, e.g., a lid **3. BINDING OF BOOK OR MAGAZINE** the protective binding, thick paper, or boards at the front and back of a book or magazine

4. CLOTH THAT COVERS FURNITURE a cloth or plastic covering for bedding or a piece of furniture **5. SHELTER FROM WEATHER** shelter from the weather, or the providing of shelter from the weather **6. SHELTER FROM DANGER** concealment or protection, especially that provided by undergrowth where animals can hide or by a shelter from attack ○ *took cover under the trees* **7. VEGETATION** the plants that cover an area of land **8. DEFENSE AGAINST ATTACK** protection provided, especially to an attacking force, by other forces located nearby or in the air ○ *air cover* **9. PROTECTIVE PRETENSE** a false identity or a pretext that provides protection for somebody such as a spy or detective **10. SUBSTITUTES FOR WORKERS** people who are available to do other people's jobs when they are absent ○ *24-hour emergency cover* **11. PLACE SET AT TABLE** a place set at a table, e.g., in a restaurant ○ *covers laid for 16 guests* **12.** COMM same as **cover charge** **13.** *UK* INSUR same as **coverage** (sense 2) **14.** MUSIC **NEW RECORDING OF WELL-KNOWN SONG** a recording by a performer of a song that was first sung or popularized by another performer **15.** STAMPS **ENVELOPE** a postmarked envelope ■ **cov·ers** *npl* **COVERINGS ON BED** the sheets, blankets, and other coverings on a bed [13C. Via Old French *covrir* < Latin *cooperire* "cover completely" < *operire* "to cover"] —**cov·er·a·ble** *adj*—**cov·er·er** *n*—**cov·er·less** *adj* ◇ **blow somebody's cover** to expose a disguise, lie, or pretense that somebody has been using to conceal something ◇ **under cover of something** hidden or protected by something

cover up *v* **1.** *vt* **COVER SOMETHING COMPLETELY** to cover somebody or something completely **2.** *vt* **CONCEAL SOMETHING BAD** to try to conceal that something illegal, immoral, or undesirable has happened or how or why it happened **3.** *vi* BOXING **PROTECT HEAD AND UPPER BODY** to hide the head and upper body behind the arms as protection against another boxer's blows

cov·er·age /kúvvərij/ *n* **1. MEDIA ATTENTION** the attention given to an event or topic by newspapers, radio, and television in their reporting ○ *extensive news coverage* **2.** INSUR **INSURANCE PROTECTION** the amount or type of protection provided by an insurance policy ○ *improved health coverage for employees* **3. DEGREE OF COVERING** the degree to which something is covered by something else ○ *Thicker paint will give better coverage.* **4. MEDIA AUDIENCE** the percentage of all the people in a given area who are reached by a newspaper or radio or television station **5.** FIN **AVAILABLE FUNDS** the amount of funds available to cover financial liabilities or commitments

cov·er·alls /kúvvər àwlz/ *npl* a one-piece outer garment that covers and protects the clothes

cov·er boy *n* a young man, especially a handsome model, whose picture is on a magazine cover

cov·er charge *n* a fixed charge that is added per head to the cost of drinks and food in a nightclub or restaurant, e.g., for bread or entertainment

cov·er crop *n* a crop planted between main crops to prevent erosion or to be plowed in to enrich the soil

cov·ered bridge /kúvvərd-/ *n* a bridge with a roof and walls that protect it against the weather

cov·ered-dish, cov·er·dish /kúvvər dìsh/ *adj regional* describes a community meal of hot dishes ○ *a covered-dish supper*

REGIONAL NOTE ***Covered-dish*** is in widespread regional use, from New York State westward across the North and South. It is absent from the Rocky Mountain and Pacific Coast states.

cov·ered wag·on *n* a large wagon with a canvas roof stretched over arched supports, formerly used by pioneers crossing the plains of North America

cov·er girl *n* a young woman, usually a glamorous model, whose picture is on the cover of a magazine

cov·er glass *n US* a piece of thin glass used to cover a specimen on a microscope slide. Can term **cover slip**

cov·er·ing /kúvvəring/ *n* something that protects, hides, or covers something

cov·er·ing fire *n* weapon fire used to protect friendly troops from direct fire from the enemy's weapons

cov·er·ing let·ter *n UK* same as **cover letter**

cov·er·let /kúvvərlət/ *n* a usually decorative cover for a bed, placed over the other covers when the bed is not being used [13C. < Old French *couvre lit* "bed cover"]

cov·er let·ter *n* a letter sent with another document or package, providing necessary or additional information

cov·er page, cov·er sheet *n* a form sent along with a fax that gives information about the sender, e.g., the name, address, telephone number, and fax number

cov·er slip *n Can, UK* same as **cover glass**

cov·er sto·ry *n* **1.** a magazine feature that is illustrated on the front cover and is the most important article in the issue **2.** a story made up to deceive somebody, e.g., to provide a false identity for an undercover investigator

cov·ert /kúvvərt, kṓ-/ *adj* **SECRET** not intended to be known, seen, or found out ■ *n* **1. UNDERGROWTH PROVIDING COVER** a thicket, or undergrowth, in which game can shelter or hide **2. SHELTER** a shelter or hiding place **3. SMALL FEATHER** a small feather around the base of a quill on the wing or tail of a bird **4.** *also* **cov·ert cloth** TEXTILES **TWILLED CLOTH** a hard-wearing twilled cloth. Use: suits. [13C. < Old French, past participle of *covrir* (see COVER)] —**cov·ert·ly** *adv* —**cov·ert·ness** *n*

SYNONYMS See ***secret.***

cov·er·ture /kúvvər chŏŏr, -chər/ *n* **1.** a shelter or covering **2.** the condition of being a married woman [13C. < Old French < *covrir* (see COVER)]

cov·er-up *n* **1.** a concealment of something illegal, immoral, or undesirable **2.** a loose item of clothing worn over another garment, e.g., a wrap over an evening dress or a T-shirt over a bathing suit

cov·er ver·sion *n* MUSIC same as **cover** *n* (sense 14)

cov·et /kúvvət/ (**-et·ed, -et·ing, -ets**) *v* **1.** *vti* to have a strong desire to possess something that belongs to somebody else **2.** *vt* to want to have something very much [13C. < Old French *coveitier* < Latin *cupiditas* (see CUPIDITY)] —**cov·et·a·ble** *adj* —**cov·et·er** *n* —**cov·et·ing·ly** *adv* —**cov·et·ous** *adj* —**cov·et·ous·ly** *adv* —**cov·et·ous·ness** *n*

SYNONYMS See ***want.***

cov·ey /kúvvee/ (*plural* **-eys**) *n* **1.** a small group of game birds such as partridge, grouse, or quail **2.** a small group of people or things [14C. < French *covée* "brood" < Latin *cubare* "lie down"]

Co·vic /chṓ vich/, **Dragan** (*b.* 1956) Croat representative of the presidency of Bosnia and Herzegovina (2002–), which rotates among a Serb, a Bosnian Muslim, and a Croat

Co·vi·na /kō vēénə/ city in southwestern California, an eastern suburb of Los Angeles. Population: 48,019 (2002 estimate).

cov·ing /kṓving/ *n* ARCHIT same as **cove** *n* (sense 3)

Cov·ing·ton /kúvvingtən/ city in northern Kentucky, directly north of Lexington, across the Kentucky-Ohio border from Cincinnati, Ohio. Population: 42,983 (2002 estimate).

cow

cow[1] /kow/ *n* **1. LARGE FEMALE QUADRUPED** an adult female grazing quadruped. Raised for: milk, meat, breeding. Genus: *Bos.* **2. MALE OR FEMALE OF DOMESTIC CATTLE** an animal of either sex and any age belonging to any breed of domestic cattle. Genus: *Bos.* **3. LARGE FEMALE MAMMAL** an adult female of large mammal species such as whales, elephants, seals, or moose [Old English *cū* < Indo-European] ◇ **have a cow** to become suddenly and greatly excited or angry (*slang*) ◇ **till** *or* **until the cows come home** until an extremely long time has elapsed (*informal*)

cow[2] /kow/ (**cowed, cow·ing, cows**) *vt* to frighten somebody into submission or obedience [Late 16C. Probably < Old Norse *kúga* "oppress"]

Cow·an /ków ən/ salt lake in southern Western Australia. Area: 359 sq. mi./940 sq. km.

cow·ard /ków ərd/ *n* **1. SOMEBODY LACKING COURAGE** somebody regarded as fearful and uncourageous **2. BULLY** somebody who harms or attacks people who are weaker or unable to defend themselves **3. ANONYMOUS ENEMY** somebody who anonymously attacks those who cannot defend themselves [13C. < Old French *cuard* < Latin *cauda* "tail"]

Cow·ard /ków ərd/, **Sir Noel** (1899–1973) British dramatist, actor, and songwriter. He was the author of *Private Lives* (1930), *Blithe Spirit* (1941), and *Brief Encounter* (1946).

> "We have no reliable guarantee that the afterlife will be any the less exasperating than this one, have we?"
> [Sir Noel Coward, *Blithe Spirit*; 1941]

cow·ard·ice /ków ərdiss/ *n* an absence of courage, or behavior that is cowardly

cow·ard·ly /ków ərdlee/ *adj* **1.** showing a lack of physical or moral courage, or too scared to do a particular thing ○ *a cowardly attempt to avoid blame* **2.** showing meanness or cruelty to people who are weaker or unable to defend themselves and fear of those who are equal or stronger ○ *a cowardly attack on an undefended village* —**cow·ard·li·ness** *n* —**cow·ard·ly** *adv*

SYNONYMS ***cowardly, faint-hearted, spineless, gutless, pusillanimous, craven, chicken***

CORE MEANING: lacking in courage

cowardly showing a lack of physical or moral courage, or too scared to do a particular thing ○ *a wicked and cowardly attack* ○ *too cowardly to admit his mistake* **faint-hearted** lacking resolve, boldness, or enthusiasm ○ *The gift trade's huge International Spring Fair is not for the faint-hearted.* **spineless** seriously lacking in willpower or strength of character ○ *criticized the president as spineless for withdrawing the nomination* ○ *their spineless acceptance of the imposition of new rules* **gutless** seriously lacking in resolve and determination ○ *They're too gutless to oppose the measure in public.* **pusillanimous** (*formal*) showing a contemptible lack of boldness and resolve ○ *The general couldn't tolerate pusillanimous performance in battle.* **craven** so weak and lacking in courage as to be worthy of contempt ○ *an act of craven stupidity* ○ *a craven surrender to pressure from big business* **chicken** (*informal*, often used by children and young people) showing a lack of courage, or too scared to do a particular thing ○ *The boy got called chicken by the other kids.* ○ *I'll show him who's chicken!* ○ *too chicken to tell him face to face*

cow·bane /ków bàyn/ (*plural same*) *n* **1.** a poisonous marsh plant. Native to: North America. Latin name: *Oxypolis rigidior.* **2.** a poisonous plant of the parsley family. Native to: marshy areas of Europe. Genus: *Cicuta.*

cow·bell /ków bèl/ *n* **1.** a bell fastened to a collar around a cow's neck that clangs as the cow moves, making the animal easier to find **2.** a bell without a clapper, played as a percussion instrument by being struck with a drumstick

cow·ber·ry /ków bèrree/ *n* **1.** (*plural* **cow·ber·ries**) a small red fruit with a smooth skin and a tart taste **2.** (*plural* **cow·ber·ries** or *same*) a creeping flowering bush that produces cowberries. Native to: northern temperate areas. Latin name: *Vaccinium vitis-idaea.*

cow·bird /ków bùrd/ *n* a blackbird that lays its eggs in the nests of other birds and often feeds alongside grazing cattle. Native to: North America. Genus: *Molothrus.*

cow·boy /ków bòy/ *n* **1. MAN WHO TENDS CATTLE** a man hired to round up, drive, and tend cattle, especially in the western United States. Cowboys traditionally work on horseback, but now also use motor vehicles. **2.** MALE CHARACTER IN WESTERNS a male character in stories and movies about the West in the late 1800s, often shown fighting Native Americans or outlaws **3.** MALE RODEO PERFORMER a man who performs or competes in shows such as rodeos **4.** RECKLESS PERSON a reckless person, especially a driver or pilot (*slang disapproving*)

cow·boy boot *n* a high-heeled boot, like those originally worn by cowboys, usually with pointed toes and ornamental stitching

cow·boy hat *n* a hat, usually felt, with a high crown and a wide brim, originally worn by cowboys and now widely worn in the Southwest and Midwest

cow·boys and In·di·ans *n* a children's game involving two sides pretending to be cowboys and Native Americans fighting against each other (*takes a singular verb*)

Cow·boy State *n* a nickname for Wyoming

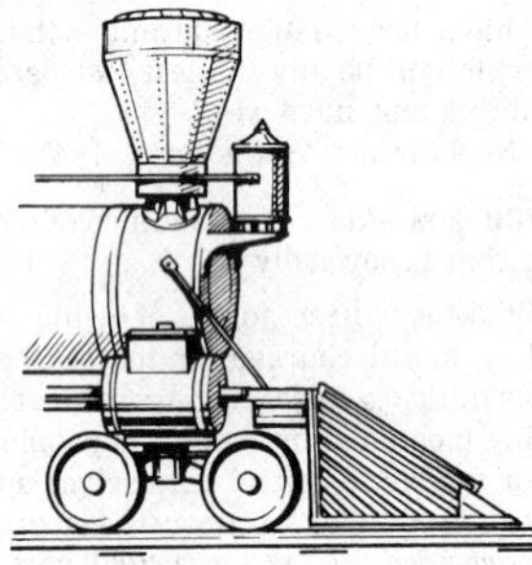

cowcatcher

cow·catch·er /ków kàchər/ *n* an angled metal frame formerly fixed to the front of a steam locomotive to clear animals and other obstructions from the track

cow·chip /ków chìp/ *n* a dried cowpat (*informal*)

cow col·lege *n* (*informal*) **1.** an agricultural college or university **2.** a small college or university in a rural area, regarded as unsophisticated

cow·er /ków ər/ (**-ered, -er·ing, -ers**) *vi* to cringe or move backward defensively in fear [13C. < Middle Low German *kūren* "lie in wait"]

cow·fish /ków fìsh/ (*plural same* or **-fish·es**) *n* **1.** a small brightly colored warm-water ocean fish with spines that resemble horns above the eyes. Family: Ostraciidae. **2.** an ocean mammal such as some species of dolphin or porpoise, or a manatee

cow·girl /ków gùrl/ *n* **1.** WOMAN WHO TENDS CATTLE a woman hired to round up, drive, and tend cattle, especially in the western United States **2.** WOMAN CHARACTER IN WESTERNS a woman character in stories and movies about the West in the late 1800s, usually accompanying or assisting a cowboy in his exploits **3.** FEMALE RODEO PERFORMER a woman who performs or competes in shows such as rodeos

cow·hand /ków hànd/ *n* somebody hired to tend cattle

cow·herb /ków ùrb, -hùrb/ *n* an annual European plant with clusters of pink flowers that has become a weed in North America. Latin name: *Vaccaria pyramidata*.

cow·herd /ków hùrd/ *n* somebody who tends cattle, usually on foot (*archaic or literary*)

cow·hide /ków hìd/ *n* **1.** SKIN OF COW the skin of a cow or bull, removed and processed **2.** LEATHER leather made from a cowhide **3.** LEATHER WHIP a whip made of braided leather or rawhide ■ *vt* (**-hid·ed, -hid·ing, -hides**) WHIP SOMEBODY to beat somebody with a whip made of braided leather or rawhide

cow horse *n* AGRIC same as **cow pony**

Cow·ich·an sweat·er /kówichən-/ *n* a heavy homespun sweater, originally black and white and knitted with symbolic designs by Native American peoples of the Pacific Northwest coast [After a people of Canada]

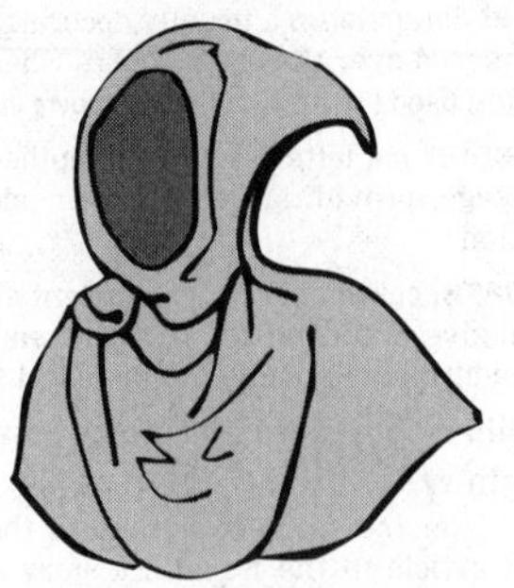

cowl

cowl /kowl/ *n* **1.** CLOTHING, CHR MONK'S HOOD the hood on a monk's cloak, or a monk's hooded cloak **2.** CLOTHING same as **cowl neck** **3.** HOOD FOR CHIMNEY a hood-shaped, sometimes revolving, cover fitted to a chimney or vent to improve ventilation and prevent downdrafts **4.** PART OF VEHICLE BODY the part of the body of an automobile to which the windshield, hood, and dashboard are attached **5.** ENG same as **cowling** [Pre-12C. Via Germanic < Latin *cucullus* "hood"]

cow·lick /ków lìk/ *n* a tuft of hair growing in a different direction from the rest of the hair on somebody's head and usually sticking up [< its resemblance to a ridge of hair on a cow's hide that is thought to be caused by the animal licking itself]

cowl·ing /kówling/ *n* a streamlined removable metal covering for an aircraft engine, fuselage, or nacelle

cowl neck *n* a collar on a woman's garment such as a sweater that drapes in large folds around the neck (*hyphenated when used before a noun*)

cow·man /kówmən, -màn/ (*plural* **-men** /-mən, -mèn/) *n* **1.** a man who owns cattle or a cattle ranch **2.** a man who is hired to tend cattle **3.** AGRIC same as **cowboy** (sense 1)

cow pars·nip *n* a tall perennial plant with a thick stem. Flowers: tiny, white and purple, in flattened clusters. Native to: northern temperate regions. Genus: *Heracleum*.

cow·pat /ków pàt/ *n* a circular flat mass of dung excreted by a cow

cow·pea /ków pee/ *n* PLANTS same as **black-eyed pea**

Cow·per's gland /kówpərz-, kóop-/ *n* either of two small glands, just below the prostate, that secrete into the urethra a lubricant fluid that is released just prior to ejaculation of semen [Mid-18C. After William *Cowper* (1666–1709), English anatomist]

cow·per·son /ków pùrss'n/ (*plural* **-per·sons** or **-peo·ple** /-peep'l/) *n* **1.** somebody who owns cattle or a cattle ranch **2.** AGRIC same as **cowhand**

cow·pie /ków pī/ *n* same as **cowpat** (*slang*)

cow·poke /ków pōk/ *n* a cowboy or cowgirl (*informal*)

cow pon·y *n* a horse trained for use in cattle herding

cow·pox /ków pòks/ *n* a mild viral skin disease in cattle, usually affecting the udder with a pustular rash. Cowpox virus was once used to inoculate humans against smallpox. Technical name **vaccinia**

cow·punch·er /ków pùnchər/ *n* a cowboy or cowgirl (*informal*)

cow·rie /kówree/, **cow·ry** (*plural* **-ries**) *n* **1.** a tropical invertebrate sea animal that has a glossy brightly colored shell with a long central toothed opening. Family: Cypraeidae. **2.** the shell of a cowrie, formerly used as money in parts of Africa, South Asia, and the South Pacific [Mid-17C. < Hindi *kaurī*]

cow shark *n* a large flabby bottom-dwelling shark that has a weak jaw and small teeth. Native to: warm and temperate seas. Family: Hexanchidae.

cow·shed /ków shèd/ *n* a building in which cattle are housed

cow·slip /ków slìp/ *n* **1.** a small plant of the primrose family. Flowers: long-stemmed, drooping, fragrant, yellow. Native to: grassy areas in temperate regions of Europe, Africa, Asia. Latin name: *Primula veris*. **2.** PLANTS same as **marsh marigold** [Old English *cūslyppe* "cow dung," probably from a belief that it grew where a cow pat had fallen]

cow town *n* **1.** a small town in a cattle-breeding area, sometimes regarded as unsophisticated (*informal*) **2.** a city or town that is a main market center or shipping point for cattle

cox /koks/ ROWING *n* same as **coxswain** *n* (sense 1) ■ *vti* (**coxed, cox·ing, cox·es**) same as **coxswain** *v* [Late 19C. Shortening of COXSWAIN] —**cox·less** *adj*

Cox /koks/, **James Middleton** (1870–1957) US politician. He was governor of Ohio (1913–15 and 1917–21), and ran for the US presidency in 1920.

cox·a /káksə/ (*plural* **-ae** /-ee/) *n* **1.** the base segment of the leg in most insects and other arthropods **2.** the hipbone or hip joint (*technical*) [Early 19C. < Latin, "hip"] —**cox·al** *adj*

cox·al·gi·a /kok sáljə/ *n* pain in the hip, or disease of the hip —**cox·al·gic** *adj*

cox·comb /kóks kōm/ *n* (*archaic*) **1.** a conceited man with an excessive interest in clothes and fashion **2.** the cap worn by a medieval jester, shaped like a rooster's comb [Mid-16C. Alteration of COCKSCOMB] —**cox·comb·ry** /kóks kōmree, kókskəmree/ *n*

cox·sack·ie vi·rus /kook saakee-, kok sákee-/, **Cox·sack·ie vi·rus** *n* a virus belonging to a group that occurs in the human intestinal tract and causes respiratory, neurological, and muscular diseases such as viral meningitis and a condition similar to poliomyelitis [Mid-20C. After *Coxsackie*, New York]

cox·swain /kóks'n, -swàyn/, **cock·swain** *n* **1.** SOMEBODY IN CHARGE OF ROWING BOAT the member of a rowing crew who faces forward, steers the boat, and directs the speed and rhythm of the rowers **2.** SOMEBODY IN CHARGE OF SHIP'S BOAT somebody who oversees a ship's boat and its crew, and who usually steers it ■ *vti* (**-swained, -swain·ing, -swains**) BE COXSWAIN to be the coxswain of a boat [14C. < *cock* "ship's boat" + SWAIN]

coy /koy/ *adj* **1.** EVASIVE annoyingly reluctant to make a commitment or to divulge something **2.** PRETENDING TO BE SHY pretending, in a teasing or provocative way, to be reserved or modest **3.** SHY shy or reserved in social situations [14C. Via French *coi* "quiet" < Latin *quietus*] —**coy·ish** *adj* —**coy·ly** *adv* —**coy·ness** *n*

coy·dog /kī dàwg, -dòg, kóy-/ *n* the supposed offspring of a coyote and feral dog, despite a lack of evidence that they interbreed in the wild [Mid-20C. Blend of COYOTE + DOG]

coy·o·te /kī ótee, kī ōt/ (*plural* **-tes** or *same*) *n* **1.** a carnivorous canine mammal, similar to but smaller than the wolf. Native to: North America. Latin name: *Canis latrans*. **2.** a smuggler who brings illegal immigrants into the United States (*slang*) [Mid-18C. Via Mexican Spanish < Nahuatl *coyotl*]

Coy·o·te State *n* a nickname for South Dakota

coy·o·til·lo /kòy ə tíllō, -teeyō, kī ə tíllō, -teeyō/ (*plural* **-los**) *n* a thorny bush with small green flowers and poisonous black berries. Native to: Mexico, southwestern United States. Latin name: *Karwinskia humboldtiana*. [Late 19C. < Mexican Spanish, "little coyote"]

coypu

coy·pu /kóy poo/ (*plural* **-pus** or *same*) *n* a large rodent with webbed feet for swimming and a long tail. Raised for: fur. Native to: South America. [Late 18C. < Araucanian]

coz /kuz/ *n* FAMILY same as **cousin** (*informal*) [Mid-16C. Shortening]

coz·en /kúzz'n/ (**-ened, -en·ing, -ens**) *vti* to deceive, cheat, or defraud somebody [Late 16C. Origin ?] —**coz·en·er** *n*

coz·en·age /kúzz'nij/ *n* a getting of something, or persuading of somebody to do something, by trickery or wheedling persuasion

co·zy /kózee/ *adj* (**-zi·er, -zi·est**) **1. SNUG** warm, comfortable, and snug **2. FRIENDLY** friendly and intimate **3. UNETHICALLY CLOSE** close and friendly, but for mutually beneficial or underhanded purposes (*disapproving*) ■ *n* (*plural* **-zies**) **COVERING TO KEEP SOMETHING WARM** a covering, often knitted or padded, put over something, especially a teapot, to keep it or its contents warm [Early 18C. Origin ?] —**co·zi·ly** *adv* —**co·zi·ness** *n*

cozy up *v* **1.** *vi* to sit or lie as close as possible to somebody for warmth or affection **2.** to try to ingratiate yourself, or become friendly or intimate, with somebody (*informal*)

cP *symbol* MEASURE centipoise

CP *abbr* **1.** MEDIA Canadian Press **2.** ONLINE chat post (*used in e-mails*) **3.** CHEM chemically pure **4.** command post **5.** POL Communist Party

cp. *abbr* **1.** compare **2.** COMM coupon

C.P. *abbr* MIL command post

CPA *abbr* **1.** *also* **C.P.A.** ACCT certified public accountant **2.** COMPUT critical path analysis

CPB, C.P.B. *abbr* BROADCAST Corporation for Public Broadcasting

cpd. *abbr* CHEM compound

CPFF *abbr* COMM cost plus fixed fee

CPI *abbr* ECON consumer price index

Cpl. *abbr* MIL Corporal

CPM, C.P.M., cpm *abbr* **1.** cost per thousand **2.** cycles per minute

CPO *abbr* NAVY Chief Petty Officer

CPR *abbr* **1.** RAIL Canadian Pacific Railway **2.** MED cardiopulmonary resuscitation

cps *abbr* COMPUT characters per second

CPS, C.P.S. *abbr* HR certified professional secretary

CPSC *abbr* SOC SCI Consumer Product Safety Commission

Cpt., CPT *abbr* MIL Captain

CPU *abbr* COMPUT central processing unit

CQ[1] *n* a set of code letters transmitted at the start of a radio message indicating that the message is meant for all receivers and requesting a response

CQ[2] *abbr* MIL **1.** call to quarters **2.** charge of quarters

cr *abbr* Costa Rica (*used in Internet addresses*) See table at **domain name**

Cr *symbol* CHEM ELEM chromium

CR *abbr* PSYCHOL **1.** conditioned reflex **2.** conditioned response

cr. *abbr* **1.** FIN credit **2.** FIN creditor **3.** creek **4.** crown

CRA *abbr* GOV Canada Revenue Agency

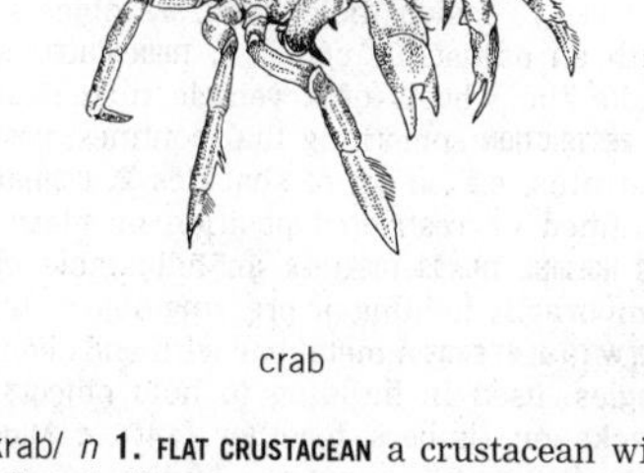

crab

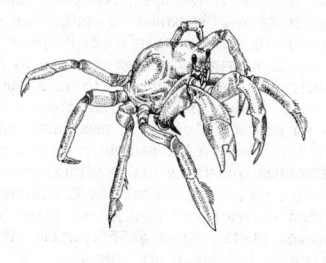

crab[1] /krab/ *n* **1. FLAT CRUSTACEAN** a crustacean with a broad flat shell, antennae, a small abdomen, and five pairs of legs, the front two of which are in the form of grasping pincers. Suborder: Brachyura. **2. CRUSTACEAN LIKE CRAB** an animal similar or related to the true crab, e.g., the hermit crab, horseshoe crab, or king crab **3. FLESH OF CRAB** the flesh of a crab used as food **4. PARASITIC LOUSE IN PUBIC HAIR** a parasitic louse resembling a tiny crab that infests the pubic hair of humans, causing inflammation and itching of the skin. Latin name: *Phthirius pubis*. **5.** MECH ENG **CRANE** a machine similar to a crane designed to lift and move heavy weights **6.** AVIAT **FLYING MANEUVER** a flying maneuver in which an aircraft is steered slightly into a crosswind to compensate for drifting off course ■ **crabs** *npl* **LICE INFESTATION** an infestation of crab lice (*informal*) ■ *v* (**crabbed, crab·bing, crabs**) **1.** *vi* **CATCH CRABS** to go fishing or hunting for crabs **2.** *vti* **SCURRY SIDEWAYS** to move sideways as a crab does, or cause something to move in this way **3.** *vti* AVIAT **FLY INTO CROSSWIND** to steer an aircraft slightly into a crosswind to compensate for drifting off course **4.** *vi* NAUT **SAIL WITH SIDEWAYS DRIFT** to sail forward with a slight sideways drift caused by a current [Old English *crabba* < Indo-European, "scratch"] —**crab·ber** *n* —**crab·like** *adj* ◇ **catch a crab** in rowing, to make a faulty stroke by failing to make contact with the water or plunging the oar blade in too deeply

crab[2] /krab/ *n* TREES same as **crab apple** [15C. Origin ?]

crab[3] /krab/ *n* **OFFENSIVE TERM** an offensive term for somebody regarded as bad-tempered or disagreeable (*informal insult*) ■ *v* (**crabbed, crab·bing, crabs**) **1.** *vi* **CRITICIZE SOMEBODY OR SOMETHING** to criticize or grumble about somebody or something (*informal*) **2.** *vt* **SPOIL SOMETHING** to ruin or spoil something through interference (*informal*) **3.** *vt* **MAKE SOMEBODY BAD-TEMPERED** to make somebody bad-tempered or bitter [Late 16C. Probably back-formation < CRABBED]

Crab *n* ZODIAC same as **Cancer** (senses 2–3) [CRAB[1]]

crab ap·ple, crab·ap·ple /kráb àpp'l/ *n* **1.** a small sour apple. Use: in jellies. **2.** a tree that produces crab apples. Genus: *Malus*. [< CRAB[2]]

crab·bed /krábbəd/ *adj* **1. GROUCHY** bad-tempered, irritable, or disagreeable by nature **2. HARD TO READ** hard to read, because the words and letters are compressed **3. COMPLICATED** complicated and hard to follow (*dated*) ○ *crabbed logic* [13C. < CRAB[1] because the way crabs threaten with their claws and their sideways walk suggest bad temper; reinforced by the idea of "sourness" found in CRAB[2]] —**crab·bed·ly** *adv*

crab·bing /krábbing/ *n* fishing or hunting for crabs [Mid-17C. < CRAB[1]]

crab·by /krábbee/ (**-bi·er, -bi·est**) *adj* bad-tempered or irritable in character (*informal*) [Mid-16C. < CRAB[1], CRAB[2]] —**crab·bi·ly** *adv* —**crab·bi·ness** *n*

crab cac·tus *n* PLANTS same as **Christmas cactus**

crab·grass /kráb gràss/ *n* a coarse grass that grows in warm regions, has creeping stems that root freely, and is considered a weed in lawns and gardens. Genus: *Digitaria*. [Late 16C. < CRAB[1]]

crab louse *n* ZOOL same as **crab**[1] *n* (sense 4) [< CRAB[1]]

crab·meat /kráb meet/ *n* the flesh of a crab used as food [< CRAB[1]]

Crab Neb·u·la *n* the gaseous remains of an exploded star in the constellation Taurus, about 5,000 light years from Earth

crab's eye *n* PLANTS same as **rosary pea** (sense 1)

crab stick *n* a stick-shaped piece of processed fish that has been flavored and colored to resemble crabmeat [< CRAB[1]]

crab·stick /kráb stik/ *n* **1.** a stick or club made from the wood of a crab apple **2.** somebody bad-tempered or irritable (*informal*) [< CRAB[2], CRAB[3]]

crab·wise /kráb wīz/ *adv, adj* **1.** sideways, as crabs usually move **2.** in a roundabout and cautious way [Early 20C. < CRAB[1]]

crack /krak/ *v* (**cracked, crack·ing, cracks**) **1.** *vti* **BREAK WITHOUT COMING FULLY APART** to break in such a way that a fine split or splits appear but the split sections do not come apart, or make something break in this way ○ *cracked a rib in falling* **2.** *vti* **BREAK INTO PIECES** to break into pieces, or break something into pieces **3.** *vti* **BREAK WITH SHARP NOISE** to break with a sudden sharp noise, or make something break in this way ○ *cracked some eggs into a saucepan* **4.** *vti* **MAKE SHARP NOISE** to make a loud sharp sound, or cause something such as a whip or a rifle to make a loud sharp sound ○ *thunder cracked overhead* **5.** *vt* **HIT SOMETHING HARD** to hit something with a powerful impact ○ *cracked his head on the beam* **6.** *vti* **BREAK OPEN UNDER PRESSURE** to break open because of pressure, or make something such as a nut break or open by pressure **7.** *vti* **FAIL OR MAKE SOMETHING FAIL** to fail, give way, or break down, or make somebody or something do so ○ *The champion was two sets down, but he didn't crack.* **8.** *vti* **BREAK DOWN PSYCHOLOGICALLY** to break down psychologically, or cause somebody to break down psychologically, e.g., under stress or torture **9.** *vi* **BECOME HOARSE OR CHANGE IN PITCH** to become slightly hoarse or suffer from uncontrollable changes in pitch, especially because of emotion or stress (*refers to voices*) **10.** *vt* **BEAT RECORD** to break through something such as an obstacle or barrier, or break a record ○ *Three cyclists cracked the 10-second barrier.* **11.** *vt* **OPEN SOMETHING SLIGHTLY** to open something such as a window slightly **12.** *vt* **DECODE OR SOLVE SOMETHING** to decipher or solve something such as a code, puzzle, or problem ○ *Police are under pressure to crack the case.* **13.** *vt* **BREAK INTO SOMETHING** to force a way into something, especially a safe (*informal*) **14.** *vt* **OPEN SOMETHING TO USE** to open something such as a can or book, in order to get access to its contents (*informal*) **15.** *vt* INDUST **BREAK MOLECULES DOWN INTO SMALLER MOLECULES** to break down something, especially the heavier hydrocarbons in petroleum, into smaller molecules by using heat or catalysis **16.** *vt* COMPUT **DISABLE COPY PROTECTION** to defeat the copy protection that is intended to prevent somebody from illegally copying and distributing a software product, music CD, or DVD (*slang*) **17.** *vt* COMPUT **BREAK INTO COMPUTER SYSTEM** to gain unauthorized access to a computer system with the intention of doing damage or committing a crime (*slang*) ■ *n* **1. THIN BREAK** a break or flaw in something such as a mirror that is visible as a fine line ○ *cracks in the ice* **2. LONG NARROW OPENING** a relatively long narrow break, hole, or opening in something ○ *peeked through a crack in the fence* **3. SHARP NOISE** a sudden loud sharp noise ○ *the crack of a rifle* **4. WEAKNESS** a flaw, defect, or weak spot **5. UNEVEN VOICE TONE** a hoarseness or uncontrollable change in pitch in somebody's voice **6. PURIFIED FORM OF COCAINE** a purified and extremely addictive form of cocaine **7. BLOW** a hard blow from somebody or something (*informal*) ○ *a crack over the head* **8. SARCASTIC COMMENT** a sarcastic, funny, or rude remark, especially at somebody else's expense (*informal*) **9. ATTEMPT** an attempt at something (*informal*) ■ *adj* **EXCELLENT** excellent, expert, or trained to a high degree of efficiency ○ *She's a crack shot.* [Old English *cracian* < Germanic, "make a loud noise"] ◇ **be not all he's** *or* **she's** *or* **it's cracked up to be** to be not as good as promised or reputed ◇ **crack a joke** to tell a joke ◇ **fall between** *or* **through the cracks** to be overlooked or forgotten

crack down *vi* to take strong and decisive action against something undesirable or illegal or against somebody involved in such activity (*informal*)

crack up *v* **1.** *vi* **HAVE BREAKDOWN** to experience a psychological or, sometimes, physical breakdown, usually because of stress (*informal*) **2.** *vi* **BREAK INTO PIECES** to crack and break into pieces **3.** *vti* **LAUGH UNCONTROLLABLY** to laugh uncontrollably, or cause somebody to laugh uncontrollably (*informal*) **4.** *vti* **CRASH** to crash a car, boat, or aircraft (*informal*) ○ *a plane that cracked up*

crack·brained /krák brày̆nd/ *adj* extremely irrational or eccentric (*informal*) ○ *a crackbrained idea*

crack co·caine *n* DRUGS same as **crack** *n* (sense 6)

crack·down /krák dòwn/ *n* a strong and decisive measure taken against an undesirable or illegal activity or against somebody involved in such activity (*informal*)

cracked /krakt/ *adj* **1. HAVING CRACKS** marked with a crack or cracks ○ *dry cracked lips* **2. COARSELY CRUSHED** broken or crushed into coarse pieces ○ *cracked ice* **3. HOARSE** sounding rough or hoarse vocally, often because of emotion or stress **4. IRRATIONAL** extremely irrational (*informal*)

cracked wheat *n* whole grains of wheat that have been chopped into little pieces

crack·er /krákər/ *n* **1. FLAT CRISP WAFER** a thin crisp flatbread, usually unsweetened and sometimes salted, often eaten with cheese **2.** OFFENSIVE TERM an offensive term for a white person living on a relatively small income in a rural area, especially in the South **3.** *Southern US* SOMEBODY FROM GEORGIA OR FLORIDA somebody who comes from Georgia or Florida (*informal humorous*) **4.** INDUST DEVICE FOR CRACKING PETROLEUM COMPOUNDS a device in which petroleum oils and tars are broken down to yield more valuable light fuels **5.** LEISURE same as **firecracker** **6.** COMPUT SOMEBODY WHO ACCESSES COMPUTER SYSTEM ILLICITLY a user who gains unauthorized access to a computer system, especially to acquire or interfere with data **7.** *UK* CARDBOARD TUBE HOLDING PARTY FAVOR a cardboard tube, containing a party favor, and wrapped in colored paper, that opens with an explosive noise when both its ends are pulled **8.** COMPUT SOMEBODY WHO DISABLES COPY PROTECTION somebody who defeats the copy protection of a software product, music CD, or DVD (*slang*) **9.** COMPUT SOMEBODY WHO BREAKS INTO COMPUTER SYSTEM somebody who gains unauthorized access to a computer system with the intention of doing damage or committing a crime (*slang*)

crack·er-bar·rel *adj* expressing unsophisticated but practical sense or wisdom of the kind often associated with a rural community [< the idea of the village store as a social center]

crack·head /krák hèd/ *n* an addict of crack cocaine (*slang*)

crack house *n* a house or apartment where crack cocaine is sold to addicts and where, sometimes, it is also made (*slang*)

crack·ing /kráking/ *adj* very fast (*informal*) ○ *at a cracking pace* ■ *adv* same as **extremely** (*informal*) ○ *did a cracking good job* ■ *n* the breaking down of something, especially the heavier hydrocarbons in petroleum, into smaller molecules using heat or catalysis ◇ **get cracking** to start moving or doing something quickly or more quickly (*informal*)

crack·le /krák'l/ *v* (**-led, -ling, -les**) **1.** *vi* MAKE RAPID SNAPPING NOISE to make repeated short sharp snapping or popping noises such as dry wood makes when burning, or cause something to make such noises **2.** *vi* SCINTILLATE to be lively, energetic, or scintillating ○ *The play crackles with wit.* **3.** *vt* DECORATE POTTERY WITH CRACKS to decorate a piece of pottery or porcelain with a network of fine cracks in the surface of its glaze ■ *n* **1.** REPEATED SNAPPING NOISES a series of repeated short sharp snapping or popping noises **2.** FINE DECORATIVE CRACKS a network of fine cracks created as decoration in the surface of the glaze of pottery or porcelain **3.** *also* **crack·le·ware** /krák'l wèr/ PORCELAIN DECORATED WITH FINE CRACKS pottery or porcelain decorated with a network of fine cracks in the surface of its glaze

crack·ling /krákling/ *n* a series of repeated short sharp snapping or popping noises ■ **crack·lings** *npl* the crisp pieces left after the fat has been rendered from fatty pieces of meat or skin, especially of pork

crack·ly /kráklee/ (**-li·er, -li·est**) *adj* **1.** brittle or crisp **2.** making or consisting of a series of repeated short sharp snapping or popping noises

crack·nel /kráknəl/ *n* a hard light brittle cookie ■ **crack·nels** *npl* FOOD same as **cracklings** (*see* **crackling**) [14C. Via Old French *craquelin* < Middle Dutch *krākeline*, a small cake < *krāken* "to crack"]

crack·pot /krák pòt/ *n* somebody regarded as eccentric or wildly imaginative (*informal insult*) ■ *adj* extremely eccentric or unrealistic (*informal*) ○ *another of his crackpot money-making schemes*

crack-up *n* (*informal*) **1.** a motor vehicle or aircraft crash **2.** a psychological or sometimes physical breakdown

Cra·cow another spelling of **Kraków**

-cracy *suffix* rule, government, power ○ *technocracy* [< French *-cratie* < Greek *kratos* "power, strength" < Indo-European, "hard"]

cra·dle /kráyd'l/ *n* **1.** BABY'S BED a small bed for a baby, with rockers and enclosing sides **2.** STARTING PLACE the place where something begins or develops in its early stages ○ *the cradle of civilization* **3.** SUPPORT FOR TELEPHONE HANDSET the part of a telephone on which the handset rests or hangs **4.** AUTOMOT MECHANIC'S BOARD ON WHEELS a flat board on wheels or casters on which a mechanic can slide under a vehicle **5.** CIV ENG SUPPORTING FRAMEWORK a framework for supporting something such as a ship that is being built or repaired **6.** CIV ENG HANGING PLATFORM a movable platform or cage hung on the side of something such as a building or ship, to hold a worker **7.** MED PROTECTIVE FRAME SUPPORTING SHEET OR BLANKET a frame placed beneath a top sheet or blanket covering a patient to keep it from touching a sensitive part of the body, e.g., after an injury or operation **8.** MIN EXTRACT PANNING DEVICE a rocking device like a box used in panning for gold ■ *vt* (**-dled, -dling, -dles**) **1.** HOLD SOMEBODY OR SOMETHING CAREFULLY to hold or support somebody or something tenderly, carefully, or protectively, especially in a hollow formed with the arms or hands **2.** PUT SOMEBODY OR SOMETHING INTO CRADLE to put somebody or something into a cradle or something like a cradle **3.** CIV ENG SUPPORT SOMETHING IN FRAMEWORK to support something such as a ship that is being built or repaired in a framework **4.** NURTURE SOMEBODY OR SOMETHING to look after a young child or support something in the early stages of its development **5.** MIN EXTRACT WASH SOIL FOR GOLD to wash gold-bearing soil in a cradle [Old English *cradol*] —**cra·dler** *n* ◇ **rob the cradle** to be romantically or sexually involved with somebody who is much younger (*informal*)

cra·dle·board /kráyd'l bàwrd/ *n* a wooden frame supporting a cloth enclosure for a baby, traditionally worn on the back by some Native North Americans in order to carry a baby while working or traveling. Cradleboards are often highly decorated with beadwork.

cra·dle cap *n* a skin condition that commonly affects the scalp of young babies, causing scaling and flaking

cra·dle-rob·ber *n* somebody who has a romantic or sexual relationship with a much younger person (*disapproving*)

cra·dle·song /kráyd'l sàwng/ *n* MUSIC same as **lullaby** *n* (sense 1)

craft /kraft/ *n* **1.** MAKING THINGS BY HAND a profession or activity involving the skillful making of decorative or practical objects by hand, e.g., weaving, pottery, or woodcarving (*often used in combination*) **2.** OBJECT PRODUCED BY SKILLFUL HANDWORK something produced skillfully by hand, especially in a traditional manner, e.g., a piece of pottery or carving (*often used in the plural*) **3.** SKILL skill in making or doing things, especially by hand **4.** SKILLED PROFESSION OR ACTIVITY a profession or activity that requires skill and training, or experience or specialized knowledge (*often used in combination*) ○ *his love for the craft of moviemaking* **5.** GUILD the people engaged in a skilled trade or profession, considered as a group (*dated*) **6.** DEVIOUSNESS skill in trickery or deceiving others (*archaic*) **7.** (*plural same*) VESSEL a vessel used for traveling, e.g., a boat, ship, airplane, or space vehicle (*often used in combination*) ■ *vt* (**craft·ed, craft·ing, crafts**) **1.** MAKE SOMETHING WITH SKILL to produce or create something with skill and care **2.** MAKE SOMETHING BY HAND to make something skillfully by hand [Old English *cræft* "strength, power" < Germanic] —**craft·er** *n*

craft beer *n* a beer that is brewed on a small scale and only distributed locally

craft-brewed *adj* made by a small-scale brewery in small quantities

craft food *n* food for sale to consumers that is prepared carefully using high-quality ingredients, especially as contrasted with fast food

crafts·man /kráftsmən/ (*plural* **-men** /-mən/) *n* **1.** somebody who makes decorative or practical objects skillfully by hand **2.** somebody who does something with great skill and expertise —**crafts·man·like** *adj* —**crafts·man·ly** *adj* —**crafts·man·ship** *n*

crafts·per·son /kráfts pùrss'n/ (*plural* **-per·sons** or **-peo·ple** /-pèep'l/) *n* a skillful maker of decorative or practical objects by hand

crafts·wom·an /kráfts wòòmmən/ (*plural* **-wom·en** /-wìmmin/) *n* a woman who makes decorative or practical objects skillfully by hand

craft un·i·on *n* a labor union for people who work at a specific skilled trade, as distinct from an organization for those employed in a specific industry

craft·work /kráft wùrk/ *n* **1.** activity that involves the skillful making of decorative or practical objects by hand, e.g., weaving, pottery, or woodcarving **2.** an example of craftwork —**craft·work·er** *n*

craft·y /kráftee/ (**-i·er, -i·est**) *adj* using or involving cunning or trickery to deceive other people —**craft·i·ly** *adv* —**craft·i·ness** *n*

crag /krag/ *n* a steep rough mass of rock forming part of a cliff or mountain peak [14C. < Celtic, probably Welsh *craig* or Gaelic *creagh*] —**crag·ged** *adj*

crag·gy /krággee/ (**-gi·er, -gi·est**) *adj* **1.** steep and rocky, and forming part of a cliff or mountain peak **2.** rugged-looking with strong prominent masculine features —**crag·gi·ly** *adv* —**crag·gi·ness** *n*

Craig /krayg, kreg/, **Sir James Henry** (1748–1812) British-born Canadian politician and military leader. He served as governor-general of Canada (1807–11).

Cra·io·va /krə yṓvə/ city and capital of Dolj County, southwestern Romania. It is an important industrial center. Population: 310,838 (1997).

crake /krayk/ *n* a marsh bird with a short beak. Native to: Europe, Asia, Africa. [14C. < Old Norse *kráka* "crow," *krákr* "raven" < an imitation of its sound]

cram /kram/ *v* (**crammed, cram·ming, crams**) **1.** *vt* FORCE SOMETHING INTO SMALL SPACE to force objects or people into a space or container that is too small to hold them comfortably **2.** *vt* EAT FOOD GREEDILY to eat food hastily and greedily **3.** *vt* FORCE SOMEBODY TO EAT to encourage or force a person or animal to eat more than is necessary **4.** *vti* STUDY INTENSIVELY to study a subject intensively, e.g., for an imminent exam (*informal*) ■ *n* **1.** TIGHTLY PACKED STATE a situation in which a group of people or things are crushed, crowded, or tightly packed together **2.** PERIOD OF INTENSIVE STUDY a period of intensive study, e.g., for an imminent exam (*informal*) [Old English *(ge)crammian* < Germanic] —**cram·mer** *n*

Cram /kram/, **Ralph Adams** (1863–1942) US architect. He was a leading exponent of the Gothic Revival, particularly in US university buildings.

Cram, Steve (*b.* 1960) British middle-distance runner. In 1984 he was Olympic silver medalist in the 1,500 meters. Over 19 days in 1985, he set new world records for the mile, the 1,500 meters, and the 2,000 meters. Full name **Cram, Steven**

cram·bo /krámbō/ (*plural* **-boes** or **-bos**) *n* a game in which one player gives a word or a line of verse for which the other players must find a rhyming word or line (*dated*) [Mid-17C. Alteration of obsolete *crambe* "cabbage, distasteful repetition," via Latin < Greek *krambē* "cabbage"]

cramp[1] /kramp/ *n* **1.** PAINFUL MUSCLE CONTRACTION a sudden painful involuntary contraction of a muscle **2.** MUSCLE PARALYSIS temporary loss of function in a muscle or muscle group caused by repetitive use or overexertion ○ *writer's cramp* ■ **cramps** *npl* ABDOMINAL PAIN severe pain in the abdomen or adjoining areas, usually of gastrointestinal or uterine origin ■ *vi* (**cramped, cramp·ing, cramps**) BE AFFECTED WITH CRAMP to experience a muscular cramp [14C. Via French < Middle Dutch *krampe*]

cramp[2] /kramp/ *vt* (**cramped, cramp·ing, cramps**) **1.** CONFINE SOMEBODY OR SOMETHING to confine or enclose somebody or something in a small space (*usually passive*) **2.** HAMPER SOMEBODY OR SOMETHING to hamper or obstruct somebody or something **3.** HOLD THINGS TOGETHER to fasten, hold, or press objects together with an adjustable clamp **4.** TURN WHEELS SHARPLY to make the wheels of a vehicle turn sharply ■ *n* **1.** RESTRICTION something that confines, restricts, or restrains, e.g., a set of shackles **2.** CONFINED PLACE a confined or restricted position or place **3.** DEVICE FOR HOLDING THINGS TOGETHER an adjustable clamp for temporarily holding or pressing objects together **4.** BAR WITH BENT ENDS a metal bar with ends bent at right angles, used in building to hold objects such as bricks or timbers together [14C. < Middle Dutch *krampe*]

cramped /krampt/ *adj* **1.** LACKING SPACE inconveniently or uncomfortably small and confining **2.** PACKED IN packed into too small a space for comfort **3. HARD TO READ** written or printed in small characters that are close together and hard to read [Late 17C. < CRAMP[2]]

cramp·fish /krámp fìsh/ (*plural same* or **-fish·es**) *n* FISH same as **electric ray**

cramp i·ron *n* CONSTR same as **cramp**[2] *n* (sense 4)

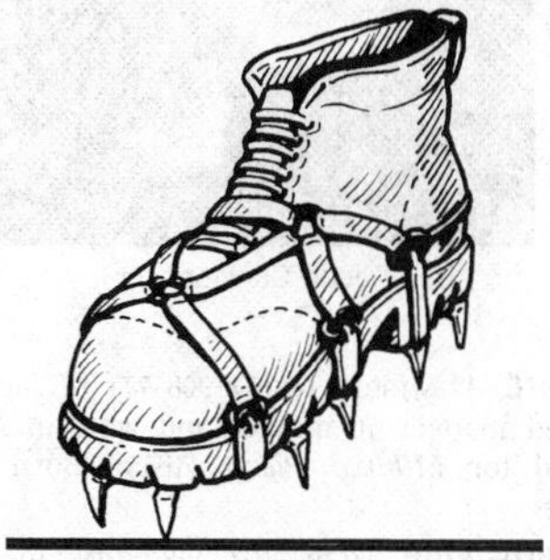

crampon

cram·pon /krám pòn/ *n* a framework of metal spikes fastened to the sole of a boot or shoe to provide better traction on ice or snow (*usually used in the plural*) [13C. Via French < Frankish]

Cra·nach /kraá naakh/, **Lucas, the Elder** (1472–1553) German painter and engraver. He was known for paintings of stylized sensuous nudes; he was also a friend of Martin Luther, whose portrait he painted, as well as a propagandist for the Reformation. Born **Müller** *or* **Sunder, Lucas**

cran·ber·ry /krán bèrree/ (*plural* **-ries**) *n* **1.** a sour red or reddish berry. Use: fruit juice, sauce for roast turkey. **2.** a low-growing evergreen plant of the heath family that yields cranberries. Genus: *Vaccinium*. [Mid-17C. < German *Kranbeere* "crane berry," because the stamens are said to look like a crane's beak]

cran·ber·ry bush, cran·ber·ry tree *n* a bush that produces acid red fruit. Native to: North America. Latin name: *Viburnum trilobum*.

Cran·brook /krán brŏŏk/ city in southeastern British Columbia, Canada, some 30 mi./60 km north of the US border. Population: 18,528 (2001).

crane (sense 4)

crane /krayn/ *n* **1. LIFTING MACHINE** a large machine used to lift and move heavy objects by means of a hook attached to cables suspended from a supporting, usually movable, beam **2. MOVING SUPPORT FOR CAMERA** a moving platform with a long support for a motion-picture or television camera **3. MOVABLE SUPPORT WITH LONG ARM** a device with a long arm for supporting something, e.g., one for swinging and holding a pot or kettle over a fire **4.** BIRDS **LONG-LEGGED BIRD** a bird with long legs and a long neck that lives on plains and in marshes. Family: Gruidae. **5.** BIRDS **BIRD LIKE CRANE** any bird that looks like a true crane, e.g., a heron or stork ■ *v* (**craned, cran·ing, cranes**) **1.** *vti* **STRETCH NECK** to stretch the neck in order to get a better view of something **2.** *vt* **MOVE SOMETHING BY CRANE** to lift or move something using a crane [Old English *cran* < Indo-European, probably an imitation of the bird's cry]

Crane /krayn/, **Hart** (1899–1932) US poet. He celebrated modern civilization in poems such as *The Bridge* (1930). Full name **Crane, Harold Hart**

> "We have all seen / The moon in lonely alleys make / A grail of laughter of an empty ash can."
> [Hart Crane, "Chaplinesque"; 1926]

Crane, Stephen (1871–1900) US writer. He is known for his novel *The Red Badge of Courage* (1895) and other fiction and poetry. See Cultural note at **courage**

> "A singular disadvantage of the sea lies in the fact that after successfully surmounting one wave you discover that there is another behind it just as important and just as nervously anxious to do something effective in the way of swamping boats."
> [Stephen Crane, "The Open Boat," *The Open Boat and Other Stories*; 1898]

Crane, Walter (1845–1915) British painter and illustrator. A leading member of the Arts and Crafts movement, he is known for his illustrations of children's books and his watercolors of mythological scenes.

crane fly *n* a large two-winged fly with a long thin body and long legs. Family: Tipulidae.

cranes·bill /kráynz bìl/ *n* PLANTS same as **geranium** (sense 2)

crani- *prefix* same as **cranio-** (*used before vowels*)

cra·ni·a ANAT plural of **cranium**

cra·ni·al /kráynee əl/ *adj* relating to, involving, or located in the skull, especially the part covering the brain

cra·ni·al in·dex *n* ANTHROP same as **cephalic index**

cra·ni·al nerve *n* either of a pair of nerves that originate in the brain stem and pass out of the skull to the surface of the body. There are 12 pairs of cranial nerves in mammals, birds, and reptiles, and usually 10 in fish and amphibians.

cra·ni·al os·te·op·a·thy *n* gentle manipulation of the bones of the cranium and face to relieve tension and headache. It is also used for relieving pressure on the brain in newborn babies.

cra·ni·ate /kráynee ət, -àyt/ *adj* having a skull or cranium

cranio- *prefix* cranium, skull ○ *craniometry* [< CRANIUM]

cra·ni·o·fa·cial /kràynee ō fáysh'l/ *adj* relating to or involving both the cranium and the face

cra·ni·ol·o·gy /kràynee óllәjee/ *n* the scientific study of the shapes, sizes, and other characteristics of human skulls —**cra·ni·o·log·i·cal** /-ə lójjik'l/ *adj* —**cra·ni·o·log·i·cal·ly** *adv* —**cra·ni·ol·o·gist** *n*

cra·ni·om·e·try /kràynee ómmәtree/ *n* the scientific measurement of skulls —**cra·ni·om·e·ter** *n* —**cra·ni·o·met·ric** /-ə méttrik/ *adj* —**cra·ni·o·met·ri·cal** *adj* —**cra·ni·o·met·ri·cal·ly** *adv* —**cra·ni·om·e·trist** *n*

cra·ni·o·sac·ral /kràynee ō sákrəl, -sáy-/ *adj* ANAT same as **parasympathetic**

cra·ni·o·sac·ral ther·a·py *n* gentle manipulation of the bones of the face, skull, and spine, intended to relieve conditions including migraine, sinusitis, and musculoskeletal problems

cra·ni·ot·o·my /kràynee óttəmee/ (*plural* **-mies**) *n* cutting open the skull to expose the brain, especially for brain surgery

cra·ni·um /kráynee əm/ (*plural* **-ni·ums** or **-ni·a** /-nee ə/) *n* the skull of a vertebrate, especially the part that covers the brain [15C. Via medieval Latin < Greek *kranion*]

crank[1] /krangk/ *n* **1. MECHANICAL DEVICE FOR TRANSMITTING MOTION** a device consisting of an arm or handle that is connected to a shaft at right angles, enabling the transmission of motion to or from the shaft. A crank may be used for changing rotary motion to reciprocating motion or vice versa. **2. ECCENTRIC PERSON** somebody regarded as having unusual ideas and opinions (*informal insult*) **3. GROUCH** somebody regarded as disagreeable and bad tempered (*informal*) **4.** DRUGS **ILLEGAL DRUG** powdered methamphetamine used as an illegal drug (*slang*) ■ *v* (**cranked, crank·ing, cranks**) **1.** *vti* **USE CRANK ON SOMETHING** to start, move, or operate something by turning a crank **2.** *vt* **FORM SOMETHING INTO CRANK SHAPE** to form something into the right-angled shape of a crank ■ *adj* **1. ECCENTRIC** associated with or done by somebody who has unusual, often strongly held, ideas and opinions (*disapproving*) **2. FROM SOMEBODY MALICIOUS** associated with or done by somebody who is malicious or playing a prank [Old English *cranc* < Germanic, "crooked"]

crank out *vt* to produce something quickly, mechanically, regularly, and in large quantities (*informal*)

crank up *v* **1.** *vti* **START SOMETHING WITH CRANK** to start something, especially an engine, with a crank **2.** *vt* **INCREASE SOMETHING** to increase the force, volume, or intensity of something (*informal*) **3.** *vt* **START SOMETHING** to get something to begin to operate or happen (*informal*) **4.** *vi* **TAKE DRUGS** to take or inject an illegal drug (*slang*)

crank[2] /krangk/ *adj* describes a vessel that is unsteady on the water and likely to capsize [Early 17C. Origin ?]

crank·case /krángk kàyss/ *n* the metal casing that encloses the crankshaft in some engines, especially internal-combustion engines

crank·pin /krángk pìn/ *n* a short cylindrical bearing piece in the arm of a crank, attached to a connecting rod

crank·shaft /krángk shàft/ *n* a shaft that drives or is driven by a crank, e.g., one attached to a connecting rod in an internal-combustion engine

crank·y[1] /krángkee/ (**-i·er, -i·est**) *adj* **1. GROUCHY** disagreeable and easily irritated (*informal*) **2. WORKING UNPREDICTABLY** not working well and likely to break down or operate unreliably **3. ECCENTRIC** eccentric or obsessive (*informal*) **4. CROOKED** characterized by twists and turns —**crank·i·ly** *adv* —**crank·i·ness** *n*

crank·y[2] /krángkee/ *adj* NAUT same as **crank**[2]

cran·nog /kránnəg/ *n* an ancient Celtic settlement in Scotland or Ireland, built on a natural or constructed island in a lake or swamp and usually fortified [Early 17C. < Irish *crannóg* or Gaelic *crannag* "timber structure" < *crann* "tree"]

cran·ny /kránnee/ (*plural* **-nies**) *n* a small narrow crack, hole, or opening in a wall or rock [15C. < French *crané* "notched" < popular Latin *crena* "small notch"] —**cran·nied** *adj*

Cran·ston /kránstən/ city in eastern Rhode Island; a southwestern suburb of Providence. Population: 81,113 (2002 estimate).

crap[1] /krap/ (*slang*) *n* **1.** an offensive term for nonsense, or something worthless or annoying **2.** an offensive term for an act of passing solid waste matter out of the body through the anus **3.** an offensive term for excrement ■ *adj* an offensive term meaning worthless, useless, or lacking in ability ■ *vti* (**crapped, crap·ping, craps**) an offensive term meaning to pass solid waste matter out of the body through the anus [15C. Probably < Middle Dutch]

crap[2] /krap/ *n* **1.** a losing throw at craps **2.** GAMBLING same as **craps** (sense 1) (*usually used before a noun*) [Late 19C. Back-formation < CRAPS]

crap out *vi* (*slang*) **1. MAKE LOSING THROW** to make a losing throw in the game of craps **2. AVOID DOING SOMETHING** to avoid or discontinue an activity, especially out of fear **3. RENEGE** to fail to fulfill a promise

crape /krayp/ *n* **1.** TEXTILES same as **crepe** (sense 2) **2.** a band of crepe worn as a sign of mourning around the arm or, formerly, around a hat [Early 16C. < French *crêpe* (see CREPE)]

crape myr·tle *n* a deciduous bush or tree, cultivated for its white, pink, or red flowers. Native to: Asia. Latin name: *Lagerstroemia indica*.

crap·per /kráppər/ *n* an offensive term for a toilet (*slang*) [Mid-20C. < CRAP[1]]

crap·pie /kráppee/ (*plural* **-pies** or *same*) *n* a freshwater sunfish with equal-sized anal and dorsal fins. Native to: lakes and ponds in North America. Genus: *Pomoxis*. [Mid-19C. Origin ?]

crap·py /kráppee/ (**-pi·er, -pi·est**) *adj* an offensive term meaning worthless, useless, of poor quality, or badly made or done (*slang*)

craps /kraps/ *n* **1.** a US gambling game played with two dice **2.** GAMBLING same as **crap**[2] (sense 2) [Early 18C. Probably < French, variant of *crabs* "score of two ones at dice" < English, plural of CRAB[1]]

crap·shoot /kráp shoòt/ *n* **1.** something that is a matter of chance or is risky (*informal*) **2.** a game of craps —**crap·shoot·er** *n*

crap·u·lence /kráppyələnss/ *n* **1.** overindulgence, especially in alcoholic drink **2.** sickness caused by overindulgence in good food and, especially, alcoholic drink (*dated*) —**crap·u·lent** *adj*

crap·u·lous /kráppyələss/ *adj* regularly overindulging in food or alcohol (*literary*) [Mid-17C. < late Latin *crapulentus* "very drunk" < Greek *kraipalē* "drunken headache"] —**crap·u·lous·ly** *adv*

cra·que·lure /kra klòor/ *n* a network of small cracks that sometimes appear on the surface of an oil painting as it ages [Early 20C. < French]

crash[1] /krash/ *n* **1.** VEHICLE COLLISION a collision involving a moving vehicle or aircraft **2.** LOUD NOISE a loud noise such as that made by thunder or by something breaking violently into pieces **3.** COMPUTER BREAKDOWN a sudden complete failure of a computer system, device, or program, usually with an accompanying loss of data ○ *a system crash* **4.** FINANCIAL COLLAPSE the financial collapse or failure of something such as a stock market, involving a massive drop in stock prices, or the collapse of a commercial business ■ *v* (**crashed, crash·ing, crash·es**) **1.** *vti* COLLIDE VIOLENTLY to strike against something with great force, causing damage or destruction, or cause something such as a car to strike against something in this way **2.** *vti* MAKE LOUD NOISE to make a loud noise, or cause something to make a loud noise **3.** *vti* BREAK INTO PIECES NOISILY to break into pieces violently and noisily, or break an object in this way **4.** *vti* MOVE NOISILY to move noisily, destructively, or violently, or cause something to move in this way **5.** *vti* HAVE OR CAUSE COMPLETE COMPUTER FAILURE to experience a sudden complete failure, or cause a computer system to have a sudden complete failure **6.** *vi* COLLAPSE FINANCIALLY to suffer financial collapse or failure **7.** *vi* DROP SHARPLY to decrease in value rapidly and steeply ○ *Stock prices crashed.* **8.** *vti* ATTEND UNINVITED to attend an event such as a party without an invitation (*informal*) **9.** *vi* SLEEP to sleep, especially somewhere other than usual when exhausted, or stay temporarily somewhere other than at home (*slang*) **10.** *vi* BECOME DEPRESSED AFTER DRUG to become depressed as the effects of a drug-induced high wear off (*slang*) ■ *adj* **1.** RAPID AND INTENSIVE done intensively over a short period of time in order to achieve the desired results quickly ○ *crash course* ○ *crash diet* **2.** FOR EMERGENCIES designed to be used during emergencies ○ *a crash cast in the ER* [14C. Origin ?] —**crash·er** *n* ◇ **crash and burn** (*slang*) **1.** to fail utterly **2.** to fall asleep or collapse from exhaustion

crash[2] /krash/ *n* a coarse linen or cotton cloth. Use: towels, curtains, book bindings. [Early 19C. < Russian *krashenina* "dyed coarse linen"]

crash ax *n* a tool similar to an ax, used by aircrews to cut an escape route through the skin of a commercial aircraft cockpit in case of an on-ground emergency

crash bar·ri·er *n* a safety barrier at the edge of a road or racetrack or between the lanes of a highway

crash dive *n* a steep rapid dive from the surface of a body of water by a submarine

crash-dive *vti* **1.** to dive steeply through the air and crash, or cause an aircraft to do this **2.** to make a steep rapid descent from the surface of a body of water, or cause a submarine to do this

crash hel·met *n* a hard padded helmet worn by cyclists, racing drivers, and others to protect the head in case of an accident

crash·ing /kráshing/ *adj* complete and utter (*informal*) ○ *a crashing bore*

crash land·ing *n* an emergency landing by an aircraft, usually causing damage to the aircraft —**crash-land** /krásh lànd/ *vti*

crash pad *n* **1.** padding inside a vehicle that is designed to protect the occupants in a crash **2.** a place other than home where somebody sleeps or stays temporarily (*dated slang*)

crash-test *vt* **1.** to test a vehicle by deliberately crashing it into a wall to learn how it and its occupants will be affected in an accident **2.** to establish the safety and reliability of something by subjecting it to tests, e.g., using heat, pressure, or strain, until it reaches its breaking point

crash·wor·thy /krásh wùrthee/ *adj* able to withstand a crash —**crash·wor·thi·ness** *n*

crass /krass/ *adj* **1.** so thoughtless, vulgar, and insensitive as to lack all refinement or delicacy **2.** extreme or flagrant ○ *crass stupidity* [15C. < Latin *crassus* "thick"] —**crass·i·tude** *n* —**crass·ly** *adv* —**crass·ness** *n*

-crat *suffix* a supporter or member of a particular form of government or hierarchy ○ *technocrat* [< French *-crate* < Greek *kratos* "strength"]

crate /krayt/ *n* **1.** BOX a large open sturdy box used to carry or store objects or built to fit and protect something during shipping **2.** OLD VEHICLE an old rickety airplane or automobile (*dated informal*) ■ *vti* (**crat·ed, crat·ing, crates**) PUT SOMETHING IN CRATE to put or pack something in a crate [14C. Origin ?]

cra·ter /kráytər/ *n* **1.** VOLCANO SUMMIT a circular funnel-shaped depression produced by volcanic eruption **2.** EXPLOSION HOLE a large hole in the ground or a surface caused by an explosion **3.** METEORITE IMPACT AREA a bowl-shaped hole on the surface of the Moon or a planet caused by the impact of a meteorite ■ *vti* (**-tered, -ter·ing, -ters**) FORM CRATERS to form craters, or make craters form in something [Early 17C. Via Latin < Greek *kratēr* "(mixing) bowl"] —**cra·ter·like** *adj*

Cra·ter *n* a small constellation of the southern hemisphere. See illustration at **constellation**

Cra·ter Lake Na·tion·al Park /kráytər-/ national park in southern Oregon. Established in 1902, the park includes the circular Crater Lake, situated in the crater of an extinct volcano. At 1,932 ft./589 m, it is the deepest lake in the United States. Area: 286 sq. mi./741 sq. km.

C ra·tion *n* a canned field ration formerly issued to US soldiers [< *canned*]

cra·ton /kráy tòn/ *n* the extensive interior of a large block of the Earth's crust that has been relatively stable for many millions of years [Mid-20C. Either alteration of *kratogen* < Greek *kratos* "strength"; or < German *Kraton*, alteration of Greek *kratos*] —**cra·ton·ic** /kray tónnik/ *adj*

cra·vat /krə vát/ *n* a scarf or band of fabric worn around a man's neck and tied in front. A cravat may be worn on formal occasions instead of a bow tie. [Mid-17C. < French *cravate* < *Cravate* "Croatian" < German *Krabat(e)* < Serbo-Croat *Hrvāt* "a Croat"]

crave /krayv/ (**craved, crav·ing, craves**) *v* **1.** *vti* to have a strong desire for something **2.** *vt* to beg somebody to do or give something (*archaic*) [Old English *crafian* "to demand" < Germanic] —**crav·er** *n* —**crav·ing·ly** *adv*

SYNONYMS See ***want***.

cra·ven /kráyvən/ *adj* so lacking in courage as to be worthy of contempt [12C. Origin ?] —**cra·ven·ly** *adv* —**cra·ven·ness** *n*

SYNONYMS See ***cowardly***.

crav·ing /kráyving/ *n* a strong desire for something

craw /kraw/ *n* **1.** ZOOL, INSECTS same as **crop** *n* (senses 7–8) **2.** the stomach of an animal (*informal*) **3.** *Ireland* the throat or gullet [14C. Related to Middle Low German *krage* or Middle Dutch *crāghe* "neck, throat"]

craw·dad /kráw dàd/ *n Southern US* MARINE BIOL same as **crayfish** (sense 1) [Early 20C. Probably alteration of CRAWFISH]

craw·fish /kráw fìsh/ *n* (*plural same* or **-fish·es**) MARINE BIOL same as **crayfish** (sense 1) ■ *vi* to withdraw from an undertaking or enterprise (*informal*) [Early 17C. Variant]

Joan Crawford

Craw·ford /kráwfərd/, **Joan** (1908–77) US actor. She starred in over 70 movies and won an Academy Award for *Mildred Pierce* (1945). Born **LeSueur, Lucille**

Craw·fords·ville /kráwfərdz vìl/ city in western Indiana, northwest of Indianapolis. Population: 15,330 (2002 estimate).

crawl /krawl/ *vi* (**crawled, crawl·ing, crawls**) **1.** MOVE CLOSE TO GROUND to move slowly along on hands and knees or with the body close to the ground or a surface **2.** MOVE SLOWLY CLOSE TO SURFACE to move slowly across something with the body close to or touching the surface **3.** MOVE VERY SLOWLY to move forward at a slow pace **4.** BE OVERRUN to be filled with large numbers of moving people or things ○ *The place was crawling with reporters.* **5.** FEEL CREEPY to feel a sensation of being covered with moving insects, usually in reaction to something frightening or disgusting ○ *made his skin crawl* **6.** BE SERVILE to try to please somebody by behaving in a servile way (*informal*) **7.** BOT GROW ACROSS SURFACE to grow and spread along a surface by means of tendrils or clinging stems (*refers to vines or low-growing plants*) ■ *n* **1.** SLOW SPEED a very slow pace **2.** OVERARM SWIMMING STROKE a fast swimming stroke in which the swimmer lies face down and uses a flutter kick and an overarm stroke **3.** PROGRESS ON HANDS AND KNEES slow movement on hands and knees or with the body close to the ground or a surface **4.** MOVING WORDS ON TELEVISION OR FILM words or figures that are scrolled across a television or movie screen to convey information, e.g., programming credits or news bulletins [14C. Probably < Old Norse *krafla* "paw with the hands"] —**crawl·ing·ly** *adv*

crawl·er /kráwlər/ *n* **1.** SOMETHING THAT CRAWLS an insect or other animal that crawls **2.** VEHICLE WITH TRACKS a vehicle that has continuous tracks of linked plates instead of wheels **3.** ONLINE, COMPUT PROGRAM COLLECTING ONLINE DOCUMENTS a computer program that collects online documents and reference links

crawl space *n* a low unfinished space under a floor or above a ceiling in a building that gives access to plumbing, wiring, and ductwork

crawl·y /kráwlee/ (**-i·er, -i·est**) *adj* causing a shuddery disgust or unease (*informal*)

Cra·xi /kráaksee/, **Bettino** (1934–2000) Italian politician. He was Italy's first socialist prime minister (1983–87). Indicted for corruption in 1993, he was convicted and sentenced to 14 years' imprisonment.

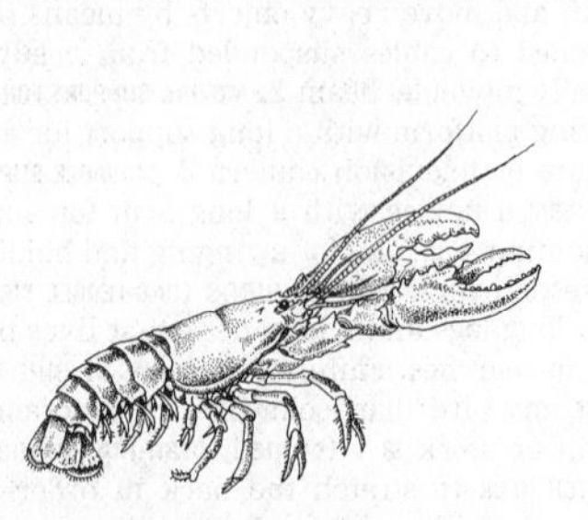

crayfish

cray·fish /kráy fìsh/ (*plural same* or **-fish·es**) *n* **1.** a freshwater crustacean with large claws like those of a lobster. It is prized for its tail meat. Superfamily:

Astacoidea. **2.** MARINE BIOL same as **spiny lobster** **3.** a crayfish used as food [14C. By folk etymology < French *crevice* < Indo-European, "to scratch"]

cray·on /kráy òn/ *n* **1.** COLORED DRAWING STICK a stick of colored wax, chalk, or charcoal, used for drawing and coloring **2.** DRAWING a drawing made using crayons ■ *vti* **(-oned, -on·ing, -ons)** USE CRAYONS to draw or color something with crayons [Mid-17C. < French, "pencil" < *craie* "chalk" < Latin *creta* "chalk, clay"] —**cray·on·ist** *n*

craze /krayz/ *n* **1.** FAD a fashion that is extremely popular for a short time **2.** CERAMICS FINE CRACK a fine crack in the glaze of pottery. It happens when the glaze cools and contracts at a different temperature from the clay. ■ *vti* **(crazed, craz·ing, craz·es)** **1.** BECOME OR MAKE IRRATIONAL to become, or make somebody become, irrational or highly excited (*often considered offensive*) **2.** CERAMICS PRODUCE OR SUSTAIN CRACKS to produce fine cracks in the glaze of pottery, or become covered with such cracks [14C. Probably < assumed Old Norse *krasa* "shatter"] —**crazed** *adj*

craz·ing /kráyzing/ *n* fine cracks in the glaze of a piece of pottery, produced when the glaze cools and contracts at a different temperature from the clay. When the effect is deliberate, it is often called "crackle."

cra·zy /kráyzee/ *adj* **(-zi·er, -zi·est)** (*informal*) **1.** OFFENSIVE TERM an offensive term meaning affected by a psychiatric disorder **2.** RIDICULOUS not showing good sense or practicality **3.** VERY FOND extremely fond of somebody or something ○ *crazy about tennis* ■ *n* (*plural* **-zies**) OFFENSIVE TERM an offensive term for somebody with a psychiatric disorder —**cra·zi·ly** *adv* —**cra·zi·ness** *n*

cra·zy bone *n* ANAT same as **funny bone** (*informal*)

Cra·zy Horse /kráyzee hàwrss/ (1849?–77) Oglala Sioux leader. He opposed and fought against white settlement. Born **Tashunca Witco**

"It is a good day to fight! It is a good day to die! Strong hearts, brave hearts to the front! Weak hearts and cowards to the rear!"
[Crazy Horse, Address to Sioux warriors at the Battle of Little Bighorn; June 25, 1876]

cra·zy quilt *n* **1.** a quilt made of irregularly shaped and patterned pieces of cloth sewn together **2.** a confusing mix of things that do not belong or fit together ○ *a crazy quilt of confusing ideas and contradictory suggestions*

cra·zy·weed /kráyzee wèed/ (*plural same* or **-weeds**) *n* PLANTS same as **locoweed**

creak /kreek/ *vi* **(creaked, creak·ing, creaks)** **1.** SQUEAK to make a prolonged squeaking noise **2.** MOVE WITH SQUEAKING to move along while making prolonged squeaking noises ■ *n* PROLONGED SQUEAK a prolonged squeaking noise [14C. An imitation of the sound] —**creak·ing·ly** *adv*

SPELLCHECK Do not confuse the spelling of ***creak*** and ***creek*** ("a stream"), which sound similar.

creak·y /kréekee/ **(-i·er, -i·est)** *adj* **1.** CREAKING making a prolonged squeaking noise **2.** STIFF not able to move easily, especially as a result of aging (*informal*) **3.** OLD OR OLD-FASHIONED showing signs of having deteriorated over time or of being old-fashioned (*informal*) —**creak·i·ly** *adv* —**creak·i·ness** *n*

cream /kreem/ *n* **1.** FATTY PART OF MILK a high-fat liquid product separated from milk. Use: in cooking, accompaniment to desserts. **2.** CREAMY FOOD a food that contains cream or has a consistency like cream **3.** CREAMY LOTION a cosmetic or medicinal preparation that has a thick smooth consistency like cream **4.** BEST PART the best part of something ○ *the cream of society* **5.** YELLOW-TINGED WHITE an off-white color with a yellow tinge **6.** SOFT-CENTERED CHOCOLATE a chocolate with a soft smooth filling ■ *adj* WHITE WITH SOME YELLOW of a yellowish white color ■ *v* **(creamed, cream·ing, creams)** **1.** *vt* COMBINE INGREDIENTS to mix ingredients together to soften and combine them **2.** *vt* PREPARE SOMETHING WITH CREAM to add cream to something while cooking it or on serving it **3.** *vti* FORM FOAM ON TOP to form a frothy layer resembling cream on the surface of a liquid, or cause such a layer to form **4.** *vt* REMOVE CREAM FROM MILK to separate the cream from milk **5.** *vti* FORM CREAM to form cream, or allow milk to form cream **6.** *vt* DEFEAT SOMEBODY to defeat somebody thoroughly (*slang*) ○ *We creamed them!* **7.** *vt* WRECK SOMETHING BY SMASHING to wreck or damage something by smashing it into a hard object (*slang*) ○ *She creamed her car against the stone wall.* **8.** *vti* TABOO TERM a highly offensive term meaning to ejaculate (*taboo*) [14C. < French *creme,* blend of late Latin *cramum* + ecclesiastical Latin *chrisma* "ointment" (< Greek *khrisma*)]

cream off *vt* **1.** to take away the best part of something **2.** to take and use something for an illicit or unintended purpose (*informal*)

cream cheese *n* a soft white unmatured cheese with a high fat content

cream·cups /kréem kùps/ *npl* an annual plant of the poppy family. Flowers: small, pale yellow, or cream. Native to: southwestern United States, Mexico. Latin name: *Platystemon californicus.*

cream·er /kréemər/ *n* **1.** a small pitcher for serving cream **2.** a cream substitute, used especially in coffee or tea

cream·er·y /kréeməree/ (*plural* **-ies**) *n* a place at which milk is processed and dairy products are produced

cream of tar·tar *n* potassium bitartrate, when used as a leavening agent in cooking

cream puff *n* **1.** CREAM-FILLED PASTRY a sweet pastry made of a flaky shell filled with whipped cream and dusted with powdered sugar **2.** OFFENSIVE TERM an offensive term for a man regarded as effeminate (*slang*) **3.** GOOD CAR a used car in very good condition (*slang*) ■ *adj* UNIMPORTANT of little consequence or difficulty

cream sauce *n* sauce made with cream, especially one based on milk, white wine, or a light-colored broth

cream sher·ry *n* a smooth sweet sherry

cream so·da *n* a carbonated soft drink flavored with vanilla

cream·ware /kréem wèr/ *n* glazed earthenware of a deep creamy color, first produced in Britain in about 1720

cream·y /kréemee/ **(-i·er, -i·est)** *adj* **1.** with a texture, color, taste, or consistency like cream **2.** containing a large amount of cream —**cream·i·ly** *adv* —**cream·i·ness** *n*

crease /kreess/ *n* **1.** FOLD PUT IN FABRIC a straight line formed in clothing or fabric by pressing **2.** UNWANTED FABRIC FOLD an unwanted line in clothing or fabric that has been crushed or folded **3.** SKIN WRINKLE a line or wrinkle on the skin **4.** HOCKEY HOCKEY GOAL AREA the rectangular area in front of a hockey goal **5.** SPORTS GOAL AREA the semicircular area surrounding a lacrosse goal ■ *v* **(creased, creas·ing, creas·es)** **1.** *vti* MAKE OR ACQUIRE CREASES to form lines, folds, or wrinkles in something, or become lined, folded, or wrinkled ○ *This fabric creases badly.* ○ *His face creased into a smile.* **2.** *vt* GRAZE SKIN to graze the skin and inflict a superficial wound [Late 16C. Probably < CREST] —**creas·er** *n* —**creas·y** *adj*

cre·ate /kree áyt/ **(-at·ed, -at·ing, -ates)** *v* **1.** *vt* MAKE SOMETHING to bring something into existence **2.** *vt* GIVE RISE TO SOMETHING to result in something or make something happen **3.** *vti* PRODUCE INVENTIONS OR ART to use imagination to invent things or produce works of art **4.** *vt* APPOINT SOMEBODY to give somebody a new title, role, or office **5.** *vt* ARTS PERFORM ROLE FOR FIRST TIME to be the first person to perform a particular role in a theatrical production [14C. < Latin *creat-,* past participle of *creare* "bring forth"]

SYNONYMS See ***make.***

cre·a·tine /kreé ə teen, -tin/, **cre·a·tin** /-tin/ *n* an amino acid that provides energy to muscles, usually as phosphocreatine. Formula: $C_4H_9N_3O_2$. [Mid-19C. < assumed Greek *kreat-* "flesh"]

cre·a·tine ki·nase *n* an enzyme that breaks down phosphocreatine into creatine and phosphoric acid, releasing energy

cre·a·tine phos·phate *n* BIOCHEM same as **phosphocreatine**

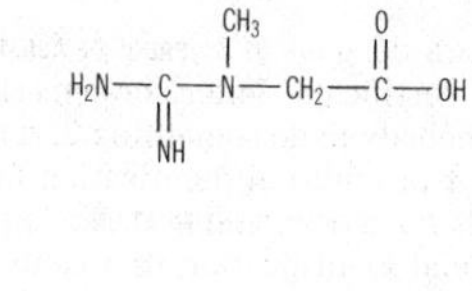

creatine

cre·at·i·nine /kree átt'n een/ *n* a derivative of creatine found in muscle, blood, and urine. Formula: $C_4H_7ON_3$. [Mid-19C. < CREATINE]

cre·a·tion /kree áysh'n/ *n* **1.** MAKING SOMETHING the bringing of something into existence **2.** EARTH AND ITS INHABITANTS the world and everything in it **3.** SOMETHING CREATED BY SOMEBODY a product of human imagination or invention **4.** ELABORATE GARMENT an elaborate or striking item of clothing —**cre·a·tion·al** *adj*

Cre·a·tion *n* **1.** according to the Bible, the act of God that brought the universe and all living beings into existence **2.** according to the Bible, the universe as created by God

cre·a·tion·ism /kree áysh'n ìzzəm/ *n* the belief that God created the universe —**cre·a·tion·ist** *adj, n*

cre·a·tion sci·ence *n* the attempt to provide scientific proof for the account of God's creation of the world that is described in the Bible

cre·a·tive /kree áytiv/ *adj* **1.** ABLE TO CREATE able to create things ○ *Humans are a creative species.* **2.** NEW AND ORIGINAL using or showing use of the imagination to create new ideas or things ○ *a creative approach to the problem of lack of space* **3.** RESOURCEFUL making imaginative use of the limited resources available ○ *a creative cook* **4.** FIN DECEPTIVE IN PRESENTING FINANCIAL INFORMATION employing deceptive methods to distort financial records (*ironic*) ○ *creative accounting* ○ *creative bookkeeping* ■ *n* IDEAS PERSON a creator of new ideas and concepts for sales campaigns (*informal*) ○ *ad agency creatives hard at work on a TV infomercial* —**cre·a·tive·ly** *adv* —**cre·a·tive·ness** *n*

cre·a·tive writ·ing *n* **1.** the writing of fiction, poetry, or drama, often as an exercise **2.** works of fiction, poetry, or drama

cre·a·tiv·i·ty /krée ay tívvətee/ *n* **1.** the quality of being creative **2.** the ability to use the imagination to develop new and original ideas or things, especially in an artistic context

cre·a·tor /kree áytər/ *n* somebody who produces or initiates something —**cre·a·tor·ship** *n*

Cre·a·tor *n* God regarded as creator of the universe

crea·ture /kréechər/ *n* **1.** LIVING BEING any living person or animal **2.** UNPLEASANT LIVING BEING an unpleasant or frightening living thing **3.** CREATED THING somebody or something that has been created ○ *a creature of your imagination* **4.** TYPE OF PERSON somebody of a particular type ○ *He's a creature of habit.* **5.** SUBSERVIENT PERSON somebody who owes his or her status to another person and is thereby subject to undue influence ○ *The senator is a creature of the party boss who got him elected.* [13C. Directly or via French < late Latin *creatura* < Latin *creat-* (see CREATE)] —**crea·tur·al** *adj* —**crea·ture·hood** *n*

crea·ture com·forts *npl* things considered necessary for a comfortable life

crèche /kresh, kraysh/ *n* **1.** NATIVITY SCENE a three-dimensional representation of the scene at the birth of Jesus Christ **2.** HOSPITAL FOR FOUNDLINGS formerly, a hospital for abandoned children **3.** *UK* CHILDCARE FACILITY a place where small children are looked after while their parents or guardians are working or busy with other tasks [Late 18C. Via French, "crib" < assumed Vulgar Latin *creppia* < Germanic]

cre·dence /kréed'nss/ *n* **1.** ACCEPTANCE acceptance based on the degree to which something is believable **2.** TRUSTWORTHINESS the power to inspire belief or trust

3. *also* **cre·dence ta·ble** CHR **CHURCH TABLE FOR BREAD AND WINE** a small shelf or table in a church where the bread, wine, and containers used for Communion are kept [14C. Directly or via French < medieval Latin *credentia* "belief" < Latin *credent-*, present participle of *credere* "believe"]

cre·den·tial /krə dénshəl/ *n* 1. **PROOF OF ABILITY OR TRUSTWORTHINESS** a certificate, letter, or experience that qualifies somebody to do something 2. **AUTHENTICATION** anything that provides authentication for a claim ■ **cre·den·tials** *npl* **OFFICIAL IDENTIFICATION** a letter, badge, or other official identification that confirms somebody's position or status ■ *vt* (**-tialed, -tial·ing, -tials**) **GIVE SOMEBODY CREDENTIALS** to provide somebody with official credentials [15C. < medieval Latin *credentialis* "entitling confidence" < *credentia* (see CREDENCE)]

cre·den·tialed /krə dénshəld/ *adj* 1. trained and licensed in a particular profession ○ *a credentialed medical practitioner* 2. having or carrying credentials that allow somebody to do something or participate in something (*informal*) ○ *spoke to all the credentialed reporters at the event*

cre·den·tial·ism /krə dénsh'l ìzzəm/ *n* an overemphasis on educational credentials when assessing somebody's qualifications, e.g., for a job

cre·den·za /krə dénzə/ *n* 1. a buffet or sideboard, usually without legs 2. a low piece of office furniture that has enclosed shelf space [Late 19C. Via Italian < medieval Latin *credentia* (see CREDENCE)]

cred·i·bil·i·ty /krèddə bíllətee/ *n* 1. the ability to inspire belief or trust 2. a willingness to accept something as true

cred·i·bil·i·ty gap *n* 1. **DISTRUST OF OFFICIAL STATEMENTS** a situation in which the public distrusts the accuracy of official statements 2. **LACK OF TRUST** any situation in which a lack of trust exists between two groups 3. **DISCREPANCY BETWEEN CLAIM AND TRUTH** an apparent difference between what is claimed to be true and what is in fact true

cred·i·ble /kréddəb'l/ *adj* 1. **BELIEVABLE** easy to believe 2. **TRUSTWORTHY** inspiring trust and confidence 3. **MILITARILY EFFECTIVE** of sufficient strength to function effectively as a military force [14C. < Latin *credibilis* < *credere* "believe"] —**cred·i·ble·ness** *n* —**cred·i·bly** *adv*

USAGE credible, credulous, or **creditable**? These three adjectives, and the corresponding nouns *credibility, credit,* and *credulity,* are sometimes confused. A person or thing is ***credible*** when he, she, or it can be easily or readily believed: *My story may sound barely credible but I assure you it's true.* ***Credible*** also has the newer meaning "inspiring confidence": *The government needs to develop a credible monetary policy.* Somebody is ***credulous*** when he or she is all too ready to believe: *Only the most credulous person would believe such a feeble excuse.* ***Creditable*** is connected with the word *credit* and means "bringing credit": *An excellent squash player, she plays a creditable game of tennis as well.*

cred·it /kréddit/ *n* 1. **RECOGNITION** praise or recognition for something done 2. **SOURCE OF PRIDE** a source of pride or honor 3. **GOOD REPUTATION** somebody's good reputation among or influence with other people ○ *She has a lot of credit with this community.* 4. **PAY-LATER SYSTEM** an arrangement by which a buyer can take possession of something now and pay for it later or over time ○ *offer credit* ○ *buy on credit* 5. **TIME TO PAY** the time allowed for payment of something by credit 6. **FINANCIAL STATUS** somebody's financial status or reputation 7. **SPENDING ENTITLEMENT AT STORE** money that a customer is owed by a store and is entitled to spend there 8. **BALANCE IN ACCOUNT** the amount of money in an account after debts have been charged against it 9. **MONEY PAID INTO ACCOUNT** an amount of money paid into an account 10. **AMOUNT BANK WILL LEND** the amount of money that a financial institution is prepared to lend somebody 11. **ACKNOWLEDGMENT OF SOMEBODY'S ROLE** a mention of the role that somebody played in an endeavor, especially an artistic one 12. **DEDUCTION OF PAYMENT FROM OWED AMOUNT** the deduction from a business account of an amount owed that has been paid 13. **ACCOUNT PAYMENTS COLUMN** the right-hand side of an account record, where payments to the account are recorded 14. **PAYMENT RECORDED** a payment recorded against an amount owed 15. **COURSE UNIT** a unit of study, often equivalent to an hour of class time, in a course of higher education 16. **RECOGNITION OF COURSE COMPLETION** official recognition that a student has successfully completed a course of study ○ *get credit for a course* ■ **cred·its** *npl* MOVIES, MEDIA **LIST OF ACKNOWLEDGMENTS** a listing of the people involved in a movie or television production, together with their roles or jobs ■ *vt* (**-it·ed, -it·ing, -its**) 1. **BELIEVE SOMETHING** to accept that something is true 2. **RECOGNIZE SOMEBODY AS RESPONSIBLE** to recognize somebody as the person responsible for an achievement 3. **ATTRIBUTE SOMETHING TO SOMEBODY** to ascribe something such as a personal quality to somebody 4. **ADD MONEY TO BANK ACCOUNT** to add an amount of money to somebody's bank or savings account 5. **RECORD PAYMENT OF MONEY** to record an amount of money as a payment in an accounting record 6. EDUC **SAY OFFICIALLY THAT STUDENT PASSED** to award a credit to a student for successful completion of a course of study [Mid-16C. Via French < Latin *creditum* "loan" < past participle of *credere* "entrust, believe"] ◇ **to somebody's credit** something for which somebody should be commended

ORIGIN The Latin word *credere*, "to believe," from which ***credit*** is derived, is also the source of English *credible, creed, grant,* and *miscreant.*

cred·it·a·ble /krédditəb'l/ *adj* bringing credit, or worthy of praise —**cred·it·a·bil·i·ty** /krèdditə bíllətee/ *n* —**cred·it·a·ble·ness** *n* —**cred·it·a·bly** *adv*

USAGE See ***credible.***

cred·it ac·count *n UK* same as **charge account**

cred·it bu·reau *n* a business that provides information concerning somebody's creditworthiness to companies or banks

cred·it card *n* a card issued by a bank or business that allows somebody to purchase goods and services and pay for them later, often with interest

cred·it hour *n* a credit at a school or college that represents one hour of classroom study per week over the period of time that the course is taught

cred·it line *n* 1. the maximum amount of credit that a lending institution or a credit card company will extend to a client 2. a printed acknowledgment of the author or source of material that was included in a publication

cred·it note *n Can, UK* FIN same as **credit slip**

cred·i·tor /krédditər/ *n* a person or organization owed money by another

cred·it rat·ing *n* an estimate of somebody's ability to repay money given on credit

cred·it-ref·er·ence a·gen·cy *n UK* FIN same as **credit bureau**

cred·it slip *n US* a slip of paper stating that somebody is owed an amount of money by a store and is entitled to merchandise valued at that amount. Can term **credit note**

cred·it squeeze *n* a reduction in the availability of credit or an increase in the interest charged for credit

cred·it un·ion *n* a cooperative savings association that makes loans to its members at reduced interest rates

cred·it·wor·thy /kréddit wùrthee/ *adj* considered to be financially reliable enough to be given credit or lent money —**cred·it·wor·thi·ness** *n*

cre·do /kreédō/ (*plural* **-dos**) *n* a statement of principles or beliefs, especially one that is professed formally [12C. < Latin, "I believe" (first words of the Apostles' and Nicene creeds), form of *credere* "believe"]

Cre·do (*plural* **-dos**) *n* 1. the Apostles' Creed or Nicene Creed, both of which are ancient statements of the basic doctrines of Christianity 2. a musical setting, especially in a Mass, of the Credo

cre·du·li·ty /krə dóolətee/ *n* the tendency to believe something too readily

cred·u·lous /kréjjələss/ *adj* 1. too easily convinced that something is true 2. resulting from a tendency to believe things too readily [Late 16C. < Latin *credulus* < *credere* "believe"] —**cred·u·lous·ly** *adv* —**cred·u·lous·ness** *n*

USAGE See ***credible.***

Cree /kree/ (*plural same* or **Crees**) *n* 1. a member of a Native North American people who live in central Canada and Montana. The Cree are the largest group of the Native Americans in Canada. 2. the Algonquian language of the Cree people. Native speakers: 62,000. [Mid-18C. < Canadian French *Cris*, shortening of *C(h)ristinaux*, alteration of an Algonquian word (modern *kinistiono*)] —**Cree** *adj*

creed /kreed/ *n* 1. **STATEMENT OF BELIEFS** a formal summary of the principles of the Christian faith 2. **RELIGION** a set of religious beliefs 3. **SET OF PRINCIPLES** any set of beliefs or principles [Pre-12C. < Latin *credo* (see CREDO)]

creek /kreek, krik/ *n* a stream, especially one that flows into a river [15C. Directly or via French *crique* < Old Norse *kriki* "nook, corner"] ◇ **up the creek (without a paddle)** in a difficult situation, or in trouble (*informal*)

REGIONAL NOTE See ***run.***

Creek /kreek/ (*plural same* or **Creeks**) *n* 1. a member of a Native North American people who once lived in Alabama, Georgia, and Florida, and who now live mainly in central Oklahoma and southern Alabama. The Creek were one of the Five Civilized Nations who, under the Removal Act of 1830, were sent to live on reservations in Oklahoma. 2. the Muskogean language of the Creek people. Native speakers: 50,000. [Early 18C. < CREEK; from the large number of creeks in their country] —**Creek** *adj*

creel /kreel/ *n* 1. **WICKER BASKET FOR FISH** a wicker basket used by anglers for holding fish 2. **WICKER FISH TRAP** a wicker trap for catching fish or lobsters 3. **BOBBIN HOLDER** a framework in a spinning machine that holds the bobbins [14C. Origin ?]

creep /kreep/ *vi* (**crept** /krept/ or **creeped, creep·ing, creeps**) 1. **MOVE QUIETLY** to move along silently and stealthily 2. **MOVE NEAR GROUND** to move along with the body close to the ground 3. **PROCEED SLOWLY** to move along very slowly 4. **GRADUALLY DEVELOP** to appear, approach, or develop gradually 5. **SHIVER WITH DISGUST** to tingle uncomfortably as if covered with crawling insects, especially from fear or disgust 6. **SPREAD OVER SURFACE** to grow along a surface by sending out tendrils, suckers, or roots 7. **BE DISPLACED SLIGHTLY** to move slightly from the original or proper position 8. INDUST **DEFORM FROM STRESS OR HEAT** to become deformed over a period of time due to stress or heat ■ *n* 1. **CREEPING MOVEMENT** a slow or stealthy pace or movement 2. **SOMEBODY REPELLENT** somebody considered obnoxious or disliked (*informal*) 3. **SLIGHT DISPLACEMENT** the slight movement of something 4. GEOL **MOVEMENT OF ROCK** a gradual movement of rock and debris down a slope 5. GEOL **DEFORMATION OF ROCKS UNDER STRESS** a slow deformation of rocks and minerals in response to prolonged stress 6. METALL **DEFORMATION OF METAL UNDER STRESS** a gradual deformation of a hard material, especially metal, as a result of heat or stress ■ **creeps** *npl* **UNEASY FEELING** an uneasy or unnerving feeling usually caused by fear or disgust (*informal*) [Old English *crēopan* < Germanic]

creep out *vt* to make somebody feel fear, disgust, or another emotion that produces extreme uneasiness (*slang*) ○ *It creeps me out to watch a horror film.*

creep up on *vt* 1. to approach somebody or something stealthily 2. to enter somebody's consciousness or feelings gradually

creep·back /kreép bàk/ *n* the tendency for employers to recruit new employees surreptitiously after excessive or heavy layoffs

creep·er /kreépər/ *n* 1. **CLINGING PLANT** a plant that grows by means of tendrils, suckers, or roots that anchor it to a surface 2. **SMALL CLIMBING BIRD** a small climbing bird with a slender curved beak and short legs. Native to: forests of North America, Europe, Asia, and Africa. Family: Certhiidae. 3. **SOMEBODY OR SOMETHING THAT CREEPS** a person or animal that moves by creeping 4. CLOTHING **INFANT'S ONE-PIECE GARMENT** an infant's one-piece garment that has short or no pant legs and can be unsnapped at the crotch 5. AUTOMOT same as **cradle** *n* (sense 4) 6. **UNDERWATER GRAPPLING DEVICE** a device with hooks that is used to drag for submerged objects in deep water 7. *Northeast US*

SHOE SPIKES a spiked or toothed device that is attached to the sole of a boot to provide traction on ice

creep·ing /kréeping/ *adj* **1.** developing or advancing gradually over a period of time **2.** growing and spreading by sending out tendrils, suckers, or roots

creep·ing Char·lie (*plural* **creep·ing Char·lies** or *same*) *n* PLANTS same as **moneywort**

creep·ing e·rup·tion *n* a skin disease caused by hookworm or roundworm larvae, producing itching and eruptions in the form of spreading red lines on the skin

creep·ing Jen·nie, **creep·ing Jen·ny** *n Can, UK* an evergreen creeping plant with round leaves. Flowers: yellow. Native to: Europe, eastern North America. Latin name: *Lysimachia nummularia*. US term **moneywort**

creep·ing this·tle *n UK* same as **Canada thistle**

creep·y /kréepee/ (**-i·er, -i·est**) *adj* unsettling because of causing fear, disgust, or uneasiness (*informal*) —**creep·i·ly** *adv* —**creep·i·ness** *n*

creep·y-crawl·y (*plural* **creep·y-crawl·ies**) *n* a crawling insect or small animal (*informal*)

cre·mains /kri máynz/ *npl* the ashes that remain after a corpse has been cremated [Mid-20C. Contraction of *cremated remains*]

cre·mate /krée màyt/ (**-mat·ed, -mat·ing, -mates**) *vt* to burn a corpse until only ashes are left [Late 19C. Either < Latin *cremat-* (see CREMATION), or back-formation < CREMATION] —**cre·ma·tor** *n*

cre·ma·tion /kri máysh'n/ *n* **1.** the burning of a corpse until only ashes are left **2.** a funeral ceremony during which a cremated decedent's ashes are interred [Early 17C. < Latin *cremation-* < *cremat-*, past participle of *cremare* "burn"]

cre·ma·to·ri·um /kreémə táwree əm/ (*plural* **-ri·ums** or **-ri·a** /-ree ə/) *n* a building or furnace where corpses are incinerated [Late 19C. < modern Latin < Latin *cremat-* (see CREMATION)]

cre·ma·to·ry /kreémə tàwree, krémmə-/ *n* (*plural* **-ries**) same as **crematorium** ■ *adj* relating to or used for cremation

Cré·ma·zie /krày maa zeé/, **Octave** (1827–79) Canadian poet. Considered the founder of French-Canadian poetry, his works include *Chant du vieux soldat canadien* (*Song of the Old Canadian Soldier*) (1855).

crème brû·lée /krèm broo láy/ (*plural* **crème brû·lées** /krèm broo láyz/ or **crèmes brû·lées** /krèm broo láy/) *n* a rich baked custard with caramelized sugar on top [< French, "burned cream"]

crème car·a·mel /krèm kaarə mél, -karrə-/ (*plural* **crème car·a·mels** /krèm kaarə mélz, -karrə-/ or **crèmes car·a·mel** /krèm-, krèmz-/) *n* a custard coated with caramelized sugar, which forms a sauce, cooked in a mold. It is chilled and removed from the mold before serving. [< French, "caramel cream"]

crème de ca·cao /krèm də kə kṓ, -kaa kaa ṓ/ (*plural* **crème de ca·caos** /krèm də kəkṓz, -kaa kaa ṓz/ or **crèmes de ca·cao** /krèm də kəkṓ, -kaa kaa ṓ/) *n* a sweet chocolate-flavored liqueur [< French, "cream of cacao"]

crème de la crème /krèm də laa krém/ *n* the very best of a group of people or things [< French, "cream of the cream"]

crème de menthe /krèm də ménth, -maáNt/ (*plural* **crème de menthes** or **crèmes de menthe** /*pronunc. same*/) *n* a sweet mint-flavored liqueur [< French, "cream of mint"]

crème fraîche /krèm frésh/ *n* a thickened French sour cream, used in cooking or served with other foods [< French, "fresh cream"]

Cre·mo·na /krə mṓnə/ capital of Cremona Province, Lombardy, northern Italy. It is situated on the Po River, southeast of Milan. Population: 70,887 (2001).

cre·nate /krée nàyt/, **cre·nat·ed** /-nàytəd/ *adj* having a scalloped edge or a surface with rounded projections (*technical*) [Late 18C. < modern Latin *crenatus* < Latin *crena* "small notch"] —**cre·nate·ly** *adv*

cre·na·tion /kri náysh'n/ *n* **1.** ROUNDED PROJECTION a rounded projection from the edge or surface of something such as a plant leaf or a coin **2.** SCALLOPED EDGE OR SURFACE a scalloped edge, or a surface with rounded projections **3.** SHRINKAGE OF RED BLOOD CELLS a medical condition in which the red blood cells shrink and develop multiple indentations and protrusions

WORLD ENGLISH ***Creole*** languages are found in communities where a pidgin language earlier served as a useful lingua franca. Creoles are often the sole language of a community and so are capable of fulfilling all their speakers' linguistic needs. In being transformed into a creole, a pidgin's vocabulary is expanded and its structures made increasingly subtle, flexible, and precise.

Creoles, which involve a language shift, are often caused by the disruption of normal speech communities. The best-known examples are found in the Caribbean. Caribbean creoles evolved as a result of the slave trade, when as many as ten million Africans, speaking perhaps 500 different mother tongues, were sold into slavery. Africans working on plantations were obliged to relinquish their ancestral languages and communicate in pidgin forms of a European tongue. Children born into slave communities used the pidgin for all their communication needs and thus transformed it into a creole.

More recently, creoles related to English have developed in many other places including Cameroon, Nigeria, Hawaii, and Papua New Guinea. In such areas, speakers found that the pidgin lingua franca helped communication between different groups so much that it was increasingly spoken at home and children acquired it as a mother tongue.

The name *creole* comes from Spanish *criollo* meaning "native." In the 16th century, a "creole" was a person of European ancestry born in the New World. Over the next two centuries, it was applied to children of mixed race and then to Africans born in the Americas. By the early 1800s, "creole" could be applied to a language.

There are clear historical, geographic, and linguistic factors linking all the Creole Englishes in West Africa, the Caribbean, Central America, and the United States. There are four main creoles in the United States: (1) *Gullah*, or *Geechee*, is spoken mainly in the Sea Islands, Florida, Carolina (especially the Carline Low Country), and Georgia. It is the language used at home by perhaps a quarter of a million people in this region and several thousand more who have migrated to New York. Its names probably come from either the Gola people of Liberia or from the Ogeechee River plantations of Georgia. (2) *Afro-Seminole* is a Creole English spoken mainly in parts of Texas and Mexico. It is almost certainly derived from Gullah when 18th-century slaves escaped from Florida and Georgia and settled with Seminoles. (3) *African American Vernacular English*, or *US Black English*, covers the entire spectrum from standard US English to varieties similar to Gullah, which probably developed on plantations in the southern states from Texas to Virginia (at the time of the Civil War, over 90% of African Americans lived in the South). (4) *Native American Pidginized English* is a form of pidgin English that was probably used between some Native Americans and English speakers and there may be relics of it in the words of Native American languages that were common currency both in US English and Native American languages, for example *papoose* and *chuck* (food).

Here is an example of Hawaiian Creole English: "God, you our Fadda./ You stay inside da sky./ We like all da peopo know fo shua how you stay,/ An dat you stay good and spesho,/ An we like dem give you plenny respeck. Da Jesus Book, Matthew 6:9–10" (Joseph E. Grimes *et al.*)

(God, you are our Father./ You are in heaven./ We want everyone to be certain how you are, and that you are good and special,/ and we want them to give you plenty of respect.)

See also ***pidgin***.

cren·el /krénn'l/, **cren·elle** /krə nél/ *n* a gap in the top of a castle wall or parapet, used for firing missiles or shooting [15C. < Old French, "small notch" < Latin *crena*]

cren·e·late /krénn'l àyt/ (**-lat·ed, -lat·ing, -lates**), **cren·el·late** *vt* to provide a structure with battlements or decorative features resembling battlements [Early 19C. < French *créneler* < Old French *crenel* (see CRENEL)] —**cren·e·lat·ed** *adj* —**cren·e·la·tion** /krènn'l áysh'n/ *n*

cren·elle *n* ARCHIT another spelling of **crenel**

cren·shaw /krén shàw/ *n* a variety of melon with a green rind and sweet salmon-pink flesh that is closely related to the casaba, honeydew, and winter melons [Late 20C. Origin ?]

cren·u·late /krénnyələt, -làyt/, **cren·u·lat·ed** /-làytəd/ *adj* describes plant leaves or shorelines that have a finely scalloped or notched wavy edge (*technical*) [Late 18C. < modern Latin *crenulatus* < *crenula* "small notch" < Latin *crena*]

cren·u·la·tion /krènnyə láysh'n/ *n* (*technical*) **1.** a very small notch or indentation, e.g., on a plant's leaf **2.** the condition of having very fine notching or indentations along an edge

cre·o·dont /kreé ə dònt/ (*plural* **-donts** or **-don·ta** /-dòntə/) *n* an extinct carnivorous mammal that lived during the Tertiary period. Suborder: Creodonta. [Late 19C. < modern Latin *Creodonta* "flesh-toothed ones" < Greek *kreas* "flesh" + *odont-* "tooth"]

cre·ole /kreé ṑl/ *n* **1.** LANGUAGE OF MIXED ORIGIN a language that has evolved from the mixture of two or more languages and has become the first language of a group **2.** PEOPLES another spelling of **Creole** (sense 3) ■ *adj* **1.** COOKED NEW ORLEANS STYLE cooked in a spicy flavorful way associated with the French Creoles of New Orleans. Tomatoes, hot peppers, onions, and rice are characteristic ingredients. **2.** OF CREOLE relating to or belonging to a creole language [Late 19C. < CREOLE]

Cre·ole *n* **1.** SOMEBODY OF FRENCH ANCESTRY somebody who comes from the southern United States, especially southern Louisiana, and is descended from early French settlers **2.** LANGUAGE OF LOUISIANA the creolized French language spoken by the Creoles of New Orleans and southern Louisiana **3.** AFRICAN DESCENDANT BORN IN AMERICAS somebody of African or mixed African descent born in the Americas **4.** LANGUAGE OF CARIBBEAN ISLANDS a group of creolized languages, based on English and French, spoken on some islands of the Caribbean **5.** CARIBBEAN PERSON OF EUROPEAN ANCESTRY somebody who comes from a Caribbean or Latin American country and is of European, especially Spanish descent **6.** CREOLE SPEAKER somebody of both European and African ancestry who speaks a form of Creole [Mid-18C. < French < Spanish *criollo* "native" < Portuguese *crioulo* < *criar* "bring up" < Latin *creare* "bring forth"] —**Cre·ole** *adj*

cre·o·lize /kreé ə lìz/ (**-liz·ed, -liz·ing, -lizes**) *vt* to form a new mixed language from two or more other languages —**cre·o·liz·a·tion** /krèe əli záysh'n/ *n* —**cre·o·lized** *adj*

Cre·on /kreé òn/ *n* in Greek mythology, the brother of Jocasta and the successor of Oedipus as king of Thebes. He was also the uncle of Antigone and issued an edict forbidding the burial of the body of her brother Polynices, which she defied.

cre·o·sol /kreé ə sàwl/ *n* a pale yellow or colorless oily liquid. Source: creosote. Formula: $C_8H_{10}O_2$. [Mid-19C. < CREOSOTE]

cre·o·sote /kreé ə sṑt/ *n* **1.** WOOD PRESERVATIVE a thick yellowish-to-brown oily substance. Source: coal tar. Use: wood preservative. **2.** ANTISEPTIC a yellow to colorless oily substance. Source: wood tar. Use: antiseptic. **3.** CHIMNEY TAR a dark brown to black flammable tar deposited inside a chimney flue when wood, especially pine or other resinous wood, is burned ■ *vt* (**-sot·ed, -sot·ing, -sotes**) APPLY CREOSOTE TO SOMETHING to apply creosote to wood as a preservative [Mid-19C. < German *Kreosote* < Greek *kreas* "flesh" + *sōtēr* "preserver"; from its antiseptic properties]

cre·o·sote bush *n* a resinous evergreen bush with leaves that smell like creosote. Native to: deserts of southwestern United States and Mexico. Latin name: *Larrea tridentata*.

crepe /krayp/, **crêpe** *n* **1.** FOOD a thin pancake usually served rolled up or folded with a filling **2.** TEXTILES a light fine fabric with a crinkled surface **3.** TEXTILES same as **crape** (sense 2) **4.** PAPER same as **crepe paper**

5. INDUST same as **crepe rubber** [Late 18C. < French < Old French *crespe* "curled" < Latin *crispus*] —**crep·y** *adj*

crêpe de Chine /kràyp də sheen/, **crepe de Chine** *n* a light smooth silk fabric. Use: delicate articles of clothing. [< French, "crepe of China"]

crepe myr·tle *n* PLANTS another spelling of **crape myrtle**

crepe pa·per, **crêpe pa·per** *n* a thin, slightly stretchy, crinkled colored paper, used for wrapping presents or making decorations (*hyphenated when used before a noun*)

crêp·e·rie /kráypəree, kréppə-/, **crep·e·rie** *n* a restaurant that specializes in thin pancakes (**crepes**) with fillings [< French *crêperie* < *crêpe* (see CREPE)]

crepe rub·ber, **crêpe rub·ber** *n* rubber in the form of thin crinkled sheets, used especially for the soles of shoes

crêpe suz·ette /kràyp soo zét/ (*plural* **crêpes suz·ette** /*pronunc. same*/ or **crêpe suz·ettes** /kràyp soo zéts/) *n* a pancake prepared with orange sauce and flambéed with an orange-flavored liqueur or brandy [< French, probably after *Suzanne* Reichenberg (1853–1924), French actress]

crep·i·tate /kréppi tàyt/ (**-tat·ed, -tat·ing, -tates**) *v* **1.** *vi* to make a crackling or grating sound (*formal or literary*) **2.** to make the crackling or grating sound of crepitus [Early 17C. < Latin *crepitat-*, past participle of *crepitare* "crackle" < *crepare* "to rattle," an imitation of the sound] —**crep·i·tant** *adj* —**crep·i·ta·tion** /krèppi táysh'n/ *n*

crep·i·tus /kréppitəss/ *n* **1.** the grating sound heard when the broken ends of a bone rub together **2.** a crackling sound heard in the chest of somebody who has a lung disease such as pneumonia [Early 19C. < Latin, "rattling" < *crepare* (see CREPITATE)]

crept past participle, past tense of **creep**

cre·pus·cu·lar /krə púskyələr/ *adj* **1.** relating to or resembling the fading light of dusk (*literary*) **2.** describes fish and land mammals that are active at dusk and dawn, when the light level is low (*technical*) [Mid-17C. < Latin *crepusculum* "twilight"]

Cre·rar /kree raar/, **Henry Duncan Graham** (1888–1965) Canadian military leader. He headed the Canadian army in Europe (1944–45) during World War II.

cresc. *abbr* MUSIC crescendo

cres·cen·do /krə shéndō/ *n* (*plural* **-dos** or **-does** or **-di** /-dee/) **1.** MUSIC **INCREASE IN LOUDNESS** a gradual increase in the volume of a passage of music **2.** MUSIC **MUSIC PLAYED INCREASINGLY LOUDLY** a passage of music in which there is a gradual increase in volume **3. INTENSIFICATION** an increase in volume or intensity similar to a crescendo in music **4.** ⚠ **CLIMAX** the climax of an increase in volume or intensity ■ *adj* **BECOMING LOUDER OR MORE INTENSE** gradually increasing in volume or intensity ■ *adv* MUSIC **WITH INCREASING LOUDNESS** with a gradual increase in volume ■ *vi* (**-doed, -do·ing, -does**) **BECOME LOUDER OR STRONGER** to increase in volume or intensity [Late 18C. < Italian, present participle of *crescere* "increase" < Latin, "grow"]

USAGE A *crescendo* is properly a process and not the end of a process. This is usually well understood in musical contexts, where the word is a technical term. In figurative uses, however, it tends to be used as an alternative for *climax*, which is indeed the end point or culmination of a process. In careful usage, noise or feeling can increase *to* a climax but it does so *in* a *crescendo*. Correct: *The bird's calls rose in a crescendo.* Avoid: *The annoying telemarketing calls reached a crescendo the following week.*

cres·cent /kréss'nt/ *n* **1. LESS THAN HALF VISIBLE MOON** the Moon or a planet before and after it is full, when it has less than half its disk illuminated **2. ARC SHAPE** a curved shape like that of the Moon when it is less than half illuminated **3. ARC-SHAPED THING** something shaped like a crescent **4.** *also* **Cres·cent ARC-SHAPED STREET** a curved street, especially one that opens onto the same street at each end **5.** *also* **Cres·cent ISLAMIC SYMBOL** the emblem of Islam or Turkey, shaped like a crescent moon **6.** *also* **Cres·cent ISLAMIC POWER** Islamic or Turkish power **7. HERALDIC SYMBOL FOR SECOND SON** in heraldry, a crescent moon, used to signify a second son ■ *adj* **1. ARC-SHAPED** shaped like a crescent **2. GROWING** gradually increasing in size (*literary*) [14C. Via Anglo-Norman < Latin *crescent-*, present participle of *crescere* "grow"] —**cres·cen·tic** /krə séntik/ *adj*

ORIGIN The Latin word *crescere*, "to grow," from which ***crescent*** is derived, is also the source of English *accrete*, *concrete*, *create*, *crescendo*, *crew*[1], *croissant*, *increase*, and *recruit*.

cre·sol /kree sàwl/ *n* a colorless compound. Source: wood or coal tar. Use: antiseptic, disinfectant. Formula: C_7H_8O. [Mid-19C. Alteration of CREOSOL]

cress /kress/ (*plural same* or **cress·es**) *n* **1.** small pungently flavored leaves. Use: in salads, as a garnish. **2.** a plant of the mustard family whose leaves are cress [Old English *cressa* < Germanic]

Cres·si·da /kréssədə/ *n* **1.** in medieval retellings of the Trojan War, a Trojan woman captured by the Greeks who was unfaithful to her Trojan lover, Troilus, by giving herself to the Greek Diomedes **2.** a small natural satellite of Uranus, discovered by the Voyager 2 planetary probe in 1986

crest /krest/ *n* **1. TOP OF CURVE OR SLOPE** the top part of something that slopes or rises upward, e.g., a wave or a hill **2. CULMINATION** the highest stage or culminating point in an activity or achievement **3.** ZOOL **TUFT ON ANIMAL'S HEAD** a tuft or other growth on the top of the head of a bird or other animal **4. SOMETHING RESEMBLING HEAD TUFT** something resembling the crest of a bird or other animal **5.** ZOOL **NECK RIDGE** a ridge along the neck of a horse, lion, or other mammal, from which hair grows **6.** ARMS **HELMET ORNAMENT** a plume or other decoration on the top of a helmet **7.** HERALDRY **SYMBOL OF FAMILY OR OFFICE** a small animal, bird, or other heraldic symbol of a family or office, placed above the shield in a coat of arms or used alone on a helmet ■ *v* (**crest·ed, crest·ing, crests**) **1.** *vi* **RISE UP TO TOP** to reach or rise to a crest **2.** *vt* **REACH TOP OF SOMETHING** to reach the crest of something such as a hill **3.** *vt* **TOP SOMETHING** to be at the top of something [14C. Via French *creste* < Latin *crista* "tuft"] —**crest·ed** *adj*

crest·ed wheat·grass /krèstəd-/ *n* a perennial grass grown for forage, hay, and erosion control in North America. Native to: Europe, Asia. Genus: *Agropyron*.

crest·fall·en /krést fàwlən/ *adj* disappointed or humiliated, especially after being enthusiastic or confident [Late 16C. < the drooping of somebody's head when disappointed] —**crest·fall·en·ly** *adv*—**crest·fall·en·ness** *n*

crest·ing /krésting/ *n* **1.** an ornamental ridge on a roof **2.** an ornamental carving or rail on the top of a piece of furniture

cre·syl·ic ac·id /kri síllik-/ *n* CHEM same as **cresol** [< *cresyl*, isomeric radical < CRESOL]

cre·ta·ceous /krə táyshəss/ *adj* consisting of or resembling chalk (*technical*) [Late 17C. < Latin *cretaceus* "chalky" < *creta* "chalk"] —**cre·ta·ceous·ly** *adv*

Cre·ta·ceous *n* the period of geologic time, 142 million to 65 million years ago, during which the dinosaurs became extinct, layers of chalk were laid down, and flowering plants arose —**Cre·ta·ceous** *adj*

Crete /kreet/ largest Greek island in the southern Aegean Sea. The chief town is Heraklion. Population: 540,054 (1991). Area: 3,190 sq. mi./8,261 sq. km. —**Cre·tan** /kreet'n/ *adj, n*

cre·tic /kreetik/ *n* LITERAT same as **amphimacer** [Late 16C. Via Latin, "Cretan" < Greek *krētikos* < *Krētē* "Crete"]

cre·tin /kreet'n/ *n* **1.** an offensive term for somebody considered unintelligent (*insult*) **2.** an offensive term for somebody affected by congenital myxedema (*dated insult*) [Late 18C. Via French < Swiss French *creitin* "mentally challenged person" < Latin *Christianus* (see CHRISTIAN)] —**cre·tin·ism** *n* —**cre·tin·oid** *adj*—**cre·tin·ous** *adj*

cre·tonne /kree tòn, krə tón/ *n* a heavy cotton, linen, or rayon fabric, usually printed with a colorful design. Use: upholstery. [Late 19C. < French, after *Creton*, village in Normandy]

cre·tons /krə tóN/ *npl Can* in Quebec, a dish of spiced shredded pork cooked with onions in lard [< Canadian French, probably < Middle Dutch *kerte* "cut"]

Creutz·feldt-Ja·kob dis·ease /kròyts felt yaa kawb-/ *n* a rare fatal brain disease, a form of spongiform encephalopathy, that develops slowly, causing dementia and loss of muscle control. A transmissible protein particle (**prion**) is the suspected cause. A new variant of the disease, which develops rapidly and affects younger people, appeared in the late 1980s. [Late 20C. After H. G. *Creutzfeldt* (1885–1964) and A. M. *Jakob* (1884–1931), German neurologists]

cre·val·le /krə vállee, -vállə/ (*plural same* or **-les**) *n* a spiny-finned ocean fish related to the pompano, found in the western Atlantic and the Pacific. Family: Carangidae. [Late 19C. Alteration of CAVALLA]

cre·val·le jack (*plural same* or **cre·val·le jacks**) *n* FISH same as **jack crevalle**

cre·vasse /krə váss/ *n* **1. DEEP CRACK** a deep crack, e.g., in the ice of a glacier **2. LEVEE CRACK** a crack in a levee or dike ■ *vti* (**-vassed, -vass·ing, -vass·es**) **FORM CREVASSES** to develop crevasses, or make something develop crevasses [Early 19C. < French, modern form of Old French *crevace* (see CREVICE)]

crev·ice /krévviss/ *n* a narrow crack or opening, especially in rock [14C. < Old French *crevace* "a burst" < *crever* "to burst" < Latin *crepare* "to rattle," an imitation of the sound] —**crev·iced** *adj*

crew[1] /kroo/ *n* **1. PEOPLE WORKING TOGETHER** a group of people who work together on a project or task **2. ONBOARD STAFF** the people who work on a ship, aircraft, or spacecraft **3.** NAUT **SHIP'S STAFF EXCLUDING OFFICERS** the members of a ship's staff who are not officers **4. SPECIALIZED STAFF ON CRAFT** a smaller group within the overall staff of a ship, aircraft, or spacecraft who are assigned a particular task ○ *cabin crew* **5. GROUP OF FRIENDS** a group of people who spend much time together or are somehow associated with one another (*informal*) **6. URBAN GANG** a group of youths who operate as a city gang (*slang*) **7. ROWERS** the rowers and coxswain of a racing shell **8. SPORT OF SHELL RACING** the sport of rowing racing shells ■ *v* (**crewed, crew·ing, crews**) **1.** *vi* **BE ON CREW** to be a member of a crew **2.** *vt* **BE ON STAFF OF VESSEL** to serve as a member of the personnel of a ship, aircraft, or spacecraft (*often passive*) [15C. < French *creüe* "increase, recruit" < the past participle of *croistre* "grow" < Latin *crescere*]

crew[2] *UK* past tense of **crow**[2]

crew chief *n* **1.** a noncommissioned officer in the Air Force who is in charge of the maintenance and ground handling of an aircraft **2.** the head of the maintenance crew that fuels and repairs an automobile or other motor vehicle during a race

crew cut *n* a haircut, usually worn by men and boys, with the hair cut close to the head [Probably because adopted by boat crews at Harvard and Yale in the mid-20C]

Crewe /kroo/ city and major rail junction in Cheshire, northwestern England. Population: 63,351 (1991).

crewed /krood/ *adj* operated by onboard personnel ○ *a crewed mission to the Moon*

crew·el /kroo əl/ *n* **1.** a loosely twisted woolen yarn used in embroidery **2.** HANDICRAFT same as **crewelwork** [15C. Origin ?] —**crew·el·ist** *n*

crew·el·work /kroo əl wùrk/ *n* embroidery work done with crewel yarn

crew·mate /kroo màyt/ *n* a fellow member of a crew, especially on board a ship or spacecraft

crew neck *n* **1.** a close-fitting round neckline on a sweater, sweatshirt, or other garment **2.** a sweater with a close-fitting round neck [< the sweaters with such a neckline worn by boat crews] —**crew-neck** *adj*

crew sock *n* a thick short sock that is ribbed above the ankle

crib /krib/ *n* **1. BABY'S BED** a bed for a baby or small child that has high, usually vertically barred, sides to keep the child from falling out **2.** AGRIC **GRAIN STORE** a small building with slatted sides used for storing grain, especially corn **3.** AGRIC **ANIMAL'S STALL** a stall for cattle or horses **4.** AGRIC **HAY RACK** a trough or box for hay or other fodder from which livestock can feed **5.** EDUC same as **crib sheet** (*informal*) **6. PLAGIARISM** a theft of material from an intellectual or artistic work **7. PETTY THEFT** a theft of something of insignificant value **8. SOMEBODY'S HOME** somebody's home, especially an urban apartment (*slang*) **9. PROSTITUTE'S ROOM** a run-down house or room used by a prostitute (*slang*) **10. BASKET** a wicker basket **11.** CARDS **DEALER'S CARDS** in cribbage, the cards used by the dealer consisting of cards discarded by the other players **12.** CARDS same as **cribbage** (*informal*) ■ *v* **(cribbed, crib·bing, cribs) 1.** *vti* **PLAGIARIZE** to steal somebody's ideas or work **2.** *vi* EDUC **USE CRIB SHEET** to use a crib sheet in an examination (*informal*) **3.** *vt* **PUT SOMEBODY OR SOMETHING IN CRIB** to put somebody or something such as an infant or hay into a crib **4.** *vt* **PROVIDE CRIB FOR SOMETHING** to construct or provide a crib for something [Old English *crib(b)* "manger, trough" < Germanic] —**crib·ber** *n*

crib·bage /kríbbij/ *n* a card game for two to four players in which the score is kept by moving pegs along rows of holes in a small board **(cribbage board)** [Mid-17C. Probably < CRIB + -AGE]

crib·bing /kríbbing/ *n* **1.** EDUC the use of a crib sheet to cheat in an examination (*informal*) **2.** CONSTR the timbers used for a framework, e.g., of a mineshaft or foundation **3.** VET same as **crib-biting**

crib-bit·ing *n* a behavioral pattern that develops in horses kept in stables, marked by chewing of the stalls and salivating excessively. The disorder is partly an inherited condition and partly an expression of boredom. —**crib-bit·er** *n*

crib death *n* the sudden and unexplained death of a small baby while sleeping

crib·ri·form /kríbbrə fàwrm/ *adj* describes a part with small holes like a sieve, especially the top part **(cribriforum plate)** of the ethnoid bone forming the roof of the nasal cavity (*technical*) [Mid-18C. < Latin *cribrum* "sieve"]

crib sheet *n* a list of answers or a translation of a foreign text used for cheating in examinations or work in class

cri·ce·tid /krī seétid, -séttid/ (*plural* **-tids** or *same*) *n* a small rodent of the family that includes the hamster, gerbil, muskrat, and vole. Family: Cricetidae. [Mid-20C. < modern Latin *Cricetidae* < *Cricetus* (genus name of hamsters) < medieval Latin *cricetus* "hamster"] —**cri·ce·tid** *adj*

Crich·ton /krīt'n/, **Michael** (*b.* 1942) US writer. He is known for his science fiction thrillers including *Jurassic Park* (1990), which was made into a movie in 1993.

crick[1] /krik/ *n* a painful stiffness or muscle spasm in the neck or back ■ *vt* **(cricked, crick·ing, cricks)** to cause a painful stiffness or muscle spasm in the neck or back [15C. Origin ?]

crick[2] /krik/ *n regional* GEOG same as **creek** [Variant]

Crick /krik/, **Francis H. C.** (*b.* 1916) British biophysicist. He worked with James D. Watson and Maurice Wilkins in exploring the structure of the DNA molecule, for which they shared the Nobel Prize in physiology or medicine (1962). Full name **Francis Henry Compton Crick**

crick·et[1] /kríkət/ *n* **1.** a leaping insect that has biting mouthparts, long legs, and antennae. The male produces a chirping sound by rubbing its forewings together. Family: Gryllidae. **2.** a small metal toy or noisemaker that produces a sharp clicking sound when it is pressed [14C. < French *criquet* "grasshopper, locust" < Old French *criquer* "to click," an imitation of the sound]

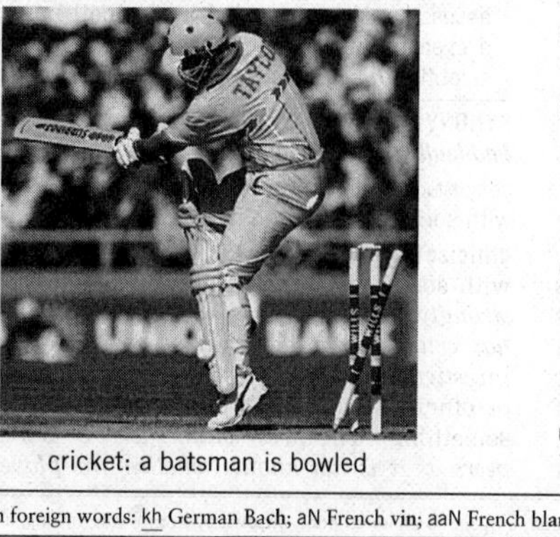

cricket: a batsman is bowled

crick·et[2] /kríkət/ *n* an outdoor sport played chiefly in England and Commonwealth countries by two teams of 11 players using a flat bat, a small hard ball, and wickets. A player scores by batting the ball and running, while the defenders can get a player out by bowling and hitting the wicket, catching a hit ball, or running the player out. ■ *vi* **(crick·et·ed, crick·et·ing, crick·ets)** to play cricket [Late 16C. Origin ?] —**crick·et·er** *n*

crick·et[3] /kríkət/ *n* a wooden footstool [Mid-17C. Origin ?]

cri·coid /krī kòyd/ *adj* relating to or in the region of the lowermost cartilage of the larynx [Mid-18C. Via modern Latin, "ring-shaped" < Greek *krikoeidēs* < *krikos* "ring"]

cri·coid car·ti·lage *n* the lowermost cartilage of the larynx, which has a shape like a signet ring

cri de coeur /kreè də kúr/ (*plural* **cris de coeur** /*pronunc. same*/) *n* a heartfelt, usually anguished appeal [< French, "cry from the heart"]

cri·er /krīər/ *n* **1. CRYING PERSON OR ANIMAL** a person or animal that cries **2.** PUBLIC ADMIN same as **town crier** (sense 2) **3. LAW COURT ANNOUNCER** an official who makes public announcements of the orders of a court of law **4. VENDOR SHOUTING WARES** a vendor who makes public announcements about the goods that he or she has for sale

crime /krīm/ *n* **1. ILLEGAL ACT** an action prohibited by law or a failure to act as required by law **2. ILLEGAL ACTIVITY** activity that involves breaking the law ○ *measures to combat crime* **3. IMMORAL ACT** an act considered morally wrong **4. UNACCEPTABLE ACT** a shameful, unwise, or regrettable act (*informal*) ○ *It's a crime the way some people waste food.* [13C. Via French < Latin *crimen* (stem *crimin-*) "judgment" < *cernere* "decide"] —**crime·less** *adj*

CULTURAL NOTE ***Crime and Punishment***, a novel (1866) by Russian writer Fyodor Dostoyevsky. Set in St. Petersburg, it describes how a young student, Raskolnikov, plans and carries out the murder of a woman pawnbroker, ostensibly for money, but in reality to prove that some individuals are above the law. Ultimately, however, his conscience forces him to confess his crime.

Cri·me·a /krī meé ə/ peninsula in southeastern Ukraine between the Black Sea and the Sea of Azov. Area: 10,036 sq. mi./25,993 sq. km. —**Cri·me·an** *n, adj*

crime a·gainst hu·man·i·ty *n* a cruel and immoral act such as torture, murder, or expulsion, committed against a large number of people

crime of pas·sion *n* a crime that is motivated by an extreme emotion, especially sexual jealousy

crime scene tape *n* barricade tape that is used to cordon off an area and warn people of a crime scene

crime wave *n* a period during which more crimes than usual are committed

crim·i·nal /krímmin'l/ *n* **SOMEBODY ACTING ILLEGALLY** somebody who has committed a crime ■ *adj* **1. PUNISHABLE AS CRIME** punishable as a crime under the law **2. PROSECUTING CRIMINALS** relating to or involved in the prosecution and punishment of people accused of committing crimes **3. RELATING TO CRIMINALS** relating to or done by criminals **4. MORALLY WRONG** morally wrong, whether illegal or not **5. UNACCEPTABLE** shameful, unwise, or regrettable (*informal*) ○ *a criminal waste of resources* [15C. Directly or via French < late Latin *criminalis* "of crime" < Latin *crimin-* (see CRIME)] —**crim·i·nal·ly** *adv*

crim·i·nal con·ver·sa·tion *n* adultery considered as a legal breach of the marriage contract (*technical*)

crim·i·nal·i·ty /krìmmi nállətee/ (*plural* **-ties**) *n* **1. CRIMINAL QUALITY** a criminal character or quality **2. TENDENCY TO BREAK LAW** a tendency to commit crimes **3. CRIME** a criminal act or practice (*often used in the plural*)

crim·i·nal·ize /krímmin'l īz/ (**-ized, -iz·ing, -iz·es**) *vt* **1.** to make an action punishable as a crime under the law **2.** to make somebody become a criminal or treat somebody as a criminal —**crim·i·nal·i·za·tion** /krìmmin'li záysh'n/ *n*

crim·i·nal neg·li·gence *n* the crime of causing injury or harm to a person or property as the result of doing something or failing to provide a proper or reasonable level of care

crim·i·nal rec·ord *n* a record of somebody's previous convictions for crime

crim·i·nol·o·gy /krìmmi nólləjee/ *n* the sociological study of crime, criminals, and the punishment of criminals —**crim·i·no·log·i·cal** /krìmminə lójjik'l/ *adj* —**crim·i·no·log·i·cal·ly** *adv* —**crim·i·nol·o·gist** *n*

crimp /krimp/ *vt* **(crimped, crimp·ing, crimps) 1. FOLD OR PRESS ENDS TOGETHER** to fold or press the ends or edges of something together **2. INTERFERE WITH SOMETHING** to hinder, obstruct, or otherwise interfere with something such as a plan or process ○ *A slowdown in sales crimped the company's cash flow.* **3. PLEAT SOMETHING** to press or gather something such as a piece of fabric into small folds **4. CURL HAIR** to make somebody's hair wavy, usually with a curling iron **5. PINCH EDGES AS DECORATION** to pinch or press together the edges of pastry to form a seal or for decoration **6.** MANUF **MOLD LEATHER** to mold or form leather into a shape **7. JOIN METAL INTO SEAM** to bend or fold the edges of sheet metal to form a seam for a tube or between two pieces ■ *n* **1. CRIMPING** an act of crimping something **2. HINDRANCE** a hindrance, obstruction, or interference, or somebody who causes it **3. TIGHT HAIR WAVE** a tight artificial wave in somebody's hair, usually made with a curling iron **4. PINCHED EDGE** a fold or crease made by pinching together two edges, e.g., of fabric or pastry **5.** INDUST **CREASE FORMED BY BENDING** a fold or crease formed by bending something such as sheet metal **6. CURL OF WOOL FIBERS** the curl or wave of wool fibers [Late 17C. Probably < Dutch or Low German *krimpen* "shrink, crimp" < Germanic] —**crimp·er** *n*

crimp·y /krímpee/ (**-i·er, -i·est**) *adj* having many small waves, folds, or wrinkles —**crimp·i·ness** *n*

crim·son /krímz'n/ *n* **DEEP RED COLOR** a deep rich purplish red color ■ *v* **(-soned, -son·ing, -sons) 1.** *vti* **BECOME OR MAKE CRIMSON** to become a deep rich purplish red color, or make something become this color **2.** *vi* **REDDEN IN FACE** to blush with embarrassment, shyness, or shame [15C. Via Old Spanish *cremesín* < Arabic *ḳirmizī* "red color" < *ḳirmīz* "kermes insect"] —**crim·son** *adj*

cringe /krinj/ *vi* **(cringed, cring·ing, cring·es) 1. CROUCH OR MOVE BACK SUDDENLY** to pull the head and body quickly away from somebody or something in a frightened or servile way **2. BE EMBARRASSED OR UNCOMFORTABLE** to react to something with embarrassment or discomfort, often by physically flinching (*informal*) ○ *We always cringe at his jokes.* **3. ACT HUMBLY** to behave in a very humble or servile way (*disapproving*) ■ *n* **FRIGHTENED OR SERVILE MOVEMENT** a quick pulling away of the head and body from somebody or something in a frightened or servile way [13C. Probably < Old English *crincan* "to yield"] —**cring·er** *n*

crin·gle /kríng g'l/ *n* a piece of rope with a metal ring **(grommet)** in it, fitted into the main rope **(boltrope)** around the edge of a sail [Early 17C. < Low German *kringel* "small ring"]

crin·kle /kríngk'l/ *vti* (**-kled, -kling, -kles**) **1. CREASE OR BE CREASED** to become, or make something become, finely folded, wrinkled, or wavy, e.g., by crushing or pressing it **2. MAKE SOFT CRACKLING SOUND** to make little crunching or rustling noises, like the sound of paper being crushed, or cause something to make these noises ■ *n* **TINY CREASE OR WAVE** a little crease, fold, or wave, especially in paper or cloth [14C. Origin ?] —**crin·kli·ness** *n* —**crin·kly** *adv*

crin·kle·root /kríngk'l ro͝ot/ (*plural same* or **-roots**) *n* a plant that has pungent fleshy roots. Flowers: pink or white, in clusters. Native to: woodlands of eastern North America. Genus: *Dentaria*.

cri·noid /krī nòyd/ *n* a primitive invertebrate sea animal **(echinoderm)** with a cup-shaped body and five feathery radiating arms, related to starfish and sea urchins. Class: Crinoidea. [Mid-19C. < Greek *krinoidēs* "like a lily" < *krinon* "lily"] —**cri·noid** *adj*

crin·o·line /krínn'lin/ *n* **1. FABRIC FOR STIFFENING THINGS** a stiff fabric made of horsehair and cotton or linen. Use: formerly, linings, petticoats. **2. STIFF PETTICOAT** a petticoat of crinoline fabric or net, worn to expand a skirt **3. HOOPED SKIRT** a skirt or petticoat containing wire hoops, worn to expand the skirt [Mid-19C. Via French < Italian *crinolino* < *crino* "horsehair" + *lino* "flax"] —**crin·o·lined** *adj*

cri·num /krīnəm/ (*plural same* or **-nums**) *n* a plant that grows from a bulb and has long thin leaves and clusters of flowers in various colors. Native to: tropics. Genus: *Crinum*. [Via modern Latin < Greek *krinon* "lily"]

cri·ol·lo /kree ṓlō/ (*plural* **-los**) *n* **1.** *Hispanic* somebody who comes from a Latin American country and is of European, especially Spanish, descent **2.** a domestic mammal such as a horse belonging to a Latin American breed [Late 19C. < Spanish (see CREOLE)] —**cri·ol·lo** *adj*

cri·o·sphinx /krée ə sfingks/ (*plural* **-sphinx·es** or **-sphing·es** /krée ə sfín jeez/) *n* in Egyptian mythology and art, a figure that is like a sphinx in having a lion's body but has the head of a ram instead of a human head [Mid-19C. < Greek *krios* "ram"]

cripes /krīps/ *interj* used to express surprise or concern (*dated slang*) [Early 20C. Alteration of CHRIST]

crip·ple /kríppʼl/ *n* **1.** OFFENSIVE TERM an offensive term for somebody whose use of a limb or limbs is impaired **2.** OFFENSIVE TERM an offensive term for somebody who is challenged in a particular area or aspect, e.g., financially ■ *vt* (**-pled, -pling, -ples**) **1.** OFFENSIVE TERM an offensive term meaning to impair the ability of somebody to move, e.g., as a result of an accident or medical condition **2.** IMPAIR FUNCTIONING OR PROGRESS to impair the functioning or progress of something such as a machine or project ○ *Dissent has crippled corporate decision-making.* [Old English *crypel* < Germanic, "bent"] —**crip·pled** *adj* —**crip·pling** *adj* —**crip·pling·ly** *adv*

Crip·ple Creek /krìppʼl-/ town in Colorado and administrative seat of Teller County. It was a major gold-mining center (1891–1920). Population: 1,100 (2002 estimate).

cris de coeur plural of **cri de coeur**

cri·sis /krī́ssiss/ (*plural* **cri·ses** /krī́ seez/) *n* **1.** DANGEROUS OR WORRYING TIME a situation or period in which things are very uncertain, difficult, or painful, especially a time when action must be taken to avoid complete disaster or breakdown **2.** CRITICAL MOMENT a time when something very important for the future happens or is decided **3.** MED TURNING POINT IN DISEASE a point in the course of a disease when the patient suddenly begins to get worse or better [15C. Via Latin < Greek *krisis* "decisive moment" < *krinein* "decide"]

cri·sis man·age·ment *n* the business or process of working through a crisis to solve or cope with problems as they arise

crisp /krisp/ *adj* **1.** HARD BUT EASILY BROKEN dry and firm, and of a texture that breaks easily ○ *The snow had frozen overnight and was crisp underfoot.* **2.** FRESH AND CRUNCHY fresh and firm enough to snap when bitten into ○ *a crisp apple* **3.** STIFF AND CLEAN with a stiff, uncreased, or unspoiled surface ○ *a crisp white tablecloth* **4.** DISTINCT distinct and clear, without ambiguity or distortion ○ *She was pleased with the crisp image of the print.* **5.** SHARP AND CONCISE sharp and concise, often to the point of brusqueness ○ *a crisp reply* **6.** INVIGORATING invigorating and fresh ○ *It was a beautiful crisp frosty morning.* **7.** QUICK AND PRECISE performed in a quick and precise way ○ *crisp marching* ■ *n* **1.** DESSERT WITH CRUNCHY TOPPING a dish of prepared fruit covered with a mixture of flour, sugar, and fat baked until the top is crunchy **2.** *UK* FOOD same as **potato chip** ■ *vti* (**crisped, crisp·ing, crisps**) BECOME OR MAKE CRISP to become or make something crisp or crisper, usually in an oven [Mid-16C. < Latin *crispus* "curled" (the original sense in English)] —**crisp·ly** *adv* —**crisp·ness** *n* ◇ **to a crisp** until hard and crunchy, usually excessively so (*informal*) ○ *toast burned to a crisp*

cris·pate /kríss pàyt/ *adj* describes leaves that have curled or wavy edges (*technical*) [Mid-19C. < Latin *crispatus*, past participle of *crispare* "curl" < *crispus* "curled"]

cris·pa·tion /kriss páysh'n/ *n* a minor convulsive muscle contraction that produces a creeping feeling in the skin [Early 17C. < Latin *crispat-*, past participle of *crispare* (see CRISPATE)]

crisp·bread /krísp brèd/ *n* a flat crisp usually rectangular cracker made from rye, wheat, corn, or other grain

crisp·er /kríspər/ *n* a covered compartment in a refrigerator, where fruits and vegetables are placed to keep them fresh and crisp

crisp·y /kríspee/ (**-i·er, -i·est**) *adj* having a pleasantly light, crunchy texture ○ *Do you like your bacon crispy?* —**crisp·i·ness** *n*

cris·sa ZOOL plural of **crissum**

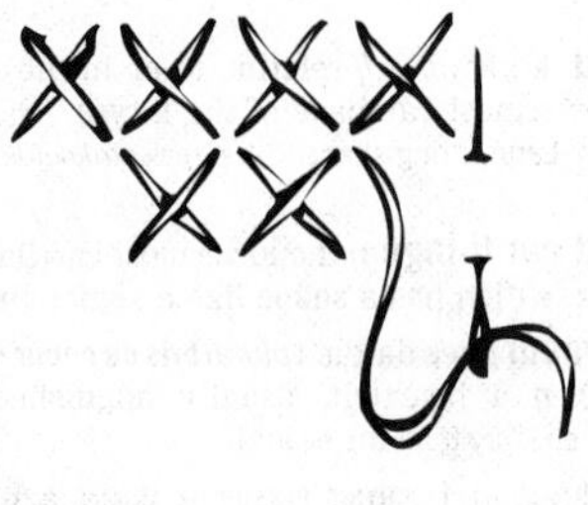

crisscross: crisscross stitches

criss·cross /kríss kràwss/ *n* CROSS OR LATTICE ARRANGEMENT a pattern of lines that cross each other ■ *adj* HAVING VERTICAL AND HORIZONTAL CROSSED LINES running in different directions across each other, or made up of lines like this ■ *adv* BACK AND FORTH in a way that makes a crisscross pattern of crossing lines ■ *v* (**-crossed, -cross·ing, -cross·es**) **1.** *vti* MAKE PATTERN OF CROSSED LINES to create a crisscross pattern on something **2.** *vt* GO TO AND FRO ACROSS SOMETHING to travel or move backward and forward or in all different directions over something [Early 17C. Alteration of obsolete *Christcross*, the figure of a cross, contraction of *Christ's cross*]

cris·sum /kríssəm/ (*plural* **-sa** /-sə/) *n* the feathers beneath the tail of a bird [Late 19C. < modern Latin < Latin *crissare* "wiggle the hips"] —**cris·sal** *adj*

cris·ta /krístə/ (*plural* **-tae** /-tee/) *n* **1.** a crest or ridge, e.g., the border of a bone **2.** a fold in the inner membrane of a mitochondrion, providing a large surface area over which the enzymes responsible for energy metabolism are located [Mid-19C. < Latin, "tuft of hair, ridge"] —**cris·tate** *adj*

cris·to·ba·lite /kri stṓbə līt/ *n* a white form of quartz. Source: volcanic rocks. [Late 19C. After the hill of San *Cristóbal*, near Pachuca de Soto, Mexico]

crit /krit/ *n* ARTS same as **critique** *n* (sense 1) (*informal*) ○ *I haven't seen the film but I've read a couple of crits.* [Early 20C. Shortening]

crit. *abbr* **1.** ARTS critic **2.** MED critical **3.** ARTS criticism

cri·te·ri·on /krī téeree ən/ (*plural* **-ri·a** /-ree ə/ or **-ri·ons**) *n* an accepted standard used in making a decision or judgment about something (*often used in the plural*) [Early 17C. < Greek *kritērion* < *kritēs* (see CRITIC)] —**cri·te·ri·al** *adj*

USAGE criterion or **criteria**? ***Criterion*** is singular and ***criteria*** is plural; it is generally regarded as incorrect to use ***criteria*** as a singular noun (with *criterias* as a bogus plural), though it is commonly seen and heard in the print and electronic media, and in some law contexts as well. The phrase *set of criteria* is often used when a singular expression is required.

crit·ic /kríttik/ *n* **1.** SOMEBODY JUDGING SOMETHING somebody who judges or appraises somebody or something ○ *an eminent critic of postwar government* **2.** WRITER OF REVIEWS somebody, especially a journalist, who writes or broadcasts opinions on the quality of things such as drama productions, art exhibitions, literary works, and society as a whole ○ *the newspaper's TV critic* **3.** FAULT-FINDER somebody who habitually finds fault [Mid-16C. Via Latin < Greek *kritikos* "discerning" < *kritēs* "judge" < *krinein* "decide"]

crit·i·cal /kríttik'l/ *adj* **1.** NOT APPROVING tending to find fault with somebody or something, or with people and things in general **2.** GIVING COMMENTS OR JUDGMENTS containing or involving comments and opinions that analyze or judge something, especially in a detailed way ○ *a critical analysis of modern economic theory* **3.** CRUCIAL extremely important because of being or happening at a time of special difficulty, trouble, or danger, when matters could quickly get either worse or better ○ *The decision was a critical one for the country.* **4.** ESSENTIAL absolutely necessary for the success of something ○ *Their support is critical to our campaign.* **5.** LIFE-THREATENING medically life-threatening or in danger ○ *a patient in a critical condition* **6.** UNDERGOING CHANGE relating to a property of a system that is undergoing a sudden change ○ *critical temperature* **7.** SUSTAINING NUCLEAR CHAIN REACTION designed or having the mass to sustain a nuclear chain reaction —**crit·i·cal·ly** *adv* —**crit·i·cal·ness** *n*

crit·i·cal an·gle *n* **1.** the angle between a ray of light and a surface at which the ray will be completely reflected by the surface **2.** AEROSP same as **stalling angle**

crit·i·cal care *n* the highest level of monitoring and intensive care in a hospital of patients with life-threatening failure of several organs or body systems. ◊ **intensive care** (sense 2)

crit·i·cal·i·ty /krìtti kállətee/ *n* **1.** the condition of being crucial, decisive, or extremely serious **2.** the point in an intensifying nuclear reaction at which it becomes self-sustaining

crit·i·cal list *n* the list of those patients in a hospital who are in a medically life-threatening condition

crit·i·cal mass *n* **1.** POINT OF CHANGE a point or situation at which change occurs ○ *Support for the measure has reached critical mass.* **2.** NECESSARY SIZE OR AMOUNT the size or amount of something that is required before an activity or event can take place **3.** AMOUNT OF FISSIONABLE MATERIAL the smallest amount of fissionable material needed to maintain a nuclear chain reaction **4.** BUSINESS NECESSARY NUMBER OF CUSTOMERS the number of customers or size of market share that allows a business enterprise to become profitable **5.** COMPUT POINT OF EXCESSIVE SOFTWARE FEATURES the point in software development at which a piece of software acquires so many features that it ceases to be useful

crit·i·cal point *n* **1.** the point at which two or more phases of a substance such as liquid and gas are identical or in equilibrium **2.** a point on a graph at which the tangent to a curve is parallel to either the horizontal or vertical axis

crit·i·cal re·gion *n* the possible results of a statistical test that are outside the range of acceptable probabilities and, if observed, would lead to their rejection

cri·ti·cal sec·tion *n* in surfing, the most difficult part of a wave to surf

crit·i·cal state *n* CHEM same as **critical point** (sense 1)

crit·i·cal tem·per·a·ture *n* the temperature of a substance at the critical point when it is between liquid and vapor phases

crit·i·cal think·ing *n* disciplined intellectual criticism that combines research, knowledge of historical context, and balanced judgment

crit·i·cism /krítti sìzzəm/ *n* **1.** ACT OF CRITICIZING a spoken or written opinion or judgment of what is wrong or bad about somebody or something **2.** DISAPPROVAL spoken or written opinions that point out one or more faults of somebody or something **3.** ASSESSMENT OF CREATIVE WORK considered judgment of or discussion about the qualities of something, especially a creative work **4.** MEDIA same as **critique** *n* (sense 1)

crit·i·cize /krítti sīz/ (**-cized, -ciz·ing, -ciz·es**) *vti* **1.** to express disapproval of or dissatisfaction with somebody or something **2.** to make a considered assessment of the qualities of something, especially a creative work —**crit·i·ciz·a·ble** /krítti sīzəb'l, krìtti sīzəb'l/ *adj* —**crit·i·ciz·er** *n*

SYNONYMS ***criticize, censure, castigate, blast, condemn, find fault with, pick holes in, nitpick***

CORE MEANING: to express disapproval of or dissatisfaction with somebody or something

criticize to express disapproval of or dissatisfaction with somebody or something ○ *The new policy was strongly criticized by two special-interest groups.* ○ *He has criticized the government for not launching an investigation.* **censure** to make a formal, often public or official statement of disapproval of somebody or something ○ *The three senators were censured by their peers.* ○ *It is not known whether the player will be* *censured for his bad sportsmanship.* **castigate** (*formal*) to criticize or rebuke somebody or somebody's behavior severely ○ *She castigated her political opponent on Tuesday for exaggerating the problem.* ○ *He was castigated as an alarmist by the country's president.* **blast** (*informal*) to criticize somebody or something severely ○ *She blasts homeowners who waste water during droughts.* ○ *The Olympic champion yesterday blasted critics who label sports as endorsement-driven.* **condemn** to state that something or somebody is in some way wrong or unacceptable ○ *When is world opinion going to condemn the rogue nation's actions?* ○ *This breach of medical confidentiality was strongly condemned by the patient's attorney.* **find fault with** to criticize somebody or something, often unfairly ○ *He finds fault with everything I do.* ○ *It is difficult to find fault with this eccentric and lively account.* **pick holes in** to look for and find minor mistakes in something, particularly in an argument ○ *pick holes in someone's ideas* ○ *It's almost impossible to pick holes in their claim.* **nitpick** to find insignificant details of something unsatisfactory, often unjustifiably. ○ *Moira said her brother was still nitpicking over the contract.* ○ *We're just nitpicking – both proposals are generally sensible and workable.*

---

cri·tique /kri te̋ek/ *n* **1.** a written or broadcast assessment of something, usually a creative work, with comments on its good and bad qualities **2.** MEDIA same as **criticism** (sense 3) ■ *vt* (**-tiqued, -tiqu·ing, -tiques**) to discuss or comment on something such as a creative work, giving an assessment of its good and bad qualities [Mid-17C. Via French < Greek *kritikē (tekhnē)* "art of criticism" < *kritikos* (see CRITIC)]

~~**critisism**~~ incorrect spelling of **criticism**

crit·ter /kríttər/ *n* a living thing, especially an animal (*informal or regional*) ○ *That dog was a funny old critter.* [Early 19C. Alteration of CREATURE]

croak /krōk/ *n* **1.** CRY OF ANIMAL OR BIRD a rough, usually low-pitched, vibrating sound, especially the characteristic cry of a frog or crow **2.** ROUGH VOICE OF PERSON a rough low uneven sound or voice of somebody with a dry or sore throat ■ *v* (**croaked, croak·ing, croaks**) **1.** *vi* MAKE LOW-PITCHED CALL to make a rough, usually low-pitched, vibrating sound, especially the characteristic cry of a frog or crow **2.** *vti* SPEAK HOARSELY to speak or say something in a rough low uneven voice because of a dry or sore throat **3.** *vi* GRUMBLE to grumble or mutter gloomily (*informal*) **4.** *vti* KILL OR DIE to kill somebody, or be killed (*slang*) [Mid-16C. Probably an imitation of the sound] —**croak·i·ly** *adv* —**croak·y** *adj*

croak·er /krṓkər/ *n* **1.** FISH THAT MAKES CROAKING SOUND a fish that makes croaking or grunting noises. Family: Sciaenidae. **2.** CROAKING ANIMAL a bird or other animal that croaks when it calls **3.** PHYSICIAN a medical doctor (*slang; humorous*)

Cro·at /krṓ a̋at, krṓ àt/ *n* **1.** somebody who comes from Croatia **2.** LANG same as **Croatian** (sense 1) [Mid-17C. Via modern Latin *Croata* < Serbo-Croatian *Hrvāt*] —**Cro·at** *adj*

Croatia

Cro·a·tia /krō áyshə, -shee ə/ country in southeastern Europe, on the Balkan Peninsula, bordering the Adriatic Sea. Language: Croatian. Currency: kuna. Capital: Zagreb. Population: 4,422,248 (2003). Area: 21,819 sq. mi./56,510 sq. km. Official name **Republic of Croatia**

Cro·a·tian /krō áysh'n/ *n* **1.** the Slavic language that is the official language of Croatia, closely related to Bosnian and Serbian. Native speakers: 5 million. **2.** PEOPLES same as **Croat** (sense 1) —**Cro·a·tian** *adj*

croc /krok/ *n* REPT same as **crocodile** (sense 1) (*informal*) [Late 19C. Shortening]

Cro·ce /krṓ chay/, **Benedetto** (1866–1952) Italian philosopher, historian, and political leader. He opposed fascism and made important contributions to idealistic philosophy.

cro·ce·in /krṓssee in/ *n* a red or orange acid azo dye [20C. < Latin *croceus* "saffron-colored" < *crocus* (see CROCUS)]

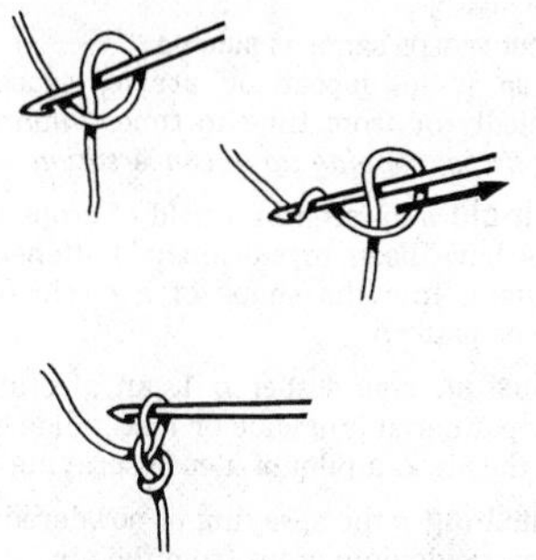

crochet: a hooked needle is used to catch thread (top), which is twisted and pulled to create a loop (center and bottom)

cro·chet /krō sháy/ *n* a form of needlework used to make clothes or decorative items from wool or thick stiff thread by looping the wool or thread through itself with a hooked needle (**crochet hook**) ■ *vti* (**-cheted** /-sháyd/, **-chet·ing** /-sháy ing/, **-chets** /-sháyz/) to make something using the technique of crochet [Mid-19C. < French, literally "little hook" < *croche* "hook" < Germanic] —**cro·chet·er** /krō sháy ər/ *n*

cro·ci PLANTS plural of **crocus**

cro·cid·o·lite /krō síddə lìt/ *n* a fibrous purplish blue form of the mineral riebeckite [Mid-19C. < Greek *krokid-* "nap of woolen cloth"]

crock /krok/ *n* **1.** CLAY POT a pot made of clay **2.** POTTERY FRAGMENT a fragment of clay pottery **3.** FALSEHOOD something, especially a story, that is ridiculous or untrue (*slang*) ○ *His story about working until midnight is just a crock!* [Old English *crocc* < Germanic]

crocked /krokt/ *adj* same as **drunk** *adj* (sense 1) (*slang*) [Early 20C. Origin ?]

crock·er·y /krókəree/ *n* plates, cups, saucers, and other household items made of earthenware [Early 18C. < *crocker* "potter" < CROCK]

crock·et /krókət/ *n* a leaf shape carved as a decoration in Gothic architecture [Late 17C. < Old French dialect *croquet* "shepherd's crook," variant of Old French *crochet* (see CROCHET)]

Crock·ett /krókət/, **Davy** (1786–1836) US frontiersman. He fought against the Creek Native Americans and joined Congress in 1827. A member of the Texas revolutionaries fighting against Mexico, he died at the battle of the Alamo. Full name **Crockett, David**

> "I leave this rule for others when I'm dead,/Be always sure you're right—then go ahead."
> [Davy Crockett, *Narrative of the Life of David Crockett, of the State of Tennessee*; 1834]

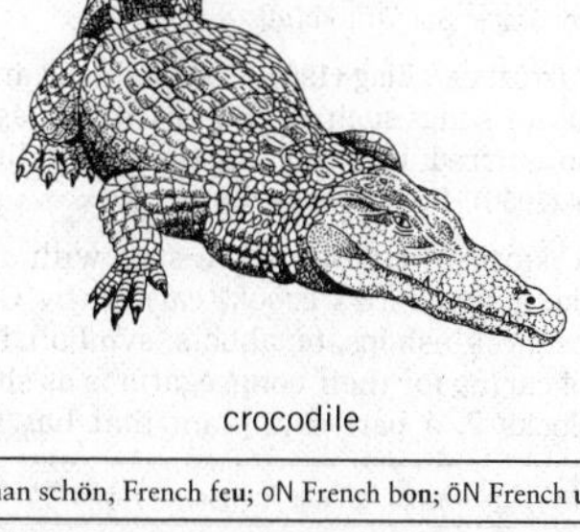

crocodile

croc·o·dile /krókə dìl/ (*plural* **-diles** or *same*) *n* **1.** a large carnivorous reptile that lives near water, and has a long thick-skinned body and a broad head with strong jaws. Native to: tropical or subtropical regions. Family: Crocodylidae. **2.** REPT same as **crocodilian 3.** leather made from the skin of a crocodile ○ *crocodile shoes* [13C. Via Old French *cocodril* < Greek *krokodilos*, a small lizard]

croc·o·dile bird *n* same as **Egyptian plover**

croc·o·dile clip ELEC ENG *n UK* same as **alligator clip**

croc·o·dile tears *npl* false tears or an insincere show of grief [Because crocodiles were believed to make sounds like weeping to attract prey, and to shed hypocritical tears over their victims]

croc·o·dil·i·an /kròkə díllee ən/ *n* a large predatory reptile belonging to a group that includes the alligator, caiman, crocodile, gavial, and related extinct animals. Order: Crocodylia. —**croc·o·dil·i·an** *adj*

croc·o·ite /krókō ìt/, **croc·oi·site** /krókwə zìt/ *n* a rare orange or red mineral consisting of lead chromate. Formula: $PbCrO_4$. [Mid-19C. Alteration of French *crocoise* < Greek *krokoeis* "saffron-colored" < *krokos* "saffron"]

cro·cus /krṓkəss/ (*plural* **-cus·es** or **-ci** /-sì, -kee/) *n* **1.** SPRING FLOWER a small perennial spring-flowering plant that grows from a corm. Flowers: white, red, purple, or yellow. Genus: *Crocus*. **2.** FLOWER LIKE CROCUS a plant that has a flower like a true crocus, e.g., the autumn crocus **3.** *US* METAL POLISH powdered ferric oxide. Use: polishing metal. Can term **jeweller's rouge** [14C. Via Latin < Greek *krokos* "saffron, crocus"]

cro·cus sack, **cro·cus bag** *n Southern US* same as **gunnysack**

REGIONAL NOTE *Crocus sack* is a Virginian Piedmont term that spreads southward below the South Midland territory, where *tow sack* prevails. In Southern regions, the spelling form *croker sack* recurs and has become far more common there than the original form.

Croe·sus /kre̋essəss/ *n* a very wealthy man [After CROESUS]

Croe·sus /kre̋essəss/, **king of Lydia** (*fl* 6th century B.C.) Lydian monarch. A proverbially wealthy ruler, he reigned from about 560 B.C. to 546 B.C. when he was defeated and probably captured by Cyrus the Great.

croft /kroft/ *n* a small plot of land, often with a house on it, that the owner or occupier farms, especially in Scotland [Old English, origin ?] —**croft·er** *n*

Crohn's dis·ease /krṓnz-/ *n* a chronic inflammatory disease, usually of the lower intestinal tract, marked by scarring and thickening of the intestinal wall and obstruction [Mid-20C. After B. B. *Crohn* (1884–1983), US pathologist]

crois·sant /krwaa sa̋ant, -sa̋an, -sa̋aN/ *n* a piece of baked dough or pastry shaped into a crescent, usually moist, flaky, and very rich in fat, originally made in France [Late 19C. < French, "crescent"]

Croix de Guerre /krwa̋a də gér/ (*plural same*) *n* a French military medal awarded for bravery in war [< French, "war cross"]

cro·ker sack /krṓkər-/ *n Southern US* same as **gunnysack** [Alteration of CROCUS SACK]

REGIONAL NOTE See *crocus sack*.

Cro-Mag·non /krō mágnən, -mánnyən/ *n* the earliest known form of modern human being found in Europe, dating from about 50,000 to 30,000 years ago [Mid-19C. After a hill in the Dordogne, France]

crom·lech /króm lèk/ *n* **1.** a group of prehistoric standing stones arranged in a circle **2.** an ancient stone burial chamber [Late 17C. < Welsh < *crwm* "arched" + *llech* "flat stone"]

Crom·well /króm wèl, krómmwəl/, **Oliver** (1599–1658) English soldier and politician. He led the Parliamentarians to victory in the English Civil War (1642–49) and, after the execution of Charles I, ruled as Lord Protector of England (1653–58).

> "A few honest men are better than numbers."
> [Oliver Cromwell, *Letter to Sir W. Spring*; September 1643]

crone /krōn/ *n* **1.** an offensive term that deliberately insults a woman's age, appearance, and temperament (*insult*) **2.** a woman aged over 40 (*approving; used by one woman to another*) [14C. < Old N French *carogne* "withered old woman," literally "carrion" < Latin *caro* "flesh"]

USAGE See *insult*.

~~cronic~~ incorrect spelling of **chronic**

Cro·nin /krónin/, **A. J.** (1896–1981) Scottish novelist and physician. His bestsellers, including *The Stars Look Down* (1935), drew on his medical background. Full name **Cronin, Archibald Joseph**

Cron·kite /krón kīt, króng-/, **Walter** (*b.* 1916) US broadcast journalist. He made his name covering World War II and the Nuremberg trials. As the longtime anchor of the nightly "CBS Evening News" (1962–81) his sound journalism and reportage through the controversial Vietnam War and the Watergate scandal led him to be voted the man most trusted by Americans. Full name **Cronkite, Jr., Walter Leland**

"And that's the way it is."
[Walter Cronkite, sign-off signature, *CBS Evening News*; 1962–81]

~~cronology~~ incorrect spelling of **chronology**

Cro·nus /krṓnəss/ *n* in Greek mythology, a Titan who ruled the world until his son Zeus dethroned him. Roman equivalent **Saturn**

cro·ny /krṓnee/ (*plural* **-nies**) *n* a close friend, especially one of long standing [Mid-17C. < Greek *khronios* "long-lasting" < *khronos* "time"]

cro·ny cap·i·tal·ism *n* the flow of wealth to a small group of people who are already wealthy and well connected

cro·ny·ism /krṓnee ìzzəm/ *n* special treatment and preference given to friends or colleagues, especially in politics (*disapproving*)

Cro·nyn /krṓnin/, **Hume** (1911–2003) Canadian-born US stage and screen actor who starred in many movies, including *Cocoon* (1985). In 1994 Cronyn and his wife, Jessica Tandy, were awarded the first Tony Award for lifetime theatrical achievement.

crook /krŏŏk/ *n* **1.** HOOK-SHAPED DEVICE a curved or hooked tool, instrument, or part in a mechanism **2.** AGRIC SHEPHERD'S HOOKED STICK a long stick with a curved end used by a shepherd to catch or guide a sheep **3.** CHR same as **crosier** (sense 1) **4.** BEND IN SOMETHING a bent or curved part of something, e.g., the curve made by somebody's arm when the elbow is bent **5.** DISHONEST PERSON a thief, cheat, or criminal (*informal*) ■ *vti* (**crook·ed, crook·ing, crooks**) FORM BEND to curve, or make something such as a finger take on a hooked or curved shape [12C. < Old Norse *krókr* "hook"] —**crook·er·y** *n*

crook·ed /krŏŏkəd/ *adj* **1.** WITH BENT SHAPE sharply curved, bent, or twisted, often in more than one place **2.** ALIGNED INCORRECTLY not aligned properly or set at an angle ○ *That picture is crooked.* **3.** NOT LEGAL illegal or dishonest (*informal*) —**crook·ed·ly** *adv* —**crook·ed·ness** *n*

crook·neck /krŏŏk nèk/, **crook·neck squash, crook·necked squash** /krŏŏk nèkt-/ *n* a yellow summer squash with a long curved neck

croon /kroon/ *vti* (**crooned, croon·ing, croons**) **1.** SING OR MURMUR GENTLY to sing or murmur something in a soft low voice, especially to yourself or to a sleepy child **2.** SING SENTIMENTALLY to perform a song or songs in a smooth sentimental style ■ *n* GENTLE SINGING singing in a soft low voice, or something sung in this way [15C. < Middle Dutch *krōnen* "to lament"] —**croon·er** *n*

crop /krop/ *n* **1.** AGRIC, BOT PLANTS GROWN FOR USE a group of plants grown by people for food or other use, especially on a large scale in farming or horticulture **2.** AGRIC AMOUNT HARVESTED the amount harvested from a plant or area of land, during one particular period of time ○ *a good crop of tomatoes* **3.** AGRIC ANIMALS REARED FOR PRODUCE a group of animals reared in farming, or something produced from them ○ *a poor crop of lambs* **4.** GROUP OF PEOPLE OR THINGS a number of people or things doing something or being done at the same time ○ *last year's crop of students* **5.** WHIP HANDLE the handle of a whip **6.** SHORT HAIRSTYLE a short hairstyle, usually for a woman **7.** POUCH IN BIRD'S THROAT a pouch in the throat of many birds in which they store food before regurgitating it to feed their young **8.** POUCH IN DIGESTIVE SYSTEM a pouch in the digestive tract of an insect or earthworm ■ *v* (**cropped, crop·ping, crops**) **1.** *vt* CUT SOMETHING SHORT to cut something short, e.g., hair or a lawn **2.** *vti* AGRIC GRAZE to eat the top parts of growing plants, especially grass **3.** *vt* CUT PART OF PHOTO to cut off or conceal unwanted parts of an image, especially a photograph [Old English *cropp* "ear of grain" < Germanic, "round mass"]

crop out *vi* GEOL same as **outcrop**

crop up *vi* to appear or arrive, especially unexpectedly or from time to time (*informal*) ○ *Her name keeps cropping up in conversation.*

crop cir·cle *n* an area in a field of crops where the plants have been mysteriously flattened, usually overnight, into the shape of a circle or a more complex pattern

crop-dust·er, crop dust·er *n* **1.** an aircraft used to spray powdered fungicide or insecticide onto crops from the air **2.** a pilot of a crop-spraying aircraft

crop-dust·ing *n* the spraying of powdered fungicide or insecticide onto crops from the air

crop·land /króp lànd/ *n* agricultural land that is suitable or used for growing crops

crop pants, cropped pants /krópt-/ *npl* pants that end between the knee and the ankle

crop·per /króppər/ *n* AGRIC same as **sharecropper** ◇ **come a cropper** (*informal*) **1.** to fail completely **2.** to experience a hurtful or embarrassing fall

crop ro·ta·tion *n* a system of farming in which a piece of land is planted with different crops in succession, in order to improve soil fertility and control crop pests and diseases

crop top *n* **1.** a piece of clothing for women or girls, covering the upper body but cut short to end above the navel **2.** somebody with a very short haircut (*informal*)

croqu·em·bouche /krōk aam bŏŏsh/ *n* a tall cone-shaped cake or dessert constructed from balls of choux pastry filled with custard and coated with a hard caramel glaze [< French *croque en bouche* "crunch in the mouth"]

croque mon·sieur /krōk mə syúr/ *n* a toasted, grilled, or fried cheese and ham sandwich [< French, "bite (a) man"]

cro·quet /krō káy/ *n* **1.** LAWN GAME WITH BALLS AND MALLETS an outdoor game, usually played on a lawn, in which the players use long-handled wooden mallets to hit large wooden balls through a series of hoops (**wickets**) **2.** STROKE IN LAWN GAME a stroke played in the game of croquet whereby a player knocks away an opponent's ball by hitting his or her own ball when the two are touching ■ *vti* (**-queted** /-káyd/, **-quet·ing** /-káying/, **-quets** /-káyz/) KNOCK SOMEBODY'S CROQUET BALL AWAY to knock away an opponent's ball in the game of croquet by hitting your own ball when the two are touching [Mid-19C. Origin ?]

cro·quette /krō két/ *n* a little flat cake or ball of tasty mixture coated in egg and breadcrumbs, and fried [Early 18C. < French < *croquer* "to crunch," an imitation of the sound]

cro·quis /krō kée/ (*plural same*) *n* a rough sketch or draft of something (*technical*) [Early 19C. < French < *croquer* "to sketch"]

crore /krawr/ (*plural* **crores** or *same*) *n* S Asia ten million, especially ten million rupees or the equivalent, one million pounds, in UK sterling [Early 17C. Via Hindi *kroṛ* < Sanskrit *koṭiḥ*]

Cros·by /krózbee/, **Bing** (1904–77) US singer and actor. Famous for songs such as "White Christmas" (1942), he also starred in many movies, including *High Society* (1956). Born **Crosby, Harry Lillis**

cro·sier /krṓzhər/, **cro·zier** *n* **1.** a staff with a hooked end like a shepherd's crook, carried by Christian bishops, archbishops, or abbots, symbolizing their roles of caring for their congregations as shepherds tend flocks **2.** a part of a plant that has a curled end, e.g., the frond of a fern [13C. < Old French *crosier* "crook bearer" < *croce* "crook"]

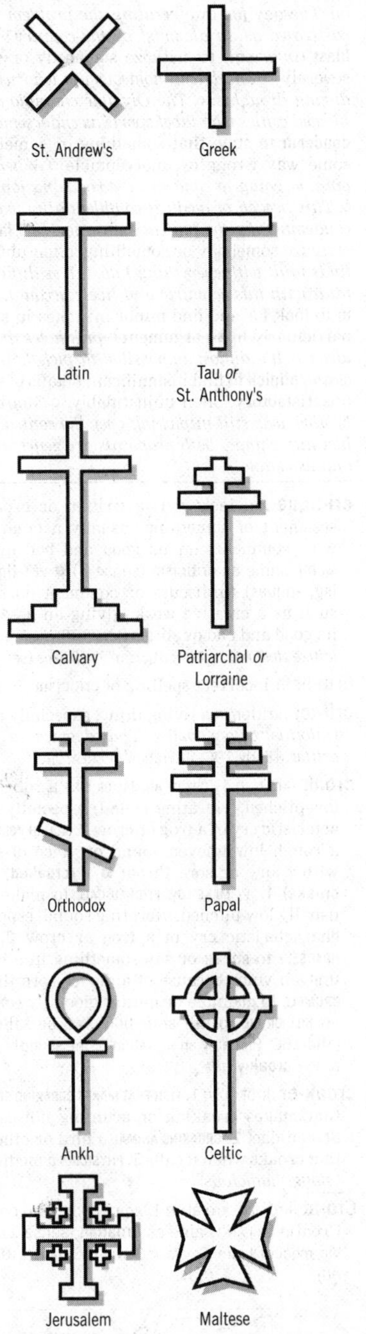

cross

cross /krawss/ *n* **1.** CHRISTIAN SYMBOL a long vertical bar intersected at right angles, usually about two-thirds up, by a shorter horizontal bar, used as a symbol of Christianity or of the Crucifixion. The shape refers to the cross on which Jesus Christ was crucified. **2.** *also* **Cross** WOODEN STRUCTURE JESUS CHRIST DIED ON the wooden cross on which, according to the Bible, Jesus Christ was crucified and died **3.** CROSS-SHAPED MEDAL OR INSIGNIA a medal or insignia shaped like a cross **4.** WOODEN EXECUTION POST WITH CROSSBAR an upright wooden post with a shorter post fixed across it at right angles toward the top, on which, formerly, people were nailed or hanged in public executions **5.** CROSS-SHAPED SYMBOL a symbol or emblem in the form of a stylized cross. A cross is usually formed by two intersecting lines or bands, of any length and meeting at any angle, but sometimes by a main line or band intersected by shorter ones. (*often used in combination*) **6.** TWO INTERSECTING LINES a sign or mark (X) made of two straight lines that bisect each other, used to mark or cancel something, or as a signature by people who cannot write **7.** MIXTURE somebody or something that is a blend of two different types or characteristics ○ *a cross between a mystery and a historical novel* **8.** GENETICS HYBRID INDIVIDUAL an animal or plant produced by interbreeding two genetically different individuals **9.** BOXING SIDEWAYS BLOW a punch thrown at a boxing opponent from the side, in response to and evading the opponent's jab or lead **10.** SOCCER, HOCKEY PASS ACROSS FIELD in soccer or field hockey, a pass sent across the field, usually in the air **11.** SPORTS PASS ACROSS GOAL a pass that sends the ball across the field in a team game such as field hockey **12.** DIFFICULTY a difficulty in somebody's personal life that is particularly testing, troubling, or painful ○ *His daughter's death was a particularly difficult cross to bear.* **13.** CONSTR PIPE CONNECTION a cross-shaped joint used to connect four pipes **14.** LAW CROSS-EXAMINATION cross-examination of a witness ○ *On cross, the witness admitted he had lied.* **15.** SOMETHING DISHONEST something dishonest or fraudulent, especially a sports contest in which the outcome has been dishonestly decided before it begins (*slang*) ■ *v* (**crossed, cross·ing, cross·es**) **1.** *vti* GO ACROSS to move or move somebody or something from one side of something to the other ○ *We've already crossed the border.* ○ *The river's too swift to cross the horses here.* **2.** *vi* EXTEND ACROSS to extend from one side of something to the other ○ *Numerous fallen trees cross the stream.* **3.** *vt* PLACE THINGS ONE ACROSS OTHER to put two things so that one lies across the other ○ *crossed her legs* **4.** *vti* MEET AT ONE POINT to meet at a particular place or time and then continue separately again ○ *A settlement grew up where two trade routes crossed.* **5.** *vt* GENETICS INTERBREED PLANTS OR ANIMALS to interbreed or hybridize plants or animals that are genetically different **6.** *vt* CHR MAKE CHRISTIAN BLESSING GESTURE WITH HAND to draw the shape of a Christian cross in the air over somebody or something as a symbol of God's blessing **7.** *vti* SPORTS PASS BALL ACROSS FIELD in soccer and some other games, to make a pass that sends the ball across, rather than up or down, the field **8.** *vt* THWART SOMEBODY to do something that goes against somebody's wishes or that annoys or frustrates somebody ○ *I wouldn't cross her unless you want to make life difficult for yourself.* **9.** *vt* WRITE LINE ACROSS LETTER "T" to draw a horizontal line across the vertical line of a letter "T," to complete the letter ■ *adj* ANGRY feeling or indicating anger ○ *exchanged a few cross words* [Pre-12C. Via Old Norse *kross* < Old Irish *cros* < Latin *crux*] —**cross·er** *n* —**cross·ly** *adv* —**cross·ness** *n*

cross off *vt* to remove something, especially a name or item written on a list, by drawing a line through it

cross out *vt* to cancel something, especially a word or item that is wrong or not wanted, by drawing a line through it

cross- *prefix* **1.** crossing ○ *crossover* **2.** opposing, opposite ○ *crosscurrent* **3.** reciprocal, mutual ○ *cross-link* [< CROSS]

cross ac·tion *n* a legal proceeding brought by somebody who has been sued against the person who brought the original action or against a codefendant

cross·bar /kráwss baar/ *n* **1.** LEVEL POLE a bar that runs horizontally between two vertical posts, e.g., between goalposts or the uprights of a jump **2.** LEVEL BAR IN BICYCLE FRAME a horizontal metal bar that runs from below the handlebars to below the saddle, traditionally on a man's or boy's bicycle **3.** TRANSVERSE STRIPE a transverse bar, stripe, or band

cross·beam /kráwss beem/ *n* a beam that passes between two supports in the structure of a building

cross·bear·er /kráwss bèrrər/, **cross-bear·er** *n* somebody who bears a cross in front of a bishop or archbishop in a ceremonial procession

cross-bed·ding *n* **1.** layers of geologic strata in which deposits were laid down at an angle with respect to those above and below, commonly seen in sandstone deposited as dunes **2.** the layering of geologic strata transverse to the main beds of stratified rock —**cross-bed·ded** *adj*

cross·bill /kráwss bil/ *n* a large finch that has a beak with crossed tips that it uses to extract seeds from conifer cones. Native to: coniferous forests. Genus: *Loxia.*

cross·bones /kráwss bōnz/ *npl* a representation of two human thighbones crossing each other in the middle, traditionally placed beneath a skull as a symbol of death. The image of crossbones lying below a skull was traditionally used by pirates on their flag (**Jolly Roger**) and in modern times is used to show that something is poisonous.

cross·bow /kráwss bō/ *n* a medieval weapon, or its modern sports successor, consisting of a bow attached crosswise to a stock with a cranking mechanism and a trigger. A crossbow fires short heavy arrows called bolts or quarrels. —**cross·bow·man** *n*

cross·breed /kráwss breed/ *vti* (**-bred** /-brèd/, **-breed·ing, -breeds**) to breed new strains of plants or animals from genetically different individuals ■ *n* an animal or plant produced by crossbreeding —**cross·bred** /-brèd/ *adj, n*

cross·check /kráwss chèk/ (**-checked, -check·ing, -checks**), **cross-check** *vt* **1.** to make sure that something such as a fact or figure is correct by looking it up in other sources or asking another person **2.** in field hockey, ice hockey, and lacrosse, to obstruct an opposing player by using both hands to thrust a playing stick across his or her body —**cross·check** *n*

cross-claim *n* a claim made against another party on the same side of a lawsuit such as a codefendant

cross-coun·try *adj* **1.** NOT ON ROAD OR TRACK done over fields or hills, or through woods, not on roads or a specially prepared area ○ *a cross-country run* **2.** ACROSS WHOLE COUNTRY from one side of a country to another, or throughout a country ○ *The band embarked on a cross-country tour.* **3.** OPERATING OFF ROADS designed or able to operate without roads ○ *a cross-country vehicle* ■ *n* RACING OVER FIELDS a sports activity or event such as running, cycling, or racing that is done off the roads

cross-coun·try ski·ing *n* skiing on long narrow skis across open countryside on fairly level ground

cross·court /kráwss kàwrt/ *adj* hit or thrown from one side of a playing court toward the other, especially in tennis or basketball

cross cous·in, cross-cous·in *n* a cousin who is related to somebody through a brother and sister, being either a father's sister's child or a mother's brother's child

cross-cul·tur·al *adj* relating to or comparing two or more different cultures ○ *cross-cultural research on community activism* —**cross-cul·tur·al·ly** *adv*

cross·cur·rent /kráwss kùrrənt, -kùr ənt/ *n* **1.** a current that flows across another current, mainly in water but also in air **2.** a movement or trend that conflicts with the general one, especially a trend in people's ideas or opinions

cross·cut /kráwss kùt/ *adj* **1.** CUT AT ANGLE describes something such as wood, meat, or fabric that is cut across its main grain **2.** FOR CUTTING ACROSS made or used for cutting across the grain of wood ■ *v* (**-cut, -cut·ting, -cuts**) **1.** *vt* CUT WOOD ACROSS GRAIN to cut across the grain of wood using a crosscut saw **2.** *vti* MOVIES ALTERNATE MOVIE SHOTS to alternate repeatedly brief scenes from one filmed sequence with scenes from another to give the impression that the events they show are happening at the same time ■ *n* **1.** CUT MADE ACROSS a cut made across something such as a long piece of timber **2.** TUNNEL ACROSS VEIN OF ORE a tunnel in a mine that cuts across a vein of ore **3.** MOVIES EXAMPLE OF MOVIE ALTERNATING SHOTS an example of the movie technique in which short segments of two or more scenes are alternated **4.** SHORTCUT a shorter and more direct route to a place

cross·cut saw *n* a saw used for cutting wood across the grain

cross·cut·ting /kráwss kùtting/ *n* repeated alternation between brief filmed sequences to give the impression that the events they show are happening at the same time

cross-dress *vi* to wear clothes usually worn by somebody of the opposite sex —**cross-dress·er** *n* —**cross-dress·ing** *n*

crosse /krawss, kross/ *n* a wooden stick used in the game of lacrosse, curved at the top into a triangular frame that supports a tough leatherwork net [Mid-19C. < French, "bishop's crook"]

cross-ex·am·ine *vt* **1.** to question a witness for the opposing side in a hearing or trial **2.** to ask somebody a lot of detailed questions in a persistent or aggressive way (*informal*) —**cross-ex·am·i·na·tion** *n* —**cross-ex·am·in·er** *n*

SYNONYMS See ***question.***

cross-eyed *adj* an offensive term meaning having one or both eyes turned in toward the nose

cross-fade *vti* in movie or television editing, to gradually introduce a new sound or picture while causing another one to disappear

cross-fer·til·i·za·tion *n* **1.** the fertilization of a female sex cell (**gamete**) of one individual by a male sex cell from a different individual, usually of the same species **2.** BOT same as **cross-pollination** **3.** the exchange of ideas between two groups, especially cultures, that produces benefits for both —**cross-fer·til·ize** *vti*

cross·field /kráwss feeld/ *adj* kicked or thrown from one side of a playing field toward the other, especially in soccer or rugby ○ *a crossfield pass*

cross·fire /kráwss fīr/ *n* **1.** gunshots that come from more than one place, in such a way that the lines of fire converge **2.** heated or lively conversation, with different and opposing views and ideas being put forward, or an example of this

cross-grained *adj* **1.** with an irregular grain or a grain that runs across the length **2.** difficult to deal with because of stubbornness, contrariness, or bad temper (*informal*)

cross hairs, cross·hairs /kráwss hèrz/ *npl* a pair of fine lines or wires that cross at right angles inside a lens or sight, used, e.g., in focusing an optical instrument or aiming a rifle

cross·hatch /kráwss hàch/ (**-hatched, -hatch·ing, -hatch·es**) *vti* to draw parallel or intersecting lines across part of a drawing or diagram, usually diagonally, especially to give the effect of shadow or different texture —**cross·hatch·ing** *n*

cross·head /kráwss hèd/ *n* a sliding metal block securing one end of a piston rod to a connecting rod

cross-hedg·ing *n* the process of securing a future financial position against unfavorable economic events by taking out a position in a different financial transaction that would benefit by the same unfavorable events

cross-in·dex *v* **1.** *vt* to give a particular item one or more additional entries in an index, under different headings, as cross-references to it **2.** *vti* to supply cross-references in something

cross·ing /kráwssing/ *n* **1.** POINT WHERE SOMEBODY CAN CROSS SOMETHING a place that has been specially constructed, chosen, or marked out as somewhere where something such as a road or a border may be crossed **2.** POINT WHERE ROUTES CROSS a place where a railroad track and a road, or two railroad tracks, roads, or similar routes go across each other **3.** JOURNEY ACROSS WATER a journey across a body of water **4.** CENTRAL AREA OF CROSS-SHAPED CHURCH the place in a cross-shaped church where the nave and the transept meet

cross·ing o·ver, cross·ing-o·ver *n* the interchange of segments between homologous chromosomes during cell division (**meiosis**), resulting in new combinations of gene types (**alleles**) and therefore variability in inherited characteristics

cross·jack /kráwss jàk/ *n* a sail on the mizzenmast of a ship

cross-leg·ged /kràwss léggəd, -légd/ *adj* in a sitting position with the legs bent so that the knees are apart and the ankles are crossed in front ■ *adv* with one leg lying over the other ○ *sitting cross-legged*

cross·let /kráwsslət/ *n* on coats of arms, a cross that has a smaller cross at the end of each of its arms

cross-link *n also* **cross-link·age** a transverse connecting element, e.g., an atom, chemical group, or covalent bond between parallel chains of a complex organic molecule, especially a polymer or protein ■ *vt* to join polymer chains by a cross-link

cross match·ing *n* the process of testing for the compatibility of a donor's and recipient's tissues before blood transfusion or tissue transplantation —**cross-match** *vt*

cross-mul·ti·ply *vi* to multiply each numerator of two fractions by the denominator of the other —**cross-mul·ti·pli·ca·tion** *n*

cross of Lor·raine *n* a cross with two horizontal bars (**patriarchal cross**) that was adopted as the symbol of the duchy of Lorraine [After LORRAINE]

Cross of Val·our *n* the highest Canadian decoration for courage

cros·sop·te·ryg·i·an /kro sòptə ríjjee ən, -jən/ (*plural* **-ans** or *same*) *n* a bony fish with paired fleshy pectoral fins like limbs that is thought to be ancestral to amphibians and other land vertebrates. All except the coelacanth are extinct. Subclass: Crossopterygii. [Mid-19C. < modern Latin *Crossopterygii* < Greek *krossoi* "fringe" + *pterux* "wing"] —**cros·sop·te·ryg·i·an** *adj*

cross·o·ver /kráwss ṑvər/ *n* **1. CROSSING OR TRANSFER POINT** a place for crossing from one side of something to the other, or from one line, system, or vehicle to another **2.** AUTOMOT same as **sport tourer 3. SOMETHING NOW POPULAR WITH DIFFERENT AUDIENCE** an artist, musician, artistic creation, or piece of music that has become popular outside one original category **4. WIDENING OF POPULARITY** the process by which an artistic work becomes popular outside the category in which it originated **5.** POL **SOMEBODY VOTING AGAINST OWN PARTY** a supporter of one political party who votes for a candidate of another party, especially in a primary election **6.** GENETICS same as **crossing over** ■ *adj* **VOTING FOR OTHER PARTY** describes a voter who crosses party lines to vote for another party's candidate

cross-par·ty *adj* involving two or more political parties

cross·patch /kráwss pàch/ *n* somebody who is considered to be bad-tempered and touchy (*dated informal*) [Late 17C. < CROSS "annoyed" + PATCH "fool"]

cross·piece /kráwss peess/ *n* a piece that crosses a structure or implement from one side to the other, e.g., a beam in a building or part of the handle of a tool

cross-plat·form *adj* available for more than one type of computer or operating system

cross-pol·li·na·tion *n* the transfer of pollen from an anther of one flower to the stigma of another —**cross-pol·li·nate** *vti*

cross-post *vti* to post a single electronic message or article simultaneously to multiple newsgroups, an action generally considered a serious breach of netiquette

cross prod·uct *n* MATH same as **vector product**

cross-pur·pose *n* a conflicting or contrary purpose ◇ **at cross-purposes** not understanding each other, usually through not realizing that the other person means or intends something different ○ *The PTO and the school board have been working at cross-purposes.*

cross-ques·tion *vt* LAW same as **cross-examine** (sense 1) ■ *n* a lawyer's question to a witness being cross-examined in a court case —**cross-ques·tion·ing** *n*

cross-re·ac·tion *n* the immunological reaction of one antigen with the antibodies developed against another similar antigen —**cross-re·act** *vi* —**cross-re·ac·tive** *adj* —**cross-re·ac·tiv·i·ty** *n*

cross-re·fer *vti* to give a note that tells a reader of a book, index, or library catalog to look in another specified part or on another page of the same work

cross-ref·er·ence *n* a note, especially one printed in a book, index, or library catalog, that tells a reader to look in another specified place for information ■ *v* **1.** *vt* to provide a text, index, or library catalog with cross-references **2.** *vti* INFO SCI same as **cross-refer**

cross-re·sis·tance *n* resistance developed by an organism to the effects of a toxin as a result of being exposed to a similar toxin

cross·road /kráwss rṑd/ *n* a road that runs across another one or that links two main roads

cross·roads /kráwss rṑdz/ (*plural same*) *n* **1. INTERSECTION** a place where two or more roads meet or cross each other, especially in a rural or quiet area **2. RURAL COMMUNITY** a small town or community located at a crossroads (*takes a singular verb*) **3. MEETING PLACE** a central meeting place that has a lot of activity (*takes a singular verb*) **4. DECISIVE MOMENT** a time when an important decision must be made

cross·ruff /kráwss rùf/ *n* in whist and bridge, a tactic in which two partners alternately trump each other's first card (**lead**) in each round ■ *vti* (**-ruffed, -ruff·ing, -ruffs**) in whist or bridge, to play a crossruff, or trump a card in a crossruff [Late 16C. < CROSS- + RUFF²]

cross sec·tion, cross-sec·tion *n* **1. PLANE CUTTING THROUGH OBJECT** a plane surface formed by cutting through an object at right angles to an axis, especially the longest axis **2. SOMETHING CUT IN CROSS SECTION** a piece cut as part of a cross section, or an image of such a piece ○ *draw a cross section of a cone* **3. REPRESENTATIVE SAMPLE** a sample of something that represents all or most of the different parts that the whole contains ○ *polled a cross section of the residents* **4.** PHYS **PROBABILITY OF PARTICLE INTERACTION** a measure of the probability of an interaction such as fission or ionization occurring between two elementary particles —**cross-sec·tion·al** *adj*

cross-stitch *n* **1. EMBROIDERY STITCH** a stitch made up of two diagonal stitches crossing each other **2. EMBROIDERY IN CROSS-SHAPED STITCHES** pictures, designs, or items of needlework sewn using cross-stitches ■ *vti* **SEW USING CROSS-STITCH** to embroider using cross-stitches, or make something in cross-stitch

cross·talk /kráwss tàwk/ *n* **1.** unwanted sounds or other signals picked up by one channel of an electronic communications system from another channel, e.g., between telephones or loudspeakers **2.** talking that is not part of the main conversation and may distract from it

cross·tie /kráwss tī/ *n* **1.** a transverse supporting part of a structure, e.g., a beam or rod **2.** RAIL same as **tie** *n* (sense 5)

cross·town /kráwss tòwn/, **cross-town** *adj* **1.** traveling or extending across a city or town ○ *a crosstown bus* **2.** situated in or relating to the other side of a town ○ *playing their crosstown rivals* —**cross·town** *adv*

cross-train *v* **1.** *vi* to train for more than one competitive sport at a time **2.** *vti* to learn one or more tasks or skills at a time, or teach somebody one or more skills

cross·train·er /kráwss tràynər/ *n* **1. ATHLETIC SHOE** an athletic shoe designed for more than one sporting activity **2. SOMEBODY TRAINING FOR DIFFERENT SPORTS** an athlete who trains for more than one competitive sport at a time **3. EXERCISING MACHINE** an exercise machine intended to help develop many different groups of muscles

cross train·ing *n* fitness training in different sports, e.g., running and weightlifting, usually undertaken to enhance performance in one of the sports

cross-train·ing *adj* designed to be used for more than one kind of sporting activity ○ *a cross-training bike*

cross·tree /kráwss tree/ *n* either of a pair of horizontal pieces of wood or metal on a ship's mast to which ropes or wires are fixed to support the mast

cross vault, cross vault·ing *n* a ceiling created by the crossing of two or more simple arched vaults (**barrel vaults**)

cross vine *n* PLANTS same as **bignonia**

cross·walk /kráwss wàwk/ *n* a place marked on a street where pedestrians can cross the street safely

cross·way /kráwss wày/ *n* ROADS same as **crossroad**

cross·ways /kráwss wàyz/ *adv* **1.** same as **crosswise 2.** from one side or corner to another, in a slanting line

cross·wind /kráwss wìnd/ *n* a wind that blows across a route, flight path, or direction of travel

cross·wise /kráwss wīz/ *adv* in such a way as to cross something or be positioned across it ■ *adj* crossing or lying across something else

cross·word /kráwss wùrd/, **cross·word puz·zle** *n* a puzzle in which numbered clues are solved and words that form the answers entered horizontally or vertically into a correspondingly numbered grid of squares

cros·ti·ni /kro steenee/ *npl* small canapés made from toasted bread with a topping such as olive paste or mushrooms [< Italian, "little crusts"]

crotch /kroch/ *n* **1. PLACE WHERE LEGS JOIN BODY** the part of the human body where the legs join the trunk **2. PART OF GARMENT COVERING GENITALS** the area of a pair of pants or underpants that covers the wearer's genitals **3. PLACE WHERE TREE DIVIDES** a part of a tree where it forks into two branches **4. FORK IN STICK** a fork in a pole or stick [Mid-16C. Probably variant of CRUTCH] —**crotched** *adj*

crotch·et /króchət/ *n* **1.** a whim, or a perverse idea or opinion **2.** *UK* MUSIC same as **quarter note** [14C. < Old French *crochet* (see CROCHET)]

crotch·et·y /króchətee/ *adj* irritable and difficult to please (*informal*) —**crotch·et·i·ness** *n*

cro·ton /krṓt'n/ (*plural same* or **-tons**) *n* **1.** a bush or tree of the spurge family, some types of which are noted for their medicinal properties. Native to: tropics. Genus: *Croton.* **2.** an evergreen plant grown for its leathery variegated foliage. Native to: tropics. Latin name: *Codiaeum variegatum.* [Mid-18C. Via modern Latin < Greek *krotōn* "sheep-tick"; from the shape of its seeds (sense 1)]

Cro·ton bug /krṓt'n-/ *n* INSECTS same as **German cockroach** [Mid-19C. After the *Croton* River, New York, which supplied water for New York City]

cro·ton·ic ac·id /krō tónnik-/ *n* a colorless crystalline organic acid. Use: organic synthesis, manufacture of drugs and resins. Formula: $C_4H_6O_2$. [< CROTON]

cro·ton oil *n* a yellowish brown oil extracted from the seeds of a croton tree. Use: formerly, purgative, counterirritant.

crouch /krowch/ *vi* (**crouched, crouch·ing, crouch·es**) **1. BEND DOWN LOW** to squat down on the balls of the feet with knees bent and body hunched over ○ *I had to crouch to get under the table.* **2. BEND IN PREPARATION TO POUNCE** to stay down close to the ground with legs bent, waiting to spring or run forward (*refers to animals*) ■ *n* **CROUCHING POSITION** the position of a human squatting with back and knees bent or of an animal with the body pressed low to the ground in readiness to spring [14C. Probably < variant of Old French *crochir* "be crooked" < *croche* (see CROCHET)]

croup¹ /kroop/ *n* an inflammatory condition of the larynx and trachea, especially in young children, marked by a cough, hoarseness, and difficulty in breathing [Mid-18C. < *croup* "to croak," probably an imitation of the sound] —**croup·ous** *adj* —**croup·y** *adj*

croup² /kroop/, **croupe** *n* the hindquarters of a four-legged animal, especially a horse [13C. < French *croupe*]

crou·pi·er /kro͝opee ər, -ee ày/ *n* somebody in charge of a gaming table who collects and pays out the players' money and chips, and deals the cards or spins the roulette wheel [Mid-18C. < French, "person who rides behind" < *croupe* "rump"]

crous·tade /kroo staad/ *n* an edible casing for a tasty filling [Mid-19C. < French < Latin *crusta* "rind"]

crou·ton /kro͞o tòn/ *n* a small piece, usually a cube, of fried bread used as a garnish for soups, salads, and other dishes (*usually used in the plural*) [Early 19C. < French *croûton*, "little crust" < *croûte* "crust" < Latin *crusta* "rind, shell"]

crow¹ /krō/ *n* a large bird with shiny black feathers and a raucous cry, of a family whose members include rooks and ravens. Native to: found worldwide. Genus: *Corvus.* [Old English *crāwe* < Germanic] ◇ **as the crow flies** in a straight line ◇ **eat crow** to be forced to admit that you have been wrong or have been humiliatingly defeated (*informal*)

crow² /krō/ *vi* (**crowed, crow·ing, crows**) **1. CRY LIKE ROOSTER** to give the loud shrill cry of a rooster **2. CRY OUT HAPPILY** to cry out with pleasure in the way that babies do **3. BRAG ABOUT SOMETHING** to boast about personal success or celebrate about something another person has failed to do in a noisy and exuberant way ■ *n* **ROOSTER'S LOUD CRY** a long shrill call made by a bird, especially a rooster [Old English *crāwan* < Germanic]

Crow /krō/ (*plural same* or **Crows**) *n* **1.** a member of a Native North American people who once lived on the plains of North Dakota and who now live in southern Montana and Wyoming **2.** the Siouan language of the Crow people. Native speakers: 5,000. [Early 19C. Translation of French *(gens de) corbeaux* "raven people," translation of a Native American name] —**Crow** *adj*

crow·bar /krṓ baar/ *n* an iron or steel bar with one flattened end, often also bent or forked. Use: as a lever for raising or moving things. [Mid-18C. Because the flattened end resembles a crow's foot] —**crow·bar** *vt*

crow·ber·ry /krṓ bèrree/ (*plural* **-ries**) *n* **1.** a low-growing evergreen bush with edible black berries. Native to: colder regions. Latin name: *Empetrum nigrum.* **2.** the flavorless edible berry of the crowberry bush

crowd[1] /krowd/ *n* **1.** PEOPLE GATHERED TOGETHER a large group of people gathered in one place **2.** AUDIENCE OR SPECTATORS a group of people attending the same public event or entertainment ○ *performing in front of a sellout crowd* **3.** SET OF PEOPLE a group of people with something in common **4.** MASSES the mass or majority of people **5.** LARGE GROUP OF THINGS a large number of things put or found together ■ *v* (**crowd·ed, crowd·ing, crowds**) **1.** *vi* THRONG TOGETHER to assemble or move in large numbers **2.** *vti* HERD OR CRAM to urge, herd, or force a closely packed group of people, animals, or things into a place, or move into a place in a closely packed group **3.** *vti* ADVANCE BY SHOVING to move forward by pushing and shoving, or shove past a person or barrier **4.** *vt* FILL OR PACK SOMETHING to fill or cover something or a place in large numbers or to capacity **5.** *vti* PRESS NEAR SOMEBODY to stand or move uncomfortably close to somebody or something **6.** *vt* PRESSURE SOMEBODY to put pressure on somebody to do something, or make somebody feel forced into an act [Old English *crūdan* "to press" < W Germanic] —**crowd·ed** *adj* —**crowd·ed·ness** *n* —**crowd·er** *n*
crowd out *vt* to exclude or push out somebody or something by force of numbers

crowd[2] /krowd/ *n* an ancient Celtic stringed instrument that was bowed or plucked [14C. < Welsh *crwth*]

crowd pleas·er *n* a person, object, event, or occasion that has great popular appeal (*informal*) —**crowd-pleas·ing** *adj*

crow·foot /krṓ fòot/ *n* **1.** PLANT WITH LEAVES LIKE CROW'S FOOT a plant related to the buttercup that has divided leaves resembling the feet of a crow. Flowers: small, yellow or white. Genus: *Ranunculus.* **2.** PLANT LIKE CROWFOOT a plant that has leaves resembling a bird's foot **3.** (*plural* **crow·feet** /-feet/) NAUT ROPES SUPPORTING AWNING a set of ropes to support an awning on a boat

crown /krown/ *n* **1.** HEADDRESS SYMBOLIZING ROYALTY an ornate headdress worn as a symbol of sovereignty, often made of gold and set with gems **2.** SYMBOL OF ACHIEVEMENT a wreath or circlet worn on the head as a symbol of victory, success, or high achievement **3.** TOP-RANKING TITLE a title or distinction that signifies victory or supreme achievement **4.** UPPERMOST PART the top part of something, especially a hill **5.** PINNACLE the highest point of quality, achievement, or fame **6.** ANAT TOP OF HEAD the top part of the head **7.** CLOTHING TOP OF HAT the top part of a hat **8.** BIRDS TOP OF BIRD'S HEAD the top part of the head of a bird **9.** DENT VISIBLE PART OF TOOTH the visible part of a tooth, covered by enamel **10.** DENT ARTIFICIAL TOOTH an artificial replacement for the visible part of a tooth that has decayed or been damaged **11.** BOT UPPER PART OF PLANT the upper part of a tree or bush, consisting of the foliage and branches **12.** BOT ROOTS AND LOWER STEM OF PLANT the roots and lower stem of a plant, or a plant consisting only of these parts, used especially for propagation **13.** BOT same as **corona** (sense 3) **14.** *also* **Crown** POL MONARCH the reigning monarch of a country **15.** *also* **Crown** POL MONARCH'S POWER the power or authority vested in a monarch **16.** COINS EUROPEAN COIN a European coin whose name is translated as "crown," e.g., the Norwegian and Danish krone or the Swedish krona **17.** HIST, COINS BRITISH COIN a former British coin worth five shillings **18.** TOP OF GEMSTONE the upper part of a cut gemstone **19.** NAUT JUNCTION OF ANCHOR ARMS AND SHANK the junction where the arms of an anchor join the shank ■ *v* (**crowned, crown·ing, crowns**) **1.** *vt* CONFER ROYAL STATUS ON SOMEBODY to make a person a monarch, or place a crown on a person's head to symbolize monarchy **2.** *vt* REWARD SOMEBODY WITH CROWN to place a crown on somebody's head, especially in recognition of a victory, success, or achievement **3.** *vt* RANK SOMEBODY HIGHEST to confer the top rank on somebody ○ *crowned him champion* **4.** *vt* BE SUMMIT OF SOMETHING to be or form the top of something **5.** *vt* PUT FINISHING TOUCH TO SOMETHING to complete or be the consummation or confirmation of something **6.** *vt* DENT FIT CROWN TO TOOTH to fit an artificial crown to a damaged or decayed tooth **7.** *vt* BOARD GAMES MAKE CHECKER KING to promote an ordinary checkers piece to the status of king **8.** *vt* TOP SOMETHING WITH SOMETHING ELSE to put something on or at the top of something else **9.** *vt* HIT SOMEBODY ON HEAD to hit somebody over the head (*informal*) **10.** *vi* BECOME VISIBLE DURING CHILDBIRTH to progress during childbirth through the birth canal to the point where part of the head is showing at the vaginal opening (*informal*) ○ *The baby is crowning.* [12C. Via Anglo-Norman *corune*, Old French *corone* < Latin *corona* "wreath, garland" < Greek *korōnē* "something curved" < *korōnis* "curved"]

Crown at·tor·ney *n Can* a lawyer who undertakes criminal prosecutions on behalf of a federal, provincial, or territorial government

Crown Col·o·ny *n* a British colony in which the Crown has a whole or partial governing power

Crown cor·po·ra·tion *n Can* in Canada, a commercial company owned by the government but independently managed

crowned head /krównd-/ *n* a reigning monarch

crown gall *n* a disease of fruit and roses that results in swellings on the roots or stems and is caused by the bacterium *Agrobacterium tumefaciens*

crown glass *n* **1.** high-quality glass with a low index of refraction. Use: lenses. **2.** a traditional window glass made by spinning a bubble of molten glass on the end of a rod until it forms a flat disk

crown·ing /krówning/ *adj* **1.** ULTIMATE IN ACHIEVEMENT representing supreme achievement or the ultimate moment in something **2.** FORMING SUMMIT forming a crown or summit ■ *n* **1.** POL INVESTITURE OF MONARCH the process or ceremony of making somebody a monarch **2.** MED STAGE IN LABOR the stage in giving birth at which an infant's head passes through the vaginal opening

crown·ing glo·ry *n* **1.** the most impressive feature or achievement of a particular person or thing **2.** somebody's hair (*humorous*)

crown jew·el *n* the most valuable part of something, or the most prized asset ■ **crown jew·els** *npl* the jewelry and regalia that a monarch wears on state occasions

crown land *n Can* public land, especially forests, that is owned and regulated by a Canadian federal or provincial government

crown lens *n* a lens made of crown glass, especially the converging component of an achromatic lens

crown-of-thorns (*plural same*) *n* **1.** MARINE BIOL SPINY STARFISH a spiny starfish that feeds on live coral. Native to: Pacific. Latin name: *Acanthaster planci.* **2.** PLANTS THORNY BUSH WITH SCARLET BRACTS a thorny spurge bush with scarlet bracts grown as a house plant or as a hedge in tropical regions. Native to: Madagascar. Latin name: *Euphorbia milii.* **3.** HEAVY BURDEN a painful or onerous burden (*literary*) [< the biblical accounts of the wreath of thorns placed on the head of Jesus Christ]

crown·piece /krówn peess/ *n* **1.** a bridle strap that fits over a horse's head behind the ears **2.** *UK* a part that fits over or forms the top of something

crown prince *n* the principal male heir in a monarchy

crown prin·cess *n* **1.** the principal female heir in a monarchy **2.** the wife of a crown prince

Crown pros·e·cu·tor *n Can* LAW same as **Crown attorney**

crown roast *n* a cut of meat consisting of two rib sections sewn together to form a circle

crown saw *n* a cylindrical saw with a row of teeth along one edge, designed for cutting round holes

crown vetch *n* a leguminous plant that is cultivated for garden borders and erosion control. Flowers: small, pink or white. Native to: Europe. Latin name: *Coronilla varia.*

crown wheel *n* a wheel in a clock or watch next to the winding knob, formed from two sets of teeth at right angles to each other

crow's feet *npl* a network of wrinkles radiating from the outer corner of the human eye [Because they resemble the footprints of crows]

crow's-foot *n* **1.** HANDICRAFT a sewing stitch with three points, used especially for finishing off a seam **2.** AVIAT a set of short ropes that redistributes the pull of a single rope, used in airships and ballooning **3.** MIL same as **caltrop** (sense 4) [< the shape]

crow's-nest *n* **1.** a lookout point consisting of a railed platform at the top of a ship's mast or superstructure **2.** a high enclosed lookout point on land

crow·step /krṓ stèp/ *n* ARCHIT same as **corbie-step** [Because only a small or perching animal could use it]

croze /krōz/ *n* **1.** a groove at the top of a barrel or cask into which the flat surface is fitted **2.** a cooper's tool used to cut grooves at the top of barrels and casks [Early 17C. < French *creux* "hollow, groove," probably < Celtic]

cro·zier *n* CHR, BOT another spelling of **crosier**

CRT[1] *n* a computer monitor containing a cathode-ray tube [< CRT[2]]

CRT[2] *abbr* ELECTRONICS cathode-ray tube

cru /kroo/ *n* **1.** a vineyard or wine-growing area in France that meets specific standards of quality **2.** an official grade of French wine [Early 19C. < French *crû*, past participle of *croître* "grow" < Latin *crescere*]

cru·ces plural of **crux**

cru·cial /króosh'l/ *adj* **1.** most vital and of the greatest significance in determining an outcome **2.** ⚠ very important or significant (*informal*) [Early 18C. < French < Latin *cruc-* "cross"] —**cru·cial·ly** *adv*

USAGE ***Crucial*** has the core meaning of decisive: *Her tie-breaking vote was crucial.* However, ***crucial*** has been trivialized to the point that it often means nothing more than "important." This is especially true in media reports in which a hard-hitting word is often more attractive to the reporter: *If proportional representation is adopted, it is crucial (= important) to choose the best method.* Avoid overusing ***crucial*** in formal college writing; it is better reserved for superlatives.

cru·ci·ate /króoshee àyt/ *adj* **1.** same as **cruciform** **2.** describes insect wings that form a cross shape when at rest [Late 17C. < medieval Latin *cruciata* < Latin *crux* "cross"]

cru·ci·ble /króossəb'l/ *n* **1.** METALL CONTAINER FOR MELTING SOMETHING a heat-resistant container in which ores or metals are melted **2.** METALL BOTTOM OF FURNACE the hollow part at the bottom of a furnace where molten metal collects **3.** TESTING CIRCUMSTANCES a place or set of circumstances where people or things are subjected to forces that test them and often make them change **4.** ORDEAL a severe trial or ordeal [15C. < medieval Latin *crucibulum* "nightlight, crucible"]

CULTURAL NOTE ***The Crucible***, a play (1953) by Arthur Miller. Intended as a metaphor for the "un-American" McCarthy hearings of the 1950s, the play is set in Salem, Massachusetts, in 1692 and describes how the social fabric of a small town is ripped apart when a group of young girls starts to denounce townsfolk as witches. It was made into a movie by Nicholas Hytner in 1996.

cru·ci·ble steel *n* a high-grade steel made by mixing steel and additives in a furnace

cru·ci·fer /króossəfər/ *n* **1.** a plant with long narrow seedpods, e.g., the cabbage, turnip, broccoli, or wallflower. Flowers: with four petals in the shape of a cross. Family: Cruciferae. **2.** somebody who bears a cross, especially in a Christian ceremony [Mid-16C. < ecclesiastical Latin < Latin *cruc-* "cross" + *-fer* "bearer"] —**cru·cif·er·ous** *adj*

~~**crucifiction**~~ incorrect spelling of **crucifixion**

cru·ci·fix /krŏŏssə fiks/ *n* a model or image of Jesus Christ on the cross [12C. Via French < ecclesiastical Latin *crucifixus* < Latin *cruci fixus* "fixed to a cross"]

cru·ci·fix·ion /krŏŏssə fíksh'n/ *n* **1. EXECUTION BY HANGING ON CROSS** a form of execution used in ancient times that involved binding or nailing the victim to an upright cross until death **2. EXECUTION** an execution involving crucifixion **3. ORDEAL** a painful ordeal or victimization

Cru·ci·fix·ion *n* **1.** the agony and death of Jesus Christ on the cross at Calvary **2.** a depiction of Jesus Christ on the cross

cru·ci·form /krŏŏssi fàwrm/ *adj* shaped like a cross [Mid-17C. < Latin *cruc-* "cross"]

cru·ci·fy /krŏŏssi fī/ (**-fied, -fy·ing, -fies**) *v* **1.** *vt* **EXECUTE SOMEBODY ON CROSS** to execute somebody by crucifixion **2.** *vt* **CRITICIZE SOMEBODY HARSHLY** to criticize somebody unsparingly **3.** *vt* **TREAT SOMEBODY CRUELLY** to defeat, torment, or victimize somebody in a thorough or cruel way **4. cru·ci·fy your·self** *vr* **SEVERELY DISCIPLINE YOUR BODY** to subject yourself to hard physical discipline [14C. Via French *crucifier* < ecclesiastical Latin *crucifigere* < Latin *cruci figere* "fix to a cross"] —**cru·ci·fi·er** *n*

crud /krud/ *n* **1. FILTH** a messy, dirty, or sticky substance (*slang*) **2. SOMEBODY OR SOMETHING CONTEMPTIBLE** a person or thing that is considered disgusting or worthless (*slang*) **3. NONSENSE** absolute nonsense (*slang*) **4.** INDUST **WASTE PRODUCT** an unwanted by-product, especially in the nuclear industry **5.** SKIING **SLUSHY SNOW** slushy snow that is unfit for good skiing (*informal*) [14C. Earlier form of CURD] —**crud·dy** *adj*

crude /krood/ *adj* (**crud·er, crud·est**) **1.** roughly or unskillfully made or conceived ○ *a crude model of a ship* **2. VULGAR** vulgar or obscene ○ *a crude gesture* **3. IN RAW STATE** in an unprocessed condition ○ *crude ore* **4. APPROXIMATE** not precisely accurate ○ *a crude estimate* **5. UNCORRECTED OR UNEMBELLISHED** describes numerical results or collected data that have not been organized, adjusted, or altered in any way ○ *crude data* ○ *crude facts* ■ *n* INDUST same as **crude oil** [14C. < Latin *crudus* "raw, rough"] —**crude·ly** *adv* —**crude·ness** *n* —**cru·di·ty** *n*

crude oil *n* petroleum that has not yet been refined

cru·di·tés /krŏŏdi táy/ *npl* small pieces of raw vegetables e.g., carrots and cucumbers, eaten as an appetizer or snack, often served with a dip [Mid-20C. < French, plural of *crudité* < Latin *cruditas* < *crudus* "raw"]

cru·el /krŏŏ əl/ *adj* **1.** deliberately and remorselessly causing pain or anguish **2.** bringing about pain and distress [12C. Via French < Latin *crudelis*] —**cru·el·ly** *adv* —**cru·el·ness** *n*

cru·el·ty /krŏŏ əltee/ (*plural* **-ties**) *n* **1. CONDITION OF BEING CRUEL** the quality or condition of being cruel **2. DELIBERATELY CRUEL ACT** an act that deliberately causes pain and distress **3.** LAW **PSYCHOLOGICAL OR PHYSICAL PAIN** the infliction of pain, distress, or anguish, especially when it is long-term and considered extreme enough to be grounds for divorce [13C. Via Old French *crualté* < Latin *crudelitas* < *crudelis* "cruel"]

cru·et /krŏŏ ət/ *n* **1.** a small container for holding a condiment such as oil or vinegar **2.** either of two containers that hold the water and wine used in the Christian Communion service [13C. < Anglo-Norman, "little flask" < Old French *crue* "flask" < Germanic]

cruise /krooz/ *v* (**cruised, cruis·ing, cruis·es**) **1.** *vti* **TRAVEL BY SEA** to travel by ship over a sea or other large body of water, usually calling at several places **2.** *vi* **TRAVEL AT EASY RATE** to travel at a steady efficient rate, below top speed **3.** *vi* **PROCEED CASUALLY** to proceed in a leisurely casual way or with no particular destination ○ *We've just been cruising around in the car.* **4.** *vi* **TRAVEL WHILE LOOKING FOR SOMETHING** to travel at a slow steady rate while searching or watching for something ○ *The police cruised the streets looking for the suspect.* **5.** *vi* **ACHIEVE OBJECTIVE IN SPORT** to progress or achieve a goal with very little effort, especially in sport ○ *cruised to the semifinals* **6.** *vti* **SEEK SEXUAL PARTNER** to go out looking for a sexual partner, or frequent a public place in search of one (*slang*) ■ *n* **TRIP BY SEA** a journey by ship for pleasure or for naval purposes [Mid-17C. < Dutch *kruisen* "to cross" < *kruis* "cross" < Latin *crux*]

Cruise /krooz/, **Tom** (*b.* 1962) US actor. He has starred in many Hollywood movies, including *Jerry Maguire* (1996). Born **Mapother IV, Thomas Cruise**

cruise con·trol *n* an electronic device in a motor vehicle that allows a selected speed to be maintained consistently

cruise lin·er *n* same as **cruise ship**

cruise mis·sile *n* a long-range jet-propelled guided missile that flies low

cruis·er /krŏŏzər/ *n* **1. SMALL WARSHIP** a fast and easily maneuverable warship that is smaller and less heavily armored than a battleship **2.** BOAT same as **cabin cruiser** **3. POLICE CAR** a police car, especially one used to patrol an area **4. SOMEBODY SEEKING SEXUAL PARTNER** somebody who seeks a sexual partner in a public place (*slang*) [Late 17C. < Dutch *kruiser* < *kruisen* (see CRUISE)]

cruis·er·weight /krŏŏzər wàyt/ *n* **1.** in professional boxing, a weight category for competitors whose weight does not exceed 190 lb./86 kg **2.** a professional boxer who competes at cruiserweight level

cruise ship *n* a large luxurious passenger ship equipped with many leisure facilities, used for going on cruises

cruise·wear /krŏŏz wèr/ *n* light casual clothing appropriate for pleasure cruises or hot weather while on vacation

cruis·ing ra·di·us *n* the maximum distance that a vessel or aircraft can travel without needing to refuel

crul·ler /krúllər/, **krul·ler** *n* **1.** a small ring-shaped deep-fried cake **2.** an unraised doughnut, usually twisted in shape [Early 19C. < Dutch *kruller* < *krullen* "to curl"]

REGIONAL NOTE In the sense of "deep-fried small cake," ***cruller*** belongs primarily to New England and the Middle Atlantic and North Central states, but is common also in California. The sense "unraised doughnut" is found most frequently in New England and Pennsylvania.

crumb /krum/ *n* **1. SMALL FRAGMENT OF BAKED FOOD** a very small fragment of bread, cake, cookie, or similar food **2. SMALL AMOUNT** a tiny amount of something **3. INNER PART OF LOAF** the soft middle part of a loaf of bread **4. CONTEMPTIBLE PERSON** somebody regarded as contemptible (*dated slang*) ■ *v* (**crumbed, crumb·ing, crumbs**) **1.** *vt* COOK **PUT CRUMBS ON OR IN FOOD** to coat or thicken food with crumbs, especially breadcrumbs **2.** *vti* COOK **CRUMBLE** to break bread, cake, or cookies into small bits, or be broken in this way **3.** *vt* **CLEAN CRUMBS FROM SOMETHING** to clear away crumbs from something [Old English *cruma* < Germanic]

crum·ble /krúmb'l/ *v* (**-bled, -bling, -bles**) **1.** *vti* to break up into tiny bits, or make something break into tiny bits **2.** *vi* to disintegrate or fall apart ■ *n UK* FOOD same as **crisp** *n* (sense 1) [15C. Probably < Old English *gecrymmian* "break into crumbs" < *cruma* (see CRUMB)]

crum·bly /krúmblee/ (**-bli·er, -bli·est**) *adj* **1.** tending to crumble readily **2.** containing or covered with many crumbs —**crum·bli·ness** *n*

crumb·y /krúmmee/ (**-i·er, -i·est**) *adj* **1.** full of or covered with crumbs **2.** soft and spongy in texture, like the inside of a loaf of bread **3.** same as **crummy** (*informal*)

crum·horn /krúm hàwrn/, **krumm·horn** *n* a medieval double-reed woodwind instrument with an upward-curving tube [Late 17C. < German *Krummhorn* "crooked horn"]

crum·my /krúmmee/ (**-mi·er, -mi·est**) *adj* (*informal*) **1.** inferior or of little worth ○ *a crummy hotel* **2.** miserable or unwell ○ *had a headache and felt crummy* [Mid-19C. Variant of CRUMBY]

crump /krump/ *n* **SOUND OF BURSTING BOMB** the thudding sound of an exploding shell or bomb ■ *vi* (**crumped, crump·ing, crumps**) **1. MAKE THUDDING NOISE** to make a thudding noise like the sound of an exploding shell or bomb **2. MAKE CRUNCHING NOISE** to make a crunching noise like the sound of footsteps in crisp snow [Mid-17C. An imitation of the sound]

crum·pet /krúmpət/ *n* a solid cake with a slightly elastic texture and small holes that is eaten toasted with butter [Late 17C. Origin ?]

crum·ple /krúmp'l/ *v* (**-pled, -pling, -ples**) **1.** *vti* **CREASE AND WRINKLE** to become full of irregular creases and wrinkles, or make something full of creases **2.** *vti* **COLLAPSE** to collapse, or make something collapse **3.** *vi* **LOOK UPSET OR DISAPPOINTED** to lose the appearance of equanimity and control, especially when upset or disappointed and close to tears ■ *n* **WRINKLE** a crease or wrinkle in something [14C. < Old English *crump* "crooked, curled up"] —**crum·ply** *adj*

crunch /krunch/ *v* (**crunched, crunch·ing, crunch·es**) **1.** *vt* **MUNCH FOOD NOISILY** to crush crisp foods audibly with the teeth **2.** *vti* **SCRUNCH** to make a noisy scrunching sound, or cause something to make such a sound **3.** *vt* COMPUT **RAPIDLY PROCESS DATA** to process data or numbers at high speed (*informal*) ■ *n* **1. SCRUNCHING NOISE** a loud short sound made when something is crushed ○ *the crunch of footsteps on gravel* **2. DECISIVE MOMENT** a critical time or situation, especially one when a decision or action must be taken ○ *when it comes to the crunch* **3. CRISIS** an emergency or crisis, especially one caused by a shortage of money or other resources **4.** FITNESS **SIT-UP EXERCISE** a form of sit-up in which the body is only partially raised, intended to strengthen the abdominal muscles ■ *adj* **NEEDING DECISIVE ACTION** requiring a decision or action [Early 19C. An imitation of the sound] —**crunch·a·ble** *adj* —**crunch·er** *n*

crunch·y /krúnchee/ (**-i·er, -i·est**) *adj* crisp and making a crunching sound when eaten or walked upon —**crunch·i·ly** *adv* —**crunch·i·ness** *n*

crup·per /krúppər/ *n* **1.** a strap that passes under the tail of a horse and is attached to a saddle or harness to prevent it from sliding forward **2.** the hindquarters of a horse [14C. < Anglo-Norman *cropere*, Old French *cropiere*]

crus /krooss, kruss/ (*plural* **cru·ra** /krŏŏrə/) *n* **1.** the leg between the knee and ankle **2.** a body part shaped like a leg or pair of legs [Late 16C. < Latin, "leg"] —**cru·ral** /krŏŏrəl/ *adj*

cru·sade /kroo sáyd/ *n* **1. CONCERTED EFFORT** a vigorous concerted action to promote or eliminate something **2. RELIGIOUSLY MOTIVATED EFFORT** a war or campaign that is religiously motivated, e.g., one with papal sanction **3.** *also* **Cru·sade RELIGIOUS WAR** in the 11th, 12th, and 13th centuries, a military expedition by European Christians to retake areas in the Holy Land captured by Muslim forces ■ *vi* (**-sad·ed, -sad·ing, -sades**) **1. CAMPAIGN VIGOROUSLY** to make a vigorous or concerted effort to promote or eliminate something **2. FIGHT FOR RELIGION** to fight in a religious crusade [15C. < medieval Latin *cruciata* < Latin *crux* "cross"]

cru·sad·er /kroo sáydər/ *n* **1.** a vigorous campaigner for or against something **2.** *also* **Cru·sad·er** a soldier who took part in any of the crusades to the Holy Land

cru·sa·do /kroo zaádō, -saádō, -sáydō/ (*plural* **-does** or **-dos**) *n* a gold or silver coin with a cross imprinted on it that was a unit of currency in Portugal between the 15th and 20th centuries [Mid-16C. < Portuguese *cruzado* (see CRUZADO)]

crush /krush/ *v* (**crushed, crush·ing, crush·es**) **1.** *vti* **COMPRESS** to compress somebody or something, causing injury, damage, or distortion, or become compressed in this way **2.** *vti* **CREASE** to crease a fabric or item of clothing, or become creased **3.** *vti* **GRIND** to grind something into small pieces, or be ground in this way **4.** *vt* **QUELL PROTEST** to put down a protest or movement using force **5.** *vt* **OVERWHELM SOMEBODY OR SOMETHING** to defeat, subdue, or suppress somebody or something overwhelmingly **6.** *vt* **MASH FRUIT** to reduce fruit or vegetables to juice and pulp by pressing **7.** *vt* **PHYSICALLY PRESS SOMEBODY HARD** to exert physical pressure on somebody by hugging, pressing, or pushing **8.** *vt* **HUMILIATE SOMEBODY** to humiliate somebody by the force of a remark, criticism, or argument **9.** *vi* **CROWD TOGETHER** to move in a mass or crowd ■ *n* **1. CROWD OF PEOPLE** a crowd or mass, especially of people **2. CROWDED SITUATION** a crowded situation, or an action that results in this **3.** BEVERAGES **FRUIT DRINK** a drink containing the juice from crushed fruit **4. SHORT-LIVED LOVE** a temporary romantic attraction, especially in teenagers and young people (*informal*) 5. **OBJECT OF SOMEBODY'S TEMPORARY ROMANTIC ATTRACTION** the person who is the object of somebody's temporary romantic infatuation (*informal*) [14C. < Anglo-Norman *crussier*, Old French *croissir*] —**crush·a·ble** *adj* —**crush·er** *n* —**crush·ing** *adj* —**crush·ing·ly** *adv*

SYNONYMS See *love*.

crushed /krusht/ *adj* **1.** extremely upset, saddened, or depressed ○ *was totally crushed upon hearing the news of the accident* **2.** describes a fabric or material that has been manufactured or treated to create permanent creases in it ○ *crushed velvet*

crush·proof /krúsh proòf/ *adj* made to resist being crushed, creased, or wrinkled

crust /krust/ *n* **1. OUTER PART OF BREAD** the thin, usually hard or crisp outer part of a loaf or slice of bread **2. PIECE OF BREAD** a piece of bread that is mostly crust or is stale and dry **3. PASTRY FOR PIE** the pastry that wholly or partly encases a pie or tart **4. HARD UPPER LAYER** a crisp, hard, or thick outer layer or coating that develops on something **5.** GEOL **SOLID OUTER LAYER OF EARTH** the thin outermost layer of Earth, approximately one percent of Earth's volume, that varies in thickness and has a different composition from the interior. Other terrestrial planets are believed to have crusts. **6.** MED **SCAB** a dry hardened outer layer of blood, pus, or other bodily secretion that forms over a cut or sore **7.** WINE **LAYER OF POTASSIUM TARTRATE** a thin layer of potassium tartrate that forms on the inside of some wine and port bottles as the contents mature **8.** BIOL **BODY COVERING** the hard outermost body covering in some living organisms such as lichens and crustaceans ■ *v* (**crust·ed, crust·ing, crusts**) **1.** *vi* **DEVELOP AS CRUST** to form into a crust **2.** *vti* **MAKE OR BECOME ENCRUSTED** to cover something with a crust or become covered with a crust [14C. Via Old French *crouste* < Latin *crusta* "rind, shell"]

crus·ta·cean /kru stáysh'n/ *n* an invertebrate animal with several pairs of jointed legs, a hard protective outer shell, two pairs of antennae, and eyes at the ends of stalks. Lobsters, crabs, shrimp, crayfish, water fleas, barnacles, and wood lice are crustaceans. Subphylum: Crustacea. [Mid-19C. < modern Latin *Crustacea* (plural) "(things) having a shell" < Latin *crusta* "shell"] —**crus·ta·cean** *adj* —**crus·ta·ceous** *adj*

crust·al /krúst'l/ *adj* describes the crust of Earth or another astronomical object [Mid-19C. < Latin *crusta* "shell"]

crus·tose /krúss tōss/ *adj* describes lichens or algae that resemble a crust on the surface they adhere to [Late 19C. < Latin *crustosus* < *crusta* "shell"]

crust·y /krústee/ (**-i·er, -i·est**) *adj* **1.** having a crisp crust ○ *crusty bread* **2.** gruff, curt, and candid in speech —**crust·i·ly** *adv* —**crust·i·ness** *n*

crutch /kruch/ *n* **1. SOMETHING PROVIDING HELP OR SUPPORT** something that sustains or supports somebody or something that is otherwise liable to collapse, fail, or falter **2.** MED **WALKING AID** a staff with a handgrip and a rest for the forearm or armpit, used to help a person who is unable to walk unassisted **3.** ANAT same as **crotch** (sense 1) **4.** NAUT **FORKED SUPPORT** a forked supporting piece for a boom, oar, or spar **5.** RIDING **LEG REST ON SIDESADDLE** a forked leg support on a sidesaddle ■ *vt* (**crutched, crutch·ing, crutch·es**) **HOLD SOMETHING UP WITH CRUTCH** to support something with a crutch or similar object [Old English *cryc(c)* < Germanic]

crux /kruks/ (*plural* **crux·es** or **cru·ces** /kroò seez/) *n* **1. CRUCIAL POINT** an essential or deciding point or element in something, e.g., in an argument **2. PUZZLING PROBLEM** an extremely difficult or puzzling problem **3.** CLIMBING **ARDUOUS PART OF CLIMB** the most demanding part of a climb up a mountain or rocks [Mid-17C. < Latin, "cross"]

Crux *n* ASTRON same as **Southern Cross**. see illustration at **constellation**

crux an·sa·ta /krùks an sáytə, -saátə/ (*plural* **cru·ces an·sa·tae** /kroò seez an sáytee, -saátee/) *n* ANCIENT HIST same as **ankh** [< Latin, "cross with a handle"]

Celia Cruz

Cruz /krooz/, **Celia** (1924–2003) Cuban-born US vocalist. She was one of the leading singers of the popular Latin dance music called salsa. Known as **the Queen of Salsa**

cru·za·do /kroo zaádō/ (*plural* **-does** or **-dos**) *n* **1.** a unit of currency used in Brazil between 1986 and 1990, equivalent to 100 centavos **2.** a coin or bill worth one cruzado **3.** MONEY another spelling of **crusado** [Mid-16C. < Portuguese < past participle of *cruzar* "mark with a cross" < Latin *crux* "cross"]

Cru·zan /kroo zán, kroò zàn/ *n Carib* somebody who comes from St. Croix in the US Virgin Islands [Mid-20C. < assumed American Spanish *cruzano* < Spanish *Santa Cruz* "St. Croix"]

Crven·kov·ski /kùrv'n kóvskee/, **Branko** (*b.* 1962) prime minister of the Former Yugoslav Republic of Macedonia. He was elected as Macedonia's first prime minister in 1992, lost office in 1998, and was reelected in 2002.

cry /krī/ *v* (**cried, cry·ing, cries**) **1.** *vti* **SHED TEARS** to shed tears as the result of a strongly felt emotion **2.** *vti* **SHOUT** to call or shout out loudly **3.** *vi* ZOOL **MAKE DISTINCTIVE SOUND** to make a natural high-pitched characteristic call (*refers to birds or animals*) **4.** *vt* **GIVE SOMETHING AS REASON** to plead or profess something as a reason or explanation ○ *cry hardship* **5.** *vt* **ANNOUNCE FOR SALE** to proclaim something publicly as being for sale (*archaic*) ■ *n* (*plural* **cries**) **1. INARTICULATE SOUND** a loud inarticulate expression of rage, pain, or surprise **2. CALL OF BIRD OR ANIMAL** the natural high-pitched characteristic call of a bird or animal **3. PERIOD OF WEEPING** an act or period of shedding tears **4. PUBLIC DEMAND** a public demand, especially an urgent one **5.** HUNTING **BAYING OF HOUNDS** the sound of hounds baying as they chase their quarry **6.** HUNTING **HOUNDS** a pack of hounds **7. UNIFYING CALL** a call to rally or unite **8. PROCLAMATION** an announcement or advertisement called out in public (*archaic*) [13C. Via French *crier* < Latin *quiritare* "raise a public outcry" < *Quirites* "Roman citizens"] ◇ **for crying out loud!** used to express annoyance, impatience, frustration, or surprise (*informal*) ◇ **in full cry** in enthusiastic pursuit of something

CULTURAL NOTE ***Cry, the Beloved Country,*** a novel (1948) by South African writer Alan Paton. It tells of a Black man's search for his sister and his son in Johannesburg, where he encounters the underside of life and the racial hatred that divides the country. His sister has become a prostitute and his son is condemned to death for the murder of a white farmer's son. The novel ends on a note of optimism on the issue of racial harmony, as the two fathers are reconciled.

cry down *vt* to say disparaging or belittling things about somebody or something

cry off *vi* to withdraw from an arrangement or activity previously agreed to (*informal*)

cry out *v* **1.** *vti* to exclaim something loudly because of pain, shock, or fear **2.** *vi* to be in obvious and urgent need

cry up *vt* to praise somebody or something highly

cry·ba·by /krī bàybee/ (*plural* **-bies**) *n* an offensive term for somebody, especially a child, who cries or complains a lot (*insult*)

cry·ing /krī ing/ *adj* desperate or deplorable and demanding a remedy ○ *a crying shame*

cryo- *prefix* freezing, cold ○ *cryosurgery* [< Greek *kruos* "icy cold" < Indo-European, "freeze over"]

cry·o·bank /krī ə bàngk/ *n* a place where biological material such as semen and body tissue can be stored at extremely low temperatures

cry·o·bi·ol·o·gy /krì ō bī óllajee/ *n* the branch of biology that studies how extremely low temperatures affect organisms —**cry·o·bi·o·log·i·cal** /-bī ə lójjik'l/ *adj* —**cry·o·bi·o·log·i·cal·ly** *adv* —**cry·o·bi·ol·o·gist** *n*

cry·o·gen /krī ə jèn/ *n* a substance such as liquid nitrogen used in producing extremely low temperatures

cry·o·gen·ic /krì ə jénnik/ *adj* relating to extremely low temperatures —**cry·o·gen·i·cal·ly** *adv*

cry·o·gen·ics /krì ə jénniks/ *n* the branch of physics that studies the causes and effects of extremely low temperatures (*takes a singular verb*)

cry·o·lite /krī ə līt/ *n* an uncommon white fluoride mineral containing sodium and aluminum. Use: source of aluminum. [Early 19C. < CRYO-; because first found in Greenland]

cry·om·e·ter /krī ómmətər/ *n* a thermometer that measures very low temperatures —**cry·om·e·try** *n*

cry·on·ics /krī ónniks/ *n* the study or practice of keeping a newly dead body at an extremely low temperature in the hope of restoring it to life later with the help of future medical advances (*takes a singular verb*) ■ *npl* the collective techniques involved in cryogenics (*takes a plural verb*) [Mid-20C. Contraction of CRYOGENICS] —**cry·on·ic** *adj*

cry·o·phil·ic /krì ə fíllik/ *adj* capable of living at low temperatures

cry·o·phyte /krī ə fīt/ *n* an organism that can live or grow on snow or ice, e.g., an alga

cry·o·pre·cip·i·tate /krì ō pri síppə tàyt, -tət/ *n* a substance that is precipitated at low temperatures, especially a precipitate of blood containing a blood-clotting factor

cry·o·pres·er·va·tion /krì ō prezər váysh'n/ *n* the process of storing semen, ova, corneas, embryos, or body tissue at extremely low temperatures for future use —**cry·o·pre·serve** /krì ō pri zúrv/ *vt*

cry·o·probe /krī ə prōb/ *n* an instrument used in cryosurgery for cooling body tissue to low temperatures

cry·o·pro·tec·tant /krì ō prə téktənt/ *n* a substance such as glycerol used to protect stored living tissue from the effects of freezing

cry·o·scope /krī ə skōp/ *n* an instrument used for determining the temperature at which a liquid freezes

cry·os·co·py /krī óskəpee/ *n* the study or practice of determining the freezing point of liquids —**cry·o·scop·ic** /krì ə skóppik/ *adj*

cry·o·stat /krī ə stàt/ *n* a regulating device for maintaining a constant low temperature

cry·o·sur·ger·y /krì ō súrjəree/ *n* surgery in which low temperatures are applied, e.g., to destroy diseased tissue or to seal down detached retinas —**cry·o·sur·geon** *n* —**cry·o·sur·gi·cal** *adj*

cry·o·ther·a·py /krì ō thérrəpee/ (*plural* **-pies**) *n* medical treatment that involves cooling the body, especially by applying ice packs

crypt /kript/ *n* **1.** an underground room or vault, often below a church, used as a burial chamber or chapel, or for storing religious artifacts **2.** a small recess, tubular gland, or follicle in the body [Late 18C. Via Latin < Greek *kruptē* "vault," feminine of *kruptos* "hidden"]

crypt- *prefix* same as **crypto-** (*used before vowels*)

crypt·a·nal·y·sis /krìptə nálləssiss/ *n* **1.** the process or science of deciphering coded texts or messages **2.** the techniques and methods used in deciphering coded texts and messages, or the study of such methods —**crypt·an·a·lyst** /krip tánn'list/ *n* —**crypt·an·a·lyt·ic** /krìp tanə líttik/ *adj* —**crypt·an·a·lyt·i·cal** *adj*

cryp·tic /kríptik/ *adj* **1. AMBIGUOUS OR OBSCURE** deliberately mysterious and seeming to have a hidden meaning **2. SECRET** secret or hidden in some way **3. INDICATING SOLUTION INDIRECTLY** describes crossword puzzles, clues, or anagrams with an indirect solution **4. USING CODES** relating to or using codes or similar techniques **5.**

ZOOL PROTECTIVE describes body markings or coloring that camouflages an animal [Early 17C. Via late Latin < Greek *kruptikos* < *kruptē* (see CRYPT)] —**cryp·ti·cal·ly** *adv* —**cryp·tic·ness** *n*

SYNONYMS See ***obscure***.

cryp·tic cross·word *n* a crossword which uses obscure clues to indicate the solutions indirectly

crypto- *prefix* secret, hidden ○ *cryptogram* ○ *cryptanalysis* [< Greek *kruptos* < *kruptein* "to hide"]

cryp·to·clas·tic /krìptə klástik/ *adj* describes rock composed of microscopic mineral fragments

cryp·to·coc·co·sis /krìptō ko kóssiss/ *n* an infectious disease that affects parts of the body, especially the brain and central nervous system, with lesions or abscesses caused by the fungus *Cryptococcus neoformans* [Mid-20C. < CRYPTOCOCCUS]

cryp·to·coc·cus /krìptə kókəss/ (*plural* **-ci** /-kók sī, -kó kī/) *n* a fungus that resembles a yeast, some types of which cause illnesses such as cryptococcosis. Genus: *Cryptococcus*. [Early 20C. < modern Latin, "hidden coccus"]

cryp·to·crys·tal·line /krìptō krístə līn, -lin/ *adj* describes rocks that are composed of crystals too small to be seen with a petrological microscope

cryp·to·gam /kríptə gàm/ *n* an organism such as a fern, moss, alga, or fungus that reproduces by means of spores instead of seeds [Late 18C. Via French < modern Latin *cryptogamus* "hidden marriage"; because the means of reproduction is not apparent] —**cryp·to·gam·ic** /krìptə gámmik/ *adj* —**cryp·tog·a·mous** /krip tóggəməss/ *adj*

cryp·to·gen·ic /krìptə jénnik/ *adj* MED same as **idiopathic**

cryp·to·gram /kríptə gràm/ *n* **1.** a text or message that is in code or cipher **2.** a symbol with a secret meaning or significance

cryp·to·graph·ic /krìptə gráffik/ *adj* relating to or using cryptography —**cryp·to·graph·i·cal** /krìptə gráffik'l/ *adj* —**cryp·to·graph·i·cal·ly** /krìptə gráffiklee/ *adv*

cryp·to·graph·ic key *n* a parameter that determines the transformation of computer data to encrypted format, measured in bits (*used in e-commerce*)

cryp·tog·ra·phy /krip tóggrəfee/ *n* **1.** the study or analysis of codes and coding methods **2.** coded or secret writing —**cryp·to·graph** /kríptə gràf/ *n* —**cryp·tog·ra·pher** *n*

cryp·tol·o·gy /krip tólləjee/ *n* COMMUNICATION **1.** same as **cryptography** (sense 1) **2.** same as **cryptanalysis** —**cryp·to·log·ic** /krìptə lójjik/ *adj* —**cryp·to·log·i·cal** *adj* —**cryp·tol·o·gist** *n*

cryp·to·me·ri·a /krìptə méeree ə/ *n Can, UK* a tall coniferous tree with curved needle-shaped leaves arranged in spirals. Native to: China, Japan. Latin name: *Cryptomeria japonica*. US term **Japanese cedar** [Mid-19C. < modern Latin, "hidden part," because its seeds are hidden by scales]

crypt·or·chid /krip táwrkid/ *n* a man, boy, or male animal with one or both testicles that have failed to descend into the scrotum [Late 19C. < CRYPTORCHISM]

crypt·or·chism /krip táwr kìzzəm/, **crypt·or·chi·dism** /krip táwrki dìzzəm/ *n* a developmental condition affecting some men, boys, or male animals in which one or both testicles fail to descend into the scrotum [Late 19C. < CRYPTO- + Latin *orchis* "testicle" < Greek *orkhis*]

cryp·to·spor·i·di·o·sis /krìptō spawridee óssiss/ *n* an infectious condition of humans and domestic animals, characterized by fever, diarrhea, and stomach cramps, and spread by a protozoan of the genus *Cryptosporidium* [< CRYPTOSPORIDIUM]

cryp·to·spor·i·di·um /krìptō spə ríddee əm/ (*plural* **-di·a** /-dee ə/) *n* a water-borne protozoan parasite that contaminates drinking water supplies, causing intestinal infections in human beings and domestic animals [Late 20C. < modern Latin < Greek *kruptos* "hidden" + *sporidium* "little spore" < *spora* "seed"]

cryp·to·zo·ic /krìptə zó ik/ *adj* describes invertebrates that live in dark or concealed places such as under stones or in caves or holes

Cryp·to·zo·ic *adj* GEOL same as **Precambrian** —**Cryp·to·zo·ic** *n*

cryp·to·zo·ite /krìptə zó ìt/ *n* a malarial parasite at the stage in its life cycle when it is present in the host's body tissue but before it invades the red blood cells [< CRYPTO- + Greek *zōion* "animal"]

cryp·to·zo·ol·o·gy /krìptō zō óllәjee/ *n* the study of imaginary creatures or fabled creatures such as the Loch Ness monster or the yeti —**cryp·to·zo·o·log·i·cal** /krìptō zō ə lójjik'l/ *adj* —**cryp·to·zo·ol·o·gist** *n*

cryst. *abbr* CHEM, MINERALS, ELECTRONICS **1.** crystalline **2.** crystallography

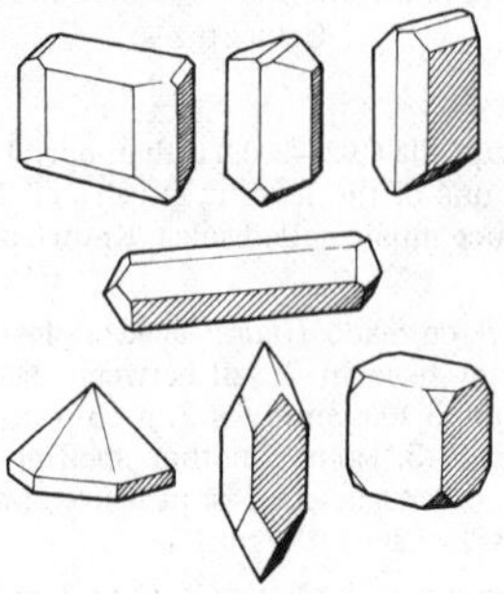

crystal

crys·tal /kríst'l/ *n* **1.** CHEM **SOLID WITH REPETITIVE INTERNAL STRUCTURE** a solid containing an internal pattern of atoms, molecules, or ions that is regular, repeated, and geometrically arranged **2.** MINERALS **QUARTZ** a clear colorless mineral, especially quartz **3.** MINERALS **PIECE OF CRYSTAL** a piece of a mineral in crystal form **4.** ELECTRONICS **ELECTRONIC COMPONENT** a crystalline substance that has semiconducting or piezoelectric properties and is used as an electronic component, or the electrical device using it **5. OBJECT LIKE CRYSTAL** something that has the form of a crystal, e.g., a frozen snowflake or a grain of salt ○ *snow crystals* ○ *crystals of salt* **6.** GLASS **HEAVY GLASS** a heavy transparent sparkling glass **7.** HOUSEHOLD **CRYSTAL GLASS OBJECTS** objects made from heavy transparent sparkling glass **8.** JEWELRY **GLASS OVER WATCH FACE** a transparent glass or plastic cover for the face of a clock or watch **9.** DRUGS same as **crystal meth** (*slang*) ■ *adj* **VERY CLEAR** clear and sparkling [Pre-12C. Via French < Latin *crystallum* < Greek *krustallos* "ice"]

Crys·tal /kríst'l/ city in southeastern Minnesota, near the Mississippi River; a northwestern suburb of Minneapolis. Population: 22,524 (2002 estimate).

crys·tal ball *n* **1.** a clear solid sphere of glass or rock crystal that is used by a fortune teller for supposedly predicting the future **2.** a means of supposedly predicting future events

crys·tal clear *adj* **1.** clear or obvious to the understanding **2.** clean and sparkling

crys·tal gaz·ing *n* the prediction of future events by questionable means, most commonly by staring into a crystal ball in the belief that images of future events will appear there —**crys·tal gaz·er** *n*

crys·tal heal·ing *n* the use of pieces of crystal in the belief that they can promote health and increase well-being

crys·tal·ize *vti* CHEM, COOK another spelling of **crystallize**

crystall- *prefix* same as **crystallo-** (*used before vowels*)

Crys·tal Lake town in northeastern Illinois, east of Rockford and northwest of Chicago. Population: 39,594 (2002 estimate).

crys·tal lat·tice *n* the regular array of points in space that are occupied by the atoms, ions, or molecules that make up a crystal

crys·tal·lif·er·ous /krìstə líffərəss/, **crys·tal·lig·er·ous** /krìstə líjjərəss/ *adj* forming or containing crystals

crys·tal·line /krístə līn, -lin/ *adj* **1. RESEMBLING OR BEING CRYSTALS** relating to, made of, containing, or resembling crystals **2. VERY CLEAR** clear and sparkling **3. HAVING DEFINITE SHAPE** clear and definite in shape —**crys·tal·lin·i·ty** /krìstə línnətee/ *n*

crys·tal·line lens *n* the transparent lens behind the iris in the eyes of vertebrates

crys·tal·lite /krístə līt/ *n* a tiny rudimentary crystal, e.g., of a type found in some igneous rocks —**crys·tal·lit·ic** /krìstə líttik/ *adj*

crys·tal·lize /krístə līz/ (**-lized, -liz·ing, -liz·es**), **crys·tal·ize** (**-ized, -iz·ing, -iz·es**) *vti* **1. MAKE OR BECOME WELL-DEFINED** to make an idea or feeling become fixed or definite, or become fixed or definite **2. FORM CRYSTALS** to form crystals, or make something do this **3.** COOK **COAT WITH SUGAR CRYSTALS** to coat or impregnate something with crystals, especially sugar crystals, or become coated or impregnated in this way —**crys·tal·liz·a·bil·i·ty** /krìstə līzə bílləte e/ *n* —**crys·tal·liz·a·ble** *adj* —**crys·tal·li·za·tion** /krìstəli záysh'n/ *n* —**crys·tal·liz·er** *n*

crystallo- *prefix* crystal, crystalline ○ *crystallography* ○ *crystalliferous* [< Greek *krustallos* "ice"]

crys·tal·log·ra·phy /krìstə lóggrəfee/ *n* the branch of science dealing with the formation and properties of crystals —**crys·tal·log·ra·pher** *n* —**crys·tal·lo·graph·ic** /krìstələ gráffik/ *adj* —**crys·tal·lo·graph·i·cal·ly** *adv*

crys·tal·loid /krístə lòyd/ *n* **1.** PHYS **SUBSTANCE PASSING THROUGH SEMIPERMEABLE MEMBRANE** a substance that in solution can pass through a semipermeable membrane **2.** BOT **PROTEIN IN PLANT CELL** a mass of protein resembling a crystal that commonly occurs in seeds and other storage organs ■ *adj* **RESEMBLING CRYSTAL** having the structure, properties, or appearance of a crystal —**crys·tal·loi·dal** /krìstə lóyd'l/ *adj*

crys·tal meth *n* powdered methamphetamine used as an illegal drug (*slang*)

crys·tal pleat *n* any of a series of permanently pressed pleats of varying widths, often in a sheer fabric

crys·tal set *n* an early form of radio receiver that used a quartz crystal as a detector

Cs *symbol* CHEM ELEM cesium

CS *abbr* **1.** FIN capital stock **2.** CIV ENG chartered surveyor **3.** MIL chief of staff **4.** CHR Christian Science **5.** CHR Christian Scientist

cs. *abbr* **1.** case **2.** SOC SCI census

C.S.A. *abbr* Confederate States of America

csar·das *n* DANCE, MUSIC another spelling of **czardas**

csc *abbr* MATH cosecant

C-sec·tion *n* MED same as **cesarean**

CSF *abbr* MED cerebrospinal fluid

CS gas *n* a gas that causes tears, salivation, and painful breathing. Formula: $C_9H_5ClN_2$. [Abbreviation of *Corson-Stoughton*, after B. B. *Corson* (b. 1896) and R. W. *Stoughton* (1906–57), US chemists]

CSH /kash/ *n* MED a military field hospital. Full form **Combat Support Hospital**

CSO *abbr UK* Central Statistical Office

C-SPAN /sée spàn/ *n* a cable TV channel that focuses chiefly on public affairs such as Congressional hearings and cultural and social issues [Acronym < *Cable Satellite Public Affairs Network*]

CST *abbr* **1.** TIME Central Standard Time **2.** PSYCHIAT convulsive shock treatment

c-store, **C-store** *n* COMM same as **convenience store** (*informal*)

CT *abbr* **1.** TIME Central Time **2.** MED computed tomography **3.** Connecticut

ct. *abbr* **1.** FIN cent **2.** EDUC certificate

Ct. *abbr* **1.** Connecticut **2.** Count (*used in titles*)

CTD *abbr* MED cumulative trauma disorder

cte·nid·i·um /tə níddee əm/ (*plural* **-i·a** /-ee ə/) *n* a gill found in mollusks that has a central axis with a fringe of filaments on each side. It is used in gas exchange and filter feeding. [Late 19C. Via modern Latin < Greek *ktenidion* "little comb" < *kteis* "comb"]

cten·oid /té nòyd, tée-/ *adj* describes fish scales that have tiny projections like the teeth of combs, or fish that have such scales [Mid-19C. < Greek *kten-* "comb"]

cten·o·phore /ténnə fàwr/ *n* a invertebrate ocean animal resembling a jellyfish, with eight rows of undulating filaments used for swimming. Sea gooseberries and sea walnuts are ctenophores. Phylum: Ctenophora. [Late 19C. < modern Latin *ctenophorus* < Greek *kten-* "comb"] —**cte·noph·o·ran** /tə nóffərən/ *adj, n*

CTI *abbr* COMPUT, TELECOM computer-telephony integration

ctn *abbr* MATH cotangent

CTO *adj* describes stamps that are bought by private collectors and postmarked in sheets. Full form **canceled to order**

C to C /seè tə seè/, **C. to C.**, **C2C** *adj* **1.** between two centers. Full form **center to center** **2.** relating to Internet transactions between two consumers. Full form **consumer-to-consumer**

ctr. *abbr* **1.** center **2.** counter

CTRL, **Ctrl.** *abbr* COMPUT control key

CTRL-ALT-DEL, **Ctrl-Alt-Del** *n* a combination of three computer keys, labeled control (CTRL), alternate (ALT), and delete (DEL), that are struck together to reboot a computer

cts. *abbr* cents

CT scan *n UK* MED same as **CAT scan** (sense 1)

CT scan·ner *n UK* MED same as **CAT scanner**

CTV *abbr* Canadian Television Network Limited

cu *abbr* Cuba (*used in Internet addresses*) See table at **domain name**

Cu *symbol* CHEM ELEM copper[1]

CU *abbr* see you (*used in e-mails or text messages*)

cu. *abbr* MEASURE cubic

cua·dril·la /kwaa dreéyə/ *n* a group of three banderilleros and two picadors who assist a matador in the bullring [Mid-19C. < Spanish, "little square" (from a formation used) < *cuadra* "square" < Latin *quadr-*]

cua·tro /kwaátrō/ *n Carib* a small four-stringed guitar [Mid-20C. < Spanish, "four"]

cub /kub/ *n* an offspring of a carnivorous mammal such as a bear, lion, or tiger ■ *vi* (**cubbed, cub·bing, cubs**) to give birth to an animal cub [Mid-16C. Origin ?] —**cub·bish** *adj* —**cub·bish·ly** *adv*

Cub *n* YOUTH ORG same as **Cub Scout**

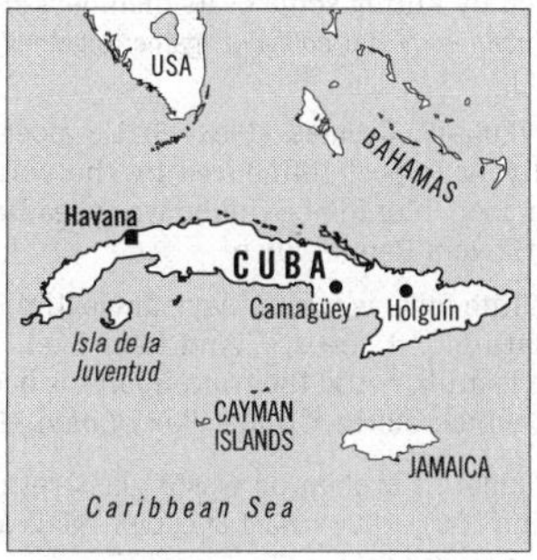

Cuba

Cu·ba /kyoóbə/ country in the Caribbean Sea comprising two main islands and over 1,000 islets. Language: Spanish. Currency: peso. Capital: Havana. Population: 11,263,429 (2003). Area: 44,218 sq. mi./114,525 sq. km. Official name **Republic of Cuba** —**Cu·ban** *adj, n*

cub·age /kyoóbij/ *n UK* MEASURE same as **cubature** (sense 2)

Cu·ba li·bre /kyoóbə leébrə/ *n* a drink made by mixing rum, cola, ice, and lime juice [< American Spanish, "free Cuba" (a toast used during the Cuban War of Independence, 1895–98)]

Cu·ban heel *n* a straight broad heel of medium height for a shoe

Cu·ban sand·wich *n Southern US* a long narrow sandwich of Cuban origin, filled with ham, pork, cheese, and pickles, and often grilled

cu·ba·ture /kyoóbə choòr, -chər/ *n* **1.** the process of working out the cubic content or volume of a solid **2.** the cubic content or volume of a solid [Late 17C. < CUBE[1]]

cub·by·hole /kúbbee hōl/, **cub·by** /kúbbee/ (*plural* **-bies**) *n* **1.** a small space or room **2.** a small storage compartment

cube[1] /kyoob/ *vt* (**cubed, cub·ing, cubes**) **1.** DICE FOOD to cut or shape food into cubes **2.** COOK TENDERIZE MEAT to score meat with a pattern of squares in order to make it more tender **3.** MULTIPLY ITEM BY ITSELF TWICE to multiply a number or quantity by itself twice, e.g., 6 cubed is 6 x 6 x 6 **4.** WORK OUT CUBIC CONTENT OF SOMETHING to calculate the cubic content of something ■ *n* **1.** SOLID FIGURE OF SIX EQUAL SIDES a three-dimensional geometric figure formed of six equal square plane faces, each set at right angles to the four sides adjacent to it **2.** CUBE-SHAPED OBJECT a solid shaped like a cube **3.** PRODUCT OF THREE EQUAL NUMBERS the product of three equal numbers or quantities multiplied together, usually written in mathematical notation as a raised 3, e.g., 4^3 means $4 \times 4 \times 4$ **4.** MEASURE, MECH ENG CUBIC INCHES cubic inches, especially of an internal-combustion engine (*informal*) [Mid-16C. Directly or via French < Latin *cubus* < Greek *kubos* "cube, pelvis"] —**cub·er** *n*

cu·be[2] /kyoó bày, kyoo báy/, **cu·bé** *n* a leguminous woody plant. Use: source of rotenone. Native to: tropical America. Genus: *Lonchocarpus*. [Early 20C. < American Spanish]

cu·beb /kyoó bèb/ *n* **1.** a small unripe brownish spicy berry of a climbing plant. Use: formerly, to treat respiratory and urinary disorders. **2.** a climbing plant with heart-shaped leaves, spikes of small flowers, and brownish spicy berries. Native to: Southeast Asia. Latin name: *Piper cubeba*. [13C. Via French *cubèbe* < Arabic *kubāba*]

cube root *n* a number or quantity that, when multiplied by itself twice, equals a given number or quantity

cube steak *n* a thin slice of beef that has been scored with squares to make it more tender

cube van *n Can* a small truck with a cube-shaped storage compartment at the rear

cu·bic /kyoóbik/, **cu·bi·cal** /-bik'l/ *adj* **1.** THREE-DIMENSIONAL having three measurable dimensions **2.** EQUAL TO VOLUME OF CUBE describes a volume or capacity that is equal to that of a particular cube **3.** CUBE-SHAPED shaped like a cube **4.** MATH RELATING TO OR CONTAINING CUBED VARIABLE describes a mathematical expression or equation in which at least one variable is cubed but no variable is to be multiplied by itself more than two times ○ *a cubic equation* **5.** CRYSTALS HAVING THREE EQUAL AXES describes a crystal that has three equal perpendicular axes. Symbol **c** ■ *n* MATH MATHEMATICAL EXPRESSION a cubic expression, equation, or curve —**cu·bi·cal·ly** *adv*

cu·bi·cle /kyoóbik'l/ *n* **1.** a work area that is partly separated from the rest of a room in an office or library **2.** a small partitioned area for private use in a larger, more public room such as a locker room or dormitory [15C < Latin *cubiculum* "bedroom" < *cubare* "lie down"]

cu·bic meas·ure *n* a unit or system for measuring volume or capacity

cu·bic zir·co·ni·a *n* a synthetic gemstone resembling a diamond. Use: jewelry.

cu·bi·form /kyoóbi fàwrm/ *adj* shaped like a cube (*technical*)

cub·ism /kyoó bìzzəm/, **Cub·ism** *n* an artistic style, chiefly in painting and sculpture, that developed in the early 20th century and emphasizes the representation of natural forms as geometric shapes seen from several angles [Early 20C. < French *cubisme* < *cube* (see CUBE[1])] —**cub·ist** *n* —**cu·bis·tic** /kyoo bístik/ *adj* —**cu·bis·ti·cal·ly** *adv*

cu·bit /kyoóbit/ *n* an ancient unit of length, equal to the distance from the elbow to the tip of the middle finger, approximately 17–22 in./43–56 cm [14C. < Latin *cubitum* "elbow, forearm"]

cu·bit·al /kyoóbit'l/ *adj* relating to the elbow, ulnar bone, or forearm [15C. < Latin *cubitalis* < *cubitum* "elbow, forearm"]

cu·boid /kyoó bòyd/ *n* **1.** MATH SOLID FIGURE OF SIX RECTANGULAR PLANES a three-dimensional geometric figure formed of six rectangular plane faces, each set at right angles to the four sides adjacent to it **2.** ANAT BONE IN FOOT the outermost tarsal bone of the foot in vertebrates ■ *adj* MATH CUBE-SHAPED shaped like a cube —**cu·boi·dal** /kyoo bóyd'l/ *adj*

cub re·port·er *n* an inexperienced young newspaper reporter

Cub Scout *n* a member of the branch of the Boy Scouts for younger children, generally 8 to 11 years of age

cuck·ing stool /kúking-/ *n* a punishment used in medieval times in which somebody was tied to a stool and pelted with rotting food [< obsolete *cuck* "defecate" < N Germanic; because a commode was sometimes used]

cuck·old /kúk'ld/ *n* a husband whose wife has been unfaithful to him ■ *vt* (**-old·ed, -old·ing, -olds**) to make a cuckold of a husband [Pre-12C. < Old N French, variant of Old French *cucuault* < *cucu* "cuckoo"] —**cuck·old·ry** *n*

cuckoo

cuck·oo /koó koò, koó-/ *n* (*plural* **-oos**) **1.** BIRD LAYING IN OTHERS' NESTS a bird that lays its eggs in the nests of other birds that bring the nestlings up as their own. Native to: Europe. Latin name: *Cuculus canorus*. **2.** BIRD RELATED TO TRUE CUCKOO a bird that is a member of the cuckoo family **3.** CUCKOO'S CALL the characteristic two-note call of the European cuckoo **4.** SOMEBODY REGARDED AS ECCENTRIC somebody regarded as eccentric or unconventional (*informal; sometimes offensive*) ■ *adj* ECCENTRIC eccentric or unconventional (*informal*) ■ *vi* (**-ooed, -oo·ing, -oos**) GIVE CALL OF CUCKOO to make the characteristic two-note call of the cuckoo [13C. < Old French *cucu*, an imitation of its call]

CULTURAL NOTE ***One Flew Over the Cuckoo's Nest***, a movie (1975) by US director Milos Forman. Based on Ken Kesey's 1962 novel, it describes how mischievous convict Randle McMurphy inspires his fellow inmates at a mental health facility to rebel against the disciplinarian Nurse Ratched. The movie can be seen as a metaphor for the conflict between individuality and creativity and society's pressure to conform.

cuck·oo clock *n* a clock that indicates the hour with sounds like a cuckoo's call, usually accompanied by the appearance of a mechanical bird from behind a door

cuck·oo·flow·er /koó koò flòwr, koó-/ *n* **1.** a plant often found in moist meadows. Flowers: light purple or occasionally white, with yellow anthers. Latin name: *Cardamine pratensis*. **2.** PLANTS same as **ragged robin** [Late 16C. Because the plant is in flower at about the time of year when the European cuckoo is first heard]

cuck·oo·pint /koó koo pìnt, koó-/ *n* a perennial plant with leaves shaped like arrowheads and flowering stems consisting of a yellowish green cone around a reddish purple spike that later carries poisonous scarlet berries. Native to: Europe. Latin name: *Arum maculatum*. [15C. Shortening of *cuckoo pintle* "cuckoo penis"; from the shape of the spadix]

cuck·oo spit *n* **1.** a white frothy secretion found on the stems and leaves of plants, produced by the larvae of insects such as the spittlebug **2.** an insect that produces cuckoo spit [Because it was believed to have been spat out by cuckoos]

cu·cum·ber /kyoó kùmbər/ (*plural* **-bers** or *same*) *n* **1.** a long fruit with dark green peel and crisp white watery flesh that is usually eaten raw in salads and sandwiches or pickled **2.** a climbing or trailing annual plant of the gourd family that produces cucumbers. Latin name: *Cucumis sativus.* [14C. < Latin *cucumer-*, by association with Old French *cocombre*] ◇ **cool as a cucumber** calm and composed, especially under pressure

cu·cum·ber tree *n* a small tree with greenish yellow flowers and cucumber-shaped fruit. Native to: central and eastern North America. Genus: *Magnolia.*

cu·cur·bit /kyoo kúrbit/ *n* a climbing or trailing plant of the gourd family with large, fleshy, tough-skinned or hard-skinned fruits, e.g., the cucumber, watermelon, or squash. Native to: tropical or subtropical regions. Family: Cucurbitaceae. [14C. Via French < Latin *cucurbita* "gourd"]

Cú·cu·ta /kóokətə/ city in northeastern Colombia and the capital of Norte de Santander Department, situated near the Venezuelan frontier. Population: 624,000 (1999).

cud /kud/ *n* partly digested food that cows and other ruminants return to the mouth, after it has passed into the first stomach, to chew again as an aid to digestion [Old English *cudu* < Indo-European, "sticky substance"]

cud·dle /kúdd'l/ *v* (**-dled, -dling, -dles**) **1.** *vti* **TENDERLY HUG OR NESTLE** to nestle together or hold somebody or something close for affection, warmth, or comfort **2.** *vi* **ASSUME COMFORTABLE POSITION** to get into a warm comfortable position ■ *n* **TENDER HUG** a prolonged hug or embrace given to comfort or show affection [Early 16C. Origin ?] —**cud·dler** *n* —**cud·dle·some** *adj*
cuddle up *vi* to assume a relaxed comfortable position alone or close to another person

cud·dly /kúddlee/ (**-dlier, -dli·est**) *adj* pleasant to hold because of being soft, warm, or endearingly attractive

cud·dy /kúddee/ (*plural* **-dies**) *n* a small cabin or galley on a boat [Mid-17C. Probably via early modern Dutch *kajute* < French *cahute* "shanty"]

cudg·el /kújjəl/ *n* a heavy stick used as a weapon ■ *vt* (**-eled, -el·ing, -els**) to beat somebody with a cudgel [Old English *cycgel*, origin ?] ◇ **take up the cudgels** to defend or support a person or cause actively and energetically

cud·weed /kúd weed/ (*plural* **-weeds** or *same*) *n* a plant of the daisy family that has woolly leaves. Flowers: white or yellow, in clusters. Native to: temperate regions worldwide. Genera: *Gnaphalium* or *Filago.*

cue[1] /kyoo/ *n* **1. SIGNAL TO SPEAK OR ACT** something said or done that provides the signal for somebody, especially an actor or performer, to say or do something **2. PROMPT OR REMINDER** something that prompts or reminds somebody to do something ○ *I took my cue from my brother and said nothing.* **3.** PSYCHOL **RESPONSE-PRODUCING STIMULUS** a stimulus or pattern of stimuli, often not consciously perceived, that results in a specific learned behavioral response ■ *vt* (**cued, cu·ing, cues**) **GIVE SIGNAL OR PROMPT TO SOMEBODY** to give somebody, especially an actor or performer, a signal to say or do something [Mid-16C. Origin ?]
cue in *vt* **1. GIVE SIGNAL TO SOMEBODY** to signal that it is time for somebody, especially a performer, to say or do something ○ *The conductor will cue you in.* **2. INSTRUCT OR REMIND SOMEBODY** to give somebody information, instructions, or a reminder **3. INSERT SOMETHING INTO PERFORMANCE** to insert something such as a speech or song into a performance

cue[2] /kyoo/ *n* **1.** CUE GAMES **STICK USED TO HIT BALL** in games such as billiards, snooker, and pool, a long tapering stick used to strike the cue ball **2.** LEISURE **LONG STICK USED IN SHUFFLEBOARD** a long stick with a semicircular piece attached at the end, used to push shuffleboard disks **3.** HAIR, HIST same as **queue** *n* (sense 4) ■ *vt* (**cued, cu·ing, cues**) **1.** CUE GAMES **STRIKE BALL WITH CUE** in games such as billiards, snooker, and pool, to strike a cue ball with a cue **2. TIE HAIR IN BRAID** to tie the hair at the back of the head in a braid [Mid-18C. Variant of QUEUE]

cue[3] /kyoo/ *n* the letter q [Mid-18C. < the pronunciation of *q*]

cue ball *n* in games such as billiards, snooker, and pool, the white ball struck with the cue so that it strikes the object ball in turn

cue bid *n* in bridge, a bid made to show a partner that the bidder has either an ace or no cards in a particular suit

cue card *n* in broadcasting, a large card containing the words that somebody is to say, held up out of sight of the viewing audience

cued speech /kyood speech/ *n* a series of hand movements used to differentiate ambiguous mouth positions as an aid in lip reading

cue game *n* a game such as billiards, snooker, or pool in which a long tapering stick is used to strike a cue ball

Cuen·ca /kwéng kaa, -kə/ city in a valley of the Andes Mountains in southern Ecuador. It is the capital of Azuay Province. Population: 278,035 (2000).

Cuer·na·va·ca /kwèrnə vaakə/ tourist resort and capital city of Morelos State, south central Mexico. Population: 338,706 (2000).

cues·ta /kwéstə/ *n* a ridge with a steep face on one side and a gentle slope on the other, especially in the southwestern United States [Early 19C. Via Spanish, "slope" < Latin *costa* "rib, side"]

cuff[1] /kuf/ *n* **1. END OF SLEEVE NEAREST WRIST** the part of a sleeve that covers the wrist, either turned back or with a band of fabric attached **2. FOLD AT BOTTOM OF PANT LEG** a turned-up fold at the bottom of a pant leg **3. PART OF GLOVE COVERING LOWER ARM** the part of a glove or gauntlet that extends up the arm beyond the wrist **4. BAND ON SOCK** a ribbed or elasticized band at the top of a sock that serves to hold it up **5.** MED **BAND USED IN MEASURING BLOOD PRESSURE** an inflatable band fastened around a patient's arm when measuring blood pressure **6.** POLICE same as **handcuff** (*informal; often used in the plural*) ■ *vt* (**cuffed, cuff·ing, cuffs**) **1. PUT CUFF ON PANTS** to give pants a cuff **2. HANDCUFF SOMEBODY** to put handcuffs on somebody (*informal*) [14C. Origin ?] —**cuff·less** *adj*

cuff[2] /kuf/ *vt* (**cuffed, cuff·ing, cuffs**) to hit somebody lightly with an open hand ■ *n* a light blow with an open hand [Mid-16C. Probably an imitation of the sound of hitting]

cuff link *n* an ornamental fastener for a shirt cuff, used as an alternative to a button (*often used in the plural*)

Cu·fic *adj, n* LANGUAGE another spelling of **Kufic**

Cu·ia·bá /kooyə baa/ city in southwestern Brazil on the Cuiabá River. It is the capital of Mato Grosso State. Population: 433,355 (1996).

cui bo·no /kwee bṓnō/ *n* **1.** the legal principle that somebody who would gain something from a particular action or event is probably responsible for it **2.** the usefulness of something used to measure its value [Early 17C. < Latin, "to whom is the benefit"]

cui·rass /kwi ráss/ *n* **1. ARMOR FOR UPPER BODY** a piece of body armor made of metal or leather, covering the chest and sometimes the back **2. PROTECTION** a protective covering, or a means of protection **3.** ZOOL **ANIMAL'S HARD PROTECTIVE COVERING** a protective outer covering on some animals, e.g., scales or a shell [15C. Via Old French *cuirace* < Latin *coriaceus* "made of leather" < *corium* "leather"]

cui·ras·sier /kweerə seer, kyoorə-/ *n* a mounted soldier wearing a cuirass, especially in 16th-century Europe [Mid-16C. < French < *cuirasse*, modern form of Old French *cuirace* (see CUIRASS)]

cuish *n* ARMS same as **cuisse**

cui·sine /kwi zeen/ *n* **1.** a style of cooking, especially one that is notable for high quality **2.** the range of food prepared by a restaurant, country, or person [Late 18C. Via French, "kitchen" < Latin *coquina* < *coquere* "to cook"]

cui·sine min·ceur /-maN súr/ *n* a low-calorie form of cooking originating in France [< French, "slimness cooking"]

cuisse /kwiss/, **cuish** /kwish/ *n* a piece of armor formerly worn in battle to protect the thigh [13C. < Old French *cuiss(i)eus*, plural of *cuissel* < late Latin *coxale* < Latin *coxa* "hip"]

cuke /kyook/ *n* FOOD same as **cucumber** (*informal*) [Early 20C. Shortening]

CUL *abbr* see you later (*used in e-mails or text messages*)

Cul·bert·son /kúlbərtsən/, **Ely** (1891–1955) Romanian-born US bridge player. He invented a contract-bridge bidding system, and wrote widely about the game.

> "Power politics is the diplomatic name for the law of the jungle."
> [Ely Culbertson, *Must We Fight Russia?*; 1946]

cul-de-sac /kùl də sák/ (*plural* **culs-de-sac** /*pronunc. same*/ or **cul-de-sacs**) *n* **1. STREET CLOSED AT ONE END** a road with no exit at one end, often in a residential area **2. IMPASSE** a situation in which further progress is impossible **3.** ANAT **BODY CAVITY RESEMBLING POUCH** a body cavity or tubular structure open at one end only [< French, "bottom of a sack"]

Cu·le·bra, Is·la de /koo láybrə/ island and wildlife refuge off the eastern coast of Puerto Rico. Area: 10 sq. mi./26 sq. km. Population: 1,542.

CUL8R *abbr* see you later (*used in e-mails or text messages*)

cu·le·ro /koo lérrō/ *n* a highly offensive term for somebody viewed with dislike or contempt (*taboo*)

cu·let /kyoolət/ *n* the flat face at the base of a faceted gemstone [Late 17C. < French, "little base" < *cul* (see CULOTTES)]

Cu·lia·cán /koolyə kaan/ city in western Mexico, the capital of Sinaloa State. Population: 745,537 (2000).

cu·li·nar·y /kúllə nèrree, kyoo-/ *adj* relating to food or cooking [Mid-17C. < Latin *culinarius* < *culina* "kitchen"] —**cu·li·nar·i·ly** *adv*

cull /kul/ *vt* (**culled, cull·ing, culls**) **1. REMOVE SOMEBODY OR SOMETHING AS WORTHLESS** to remove an inferior person or thing from a group **2. SELECT SOMEBODY OR SOMETHING** to select or gather people or things, especially those that are good examples of their kind ○ *The following cases are culled from the police reports.* **3. REMOVE ANIMAL FROM HERD** to remove an animal, especially a sick or weak one, from a herd or flock ■ *n* **1. SOMETHING WITHOUT VALUE** something regarded as worthless, especially an unwanted or inferior animal removed from a herd **2.** VET **REDUCTION OF ANIMAL NUMBERS** a reduction of the numbers of an animal population achieved by killing some of its members [12C. < Old French *coillier* < Latin *colligere* "gather together" < *legere* "gather"]

Cul·len /kúllən/, **Countee** (1903–46) US poet. An essentially lyric poet influenced by the work of the British poet John Keats, Cullen was a leading figure of the Harlem Renaissance.

> "'White folks is white,' says uncle Jim; / 'A platitude,' I sneer; / And then I tell him so is milk, / And the froth upon his beer."
> [Countee Cullen, "Uncle Jim," *Color*; 1925]

cul·let /kúllət/ *n* broken or waste glass returned for recycling [Early 19C. Variant of COLLET "glass left on the end of a blowing iron"]

Cul·lo·den /kə lódd'n, -láwd'n/ moors near Inverness, in northeastern Scotland. It was the scene of a battle in 1746 that ended the second Jacobite Rebellion.

culm[1] /kulm/ *n* **1. MINE WASTE** waste from a coal mine **2. SHALE WITH COAL** shale that contains much coal **3. INFERIOR ANTHRACITE** anthracite coal of poor quality [14C. Probably < Old English *col* (see COAL)]

culm[2] /kulm/ *n* the jointed hollow stem of a grass or similar plant [Mid-17C. < Latin *culmus*]

cul·mi·nant /kúlmənənt/ *adj* **1.** describes a planet or other astronomical object that is at its highest altitude **2.** reaching a climax or point of highest development (*formal*) [Early 17C. < late Latin *culminant-*, present participle of *culminare* (see CULMINATE)]

cul·mi·nate /kúlmə nàyt/ (**-nat·ed, -nat·ing, -nates**) *v* **1.** *vti* **COME OR BRING TO HIGHEST POINT** to reach a climax or point of highest development, or make something do this ○ *a general feeling of dissatisfaction that culminated in his resignation* **2.** *vti* **FINISH SPECTACULARLY** to come or bring something to an end, especially a climactic one ○ *The festivities culminated in a procession through the town.* **3.** *vi* **HAVE SOMETHING AT HIGHEST END** to have something at the apex ○ *The tower* *culminates in a point.* **4.** *vi* ASTRON **REACH HIGHEST OR LOWEST POINT** to reach the highest or, less commonly, the lowest point in the sky relative to an observer's horizon (*refers to astronomical objects*) [Mid-17C. < late Latin *culminat-*, past participle of *culminare* "exalt" < *culmen* "summit"]

cul·mi·na·tion /kùlmə náysh'n/ *n* **1. HIGHEST POINT** the highest, most important, or final point of an activity **2. ACT OF CULMINATING** the arrival at, or the bringing of something to, a climax **3.** ASTRON **HIGHEST OR LOWEST ALTITUDE** the highest or, less commonly, the lowest point in the sky that an astronomical object reaches relative to an observer's horizon

cu·lottes /koo lóts, ko͝o lòts/ *npl* a pair of women's knee-length shorts, cut to resemble a skirt [Mid-19C. < French, "knee breeches," literally "small bottom" < *cul* "bottom, rump" < Latin *culus*]

cul·pa·ble /kúlpəb'l/ *adj* deserving blame or punishment for a wrong [13C. Via French < Latin *culpabilis* < *culpare* "to blame" < *culpa* "fault, blame"] —**cul·pa·bil·i·ty** /kùlpə bíllətee/ *n* —**cul·pa·bly** *adv*

Cul·pep·er /kúl pèppər/, **Thomas, 2nd Baron Culpeper** (1635–89) English-born colonial administrator. He was the governor of Virginia (1680–83).

cul·prit /kúlprit/ *n* **1. WRONGDOER** somebody who is responsible for or guilty of an offense or misdeed **2. ACCUSED PERSON** somebody charged with a crime and awaiting trial **3. ORIGIN OF PROBLEM** a cause of a problem (*informal*) ○ *A faulty connection proved to be the culprit.* [Late 17C. Probably misunderstanding of *cul. prist* < Anglo-Norman *Culpable: prest d'averrer* "You are guilty; we are ready to prove it"]

cult /kult/ *n* **1. RELIGION** a system of religious or spiritual beliefs, especially an informal and transient belief system regarded by others as misguided, unorthodox, extremist, or false, and directed by a charismatic, authoritarian leader **2. RELIGIOUS GROUP** a group of people who share religious or spiritual beliefs, especially beliefs regarded by others as misguided, unorthodox, extremist, or false **3. IDOLIZATION OF SOMEBODY OR SOMETHING** an extreme or excessive admiration for a person, philosophy of life, or activity (*often used before a noun*) ○ *the cult of youth* ○ *a cult hero* **4. OBJECT OF IDOLIZATION** a person, philosophy, or activity regarded with extreme or excessive admiration **5. FAD** something popular or fashionable among a devoted group of enthusiasts (*often used before a noun*) ○ *has taken on cult status* **6.** CULTL ANTHROP **SYSTEM OF SUPERNATURAL BELIEFS** a body of organized practices and beliefs supposed to involve interaction with and control over supernatural powers **7.** SOCIOL **ELITE GROUP** a self-identified group of people who share a narrowly defined interest or perspective [Early 17C. Directly or via French < Latin *cultus* "worship" < *colere* "cultivate"] —**cult·ic** *adj* —**cult·ish** *adj* —**cult·ish·ly** *adv* —**cult·ish·ness** *n* —**cult·ism** *n* —**cult·ist** *n*

cul·ti RELIG plural of **cultus**

cul·ti·var /kúltə vaar/ *n* a variety of a cultivated plant that is developed by breeding and has a designated name [Early 20C. Blend of CULTIVATE + VARIETY]

cul·ti·vate /kúltə vàyt/ (**-vat·ed, -vat·ing, -vates**) *vt* **1. PREPARE LAND FOR CROPS** to work land or prepare soil for growing crops **2. GROW PLANT** to grow a plant or crop **3. LOOSEN SOIL** to break up soil with a tool or machine, especially before sowing or planting **4. NURTURE SOMETHING** to improve or develop something, usually by study or education ○ *cultivating her interest in science* **5. DEVELOP ACQUAINTANCE WITH SOMEBODY** to develop an acquaintance or intimacy with somebody, often for personal advantage **6. MAKE SOMEBODY CULTURED** to civilize or educate a person or group [Mid-17C. < medieval Latin *cultivat-*, past participle of *cultivare* < *cultivus* "cultured" < Latin *cult-* (see CULTURE)] —**cul·ti·va·ble** *adj* —**cul·ti·vat·a·ble** *adj* —**cul·ti·vat·ed** *adj*

Cul·ti·vat·ed Aus·tra·lian *n* the prestige form of Australian English, spoken with a standard British English accent

WORLD ENGLISH See ***Australian English.***

cul·ti·va·tion /kùltə váysh'n/ *n* **1. PREPARATION OF LAND OR GROWING CROPS** the planting, growing, and harvesting of crops or plants, or the preparation of land for this purpose **2. IMPROVEMENT** improvement or development, especially through study or education **3. SOPHISTICATION** educated taste or sophistication

cul·ti·va·tor /kúltə vàytər/ *n* **1.** somebody who grows, nurtures, or encourages something ○ *an enthusiastic cultivator of roses* ○ *a cultivator of useful political contacts* **2.** a gardening or farm tool or machine for breaking up soil

cul·tur·al /kúlchərəl/ *adj* **1.** relating to a culture or civilization **2.** relating to the arts and intellectual activity —**cul·tur·al·ly** *adv*

cul·tur·al an·thro·pol·o·gy *n* the scientific study of human culture or the culture of specific societies, including social structure, language, religion, art, and technology —**cul·tur·al an·thro·pol·o·gist** *n*

cul·tur·al di·ver·si·ty *n* ethnic variety, as well as socioeconomic and gender variety, in a group, society, or institution

cul·tur·al lag *n* a slower rate of change in one part of a culture or one society compared with another

cul·tur·al ma·te·ri·al·ism *n* the anthropological theory that environment, resources, technology, and other material things are the major influences on cultural change

cul·tur·al rel·a·tiv·ism *n* the principle that people should not judge the behavior of others using the standards of their own culture, and that each culture must be analyzed on its own terms

Cul·tur·al Rev·o·lu·tion *n* a political and cultural reform movement in the People's Republic of China from 1965 to 1968 that was intended to revolutionize political opinion and behavior. It was characterized by social upheaval. The Red Guard played a prominent role in the movement, which was aimed at restoring principles associated with Mao Zedong.

cul·tur·al stud·ies *n* (*takes a singular verb*) **1.** the study of culture from a sociological rather than an aesthetic viewpoint. It draws on the social sciences such as politics and semiotics, rather than traditional forms of literary, artistic, or musical criticism. **2.** a wide-ranging educational course, especially at college or university level, covering all aspects of culture, the arts, sciences, and social science. It is often intended as a foundation for other courses.

cul·ture /kúlchər/ *n* **1. ARTS COLLECTIVELY** art, music, literature, and related intellectual activities, considered collectively ○ *Culture is necessary for a healthy society.* ○ *popular culture* **2. KNOWLEDGE AND SOPHISTICATION** enlightenment and sophistication acquired through education and exposure to the arts ○ *They are people of culture.* **3. SHARED BELIEFS AND VALUES OF GROUP** the beliefs, customs, practices, and social behavior of a particular nation or people ○ *Southeast Asian culture* **4. PEOPLE WITH SHARED BELIEFS AND PRACTICES** a group of people whose shared beliefs and practices identify the particular place, class, or time to which they belong **5. SHARED ATTITUDES** a particular set of attitudes that characterizes a group of people ○ *The company tries hard to avoid a blame culture.* **6. GROWING OF BIOLOGICAL MATERIAL** the growing of biological material, especially plants, microorganisms, or animal tissue, in a nutrient substance (**culture medium**) in specially controlled conditions for scientific, medical, or commercial purposes **7.** BIOTECH **BIOLOGICAL MATERIAL GROWN IN SPECIAL CONDITIONS** biological material, especially plants, microorganisms, or animal tissue, grown in a nutrient substance (**culture medium**) in specially controlled conditions for scientific, medical, or commercial purposes **8. TILLAGE** the cultivation of the land or soil in preparation for growing crops or plants **9. IMPROVEMENT** the development of a skill or expertise through training or education ○ *physical culture* ■ *vt* (**-tured, -tur·ing, -tures**) **1. GROW BIOLOGICAL MATERIAL IN SPECIAL CONDITIONS** to grow biological material, especially plants, microorganisms, or animal tissue, in a nutrient substance (**culture medium**) in specially controlled conditions, for scientific, medical, or commercial purposes **2.** AGRIC **CULTIVATE PLANTS** to cultivate plants or crops **3. NURTURE SOMEBODY OR SOMETHING** to nurture somebody or something, especially in order to advance your own interests ○ *She spent a great deal of time culturing new contacts on Capitol Hill.* [13C. Via French < Latin *cultura* "tillage" < *cult-*, past participle of *colere* "inhabit, cultivate"]

cul·tured /kúlchərd/ *adj* **1. EDUCATED AND SOPHISTICATED** educated and informed about the arts and related intellectual activity **2. GROWN IN NUTRIENT SUBSTANCE** grown in a nutrient substance (**culture medium**) in a laboratory **3. ARTIFICIALLY PRODUCED** created artificially, and not by natural or organic processes

cul·tured pearl *n* a pearl created artificially by introducing a foreign body into an oyster or clam shell to attract layers of mother-of-pearl around it

cul·ture lag *n* SOCIOL same as **cultural lag**

cul·ture me·di·um (*plural* **cul·ture me·dia** or **cul·ture me·di·ums**) *n* a nutrient substance such as a broth or an agar gel in which scientists grow selected microorganisms, fungi, cells, or tissue in a laboratory

cul·ture shock *n* the feelings of confusion and anxiety experienced by somebody suddenly encountering an unfamiliar cultural environment

cul·ture vul·ture *n* somebody who has a strong or obsessive interest in the arts (*informal*)

cul·ture war *n* public debate reflecting the division over religious, educational, political, and moral issues within a multicultural society —**cul·ture war·ri·or** *n*

cul·tus /kúltəss/ (*plural* **-tus·es** or **-ti** /-tī/) *n* a religious group, especially a cult and its system of beliefs (*formal*) [Early 17C. < Latin *cultus* (see CULT)]

Cul·ver Cit·y /kùlvər-/ city in southwestern California, southwest of Los Angeles. It is a center for the film industry. Population: 39,698 (2002 estimate).

cul·ver·in /kúlvərin/ *n* **1.** a long-range cannon used between the 15th and 17th centuries **2.** a musket used in the 15th and 16th centuries [15C. < French *coulevrine* < *couleuvre* "snake" < Latin *colubra*]

cul·vert /kúlvərt/ *n* **1.** a covered channel that carries water or cabling under a road or railroad, or through an embankment **2.** an arch, bridge, or part of a road that covers a culvert [Late 18C. Origin ?]

cum /kum/ *prep* together with, along with, in combination with, or functioning as (*informal*) ○ *He lives and works in an apartment cum office.* [Late 19C. < Latin, "with"]

cum. *abbr* STATS cumulative

cum·ber /kúmbər/ *vt* (*archaic or literary*) **1.** to hamper or hinder somebody or something **2.** to burden or encumber somebody or something [14C. Probably shortening of ENCUMBER]

Cum·ber·land /kúmbərlənd/ **1.** river in southern Kentucky and northern Tennessee, formed in southeastern Kentucky and emptying into the Ohio River. Length: 720 mi./1,160 km. **2.** city in the northwestern corner of Maryland, on the Potomac River, west of Hagerstown. Population: 21,082 (2002 estimate). **3.** town in northeastern Rhode Island, on Blackstone River, a northern suburb of Providence. Population: 33,104 (2002 estimate).

Cum·ber·land Falls waterfall in Kentucky. It is situated in Cumberland Falls State Resort Park. Height: 68 ft./21 m.

Cum·ber·land Gap pass through the Cumberland Mountains near the meeting point of Tennessee, Virginia, and Kentucky. Height: 1,650 ft./503 m.

cum·ber·some /kúmbərssəm/ *adj* **1.** awkward to carry or handle because of weight, size, or shape **2.** difficult to use or deal with because of length or complexity —**cum·ber·some·ly** *adv* —**cum·ber·some·ness** *n*

cum·bi·a /kúm bee ə/ *n Hispanic* a type of music and dance possibly of Columbian origin, now common in Mexico and other Latin American countries

Cum·bri·a /kúmbree ə/ county in northwestern England, formed in 1974, incorporating mainly the former counties of Cumberland and Westmorland. Carlisle is the county town. Population: 487,607 (2001). Area: 2,629 sq. mi./6,810 sq. km. —**Cum·bri·an** /kúmbree ən/ *n, adj*

cum·brous /kúmbrəss/ *adj* large and unwieldy (*archaic or literary*) ○ *"this cumbrous and creaking structure"* (Thomas Hardy, *Tess of the d'Urbervilles;*

1891) [14C. < *cumber* "encumbrance, hindrance, obstruction," probably < CUMBER] —**cum·brous·ly** *adv* —**cum·brous·ness** *n*

cu·mene /kyoo͝ meen/ *n* an oily colorless liquid hydrocarbon. Use: fuel additive, synthesis of chemicals. Formula: $C_6H_5CH(CH_3)_2$. [Mid-19C. Via French < Latin *cuminum* (see CUMIN)]

cum·in /kúmmin, ko͝omin/ *n* **1.** the aromatic seeds of a plant of the carrot family. Use: whole or ground as a spice. **2.** the plant that produces cumin seeds. Native to: Mediterranean. Latin name: *Cuminum cyminum*. [Pre-12C. Via Latin *cuminum* < Greek *kuminon* < Semitic]

cum lau·de /ko͝om lów dày, -dee/ *adv, adj* with academic honors [< Latin, "with praise"]

cum·mer·bund /kúmmər bùnd/ *n* a pleated sash, often brightly colored, worn around the waist by men as part of formal dress [Early 17C. < Urdu *kamar-band* "loin-band, waistband"]

cum·mings /kúmmingz/, **e. e.** (1894–1962) US poet. He is known for his experimental poetry, which was written mostly in lowercase letters. Full name **Cummings, Edward Estlin**

> "The churches are drowning with stars, everywhere stars blossom, frank and gold and keen...Now (touched by a resonance of sexually celestial forms) the little murdered adventure called Humanity becomes a selfless symbol."
> [e. e. cummings, *Eimi*; 1933]

cum·quat *n* TREES, FOOD another spelling of **kumquat**

cu·mu·late *v* /kyoo͝myə làyt/ (**-lat·ed, -lat·ing, -lates**) **1.** *vti* same as **accumulate** (sense 1) **2.** *vt* to combine two or more items into one ■ *adj* /kyoo͝myə lət, -làyt/ heaped up in a pile or mass [Mid-16C. < Latin *cumulat-*, past participle of *cumulare* "gather in a heap" < *cumulus* "heap, pile"] —**cu·mu·la·tion** /kyoo͝myə láysh'n/ *n*

cu·mu·la·tive /kyoo͝myə làytiv, -lət-/ *adj* **1.** GRADUALLY BUILDING UP becoming successively larger, stronger, or more effective ○ *Many drugs have a cumulative effect on the body.* **2.** CREATED BY GRADUAL ADDITIONS resulting from successive additions **3.** FIN ADDED TO NEXT PAYMENT describes an interest or dividend payment that is added to the next payment rather than being paid out when it falls due **4.** FIN ENTITLING SHAREHOLDER TO CLAIM DIVIDEND ARREARS describes preferred stocks whose holder has the right to claim dividend arrears before dividends are distributed to holders of common stock **5.** LAW MORE SEVERE FOR REPEAT OFFENDER describes a more severe punishment imposed on somebody who has previously committed the same crime **6.** LAW CONSECUTIVE used to describe a sentence or prison term that follows another consecutively **7.** STATS INCLUDING ALL GIVEN VALUES OF VARIABLE relating to the sum of the number of times a variable has a specific value totaled over all the values of the variable that are less than a given value **8.** STATS INCREASING WITH SUCCESSIVE MEASUREMENTS describes an error that increases as more measurements are taken —**cu·mu·la·tive·ly** *adv* —**cu·mu·la·tive·ness** *n*

cu·mu·la·tive dis·tri·bu·tion func·tion *n* a procedure that assigns to each possible value of a random variable the probability that this value will be found. If each value is equally likely to be found, the distribution is said to be uniform.

cu·mu·la·tive trau·ma dis·or·der *n* US a painful condition affecting some people who overuse muscles as a result of, e.g., regularly operating a computer keyboard and mouse or playing the piano. ◊ **tenosynovitis**. Can term **RSI**

cu·mu·li METEOROL plural of **cumulus**

cu·mu·lo·nim·bus /kyoo͝myəlō nímbəss/ (*plural* **-bi** /-bī/ or **-bus·es**) *n* a tall dark cumulus cloud in the shape of an anvil, often bringing thunderstorms [Late 19C. < CUMULUS]

cu·mu·lus /kyoo͝myələss/ (*plural* **-li** /-lī/) *n* **1.** a large white or gray cloud with a flat base and a rounded fluffy top, or a mass of such clouds, developing as a result of rising hot air currents **2.** a mass or heap [Mid-17C. < Latin, "heap, pile"] —**cu·mu·lous** *adj*

Cu·na /ko͝onə/ (*plural same* or **-nas**), **Ku·na** *n* **1.** a member of a Native Central American people of the isthmus of Panama and northwestern Colombia **2.** the Chibchan language of the Cuna people. Native speakers: 30,000 to 50,000. [Mid-19C. < Cuna] —**Cu·na** *adj*

cu·ne·al /kyoo͝nee əl/ *adj* having the shape of a wedge (*technical*) [Late 16C. Directly or via modern Latin < medieval Latin *cunealis* < Latin *cuneus* "wedge"]

cu·ne·ate /kyoo͝nee àyt, -ət/ *adj* describes a leaf that is more or less triangular with the narrowest point of the triangle forming the tip [Early 19C. < Latin *cuneus* "wedge"] —**cu·ne·ate·ly** *adv*

AKG London
Cuneiform: Sumerian clay tablet (18th century B.C.)

cu·ne·i·form /kyoo͝ni fàwrm, kyoo née ə-/ *adj* **1.** WEDGE-SHAPED with the narrowly triangular shape of a wedge **2.** USED IN ANCIENT WRITING SYSTEM relating or belonging to a writing system in which wedge-shaped impressions were made in soft clay. There were several such writing systems in ancient Southwest Asia, including one for Sumerian. **3.** USED FOR CUNEIFORM WRITING describes the clay tablets on which cuneiform script was written **4.** ANAT OF ANKLE describes any of three wedge-shaped bones of the ankle ■ *n* **1.** CUNEIFORM SCRIPT writing that uses small wedge-shaped characters **2.** ANAT WEDGE-SHAPED ANKLE BONE any of the three cuneiform bones of the ankle [Late 17C. < French *cunéiforme* or modern Latin *cuneiformis* < Latin *cuneus* "wedge"]

cun·ner /kúnnər/ (*plural same* or **-ners**) *n* a small fish of the wrasse family. Native to: North Atlantic Ocean. Latin name: *Tautogolabrus adspersus*. [Early 17C. Origin ?]

cun·ni·lin·gus /kùnni líng gəss/ *n* sexual stimulation of a woman's genitals using the tongue and lips [Late 19C. < Latin, "vulva-licker"]

cun·ning /kúnning/ *adj* **1.** CRAFTY AND DECEITFUL clever or artful in a way that is intended to deceive **2.** CLEVERLY THOUGHT OUT showing skill, shrewdness, and ingenuity in planning or doing something **3.** CUTE attractive in a pleasant delicate way (*dated informal*) ■ *n* **1.** CRAFTINESS AND DECEITFULNESS the ability to deceive in a clever subtle way **2.** SKILLFUL PERFORMANCE skillful ingenuity or grace in doing something [13C. Probably < Old Norse *kunna* "know"] —**cun·ning·ly** *adv* —**cun·ning·ness** *n*

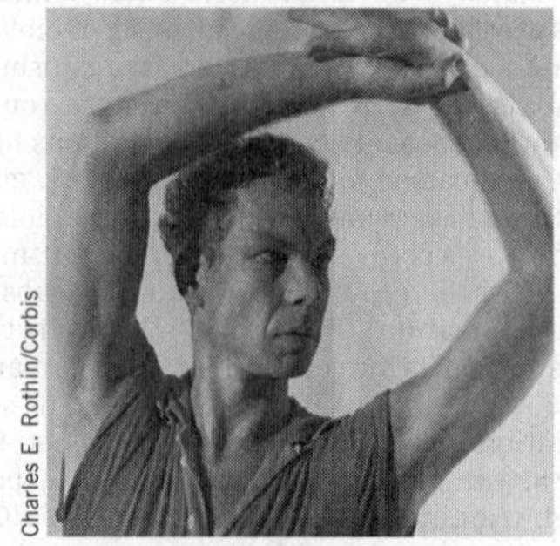
Charles E. Rothin/Corbis
Merce Cunningham

Cun·ning·ham /kúnning hàm/, **Merce** (*b.* 1919) US dancer and choreographer. He formed his own dance company in 1953 and has played an important role in the development of avant-garde dance.

> "I compare...dance...to water...Everyone knows what water is or what dance is, but...fluidity makes them intangible...Music at least has a literature, a notation."
> [Merce Cunningham. Quoted in *The Dancer and the Dance*, in conversation with Jacqueline Lesschaeve; 1991]

cunt /kunt/ *n* **1.** a highly offensive term for a woman's genitals (*taboo*) **2.** a highly offensive term for a woman (*taboo*) **3.** a highly offensive term for somebody who is viewed with great dislike or contempt, especially a man (*taboo insult*) **4.** a highly offensive term for sexual intercourse with a woman (*taboo*) [13C. Ultimately < Germanic]

cup /kup/ *n* **1.** DRINKING CONTAINER a small container, usually with a handle, used to hold liquids for drinking **2.** AMOUNT CUP HOLDS the contents of a cup ○ *Will you have another cup?* **3.** MEASURE MEASURE USED IN COOKING a unit of volume used especially in cooking, equal to 8 fl oz/237 ml **4.** WINNER'S PRIZE an ornamental trophy, typically a large two-handled silver goblet, awarded as a prize in a competition, especially a sports competition **5.** SPORTS CONTEST a sports competition in which the winner's prize is a large ornamental goblet **6.** BOWL-SHAPED OBJECT something that has an open hollow rounded shape **7.** CLOTHING PART OF BRA either of the shaped sections of a bra that support and cover the breasts **8.** SPORTS, CLOTHING ATHLETIC SUPPORT an athletic support reinforced with plastic or metal, worn to protect the male genitals during team sports **9.** BOT, ANAT BOWL-SHAPED PLANT OR BODY PART an open hollow rounded part or structure in a plant or in the body **10.** BEVERAGES PARTY PUNCH a mixed drink with a particular ingredient as its base, usually served from a large bowl at parties ○ *a champagne cup* **11.** FOOD DISH SERVED IN CUP-SHAPED CONTAINER a dessert or appetizer served in a small bowl or glass dish **12.** CHR COMMUNION CHALICE OR WINE the vessel from which the consecrated wine is drunk during the Christian service of Communion, or the wine itself **13.** GOLF HOLE ON GOLF COURSE the hole on a green that is the target in golf, or the metal lining of a golf hole **14.** SOMEBODY'S LOT IN LIFE what a person is destined to receive, suffer, or enjoy in life (*literary*) ■ *vt* (**cupped, cup·ping, cups**) **1.** MAKE HANDS INTO CUP to form one or both of the hands into an open hollow rounded shape, usually to hold or receive something such as water **2.** HOLD SOMETHING IN HANDS to hold something in cupped hands **3.** DRAW BLOOD TO SKIN'S SURFACE formerly, to use a cupping glass to increase the blood supply to an area of the skin [Pre-12C. < late Latin *cuppa*, probably < Latin *cupa* "tub"] ◇ **in your cups** drinking or having drunk too much alcohol (*archaic or humorous*)

cup-and-sau·cer plant *n* a climbing plant. Flowers: large, brightly colored. Native to: Mexico. Latin name: *Cobaea scandens*.

cup·bear·er /kúp bèrrər/ *n* a servant who pours wine, especially one employed in a royal household

cup·board /kúbbərd/ *n* a piece of furniture, either built-in or freestanding, used for storing food or kitchen and domestic items

cup·cake /kúp kàyk/ *n* a small individual iced cake, baked in a paper or foil cup or in a cup-shaped mold

cu·pel /kyoo͝p'l, kyoo pél/ *n* a small container in which precious metals are refined, especially one in which gold and silver are separated from base metals during assaying ■ *vt* (**-peled, -pel·ing, -pels**) to separate gold or silver from a base metal using a cupel [Early 17C. < French *coupelle* "little cup" < *coupe* "cup" < late Latin *cuppa* (see CUP)] —**cu·pel·la·tion** /kyoo͝pə láysh'n/ *n* —**cu·pel·ler** *n*

Cu·per·ti·no /koopər teénō/ city in western California, a western suburb of San Jose. Population: 50,005 (2002 estimate).

cup·ful /kúp fo͝ol/ *n* **1.** the amount held by a cup ○ *There's only about a cupful of water left.* **2.** MEASURE same as **cup** *n* (sense 3)

cup fun·gus *n* an often bright red, orange, or yellow fungus with a cup-shaped spore-bearing structure on its surface. Subdivision: *Ascomycotina*.

cup hold·er *n* **1.** a device for holding a container for drinks to keep it from tipping, especially one installed in a vehicle **2.** the tray of a compact disk drive in a computer, or the drive itself

cu·pid /kyóopid/ *n* a representation of the god Cupid as a symbol of love in painting or sculpture [Early 17C. < CUPID]

Cu·pid /kyóopid/ *n* in Roman mythology, the god of love, the son of Venus, usually represented as a young boy with wings and a bow and arrow. Greek equivalent **Eros** [14C. < Latin *Cupido*, literally "desire" < *cupere* "to desire"]

cu·pid·i·ty /kyoo píddətee/ *n* greed, especially for money or possessions (*formal*) [15C. Directly or via French < Latin *cupiditas* < *cupere* "to desire"]

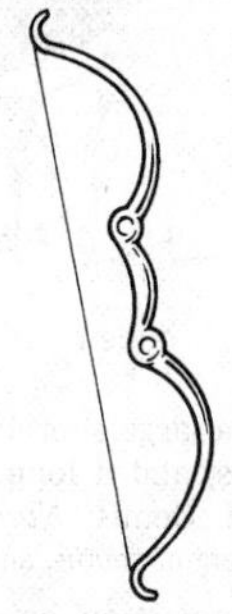

Cupid's bow (sense 2)

Cu·pid's bow *n* **1.** a double curve, especially the curves of the upper lip **2.** a bow with two curves used in archery [< the traditional representation of the bow used by Cupid]

cup of tea *n* (*informal*) **1.** what somebody likes or prefers ○ *This is more my cup of tea.* **2.** something to be dealt with

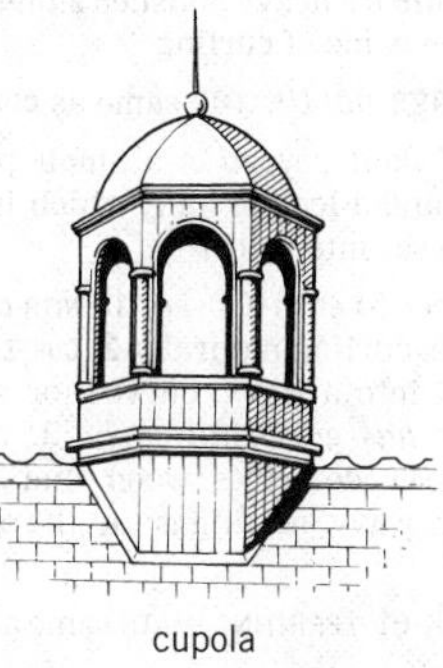

cupola

cu·po·la /kyóopələ/ *n* **1.** ARCHIT **DOME-SHAPED ROOF** a roof or ceiling in the form of a dome **2.** ARCHIT **STRUCTURE ON ROOF** a small structure on a roof, sometimes made of glass and providing natural light inside **3.** MIL **GUN TURRET** a domed structure protecting a gun, e.g., on a warship **4.** MIL, RAIL **SMALL OBSERVATION DOME** a glass observation dome on the roof of an armored vehicle or railroad caboose **5.** METALL **BLAST FURNACE** a cylindrical blast furnace used in foundries for remelting iron or other metals [Mid-16C. Via Italian < late Latin *cupula* "little cask, vault" < *cupa* "cask"]

cup·pa /kúppə/ *n* a cup of tea or coffee (*informal*) ○ *started the day with a cuppa joe* [Mid-20C. < an informal pronunciation of *cup of*]

cup·ping /kúpping/ *n* a historical medical practice in which a cupping glass was used to increase the blood supply to an area of the skin

cup·ping glass *n* a glass container in which a partial vacuum is created by heat or suction that is applied to the skin to increase the blood supply in the tissues below

cup·py /kúppee/ (**-pi·er, -pi·est**) *adj* **1.** with the shape of a cup **2.** with many small shallow hollows in the surface

cupr- *prefix* same as **cupro-** (*used before vowels*)

cu·prate /kóo pràyt/ *n* a salt containing an anionic grouping of copper and oxygen

cu·pre·ous /kóopree əss/ *adj* **1.** consisting of or containing copper **2.** of a reddish brown color [Mid-17C. < late Latin *cupreus* < *cuprum* (see COPPER[1])]

cu·pric /kóoprik/ *adj* containing copper with a valence of 2 [Late 18C. < late Latin *cuprum* (see COPPER[1])]

cu·prif·er·ous /koo prífferəss/ *adj* having copper as a constituent [Late 18C. < late Latin *cuprum* (see COPPER[1])]

cu·prite /kóo prìt/ *n* a reddish brown or black mineral that is an ore of copper and consists of copper oxide [Mid-19C. < late Latin *cuprum* (see COPPER[1])]

cupro- *prefix* copper ○ *cupronickel* [< late Latin *cuprum* (see COPPER[1])]

cu·pro·nick·el /kóo prō níkʼl/ *n* a corrosion-resistant alloy of copper containing up to 40 percent nickel

cu·prous /kóoprəss/ *adj* containing copper with a valence of 1 [Mid-17C. < late Latin *cuprum* (see COPPER[1])]

cu·pule /kyóo pyool/ *n* a cup-shaped body part or plant part, e.g., that enclosing the base of an acorn [15C. < late Latin *cupula* "little cask, vault" < *cupa* "cask"]

Cu·que·nan Wa·ter·fall /kóo kay nan-/ waterfall in Venezuela, one of the highest in the world. Height: 2,000 ft./610 m.

cur /kur/ *n* **1.** a mixed-breed dog, especially one that is ill-natured or in poor condition **2.** an offensive term for somebody regarded as mean, cowardly, or otherwise unpleasant (*dated insult*) [12C. Originally in *cur-dog*, origin ?]

cur·a·ble /kyóorəbʼl/ *adj* **1.** describes a condition that is capable of being treated by medical procedures **2.** having a condition that can be treated by medical procedures —**cur·a·bil·i·ty** /kyòorə bíllətee/ *n* —**cur·a·bly** *adv*

cu·ra·çao /kóorə sów, -sō, kyóorə-/ *n* an orange-flavored liqueur that originated on the Caribbean island of Curaçao [Early 19C. < CURAÇAO]

Cu·ra·çao /kóorə sów, -sō, kyóorə-/ island in the Netherlands Antilles, in the Caribbean Sea, and the largest of the island group. Area: 171 sq. mi./444 sq. km.

cu·ra·cy /kyóorəssee/ (*plural* **-cies**) *n* the position or term of office of a curate [15C. < CURATE[1]]

cu·ra·re /kyoo ráaree/, **cu·ra·ri** *n* **1.** a dark resin from some South American plants. Use: muscle relaxant, traditional arrow poison. **2.** a tropical vine from which curare is obtained. Native to: South America. Genera: *Strychnos* or *Chondodendron*. [Late 18C. Via Spanish, Portuguese < Carib *kurari*]

cu·ra·rize /kyóorə rìz/ (**-rized, -riz·ing, -riz·es**) *vt* to treat somebody with curare —**cu·ra·ri·za·tion** /kyòorəri záysh'n/ *n*

cu·ras·sow /kyóorə sō/ *n* a large crested game bird with a long tail and a brightly colored beak. Native to: South and Central America. Family: Cracinae. [Late 17C. Alteration of CURAÇAO]

cu·rate[1] /kyóorət/ *n* **1.** a member of the Christian clergy who assists a vicar, rector, or priest **2.** a member of the Christian clergy in charge of a parish [14C. < medieval Latin *curatus* "somebody who cares for a parish" < Latin *cura* "care"]

cu·rate[2] /kyoor àyt/ (**-rat·ed, -rat·ing, -rates**) *v* **1.** *vti* to be the curator of a museum, gallery, or other collection **2.** *vt* to organize and choose the items in an exhibition at a museum or gallery (*usually passive*) [Early 18C. Back-formation < CURATOR]

cu·ra·tive /kyóorətiv/ *adj* able to restore health ■ *n* a substance or treatment that can restore health —**cu·ra·tive·ly** *adv* —**cu·ra·tive·ness** *n*

cu·ra·tor /kyə ráytər, kyoo ràytər/ *n* **1.** the administrative head of a museum, gallery, or other collection **2.** somebody who organizes and chooses the items in an exhibition at a museum or gallery [14C. < Latin < *curare* (see CURE)] —**cu·ra·to·ri·al** /kyòorə táwree əl/ *adj* —**cu·ra·tor·ship** *n*

curb /kurb/ *n* **1.** ROADS **EDGE OF STREET** a line of concrete or asphalt that forms part of the gutter at the edge of a street **2.** **EDGING FOR LAWN** a line of stones that forms the edge of an area of lawn **3.** **IMPOSED LIMITATION** something that controls or limits something else ○ *sought a curb on drug trafficking* **4.** **RAISED PART THAT SURROUNDS SOMETHING** an enclosing frame or raised margin, e.g., around a skylight or a well **5.** RIDING **HORSE'S BIT AND ATTACHED CHAIN** a horse's bit with a chain or strap attached, passed under the horse's jaw ■ *vt* (**curbed, curb·ing, curbs**) **1.** **HOLD SOMETHING BACK** to restrain, control, or limit something ○ *hope to curb inflation* **2.** ROADS **EDGE STREET WITH CURB** to provide a street with a curb **3.** **LEAD DOG OFF SIDEWALK TO DEFECATE** to lead a dog off the sidewalk onto the curb or into the gutter to let it defecate [15C. Probably variant of *courb* "to curve," via French *courber* < Latin *curvare*]

curb ap·peal *n* the attractive appearance of a property for sale as seen from the roadside, creating a favorable first impression on a potential buyer

curb bit *n* RIDING same as **curb** *n* (sense 5)

curb cut *n* a small ramp built on a curb to make it easier for people in wheelchairs or people pushing strollers to move between the street and sidewalk

curb·ing /kúrbing/ *n* **1.** the material used to make a curb **2.** the whole length of curb along a street or all the curbs

curb roof *n* a roof that has two or more different angles of slope on each side, e.g., a mansard or gambrel roof

curb ser·vice *n* service to customers who remain in their vehicles, especially at fast food outlets

curb·side /kúrb sìd/ *n* **1.** the edge of a street or a sidewalk bordered by a curb. UK spelling **kerbside** **2.** ROADS same as **sidewalk**

curb·side ser·vice *n* COMM same as **curb service**

curb·stone /kúrb stōn/ *n* any of the stones or pieces of concrete that form a curb. UK spelling **kerbstone**

cur·cu·li·o /kur kyóolee ō/ (*plural* **-os**) *n* a weevil that damages fruit trees, vegetables, and other plants. Genus: *Conotrachelus*. [Mid-18C. < Latin, "corn weevil"]

cur·cu·ma /kúrkyəmə/ *n* a tropical plant from which turmeric and zedoary are obtained. Native to: South Asia. Genus: *Curcuma*. [15C. Via medieval Latin < Arabic *kurkum* "turmeric" < Sanskrit *kuṇkuma* "saffron"]

curd /kurd/ *n* **1.** **SOLID PART OF SOUR MILK** the solid substance formed when milk coagulates. Use: for making cheese. **2.** **SUBSTANCE LIKE MILK CURD** a food substance with a consistency similar to milk curd ■ *vti* (**curd·ed, curd·ing, curds**) **CURDLE** to turn something into curd, or to become curd [14C. Origin ?] —**curd·y** *adj*

curd cheese *n UK* a mild soft cheese made from skim milk curds

cur·dle /kúrd'l/ (**-dled, -dling, -dles**) *vti* **1.** to separate into curds and whey, or cause a liquid such as milk to separate into curds and whey, e.g., by permitting or encouraging bacterial action **2.** to go bad or wrong, or spoil something (*informal*) [Late 16C. < CURD]

cur dog *n Southern US* a mixed-breed mongrel dog

REGIONAL NOTE *Cur dog* is common throughout the South, except in Louisiana, where the intrepid *Catahoula cur*, which guards hogs and other stock, is the official state dog.

cure /kyoor/ *v* (**cured, cur·ing, cures**) **1.** *vti* **HEAL SOMEBODY** to restore a sick person or animal to health ○ *Six months later she was completely cured.* **2.** *vt* **TREAT ILLNESS SUCCESSFULLY** to bring an end to an illness, disorder, or injury by medical treatment ○ *Diseases like this are not easily cured.* **3.** *vt* **RESOLVE PROBLEM** to bring an end to a problem ○ *curing unemployment* **4.** *vti* **PRESERVE FOOD** to preserve food, especially meat or fish, usually by smoking, drying, or salting it, or to be preserved by one of these methods **5.** *vt* **PRESERVE SOMETHING BY DRYING** to preserve a substance, especially leather or tobacco, by drying it **6.** *vt* MANUF **FINISH SOMETHING WITH CHEMICAL PROCESS** to finish a material by applying chemicals **7.** *vt* INDUST **MAKE RUBBER STRONGER** to strengthen rubber with additives in the presence of heat and pressure **8.** *vti* CONSTR **HARDEN SOMETHING** to make a material, especially concrete or cement, harden ■ *n* **1.** **SOMETHING THAT RESTORES HEALTH** a medication or treatment that brings about a full recovery from an illness or injury ○ *working to find a cure for the disease* **2.** **RECOVERY** restoration or return to health ○ *I managed to achieve a complete cure.* **3.** **PROBLEM'S SOLUTION** something that resolves a problem **4.** **FOOD PRESERVATION PROCESS** the preservation of meat or fish, especially by smoking, drying, or salting **5.** **SPIRITUAL CARE** in the Christian Church, the spiritual and pastoral responsibility of the clergy for laypeople [13C. Via French < Latin *curare* "care for" < *cura* "care, concern"] —**cur·er** *n*

ORIGIN The Latin word *cura*, "care," "concern," from which ***cure*** is derived, is also the source of English *curate*[1], *curious*, *scour*[1], *secure*, and *sinecure*.

cu·ré /kyoo ráy, kyə-/ *n* a parish priest [Mid-17C. Via French < medieval Latin *curatus* (see CURATE[1])]

cure-all *n* a treatment or remedy that is believed to be able to cure every ailment or problem

~~**curency**~~ incorrect spelling of **currency**

cu·ret *n, vt* SURG another spelling of **curette**

cu·ret·tage /kyo͝orə ta͝azh/ *n* a surgical procedure that involves scraping the inside surface of a body cavity with an instrument shaped like a spoon (**curette**) to remove unwanted growths or other tissue [Late 19C. < French < *curette* (see CURETTE)]

cu·rette /kyoo rét/, **cu·ret** *n* a spoon-shaped surgical instrument used to remove tissue from the inner surface of a body cavity ■ *vt* (**-ret·ted, -ret·ting, -rettes; -rets**) to scrape tissue from the inner surface of a body cavity using a curette [Mid-18C. < French < *curer* "clean out" < Latin *curare* (see CURE)]

cu·rette·ment /kyoo rétmənt/ *n* SURG same as **curettage**

cur·few /kúr fyo͞o/ *n* **1.** RESTRICTION ON PEOPLE'S MOVEMENTS an official restriction on people's movements, requiring them to remain indoors after a specific time **2.** TIME OR SIGNAL FOR CURFEW the time at which a curfew takes effect, or the signal given at this time **3.** LENGTH OF CURFEW the duration of a curfew **4.** MEDIEVAL REMINDER TO EXTINGUISH LIGHTS in the Middle Ages, the ringing of a bell in the evening as a reminder to put out fires and lights ○ *"The curfew tolls the knell of parting day"* (Thomas Gray, *Elegy written in a Country Churchyard*; 1751) [13C. < Anglo-Norman *coeverfu*, Old French *cuevrefeu*, literally "cover fire"]

cu·ri·a /kyo͝oree ə/ (*plural* **-ri·ae** /kyo͝ori ee/) *n* **1.** PAPAL COURT the administrative body at the Vatican, by which the pope governs the Roman Catholic Church **2.** SUBDIVISION OF ANCIENT ROMAN TRIBE in ancient Rome, a subdivision of each tribe, or the place where it met **3.** ANCIENT ROMAN SENATE the senate or senate house in an ancient Roman city **4.** MEDIEVAL COURT a medieval monarch's court of justice [Early 17C. < Latin, "council"] —**cu·ri·al** *adj*

~~**curiculum**~~ incorrect spelling of **curriculum**

cu·rie /kyo͝oree, kyoor ée/ *n* a unit of radioactivity equal to 3.7 times 10^{10} disintegrations per second [Early 20C. After Pierre CURIE and Marie CURIE]

Cu·rie /kyo͝oree, kyoor ée/, **Irène** ♦ **Joliot-Curie, Irène**

AKG London

Marie Curie

Cu·rie, Marie (1867–1934) Polish-born French chemist and physicist. She pioneered research into radioactivity and was twice awarded the Nobel Prize (in Physics in 1903 and in Chemistry in 1911). Her husband Pierre Curie collaborated with her and was jointly awarded the 1903 Nobel Prize. Born **Skłodowska, Marja**

> "All my life through, the new sights of Nature made me rejoice like a child."
> [Attributed to Marie Curie]

Cu·rie, Pierre (1859–1906) French physicist. A professor of physics at the Sorbonne in Paris, his research with his wife, Marie Curie, on radioactivity led to the discovery of polonium and radium. They shared the Nobel Prize in physics (1903).

Cu·rie point *n* the temperature at which in some substances such as iron there is a change in the magnetic characteristics from ferromagnetic to paramagnetic behavior [After Pierre CURIE]

Cu·rie's law *n* the law of physics stating that there is an inverse proportionality between the effect of a magnetic field on a paramagnetic material and its absolute temperature [After Pierre CURIE]

Cu·rie tem·per·a·ture *n* PHYS same as **Curie point**

Cu·rie-Weiss law /-vīss-/ *n* a variation of Curie's law in which the temperature term is reduced by an amount equal to the Curie point [After Pierre CURIE and Pierre Ernest *Weiss* (1865–1940) French physicist]

cu·ri·o /kyo͝oree ō/ (*plural* **-os**) *n* an object that is valued and often collected for its interest or rarity [Mid-19C. Shortening of CURIOSITY]

cu·ri·o·sa /kyo͝oree ṓssə, -ṓzə/ *npl* **1.** books or other texts dealing with unusual topics, especially erotica **2.** interesting and unusual objects [Late 19C. < Latin, neuter plural of *curiosus* (see CURIOUS)]

cu·ri·os·i·ty /kyo͝oree óssətee/ (*plural* **-ties**) *n* **1.** DESIRE TO KNOW SOMETHING eagerness to know about something or to get information **2.** TENDENCY TO PRY an excessive interest in other people's affairs **3.** SOMEBODY OR SOMETHING THOUGHT STRANGE an interesting and unusual object, person, or phenomenon [14C. Via French < Latin *curiositas* < *curiosus* (see CURIOUS)]

cu·ri·ous /kyo͝oree əss/ *adj* **1.** EAGER TO KNOW SOMETHING eager to know about something or to get information ○ *I'm curious to know how they found out about the party.* **2.** TOO INQUISITIVE excessively eager to find out about other people's affairs **3.** ODD strange, unexpected, or hard to explain ○ *several curious events* **4.** VERY INTRICATE intricate or detailed (*archaic or literary*) [14C. Via French < Latin *curiosus* "careful, inquisitive" < *cura* "care"] —**cu·ri·ous·ly** *adv* —**cu·ri·ous·ness** *n*

~~**curiousity**~~ incorrect spelling of **curiosity**

Cur·i·ti·ba /ko͝ori téebə/ city in southern Brazil. It is the capital of Paraná State. Population: 1,476,253 (1996). Former name **Curityba**.

Cu·ri·ty·ba /ko͝ori téebə/ former name for **Curitiba**

cu·ri·um /kyo͝oree əm/ *n* a silvery white metallic radioactive element. Source: produced artificially from plutonium. Symbol **Cm**. See table at **element** [Mid-20C. After Pierre CURIE and Marie CURIE]

curl /kurl/ *v* (**curled, curl·ing, curls**) **1.** *vti* MAKE HAIR CURLY to put hair into waves, coils, or spirals, or be naturally like this **2.** *vti* MAKE SOMETHING CURVED OR COILED to bend, twist, or wind something into a curved or spiral shape, or become curved or coiled ○ *He curled the silver ribbon into spirals.* ○ *The paper had begun to curl at the edges.* **3.** *vi* MOVE IN SPIRAL MOTION to move in a curve or spiral ○ *Smoke curled into the sky.* **4.** *vi* SPORTS PARTICIPATE IN CURLING to play the game of curling ■ *n* **1.** CURVED OR COILED HAIRS a lock of hair curved into a round or spiral shape (*often used in the plural*) **2.** TENDENCY TO CURL the tendency of hair to grow or stay in ringlets ○ *My hair doesn't have much curl.* **3.** CURVED OR COILED THING something with a curved or coiled shape, e.g., a wood shaving or the crest of a breaking wave **4.** ADOPTION OF CURVED SHAPE the formation of something into a curved or round shape **5.** GYM WEIGHTLIFTING MANEUVER a weightlifting move in which a barbell is held at thigh height with the underarms facing outward, then raised to the chest, and lowered without moving the shoulders, upper arms, or legs **6.** MARKING ON WOOD a curved or spiral marking in wood grain [14C < Middle Dutch *krul* "curly" < Germanic]

curl up *v* **1.** *vi* CURVE BODY AND DRAW UP LEGS to sit or lie with the body curved and the legs tucked up ○ *curl up in bed with a good novel* **2.** *vti* COIL to become curved or coiled, or bend, twist, or wind something into a curved or spiral shape ○ *The paper curled up in the fire before it burst into flames.* **3.** *vi* FEEL EXTREMELY EMBARRASSED to be overcome with embarrassment, revulsion, or some other strong feeling (*informal*) ○ *When I realized my mistake I just wanted to curl up and disappear.*

Curl /kurl/, **Robert Floyd** (*b.* 1933) US chemist. Together with Richard Smalley and Harold Kroto, he discovered the family of carbon molecules called fullerenes, and shared a Nobel Prize in chemistry (1996).

curl·er /kúrlər/ *n* **1.** a roller or other device used to curl hair **2.** somebody who plays the game of curling

curlew

cur·lew /kúr lo͞o/ *n* a large shorebird with brownish feathers, long legs, and a long slender beak that curves downward. Genus: *Numenius*. [14C. < Old French *courlieu*, variant of *courlis*, an imitation of its cry]

curl·i·cue /kúrli kyo͞o/ *n* an ornamental twist, especially in calligraphy or design [Mid-19C. < CURLY + CUE[2] "pigtail"] —**curl·i·cued** *adj*

curl·ing /kúrling/ *n* a team game played on an ice rink, in which a heavy polished stone with a handle is slid toward a circular target (**tee**) [Early 17C. < the curving path of the stone as it reaches the target]

curl·ing i·ron *n* a device consisting of a heated rod around which the hair is twisted to form a curl

curl·ing stone *n* a heavy polished stone with a handle used in the game of curling

curl·ing tongs *npl UK* HAIR same as **curling iron**

curl·pa·per /kúrl pàypər/ *n* a small piece of paper rolled around a lock of hair, which is then twisted and left to set into a curl

curl·y /kúrlee/ (**-i·er, -i·est**) *adj* **1.** WITH CURLS arranged in curls, or curling naturally **2.** CURVED OR COILED bent or twisted into a wavy, curved, or spiral shape ○ *The paper has gotten all curly.* **3.** WOODWORK WITH CURVES IN GRAIN describes wood that has irregular curved or wavy markings in the grain —**curl·i·ness** *n*

curl·y brack·et *n* PRINTING, MATH same as **brace**[1] (sense 7)

curl·y top *n* a viral disease of beets, tomatoes, beans, and other plants that makes the leaves curl

cur·mudg·eon /kur mújjən/ *n* somebody considered to be bad-tempered, disagreeable, or stubborn [Late 16C. Origin ?] —**cur·mudg·eon·ly** *adj* —**cur·mud·geon·ry** *n*

cur·rach /kúrrə/, **cur·ragh** *n Ireland, Scotland* a boat like a coracle, formerly used on Scottish and Irish lakes and rivers [15C. < Irish, Gaelic *curach* "small boat"]

cur·rant /kúrrənt, kúr ənt/ *n* **1.** SMALL DRIED GRAPE a small dark dried seedless grape. Use: in cooking. Native to: Mediterranean. **2.** SMALL JUICY FRUIT a small round juicy fruit of a small deciduous bush, especially a red currant or black currant **3.** FRUIT-BEARING BUSH the bush, cultivated in temperate regions, that produces currants, especially red currants or black currants. Genus: *Ribes*. [Early 16C. Shortening of Anglo-Norman *raisins de Corauntz*, variant of Old French *raisins de Corinthe* "grapes from Corinth," where they originated]

USAGE currant or **current**? Do not confuse ***currant*** with ***current***, which has the same pronunciation. The word ***currant*** is used only as a noun, denoting a small dried grape, or a fruit or plant such as a black currant or red currant. The word ***current*** can be used as a noun, denoting a flow of water, air, or electricity, or as an adjective, meaning "of the present" (as in *current affairs*).

cur·ren·cy /kúrrənssee, kúr ənssee/ (*plural* **-cies**) *n* **1.** MONEY a system of money, or the bills and coins themselves, used in a country. See table on next page **2.** ACCEPTANCE OF IDEA OR TERM widespread acceptance or use of an idea, theory, word, or phrase

ALPHABETICAL CURRENCY TABLE

Unit	Country
afghani	Afghanistan
agora	Israel
avo	Macau
baht	Thailand
baisa	Oman
balboa	Panama
ban	Moldova
	Romania
birr	Ethiopia
bolivar	Venezuela
boliviano	Bolivia
butut	Gambia
cedi	Ghana
cent	Antigua and Barbuda
	Australia
	Austria
	Bahamas
	Barbados
	Belgium
	Belize
	Brunei
	Canada
	Cyprus
	Dominica
	Ecuador
	Eritrea
	Ethiopia
	Fiji
	Finland
	France
	Germany
	Greece
	Grenada
	Guyana
	Hong Kong
	Ireland
	Italy
	Jamaica
	Kenya
	Kiribati
	Liberia
	Luxembourg
	Malta
	Marshall Islands
	Mauritius
	Micronesia
	Namibia
	Nauru
	Netherlands
	New Zealand
	Palau
	Portugal
	St. Kitts and Nevis
	St. Lucia
	St. Vincent and the Grenadines
	Seychelles
	Sierra Leone
	Singapore
	Solomon Islands
	Somalia
	South Africa
	Spain
	Sri Lanka
	Suriname
	Swaziland
	Taiwan
	Tanzania
	Trinidad and Tobago
	Tuvalu
	Uganda
	United States
	Zimbabwe
centas	Lithuania
centavo	Argentina
	Bolivia
	Brazil
	Cape Verde
	Chile
	Colombia
	Cuba
	Dominican Republic
	El Salvador
	Guatemala
	Honduras
	Mexico
	Mozambique
	Nicaragua
	Philippines
centesimo	Panama
	Uruguay
centime	Algeria
	Benin
	Burkina Faso
	Burundi
	Cameroon
	Central African Republic
	Chad
	Comoros
	Congo (Dem. Rep. of the)
	Congo (Rep. of the)
	Côte d'Ivoire
	Djibouti
	Equatorial Guinea
	Gabon
	Guinea
	Guinea-Bissau
	Haiti
	Liechtenstein
	Madagascar
	Mali
	Monaco
	Morocco
	Niger
	Rwanda
	Senegal
	Switzerland
	Togo
centimo	Costa Rica
	Paraguay
	Peru
	São Tomé and Príncipe
	Venezuela
CFA franc	Benin
	Burkina Faso
	Cameroon
	Central African Republic
	Chad
	Congo (Rep. of the)
	Côte d'Ivoire
	Equatorial Guinea
	Gabon
	Guinea-Bissau
	Mali
	Niger
	Senegal
	Togo
chetrum	Bhutan
chon	North Korea
	South Korea
colón	Costa Rica
	El Salvador
Congo franc	Congo (Dem. Rep. of the)
cordoba	Nicaragua
dalasi	Gambia
denar	Macedonia, Former Yugoslav Rep. of
dinar	Algeria
	Bahrain
	Iraq
	Jordan
	Kuwait
	Libya
	Serbia and Montenegro
	Sudan
	Tunisia
dinar	Iran
dirham	Morocco
	United Arab Emirates
dirham	Libya
	Qatar
dobra	São Tomé and Príncipe
dollar	Antigua and Barbuda
	Australia
	Bahamas
	Barbados
	Belize
	Brunei
	Canada
	Dominica
	Ecuador
	Fiji
	Grenada
	Guyana
	Hong Kong
	Jamaica
	Kiribati
	Liberia
	Marshall Islands
	Micronesia
	Namibia
	Nauru
	New Zealand
	Palau
	St. Kitts and Nevis
	St. Lucia
	St. Vincent and the Grenadines
	Singapore
	Solomon Islands
	Taiwan
	Trinidad and Tobago
	Tuvalu
	United States
	Zimbabwe
dong	Vietnam
dram	Armenia
escudo	Cape Verde
euro	Austria
	Belgium
	Finland
	France
	Germany
	Greece
	Ireland
	Italy
	Luxembourg
	Netherlands
	Portugal
	Spain
eyrir	Iceland
filler	Hungary
fils	Bahrain
	Iraq
	Jordan
	Kuwait
	United Arab Emirates
	Yemen
forint	Hungary
franc	Burundi
	Comoros
	Djibouti
	Guinea
	Liechtenstein
	Madagascar
	Monaco
	Rwanda
	Switzerland
gourde	Haiti
grosz	Poland
guarani	Paraguay
guilder	Suriname
halala	Saudi Arabia
haler	Czech Republic
halier	Slovakia
hao	Vietnam
hryvnia	Ukraine
jiao	China
khoum	Mauritania
kina	Papua New Guinea
kip	Laos
kobo	Nigeria
kopek	Russia
kopiyka	Ukraine
koruna	Czech Republic
	Slovakia
krona	Faroe Islands
	Iceland
	Sweden
krone	Denmark
	Norway
kroon	Estonia
kuna	Croatia
kwacha	Malawi
	Zambia
kwanza	Angola
kyat	Myanmar
laari	Maldives
lari	Georgia
lat	Latvia
lek	Albania
lempira	Honduras
leone	Sierra Leone
leu	Moldova
	Romania
lev	Bulgaria
lilangeni	Swaziland
lipa	Croatia
lira	Malta
	Turkey
litas	Lithuania
loti	Lesotho
lumma	Armenia
lwei	Angola
manat	Azerbaijan
	Turkmenistan
marka	Bosnia and Herzegovina
markka	Finland
metical	Mozambique
millime	Tunisia
mongo	Mongolia
naira	Nigeria
nakfa	Eritrea
ngultrum	Bhutan
ngwee	Zambia
øre	Denmark
	Norway
öre	Sweden
ouguiya	Mauritania
pa'anga	Tonga
paisa	India
	Nepal
	Pakistan
para	Yugoslavia
pataca	Macau
penny	United Kingdom
peseta	Andorra
pesewa	Ghana
peso	Argentina
	Chile
	Colombia
	Cuba
	Dominican Republic
	Mexico
	Philippines
	Uruguay
piaster	Egypt
	Jordan
	Lebanon
	Syria
poisha	Bangladesh
pound	Cyprus
	Egypt
	Lebanon
	Syria
	United Kingdom
pound	Sudan
pul	Afghanistan
pula	Botswana
pya	Myanmar
qindar	Albania
quetzal	Guatemala
rand	South Africa
real	Brazil
rial	Iran
	Oman
	Yemen
riel	Cambodia
ringgit	Malaysia
riyal	Qatar
	Saudi Arabia
rubel	Belarus
ruble	Russia
	Tajikistan
rufiyaa	Maldives
rupee	India
	Mauritius
	Nepal
	Pakistan
	Seychelles
	Sri Lanka
rupiah	Indonesia
santim	Latvia
satang	Thailand
sen	Cambodia
	Indonesia
	Japan
	Malaysia
sene	Samoa
seniti	Tonga
sent	Estonia
sente	Lesotho
shekel	Israel
shilling	Kenya
	Somalia
	Tanzania
	Uganda
sol	Peru
som	Kyrgyzstan
	Uzbekistan
stotin	Slovenia
stotinka	Bulgaria
taka	Bangladesh
tala	Samoa
tambala	Malawi
tenge	Kazakhstan
tetri	Georgia
thebe	Botswana
toea	Papua New Guinea
tolar	Slovenia
tughrik	Mongolia
tyiyn	Kyrgyzstan
vatu	Vanuatu
won	North Korea
	South Korea
yen	Japan
yuan	China
zloty	Poland

= main unit

= subunit

3. CIRCULATION the transmitting of something, especially money, from person to person 4. TIME WHEN SOMETHING IS CURRENT the period of time during which something is current [Mid-17C. < CURRENT]

cur·ren·cy-sta·bi·li·za·tion fund *n* a fund set aside for use in stabilizing the foreign exchange rate for a national currency in international markets

cur·rent /kúrrənt, kúr ənt/ *adj* 1. EXISTING NOW happening, existing, or in force at the present ○ *In my current job, I am in charge of 25 people.* 2. VALID accepted as legally valid 3. PRESENTLY ACCEPTED widely known, accepted, or believed ○ *The theory is no longer current.* 4. FIN UP-TO-DATE WITH PAYMENTS having made all the payments required for the present time ■ *n* 1. FLOW OF WATER OR AIR a steady flow of water or air in one direction 2. STREAM a mass of water or air flowing steadily in one direction 3. FLOW OF ELECTRIC CHARGE the flow of electricity through a cable, wire, or other conductor 4. RATE OF FLOW OF ELECTRICITY the rate of flow of an electric charge through a conductor 5. TENDENCY a trend or tendency ○ *going against the current and moving out of the city upstate* [13C. < Old French *corant*, present participle of *courre* "run" < Latin *currere*] —**cur·rent·ness** *n*

USAGE See ***currant***.

ORIGIN The Latin word *currere*, "to run," from which ***current*** is derived, is also the source of English *corridor, courier, course, occur,* and *succor.*

cur·rent ac·count *n Can, UK* an account at a bank or building society from which money may be drawn on demand. US term **checking account**

cur·rent af·fairs *npl UK* same as **current events**

cur·rent as·sets *npl* available cash and other assets that could be converted to cash within a year

cur·rent-cost ac·count·ing *n* a method of accounting that assesses the value of assets as the cost of replacing them rather than as their original cost

cur·rent den·si·ty *n* the ratio of the amount of current flowing through a conductor to the cross-sectional area of the conductor. Symbol *j, J*

cur·rent ef·fi·cien·cy *n* in an electrolytic process, the mass of the substance liberated by a current divided by the theoretical mass, as predicted by Faraday's law

cur·rent e·vents *npl* important political and social events or issues of the present time

cur·rent li·a·bil·i·ties *npl* business liabilities that are due to be cleared before the end of the financial year

cur·rent·ly /kúrrəntlee, kúr əntlee/ *adv* at the present time ○ *They are currently living abroad.*

cur·rent ra·tio *n* the ratio of current assets to current liabilities

cur·ri·cle /kúr ik'l/ *n* a light two-wheeled open carriage drawn by a pair of horses side by side [Mid-18C. < Latin *curriculum* "racing chariot"]

cur·ric·u·lum /kə ríkyələm/ (*plural* **-la** /-lə/ or **-lums**) *n* the subjects taught at an educational institution, or the topics taught within a subject [Early 19C. < Latin, "running, course" < *currere* "to run"] —**cur·ric·u·lar** *adj*

cur·ric·u·lum vi·tae /kə rìkyələm veé tī, -vítee/ (*plural* **cur·ric·u·la vi·tae** /kə rìkyələ-/) *n UK* full form of **CV**[2] [Early 20C. < Latin, "course of life"]

cur·ri·er /kúrree ər, kúr ee ər/ *n* somebody who dresses and finishes leather after it has been tanned [14C. Via Old French *corier* < Latin *coriarius* < *corium* "leather"]

Cur·ri·er /kúrree ər, kúr ee ər/, **Nathaniel** (1813–88) US lithographer. He formed half of Currier and Ives, noted for their colored prints of Victorian American life.

cur·rish /kúr ish/ *adj* having a hostile or disagreeable disposition (*literary*) [15C. < CUR] —**cur·rish·ly** *adv* —**cur·rish·ness** *n*

cur·ry[1] /kúrree, kúr ee/ *n* (*plural* **-ries**) 1. HIGHLY SPICED DISH a dish containing meat, fish, or vegetables in a highly spiced sauce ○ *chicken curry* 2. SEASONING FOR CURRY a mixture of spices used to prepare curry. It may be a sauce, paste, powder, or other form. (*often used before a noun*) ○ *curry paste* ■ *vt* (**-ried, -ry·ing, -ries**) PREPARE FOOD IN SPICY SAUCE to cook meat, fish, or vegetables in a highly spiced sauce [Late 16C. < Tamil *kari* "sauce"]

cur·ry[2] /kúrree, kúr ee/ (**-ried, -ry·ing, -ries**) *vt* 1. to groom a horse 2. to make leather flexible and waterproof as the final stage in its processing [13C. < Old French *correier* "prepare" < Latin *con* "with" + Germanic ancestor of READY]

Cur·ry /kúrree, kúr ee/, **John Steuart** (1897–1946) US artist. He is known for his easel paintings and murals. Some of his murals adorn federal buildings in Washington, D.C.

cur·ry·comb /kúrree kōm, kúr ee-/ *n* a comb with metal or rubber teeth, used to groom horses ■ *vt* (**-combed, -comb·ing, -combs**) to groom a horse with a currycomb [Late 16C. < CURRY[2]]

cur·ry pow·der *n* a mixture of finely ground spices, usually turmeric, cumin, coriander, chili, and ginger, used to make curry [< CURRY[1]]

curse /kurss/ *n* 1. SWEARWORD a swearword, obscenity, or blasphemous oath 2. EVIL PRAYER a malevolent appeal to a supernatural being for harm to come to somebody or something, or the harm that is thought to result from this 3. SOURCE OF HARM a cause of unhappiness or harm ○ *the curse of poverty* 4. MENSTRUATION menstruation or a menstrual period (*dated slang*) 5. CHR, HIST RELIGIOUS BAN an ecclesiastical pronouncement of censure or excommunication ■ *interj* **curs·es** USED AS OATH used to express irritation or annoyance ■ *v* (**cursed, curs·ing, curs·es**) 1. *vti* SWEAR to utter swearwords or obscenities at somebody 2. *vt* WISH EVIL ON SOMEBODY to appeal malevolently to a supernatural being for harm to come to somebody or something [Old English *curs*, origin ?] —**curs·er** *n*

curs·ed /kúrssəd, kurst/ *adj* 1. HAVING BEEN WISHED EVIL afflicted with harm thought to result from a curse 2. WICKED OR HATEFUL evil to the point of being despicable 3. ANNOYING OR FRUSTRATING stubborn to the point of causing irritation or annoyance (*informal*) —**curs·ed·ly** /kúrsədlee/ *adv* —**curs·ed·ness** /-nəss/ *n*

cur·sive /kúrssiv/ *adj* WRITTEN IN FLOWING STYLE describes writing or a style of writing in a flowing style with the letters joined together ■ *n* 1. FLOWING SCRIPT cursive writing, or a cursive script 2. MANUSCRIPT WRITTEN IN FLOWING STYLE an ancient manuscript or other piece of writing in a flowing hand 3. PRINTING TYPEFACE a typeface in which the letters are joined together [Late 18C. < medieval Latin *cursivus* < Latin *currere* "to run"] —**cur·sive·ly** *adv* —**cur·sive·ness** *n*

cur·sor /kúrssər/ *n* a moving marker on a computer screen that marks the point at which keyed characters will appear or be deleted ■ *vi* (**-sored, -sor·ing, -sors**) to move the cursor in a particular direction on a computer screen ○ *Cursor down to "properties."* [14C. < Latin (see CURSORY)]

cur·so·ri·al /kur sáwree əl/ *adj* having a body or body parts particularly well-adapted for running [Mid-19C. < Latin *cursor* (see CURSORY)]

cur·so·ry /kúrssəree/ *adj* done in a quick or superficial way [Early 17C. < Latin *cursorius* < *cursor* "runner" < *currere* "to run"] —**cur·so·ri·ly** *adv* —**cur·so·ri·ness** *n*

curt /kurt/ *adj* 1. rude or abrupt 2. using few words [14C. < Latin *curtus* "cut short"] —**curt·ly** *adv* —**curt·ness** *n*

cur·tail /kur táyl/ (**-tailed, -tail·ing, -tails**) *vt* to reduce the length or duration of something [15C. Alteration of CURTAL] —**cur·tail·ment** *n*

cur·tail step /kùr tayl-/ *n* a wider lowest step on some flights of stairs, often rounded at one or both ends [Mid-18C. Origin ?]

cur·tain /kúrt'n/ *n* 1. CLOTH HUNG TO COVER SOMETHING a piece of cloth hung at a window, in a doorway, or around a bed, usually for privacy or to exclude light or drafts 2. CLOTH AT FRONT OF STAGE in a theater, a hanging cloth that is raised and lowered or pulled back and forth at the front of the stage 3. BEGINNING OR END OF SHOW the beginning or end of a performance, act, or scene, as marked by the raising or lowering or opening and closing of the curtain 4. BARRIER OR SCREEN something that acts as a barrier or screen to divide, protect, or conceal something 5. SOMETHING LIKE CURTAIN something that resembles a curtain in appearance ○ *a curtain of water* 6. BUILDINGS WALL CONNECTING OTHER STRUCTURES a length of wall, especially one that connects two towers or gates ■ *vt* (**-tained, -tain·ing, -tains**) 1. HIDE OR DIVIDE SOMETHING WITH CURTAIN to surround, separate, or conceal something with a curtain 2. FIT SOMETHING WITH CURTAINS to provide something, especially a window, with curtains [13C. Via French < late Latin *cortina*, translating Greek *aulaia*] ◇ **bring down the curtain on something** to bring an end to something (*informal*)

cur·tain call *n* an appearance by actors, dancers, or singers at the front of the stage to receive the audience's applause at the end of a performance

cur·tain lec·ture *n* a private reprimand given to a man by his wife (*dated*) [Because originally delivered within the privacy of drawn bed curtains]

cur·tain rais·er *n* 1. a short performance put on immediately before the main performance 2. a smaller or less important event that takes place before the main event

cur·tain speech *n* 1. a speech addressed to the audience by somebody in front of the curtain after a play has ended 2. the speech before the final curtain of an act or play

cur·tain time *n* the time when a play starts or is set to start

cur·tain wall *n* 1. an external wall that does not bear any of the load of the building it is attached to 2. a low wall outside a castle built for defense

cur·tal /kúrt'l/ *n* an animal whose tail has been docked (*archaic*) [Early 16C. < obsolete French *courtault* < *court* "short" + *-ault*, pejorative suffix]

~~curtesy~~ incorrect spelling of **courtesy**

cur·ti·lage /kúrt'lij/ *n* an enclosed area occupied by a dwelling, grounds, and outbuildings [14C. < Old French *co(u)rtillage* < *co(u)rtil* "kitchen garden," literally "small court" < *cort* "court"]

Cur·tin /kúrt'n/, **John Joseph** (1885–1945) Australian journalist and politician. He was an Australian Labor Party politician and prime minister of Australia (1941–45). See table at **prime minister**

~~curtious~~ incorrect spelling of **courteous**

Cur·tis /kúrtiss/, **Charles Brent** (1860–1936) US politician. He was a Republican senator who served as vice president under President Hoover (1929–33).

Cur·tis, Cyrus H. K. (1850–1933) US publisher. He built the *Saturday Evening Post* into one of the most successful US magazines of its time. Full name **Curtis, Cyrus Hermann Kotzschmar**

Cur·tiss /kúrtiss/, **Glenn Hammond** (1878–1930) US aviator. He made the first domestic public air flight (1908) and invented the first successful seaplane (1911).

Cur·tiz /kúrtiss/, **Michael** (1888–1962) Hungarian-born US movie director. He won an Academy Award for *Casablanca* (1942) and directed over 160 movies.

curt·sy /kúrtsee/, **curt·sey** *vi* (**-sied, -sy·ing, -sies; -seyed, -sey·ing, -seys**) to bend the knees, with one foot behind the other, as a gesture of respect. Women curtsy in formal situations where men bow, e.g., when acknowledging the applause of an audience after performing on stage, or when meeting royalty. ■ *n* (*plural* **-sies;** *plural* **-seys**) a movement made by a woman as a sign of respect for somebody in which she bends her knees with one foot behind the other [Early 16C. Variant of COURTESY]

cu·rule /kyŏor ŏol/ *adj* in ancient Rome, having the status to sit on an official chair (**curule chair**) and the privileges associated with this status [Mid-16C. < Latin *curulis* < *currus* "chariot" < *currere* "to run"; because the chief Roman magistrate was conveyed in a chariot]

cu·rule chair *n* a folding chair with heavy legs and no back, used by high officials of ancient Rome

cur·va·ceous /kur váyshəss/ *adj* having an attractive body with rounded hips and breasts —**cur·va·ceous·ly** *adv* —**cur·va·ceous·ness** *n*

cur·va·ture /kúrvə chŏor, -chər/ *n* 1. BEING CURVED the quality of being curved 2. DEGREE OF CURVE the degree of curving in a line or surface ○ *the slight curvature of the land* 3. MATH RECIPROCAL OF RADIUS the reciprocal of the radius of the circle that best matches a curve at a given point [15C. < Latin *curvatura* "bending" < *curvus* "curved"]

curve /kurv/ *n* **1. ROUNDED LINE** a line that bends smoothly and regularly from being straight or flat, like part of a circle or sphere **2. SOMETHING SHAPED IN CURVE** something with a smooth round shape, e.g., a bend in a road **3.** STATS **PLOTTED LINE** a line plotted on a graph from statistical data **4.** EDUC **STATISTICAL METHOD OF GRADING** a method of distributing students' grades by plotting each person's score on a graph and then dividing this line into grades **5.** MATH **LINE REPRESENTING EQUATION** a line whose points are defined by an equation and whose coordinates are functions of an independent variable **6.** BASEBALL same as **curveball** ■ *v* **(curved, curv·ing, curves) 1.** *vti* **MOVE IN CURVE** to move or bend in a curve, or make something move or bend in a curve **2.** *vt* BASEBALL **THROW CURVE BALL** to pitch somebody a curve ball **3.** *vt* **GRADE STUDENTS RELATIVELY TO ONE ANOTHER** to grade students' work by plotting scores on a graph and then assigning individual grades according to a standard distribution [15C. < Latin *curvus* "curved, crooked"] —**curved** *adj* ◇ **ahead of the curve** forward-thinking and ahead of a trend or trends ◇ **behind the curve** reactive, or slow to react, to a trend or trends ◇ **pitch** *or* **throw somebody a curve** to surprise somebody, usually with an unexpected and unwelcome question or response (*informal*)

curve·ball /kúrv bàwl/ *n* in baseball, a ball that when pitched drifts to the left if thrown by a right-handed pitcher and to the right if thrown by a left-handed pitcher

cur·vet /kur vét/ *n* a leap by a horse in dressage in which its hind legs are raised just before the forelegs touch the ground ■ *vti* **(-vet·ed** or **-vet·ted, -vet·ing** or **-vet·ting, -vets)** to perform a curvet in dressage, or make a horse perform a curvet [Late 16C. < Italian *corvetta* "small curve" < *corve* "curve" < Latin *curvus* "curved"]

cur·vi·lin·e·ar /kùrvə línnee ər/, **cur·vi·lin·e·al** /-əl/ *adj* **1.** being a curve, or having a curved part or parts ○ *a curvilinear polygon* **2.** moving along a curved path or line ○ *The ball followed a curvilinear trajectory.* [Early 18C. < Latin *curvus* "curved," after RECTILINEAR] —**cur·vi·lin·e·ar·i·ty** /kùrvə linee árrətee/ *n* —**cur·vi·lin·e·ar·ly** *adv*

curv·y /kúrvee/ **(-i·er, -i·est)** *adj* **1.** with a rounded shape **2.** having many curves or bends

cus·cus /kúss kùss/ *n* a tree-dwelling nocturnal marsupial with a round head, large eyes, large curved claws, and thick fur. Native to: rain forests of northeastern Australia and New Guinea. Genus: *Phalanger.* [Mid-17C. Via French *couscous* or modern Latin *cuscus* < Dutch *koeskoes* < a language of New Guinea]

cu·sec /kyoo sèk/ *n* a unit of flow equal to one cubic foot per second, no longer in common use [Early 20C. Shortening of *cubic foot per second*]

C·U·See·Me /see yoo see mee/ *n* a computer program that enables users to engage in real-time video conferencing over the Internet [Late 20C. < play on abbreviation of *Cornell University*, Ithaca, New York, where it was developed]

Cush /kōōsh/, **Kush** *n* **1.** in the Bible, the oldest son of Ham and brother of Canaan (Genesis 10:6) **2.** a region of northeastern Africa thought to be where the descendants of Cush settled. It is roughly equivalent to modern Ethiopia, part of northern Sudan, and southern Egypt.

Cush·ing /kōōshing/, **Harvey** (1869–1939) US neurosurgeon. He was a Harvard professor (1912–33) and in 1925 won the Pulitzer Prize for his *Life of Sir William Osler*.

> "There is only one ultimate and effectual preventive for the maladies to which flesh is heir, and that is death."
> [Harvey Cushing, "Medicine at the Crossroads," *The Medical Career and Other Papers*; 1928]

Cush·ing, Peter (1913–94) British actor. He was noted for his Baron Frankenstein and other roles in Hammer Studio's Gothic horror movies (1957–73).

Cush·ing's dis·ease /kōōshingz-/ *n* a form of Cushing's syndrome caused by excessive production of the hormone ACTH by the pituitary gland [Mid-20C. After US surgeon Harvey CUSHING]

Cush·ing's syn·drome *n* a condition caused by excessive production of corticosteroids by the adrenal cortex or pituitary gland and marked by obesity, muscular weakness, hypertension, striated skin, and fatigue [Mid-20C. See CUSHING'S DISEASE]

cush·ion /kōōsh'n/ *n* **1. SOFT FILLED BAG FOR SITTING ON** a fabric case filled with soft material, used to sit or lean on **2. SOFT PROTECTIVE PAD** a pad that is used for support, to rest against, to protect against damage, or as a shock absorber **3. SOMETHING SOFT AND YIELDING** something that gives slightly when pressed ○ *a cushion of moss at the foot of the tree* **4. SOMETHING HELPFUL** something that limits the effect of an unpleasant situation ○ *An unexpected inheritance provided a cushion when her savings ran out.* **5.** CUE GAMES **BILLIARD TABLE RIM** the raised rim around the top of a billiard table that borders its playing surface **6.** HANDICRAFT **ACCESSORY FOR MAKING LACE** a pillow for supporting the tools used in making lace ■ *vt* **(-ioned, -ion·ing, -ions) 1. PROTECT SOMEBODY OR SOMETHING AGAINST IMPACT** to protect somebody or something against the effects of physical impact ○ *A pile of sand cushioned his fall.* **2. REDUCE UNPLEASANTNESS** to lessen the effect of an unpleasant situation ○ *a generous payout to cushion the blow of early retirement* **3. SUPPORT SOMETHING WITH CUSHION** to support or rest something on a cushion or other soft object **4. PAD SOMETHING** to pad something with cushions or some other soft spongy material [14C. < French *coussin*, literally "(support for the) hip" < Latin *coxa* "hip"] —**cush·ion·y** *adj*

Cush·it·ic /kōō shíttik/ *n* a branch of the Afro-Asiatic family of languages spoken in Ethiopia, Somalia, and Kenya. Native speakers: 13 million. [Early 20C. < CUSH] —**Cush·it·ic** *adj*

Cush·man /kōōshmən/, **Charlotte** (1816–76) US stage actor, known for her tragic roles such as Lady Macbeth. Full name **Cushman, Charlotte Saunders**

cush·y /kōōshee/ **(-i·er, -i·est)** *adj* (*informal*) **1.** requiring little or no hard work, and often providing a good salary and many perks ○ *a cushy job* **2.** luxuriously styled and crafted ○ *cushy sedans for executive types* [Early 20C. < Hindi *khūsh* "pleasant"] —**cush·i·ly** *adv* —**cush·i·ness** *n*

cusk /kusk/ (*plural same* or **cusks**) *n* **1.** a large food fish of the cod family. Native to: the North Atlantic. Latin name: *Brosme brosme.* **2.** FISH same as **burbot** [Early 17C. Origin ?]

cusp /kusp/ *n* **1. POINTED END** a point or pointed end of something **2.** DENT **RIDGE ON MOLAR TOOTH** a ridge on the grinding surface of a molar tooth that helps in grinding and chewing food **3.** ANAT **FLAP OF VALVE** a triangular fold or flap of a valve in the heart or in lymph vessels that allows the flow of blood or lymph in one direction only **4.** MATH **POINT OF INTERSECTION** a point where two arcs or branches of a curve intersect and the two tangents to the curve coincide **5.** ASTROL **BORDER BETWEEN ZODIAC SIGNS** the border between two astrological star signs **6.** ARCHIT **POINTED PROJECTION IN GOTHIC ARCHITECTURE** a pointed projection formed by the intersection of two arcs, found especially in Gothic architecture **7.** ASTRON **POINTED END OF CRESCENT MOON** either of the pointed ends of a crescent moon or of any astronomical object appearing with the same curved shape [Late 16C. < Latin *cuspis* "point"] —**cusped** *adj* —**cus·pi·date** /kúspi dàyt/ *adj*

cus·pid /kúspid/ *n* DENT same as **canine** *n* (sense 1) [Mid-18C. < Latin *cuspid-* "point"]

cus·pi·dor /kúspi dàwr/ *n* same as **spittoon** [Mid-18C. < Portuguese < *cuspir* "to spit" < Latin *conspuere* < *spuere*]

cuss /kuss/ (*informal*) *vti* **(cussed, cuss·ing, cuss·es)** same as **curse** *v* (sense 1) ■ *n* **1.** a person or animal with a particular, usually irritating, trait **2.** an instance of vulgar or offensive language [Late 18C. Variant of CURSE]

cuss out *vt* to rebuke somebody using angry, foul language (*informal*)

cuss·ed /kússəd/ *adj* (*informal*) **1.** causing annoyance and anger, especially by being uncooperative **2.** same as **cursed** (senses 1–2) [Mid-19C. Variant of CURSED] —**cuss·ed·ly** *adv* —**cuss·ed·ness** *n*

cuss·word /kúss wùrd/ *n* same as **swearword** (*informal*)

cus·tard /kústərd/ *n* **1.** a cooked mixture of sugar, eggs, and milk **2.** *UK* a sweet sauce made with eggs, milk, sugar, and a thickening agent, or with milk and custard powder [15C. < Anglo-Norman *crustade* < Old French *crouste* "crust"] —**cus·tard·y** *adj*

ORIGIN A ***custard*** was originally an open pie of meat or fruit (the name referred to the pie's pastry shell or crust). The filling included stock or milk, often thickened with eggs. By around 1600 the term indicated a dish in its own right made of eggs beaten into milk and cooked.

cus·tard ap·ple *n* **1. HEART-SHAPED GREEN FRUIT** a large heart-shaped fruit with large black seeds and soft whitish flesh inside a green skin **2. CARIBBEAN TREE** a tree that bears custard apples. Native to: Caribbean. Latin name: *Annona reticulata.* **3. TREE RELATED TO CUSTARD APPLE** a fruit-bearing tree related to a true custard apple tree, e.g., the papaw, cherimoya, or sweetsop

cus·tard pie *n* a pie filled with custard, whipped cream, or a substance resembling either of these. Custard pies are traditionally thrown at people in slapstick comedy routines.

Cus·ter /kústər/, **George Armstrong** (1839–76) US soldier. He was killed fighting against Native Americans at the Battle of Little Bighorn (1876).

cus·to·di·al /ku stōdee əl/ *adj* **1. RELATING TO LEGAL CUSTODY** relating to the legal custody of, and responsibility for, a child ○ *a custodial parent* **2. JANITORIAL** connected with the work of a custodian or janitor **3. INVOLVING DETENTION** involving or consisting of detention in a prison ○ *a custodial sentence*

cus·to·di·al care *n* assistance, usually on a long-term basis, with the tasks of daily living, provided to people who are unable to look after themselves

cus·to·di·an /ku stōdee ən/ *n* **1. PERSON RESPONSIBLE FOR SOMETHING VALUABLE** somebody responsible for holding or looking after valuable property on behalf of a company or another person **2. UPHOLDER OF SOMETHING VALUABLE** a protector and upholder of something seen as valuable and endangered such as traditions or moral values **3. JANITOR** somebody responsible for general maintenance and cleaning, especially of a school or other public building [Late 18C. < CUSTODY] —**cus·to·di·an·ship** *n*

cus·to·dy /kústədee/ *n* **1. RIGHTS OVER CHILD** the legal right and responsibility for raising a child and personally supervising the child's upbringing, especially a person's right to keep the child in his or her home **2. DETENTION** detention by the police or other authorities ○ *arrested and in custody* ○ *Police have taken a man into custody.* **3. PROTECTION** the state of being held in another person's care or protection [15C. < Latin *custodia* "guarding" < *custos* "guardian"]

cus·tom /kústəm/ *n* **1. TRADITION** something that people always do or always do in a particular way by tradition **2. HABIT** the way somebody usually or routinely behaves in a particular situation **3.** LAW **TRADITION LIKE LAW** a traditional practice that is so long-established and universal that it has acquired the force of law **4.** *UK* COMM same as **patronage** ■ *adj* **1. MADE TO ORDER** made or built to order **2. MAKING GOODS TO ORDER** making, building, or selling goods to order ○ *a custom tailor* **3. CHANGED TO SUIT BETTER** altered in order to fit somebody's requirements better [12C. Via Old French *costume* "habitual practice" < Latin *consuetudin-* < *consuescere*, literally "accustom completely" < *suescere* "become accustomed"]

SYNONYMS See *habit*.

cus·tom·a·ble /kústəməb'l/ *adj* liable for import or export duties

cus·tom·ar·y /kústə mèrree/ *adj* **1. USUAL** conforming to what is usual or normal **2. CHARACTERISTIC** usual for somebody or characteristic of somebody's usual behavior ○ *his customary good humor* **3.** LAW **BASED ON CUSTOM** based on custom and tradition rather than written law —**cus·tom·ar·i·ly** /kùstə mérrəlee/ *adv*

SYNONYMS See *usual*.

cus·tom-built *adj* designed and built to meet the requirements of an individual customer —**cus·tom-build** *vt*

cus·tom drug *n* a drug that targets a specific condition, especially a drug that is tailored to an individual patient's genetic requirements

cus·tom·er /kústəmər/ *n* **1.** a person or company that buys goods or services **2.** somebody who interacts with others in a particular way (*informal*) ○ *a cool customer* [15C. < the idea of "customary business practice"]

cus·tom·er rage *n* extreme frustration and anger on the part of a consumer-caller with the quality of a product or service, exhibited by shouting or cursing at a customer-service representative over the telephone

cus·tom·er serv·ice *n* a department of a business that deals with routine inquiries and complaints from or disputes with customers ○ *You can call customer service toll-free.*

cus·tom·house /kústəm hòwss/ (*plural* **-hous·es** /-hòwzəz/) *also* **cus·toms·house** /kústəmz hòwss/ *n* an office at a port where customs are collected and where ships are given permission to enter or leave

cus·tom·ize /kústə mīz/ (**-ized, -iz·ing, -iz·es**) *vt* to alter something in order to make it fit somebody's requirements better ○ *She has customized the software to suit our needs.* —**cus·tom·i·za·tion** /kùstəmi záysh'n/ *n* —**cus·tom·iz·er** *n*

cus·tom-made *adj* designed and made to meet the requirements of an individual customer ○ *custom-made shoes*

cus·toms /kústəmz/ *n* (*takes a singular or plural verb*) **1.** *also* **Cus·toms** PLACE WHERE DUTIABLE GOODS ARE EXAMINED a place where goods and baggage are examined on entering a country to see what duty is payable on them and to check for smuggled goods ○ *pass through customs* **2.** *also* **Cus·toms** GOVERNMENT AGENCY a government department responsible for collecting taxes on imports and for preventing illegal imports **3.** DUTIES ON GOODS taxes payable on imports and exports [14C. < CUSTOM "customary tax"]

cus·toms·house *n* FIN, SHIPPING same as **customhouse**

cus·toms un·ion *n* an association of countries that enjoy free trade among themselves and agree on tariffs for nonmembers

cus·tom-tai·lor (**cus·tom-tai·lored, cus·tom-tai·lor·ing, cus·tom-tai·lors**) *vt* to plan, build, or change something so that it fits somebody's individual requirements

cut /kut/ *v* (**cut, cut·ting, cuts**) **1.** *vti* DIVIDE SOMETHING WITH SHARP TOOL to divide something into pieces using a knife, scissors, or a similar sharp-edged tool **2.** *vt* SEVER PART USING SHARP TOOL to sever something or separate a part of something using a sharp-edged tool such as a knife, scissors, or a saw ○ *cut a slice of bread* **3.** *vti* MAKE HOLE IN SOMETHING to pierce or make a hole in something using a sharp instrument **4.** *vi* BE SHARP to be sharp enough to slice or pierce things easily ○ *These scissors won't cut.* **5.** *vi* YIELD TO BLADE to be easily sliced or pierced by a sharp tool such as a knife ○ *bread that cuts easily* **6.** *vt* INJURE SOMEBODY WITH SHARP EDGE to injure somebody or yourself with something sharp, usually enough to draw blood **7.** *vt* SHORTEN SOMETHING WITH SHARP TOOL to make something shorter by removing some of it with a sharp tool such as scissors ○ *I'm having my hair cut this afternoon.* **8.** *vt* SHAPE GARMENT to shape fabric in a particular way in order to fashion a garment ○ *a skirt cut on the bias* **9.** *vt* REDUCE QUANTITY to reduce an amount, e.g., of money or time, or remove an amount from something ○ *cut a budget* **10.** *vt* STOP PROVIDING SOMETHING to stop providing a service or supply of something ○ *cut the supply of water to the farmers* **11.** *vt* TURN DEVICE OFF to stop something from operating ○ *cut the engine* **12.** *vi* TAKE OR BE SHORTCUT to cross, travel, or make a line through or across an area, especially in order to save time ○ *This path cuts through the woods.* **13.** *vti* INTERSECT to cross something or cross each other at a particular point ○ *The road cuts the river in three places.* **14.** *vi* CHANGE DIRECTION SHARPLY to make a sharp change in direction ○ *You need to cut to the right here.* **15.** *vti* DELETE DATA to delete data on a computer, often in order to insert it somewhere else. ◊ **paste**[1] *v* (sense 3) **16.** *vt* SHORTEN SOMETHING BY EDITING to make something such as a movie, text, or speech shorter by removing parts of it, or remove a part to make it shorter **17.** *vti* MOVIES, BROADCAST EDIT MOVIE OR VIDEO to edit a movie or other work intended for performance or broadcast **18.** *vi* MOVIES STOP FILMING to stop filming a particular scene (*usually used as a command*) **19.** *vi* MOVIES CHANGE SCENE to switch suddenly from one scene to another when filming or showing a film **20.** *vt* MAKE RECORDING to make a recording of a song or group of songs (*informal*) ○ *The band cut 12 new tracks for the album.* **21.** *vti* DIVIDE DECK OF CARDS to divide a deck of cards in two, usually after shuffling them **22.** *vt* DILUTE to add a substance to another, especially to a drug or an alcoholic drink, usually in order to make it weaker or cheaper **23.** *vti* REMOVE GRIME to dissolve something such as dirt or grease from something else in the process of cleaning it **24.** *vt* GROW TEETH THROUGH GUMS to produce a tooth through the surface of the gums ○ *The baby's cutting a tooth.* **25.** *vt* SNUB SOMEBODY to pay no attention to somebody in a public place or in an obvious way **26.** *vti* UPSET SOMEBODY to hurt somebody's feelings ○ *a cruel remark that cut me deeply* **27.** *vt* STOP DOING SOMETHING to stop doing something that is annoying somebody (*informal*) ○ *Cut that racket!* **28.** *vt* NOT ATTEND EVENT to fail to attend a scheduled event as expected, e.g., not go to school (*informal*) ○ *expelled for cutting classes* **29.** *vt* NEGOTIATE SOMETHING to negotiate an agreement (*informal*) ○ *cut a deal* **30.** *vt* RACKET GAMES HIT BALL SO IT SPINS to hit a ball with a racket in such a way that it spins as it flies through the air ■ *n* **1.** WOUND IN SKIN an injury made when something sharp pierces the skin **2.** INCISION an incision made in something with a knife or other sharp-edged tool **3.** REDUCTION a reduction in the amount of something ○ *cuts in taxes and interest rates* **4.** STOPPING OF SUPPLY a stopping of a supply, e.g., of electricity ○ *power cuts* **5.** HAIRCUT a haircut or hairstyle **6.** GARMENT STYLE the way of cutting a garment from fabric that determines its shape and fit ○ *a dress with a flattering cut* **7.** PRUNING OF TEXT a removal of a section of something such as a movie, text, or speech in order to make it shorter or improve it, or a section removed ○ *The editor advised me to make some cuts in the final chapter.* **8.** MOVIES VERSION a particular edited version of a movie ○ *the director's final cut of the film* **9.** RECORDING SINGLE RECORDING a track on a musical recording **10.** PARTICULAR SEGMENT OF MEAT a piece of meat cut in a standard way, ready to be cooked ○ *buys the cheapest cuts* **11.** SHARE a share of an amount of money or something else to be divided (*informal*) **12.** NON-ATTENDANCE an unauthorized absence from a scheduled event, especially a class ○ *expelled for too many cuts* **13.** BASEBALL SWING OF BAT a swing of a baseball bat **14.** CARDS DIVIDING OF DECK OF CARDS the action of dividing a deck of cards in two **15.** PRINTING PRINTING DEVICE a block for printing that has a design engraved, incised, or cut in relief on it (*often used in combination*) **16.** HURTFUL STATEMENT OR ACTION a statement or action intended to insult or hurt **17.** same as **snub** ■ *adj* **1.** INJURED WITH SOMETHING SHARP injured or damaged by something sharp, usually enough to draw blood ○ *nursing a cut finger* **2.** SEPARATED WITH KNIFE separated or severed using a knife, scissors, or similar sharp tool ○ *cut flowers* **3.** BOT DIVIDED describes a leaf that is divided into segments [13C. < assumed Old English *cytan*] —**cut·ta·ble** *adj* ◇ **cut and run** to leave a place quickly to avoid being caught or detained ◇ **cut both ways** to have both advantages and disadvantages ◇ **cut it close** to allow barely enough of something, often time, for what has to be done ◇ **cut loose** (*informal*) **1.** to behave in an unrestrained and relatively uncontrolled way **2.** to break away from the influence or control of somebody or something ◇ **cut somebody dead** to ignore somebody deliberately and completely ◇ **cut somebody short** to interrupt somebody who is speaking ◇ **cut somebody some slack** to allow somebody a degree of freedom or latitude to do something ◇ **cut something short** to end something earlier than expected or desired ◇ **not (be able to) cut it** to fall short of requirements, or be unable to cope with a situation (*informal*) ○ *His usual excuses just don't cut it with me.*

cut across *vt* to affect a widely differing group of people or things equally

cut back *v* **1.** *vti* to reduce the amount of something ○ *cut back on spending* **2.** *vt* to cut the tops or all of the stems or branches off a plant in order to remove dead growth or produce bushier growth ○ *cut back the roses*

cut down *v* **1.** *vti* REDUCE SOMETHING to consume, use, or do less of something, especially because it is considered harmful ○ *The doctor says I have to cut down on fried foods.* **2.** *vt* FELL OR CLEAR AWAY PLANTS to cut through the trunk or stem of a plant so that it can be removed or harvested **3.** *vt* KILL SOMEBODY to kill somebody, especially suddenly or unexpectedly (*usually passive*) **4.** *vt* MAKE CLOTHING SMALLER to alter a piece of clothing so that it will fit somebody smaller **5.** *vt* AUTOMOT REMODEL CAR BY REMOVING EXTRAS to remodel a car by removing unnecessary extras, especially in order to make it more suitable for racing

cut in *v* **1.** *vti* INTERRUPT to interrupt when somebody is speaking **2.** *vti* JOIN MIDDLE OF LINE to enter a line of people by pushing in front of others who have been waiting **3.** *vi* JOIN TRAFFIC DANGEROUSLY to join a lane of traffic too close in front of another car so that it has to brake sharply **4.** *vi* START TO OPERATE to start working as part of a machine or electrical device **5.** *vi* PARTNER SOMEBODY ALREADY DANCING to interrupt a dancing couple and take one of them as your own partner **6.** *vt* COOK MIX FAT WITH FLOUR to mix shortening into flour using a metal blade **7.** *vt* ALLOW SOMEBODY TO SHARE to allow somebody to have a share in something, especially money (*informal*) ○ *cut us in on the profits*

cut off *v* **1.** *vt* REMOVE PART OF SOMETHING to remove something that is part of something else by cutting it **2.** *vt* STOP SUPPLY to stop supplying something ○ *cut off the electricity* **3.** *vt* ISOLATE SOMEBODY OR SOMETHING to separate a person, group, or place from usual communication or contact ○ *a town cut off by the blizzard* **4.** *vt* DISCONNECT SOMEBODY ON TELEPHONE to disconnect somebody who is talking on the telephone **5.** *vt* STOP SOMEBODY TALKING to interrupt what somebody is saying and stop him or her from talking ○ *cut him off in mid-sentence* **6.** *vt* DISINHERIT SOMEBODY to exclude somebody from an inheritance ○ *They cut their son off without a penny.* **7.** *vti* BRING SOMETHING TO ABRUPT END to bring something to an abrupt end, or be brought to an abrupt end ○ *The machine cut off suddenly.*

cut out *v* **1.** *vt* REMOVE SOMETHING BY CUTTING to remove part of something using a cutting tool **2.** *vt* CUT SHAPE FROM SOMETHING to cut a shaped piece from a larger part or whole **3.** *vt* REMOVE PART FROM TEXT to remove part of a text or broadcast **4.** *vt* STOP DOING SOMETHING to stop doing something, especially because it is considered harmful ○ *I've cut out all dairy products.* **5.** *vt* EXCLUDE SOMEBODY to exclude or eliminate somebody from a group or activity ○ *cut them out of future negotiations* **6.** *vt* OMIT SOMETHING to exclude, eliminate, or omit something ○ *I followed the recipe but cut out the walnuts.* **7.** *vt* DISINHERIT SOMEBODY to change a will so that somebody will no longer inherit **8.** *vi* CEASE FUNCTIONING to stop functioning suddenly, especially to stop providing power ○ *The engine cut out.* **9.** *vt* SEPARATE ANIMAL FROM HERD to separate an animal, especially a cow, from a herd **10.** *vt Southern US* TURN SOMETHING OFF to turn off a light or electrical appliance ○ *cut the lights out* **11.** *vt* STOP SOMETHING ANNOYING to stop doing something that is annoying somebody (*informal; often used as a command*) ○ *Cut out the wisecracks.* **12.** *vi* LEAVE QUICKLY to leave a location or place hastily (*slang*) ○ *Let's cut out of here.* ■ *adj* NATURALLY SUITED naturally suited for a particular activity or profession ○ *I wasn't cut out to be a driving instructor.*

cut over *vt* to transfer existing data, functions, or users of a computer system to new facilities or equipment in a synchronized manner

cut through *vt* to deal with a problem or obstacle in a way that reduces or eliminates it ○ *Can't we cut through the formalities?*

cut up *v* **1.** *vt* CUT SOMEBODY OR SOMETHING INTO PIECES to divide somebody or something into pieces by cutting **2.** *vt* INJURE SOMEBODY to injure somebody, especially enough to draw blood **3.** *vi* MISBEHAVE to behave in a humorous and disruptive way (*slang*) ○ *cutting up in class* ■ *adj* UPSET upset and distressed (*informal*) ○ *He was all cut up over his mother's death.*

cut-and-cov·er *adj* describes a method of constructing a tunnel by digging a trench down from ground level and then roofing it

cut-and-dried *adj* **1.** clear, settled, and not needing changes or further work ○ *The ethics of organ transplants aren't exactly cut-and-dried.* **2.** obvious or conforming to what is expected ○ *a cut-and-dried press conference* [Originally of herbs on sale]

cut-and-paste *n* a facility of computers allowing data to be deleted in one place and inserted in another ○ *Use cut-and-paste to move that paragraph into the new document.* —**cut-and-paste** *vt*

cut-and-try *adj* done by trial and error, using experimental procedures ○ *a cut-and-try approach*

cu·ta·ne·ous /kyoo táynee əss/ *adj* relating to the skin [Late 16C. < modern Latin *cutaneus* < Latin *cutis* "skin"] —**cu·ta·ne·ous·ly** *adv*

cu·ta·ne·ous an·thrax *n* skin ulceration caused by anthrax bacteria

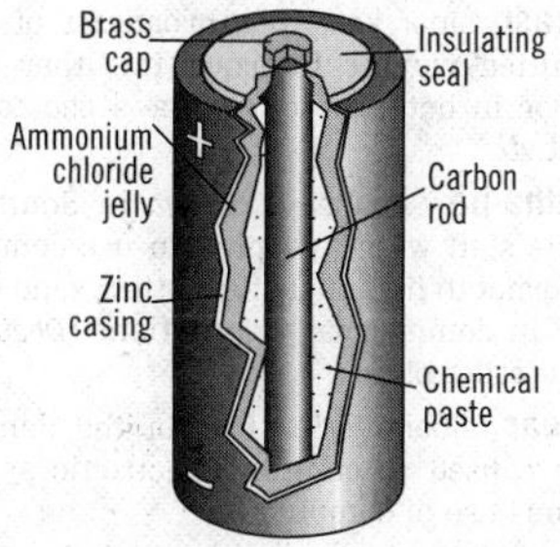

cutaway: cutaway view of a battery

cut·a·way /kúttə wày/ *n* **1.** MODEL WITH INSIDE VIEW a drawing or model of something with part of its outside removed to give a view of the inside **2.** CLOTHING MEN'S FORMAL COAT WITH TAILS a formal coat for men, cut short at the front and with two long tails at the back **3.** MOVIES, MEDIA SECONDARY SHOT WITH CAMERA in a filmed sequence, a short shot that shows an action separate from the main action ■ *adj* **1.** GIVING INSIDE VIEW constructed or represented so as to give a view of the inside **2.** CLOTHING CUT DIAGONALLY having the front cut diagonally away from the center, e.g., in the part of a tailcoat below the waist

cut·back /kút bàk/ *n* a reduction in the amount of something ○ *cutbacks in public spending*

cutch /kuch/ *n* TREES same as **catechu** [Mid-18C. < Malay *kachu* "astringent vegetable extract" < Dravidian]

cute /kyoot/ (**cut·er, cut·est**) *adj* **1.** ATTRACTIVE IN CHILDLIKE WAY endearingly attractive in the way that some children and young animals are **2.** PHYSICALLY ATTRACTIVE young and physically attractive **3.** PLEASING smaller than the usual size but nicely arranged or appointed ○ *an apartment with a cute little kitchen* **4.** SHREWD sharply intelligent or wily [Early 18C. Shortening of ACUTE] —**cute·ly** *adv* —**cute·ness** *n* ◇ **get cute (with somebody)** to show insolence to somebody (*informal*)

cu·tes ANAT plural of **cutis**

cute·sy /kyóotsee/ (**-si·er, -si·est**) *adj* too obviously attempting to be charming (*informal*) —**cute·si·ness** *n*

cut·ey *n* another spelling of **cutie** (*informal*)

cut glass *n* glass with a decorative pattern cut into its surface (*hyphenated before a noun*) ○ *a cut-glass bowl*

cut·grass /kút gràss/ *n* a marsh grass with rough or sharp edges along the leaf margin. Genus: *Leersia*.

cu·ti·cle /kyóotik'l/ *n* **1.** SKIN AT BASE OF NAILS an edge of hard skin at the base of a fingernail or toenail **2.** ANAT same as **epidermis** (sense 1) **3.** ANAT DEAD EPIDERMIS dead or hardened epidermis **4.** ZOOL HARD COVERING OF INVERTEBRATES a hardened noncellular layer secreted by and covering the epidermis in many invertebrates **5.** BOT PROTECTIVE PLANT LAYER the thin outermost noncellular layer covering the parts of plants that are above the ground and helping to prevent water loss [15C. < Latin *cuticula* "little skin" < *cutis* "skin"] —**cu·tic·u·lar** /kyoo tíkyələr/ *adj*

cut·ie /kyóotee/, **cut·ey** (*plural* **-eys**) *n* a cute person or animal (*informal*)

cu·tin /kyóot'n/ *n* a waxy mixture of fats and soaps forming the protective layer (**cuticle**) of plants [Mid-19C. < CUTIS]

cut-in *n* in a filmed sequence, a camera shot that focuses in on a smaller portion of a scene already established

cu·tin·ize /kyóot'n ìz/ (**-ized, -iz·ing, -iz·es**) *vti* to deposit cutin in the cell walls of the parts of plants that are above the ground —**cu·tin·i·za·tion** /kyòot'ni záysh'n/ *n*

cu·tis /kyóotiss/ (*plural* **-tes** /-teez/) *n* ANAT same as **dermis** [Early 17C. < Latin, "skin"]

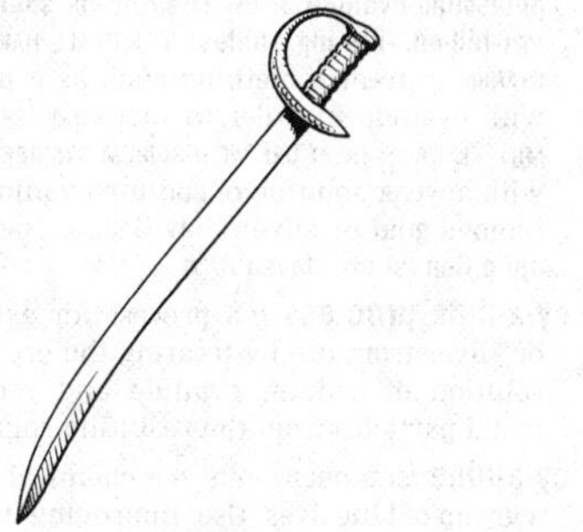
cutlass

cut·lass /kúttləss/ *n* **1.** a short thrusting sword with a flat and slightly curved blade, used in the past especially by sailors **2.** *Carib* a machete [Late 16C. Via French *cutelas* "large knife" < Latin *cultellus* "small knife" < *culter* (see COULTER)]

cut·lass fish *n* a sea fish with a long slender body and long sharp teeth. Genus: *Trichiurus*.

cut·ler·y /kúttləree/ *n* **1.** *Can, UK* knives, forks, and spoons used for eating. US term **flatware 2.** knives and other instruments with a blade

cut·let /kúttlət/ *n* **1.** a mixture of chopped meat, fish, nuts, vegetables, or other foods, made into a flat round shape, covered with breadcrumbs, and fried **2.** a flat, boneless piece of meat that will serve one person [Early 18C. < French *côtelette* "little rib" < Latin *costa* "rib"]

cut·line /kút lìn/ *n* a caption to an illustration

cut·off /kút àwf, -òf/ *n* **1.** LIMIT a limit or date beyond which something is stopped **2.** END OF SUPPLY an end to the supply of something ○ *a cutoff in oil imports* **3.** ENG VALVE a valve that controls the flow of fluid or gas through a pipe **4.** SHORTCUT a shorter route or bypass **5.** BASEBALL RELAYED THROW in baseball, a throw from the outfield to home plate or a base in two stages, using an infielder as an intermediary **6.** MUSIC BREAK IN MUSIC the end of a note, passage, or piece of music, especially when indicated by a sign from the conductor **7.** MUSIC SIGNAL FROM MUSIC CONDUCTOR a sign given by a conductor to indicate a break in the music **8.** ELECTRONICS ELECTRICAL THRESHOLD the value of voltage, frequency, or other variable that represents a minimum or maximum for effective operation **9.** GEOG NEW RIVER CHANNEL a short channel cut by a river across a bend in the river, forming an oxbow lake ■ **cut·offs** *npl* SHORTS MADE FROM PANTS shorts made by cutting off the legs of a pair of pants, especially jeans

cut·off man *n* in baseball, an infielder who catches a throw from an outfielder and relays it to home plate or a base

cut·out /kút òwt/ *n* **1.** SILHOUETTE SHAPE a two-dimensional shape of somebody or something, usually made from stiff cardboard **2.** SOMETHING CUT OUT something that has been cut out from something else **3.** ELEC SAFETY DEVICE FOR ELECTRIC CIRCUIT a device that switches off an electric circuit or supply, e.g., to a machine, as a safety measure **4.** RECORDING OUTDATED AUDIO RECORDING a recording sold at a discount because it is out-of-date and supply exceeds demand **5.** SPIES' GO-BETWEEN somebody trusted to pass messages between espionage agents (*informal*)

cut·o·ver /kút òvər/ *n* the transfer of a system such as a computer network to new facilities or equipment including the transitional period when old and new systems are operating concurrently ■ *adj* describes forest land with the trees cut down for selling as timber

cut·purse /kút pùrss/ *n* CRIME same as **pickpocket** (*archaic*)

cut-rate *adj* on sale or selling for less than the standard price, and often regarded as shoddy

CUTS *abbr* COMPUT Computer Users' Tape System

Cut·tack /kúttək/ city in eastern Orissa State, eastern India. It is situated at the head of a delta formed by the Mahanadi River on the Bay of Bengal. Population: 587,637 (2001).

cut·ter /kúttər/ *n* **1.** SHARP TOOL a tool used to cut through something (*often used in the plural*) ○ *wire cutters* **2.** SOMEBODY WHO CUTS SOMETHING somebody whose work involves cutting things such as fabrics to be made into clothing **3.** SOMEBODY WHO REDUCES SOMETHING somebody who cuts or reduces something **4.** SMALL ARMED PATROL BOAT a small lightly armed patrol boat used especially by the Coast Guard **5.** SINGLE-MASTED SAILBOAT a single-masted sailing vessel on which the mast is positioned farther aft than on a sloop **6.** BOAT FOR TRANSPORTING PASSENGERS a ship's boat, powered by a motor or by oars, that is used to transport passengers and light cargo **7.** SMALL SLEIGH formerly, a small sleigh pulled by one horse

cut·throat /kút thròt/ *adj* **1.** WITH NO HOLDS BARRED aggressive and merciless in striving for supremacy **2.** MURDEROUS capable of murder or characteristic of a murderer (*archaic*) **3.** FOR 3 PLAYERS describes games for three players that are adapted from games for four partnered players ○ *cutthroat bridge* ■ *n* **1.** DANGEROUS PERSON a murderer or an aggressive dangerous person **2.** (*plural same* or **cut·throats**) FISH same as **cutthroat trout**

cut·throat ra·zor *n UK* same as **straight razor**

cut·throat trout *n* a trout that resembles the rainbow trout but has reddish orange markings on each side of the throat. Native to: western North America. Latin name: *Salmo clarkii*.

cut time *n* a musical meter in which two half notes receive the beat in each bar, notated in the time signature by a "C" with a slash through it

cut·ting /kútting/ *n* **1.** PART OF PLANT FOR PROPAGATION a piece taken from a stem, leaf, or root that will grow into a new plant **2.** EDITING PROCESS the process of editing a text, film, or recording **3.** MOVIES CHANGING OF SHOTS IN MOVIE the technique of changing from one shot to another in the editing of a movie **4.** *UK* MEDIA same as **clipping** (sense 1) ■ *adj* **1.** ABRASIVE AND HURTFUL sharply expressed and likely to upset somebody's feelings ○ *a cutting remark* **2.** VERY COLD piercingly cold ○ *a cutting wind* —**cut·ting·ly** *adv*

cut·ting board *n* a piece of flat wood or rigid plastic used to protect a countertop or table while cutting food

cut·ting edge *n* the most advanced and modern stage of something (*hyphenated when used before a noun*)

cut·ting horse *n* a horse trained to separate cows, calves, or steers from a herd on the commands of its rider

cut·ting room *n* a room where motion picture film is edited, usually by hand and by being physically cut

cut·tle·bone /kútt'l bòn/ *n* the white internal shell of a cuttlefish. Use: whole as a mineral supplement for caged birds, in powdered form for polishing. [Late 16C. < Old English *cudele* (see CUTTLEFISH)]

cut·tle·fish /kútt'l fish/ (*plural same* or **-fish·es**) *n* an invertebrate sea animal that lives on the ocean floor and has ten arms, a flattened body, and an internal shell. Cuttlefish eject a dark inky fluid as a defense mechanism. Genus: *Sepia*. [Late 16C. < Old English *cudele*, related to COD[2] "bag"; from its shape]

cut·up /kút ùp/ *n* somebody known for telling jokes, showing off, and playing pranks (*informal*)

cut·wa·ter /kút wàwtər/ *n* **1.** the foremost part of a ship's prow **2.** a pointed or wedge-shaped upstream face of a bridge pier at water level, designed to minimize the effects of moving water, ice floes, and debris

cuttlefish

cut·work /kút wùrk/ *n* openwork embroidery in which the design is outlined in buttonhole stitch, after which some parts of the fabric within the outlines are cut away

cut·worm /kút wùrm/ *n* a nocturnal moth caterpillar that feeds on and eats through the base of young plant stems. Family: Noctuidae.

cu·vée /koo váy/ *n* a single batch of wine [Mid-19C. < French, "contents of a vat" < *cuve* "cask, vat" < Latin *cupa*]

cu·vette /koo vét/ *n* a transparent tubular laboratory vessel or dish for holding a liquid [Late 17C. < French, "small cask" < *cuve* (see CUVÉE)]

Cu·vier /kóovee ày, kyóo-/, **Georges, Baron** (1769–1832) French zoologist and anatomist. He devised animal classification systems and established the fields of comparative anatomy and paleontology. Full name **Georges Léopold Chrétien Frédéric Dagobert, Baron Cuvier**

Cuy·a·ho·ga /kī ə hṓgə, -háw-/ river in northeastern Ohio, flowing southwest and then sharply north into Lake Erie. Length: 100 mi./161 km.

Cuy·a·ho·ga Falls city in northeastern Ohio, on the northern shore of the Cuyahoga River, northeast of Akron. Population: 49,236 (2002 estimate).

cuz /kəz/ *conj* same as **because** (*nonstandard*)

Cuz·co /kóozkō, kóoss-/ city in southern Peru, and capital of Cuzco Department. It was the capital of the Inca empire until 1533. Population: 278,590 (1998).

cv *abbr* Cape Verde (*used in Internet addresses*) See table at **domain name**

CV[1] *abbr* **1.** MED cardiovascular **2.** MIL Cross of Valour

CV[2], **cv** *n* HR same as **résumé** (sense 1)

C.V. *abbr* Cape Verde

CVA *abbr* **1.** MED cerebrovascular accident **2.** Columbia Valley Authority

CVS *abbr* MED chorionic villus sampling

cw *abbr* PHYS continuous wave

CW *abbr* **1.** MIL chemical warfare **2.** ARMS chemical weapons **3.** PHYS continuous wave

CWD *abbr* VET, MED chronic wasting disease

cwm /koom/ *n UK* GEOL same as **cirque** [Mid-19C. < Welsh, "valley"]

CWO *abbr* **1.** MIL Chief Warrant Officer **2.** BUSINESS chief Web officer

cwt., **cwt** *abbr* MEASURE hundredweight [*C* the roman numeral for "hundred"]

cx *abbr* Christmas Island (*used in Internet addresses*) See table at **domain name**

cXML *abbr* E-COMMERCE commerce XML (*used in e-commerce*)

cy *abbr* Cyprus (*used in Internet addresses*) See table at **domain name**

-cy *suffix* **1.** condition, quality ○ *buoyancy* **2.** action ○ *advocacy* **3.** rank, office ○ *baronetcy* [Via Old French *-cie, -tie* < Latin *-cia, -tia*, Greek *-k(e)ia, -t(e)ia*]

CYA *abbr* ONLINE see ya (*used in e-mails or text messages*)

cy·an /sī ən, -àn/ *n* a deep greenish blue color that, together with yellow and magenta, is one of the three subtractive colors [Late 19C. < Greek *kuanos* "dark blue"] —**cy·an** *adj*

cyan- *prefix* same as **cyano-** (*used before vowels*)

cy·an·am·ide /sī ánnə mīd/, **cy·an·am·id** /-mid/ *n* **1.** a white crystalline caustic compound. Formula: CH_2N_2. **2.** CHEM same as **calcium cyanamide**

cy·a·nate /sī ə nàyt, -nət/ *n* a salt or ester of cyanic acid

cy·an·ic /sī ánnik/ *adj* of a greenish blue color

cy·an·ic ac·id *n* a weak colorless unstable acid. Formula: HOCN.

cy·a·nide /sī ə nīd/ *n* **1.** COMPOUND CONTAINING CARBON AND NITROGEN a compound containing carbon and nitrogen as a CN group or CN^- ion **2.** CHEM same as **potassium cyanide 3.** CHEM same as **sodium cyanide** ■ *vt* (**-nid·ed, -nid·ing, -nides**) **1.** METALL HARDEN METAL WITH CYANIDE to treat something such as a metal surface with cyanide in order to increase its hardness **2.** MIN EXTRACT TREAT ORE WITH SODIUM CYANIDE to treat ore with a weak solution of sodium cyanide in order to remove gold or silver [Early 19C. < CYANOGEN] —**cy·a·nid·a·tion** /sī əni dáysh'n/ *n*

cy·a·nide proc·ess *n* a process for extracting gold or silver from ore by treating the ore with a weak solution of sodium cyanide and recovering the metal particles from the resulting solution

cy·a·nine /sī ə neen, -nin/ *n* a chemical belonging to a group of blue dyes. Use: improving the sensitivity of photographic film to green, yellow, red, and infrared light.

cy·a·nite /sī ə nīt/ *n* MINERALS another spelling of **kyanite**

cyano- *prefix* **1.** blue ○ *cyanosis* **2.** cyanide ○ *cyanogenesis* **3.** cyanogen ○ *cyanic acid* [< Greek *kuanos* "dark blue"]

cy·a·no·ac·ry·late /sī ənō ákrə làyt, -ákrələt/ *n* a liquid acrylate monomer belonging to a group with adhesive properties. Use: industry and medicine.

cy·a·no·bac·te·ri·a /sī ənō bak téeree ə/ *npl* bacteria belonging to a large group that have a photosynthetic pigment and carry out photosynthesis. They were formerly classified as blue-green algae. Family: Cyanophyta.

cy·a·no·co·bal·a·min /sī ə nō kō bálləmin/ *n* BIOCHEM same as **vitamin** B_{12}

cy·an·o·gen /sī ánnəjən, -jèn/ *n* **1.** a flammable colorless poisonous gas. Use: organic synthesis. Formula: C_2N_2. **2.** a univalent radical. Source: cyanide compounds. Formula: CN. [Early 19C. < French *cyanogène* < Greek *kuanos* "dark blue"; from its being a constituent of Prussian blue]

cy·a·no·gen·e·sis /sī ənō jénnəssiss/ *n* the natural generation and release of hydrogen cyanide that occurs in some plants —**cy·a·no·ge·net·ic** /-jə néttik/ *adj* —**cy·a·no·gen·ic** *adj*

cy·a·no·hy·drin /sī ənō hīdrin/ *n* an organic compound belonging to a group that contain both nitrile and hydroxyl groups

cy·a·no·sis /sī ə nṓssiss/ *n* a condition in which the skin and mucous membranes take on a bluish color because there is not enough oxygen in the blood [Mid-19C. Via modern Latin < Greek *kuanōsis* "blueness" < *kuanos* "dark blue"] —**cy·a·not·ic** /-nóttik/ *adj*

cy·an·o·type /sī ánnə tīp/ *n* PRINTING same as **blueprint** *n* (sense 1)

Cyb·e·le /síbbəlee/ *n* in the mythology of ancient Phrygia, the goddess of nature. She was worshiped by the Romans as the Great Mother of the Gods.

cyber- *prefix* **1.** computers and information systems ○ *cyberlaw* **2.** virtual reality ○ *cyberspace* **3.** the Internet ○ *cybercafé* [< CYBERNETICS, CYBERSPACE]

cy·ber·art *n*
cy·ber·art·ist *n*
cy·ber·at·tack *n*
cy·ber·bab·ble *n*
cy·ber·bank *n*
cy·ber·bank·ing *n*
cy·ber·brain *n*
cy·ber·com·merce *n*
cy·ber·crime *n*
cy·ber·cul·ture *n*
cy·ber·date *n*
cy·ber·dat·ing *n*
cy·ber·fem·i·nism *n*
cy·ber·fem·i·nist *n, adj*
cy·ber·fo·ren·sics *n*
cy·ber·fraud *n*
cy·ber·hack·er *n*
cy·ber·hack·ing *n*
cy·ber·hip·pie *n*
cy·ber·in·sur·ance *n*
cy·ber·in·vest·or *n*
cy·ber·land *n*
cy·ber·mar·ket·ing *n*
cy·ber·mass·es *npl*
cy·ber·naut *n*
cy·ber·pho·bi·a *n*
cy·ber·pho·bic *n, adj*
cy·ber·porn *n*
cy·ber·proph·et *n*
cyb·er·ro·mance *n*
cy·ber·safe·ty *n*
cy·ber·sales *npl*
cy·ber·se·cu·ri·ty *n*
cy·ber·sex *n*
cy·ber·shop·per *n*
cy·ber·shop·ping *n*
cy·ber·snoop·er *n*
cy·ber·snoop·ing *n*
cy·ber·suit *n*
cy·ber·theft *n*
cy·ber·thief *n*
cy·ber·van·dal·ism *n*
cy·ber·war *n*
cy·ber·war·fare *n*
cy·ber·wid·ow *n*
cy·ber·world *n*

cy·ber age *n* the present age, thought of as a period characterized by the growth and importance of computer technology and electronic communications

cy·ber·ca·fé /sībər ka fày, -kə fày/ *n* **1.** a coffeehouse where people can browse the Internet for a fee **2.** an area on the Internet where people communicate using a chat program or a bulletin board

cy·ber·cast /sībər kàst/ *n* a broadcast of an event transmitted via the Internet, in either sound or vision or in both [Blend of CYBER- + BROADCAST] —**cy·ber·cast** *vti*

cy·ber dha·ba /-daabə/ *n S Asia* in South Asia, a roadside stall where people can use computers or the Internet to find out information, send e-mail, or engage in commercial transactions [*Dhaba* < Hindi, "roadside eating place"]

cy·ber·fear /sībər feer/ *n* fear of the damage that can be caused to complex electronic systems by malicious use of computers

cy·ber·law /sībər làw/ *n* the body of laws relating to computers, information systems, and networks —**cy·ber·law·yer** *n*

cy·ber mall *n* a shared portal on the Internet providing information and links for a number of online businesses

cy·ber·med·i·ar·y /sībər meedee èrree/ (*plural* **-ies**) *n* an organization that facilitates online transactions without owning the products or services [Late 19C. Blend of CYBER- + INTERMEDIARY]

cy·ber·nate /sībər nàyt/ (**-nat·ed, -nat·ing, -nates**) *vt* to control a manufacturing process with a servomechanism or computer [Mid-20C. < CYBERNETICS] —**cy·ber·nat·ed** *adj* —**cy·ber·na·tion** /sībər náysh'n/ *n*

cy·ber·net·ics /sībər néttiks/ *n* (*takes a singular verb*) **1.** the science or study of communication in organisms, organic processes, and mechanical or electronic systems **2.** the replication or imitation of biological control systems with the use of technology [Mid-20C. < Greek *kubernētēs* "steersman" < *kubernan* "to steer"] —**cy·ber·net·ic** *adj* —**cy·ber·net·i·cal·ly** *adv*—**cy·ber·ne·ti·cian** /sībərnə tísh'n/ *n*—**cy·ber·net·i·cist** *n*

cy·ber·punk /sībər pùngk/ *n* science fiction featuring characters living in a darkly frightening futuristic world dominated by computer technology

cy·ber·self /sībər sèlf/ (*plural* **-selves** /-sèlvz/) *n* a false identity assumed by somebody in an Internet chat room or in interactive Internet role-play

cy·ber·slack·er /sībər slàker/ *n* an employee who makes unauthorized use of the Internet during work time (*informal*) —**cy·ber·slack·ing** /sībər slàking/ *n*

cy·ber·space /sībər spàyss/ *n* **1.** the notional realm in which electronic information exists or is exchanged ○ *an e-mail message lost in cyberspace* **2.** the imagined world of virtual reality

cy·ber·squat·ting /sībər skwòtting/ *n* the registering of an Internet domain name containing a trademark with the intent to sell it to the trademark owner —**cy·ber·squat·ter** *n*

cy·ber·stalk·er /sībər stàwkər/ *n* **1.** a pedophile who uses the Internet to seek sex with children **2.** a stalker who uses the Internet to harass a victim —**cy·ber·stalk·ing** *n*

cy·ber·surf·er /sībər sùrfər/ *n* somebody who spends a lot of time surfing the Internet (*slang*) —**cy·ber·surf·ing** *n*

cy·ber·ter·ror·ism /sībər térrə rìzzəm/ *n* the use of techniques that disrupt or damage computer-based information systems to cause fear, injury, or economic loss —**cy·ber·ter·ror·ist** *n, adj*

cy·ber·thrill·er /sībər thrìllər/ *n* a story or script in which computers are central to the action

cy·ber·wooz·ling /sībər wo͞ozling/ *n* the gathering of data from the computer of a visitor to a website without his or her knowledge or authorization (*slang*) [Late 20C. < CYBER- + *woozle,* after a scary animal in the Winnie the Pooh stories of A. A. MILNE]

cy·borg /sī bàwrg/ *n* a fictional being that is part human, part robot [Mid-20C. Blend of CYBERNETICS + ORGANISM]

cy·brar·y /sī brèrree/ (*plural* **-ies**) *n* a guide to the information available on the World Wide Web on a particular topic, or an information-gathering service using the Internet [Late 20C. Blend of CYBER- + LIBRARY] —**cy·brar·i·an** /sī brérree ən/ *n*

cy·cad /sīkəd, -kàd/ *n* a tropical tree that has a thick trunk, sharp-pointed leaves like palm leaves, and cones. Order: Cycadales. [Mid-19C. < modern Latin *Cycad-* < Greek *kukas,* miswriting of *koikas,* plural of *koix,* a palm tree]

cycl- *prefix* same as **cyclo-** (*used before vowels*)

Cyc·la·des /síklə dee̅z/ large group of Greek islands in the southern Aegean Sea. The largest island is Naxos and the chief town is Hermoupolis on the island of Syros. Population: 88,485 (1981). Area: 993 sq. mi./2,572 sq. km.

cy·cla·mate /sīklə màyt/ *n* a salt or ester of cyclamic acid, especially sodium cyclamate. Use: artificial sweetener. [Mid-20C. Contraction of *cyclohexylsulfamate*]

cy·cla·men /síkləmən/ *n* a small plant with heart-shaped leaves that grows wild under trees in parts of Europe, and is also cultivated. Flowers: white, pink. Genus: *Cyclamen.* [Mid-16C. Via Latin *cyclaminos* < Greek *kuklaminos,* probably < *kuklos* "circle"; from its bulbous root] —**cy·cla·men** *adj*

cy·cla·mic ac·id /sìkləmik-, sī-/ *n* a synthetic crystalline acid. Use: production of cyclamates, food additive. Formula: $C_6H_{13}NO_3S$. [Contraction of *cyclohexylsulfamic acid*]

cy·clase /sī klàyss, -klàyz/ *n* an enzyme that aids the formation of hydrocarbon rings (**cyclization**) in a compound

cy·cle /sīk'l/ *n* **1. REPEATED SEQUENCE OF EVENTS** a sequence of events that is repeated again and again, especially a causal sequence ○ *breaking the cycle of violence and bloodshed* **2. TIME BETWEEN REPEATED EVENTS** a period of time during which one complete sequence of a recurring series of events occurs ○ *a seven-year economic cycle* **3. COMPLETE PROCESS** a complete process or sequence of processes in a machine or electronic device, or the time that this takes **4.** PHYS **ONE COMPLETE OSCILLATION** one complete continuous change in the magnitude of an oscillating quantity or system that brings the system back to its original energy state ○ *running at 100 cycles per second* **5.** ARTS **LINKED ARTWORKS** a series of linked songs, poems, stories, plays, or operas that deal with the same story, events, or characters ○ *Wagner's Ring cycle* **6.** TIME **LONG TIME** a very long period of time **7.** ASTRON **ORBIT** one complete orbit of an astronomical object **8.** COMPUT **SET OF OPERATIONS** a set of instructions completed as a unit by a computer, or the time that completion takes **9. BICYCLE** a bicycle, motorcycle, or other such vehicle **10.** AUTOMOT same as **motorcycle** ■ *v* (**-cled, -cling, -cles**) **1.** *vti* **GO THROUGH CYCLE** to put something through or go through a sequence of events ○ *programmed to cycle every hour* **2.** *vi* **RIDE BICYCLE** to ride a bicycle, motorcycle, or other such vehicle [14C. Directly or via French < Latin *cyclus* < Greek *kuklos* "circle"]

cy·cle path *n UK* ROADS same as **bikeway**

cy·cle rick·shaw *n* a three-wheeled vehicle like a large tricycle with a wide back seat for passengers, used as hired transportation

cy·clic /sīklik, sík-/, **cy·cli·cal** /sīklik'l, sík-/ *adj* **1. IN CYCLES** occurring or repeated in cycles **2.** CHEM **ARRANGED IN RING** describes organic compounds that are composed of a closed ring of atoms **3.** MUSIC **WITH RECURRENT THEME** describes music containing a recurrent theme or motif —**cy·cli·cal·i·ty** /sīkli kállətee, sìkli-/ *n* —**cy·cli·cal·ly** *adv* —**cy·cli·cit·y** /sī klíssətee, si-/ *n*

cy·cli·cal un·em·ploy·ment *n* the fluctuation in the level of unemployment that coincides with a business cycle

cy·clic AMP *n* a cyclic form of AMP that activates enzymes in many hormone-induced biochemical reactions

cy·clic GMP *n* a cyclic form of GMP that is responsible for aspects of cell division and growth

cy·clist /sīklist/ *n* somebody who rides a bicycle, motorcycle, or other such vehicle

cy·cli·za·tion /sīklə záysh'n, sìklə-/ *n* the formation of one or more hydrocarbon rings in an organic compound

cyclo- *prefix* **1.** circle, cycle ○ *cyclometer* **2.** cyclic compound ○ *cyclopropane* [< Greek *kuklos* "circle"]

cy·clo·ad·di·tion /sīklō ə dísh'n/ *n* the creation of a ring structure in a chemical compound

cy·clo·al·i·phat·ic /sīklō alə fáttik/ *adj* CHEM same as **alicyclic**

cy·clo·al·kane /sīklō ál kàyn/ *n* CHEM an alicyclic hydrocarbon

cy·clo·gen·e·sis /sīklō jénnəssiss/ *n* the formation and development of a cyclone [Mid-20C. < CYCLONE]

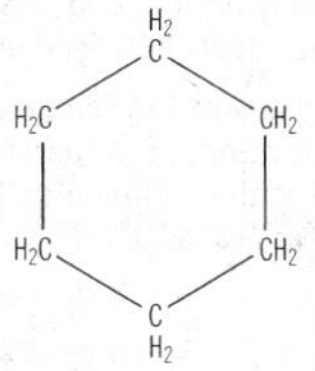

cyclohexane

cy·clo·hex·ane /sīklō hék sàyn/ *n* a colorless, pungent, flammable liquid hydrocarbon. Source: benzene. Use: paint thinner, solvent, in organic synthesis. Formula: C_6H_{12}.

cy·clo·hex·a·none /sīklō héksə nōn/ *n* a colorless liquid ketone. Use: solvent, organic synthesis. Formula: $C_6H_{10}O$.

cy·clo·hex·i·mide /sīklō héksə mīd/ *n* a colorless crystalline compound. Source: the bacterium *Streptomyces griseum.* Use: fungicide. Formula: $C_{15}H_{23}NO_4$.

cy·cloid /sī klòyd/ *adj* **1. LIKE CIRCLE** resembling a circle **2.** FISH **CIRCULAR AND THIN** describes fish scales that are circular and thin with smooth edges **3.** PSYCHOL **MOODY** changing between states of depression and elation (*technical*) ■ *n* **1.** MATH **GEOMETRIC CURVE** a geometric curve formed by a point on the circumference of a circle that rolls along a straight line **2.** FISH **FISH WITH CYCLOID SCALES** a fish with scales that are circular and thin with smooth edges —**cy·cloi·dal** *adj*

cy·clom·e·ter /sī klómmətər/ *n* an instrument that counts the number of times a wheel rotates and can, therefore, show the distance a vehicle has traveled —**cy·clo·met·ric** /sīklə méttrik/ *adj*—**cy·clom·e·try** *n*

cy·clone /sīklōn/ *n* **1.** METEOROL **LARGE-SCALE STORM SYSTEM** a large-scale storm system with heavy rain and winds that rotate counterclockwise in the northern hemisphere around and clockwise in the southern hemisphere around and toward a low-pressure center **2.** METEOROL **VIOLENT STORM** a violent rotating windstorm or tornado **3.** TECH **ROTATING DEVICE** a device that rotates rapidly, using centrifugal force to separate materials, e.g., particles from a gas [Mid-19C. < Greek *kuklōma* "wheel, coil" < *kuklos* "circle"] —**cy·clon·ic** /sī klónnik/ *adj*—**cy·clon·i·cal·ly** *adv*

cy·clone cel·lar *n* BUILDINGS same as **storm cellar**

cy·clo·pae·di·a *n* PUBL another spelling of **cyclopedia**

cy·clo·pe·an /sīklə pée ən, sī klōpee ən/ *adj* **1.** *also* **Cy·clo·pe·an** MYTHOL **LIKE CYCLOPS** relating to or resembling a Cyclops **2.** ARCHIT **MADE OF BIG STONES** constructed of massive irregular stone blocks without mortar **3. ENORMOUS OR MASSIVE** of enormous size or great mass **4.** OPTICS **DESCRIBING VISION** describes the phenomenon of apparent unity in binocular vision

cy·clo·pe·di·a /sīklə pe̅edee ə/, **cy·clo·pae·di·a** *n* PUBL same as **encyclopedia** [Early 18C. Shortening] —**cy·clo·pe·dic** *adj*—**cy·clo·pe·dist** *n*

cy·clo·pen·tane /sīklō pén tàyn/ *n* a colorless, flammable, pungent, liquid cycloalkane. Use: paint remover, fuel, solvent. Formula: C_5H_{10}.

cy·clo·pes ZOOL plural of **cyclops**

Cy·clo·pes MYTHOL plural of **Cyclops**

cy·clo·phos·pha·mide /sīklō fósfə mīd/ *n* a toxic drug that suppresses immunity. Use: treatment of leukemia, lymphoma, Hodgkin's disease, tumors.

cy·clo·ple·gia /sīklō ple̅ejə, -klə-/ *n* loss of movement in the eye muscles that adjust the size of the lens and are used for focusing —**cy·clo·ple·gic** *adj*

cy·clo·pro·pane /sīklō prō pàyn/ *n* a flammable hydrocarbon gas. Use: general anesthetic, in organic synthesis. Formula: C_3H_6.

cy·clops /sī klòps/ (*plural* **cy·clo·pes** /sī klō pe̅ez/ or *same*) *n* a freshwater crustacean (**copepod**) with a single eye. Genus: *Cyclops.* [Mid-19C. < modern Latin < Latin "Cyclops" (see CYCLOPS)]

Cy·clops /sī klòps/ (*plural* **Cy·clo·pes** /sī klō pe̅ez/ or *same* or **-clops·es**) *n* in Greek mythology, of a race of giants who had only one eye in the middle of the forehead [Early 16C. Via Latin < Greek *Kuklōps* < *kuklos* "circle" + *ōps* "eye"]

cy·clo·ram·a /sīklə rámmə/ *n* **1.** a picture painted all the way around the wall of a circular room **2.** a large concave curtain or wall behind a stage [Mid-19C < CYCLO- after PANORAMA] —**cy·clo·ram·ic** *adj*

cy·clo·sis /sī klōssiss/ *n* the rotary flow of protoplasm within some cells and protozoans [Mid-19C. < Greek *kuklōsis* "encirclement" < *kuklos* "circle"]

cy·clo·spor·in /sīklō spáwrin/, **cy·clo·spor·ine** /-re̅en, -rin/ *n* a drug obtained from a soil fungus. Use: suppression of tissue rejection following transplant surgery. [Late 20C. < CYCLO- + *polysporum,* fungus that produces the drug]

cy·clo·stome /sīklə stōm/ *n* a jawless fish with a circular sucking mouth and without true teeth. Lampreys and hagfish are cyclostomes. Class: Cyclostomata. [Mid-19C. < CYCLO- + Greek *stoma* "mouth"] —**cy·clos·to·mate** /sī klóstəmət, sīklō stō màyt/ *adj* —**cy·clo·stom·a·tous** /sīklə stómmətəss, -stōmətəss/ *adj*

cy·clo·thy·mi·a /sīklə thīmee ə/ *n* a psychiatric disorder in which the patient has frequent, relatively mild mood swings between elation and depression —**cy·clo·thy·mic** *adj*

cy·clo·tron /sīklə tròn/ *n* a circular particle accelerator in which charged particles are confined by a vertical magnetic field and accelerated by an alternating high-frequency applied voltage. It is used to study the way particles interact.

cyg·net /sígnət/ *n* a young swan [15C. Old French *cigne* "swan" < Greek *kuknos*]

Cyg·nus /sígnəss/ *n* a constellation of the northern hemisphere containing the star Deneb. See illustration at **constellation**

CYL *abbr* ONLINE see you later (*used in e-mails or text messages*)

cyl. *abbr* **1.** cylinder **2.** cylindrical

cyl·in·der /síllindər/ *n* **1. OBJECT SHAPED LIKE TUBE** an object or shape with straight sides and circular ends of equal size **2.** MECH ENG **CHAMBER FOR PISTON** a chamber in an internal-combustion engine or a pump within which a piston moves back and forth **3.** ARMS **ROTATING PART OF REVOLVER** the rotating part of a revolver, containing chambers into which cartridges are loaded **4. LONG THIN CONTAINER** a long thin sealed container, e.g., one in which gas is kept under pressure **5.** MATH **GEOMETRIC SOLID** a three-dimensional geometric solid bounded by two equal parallel circles and a curved surface formed by moving a straight line so that its ends lie on the circles **6.** MATH **GEOMETRIC SURFACE** a three-dimensional geometric surface formed by a straight line moving in a circle around and parallel to a fixed straight line, forming a hollow tube shape **7.** PRINTING **ROTATING PART OF PRINTING PRESS** a revolving drum of a printing press that produces or receives the impression **8.** HIST same as **cylinder seal** [Late 16C. Via Latin < Greek *kulindros* "roller" < *kulindein* "to roll"] —**cyl·in·dered** *adj*

cyl·in·der block *n UK* AUTOMOT same as **engine block**

cyl·in·der head *n* the closed detachable end of a cylinder in an internal-combustion engine

cyl·in·der press *n* a printing press in which a flat bed holding the type moves under a revolving cylinder carrying the paper

cyl·in·der seal *n* an engraved cylindrical clay or stone object used in ancient times, especially in Mesopotamia, as a seal that was rolled in wet clay to leave an impression

cy·lin·dri·cal /sə líndrik'l/, **cy·lin·dric** /sə líndrik/ *adj* having straight sides, circular ends of equal size, and a constant circular cross section —**cy·lin·dri·cal·i·ty** /sə lìndri kállətee/ *n* —**cy·lin·dri·cal·ly** *adv*

cy·lin·dri·cal pro·jec·tion *n* a method of making a map by projecting the globe onto a surrounding cylinder. The Mercator projection is a type of cylindrical projection.

cy·ma /sīmə/ (*plural* **-mae** /-mee/ or **-mas**) *n* a projecting molding with an S-shaped profile [Mid-16C. Via modern Latin < Greek *kuma* "swelling, wave" < *kuein* "become pregnant"]

cym·bal /símb'l/ *n* a circular brass percussion instrument played with a stick or in pairs by striking them together [Pre-12C. Directly or via French < Latin *cymbalum* < Greek *kumbalon* < *kumbē* "bowl, cup"]

SPELLCHECK cymbal or **symbol**? Do not confuse the spelling of ***cymbal*** and ***symbol***, which sound similar. A ***cymbal*** is a round brass percussion instrument, as in *play the cymbals*. ***Symbol***, the more frequent of the two words, denotes an object, sign, or character that represents something else, as in *mathematical symbols*.

cym·bid·i·um /sim bíddee əm/ (*plural* **-bid·i·a** /-bíddee ə/ or **-bid·i·ums**) *n* an orchid with long narrow leaves. Flowers: brightly colored with boat-shaped lower petals. Native to: tropical Asia, Australia. Genus: *Cymbidium*. [Early 19C. < modern Latin < Greek *kumbē* "cup"]

cyme /sīm/ *n* a flower cluster in which each flower stem ends in a single flower and other flower stems form below and to the side [Early 18C. Via French, "summit" < Latin *cyma* (see CYMA)] —**cy·mif·er·ous** /sī míffərəss/ *adj* —**cy·moid** *adj*

cy·mene /sī meen/ *n* a colorless liquid benzene derivative, existing in three isomers. Use: solvents, manufacture of resins. Formula: $(CH_3)_2CHC_6H_4CH_3$. [Mid-19C. < Greek *kummon* "cumin"]

cy·mo·phane /sīmə fàyn/ *n* an opalescent variety of chrysoberyl. Use: gems. [Early 19C. < Greek *kuma* (see CYMA) + *-phanēs* "showing"]

cy·mose /sī mòss/, **cy·mous** /sīməss/ *adj* relating to, like, or being a cyme —**cy·mose·ly** *adv*

Cym·ric /kúmmrik/ *adj* **1.** relating to Wales **2.** relating to the Welsh language (*dated*) ■ *n* LANG same as **Welsh** (*dated*) [Mid-19C. < Welsh *Cymry* "the Welsh" < *Cymru* "Wales"]

Cym·ru /kúmree/ ♦ **Wales**

Cyn·e·wulf /kínnə wòolf/, **Cyn·wulf** /kín-/ (*fl* 750?) English poet and probable author of four important Old English poems. He may have been a monk in northeastern England.

cyn·ic /sínnik/ *n* **1.** somebody who believes that human actions are insincere and motivated by self-interest **2.** somebody sneering and sarcastic [Late 16C. < CYNIC]

Cyn·ic /sínnik/ *n* a member of a group of ancient Greek philosophers who believed that virtue is the only good and that the only means of achieving it is self-control. The sect was founded by Antisthenes in the 4th century B.C. ■ *adj* belonging to, characteristic of, or relating to the Cynics [Mid-16C. Via Latin < Greek *Kunikos*]

cyn·i·cal /sínnik'l/ *adj* **1.** doubting or contemptuous of human nature or the motives, goodness, or sincerity of others ○ *Many people have developed a cynical distrust of politicians.* **2.** mocking, scornful, or sneering ○ *They were made the butt of many cynical jokes.* —**cyn·i·cal·ly** *adv* —**cyn·i·cal·ness** *n*

cyn·i·cism /sínni sìzzəm/ *n* **1.** the state or fact of having cynical attitudes or beliefs, or a cynical character or quality **2.** a cynical action, comment, or idea

Cyn·i·cism *n* the beliefs or philosophy of the ancient Greek Cynics

cy·no·sure /sīnə shòor/ *n* (*formal*) **1.** the center of admiration, attention, or attraction **2.** somebody or something acting as a guide or used for direction ○ *Guidebooks are the cynosure of the inexperienced traveler.* [Late 16C. Via Latin *Cynosura* "Ursa Minor" (which contains Polaris) < Greek *kunosoura*, literally "dog's tail"] —**cy·no·sur·al** /sīnə shóorəl/ *adj*

Cyn·thi·a /sínthee ə/ *n* **1.** the Moon personified as a goddess (*literary*) **2.** MYTHOL same as **Diana** [Late 16C. After Mount *Cynthus* in Delos, where the goddess Diana was supposedly born]

Cyn·wulf ♦ **Cynewulf**

CYO *abbr* CHR Catholic Youth Organization

cy·pher *n* COMMUNICATION another spelling of **cipher**

cy·pher·punk /sīfər pùngk/ *n* an experienced computer hacker who breaks codes and enters secure computer systems [Late 20C. < CYPHER, after CYBERPUNK]

cy pres /sèe práy/ *adv* in law, as nearly as possible to the will or intention of a person whose wishes cannot be executed literally [Via Anglo-Norman < French *si près* "as near as"]

cypress

cy·press[1] /sīprəss/ *n* **1.** **CONIFER** a coniferous evergreen tree with dark green leaves resembling scales. Native to: Europe, Asia, North America. Genus: *Cupressus*. **2. TREE OR BUSH LIKE CYPRESS** a coniferous tree or bush that is similar to a true cypress, e.g., a bald or swamp cypress **3. WOOD** the hard wood of a cypress tree **4. SYMBOL OF MOURNING** the branches of a cypress tree as a symbol of mourning [12C. Via French < late Latin *cypressus* < Greek *kuparissos*]

cy·press[2] /sīprəs/, **cy·prus** *n* a fine silk or cotton fabric, usually black. Use: mourning clothes. [15C. Via Anglo-Norman *cipres* < Old French *Cipre* "Cyprus"]

Cy·press /sīprəss/ city in southwestern California, a southeastern suburb of Los Angeles. Population: 47,249 (2002 estimate).

cy·press vine *n* a climbing plant related to morning glory with leaves divided into many thin segments. Flowers: scarlet, orange, or white, tubular. Native to: tropical America. Latin name: *Ipomoea quamoclit*.

Cyp·ri·an /síppree ən/, **St.** (200?–258) African-born Roman lawyer, bishop, and martyr. He was a Carthaginian bishop, and his works, including *On the Unity of the Catholic Church* (251), influenced St. Augustine. Full name **Caecilius Cyprianus, Thascius**

cyp·ri·nid /síppranid, sə prínnid/ (*plural same* or **-nids**) *n* a freshwater fish of the family that includes the carps and minnows, typically with rounded scales, soft fins, and toothless jaws. Family: Cyprinidae. [Late 19C. < Latin *cyprinus* (see CYPRINOID)] —**cyp·ri·nid** *adj*

cy·prin·o·dont /sə prínnə dònt, -prīnə-/ *n* a small freshwater fish with soft fins and a toothed jaw, e.g., a killifish or guppy. Native to: North America, Europe, Asia, Africa. Family: Cyprinodontidae. [Mid-19C. < CYPRINOID] —**cy·prin·o·dont** *adj*

cyp·ri·noid /síppra nòyd/ *n* any fish belonging to a large group that includes carp [Mid-19C. < Latin *cyprinus* "carp" < Greek *kuprinos*] —**cyp·ri·noid** *adj*

Cyp·ri·ot /síppree ət/, **Cyp·ri·ote** *n* **SOMEBODY FROM CYPRUS** somebody who comes from Cyprus ■ *adj* **1. OF CYPRUS** relating to Cyprus **2. OF LANGUAGES OF CYPRUS** relating to the dialects of Greek and Turkish that are spoken on Cyprus [Late 16C. < Greek *Kupriōtēs* < *Kupros* "Cyprus"]

cy·pro·hep·ta·dine /sīprō héptə deen/ *n* an antihistamine drug. Use: treatment of asthma, allergies, skin disorders. [Late 20C. < CYCLIC + HEPTA- + PIPERIDINE]

cy·prus *n* TEXTILES another spelling of **cypress**[2]

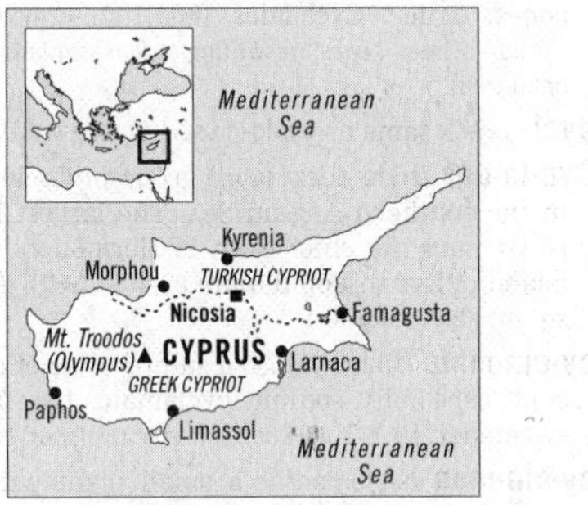

Cyprus

Cy·prus /sīprəss/ island country in the eastern Mediterranean Sea. Since 1974, it has been partitioned between the Greek Cypriot south and the officially unrecognized Turkish Republic of Northern Cyprus. It became an independent member of the British Commonwealth in 1961 and a member of the European Union in 2004. Principal language: Greek. Currency: Cyprus pound, Turkish lira. Capital: Nicosia. Population: 771,657 (2003). Area: 3,572 sq. mi./9,251 sq. km. Official name **Republic of Cyprus**

cyp·se·la /sípsələ/ (*plural* **-lae** /-lee/) *n* a small hard one-seeded fruit with an attached calyx that does not split during seed dispersal, as in the daisy and dandelion. Family: Compositae. [Late 19C. Via modern Latin < Greek *kupselē* "hollow vessel"]

Cy·ra·no de Ber·ge·rac /sírrənō də búrzhə ràk/, **Savinien** (1619–55) French poet and dramatist. He fought in over 1,000 duels, often on account of insults relating to his extraordinarily long nose. His satirical accounts of journeys to the Sun and the Moon suggested the character of Lemuel Gulliver to Jonathan Swift.

> "Perish the Universe, provided I have my revenge."
> [Savinien Cyrano de Bergerac, *La Mort d'Agrippine (The Death of Agripinna)*; 1654]

Cyr·e·na·ic /sìrrə náy ik/ *adj* **1.** PEOPLES **OF CYRENE** relating to ancient Cyrene or Cyrenaica **2.** PHILOSOPHY **OF PHILOSOPHY OF PLEASURE** relating to or advocating the philosophical doctrines of Aristippus of Cyrene, who believed pleasure is the supreme good ■ *n* **1.** PEOPLES **SOMEBODY FROM CYRENE** somebody who came from ancient Cyrene or Cyrenaica **2.** PHILOSOPHY **BELIEVER IN CYRENAIC PHILOSOPHY** an adherent of the Cyrenaic school of philosophy **3.** PHILOSOPHY **HEDONIST** somebody who believes that pleasure is the sole good in life [Late 16C. Via Latin < Greek *Kurēnaikos* < *Kurēnē* "Cyrene"] —**Cyr·e·na·i·cism** /-i sìzzəm/ *n*

Cyr·e·na·i·ca /sìrrə náy ikə, sīrə-/ historic region settled by the ancient Greeks that occupied the eastern half of Libya

Cy·re·ne /sī reenee/ ancient Greek town in Libya and the original capital of Cyrenaica, founded in about 630 B.C. The ruins are situated about 140 mi./225 km from Benghazi in northeastern Libya.

Cyr·il /sírrəl/, **St.** (827–869) Greek missionary. With his brother Methodius he brought Christianity to the Slavs of southeastern Europe, and is said to have devised the Cyrillic alphabet.

Cy·ril·lic /sə ríllik/ *adj* relating to an old alphabet derived from Greek script and attributed to St. Cyril, or a modified form used in writing modern Slavic languages such as Bulgarian and Russian. The Cyrillic alphabet is also used in writing the non-Slavic languages of some republics of the former Soviet Union. ■ *n* the Cyrillic alphabet [Early 19C. After St. CYRIL]

Cy·rus II /sī́rəss/ (600?–529 B.C.) king of Persia (550–529 B.C.). He founded the Persian Empire and was known for his tolerance, allowing the Jews to return from exile in Babylon.

cyst /sist/ *n* **1. SPHERICAL SWELLING** a closed, usually spherical, membranous sac that develops in human or other animal tissue and contains fluid or semisolid material. Some types of cysts form when glands are blocked, and most cysts are benign. **2.** ANAT **HOLLOW ORGAN OR CAVITY** a thin-walled bladder, sac, or vesicle in an animal **3.** BOT, FUNGI **RESTING SPORE** in some algae and fungi, a spore that is not undergoing cell division **4.** BOT **AIR-FILLED CAVITY IN SEAWEEDS** a small air-filled cavity resembling a bladder that occurs in some seaweeds such as the bladder wrack **5.** ZOOL **PROTECTIVE SAC ENCLOSING ORGANISM** a sac or capsule that encloses and protects some organisms in a dormant or larval stage **6.** ZOOL **PROTECTIVE COVERING AROUND PARASITE** a protective covering around a parasite, produced by a host or by the parasite itself [Early 18C. Via late Latin < Greek *kustis* "bladder, cyst"] —**cys·toid** *adj, n*

cyst- *prefix* same as **cysto-** (*used before vowels*)

cys·tec·to·my /siss téktəmee/ (*plural* **-mies**) *n* **1.** surgical removal of a cyst **2.** surgical removal of the urinary bladder

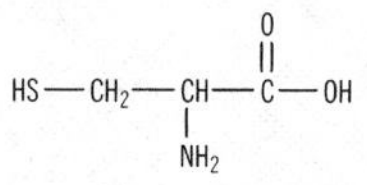

cysteine

cys·te·ine /sís tee̅n, sístee e̅en/ *n* a sulfur-containing amino acid that is converted to cystine during metabolism. Formula: $C_3H_7NO_2S$. [Late 19C. < CYSTINE + *-eine*, variant of -EIN]

cys·tic /sístik/ *adj* **1. FORMING CYST** forming, of the nature of, or consisting of a cyst **2. CONTAINING CYST** containing a cyst or cysts **3. WITHIN CYST** enclosed within a cyst **4. RELATING TO BLADDER** relating to a bladder, especially the urinary bladder

cys·tic duct *n* the duct of the gall bladder that joins the bile duct from the liver to form the common bile duct

cys·ti·cer·cus /sìstə súrkəss/ (*plural* **-ci** /-sī/) *n* the larva of some tapeworms that consists of a folded inverted head encapsulated in a fluid-filled sac. It is found in the body tissues of infested people and animals. [Mid-19C. < modern Latin *cysticercus* < Greek *kustis* "bladder" + *kerkos* "tail"]

cys·tic fi·bro·sis /-fī brṓsiss/ *n* a hereditary disease starting in infancy that affects various glands and results in secretion of thick mucus that blocks internal passages, including those of the lungs, causing respiratory infections. The pancreas is also affected, resulting in a deficiency of digestive enzymes and impaired nutrition.

cys·tine /sí stee̅n, sístin/ *n* an amino acid found in many proteins, especially keratin [Mid-19C. < Greek *kustis* "bladder"]

cys·tin·u·ri·a /sìstə nyŏŏree ə/ *n* the excessive excretion of cystine in the urine and the formation of cystine stones in the kidney, characteristic of an inherited disorder of the metabolism

cys·ti·tis /si stī́tiss/ *n* inflammation of the urinary bladder, often caused by infection

cysto- *prefix* hollow structure, sac, cyst ○ *cystocarp* [Via modern Latin, "bladder" < Greek *kustis*]

cys·to·carp /sístə kaarp/ *n* the reproductive body of red algae produced after fertilization and consisting of a mass of asexual spores borne on filaments

cys·to·cele /sístə see̅l/ *n* a hernia of a woman's urinary bladder that protrudes through the vaginal wall

cys·tog·ra·phy /sis tóggrəfee/ *n* X-ray examination of the urinary bladder after the introduction of a liquid that is partially opaque to X-rays

cys·to·lith /sístə lith/ *n* **1.** a hard mineral deposit, usually of calcium carbonate, that occurs in the epidermal cells of some plants such as figs or stinging nettles **2.** a stone that occurs in the bladder

cys·to·scope /sístə skōp/ *n* a narrow tubular instrument that is passed through the urethra to examine the interior of the urethra and the urinary bladder —**cys·to·scop·ic** /sìstə skóppik/ *adj* —**cys·tos·co·py** /si stóskəpee/ *n*

cys·tos·to·my /sis tóstəmee/ (*plural* **-mies**) *n* the surgical construction of an opening into the urinary bladder to permit the removal of stones

cyt- *prefix* same as **cyto-** (*used before vowels*)

-cyte *suffix* cell ○ *phagocyte* [Via modern Latin *-cyta* < Greek *kutos* "hollow vessel"]

Cyth·e·re·a /sə the̅eree ə/ *n* MYTHOL same as **Aphrodite**

Cyth·e·re·an /sə the̅eree ən/ *adj* **1.** relating to the planet Venus **2.** relating to Cytherea

cy·ti·dine /síttə de̅en/ *n* a compound (**nucleoside**) formed from cytosine and ribose. Formula: $C_9H_{13}N_3O_5$. [Early 20C. < CYTO- + -IDINE]

cy·ti·dy·lic ac·id /sìttə díllik-/ *n* a nucleotide derived from cytosine and found in DNA and RNA. Formula: $C_9H_{14}N_3O_8P$. [Mid-20C. < CYTIDINE]

cyto- *prefix* cell ○ *cytotoxin* [< Greek *kutos* "hollow vessel" < Indo-European, "thing that hides"]

cy·to·cha·la·sin /sītō kə láyzin/ *n* a substance derived from fungi that inhibits the formation of microscopic filaments within living cells, thereby interfering with various cell activities, as in the cleavage of cytoplasm following nuclear division. Cytochalasins are used in cell biology to investigate phenomena such as cytoplasmic movement and cell motility. [Mid-20C. < CYTO- + Greek *khalasis* "dislocation"]

cy·to·chem·is·try /sītō kémmistree/ *n* a branch of biochemistry dealing with the chemistry of the cells of organisms —**cy·to·chem·i·cal** *adj* —**cy·to·chem·i·cal·ly** *adv*

cy·to·chrome /sītə krōm/ *n* a protein belonging to a group that contains iron and plays a role in cell respiration

cy·to·chrome ox·i·dase *n* an enzyme complex that is involved in the electron transport phase of cell respiration

cy·to·gen·e·sis /sītō jénnəsiss/ *n* the origin, development, and variation of living cells

cy·to·ge·net·ics /sītō jə néttiks/ *n* the study of the relationship between inheritance and the structure and function of cell components (*takes a singular verb*) —**cy·to·ge·net·ic** *adj* —**cy·to·ge·net·i·cal·ly** *adv* —**cy·to·ge·net·i·cist** *n*

cy·tog·e·ny /sī tójjənee/ *n* BIOL same as **cytogenesis**

cy·to·kine /sītə kīn/ *n* any protein secreted by lymph cells that affects cellular activity and controls inflammation [Mid-20C. < CYTO- + Greek *kinein* "to move"]

cy·to·ki·ne·sis /sītō ki ne̅essiss, -kī-/ *n* division of the cytoplasm of a cell during mitosis or meiosis —**cy·to·ki·net·ic** /sītō ki néttik, -kī-/ *adj*

cy·to·ki·nin /sītə kīnin/ *n* a plant growth hormone that encourages cell division

cy·tol·o·gy /sī tólləjee/ *n* **1.** a branch of biology dealing with the study of cells, especially their structures and functions **2.** the examination of cells obtained from body tissue or fluids, especially to establish if they are cancerous —**cy·to·log·ic** /sītə lójjik/ *adj* —**cy·to·log·i·cal** *adj* —**cy·to·log·i·cal·ly** *adv* —**cy·tol·o·gist** *n*

cy·tol·y·sis /sī tólləssiss/ *n* the destruction or dissolution of cells, e.g., by the immune system —**cy·to·lyt·ic** /sītə líttik/ *adj*

cy·to·me·gal·ic /sītō mə gállik/ *adj* characterized by, producing, or relating to enlarged cells [Mid-20C. < CYTO- + MEGALO-]

cy·to·me·gal·ic in·clu·sion dis·ease *n* a serious disease of newborn babies affecting the brain, liver, kidneys, and lungs. It is caused by cytomegalovirus infection of pregnant mothers and leads to enlargement of the affected cells.

cy·to·meg·a·lo·vi·rus /sītō meggələ vīrəss/ *n* a virus that causes enlargement of epithelial cells, usually resulting in mild infections but causing more serious disorders in AIDS patients and in newborn babies

cy·to·path·o·gen·ic /sītō pathə jénnik/, **cy·to·path·ic** /sītō páthik/ *adj* relating to or causing damage or disease to cells —**cy·to·path·o·ge·nic·i·ty** /-pathə jə níssətee/ *n*

cy·to·pa·thol·o·gy /sītō pə thólləjee/ (*plural* **-gies**) *n* **1.** a branch of pathology dealing with cell disease and damage **2.** the set of features or conditions associated with a diseased cell or cells —**cy·to·path·o·log·ic** /-pathə lójjik/ *adj* —**cy·to·path·o·log·i·cal** *adj* —**cy·to·pa·thol·o·gist** *n*

cy·top·a·thy /sī tóppəthee/ *n* deterioration or disease in a living cell

cy·to·phar·ynx /sītō férringks/ (*plural* **-pha·ryn·ges** /-fə rin je̅ez/ or **-phar·ynx·es**) *n* a tube in some protozoans extending from the cytoplasm into the endoplasm

cy·to·pho·tom·e·ter /sītō fō tómmətər/ *n* an instrument that uses the variations in light intensity produced by stained cell cytoplasm to identify and locate chemical compounds within cells —**cy·to·pho·to·met·ric** /sītō fōtə méttrik/ *adj* —**cy·to·pho·to·met·ri·cal·ly** *adv* —**cy·to·pho·tom·e·try** *n*

cy·to·plasm /sītō plàzzəm/ *n* the complex of chemical compounds and structures within a plant or animal cell excluding the nucleus. Cytoplasm contains the cytosol, organelles, vesicles, and cytoskeleton. —**cy·to·plas·mic** /sītō plázmik/ *adj* —**cy·to·plas·mi·cal·ly** *adv*

cy·to·plas·mic in·her·i·tance *n* the inheritance of genes from the female parent that are not in the nucleus but in organelles such as mitochondria that are found in the cytoplasm. This type of inheritance is not controlled by Mendel's laws.

cy·to·plas·mic stream·ing *n* the movement of cytoplasm within living cells resulting in the transport of nutrients and enzymes, and in the case of one-celled organisms, locomotion of the cell itself

cy·to·plast /sītō plàst/ *n* a plant or animal cell that has had the nucleus removed —**cy·to·plas·tic** /sītō plástik/ *adj*

cy·to·sine /sītə se̅en, -sin/ *n* a pyrimidine base that pairs with guanine in DNA and RNA. Symbol **C** [Late 19C. < CYTO- + -OSE[1]]

cy·to·skel·e·ton /sītō skéllət'n/ *n* the internal network of protein filaments and microtubules in an animal or plant cell that controls the cell's shape and movement —**cy·to·skel·e·tal** *adj*

cy·to·sol /sītə sòl, sītə sàwl/ *n* the fluid component of a cell's cytoplasm excluding organelles and other structures —**cy·to·sol·ic** /sītə sóllik/ *adj*

cy·to·some /sītə sòm/ *n* the cytoplasm in a cell, excluding the nucleus

cy·to·stat·ic /sītə státtik/ *adj* suppressing cell growth and multiplication ■ *n* a cytostatic agent —**cy·to·stat·i·cal·ly** *adv*

cy·to·tax·is /sītō táksiss/ *n* the movement of cells or cell masses in relation to one another

cy·to·tax·on·o·my /sītō tak sónnəmee/ *n* the classification of organisms according to cell structure, especially the number, structure, and shape of chromosomes —**cy·to·tax·o·nom·ic** /-taksə nómmik/ *adj* —**cy·to·tax·o·nom·i·cal·ly** *adv* —**cy·to·tax·on·o·mist** *n*

cy·to·tech·nol·o·gist /sìtō tek nóllǝjist/ *n* somebody trained to prepare cell samples and identify irregularities —**cy·to·tech·nol·o·gy** *n*

cy·to·tox·ic /sìtō tóksik/ *adj* **1.** describes a drug that prevents cell division **2.** describes a type of cell in the immune system that destroys other cells —**cy·to·tox·ic·i·ty** /-tok síssǝtee/ *n*

cy·to·tox·ic T cell *n* BIOL same as **killer cell** (*technical*)

cy·to·tox·in /sìtō tóksin/ *n* any substance that kills living cells

cy·to·trop·ic /sìtō tróppik/ *adj* describes motile cells that are mutually attracted to each other

cy·to·trop·ism /sī tóttrǝ pìzzǝm/ *n* the movement or turning of cells or cell masses toward or away from one another

CZ, **C.Z.** *abbr* Canal Zone

czar, etc. *n* HIST another spelling of **tsar, etc.**

czar·das /chaár daàsh/, **csar·das** *n* **1.** a Hungarian dance with a slow section followed by a faster one **2.** the music for a czardas [Mid-19C. < Hungarian *csárdás* < *csárda* "inn"]

Czech /chek/ *n* **1.** SOMEBODY FROM CZECH REPUBLIC somebody who comes from the Czech Republic **2.** SOMEBODY FROM CZECHOSLOVAKIA somebody who came from the former Czechoslovakia **3.** LANGUAGE OF CZECH REPUBLIC the official language of the Czech Republic, belonging to the West Slavic group of Indo-European languages. Native speakers: 10 million. [Early 19C. Via Polish < Czech *Čech*] —**Czech** *adj*

Czech·o·slo·va·ki·a /chèkǝsslǝ vaákee ǝ, chèkō slō-/ former country in central Europe that was divided into the Czech Republic and the Slovak Republic, or Slovakia, on January 1, 1993

Czech·o·slo·vak·i·an /chèkǝslǝ vaákee ǝn, chèkō slō vaákee ǝn/ *n* **1.** PEOPLES same as **Czech** (sense 2) **2.** LANGUAGE either Czech or Slovak, the languages of the former Czechoslovakia ■ *adj* PEOPLES relating to the former Czechoslovakia, or its peoples, languages, or cultures

Czech Re·pub·lic /chèk-/ country in central Europe created in 1993 when the former Czechoslovakia was divided into the Czech Republic and the Slovak Republic, or Slovakia. It became a member of the European Union in 2004. Language: Czech. Currency: Czech koruna. Capital: Prague. Population: 10,249,216 (2003). Area: 30,450 sq. mi./78,864 sq. km.

Czech Republic

Czer·ny /cháirnee/, **Karl** (1791–1857) Austrian pianist and composer. He was a pupil of Ludwig van Beethoven and the teacher of Franz Liszt. Of his many compositions, his teaching studies for the piano are best known.

Czę·sto·cho·wa /chènstǝ kṓvǝ/ city in south central Poland, north of Katowice. Population: 258,100 (1997).

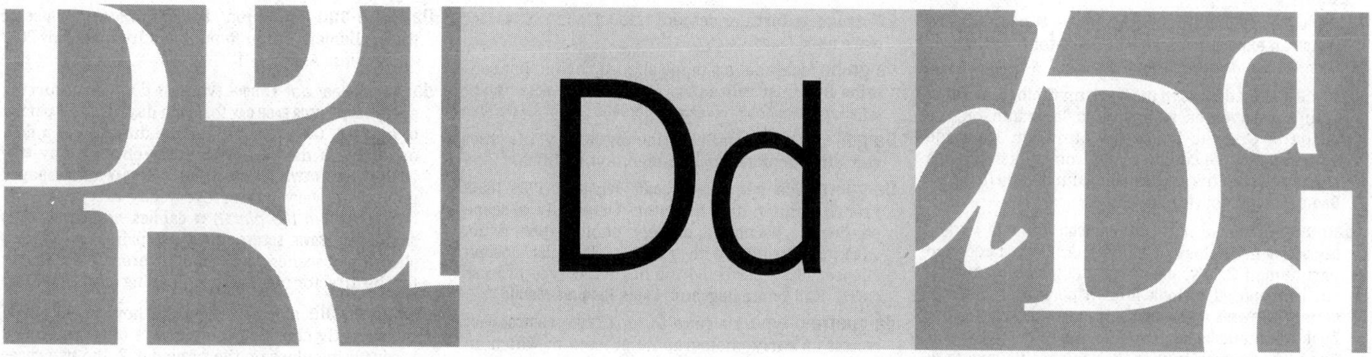

d[1] /dee/ (*plural* **d's**), **D** (*plural* **D's** or **Ds**) *n* **1. 4TH LETTER OF ENGLISH ALPHABET** the fourth letter of the English alphabet, representing a consonant sound **2. LETTER "D" WRITTEN** a written representation of the letter "d" **3. ROMAN NUMERAL** the Roman numeral for 500

d[2] *symbol* **1.** PHYS deuteron **2.** PHYS relative density **3.** CHESS **FOURTH VERTICAL ROW OF CHESSBOARD** used to refer to the fourth vertical row of squares from the left on a chessboard

'd *contr* **1.** did ○ *Where'd she get that hat?* **2.** had ○ *We'd already finished supper.* **3.** would ○ *I'd like to stop at the store.*

d', D' see also under surname

D[1] /dee/ (*plural* **D's** or **Ds**) *n* **1. "D"-SHAPED OBJECT** something shaped like a letter "D" **2.** MUSIC **2ND NOTE IN C MAJOR** the second note of a scale in C major **3.** MUSIC **SOMETHING THAT PRODUCES D** a string, key, or pipe tuned to produce the note D **4.** MUSIC **SCALE BEGINNING ON D** a scale or key that starts on the note D **5.** MUSIC **WRITTEN SYMBOL OF D** a graphic representation of the tone of D **6.** EDUC **4TH HIGHEST GRADE** the fourth highest grade in a series, e.g., a below-average grade for academic work **7.** FIELD HOCKEY **SEMICIRCLE AROUND FIELD HOCKEY GOAL** in field hockey, the semicircle surrounding the goal, from which a player may try to score

D[2] *symbol* **1.** CHEM deuterium **2.** OPTICS diopter **3.** PHYS dispersion **4.** AEROSP drag **5.** MATH used to refer to the first derivative of a function

D[3] *abbr* **1.** CALENDAR December **2.** POL Democrat **3.** Department **4.** deputy **5.** JUD-CHR Deus **6.** PHYS, MATH diameter **7.** dinar **8.** Director **9.** JUD-CHR Dominus **10.** Don **11.** CARS drive (*used on gearshifts of automatic transmissions*) **12.** Duchess **13.** Duke

d. *abbr* **1.** ZOOL dam[2] **2.** CALENDAR date **3.** daughter **4.** TIME day **5.** MEASURE degree **6.** TRAVEL departs **7.** depth **8.** deputy **9.** MATH, PHYS diameter **10.** died **11.** dollar **12.** drachma

da[1] *symbol* MEASURE deca-

da[2] see also under surname

DA[1] *abbr* **1.** COMM deed of arrangement **2.** ARMS delayed action **3.** GOV Department of Agriculture **4.** BANKING deposit account **5.** COMPUT digital-to-analog **6.** *also* **D.A.** LAW district attorney **7.** COMMUNICATION don't answer (*used in telegraphy*)

DA[2] *n* a man's hairstyle popular in the 1950s in which the hair is slicked back and drawn into a point at the back of the neck (*informal*) [Abbreviation of *duck's ass*; because it looks like a duck's tail]

D/A *abbr* **1.** COMM days after acceptance **2.** COMM delivery on acceptance **3.** BANKING deposit account **4.** COMPUT digital-to-analog **5.** COMM documents against acceptance

dab[1] /dab/ *vt* (**dabbed, dab·bing, dabs**) **1. TAP SOMETHING GENTLY** to pat or touch something lightly or gently ○ *She dabbed the tears from her eyes.* **2. APPLY SOMETHING GENTLY** to apply a substance using a quick light tapping action ○ *The nurse dabbed some ointment on the cut.* ■ *n* **1. SMALL QUANTITY** a small quantity, especially of a moist or soft substance ○ *a dab of butter* **2. GENTLE TAP** a light gentle tap, e.g., with the hand or a soft material [14C. Suggestive of the action]

dab[2] /dab/ (*plural* **dabs** or *same*) *n* **1.** a small brown flatfish. Native to: Europe. Latin name: *Limanda limanda.* **2.** the flesh of a dab as food [15C. Origin ?]

dab·ber /dábbər/ *n* a pad used by engravers and printers to apply ink or color [Late 18C. < DAB[1]]

dab·ble /dább'l/ (**-bled, -bling, -bles**) *v* **1.** *vi* **BECOME INVOLVED SUPERFICIALLY** to have a casual or superficial interest in something ○ *He dabbled in local politics for a few years.* **2.** *vi* **SPLASH** to paddle, play, or splash in water **3.** *vt* **DIP SOMETHING** to wet something by dipping it in a liquid ○ *We sat by the pool, dabbling our feet in the water.* **4.** *vt* **SPLASH SOMETHING WITH LIQUID** to daub, splash, or spatter somebody or something with a liquid **5.** *vi* ZOOL **MOVE UNDER WATER FOR FOOD** to move the bill to the bottom of shallow water in order to reach food (*refers to ducks*) [Mid-16C. Probably < Dutch *dabbelen* "keep tapping" < *dabben* "to tap"] —**dab·bler** *n*

dab·chick /dáb chìk/ *n* a small diving water bird, the smallest of the European grebes. Latin name: *Tachybaptus ruficollis.* [Mid-16C. Origin ?]

da ca·po /daa kaápō/ *adv* to be played or sung again from the beginning of the passage or piece (*used as a musical direction*) [Early 18C. < Italian, "from the head"] —**da ca·po** *adj*

Dac·ca ➧ **Dhaka**

dace /dayss/ (*plural same* or **dac·es**) *n* **1.** a small freshwater fish. Native to: North America. Family: Cyprinidae. **2.** a small freshwater fish with a slim olive green body. Native to: Europe. Latin name: *Leuciscus leuciscus.* [15C. < Old French *dars* "dace, dart"]

da·cha /daáchə/ *n* a Russian cottage or house in the suburbs or countryside [Mid-19C. < Russian, "grant of land"]

Da·chau /daá kòw, -k̲h̲òw/ site of a World War II Nazi concentration camp (1939–45) in Bavaria, about 10 mi./16 km northwest of Munich, southwestern Germany. It is now a memorial to those who died there.

dachshund

dachs·hund /daáks hòond, daáksənt/ *n* a small dog belonging to a breed that has a long body, short legs, and drooping ears [Late 19C. < German, "badger dog"]

~~**dachsund**~~ incorrect spelling of **dachshund**

da·coit /də kóyt/, **da·koit** *n* a member of a gang of armed robbers in South Asia and Myanmar [Late 18C. < Hindi *dakait* < *dākā* "gang robbery"]

dac·tyl /dákt'l/ *n* **1.** a metrical foot of one long syllable followed by two short syllables in classical verse or one stressed syllable followed by two unstressed syllables in modern verse **2.** a finger, toe, or related body part [14C. Via Latin < Greek *daktulos* "finger"]

dactyl- *prefix* same as **dactylo-** (*used before vowels*)

-dactyl *suffix* an animal with fingers or toes of a particular type or number ○ *polydactyl* [< Greek *daktulos* "finger"] —**-dactylous** *suffix*

dac·tyl·ic /dak tíllik/ *adj* relating to a metrical dactyl, or containing dactyls ■ *n* LITERAT same as **dactyl** (sense 1) —**dac·tyl·i·cal·ly** *adv*

dac·tyl·ic hex·am·e·ter *n* a line of verse consisting of six feet, the fifth of which is a dactyl, the first four dactyls or spondees, and the sixth a spondee or trochee. It is the meter of Greek and Roman epic poetry.

dactylo- *prefix* finger, toe ○ *dactylology* [< Greek *daktulos* "finger"]

dac·ty·log·ra·pher /dàktə lóggrəfər/ *n* a qualified person who examines or takes fingerprints

dac·ty·log·ra·phy /dàktə lóggrəfee/ *n* the scientific examination of fingerprints for identification purposes —**dac·ty·lo·graph·ic** /dàktəlō gráffik, dak tìllə-/ *adj*

dac·ty·lol·o·gy /dàktə lóllәjee/ *n* communication using signs made with the hands, often used by hearing-impaired people

dad /dad/ *n* a person's father (*informal*; *often used as a form of address*) [Mid-16C. Origin ?]

Da·da /daá daá/, **da·da, Da·da·ism** /daá daa ìzzəm/, **da·da·ism** *n* a European artistic and literary movement of the early 20th century whose work was characterized by anarchy, irrationality, and irreverence [Early 20C. < French, "hobbyhorse"] —**Da·da·ist** *n, adj*

dad-blamed *adj* used to express surprise or mild annoyance (*informal*) [Euphemistic alteration of *God-damned*]

dad·dy /dáddee/ (*plural* **-dies**) *n* **1.** a person's father, especially a young child's (*informal*; *often used as a form of address*) **2.** the earliest or finest example of something (*informal*) ○ *He was a fine trumpet player, the daddy of them all.* **3.** same as **sugar daddy** (*slang*)

dad·dy long·legs /-láwng lègz/ (*plural same*) *n* **1.** an arachnid with long legs and an oval body. Order: Opiliones. **2.** *UK* same as **crane fly**

da·do /dáydō/ *n* (*plural* **-does** or **-dos**) **1.** CONSTR **LOWER PART OF INTERIOR WALL** the lower part of an interior wall, decorated or faced in a different manner from the upper part, usually with panels, paint, or wallpaper **2.** ARCHIT same as **die**[2] (sense 5) **3.** CONSTR **RECTANGULAR GROOVE IN BOARD** a rectangular groove cut into a board so that a matching piece can be fitted into it to form a joint ■ *vt* (**-doed, -do·ing, -does**) CONSTR **1. PUT DADO ON WALL** to fit a wall with a dado **2. CUT DADO IN SOMETHING** to cut a rectangular groove in something so that a matching piece can be fitted into it to form a joint **3. INSERT SOMETHING INTO DADO** to insert something into a rectangular groove to form a joint [Mid-17C. < Italian, "die (of a pedestal), cube"]

da·do ra·il *n* a decorative rail fitted around an interior wall, usually at middle height

Da·dra and Na·gar Ha·ve·li /daádrə ən naágər haa váylee/ Union Territory in western India, between the states of Maharashtra and Gujarat. Capital: Silvassa. Population: 220,451 (2001). Area: 189 sq. mi./491 sq. km.

dae·dal /deéd'l/, **de·dal** *adj* (*literary*) **1. INTRICATE** complex or intricate **2. INGENIOUS** skillful or ingenious **3. DECORATED WITH MANY THINGS** decorated with many things, especially natural wonders ■ *n* **INGENIOUS INVENTOR** an expert or ingenious inventor [Late 16C. Via Latin < Greek *daidalos* "skillful"]

Dae·da·lus /déddʹləss/ *n* in Greek mythology, a craftsman and inventor who built a labyrinth on the island of Crete to house the Minotaur. He made wings so that he could escape from Crete with his son Icarus, but his son perished during the flight. —**Dae·da·li·an** /di dáylee ən/ *adj*

dae·mon /deéemən/ *n* **1.** *also* **dai·mon** /dī mōn/ MYTHOL **DEMIGOD** a mythological being that is part-god and part-human **2.** *also* **dai·mon** MYTHOL **GUARDIAN SPIRIT** a spirit supposed to look after a person or place **3.** COMPUT **SOFTWARE** a piece of software that carries out background tasks such as filtering or debugging, at fixed intervals or in response to specific events **4.** same as **demon** (sense 1) (*archaic*) [Variant of DEMON] —**dae·mon·ic** /di mónnik/ *adj*

daff /daf/ *n* PLANTS same as **daffodil** (sense 1) (*informal*) [Early 20C. Shortening]

daffodil

daf·fo·dil /dáffə dil/ *n* **1.** a plant with long slender leaves growing from a bulb. Flowers: yellow, trumpet-shaped. Native to: Europe. Latin name: *Narcissus pseudonarcissus*. **2.** a brilliant yellow color, like that of a daffodil [Mid-16C. < medieval Latin *affodilus* "asphodel"] —**daf·fo·dil** *adj*

daf·fy /dáffee/ (**-fi·er, -fi·est**) *adj* silly in an amusing or harmless way (*informal*) [Late 19C. < alteration of DAFT] —**daf·fi·ly** *adv* —**daf·fi·ness** *n*

daft /daft/ *adj* **1.** obviously silly or unreasonable (*informal*) ○ *a daft idea* **2.** *Scotland* thoughtless or frivolous [Old English *gedæfte* "fitting" < Germanic, "fit, suitable"] —**daft·ly** *adv* —**daft·ness** *n*

dag[1] /dag/ *n* a decorative edging for garments, used especially in medieval times [Early 17C. Shortening of DAGLOCK]

dag[2] *symbol* MEASURE decagram [Shortening and alteration]

da Ga·ma /də gaámə/ ➧ **Gama, Vasco da**

Da·gan /daágən/ *n* in Babylonian mythology, the god of the Earth

Dag·e·stan /daági staán/ autonomous republic in the Caucasus region of southern Russia, bordered by Kalmykia to the north, the Caspian Sea to the east, Azerbaijan to the south, and Chechnya and Georgia to the west. The administrative center is Makhachkala. Area: 19,400 sq. mi./50,300 sq. km. Population: 2,121,000 (1997).

Da·ges·tan·i·an /daágə staánee ən/ *n* **1.** a group of North Caucasian languages spoken in Dagestan. Native speakers: 3,000. **2.** somebody who comes from Dagestan —**Da·ges·tan·ian** *adj*

dag·ger /dággər/ *n* **1. SHORT POINTED KNIFE** a short pointed knife used as a weapon **2. IRRITATION** something that torments or wounds somebody ○ *Such cutting words were a dagger to my heart.* **3. SIGN USED AS REFERENCE MARK** a sign (†) that is used as a reference mark, especially to a footnote ■ *vt* (**-gered, -ger·ing, -gers**) PRINTING **MARK SOMETHING WITH REFERENCE SIGN** to mark text with a dagger sign [14C. Origin ?] ◇ **be at daggers drawn** *UK* to be hostile to each other and ready to defend a strongly held opposing view ◇ **look daggers at somebody** to look at somebody in an angry or hostile way

da·go /dáygō/ (*plural* **-gos** or **-goes**), **Da·go** *n* a highly offensive term for somebody of Italian, Spanish, or Portuguese birth or descent (*taboo*) [Mid-19C. Variant of the name *Diego*]

da·go·ba /daágəbə/ *n* a dome-shaped shrine that contains Buddhist relics [Early 19C. Via Sinhalese *dāgaba* < Pali *dhātu-gabbha* "receptacle for relics"]

Da·gon /dáy gòn/ *n* in Philistine mythology, the chief god, often depicted as half man and half fish

Da·guerre /də gér, daa-/, **Louis Jacques** (1789–1851) French painter and inventor. Originally a scene painter, he became a pioneer photographer who, working initially with French physicist Joseph Niépce (1829), perfected the daguerreotype process (1837). Full name **Daguerre, Louis Jacques Mandé**

da·guerre·o·type /də gérrə tīp/ *n* **1. EARLY PHOTOGRAPHIC PROCESS** an early photographic process in which an image was produced on a light-sensitive silver or silver-coated plate and developed in mercury vapor **2. EARLY PHOTOGRAPH** a photograph produced by the daguerreotype process ■ *vt* (**-typed, -typ·ing, -types**) **PHOTOGRAPH SOMEBODY OR SOMETHING** to make a daguerreotype of something or somebody [Mid-19C. < French *daguerréotype*, after L. J. DAGUERRE] —**da·guerre·o·typ·er** *n* —**da·guerre·o·typ·y** *n*

Da·gu·pan /daa goŏ paàn/ port and city on Luzon island in the northwestern Philippines. Population: 116,211 (1990).

Dag·wood sand·wich /dág wŏŏd-/, **Dag·wood** *n* a thick sandwich filled with a variety of meats and cheeses together with different dressings and seasonings [Late 20C. After *Dagwood* Bumstead, comic-strip character]

dah /daa/ *n* the spoken representation of a dash in Morse code and other telegraphic codes [Mid-20C. An imitation of the sound made by a Morse code transmitter]

da·hi /daáhee/ *n S Asia* FOOD same as **yogurt** [< Hindi *dahī* "curds"]

dahl /daal/ *n* a thick stew made from lentils, onions, and spices, originating in South Asia [Late 17C. < Hindi *dāl*]

Dahl /daal/, **Roald** (1916–90) British writer. He is best known for his many children's books, including *James and the Giant Peach* (1961) and *Charlie and the Chocolate Factory* (1964). His books for adults include *Kiss, Kiss* (1960).

> "Do you *know* what breakfast cereal is made of? It's made of all those little curly wooden shavings you find in pencil sharpeners!"
> [Roald Dahl, *Charlie and the Chocolate Factory*, 1964]

dahlia

dahl·ia /daályə, dál-/ *n* a tall perennial plant with tuberous roots. Flowers: large, brightly colored. Genus: *Dahlia*. [Early 19C. After Andreas *Dahl* (1751–89), Swedish botanist]

Da·ho·mey /də hṓmee, -may/ former name for **Benin** (until 1975)

da·hoon /də hoón/ *n* an evergreen tree of the holly family with leathery, dark-green leaves that produces orange, red, or yellow fruits. Native to: southern United States. Latin name: *Ilex cassine*.

daid·zein /dídzin/ *n* an isoflavone derivative found in soy products that is a possible natural cancer preventative

dai·kon /dī kòn, dīkən/ *n* a long sweet white radish used in Asian cuisines. Latin name: *Raphanus sativus longipinnatus*. [Late 19C. < Japanese < *dai* "big" (< Middle Chinese *daj*) + *kon* "root" (< Middle Chinese *kən*)]

Dáil Éire·ann /dòyl érrən/, **Dáil** *n* the lower house of the parliament of the Republic of Ireland [Early 20C. < Irish, "Irish Assembly"]

dai·ly /dáylee/ *adj* **1. DONE EVERY DAY** done or occurring every day **2. FOR EACH DAY** for each day, or for a period of a day **3. LASTING ONE DAY** for the duration of a day, or during a day ■ *adv* **EVERY DAY** on each day ■ *n* (*plural* **-lies**) **NEWSPAPER PUBLISHED EVERY DAY** a newspaper published every day or every day except Sunday (*often used in the plural*) ■ **dai·lies** *npl* MOVIES **DAY'S SHOOTING OF MOVIE SCENES** unedited prints of a day's shooting of scenes from a movie, prepared each day for the director to view the following day [15C. < DAY]

dai·ly dou·ble *n* **1.** a bet, e.g., in horseracing, won by correctly choosing the winners of two specified races taking place on the same day **2.** the two races specified for a daily double bet

dai·ly doz·en *n* a set of physical exercises to be done each day

dai·mi·o *n* HIST another spelling of **daimyo**

Daim·ler /dímlər/, **Gottlieb** (1834–1900) German engineer and inventor. His high-speed gasoline-burning internal-combustion engine powered the first motorcycle and one of the earliest successful automobiles (1887).

dai·mon *n* MYTHOL another spelling of **daemon** (senses 1–2)

dai·my·o /dímyō/ (*plural same* or **-os**), **dai·mi·o** *n* a great Japanese feudal lord who was a vassal of the emperor [Early 18C. < Japanese, "great name"]

Dain·tree Na·tion·al Park /dàyn tree-/ national park in northeastern Queensland, Australia, that forms part of the Wet Tropics of Queensland World Heritage Area. Area: 2,734 sq. mi./7,080 sq. km.

dain·ty /dáyntee/ *adj* (**-ti·er, -ti·est**) **1. PRETTY** delicate and pretty ○ *dainty slippers* **2. TASTY** choice, delicious, or tasty ○ *a dainty morsel* **3. REFINED IN TASTE** having refined taste or manners **4. OVERLY FASTIDIOUS** excessively fastidious or particular ■ *n* (*plural* **-ties**) **DELICACY** something delicious, especially a small piece of food [13C. Via Anglo-Norman *dainte*, Old French *daintie* < Latin *dignitas* (see DIGNITY)] —**dain·ti·ly** *adv* —**dain·ti·ness** *n*

dai·qui·ri /dákəree/ (*plural* **-ris**) *n* an iced cocktail made from rum, lemon or lime juice, and sugar or syrup [Early 20C. After *Daiquiri*, Cuba]

dair·y /dérree/ *n* (*plural* **-ies**) **1. FARM FOR MILK PRODUCTION** a farm that produces milk and milk products **2. PLACE TO STORE MILK AND CREAM** a room or building where milk and cream and sometimes other perishables are stored **3. PLACE TO MAKE BUTTER AND CHEESE** a room or building where butter and cheese are made **4. ESTABLISHMENT THAT SELLS OR PROCESSES MILK** a commercial establishment that processes, sells, or distributes milk and milk products **5. DAIRY PRODUCTS** dairy products collectively **6.** *regional* **DUG-OUT HOLE** a space dug out in the side of a hill ■ *adj* **1. RELATING TO MILK PRODUCTS** relating to, producing, or containing milk or milk products **2.** JUDAISM **CONCERNING FOODS IN JEWISH DIETARY LAW** relating to those foods, including milk products, eggs, fish, and vegetables, that Jewish dietary law allows on occasions when milk is consumed [13C. < obsolete *deie* "woman servant, dairy worker" < Old English *dæge* "kneader (of bread)"]

SPELLCHECK dairy or **diary**? Do not confuse the spelling of ***dairy*** and ***diary***. The word ***dairy*** is a noun and adjective referring to milk, cream, butter, etc., as in *buy milk from the dairy, dairy farming, cheese and other dairy products*. The word ***diary*** is a noun denoting a personal record of events or appointments, or a book used for this purpose.

REGIONAL NOTE In the sense "storage house or shed for storing milk and other perishables," ***dairy*** competes with *dairy house, milk house, safe, spring,* and *springhouse*. In the mountains, as in eastern Tennessee, the term ***dairy*** may signal a hole dug out in the side of a hill.

dair·y cat·tle *npl* cattle bred and raised for milk production

dair·y house *n regional* a storage house or shed for storing milk and other perishables

REGIONAL NOTE See ***dairy***.

dair·y·ing /dérree ing/ *n* the business of operating a dairy or dairy farm

dair·y·man /dérrimən, -màn/ (*plural* **-men** /dérrimən, -mèn/) *n* a man who owns or is employed at a dairy

dai·ry·per·son /dérree pùrss'n/ (*plural* **-per·sons** or **-peo·ple** /-peep'l/) *n* an owner or employee of a dairy

dai·ry·wo·man /dérree wŏŏmmən/, **dai·ry·wo·man** /-wìmmin/ *n* a woman who owns or is employed at a dairy

da·is /dáy iss, dī-/ *n* a raised platform at the end of a hall or large room [13C. Via French < Latin]

dai·shi·ki *n* CLOTHING another spelling of **dashiki**

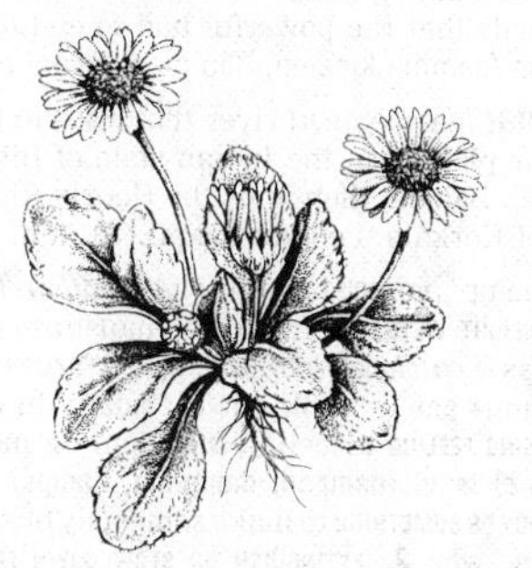

daisy

dai·sy /dáyzee/ (*plural* **-sies**) *n* **1. TALL PLANT** a tall flowering plant. Flowers: large white petals around a yellow center. Native to: Europe, Asia, North America. Latin name: *Chrysanthemum leucanthemum*. **2. LOW-GROWING FLOWERING PLANT** a low-growing wild plant, with cultivated varieties. Flowers: white or pinkish white petals, yellow center. Native to: Europe. Latin name: *Bellis perennis*. **3. YOUNG GIRL SCOUT** a preschool-age member of the Girl Scouts **4. EXCELLENT PERSON OR THING** a person or thing regarded as first-rate or excellent (*slang*) [Old English *dæges eage* "day's eye"; because the flower opens in daylight and closes at night]

dai·sy chain *n* **1.** a garland made by threading the stems of daisies together **2.** a series of connected things, events, or people (*slang*)

dai·sy·cut·ter /dáyzee kùttər/ *n* **1.** a bomb that detonates just above ground level, used against personnel and to destroy vegetation in order to create a landing zone for helicopters **2.** a batted baseball that skims the ground (*dated*)

dai·sy ham *n* a small cut of pork shoulder that has been boned, salted, and smoked

dai·sy wheel *n* in some electronic typewriters and printers, a wheel with type elements at the ends of spokes radiating from a central hub

Dak. *abbr* Dakota

Da·kar /dá kaar, də kaar/ capital and largest city of Senegal. It is situated on Cape Verde Peninsula, close to the westernmost tip of mainland Africa, and is one of West Africa's leading ports. Population: 1,708,000 (1995).

da·koit *n* CRIME another spelling of **dacoit**

Da·ko·ta[1] /də kṓtə/ (*plural* **-tas** or *same*) *n* **1.** a member of the Sioux people, especially the Santee branch **2.** a Siouan language spoken in the United States and the Canadian province of Manitoba. Native speakers: 10,000–20,000. [Early 19C. < Dakota *Dakhōta* "allies"] —**Da·ko·ta** *adj*

Da·ko·ta[2] /də kṓtə/ ➧ **North Dakota, South Dakota** —**Da·ko·tan** *n, adj*

dal *symbol* MEASURE decaliter

Da·lai La·ma /daa lī laamə/ *n* in Tibetan Buddhism, the highest priest and, until the Chinese occupation of Tibet in 1959, the traditional spiritual and secular ruler of Tibet [Late 17C. < Mongolian, "ocean lama"]

da·la·si /daa laassee/ (*plural* **-sis**) *n* the main unit of Gambian currency. See table at **currency** [Late 20C. < name of an earlier Gambian coin]

dale /dayl/ *n* a broad lowland valley ○ *walked over hill and dale* [Old English *dæl* < Indo-European, "bend, curve"]

Dale /dayl/, **Sir Henry Hallett** (1875–1968) British physiologist and pharmacist. With Otto Loewi, he established the role of the chemical acetylcholine in the transmission of nerve impulses. He and Loewi were joint Nobel laureates (1936).

da·led *n* same as **daleth**

Dales, York·shire ➧ **Yorkshire Dales**

da·leth /daa lèth, daalət/, **da·led** /-lèd, -ləd/, **da·let** /-lèt, -lət/ *n* the fourth letter of the Hebrew alphabet, represented in the English alphabet as "d." See table at **alphabet**

Da·ley /dáylee/, **Richard J.** (1902–76) US politician. He was the Democratic mayor of Chicago (1955–76) and was known for exerting strong personal control over local Democratic Party politics. Full name **Daley, Richard Joseph**

AKG London

Salvador Dali

Da·li /daalee/, **Da·lí, Salvador** (1904–89) Spanish surrealist painter. He is known for the dreamlike imagery and almost photographic realism of his work. After settling in New York (1940), he adopted other styles and wrote *The Secret Life of Salvador Dali* (1942). —**Da·li·esque** /daalee ésk/ *adj*

> "Those who do not want to imitate anything, produce nothing."
> [Salvador Dali, *Dalí by Dalí*; 1970]

~~dalia~~ incorrect spelling of **dahlia**

Da·lian /daa lyaan/ industrial seaport on the southern peninsula in Liaoning Province, northeastern China. Population: 2,560,000 (1995).

Dal·it /daalit/ *n* in parts of South Asia, a member of the lowest caste within the traditional Hindu caste system [Via Hindi < Sanskrit *dalita* "oppressed"]

Dal·las /dálləss/ city in northeastern Texas, on the Trinity River, east of Fort Worth. It is an important commercial, financial, and distribution center. Population: 1,211,467 (2002 estimate).

Dal·las, George (1792–1864) vice president of the United States. He was vice president (1845–49) under President James K. Polk. The city of Dallas, Texas, is named for him. Full name **Dallas, George Mifflin**

dalles /dalz/ *npl* rapids where a river flows between the steep narrow walls of a canyon or ravine [Late 18C. < French, "tubes, conduits"]

dal·li·ance /dállee ənss/ *n* (*literary*) **1.** a flirtation or flirtatious episode, or an affair **2.** the frivolous or idle wasting of time

Dal·lis grass /dálləss-/ *n* a tall perennial grass, grown as a pasture grass in the southern United States. Native to: South America. Latin name: *Paspalum dilatatum*. [Early 20C. Origin ?]

Dall sheep /dáwl-/, **Dall's sheep** *n* a wild mountain sheep with curved horns and a coat varying from white to black. Native to: Alaska, Canada. Latin name: *Ovis dalli*. [After William H. *Dall* (1845–1927), US naturalist]

dal·ly[1] /dállee/ (**-lied, -ly·ing, -lies**) *vi* **1. FLIRT** to act in an amorous, flirtatious, or playful manner **2. TOY** to trifle or deal lightly with something or somebody **3. WASTE TIME** to dawdle, loiter, or waste time [14C. < Anglo-Norman *dalier* "amuse yourself"] —**dal·li·er** *n*

dal·ly[2] /dá lee/ (*plural* **-lies**) *n Southwest US* a temporary twist of a rope around a saddle horn, used by a cowhand in roping an animal [Early 20C. < *dally* "twist a rope around a saddle horn" < Spanish *dale (vuelta)!* "give it a turn!"]

Dal·ma·tia /dal máyshə/ region of Croatia, consisting of a coastal area and offshore islands. It is bordered inland by the Dinaric Alps and includes the major cities of Dubrovnik and Split. Area: 5,000 sq. mi./12,950 sq. km.

Dal·ma·tian /dal máysh'n/ *n* **1.** *also* **dal·ma·tian SPOTTED DOG** a dog belonging to a breed that has a white coat with black or brown spots **2. SOMEBODY FROM DALMATIA** somebody who comes from Dalmatia **3. EXTINCT ROMANCE LANGUAGE** an extinct Romance language formerly spoken along the Adriatic coast in the region of Dubrovnik —**Dal·ma·tian** *adj*

Dal·ma·tian coast *n* a coastline characterized by chains of islands close to the mainland, formed when rising sea levels flood a series of valleys and ridges parallel to the coast

dal·mat·ic /dal máttik/ *n* **1.** a vestment with slit sides and wide sleeves, worn by a priest or deacon of the Roman Catholic Church **2.** a robe with slit sides and wide sleeves, worn by British sovereigns at their coronation [15C. Directly or via Old French *dalmatique* < Latin *dalmatica* "(robe) made of Dalmatian wool" < *Dalmaticus* "of Dalmatia"]

dal se·gno /daal sáynyō/ *adv* to be played or sung again from the point marked with the sign 𝄋 to the point marked "fine" (*used as a musical direction*) [Late 19C. < Italian, "from the sign"]

dal·ton /dáwlt'n/ *n* CHEM same as **atomic mass unit** [Mid-20C. After John DALTON]

Dal·ton /dáwlt'n/, **John** (1766–1844) British physicist and meteorologist. His experiments with gases (1803) laid the foundations for modern atomic theory. He also first described color blindness (1794).

dal·ton·ism /dáwlt'n ìzzəm/, **Dal·ton·ism** *n* color blindness, especially an inability to distinguish between red and green [Mid-19C. < French *daltonisme*, after John DALTON] —**dal·ton·ic** /dawl tónnik/ *adj*

Dal·ton plan /dáwlt'n-/, **Dal·ton sys·tem** *n* a system of teaching and learning whereby the student is free to continue without interruption on any subject that may arise in the course of his or her study [Early 20C. After *Dalton*, Massachusetts]

Dal·ton's law *n* the principle that mixed gases in a given volume exert a pressure equal to the sum of the pressures they would exert individually in the same volume [After John DALTON]

Dal·ton sys·tem *n* EDUC same as **Dalton plan**

Da·ly Cit·y /dàylee-/ city in western California on the Pacific Ocean, south of San Francisco. Population: 101,901 (2002 estimate).

NevadaBarnaby's

dam: Hoover dam (completed 1936), Arizona

dam[1] /dam/ *n* **1. BARRIER CONTROLLING FLOW OF WATER** a barrier of concrete or earth that is built across a river or stream to obstruct or control the flow of water, especially in order to create a reservoir **2. RESERVOIR CONFINED BY DAM** a reservoir of water created, confined, or controlled by a dam **3. SOMETHING LIKE DAM** a barrier that resembles or acts as a dam ■ *vt* (**dammed, dam·ming, dams**) **1. CONFINE SOMETHING WITH DAM** to confine, provide, or restrain something with a dam **2. OBSTRUCT SOMETHING** to obstruct or restrict something [14C. < Middle Dutch]

dam[2] /dam/ *n* the female parent of an animal, especially of four-legged domestic livestock [14C. Variant of DAME]

dam[3] *symbol* MEASURE decameter

Dam /dam, daam/, **Henrik** (1895–1976) Danish biochemist. Working with Edward A. Doisy, he isolated vitamin K, a fat-soluble substance necessary for blood coagulation. The pair shared a Nobel Prize (1943). Full name **Dam, Carl Peter Henrik**

da·ma /dámmə/ *n Hispanic* a girl who is another young girl's formal escort in a court of honor (**corte de honor**) during her rite of passage (**quinceañera**) welcoming her into adulthood [< Spanish, "lady"]

dam·age /dámmij/ *n* **1. HARM OR INJURY** physical injury that makes something less useful, valuable, or able to function ○ *Damage to the vehicle was slight.* **2. ADVERSE EFFECT** a harmful effect on somebody or something ○ *did untold damage to her standing in the community* ○ *suffered psychological damage as a result of the harassment* **3. COST** the cost or price of something (*informal*) ○ *What's the damage?* ■ **dam·ag·es** *npl* LAW **MONEY PAID AS COMPENSATION** money paid or claimed as compensation for harm, loss, or injury ■ *v* (**-aged, -ag·ing, -ag·es**) **1.** *vt* **HARM SOMEBODY OR SOMETHING** to cause damage to something or somebody **2.** *vi* **BE HARMED** to suffer damage ○ *Soft fruit damages easily.* [13C. < Old French, "loss through injury" < *dam* "loss, damage" < Latin *damnum*] —**dam·age·a·bil·i·ty** /dàmmijə bíllətee/ *n* —**dam·age·a·ble** *adj*

SYNONYMS See *harm.*

dam·age con·trol *n* **1.** containment and neutralization of difficulties caused by an event, e.g., public relations problems caused by a scandal, legal case, or other controversial matter (*informal*) ○ *As soon as the scandal broke, the Party's damage control kicked in.* **2.** shipboard measures to control, contain, and offset damages to a vessel, e.g., by collision, attack, fire, or an explosion

dam·ag·ing /dámmijing/ *adj* causing or capable of causing harm, injury, or loss ○ *a damaging report* —**dam·ag·ing·ly** *adv*

Da·man /də maán/ capital of the Union Territory of Daman and Diu, western India. Population: 26,905 (1991).

Da·man and Di·u /-dée oo/ Union Territory of western India, comprising the coastal town of Daman and the island of Diu off the coast of Gujarat. Capital: Daman. Population: 158,059 (2001). Area: 43 sq. mi./112 sq. km.

dam·ar *n* INDUST another spelling of **dammar**

Dam·ar·a /də maárə/ (*plural* **-as** *or same*) *n* **1.** a member of a people living in southwestern Africa, mainly in Namibia **2.** a dialect of the Nama language spoken in Namibia. Native speakers: 160,000. [Early 19C. < Nama] —**Dam·ar·a** *adj*

Da·ma·ra·land /də maárə lànd, dámmərə-/ historic region in north central Namibia, named for the Damara people

dam·as·cene /dámmə seén, dàmmə seén/ *vt* (**-cened, -cen·ing, -cenes**) **DECORATE METAL WITH WAVY PATTERNS** to decorate metal such as iron or steel with wavy patterns of etching or inlays of precious metals, especially gold or silver ■ *n* **DESIGN OR OBJECT CREATED BY DAMASCENING** a design or object created by the process of damascening ■ *adj* **1. RELATING TO DAMASCENING** relating to the art or process of damascening metal **2. OF OR LIKE DAMASK** made of or resembling damask [Mid-19C. < DAMASCENE (adj)] —**dam·a·scen·er** *n*

Dam·as·cene /dámmə seén, dàmmə seén/ *n* somebody who comes from Damascus ■ *adj* relating to Damascus [15C. < Via Latin *Damascenus* "of Damascus" < Greek *damaskēnos*]

Da·mas·cus /də máskəss/ capital city of Syria on the Baradá River in the southwestern part of the country. Thought to have been inhabited since 2000 B.C., it is one of the oldest cities in the world. Population: 2,036,000 (1995).

dam·ask /dámməsk/ *n* **1. PATTERNED FABRIC** a reversible cotton, linen, or silk fabric with a pattern woven into it. Use: table linen. **2. TABLE LINEN** table linen made from damask **3. GRAYISH-PINK COLOR** a grayish-pink color, like that of the damask rose ■ *vt* (**-asked, -ask·ing, -asks**) **DECORATE FABRIC WITH PATTERN** to decorate or weave a fabric with an elaborate pattern [14C. < Latin *Damascus* "Damascus"] —**dam·ask** *adj*

dam·ask rose *n* a large hardy rose. Flowers: fragrant, pink or red. Use: essential oil. Native to: Asia. Latin name: *Rosa damascena.* [< *Damask* "of Damascus"]

Dam·a·vand /dámmə vànd/ mountain in Iran, northeast of Tehran. It is the highest peak in the Elburz Mountains and in the country. Height: 18,602 ft./5,670 m.

dame /daym/ *n* **1.** a term for a woman or girl (*often considered offensive*) **2.** the woman in charge of a household (*archaic*) **3.** THEATER same as **pantomime dame** [13C. Via Old French and late Latin *domna* < Latin *domina* "woman in charge of the house"]

Dame *n* **1.** the title of a woman awarded any of various orders of chivalry or merit such as the Order of the British Empire by a sovereign or government **2.** the official title of the wife of a baronet or knight

dame's vi·o·let, **dame's rock·et** *n* a perennial plant of the mustard family. Flowers: fragrant, purple or white. Native to: Europe, Asia. Latin name: *Hesperis matronalis.* [Translation of the Latin name in old herbals, *Viola matronalis*]

Da·mi·en /dáymee ən, daa myáN/, **Father** (1840–89) Belgian Roman Catholic priest. From 1873 until his death from leprosy, he lived among lepers isolated on Molokai Island, Hawaii, attending to their spiritual and material needs. Full name **de Veuster, Joseph Damien**

Dam·i·et·ta /dàmmee éttə/ city in the northeastern corner of the Nile delta, Egypt. It is situated near the mouth of the Damietta River, a tributary of the Nile. Population: 89,498 (1986).

dam·mar /dámmər/, **dam·ar**, **dam·mer** *n* a hard resin obtained from various trees of Southeast Asia. Use: inks, lacquers, oil paints, varnishes. [Late 17C. < Malay *damar* "resin"]

dam·mit /dámmit/ *interj* used as a swearword to express irritation, displeasure, disappointment, or frustration with somebody or something (*informal*; *sometimes offensive*) [Mid-19C. Variant of *damn it*]

damn /dam/ *interj, adj, adv* **USED TO EXPRESS ANNOYANCE** used emphatically or as a swearword to express annoyance, disappointment, or frustration with somebody or something (*informal*; *sometimes considered offensive*) ■ *v* (**damned, damn·ing, damns**) **1.** *vt* **SAY SOMEBODY OR SOMETHING IS BAD** to express disapproval of somebody or something, especially in public **2.** *vt* **DOOM SOMEBODY OR SOMETHING TO FAILURE** to cause somebody or something to fail **3.** *vt* **CONDEMN SOMEBODY TO HELL** in Christian belief, to condemn somebody to hell or to eternal punishment **4.** *vti* **SWEAR AT SOMEBODY OR SOMETHING** to curse or swear at somebody or something, using the word "damn" [13C. Via Old French *damner* "condemn" < Latin *damnare* < *damnum* "damage"] —**damn·er** *n* ◇ **not give** *or* **care a damn** to be not at all concerned or worried about something ◇ **not worth a damn** completely worthless

dam·na·ble /dámnəb'l/ *adj* **1.** detestable, hateful, or extremely bad **2.** in Christian belief, deserving divine condemnation or damnation (*dated*) —**dam·na·bil·i·ty** /dàmnə bíllətee/ *n* —**dam·na·ble·ness** *n* —**dam·na·bly** *adv*

dam·na·tion /dam náysh'n/ *n* **1. CONDEMNATION** in Christian belief, condemnation to hell or eternal punishment **2. PUNISHMENT** in Christian belief, eternal punishment in hell **3. SIN** in Christian belief, something that causes condemnation to hell or eternal punishment ■ *interj* **ANGRY EXCLAMATION** used as a swearword to express anger or disappointment

dam·na·to·ry /dámnə tàwree/ *adj* causing, expressing, or threatening condemnation (*formal*)

damned /damd/ *adj* **1. CONDEMNED** in Christian belief, condemned to hell or to eternal punishment **2. EXPRESSION OF ANNOYANCE** used emphatically or as a swearword to express annoyance (*informal*) ■ *adv* **VERY** extremely (*informal*) ○ *a damned good saxophone player* ■ *npl* **PEOPLE CONDEMNED TO HELL** in Christian belief, those condemned to hell or doomed to suffer eternal punishment

damned·est /dámdəst/ *n* everything possible (*slang*) ○ *She did her damnedest to persuade them to stay.* ■ *adj* most amazing or extraordinary (*informal*) ○ *It was the damnedest thing I'd ever seen.*

dam·ni·fy /dámni fì/ (**-fied, -fy·ing, -fies**) *vt* to cause damage or loss to somebody or something [Early 16C. Via Old French *damnifier* < Latin *damnificare* "injure, condemn" < *damnare* (see DAMN)] —**dam·ni·fi·ca·tion** /dàmnifi káysh'n/ *n*

damn·ing /dámming/ *adj* **1.** proving or showing that somebody or something is guilty, wrong, or very bad **2.** very critical or unfavorable ○ *The reviewer made some very damning comments about the show.* —**damn·ing·ly** *adv*

Dam·o·cles /dámmə kleez/ (*fl* 4th century B.C.) Syracusan Greek courtier. Dionysius of Syracuse, tired of his envious flattery, had him seated beneath a sword hanging from a hair in order to show him the perils that the powerful had to endure. —**Dam·o·cle·an** /dàmmə klee ən, dámmə klee ən/ *adj*

Da·mo·dar /daámə daar/ river that rises in the Chota Nagpur plateau in the Indian state of Bihar, flows through Bangla, then joins the Hoogly River southwest of Korkata. Length: 368 mi./592 km.

damp /damp/ *adj* **MOIST** slightly wet ○ *damp laundry* ■ *n* **1. SLIGHT WETNESS** humidity, moisture, or slight wetness ○ *patches of damp* **2.** MIN EXTRACT **HARMFUL GAS** poisonous gas or rank air, especially in a mine **3. DEPRESSING FEELING** a feeling of gloom or melancholy (*archaic*) ■ *vt* (**damped, damp·ing, damps**) **1. DAMPEN SOMEBODY OR SOMETHING** to make somebody or something slightly wet **2. EXTINGUISH OR SLOW DOWN FIRE** to extinguish a fire or make it burn more slowly by reducing its supply of air **3.** MUSIC **REDUCE VIBRATION OF STRING** to reduce the vibration of a string on a piano **4.** MUSIC **MUFFLE BRASS OR WOODWIND INSTRUMENT** to muffle the sound of a brass or woodwind instrument **5. DISCOURAGE SOMEBODY OR SOMETHING** to discourage somebody or stifle a feeling ○ *Rain damped the picnickers' enthusiasm.* **6.** PHYS **REDUCE OSCILLATION** to decrease the amplitude of an oscillation or wave [14C. < Middle Low German < Germanic] —**damp·ly** *adv* —**damp·ness** *n*

SYNONYMS See *wet.*

damp down *vt* **1.** to cause a fire to burn more slowly by adding ash or by reducing the flow of air **2.** to control, restrain, or reduce the intensity of something

damp off *vi* to decline in power, wealth, or strength

damp course *n* a layer of waterproof material near the ground in a brick wall that prevents damp from rising

damp·en /dámpən/ (**-ened, -en·ing, -ens**) *vti* **1.** to make something slightly wet, or become slightly wet **2.** to deaden or stifle something, or become deadened or stifled —**damp·en·er** *n*

dampen down *vt* same as **damp down**

dampen off *vi* same as **damp off**

damp·er /dámpər/ *n* **1. SOMEBODY OR SOMETHING DISCOURAGING** somebody or something that causes discouragement or inhibition **2. PLATE TO CONTROL FIRE** a metal plate that controls the draft in a furnace or stove **3.** MUSIC **PIANO MUTE** a felt-covered block in a piano that stops the vibration of strings **4.** MUSIC **HORN OR WOODWIND MUTE** a mute to muffle the sound of a brass or woodwind instrument **5.** ELEC ENG **DEVICE TO CONTROL VIBRATION** a device for controlling the excessive vibration of a suspended magnetic needle **6.** ELEC ENG **DEVICE IN ELECTRIC MOTOR** a piece of copper embedded in or near the poles of an electric motor to reduce any tendency to pulsate to speeds above or below its intended speed ◇ **put a damper on something** to make something less fun and more inhibited ○ *The sudden arrival of the adults put a damper on the kids' party.*

Dam·pi·er /dámpee ər/, **William** (1652–1715) English explorer. He was one of the first Europeans to visit Australia and published numerous surveys, logs, and charts of his voyages around the world.

damp·ing off /dámping-/ *n* a fatal disease of seedlings grown under very damp conditions that is caused by various fungi

damp-proof *adj* impervious or resistant to damp or moisture ■ *vt* to make something such as a building damp-proof

damp-proof course *n* CONSTR same as **damp course**

Dam·rosch /dám ròsh/, **Walter Johannes** (1862–1950) German-born US conductor and composer. He conducted several noted orchestras, most notably the NBC Symphony Orchestra in New York (1928–42).

dam·sel /dámzəl/ *n* a girl or young unmarried woman, originally one of noble birth (*archaic or literary*) [13C. < Old French *dameisele*, alteration (after *dame*) of *donsele* < Vulgar Latin *dominicella* "little lady" < Latin *domina* "woman in charge of the house"]

dam·sel·fish /dámzəl fish/ (*plural same* or **-fish·es**) *n* a small brightly colored ocean fish that lives along coral reefs. Native to: tropics. Family: Pomacentridae.

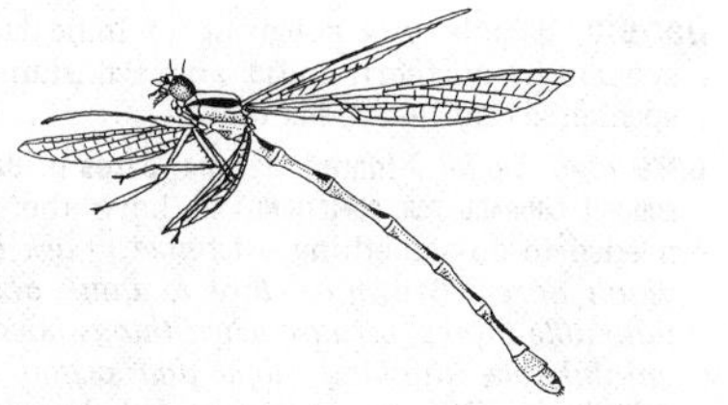

damselfly

dam·sel·fly /dámzəl flī/ (*plural* **-flies**) *n* a slender insect, related to the dragonfly but smaller in size, that folds its wings together above its body when resting and has eyes facing sideways. Suborder: Zygoptera.

dam·son /dámzən/ *n* **1.** a small sour dark purple fruit, usually eaten cooked or made into jelly **2.** a fruit tree related to the plum that produces damsons. Latin name: *Prunus insititia.* [15C. Alteration of DAMASCENE (adj)]

dan[1] /dan/, **Dan** *n* **1.** one of the numbered black-belt levels of proficiency in martial arts such as judo and karate **2.** somebody who has achieved a dan [Mid-20C. Via Japanese < Middle Chinese *nam* "male"]

dan[2] /dan/ *n* a small buoy, often with a flag attached, used as a marker [Late 17C. Origin ?]

Dan /dan/ *n* in the Bible, the son of Jacob and Bilhah and the founder of the tribe of Dan (Genesis 30:6)

Dan. *abbr* **1.** BIBLE Daniel **2.** Danish

Da·na /dáynə/, **James Dwight** (1813–95) US mineralogist. He was appointed professor of natural history (1849) and professor of geology and mineralogy (1864) at Yale University, and is known for his work *Manual of Mineralogy* (1848).

Da·na·i·des /də náy ə deez/, **Da·na·ï·des** *npl* in Greek mythology, the 50 daughters of Danaüs, king of Argos, who were ordered by their father to kill their bridegrooms, but one, Hypermnestra, refused

Da Nang /də náng, daa naang/, **Da·nang** city and port in east central Vietnam. It was a major US military base during the Vietnam War. Population: 382,674 (1992).

Da·na Point /dáynə-/ town in southwestern California on the Pacific Ocean, southeast of Los Angeles. Population: 35,804 (2002 estimate).

dan buoy *n* NAVIG same as **dan**[2]

Dan·bur·y /dán bèrree/ city in southwestern Connecticut. It was an important military supply base during the American Revolution and is now an industrial and commercial center. Population: 76,917 (2002 estimate).

dance /danss/ *v* (**danced, danc·ing, danc·es**) **1.** *vi* **MOVE RHYTHMICALLY TO MUSIC** to move the feet and body rhythmically, usually in time to music **2.** *vt* **PERFORM PARTICULAR STEPS TO MUSIC** to perform or participate in a particular series of rhythmical steps and movements, usually to music ○ *to dance a lively polka* **3.** *vt* **MAKE SOMEBODY DANCE** to cause somebody to dance ○ *He danced her across the floor.* **4.** *vi* **JUMP UP AND DOWN** to leap or skip, especially in an emotional manner ○ *The children danced with glee.* **5.** *vi* **MOVE ABOUT QUICKLY** to bob up and down or move quickly about ○ *The leaves danced across the lawn.* **6.** *vi* **EVADE ISSUE** to talk misleadingly so as to avoid facing an issue squarely (*informal*) ○ *They danced around the issue of employee bonuses.* ○ *Don't dance around on the question of fairness.* **7.** *vt* **ACHIEVE SOMETHING BY DANCING** to achieve or proceed through something by dancing ○ *She danced her way to fame and fortune.* **8.** *vi* BOARD GAMES **FAIL TO ROLL REENTRY NUMBER** in backgammon, to fail to roll a number that reenters a piece from the bar ○ *He rolled a 6–6 and danced.* ■ *n* **1. RHYTHMIC BODY MOVEMENTS TO MUSIC** a series of rhythmic steps and movements, usually performed to music **2. PERIOD OF DANCING** a session of dancing **3. OCCASION FOR DANCING** a social gathering for dancing **4. ART OF DANCING** dancing as a performance art **5.** MUSIC **MUSIC FOR DANCING** a piece of music for a dance **6. EVASION** evasive talk (*informal*) **7.** ZOOL **PATTERN OF ANIMAL MOVEMENTS** a pattern of animal movements used, e.g., by birds in courtship or by bees in giving information about food ■ *adj* **OF OR FOR DANCING** relating to, involving, or created for dancing [13C. < Old French] —**dance·a·ble** *adj* —**danc·er** *n*

dance band *n* a band that plays music for dancing

dance floor *n* an area of bare floor for dancing

dance hall *n* **1.** an enclosed space where public dances are held **2.** electronically produced dance music combining different musical styles with a disk jockey talking or rapping to the rhythm

dance mu·sic *n* **1.** music suitable for dancing **2.** pop music that uses repeated electronic rhythms

dance of death, Dance of Death *n* an allegorical representation in medieval art, literature, and music of a dance in which Death, personified as a skeleton, leads people to the grave

danc·er·cise /dánssər sīz/ *n* aerobic exercise in the form of dance [Mid-20C. Blend of DANCE + EXERCISE]

danc·ing /dánssing/ *n* the performance of or participation in a dance ■ *adj* performing, used for, or participating in dance or a dance ○ *my dancing partner* ○ *dancing shoes*

danc·ing der·vish *n* a member of an ascetic Muslim religious group known for very energetic dancing

D and C *n* a gynecological surgical procedure in which the cervix is widened and some of the womb lining is scraped out for diagnostic or treatment purposes or in an abortion. Full form **dilation and curettage**

dandelion

dan·de·li·on /dánd'l ī ən/ *n* a weed with bright yellow flowers on hollow stalks that produce fluffy white seed heads. Use: leaves in salads, medicine, winemaking. Latin name: *Taraxacum officinale.* [15C. < French *dent de lion* "lion's tooth"]

dan·de·li·on greens *npl* the tender leaves of young dandelion plants, eaten raw in salads or cooked as a vegetable

dan·der /dándər/ *n* **1.** minute particles or scales shed from the feathers, hair, or skin of various animals **2.** *Ireland* same as **dandruff** [Late 18C. Origin ?] ◇ **get somebody's dander up** to make somebody angry

Dan·die Din·mont /dàndee dín mònt, -dínmənt/, **Dan·die Din·mont ter·ri·er** *n* a small terrier belonging to a breed from the Scottish Borders with a long body, short legs, drooping ears, and a long, wiry, grayish or brownish coat [Early 19C. After the fictional owner of such dogs in *Guy Mannering* by Sir Walter Scott]

dan·di·fy /dándə fī/ (**-fied, -fy·ing, -fies**) *vt* to dress somebody as or cause somebody to resemble a dandy —**dan·di·fi·ca·tion** /dàndəfi káysh'n/ *n* —**dan·di·fied** *adj*

dan·dle /dánd'l/ (**-dled, -dling, -dles**) *vt* **1.** to move a

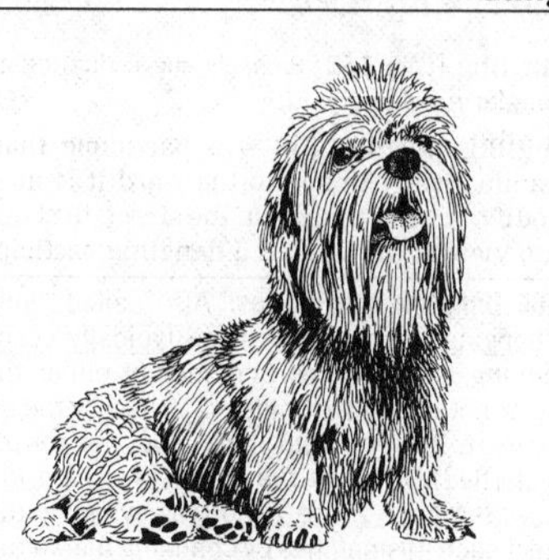

Dandie Dinmont

baby or small child gently up and down in your arms or on your knees **2.** to fondle or pet somebody or something [Mid-16C. Origin ?] —**dan·dler** *n*

dan·druff /dándrəf/ *n* loose dry scales of dead skin that are shed from the scalp [Mid-16C. < *dand-*, origin ? + *-ruff*, origin ?] —**dan·druff·y** *adj*

dan·dy /dándee/ *adj* (**-di·er, -di·est**) **1. EXCELLENT** very good, excellent, or first-rate (*informal*) **2. TOO CONCERNED WITH APPEARANCE** characteristic of a man who is excessively concerned with his elegant appearance (*dated*) ■ *n* (*plural* **-dies**) **1. EXCELLENT PERSON OR THING** somebody or something considered to be very good or the best in its class (*informal*) **2. MAN TOO CONCERNED WITH APPEARANCE** a man who is excessively concerned with his elegant appearance (*dated*) **3. SAILBOAT** a ketch or yawl **4.** PAPER same as **dandy roll** [Late 18C. Shortening of Scottish *Jack-a-dandy* "affected man"] —**dan·di·ly** *adv* —**dan·dy·ish** *adj* —**dan·dy·ism** *n*

dan·dy fe·ver *n* MED same as **dengue**

dan·dy roll, dan·dy roll·er *n* a wire cylinder used in paper manufacture to produce a watermark

Dane /dayn/ *n* somebody who comes from Denmark [14C. < Old Norse *Danir* (plural) "Danes"]

Dane·geld /-gèld/, **Dane·gelt** /dáyn gèlt/ *n* **1.** an annual tax first levied in the 10th century in England to buy off Danish invaders. It continued until the 12th century as a land tax. **2.** a payment made in order to avoid trouble or to prevent attack from a stronger enemy [Pre-12C. < assumed Old Norse *Danagiald* < *Danir* (plural) "Danes" + *giald* "payment"]

Dane·law /dáyn làw/ *n* **1.** the body of laws established in the parts of England settled in the 9th century by Danish invaders **2.** the parts of Anglo-Saxon England that came under Danish law and where Danish customs were observed [Old English *Dena lagu* "Danes' law"]

dang /dang/ *interj, adj, adv* same as **damn** (*informal; euphemistic*) [Late 18C. Alteration]

danged /dangd/ *adj, adv* same as **damned** *adj* (sense 2), *adv* (*informal; euphemistic*)

dan·ger /dáynjər/ *n* **1.** exposure or vulnerability to harm, injury, or loss ○ *Their lives were in danger.* ○ *His reckless behavior had put them all in danger.* **2.** somebody or something that may cause harm, injury, or loss (*often used in the plural*) ○ *the dangers of smoking* [13C. Via Anglo-Norman *daunger* < assumed Vulgar Latin *domniarium* "power to do harm" < Latin *dominium* "sovereignty" < *dominus* "lord"]

dan·ger mon·ey *n UK* same as **hazard pay**

dan·ger·ous /dáynjərəss/ *adj* **1.** likely to cause or result in harm or injury **2.** involving risk or difficulty ○ *The business is in a dangerous financial position.* —**dan·ger·ous·ly** *adv* —**dan·ger·ous·ness** *n*

dan·gle /dáng g'l/ *v* (**-gled, -gling, -gles**) **1.** *vti* **HANG LOOSELY** to swing or hang loosely, or cause something to swing or hang loosely ○ *The children dangled their legs over the side of the swimming pool.* **2.** *vt* **OFFER SOMETHING AS INDUCEMENT** to offer or display something as an enticement or inducement ○ *The possibility of promotion was dangled before her.* **3.** *vi* **HANG AROUND SOMEBODY** to hang around somebody ○ *The famous film director had many aspiring actors dangling after her.* ■ *n* **1. DANGLING THING** something that dangles, especially a charm from a bracelet or necklace **2. ACT OF DANGLING** the act or an instance of dangling [Late 16C. Probably suggesting the action] —**dan·gler** *n* —**dan·gly** *adj*

dan·gling par·ti·ci·ple *n* a participle that is not grammatically linked to the word it is intended to modify. In "Driving down the street, the house came into view," "driving" is a dangling participle.

USAGE Dangling participles: Also called "misplaced" or "hanging" participles, these typically occur at the beginning of sentences and modify either the wrong thing or nothing in particular: *Startled by the noise, her book fell to the floor* (but it was she, not her book, who was startled). *Lying in the sun, it was hard to imagine the winter back home* (who was lying in the sun?). Correct such mismatches by changing the wording: *Startled by the noise, she dropped her book* and *Lying in the sun, he found it hard to imagine the winter back home.* A number of dangling participles, however, are well established and idiomatic, for example, *given, considering,* and *regarding.* These are so well established that they are generally thought of as independent of the verbs from which they sprang and are now said to be prepositions.

dan grade *n* MARTIAL ARTS same as **dan**[1] (sense 1)

Dan·iel /dánnyəl/ *n* **1. BIBLICAL PROPHET** in the Bible, a prophet whose faith in God protected him in the lion's den **2. BOOK OF BIBLE** the book of the Bible that tells the story of Daniel. See table at **Bible 3. WISE PERSON** a wise and honorable person

Dan·iels /dánnyəlz/, **Josephus** (1862–1948) US editor, publisher, and politician. He served as secretary of the navy (1913–21) and US ambassador to Mexico (1933–41).

da·ni·o /dáynee ō/ (*plural* **-os**) *n* a brightly colored freshwater fish that is kept as an aquarium fish. Native to: India, Sri Lanka. Genera: *Danio* or *Brachydanio.* [Late 19C. < modern Latin]

Dan·ish /dáynish/ *adj* **OF DENMARK** relating to Denmark or its people, language, or culture ■ *n* LANG **LANGUAGE OF DANES** the official language of Denmark, also an official language of the Faroe Islands and Greenland, belonging to the North Germanic group of Indo-European languages. Native speakers: 5 million. ■ *npl* PEOPLES **PEOPLE FROM DENMARK** people who come from Denmark [14C. < Anglo-Norman *Danes* (plural) "Danes" < Old Icelandic *Danir*]

LANGUAGE HERITAGE See ***Scandinavian.***

Dan·ish blue *n* a blue-veined cheese with a strong taste, originally produced in Denmark

Dan·ish pas·try *n* a rich puff pastry made from a yeast dough with a sweet filling containing fruit or nuts

Dan·ite /dá nīt/ *n* in the Hebrew Bible, a member of the tribe descended from Dan, the son of Jacob —**Dan·ite** *adj*

dank /dangk/ *adj* unpleasantly damp and cold [14C. Probably < N Germanic] —**dank·ly** *adv* —**dank·ness** *n*

SYNONYMS See ***wet.***

Dank·worth /dángkwərth/, **Johnny** (*b.* 1927) British jazz musician, bandleader, and composer. From traditional jazz in the 1950s, he moved through bebop to chamber jazz. Full name **Dankworth, John Philip William**

danse ma·ca·bre /daanss mə kaábrə/ (*plural* **danses ma·ca·bres** /*pronunc. same*/) *n* ARTS same as **dance of death** [Late 19C. < French, "macabre dance"]

dan·seur /dan súr, daaN-/ *n* a male ballet dancer [Early 19C. < French, "male dancer"]

dan·seuse /dan sőoz, daaN sőz/ *n* a female ballet dancer [Early 19C. < French, "woman dancer"]

Dan·te /daán tay/ (1265–1321) Italian poet. One of the greatest poets in world literature, he is best known for his epic masterpiece *The Divine Comedy*, which he began writing in 1307 and completed shortly before his death. He was involved in the political struggles of his time, and his involvement in politics forced him to leave his native Florence. He finally settled in Ravenna. See Cultural note at **inferno.** Full name **Alighieri, Dante** —**Dan·te·an** /dántee ən, daántee-/ *adj, n*

"Consider your origins: you were not made to live as brutes, but to follow virtue and knowledge."
[Dante, "Inferno," *The Divine Comedy*; 1307?–21?]

Dan·tesque /dan tésk, daan-/ *adj* in the style of the works of Dante Alighieri

dan·tho·ni·a /dan thṓnee ə/ *n* a perennial tufted grass that has narrow leaves and small flowers growing closely together along the stem. Native to: Australia, New Zealand. Genus: *Danthonia.* [Early 20C. < modern Latin, after Étienne Danthoine, 19C French botanist]

Dan·ton /daan táwN/, **Georges Jacques** (1759–94) French lawyer. Minister of justice in Revolutionary France, he was overthrown in the Reign of Terror (1793) and guillotined the following year.

"Thou wilt show my head to the people: it is worth showing."
[Georges Jacques Danton, *The French Revolution*, Thomas Carlyle; 1837]

Dan·ube /dán yoob/ longest river in western Europe. It rises in the Black Forest in southwestern Germany and flows through Austria, the Czech Republic, Slovakia, Hungary, Croatia, Yugoslavia, Bulgaria, Romania, and Ukraine. It empties into the Black Sea. Length: 1,770 mi./2,850 km. —**Dan·u·bi·an** /də nyóobee ən/ *adj*

Dan·vers /dánvərz/ town in northeastern Massachusetts, southwest of Gloucester and northeast of Boston. Population: 25,446 (2002 estimate).

Dan·ville /dán vìl/ **1.** town in Illinois directly east of the Illinois-Indiana border, east of Urbana. Population: 33,365 (2002 estimate). **2.** city in southern Virginia near the North Carolina border. It was the last capital of the Confederacy. Population: 47,596 (2002 estimate).

Dan·zig /dánssig, daánt sik/ ➧ **Gdansk**

dap /dap/ (**dapped, dap·ping, daps**) *v* **1.** *vi* to fish by bobbing the bait lightly on the surface of the water **2.** *vt* to cut a notch in timber in order to join it to another piece [Mid-17C. Probably suggesting the action]

daph·ne /dáfnee/ (*plural* **-nes** or *same*) *n* a cultivated bush with glossy evergreen leaves. Flowers: fragrant, bell-shaped, pink or purplish. Native to: Europe, Asia. Genus: *Daphne.* [15C. < Greek *daphnē* "laurel, bay tree"]

daph·ni·a /dáfnee ə/ (*plural* **-as** or *same*) *n* a tiny freshwater flea with a transparent shell and branched antennae for swimming. Some types are used as food for aquarium fish. Genus: *Daphnia.* [Mid-19C. < modern Latin < *Daphne*, nymph in Greek mythology]

Da Pon·te /də póntee/, **Lorenzo** (1749–1838) Italian librettist and poet. He wrote the librettos for Wolfgang Amadeus Mozart's *Don Giovanni* (1787) and other operas. He moved to New York City in 1805. Born **Conegliano, Emanuele**

dap·per /dáppər/ *adj* **1. TRIM** describes a man who is neat and elegant in dress and manner **2. LIVELY** alert and lively or brisk **3. NIMBLE** small and active or nimble [15C. < Middle Dutch or Middle Low German, "bold, heavy"] —**dap·per·ly** *adv* —**dap·per·ness** *n*

dap·ple /dápp'l/ *vti* (**-pled, -pling, -ples**) **MARK SOMETHING WITH PATCHES OF COLOR** to mark something with patches or spots of a different color or with light and shade, or be marked in this way ○ *Sunlight dappled the path through the trees.* ■ *adj* same as **dappled** ■ *n* **1. COLORED MARKINGS** spots or patches of a different color, especially on a horse, or of light and shade **2. SPOT OF COLOR** an individual spot or patch of color, light, or shade **3. DAPPLED ANIMAL** an animal, especially a horse, with a dappled coat [Late 16C. Back-formation < DAPPLED]

dap·pled /dápp'ld/ *adj* marked with spots or patches of a different color or with light and shade ○ *in the dappled shade of the chestnut tree* [15C. Origin ?]

dap·ple-gray *adj* describes a horse or pony of a light gray or white color with darker gray spots or patches ■ *n* a dapple-gray horse or pony [14C. Origin ?]

dap·sone /dáp sōn/ *n* an antibacterial drug containing sulfur. Use: treatment of leprosy and dermatitis. [Mid-20C. Contraction of *dipara-amino-phenylsulfone*]

DAR *abbr* **1.** MIL damage assessment routine **2.** Daughters of the American Revolution

Dar·by and Joan /daárbee ən jṓn/ *n UK* a man and woman who are devoted to each other and have long lived together in domestic harmony [Late 18C. < a couple in a poem published in the *Gentleman's Magazine* in 1735]

Dard /daard/ *n* somebody who speaks a Dardic language [Mid-19C. < Dardic]

Dar·dan·elles /daárd'n élz/ strait that separates Asian Turkey from the Gallipoli peninsula of European Turkey, and links the Aegean Sea with the Sea of Marmara. Its ancient name is the Hellespont. Length: 43 mi./70 km.

Dar·dic /daárdik/ *n* a subgroup of Indic languages spoken in northern India and Pakistan. Native speakers: 7 million. —**Dar·dic** *adj*

dare /der/ *modal v* (**dared, dar·ing, dares** or **dare**) **HAVE ENOUGH COURAGE FOR SOMETHING** to have the courage needed to do something ○ *wanted to ask but then didn't dare* ○*"We must dare to think about 'unthinkable things' because when things have become unthinkable, thinking stops and action becomes mindless."* (William Fulbright *US Senate Speech*; March 27, 1965) ■ *v* **1.** *vti* **HAVE AUDACITY TO DO SOMETHING** to do something that angers or outrages somebody (*sometimes used as an auxiliary*) ○ *Don't you dare do that!* ○ *How dare you?* **2.** *vt* **CHALLENGE SOMEBODY** to challenge somebody to do something, usually something dangerous or frightening ○ *daring each other to jump first* ■ *n* **CHALLENGE** a challenge to somebody to do something dangerous or frightening, or a response to such a challenge ○ *did it for a dare* [Old English *darr, dearr*, forms of *durran* "dare" < Germanic] —**dar·er** *n*

Dare /der/, **Virginia** (1587–?) American colonist. She was the first child born to English colonists in North America. She had disappeared with the Roanoke Island colonists by 1590.

dare·dev·il /dér dèvv'l/ *n* **RISK-TAKER** a daring risk-taker, especially somebody who performs dangerous stunts ■ *adj* **1. UNMINDFUL OF DANGER** showing a carefree disregard for risk or danger, especially by performing dangerous stunts **2. DANGEROUS** involving a high degree of risk or danger ○ *a daredevil stunt*

dare·dev·il·ry /dér dèvv'lree/, **dare·dev·il·try** /-tree/ *n* **1.** a carefree disregard for risk or danger **2.** dangerous acts or stunts performed by a daring person

Dar el-Baid·a /daár el bīdə/ ➧ **Casablanca**

dare·say /dér sày/ ◇ **I daresay 1.** *UK* used, often in an irritable tone, to express the fact that the speaker considers something to be likely or possible ○ *And that, I daresay, is the last we'll see of him.* **2.** used impatiently to dismiss something that is true but irrelevant ○ *"That's what they told me at the office."–"I daresay, but they often get things wrong."* ○ *The press will make an issue out of that comment, I daresay, but the story will die the next day.*

Dar es Sa·laam /daár ess sə laám/ largest city, leading port, and former capital of Tanzania. The name means "haven of peace." Population: 2,545,000 (1999).

dar·gah /daárgə/ *n* **1.** a site where a Muslim holy man was buried or cremated **2.** a shrine built at a dargah [< Persian]

dar·ing /dérring/ *adj* **1. BRAVE AND ADVENTUROUS** showing a courageous or reckless disregard for danger ○ *The officer led a daring assault on the enemy machine-gun nest.* **2. RISKY** involving an element of risk or danger ○ *a daring move* **3. SHOCKING** unconventional, different, or innovative in a way that is likely to shock, upset, or offend ■ *n* **BOLDNESS** courage combined with a willingness to take risks or attempt difficult or unconventional things —**dar·ing·ly** *adv* —**dar·ing·ness** *n*

dar·i·ole /dárree ōl/ *n* **1.** *also* **dar·i·ole mold** a small cup-shaped mold in which individual portions of a dish can be cooked and then served **2.** a dish cooked and served in a dariole [14C. < French, "custard tart"]

Da·ri·us I /də rī́ əss/ (558–486 B.C.) king of Persia. He reorganized the administration of the Persian Empire during his reign (521–486 B.C.). His army invaded Greece in 490 but was defeated at the battle of Marathon.

Da·ri·us III (380?–330 B.C.) king of Persia. He was defeated by Alexander the Great at the battles of Issus (333 B.C.) and Guagamela (331 B.C.), and was assassinated by one of his own satraps.

Dar·jee·ling[1] /daar jeéling/ *n* a high-quality black tea grown around Darjeeling in India, or a hot drink made from its leaves

Dar·jee·ling[2] /daar jeéling/ city in northern Bangla, India, close to the border with Nepal. Under British rule, it was the summer capital of the government of Bengal. It is famous for its tea plantations. Population: 73,062 (1991).

dark /daark/ *adj* **1.** NOT LIGHT OR LIT having little or no light ○ *It's getting dark; do you mind if I put the light on?* ○ *It was a dark and stormy night.* **2.** NOT LIGHT IN COLOR reflecting less light than other colors or shades and therefore appearing deeper, richer, or more somber ○ *The curtains are dark green.* **3.** BROWNISH OR BLACKISH not pale or fair, but brown to black in hair or eye color ○ *She has darker eyes than her brother.* **4.** MISERABLE characterized by unhappiness, misfortune, or pessimism ○ *in the dark days after her brother's death* **5.** ANGRY suggesting hostility or anger ○ *dark looks* **6.** NASTY evil or wicked ○ *the dark side of his character* **7.** MYSTERIOUS little known or kept hidden from others ○ *dark secrets* **8.** UNENLIGHTENED lacking enlightenment, learning, and artistic or scientific achievement (*formal*) **9.** THEATER CLOSED not open for the presentation of theatrical performances **10.** LAW NOT IN SESSION not in session for hearings, trials, or other proceedings ○ *The courtroom is dark today because the judge has declared a Friday recess.* **11.** MELLOW deep and rich in sound ■ *n* **1.** LACK OF LIGHT a place, time, or situation in which there is too little light to see properly ○ *I don't like driving in the dark.* **2.** NIGHTFALL the beginning of night ○ *We left early to be home before dark.* **3.** SHADED AREA a darker color or a darker-colored or shaded part ○ *the contrast between the darks and the lights in the picture* [Old English *deorc* < Indo-European] ◇ **in the dark** ignorant, unaware, or not informed about something ○ *She kept everyone in the dark about her plans.* ◇ **whistle in the dark** to attempt to or pretend to keep up your courage when afraid

dark ad·ap·ta·tion, dark a·dap·tion *n* the reflex changes that enable the eye to continue to see in dim light, e.g., dilation of the pupil and increased sensitivity of the retina —**dark-a·dapt·ed** *adj*

Dark-Age *adj* relating to, dating from, belonging to, or typical of the Dark Ages

Dark Ag·es *npl* **1.** the period of European history between the fall of the Roman Empire in A.D. 476 and about A.D. 1000, for which there are few historical records and during which life was comparatively uncivilized **2.** an undeveloped state, way of life, or way of doing things (*informal*) ○ *Computers were in their Dark Ages a few decades ago.*

dark choc·o·late *n* chocolate that has no added milk and is darker and less sweet than milk chocolate

dark·en /daárkən/ (**-ened, -en·ing, -ens**) *vti* **1.** to become darker, or make something darker ○ *I mixed a little blue and brown with the red to darken it.* **2.** to become unhappy, less hopeful, or angry, or cause such a change in somebody or something ○ *The outlook has darkened considerably since the last update.* —**dark·en·er** *n*

dark en·er·gy *n* a hypothetical force that opposes the attraction of gravity throughout the universe and causes the expansion of the universe to accelerate

dark fib·er *n* a fiber optic cable that is not transmitting a signal

dark-field il·lu·mi·na·tion *n* the lighting of a specimen in a microscope from the side so that it can be seen against a dark background

dark-field mi·cro·scope *n* OPTICS same as **ultramicroscope**

dark glass·es *npl* eyeglasses with dark-tinted lenses, especially sunglasses

dark horse *n* **1.** LITTLE-KNOWN PERSON somebody about whom very little is known or who tends to be reticent, especially somebody who subsequently reveals unexpected talents **2.** POL UNEXPECTEDLY SUCCESSFUL CANDIDATE a candidate who gains an unexpected amount of support in an electoral campaign **3.** SPORTS UNEXPECTEDLY SUCCESSFUL CONTESTANT a little-known competitor who achieves unexpected success in a race or other sports contest [< the idea of a little-known racehorse making a surprisingly good showing in a race]

dark·ish /daárkish/ *adj* fairly dark in color or shading ○ *a woman with darkish hair*

dark lan·tern *n* a lantern with a sliding panel that is used to dim or hide its light

dar·kle /daárk'l/ (**-kled, -kling, -kles**) *vi* (*archaic or literary*) **1.** to grow dark **2.** to appear indistinctly [Early 19C. Back-formation < DARKLING]

dar·kling /daárkling/ (*archaic or literary*) *adv* IN DARKNESS in the dark ○ *"Darkling I listen, and full many a time..."* (John Keats, *Ode to a Nightingale*; 1820) ■ *adj* **1.** LACKING CLARITY dark, dim, or obscure **2.** OCCURRING IN DARKNESS done or happening in the night [15C. < DARK + -LING[2]]

dar·kling bee·tle *n* a beetle with a hard black or brown body whose larvae feed on decaying vegetable matter, living plants, and grain. Family: Tenebrionidae.

dark·ly /daárklee/ *adv* **1.** in a way that conveys a threat or a sense of foreboding **2.** in or with black or as a dark-colored shape ○ *trees darkly outlined against the horizon*

dark mat·ter *n* matter postulated to exist in the universe because of observed gravitational effects. It is thought to comprise a substantial part of the mass of the universe but remains as yet undetected by direct observation.

dark meat *n* meat from the legs and thighs of poultry, which is a darker color than the meat of the breast

dark·ness /daárknəss/ *n* **1.** the absence or lack of light ○ *He flicked a switch and the room was plunged into darkness.* **2.** same as **nighttime 3.** the comparative depth of a color or its closeness to black

dark re·ac·tion *n* the second phase of photosynthesis, which does not require light

dark·room /daárk ròom, -ròom/ *n* a room from which natural light is excluded so that light-sensitive photographic materials can be safely handled and photographs can be developed

dark·some /daárksəm/ *adj* lacking light and therefore gloomy or unpleasant (*archaic or literary*) ○ *doomed to die in a darksome dungeon*

dark star *n* a star that is not visible and is usually detectable only by its radio or infrared emissions or by its gravitational effect on other astronomical objects. It is often a component of a binary star and can cause the brightness of its visible partner to vary periodically.

dar·ling /daárling/ *n* **1.** LOVING TERM OF ADDRESS used as an affectionate form of address to a loved one, or as a general, informal, and sometimes slightly affected form of address to a social acquaintance **2.** SOMEBODY CONSIDERATE somebody who is kind, helpful, or likable **3.** INFORMAL TERM OF ADDRESS an extremely informal and usually suggestive term of address, often to a stranger (*informal*) **4.** FAVORITE somebody who is especially popular with somebody else or a group ○ *She's the darling of the literary reviews.* **5.** BELOVED PERSON a much-loved person or sweetheart (*dated*) ○ *She is my darling.* ■ *adj* **1.** DEARLY LOVED loved very much **2.** NICE pretty and charming (*informal*) [Old English *deorling* "dear person, dear one" < DEAR]

Dar·ling /daárling/ river in southeastern Australia that rises near Toowoomba in southern Queensland and joins the Murray River in New South Wales, forming the country's longest river system. Length: 1,702 mi./2,739 km.

Dar·ling, Grace (1815–42) British hero. The daughter of a lighthouse keeper on the Farne Islands off the coast of Northumberland, England, she rowed with her father in a storm to rescue shipwrecked sailors (1838). Full name **Darling, Grace Horsley**

Dar·ling Range range of hills near Perth in Western Australia. Its highest peak is Mount Cooke, 1,910 ft./582 m.

Dar·ling·ton /daárlingtən/ city and borough in County Durham, northern England. The Stockton and Darlington Railway, the world's first public steam railroad line, opened there in 1825. Population: 97,838 (2001).

darm·stad·ti·um /daárm státtee əm/ *n* a highly unstable radioactive chemical element, produced artificially by nuclear fusion. Symbol **Ds**. See table at **element**

darn[1] /daarn/ *vti* (**darned, darn·ing, darns**) to mend a hole in a piece of clothing or fabric using long interwoven stitches to fill the gap ○ *sat there darning socks* ■ *n* a repair to a piece of clothing or fabric using long interwoven stitches [Early 17C. Probably < French dialect *darner* "mend" < *darne* "piece"] —**darn·er** *n*

darn[2] /daarn/ (*informal; euphemistic*) *interj* EXCLAMATION used instead of a swearword to express irritation, displeasure, or surprise ■ *adj, adv* EMPHATIC TERM used instead of a swearword to give emphasis or to indicate irritation or displeasure with somebody or something ○ *a darn good movie* ■ *vt* (**darned, darn·ing, darns**) CONDEMN SOMEBODY OR SOMETHING used to express annoyance or frustration with somebody or something ○ *Darn it, I told you not to go in there.* [Late 18C. Alteration of DAMN]

darned /daarnd/ *adj* used instead of a swearword to express annoyance, surprise, or refusal (*informal; euphemistic*) ○ *I'll be darned if I know.* ○ *The darned car won't start.*

darned·est /daárndəst/ *adj* most amazing or extraordinary (*informal; euphemistic*)

dar·nel /daárn'l/ *n* a grass commonly found growing as a weed in grain fields. Native to: Europe, Asia. Genus: *Lolium*. [Early 14C. Origin ?]

darn·ing /daárning/ *n* **1.** the work of repairing holes in clothing or fabric with long interwoven stitches **2.** clothing or fabric that needs to be darned

darn·ing nee·dle *n* **1.** a long needle with a large eye, used in darning **2.** *US regional, Can* INSECTS same as **dragonfly**

REGIONAL NOTE In the sense "dragonfly," ***darning needle*** is a northern term, being found from New England to the Pacific states including California. The expanded form *devil's darning needle* occurs across the same territory, but less frequently. See also ***snake doctor***.

Darn·ley /daárnlee/, **Henry Stewart, Lord** (1545–67) Scottish nobleman. He was the second husband of Mary, Queen of Scots, and father of James VI of Scotland, who later became James I of England.

Dar·row /dárrō/, **Clarence** (1857–1938) US lawyer. A defender of the underdog in controversial legal cases, he is best known for his defense of John T. Scopes, a schoolteacher charged in Tennessee with having violated a law banning the teaching of evolutionary theory in the public schools (1925). Full name **Darrow, Clarence Seward**

> "The history of the past is a record of man's cruel inhumanity to man—of one imperfect vessel accusing and shattering another for the faults of both...There might be some excuse if man could turn from the frail, cracked vessels, and bring to trial the great potter for the imperfect work of his hand."
> [Clarence Darrow. Quoted in *The Meaning of History*, N. Gordon and Joyce Carper; 1991]

dart /daart/ *n* **1.** LEISURE MISSILE USED IN GAME a short weighted arrow with a long slender point, a tapered tubular body, and plastic or metal fins that is thrown at a dartboard in the game of darts **2.** ARMS MISSILE USED AS WEAPON a small arrow with a point at one end and feathers or fins at the other that can be thrown, shot from a blowgun, or scattered by an exploding bomb **3.** ZOOL POINTED PROJECTING PART OR ORGAN a pointed projecting body part used, e.g., to penetrate tissue, or, in some species of snails, in mating **4.** FAST MOVE a sudden quick movement ○ *He made a dart for the door.* **5.** HANDICRAFT STITCHED TAPERING FOLD a tapering fold sewn into a garment to make it fit, e.g., at the waist or bust ■ *v* (**dart·ed, dart·ing, darts**) **1.** *vi* MOVE SWIFTLY to move suddenly and quickly ○ *The little fish darted under a stone.* **2.** *vt* MAKE SOMETHING MOVE QUICKLY to move, extend, or direct something suddenly and quickly ○ *She darted a meaningful glance at her press secretary during the meeting* *with reporters.* [14C. < Old French < Germanic < Indo-European, "sharp"]

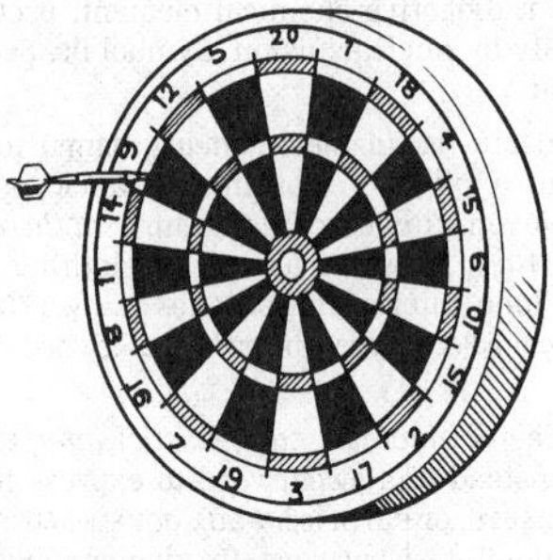

dartboard

dart·board /da͡art ba̓wrd/ *n* a round piece of wood or similar material marked with 20 radiating numbered segments and a bull's eye in the center, used as a target in the game of darts. The bull's eye has an inner and an outer ring, and the radiating segments have concentric bands representing a triple and a double score.

dart·er /da͡artər/ *n* **1.** N AMERICAN FISH a brightly colored fast-moving freshwater fish of the perch family. Native to: eastern North America. Family: Percidae. **2.** *Can, UK* BIRDS **TROPICAL FISH-EATING BIRD** a fish-eating diving bird with a long neck and sharp beak. Native to: warmer freshwater regions of the Americas, Africa, Asia, and Australia. Family: Anhingidae. US term **anhinga** **3.** SOMEBODY OR SOMETHING THAT DARTS somebody or something that moves suddenly and quickly

dart·ing /da͡arting/ *adj* swift and sudden, or making swift and sudden movements ○ *the darting movements of the dancers' feet* —**dart·ing·ly** *adv*

Dart·moor /da͡art mo͝or, -ma̓wr/ area in Devon, Southwestern England, now a national park The highest point is High Wilhays, 2,038 ft./621 m. Area: 368 sq. mi./954 sq. km. [Mid-19C. After *Dartmoor*, England]

Dart·mouth /da͡artməth/ **1.** town and seaport in Devon, England. The British Royal Naval College is located there. Population: 28,503 (1998). **2.** city in southern Nova Scotia, Canada, on Halifax Harbour opposite Halifax. Population: 65,629 (1996).

darts /daarts/ *n* an indoor game in which players take turns throwing arrow-shaped missiles (**darts**) from a set distance at a circular board (**dartboard**) placed at about eye level on a wall (*takes a singular verb*)

Dar·win /da͡arwin/ coastal city in northern Australia, capital of the Northern Territory. Population: 86,600 (1998).

Dar·win, Charles (1809–82) British naturalist. He laid the foundation for modern evolutionary theory and wrote *On the Origin of Species by Means of Natural Selection* (1859). He wrote many other books on the natural sciences, including *The Volcanic Islands* (1844) and *The Descent of Man* (1871). Full name **Darwin, Charles Robert**

> "We must, however, acknowledge, as it seems to me, that man with all his noble qualities...still bears in his bodily frame the indelible stamp of his lowly origin."
> [Charles Darwin, *The Descent of Man*; 1871]

Dar·win·i·an /daar wínnee ən/ *adj* **1.** RELATING TO DARWIN OR HIS THEORY relating to the 19th-century British naturalist Charles Darwin or his theory of evolution **2.** OF DARWIN, AUSTRALIA relating to the city of Darwin, Australia ■ *n* **1.** DARWINIST somebody who believes in or advocates Charles Darwin's theory of evolution **2.** *also* **Dar·win·ite** /da͡arwi nīt/ SOMEBODY FROM DARWIN somebody who comes from the city of Darwin, Australia

Dar·win·i·an the·o·ry *n* the theory, first developed by the 19th-century British naturalist Charles Darwin, that species of living things originate, evolve, and survive through natural selection in response to environmental forces

Dar·win·ism /da͡arwi nìzzəm/ *n* **1.** BIOL same as **Darwinian theory** **2.** belief in or advocacy of Charles Darwin's theory of evolution —**Dar·win·ist** *n, adj*

Dar·wi·nite /da͡arwi nīt/ *n* PEOPLES same as **Darwinian** *n* (sense 2)

Dar·win's finch·es *npl* the birds of the Galapagos Islands on which Charles Darwin based his theory of natural selection through observation of their feeding habits and corresponding differences in beak structure. Subfamily: Geospizinae.

dash /dash/ *n* **1.** RUSHING MOVEMENT a quick purposeful movement by a person or a group of people in a particular direction ○ *There was a dash for the exit as soon as the alarm was raised.* **2.** SMALL QUANTITY ADDED a small quantity of something added to something else, e.g., to improve the flavor of food or drink or to enliven speech or writing ○ *A dash of common sense would make the arguments a lot more convincing.* **3.** VIGOR AND VERVE a combination of vigor, daring, and style in the way somebody acts ○ *She carried it off with a certain amount of dash.* **4.** QUICK STROKE a quick and often violent movement, blow, or stroke ○ *with a dash of her arm* **5.** TRACK AND FIELD RACE a short-distance running race **6.** GRAM PUNCTUATION MARK a short horizontal line (–) used as a punctuation mark, often in place of a comma or colon, or as a sign that a letter or word has been omitted **7.** COMMUNICATION MORSE SYMBOL a short horizontal line representing a long sound or flash of light in written transcriptions of Morse code **8.** AUTOMOT DASHBOARD the instrument panel of a car (*informal*) ■ *v* (**dashed, dash·ing, dash·es**) **1.** *vi* HURRY OFF to run, move, or travel fast or hastily ○ *He dashed off to catch his plane.* **2.** *vt* KNOCK OR THROW SOMETHING VIOLENTLY to knock or throw something with a sudden violent sweep or blow (*formal*) ○ *She dashed the papers down on the desk in anger.* **3.** *vti* SMASH SOMETHING to break or throw something, or be broken or thrown, usually against a hard surface (*formal*) ○ *The waves were dashing against the sea wall.* **4.** *vt* RUIN SOMETHING to frustrate or destroy something (*often passive*) ○ *The new crisis has dashed all hopes of a speedy return to democratic government.* **5.** *vt* DISCOURAGE SOMEBODY to make somebody feel discouraged or intimidated (*usually passive*) ○ *I felt more than a little dashed by the ease with which she had refuted my arguments.* **6.** *vt* ADD SMALL AMOUNT TO SOMETHING to alter, improve, or flavor something with a small amount of another substance (*often passive*) ○ *tonic water dashed with bitters* **7.** *vt UK* EXPRESS IRRITATION WITH SOMEBODY OR SOMETHING used to express annoyance or dissatisfaction with somebody or something (*dated informal*) ○ *Dash it, I've already paid the man!* [13C. Origin ?]

USAGE ***Dashes*** are used in pairs around text that adds extra information and can be omitted without affecting the structure of the sentence: *He drives to Portland and back – a round trip of 600 miles – at least once a week.* Commas and parentheses can be used for the same purpose, and are often preferable in formal contexts, but dashes (used sparingly) are a stronger means of separating and have the effect of drawing attention to the extra information. Similarly, a dash may be used instead of a *colon* to introduce something that explains or elaborates on what has gone before: *Unemployment in the town has fallen to 3000 – a drop of almost 20%.* This short dash is called an ***en dash*** and usually has a space on either side; a longer ***em dash*** may be used in the same way but without spaces: *Unemployment in the town has fallen to 3000—a drop of almost 20%.* An em dash can also be used in place of omitted letters, e.g., to avoid mentioning a person's full name: *Mr. J— accused Ms. D— of lying.*

dash off *vt* to write, draw, or compose something in a great hurry (*informal*) ○ *She dashed off a note to her secretary before leaving the office.*

dash·board /dásh ba̓wrd/ *n* **1.** a panel in front of the driver of a vehicle or the pilot of a small aircraft or boat that contains various indicator dials, switches, and controls **2.** a board, panel, or screen to protect the driver of a horse-drawn carriage from being splashed with mud [Mid-19C. < DASH in the obsolete sense "splash, spatter"]

da·sheen /da she͡en/ *n Carib* **1.** tubers of the taro plant, usually boiled for eating **2.** PLANTS same as **taro** [Late 19C. Origin ?]

da·she·ki *n* CLOTHING another spelling of **dashiki**

dash·er /dáshər/ *n* a device that agitates or stirs the contents of a churn or ice-cream maker

da·shi /da͡ashee/ *n* a clear broth or stock, usually made from fish [Mid-20C. < Japanese]

da·shi·ki /də she͡ekee/, **dai·shi·ki** /dī-/, **da·she·ki** /-shékee/ *n* a brightly colored loose-fitting garment resembling a long shirt without buttons, worn mainly by men in Africa, the Caribbean, and the United States [Mid-20C. Probably < Yoruba *danshiki*]

dash·ing /dáshing/ *adj* (*dated*) **1.** smartly dressed and stylish ○ *That's a rather dashing outfit, even if I do say so.* **2.** confident and full of bravado and spirit ○ *a dashing young officer* —**dash·ing·ly** *adv* —**dash·ing·ness** *n*

dash·pot /dásh pòt/ *n* a device consisting of a piston inside a fluid-filled cylinder that absorbs or dampens vibrations in a mechanism

das·sie /dássee/ *n* ZOOL same as **rock hyrax** [Late 18C. Via Afrikaans < Dutch *dasje* "small badger" < *das* "badger"]

das·tard·ly /dástərdlee/ *adj* mean, treacherous, or cowardly (*dated or humorous*) ○ *a dastardly deed* [Late 16C. < *dastard*, probably < *dast*, a past participle of DAZE] —**das·tard·li·ness** *n*

das·y·ure /dássee yo͝or/ *n* a small usually carnivorous marsupial. Native to: Australia, Tasmania, neighboring islands. Subfamily: Dasyurinae. [Mid-19C. Via French < modern Latin *dasyurus* < Greek *dasus* "rough, hairy" + *oura* "tail"]

DAT /dat, de͡e ay te͡e/ *abbr* COMPUT digital audiotape

da·ta /dáytə, dáttə/ *n* (*takes a singular or plural verb*) **1.** ⚠ information, often in the form of facts or figures obtained from experiments or surveys, used as a basis for making calculations or drawing conclusions **2.** ⚠ information, e.g., numbers, text, images, and sounds, in a form that is suitable for storage in or processing by a computer ■ plural of **datum** [Mid-17C. < plural of Latin *datum*, neuter past participle of *dare* "give, grant"]

USAGE Data – singular or plural? Because the meaning ***data*** is much like that of the singular noun *information*, and because its Latin *-a* plural announces the word's plural status less plainly than a final *s* would, it is often treated as if it were singular. This use is extremely common, and few perceive it as wrong these days, especially given the word's connotation of a collection or single unit made up of many informational subunits. All the same, in formal English, *Our data have been assembled over a number of years* would be regarded as correct, and commonly used constructions such as *very little data, the data shows...*, and *a great deal of data* would be regarded as incorrect.

da·ta bank *n* **1.** a large store of information, especially kept in or available to a computer, sometimes consisting of several databases **2.** COMPUT same as **database**

da·ta·base /dáytə bàyss/ *n* a systematically arranged collection of computer data, structured so that it can be automatically retrieved or manipulated ■ *vt* (**-based, -bas·ing, -bas·es**) to input data into a database

da·ta·base man·age·ment sys·tem *n* a computer program devised to create, store, and manipulate databases

da·ta cap·ture *n* the collecting and entering of data in a computer, or the conversion of data into a form compatible with computers

da·ta com·pres·sion *n* the encoding of data so that it requires less disk space for storage and less time for transmission

da·ta el·e·ment *n* the smallest meaningful piece of information in an electronic business transaction (*used in e-commerce*)

da·ta fu·sion *n* the integration of data and knowledge collected from disparate sources by different methods into a consistent, accurate, and useful whole

da·ta·glove /dáytə glùv, dáttə-/ *n* a glove with sensors that feed spatial and tactile data to a computer, allowing the wearer to manipulate and explore virtual reality

da·ta min·ing *n* the locating of previously unknown patterns and relationships within data using a database application, e.g., the locating of customers with common interests in a retail establishment's database

da·ta·port /dáytə pàwrt, dáttə-/ *n* a socket for connecting a laptop computer to the Internet

da·ta proc·ess·ing *n* the entering, storing, updating, and retrieving of information using a computer

da·ta pro·tec·tion *n* **1.** legal safeguards to prevent misuse of information stored on computers, particularly information about individual people **2.** the adoption of administrative, technical, or physical deterrents to safeguard computer data

da·ta set *n* a computer file

da·ta·sheet /dáytə shèet, dáttə-/ *n* a document accessible on the Internet that gives a detailed description of something, especially a product

da·ta ware·house *n* a database used for analyzing overall business strategy rather than routine operations

date[1] /dayt/ *n* **1.** DAY, MONTH, AND YEAR a phrase or string of numbers that denotes a specific day of the month or year. It usually consists of the name or number of the month, the number of the day, and the number of the year. **2.** TIME OF EVENT a date used to locate a past or future event in time ○ *The concert has been postponed to a later date.* **3.** VISUAL REPRESENTATION OF DATE the words or numbers of a date in the form of a written statement or inscription, e.g., on a document or coin ○ *There's no date on this letter.* **4.** PERIOD OF TIME the period during which something such as a work of art was created ○ *This has much in common with other artifacts of the same date.* **5.** APPOINTMENT an appointment to meet somebody for a social or business activity ○ *I've got a dinner date with a client.* **6.** ROMANTIC APPOINTMENT a romantic engagement with somebody ○ *I thought we had a date tonight.* **7.** PARTNER ON DATE somebody with whom a date has been arranged ○ *My date stood me up.* **8.** ARTS COMMITMENT TO PERFORM an engagement to give a performance ○ *Our band has a date to play at the Coliseum.* ■ **dates** *npl* DATES OF BIRTH AND DEATH the years of somebody's birth and death ○ *Do you happen to know Thomas Jefferson's dates?* ■ *v* (**dat·ed, dat·ing, dates**) **1.** *vt* PUT DATE ON SOMETHING to mark something with a date, usually the current date ○ *Please sign and date the contract.* **2.** *vt* ASSIGN DATE TO SOMETHING to find out or state the time or period when something was made ○ *The early works of Shakespeare are difficult to date precisely.* **3.** *vi* ORIGINATE to have an origin in a particular time in the past ○ *We have family records dating back to the 16th century.* **4.** *vi* GO OUT OF STYLE to become old-fashioned ○ *This is a classic style and won't date.* **5.** *vt* MAKE SOMEBODY OR SOMETHING SEEM OLD to reveal the age of somebody or something, or make somebody or something seem old-fashioned ○ *The shape of the headlights dates the car.* **6.** *vti* GO ON DATES WITH SOMEBODY to go out regularly with somebody as a romantic partner ○ *We dated for a few months.* [14C. < medieval Latin *data* < past participle of Latin *dare* "give, grant"; from uses such as *(epistola) data Romae* "(letter) given at Rome," with the day and month appended] —**dat·a·ble** *adj* ◇ **to date** up to the present time

date[2] /dayt/ *n* **1.** a dark-colored oval fruit that has sweet flesh and a single hard narrow seed **2.** TREES same as **date palm** [13C. Via Old French < Greek *daktulos* "finger or toe, date"]

date·book /dáyt bòok/ *n* a diary in which social engagements and other things to be remembered are noted

dat·ed /dáytəd/ *adj* **1.** no longer used or in vogue, often having been current or fashionable in the recent past **2.** marked with a date

date·less /dáytləss/ *adj* **1.** unlikely to become old-fashioned or obsolete **2.** limitless in time (*archaic or literary*) ○ *"For precious friends hid in death's dateless night"* (William Shakespeare, *Sonnets*; 1609)

date·line /dáyt lìn/ *n* a line at the head of a newspaper article or similar item giving the date and place of writing

Date Line *n* TIME same as **International Date Line**

date palm *n* a tall palm tree with feathery fronds, cultivated for its fruit. Native to: North Africa, western Asia. Latin name: *Phoenix dactylifera.*

date rape *n* an act of rape committed against somebody during or after a date —**date-rape** *vt*

date rape drug *n* a drug that causes unconsciousness and memory loss, sometimes used in the commission of date rape (*informal*)

date stamp *n* a rubber stamp used to mark the date on something, or the date marked by such a stamp —**date-stamp** *vt*

Da·tin /daá tìn/ *n* in Malaysia, the title of a woman member of a senior order of chivalry [< Malay]

dat·ing bar *n* LEISURE same as **singles bar**

dat·ing ser·vice *n* a business that finds potential romantic partners for people

da·tive /dáytiv/ *n* **1.** a grammatical form (**case**) that identifies the source, agent, or instrument of action of the verb in some inflected languages and that affects nouns, pronouns, and adjectives **2.** a word or phrase in the dative [15C. < Latin *dativus* "of giving" < *dat-*, past participle of *dare* "give, grant"] —**da·tive** *adj*

da·tive bond *n* CHEM same as **coordinate bond** [Because one atom gives up electrons to another]

da·to·lite /dátt'l ìt/ *n* a hydrated silicate containing calcium and boron. Source: igneous rocks. [Early 19C. < Greek *dateisthai* "divide"; from the divisions between its crystals]

Da·tuk /daá tòok/ *n* in Malaysia, the title of a man who is a member of a senior order of chivalry [Mid-19C. < Malay *datok*]

da·tum /dáytəm, dáttəm/ (*plural* **-ta** /dáytə, dáttə/) *n* **1.** ITEM OF INFORMATION a piece of information **2.** LOGIC GIVEN FACT a known or assumed fact that is used as the basis for a theory, conclusion, or inference **3.** (*plural* **da·tums**) MAPS POINT OF REFERENCE a point, line, or surface used as a basis for measurement or calculation in mapping or surveying [Mid-18C. < Latin (see DATA)]

da·tum line, da·tum lev·el, da·tum plane *n* the horizontal line or plane from which all other heights and depths are measured or calculated on a map or chart

DATV /dày tee veé/ *abbr* MEDIA digitally assisted television

daub /dawb/ *v* (**daubed, daub·ing, daubs**) **1.** *vt* APPLY SOMETHING BLOTCHILY to put or spread a semiliquid substance such as mud, paint, or cream, on a surface in a crude, hurried, or irregular way ○ *They had daubed slogans all over the walls.* **2.** *vti* PAINT CRUDELY to paint or apply paint crudely and inexpertly ■ *n* **1.** BLOTCH OF SUBSTANCE a patch, splash, or smear of a semiliquid substance applied to something in a crude, hurried, or irregular way **2.** BAD PAINTING a painting that is considered to be crudely or inexpertly done ○ *"When he first came to Rome he painted worthless daubs and gave no promise of talent."* (Henry James, *Roderick Hudson*; 1876) **3.** CONSTR SUBSTANCE FOR DAUBING a mixture of clay, lime, and chopped straw plastered onto interwoven rods or twigs to make a wall [14C. Via Old French *dauber* < Latin *dealbare* "whiten over, plaster" < *albare* "whiten" < *albus* "white"] —**daub·er** *n* —**daub·y** *adj*

daube /dōb/ *n* in French cuisine, a dish of braised meat or vegetables, especially a traditional French dish of beef braised in wine [Early 18C. < French, via Italian *dobba* < Catalan *a la adoba* "stewed" < Germanic, "to strike"]

Dau·bi·gny /dō bee nyeé/, **Charles-François** (1817–78) French painter and etcher. He was a landscape painter associated with the Barbizon School whose work influenced the impressionists.

Dau·det /dō dáy/, **Alphonse** (1840–97) French writer. His works include *Letters from my Mill* (1869). Full name **Daudet, Louis Marie Alphonse**

> "During the day beings live, at night things live."
> [Alphonse Daudet, "Les Étoiles" ("The Stars,") *Lettres de mon moulin (Letters from my Mill)*; 1869]

daugh·ter /dáwtər/ *n* **1.** FEMALE CHILD somebody's female child **2.** WOMAN OR GIRL CONNECTED WITH PLACE a woman or girl considered as a product of a place or institution (*formal*) ○ *daughter of the church* **3.** PRODUCT OF SOMETHING something produced by or issuing from something else (*literary*) ○ *Truth is the daughter of time.* **4.** DESCENDANT a woman or girl descendant (*literary*) ○ *a daughter of Eve* **5.** PHYS NUCLIDE FORMED BY RADIOACTIVE DECAY a nuclide formed from an element by radioactive decay ■ *adj* **1.** FORMED FROM SOMETHING ELSE formed by or from a similar thing, usually retaining close links with it and sometimes remaining subordinate to it **2.** BEING OFFSPRING produced by a process of reproduction, replication, or division [Old English *dohtor* < Indo-European] —**daugh·ter·less** *adj*

daugh·ter·board /dáwtər bàwrd/ *n* a printed circuit board that plugs into a motherboard, usually to improve the performance of a system or add function

daugh·ter cell *n* either of the identical cells produced when a living cell divides

daugh·ter-in-law (*plural* **daugh·ters-in-law**) *n* the wife of somebody's son

daugh·ter·ly /dáwtərlee/ *adj* typical or expected of a daughter ○ *She came to regard the distinguished professor with an almost daughterly affection.* —**daugh·ter·li·ness** *n*

Daugh·ters of the A·mer·i·can Rev·o·lu·tion *npl* a women's patriotic society founded in 1890 by descendants of those who fought in the American Revolution. It has about 200,000 members and is based in Washington, D.C.

Dau·mier /dō myáy/, **Honoré** (1808–79) French painter and caricaturist. He is known for his satirical caricatures of contemporary society and politics.

daunt /dawnt/ (**daunt·ed, daunt·ing, daunts**) *vt* to make somebody feel anxious, intimidated, or discouraged (*usually passive*) ○ *The scale of the task would have daunted even the most experienced organizer.* [13C. Via Anglo-Norman *daunter* < Latin *domitare* "to tame"] —**daunt·er** *n*

daunt·ing /dáwnting/ *adj* likely to discourage, intimidate, or frighten somebody ○ *You'll find the task less daunting if you divide it up into manageable sections.* —**daunt·ing·ly** *adv*

daunt·less /dáwntləss/ *adj* unlikely or unable to be frightened or discouraged ○ *We remember with admiration their dauntless courage and optimism.* —**daunt·less·ly** *adv* —**daunt·less·ness** *n*

dau·phin /dáwfin, dṓ-/ *n* in former times, the eldest son of the king of France and the direct heir to the throne [15C. < French, in Old French *daulphin* (see DOLPHIN); because of dolphins on a relevant coat of arms]

dau·phine /daw feén, dō feén/ *n* (*plural* **-phines** /*pronunc. same*/) the wife of the dauphin ■ *adj* prepared by mixing mashed potato with choux pastry dough and forming the mixture into balls or cylinders, which are then deep-fried ○ *dauphine potatoes* [Mid-19C. < French, feminine form of *dauphin* (see DAUPHIN)]

dau·phin·ois /dàwfin waáz/, **dau·phin·oise** *adj* thinly sliced and baked in milk or cream, sometimes with garlic or cheese ○ *potatoes dauphinoise* [< French, "from the Dauphiné province"]

DAV *abbr* Disabled American Veterans

Da·vao /daá vòw/ city on Mindanao island in the southern Philippines. Population: 1,191,000 (1995)

da·ven /daávən/ (**dav·ened, dav·en·ing, dav·ens**) *vti* to recite prayers from the Jewish liturgies [Mid-20C. < Yiddish *davnen* "pray"]

Dav·e·nant /dávvənənt/, **Sir William** (1606–68) English poet and dramatist. His works include the comic play *The Wits* (1633) and the epic poem *Gondibert* (1651). His notable theatrical innovations include an early English opera, movable scenery, and the introduction of women actors. He was appointed English poet laureate in 1638.

dav·en·port /dávvən pàwrt/ *n* **1.** a large well-upholstered sofa, especially one that can be converted into a bed **2.** an ornamental writing desk with a sloping top and drawers in its sides [Mid-19C. Origin ?]

Dav·en·port /dávvən pàwrt/ city in eastern Iowa, on the western bank of the Mississippi River. Population: 97,777 (2002 estimate).

Da·vid /dáyvid/ (*d.* 962 B.C.) king of Judah. During his reign (1000–962 B.C.), he defeated the Philistines, conquered Jerusalem, and became the ruler of Israel.

Da·vid, Elizabeth (1913–92) British food researcher and writer. Her many books include *Mediterranean Food* (1950) and *English Bread and Yeast Cookery* (1977).

Da·vid·son /dáyvidssən/, **Jo** (1883–1952) US sculptor. He is known for his busts of Woodrow Wilson and Albert Einstein.

Da·vies /dáyveez/, **Arthur B.** (1862–1928) US painter. He was one of the early exponents of modern art, including cubism, and a member of an antiacademic group of artists known as The Eight. Full name **Davies, Arthur Bowen**

Da·vies, Robertson (1913–95) Canadian novelist, essayist, and playwright. His books include *The Salterton Trilogy* (1951–58), *The Deptford Trilogy* (1970–75), and *The Cornish Trilogy* (1981–88). *What's Bred in the Bone* (1985) was short-listed for the Booker Prize.

> "Our age has robbed millions of the simplicity of ignorance, and has so far failed to lift them to simplicity of wisdom."
> [Robertson Davies, *A Voice from the Attic*; 1960]

da Vin·ci ➧ **Leonardo da Vinci**

Da·vis /dáyviss/ city in central California, west of Sacramento and northeast of San Francisco. Population: 64,221 (2002 estimate).

Da·vis, Alexander Jackson (1803–92) US architect. He was in the vanguard of the Greek Revival movement, designing many public buildings and state capitols in neoclassical style.

Da·vis, Benjamin Oliver, Jr. (1912–2002) US pilot. He flew with the Tuskegee Airmen in World War II and became the first African American general in the US Air Force (1954).

Bette Davis

Da·vis, Bette (1908–89) US movie actor. She won the Academy Award for best actress for *Dangerous* (1935) and *Jezebel* (1938). Full name **Davis, Ruth Elizabeth**

Da·vis, Jefferson (1808–89) US politician. He was the first and only president of the Confederate States of America (1861–65).

> "All we ask is to be let alone."
> [Jefferson Davis. *Inaugural Address as president of the Confederate States of America*; February 18, 1861]

Da·vis, Da·vys, John (1550?–1605) English navigator. While searching for a northwestern route between Europe and the Indies, he sailed through the present-day Davis Strait (1587).

Da·vis /dáyviss/, **Miles** (1926–91) US jazz trumpeter and composer. A consummate improviser, he pioneered a more understated form of bebop known as "cool jazz." He was also noted for incorporating electronic instruments into jazz and combining jazz and rock. Full name **Miles Dewey Davis III**

> "You can tell the way I play by the way I stand."
> [Miles Davis. Quoted in *Black Talk*, Ben Sidan; 1971]

Popperfoto

Miles Davis

Da·vis, Ossie (*b.* 1917) US actor and playwright. He starred in the movie *The Hill* (1965) and wrote the play *Purlie Victorious* (1961).

Da·vis, Sammy, Jr. (1925–90) US singer, actor, and dancer. One of the most popular and successful US entertainers of his time, he was well known for his exuberant performances on stage and in movies such as *Ocean's Eleven* (1960), as well as for his encounters with racism.

Da·vis, Stuart (1894–1964) US painter. Known as the first abstract painter in the United States, he developed his distinctive style from Cubism and his love of jazz.

Da·vis Cup *n* **1.** an annual international men's tennis competition for which a trophy is awarded to the winning nation **2.** the trophy awarded to the winning nation in the Davis Cup competition [Early 20C. After Dwight Filley *Davis*, who donated the trophy]

Da·vis Strait body of water separating Baffin Island, Canada, from Greenland, and forming the entrance to Baffin Bay. Depth: 11,900 ft./3,660 m.

dav·it /dávvit/ *n* a small crane at the side of a ship's deck, especially one of a pair of curved metal posts with tackle attached for suspending and lowering a lifeboat [15C. < Anglo-Norman *daviot, daviet* < the name *Davi* "David"]

Dav·itt /dávvit/, **Michael** (1846–1906) Irish nationalist leader. He was imprisoned (1870–77) for nationalist activities, and founded the antiabsentee landlord Land League (1879).

Dav·os /daa vṓss/ mountain resort in Graubünden Canton, eastern Switzerland. Population: 11,325 (1998).

Da·vy /dáyvee/, **Sir Humphry** (1778–1829) British chemist. He is best known as the inventor of the miner's safety lamp (**Davy lamp**)(1815). He also discovered the use of nitrous oxide as an anesthetic and identified several metallic elements.

Da·vy Jones /dàyvee jṓnz/ *n* the personification of the sea

Da·vy Jones's lock·er *n* the bottom of the sea, especially considered as the final resting place of drowned sailors or sunken ships (*informal*)

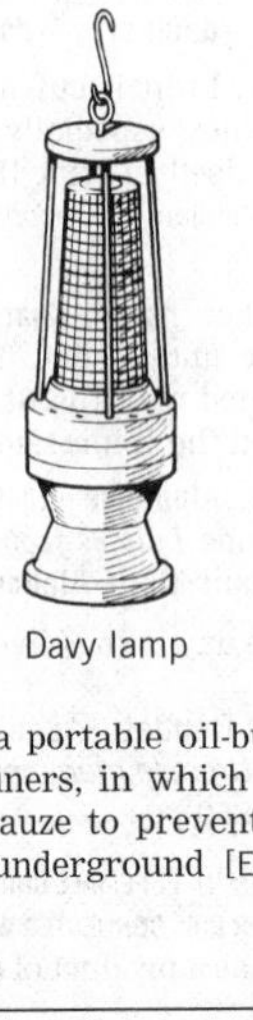

Davy lamp

Da·vy lamp *n UK* a portable oil-burning lamp, formerly used by miners, in which the flame is protected by metal gauze to prevent it from igniting explosive gases underground [Early 19C. After Sir Humphry DAVY]

Da·vys ➧ **Davis, John**

daw /daw/ *n* BIRDS same as **jackdaw** (*archaic or regional*) [15C. Probably < assumed Old English *dawe* < Germanic]

daw·dle /dáwd'l/ (**-dled, -dling, -dles**) *vi* **1.** to walk or move slowly and reluctantly or idly ○ *We'll get there in time if you don't dawdle.* **2.** to spend far more time than is necessary in doing something ○ *We dawdled over lunch.* [Mid-17C. Origin ?] —**daw·dler** *n* —**daw·dling** *n, adj* —**daw·dling·ly** *adv*

Dawes /dawz/, **Charles Gates** (1865–1951) vice president of the United States. Originally a banker, he served as vice president (1925–29) under President Calvin Coolidge.

Daw·kins /dáwkinz/, **Richard** (*b.* 1941) British evolutionary biologist. He is best known for his book *The Selfish Gene* (1976), which describes the gene's strategy for survival. He developed his arguments in *The Blind Watchmaker* (1986).

> "It is raining DNA outside. On the bank of the Oxford canal at the bottom of my garden is a large willow tree, and it is pumping downy seeds into the air...It is raining instructions out there; it's raining programs; it's raining tree-growing, fluff-spreading algorithms. That is not a metaphor, it is the plain truth. It couldn't be any plainer if it were raining floppy disks."
> [Richard Dawkins, *The Blind Watchmaker*; 1986]

dawn /dawn/ *n* **1.** DAYBREAK the first appearance of light in the sky as the Sun rises at the beginning of a new day **2.** BEGINNING the beginning of something, especially a period of time or history ○ *the dawn of the industrial era* ■ *vi* (**dawned, dawn·ing, dawns**) **1.** BEGIN to begin, as the sun rises and light appears in the sky (*refers to a new day*) ○ *The day dawned cloudy and wet.* **2.** BECOME APPARENT to begin to be perceived ○ *The realization dawned that few would survive.* **3.** START TO EXIST to begin to develop or exist (*literary*) [15C. Back-formation (as verb) < DAWNING]
dawn on *vt* to come into the mind or consciousness of somebody ○ *It was some time before the seriousness of the situation dawned on them.*

dawn cho·rus *n* **1.** the loud singing of many birds as the first light of day appears in the sky **2.** any loud sound, especially from a number of different sources, occurring very early in the morning (*humorous*) ○ *a dawn chorus of power drills and hammering*

dawn·ing /dáwning/ *n* the beginning of a new day or of a new period of time or history ○ *with the dawning of the computer age* ■ *adj* beginning to appear, develop, or be perceived [13C. Alteration of obsolete *dawing* < Old English *dagian* "dawn, become day" < Germanic]

dawn raid *n* **1.** a surprise attack on enemy troops at dawn **2.** a surprise attempt to buy a large number of a company's shares at the start of a day's trading, especially as a first stage in a takeover bid

dawn red·wood *n* a deciduous tree with flat leaves and small round cones, widely grown as an ornamental. Native to: China. Latin name: *Metasequoia glyptostroboides.*

Daw·son /dáwss'n/, **Sir John William** (1820–99) Canadian geologist. He worked mainly with plant fossils and wrote *Acadian Geology* (1855).

Daw·son Creek city located on the British Columbia-Alberta border, Canada. It is the starting point of the Alaska Highway. Population: 10,754 (2001).

DAX /daks/ *n* a stock index on the Frankfurt Stock Exchange. Full form **Deutsche Aktienindex**

day /day/ *n* **1.** 24 HOURS a period of 24 hours, usually beginning and ending at midnight **2.** SUNRISE TO SUNSET the part of a 24-hour period when it is light, between sunrise and sunset **3.** TIME OF ACTIVITY the part of a 24-hour period when somebody is working or active ○ *I work an 8-hour day.* **4.** INDEFINITE PERIOD OR POINT IN TIME a time or period of time in the past, present, or future ○ *One of these days we'll get around to painting the house.* **5.** TIME OF FAME the time when a particular person or thing is well known, popular, successful, or effective ○ *In her day she was one of our best-known Shakespearean actors.* **6.** LIFE OR EXISTENCE the time when a particular person or thing is active or in existence ○ *In my day we had to work on Saturday mornings.* **7. PERIOD OF EARTH'S ROTATION ABOUT AXIS** a unit of time equal to the Earth's period of rotation about its axis, measured either relative to the Sun (**solar day**) or the stars (**sidereal day**) **8.** ASTRON **PERIOD OF PLANET'S ROTATION ABOUT AXIS** the period of time in which a planet revolves once on its axis [Old English *dæg* < Indo-European] ◇ **call it a day** to finish work or stop doing something ◇ **carry** *or* **win the day** to gain a victory ◇ **day after day** for several or many days in a row ◇ **day by day 1.** each consecutive day **2.** progressively ◇ **day in, day out** every day without exception and all day long ◇ **have a nice day** used for wishing somebody well when parting ◇ **have seen better days** to be in a less prosperous or less good condition than previously ◇ **in this day and age** nowadays, as opposed to past times and customs ◇ **make somebody's day** to make somebody very happy ◇ **name the day** to set a date for something, typically a wedding ◇ **save the day** to prevent defeat or disaster ◇ **somebody's** *or* **something's days are numbered** expresses the opinion that somebody or something will not survive much longer ◇ **that'll be the day!** expresses the opinion that something is most unlikely to happen (*informal*) ○ *You think they'll offer me Mike's job? That'll be the day!* ◇ **the other day** not long ago ◇ **those were the days!** expresses affection and nostalgia for past times

Day /day/, **Benjamin Henry** (1810–89) US publisher. In 1883 he founded the *New York Sun*, the first penny daily newspaper in the United States.

Day, Clarence (1874–1935) US humorist and essayist. He is known for the humorous autobiographical works *Life with Father* (1935) and *Life with Mother* (1937). Full name **Day, Clarence Shepard**

> "The artistic impulse seems not to wish to produce finished work. It certainly deserts us halfway, after the idea is born; and if we go on, art is labor."
> [Clarence Day, *This Simian World*; 1920]

Day, Doris (*b.* 1924) US film actor and singer. She came to fame in the late 1950s with roles in light musicals and romantic comedies such as *Calamity Jane* (1953) and *Pillow Talk* (1959), for which she received an Academy Award nomination. Born **Kappelhoff, Doris von**

Day·ak /dī àk/ (*plural* **-aks** or *same*), **Dy·ak** *n* a member of a Malaysian people who live in the interior of Borneo and are noted for their communal long houses [Mid-19C. < Malay, "up-country"] —**Day·ak** *adj*

Da·yan /daa yaán/ *n* the judge of the Beth Din, a Jewish religious court [Late 19C. < Hebrew < *dān* "to judge"]

Da·yan /daa yaán/, **Moshe** (1915–81) Israeli general and politician. He was chief of Israel's general staff (1953–58) and defense minister (1967–74). He resigned after criticism over the Yom Kippur War (1973–74), but became foreign minister in 1977, resigning again in 1979 in protest over Menachem Begin's policies concerning the West Bank.

> "Whenever you accept our views we shall be in full agreement with you."
> [Moshe Dayan, *Observer (London)*; August 14, 1977]

day bed *n* **1.** a couch or bed for reclining on during the day **2.** a sofa that can be converted into a bed

day blind·ness *n* the inability to see clearly in bright light with comparatively good vision in dim light. Technical name **hemeralopia**

day·book /dáy bòòk/ *n* **1.** a book in which financial transactions are recorded day by day **2.** a diary or journal

day·break /dáy bràyk/ *n* the time when light first appears in the sky at the beginning of a day

day camp *n* a camp that provides activities and meals for children during the day but has no overnight accommodations

day·care /dáy kèr/ *n* daytime supervision and recreational or medical facilities for preschool children, physically challenged people, or seniors wanting special assistance

day·dream /dáy drèem/ *n* **1. DREAM EXPERIENCED WHILE AWAKE** a series of often distracting and usually pleasant thoughts and images that pass through the mind while awake **2. UNREALIZABLE HOPE OR FANTASY** a pleasant wish or hope that is unlikely to be fulfilled ■ *vi* (**-dreamed** or **-dreamt** /-drèmt/, **-dream·ing, -dreams**) **THINK DISTRACTING THOUGHTS** to have or indulge in daydreams —**day·dream·er** *n* —**day·dream·ing** *n* —**day·dream·y** *adj*

day·fly /dáy flī/ (*plural* **-flies**) *n* INSECTS same as **mayfly** (sense 1) [Early 17C. Because it lives for only one day]

Day-Glo /dáy glō/ *tdmk* a trademark for fluorescent dyes and coloring agents

day·hop /dáy hòp/ *n* (*informal*) **1.** a journey or distance that can be traveled within a day **2.** a student at a boarding school or college who does not board there

day job *n* a job that somebody does merely to earn an income while trying to achieve success in another field, especially the arts

day la·bor·er *n* a manual worker who is hired and paid on a day-to-day basis —**day la·bor** *n*

Day-Lew·is /day lòò iss/, **Cecil** (1904–72) Irish-born British poet and novelist. His poetry includes *A Time to Dance* (1935) and *Poems in Wartime* (1940). The British poet laureate (1968–72), he also wrote works of literary criticism, and published detective stories under the name Nicholas Blake.

> "Now the peak of summer's past, the sky is overcast / And the love we swore would last for an age seems deceit."
> [Cecil Day-Lewis, *Hornpipe*; 1943]

Day-Lew·is, Daniel (*b.* 1957) British-born Irish stage and movie actor. He won an Academy Award for best actor in *My Left Foot* (1989).

day·light /dáy līt/ *n* **1. SUNLIGHT** natural light from the sun ○ *Open the curtains and let in some daylight.* **2. DAYTIME** the part of the day when it is light **3. DAYBREAK** the time when light first appears in the sky at the beginning of a day **4. PUBLIC AWARENESS** public knowledge, notice, or scrutiny ○ *There are some secrets that they would prefer not to have exposed to daylight.* **5. VISIBLE GAP** a visible gap between competitors in a race, showing the lead that one has over the other ○ *There's definitely daylight now between the two boats as they approach the halfway mark.* ◇ **beat** *or* **knock** *or* **scare** *or* **frighten the living daylights out of somebody** to beat or frighten somebody very severely (*informal*) ◇ **in broad daylight** in open daylight for all to see

day·light rob·ber·y *n UK* same as **highway robbery** (*informal*)

day·light-sav·ing time, day·light time *n* an adjustment of clock time to allow more hours of normal daylight. Clocks are usually set one hour ahead of standard time to achieve this.

day lil·y *n* a perennial summer flowering plant with long slender leaves. Flowers: large yellow, red, or orange, resembling those of the lily, usually dying after one day. Genus: *Hemerocallis.*

day·long /dáy làwng/ *adj, adv* throughout the entire day

day-neu·tral *adj* used to describe plants that mature and flower unaffected by the length of the daylight period they grow in

day nurs·er·y *n* a place where preschool children are looked after during the daytime, usually while their parents are at work

Day of A·tone·ment *n* JUDAISM same as **Yom Kippur**

day off (*plural* **days off**) *n* a day on which somebody does not have to work

Day of Judg·ment *n* JUD-CHR same as **Judgment Day**

day of reck·on·ing *n* a time when somebody is made to answer for crimes or mistakes

day one *n* the first day or the very beginning of something (*informal*) ○ *It's day one of the electoral campaign.*

day out (*plural* **days out**) *n* a day of leisure spent away from home

day·pack /dáy pàk/ *n* a small backpack or bag for carrying things needed during the day

day room *n* a communal recreation room in an institution such as a hospital or barracks

days /dayz/ *adv* during the day or every day ○ *I work days one week and nights the next.*

day sail·er *n* a small sailboat without sleeping accommodations

day school *n* **1.** a private school that does not take boarders **2.** a school that holds classes during the daytime but not during the evening

day shift *n* **1.** a shift that is worked during the day or part of the day **2.** a group of employees who work during the day at a place where others work during the night

day·side /dáy sīd/ *n* the side of a planet that faces the Sun

Days of Awe *npl* JUDAISM same as **High Holidays**

days of grace *npl* the extra days, customarily three, allowed for the settlement of a note or bill after it falls due

day spa *n* HEALTH same as **health spa** (sense 2)

day·spring /dáy sprìng/ *n* the first light of day (*literary*)

day·star /dáy staar/ *n* ASTRON **1.** same as **morning star** (*literary*) **2.** same as **sun** *n* (sense 1) (*archaic or literary*)

day stu·dent *n* a student at a school, college, or university who does not board there

day·time /dáy tīm/ *n* the part of the day when there is natural light ■ *adj* occurring, done, or used during the daytime

day-to-day *adj* **1.** occurring or tending to be the same every day ○ *the day-to-day business of earning a living* **2.** planning or providing for one day at a time ○ *We do everything on a day-to-day basis – we can never plan ahead.*

Day·ton /dáyt'n/ city in Ohio on the Great Miami River, southwest of Columbus and northeast of Cincinnati. Population: 162,669 (2002 estimate).

Day·to·na Beach /day tṓnə-/ city and resort on the Atlantic coast of northeastern Florida, situated on the Halifax River. Its hard white-sand beach, long the site of car speed trials and races, is a popular spring vacation destination for students. Population: 64,605 (2002 estimate).

Day·ton Ac·cords *npl* an agreement signed by the presidents of Bosnia, Croatia, and Serbia in 1995, containing measures to end hostilities in the former Yugoslavia

day trad·ing *n* the purchase and subsequent sale of securities on the same day, used as a way of making quick profits on price movements —**day trad·er** *n*

day trip *n* a journey or outing to and from a place within a day —**day trip·per** *n*

day·wear /dáy wèr/ *n* clothes for wearing during the day

daze /dayz/ *n* **CONFUSED STATE** a state of confusion and unclear thinking, often the result of a blow or shock ○ *Things happened so quickly I was left in a daze.* ■ *vt* (**dazed, daz·ing, daz·es**) **1. STUN SOMEBODY** to leave somebody wholly or partly unconscious or unable to think clearly, especially as a result of a blow or shock ○ *The blow seemed to have dazed her.* **2. BEWILDER SOMEBODY** to leave somebody feeling confused or amazed [14C. Back-formation < *dazed* < Old Norse *dasaðr* "weary from cold or exertion"] —**dazed** *adj*

daz·zle /dázz'l/ *vti* (**-zled, -zling, -zles**) **1. DEPRIVE OF SIGHT TEMPORARILY** to make somebody temporarily unable to see ○ *The glare of the oncoming headlights dazzled me.* **2. AMAZE SOMEBODY** to amaze somebody with brilliance or skill or with a wonderful spectacle or display (*often passive*) ○ *She dazzled the spectators with a triple somersault.* ■ *n* **LIGHT THAT DAZZLES** very bright light that deprives somebody of sight temporarily ○ *a lot of dazzle from the white-painted walls of the house* [15C. < DAZE]

dazzle up *vt* to make something more attractive and colorful (*informal*)

daz·zling /dázzling/ *adj* **1.** bright enough to deprive somebody of sight temporarily **2.** spectacularly skillful or impressive ○ *a dazzling lineup of stars* —**daz·zling·ly** *adv*

dB *symbol* MEASURE decibel

Db *symbol* CHEM ELEM dubnium

DB, D.B. *abbr* ACCT daybook

d.b.a. *abbr* doing business as

D.B.A., DBA *abbr* Doctor of Business Administration

DB con·nec·tor *n* a connector that facilitates serial and parallel input and output. Full form **data bus connector**

D.B.E. *abbr* Dame Commander of the Order of the British Empire

d.b.h. *abbr* FORESTRY diameter at breast height

D.Bib. *abbr* BIBLE Douay Bible

dbl., dble. *abbr* double

DBMS *abbr* COMPUT database management system

DBS *abbr* BROADCAST **1.** direct broadcasting by satellite **2.** direct broadcasting satellite

dc *abbr* ELEC ENG direct current

DC *abbr* **1.** MUSIC da capo **2.** ELEC ENG direct current **3.** District of Columbia

D.C. *abbr* **1.** MUSIC da capo **2.** ELEC ENG direct current **3.** District of Columbia

DCC *abbr* RECORDING digital compact cassette

DCD *abbr* RECORDING digital compact disc

D.C.L. *abbr* Doctor of Civil Law

dd. *abbr* **1.** dated **2.** delivered

D.D. *abbr* **1.** BANKING demand draft **2.** MIL dishonorable discharge **3.** CHR, EDUC Doctor of Divinity

D-day *n* **1.** BEGINNING OF LIBERATION OF EUROPE June 6, 1944, the day on which Allied forces landed in northern France to begin the liberation of occupied Europe in World War II **2.** DAY WHEN OPERATION IS TO BEGIN a day chosen for the beginning of a military operation or other major venture **3.** MIL START OF 2003 IRAQ GROUND WAR March 19, 2003, the day on which ground operations began during the War in Iraq, involving invading Coalition forces of the United States, the United Kingdom, Spain, and some other countries

DDD *abbr* direct distance dialing

DDR SDRAM *abbr* COMPUT double data rate synchronous dynamic random-access memory

D.D.S. *abbr* **1.** LIBRARIES Dewey decimal system **2.** DENT, EDUC Doctor of Dental Science **3.** DENT, EDUC Doctor of Dental Surgery

DDT *n* an insecticide effective especially against malaria-carrying mosquitoes. It has been banned in many countries since 1974 because of its toxicity, its persistence in the environment, and its ability to accumulate in living tissue. Formula: $C_{14}H_9Cl_5$. Full form **dichlorodiphenyltrichloroethane**

de[1], **De** see also under surname

de[2] *abbr* Germany (*used in Internet addresses*) See table at **domain name**

DE *abbr* Delaware[2] (sense 1)

de- *prefix* **1.** opposite, reverse ○ *decertify* **2.** remove ○ *decaffeinate* ○ *delist* **3.** derived from ○ *denominative* **4.** reduce ○ *degrade* **5.** get off ○ *deplane* **6.** formed by removing one or more atoms from a particular element ○ *deoxy-* [Via Old French *de-, des-* < Latin *de-, dis-* "apart, away"]

DEA *abbr* GOV Drug Enforcement Administration

de·ac·ces·sion /dee ak sésh'n/ (**-sioned, -sion·ing, -sions**) *vti* to remove a book or work of art from the collection of a library or museum and sell it

de·a·cid·i·fy /dee ə siddə fī/ (**-fied, -fy·ing, -fies**) *vt* to remove the acid from something, or reduce the acid content of something —**de·a·cid·i·fi·ca·tion** /dee ə sidəfi káysh'n/ *n*

dea·con /deekən/ *n* **1.** in the Roman Catholic, Orthodox, and Episcopal Churches, an ordained member of the clergy who ranks below a priest **2.** in many Protestant churches, a layperson who is appointed or elected to assist the minister [Pre-12C. Via Latin *diaconus* < Greek *diakonos* "servant, messenger"]

dea·con·ess /deekənəss/ *n* **1.** a woman who ranks below a priest **2.** a woman who is appointed to assist a minister (*dated*)

dea·con·ry /deekənree/ (*plural* **-ries**) *n* **1.** the position or rank of deacon **2.** deacons considered as a group

de·ac·ti·vate /dee ákti vàyt/ (**-vat·ed, -vat·ing, -vates**) *vt* **1.** MAKE SOMETHING INACTIVE to prevent something that is active or live, especially an explosive device, from operating **2.** STOP ACTIVE COMPOUND FROM WORKING to render a biologically active compound such as an enzyme inactive or ineffective **3.** END ACTIVE MILITARY STATUS to make a military unit no longer active —**de·ac·ti·va·tion** /dee àkti váysh'n/ *n* —**de·ac·ti·va·tor** *n*

dead /ded/ *adj* **1.** NO LONGER ALIVE having passed from the living state to being no longer alive ○ *a dead bird* **2.** INANIMATE never having been alive and having none of the characteristics of a living thing **3.** WITHOUT LIVING THINGS having no living things, or unable to support life ○ *a dead planet* **4.** WITHOUT PHYSICAL SENSATION having lost normal sensitivity to touch or pain, e.g., from the effects of cold, disease, or anesthesia ○ *My fingers have gone completely dead.* **5.** INSENSITIVE unable or unwilling to respond to, understand, or appreciate something ○ *She seemed completely dead to her surroundings.* **6.** LACKING ANY SIGNS OF LIFE showing little indication of feeling or vitality ○ *His eyes were dead.* **7.** LIKE CORPSE having the appearance of a dead person **8.** LACKING ACTIVITY OR INTEREST without human activity or anything interesting or entertaining ○ *This town is dead after seven o'clock at night.* **9.** NO LONGER CURRENT no longer in use, or no longer relevant, appropriate, or important ○ *That issue is now dead, despite attempts to revive it.* **10.** BROKEN DOWN no longer able to operate because of a fault, breakdown, or loss of power ○ *The phone went dead.* **11.** NOT BURNING no longer burning or able to burn **12.** NONRESONANT not resonant or producing sounds that are not resonant ○ *"To where Saint Mary Woolnoth kept the hours / With a dead sound on the final stroke of nine"* (T. S. Eliot, *The Waste Land*; 1922) **13.** TOTAL sudden, abrupt, and complete ○ *came to a dead stop in the middle of the road* ○ *There was a dead silence for a few seconds.* **14.** EXACT precise or exact in position or character ○ *dead center* **15.** EXHAUSTED very tired or completely without energy (*informal*) **16.** DOOMED certain to face a very unpleasant fate (*informal*) ○ *If I don't get this report in by tomorrow, I'm dead.* **17.** WITH NO RETURN producing or yielding no return ○ *dead capital* **18.** SPORTS OUT OF PLAY in some sports, used to describe a ball that has crossed the boundary of the playing area **19.** GOLF LANDING CLOSE TO GOLF HOLE in golf, used to describe a shot in which the ball comes to rest so close to the hole that the next shot cannot miss ■ *npl* DEAD PEOPLE people who have died or been killed ○ *respect for the dead* ■ *adv* **1.** PRECISELY emphasizes that an approximate-sounding description or instruction, e.g., concerning a time, a position, or a straight line, is in fact precise or to be followed precisely ○ *Keep going dead ahead for another 300 yards.* **2.** ENTIRELY completely or absolutely ○ *You can be dead sure that he won't make the same mistake again.* **3.** WITH SUDDENNESS abruptly or immediately ○ *stopped dead in her tracks* [Old English *dēad* < Germanic, "died"] —**dead·ness** *n* ◇ **the dead of night** *or* **winter** the most extreme point of night or winter

---

SYNONYMS ***dead, deceased, departed, late, lifeless, defunct, extinct***

CORE MEANING: no longer living, functioning, or in existence

dead having passed from the living state to being no longer alive ○ *He was dead before his body hit the floor.* ○ *A father of four was shot dead by soldiers last night.* ○ *The dead fox had been hit on the road and run over.* **deceased** (*formal*, of people only, especially in legal or other technical contexts, or as a euphemism) no longer living ○ *the heirs of a deceased partner* ○ *His grandmother, now deceased, came from Glasgow.* **departed** (*literary*, restricted to people) no longer living ○ *sweet departed spirit* ○ *the soul of our dear brother here departed* **late** (of people) having died recently or within living memory ○ *the late Iranian leader Ayatollah Khomeini* **lifeless** not living, or apparently not living ○ *She lay lifeless in the snow.* ○ *They found the baby cold and seemingly lifeless.* **defunct** no longer operative, valid, or functional, or no longer in existence ○ *attempts to revive a defunct ceasefire* ○ *former editor-in-chief of a now defunct newspaper* **extinct** no longer in existence, or no longer active ○ *an animal that was declared extinct in 1936* ○ *small houses clinging to the lower slopes of extinct volcanoes*

---

dead air *n* an unintentional period of silence during a broadcast

dead-air space *n* a space that is sealed or has no ventilation

dead·beat /déd bèet/ *n* **1.** SOMEBODY WHO DOES NOT PAY DEBTS a debtor who does not repay money that is owed (*slang*) **2.** LOAFER somebody regarded as irresponsible, lazy, and disreputable (*slang insult*) ■ *adj* PHYS DAMPED AND NOT OSCILLATING describes an instrument that gives a true reading without oscillation

dead·beat dad *n* a man who, upon divorce, separation, or desertion of his family, avoids or refuses payment of child support (*slang insult*)

dead·beat mom *n* a woman who, upon divorce, separation, or desertion of her family, avoids or refuses payment of child support (*slang insult*)

dead bolt *n* a bolt that is operated directly by the turning of a key or knob and not by a spring mechanism

dead cat bounce *n* an apparent recovery from a major decline in stock prices resulting from speculators rebuying stock that they previously sold rather than from a genuine upturn in the market (*slang*)

dead cen·ter *n* **1.** MIDDLE the exact center of something **2.** TOP OR BOTTOM OF PISTON STROKE the position at the top or bottom of a piston stroke in a reciprocating engine or pump, at which point the piston and the connecting rod are in a straight line **3.** POINTED ROD IN LATHE a nonrotating pointed shaft mounted at both ends or one end of a lathe to support the workpiece and hold it in place

dead duck *n* something or somebody with no chance of success or survival (*slang*)

dead·en /dédd'n/ (**-ened, -en·ing, -ens**) *vt* **1.** MAKE SOMETHING LESS INTENSE to lessen the intensity of something such as pain or sound ○ *The snow deadened the sound of their footsteps.* **2.** DESENSITIZE SOMEBODY OR SOMETHING to make something or somebody less sensitive to pain or other stimuli ○ *A local anesthetic will deaden the nerves.* **3.** MAKE SOMETHING LESS RESONANT to make an area soundproof or less resonant —**dead·en·er** *n*

dead end *n* **1.** POINT AT WHICH SOMETHING ENDS ABRUPTLY an end of a street, path, road, or passage beyond which it is impossible to proceed **2.** PASSAGE THAT ENDS ABRUPTLY a street, path, or passage beyond which somebody or something cannot proceed **3.** SITUATION THAT LEADS NOWHERE a situation or course of action in which further progress or development is impossible ○ *a line of research that proved to be a dead end*

dead-end *adj* **1.** WITH CLOSED END with no exit at one end **2.** WITHOUT PROSPECTS offering no prospects of progress, development, or improvement ○ *stuck in a dead-end job* **3.** WITH NO PROSPECTS describes young people, usually from underprivileged backgrounds, whose behavior makes them unlikely to succeed in life (*informal*) ■ *vi* (**dead-end·ed, dead-end·ing, dead-ends**) COME TO DEAD END to have no exit or prospect of further progress or development ○ *A half a mile from here the road dead-ends.*

dead-end·er *n* (*informal*) **1.** same as **loser** (sense 3) **2.** MIL a person who is too fanatical in the belief of a cause to accept the reality of defeat and to surrender, typically engaging in insurgency and terroristic acts against conquering forces

dead·en·ing /dédd'ning/ *n* material used to make a room or building soundproof or less resonant

dead·eye /déd ī/ *n* **1.** a rounded block of wood, pierced by three holes with a groove around its edge, used to tighten shrouds on sailing vessels **2.** a skilled marksman or markswoman (*informal*)

dead·fall /déd fàwl/ *n* a simple trap consisting of a heavy weight that falls on and crushes its victim when a support is removed

dead fin·gers *n* a condition that can affect people who work with pneumatic drills, causing loss of sensation and reduced blood circulation in the fingers (*takes a singular verb*)

dead hand *n* **1.** a negative or oppressive influence exerted over an activity or a group of people ○ *remove the dead hand of bureaucracy* **2.** LAW same as **mortmain**

dead·head /déd hèd/ *n* **1.** SOMEBODY INCOMPETENT somebody regarded as unintelligent, useless, or ineffectual (*informal insult*) **2.** SOMEBODY WITH FREE TICKET somebody who uses a free ticket for travel or to attend an event (*informal*) 3. **VEHICLE WITH NO PASSENGERS** a vehicle or aircraft that is carrying no passengers or freight (*informal*) ■ *v* (**-head·ed, -head·ing, -heads**) 1. *vt* **REMOVE DEAD FLOWERS FROM PLANT** to remove dead flower heads from a plant to improve its appearance or stimulate further flowering 2. *vti* **DRIVE EMPTY VEHICLE** to drive or pilot a vehicle or aircraft that is carrying no passengers or freight ○ *Williams deadheaded it from New Jersey to California last weekend.*

dead heat *n* a race or other competition in which two or more contestants finish together or with the same score

dead-heat (**dead-heat·ed, dead-heat·ing, dead-heats**) *vi* to finish a race or other competition together or with the same score

dead let·ter *n* 1. **LETTER THAT CANNOT BE DELIVERED** a letter that the postal service cannot deliver, usually because the address is inadequate or the addressee does not claim it 2. **UNENFORCED OR INEFFECTIVE RULE** a law or regulation that still applies but is not enforced or uniformly obeyed 3. **SOMETHING NOW IRRELEVANT OR UNIMPORTANT** something that is no longer considered relevant or important

dead let·ter box, **dead let·ter drop** *n* a place where a message or other item can be left in secret by one person and collected later by another, so that the two people do not meet

dead lift *n* a weightlifting event in which a weight is raised from the floor to the level of the hips and lowered again in a controlled manner

dead·light /déd lìt/ *n* 1. a protective shutter or plate fastened over a porthole or cabin window in bad weather 2. a thick glass window set in the deck or side of a ship to let light into a cabin

dead·line /déd lìn/ *n* 1. the time by which something must be done or completed 2. formerly, a line in a prison or prison camp marking a boundary beyond which prisoners were forbidden to go on pain of death

dead load *n* the permanent weight of a structure such as a bridge, exclusive of its load

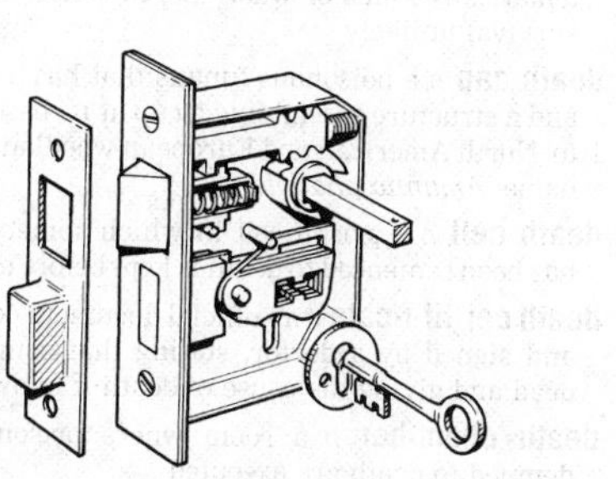

deadlock (sense 3)

dead·lock /déd lòk/ *n* 1. **STALLED SITUATION** a situation in which no further progress is possible in a dispute, usually because the people involved are unwilling to change their positions or to compromise ○ *try to break the deadlock in negotiations* 2. **TIED SCORE** in sports, a tied score 3. **TYPE OF LOCK** a lock that can be opened or closed only with a key —**dead·lock** *vti*

dead loss *n* a complete loss for which no form of compensation is available

dead·ly /déddlee/ *adj* (**-li·er, -li·est**) 1. **CAUSING DEATH** able or likely to cause death 2. **PRECISE** very accurate, especially in shooting ○ *deadly aim* 3. **EXTREMELY HOSTILE** involving or having an intense desire for the defeat, downfall, or death of somebody ○ *deadly enemies* 4. **CAUSING OFFENSE** causing or intended to cause great offense to another person ○ *a deadly insult* 5. **COMPLETE** used to emphasize the intensity of something ○ *in deadly earnest* 6. **DULL** extremely boring (*informal*) ○ *back to the deadly routine of daily life* ■ *adv* 1. same as **deathly** ○ *deadly pale* 2. **COMPLETELY** to the greatest extent possible ○ *I was being deadly serious when I made that suggestion.* —**dead·li·ness** *n*

SYNONYMS ***deadly, fatal, mortal, lethal, terminal***
CORE MEANING: causing death
deadly likely or designed to cause death ○ *Cannons are extremely deadly weapons.* ○ *a killer bee whose sting is ten times more deadly than the garden varieties* **fatal** used to describe accidents or illnesses that result in death ○ *a fatal road accident* ○ *an acute form of pneumonia which may prove fatal* **mortal** causing death ○ *mortal wounds* ○ *His face was drawn as if he realized the mortal danger they were now in.* **lethal** certain to or intended to cause death ○ *sentenced to death by lethal injection* ○ *Any sharply pointed object is potentially a lethal weapon.* **terminal** used to describe illnesses that result in death ○ *diagnosed with terminal cancer*

dead·ly night·shade *n UK* same as **belladonna** (sense 2)

dead·ly sins *npl* according to some Christian beliefs, the sins that lead to damnation, specifically the seven deadly sins of anger, avarice, envy, gluttony, lechery, pride, and sloth

dead·man /déd màn/ (*plural* **-men** /-mèn/) *n* 1. a heavy block or plate buried in the ground that serves as an anchor to a connected structure such as a retaining wall 2. a belaying point for use in firm snow, consisting of a metal plate with a wire loop attached to it [Mid-19C. Because buried securely, like a coffin]

dead man's float *n* a floating position in which a swimmer is face down with arms extended forward and legs kept together

dead man's han·dle, **dead man's ped·al** *n* a safety device on an electric or diesel train that automatically cuts off the power and applies the brakes when the driver releases pressure on it

dead march *n* a piece of solemn music played to accompany a procession at a funeral, especially a military funeral

dead men's shoes *npl* a situation in which the only prospect of promotion is the death or retirement of more senior employees

dead net·tle *n* a flowering plant that resembles a nettle but does not sting. Genus: *Lamium.*

dead-on *adj* very accurate or correct (*informal; not hyphenated when used after a verb*) ○ *a dead-on prediction*

dead·pan /déd pàn/ *adj* **PURPOSELY IMPASSIVE** deliberately expressing no emotion ■ *adv* **EXPRESSIONLESS** without showing any expression or emotion ○ *delivered the line absolutely deadpan* ■ *n* **EXPRESSIONLESS FACE OR PERFORMER** an expressionless face, or a performer with an expressionless face ■ *vti* (**-panned, -pan·ning, -pans**) **SPEAK OR ACT IN DEADPAN MANNER** to speak or do something in a deliberately expressionless way [Early 20C. < US slang *pan* "face"]

dead pea·sants' in·sur·ance *n* INSUR same as **corporate-owned life insurance** (*slang*)

dead pres·i·dents *npl* money in the form of cash, especially bills (*slang*) [< the portraits of US past presidents on bills]

dead reck·on·ing *n* a simple method of determining the position of a ship or aircraft by charting its course and speed from a previously known position

dead ring·er *n* 1. somebody or something that exactly resembles another (*informal*) 2. an automatically dialed telemarketing call that cuts off when answered because there is nobody at the sender's end available to deal with it

Dead Sea /dèd-/ salt lake on the border between Israel and Jordan, in southwestern Asia. Its surface, at 1,312 ft./400 m below sea level, marks the lowest point on Earth. Area: 394 sq. mi./1,020 sq. km.

Dead Sea Scrolls *npl* a collection of ancient manuscripts, discovered in caves near the Dead Sea, that provide important evidence for biblical scholars and historians. They were discovered between 1947 and 1956, and are generally held to have been written between 100 B.C. and A.D. 68.

dead set *n* the rigid motionless position of a hunting dog pointing with its muzzle at game

dead shot *n* an expert shooter

dead spot *n* an area within the range of a radio transmitter where reception of the signal is weak or dead

dead·start /déd staart/ *vti* COMPUT same as **coldboot**

dead time *n* an interval during which an electrical device or component, having just responded to one stimulus, is unable to respond to another

dead weight *n* 1. **HEAVY WEIGHT** a heavy motionless weight bearing down on something or somebody ○ *a foundation slab carrying the dead weight of the building* 2. **OPPRESSIVE BURDEN** somebody or something that weighs somebody else down or hinders progress 3. **TOTAL WEIGHT** the total weight of everything carried on a ship, equal to the difference between the laden and unladen weight 4. CIV ENG same as **dead load**

Dead White Eur·o·pe·an Male, **Dead White Male** *n* a conventionally important historical figure, especially one of the writers and thinkers whose works have traditionally formed the basis of academic study in Europe and North America (*informal disapproving*)

dead·wood /déd wòod/ *n* 1. **DEAD TREE PARTS** dead trees and branches 2. **SOMEBODY OR SOMETHING UNNECESSARY** people or things regarded as useless or superfluous 3. **PLANKS BETWEEN KEEL AND STERN** vertical planks filling the gap between the keel and the stern of a sailing vessel

dead zone *n* an area in which cell phone users are unable to receive signals

dead·zone /déd zōn/ *n* an area of slow-moving or stagnant water close to the bank of a river

deaf /def/ *adj* 1. **HARD OF HEARING** completely or partially unable to hear in one or both ears 2. **UNRESPONSIVE OR INDIFFERENT** unwilling to respond to something as if unable to hear it ○ *They remained deaf to all our entreaties.* ■ *npl* **PEOPLE WHO CANNOT HEAR** people who are hard of hearing [Old English *dēaf* < Indo-European] —**deaf·ness** *n*

USAGE The adjective and noun ***Deaf***, when capitalized, refer to the community of hearing-impaired people who use American Sign Language to communicate, and who use ***Deaf*** to refer to themselves. Avoid using ***deaf*** in lowercase in such contexts because it is taken to be offensive. A preferred substitute is *hearing-impaired.*

deaf·blind /déf blìnd/ *adj* unable either to hear or to see

deaf·en /déffən/ (**-ened, -en·ing, -ens**) *vt* 1. to make somebody temporarily or permanently unable to hear ○ *I was momentarily deafened by the noise of the explosion.* 2. to soundproof a room, wall, or building

deaf·en·ing /déff'ning/ *adj* extremely or unbearably loud ○ *She turned up the volume until the noise was absolutely deafening.* —**deaf·en·ing·ly** *adv*

deaf-mute (*dated*) *adj* ⚠ an offensive term meaning unable to hear or speak ■ *n* an offensive term for somebody who is unable to hear or speak

USAGE ***Deaf-mute*** and ***mute*** in reference to people who are unable to hear or speak are highly offensive and should be avoided. Preferred substitutes are *hearing-impaired* or *hearing-and-speech-impaired.*

Deak·in /deekin/, **Alfred** (1856–1919) Australian Liberal politician. He was prime minister of Australia (1903–04, 1905–08, and 1909–10). See table at **prime minister**

deal[1] /deel/ *n* 1. **BUSINESS TRANSACTION** an agreement, arrangement, or transaction, usually one that benefits all the parties involved 2. **BARGAIN** something offered for sale on favorable terms (*informal*) 3. **TREATMENT** the particular treatment given to somebody or received from somebody (*informal*) ○ *They got a pretty raw deal from their employer.* 4. **DISTRIBUTION OF CARDS** the distribution of the cards needed to play a card game 5. **PLAYER'S TURN TO DISTRIBUTE CARDS** a particular player's right or turn to distribute the cards for a card game ○ *Whose deal is it?* 6. **ROUND OF GAME** a round of a card game following a specific distribution of the cards 7. **CARDS DISTRIBUTED OR RECEIVED** the cards distributed or received for a particular round of a card game ■ *v* (**dealt** /delt/, **deal·ing, deals**) 1. *vti* **DISTRIBUTE CARDS** to distribute the cards for a round of a card game ○ *You deal seven cards to each player.* 2. *vti* **GIVE OUT PARTICULAR CARD** to give a particular card or cards to a player when distributing them ○

I was dealt five clubs and no hearts. **3.** *vti* **SELL SOMETHING** to sell something, especially illegal drugs **4.** *vt* **MAKE SOMEBODY EXPERIENCE SOMETHING** to cause somebody to experience or suffer something, often as a reward or punishment ○ *The latest opinion poll has dealt a severe blow to her hopes of re-election.* [Old English *dǣl* "part, share, amount," *dǣlan* "divide" < Germanic] ◇ **a done deal** something that has already been settled or finalized ◇ **cut a deal** to negotiate an agreement ◇ **make a big deal out of something** to make a fuss about something unimportant (*informal*) ◇ **the real deal** the ultimate example of its kind, or somebody regarded as the epitome of a particular trait or characteristic

deal in *vt* **1.** to buy and sell something as a business ○ *We deal mainly in second-hand goods.* **2.** to let somebody join in a card game or some other form of joint activity (*informal*) ○ *Deal me in.*

deal out *vt* to give something, or a share of something, to each of a number of people ○ *She dealt out compliments to all the actors.*

deal with *vt* **1. HANDLE SOMETHING** to take action with regard to something or somebody, e.g., to solve a problem or to help somebody **2. BE ABOUT SOMETHING** to write or speak about something or to have something as the subject of written or spoken material ○ *I was intending to deal with the Metaphysical poets in my next lecture.* **3. TREAT SOMEBODY IN PARTICULAR WAY** to treat or behave toward somebody in a particular way, especially in a business context ○ *People who break the regulations will be dealt with severely.* **4. HAVE BUSINESS DEALINGS WITH SOMEBODY** to do business with somebody or an organization

deal[2] /deel/ *n* **1.** fir or pine wood, especially when cut to a standard size **2.** a plank or board of deal [15C. < Middle Low German or Middle Dutch *dele* "plank"]

de·a·late /dee áy làyt, -áylət/, **de·a·lat·ed** /-áy làytəd/ *adj* used to describe an insect such as an ant or termite that has lost or shed its wings, usually after mating —**de·a·la·tion** /dèe ay láysh'n/ *n*

de·al·co·hol·ize /dee álkə haw lìz/ (**-ized, -iz·ing, -iz·es**) *vt* to remove some or all of the alcohol from a drink —**de·al·co·hol·i·za·tion** /dee àlkə hawli záysh'n/ *n*

deal·er /déelər/ *n* **1. SELLER OR TRADER** a person or company whose business is buying and selling **2. SELLER OF DRUGS** somebody who sells illegal drugs **3. SOMEBODY WHO DEALS CARDS** somebody who deals cards in a card game

deal·er plates *npl* temporary license plates given to a vehicle before it is registered

deal·er·ship /déelər shìp/ *n* **1.** a franchise to sell a specific brand of product or service **2.** the premises from which a dealer, especially a car dealer, operates

deal·fish /déel fish/ (*plural same* or **-fish·es**) *n* a deep-sea fish with a long flat silvery body. Native to: northeastern Atlantic. Genus: *Trachipterus.* [Mid-19C. < DEAL[2]; because it resembles a thin plank]

deal·ing /déeling/ *n* conduct toward or treatment of other people, especially in business matters ○ *The firm's reputation for fair dealing is at stake.* ■ **deal·ings** *npl* contact and interaction with other people or organizations for business purposes

deal·ing room *n* a room at a stock exchange where the buying and selling of stocks and shares takes place

deal·mak·er /déel màykər/ *n* somebody who arranges deals, especially in business or politics —**deal·mak·ing** *n*

dealt past participle, past tense of **deal**[1]

de·am·i·nase /dee ámmi nàyss, -nàyz/ *n* an enzyme that breaks down amino compounds such as amino acids

de·am·i·nate /dee ámmi nàyt/ (**-nat·ed, -nat·ing, -nates**), **de·am·i·nize** /dee ámmi nìz/ (**-nized, -niz·ing, -niz·es**) *vt* to remove an amino group from a molecule —**de·am·i·na·tion** /dee àmmi náysh'n/ *n* —**de·am·i·ni·za·tion** /dee àmmini záysh'n/ *n*

dean /deen/ *n* **1. ACADEMIC ADMINISTRATOR** a senior member of the academic staff of a university or college who manages the whole institution or a department, faculty, or group of students **2. COLLEGE ADVISER OR RULE ENFORCER** a member of the academic staff of a university, college or, sometimes, high school, responsible for the counseling and welfare of students, and sometimes for discipline **3. SENIOR CLERIC** a senior member of the clergy who holds an administrative position in a cathedral or collegiate church, or in a division in a diocese [14C. Via Old French *deien* < late Latin *decanus* "person in charge of ten others" < Latin *decem* "ten"] —**dean·ship** *n*

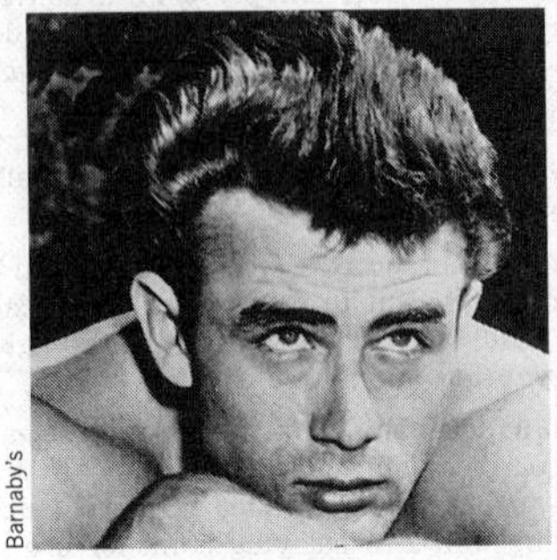

Barnaby's

James Dean

Dean /deen/, **James** (1931–55) US movie actor. He became a symbol of misunderstood youth through his roles in *East of Eden* (1955) and *Rebel Without a Cause* (1955).

Deane /deen/, **Silas** (1737–89) US diplomat. He negotiated a US treaty with France (1778) during the American Revolution, but later denounced the war.

dean·er·y /déenəree/ (*plural* **-ies**) *n* **1.** a dean's jurisdiction, office, or residence **2.** a group of parishes administered by a rural dean

Dean of Fac·ul·ty *n* the administrator of a university or college faculty

dean's list *n* a list of students who have achieved a high standard in their work at a high school, college, or university

dear /deer/ *adj* **1. BELOVED** loved or especially valued ○ *a dear friend* **2. COSTLY** high in price **3. CHARGING A LOT** charging high prices ■ *n* **1. SOMEBODY BELOVED** somebody who is loved or valued, especially for being kind or thoughtful **2. TERM OF ENDEARMENT** used as an affectionate term of address ■ *interj* **EXPRESSES SHOCK** used to express shock or consternation ○ *Oh dear!* ■ *adv* **DEARLY** at a high cost ○ *This will cost you dear.* [Old English *deore* < Germanic] —**dear·ness** *n*

SPELLCHECK Do not confuse the spelling of ***dear*** and ***deer***, which sound similar. The word ***dear*** as a noun denotes somebody loved. The noun ***deer*** denotes a widespread animal notable for the male's branched antlers.

Dear *adj* used before a name or title to begin a letter

Dear·born /déer bàwrn/ city in southeastern Michigan, a western suburb of Detroit, noted as an automobile manufacturing center. Population: 97,833 (2002 estimate).

Dear·born Heights city in southeastern Michigan, northwest of Dearborn and a western suburb of Detroit. Population: 58,047 (2002 estimate).

dear·ie /déeree/, **dear·y** (*plural* **-ies**) *n* used to address somebody in an affectionate way (*informal*)

Dear John let·ter, Dear John *n* a letter from a woman ending a romantic or sexual relationship (*informal*) [< the salutation opening such a letter, *John* being a common man's given name]

dear·ly /déerlee/ *adv* **1.** with great affection or intensity **2.** at a high cost ○ *He paid dearly for his mistake.*

dearth /durth/ *n* a scarcity of something ○ *a dearth of new ideas* [13C. < DEAR]

SYNONYMS See ***lack***.

dea·sil /déez'l/ *adv Scotland* in a clockwise direction [Late 18C. < Gaelic *deiseil*]

death /deth/ *n* **1. END OF BEING ALIVE** the ending of all vital functions or processes in an organism or cell **2. WAY OF DYING** a manner of dying ○ *an easy death* **3. SOMEBODY'S DYING** an instance of somebody's dying **4. END OF SOMETHING** the destruction or extinction of something **5. CONDITION OF BEING DEAD** the condition or quality of being dead ○ *In death she looked peaceful and composed.* [Old English *dēa* < Germanic] ◇ **at death's door** so ill or injured as to be almost dead ◇ **be in at the death** to be present at the end or culmination of something ◇ **be the death of somebody** to cause somebody's death (*often used figuratively for emphasis*) ○ *All this homework will be the death of me!* ◇ **beat something to death** to repeat something, such as a story or idea, so often that people become bored with it ◇ **catch your death (of cold)** to get a very bad cold ◇ **like death warmed over** looking very sick ◇ **put somebody to death** to kill somebody, especially in accordance with a legal death sentence ◇ **sick to death of something** tired of hearing about something or having to deal with it ◇ **to death 1.** until somebody or something dies **2.** used to add emphasis ○ *bored to death* ◇ **to the death** until one opponent in a fight is killed

SYNONYMS See ***kill***[1].

Death *n* a personification of death, usually represented as a ghostly form or skeleton holding a scythe

death ad·der *n* a poisonous snake with a body like an adder. Native to: Australia. Latin name: *Acanthopis antarcticus.*

death an·gel *n* FUNGI same as **death cap**

death·bed /déth bèd/ *n* the bed on which somebody dies ■ *adj* said, done, or made by somebody while near death ○ *deathbed confessions*

death ben·e·fit *n* a sum of money that is paid to the beneficiary of a life insurance policy after the death of the insured

death·blow /déth blō/ *n* **1.** an action or event that destroys or ends something **2.** a blow that kills somebody

death cam·as *n* a plant of the lily family whose roots are poisonous to livestock. Flowers: greenish white, in clusters. Native to: western North America. Genus: *Zigadenus.*

death camp *n* a place where prisoners are systematically killed or where harsh conditions make survival unlikely

death cap *n* a poisonous fungus that has a pale cap and a structure resembling a cup at its base. Native to: North American and European woodlands. Latin name: *Amanita phalloides.*

death cell *n* a prison cell in which somebody who has been sentenced to death is kept before execution

death cer·tif·i·cate *n* an official document completed and signed by a doctor, stating that somebody is dead and giving the cause of death if known

death cham·ber *n* a room where prisoners condemned to death are executed

death-deal·ing *adj* causing or liable to cause death

death-de·fy·ing *adj* taking the risk of being killed

death fu·tures *npl* a financial investment in the form of the purchase at a reduced rate of the life insurance of somebody who has a terminal illness. This both provides necessary income for the dying person to meet medical costs and guarantees a good return for the purchaser. (*hyphenated when used before a noun*)

death grip *n* a sudden powerful grip, especially one made by somebody who is dying

death house *n* a building where prisoners condemned to death are housed prior to execution

death in·stinct *n* an inherent and unconscious tendency, proposed in some theories of the mind, toward self-destruction

death knell *n* **1.** a sign that something is dead, destroyed, or coming to an end ○ *The bankruptcy notice was the company's death knell.* **2.** the ringing of a bell to announce that somebody has died

death·less /déthləss/ *adj* immortal, usually because of being excellent (*literary or humorous*) ○ *deathless prose* —**death·less·ly** *adv* —**death·less·ness** *n*

death·ly /déthlee/ *adj* **1. LIKE DEATH** resembling death or somebody who is dead ○ *deathly pallor* **2. EXTREME** high in degree or intensity ○ *a deathly hush* ■ *adv* **EXTREMELY** extremely or intensely —**death·li·ness** *n*

death mask: "Mask of Agamemnon," discovered in a grave at Mycenae, Greece, in 1876

death mask *n* a cast made of somebody's face soon after death

death·match /déth màch/ *n* in a computer game, a fight that ends in the death of a character

death met·al *n* heavy metal music characterized by satanic and horror film iconography

death pen·al·ty *n* LAW same as **capital punishment**

death-qual·i·fy (**death-qual·i·fied, death-qual·i·fy·ing, death-qual·i·fies**) *vt* to excuse somebody who rejects the death penalty from being on a jury whose verdict might entail a sentence of death —**death-qual·i·fi·ca·tion** *n*

death rate *n* the proportion of deaths to the population of an area or group

death rat·tle *n* a rough gurgling noise that sometimes comes from somebody's throat at the moment of death, caused by breath passing through mucus

death ray *n* an imaginary power beam that can kill

death row /-rō/ *n* a row of prison cells, or an area in a prison, housing prisoners that have been sentenced to death

death seat *n US* the seat next to the driver in a motor vehicle, considered to be especially dangerous (*informal*)

death sen·tence *n* **1.** the punishment of death, received in a court of law **2.** a diagnosis or decision that has a fatal effect

death's head *n* a human skull or its representation in art, often a symbol of mortality

death's head moth, death's head hawk-moth *n* a large moth with pale markings on the back of its thorax that look like a human skull. Native to: Europe. Latin name: *Acherontia atropos.*

death squad *n* an unofficial but organized group of people who seek out and murder political opponents or other people they consider as enemies

death tax *n* FIN **1.** same as **estate tax 2.** same as **inheritance tax**

death toll *n* the total number of people killed as a result of an event such as a road accident or natural disaster

death·trap /déth tràp/ *n* a building, structure, or vehicle that is extremely unsafe (*informal*)

Death Val·ley /dèth-/ low-lying desert region in southeastern California. It contains the lowest point in the United States, 282 ft./86 m below sea level.

Death Val·ley Na·tion·al Park national park in southeastern California and southwestern Nevada that includes Death Valley and the surrounding mountains. Area: 5,262 sq. mi./13,628 sq. km.

death war·rant *n* **1.** an official document that authorizes somebody's execution **2.** something that ends hope or expectation

death·watch /déth wòch/ *n* **1.** a vigil near a dead or dying person, sometimes a traditional or religious custom **2.** INSECTS same as **deathwatch beetle**

death·watch bee·tle *n* a small beetle whose larva bores into wood and makes a ticking sound. Latin name: *Xestobium rufovillosum.*

death wish *n* **1.** a desire to die or, less commonly, a desire for the death of somebody else **2.** a desire for self-destruction or personal misery

de·at·tri·bu·tion /dee àttrə byóosh'n/ *n* a change in an official or agreed opinion about the attribution of a work of art

deb /deb/ *n* same as **debutante** (*informal*) [Early 20C. Shortening]

deb. *abbr* **1.** FIN debenture **2.** BANKING debit

de·ba·cle /də baák'l, -bák'l/ *n* **1.** a sudden disaster, defeat, or humiliating failure **2.** a sudden breakup of river ice in the spring thaw, causing a violent rush of water and ice [Early 19C. < French < *débâcler* "unbar" (of ice breaking on a river) < Latin *bacculus* "stick"]

De·Ba·key /də báykee/, **Michael Ellis** (*b.* 1908) US cardiac surgeon. He performed the first coronary artery bypass operation (1966).

de·bar /dee baár/ (**-barred, -bar·ring, -bars**) *vti* to exclude somebody from entering or taking part in something [15C. < Old French *desbarrer* < *barrer* "to bar"] —**de·bar·ment** *n*

de·bark[1] /di baárk/ (**-barked, -bark·ing, -barks**) *v* **1.** *vi* TRANSP same as **disembark** (senses 1–2) **2.** *vt* to unload something from a vehicle (*formal*) [Mid-17C. < French *débarquer* "get out of a boat"] —**de·bar·ka·tion** /dèe baar káysh'n/ *n*

de·bark[2] /dee baárk/ (**-barked, -bark·ing, -barks**) *vt* to remove the bark from wood [Mid-18C. < DE- + BARK[2]]

de·base /di báyss/ (**-based, -bas·ing, -bas·es**) *vt* **1.** to reduce something in value or quality **2.** to reduce somebody in status, significance, or moral worth —**de·base·ment** *n* —**de·bas·er** *n*

de·bat·a·ble /di báytəb'l/ *adj* **1.** liable to be questioned or disputed ○ *It's debatable whether this is actually an improvement.* **2.** *UK* claimed by more than one country or party (*formal*)

de·bat·a·bly /di báytəblee/ *adv* used to show that the speaker or writer is aware that some people might disagree with the statement about to be made ○ *He was debatably the best orator of his generation.*

de·bate /di báyt/ *vti* (**-bat·ed, -bat·ing, -bates**) **1.** TALK OR ARGUE ABOUT SOMETHING to talk about something at length and in detail, especially as part of a formal exchange of opinion **2.** THINK ABOUT SOMETHING to ponder something carefully ■ *n* **1.** PUBLIC MEETING FOR DISCUSSION an organized or public discussion of something **2.** ARGUMENT argument or prolonged discussion ○ *The matter is not open to debate.* **3.** CONSIDERATION a prolonged consideration of something [13C. < Old French *debat* < Latin *battere* "to fight"] —**de·bat·er** *n*

de·bat·ing so·ci·e·ty /di báyting-/ *n* an organization whose main purpose is to hold regular formal debates on different topics

de·bauch /di báwch/ (*formal*) *vt* (**-bauched, -bauch·ing, -bauch·es**) **1.** LEAD SOMEBODY INTO IMMORAL BEHAVIOR to persuade somebody to behave in an immoral way **2.** SEDUCE SOMEBODY to seduce somebody sexually ■ *n* EPISODE OF DISSIPATION a period of indulgence in immoral behavior [Late 16C. < French *débaucher*] —**de·bauch·er** *n*

de·bauched /di báwcht/ *adj* unrestrainedly and immorally self-indulgent —**de·bauch·ed·ness** /-báwch ədnəss, -báwcht-/ *n*

de·bauch·ee /di bàw chée, dèbbə shée/ *n* somebody regarded as immoral, unrestrained, and self-indulgent

de·bauch·er·y /di báwchəree/ (*plural* **-ies**) *n* unrestrained self-indulgent immoral behavior, or an instance of this

de Beau·voir, Simone ♦ **Beauvoir, Simone de**

de·ben·ture /də bénchər/ *n* **1.** *also* **de·ben·ture bond** UNSECURED BOND a bond backed only by the credit standing of the issuer, sometimes convertible into stock **2.** CERTIFICATE OF DEBT a certificate that acknowledges the existence of a debt of a particular amount owed to somebody **3.** CUSTOMS REFUND CERTIFICATE a certificate issued by customs officials that provides for a refund of duty previously paid [15C. < Latin *debentur* "they are owed," form of *debere* "owe"] —**de·ben·tured** *adj*

de·bil·i·tate /di bílli tàyt/ (**-tat·ed, -tat·ing, -tates**) *vt* to sap the strength or energy of somebody or something [Mid-16C. < Latin *debilitat-*, past participle of *debilitare* "weaken" < *debilitas* "weakness" (see DEBILITY)] —**de·bil·i·ta·tion** /di bìlli táysh'n/ *n* —**de·bil·i·ta·tive** *adj*

de·bil·i·tat·ed /di bílli tàytəd/ *adj* with reduced strength or energy

SYNONYMS See *weak.*

de·bil·i·tat·ing /di bílli tàyting/ *adj* reducing somebody's strength or energy

de·bil·i·ty /di bíllətee/ (*plural* **-ties**) *n* a general lack of strength or energy [15C. Via French < Latin *debilitas* < *debilis* "weak"]

deb·it /débbit/ *n* **1.** RECORDED DEBT OR EXPENSE an entry showing a debt or expense in a record of accounts **2.** SUM OF MONEY DEDUCTED an amount of money taken out of an account **3.** TOTAL OF DEBTS OR EXPENSES the total of individual debit entries in an account **4.** COLUMN FOR RECORDING DEBTS OR EXPENSES a column on the left of an accounting statement where debts and expenses are recorded **5.** DRAWBACK something that is disadvantageous or unfavorable ○ *The pay's better, but on the debit side there's a lot more work to do.* ■ *vt* (**-it·ed, -it·ing, -its**) **1.** RECORD DEBIT to make, enter, or record a debit in an account **2.** CHARGE SOMEBODY MONEY to remove a sum of money from somebody's account in payment for something [15C. < Latin *debitum* (see DEBT)]

deb·it card *n* a plastic card that the holder can use to pay for purchases, the money being transferred directly from the holder's bank account to the seller

deb·o·nair /dèbbə nér/ *adj* **1.** looking well-dressed, sophisticated, and at ease **2.** characterized by ease of manner, elegance, or sophistication [13C. < Old French < *de bon aire* "of good disposition"] —**deb·o·nair·ly** *adv*

de·bone /dee bṓn/ (**-boned, -bon·ing, -bones**) *vt* to remove the bones from meat or fish

de·bouch /di bówch, -bóosh/ (**-bouched, -bouch·ing, -bouch·es**) *vi* **1.** to move from an enclosed or confined area into more open terrain **2.** to widen out, or flow out, from a valley or ravine into a broader area (*refers to a geographic feature such as a valley or a flow of water*) [Mid-18C. < French *déboucher* "come out of the mouth" < Latin *bucca* "cheek, mouth"] —**de·bouch·ment** *n*

De·bre·cen /débbrət sèn/ capital of Hajdú-Bihar County, eastern Hungary. Population: 205,032 (1999).

dé·bride·ment /day breédmənt, di-, dày breéd maaN/ *n* the removal of dead, damaged, or infected tissue from a wound [Mid-19C. < French, "unbridling"] —**dé·bride** *vti*

de·brief (**-briefed, -brief·ing, -briefs** /dee breéf/) *vt* **1.** to question somebody closely about a task, mission, or event after it has ended **2.** to supply somebody with information about a task, mission, or event after it has ended —**de·brief** /deé breef/ *n*

de·brief·ing /dee breéfing/ *n* an interview in which somebody is asked about or reports on a task, mission, or event after it has ended

de·bris /də breé, day-, dáy breè/, **dé·bris** *n* fragments of something that has been destroyed or broken into pieces [Early 18C. < French *débris* "broken up" < Old French *brisier* "break"]

de Bro·glie wave·length /də bràw gleé-/ *n* the wavelength of the wave associated with the motion of an atomic or subatomic particle (**de Broglie wave**) that produces diffraction. The de Broglie wavelength is given by Planck's constant divided by the mass and velocity of the particle. [Early 20C. After Louis Victor *de Broglie* (1892–1987), French physicist]

Debs /debz/, **Eugene** (1855–1926) US Socialist leader, pacifist, and labor organizer. He helped establish the Social Democratic Party of America and ran five times as Socialist candidate for US president (1900–20). He was imprisoned from 1918 until 1921 for his pacifist beliefs. Full name **Debs, Eugene Victor**

> "When great changes occur in history, when great principles are involved, as a rule the majority are wrong. The minority are right."
>
> [Eugene Debs, *Speeches*; 1928]

debt /det/ *n* **1.** SOMETHING OWED an amount of money, a service, or an item of property that is owed to somebody **2. STATE OF OWING SOMETHING** the condition of owing something to somebody **3. OBLIGATION** an obligation or borrowing ○ *Her poetry shows a great debt to the works of Lorca.* **4. SIN** a sin or trespass (*archaic*) [13C. Via French *dette* < Latin *debitum* < past participle of *debere* "owe"] —**debt·less** *adj* —**debt·or** /déttər/ *n*

ORIGIN The Latin word *debere* "to owe," from which ***debt*** is derived, is also the source of English *debenture, debit, due, duty,* and *endeavor.*

debt col·lector *n* somebody who is employed to recover money owed to somebody else

debt of hon·or *n* a debt that somebody is morally, but not legally, obliged to pay

debt re·lief *n* a policy that advocates the cancellation of debts owed by poorer developing countries to richer countries

debt swap *n* an exchange of financial obligations, especially between corporations or governments, in order to gain profit or a more convenient repayment schedule

de·bud /dee búd/ (**-bud·ded, -bud·ding, -buds**) *vt* BOT same as **disbud** (sense 1)

de·bug /dee búg/ (**-bugged, -bug·ging, -bugs**) *vt* **1. FIND AND REMOVE ERRORS FROM SOMETHING** to find and remove errors in a system, especially a computer program or device **2. REMOVE SECRET LISTENING DEVICES FROM PLACE** to find and take away any electronic listening devices that are concealed in a place **3. CLEAR PLACE OF INSECTS** to remove or destroy insects that are in a place (*informal*)

de·bug·ger /dee búggər/ *n* a computer utility program that helps find software errors by allowing the user to access the source code

de·bunk /dee búngk/ (**-bunked, -bunk·ing, -bunks**) *vt* to show that something is wrong or false [Early 20C. < BUNK[2]] —**de·bunk·er** *n*

de·burr /dee búr/ (**-burred, -bur·ring, -burrs**) *vt* to remove rough edges (**burrs**) from a piece of machined metal

De·bus·sy /də byóossee, dèbbyoo sée/, **Claude** (1862–1918) French composer. His works include the opera *Pelléas et Mélisande* (1902) and the orchestral poem *La mer* (1905). He developed a style known as musical impressionism. Full name **Debussy, Achille Claude**

> "Music is the arithmetic of sounds as optics is the geometry of light."
> [Claude Debussy. Quoted in *The Penguin Dictionary of Modern Quotations*, J. M Cohen (ed.); 1971]

de·but /day byóo, dáy byòo/ *n* **1. FIRST PUBLIC APPEARANCE** the first public appearance or presentation of a performer, program, or performance **2. YOUNG WOMAN'S FIRST OFFICIAL SOCIAL ENGAGEMENT** a young woman's first appearance in public at a formal social event ■ *vti* (**-buted, -but·ing, -buts**) **MAKE FIRST FORMAL PUBLIC APPEARANCE** to show or perform formally and publicly for the first time, or make something do this [Mid-18C. < French < *débuter* "lead off" < *de-* "from" + *but* "goal, target"]

deb·u·tante /débbyə taànt/ *n* a young woman who is being introduced formally into society by appearing at a formal social event such as a dance or party for the first time [Early 19C. < French, "leading off" < present participle of *débuter* (see DEBUT)]

de·bye /də bī/ *n* a unit of electric dipole moment [After Peter J. *Debye* (1884–1966), US chemical physicist]

dec. *abbr* **1.** deceased **2.** declaration **3.** GRAM declension **4.** ASTRON declination **5.** decrease

Dec. *abbr* December

dec- *prefix* same as **deca-** (*used before vowels*)

deca-, **deka-** *prefix* ten ○ *decagram* Symbol **da** [< Greek *deka* < Indo-European, "ten"]

dec·ade /dé kàyd, de káyd, də káyd/ *n* **1.** a period of ten years **2.** a group, set, or series of ten [15C. Via French < late Latin *decad-* < Greek *deka* "ten"] —**dec·a·dal** /dékəd'l/ *adj*

dec·a·dence /dékəd'nss/, **dec·a·den·cy** /dékəd'nsee/ *n* **1. PROCESS OF CIVILIZATION'S DECLINE** a process of decline or decay in a society, especially in its morals **2. STATE OF DECLINE** the condition of a civilization in decline **3. IMMORALITY** a state of uninhibited immoral self-indulgence [Mid-16C. Via French *décadence* < medieval Latin *decadentia* < Latin *decidere* "fall down or away" (see DECAY)]

dec·a·dent /dékəd'nt/ *adj* **1.** undergoing a process of decline or decay, especially in morals **2.** showing uninhibitedly or immorally self-indulgent behavior [Mid-19C. < French *décadent* < *décadence* (see DECADENCE)] —**dec·a·dent·ly** *adv*

de·caf /dée kàf/ (*informal*) *n* **1.** *UK* a decaffeinated drink, especially coffee **2.** decaffeinated coffee ■ *adj* BEVERAGES same as **decaffeinated** [Late 20C. Shortening]

de·caf·fein·at·ed /dee káffə nàytəd/ *adj* having had all or most of the caffeine taken out —**de·caf·fein·ate** *vt* —**de·caf·fein·a·tion** /dee kàffə náysh'n/ *n*

dec·a·gon /dékə gòn/ *n* a polygon with ten straight sides and ten angles [Mid-17C. Via medieval Latin < Greek *dekagōnos* "ten-angled"] —**de·cag·o·nal** /də kággən'l/ *adj*

dec·a·gram /dékə gràm/, **dek·a·gram** *n* a unit of weight equal to ten grams. Symbol **dag** [Early 19C. < French *décagramme*]

dec·a·he·dron /dèkə heédrən/ *n* a three-dimensional geometric figure formed of ten flat outer surfaces —**dec·a·he·dral** *adj*

de·cal /dée kàl, di kál/ *n* **1.** a picture or design on specially treated paper that allows it to be transferred to a surface such as glass, wood, or metal **2.** a decorative paper or plastic sticker [Mid-20C. Shortening of DECALCOMANIA]

de·cal·ci·fy /dee kálssə fī/ (**-fied, -fy·ing, -fies**) *vti* to lose calcium or a calcium compound, or remove calcium or a calcium compound from bones or teeth —**de·cal·ci·fi·ca·tion** /dee kàlssəfi káysh'n/ *n* —**de·cal·ci·fi·er** *n*

de·cal·co·ma·ni·a /dee kàlkə máynee ə/ *n* **1.** the process of fixing a picture or design to the surface of something such as glass, wood, or metal by transferring it from specially treated paper **2.** DESIGN same as **decal** [Mid-19C. < French *décalcomanie* < *décalquer* "transfer a tracing" + *-manie* "mania, craze"; from its popularity in the 19C]

de·ca·les·cence /deèkə léss'nss/ *n* the absorption of heat without temperature increase at specific conditions during the heating of a metal, caused by changes in the crystalline composition [Late 19C. < *calescence* "increasing warmth or heat"] —**de·ca·les·cent** *adj*

dec·a·li·ter /dékə leètər/, **dek·a·li·ter** *n* a unit of volume equal to ten liters. Symbol **dal** [Early 19C. < French *décalitre*]

dec·a·li·tre *n* MEASURE Can, UK spelling of **decaliter**

Dec·a·logue /dékə lòg/ *n* BIBLE same as **Ten Commandments** [14C. Directly or via French < ecclesiastical Latin *decalogus* < Greek *dekalogos (biblos)* "(book of) ten pronouncements" < *deka* "ten" + *logos* "word, pronouncement"]

dec·a·me·ter /dékə meètər/, **dek·a·me·ter** *n* a unit of length equal to ten meters. Symbol **dam** [Early 19C. < French *décamètre*]

dec·a·me·tre *n* MEASURE Can, UK spelling of **decameter**

dec·a·met·ric /dèkə méttrik/ *adj* having radio waves of high frequency, between 10 and 100 meters

de·camp /di kámp/ (**-camped, -camp·ing, -camps**) *vi* **1.** to leave a place abruptly or secretly **2.** to pack up and leave a camp or camping site [Late 17C. < French *décamper* < *camp* "camp"] —**de·camp·ment** *n*

de·ca·nal /di káyn'l, dékən'l/ *adj* relating to a dean or deanery (*formal*) [Early 18C. < medieval Latin *decanalis* < late Latin *decanus* (see DEAN)]

dec·ane /dé kàyn/ *n* an isomeric liquid alkane. Formula: $C_{10}H_{22}$. [Late 18C. < DECA- + -ANE]

de·ca·ni /di káy nī/ *adj* relating to or sung by the half of a church choir that sits on the south side of the chancel. ◊ **cantoris** [Mid-18C. < late Latin, form of *decanus* (see DEAN), referring to the side of the church the dean usually sits on]

dec·a·no·ic ac·id /dekə nō ik-/ *n* CHEM same as **capric acid** [< *decane*, liquid hydrocarbon]

de·cant /di kánt/ (**-cant·ed, -cant·ing, -cants**) *vt* to pour a liquid gently and carefully from one container to another so as not to disturb sediment [Mid-17C. < medieval Latin *decanthare* < Latin *canthus* "lip of a jug" < Greek *kanthos* "corner of the eye" (from the supposed similarity in shape)]

decanter

de·cant·er /di kántər/ *n* a decorative bottle with a stopper, used for holding and serving alcoholic drinks

de·cap·i·tate /di káppi tàyt/ (**-tat·ed, -tat·ing, -tates**) *vt* to cut off the head of somebody or something [Early 17C. < late Latin *decapitat-*, past participle of *decapitare* < Latin *caput* "head"] —**de·cap·i·ta·tion** /di kàppi táysh'n/ *n* —**de·cap·i·ta·tor** *n*

dec·a·pod /dékə pòd/ *n* **1.** an invertebrate animal with stalked eyes and five pairs of legs, one or more with pincers, attached to the thorax. Many decapods are marine crustaceans and they include shrimp, lobsters, and crabs. Order: Decapoda. **2.** a ocean mollusk with ten tentacles, e.g., a cuttlefish or squid. Class: Cephalopoda. [Early 19C. Via French *décapode* < modern Latin *Decapoda*, literally "ten legs"] —**de·cap·o·dal** /di káppəd'l/ *adj* —**de·cap·o·dan** /di káppəd'n/ *adj* —**de·cap·o·dous** /di káppədəss/ *adj*

de·cap·su·late /dee kápsə làyt/ (**-lat·ed, -lat·ing, -lates**) *vt* to remove a capsule from a body part or organ such as the kidney —**de·cap·su·la·tion** /dee kàpsə láysh'n/ *n*

de·car·bon·ate /dee kaárbə nàyt/ (**-at·ed, -at·ing, -ates**) *vt* to remove carbon dioxide or carbonic acid from something —**de·car·bon·a·tion** /-kaàrbə náysh'n/ *n* —**de·car·bon·a·tor** *n*

de·car·bon·ize /dee kaárbə nīz/ (**-ized, -iz·ing, -iz·es**) *vt* to remove the carbon from something, e.g., the carbon deposits from an internal-combustion engine —**de·car·bon·i·za·tion** /-kaàrbəni záysh'n/ *n* —**de·car·bon·iz·er** *n*

de·car·box·yl·ase /deè kaar bóksə làyss, -làyz/ *n* an enzyme that removes a carboxyl group from a molecule

de·car·box·yl·a·tion /deè kaar bòksə láysh'n/ *n* the removal or loss of a carboxyl group from an organic compound —**de·car·box·y·late** /deè kaar bóksə làyt/ *vt*

de·car·bu·rize /dee kaárbə rīz/ (**-rized, -riz·ing, -riz·es**) *vt* CHEM, ENG same as **decarbonize**

de·ca·style /dékə stīl/ *n* a portico that has ten columns ■ *adj* consisting of or having ten columns [Early 18C. < Greek *dekastulos* "having ten columns"]

dec·a·syl·la·ble /dékə sìlləb'l/ *n* a line of verse or a word made up of ten syllables —**dec·a·syl·lab·ic** /dèkə si lábbik/ *adj*

de·cath·lete /di káthleet/ *n* an athlete who competes in a decathlon

de·cath·lon /di káthlən, -lòn/ *n* a contest in which athletes compete in ten different track-and-field events and are awarded points for each to find the best all-around athlete. The events are long jump, high jump, pole vault, shot put, discus, javelin, 110-meter hurdles, and running over 100 meters, 400 meters, and 1,500 meters. [Early 20C. < DECA- + Greek *athlon* "contest"]

De·ca·tur /di káytər/ **1.** city in northern Alabama, on the southern bank of the Tennessee River, southwest of Huntsville. Population: 53,941 (2002 estimate). **2.** city in central Illinois, on the northern bank of the Sangamon River, southwest of Champaign and east of Springfield. Population: 79,842 (2002 estimate).

De·ca·tur, Stephen (1779–1820) US naval officer. He commanded the *United States* in the War of 1812, defeating the British vessel *Macedonian.*

"Our country! In her intercourse with foreign nations, may she always be in the right; but our country, right or wrong."
[Stephen Decatur, *Speech, Norfolk, Virginia*; 1816]

de·cay /di káy/ *v* (**-cayed, -cay·ing, -cays**) **1.** *vti* **BECOME ROTTEN** to decompose and become soft, crumbly, or liquefied, or make something do this **2.** *vti* **DECLINE OR CAUSE DECLINE** to decline in quality gradually and steadily, or make something do this **3.** *vi* PHYS **DISINTEGRATE** to undergo spontaneous disintegration (*refers to radioactive material*) **4.** *vi* PHYS **DECREASE** to decrease gradually in magnitude (*refers to a physical quantity or effect*) **5.** *vi* ASTRON **DESCEND** to decrease gradually in altitude (*refers to an artificial satellite in orbit*) ■ *n* **1. REDUCTION** a decline in quality ○ *"A state too extensive in itself, or by virtue of its dependencies, ultimately falls into decay."* (Simón Bolívar, *Letter from Jamaica*; 1815) **2. PROCESS OF BIOLOGICAL DETERIORATION** the process of decomposition that affects plant material and the bodies of animals after they die and are invaded by bacteria or fungi **3. ROTTEN OR SPOILED PART** the areas of something that are decomposed or rotted ○ *cut out the decay* **4.** PHYS **DISINTEGRATION OF RADIOACTIVE MATERIAL** the spontaneous disintegration of a radioactive material along with the emission of one or more elementary particles or radiation **5.** PHYS **GRADUAL DECREASE** a gradual decrease in the magnitude of a physical quantity or effect such as current, stored charge, or phosphorescence **6.** ASTRON **DESCENT OF ARTIFICIAL SATELLITE** the gradual decrease in altitude of an orbiting artificial satellite **7.** MUSIC **DECLINE IN SOUND OF NOTE** the fading away of a musical note [15C. Via French *decair* < Latin *decidere* "fall off or away" < *cadere* "to fall"]

de·cay con·stant *n* the probability that an unstable radioactive nucleus will decay in a standard unit of time

Dec·can /dékən/ triangular plateau that makes up much of southern India, south of the Sātpura Range. It is bordered by the mountainous Eastern and Western Ghats ranges.

decd. *abbr* deceased

de·cease /di seéss/ (*formal*) *n* same as **death** ■ *vi* (**-ceased, -ceas·ing, -ceas·es**) same as **die**[1] [14C. Via French < Latin *decessus* "death, departure" < past participle of *decedere* "go away" < *cedere* "give way"]

de·ceased /di seést/ (*formal*) *adj* no longer living ■ *n* somebody who has died recently

SYNONYMS See *dead.*

de·ce·dent /di seéd'nt/ *n* LAW same as **deceased** [Late 16C. < Latin *decedent-*, present participle of *decedere* (see DECEASE)]

de·ceit /di seét/ *n* **1.** the act or practice of deceiving or misleading somebody **2.** something that is done to deceive or mislead somebody [13C. < Old French < *deceveir* (see DECEIVE)]

de·ceit·ful /di seétfəl/ *adj* intentionally misleading or fraudulent —**de·ceit·ful·ly** *adv* —**de·ceit·ful·ness** *n*

de·ceive /di seév/ (**-ceived, -ceiv·ing, -ceives**) *v* **1.** *vt* **INTENTIONALLY TRICK OR MISLEAD SOMEBODY** to mislead or deliberately hide the truth from somebody **2. de·ceive your·self** *vr* **FOOL YOURSELF** to convince yourself of something that is not true **3.** *vt* **BE SEXUALLY UNFAITHFUL TO SOMEBODY** to be sexually unfaithful to a spouse or sexual partner [13C. Via Old French *deceveir* < Latin *decipere* "ensnare, take in" < *capere* "take, seize"] —**de·ceiv·a·ble** *adj* —**de·ceiv·er** *n*

de·ceiv·ing /di seéving/ *adj* liable or meant to deceive or mislead —**de·ceiv·ing·ly** *adv*

de·cel·er·ate /dee séllə ràyt/ (**-at·ed, -at·ing, -ates**) *vti* to reduce speed, or make something do this [Late 19C. < DE- + ACCELERATE] —**de·cel·er·a·tion** /dee sèllə ráysh'n/ *n* —**de·cel·er·a·tor** *n*

De·cem·ber /di sémbər/ *n* in the Gregorian calendar, the 12th month of the year, lasting 31 days. See table at **calendar** [13C. Via French < Latin < *decem* "ten"; because the tenth month of the Roman year]

De·cem·brist /di sémbrist/ *n* a member of a group of Russian officers who tried unsuccessfully to overthrow Tsar Nicholas I of Russia in December 1825

de·cem·vir /di sémvər/ *n* **1.** in ancient Rome, one of a group of ten magistrates, especially those who drew up the laws of the Twelve Tables in 451–450 B.C. **2.** a member of an official body that consists of ten people (*archaic*) [15C. < Latin *decem viri* "ten men"] —**de·cem·vi·ral** *adj*

de·cem·vi·rate /di sémvərət, -sémvə ràyt/ *n* a group of ten people who hold power or office together

de·cen·cy /deéss'nssee/ *n* (*plural* **-cies**) **1. CONFORMITY WITH MORAL STANDARDS** behavior or an attitude that conforms to the commonly accepted standards of what is right and respectable **2. MODESTY** modesty or propriety ■ **de·cen·cies** *npl* **MORAL BEHAVIOR** the commonly accepted standards of good behavior (*formal*)

de·cen·na·ry /di sénnəree/ *n* (*plural* **-ries**) a ten-year period (*formal*) ■ *adj* CALENDAR same as **decennial** [Early 19C. < DECENNIUM]

de·cen·ni·a /di sénnee ə/ *n* plural of **decennium**

de·cen·ni·al /di sénnee əl/ *adj* lasting for, consisting of, or happening every ten years ■ *n* an anniversary celebrated ten years after something or every ten years —**de·cen·ni·al·ly** *adv*

de·cen·ni·um /di sénnee əm/ (*plural* **-ni·ums** or **-ni·a** /-nee ə/) *n* a ten-year period [Late 17C. < Latin < *decennis* < *decem* "ten" + *annus* "year"]

de·cent /deéss'nt/ *adj* **1. MORAL** conforming to accepted standards of moral behavior ○ *It was decent of her to apologize.* **2. GOOD** above average in quality or quantity ○ *one of the few decent restaurants around here* **3. SATISFACTORY** adequate or sufficient in quality ○ *did a decent job* **4. KIND** kind, considerate, or generous **5. SUFFICIENTLY DRESSED** fully dressed, as opposed to being naked or wearing only underwear (*informal*) ○ *Don't come in; I'm not decent!* [Mid-16C. Directly or via French < Latin *decent-*, present participle of *decere* "be fitting"] —**de·cent·ness** *n*

de·cent·ly /deéss'ntlee/ *adv* in a way that conforms to accepted standards of moral behavior or appearance

de·cen·tral·ize /dee séntrə lìz/ (**-ized, -iz·ing, -iz·es**) *vti* to reorganize something such as a political unit so that power is shifted from a central or upper location to another less central place, or be reorganized in this way —**de·cen·tral·i·za·tion** /dee sèntrəli záysh'n/ *n*

de·cep·tion /di sépsh'n/ *n* **1.** the practice of deliberately making somebody believe things that are not true **2.** an act, trick, or device intended to deceive or mislead somebody [15C. Directly or via French < Latin *deception-* < *decept-*, past participle of *decipere* (see DECEIVE)]

de·cep·tive /di séptiv/ *adj* **1.** liable or meant to deceive or mislead somebody **2.** capable of being mistaken for something else ○ *a deceptive barking noise* [Early 17C. Directly or via French < late Latin *deceptivus* < Latin *decept-* (see DECEPTION)] —**de·cep·tive·ness** *n*

de·cep·tive·ly /di séptivlee/ *adv* in a way that deceives or misleads, or is contrary to appearances ○ *a deceptively easy task*

USAGE Although *deceptively simple* almost invariably means "complex despite apparent simplicity," that is not a model from which to generalize about the meaning of ***deceptively.*** When people are asked whether, for example, *a deceptively dangerous place to stand* is a place that is more or less dangerous than it appears, they respond variously, with a substantial minority admitting they have no idea what ***deceptively*** is intended to convey. Sometimes context clarifies the meaning: *It was a small house, but it had deceptively large rooms.* Unless the context makes the meaning clear, ***deceptively*** is best avoided.

de·cer·e·brate *adj* /dee sérrə bràyt, -brət/ having lost all cerebral function, vision, hearing, and other senses, and voluntary motor activity, e.g., as a result of a severe stroke ■ *vt* /dee sérrə bràyt/ (**-brat·ed, -brat·ing, -brates**) to remove the cerebrum or brain stem from an animal surgically [Late 19C. < DE- + CEREBRUM] —**de·cer·e·bra·tion** /dee sèrrə bráysh'n/ *n*

de·cer·ti·fy /dee súrtə fì/ (**-fied, -fy·ing, -fies**) *vt* to withdraw certification from somebody or something —**de·cer·ti·fi·ca·tion** /dee sùrtəfi káysh'n/ *n*

de·chan·nel·ize /dee chánn'l ìz/ (**-ized, -iz·ing, -iz·es**) *vt* to reroute a river to its original location and configuration of flow

deci- *prefix* a tenth ○ *decigram* Symbol **d** [< French < Latin *decimus* (see DECIMAL)]

de·ci·bel /déssəb'l, déssə bèl/ *n* a unit of relative loudness, electric voltage, or current equal to ten times the common logarithm of the ratio of two readings. For sound, the decibel scale runs from zero for the least perceptible sound to 130 for sound that causes pain. Symbol **dB**

de·cide /di síd/ (**-cid·ed, -cid·ing, -cides**) *v* **1.** *vti* **CHOOSE** to make a choice or come to a conclusion about something ○ *We decided not to go in the end.* **2.** *vt* **LEAD SOMEBODY TO CHOOSE** to make somebody choose what to do or come to a conclusion about something (*informal*) ○ *His encouraging letter decided me against dropping the course.* **3.** *vt* **END SOMETHING CLEARLY** to bring something to an end in a definite or obvious way ○ *The final goal decided the contest.* **4.** *vi* **ARRIVE AT VERDICT** to come to a verdict or judgment [14C. Directly or via French *décider* < Latin *decidere* "cut off" < *caedere* "cut"] —**de·cid·a·ble** *adj*

de·cid·ed /di sídəd/ *adj* **1.** clearly seen, felt, or noticed ○ *a decided slant* **2.** free of uncertainty or doubt ○ *a person of decided opinions*

de·cid·ed·ly /di sídədlee/ *adv* without any doubt or question

de·cid·er /di sídər/ *n* something that settles the outcome of a contest or argument, especially, in sports, a final scoring play or a game played to determine the ultimate winner

de·cid·ing /di síding/ *adj* acting to settle the result of a contest or debate, or to make clear what must be done next

de·cid·u·a /di síjjoo ə/ (*plural* **-ae** /-ee/) *n* a specialized part of the mucous membrane (**endometrium**) that lines the womb during pregnancy and is shed with the placenta at birth [Late 18C. < modern Latin *decidua (membrana)* "deciduous (membrane)"] —**de·cid·u·al** *adj*—**de·cid·u·ate** *adj*

de·cid·u·ous /di síjjoo əss/ *adj* **1. SHEDDING LEAVES IN FALL** describes trees and bushes that shed their leaves in the fall **2. OF DECIDUOUS TREES** describes a forest or wood that is composed mostly of deciduous trees **3. SHED AFTER DEVELOPMENTAL STAGE** describes the teeth, antlers, or wings of animals and birds that are shed after a stage of development **4. SHED EASILY OR AT INTERVALS** describes the scales of fish that are shed easily or at intervals [Mid-17C. < Latin *deciduus* < *decidere* "fall down" < *cadere* "fall, die"] —**de·cid·u·ous·ness** *n*

~~**decieve**~~ incorrect spelling of **deceive**

dec·i·gram /déssi gràm/, **dec·i·gramme** *n* a metric unit of mass equal to one-tenth of a gram. Symbol **dg** [Early 19C. < French *décigramme*]

dec·ile /dé sìl, déss'l/ *n* **1.** one of ten groups containing an equal number of the items that make up a frequency distribution **2.** one of the nine values that divide the total number of items in a frequency distribution into ten groups, each containing an equal number of items

dec·i·li·ter /déssə leètər/ *n* a unit of volume equal to 0.1 liter. Symbol **dl** [Early 19C. < French *décilitre*]

dec·i·li·tre *n* MEASURE Can, UK spelling of **deciliter**

dec·i·mal /déssəm'l/ *adj* relating to the number ten as a base and counted or ordered in units of ten ■ *n* a number expressed in a counting system that uses units of 10, especially a decimal fraction [Early 17C. < modern Latin *decimalis* < Latin *decimus* "tenth" < *decem* "ten"] —**dec·i·mal·ly** *adv*

dec·i·mal clas·si·fi·ca·tion *n* LIBRARIES same as **Dewey decimal system**

dec·i·mal cur·ren·cy *n* currency based on units of ten or multiples of ten

dec·i·mal frac·tion *n* a numerical fraction with ten as its denominator, written showing the fractional elements after a decimal point

dec·i·mal·ize /déssəmə lìz/ (**-ized, -iz·ing, -iz·es**) *vti* to convert something such as a country's currency or measurement system into a decimal or metric system, or convert to a decimal or metric system —**dec·i·mal·i·za·tion** /dèssəməli záysh'n/ *n*

dec·i·mal place *n* the place or a specific number of digits to the right of the decimal point in a line of numbers

dec·i·mal point *n* a printed or written dot in a decimal number that divides the whole numbers from the tenths, hundredths, and smaller divisions of ten

dec·i·mal sys·tem *n* a numerical system that has the number ten as the basic unit with other units as powers or multiples of ten. The metric system of measurement and most currency systems are based on a decimal system.

dec·i·mate /déssə màyt/ (**-mat·ed, -mat·ing, -mates**) *vt* **1.** ⚠ DESTROY LARGE PROPORTION OF SOMETHING to kill off or remove a large proportion of a group of people, animals, or things **2.** ⚠ ALMOST DESTROY SOMETHING to inflict so much damage on something that it is seriously reduced in effectiveness ○ *A boycott of products could decimate the industry.* **3.** KILL ONE PERSON IN 10 to kill one out of every ten people in a group, especially in a body of mutinous soldiers (*archaic*) [Late 16C. < Latin *decimat-*, past participle of *decimare* "take a tenth" < *decimus* (see DECIMAL)] —**dec·i·ma·tion** /dèssə máysh'n/ *n* —**dec·i·ma·tor** *n*

USAGE The popular meaning of ***decimate***, "to destroy," now predominates because the need for a word meaning "to kill one person in ten" has greatly diminished. Even so, the popular meaning is not accepted by everyone, and it is often better to use *annihilate*, *exterminate*, *destroy*, or *devastate*.

dec·i·me·ter /déssə meetər/ *n* a unit of length equal to 0.1 meter. Symbol **dm**

dec·i·me·tre *n* MEASURE Can, UK spelling of **decimeter**

de·ci·pher /di sífər/ (**-phered, -pher·ing, -phers**) *vt* **1.** to succeed in establishing what a word or piece of writing says when it is difficult or almost impossible to read **2.** to study something that is written in code or in an unknown form of writing until it can be understood and read normally —**de·ci·pher·a·ble** *adj* —**de·ci·pher·er** *n* —**de·ci·pher·ment** *n*

de·ci·sion /di sízh'n/ *n* **1.** SOMETHING SOMEBODY HAS CHOSEN something that somebody chooses or makes up his or her mind about, after considering it and other possible choices ○ *made a final decision on the guest list* **2.** FIRMNESS IN CHOOSING SOMETHING the ability to choose or decide about things in a clear and definite way without too much hesitation or delay ○ *a man of decision* **3.** PROCESS OF CHOOSING the process of coming to a conclusion or determination about something **4.** BOXING VICTORY DECIDED ON POINTS a win in a boxing match that is awarded to the fighter who is given the higher total of points by the judges ○ *He won a 10-round decision.* [15C. Directly or via French < Latin *decision-* < past participle of *decidere* (see DECIDE)] —**de·ci·sion·al** *adj*

de·ci·sion-mak·ing *n* the process of making choices or reaching conclusions, especially on important political or business matters —**de·ci·sion-mak·er** *n*

de·ci·sion the·o·ry *n* the study of the best possible outcomes for decisions made under varying conditions

de·ci·sion tree *n* a diagram set out like the branches of a tree that shows the consequences of a decision, each decision entailing a course of action that requires various other decisions

de·ci·sive /di sísiv/ *adj* **1.** settling or ending something such as a debate, controversy, or contest ○ *a decisive victory* **2.** showing an ability to make decisions quickly, firmly, and clearly [Early 17C. Via French < medieval Latin *decisivus* < past participle of Latin *decidere* (see DECIDE)] —**de·ci·sive·ly** *adv* —**de·ci·sive·ness** *n*

deck /dek/ *n* **1.** FLOOR SURFACE ACROSS SHIP a level surface that runs from one side of a ship to the other, forming a floor **2.** LEVEL OF SHIP OR VEHICLE a floored, self-contained area of a ship or a passenger vehicle such as a bus or tram **3.** LEVEL OF STRUCTURE a tier or level of a building or other structure **4.** BUILDINGS TERRACE OF HOUSE an open unroofed area of wooden floor extending from the back of a house **5.** FLOOR OF ROADWAY OR BRIDGE the floor or platform of a roadway or bridge **6.** AUDIO UNIT a wide flat piece of audio equipment that contains a player for compact disks, records, cassettes, or tapes **7.** PACK OF CARDS a pack of playing cards **8.** GROUND the ground or floor (*informal*) ■ *vt* (**decked, deck·ing, decks**) **1.** KNOCK SOMEBODY DOWN to strike and knock somebody down deliberately (*informal*) **2.** DECORATE SOMEBODY OR SOMETHING to decorate or ornament somebody or something (*literary*) ○ *deck the halls with boughs of holly* **3.** BUILD DECK FOR SOMETHING to make a deck for a ship or other structure ■ *n* SKATEBOARD PLATFORM the platform of a skateboard on which the rider stands (*slang*) ■ *adj* TRENDSETTING very fashionable or trendsetting (*slang*) [15C. < Middle Dutch *dec* "roof, covering, cloak" < Germanic] —**decked** *adj* —**deck·er** *n* ◇ **clear the deck** *or* **decks** to get rid of all obstacles, especially pending work, prior to beginning a new task ◇ **hit the deck** (*informal*) **1.** to fall on the floor or ground, often as self-protection **2.** to get out of bed ◇ **on deck 1.** on the top external surface of a ship or boat **2.** scheduled to appear next **3.** prepared and available to take part in an event or activity (*informal*) ◇ **play with a full deck** to be rational and intelligent (*slang*)

deck out *vt* to decorate something, or dress somebody up in fancy clothes

deck over *vt* to complete the construction of an upper deck on a ship

deck bridge *n* a bridge designed so that the roadway or track is supported by the upper horizontal part of the structural framework

deck chair *n* a collapsible adjustable outdoor chair with a lightweight framework and a seat made from strong fabric

deck hand *n* a laborer on a ship, yacht, or other vessel

deck·house /dék hòwss/ (*plural* **-hous·es** /-hòwzəz/) *n* a structure built on the main deck of a ship or other vessel

deck·ing /déking/ *n* a waterproof covering for the deck or roof of a house

deck·le /dék'l/ *n* **1.** a metal frame used to contain pulp in a mold during the making of handmade paper **2.** PAPER same as **deckle edge** [Mid-18C. < German *Deckel* "little covering" < *Decke* "covering"]

deck·le edge *n* a rough, irregular, or feathery edge on handmade paper —**deck·le-edged** *adj*

deck of·fi·cer *n* an officer responsible for tasks such as navigation that take place on a ship's main deck

deck shoe *n* a flat canvas shoe with a thick nonslip sole, typically worn on a yacht

deck ten·nis *n* a game based on lawn tennis, using a small court with a net and a ring made of rubber or rope that the players throw back and forth

de·claim /di kláym/ (**-claimed, -claim·ing, -claims**) *v* **1.** *vti* to make a formal or theatrical speech or statement about something **2.** *vi* to deliver a recitation [14C. Directly or via French < Latin *declamare* "cry out" < *clamare* "cry, call"] —**de·claim·er** *n*

dec·la·ma·tion /dèklə máysh'n/ *n* **1.** a speech or presentation spoken in a formal or theatrical style **2.** the art or process of declaiming ○ *"The air of the New World seems favorable to the art of declamation."* (Joseph Conrad, *Nostromo*; 1904) [15C. Directly or via French < Latin *declamation-* < past participle of *declamare* (see DECLAIM)]

de·clam·a·to·ry /di klámmə tàwree/ *adj* **1.** spoken or written in a formal or theatrical style **2.** loud and rhetorical but without very meaningful content

de·clar·ant /di klérrənt/ *n* **1.** somebody who makes a legal or formal, statement **2.** a noncitizen of the United States who has formally declared the intention of becoming a US citizen [Late 17C. < French *déclarant*, present participle of *déclarer* "declare"]

dec·la·ra·tion /dèklə ráysh'n/ *n* **1.** FORMAL STATEMENT a formal document giving explicit details such as the terms of a business agreement or plan, or information on goods or assets for tax purposes **2.** OFFICIAL PROCLAMATION an emphatic formal public statement, especially by a government or public body **3.** MAKING OF DECLARATION the process or act of declaring something in an official or public way **4.** LAW UNSWORN BUT SOLEMN LEGAL STATEMENT a formal statement of facts that is allowed in a legal case in place of a statement made under oath **5.** LAW PLAINTIFF'S OFFICIAL WRITTEN CLAIM a formal document in which a plaintiff lays out precise details of the circumstances leading to the legal action being taken **6.** CARDS ANNOUNCEMENT OF BID in bridge, the act of naming a suit as trump or of declaring no-trump by the player who makes the final bid [14C. < Latin *declaration-* < past participle of *declarane* (see DECLARE)]

Dec·la·ra·tion of Hu·man Rights *n* a United Nations document approved on December 10, 1948, by the General Assembly, affirming the rights of all human beings. It proclaimed their right to free movement in search of truth and justice and their right to live their lives in dignity.

dec·la·ra·tion of in·de·pen·dence *n* a proclamation by which a country, group, or people asserts publicly that it has become independent of a governing power

Dec·la·ra·tion of In·de·pen·dence *n* a written statement, issued and adopted by the Continental Congress in 1776, proclaiming that the 13 North American colonies henceforward would govern themselves instead of being ruled by Great Britain. The Declaration of Independence was formally endorsed on July 4, 1776. ○ *"If the American Revolution had produced nothing but the Declaration of Independence, it would have been worthwhile."* (Samuel Eliot Morison, *The Oxford History of the American People*; 1965)

de·clar·a·tive /di klérrətiv, -klárrətiv/ *adj* **1.** containing a statement **2.** in the form of a statement ○ *a declarative sentence* —**de·clar·a·tive** *n* —**de·clar·a·tive·ly** *adv*

de·clar·a·to·ry /di klérrə tàwree/ *adj* **1.** stating and clarifying something, especially a legal right, status, decree, or judgment **2.** same as **declarative** —**de·clar·a·to·ri·ly** *adv*

de·clare /di klér/ (**-clared, -clar·ing, -clares**) *v* **1.** *vti* ANNOUNCE SOMETHING CLEARLY OR LOUDLY to state something in a plain, open, or emphatic way **2.** *vt* STATE SOMETHING FORMALLY OR OFFICIALLY to make an official or public announcement about somebody or something, especially on a legal or medical matter ○ *The doctors declared her fit to work.* ○ *The chairperson declared the meeting open.* **3.** *vt* REVEAL SOMETHING AS TAXABLE to inform customs or tax authorities about goods on which duty is owed or about income that is taxable **4.** *vt* ANNOUNCE ACTION OR STATUS to make an official statement that a particular course of action or status is in effect ○ *to declare independence* **5.** *vi* MAKE DECISION KNOWN to announce a choice or decision formally and publicly (*formal*) ○ *declared for the presidency* **6. de·clare your·self** *vr* PROPOSE MARRIAGE to make a formal or open statement of love for and a wish to marry somebody (*archaic*) **7.** *vti* CARDS SAY WHICH SUIT IS TRUMPS in bridge, to announce to the other players the suit that will be trumps for the hand or that there will be no trump suit **8.** *vti* CARDS LAY CARDS ON TABLE in a card game such as bezique, to show that you have a specific score by displaying the cards face up on the table and claiming your score [14C. < Latin *declarare* "make clear" < *clarus* "clear"] —**de·clar·a·ble** *adj* ◇ **declare war 1.** to make a formal public announcement that the country represented is now at war with another country and will begin military action against it ○ *"Older men declare war, but it is the youth that must fight and die."* (Herbert Hoover, *Speech, Republican National Convention*; June 27, 1944) **2.** to begin a fierce campaign to get rid of or defeat something, or start fighting it in earnest

de·class /dee klάss/ (**-classed, -class·ing, -class·es**) *vt* to give somebody a lower status or class in society

dé·clas·sé /dày klaa sáy/ *adj* reduced to or having a low class or status in society [Late 19C. < French, past participle of *déclasser* "declass"]

de·clas·si·fy /dee klάssi fì/ (**-fied, -fy·ing, -fies**) *vt* to remove something from an official list of confidential or top-secret material so that anyone may see it —**de·clas·si·fi·ca·tion** /dee klàssifi káysh'n/ *n*

de·claw /dee kláw/ (**-clawed, -claw·ing, -claws**) *vt* **1.** to remove the claws from the paws of an animal **2.** to remove the power, authority, or force from somebody or something ○ *The acerbic comedy has been declawed by the demands of network TV.*

de·clen·sion /di klénshən/ *n* 1. GRAM **SET OF WORDS THAT BEHAVE SIMILARLY** a group of nouns, adjectives, or pronouns that all change their form or word endings in the same way according to gender, number, or grammatical case 2. GRAM **PROCESS OF ENDING WORDS** the process by which some sets of nouns, adjectives, and pronouns vary in form to show gender, number, or grammatical case 3. **WORSENING OR FALLING AWAY** the process of gradually declining or deteriorating (*formal*) 4. GEOL **DOWNWARD SLOPE** a downward slope, especially of terrain [15C. Via French *déclinaison* < Latin *declination-* < *declinare* "bend away" (see DECLINE), from the idea of inflections deviating from the pure form] —**de·clen·sion·al** *adj*

de·clin·able /di klīnəb'l/ *adj* used to describe a noun, adjective, or pronoun having different grammatical forms according to number, case, or gender [Mid-16C. Via French < Latin *declinabilis* < *declinare* (see DECLINE)]

dec·li·na·tion /dèklə náysh'n/ *n* 1. the angular distance of an astronomical object measured in degrees from the celestial equator along the great circle passing through it and the celestial poles 2. PHYS, GEOG same as **magnetic declination**

de·cline /di klīn/ *v* (-**clined, -clin·ing, -clines**) 1. *vti* **REFUSE INVITATION** to give a polite refusal to an invitation 2. *vi* **REFUSE PARTICIPATION** to refuse to respond or take part in something 3. *vi* **DIMINISH** to decrease in number, amount, value, or quality ○ *stocks declining in value* 4. *vi* **GET WEAKER** to become physically or mentally less vigorous, especially because of illness or advancing years ○ *His health had declined.* 5. *vt* GRAM **LIST VARIOUS FORMS** to state the grammatical forms of a noun, adjective, or pronoun 6. *vi* GRAM **HAVE INFLECTIONS** to exist in various inflected forms (*refers to a noun, adjective, or pronoun*) 7. *vi* **SLOPE DOWN** to bend something downward, or slope downward ■ *n* 1. **DETERIORATION OR REDUCTION** a decrease in number, amount, value, or quality 2. **PERIOD NEAR END** the terminal period of somebody or something, ending in death or disappearance ○ *at the decline of the empire* 3. **DOWNWARD SLOPE** a downward slope or movement [14C. Directly or via French < Latin *declinare* "turn aside, bend away" < *clinare* "bend"] —**de·clin·er** *n* ◇ **be on the decline** 1. to show a gradual decrease in number, amount, value, or quality 2. to show a gradual worsening of health

dec·li·nom·e·ter /dèklə nómmətər/ *n* an instrument that measures the difference between magnetic north or south and true north or south at a specific point on the Earth's surface [Mid-19C. < DECLINATION]

de·cliv·i·tous /di klívvətəss/ *adj* sloping downward

de·cliv·i·ty /di klívvətee/ (*plural* **-ties**) *n* 1. a surface, especially a piece of land, that slopes downward 2. a downward inclination, especially of a piece of land [Early 17C. < Latin *declivitas* < *clivus* "slope"]

Dec·o /dékō/, **dec·o** *adj* DESIGN same as **art deco** [Mid-20C. Shortening]

de·coct /di kókt/ (-**coct·ed, -coct·ing, -cocts**) *vt* to extract the essence or active ingredient from a substance by boiling it [15C. < Latin *decoct-*, past participle of *decoquere* "boil down" < *coquere* "cook"]

de·coc·tion /di kóksh'n/ *n* 1. the extraction of an essence or active ingredient from a substance by boiling 2. a concentrated substance that results from decoction

de·code /dee kṓd/ (-**cod·ed, -cod·ing, -codes**) *vt* 1. **DECIPHER CODE** to transform an encoded message into an understandable form 2. **TRANSFORM ELECTRONIC SIGNAL FOR USE** to transform an electronic signal into a usable form 3. **FIND MEANING OF INDIRECT LANGUAGE** to find the direct meaning of cryptic or indirect language 4. **DISCOVER UNDERLYING MEANING OF IMAGE** to understand the underlying meaning of something such as a painting —**de·cod·a·ble** *adj*—**de·cod·er** *n*

de·cod·er /dee kṓdər/ *n* a person, device, or computer program that decodes something

de·col·late /dékə làyt, dee kṓ làyt/ (-**lat·ed, -lat·ing, -lates**) *vt* to separate continuous paper into single sheets —**de·col·la·tion** /dèkə láysh'n, dèekō-/ *n* —**de·col·la·tor** *n*

dé·colle·tage /dày kawl taázh, dày kolə-/ *n* 1. the top front part of a woman's low-cut garment 2. a piece of women's clothing with a décolletage [Late 19C. < French < *décolleté* (see DÉCOLLETÉ)]

dé·colle·té /dày kawl táy, -kolə táy/ *adj* 1. **WITH LOW NECKLINE** having a low-cut front neckline ○ *a décolleté dress* 2. **WEARING LOW-CUT GARMENT** wearing a décolleté garment ■ *n* **CHEST AREA** the upper part of a woman's chest, below the neck [Mid-19C. < French, past participle of *décolleter* "lower the neckline" < *collet* "collar" < Latin *collum* "neck"]

de·col·o·nize /dee kóllə nīz/ (-**nized, -niz·ing, -niz·es**) *vt* to grant independence to a colony —**de·col·o·ni·za·tion** /dee kòlləni záysh'n/ *n*

de·col·or /dee kúllər/ (-**ored, -or·ing, -ors**) *vt* INDUST same as **decolorize** —**de·col·or·a·tion** /dee kùllə ráysh'n/ *n*

de·col·or·ant /dee kúllərənt/ *n* a chemical that removes the color from a fabric or other substance —**de·col·or·ant** *adj*

de·col·or·ize /dee kúllə rīz/ (-**ized, -iz·ing, -iz·es**) *vt* to remove the color from a fabric or other substance, e.g., by chemical means —**de·col·or·i·za·tion** /dèe kùlləri záysh'n/ *n*

de·com·mis·sion /dèe kə mísh'n/ (-**sioned, -sion·ing, -sions**) *vt* to remove something such as a ship, nuclear power station, machinery, or weapons from service

de·com·pen·sa·tion /dèe kompən sáysh'n/ *n* 1. the deterioration of existing psychological defenses in a patient already exhibiting pathological behavior 2. the failure of the heart to maintain adequate circulation because of various stresses upon it

de·com·pil·er /dèe kəm pīlər/ *n* a computer program that translates basic machine code back into high-level source code

de·com·pose /dèe kəm pṓz/ (-**posed, -pos·ing, -pos·es**) *vti* 1. **ROT** to break down organic matter from a complex to a simpler form, mainly through the action of fungi and bacteria, or be broken down in this way 2. **BREAK DOWN INTO PIECES** to break something down into smaller or simpler parts, or be broken down in this way 3. CHEM **BREAK DOWN INTO CONSTITUENT PARTS** to separate into constituent parts, or cause something to separate into its constituent parts —**de·com·pos·a·bil·i·ty** /dèe kəm pōzə bílləteе/ *n* —**de·com·pos·a·ble** *adj* —**de·com·pos·er** *n* —**de·com·po·si·tion** /dèe kompə zísh'n/ *n*

de·com·press /dèe kəm préss/ (-**pressed, -press·ing, -press·es**) *v* 1. *vti* **REDUCE PRESSURE** to cause a reduction in the atmospheric pressure of an enclosed space, or experience such a reduction 2. *vti* **ALLOW EXPANSION** to allow a substance to expand to normal dimensions or volume by the removal of pressure, or undergo this process 3. *vi* **RELAX** to relax or unwind, especially after being busy or stressed (*informal*) 4. *vt* COMPUT **EXPAND COMPUTER DATA** to expand compressed electronic data to its normal extent, or undergo this process —**de·com·pres·sive** *adj*

de·com·pres·sion /dèe kəm présh'n/ *n* 1. **PRESSURE DECREASE** a decrease in surrounding or inherent pressure, especially the controlled decrease in pressure that divers undergo to prevent decompression sickness 2. COMPUT **COMPUTER DATA EXPANSION** the expansion to full size of compressed electronic data 3. SURG **SURGERY TO REDUCE PRESSURE IN ORGAN** a surgical procedure to reduce pressure in an organ or part of the body caused, e.g., by fluid on the brain, or to reduce the pressure of tissues on a nerve

de·com·pres·sion cham·ber *n* a sealed room where divers undergo decompression

de·com·pres·sion sick·ness *n* a condition marked by joint pain, nausea, loss of motion, and breathing difficulties experienced by divers and others who emerge too quickly from a pressurized environment. It is caused by the formation of nitrogen bubbles in the blood and tissues.

de·con /dée kòn/ (-**conned, -con·ning, -cons**) *vt* same as **decontaminate** (*informal*) [Late 19C. [shortening]]

de·con·cen·trate /dee kónss'n tràyt/ (-**trat·ed, -trat·ing, -trates**) *v* 1. *vti* to experience a reduction in concentration or density, or cause something to experience such a reduction 2. *vt* POL same as **decentralize** —**de·con·cen·tra·tion** /dèe kònss'n tráysh'n/ *n*

de·con·di·tion /dèe kən dísh'n/ (-**tioned, -tion·ing, -tions**) *v* 1. *vt* to cause or teach a person or animal to stop exhibiting a conditioned response 2. *vti* to lose physical fitness through lack of exercise, illness, or a period of weightlessness in space flight, or cause somebody to do this

de·con·gest /dèe kən jést/ (-**gest·ed, -gest·ing, -gests**) *vt* 1. to loosen mucus in the nasal passages, sinuses, or bronchi 2. to increase the flow in something that is compacted or congested, especially with traffic

de·con·ges·tant /dèe kən jéstənt/ *n* an agent that relieves nasal congestion —**de·con·ges·tant** *adj* —**de·con·ges·tive** *adj*

de·con·se·crate /dee kónssə kràyt/ (-**crat·ed, -crat·ing, -crates**) *vt* to convert a sacred place, building, or object to secular use —**de·con·se·cra·tion** /dee kònssə kráysh'n/ *n*

de·con·struct /dèe kən strúkt/ (-**struct·ed, -struct·ing, -structs**) *vt* to subject a text to critical analysis using the theories of deconstruction

de·con·struc·tion /dèe kən strúksh'n/ *n* a method of analyzing texts based on the ideas that language is inherently unstable and shifting and that the reader rather than the author is central in determining meaning. It was introduced by the French philosopher Jacques Derrida in the late 1960s. —**de·con·struc·tion·ism** *n* —**de·con·struc·tion·ist** *n, adj*

de·con·tam·i·nate /dèe kən támmə nàyt/ (-**nat·ed, -nat·ing, -nates**) *vt* to remove unwanted chemical, radioactive, or biological impurities or toxins from a person, object, or place —**de·con·tam·i·nant** *n* —**de·con·tam·i·na·tion** /dèekən tàmmə náysh'n/ *n*

de·con·trol /dèe kən trṓl/ *vt* (-**trolled, -trol·ling, -trols**) to remove official restraints or regulations on something, especially prices or rents ■ *n* the removal of restraints, especially by a government on prices or rents

de·cor /day káwr, dáy kawr/, **dé·cor** *n* 1. the style of furnishings and decorative items chosen for a room or house 2. the scenery of a stage [Late 19C. < French < *décorer* "decorate" < Latin *decorare* (see DECORATE)]

dec·o·rate /dékə ràyt/ (-**rat·ed, -rat·ing, -rates**) *vt* 1. to make something more attractive by adding nonfunctional features to it ○ *decorated the hat with a couple of feathers* 2. to give a medal or other honor or award to somebody to acknowledge bravery, dedication, or achievement [Mid-16C. < Latin *decorat-*, past participle of *decorare* "beautify" < *decus* "ornament"]

Dec·o·rat·ed ar·chi·tec·ture /dékə raytəd-/, **Dec·o·rat·ed style** *n* the second, more ornate stage of English Gothic architecture, characterized by an increased use of geometric tracery and floral motifs

dec·o·ra·tion /dèkə ráysh'n/ *n* 1. **ATTRACTIVE ITEM** an item, usually one of a group, attached to something to make it look more attractive or to mark a special occasion 2. **ORNAMENTATION** the addition of ornaments to make something more attractive 3. **AWARD** a medal or other honor or award given to somebody to acknowledge bravery, dedication, or achievement

Dec·o·ra·tion Day *n* CALENDAR same as **Memorial Day** (*dated*)

dec·o·ra·tive /dékərətiv, -ràytiv/ *adj* 1. serving merely to look attractive rather than having a functional purpose 2. serving to make something look more attractive, especially by adding nonfunctional embellishments —**dec·o·ra·tive·ly** *adv* —**dec·o·ra·tive·ness** *n*

dec·o·ra·tive art *n* 1. art concerned with the design and production of functional but decorative items for home use such as ceramics, furniture, and fabrics (*often used in the plural*) 2. the products of decorative art, collectively

dec·o·ra·tor /dékə ràytər/ *n* 1. **INTERIOR DECORATOR** somebody whose job is to plan the decoration and furnishings of a room or building 2. **SOMEBODY WHO DECORATES** somebody whose job is to decorate something (*often used in combination*) 3. *UK* **SOMEBODY WHO PAINTS AND WALLPAPERS** somebody whose job is painting and wallpapering houses and other buildings ■ *adj* **FOR HOME DECOR** describes colors, fabrics, and accessories suitable for use in home decor

dec·o·rous /dékərəss, di káwrəss/ *adj* 1. conforming to what is acceptable or expected in formal or solemn settings, especially in dress or behavior ○ *"They began to talk politely, in decorous half-completed sentences, with little gasps of agreement."* (William Faulkner, *Sanctuary*; 1931) **2.** understated and dignified [Mid-17C. < Latin *decorus* "seemly" < *decor* "attractiveness"] —**dec·o·rous·ly** *adv* —**dec·o·rous·ness** *n*

de·cor·ti·cate *vt* /dee káwrti kàyt/ (**-cat·ed, -cat·ing, -cates**) **1.** BOT **REMOVE OUTER LAYER FROM PLANT** to remove an outer layer such as bark, rind, or a husk from a plant or part of a plant **2.** SURG **SURGICALLY REMOVE LAYER FROM ORGAN** to remove surgically the outer layer of an organ or structure such as the brain or kidney ■ *adj* /dee káwrti kàyt, -kət/ MED **WITHOUT CORTEX FUNCTION** describes a brain that has lost the function of its cerebral cortex as a result of disease or surgery [Early 17C. < Latin *decorticat-*, past participle of *decorticare* < *cortex* (see CORTEX)] —**de·cor·ti·ca·tion** /dee kàwrti káysh'n/ *n* —**de·cor·ti·ca·tor** *n*

de·co·rum /di káwrəm/ *n* **1.** dignity or good taste that is appropriate to a specific occasion **2.** the compatibility of an element such as character, form, style, or plot in a literary or artistic work with the work as a whole [Mid-16C. < Latin < *decorus* (see DECOROUS)]

de·cou·page /dàykoo paázh/, **dé·cou·page** *n* **1.** a decorative technique in which a design is made of cut-out pieces of printed paper glued onto a flat base and then varnished **2.** a picture or other form of decoration made using decoupage [Mid-20C. < French < *découper* "cut up, cut out" < *couper* "cut"]

de·cou·ple /dee kúpp'l/ (**-pled, -pling, -ples**) *vt* **1.** **SEPARATE OBJECTS** to separate or disengage one thing from another **2.** **REDUCE INTERDEPENDENCE** to remove or weaken the interaction between two electronic circuits, subsystems, or systems so that there is little or no transfer or feedback of energy between them **3.** PHYS **LESSEN STRENGTH OF SHOCK WAVES** to reduce or eliminate airborne shock waves from a nuclear or other explosion by detonating a device deep underground —**de·cou·pler** *n*

de·coy *n* /deé kòy, di kóy/ **1.** **DISTRACTOR** somebody or something used to deceive or divert attention, especially in order to lure somebody into a trap **2.** HUNTING **LURE TO ATTRACT ANIMAL** a bird or other animal, or a realistic replica, used by hunters to attract wildlife to a place for trapping or shooting **3.** HUNTING **ENTRAPMENT AREA** an enclosed area or stretch of water that game or fowl are driven or lured into so that they can be easily shot or captured ■ *vt* /di kóy, deé kòy/ (**-coyed, -coy·ing, -coys**) **DECEIVE** to deceive or entrap a person or animal by using a decoy [Mid-16C. < Dutch *de kooi* "the cage" < Latin *cavea* "cage"]

de·crease *vti* /di kreéss/ (**-creased, -creas·ing, -creas·es**) **DIMINISH** to lessen in size, strength, or amount, or cause something to do this ■ *n* /deé kreèss/ **1.** **PROCESS OF DIMINISHING** the process of diminishing in size, strength, or amount ○ *street crime is on the decrease* **2.** **REDUCTION** a reduction in the size, strength, or amount of something ○ *a 2% decrease in revenue* [14C. Via Old French *decreiss-* < Latin *decrescere* < *crescere* "grow"] —**de·creas·ing** *adj* —**de·creas·ing·ly** *adv*

de·cree /di kreé/ *n* **1.** **OFFICIAL ORDER** an order with the power of legislation issued by a ruler or other person or group with authority **2.** LAW **COURT RULING** a ruling given by a court, especially a divorce, equity, or probate court **3.** RELIG **DIVINE WILL** in Christian belief, the will or purpose of God, interpreted through events considered to be God's doing ■ *vt* (**-creed, -cree·ing, -crees**) **ISSUE ORDER FOR SOMETHING TO HAPPEN** to make an official order, pronouncement, or legal ruling to effect something [14C. Via Old French *decré* < Latin *decretum*, neuter past participle of *decernere* "decide, pronounce a decision"]

de·cree ni·si /-ní sī/ (*plural* **de·crees ni·si**) *n* an interim ruling of a divorce court that will become absolute in the absence of objections arising

dec·re·ment /dékrəmənt/ *n* **1.** the amount by which a quantity or quality gradually decreases **2.** the process by which a quantity or quality gradually decreases (*formal*) [Late 16C. < Latin *decrementum* < *decrescere* (see DECREASE)] —**dec·re·ment·al** /dèkrə mént'l/ *adj*

de·crep·it /di kréppit/ *adj* **1.** in poor condition, especially as a result of being old, overused, or not working efficiently **2.** with strength lessened by the effects of age (*informal*) [15C. < Latin *decrepitus* < *crepitus*, past participle of *crepare* "crack, creak"] —**de·crep·it·ly** *adv*

SYNONYMS See ***weak***.

de·crep·i·tate /di kréppi tàyt/ (**-tat·ed, -tat·ing, -tates**) *vti* to heat a substance, especially a salt, until it crackles or stops crackling, or be heated in this way (*technical*) [Mid-17C. < DE- + Latin *crepitare* "crackle" < *crepitus* "cracked" (see DECREPIT)] —**de·crep·i·ta·tion** /di krèppi táysh'n/ *n*

de·crep·i·tude /di kréppi tòod/ *n* the condition of being old, worn out, or in poor working order

decresc. *abbr* MUSIC decrescendo

de·cre·scen·do /dày krə shéndō, deè-/ *adv* with decreasing loudness (*used as a musical direction*) ■ *n* (*plural* **-dos**) a piece of music, or a section of a piece, played decrescendo [Early 19C. < Italian, "decreasing"] —**de·cre·scen·do** *adj*

de·cres·cent /di kréss'nt/ *adj* describes the moon when it is waning (*technical*) [Early 17C. < Latin *decrescent-*, present participle of *decrescere* (see DECREASE)] —**de·cres·cence** *n*

de·cre·tal /di kreét'l/ *n* a papal decree or edict that relates to an aspect of Roman Catholic law or doctrine [14C. < late Latin *decretale* < Latin *decret-*, past participle of *decernere* "decide, pronounce a decision"] —**de·cre·tal** *adj*

dec·re·to·ry /dékrə tàwree, di kreétəree/ *adj* relating to or having the force of a decree [Late 16C. < Latin *decretorius* < *decret-* (see DECRETAL)]

de·crim·i·nal·ize /dee krímmənə līz/ (**-ized, -iz·ing, -iz·es**) *vt* to make legal an action or substance that was formerly illegal —**de·crim·i·nal·i·za·tion** /dee krìmmənəli záysh'n/ *n* —**de·crim·i·nal·ized** *adj*

SYNONYMS See ***legal***.

de·cry /di krī́/ (**-cried, -cry·ing, -cries**) *vt* to express strong disapproval of or openly criticize somebody or something ○ *critics decrying lowered standards in education* [Early 17C. After French *décrier* "cry down"] —**de·cri·al** *n* —**de·cri·er** *n*

de·crypt /dee krípt/ (**-crypt·ed, -crypt·ing, -crypts**) *vt* same as **decode** (senses 1, 3) [Mid-20C. < DE- + CRYPTOGRAM] —**de·cryp·tion** *n*

de·cu·bi·tus /di kyóobitəss/ *n* the position of a person's body when he or she is lying down, usually on the front, back, or side (*technical*) [Late 19C. < modern Latin < Latin *decumbere* (see DECUMBENT)] —**de·cu·bi·tal** *adj*

de·cu·bi·tus ul·cer *n* MED same as **bedsore** (*technical*)

de·cum·bent /di kúmbənt/ *adj* **1.** describes plants that lie along the ground but have a tip growing upward **2.** describes hair or bristles that lie or grow flat along a surface [Early 17C. < Latin *decumbent*, present participle of *decumbere* "lie down" < *cubare* "lie down"] —**de·cum·bence** *n* —**de·cum·bent·ly** *adv*

de·cu·ri·on /di kyóoree ən/ *n* **1.** in ancient Rome, an officer in command of ten soldiers **2.** a council member in the Roman Empire [14C. < Latin *decurion-* < *decuria* (see DECURY), after *centurion*]

de·cur·rent /di kúr ənt/ *adj* describes plant leaves that curve down at the edges, or trees with a rounded shape [15C. < Latin *decurrent-*, present participle of *decurrere* "run down" < *currere* "run"] —**de·cur·rent·ly** *adv*

de·cur·y /dékyəree/ (*plural* **-ies**) *n* in ancient Rome, a company of ten soldiers [Mid-16C. < Latin *decuria* < *decem* "ten," after *centuria* "century"]

de·cus·sate /di kú sàyt, dékə sàyt/ *adj* **1.** having the shape of a cross **2.** describes leaves that form pairs opposite each other and at right angles to the pair above and the pair below, as in the horse chestnut [Early 19C. < Latin *decussatus*, past participle of *decussare* "divide crosswise" < *decussis*, the numeral ten (written "X") < *decem* "ten" + *assis*, a coin] —**de·cus·sate·ly** *adv* —**dec·us·sa·tion** /dèkə sáysh'n, deè kə-/ *n*

de·dal *adj, n* another spelling of **daedal** (*literary*)

de·dans /də daáN/ *n* (*plural same*) in court tennis, the open end of the court just behind the serving area where spectators can watch the match ■ *npl* the spectators who watch from the dedans [Early 18C. < French, "inside, interior"]

Ded·ham /déddəm/ town in eastern Massachusetts, on the southern bank of the Charles River, southwest of Boston. It was settled in 1635. Population: 23,378 (2002 estimate).

ded·i·cate /déddi kàyt/ (**-cat·ed, -cat·ing, -cates**) *vt* **1.** **DEVOTE ATTENTION TO SOMETHING** to spend time or energy doing something **2.** **COMMIT YOURSELF TO SOMETHING** to commit yourself or your life to something **3.** **ADDRESS WORK OF ART TO SOMEBODY** to associate a book, piece of music, or other art form with somebody as a token of friendship or esteem or as an acknowledgment of help received **4.** **PLAY MUSIC ADDRESSED TO SOMEBODY** to play a piece of music, or request the playing of a piece of music, as a tribute, especially on the radio **5.** **SET SOMETHING ASIDE FOR PURPOSE** to set something aside for a particular purpose ○ *an entire TV series dedicated to birds* **6.** **SET SOMETHING APART AS HOLY** to set something apart for a sacred purpose or to the memory of a holy person, saint, or god, especially in a ceremony for this purpose ○ *"We cannot dedicate – we cannot consecrate – we cannot hallow – this ground. The brave men...who struggled here have consecrated it."* (Abraham Lincoln, *Gettysburg Address*; November 19, 1863) [15C. < Latin *dedicat-*, past participle of *dedicare* "consecrate" < *dicare* "proclaim"] —**ded·i·ca·tee** /dèddi kay teé/ *n* —**ded·i·ca·tive** *adj* —**ded·i·ca·tor** *n*

ded·i·cat·ed /déddi kàytəd/ *adj* **1.** wholeheartedly devoted or committed to a goal, cause, or job **2.** designed to carry out only one task, or set aside for a specific purpose ○ *relayed via a dedicated satellite link* —**ded·i·cat·ed·ly** *adv*

ded·i·cat·ed line *n* a telephone line assigned to a designated user, usually to provide a permanent connection to the Internet

ded·i·ca·tion /dèddi káysh'n/ *n* **1.** **DEVOTION** the quality of being devoted or committed to something ○ *her dedication to duty* **2.** **INSCRIPTION** a short printed text at the beginning of a written or musical work associating it with somebody esteemed by the author **3.** **PIECE OF MUSIC** a piece of music played or requested as a tribute, especially on the radio **4.** **SETTING ASIDE** an act of setting something aside for a purpose, often in a special ceremony —**ded·i·ca·tion·al** *adj*

de·dif·fer·en·ti·a·tion /deè diffə renshee áysh'n/ *n* BIOL same as **anaplasia**

de·duce /di dóoss/ (**-duced, -duc·ing, -duc·es**) *vt* **1.** to come to a conclusion, often without all the necessary or relevant information, but using what is known in a logical way **2.** to come to a conclusion by inference from a general principle [15C. < Latin *deducere* "lead out" < *ducere* "to lead"] —**de·duc·i·ble** *adj*

SYNONYMS ***deduce, infer, assume, reason, conclude, work out, figure out***

CORE MEANING: to reach a logical conclusion on the basis of information

deduce to come to a conclusion, often without all the necessary or relevant information, but using what is known in a logical way ○ *While it is relatively easy to deduce a cause from an effect, it is more difficult to predict effects from causes.* ○ *It didn't take a rocket scientist to deduce that they were having an affair.* **infer** to come to a conclusion or form an opinion about something on the basis of evidence or reasoning ○ *It has been inferred from his poetry that he was homosexual.* ○ *Negligence may be inferred from the fact that the product left the manufacturer in a defective state.* **assume** to accept something as true without checking or confirming it ○ *She had always assumed that her mother was born in Paris.* ○ *He could reasonably have assumed from what was said that his employment prospects were good.* **reason** to consider information and use it to reach a conclusion in a logical way ○ *Scott reasoned that if Annabel were having a heart attack, she wouldn't be able to talk on the telephone.* ○ *Either, he reasoned, there was no burglar, or else the burglar was not interested in diamonds.* **conclude** to form an opinion or make a logical judgment about something after considering everything known about it ○ *The report concluded that a world recession was unlikely.* ○ *They were forced to conclude from the evidence that the case had been mishandled.* **work out** to solve a problem or find an answer to a question by reasoning or calculation ○ *Try and work out what the poem is about.* ○ *It took me a long time to work out the* *answers in the math section* **figure out** to find a solution or reach a conclusion by careful thought or reasoning ○ *Your task is to figure out what this answer means in terms of likely delay.* ○ *I can't figure out why he got into foreign investment.*

de·duct /di dúkt/ (**-duct·ed, -duct·ing, -ducts**) *vt* to subtract an amount for some purpose [15C. < Latin *deduct-*, past participle of *deducere* (see DEDUCE)]

de·duct·i·ble /di dúktəb'l/ *n* **UNINSURED AMOUNT** an agreed amount that must be paid by an insured person making a claim against an insurance policy before an insurer will pay any compensation ○ *a $500 deductible* ■ *adj* **1. ALLOWABLE AGAINST TAX** allowed by tax authorities as a legitimate expense not subject to tax **2. LIABLE TO DEDUCTION** capable of being, or liable to be, subtracted from something for some purpose —**de·duct·i·bil·i·ty** /di dùktə bíllətee/ *n*

de·duc·tion /di dúksh'n/ *n* **1. AMOUNT DEDUCTED** an amount that is subtracted from something, especially as an allowance against tax **2. SUBTRACTION OF AMOUNT** the act of subtracting an amount for a purpose **3. CONCLUSION DRAWN** a conclusion drawn from available information **4. DRAWING CONCLUSION** the process of drawing a conclusion from available information **5.** LOGIC **LOGICAL CONCLUSION** a conclusion reached by applying the rules of logic to a premise **6.** LOGIC **REASONING** the forming of conclusions by applying the rules of logic to a premise

de·duc·tive /di dúktiv/ *adj* based on logical or reasonable deduction ○ *deductive reasoning* —**de·duc·tive·ly** *adv*

deed /deed/ *n* **1. SOMETHING DONE** an intentional act ○*"The last temptation is the greatest treason / To do the right deed for the wrong reason."* (T. S. Eliot, *Murder in the Cathedral*; 1935) **2. DOCUMENT** a signed document that outlines the terms of an agreement, especially one that details a change in ownership of property **3.** LAW same as **title deed** ■ **deeds** *npl* **ACTIONS** action in general, especially as contrasted with speech ■ *vt* (**deed·ed, deed·ing, deeds**) LAW **TRANSFER PROPERTY TO SOMEBODY** to sign over or transfer something, especially real estate, to another person ○ *deeded her cabin to her grandson* [Old English *dēd* < Germanic, "a doing" < Indo-European]

deed·ed /déedəd/ *adj* associated with a deed that shows clear ownership ○ *a ranch consisting of 640 deeded acres*

dee·jay /dée jày/ *n* same as **DJ** (sense 1) (*informal*) [Mid-20C. Respelling] —**dee·jay** *vi*

deem /deem/ (**deemed, deem·ing, deems**) *vt* to judge or consider something in a particular light (*formal; often used in the passive*) ○ *a plan that was deemed impractical from the very start* [Old English *dēman* < Germanic, "to judge"]

de·em·pha·size /dee émfə sìz/ *vt* to make something seem or be less important or central —**de·em·pha·sis** /dee émfəssiss/ *n*

de·en·er·gize /dee énnər jìz/ *v* **1.** *vt* to cut off an electrical circuit from its source of power **2.** *vti* to have less energy or vitality, or cause somebody to have less energy or vitality —**de·en·er·gi·za·tion** /dee ènnərji záysh'n/ *n*

deep /deep/ *adj* **1. DOWN FROM SURFACE** extending from a surface downward or inward ○ *very deep mud* ○ *a deep wound* **2. FAR FROM TOP TO BOTTOM** extending a long way from top to bottom ○ *a deep well* ○*"The deep dark-shining / Pacific leans on the land."* (Robinson Jeffers, *Night*; 1925) **3. FAR FROM FRONT TO BACK** extending a long way from front to back ○ *a cupboard with deep shelves* **4. FAR FROM EDGE** extending a long way from a surface or boundary inward ○ *deep woods* **5. MADE UP OF UNITS** standing or lining up in a particular number of rows ○ *people six deep on the sidewalk* **6. FAR DOWN OR IN** relatively far down, in, or inside something ○ *a nagging pain deep inside his chest* **7. COMING FROM OR REACHING INSIDE BODY** coming from or reaching far down inside the body ○ *take a deep breath* **8. LOW IN PITCH** low in pitch and rounded in tone ○ *a deep booming voice* **9. DARK IN COLOR** relatively dark, rich, or intense in color ○ *deep purple* **10. EXTREME** extreme, severe, or intense ○ *deep suspicion* ○ *deep discounts* **11. PROFOUND** intellectually profound ○ *no evidence of deep thinking* ■ *adj, adv* **1.** SPORTS **NEAR OWN GOAL** in sports such as football, nearer to the goal a team is defending than the goal it is attacking ○ *Chicago played with two deep defenders.* ○ *deep in their own territory* **2.** BASEBALL **NEAR BOUNDARY** in baseball, playing or played near the boundary of the playing area, farther from home plate or one of the bases than is usual ○ *a fly ball to deep left field* ■ *adv* **FAR** far, especially from a surface or point of entry ○ *The expedition went deep into the jungle.* ■ *n* **1. OCEAN** the ocean depths **2. INTENSE PART** the middle or most intense part of something (*literary*) ○ *the deep of night* [Old English *dēop* < Indo-European, "deep, hollow"] —**deep·ness** *n* ◇ **deep down (inside)** in your innermost being ◇ **deep in something** completely overwhelmed by or absorbed in something ○ *deep in a new novel* ○ *She sat silent, deep in thought.* ◇ **in deep** very involved

deep-dis·count bond *n* a bond sold at a large discount because it bears little or no interest although it provides a capital gain on redemption

deep-dish *adj* baked in a deep dish and so thicker than normal ○ *deep-dish pizza*

deep-dyed *adj* **1.** describes fabric that has been dyed with a concentrated fade-resistant dye **2.** same as **dyed-in-the-wool** (sense 1)

deep·en /déepən/ (**-ened, -en·ing, -ens**) *vti* **1.** to become deep or deeper, or make something deep or deeper **2.** to become more intense, or make something more intense ○ *the recession was deepening* —**deep·en·er** *n*

deep end *n* the part of a swimming pool, lake, or other body of water where the water is deepest ◇ **be thrown in at the deep end** to have to learn something new or difficult with very little experience or warning ◇ **go off the deep end 1.** to fly into a rage or lose your emotional equilibrium **2.** to behave irrationally (*informal*)

deep-fat fry·er *n* same as **deep fryer**

deep-freeze *vt* **1. FREEZE SOMETHING QUICKLY** to freeze something such as food quickly in order to prolong its freshness or nutritional value **2. KEEP SOMETHING VERY COLD** to store something at very low temperatures **3. SUSPEND ACTIVITY** to put off or suspend activity (*informal*) —**deep-fro·zen** *adj*

deep-fry *vt* to cook food in fat or oil that is deep enough to cover the food completely —**deep-fried** *adj*

deep fry·er *n* an electrical appliance for deep-frying food

deep·ly /déeplee/ *adv* **1.** profoundly or intensely ○ *deeply offended* **2.** far down inside ○ *breathe deeply* ○ *deeply felt pain*

deep-root·ed *adj* **1.** firmly held or established, usually over a long period of time, and so unlikely to change **2.** having roots that grow deep in the soil

deep-sea *adj* relating to the deep waters of the ocean far away from land

deep-seat·ed *adj* firmly established and difficult to change or eradicate ○ *deep-seated fear*

deep-set *adj* describes eyes with deep sockets

deep six *n* the disposal or destruction of something (*slang*) [< naval slang, "burial at sea," origin ?]

deep-six (**deep-sixed, deep-six·ing, deep-six·es**) *vt* to dispose of or destroy something (*slang*)

Deep South /dèep sówth/ a part of the southeastern United States, usually considered to comprise Alabama, Georgia, Louisiana, Mississippi, and South Carolina, regarded as the heartland of traditional Southern culture

deep space *n* space beyond the Earth's gravitational influence or beyond the orbit of the Moon

deep struc·ture *n* the underlying form of a language, conceived as containing all the information needed to make any sentence in that language

deep vein throm·bo·sis *n* a potentially fatal condition in which a blood clot forms in a vein or artery and may partially or completely block blood flow. It is often the result of long periods of immobility.

deep-wa·ter *adj* **1.** describes a port or anchorage that is deep enough to accommodate large oceangoing vessels **2.** *regional* designed or trained to travel on the oceans

REGIONAL NOTE In the sense "seagoing," as in *deep-water ship* or *deep-water sailor*, ***deep-water*** is most commonly found in coastal Maine but is also recorded in coastal Massachusetts and New York.

deer /deer/ (*plural same*) *n* an animal distinguished by the branched antlers on males. More than forty species of deer exist, of different sizes and with different markings, and they are found wild on all continents except Australia and Antarctica. Family: Cervidae. [Old English *dēor* "animal" < Germanic, "breathing creature" < Indo-European, "breath, vapor"]

SPELLCHECK See ***dear.***

Deere /deer/, **John** (1804–86) US inventor. He founded a company that manufactured agricultural equipment, including a revolutionary steel plow.

Deer·field Beach /deer feeld-/ city in southeastern Florida on the coast of the Atlantic Ocean. Population: 65,635 (2002 estimate).

deer fly *n* a biting fly that infests deer and other animals, sucking blood and spreading the infectious disease tularemia. It also delivers a stinging bite to humans. Genus: *Chrysops.*

deer·grass /deér gràss/ (*plural same*) *n* a perennial flowering plant that grows in thick tufts. Native to: temperate peat bogs. Latin name: *Trichophorum caespitosum.*

deer·hound /deér hòwnd/ *n* a large long-legged dog with a very shaggy coat, belonging to a breed developed in Scotland as a hunting dog from a Mediterranean strain of greyhound

deer lick *n* a naturally occurring or artificial salty patch of ground where deer come to lick salt

deer mouse *n* a mouse that lives in natural surroundings rather than buildings, often making its nest in a tree or tree stump. Native to: North and Central America. Genus: *Peromyscus.*

Deer Park /deér paárk/ city in southwestern Texas, on Buffalo Bayou near Galveston Bay. It is a western suburb of Houston. Population: 28,992 (2002 estimate).

deer·skin /deér skìn/ *n* the treated hide of a deer used as a fabric

deer·stalk·er /deér stàwkər/, **deer·stalk·er hat** *n* a tweed hat with visors at the front and back and earflaps that can either be tied together on its crown or fastened under the chin

deer·stalk·ing /deér stàwking/ *n* the activity of hunting wild deer by stealthily following them on foot

deer tick *n* a tick that is a parasite of humans and other animals and transmits the bacterium that causes Lyme disease. Latin name: *Ioxides dammini.*

de·es·ca·late /dee éskə làyt/ *vt* to reduce the level or intensity of a difficult or dangerous situation —**de·es·ca·la·tion** /dee èskə láysh'n/ *n*

deet /deet/ *n* an oily colorless chemical that is the active ingredient in the most widely used insect repellents applied to the skin. Formula: $C_{12}H_{17}NO$. [Mid-20C. Contraction and alteration of DIETHYL TOLUAMIDE]

def. *abbr* **1.** LAW defendant **2.** MIL, SPORTS, LAW defense **3.** FIN deferred **4.** GRAM definite **5.** LING definition

de·face /di fáyss/ (**-faced, -fac·ing, -fac·es**) *vt* to spoil the appearance of something, especially intentionally [14C. < French *défacer* < *face* (see FACE)] —**de·face·a·ble** *adj* —**de·face·ment** *n* —**de·fac·er** *n*

de fac·to /di fáktō, day-/ *adv* in fact, whether with a legal right or not ■ *adj* acting or existing in fact but without legal sanction ○ *the de facto rules of the country* [Early 17C. < Latin, "in fact," literally "from what is done"]

de·fal·cate /di fál kàyt, -fáwl-, déff'l-/ (**-cat·ed, -cat·ing, -cates**) *vt* to misuse something, especially money or property, that belongs to somebody else and is held in trust [Mid-16C. < medieval Latin *defalcat-*, past participle of *defalcare* "deduct" < Latin *falx* "scythe"] —**de·fal·ca·tion** /dèe fal káysh'n, -fawl-, déff'l-/ *n* —**de·fal·ca·tor** *n*

de·fame /di fáym/ (**-famed, -fam·ing, -fames**) *vt* to attack somebody or somebody's reputation, character, or good name by making slanderous or libelous statements [14C. Via Old French *deffamer* < Latin *diffamare* "spread about as an insulting report" < *fama* "talk, report, reputation"] —**def·a·ma·tion** /dèffə máysh'n/ *n* —**de·fam·a·to·ry** /di fámmə tàwree/ *adj* —**de·fam·er** *n*

SYNONYMS See *malign*.

de·fang /dee fáng/ (**-fanged, -fang·ing, -fangs**) *vt* **1.** to weaken the power or harmful effect of something **2.** to remove the fangs from a snake or other animal

de·fat /dee fát/ (**-fat·ted, -fat·ting, -fats**) *vt* to remove the fat or fats from something

de·fault /di fáwlt/ *n* **1.** PRESET OPTION an option that will automatically be selected by a computer if the user does not choose one **2.** FAILURE TO DO SOMETHING a failure to meet an obligation, especially a financial one **3.** LAW NONAPPEARANCE IN COURT a failure to make a summoned court appearance **4.** SPORTS NONPARTICIPATION IN COMPETITION a failure to appear for or complete a competition ■ *vi* (**-fault·ed, -fault·ing, -faults**) **1.** FAIL TO PAY DEBT to fail to pay a debt or other financial obligation **2.** LAW FAIL TO APPEAR IN COURT to fail to make an appearance in court although summoned to do so **3.** SPORTS FAIL TO COMPETE to fail to appear for a game or contest **4.** COMPUT USE PRESET OPTION to use a device, command, or file when no other is specified [13C. < Old French *defaute*, past participle of *defaillir* "fail" < *faillir* (see FAIL)] ◇ **by default 1.** having come about because some other thing, often something expected, did not happen **2.** having come about because somebody failed to appear as expected **3.** according to a computer's preset configuration ◇ **in default of something** *or* **somebody** because of a lack of something or the absence of somebody (*formal*)

de·fault·er /di fáwltər/ *n* **1.** NONPAYER a debtor who defaults on a financial obligation **2.** LAW ABSENTEE FROM COURT somebody who fails to respond to a court summons **3.** SPORTS ABSENTEE FROM COMPETITION a person or team failing to appear for a game or contest

de·fea·sance /di féez'nss/ *n* LAW **1.** ACT OF MAKING SOMETHING VOID the declaration of something as null and void **2.** LEGAL CLAUSE a clause in a legal document that states that, in the event of a condition being fulfilled, the document will become null and void **3.** LEGAL DOCUMENT a document containing a defeasance [15C. < Old French *defesance* < *defaire* < medieval Latin *disfacere* (see DEFEAT)]

de·fea·si·ble /di féezəb'l/ *adj* **1.** capable of being made or declared null and void **2.** liable to be forfeited —**de·fea·si·bil·i·ty** /di fèezə bíllətee/ *n* —**de·fea·si·ble·ness** *n*

de·feat /di féet/ *vt* (**-feat·ed, -feat·ing, -feats**) **1.** BEAT COMPETITOR to win a victory over a competitor, e.g., in sports or business **2.** WIN VOTE to win a victory over another person or group in a debate or vote **3.** BEAT ENEMY to win a victory over enemy forces in a battle or war **4.** CAUSE FAILURE OF SOMETHING to cause something to fail or to fall short of realization ○ *The truck defeated all my attempts to get it to start.* **5.** BAFFLE SOMEBODY to leave somebody in a baffled or uncomprehending state ○ *His logic defeats me.* **6.** LAW MAKE SOMETHING VOID to make or declare something null and void ■ *n* **1.** FACT OF LOSING TO OPPONENT the fact or an instance of losing to an enemy in battle or an opponent in a competition ○ *the home team's humiliating defeat* **2.** FAILURE failure to win or to realize a goal ○ *She refused to admit defeat and appealed.* [14C. Via Anglo-Norman *defeter* "disfigure, destroy" < medieval Latin *disfacere* "unmake" < Latin *facere* "do, make"] —**de·feat·er** *n* ◇ **defeat the object** *or* **purpose of something** make the desired outcome less likely or possible while appearing to have the intent of pursuing it

SYNONYMS *defeat, beat, conquer, vanquish, overcome, triumph, thrash, trounce*

CORE MEANING: to win a victory

defeat to win a victory over an enemy or competitor, or to cause somebody or something to fail ○ *The Spartans succeeded in defeating their enemies.* ○ *She played a major role in defeating the proposal.* **beat** to defeat somebody in a contest, or to succeed in the face of difficulty ○ *"I am the champion of the world and will beat him again," he said.* ○ *After a paralyzing accident a month ago, his goal is to walk again, though he realizes he will have to beat some big odds to do it.* **conquer** to defeat and take control of a people in war, or to succeed despite difficulty ○ *their vow to retake their conquered land* ○ *He's already conquered his toughest challenge.* **vanquish** to defeat somebody decisively in a battle or competition ○ *The Patriots emerge victorious and the Bears are once again vanquished.* **overcome** to defeat somebody or something, especially in a conflict or competition ○ *The French quickly overcame the opposing forces* ○ *The home team overcame their longtime rivals to move to the top of the league* **triumph** to be successful, especially against an adversary or against difficult odds ○ *Foreknowledge will help a wise general to triumph over his enemies.* ○ *It seemed that scientific investigation was triumphing over ignorance.* **thrash** to defeat a person or team decisively, especially in a sports competition ○ *The Red Sox, who were thrashed in the last game by the Yankees, took the lead.* **trounce** to defeat an opponent or team convincingly ○ *In the first round match the Japanese player fired powerful and well-placed ground strokes to trounce the American veteran.*

de·feat·ist /di féetist/ *adj* showing a tendency to expect failure or accept it too readily ■ *n* somebody who consistently expects or accepts failure —**de·feat·ism** *n*

def·e·cate /déffə kàyt/ (**-cat·ed, -cat·ing, -cates**) *v* **1.** *vi* to expel feces from the bowel through the rectum (*formal or technical*) **2.** *vt* to remove impurities from a solution, especially a solution that contains sugar [15C. < Latin *defaecat-*, past participle of Latin *defaecare* "remove waste" < *faex* "dregs, waste"] —**def·e·ca·tion** /dèffə káysh'n/ *n* —**def·e·ca·tor** *n*

de·fect *n* /dée fèkt, di fékt/ **1.** FLAW IN SOMETHING a physical problem in a machine, structure, or system, especially one that prevents it from functioning correctly **2.** INADEQUATE FEATURE a feature of something that is regarded as inadequate **3.** IMPERFECTION IN CRYSTAL an imperfection in the internal structure of a crystal, e.g., an atom of a different substance ■ *vi* /di fékt/ (**-fect·ed, -fect·ing, -fects**) **1.** REJECT HOMELAND to leave your native country or the country you are living in and refuse to return there, usually for political or moral reasons **2.** ABANDON ALLEGIANCE to abandon allegiance to a cause or party, especially when this also involves supporting something previously opposed [15C. < Latin *defect-*, past participle of *deficere* "be wanting, desert" < *facere* "do, make"] —**de·fec·tion** *n* —**de·fec·tor** *n*

SYNONYMS See *flaw*[1].

de·fec·tive /di féktiv/ *adj* **1.** FAULTY imperfect or faulty, so not functioning properly or at all **2.** OFFENSIVE TERM an offensive term that means having learning difficulties or problems in coping with emotions (*insult*) **3.** GRAM INCOMPLETE lacking the usual or expected range of grammatical inflections ■ *n* OFFENSIVE TERM an offensive term for somebody who has learning difficulties or problems in coping with emotions (*insult*) —**de·fec·tive·ly** *adv* —**de·fec·tive·ness** *n*

USAGE defective or **deficient**? ***Defective*** is normally used in reference to processes, machines, or to other functional things such as the human senses: *If the workmanship is defective, they'll replace the shoes with a new pair. Artillery officers sometimes have defective hearing.* ***Deficient*** is used to describe things that lack a quality, element, or ingredient, without this amounting to actual failure to work or function: *Her voice is beautiful but a little deficient in power. Their diet is deficient in vitamin D.*

de·fem·i·nize /dee fémmə nīz/ (**-nized, -niz·ing, -niz·es**) *vt* to remove or diminish characteristics of somebody or something that are traditionally regarded as associated with women or girls

de·fence *n* Can, UK spelling of **defense**

de·fend /di fénd/ (**-fend·ed, -fend·ing, -fends**) *v* **1.** *vt* PROTECT SOMEBODY OR SOMETHING to protect somebody or something from attack, harm, or danger **2.** *vti* REPRESENT SOMEBODY IN COURT to represent and speak on behalf of an accused person in court **3.** *vt* SUPPORT POSITION to offer support for something or somebody, especially by arguing against the objections or criticism of others **4.** *vi* RESIST OPPONENT in sports, to resist the attacks of an opposing player or team and try to prevent them from scoring **5.** *vt* TRY TO KEEP TITLE to try to retain a title, especially a sporting one, by competing in the relevant competitions **6.** *vt* PROTECT GOAL in sports, to protect the goal and goal area from the attacks of the opposition [13C. Via French < Latin *defendere* "ward off" < Indo-European, "strike, kill"] —**de·fend·a·ble** *adj*

SYNONYMS See *safeguard*.

de·fen·dant /di féndənt/ *n* a person or company required to answer charges in a court

~~**defendent**~~ incorrect spelling of **defendant**

de·fend·er /di féndər/ *n* **1.** *UK* DEFENSIVE PLAYER in sports, somebody whose role is to try to prevent the opposition from scoring or getting into a scoring position **2.** SUPPORTER somebody who supports or justifies something or somebody **3.** PROTECTOR a protector of a person or place against attack **4.** HOLDER OF TITLE the holder of a title that is challenged recurrently

De·fend·er of the Faith *n* a title given by Pope Leo X in 1521 to King Henry VIII and held by English and British monarchs ever since

de·fend·ing /di fénding/ *adj* holding a title that is subject to recurring competition ○ *the defending champions*

de·fen·es·trate /dee fénnə strȧyt/ (**-trat·ed, -trat·ing, -trates**) *vt* to throw something or somebody out of a window (*formal or humorous*) [Early 17C. < DE- + Latin *fenestra* "window"] —**de·fen·es·tra·tion** /dee fènnə stráysh'n/ *n*

de·fense /di fénss/ *n* **1.** PROTECTION the protection of something, especially from attack by an enemy **2.** SOMETHING THAT PROTECTS a method or object for protecting something ○ *Prevention is our strongest defense against the disease.* **3.** ARMED FORCES a country's armed forces **4.** JUSTIFICATION an excuse or justification for something ○ *spoke in defense of the motion* **5.** LAW REASONS OFFERED the set of reasons that a defendant offers in court in denial of a charge **6.** LAW DEFENDANT'S CASE the facts and their presentation as they relate to the defendant in a court case **7.** LAW COUNSEL AND DEFENDANT the counsel and the defendant in a court case **8.** /dée fènss/ SPORTS DEFENSIVE PLAY in sports, the method or maneuvers that prevent the other team from scoring **9.** /dée fènss/ SPORTS DEFENSIVE PLAYERS the sports team members who play defense ■ **de·fens·es** *npl* **1.** PROTECTIVE QUALITIES the qualities of the body or mind that protect somebody from attack, injury, or illness **2.** FORTIFICATIONS the fortifications that protect a place from enemies or the forces of nature [14C. < Old French *defens(e)* < Latin *defens-*, past participle of *defendere* (see DEFEND)]

de·fense·less /di fénssləss/ *adj* lacking any form of protection and therefore vulnerable ■ *npl* people who are unable to defend themselves and their interests ○ *working as a shield for the defenseless* —**de·fense·less·ly** *adv* —**de·fense·less·ness** *n*

de·fense·man /dée fenss màn/ (*plural* **-men** /-mèn/) *n* a team member who plays a defensive position, especially in hockey

de·fense mech·a·nism *n* **1.** any means of avoiding emotional distress, destructive impulses, or a threat to self-esteem, especially the suppression of unwanted thoughts or memories **2.** a natural protective response to danger or attack used by an organism, e.g., when faced with a predator or invaded by a disease agent

de·fense-mind·ed *adj* giving emphasis to building a team with strong defensive skills

de·fen·si·ble /di fénssəb'l/ *adj* **1.** capable of being protected from attack **2.** able to be explained, justified, or excused —**de·fen·si·bil·i·ty** /di fènssə bíllətee/ *n* —**de·fen·si·ble·ness** *n* —**de·fen·si·bly** *adv*

de·fen·sin /dee fénssin/ *n* a peptide in a set of three present in human white blood cells that appear to play a role in the prevention or elimination of infection

de·fen·sive /di fénssiv/ *adj* **1.** QUICK TO JUSTIFY aiming to deflect or avoid perceived criticism **2.** SERVING TO PROTECT designed for protection or defense **3.** FAVORING DEFENSE AS PLAYING STRATEGY concentrating more on preventing an opponent from gaining an advantage than on scoring **4.** OF DEFENSE TEAM relating to the team that plays defense, especially in football —**de·fen·sive·ness** *n* ◇ **on the defensive 1.** expecting criticism or aggression and prepared to respond **2.** having assumed a position that indicates readiness to play defensively

de·fen·sive·ly /di fénssivlee/ *adv* **1.** in a defensive way **2.** as regards defense, especially defensive play ○ *Defensively they played well, but they didn't manage to score.*

de·fen·sive med·i·cine *n* medical treatment that involves carrying out extensive diagnostic testing in order to minimize the chances of a patient's suing the doctor or hospital for negligence

de·fer[1] /di fúr/ (**-ferred, -fer·ring, -fers**) *vti* **1.** to put something off until a later time **2.** to allow somebody to postpone conscription into the armed forces [14C. < French *différer* "put aside, differ"] —**de·fer·ment** *n* —**de·fer·ra·ble** *adj* —**de·fer·ral** *n* —**de·fer·rer** *n*

de·fer[2] /di fúr/ (**-ferred, -fer·ring, -fers**) *vi* to give way to, and usually acknowledge the merit of, somebody else's judgment, opinion, wishes, or action ○ *I defer to your superior knowledge.* [15C. Via French < Latin *deferre* "carry away" < *ferre* "carry" (see FERTILE)] —**de·fer·rer** *n*

~~defered~~ incorrect spelling of **deferred**

def·er·ence /défførənss/ *n* **1.** polite respect, especially putting another person's interests first **2.** submission to the judgment, opinion, or wishes of another person [Mid-17C. < DEFER[2]] ◇ **in deference to** out of respect or courtesy to somebody or something

def·er·ent[1] /déffərənt/ *adj* same as **deferential** [Early 19C. < DEFER[2], DEFERENCE]

def·er·ent[2] /déffərənt/ *adj* describes a duct, nerve, or vessel in the body that is capable of carrying impulses or fluid away, down, or outward [Early 17C. Via French < Latin *deferent-*, present participle of *deferre* (see DEFER[2])]

def·er·en·tial /dèffə rénsh'l/ *adj* showing or expressing polite respect or courtesy [Early 19C. < DEFERENCE] —**def·er·en·tial·ly** *adv*

de·ferred an·nu·i·ty /di fúrd-/ *n* an investment that does not pay out until at least one year after the final premium has been paid

de·ferred month *n* a more distant month in which futures or options trading is taking place, as opposed to a month that is nearer in time

de·ferred sen·tence *n* a sentence that is not passed until a specific period has elapsed in order to allow the court time to assess the behavior of the convicted person

de·fer·ves·cence /dee fər véss'nss/ *n* **1.** a decrease in a fever **2.** the stage of an illness during which fever subsides [Early 18C. < Latin *defervescere* "stop boiling" < *fervere* "be hot, boil"] —**de·fer·vesce** *vti* —**de·fer·ves·cent** *adj*

~~defferred~~ incorrect spelling of **deferred**

de·fi·ance /di fī ənss/ *n* open, bold, or hostile refusal to obey or conform ◇ **in defiance of 1.** with complete disregard for a rule, law, or person in authority **2.** notwithstanding a rule or expectation

De·fi·ance /di fī ənss/ city in northwestern Ohio, southwest of Toledo and northwest of Lima. Population: 16,274 (2002 estimate).

de·fi·ant /di fī ənt/ *adj* **1.** deliberately and openly disobedient **2.** tending to confront and challenge [Late 16C. < French *défiant*, present participle of *défier* < assumed Vulgar Latin *disfidare* "renounce your faith"] —**de·fi·ant·ly** *adv*

de·fib·ril·late /dee fíbbrə làyt, -fībrə-/ (**-lat·ed, -lat·ing, -lates**) *vt* to apply an electric shock to the chest, or sometimes directly to the heart itself, in order to restore a regular heartbeat after a critically irregular beat has developed —**de·fib·ril·la·tion** /dee fibbrə láysh'n, -fībrə-/ *n*

de·fib·ril·la·tor /dee fíbbrə làytər, -fībrə-/ *n* a machine that administers a controlled electric shock to the chest or heart to correct a critically irregular heartbeat that cannot drive the circulation

de·fi·cien·cy /di físh'nsee/ (*plural* **-cies**) *n* **1.** SHORTAGE an inadequate supply of something necessary, especially a nutrient **2.** POOR PROVISION a weakness in the provision or performance of something ○ *serious deficiencies in the provision of cleaning services* **3.** AMOUNT LACKING the amount by which something falls short of being complete

SYNONYMS See *lack*.

de·fi·cien·cy dis·ease *n* a disease resulting from lack of a nutrient or other substance required by a human being or other animal or a plant for growth, development, or general health. The deficiency may be caused either by an inadequate supply of the required substance or by an inability to process it.

de·fi·cient /di físh'nt/ *adj* **1.** lacking a particular quality, element, or ingredient, especially one that is expected or necessary ○ *deficient in tact* **2.** inadequate or not good enough [Late 16C. < Latin *deficient-*, present participle of *deficere* "leave undone, fail" < *facere* "do, make"] —**de·fi·cient·ly** *adv*

USAGE See *defective*.

def·i·cit /déffissit/ *n* **1.** the amount by which expenditures exceed income or budget **2.** the amount by which a total is less than it should be [Late 18C. < French *déficit* < Latin *deficit* "it is lacking" < *deficere* (see DEFICIENT)]

SYNONYMS See *lack*.

def·i·cit fi·nanc·ing *n* the practice of deliberately allowing government spending to exceed its revenues in order to try to boost economic activity and lower unemployment

def·i·cit spend·ing *n* government spending that is financed by borrowing money rather than through money raised by taxation

def·i·lade /déffi làyd, -laad/ *n* fortifications or protection against enemy gunfire that might be aimed at a line of troops ■ *vt* (**-lad·ed, -lad·ing, -lades**) to set up protective fortifications to protect troops or a position [Early 19C. < French *défiler* (see DEFILE[2]), after ENFILADE]

de·file[1] /di fīl/ (**-filed, -fil·ing, -files**) *vt* **1.** CORRUPT SOMETHING to corrupt or ruin something (*formal*) **2.** DAMAGE REPUTATION to damage somebody's reputation or good name **3.** DESTROY SANCTITY OF SOMETHING to make a holy or sacred thing or place no longer fit for ceremonial use **4.** POLLUTE SOMETHING to make something dirty or polluted (*formal*) **5.** DEPRIVE WOMAN OF VIRGINITY to be the first man to have sexual intercourse with a woman, usually outside marriage (*archaic*) [14C. Alteration of French *defouler* "trample" < *fouler* "trample under foot"] —**de·file·ment** *n* —**de·fil·er** *n*

de·file[2] /di fīl/ *n* **1.** MOUNTAIN PASS a narrow pass between mountains **2.** PASSAGE a passage only wide enough for people to pass single-file ■ *vi* (**-filed, -fil·ing, -files**) MARCH SINGLE-FILE to march or go in single file, especially when the way is too narrow to march in any other formation [Late 17C. < French *défiler* "march in a line" < *file* (see FILE[1])]

~~definate~~ incorrect spelling of **definite**

~~definately~~ incorrect spelling of **definitely**

de·fine /di fīn/ (**-fined, -fin·ing, -fines**) *v* **1.** *vt* STATE SOMETHING to state or describe something exactly ○ *clearly defined objectives* **2.** *vt* CHARACTERIZE SOMEBODY OR SOMETHING to identify somebody or something by a distinctive characteristic quality or feature ○ *The age we live in is defined by a deep sense of uncertainty.* **3.** *vt* SHOW SOMETHING CLEARLY to show something clearly, especially in shape or outline (*usually passive*) ○ *The tire marks were clearly defined in the snow.* **4.** *vt* MARK LINE to mark a boundary, edge, or limit ○ *That row of trees defines the eastern boundary of the estate.* **5.** *vti* GIVE MEANING OF WORD to give the precise meaning of a word or expression [14C. Via French < Latin *definire* "limit, determine" < *finis* "final moment, end"] —**de·fin·a·bil·i·ty** /di fīnə bíllətee/ *n* —**de·fin·a·ble** *adj* —**de·fin·a·bly** *adv* —**de·fin·er** *n*

de·fin·i·en·dum /də finnee éndəm/ (*plural* **-da** /-də/) *n* the word or expression defined by a definition, e.g., in a dictionary or glossary (*technical*) [Late 19C. < Latin, "thing to be defined" < *definire* (see DEFINE)]

de·fin·i·ens /də fínnee ènz/ (*plural* **-en·tia** /də finnee énshə, -énshee ə/) *n* the words used to define a word or expression, e.g., in a dictionary or glossary (*technical*) [Late 19C. < medieval Latin, "something that defines" < present participle of Latin *definire* (see DEFINE)]

de·fin·ing /di fīning/ *adj* giving a distinctive character to something or encapsulating its character ○ *That was the defining act of his election campaign.*

def·i·nite /déffənit/ *adj* **1.** CLEAR precise and distinct ○ *a definite age range* ○ *the definite outline of a building amongst the trees* **2.** FIXED fixed, certain, and not to be altered ○ *Do we have a definite date for the meeting?* **3.** ABSOLUTELY SET ON SOMETHING certain about something and unlikely to have a change of mind ○ *I'm definite about this.* **4.** OBVIOUS unquestionable and unmistakable ○ *a definite turn for the better* **5.** BOT WITH TERMINAL FLOWER describes a flower head in which the first-formed flower is at the stalk's end with subsequent flowers developing lower down on one or both sides of the stalk [Mid-16C. < Latin *definitus*, past participle of *definire* (see DEFINE)] —**def·i·nite·ness** *n*

USAGE **definite** or **definitive**? ***Definite*** describes something as being distinct or precise without making any strong judgment about it: *He has definite ideas on the subject.* ***Definitive*** denotes something authoritative, conclusive, or decisive; it is therefore a more evaluative word: *She wrote the definitive book on the subject.*

def·i·nite ar·ti·cle *n* a word that designates a noun as being specific and identifiable, e.g., "the"

def·i·nite in·te·gral *n* a determination of the difference in values of an integral between two limits, expressed using symbols

def·i·nite·ly /déffənitlee/ *adv* **1.** CERTAINLY without a doubt ○ *He definitely had a Swedish accent.* **2.** FINALLY AND UNCHANGEABLY as a conclusion after some thought or hesitation ○ *Once she had definitely decided to go, she started packing.* **3.** EXACTLY in a precise way ○ *Without knowing definitely what it was, he just felt that something was wrong.* **4.** OBVIOUSLY in a distinct and unmistakable way ○ *Her attitude suddenly became more definitely critical.* **5.** ABSOLUTELY with no exceptions ○ *The sign read, "Definitely no admittance."* ■ *interj* YES used to say "yes" in an emphatic and enthusiastic way ○ *"Are you going to come to the party?" "Definitely!"*

def·i·ni·tion /dèffə nísh'n/ *n* **1.** MEANING OF WORD a brief precise statement of what a word or expression means, e.g., in a dictionary **2.** ACT OF DEFINING WORD the act or process of defining what a word or expression means, e.g., in writing a dictionary **3.** CLARIFICATION the act of describing or stating something clearly and unambiguously **4.** MEDIA, PHOTOGRAPHY CLARITY the degree of clarity of an image. It is related to the sharpness and degree of contrast in the image. **5.** EMBODIMENT OF SOMETHING somebody or something believed to represent or embody a particular idea or quality (*formal*) ○ *His behavior has always seemed to me the very definition of courtesy.* **6.** SHARPNESS OF SOUND the degree of distinctiveness of a sound [14C. Via French < Latin *definition-* < *definire* (see DEFINE)] —**def·i·ni·tion·al** *adj* ◇ **by definition** used to emphasize that somebody or something is considered to have a particular intrinsic quality

de·fin·i·tive /di fínnətiv/ *adj* **1.** CONCLUSIVE AND FINAL providing a final decision that will not be questioned or changed ○ *We need a definitive answer.* **2.** MOST AUTHORITATIVE recognized as being the most authoritative and of the highest standard ○ *the definitive study of the subject* **3.** STAMPS SOLD FOR LONG TIME describes postage stamps sold for an extended or indefinite period, often as part of a set sharing common design elements **4.** BIOL FULLY GROWN fully formed or completely developed ■ *n* STAMPS DEFINITIVE STAMP a postage stamp sold for an extended or indefinite period [14C. < French *définitif* < Latin *definire* (see DEFINE)] —**de·fin·i·tive·ly** *adv* —**de·fin·i·tive·ness** *n*

USAGE See *definite*.

de·fin·i·tive host *n* the plant or animal in or on which a parasitic organism reaches sexual maturity

~~definitly~~ incorrect spelling of **definitely**

def·la·grate /défflə gràyt/ (**-grat·ed, -grat·ing, -grates**) *vti* to burn violently, or make something burn violently (*technical*) [Early 17C. < Latin *deflagrat-*, past participle of *deflagrare* "burn up" < *flagrare* "burn"] —**def·la·gra·tion** /dèfflə gráysh'n/ *n*

de·flate /di fláyt/ (**-flat·ed, -flat·ing, -flates**) *v* **1.** *vti* LET AIR OUT to let out air or gas from an inflatable object with the result that it shrinks or collapses, or lose air or gas **2.** *vt* MAKE SOMEBODY LESS CONFIDENT to destroy somebody's confidence or make somebody less self-assured or conceited **3.** *vt* **DESTROY THEORY** to show that a theory or argument is wrong **4.** *vt* ECON **CAUSE DEFLATION IN ECONOMY** to bring about deflation in the economy or the money supply [Late 19C. < DE- + INFLATE] —**de·flat·ed** *adj* —**de·fla·tor** *n*

de·fla·tion /di fláysh'n/ *n* **1. COLLAPSE BECAUSE OF AIR LOSS** the release or escape of air or gas from something, resulting in its shrinking or collapsing **2. LOSS OF SELF-ESTEEM** a sudden loss of confidence, self-assurance, or conceit **3.** ECON **REDUCED ECONOMIC ACTIVITY** the reduction of general economic activity, including lower prices and a reduced supply of money and credit **4.** GEOL **EROSION** the erosion of land by wind

de·fla·tion·ar·y /di fláysh'n èrree/ *adj* **1.** undergoing or creating a lower level of general economic activity **2.** serving to reduce or destroy somebody else's self-assurance or confidence

de·fla·tion·ist /di fláysh'nist/ *adj* in favor of economic deflation —**de·fla·tion·ist** *n*

de·flect /di flékt/ (**-flect·ed, -flect·ing, -flects**) *v* **1.** *vti* **CHANGE COURSE** to change course because of hitting something, or change something's course by coming into contact with it ○ *The pitcher's arm deflected the ball into the outfield.* **2.** *vt* **DIRECT ATTENTION AWAY** to direct people's attention or criticism away from a subject or issue to something else **3.** *vt* **FORCE ALTERATION OF PLANS** to force somebody to change what he or she is doing or planning to do [Mid-16C. < Latin *deflectere* "bend away" < *flectere* "bend"] —**de·flect·a·ble** *adj* —**de·flec·tive** *adj* —**de·flec·tor** *n*

de·flec·tion /di fléksh'n/ *n* **1. CHANGE OF COURSE** a change of course that results from hitting somebody or something **2. AMOUNT SOMETHING DEFLECTS** the amount or distance by which something is deflected **3. ACT OF DIVERTING ATTENTION** the act of directing people's attention or criticism away from something **4. MOVEMENT OF NEEDLE AWAY FROM ZERO** a definite movement of the indicator on a measuring instrument **5.** ENG **MOVEMENT OF STRUCTURE UNDER LOAD** the movement of a structure or a part of a structure when it is bearing a load

de·flexed /di flékst/ *adj* describes petals or leaves that bend sharply downward [Late 18C. < Latin *deflexus*, past participle of *deflectere* (see DEFLECT)]

def·lo·ra·tion /dèfflə ráysh'n/ *n* an act of having sex with a woman and so ending her virginity (*literary*) [14C. Directly or via French < late Latin *defloration-* < *deflorare* (see DEFLOWER)]

de·flow·er /dee flówr/ (**-ered, -er·ing, -ers**) *vt* to have sex with a woman and so end her virginity (*literary*) [14C. Via Old French *deflourer* < late Latin *deflorare* < Latin *flos* "flower"] —**de·flow·er·er** *n*

de·fo·cus /dee fṓkəss/ *v* (**-cused, -cused** or **-cussed, -cus·ing** or **-cus·sing, -cus·es** or **-cus·ses**) **1.** *vt* **SOFTEN PICTURE** to soften or blur an image by focusing away from the exact plane of focus of the object in the image **2.** *vti* **STOP FOCUSING** to stop focusing on something, or cause the eyes to stop focusing on something ■ *n* **CONDITION OF DEFOCUSING** the condition or state caused by defocusing, e.g., the blurring of a photographic image

De·foe /də fṓ/, **Daniel** (1660?–1731) English novelist and journalist. His novels were among the earliest in the English language, and include *Robinson Crusoe* (1719) and *Moll Flanders* (1722). Born **Daniel Foe**

> "He bade me observe it, and I should always find, that the calamities of life were shared among the upper and lower part of mankind; but that the middle station had the fewest disasters."
> [Daniel Defoe, *Robinson Crusoe*; 1719]

de·fog /dee fáwg, -fóg/ (**-fogged, -fog·ging, -fogs**) *vti* **1.** to remove condensation from the windshield, mirror, and windows of a motor vehicle, or lose condensation **2.** to remove condensation from the lens of a camera or other optical equipment, especially by allowing it to warm up, or lose condensation in this way

de·fog·ger /dee fáwgər, -fóggər/ *n* **1.** a device that clears condensation from the windshield of a motor vehicle, especially heating vents in the dashboard or heating elements on or in the windshield glass **2.** a liquid used to clean and remove condensation from goggles or eyeglasses

de·fo·li·ant /dee fṓlee ənt/ *n* a chemical that strips trees and plants of their leaves and is sometimes used in warfare to deny cover to enemy forces

de·fo·li·ate /dee fṓlee àyt/ (**-at·ed, -at·ing, -ates**) *vti* to strip trees and plants of their leaves, e.g., by using chemicals or through pollution or attack by pests, or lose leaves in any of these ways [Late 18C. < late Latin *defoliat-*, past participle of *defoliare* < Latin *folium* "leaf, page"] —**de·fo·li·a·tion** /dee fṓlee áysh'n/ *n* —**de·fo·li·a·tor** *n*

de·force /dee fáwrss/ (**-forced, -forc·ing, -forc·es**) *vt* to keep the rightful owner of property away from it, or keep the property away from its owner, by force or violence (*formal*) [14C. < Anglo-Norman *deforcer* "force away from" < *forcier* < Latin *fortis* "strong"] —**de·force·ment** *n*

de·for·est /dee fáwrəst/ (**-est·ed, -est·ing, -ests**) *vt* to remove the trees from an area of land —**de·for·es·ta·tion** /dee fàwrə stáysh'n/ *n* —**de·for·est·er** *n*

De For·est /di fáwrəst/, **Lee** (1873–1961) US inventor. He invented the audion, a vacuum tube that revolutionized the radio industry (1906).

de·form /di fáwrm/ (**-formed, -form·ing, -forms**) *vti* **1. DISTORT** to become, or make something become, distorted, damaged, or disfigured **2. SPOIL** to spoil the appearance of something and make it ugly, or become spoiled and ugly ○ *The new office buildings have deformed the whole area.* **3.** PHYS **CHANGE SHAPE** to change the shape of something through stress, or become changed in this way [15C. Via French < Latin *deformare* < *forma* "mold, shape, beauty"] —**de·form·a·bil·i·ty** /di fàwrmə bíllətee/ *n* —**de·form·a·ble** *adj* —**de·formed** *adj* —**de·form·er** *n*

de·for·mal·ize /dee fáwrm'l ìz/ (**-ized, -iz·ing, -iz·es**) *vt* to make something such as a meeting or report less formal —**de·for·mal·i·za·tion** /dee fàwrməli záysh'n/ *n*

de·for·ma·tion /dèe fawr máysh'n, dèffər-/ *n* **1. ACT OF DEFORMING OR BEING DEFORMED** the act or process of damaging, disfiguring, or spoiling the look of something, or the condition of being damaged, disfigured, or spoiled **2. CHANGE IN SHAPE** a change in the shape of something, especially one that suggests damage or disfigurement **3. UNPLEASANT RESULT OF CHANGE** the harmful or disfiguring result of a change in form **4. CHANGE IN SHAPE BECAUSE OF STRESS** a change in shape resulting from the application of stress

de·for·mi·ty /di fáwrmətee/ (*plural* **-ties**) *n* **1. DISFIGUREMENT** the condition of being disfigured or badly formed ○ *the deformity of the pine trees at such a high altitude in the mountains* **2. STRUCTURAL CHANGE FROM NORMAL** a permanent change from normal body structure **3. SOMETHING WITH SHAPE FAR FROM NORMAL** something that has a shape not normal for its kind or nature

de·frag /dee frág/ (**-fragged, -frag·ging, -frags**) *vt* COMPUT same as **defragment** (*informal*) [Late 20C. Shortening]

de·frag·ment /dee frágmənt/ (**-ment·ed, -ment·ing, -ments**) *vt* to reorganize the storage space on a hard disk and optimize its performance by consolidating related files

de·fraud /di fráwd/ (**-fraud·ed, -fraud·ing, -frauds**) *vt* to deprive somebody of money or property by dishonest means [14C. Directly or via French < Latin *defraudare* < *fraudare* "to cheat"] —**de·fraud·a·tion** /dèe fraw dáysh'n/ *n* —**de·fraud·er** *n* —**de·fraud·ment** *n*

de·fray /di fráy/ (**-frayed, -fray·ing, -frays**) *vt* to provide money to pay for part or all of the cost of something ○ *The company will defray the cost of your training.* [Mid-16C. < French *défrayer* < *frais* "expenses"] —**de·fray·a·ble** *adj* —**de·fray·al** *n* —**de·fray·er** *n* —**de·fray·ment** *n*

de·frock /dee frók/ (**-frocked, -frock·ing, -frocks**) *vt* to take away the status, job, and authority of a priest or other member of the clergy, especially as a punishment for wrongdoing [Early 17C. < French *défroquer* < *froc* "frock"]

de·frost /dee fráwst/ *vti* (**-frost·ed, -frost·ing, -frosts**) **1.** to remove frost or ice from something, or become free of frost or ice **2.** to thaw frozen food, or become thawed ■ *n* AUTOMOT, HOUSEHOLD same as **defroster** (sense 1)

de·frost·er /dee fráwstər/ *n* **1.** a device that removes frost and ice or condensation from the windshield, windows, and mirror of a motor vehicle **2.** a device used to thaw frozen foods

deft /deft/ *adj* **1.** moving or acting in a quick, smooth, and skillful way **2.** showing good sense and skill in achieving or acquiring things [13C. Variant of DAFT] —**deft·ly** *adv* —**deft·ness** *n*

de·funct /di fúngkt/ *adj* **1.** no longer operative, valid, or functional **2.** no longer alive or in existence (*humorous*) [Mid-16C. < Latin *defunctus*, past participle of *defungi* "finish" < *fungi* "perform"] —**de·funct·ness** *n*

SYNONYMS See ***dead***.

de·fuse /dee fyóoz/ (**-fused, -fus·ing, -fus·es**) *vt* **1.** to make a situation less tense, dangerous, or uncomfortable ○ *The diplomats tried to defuse the escalating crisis.* **2.** to make a bomb or mine harmless by removing its detonating device

SPELLCHECK defuse or **diffuse**? Do not confuse the spelling of ***defuse*** and ***diffuse***, which sound similar. ***Defuse*** is only used as a verb, meaning "make something less dangerous or less tense," as in *defuse a bomb, defuse the situation*. ***Diffuse*** can be used as a verb or, with a slightly different pronunciation, as an adjective. The verb ***diffuse*** means "spread or scatter" or "make less intense," as in *diffuse propaganda, diffuse the light*.

de·fy /di fí/ (**-fied, -fy·ing, -fies**) *vt* **1. OPENLY RESIST SOMEBODY OR SOMETHING** to challenge openly somebody's or something's authority or power by refusing to obey a command or regulation ○ *He defied all orders from headquarters.* **2. CHALLENGE SOMEBODY** to challenge or dare somebody to do something ○ *I defy you to find a better deal than this.* **3. NOT BE EXPLAINED BY SOMETHING** to fail to be explained or clarified by something such as logic or analysis ○ *a decision that defies all logic* [14C. Via French *défier* < assumed Vulgar Latin *disfidare* "renounce your faith" < Latin *fides* "trust, belief"] —**de·fi·er** *n*

deg. *abbr* degree

dé·ga·gé /dày gaa zháy/ *adj* (*formal*) **1.** casual and relaxed **2.** detached and without emotional involvement [Late 17C. < French, "disengaged"]

de·gas /dee gáss/ (**-gassed, -gas·sing, -gas·es**) *vt* to remove gas from a liquid or solid or from a vacuum system

AKG London

Edgar Degas: self-portrait (1854–5)

De·gas /də gaá/, **Edgar** (1834–1917) French painter and sculptor. A leading impressionist, he often depicted the human figure in movement, particularly ballet dancers. Full name **Degas, Hilaire Germain Edgar**

> "It is very good to copy what one sees; it is much better to draw what you can't see any more but is in your memory. It is a transformation in which imagination and memory work together. You only reproduce what struck you, that is to say the necessary."
> [Edgar Degas, *Degas by Himself: Drawings, Prints, Paintings, Writings*, Richard Kendall (ed.); 1987]

de Gaulle /də gáwl/, **Charles, General** (1890–1970) French general and politician. He became leader of the Free French in London after the fall of France in World War II, taking over as head of the provisional government in 1945. He served as French president from 1959 to 1969. Full name **de Gaulle, Charles André Joseph Marie**. See illustration on next page

Charles de Gaulle

"The French will only be united under the threat of danger. Nobody can simply bring together a country that has 265 kinds of cheese."
[Charles de Gaulle, *Election speech*; 1951]

de·gauss /dee gówss/ (**-gaussed, -gauss·ing, -gauss·es**) *vt* to remove or counteract a magnetic field in something such as electrical equipment or a ship's hull —**de·gauss·er** *n*

de·gen·der·ize /dee jéndə rīz/ (**-ized, -iz·ing, -iz·es**), **de·gen·der** /dee jéndər/ (**-dered, -der·ing, -ders**) *vt* to remove references to people's gender from language or a text in order to make it more neutral or less biased —**de·gen·der·i·za·tion** /dee jèndəri záysh'n/ *n*

de·gen·er·a·cy /di jénnərəssee/ *n* **1.** (*plural* **de·gen·er·a·cies**) **BAD BEHAVIOR** immoral, depraved, or corrupt behavior, or an instance of this **2. WORSENED CONDITION** a condition that is worse than normal or worse than before **3. WORSENING OF CONDITION** the process of becoming physically, morally, or mentally worse **4.** QUANTUM PHYS **STATE OF EQUAL ENERGY** the condition of two or more quantum states that have the same energy

de·gen·er·ate *vi* /di jénnə ràyt/ (**-at·ed, -at·ing, -ates**) **1. BECOME WORSE** to develop into a condition that is worse than before, worse than normal, or not as good as it should be **2.** BIOL **BECOME USELESS** to become less specialized or lose the ability to function (*refers to organisms or body parts*) ■ *adj* /di jénnərət/ **1. IN WORSENED CONDITION** in a condition that is worse than normal or worse than before **2. INFERIOR** in a condition that is worse than an original or previous state **3.** QUANTUM PHYS **EQUAL IN ENERGY** describes a system in which different quantum states have equal energy **4.** BIOL **WITH REDUCED OR ABSENT PART** describes a part, or an organism with a part, that has become reduced in size or function or lost completely during the history of its species or compared to related species ■ *n* /di jénnərət/ **SOMEBODY IMMORAL** somebody regarded as immoral or corrupt [15C. < Latin *degenerat-*, past participle of *degenerare* "depart from your own kind" < *genus* "race, kind"] —**de·gen·er·ate·ly** *adv*—**de·gen·er·ate·ness** /-ətnəss/ *n*

de·gen·er·ate mat·ter *n* highly compressed matter consisting of elementary particles that are not combined to form atoms, occurring in the final stage of a star's development into a white dwarf

de·gen·er·a·tion /di jènnə ráysh'n/ *n* **1. WORSENING OF CONDITION** the process of becoming physically, morally, or mentally worse **2.** MED **DETERIORATION** a disease process that causes a gradual deterioration in the structure of a body part with a consequent loss of the ability to function **3.** EVOLUTION **LOSS OF FUNCTION** the gradual loss of the biological function, specialization, or adaptation of a part of the body over many generations

de·gen·er·a·tive /di jénnərətiv/ *adj* causing or showing a gradual deterioration in the structure of a body part with a consequent loss of the part's ability to function

de·gen·er·a·tive joint dis·ease *n* MED same as **osteoarthritis**

de·glam·or·ize /dee glámmə rīz/ (**-ized, -iz·ing, -iz·es**), **de·glam·our·ize** *vt* to make something less attractive or exciting than it sometimes appears —**de·glam·or·i·za·tion** /dee glàmməri záysh'n/ *n*

de·glaze /dee gláyz/ (**-glazed, -glaz·ing, -glaz·es**) *vt* **1.** to remove the glaze from pottery to leave a dull finish **2.** to dissolve fragments remaining in a frying or roasting pan by heating them and adding a liquid so as to make a sauce

de·glu·ti·nate /dee gloót'n àyt/ (**-nat·ed, -nat·ing, -nates**) *vt* to remove the gluten from cereal or flour [Late 19C. < DE- + Latin *glutin-*, stem of *gluten* "glue"] —**de·glu·ti·na·tion** /dee gloót'n áysh'n/ *n*

de·glu·ti·tion /dèe gloo tísh'n/ *n* the act or process of swallowing (*technical*) [Mid-17C. < French *déglutition* < Latin *degluttire* "swallow down" < *gluttire* (see GLUTTON)]

de·grad·a·ble /di gráydəb'l/ *adj* **1.** able to undergo chemical or biological decomposition **2.** able to be degraded in any way —**de·grad·a·bil·i·ty** /di gràydə bíllətee/ *n*

deg·ra·da·tion /dèggrə dáysh'n/ *n* **1. GREAT HUMILIATION** great humiliation brought about by loss of status, reputation, or self-esteem ○ *suffered the degradation of overwhelming defeat at the polls* **2. ACT OF HUMILIATING SOMEBODY** the act of humiliating somebody, causing him or her a loss of status, reputation, or self-esteem ○ *the constant degradation and undermining of other members of the staff* **3. BAD LIVING CONDITIONS** a way of life without dignity, health, or social comforts **4. LOSS OF QUALITY** a decline in the quality or performance of something ○ *a rapid degradation in the engine's horsepower* **5. PROCESS OF DECLINE** the process by which a decline in quality or performance is brought about **6.** GEOL, GEOG **EROSION** erosion of the Earth's land surface by water, wind, or ice **7.** CHEM **BREAKDOWN OF COMPOUND** the breakdown of a chemical compound into atoms or simpler compounds **8.** PHYS **DECREASE OF ENERGY** the process by which the energy available for doing work is irreversibly decreased

de·grade /di gráyd/ (**-grad·ed, -grad·ing, -grades**) *v* **1.** *vt* **TREAT SOMEBODY HUMILIATINGLY** to cause somebody a humiliating loss of status, self-esteem, or reputation **2.** *vti* **WORSEN** to become worse, or make something become worse, especially in quality or performance ○ *Using the wrong fuel had significantly degraded the engine's power.* **3.** *vt* **LOWER SOMEBODY IN GRADE** to lower somebody in rank, grade, or level **4.** *vti* GEOL, GEOG **ERODE** to erode the land surface or a river bed, or be eroded by the action of wind, ice, or water **5.** *vt* ENVIRON **DESTROY OR DAMAGE ENVIRONMENT** to cause damage or destruction to part of the environment as a result of human activity **6.** *vti* PHYS **REDUCE AVAILABLE ENERGY** to reduce irreversibly the energy available in matter, or be reduced irreversibly [14C. Via French < ecclesiastical Latin *degradare* "reduce in rank" < Latin *gradus* "step, stage"] —**de·grad·ed** *adj* —**de·grad·er** *n*

de·grad·ing /di gráyding/ *adj* causing somebody to feel shame and humiliation —**de·grad·ing·ly** *adv*

de·grease /dee gréess/ (**-greased, -greas·ing, -greas·es**) *vt* to remove grease from something such as an engine, especially using chemicals —**de·greas·er** *n*

de·gree /di grée/ *n* **1. EXTENT OR AMOUNT** the relative extent, amount, intensity, or level of something, especially when compared with other things ○ *showed a high degree of awareness of the issues* **2. EDUCATIONAL TITLE** a title awarded by a university or college following successful completion of a course of study or period of research, or a similar title granted as an honor **3. UNIT OF TEMPERATURE MEASUREMENT** a unit of measurement for temperature on a scale such as Celsius or Fahrenheit ○ *degrees Celsius* Symbol ° **4. UNIT FOR MEASURING ANGLES** a unit of measurement for planar angles, equal to a 360th of a full revolution. Symbol ° **5. UNIT OF LATITUDE OR LONGITUDE** a unit of latitude or longitude, equal to 1/360 of a circle, used to locate and designate places on the Earth ○ *27 degrees north* Symbol ° **6.** LAW **CLASSIFICATION OF MURDER** a level of classification of murder according to its seriousness, first-degree murder being the most serious **7.** MED **SEVERITY OF BURNS ON BODY** a level of classification of the seriousness of the damage to tissue caused by a burn, third-degree burns being the most serious **8.** MEASURE **UNIT OF MEASUREMENT ON SCALE** a unit on any of various measurement scales, e.g., that used to measure specific gravity or that used to specify the alcohol content of drinks. Symbol ° **9.** GRAM **STATE OF ADJECTIVE OR ADVERB** a state of an adjective or adverb, either the positive, the comparative, or the superlative **10.** SOC SCI **CLOSENESS OF RELATIONSHIP** an indication of the genealogical closeness of a relationship within a family **11.** SOC SCI **STATUS** rank, position, or status in society (*formal or literary*) ○ *of high degree* **12.** MUSIC **POSITION OF NOTE ON MUSICAL SCALE** the relative position of a note on a musical scale **13.** MATH **HIGHEST EXPONENT OF DERIVATIVE** in a differential equation, the exponent of the derivative of highest order, e.g., $4x^2y^2$ is of degree four **14.** MATH **SUM OF POLYNOMIAL VARIABLE EXPONENTS** in a polynomial equation, the sum of the exponents of the variables in the term with the highest power, e.g., $4x^3y^2 + 3y^2 + 2$ is of degree five [13C. Via French *degré* < assumed Vulgar Latin *degradus*, literally "step down" < Latin *gradus* "step, stage"]

de·gree-day *n* a unit of measurement for heating systems, used to estimate fuel requirements and representing one degree of variation from the mean daily temperature outside

de·gree of free·dom *n* **1.** STATS **INDEPENDENT VARIABLE** an independent variable in a statistical measure or frequency distribution **2.** PHYS, CHEM **VARIABLE SPECIFYING ENERGY** an independent variable needed to specify the energy state of an atom, molecule, or system **3.** CHEM **VARIABLE SPECIFYING STATE** any of the independent variables such as pressure that are needed to specify the state of a system according to the phase rule

de·gres·sion /di grésh'n/ *n* **1.** a gradual decrease or downward movement (*formal*) **2.** a gradual lowering of the tax rate on sums below a specific amount [15C. < medieval Latin *degression-* < Latin *degress-*, past participle of *degredi* "step down" < *gradus* "step, stage"] —**de·gres·sive** *adj*

de Ha·vil·land /də hávvilənd/, **Olivia** (*b.* 1916) British-born US movie actor. She won Academy Awards for *To Each His Own* (1946) and *The Heiress* (1949). Full name **de Havilland, Olivia Mary**

De Ha·vil·land /də hávvilənd/, **Sir Geoffrey** (1882–1965) British aviation pioneer and aircraft designer. Aircraft designed by him include the Tiger Moth (1931), Mosquito (1940), and Comet airliner (1952).

de·hire /dee hīr/ (**-hired, -hir·ing, -hires**) *vt* to dismiss somebody from employment (*used euphemistically*)

de·hisce /di híss/ (**-hisced, -hisc·ing, -hisc·es**) *vi* **1.** to burst open, releasing seeds, pollen, or spores (*refers to dry fruits, seed pods, anthers, or spore-bearing structures*) **2.** to open along the joined edges (*technical*; *refers to a wound that has been stitched*) [Mid-17C. < Latin *dehiscere* "open up" < *hiscere* "begin opening" < *hiare* "gape"] —**de·his·cence** /di híss'nss/ *n*—**de·his·cent** *adj*

de·horn /dee háwrn/ (**-horned, -horn·ing, -horns**) *vt* to remove or prevent the growth of the horns of an animal by surgery or cauterization —**de·horn·er** *n*

Deh·ra Dun /dàyrə doón/, **Deh·ra Dūn** capital city of Uttaranchal state in northern India. Population: 527,859 (2001).

de·hu·man·ize /dee hyoómə nīz/ (**-ized, -iz·ing, -iz·es**) *vt* **1. MAKE SOMEBODY LESS HUMAN** to make somebody less human by taking away his or her individuality, the creative and interesting aspects of his or her personality, or his or her compassion and sensitivity toward others **2. REMOVE PEOPLE-FRIENDLY FEATURES OF SOMETHING** to take away the qualities or features of something that make it able to meet human needs and desires or enhance people's lives **3. MAKE SOMETHING BORINGLY ROUTINE** to remove creativity and interest from a process and make it dull, routine, and mechanical —**de·hu·man·i·za·tion** /dee hyoòməni záysh'n/ *n* —**de·hu·man·ized** *adj* —**de·hu·man·iz·ing** *adj*

de·hu·mid·i·fi·er /dèe hyoo míddə fī ər/ *n* an electrical appliance for removing excess humidity from the air in a room or building. See illustration on next page

de·hu·mid·i·fy /dèe hyoo míddə fī/ (**-fied, -fy·ing, -fies**) *vt* to remove excess humidity from the air in a room or building —**de·hu·mid·i·fi·ca·tion** /dèe hyoo mìddəfi káysh'n/ *n*

de·hy·drate /dee hī dràyt/ (**-drat·ed, -drat·ing, -drates**) *v* **1.** *vt* FOOD INDUST **PRESERVE FOOD BY DRYING** to remove moisture from food as a way of preserving it **2.** *vti* MED **LOSE BODY FLUIDS** to lose water or fluids from the body or its tissues, or cause the body or its tissues to do this **3.** *vt* CHEM **TAKE AWAY WATER FROM COMPOUND** to

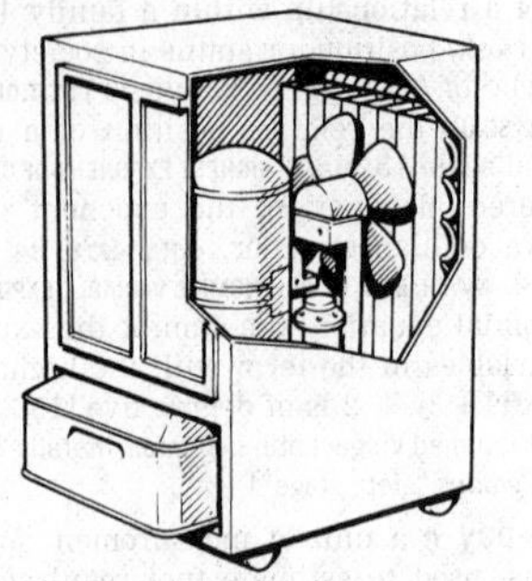

dehumidifier: cutaway view showing filters for removal of moisture from the air

deprive a chemical compound of water molecules or of the proportion of hydrogen and oxygen atoms present in water

de·hy·drat·ed /dee hī̄ dràytəd/ *adj* **1.** FOOD INDUST **DRIED** preserved by the removal of all moisture **2.** MED **EXPERIENCING FLUID LOSS** lacking water in the body, as the result of loss of bodily fluids or from being deprived of liquid **3.** CHEM **WITH WATER MOLECULES REMOVED** describes a chemical compound that has had water molecules removed or the proportion of hydrogen and oxygen atoms that would be present in a water molecule removed

SYNONYMS See *dry.*

de·hy·dra·tion /dee hī dráysh'n, dee hī-/ *n* **1.** FOOD INDUST **REMOVAL OF MOISTURE FROM FOOD** the removal of moisture from food as a way of preserving it **2.** MED **LOSS OF BODY FLUID** a dangerous lack of water in the body resulting from inadequate intake of fluids or excessive loss through sweating, vomiting, or diarrhea **3.** CHEM **LOSS OF WATER BY CHEMICAL COMPOUND** the process by which a chemical compound loses water molecules or the proportion of hydrogen and oxygen atoms present in water

de·hy·dra·tor /dee hī dràytər/ *n* an electrical appliance for drying food, consisting of a stack of interlocking trays through which heated air is circulated

de·hy·dro·chlo·rin·ase /dee hīdrə kláwrə nàyss, -nàyz/ *n* an enzyme that removes hydrogen and chlorine from compounds. Its presence accounts for the resistance shown by some insects to DDT.

de·hy·dro·chlo·rin·ate /dee hīdrə kláwrə nàyt/ (**-at·ed, -at·ing, -ates**) *vt* to chemically remove hydrogen and chlorine or hydrogen chloride from a substance —**de·hy·dro·chlo·ri·na·tion** /dee hīdrə klawrə náysh'n/ *n*

de·hy·dro·gen·ase /dee hīdrəjə nàyz/ *n* an enzyme that speeds up the transfer of hydrogen between compounds

de·hy·dro·gen·ate /dee hīdrəjə nàyt, dee hī drójjə-/ (**-at·ed, -at·ing, -ates**) *vt* to remove hydrogen from a compound, e.g., by means of a catalyst or in an enzyme-controlled process in cells —**de·hy·dro·gen·a·tion** /dee hīdrəjə náysh'n, dee hī drojə-/ *n*

de·hy·dro·gen·ize /dee hīdrəjə nīz, dee hī drójjə-/ (**-ized, -iz·ing, -iz·es**) *vt* CHEM same as **dehydrogenate** —**de·hy·dro·gen·i·za·tion** /dee hīdrəjəni záysh'n, dee hī dròjjəni-/ *n*

de·hyp·no·tize /dee hípnə tīz/ (**-tized, -tiz·ing, -tiz·es**) *vt* to bring somebody out of a hypnotic state —**de·hyp·no·sis** /dee hip nṓssiss/ *n* —**de·hyp·no·ti·za·tion** /dee hìpnəti záysh'n/ *n*

de·ice /dee īss/ (**-iced, -ic·ing, -ic·es**) *vt* to remove ice from something such as a windshield, or prevent ice from forming on it

de·ic·er /dee īssər/ *n* a device or chemical substance that removes ice or prevents it forming, e.g., on the windshield of a motor vehicle or the wings of an aircraft. One of the commonest de-icers is ethylene glycol, which is used in antifreeze.

de·i·cide /dee i sīd/ *n* **1.** the act of killing a god or goddess **2.** somebody who kills a god or goddess [Early 17C. Partly < ecclesiastical Latin *deicida* "god-killer," partly < Latin *deus* "god" + -CIDE] —**de·i·ci·dal** /dee i sīd'l/ *adj*

deic·tic /dīktik/ *adj* describes a word or expression such as "you," "this," "now," and "there" that depends for its full meaning on the context in which it is used [Early 19C. < Greek *deiktikos* < *deiknunai* "to show"] —**deic·ti·cal·ly** *adv*

de·i·fy /dee i fī/ (**-fied, -fy·ing, -fies**) *vt* **1.** to make somebody into a god **2.** to honor or adore somebody or something as if he, she, or it were divine [14C. Via French *déifier* < ecclesiastical Latin *deificare* < Latin *deus* "god"] —**de·i·fi·ca·tion** /dee ifi káysh'n/ *n* —**de·i·fi·er** *n*

Deigh·ton /dáyt'n/, **Len** (*b.* 1929) British writer. He is best known for spy thrillers, including *The Ipcress File* (1962). He has also written on cooking and military history. Full name **Deighton, Leonard Cyril**

deign /dayn/ (**deigned, deign·ing, deigns**) *vi* to do something in a way that shows that it is considered a great favor ○ *I don't suppose he'll deign to accept our invitation.* [13C. Via Old French *deignier* < Latin *dignare* "deem worthy" < *dignus* "worthy"]

Dei·mos /dī mòss/ *n* the outermost of the two natural satellites of Mars, both of which are small. It was discovered in 1877 and there is evidence suggesting that it is a captured asteroid. [After one of the sons of Ares in Greek mythology]

de·in·dus·tri·al·i·za·tion /dee in dùstree əli záysh'n/ *n* the removal or reduction of industrial activity in a country or region, especially heavy industry or manufacturing industry

de·in·dus·tri·al·ize /dee in dústree ə līz/ (**-ized, -iz·ing, -iz·es**) *vti* to take away or lose industries, especially the heavy industries and manufacturing industries, from a country or region

de·in·sti·tu·tion·al·ize /dee instə tóoshən'l īz, -shnə līz/ (**-ized, -iz·ing, -iz·es**) *vt* to discharge a patient or client from institutional care, often in order to treat the person in his or her community —**de·in·sti·tu·tion·al·i·za·tion** /-tòoshən'li záysh'n, -tòoshnəli-/ *n*

de·i·on·ize /dee ī ə nīz/ (**-ized, -iz·ing, -iz·es**) *v* to remove ions from a solution —**de·i·on·i·za·tion** /dee ī əni záysh'n/ *n* —**de·i·on·iz·er** *n*

de·ism /dee ìzzəm/ *n* a belief in God based on reason rather than revelation and involving the view that God has set the universe in motion but does not interfere with how it runs. Deism was especially influential in the 17th and 18th centuries. [Late 17C. < Latin *deus* "god"] —**de·ist** *n* —**de·is·tic** /dee ístik/ *adj* —**de·is·ti·cal·ly** *adv*

de·i·ty /dee ətee/ (*plural* **-ties**) *n* **1.** **GOD OR GODDESS** a god, goddess, or other being regarded as divine **2.** **DIVINE STATE** the condition or status of a god or goddess **3.** **SOMEBODY OR SOMETHING RESEMBLING GOD** somebody or something that is treated like a god [14C. Via French < ecclesiastical Latin *deitas* "divine nature" < Latin *deus* "god"]

De·i·ty *n* in monotheistic belief, God

deix·is /dīksiss/ *n* the use of a word or expression such as "he," "that," "now," or "here," whose full meaning depends on the context in which it is used [Mid-20C. < Greek, "reference" < *deiknunai* "to show"]

dé·jà vu /dày zhaa vóo/ *n* **1.** a feeling of having experienced something before, although in fact it is the first time that it has been experienced **2.** a state of boring familiarity or repetitiveness [Early 20C. < French, "already seen"]

USAGE ***Déjà vu*** once referred exclusively to the illusion of having been somewhere before or having done something before: *Entering the house for the first time, she had an eerie sense of déjà vu.* Recently, however, it has come to encompass as well the reality of repetitiveness in events or actions: *As they began to discuss which route was best, he had a distinct sense of déjà vu.* This sense of the word has been extended still further, until the turnaround from the original meaning is almost complete and ***déjà vu*** is sometimes also used to describe tedium: *Gray winter days bring on déjà vu.*

de·ject·ed /di jéktəd/ *adj* feeling or showing sadness and lack of hope, especially because of disappointment [Late 16C. < archaic *deject* < Latin *deject-*, past participle of *dejicere* "throw down" < *jacere* "throw"] —**de·ject·ed·ly** *adv* —**de·ject·ed·ness** *n*

de·jec·tion /di jéksh'n/ *n* **1.** **GREAT UNHAPPINESS** sadness and lack of hope, especially as a result of disappointment **2.** **DEFECATION** the act of passing solid waste matter out of the anus (*technical*) **3.** **EXCREMENT** solid waste matter passed out through the anus (*technical*)

de ju·re /dee jóoree, day yóo ràyl/ *adv, adj* by right according to the law [Mid-16C. < Latin, "from the law"]

deka- *prefix* another spelling of **deca-**

dek·a·gram *n* another spelling of **decagram**

De Kalb /di kálb/ town in northern Illinois, west of Chicago and southeast of Rockford. Population: 36,094 (1998).

dek·a·li·ter *n* MEASURE another spelling of **decaliter**

dek·a·me·ter *n* MEASURE another spelling of **decameter**

deke /deek/ (*informal*) *vt* (**deked, dek·ing, dekes**) to deceive an opponent in hockey by making a deceptive move ○ *He deked two defensemen as he crossed the blue line.* ■ *n* in hockey, a deceptive move that lures a player out of position [Mid-20C. Shortening of DECOY]

Dek·ker /dékər/, **Thomas** (1572?–1632) English dramatist and pamphleteer. He wrote over 40 plays, including *The Honest Whore* (1604; part II 1630). He also wrote in collaboration with other Elizabethan dramatists including Philip Massinger, Thomas Middleton, and William Rowley.

> "Golden slumbers kiss your eyes, / Smiles awake you when you rise."
> [Thomas Dekker, *Patient Grissil*; 1603]

de Klerk /də klúrk/, **F. W.** (*b.* 1936) South African politician. He introduced reforms during his presidency (1989–94) that led to the end of apartheid. He shared the Nobel Peace Prize with Nelson Mandela (1993). Full name **de Klerk, Frederick Willem**

> "There is no such thing as a nonracial society in a multiracial country."
> [F. W. de Klerk, *Time*; 1994]

de Koo·ning /də kóoning/, **Elaine** (1920–89) US artist. She is known for her portraits of John F. Kennedy. Full name **de Kooning, Elaine Marie Catherine Fried**

de Koo·ning, Willem (1904–97) Dutch-born US artist. He is known for his abstract expressionist paintings, including the series of six paintings entitled *Woman* (1953).

> "The trouble with being poor is that it takes up all your time."
> [Attributed to Willem de Kooning]

del *abbr* COMPUT, PRINTING delete

del. *abbr* **1.** delegate **2.** POL delegation **3.** POL delete

Del. *abbr* Delaware[2] (sense 1)

de la see also under surname

De·la·croix /də laa krwaá, dèllə-/, **Eugène** (1798–1863) French painter and lithographer. His romantic works, e.g., *Liberty Guiding the People* (1830), are characterized by melodrama and vivid color. Full name **Delacroix, Ferdinand Victor Eugène**

> "Painting is only a bridge linking the painter's mind with that of the viewer."
> [Eugène Delacroix, *Journal*; 1850]

Del·a·go·a Bay /dèllə gṓ ə-/ bay on the southern Mozambique coast. Mozambique's capital, Maputo, is situated near the head of the bay.

de·laine /də láyn/ *n* a fine woolen or woolen and cotton fabric resembling muslin [Mid-19C. Shortening of MOUSSELINE DE LAINE]

de la Mare /dèllə mér/, **Walter** (1873–1956) British poet, anthologist, and novelist. The works of this prolific writer include *The Listeners and Other Poems* (1912) and *Memoirs of a Midget* (1921).

> "This Prince of Commerce spent his days / In crafty, calm, cold, cozening strife: / He thus amassed a million pounds, / And bought a pennyworth of life."
> [Walter de la Mare, "Hard Labor," *The Complete Poems of Walter de la Mare*; 1969]

de·lam·i·nate /dee lámmə nàyt/ (**-nat·ed, -nat·ing, -nates**) *vti* to separate or peel off in thin layers, or cause something to do this —**de·lam·i·na·tion** /dee làmmə náysh'n/ *n*

~~de·lap·i·dat·ed~~ incorrect spelling of **dilapidated**

de la Roche /də laa rṓsh, dèllə-/, **Mazo** (1885–1961) Canadian writer. She is known for her series of novels about the Whiteoak family, the first being *Jalna* (1927).

de la Tour, Georges ➧ **La Tour, Georges de**

De·lau·nay /də làw náy/, **Sonia** (1885–1980) Russian-born French painter and designer. Her paintings and designs for textiles, bookbindings, and theatrical costumes in the 1920s were characterized by bright colors and geometric forms. Born **Terk, Sonia**

> "If you are an artist...You must do what you want and be ready not to sell. You can't be too ambiguous for money."
> [Sonia Delaunay. Quoted in *Art Talk: Conversations with 15 Women Artists*, Cindy Nemser; 1975]

Del·a·ware[1] /déllə wèr/ (*plural same* or **-wares**) *n* **1.** a member of a group of Native North American peoples who once lived between the Delaware and Hudson rivers, and now live mostly in Oklahoma, Wisconsin, Kansas, and Ontario **2.** a sweet, light red grape variety grown mainly in the United States [Early 18C. After the *Delaware* River, E United States] —**Del·a·ware** *adj*

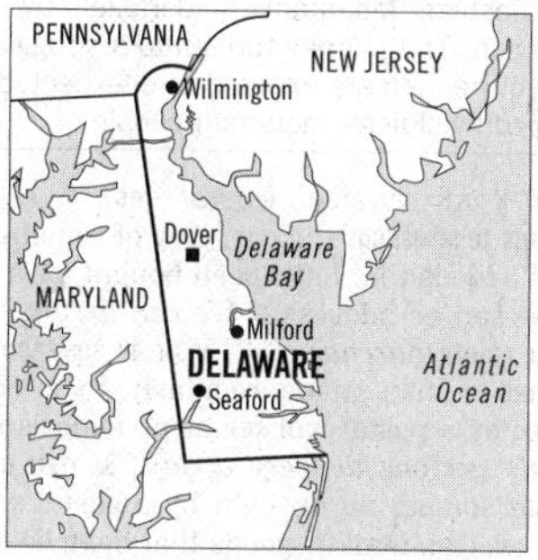

Delaware

Del·a·ware[2] /déllə wèr/ **1.** first US state, bordered by the Atlantic Ocean, Maryland, Pennsylvania, and New Jersey. Capital: Dover. Population: 807,385 (2002 estimate). Area: 2,396 sq. mi./6,206 sq. km. **2.** major river of the eastern United States, with its source in southern New York. Length: 390 mi./630 km.

Del·a·ware Bay arm of the Atlantic Ocean between eastern Delaware and southwestern New Jersey. It extends northwestward from the Atlantic to the Delaware River estuary.

Del·a·ware Wa·ter Gap /-wáwtər gàp/ scenic gorge on the Delaware River, cutting through the Kittatinny Mountains. Length: 2 mi./3 km.

De la Warr /déllə wèr/, **Thomas West, 3rd Baron** (1577–1618) English-born colonial governor. In 1610 he arrived at Jamestown in time to save the settlement of Virginia from being disbanded. The state of Delaware is named for him. Known as **Lord Delaware**

de·lay /di láy/ *v* (**-layed, -lay·ing, -lays**) **1.** *vti* PUT SOMETHING OFF UNTIL LATER to postpone something, or wait until later before doing something **2.** *vt* MAKE SOMEBODY OR SOMETHING LATE to make somebody or something late or slow ○ *I was delayed at the office.* ■ *n* **1.** LATENESS a failure to happen or to do something at the intended or expected time ○ *All services are subject to delay or cancellation.* **2.** EXTENT OF LATENESS the extent of the period of time by which somebody or something is made late or slowed down ○ *long delays on the beltway* **3.** PROCRASTINATION procrastination or failure to do something quickly enough ○ *This must be done without delay.* [13C. < Anglo-Norman *delaier* "leave off" < *laier* "leave"] —**de·lay·er** *n*

de·lay ac·tion *n* MECH ENG same as **delayed action** (sense 1)

de·layed /di láyd/ *adj* **1.** made to happen later than intended or expected **2.** happening after a period of time ○ *causing delayed damage to the kidneys*

de·layed ac·tion *n* **1.** the activation of a mechanism a short time after it has been set (*hyphenated when used before a noun*) **2.** a mechanism used to produce delayed action

de·layed neu·tron *n* a neutron emitted after a measurable time delay in the process of nuclear fission

de·layed-re·lease *adj* formulated to release an active ingredient gradually to prolong its effect

de·lay·er·ing /dee láy əring/ *n* the process of simplifying the structure of an organization to make it more efficient —**de·lay·er** *vti*

de·lay·ing ac·tion, **de·lay·ing op·er·a·tion** *n* a maneuver used to gain time or allow a retreat when there are not enough resources to confront an opponent directly

de·lay·ing tac·tic *n* a deliberate attempt to delay something in order to gain time or another advantage

de·lay line *n* a device designed to cause a delay in transmitting an electronic signal

Del·brück /dél brŏŏk/, **Max** (1906–81) German-born US biologist. He shared the Nobel Prize in physiology or medicine (1969) for his work on the replication of viruses and their genetic structure.

Del City /dél-/ city in central Oklahoma. It is an eastern suburb of Oklahoma City. Population: 22,181 (2002 estimate).

de·le /deélee/ (*informal*) *n* a mark used in the margin of printed material to show that something is to be deleted ■ *vt* (**-led, -le·ing, -les**) to mark a passage of printed material for deletion [Early 18C. < Latin, "delete!"]

de·lec·ta·ble /di léktəb'l/ *adj* **1.** DELICIOUS having a delicious taste **2.** DELIGHTFUL absolutely delightful, very pleasing, or very attractive ■ *n* SOMETHING VERY TASTY an appetizing food or dish [14C. < French *delectable* < Latin *delectare* (see DELIGHT)] —**de·lec·ta·bil·i·ty** /di lèktə bílləteé/ *n* —**de·lec·ta·ble·ness** *n* —**de·lec·ta·bly** *adv*

de·lec·ta·tion /dee lek táysh'n/ *n* pleasure or enjoyment (*formal*) [14C. < Old French < Latin *delectare* (see DELIGHT)]

del·e·gate *n* /délləgət, déllə gàyt/ **1.** REPRESENTATIVE OR DEPUTY somebody who is chosen to represent or given the authority to act on behalf of another person, group, or organization, e.g., at a meeting or conference **2.** MEMBER OF HOUSE OF DELEGATES a member of a House of Delegates, the lower house of the legislature in Maryland, Virginia, or West Virginia **3.** REPRESENTATIVE OF US TERRITORY a representative of a territory or of the District of Columbia in the US House of Representatives, who may speak on issues but not vote ■ *vti* /déllə gàyt/ (**-gat·ed, -gat·ing, -gates**) **1.** GIVE TASK TO SOMEBODY ELSE to give a task to somebody else with responsibility to act on your behalf ○ *She delegates that responsibility to her assistant.* **2.** GIVE AUTHORITY TO SOMEBODY ELSE to give somebody else the power to act, make decisions, or allocate resources on your behalf ○ *an executive who was unafraid to delegate* ■ *n* /délləgət, déllə gàyt/ SOMEBODY ASSIGNED A TASK somebody to whom a task or responsibility is delegated (*informal*) [15C. < Latin *delegat-*, past participle of *delegare* "send away" < *legare* "send"] —**del·e·ga·ble** *adj* —**del·e·ga·tor** *n*

del·e·ga·tion /dèllə gáysh'n/ *n* **1.** GIVING OF RESPONSIBILITY TO SOMEBODY ELSE the giving of some power, responsibility, or work to somebody else **2.** CONDITION OF BEING GIVEN RESPONSIBILITY the condition of being given to somebody else as a duty or responsibility **3.** GROUP REPRESENTING SOMEBODY a group of people chosen to represent or act on behalf of somebody **4.** STATE REPRESENTATIVES all the members of the US Congress who represent one state **5.** CONGRESSIONAL GROUP a group of members of the US Congress who represent the nation while traveling officially at home or abroad ○ *A delegation of five senators toured the military hospital.*

de·le·git·i·mize /deélə jíttə mīz/ (**-mized, -miz·ing, -miz·es**) *vt* to take away the legitimacy or legal status of somebody or something —**de·le·git·i·mi·za·tion** /deélə jìttəmi záysh'n/ *n*

~~delemma~~ incorrect spelling of **dilemma**

de·lete /di leét/ *vt* (**-let·ed, -let·ing, -letes**) **1.** to score out or erase something that is printed or written **2.** to erase or remove something from a computer file or disk ■ *n* same as **delete key** ○ *Click on the icon for that file and then hit delete.* [15C. < Latin *delet-*, past participle of *delere* "blot out, efface"]

de·lete key *n* a computer key that moves the cursor to erase characters, or removes highlighted text

del·e·te·ri·ous /dèllə teéree əss/ *adj* having a harmful or damaging effect on somebody or something [Mid-17C. Via medieval Latin < Greek *dēlētērios* "noxious"] —**del·e·te·ri·ous·ly** *adv* —**del·e·te·ri·ous·ness** *n*

de·le·tion /di leésh'n/ *n* **1.** REMOVAL OR ERASURE OF SOMETHING the action or process of erasing, scoring out, or removing something written, printed, or shown or stored on a computer **2.** SOMETHING REMOVED OR ERASED something erased, scored out, or removed from a text or a computer file or directory **3.** GENETICS ABSENCE OF GENETIC MATERIAL the loss or absence of part of a chromosome, ranging from a pair of chemicals (**base pair**) to a whole chromosomal arm. Some medical conditions are the result of deletion.

de·lev·er·age /dee lévvərij/ (**-aged, -ag·ing, -ag·es**) *vti* to reduce the amount of debt that a company owes, usually by laying off workers, selling off unprofitable divisions, and other cost-cutting measures

delft /delft/, **Delft**, **delft·ware** /délft wàir/, **Delft·ware** *n* earthenware with an opaque white glaze, usually with blue decoration [Late 17C. After DELFT]

Delft /delft/ city in the province of Zuid-Holland, in the western Netherlands, known as a center of production of glazed earthenware. Population: 96,370 (2000).

delft·ware /délft wèr/, **Delft·ware** *n* CERAMICS same as **delft**

Del·ga·do, Cape /del gaádō/ cape in northeastern Mozambique, just south of the border with Tanzania

Del·hi /déllee/ city in northern India. It is a major political, transportation, commercial, and industrial center, and contains New Delhi, the national capital. Population: 13,782,976 (2001).

del·i /déllee/ (*plural* **-is**) *n* FOOD (*informal*) **1.** same as **delicatessen** (sense 1) **2.** same as **delicatessen** (sense 2) [Mid-20C. Shortening]

De·li·an /deéljən/ *adj* relating to the Greek island of Delos ■ *n* somebody who comes from Delos [Late 16C < Latin *Delios* "of Delos"]

De·li·an League /deélee ən-/, **De·li·an Con·fed·er·a·cy** *n* an alliance of Greek states set up in 477 B.C. to oppose Persia

de·lib·er·ate *adj* /di líbbərət/ **1.** INTENTIONAL carefully thought out and done intentionally **2.** CAREFUL slow, careful, and methodical ■ *vti* /di líbbə ràyt/ (**-at·ed, -at·ing, -ates**) THINK to consider something carefully and in detail [15C. < Latin *deliberatus*, past participle of *deliberare* "weigh carefully" < *librare* "weigh" < *libra* "balance"] —**de·lib·er·ate·ly** *adv* —**de·lib·er·ate·ness** *n* —**de·lib·er·a·tor** *n*

de·lib·er·a·tion /di lìbbə ráysh'n/ *n* (*formal*) **1.** CAREFUL THOUGHT long careful consideration of something **2.** DISCUSSION formal or official discussion or debate ○ *The planning committee's deliberations went on all night.* **3.** CARE slowness and methodical carefulness

de·lib·er·a·tive /di líbbə ràytiv, -rətiv/ *adj* (*formal*) **1.** involved in or organized for careful discussion and debate **2.** relating to or resulting from discussion and debate —**de·lib·er·a·tive·ly** *adv* —**de·lib·er·a·tive·ness** *n*

De·libes /də leéb/, **Léo** (1836–91) French composer. His works include the grand opera *Lakmé* (1883) and the ballet *Coppélia* (1870). Full name **Delibes, Clément Philibert Léo**

del·i·ca·cy /déllikəssee/ (*plural* **-cies**) *n* **1.** SOMETHING NICE TO EAT a delicious, rare, or highly prized item of food **2.** SENSITIVITY sensitivity to the feelings of others **3.** NEED FOR TACT the quality of requiring great tact or sensitivity ○ *a matter of extreme delicacy* **4.** GREAT SENSITIVITY IN FEELINGS excessive sensitivity with regard to something offensive or embarrassing ○ *his delicacy on matters of a medical nature* **5.** SUBTLETY AND REFINEMENT pleasing subtlety in something such as taste, smell, or color ○ *the delicacy of her perfume* **6.** FINENESS fineness and subtlety of feeling, observation, or execution ○ *the delicacy of the brushwork in his later paintings* **7.** FRAGILITY the quality of being easily damaged or broken **8.** LACK OF PHYSICAL STRENGTH lack of physical strength or health **9.** SENSITIVITY OF RESPONSE IN EQUIPMENT sensitivity in the way something such as scientific equipment or a musical instrument responds to use

del·i·cate /déllikət/ *adj* 1. FRAGILE having a fine structure that is easily damaged or broken 2. FRAIL not having much resistance to illness or injury ○ *in delicate health* 3. SUBTLE mild, gentle, pale, or soft, and pleasant to the senses ○ *a delicate shade of blue* 4. FINE finely made and containing small parts or details ○ *delicate tracery* 5. SKILLFUL showing or characterized by great skill or craft, especially in producing or containing finely detailed intricate work or gentle or adroit movements ○ *a filigree of delicate shimmering brushstrokes* 6. NEEDING TACT needing to be dealt with using tact and sensitivity ○ *The negotiations were at a delicate stage.* 7. REFINED having or showing a refined and sensitive taste 8. EASILY OFFENDED easily shocked or upset by offensive or embarrassing things 9. ACCURATE describes instrumentation that is very precise and able to give exact readings ■ **del·i·cates** *npl* CLOTHES NEEDING SPECIAL WASHING AND DRYING clothes that need careful washing and drying, e.g., using a special washing machine cycle [14C. Directly or via French < Latin *delicatus*, related to *delicere* (see DELIGHT)] —**del·i·cate·ness** *n*

SYNONYMS See ***fragile***.

del·i·cate·ly /déllikətlee/ *adv* 1. FINELY in a way that shows skill in producing fine detail 2. SUBTLY in a pleasingly mild and subtle way ○ *delicately flavored* 3. GENTLY AND CAREFULLY gently and carefully, with no rough or sudden movements 4. WITH TACT tactfully and sensitively ○ *a matter that must be handled very delicately* 5. PRECARIOUSLY in a way that seems precarious or sensitive to even a slight change or disturbance ○ *delicately balanced on its edge*

del·i·ca·tes·sen /dèllikə téss'n/ *n* 1. a store specializing in imported or unusual foods and ingredients such as cooked meats, cheeses, and pickles 2. prepared food sold in a delicatessen, e.g., cooked meats, cheeses, pickles, and salads [Late 19C. Via German and French < Italian *delicatezza* "delicacy" < Latin *delicatus* (see DELICATE)]

de·li·cious /di líshəss/ *adj* 1. having an appealing or enjoyable taste or smell 2. highly amusing, pleasing, or enjoyable [13C. < Old French < Latin *delicia* "pleasure" < *delicere* (see DELIGHT)] —**de·li·cious·ness** *n*

de·li·cious·ly /di líshəsslee/ *adv* 1. TASTILY in a way that appeals to the sense of taste or smell ○ *a deliciously sweet and crunchy apple* 2. APPETIZINGLY in an appetizing way ○ *steaks sizzling away deliciously on the grill* 3. ENJOYABLY in an amusing, pleasing, or enjoyable way

de·lict /di líkt/ *n* in civil and criminal law, a wrong or injury done to somebody [Early 16C. < Latin *delictum*, neuter past participle of *delinquere* "offend" (see DELINQUENT)]

de·light /di lít/ *n* 1. JOY great enjoyment and pleasure ○ *To my delight, he accepted.* 2. SOMEBODY OR SOMETHING GIVING JOY somebody or something that brings somebody great enjoyment and pleasure ○ *That's one of the delights of traveling to interesting places.* ■ *v* (**-light·ed, -light·ing, -lights**) 1. *vti* GIVE JOY TO SOMEBODY to give somebody great enjoyment and pleasure 2. *vi* DERIVE JOY FROM SOMETHING to gain great enjoyment and pleasure from something ○ *She delighted in outwitting her competitors.* [13C. < Old French *delit* < Latin *delectare* "keep enticing" < *delicere* "allure" < *lacere* "entice"] —**de·light·ed** *adj* —**de·light·ed·ly** *adv* —**de·light·er** *n*

de·light·ful /di lítfəl/ *adj* giving great enjoyment and pleasure, especially by being pleasant, good to look at, or amusing —**de·light·ful·ly** *adv* —**de·light·ful·ness** *n*

De·li·lah /di lílə/ *n* in the Bible, the mistress of Samson who betrayed him to the Philistines. Having discovered that the source of his strength was his hair, she cut it off while he slept.

De·Lil·lo /də leélō/, **Don** (*b.* 1936) US novelist. One of the foremost postmodernist writers in the United States, he is author of *White Noise* (1985), which won the National Book Award for Fiction, and *Underworld* (1997).

> "I've come to think of Europe as a hard-cover book, America as the paperback version."
> [Don DeLillo, *The Names*; 1982]

de·lim·it /di límmit/ (**-it·ed, -it·ing, -its**), **de·lim·i·tate** /di límmə tàyt/ (**-tat·ed, -tat·ing, -tates**) *vt* to set out or establish the limits or boundaries of something (*formal*) [Mid-19C. Via French < Latin *delimitare* < *limit-* (see LIMIT)] —**de·lim·i·ta·tion** /di lìmmə táysh'n/ *n* —**de·lim·i·ta·tive** *adj*

de·lim·it·er /di límmitər/ *n* a character or space marking the beginning or end of a data element

de·lin·e·ate /di línnee àyt/ (**-at·ed, -at·ing, -ates**) *vt* 1. DESCRIBE SOMETHING to describe or explain something in detail (*formal*) 2. DRAW SOMETHING to sketch or draw something in outline 3. PORTRAY SOMETHING VISUALLY to represent something visually using something such as a chart or graph 4. DEMARCATE BOUNDS OF SOMETHING to indicate the physical boundaries of something [Mid-16C. < Latin *delineat-*, past participle of Latin *delineare* "sketch out" < *linea* (see LINE[1])] —**de·lin·e·a·ble** *adj* —**de·lin·e·a·tion** /di lìnnee áysh'n/ *n* —**de·lin·e·a·tive** *adj*

de·lin·e·a·tor /di línnee àytər/ *n* 1. an adjustable pattern that a tailor uses to cut garments of different sizes 2. somebody or something that outlines or describes something

de·lin·quen·cy /di língkwənsee/ *n* 1. UNLAWFUL BEHAVIOR antisocial or illegal behavior or acts, especially by young people 2. NEGLECT OF DUTY failure to fulfill a duty, commitment, or responsibility (*formal*) 3. FIN SOMETHING OVERDUE something that is overdue for payment, e.g., a debt or tax (*formal*)

de·lin·quent /di língkwənt/ *n* YOUTHFUL OFFENDER somebody, especially a young person, who has acted antisocially or broken the law ■ *adj* 1. ANTISOCIAL OR UNLAWFUL relating to antisocial behavior or lawbreaking 2. IGNORING DUTY neglecting a duty, commitment, or responsibility (*formal*) 3. FIN UNPAID unpaid and overdue for payment [15C. < Latin *delinquent-*, past participle of *delinquere* "offend" < *linquere* "leave"] —**de·lin·quent·ly** *adv*

del·i·quesce /dèlli kwéss/ (**-quesced, -quesc·ing, -quesc·es**) *vi* 1. CHEM DISSOLVE to dissolve gradually by absorbing moisture from the air 2. BOT FORM BRANCHES to form many branches without a main stem 3. FUNGI BECOME LIQUID to become soft or liquid after the release of spores [Mid-18C. < Latin *deliquescere* "start melting away" < *liquere* "be liquid"] —**del·i·ques·cence** *n* —**del·i·ques·cent** *adj*

de·lir·i·ous /di leéree əss/ *adj* 1. irrational as a temporary result of a physical condition such as fever, poisoning, or brain injury 2. extremely excited or emotional ○ *delirious with joy* [Late 16C. < DELIRIUM] —**de·lir·i·ous·ly** *adv* —**de·lir·i·ous·ness** *n*

de·lir·i·um /di leéree əm/ *n* 1. a state marked by extreme restlessness, confusion, and sometimes hallucinations, caused by fever, poisoning, or brain injury 2. a state of extreme excitement or emotion [Mid-16C. < Latin < *delirare* "be deranged," literally "be out of your track" < *lira* "ridge between furrows"]

de·lir·i·um tre·mens /-treémənz/ *n* agitation, tremors, and hallucinations caused by alcohol dependence and withdrawal [< Latin, "trembling delirium"]

del·ish /di lísh/ *adj* same as **delicious** (*slang*) [Early 20C. Shortening]

de·list /dee líst/ (**-list·ed, -list·ing, -lists**) *vt* 1. to remove a security from a listing on a stock exchange 2. to remove somebody or something from an official list

De·li·us /deélee əss/, **Frederick** (1862–1934) British composer. His music is characterized by rich orchestration and the subtle evocation of moods, e.g., as in *On Hearing the First Cuckoo in Spring* (1912).

de·liv·er /di lívvər/ (**-ered, -er·ing, -ers**) *v* 1. CARRY SOMETHING TO SOMEBODY to take something such as mail, goods that have been bought, or a message to a person or an address 2. *vt* HELP BABY TO BE BORN to give medical help to a baby human or animal when it is being born 3. *vt* PRODUCE BABY to give birth to a baby (*often passive*) 4. *vt* MAKE SPEECH to make a speech or give a talk to an audience 5. *vt* ANNOUNCE SOMETHING to announce something formally such as an opinion, decision, or judgment ○ *The jury delivered its verdict.* 6. *vt* THROW BALL to toss or throw a ball to somebody or at something 7. *vt* INFLICT BLOW to inflict a blow on somebody or something 8. *vi* DO THING PROMISED to do what has been promised ○ *He has yet to deliver anything that was promised in his speeches.* 9. *vt* POL ACHIEVE SUPPORT FOR SOMEBODY to organize and obtain the support of a place or people for a candidate or political party (*informal*) 10. *vt* PROVIDE SOMETHING to provide or produce something ○ *Note the total dosage of antibiotics delivered.* 11. *vt* RELEASE SOMEBODY to free or save somebody from captivity, hardship, or evil (*literary*) 12. *vt* GIVE SOMEBODY SOMETHING to hand somebody or something over to somebody else ○ *You have 48 hours to deliver the payment.* [13C. Via French *délivrer* < Latin *deliberare* "free completely" < *liberare* (see LIBERATE)] —**de·liv·er·a·bil·i·ty** /di lìvvərə bíllətee/ *n* —**de·liv·er·er** *n*

de·liv·er·a·ble /di lívvərəb'l/ *adj* able to be delivered as promised ■ *n* something that has been promised to a customer or client, especially a piece of work that is part of a larger project, often contractually identified both in time and content (*usually used in the plural*)

de·liv·er·ance /di lívvərənss/ *n* 1. rescue from captivity, hardship, or domination by evil (*formal*) ○ *He sought deliverance from his imprisonment.* 2. a formal announcement of a decision, judgment, or opinion

CULTURAL NOTE ***Deliverance***, a movie (1972) by British director John Boorman. Based on the novel by James Dickey (1972), it is the story of a canoe trip through the Appalachian Mountains undertaken by four city businessmen. The journey turns into a struggle for survival when the men are exposed to unexpected dangers and harried by sinister mountain people.

de·liv·er·y /di lívvəree/ (*plural* **-ies**) *n* 1. TAKING OF SOMETHING TO SOMEBODY the carrying of something such as mail, goods that have been bought, or a message to a person or address ○ *We can arrange delivery of any items purchased.* 2. VISIT BY SOMEBODY BRINGING SOMETHING a visit made regularly to a person or address by a postal worker or a vendor's vehicle ○ *We only get one delivery a day.* 3. ITEM BROUGHT TO SOMEBODY something brought by a postal worker or a vendor, e.g., mail or goods that have been bought 4. BIRTH PROCESS the process of giving birth to a baby 5. MANNER OF SPEAKING the action or manner in which somebody speaks to an audience ○ *She needs to work on her vocal delivery.* 6. RESCUE OF VICTIM the rescue or saving of somebody from captivity, hardship, or evil ○ *He prayed for delivery from his oppressors.* 7. WAY OF PUTTING BALL IN MOTION the action or manner of throwing, tossing, or rolling a ball or aiming a punch 8. LAW ACTION NEEDED TO EFFECT PROPERTY TRANSFER a formal action needed to accomplish a transfer of property

de·liv·er·y room *n* a specially equipped room in a hospital where women give birth

dell /del/ *n* a small, usually wooded valley or hollow [Old English < Germanic]

Del·la Falls /déllə-/ falls, located in central Vancouver Island, British Columbia, Canada. Height: 1,445 ft./440 m. Flowing from a glacier-fed lake, Della Falls are Canada's highest falls.

Del·la Rob·bi·a /déllə róbee ə/, **Luca** (1400?–82) Italian sculptor and ceramist. He is best known for his early Renaissance panels in Florence Cathedral. He invented a technique for making glazed terra cotta figures.

Del·mar·va Pen·in·su·la /del maárvə-/ peninsula in the states of Delaware, Maryland, and Virginia. Length: 180 mi./290 km.

Del·mon·i·co steak /del mònnikō-/ *n* a small steak cut from the front end of a short loin of beef [Early 20C. After the *Delmonico* Restaurant in New York City]

de·lo·cal·ize /dee lṓkə lìz/ (**-ized, -iz·ing, -iz·es**) *vt* 1. to remove something from its locality 2. to remove something from local influences, and broaden its range or scope —**de·lo·cal·i·za·tion** /dee lṑkəli záysh'n/ *n*

De·lon /də láwN/, **Alain** (*b.* 1935) French actor, producer, director, and screenwriter. His notable movies include the film noir classic *The Godson* (1967).

De·los /deé lòss/ island of Greece, the smallest island of the Cyclades group in the southern Aegean Sea, now almost uninhabited. Area: 2 sq. mi./5 sq. km.

de·louse /dee lówss/ (**-loused, -lous·ing, -lous·es**) *vt* to give a person or animal treatment to remove lice

Del·phi /dél fī/ ancient Greek town on the southern slopes of Mount Parnassus, about 6 mi./9.5 km north of the Gulf of Corinth. It is the site of the Temple of Apollo and the Delphic oracle.

Del·phic *adj* **1. Del·phic** /délfik/, **Del·phi·an** /délfee ən/ relating to Delphi or its temple or oracle **2.** *also* **del·phic** obscure and open to more than one interpretation —**Del·phi·cal·ly** *adv*

Del·phic or·a·cle *n* in ancient Greece, an oracle of great authority and notorious ambiguity at Delphi, where it was believed the god Apollo spoke through a priestess

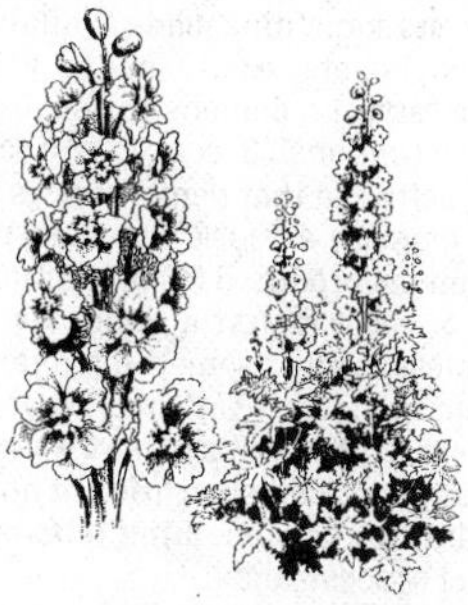

delphinium

del·phin·i·um /del fínnee əm/ *n* a tall ornamental plant. Flowers: blue or white in long spikes. Genus: *Delphinium.* [Early 17C. Via modern Latin < Greek *delphinion* "larkspur" < *delphis* "dolphin"; from the shape of the flower]

Del·phi·nus /del fínəss/ *n* a small faint constellation of the northern hemisphere lying on the Milky Way, situated between Pegasus and Aquila. See illustration at **constellation**

Del·phi tech·nique *n* a process used in business forecasting of reaching a consensus by the anonymous solicitation and comparison of the views of experts [< the oracle of DELPHI]

Del·ray Beach /dèl ray-/ city on the Atlantic Ocean coast in southeastern Florida. Population: 62,272 (2002 estimate).

Del Ri·o /del rée ō/ town in southwestern Texas on the Río Grande, directly opposite Ciudad Acuña, Mexico. Population: 34,611 (2002 estimate).

del·ta /déltə/ *n* **1.** **TRIANGULAR LAND AREA AT RIVER MOUTH** a triangular deposit of sand and soil at the mouth of a river or inlet **2.** *also* **Del·ta AREA IN RIVER DELTA** an area in or around the delta of a river **3. 4TH LETTER OF GREEK ALPHABET** the fourth letter of the Greek alphabet, represented in the English alphabet as "d." See table at **alphabet 4. SOMETHING TRIANGULAR** something shaped like a triangle or delta **5.** MATH **CHANGE IN VARIABLE** a change in the value of a variable. Symbol Δ [Pre-12C. Via Latin < Greek < Phoenician]

Del·ta *n* **1.** a code word for the letter "D," used in international radio communications **2.** the fourth brightest star in a constellation (*followed by the Latin genitive*)

Del·ta Force *n* the US Army 1st Special Forces Operational Detachment, a military and counterterrorist force

del·ta ray *n* a low-energy particle, e.g., an electron, emitted by matter when subjected to ionizing radiation

del·ta wave, del·ta rhythm *n* a slow brain wave that is produced by adults in deep sleep. Delta waves are produced in the front of the brain and have a frequency of 3.5 cycles per second.

del·ta wing *n* an airplane wing that has a triangular swept-back shape

del·ti·ol·o·gy /dèltee óllәjee/ *n* the collection and study of postcards [Mid-20C. < Greek *deltion* "little writing tablet" < *deltos* "writing tablet"] —**del·ti·ol·o·gist** *n*

del·toid /dél tòyd/ *n* a thick triangular muscle that covers the shoulder joint ■ *adj* triangular in shape (*technical*) [Mid-18C. Directly or via French < modern Latin *deltoides* "delta-shaped" < Greek *delta*]

Del·to·na /del tṓnə/ city in east central Florida, southwest of Daytona Beach. Population: 73,788 (2002 estimate).

delts /delts/ *npl* the deltoid muscles (*informal*) [Shortening]

de·lude /di lóod/ (**-lud·ed, -lud·ing, -ludes**) *vt* to persuade somebody to believe something that is untrue or unreal [15C. < Latin *deludere* "play to your detriment" < *ludere* "play" (see LUDIC)] —**de·lud·a·ble** *adj* —**de·lud·ed** *adj* —**de·lud·er** *n* —**de·lud·ing·ly** *adv*

del·uge /déllyooj/ *n* **1. SUDDEN HEAVY DOWNPOUR** a sudden heavy downpour of rain or torrent of water **2. VAST QUANTITY** an overwhelming amount of something ■ *vt* (**-uged, -ug·ing, -ug·es**) **1. INUNDATE SOMEBODY WITH SOMETHING** to overwhelm somebody with a large amount of something **2. OVERWHELM SOMEBODY OR SOMETHING WITH WATER** to flood or soak somebody or something with heavy rain or a sudden torrent of water [15C. < Old French < Latin *diluere* "wash away" < *lavare* "wash"]

Del·uge *n* BIBLE same as **Flood**

de·lu·sion /di lóozh'n/ *n* **1.** a persistent false belief held in the face of strong contradictory evidence, especially as a symptom of a psychiatric condition **2.** a false or mistaken belief or idea about something [15C. < Latin *delusion-* < past participle of *deludere* (see DELUDE)] —**de·lu·sion·al** *adj*

USAGE See ***allusion.***

de·lu·sions of gran·deur *npl* gross and false overestimation of personal worth, importance, powerfulness, or attractiveness

de·lu·sive /di lóossiv/ *adj* leading to a belief in something untrue or unreal [Early 17C. < Latin *delus-*, past participle of *deludere* (see DELUDE)] —**de·lu·sive·ly** *adv* —**de·lu·sive·ness** *n*

de·lu·so·ry /di lóossəree/ *adj* deceptive in nature or character and likely to mislead or delude somebody [15C. < late Latin *delusorius* < past participle of Latin *deludere* (see DELUDE)]

de·luxe /di lúks/, **de luxe** *adj* of a luxurious standard and surpassing all others of the same type [Early 19C. < French *de luxe* "of luxury"]

delve /delv/ *v* (**delved, delv·ing, delves**) **1.** *vi* **DIG FOR INFORMATION** to investigate or research something thoroughly in order to obtain information **2.** *vti* **EXCAVATE SOMETHING** to dig something such as a ditch, hole, or burrow (*archaic*) ■ *n* **RUMMAGING SEARCH** a rummaging or a digging into something to find something that is hidden or difficult to reach [Old English *delfan* < Germanic] —**delv·er** *n*

dem /dem/ *pron Carib* same as **them** ◇ **an** *or* **and dem** *or* **an them** *Carib* **1.** used to form a plural ○ *di man an dem a come* **2.** and others

Dem /dem/ *n* POL same as **Democrat** (*informal*) [Late 19C. Shortening]

Dem. *abbr* POL **1.** Democrat **2.** Democratic

de·mag·net·ize /dee mágnə tīz/ (**-ized, -iz·ing, -iz·es**) *vt* to remove the magnetic properties from something —**de·mag·net·i·za·tion** /dee màgnəti záysh'n/ *n* —**de·mag·net·iz·er** *n*

dem·a·gog *n, vti* POL another spelling of **demagogue**

dem·a·gog·ic /dèmmə gójjik, -góggik/, **dem·a·gog·i·cal** /-ik'l/ *adj* making an appeal to people's emotions, instincts, and prejudices in a way that is considered to be politically manipulative and dangerous [Mid-19C. < Greek *dēmagōgikos* < *dēmagōgos* (see DEMAGOGUE)] —**dem·a·gog·i·cal·ly** *adv*

dem·a·gogue /démmə gòg/, **dem·a·gog** *n* **1. EMOTIVE DICTATOR** a political leader who gains power by appealing to people's emotions, instincts, and prejudices in a way that is considered manipulative and dangerous **2. POPULAR LEADER IN ANCIENT TIMES** in ancient times, a popular leader who represented the ordinary people ■ *v* (**-gogued, -gogu·ing, -gogues; -goged, -gog·ing, -gogs**) **1.** *vi* **ENGAGE IN DEMAGOGUERY** to act like a demagogue in gaining power by appealing to people's emotions and prejudices **2.** ⚠ *vti* **ELICIT EMOTIVE BIAS ON ISSUES** to elicit people's emotional and prejudicial biases on an issue [Mid-17C. < Greek *dēmagōgos* "leader of the people" < *agōgos* "leader" < *agein* "lead"] —**dem·a·gog·ism** *n* —**dem·a·gogu·er·y** *n*

USAGE See ***functional shift.***

de Man /də mán/, **Paul** (1919–83) Belgian-born US philosopher and theorist. He moved to the United States in 1947 and taught at Cornell, Johns Hopkins, and Yale universities. He is most famous for his essays on deconstructionism, e.g., *Blindness and Insight: Essays in the Rhetoric of Contemporary Criticism* (1971).

de·mand /di mánd/ *n* **1. FORCEFUL REQUEST** a clear and firm request that is difficult to ignore or deny **2. CUSTOMER INTEREST IN ACQUIRING SOMETHING** the level of desire or need that exists for particular goods or services ○ *Demand for that model is outstripping supply.* **3. NEED FOR RESOURCES OR ACTION** an urgent requirement for time, facilities, resources, or action **4.** LAW **LEGALLY ENFORCEABLE REQUEST** a formal request that must be complied with by law ■ *v* (**-mand·ed, -mand·ing, -mands**) **1.** *vt* **REQUEST SOMETHING FORCEFULLY** to request something clearly and firmly in a way that is difficult to ignore or deny **2.** *vt* **ASK FORCEFULLY FOR ANSWER** to ask for an answer to a question in an extremely forceful way **3.** *vti* **CALL FOR RESOURCES** to require something such as time, facilities, resources, or action in order to function or succeed [14C. Via French < Latin *demandare* "entrust completely" < *mandare* "entrust, order" (see MANDATE)] —**de·mand·a·ble** *adj* —**de·mand·er** *n* ◇ **in demand** wanted or sought by many people ◇ **on demand** promptly, whenever a request is received

de·mand de·pos·it *n* a bank deposit that can be withdrawn at any time without notice

de·mand draft *n* FIN same as **sight draft**

de·mand feed·ing *n* the practice of feeding a baby when it cries to be fed, rather than at set times

de·mand·ing /di mánding/ *adj* requiring a lot of time, attention, energy, or resources

de·mand·ing·ly /di mándinglee/ *adv* in a highly insistent manner

de·mand loan *n* FIN same as **call loan**

de·mand note *n* same as **sight draft**

de·mand-pull, de·mand-pull in·fla·tion *n* inflation caused by demand for goods and services outstripping supply

de·mand-side *adj* relating to an economic policy that emphasizes the importance of demand and consumption

de·man·toid /di mán tòyd/ *n* a transparent green variety of garnet. Use: gems. [Late 19C. < German, "diamond-shaped" < *Demant* "diamond"]

de·mar·cate /di maar kàyt, dee maar kàyt/ (**-cat·ed, -cat·ing, -cates**) *vt* **1.** to decide on and set the boundaries of a piece of land **2.** to state in a clear way where something begins and ends [Early 19C. Back-formation < DEMARCATION] —**de·mar·ca·tor** *n*

de·mar·ca·tion /dee maar káysh'n/ *n* **1.** the process of deciding on and setting the boundaries of a piece of land **2.** the division of something so that its divided parts are separate and identifiable [Early 18C. < Spanish *demarcación* "marking off" < *marcar* "to mark" < Germanic]

de·mar·ca·tion dis·pute *n* a disagreement over where a land boundary lies

dé·marche /day maarsh/ (*plural* **-march·es**) *n* **1. DIPLOMATIC REPRESENTATION** a diplomatic representation, especially a move, maneuver, or protest made orally **2. CITIZENS' PROTEST STATEMENT** a statement of protest made by or on behalf of the citizens of a nation to their government or to a controlling authority **3. MOVE OR COUNTERMOVE** a move, step, or countermove [Mid-17C. < French *démarcher* "take steps" < *marcher* "march"]

De Ma·ri·a /də ma rée ə/, **Walter** (*b.* 1935) US artist. A prominent conceptual artist and pioneer of the Land Art movement, he is best known for *New York Earth Room* (1977) and for his large-scale sculpture on a plateau in New Mexico *The Lightning Field* (1977).

de·ma·te·ri·al·ize /deemə teeree ə līz/ (**-ized, -iz·ing, -iz·es**) *vti* to disappear, or cause something to disappear —**de·ma·te·ri·al·i·za·tion** /deemə teeree əli záysh'n/ *n*

deme /deem/ *n* **1.** a township in Attica in ancient Greece **2.** a local population of closely related interbreeding species [Mid-19C. < Greek *dēmos* (see DEMOS)]

de·mean /di meén/ (**-meaned, -mean·ing, -means**) *vt* to reduce somebody to a much lower status in a humiliating way [Early 17C. < DE- "down" + MEAN[2] "inferior in rank"] —**de·mean·ing** *adj*

de·mean·or /di meénər/ *n* somebody's behavior, manner, or appearance, especially as it reflects on character

de·mean·our *n* Can, UK spelling of **demeanor**

de·ment·ed /di méntəd/ *adj* **1.** completely unreasonable or lacking any sense of the consequences of actions taken (*informal*) **2.** affected by the loss of intellectual functions that is associated with dementia [Mid-17C. Past participle of obsolete *dement* "deprive of reason" < Latin *dementare* < *ment-* "mind"] —**de·ment·ed·ly** *adv* —**de·ment·ed·ness** *n*

de·men·tia /di ménshə/ *n* the usually progressive deterioration of intellectual functions such as memory that can occur while other brain functions such as those controlling movement and the senses are retained [Late 18C. < Latin < *dement-* < *de-* "away" + *ment-* "mind"]

de·men·tia prae·cox /-preé kòks/ *n* PSYCHIAT same as **schizophrenia** (sense 1) (*archaic*) [< Latin, "premature loss of mind"]

Dem·e·rar·a win·dow *n Carib* a louvered window, hinged at the top and pushed up and held with a stick [After a region of Guyana]

de·merg·er /dee múrjər/ *n UK* a merger between two or more companies that is dissolved, or the separation of one company from a larger company or group —**de·merge** *vti*

de·mer·it /di mérrit/ *n* **1.** a mark against somebody such as a student or cadet for a deficiency or misconduct **2.** a negative feature or disadvantage of something, especially when contrasted with its positive features or advantages (*often used in the plural*) [14C. Directly or via French < Latin *demeritum* < *demereri* "deserve thoroughly" < *mereri* "deserve"] —**de·mer·i·to·ri·ous** /di mèrrə táwree əss/ *adj*—**de·mer·i·to·ri·ous·ly** *adv*

Dem·er·ol /démmə rōl/ *tdmk* a trademark for the painkiller meperidine

de·mer·sal /di múrss'l/ *adj* living or found in the deepest part of a body of water [Late 19C. < Latin *demersus*, past participle of *demergere* "submerge" < *mergere* "plunge"]

de·mesne /di máyn/ *n* **1. POSSESSION OF OWN LAND** the possession and use of your own land, as opposed to the ownership of land that is occupied by tenants (*formal*) **2. ESTATE** an extensive landed property (*formal*) **3. REALM OF MONARCH** the realm under the rule of a monarch (*formal*) **4. PRIVATE GROUNDS OF MANSION** the grounds attached to a mansion for the private use of the owner (*archaic*) **5. FEUDAL MANORIAL LAND** manorial land that a feudal lord kept for his own private use (*archaic*) [14C. Via Old French *demeine* "belonging to a lord" < Latin *dominicus* < *dominus* "lord"]

De·me·ter /də meétər/ *n* in Greek mythology, the goddess of corn and the harvest, daughter of Cronus and Rhea and mother of Persephone. Roman equivalent **Ceres**[1] (sense 1)

demi- *prefix* **1.** half ○ *demivolte* **2.** partly ○ *demigod* [Via Old French < Latin *dimidius* "split in two" < *dis-* "apart" + *medius* "half"]

dem·i·bas·tion /dèmmee básch'n, -bástee ən/ *n* a two-sided fortification that consists of a wall facing forward and a wall facing a flank

dem·i·god /démmee gòd/ *n* **1. MAN TREATED LIKE GOD** an important or revered man who is treated like a god **2. HUMAN WITH POWERS OF GOD** a mythological being who is half human and half god **3. MINOR GOD** a god regarded as minor in a hierarchy of other gods

dem·i·god·dess /démmee gòddəss/ *n* **1.** an important or revered woman who is treated like a goddess **2.** a mythological being who is half woman and half goddess

dem·i·john /démmee jòn/ *n* a large bottle that has a short narrow neck and is often used for making wine. Demijohns may also be made of earthenware and are sometimes encased in a wickerwork covering. [Mid-18C. By folk etymology < French *dame-jeanne* "Lady Jane," its popular name in France]

de·mil·i·ta·rize /dee míllitə rīz/ (**-rized, -riz·ing, -riz·es**) *vt* to remove or prohibit the presence of soldiers, weapons, and military installations in an area after an agreement has been made to stop fighting —**de·mil·i·ta·ri·za·tion** /dee mìllitəri záysh'n/ *n*

de·mil·i·ta·rized zone *n* an officially recognized area from which all soldiers, weapons, and military installations have been removed after an agreement to stop fighting

De Mille /də míl/, **Agnes** (1909–93) US dancer and choreographer. She was known for integrating popular dance styles with ballet in classical productions and musicals. Full name **de Mille, Agnes George**

> "It is the one physical performance possible to women that does not carry with it either moral responsibility or physical hazard. It constitutes a true recapturing of pagan freedom and childish play. It can be even a complete although unconscious substitute for physical love, and in the lives of the greatest dancers it usually assumes this function."
>
> [Agnes de Mille, "Ballet and Sex," *Dance to the Piper*, 1987]

De·Mille /də míl/, **Cecil B.** (1881–1959) US movie director and producer. He was known for his lavish epic movies. Full name **DeMille, Cecil Blount**

dem·i·mon·daine /dèmmee mon dáyn/ *n* a woman who is financially supported by a wealthy lover [Late 19C. < French < *demi-monde* "half world"]

dem·i·monde /démmee mònd, dèmmee mónd/ *n* (*literary*) **1.** people who are not considered to be entirely respectable **2.** a class of women who were financially supported by wealthy lovers, especially in the 19th and early 20th centuries [Mid-19C. < French *demi-monde* "half world"]

de·min·er·al·ize /dee mínnərə līz/ (**-ized, -iz·ing, -iz·es**) *vt* to remove minerals or mineral salts from something such as bone or a liquid —**de·min·er·al·i·za·tion** /dee mìnnərəli záysh'n/ *n* —**de·min·er·al·i·zer** *n*

Dem·ing /démming/ town in southwestern New Mexico, west of Las Cruces. Population: 14,126 (2002 estimate).

dem·i·pen·sion /dèmmee paan syàwn/ *n UK* TRAVEL same as **half board**

De·mir·el /dèmmi rél/, **Süleyman** (*b.* 1924) Turkish politician. He served four terms as prime minister (1965–93) and was the ninth president of Turkey (1993–2000).

dem·i·re·lief /démmee ri leéf/ *n* same as **half relief**

de·mise /di mīz/ (*formal*) *n* **1. SOMEBODY'S DEATH** the death of somebody, especially when it happens slowly and predictably **2. END OF SOMETHING** the end of something that used to exist, especially when it happens slowly and predictably ■ *v* (**-mised, -mis·ing, -mis·es**) **1.** *vi* **CEASE LIVING** to die, especially slowly and predictably **2.** *vti* LAW **TRANSFER LEGALLY** to transfer something through a line of descent or according to a will, or be transferred in this way [15C. < Anglo-Norman < Old French *demis* "sent away" < Latin *dimittere* (see DEMIT)] —**de·mis·a·ble** *adj*

dem·i·sec /dèmmee sék/ *adj* describes champagne or sparkling wine that is more sweet than dry [< French, "half dry"] —**dem·i·sec** *n*

dem·i·sem·i·qua·ver /dèmmee semmee kwáyvər/ *n UK* same as **thirty-second note**

de·mis·sion /di mísh'n/ *n* resignation from an important official post [Mid-16C. Via French < Latin *dimission-* "dismissal" < past participle of *dimittere* (see DEMIT)]

de·mist /dee míst/ *vti UK* same as **defog**

de·mist·er /dee místər/ *n UK* same as **defogger**

de·mit /di mít/ (**-mit·ted, -mit·ting, -mits**) *vti* to resign from or give up an important official post (*formal*) [15C. Via French < Latin *dimittere* "send away" < *mittere* "send"]

dem·i·tasse /démmee tàss, -taàss/ *n* a small cup of coffee, or the cup in which such coffee is served [Mid-19C. < French, "half cup"]

dem·i·urge /démmee ùrj/ *n* **1.** a very strong, driving, and influential force or personality (*formal*) **2.** a public magistrate in some ancient Greek states [Early 17C. Via ecclesiastical Latin < Greek *dēmiourgos* "skilled person" < *dēmios* "of the people" + *-ergos* "working"] —**dem·i·ur·geous** /dèmmee úrjəss/ *adj*—**dem·i·ur·gic** *adj* —**dem·i·ur·gi·cal** *adj* —**dem·i·ur·gi·cal·ly** *adv*

Dem·i·urge *n* in Gnostic and Platonic philosophies, the creator and controller of the material world

dem·i·volte /démmee vōlt/ *n* in dressage, a half turn made by a horse with its forelegs raised [Mid-17C. < French, "half turn"]

dem·i·world /démmee wùrld/ *n* same as **demimonde** (sense 1)

dem·o /démmō/ *n* (*plural* **de·mos**) **1. DEMONSTRATION OF PRODUCT FEATURES** something made available for testing by potential buyers, e.g., a motor vehicle **2. DEMONSTRATION OF PRODUCT** a demonstration, especially of a new product (*informal*) **3.** COMPUT **TRIAL SOFTWARE** a trial version of software that demonstrates its principle features (*informal*) **4.** MUSIC **MUSIC SAMPLE** a recorded sample of music produced for promotional purposes (*informal*) **5. PUBLIC PROTEST** a public event in which people protest against something, often by marching through the streets (*informal*) ■ *vt* (**de·moed, de·mo·ing, de·mos**) **SHOW HOW SOMETHING WORKS** to explain, describe, or give a demonstration of how something works or how to do something (*informal*) [Mid-20C. Shortening of DEMONSTRATION]

de·mob /dee mób/ (**-mobbed, -mob·bing, -mobs**) *vti UK* same as **demobilize** (*informal*) [Early 20C. Shortening]

de·mo·bil·ize /dee mṓbə līz/ (**-ized, -iz·ing, -iz·es**) *vti* to discharge somebody from the armed forces and send him or her home, usually after a war, or be discharged in this way —**de·mo·bil·i·za·tion** /dee mōbəli záysh'n/ *n*

de·moc·ra·cy /di mókrəssee/ (*plural* **-cies**) *n* **1. FREE AND EQUAL REPRESENTATION OF PEOPLE** the free and equal right of every person to participate in a system of government, often practiced by electing representatives of the people by the majority of the people ○ *"Democracy is like the experience of life itself – always changing, infinite in its variety, sometimes turbulent and all the more valuable for having been tested for adversity."* (Jimmy Carter, *Speech to Parliament of India*; June 2, 1978) **2. DEMOCRATIC NATION** a country with a government that has been elected freely and equally by all its citizens **3. DEMOCRATIC SYSTEM OF GOVERNMENT** a system of government based on the principle of majority decision-making **4. CONTROL OF ORGANIZATION BY MEMBERS** the control of an organization by its members, who have a free and equal right to participate in decision-making processes [Late 16C. Directly or via French < medieval Latin *democratia* < Greek *dēmokratia* "rule of the people" < *dēmos* "people" + *kratos* "rule"]

dem·o·crat /démmə kràt/ *n* somebody who believes in or supports democracy or the democratic system of government

Dem·o·crat *n* a member of the Democratic Party, one of the two major political parties in the United States

dem·o·crat·ic /dèmmə kráttik/ *adj* characterized by free and equal participation in government or in the decision-making processes of an organization or group —**dem·o·crat·i·cal·ly** *adv*

Dem·o·crat·ic *adj* relating to or associated with the Democratic Party of the United States

dem·o·crat·ic def·i·cit *n* a situation in which political structures, organizations, or decision-making processes lack democratic legitimacy, especially as discussed in the European Union

Dem·o·crat·ic Par·ty *n* one of the two major political parties in the United States, formed after a split in the former Democratic-Republican Party under Andrew Jackson in 1828

Dem·o·crat·ic-Re·pub·li·can Par·ty *n* a US political party that was founded by Thomas Jefferson in 1792 and was dissolved in 1828 under Andrew Jackson. Its main opponent was the Federalist Party, originally led by Alexander Hamilton.

Dem·o·crat·ic Un·i·on·ist Par·ty *n* a Northern Ireland political party, established by the Reverend Ian Paisley in 1971, and strongly committed to the maintenance of the union between Great Britain and Northern Ireland

de·moc·ra·tize /di mókrə tīz/ (**-tized, -tiz·ing, -tiz·es**) *vt* **1. GIVE CONTROL OF COUNTRY TO CITIZENRY** to put a country under the control of its citizens by allowing them to participate in government or decision-making processes in a free and equal way **2. INTRODUCE DEMOCRACY TO STATE** to take steps toward establishing the features of liberal democracy in a state **3. GIVE CONTROL OF ORGANIZATION TO MEMBERS** to put an organization under the control of its members by giving them free and equal decision-making powers **4. GIVE SOMETHING POPULAR APPEAL** to make something accessible to everybody —**de·moc·ra·ti·za·tion** /di mòkrəti záysh'n/ *n*

De·moc·ri·tus /di mókritəss/ (460?–370? B.C.) Greek philosopher. A prolific writer, he first propounded the atomic theory of the universe. Only a few fragments of his work remain.

> "In reality we apprehend nothing for certain, but only as it changes according to the condition of our body, and of the things that impinge or offer resistance to it."
> [Attributed to Democritus]

dé·mo·dé /dày mō dáy/ *adj* no longer fashionable [Late 19C. < French, past participle of *démoder* "go out of fashion" < *mode* "fashion"]

de·mod·u·late /dee mójjə làyt/ (**-lat·ed, -lat·ing, -lates**) *vt* to extract a signal carrying information from a radio wave (**carrier**) —**de·mod·u·la·tion** /dee mòjjə láysh'n/ *n* —**de·mod·u·la·tor** *n*

dem·o·graph·ic /dèmmə gráffik/ *adj* **OF HUMAN POPULATIONS** relating to demography or demographics ■ *n* MARKETING **PART OF POPULATION** a part of a population identified as a group, especially as a target for sales or advertising ■ **dem·o·graph·ics** *npl* **CHARACTERISTICS AND STATISTICS OF HUMAN POPULATION** the characteristics of a human population or part of it, especially its size, growth, density, distribution, and statistics regarding birth, marriage, disease, and death —**dem·o·graph·i·cal** *adj* —**dem·o·graph·i·cal·ly** *adv*

de·mog·ra·phy /di móggrəfee/ *n* **1.** the study of human populations, including their size, growth, density, and distribution, and statistics regarding birth, marriage, disease, and death **2.** the makeup of a particular human population [Late 19C. < Greek *dēmos* "people"] —**de·mog·ra·pher** *n* —**de·mog·ra·phist** *n*

dem·oi·selle /dèmwə zél/ *n* **1.** a young woman or girl (*literary*) **2.** *also* **dem·oi·selle crane** BIRDS a small crane with a slender gray body, black plumes, and white ear tufts. Native to: northern Africa, Asia. Latin name: *Anthropoides virgo*. **3.** FISH same as **damselfish** **4.** INSECTS same as **damselfly** [Early 16C. < French, modern form of Old French *dameisele* (see DAMSEL)]

de·mol·ish /di móllish/ (**-ished, -ish·ing, -ish·es**) *vt* **1. WRECK STRUCTURE** to destroy a building or other structure completely **2. DAMAGE SOMETHING IRREPARABLY** to damage something so severely that it cannot be repaired or restored **3. BEAT OPPONENT SOUNDLY** to beat an opponent very convincingly, especially in sports or debate (*informal*) **4. EAT FOOD FAST** to eat a large amount of food very quickly (*informal*) [Mid-16C. < Old French *démoliss-*, stem of *démolir* < Latin *demolire* "undo construction of a mass" < *moles* "mass"] —**de·mol·ish·er** *n*

dem·o·li·tion /dèmmə lísh'n/ *n* **1. DESTRUCTION OF BUILDING** the complete destruction of a building or other structure ○ *The old hospital is scheduled for demolition.* **2. ANNIHILATION** the destruction or annihilation of somebody or something ■ **dem·o·li·tions** *npl* **EXPLOSIVES** explosives, especially those used by the military [Mid-16C. Via French < Latin *demolition-* < *demolire* (see DEMOLISH)]

dem·o·li·tion der·by *n* an entertainment and sporting event held at a fair or on a speedway at which drivers crash old cars, the winner being the driver of the last car running

dem·o·li·tion·ist /dèmmə lísh'nist/ *n* a person or company whose job it is to demolish buildings

de·mon /deémən/ *n* **1. SUPPOSED EVIL SPIRIT** a supposed ghost or spirit regarded as evil **2. PERSONAL FEAR OR ANXIETY** a fear or anxiety that torments somebody ○ *We all have our own personal demons.* **3. EXPERT** somebody who is very skilled at something (*informal*) [13C. Via Latin *daemon*, medieval Latin *demon* "evil spirit" < Greek *daimōn* "divine power, guiding spirit"]

de·mon·e·tize /dee mónnə tīz/ (**-tized, -tiz·ing, -tiz·es**) *vt* **1.** to stop using a particular metal to make coins **2.** to withdraw units of money from circulation [Mid-19C. < French *démonétiser* "refrain from using money" < Latin *moneta* "money"] —**de·mon·e·ti·za·tion** /dee mònnəti záysh'n/ *n*

de·mo·ni·ac /di mṓnee àk/, **de·mo·ni·a·cal** /deèmə nī́ ək'l/ *adj* **1.** resembling or characteristic of a supposed evil spirit **2.** evil or wicked in character or nature **3.** same as **demonic** (sense 2) [14C. < late Latin *daemoniacus* < Latin *daemon* (see DEMON)]

de·mon·ic /di mónnik/ *adj* **1.** relating to or resembling a demon, especially in wickedness **2.** intense, frantic, or wild, as if driven or possessed by a demon —**de·mon·i·cal·ly** *adv*

de·mon·ize /deémə nīz/ (**-ized, -iz·ing, -iz·es**) *vt* to cause somebody or something to appear evil or threatening in the eyes of others —**de·mon·i·za·tion** /deèməni záysh'n/ *n*

de·mon·o·la·try /deèmə nóllətree/ *n* the worship of demons or of the devil —**de·mon·o·lat·er** *n*

de·mon·ol·o·gy /deèmə nólləjee/ *n* the study of demons, especially those that are frequent in the folklore of some societies —**de·mon·o·log·i·cal** /deèmənə lójjik'l/ *adj* —**de·mon·ol·o·gist** *n*

de·mon·stra·ble /di mónstrəb'l/ *adj* **1.** so obvious as to be readily recognized ○ *a demonstrable need for rail service* **2.** capable of being shown to exist or be true ○ *demonstrable proof* [14C. Directly or via French < Latin *demonstrabilis* < *demonstrare* (see DEMONSTRATE)] —**de·mon·stra·bil·i·ty** /di mònstrə bíllətee/ *n* —**de·mon·stra·ble·ness** *n* —**de·mon·stra·bly** *adv*

dem·on·strate /démmən stràyt/ (**-strat·ed, -strat·ing, -strates**) *v* **1.** *vt* **EXPLAIN WORKINGS OF SOMETHING** to explain or describe how something works or how to do something **2.** *vt* **SHOW VALIDITY OF SOMETHING** to show or prove something clearly and convincingly **3.** *vi* **PROTEST OR SUPPORT SOMEBODY OR SOMETHING** to make a public show as a group for or against an issue, cause, or person, often by marching through the streets [Mid-16C. < Latin *demonstrat-*, past participle of *demonstrare* < *monstrare* "show" < *monstrum* "omen"]

dem·on·stra·tion /dèmmən stráysh'n/ *n* **1. DISPLAY SHOWING HOW TO DO SOMETHING** a presentation to others of the way in which something works or is done **2. GROUP DISPLAY OF OPINION** a public show as a group for or against an issue, cause, or person **3. SHOW OF MILITARY PREPAREDNESS** a show of military force or readiness for combat **4. CONCLUSIVE PROOF** evidence or proof that allows no doubt as to the validity or soundness of something

dem·on·stra·tion sport *n* a sport that is contested in the Olympics on a trial basis and has yet to be accepted as a permanent medal sport

de·mon·stra·tive /di mónstrətiv/ *adj* **1. OBVIOUSLY AFFECTIONATE** unrestrained in showing love and affection toward somebody **2. PROVING** serving as proof ○ *demonstrative evidence* **3.** GRAM **SPECIFYING WHICH PERSON OR THING** describes a word such as "this" or "those" specifying which person or thing is being referred to ■ *n* GRAM **WORD SPECIFYING WHICH PERSON OR THING** a demonstrative word or phrase, e.g., "this," "that," "these," or "those" —**de·mon·stra·tive·ly** *adv* —**de·mon·stra·tive·ness** *n*

dem·on·stra·tor /démmən stràytər/ *n* **1.** a public protester or supporter of something, usually a member of a group **2.** somebody who shows or explains how to do something, or how something works **3.** *UK* same as **demo** *n* (sense 1)

de·mor·al·ize /di máwrə līz/ (**-ized, -iz·ing, -iz·es**) *vt* **1. ERODE MORALE OF SOMEBODY** to erode or destroy the courage, confidence, or hope of a person or group **2. CAUSE CONFUSION IN SOMETHING** to throw something into disorder or chaos **3. RUIN SOMEBODY MORALLY** to corrupt somebody morally —**de·mor·al·i·za·tion** /di màwrəli záysh'n/ *n* —**de·mor·al·iz·er** *n* —**de·mor·al·iz·ing·ly** *adv*

de·mos /deéməss/ *n* **1.** the ordinary people of a community or nation (*formal*) **2.** the common people in an ancient Greek city-state [Late 18C. < Greek *dēmos* "district, people living in a district"]

De·mos·the·nes /di mósthə neéz/ (384–322 B.C.) Greek orator. His reputation as the greatest Greek orator is based mainly on the *Philippics* (351, 344, 341 B.C.), a series of orations urging the Athenians to oppose the growing power of Philip II of Macedon.

de·mote /dee mṓt/ (**-mot·ed, -mot·ing, -motes**) *vt* to reduce somebody or something to a lower rank, status, or position [Late 19C. < DE- + PROMOTE]

de·mot·ic /di móttik/ *adj* **1.** relating to or involving ordinary people (*formal*) **2.** relating to a simplified form of Egyptian hieroglyphics [Early 19C. < Greek *dēmotikos* "popular, common" < *dēmos* "people"]

De·mot·ic *n* **1.** the colloquial form of modern Greek, adopted as the official variety of the language **2.** the later form of the ancient Egyptian language, written in the demotic script that was current in the first millennium B.C. —**De·mot·ic** *adj*

de·mo·tion /di mṓsh'n/ *n* a reduction in the rank, status, or position of somebody or something

de·mo·ti·vate /dee mṓti vàyt/ (**-vat·ed, -v·at·ing, -vates**) *vt* to make somebody feel less interested in working or studying effectively —**de·mo·ti·va·tion** /dee mòti váysh'n/ *n*

de·mount /dee mównt/ (**-mount·ed, -mount·ing, -mounts**) *vt* **1.** to take a piece of equipment away from its supports **2.** to take something apart, usually with the intention of reassembling it later —**de·mount·a·ble** *adj*

Demp·sey /démpsee/, **Jack** (1895–1983) US boxer. He won the world heavyweight title in 1919, which he lost to Gene Tunney in 1926. Full name **Dempsey, William Harrison**. Known as **the Manassa Mauler**

> "Kill the other guy before he kills you."
> [Jack Dempsey, *Times (London)*; June 2, 1983]

de·mul·cent /di múlssənt/ *n* a substance that soothes irritated or inflamed skin or mucous membranes. Lanoline and glycerin are demulcents. [Mid-18C. < Latin *demulcent-*, present participle of *demulcere* "soothe down" < *mulcere* "soothe"] —**de·mul·cent** *adj*

de·mul·si·fy /di múlssə fī/ (**-fied, -fy·ing, -fies**) *vti* to break an emulsion down permanently into its components, or be broken down permanently —**de·mul·si·fi·ca·tion** /di mùlssəfi káysh'n/ *n* —**de·mul·si·fi·er** *n*

de·mur /di múr/ (**-murred, -mur·ring, -murs**) *v* **1.** *vi* **SHOW RELUCTANCE** to delay or try to avoid doing something because of personal reservations or objections ○ *"While I acknowledged it might come to that [the use of force in the Persian Gulf], I demurred, saying it was too early to contemplate such action."* (George Bush, *A World Transformed*; 1998) **2.** *vi* **OBJECT SOMEWHAT** to object mildly to something that you do not want to do but have been asked to do **3.** *vti* LAW **MAKE LEGAL OBJECTION** to admit the facts of an opposing argument, but object that those facts alone are not by themselves adequate to make the case **4.** *vt* **SAY SOMETHING AS OBJECTION** to state something as a mild objection or a legal demurrer [13C. Via Old French *demorer* "delay, stay" < Latin *demorare*] —**de·mur·ra·ble** *adj* —**de·mur·ral** *n*

SYNONYMS See ***object***.

de·mure /di myŏor/ (**-mur·er, -mur·est**) *adj* **1.** looking or behaving in a modest manner, with reserve or seriousness **2.** acting in an affectedly shy or modest way [14C. < past participle of Old French *demorer* (see DEMUR)] —**de·mure·ly** *adv* —**de·mure·ness** *n*

de·mur·rage /di múr ij/ *n* **1.** detention or delay of a cargo carrier during its loading or unloading process, beyond its scheduled time of departure **2.** compensation paid when there is a delay in loading or unloading a carrier causing a delay in the carrier's departure [Mid-17C. < Old French *demo(u)rage* < *demorer* (see DEMUR)]

de·mur·rer /di múr ər/ *n* a legal objection that admits the facts of an opposing argument but asserts that those facts alone are not adequate to make the case [Early 16C. < French *demorer* (see DEMUR)]

De·muth /di mŏoth/, **Charles** (1883–1935) US painter. He was known for his still-life watercolors, and his oil-and-tempera architectural scenes such as *Business* (1921).

de·mu·tu·al·ize /dee myo͝ochoo ə lìz/ (**-ized, -iz·ing, -iz·es**) *vti* to convert a mutual organization such as an insurance company to a public corporation, or be converted in this way —**de·mu·tu·al·i·za·tion** /dee myo͝ochoo əli záysh'n/ *n*

de·my /di mī/ *adj* describes printing paper that is 17.5 in./444.5 mm by 22.5 in./571.5 mm or writing paper that is 16 in./406.4 mm by 21 in./533.4 mm [15C. Alteration of DEMI-]

de·my·e·lin·a·tion /dee mī əli náysh'n/ *n* the loss of the fatty covering (**myelin**) of nerve fibers —**de·my·e·lin·ate** /dee mī əli nàyt/ *vt*

de·mys·ti·fy /dee místə fī/ (**-fied, -fy·ing, -fies**) *vt* to remove the mystery surrounding something, e.g., by explaining it in simple language —**de·mys·ti·fi·ca·tion** /dee mìstəfi káysh'n/ *n* —**de·mys·ti·fi·er** *n*

de·my·thol·o·gize /dèemi thóllə jīz/ (**-gized, -giz·ing, -giz·es**) *vt* to reveal and understand the true character, nature, or meaning of something by ridding it of all mythical or mysterious aspects —**de·my·thol·o·gi·za·tion** /dèemi thòlləji záysh'n/ *n* —**de·my·thol·o·giz·er** *n*

den /den/ *n* **1.** ROOM FOR RELAXING a room in a house where family members and guests relax **2.** PLACE OF CRIME a place where illegal or secret activities take place **3.** WILD ANIMAL'S LAIR the hidden home of a wild animal **4.** CUB SCOUT GROUP a group of Cub Scouts typically made up of eight to ten youths **5.** SQUALID ROOM a squalid small room or place to live **6.** CHILDREN'S HIDEOUT a secret place where children play [Old English *denn* "wild animal's lair" < Indo-European, "flat surface"]

De·na·li /də naalee/ ➧ **McKinley, Mount**

De·na·li Na·tion·al Park and Pre·serve national park in central Alaska. It is home to Mount McKinley, the highest point in North America, at 20,320 ft./6,194 m. It was combined with Denali National Monument in 1980. Area: 9,492 sq. mi./24,585 sq. km.

de·nar /dée naar/ *n* the main unit of currency in the Former Yugoslav Republic of Macedonia. See table at **currency** [Late 20C. Alteration of Serbo-Croatian *dinar* "dinar" after Latin *denarius* (see DENARIUS)]

de·nar·i·us /di nérree əss/ (*plural* **-i·i** /-ee ī/) *n* **1.** an ancient Roman silver coin originally worth ten asses **2.** an ancient Roman gold coin worth 25 silver denarii [14C. < Latin, literally "containing ten" < *deni* "ten at a time"]

den·a·ry /dénnəree/ *adj* relating to a number system that has ten as its base, as in the decimal system [Mid-19C. < Latin *denarius* (see DENARIUS)]

de·na·tion·al·ize /dee náshən'l īz, -náshnə līz/ (**-ized, -iz·ing, -iz·es**) *vt* **1.** to sell an industry or other major asset owned by the state to private investors **2.** to deprive a people or nation of national rights or characteristics —**de·na·tion·al·i·za·tion** /dee nàshən'li záysh'n, -nàsh nəli-/ *n*

de·nat·u·ral·ize /dee náchərə līz/ (**-ized, -iz·ing, -iz·es**) *vt* **1.** to take away a naturalized citizen's citizenship, e.g., for having entered the country illegally **2.** to take away the original nature of something ○ *once-verdant jungles that were denaturalized by defoliants* —**de·nat·u·ral·i·za·tion** /dee nàchərəli záysh'n/ *n*

de·na·ture /dee náychər/ (**-tured, -tur·ing, -tures**) *vt* **1.** MAKE SOMETHING UNPALATABLE to make food or drink, especially alcohol, unsuitable for human consumption, by adding poison, dye, or unpleasant flavors **2.** BIOCHEM MODIFY MOLECULE'S STRUCTURE to change the molecular structure and characteristics of a molecule by chemical or physical means **3.** INDUST REMOVE WEAPON POTENTIAL OF NUCLEAR MATERIAL to make nuclear material unsuitable for use in a weapon by adding an isotope that cannot be split —**de·na·tur·ant** *n* —**de·na·tur·a·tion** /dee nàychə ráysh'n/ *n*

de·naz·i·fy /dee naatsə fī/ (**-fied, -fy·ing, -fies**) *vt* to remove something or somebody connected to Nazis or Nazism —**de·naz·i·fi·ca·tion** /dee naatsəfi káysh'n/ *n*

Den·bigh·shire /dénbee sheer, -shər/ county in north Wales. Population: 93,065 (2001).

Dench /dench/, **Dame Judi** (*b.* 1934) British actor. She has played leading roles with Britain's major stage companies and in award-winning films. She won an Academy Award for her performance in *Shakespeare in Love* (1999). Full name **Dench, Dame Judith Olivia**

dendr- *prefix* same as **dendro-** (*used before vowels*)

dendri- *prefix* same as **dendro-**

den·dri·form /déndri fàwrm/ *adj* shaped like a tree

den·dri·mer /déndrimər/ *n* a copolymer with a regular branching structure attached to a central chain of carbon atoms —**den·dri·mer·ic** /dèndri mérrik/ *adj*

den·drite /dén drīt/ *n* **1.** a branched extension of a nerve cell (**neuron**) that receives electrical signals from other neurons and conducts those signals to the cell body **2.** a mineral crystallized in the shape of a tree [Early 18C. Directly or via French < Greek *dendritēs* "of a tree" < *dendron* "tree"] —**den·drit·ic** /den dríttik/ *adj* —**den·drit·i·cal** *adj* —**den·drit·i·cal·ly** *adv*

dendro- *prefix* tree, resembling a tree ○ *dendrology* ○ *dendrite* [< Greek *dendron* < Indo-European, "be solid"]

den·dro·chro·nol·o·gy /dèndrō krə nóllәjee/ *n* the study of the annual growth rings in trees, wood, or wooden objects, especially as a way of dating wooden remains or determining past climatic conditions —**den·dro·chron·o·log·i·cal** /dèndrō krònnə lójjik'l/ *adj* —**den·dro·chro·nol·o·gist** *n*

den·dro·gram /déndrə gràm/ *n* a diagram showing the relationships of items arranged like the branches of a tree

den·droid /dén dròyd/, **den·droid·al** /den dróyd'l/ *adj* **1.** WITH STEM RESEMBLING TREE TRUNK describes plants with an erect main stem like a tree trunk **2.** MULTIBRANCHED describes plants with many branches, like those of a tree **3.** RESEMBLING TREE generally resembling a tree in shape or form

den·drol·o·gy /den dróllәjee/ *n* the study of trees and other woody plants —**den·dro·log·ic** /dèndrə lójjik/ *adj* —**den·dro·log·i·cal** *adj* —**den·drol·o·gist** *n* —**den·drol·o·gous** /-gəss/ *adj*

den·dron /dén dròn/ *n* ANAT same as **dendrite** (sense 2) (*dated*) [Late 19C. < DENDRITE + -ON[2]]

De·ne /day náy/ *npl* a group of Athabaskan-speaking Native North Americans who live in northern Canada, chiefly in the Northwest Territories [Late 19C. Via Canadian French < Athabaskan]

Den·eb /dénneb/ *n* the brightest star in the constellation Cygnus. Deneb is a white giant located over 1600 light-years from Earth.

de·ner·vate /dee núr vàyt/ (**-vat·ed, -vat·ing, -vates**) *vt* to deprive an organ or body part of nerves, either by cutting them or by blocking them with drugs, e.g., to control pain —**de·ner·va·tion** /dèenər váysh'n/ *n*

De·neuve /də no͝ov, də nōv/, **Catherine** (*b.* 1943) French movie actor. Her movies include *Repulsion* (1965) and *Belle de Jour* (1967). Born **Dorléac, Catherine**

den·gue /déng gee, -gày/, **den·gue fe·ver** *n* a tropical disease caused by a virus that is transmitted by mosquitoes and marked by high fever and severe muscle and joint pains [Early 19C. < Caribbean Spanish]

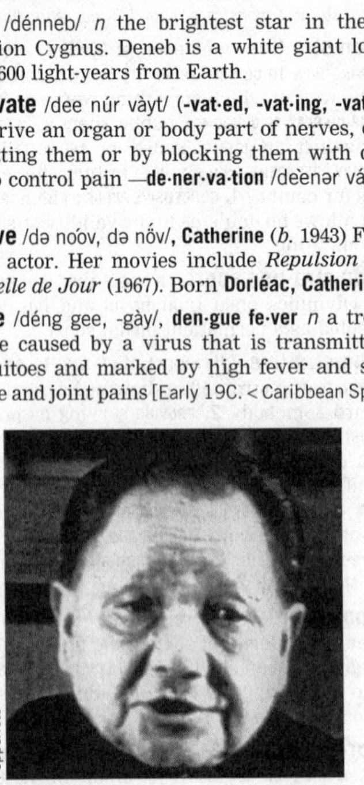

Deng Xiaoping

Deng Xiao·ping /dèng show píng, dùng-/ (1904–97) Chinese political leader. Purged twice from the Communist Party, he was reinstated in 1977 and was the undisputed leader of China until his death. He introduced reforms that led to greater economic freedom in China.

> "No individual in the present Chinese leadership can determine any of our policies on his own. All important decisions are made through collective discussions."
> [Deng Xiaoping, *Interview with Robert Maxwell*; 1984]

de·ni /dénnee/ (*plural same*) *n* a subunit of currency in the Former Yugoslav Republic of Macedonia. See table at **currency** [Late 20C. < Macedonian]

de·ni·a·ble /di nī əb'l/ *adj* **1.** able to be disclaimed or declared untrue ○ *deniable allegations* **2.** describes an activity planned and carried out in such a way that disavowal of it would probably be believed ○ *deniable covert operations* —**de·ni·a·bil·i·ty** /di nī ə bíllətee/ *n* —**de·ni·a·bly** *adv*

de·ni·al /di nī əl/ *n* **1.** DISAVOWAL a statement saying that something is not true or not correct ○ *her continued denial of the story* **2.** REFUSAL TO ALLOW SOMEBODY SOMETHING a refusal to grant something desired or believed to be a right ○ *a denial of justice* **3.** REFUSAL TO ACKNOWLEDGE EXISTENCE OF SOMETHING a refusal to believe in something or admit that something exists **4.** PSYCHOL REFUSAL TO FACE UNPLEASANT FACTS a state of mind marked by a refusal or an inability to recognize and deal with a serious personal problem ○ *She's in denial.* **5.** LAW OPPOSITION TO ALLEGATION in a court of law, a statement denying an accusation of wrongdoing

de·ni·al-of-ser·vice at·tack *n* an illegal attempt to put a computer system out of action by overloading it with data from many sources simultaneously

den·i·er[1] /dénnyər/ *n* **1.** a unit of fineness of silk and some artificial fibers such as nylon equal to one gram per 9,000 m of yarn. It is now largely superseded by other units. **2.** a silver coin, formerly used in several European countries [15C. Via French < Latin *denarius* (see DENARIUS)]

de·ni·er[2] /di nīr/ *n* somebody who denies something [15C. < DENY]

den·i·grate /dénni gràyt/ (**-grat·ed, -grat·ing, -grates**) *vt* **1.** to attack somebody's character or reputation **2.** ⚠ to disparage or criticize somebody or something, or make something seem unimportant [15C. < Latin *denigrat-*, past participle of *denigrare* "blacken completely" < *niger* "black"] —**den·i·gra·tion** /dènni gráysh'n/ *n* —**den·i·gra·tor** *n*

USAGE In its best-established sense ***denigrate*** means "attack a reputation." However, it is now often found in sentences like *I don't mean to denigrate the problem,* where its meaning has become closer to "disparage or belittle somebody or something." In this, it is following in the footsteps of *deprecate,* whose traditional meaning is "express condemnation of somebody or something," but which in *self-deprecating* has taken on the additional sense of "belittle."

den·im /dénnim/ *n* a durable woven cotton cloth. Use: clothing, especially jeans. ■ **den·ims** *npl* clothes made of denim, especially jeans, jackets, shirts, or skirts [Late 17C. < French *(serge) de Nîmes* "(serge) of Nîmes," France]

De Ni·ro /də neerō/, **Robert** (*b.* 1943) US actor. He won Academy Awards for *The Godfather II* (1974) and *Raging Bull* (1980).

> "Are you talking to me? / Are you talking to me? / Are you talking to me? / ...Well, I'm the only one here."
> [Robert De Niro. Words of lines for a main character *Taxi Driver*; 1976]

Den·i·son /dénniss'n/ city in northeastern Texas, near the Red River and the Texas-Oklahoma border, north of Dallas. Population: 23,169 (2002 estimate).

den·i·trate /dee nī tràyt/ (**-trat·ed, -trat·ing, -trates**) *vti* to remove a nitro or nitrate group, nitrogen compound, or nitrous acid from a chemical compound, or lose such components —**den·i·tra·tion** /dèe nī tráysh'n/ *n*

de·ni·tri·fy /dee nītrə fī/ (**-fied, -fy·ing, -fies**) *vt* **1.** to remove nitrogen or a nitrogen compound from a substance **2.** to convert nitrates into nitrites and ammonia —**de·ni·tri·fi·ca·tion** /dee nītrəfi káysh'n/ *n*

den·i·zen /dénniz'n/ *n* **1.** RESIDENT a resident of a specific country or area **2.** HABITUAL VISITOR a habitual visitor to a place ○ *denizens of cyberspace chat rooms* **3. NONNATIVE PLANT OR ANIMAL** a nonnative plant or animal that grows or lives in an area **4. FOREIGNER WITH RIGHTS OF RESIDENCE** a new resident in a foreign country who is given some legal rights there [15C. < Anglo-Norman *deinzein* < Old French *deinz* "inside" < Latin *de intus* "from inside"]

Denmark

Den·mark /dén maark/ southernmost and smallest country in Scandinavia, comprising the Jutland peninsula and about 480 islands. Language: Danish. Currency: krone. Capital: Copenhagen. Population: 5,384,384 (2003). Area: 16,639 sq. mi./43,094 sq. km. Official name **Kingdom of Denmark**

den moth·er *n* **1.** a woman who is in charge of a den of Cub Scouts **2.** a woman who has responsibility for a group of people

Den·nis /dénniss/ resort town in southeastern Massachusetts, on the north shore of Cape Cod on Cape Cod Bay, northeast of Yarmouth. Population: 16,194 (2002 estimate).

de·nom·i·nal /di nómmən'l/ *adj* describes parts of speech that are formed from or have the same form as a noun, e.g., the verb "to butter" —**de·nom·i·nal** *n*

de·nom·i·nate /di nómmə nàyt/ (**-nat·ed, -nat·ing, -nates**) *vt* **1.** to define something in terms of a particular unit of currency **2.** to give something a particular name or description (*formal*) [Mid-16C. < Latin *denominat-*, past participle of *denominare*, literally "name completely" < *nominare* "to name"] —**de·nom·i·na·ble** *adj*

de·nom·i·na·tion /di nòmmə náysh'n/ *n* **1. RELIGIOUS GROUPING** a religious grouping within a faith that has its own system of organization **2. UNIT OF VALUE OR MEASURE** a unit in a scale of value, especially monetary value, weight, measure, or size **3. NAME OR DESIGNATION** a name or designation given to a class, group, or type [14C. Directly or via French < Latin *denomination-* < *denominat-* (see DENOMINATE)] —**de·nom·i·na·tion·al** *adj*

de·nom·i·na·tive /di nómmə nàytiv, -nətiv/ *adj* GRAM same as **denominal** [Late 16C. < late Latin *denominativus* < Latin *denominat-* (see DENOMINATE)] —**de·nom·i·na·tive** *n* —**de·nom·i·na·tive·ly** *adv*

de·nom·i·na·tor /di nómmə nàytər/ *n* **1. NUMBER BELOW LINE IN FRACTION** the number below the line in a simple fraction, which indicates the number of parts making up the whole **2. COMMON CHARACTERISTIC** something held in common **3. AVERAGE LEVEL** an average standard, degree, or level of quality or taste

Den·on·ville /də noN veél/, **Jacques-René de Brisay, Marquis de** (1642–1710) French-born Canadian colonial administrator. He was governor-general of New France from 1685 to 1689, leading expeditions against the Iroquois in 1687 and 1689.

de nos jours /də nō zhoór/ *adj* of our time [< French]

de·no·ta·tion /deènō táysh'n/ *n* **1. BASIC MEANING** the most specific or literal meaning of a word, as opposed to its figurative senses or connotations **2. INDICATOR OF SOMETHING** a sign, symbol, or indication of something **3. REFERENCE OF TERM** in logic, the reference of a term

de·note /di nṓt/ (**-not·ed, -not·ing, -notes**) *vt* **1. MEAN SOMETHING** to have something as a meaning, especially a specific or literal one **2. REFER TO SOMEBODY OR SOMETHING** to designate or refer to somebody or something **3. SIGNIFY SOMETHING** to be a sign or indication of something [Late 16C. Via French < Latin *denotare*, literally "mark completely" < *notare* "to mark"] —**de·no·ta·tive** /deè nō tàytiv, di nṓtətiv/ *adj* —**de·no·tive** *adj*

USAGE denote or **represent**? Use ***denote*** when you want to say "to mean," "to refer to," or "to signify": *That word denotes "life" in Spanish. For our purposes, the word "corporation" will denote the XYZ Foundation. The tiny points of light in the sky denote the Big Dipper.* Use ***represent*** when you mean "to symbolize something else": *The red maple leaf represents* [not *denotes*] *Canada.*

USAGE See ***connote.***

---

de·noue·ment /dàynoo maaN/ *n* **1.** a final part of a story or drama in which everything is made clear and no questions or surprises remain **2.** the final stage or climax of a series of events ○ *the gripping denouement of the championship* [Mid-18C. < French < *dénouer* "untie" < *nouer* "to tie" < Latin *nodus* "knot"]

de·nounce /di nównss/ (**-nounced, -nounc·ing, -nounc·es**) *vt* **1. CRITICIZE SOMETHING PUBLICLY** to criticize or condemn something publicly and harshly **2. CHARGE SOMEBODY WITH WRONGDOING** to accuse somebody publicly of something such as disloyalty, or inform against somebody **3. ANNOUNCE TERMINATION OF AGREEMENT** to make a formal announcement of the end of a treaty or other agreement (*formal*) [14C. Via Old French *denoncier* < Latin *denuntiare* < *nuntiare* "proclaim, announce" < *nuntius* "messenger"] —**de·nounce·ment** *n* —**de·nounc·er** *n*

SYNONYMS See ***disapprove.***

---

de nov·o /də nṓvō, day-/ *adv* anew, afresh, or over again from the beginning ○ *Having found the lower court's analysis wrong, the appellate court undertook a review de novo.* [Mid-16C. < Latin, "from new"]

Den·pa·sar /den paá saar/ city in Indonesia and capital of the island province of Bali, located near Bali's southernmost point. Population: 373,272 (1997).

dense /denss/ (**dens·er, dens·est**) *adj* **1. TIGHTLY PACKED** so close together that there is little sense of open or unoccupied space ○ *a dense jungle* ○ *a dense population of 2 million* **2. VERY THICK** so thick that it is difficult or impossible to see through ○ *dense summer haze* **3. HARD TO PENETRATE INTELLECTUALLY** so complex and intricate that it is difficult to assimilate and understand **4. SLOW TO LEARN OR UNDERSTAND** considered to lack the ability to learn or understand quickly (*informal insult*) **5. WITH HIGH MASS** with a relatively high mass per unit volume [15C. Directly or via French < Latin *densus* "thick, dense"] —**dense·ly** *adv* —**dense·ness** *n*

den·sim·e·ter /den símmətər/ *n* an instrument that measures density or specific gravity [Mid-19C. < Latin *densus* "thick, dense"] —**den·si·met·ric** /dènssi méttrik/ *adj* —**den·sim·e·try** *n*

den·si·tom·e·ter /dènssi tómmətər/ *n* **1.** an instrument for measuring optical density, e.g., that of a photographic negative **2.** PHYS same as **densimeter** [Early 20C. < DENSITY] —**den·sit·o·met·ric** /dènssitə méttrik/ *adj* —**den·si·tom·e·try** *n*

den·si·ty /dénssətee/ (*plural* **-ties**) *n* **1.** the concentration of people or things within an area in relation to its size **2.** PHYS a measure of a quantity such as mass or electric charge per unit volume. Symbol ρ **3.** ELEC same as **charge density 4.** ELEC same as **current density**

den·si·ty func·tion *n* STATS same as **probability density function** (sense 2)

dent /dent/ *v* (**dent·ed, dent·ing, dents**) **1.** *vti* **MAKE DEPRESSION IN SOMETHING BY HITTING** to make a shallow depression in the surface of something by hitting it or putting pressure on it, or receive a depression through pressure **2.** *vt* **HARM SOMETHING ABSTRACT** to do nonphysical, usually minor, damage to something ○ *dented their championship hopes* ■ *n* **1. AREA IN DEPRESSED SURFACE** a shallow depression in the surface of something that is made by hitting it or putting pressure on it **2. ADVANCE** progress in reaching a goal (*informal*) ○ *make a dent in the backlog* **3. REDUCTION** a reduction in an amount of something such as resources (*informal*) ○ *a dent in the budget* **4. NONPHYSICAL DAMAGE** nonphysical, usually minor, damage, e.g., to somebody's reputation or pride [13C. Variant of DINT]

dent. *abbr* DENT **1.** dental **2.** dentistry

den·tal /dént'l/ *adj* **1. OF DENTISTRY** relating to or used in dentistry **2. OF TEETH** relating or belonging to the teeth **3.** DENT **NEAR TOOTH** affecting or located in or near a tooth ○ *dental abscess* **4.** PHON **MADE BY TONGUE AND TEETH** describes a consonant that is formed by placing the tongue against the back of the top front teeth ■ *n* PHON **DENTAL CONSONANT** a consonant formed by placing the tongue against the back of the top front teeth [Late 16C. < late Latin *dentalis* < Latin *dent-* "tooth"]

den·tal car·ies *n* decay of teeth caused by the action of acid-forming bacteria and improper dental care

den·tal floss *n* thread that is used to remove food and plaque from between the teeth

den·tal hy·giene *n* the care people take of their teeth and gums to prevent tooth and gum diseases

den·tal hy·gien·ist *n* somebody licensed to provide dental care under the supervision of a dentist, especially cleaning and scaling teeth and taking X-rays

den·tal sur·geon *n* a dentist who is trained and licensed to practice oral surgery such as tooth extractions, and who is usually licensed to use general anesthesia

den·tal tech·ni·cian *n* somebody trained to make dental appliances such as caps, dentures, and bridges

den·tate /dén tàyt/ *adj* edged with pointed or tooth-shaped projections [15C. < Latin *dentatus* < *dent-* "tooth"] —**den·tate·ly** *adv* —**den·ta·tion** /den táysh'n/ *n*

dent corn *n US* a type of corn widely grown in the United States, with kernels that are indented at the tip when mature. Latin name: *Zea mays.*

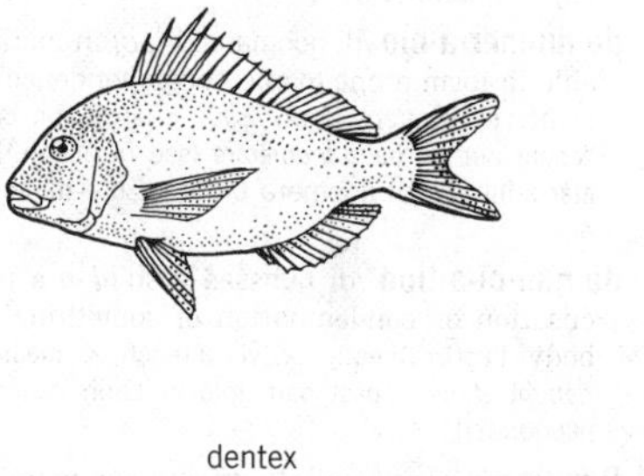

dentex

den·tex /dén tèks/ (*plural* **-tex·es** or *same*) *n* a red game fish, about 4 ft./1.2 m long. Native to: Cape of Good Hope, South Africa. Latin name: *Dentex rupestris.* [Mid-19C. Via modern Latin < Latin, type of fish]

denti- *prefix* tooth, dental ○ *dentiform* [< Latin *dent-* "tooth" < Indo-European]

den·ti·cle /déntik'l/ *n* **1.** a small tooth or tooth-shaped projection **2.** a small tooth-shaped scale with a projecting spine, typical of cartilaginous fish [15C. < Latin *denticulus* "small tooth" < *dent-* "tooth"] —**den·tic·u·lar** /den tíkyələr/ *adj*

den·tic·u·late /den tíkyə lət/ *adj* **1.** with fine teeth or pointed projections **2.** describes a building or part of a building decorated with small rectangular blocks (**dentils**) that look like a row of teeth [Mid-17C. < Latin *denticulatus* < *denticulus* (see DENTICLE)] —**den·tic·u·late·ly** *adv*

den·ti·form /déntə fàwrm/ *adj* shaped like a tooth

den·ti·frice /déntə friss/ *n* a paste or similar compound for cleaning teeth [15C. Via French < Latin *dentifricium* < *dent-* "tooth" + *fricare* "rub"]

den·til /dént'l, dén tìl/ *n* a small rectangular block that is arranged with others to look like a row of teeth, used as a form of architectural decoration [Late 16C. < Italian *dentello* or obsolete French *dentille* "small tooth" < Latin *dent-* "tooth"]

den·ti·lin·gual /dènti líng gwəl/ *adj* describes a speech sound pronounced or articulated with the tongue touching the teeth on the top jaw

den·tine /dén teèn/, **den·tin** /-tin/ *n* the hard part of a tooth that lies underneath the enamel and surrounds the pulp and root canals [Mid-19C. < Latin *dent-* "tooth"] —**den·tin·al** /den tée'n'l, déntən'l/ *adj*

den·tist /déntist/ *n* somebody trained and licensed to practice general dentistry or a specialty such as orthodontics or dental surgery [Mid-18C. < French *dentiste* < *dent* "tooth" < Latin *dent-*]

den·tist·ry /déntistree/ *n* the medical science concerned with the prevention and treatment of tooth and gum disorders and diseases, requiring graduation from dental school and appropriate licensing

den·ti·tion /den tísh'n/ *n* **1.** the type, number, and arrangement of a set of teeth **2.** the process of developing and cutting new teeth [Late 16C. < Latin *dent-* "tooth"]

Den·ton /dént'n/ city in northern Texas, north of Fort Worth and northwest of Dallas. Population: 90,349 (2002 estimate).

den·ture /dénchər/ *n* a partial or complete set of artificial teeth for the upper or lower jaw, usually attached to a plate [Late 19C. < French < *dent* "tooth" (see DENTIST)]

den·tur·ist /dénchərist/ *n* a dental technician who makes and fits dentures that are sold directly to the public rather than through a dentist

de·nu·cle·ar·ize /dee no͝oklee ə rīz/ (**-ized, -iz·ing, -iz·es**) *vt* to remove, ban, or eliminate nuclear weapons or nuclear power sources from a place, industry, or organization —**de·nu·cle·ar·i·za·tion** /dee no͝oklee əri záysh'n/ *n*

de·nude /di no͝od/ (**-nud·ed, -nud·ing, -nudes**) *vt* **1. REMOVE SOMEBODY'S OR SOMETHING'S COVERING** to strip somebody or something bare **2. DESTROY GROUND COVER OF PLACE** to strip away the covering vegetation from an area **3. STRIP AREA BY EROSION** to remove soil from an area, or expose underlying layers of rock by weathering and erosion [15C. < Latin *denudare* "strip away" < *nudare* "strip" < *nudus* "nude"] —**de·nu·da·tion** /dèe noo dáysh'n, dènnyə-/ *n*

de·nu·mer·a·ble /di no͝omərəb'l/ *adj* in mathematics, able to form a one-to-one correspondence with the positive integers [Early 20C. < late Latin *denumerare* "count out" < Latin *numerare* (see NUMERATE)] —**de·nu·mer·a·bil·i·ty** /di no͝omərə bíllətee/ *n* —**de·nu·mer·a·bly** *adv*

de·nun·ci·a·tion /di nùnssee áysh'n/ *n* a public accusation or condemnation of something or somebody [15C. Directly or via French < medieval Latin *denunciation-* < past participle of Latin *denuntiare* (see DENOUNCE)]

Den·ver /dénvər/ capital city and commercial center of the state of Colorado, in the Rocky Mountains. It is home to the Denver campus of the University of Colorado. Population: 560,415 (2002 estimate).

Den·ver boot *n* a locking device fastened to one of the wheels of a vehicle so that it cannot be moved until a fine or other charge has been paid

de·ny /di nī/ (**-nied, -ny·ing, -nies**) *v* **1.** *vt* **SAY SOMETHING IS NOT TRUE** to declare that something is not true or not the case **2.** *vt* **REFUSE REQUEST** to refuse to let somebody have or do something **3.** *vt* **DISAVOW SOMEBODY** to refuse to acknowledge somebody **4. de·ny your·self** *vr* **NOT ALLOW YOURSELF SOMETHING** to refuse to gratify your own needs or desires [13C. Via Old French *deneier* < Latin *denegare* "negate completely" < *negare* "deny"]

de·och an dor·uis /dyòkh ən dáwriss/, **doch-an-dor·ris** /dòkh ən dáwriss/, **doch an dor·is** *n Scotland* a parting drink [Late 17C. < Scottish Gaelic *deoch an doruis* "a drink at the door"]

de·o·dar /dée ə daar/ (*plural* **-dars** or *same*) *n* **1.** the hard sweet-smelling wood of a Himalayan tree. Use: timber. **2.** a cedar tree with dark blue green leaves and drooping branches that is the source of deodar wood. Native to: Himalayan range. Latin name: *Cedrus deodara*. [Early 19C. Via Hindi *deodār* < Sanskrit *devadāru* "divine wood"]

de·o·dor·ant /dee ṓdərənt/ *n* **1.** a substance applied to the body, especially under the arms, to mask or prevent body odor **2.** a substance that is used to disguise unpleasant smells [Mid-19C. < DE- + Latin *odor* "smell"]

de·o·dor·ize /dee ṓdə rīz/ (**-ized, -iz·ing, -iz·es**) *vt* to disguise or eliminate unpleasant odors in a place [Mid-19C. < DE- + Latin *odor* "smell"] —**de·o·dor·i·za·tion** /dee ōdəri záysh'n/ *n* —**de·o·dor·iz·er** *n*

De·o gra·ti·as /dày ō graatee əss/ *interj* thanks be to God (*used in various Christian choral and liturgical contexts*) [< Latin]

de·on·tic /dee óntik/ *adj* relating to the concept of moral obligation [Mid-19C. < Greek *deont-*, present participle of *dein* "be wanting, be needful"]

de·on·to·log·i·cal /dee òntə lójjik'l/ *adj* relating to philosophical theories that state that the moral content of an action is not wholly dependent on its consequences —**de·on·to·log·i·cal·ly** *adv*

de·on·tol·o·gy /dèe on tólləjee/ *n* the study of what is morally obligatory, permissible, right, or wrong [Early 19C. < Greek *deont-* (see DEONTIC)] —**de·on·tol·o·gist** *n*

de·or·bit /dee áwrbit/ (**-bit·ed, -bit·ing, -bits**) *vti* to put something out of orbit, or go out of orbit

De·o vo·len·te /dày ō və léntee, -vō lén tày/ *interj* God willing [< Latin]

de·ox·i·dize /dee óksi dīz/ (**-dized, -diz·ing, -diz·es**) *vt* **1.** to remove the oxygen from a compound or molecule **2.** CHEM same as **reduce** (sense 9) —**de·ox·i·di·za·tion** /dee òksidi záysh'n/ *n* —**de·ox·i·diz·er** *n*

deoxy- *prefix* containing less oxygen than a related compound ○ *deoxyribose*

de·ox·y·gen·ate /dee óksijə nàyt/ (**-at·ed, -at·ing, -ates**) *vt* to remove dissolved oxygen from a substance —**de·ox·y·gen·a·tion** /dee òksijə náysh'n/ *n*

de·ox·y·gen·ize /dee óksijə nīz/ (**-ized, -iz·ing, -iz·es**) *vt* CHEM same as **deoxygenate**

de·ox·y·ri·bo·nu·cle·ase /dee òksee rībō no͝oklee àyss, -àyz/ *n* GENETICS full form of **DNase** [Mid-20C. < DEOXYRIBONUCLEIC ACID]

de·ox·y·ri·bo·nu·cle·ic ac·id /dee òksee rībō noo klée ik-/ *n* GENETICS full form of **DNA**[1] (sense 1) [Mid-20C. < DEOXYRIBOSE]

de·ox·y·ri·bo·nu·cle·o·tide /dee òksee rībō no͝oklee ə tīd/ *n* a nucleotide containing deoxyribose that is a component of DNA [Mid-20C. < DEOXYRIBOSE]

de·ox·y·ri·bose /dee òksee rī bòss/ *n* a five-carbon simple sugar that is a structural component of DNA

DEP *abbr* GOV Department of Environmental Protection

dep. *abbr* **1.** GOV, BUSINESS department **2.** TRANSP departs **3.** TRANSP departure **4.** GRAM deponent **5.** LAW deposed **6.** FIN deposit **7.** TRANSP depot **8.** *also* **Dep.** deputy

de·pan·neur /dáypə núr/ *n Can* a convenience store in French-speaking Canada [< Canadian French < French *dépanner* "repair, help out"]

De·par·dieu /də paar djṓ/, **Gérard** (*b.* 1948) French actor. His films include *The Last Metro* (1980), *Cyrano de Bergerac* (1990), and *Green Card* (1990).

> "I appreciate teamwork. I don't like a one-man show. I'm an interpreter, a sort of tool—I don't mean an object. The right tool is quite essential. Try pounding a nail in with a screwdriver."
> [Attributed to Gérard Depardieu]

de·part /di paart/ (**-part·ed, -part·ing, -parts**) *v* **1.** *vi* **SET OFF** to leave, especially at the beginning of a journey **2.** *vt* **LEAVE PLACE** to leave from a place **3.** *vi* **CHANGE** to change or vary from a pattern **4.** *vt* **DIE** to reach the end of your life (*literary*) ○ *depart this life* [13C. < French *départir* "end your life" < Latin *partire* "divide into parts" < *pars* "part"]

de·part·ed /di paartəd/ *n* somebody who has died, especially recently (*formal or literary*) ■ *adj* having died (*archaic or literary*)

SYNONYMS See ***dead***.

---

de·part·ment /di paartmənt/ *n* **1. SECTION OF ORGANIZATION** a division of a large organization such as a university or store that has its own function **2. PART OF GOVERNMENT** a major division of government that is responsible for dealing with a specific area of policy or administration **3. SPECIALTY** somebody's specialty or area of responsibility (*informal*) **4. CATEGORY** a particular quantifiable or qualifiable category (*informal*) **5.** POL **FRENCH DISTRICT** an administrative district in France

de·part·men·tal /di paart mént'l/ *adj* relating to a department in a government or an organization —**de·part·men·tal·ly** *adv*

de·part·men·tal·ism /di paart mént'l ìzzəm/ *n* **1.** the division of organizations into departments, particularly as a deliberate policy that is taken to excess **2.** the tendency of government departments to follow their own interests

de·part·men·tal·ize /dèe paart mént'l īz/ (**-ized, -iz·ing, -iz·es**) *vt* to divide an organization into departments, especially as a policy or to an excessive degree —**de·part·men·tal·i·za·tion** /dèe paart ment'li záysh'n/ *n*

De·part·ment of De·fense *n* the executive department of the federal government that is mainly responsible for maintaining national security and overseeing the armed forces

De·part·ment of En·er·gy *n* the executive department of the federal government that is mainly responsible for developing energy technology and regulating energy production and use

De·part·ment of En·vi·ron·men·tal Pro·tec·tion *n* a state agency responsible for protecting human health by ensuring clean air and water and safe management of hazardous waste materials

De·part·ment of Fi·nance Can·a·da *n* the Canadian government department that is responsible for preparing the federal budget, overseeing tax policies and legislation, and regulating the country's banks and financial institutions

De·part·ment of Home·land Se·cu·ri·ty *n* the executive department of the federal government that was established in the aftermath of September 11, 2001, to protect the country against future terrorist attacks

De·part·ment of Hous·ing and Ur·ban De·vel·op·ment *n* the executive department of the federal government that is mainly responsible for promoting community development and enforcing fair housing laws

De·part·ment of Hu·man Re·sourc·es and Skills De·vel·op·ment *n* the Canadian government department that is responsible for developing and administering policies relating to labor and homelessness

De·part·ment of Jus·tice *n* the executive department of the federal government that is mainly responsible for supervising US district attorneys, administering federal prisons, and representing the US government in legal matters

De·part·ment of Jus·tice Can·a·da *n* the Canadian government department that is mainly responsible for developing policies affecting the justice system and providing legal services to the federal government

De·part·ment of Na·tion·al De·fence and the Ca·na·di·an Forc·es *n* the Canadian government department that is mainly responsible for national security and overseeing the armed forces

De·part·ment of So·cial Ser·vic·es *n* a state agency responsible for providing services and protection to people living in poverty or situations of abuse or neglect

De·part·ment of the In·te·ri·or *n* the executive department of the federal government that is mainly responsible for developing the nation's natural resources, managing national parks, and overseeing Native American reservations and outlying territories

de·part·ment store *n* a large store that sells a wide range of goods in separate departments

de·par·ture /di paarchər/ *n* **1. SETTING OFF** the action of setting off on a journey **2. CHANGE FROM USUAL** a change from the usual or expected way **3. COURSE** a course of action, or the beginning of one **4.** NAUT **EAST OR WEST TRAVEL** the distance traveled due east or west by a ship, as a change in longitude

de·par·ture lounge *n* an area where departing passengers can wait until their aircraft or other transport is ready

de·pas·ture /di páschər/ (**-tured, -tur·ing, -tures**) *vt* to allow animals to graze on an area

de·pau·pe·rate /di páwpərət/ *adj* **1.** lacking or depleted in the variety of plant or animal species **2.** less than fully grown or developed [Mid-19C. < medieval Latin *depauperatus,* past participle of *depauperare* "impoverish" < Latin *pauper* (see PAUPER)] —**de·pau·pe·ra·tion** /di pàwpə ráysh'n/ *n*

de·pend /di pénd/ (**-pend·ed, -pend·ing, -pends**) *vi* **1.** BE CONTINGENT to be affected or decided by other factors **2.** VARY to vary according to the circumstances **3.** HANG DOWN to hang down or be suspended from something (*archaic*) [15C. Via French < Latin *dependere* "hang down" < *pendere* "hang"]

USAGE The verb ***depend*** should be followed by *on* when it introduces a clause beginning with *how, what, where, whether, who,* or *why*: *It depends on how you interpret the word "liberal." The amount you pay depends on what you earn.* The omission of *on* in sentences of this type is more acceptable in speech than in writing, as in *"Are you planning to go?" "It just depends."*

depend on, depend upon *vt* **1.** to need something in order to exist or survive **2.** to have complete confidence in somebody or something

de·pend·a·ble /di péndəb'l/ *adj* able to be trusted or depended on ○ *a dependable employee* ○ *a dependable source of power* —**de·pend·a·bil·i·ty** /di pèndə bíllətee/ *n*

de·pend·a·bly /di péndəblee/ *adv* **1.** used to indicate that somebody or something is behaving as usual or expected ○ *Sam was, dependably, the last to arrive.* **2.** in a way that inspires trust or confidence

de·pend·ance *n US* another spelling of **dependence**

de·pend·an·cy *n US* POL, BUILDINGS another spelling of **dependency**

de·pend·ant *n* same as **dependent**

USAGE **dependant** or **dependent**? Do not confuse ***dependant*** with ***dependent,*** which has the same pronunciation. The adjective derived from the verb *depend* is always spelled ***dependent,*** in both US and British English: *The young birds are still dependent on their parents.* The noun meaning "somebody who is supported financially by another," as in *an unmarried woman with no dependants,* is usually spelled ***dependent*** in US English and ***dependant*** in British English.

de·pend·ence /di péndənss/, **de·pend·ance** *n* **1.** RELIANCE ON SOMEBODY OR SOMETHING reliance on or trust in somebody or something for help or support ○ *dependence on public transportation* ○ *mutual dependence* **2.** STATE OF BEING CONTINGENT the state of being affected or decided by particular factors or circumstances ○ *agriculture's dependence on the weather* **3.** PHYSICAL OR PSYCHOLOGICAL NEED a physical or psychological need to use a drug or other substance regularly, despite the fact that it is likely to have a damaging effect

de·pend·en·cy /di péndənssee/ (*plural* **-cies**), **de·pend·an·cy** *n* **1.** a country or state that belongs to another nonadjacent country **2.** a building near to and associated with a larger main building **3.** same as **dependence**

de·pend·en·cy the·o·ry *n* a theory of international relations holding that major states influence other states though their economic power

de·pend·ent /di péndənt/ *n also* **de·pend·ant** *US* FAMILY MEMBER a family member or other person who is supported financially by another, especially one living in the same house ■ *adj* **1.** NEEDING SOMETHING having a physical or psychological need to use a drug or other substance regularly (*usually used in combination*) ○ *alcohol-dependent* **2.** NOT SELF-RELIANT needing to rely on or trust in somebody or something for help or support, especially financial support ○ *countries dependent on oil revenues* ○ *dependent children* **3.** CONTINGENT affected or decided by particular factors or circumstances (*often used in combination*) ○ *age-dependent* —**de·pend·ent·ly** *adv*

USAGE See ***dependant.***

de·pend·ent clause *n* GRAM same as **subordinate clause**

de·pend·ent var·i·a·ble *n* an element in a mathematical expression that changes its value according to the value of other elements present

de·per·son·al·ize /dee púrssən'l ìz, -snəl-/ (**-ized, -iz·ing, -iz·es**) *vt* **1.** to take away or omit the qualities from something that make a person feel welcome or important ○ *a depersonalized workplace* **2.** to make somebody lose his or her sense of personal identity and external reality —**de·per·son·al·i·za·tion** /dee pùrssən'li záysh'n, -snəli-/ *n*

de·pict /di píkt/ (**-pict·ed, -pict·ing, -picts**) *vt* **1.** to describe or portray something in words **2.** to show something in a picture, painting, or sculpture [15C. < Latin *depict-,* past participle of *depingere* "portray" < *pingere* "to paint"] —**de·pict·er** *n* —**de·pic·tive** *adj*

de·pic·tion /di píksh'n/ *n* a picture, description, or other representation of something

de·pig·men·ta·tion /dee pìgmən táysh'n/ *n* partial or total absence in the body of the pigment melanin, especially in the skin, hair, and eyes

dep·i·late /déppi làyt/ (**-lat·ed, -lat·ing, -lates**) *vti* to remove hair from the body, usually from the legs or underarms [Mid-16C. < Latin *depilat-,* past participle of Latin *depilare* < *pilus* "hair"] —**dep·i·la·tor** *n*

dep·i·la·tion /dèppi láysh'n/ *n* the removal of hair, including its roots, from the body or from hides or leather

de·pil·a·to·ry /di píllə tàwree/ *adj* used for removing hair from the body ■ *n* (*plural* **-ries**) a substance that removes hair from the body

de·plane /dee pláyn/ (**-planed, -plan·ing, -planes**) *vi* to disembark from an airplane

de·plete /di pleét/ (**-plet·ed, -plet·ing, -pletes**) *vt* **1.** to use up or reduce something such as supplies, resources, or energy **2.** to use up or remove all the contents of something [Early 19C. < Latin *deplet-,* past participle of *deplere* "empty out" < *plere* "fill"] —**de·plet·a·ble** *adj* —**de·ple·tion** /di pleésh'n/ *n* —**de·ple·tive** *adj*

de·plet·ed u·ra·ni·um *n* uranium containing an unusually low amount of the U-235 isotope, usually as a result of having been used as fuel in a nuclear reactor

de·ple·tion lay·er *n* a layer in a semiconductor that has few charge carriers transporting electric charge between zones of different conductivity

de·plor·a·ble /di pláwrəb'l/ *adj* **1.** worthy of severe condemnation **2.** wretched because of neglect, poverty, or other misfortune —**de·plor·a·bil·i·ty** /di plàwrə bíllətee/ *n* —**de·plor·a·ble·ness** *n* —**de·plor·a·bly** *adv*

de·plore /di pláwr/ (**-plored, -plor·ing, -plores**) *vt* **1.** to disapprove of something very strongly **2.** to regret or feel grief about something [Mid-16C. Via French or Italian < Latin *deplorare* "lament, regret" < *plorare* "wail"] —**de·plor·ing·ly** *adv*

SYNONYMS See ***disapprove.***

de·ploy /di plóy/ (**-ployed, -ploy·ing, -ploys**) *v* **1.** *vti* to position troops, weapons, or resources in a specific area in readiness for action, or take up position in this way **2.** *vt* to put something to use [15C. Via French *déployer* < Latin *displicare* "unfold" < *plicare* "to fold"] —**de·ploy·a·ble** *adj* —**de·ploy·er** *n* —**de·ploy·ment** *n*

de·plume /dee ploóm/ (**-plumed, -plum·ing, -plumes**) *vt* to remove the feathers from a bird [15C. Via French < medieval Latin *deplumare* < Latin *pluma* "down, feather"] —**de·plu·ma·tion** /deè ploo máysh'n/ *n*

de·po·lar·ize /dee pṓlə rìz/ (**-ized, -iz·ing, -iz·es**) *vti* to remove or reduce the polarization or polarity of something, or lose polarization or polarity —**de·po·lar·i·za·tion** /dee pṑləri záysh'n/ *n* —**de·po·lar·iz·er** *n*

de·po·lit·i·cize /deèpə lítti sìz/ (**-cized, -ciz·ing, -ciz·es**) *vt* to remove the political aspect of something —**de·po·lit·i·ci·za·tion** /deèpə lìttissi záysh'n/ *n*

de·pol·lu·tion /deèpə loósh'n/ *n* the removal of pollution from something —**de·pol·lute** *vt*

de·pol·y·mer·ize /dee póllәmə rìz/ (**-ized, -iz·ing, -iz·es**) *vti* to break down a polymer into simpler monomers, or undergo this process —**de·pol·y·mer·i·za·tion** /dee pòlləməri záysh'n/ *n*

de·pone /di pṓn/ (**-poned, -pon·ing, -pones**) *vti* to testify or declare something under oath [15C. < medieval Latin *deponere* (see DEPOSE)]

de·po·nent /di pṓnənt/ *adj* GRAM PASSIVE AND ACTIVE describes a verb that inflects like a passive verb but is active in meaning ■ *n* **1.** GRAM ACTIVE VERB WITH PASSIVE FORM a verb that inflects like a passive verb but is active in meaning **2.** LAW TESTIFYING WITNESS somebody who signs an affidavit or testifies under oath [15C. < Latin *deponent-,* present participle of *deponere* (see DEPOSE)]

de·pop·u·late /dee póppyə làyt/ (**-lat·ed, -lat·ing, -lates**) *vt* to cause a reduction in the number of residents in an area, e.g., through disease, war, famine, or enforced relocation [Mid-16C. < Latin *depopulat-,* past participle of *depopulare* "ravage completely, reduce in population" < *populari* "lay waste" < *populus* "people"] —**de·pop·u·la·tion** /dee pòppyə láysh'n/ *n* —**de·pop·u·la·tor** *n*

de·port[1] /di páwrt/ (**-port·ed, -port·ing, -ports**) *vt* **1.** to force a foreign national to leave a country **2.** to expel or banish somebody from his or her own country [Mid-17C. Via French < Latin *deportare* "carry off" < *portare* "carry"] —**de·port·a·ble** *adj* —**de·por·ta·tion** /deè pawr táysh'n/ *n*

de·port[2] /di páwrt/ (**-port·ed, -port·ing, -ports**) *vr* **de·port your·self** to conduct yourself in a particular way ○ *deports herself with dignity* [15C. < Old French *deporter* "behave, conduct yourself" < *porter* < Latin *portare* "carry"]

de·port·ee /deè pawr teé/ *n* somebody subject to deportation

de·port·ment /di páwrtmənt/ *n* the manner in which a person behaves [Early 17C. < French *déportement* < Old French *deporter* (see DEPORT[2])]

de·pose /di pṓz/ (**-posed, -pos·ing, -pos·es**) *v* **1.** *vt* REMOVE FROM OFFICE to remove somebody from office or from a position of power **2.** *vti* GIVE EVIDENCE to give evidence or testify under oath, either in a written or verbal form **3.** *vt US* TAKE EVIDENCE to request and record evidence from a witness [13C. < French *déposer,* alteration (influenced by *poser* "put") of Latin *deponere* "put down," in medieval Latin "testify" < *ponere* "to place"] —**de·pos·a·ble** *adj* —**de·pos·al** *n* —**de·pos·er** *n*

de·pos·it /di pózzit/ *v* (**-it·ed, -it·ing, -its**) **1.** *vt* PUT SOMETHING SOMEWHERE to put or drop something somewhere ○ *She deposited her coat on the couch.* **2.** *vt* LEAVE SOMETHING IN SAFE PLACE to leave something somewhere for safekeeping ○ *deposit valuables in the hotel safe* **3.** *vt* PUT MONEY IN BANK to pay money into an account in a bank or other financial institution **4.** *vt* GIVE PAYMENT AS SECURITY to give a sum of money as part-payment or security ○ *deposited $1000 as a down payment* **5.** *vti* FORM LAYER to leave or form a layer of sand, sediment, or other substance, as a gradual process in one place, or be left in this way ○ *layers of silt deposited by the river* ■ *n* **1.** PUTTING MONEY IN BANK an act of placing money or a valuable item in a bank or other financial institution ○ *make a monthly deposit* **2.** MONEY IN BANK an amount of money or a valuable item that is paid into or left in a bank or other financial institution ○ *Deposits made after 2 pm are credited the following day.* **3.** SECURITY MONEY a partial payment or security on something that is going to be bought ○ *You need to pay a deposit.* **4.** SURETY MONEY money that is given as security against possible damage or loss, e.g., on something rented **5.** COATING a coating or crust that is left on a surface by a process such as evaporation or electrolysis **6.** ACCUMULATION OF NATURAL MATERIALS an accumulation of sand, sediment, minerals, or other substances that has built up over a period of time through a natural process ○ *a land rich in mineral deposits* **7.** DEPOSITED THING something put or left in a place [Late 16C. < Latin *depositum* < *deposit-,* past participle of *deponere* (see DEPOSE)] —**de·pos·i·tor** *n*

de·pos·it ac·count *n* a bank account that earns interest

de·pos·i·tar·y /di pózzi tèrree/ (*plural* **-ies**) *n* **1.** a person or institution that is entrusted with something for safekeeping **2.** same as **depository** (sense 1)

dep·o·si·tion /dèppə zísh'n/ *n* **1.** WITNESS'S TESTIMONY testimony that is given under oath, especially a statement given by a witness that is read out in court in the witness's absence **2.** OUSTING FROM OFFICE the act of removing somebody from high office or power **3.** DEPOSIT something that has been deposited somewhere **4.** BUILD-UP OF DEPOSITS the accumulation of natural materials by a gradual process [14C. Via French < Latin *deposition-* < *deponere* (see DEPOSE)] —**dep·o·si·tion·al** *adj*

de·pos·i·to·ry /di pózzi tàwree/ (*plural* **-ries**) *n* **1.** a place where something is kept for safekeeping or storage, e.g., a warehouse or store for furniture or valuables **2.** same as **depositary** (sense 1)

de·pos·it slip *n* a form for listing the contents of a bank deposit

de·pot /deépō, déppō/ *n* **1. WAREHOUSE** a warehouse or other place used for storing things **2.** TRANSP **STATION** a railroad or bus station **3.** MIL **MILITARY STORAGE** a place where military supplies are stored **4.** MIL **MILITARY TRAINING BASE** a place where military recruits are gathered together and trained [Late 18C. Via French *dépôt* < Latin *depositum* (see DEPOSIT)]

de·prave /di práyv/ (**-praved, -prav·ing, -praves**) *vt* to have a morally bad or corrupting influence on somebody (*often passive*) [14C. Directly or via French < Latin *depravare* "to corrupt" < *pravus* "crooked"] —**de·prav·er** *n*

de·praved /di práyvd/ *adj* showing great moral corruption or wickedness —**de·prav·ed·ly** /di práyvədlee, -práyvd-/ *adv*

de·prav·i·ty /di právvətee/ (*plural* **-ties**) *n* **1.** a state of moral corruption **2.** a morally corrupt or wicked act [Mid-17C. Alteration (after DEPRAVE) of obsolete *pravity* < Latin *pravitas* < *pravus* "crooked"]

dep·re·cate /déppra kàyt/ (**-cat·ed, -cat·ing, -cates**) *vt* **1.** to express condemnation of something or somebody ○ *The spokesman deprecated the use of violence.* **2.** ⚠ same as **depreciate** (sense 3) **3.** COMPUT to state that a computational method or computer feature is superseded [Early 17C. < Latin *deprecat-*, past participle of *deprecari*, literally "pray against" < *precari* (see PRAY)] —**dep·re·ca·tion** /dèppra káysh'n/ *n* —**dep·re·ca·tor** *n*

USAGE deprecate or **depreciate**? To ***deprecate*** something is to condemn it as wrong in itself: *We deprecate the use of public money for nonessential purposes.* To ***depreciate*** something is to belittle or disparage it, even though it may not be wrong or bad in itself: *They were constantly depreciating our attempts to speak Italian.* This use is increasingly rare. Admittedly, *self-deprecate* goes a long way toward blurring the distinction, for it means "belittle yourself," not "condemn yourself"; in this sense it is well established, but it may be best regarded as the exception rather than the rule. Both words have more common synonyms: *condemn, deplore,* and *disapprove of* for ***deprecate***, and *belittle, disparage,* and *decry* for ***depreciate***. ***Depreciate*** is also commonly used intransitively (without an object), in financial contexts, to mean "lose value": *The value of the yen has depreciated 20 percent in real terms.*

dep·re·cat·ing /déppra kàyting/ *adj* **1.** showing or expressing disapproval **2.** showing or expressing apology —**dep·re·cat·ing·ly** *adv*

dep·re·ca·to·ry /déppraka tàwree/, **dep·re·ca·tive** /déppra kàytiv/ *adj* **1.** disapproving and critical **2.** showing or expressing apology —**dep·re·ca·to·ri·ly** *adv*

de·pre·ci·ate /di preéshee àyt/ (**-at·ed, -at·ing, -ates**) *v* **1.** *vti* **LOSE VALUE** to become less valuable, or lessen the value of something **2.** *vt* **TREAT SOMETHING AS DECREASINGLY VALUABLE** to consider something as having less value each year over a fixed period, for the calculation of income tax **3.** *vt* **BELITTLE SOMETHING OR SOMEBODY** to speak critically or disparagingly about something or somebody [15C. < late Latin *depreciat-*, past participle of *depreciare*, alteration of Latin *depretiare* "lower the price of" < *pretium* "price, money"] —**de·pre·cia·ble** *adj* —**de·pre·ci·at·ing·ly** *adv* —**de·pre·ci·a·tor** *n*

USAGE See *deprecate*.

de·pre·ci·a·tion /di preéshee áysh'n/ *n* **1. DROP IN VALUE** the decrease in value of an item over time **2. AMOUNT OF DECREASE** the amount or percentage by which something decreases in value over time, usually one year **3. BELITTLEMENT** critical commentary or strong disparagement of somebody or something

de·pre·cia·tive /di preéshətiv, -shee àytiv/ *adj* **1.** reducing or tending to reduce something in value **2.** losing or tending to lose value

de·pre·cia·to·ry /di preéshee ə tàwree/ *adj* **1.** FIN same as **depreciative 2.** belittling or critical

dep·re·da·tion /dèppra dáysh'n/ *n* an attack involving plunder and pillage [15C. Via French < late Latin *depraedation-* < past participle of Latin *depraedari*, literally "plunder thoroughly" < *praedari* (see PREDATORY)]

de·press /di préss/ (**-pressed, -press·ing, -press·es**) *vt* **1. MAKE SOMEBODY UNHAPPY** to make somebody feel very sad or hopeless ○ *"There's nothing that depresses me more than seeing a planet being destroyed."* (Douglas Adams, *Life, The Universe, and Everything*; 1982) **2. WEAKEN SOMETHING** to weaken something, or make something less active **3. DEVALUATE SOMETHING** to decrease the value of something **4. PUSH ON SOMETHING** to press something such as a button or lever [14C. Via French < Latin *depress-*, past participle of *deprimere* "press down" < *premere* "press"] —**de·press·i·ble** *adj*

de·pres·sant /di préss'nt/ *n* a drug or agent that slows the body's vital functions ■ *adj* able to sedate or lower the rate of the body's vital functions

de·pressed /di prést/ *adj* **1. SAD** unhappy or hopeless **2. HAVING DEPRESSION** having the psychiatric disorder depression **3. ECONOMICALLY LACKING** lacking economic resources or activities ○ *a depressed area* **4. WEAK** less active or strong than usual ○ *the depressed dollar* **5. LOWER** lower than the surrounding area **6.** BIOL **FLATTENED** flattened, as if from downward pressure

de·press·ing /di préssing/ *adj* making somebody feel sad or disheartened —**de·press·ing·ly** *adv*

de·pres·sion /di présh'n/ *n* **1. SADNESS** a state of unhappiness and hopelessness **2. PSYCHIATRIC DISORDER** a psychiatric disorder showing symptoms such as persistent feelings of hopelessness, dejection, poor concentration, lack of energy, inability to sleep, and, sometimes, suicidal tendencies **3. ECONOMIC SLUMP** a period in which an economy is greatly affected by unemployment, low output, and poverty **4. REDUCED ACTIVITY** a lowering of activity, quality, vitality, or force **5. HOLLOW** an area on the surface of something that is lower than the surface surrounding it **6.** METEOROL **LOW PRESSURE AREA** an area of low barometric pressure that often brings rain

De·pres·sion glass *n* decorative colored glassware that was produced in large quantities in the United States during the 1920s and 1930s

de·pres·sive /di préssiv/ *adj* **1. CAUSING DEPRESSION** relating to or causing depression ○ *the depressive atmosphere of a gray, cold marshland* **2.** PSYCHIAT **HAVING DEPRESSION** experiencing or with a history of depression ■ *n* PSYCHIAT **DEPRESSED PERSON** a habitually depressed person —**de·pres·sive·ly** *adv* —**de·pres·sive·ness** *n*

de·pres·sor /di préssər/ *n* **1. MEDICAL INSTRUMENT** a medical or surgical instrument that is used to move aside or press down an organ or part of the body **2. PULLING MUSCLE** a muscle that acts to pull down a part of the body **3. APPLIER OF PRESSURE** somebody or something that presses down

de·pres·sor nerve *n* a nerve that, when stimulated, decreases activity in an organ, lowers blood pressure, or slows the heart

de·pres·sur·ize /dee préshə rīz/ (**-ized, -iz·ing, -iz·es**) *vt* **1.** to reduce the pressure of air or gas within a container, cabin, or other enclosed space **2.** to make a situation less tense —**de·pres·sur·i·za·tion** /dee prèshəri záysh'n/ *n*

dep·ri·va·tion /dèppra váysh'n/ *n* **1.** the state of being without or denied something, especially of being without adequate food or shelter **2.** the act of taking something away from somebody or preventing somebody from having something

de·prive /di prīv/ (**-prived, -priv·ing, -prives**) *vt* **1.** to prevent somebody from having something **2.** to take something away from somebody ○ *They have no right to deprive you of your own property.* [14C. Via French < medieval Latin *deprivare* "deprive completely" < Latin *privare* (see PRIVATION)] —**de·priv·a·ble** *adj* —**de·priv·er** *n*

de·prived /di prīvd/ *adj* lacking the things needed for a comfortable or successful life

de pro·fun·dis /dày prə foōndiss/ *adv* out of the depths of misery or despair [13C. < Latin, "out of the depths," first words of Psalm 130]

de·pro·gram /dee prō gràm/ (**-grammed** or **-gramed, -gram·ming** or **-gram·ing, -grams**) *vt* to undo the effects of indoctrination on somebody, especially somebody under the influence of a religious group

de·pro·gramme *vt* RELIG UK spelling of **deprogram**

dept. *abbr* **1.** department **2.** deputy

depth /depth/ *n* **1. HOW DEEP SOMETHING IS** the distance or measurement from the top of something to its bottom, from front to back, or from the outside in **2. BEING DEEP** the quality of being deep **3. INTENSITY** the strength of a feeling **4. COMPLEXITY** complexity or profundity of character or thought ○ *a woman of great depth* ○ *the depths of knowledge* **5. BREADTH** wideness in scope **6. COLOR QUALITY** the richness of a color **7. LOWNESS** the low tone or pitch of a sound ■ **depths** *npl* **1. LOWEST POINT** the lowest or worst point or moment ○ *the depths of despair* **2. DEEP PART** a deep or remote part of something ○ *the ocean depths* **3. MIDDLE PART** the middle part of something long, monotonous, and possibly unpleasant ○ *in the depths of tedious research* **4. DEBASEMENT** a state of great moral debasement ○ *having fallen to such depths* [14C. < DEEP] ◇ **hidden depths INTERESTING CHARACTERISTICS** interesting or serious aspects of somebody's character that are not immediately obvious ◇ **out of your depth 1.** unable to understand or do something because it is outside the range of your knowledge or skills **2.** unable to stand because the water is too deep

depth charge *n* a bomb that is designed to explode at a particular depth under water, often used against submarines

depth gauge, depth find·er *n* an instrument that measures the depth of water or other liquid

depth of field *n* the total focused area in front of and behind an object held in the focus of a camera or lens

depth of fo·cus *n* the distance that a camera lens can be moved closer to or further from the film, without the resulting image being blurred

depth per·cep·tion *n* the ability to perceive objects and their spatial relationship in three dimensions

depth psy·chol·o·gy *n* **1.** the study and psychology of the unconscious mind **2.** PSYCHOANAL same as **psychoanalysis**

depth sound·er *n* an ultrasonic instrument that measures the depth of water under a ship

dep·u·rate /déppyə ràyt/ (**-rat·ed, -rat·ing, -rates**) *vt* to cleanse or purify something, especially by removing toxins [Early 17C. < medieval Latin *depurat-*, past participle of *depurare* < Latin *purus* "pure"] —**dep·u·ra·tion** /dèppyə ráysh'n/ *n* —**dep·u·ra·tive** *adj* —**dep·u·ra·tor** *n*

dep·u·ta·tion /dèppyə táysh'n/ *n* **1.** a group of people who have been chosen to represent a larger group of people and act on their behalf **2.** the act of appointing a deputy or deputation

de·pute /di pyoōt/ (**-put·ed, -put·ing, -putes**) *v* (*formal*) **1.** *vt* **CHOOSE REPRESENTATIVE** to choose somebody to be your agent, substitute, or representative **2.** *vt* **DELEGATE SOMETHING** to delegate work, authority, or duties to somebody else **3.** *vi* **ACT AS DEPUTY** to act as deputy for somebody [14C. Via French *députer* < Latin *deputare* "assign" < *putare* "consider"]

dep·u·tize /déppyə tīz/ (**-tized, -tiz·ing, -tiz·es**) *v* **1.** *vi* to act as somebody's deputy **2.** *vt* to choose somebody to act as a deputy —**dep·u·ti·za·tion** /dèppyəti záysh'n/ *n*

dep·u·ty /déppyətee/ (*plural* **-ties**) *n* **1. SOMEBODY'S REPRESENTATIVE** somebody fully authorized or appointed to act on behalf of somebody else **2. SECOND-IN-COMMAND** an assistant who is authorized to act in a superior's place **3. MEMBER OF PARLIAMENT** a parliamentary representative in some countries, e.g., in France, Germany, or Italy **4.** POLICE same as **deputy sheriff** [15C. < French *député*, past participle of *députer* (see DEPUTE)]

SYNONYMS See *assistant*.

dep·u·ty min·is·ter *n Can* the most senior civil servant in a Canadian government department

dep·u·ty sher·iff *n* a sheriff's assistant, authorized to take charge when the sheriff is absent

de Quin·cey /də kwínssee/, **Thomas** (1785–1859) British essayist and critic. He was a friend of William Wordsworth and Samuel Taylor Coleridge, and author of *Confessions of an English Opium Eater* (1821).

"All that is literature seeks to communicate power; all that is not literature, to communicate knowledge."
[Thomas de Quincey, "Letters to a Young Man Whose Education has been Neglected," *London Magazine*; 1823]

de·rac·i·nate /di ráss'n àyt/ (**-nat·ed, -nat·ing, -nates**) *vt* to remove somebody or something from a natural environment, especially people from their native culture (*literary*) [Late 16C. < French *déraciner* < *racine* "root" < late Latin *radicina* < Latin *radix*] —**de·rac·i·na·tion** /di ràss'n áysh'n/ *n*

de·rail /dee ráyl/ (**-railed, -rail·ing, -rails**) *vti* **1.** to make a train or tram come off the rails, or come off the rails **2.** to send something off course, or go off course ○ *plans to derail the Republican campaign* [Mid-19C. < French *dérailler* < *rail* (see RAIL[1])] —**de·rail·ment** *n*

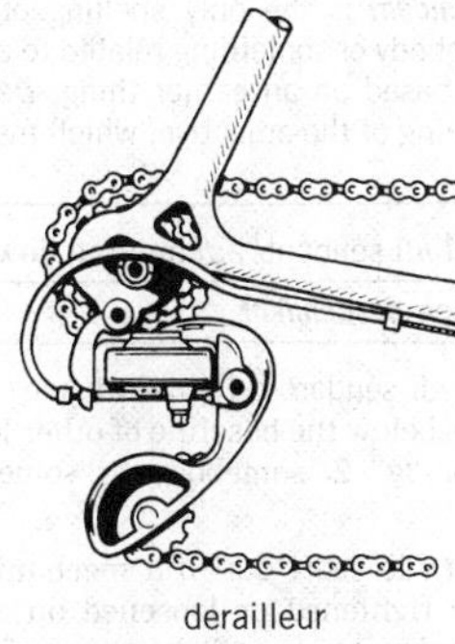
derailleur

de·rail·leur /di ráylər/ *n* a device for changing gears on a bicycle that lifts the chain from one sprocket wheel to another [Mid-20C. < French *dérailleur* < *dérailler* (see DERAIL)]

De·rain /də ráN/, **André** (1880–1954) French painter, illustrator, and stage designer. A leader in several art movements of the early 20th century, he is particularly noted for the paintings of his Fauve period (1905–08).

de·range /di ráynj/ (**-ranged, -rang·ing, -rang·es**) *vt* **1.** MAKE SOMEBODY IRRATIONAL to make somebody irrational or extraordinarily angry **2.** DISTURB ROUTINE to disturb the normal way in which something works **3.** THROW SOMETHING INTO DISORDER to throw something into disorder and confusion [Late 18C. < French *déranger* "put out of line" < *rang* "line"] —**de·ranged** *adj* —**de·range·ment** *n*

de·rate /dee ráyt/ (**-rat·ed, -rat·ing, -rates**) *vt* to lower the rated capability of an electrical apparatus

de·ra·tion /dee rásh'n/ (**-tioned, -tion·ing, -tions**) *vt* to stop rationing a commodity, usually because the supply has become adequate

der·by /dúrbee/ (*plural* **-bies**) *n* **1.** HORSERACE a horserace run annually, usually for three-year-olds **2.** RACE any race or contest open to qualified competitors **3.** ROUND FELT HAT a stiff felt hat with a round crown and a small, curved brim [Late 19C. After DERBY[1]]

Der·by[1] *n* a horserace held each spring at Churchill Downs in Louisville, Kentucky, or one run annually at Epsom Downs, Surrey, England [Early 19C. After the 12th Earl of *Derby*, who founded the English race]

Der·by[2] /dúrbee, daárbee/ **1.** cathedral city in Derbyshire, England. Population: 221,708 (2001). **2.** port in northwestern Western Australia, situated on King Sound near the mouth of the Fitzroy River. Population: 8,517 (2002 estimate).

Der·by /dúrbee/, **23rd Earl of** (1799–1869) British politician. Three times prime minister (1852, 1858–59, and 1866–68), he carried the second Reform Act for the emancipation of West Indian slaves (1867) through Parliament. Full name **Stanley, Edward George Geoffrey Smith**

Der·by·shire /dúrbee sheer, -shər, daár-/ county in central England, including most of the Peak District. Matlock is the administrative center. Population: 734,585 (2001). Area: 1,016 sq. mi./2,631 sq. km.

de·re·cho /de ráy chō/ (*plural* **-chos**) *n Southwest US* **1.** a share of water from an irrigation canal (**acequia**), allocated to users according to the amount of land owned **2.** a destructive windstorm that is associated with a line of severe thunderstorms and is caused by winds blowing in a straight line, rather than the rotary winds of a tornado [< American Spanish < Spanish, "right, straight"]

de·rec·og·nize /dee rékəg nīz/ (**-nized, -niz·ing, -niz·es**) *vt* to stop accepting the legitimacy of something, especially a diplomatic mission —**de·rec·og·ni·tion** /dee rèkəg nísh'n/ *n*

de·reg·is·ter /dee réjjistər/ (**-tered, -ter·ing, -ters**) *vti* to remove a name or other item from a register or official list —**de·reg·is·tra·tion** /dee rèjji stráysh'n/ *n*

de·reg·u·late /dee réggyə làyt/ (**-lat·ed, -lat·ing, -lates**) *vt* to free something such as an organization or industry from regulation —**de·reg·u·la·tion** /dee règgyə láysh'n/ *n* —**de·reg·u·la·tor** *n* —**de·reg·u·la·to·ry** *adj*

der·e·lict /dérrə likt/ *adj* **1.** DESERTED no longer lived in **2.** NEGLECTED in poor condition because of neglect **3.** LAW ABANDONING DUTY neglectful of duty or obligations ■ *n* **1.** HOMELESS PERSON somebody without a home or employment **2.** ABANDONED PROPERTY a building, ship, or other property that has been abandoned **3.** LAW NEGLECTFUL PERSON somebody who is neglectful of duty or obligations [Mid-17C. < Latin *derelictus*, past participle of *derelinquere* "abandon utterly" < *relinquere* (see RELINQUISH)]

der·e·lic·tion /dèrrə líkshən/ *n* **1.** LAW NEGLECT OF DUTY deliberate neglect of duty or obligations **2.** ABANDONMENT the act of abandoning a building **3.** STATE OF NEGLECT a state of abandonment or neglect **4.** LAW LAND GAINED FROM SEA land gained because water has receded from it

de·re·press /dee ri préss/ (**-pressed, -press·ing, -press·es**) *vt* to activate a gene by deactivating the repressor —**de·re·pres·sion** *n*

de·re·pres·sor /dee ri préssər/ *n* an agent, e.g., a protein, that begins or enhances gene transcription by removing the repression of an operon

de·req·ui·si·tion /dee rèkwi zísh'n/ (**-tioned, -tion·ing, -tions**) *vt* to return something to civilian use that was earlier requisitioned by the military or a government

de·re·strict /dee ri stríkt/ (**-strict·ed, -strict·ing, -stricts**) *vt* to remove the restrictions from something —**de·re·stric·tion** *n*

de·ride /di ríd/ (**-rid·ed, -rid·ing, -rides**) *vt* to show contempt for somebody or something [Mid-16C. < Latin *deridere* "laugh down" < *ridere* "laugh"] —**de·rid·er** *n* —**de·rid·ing·ly** *adv*

SYNONYMS See ***ridicule***.

~~**de rigeur**~~ incorrect spelling of **de rigueur**

de ri·gueur /də ree gúr/ *adj* strictly required by the current fashion or by etiquette [Mid-19C. < French, "of strictness"]

de·ri·sion /di rízh'n/ *n* **1.** contempt and mockery **2.** the state of being derided [14C. < French *dérision* < Latin *deridere* (see DERIDE)] —**de·ris·i·ble** /di rízəb'l/ *adj*

de·ri·sive /di ríssiv, -zìv/ *adj* showing contempt or ridicule [Mid-17C. < DERISION] —**de·ri·sive·ly** *adv* —**de·ri·sive·ness** *n*

USAGE **derisive** or **derisory**? ***Derisive*** means "showing contempt or ridicule": *He gave a derisive laugh.* ***Derisory*** means "so small or inadequate as to deserve contempt or ridicule": *a derisory offer*, though it sometimes is used as a synonym of ***derisive***, as in *looked at me with a derisory smile.* Careful writers do try to maintain the distinction and the use of ***derisory*** where ***derisive*** is appropriate is best avoided.

de·ri·so·ry /di rísseree, -ríza-/ *adj* **1.** so small or inadequate as to deserve contempt or ridicule **2.** ⚠ same as **derisive** [Early 17C. < late Latin *derisorius* < Latin *deridere* (see DERIDE)]

USAGE See ***derisive***.

deriv. *abbr* **1.** LING, MATH, LOGIC derivation **2.** LING, MATH, CHEM derivative

der·i·vate /dérrivət, -vàyt/ *n, adj* same as **derivative** [15C. < Latin *derivatus*, past participle of *derivare* (see DERIVE)]

der·i·va·tion /dèrri váysh'n/ *n* **1.** SOURCE the origin or source of something such as a word or somebody's name **2.** LING WORD FORMATION the formation of a word or term from another word or from a basic form **3.** MATH, LOGIC PROOF a mathematical or logical argument whose steps show that the conclusion follows necessarily from initial assumptions **4.** ACT OF DERIVING SOMETHING the act of obtaining something from a source or issuing from a source —**der·i·va·tion·al** *adj*

SYNONYMS See ***origin***.

de·riv·a·tive /di rívvətiv/ *adj* UNORIGINAL copied from somewhere and not original ■ *n* **1.** DERIVED THING an idea, language, term, or other thing that has developed from something else that is similar to it **2.** LING DERIVED WORD a word that is formed from another word, e.g., "quickly" from "quick" **3.** CHEM RELATED CHEMICAL PRODUCT a chemical substance that is formed from a related substance ○ *an opium derivative* **4.** MATH CHANGE OF FUNCTION the limit approached in the ratio of a function and its variable, as the variable is changed ever more infinitesimally **5.** FIN FINANCIAL PRODUCT a tradable financial product whose value depends on the value of some other asset or combination of assets —**de·riv·a·tive·ly** *adv* —**de·riv·a·tive·ness** *n*

de·rive /di rív/ (**-rived, -riv·ing, -rives**) *v* **1.** *vti* GET OR COME FROM SOMETHING to obtain something from a source, or come from a source **2.** *vt* LOGIC DEDUCE SOMETHING to reach a conclusion about something by reasoning **3.** *vi* LING COME FROM SOURCE to develop from another word or a source word or term **4.** *vt* LING FORM ONE WORD FROM ANOTHER form a word or term from another, or state that a word or term developed from another **5.** *vt* CHEM MAKE COMPOUND to create a chemical substance from another **6.** *vt* MATH OBTAIN FUNCTION to obtain a function by differentiation [14C. Directly or via French < Latin *derivare* "draw off water through a channel" < *rivus* "stream"] —**de·riv·a·ble** *adj* —**de·riv·er** *n*

de·rived u·nit *n* a unit of measurement that is a multiple or fraction of a base unit

derm- *prefix* same as **derma-** (*used before vowels*)

-derm *suffix* skin ○ *ectoderm* [< Greek *derma*]

der·ma /dúrmə/ *n* same as **kishke** [Probably via Yiddish *gederem* "intestines" < Old High German *darm* "gut"]

derma- *prefix* skin ○ *dermatome* [Early 18C. Via modern Latin < Greek, "skin"]

der·ma·bra·sion /dúrmə bráyzh'n/ *n* a surgical process that removes scars or other imperfections of the skin by scraping the skin's surface with wire brushes or very fine sandpaper [Mid-20C. < Greek *derma* "skin" + ABRASION]

der·mal /dúrm'l/, **der·mic** /-mik/ *adj* involving, located in, or made up of skin or its main layer (**dermis**) [Early 19C. < Greek *derma* "skin"]

der·map·ter·an /dər máptərən/ *n* an insect that has strong sharp sensory appendages coming from the end of its abdomen, e.g., an earwig [Late 19C. < modern Latin *Dermaptera* < Greek *derma* "skin" + *pteron* "wing"] —**der·map·ter·an** *adj*

dermat- *prefix* same as **dermato-** (*used before vowels*)

der·ma·ti·tis /dùrmə títiss/ *n* inflammation of the skin from any cause, resulting in a range of symptoms such as redness, swelling, itching, or blistering

dermato- *prefix* skin ○ *dermatoplasty* [< Greek *dermat-*, stem of *derma* "skin"]

der·mat·o·glyph·ics /dùrmətə glíffiks/ *npl* the lines that form a pattern on the skin, e.g., on the fingers and palms of the hands (*takes a plural verb*) ■ *n* the study of dermatoglyphics (*takes a singular verb*) [Early 20C. < DERMATO- + Greek *gluphē* "carving" (see GLYPH)] —**der·mat·o·glyph·ic** *adj*

der·ma·toid /dúrmə tòyd/ *adj* resembling skin

der·ma·tol·o·gy /dùrmə tólləjee/ *n* the branch of medicine that deals with the skin and diseases affecting the skin —**der·ma·to·log·i·cal** /dùrmətə lójjik'l/ *adj* —**der·ma·to·log·i·cal·ly** *adv* —**der·ma·tol·o·gist** *n*

der·ma·tome /dúrmə tōm/ *n* **1.** an area of skin that has nerve fibers coming from a single spinal nerve **2.** an instrument used to slice thin layers of skin for skin grafting —**der·ma·tom·ic** /dùrmə tómmik/ *adj*

der·ma·to·pa·thol·o·gy /dùrmatō pə thólləjee/ *n* the medical study of the skin and its reaction to disease and pathogens at the cellular level —**der·ma·to·path·o·log·ic** /-pathə lójjik/ *adj* —**der·ma·to·path·o·log·i·cal** *adj*

der·mat·o·phyte /dur máttə fīt, dúrmətə fīt/ *n* a parasitic fungus that affects the skin, hair, or nails —**der·mat·o·phyt·ic** /dur màttə fíttik, dùrmətə fíttik/ *adj*

der·ma·to·phy·to·sis /dùrmatō fī tōssiss/ *n* a fungal infection of the skin, hair, or nails

der·ma·to·plas·ty /dúrmatō plàstee/ *n* any operation on the skin, especially skin grafting (*technical*) —**der·ma·to·plas·tic** /dùrmatō plástik/ *adj*

der·ma·to·sis /dùrmə tōssiss/ (*plural* **-to·ses** /-tō seez/) *n* any disease affecting the skin

-dermatous *suffix* having a particular kind of skin ○ *sclerodermatous* [< Greek *dermat-* (see DERMATO-)]

der·mes·tid /dur méstid/ *n* a beetle with clubbed antennae that eats organic materials, e.g., cabinet and carpet beetles. Family: Dermestidae. [Late 19C. < modern Latin *Dermestidae* < Greek *derma* "skin" + *esthiein* "eat"]

der·mic *adj* BIOL same as **dermal**

der·mis /dúrmiss/ *n* the thick sensitive layer of skin or connective tissue beneath the epidermis that contains blood, lymph vessels, sweat glands, and nerve endings [Mid-19C. < modern Latin, back-formation < EPIDERMIS]

-dermis *suffix* skin ○ *endodermis* [Back-formation < EPIDERMIS]

der·moid /dúr mòyd/, **der·moid cyst** *n* a benign tumor that contains skin or skin derivatives, found in the ovaries or on the face, especially around the eyes [Early 19C. < Greek *derma* "skin"]

der·nier cri /dèr nyay kreé/ *n* the latest thing in fashion [Late 19C. < French, "latest cry"]

der·o·gate /dérrə gàyt/ (**-gat·ed, -gat·ing, -gates**) *v* **1.** *vi* DEVIATE FROM CONDITIONS to deviate from a norm, rule, law, or set of conditions, e.g., by refusing to be bound by part of a treaty **2.** *vi* MAKE SOMETHING SEEM INFERIOR to make something seem inferior or less significant (*formal*) ○ *conduct that will derogate from your good name* **3.** *vt* CRITICIZE SOMEBODY OR SOMETHING to criticize somebody or something severely **4.** *vt* REPEAL LAW PARTIALLY to repeal or abolish part of a law or decree [15C. < Latin *derogat-*, past participle of *derogare* "repeal a law, detract from, impair" < *rogare* "ask, propose a law"]

der·o·ga·tion /dèrrə gáysh'n/ *n* **1.** DEVIATION a deviation from a rule or law, especially one specifically provided for **2.** EXEMPTION FROM RULE an exemption from a law or ruling given to a state **3.** DISPARAGEMENT the act of belittling or criticizing somebody or something —**de·rog·a·tive** /di róggətiv, dérrə gàytiv/ *adj*

de·rog·a·to·ry /di róggə tàwree/ *adj* expressing criticism or a low opinion —**de·rog·a·to·ri·ly** /di rògge táwrəlee/ *adv* —**de·rog·a·to·ri·ness** /di róggə tàwreenəss/ *n*

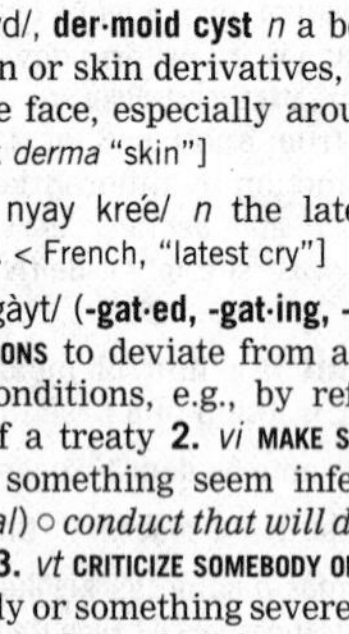

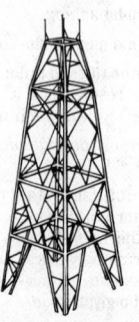

derrick (sense 2)

der·rick /dérrik/ *n* **1.** a simple crane that is typically used for moving cargo onto or from a ship **2.** a structure placed over an oil well that is used to raise and lower piping, drills, and other boring equipment [Early 17C. After a London hangman called *Derrick*; originally "hangman, gallows"]

Der·ri·da /dérri daá/, **Jacques** (*b.* 1930) Algerian-born French philosopher. He introduced deconstruction, a controversial technique for textual analysis.

> "The writer writes *in* a language and *in* a logic whose proper system, laws, and life his discourse by definition cannot dominate absolutely."
> [Jacques Derrida, *Of Grammatology*; 1967]

der·ri·ère /dèrree ér/ *n* somebody's buttocks (*humorous*) [Late 18C. < French, "behind"]

der·ring-do /dèrring doó, dérring doó/ *n* boldness or acts of great daring (*dated*) [Late 16C. Alteration and misinterpretation of *dorring don* "daring to do"]

der·rin·ger /dérrinjər/ *n* a pocket-sized, short-barreled, large-caliber pistol [Mid-19C. After Henry *Deringer* (1786–1868), US gunsmith]

der·ris /dérriss/ *n* **1.** an insecticide made from a tropical plant. It contains the natural toxin rotenone. **2.** a woody climbing plant with a tuberous root that produces derris. Native to: South Asia. Genus: *Derris.* [Mid-19C. Via modern Latin < Greek, "leather covering"]

Der·ry /dérree/ district council in County Londonderry, Northern Ireland. Population: 105,066 (2002).

der·vish /dúrvish/ *n* **1.** a member of any of several ascetic Muslim religious groups, some of which are known for their practices of very energetic dancing, whirling, chanting, or singing. They are known as whirling, dancing, or howling dervishes according to the group they belong to. **2.** a very energetic person [Late 16C. Via Turkish *derviş* < Persian *darvīš* "poor, mendicant"]

DES *abbr* **1.** E-COMMERCE data encryption standard **2.** PHARM diethylstilbestrol

de·sa·cral·ize /dee sákrə līz/ (**-ized, -iz·ing, -iz·es**) *vt* to remove the sacred, religious, or supernatural qualities or status from something

De·sai /də sī/, **Anita** (*b.* 1937) Indian writer. Her novels include *Cry, the Peacock* (1963) and *In Custody* (1984).

de·sal·i·nate /dee sállə nàyt/ (**-nat·ed, -nat·ing, -nates**) *vt* to remove the salt from something —**de·sal·i·na·tion** /dee sàllə náysh'n/ *n* —**de·sal·i·na·tor** *n*

de·sal·i·nize /dee sállə nīz/ (**-nized, -niz·ing, -niz·es**) *vt* CHEM same as **desalinate** —**de·sal·i·ni·za·tion** /dee sàlləni záysh'n/ *n*

de·salt /dee sáwlt/ (**-salt·ed, -salt·ing, -salts**) *vt* CHEM same as **desalinate** —**de·salt·er** *n*

de·sat·u·ra·tion /dee sàchə ráysh'n/ *n* the addition of white to a saturated color in order to achieve a paler shade

de·scale /dee skáyl/ (**-scaled, -scal·ing, -scales**) *vt UK* to remove the lime scale that has accumulated in a household appliance such as a kettle

des·cant /dés kànt, dís-/, **dis·cant** /dís-/ *n* **1.** HIGH MELODY a melody that is sung or played above the basic melody of a piece of music **2.** COMMENT a comment, remark, or criticism on a particular subject (*literary*) ■ *vi* (**-cant·ed, -cant·ing, -cants**) DISCOURSE ON SOMETHING to comment at length on a particular subject (*literary*) [14C. Via Anglo-Norman *descaunt* < medieval Latin *discantus* "part song, refrain" < Latin *cantus* "song"] —**des·cant·er** *n*

Des·cartes /day kaárt/, **René** (1596–1650) French philosopher and mathematician. He is often called the father of modern philosophy, and his *Discourse on Method* (1637) introduced his technique of philosophical inquiry. His work on analytic geometry resulted in the Cartesian system of coordinates.

> "There is a great difference between the mind and the body, inasmuch as the body is by its very nature always divisible, while the mind is utterly indivisible."
> [René Descartes, *Meditations on First Philosophy*; 1641]

de·scend /di sénd/ (**-scend·ed, -scend·ing, -scends**) *v* **1.** *vti* GO DOWN to go down a staircase, hill, valley, or other downward incline **2.** *vi* COME NEARER GROUND to come nearer the ground, especially in an aircraft in preparation for landing **3.** *vi* SLOPE to slope downward **4.** *vti* BE RELATED to be connected by blood to an ancestor ○ *be descended from Vikings* **5.** *vi* BE INHERITED to be inherited from or passed down by parents or ancestors **6.** *vi* ARRIVE SUDDENLY to arrive at a place suddenly, especially in large numbers ○ *tourists descending on unspoiled areas* **7.** *vi* BECOME ESTABLISHED to become more evident or established, suddenly or by degrees ○ *An atmosphere of gloom descended on the assembled crowd.* **8.** *vi* LOWER ONESELF to behave in a way that is disappointing and below somebody's usual standards [14C. Via French *descendre* < Latin *descendere* "climb down" < *scandere* "climb"] —**de·scend·a·ble** *adj*

de·scen·dant /di séndənt/ *n* **1.** a person, animal, or plant related to one that lived in the past **2.** something that is based in design, form, or concept on an earlier thing ■ *adj* another spelling of **descendent**

SPELLCHECK descendant or **descendent**? Do not confuse the spelling of ***descendant*** and ***descendent***, which sound similar. ***Descendant*** is the only spelling of the noun, denoting somebody or something related to an ancestor, or something based on an earlier thing. ***Descendent*** is the usual spelling of the adjective, which means "going downward."

de·scen·dent /di séndənt/ *adj* moving downward

SPELLCHECK See ***descendant.***

de·scend·er /di séndər/ *n* **1.** the tail part of a letter that extends below the baseline of other letters, e.g., on a "y" or "g" **2.** somebody or something that descends

de·scen·deur /dè saaN dúr/ *n* a mechanical device that can be tightened or loosened on a rope, enabling a climber to control the speed of his or her descent [Late 20C. < French, "descender" < *descendre* (see DESCEND)]

de·scend·i·ble /di séndəb'l/ *adj* **1.** able to be inherited **2.** allowing descent or downward movement

de·scend·ing /di sénding/ *adj* going or arranged from highest to lowest, greatest to smallest, or latest to earliest ○ *in descending order*

de·scent /di sént/ *n* **1.** GOING DOWN an act of going from the top to the bottom or from a higher position to a lower position **2.** WAY DOWN a path or other way down something such as a mountain **3.** DECLINE a decline or change from something better to something worse **4.** SUDDEN ARRIVAL the sudden arrival of a person or group of people **5.** ANCESTRAL BACKGROUND the connection somebody has to an ancestor or group of ancestors **6.** INHERITED DEVELOPMENT characteristics or developments that can be traced to an earlier source **7.** ONE GENERATION a step of one generation in a lineage **8.** LAW INHERITANCE the transmission of property by inheritance [13C. < French *descente* < *descendre* (see DESCEND)]

SPELLCHECK descent or **dissent**? Do not confuse the spelling of ***descent*** and ***dissent***, which sound similar. The word ***descent*** is only used as a noun, meaning "the act of descending," "a way down," "ancestral background," "a decline," etc., as in *a steep descent, people of Spanish descent.* The word ***dissent*** can be a noun or a verb, referring to disagreement or nonconformity, as in *dissent from official party policy, to dissent from orthodox religious doctrine.*

Des·champs /day shaáN/, **Eustache** (1340?–1407?) French poet. He wrote many ballads and poems, and the first treatise on French versification.

> "Who will bell the cat?"
> [Eustache Deschamps, "Ballade: Le Chat et les souris" "(Ballad: The Cat and the Mice)"; 14th century]

de·school /dee skoól/ (**-schooled, -school·ing, -schools**) *vti* to reduce somebody's involvement with education within the school system, or undergo this process —**de·school·ing** *n*

Des·chutes /day shoót, də shoóts/ river in northern Oregon that rises in the Cascade Range and flows northeastward to the Columbia River. Length: 250 mi./402 km.

de·scram·ble /dee skrámb'l/ (**-bled, -bling, -bles**) *vt* to make intelligible a message transmitted in code form —**de·scram·bler** *n*

de·scribe /di skrī́b/ (**-scribed, -scrib·ing, -scribes**) *vt* **1. EXPLAIN SOMETHING** to give an account of something by giving details of its characteristics **2. CHARACTERIZE SOMEBODY OR SOMETHING** to label or typify somebody or something **3. DRAW SHAPE** to make a shape or outline in the air (*formal*) ○ *The plane described a perfect figure eight.* **4. REPRESENT SOMETHING** to represent something pictorially or with a model [15C. < Latin *describere* "write down" < *scribere* "write"] —**de·scrib·a·ble** *adj* —**de·scrib·er** *n*

de·scrip·tion /di skrípshən/ *n* **1. EXPLANATION** a written or verbal account, representation, or explanation of something **2. PROCESS OF DESCRIBING** the process of giving an account or explanation of something **3. SORT** a kind or variety of something ○ *cars of every description* [14C. Via French < Latin *description-* < *descript-*, past participle of *describere* (see DESCRIBE)]

de·scrip·tive /di skríptiv/ *adj* **1. BEING DESCRIPTION** containing or consisting of description **2. CLASSIFYING** serving mainly to label, describe, or classify **3. ATTRIBUTIVE** expressing an attribute or quality of a noun ○ *descriptive adjective* [Mid-18C. < late Latin *descriptivus* < Latin *descript-* (see DESCRIPTION)] —**de·scrip·tive·ly** *adv* —**de·scrip·tive·ness** *n*

de·scrip·tive clause *n* GRAM same as **nonrestrictive clause**

de·scrip·tive lin·guis·tics *n* the study of a language limited to a comprehensive account of its grammar at a given time, omitting historical or comparative features and not attempting to formulate prescriptive rules (*takes a singular verb*)

de·scrip·tiv·ism /di skrípti vìzzəm/ *n* **1.** adherence to the practices and tenets of descriptive linguistics **2.** the notion or thesis that descriptive statements can be true and accurate reflections of phenomena —**de·scrip·tiv·ist** *n, adj*

de·scrip·tor /di skríptər/ *n* a word or phrase used to categorize records in a database so that all records containing the key can be retrieved together [Mid-20C. < Latin, "describer" < *descript-* (see DESCRIPTION)]

de·scry /di skrī́/ (**-scried, -scry·ing, -scries**) *vt* to catch sight of something (*literary*) [14C. < Old French *descrier* "cry out, proclaim" < *crier* (see CRY)] —**de·scri·er** *n*

Des·de·mo·na /dèzdə mṓnə/ *n* a small satellite of Uranus, discovered in 1986 by Voyager 2

~~desease~~ incorrect spelling of **disease**

des·e·crate /déssə kràyt/ (**-crat·ed, -crat·ing, -crates**) *vt* **1.** to damage something sacred, or do something that is offensive to the religious nature of something **2.** to damage something that is held dear or revered [Late 17C. < DE- + CONSECRATE] —**des·e·crat·er** *n* —**des·e·cra·tion** /dèssə kráysh'n/ *n* —**des·e·cra·tor** *n*

de·seed /dee seéd/ (**-seed·ed, -seed·ing, -seeds**) *vt* to remove the seeds from a fruit, vegetable, or plant

de·seg·re·gate /dee séggrə gàyt/ (**-gat·ed, -gat·ing, -gates**) *vti* to put an end to a customary or enforced separation of ethnic or racial groups in a place or institution, e.g., in a workplace or school —**de·seg·re·ga·tion** /dee sèggrə gáysh'n/ *n* —**de·seg·re·ga·tion·ist** *n*

de·se·lect /deè sə lékt/ (**-lect·ed, -lect·ing, -lects**) *vt* **1.** to remove selection status from an option or data on a menu or list on a computer screen **2.** *US* to end the training of an unsuitable trainee before the training program is completed —**de·se·lec·tion** *n*

~~desend~~ incorrect spelling of **descend**

de·sen·si·tize /dee sénssə tī́z/ (**-tized, -tiz·ing, -tiz·es**) *vt* **1. MAKE SOMEBODY LESS ALLERGIC** to make somebody less sensitive to a known allergen by injecting increasing amounts of the allergen over time, building up resistance **2. MAKE SOMEBODY LESS SENSITIVE TO FEAR** to make somebody less responsive to an overwhelming fear by repeated exposure to the feared situation or object, either in natural or artificial circumstances **3. MAKE SOMEBODY OR SOMETHING LESS SENSITIVE** to make somebody or something less sensitive in other respects —**de·sen·si·ti·za·tion** /dee sènssəti záysh'n/ *n* —**de·sen·si·tiz·er** *n*

~~desent~~[1] incorrect spelling of **decent**

~~desent~~[2] incorrect spelling of **descent**

WORLD'S LARGEST DESERTS

1		Sahara Desert
	Area	[3.5 million sq. mi./9.1 million sq. km]
	Location	*North Africa*
2		Gobi Desert
	Area	[0.5 million sq. mi./1.3 million sq. km]
	Location	*Central Asia/Mongolia*
3		Patagonian Desert
	Area	[0.26 million sq. mi./0.67 million sq. km]
	Location	*South America/Argentina*
=4		Rub' al-Khali Desert
	Area	[0.25 million sq. mi./0.65 million sq. km]
	Location	*Southwestern Asia/Arabia*
=4		Great Victoria Desert
	Area	[0.25 million sq. mi./0.65 million sq. km]
	Location	*Australia*
6		Great Basin Desert
	Area	[0.21 million sq. mi./0.54 million sq. km]
	Location	*North America*
7		Kalahari Desert
	Area	[0.2 million sq. mi./0.5 million sq. km]
	Location	*Southwestern Africa*
8		Great Sandy Desert
	Area	[0.15 million sq. mi./0.39 million sq. km]
	Location	*Australia*
9		Garagum Desert
	Area	[0.14 million sq. mi./0.35 million sq. km]
	Location	*Central Asia/Turkmenistan*
10		Sonoran Desert
	Area	[0.12 million sq. mi./0.31 million sq. km]
	Location	*Mexico and United States*

des·ert[1] /dézzərt/ *n* **1. DRY AREA** an area of land, usually in very hot climates, that consists only of sand, gravel, or rock with little or no vegetation, no permanent bodies of water, and erratic rainfall **2. DEPRIVED PLACE** a place or situation that is devoid of some desirable thing or overwhelmed by an undesirable thing ○ *a cultural desert* **3. LIFELESS PLACE** a place devoid of life [12C. Via French *désert* < late Latin *desertum* "abandoned place" < Latin *desert-* (see DESERT[2])]

USAGE desert or **dessert**? ***Dessert*** is a noun, is pronounced with the stress on the second syllable, and has only one modern meaning: "a sweet course eaten at the end of a meal." ***Desert*** is pronounced with the stress on the first syllable when it is a noun meaning "an arid area," and with the stress on the second syllable when it is a noun meaning "something somebody deserved," as in *just deserts* and similar expressions. The stress is also on the second syllable when ***desert*** is used as a verb, meaning "abandon something" or "run away."

de·sert[2] /di zúrt/ (**-sert·ed, -sert·ing, -serts**) *v* **1.** *vt* **ABANDON PLACE** to leave a place with no one staying behind **2.** *vt* **ABANDON PERSON** to leave or abandon somebody, especially somebody to whom a duty or obligation is owed **3.** *vti* MIL **LEAVE ARMY WITHOUT PERMISSION** to run away from an armed force or military post without permission and intending never to go back **4.** *vt* **BE UNAVAILABLE TO SOMEBODY** to be absent from somebody when needed ○ *Her sense of humor appeared to have deserted her.* [14C. Via French *déserter* < Latin *desert-*, past participle of *deserere* "abandon" < *serere* "join"] —**de·sert·ed** *adj* —**de·sert·er** *n*

USAGE See ***desert***[1].

de·sert[3] /di zúrt/ *n* something deserved, either punishment or reward (*usually used in the plural*) ○ *He'll get his just deserts.* [13C. < Old French, "what is deserved" < past participle of *deservir* (see DESERVE)]

USAGE See ***desert***[1].

des·ert boot *n* a laced ankle boot of beige or brown suede with a crepe-rubber sole

de·sert·i·fi·ca·tion /di zùrtəfi káysh'n/ *n* a process by which land becomes increasingly dry until almost no vegetation grows on it, making it a desert

de·ser·tion /di zúrsh'n/ *n* the act or an instance of deserting from the armed forces

des·ert is·land *n* a small isolated unpopulated tropical island

des·ert pave·ment *n* a layer of gravel that remains when the finer-grained particles of a desert soil have been blown away

des·ert rat *n* **1.** any rodent that lives in a desert **2.** *Can, Southwest US* a person who lives and works in a desert, e.g., a prospector

des·ert var·nish *n* a very thin dark surface coating of iron and manganese oxides that forms on exposed rock surfaces in deserts

de·serve /di zúrv/ (**-served, -serv·ing, -serves**) *vt* to have earned or be worthy of something [13C. Via Old French *deservir* < Latin *deservire* "serve well" < *servire* (see SERVE)] —**de·served** *adj* —**de·serv·er** *n*

de·serv·ed·ly /di zúrvədlee/ *adv* in a way that is justly and fully earned or merited ○ *She was deservedly popular as a teacher.*

de·serv·ing /di zúrving/ *adj* worthy to receive something because of need, merit, or justice ○ *I can think of no more deserving cause.* ■ *npl* people who have earned something justly through merit or need —**de·serv·ing·ly** *adv* —**de·serv·ing·ness** *n*

de Se·ver·sky /də sə vérskee/, **Alexander Procofieff** (1894–1974) Russian-born US aeronautical engineer. He set up and ran the Seversky Aircraft Corporation (1931–39) and invented the automatic bombsight.

de·sex /dee séks/ (**-sexed, -sex·ing, -sex·es**) *vt* **1.** to remove the sex organs from an animal or person **2.** BIOL, SOC SCI same as **desexualize**

de·sex·u·al·ize /dee sékshoo ə lī́z/ (**-ized, -iz·ing, -iz·es**) *vt* **1.** to suppress or diminish the sexual characteristics of an animal or person **2.** *US* to remove sexist features from something —**de·sex·u·al·i·za·tion** /dee sèkshoo əli záysh'n/ *n*

des·ha·bille *n* CLOTHING another spelling of **dishabille**

de·si /dáyssee/, **de·shi** /dáyshee/ *adj* **1.** *S Asia* **LOCAL** produced or made locally **2.** *S Asia* **RUSTIC** characteristic of rural areas, especially those considered to be unsophisticated **3. OF S ASIA** relating to or characteristic of South Asia ■ *n* **S ASIAN N AMERICAN** a North American of South Asian descent [< Hindi]

De Si·ca /də seékə/, **Vittorio** (1901–74) Italian movie director and actor. He made Italian neorealism internationally known through his *Bicycle Thieves* (1948).

des·ic·cant /déssikənt/ *n* a substance that absorbs water. Use: removal of moisture. [Late 17C. < Latin *desiccant-*, present participle of *desiccare* (see DESICCATE)] —**des·ic·cant** *adj*

des·ic·cate /déssi kàyt/ (**-cat·ed, -cat·ing, -cates**) *v* **1.** *vt* **REMOVE OR LOSE MOISTURE** to remove the moisture from something, or become free of moisture **2. PRESERVE FOOD BY DRYING** to preserve food by removing its moisture **3.** *vt* **MAKE UNINTERESTING** to remove vitality from something [Late 16C. < Latin *desiccat-*, past participle of *desiccare* "dry out" < *siccus* "dry"] —**des·ic·ca·tion** /dèssi káysh'n/ *n* —**des·ic·ca·tive** /déssi kàytiv/ *adj* —**des·ic·ca·tor** *n*

des·ic·cat·ed /déssi kàytəd/ *adj* **1.** free from moisture, or preserved by drying (*used of products, especially food*) **2.** describes something, especially a literary work, lacking in energy or vitality

SYNONYMS See *dry*.

de·sid·er·a·ta plural of **desideratum**

de·sid·er·a·tive /disíddə ràytiv, di síddərətiv/ *adj* **1.** having a desire for something (*formal*) **2.** describes a verb that, in some languages, expresses a desire to perform the action indicated by a related verb

de·sid·er·a·tum /di sìddə raátəm, -ráytəm/ (*plural* **-ta** /-tə/) *n* something that is desired or felt to be essential (*formal*) [Mid-17C. < Latin, neuter past participle of *desiderare* "desire, wish for"]

de·sign /di zī́n/ *v* (**-signed, -sign·ing, -signs**) **1.** *vti* **CREATE DETAILED PLAN OF SOMETHING** to make a detailed plan of the form or structure of something, emphasizing features such as its appearance, convenience, and efficient functioning ○ *a well-designed car interior* **2.** *vti* **PLAN AND MAKE SOMETHING** to plan and make something in a skillful or artistic way **3.** *vt* **INTEND SOMETHING FOR PARTICULAR USE** to intend something for a particular purpose ○ *The scholarship was designed to aid foreign students.* **4.** *vt* **INVENT SOMETHING** to contrive, devise, or plan something ■ *n* **1. PICTURE OF SOMETHING'S FORM AND STRUCTURE** a drawing or other graphical representation of something that shows how it is to function or be made **2. WAY SOMETHING IS MADE** the way in which something is planned and made ○ *the elegant design of the aircraft's wings* **3. DECORATIVE PATTERN** a pattern or shape, sometimes repeated, used for decoration ○ *a geometric design* **4. PROCESS OF DESIGNING** the process, techniques, or art of designing things ○ *studied architecture and design* **5. INTENTION** an underlying sense of purpose or planning (*formal*) ■ **de·signs** *npl* **SELFISH OR DISHONEST PLAN** a secretive plan undertaken for selfish or dishonest motives ○ *They had designs on her job.* [14C. < Latin *designare* (see DESIGNATE)] —**de·sign·a·ble** *adj* ◇ **by design** intentionally or on purpose

des·ig·nate *vt* /dézzig nàyt/ (**-nat·ed, -nat·ing, -nates**) **1. DESCRIBE SOMEBODY OR SOMETHING FORMALLY** to give somebody or something a formal description or name (*often passive*) **2. CHOOSE SOMETHING FOR USE** to choose something for a particular purpose (*usually passive*) **3. NAME SOMEBODY TO POSITION** to formally choose somebody for a job, position, or duty **4. MARK SOMETHING** to mark or indicate something ○ *Colored pins on the map designated the new buildings.* ■ *adj* /dézzignət/ **CHOSEN FOR FUTURE POST** chosen for a particular position, while not yet actually in office [Late 18C. < Latin *designat-*, past participle of *designare* "mark out" < *signum* "mark"] —**des·ig·na·tive** *adj* —**des·ig·na·tor** *n* —**des·ig·na·to·ry** *adj*

des·ig·nat·ed driv·er *n* a driver of a motor vehicle who abstains from alcoholic drinks on a social occasion in order to drive people home safely

des·ig·nat·ed hit·ter *n* a player in baseball who does not play defensively but substitutes for a pitcher in the batting order

des·ig·na·tion /dèzzig náysh'n/ *n* **1.** a name, label, or description given to something or somebody **2.** the act or process of being named or specified

de·sign·ed·ly /di zínədlee/ *adv* intentionally or on purpose

des·ig·nee /dèzzig neé/ *n US* somebody chosen to perform a job, duty, or task

de·sign·er /di zínər/ *n* **SOMEBODY WHO DESIGNS** somebody who designs things, especially fashionable and expensive clothes ■ *adj* **1. DESIGNED BY SOMEBODY FAMOUS** created or produced by a famous designer ○ *designer jeans* **2. FASHIONABLE** trendy, popular, and usually expensive ○ *designer foods* **3. SPECIALLY MADE** created for a specific purpose, requirement, or need

de·sign·er ba·by *n* a baby preselected at the embryo stage for desirable characteristics (*informal*)

de·sign·er drug *n* a drug that has been chemically altered to enhance its properties or to evade a legal prohibition

de·sign·er gene *n* a gene that is introduced into an organism to control the presence or absence of a specific characteristic

de·sign·er la·bel *n* a label attached to clothing to display the name of the designer

de·sign·er stub·ble *n* beard growth that is kept deliberately short to create a look that suggests a nonchalant attitude to grooming that belies the effort taken to achieve it (*informal*)

de·sign·ing /di zíning/ *adj* tending to scheme and make secret plans for personal benefit —**de·sign·ing·ly** *adv*

des·i·nence /déssinənss, dézz-/ *n* an ending or suffix of a word (*technical*) [Late 16C. Via French *désinence* < medieval Latin *desinentia* < Latin *desinere* "leave off, end" < *sinere* "leave"] —**des·i·nen·tial** /dèssi nénsh'l, dèzz-/ *adj*

de·sir·a·ble /di zírəb'l/ *adj* **1. WORTHY OF DESIRE** worth having or doing **2. ATTRACTIVE** sexually attractive or pleasing ■ *n* **SOMEBODY OR SOMETHING DESIRED** somebody who or something that is desired —**de·sir·a·bil·i·ty** /di zìrə bíllətee/ *n* —**de·sir·a·bly** *adv*

de·sire /di zír/ *vt* (**-sired, -sir·ing, -sires**) **1. WISH FOR SOMETHING** to want something very strongly **2. FIND SOMEBODY SEXUALLY ATTRACTIVE** to want to have sexual relations with somebody **3. REQUEST SOMETHING** to wish for and request something (*formal*) ■ *n* **1. CRAVING** a wish, craving, or longing for something **2. SOMETHING WISHED FOR** something that or somebody who is wished for (*formal*) **3. SEXUAL CRAVING** a strong wish for sexual relations with somebody [13C. Via French *désirer* < Latin *desiderare*] —**de·sir·er** *n*

SYNONYMS See ***want.***

~~desireable~~ incorrect spelling of **desirable**

de·sir·ous /di zírəss/ *adj* seeking or wishing for something very much (*formal*) —**de·sir·ous·ly** *adv* —**de·sir·ous·ness** *n*

de·sist /di síst, -zíst/ (**-sist·ed, -sist·ing, -sists**) *vi* to stop doing something [15C. Via French < Latin *desistere* < *sistere* "bring to a standstill" < *stare* "stand"] —**de·sis·tance** *n*

desk /desk/ *n* **1. TABLE USED FOR WORK** a table with a broad flat or sloping top, often with drawers and compartments, used for writing, reading, drawing, or computing **2. COUNTER OFFERING SERVICE TO CUSTOMERS** a counter where a service is provided, e.g., in a hotel or an airport **3. DEPARTMENT OF ORGANIZATION** a division of a communications company or other organization that specializes in a particular area of interest **4. STAND FOR SUPPORTING MUSIC** a stand for supporting a musical score that is shared by two players in an orchestra, or the two players who share it **5. BOOK STAND IN CHURCH** a stand for the book from which a service is read in church ■ *adj* **OF DESK** done at a desk, or designed to be kept on a desk ○ *a desk diary* [14C. Via medieval Latin *desca* < Latin *discus* "disk, dish, tray" (see DISH)]

desk·bound /désk bòwnd/ *adj* working at a desk rather than at a physically active or practical task

desk clerk *n* a hotel receptionist

desk din·ing *n* eating lunch at your desk at your place of work, in order to save time (*informal*)

desk·fast /désk fəst/ *n* breakfast eaten while at work, especially at a desk in an office (*informal*)

de·skill /dee skíl/ (**-skilled, -skil·ling, -skills**) *vt* to remove the need for skill or judgment in the performance of a task, often because of increasingly sophisticated production methods

desk job *n* a job in which most duties or tasks are undertaken while sitting at a desk in an office

desk·man /désk màn, -mən/ (*plural* **-men** /-mèn, -mən/) *n* a man who works at a desk, especially one who edits copy at a newspaper desk

desk or·gan·iz·er *n* a small container with several compartments used on a desk to keep pens, paper clips, and other small items organized and handy for use

desk·per·son /désk pùrss'n/ *n* a worker at a desk, especially one who edits copy at a newspaper desk

desk ser·geant *n* a police sergeant who works in administration at a police station

desk stu·dy *n* an investigation of the available facts and figures relevant to a specific issue, often before starting a new or more detailed study of it

desk ti·dy *n UK* COMM same as **desk organizer**

desk·top /désk tòp/ *n* **1. GRAPHICAL COMPUTER REPRESENTATION OF OFFICE DESK** a display on a computer screen comprising background and icons representing equipment, programs, and files **2. SURFACE OF DESK** the working surface of a desk ■ *adj* **USABLE ON TOP OF DESK** small and compact enough for the top of a desk

desk·top pub·lish·ing *n* the use of a personal computer and specialist software to lay out and produce typeset-quality documents for printing. Desktop publishing systems can mix text and graphics on the same page and are used to produce a variety of documents from flyers and newsletters to brochures and books.

desm- *prefix* same as **desmo-** (*used before vowels*)

des·man /déssmən/ *n* **1.** an amphibious mammal resembling a mole that has dense fur, webbed feet, and a flat scaly tail. Native to: Pyrenees. Latin name: *Galemys pyrenaicus*. **2.** an amphibious mammal related to the Pyrenean desman. Native to: Russia. Latin name: *Desmana moschata*. [Late 18C. Shortening of Swedish *desmanråtta* "muskrat" < *desman* "musk" + *råtta* "rat"]

De Smet /də smét/, **Pierre Jean** (1801–73) Belgian-born US Jesuit missionary. He was known for mediating between Native American peoples and European settlers. Also known as **Blackrobe**

des·mid /déssmid, déz-/ *n* a green, usually one-celled, freshwater alga composed of two symmetrical half-cells. It forms branching colonies like mats and is found in unpolluted water. Family: Desmidiaceae. [Mid-19C. < modern Latin *Desmidium* < Greek *desmos* "bond, chain"] —**des·mid·i·an** /dess míddee ən, dez-/ *adj*

desmo- *prefix* ligament, bond ○ *desmosome* [< Greek *desmos* < *dein* "bind"]

Des Moines /di móyn/ **1.** capital, largest city, and commercial center of Iowa, situated where the Raccoon River meets the Des Moines River in the south central part of the state. Population: 198,076 (2002 estimate). **2.** the longest river in Iowa, formed by the junction of its east and west branches near Humboldt. Length: 327 mi./526 km.

des·mo·some /dézmə sòm/ *n* a small patch of interlocking fibers between the outer membranes of adjacent cells that helps to hold cells together in tissues such as skin

Des·mou·lins /dày moo láN/, **Camille** (1760–94) French revolutionary and journalist. An effective pamphleteer and orator, he incurred the wrath of Maximilien Robespierre and was guillotined. Full name **Desmoulins, Lucie-Simplice-Camille-Benoist**

des·o·late *adj* /déssələt/ **1. EMPTY** bare, uninhabited, and deserted **2. ALONE** solitary, joyless, and without hope **3. GRIM** dismal and gloomy ■ *vt* /déssə làyt/ (**-lat·ed, -lat·ing, -lates**) **1. DEVASTATE PLACE** to make a place barren or deserted **2. MAKE SOMEBODY WRETCHED** to make somebody feel sad and lonely [14C. < Latin *desolatus*, past participle of *desolare* "leave alone" < *solus* "alone"] —**des·o·lat·ed** *adj* —**des·o·late·ly** *adv* —**des·o·late·ness** *n* —**des·o·la·ter** *n* —**des·o·la·tion** /dèssə láysh'n/ *n*

de·sorp·tion /di sáwrpsh'n, di záwrpsh'n/ *n* the action or process of releasing an absorbed substance from something, e.g., gas from rocks [Early 20C. < DE- + ABSORPTION]

de So·to /də sṓtō/, **Hernando** (1500?–42?) Spanish explorer. He explored parts of South America (1519–32) and southeastern North America (1539–42).

De So·to /də sṓtō/ city in northeastern Texas. It is a southern suburb of Dallas. Population: 39,440 (2002 estimate).

de·spair /di spér/ *n* **1. FEELING OF HOPELESSNESS** a profound feeling that there is no hope **2. CAUSE OF HOPELESSNESS** somebody or something that makes somebody feel hopeless or exasperated ○ *He was the despair of his soccer coach.* ■ *vi* (**-spaired, -spair·ing, -spairs**) **LOSE HOPE** to feel that there is no hope [14C. Via French < Latin *desperare* "stop hoping" < *sperare* "to hope" < *spes* "hope"]

de·spair·ing /di spérring/ *adj* feeling or showing loss of hope —**de·spair·ing·ly** *adv*

~~desparate~~ incorrect spelling of **desperate**

des·patch *vti, n* another spelling of **dispatch**

des·per·a·do /dèspə raádō/ (*plural* **-does** or **-dos**) *n* a reckless and violent criminal, especially in the early settlement of the western United States [Early 17C. Alteration of obsolete *desperate* "desperate person," after Spanish *desesperado*]

des·per·ate /déspərət/ *adj* **1. DESPAIRING** overwhelmed with urgency and anxiety, to the point of losing hope **2. AS LAST RESORT** so drastic or reckless as to be suitable only for a last resort **3. EXTREME** extremely difficult, serious, or dangerous ○ *a desperate shortage of food and water* **4. IN GREAT NEED** wanting or needing something very much ○ *Desperate for an answer, she phoned again.* **5. BEYOND HOPE** so wicked as to allow no hope of redemption **6. AWFUL** extremely bad (*informal*) ○ *The food was desperate!* [14C. < Latin *desperatus*, past participle of *desperare* (see DESPAIR)] —**des·per·ate·ly** *adv* —**des·per·ate·ness** *n*

des·per·a·tion /dèspə ráysh'n/ *n* **1.** recklessness brought on by great urgency and anxiety **2.** a condition of being without hope

~~**desperatly**~~ incorrect spelling of **desperately**

des·pi·ca·ble /di spíkəb'l/ *adj* fully deserving of contempt [Mid-16C. < late Latin *despicabilis* < Latin *despicari* "look down on"] —**des·pi·ca·bil·i·ty** /di spìkə bíllətee/ *n* —**des·pi·ca·ble·ness** *n* —**des·pi·ca·bly** *adv*

De·spi·na /de spéenə/ *n* a small natural satellite of Neptune, discovered in 1989 by the Voyager 2 planetary probe

de·spise /di spíz/ (**-spised, -spis·ing, -spis·es**) *vt* to dislike somebody or something intensely and with contempt [13C. < Old French *despis-*, stem of *despire* < Latin *despicere* "look down on" < *specere* "look"] —**de·spis·er** *n*

de·spite /di spít/ *prep* **1.** although it might have been prevented by something ○ *The mission blasted off today despite bad weather.* **2.** indicates that something is done unexpectedly or unintentionally ○ *She blushed deeply despite herself.* [13C. Via Old French *despit* "spite" < Latin *despect-*, past participle of *despicere* (see DESPISE)] ◇ **in despite of** in spite of or notwithstanding (*archaic*)

Des Plaines /dess pláynz/ city in northeastern Illinois, on the Des Plaines River. It is a northwestern suburb of Chicago. Population: 58,732 (2002 estimate).

de·spoil /di spóyl/ (**-spoiled, -spoil·ing, -spoils**) *vt* to rob a place of everything of value [13C. Via Old French *despoillier* < Latin *despoliare* "strip entirely of booty" < *spolium* "booty"] —**de·spoil·er** *n* —**de·spoil·ment** *n* —**de·spo·li·a·tion** /di spòlee áysh'n/ *n*

de·spond /di spónd/ (*archaic or literary*) *vi* (**-spond·ed, -spond·ing, -sponds**) to become discouraged or lose hope ■ *n* a feeling of extreme unhappiness and hopelessness ○ *a slough of despond* [Mid-17C. < Latin *despondere* "give up (your vitality)" < *spondere* "to promise"] —**de·spond·ing·ly** *adv*

de·spon·dent /di spóndənt/ *adj* extremely unhappy and discouraged —**de·spon·dence** *n* —**de·spon·den·cy** *n* —**de·spon·dent·ly** *adv*

des·pot /dés pòt, déspət/ *n* **1.** POWERFUL RULER a tyrant or ruler with absolute powers **2.** TYRANNICAL PERSON somebody who behaves in a tyrannical way toward other people **3.** ROMAN, BYZANTINE, OR OTTOMAN RULER a minor emperor or prince of the later Roman, Byzantine, or Ottoman empires [Mid-16C. Via French < Greek *despotēs* "absolute ruler"]

des·pot·ic /di spóttik/, **des·pot·i·cal** /-k'l/ *adj* relating to, carried out by, or behaving like a despot —**des·pot·i·cal·ly** *adv*

des·pot·ism /déspə tìzzəm/ *n* **1.** rule by a despot or tyrant **2.** cruel and arbitrary use of power

de·spu·mate /déspyə màyt, di spyóo-/ (**-mated, -mat·ing, -mates**) *v* **1.** *vi* to form froth or scum on the surface **2.** *vt* to remove the scum or froth on the surface of a liquid [Mid-17C. < Latin *despumat-*, past participle of *despumare* "skim off (scum)" < *spuma* "foam, scum"] —**de·spu·ma·tion** /dèspyə máysh'n/ *n*

des·qua·mate /déskwə màyt/ (**-mat·ed, -mat·ing, -mates**) *v* **1.** *vi* to flake or peel off naturally in small pieces (*refers especially to skin*) **2.** *vt* to remove a thin layer of skin, especially as a treatment for acne [Early 18C. < Latin *desquamat-*, past participle of *desquamare* "scale off" < *squama* "scale"] —**des·qua·ma·tion** /dèskwə máysh'n/ *n*

Des·sau /déss ow/ industrial city in Halle District, Saxony-Anhalt State, east central Germany. It is situated north of Leipzig. Population: 92,535 (1997).

des·sert /di zúrt/ *n* a sweet course eaten at the end of a meal [Mid-16C. < French, "(course following) clearing the table" < past participle of *desservir* "remove what has been served" < *servir* (see SERVE)]

USAGE See ***desert***[1].

des·sert·spoon /di zúrt spòon/ *n* **1.** a medium-sized spoon, larger than a teaspoon but smaller than a tablespoon, used for eating dessert **2.** *also* **des·sert·spoon·ful** the amount a dessertspoon contains

des·sert wine *n* a sweet wine served with dessert or after a meal

~~**dessicated**~~ incorrect spelling of **desiccated**

de·sta·bi·lize /dee stáybə lìz/ (**-lized, -liz·ing, -liz·es**) *vt* to make something, especially a government or economy, unstable in order to impair its functioning or bring about its collapse —**de·sta·bi·li·za·tion** /dee stàybəli záysh'n/ *n*

De Stijl /də stíl/ *n* an artistic movement founded in the Netherlands in 1917 that advocated the reduction of forms to geometric shapes and the use of primary colors along with black and white [Mid-20C. < Dutch, "the style," title of the periodical that represented the movement]

des·ti·na·tion /dèsti náysh'n/ *n* **1.** PREDETERMINED END OF TRIP the place to which somebody or something is going or must go **2.** INTENDED OR DESTINED END a purpose for which somebody or something is intended ■ *adj* INVOLVING PARTICULAR PLACE involving or relating to an establishment such as a restaurant or store that people make a point of going to, usually because of its reputation (*informal*) ○ *destination dining* [14C. < Latin *destination-* "appointment" < *destinare* (see DESTINE)]

des·ti·na·tion wed·ding *n* a wedding for which the couple travel to an exotic location to have their marriage ceremony

des·tine /déstin/ (**-tined, -tin·ing, -tines**) *vt* to intend or decide that somebody will have a particular fate or something will have a particular use [14C. Via French < Latin *destinare* "set up, decree, determine" < *-stinare* "cause to stand"]

des·tined /déstind/ *adj* **1.** sure, preordained, or intended ○ *She seemed destined for great things.* **2.** traveling toward a particular destination

des·ti·ny /déstinee/ (*plural* **-nies**) *n* **1.** SOMEBODY'S PREORDAINED FUTURE the apparently predetermined and inevitable series of events that happen to somebody or something **2.** INNER REALIZABLE PURPOSE OF LIFE the inner purpose of a life that can be discovered and realized **3.** *also* **Des·ti·ny** SOMETHING THAT PREDETERMINES EVENTS a force or agency that predetermines what will happen [14C. < Old French *destinee* < Latin *destinare* (see DESTINE)]

des·ti·tute /désti tòot/ *adj* **1.** lacking all money, resources, and possessions necessary for subsistence **2.** lacking a particular quality ○ *destitute of ideas* [14C. < Latin *destitutus*, past participle of *destituere* "set down, abandon" < *statuere* "set" < *status* "position"] —**des·ti·tute·ness** *n* —**des·ti·tu·tion** /dèsti tóosh'n/ *n*

de·stroy /di stróy/ (**-stroyed, -stroy·ing, -stroys**) *v* **1.** *vti* DEMOLISH to demolish something or reduce something to fragments **2.** *vti* RUIN to ruin something or make something useless **3.** *vti* ABOLISH to abolish, rescind, or end something **4.** *vt* DEFEAT SOMEBODY to defeat somebody in a crushing way **5.** *vt* KILL ANIMAL to kill something or somebody, especially an animal (*usually passive*) ○ *Afterward, the dog could not be cured and so had to be destroyed.* [12C. Via Old French *destruire* < Latin *destruere* "undo results of building" < *struere* "build"] —**de·stroy·a·ble** *adj*

USAGE Risk of redundancy: Like the qualities described by adjectives such as *unique* and *crucial*, the actions that many verbs signify do not occur by degrees. Ones having to do with destruction are cases in point. A house, for example, cannot be *slightly destroyed, a little bit ruined*, or *moderately demolished*. Either it has been ***destroyed***, *demolished*, or *ruined* or it hasn't. (*Partly destroy* and *partly demolish* are special cases, in that they signify the destruction of a part of something, not the damaging of all of it.) Although it is common to see expressions like *completely destroyed* and *totally demolished* used for emphasis, the adverb is strictly speaking redundant.

de·stroy·er /di stróy ər/ *n* **1.** a fast highly maneuverable warship, smaller than a cruiser and bigger than a frigate, that is used to escort convoys and attack submarines **2.** somebody or something that causes destruction

de·stroy·ing an·gel *n* a highly poisonous large white mushroom with a frill near the top of its stalk. It grows in moist woodlands in temperate regions. Latin name: *Amanita virosa.*

de·struct /di strúkt/ *n* the intentional destruction of a malfunctioning missile or rocket after its launch ■ *vti* (**-struct·ed, -struct·ing, -structs**) to intentionally destroy a malfunctioning missile or rocket after its launch, or be destroyed in this way [Mid-20C. Back-formation < DESTRUCTION]

de·struc·ti·ble /di strúktəb'l/ *adj* capable of being destroyed or liable to be destroyed [Mid-18C. Via French < late Latin *destructibilis* < Latin *destruct-* (see DESTRUCTION)] —**de·struc·ti·bil·i·ty** /di strùktə bíllətee/ *n*

de·struc·tion /di strúksh'n/ *n* **1.** PROCESS OF DESTROYING the act or process of destroying something **2.** DESTROYED STATE the condition of having been destroyed **3.** MEANS OF DESTROYING a cause or means of destroying something ○ *A love of fast cars was his destruction.* [13C. < Latin *destruction-* < *destruct-*, past participle of *destruere* (see DESTROY)]

de·struc·tive /di strúktiv/ *adj* **1.** causing or capable of causing destruction **2.** intended to damage or hurt rather than be helpful or instructive [15C. Via French < late Latin *destructivus* < Latin *destruct-* (see DESTRUCTION)] —**de·struc·tive·ly** *adv* —**de·struc·tive·ness** *n* —**de·struc·tiv·i·ty** /dèe struk tívvətee, di strùk-/ *n*

de·struc·tive dis·til·la·tion *n* the process of heating solid substances in the absence of air to decompose them in order to obtain useful products from the vapor and residues

de·struc·tor /di strúktər/ *n* **1.** an onboard explosive device used to destroy a missile or rocket if it malfunctions dangerously after its launch **2.** an incinerator used to burn garbage

des·ue·tude /désswi tòod/ *n* the condition of not being in use (*formal*) [Early 17C. Via French < Latin *desuetudo* < *desuescere* "become unaccustomed" < *suescere* "be accustomed"]

de·sul·fur·ize /dee súlfə rìz/ (**-ized, -iz·ing, -iz·es**) *vti* to remove sulfur and its compounds from something, typically from petroleum products or from flue gases when coal or another fuel is burned, or lose sulfur in this way —**de·sul·fur·i·za·tion** /-sùlfəri záysh'n/ *n* —**de·sul·fur·iz·er** *n*

de·sul·phur·ize INDUST Can, UK spelling of **desulfurize**

des·ul·to·ry /déss'l tàwree/ *adj* **1.** aimlessly passing from one thing to another ○ *conversing in a desultory fashion* **2.** happening in a random, disorganized, or unmethodical way ○ *The soldiers were subject to desultory fire from the enemy position.* [Late 16C. < Latin *desultorius* "leaping" < *desilire* "leap down" < *salire* "leap"] —**des·ul·to·ri·ly** *adv* —**des·ul·to·ri·ness** *n*

det., **det** *abbr* **1.** MIL detached **2.** MIL detachment **3.** detail **4.** GRAM determiner

de·tach /di tách/ (**-tached, -tach·ing, -tach·es**) *v* **1.** *vti* to separate, disconnect, or unfasten something, or become separated, disconnected, or unfastened **2.** *vt* to separate a military unit or an individual person from a larger unit for special duties [Late 17C. Via French *détacher* < Old French *destachier* < *attachier* (see ATTACH)] —**de·tach·a·ble** *adj* —**de·tach·a·bly** *adv* —**de·tach·er** *n*

de·tached /di tácht/ *adj* **1.** NOT ATTACHED not attached to something **2.** SEPARATE describes a building that stands on its own and is not joined to another building **3.** FREE FROM EMOTIONAL INVOLVEMENT unaffected by emotional involvement or any form of bias —**de·tach·ed·ly** /di táchədlee, di táchtlee/ *adv* —**de·tach·ed·ness** /de táchədnəss, di táchtnəss/ *n*

de·tached ret·i·na *n* an eye condition in which the retina becomes separated from the eyeball, causing loss of vision

de·tach·ment /di táchmənt/ *n* **1.** ALOOFNESS lack of interest in or involvement with other people or with worldly concerns **2.** DISINTERESTEDNESS a lack of bias, prejudice, or emotional involvement **3.** SEPARATION the condition of being separated from something, or the process of separating one thing from another **4.** MILITARY UNIT a military unit separated from its normal, larger unit for special duties **5.** SPECIALIZED GROUP any specialized and separately employed unit of a group or organization **6.** *Can* CANADIAN POLICE UNIT an organizational unit of the Royal Canadian Mounted Police

de·tail *n* /di táyl, dée tàyl/ **1.** INDIVIDUAL PART an individual separable part of something, especially one of several items of information ○ *No details of the proposed legislation are available yet.* **2.** EVERY ELEMENT OF WHOLE all of the individual parts that together make up a whole ○ *attention to detail* **3.** INCLUSION OF

ALL ELEMENTS the treatment and inclusion of all of the individual parts that make up something ○ *Your description of the item needs more detail.* **4.** INSIGNIFICANT PART something that is insignificant or a minor part of something else ○ *Safety in the sport is not a mere detail.* **5.** ARTS, ARCHIT SMALL ELEMENT OF ARTWORK OR STRUCTURE a small element of a work of art or building structure, considered separately **6.** GROUP WITH SPECIAL TASK a group of people, especially in the armed services, given a specific task ■ **de·tails** *npl* PERSONAL FACTS facts about somebody, e.g., his or her name and address ■ *vt* /di táyl/ (**-tailed, -tail·ing, -tails**) **1.** LIST THINGS to list or enumerate a series of items or events **2.** MIL GIVE MILITARY UNIT SPECIALIZED ASSIGNMENT to assign a military unit to a specialized task (*often passive*) **3.** DECORATE SOMETHING to add refinements or decorations to something, especially a motor vehicle [Early 17C. < French *détail* "piece cut off" < *détaillir* "cut up" < *taillier* "cut"] ◇ **go into detail** to be very specific and include all of the particulars ◇ **in detail** covering every item or particular

de·tail draw·ing *n* a large-scale drawing that shows part of a machine, device, or building

de·tailed /di táyld, dée tàyld/ *adj* including all or many of the distinguishing features of something

de·tail·er /di táylər, dée tàylər/ *n* **1.** a person or shop that specializes in adding decorative details to motor vehicle bodies **2.** somebody in the Department of the Navy who assigns officers and enlisted personnel to specific billets

de·tail·ing /di táyling/ *n* details or small decorative features added to something such as a garment or piece of artwork ○ *exquisite detailing*

de·tain /di táyn/ (**-tained, -tain·ing, -tains**) *vt* **1.** to hold back or delay somebody or something **2.** to restrain or keep somebody or something in custody [15C. Via Old French *detenir* < Latin *detinere* "hold back" < *tenere* "hold, keep"] —**de·tain·a·ble** *adj* —**de·tain·ment** *n*

de·tain·ee /dée tay née, di-/ *n* somebody who is held in custody

de·tain·er /di táynər/ *n* **1.** a writ authorizing that somebody in custody may be confined for a further period **2.** the wrongful withholding of somebody's property or freedom

de·tect /di tékt/ (**-tect·ed, -tect·ing, -tects**) *v* **1.** *vt* to notice or discover the existence of something **2.** *vt* ELECTRONICS same as **demodulate** **3.** *vti* to investigate crimes or other matters as a detective [15C. < Latin *detect-*, past participle of *detegere* "uncover" < *tegere* "cover"] —**de·tect·a·bil·i·ty** /di tèktə bíllətee/ *n* —**de·tect·a·ble** *adj* —**de·tect·a·bly** *adv*

de·tec·tion /di téksh'n/ *n* **1.** PERCEPTION OF SOMETHING'S EXISTENCE the act of noticing or discovering the existence of something, or the state of having been noticed or discovered **2.** DETECTIVE WORK the work of a detective in investigating crime or wrongdoing **3.** TELECOM SIGNAL EXTRACTION the extraction of a signal carrying information from a radio wave (**carrier**)

de·tec·tive /di téktiv/ *n* somebody who investigates and gathers evidence about possible crimes or wrongdoing ■ *adj* acting to detect something ○ *detective devices*

de·tec·tor /di téktər/ *n* **1.** a device for sensing the presence of or changes in something such as radiation or pressure **2.** somebody or something that detects

de·tent /di tént/ *n* a locking device that permits movement of a machine part in one direction only, e.g., a lever or spring-loaded catch [Late 17C. < French *détente* "release" < Latin *tendere* "to stretch"]

dé·tente /day taánt, -taáNt/, **de·tente** *n* a relaxation of tension or hostility between nations [Early 20C. < French, "relaxation" (see DETENT)]

de·ten·tion /di ténshən/ *n* **1.** the act of keeping somebody in custody, or the state of being kept in custody **2.** a form of punishment for school students in which they are made to stay in class at a break or at school after normal hours [15C. < late Latin *detention-* < Latin *detinere* (see DETAIN)]

de·ten·tion cen·ter *n* **1.** *Can* CRIME same as **detention home** **2.** a place where people wishing to enter a country without prior approval can be held until their claim is processed **3.** a county jail

de·ten·tion home *n* a place where young people are held in custody, usually while awaiting disposition of their cases by a juvenile court. Can term **detention centre**

de·ter /di túr/ (**-terred, -ter·ring, -ters**) *vti* to discourage somebody from taking action or prevent something from happening, especially by making somebody feel afraid or anxious [Mid-16C. < Latin *deterrere* "scare off" < *terrere* "scare"] —**de·ter·ment** *n* —**de·ter·ra·ble** *adj*

de·terge /di túrj/ (**-terged, -terg·ing, -terg·es**) *vt* to cleanse something, especially a wound (*technical*) [Early 17C. Directly or via French < Latin *detergere* "wipe off" < *tergere* "wipe"]

de·ter·gent /di túrjənt/ *n* a cleansing substance, especially a synthetic liquid that dissolves dirt and oil ■ *adj* having the properties of a detergent —**de·ter·gen·cy** *n*

de·te·ri·o·rate /di téeree ə ràyt/ (**-rat·ed, -rat·ing, -rates**) *vti* to become or make something worse in quality, value, or strength [Late 16C. < late Latin *deteriorat-*, past participle of *deteriorare* < Latin *deterior* "worse"] —**de·te·ri·o·ra·tion** /-tèeree ə ráysh'n/ *n* —**de·te·ri·o·ra·tive** *adj*

de·ter·min·a·ble /di túrminəb'l/ *adj* **1.** able to be worked out, decided, or found **2.** able to be terminated (*technical*) —**de·ter·min·a·bil·i·ty** /di tùrminə bíllətee/ *n* —**de·ter·min·a·bly** *adv*

de·ter·mi·nant /di túrminənt/ *n* **1.** CAUSE a factor that causes or influences something **2.** MATH ARRAY OF MATHEMATICAL ELEMENTS a square array of elements that itself has a numerical value, used in various mathematical processes such as solving simultaneous equations and studying linear transformations ■ *adj* CAUSAL causing or influencing something

de·ter·mi·nate /di túrminət/ *adj* **1.** having exact and definite limits **2.** same as **determined** (*formal*) **3.** BOT describes a pattern of flowering in which primary and secondary stems end in a flower bud and stop growing —**de·ter·mi·na·cy** /di túrminəssee/ *n* —**de·ter·mi·nate·ly** *adv* —**de·ter·mi·nate·ness** *n*

de·ter·mi·na·tion /di tùrmi náysh'n/ *n* **1.** FIRMNESS OF PURPOSE firmness of purpose, will, or intention ○ *full of ambition and determination* **2.** FIXED PURPOSE a fixed purpose or resolution ○ *her determination to succeed* **3.** ACT OF DISCOVERING SOMETHING an act of finding out or ascertaining something, especially as a result of investigation or research (*formal*) ○ *determination of the cause of death* **4.** DECISION ON COURSE OF ACTION the process of deciding on or establishing a course of action (*formal*) ○ *They were entrusted with the determination of future policy.* **5.** SETTLEMENT OF DISPUTE OR CONTEST the authoritative settlement of a dispute, especially by a judicial body **6.** LAW END OF ESTATE, INTEREST, OR RIGHT the conclusion or termination of an estate, interest, or right **7.** LOGIC QUALIFYING OF CONCEPT the qualifying of a concept or proposition by defining its attributes **8.** BIOL STAGE IN DEVELOPMENT OF EMBRYONIC TISSUE the stage in the development of embryonic tissue after which it can only develop as one specific type of tissue and no longer has the potential to develop into different types

de·ter·mi·na·tive /di túrmi nàytiv, di túrminətiv/ *adj* able to determine something ■ *n* **1.** a factor that determines something **2.** GRAM same as **determiner** (sense 1) —**de·ter·mi·na·tive·ly** *adv* —**de·ter·mi·na·tive·ness** *n*

de·ter·mine /di túrmin/ (**-mined, -min·ing, -mines**) *v* **1.** *vt* DECIDE SOMETHING to decide or settle something conclusively **2.** *vt* FIND OUT SOMETHING to find out or ascertain something, usually after investigation **3.** *vt* INFLUENCE SOMETHING to influence or form something **4.** *vt* SET LIMITS OF SOMETHING to establish and set the limits or form of something **5.** *vti* ADOPT PURPOSE to adopt a set purpose, or make somebody do this ○ *determined to leave as soon as possible* **6.** *vti* LAW END to end something, or come to an end [14C. Via French < Latin *determinare* "set the limits of" < *terminus* "limit, boundary"]

de·ter·mined /di túrmind/ *adj* feeling or showing firmness or a fixed purpose —**de·ter·mined·ly** *adv* —**de·ter·mined·ness** *n*

de·ter·min·er /di túrminər/ *n* **1.** a word that appears before any descriptive adjective and decides the kind of reference that a noun has, e.g., "a," "the," "this," "each," "some," "either," "my," and "your" **2.** somebody or something that determines something

de·ter·min·ing /di túrmining/ *adj* causing or deciding something ○ *the determining factor*

de·ter·min·ism /di túrmi nìzzəm/ *n* the doctrine or belief that everything, including every human act, is caused by something and that there is no real free will —**de·ter·min·ist** *n*

de·ter·min·is·tic /di tùrmi nístik/ *adj* **1.** relating to the doctrine or belief that everything, including every human act, is caused by something and that there is no real free will **2.** having an outcome that can be predicted because all of its causes are either known or the same as those of a previous event —**de·ter·min·is·ti·cal·ly** *adv*

de·ter·rent /di túr ənt, di túrrənt/ *n* **1.** SOMETHING THAT DETERS something that deters somebody or something **2.** WEAPONS THAT DETER ATTACK weapons, particularly nuclear weapons, held as a retaliatory threat ■ *adj* ACTING TO DETER capable of deterring somebody or something —**de·ter·rence** *n*

de·test /di tést/ (**-test·ed, -test·ing, -tests**) *vt* to dislike somebody or something very much [15C. Via French < Latin *detestari* "bear witness against, denounce" < *testis* "witness"] —**de·test·er** *n*

de·test·a·ble /di téstəb'l/ *adj* causing or deserving intense dislike —**de·test·a·bil·i·ty** /di tèstə bíllətee/ *n* —**de·test·a·bly** *adv*

de·tes·ta·tion /dèe te stáysh'n/ *n* **1.** an intense dislike of somebody or something **2.** somebody or something that is detested ○ *Neckties are a real detestation for him.*

de·throne /dee thrṓn/ (**-throned, -thron·ing, -thrones**) *vt* **1.** to remove a ruler, especially a monarch, from power **2.** to remove somebody from a high or powerful position, especially a champion in a sport —**de·throne·ment** *n* —**de·thron·er** *n*

det·i·nue /détt'noo/ *n* a legal action to reclaim wrongfully withheld personal property [15C. < Old French, "detention" < *detenir* (see DETAIN)]

det·o·nate /détt'n àyt/ (**-nat·ed, -nat·ing, -nates**) *vti* to explode, or make something explode [Early 18C. < Latin *detonat-*, past participle of *detonare* "thunder down" < *tonare* "to thunder"] —**det·o·na·tive** *adj*

det·o·na·tion /dètt'n áysh'n/ *n* **1.** an explosion, or an act of making something explode **2.** a premature spontaneous burning of a fuel-air mixture inside an internal-combustion engine

det·o·na·tor /détt'n àytər/ *n* a device or small quantity of explosive used to make a bomb or larger quantity of explosive explode

de·tour /dée to͝or, di to͝or/ *n* **1.** DEVIATION FROM MORE DIRECT ROUTE a deviation from a shorter, more direct route **2.** ROADS ALTERNATIVE ROUTE a route to be taken by traffic as an alternative to the normal route when the normal route cannot be used **3.** DEVIATION FROM NORMAL COURSE a deviation from a direct, expected, or previously decided course of action ■ *vti* (**-toured, -tour·ing, -tours**) DEVIATE OR MAKE DEVIATE to deviate from a shorter route, or make somebody or something do this [Mid-18C. < French *détour* < Old French *destorner* "turn away" < *torner* < Latin *tornare* (see TURN)]

de·tox /dée tòks/ (*informal*) *n* **1.** a medical facility in which alcoholics or drug addicts are detoxified **2.** the detoxification of an alcoholic or drug addict ■ *vti* (**-toxed, -tox·ing, -tox·es**) MED same as **detoxify** (sense 1) [Late 20C. Shortening of DETOXIFICATION, DETOXIFY]

de·tox·i·cate /dee tóksi kàyt/ (**-cat·ed, -cat·ing, -cates**) *vt* MED same as **detoxify** (sense 1) —**de·tox·i·cant** *n, adj*

de·tox·i·fi·ca·tion /dee tòksəfi káysh'n/, **de·tox·i·ca·tion** /dee tòksi káysh'n/ *n* **1.** the process of removing a toxic substance from something or counteracting its toxic effects **2.** the process of subjecting somebody or yourself to withdrawal from a toxic or addictive substance such as alcohol or drugs

de·tox·i·fy /dee tóksi fī/ (**-fied, -fy·ing, -fies**) *v* **1.** *vti* to subject somebody or yourself to withdrawal from a toxic or addictive substance such as alcohol or drugs **2.** *vt* to remove a toxic substance from something or counteract its toxic effects [Early 20C. < DE- + TOXIC]

de·tract /di trákt/ (**-tract·ed, -tract·ing, -tracts**) *vi* to reduce the quality, value, or importance of something by taking something away from it [15C. < Latin *detract-*, past participle of *detrahere* "take or pull away" < *trahere* "pull"] —**de·trac·tive** *adj* —**de·trac·tive·ly** *adv*

de·trac·tion /di tráksh'n/ *n* **1. REDUCTION IN EFFECT OR FORCE** a reduction or taking away of quality, value, or importance from something **2. SOMEBODY OR SOMETHING THAT DETRACTS** somebody or something that detracts from the quality, value, or importance of something **3. REPUTATION DAMAGE** the act of damaging somebody's reputation, especially by making discrediting comments (*formal*)

de·trac·tor /di tráktər/ *n* somebody who disparages or devalues somebody or something

de·train /dee tráyn/ (**-trained, -train·ing, -trains**) *vti* to get out of or remove people from a railroad train —**de·train·ment** *n*

de·trib·al·ize /dee tríb'l ìz/ (**-ized, -iz·ing, -iz·es**) *vti* to abandon tribal practices, usually as a result of exposure to another culture, or make somebody do this —**de·trib·al·i·za·tion** /dee tríb'li záysh'n/ *n*

det·ri·ment /déttrimənt/ *n* **1.** damage, harm, or disadvantage **2.** something that causes damage, harm, or disadvantage (*formal*) [15C. Via French < Latin *detrimentum* < *deterere* "wear away" < *terere* "rub, wear"]

det·ri·men·tal /dèttri mént'l/ *adj* causing damage, harm, or disadvantage —**det·ri·men·tal·ly** *adv*

de·tri·tion /di trísh'n/ *n* the process of wearing something away by friction [Late 17C. < medieval Latin *detrition-* < Latin *deterere* (see DETRIMENT)]

de·tri·ti·vore /di trítə vàwr/, **de·tri·to·vore** *n UK* an organism that feeds on decaying animal or plant material. Detritivores such as bacteria, earthworms, and many insects aid in breaking down soil. [Mid-20C. < DETRITUS]

de·tri·tus /di trítəss/ *n* **1. DEBRIS** debris or discarded material **2.** GEOL **ROCK FRAGMENTS** fragments of rock that have been worn away **3.** ECOL **ORGANIC MATTER** organic debris formed by the decomposition of plants or animals [Late 18C. < Latin < past participle of *deterere* (see DETRIMENT)] —**de·tri·tal** *adj*

De·troit /də tróyt/ city in southeastern Michigan, on the Detroit River and Lake St. Clair. It is one of the most important car manufacturing centers in the world. Population: 925,051 (2002 estimate).

de trop /də tró/ *adj* superfluous or excessive (*literary*) [Mid-18C. < French]

de·tu·mes·cence /dèe too méss'nss/ *n* a gradual reduction in a swelling, especially of a penis [Late 17C. < Latin *detumescere* "stop swelling" < *tumere* "swell"] —**de·tu·mesce** *vi* —**de·tu·mes·cent** *adj*

deuce[1] /dooss/ *n* **1. CARD WITH TWO SPOTS** a playing card with two pips or the face of a die with two spots **2. TIE-BREAKING SITUATION** in tennis, badminton, and other racket games, a situation in which a player must score two successive points to win after the score is tied **3. NUMBER 2** the number 2 (*slang*) **4. TWO DOLLARS** two dollars, or a two-dollar bill (*slang*) [15C. Via Old French *deus* "two" < Latin *duos*]

deuce[2] /dooss/ (*dated slang*) *n* something that is bad or unpleasant ■ *interj* used instead of a swearword to show displeasure, irritation, or surprise [Mid-17C. Via Dutch or Low German *duus* "throw of two on two dice" (the lowest score) < Latin *duos* "two"]

deuc·ed /doossəd, doost/ (*dated slang*) *adj* used instead of a swearword to give emphasis or to show displeasure, irritation, or surprise ■ *adv* decidedly or extremely —**deuc·ed·ly** *adv*

deuc·es wild *n* a form of poker or another card game in which a deuce can represent a card of any suit and denomination a player chooses

De·us /dáy əss/ *n* JUD-CHR same as **God** [13C. < Latin]

de·us ex ma·chi·na /dày əss eks maákinə/ *n* **1.** an improbable character or unconvincing event used to resolve a plot **2.** in ancient Greek and Roman theater, a god introduced to resolve a complicated plot [< modern Latin, "god from the machinery" (used in Greek theater to lower actors onto the stage)]

Deut. *abbr* BIBLE Deuteronomy

deuter- *prefix* same as **deutero-** (*used before vowels*)

deu·ter·ag·o·nist /dootə rággənist/ *n* a character second in importance to the leading character (**protagonist**) in ancient Greek drama [Mid-19C. < Greek *deuteragōnistēs* < *deuteros* "second" + *agōnistēs* "actor" (see PROTAGONIST)]

deu·ter·a·no·pi·a /dootərə nópee ə/ *n* colorblindness in which red and green are confused —**deu·ter·a·nop·ic** /-nóppik, -nópik/ *adj*

deu·ter·ate /dootə ràyt/ (**-at·ed, -at·ing, -ates**) *vt* to add deuterium to a chemical compound [Mid-20C. < DEUTERIUM] —**deu·te·ra·tion** /dootə ráysh'n/ *n*

deu·ter·ide /dootə rìd/ *n* a compound of hydrogen (**hydride**) in which hydrogen has been replaced by its heavier isotope deuterium [Mid-20C. < DEUTERIUM]

deu·te·ri·um /doo teeree əm/ *n* an isotope of hydrogen that has double the mass of ordinary hydrogen because it contains a neutron in its nucleus. Use: tracer in experiments. Symbol **D** [Mid-20C. < Greek *deuteros* "second"]

deu·te·ri·um ox·ide *n* CHEM same as **heavy water**

deutero- *prefix* second, secondary ○ *deuterocanonical* [< Greek *deuteros*]

deu·ter·o·ca·non·i·cal /dootə rō kə nónnik'l/ *adj* relating or belonging to a secondary, less well-regarded, or disputed collection of religious scripture, especially the Apocrypha

deu·ter·o·my·cete /dyootərō mí seet/ *n* a fungus in which sexual reproduction apparently never occurs. Such fungi, which include the penicillin fungus and the agent responsible for thrush, reproduce entirely asexually by spores or budding.

deu·ter·on /dootə ròn/ *n* the nucleus of a deuterium atom, consisting of one proton and one neutron. It is used mainly as a bombarding particle in particle accelerators such as cyclotrons. Symbol D^+ [Mid-20C. < DEUTERO-, after PROTON]

Deu·ter·on·o·my /dootə rónnəmee/ *n* a book of the Bible that repeats the Ten Commandments and records much of mosaic law. It is the fifth book of the Pentateuch. See table at **Bible** [14C. Via late Latin < Greek *Deuteronomion* "second law"; because the book contains a repetition of the Decalogue and of parts of *Exodus*] —**Deu·ter·o·nom·ic** /dootərə nómmik/ *adj*

deu·ter·o·stome /dyootərə stōm/ *n* an animal whose mouth develops from a second opening in the early embryo, opposite to the initial opening (**blastopore**) of the rudimentary gut. Chordates and echinoderms are deuterostomes.

deu·to·plasm /dootə plàzzəm/ *n* nutrient matter contained in some reproductive cells, e.g., the yolk in a bird's egg —**deu·to·plas·mic** /dootə plázmik/ *adj*

deut·sche mark /dóychə maark/, **deut·sche·mark** *n* the main unit of the former German currency. Symbol **DM** [Mid-20C. < German, "German mark" < *deutsch* "German" + *Mark* (see MARK[2])]

deut·zi·a /dootsee ə, dóyt-/ (*plural* **-as** or *same*) *n* a bush with clusters of white to pink or lavender flowers. Native to: Asia, Central America. Genus: *Deutzia*. [Mid-19C. < modern Latin, after Johann van der Deutz, 18C Dutch patron of botany]

dev. *abbr* deviation

de·va /dáyvə/ *n* a Hindu or Buddhist god [Early 19C. < Sanskrit, "god"]

De Va·le·ra /dèvvə lérrə/, **Eamon** (1882–1975) US-born Irish politician. He was a key figure in establishing the Irish Republic. He formed a dissident faction of Sinn Fein, the Fianna Fáil party (1926), was prime minister (1932–48, 1951–54, and 1957–59), and served as president (1959–73).

> "Whenever I wanted to know what the Irish people wanted, I had only to examine my own heart and it told me straight off what the Irish people wanted."
> [Eamon De Valera, *Speech to the Irish Parliament*, January 6, 1922]

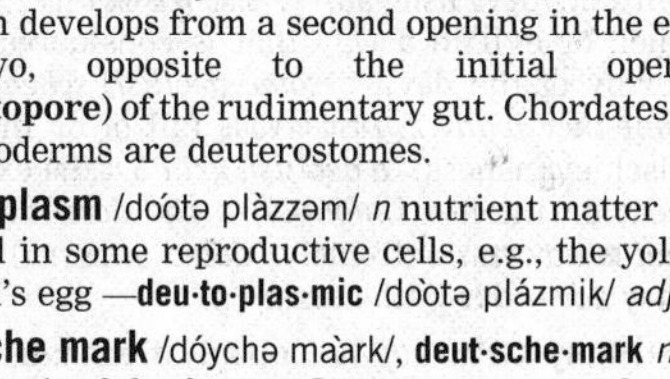
Popperfoto
Eamon De Valera

de·val·u·ate /dee vállyoo àyt/ (**-at·ed, -at·ing, -ates**) ECON same as **devalue** (sense 1)

de·val·ue /dee vállyoo/ (**-ued, -u·ing, -ues**) *vti* **1.** to lower the value of a nation's currency by government action, or become lowered in value **2.** to cause the value or importance of somebody or something to be reduced, or to become reduced in value or importance —**de·val·u·a·tion** /dee vàllyoo áysh'n/ *n*

De·va·na·ga·ri /dàyvə naágəree/ *n* the alphabet that is used to write Hindi, Marathi, Nepali, and several languages of northern India, as well as classical Sanskrit [Late 18C. < Sanskrit < *deva* "god" + *Nāgarī*, earlier name for the script]

dev·as·tate /dévvə stàyt/ (**-tat·ed, -tat·ing, -tates**) *vt* **1.** to cause severe or widespread damage to something ○ *an area devastated by floods* **2.** to shock or upset somebody greatly (*often passive*) [Mid-17C. < Latin *devastat-*, past participle of *devastare* "lay waste completely" < *vastare* "lay waste" < *vastus* "waste"] —**dev·as·ta·tion** /dèvvə stáysh'n/ *n* —**dev·as·ta·tive** *adj* —**dev·as·ta·tor** *n*

dev·as·tat·ing /dévvə stàyting/ *adj* **1. DAMAGING** causing severe or widespread damage ○ *policies that have a devastating effect on economic growth* **2. VERY UPSETTING** causing great shock or upset ○ *The news was devastating.* **3. SHARPLY CRITICAL** containing criticism that is very sharp and very effective or damaging, often as a result of its precise detail or caustic wit **4. REMARKABLE** startlingly impressive or attractive (*informal*) ○ *the devastating speed of her forehand return* —**dev·as·tat·ing·ly** *adv*

de·vein /dee váyn/ (**-veined, -vein·ing, -veins**) *vt* to remove the dark thready gut (**vein**) from the back of the tail meat of a shrimp

de·vel·op /di vélləp/ (**-oped, -op·ing, -ops**) *v* **1.** *vti* **CHANGE AND GROW** to change and become larger, stronger, or more impressive, successful, or advanced, or cause somebody or something to change in this way **2.** *vi* **ARISE AND INCREASE** to arise and then increase or progress to a more complex state ○ *Tension was developing between the two nations.* **3.** *vt* **ADOPT OR ACQUIRE SOMETHING** to acquire a feature, habit, or illness that then becomes more marked or extreme ○ *The baby is developing a cold.* **4.** *vt* **ENLARGE ON SOMETHING** to add details to a basic plan or idea **5.** *vt* **BECOME CLEAR** to become apparent and thus resolve a question or clarify a situation ○ *It developed that we didn't need reservations.* **6.** *vti* **PRESENT OR BE REVEALED IN STAGES** to present the sequential events or successive stages of a story or argument, or have such events or stages revealed ○ *The theory is developed at length in her new book.* **7.** *vt* **USE RESOURCES FOR HUMAN PURPOSES** to use or make available land, minerals, or other natural resources for human purposes such as housing **8.** *vt* **BUILD STRUCTURES** to plan and construct buildings, roads, or other technological structures ○ *develop a global communications system* **9.** *vt* **TURN FILM INTO NEGATIVES OR PRINTS** to treat photographic film with chemicals in order to produce a negative or print (*often passive*) ○ *Send the rolls off to be developed.* **10.** *vi* **ACHIEVE SEXUAL MATURITY** to become sexually mature **11.** *vt* CHESS **BRING PIECE INTO PLAY** to bring a chess piece into play **12.** *vt* MUSIC **VARY MUSICAL THEME** to add to a musical theme by using variation or ornamentation, especially by breaking it down into motifs and using other musical techniques [Mid-17C. < French *développer* "unwrap" < Old French *voloper* "wrap"] —**de·vel·op·a·ble** *adj*

~~develope~~ incorrect spelling of **develop**

de·vel·oped /di vélləpt/ *adj* wealthy and technologically advanced, with sophisticated manufacturing and service industries

~~developement~~ incorrect spelling of **development**

de·vel·op·er /di vélləpər/ *n* **1. SOMEBODY WHO DEVELOPS**

somebody or something that develops something ○ *the developer of a new manufacturing process* **2. BUYER OF LAND FOR BUILDING** a person or company that buys land in order to build on it or sell it to others who want to build on it **3.** PHOTOGRAPHY **CHEMICAL FOR MAKING NEGATIVES OR PRINTS** a chemical used to turn exposed film into negatives or prints

de·vel·op·ing /di vélləping/ *adj* using or involving small-scale agriculture and industry of the kind that characterized the earlier economic stages of technologically advanced nations

de·vel·op·ment /di véllәpmәnt/ *n* **1. EVENT CAUSING CHANGE** an incident that causes a situation to change or progress (*often used in the plural*) ○ *Have there been any political developments since last week?* **2. PROCESS OF CHANGE** the process of changing and becoming larger, stronger, or more impressive, successful, or advanced, or of causing somebody or something to change in this way ○ *sustained economic development* **3. INCOMPLETE STATE** a state in which the developing of something is not yet completed ○ *The prototype is in development.* **4. HOUSES OR OTHER BUILDINGS** a group of houses or other buildings that are built as a single construction project **5.** MUSIC **VARIATION OF MUSICAL THEME** the process of varying and ornamenting a musical theme **6.** MUSIC **MUSICAL SECTION WHERE THEME IS DEVELOPED** one of the three main sections of the sonata form, in which the musical themes presented in the exposition are rhythmically and melodically elaborated **7.** CHESS **BRINGING OF PIECE INTO PLAY** the bringing of a chess piece into play —**de·vel·op·men·tal** /-vèllәp mént'l/ *adj* —**de·vel·op·men·tal·ly** *adv*

de·vel·op·men·tal psy·chol·o·gy *n* the branch of psychology that deals with the ways that personality, cognitive ability, and behavior change during somebody's life span, with particular concentration on childhood development

dé·vel·op·pé /di vèllә páy, dàyvәlō páy/ *n* a ballet movement in which the foot of one leg is drawn up to the knee of the other and then extended slowly out into the air [Early 20C. < French, past participle of *développer* (see DEVELOP)]

de·verb·a·tive /dee vúrbәtiv/, **de·ver·bal** /-vúrb'l/ *adj* derived from a verb, e.g., as the noun "driver" is derived from the verb "drive," and the adjective "clingy" from the verb "cling" [Early 20C. After DENOMINATIVE]

De·vi /dáyvee/ *n* the supreme Hindu goddess, wife of the god Shiva, manifested in the different forms and characters of Durga, Kali, Parvati, and Sati [Late 20C. < Sanskrit, "goddess"]

de·vi·ance /deévee әnss/, **de·vi·an·cy** /deévee әnssee/ *n* behavior that is sharply different from a customary, traditional, or generally accepted standard

de·vi·ant /deévee әnt/ *adj* diverging sharply from a customary, traditional, or generally accepted standard, or displaying such divergent behavior ○ *abstract paintings, once thought deviant, now worth millions* ■ *n* an offensive term for somebody whose behavior is different from a customary, traditional, or generally accepted standard [14C. < late Latin *deviant-*, present participle of *deviare* (see DEVIATE)]

de·vi·ate *vi* /deévee àyt/ (**-at·ed, -at·ing, -ates**) **1.** to be different or behave differently **2.** to turn off from a course or path ■ *adj* /deévee әt/ PSYCHOL same as **deviant** ■ *n* /deévee әt/ PSYCHOL same as **deviant** [Mid-17C. < late Latin *deviat-*, past participle of *deviare* "depart from the way" < Latin *via* "way, road"] —**de·vi·a·tor** *n* —**de·vi·a·to·ry** *adj*

de·vi·a·tion /deévee áysh'n/ *n* **1. CHANGE OR DIFFERENCE** a change or difference from what is usual, accepted, expected, or planned ○ *These rituals represented a deviation from established practices.* **2.** PSYCHOL **UNACCEPTABLE BEHAVIOR OR ATTITUDE** behavior or an attitude that is sharply different from a customary, traditional, or generally accepted standard **3.** STATS **DIFFERENCE FROM STATISTICAL AVERAGE** the difference between any individual value and a fixed value such as the average of all the other values in its series **4.** NAVIG **COMPASS ERROR** an error in a compass reading caused by local magnetic fields, especially on a ship at sea

de·vi·a·tion·ism /deévee áysh'n ìzzәm/ *n* departure from accepted or established political views, especially from orthodox communism —**de·vi·a·tion·ist** *n, adj*

de·vice /di víss/ *n* **1. TOOL OR MACHINE** a tool or machine designed to perform a particular task or function **2. PLOY** a way of achieving something, especially a clever or dishonest way **3. EXPLOSIVE OBJECT** a bomb or something that causes an explosion or fire **4. LITERARY OR DRAMATIC TOOL** something designed to create a particular effect in a literary or dramatic work, or to evoke a particular response from a reader, listener, or viewer ○ *a familiar cinematic device* **5. EMBLEM OR MOTTO** an emblem or motto, or a combination of the two, especially when used in heraldry ○ *a heraldic device* **6. ORNAMENTAL DESIGN** an ornamental pattern or design, e.g., in embroidery [13C. < Old French *devis* "division, contrivance," *devise* "plan" < Latin *dividere* (see DIVIDE)] ◇ **leave somebody to his** *or* **her own devices** to let somebody do as he or she wishes, instead of giving the person direction or assistance

~~devide~~ incorrect spelling of **divide**

dev·il /dévv'l/ *n* **1.** *also* **Dev·il GOD'S ENEMY** in Christianity and some other religions, the enemy of God, who rules Hell, tempts people to sin, and personifies the spirit of evil as Satan **2. EVIL SPIRIT** an evil spirit, particularly a subordinate of Satan **3. OFFENSIVE TERM** somebody who is regarded as evil, unpleasant, or violent (*insult*) **4. MISCHIEVOUS PERSON OR ANIMAL** a mischievous, troublesome, or high-spirited person or animal **5. PERSON OR ANIMAL** a person or animal of the sort described ○ *You lucky devil!* **6.** METEOROL same as **dust devil** **7. DIFFICULT OR UNPLEASANT CASE** an extremely difficult or unpleasant instance of something (*informal*) **8. INTENSIFIER** used as an intensifier in questions and exclamations (*slang*) ○ *Who the devil does he think he is?* **9.** PRINTING same as **printer's devil** (*archaic*) ■ *vt* (**-iled, -il·ing, -ils**) **1. MAKE FOOD SPICY** to cook or prepare a food with spicy seasonings **2. PESTER SOMEBODY** to annoy, worry, or pester somebody, especially by making repeated requests for something (*informal*) ○ *He's been deviling me with requests for an interview.* [Old English *dēofol*, via Latin *diabolus* < Greek *diabolos* "devil, Satan"] ◇ **between the devil and the deep blue sea** faced with two equally undesirable choices

dev·il·fish /dévv'l fish/ (*plural same* or **-fish·es**) *n* a fish that is thought to have an evil or frightening appearance, e.g., a manta ray or octopus

dev·il·ish /dévv'lish/ *adj* **1. SINISTER OR CRUEL** sinister, cruel, or evil in a way that is considered like or worthy of the devil ○ *some devilish scheme to get what they want* **2. MISCHIEVOUS** full of or indicating mischievousness ○ *a devilish grin* **3. GREAT** extremely great or intense (*informal*) ○ *the devilish midday heat* ■ *adv* **VERY** extremely (*dated informal*) —**dev·il·ish·ly** *adv* —**dev·il·ish·ness** *n*

dev·il-may-care *adj* **1.** foolishly nonchalant about risk or danger **2.** tending to enjoy the present and not think or worry about the future

dev·il·ment /dévv'lmәnt/ *n* troublesome, mischievous, or devilish behavior ○ *always getting up to some devilment or other*

dev·il·ry *n* same as **deviltry**

dev·il's ad·vo·cate *n* **1.** somebody who argues about something merely to provoke discussion **2.** a Roman Catholic official appointed to argue against the canonization or beatification of a candidate

dev·il's club *n* a prickly bush with greenish white flowers and clusters of red berries. Native to: western North America. Latin name: *Oplopanax horridus.* [< its prickles]

dev·il's darn·ing nee·dle *n* INSECTS **1.** *regional* same as **dragonfly** **2.** same as **damselfly** (*informal*) [< its long thin body]

REGIONAL NOTE See *darning needle.*

dev·il's food cake *n* a rich dark chocolate cake [< the contrast with the paleness of ANGEL FOOD CAKE]

Dev·il's Is·land /dévv'lz-/ rocky islet off the coast of French Guiana in the Atlantic Ocean. It was used as a penal colony from 1852 to 1946.

Dev·il's Mar·bles mound of granite boulders and sacred Aboriginal site in central Australia, near Tennant Creek in the Northern Territory. The boulders are about 1,500 million years old.

dev·il's paint·brush *n* PLANTS same as **orange hawkweed** [< the fiery color of the flowers]

dev·il's walk·ing stick *n* PLANTS same as **Hercules' club** (sense 1) [< its prickly leaves]

dev·il·try /dévv'ltree/ (*plural* **-tries**), **dev·il·ry** /dévv'lree/ *n* **1.** cruel or evil behavior or actions **2.** evil act or acts supposedly performed by calling on the powers of the devil or evil spirits

dev·il·wood /dévv'l wòod/ *n* a tree with hard wood, whitish bark, and fragrant greenish flowers. Native to: southern United States. Latin name: *Osmanthus americanus.* [Early 19C. Because it is extremely difficult to cut]

de·vi·ous /deévee әss/ *adj* **1. SECRETIVE AND CALCULATING** not straightforward, sincere, or honest about intentions or motives **2. UNFAIR OR UNDERHAND** not adhering to the right or usual course, procedures, or standards **3. RAMBLING** circuitous and roundabout, usually changing direction many times ○ *got here by a devious route* [Late 16C. < Latin *devius* "out of the way" < *via* "way, road"] —**de·vi·ous·ly** *adv* —**de·vi·ous·ness** *n*

de·vis·al /di víz'l/ *n* **1.** the inventing or contriving of something **2.** the handing down of property through a will

de·vise /di víz/ *vt* (**-vised, -vis·ing, -vis·es**) **1. THINK SOMETHING UP** to conceive of the idea for something and figure out how it will work **2. PASS ON PROPERTY** to pass on property through a will ■ *n* **1. CLAUSE BEQUEATHING PROPERTY** a clause in a will stating that an item of property is to be given to somebody or something **2.** LAW **BEQUEATHING OF PROPERTY** the bequeathing of an item of property **3.** LAW **SOMETHING BEQUEATHED** an item of property bequeathed through a will [13C. < French *deviser* "divide, order, form a plan" < Latin *dividere* (see DIVIDE)] —**de·vis·a·ble** *adj* —**de·vis·er** *n*

de·vi·see /di vì zeé/ *n* somebody to whom property has been bequeathed in a will

de·vi·sor /di vízәr/ *n* somebody who bequeaths property in a will [15C. < Anglo-Norman *devisour*, Old French *deviseor* < Old French *deviser* (see DEVISE)]

de·vi·tal·ize /dee vít'l ìz/ (**-ized, -iz·ing, -iz·es**) *vt* to deprive something of its strength or vigor —**de·vit·al·i·za·tion** /dee vìt'li záysh'n/ *n*

de·vit·ri·fy /dee víttrә fì/ (**-fied, -fy·ing, -fies**) *vti* to change from a glassy to a crystalline state and become brittle and opaque, or cause a material to do this —**de·vit·ri·fi·ca·tion** /dee vìttrәfi káysh'n/ *n*

de·vo·cal·ize /dee vṓkә lìz/ (**-ized, -iz·ing, -iz·es**) *vt* PHON same as **devoice** —**de·vo·cal·i·za·tion** /di vṑkәli záysh'n/ *n*

de·voice /dee vóyss/ (**-voiced, -voic·ing, -voic·es**) *vt* to pronounce a usually voiced speech sound without vibration of the vocal cords

de·void /di vóyd/ *adj* completely lacking in something ○ *a house devoid of charm* [14C. < past participle of obsolete *devoid* "remove, vacate" < Old French *devoidier* "empty out" < *vuidier* "to empty" < Latin *vacare* "be empty"]

de·voirs /dev waár/ *npl* expressions or acts of courtesy and respect (*archaic or literary*) [15C. < Old French *deveir* "owe" < Latin *debere*]

de·vol·a·til·ize /dee vóllәt'l ìz/ (**-ized, -iz·ing, -iz·es**) *vt* to remove volatile material from a substance, usually by means of heat or a vacuum and sometimes by both —**de·vol·a·til·i·za·tion** /dee vòllәt'li záysh'n/ *n*

dev·o·lu·tion /dèvvә lóosh'n/ *n* **1. DELEGATING OF RESPONSIBILITIES** the delegation of responsibilities from a superior to a subordinate, deputy, or substitute **2. DELEGATION OF POWER** the transfer of power from a central to a subordinate level or organization, particularly from a central government to regional or local governments **3. INHERITANCE OF PRIVILEGES** the transfer or inheritance of authority, rights, or property, e.g., from a monarch to his or her successors **4.** BIOL same as **degeneration** (sense 3) [15C. < late Latin *devolution-* < Latin *devolvere* (see DEVOLVE)] —**dev·o·lu·tion·ar·y** *adj*

dev·o·lu·tion·ist /dèvvә lóosh'nist/ *n* somebody who favors transferring power from a central government to smaller political units —**dev·o·lu·tion·ist** *adj*

de·volve /di vólv/ (**-volved, -volv·ing, -volves**) *v* **1.** *vti* TRANSFER OR BE TRANSFERRED TO ANOTHER to transfer power, responsibility, or rights to somebody or something, e.g., from a central government to a regional government, or be transferred in this way **2.** *vi* BECOME SOMEBODY ELSE'S OBLIGATION to become the duty or responsibility of somebody else **3.** *vi* DETERIORATE to deteriorate slowly over time ○ *Order has devolved into anarchy.* **4.** *vi* LAW BE GIVEN OR BEQUEATHED to be given to somebody under the terms of a will or other legal instruction [15C. < Latin *devolvere* "roll down" < *volvere* "roll"] —**de·volve·ment** *n*

Dev·on /dévvən/ county in southwestern England, bordered on the north by the Bristol Channel and on the south by the English Channel. It is a popular vacation area. Population: 704,493 (2001). Area: 2,591 sq. mi./6,711 sq. km.

De·vo·ni·an /də vṓnee ən/ *n* the geologic period, 410 million to 360 million years ago, during which forests and amphibians first appeared, and fish became abundant. See table at ■ *adj* relating to the Devonian period of geologic time [Early 17C. < medieval Latin *Devonia* < Old English *Defenascīr* "Devonshire," former name of the county of Devon, England]

De·von·shire cream /dévvən sheer-, -shər-/ *n UK* FOOD same as **clotted cream** [Because a specialty of the county of *Devon*, England, formerly *Devonshire*]

de·vo·ré /də váw ray/, **dé·vo·ré** *n* **1.** the use of a chemical paste to create patterns in fabrics such as velvet by dissolving the natural fibers and revealing the synthetic warp and weft threads **2.** fabric created using the devoré technique [< French, past participle of *dévorer* (see DEVOUR)]

de·vote /di vṓt/ (**-vot·ed, -vot·ing, -votes**) *vt* to commit yourself to, or allot or use something for, a particular activity, aim, or purpose ○ *She devoted her whole life to the cause.* [Late 16C. < Latin *devot-*, past participle of *devovere* "dedicate by a vow" < *vovere* "to vow"]

de·vot·ed /di vṓtəd/ *adj* **1.** feeling or showing great love, commitment, or loyalty to somebody or something, especially over a long period of time **2.** feeling or showing great dedication to something —**de·vot·ed·ly** *adv* —**de·vot·ed·ness** *n*

dev·o·tee /dèvvə tée, dèvvō-/ *n* **1.** a very ardent enthusiast or follower of something **2.** a dedicated member of a religious or spiritual group

de·vo·tion /di vṓsh'n/ *n* **1.** COMMITTED LOVE deep love and commitment **2.** DEDICATION great dedication and loyalty **3.** ENTHUSIASM strong enthusiasm and admiration for somebody or something **4.** RELIGIOUS FERVOR fervent religious or spiritual feeling **5.** ACT OF DEVOTING the act of devoting something or being devoted to a particular purpose ■ **de·vo·tions** *npl* PRAYERS prayers or other religious observances, especially somebody's private prayers or observances —**de·vo·tion·al** *adj*

De·Vo·to /də vṓtō/, **Bernard Augustine** (1897–1955) US historian and critic. He was known for his articles in *Harper's Magazine* (1935–55) and his three-volume work on the American West (1943–52).

> "Art is the terms of an armistice signed with fate."
> [Bernard Augustine DeVoto, *Mark Twain at Work*; 1942]

de·vour /di vówr/ (**-voured, -vour·ing, -vours**) *vt* **1.** EAT SOMETHING QUICKLY to eat something quickly and hungrily ○ *They devour in minutes what it's taken you all afternoon to prepare.* **2.** TAKE SOMETHING IN EAGERLY to read, look at, watch, or listen to something eagerly ○ *Young children seem to devour her stories.* **3.** DESTROY SOMETHING to destroy something rapidly and completely (*literary; often passive*) ○ *a house devoured by the flames* **4.** WASTE SOMETHING to use up something unwisely or wastefully (*literary*) **5.** OVERWHELM SOMEBODY to become an overwhelming and destructive passion or obsession for somebody (*literary; usually passive*) ○ *was devoured by jealousy* [14C. Via Old French *devour-*, stressed stem of *devorer* < Latin *devorare* "swallow down" < *vorare* "swallow"] —**de·vour·er** *n* —**de·vour·ing** *adj* —**de·vour·ing·ly** *adv*

de·vout /di vówt/ *adj* **1.** VERY RELIGIOUS deeply religious **2.** DEVOTED TO SOMETHING devoted to a particular personal interest or cause ○ *a devout baseball fan* **3.** VERY SINCERE deeply and sincerely felt or meant (*formal*) [12C. Via French < Latin *devotus*, past participle of *devovere* (see DEVOTE)] —**de·vout·ly** *adv* —**de·vout·ness** *n*

De Vries /də vréess/, **Hugo** (1848–1935) Dutch botanist and geneticist. He independently discovered the laws of heredity and introduced the theory of mutation in plant evolution. Full name **De Vries, Hugo Marie**

dew /doo/ *n* **1.** WATER DROPLETS ON COOL OUTDOOR SURFACES moisture from the air that has condensed as tiny drops on outdoor objects and surfaces that have cooled, especially during the night **2.** SMALL DROPS drops of moisture of any kind, e.g., tears or sweat (*literary*) **3.** FRESHNESS AND PURITY a fresh and pure or refreshing quality in something (*literary*) ■ **dews** *npl* DEWDROPS drops of dew (*literary*) ■ *vt* (**dewed, dew·ing, dews**) COAT SOMETHING WITH DEW to coat or moisten something with drops of dew (*literary*) [Old English *dēaw* < Germanic]

SPELLCHECK dew, do, or **due**? Do not confuse the spelling of ***dew, do,*** and ***due***, which sound similar. ***Dew*** is chiefly used as a noun, denoting droplets of moisture, as in *the morning dew on the grass*. ***Do*** is a very common verb with a wide range of meanings, principally "perform an action" (as in *do the housework*), and is occasionally used as a noun (as in *dos and don'ts*). ***Due*** is used as an adjective, meaning "expected," "ready," "appropriate," or "owed" (as in *due for promotion, after due consideration*), or as a noun denoting something due (as in *give him his due, pay your dues*).

DEW *abbr* MIL distant early warning

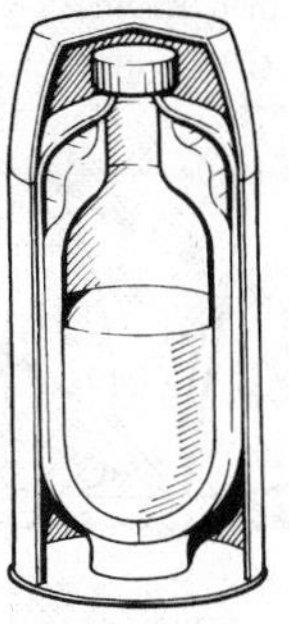

Dewar flask

Dew·ar flask /doo ər-/, **Dew·ar vac·u·um flask** *n* a double-walled silvered glass or metal flask with a vacuum between the walls, providing thermal insulation. It is frequently used to store liquefied gases. [Mid-20C. After Sir James *Dewar* (1824–1923), British physicist and chemist]

de·wa·ter /dee wàwtər/ (**-tered, -ter·ing, -ters**) *vt* to remove water from a substance, especially sewage or crude oil, or from a place

dew·ber·ry /doo bèrree/ (*plural* **-ries**) *n* **1.** an edible bluish black blackberry **2.** a variety of the bramble with trailing stems and bluish black fruit. Genus: *Rubus*.

dew·claw /doo klàw/ *n* a functionless shorter digit or claw on the foot of a dog or other mammal [Late 16C. Origin ?] —**dew·clawed** *adj*

dew·drop /doo dròp/ *n* a drop of water that has condensed on a cool outdoor surface

Dew·ey /doo ee/, **George** (1837–1917) US naval officer. He defeated the Spanish fleet at the Battle of Manila Bay (1898) in the Philippines.

> "You may fire when you are ready, Gridley."
> [Attributed to George Dewey]

Dew·ey, John (1859–1952) US philosopher, psychologist, and educator. He developed the philosophy of pragmatism and was a leading educational theorist.

> "In the traditional method the child must say something that he has merely learned. There is all the difference in the world between having something to say, and having to say something."
> [John Dewey, *Dewey on Education*; 1959]

Dew·ey, Melvil (1851–1931) US librarian and educator. He formulated the Dewey decimal system (1876), which revolutionized the way books were cataloged.

Dew·ey, Thomas Edmund (1902–71) US lawyer and politician. He was the governor of New York State (1942–55) and the Republican nominee for US president (1944 and 1948).

Dew·ey dec·i·mal sys·tem, Dew·ey dec·i·mal clas·si·fi·ca·tion *n* a system of classifying library books that divides them into ten main classes, divided in turn into categories with three-digit numbers and subcategories with numbers after a decimal point [After Melvil DEWEY]

dew·fall /doo fàwl/ *n* **1.** the formation of dew, or the time when dew begins to form **2.** the amount of dew that has condensed on objects and surfaces

De Witt /də wít/, **Jan** (1625–72) Dutch politician. The chief minister of the Netherlands (1653–72) and a leading republican, he secured Dutch victory in the Second Anglo-Dutch War (1664–67).

dew·lap /doo làp/ *n* **1.** a loose fold of skin hanging from the neck of some animals such as cows **2.** a loose fold of skin on somebody's throat, often forming later in life [14C. < obsolete *dew*, origin ? + LAP[1] "loose piece"] —**dew·lapped** *adj*

DEW line /doo-/ *n* a line of radar stations across the Arctic regions of North America, designed to give an early warning of approaching enemy aircraft and missiles [Acronym < *distant early warning*]

de·worm /dee wúrm/ (**-wormed, -worm·ing, -worms**) *vt* to cure an animal of an infestation of worms —**de·worm·er** *n*

dew point *n* the temperature at which the air cannot hold all the moisture in it and dew begins to form. If objects and surfaces have cooled to below freezing point when the moisture in the air begins to condense, frost is formed instead.

dew worm *n* a common earthworm used as fishing bait

dew·y /doo ee/ (**-i·er, -i·est**) *adj* **1.** COVERED WITH DEW covered with dew or characterized by the presence of dew **2.** MOIST moist or moist-looking **3.** LIKE DEW like dew, especially in having a fresh, pure, or refreshing quality (*literary*) **4.** NAIVE childishly pure or innocent (*literary*) ○ *a dewy outlook on life* —**dew·i·ly** *adv* —**dew·i·ness** *n*

dew·y-eyed *adj* childishly innocent, inexperienced, or trusting ○ *full of dewy-eyed optimism*

dex /deks/ *n* dexamphetamine, or a tablet containing it (*slang*) [Mid-20C. Shortening]

dex·a·meth·a·sone /dèksə méthə sōn/ *n* a synthetic steroid. Use: treatment of inflammatory conditions and hormonal imbalances. [Mid-20C. < *dexa-* (blend of HEXA- + DECA-) + *-methasone*, INN stem]

dex·am·phet·a·mine /dèk sam féttə meen/ *n UK* PHARM same as **dextroamphetamine**

Dex·e·drine /déksə dreen/ *tdmk* a trademark for the sulfate of dextroamphetamine

dex·ie /déksee/ *n* a tablet containing dexamphetamine (*slang*) [Mid-20C. Shortening]

dex·i·o·trop·ic /dèksee ō tróppik/ *adj* describes the cleavage of a fertilized egg in which the newly dividing cells form a pattern that spirals to the right when viewed from above [Late 19C. < Greek *dexios* "on the right side"]

dex·ter /dékstər/ *adj* placed on the right-hand side of a coat of arms, that is, on the left from the point of view of somebody looking at it (*technical; usually used after nouns*) [Mid-16C. < Latin, "on the right"]

dex·ter·i·ty /dek stérrətee/ *n* **1.** ease and skill in physical movement, especially in using the hands and manipulating objects ○ *manual dexterity* **2.** sharpness or quickness of mind

dex·ter·ous /dékstərəss, dékstrəss/, **dex·trous** /dékstrəss/ *adj* **1.** characterized by ease and skill in physical movement, especially in using the hands and manipulating objects **2.** mentally sharp or quick [Early 17C. < Latin *dexter* "skillful, on the right"] —**dex·ter·ous·ly** *adv* —**dex·ter·ous·ness** *n*

dextr- *prefix* same as **dextro-** (*used before vowels*)

dex·tral /dékstrəl/ *adj* (*technical*) **1.** on or relating to the right-hand side, especially of the body **2.** same as **right-handed** *adj* (sense 1) **3.** describes the clockwise spiraling of the shell of an invertebrate sea animal [Mid-17C. < medieval Latin *dextralis* < Latin *dextra* "right hand" < *dexter* "on the right"] —**dex·tral·i·ty** /dek strálləteé/ *n* —**dex·tral·ly** *adv*

dex·tran /dék stràn, dékstrən/ *n* a branched polysaccharide produced by the action of bacteria on sucrose. Use: blood plasma substitute, food additive. [Late 19C. < DEXTRO- + -AN[2]]

dex·trin /dékstrin/, **dex·trine** /dék streen, -strin/ *n* a product that is an intermediate in the formation of maltose. Source: heating of starch. Use: adhesive, sizing, in syrups and beers. Formula: $(C_6H_{10}O_5)_n$. [Mid-19C. < DEXTRO-]

dex·tro /dék strō/ *adj* CHEM same as **dextrorotatory** [Early 20C. Shortening]

dextro- *prefix* **1.** right, on the right ○ *dextrocardia* **2.** dextrorotatory ○ *dextroglucose* [< Latin *dexter* "on the right"]

dex·tro·am·phet·a·mine /dèkstrō am féttə meen/, **dex·tro·am·fet·a·mine** *technical n* a form of amphetamine. Use: stimulant, antidepressant.

dex·tro·car·di·a /dèkstrō kaárdee ə/ *n* a medical condition in which the heart inclines to the right side of the center of the chest instead of the left, often with a similar reversal of all abdominal organs

dex·tro·glu·cose *n* BIOCHEM same as **dextrose**

dex·tro·ro·ta·ry /dèkstrō rṓtəree/ *adj* CHEM same as **dextrorotatory**

dex·tro·ro·ta·tion /dèkstrə rō táysh'n/ *n* a rotation to the right or clockwise, particularly of the plane of polarization of light passing through a crystal or solution. Substances that cause dextrorotation are said to be optically active.

dex·tro·ro·ta·to·ry /dèkstrə rṓtə tàwree/, **dex·tro·ro·ta·ry** /dèkstrə rṓtəree/ *adj* rotating the plane of polarization of light passing through it to the right or clockwise

dex·trose /dék strōss/ *n* a sugar produced during cellular metabolism in plant and animal tissue. It is found in many fruits, especially grapes, and is a major component of honey and corn syrup.

dex·trous *adj* same as **dexterous**

dey /day/ (*plural* **deys**) *n* **1.** the governor of Algiers under the Ottoman Empire **2.** a title sometimes used for ruling officials in Tunis and Tripoli in North Africa under the Ottoman Empire [Mid-17C. Via French < Turkish *dayi* "maternal uncle," also a courtesy title]

DF *abbr* TELECOM direction finder

D.F.A. *abbr* Doctor of Fine Arts

DFC *abbr* MIL Distinguished Flying Cross

dg *symbol* MEASURE decigram

D.G. *abbr* CHR Deo gratias

DH, **dh** *abbr* BASEBALL designated hitter

D.H. *abbr* EDUC Doctor of Humanities

DHA *n* a polyunsaturated essential fatty acid found in cold-water fish and some algae that has been linked to the reduction of cardiovascular disease and other health benefits. Full form **docosahexaenoic acid**

dha·ba /daábə/ *n S Asia* a roadside stall where food is sold [< Hindi]

Dha·ka /daákə, dákə/, **Dac·ca** capital and largest city of Bangladesh. It is situated in the center of the country, on the Buriganga, one of the tributary rivers of the Ganges delta. Population: 3,368,940 (1991).

dhan·sak /dán saàk/ *n* a curry made from meat or vegetables mixed with lentils, originating in South Asia [Late 20C. < Gujarati]

dhar·ma /daárməl/ *n* **1.** in Hinduism, somebody's duty to behave according to strict religious and social codes, or the righteousness earned by performing religious and social duties **2.** in Buddhism, the truth about the way things are and will always be in the universe or in nature, especially when contained in scripture [Late 18C. < Sanskrit, "something established, decree, custom"] —**dhar·mic** *adj*

dhar·ma·sha·la /daármə shaálə/ (*plural* **-las**), **dharm·sa·la** /-saálə/ *n* in South Asia, a building that has a religious or charitable purpose, often used as a place where travelers may rest without payment [Early 19C. < Sanskrit *dharmaśālā* "virtue house"]

dhar·na /daárnə/, **dhur·na** /dúrnə/ *n* in parts of South Asia, the practice of protesting against an injustice by sitting and fasting outside the door of the offender [Late 18C. < Hindi, "placing, act of sitting in restraint"]

Dhar·uk /dúrrŏŏk/ (*plural same* or **-uks**) *n* **1.** a member of an Australian Aboriginal people that formerly inhabited the area around present-day Sydney **2.** the language of the Dharuk people, now extinct [Probably < an Aboriginal language] —**Dhar·uk** *adj*

Dhau·la·gi·ri /dòwlə geeree/ one of the world's highest mountains. It is situated in the Himalayan range in northern Nepal. Height: 26,811 ft./8,172 m.

dho·bi itch *n UK* same as **jock itch**

dhol /dōl/ *n* a large, barrel-shaped, often double-ended drum used in South Asian music [Mid-19C. < Hindi *ḍhol*]

dho·lak /dṓlək/ *n* a small barrel-shaped drum used in South Asian music [Mid-19C. < Hindi *ḍholak*]

dhole /dōl/ *n* a wild dog with a reddish coat and bushy tail that hunts large animals in packs. Native to: South Asia. Latin name: *Cuon alpinus*. [Early 19C. Probably < Kannada *tōḷa* "wolf"]

dho·ti /dṓtee/, **dhoo·tie** /dóotee/, **dho·tie** /dṓtee/, **dhu·ti** /dóotee/ *n* **1.** a loincloth worn by some Hindu men **2.** the cotton cloth used to make the loincloths worn by some Hindu men [Early 17C. < Hindi]

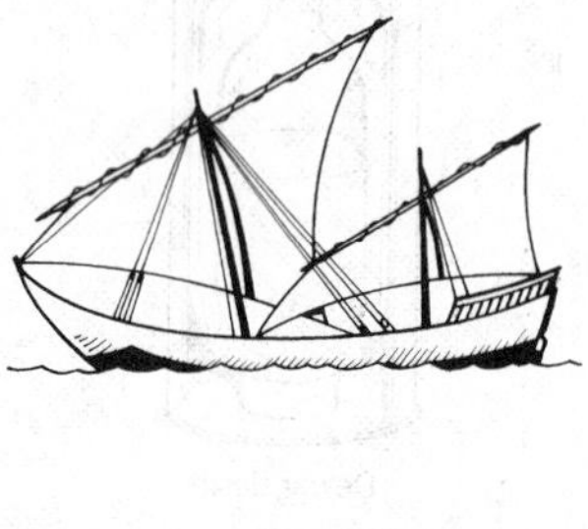

dhow

dhow /dow/ *n* a low-sided ship with one or two masts and triangular curving sails, used by Arab sailors in the Indian Ocean [Late 18C. Probably < Persian]

DHS *abbr* Department of Homeland Security

Dhu al-Hij·jah /dool hí jaà/ *n* in the Islamic calendar, the 12th month of the year, during which the holiday of Yom Arafat is celebrated. See table at **calendar** [Late 18C. < Arabic, "the one of the pilgrimage"]

Dhu al-Qa'·dah /dool kaà daà/ *n* in the Islamic calendar, the 11th month of the year. See table at **calendar** [Late 18C. < Arabic, "the one of the sitting"]

Dhur·ga /dúrgə/ *n* an Australian Aboriginal language of New South Wales, now extinct or almost extinct [Mid-20C. < Dhurga] —**Dhur·ga** *adj*

dhur·na *n* another spelling of **dharna**

dhur·rie /dúrree/, **dur·rie** *n* a flat-woven cotton rug made in South Asia [Late 19C. < Hindi *darī*]

dhu·ti *n* CLOTHING, TEXTILES another spelling of **dhoti**

di-[1] *prefix* **1.** two, twice, double ○ *dicephalous* **2.** containing two atoms, radicals, or groups ○ *dimethyl* [< Greek. < Indo-European "two"]

di-[2] *prefix* same as **dia-** (*used before vowels*)

dia- *prefix* through, across ○ *diachronic* ○ *diadromous* [< Greek *dia*]

di·a·base /dī ə bàyss/ *n* an igneous rock of fine to medium grain size [Mid-19C. < French] —**di·a·ba·sic** /dī ə báyssik/ *adj*

Di·a·be·si·ty /dī ə beé sətee/ *tdmk* a trademark for diabetes caused by obesity

di·a·be·tes /dī ə beé teez, -beétiss/ *n* a medical disorder, especially diabetes mellitus, that causes the body to produce an excessive amount of urine [Mid-16C. Via Latin < Greek, "passer through, siphon" < *diabainein* "go through"]

di·a·be·tes in·sip·i·dus /-in síppidəss/ *n* a disorder of the pituitary gland that causes the body to produce large amounts of urine [< modern Latin, "bland diabetes"]

di·a·be·tes mel·li·tus /-mə lī́təss, -méllitəss/ *n* a disorder in which there is no control of blood sugar, through inadequate insulin production (**Type 1**) or decreased sensitivity to insulin (**Type 2**), causing kidney, eye, and nerve damage. Type 1 usually develops in childhood and requires lifelong injection of insulin, while Type 2 typically develops in middle age and can usually be controlled by diet and drugs. [< modern Latin, "honey-sweet diabetes"]

di·a·bet·ic /dī ə béttik/ *adj* **1.** HAVING DIABETES having diabetes, especially diabetes mellitus **2.** RELATING TO DIABETES relating to or caused by diabetes, especially diabetes mellitus **3.** INTENDED FOR SOMEBODY WITH DIABETES made without sugar and therefore suitable for somebody who has diabetes mellitus ■ *n* SOMEBODY WITH DIABETES somebody who has diabetes, especially diabetes mellitus

di·a·ble·rie /dee aábləree/ *n* **1.** witchcraft or magic **2.** stories, traditions, and practices associated with magic or devil worship **3.** same as **mischief** (*literary*) [Mid-18C. < French < *diable* "devil" < Latin *diabolus* (see DEVIL)]

di·ab·lo /dee aáblō, dyaáblō/ *adj* describes a food that is seasoned with hot pepper (*usually used after nouns*) [Late 20C. < French *diable* "flavored with hot spices" < *diable* (see DIABLERIE)]

di·a·bol·i·cal /dī ə bóllik'l/, **di·a·bol·ic** /-bóllik/ *adj* **1.** connected with the devil or devil worship **2.** extremely cruel or evil [14C. < French *diabolique* < late Latin *diabolicus* < Latin *diabolus* (see DEVIL)] —**di·a·bol·i·cal·ly** *adv*

di·ab·o·lism /dī ábbə lìzzəm/ *n* **1.** worship of the devil or devils **2.** evil behavior or character (*literary*) —**di·ab·o·list** *n*

di·ab·o·lize /dī ábbə līz/ (**-lized, -liz·ing, -liz·es**) *vt* **1.** to cause somebody or something to appear evil **2.** to make somebody or something evil

di·a·ce·tyl·mor·phine /dī àssət'l máwr feen/ *n* DRUGS same as **heroin** (*technical*)

di·a·chron·ic /dī ə krónnik/ *adj* relating to or involving the study or development of something, especially a language, through time ○ *diachronic linguistics* [Mid-19C. < DIA- + Greek *khronos* "time"] —**di·a·chron·i·cal·ly** *adv*

di·ach·ro·nism /dī ákrə nìzzəm/ *n* the existence within a single geologic formation of regions of rock that were laid down at different times, e.g., by a sea that gradually covered a landmass —**di·ach·ro·nous** *adj*

di·ach·ro·ny /dī ákrənee/ *n* change or development over time

di·ac·id /dī ássid/ *adj* having two acidic hydrogen atoms that may be replaced by metal or acid ions to form a salt or an ester ■ *n* an acid that has two acidic hydrogen atoms

di·ac·o·nal /dī ákən'l, dee-/ *adj* relating to a deacon or deaconess or to the position of deacon or deaconess [Early 17C. < late Latin *diaconalis* < Latin *diaconus* (see DEACON)]

di·ac·o·nate /dī ákənət, dee-/ *n* the position of deacon or deaconess, or the term of office of a deacon or deaconess [Early 18C. < late Latin *diaconatus* < Latin *diaconus* (see DEACON)]

di·a·crit·ic /dī ə kríttik/ *adj* LANGUAGE same as **diacritical** ■ *n* a mark above or below a printed letter that indicates a change in the way it is to be pronounced or stressed. Acute and grave accents, tildes, and cedillas are examples of diacritics. See table on next page [Late 17C. < Greek *diakritikos* "that distinguishes or separates" < *krinein* "separate, decide"]

di·a·crit·i·cal /dī ə kríttik'l/ *adj* indicating a change or modification in something, especially in the way a printed letter is to be pronounced or stressed —**di·a·crit·i·cal·ly** *adv*

di·a·crit·i·cal mark *n* LANGUAGE same as **diacritic**

di·a·cyl·glyc·er·ol /dī àss'l glíssə ràwl/ *n* an inter-

COMMON DIACRITICS

Name	Mark		Word/Phrase
grave	À	à	à la mode
acute	Á	á	Cádiz
circumflex	Â	â	château
tilde	Ã	ã	São Paulo
umlaut	Ä	ä	Fräulein
angstrom	Å	å	Århus
cedilla	Ç	ç	façade
grave	È	è	crèche
acute	É	é	purée
circumflex	Ê	ê	fête
dieresis	Ë	ë	Noël
grave	Ì	ì	Forlì
acute	Í	í	Valparaíso
circumflex	Î	î	maître d'hôtel
dieresis	Ï	ï	faïence
haček	Ň	ň	Plzeň
tilde	Ñ	ñ	mañana
acute	Ó	ó	Kraków
circumflex	Ô	ô	maître d'hôtel
umlaut	Ö	ö	rösti
haček	Ř	ř	Dvořák
acute	Ú	ú	Setúbal
circumflex	Û	û	crêpe
krouzek	Ů	ů	domů ("home")
umlaut	Ü	ü	gemütlich

mediate signaling molecule produced during intracellular processes

Dí·a de la Ra·za /dee ə də laa raa saa/ *n Hispanic* in Spanish-speaking regions, a holiday in commemoration of Christopher Columbus. Date: October 12. [< American Spanish, "day of the race (of people)"]

di·a·del·phous /dī ə délfəss/ *adj* describes stamens or flowers that have the stamen filaments grouped into two bundles [Early 19C. < DI-[1] + Greek *adelphos* "brother"]

di·a·dem /dī ə dèm, dī ədəm/ *n* **1. CROWN** a jeweled headband used as a royal crown **2. JEWELED HEADBAND** any jeweled headband **3. REGAL POWER** royal power or dignity (*literary*) [14C. Via French < Greek *diadēma* "(regal) headband" < *diadein* "bind around" < *dein* "bind"]

di·a·dem spi·der *n* a garden spider that spins orbed webs. Native to: Europe, Asia. Latin name: *Araneus diadematus*. [< its webs]

Di·ad·o·chi /dī áddəkee/ *npl* the six Macedonian generals who divided up and then fought over the empire of Alexander the Great after his death [Mid-19C. < Greek *diadokhoi* "successors" < *diadekhesthai* (see DIADOCHY)]

di·ad·o·chy /dī áddəkee/ *n* the replacement of one element by another within the structure of a crystal [Early 18C. < Greek *diadokhē* "succession" < *diadekhesthai* "succeed one another" < *dekhesthai* "take, accept"]

di·ad·ro·mous /dī áddrəməss/ *adj* describes fish that migrate between fresh and salt water [< Greek *dia* "through, across" + *dromos* "running"]

di·aer·e·sis *n* LING another spelling of **dieresis**

diag. *abbr* MATH **1.** diagonal **2.** diagram

di·a·gen·e·sis /dī ə jénnəssiss/ *n* the changes that take place in a sediment as a result of increased temperatures and pressures, causing solid rock to form, e.g., as sand becomes sandstone —**di·a·ge·net·ic** /dī əjə néttik/ *adj*

di·a·ge·ot·ro·pism /dī əjee óttrə pìzzəm/ *n* a response of a plant to gravity in which a part of the plant adopts a horizontal position —**di·a·ge·o·trop·ic** /-əjee ə tróppik/ *adj*

Di·a·ghi·lev /dee áagə lèf/, **Sergei** (1872–1929) Russian ballet impresario. His Ballets Russes company, founded in Paris, France in 1909, revolutionized ballet as an art, unifying dance, music, drama, and painting. Full name **Diaghilev, Sergei Pavlovich**

di·ag·nose /dī əg nōss, -nōz/ (**-nosed, -nos·ing, -nos·es**) *vt* **1.** to identify an illness or disorder in a patient through an interview, physical examination, and medical tests and other procedures **2.** to identify the nature or cause of something, especially a problem or fault [Mid-19C. Back-formation < DIAGNOSIS] —**di·ag·nos·a·ble** /dī əg nṓzəb'l, -nṓssəb'l/ *adj*

di·ag·no·sis /dī əg nṓssiss/ (*plural* **-no·ses** /-nō seez/) *n* **1. IDENTIFICATION OF ILLNESS** the identifying of an illness or disorder in a patient through physical examination, medical tests, or other procedures **2. IDENTIFICATION OF PROBLEM** the identifying of the nature or cause of something, especially a problem or fault **3. DECISION REACHED BY DIAGNOSIS** a decision or conclusion reached by medical or other diagnosis ○ *The diagnosis is flu.* [Late 17C. Via modern Latin < Greek *diagnōsis* < *diagignōskein* "distinguish" < *gignōskein* "know, perceive"]

di·ag·nos·tic /dī əg nóstik/ *adj* identifying, or used in identifying, the nature or cause of an illness, disorder, or problem ■ *n* a test, procedure, or instrument used to identify the nature or cause of an illness, disorder, or problem —**di·ag·nos·ti·cal·ly** *adv* —**di·ag·nos·ti·cian** /dī əg no stísh'n/ *n*

di·ag·nos·tics /dī əg nóstiks/ *n* the art of identifying illnesses or disorders in patients through diagnosis, or procedures for diagnosis (*takes a singular verb*)

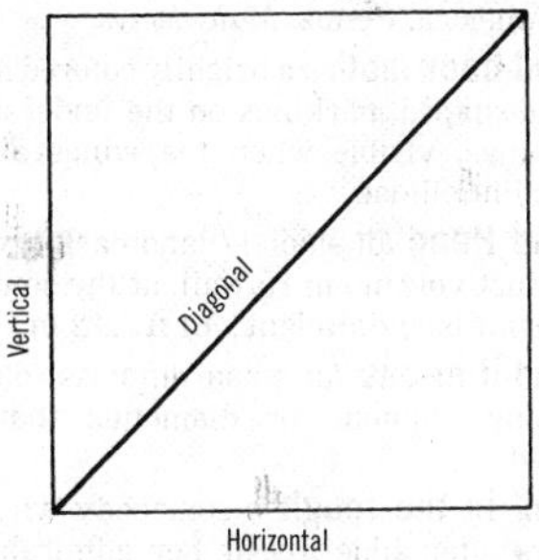

diagonal

di·ag·o·nal /dī ággən'l, dī ágn'l/ *adj* **1. SLANTING OR OBLIQUE** running from one side to another in a slanting or oblique way **2. WITH SLANTING LINES** having slanting lines or markings **3.** MATH **JOINING ANGLES OR CORNERS** describes a line that joins two opposite or nonadjacent angles or corners of a straight-sided geometric figure ■ *n* **1. SLANTING LINE** a slanting line or direction **2. LINE JOINING ANGLES** a line that joins two opposite or nonadjacent angles or corners of a straight-sided geometric figure **3.** PRINTING same as **slash** *n* (sense 5) [Mid-16C. < Latin *diagonalis* < Greek *diagōnios* "from angle to angle" < *gōnia* "angle"] —**di·ag·o·nal·ly** *adv*

di·a·gram /dī ə gràm/ *n* **1. SIMPLE EXPLANATORY DRAWING** a simple drawing showing the basic shape, layout, or workings of something **2. CHART** a chart or graph that illustrates something such as a statistical trend **3.** MATH **MATHEMATICAL DRAWING** a line drawing that presents mathematical information ■ *vt* (**-grammed** or **-gramed, -gram·ming** or **-gram·ing, -grams**) INFO SCI, MATH **ILLUSTRATE SOMETHING** to make a diagram that represents or illustrates something [Early 17C. Via Latin < Greek *diagramma* "geometric figure, written list, scale in music" < *diagraphein* "mark out by lines, draw" < *graphein* "write"] —**di·a·gram·ma·ble** *adj*

di·a·gram·mat·ic /dī əgrə máttik/, **di·a·gram·mat·i·cal** /-máttik'l/ *adj* in the form of an explanatory drawing or chart —**di·a·gram·mat·i·cal·ly** *adv*

di·a·graph /dī ə gràf/ *n* a mechanical instrument used for producing scale copies of diagrams and maps [Late 19C. < French *diagraphe* < Greek *diagraphein* (see DIAGRAM)]

di·a·ki·ne·sis /dī əki neessiss, -kī-/ *n* the final stage in cell reduction division (**meiosis**), during which the paired chromosomes begin to shorten, thicken, and separate [Early 20C. < modern Latin < Greek *dia* "through, across" + *kinēsis* "motion" (see KINESIS)] —**di·a·ki·net·ic** /-néttik, -néttik, -/ *adj*

di·al /dī əl/ *n* **1. INDICATOR WITH MOVABLE POINTER** an instrument with a movable pointer that displays a measurement such as the current speed of a vehicle or the level of steam pressure inside a boiler **2. CONTROL KNOB** a round control knob or disk turned with the fingers to adjust a piece of electrical or mechanical equipment such as a radio **3. STATION INDICATOR ON RADIO** a numbered panel with a movable pointer on a radio, used for tuning in to different stations **4. CLOCK FACE** the round face of a traditional clock **5. DISK WITH HOLES ON TELEPHONE** a disk with numbered finger holes on the front of an old telephone, turned with a finger to select the required telephone number **6. SUNDIAL** a sundial or its face (*dated or literary*) ■ *vti* (**-aled, -al·ing, -als**) **1. CALL BY TELEPHONE** to call a number or a person on the telephone **2. SELECT RADIO OR TELEVISION STATION** to tune in a radio or television station or program using a dial [14C. < Old French, "wheel in clockwork that makes a revolution once a day" < Latin *dies* "day"] —**di·al·er** *n*

dial. *abbr* **1.** LING dialect **2.** LING dialectal **3.** PHILOSOPHY dialectic **4.** LING, PHILOSOPHY dialectical **5.** LITERAT dialogue

di·a·lect /dī ə lèkt/ *n* LING **1. REGIONAL VARIETY OF LANGUAGE** a regional variety of a language, with differences in vocabulary, grammar, and pronunciation **2. LANGUAGE SPOKEN BY CLASS OR PROFESSION** a form of a language spoken by members of a social class or profession **3. NONSTANDARD SPEECH** nonstandard spoken language **4. MEMBER OF LANGUAGE FAMILY** one of a family of related languages ○ *Romance dialects such as French and Italian* [Mid-16C. Directly or via French < Latin *dialectus* "way of speaking, dialect" < Greek *dialektos* "conversation, language, local speech" < *dialegesthai* (see DIALOGUE)] —**di·a·lec·tal** /dī ə lékt'l/ *adj* —**di·a·lec·tal·ly** *adv*

SYNONYMS See *language*.

di·a·lec·tic /dī ə léktik/ *n* **1. TENSION BETWEEN CONFLICTING IDEAS** the tension that exists between two conflicting or interacting forces, elements, or ideas **2. INVESTIGATION OF TRUTH THROUGH DISCUSSION** the investigation of the truth through discussion, or the art of investigating truths through discussion **3.** *also* **di·a·lec·tics DEBATE RESOLVING CONFLICT** debate intended to resolve a conflict between two contradictory or apparently contradictory ideas or parts logically, establishing truths on both sides rather than disproving one argument (*takes a singular verb*) **4. HEGELIAN PROCESS** the process, in Hegelian and Marxist thought, in which two apparently opposed ideas, the thesis and antithesis, become combined in a unified whole, the synthesis **5. SOCRATIC METHOD FOR REVEALING TRUTH** the methods used in Socratic philosophy to reveal truth through disputation [Late 16C. Via Latin *dialectica* < Greek *dialektikē (tekhnē)* "(art) of discussion or debate" < *dialektikos* "of conversation" < *dialektos* (see DIALECT)] —**di·a·lec·ti·cian** /dī ə lek tísh'n/ *n*

di·a·lec·ti·cal /dī ə léktik'l/ *adj* **1.** PHILOSOPHY **ACHIEVED BY DIALECTIC** achieved or attempted by dialectic **2.** PHILOSOPHY **INVOLVING DIALECTIC** involving or depending upon dialectic **3.** LING **DIALECTAL** relating to or belonging to a dialect —**di·a·lec·ti·cal·ly** *adv*

di·a·lec·ti·cal ma·te·ri·al·ism *n* the Marxian concept of reality in which material things are in the constant process of change brought about by the tension between conflicting or interacting forces, elements, or ideas —**di·a·lec·ti·cal ma·te·ri·al·ist** *n*

di·a·lec·tics /dī ə léktiks/ *n* PHILOSOPHY same as **dialectic** (sense 3)

di·a·lec·tol·o·gy /dī ə lek tólləjee/ *n* the study of the dialects of a language —**di·a·lec·to·log·i·cal** /dī ə lektə lójjik'l/ *adj* —**di·a·lec·to·log·i·cal·ly** *adv* —**di·a·lec·tol·o·gist** *n*

di·al gauge *n* a sensitive measuring device that indicates small displacements of a plunger by means of a pointer moving over a circular scale. It is usually used for measuring pressure or a vacuum.

di·al·ling tone *n UK* same as **dial tone**

di·a·log *n, vi* LITERAT, POL another spelling of **dialogue**

di·a·log box *n* a small rectangular window displayed on a computer screen that conveys information to, or requires a response from, the user

di·a·log *n, vi* LITERAT, POL another spelling of **dialogue**

di·a·log box *n* a small rectangular window displayed on a computer screen that conveys information to, or requires a response from, the user

di·a·log·ic /dī ə lójjik/, **di·a·log·i·cal** /dī ə lójjik'l/ *adj* **1.** written in the form of a conversation **2.** relating to dialogues

di·al·o·gist /dī állәjist/ *n* **1.** a writer of dialogue for movies, television, or radio **2.** a participant in a dialogue —**di·a·lo·gis·tic** /dì ələ jístik/ *adj*

di·a·logue /dī ə lòg/, **di·a·log** *n* **1. CHARACTERS' WORDS** the words spoken by characters in a book, movie, or play, or a section of a work that contains spoken words **2. FORMAL DISCUSSION** a formal discussion or negotiation, especially between opposing sides in a political or international context **3. CONVERSATION** talk of any kind between two or more people (*formal*) **4. LITERARY WORK IN CONVERSATION FORM** a work of literature in the form of a conversation ■ *vi* (**-logued, -logu·ing, -logues; -loged, -log·ing, -logs**) **TAKE PART IN TALK** to take part in a conversation, discussion, or negotiation [12C. Via French < Greek *dialogos* < *dialegesthai* "speak with each other" < *legein* "speak"] —**di·a·log·uer** *n*

di·a·logue box *n* COMPUT UK spelling of **dialog box**

di·al tone *n* a continuous sound that you hear when you lift a telephone receiver. It indicates that a number can be dialed.

di·al-up *adj* requiring a computer modem and telephone line to establish communication with another computer or a network

di·al·y·sis /dī állәssiss/ *n* **1.** the process of filtering the accumulated waste products of metabolism from the blood of a patient whose kidneys are not functioning properly, using a kidney machine **2.** the separation of dissolved substances from a solution by allowing the solution to diffuse through a semipermeable membrane [Mid-19C. Via Latin, "set of propositions without a connecting conjunction" < Greek *dialusis* "separation, loosening" < *luein* "loosen"] —**di·a·lyt·ic** /dì ə líttik/ *adj* —**di·a·lyt·i·cal·ly** *adv*

di·a·lyze /dí ə līz/ (**-lyzed, -lyz·ing, -lyz·es**) *vti* **1.** to remove the accumulated waste products of metabolism from the blood of a patient whose kidneys are not functioning, or undergo such a procedure **2.** to separate dissolved substances from a solution by diffusing it through a semipermeable membrane, or be subjected to this process [Mid-19C. < DIALYSIS, after ANALYZE] —**di·a·lyz·a·bil·i·ty** /dí ə līzə bíllətee/ *n* —**di·a·lyz·a·ble** *adj* —**di·a·ly·za·tion** /dì əli záysh'n/ *n* —**di·a·lyz·er** *n*

di·a·mag·net /dì ə mágnət/ *n* a substance that is repelled by magnetic fields, e.g., a noble gas, halogen, and alkali or alkaline earth metal —**di·a·mag·net·ic** /-mag néttik/ *adj* —**di·a·mag·net·i·cal·ly** *adv*

di·a·mag·ne·tism /dì ə mágnə tìzzəm/ *n* a tendency in materials with a relative permeability of less than one to be repelled by a magnetic field and align themselves at right angles to it

di·a·man·té /dee ə maan tày/ *adj* **COVERED WITH IMITATION DIAMONDS** decorated with colorless imitation gems (**rhinestones**) that look like diamonds ■ *n* **1. IMITATION DIAMONDS** colorless imitation gems that look like diamonds. Use: jewelry. **2. CLOTHES WITH IMITATION DIAMONDS** clothing or fabric decorated with diamanté [Early 20C. < French, past participle of *diamanter* "set with diamonds" < *diamant* (see DIAMOND)]

di·a·man·tine /dì ə mán tīn, -teen, -mánt'n/ *adj* **1.** resembling diamonds **2.** made of diamond or consisting of diamonds [Early 17C. < French *diamantin* < *diamant* (see DIAMOND)]

di·am·e·ter /dī ámmətər/ *n* **1. LINE THROUGH CENTER OF CIRCLE** a straight line running from one side of a circle or other rounded geometric figure through the center to the other side, or the length of this line **2. WIDTH** the width or thickness of something, especially something circular or cylindrical ○ *10 inches in diameter* **3. MAGNIFYING POWER OF LENS** the unit of measurement for the magnifying power of a lens [14C. Via French < Latin *diametrus* < Greek *diametros (grammē)* "(line) that measures through" < *metron* "measure"] —**di·am·e·tral** *adj*

di·a·met·ric /dì ə méttrik/, **di·a·met·ri·cal** /dì ə méttrik'l/ *adj* complete in respect of being opposite or different

di·a·met·ri·cal·ly /dì ə méttrikəlee/ *adv* used to emphasize that a difference or contrast is as great as it can be ○ *diametrically opposite concepts*

di·am·ine /dì ə meen, dī á meen/ *n* an organic chemical compound that contains two amino groups

di·a·mond /dí əmənd, dímənd/ *n* **1.** MINERALS **HARD COLORLESS MINERAL** a hard transparent precious stone that is a variety of carbon. Use: gems, abrasives, cutting tools. **2.** MATH **SHAPE LIKE SQUARE RESTING ON CORNER** a two-dimensional geometric figure formed of four sides, like a square standing on one of its corners **3.** CARDS **CARD WITH DIAMOND-SHAPED SYMBOL** a playing card with a diamond-shaped symbol on it **4.** BASEBALL **INFIELD** the area of a baseball field bounded by home plate and the three bases **5.** BASEBALL **PLAYING AREA** an area for playing baseball including the infield and the outfield ■ *vt* (**-mond·ed, -mond·ing, -monds**) **DECORATE SOMETHING WITH DIAMONDS** to decorate something with diamonds or similar gemstones [13C. Via French *diamant* "hardest metal" < medieval Latin *diamant-*, alteration of Latin *adamant-* (see ADAMANT)]

di·a·mond an·ni·ver·sa·ry *n* an anniversary celebrating 60, or sometimes 75, years of something such as marriage [< the custom of marking the occasion with gifts containing diamonds]

di·a·mond·back /dí əmənd bàk, dímənd-/ *n* **1.** a large poisonous rattlesnake with diamond-shaped markings on its back. Native to: southwestern United States, Mexico. Latin name: *Crotalus adamantus* or *Crotalus atrox*. **2.** a terrapin with diamond-shaped markings on its shell. Native to: salt marshes of the Atlantic and the Gulf coasts of North America. Genus: *Malaclemys*.

di·a·mond·back moth *n* a brightly colored moth with diamond-shaped markings on the underside of the front wings, visible when the wings are folded. Family: Plutellidae.

Di·a·mond Head /dí əmənd-/ landmark promontory and extinct volcano in Hawaii, at the southeastern tip of Oahu Island. Height: 761 ft./232 m.

di·a·mond·if·er·ous /dì əmən díffərəss, dìmən-/ *adj* containing diamond or diamonds that can be extracted

di·a·mond in the rough *n* somebody whose rough manners often hide his or her admirable or undeveloped qualities

di·a·mond ju·bi·lee *n* same as **diamond anniversary** [< the custom of marking the occasion with gifts containing diamonds]

dia·mond lane *n* TRANSP same as **carpool lane** (*informal*) [From the diamond symbol marking the lane]

di·a·mond point *n* a cutting tool in which two cutting edges meet at an acute angle, forming a diamond shape

di·a·monds /dí əməndz, díməndz/ *n* one of the four suits used in cards, with a red diamond shape as its symbol (*takes a singular or plural verb*)

Di·a·mond State *n* a nickname for the US state of Delaware

di·a·mond wed·ding *n UK* same as **diamond anniversary** [< the custom of marking the occasion with gifts containing diamonds]

di·a·mor·phine /dì ə máwr feen/ *n* PHARM same as **heroin** (*technical*) [Early 20C. Contraction of DIACETYLMORPHINE]

Di·an·a /dī ánnə/ *n* in Roman mythology, the goddess of hunting, virginity, and the moon. Greek equivalent **Artemis**

Barnaby's

Diana, Princess of Wales

Di·an·a /dī ánnə/, **Princess of Wales** (1961–97) British princess. She married Prince Charles in 1981, had two sons, and was divorced in 1996. She was killed in a car crash in Paris. Born **Spencer, Diana Frances**

> "The vicious circle of fear, prejudice and ignorance has increased the spread of AIDS to an alarming level. Due to fear and prejudice, many still do not want to listen. After all, AIDS is a killer."
> [Diana, *Independent (London)*; February 17, 1993]

di·an·drous /dī ándrəss/ *adj* describes flowers that have two stamens, or fungi and nonseeding plants that have two antheridia [Late 18C. < DI-[1] + Greek *andr-* "man"]

di·an·thus /dī ánthəss/ *n* a flowering plant belonging to the group that includes carnations, pinks, and sweet william. Genus: *Dianthus*. [Late 18C. < modern Latin < Greek *Dios* "of Zeus" + *anthos* "flower"]

di·a·pa·son /dì ə páyz'n, -pàyss'n/ *n* MUSIC **1. PIPE ORGAN'S MAIN STOP** one of two main stops on a pipe organ that control the organ's tone and characteristic sound **2. MUSICAL RANGE** the range of a musical instrument or of somebody's singing voice (*technical*) **3. TUNING DEVICE** a tuning fork or pitch pipe (*technical*) [14C. Via Latin < Greek *dia pasōn khordōn* "across all the notes of the scale"] —**di·a·pa·son·al** *adj* —**di·a·pa·son·ic** /dì əpə zónnik, -sónnik/ *adj*

di·a·pause /dí ə pàwz/ *n* a period during which the metabolism of some animals or insects slows down, temporarily suspending their bodily development and growth. Such periods are linked to seasonal or environmental changes.

di·a·pe·de·sis /dì əpə deessiss/ *n* a condition in which blood leaks through the apparently unruptured walls of blood vessels into surrounding tissue, as a reaction to severe inflammation or injury [Early 17C. < modern Latin < Greek *dia-* "through" + *pēdan* "to leap"] —**di·a·pe·det·ic** /-déttik/ *adj*

di·a·per /dí əpər, dípər/ *n* **1. ABSORBENT BABY CLOTHING** a piece of soft absorbent material that is worn by a baby as underwear to absorb bodily waste **2. PATTERN OF SMALL MOTIFS** a pattern woven into or printed on fabric, consisting of a small motif, often a diamond, repeated to cover an entire surface **3.** TEXTILES **FABRIC WITH DIAPER PATTERN** cotton or linen fabric with a diaper pattern woven into or printed on it ■ *vt* (**-pered, -per·ing, -pers**) **1. DRESS BABY IN DIAPER** to put a diaper on a baby **2. PUT DIAPER PATTERN ON SOMETHING** to decorate something, especially fabric, with a diaper pattern [14C. Via Old French *diapre* "ornamental cloth" < medieval Greek *diaspros* "thoroughly white"]

di·a·per rash *n* a sensitive red area or spotted rash on a baby's bottom, usually caused by irritation from urine, feces, or chemical irritants in diapers

di·aph·a·nous /dī áffənəss/ *adj* **1.** delicate or gauzy, so as to be transparent ○ *the insect's diaphanous wings* **2.** fragile or insubstantial because extremely faint or slight (*literary*) ○ *diaphanous breezes* [Early 17C. Via Latin *diaphanus* < Greek *diaphanēs* "shown through" < *phainein* "to show"] —**di·a·pha·ne·i·ty** /dì àffə nee ətee/ *n* —**di·aph·a·nous·ly** *adv* —**di·aph·a·nous·ness** *n*

di·a·phone /dí ə fōn/ *n* **1.** a set of all the different ways that a speech sound is pronounced in all the dialects of a language, or a member of this set **2.** a foghorn with a two-note sound

di·a·pho·re·sis /dì əfə reessiss/ *n* sweating, especially sweating induced for medical reasons (*technical*) [Late 17C. < late Latin < Greek *diaphorein* "dissipate by sweating" < *phorein* "carry"]

di·a·pho·ret·ic /dì əfə réttik/ *adj* describes agents that induce sweating, or their effect —**di·a·pho·ret·ic** *n*

di·a·phragm /dí ə fràm/ *n* **1.** ANAT **MUSCULAR WALL BELOW RIB CAGE** a curved muscular membrane in humans and other mammals that separates the abdomen from the area around the lungs **2.** MED **DOME-SHAPED CONTRACEPTIVE** a dome-shaped rubber or plastic contraceptive device for women, placed inside the vagina over the entrance to the womb to prevent sperm from entering **3.** PHOTOGRAPHY **CAMERA'S MECHANISM CONTROLLING OPENING FOR LIGHT** a disk with a fixed or variable opening that controls the amount of light that enters a camera or other optical instrument **4.**

ACOUSTICS **VIBRATING DISK IN SOUND EQUIPMENT** a thin disk in a microphone, telephone receiver, or other sound device that vibrates in response to sound waves or electrical signals, converting one into the other **5.** **THIN MEMBRANE** a thin separating membrane, e.g., the porous plate dividing the sections of an electrolytic cell or the plate of cells across the stems of some water plants [14C. < late Latin *diaphragma* < Greek *diaphrassein* "to barricade" < *phrassein* "fence in"] —**di·a·phrag·mat·ic** /dī ə frag máttik, -frə máttik/ *adj* —**di·a·phrag·mat·i·cal·ly** *adv*

~~diaphram~~ incorrect spelling of **diaphragm**

di·aph·y·sis /dī áffississ/ (*plural* **-y·ses** /-i seèz/) *n* the central section of a long bone, between the growth areas at each end [Mid-19C. < Greek *diaphusis* "growing through" < *phusis* "growth"] —**di·a·phys·i·al** /dī ə fízzee əl/ *adj*

di·a·pir /dí ə peèr/ *n* a dome-shaped body of rock that migrates upward through denser overlying rock, e.g., a salt deposit [Early 20C. < Greek *diapeirainein* "pierce through" < *peirainein* "pierce"] —**di·a·pir·ic** /dī ə peèrik/ *adj*

di·a·pos·i·tive /dì ə pózzitiv/ *n* PHOTOGRAPHY same as **transparency** (sense 2)

di·ar·chy /dí aarkee/ (*plural* **-chies**), **dy·ar·chy** *n* **1.** a form of government in which power is held by two supreme rulers or two governing bodies **2.** a country ruled or run by two supreme rulers or two governing bodies [Mid-19C. < DI-[1] after MONARCHY] —**di·ar·chal** /dī aark'l/ *adj* —**di·arch·ic** /dī aar kik/ *adj* —**di·arch·i·cal** *adj*

~~diarhea~~ incorrect spelling of **diarrhea**

di·a·rist /dí ərist/ *n* the writer of a diary, especially one that is published

di·a·rize /dí ərīz/ (**-rized, -riz·ing, -riz·es**) *v* **1.** *vt* to enter an appointment or date to remember in a diary **2.** *vi* to keep a record of events in a diary (*archaic*)

di·ar·rhe·a /dì ə reè ə/ *n* **1.** frequent and excessive discharging of the bowels producing thin watery feces, usually as a symptom of gastrointestinal upset or infection **2.** thin watery feces [Early 16C. Via Latin < Greek *diarrhoia* < *diarrhein* "flow through" < *rhein* "to flow"] —**di·ar·rhe·al** *adj*—**di·ar·rhe·ic** *adj*

di·ar·thro·sis /dī aar thróssiss/ *n* the ability of some joints of the body to move in several directions [Late 16C. < Greek *diarthroun* "fasten by a joint" < *arthroun* "fasten"] —**di·ar·thro·di·al** *adj*

di·a·ry /dí əree/ (*plural* **-ries**) *n* **1.** **PERSONAL RECORD OF LIFE'S EVENTS** a personal record of events in somebody's life, often including personal thoughts and observations **2.** **BLANK BOOK** a book with blank or lined paper for keeping a diary in **3.** *Can, UK* a book, usually with pages labeled according to the days of a given year, in which people keep notes of appointments. US term **appointment book** [Late 16C. < Latin *diarium* < *dies* "day"]

USAGE See *dairy.*

Di·as /deè əss/, **Di·az, Bartolomeu** (1450?–1500) Portuguese navigator and explorer. He was the first European to round the Cape of Good Hope (1488), establishing a sea route from Europe to Asia.

di·as·po·ra /dī áspərə/ *n* a dispersion of a people, language, or culture that was formerly concentrated in one place ○ *the African diaspora* [Late 19C. < Greek < *diaspeirein* "disperse" < *speirein* "sow, scatter"]

Di·as·po·ra *n* **1.** the dispersion of the Jews from Palestine following the Babylonians' conquest of the Judean Kingdom in the 6th century B.C. and again following the Romans' destruction of the Second Temple in A.D. 70 **2.** the Jewish communities living outside either the present-day state of Israel or the ancient biblical kingdom of Israel

di·a·spore /dí ə spàwr/ *n* **1.** a white, gray, or pink form of aluminum oxide mineral. Source: bauxite. Use: abrasives, heat-resistant materials. **2.** a seed or spore that is dispersed from a plant [Early 19C. < Greek *diaspora* (see DIASPORA); from its dispersion when heated]

di·a·stase /dí ə stàyss, -stàyz/ *n* BIOCHEM former name for **amylase** [Mid-19C. < modern Latin *diastasis* (see DIASTASIS) + -ASE] —**di·a·sta·sic** /dī ə stáyzik, -stáyssik/ *adj*

di·as·ta·sis /dī ástəssiss/ (*plural* **-ta·ses** /-tə seèz/) *n* the dislodging of the end (**epiphysis**) of a long bone from its shaft without a fracturing of the bone itself (*technical*) [Early 18C. Via modern Latin < Greek, "separation" < *stasis* "placing"] —**di·a·stat·ic** /dī ə státtik/ *adj*

di·a·ste·ma /dī ə steèmə/ (*plural* **-ma·ta** /-mətə/) *n* a larger than usual gap between two adjacent teeth (*technical*) [Mid-19C. Via late Latin < Greek, "gap" < *diistanai* "place apart" < *histanai* "to place"] —**di·a·ste·mat·ic** /-əstə máttik/ *adj*

di·a·ste·re·o·is·o·mer /dī ə steree ō íssəmər/, **di·a·ste·re·o·mer** /dī ə stérree ōmər/ *n* a molecule that has the same formula and structure as another (**stereoisomer**), but is arranged differently in space and is therefore not a mirror image

di·as·to·le /dī ástəlee/ *n* the rhythmic expansion of the chambers of the heart at each heartbeat, during which they fill with blood [Late 16C. Via late Latin < Greek, "separation, expansion" < *diastellein* "to place apart" < *stellein* "to place"] —**di·a·stol·ic** /dī ə stóllik/ *adj*

di·a·style /dí ə stīl/ *adj* describes classical buildings with columns set at intervals equal to three or sometimes four times the diameter of a column, slightly farther apart than in the Doric order ■ *n* a diastyle building or colonnade [Mid-16C. Directly or via Latin < Greek *diastulos* "between columns" < *stulos* "column"]

di·a·ther·mi·a /dī ə thúrmee ə/ *n* MED same as **diathermy** [Early 20C. < modern Latin < Greek *dia* "across, through" + *thermē* "heat"]

di·a·ther·mic /dì ə thúrmik/ *adj* **1.** relating to diathermy **2.** able to conduct or transmit heat or infrared radiation [Early 20C. < French *diathermique* < Greek *dia* "across, through" + *thermē* "heat"]

di·a·ther·my /dí ə thùrmee/ *n* the treatment of organs or tissues by passing high-frequency electric currents through them in order to generate heat, thus increasing circulation [Early 20C. < modern Latin *diathermia* (see DIATHERMIA)]

di·ath·e·sis /dī áthəssiss/ (*plural* **-e·ses** /-ə seèz/) *n* a susceptibility to a disease or set of diseases such as allergies or gout [Mid-17C. < modern Latin < Greek *diatithenai* "arrange, dispose" < *tithenai* "put"] —**di·a·thet·ic** /dī ə théttik/ *adj*

di·a·tom /dí ə tòm/ *n* a microscopic one-celled alga that has silica-filled cell walls or shells divided into two halves. Diatoms are responsible for the formation of diatomite in water. Class: Bacillariophyceae. [Mid-19C. < modern Latin *Diatoma* < Greek *diatomos* "cut in two" < *diatemnein* "to cut through" < *temnein* "to cut"] —**di·a·to·ma·ceous** /dī ətə máyshəss/ *adj*

di·a·to·ma·ceous earth *n* **1.** GEOL same as **diatomite** **2.** a form of unrefined diatomite. Use: insecticide.

di·a·tom·ic /dì ə tómmik/ *adj* having two atoms per molecule —**di·a·tom·ic·i·ty** /-atə míssətee/ *n*

di·at·o·mite /dī áttə mīt/ *n* a soft powdery porous rock. Source: accumulated shells of diatoms. Use: in fireproof cements, insulating materials, dynamite, as insecticide

di·a·ton·ic /dì ə tónnik/ *adj* relating to or based on musical scales consisting of five tones and two semitones, e.g., a major or minor scale with no extra sharps or flats added ■ *n* the interval between any two notes of a diatonic scale [Early 17C. Via French or late Latin < Greek *diatonikos* "at intervals of a tone" < *tonos* "tone"] —**di·a·ton·i·cal·ly** *adv* —**di·a·ton·i·cism** /-tónni sìzzəm/ *n*

di·a·tribe /dí ə trìb/ *n* a bitter verbal or written attack on somebody or something ○ *a diatribe against falling standards* [Late 16C. Via French < Greek *diatribē* "act of spending time (in discourse)"]

di·at·ro·pism /dī áttrə pìzzəm/ *n* the tendency of a plant or plant part to grow at right angles in response to an external stimulus such as light —**di·a·trop·ic** /dī ə tróppik/ *adj*

Di·az another spelling of **Dias**

Dí·az /deè aaz, -aass/, **Porfirio** (1830–1915) Mexican politician and military leader. The president of Mexico (1876–80, 1884–1911), he was forced out of office during the Mexican revolution. Full name **Díaz, José de la Cruz Porfirio**

> "Poor Mexico, so far from God and so near to the United States."
> [Attributed to Porfirio Díaz]

di·az·e·pam /dī ázzə pàm/ *n* a tranquilizer that has habit-forming potential. Use: short-term relief of anxiety or tension, muscle relaxant. [Mid-20C. < *di-* + *-azepam*, INN stem]

di·a·zine /dí ə zeèn, dī ázzin/ *n* a chemical compound in which the molecules contain a hexagonal ring of four carbon atoms and two nitrogen atoms, existing in three isomeric forms. Formula: $C_4N_2H_4$.

di·a·zo /dī ázzō, -áyzō/ *adj* describes an organic compound containing two adjacent nitrogen atoms, e.g., an azo compound or a diazonium salt ■ *n* (*plural* **-zos** or **-zoes**) a photograph or photocopy made using a diazo compound or the diazotype process

di·a·zole /dí ə zōl, dī á zōl/ *n* an organic chemical compound with a five-sided ring structure containing three carbon atoms and two nitrogen atoms

di·a·zo·ni·um salt *n* a salt containing two adjacent nitrogen atoms as an (**azo**) group. Use: manufacture of azo dyes.

Dí·az Or·daz /deè az áwr dàz, deè aass áwr daàss/, **Gustavo** (1911–79) Mexican politician. He served as senator (1946–52), minister of the interior (1958–63), and president (1964–70).

> "My government will protect all liberties but one—the liberty to do away with other liberties."
> [Gustavo Díaz Ordaz, *Inaugural speech as president*; 1964]

di·a·zo·tize /dī ázzə tīz/ (**-tized, -tiz·ing, -tiz·es**) *vt* to transform an amine into a diazo compound using nitrous acid —**di·a·zo·ti·za·tion** /dī àzzəti záysh'n/ *n*

di·a·zo·type /dī ázzə tīp/ *n* a printing or photographic process that exploits the light-sensitive properties of diazo compounds

di·ba·sic /dī báyssik/ *adj* **1.** describes an acid that has two replaceable hydrogen atoms **2.** describes a salt or an acid that is formed with two atoms of a monovalent metallic element —**di·ba·sic·i·ty** /dī bay síssətee/ *n*

dib·ber /díbbər/ *n* a small pointed gardening tool used to make holes in the soil for planting seeds, bulbs, or seedlings [Mid-18C. < *dib*, related to DIBBLE]

dib·ble /díbb'l/ *n* GARDENING same as **dibber** ■ *vt* (**-bled, -bling, -bles**) to make planting holes in soil with a pointed tool, or put plants or seeds in such holes [14C. Origin ?] —**dib·bler** *n*

di·bro·mide /dī brṓ mīd/ *n* a chemical compound whose molecules contain two bromine atoms

dibs /dibz/ *npl* **CLAIM OF RIGHTS** a claim of exclusive rights to take or use something (*informal; (takes a singular verb)*) ○ *called dibs on the front seat* ■ *n* **MONEY** money, especially in small amounts (*dated informal*) ■ *interj* **EXPRESSION OF CLAIM** used to express a claim to take or use something (*informal*) ○ *Dibs on the red bike!* [Early 19C. < shortening of *dibstones* "game played with pebbles"]

di·car·box·yl·ic ac·id /dī kaar bok sìllik-/ *n* any acid that contains two carboxyl groups

dice /dīss/ LEISURE plural of **die**[2] (sense 1) ■ *n* **GAME PLAYED WITH DICE** a gambling game played with dice, e.g., craps (*takes a singular or plural verb*) ■ *also* **dic·es** *npl* **CHUNKS** cube-shaped pieces, especially of meat (*takes a plural verb*) ■ *v* (**diced, dic·ing, dic·es**) **1.** *vt* **CUT UP FOOD** to cut food into cubes ○ *diced carrots* **2.** *vti* **PLAY WITH DICE** to gamble using dice, or win or lose something playing dice **3.** *vi* **TAKE RISKS** to challenge or take risks with somebody or something dangerous ○ *dicing with death* **4.** *vt* **DECORATE SOMETHING WITH SQUARE PATTERN** to decorate something with a pattern of squares or cubes [14C. < French *dé* (plural *dés*) < Latin *datum*, past participle of *dare* "give, play"] —**dic·er** *n* ◇ **load the dice 1.** to manipulate a situation unfairly in order to obtain a desired result **2.** to add weight to a die so that it always falls on the same side (*informal*) ◇ **no dice** used to indicate that there is no chance of something happening (*informal*)

USAGE Dice – singular or plural? ***Dice***, used with a plural verb, means "small cubes with the numbers 1 to 6 marked in dots on the sides, used in gambling." ***Dice***, used with a singular verb, means a gambling game in which these cubes are used. ***Dice*** (plural) can also refer to cube-shaped pieces, especially of food.

di·cen·tra /dī séntrə/ *n* a perennial plant that grows best in shade. Flowers: small, drooping, in arching sprays. Genus: *Dicentra.* [Mid-19C. < modern Latin < Greek *dikentros* "two-pointed" < *kentron* "center, point"; from the shape of its leaves]

di·ceph·a·lous /dī séffələss/ *adj* having two heads

dic·ey /dīssee/ (**-i·er, -i·est**), **dic·y** *adj* uncertain and involving danger or risk (*informal*)

di·cha·si·um /dī káy zee əm, -káyzhəm/ (*plural* **-si·a** /-zee ə, -káyzhə/) *n* a flowering stem that has a single flower growing on the end (**cyme**) and later sprouts two single-flower branches, one on each side of and below the first flower [Late 19C. < Greek *dikhasis* "division" < *dikha* "apart"] —**di·cha·si·al** *adj* —**di·cha·si·al·ly** *adv*

di·chlo·ro·di·fluor·o·meth·ane /dī klàwrō dī flòorō mé thàyn, -flàwrō-/ *n* a colorless, nonflammable, gaseous CFC. Use: propellant in aerosols, refrigerant, in fire extinguishers. Formula: CCl_2F_2.

di·chlo·ro·di·phen·yl·tri·chlo·ro·eth·ane /dī klàwrō dī fènn'l trī klàwrō é thàyn, -trī klàwrō é thàyn/ *n* CHEM full form of **DDT**

di·chlo·ro·meth·ane /dī klàw rō mé thàyn/ *n* a colorless, nonflammable, toxic gas. Use: in paint strippers, degreasing, plastics processing. Formula: CH_2Cl_2.

di·chlo·ro·phe·nox·y·ac·et·ic ac·id /dī klàwrō fə noksee ə seetik-/ *n* CHEM same as **2,4-D**

di·chog·a·my /dī kóggəmee/ *n* a plant's production of male and female parts at different times, in order to prevent self-pollination and ensure cross-fertilization [Mid-19C. < Greek *dikho-* "apart" + *gamos* "marriage"] —**di·cho·gam·ic** /dìkō gámmik/ *adj* —**di·chog·a·mous** *adj*

di·chon·dra /dī kóndrə/ *n* a low-growing plant of the morning glory family. Use: substitute for lawn grass in warm areas. Native to: United States. Genus: *Dichondra.* [Mid-20C. < modern Latin < Greek *dikho-* "apart" + *khondros* "grain"]

di·chot·ic /dī kóttik/ *adj* involving or relating to the simultaneous stimulation of each ear with different sounds [Mid-20C. < Greek *dikho-* "apart" + *ōt-* "ear"]

di·chot·o·mize /dī kóttə mīz/ (**-mized, -miz·ing, -miz·es**) *vti* to divide something into two classes or groups, or become divided into two —**di·chot·o·mi·za·tion** /dī kòttəmi záysh'n/ *n*

di·chot·o·my /dī kóttəmee/ (*plural* **-mies**) *n* **1. SEPARATION OF DIFFERENT OR CONTRADICTORY THINGS** a separation into two divisions that differ widely from or contradict each other **2.** BOT **BRANCHING OF PLANTS** the division of each of a plant's branches into two more branches **3.** ASTRON **MOON PHASE WHEN HALF VISIBLE** the phase of the Moon or a planet when half of its surface appears illuminated by the Sun [Late 16C. Via modern Latin < Greek *dikhotomia* "cutting in two" < *dikho-* "apart, in two" + *temnein* "to cut"] —**di·chot·o·mic** /dìkə tómmik/ *adj* —**di·chot·o·mous** *adj* —**di·chot·o·mous·ly** *adv*

di·chro·ic /dī krṓ ik/ *adj* describes a crystal that appears to be a different color when viewed along a different axis [Mid-19C. < Greek *dikhroos* "two-colored" < *khrōs* "color"] —**di·chro·ism** *n*

di·chro·ite /dī krṓ īt/ *n* MINERALS same as **cordierite** [Early 19C. < Greek *dikhroos* (see DICHROIC)]

di·chro·it·ic /dìkrō íttik/ *adj* CHEM same as **dichroic**

di·chro·mate /dī krṓ màyt/ *n* a salt of dichromic acid, characteristically orange red in color

di·chro·mat·ic /dì krō máttik/ *adj* **1. WITH TWO COLORS** having two colors **2.** OPHTHALMOL **PARTIALLY COLORBLIND** able to distinguish only two of the three primary colors and their combinations **3.** ZOOL **WITH DIFFERENT COLOR PHASES** describes animals, especially birds, that have two different colors in phases that are not associated with the normal variations in color that occur with sex and age

di·chro·ma·tism /dī krṓmə tìzzəm/ *n* **1.** the presence of only two colors in something **2.** colorblindness in which only two of the three primary colors and their combinations can be distinguished

di·chro·mic /dī krṓmik/ *adj* OPHTHALMOL same as **dichromatic** (sense 2) [Mid-19C. < Greek *dikhrōmos* "two-colored" < *khrōma* "color"]

di·chro·mic ac·id *n* an unstable acid found only in solution and in the form of dichromate salts. Formula: $H_2Cr_2O_7$.

di·chrom·ism /dī krṓ mìzzəm/ *n* OPHTHALMOL same as **dichromatism** (sense 2)

~~**dicision**~~ incorrect spelling of **decision**

dick[1] /dik/ *n* an offensive term for the penis (*slang*) [Mid-16C. < the male first name *Dick*]

dick[2] /dik/ *n* same as **detective** (*dated slang*) [Early 20C. Origin ?]

Dick and Jane /dìk ənd jáyn/ *npl* the stereotypes of middle-class white Americans (*informal; hyphenated when used before a noun*)

dick·ens /díkənz/ *n* used for emphasis in a variety of expressions, especially expressions of surprise or annoyance (*informal*) ○ *What the dickens is going on here?* ○ *scared the dickens out of me* [Late 16C. Probably < the surname *Dickens*]

Dick·ens /díkənz/, **Charles** (1812–70) British novelist. His career began with magazine sketches, written under the pseudonym "Boz," before *Pickwick Papers* (1837) brought him greater popularity. His many subsequent novels, appearing in monthly installments and often depicting poverty and social injustice in Victorian England, have remained popular. Full name **Dickens, Charles John Huffam.** See Cultural note at **bleak, carol, expectation, hard, twist**

> "It was the best of times, it was the worst of times."
> [Charles Dickens, *A Tale of Two Cities*; 1859]

> "In the little world in which children have their existence, whosoever brings them up, there is nothing so finely perceived and so firmly felt, as injustice."
> [Charles Dickens, *Great Expectations*; 1860–6]

Dick·en·si·an /di kénzee ən/ *adj* **1. OF CHARLES DICKENS** relating to the 19th-century British novelist Charles Dickens **2. REMINISCENT OF POVERTY-STRICKEN VICTORIAN BRITAIN** typical or reminiscent of the harsh poverty-stricken living conditions described in the works of Dickens **3. JOLLY AND GENIAL** jolly and cordial, like some of the scenes and characters featured in the novels of Dickens **4. FULL OF TWISTS AND AMAZING COINCIDENCES** full of twists and remarkable coincidences, like the plots of some of the novels of Dickens ○ *an episode too Dickensian for most modern audiences to swallow*

dick·er /díkər/ *vi* (**-ered, -er·ing, -ers**) to bargain for goods or services (*informal*) ○ *collectors dickering at antique sales* ■ *n* bargaining in general, or something settled, achieved, or obtained through bargaining [Early 19C. Probably < Latin *decuria* "group of ten, ten hides for sale" < *decem* "ten" + *vir* "man"]

dick·ey /díkee/ (*plural* **-eys** or **-ies**), **dick·y** (*plural* **-ies**), **dick·ie** *n* **1.** a garment that is only the front or neck of a shirt, worn under a shirt, jacket, or sweater **2.** *UK regional* a donkey, especially a male [Mid-18C. Origin ?]

Dick·ey /díkee/, **James** (1923–97) US writer. He is known for his poetry and the novel *Deliverance* (1970). Full name **Dickey, James Lafayette**

> "We have all been in rooms we cannot die in."
> [James Dickey, *Adultery*; 1967]

dick·head /dík hèd/ *n* an offensive term for a man who is regarded as unintelligent or annoying (*slang insult*)

dick·ie *n* CLOTHING, AUTOMOT another spelling of **dickey**

CORBIS/Bettmann

Emily Dickinson

Dick·in·son /díkinssən/, **Emily** (1830–86) US poet. She is considered one of America's greatest writers. Most of her poems were published posthumously. Full name **Dickinson, Emily Elizabeth**

Dick·in·son, John (1732–1808) American founding father. He led opposition to British tax policy and wrote *Letters from a Farmer in Pennsylvania* (1767–68).

> "Then join hand in hand, brave Americans all! / By uniting we stand, by dividing we fall."
> [John Dickinson, "The Liberty Song"; 1768]

dick·y[1] /díkee/ (**-ier, -iest**) *adj UK* (*informal*) **1.** not well in health **2.** faulty or unreliable [Late 18C. Origin ?]

dick·y[2] *n* CLOTHING another spelling of **dickey**

di·cli·nous /dī klīnəss/ *adj* describes plants that have stamens and pistils in separate flowers, rather than in the same flower [Early 19C. < modern Latin *diclines* "two beds" < Greek *klinē* "bed"] —**di·clin·ism** *n* —**di·cli·ny** /dī klīnee/ *n*

di·cot·y·le·don /dī kòtt'l éed'n/ *n* a flowering plant that produces two seed leaves (**cotyledons**) when it germinates and whose subsequent leaves have a network of veins. Most herbaceous plants, trees, and bushes are dicotyledons. Subclass: Dicotyledonae. [Early 18C. < modern Latin *Dicotyledonae*, literally "two cotyledons"] —**di·cot·y·le·don·ous** *adj*

di·cro·tism /díkrə tìzzəm/ *n* a physiological condition in which each heartbeat produces a double pulse, occurring in typhoid fever and other conditions [Mid-19C. < Greek *dikrotos* "double-beating"] —**di·cro·tal** /dī krṓt'l/ *adj* —**di·crot·ic** /dī króttik/ *adj*

dict. *abbr* **1.** dictation **2.** POL dictator **3.** PUBL dictionary

dic·ta plural of **dictum**

Dic·ta·phone /díktə fōn/ *tdmk* a trademark for a small hand-held tape recorder used for dictation

dic·tate *v* /dík tàyt, dik táyt/ (**-tat·ed, -tat·ing, -tates**) **1.** *vti* **SPEAK ALOUD WORDS TO BE WRITTEN** to speak the words of a text or letter to be written, either to somebody writing it down as it is spoken, or into a tape recorder for later transcription **2.** *vti* **RULE OR CONTROL OTHER PEOPLE** to rule over or make decisions for others with absolute authority, or attempt to do so ○ *dictates their every move* **3.** *vt* **CONTROL SOMETHING** to have control over something (*usually passive*) ○ *The decision to go will be dictated by the weather conditions.* ■ *n* /dík tàyt/ **1. COMMAND GIVEN** an order telling people what they must do ○ *dictates received from their superiors* **2. GOVERNING PRINCIPLE** a rule or principle that governs how people behave ○ *the dictates of fashion* [Late 16C. < Latin *dictat-*, past participle of *dictare* "say often" < *dicere* "to say"]

dic·ta·tion /dik táysh'n/ *n* **1. ACT OF DICTATING** the act of dictating a text or letter, or of writing down what is being dictated **2. STUDENTS' WRITING OF WORDS SPOKEN** a test or exercise of language comprehension in which students write down words spoken aloud by a teacher ○ *a Spanish dictation* **3. WORDS WRITTEN DOWN** words written down that have been dictated —**dic·ta·tion·al** *adj*

dic·ta·tor /dík tàytər/ *n* **1.** POL **POWERFUL RULER** a leader who rules a country with absolute power, usually by force **2. BOSSY PERSON** somebody who is regarded as behaving in an autocratic or domineering way

3. **AUTHORITY ON SUBJECT** somebody whose opinions on a subject are listened to and followed by society at large ○ *one of the great dictators of modern music* 4. **SOMEBODY WHO GIVES DICTATION** a speaker of words out loud so that somebody else can transcribe them 5. ANCIENT HIST **TEMPORARY ROMAN RULER** in ancient Rome, a temporary appointed leader with absolute power to deal with a crisis or an emergency

dic·ta·to·ri·al /dìktə táwree əl/ *adj* 1. fond of telling others what to do or of using power or authority to make them do it 2. relating to or ruled by dictators —**dic·ta·to·ri·al·ly** *adv*

dic·ta·tor·ship /dik táytər shìp/ *n* 1. **DICTATOR'S POWER OR RULE** a dictator's power or authority, or the period of time during which a dictator rules 2. **GOVERNMENT BY DICTATOR** government by a dictator, usually by force 3. **COUNTRY RULED BY DICTATOR** a country ruled by a dictator 4. **ABSOLUTE AUTHORITY** absolute power or authority

dic·tion /díksh'n/ *n* 1. the clarity with which somebody pronounces words when speaking or singing 2. choice of words to fit their context ○ *"a tendency to identify the poetic impulse with melancholy moods and sonorous diction"* (Northrop Frye, *The Bush Garden*; 1972) [Mid-16C. < Latin *diction-* < *dicere* "to say"] —**dic·tion·al** *adj* —**dic·tion·al·ly** *adv*

dic·tion·ar·y /díkshə nèrree/ (*plural* **-ies**) *n* 1. **BOOK OF WORD MEANINGS** a reference book that contains alphabetically ordered words, with explanations of their meanings, often with information about grammar, pronunciation, and etymology 2. **FOREIGN-LANGUAGE REFERENCE BOOK OF WORDS** a reference book that alphabetically arranges and translates words and phrases in two or more languages ○ *a Spanish-English dictionary* 3. **SPECIALIZED REFERENCE BOOK** a reference book that alphabetizes and explains terms relating to a subject or topic ○ *a dictionary of music* 4. **LIST OF INFORMATION** a book that lists examples or information arranged alphabetically or in some other way, e.g., by author ○ *a dictionary of quotations* 5. COMPUT **WORD-PROCESSING REFERENCE** a file used as a reference by a word-processing program for correct spelling and hyphenation 6. COMPUT **ALPHABETICAL LIST OF COMPUTER CODES** an alphabetized list of keys or code names used in a program, each briefly defined [Early 16C. < medieval Latin *dictionarius* "of words" < Latin *diction-* (see DICTION)]

dic·tum /díktəm/ (*plural* **-tums** or **-ta** /-tə/) *n* 1. an authoritative saying, statement, or pronouncement 2. LAW same as **obiter dictum** (sense 1) [Late 16C. < Latin < past participle of *dicere* "say"]

dic·ty·op·ter·an /dìktee óptərən/ *n* an insect with, typically, a flattened body, long legs, and leathery front wings held flat over the membranous hind wings, e.g., a cockroach or mantis. Order: Dictyoptera. [< modern Latin *Dictyoptera* < Greek *diktuon* "net" + *pteron* "wing"]

dic·y *adj* another spelling of **dicey** (*informal*)

di·cyn·o·dont /dī sínnə dònt/ *n* an extinct plant-eating reptile with teeth like tusks. Suborder: Dicynodontia. [Mid-19C. < modern Latin *Dicynodontia*, literally "two canine teeth" < Greek *kun-* "dog" + *odont-* "tooth"]

did past tense of **do**[1]

DID *abbr* PSYCHIAT dissociative identity disorder

di·dac·tic /dī dáktik/ *adj* 1. containing a political or moral message ○ *didactic theater* 2. tending to give instruction or advice, even when it is not welcome or not needed [Mid-17C. < Greek *didaktikos* < *didaskein* "teach"] —**di·dac·ti·cal·ly** *adv*

di·dac·ti·cism /dī dákti sìzzəm/ *n* the instructional quality of something such as a piece of writing, or the attitude of somebody who likes to instruct others or give them advice ○ *the welcome absence of didacticism in modern poetry*

di·dac·tics /dī dáktiks/ *n* the science or profession of teaching (*takes a singular verb*)

did·dle[1] /dídd'l/ (**-dled, -dling, -dles**) *vt* 1. **CHEAT SOMEBODY** to cheat or swindle somebody (*slang; often passive*) 2. COMPUT **MANIPULATE DATA ILLEGALLY** to manipulate computer data illegally (*informal*) 3. COMPUT **MANIPULATE PROGRAM** to manipulate a computer program in an informal or a not particularly serious manner (*informal*) [Early 19C. Probably < Jeremy *Diddler*, character who constantly borrowed and failed to repay money in *Raising the Wind* (1803) by James Kenney (1780–1849)] —**did·dler** *n*

did·dle[2] /dídd'l/ (**-dled, -dling, -dles**) *v* 1. *vi* **SPEND TIME IDLY** to spend time doing nothing in particular (*slang*) ○ *spent the morning diddling around* 2. *vi* **TOUCH OR PLAY WITH SOMETHING REPEATEDLY** to spend time touching, fiddling with, or adjusting something repeatedly (*slang*) 3. *vt* **JERK REPEATEDLY** to jerk something up and down or back and forth (*informal*) 4. *vt* **OFFENSIVE TERM** an offensive term meaning to have sexual intercourse with a woman (*slang*) 5. *vti* **OFFENSIVE TERM** an offensive term meaning to masturbate (*slang*) [Mid-17C. Origin ?] —**did·dler** *n*

did·dly·squat /díddlee skwòt/, **did·dly** *n* nothing at all (*informal*) ○ *And what did I get? Diddlysquat!* [Mid-20C. Probably alteration of *doodlysquat*, origin ?]

~~**dident**~~ incorrect spelling of **didn't**

did·ger·i·doo /dìjjəree dóo/ (*plural* **-doos**), **did·jer·i·doo** *n* an Australian Aboriginal musical instrument with a long thick wooden pipe that is blown to create a deep reverberating humming sound [Early 20C. < an Aboriginal language, an imitation of the sound]

di·di /dée dee/ *n S Asia* 1. somebody's older sister or female cousin (*often used as a form of address*) 2. used as a form of address for an older woman [< Hindi]

di di mau /dée dee mów/ *vi* to leave a place quickly and unceremoniously [< Vietnamese, "go away fast"]

Did·i·on /díddee ən/, **Joan** (*b.* 1934) US writer. She expresses concern for North American cultural and political values in her journalism, screenplays, and novels such as the bestselling *Play It as It Lays* (1970).

did·n't /dídd'nt/ *contr* did not ○ *I didn't want to go.*

Di·do /dídō/ *n* in Roman mythology, the queen and founder of Carthage who killed herself when abandoned by her lover, Aeneas

Did·rik·son /díddriksən/, **Babe** ➧ **Zaharias, Babe Didrikson**

didst /didst/ *vti* second person present singular of "did," used with "thou" (*archaic*)

di·dym·i·um /dī dímmee əm/ *n* a mixture of metallic elements from the rare-earth, or lanthanide, series of elements, consisting chiefly of neodymium and praseodymium. Use: production of colored glass, optical filters. [Mid-19C. < Greek *didumos* "twin"]

die[1] /dī/ (**died, dy·ing, dies**) *v* 1. *vi* **STOP LIVING** to cease to be alive (*refers to a person, plant, or animal*) 2. *vi* **STOP EXISTING** to cease to exist, especially gradually ○ *feelings I thought had died long ago* 3. *vi* **STOP WORKING** to stop functioning ○ *The engine suddenly died.* 4. *vti* **DIE AS STATED** to experience a particular kind of death ○ *The villain, of course, dies a gruesome death.* 5. *vi* **EMPHASIZING DESIRE** used to indicate how strongly the speaker wishes to do or have something ○ *I'm dying to tell them!* [12C. Probably < Old Norse *deyja* < Indo-European] ◇ **die hard** to give up or come to an end only after long, difficult, and sustained resistance ◇ **to die for** highly desirable and hence worth sacrificing something to obtain (*informal*)

SPELLCHECK die or **dye**? Do not confuse the spelling of ***die*** and ***dye***, which sound similar. ***Die*** is a verb meaning "stop living or existing": *Her mother died last year. The sound died away.* There is also a noun spelled ***die***, which is used in the saying *the die is cast* and which denotes a small cube used in games, a mold, or a stamping or cutting tool. ***Dye*** is a noun or verb referring to a substance used to change the color of something, as in *vegetable dyes, to dye your hair, a dyed-in-the-wool conservative.* Note also that the present participle of ***die*** is spelled *dying*, whereas the present participle of ***dye*** is spelled *dyeing*.

USAGE A person can *die of* an illness, or *die in* an earthquake or a fire. In careful usage, *die from* is reserved for indirect causes of death, e.g., refusal to leave a flooded area or failure to wear a seat belt: *The study found that people with the lowest cholesterol levels were more likely to die from tragic causes, such as car crashes or suicide.*

die away *vi* to fade or grow faint

die back *vi* to wither or die from the tips of new shoots back to the established stem or old wood of the plant, as a result of disease, seasonal change, or poor conditions

die down *vi* to become quieter, weaker, or less intense

die off *vi* to die gradually one by one, until none is left

die out *vi* 1. to become extinct, or gradually cease to exist ○ *entire species that have died out in our century* 2. to fade and finally disappear gradually ○ *Over the years, opposition to the plan had died out.*

die[2] /dī/ *n* 1. (*plural* **dice** /dīss/) LEISURE **NUMBERED CUBE USED IN GAMES** a small cube with the numbers 1 to 6 marked in dots on the sides, used in gambling and in a wide variety of games of chance ○ *throw each die once* 2. ENG **STAMPING OR PRESSING TOOL** the metal tool on a stamping or pressing machine that gives the finished object its shape and design 3. ENG **MOLD** a tool for molding substances such as metal or plastic 4. ENG **TOOL FOR CUTTING** a tool that cuts screw threads on metal rods, consisting of a metal block with an internally threaded hole into which blank rods are screwed to cut external threads 5. ARCHIT **PART OF PEDESTAL** the part of a pedestal that lies between the base and the cornice, especially when it is cubic in shape [12C. < French *dé* (see DICE)]

die·back /dī bàk/ *n* gradual decay that sets in at a plant's young shoots then works back to established stems or old wood, as a result of disease, seasonal change, or poor conditions

die-cast *vt* to make a metal or plastic object by pouring or forcing molten metal or plastic into a mold —**die-cast** *adj*

di·e·cious *adj* PLANTS another spelling of **dioecious**

Die·fen·ba·ker /déefən bàykər/, **John George** (1895–1979) Canadian politician. He headed the Progressive Conservative Party (1956–67) and served as prime minister of Canada (1957–63). See table at **prime minister**

> "Freedom is the right to be wrong, not the right to do wrong."
> [John George Diefenbaker. Quoted in *Reader's Digest*; September 1979]

di·ef·fen·bach·i·a /dèefən baákee ə, -bákee ə, dèefən baákee ə, -bàkee ə/ *n* an evergreen plant with poisonous sap, widely cultivated as a house plant for its large many-colored leaves. Native to: tropical America. Genus: *Dieffenbachia*. [Late 19C. < modern Latin, after Ernst *Dieffenbach* (1794–1855), German botanist]

~~**diegn**~~ incorrect spelling of **deign**

Di·e·go same as **Diego Garcia** (*informal*)

Di·e·go Gar·cia /dee àygō gaar sée ə/ largest island in the disputed island territory of the Chagos Archipelago, in the central Indian Ocean. It is the site of a US communications center and naval base. Area: 10.5 sq. mi./27 sq. km.

die·hard /dī haard/ *adj* resistant to any kind of change, and reluctant to give up beliefs, positions, or attitudes ○ *diehard football fans* ■ *n* somebody who resists change or stubbornly persists in a belief or opinion ○ *with the old diehards holding out to the bitter end* —**die·hard·ism** *n*

~~**dieing**~~ incorrect spelling of **dying**

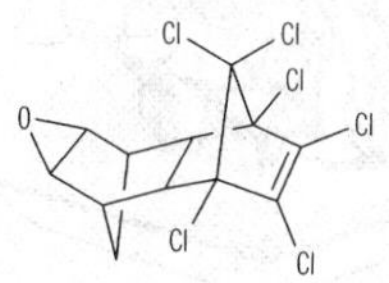

dieldrin

diel·drin /déeldrin/ *n* an insecticide based on a chlorinated naphthalene derivative, now widely banned. Formula: $C_{12}H_{10}OCl_6$. [Mid-20C. After Otto *Diels* (1876–

1954), German chemist + *aldrin*, toxic insecticide, after Kurt *Alder* (see DIELS-ALDER REACTION)]

di·e·lec·tric /dī i léktrik/ *adj* not able to conduct direct electric current, and therefore useful as an insulator ■ *n* a dielectric substance [Mid-19C. < DIA-] —**di·e·lec·tri·cal·ly** *adv*

di·e·lec·tric con·stant *n* PHYS same as **relative permittivity**

di·e·lec·tric heat·ing *n* the heating of an insulating material by placing it in a rapidly changing electric field. The technique is used in the manufacture of foam rubber, plastics, and other materials.

di·e·lec·tric lens *n* a lens made of insulating material that deflects radio waves passing through it in the way that a glass lens deflects light. Use: to shape beams emitted from radar and microwave antennas.

Diels-Al·der re·ac·tion /deélz áaldər-/ *n* a chemical reaction in which an organic compound with two double bonds between carbon atoms (**diene**) and a compound containing a double or triple bond combine to form a ring compound [Mid-20C. After Otto *Diels* (see DIELDRIN) and Kurt *Alder* (1902–58), German chemist]

Di·em /dee ém, dyem/, **Ngo Dinh** (1901–63) Vietnamese politician. He was supported by the United States as the first president of South Vietnam (1955–63). He was assassinated after large antigovernment demonstrations.

di·en·ceph·a·lon /dī en séffə lòn/ *n* the area in the center of the brain just above the brain stem that includes the thalamus and hypothalamus [Late 19C. < DIA- + Greek *enkephalos* "brain"] —**di·en·ce·phal·ic** /-enssə fállik/ *adj*

di·ene /dī́ een/ *n* an unsaturated hydrocarbon (**alkene**) containing two carbon-to-carbon double bonds

Di·eppe /dee ép/ seaport and resort on the English Channel in the Seine-Maritime department, Haute-Normandie region, in northwestern France. It is situated about 60 mi./97 km west of Amiens. Population: 34,653 (1999).

di·er·e·sis /dī érrəssiss/ (*plural* **-ses** /-seez/), **di·aer·e·sis** (*plural* **-ses** /dī érrəssiss/) *n* **1.** a mark (¨) placed above a vowel to show that it should be pronounced. It may be above the second of two adjacent vowels to show that it is a separate syllable, as in the word "naïve," or above a single vowel, as in the name "Brontë." See table at **diacritic 2.** a pause in a line of poetry that occurs when the end of a metrical foot coincides with the end of a word [Late 16C. Via Latin < Greek *diairesis* < *diairein* "separate, divide" < *hairein* "take"] —**di·e·ret·ic** /dī ə réttik/ *adj*

Dier·i /deéree/, **Diyar·i** *n* an Aboriginal language of South Australia, now almost extinct [Late 19C. < Dieri] —**Di·e·ri** *adj*

die·sel /deéz'l, deéss'l/ *n* **1.** AUTOMOT same as **diesel engine 2.** a vehicle, e.g., a car or train, that is powered by a diesel engine **3.** AUTOMOT same as **diesel fuel** [Late 19C. After Rudolf *Diesel* (1858–1913), German engineer]

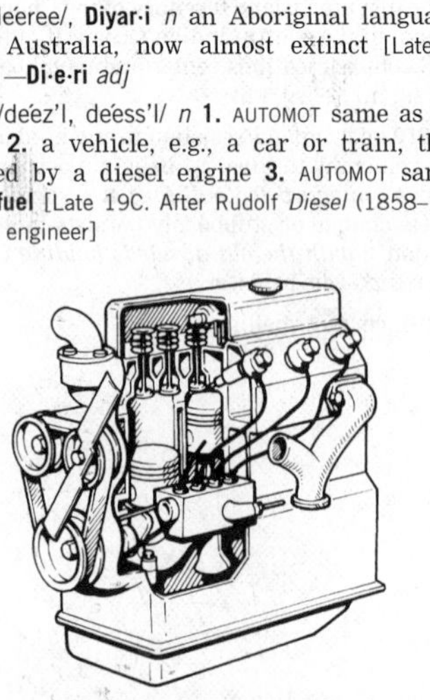

diesel engine: cutaway view showing compression chambers

die·sel en·gine *n* an internal-combustion engine that ignites diesel fuel using compression alone, rather than using an electrical spark

die·sel fu·el *n* a thick oily fuel that is obtained from the distillation of petroleum. It has an ignition temperature of 540°C and is ignited by the heat of compression.

die·sel oil *n UK* same as **diesel fuel**

Di·es I·rae /deè ayss eè rày/ *n* **1.** a 13th-century Latin hymn that describes the Day of Judgment, used in a Requiem Mass **2.** a musical setting of the Dies Irae, usually as part of a Requiem Mass [< Latin, "day of wrath"]

di·e·sis /dī́ əssiss/ (*plural* **-e·ses** /-ə seez/) *n* PRINTING same as **double dagger** [14C. Via Latin < Greek, "quarter tone" (which the symbol originally indicated)]

die·stock /dī́ stòk/ *n* a device for holding the dies that are used for cutting threads on screws [Mid-19C. < DIE[2]]

di·es·trus /dī éstrəss/ *n* a stage of the estrous cycle, following estrus, in which the ovary is functional and the predominant ovarian hormone produced is progesterone —**di·es·trous** *adj*

di·et[1] /dī́ ət/ *n* **1.** WHAT PERSON OR ANIMAL EATS the food that a person or animal usually consumes **2.** CONTROLLED INTAKE OF FOOD a controlled intake of food and drink designed for weight loss, for health or religious reasons, or to control or improve a medical condition ○ *a wheat-free diet* **3.** REGULAR INTAKE OF SOMETHING a continuous or daily experience of, or indulgence in, something other than food ○ *living on a diet of soap operas and game shows* ■ *adj* DESIGNED OR PROMOTED FOR WEIGHT LOSS describes a food or drink that is intended for people trying to lose weight, usually because it is low in calories or fat, or contains a sugar substitute ○ *a diet soda* ■ *vi* (**-et·ed, -et·ing, -ets**) EAT LESS to follow a restricted pattern of eating or drinking in order to lose weight [Pre-12C. Via Old French *diete* < Greek *diaita* "course of life"] —**di·e·tar·y** *adj* —**di·et·er** *n*

di·et[2] /dī́ ət/ *n* **1.** POL LEGISLATIVE ASSEMBLY a legislative assembly in some countries such as Japan **2.** HIST ASSEMBLY IN HOLY ROMAN EMPIRE a general assembly of the estates of the Holy Roman Empire **3.** LAW COURT SESSION IN SCOTLAND in Scotland, a session of a court, or the date fixed for a court hearing [15C. < medieval Latin *dieta* "day's journey, work," (by association with Latin *dies* "day") "day for a meeting (of legislators)," probably < Greek *diaita* "course of life"]

di·e·tar·y fi·ber *n* same as **fiber** (sense 5)

di·e·tar·y laws *npl* the rules governing which items of food observant Jews are permitted to eat, derived from Leviticus 11 and Deuteronomy 14

di·e·tet·ic /dī ə téttik/ *adj* **1.** relating to what people eat and drink **2.** prepared to suit the requirements of a special diet —**di·e·tet·i·cal·ly** *adv*

di·e·tet·ics /dī ə téttiks/ *n* the study of food and nutrition and its relation to people's health (*takes a singular verb*)

di·eth·yl·car·bam·a·zine /dī èth'l kaar bámmə zeen-/ *n* a white water-soluble substance in the form of crystals. Use: to treat worms in humans, dogs, and cats. [< DI-[1] + ETHYL + CARBO- + AMIDE + AZINE]

di·eth·yl eth·er /dī èth'l-/ *n* CHEM same as **ether** (sense 1)

di·eth·yl·stil·bes·trol /dī èthəl stil béstrawl/ *n* a synthetic estrogen. Use: formerly, for hormone replacement. [Mid-20C < DI-[1] + ETHYL + STILBENE + OESTROGEN + -OL[1]]

di·eth·yl tol·u·am·ide /dī èth'l tollyoo á mīd, -ámmid/ *n* CHEM same as **deet**

~~**dieties**~~ incorrect spelling of **deities**

di·e·ti·tian /dī ə tish'n/, **di·e·ti·cian** *n* a specialist in the study of food and nutrition in relation to health

Marlene Dietrich

Die·trich /deétrik/, **Marlene** (1901–92) German-born US singer and movie actor. She starred in movies from the 1930s to the 1970s, including *The Devil is a Woman* (1935) and *Witness for the Prosecution* (1957). Full name **von Losch, Maria Magdalene Dietrich**

> "Once a woman has forgiven her man, she must not reheat his sins for breakfast."
> [Marlene Dietrich, *Cosmopolitan*; February 1980]

~~**diferent**~~ incorrect spelling of **different**

diff. *abbr* **1.** difference **2.** different

dif·fer /díffər/ (**-fered, -fer·ing, -fers**) *vi* **1.** to be dissimilar or unlike ○ *new models that differ greatly from the early prototypes* **2.** to have different opinions about something ○ *We agreed to differ.* [14C. Via French, "differ, defer" < Latin *differre* "differ" < *ferre* "carry"]

SYNONYMS See *disagree*.

dif·fer·ence /díffərənss, díffrənss/ *n* **1.** STATE OF BEING UNLIKE OTHERS the quality of being different from or unlike something or somebody else ○ *There's no real difference between going by train and going by car.* **2.** DISTINGUISHING FEATURE a feature that distinguishes one person or thing from another ○ *Can you spot the differences between the two?* **3.** SIGNIFICANT CHANGE a change that has an effect ○ *a noticeable difference in her moods* **4.** DISAGREEMENT a disagreement, argument, or divergence of opinions ○ *settle our differences* **5.** MATH ANSWER TO SUBTRACTION EQUATION the amount by which one quantity is greater or smaller than another ○ *What's the difference between 16 and 6?* **6.** LOGIC DEFINING FEATURE a distinguishing feature that marks out a thing being defined or discussed from others that are more general ○ *being divisible by two is the difference between even numbers and other whole numbers* ◇ **make all the difference** to have an enormous, usually positive, effect or influence ◇ **make no difference** to be of no importance or not matter ◇ **split the difference** to take the average of two amounts, or agree on something that is halfway between two extremes ◇ **tell the difference** to distinguish or figure out the features that make things unlike each other

USAGE difference or **differentiation**? These two words do not share a single meaning, so careful writers avoid using them interchangeably. ***Difference*** denotes the quality of being different or an instance of this. ***Differentiation*** denotes becoming different in the course of development. *My paper explores the difference* [not *differentiation*] *between the world of the adult and the world of the child.* Conversely, do not use ***difference*** when ***differentiation*** is called for: *studied the history of the differentiation* [not *difference*] *of Latin into vernaculars.*

dif·fer·ent /díffərənt, díffrənt/ *adj* **1.** UNLIKE SOMETHING OR SOMEBODY ELSE not the same as something or somebody else ○ *This is certainly different from anything I've ever experienced before.* **2.** DISTINCT separate or distinct from another or others ○ *She wore a different pair of shoes every day.* **3.** UNUSUAL contrary to norms or expectations ○ *What do you think of my hat? – Well, it's certainly different.* [14C. Via French < Latin *different-*, present participle of *differre* (see DIFFER)] —**dif·fer·ent·ly** *adv*

USAGE Different from or **different than**? ***Different from*** and ***different than*** are both common in US English, though critics for 300 years have objected to *different than*. If you are drawing distinctions directly between two people or items, then *from* is the safer choice: *Their attitudes are very different from those of their contemporaries.*

dif·fer·en·ti·a /díffə rénshee ə, -rénshə/ (*plural* **-ti·ae** /-shee ee/) *n* an element that separates one thing from another, especially a trait that distinguishes one subclass from another, e.g., one species from another in the same genus

dif·fer·en·tial /díffə rénshəl/ *n* **1.** DIFFERENCE BETWEEN POINTS ON SCALE a difference between two values on a scale, e.g., a difference in the rates of pay for different jobs in the same line of work **2.** AUTOMOT same as **differential gear 3.** MATH CHANGE IN VARIABLE an infinitesimal change in a variable ■ *adj* **1.** OF

DIFFERENCES relating to or based on differences **2.** MATH RELATING TO CHANGE IN VARIABLES relating to or involving infinitesimal changes in a variable with respect to another variable

dif·fer·en·tial cal·cu·lus *n* the branch of mathematics dealing with continuously varying quantities, with applications in the determination of maximum and minimum points, and with rates of change through the use of derivatives and differentials

dif·fer·en·tial co·ef·fi·cient *n* MATH same as **derivative** *n* (sense 4)

dif·fer·en·tial e·qua·tion *n* a mathematical equation that relates functions and their derivatives

dif·fer·en·tial gear *n* an arrangement of gears that allows two shafts driven by a third to turn at different speeds, e.g., in a motor vehicle

dif·fer·en·ti·ate /dìffə rénshee àyt/ (**-at·ed, -at·ing, -ates**) *v* **1.** *vti* SEE DIFFERENCES BETWEEN THINGS to see or show the differences between two or more things **2.** *vt* BE DIFFERENCE to establish a difference between two things or among several things **3.** *vti* MAKE OR BECOME DIFFERENT to make something different or specialized by modifying it, or become different or specialized by being modified **4.** *vi* BIOL BECOME SPECIALIZED to change from a generalized form into a form specialized for a tissue, organ, or other body part (*refers to embryo cells*) **5.** *vt* MATH CALCULATE DERIVATIVE OF FUNCTION to calculate the mathematical derivative of a function [Early 19C. < medieval Latin *differentiat-*, past participle of *differentiare* < Latin *differre* (see DIFFER)] —**dif·fer·en·tia·ble** *adj* —**dif·fer·en·ti·a·tor** *n*

dif·fer·en·ti·a·tion /dìffə renshee áysh'n/ *n* **1.** DEVELOPMENT FROM ONE INTO MANY a developmental process from a single unit or whole into many other derived things, or from a simple to a complex state **2.** VISIBLE DIFFERENCES the complex of visible differences exhibited among two or more things **3.** ESTABLISHMENT OF DIFFERENCES the establishment of differences or a difference among two or more things **4.** BIOL SPECIALIZATION change from a generalized form to another, specialized, form for a tissue, organ, or other body part **5.** MATH CALCULATION OF DERIVATIVE calculation of the derivative of a mathematical function

USAGE See *difference.*

dif·fi·cult /díffikəlt/ *adj* **1.** HARD TO DO requiring a lot of planning or effort to do, understand, or deal with ○ *a difficult job* ○ *a difficult question* **2.** FULL OF PROBLEMS full of problems, trouble, or aspects that are hard to endure ○ *a difficult birth* **3.** HARD TO PLEASE hard to please or control ○ *a difficult audience* **4.** HARD TO CONVINCE hard to convince or persuade ○ *If they're difficult, offer them more.* [14C. Back-formation < DIFFICULTY] —**dif·fi·cult·ness** *n*

SYNONYMS See *hard.*

dif·fi·cul·ty /díffikəltee/ *n* (*plural* **-ties**) **1.** QUALITY OF BEING DIFFICULT the quality of being hard to do, understand, or deal with **2.** SOMETHING NOT EASILY DONE something that is hard to do, understand, or deal with **3.** EFFORT a great effort or struggle to do something **4.** DISPUTE a dispute or controversy ■ **dif·fi·cul·ties** *npl* **1.** TROUBLE a situation full of trouble, danger, or embarrassment ○ *Even a strong swimmer can get into difficulties in this river.* **2.** OBJECTIONS objections or attempts to prevent the progress of something ○ *You're supposed to be here to help, not make difficulties.* [14C. < Latin *difficultas* < *difficilis* "not easy" < *facilis* (see FACILE)]

dif·fi·dent /díffid'nt/ *adj* **1.** lacking self-confidence and rather shy **2.** reserved or restrained in behavior [15C. < Latin *diffident-*, present participle of *diffidere* "to distrust" < *fidere* "to trust"] —**dif·fi·dence** *n* —**dif·fi·dent·ly** *adv*

dif·fract /di frákt/ (**-fract·ed, -fract·ing, -fracts**) *vti* to produce diffraction in waves such as light or sound waves, or undergo diffraction [Early 19C. < Latin *diffract-*, past participle of *diffringere* "to break apart" < *frangere* "to break"] —**dif·frac·tive** *adj* —**dif·frac·tive·ly** *adv*

dif·frac·tion /di frákshən/ *n* the bending or spreading out of waves, e.g., of sound or light, as they pass around the edge of an obstacle or through a narrow aperture

dif·frac·tion grat·ing *n* a glass plate or metal mirror engraved with a large number of parallel lines or grooves, used to produce a spectrum by diffraction or interference

dif·frac·tion ring *n* a circular pattern of light that surrounds a particle under a microscope, resulting from diffraction

dif·frac·tom·e·ter /dì frak tómmətər/ *n* an instrument that uses diffraction, usually of X-rays or electrons by crystals, to investigate the atomic structure of a material

~~**diffrent**~~ incorrect spelling of **different**

dif·fuse[1] /di fyóoz/ (**-fused, -fus·ing, -fus·es**) *vti* **1.** SPREAD THROUGH to spread something throughout something else, or become spread throughout something else **2.** SCATTER OR BECOME SCATTERED to scatter something over an area, or become scattered over an area **3.** MAKE SOMETHING LESS INTENSE to make something, especially light, less bright or intense, or become less bright or intense **4.** UNDERGO OR SUBJECT TO DIFFUSION to subject something to diffusion, or undergo diffusion [14C. < Latin *diffus-*, past participle of *diffundere* "pour in every direction" < *fundere* "pour"] —**dif·fus·i·ble** *adj*

SPELLCHECK See *defuse.*

dif·fuse[2] /di fyóoss/ *adj* **1.** spread throughout a wide area **2.** lacking organization and conciseness, especially in writing or speech [15C Directly or via French < Latin *diffusus* "spread out," past participle of *diffundere* (see DIFFUSE[1])] —**dif·fuse·ly** *adv* —**dif·fuse·ness** *n*

SPELLCHECK See *defuse.*

SYNONYMS See *wordy.*

dif·fus·er /də fyóozər/ *n* **1.** PERSON OR THING THAT DIFFUSES somebody or something that diffuses **2.** HOUSEHOLD DEVICE THAT DIFFUSES LAMP LIGHT a piece of translucent or reflective material fixed to a light source such as a lamp in order to soften or spread the light over a wide area **3.** PHOTOGRAPHY, MOVIES DEVICE THAT SOFTENS PHOTOGRAPHER'S LIGHT a cloth screen, piece of frosted glass, or other material that is used to soften the brightness of the lighting in photography or cinematography **4.** ACOUSTICS CONE TO DISPERSE SOUND WAVES a device, e.g., a cone or wedge, fixed inside a loudspeaker to diffuse sound waves

dif·fu·sion /də fyóozh'n/ *n* **1.** PROCESS OF DIFFUSING a process during which something diffuses or is diffused **2.** RESULT OF DIFFUSING the result of something diffusing or being diffused **3.** CULTL ANTHROP SPREAD OF CULTURAL FEATURES the spread of tools, practices, or other features from one culture to another **4.** PHYS SCATTERING OF LIGHT the scattering of light in many directions as the result of reflection from an uneven surface or passage though a translucent material **5.** PHYS INTERMINGLING OF SUBSTANCES the random movement of atoms, molecules, or ions from one site in a medium to another, resulting in complete mixing —**dif·fu·sion·al** *adj*

dif·fu·sion·ism /də fyóozhə'n ìzzəm/ *n* the anthropological theory that similarities in tools, practices, or other features between cultures result from their being spread from one culture to another rather than being arrived at independently —**dif·fu·sion·ist** *adj, n*

dif·fu·sive /də fyóossiv/ *adj* **1.** relating to, involving, or characteristic of diffusion **2.** same as **diffuse**[2] (sense 2) —**dif·fu·sive·ly** *adv* —**dif·fu·sive·ness** *n*

~~**dificult**~~ incorrect spelling of **difficult**

dig /dig/ *v* (**dug** /dug/, **dig·ging, digs**) **1.** *vti* BREAK UP OR REMOVE EARTH to break up, overturn, or remove something, especially soil, with the hands, paws, a tool, or a machine ○ *The excavator dug the rock out of the hole.* **2.** *vt* CREATE SOMETHING BY DIGGING to make something by removing material, especially earth, with the hands, paws, a tool, or a machine ○ *digging a hole* **3.** *vti* OBTAIN OR FREE BY DIGGING to obtain, uncover, or free something by removing the material covering it using the hands, paws, a tool, or a machine ○ *dig the car out of the snow* **4.** *vi* SEARCH BY DIGGING to try to find something by digging ○ *dig for buried treasure* **5.** *vti* MOVE THROUGH SOMETHING BY DIGGING to move through something by digging a way through it **6.** *vti* DISCOVER SOMETHING BY RESEARCH to find out something by research or questioning ○ *See what you can dig up about her past.* **7.** *vi* SEARCH CAREFULLY to search carefully or persistently ○ *digging through the papers in the file* **8.** *vti* PUSH INTO SOMETHING FORCEFULLY to push something into something else with force, or be pushed with force into something ○ *dug his teeth into the steak* ○ *dug her elbow into my side* **9.** *vti* UNDERSTAND SOMETHING to understand something fully or with sympathy (*dated slang*) ○ *I dig what you're saying.* **10.** *vt* LIKE SOMEBODY OR SOMETHING to like or appreciate somebody or something (*dated slang*) ○ *They don't dig jazz.* ■ *n* **1.** PROD a push with something fairly sharp ○ *a dig in the ribs* **2.** CUTTING REMARK a remark intended to hurt or make fun of somebody ○ *a dig about her new hairstyle* **3.** ACT OF DIGGING the act of digging or excavating something **4.** ARCHAEOL ARCHAEOLOGICAL EXCAVATION an archaeological or paleontological excavation ○ *a dig in Egypt* ■ **digs** *npl UK* LODGINGS a room or rooms that somebody rents in another person's house (*dated informal*) [12C. Origin ?]

dig in *v* **1.** *vti* TAKE UP DEFENSIVE POSITIONS to prepare trenches or other defensive structures, or establish a force or equipment in a defensive position **2.** *vi* RESIST ATTACK to put up a stubborn resistance to an attack **3.** *vi* MAINTAIN OPINION STUBBORNLY to stick to an established position, e.g., in an argument, and fight stubbornly to maintain it **4.** *vi* START EATING to start eating, especially in an enthusiastic way (*informal*) **5.** *vi* SET TO WORK to begin work with great determination (*informal*) **6.** *vt* AGRIC, GARDENING BURY PLANTS to cover plants or the remains of a crop by turning over the soil in which they are growing and burying them

dig out *vt* **1.** UNCOVER SOMETHING to obtain, uncover, or free something by removing the material covering it using the hands, paws, a tool, or a machine **2.** RETRIEVE SOMETHING to retrieve something from where it is kept (*informal*) **3.** DISCOVER SOMETHING to find something out by research or questioning (*informal*)

dig up *vt* **1.** TAKE SOMETHING OUT OF GROUND to dig for something that is buried in the ground and remove it **2.** TURN OVER EARTH to dig into and turn over the soil in an area **3.** INVESTIGATE SOMETHING to find out something by research or investigation (*informal*)

di·gam·ma /dī gámmə/ *n* a letter of the ancient Greek alphabet that became obsolete in the classical period, represented in the English alphabet as "w." See table at **alphabet** [Late 17C. Via Latin < Greek, "double gamma"; from its resemblance to two capital gammas, one above the other]

dig·a·my /díggəmee/ (*plural* **-mies**) *n* a second marriage that, unlike bigamy, is legal because the first husband or wife is dead or has been divorced (*formal*) [Early 17C. Via late Latin < Greek *digamia*, < *digamos* "married to two people" < *gamos* "marriage"] —**dig·a·mous** *adj*

di·gas·tric /dī gástrik/ *adj* describes a muscle, especially the muscle on either side of the lower jaw, in which two fleshy parts are connected by a tendon [Early 18C. < modern Latin *digastricus* < *gastricus* (see GASTRIC); from an analogy between "fleshy parts" and "stomachs"]

di·ge·ra·ti /dìjjə raátee/, **di·gi·ter·a·ti** /dìjjitə raátee/ *npl* people with expertise in computers, the Internet, or the World Wide Web (*informal*) [Late 20C. < DIGITAL after LITERATI]

di·gest *v* /dī jést, di-/ (**-gest·ed, -gest·ing, -gests**) **1.** *vt* PROCESS FOOD to process food in the body into a form that can be absorbed and used or excreted **2.** *vt* ABSORB SOMETHING MENTALLY to think about something and come to understand or appreciate what it means **3.** *vt* ORGANIZE SOMETHING SYSTEMATICALLY to organize something into a system, often through selective condensing of the various items **4.** *vt* ABRIDGE SOMETHING to make a summary of something, often a written work **5.** *vti* CHEM BREAK DOWN to soften or break down a substance through exposure to heat, water, chemicals, enzymes, or bacteria, or be broken down in this way ■ *n* /dī jèst/ **1.** SUMMARY a shortened version of a work that contains the most important or interesting information from the original version **2.** COLLECTION OF ABRIDGED PIECES a magazine, book, or broadcast that contains shortened versions of articles or stories originally from different sources **3.** LAW COLLECTION OF LEGAL OPINIONS a systematic compilation of laws or legal opinions [14C. < Latin *digest-*, past participle of *digerere* "carry apart" < *gerere* "carry"]

di·gest·er /dī jéstər, di-/ *n* **1.** somebody or something that digests something **2.** a vessel or device in which chemical digestion takes place

di·gest·i·ble /dī jéstəb'l, di-/ *adj* easily digested —**di·gest·i·bil·i·ty** /dī jèstə bíllətee, di-/ *n* —**di·gest·i·bly** *adv*

di·ges·tif /deè zhe steéf/ *n* an alcoholic drink, e.g., a brandy or liqueur, drunk after a meal, supposedly to help the digestion of food [Early 20C. < French, "digestive" < Latin *digestivus* < *digerere* (see DIGEST)]

di·ges·tion /dī jéschən, di-/ *n* **1.** PROCESSING OF FOOD IN BODY the breaking down of foodstuffs in the body into a form that can be absorbed and used or excreted **2.** ABILITY TO DIGEST FOOD the ability to process food in the body into a form that can be absorbed and used or excreted **3.** ABILITY TO ABSORB IDEAS the ability to think about something and come to understand or appreciate what it means, or the process of doing so **4.** CHEM BREAKING DOWN the softening or breaking down of a substance through exposure to heat, water, chemicals, enzymes, or bacteria

di·ges·tive /dī jéstiv, di-/ *adj* relating to or aiding in the digestion of food ■ *n* something that aids or promotes the digesting of food —**di·ges·tive·ly** *adv*

di·ges·tive gland *n* a gland that secretes digestive enzymes, e.g., the pancreas in vertebrates

di·ges·tive tract *n* ANAT same as **alimentary canal**

dig·ger /díggər/ *n* **1.** somebody or something that digs **2.** a tool, machine, or part of a machine that is used for digging or excavation **3.** another spelling of **Digger**

Dig·ger (*plural* **Dig·gers** or **dig·gers**) *n* **1.** a member of a Native North American people who gathered food mainly by digging for roots (*sometimes used disparagingly*) **2.** somebody from Australia, especially a soldier who served in World War I, or somebody from New Zealand, especially a soldier who served in World War I or II (*informal*)

dig·gings /díggingz/ *n* a place where something is mined, especially precious metals or gems ■ *npl* material that has been dug out of a hole or mine

dight /dīt/ (**dight·ed** or **dight, dight·ing, dights**) *vt* to equip, dress, or adorn somebody (*archaic*) [Old English *dihtan*, via Germanic < Latin *dictare* "say often," (see DICTATE)]

dig·i·cam /díjee kàm/ *n* PHOTOGRAPHY same as **digital camera**

dig·it /díjjit/ *n* **1.** MATH NUMERAL IN DECIMAL SYSTEM one of the ten Arabic numerals, 0 through 9, that are used to represent numbers in the decimal system **2.** MATH NUMERAL IN ANY NUMBER SYSTEM in any system of numbering, a symbol that represents a number **3.** ANAT HUMAN FINGER OR TOE a finger or toe of a human **4.** ZOOL ANIMAL FINGER OR TOE a finger, toe, or similar part on a terrestrial vertebrate **5.** MEASURE FINGER WIDTH the width of a finger used as a unit of length, equal to approximately ¾ in./2 cm [14C. < Latin *digitus* "finger, toe"]

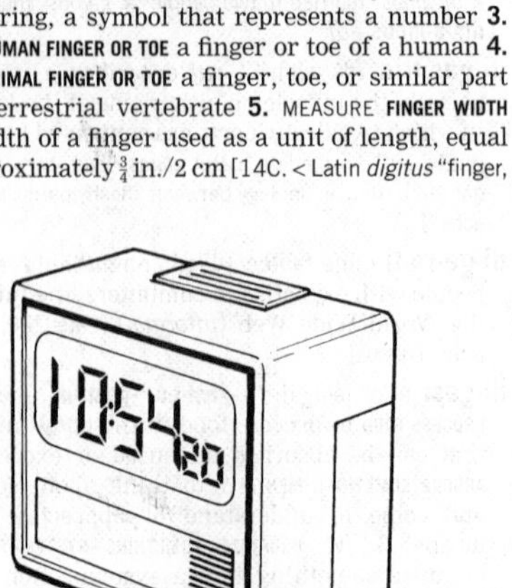

digital: clock displaying the time in numerical form

dig·i·tal /díjjit'l/ *adj* **1.** REPRESENTING DATA AS NUMBERS processing, storing, transmitting, representing, or displaying data in the form of numerical digits, as in a digital computer **2.** REPRESENTING SOUND/LIGHT WAVES AS NUMBERS representing a varying physical quantity such as sound or light waves by means of discrete signals interpreted as numbers, usually in the binary system, as in a digital recording or digital television **3.** ECON OF E-COMMERCE relating to, used in, or characterized by e-commerce **4.** LIKE FINGER like a finger or toe **5.** DONE WITH FINGERS using or operated by a finger or fingers [15C. < Latin *digitalis* < *digitus* "finger, toe"] —**dig·i·tal·ly** *adv*

dig·i·tal au·di·o·tape *n* a magnetic tape used in the digital recording of music

dig·i·tal cam·er·a *n* a camera that records and stores photographic images in digital form. The images can be viewed and manipulated by the camera, loaded onto a computer, and printed as a photograph or e-mailed as an image.

dig·i·tal cash *n* credit in the form of an encoded bank authorization that can be used for buying goods or services on the Internet

dig·i·tal cer·tif·i·cate *n* a unique code assigned to a buyer, merchant, or bank in online business transactions that allows the recipient to verify the sender's identity and encrypt a response

dig·i·tal coins *npl* electronic payment in small denominations (*used in e-commerce*)

dig·i·tal com·put·er *n* a computer that stores and performs a series of mathematical and logical operations on data expressed as discrete signals interpreted as numbers, usually in the form of binary notation

dig·i·tal dis·play *n* a video display that renders a limited number of colors and shades of gray

dig·i·tal di·vide *n* the difference in opportunities available to people who have access to modern information technology and those who do not

dig·i·tal en·cryp·tion stan·dard *n* a standard for private key data encryption that uses 56-bit encryption (*used in e-commerce*)

dig·i·tal im·age·ry, dig·i·tal im·ag·ing *n* the process of altering a digital image on a computer

dig·i·tal·is /díjji tálliss/ (*plural* **-tal·is·es** or **-tal·is**) *n* **1.** a drug containing glycoside, prepared from dried foxglove leaves. Use: heart stimulant. **2.** a plant such as the foxglove. Native to: Europe, Asia. Genus: *Digitalis*. [Early 17C. Via modern Latin, "foxglove" < Latin, "of or like a finger" (see DIGITAL); from the shape of the flowers]

dig·i·tal·ize[1] /díjjit'l īz/ (**-ized, -iz·ing, -iz·es**), **dig·i·tal·ise** *vt* COMPUT same as **digitize** [Mid-20C. < DIGITAL] —**dig·i·tal·i·za·tion** /dìjjit'l záysh'n/ *n*

dig·i·tal·ize[2] /díjjit'l īz/, **dig·i·tal·ise** *n* to treat somebody with digitalis [Mid-20C. < DIGITAL]

dig·i·tal log·ic *n* the use of digital circuitry to determine if a condition is true or false

dig·i·tal ob·ject i·den·ti·fi·er *n* an identifying symbol for a web file that redirects users to any new Internet location for that file

dig·i·tal re·cord·ing *n* **1.** audio recording in which sounds are stored as numbers, producing purer sound **2.** a recording made using the digital method

dig·i·tal sig·na·ture *n* a digital signal or pattern that identifies the user or the user's habits

Dig·i·tal Sub·scrib·er Line *n* full form of **DSL**

dig·i·tal tab·let *n* COMPUT same as **graphics tablet**

dig·i·tal tel·e·vi·sion *n* **1.** television broadcasting in which the picture is transmitted as discrete signals represented as numbers **2.** a television set specially constructed or adapted for receiving such signals

dig·i·tal vid·e·o disk, dig·i·tal ver·sa·tile disk *n* TECH full form of **DVD**

dig·i·tal vid·e·o disk-ROM *n* TECH full form of **DVD-ROM**

dig·i·tal wal·let *n* an item of software that stores information about an online shopper's payment options and may contain credit in the form of digital cash, or credit card or bank information

dig·i·tal watch *n* a watch that shows the time in numerical form, instead of by hands on a dial

dig·i·tate /díjji tàyt/, **dig·i·tat·ed** /díjji tàytəd/ *adj* **1.** having fingers or toes, or having parts that are like fingers or toes **2.** describes leaves that have divisions or parts arrayed from a central point like the spread fingers of a hand —**dig·i·ta·tion** /dìjji táysh'n/ *n*

di·gi·ter·a·ti *npl* COMPUT same as **digerati** (*informal*)

dig·i·ti·grade /díjjitə gràyd/ *adj* describes the gait of animals such as cats and deer that walk with only the tips of the digits touching the ground, the rest of the foot being raised ■ *n* an animal such as a cat or deer that walks with its weight on its digits and the back of its foot raised [Mid-19C. < French < Latin *digitus* "finger, toe" + *gradus* "step"]

dig·i·tize /díjji tīz/ (**-tized, -tiz·ing, -tiz·es**) *vt* to convert an image, graph, or other data into digital form for processing on a computer —**dig·i·ti·za·tion** /dìjjiti záysh'n/ *n* —**dig·i·tiz·er** *n*

dig·i·ti·zing tab·let /díjjitīzing-/ *n* COMPUT same as **graphics tablet**

dig·i·tox·in /díjji tóksin/ *n* a bitter white glycoside found in foxglove leaves. Use: heart stimulant. Formula: $C_{41}H_{64}O_{13}$. [Late 19C. Blend of DIGITALIS + TOXIN]

dig·i·zine /díjji zeèn/ *n* a magazine that is delivered in digital form either on the Internet or on a CD-ROM (*informal*) [Blend of DIGITAL + MAGAZINE]

di·glos·si·a /dī gláwssee ə, -glóssee ə/ *n* the existence of a formal literary form of a language, considered more prestigious, along with a colloquial form used by most speakers and considered of lower status [Mid-20C. < Greek *diglōssos* "bilingual" < *glōssa* "language"]

dig·ni·fied /dígnə fīd/ *adj* showing self-respect or behaving in a proper and respectable way

dig·ni·fy /dígnə fī/ (**-fied, -fy·ing, -fies**) *vt* **1.** GIVE DISTINCTION TO SOMETHING to give honor or an aura of importance to something **2.** GIVE UNDESERVED ATTENTION TO SOMETHING to treat somebody or something as honorable or worthy of attention when this treatment is undeserved ○ *I won't dignify his insult with a response.* **3.** ENNOBLE SOMEBODY to award an honor to somebody, or raise somebody to noble rank [15C. Via obsolete French *dignifier* < late Latin *dignificare* "make worthy" < Latin *dignus* "worthy"]

dig·ni·tar·y /dígnə tèrree/ (*plural* **-ies**) *n* somebody who holds a high rank or position

dig·ni·ty /dígnətee/ (*plural* **-ties**) *n* **1.** SELF-RESPECT a proper sense of pride and self-respect **2.** SERIOUSNESS IN BEHAVIOR seriousness, respectfulness, or formality in somebody's behavior and bearing **3.** WORTHINESS the condition of being worthy of respect, esteem, or honor **4.** DUE RESPECT the respect or honor that a high rank or position should be shown **5.** HIGH OFFICE a high rank, position, or honor [12C. Via French < Latin *dignitas* < *dignus* "worthy"]

dig·ox·in /dī jóksin/ *n* a glycoside extracted from foxglove leaves. Use: heart stimulant. [Mid-20C. Contraction of DIGITOXIN, a similar glycoside]

di·graph /dī gràf/ *n* **1.** a pair of letters that represents a single speech sound, e.g., "ng" in "ring" or "ch" in "child" **2.** PRINTING same as **ligature** (sense 5) —**di·graph·ic** /dī gráffik/ *adj*

di·gress /dī gréss/ (**-gressed, -gress·ing, -gress·es**) *vi* to move away from the central topic or line of argument in speaking or writing, usually temporarily [Early 16C. < Latin *digress-*, past participle of *digredi* "step aside" < *gradus* "step"]

di·gres·sion /dī grésh'n/ *n* **1.** an act or instance of departing from the central topic or line of argument while speaking or writing, usually temporarily **2.** a part of something spoken or written that departs from the central topic or line of argument, usually temporarily —**di·gres·sion·al** *adj* —**di·gres·sion·ar·y** *adj*

di·gres·sive /dī gréssiv/ *adj* tending to depart from the central topic or line of argument —**di·gres·sive·ly** *adv* —**di·gres·sive·ness** *n*

di·he·dral /dī heédrəl/ *n* **1.** *also* **di·he·dral an·gle** the angle contained between two planes that intersect, measured by the angle made by any two lines at right angles to the two planes **2.** the angle between an upwardly inclined aircraft wing and a horizontal line [Late 18C. < DI-[1] + Greek *hedra* "seat, base"]

di·hy·brid /dī hībrid/ *n* an organism that is heterozygous for two genes, so that each gene is represented by two variant forms (**alleles**) —**di·hy·brid·ism** *n*

di·hy·dric /dī hídrik/ *adj* containing two hydroxyl groups

Di·jon /dee zháwN/ capital of the Côte d'Or Department in east central France. It is situated at the foot of the Côte d'Or hills, about 155 mi./249 km southeast of Paris. Population: 149,867 (1999).

dik-dik

dik-dik /dík dik/ (*plural* **dik-diks** or *same*) *n* a small long-muzzled antelope. Native to: dry regions of eastern Africa. Genus: *Madoqua.* [Late 19C. An imitation of the animal's cry]

dike[1] /dīk/, **dyke** *n* **1. EMBANKMENT TO PREVENT FLOODS** an embankment built along the shore of a sea or lake or beside a river to hold back the water and prevent flooding **2. BARRIER** a barrier or obstacle meant to keep something out **3. CAUSEWAY** a raised roadway across a swamp or body of water **4. DITCH** a drainage ditch or other artificial watercourse **5.** GEOL **LONG MASS OF IGNEOUS ROCK** a vertical or near-vertical mass of igneous rock that has forced its way upward through overlying strata ■ *vt* (**diked, dik·ing, dikes; dyked, dyk·ing, dykes**) **1. PROTECT LAND WITH DYKES** to enclose or protect an area of land with a dike or series of dikes **2. DRAIN LAND WITH DITCHES** to drain an area of land using ditches [13C. Probably < Old Norse *dík* < Germanic, "hole and mound resulting from digging"] —**dik·er** *n*

dike[2] *n* SOC SCI another spelling of **dyke**[1] (*slang offensive*)

dik·tat /dik taát/ *n* **1.** a statement or order that cannot be opposed **2.** a harsh settlement imposed on a defeated opponent or enemy [Mid-20C. Via German < Latin *dictatum* < past participle of *dictare* (see DICTATE)]

di·lap·i·date /di láppə dàyt/ (**-dat·ed, -dat·ing, -dates**) *vti* to become, or make something become, partly ruined or decayed, especially through neglect [Early 16C. < Latin *dilapidat-*, past participle of *dilapidare* "squander" < *lapis* "stone"] —**di·lap·i·da·tion** /-làppi dáysh'n/ *n*

di·lap·i·dat·ed /di láppi dàytəd/ *adj* partly ruined or decayed, especially as a result of neglect

di·la·tan·cy /dī láyt'nsee, di-/ *n* the tendency of a substance to become more viscous or solid when affected by an outside force or agitation

di·la·tant /dī láyt'nt, di-/ *adj* **1. ABLE TO EXPAND** able or likely to expand **2.** CHEM **BECOMING MORE VISCOUS** tending to become more viscous or solid when affected by an outside force or agitation ■ *n* **SUBSTANCE CAUSING EXPANSION** a substance that causes another to expand

dil·a·ta·tion /dìlə táysh'n, dìllə-/ *n* **1.** same as **dilation** (senses 1–2) **2.** a lengthy detailed explanation or discussion of a subject by a speaker or writer —**dil·a·ta·tion·al** *adj*

dil·a·ta·tor /dílə tàytər, díllə-/ *n* MED same as **dilator** (sense 2)

di·late /dī láyt, di-, dī làyt/ (**-lat·ed, -lat·ing, -lates**) *v* **1.** *vti* to become, or cause something to become, wider, larger, or stretched **2.** *vi* to talk or write at great length [14C. Via French < Latin *dilatare* "spread widely apart" < *latus* "wide"] —**di·lat·a·ble** *adj* —**di·la·tive** *adj*

di·la·tion /dī láysh'n, di-/ *n* **1. EXPANDING OF SOMETHING** the act or process of widening or being widened, enlarging or being enlarged, or stretching or being stretched **2. EXPANDED CONDITION** a condition in which something is widened, enlarged, or stretched **3. EXPANDED THING** something, especially a part of something else, that has become widened, enlarged, or stretched **4.** MED **ENLARGEMENT OF BODY PART** the stretching or enlargement of a hollow organ or body cavity

di·la·tion and cu·ret·tage *n* SURG full form of **D and C**

dil·a·tom·e·ter /dìllə tómmətər, dìlə-/ *n* an instrument used to measure expansion, e.g., in the volume of a liquid —**dil·a·to·met·ric** /dìllətə méttrik, dìlə-/ *adj* —**dil·a·tom·e·try** *n*

di·la·tor /dī láytər, di-, dī làytər/ *n* **1.** a muscle or muscle group that expands a part of the body **2.** something that makes something else wider or larger, especially a medical instrument used to widen a body passage

dil·a·to·ry /díllə tàwree/ *adj* **1.** tending to waste time or move slowly **2.** intended to cause a delay or waste time [15C. < late Latin *dilatorius* < Latin *dilat-*, past participle of *differre* "to delay"] —**dil·a·to·ri·ly** /dìllə táwrəlee/ *adv* —**dil·a·to·ri·ness** *n*

dil·do /díldō/ (*plural* **-dos**), **dil·doe** (*plural* **-does**) *n* an object shaped like a penis, used in sexual activity [Late 16C. Origin ?]

~~dilema~~ incorrect spelling of **dilemma**

di·lem·ma /di lémmə/ *n* **1.** a situation in which somebody must choose one of two or more unsatisfactory alternatives **2.** in logic, a form of reasoning that, though valid, leads to two undesirable alternatives [Early 16C. Via Latin < Greek *dilēmma* "double proposition" < *lēmma* "proposition"]

dil·et·tante /dìllə taánt/ *n* (*plural* **-tantes** or **-tan·ti** /-taántee/) **1. DABBLER IN ART OR KNOWLEDGE** somebody who takes up a subject or interest in a superficial or desultory way **2. ART LOVER** somebody who is very interested in the fine arts (*dated*) ■ *adj* **SUPERFICIAL** relating to somebody who has only a superficial understanding of something [Mid-18C. < Italian < *dilettare* "to delight" < Latin *delectare* (see DELIGHT)] —**dil·et·tan·tish** *adj* —**dil·et·tan·tism** *n*

dil·i·gence[1] /díllәjәnss/ *n* **1.** persistent and hard-working effort in doing something **2.** the care or attention expected by the law in doing something such as fulfilling the terms of a contract [14C. Via French < Latin *diligentia* < *diligent-* (see DILIGENT)]

dil·i·gence[2] /díllәjәnss/ *n* a stagecoach, especially in France [Late 17C. < French, shortening of *carrosse de diligence* "coach of speed"]

dil·i·gent /díllәjәnt/ *adj* showing persistent and hard-working effort in doing something [14C. Via French < Latin *diligent-*, present participle of *diligere* "value highly, love" < *legere* "choose"] —**dil·i·gent·ly** *adv*

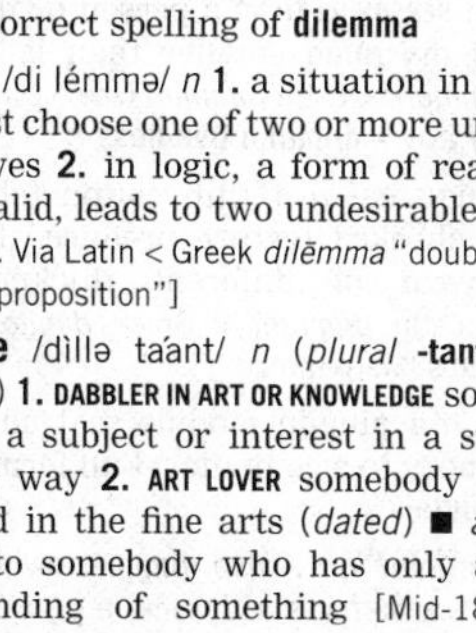

dill

dill /dil/ *n* **1.** the leaves or seeds of an aromatic herb. Use: as flavoring or garnish. **2.** an herb with fine feathery leaves and flat flower heads that produces dill. Latin name: *Anethum graveolens.* [Old English *dile*, origin ?] —**dilled** *adj*

dill pick·le *n* a cucumber that has been pickled in dill-flavored vinegar or brine

dil·ly /díllee/ (*plural* **-lies**) *n* a remarkable thing or a person (*slang*)

dil·ly-dal·ly /díllee dàllee/ (**dil·ly-dal·lied, dil·ly-dal·ly·ing, dil·ly-dal·lies**) *vi* to waste time by being too slow, doing nothing, or being unable to decide what to do (*informal*) [Doubled < DALLY[1]]

dil·u·ent /díllyoo әnt/ *adj* used for diluting something ■ *n* a substance that dilutes another substance [Early 18C. < Latin *diluent-*, present participle of *diluere* (see DILUTE)]

di·lute /dī lo͞ot, di-/ *v* (**-lut·ed, -lut·ing, -lutes**) **1.** *vt* **MAKE OR BECOME THINNER** to make something thinner or weaker by adding water or another liquid, or to become thinner or weaker in this way **2.** *vti* **LESSEN STRENGTH** to reduce the strength or effect of something, or become reduced in strength or effect **3.** *vt* FIN **REDUCE VALUE OF STOCK** to decrease the value of a stock by issuing additional shares ■ *adj* **THINNED** thinner or weaker than at full concentration because of the addition of water or another liquid [Mid-16C. < Latin *dilut-*, past participle of *diluere* "to wash away" < *lavare* "to wash"] —**di·lute·ness** *n* —**di·lut·er** *n* —**di·lu·tive** *adj*

di·lu·tion /dī lo͞osh'n, di lo͞osh'n/ *n* **1. ACT OF THINNING OR WEAKENING** a thinning or weakening of a substance, usually a liquid, by the addition of another substance such as water **2. LESS CONCENTRATED LIQUID** a substance, especially a liquid, that has been made thinner or weaker by the addition of water or another liquid **3. LESSENING OF STRENGTH** a lessening of the strength or effect of something **4. THINNED OR WEAKENED STATE** a thinned or weakened condition **5.** FIN **DECREASE IN STOCK VALUE** a decrease in the value of a stock caused by the issue of additional shares

di·lu·vi·al /di lo͞ovee әl/, **di·lu·vi·an** /-vee әn/ *adj* relating to the great Flood described in the Bible [Mid-17C. < late Latin *diluvialis* < Latin *diluvium* "flood" < *diluere* (see DILUTE)]

dim /dim/ *adj* (**dim·mer, dim·mest**) **1. NOT WELL LIT** not easy to see in or into because of inadequate light **2. PRODUCING LITTLE LIGHT** not producing very much light, or less bright than is usual **3. DULL IN COLOR** dull or subdued in color or brightness **4. NOT CLEARLY VISIBLE** not clearly visible or distinct **5. NOT EASY TO PERCEIVE** difficult to understand or perceive with the senses **6. NOT CLEAR TO MIND** not clearly recalled or perceived **7. NOT SEEING CLEARLY** not able to see clearly **8. IMPROBABLE** unlikely to be successful or fulfilled **9. UNINTELLIGENT** regarded as lacking in intelligence or mental sharpness (*informal*) ■ *v* (**dimmed, dim·ming, dims**) **1.** *vti* **MAKE OR BECOME DIM** to make something less bright, clear, or keen, or become less bright, clear, or keen **2.** *vt* **SWITCH HEADLIGHTS TO LOW BEAMS** to switch the headlights of a motor vehicle from high beams to low beams ■ **dims** *npl* **LOW BEAMS** the low beams of a motor vehicle's headlights [Old English < Germanic] —**dim·ly** *adv* —**dim·ma·ble** *adj* —**dim·ness** *n*

dim. *abbr* **1.** dimension **2.** MUSIC diminuendo **3.** GRAM diminutive

Di·Mag·gio /də maázhee ō, də májjee ō/, **Joe** (1914–99) US baseball player. Considered one of the greatest hitters and center fielders of all time, he played with the New York Yankees from 1936 to 1951 and was elected to the Baseball Hall of Fame in 1955. Full name **DiMaggio, Joseph Paul.** Known as **Joltin' Joe, Yankee Clipper**

> "A ball player's got to be kept hungry to become a big-leaguer. That's why no boy from a rich family ever made the big leagues."
> [Attributed to Joe DiMaggio]

dim bulb (*slang*) *n* an offensive term for somebody who is regarded as having little or no intelligence ■ *adj* inadequately thought out or planned with no intelligent input (*disapproving*) [Early 20C]

dime /dīm/ *n* a US or Canadian coin worth ten cents [14C. Via French, "tithe, tenth part" < Latin *decima*, form of *decimus* "tenth" < *decem* "ten"] ◇ **a dime a dozen** very numerous or common, and therefore of little value (*informal*) ◇ **one thin dime** a very small amount of money

dime bag *n* a quantity of an illegal drug sold for a set price, originally ten dollars (*slang*)

di·men·hy·dri·nate /dī men hídrə nàyt, -mən-/ *n* an antihistamine drug. Use: treatment of motion sickness. [Mid-20C. < DIMETHYL + HYDR- + AMINE]

dime nov·el *n* a cheap paperback novel with a melodramatic or romantic story, especially one published in the United States from the mid-1800s to the early 1900s

di·men·sion /di ménshən, dī-/ *n* **1. MEASUREMENT OF SIZE OF SOMETHING** a measurement of something in one or more directions such as length, width, or height ○ *the dimensions of the room* **2. SIZE** the size or extent of something (*usually used in the plural*) ○ *discussed the dimensions of the problem* 3. **ASPECT** a feature or distinctive part of something ○ *the spiritual dimension of life* 4. **LIFELIKE QUALITY** the artistic quality of appearing to be convincing and lifelike ○ *The characters in this novel lack dimension.* 5. **LEVEL OF REALITY** a level of consciousness, existence, or reality 6. MATH **COORDINATE FOR SPACE AND TIME** a coordinate used with others to locate a point in space and time 7. PHYS **PROPERTY DEFINING PHYSICAL QUANTITY** one of a group of properties or magnitudes such as mass or time that collectively define a physical quantity ■ *vt* (**-sioned, -sion·ing, -sions**) 1. **MAKE SOMETHING TO REQUIRED SIZE** to cut or make something to a specific size 2. **INDICATE SIZE OF SOMETHING** to specify the size of something [14C. Via French < Latin *dimension-* < *dimetiri* "to measure out" < *metiri* "to measure"] —**di·men·sion·al** *adj* —**di·men·sion·al·i·ty** /di mènshə nállətee, dī-/ *n* —**di·men·sion·al·ly** *adv* —**di·men·sion·less** *adj*

di·men·sion·al a·nal·y·sis *n* 1. the procedure of checking or ensuring that the terms in a physical equation have the same dimensions 2. the application of knowledge of the physical dimensions of a system to infer information mathematically too complex to calculate

di·mer /dīmər/ *n* a molecule made up of two simpler identical molecules —**di·mer·ic** /dī mérrik/ *adj*

di·mer·cap·rol /dīmər ká prawl/ *n* a colorless oily substance with an unpleasant smell. Use: antidote to heavy metal poisoning. [Mid-20C. < DI-[1] + MERCAPTAN + PROPANE]

dime store *n* a store that sells a range of inexpensive goods [The maximum price of goods sold there being, originally, one dime]

dime-store *adj* 1. not costing very much money 2. of low or second-rate quality

dim·e·ter /dímmətər/ *n* 1. a line of verse consisting of two metrical feet 2. verse made up of lines consisting of two metrical feet [Late 16C. < late Latin < Greek *dimetros* "having two measures" < *metron* "measure"]

di·meth·o·ate /dī méthō àyt/ *n* a white crystalline compound. Use: insecticide. Formula: $C_5H_{12}NO_3PS_2$. [Mid-20C. < DIMETHYL + THIO-]

di·meth·yl /dī méth'l/ *adj* having two methyl groups in a molecule

di·meth·yl·a·mine /dī mèth'l á meen/ *n* a soluble flammable gas with an odor like ammonia. Use: solvent, in drugs, synthesis of chemicals. Formula: C_2H_7N.

di·meth·yl·gly·ox·ime /dī mèth'l glī ók seem/ *n* a white powdery or crystalline substance soluble in alcohol. Use: reagent, biochemical research.

di·meth·yl·ni·tros·a·mine /dī mèth'l nī tróssə meen, -nītrō sá-/ *n* a yellow carcinogenic compound. Source: tobacco smoke, some foods. Formula: $C_2H_6N_2O$.

di·meth·yl·sulf·ox·ide /dī mèth'l sul fók sīd/ *n* CHEM full form of **DMSO**

dimin. *abbr* 1. MUSIC diminuendo 2. GRAM diminutive

di·min·ish /di mínnish/ (**-ished, -ish·ing, -ish·es**) *v* 1. *vti* **MAKE OR BECOME SMALLER** to make something smaller or less important, or become smaller or less important 2. *vti* **SEEM OR MAKE SEEM SMALLER** to appear smaller, or make something appear smaller 3. *vti* ARCHIT **TAPER FROM BOTTOM TO TOP** to taper from the lower part to the upper part, or make something taper in this way 4. *vt* MUSIC **CONTRACT MUSICAL INTERVAL** to contract a perfect or minor musical interval by one semitone [15C. Blend of obsolete *diminue* (< Latin *minuere* "lessen") + *minish* "diminish" (< Latin *minutia* "smallness")] —**di·min·ish·ing·ly** *adv* —**di·min·ish·ment** *n*

di·min·ished /di mínnisht/ *adj* describes a musical interval or chord reduced by one semitone

di·min·ished re·spon·si·bil·i·ty *n* in criminal law, a partial defense where the defendant seeks to argue reduced culpability on the grounds that a psychiatric disorder reduced responsibility for his or her actions

di·min·ish·ing re·turns /di mìnishing-/ *npl* additional increases in something such as profits or benefits that do not rise in proportion to the additional effort or investment necessary to produce them

di·min·u·en·do /di mìnnyoo éndō/ MUSIC *adv* same as **decrescendo** ■ *n* (*plural* **-dos**) same as **decrescendo** [Late 18C. < Italian, present participle of *diminuire* "diminish" < Latin *diminuere* (see DIMINUTION)] —**di·min·u·en·do** *adj*

dim·i·nu·tion /dìmmə nóosh'n/ *n* 1. a lessening, decreasing, or reduction of something, or the result of such a reduction 2. the repetition of a musical phrase, using notes that are of a shorter duration than in the original phrase [14C. < Latin *diminut-*, past participle of *diminuere* "break into small pieces" < *minuere* "lessen"]

di·min·u·tive /di mínnyətiv/ *adj* 1. **VERY SMALL** very small or much smaller than is usual 2. **INDICATING SMALLNESS** describes a suffix such as "-ette" or "-let" that indicates small size, youth, familiarity, or fondness or a word or name formed with such a suffix ■ *n* 1. **WORD INDICATING SMALLNESS** a word or name that indicates small size, youth, familiarity, or fondness, e.g., "kitchenette" or "booklet" 2. **SUFFIX INDICATING SMALLNESS** a suffix, e.g., "-ette," or "-let," that indicates small size, youth, familiarity, or fondness 3. **VERY SMALL PERSON OR THING** a person or thing that is very small or much smaller than is usual [14C. < French *diminutif* < Latin *diminut-* (see DIMINUTION)] —**di·min·u·tive·ly** *adv* —**di·min·u·tive·ness** *n*

dim·i·ty /dímmətee/ *n* a thin cotton fabric with a striped or checked texture produced by weaving together yarn of different thicknesses [15C. < medieval Latin *dimitum* < Greek *dimitos* "of double thread" < *mitos* "warp thread"]

DIMM /dim/ *n* a plug-in module that adds random-access memory to a computer. Full form **dual in-line memory module**

dim·mer /dímmər/ *n* 1. *also* **dim·mer switch** **DEVICE FOR VARYING LIGHT'S BRIGHTNESS** a device, e.g., a variable resistor, that can be used to vary the brightness of a light by regulating the amount of current supplied to it 2. **SWITCH FOR DIMMING HEADLIGHTS** a control used to lower a car's headlights or raise them to full beam ■ **dim·mers** *npl* **LOW BEAMS** the low beams of a motor vehicle's headlights

di·mor·phism /dī máwr fìzzəm/ *n* 1. BIOL **EXISTENCE OF DIFFERENT FORMS WITHIN SPECIES** the existence of two or more different forms within a biological species. In sexual dimorphism, male and female may vary in color, size, or some other trait. 2. BOT **EXISTENCE OF DIFFERENT PLANT PART FORMS** the existence in a plant of two different forms of the same organ or part, as when there are two forms of flowers 3. CHEM **EXISTENCE OF DIFFERENT CRYSTALLINE FORMS** the existence of a substance in two different crystalline forms —**di·mor·phic** *adj* —**di·mor·phous** *adj*

dim-out *n* 1. a restriction on the use of lights at night, ordered by a government or the military, in order to make a city less visible to nighttime air raids 2. the partial darkness caused when the use of lights at night is restricted, e.g., for military reasons

dim·ple /dímp'l/ *n* 1. **INDENTED AREA IN SKIN** a naturally occurring slightly indented area in the skin and flesh of the cheek, chin, or other part of the body 2. **INDENTED SURFACE AREA** an indented, hollowed, or depressed area in the surface of something ■ *v* (**-pled, -pling, -ples**) 1. *vt* **PRODUCE DIMPLES IN CHEEKS** to cause dimples to appear in the cheeks by smiling 2. *vti* **FORM DIMPLE** to form a dimple or dimples in something, or have a dimple or dimples ○ *This mold dimples the surface of the golf ball.* [14C. < assumed Old English *dympel* < Germanic] —**dim·ply** *adj*

dim sum /dìm sóom/ *n* dumplings, spring rolls, and various other traditional Chinese dishes served in small portions as a meal [< Chinese (Cantonese) *tím sam* "small center"]

dim·wit /dím wìt/ *n* an offensive term that deliberately insults somebody's intelligence (*informal*) —**dim·wit·ted** *adj*

din[1] /din/ *n* **LOUD PERSISTENT NOISE** a loud persistent noise, especially one composed of confused sounds ■ *v* (**dinned, din·ning, dins**) 1. *vi* **BE NOISY** to make a loud persistent noise 2. *vt* **INSTILL SOMETHING THROUGH REPETITION** to fix something in somebody's mind by repeating it over and over again [Old English *dyne* < Indo-European]

din[2] *symbol* MONEY dinar

di·nar /di náar, dee náar/ *n* a currency unit in some North African, southwestern Asian, and southeastern European countries. See table at **currency** [Mid-17C. Via late Greek < Latin *denarius* (see DENARIUS)]

Di·nar·ic Alps /di nàrrik-/ southeastern extension of the Eastern Alps that runs parallel to the Adriatic coast through Slovenia, Croatia, Bosnia-Herzegovina, and Yugoslavia, as far south as Albania. Highest peak: Bobotov Kuk 8,274 ft./ 2,522 m.

dine /dīn/ (**dined, din·ing, dines**) *v* 1. *vi* **EAT DINNER** to eat the main meal of the day ○ *We dine early.* 2. *vi* **EAT** to have a particular food or type of food in a meal ○ *We dined on vegetables and rice.* 3. *vt* **PROVIDE DINNER FOR SOMEBODY** to provide dinner for somebody, or take somebody out to dinner (*informal*) [13C. < Old French *di(s)ner*]

dine out *vi* to eat dinner somewhere other than at home, especially in a restaurant

din·er /dīnər/ *n* 1. a small inexpensive restaurant, often resembling a railroad dining car, where customers eat at the counter or in booths 2. somebody eating a meal, especially dinner

di·ne·ro /di nérrō/ *n Hispanic* same as **money** (*informal*) [Mid-19C. < Spanish]

Di·nes·en /deenəss'n/, **Isak** (1885–1962) Danish writer. A much-traveled author, she is best known for her short stories such as *Seven Gothic Tales* (1934) and her semiautobiographical work, *Out of Africa* (1938). Pseudonym of **Blixen-Finecke, Karen Christence, Baroness.** Born **Dinesen, Karen Christence**

> "What is man, when you come to think upon him, but a minutely set, ingenious machine for turning, with infinite artfulness, the red wine of Shiraz into urine?"
> [Isak Dinesen, "The Dreamers," *Seven Gothic Tales*; 1934]

di·nette /dī nét/ *n* 1. an alcove or part of a room where meals are eaten, especially in or near a kitchen 2. a table and chairs used to furnish a dinette

ding[1] /ding/ *v* (**dinged, ding·ing, dings**) 1. *vti* **RING OR MAKE RING** to ring with a high-pitched sound, or make something do this 2. *vt* same as **din**[1] *v* (sense 2) 3. *vi* **TALK REPEATEDLY** to talk repeatedly or wearyingly about something ■ *n* **RINGING** a ringing sound, especially one made by a bell [Mid-16C. An imitation of the sound]

ding[2] /ding/ (*informal*) *vt* (**dinged, ding·ing, dings**) to make a dent or cause other surface damage in something ■ *n* a dent or other surface damage in something [14C. Probably < Old Norse]

ding-a-ling /díngə lìng/ *n* 1. the sound of a bell, especially a small handheld bell 2. somebody who is considered odd, irrational, or incapable of serious or organized thought (*informal insult*) [Late 19C. An imitation of the sound]

ding·bat /díng bàt/ *n* 1. **PRINTER'S SYMBOL** a symbol or ornamental character used in a printed work, e.g., a star or pointing hand 2. **OBJECT USED AS MISSILE** a brick, rock, or other object that is thrown as a missile 3. **SILLY PERSON** somebody who is considered silly or lacking in intelligence (*informal insult*) 4. **THING WHOSE NAME IS NOT KNOWN** an object whose name has been forgotten or is not known (*slang*) [Mid-19C. Origin ?]

ding-dong *n* 1. **SOUND OF BELL** the sound of a bell being struck two or more times 2. **SOUND IMITATIVE OF BELL SOUND** a ringing or repeated sound that is similar to that made by a bell 3. **IRRATIONAL PERSON** somebody considered as odd, irrational, silly, or lacking in intelligence (*informal insult*) ■ *adj* **FIERCELY CONTESTED** fiercely contested, with advantage shifting continually from one side to another (*informal*) ○ *a ding-dong battle of wills* ■ *vi* (**ding-dong·ed, ding-dong·ing, ding-dongs**) **MAKE RINGING SOUND** to make a ringing sound like a bell [Mid-16C. An imitation of the sound]

dinge /dinj/ *n* a dingy state or condition [Early 19C. Probably back-formation < DINGY]

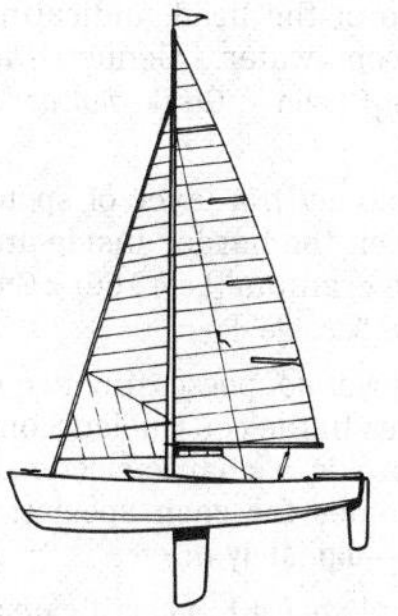

dinghy

din·ghy /díngee/ (*plural* **-ghies**) *n* **1.** a small boat, especially a small sailboat or one that is towed behind or carried on a larger boat **2.** an inflatable life raft [Early 19C. < Hindi *dīgī* "small boat" < *dēgā* "boat"]

din·gle /díng g'l/ *n* a wooded valley (*literary*) [13C. Origin ?]

din·gle·ber·ry /díng g'l bèrree/ (*plural* **-ries**) *n* a small piece of dried feces that clings to the hair or fur near the anus (*slang*) [Mid-20C. Origin ?]

din·go /díng gō/ (*plural* **-goes**) *n* a wild dog with a reddish brown coat. Native to: Australia. Latin name: *Canis dingo*. [Late 18C. < Aboriginal *dingu*]

din·gus /díng gəss/ (*plural* **-gus·es**) *n* something whose name has been forgotten or is not known (*informal*) [Late 19C. Via Dutch, "what's-its-name" < German, form of *Ding* "thing"]

din·gy /dínjee/ (**-gi·er, -gi·est**) *adj* **1. DARK** lacking light in a gloomy or unpleasant way **2. DIRTY OR FADED** dirty-looking, discolored, or faded **3. SHABBY** shabby and uninviting [Mid-18C. Origin ?] —**din·gi·ly** *adv* —**din·gi·ness** *n*

din·ing car /dī́ning-/ *n* a railroad car where meals are served to a train's passengers

din·ing room *n* a room where meals are eaten, especially in a home or hotel

din·ing ta·ble *n* a table on which meals are served, usually in a dining room

di·ni·tro·ben·zene /dī nī trō bén zeen/ *n* a yellow crystalline compound that occurs in three isomeric forms. Use: manufacture of dyes and plastics. Formula: $C_6H_4(NO_2)_2$.

dink /dingk/ *n* SPORTS same as **drop shot** [Mid-20C. An imitation of the sound of the ball being hit]

DINK /dingk/, **dink** *n* a member of a couple who both have careers, usually in well-paid fields, and have no children (*informal*) [Late 20C. Acronym < *dual* (or *double*) *income, no kids*]

Din·ka /díngkə/ (*plural* **-kas** or *same*) *n* **1.** a member of a people who live in the Nile Valley in southern Sudan **2.** a language of the Nilo-Saharan family, spoken in southern Sudan. Native speakers: 1.4 million. [Mid-19C. < Dinka *Jieng* "people"] —**Din·ka** *adj*

din·key /díngkee/ (*plural* **-keys**), **din·ky** (*plural* **-kies**) *n* a small locomotive, used for tasks like shunting rather than long-distance journeys [Mid-19C. Variant of DINKY]

din·ky /díngkee/ *adj* (**-ki·er, -ki·est**) small in size, or of almost no importance (*informal*) ■ *n* (*plural* **-kies**) RAIL another spelling of **dinkey** [Late 18C. < Scots dialect *dink* "finely dressed, trim," origin ?]

din·ner /dínnər/ *n* **1. MAIN MEAL** the main meal of the day, usually eaten in the evening or sometimes in the early afternoon **2. BANQUET** a formal evening meal given in honor of somebody or something **3. RESTAURANT MEAL** a meal that is eaten in a restaurant and consists of several courses, often offered together for a set price **4. FOOD FOR DINNER** the food served during or for a dinner [13C. < Old French *di(s)ner* "dine"]

din·ner dance *n* a formal social occasion at which dancing follows a dinner

din·ner jack·et *n UK* same as **tuxedo** (sense 2)

din·ner tab·le *n* **1.** a table at which meals are eaten, often large and capable of seating a group of people **2.** the occasion at which people are seated at a table to eat a meal together

din·ner the·a·ter *n* a restaurant where a play is performed for customers during or after their dinner

din·ner·time /dínnər tīm/ *n* the time of the day when dinner is usually eaten

din·ner·ware /dínnər wèr/ *n* dishes used for serving or eating a meal, or a set of these dishes

Di·no /dī́nō/ (*plural* **-nos**) *n* a member of the Democratic Party, especially a member of Congress, who usually does not vote the party line and who disagrees with colleagues on issues (*slang*) [20C. Acronym of *Democrat in name only*.]

di·no·flag·el·late /dīnō flájjə làyt, -flájjələt/ *n* a tiny single-celled sea organism with two long slender appendages (**flagella**), occurring in large numbers in plankton. Some types are luminescent and some are toxic, especially when they multiply prolifically to cause a brownish red discoloration (**red tide**). Latin name: *Dinoflagellata*. [Late 19C. < modern Latin *Dinoflagellata* < Greek *dinos* "a whirling" + Latin *flagellum* "whip" (see FLAGELLUM)]

di·no·saur /dī́nə sàwr/ *n* **1.** an extinct, chiefly terrestrial reptile that lived in the Mesozoic Era. Some dinosaurs were the largest known land animals. Order: Ornithischia or Saurischia. **2.** somebody or something that is hopelessly out of date or incapable of adapting to change [Mid-19C. < modern Latin *dinosaurus* < Greek *deinos* "terrible" + *sauros* "lizard"] —**di·no·sau·ri·an** /dīnə sáwree ən/ *adj*

dint /dint/ *n* same as **dent** ■ *vt* (**dint·ed, dint·ing, dints**) **1.** same as **dent 2.** to drive something in forcefully [Old English *dynt* "blow, stroke (especially of a weapon)" < Germanic] ◇ **by dint of** using something, or by the force of something

di·o·cese /dī́ əssiss, -ə seez/ *n* the Christian churches that are under the authority of one bishop, or the district containing them [14C. < Greek *dioikēsis* "administration" < *dioikein* "manage" < *oikos* "house"] —**di·oc·e·san** /dī óssəss'n/ *adj*

Di·o·cle·tian /dī ə kleesh'n/ (245–313) emperor of Rome. Proclaimed emperor in 284, he instituted successful administrative reforms, but his attempt to restore traditional religion by persecuting Christians failed. He abdicated in 305. Full name **Gaius Aurelius Valerius Diocletianus**

di·ode /dī́ ōd/ *n* an electronic device that has two electrodes and is used to convert alternating current to direct current

di·oe·cious /dī eeshəss/, **di·e·cious** *adj* having male and female flowers on different plants of the same species [Mid-18C. < modern Latin *Dioecia*, literally "two houses" < Greek *oikos* "house"] —**di·oe·cism** /-ée sìzzəm/ *n*

di·oes·trus *n, adj* ZOOL Can, UK spelling of **diestrus**

Di·og·e·nes /dī ójjə neez/ (412?–323 B.C.) Greek philosopher. He was a founder of Cynicism, an ancient school of philosophy. He is said to have lived in a tub in Athens and to have wandered the streets with a lamp, seeking an honest man.

> "The mountains too, at a distance, appear airy masses and smooth, but seen near at hand they are rough."
> [Diogenes. Quoted in "Pyrrho," *Lives of the Philosophers*, Diogenes Laërtius; 3rd century A.D.]

di·ol /dī́ àwl/ *n* an alcohol with two hydroxyl groups in each molecule

Di·o·me·des /dī ə meedeez/ *n* in Greek mythology, a former suitor of Helen of Troy who joined the Greek army and became a hero of the Trojan War

Di·o·ne /dī ōnee/ *n* a natural satellite of Saturn discovered in 1684. It has a radius of 348 mi./560 km and the surface exhibits several distinct terrain types.

Di·o·nys·i·ac *adj* MYTHOL same as **Dionysian**

di·o·nys·i·an /dī ə nísh'n, -nízh'n, dī ə nissee ən/ *adj* **1.** relating to or involving drunkenness and sexual activity **2.** in the philosophical writings of Nietzsche, spontaneous and intuitive rather than rational

Di·o·nys·i·an /dī ə nísh'n, -nízh'n, -nissee ən/, **Di·o·nys·i·ac** /dī ə nissee àk, -nízzee àk/ *adj* **1.** relating to the Greek god Dionysus **2.** relating to the worship of the Greek god Dionysus [Early 17C. < Greek *Dionusos* "Dionysus"]

Di·o·ny·si·us Ex·ig·u·us /dī ə níshəss eg zíggyoo əss, dī ə nissee əss-/ (500?–556) Scythian Roman scholar. He introduced the Christian era of dating in his *Cyclus Paschalis* (525). He adopted the name *Exiguus*, "little," as a token of humility.

Di·o·ny·si·us the A·re·o·pa·gite /-àrree óppə jìt, -gìt/ (*fl* 1st century A.D.) Greek religious leader. He converted to Christianity through the preaching of St. Paul, as recorded in the Bible in Acts 17:34, and is thought to have been the first bishop of Athens. He was formerly thought to be the author of influential theological texts that were actually written in about A.D. 500.

Di·o·ny·sus /dī ə nī́səss, -née-/ *n* in Greek mythology, the god of wine, identified with Bacchus

Di·o·phan·tine e·qua·tion /dī ə fàn tīn-, -fàntin-/ *n* an algebraic equation that contains two or more variables, has only whole-number (**integral**) coefficients, and has integral solutions for the variables [After *Diophantus* (fl. 3C B.C.), Greek mathematician]

di·op·side /dī óp sīd/ *n* a pale green mineral consisting of calcium magnesium silicate. Source: igneous rocks. [Early 19C. < DI-[1] + Greek *opsis* "aspect"]

di·op·ter /dī óptər/ *n* a unit of measurement for the power of a lens, especially a spectacle lens, equal to the reciprocal of the focal length of the lens in meters. Symbol **D** [Late 19C. Via French < Latin *dioptra* "instrument for measuring angles" < Greek < *dia-* "through" + *optos* "visible"] —**di·op·tral** *adj*

di·op·tric /dī óptrik/, **di·op·tri·cal** /-óptrik'l/ *adj* **1.** relating to the study of how images are formed by lenses **2.** relating to the refractive powers of light or the measurement of the refractive power of a lens [Mid-17C. < Greek *dioptrikos* < *dioptra* (see DIOPTER)]

di·op·trics /dī óptriks/ *n* the branch of optics that studies the refraction of light by lenses or within the eye (*takes a singular verb*)

Di·or /dee áwr/, **Christian** (1905–57) French couturier. In 1946 he founded the fashion house bearing his name. He achieved worldwide fame by introducing the "New Look" in 1947, which featured narrow shoulders and calf-length skirts.

> "My models—they're the life of my dresses, and I want my dresses to be happy."
> [Christian Dior. Quoted in *Dior*, Françoise Giroud; Stewart Spencer, tr.; 1987]

di·o·ram·a /dī ə ráamə, -rámmə/ *n* **1.** a three-dimensional representation of a scene in which objects or models are arranged in a natural setting against a realistic background, e.g., in a museum **2.** a representation of a scene that is made to appear three-dimensional, e.g., one in which the viewer looks through a hole at objects painted on layers of translucent material [Early 19C. < French, literally "sight through"; < Greek *dia-* "through" after *panorama*] —**di·o·ram·ic** /-rámmik/ *adj*

di·o·rite /dī́ ə rīt/ *n* a dark granular igneous rock that consists of plagioclase and a ferromagnesian mineral such as hornblende. Use: surfacing roads. [Early 19C. < Greek *diorizein* "distinguish" < *orizein* "to limit"] —**di·o·rit·ic** /dī ə ríttik/ *adj*

Di·os·cu·ri /dī ə skyoor ī/ *npl* in Greek mythology, the twin gods Castor and Pollux, who were the sons of Zeus and Leda [Early 20C. < Greek *Dioskouroi* < *Dios* "of Zeus" + *kouros* "boy, son"]

di·ox·ane /dī ók sàyn/ *n* a toxic flammable colorless liquid. Use: solvent for waxes and resins, paints, lacquers, cosmetics, deodorants, textile manufacture. Formula: $C_4H_8O_2$.

di·ox·ide /dī ók sīd/ *n* an oxide that has two oxygen atoms in each molecule

di·ox·in /dī óksin/ *n* a heterocyclic hydrocarbon that is a carcinogen and toxic environmental pollutant. Source: byproduct of combustion processes, manufacture of herbicides and bactericides, chlorine bleaching of paper.

dip /dip/ *v* (**dipped, dip·ping, dips**) **1.** *vt* PUT SOMETHING BRIEFLY IN LIQUID to put something briefly into a liquid or soft mixture and take it out again ○ *She dipped her fingers in the water.* **2.** *vi* MOVE DOWNWARD to sink to a lower level ○ *The plane dipped and then flew on.* **3.** *vt* LOWER SOMETHING to lower something and raise it again ○ *The horse dipped its head.* **4.** *vt* LOWER SOMEBODY OVER ONE ARM while dancing, to lower a partner toward the floor over one arm **5.** *vi* BECOME LESS to fall to a lower level or amount, especially for a short time ○ *Prices dipped at the beginning of October.* **6.** *vti* PUT YOUR HAND IN to put your hand into something in order to take something out ○ *He dipped his hand into his pocket.* **7.** *vt* SCOOP SOMETHING to take up liquid or small pieces of a substance with something such as a spoon or cup ○ *She was dipping soup from the pot.* **8.** *vt* UK AUTOMOT same as **dim** *v* (sense 2) **9.** *vt* DISINFECT ANIMAL to put an animal such as a sheep or dog into a bath of disinfectant **10.** *vi* SLOPE DOWNWARD to slope downward from the horizontal ○ *The road dipped toward the river.* **11.** *vt* MAKE CANDLE FROM WAX to make a candle by repeatedly putting a wick into melted wax ○ *dip a candle* ■ *n* **1.** LOWERING an act of sinking lower, of lowering something, or of putting something in liquid ○ *She acknowledged him with a dip of her head.* **2.** PUTTING HAND IN the action of putting the hand into something to take something out or of scooping up liquid or small pieces of a substance **3.** SWIM a quick swim ○ *There's time for a dip before lunch.* **4.** SLIGHT DECREASE a temporary decrease in the amount or level of something ○ *a dip in sales* **5.** LOWER PLACE a place where the ground slopes, especially to form a hollow ○ *We came to a dip in the road.* **6.** MIXTURE FOR DIPPING FOOD INTO a creamy mixture into which pieces of food can be dipped, often served with crackers or chips ○ *sour cream and onion dip* **7.** CANDLE a candle made by dipping a wick repeatedly in wax **8.** DISINFECTANT FOR ANIMALS a mixture of chemicals used to disinfect animals ○ *sheep dip* **9.** LIQUID CHEMICAL PREPARATION a chemical mixture in which something can be immersed, e.g., a dye or preservative **10.** OFFENSIVE TERM an offensive term that deliberately insults somebody's intelligence or common sense (*slang insult*) **11.** THIEF WHO PICKS POCKETS a pickpocket (*slang*) **12.** GEOG ANGLE OF MAGNETIC NEEDLE the angle that a magnetic needle makes with the horizontal plane **13.** GEOL ANGLE OF ROCK LAYER the angle a sloping rock layer makes to the horizontal ○ *The rock bed has a dip of ten degrees.* **14.** GYMNASTICS PARALLEL BARS EXERCISE an exercise on parallel bars in which the elbows are bent until the gymnast's chin is level with the bars, and the body is raised by straightening the arms [Old English *dyppan* < Germanic]

dip into *vt* **1.** to read parts of a text such as a book or magazine rather than the whole of it **2.** to use some of the money that has been saved

dip., Dip. *abbr* EDUC diploma

di·pep·ti·dase /dī pépti dàyss, -dàyz/ *n* an enzyme that breaks down dipeptides in the final stage of protein digestion

di·pep·tide /dī pép tīd/ *n* a compound composed of two amino acids

di·pha·sic /dī fáyzik/, **di·phase** /dī fàyz/ *adj* describes parasites that have an independent stage in their life cycle

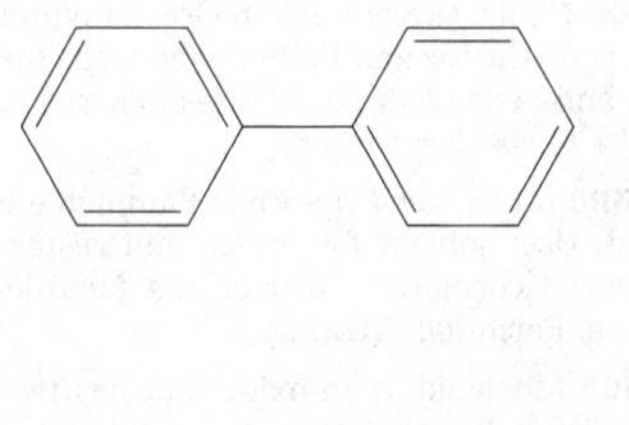

diphenyl

di·phen·yl /dī fénn'l, -feen'l/ *n* a white crystalline substance. Use: fungicide, in organic synthesis, as a heat transfer agent. Formula: $C_{12}H_{10}$.

di·phen·yl·a·mine /dī fènn'lə meen, dī feen'l-/ *n* a colorless toxic crystalline substance. Use: in solid rocket propellants, dyes, manufacture of plastics. Formula: $(C_6H_5)_2NH$.

di·phen·yl·ke·tone /dī feen'l kee tōn, dī fènn'l-/ *n* CHEM same as **benzophenone**

di·phos·gene /dī fóz jeen/ *n* a colorless oily liquid with an extremely poisonous vapor. Use: in gas warfare during World War I. Formula: $ClCOOCCl_3$.

di·phos·phate /dī fóss fàyt/ *n* a chemical compound that contains two phosphate groups per molecule

di·phos·pho·gly·cer·ic ac·id /dī fòsfə gli sèrrik-/ *n* a compound in red blood cells that allows the release of oxygen from hemoglobin

diph·the·ri·a /dif theeree ə, dip-/ *n* a serious infectious disease, caused by a bacterium, *Corynebacterium diphtheriae*, that attacks the membranes of the throat and releases a toxin that damages the heart and the nervous system. The main symptoms are fever, weakness, and severe inflammation of the affected membranes. [Mid-19C. < modern Latin < Greek *diphthera, diphtheris* "hide, skin," indicating the tough membrane developed in the throat] —**diph·the·ri·al** *adj* —**diph·ther·ic** /-thérrik/ *adj* —**diph·the·rit·ic** /dìfthə ríttik, dìpthə-/ *adj* —**diph·ther·oid** /dífthə ròyd, dípthə-/ *adj*

diph·thong /díf thàwng, díp-/ *n* **1.** a complex vowel sound in which the first vowel gradually moves toward a second vowel so that both vowels form one syllable, e.g., "a" and "i" in "rail" **2.** a character formed by joining the two letters "a" and "e" as "æ" or the two letters "o" and "e" as "œ" [15C. Via French < Latin *diphthongus* "two sounds" < Greek *phthoggos* "sound"] —**diph·thon·gal** /dif tháwng g'l, dip-/ *adj*

diph·thong·ize /díf thawng īz, díp-/ (**-ized, -iz·ing, -iz·es**) *vti* to become a diphthong, or make a vowel into a diphthong —**diph·thong·i·za·tion** /dìf thawngi záysh'n, dìp-/ *n*

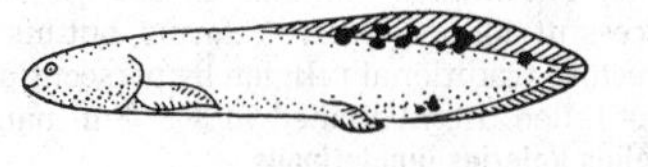

diphycercal

diph·y·cer·cal /dìffi súrk'l/ *adj* describes a tail fin, on some young fish and some adult fish such as lampreys and lungfish, that is found above and below the backbone [Mid-19C. < Greek *diphu-* "of double form" + *kerkos* "tail"]

di·phy·o·dont /dī fī ə dònt/ *adj* used to describe a mammal that grows two sets of teeth in a lifetime [Mid-19C. < Greek *diphu-* "double form" + *odont-* "tooth"]

dipl. *abbr* **1.** diplomat **2.** diplomatic

dipl- *prefix* same as **diplo-** (*used before vowels*)

di·ple·gia /dī pleejə, -jee ə/ *n* inability to move corresponding parts on both the right and left sides of the body [Late 19C. < DI-[1] after PARAPLEGIA] —**di·ple·gic** *adj, n*

di·plex /dī plèks/ *adj* capable of simultaneously transmitting or receiving two signals in the same direction along a telecommunications channel [Late 19C. Alteration of DUPLEX] —**di·plex·er** *n*

diplo- *prefix* **1.** double, twin ○ *diplopod* **2.** having twice the basic number of chromosomes ○ *diplont* [< Greek *diploos* "double"]

dip·lo·blas·tic /dìpplō blástik/ *adj* used to describe an invertebrate animal in which the adult tissues are derived from just two layers of embryonic germ tissue, namely endoderm and ectoderm. Cnidarians are diploblastic.

di·plod·o·cus /di plóddəkəss/ *n* a large herbivorous dinosaur of the late Jurassic Period that had four legs and a very long neck and tail. It had nostrils near the top of the head, indicating that it spent time in deep water. Genus: *Diplodocus.* [Late 19C. < modern Latin < Greek *diploos* "double" + *dokos* "beam"]

dip·lo·ë /dípplō ee/ *n* a layer of spongy bone tissue found between the harder inside and outside bone layers of the cranium [Late 16C. < Greek *diploē* "doubling" < *diploos* "double"]

dip·loid /díp lòyd/ *adj* possessing two matched sets of chromosomes in the cell nucleus, one set from each parent. There is a characteristic diploid number of chromosomes for each species. —**dip·loid·ic** /di plóydik/ *adj* —**dip·loi·dy** *n*

di·plo·ma /di plṓmə/ *n* **1.** a certificate given by a high school, college, university, or professional organization, indicating that somebody has completed a course of education or training and reached the required level of competence **2.** a written document or charter, especially one that confers specific rights or privileges [Mid-17C. Via Latin < Greek, "folded paper" < *diploun* "fold, make double" < *diploos* "double"]

di·plo·ma·cy /di plṓməssee/ *n* **1.** INTERNATIONAL RELATIONS the management of communication and relationships between nations by members and employees of each nation's government **2.** SKILL IN INTERNATIONAL DEALINGS skill in managing communication and relationships between nations **3.** TACT skill and tact in dealing with other people

dip·lo·mat /dípplə màt/ *n* **1.** a member or employee of a government who represents his or her country in dealings with other nations, especially by working in an embassy or consulate abroad **2.** somebody who is tactful and sensitive in dealings with other people [Early 19C. < French *diplomate*, back-formation < *diplomatique* (see DIPLOMATIC)]

dip·lo·mate /dípplə màyt/ *n* somebody who holds a professional diploma ○ *diplomate of the National Board of Medical Examiners*

dip·lo·mat·ic /dìpplə máttik/ *adj* **1.** INVOLVING DIPLOMACY concerned with or involving international diplomacy or the work of diplomats **2.** TACTFUL showing tact and skill in dealing with people **3.** RELATING TO DIPLOMATICS relating to the study of old documents **4.** COPIED ACCURATELY accurately reproducing an original document or printed text [Early 18C. < French *diplomatique* and modern Latin *diplomaticus* < Latin *diploma* (see DIPLOMA)] —**dip·lo·mat·i·cal·ly** *adv*

dip·lo·mat·ic bag *n* a bag in which official correspondence travels between a government office and an embassy of that government in another country, carried by a special messenger. The bag is not subject to the regulations governing ordinary mail.

dip·lo·mat·ic corps *n* all the diplomats from other countries who reside in another nation

dip·lo·mat·ic im·mu·ni·ty *n* the legal status of diplomats, who are not subject to the legal and taxation systems of a country in which they are resident as accredited representatives

dip·lo·mat·ics /dìpplə máttiks/ *n* the study and verification of very old documents (*takes a singular verb*)

di·plo·ma·tist /di plṓmətist/ *n* a professional diplomat

dip·lont /díp lònt/ *n* an organism whose cells, other than reproductive cells, have a diploid number of chromosomes in their nuclei —**dip·lont·ic** /di plóntik/ *adj*

dip·lo·pi·a /di plṓpee ə/ *n* OPHTHALMOL same as **double vision** (*technical*) —**dip·lo·pic** /di plóppik, -plṓpik/ *adj*

dip·lo·pod /dípplə pòd/ *n* a millipede that has two pairs of legs on each body segment. Class: Diplopoda. [Mid-19C. < modern Latin *Diplopoda* < Greek *diploos* "double" + *pod-* "foot"] —**dip·lop·o·dous** /di plóppədəss/ *adj*

dip·lo·tene /dípplō teen/ *n* a stage in the first part of reproductive cell division (**meiosis**) in which paired chromosomes start to move apart from one another but remain connected at points. At these connecting points, genetic information is exchanged. [Early 20C. < DIPLO- + Greek *tainia* "band, ribbon"]

dip·o·dy /díppədee/ (*plural* **-dies**) *n* a line of verse consisting of two stressed units or feet [Late 19C. < Greek *dipod-* "two-footed"]

di·pole /dī pōl/ *n* two equal and opposite magnetized or electrically charged poles that are separated by a short distance —**di·pol·ar** /dī pōlər/ *adj*

di·pole mo·ment *n* **1.** the product of one of the equal but opposite charges on two atoms in a molecule, and the distance separating them **2.** the product of two equal and opposite magnetic poles or electric charges that are separated by a short distance

dip·per /díppər/ *n* **1.** SCOOP a cup or ladle for dipping into liquid **2.** SMALL WATER BIRD a small plain-colored bird that lives beside rivers and can swim and dive. Family: Cinclidae. **3.** SOMETHING THAT DIPS somebody or something that dips objects in a liquid, e.g., a machine operating an industrial process **4.** SMALL PAINT HOLDER a small container to hold paint on an artist's palette

dip·py /díppee/ (**-pi·er, -pi·est**) *adj* silly or eccentric, especially in an amusing or harmless way (*informal*) [Early 20C. Origin ?] —**dip·pi·ly** *adv* —**dip·pi·ness** *n*

di·pro·pel·lant /dī prə péllənt/ *n* AEROSP same as **bipropellant**

di·prot·ic /dī próttik/ *adj* with two transferable hydrogen protons [< DI-[1] + PROTON]

di·pro·to·dont /dī prṓtə dònt/ *adj* describes a marsupial that has the first pair of incisor teeth in each jaw enlarged ■ *n* a marsupial with enlarged incisors, e.g., a kangaroo or a wallaby. Order: Diprotodontia.

dip·shit /díp shìt/ *n* an offensive term that deliberately insults somebody's intelligence or value (*slang insult*)

dip·so /dípsō/ (*plural* **-sos**) *n* same as **alcoholic** (*slang insult*) [Late 19C. Shortening of DIPSOMANIAC]

dip·so·ma·ni·a /dìpsə máynee ə/ *n* a habitual and uncontrollable craving for alcohol (*dated*) [Mid-19C. < Greek *dipsa* "thirst"]

dip·so·ma·ni·ac /dìpsə máynee àk/ *n* somebody with a habitual and uncontrollable craving for alcohol (*dated*) —**dip·so·ma·ni·a·cal** /dìpsō mə nī ək'l/ *adj*

dip·stick /díp stìk/ *n* a measuring rod that is dipped into a container to indicate the depth of liquid in it, especially one used to measure the amount of oil in a car's engine

DIP switch /díp-/, **dip switch** *n* a switch that turns optional settings on or off on a computer component. Full form **dual in-line package switch**

dip·ter·an /díptərən/, **dip·ter·on** /-ròn/ *n* a two-winged insect. Flies, gnats, mosquitoes, and midges are dipterans. Order: Diptera. [Mid-19C. < modern Latin *Diptera* < Greek *dipteros* "two-winged"] —**dip·ter·al** *adj* —**dip·ter·ous** *adj*

~~**diptheria**~~ incorrect spelling of **diphtheria**

~~**dipthong**~~ incorrect spelling of **diphthong**

dip·tych /díptik/ *n* **1.** a pair of paintings, especially religious paintings on two hinged panels **2.** a pair of writing tablets joined by a hinge and having wooden backs and waxed writing surfaces, used especially in ancient Greece and Rome [Early 17C. Via late Latin < late Greek *diptukha* "pair of writing tablets," plural of *diptukhos* "folded in two" < *ptukhē* "fold"]

di·pyr·id·a·mole /dī peéridə mōl, dīpə ríddə-/ *n* a drug that widens the blood vessels. Use: treatment of angina, prevention of blood clots. [Mid-20C. < DI-[1] + PYRIMIDINE + PIPERIDINE + AMINO- + -OL[1]]

di·quat /dī kwòt/ *n* a biodegradable herbicide used to control weeds in water [Mid-20C. < DI-[1] + QUATERNARY; because based on a quaternary amine]

Di·rac /di rák/, **Paul** (1902–84) British theoretical physicist. He worked on quantum theory and predicted the existence of the positron, the first particle of antimatter to be established experimentally. He shared the Nobel Prize in physics (1933). Full name **Dirac, Paul Adrien Maurice**

> "God is a mathematician of a very high order, and He used very advanced mathematics in constructing the universe."
> [Paul Dirac, *Scientific American*; May 1963]

Di·rac con·stant *n* a constant used in quantum mechanics that is Planck's constant divided by 2π

Di·rac e·qua·tion *n* an equation in quantum mechanics that describes the wave behavior of an electron in an electromagnetic field, in a manner consistent with special relativity

dire /dīr/ (**dir·er, dir·est**) *adj* **1.** characterized by severe, serious, or desperate circumstances **2.** warning of a future disaster or serious consequences [Mid-16C. < Latin *dirus* "fearful, awful, boding ill"] —**dire·ly** *adv* —**dire·ness** *n*

di·rect /di rékt, dī-/ *v* (**-rect·ed, -rect·ing, -rects**) **1.** *vt* SUPERVISE SOMEBODY to organize and control the work of an organization or a group of people ○ *I found her directing a team of rescue workers.* **2.** *vt* INSTRUCT SOMEBODY to tell somebody to do something (*formal*) ○ *The medicine should be taken only as directed.* **3.** *vt* FOCUS ATTENTION ON SOMETHING to focus attention or concentrate activities on something ○ *Please direct your attention toward the figures at the right of the screen.* **4.** *vt* AIM OR SEND SOMETHING to aim, point, or send something or somebody in a particular direction ○ *Direct the extinguisher at the base of the flames.* **5.** *vt* ADDRESS LETTER to write an address on something to be delivered ○ *The envelope was directed to our offices.* **6.** *vt* GIVE SOMEBODY DIRECTIONS to tell somebody how to get to a place ○ *Can you direct me to the station?* **7.** *vt* ADDRESS COMMENTS TO SOMEBODY to say something to somebody specifically ○ *The remarks were directed to his sister.* **8.** *vti* SUPERVISE MOVIES OR PLAYS to be responsible for supervising the creative aspects of a movie, play, or television program, giving instructions and guidance to the actors and other people involved ○ *He has directed several movies.* **9.** *vt* MUSIC same as **conduct** *v* (sense 4) ■ *adj* **1.** NOT STOPPING OR DEVIATING going straight from one place or point to another ○ *a direct flight from Paris to Miami* **2.** IMMEDIATE lacking the influence of any other factors ○ *No direct link between the two events has been established.* **3.** PERSONAL in which no person, action, or process intervenes ○ *We are in direct contact with them.* **4.** STRAIGHTFORWARD easy to understand or respond to ○ *The author makes a direct appeal to our emotions.* **5.** PRECISE having the characteristics of accuracy and precision ○ *a direct quotation* **6.** IMMEDIATELY RELATED connected by a straight and unbroken line of descent from parent to child ○ *a direct descendant of George Washington* **7.** COMPLETE OR EXACT showing complete contradiction or opposition ○ *Their conclusions were in direct contradiction to ours.* **8.** POL DIRECTLY INVOLVING ELECTORATE involving participation in government from the electorate rather than through electoral representatives ○ *direct democracy* **9.** MATH, LOGIC WORKING FROM PREMISE TO CONCLUSION working immediately from the premise to the conclusion in proving something **10.** ASTRON MOVING WEST TO EAST moving from west to east as observed from celestial north ■ *adv* **1.** STRAIGHT, WITHOUT DIVERSION straight from one place or person to another, without a stop or diversion ○ *You can fly direct from Amsterdam to Chicago.* **2.** DIRECTLY by an immediate connection, without somebody or something intervening ○ *You can dial Calcutta direct.* [14C. < Latin *directus*, past participle of *dirigere* "set straight, guide"] —**di·rect·ness** *n*

SYNONYMS See *guide*.

di·rect ac·cess *n* the ability to retrieve information directly from any part of a storage device without referring to the preceding data

di·rect ac·tion *n* a political or industrial action intended to have an immediate and noticeable effect that will influence a government or employer, e.g., a strike, a boycott, or civil disobedience

di·rect con·nec·tion *n* a fast permanent connection linking a computer or system to a network such as the Internet. It can be used at any time and is much faster than a dial-up connection.

di·rect cost *n* a cost that can be linked directly with a specific project or activity

di·rect cou·pling *n* direct connection of one part of a circuit to another without the use of transformers or capacitors, allowing both direct current and alternating current to flow along the connection —**direct-cou·pled** *adj*

di·rect cur·rent *n* electrical current that flows in only one direction and has a fairly constant average value

di·rect deb·it *n* an arrangement by which sums of money of varying amounts that are owed at regular intervals are paid to the creditor directly from the payer's bank account

di·rect de·pos·it *n* a method of transferring a payment such as a salary electronically directly from the payer's bank account into the payee's

di·rect dis·course *n* the repeating of speech by giving the exact words that were spoken, in writing conventionally inside quotation marks

di·rect dis·tance di·al·ing *n* the system by which a telephone user can dial another telephone anywhere in the system without the help of an operator

di·rect dye *n* a dye that can be used directly on a fabric without needing an extra chemical (**mordant**) to fix the color

di·rect·ed speech *n* LING same as **motherese**

di·rect e·lec·tions *npl* government elections in which the people of a country constitute the electorate rather than a small group of selected representatives

di·rect ev·i·dence *n* evidence that provides direct factual information in a trial, e.g., a photograph, a document, or a witness's account

di·rect free kick *n* in soccer, a free kick that is awarded as compensation for a foul and can be taken as a direct shot at the opponent's goal

di·rect in·jec·tion *n* the injection of fuel in liquid form into the cylinders of an internal-combustion engine, without previously passing it through a carburetor

di·rec·tion /di rékshən, dī-/ *n* **1.** MANAGEMENT instructions given by somebody who controls something or somebody **2.** WAY the way in which somebody or something goes, points, or faces ○ *They shook hands and walked off in opposite directions.* **3.** SUPERVISION OF SOMETHING the control and supervision of a group, person, or organization **4.** DEVELOPMENT the way in which something develops ○ *The organization has begun to take a new direction.* **5.** SENSE OF PURPOSE a feeling of having a definite goal or purpose ○ *He's a nice boy, but seems to lack a sense of direction.* **6.** ARTS ART OF DIRECTING the art or practice of directing a movie or play **7.** MUSIC INSTRUCTION IN MUSIC an instruction in a piece of music that shows how it should be played **8.** MUSIC CONDUCTING PERFORMERS the process of conducting an orchestra or choir ■ **di·rec·tions** *npl* INSTRUCTIONS instructions on how to get to a place or how to do something ○ *I need to stop the car and ask for directions.* —**di·rec·tion·less** *adj*

di·rec·tion·al /di rékshən'l, dī-/ *adj* **1.** RELATING TO DIRECTION showing, concerned with, or dependent on direction ○ *Use your directional lights to indicate the way you plan to turn.* **2.** RELATING TO CONTROL OF SOMETHING showing or relating to the management or control of somebody's work, behavior, or way of thinking **3.** INDICATING TREND showing the future direction in which something might go **4.** ELECTRONICS MORE EFFICIENT IN ONE DIRECTION more efficient in a specific direction for transmitting and receiving sound waves, nuclear particles, light, or radio waves ○ *a directional antenna* —**di·rec·tion·al·i·ty** /di rèkshə nállətee, dī-/ *n*

di·rec·tion·al drill·ing *n* a method of drilling for oil or gas or for installing underground utilities in which special assemblies are used to drill at any angle and around obstacles

di·rec·tion find·er *n* a device used especially in navigation to determine the direction of a transmitted radio signal —**di·rec·tion find·ing** *n*

di·rec·tive /di réktiv, dī-/ *n* ORDER an order or official instruction ■ *adj* **1.** PROVIDING GUIDANCE giving explicit guidance or instructions ○ *directive utterances* **2.** SHOWING DIRECTION indicating a direction ○ *directive signals* —**di·rec·tive·ness** *n*

di·rect la·bor *n* labor that is directly involved in the production of goods or the provision of services rather than, e.g., in administration or sales

di·rect light·ing *n* a method of lighting in which a large percentage, usually not less than 90 percent, of the emitted light is directed downward

di·rect·ly /di réktlee, dī-/ *adv* **1.** STRAIGHT straight to a place or a person, or straight in a particular direction ○ *She went directly to the filing cabinet.* ○ *Your letter was sent directly to me.* **2.** WITH NOTHING IN BETWEEN without any person, thing, or event intervening ○ *I prefer to deal directly with senior management.* **3.** COMPLETELY in every respect ○ *I am directly opposed to everything that they stand for.* **4.** CLEARLY in a clear and unambiguous manner ○ *She refuses to say directly what the trouble is.* **5.** IMMEDIATELY at once (*formal*) ○ *I'll deal with it directly.* **6.** *regional* SOON in a short while ○ *Please take a seat, and I'll be with you directly.*

di·rect mail *n* the use of mail addressed to potential customers as a way of advertising, or the promotional material that is mailed —**di·rect mail·er** *n*

di·rect-mail shot *n* a mailing of promotional literature to a number of potential customers directly ○ *We're in the middle of doing a direct-mail shot.*

di·rect mar·ket·ing *n* methods of marketing by which a company deals directly with its end customers, including mail order by catalog, direct mail, telephone sales, or the advertising of goods

di·rect ob·ject *n* the word or phrase in a sentence that indicates somebody or something directly affected by the action of the verb, e.g., "cat" in "she fed the cat"

di·rec·tor /di réktər, dī-/ *n* **1.** HEAD OF MANAGEMENT a manager of an organized group or a program of activity **2.** SOMEBODY WHO RUNS COMPANY a member of the board that controls the affairs of a company. A board may be made up of executive directors, who manage the company, and nonexecutive directors, who contribute advice. **3.** FILMMAKER a supervisor of the actual making of a movie or television program **4.** MUSICAL CONDUCTOR a supervisor of the work of a group of musicians, especially an orchestra conductor [15C. Via Anglo-Norman < late Latin < Latin *directus* (see DIRECT)] —**di·rec·to·ri·al** /di rèk táwree əl, dī-/ *adj* —**di·rec·to·ri·al·ly** *adv* —**di·rec·tor·ship** *n*

di·rec·tor·ate /di réktərət, dī-/ *n* a board of directors, e.g., of a company

di·rec·to·ri·al /di rèk táwree əl, dī-/ *adj* relating to, belonging to, or suitable for a director —**di·rec·to·ri·al·ly** *adv*

di·rec·tor's chair *n* **1.** the chair used by the director on the set of a movie **2.** a light folding chair with a wooden or metal frame with arms, and a canvas back and seat

di·rec·tor's cut *n* a cut of a movie that has not been altered by a studio and that its director has complete artistic control over, often not the version that is released commercially

di·rec·to·ry /di réktəree, dī-/ *n* (*plural* **-ries**) **1.** BOOK OF NAMES a book alphabetically listing persons and organizations, usually with information about how to contact them **2.** LIST OF TENANTS a listing in the lobby of a building of those who live or work in the building, with their floor or room numbers **3.** COMPUT INDEX OF COMPUTER FILES an index of files stored on a computer disk. A disk may have many separate directories containing different types of files. **4.** RULE BOOK a book of rules or instructions ■ *adj* GIVING DIRECTION providing direction or advice

di·rec·to·ry as·sis·tance *n* same as **information** (sense 3)

di·rect pri·mar·y *n* a primary election in which the candidates who will seek office as nominees of a political party are chosen directly by popular vote

di·rect ques·tion *n* **1.** a question directed to a specific person and requiring a response **2.** a question repeated in the exact words that were spoken, placed inside quotation marks in writing

di·rect-read·ing *adj* allowing the immediate reading of a measurement, without intervening calculations

di·rec·trix /di réktriks, dī-/ (*plural* **-trix·es** or **-tri·ces** /di réktri sēez, dī rek trī sēez/) *n* a fixed line used in constructing a curve or conic section, the distance from the midline divided by the distance from a fixed point being identical for all points on the figure [Early 16C. < medieval Latin, feminine form of late Latin *director* (see DIRECTOR)]

di·rect sell·ing *n* MARKETING same as **direct marketing**

di·rect speech *n Can, UK* same as **direct discourse**

di·rect tax *n* a tax that is levied directly on the income or capital of a person or organization, rather than as part of the price of goods or services

dire straits *npl* a situation of emergency or desperate need

dire wolf *n* a large extinct mammal of the Pleistocene Epoch, similar to a wolf. Native to: North America. Latin name: *Canis dirus.*

dirge /durj/ *n* **1.** FUNERAL HYMN a song of mourning or lament, especially one about death or intended for a funeral **2.** MOURNFUL MUSIC a song or piece of music that sounds sad or depressing **3.** FUNERAL SERVICE a funeral service that is sung [Early 15C. < Latin *dirige* "guide!" (first word of Psalm 5:8, used as the antiphon in a funeral service)]

dir·ham /də rám, dər hám/ *n* a unit of currency in some North-African and Middle-Eastern countries. See table at **currency** [Late 18C. Via Arabic < Greek *drachmē* "number of coins one hand can hold"]

dir·i·gi·ble /dírrijəb'l, di ríjjəb'l/ *n* AVIAT same as **airship** ■ *adj* able to be steered or navigated [Late 16C. < Latin *dirigere* "direct, guide"; because an airship (unlike a balloon) can be steered] —**dir·i·gi·bil·i·ty** /dìrrijə bíllətee, di rìjjə-/ *n*

di·ri·gis·me /dìrri zheézmə/ *n* full and direct government control of a country's economy and social institutions [Mid-20C. < French < *diriger* "to direct" < Latin *dirigere*] —**di·ri·giste** /dìrri zhéest/ *adj*

dirk /durk/ *n* a dagger with a long straight blade, formerly used by Scottish Highlanders ■ *vt* (**dirked, dirk·ing, dirks**) to stab somebody with a dagger [Mid-16C. Origin ?]

Dirk Har·tog Is·land /dùrk haár tog-/ uninhabited island off the western coast of Australia. It is the westernmost point on the continent, and in 1616 was the site of the first landing by a European. Area: 234 sq. mi./613 sq. km.

dirn·dl /dúrnd'l/ *n* **1.** *also* **dirn·dl skirt** a full skirt that is gathered at the waist **2.** a dress with a full gathered skirt and a tight, low bodice that is worn over a short-sleeved blouse and is part of German and Austrian national costume [Mid-20C. < German dialect, "little girl"]

dirt /durt/ *n* **1.** UNCLEAN SUBSTANCE a substance that spoils the cleanness of somebody or something ○ *There was a smear of dirt on his shirt.* **2.** EARTH earth, soil, or mud ○ *Children were playing in the dirt by the side of the road.* **3.** HARD-PACKED EARTH soil packed down to make a firm surface, especially to form a road, track, or path ○ *dirt floors* **4.** SCANDALOUS FACTS scandalous or damaging facts about somebody ○ *The local paper may have some dirt on the candidates.* **5.** CORRUPTING INFLUENCE something that is considered to have a corrupting influence, e.g., pornography or foul language [13C. < Old Norse *drit* "excrement" < Germanic] ◇ **dig the dirt on somebody** *or* **something** to search for scandalous information about somebody or something in order to make it public ◇ **treat somebody like dirt** to treat somebody with the utmost contempt (*informal*)

dirt·bag /dúrt bàg/ *n* an offensive term that deliberately insults somebody's character (*slang*)

dirt bike *n* a motorcycle designed to be ridden across country or on dirt roads

dirt·board·ing /dúrt bàwrding/ *n* EXTREME SPORTS same as **mountainboarding**

dirt-cheap *adj, adv* extremely cheap or cheaply (*informal*)

dirt daub·er *n regional* INSECTS same as **potter wasp**

REGIONAL NOTE ***Dirt dauber*** is used for the potter wasp across the entire South, and across Oklahoma and Texas, with scattered instances in the Midwest. Other terms for the potter wasp include *mud dauber* and *mud wasp.*

dirt farm·er *n* a farmer with a little land who farms it alone or with family help —**dirt farm·ing** *n*

dirt-poor *adj* having so little money that the basic needs of life can scarcely be satisfied

dirt road *n* a road that is not surfaced, but consists of hard-packed earth

dirt track *n* **1.** a road or path that is not surfaced, but consists of earth **2.** a track of earth mixed with gravel and cinders that is used for horse racing or motorcycle racing

dirt·y /dúrtee/ *adj* (**-i·er, -i·est**) **1.** NOT CLEAN marked by or covered in dirt ○ *dirty fingernails* **2.** CAUSING DIRT creating dirt or pollution ○ *a battered truck with a dirty engine* **3.** MAKING SOMEBODY GRIMY likely to cause somebody to be filthy or grimy ○ *Working on cars is a dirty job.* **4.** NOT KEPT UP lacking care and maintenance, especially of dwellings in a neighborhood **5.** NOT HONEST OR LEGAL lacking honesty or moral integrity, especially if the rules of a game or law have been broken ○ *dirty tactics* **6.** MALICIOUS characterized by extreme meanness and cruelty ○ *a dirty lie* **7.** SEXUALLY SUGGESTIVE concerned with sex, especially in a way that is obscene or suggestive **8.** ANGRY expressing anger, displeasure, or disapproval ○ *a dirty look* **9.** LACKING BRIGHTNESS OR CLARITY lacking in luster or clarity (*often used in combination*) ○ *The walls were a dirty green.* **10.** STORMY characterized by heavy rain and strong winds ○ *dirty weather* **11.** RADIOACTIVE producing radioactive contamination **12.** DESPICABLE behaving in a nasty or despicable way (*informal*) ○ *a dirty rascal* **13.** RELATING TO ILLEGAL DRUGS relating to the use or sale of illegal drugs by somebody (*slang*) ■ *adv* (**-i·er, -i·est**) **1.** UNFAIRLY in an unfair or dishonest way ○ *You have to fight dirty if you want to win.* **2.** SUGGESTIVELY in a sexually suggestive or indecent way ■ *v* (**-ied, -y·ing, -ies**) **1.** *vti* MAKE OR BECOME DIRTY to make something or somebody dirty, or become dirty ○ *He wouldn't want to dirty his hands with that kind of work.* **2.** *vt* DISHONOR SOMETHING to make something seem less honest or honorable ○ *to dirty their reputation* —**dirt·i·ly** *adv* —**dirt·i·ness** *n* ◇ **get your hands dirty 1.** to perform menial or manual labor or work very hard **2.** to perform or participate in a degrading or unpleasant act

CULTURAL NOTE ***Dirty Harry,*** a movie (1971) by Don Siegel. It is the story of San Francisco policeman Harry Callahan (Clint Eastwood), known as "Dirty" because he always gets the worst jobs, and his attempts to apprehend a serial killer, Scorpio. This and subsequent movies centering on the Callahan character resulted in *Dirty Harry* being used as an adjective meaning police who use unnecessary force, as in *Dirty Harry syndrome.* Famous lines spoken by the Callahan character have also made their way into mainstream US English. An example is "Go ahead, make my day!" from *Sudden Impact* (1983).

SYNONYMS ***dirty, filthy, grubby, grimy, soiled, squalid, unclean***

CORE MEANING: not clean

dirty marked by or covered in dirt ○ *Diesel engines have very dirty exhaust emissions.* ○ *Each year, over a million children die from diarrhea spread by dirty water.* **filthy** extremely or disgustingly dirty ○ *Just look at your shoes – they're filthy!* ○ *I was taken into a filthy room with little furniture.* **grubby** slightly dirty ○ *a rather grubby handkerchief* ○ *Traveling always made her feel grubby.* **grimy** heavily ingrained with accumulated dirt ○ *the faint light from a grimy window* ○ *The rescue workers' faces were tired and grimy.* **soiled** stained or marked, especially during normal use ○ *soiled bed linen* ○ *His white shirt was a little soiled.* **squalid** neglected, insanitary and unpleasant ○ *living in squalid conditions* ○ *She died alone in a squalid rooming house.* **unclean** dirty and insanitary, or impure in moral or religious contexts ○ *unclean water supplies* ○ *After such violent experiences, the victims often say they feel unclean.* ○ *People with leprosy were regarded as ritually unclean.*

dirt·y bomb *n* a bomb containing radioactive nuclear waste dispersed by means of conventional explosives

dirt·y den·im *n* denim that is given a dirty or discolored appearance, usually by weaving brown yarn into the fabric during the manufacturing process. Use: clothing, especially jeans.

dirt·y drug *n* a drug used in psychiatric conditions that has poorly understood effects on brain function (*informal*)

dirt·y lin·en, dirt·y laun·dry *n* personal matters that it would be embarrassing or disadvantageous to let other people know about ○ *Don't wash your dirty linen in public.*

dirt·y old man *n* an older man who shows an interest in sex that is perceived as immoral, perverted, or generally unpleasant (*informal insult*)

dirt·y pool *n* unfair or dishonest tactics used to gain an advantage (*informal*)

dirt·y re·al·ism *n* a literary genre, originating in the United States, using an unpretentious laconic style and depicting the lives of rootless and disaffected people

dirt·y trick *n* UNFAIR ACTION something unfair or dishonest that is done to gain an advantage ■ **dirt·y tricks** *npl* **1.** UNFAIR POLITICAL TACTICS tactics used in a political campaign to discredit an opponent in a way that is not completely fair or honest **2.** SPY TACTICS secret activities carried out by the spies of one government in order to disrupt or destroy the internal functioning of another nation (*informal*) **3.** COMMERCIAL ESPIONAGE the activity of stealing secret products or processes from one company and selling them to rival companies (*informal*)

dirt·y trick·ster *n* a political aide who uses unfair or dishonest ways to discredit an opponent ○ *The dirty tricksters on both sides have overreached themselves this time.*

dirt·y word *n* **1.** a swearword or offensive word **2.** something that is disapproved of ○ *Delay seems to be a dirty word in this office!*

dirt·y work *n* something that somebody wants to be done that is unpleasant, unfair, unkind, dishonest, or illegal

dis /diss/ (**dissed, diss·ing, diss·es**), **diss** *vt* (*slang*) **1.** to treat somebody without respect, e.g., by talking back or being purposely rude ○ *Don't you dis me!* ○ *Don't be dissing me!* **2.** to criticize somebody or something [Late 20C. Origin ?]

Dis /diss/ *n* **1.** MYTHOL same as **Pluto** (sense 2) **2.** in Roman mythology, the region of the dead. Greek equivalent **Hades**

dis- *prefix* **1.** to undo, do the opposite ○ *disapprove* **2.** opposite or absence of ○ *discourtesy* **3.** to deprive of, remove from ○ *dishonor* **4.** not ○ *disobedient* **5.** to free from ○ *disburden* **6.** completely ○ *dissever* [Directly or via French < Latin < *dis* "apart"]

dis·a·bil·i·ty /dìssə bíllətee/ (*plural* **-ties**) *n* **1.** RESTRICTED CAPABILITY TO PERFORM PARTICULAR ACTIVITIES an inability to perform some or all of the tasks of daily life **2.** MEDICAL CONDITION RESTRICTING ACTIVITIES a medically diagnosed condition that makes it difficult to engage in the activities of daily life **3.** PAYMENT TO PERSON WITH INABILITY a sum of money paid to somebody, usually on a monthly basis, by a government agency or insurance company because he or she is unable to work **4.** LEGAL DISQUALIFIER something that causes somebody to be regarded in law as ineligible to perform a specific transaction

dis·a·bil·i·ty clause *n* a clause in a life insurance policy indicating the conditions that will apply if the holder becomes unable to work, including release from payment of further premiums

dis·a·ble /diss áyb'l/ (**-bled, -bling, -bles**) *vt* **1.** RESTRICT SOMEBODY IN SOME ACTIVITIES to make somebody unable to perform the activities needed to earn a living or carry out the basic tasks of daily life without difficulty **2.** STOP SOMETHING FROM WORKING to prevent a device or system from working by disconnecting a part of it **3.** DISQUALIFY SOMEBODY LEGALLY to make somebody ineligible in law to perform a specific transaction —**dis·a·ble·ment** *n*

dis·a·bled /diss áyb'ld/ *adj* **1.** UNABLE TO PERFORM PARTICULAR ACTIVITIES describes somebody with a condition that makes it difficult to perform some or all of the basic tasks of daily life **2.** UNABLE TO OPERATE incapable of performing or functioning ■ *npl* PHYSICALLY CHALLENGED PEOPLE people who are physically challenged

USAGE Though *physically challenged* and *people with disabilities* are preferred over the adjectival and noun forms of ***disabled***, the adjective ***disabled*** has a long history of use by those so affected, as in the name of the organization *Disabled American Veterans.*

dis·a·bled list *n* a list of the players of a sports team who are unable to play because of an injury

dis·a·buse /dìssə byóoz/ (**-bused, -bus·ing, -bus·es**) *vt* to tell somebody or make somebody realize that an idea is not true ○ *I was quickly disabused of my idealistic notions about the campaign.* ○ *She disabused him of many old prejudices.* [Early 17C. < ABUSE in the obsolete sense "a delusion"] —**dis·a·bus·al** *n*

di·sac·cha·ride /dī sákə rīd/ *n* a sugar consisting of two linked monosaccharide units

dis·ac·cord /dìssə káwrd/ (*formal*) *n* lack of harmony or agreement ■ *vi* (**-cord·ed, -cord·ing, -cords**) to disagree or not be in accordance with one another

dis·ad·van·tage /dìssəd vántij/ *n* **1.** BAD QUALITY something that makes a situation worse or that makes somebody or something less effective or desirable **2.** BAD SITUATION a situation that is unfavorable to somebody ○ *He was at a disadvantage, having only received the documents that morning.* **3.** LOSS injury, loss, or damage (*formal*) ■ *vt* (**-taged, -tag·ing, -tag·es**) CAUSE PROBLEM FOR SOMEBODY to put somebody or something at a disadvantage

dis·ad·van·taged /dìssəd vántijd/ *adj* **1.** in a worse position than somebody else or other people **2.** unable to perform well in a competitive or military endeavor

dis·ad·van·ta·geous /diss àdvən táyjəss, dìss advən-/ *adj* not helpful or favorable —**dis·ad·van·ta·geous·ly** *adv* —**dis·ad·van·ta·geous·ness** *n*

dis·af·fect /dìssə fékt/ (**-fect·ed, -fect·ing, -fects**) *vt* to make somebody dissatisfied with somebody or something, especially somebody to whom respect or loyalty is owed —**dis·af·fect·ed** *adj* —**dis·af·fect·ed·ly** *adv* —**dis·af·fect·ed·ness** *n* —**dis·af·fec·tion** *n*

dis·af·fil·i·ate /dìssə fíllee àyt/ (**-at·ed, -at·ing, -ates**) *v* **1.** *vti* to end the affiliated status of a subsidiary group ○ *The group was formally disaffiliated from its parent body at the end of 1985.* **2.** *vi* to withdraw from affiliation or association with a larger group or organization —**dis·af·fil·i·a·tion** /dìssə filee áysh'n/ *n*

dis·af·firm /dìssə fúrm/ (**-firmed, -firm·ing, -firms**) *vt* **1.** to say that something is not true or that the opposite of it is true (*formal*) **2.** to alter a legal decision, or refuse to recognize or acknowledge something formally —**dis·af·fir·mance** *n* —**dis·af·fir·ma·tion** /diss àffər máysh'n/ *n*

dis·ag·gre·gate /diss àggrə gàyt/ (**-gat·ed, -gat·ing, -gates**) *vti* to separate something into its component parts, or break apart —**dis·ag·gre·ga·tion** /diss àggrə gáysh'n/ *n*

dis·a·gree /dìssə grée/ (**-greed, -gree·ing, -grees**) *vi* **1.** NOT AGREE to have or put forward a different view or opinion ○ *She strongly disagrees with you on this point.* **2.** NOT MATCH to fail to be in accordance with something, or to show a different result **3.** AFFECT SOMEBODY BADLY to have an unpleasant effect on somebody ○ *I love oysters, but they disagree with me.* [15C. < French *désagréer* < *agréer* "agree"]

SYNONYMS ***disagree, differ, argue, dispute, take issue with, contradict, agree to differ, be at odds***

CORE MEANING: to have or express a difference of opinion with somebody

disagree to have or put forward a different view or opinion ○ *He strongly disagrees with what was said.* ○ *I begin by disagreeing with her that the area is as suitable as she thinks it is.* **differ** to have different opinions about something ○ *People may well differ on the issue of whether this development is a good or a bad thing.* ○ *Accounts differ as to who was present and how many vehicles they had.* **argue** to express disagreement, especially continuously or angrily ○ *My husband and I argue about football all the time.* ○ *She knew better than to argue with him when he used that tone of voice.* **dispute** to disagree or argue about something ○ *For years, scholars have disputed over this text.* ○ *The two brothers had been disputing about the terms of their parents' will.* **take issue with** to disagree strongly with somebody about something ○ *I would take issue with her view.* ○ *It is with regret that I have had to take issue with a fellow member of our committee.* **contradict** to argue against the truth or correctness of a statement or claim ○ *Let her tell her story and don't contradict her.* ○ *Important witnesses are contradicting each other's accounts.* **agree to differ** to stop arguing and accept that the opposing viewpoints are irreconcilable ○ *We might as well agree to differ and get along as well as we can.* ○ *If after discussion the social worker and client agree to differ with respect to the report's content, both versions will be recorded.* **be at odds** to be in disagreement, especially over a period of time or about a particular issue ○ *The Mayor seems to be at odds with his own officials over this question.*

dis·a·gree·a·ble /dìssə grée əb'l/ *adj* **1.** causing feelings that are not pleasant or enjoyable **2.** lacking courtesy or constantly finding a reason to disagree with somebody —**dis·a·gree·a·bil·i·ty** /dìssə gree ə bíllətee/ *n* —**dis·a·gree·a·ble·ness** *n* —**dis·a·gree·a·bly** *adv*

dis·a·gree·ment /dìssə gréemənt/ *n* **1.** FAILURE TO AGREE ABOUT SOMETHING the fact of having or expressing a different opinion and failing to agree about something **2.** SLIGHT ARGUMENT a situation in which a number of people or groups argue **3.** DIFFERENCE failure to be in accordance with something

dis·al·low /dìssə lów/ (**-lowed, -low·ing, -lows**) *vt* **1.** to refuse to accept something because it is not true, valid, or correctly done (*formal*) **2.** to cancel a privilege or entitlement, or refuse to allow something that was previously allowed —**dis·al·low·a·ble** *adj* —**dis·al·low·ance** *n*

~~**disallusion**~~ incorrect spelling of **disillusion**

dis·am·big·u·ate /dìss am bíggyoo àyt/ (**-at·ed, -at·ing, -ates**) *vt* to establish the true meaning of an expression, regulation, or ruling that is confusing or that could be interpreted in more than one way —**dis·am·big·u·a·tion** /dìss am bìggyoo áysh'n/ *n*

~~**disapear**~~ incorrect spelling of **disappear**

~~**disapointed**~~ incorrect spelling of **disappointed**

dis·ap·pear /dìssə péer/ (**-peared, -pear·ing, -pears**) *v* **1.** *vi* VANISH FROM SIGHT to cease to be seen, e.g., by moving away or going behind or into something **2.** *vi* NOT BE FOUND to be gone from or no longer be seen in a place without any explanation **3.** *vi* CEASE TO EXIST to no longer exist **4.** *vt* CAUSE OPPONENT TO DISAPPEAR to make a political opponent disappear by arresting or killing the person without due process of law ○ *It wasn't the first time they had disappeared someone who was in the way.* —**dis·ap·pear·ance** *n*

dis·ap·peared /dìssə péerd/ *npl* people who have been arrested by a regime that they opposed and whose subsequent fate is not known [Late 20C. Translation of Spanish *desaparecido*]

dis·ap·pear·ing act ◇ **do a disappearing act** to be unable to be found or contacted when needed (*humorous*)

dis·ap·point /dìssə póynt/ (**-point·ed, -point·ing, -points**) *v* **1.** *vi* to be not as good, attractive, or satisfactory as was hoped or expected **2.** *vt* to let somebody down by not doing something or by not happening as hoped or expected [15C. < French *désappointer* "deprive of an appointment"]

dis·ap·point·ed /dìssə póyntəd/ *adj* unhappy because something was not as good, attractive, or satisfactory as expected, or because something hoped for or expected did not happen —**dis·ap·point·ed·ly** *adv*

dis·ap·point·ing /dìssə póynting/ *adj* not as good, attractive, or satisfactory as hoped or expected —**dis·ap·point·ing·ly** *adv*

dis·ap·point·ment /dìssə póyntmənt/ *n* **1.** FEELING OF BEING LET DOWN a feeling of sadness or frustration because something was not as good, attractive, or satisfactory as expected, or because something hoped for did not happen **2.** SOMETHING DISAPPOINTING something or somebody that disappoints somebody, or an occasion when somebody is disappointed **3.** FRUSTRATION the failure to attain hopes or wishes

dis·ap·pro·ba·tion /dìss àpprə báysh'n/ *n* the expression of moral or social disapproval (*formal*)

dis·ap·prov·al /dìssə próov'l/ *n* a negative judgment of something based on personal standards

dis·ap·prove /dìssə próov/ (**-proved, -prov·ing, -proves**) *v* **1.** *vi* to give a negative judgment of something based on personal standards **2.** *vt* to refuse to approve or agree to something (*formal*) —**dis·ap·prov·ing** *adj* —**dis·ap·prov·ing·ly** *adv*

SYNONYMS ***disapprove, frown on, object, criticize, condemn, deplore, denounce, censure***

CORE MEANING: to have an unfavorable opinion of something or somebody

disapprove to give a negative judgment of something based on personal standards ○ *Why do you disapprove so strongly of my leisure pursuits?* ○ *Her parents will disapprove if they find out where she spent the evening.* **frown on** to dislike and disapprove of something ○ *a practice which would be frowned on today* ○ *They were raised in an era when ease and convenience were frowned on.* **object** to be opposed to something, or express opposition ○ *a petition strongly objecting to the proposals* ○ *I don't object to people smoking in the open air.* **criticize** to express disapproval of or dissatisfaction with somebody or something ○ *The ministers have been sharply criticized for their conduct.* ○ *I feel that the role of the media is to criticize the government, not to defend it.* **condemn** to state that something or somebody is in some way wrong or unacceptable ○ *The present system has been widely condemned as unfair and archaic.* ○ *The rebels were forced to sign statements condemning their own actions.* **deplore** to disapprove of something very strongly ○ *We deplore all use of violence.* ○ *I deeply deplore the government's action.* **denounce** to criticize or condemn something publicly and harshly ○ *a letter denouncing the government's economic approach as ruinous* ○ *The hierarchy publicly denounced any attack on ecclesiastical privileges.* **censure** to make a formal, often public or official statement of disapproval ○ *A partner in the firm was officially censured for unprofessional conduct.*

dis·arm /diss aárm/ (**-armed, -arm·ing, -arms**) *v* **1.** *vti* GIVE UP WEAPONS to give up a supply of weapons or reduce the strength of armed forces, or force another nation to do this **2.** *vt* DEFUSE BOMB to make a bomb unable to explode, or make a weapon incapable of being fired **3.** *vt* WIN SOMEBODY OVER to make somebody less hostile or suspicious and more inclined to act in a friendly way ○ *They disarmed us with their confidence and skill.* —**dis·arm·er** *n*

dis·ar·ma·ment /diss aármәmәnt/ *n* **1.** the process of reducing a nation's supply of weapons or the strength of its armed forces ○ *a believer in negotiated mutual disarmament* **2.** the condition of having given up weapons ○ *Disarmament brought peace to the troubled region.*

dis·arm·ing /diss aárming/ *adj* making somebody feel more friendly or trusting —**dis·arm·ing·ly** *adv*

dis·ar·range /dìssә ráynj/ (**-ranged, -rang·ing, -rang·es**) *vt* to disturb the order or arrangement of something —**dis·ar·range·ment** *n*

dis·ar·ray /dìssә ráy/ *n* **1.** DISORGANIZED STATE a disorganized and confused state ○ *The meeting was thrown into disarray by the surprise announcement.* **2.** UNTIDINESS a state of untidiness, especially in dress ■ *vt* (**-rayed, -ray·ing, -rays**) **1.** MAKE SOMETHING DISORGANIZED to make something confused and disorganized **2.** UNDRESS SOMEBODY to remove somebody's clothes (*archaic*)

dis·ar·tic·u·late /dìss aar tíkyә làyt/ (**-lat·ed, -lat·ing, -lates**) *vti* to separate something at the joints, or come apart at the joints —**dis·ar·tic·u·la·tion** /dìss aar tikyә láysh'n/ *n* —**dis·ar·tic·u·la·tor** *n*

dis·as·sem·ble /dìssә sémb'l/ (**-bled, -bling, -bles**) *vt* to take something such as a piece of machinery apart —**dis·as·sem·bly** *n*

dis·as·so·ci·ate /dìssә sṓshee àyt, -sṓssee-/ (**-at·ed, -at·ing, -ates**) *vt* **1.** to end an association with another person or group **2.** to deny any connection or involvement with somebody or something ○ *In a press conference, the spokesperson attempted to disassociate himself from the scandal.*

dis·as·so·ci·a·tion /dìssә sōshee áysh'n, -sōssee-/ *n* **1.** the termination of an association with another person or group **2.** the denial of any connection or involvement with somebody or something else

USAGE **disassociation** or **dissociation**? Both these words, and the verbs (*disassociate, dissociate*) from which they come, share the meaning "separation from a relationship with another," and in this sense they are interchangeable: *sought disassociation/dissociation from the scandal; sought to dissociate/disassociate themselves from the scandal.* ***Dissociation***, however, does have two senses not shared by ***disassociation***: in psychology and psychiatry, "separation of emotions as a defense mechanism" and in chemistry, "the breaking up of a molecule into simpler components." Do not confuse the two words.

dis·as·ter /di zástәr/ *n* **1.** an event that causes serious loss, destruction, hardship, unhappiness, or death **2.** somebody or something that fails completely, especially in a way that is distressing, embarrassing, or laughable (*informal*) [Late 16C. Via French < Italian *disastro*, literally "ill-starred" < Latin *astrum* "star" < Greek *astron*]

dis·as·ter ar·e·a *n* **1.** a place that is officially declared to be in a state of emergency and in need of special assistance such as federal relief money after a natural disaster ○ *The southern half of the state has been declared a disaster area.* **2.** a very messy or disorganized place or situation (*informal*)

dis·as·ter mov·ie *n* a movie that deals with a disaster such as an earthquake or plane crash in a dramatic and spectacular way

~~disasterous~~ incorrect spelling of **disastrous**

dis·as·trous /di zástrәss/ *adj* **1.** having seriously damaging results **2.** performed in an incompetent or awkward way [Late 16C. < French *désastreux* < Italian *disastro* (see DISASTER)] —**dis·as·trous·ly** *adv* —**dis·as·trous·ness** *n*

~~disatisfied~~ incorrect spelling of **dissatisfied**

dis·a·vow /dìssә vów/ (**-vowed, -vow·ing, -vows**) *vt* to deny any knowledge of, responsibility for, or association with somebody or something —**dis·a·vow·a·ble** *adj* —**dis·a·vow·al** *n* —**dis·a·vow·ed·ly** /-әdlee/ *adv* —**dis·a·vow·er** *n*

dis·band /diss bánd/ (**-band·ed, -band·ing, -bands**) *vti* to break up as a group or organization, or cause a group or organization to break up —**dis·band·ment** *n*

dis·bar /diss baár/ (**-barred, -bar·ring, -bars**) *vt* to take away officially the right of an attorney to practice law —**dis·bar·ment** *n*

dis·be·lief /dìss bi léef/ *n* the feeling of not believing or of not being able to believe somebody or something

dis·be·lieve /dìss bi léev/ (**-lieved, -liev·ing, -lieves**) *v* **1.** *vt* to think that something somebody has said is untrue **2.** *vi* to have no belief in something, especially in God or religion —**dis·be·liev·er** *n* —**dis·be·liev·ing** *adj* —**dis·be·liev·ing·ly** *adv*

dis·ben·e·fit /diss bénnәfit/ *n* UK something that makes a situation disadvantageous or unfavorable

dis·bud /diss búd/ (**-bud·ded, -bud·ding, -buds**) *vt* **1.** to remove buds or shoots from a plant so that the remaining ones will be larger and stronger **2.** to remove the horns from a young animal, especially from cattle

dis·bur·den /diss búrd'n/ (**-dened, -den·ing, -dens**) *vt* **1.** to gain relief by telling somebody about something that is causing anxiety or guilt **2.** to free somebody or something from a burden or constraint —**dis·bur·den·ment** *n*

dis·burse /diss búrss/ (**-bursed, -burs·ing, -burs·es**) *vt* to pay out money, especially from a fund (*formal*) [Mid-16C. < Old French *desbourser* "remove from the purse" < *bourse* "purse"] —**dis·burs·a·ble** *adj* —**dis·burse·ment** *n* —**dis·burs·er** *n*

SPELLCHECK **disburse** or **disperse**? Do not confuse the spelling of ***disburse*** and ***disperse***, which sound similar. ***Disburse*** is largely restricted to formal contexts and refers specifically to paying out money: *All the funds have been disbursed.* ***Disperse***, the more frequent of the two verbs, means "scatter," "cause to go away," or "disappear": *The crowds dispersed.*

disc /disk/ *n* **1.** COMPUT another spelling of **disk** **2.** a phonograph record (*dated informal*)

disc. *abbr* **1.** COMM discount **2.** discovered

disc- *prefix* same as **disco-** (*used before vowels*)

dis·calced /diss kálst/ *adj* wearing sandals or going barefoot in accordance with the rules of some orders of monks, friars, or nuns [Mid-17C. Shortening of obsolete *discalceated* "with shoes removed" < Latin *calceare* "to shoe" < *calceus* "shoe"]

dis·cant *n, vi* MUSIC same as **descant** —**dis·cant·er** *n*

dis·card *v* /diss kaárd/ (**-card·ed, -card·ing, -cards**) **1.** *vt* THROW SOMETHING AWAY to get rid of something that is not wanted or needed **2.** *vt* REJECT CARD in some card games, to put down a card from a hand and not play it **3.** *vti* PLAY CARD in a card game such as bridge or whist, to play a card so that it has no value, because it is neither in the required suit nor a trump ■ *n* /díss kaàrd/ **1.** ACT OF DISCARDING the act of discarding a playing card **2.** SOMETHING DISCARDED somebody or something that has been discarded —**dis·card·a·ble** *adj* —**dis·card·er** *n*

dis·car·nate /diss kaárnәt, -kaár nàyt/ *adj* lacking a physical body [Mid-17C. < DIS- + Latin *carn-* "flesh"]

disc brake, **disk brake** *n* a brake that works by the friction of a caliper or pads against a rotating disk

dis·cern /di súrn/ (**-cerned, -cern·ing, -cerns**) *v* **1.** *vt* SEE OR NOTICE SOMETHING UNCLEAR to see or notice something that is not very clear or obvious **2.** *vt* UNDERSTAND SOMETHING to understand something that is not immediately obvious **3.** *vti* DISTINGUISH to be able to tell the difference between two or more things [14C. Directly or via French < Latin *discernere* "separate off" < *cernere* "separate, determine"] —**dis·cern·er** *n* —**dis·cern·i·ble** *adj*

dis·cern·i·bly /di súrnәblee/, **dis·cern·a·bly** *adv* in an obvious way or to a noticeable extent ○ *not discernibly different*

dis·cern·ing /di súrning/ *adj* showing good judgment and good taste —**dis·cern·ing·ly** *adv*

dis·cern·ment /di súrnmәnt/ *n* good taste and judgment

dis·charge *v* /diss chaárj/ (**-charged, -charg·ing, -charg·es**) **1.** *vt* DISMISS SOMEBODY FROM INSTITUTIONAL SETTING to arrange for or allow somebody to leave an institution, especially a hospital, or make the decision yourself to leave such a place after being an inpatient **2.** *vt* RELEASE SOMEBODY FROM ARMED FORCES to release somebody from service in the armed forces formally, or formally end your service **3.** *vt* RELEASE OR ACQUIT SOMEBODY to release a prisoner, or acquit somebody in a court of law **4.** *vti* EMIT OR DUMP LIQUID OR GAS to emit, give off, or dispose of a gas or liquid, or be emitted or disposed of **5.** *vt* CARRY SOMETHING OUT to carry out a duty, responsibility, or promise (*formal*) **6.** *vt* RELEASE SOMEBODY FROM DUTY to excuse somebody from a duty or obligation **7.** *vt* FIRE EMPLOYEE to dismiss somebody from a job (*formal*) **8.** *vt* PAY DEBT to pay a debt in full (*formal*) **9.** *vti* SHOOT OR GO OFF to fire a weapon or missile, or be fired (*formal*) **10.** *vt* CANCEL COURT ORDER to cancel or annul a court order **11.** *vti* OFFLOAD SHIP'S CARGO to unload cargo or passengers from a ship **12.** *vti* LOSE ELECTRIC CHARGE to lose or release electric charge by the addition or loss of electrons from a stationary body, e.g., in static electricity, or be released in this way **13.** *vi* SPARK to give off electricity suddenly in the form of a spark or arc, e.g., in the release of stored energy in a capacitor **14.** *vti* DRAIN ELECTRICITY to drain slowly of electricity, or make the electricity in a battery drain slowly **15.** *vt* RELEASE PRESSURE ON BUILDING to release the pressure on part of a building by spreading it over adjacent parts **16.** *vt* BLEACH FABRIC to remove the color from fabric by bleaching it **17.** *vi* RUN OR BLUR to undergo a running or blurring of dyes ■ *n* /díss chaàrj, diss chaárj/ **1.** DISMISSAL FROM INSTITUTION permission or orders to leave an institution, especially a hospital, after being a patient **2.** SEPARATION FROM ARMED FORCES formal and official release of somebody from the armed forces, or a document certifying this **3.** PRISONER'S RELEASE the release of a prisoner from custody **4.** MUCUS a flow of fluid from the body, especially an unusual or large flow of mucus from the bodily orifices or pus from a wound **5.** EMISSION OF SUBSTANCES the emission of gases, liquids, or chemicals **6.** RATE OF EMISSION the rate at which a gas or liquid is being emitted **7.** PERFORMANCE OF DUTY the carrying out of a duty, obligation, responsibility, or promise (*formal*) **8.** DEBT PAYMENT the payment of a debt (*formal*) **9.** FIRING the firing of a gun (*formal*) **10.** PRODUCTION OF ELECTRICITY the process of converting chemical energy into electrical energy, e.g., in a battery **11.** CONTINUOUS FLOW OF ELECTRICITY THROUGH AIR the continuous flow of electric energy through air or a gas as a result of ionization, as occurs when a spark jumps a gap, or, at a reduced pressure, as in a fluorescent lamp **12.** CARGO OFFLOADING the unloading of cargo **13.** VOLUME OF RIVER WATER FLOW the volume of water in a river flowing past a point during a specific time interval [14C. Via Old French *descharger* < late Latin *discar(r)icare* "unload" < Latin *car(ri)care* "to load"] —**dis·charge·a·ble** *adj* —**dis·charg·er** *n*

SYNONYMS See *perform.*

dis·charge lamp *n* an electric lamp that glows as a result of electricity passing through a gas

dis·charge tube *n* a tube filled with low-pressure gas that glows when it conducts electricity at a given voltage. Use: neon and fluorescent lights.

dis·ci TRACK AND FIELD plural of **discus**

dis·ci·ple /di sīp'l/ *n* **1.** somebody who believes in and follows the teachings of a leader, a philosophy, or a religion **2.** in the Bible, one of the 12 original followers of Jesus Christ [Pre-12C. < Latin *discipulus* "learner" < *discere* "learn"] —**dis·ci·ple·ship** *n* —**dis·cip·u·lar** /di síppyələr/ *adj*

Dis·ci·ple *n* **1.** CHR another spelling of **disciple** (sense 2) **2.** a member of the Disciples of Christ

Dis·ci·ples of Christ *n* a Protestant denomination of the Christian Church whose congregations regard the Bible as the sole rule of faith and living, and practice baptism by total immersion. It was founded in the United States in 1809 by Thomas and Alexander Campbell. (*takes a singular or plural verb*)

dis·ci·pli·nar·i·an /dìssəplə nérree ən/ *n* somebody who believes in or enforces strictly defined rules of behavior ■ *adj* same as **disciplinary**

dis·ci·pli·nar·y /díssəplə nèrree/ *adj* **1.** relating to the enforcement and punishment of rules of behavior **2.** relating to an academic subject ○ *Teachers tried to cut across traditional disciplinary boundaries in their lessons.* —**dis·ci·pli·nar·i·ly** /-plə nérrəlee/ *adv* —**dis·ci·pli·nar·i·ty** /-plə nárrətee/ *n*

dis·ci·pli·nar·y bar·racks *n* a military prison

dis·ci·pline /díssəplin/ *n* **1.** TRAINING TO ENSURE PROPER BEHAVIOR the practice or methods of teaching and enforcing acceptable patterns of behavior **2.** ORDER AND CONTROL a controlled orderly state, especially in a class of schoolchildren **3.** CALM CONTROLLED BEHAVIOR the ability to behave in a controlled and calm way even in a difficult or stressful situation **4.** CONSCIOUS CONTROL OVER LIFESTYLE mental self-control used in directing or changing behavior, learning something, or training for something **5.** EDUC ACTIVITY OR SUBJECT a subject or field of activity, e.g., an academic subject **6.** PUNISHMENT punishment designed to teach somebody obedience **7.** CHR CHURCH RULES the system of rules used in a religious denomination or order ■ *v* (**-plined, -plin·ing, -plines**) **1.** *vr* MAKE YOURSELF DO SOMETHING REGULARLY to make yourself act or work in a controlled or systematic way **2.** *vt* PUNISH SOMEBODY to punish somebody as a way of enforcing obedience **3.** *vt* TEACH SOMEBODY OBEDIENCE to teach somebody to obey rules or to behave in an acceptable way [13C. Directly or via French < Latin *disciplina* "instruction given to a learner" < *discipulus* (see DISCIPLE)] —**dis·ci·plin·a·ble** *adj* —**dis·ci·pli·nal** /díssəplin'l, di sípplin'l/ *adj* —**dis·ci·plined** *adj* —**dis·ci·plin·er** *n*

disc jock·ey *n* MUSIC, MEDIA full form of **DJ** (sense 1)

dis·claim /diss kláym/ (**-claimed, -claim·ing, -claims**) *v* **1.** *vt* DENY CONNECTION WITH SOMETHING to deny that you know about something or that you are responsible for something **2.** *vt* DENY VALIDITY OF SOMETHING to refuse to accept the validity or authority of something **3.** *vti* RENOUNCE LEGAL RIGHT to renounce a legal claim or right to something [15C. < Anglo-Norman *disclaimer* "not to claim" < Old French *clamer* "to claim"] —**dis·cla·ma·tion** /dìsklə máysh'n/ *n*

dis·claim·er /diss kláymər/ *n* LAW **1.** REFUSAL TO ACCEPT RESPONSIBILITY a statement refusing to accept responsibility for something, e.g., a denial of legal liability for any injury associated with a product **2.** STATEMENT RENOUNCING LEGAL RIGHT a statement saying that somebody gives up a legal right or claim to something such as damages arising from an accident **3.** DENIAL OF KNOWLEDGE a statement denying knowledge of something

dis·close /diss klṓz/ (**-closed, -clos·ing, -clos·es**) *vt* **1.** to reveal something that has been kept a secret **2.** to reveal something that has been covered or hidden (*formal*) [15C. < Old French *desclos-*, present stem of *desclore* < medieval Latin *disclaudere* "to open" < Latin *claudere* "to close"] —**dis·clos·a·ble** *adj* —**dis·clos·er** *n*

dis·clos·ing a·gent /diss klṓzing-/ *n* a dye in liquid or tablet form that colors something, especially the teeth to show plaque

dis·clo·sure /diss klṓz͟hər/ *n* **1.** MAKING OF SECRET INFORMATION PUBLIC the revelation of information that was previously kept secret **2.** SECRET INFORMATION MADE PUBLIC a piece of information that is revealed after being secret **3.** LAW PROCESS OF SHARING INFORMATION BETWEEN SIDES in a lawsuit, the legal requirement that each side must provide copies of all documents to the other side before the trial, or the process of fulfilling this requirement

dis·co /dískō/ *n* (*plural* **-cos**) **1.** CLUB OR PARTY WITH DANCING a club or party where people dance to recorded pop music, often introduced by a DJ **2.** STEADY-BEAT POP MUSIC FOR DANCING a style of pop music with a steady pronounced beat, popular in the 1970s for dancing. It developed from soul music, in response to the growing popularity of discos. **3.** DANCE DONE TO DISCO MUSIC popular dancing with hips and arms moving to the repetitive beat of disco music ■ *vi* (**-coed, -co·ing, -cos**) TAKE PART IN DISCO DANCING to dance to disco music (*informal*) [Mid-20C. Shortening of DISCOTHEQUE]

disco- *prefix* **1.** disk ○ *discoid* **2.** phonograph record ○ *discography* [Via Latin < Greek *diskos* (see DISH)]

dis·cob·o·lus /diss kóbb'ləss/ (*plural* **-li** /-ī/), **dis·cob·o·los** *n* a discus thrower in ancient Greece [Early 18C. Via Latin < Greek *diskobolos* "disk-throwing" < *diskos* (see DISH) + *-bolos* "throwing" < *ballein* "to throw"]

dis·cog·ra·phy /diss kóggrəfee/ (*plural* **-phies**) *n* a list of the recordings made by a performer, group, or of a specific category of music —**dis·cog·ra·pher** *n* —**dis·co·graph·ic** /dìskə gráffik/ *adj*

dis·coid /díss kòyd/ *n* a disk-shaped object or part ■ *adj also* **dis·coi·dal** /diss kóyd'l/ shaped like a disk [Late 18C. < Greek *diskoeidēs* < *diskos* (see DISH)]

dis·col·or /diss kúllər/ (**-ored, -or·ing, -ors**) *vti* to change from the original or desired color and take on an unpleasant, faded, darkened, or dirty appearance, or make something change in this way [14C. Directly or via French < medieval Latin *discolorare* < Latin *colorare* "to color"] —**dis·col·or·a·tion** /diss kùllə ráysh'n/ *n* —**dis·col·ored** *adj* —**dis·col·or·ment** *n*

dis·com·bob·u·late /dìskəm bóbbyə làyt/ (**-lat·ed, -lat·ing, -lates**) *vt* to throw somebody into a state of confusion (*informal*; *often passive*) [Mid-19C. Probably alteration of DISCOMPOSE or DISCOMFIT] —**dis·com·bob·u·la·tion** /dìskəm bobyə láysh'n/ *n*

dis·com·fit /diss kúmfit/ (**-fit·ed, -fit·ing, -fits**) *vt* (*formal*) **1.** to make somebody feel confused, uneasy, or embarrassed **2.** to frustrate somebody's plans [13C. < Old French *desconfit*, past participle of *desconfire* "destroy" < *confire* "make" < Latin *conficere* (see CONFECT)] —**dis·com·fit·er** *n*

dis·com·fi·ture /diss kúmfichər/ *n* frustrating feelings of embarrassment or awkwardness (*formal*)

dis·com·fort /diss kúmfərt/ *n* **1.** STATE OF PHYSICAL UNEASE very mild pain, or a feeling of being physically uncomfortable **2.** EMBARRASSMENT the state of feeling awkward, embarrassed, or uneasy **3.** CAUSE OF LACK OF COMFORT something that makes somebody feel physically or mentally uncomfortable ■ *vt* (**-fort·ed, -fort·ing, -forts**) MAKE SOMEBODY UNCOMFORTABLE to make somebody feel physically or mentally uncomfortable (*formal*) [14C. < Old French *desconfort* < *desconforter* "deprive of comfort" < *conforter* "to comfort"] —**dis·com·fort·a·ble** *adj* —**dis·com·fort·ing** *adj* —**dis·com·fort·ing·ly** *adv*

dis·com·mode /dìskə mṓd/ (**-mod·ed, -mod·ing, -modes**) *vt* to cause problems or inconvenience to somebody (*formal*) [Early 18C. < obsolete French *discommoder* "deprive of convenience" < Latin *commodus* "suitable"] —**dis·com·mo·di·ous** *adj* —**dis·com·mo·di·ous·ly** *adv*

dis·com·pose /dìskəm pṓz/ (**-posed, -pos·ing, -pos·es**) *vt* to make somebody lose his or her composure —**dis·com·pos·ed·ly** /-pṓzədlee/ *adv*

dis·com·po·sure /dìskəm pṓz͟hər/ *n* loss of the ability to remain calm and self-assured, especially under difficult or emotional circumstances

dis·con·cert /dìskən súrt/ (**-cert·ed, -cert·ing, -certs**) *vt* **1.** to make somebody feel ill at ease, slightly confused, or taken aback **2.** to upset or frustrate plans (*formal*) [Mid-17C. < French *desconcerter* "bring out of agreement" < Old Italian *concertare* "bring into agreement"] —**dis·con·cert·ed** *adj* —**dis·con·cer·tion** *n* —**dis·con·cert·ment** *n*

dis·con·cert·ing /dìskən súrting/ *adj* making somebody feel ill at ease, slightly confused, or taken aback —**dis·con·cert·ing·ly** *adv*

dis·con·firm /dìskən fúrm/ (**-firmed, -firm·ing, -firms**) *vt* to show that something such as a theory cannot be right —**dis·con·fir·ma·tion** /dìss konfər máysh'n/ *n*

dis·con·form·i·ty /dìskən fáwrmətee/ (*plural* **-ties**) *n* **1.** same as **nonconformity** (*archaic*) **2.** in geology, a break in the sedimentary record in which the rock layers remain parallel

dis·con·nect /dìskə nékt/ *v* (**-nect·ed, -nect·ing, -nects**) **1.** *vt* SHUT OFF SUPPLY OF PUBLIC UTILITY to shut off a telephone line or the supply of water, gas, or electricity to a building or customer **2.** *vti* DETACH POWER FROM APPLIANCE to break the connection between an appliance and its source of power **3.** *vt* BREAK TELEPHONE CONNECTION BETWEEN SPEAKERS to break or lose the telephone connection between two people during a conversation (*usually passive*) **4.** *vt* DETACH ONE PART FROM ANOTHER to detach something that was connected to something else **5.** *vti* BREAK OFF EMOTIONAL OR SPIRITUAL RELATIONSHIP to end, forget, or lose an emotional or spiritual connection with something or somebody ■ *n* **1.** EMOTIONAL DISINTEREST AND ISOLATION a state of emotional isolation and disinterest that may be voluntary or involuntary ○ *She's in a state of utter disconnect as far as her old school is concerned.* **2.** DISCONNECTION a disconnection of joined parts or things ○ *a disconnect between his words and his acts* —**dis·con·nect·er** *n* —**dis·con·nec·tive** *adj*

dis·con·nect·ed /dìskə néktəd/ *adj* **1.** not connected or joined **2.** showing no logical connection or relationship ○ *rambling disconnected prose* —**dis·con·nect·ed·ly** *adv* —**dis·con·nect·ed·ness** *n*

dis·con·nec·tion /dìskə nékshən/ *n* **1.** the disconnecting of a telephone line or a supply of gas, water, or electricity **2.** the separation of things that were formerly linked or connected

dis·con·so·late /diss kónssələt/ *adj* miserable or disappointed and unable to be cheered up [15C. < medieval Latin *disconsolatus* "comfortless" < Latin *consolatus*, past participle of *consolare* (see CONSOLE[1])] —**dis·con·so·late·ly** *adv* —**dis·con·so·late·ness** *n* —**dis·con·so·la·tion** /diss kònssə láysh'n/ *n*

dis·con·tent /dìskən tént/ *n* **1.** DISSATISFIED UNHAPPINESS a feeling of mild unhappiness and dissatisfaction **2.** LONGING FOR BETTER THINGS a restless desire for something better (*literary*) **3.** DISCONTENTED PERSON somebody who is mildly unhappy and dissatisfied (*literary or formal*) ■ *adj* same as **discontented** —**dis·con·tent·ment** *n*

dis·con·tent·ed /dìskən téntəd/ *adj* feeling mildly unhappy and dissatisfied —**dis·con·tent·ed·ly** *adv* —**dis·con·tent·ed·ness** *n*

dis·con·tin·ue /dìskən tínnyoo/ (**-ued, -u·ing, -ues**) *v* **1.** *vti* to come to an end after happening regularly, or end something that has been happening regularly **2.** *vt* to stop manufacturing something, usually a particular model or type of product [15C. Via French < medieval Latin *discontinuare* "not to continue" < Latin *continuare* "continue"] —**dis·con·tin·u·ance** *n* —**dis·con·tin·u·a·tion** /dìskən tinyoo áysh'n/ *n* —**dis·con·tin·ued** *adj* —**dis·con·tin·u·er** *n*

dis·con·ti·nu·i·ty /diss kòntə nóō ətee/ (*plural* **-ties**) *n* **1.** BREAK IN OTHERWISE CONTINUOUS PROCESS a break or gap in a process that would normally be continuous **2.** MATH POINT OF CHANGE the point or value of a variable at which a curve or mathematical function shows an abrupt change as the variable smoothly increases or decreases **3.** MATH LACK OF MATHEMATICAL CONTINUITY the characteristic of being discontinuous **4.** MATH MATHEMATICAL VALUE a value of a variable for which a function is not continuous **5.** GEOL BOUNDARY BETWEEN ROCK TYPES a boundary between rock types deep within the Earth's crust that is detected as a change in the speed of seismic waves

dis·con·tin·u·ous /dìskən tínnyoo əss/ *adj* **1.** having breaks or gaps in an otherwise continuous process or line **2.** describes variables and functions that have mathematical discontinuity —**dis·con·tin·u·ous·ly** *adv* —**dis·con·tin·u·ous·ness** *n*

dis·cord /díss kàwrd/ *n* **1.** LACK OF AGREEMENT disagreement or strife between people, or incompatibility or conflict between things or situations **2.** UNPLEASANT MUSICAL COMBINATION inharmonious combination of sounds, especially musical sounds **3.** MUSIC UNHARMONIOUS CHORD a musical chord or interval that is conventionally regarded as unpleasant or requiring resolution [13C. Via French < Latin *discordia* < *discord-*, stem of *discors* < *cors* "heart"]

dis·cor·dant /diss káwrd'nt/ *adj* **1.** in disagreement, or incompatible **2.** consisting of sounds, usually musical notes, that are harsh, unpleasant, or clashing —**dis·cor·dance** *n* —**dis·cor·dant·ly** *adv*

dis·co·theque /dískə tèk/ *n* LEISURE same as **disco** *n* (sense 1) [Mid-20C. < French *discothèque* < *disque* "disk, record" + *-thèque* "library"]

dis·count *n* /díss kòwnt/ **1.** REDUCTION IN PRICE a reduction in the usual price of something **2.** FIN, BANKING same as **discount rate** **3.** FIN INTEREST DEDUCTED FROM FINANCIAL INSTRUMENT the interest deducted from the face value of a financial instrument or promissory note before a sale or loan is completed **4.** FIN DEDUCTION FROM PAR VALUE OF STOCK the amount by which the par value of stock exceeds the market price actually paid by purchasers ■ *v* /diss kównt, díss kòwnt/ (**-count·ed, -count·ing, -counts**) **1.** *vt* REDUCE PRICE OF SOMETHING to offer something for sale at less than the usual price **2.** *vt* FIN TRADE INVESTMENT AT REDUCED PRICE to buy or sell a financial instrument at a reduced price that is calculated according to the interest rate and risk on the investment **3.** *vti* FIN MAKE SECURED LOAN AT REDUCED RATE to lend money on a negotiable long-term financial instrument at a reduced price that is calculated according to the instrument's risk and the interest due before its maturity **4.** *vt* DISMISS SOMETHING AS UNTRUE OR TRIVIAL to decide that something can be disregarded as unimportant, irrelevant, or untrue ○ *We had already discounted the theory that they were involved.* **5.** *vt* ANTICIPATE SOMETHING AND ALLOW FOR IT to foresee something and make adjustments to lessen or absorb its impact ■ *adj* WITH REDUCED PRICE for sale at less than the usual price, or selling goods for less than the usual price ○ *a discount warehouse* [Early 17C. < French *descompte* (noun) and Italian *discontare* (verb) < medieval Latin *discomputare*, literally "count away" < Latin *computare* "reckon together"] —**dis·count·a·ble** /díss kòwntəb'l, diss kówntəb'l/ *adj*

dis·count bro·ker *n* **1.** a stockbroker who executes trades for customers, but who in exchange for low commissions offers little advice or investment research **2.** an agent who buys and sells bills or other commercial paper at a discount —**dis·count bro·ker·age** *n*

dis·count bro·ker·age *n* a brokerage firm that charges low commissions to investors because it offers few additional services such as investment advice

dis·count card *n* a plastic card entitling the holder to a reduction on the price of goods or services bought at a specific place

dis·count·ed cash flow /diss kówntəd-/ *n* a method of valuing an investment by calculating what future cash returns will be worth at the time they are received, based on estimates of future inflation and interest rates

dis·coun·te·nance /diss kówntənənss/ (*formal*) *vt* (**-nanced, -nanc·ing, -nanc·es**) **1.** EMBARRASS SOMEBODY to make somebody embarrassed **2.** DISAPPROVE OF SOMEBODY OR SOMETHING to discourage or disapprove of somebody or something ■ *n* DISFAVOR disapproval of somebody or something

dis·count·er /díss kòwntər/; *except commerce* /diss kówntər/ *n* **1.** COMM same as **discount store** **2.** FIN SOMEBODY WHO DISCOUNTS FINANCIAL INSTRUMENTS somebody who buys, sells, or lends money on financial instruments at a reduced price **3.** SOMEBODY WHO DISMISSES SOMETHING somebody who discounts something as unimportant, irrelevant, or untrue **4.** ANTICIPATOR somebody who discounts something to lessen or absorb its impact

dis·count house /díss kownt-/ *n* COMM same as **discount store**

dis·count mar·ket /díss kownt-/ *n* the part of the financial market trading in discounted commercial bills, including banks and brokers

dis·count rate /díss kownt-/ *n* **1.** the rate at which expected cash returns from a security are converted into the security's market price **2.** the rate of interest at which member banks may borrow money from the Federal Reserve Bank

dis·count store /díss kownt-/ *n* a store that sells merchandise at prices that are reduced from those recommended by the manufacturers

dis·cour·age /diss kúr ij/ (**-aged, -ag·ing, -ag·es**) *vt* **1.** TEND TO STOP SOMETHING to tend to prevent something from happening by making it more difficult or unpleasant ○ *dirty beaches that discourage sunbathing* **2.** TRY TO DETER SOMEBODY to try to stop a person or animal from doing something **3.** MAKE SOMEBODY LESS OPTIMISTIC to make somebody feel less motivated, confident, or optimistic [15C. < Old French *descoragier* "deprive of courage" < *corage* "courage"] —**dis·cour·age·ment** *n* —**dis·cour·ag·er** *n*

dis·cour·ag·ing /diss kúr ijing/ *adj* making somebody feel less motivation, confidence, or optimism about something —**dis·cour·ag·ing·ly** *adv*

dis·course *n* /díss kàwrss/ **1.** SERIOUS SPEECH OR PIECE OF WRITING a serious and lengthy speech or piece of writing about a topic **2.** SERIOUS CONVERSATION serious discussion about something between people or groups **3.** LING LANGUAGE language, especially the type of language used in a particular context or subject ○ *political discourse* **4.** LING MAJOR UNIT OF LANGUAGE a unit of language, especially spoken language, that is longer than the sentence. The term is used by linguists when investigating features of language that extend beyond sentences. ■ *vi* /diss káwrss/ (**-coursed, -cours·ing, -cours·es**) **1.** SERIOUSLY SPEAK OR WRITE ON TOPIC to speak or write about a subject in a formal context and at length ○ *In the second part, the author discourses on ethics.* **2.** CONVERSE to have a conversation (*formal*) [15C. < Latin *discursus* "running to and fro" < *discurrere* "to run apart" < *currere* "to run"] —**dis·cours·er** /diss káwrsər/ *n*

dis·course a·nal·y·sis *n* the analysis of features of language that extend beyond the limits of a sentence

dis·cour·te·sy /diss kúrtəssee/ (*plural* **-sies**) *n* behavior or an action that is bad-mannered or impolite —**dis·cour·te·ous** /diss kúrtee əss/ *adj* —**dis·cour·te·ous·ly** *adv* —**dis·cour·te·ous·ness** *n*

dis·cov·er /diss kúvvər/ (**-ered, -er·ing, -ers**) *vt* **1.** FIND OUT ABOUT SOMETHING to find out information that was not previously known ○ *We discovered she'd known all along.* **2.** BE FIRST TO FIND OR LEARN SOMETHING to be the first person to find or learn something previously unknown ○ *Researchers discovered a new genetic link to the causes of the disease.* **3.** FIND SOMEBODY OR SOMETHING to find somebody or something unexpectedly or after a search ○ *was discovered living in Florida* **4.** FIRST NOTICE INTEREST IN SOMETHING to realize for the first time that you enjoy or have a talent for something ○ *Having discovered painting in her 50s, she ended up making a living by it.* **5.** RECOGNIZE SOMEBODY'S POTENTIAL FOR SUCCESS to realize that a musician, actor, performer, or other person has exceptional talent or unusual beauty, and help to bring him or her to prominence [14C. Via Old French *descovrir* < late Latin *discooperire* "to uncover" < Latin *cooperire* "to cover"] —**dis·cov·er·a·ble** *adj* —**dis·cov·er·er** *n*

dis·cov·ered check *n* a move in chess that creates a check previously blocked by the piece moved

dis·cov·er·y /diss kúvvəree/ (*plural* **-ies**) *n* **1.** SOMETHING LEARNED OR FOUND something new that has been learned or found ○ *These dinosaur remains were one of the most important discoveries of the century.* **2.** PROCESS OF LEARNING SOMETHING the fact or process of finding out about something for the first time ○ *the discovery of DNA* ○ *a voyage of discovery* **3.** PROCESS OF FINDING SOMETHING the process or act of finding something or somebody unexpectedly or after searching ○ *The discovery of the abandoned car provided new clues.* **4.** SOMEBODY RECOGNIZED AS POTENTIALLY SUCCESSFUL a previously unknown musician, actor, performer, or other person who has been identified by somebody as having exceptional talent or unusual beauty **5.** RECOGNITION OF POTENTIAL FOR SUCCESS the recognition of somebody's exceptional talent or beauty, leading to that person's fame **6.** LAW MUTUAL DISCLOSING OF DATA OR DOCUMENTS the stage of a legal proceeding during which each side must provide data and documents to the other side **7.** LAW DISCLOSABLE DATA AND DOCUMENTS data or materials that a party in a legal proceeding must disclose to another party before or during the proceeding

dis·cred·it /diss kréddit/ *vt* (**-it·ed, -it·ing, -its**) **1.** HARM REPUTATION OF SOMEBODY to make somebody or something appear untrustworthy or wrong **2.** CAUSE SOMETHING TO SEEM DOUBTFUL to cast doubt on the validity or accuracy of something **3.** NOT BELIEVE SOMETHING to not accept that something is accurate or true ○ *Scientists generally discredit the theory of canals on Mars.* ■ *n* **1.** LOSS OF REPUTATION the loss of somebody's or something's good name or reputation ○ *brought the game into discredit* **2.** CAUSE OF BAD REPUTATION somebody or something who causes the loss of a good name or reputation ○ *a discredit to his profession* **3.** DOUBT OR SUSPICION doubt about the validity or accuracy of something —**dis·cred·it·a·ble** *adj*

dis·creet /di skréet/ *adj* **1.** TACTFUL careful to avoid embarrassing or upsetting others **2.** GOOD AT KEEPING SECRETS careful not to speak about anything that should be secret or confidential **3.** SUBTLE AND UNOBTRUSIVE subtle and circumspect, ensuring that no undue attention is attracted ○ *wearing discreet makeup* **4.** MODEST modest, and not ostentatious or flashy [14C. Via French < Latin *discretus* "distinct," past participle of *discernere* "distinguish" (see DISCERN)] —**dis·creet·ness** *n*

USAGE discreet or **discrete**? These two words have the same pronunciation and are sometimes confused. Both are adjectives, but their meanings are quite different. ***Discreet*** is the more frequent word in general use and means "tactful," "good at keeping secrets," or "subtle and unobtrusive": *I made a few discreet inquiries.* ***Discrete*** is a more formal or technical word meaning "separate, unconnected, and distinct": *Several discrete strands of evidence were pursued.*

dis·creet·ly /diss kréetlee/ *adv* taking care to avoid upsetting or embarrassing people, giving away anything confidential, or appearing immodest or flashy

dis·crep·an·cy /di skréppənsee/ (*plural* **-cies**) *n* a distinct difference between two things such as sets of figures that should match or correspond ○ *found a discrepancy in the figures* [Early 17C. < Latin *discrepantia* < *discrepare* "differ" < *crepare* "to rattle"] —**dis·crep·ant** *adj*

dis·crete /di skréet/ *adj* **1.** completely separate and unconnected **2.** describes mathematical elements or variables that are distinct, unrelated, and have a finite number of values [14C. < Latin *discretus* (see DISCREET)] —**dis·crete·ly** *adv* —**dis·crete·ness** *n*

USAGE See *discreet.*

dis·cre·tion /di skrésh'n/ *n* **1.** TACT the good judgment and sensitivity needed to avoid embarrassing or upsetting others **2.** FREEDOM TO DECIDE the freedom or authority to judge something or make a decision about it ○ *Tipping is left to the customer's discretion.* **3.** CONFIDENTIALITY the ability to keep sensitive information secret [14C. Via French < Latin *discretion-* "separation, discernment" < *discret-*, past participle of *discernere* (see DISCERN)]

dis·cre·tion·ar·y /di skrésh'n èrree/ *adj* **1.** GIVING SOMEBODY AUTHORITY TO DECIDE giving somebody the freedom to make a decision according to individual circumstances **2.** GIVEN OR REFUSED ACCORDING TO CIRCUMSTANCES given according to the merits of an individual case, rather than being provided or awarded automatically **3.** USABLE AS WANTED able to be used as desired without any stipulations ○ *a discretionary fund* —**dis·cre·tion·ar·i·ly** *adv*

dis·cre·tion·ar·y ac·count *n* a securities account in which the broker has been given the authority to make decisions about buying and selling without the customer's prior permission

dis·cre·tion·ar·y in·come *n* income that is left over after necessary expenditure

dis·cre·tion·ar·y trust *n* **1.** a trust in which somebody other than its founder, e.g., a trustee, determines the beneficiaries' shares **2.** a trust in which the trustee has full discretion to decide which beneficiaries will receive what parts of the trust when it is distributed

dis·crim·i·na·ble /diss krímmənəb'l/ *adj* able to be perceived as different or distinct [Mid-18C. < DISCRIMINATE] —**dis·crim·i·na·bil·i·ty** /diss krìmmənə bíllətee/ *n* —**dis·crim·i·na·bly** *adv*

dis·crim·i·nant /diss krímmənənt/ *n* a relation between the coefficients *a*, *b*, and *c* of a mathematical expression of the form $ax^2 + bx + c = 0$, used in the study of roots and other properties of the expression [Mid-19C. < Latin *discriminant-*, present participle of *discriminare* (see DISCRIMINATE)]

dis·crim·i·nant func·tion *n* a statistical method used to place an item that could belong to any of two or more sets of variables in the correct set, with a minimal probability of error

dis·crim·i·nate /di skrímmə nàyt/ (**-nat·ed, -nat·ing, -nates**) *v* **1.** *vi* **TREAT GROUP UNFAIRLY BECAUSE OF PREJUDICE** to treat one person or group worse than others or better than others, usually because of a prejudice about race, ethnicity, age, religion, or gender **2.** *vti* **DISCERN DIFFERENCE** to recognize or identify a difference ○ *could not discriminate between red and green* **3.** *vi* **BE AWARE OF DIFFERENCES** to pay attention to subtle differences and exercise judgment and taste [Early 17C. < Latin *discriminat-*, past participle of *discriminare* "to divide" < *discrimin-* "division" < *discernere* (see DISCERN)] —**dis·crim·i·nate·ly** /-nətlee/ *adv* —**dis·crim·i·na·tive** *adj*

dis·crim·i·nat·ing /di skrímmə nàyting/ *adj* **1.** able to identify subtle differences and appreciate good quality or taste ○ *Discriminating customers prefer these handmade linens.* **2.** describes tariffs that are set at different rates for different importers —**dis·crim·i·nat·ing·ly** *adv*

dis·crim·i·na·tion /di skrìmmə náysh'n/ *n* **1. TREATING PEOPLE DIFFERENTLY THROUGH PREJUDICE** unfair treatment of one person or group, usually because of prejudice about race, ethnicity, age, religion, or gender **2. ABILITY TO NOTICE AND VALUE QUALITY** the ability to appreciate good quality or taste **3. AWARENESS OF SUBTLE DIFFERENTIATION** the ability to notice subtle differences **4.** ELECTRONICS **SIGNAL SELECTION** the selection of a transmitted signal with a specific characteristic, e.g., frequency, by elimination of signals with other characteristics, using a discriminator —**dis·crim·i·na·tion·al** *adj*

dis·crim·i·na·tor /diss krímmə nàytər/ *n* a device or circuit that translates phase or frequency variations into amplitude variations in a modulated signal such as a radio signal, used to select signals with specific characteristics

dis·crim·i·na·to·ry /di skrímmənə tàwree/ *adj* **1.** treating a person or group unfairly, especially because of prejudice about race, ethnicity, age, religion, or gender **2.** describes a statistical test that is unbiased because the sampling procedure avoided the systematic distortion that could be introduced by an unrepresentative population —**dis·crim·i·na·to·ri·ly** *adv*

~~**discription**~~ incorrect spelling of **description**

dis·cur·sive /di skúrssiv/ *adj* **1.** lengthy and including extra material that is not essential to what is being written or spoken about ○ *One book is concise and snappy, while the other has a more relaxed, discursive style.* **2.** using logic rather than intuition to reach a conclusion [Late 16C. < medieval Latin *discursivus* < *discurs-*, past participle of *discurrere* (see DISCOURSE)] —**dis·cur·sive·ly** *adv* —**dis·cur·sive·ness** *n*

dis·cus /dískəss/ (*plural* **-cus·es** or **-ci** /dí skī/) *n* **1. DISK THROWN IN TRACK-AND-FIELD** a weighted disk thrown in track-and-field competitions by an athlete who spins with outstretched arms to launch it from the flat of his or her hand. The ancient Greek Olympic games included the throwing of a bronze discus. **2. TRACK-AND-FIELD EVENT** a track-and-field event in which the contestants compete to throw a discus as far as possible **3. COLORFUL AQUARIUM FISH** a small colorful freshwater fish that has a compressed disk-shaped body and is popular as an aquarium fish. Native to: South America. Latin name: *Symphysodon discus.* [Mid-17C. < Latin (see DISH)]

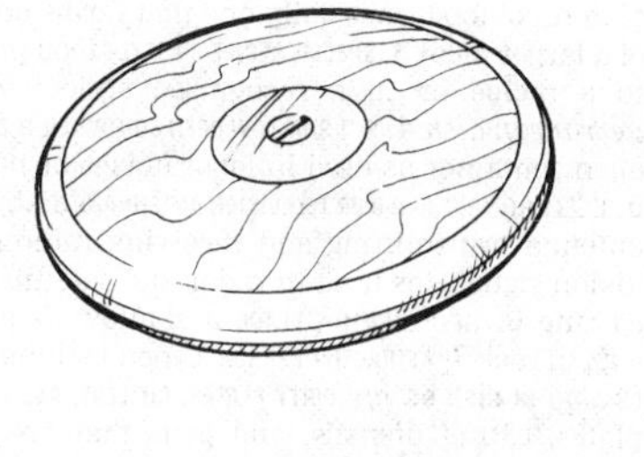

discus

dis·cuss /di skúss/ (**-cussed, -cuss·ing, -cuss·es**) *vt* **1.** to talk about a subject with others ○ *need to discuss it with them first* **2.** to consider a topic in speaking or writing ○ *Chapter 3 discusses the events leading up to the Revolutionary War.* [14C. < Latin *discuss-*, past participle of *discutere* "dash to pieces" < *quatere* "to shake"] —**dis·cuss·a·ble** *adj* —**dis·cuss·er** *n*

dis·cus·sant /di skúss'nt/ *n* a participant in a formal discussion or seminar

dis·cus·sion /di skúsh'n/ *n* **1.** a talk between two or more people about a subject, usually to exchange ideas or reach a conclusion, or talk of this kind ○ *deep in a discussion about what to do next* ○ *My decision is not open to discussion.* **2.** a detailed consideration or examination of a topic in writing or speech

dis·dain /diss dáyn/ *n* extreme contempt or disgust for something or somebody ■ *vt* (**-dained, -dain·ing, -dains**) to regard somebody or something as not worthy of respect [14C. Probably < Old French *desdeignier* "treat as unworthy" < late Latin *dedignare* < *dignare* "treat as worthy"] —**dis·dain·ful** *adj* —**dis·dain·ful·ly** *adv* —**dis·dain·ful·ness** *n*

dis·ease /di zéez/ *n* **1. MEDICAL CONDITION** a condition in humans, plants, or animals that results in pathological symptoms and is not the direct result of physical injury **2. SPECIFIC DISORDER** a disorder in humans, animals, or plants with recognizable signs and often having a known cause **3. PROBLEM IN SOCIETY** a serious problem in society or with a group of people [14C. < Old French *desaise* "lack of ease" < *aise* "ease"] —**dis·eased** *adj*

dis·e·con·o·my /dìssi kónnəmee/ (*plural* **-mies**) *n* something that contributes to increased costs

dis·em·bark /dìssəm baárk/ (**-barked, -bark·ing, -barks**) *v* **1.** *vi* to get off a passenger vehicle, especially a ship, aircraft, or train **2.** *vt* to let passengers off a ship, bus, train, or aircraft, or unload cargo (*formal*) [Late 16C. < French *désembarquer*, Spanish *desembarcar*, or Italian *disimbarcare*, < French *embarquer* or the equivalent (see EMBARK)] —**dis·em·bar·ka·tion** /diss èm baar káysh'n/ *n* —**dis·em·bark·ment** *n*

dis·em·bar·rass /dìssəm bárrəss/ (**-rassed, -rass·ing, -rass·es**) *vt* to free somebody from something embarrassing, unpleasant, or burdensome (*formal*) —**dis·em·bar·rass·ment** *n*

dis·em·bod·ied /dìssəm bóddeed/ *adj* coming from somebody who cannot be seen in a way that may be eerie or frightening ○ *a disembodied voice whispering in the darkness*

dis·em·bod·y /dìssəm bóddee/ (**-ied, -y·ing, -ies**) *vt* in some beliefs, to free the soul or spirit from the body —**dis·em·bod·i·ment** *n*

dis·em·bow·el /dìssəm bów əl/ (**-eled, -el·ing, -els**) *vt* **1.** to cut open the stomach of a person or animal and remove the internal organs, especially the intestines **2.** to remove the internal substance, elements, or parts of something (*literary*) —**dis·em·bow·el·ment** *n*

dis·em·broil /dìssəm bróyl/ (**-broiled, -broil·ing, -broils**) *vt* to free yourself or somebody else from a difficult situation (*archaic or literary*)

dis·em·pow·er /dìssəm pówr/ (**-ered, -er·ing, -ers**) *vt* to take power or influence away from somebody or from yourself —**dis·em·pow·er·ment** *n*

dis·en·a·ble /dìssi náyb'l/ (**-bled, -bling, -bles**) *vt* to prevent something, or make something unable to operate or perform a function ○ *disenabled the weapons system on the aircraft prior to landing* —**dis·en·a·ble·ment** *n*

dis·en·chant /dìssən chánt/ (**-chant·ed, -chant·ing, -chants**) *vt* **1.** to make somebody stop believing that something or somebody is worthwhile, right, or deserving of support **2.** to free somebody from an enchantment or magic spell (*literary*) [Late 16C. < French *désenchanter* "undo enchantment" < *enchanter* "enchant"] —**dis·en·chant·ed** *adj* —**dis·en·chant·er** *n* —**dis·en·chant·ing** *adj* —**dis·en·chant·ing·ly** *adv* —**dis·en·chant·ment** *n*

dis·en·cum·ber /dìssən kúmbər/ (**-bered, -ber·ing, -bers**) *vt* to relieve somebody or something of a burden or problem —**dis·en·cum·ber·ment** *n*

dis·en·dow /dìssən dów/ (**-dowed, -dow·ing, -dows**) *vt* to withdraw an endowment, especially a gift of money —**dis·en·dow·er** *n* —**dis·en·dow·ment** *n*

dis·en·fran·chise /dìssən frán chīz/ (**-chised, -chis·ing, -chis·es**) *vt* to deprive a person or organization of a privilege, immunity, or legal right, especially the right to vote —**dis·en·fran·chise·ment** /dìssən frán chīzmənt, -fránchizmənt/ *n*

dis·en·gage /dìssən gáyj/ (**-gaged, -gag·ing, -gag·es**) *v* **1.** *vti* **PHYSICALLY DISCONNECT OR BECOME DISCONNECTED** to disconnect one thing from another, or become disconnected from something **2.** *vt* **MENTALLY DETACH YOURSELF OR ANOTHER** to withdraw or mentally separate yourself or somebody else from a situation or difficulty **3.** *vti* MIL **STOP FIGHTING IN WAR** to bring troops out of a war or combat, or withdraw from a war or combat **4.** *vti* FENCING **MOVE SWORD FROM OPPONENT'S** to move the point of your sword around an opponent's sword in order to open a new line of attack

dis·en·gage·ment /dìssən gáyjmənt/ *n* **1. RELEASE FROM SOMETHING** the release of somebody or something from a physical or mental attachment **2. WITHDRAWAL OF ARMY** the withdrawal of troops or an army from a war or combat **3. CANCELING OF WEDDING PLANS** the act or process of breaking off an engagement to be married, canceling wedding plans, and returning gifts

dis·en·tail /dìssən táyl/ (**-tailed, -tail·ing, -tails**) *vt* to lift the restrictions on who may inherit specific property —**dis·en·tail·ment** *n*

dis·en·tan·gle /dìssən táng g'l/ (**-gled, -gling, -gles**) *vt* **1. UNTANGLE JUMBLE** to untangle and free things that are muddled, tied, or knotted together **2. STRAIGHTEN OUT CONFUSION** to clarify something confusing, or separate and analyze a confusion of ideas ○ *It was hard to disentangle fact from fiction in his account.* **3. EXTRICATE SOMEBODY FROM SITUATION** to free somebody or yourself from a relationship or complicated situation —**dis·en·tan·gle·ment** *n*

dis·en·tomb /dìssən tóom/ (**-tombed, -tomb·ing, -tombs**) *vt* to take a body out of a tomb or from a place like a tomb

dis·e·qui·lib·ri·um /dìss eekwə líbbree əm/ *n* a state of instability or imbalance, especially in an economy

dis·es·tab·lish /dìssə stábblish/ (**-lished, -lish·ing, -lish·es**) *vt* **1.** to undo or change something that has been established for a long time **2.** to end the official relationship between the state and a nation's established church or religion —**dis·es·tab·lish·ment** *n*

dis·es·teem /dìssə stéem/ (*formal*) *vt* (**-teemed, -teem·ing, -teems**) to have a low opinion of somebody or something ■ *n* lack of respect or esteem ○ *held in disesteem*

di·seur /dee zúr/ *n* a man, usually an actor, who is an accomplished reciter of dramatic monologues. Such recitals, often accompanied by music, were once a popular form of theatrical entertainment. [< French, "talker" < *dire* "to say" < Latin *dicere*]

di·seuse /dee zṓz/ *n* a woman, usually an actor, who is an accomplished reciter of dramatic monologues. Such recitals, often accompanied by music, were once a popular theatrical entertainment. [Late 19C. < French, feminine of *diseur* (see DISEUR)]

dis·fa·vor /diss fáyvər/ *n* **1. CONDITION OF DISAPPROVAL** the state of being disapproved of ○ *This fell into disfavor years ago.* **2. DISRESPECT OR DISAPPROVAL** a feeling of disapproval or lack of respect ○ *They were looked on with disfavor.* ■ *vt* (**-vored, -vor·ing, -vors**) **DISLIKE**

OR DISAPPROVE OF SOMETHING to regard something with dislike or disapproval (*formal*)

dis·fea·ture /diss féechər/ (-tured, -tur·ing, -tures) *vt* same as **disfigure** —**dis·fea·ture·ment** *n*

dis·fig·ure /diss fíggyər/ (-ured, -ur·ing, -ures) *vt* to mar the appearance of somebody or something [14C. < Old French *desfigurer* "deprive something of its figure" < Latin *figura* "figure"] —**dis·fig·u·ra·tion** /diss fíggyə ráysh'n/ *n* —**dis·fig·ure·ment** *n*

dis·fran·chise /diss frán chīz/ (-chised, -chis·ing, -chis·es) *vt* POL same as **disenfranchise** —**dis·fran·chise·ment** /diss frán chīzmənt, -chizmənt/ *n*

dis·frock /diss frók/ (-frocked, -frock·ing, -frocks) *vt* CHR same as **defrock**

dis·gorge /diss gáwrj/ (-gorged, -gorg·ing, -gorg·es) *vt* **1.** POUR SUBSTANCES OUT to pour out liquid, gas, or other contents in a gushing stream ○ *disgorged the contents of her purse* **2.** LET PEOPLE OUT to let a large number of people come out of a building or vehicle at the same time ○ *a cruise ship disgorging thousands of passengers* **3.** REGURGITATE OR VOMIT FOOD to vomit or regurgitate food that has been eaten or partly eaten, as some birds and mammals do to feed their young [15C. < Old French *desgorger* "expel from the throat" < *gorge* "throat"] —**dis·gorge·ment** *n*

dis·grace /diss gráyss/ *n* **1.** STATE OF BEING DISAPPROVED OF shame or loss of respect arising from bad behavior ○ *She was sent home in disgrace.* **2.** CAUSE OF SHAME OR DISRESPECT a cause of shame or loss of respect ○ *She's a disgrace to the family.* ■ *vt* (-graced, -grac·ing, -grac·es) CAUSE SOMEBODY TO LOSE RESPECT to bring shame or loss of respect on yourself or others who are associated with you by bad behavior ○ *He disgraced himself by forgetting the wedding.* [Mid-16C. Via French *disgracier* < Italian *disgraziare* < *disgrazia* "disfavor" < Latin *gratia* (see GRACE)] —**dis·grac·er** *n*

dis·grace·ful /diss gráyssfəl/ *adj* so bad or unacceptable that it should be something to be ashamed of ○ *The way they were treated was disgraceful.* —**dis·grace·ful·ly** *adv* —**dis·grace·ful·ness** *n*

dis·grun·tle /diss grúnt'l/ (-tled, -tling, -tles) *vt* to make somebody feel dissatisfied and irritated [Mid-17C. < obsolete *gruntle* "to grumble, grunt" < GRUNT[1]] —**dis·grun·tled** *adj* —**dis·grun·tle·ment** *n*

dis·guise /diss gīz/ *vt* (-guised, -guis·ing, -guis·es) **1.** CHANGE SOMEBODY'S APPEARANCE FOR CONCEALMENT to make changes in the appearance of somebody or something to avoid recognition ○ *He fled the besieged city disguised as a woman.* **2.** HIDE SOMETHING TO PREVENT OTHERS KNOWING to hide feelings or facts from other people ○ *She couldn't disguise her horror.* **3.** CHANGE SOMETHING TO PREVENT RECOGNITION to change something so that it cannot be recognized ○ *His voice has been disguised during the interview to conceal his identity.* ■ *n* **1.** SOMETHING DONE TO PREVENT RECOGNITION something worn or done in order to change somebody's appearance and prevent recognition ○ *Anyone would have seen through such a flimsy disguise.* **2.** ALTERATION OR CONCEALMENT TO PREVENT RECOGNITION the alteration or concealment of something in order to prevent it being seen or recognized by others ○ *a plot that relies on disguise* **3.** ALTERED APPEARANCE an altered appearance intended to conceal somebody's identity or make somebody look like somebody else ○ *went to the ball in disguise* [14C. < Old French *desguis(i)er* "remove your appearance" < *guise* "appearance"] —**dis·guis·a·ble** *adj* —**dis·guised** *adj* —**dis·guis·er** *n*

dis·gust /diss gúst/ *n* **1.** STRONG DISAPPROVAL OR REVULSION a feeling of horrified disapproval of something ○ *viewed the tawdry scandal with unconcealed disgust* **2.** IMPATIENT IRRITATION a feeling of impatient irritation ○ *Much to my disgust, I was compelled to hand over the documents.* ■ *vt* (-gust·ed, -gust·ing, -gusts) MAKE SOMEBODY FEEL REVOLTED to make somebody feel sickened or revolted [Late 16C. < French *desgoust* or Italian *disgusto* "have a distaste for" < Latin *gustus* "taste"] —**dis·gust·ed** *adj* —**dis·gust·ed·ness** *n*

SYNONYMS See *dislike*.

dis·gust·ing /diss gústing/ *adj* **1.** tending to repel and sicken people ○ *a disgusting smell* **2.** completely unacceptable or disgraceful ○ *a disgusting waste of money* —**dis·gust·ing·ly** *adv* —**dis·gust·ing·ness** *n*

dish /dish/ *n* **1.** SERVING BOWL a container for serving food, usually a bowl **2.** SERVING OF FOOD a serving or plateful of food, especially one that forms only part of a larger meal **3.** SPECIAL RECIPE OR STYLE food prepared to a recipe or in a recognized style ○ *a Mediterranean dish* **4.** SCI SHALLOW OPEN CONTAINER a shallow open container as used in laboratories or hospitals **5.** ELECTRONICS RADIO OR TELEVISION ANTENNA a dish-shaped antenna transmitting and receiving radio or television signals, as used in radar and satellite broadcasting **6.** GEOL HOLLOW PLACE a shallow depression, e.g., in rock **7.** ATTRACTIVE PERSON a good-looking person (*slang*) ■ **dish·es** *npl* DIRTY PLATES, CUTLERY, AND PANS the plates, eating utensils, and pans that are dirtied during the cooking and eating of a meal ○ *my turn to wash the dishes* ○ *do the dishes* ■ *vt* (dished, dish·ing, dish·es) HOLLOW SOMETHING OUT to make or form a concave shape in something [Pre-12C. Via Latin *discus* "dish, platter" < Greek *diskos* "disk, quoit, platter" < *dikein* "to throw"]

dish out *vt* **1.** to serve food to people ○ *dishing out mashed potatoes* **2.** to give something out freely, especially criticism, money, punishment, or advice (*informal*) ◇ **dish it out (but not be able to take it)** to criticize others freely (while not being able to accept criticism) (*informal*) ○ *She can really dish it out but she surely can't take it.*

dis·ha·bille /díssə béel, -bée/, **des·ha·bille** /déssə béel, -bée/ *n* a state in which somebody is partially undressed or dressed very casually or incompletely (*formal*) [Late 17C. < French *déshabillé*, past participle of *déshabiller* "undress" < *habiller* "dress"]

dish an·ten·na *n* a transmitting and receiving antenna in the form of a bowl-shaped reflector, used, e.g., in radar and in satellite television broadcasting

dis·har·mo·ny /diss háarmənee/ *n* **1.** CONFLICT BETWEEN PEOPLE disagreement or conflict between people or groups who cannot get along with each other **2.** LACK OF MUSICAL HARMONY lack of agreement in music or sounds, resulting in unpleasant sound combinations **3.** IMBALANCE lack of balance in something such as the body or the environment —**dis·har·mo·ni·ous** /diss haar mṓnee əss/ *adj* —**dis·har·mo·ni·ous·ly** *adv*

dish·cloth /dísh klàwth, -klòth/ *n* **1.** HOUSEHOLD same as **dishtowel** **2.** a cloth used for washing dishes

dish·cloth gourd *n* PLANTS same as **loofa** (sense 2)

dis·heart·en /diss háart'n/ (-ened, -en·ing, -ens) *vt* to make somebody lose hope and enthusiasm —**dis·heart·en·ment** *n*

dis·heart·en·ing /diss háart'ning/ *adj* making somebody lose hope or enthusiasm —**dis·heart·en·ing·ly** *adv*

dished /disht/ *adj* hollowed out in a shape like a dish

di·shev·el /di shévv'l/ (-eled or -elled, -el·ing or -el·ling, -els) *vt* **1.** to disarrange somebody's clothes or hair **2.** to disarrange something, making it messy [Late 16C. Probably back-formation < DISHEVELED] —**di·shev·el·ment** *n*

di·shev·eled /di shévv'ld/, **di·shev·elled** *adj* **1.** with messed-up hair or clothes **2.** disordered and untidy [14C. < Old French *deschevelé*, past participle of *descheveler* "disarrange the hair" < *des-* "apart" + *chevel* "hair"]

dis·hon·est /diss ónnəst/ *adj* meaning or meant to deceive, defraud, or trick people [14C. Via Old French *deshoneste* < Latin *dehonestus* < *honestus* "honorable"]

dis·hon·est·ly /diss ónnəstlee/ *adv* in a lying or deceitful way

dis·hon·es·ty /diss ónnəstee/ (*plural* -ties) *n* **1.** the use of lies or deceit, or the tendency to be deceitful **2.** a dishonest act

dis·hon·or /diss ónnər/ *n* **1.** LOSS OF OTHER PEOPLE'S RESPECT the loss of a good reputation **2.** CAUSE OF SHAME a cause of shame or loss of respect **3.** FIN FAILURE TO PAY CHECK failure or refusal by a bank or other financial institution to pay a check, bill of exchange, or other financial document (*formal*) ■ *vt* (-ored, -or·ing, -ors) **1.** BRING SHAME ON SOMEBODY to do something that brings shame on yourself or on people associated with you **2.** BREAK AGREEMENT to fail to keep a promise or agreement **3.** TREAT SOMEBODY DISRESPECTFULLY to treat somebody without any respect (*formal*) **4.** FIN FAIL TO PAY CHECK to fail to pay a check, bill of exchange, or other financial document **5.** DISGRACE WOMAN BY SEDUCTION OR RAPE to bring shame on a woman by having sexual intercourse with her before marriage or by raping her (*archaic or literary*) [14C. Via French < medieval Latin *dishonorare* "not to honor" < *honorare* "to honor"] —**dis·hon·or·er** *n*

dis·hon·or·a·ble /diss ónnərəb'l/ *adj* **1.** morally unacceptable and liable to make somebody lose the respect of others **2.** behaving in a dishonest or morally unacceptable way —**dis·hon·or·a·ble·ness** *n* —**dis·hon·or·a·bly** *adv*

dis·hon·or·a·ble dis·charge *n* dismissal from the armed forces as punishment for a serious offense such as desertion

dis·hon·our *n, vt* Can, UK spelling of **dishonor**

dish·pan /dísh pàn/ *n* a large pan or plastic tub used for washing dishes

dish·pan hands *n* a condition of the hands in which the skin is dry, scaly, and reddened because of sensitivity or overexposure to cleaning materials such as detergent (*takes a singular or plural verb*)

dish·rag /dísh ràg/ *n* HOUSEHOLD same as **dishcloth** (sense 2)

dish·tow·el /dísh tòw əl/ *n* a cloth used for drying dishes

dish·ware /dísh wèr/ *n* dishes used for serving food

dish·wash·er /dísh wòshər, -wàwshər/ *n* **1.** an electrically operated machine that washes, rinses, and dries dishes and utensils **2.** somebody who washes dishes, especially in a restaurant

dish·wash·ing liq·uid /dísh woshing-, -wàwshing-/ *n* a liquid detergent used for washing dishes

dish·wa·ter /dísh wàwtər/ *n* **1.** water that is or has been used for washing dishes or utensils **2.** a weak or tasteless drink

dish·wa·ter blond, dish·wa·ter blonde *adj* describes blond or yellow hair that is unattractively dull or pale in color (*informal*) —**dish·wa·ter blond** *n*

dish·y /díshee/ (-i·er, -i·est) *adj* very good-looking (*slang*)

~~**disign**~~ incorrect spelling of **design**

dis·il·lu·sion /díssi lóozh'n/ *vt* (-sioned, -sion·ing, -sions) to cause somebody to realize that an ideal is false or a belief is mistaken (*often passive*) ■ *n* same as **disillusionment** —**dis·il·lu·sioned** *adj* —**dis·il·lu·sive** /-lóossiv/ *adj*

dis·il·lu·sion·ment /díssi lóozh'nmənt/ *n* disappointment caused by a frustrated ideal or belief

dis·in·cen·tive /dissin séntiv/ *n* something that deters somebody from taking an action

dis·in·cli·na·tion /dìssinklə náysh'n/ *n* an unwillingness to do something

dis·in·cline /dìssin klīn/ (-clined, -clin·ing, -clines) *vt* to make somebody unwilling to do something (*often passive*) —**dis·in·clined** *adj*

dis·in·cor·po·rate /dìssin káwrpə ràyt/ (-rat·ed, -rat·ing, -rates) *vti* to end the corporate status of a company, organization, or community, or undergo such a process —**dis·in·cor·po·ra·tion** /dìssin kawrpə ráysh'n/ *n*

dis·in·fect /dìssin fékt/ (-fect·ed, -fect·ing, -fects) *vt* to clean something so as to destroy disease-carrying microorganisms and prevent infection [Late 16C. < French *désinfecter* < *infecter* "infect"] —**dis·in·fec·tion** *n* —**dis·in·fec·tor** *n*

dis·in·fec·tant /dìssin féktənt/ *n* a chemical that destroys or inhibits the growth of microorganisms that cause disease

dis·in·fest /dìssin fést/ (-fest·ed, -fest·ing, -fests) *vt* to free a place, person, or animal of small pests such as rodents or insects —**dis·in·fes·ta·tion** /dìssin fe stáysh'n/ *n*

dis·in·fla·tion /dìssin fláysh'n/ *n* a slowdown in the rate at which prices increase, e.g., during a recession —**dis·in·fla·tion·ar·y** *adj*

dis·in·form /dìssin fáwrm/ (-formed, -form·ing, -forms) *vt* to supply somebody with false or misleading information

dis·in·for·ma·tion /dìssinfər máysh'n/ *n* false or deliberately misleading information, often put out as propaganda

dis·in·gen·u·ous /dìssin jénnyoo əss/ *adj* **1.** withholding or not taking account of known information **2.** giving a false impression of sincerity or simplicity —**dis·in·gen·u·ous·ly** *adv*—**dis·in·gen·u·ous·ness** *n*

dis·in·her·it /dìssin hérrit/ (**-it·ed, -it·ing, -its**) *vt* **1.** to change a will so as to deprive somebody of an inheritance **2.** to deprive somebody of a natural or established right or privilege —**dis·in·her·i·tance** *n*

dis·in·hib·it /dìssin híbbit/ (**-it·ed, -it·ing, -its**) *vt* to free somebody from inhibitions (*technical*)

dis·in·hi·bi·tion /dìssinhi bísh'n/ *n* **1. LOSS OF INHIBITION** a loss of inhibition, e.g., through the influence of alcohol or drugs (*technical*) **2.** PSYCHOL **TEMPORARY LOSS OF INHIBITION** a temporary loss of inhibition caused by an outside stimulus such as a loud noise **3.** CHEM **REMOVAL OF INHIBITOR** the removal of a substance that slows or stops a chemical reaction

dis·in·te·grate /diss íntə gràyt/ (**-grat·ed, -grat·ing, -grates**) *vti* **1. BREAK INTO FRAGMENTS** to break into components or fragments, or break something into small pieces or constituent parts **2. LOSE WHOLENESS** to destroy the cohesion, unity, or wholeness of something, or undergo such destruction **3.** PHYS **SPLIT ATOM** to split the nucleus of an atom, or undergo atomic fission —**dis·in·te·gra·ble** *adj* —**dis·in·te·gra·tive** *adj*

dis·in·te·gra·tion /diss íntə gráysh'n/ *n* **1. BREAKING INTO PIECES** irreversible breaking into components or fragments **2. LOSS OF UNITY** the loss of unity, cohesion, or integrity **3.** PHYS **BREAKUP OF NUCLEUS** the breakup of an atomic nucleus or an unstable elementary particle into smaller parts, either by radioactive decay or through bombardment with high-energy particles

dis·in·te·gra·tion con·stant *n* PHYS same as **decay constant**

dis·in·te·gra·tor /diss íntə gràytər/ *n* **1.** a machine in which atoms are split as a result of being hit by accelerated particles **2.** a person, machine, or force that destroys or disintegrates something

dis·in·ter /dìssin túr/ (**-terred, -ter·ring, -ters**) *vt* **1.** to dig up or remove a dead body from a grave or tomb **2.** to expose something that was hidden (*formal*) [Early 17C. < French *désenterrer* < *enterrer* "inter"] —**dis·in·ter·ment** *n*

dis·in·ter·est /diss íntərəst, diss íntrəst/ *vt* (**-est·ed, -est·ing, -ests**) **MAKE SOMEBODY LOSE BIAS OR INTEREST** to cause somebody to lose interest or partiality ■ *n* **1. IMPARTIALITY** lack of bias or self-interest **2.** ⚠ **ABSENCE OF INTEREST** a lack of interest

USAGE See *disinterested.*

dis·in·ter·est·ed /diss íntərəstəd, diss íntrəstəd/ *adj* **1.** free from bias or self-interest **2.** ⚠ indifferent, not interested, or no longer interested —**dis·in·ter·est·ed·ly** *adv* —**dis·in·ter·est·ed·ness** *n*

USAGE disinterested or **uninterested**? ***Disinterested*** means "free from bias or self-interest," and also has a widely used but much criticized meaning, "indifferent or not interested." In formal writing you should avoid using the meaning "not interested."

dis·in·ter·me·di·a·tion /dìssintər meedee áysh'n/ *n* **1.** the elimination of intermediaries such as wholesalers or retailers in business transactions between producers and consumers **2.** the diversion of invested funds from low-yield to higher-yield areas, e.g., from depository accounts to stocks

dis·in·tox·i·cate /dìssin tóksi kàyt/ (**-cat·ed, -cat·ing, -cates**) *vt* MED same as **detoxify** (sense 1) —**dis·in·tox·i·ca·tion** /dìssin toksi káysh'n/ *n*

dis·in·vent /dìssin vént/ (**-vent·ed, -vent·ing, -vents**) *vt* to undo the invention of something ○ *Nuclear weapons cannot be disinvented.*

dis·in·vest /dìssin vést/ (**-vest·ed, -vest·ing, -vests**) *vti* to withdraw or reduce an investment —**dis·in·vest·ment** *n*

dis·in·vite /dìssin vít/ (**-vit·ed, -vit·ing, -vites**) *vt* to withdraw an invitation to somebody (*humorous*) —**dis·in·vi·ta·tion** /dìss invi táysh'n/ *n*

~~**disipline**~~ incorrect spelling of **discipline**

dis·join /diss jóyn/ (**-joined, -join·ing, -joins**) *vti* to disconnect parts, things, or ideas, or become disconnected [15C. < Old French *desjoign-*, stem of *desjoindre* < Latin *disjungere* < *jungere* "to join"] —**dis·join·a·ble** *adj*

dis·joint /diss jóynt/ (**-joint·ed, -joint·ing, -joints**) *v* **1.** *vti* **SEPARATE AT JOINTS** to separate something at the joints, or come apart at the joints **2.** *vti* **DISLOCATE** to force or move something out of its usual position, or be moved out of the usual position **3.** *vt* **DESTROY UNITY OF SOMETHING** to destroy the unity or coherence of something **4.** *vt* same as **disjoin** [15C. < Old French *desjoint*, past participle of *desjoindre* (see DISJOIN)] —**dis·joint** *adj*

dis·joint·ed /diss jóyntəd/ *adj* not connected in an easily understandable way —**dis·joint·ed·ness** *n*

dis·joint·ed·ly /diss jóyntədlee/ *adv* in a way that makes connections or order unclear

dis·junct /diss júngkt/ *adj* **1. SEPARATED** discontinuous or separated in time or space **2.** MUSIC **SEPARATED BY ONE SECOND** describes consecutive notes that are separated by an interval of a second **3.** MUSIC **WITH MELODIC LEAPS** describes a melody in which leaps are the dominant feature rather than smooth progression ■ *n* LOGIC **CLAUSE** either the p clause or the q clause in a logical proposition of the form "p or q" [15C. < Latin *disjunctus*, past participle of *disjungere* (see DISJOIN)]

dis·junc·tion /diss júngkshən/ *n* **1. DISCONNECTION** a disconnection of joined parts or things **2.** LOGIC **PROPOSITION WITH "OR"** a proposition of the form "p or q" that is false if both p and q are false, but true if at least one of them is true **3.** LOGIC same as **disjunct 4.** GENETICS **CHROMOSOME SEPARATION** the separation of like chromosomes during cell division

dis·junc·tive /diss júngktiv/ *adj* **1. DIVIDING** serving to divide things, or having the effect of dividing things (*technical*) **2.** GRAM **SHOWING CONTRAST** describes a word such as "or" that establishes a contrast between two words or linguistic elements **3.** LOGIC **OF LOGICAL DISJUNCTION** relating to or having the form of a proposition of the type "p or q" ■ *n* **1.** GRAM **CONTRAST WORD** a conjunction or other word that establishes a contrast **2.** LOGIC same as **disjunction** (sense 2) —**dis·junc·tive·ly** *adv*

dis·junc·ture /diss júngkchər/ *n* same as **disjunction** (sense 1)

disk /disk/, **disc** *n* **1. ROUND FLAT OBJECT** an object that is thin, flat, and circular **2.** COMPUT **COMPUTER STORAGE DEVICE** a device consisting of one or more thin magnetically or optically etched plates, used in a computer to store information **3.** ANAT **PART BETWEEN BONES OF SPINE** a flat round structure in the skeleton of a person or animal that separates the bones of the spine **4.** MECH ENG **BRAKE PART** a circular piece of metal around the hub of a vehicle wheel, against which the pads of a disc brake press **5.** AGRIC **STEEL BLADE** a circular steel blade with a sharpened edge that is used on a disk harrow or plow **6.** BOT **CENTER OF FLOWER HEAD** the central part of the flower head of a composite plant, made up of tiny tubular flowers [Mid-17C. Directly or via French < Latin *discus* (see DISH)] —**disk·like** *adj*

disk brake *n* AUTOMOT another spelling of **disc brake**

disk cam·er·a *n* a camera that uses film in a disk rather than a roll or cartridge

disk drive *n* a computer device that reads data from and writes data to spinning magnetic or optical disks

disk·ette /di skét/ *n* COMPUT same as **floppy disk**

disk flow·er, disk flo·ret *n* a tiny tubular flower that is one of the group that forms the center disk of the flower head of some composite plants, e.g., the daisy

disk har·row *n* a harrow with a series of disks set at an angle on one or more axles that loosen the soil when moved over plowed land

disk op·er·at·ing sys·tem *n* an operating system for personal computers that uses disks and diskettes for storage of programs and data

disk pack *n* a removable data storage device used in minicomputers and mainframes, consisting of a stack of magnetic or optical disks

disk plow *n* an agricultural implement with a cutting disk fixed in a frame, which cuts furrows in the soil and turns it up. It is drawn by a tractor.

disk sand·er *n* an electrically powered tool with a revolving abrasive disk. Use: sanding, grinding, polishing irregular surfaces.

disk wheel *n* an automobile wheel with a continuous flat outer surface instead of spokes

dis·like /diss lík/ *vt* (**-liked, -lik·ing, -likes**) **NOT LIKE SOMEBODY OR SOMETHING** to consider something or somebody disagreeable or unpleasant ■ *n* **1. DISAPPROVING FEELING** an attitude or feeling of disapproval or lack of enjoyment **2. SOMETHING NOT LIKED** something that is considered disagreeable —**dis·lik·a·ble** *adj*

SYNONYMS ***dislike, distaste, hatred, hate, disgust, loathing, repugnance, abhorrence, animosity, antipathy, aversion, revulsion***

CORE MEANING: a feeling of not liking somebody or something

dislike an attitude or feeling of disapproval or lack of enjoyment ○ *a dislike for sudden change* ○ *She took a dislike to the dress and refused to wear it.* ○ *He didn't try to hide his dislike of his brother's wife.* **distaste** disapproval of something or somebody's behavior ○ *He wrinkled his nose in distaste at the acrid smell.* ○ *a distaste for inactivity* **hatred** *or* **hate** intense hostility toward somebody or something ○ *violent verbal expressions of hatred* ○ *Even the children's hearts were full of hate.* **disgust** a feeling of horrified disapproval ○ *I like to go poking around in thrift shops, much to my husband's disgust.* ○ *He took early retirement from the university in disgust at the drop in standards.* **loathing** intense dislike of somebody or something ○ *A passionate loathing of materialism is evident in his writing.* ○ *I developed an irrational loathing for the man sent to meet me.* **repugnance** a very strong feeling of disgust, mainly for behavior and activities ○ *He expressed his repugnance at the assault.* ○ *international repugnance of the past week's violence* **abhorrence** a feeling of intense disapproval, mainly of behavior and activities ○ *our deep and abiding abhorrence of the current system* ○ *They declared an absolute abhorrence of receiving money from gambling in any form.* **animosity** a feeling or spirit of hostility and resentment ○ *a nation with a history of animosity toward rival exporters* ○ *There was no personal animosity between my sister and me.* **antipathy** strong hostility or opposition toward somebody or something ○ *his well-known antipathy to the nationalist cause* ○ *These rumors fueled the crowd's antipathy towards the government.* **aversion** strong hostility or opposition toward somebody or something ○ *had always shown a total aversion to most forms of exercise* ○ *his instinctive aversion to being ordered about* **revulsion** a sudden violent feeling of disgust ○ *The case sent a wave of revulsion against political corruption through the country.*

dis·lo·cate /dísslō kàyt/ (**-cat·ed, -cat·ing, -cates**) *vt* **1. PUT SOMETHING OUT OF PLACE** to put or force something out of its usual place or position **2. DISPLACE BODY PART** to move or force a bone out of the joint into which it fits **3. THROW SOMETHING INTO CONFUSION** to disrupt, upset, or disturb the order of something [Late 16C. Probably back-formation < DISLOCATION] —**dis·lo·cat·ed** *adj*

dis·lo·cat·ed work·er *n* a worker who has lost a job because his or her employer has moved, shut down, or reduced its work force

dis·lo·ca·tion /dìsslō káysh'n/ *n* **1. DISLOCATING OR BEING DISLOCATED** the displacement of something from its usual or proper position **2.** MED **DISPLACEMENT OF BODY PART** the displacement of a body part, especially of a bone from its usual fitting in a joint **3.** CHEM **IMPERFECTION IN CRYSTAL** an irregularity in the fine structure (**lattice**) of an otherwise normal crystal [14C. Directly or via French < medieval Latin *dislocation-* < Latin *locat-* (see LOCATE)]

dis·lodge /diss lój/ (**-lodged, -lodg·ing, -lodg·es**) *vti* to force something or somebody from a previously fixed or secure position, or leave such a position [15C. < Old French *dislogier* < *logier* < *loge* "hut"] —**dis·lodg·ment** *n*

dis·loy·al /diss lóy əl/ *adj* showing a lack of faith in or loyalty to somebody or something [15C. < Old French *desloial* < *loial* (see LOYAL)] —**dis·loy·al·ly** *adv*

dis·loy·al·ty /diss lóy əltee/ (*plural* **-ties**) *n* **1.** a lack of loyalty to a person, vow, organization, or state **2.** a disloyal or unfaithful act

dis·mal /dízməl/ *adj* **1. DEPRESSING** depressing to the spirit or outlook **2. HOPELESS** showing a lack or failure of hope **3. OF POOR QUALITY** very poor or inadequate ○ *a dismal performance* [14C. < obsolete noun, "unlucky days," via Anglo-Norman < medieval Latin *dies mali*] —**dis·mal·ly** *adv* —**dis·mal·ness** *n*

dis·mal sci·ence *n UK* SOC SCI same as **economics** (*humorous*)

Dis·mal Swamp former name for **Great Dismal Swamp**

dis·man·tle /diss mánt'l/ (**-tled, -tling, -tles**) *v* **1.** *vt* **BREAK SOMETHING DOWN INTO PARTS** to take something apart in a way that causes it to stop working **2.** *vi* **COME APART** to be able to be separated into components **3.** *vt* **DESTROY SOMETHING BY REMOVING KEY ELEMENTS** to destroy something such as an institution or system by removing essential parts **4.** *vt* **EMPTY PLACE OF EQUIPMENT** to strip a room or building of furniture or equipment [Late 16C. < Old French *desmanteler* "tear down a fortress wall" < *emmanteler* "shelter, fortify" < *mantel* "cloak" (see MANTLE)] —**dis·man·tle·ment** *n* —**dis·man·tler** *n*

dis·mast /dìss mást/ (**-mast·ed, -mast·ing, -masts**) *vt* to break off or remove the mast or masts of a boat or ship —**dis·mast·ment** *n*

dis·may /diss máy/ *vt* (**-mayed, -may·ing, -mays**) (*usually passive*) **1. DISCOURAGE SOMEBODY** to cause somebody to feel discouraged or disappointed **2. ALARM SOMEBODY** to fill somebody with alarm, apprehension, or distress ■ *n* **1. FEELING OF DISCOURAGEMENT** a feeling of hopelessness, disappointment, or discouragement **2. LOSS OF COURAGE** a sudden loss of courage or confidence [14C. < assumed Anglo-Norman *desmaiier*] —**dis·may·ing·ly** *adv*

disme /dīm/ *n* a United States coin first minted in 1792, worth a tenth of a dollar [Late 18C. < obsolete French, variant of *dime* (see DIME)]

dis·mem·ber /diss mémbər/ (**-bered, -ber·ing, -bers**) *vt* **1. REMOVE LIMB FROM BODY** to cut off or remove a limb or other part of a person or animal **2. DIVIDE SOMETHING UP** to cut or tear something into pieces **3. DESTROY SOMETHING BY TAKING IT APART** to destroy something by taking it apart ○ *dismembered the alliance* [14C. Via French < assumed Vulgar Latin *dismembrare* < Latin *membrum* "limb, part"] —**dis·mem·ber·er** *n* —**dis·mem·ber·ment** *n*

dis·miss /diss míss/ (**-missed, -miss·ing, -miss·es**) *vt* **1. REFUSE TO CONSIDER SOMETHING** to refuse to give consideration to something **2. REJECT SOMEBODY OR SOMETHING** to consider somebody or something as unsuitable for a particular reason ○ *dismissed the idea as ridiculous* **3. END EMPLOYMENT OF SOMEBODY** to stop employing somebody, e.g., because of unsatisfactory work or wrongdoing **4. SEND SOMEBODY AWAY** to order or allow somebody to leave **5.** LAW **REFUSE CASE FURTHER HEARING IN COURT** to refuse to give further hearing to a case in court [15C. < medieval Latin *dismiss-*, past participle of *dismittere* "send away" < Latin *mittere* "send off"] —**dis·miss·i·ble** *adj*

dis·miss·al /diss míss'l/ *n* **1. TERMINATION OF SOMEBODY'S EMPLOYMENT** the removal of somebody from employment or service **2. ACT OF SENDING AWAY** the formal sending away of a person or group ○ *didn't report the incident till after the class's dismissal* **3. REJECTION FROM CONSIDERATION** the rejection of something from consideration

dis·mis·sive /diss míssiv/ *adj* indicating rejection, especially in a contemptuous or indifferent way —**dis·mis·sive·ly** *adv* —**dis·mis·sive·ness** *n*

dis·mount *v* /diss mównt/ (**-mount·ed, -mount·ing, -mounts**) **1.** *vi* **GET OFF ANIMAL** to get down from the back of an animal such as a horse or camel **2.** *vi* **GET OFF CYCLE** to get off a bicycle or motorcycle **3.** *vt* **REMOVE ITEM FROM FRAME** to remove something from a frame, mounting, stand, or support ■ *n* /díss mòwnt/ **ACT OF DISMOUNTING** an act of dismounting or of being dismounted —**dis·mount·a·ble** *adj*

Walt Disney

Dis·ney /dízneе/, **Walt** (1901–66) US animator and producer. He created Mickey Mouse and Donald Duck, and originated the feature-length cartoon with *Snow White and the Seven Dwarfs* (1937). Full name **Disney, Walter Elias**

> "Too many people grow up. That's the real trouble with the world, too many people grow up. They forget. They don't remember what it's like to be 12 years old. They patronize, they treat children as inferiors. Well I won't do that."
> [Attributed to Walt Disney]

Dis·ney·esque /dìznee ésk/ *adj* reminiscent of or in the style of the sometimes whimsical movies and cartoons created by Walt Disney or the Disney studios

dis·o·be·di·ence /dìssə beédee ənss/ *n* a refusal or failure to obey

dis·o·be·di·ent /dìssə beédee ənt/ *adj* refusing or failing to obey, especially habitually [15C. Via French < assumed Vulgar Latin *desobedient-* < Latin *oboedient-*, present participle of *oboedire* (see OBEY)] —**dis·o·be·di·ent·ly** *adv*

dis·o·bey /dìssə báy/ (**-beyed, -bey·ing, -beys**) *vti* to refuse or fail to obey a rule, instruction, or authority, or somebody giving an instruction or in authority [14C. Via French *désobéir* < assumed Vulgar Latin *desobedir* < Latin *oboedire* (see OBEY)] —**dis·o·bey·er** *n*

dis·o·blige /dìssə blíj/ (**-bliged, -blig·ing, -blig·es**) *vt* to be unwilling to help somebody [Late 16C. < French *désobliger* < Latin *obligare* (see OBLIGE)]

dis·o·blig·ing /dìssə blíjing/ *adj* selfishly or rudely unwilling to help —**dis·o·blig·ing·ly** *adv*

~~**disolve**~~ incorrect spelling of **dissolve**

di·som·ic /dī sṓmik/ *adj* having chromosomes occurring in pairs [Early 20C. < DI-[1] + -SOME[1]] —**dis·om·y** *n*

dis·or·der /diss áwrdər/ *n* **1. ILLNESS** a medical condition involving a disturbance to the usual functioning of the mind or body **2. LACK OF ORDER** a lack of systematic or orderly arrangement **3. MESSINESS** a state of messiness ○ *found the room in complete disorder* **4.** LAW **UNRULY BEHAVIOR** a public disturbance or breach of peace ■ *vt* (**-dered, -der·ing, -ders**) **UPSET ARRANGEMENT** to disarrange or disturb the order of something

dis·or·dered /diss áwrdərd/ *adj* **1.** marked by confusion or disarray **2.** affected by a disturbance to the usual physical functioning or the mind or body ○ *disordered sleep* —**dis·or·dered·ness** *n*

dis·or·der·ly /diss áwrdərlee/ *adj* **1. LACKING ORDER** lacking order or organization **2. UNRULY** unruly and resisting authority **3.** LAW **DISTURBING PEACE** disturbing the peace or violating public order —**dis·or·der·li·ness** *n*

dis·or·der·ly con·duct *n* a minor offense likely to cause a breach of the peace

dis·or·gan·i·za·tion /diss àwrgəni záysh'n/ *n* **1.** a lack of organization or orderly arrangement **2.** the destruction or disruption of the organization, system, or unity of something

dis·or·gan·ize /diss áwrgə nīz/ (**-ized, -iz·ing, -iz·es**) *vt* to destroy or disrupt the organization, system, or unity of something [Late 18C. < French *désorganiser* < *organiser* (see ORGANIZE)] —**dis·or·gan·ized** *adj* —**dis·or·gan·iz·er** *n*

dis·o·ri·ent /diss áwree ènt/ (**-ent·ed, -ent·ing, -ents**), **dis·o·ri·en·tate** /diss áwree ən tàyt/ (**-tated, -tat·ing, -tates**) *vt* **1.** to cause somebody to feel lost or confused, especially with regard to direction or position **2.** to confuse somebody by giving misleading information —**dis·o·ri·en·ta·tion** /diss àwree ən táysh'n/ *n*

dis·own /diss ṓn/ (**-owned, -own·ing, -owns**) *vt* to refuse or no longer acknowledge a connection with somebody or something —**dis·own·er** *n* —**dis·own·ment** *n*

~~**dispair**~~ incorrect spelling of **despair**

dis·par·age /di spárrij/ (**-aged, -ag·ing, -ag·es**) *vt* to refer disapprovingly or contemptuously to somebody or something —**dis·par·age·ment** *n* —**dis·par·ag·er** *n*

dis·par·ag·ing /di spárrijing/ *adj* showing or expressing disapproval or contempt —**dis·par·ag·ing·ly** *adv*

dis·pa·rate /díspərət, di spárrət/ *adj* describes people or things so completely unlike one another that they cannot be compared [15C. < Latin *disparatus*, past participle of *disparare* "separate" < *parare* "prepare"] —**dis·pa·rate·ly** *adv* —**dis·pa·rate·ness** *n*

~~**disparitry**~~ incorrect spelling of **disparity**

dis·par·i·ty /di spárrətee/ (*plural* **-ties**) *n* **1.** a lack of equality between people or things **2.** dissimilarity or incongruity [Mid-16C. Via French < late Latin *disparitas* < *paritas* (see PARITY[1])]

dis·pas·sion /diss pásh'n/ *n* the state of not being influenced by emotion or personal feelings ○ *viewed the chaos around her with dispassion*

dis·pas·sion·ate /diss pásh'nət/ *adj* not influenced by emotion or personal feelings —**dis·pas·sion·ate·ly** *adv* —**dis·pas·sion·ate·ness** *n*

dis·patch /di spách/ *vt* (**-patched, -patch·ing, -patch·es**) **1. SEND SOMETHING TO PLACE** to send off something such as a letter or package to a destination **2. SEND SOMEBODY AWAY TO DO SOMETHING** to instruct somebody to go somewhere in order to carry out a task **3. DEAL WITH SOMETHING QUICKLY** to complete or deal with something quickly or efficiently **4. KILL SOMEBODY** to kill a person or animal ■ *n* **1. SEND-OFF** the sending of somebody or something such as a messenger or a letter **2. FULFILLMENT OF ACTIVITY** the carrying out of an activity **3. EFFICIENT SPEED** speed and efficiency ○ *carried out her duties with dispatch* **4. OFFICIAL MESSAGE** a message or report, especially an official communication from a diplomat or an officer in the armed forces **5.** MEDIA **NEWS REPORT** a news item or report sent by a journalist or news agency ○ *dispatches from the scene of the fire* **6. ACT OF KILLING** the killing of a person or animal [Early 16C. Via Italian *dispacciare* < negative form of assumed Vulgar Latin *impactare* "impede" < Latin *impact-*, past participle of *impingere* (see IMPINGE)] —**dis·patch·er** *n*

dis·pel /di spél/ (**-pelled, -pel·ling, -pels**) *vt* **1.** to rid somebody's mind of a thought or an idea, especially an erroneous one **2.** to disperse or drive away something ○ *clouds and mist that the sun soon dispelled* [15C. < Latin *dispellere* "drive away" < *pellere* "beat"] —**dis·pel·ler** *n*

dis·pen·sa·ble /di spénssəb'l/ *adj* able to be dispensed with or replaced —**dis·pen·sa·bil·i·ty** /di spènssə bíllətee/ *n* —**dis·pen·sa·ble·ness** *n*

dis·pen·sa·ry /di spénssəree/ (*plural* **-ries**) *n* **1.** a place where medical supplies are stored and distributed to patients by a pharmacist **2.** a place where temporary medical treatment is provided

dis·pen·sa·tion /dìspən sáysh'n/ *n* **1. EXEMPTION** exemption or release from a rule or obligation, especially a religious one **2. DOCUMENT GIVING EXEMPTION** an official document authorizing dispensation, especially religious dispensation **3. RELIGIOUS SYSTEM** in Christian belief, a divinely ordained religious system **4. DIVINE ORDERING** in Christian belief, a divine ordering or management of affairs and events in the world **5. RELIGIOUS EPOCH** the time during which a religious doctrine or practice is believed to be in force **6. DISTRIBUTION OF THINGS** the distribution or giving out of something ○ *dispensation of emergency supplies* —**dis·pen·sa·tion·al** *adj* —**dis·pen·sa·to·ry** /di spénssə tàwree/ *adj*

dis·pense /di spénss/ (**-pensed, -pens·ing, -pens·es**) *vt* **1.** PROVIDE SERVICE to give a service or advice to several recipients **2.** SUPPLY PRODUCT to supply something such as food, drink, or money automatically on insertion of payment or a card **3.** PHARM SUPPLY MEDICINES to supply medicine according to a prescription [14C. Via French < Latin *dispensare* < *dispendere* "weigh out" < *pendere* "weigh"]

SYNONYMS See ***share***[1].

dispense with *vt* **1.** to manage without something ○ *Since it's sunny, we can dispense with the rain gear.* **2.** to get rid of something not wanted or needed ○ *Let's dispense with all these convoluted rules and regulations.*

dis·pens·er /di spénssər/ *n* **1.** DEVICE FOR DISPENSING GOODS a device that releases its contents in convenient or measured quantities when operated (*usually used in combination*) **2.** PROVIDER OF SOMETHING somebody or something that distributes something **3.** PHARM MEDICINE SUPPLIER somebody who supplies medicine according to a prescription

~~dispensible~~ incorrect spelling of **dispensable**

dis·pens·ing op·ti·cian /di spènssing op tísh'n/ *n UK* OPHTHALMOL same as **optician** (sense 1)

dis·per·sal /di spúrss'l/ *n* **1.** DISTRIBUTION the distribution or scattering of people or things over an area **2.** BIOL NATURAL SPREAD OF SEED the natural distribution of plant seeds and the offspring of organisms that are not mobile over a wide area by various methods **3.** BIOL MOVEMENT OF ORGANISMS the movement of organisms away from their place of birth or from centers of population density **4.** DISAPPEARANCE disappearance as a result of scattering or going away in different directions

dis·per·sant /di spúrss'nt/ *n* a liquid or gas that facilitates or improves the dispersion of small particles or droplets, e.g., in an aerosol —**dis·per·sant** *adj*

dis·perse /di spúrss/ (**-persed, -pers·ing, -pers·es**) *vti* **1.** SCATTER to cause something to scatter in different directions, or scatter in this way **2.** DISTRIBUTE WIDELY to distribute something over a wide area, or become widespread **3.** CAUSE TO DISAPPEAR to cause something to disappear, or disappear **4.** CHEM DISTRIBUTE EVENLY to distribute particles evenly throughout a medium, or become distributed in this way **5.** PHYS SEPARATE INTO COLORS to separate white light into the component colors of the spectrum, or undergo this process [14C. < Old French *disperser* < Latin *dispers-*, past participle of *dispergere* "scatter around" < *spargere* "scatter"] —**dis·pers·er** *n*

SPELLCHECK See ***disburse***.

dis·per·sion /di spúrsh'n/ *n* **1.** DISPERSAL the scattering or distribution of something within an area or space **2.** CONDITION OF BEING DISPERSED the fact or state of being spread, scattered, or distributed **3.** STATS DISTRIBUTION OF VALUES the distribution of a statistical frequency distribution about an average or median **4.** CHEM MEDIUM WITH DISPERSED PARTICLES a chemical system consisting of a gas, liquid, or colloid containing dispersed particles

Dis·per·sion /di spúrsh'n/ *n* JUDAISM same as **Diaspora** (sense 1)

dis·per·sive /di spúrssiv/ *adj* tending to cause dispersion —**dis·per·sive·ly** *adv* —**dis·per·sive·ness** *n*

dis·pir·it /di spírrət/ (**-it·ed, -it·ing, -its**) *vt* to discourage or dishearten somebody —**dis·pir·it·ed** *adj* —**dis·pir·it·ed·ly** *adv* —**dis·pir·it·ed·ness** *n*

dis·pir·it·ing /di spírrəting/ *adj* discouraging or disheartening —**dis·pir·it·ing·ly** *adv*

dis·place /diss pláyss/ (**-placed, -plac·ing, -plac·es**) *vt* **1.** MOVE SOMETHING FROM USUAL PLACE to move something from its usual or correct place **2.** FORCE SOMEBODY TO LEAVE HOME to force somebody to leave his or her home or country, e.g., because of war **3.** REMOVE SOMEBODY FROM POST to discharge or remove somebody from an office, position, or job **4.** REPLACE SOMEBODY OR SOMETHING to take the place of somebody or something **5.** CHEM TAKE PLACE OF ATOM to take the place of another atom or group in a compound **6.** PHYS REPLACE FLUID WITH OBJECT to replace a volume of fluid with a floating or submerged object, forcing the original fluid to move elsewhere —**dis·place·a·ble** *adj* —**dis·plac·er** *n*

dis·placed per·son /diss pláyst-/ *n* somebody who has been forced to leave his or her home or country, especially because of war or political oppression

dis·place·ment /diss pláyssmənt/ *n* **1.** MOVEMENT FROM USUAL SITE the movement of something from its usual or correct place **2.** PHYS, NAUT FLUID DISPLACED the amount of fluid such as water that is forced to move by an object floating or submerged in it, often used as a measure of a ship's size **3.** PSYCHOL TRANSFER OF EMOTIONS OR BEHAVIOR the transfer of emotion from the original focus to another less threatening person or object, or the substitution of one response or piece of behavior for another **4.** PHYS AMOUNT OF MOVEMENT IN PARTICULAR DIRECTION the amount of movement of an object measured in a particular direction **5.** CHEM CHEMICAL REPLACEMENT a chemical reaction in which one atom or chemical group takes the place of another in a compound **6.** GEOL MOVEMENT OF GEOLOGIC FAULT the distance that a point on one side of a geologic fault has moved, relative to a corresponding point on the other side **7.** AUTOMOT ENGINE VOLUME the total volume displaced by the pistons in an internal combustion engine

dis·place·ment ton *n* a unit of measure for the displacement of a floating ship, equivalent to 35 cu. ft./0.99 cu. m or 2,240 lb

dis·play /di spláy/ *v* (**-played, -play·ing, -plays**) **1.** *vt* MAKE SOMETHING VISIBLE to make something visible or available for others to see **2.** *vt* MAKE SOMETHING EVIDENT to reveal or make evident a quality or feeling **3.** *vti* COMPUT SHOW DATA to show messages, data, or graphics on a monitor, or appear on a monitor **4.** *vti* ZOOL SHOW STYLIZED BEHAVIOR to show a pattern of animal behavior, e.g., to attract a mate or defend a territory ■ *n* **1.** VISUAL ARRANGEMENT a collection of things arranged or done for others to see, especially something considered attractive, interesting, or entertaining (*often used in combination*) **2.** STATE OF BEING VIEWABLE the state of being clearly and easily visible or placed for people to view ○ *new work on display* **3.** SHOW OF FEELING OR QUALITY an act of showing a feeling or quality ○ *a display of courage* **4.** PRINTING, MARKETING GRAPHIC ADVERTISING printed advertising that uses attractive pictures, typography, or other features **5.** ELECTRONIC SCREEN an electronic device that presents visual information **6.** INFORMATION ON SCREEN the information shown on a computer monitor or other electronic device **7.** ZOOL STYLIZED BEHAVIOR a pattern of animal behavior used to produce a response in other animals, especially of the same species, e.g., when courting or defending territory ■ *adj* INTENDED FOR ADVERTISING describes typefaces that are designed for prominent use in advertising [Late 16C. Via Old French *despleier* < Latin *displicare* "unfold" < *plicare* "to fold"] —**dis·play·er** *n*

dis·play cab·i·net, dis·play case *n* a case or stand with glass panels, used for showing items of interest

dis·please /diss pléez/ (**-pleased, -pleas·ing, -pleas·es**) *vti* to annoy or dissatisfy somebody [14C. < Old French *desplais-*, stem of *desplaire* < assumed Vulgar Latin *displacere* < Latin *placere* "to please"] —**dis·pleased** *adj*

dis·pleas·ing /diss pléezing/ *adj* causing annoyance or dissatisfaction —**dis·pleas·ing·ly** *adv*

dis·pleas·ure /diss plézhər/ *n* a feeling of annoyance or dissatisfaction [15C. < Old French *desplaisir* "displease, displeasure" < *plaisir* "pleasure"]

dis·port /di spáwrt/ *vi* (**-port·ed, -port·ing, -ports**) to behave in a playful manner (*archaic or humorous*) ■ *n* a form of lively entertainment or diversion [14C. < Old French *desporter* "divert" < *des-* "apart" + *porter* "carry"]

dis·pos·a·ble /di spṓzəb'l/ *adj* **1.** THROWAWAY designed to be thrown away after use **2.** AVAILABLE FOR USE describes money or assets that are available for use ■ *n* SOMETHING TO BE USED ONLY ONCE something that is designed to be thrown away after use, e.g., a paper cup (*often used in the plural*) —**dis·pos·a·bil·i·ty** /di spṓzə bíllətee/ *n* —**dis·pos·a·ble·ness** *n*

dis·pos·a·ble in·come *n* **1.** income that remains available for spending after deductions for taxes and other obligations **2.** the total amount of money that a country or community has available for spending

dis·pos·al /di spṓz'l/ *n* **1.** PROCESS OF GETTING RID OF SOMETHING the process of throwing away or getting rid of something **2.** ORDERLY ARRANGEMENT an orderly arrangement, distribution, or placement **3.** TRANSFERENCE OF SOMETHING TO SOMEBODY ELSE the transferring of something valuable to somebody else by sale or gift **4.** HOUSEHOLD same as **garbage disposal** (*informal*)

dis·pose /di spṓz/ (**-posed, -pos·ing, -pos·es**) *v* **1.** *vt* MAKE SOMEBODY WILLING to make somebody willing or receptive to something (*often passive*) ○ *The President is not disposed to sign the bill.* **2.** *vt* INCLINE SOMEBODY to make somebody likely to experience something **3.** *vt* PUT SOMETHING IN PLACE to arrange or position something for use or for a particular purpose (*formal; often passive*) ○ *The commander disposed his forces along the coast.* **4.** *vti* SETTLE MATTER to settle a matter by putting it into its correct or definitive form (*formal*) ○ *an outcome to be disposed by the court* [14C. < French *disposer*, alteration (after *poser* "to place") of Latin *disponere* "set out" < *ponere* "to place"] —**dis·pos·er** *n*

dispose of *vt* **1.** GET RID OF SOMETHING to throw away or get rid of something **2.** TRANSFER SOMETHING to transfer something to the ownership of somebody else, by sale or gift **3.** KILL SOMEBODY OR SOMETHING to kill a person or animal **4.** ATTEND TO MATTER to deal with a matter in order to settle it (*formal*)

dis·posed /di spṓzd/ *adj* **1.** inclined or tending to something **2.** having a particular attitude toward somebody or something ○ *favorably disposed to us*

dis·po·si·tion /dìspə zísh'n/ *n* **1.** PERSONALITY somebody's usual mood or temperament **2.** BEHAVIORAL TENDENCY an inclination or tendency to act in a particular way **3.** SETTLEMENT settlement of a business or legal matter (*formal*) **4.** same as **disposal** (senses 2–3) [14C. Via French < Latin *disposition-* < *disponere* (see DISPOSE)] —**dis·po·si·tion·al** *adj*

dis·pos·i·tive /diss pózzitiv/ *adj* deciding the final outcome of a court case [Early 17C. Directly or via French < medieval Latin *dispositivus* < *disposit-*, past participle of Latin *disponere* (see DISPOSE)]

dis·pos·sess /dìspə zéss/ (**-sessed, -ses·sing, -sess·es**) *vt* to deprive somebody of the possession or occupancy of something, especially property [15C. < Old French *despossesser* < *possesser* (see POSSESS)] —**dis·pos·ses·sor** *n* —**dis·pos·ses·so·ry** *adj*

dis·pos·sessed /dìspə zést/ *adj* deprived of property or rights ■ *npl* people who have been deprived of their property or rights ○ *defended the rights of the dispossessed*

dis·pos·ses·sion /dìspə zésh'n/ *n* **1.** the act of depriving somebody of what he or she owns, especially land or money **2.** the state of being deprived of what you own, especially land or money

dis·praise /diss práyz/ (*literary*) *vt* (**-praised, -prais·ing, -prais·es**) to express disapproval of somebody ■ *n* disapproval, or an instance or expression of it ○ *"Praise and dispraise play their part in the quality control of literary journalism..."* (Martin Amis *Atlantic Monthly*; December 2003) —**dis·prais·er** *n*

dis·proof /diss próof/ *n* **1.** the disproving of a legal argument or point **2.** evidence that disproves something

dis·pro·por·tion /dìsprə páwrsh'n/ *n* something that is out of proportion or unequal ■ *vt* (**-tioned, -tion·ing, -tions**) to make something disproportionate

dis·pro·por·tion·ate /dìsprə páwrsh'nət/, **dis·pro·por·tion·al** /dìsprə páwrsh'nəl/ *adj* unequal or out of proportion in quantity, shape, or size —**dis·pro·por·tion·al·ly** *adv* —**dis·pro·por·tion·ate·ly** *adv* —**dis·pro·por·tion·ate·ness** *n*

dis·pro·por·tion·a·tion /dìsprə pawrsh'n áysh'n/ *n* a chemical reaction in which a single substance acts as both oxidizing and reducing agent, resulting in the production of dissimilar substances

dis·prove /diss próov/ (**-proved, -prov·ing, -proves**) *vt* to show that something is not true or correct [14C. < Old French *desprover* < *prover* (see PROVE)] —**dis·prov·a·ble** *adj* —**dis·prov·al** *n*

Dis·pur /diss póor/ capital city of Assam state, northeastern India. Population: 584,342 (1991).

dis·put·a·ble /di spyóotəb'l/ *adj* not definitely true or valid and therefore debatable or open to argument —**dis·put·a·bil·i·ty** /di spyòotə bíllətee/ *n* —**dis·put·a·ble·ness** *n*

dis·put·a·bly /di spyóotəblee/ *adv* used to suggest that the speaker or writer thinks that something is true and could defend that view against those who disagree

dis·pu·tant /di spyóot'nt, díspyət'nt/ *n* somebody involved in an argument or a legal dispute ■ *adj* involved in an argument or a legal dispute

dis·pu·ta·tion /dìspyə táysh'n/ *n* (*formal*) **1.** argumentation or disagreement **2.** a formal academic debate in defense of a thesis

dis·pu·ta·tious /dìspyə táyshəss/, **dis·pu·ta·tive** /di spyóotətiv/ *adj* tending to argue or disagree without adequate cause (*formal*) —**dis·pu·ta·tious·ly** *adv* —**dis·pu·ta·tious·ness** *n*

dis·pute /di spyóot/ *v* (**-put·ed, -put·ing, -putes**) **1.** *vti* QUESTION SOMETHING to question or doubt the truth or validity of something **2.** *vi* DISAGREE ABOUT SOMETHING to disagree or argue about something **3.** *vt* STRUGGLE FOR SOMETHING to fight for or strive to win something (*formal*) **4.** *vt* OPPOSE SOMETHING to strive against or resist something (*formal*) ■ *n* **1.** ARGUMENT a serious argument or disagreement **2.** INDUSTRIAL DISAGREEMENT a prolonged disagreement between management and workers or a labor union, often involving a strike ○ *a labor dispute* [Late 16C. Via French < Latin *disputare*, literally "argue out" < *putare* "consider"] —**dis·put·ed** *adj* —**dis·put·er** *n*

SYNONYMS See *disagree*.

---

dis·qual·i·fi·ca·tion /diss kwòlləfi káysh'n/ *n* **1.** INELIGIBILITY the condition of being or becoming ineligible to do or take part in something **2.** ACT OF BEING DISQUALIFIED an instance of being disqualified **3.** SOMETHING THAT DISQUALIFIES something that makes somebody ineligible to do or take part in something

dis·qual·i·fy /diss kwóllə fì/ (**-fied, -fy·ing, -fies**) *vt* **1.** to make or declare somebody unfit, unqualified, or ineligible to do or take part in something **2.** to deprive somebody of a legal or other right or privilege —**dis·qual·i·fi·able** *adj* —**dis·qual·i·fied** *adj* —**dis·qual·i·fi·er** *n*

dis·qui·et /diss kwí ət/ *n* a feeling of anxiety or uneasiness ■ *vt* (**-et·ed, -et·ing, -ets**) to make somebody anxious or uneasy (*archaic or literary*) —**dis·qui·et·ly** *adv* —**dis·qui·et·ness** *n*

dis·qui·et·ing /diss kwí əting/ *adj* causing a feeling of anxiety or uneasiness —**dis·qui·et·ing·ly** *adv*

dis·qui·e·tude /diss kwí ə tòod/ *n* same as **disquiet**

dis·qui·si·tion /dìskwi zísh'n/ *n* a long formal essay or discussion on a subject (*formal*) [Early 17C. Via French < Latin *disquisition-* < *disquirere* "inquire" < *quaerere* "seek, ask"] —**dis·qui·si·tion·al** *adj*

Benjamin Disraeli

Dis·rae·li /diz ráylee/, **Benjamin, 1st Earl of Beaconsfield** (1804–81) British politician and novelist. He was prime minister (1868, 1874–80), and author of *Coningsby* (1844) and *Sybil* (1845).

> "I repeat...that all power is a trust—that we are accountable for its exercise—that, from the people, and for the people, all springs, and all must exist."
> [Benjamin Disraeli, *Vivian Grey*; 1826]

> "There are three kinds of lies: lies, damned lies, and statistics."
> [Attributed to Benjamin Disraeli]

dis·rate /dìss ráyt/ (**-rat·ed, -rat·ing, -rates**) *vt* to demote somebody in the military to a lower rank

dis·re·gard /dìssri gáard/ *vt* (**-gard·ed, -gard·ing, -gards**) **1.** IGNORE SOMEBODY OR SOMETHING to ignore or pay no attention to somebody or something **2.** TREAT SOMEBODY OR SOMETHING DISRESPECTFULLY to treat somebody or something with contempt or without respect ■ *n* NEGLECT a lack of attention or respect —**dis·re·gard·er** *n* —**dis·re·gard·ful** *adj*

dis·re·mem·ber /dìssri mémbər/ (**-bered, -ber·ing, -bers**) *vti* to forget or fail to remember something (*informal*)

dis·re·pair /dìssri páir/ *n* poor working order or condition as a result of neglect

dis·rep·u·ta·ble /diss réppyətəb'l/ *adj* lacking respectability on the basis of past or present actions —**dis·rep·u·ta·bil·i·ty** /diss rèppyətə bíllətee/ *n* —**dis·rep·u·ta·ble·ness** *n* —**dis·rep·u·ta·bly** *adv*

dis·re·pute /dìssri pyóot/ *n* a lack or loss of good reputation or respect

dis·re·spect /dìssri spékt/ *n* a lack of respect ■ *vt* (**-spect·ed, -spect·ing, -spects**) to show a lack of respect for somebody or something —**dis·re·spect·ful** *adj* —**dis·re·spect·ful·ly** *adv*

dis·robe /diss rṓb/ (**-robed, -rob·ing, -robes**) *vti* to remove clothing from yourself or somebody else (*formal*) [Late 16C. < Old French *desrober* < *robe* (see ROBE)] —**dis·robe·ment** *n* —**dis·rob·er** *n*

dis·rupt /diss rúpt/ (**-rupt·ed, -rupt·ing, -rupts**) *vt* **1.** to interrupt the usual course of a process or activity **2.** to destroy the order or orderly progression of something [15C. < Latin *disrupt-*, past participle of *disrumpere* "break apart" < *rumpere* "break"] —**dis·rupt·er** *n*

dis·rup·tion /diss rúpshən/ *n* **1.** UNWANTED BREAK an unwelcome or unexpected break in a process or activity **2.** SUSPENSION the interruption or suspension of usual activity or progress **3.** STATE OF DISORDER a state of disorder caused by outside influence

dis·rup·tive /diss rúptiv/ *adj* interrupting usual order or progress —**dis·rup·tive·ly** *adv* —**dis·rup·tive·ness** *n*

diss *vt* another spelling of **dis** (*slang*)

~~dissapear~~ incorrect spelling of **disappear**

~~dissapointed~~ incorrect spelling of **disappointed**

dis·sat·is·fac·tion /diss sàttəss fáksh'n/ *n* **1.** a state or feeling of not being satisfied **2.** something that causes a feeling of not being satisfied

dis·sat·is·fac·to·ry /diss sàttəss fáktəree/ *adj* not satisfactory

dis·sat·is·fy /dìss sáttəss fì/ (**-fied, -fy·ing, -fies**) *vt* to fail to satisfy somebody —**dis·sat·is·fied** *adj*

dis·sect /di sékt/ (**-sect·ed, -sect·ing, -sects**) *v* **1.** *vti* to cut and separate the parts of animal or plant specimens for scientific or medical study **2.** *vt* to examine or analyze a person or subject in detail ○ *dissected the speech* [Late 16C. < Latin *dissect-*, past participle of *dissecare* "cut apart" < *secare* "cut"] —**dis·sec·ti·ble** *adj* —**dis·sec·tor** *n*

dis·sect·ed /di séktəd/ *adj* **1.** describes a leaf that is divided into narrow lobes or segments **2.** describes a landscape that has been eroded into hills and valleys

dis·sect·ing a·or·tic an·eu·rysm *n* an aneurysm, often fatal, that leaks or ruptures, causing sharp stabbing pain in the middle of the back, sweating, and vomiting

dis·sec·tion /di sékshən/ *n* **1.** CUTTING AND EXAMINING the cutting and separating of the parts of animal or plant specimens for scientific or medical study **2.** DISSECTED SPECIMEN something that has been dissected, e.g., an anatomical specimen **3.** EXAMINATION a thorough and detailed analysis or examination of something such as a policy or plan

dis·seize /diss séez/ (**-seized, -seiz·ing, -seiz·es**) *vi* to deprive somebody wrongfully of possession of land [14C. < Anglo-Norman *disseisir*, variant of Old French *dessaisir* "dispossess" < *saisir* (see SEIZE)] —**dis·sei·sor** *n*

dis·sei·zin /diss séezin/ *n* the act of wrongfully depriving somebody of land [14C. < Anglo-Norman *disseisine*, variant of Old French *dessaisine* < *dessaisir* (see DISSEIZE)]

dis·sem·ble /di sémb'l/ (**-bled, -bling, -bles**) *v* **1.** *vi* PUT ON FALSE APPEARANCE to put on a false appearance in order to conceal facts, feelings, or intentions **2.** *vt* GIVE APPEARANCE OF SOMETHING to put on the appearance of something not actually felt or true (*formal*) **3.** *vt* HIDE SOMETHING BY PRETENSE to hide real beliefs, feelings, or intentions through misleading speech or behavior (*formal*) [15C. < Old French *dessembler* "be different" < *sembler* "seem"] —**dis·sem·blance** *n* —**dis·sem·bler** *n*

dis·sem·bling /di sémbling/ *n* the creation or adoption of a false appearance in order to conceal facts, feelings, or intentions ■ *adj* feigning or pretending —**dis·sem·bling·ly** *adv*

dis·sem·i·nate /di sémmi nàyt/ (**-nat·ed, -nat·ing, -nates**) *vti* to distribute or spread something, especially information, widely, or become widespread [15C. < Latin *disseminat-*, past participle of *disseminare* "sow abroad" < *semin-* "seed"] —**dis·sem·i·na·tion** /di sèmmi náysh'n/ *n* —**dis·sem·i·na·tive** *adj* —**dis·sem·i·na·tor** *n*

dis·sen·sion /di sénshən/ *n* disagreement or difference of opinion, especially when leading to open conflict [14C. Via French < Latin *dissension-* < *dissentire* (see DISSENT)]

dis·sen·sus /di sénssəss/ *n* disagreement or difference of opinion [Mid-20C. Blend of DISSENT + CONSENSUS]

dis·sent /di sént/ *vi* (**-sent·ed, -sent·ing, -sents**) **1.** DISAGREE to disagree with a widely held or majority opinion **2.** ISSUE MINORITY COURT OPINION to disagree with a majority court opinion and put those views into writing (*refers to judges*) ○ *Two Supreme Court justices dissented.* **3.** CHR NOT SUPPORT RELIGIOUS PRACTICES to refuse to conform to the authority, doctrines, or practices of an established church **4.** WITHHOLD ASSENT to withhold assent or approval ■ *n* **1.** DISAGREEMENT disagreement from a widely held or majority opinion **2.** CHR RELIGIOUS NONCONFORMITY refusal to conform to the authority, doctrines, or practices of an established church **3.** LAW MINORITY OPINION an opinion of a judge that is not in agreement with that of other judges **4.** POL REFUSAL TO ACCEPT POLITICAL RULES opposition to the laws, norms, and structures of a political regime, especially on moral grounds [15C. < Latin *dissentire* "feel differently" < *sentire* "feel"]

SPELLCHECK See *descent*.

---

dis·sent·er /di séntər/ *n* somebody who disagrees with the beliefs or opinions of a majority

Dis·sent·er *n* somebody who rejects the authority, doctrines, or practices of an established church, especially a Protestant who did not accept the Church of England in the 17th and 18th centuries

dis·sen·tient /di sénshee ənt/ *adj* showing or expressing disagreement with the beliefs or opinions of a majority (*formal*) [Early 17C. < Latin *dissentient-*, present participle of *dissentire* (see DISSENT)] —**dis·sen·tience** *n* —**dis·sen·tien·cy** *n* —**dis·sen·tient** *n* —**dis·sen·tient·ly** *adv*

dis·sent·ing /di sénting/ *adj* **1.** EXPRESSING OR SHOWING DISAGREEMENT disagreeing with the beliefs or opinions of a majority **2.** *also* **Dis·sent·ing** CHR OF DISSENTERS relating or belonging to a group of religious nonconformists, especially an English Protestant denomination of the 17th and 18th centuries **3.** LAW DISAGREEING WITH OTHER JUDGES disagreeing with the majority verdict or opinion of other judges —**dis·sent·ing·ly** *adv*

dis·sep·i·ment /di séppəmənt/ *n* a dividing wall or membrane separating an organ such as a plant ovary, into distinct chambers [Early 18C. < Latin *dissaepimentum* < *dissaepire* "make separate" < *saepire* "divide off" < *saepes* "hedge"] —**dis·sep·i·men·tal** /di sèppə mént'l/ *adj*

dis·ser·ta·tion /dìssər táysh'n/ *n* **1.** a lengthy formal written treatment of a subject, especially a long paper submitted as a requirement for a degree **2.** a formal spoken or written discourse —**dis·ser·ta·tion·al** *adj* —**dis·ser·ta·tion·ist** *n*

dis·serv·ice /di súrviss/ *n* an action that causes harm or difficulty

dis·sev·er /di sévvər/ (**-ered, -er·ing, -ers**) *v* (*formal*) **1.** *vt* SEPARATE SOMETHING to separate or sever something **2.** *vt* BREAK UP SOMETHING to break up or divide something **3.** *vi* COME APART to come apart or become disunited [13C. Via Anglo-Norman *deseverer* < late Latin *disseparare* "split apart" < Latin *separare* (see SEPARATE)] —**dis·sev·er·ance** *n* —**dis·sev·er·a·tion** /di sèvvə ráysh'n/ *n* —**dis·sev·er·ment** *n*

dis·si·dence /díssidənss/ *n* disagreement with authority or with prevailing opinion

dis·si·dent /díssidənt/ *n* somebody who publicly disagrees with an established political or religious system or organization [Mid-16C. < Latin *dissident-*, present participle of *dissidere* "sit apart" < *sedere* "sit"] —**dis·si·dent** *adj* —**dis·si·dent·ly** *adv*

dis·sim·i·lar /di símmələr/ *adj* differing in one or more respects —**dis·sim·i·lar·ly** *adv*

dis·sim·i·lar·i·ty /di sìmə lárrətee/ (*plural* **-ties**) *n* **1.** the fact or state of being different in one or more respects **2.** a point of difference or distinction

dis·sim·i·late /di símmə làyt/ (**-lat·ed, -lat·ing, -lates**) *vti* **1.** to make something dissimilar, or become dissimilar **2.** to undergo linguistic dissimilation, or change a consonant or consonants by this process [Mid-19C. < DIS- + ASSIMILATE] —**dis·sim·i·la·tive** *adj* —**dis·sim·i·la·to·ry** *adj*

dis·sim·i·la·tion /di sìmmə láysh'n/ *n* **1.** the process of becoming dissimilar **2.** the development of a dissimilarity between two consonant sounds in a word that were originally identical

dis·sim·i·la·to·ry /di símmələ tàwree/ *adj* describes a chemical process involving the production of an inorganic compound or element from an organic one, or a product resulting from this process

dis·si·mil·i·tude /dìssi mílli tòod/ *n* the condition or quality of differing in one or more respects from something else (*formal*) [15C. < Latin *dissimilitudo* < *dissimilis* "unlike" < *similis* "like, similar"]

dis·sim·u·late /di símmyə làyt/ (**-lat·ed, -lat·ing, -lates**) *vti* to disguise or hide true feelings, thoughts, or intentions [15C. < Latin *dissimulat-*, past participle of *dissimulare* "disguise completely" < *simulare* (see SIMULATE)] —**dis·sim·u·la·tion** /di sìmmyə láysh'n/ *n* —**dis·sim·u·la·tive** *adj*—**dis·sim·u·la·tor** *n*

dis·si·pate /díssə pàyt/ (**-pat·ed, -pat·ing, -pates**) *v* **1.** *vti* to fade or disappear, or make something do this ○ *storm clouds dissipating* **2.** *vt* to spend or use something wastefully [15C. < Latin *dissipat-*, past participle of *dissipare* "scatter around"] —**dis·si·pat·er** *n*— **dis·si·pa·tive** *adj*—**dis·si·pa·tor** *n*

dis·si·pat·ed /díssə pàytəd/ *adj* **1.** OVERINDULGING overindulging in the pursuit of physical pleasure **2.** SQUANDERED lost through squandering, as money sometimes is ○ *a dissipated inheritance* **3.** SHOWING OVERINDULGENCE resulting from or suggesting overindulgence in the pursuit of physical pleasure ○ *dissipated features* —**dis·si·pat·ed·ly** *adv* —**dis·si·pat·ed·ness** *n*

dis·si·pa·tion /díssə páysh'n/ *n* **1.** OVERINDULGENCE overindulgence in the pursuit of physical pleasures **2.** WASTEFUL USE the squandering of resources such as money or fuel (*formal*) **3.** DISPERSAL the scattering or dispersal of something ○ *dissipation of early morning fog* **4.** ABATING OF FEELING OR EMOTION the disappearance of a feeling or emotion such as anger or anxiety

dis·so·ci·ate /di sṓshee àyt, -sṓssi-/ (**-at·ed, -at·ing, -ates**) *v* **1.** *vt* REGARD SOMEBODY OR SOMETHING AS DISTINCT to treat somebody or something as distinct from or unconnected with somebody or something else **2.** *vt* same as **disassociate 3.** *vti* CHEM SPLIT SOMETHING INTO SIMPLER PARTS to cause the molecules of a compound to break down into simpler molecules, atoms, or ions, usually in a reversible reaction, or break down in this way **4.** *vi* PSYCHIAT SEPARATE OFF AREAS OF MIND to separate a group of mental processes from the rest of the mind, causing them to lose their usual relationship with it [Mid-16C. < Latin *dissociat-*, past participle of *dissociare*, literally "separate from fellowship" < *sociare* "join together" < *socius* "companion"] —**dis·so·cia·ble** *adj* —**dis·so·ci·a·tive** *adj*

dis·so·ci·a·tion /di sṑshee áysh'n, -sṑssee áysh'n/ *n* **1.** TREATMENT OF SOMETHING AS UNCONNECTED the treatment of somebody or something as distinct or unconnected, or the fact of being treated in this way **2.** same as **disassociation 3.** CHEM DIVISION OF MOLECULE the breaking up of a molecule into simpler components **4.** PSYCHIAT SEPARATION OF EMOTIONS the separation of a group of usually connected mental processes such as emotion and understanding from the rest of the mind as a defense mechanism

USAGE See ***disassociation.***

dis·so·ci·a·tive i·den·ti·ty dis·ord·er *n* PSYCHIAT same as **multiple personality disorder**

dis·sol·u·ble /di sóllyəb'l/ *adj* able to be dissolved, separated, or ended [Mid-16C. Directly or via French < Latin *dissolubilis* < *dissolvere* (see DISSOLVE)] —**dis·sol·u·bil·i·ty** /di sòllyə bíllətee/ *n* —**dis·sol·u·ble·ness** *n*

dis·so·lute /díssə lòot/ *adj* overindulging in physical pleasures in a way that is considered immoral or harmful [14C. < Latin *dissolutus*, past participle of *dissolvere* (see DISSOLVE)] —**dis·so·lute·ly** *adv* —**dis·so·lute·ness** *n*

dis·so·lu·tion /dìssə lóosh'n/ *n* **1.** ACT OF BREAKING SOMETHING DOWN the separating, decomposing, or disintegrating of something into smaller or more basic constituents **2.** BREAKUP OF SOMETHING the process of breaking up or destroying an organization or institution **3.** FORMAL ENDING OF MEETING the formal closing of a meeting or assembly **4.** LAW TERMINATION OF LEGAL RELATIONSHIP the termination of a legal relationship such as a business partnership or a marriage **5.** DEMISE somebody's death (*formal*)

dis·solve /di zólv/ *v* (**-solved, -solv·ing, -solves**) **1.** *vti* BECOME ABSORBED IN LIQUID to become absorbed in a liquid solution, or make a solid do this ○ *Dissolve two tablets in a glass of water.* **2.** *vti* DISAPPEAR to fade away gradually and disappear, or make something do this ○ *All his fears dissolved.* **3.** *vti* BREAK UP to break up into smaller or more basic parts, or make something do this **4.** *vi* START LAUGHING OR CRYING to begin to laugh or cry uncontrollably ○ *He dissolved into tears.* **5.** *vt* CLOSE FORMALLY to bring something such as a meeting or a political assembly to a formal close **6.** *vt* LAW END LEGAL RELATIONSHIP to bring a legal relationship such as a business partnership or a marriage formally to an end **7.** *vi* MOVIES, MEDIA SIMULTANEOUSLY FADE OUT AND IN to fade out slowly as a second image fades in, briefly merging one with the other ■ *n* MOVIES, MEDIA SIMULTANEOUS FADE-IN AND FADE-OUT a change from one scene to another, with the first scene gradually fading out and the next one gradually fading in over it [14C. < Latin *dissolvere*, literally "loosen asunder" < *solvere* "loosen"] —**dis·solv·a·ble** *adj*—**dis·sol·vent** *adj* —**dis·solv·er** *n*

dis·so·nance /díssənənss/ *n* **1.** UNPLEASANT NOISE a combination of sounds that is unpleasant to listen to **2.** INCONSISTENCY lack of consistency or compatibility between actions or beliefs **3.** MUSIC UNSTABLE COMBINATION OF MUSICAL NOTES a combination of notes that, when played simultaneously, sounds displeasing and needs to be resolved to a consonance

dis·so·nant /díssənənt/ *adj* **1.** UNPLEASANT TO HEAR making or involving a combination of sounds that is unpleasant to listen to **2.** CONFLICTING incompatible or inconsistent (*formal*) **3.** MUSIC CONTAINING UNPLEASANT COMBINATION OF NOTES containing unpleasant combinations of notes that need to be resolved to a consonance [15C. < Latin *dissonant-*, present participle of *dissonare* "be apart in sound" < *sonare* "to sound"] —**dis·so·nant·ly** *adv*

dis·suade /di swáyd/ (**-suad·ed, -suad·ing, -suades**) *vt* to persuade somebody not to do something [Early 16C. < Latin *dissuadere* "advise against" < *suadere* "advise, persuade"] —**dis·suad·a·ble** *adj*—**dis·suad·er** *n*

dis·sua·sion /di swáyzh'n/ *n* persuasion not to do something [15C. Directly or via French < Latin *dissuasion-* < *dissuas-*, past participle of *dissuadere* (see DISSUADE)]

dis·sua·sive /di swáyssiv/ *adj* convincing enough to persuade somebody not to do something [Early 16C. < Latin *dissuas-* (see DISSUASION)] —**dis·sua·sive·ly** *adv*— **dis·sua·sive·ness** *n*

dis·syl·la·ble *n* LING, LITERAT another spelling of **di-syllable**

dis·sym·met·ric /dìssi méttrik/, **dis·sym·met·ri·cal** /dìssi méttrik'l/ *adj* same as **asymmetric** (sense 1) —**dis·sym·met·ri·cal·ly** *adv*

dis·sym·me·try /di símmətree/ (*plural* **-tries**) *n* same as **asymmetry** (sense 1)

dist. *abbr* **1.** distance **2.** PUBLIC ADMIN district

dis·taff /dí stàf/ *n* **1.** work or other matters regarded as the concern of women (*literary; sometimes considered offensive*) **2.** a rod on which wool or flax is wound for somebody to use when spinning by hand, or the corresponding rod on a spinning wheel [Old English *distæf* < Germanic, "bunch of flax" + STAFF[1]]

dis·taff side *n* the wife's or mother's side of a family (*literary*)

dis·tal /díst'l/ *adj* describes a body part situated away from a point of attachment or origin. For example, the elbow is distal to the shoulder. [Early 19C. < DISTANT + -AL[1]] —**dis·tal·ly** *adv*

dis·tance /dístənss/ *n* **1.** LENGTH BETWEEN TWO THINGS the length of the space separating two people, places, or things ○ *What's the distance between Paris and New York?* **2.** FAR-OFF PLACE a place or position far away or not very close ○ *It's best seen from a distance.* **3.** CLOSENESS ALLOWING SOME ACTIVITY the space between two people, places, or things with regard to activity carried on between the two ○ *We can do nothing until they're within hailing distance.* **4.** AMOUNT OF SEPARATION the amount by which two places are separated, especially when thought of in terms of the time or inconvenience of a journey between the two ○ *She lives some distance away.* **5.** COOLNESS OR ALOOFNESS a cool or slightly aloof response to another person or group ○ *He suddenly felt the need to put some distance between himself and his friends.* **6.** INTERVAL OF TIME the interval between one point in time and another, especially a long interval ○ *You can't expect to remember all the details at a distance of more than 20 years.* **7.** AMOUNT OF PROGRESS the amount of progress that has been made or that is still to be made ○ *still some distance to go before we can reach an agreement* **8.** IDEOLOGICAL GULF difference of opinion or ideology ○ *There's still some distance between us with regard to the basic issues.* **9.** HORSERACING SPACE GREATER THAN 20 LENGTHS a space of more than twenty lengths between two racehorses, usually the winner and the horse finishing second ○ *win by a distance* ■ *v* (**-tanced, -tanc·ing, -tanc·es**) **1.** *vt* RESTRAIN SOMEBODY FROM EMOTIONAL INVOLVEMENT to stop yourself or somebody else from becoming emotionally involved in something ○ *Try to distance yourself from past experiences.* **2. dis·tance your·self** *vr* AVOID GIVING SUPPORT to deny that you support or are involved with somebody or something, or withdraw support from somebody or something ○ *He was trying to distance himself from the allegations.* **3.** *vt* HORSERACING BEAT HORSE BY DISTANCE to beat another racehorse by more than twenty lengths [13C Directly or via French < Latin *distantia* < *distant-* "standing apart" (see DISTANT)] ◇ **go the distance** to continue until you have completed something

dis·tance learn·ing *n* education for students working at home, with little or no face-to-face contact with teachers and with material provided remotely, e.g., by e-mail, television, or correspondence

dis·tant /dístənt/ *adj* **1.** NOT PHYSICALLY CLOSE situated, living, or happening far away ○ *a distant galaxy* **2.** REMOTE IN TIME remote in time, either in the future or the past ○ *at some time in the distant future* **3.** REMOTE IN RELATIONSHIP remote in relationship or connection ○ *a distant relative* **4.** ALOOFLY RESERVED showing that somebody does not want to be friendly or intimate **5.** HARD TO DISTINGUISH CLEARLY so slight as to be hard to discern, see, or distinguish ○ *a distant resemblance* [14C. Directly or via French < Latin *distant-*, present participle of *distare* "stand apart" < *stare* "to stand"]

dis·tant·ly /dístəntlee/ *adv* **1.** FAR AWAY far away or from far away ○ *We could distantly make out figures dancing in the village square.* **2.** FAR AWAY MENTALLY not concentrating on the immediate surroundings **3.** ALOOFLY in a detached, cold, or formal way ○ *He smiled at her distantly as she walked past.* **4.** NOT CLOSELY not closely in terms of family or blood relations ○ *distantly related*

dis·taste /diss táyst/ *n* a feeling of dislike, disapproval, or mild disgust

SYNONYMS See ***dislike.***

dis·taste·ful /diss táystf'l/ *adj* provoking dislike, disapproval, or mild disgust —**dis·taste·ful·ly** *adv* —**dis·taste·ful·ness** *n*

Dist. Atty. *abbr* LAW district attorney

dis·tem·per[1] /diss témpər/ *n* a viral disease that affects various animals, especially dogs and cats [Mid-16C. < obsolete verb < late Latin *distemperare* "combine awry" (referring to an imbalance of bodily "humors") < Latin *temperare* (see TEMPER)]

dis·tem·per[2] /diss témpər/ *n* **1.** paint in which the coloring material is mixed with water and a substance such as glue, size, or egg yolk or white, instead of with oil. Distemper is often used for painting walls, theatrical scenery, and posters. **2.** the use of distemper in painting posters and murals [14C. Directly or via Old French *destremper* "soak, mix" < late Latin *distemperare* (see DISTEMPER[1])] —**dis·tem·per** *vt*

dis·tend /di sténd/ (**-tend·ed, -tend·ing, -tends**) *vti* to expand, swell, or inflate as if by pressure from within, or cause something to do this [14C. < Latin *distendere* "stretch apart" < *tendere* "stretch"] —**dis·ten·der** *n* —**dis·ten·si·bil·i·ty** /di stènssə bíllətee/ *n* —**dis·ten·si·ble** /di sténssəb'l/ *adj* —**dis·ten·sion** /di sténsh'n/ *n*

dis·tich /dístik/ *n* two lines of poetry, sometimes rhyming, that form a complete unit in themselves [Early 16C. Via Latin < Greek *distikhon*, form of *distikhos* "of two rows or verses" < *stikhos* "row, line of verse"] —**dis·tich·al** *adj*

dis·ti·chous /dístəkəss/ *adj* describes leaves that grow in vertical rows on opposite sides of a stem —**dis·ti·chous·ly** *adv*

dis·till /di stíl/ (**-tilled, -till·ing, -tills**), **dis·til** (**-tilled, -till·ing, -tils**) *v* **1.** *vt* MAKE ALCOHOLIC SPIRITS to produce alcoholic spirits using the process of boiling liquid and condensing its vapor **2.** *vti* PURIFY LIQUID WITH HEAT to purify a liquid by boiling it and then condensing its vapor, or undergo purification in this way **3.** *vt* CREATE SOMETHING FROM ESSENTIAL ELEMENTS to create something from the essential or most important parts of something larger or longer **4.** *vi* EMERGE SLOWLY to be emitted slowly or in small quantities ○ *"Then slowly from the silence there distilled drops of music"* (John Buchan, *Greenmantle*; 1916) [14C. < Latin *distillare*, alteration of *destillare*, literally "drip apart" < *stillare* "to drip" < *stilla* "drop"] —**dis·till·a·ble** *adj*

dis·til·late /díst'l àyt, díst'lət/ *n* **1.** a concentrated liquid produced by boiling a liquid mixture and then condensing its vapor **2.** the concentrated essence of something

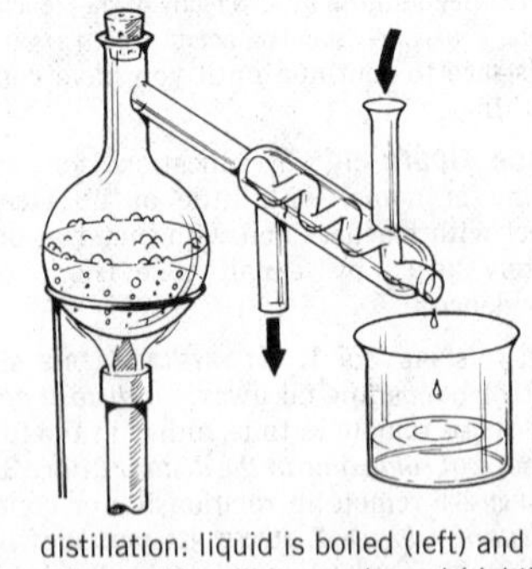

distillation: liquid is boiled (left) and the resulting vapor condensed (right)

dis·til·la·tion /dìst'l áysh'n/ *n* **1.** the process of separating, concentrating, or purifying liquid by boiling it and then condensing the resulting vapor. Alcoholic liquors, such as, whiskey and vodka are made in this way. **2.** something that consists of the essential points, aspects, or implications of something larger or longer **3.** CHEM same as **distillate** (sense 1) —**dis·til·la·to·ry** /di stíllə tàwree/ *adj*

dis·til·la·tion col·umn *n* a hollow vertical column, fitted inside with perforated trays or packing material, in which liquid mixtures are separated into their components by boiling the mixture and condensing the resulting vapor

dis·tilled /di stíld/ *adj* **1.** derived from or encapsulating a wider experience or larger set of ideas **2.** describes liquids that have been purified or concentrated by distillation

dis·till·er /di stíllər/ *n* a person or company that produces hard liquor such as whiskey, vodka, and gin

dis·till·er·y /di stílləree/ (*plural* **-ies**) *n* a place where strong alcoholic liquors such as whiskey, vodka, and gin are made by distillation

dis·tinct /di stíngkt/ *adj* **1.** CLEARLY DIFFERENT clearly different and separate from others ○ *The word has two distinct senses.* **2.** APPARENT TO SENSES easy to hear, see, smell, or understand ○ *I have a very distinct memory of that day.* **3.** CERTAIN definite or undeniable ○ *I had the distinct impression they'd been arguing.* **4.** NOTICEABLE strong enough, large enough, or definite enough to be noticed ○ *There's a distinct smell of gasoline in the car.* **5.** EMPHATIC very great in degree, e.g., as an honor felt or experienced ○ *a distinct privilege* [14C. Directly or via French < Latin *distinctus*, past participle of *distinguere* "to separate" (see DISTINGUISH)] —**dis·tinct·ly** *adv* —**dis·tinct·ness** *n*

dis·tinc·tion /di stíngkshən/ *n* **1.** DIFFERENCE a difference between two or more people or things, or the recognition of such a difference **2.** HIGH QUALITY excellence in quality or talent ○ *tailors of distinction* **3.** SOMETHING TO BE PROUD OF something done or given as a mark of respect or honor ○ *I had the distinction of giving the opening address.* **4.** DISTINGUISHING FEATURE a feature or quality that characterizes or singles out somebody or something ○ *She has the dubious distinction of being the administration's staunchest defender.* **5.** EDUC MARK OF HIGH ACHIEVEMENT recognition of high achievement or a grade that signifies this ○ *graduated from the university with distinction*

dis·tinc·tive /di stíngktiv/ *adj* **1.** uniquely characteristic of a person, group, or thing **2.** describes a feature of a phoneme that can distinguish it from other similar phonemes, e.g., the fact that it is labial, fricative, or nasal —**dis·tinc·tive·ly** *adv* —**dis·tinc·tive·ness** *n*

dis·tin·gué /dee stang gáy, di stáng gày/ *adj* having the confidence and dignity of somebody who is used to being respected (*formal*) [Early 19C. < French, past participle of *distinguer* (see DISTINGUISH)]

dis·tin·guish /di stíng gwish/ (**-guished, -guish·ing, -guish·es**) *v* **1.** *vti* RECOGNIZE DIFFERENCES BETWEEN PEOPLE OR THINGS to be aware of a difference between two or more people, groups, or things, or show that they are different from each other ○ *to distinguish between fact and fiction* **2.** *vt* BE DIFFERENCE BETWEEN PEOPLE OR THINGS to be the feature or characteristic that shows that one person, group, or thing is different from another ○ *What distinguishes dogs from wolves?* **3.** *vt* MAKE SOMEBODY OR SOMETHING OUT to be able to recognize or identify somebody or something ○ *I could barely distinguish people's faces in the fog.* **4. dis·tin·guish your·self** *vr* PERFORM WELL AND ACHIEVE RECOGNITION to make yourself well known because of excellence, especially in a profession, art, or organization ○ *He distinguished himself on the field of battle.* [Late 16C. < French *distinguer* or Latin *distinguere* "to separate" < *stinguere* "quench"] —**dis·tin·guish·a·ble** *adj* —**dis·tin·guish·a·bly** *adv* —**dis·tin·guish·er** *n*

dis·tin·guished /di stíng gwisht/ *adj* **1.** RECOGNIZED FOR EXCELLENCE well known and respected for an achievement, skill, knowledge, or talent ○ *a distinguished composer* **2.** CONFIDENT AND DIGNIFIED showing the confident and dignified appearance and manners of somebody who is used to respect **3.** SUCCESSFUL showing or involving a great deal of skill, talent, or success

Dis·tin·guished Fly·ing Cross *n* a US military medal awarded for extraordinary achievement or for heroism in air combat

Dis·tin·guished Ser·vice Cross *n* **1.** a US Army medal awarded for extraordinary heroism against an enemy. It is the US Army's second highest award for bravery, the highest being the Congressional Medal of Honor. **2.** a British medal awarded in all branches of the armed forces for distinguished service in action

Dis·tin·guished Ser·vice Or·der *n* a British medal awarded to commissioned officers in all branches of the armed forces for distinguished service in action

dis·tin·guish·ing /di stíng gwishing/ *adj* allowing one person, group, or thing to be told apart from another ○ *distinguishing characteristics*

dis·tort /di stáwrt/ (**-tort·ed, -tort·ing, -torts**) *v* **1.** *vti* ALTER SHAPE to bend, twist, stretch, or force something out of its usual or natural shape, or be made to do this **2.** *vt* GIVE INACCURATE REPORT OF SOMETHING to describe or report something in an inaccurate or misleading way **3.** *vt* MAKE SOMETHING UNCLEAR OR UNRECOGNIZABLE to change something such as an image in such a way that it becomes unclear or unrecognizable **4.** *vt* ELECTRONICS REPRODUCE SIGNAL INACCURATELY to amplify or reproduce something such as a radio or television signal inaccurately to the extent that it becomes unclear or unrecognizable [15C. < Latin *distort-*, past participle of *distorquere* "twist completely" < *torquere* "twist"] —**dis·tort·ed** *adj* —**dis·tort·er** *n* —**dis·tor·tive** *adj*

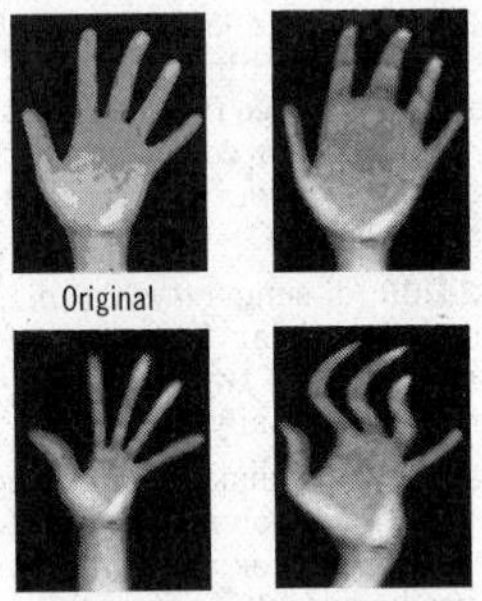

distortion: electronically manipulated images of a hand

dis·tor·tion /di stáwrsh'n/ *n* **1.** MISLEADING ALTERATION the describing or reporting of something in a way that is inaccurate or misleading **2.** RECONFIGURATION FROM CORRECT SHAPE the bending, twisting, stretching, or forcing of something out of its usual or natural shape **3.** MISSHAPEN PART a part of something that has been bent, twisted, stretched, or forced out of its usual or natural shape **4.** ALTERATION FROM CLARITY the altering of something such as a radio or television signal to the extent that it becomes unclear or unrecognizable **5.** OPTICS ALTERATION IN OPTICAL IMAGE an alteration in an image in which the original proportions are changed, resulting from a defect in a lens or optical system —**dis·tor·tion·al** *adj* —**dis·tor·tion·ar·y** *adj*

distr. *abbr* **1.** COMM, STATS, LOGIC distribution **2.** COMM, STATS, MATH distributor

dis·tract /di strákt/ (**-tract·ed, -tract·ing, -tracts**) *vt* **1.** CATCH SOMEBODY'S ATTENTION to take somebody's attention away from what he or she is doing or thinking or from what is happening **2.** AMUSE SOMEBODY to amuse or entertain somebody, especially as a means of taking his or her mind off something unpleasant **3.** MAKE SOMEBODY UNEASY to unsettle somebody's mind with disturbing, confusing, or conflicting emotions (*archaic*) ○ *"O Husband, Husband, my Heart long'd to see thee; but to see thee thus distracts me."* (John Gay, *The Beggar's Opera*; 1728) [14C. < Latin *distract-*, past participle of *distrahere* "draw away" < *trahere* "draw, drag"] —**dis·tract·i·bil·i·ty** /di stràktə bíllətee/ *n* —**dis·tract·i·ble** *adj* —**dis·trac·tive** *adj*

dis·tract·ed /di stráktəd/ *adj* **1.** showing a lack of concentration **2.** so worried or upset as to be unable to think clearly or act sensibly —**dis·tract·ed·ly** *adv* —**dis·tract·ed·ness** *n*

dis·tract·er *n* another spelling of **distractor**

dis·tract·ing /di strákting/ *adj* **1.** taking somebody's attention away from what he or she wants to do or ought to be doing **2.** helping somebody to relax and forget work or worries —**dis·tract·ing·ly** *adv*

dis·trac·tion /di strákshən/ *n* **1.** SOMETHING THAT DIVERTS ATTENTION something that interferes with concentration or takes attention away from something else **2.** AMUSEMENT something providing entertainment or amusement, especially something that takes the mind off work or worries and helps relaxation **3.** EMOTIONAL UPSET a state of great mental upset or emotional intensity ○ *Those pop-up Internet ads drive me to distraction.*

dis·tract·or /di stráktər/, **dis·tract·er** *n* **1.** an incorrect option shown as a possible answer to a multiple-choice question **2.** a person or thing that distracts somebody's attention

dis·train /di stráyn/ (**-trained, -train·ing, -trains**) *vt* to seize somebody's moveable property either in lieu of payment of a debt or in order to force the person to pay [14C. < Old French *destreign-*, present stem of *destreindre* < Latin *distringere* "draw asunder"] —**dis·train·a·ble** *adj* —**dis·train·ee** /di stràyn née/ *n* —**dis·train·er** *n* —**dis·train·ment** *n*

dis·traint /di stráynt/ *n Can, UK* same as **distress** *n* (sense 5) [Mid-18C. < DISTRAIN, after CONSTRAINT]

dis·trait /di stráy/ *adj* inattentive and slightly distracted or absent-minded (*literary*) [14C. < French < past participle of Old French *destraire* "distract" < Latin *distrahere* (see DISTRACT)]

dis·traught /di stráwt/ *adj* extremely upset and distressed [14C. Alteration of archaic *distract* "perplexed" < Latin *distractus*, past participle of *distrahere* (see DISTRACT)] —**dis·traught·ly** *adv*

dis·tress /di stréss/ *n* **1.** MENTAL SUFFERING mental suffering, e.g., that caused by grief, anxiety, or unhappiness **2.** HARDSHIP hardship or problems caused by a lack of basic necessities **3.** PHYSICAL PAIN physical pain or discomfort **4.** DANGER OR DIFFICULTY great danger or difficulty, with a need for immediate assistance ○ *a ship in distress* **5.** *US* LAW SEIZURE OF BAD DEBTOR'S PROPERTY the seizing of somebody's movable property either in lieu of payment of a debt or in order to force the person to pay. Can term **distraint** ■ *vt* (**-tressed, -tress·ing, -tress·es**) **1.** UPSET SOMEBODY to make somebody extremely upset, anxious, or alarmed **2.** MAKE FURNITURE OR FABRIC LOOK OLD to give a new piece of furniture or fabric an old or worn appearance [13C. Via Old French *destresce* < assumed Vulgar Latin *districtia* < Latin *district-*, past participle of *distringere* "draw asunder"]

dis·tressed /di strést/ *adj* **1.** VERY UPSET extremely upset, anxious, or unhappy **2.** MADE TO LOOK OLDER artificially given an old or worn appearance **3.** LAW REPOSSESSED FROM BAD DEBTOR repossessed by a bank or other lender from the borrower and offered for sale at a reduced price ○ *foreclosures and other distressed properties* **4.** OF DAMAGED GOODS describes goods that have been damaged or used ○ *They had a sale of distressed inventory.*

dis·tress·ing /di stréssing/, **dis·tress·ful** /-fəl/ *adj* causing somebody to feel extremely upset —**dis·tress·ing·ly** *adv*

dis·tress sig·nal *n* a signal, e.g., a radio message or a flare, sent by a ship or aircraft in urgent need of assistance

dis·trib·u·tar·y /di stríbbyə tèrree/ (*plural* **-ies**) *n* a channel leading water away from a main single channel

dis·trib·ute /di strí byóot/ (**-ut·ed, -ut·ing, -utes**) *v* **1.** *vt* GIVE SOMETHING OUT to give out something to a number of people ○ *distributed prizes* **2.** *vt* SHARE SOMETHING OUT to divide something into shares and give the shares to a number of people **3.** *vt* COMM SELL AND DISPATCH GOODS to sell and deliver merchandise, especially wholesale goods to a retailer **4.** *vt* SPREAD SOMETHING to scatter something or spread it throughout a particular area or place **5.** *vt* DIVIDE SOMETHING INTO CLASSES to divide something up into different classes or categories **6.** *vt* LOGIC MAKE TERM APPLY TO ALL to apply a term to all the members of the class it designates **7.** *vti* MATH MAKE MATHEMATICAL OPERATION APPLY THROUGHOUT to make an operation such as multiplication or division apply to each part of a mathematical expression [15C. < Latin *distribut-*, past participle of *distribuere* "assign separately" < *tribuere* (see TRIBUTE)] —**dis·trib·ut·a·ble** *adj*

dis·trib·ut·ed /di stríbbyətəd/ *adj* describes computer systems in which two or more computers have a telecommunications link to each other but can also operate independently

dis·trib·u·tee /di strìbbyoo tée/ *n* somebody entitled to a share of the estate of a person who has died without making a will

dis·trib·ut·er *n* another spelling of **distributor**

dis·tri·bu·tion /dìstrə byóosh'n/ *n* **1.** GIVING OUT the handing out or delivery of things to a number of people ○ *the distribution of leaflets* **2.** SHARING the process of dividing up and giving out something shared by a number of people ○ *the distribution of wealth* **3.** SCATTERING the scattering or spreading of something over an area **4.** COMM SELLING AND DELIVERY the selling and delivery of goods to retailers **5.** COMPUT SET OF RECIPIENTS a topic-oriented controlled subset of the total number of potential recipients to which a message, article, or posting to a mailing list or newsgroup is sent **6.** ECOL ENTIRE AREA WHERE SPECIES IS FOUND the area or areas taken together where something is located or where a species lives and reproduces **7.** STATS SPREAD OF STATISTICS the spread of statistics within known or possible limits, especially in relation to the norm or to expectations **8.** LAW SHARING OUT OF SOMEBODY'S ESTATE the dividing up of the estate of somebody who has died intestate among people who are entitled to receive a share **9.** LOGIC RECOMBINING OF TWO PROPOSITIONS the recombining of two operations from one proposition in another equivalent proposition, e.g., "p and (q or r)" is equivalent to "(p and q) or (p and r)" —**dis·tri·bu·tion·al** *adj*

dis·trib·u·tive /di stríbbyətiv/ *adj* **1.** INVOLVING DISTRIBUTION relating to or involving the handing out, sharing out, or scattering about of things **2.** COMM INVOLVED WITH DELIVERIES relating to or involved in the delivery of merchandise **3.** GRAM REFERRING TO EACH MEMBER OF GROUP referring to each member of a set or group individually and separately. "Each," "every," and "either" are examples of distributive words in English. **4.** LOGIC REFERRING TO INDIVIDUALS, NOT CLASSES referring to an individual member of a class, or to each member individually **5.** MATH PRODUCING EQUAL RESULTS describes a mathematical expression with two operators whose expansion produces the same results whether operated on as a whole or as a sum of the parts ■ *n* GRAM DISTRIBUTIVE WORD a word that refers to every member of a set or group individually and separately —**dis·trib·u·tive·ly** *adv*

dis·trib·u·tive ed·u·ca·tion *n* educational courses in vocational subjects that combine classroom teaching with on-the-job training

dis·trib·u·tor /di stríbbyətər/, **dis·trib·ut·er** *n* **1.** SOMEBODY WHO DISTRIBUTES SOMETHING a person, organization, or device that distributes something **2.** COMM WHOLESALER a wholesaler who sells merchandise to retailers, usually within a specific geographic area **3.** AUTOMOT DEVICE CONVEYING ELECTRICITY TO SPARK PLUGS the device in a motor vehicle's engine that transfers electric current from the induction coil to the spark plugs **4.** MOVIES ORGANIZATION ARRANGING SCREENING OF MOTION PICTURES an organization that advertises movies and arranges with owners of movie theaters to have them shown

dis·trict /dístrikt/ *n* an area of a town or country, especially one with a distinguishing feature or one that is an administrative division ○ *a fruit-growing district* ■ *vt* (**-trict·ed, -trict·ing, -tricts**) to divide an area into distinct geopolitical or cultural sectors ○ *districting the county for voting purposes* [Early 17C. Via French < medieval Latin *districtus* "(area of) jurisdiction" < Latin *district-* (see DISTRESS)]

dis·trict at·tor·ney *n* the prosecuting officer of a jurisdiction

dis·trict court *n* the trial court in either a state or a federal district in the United States

Dis·trict of Co·lum·bi·a /dìstrikt əv kə lúmbee ə/ federal district of the United States, situated on the Potomac and Anacostia rivers, coextensive with the city of Washington, D.C., the nation's capital. It was created in 1790–91. Area: 68 sq. mi./176 sq. km.

~~**distroy**~~ incorrect spelling of **destroy**

dis·trust /diss trúst/ *n* a feeling that somebody or something is dishonest or unreliable ■ *vt* (**-trust·ed, -trust·ing, -trusts**) to have a feeling that somebody or something is dishonest or unreliable —**dis·trust·ful** *adj*

dis·turb /di stúrb/ (**-turbed, -turb·ing, -turbs**) *vt* **1.** INTERRUPT SOMEBODY to interrupt or distract somebody when he or she is doing something **2.** UPSET SOMEBODY to make somebody feel anxious or slightly troubled **3.** CHANGE SHAPE OR POSITION to move something so that it is not in its usual, expected, or correct position or shape ○ *Nothing on my desk had been disturbed.* **4.** SPOIL PEACE AND QUIET to spoil the quietness, stillness, or peacefulness of something **5.** WAKEN SOMEBODY OR SOMETHING to rouse a person or animal from sleep [12C. Directly or via French < Latin *disturbare* "disturb completely" < *turbare* "disturb"] —**dis·turb·er** *n* —**dis·turb·ing** *adj* —**dis·turb·ing·ly** *adv*

SYNONYMS See ***bother.***

dis·tur·bance /di stúrbənss/ *n* **1.** COMMOTION noisy and violent behavior in a public place, or an incident involving such behavior **2.** DISRUPTION OF PEACE the disruption of a peaceful or ordered environment, or something that causes such disruption **3.** DISRUPTION OF CONCENTRATION the disruption of somebody's concentration, or something that disrupts somebody's ability to continue with a task in hand **4.** MOVEMENT FROM USUAL PLACE the act of altering or moving something so that it is not in its usual, expected, or correct position or shape ○ *visible disturbance of the archaeological site* **5.** MENTAL UPSET psychological or emotional upset **6.** GEOL EARTH TREMOR a minor movement of the ground that falls short of an earthquake **7.** METEOROL LOW-PRESSURE AREA a small area of low pressure **8.** LAW INTERFERENCE WITH SOMEBODY'S RIGHTS an act that causes disruption to others or hinders them from pursuing normal legal activities

dis·turbed /di stúrbd/ *adj* **1.** worried or concerned **2.** affected by or displaying symptoms of psychiatric disorder

di·sul·fide /dī súl fīd/ *n* a chemical compound that has two atoms of sulfur combined with one or more other elements

di·sul·fi·ram /dī súlfə ràm/ *n* a drug used in the treatment of alcoholism [Mid-20C. < DISULFIDE + *thiuram*, a radical]

di·sul·fo·ton /dī súlfə tòn/ *n* a systemic organophosphate insecticide. Use: agriculture. [Mid-20C. < DI-[1] + *sulfo-* + *-ton*, origin ?]

dis·un·ion /diss yóonyən/ *n* **1.** the splitting up of something into separate smaller parts or groups **2.** disagreement or discord

dis·u·nite /dìssyoo nīt/ (**-nit·ed, -nit·ing, -nites**) *v* **1.** *vt* to create or be a source of disagreement between different people or factions within a group **2.** *vti* to divide something into smaller parts or groups, or become divided in this way —**dis·u·nit·ed** *adj*

dis·u·ni·ty /diss yóonətee/ *n* a lack of unity within a group, especially one caused by a disagreement or a difference of opinion

dis·use /diss yóoss/ *n* the fact or condition of not being used, applied, or followed, especially for a long time

dis·used /diss yóozd/ *adj* no longer in use, or no longer used for its original purpose ○ *a disused airfield*

dis·u·til·i·ty /dìssyoo tíllətee/ *n* a state of causing a counterproductive result, inconvenience, or harm (*formal*)

dis·val·ue /diss vállyoo/ *vt* (**-ued, -u·ing, -ues**) same as **undervalue** (sense 1) ■ *n* negative worth or value

di·syl·la·ble /dī sílləb'l, di-/, **dis·syl·la·ble** *n* **1.** a word composed of two syllables **2.** a two-syllable unit of rhythm in poetry —**di·syl·lab·ic** /dī si lábbik, dì-/ *adj*

dit /dit/ *n* the spoken form of the short sound used in Morse and other telegraphic codes [Mid-20C. An imitation of the sound]

ditch /dich/ *n* **1.** NARROW CHANNEL a long narrow channel dug in the ground, usually used for drainage or irrigation but sometimes used as a boundary marker **2.** *UK* SMALL BROOK a small natural stream or brook ■ *v* (**ditched, ditch·ing, ditch·es**) **1.** *vti* DIG DITCHES to enclose, drain, or irrigate an area with ditches **2.** *vti* MAKE EMERGENCY LANDING ON WATER to land, or make an aircraft land, on water in an emergency (*informal*) **3.** *vt* ABANDON SOMETHING OR SOMEBODY to abandon something or somebody as no longer wanted, liked, or needed (*slang*) [Old English *dīc* < Germanic, "hole and mound produced by digging"] —**ditch·er** *n*

di·the·ism /díthee ìzzəm, dī thée-/ *n* **1.** belief in two equal gods **2.** the belief that the world is ruled by two equal and opposing forces or gods, one good and one evil —**di·the·ist** *n* —**di·the·is·tic** /dìthee ístik/ *adj*

dith·er /díthər/ *vi* (**-ered, -er·ing, -ers**) to behave in a nervous and indecisive way ■ *n* a state of nervous agitation or indecisiveness [Mid-17C. Alteration of obsolete *didder* "tremble, shake," origin ?] —**dith·er·er** *n*

dith·er·ing /díthəring/ *n* **1.** nervously confused indecisiveness in the face of alternative possible actions **2.** the mixing of pixels of several colors on a computer display to create the illusion of extra colors or shading

dith·y·ramb /díthə ràm/ *n* **1.** a passionately emotional speech or piece of writing (*formal*) **2.** in ancient Greece, a wild and impassioned choral hymn, originally directed to the god Dionysus [Early 17C. Via Latin < Greek *dithurambos*] —**dith·y·ramb·ic** /dìthə rámbik/ *adj*

di·tran·si·tive /dī tránzitiv/ *adj* describes a verb that requires both a direct and an indirect object, e.g. "give" as in "give the dog a bone"

dit·sy /dítsee/ (**-si·er, -si·est**), **dit·zy** (**-zi·er, -zi·est**) *adj* silly or scatterbrained (*slang*) [Late 20C. Origin ?]

dit·ta·ny /dítt'nee/ (*plural* **-nies** or *same*) *n* **1.** an aromatic plant related to oregano and marjoram and cultivated as an ornamental and for its medicinal properties. Flowers: pink. Native to: southern Europe. Latin name: *Origanum dictamnus*. **2.** an aromatic plant cultivated as a kitchen herb. Latin name: *Cunila origanoides*. **3.** PLANTS same as **gas plant** [12C. < Old French *ditain*, medieval Latin *ditaneum* < Greek *diktamnon*]

dit·to /díttō/ *interj* SAME HERE used instead of repeating something that has just been said to indicate that the same thing applies to you (*informal*) ○ *"I'm bored." "Ditto!"* ■ *adv* THE SAME THING APPLIES ELSEWHERE indicating that whatever has just been said about one person or thing applies equally to somebody or something else ○ *The car will need to be cleaned; ditto the children.* ■ *n* (*plural* **-tos**) SYMBOL REPRESENTING REPEATED MATTER a pair of marks (") that together represent matter that is repeated directly from what appears above them ■ *vt* (**-toed, -to·ing, -tos**) REPEAT SOMETHING to repeat or imitate something that somebody else has said or done [Early 17C. Via Tuscan dialect variant of Italian *detto* "said" < Latin *dictus*, past participle of *dicere* "say"]

dit·ty /díttee/ (*plural* **-ties**) *n* a short simple popular song [14C. Via Old French *dité* "composition" < Latin *dictatum* "thing dictated" < *dictat-* (see DICTATE)]

dit·ty bag *n* **1.** a small canvas or leather bag used by men for holding small personal belongings **2.** a small waterproof bag used to carry toiletries when traveling

ditz /dits/ *n* somebody considered to be silly or scatterbrained (*slang insult*) [Late 20C. Back-formation < DITSY]

dit·zy *adj* another spelling of **ditsy**

di·u·re·sis /dī ə reéssiss/ *n* increased excretion of urine caused by excessive intake of fluids, a drug, or a disease [Late 17C. < modern Latin, literally "urination through" < Greek *ourēsis* "urination"]

di·u·ret·ic /dī ə réttik/ *adj* causing increased flow of urine [14C. Via late Latin < Greek *diourētikos* < *diourein*, literally "urinate through" < *ourein* "urinate"] —**di·u·ret·ic** *n*

di·ur·nal /dī úrn'l/ *adj* **1.** DAILY happening every day **2.** IN DAYTIME happening during the day as opposed to at night **3.** ZOOL ACTIVE IN DAYTIME describes animals that are active during the day rather than at night **4.** BOT OPEN ONLY IN DAYTIME describes flowers that open during the day and close at night ■ *n* CHR ROMAN CATHOLIC BOOK FOR WORSHIP in the Roman Catholic Church, a book containing the prayer and worship material for all of the set daily services except matins [14C. < late Latin *diurnalis* < Latin *diurnus* "daily" < *dies* "day"] —**di·ur·nal·ly** *adv*

di·ur·nal par·al·lax *n* the change in an astronomical object's apparent position caused by the change in the observer's position because of the motion of Earth during a day

di·u·ron /dī ə ròn/ *n* an agricultural herbicide used to clear fields of weeds before crops emerge. Formula: $C_9H_{10}Cl_2N_2O$. [< DI-[1] "two (chlorine atoms)" + UREA]

div. *abbr* **1.** OPHTHALMOL, BIOL, MATH divergence **2.** MIL diversion **3.** MATH divide **4.** FIN dividend **5.** MATH division **6.** SOC SCI divorced

di·va /deévə/ (*plural* **-vas** or **-ve** /-vay/) *n* **1.** a distinguished woman singer, especially one who sings in operas **2.** a successful woman performer [Late 19C. Via Italian < Latin, "goddess"]

di·va·gate /dívə gàyt, dívvə-/ (**-gat·ed, -gat·ing, -gates**) *vi* (*literary*) **1.** to wander off the subject under discussion **2.** to wander around somewhere [Mid-16C. < Latin *divagat-*, past participle of *divagari* "wander around" < *vagari* "wander"] —**di·va·ga·tion** /dīvə gáysh'n, dìvvə-/ *n*

di·va·lent /dī váylənt/ *adj* having a valence of 2

Di·va·li *n* HINDUISM another spelling of **Diwali**

di·van /di ván/ *n* **1.** /di ván, dī-/ BACKLESS SOFA a sofa without a back, and sometimes without arms **2.** SMOKING ROOM in former times, a smoking room attached to a coffee shop or cigar shop **3.** /di ván, dī ván, di vaán/ LITERAT ARABIC POEMS a collection of poems written in Persian or Arabic, often by a single poet [Late 16C. Via French or Italian < Turkish *dīvān* < Persian *dīvān*]

di·var·i·cate /dī várrə kàyt, di-/ (**-cat·ed, -cat·ing, -cates**) *vi* to branch or fork at a wide angle [Early 17C. < Latin *divaricat-*, past participle of *divaricare* "stretch apart" < *varicus* "straddling"] —**di·var·i·cate** *adj*

di·var·i·ca·tion /dī vàrri káysh'n, di-/ *n* **1.** WIDE BRANCHING separation into widely spread parts or branches **2.** FORK the point at which something forks or branches **3.** DISAGREEMENT a difference of opinion (*formal*)

dive /dīv/ *v* (**dived** or **dove** /dōv/, **dived, div·ing, dives**) **1.** *vi* JUMP INTO WATER to jump or throw yourself into water, usually head first, especially with your arms stretched out above your head **2.** *vi* PERFORM ACROBATIC JUMPS INTO WATER to perform a pattern of acrobatic movements in the air ending in a usually headfirst plunge into water, especially as a sport **3.** *vi* SWIM UNDER WATER to swim below the surface of a stretch of water, often with special breathing apparatus **4.** *vi* GO TOWARD BOTTOM OF WATER to go down steeply and quickly toward the bottom of a body of water, sometimes in search of something **5.** *vi* DESCEND STEEPLY AND RAPIDLY to fly or make an aircraft fly steeply and rapidly in the direction of the ground or the sea **6.** *vi* THROW YOURSELF TO GROUND to jump quickly to one side or throw yourself forward or sideways to the ground ○ *dive out of the way* **7.** *vi* MOVE FAST to move quickly and in a rush in a particular direction ○ *dive for the door* **8.** *vti* PUT HAND IN SOMETHING to put your hand or hands quickly into something such as a pocket or a closet, in order to get something out of it ○ *dived into the drawer to retrieve her ID card* **9.** *vti* NAVY CAUSE SUBMARINE TO DESCEND to cause a submarine to go below the surface of the sea **10.** *vi* DROP IN VALUE to fall sharply in value ■ *n* **1.** HEADLONG JUMP INTO WATER a jump into water, usually head first, especially with your arms stretched out above your head **2.** ACT OF SWIMMING UNDER WATER a swim below the surface of a stretch of water, often with special breathing apparatus **3.** DESCENT TOWARD BOTTOM OF WATER a steep and usually rapid descent in the direction of the bottom of a body of water **4.** STEEP DESCENT THROUGH AIR a bird's or aircraft's rapid and steep fall or flight in the direction of the ground or the sea **5.** SUBMARINE'S DESCENT a submarine's descent below the surface of the sea **6.** QUICK MOVEMENT SIDEWAYS OR DOWN a quick jump or movement to one side, forward, or sideways to the ground **7.** DISREPUTABLE BAR OR CLUB a dirty, shabby, or disreputable bar or club (*slang*) **8.** FIN SHARP FINANCIAL DROP a sharp fall in value **9.** FOOTBALL PLAYER'S DRIVE FORWARD WITH BALL in football, an offensive play in which the ball carrier drives into the opposing line of players instead of passing the ball or running with it **10.** SPORTS PLAYER'S FALL in some sports, a feigned dramatic fall by a player to try to gain a penalty (*informal*) **11.** BOXING BOXER'S FEIGNED FALL in boxing, a fall or injury feigned by a fighter in order to lose a fight dishonestly (*slang*) ■ ARTS plural of **diva** [Old English *dūfan* "to sink," *dȳfan* "to dip" < Germanic]

USAGE Dived or **dove**? Both forms are acceptable as past tenses of ***dive***. ***Dived*** is actually an earlier past tense form, but ***dove*** has become a standard alternative. This is the reverse of the general tendency of verbs to form their past tense with *-ed*, as opposed to a change in their vowel, which was more frequently the case in the Old English period. The past participle is nonetheless ***dived***.

dive in *vi* **1.** to undertake or start on some activity with great enthusiasm **2.** to begin eating quickly and with gusto (*informal*)

dive-bomb *vt* to descend steeply in a military aircraft and deliver bombs onto a target —**dive-bomb·er** *n* —**dive-bomb·ing** *n*

dive brake *n* same as **air brake** (sense 2)

Di·ve·hi /dívve eé/ *n* LANG same as **Maldivian** (sense 2) [< Divehi] —**Di·ve·hi** *adj*

div·er /dívər/ *n* **1.** somebody who goes under the surface of water for work or recreation **2.** any water bird noted for its diving skills **3.** *UK* same as **loon**[1] (sense 1)

di·verge /di vúrj, dī-/ (**-verged, -verg·ing, -verg·es**) *vi* **1.** SEPARATE to separate and go in a different direction or different directions **2.** DIFFER to differ to some extent **3.** NOT CONFORM to deviate from or not fit in with something such as a typical pattern or expressed wish [Mid-17C. < medieval Latin *divergere* "bend apart" < Latin *vergere* "bend"] —**di·verg·ing** *adj*

di·ver·gence /di vúrjənss, dī-/, **di·ver·gen·cy** /-jənssee/ (*plural* **-cies**) *n* **1.** DIFFERENCE OR DISPARITY a difference between two or more things such as opinions or attitudes **2.** FAILURE TO CONFORM OR MATCH deviation from something such as a typical pattern or expressed wish **3.** MOVING APART the process of separating or moving apart to follow different paths or different courses **4.** AMOUNT OF DIFFERENCE the amount by which something differs from something else, especially where such a difference is not expected **5.** OPHTHALMOL DEVIATION OF EYE FROM SIGHT LINE a condition in which only one eye is directed at the object of interest and the other is directed outward **6.** BIOL DIFFERENT DEVELOPMENT OF RELATED ORGANISMS the development of different characteristics by organisms that come from the same ancestor, caused by the influence of different environments **7.** MATH SEQUENCE OF NUMBERS WITHOUT LIMIT the characteristic of a series or sequence of numbers in which the value of the last term and the sum of the series are without limit **8.** METEOROL MOVEMENT OF AIR CURRENTS a set of meteorological conditions in a given area in which the air expands and the net flow of air is out of the area, usually resulting in fair dry conditions

di·ver·gent /di vúrjənt, dī-/ *adj* **1.** MOVING APART following paths or courses that become increasingly different or separate **2.** DIFFERING showing or having differences **3.** NOT MATCHING SOMETHING deviating from something such as a typical pattern or an expressed wish **4.** MATH INCREASING WITHOUT LIMIT describes a series or sequence of numbers in which each term is equal to or greater than the preceding term, and the value of the last term and the sum of the series are without limit **5.** MATH RADIATING FROM POINT describes lines radiating from a single point —**di·ver·gent·ly** *adv*

di·verg·ing lens /dī vùrjing-/ *n* a lens, usually concave, that causes a parallel beam of light to spread

di·vers /dívərz/ *adj* more than one, and of various types (*literary*) [13C. Via French < Latin *diversus*, past participle of *divertere* "separate" (see DIVERT)]

di·verse /di vúrss, dī-, dī vùrss/ *adj* **1.** CONSISTING OF DIFFERENT THINGS made up of many differing parts ○ *culturally diverse* **2.** DIFFERING FROM EACH OTHER very different or distinct from one another ○ *a person with diverse interests* **3.** SOCIALLY INCLUSIVE composed of many ethnic, as well as socioeconomic and gender, groups ○ *sought a more diverse population of students* [13C. Variant of DIVERS] —**di·verse·ness** *n*

di·verse·ly /di vúrsslee, dī-, dī vùrsslee/ *adv* in different or various ways ○ *diversely colored*

di·ver·si·fy /di vúrssə fī, dī-/ (**-fied, -fy·ing, -fies**) *vti* **1.** to become more varied, or make something more varied **2.** to expand into new areas of business, or expand a commercial organization into new areas [15C. Via Old French *diversifier* < medieval Latin *diversificare* "make unlike" < Latin *diversus* (see DIVERS)] —**di·ver·si·fi·a·bil·i·ty** /di vùrssə fī ə bíllətee, dī-/ *n* —**di·ver·si·fi·a·ble** *adj* —**di·ver·si·fi·ca·tion** /di vùrssəfi káysh'n, dī-/ *n* —**di·ver·si·fied** *adj* —**di·ver·si·fi·er** *n*

di·ver·sion /di vúrzh'n, dī-/ *n* **1. DISTRACTION** something that takes somebody's attention away from something else **2. CHANGE OF PURPOSE** a change in the purpose or use of something from what was intended or from what it was previously **3. CHANGE OF DIRECTION** a change in the direction or path of something **4. PASTIME** an activity or interest that takes somebody's mind off more routine or serious things **5.** MIL **MOCK ATTACK** a mock attack aimed at drawing enemy attention and troops away from the place of the intended main attack **6.** *UK* ROADS same as **detour** *n* (sense 2) [15C. Directly or via French < late Latin *diversion-* "turning away" < Latin *diversus* (see DIVERS)] —**di·ver·sion·al** *adj*

di·ver·sion·ar·y /di vúrzh'n èrree, dī-/ *adj* designed or carried out to divert somebody's attention away from something

di·ver·sion·ist /di vúrzh'nist, dī-/ *n* somebody who engages in disruptive actions or sabotage in order to thwart an enemy or government, e.g., an irregular soldier, guerrilla, or political operative

di·ver·si·ty /di vúrssətee, dī-/ (*plural* **-ties**) *n* **1. VARIETY** a variety of something such as opinion, color, or style ○ *a city of great cultural diversity* **2. SOCIAL INCLUSIVENESS** ethnic variety, as well as socioeconomic and gender variety, in a group, society, or institution ○ *a company committed to diversity* **3. DISCREPANCY** discrepancy, or a difference from what is normal or expected [14C. Via French < Latin *diversitas* < *diversus* (see DIVERS)]

di·vert /di vúrt, dī-/ (**-vert·ed, -vert·ing, -verts**) *vt* **1. CHANGE SOMETHING'S PATH** to change the route or path taken by something such as traffic or a river **2. DRAW ATTENTION FROM SOMETHING** to take somebody's mind off something and draw attention to something else **3. CHANGE PURPOSE OR USE** to change the purpose or use of something from what it was previously **4. AMUSE SOMEBODY** to amuse or entertain somebody or yourself [15C. Via French *divertir* < Latin *divertere* "turn aside" < *vertere* "turn"] —**di·vert·er** *n*

di·ver·tic·u·la ANAT plural of **diverticulum**

di·ver·tic·u·li·tis /dìvərtikyə lítiss/ *n* inflammation of protrusions **(diverticula)** of the lining of the large intestine, causing severe abdominal pain, often with fever and constipation

di·ver·tic·u·lo·sis /dìvərtikyə lóssiss/ *n* the presence of protrusions **(diverticula)** in the bowel, caused when the bowel muscles rupture the bowel wall

di·ver·tic·u·lum /dìvər tíkyələm/ (*plural* **-la** /-lə/) *n* a pouch or sac in the lining of the mucous membrane of a hollow organ, especially one produced in the bowel when the bowel muscle ruptures the bowel wall [Mid-17C. < medieval Latin, "byway," variant of Latin *deverticulum* < *vertere* "to turn"] —**di·ver·tic·u·lar** *adj*

di·ver·ti·men·to /di vùrtə mén tō/ (*plural* **-ti** /-tee/ or **-tos**) *n* a piece of light classical instrumental music composed in several movements for an ensemble [Mid-18C. < Italian, "diversion" < *divertire* "divert" < Latin *divertere* (see DIVERT)]

di·vert·ing /di vúrting, dī-/ *adj* amusing or entertaining, and acting as a temporary distraction from more routine or serious matters —**di·vert·ing·ly** *adv*

di·ver·tisse·ment /di vúrtissmənt/ *n* **1.** BALLET **SERIES OF UNTHEMED DANCES** in a ballet, a dance highlighting a dancer's skill rather than developing the story **2.** DANCE **DANCE INTERLUDE** a dance interlude in a play or opera **3.** MUSIC **TUNES DERIVED FROM FAMOUS MELODIES** a set of tunes that are based on well-known melodies [Early 18C. < French < *divertiss-*, stem of *divertir* "divert" (see DIVERT)]

di·vest /di vést, dī-/ (**-vest·ed, -vest·ing, -vests**) *vt* **1. TAKE SOMETHING AWAY FROM SOMEBODY** to take away something, especially status or power, from somebody or something (*often passive*) ○ *The report divested the organization of its mystique.* **2. MAKE SOMEBODY GIVE UP SOMETHING** to rid somebody or yourself of something, especially a belief or idea ○ *divested herself of the notion* **3. MAKE SOMEBODY TAKE SOMETHING OFF** to remove something, usually clothes, from somebody or yourself (*formal or humorous*) ○ *divested himself of his coat* **4.** LAW **GIVE AWAY PROPERTY RIGHTS** to lose or give away rights to the possession of property, or deprive somebody of them [Early 17C. Alteration of obsolete *devest* "deprive" < Old French *de(s)vester* "undress" < *vestir* "clothe" < Latin *vestire*] —**di·vest·ment** *n* —**di·ves·ture** *n*

di·ves·ti·ture /di vésti choor, dī-, -véstichər/ *n* **1.** the removal or deprivation of something **2.** the sale of one or more of a company's subsidiaries, divisions, or holdings, or of its stock in those holdings

di·vide /di vīd/ *v* (**-vid·ed, -vid·ing, -vides**) **1.** *vti* **SPLIT INTO PARTS** to separate or split something into two or more parts, or be separated or split into parts ○ *a dormitory divided into cubicles* **2.** *vi* **GO IN DIFFERENT DIRECTIONS** to split into two or more parts that go off in different directions **3.** *vti* **SHARE SOMETHING** to share something between two or more people or groups, or be shared ○ *divide the spoils of war* **4.** *vt* **SEPARATE TWO PLACES** to be a barrier or boundary between one place or thing and another ○ *The river divides the north of the island from the south.* **5.** *vt* **CAUSE DISAGREEMENT BETWEEN PEOPLE** to be the cause or subject of disagreement between people ○ *The zoning proposals are dividing the community.* **6.** *vt* **SEPARATE SOMEBODY FROM ANOTHER** to cause somebody to be apart from somebody else, or cause people to be apart ○ *The war divided them from their parents.* **7.** *vt* MEASURE **MARK SOMETHING OFF** to mark units or sections of a particular size on a measuring instrument such as a ruler **8.** *vt* MATH **CALCULATE OCCURRENCE OF ONE NUMBER IN ANOTHER** to calculate how many times one number contains another **9.** *vi* MATH **BE DIVISIBLE** to be able to be divided by a particular number without a remainder ■ *n* **1. BOUNDARY OR GAP** a boundary or gap that stands between two things, conditions, or groups **2.** GEOG **RIDGE SEPARATING WATERSHEDS** a long ridge separating watersheds [14C. < Latin *dividere* "separate apart" < *-videre* "to separate"] —**di·vid·a·ble** *adj*

divide up *vti* to divide, or divide something, into several parts

SYNONYMS See *share*[1].

di·vid·ed /di vīdəd/ *adj* **1. SEPARATED** separated into two or more parts or groups **2. OF TWO MINDS** drawn toward two or more different and often incompatible purposes or groups ○ *divided loyalties* **3. IN DISAGREEMENT** in a state of internal discord, strife, or disagreement ○ *remained deeply divided over the issue* **4.** BOT **SEPARATED INTO SECTIONS** describes leaves that are split into separate sections —**di·vid·ed·ly** *adv* —**di·vid·ed·ness** *n*

di·vid·ed high·way *n* a highway that has a median strip or a barrier separating the lanes going in opposite directions, usually with two or more lanes on either side

di·vid·ed skirt *n* CLOTHING same as **culottes**

div·i·dend /dívvi dènd, dívvidənd/ *n* **1. BONUS** something good or desirable that is gained as a bonus along with something else **2.** FIN **STOCKHOLDER'S SHARE OF PROFIT** company profits paid pro rata to stockholders, either in cash or in more shares **3.** MATH **NUMBER DIVIDED BY ANOTHER** a number or quantity that is to be divided by another number or quantity **4.** LAW **PROPORTION OF BANKRUPT'S ESTATE** the proportion of a bankrupt party's estate that is to be divided among the creditors [15C. Via Anglo-Norman < Latin *dividendum* "thing to be divided," form of *dividere* (see DIVIDE)]

di·vid·er /di vīdər/ *n* a device that separates something into sections, e.g., a screen that partitions a room or a sheet of card that separates the sections of a loose-leaf binder ■ **di·vid·ers** *npl* an instrument with two movable pointed legs hinged at one end, used for measuring distances on maps and charts and for transferring measurements from one map or chart to another

di·vid·ing line /di vīding-/ *n* something that marks a change or distinction between two states or qualities

div·i-div·i /dìvvee dívvee/ *n* **1.** a long seed pod that has a high tannin content. Use: tanning leather. **2.** a small tropical American tree that produces divi-divis. Latin name: *Caesalpinia coriaria.* [Mid-19C. Via American Spanish < Carib]

div·i·na·tion /dìvvi náysh'n/ *n* **1. SEEKING KNOWLEDGE BY SUPERNATURAL MEANS** the methods or practice of attempting to foretell the future or discovering the unknown through omens, oracles, or supernatural powers **2. PROPHECY** a prophecy or prediction **3. PREMONITION** a premonition or feeling of foreboding about something that is going to happen —**di·vin·a·to·ry** /di vínnə tàwree/ *adj*

di·vine /di vīn/ *adj* **1. HAVING GODLIKE NATURE** being God or a god or goddess **2. RELATING TO GOD, GODS, OR GODDESSES** connected with, coming from, or caused by God or a god or goddess **3. CONNECTED WITH WORSHIP** relating to the worship or service of God or a god or goddess **4. LOVELY** pleasing, attractive, or well performed (*informal*) ■ *v* (**-vined, -vin·ing, -vines**) **1.** *vt* **REALIZE SOMETHING** to come to understand or realize something **2.** *vt* **DISCOVER SOMETHING AS IF SUPERNATURALLY** to learn or discover something by intuition, inspiration, or other apparently supernatural means **3.** *vt* **PREDICT SOMETHING AS IF SUPERNATURALLY** to predict something by apparently supernatural means **4.** *vti* **SEARCH WITH DIVINING ROD** to search for underground water, metal, or minerals using something such as a divining rod ■ *n* **1. THEOLOGIAN** a member of the clergy, especially one who is knowledgeable about theology **2.** *also* **Di·vine GOD** God, or an underlying creative and sustaining force in the universe [14C. Via French < Latin *divinus* < *divus* "god"] —**di·vine·ly** *adv* —**di·vine·ness** *n* —**di·vin·er** *n*

CULTURAL NOTE ***The Divine Comedy,*** an epic poem (1307?–20?) by Italian poet Dante Alighieri. Generally considered to be Dante's masterpiece, it is an account of the poet's journey through Hell, Purgatory, and Paradise, rich in historical, scientific, and philosophical allusion. The poet Virgil, representing Reason, is Dante's guide in the first two sections of the work; in the final section his guide is Beatrice, an idealization of the girl he loved in his youth.

Di·vine /di vīn/, **Father** (1882?–1965) US religious leader. He advocated communal living and racial equality, and his Peace Mission Movement, founded in the 1910s, attracted many people from the Black communities in New York City and Philadelphia. Born **Baker, George**

di·vine right *n* the belief that the monarch's authority comes directly from God rather than from the people

div·ing bee·tle /dīving-/ *n* a predatory water beetle adapted for swimming that has flattened hind legs and the capacity to breathe air trapped under its wings. Family: Dytiscidae.

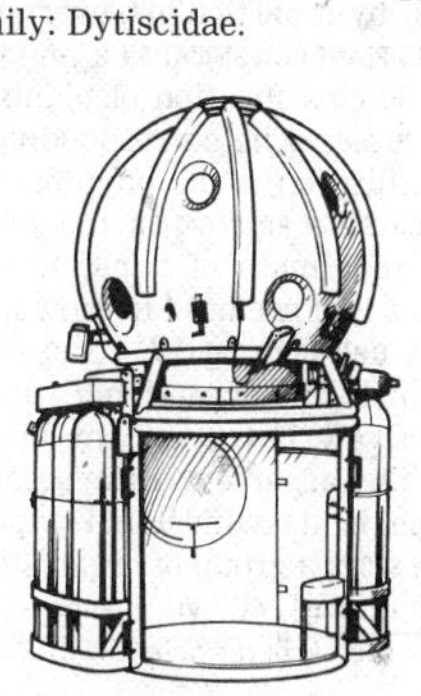

diving bell

div·ing bell *n* a metal device used for working underwater that has an open bottom and is supplied with compressed air

div·ing board *n* a raised board at the edge of a swimming pool from which to dive into the water

div·ing dress *n UK* SWIMMING same as **diving suit**

div·ing duck *n* a duck that dives for food and swims under water

div·ing re·flex *n* a reflex in mammals in which the heart rate slows and blood vessels of the skin narrow on immersion in cold water to conserve oxygen. The reflex is strongest in water animals such as seals, but is still present to a minor extent in nonaquatic animals, including humans.

div·ing suit *n* a waterproof suit, often including a helmet and an air supply, worn by divers

di·vin·ing rod /di vīning-/ *n* a forked stick used as a device for sensing underground water sources or minerals. The diviner holds an end of the rod in each hand, and the rod is said to dip sharply downward when the diviner walks over a water source or minerals.

di·vin·i·ty /di vínnətee/ (*plural* **-ties**) *n* **1.** QUALITY OF BEING GOD the quality associated with being God, a god, or a goddess **2.** *also* **Di·vin·i·ty** GOD God, a god, or a goddess **3.** THEOLOGY the study of religion, especially the Christian religion **4.** CANDY a fluffy white candy, usually made with egg white and nuts [13C. Via French < Latin *divinitas* "godhead, divinity" < *divinus* (see DIVINE)]

di·vis·i·ble /di vízzəb'l/ *adj* **1.** able to be divided, especially without leaving a remainder **2.** capable of being separated into different parts [15C. Directly or via French < late Latin *divisibilis* < Latin *divis-* (see DIVISION)] —**di·vis·i·bil·i·ty** /di vìzzə bíllətee/ *n* —**di·vis·i·bly** *adv*

di·vi·sion /di vízh'n/ *n* **1.** SPLITTING INTO PARTS the act of separating or splitting something into parts, or an instance of this ○ *the division of the region into smaller administrative districts* **2.** SHARING OF SOMETHING the separation of something into parts to be shared among people or groups ○ *the division of work among members of the group* **3.** DISAGREEMENT a disagreement or strong difference of opinion, especially when this leads to a split in a group ○ *Deep divisions exist within senior management about dealing with the problem.* **4.** SOMETHING SEPARATING something that separates things by forming a boundary between them **5.** SEPARATE PART one of the parts created when something is split **6.** MATH DIVIDING ONE NUMBER BY ANOTHER an operation used to calculate the number of times one number is contained in another **7.** SECTION OF ORGANIZATION a section of a large organization that has a specific task or function ○ *the sales division* **8.** SPORTS GROUP OF TEAMS a group of teams, usually those representing cities close to one another or of roughly similar standard in a sports league, conference, or association **9.** MIL ARMY UNIT a self-contained military unit capable of sustained operations, including a headquarters and two or more brigades in an army or several regiments in the Marines **10.** NAVY NAVAL UNIT a self-contained unit in a navy including a group of ships of the same class **11.** AIR FORCE AIR FORCE UNIT a self-contained unit in an air force including two or more fighter wings **12.** PUBLIC ADMIN GOVERNMENT UNIT a small unit of government **13.** PUBLIC ADMIN ADMINISTRATIVE AREA an area administered by a particular government unit **14.** BOT CATEGORY IN PLANT CLASSIFICATION a major category in the taxonomic classification of plants, comprising a group of classes. The corresponding category in animal classification is the phylum. **15.** GARDENING SPLITTING OF ROOTS FOR PROPAGATION the process of separating the root mass of a perennial plant into smaller pieces that are used to grow new plants **16.** BIOL same as **cell division** **17.** LOGIC LOGICAL FALLACY a fallacy in which it is argued that what is true of a whole collectively is true of any of its parts. An example is the argument that because a car is expensive, so is its windshield wiper. **18.** MUSIC GROUP OF ORGAN STOPS a group of organ stops played on the same manual [14C. Via French < Latin *division-* < *divis-*, past participle of *dividere* (see DIVIDE)] —**di·vi·sion·al** *adj*

di·vi·sion·ism /də vízh'n ìzzəm/ *n* a late-19th-century style of painting in which unmixed color is applied to the canvas in small dots that from a distance form recognizable shapes and color tones. Like pointillism, which it closely resembles, divisionism was a development of the impressionist style. —**di·vi·sion·ist** *n, adj*

di·vi·sion lob·by *n UK* POL same as **lobby** *n* (sense 4)

di·vi·sion of la·bor *n* a system of organizing production by giving separate tasks to separate workers or groups of workers

di·vi·sion sign *n* a sign (÷) placed between two numbers to show that the first number is divided by the second

di·vi·sive /di vísiv/ *adj* causing disagreement or hostility within a group so that it is likely to split [Late 16C. < late Latin *divisivus* < Latin *divis-* (see DIVISION)] —**di·vi·sive·ly** *adv* —**di·vi·sive·ness** *n*

di·vi·sor /di vízər/ *n* a number divided into another number [15C. Directly or via French < Latin < *divis-* (see DIVISION)]

di·vor·ce /di váwrss/ *n* **1.** OFFICIAL ENDING OF MARRIAGE an ending of a marriage by an official decision in a court of law **2.** SEPARATION a complete separation or split ○ *a divorce between theory and practice* ■ *v* (**-vorced, -vorc·ing, -vor·ces**) **1.** *vti* OFFICIALLY END MARRIAGE to end a marriage to somebody by an official decision in a court of law **2.** *vt* SEPARATE SOMETHING to separate or distinguish something from something else ○ *divorced truth from speculation* [14C. Via French < Latin *divortium* < *divortere*, variant of *divertere* "part, turn aside" (see DIVERT)] —**di·vorced** *adj*

di·vor·cé /di vàwr sáy, -sée/ *n* a man who is divorced [Late 19C. < French < past participle of *divorcer* "divorce" < Latin *divortium* (see DIVORCE)]

di·vor·cée /di vàwr sáy, -sée/ *n* a woman who is divorced [Early 19C. < French < feminine of *divorcé* (see DIVORCÉ)]

div·ot /dívvət/ *n* a small lump of grass and earth accidentally dug out of the ground while playing a sport, especially golf [Early 16C. Origin ?]

di·vulge /di vúlj/ (**-vulged, -vulg·ing, -vulg·es**) *vt* to reveal information, especially information that was previously secret [15C. < Latin *divulgare* "make widely known to the masses" < *vulgus* "masses"] —**di·vul·gence** *n*

div·vy /dívvee/ (*informal*) *vt* (**-vied, -vy·ing, -vies**) same as **divvy up** ■ *n* (*plural* **-vies**) **1.** somebody's share of something **2.** *UK* a dividend or share of the profits given to members of a cooperative [Late 19C. Shortening of DIVIDEND]

divvy up *vt* to divide something up and share it among a group of people (*informal*)

Di·wa·li /di wáalee/, **Di·va·li** /di váalee/ *n* a Hindu festival associated with Lakshmi, the goddess of prosperity, during which lamps are lit. Date: autumn. [Late 17C. Via Hindi *diwālī* < Sanskrit *dīpāvalī* "row of lights" < *dīpa* "light, lamp"]

Dix /diks/, **Dorothea** (1802–87) US philanthropist and reformer. She investigated conditions in prisons, almshouses, and asylums, securing legislation for their improvement. During the Civil War she was superintendent of women nurses with the Union army. Full name **Dix, Dorothea Lynde**

> "In a world where there is so much to be done, I felt strongly impressed that there must be something for me to do."
> [Dorothea Dix, *Letter*, December 31, 1844]

Dix·ie /díksee/ *n* **1.** the southern states that were members of the Confederacy during the Civil War (*informal*) **2.** the popular name for a song used as a Confederate marching tune during the Civil War [Mid-19C. Origin ?]

Dix·ie·crat /díksee kràt/ *n* a member of a group of southern Democrats who disagreed with the Democratic Party's civil rights programs and left to form the States' Rights Democratic Party in 1948 —**Dix·ie·crat·ic** /dìksee kráttik/ *adj*

Dix·ie cup *tdmk* a trademark for a small disposable paper cup

Dix·ie·land /díksee lànd/, **dix·ie·land** *n* a style of jazz, originally from New Orleans, characterized by a fast two-beat rhythm and simultaneous improvisation [Early 20C. < *Original Dixieland Jazz Band*, the first jazz band to record commercially]

DIY *abbr* ONLINE do it yourself (*used in e-mails or text messages*)

Di·yar·ba·kir /di yaárbə keér, di yaár bùkər/ city and capital of Diyarbakir Province in southeastern Turkey. Population: 479,884 (1997).

Diyar·i *n, adj* LANG another spelling of **Dieri**

di·zy·got·ic /dì zī góttik/, **di·zy·gous** /dī zígəss/ *adj* describes twins derived from two separately fertilized eggs (**zygotes**). ◊ **monozygotic**

diz·zy /dízzee/ *adj* (**-zi·er, -zi·est**) **1.** UNSTEADY AND GIDDY unsteady, as if about to lose balance, and slightly giddy **2.** EXTREME so high as to make somebody giddy ○ *the dizzy height of the tower* **3.** CONFUSED AND BEWILDERED confused, overwhelmed, and unable to think clearly **4.** FAST extremely fast ○ *dizzy speeds* **5.** FUN-LOVING BUT THOUGHTLESS fun-loving and somewhat silly or empty-headed (*informal*) ■ *vt* (**-zied, -zy·ing, -zies**) CAUSE SOMEBODY TO FEEL DIZZY to cause somebody to feel unsteady, giddy, confused, or bewildered [Old English *dysig* "foolish, stupid" < Germanic] —**diz·zi·ly** *adv* —**diz·zi·ness** *n* —**diz·zy·ing** *adj* —**diz·zy·ing·ly** *adv*

dj *abbr* Djibouti (*used in Internet addresses*) See table at **domain name**

DJ *n* **1.** somebody who plays records or other recorded music, e.g., at a live dance or on the radio. Full form **disc jockey** **2.** somebody who composes rap or techno music using samples of recorded music [Abbreviation of DISC JOCKEY] —**DJ** *vi*

D.J. *abbr* LAW district judge

dje·bel *n* GEOG another spelling of **jebel**

djel·la·ba /jə laábə/, **djel·la·bah** *n* a long loose-fitting robe with sleeves and a hood, worn especially in Islamic countries [Early 19C. < Moroccan Arabic *jellāb(a), jellābiyya*]

Djer·ba /júrbə/ island in southeastern Tunisia, lying in the Gulf of Gabes in the Mediterranean Sea. Population: 92,269 (1984). Area: 197 sq. mi./510 sq. km.

DJIA *abbr* FIN Dow Jones Industrial Average

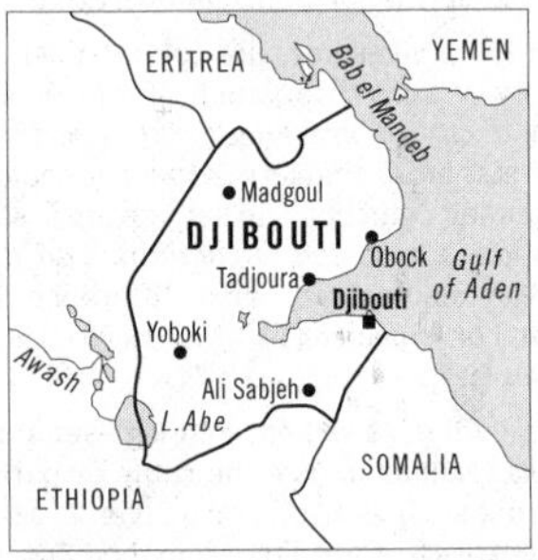

Djibouti

Dji·bou·ti /ji bóotee/ **1.** country in the Horn of Africa, bordered by the Gulf of Aden, Somalia, Ethiopia, and Eritrea. Language: Arabic, French. Currency: Djibouti franc. Capital: Djibouti. Population: 457,130 (2003). Area: 8,958 sq. mi./23,200 sq. km. Official name **Republic of Djibouti** **2.** the capital of the Republic of Djibouti. Population: 383,000 (1995 estimate).

djinn, djin·ni MYTHOL another spelling of **jinni**

DK *abbr* ONLINE don't know (*used in e-mails or text messages*)

dk. *abbr* **1.** dark **2.** NAUT deck **3.** Denmark (*used in Internet addresses*) See table at **domain name** **4.** SHIPPING dock[1]

dkg *symbol* MEASURE decagram

dkl *symbol* MEASURE decaliter

dkm *symbol* MEASURE decameter

dl *symbol* MEASURE deciliter

DL *abbr* **1.** SPORTS disabled list **2.** ONLINE download (*used in e-mails or text messages*) **3.** Down Low (*slang*)

D lay·er *n* **1.** METEOROL same as **D region** (sense 1) **2.** the lower layer of the Earth's mantle, from 450 mi./720 km deep down to the boundary with the core

D.Litt. /dee lít/, **D.Lit.** *abbr* **1.** Doctor of Letters **2.** Doctor of Literature

dlr. *abbr* FIN dealer

dm[1] *symbol* MEASURE decimeter

dm[2] *abbr* Dominica (*used in Internet addresses*) See table at **domain name**

DM *abbr* MONEY, HIST deutsche mark

D.M.A. *abbr* Doctor of Musical Arts

DMAC /dée màk, dée em ay sée/ *n* a coding system used for broadcasting color television programs via satellite. Full form **duobinary multiplexed analog component**

D.M.D. *abbr* DENT, EDUC Doctor of Dental Medicine [Latin *Dentariae Medicinae Doctor*]

DMSO *n* a clear odorless liquid compound. Use: solvent, in medicine to enable drugs to penetrate the skin. Formula: $(CH_3)_2SO$. Full form **dimethylsulfoxide**

DMU *abbr* BUSINESS decision-making unit

DMV *abbr* AUTOMOT, PUBLIC ADMIN Department of Motor Vehicles

DMZ *abbr* MIL, POL demilitarized zone

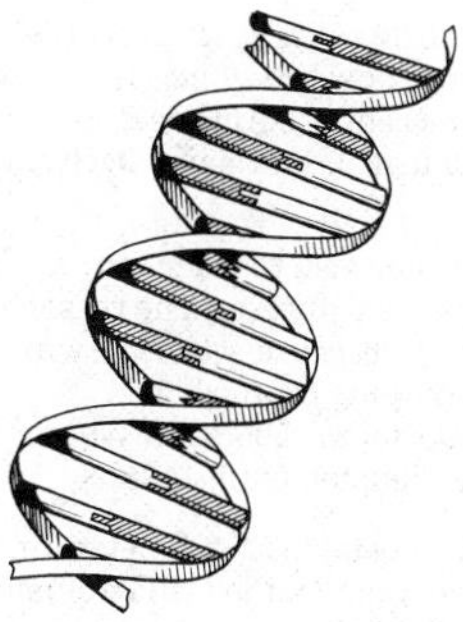

DNA

DNA[1] *n* **1.** a nucleic acid molecule in the form of a twisted double strand (**double helix**) that is the major component of chromosomes and carries genetic information. DNA, which is found in all living organisms except some viruses, reproduces itself and is the means by which hereditary characteristics pass from one generation to the next. Full form **deoxyribonucleic acid** **2.** the combination of features that make something what it is ○ *The company clearly has success in its DNA.*

DNA[2] *abbr* **1.** ONLINE did not answer (*used in e-mails or text messages*) **2.** HEALTH SERVICES did not attend

DNA chip *n* GENETICS same as **gene chip**

DNA fin·ger·print·ing *n* the analysis and use of DNA patterns from body tissues such as blood, saliva, or semen in order to establish somebody's identity — **DNA fin·ger·print** *n*

DNA li·gase *n* an enzyme (**ligase**) that joins two DNA strands during replication, repair, and recombination

DNA pol·y·mer·ase *n* an enzyme that uses single-stranded DNA to reproduce and repair DNA

DNA pro·fil·ing *n* GENETICS same as **DNA fingerprinting** —**DNA pro·file** *n*

DN·ase /dèe en áyss, dèe en áyz/ *n* an enzyme that aids the breakdown of DNA into smaller molecules. Full form **deoxyribonuclease**

DNA se·quenc·ing *n* the process of determining the exact sequence of the bases along a section length of DNA

DNA vi·rus *n* a virus with a genome containing DNA

DND/CF *abbr* GOV Department of National Defence and the Canadian Forces

Dne·pr another spelling of **Dnieper**

Dnes·tr another spelling of **Dniester**

Dnie·per /neépər/, **Dne·pr** third longest river in Europe after the Volga and Danube. It rises west of Moscow and flows southward and westward through Russia, Belarus, and Ukraine before emptying into the Black Sea. Length: 1,420 mi./2,290 km.

Dnies·ter /neéstər/, **Dnes·tr** river that rises in the Carpathian Mountains and flows through Ukraine and Moldova before emptying into the Black Sea near Odessa. Length: 870 mi./1,400 km.

DNR *abbr* MED do not resuscitate

DNS *abbr* COMPUT domain name system

do[1] /doo/ (**did** /did/, **done** /dun/, **do·ing**, **does** /duz/) CORE MEANING: a verb indicating that somebody performs an action, an activity, or a task. It is often used as an informal equivalent of more specific and less frequent verbs, e.g., "do your nails" instead of "paint your nails." ○ *He usually did the cleaning on a Sunday morning.* ○ *Why won't you let me do your hair for you?* ○ *Assuming that your terminal is properly set up, here is what you have to do to connect it.*

1. *vt* USE SOMETHING to use something in a particular way ○ *She's done absolutely nothing with the money she inherited.* **2.** *vt* TAKE ACTION to take action in a situation in order to change it or solve a problem ○ *Companies must decide what to do about their chemical waste.* **3.** *vt* CAUSE SOMETHING to cause or produce an effect or result ○ *These disputes do little to help the peace process.* **4.** *vt* WORK AT SOMETHING to work at something, especially as a job or profession, or as a course of study ○ *What does your mother do at the bank?* **5.** *vt* BE OCCUPIED WITH SOMETHING to be occupied or busy with something ○ *Are you doing anything this evening?* **6.** *vti* CONDUCT SELF to behave in a particular manner ○ *Do what you want.* ○ *Do as you please.* **7.** *vi* FARE to be successful or unsuccessful to a particular extent ○ *Automobile insurance companies are doing well this year.* **8.** *vt* PROVIDE SOMETHING to prepare or provide something ○ *I'm sorry but we don't do a lunch menu.* **9.** *vt* ACHIEVE SPEED OR RATE to achieve a particular speed or rate ○ *We were doing 55 down the freeway.* ○ *We did about 400 miles a day.* **10.** *vt* STUDY SOMETHING to study or work at doing something ○ *Have you done Nabokov yet?* ○ *I've never been able to do algebra.* **11.** *vt* PERFORM SOMETHING to perform or act a play, role, or accent ○ *They're doing "Macbeth."* ○ *I'm not very good at doing accents.* **12.** *vt* VISIT OR EXPLORE PLACE to visit or explore a country or city as a tourist (*informal*) ○ *We're doing London tomorrow.* **13.** *vti* BE ADEQUATE to be adequate in quantity or quality for somebody or something ○ *A paper cup does just as well.* ○ *Just an orange juice will do me.* **14.** *vt* SERVE TIME IN PRISON to serve a period of time in prison (*slang*) ○ *He's doing time for cheating on his taxes.* **15.** *vt* EXHAUST SOMEBODY to wear somebody out (*informal*) **16.** *vt UK* ADAPT SOMETHING to translate or adapt a play, book, or other work (*informal*) ○ *The novel was done into a feature film.* **17.** *vt* CHEAT SOMEBODY to cheat or trick somebody (*informal*) ○ *They did her out of her lunch money.* **18.** *vt* ROB SOMEBODY to rob a person or place (*slang*) ○ *They got caught while they were doing the local bank.* **19.** *vt* TAKE DRUGS to take or use a narcotic drug (*slang*) **20.** *vt* HAVE SEX WITH SOMEBODY to have sexual intercourse with somebody (*slang*) **21.** *vt* MURDER SOMEBODY to kill somebody deliberately (*slang*) **22.** *aux v* FORMS QUESTIONS AND NEGATIVES used with simple present and simple past tenses in the formation of questions and negative sentences. "Do" and "did" are often contracted to "don't" and "didn't" in negative structures. ○ *What did he want?* ○ *Don't sit there!* ○ *It doesn't matter if you can't come.* **23.** *aux v* GIVES EMPHASIS used to emphasize a positive statement or command, often as a way of politely inviting or persuading somebody to do something ○ *Yes, I do realize you can't finish the work today.* ○ *Please do be quiet!* **24.** *aux v* CHANGES EMPHASIS used to form inverted sentences in order to change the emphasis of a statement ○ *She hopes to go to college, as do her brothers.* **25.** *aux v* REPLACES ANOTHER VERB used to replace an earlier verb or verb phrase to avoid repetition, usually when comparing two things ○ *I want to have a break just as much as you do.* **26.** *n US, UK* SOCIAL GATHERING a formal social gathering, e.g., a wedding reception (*informal*) ○ *attended a big do at the White House* [Old English *dōn* < Indo-European, "to place"] ◇ **could do with** to want or need something ○ *I could do with some help.* ◇ **have to do with somebody** *or* **something** **1.** to be connected with somebody or something **2.** to concern somebody or something **3.** to involve contact or a relationship with somebody or something ◇ **that does it!** used to indicate that you are not prepared to tolerate any more (*informal*) ○ *That does it! I'm calling my lawyer!* ◇ **the dos and don'ts** the correct way to proceed or behave in a particular situation ○ *a list of dos and don'ts for the first-time investor*

SPELLCHECK See *dew.*

USAGE do ... have or **have ... got?** Both these constructions are used in questions and in negative statements: *Do you have change for a dollar?* or *Have you got change for a dollar? I don't have any change* or *I haven't got any change.* Some consider the first wording in each pair to be more proper, perceiving ***have ... got*** as colloquial and even redundant, and pointing out that *have* alone is sufficient to signify possession. But *Have you change?* and *I haven't any change* are not idiomatic, and ***do ... have*** has just as many syllables as ***have ... got.*** Therefore, it is hard to see what reasonable basis exists for preferring ***do ... have*** to ***have ... got.***

USAGE did you or **have you?** A distinction that arises in connection with questions and negative statements is represented by the wordings *Did you see the show?* or *Have you seen the show? I didn't see the show* or *I haven't seen the show.* In informal conversation, the two are used almost interchangeably. In strict usage, however, there is a difference in time perspective: the first wording (*Did you...?*) in each pair refers to a particular point in the past, whereas the second (*Have you...?*) has to do with any time in the past (thus, *ever* could be added to the second sentence in each pair without substantially changing its meaning).

SYNONYMS See ***perform.***

do away with *vt* **1.** to abolish something so that it no longer happens or exists **2.** to kill somebody (*informal*)

do for *vt* to provide for or take care of somebody ○ *You'll have to do for yourself this week – I won't be here.*

do in *vt* (*informal*) **1.** to kill or severely beat somebody **2.** to make somebody feel exhausted

do over *vt* **1.** to clean or redecorate a place such as a house or room (*informal*) **2.** *UK* to subject somebody to a violent beating (*slang*)

do up *vt* **1.** GIVE SOMETHING DECORATIVE WRAPPING to wrap or cover something with decorative material (*often passive*) **2.** DRESS FASHIONABLY to dress somebody or yourself in fashionable clothes (*informal*) **3.** FASTEN SOMETHING to fasten a piece of clothing, or be fastened ○ *did up the buttons* **4.** MAKE SOMETHING USABLE AGAIN to make something fit to use again by repairing or decorating it

do without *vti* to manage or survive without something that you want, need, or normally have

do[2] /dō/, **doh** *n* a syllable that represents the first note in a scale when singing solfeggio. In fixed solfeggio it represents the note C. [Mid-18C. < Italian]

do[3] *abbr* ONLINE Dominican Republic (*used in Internet addresses*) See table at **domain name**

DO *n* a certification for Spanish wine that guarantees its origin [Abbreviation of Spanish *denominación de origen*]

D.O. *abbr* **1.** OPHTHALMOL, EDUC Doctor of Optometry **2.** EDUC, MED Doctor of Osteopathy

D/O *abbr* COMM **1.** delivery order **2.** direct order

DOA *abbr* **1.** MED dead on arrival **2.** DRUGS drug of abuse

do·a·ble /dóo əb'l/ *adj* able to be done or achieved (*informal*)

DOB, **d.o.b.** *abbr* date of birth

dob·bin /dóbbin/, **Dob·bin** *n* a horse, especially a large heavy working horse [Late 16C. < *Dobbin*, personal name, alteration of *Robin*]

dob·by /dóbbee/ (*plural* **-bies**) *n* a part of a loom that allows small figures to be woven on it [Late 17C. Origin ?]

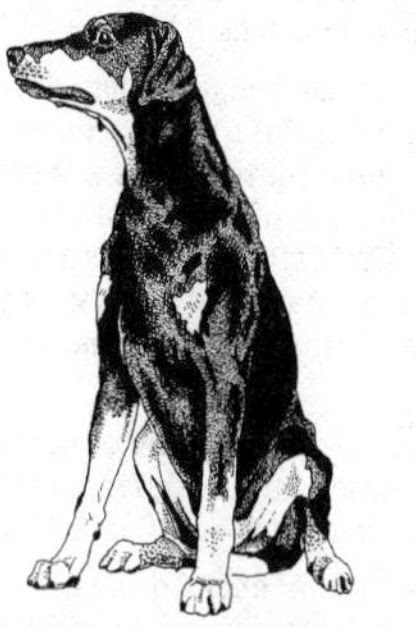

Doberman pinscher

Do·ber·man pin·scher /dṓbərmən pínshər/, **Do·ber·man** *n* a medium-sized to large powerful dog with a smooth black or dark brown coat, often used as a guard dog or for police work and belonging to a breed originating in Germany [Early 20C. After Ludwig *Dobermann*, 19C German dog breeder; *pinscher* < German, breed name]

do·bra /dṓbrə/ *n* the main unit of currency of São Tomé and Principe. See table at **currency** [Late 20C. Via Portuguese < Latin *duplus* "double"]

dob·son·fly /dóbssən flī/ (*plural* **-flies**) *n* a very large winged insect that has long slender mouthparts in the male. Its larva (**hellgrammite**) is a voracious predator of small water animals and is used by anglers as bait. Native to: North America. Latin name: *Corydalus cornutus.*

Dob·zhan·sky /dəb zhánskee/, **Theodosius** (1900–75) Russian-born US geneticist and zoologist. He made important discoveries about genetics and adaptation, from his studies of fruit flies.

doc /dok/ *n* same as **doctor** *n* (sense 1) (*informal*) [Mid-19C. Shortening]

DOC *n* a certification for Italian wine that guarantees its origin [Abbreviation of Italian *denominazione di origine controllata*]

doc. *abbr* LAW document

DOCa *n* a certification for Spanish wine that guarantees its origin and verifies that it meets production regulations [< abbreviation of Spanish *Denominación de Origen Calificada*]

do·cent /dṓss'nt, dō sént/ *n* **1.** a university lecturer or teacher, especially one who is not a full-time member of the faculty **2.** a tourist guide working in some museums or cathedrals [Late 19C. < obsolete German < Latin *docent-*, present participle of *docere* "teach"]

Do·ce·tism /dō sée tìzzəm, dṓssə-/ *n* in Christianity, an early heresy that claimed that Jesus Christ was not a real person [Mid-19C. < *Docete* "Docetist," via medieval Latin *Docetae* (plural) "Docetists" < patristic Greek *Dokētai* < Greek *dokein* "seem, appear"] —**Do·ce·tist** *n*

DOCG *n* a certification for Italian wine that guarantees its origin and verifies that it meets production regulations [Abbreviation of Italian *Denominazione di Origine Controllata e Garantita*]

doch-an-dor·ris, **doch an dor·is** *n Scotland* BEVERAGES another spelling of **deoch an doruis**

doc·ile /dóss'l/ *adj* quiet, easy to control, and unlikely to cause trouble [15C. < Latin *docilis* < *docere* "teach"] —**doc·ile·ly** *adv* —**do·cil·i·ty** /do sílləte/ *n*

dock[1] /dok/ *n* **1.** PLACE FOR SHIPS TO MOOR an area of water between two piers or next to a pier, where ships can be moored safely for loading and repair **2.** GROUP OF PIERS FOR SHIPS a group of piers in a protected area of water used as a general landing area for ships **3.** PIER OR WHARF a long narrow structure stretching out into a body of water, or a raised area of land alongside water where ships can load and unload **4.** ENCLOSED AREA OF WATER FOR SHIP an enclosed area of water for a ship in which the water level can be adjusted **5.** NAUT same as **dry dock 6.** TRANSP LOADING PLATFORM FOR TRAINS OR TRUCKS a raised platform where trains or trucks can load and unload **7.** *UK* NAUT same as **dockyard** ■ *vti* (**docked, dock·ing, docks**) **1.** MOOR to steer a ship into a dock and tie it up, or be steered in and tied up there **2.** AEROSP LINK UP WITH SPACECRAFT to link a spacecraft up with another in space, or be linked up in this way [14C. < Middle Low German *docke* or Middle Dutch *docke*]

dock[2] /dok/ *vt* (**docked, dock·ing, docks**) **1.** REDUCE WAGES to deduct a sum of money from somebody's wages, especially as a punishment **2.** REMOVE TAIL OF ANIMAL to remove the tail of a dog, sheep, or other animal, leaving a short stump ■ *n* **1.** SOLID PART OF TAIL the solid part of an animal's tail **2.** STUMP OF TAIL the stump left when an animal's tail has been docked [14C. Origin ?]

dock[3] /dok/ *n* the area in a law court where the accused person stands during a trial [Late 16C. Probably < Flemish *dok* "fowl pen, rabbit hutch"]

dock[4] /dok/ (*plural* **docks** or *same*) *n* **1.** a plant of the buckwheat family with long broad leaves and a long taproot. Flowers: greenish or reddish. Genus: *Rumex*. **2.** a broad-leafed weedy plant [Old English *docce* < Germanic]

dock·age /dókij/ *n* **1.** MOORING CHARGE a charge payable for mooring at a dock **2.** FACILITIES FOR MOORED SHIPS the facilities for ships moored at a dock **3.** DOCKING PROCESS the process of docking a ship [Mid-17C. < DOCK[1]]

dock·er /dókər/ *n UK* same as **longshoreman** [Mid-18C. < DOCK[1]]

dock·et /dókət/ *n* **1.** LAW LIST OF FUTURE COURT CASES a list of pending cases in a court **2.** LAW BOOK OF UPCOMING CASES a book in which pending court cases are kept **3.** LIST OF THINGS TO DO a list of things to do **4.** DOCUMENT SUMMARY a summary of a document **5.** CUSTOMS CERTIFICATE a customs certificate confirming payment of duty ■ *vt* (**-et·ed, -et·ing, -ets**) **1.** LAW PUT LEGAL CASE IN CALENDAR to enter a legal case in the calendar of future cases **2.** LAW SUMMARIZE COURT CASE to summarize a court case and enter the summary in the appropriate register **3.** LABEL PACKAGE to label a package with a document giving the contents or delivery details **4.** SUMMARIZE SOMETHING to attach or give a summary of something [15C. Origin ?]

dock·hand /dók hànd/ *n* SHIPPING same as **longshoreman**

dock·ing sta·tion /dóking-/ *n* a piece of hardware into which a portable computer is inserted for recharging or expanded operations [< DOCK[1]]

dock·land /dók lànd/ *n UK* the area surrounding a city's docks or port (*often used in the plural*) [Early 20C. < DOCK[1]]

dock·mack·ie /dók màkee/ (*plural* **-ies** or *same*) *n* a tall deciduous bush that produces clusters of white flowers followed by reddish black berries. Native to: China, Japan. Genus: *Viburnum acerifolium*. [Origin ?]

dock·o·min·i·um /dòkō mínnee əm/ *n* a harbor with several jetties providing permanent moorings for boats used as homes [Late 20C. Blend of DOCK[1] + CONDOMINIUM]

dock·side /dók sīd/ *n* the area of ground alongside the moorings in a dock or harbor [Late 19C. < DOCK[1]]

dock·work·er /dók wùrkər/ *n* SHIPPING same as **longshoreman** [< DOCK[1]]

dock·yard /dók yaàrd/ *n* an area of workshops, offices, and docks where ships are repaired and built [Early 18C. < DOCK[1]]

do·co·sa·hex·ae·no·ic ac·id /dōkōssə hèksənō ik-/ *n* BIOCHEM full form of **DHA** [<; Greek *do-*, form of *duo* "two" + shortening of *eikosi* "twenty" + *hexa* "six" + -ANE]

doc·tor /dóktər/ *n* **1.** HEALTH SERVICES SOMEBODY MEDICALLY QUALIFIED somebody qualified and licensed to give people medical treatment **2.** HEALTH SERVICES DENTIST, VETERINARIAN, OR OSTEOPATH a title used before the names of health professionals such as dentists, veterinarians, and osteopaths **3.** EDUC SOMEBODY WITH HIGHEST UNIVERSITY DEGREE a title given to somebody who has been awarded a doctorate, the highest level of degree awarded by a university **4.** SOMEBODY WHO CAN FIX THINGS a skilled practitioner of something, especially fixing or improving something ○ *a play doctor* **5.** CHR ROMAN CATHOLIC THEOLOGIAN in the earlier history of the Roman Catholic Church, an eminent and influential theologian **6.** EDUC TEACHER OR SCHOLAR a teacher or somebody very knowledgeable (*archaic*) ■ *v* (**-tored, -tor·ing, -tors**) **1.** *vt* CHANGE SOMETHING IN ORDER TO DECEIVE to change something in order to make it appear different from the facts or the truth ○ *doctored the figures* **2.** *vt* ADD SOMETHING TO SUBSTANCE to add something, especially a drug, alcohol, or poison, to food or drink **3.** *vti* TREAT ILL PEOPLE to treat people when they are ill **4.** *vt* FIX SOMETHING to fix something, especially in a rough or hurried way [14C. Via French < Latin, "teacher" < *doct-*, past participle of *docere* "teach"] —**doc·tor·ly** *adj* ◇ **just what the doctor ordered** something that is very welcome, pleasing, or refreshing (*informal*)

doc·tor·al /dóktərəl/, **doc·to·ri·al** /dok táwree əl/ *adj* **1.** written or done in order to obtain a doctorate, the highest degree awarded by a university ○ *a doctoral thesis* **2.** relating to or aiming for a doctorate ○ *doctoral candidate*

doc·tor-as·sist·ed su·i·cide *n UK* same as **physician-assisted suicide**

doc·tor·ate /dóktərət/ *n* the highest level of university degree, usually awarded for a lengthy piece of original research, but sometimes for other outstanding achievements

Doc·tor of Let·ters, **Doc·tor of Lit·er·a·ture** *n* the highest level of university doctorate, awarded to somebody who has made a substantial scholarly contribution to a subject, or as an honorary degree to somebody for exceptional achievement [Translation of Latin *Litterarum Doctor*]

Doc·tor of Phi·los·o·phy *n* the highest level of university degree, awarded to somebody who has successfully completed a lengthy piece of original research. A Doctor of Philosophy may be awarded in any subject except law, theology, or medicine.

Doc·tor of Vet·er·i·nar·y Med·cine *n* the highest level of university degree, awarded to somebody who has successfully completed a lengthy piece of original research in the field of veterinary medicine

Doc·tor·ow /dóktə rō/, **E. L.** (*b.* 1931) US writer. He is known for his novel *Ragtime* (1975), a critical look at turn-of-the-century America, later made into a Broadway musical. Full name **Doctorow, Edgar Laurence**

> "The writer isn't made in a vacuum. Writers are witnesses. The reason we need writers is because we need witnesses to this terrifying century."
> [E. L. Doctorow. Quoted in *Writers at Work*, George Plimpton (ed.); 1988]

doc·tri·naire /dòktrə nér/ *adj* determined to use a specific theory or method and refusing to accept that there might be a better approach —**doc·tri·naire** *n* —**doc·tri·nair·ism** *n* —**doc·tri·nar·i·an** *n*

doc·trine /dóktrin/ *n* **1.** a rule or principle that forms the basis of a belief, theory, or policy **2.** a body of ideas, particularly in religion, taught to people as truthful or correct [14C. Directly or via French < Latin *doctrina* "teaching, learning" < *doctor* (see DOCTOR)] —**doc·tri·nal** /dóktrin'l, dok trīn'l/ *adj* —**doc·tri·nal·i·ty** /dòktrə nálləte/ *n* —**doc·tri·nal·ly** *adv*

doc·u·dra·ma /dókyə draàmə, -dràmmə/ *n* a dramatized movie or television version of a true story [Mid-20C. Blend of DOCUMENTARY + DRAMA] —**doc·u·dra·mat·ic** /dòkyə drə máttik/ *adj*

doc·u·ment *n* /dókyəmənt/ **1.** FORMAL PIECE OF WRITING a formal piece of writing that provides information or acts as a record of events or arrangements **2.** LAW OBJECT CONTAINING INFORMATION an object such as a movie, photograph, or audio recording that contains information and can be used as evidence **3.** COMPUT COMPUTER FILE a computer file created using an applications program, e.g., a database, spreadsheet, illustration, or text file ■ *vt* /dókyə mènt/ (**-ment·ed, -ment·ing, -ments**) **1.** RECORD INFORMATION to make a record of something by writing about it or by filming or photographing it **2.** SUPPORT SOMETHING WITH EVIDENCE to provide evidence for a statement or claim by supplying supporting information [15C. Via French < Latin *documentum* "lesson, example" (in medieval Latin, "instruction, official paper") < *docere* "teach"] —**doc·u·ment·a·ble** /dòkyə méntəb'l/ *adj* —**doc·u·ment·al** /dòkyə mént'l/ *adj* —**doc·u·ment·er** /dókyə mèntər/ *n*

doc·u·ment·al·ist /dòkyə mént'list/ *n* a specialist in documentation

doc·u·men·ta·ry /dòkyə méntəree/ *n* (*plural* **-ries**) FACTUAL MOVIE OR TV PROGRAM a movie or TV program presenting facts and information, especially about a political, historical, or social issue ■ *adj* **1.** GIVING FACTS giving facts and information rather than telling a fictional story **2.** CONSISTING OF DOCUMENTS in the form of documents, or collected from documents —**doc·u·men·tar·i·ly** /dòkyəmən térrəlee/ *adv*

doc·u·men·ta·tion /dòkyəmən táysh'n/ *n* **1.** EVIDENTIAL OR REFERENCE DOCUMENTS documents provided or collected together as evidence or as reference material **2.** PROCESS OF PROVIDING WRITTEN INFORMATION the process of providing written details or information about something **3.** COMPUT COMPUTER SOFTWARE INFORMATION the instructions, tutorials, and reference information provided to explain how to install and use software or a computer system

doc·u·ment feed·er *n* the part of a printer, scanner, or fax machine that holds a stack of papers and feeds them through the machine so that something can be printed on them

doc·u·ment hold·er *n* a stand that holds papers in a vertical position so that they can be read easily by somebody working at a desk

doc·u·soap /dókyə sōp/ *n* a television program that combines documentary style with aspects of soap opera, e.g., by showing the personal lives of people at their workplace [Late 20C Blend of DOCUMENTARY + SOAP OPERA]

doc·u·tain·ment /dòkyə táynmənt/ *n* MEDIA same as **infotainment** [Late 20C. Blend of DOCUMENTARY + ENTERTAINMENT]

DOD *abbr* GOV Department of Defense

dod·der[1] /dóddər/ (**-dered, -der·ing, -ders**) *vi* **1.** to tremble or shake slightly as a result of age **2.** to walk slowly and unsteadily with shaking limbs as a result of age [Early 17C. Variant of obsolete and dialect *dadder* "quake, tremble," origin ?] —**dod·der·er** *n*

dod·der[2] /dóddər/ (*plural* **-ders** or *same*) *n* a leafless rootless parasitic plant of the morning glory family that lacks chlorophyll and has a reddish twining stem. Flowers: small, white. Genus: *Cuscuta*. [14C. Origin ?]

dod·dered /dóddərd/ *adj* **1.** having the top branches missing as a result of age or disease **2.** weak and unsteady [Late 17C. Probably < *dod* "lop (a tree)," origin ?]

dod·der·ing /dóddəring/, **dod·der·y** /-ree/ *adj* walking unsteadily, especially as a result of age —**dod·der·ing·ly** *adv*

dodeca- *prefix* twelve ○ *dodecasyllable* [< Greek *dōdeka* < *duō* "two" + *deka* "ten"]

do·dec·a·he·dron /dō dekə héedrən/ (*plural* **-drons** or **-dra** /-drə/) *n* a three-dimensional geometric figure formed of 12 equal pentagonal faces meeting in threes at 20 vertices [Late 16C. < Greek *dōdekaedron* < *dōdeka* "twelve" + *hedra* "seat, face"] —**do·dec·a·he·dral** *adj*

Do·de·ca·nese /dō dèkkə néez, -néess/ group of islands in the southeastern Aegean Sea that form a department of Greece. They are a major tourist destination. Capital: Rhodes. Population: 145,071 (1981). Area: 1,028 sq. mi./2,663 sq. km.

do·de·ca·no·ic ac·id /dō dekə nō ik-/ *n* CHEM same as **lauric acid** [Mid-20C. < *dodecane* "(kind of) paraffin" < DODECA-]

do·dec·a·phon·ic /dō dekə fónnik/ *adj* MUSIC same as **twelve-tone** —**do·dec·a·phon·ism** /dō dékə fō nìzzəm, -fònnizzəm, dōdə káffə-/ *n* —**do·dec·a·phon·ist** /dō dékəfənist, dōdə káffənist/ *n* —**do·dec·a·phon·y** /dō dékə fōnee, dōdə káffənee/ *n*

do·dec·a·syl·la·ble /dō dekə sílləb'l/ *n* a line of verse of 12 syllables —**do·dec·a·syl·lab·ic** /-si lábbik/ *adj*

dodge /doj/ *v* (**dodged, dodg·ing, dodg·es**) **1.** *vti* MOVE QUICKLY TO AVOID SOMETHING to move quickly and suddenly to one side to avoid being caught or hit by somebody or something ○ *He dodged the punch.* **2.** *vt* AVOID SOMETHING UNPLEASANT to avoid doing something regarded as unpleasant **3.** *vt* PHOTOGRAPHY MASK AREA OF PRINT to mask an area of a photographic print during exposure to prevent light reaching it ■ *n* **1.** TRICK TO AVOID DOING SOMETHING a clever trick or tactic to avoid doing something ○ *a tax dodge* **2.** QUICK AVOIDING MOVEMENT a sudden quick movement to one side to avoid being caught or hit by somebody or something [Mid-16C. Origin ?]

dodge ball *n* a children's game in which opponents try to avoid being hit by a large rubber ball

Dodge Cit·y /dój-/ city in southern Kansas, on the northern bank of the Arkansas River, southwest of Great Bend. Population: 25,345 (2002 estimate).

dodg·er /dójjər/ *n* **1.** SOMEBODY AVOIDING DUTY somebody who avoids a duty or responsibility, especially by using dishonest or deceitful methods **2.** SOMEBODY DISHONEST somebody cunning and untrustworthy **3.** *US* HANDBILL a small leaflet or notice **4.** SHELTERING SCREEN ON SHIP a canvas screen on a ship or yacht to protect the person at the helm from spray **5.** *Southern US* FOOD same as **corndodger**

Dodg·son /dójss'n/, **Charles Lutwidge** ➧ **Carroll, Lewis**

dodg·y /dójjee/ (**-i·er, -i·est**) *adj UK* (*informal*) **1.** suspect, dishonest, or untrustworthy **2.** dangerous or risky —**dodg·i·ly** *adv* —**dodg·i·ness** *n*

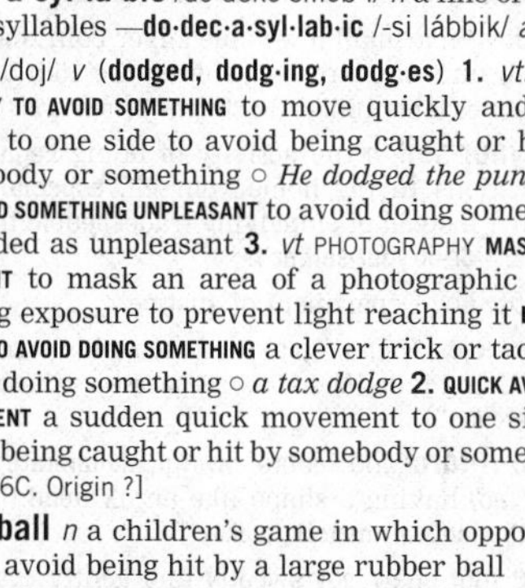

dodo

do·do /dṓ dō/ (*plural* **-dos** or **-does**) *n* **1.** EXTINCT FLIGHTLESS BIRD a large flightless bird with a hooked beak, extinct since the 17th century. Native to: formerly, Mauritius and neighboring Indian Ocean islands. Latin name: *Raphus cucullatus*. **2.** OLD-FASHIONED PERSON somebody regarded as old-fashioned and conservative (*informal insult*) **3.** UNINTELLIGENT PERSON somebody regarded as unintelligent (*informal insult*) [Early 17C. < Portuguese *doudo* "fool, simpleton"] —**do·do·ism** *n* ◇ **(as) dead as a dodo** no longer existing, functioning, flourishing, or popular

Do·do·ma /dṓdō maa, dṓdəmə/ official capital of Tanzania since 1983. It is situated in Dodoma Region, west of the former capital, Dar es Salaam. Population: 189,000 (1995).

doe /dō/ *n* a mature female of several animals, including the deer, kangaroo, rabbit, hare, and goat [Old English *dā*, origin ?]

SPELLCHECK doe or **dough**? Do not confuse the spelling of ***doe*** and ***dough***, which sound similar. A ***doe*** is a female animal such as a deer or rabbit. ***Dough*** is used to make bread or pastry.

DOE *abbr* GOV Department of Energy

doe-eyed *adj* having large appealing eyes that convey an impression of gentleness or naive innocence

do·er /dóo ər/ *n* **1.** somebody who does a particular thing (*often used in combination*) ○ *a doer of good* **2.** somebody who takes action instead of just thinking or talking about it

does 3rd person singular present of **do**[1]

doe·skin /dṓ skìn/ *n* **1.** SKIN OF DEER the skin of various animals, including a doe, deer, and goat **2.** LEATHER light supple leather made from doeskin that is particularly suitable for gloves **3.** SMOOTH WOOLEN CLOTH a densely woven smooth woolen cloth

does·n't /dúzz'nt/ *contr* does not

~~**does'nt**~~ incorrect spelling of **doesn't**

do·est /dóo əst/ 2nd person singular present of **do**[1] (*archaic*)

do·eth /dóo əth/ 3rd person singular present of **do**[1] (*archaic*)

doff /dof/ (**doffed, doff·ing, doffs**) *vt* **1.** to take off or lift and tilt a hat as a greeting or a mark of respect **2.** to take off a coat or another piece of clothing [14C. Contraction of archaic *do off* "take off"] —**dof·fer** *n*

dog /dawg, dog/ *n* **1.** DOMESTIC ANIMAL a domestic carnivorous animal with a long muzzle, a fur coat, and a long fur-covered tail, whose characteristic call is a bark. Latin name: *Canis familiaris*. **2.** MALE DOG a male dog, wolf, fox, or other member of the dog family **3.** WILD ANIMAL a wild animal such as a wolf, fox, dingo, or coyote that resembles a domestic dog and belongs to the same family. Family: Canidae. **4.** CONTEMPTIBLE PERSON somebody regarded as unpleasant or contemptible (*insult*) **5.** OFFENSIVE TERM an offensive term that deliberately insults somebody's looks (*slang insult*) **6.** PERSON somebody of a particular type (*informal*) ○ *You lucky dog!* **7.** SOMETHING USELESS OR INFERIOR something useless or of a very poor standard (*informal*) **8.** HOUSEHOLD same as **andiron** **9.** METEOROL same as **fogbow** **10.** MECH ENG GRIPPING TOOL a device for gripping or holding things ■ *vt* (**dog·ged, dog·ging, dogs**) **1.** BOTHER SOMEBODY PERSISTENTLY to bother or trouble somebody persistently (*often passive*) ○ *was dogged by bad luck* **2.** FOLLOW SOMEBODY CLOSELY to follow somebody closely in a determined way ○ *continued dogging her footsteps* **3.** MECH ENG GRIP SOMETHING WITH MECHANICAL DEVICE to grip or hold something firmly with a mechanical device [Old English *docga*, origin ?] —**dog·like** *adj* ◇ **dog in the manger** somebody who tries to prevent somebody else from having or doing something that he or she cannot have or do ◇ **a dog's life** a wretched existence ◇ **dog eat dog** ruthlessly competitive ◇ **go to the dogs** to be in the final stages of a gradual decline in standards (*informal*) ◇ **let sleeping dogs lie** to take no action in a situation that is currently peaceful but potentially troublesome ◇ **put on the dog** to make a display of wealth or knowledge ostentatiously or pretentiously (*dated informal*)

dog-and-po·ny show *n* an elaborate business presentation or promotional event (*informal*)

dog·bane /dáwg bàyn, dóg-/ *n* a plant that bears dogberries with pungent milky juice and a bitter root. Flowers: small, bell-shaped, white or pink. Genus: *Apocynum*.

dog·ber·ry[1] /dáwg bèrree, dóg-/ (*plural* **-ries**) *n* **1.** a berry of any of various plants, including dogwood **2.** a plant that produces dogberries [Mid-16C. < DOG implying inferior or inedible]

dog·ber·ry[2] /dáwg bèrree, dóg-/ (*plural* **-ries**), **Dog·ber·ry** *n* an unintelligent but self-important official [Mid-19C. After *Dogberry*, constable in *Much Ado About Nothing* by Shakespeare] —**dog·ber·ry·ism** *n*

dog bis·cuit *n* a hard biscuit made for dogs to eat

dog·cart /dáwg kaart, dóg-/ *n* a two-wheeled vehicle drawn by a horse and seating two people back to back

dog·catch·er /dáwg kàchər, dóg-/ *n* somebody who is employed to catch stray dogs

dog chew *n* a hard piece of leather or compressed material given to a dog to chew on, either as a toy or to keep its teeth in good condition

dog col·lar *n* **1.** a piece of leather or fabric worn around a dog's neck, often with the dog's name attached to it **2.** *UK* CHR same as **clerical collar** (*informal*) **3.** JEWELRY a necklace that fits closely around the neck

dog days *npl* **1.** the hottest period of the summer, roughly between early July and early September in the northern hemisphere **2.** a lazy or inactive period of time [Because in ancient times heralded by the simultaneous rising of the Dog Star and the Sun]

doge /dōj/ *n* the chief magistrate in Renaissance Venice or Genoa [Mid-16C. Via French < Venetian Italian *doze* < Latin *ducem* "leader"] —**doge·ship** *n*

dog-eared *adj* **1.** having worn and well-thumbed pages that have been creased or folded over to mark the place reached in reading **2.** shabby or well-used

do·gey *n* AGRIC another spelling of **dogie**

dog·face /dáwg fàyss, dóg-/ *n* a US infantryman (*slang*)

dog fen·nel *n* PLANTS same as **mayweed** [< its fetid smell, and from its leaves]

dog·fight /dáwg fìt, dóg-/ *n* **1.** COMBAT BETWEEN FIGHTER PLANES an aerial combat involving two or more fighter planes **2.** FIERCE FIGHT a fierce violent fight **3.** FIGHT INVOLVING DOGS a fight between dogs —**dog·fight·ing** *n*

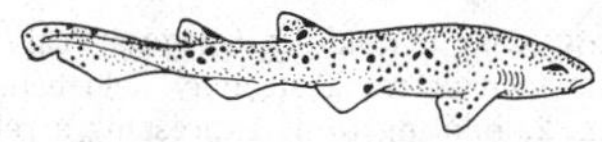

dogfish

dog·fish /dáwg fìsh, dŏg-/ (*plural* **-fish·es** or *same*) *n* **1.** a small long-tailed shark, either spiny or smooth-skinned. Native to: Pacific, Atlantic, Mediterranean waters. Families: Squalidae or Carcharhinidae or Scyliorhinidae. **2.** FISH same as **bowfin**

dog·ged /dáwgəd, dóggəd/ *adj* determined to continue without giving up in spite of difficulties —**dog·ged·ly** *adv* —**dog·ged·ness** *n*

dog·ger[1] /dáwgər, dóggər/ *n* a Dutch fishing vessel [14C. < Middle Dutch]

dog·ger[2] /dáwgər, dóggər/ *n* a large mass of calcium-containing sandstone or ironstone occurring in sedimentary rock [Late 17C. Origin ?]

dog·ger·el /dáwgərəl, dóggərəl/, **dog·grel** /dáwgrəl, dóggrəl/ *n* **1.** poetry that does not scan well and is often not intended to be taken seriously **2.** something that is badly written or makes no sense at all [14C. Probably < DOG (with its pejorative connotations)]

dog·gie *n* another spelling of **doggy**

dog·gish /dáwgish, dóggish/ *adj* **1. RESEMBLING DOG** resembling a dog, or possessing the qualities of a dog **2. BAD-TEMPERED** bad-tempered and aggressive **3. SHOWY** ostentatiously stylish —**dog·gish·ly** *adv* —**dog·gish·ness** *n*

dog·go /dáwgō, dóggō/ *adv UK* not moving or making any sound in order not to be discovered (*dated informal*) ○ *lying doggo* [Late 19C. Because dogs can lie in this manner]

dog·gone /dáwg gàwn, dóg gòn/, **dog·goned** /-gàwnd, -gònd/ (*informal*) *adv, adj* used to emphasize how bad or annoying something is ■ *interj* used to express annoyance or irritation [Early 19C. Probably alteration of GODDAMN]

dog·grel *n* LITERAT another spelling of **doggerel**

dog·gy /dáwgee, dóggee/, **dog·gie** *n* (*plural* **-gies**) same as **dog** *n* (sense 1) (*baby talk*) ■ *adj* **1.** resembling or typical of a dog in behavior or appearance **2.** fond of or interested in dogs (*informal*)

dog·gy bag *n* a container that can be used by a customer at a restaurant to take home any leftover food from his or her meal (*informal*) [< giving the food to a dog]

dog·gy pad·dle *UK* SWIMMING *n* same as **dog paddle** ■ *vi* same as **dog paddle**

dog han·dler *n* a police officer or security guard who is in charge of a specially trained working dog

dog·hanged /dáwg hàngd, dóg-/ *adj Southern US* same as **hangdog**

dog·house /dáwg hòwss, dóg-/ (*plural* **-hous·es** /-hòwzəzh) *n* a small enclosed shelter for a dog ◇ **in the doghouse** in disgrace (*informal*)

do·gie /dṓgee/, **do·gy** (*plural* **-gies**), **do·gey** (*plural* **-geys**) *n* a calf with no mother [Late 19C. Origin ?]

dog i·ron *n Southern US* an andiron

dog Lat·in *n* Latin that is incorrect in some way, especially a word or phrase that is falsely made to look or sound like Latin for humorous or satirical effect

dog·leg /dáwg lèg, dóg-/ *n* **1. SHARP BEND** a sharp bend or angle in something, especially in a road **2.** GOLF **BEND IN GOLF COURSE** in golf, a sharp bend in a fairway before a hole ■ *vi* **(-legged, -leg·ging, -legs) FORM SHARP BEND** to form a sharp bend or angle [< the bent form of a dog's hind leg] —**dog·leg·ged** /dàwg léggəd, -légd, dòg-/ *adj*

dog·ma /dáwgmə, dógmə/ (*plural* **-mas** or **-ma·ta** /-mətə/) *n* **1.** a belief or set of beliefs that a religion holds to be true **2.** a belief or set of beliefs that a political, philosophical, or moral group holds to be true [Mid-16C. Via late Latin < Greek *dogma, dogmat-* "opinion, tenet" < *dokein* "seem good, think"]

dog·mat·ic /dawg máttik, dog-/, **dog·mat·i·cal** /-k'l/ *adj* **1.** prone to expressing strongly held beliefs and opinions **2.** relating to or expressing a religious, political, philosophical, or moral dogma —**dog·mat·i·cal·ly** *adv*

dog·mat·ics /dawg máttiks, dog-/ *n* the study of religious dogmas, especially Christian dogmas (*takes a singular verb*)

dog·mat·ic the·ol·o·gy *n* same as **dogmatics**

dog·ma·tism /dáwgmə tìzzəm, dógmə-/ *n* the tendency to express strongly held opinions in a way that suggests they should be accepted without question

dog·ma·tist /dáwgmətist, dógmə-/ *n* **1.** somebody who expresses strongly held opinions and expects them to be accepted without question **2.** somebody who devises a new religious, political, philosophical, or moral dogma

dog·ma·tize /dáwgmə tīz, dógmə-/ (**-tized, -tiz·ing, -tiz·es**) *vi* to express strongly held opinions in a way that suggests they should be accepted without question —**dog·ma·ti·za·tion** /dàwgməti záysh'n, dòg-/ *n* —**dog·ma·tiz·er** *n*

dog·nap /dáwg nàp, dóg-/ (**-napped, -nap·ping, -naps**) *vt* to steal a dog, especially in order to sell it for use in medical research —**dog·nap·per** *n*

dog of·fi·cer *n* VET same as **dogcatcher**

Do·gon /dṓ gòn/ (*plural same* or **-gons**) *n* **1.** a member of a Voltaic people living on the plateaus of southeastern Mali in West Africa **2.** a Niger-Congo language of Mali and Burkina Faso. Native speakers: 500,000. —**Do·gon** *adj*

do-good·er /-gŏŏddər/ *n* somebody who sincerely tries to help others, but whose actions may be unwelcome (*informal*) —**do-good·ing** *n, adj*

dog pad·dle *n* a swimming stroke in which you lie on your front and make rapid downward movements with your arms and legs underneath your body. This stroke is often used by people learning to swim and is not used in competitions. ■ *vi* to swim using the dog paddle

dog rac·ing *n* the sport of greyhound racing in which dogs chase a mechanical rabbit around a track and spectators may bet on which dog will win

dog rose *n* a wild rose. Flowers: delicate, pink or white. Native to: Europe. Latin name: *Rosa canina*.

dogs·bod·y /dáwgz bòddee, dógz-/ (*plural* **-ies**) *n UK* a worker who does boring tasks that others do not want to do (*informal*)

dog·sled /dáwg slèd, dóg-/ *n* a vehicle mounted on runners and pulled by dogs, designed to travel over snow and ice —**dog·sled** *vi* —**dog·sled·der** *n*

Dog Star *n* ASTRON **1.** same as **Sirius 2.** same as **Procyon**

dog tag *n* **1.** a metal identification tag for a member of the military, worn on a chain around the neck (*informal*) **2.** a metal disk, attached to a dog's collar, that gives the name and address of the dog's owner and often the name of the dog

dog team *n* a team of dogs for pulling a dogsled

dog·teeth DENT, ARCHIT plural of **dogtooth**

dog-tired *adj* completely exhausted (*informal*)

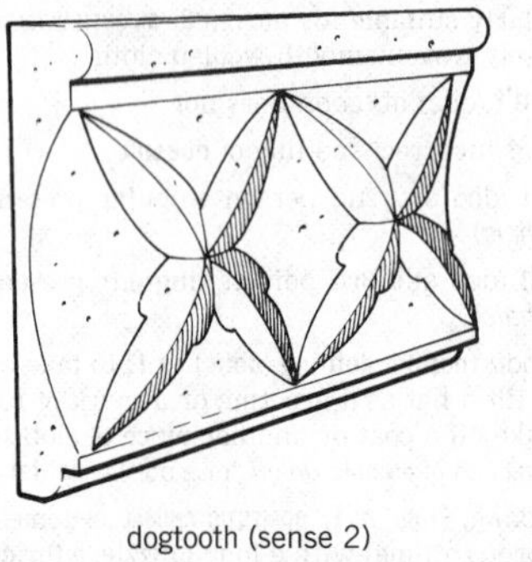

dogtooth (sense 2)

dog·tooth /dáwg tŏŏth, dóg-/ (*plural* **-teeth** /-teeth/) *n* **1.** DENT same as **canine** *n* (sense 1) (*informal*) **2.** in 13th-century English architecture, a small raised ornamental feature on a building consisting of four leaf-shaped parts arranged to form an X-shape

dog·tooth vi·o·let *n* a small spring-flowering bulbous plant with red-speckled leaves. Flowers: drooping, yellow or purple, like small lilies. Genus: *Erythronium*. [< the toothed inner segments of the perianth]

dog·trot /dáwg tròt, dóg-/ *n* **1.** a gentle trot at a steady pace **2.** *also* **dog-trot** *Southern US* a roofed corridor, similar to a breezeway, that connects two sections of a building, or a main building with a smaller one ○*"Miss Ollie had a little dog-trot house out back, with a wood stove, and table and chairs, and we used to play out in that little dog-trot house better than anything!"* (Donna Tartt *The Little Friend*; Knopf, 2003)

dog war·den *n UK* same as **dogcatcher**

dog·watch /dáwg wòch, dóg-/ *n* on a ship, the late afternoon watch from 4:00 p.m. to 6:00 p.m. or the early evening watch from 6:00 p.m. to 8:00 p.m.

dog·wood /dáwg wŏŏd, dóg-/ (*plural* **-woods** or *same*) *n* a tree or bush with clusters of small white flowers surrounded by four large white or reddish leaves (**bracts**). Genus: *Cornus*.

dog·wood an·thrac·nose *n* a fatal fungal disease of flowering dogwood trees that produces dark splotches on the leaves and cankers on the limbs and trunk

do·gy *n* another spelling of **dogie**

doh /dō/ *n* another spelling of **do**[2]

d'oh /dō/ *interj* used in humorous acknowledgment of a stupid act or remark (*slang*) [Late 20C. Origin ?]

Do·ha /dṓhə, -haà/ capital and largest city of Qatar, on the Persian Gulf. Population: 392,384 (1995).

DOI *abbr* GOV Department of the Interior

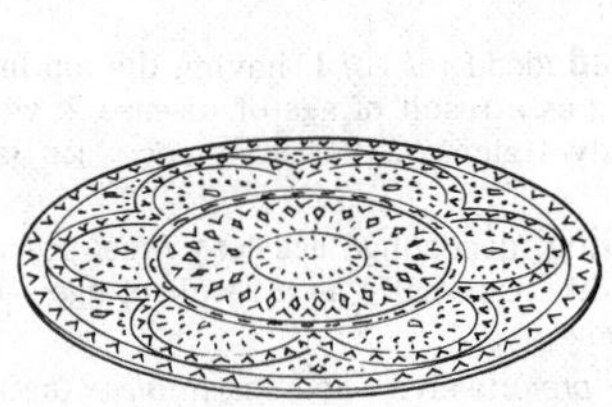

doily

doi·ly /dóylee/ (*plural* **-lies**) *n* **1.** a decorative lacy mat that is put on plates under cakes or party food to display the food attractively **2.** a small table napkin [Late 18C. After *Doiley* or *Doyley*, 17C London draper]

do·ing /dŏŏ ing/ present participle of **do**[1] ■ *n* the act of performing or carrying out something ○ *It's all your doing.*

do·ings /dŏŏ ingz/ *npl* the things that somebody has done ■ *n* social activities or events ○ *attended the holiday doings*

Doi·sy /dóyzee/, **Edward Adelbert** (1893–1986) US biochemist. Together with Henrik Dam he discovered the chemical structure of vitamin K, a fat-soluble substance necessary for blood coagulation. For this work they shared a Nobel Prize (1943).

doit /doyt/ *n* a small low-value silver coin that was a Dutch unit of currency between the 15th and 17th centuries [Late 16C. < Middle Low German *doyt*]

do-it-your·self *n* the activity of doing repairs and alterations in the home yourself, especially as a hobby, instead of employing tradespeople to do the work —**do-it-your·self·er** *n*

DOJ *abbr* GOV Department of Justice

do·jo /dṓjō/ (*plural* **-jos**) *n* a school or room for practicing judo [Mid-20C. < Japanese < *dō* "way, art" + *-jō* "ground"]

do·lab·ri·form /dō lábbrə fàwrm/, **do·lab·rate** /dō láb ràyt/ *adj* having a shape like an ax head [Mid-18C. < Latin *dolabra* "mattock, pickax"]

dol·ce /dṓl chày/ *adv* sweetly and gently (*used as a musical direction*) [Early 19C. Via Italian, "sweet" < Latin *dulcis*] —**dol·ce** *adj*

dol·ce far ni·en·te /-faar nee éntee/ *n* pleasant idleness and relaxation [Early 19C. < Italian, "sweet doing nothing"]

Dol·ce·lat·te /dōl chay laà tày/ *n* a soft creamy Italian blue cheese with a mild flavor, made from cow's milk [< Italian, literally "sweet milk"]

dol·ce vi·ta /-veétə/ *n* a life of luxury and idle self-indulgence [Mid-20C. < Italian, "sweet life"]

dol·drums /dṓldrəmz, dóldrəmz/ *npl* **1. STAGNATION** a sluggish state in which no development or improvement occurs **2. GLOOMINESS** a state of gloominess or lack of energy **3.** METEOROL **AREA NORTH OF EQUATOR** an area with no wind or light variable winds just north of the equator in the Atlantic and Pacific oceans, situated between the trade winds **4.** METEOROL, NAUT **WEATHER CONDITIONS IN DOLDRUMS** the weather conditions prevailing in the doldrums that cause sailing ships to become becalmed [Late 18C. Origin ?]

dole[1] /dōl/ *n* **1.** *UK* **GOVERNMENT UNEMPLOYMENT PAYMENT** a regular sum of money paid by the government to somebody who is unemployed (*informal*) **2. CHARITY** the giving of clothes, money, or food to somebody who is in need **3. SOMEBODY'S FATE** somebody's fate in life (*archaic*) ■ *vt* **(doled, dol·ing, doles) DISTRIBUTE SOMETHING AS CHARITY** to distribute something as charity to somebody who is in need [Old English *dāl* "portion" < Germanic]

dole out *vt* to give something to each of a group of people (*informal*)

SYNONYMS See *share*[1].

dole[2] /dōl/ *n* grief, sadness, or misery (*archaic*) [13C. Via Old French *dol* "mourning" < Vulgar Latin *dolus* < Latin *dolere* "grieve, suffer pain"]

Dole /dōl/, **Bob** (*b.* 1923) US politician and lawyer. He was the Republican nominee for US president in 1996, running against Bill Clinton after many years in the US Senate. Full name **Dole, Robert Joseph**

Dole, Elizabeth (*b.* 1936) US senator and lawyer. She served as president of the American Red Cross (1991–99). Born **Hanford, Elizabeth**

> "Sometimes I think we're the only two lawyers in Washington who trust each other."
> [Elizabeth Dole, of her husband Senator Robert Dole, *Newsweek*; August 3, 1987]

Dole, Sanford Ballard (1844–1926) US politician. He was the first and only president of the Republic of Hawaii (1894–1900), later serving as Hawaii's territorial governor (1900–03) and as a federal judge (1903–15).

dole·ful /dṓlfəl/ *adj* sad and mournful —**dole·ful·ly** *adv* —**dole·ful·ness** *n*

do·len·te /dō léntee, dō lén tày/ *adv* in a sorrowful manner (*used as a musical direction*) [< Italian, present participle of *dolere* "feel grief" < Latin] —**do·len·te** *adj*

dol·er·ite /dóllə rīt/ *n UK* GEOL same as **diabase** [Mid-19C. < French *dolérite* < Greek *doleros* "deceptive" < *dolos* "deceit"; because difficult to distinguish from diorite] —**dol·er·it·ic** /dòllə ríttik/ *adj*

dol·i·cho·ce·phal·ic /dòllikō sə fállik/, **dol·i·cho·ceph·a·lous** /-séff'ləss/ *adj* having a head disproportionately longer than it is wide, specifically one with a cephalic index of less than 75 [Mid-19C. < Greek *dolikhos* "long"] —**dol·i·cho·ceph·a·lism** /dòllikō séff'l ìzzəm/ *n*

do·li·cho·saur·us /dòllikō sáwrəss/ *n* an extinct long-necked water reptile that was common 65 million years ago [< Greek *dolikhos* "long" + *sauros* "lizard"]

do·line /do leéen/, **do·li·na** /do leénə/ *n* a large, often roughly circular basin of valley-sized proportions formed as a result of water dissolving surface limestone [Late 19C. Via German < Slovene *dolina* "valley"]

doll /dol/ *n* **1. CHILD'S TOY** a child's toy in the shape of a person or baby **2. WOMAN** a woman or girl who is pleasant to look at (*informal*; *sometimes considered offensive*) **3. HELPFUL PERSON** a nice or helpful person (*informal*) [Mid-16C. < form of the woman's name *Dorothy*] —**dol·lish** *adj* —**dol·lish·ly** *adv* —**dol·lish·ness** *n*
doll up *vt* to make yourself or somebody else such as a child look particularly elegant or stylish, usually for a special occasion (*informal*)

dol·lar /dóllər/ *n* **1. COMMON UNIT OF CURRENCY** a unit of currency used in the United States, Canada, Australia, New Zealand, and several other countries. See table at **currency 2. DOLLAR BILL** a bill worth one dollar **3.** *UK* **FORMER FIVE-SHILLING COIN** a former British coin worth five shillings (*informal*) [Mid-16C. Via early Flemish *daler* or Low German < German *Taler*, shortening of *Joachimst(h)aler*, after the silver mine of *Joachimsthal*, now Jáchymov, Czech Republic] ◇ **like a million dollars** extremely well, good-looking, or happy (*informal*) ○ *You look like a million dollars!*

dol·lar-a-year *adj* receiving only a very small token payment for work carried out

dol·lar cost av·er·ag·ing *n* the periodic and systematic purchase of a security regardless of the security price

dol·lar day *n* a day on which goods are sold at a greatly reduced price

Dol·lard des Or·meaux /dō laàr day zawr mṓ/, **Adam** (1635–60) French-born Canadian soldier and colonist. He displaced the Iroquois Native Americans from Montreal (1660).

dol·lar di·plo·ma·cy *n* **1.** the use of financial resources to facilitate foreign relations **2.** in the United States, a policy aimed at encouraging and protecting US investment abroad

dol·lar·i·za·tion /dòlləri záysh'n/ *n* **1. USE BY COUNTRY OF DOLLARS** the use of dollars by a country as its own currency **2. LINKING OF CURRENCY TO DOLLAR** the linking of a currency's value to that of the dollar **3. ACCOUNTING IN DOLLARS** the use of the dollar for accounting purposes

dol·lars-and-cents *adj* considering finance as the determining factor

dol·lar sign *n* the symbol ($) that represents a dollar

dol·lar store *n* a retail establishment selling inexpensive items, many at one dollar or less

doll·house /dól hòwss/ (*plural* **-hous·es** /-hòwzəz/) *n* a toy house containing miniature furniture

dol·lop /dólləp/ (*informal*) *n* a spoon-sized quantity of a thick liquid or a soft solid such as ice cream or cream ■ *vt* (**-loped, -lop·ing, -lops**) to spoon a quantity of a thick liquid or a soft solid [Late 16C. Origin ?]

doll's house *n UK* same as **dollhouse**

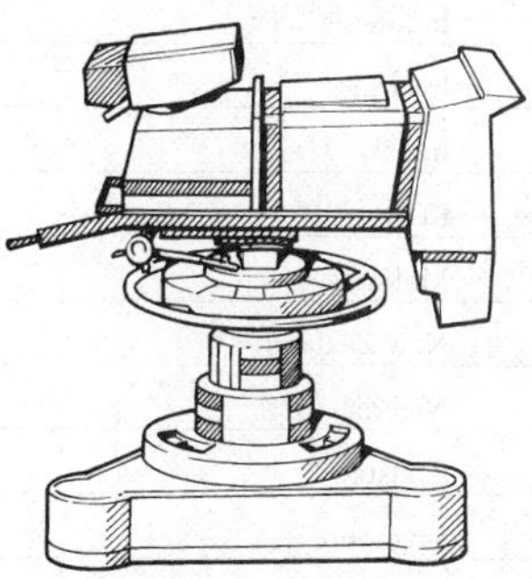

dolly: television camera on dolly

dol·ly /dóllee/ *n* (*plural* **-lies**) **1.** same as **doll** (sense 1) (*baby talk*) **2.** MEDIA, MOVIES **MOVING PLATFORM FOR CAMERA OPERATOR** a platform with wheels on which a camera operator and camera are placed in order to film moving shots for a movie or television program **3.** MECH ENG **WHEELED PLATFORM FOR MOVING THINGS** a platform on wheels used to move heavy weights **4.** CIV ENG **WEIGHT DROPPED ON POST** a heavy weight dropped on a stake or pile to force it into the ground **5.** CONSTR **TOOL FOR HOLDING RIVET** an anvil that holds one end of a rivet while the other end is being hammered **6.** METALL **HEAVY BLOCK HELD BEHIND HAMMERED METAL** a heavy block held behind sheet metal that is being hammered ■ *vti* (**-lied, -ly·ing, -lies**) **MOVE CAMERA ON DOLLY** to move a camera on a dolly in order to film moving shots

dol·ly shot *n* a shot filmed from a camera mounted on a wheeled platform

Dol·ly Var·den /dòllee vaàrd'n/ *n* (*plural same*) a trout or char with red spots found in lakes and streams. Native to: western North America, eastern Asia. Latin name: *Salvelinus malma*. [Late 19C. After a woman of colorful dress in the novel *Barnaby Rudge* by Charles Dickens]

dol·ma /dáwlmə, dáwl maà/ (*plural* **-mas** or **-ma·des** /dawl maà dèss, -deèz/) *n* a Greek or Turkish dish consisting of a grape or cabbage leaf with a stuffing, usually of meat and rice [Late 17C. < Turkish, "something stuffed"]

dol·man /dólmən, dṓl-/ *n* **1.** a woman's coat with large sleeves cut in one piece with the body of the garment **2.** a long Turkish robe [Late 16C. Via French *dol(i)man* < Turkish *dolama(n)* "robe"]

dol·man sleeve *n* a sleeve cut in one piece with the body of a garment such as a jacket or dress, particularly one fitting tightly at the wrist and wide at the armhole

dolmen

dol·men /dólmən, dṓl-/ *n* a prehistoric structure thought to have been used as a tomb that consists of a large horizontal slab of stone supported by two or more vertical slabs [Mid-19C. < French]

dol·o·mite /dṓlə mīt, dóllə-/ *n* **1.** a white, reddish, or greenish mineral consisting of calcium magnesium carbonate. Source: sedimentary rocks. Use: building stone, cement, fertilizers. **2.** a sedimentary rock consisting mainly of the mineral dolomite [Late 18C. < French, after Déodat de *Dolomieu* (1750–1801), French geologist]

Do·lo·mi·tes /dṓlə mīts, dóllə-/ mountain group in the eastern part of the northern Italian Alps. The highest peak is Marmolada, 10,964 ft./3,342 km.

do·lor /dṓlər/ *n* intense sadness (*literary*) [13C. Via French < Latin, "pain, grief, sorrow" < *dolere* "feel pain"]

do·lo·ro·so /dṑlə rṓssō/ *adv* sadly or sorrowfully (*used as a musical direction*) [Early 19C. Via Italian < late Latin *dolorosus* (see DOLOROUS)] —**do·lo·ro·so** *adj*

do·lor·ous /dṓlərəss, dóll-/ *adj* showing, causing, or involving sorrow (*literary*) [14C. Via French < late Latin *dolorosus* < Latin *dolor* (see DOLOR)] —**do·lor·ous·ly** *adv* —**do·lor·ous·ness** *n*

dol·o·stone /dṓlə stòn, dóllə-/ *n* a form of limestone having more than 50% dolomite [Mid-20C. < DOLOMITE]

do·lour *n* Can, UK spelling of **dolor**

dolphin

dol·phin /dólfin/ (*plural* **-phins** or *same*) *n* **1.** an intelligent sea mammal (**cetacean**) that resembles a large fish and has teeth and a snout similar to a beak. Found almost worldwide, dolphins are related to whales, but are smaller. Family: Delphinidae. **2.** a large ocean fish of the perch family, popular as a game fish, that has a long dorsal fin, high blunt forehead, and a brilliant green, blue, and yellow body. Latin name: *Coryphaena hippurus* or *Coryphaena equisetis*. [14C. Via Old French *daulphin* < Greek *delphin-*]

dol·phin·ar·i·um /dòlfi néree əm/ (*plural* **-ar·i·ums** or **-ar·i·a** /-érree ə/) *n* a large pool in which dolphins are kept, either for research or for public displays

dol·phin·fish /dólfin fish/ (*plural same* or **-fish·es**) *n* FISH same as **dolphin** (sense 2)

dol·phin strik·er *n* a strut extending from the front of a sailing vessel that helps to prevent upward movement of a beam such as a bowsprit

dolt /dōlt/ *n* an offensive term that deliberately insults somebody's intelligence (*informal insult*) [Mid-16C. Origin ?]

dolt·ish /dṓltish/ *adj* an offensive term meaning having or showing little or no intelligence (*dated informal*) —**dolt·ish·ly** *adv* —**dolt·ish·ness** *n*

Dol·ton /dṓlt'n/ town in northeastern Illinois, directly west of the Illinois-Indiana border. It is a southern suburb of Chicago. Population: 25,438 (2002 estimate).

dom. *abbr* **1.** domestic **2.** MUSIC dominant

D.O.M. *abbr* CHR to God, the best, the greatest [Latin *Deo Optimo Maximo*]

-dom *suffix* **1.** status, condition ○ *martyrdom* **2.** office, rank, domain ○ *dukedom* **3.** people associated with a status or rank ○ *fandom* [Old English *-dōm* < Indo-European, "put, place"]

do·main /dō máyn, də-/ *n* **1. SCOPE** the scope of a subject **2. SPHERE OF INFLUENCE** an area of activity over which

INTERNET DOMAINS

Top-level domains in Internet addresses are the final letters of the address. They indicate the country – except for the United States, where no country code is used – or type of organization, or both.

Selected Organization Domains

Domain	Organization
.ac	academic organization
.aero	aviation industry
.biz	business
.com	commercial organization
.coop	nonprofit cooperative
.edu	educational organization
.gov	government organization
.info	general use
.int	international organization
.mil	military organization
.museum	museum
.name	private individual
.net	networking organization
.org	noncommercial organization
.pro	professional practice

For countries other than the United States, country domains can be combined with organization domains, for example:

.co.uk	United Kingdom organization
.edu.au	Australian educational organization

Selected Country Domains

Domain	Country
.au	Australia
.bd	Bangladesh
.ca	Canada
.gh	Ghana
.hk	Hong Kong
.id	Indonesia
.ie	Ireland
.in	India
.ke	Kenya
.my	Malaysia
.nz	New Zealand
.ng	Nigeria
.pk	Pakistan
.sg	Singapore
.za	South Africa
.lk	Sri Lanka
.ug	Uganda
.uk	United Kingdom
.zm	Zambia
.zw	Zimbabwe

somebody has influence **3. TERRITORY GOVERNED** a territory ruled by a government or a leader **4. LAND OWNED** an area of land owned and controlled by a person, family, or organization **5.** LAW **RIGHTS OF OWNERSHIP** rights relating to the ownership of land **6.** ONLINE same as **domain name 7.** MATH **SET OF VALUES OF VARIABLE** the set of possible values specified for a given mathematical function **8.** PHYS **REGION OF UNIFORM MAGNETISM** a region in a ferromagnetic material within which all the atoms are magnetically oriented in the same direction. Increasing the magnetic field increases the size and number of the domains. [15C. < French *domaine*, alteration of *demeine* (see DEMESNE)]

do·main name *n* the sequence of words, phrases, abbreviations, or characters that serves as the Internet address of a computer or network

do·main of quan·ti·fi·ca·tion *n* the set of objects to which the quantifiers "all" and "some" apply

dome /dōm/ *n* **1. HEMISPHERICAL ROOF** a hemispherical roof, e.g., on a palace or cathedral **2. HEMISPHERICAL TOP** something that resembles a dome in shape and position, e.g., the cover of a furnace or the top of somebody's head ○ *the dome of the sky* **3. HEMISPHERICAL BUILDING STRUCTURE** a hemispherical or convex structure, especially a building ○ *a sports dome* **4. CRYSTAL FORMATION RESEMBLING ROOF** a crystal form in which two inclined surfaces intersect to form an edge like a roof **5. LARGE STATELY BUILDING** a large grand building (*archaic*) **6.** GEOL **CURVED ROCK LAYER** a semispherical topographic feature that slopes in all directions from a central point, formed by upward folding of sediments **7.** GEOL **LAVA MASS** a mass of solidified viscous lava formed above the vent of a volcano by the buildup of magma ■ *v* (**domed, dom·ing, domes**) **1.** *vti* **FORM HEMISPHERICAL SHAPE** to rise in a hemispherical shape, or form something into this shape **2.** *vt* **PUT DOME OVER SOMETHING** to cover something with a dome [Mid-17C. Via French *dôme* < Italian *duomo* "house, house of God, cathedral" < Latin *domus* "house"] —**domed** *adj*

Dome of the Rock /dōm əv th̲ə rók/ *n* a domed shrine in Jerusalem, which for Muslims is the second most holy place after the Kaaba at Mecca. It is built on the rock from which Muhammad is believed to have ascended to heaven, and where Abraham is believed to have offered the sacrifice of Isaac.

domes·day /dóomz dày/ *n* CHR same as **doomsday** (sense 1) (*archaic*)

Domes·day Book, Dooms·day Book *n* a record of all the land in England, its value, and its ownership, commissioned by William the Conqueror in 1085 [Because the ultimate authority]

do·mes·tic /də méstik/ *adj* **1. RELATING TO HOME** relating to or used in the home or everyday life within a household **2. RELATING TO FAMILY** relating to or involving a family or the people living together within a household **3. NOT WILD** kept as a farm animal or as a pet **4.** COMM **NOT FOREIGN** produced, distributed, sold, or occurring within a country ○ *domestic oil producers* **5.** POL **OF NATION'S INTERNAL AFFAIRS** relating to the internal affairs of a nation or country ○ *domestic issues such as elections* **6. ENJOYING HOME** enjoying home and family life ■ *n* **1. HOUSEHOLD SERVANT** somebody employed to do housework in somebody else's home or other duties in a large household **2.** COMM **PRODUCT NOT ORIGINATING ABROAD** a product manufactured within a country [15C. Via French < Latin *domesticus* < *domus* "house"] —**do·mes·ti·cal·ly** *adv*

do·mes·ti·cate /də mésti kàyt/ (**-cat·ed, -cat·ing, -cates**) *vt* **1. TAME ANIMAL** to accustom an animal to living with or near people, usually as a farm animal or pet **2. ACCUSTOM SOMEBODY TO HOUSEHOLD LIFE** to accustom somebody to home life or housework (*humorous*) **3.** BIOL **ADAPT PLANTS OR ANIMALS FOR HUMANS** to cultivate plants or raise animals, selectively breeding them to increase their suitability for human requirements [Mid-17C. < medieval Latin *domesticat-*, past participle of *domesticare* < Latin *domesticus* (see DOMESTIC)] —**do·mes·ti·ca·ble** *adj* —**do·mes·ti·cat·ed** *adj* —**do·mes·ti·ca·tion** /də mèsti káysh'n/ *n* —**do·mes·ti·ca·tor** *n*

do·mes·tic court *n* a court with jurisdiction over the area in which the residence or domicile of a party to a case is situated

do·mes·tic·i·ty /dō me stíssətee/ *n* **1. HOME LIFE** life as it is lived at home **2. FONDNESS FOR HOME LIFE** a liking for or familiarity with home life ■ **do·mes·tic·i·ties** *npl* **HOUSEHOLD MATTERS** the concerns of the home and family

do·mes·tic part·ner *n* a sexual partner living in the same house with somebody

do·mes·tic prel·ate *n* a Roman Catholic priest with honorary membership in the papal household

do·mes·tic vi·o·lence *n* physical violence between members of a family, especially between spouses or partners

do·mette /dō mét/ *n* a soft fleecy wool and acrylic fabric. Use: lightweight interlining. [Early 19C. Origin ?]

do·mi·cal /dṓmik'l, dómm-/ *adj* **1.** shaped like a dome **2.** having a dome or domes

dom·i·cile /dómmi sīl, dómmiss'l/ *n* **1. SOMEBODY'S HOME** the house, apartment, or other place where somebody lives (*formal*) **2.** LAW **SOMEBODY'S PLACE OF RESIDENCE** somebody's true, fixed, and legally recognized place of residence, especially in cases of prolonged absence that require them to prove a continuing and significant connection with the place ■ *vt* (**-ciled, -cil·ing, -ciles**) **GIVE SOMEBODY HOME** to establish somebody in or provide somebody with a place of residence (*formal*) ○ *The authorities domiciled the family in a nearby town.* [15C. Directly or via French < Latin *domicilium* < *domus* "house"]

dom·i·ciled /dómmi sīld, dómmiss'ld/ *adj* resident in a particular place (*formal*)

dom·i·cil·i·ar·y /dòmmə síllee èrree/ *adj* **1.** relating to a home or homes **2.** provided for or attending to people in their own homes [Late 19C. Via French *domiciliaire* < medieval Latin *domiciliarius* < Latin *domicilium* (see DOMICILE)]

dom·i·cil·i·ate /dòmmə síllee àyt/ (**-at·ed, -at·ing, -ates**) *vt* same as **domicile** (*formal*) [Late 18C. < Latin *domicilium* (see DOMICILE)]

dom·i·nance /dómmənənss/ *n* **1. POWER EXERTED OVER OTHERS** control or command wielded over others **2. FIRST IMPORTANCE** prime importance, effectiveness, or prominence **3.** GENETICS **EXPRESSION OF GENETIC FEATURE** the property of a gene that causes a parental characteristic it controls to occur in any offspring **4.** ECOL **PREPONDERANCE OF ONE SPECIES** the preponderance of a single plant or animal species in a specific community or over a specific period

dom·i·nance hi·er·ar·chy *n* BIOL same as **hierarchy** (sense 3)

dom·i·nant /dómmənənt/ *adj* **1. IN CONTROL** in control or command over others **2. MORE IMPORTANT** more important, effective, or prominent than others **3.** GENETICS **EXPRESSING SAME CHARACTERISTIC IN OFFSPRING** describes a gene that causes a parental characteristic it controls to occur in any offspring, or describes the characteristic itself **4.** ECOL **PREPONDERANT IN COMMUNITY OR PERIOD** relating to a single plant or animal species that is preponderant within a specific community or over a specific period **5.** MUSIC **RELATING TO 5TH NOTE OF SCALE** relating to the fifth note of a musical scale or the harmony based around that note ■ *n* MUSIC **1. 5TH NOTE OF SCALE** the fifth note of a musical scale **2. CHORD BASED ON 5TH NOTE** a chord or key based on the fifth note of a musical scale [15C. Via French < Latin *dominant-*, present participle of *dominari* (see DOMINATE)] —**dom·i·nant·ly** *adv*

dom·i·nant es·tate *n* property that gives its owner some rights over other property such as the right to cross land belonging to somebody else in order to reach your own house

dom·i·nant hem·i·sphere *n* the half of the brain that tends to exercise greater control over functions such as language or movement of the left or right side of the body

dom·i·nant sev·enth chord *n* a chord containing, in its most common form, the dominant as root and the major third, perfect fifth, and minor seventh above the root. It often resolves to a chord on the tonic.

dom·i·nant ten·e·ment *n UK* same as **dominant estate**

dom·i·nate /dómmə nàyt/ (**-nat·ed, -nat·ing, -nates**) *vti* **1. CONTROL** to have control, power, or authority over somebody or something **2. BE PROMINENT** to be the most important aspect or element of something

3. BE INFLUENTIAL to have a prevailing influence on somebody or something **4.** TOWER ABOVE AREA to overlook an area from a prominent and usually elevated position [Early 17C. < Latin *dominat-*, past participle of *dominari* "be lord, rule" < *dominus* "lord"] —**dom·i·na·tive** *adj* —**dom·i·na·tor** *n*

dom·i·na·tion /dòmmə náysh'n/ *n* **1.** control, power, or authority over others or another **2.** an angel of the sixth of the nine orders of angels in the traditional Christian hierarchy [14C. Via French < Latin *domination-* < *dominari* (see DOMINATE)]

dom·i·na·trix /dómmə náytriks/ (*plural* **-tri·ces** /-trə sée̲z, -nə trí̄-/) *n* a dominant woman partner in a sadomasochistic relationship [Mid-16C. < Latin, "woman ruler" < *dominari* (see DOMINATE)]

dom·i·neer /dòmmə néer, dómmə néer/ (**-neered, -neer·ing, -neers**) *vti* to rule over others tyrannically, or behave in an overbearing way [Late 16C. Via Dutch *domineren* < Latin *dominari* (see DOMINATE)]

dom·i·neer·ing /dòmmə néering, dómmə néering/ *adj* showing a desire or tendency to exercise excessive control or authority over others —**dom·i·neer·ing·ly** *adv*

~~**dominent**~~ incorrect spelling of **dominant**

Do·min·go /də míng gō/, **Plácido** (*b.* 1941) Spanish-born opera singer. He is regarded by many people as the greatest tenor voice of his time. Starting in 1990, he often appeared with José Carreras and Luciano Pavarotti as one of the "Three Tenors."

Dom·i·nic /dómminik/, **St.** (1170?–1221) Spanish priest and theologian. The founder of the Dominican order, he established priories in France, Italy, and Spain where special emphasis was placed on education. He was canonized in 1234. Born **de Guzman, Domingo**

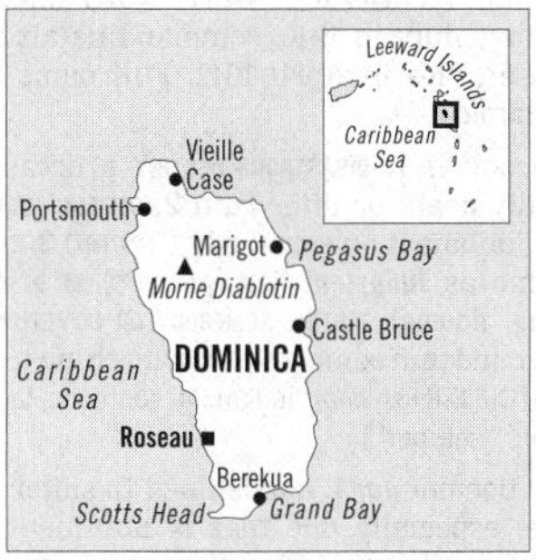

Dominica

Dom·i·ni·ca /dòmmə née̲kə, də mínnikə/ island country in the Windward Islands, in the eastern Caribbean Sea. It became an independent member of the British Commonwealth in 1978. Language: English. Currency: Eastern Caribbean dollar. Capital: Roseau. Population: 69,655 (2003). Area: 290 sq. mi./751 sq. km. Length: 29 mi./47 km. Official name **Commonwealth of Dominica**

do·min·i·cal /də mínnik'l/ *adj* (*formal*) **1.** relating to Jesus Christ as the Lord **2.** in Christianity, relating to Sunday as the day of the Lord [15C. Directly or via French < late Latin *dominicalis* < Latin *dominus* "lord"]

Do·min·i·can[1] /də mínnikən, dòmmə née̲kən/ *n* **1.** somebody who comes from the Dominican Republic **2.** somebody who comes from Dominica [Early 19C. In sense 1 < Spanish *Dominicana*, after *Santo Domingo*, early settlement and later capital of the Dominican Republic; in sense 2 < DOMINICA] —**Do·min·i·can** *adj*

Do·min·i·can[2] /də mínnikən/ *n* a member of the order of friars founded by St. Dominic in 1215. ■ *adj* relating or belonging to St. Dominic or his order of friars. [Late 16C. < medieval Latin *Dominicanus*, after St. DOMINIC]

Dom·i·ni·can Re·pub·lic /də mìnnikən-/ independent country on Hispaniola Island, off the coast of Puerto Rico in the Caribbean Sea. It was proclaimed a republic in 1844. Language: Spanish. Currency: Dominican peso. Capital: Santo Domingo. Population: 8,715,602 (2003). Area: 18,816 sq. mi./48,734 sq. km. Length: 235 mi./380 km.

do·min·ion /də mínnyən/ *n* **1.** RULING CONTROL ruling power, authority, or control **2.** SPHERE OF INFLUENCE

Dominican Republic

somebody's area of influence or control **3.** LAND RULED the land governed by a ruler (*often used in the plural*) ○ *the monarch's dominions beyond the sea* **4.** *also* **Do·min·ion** SELF-GOVERNING TERRITORY a self-governing part of the British Commonwealth or, formerly, the British Empire [15C. Via French < medieval Latin *dominion-* < Latin *dominium* "property, right of ownership" < *dominus* "lord"]

Do·min·ion Day *n* CALENDAR former name for **Canada Day**

dom·i·no /dómmə nō/ (*plural* **-noes**) *n* **1.** SMALL TILE USED IN GAME any one of a set of small oblong blocks with its face divided into two sections, each section either blank or marked with a number of dots, used in playing a game **2.** HOODED CLOAK AND MASK formerly, a hooded cloak and eye mask worn as a disguise at a party (**masquerade**), the cloak or mask alone, or the wearer of any of these **3.** COUNTRY AFFECTED BY DOMINO THEORY a country thought likely to be affected by political events in another country, particularly by the spread of Communism [Late 17C. < French, "priest's winter hood, masked cloak worn at masquerades"]

dom·i·no ef·fect *n* an inevitable succession of related and usually undesirable events, each caused by the preceding one [Because dominoes set up in a row fall in sequence once the first has fallen]

dom·i·noes /dómmə nōz/ *n* a game played using dominoes (*takes a singular verb*)

dom·i·no the·o·ry *n* a theory that political events are interrelated and that one can trigger off a chain of others. The theory was developed by US President Dwight D. Eisenhower to warn of the spread of Communism in Southeast Asia.

Do·mi·tian /də míshən/ (A.D. 51–96) Roman emperor (81–96). Although he was popular with the army and consolidated the boundaries of the Roman empire, his rule was punctuated by clashes with the senate and the aristocracy. His murder, thought to have been instigated by his wife, ended the Flavian dynasty. Full name **Titus Flavius Domitianus**

don[1] /don/ *n* **1.** LEADER OF ORGANIZED CRIME FAMILY a head of an organized crime family, especially in the Mafia **2.** *UK* UNIVERSITY OR COLLEGE TEACHER a university or college teacher, especially one at the universities of Oxford or Cambridge in England **3.** SPANISH MAN OF RANK a Spanish gentleman or aristocrat ○ *California in the days of the dons* [Late 16C. Via Spanish < Latin *dominus* "lord"]

don[2] /don/ (**donned, don·ning, dons**) *vt* to put on a garment [14C. Contraction of *do on* "put on"]

Don[1] /don/, **don** *n* a title used before a man's first name in Spain and other Spanish-speaking countries [Early 16C. < Spanish (see DON[1])]

Don[2] /don/ river rising southeast of Moscow, Russia, flowing through Volgograd and into the Sea of Azov. Length: 1,160 mi./1,870 km.

Do·na /dṓnə/ *n* a title used before a married woman's first name in Portugal and other Portuguese-speaking countries [Early 17C. Via Portuguese < Latin *domina* "lady"]

Do·ña /dṓnyə/ *n* a title used before a married woman's first name in Spain and other Spanish-speaking countries [Early 17C. Via Spanish < Latin *domina* "lady"]

do·nate /dṓ nàyt, dō náyt/ (**-nat·ed, -nat·ing, -nates**) *v* **1.** *vti* GIVE OR PRESENT SOMETHING to a contribution to a charitable organization or other good cause **2.** *vt* GIVE BODY PART to give your own blood, tissue, organs, or reproductive material to be used in the treatment of another person, either while you are alive or after your death **3.** *vt* CHEM TRANSFER ELECTRONS to transfer electrons to another atom or molecule in a chemical reaction [Late 18C. Back-formation < DONATION]

SYNONYMS See ***give***.

Don·a·tel·lo /dònnə téllō/ (1386?–1466) Italian sculptor. In his bronze statue *David* (1430–35) and other works, he revived the classical art of portraying independent functional human figures. Full name **Donato di Niccolò di Betto Bardi**

do·na·tion /dō náysh'n/ *n* **1.** a gift or contribution, especially a sum of money given to a charity ○ *All donations will be gratefully accepted.* **2.** the act of giving something, especially money to a charity [15C. Via French < Latin *donation-* < Latin *donare* "give" < *donum* "gift"]

Don·a·tist /dṓnətist, dónn-/ *n* a member of a Christian group of the 4th and 5th centuries, originating in North Africa, that placed great emphasis on sanctity [Late 16C. < late Latin *Donatista*, after *Donatus*, regarded by Donatists as the first bishop of Carthage] —**Don·a·tism** *n*

don·a·tive /dṓnətiv, dónn-/ *n* **1.** OFFICIAL DONATION a donation, especially a formal or official one (*formal*) **2.** CHR CHURCH POSITION GIVEN AS GIFT a church office (**benefice**) that is or can be presented as a gift without reference to the bishop, as opposed to one received as a right ■ *adj* MADE AS GIFT given or presented as a gift (*formal*) [15C. < Latin *donativum* < *donare* "give" (see DONATION)]

do·na·tor /dṓ nàytər/ *n* a donor of something, especially money to a charity [15C. Directly or via French < Latin < *donare* "give" (see DONATION)]

Don·cas·ter /dóngkəstər/ city on the Don River in South Yorkshire, northern England. Population: 286,866 (2001).

done /dun/ past participle of **do**[1] ■ *adj* **1.** CONCLUDED completed or finished **2.** COOKED THROUGH cooked as thoroughly as required ○ *I like my steak well done.* **3.** SOCIALLY ACCEPTABLE acceptable according to the established rules and expectations of a society ○ *It's just not done.* **4.** EXHAUSTED worn out or used up (*informal*) **5.** PREORDAINED having been decided already, therefore permitting no changes (*slang*) ○ *It's a done deal, and you can't fight it.* ■ *interj* AGREED used to confirm acceptance of a deal ■ *v Southern US, Carib* ALREADY used as an auxiliary verb to express the sense of "already" (*nonstandard*) ○ *He done leave.* ■ *adv Southern US, Carib* TRULY OR INDEED used for emphasis ○ *He's done dead.* ◇ **have done with something** *UK* to be finished with something and never return to it ○ *Why don't we just sell the house and have done with it?* ◇ **well done** used to express praise or approval of something somebody has done

REGIONAL NOTE The emphatic perfective *I done told you* extends to the adverbial usage *He's done dead* in folk speech across the Southern states and into the Caribbean.

do·nee /dō née/ *n* the recipient of a gift [Early 16C. < DONOR]

done for *adj* (*informal*) **1.** NEAR DEATH close to the point of dying **2.** EXHAUSTED extremely tired **3.** ABOUT TO BE RUINED facing defeat, ruin, or destruction

Don·e·gal /dónnə gàwl/ county in northwestern Ireland. The Atlantic Ocean lies to the west, Northern Ireland to the east. Population: 129,994 (2002). Area: 1,865 sq. mi./4,830 sq. km. Irish name **Dœn Na nGall**

Don·e·gal tweed *n* a rough tweed characterized by white flecks

done·ness /dún nəss/ *n* the state of being fully cooked or ready to serve

don·er ke·bab /dònnər-/, **don·ner ke·bab** *n UK* same as **gyro** [< Turkish *döner kebap* "rotating kebab"]

Do·nets /də néts, -nyéts/ river in Russia and Ukraine that flows into the Don River northeast of Rostov in southwestern Russia. Length: 631 mi./1,020 km.

Do·nets Ba·sin major coalfield and industrial region in southeastern Ukraine. The basin extends across the Russian border into the Rostov region.

Do·nets'k /də nyétsk/ industrial city in southeastern Ukraine. Population: 1,065,000 (1998).

dong[1] /dawng/ *n* a deep ringing sound ■ *vi* (**donged, dong·ing, dongs**) to make a deep ringing sound [Late 16C. An imitation of the sound]

dong[2] /dawng/ *n* a highly offensive term for a penis (*taboo slang*) [Mid-20C. Origin ?]

dong[3] /dawng/ *n* the main unit of Vietnamese currency. See table at **currency** [Early 19C. < Vietnamese]

Don·gen /dóngən/, **Kees van** (1877–1968) Dutch painter. The bright colors and freedom of form of his early Fauvist paintings gave way to more muted tones in his later paintings, e.g., *Aux acacias* (1916–29). Full name **Dongen, Cornelis Theodorus Marie van**

don·gle /dóng g'l, dáwng-/ *n* a small hardware device that, when plugged into a computer, enables a specific copy-protected program to run, the program being disabled on that computer if the device is not present. The device is effective against software piracy. [Late 20C. Probably arbitrary]

dong quai /dŏong kwī/ *n* **1.** an herb used in traditional Chinese medicine as a treatment for menstrual irregularities **2.** a plant of the celery family whose root is used for dong quai. Native to: China. Latin name: *Angelica sinensis*. [< Chinese]

Dong Yu·an /dŏong yoo aán/ (*fl* late 10th century) Chinese artist. He is noted for his monumental, richly colored landscapes.

Dö·nitz /dṓnits/, **Doe·nitz, Karl** (1891–1980) German naval officer. He was commander of the German submarine fleet (1936–43), naval commander in chief (1943–45), and chancellor of Germany (April-May 1945) after Adolf Hitler's suicide.

Don·i·zet·ti /dònni zéttee/, **Gaetano** (1797–1848) Italian composer. He wrote 65 operas, ranging from dramas such as *Lucia di Lammermoor* (1835) to comic works such as *Don Pasquale* (1843).

don·jon /dónjən, dún-/ *n* a fortified central tower in a medieval castle [14C. Form of DUNGEON]

Don Juan /dòn waán, -hwaán/ *n* a man who has a reputation for having casual sexual relationships with numerous women [Mid-19C. After *Don Juan* Tenorio, legendary Spanish nobleman]

donkey

don·key /dóngkee, dáwng-/ (*plural* **-keys**) *n* **1.** a small domesticated member of the horse family with a gray or brown coat, long ears, and a large head. Latin name: *Equus asinus*. **2.** somebody thought of as lacking intelligence (*informal insult*) [Late 18C. Origin ?] ◇ **donkey's years** a very long time (*dated*) ○ *I haven't seen Jack in donkey's years.* ◇ **talk the hind legs off a donkey** to chatter interminably (*slang*)

don·key en·gine *n* a small auxiliary steam engine used either to start a larger engine or independently, e.g., for pumping water on a ship

don·key's tail *n* PLANTS same as **burro's tail**

don·key·work /dóngkee wùrk, dáwngkee-/ *n* hard or boring work (*slang*)

Don·leav·y /don léevee/, **J. P.** (*b.* 1926) US-born Irish novelist, short-story writer, and playwright. His first novel, *The Ginger Man* (1955), was hailed as a comic masterpiece. Among his other novels are *A Singular Man* (1963) and *The Beastly Beatitudes of Balthazar B* (1968). Full name **Donleavy, James Patrick**

> "To more than a few, Ireland remains a glowingly sweet emerald vision having the fifteenth beer over some bereft bar counter at three a.m., in some outskirt corner of San Francisco, Hawaii, Boston, or the Bronx."
> [J. P. Donleavy, *J. P. Donleavy's Ireland*; 1986]

Don·na /dónnə/ *n* a title used before a married woman's name in Italy [Early 17C. Via Italian < Latin *domina* "lady"]

Donne /dun/, **John** (1572–1631) English poet, prose writer, and cleric, considered the greatest of the Metaphysical poets. An author of passionate love poetry, he was later ordained and appointed Dean of St. Paul's (1621). His verse includes the love poems *Songs and Sonnets*, two *Satires* (both dating from the 1590s), and *Divine Poems* (1607).

> "No man is an Island, entire of itself; every man is a piece of the Continent, a part of the main; if a clod be washed away by the sea, Europe is the less, as well as if a promontory were, as well as if a manor of thy friends or of thine own were; any man's death diminishes me, because I am involved in Mankind; And therefore never send to know for whom the bell tolls; It tolls for thee."
> [John Donne, "Meditation XVII," *Devotions upon Emergent Occasions*; 1624]

don·née /daw náy/ *n* **1.** a basic fact or assumption on which something else such as a literary or theatrical work is based and from which it develops **2.** a theme or subject, e.g., of a literary or theatrical work [Late 19C. < French, form of *donner* "give"]

Don·ner Pass /dònnər-/ pass in the Sierra Nevada, northeastern California, near Lake Tahoe. It is named for the Donner Party, a group of migrants from Illinois who are believed to have resorted to cannibalism when they were snowed in on their way to California over the winter of 1846–47.

don·nish /dónnish/ *adj UK* resembling the stereotypical image of a university professor, e.g., in displaying erudition or being absent-minded

don·ny·brook /dónni brŏŏk/ *n* a riotous brawl [Mid-19C. After *Donnybrook*, suburb of Dublin, Ireland]

do·nor /dṓnər/ *n* **1.** SOMEBODY WHO GIVES SOMETHING somebody who gives something, especially money **2.** SOMEBODY GIVING BLOOD OR BODY ORGAN somebody who voluntarily gives blood, a body organ or tissue, or reproductive material for the medical treatment of somebody else **3.** ELECTRONICS IMPURITY ADDED TO SEMICONDUCTOR an impurity (**dopant**) such as arsenic or antimony that is added to a pure semiconductor material such as silicon in order to increase its conductivity by increasing the number of carriers of negative electrical charge (**free electrons**) **4.** CHEM ATOM PROVIDING ELECTRONS FOR BOND an atom, molecule, or group that provides the pair of electrons necessary to form a chemical bond [15C. Via Anglo-Norman, Old French < Latin *donator* < *donare* "give" (see DONATION)] —**do·nor·ship** *n*

do·nor card *n* a card stating that specific organs, or sometimes the entire body, of the person carrying it may be used for the treatment of others after the donor's death

do·nor in·sem·i·na·tion *n* the introduction into a woman's vagina of sperm from a man who is not the woman's sexual partner with the intention of making the woman pregnant

do-noth·ing *adj* not inclined to engage in productive activities or to change ○ *a do-nothing committee* ■ *n* somebody who is regarded as lazy or idle (*informal insult*) —**do-noth·ing·ism** *n*

Don Qui·xo·te /dòn kee hṓtee, -kwíksət/ *n* an impractical idealist who champions hopeless causes [Mid-17C. After the hero of the satirical romance *Don Quixote de la Mancha* (1605, 1615) by Cervantes]

don't /dōnt/ *contr* do not ■ *n* something that should not be done

don't-care con·di·tion *n* a state or part of an electronic circuit that has no influence on the circuit's output

don't know *n* a voter or respondent who is undecided about an issue, e.g., during an election campaign or in an opinion survey (*slang*)

do·nut /dṓ nùt/ *n* FOOD another spelling of **doughnut**

doo·dad /dóo dàd/ *n* (*informal*) **1.** a thing whose name you cannot remember or do not know **2.** a decoration incidentally added to clothing or some other product [Early 20C. Origin ?]

doo·dah /dóo daà/ *n UK* same as **doodad** (sense 1) (*informal*) [Early 20C. Probably < *dooda(h)* in the refrain to the song *Camptown Races*]

doo·dle /dóod'l/ (**-dled, -dling, -dles**) *vti* to draw something aimlessly or absent-mindedly, usually while doing something else such as having a telephone conversation or attending a meeting [Early 17C. < Low German *dudel-* in *dudeltopf* "fool"] —**doo·dle** *n* —**doo·dler** *n*

doo·dle·bug /dóod'l bùg/ *n* **1.** the large-jawed larva of an ant lion or a similar insect larva **2.** a device to help locate minerals

doo-doo /dóo dòo/ *n* **1.** human or animal excrement (*slang humorous*) **2.** *Carib* another spelling of **dou-dou** [Mid-20C. Probably < repetition of DO[1]]

doof·er /dóofər/ *n* an object or gadget whose name you cannot remember or do not know (*slang*) [Mid-20C. Probably < *do for*]

doo·fus /dóofəss/ *n* somebody regarded as unintelligent or thoughtless (*slang insult*) [Late 20C. Origin ?]

doo·hick·ey /dóo hìkee/ (*plural* **-eys**) *n* an object or gadget whose name you cannot remember or do not know (*informal*) [Early 20C. Blend of DOODAD + HICKEY]

Doo·lit·tle /dóo lìtt'l/, **Hilda** (1886–1961) US poet. Known for her imagist poetry, she wrote *Sea Garden* (1916) and *Bid Me to Live* (1960). Pseudonym **H. D., Imagiste**

Doo·lit·tle, James H. (1896–1993) US aviator. He set many flight records after World War I and returned to military duty in 1940, commanding air raids on Japanese cities in April 1942. Full name **Doolittle, James Harold**

doom /doom/ *n* **1.** DISASTROUS DESTINY a dreadful fate, especially death or utter ruin **2.** OFFICIAL JUDGMENT an official judgment on somebody (*formal*) **3.** *also* **Doom** CHR same as **Judgment Day** (*archaic*) ■ *vt* (**doomed, doom·ing, dooms**) DESTINE SOMEBODY OR SOMETHING TO DISASTER to condemn somebody or something to a dreadful fate [Old English *dōm* "judgment, sentence, law" < Indo-European, "set, put"]

doomed /doomd/ *adj* **1.** condemned to suffer a dreadful fate, especially one that is imminent and inescapable ○ *From that time, the creature was doomed to extinction.* **2.** bound to fail or suffer something unpleasant ○ *The partnership was doomed from the start.*

doom palm *n* TREES same as **doum**

doom·say·er /dóom sày ər/ *n* somebody who frequently predicts disasters

dooms·day /dóomz dày/ *n* **1.** *also* **Dooms·day** a day of final reckoning, especially, in Christian theology, the day of the Last Judgment **2.** the final destruction or dissolution of the world

Dooms·day Book *n* HIST another spelling of **Domesday Book**

door /dawr/ *n* **1.** MOVABLE PANEL AT ENTRANCE a movable barrier used to open and close the entrance to a building, room, closet, or vehicle, usually a solid panel, hinged to or sliding in a frame **2.** GAP FORMING ENTRANCE the gap that forms the entrance to a building or room **3.** BUILDING OR ROOM a building or room considered in relation to those on either side ○ *She lives two doors down the street.* [Old English *duru* "door," *dor* "gate" < Indo-European, "entrance to the enclosure around a house"] —**door·less** *adj* ◇ **close** *or* **shut the door on something** to disallow the possibility of something happening ◇ **Katie bar the door** *regional* used as a warning that you should brace yourself for impending calamity ◇ **lay something at somebody's door** to blame something on somebody ◇ **out of doors** in the open air ◇ **show somebody the door** to tell somebody to leave

door·bell /dáwr bèl/ *n* a bell placed on or beside a door, to be rung by visitors as a sign of their arrival

door bun·dle *n* a bundle of equipment pushed out of an aircraft by hand before parachutists exit

do-or-die *adj* involving the determination to risk everything in an effort to succeed

door·frame /dáwr fràym/ *n* the frame constructed around the entrance to a building or room and into which a door is set

door·jamb /dáwr jàm/ *n* either of the vertical side pieces of a doorframe

door·keep·er /dáwr keèpər/ *n* **1.** somebody on duty at a door or gate, especially somebody who guards the entrance **2.** *also* **Door·keep·er** an officer of a legislature whose job it is to control access to the floor and the visitors' galleries

door·knob /dáwr nòb/ *n* a round handle used to open or close a door

door·knock·er /dáwr nòkər/ *n* a metal fixture attached with hinges to the door of a house, used for knocking on the door

door·man /dáwr màn, -mən/ (*plural* **-men** /-mèn, -mən/) *n* a man on duty at the door of a building such as a nightclub, hotel, or apartment building, usually employed to assist customers, e.g., by calling cabs

door·mat /dáwr màt/ *n* **1.** a mat to wipe your shoes on immediately before or after entering a building **2.** a passive person who submits to being treated inconsiderately (*informal*)

~~**doormouse**~~ incorrect spelling of **dormouse**

door·nail /dáwr nàyl/ *n* a nail with a large head formerly used to decorate or reinforce a door

door o·pen·er *n* a gift or other favor to somebody in power that brings the giver an opportunity for success (*informal*)

door·per·son /dáwr pùrss'n/ (*plural* **-per·sons** or **-peo·ple** /-peèp'l/) *n* somebody on duty at the door of a building such as a nightclub, hotel, or apartment building, usually employed to assist customers, e.g., by calling cabs

door·plate /dáwr plàyt/ *n* a plate or plaque attached to the door of a building or room, usually giving information about the person associated with the building or room

door·post /dáwr pòst/ *n* CONSTR same as **doorjamb**

door prize *n* a prize awarded to a person who, upon entry to an event, receives a ticket that subsequently wins a draw in a lottery

door·sill /dáwr sìl/ *n* same as **threshold** (sense 3)

door·step /dáwr stèp/ *n* a step at the entrance to a building ◇ **on your (own) doorstep** very near where you live

door·stop /dáwr stòp/ *n* **1.** a movable device, e.g., a wedge or heavy object, used to hold a door open **2.** a rubber stud or rubber-tipped projection on a wall, floor, or door that prevents damage to the wall when the door is opened

door to door *adv* **1.** going from one house to the next, usually in order to sell things, to collect money for charity, or to solicit support in an election **2.** from the place of departure to the place of arrival ○ *The trip took three hours door to door.*

door-to-door *adj* **1.** done or going from one house to the next (*not hyphenated when used after a verb*) **2.** from the point of departure to the point of arrival (*not hyphenated after a verb*)

door·way /dáwr wày/ *n* **1.** an entrance to a building or room, especially one that has a door **2.** a means of achieving or escaping from something

door·wo·man /dáwr wòommən/ (*plural* **-wo·men** /-wìmmin/) *n* a woman on duty at the door of a building such as a nightclub, hotel, or apartment building, usually employed to assist customers, e.g., by calling cabs

doo-wop /doò wòp/ *n* harmonized singing of nonsense syllables, with a rhythm-and-blues melody on top, popularized by street singers in the 1950s [Mid-20C. An imitation of the sound]

doo·zy /doòzee/ (*plural* **-zies**) *n* a remarkable or excellent thing (*slang*) [Early 20C. Origin ?]

do·pa /dṓpə/ *n* a natural precursor of epinephrine and dopamine. Use: in synthetic form, treatment of Parkinson's disease. [Early 20C. Acronym < DI-[1] + OXY- + PHENYL + ALANINE]

do·pa·mine /dṓpə meèn/ *n* a neurotransmitter that is also a precursor of epinephrine [Mid-20C. Blend of DOPA + AMINE]

dop·ant /dṓpənt/ *n* a substance such as arsenic or antimony that is added in small quantities to a semiconductor material in order to change its electrical characteristics. Dopants are added during the manufacture of semiconducting diodes and transistors.

dope /dōp/ *n* **1.** ILLEGAL DRUG an illegal drug, especially marijuana (*slang*) **2.** DRUG AFFECTING PERFORMANCE a drug given illegally, e.g., to racehorses or athletes, to affect performance **3.** INSIDE INFORMATION confidential information about somebody or something (*slang*) **4.** FOOL somebody who is regarded as unintelligent (*informal insult*) **5.** CHEM VISCOUS LIQUID a viscous liquid. Use: lubrication, waterproofing and strengthening fabrics, coating aircraft wings, improving the combustion of engine fuels. **6.** CHEM ABSORBENT MATERIAL an absorbent material. Use: manufacture of dynamite. **7.** ELECTRONICS same as **dopant** ■ *vt* (**doped, dop·ing, dopes**) **1.** ADD DRUG TO FOOD OR DRINK to add a drug to food or drink secretly in order to affect performance or consciousness **2.** ELECTRONICS ADD IMPURITY TO SEMICONDUCTOR to add a substance such as arsenic or antimony to a semiconductor material like silicon or germanium during the manufacturing process in order to increase its conductivity ■ *adj* EXTREME SPORTS COOL in snowboarding, cool, hip, or generally good or stylish (*slang*) [Early 19C. < Dutch *doop* "thick dipping sauce" < *doopen* "dip, mix"] —**dop·er** *n*
dope out *vt* to solve a puzzling problem by analyzing or reasoning it out (*slang*)
dope up *vt* to make somebody drowsy or semiconscious by administering a drug such as an anesthetic or an illegal narcotic (*slang*)

dope dog *n* a dog specially trained to locate by scent contraband narcotics hidden in luggage or packages or concealed on a person's body (*informal*)

dope·head /dṓp hèd/ *n* somebody who takes illegal drugs regularly or who is physiologically or mentally dependent on them (*slang*)

dope sheet *n* a booklet that gives information about the horses entered for races (*slang*)

dope·ster /dṓpstər/ *n* somebody who is able to supply information and analysis about current events and forecasts for the future, especially in the fields of sports and politics (*informal*)

dop·ey /dṓpee/ (**-i·er, -i·est**), **dop·y** *adj* **1.** half-asleep or drowsy **2.** showing a lack of good sense or intelligence (*informal insult*) —**dop·i·ly** *adv* —**dop·i·ness** *n*

dop·ing a·gent /dṓping-/ *n* ELECTRONICS same as **dopant**

dop·pel·gäng·er /dópp'l gàngər/, **dop·pel·gang·er** *n* **1.** somebody who closely resembles somebody else **2.** an apparition in the form of a double of a living person [Mid-19C. < German, literally "double-goer"]

Dop·pler ef·fect /dópplər-/, **Dop·pler shift** *n* a perceived change in the frequency of a wave as the distance between the source and the observer changes. For example, the sound of a siren on a moving vehicle appears to change as it approaches and passes an observer. [Early 20C. After Christian J. *Doppler* (1803–53), Austrian physicist]

Dop·pler ra·dar *n* a means of detecting a moving target that uses electromagnetic radiation and relies on a change in the frequency of microwave signals reflected from the target [Mid-20C. < its use of the DOPPLER EFFECT]

Dop·pler shift *n* PHYS same as **Doppler effect**

dop·y *adj* another spelling of **dopey**

dor /dawr/ *n* a European dung beetle that makes a droning sound as it flies. Latin name: *Geotrupes stercorarius.* [Old English *dora* "bumblebee," origin ?]

do·ra·do /də raádō/ (*plural* **-dos** or *same*) *n* **1.** FISH same as **dolphin** (sense 2) **2.** a fish resembling a salmon. Native to: South America. Genus: *Salminus.* [Early 17C. Via Spanish, literally "gilded" < late Latin *deauratus*, past participle of *deaurare* (see DORY[2])]

Do·ra·do *n* an inconspicuous constellation of the southern hemisphere containing part of the Large Magellanic Cloud. See illustration at **constellation**

Do·rá·ti /daw raátee/, **Antal** (1906–88) Hungarian-born US conductor and composer. He championed Hungarian music and conducted many of the world's major orchestras.

> "When I was 25, Bartók needed me, a young man who would get up on the podium, play his music and be whistled at for it."
> [Antal Doráti, *Remark*; April 1986]

dor·bee·tle /dáwr beèt'l/ *n* INSECTS same as **dor**

Dor·dogne /dawr dáwnyə/ river in southwestern France. It rises in the Massif Central and flows generally westward to join the Garonne north of Bordeaux. Length: 300 mi./483 km.

Dor·drecht /dáwr drèkt, -drèkht/ city and port in Zuid-Holland Province, southwestern Netherlands. Population: 119,811 (2000).

Do·ré /daw ráy/, **Gustave** (1833–83) French illustrator, painter, and sculptor. He is best known for his vivid wood engravings, which were used as illustrations for the works of Dante, Edgar Allan Poe, and John Milton, among others. Full name **Doré, Paul Gustave**

Dor·en ➧ **Van Doren, Mark**

Do·ri·an /dáwree ən/ *n* a member of a Greek-speaking people who overthrew the Mycenaean civilization on mainland Greece about 1100 B.C. They subsequently colonized Peloponnesus and other parts of the Mediterranean area. [Mid-16C. < Latin *Dorius* "of Doris" (region of ancient Greece) < Greek *Dōrios* < *Dōris* "Doris"] —**Do·ri·an** *adj*

Do·ri·an mode *n* a scale of notes originating in ancient Greek music and consisting of the eight notes of the diatonic scale rising from D to D

Dor·ic /dáwrik/ *n* **1.** ANCIENT GREEK DIALECT a dialect of ancient Greek spoken mainly in the area of modern Peloponnesus **2.** DIALECT OF SCOTS a rural dialect of Scots spoken in parts of northeastern Scotland ■ *adj* **1.** IN SIMPLE CLASSICAL ARCHITECTURAL STYLE relating to or built in a style of architecture characterized by fluted columns with a rounded molding at the top and no base **2.** OF DORIANS relating to the Dorians of ancient Greece **3.** OF DORIC relating to Doric [Mid-16C. Via Latin, "of Doris" (region of ancient Greece) < Greek *Dōrikos* < *Dōris* "Doris"]

Dor·ic or·der *n* the first of the five classical orders of architecture, characterized by fluted columns with a rounded molding at the top and no base. It was developed in Greece in the 7th century B.C.

dork /dawrk/ *n* **1.** an offensive term that deliberately insults somebody's intelligence, physical appearance or social skills (*slang insult*) **2.** an offensive term for a penis (*slang*) [Mid-20C. Origin ?]

Dor·king /dáwrking/ *n* a heavy domestic fowl belonging to a breed originating in England. Raised for: food. [Late 18C. After *Dorking*, town in S England]

dork·y /dáwrkee/ (**-i·er, -i·est**) *adj* regarded as being unintelligent, physically unattractive, or useless (*slang insult*)

dorm /dawrm/ *n* EDUC, TRAVEL same as **dormitory** (*informal*) [Early 20C. Shortening]

dor·mant /dáwrmənt/ *adj* **1.** NOT ACTIVELY GROWING in an inactive state, when growth and development slow or cease, in order to survive adverse environmental conditions **2.** TEMPORARILY INACTIVE temporarily inactive or not in use **3.** NOT ERUPTING describes a volcano that is not erupting, but not extinct **4.** LATENT latent and able to be aroused ○ *dormant feelings of uneasiness* **5.** HERALDRY SLEEPING in a heraldic device, portrayed in a sleeping posture [14C. < French, present participle of *dormir* "sleep" < Latin *dormire*] —**dor·man·cy** *n*

dor·mer /dáwrmər/, **dor·mer win·dow** *n* a window for a room within the roof space that is built out at right angles to the main roof and has its own gable. See illustration on next page [Late 16C. < Old French *dorměor* "sleeping room" < *dormir* (see DORMANT)]

dor·mice ZOOL plural of **dormouse**

dor·mie /dáwrmee/ *adj* in golf, as many holes up on an opponent as there are holes left to play ○ *dormie four* [Mid-19C. Origin ?]

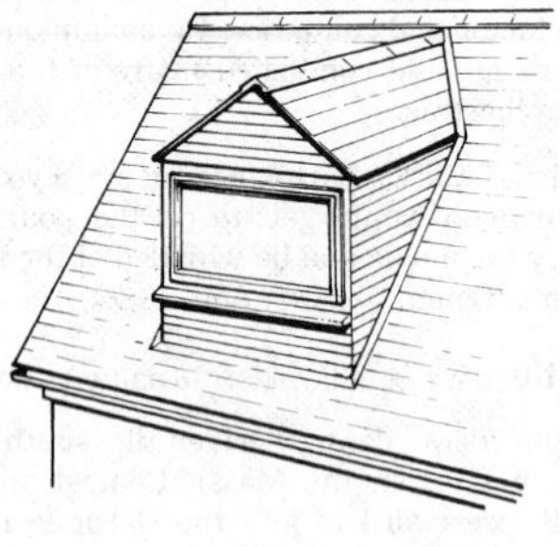

dormer

dor·mi·to·ry /dáwrmi tàwree/ (*plural* **-ries**) *n* **1.** a large room in which many people sleep, e.g., at a boarding school or in a hostel **2.** a building used as living and sleeping quarters by college students [15C. < Latin *dormitorium* < *dormire* "to sleep"]

dor·mi·to·ry town *n UK* same as **bedroom community**

dormouse

dor·mouse /dáwr mòwss/ (*plural* **-mice** /-mīss/) *n* a small nocturnal rodent resembling a mouse with reddish brown fur and a hairy tail. Dormice feed on nuts, berries, and seeds, and hibernate during the winter. Family: Gliridae. [15C. Origin ?]

dor·nick /dáwrnik/ *n regional* a small stone [Mid-19C. Probably < Irish *dornóg*]

dor·sa ANAT plural of **dorsum**

dor·sal /dáwrss'l/ *adj* **1.** relating to or situated on the back of the body **2.** describes the underside of a leaf or other surface that faces away from the stem [15C. Directly or via French < late Latin *dorsalis* < Latin *dorsum* (see DORSUM)] —**dor·sal·ly** *adv*

dor·sal fin *n* a single fin on the back of a fish or other water animal such as a dolphin that gives it stability while swimming

Dor·set /dáwrssət/ county on southern coast of England. Population: 390,980 (2001). Area: 1,025 sq. mi./2,654 sq. km.

dorsi- *prefix* same as **dorso-**

dor·si·flex·ion /dàwrssi flékshən/ *n* the bending back of a hand or foot or of the fingers or toes

dor·si·ven·tral /dàwrssi véntrəl/ *adj* **1.** describes something such as a leaf or a flatworm that is flat, with distinct upper and lower surfaces **2.** ANAT same as **dorsoventral** (sense 1) —**dor·si·ven·tral·i·ty** /-ven trállətee/ *n* —**dor·si·ven·tral·ly** *adv*

dorso- *prefix* back, upper surface ○ *dorsolateral* [< Latin *dorsum*]

dor·so·lat·er·al /dàwrssō láttərəl/ *adj* relating to or involving both the back and the side of the body —**dor·so·lat·er·al·ly** *adv*

dor·so·ven·tral /dàwrssō véntrəl/ *adj* **1.** extending from the back of the body to the front **2.** BIOL same as **dorsiventral** (sense 1)

dor·sum /dáwrssəm/ (*plural* **-sa** /-sə/) *n* the back or upper surface of a part of the body such as the hand or foot (*technical*) [Late 18C. < Latin, "the back"]

Dort·mund /dáwrtmənd, -mo͝ont/ city and inland port in North Rhine-Westphalia State in northwestern Germany. Population: 600,918 (1997).

do·ry[1] /dáwree/ (*plural* **-ries**) *n* **1.** a small boat used for various purposes such as patrolling a harbor or transporting people from a larger vessel to the shore **2.** a narrow flat-bottomed fishing boat with high sides [Early 18C. Origin ?]

do·ry[2] /dáwree/ (*plural* **-ries**) *n* a fish with a deep flat body, spiny fins, and an extendable mouth, found near the ocean bottom. Family: Zeidae. [14C. < French *dorée* < form of *dorer* "gild" < late Latin *deaurare* "gild over" < Latin *aurum* "gold"]

DOS /doss/ *abbr* COMPUT **1.** denial-of-service **2.** disk operating system

do·sa /dṓssə/ (*plural* **-sas** or **-sai** /-sī/) *n* a pancake made with rice and lentil flour that is usually stuffed with spiced vegetables and eaten with chutney, originating in South India [< Tamil *tōcai*]

dos-à-dos /dṑzə dṓ, dṑssə-/ *n* (*plural same*), *interj* DANCE same as **do-si-do** [Mid-19C. < French, "back to back"]

dos·age /dṓssij/ *n* **1.** DOSE OF DRUG the amount and frequency of drug administration ○ *Do not exceed the recommended dosage.* **2.** ADMINISTRATION OR DETERMINATION OF DOSE the administration of a measured amount of a drug, or the determination of the correct amount **3.** ADDING OF EXTRA INGREDIENT the addition of an extra ingredient to something, especially wine

dose /dōss/ *n* **1.** PRESCRIBED AMOUNT OF MEDICATION a measured quantity of medication administered once or at specific intervals **2.** EXPOSURE TO RADIATION the amount of radiation to which somebody or something is exposed during a specific time, either accidentally or as part of an experiment or medical treatment **3.** EXTRA INGREDIENT an additional ingredient such as syrup added to wine to fortify it **4.** VENEREAL DISEASE an infection with a sexually transmitted disease (*slang*) ■ *vt* (**dosed, dos·ing, dos·es**) **1.** GIVE MEDICINE TO SOMEBODY to administer medication to somebody ○ *I've been dosing myself up with flu remedies all week.* **2.** MEASURE OUT MEDICATION to prescribe or administer the required amount of medication **3.** ADD INGREDIENT TO SOMETHING to add an extra ingredient to something [15C. Via French < Greek *dosis* "prescribed portion" < *didonai* "give"] ◇ **in small doses** no more than a little at a time (*informal*) ○ *I can take their music only in small doses.*

dose·me·ter /dṓss meetər/ *n* MEASURE same as **dosimeter**

do-si-do /dṑ see dṓ/ *n* (*plural* **do-si-dos**) a movement in square dancing in which two dancers pass each other and circle back to back ■ *interj* used to instruct dancers to perform a do-si-do [Early 20C. Alteration of DOS-À-DOS] —**do-si-do** *vti*

do·sim·e·ter /dō símmətər/ *n* an instrument for measuring the amount of radiation absorbed by somebody or something, often fixed in a working area or worn by personnel who might be exposed to radiation [Late 19C. < DOSE] —**do·si·met·ric** /dṑssi méttrik/ *adj* —**do·sim·e·trist** *n* —**do·sim·e·try** *n*

Dos Pas·sos /dōss pássōss/, **John** (1896–1970) US writer. He is best known for his *U.S.A.* trilogy (1930–36), a critical portrait of US life. Full name **Dos Passos, John Roderigo**

> "They wrapped me in the stars and stripes
> I never remembered whether they brought
> me home or buried me at sea but anyway
> I was wrapped up in Old Glory."
> [John Dos Passos, *The 42nd Parallel*; 1930]

doss /doss/ *UK vi* (**dossed, doss·ing, doss·es**) to sleep or settle down to sleep, especially on an improvised bed (*slang*) ○ *Can I doss down on your floor tonight?* ■ *n* a bed for the night or a place to sleep, especially a makeshift one or one in a flophouse [Late 18C. Origin ?]

dos·sal /dóss'l/, **dos·sel** *n* a rich hanging for the back of an altar or the sides of a chancel in a church [Mid-17C. < medieval Latin *dossale* < Latin *dorsum* "the back"]

doss·house /dóss hòwss/ *n UK* same as **flophouse** (*informal*)

dos·si·er /dóssee ày/ *n* a collection of documents relating to a person or topic [Late 19C. < French (originally "bunch of papers with a label on the back") < *dos* "the back" < Latin *dorsum*]

dost /dust/ 2nd person singular present of **do**[1] (*archaic*)

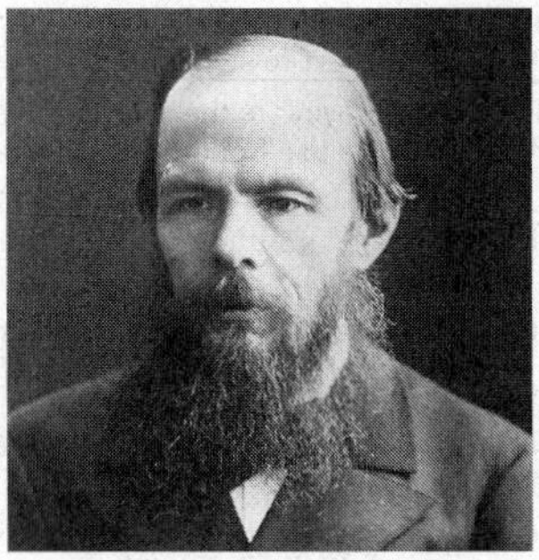

Fyodor Dostoyevsky

Dos·toy·ev·sky /dòstə yéfskee/, **Fyodor** (1821–81) Russian novelist. He is author of *Crime and Punishment* (1866) and *The Brothers Karamazov* (1879–80). Full name **Dostoyevsky, Fyodor Mikhaylovich**

> "If the devil doesn't exist but man has created him, he has created him in his own image and likeness."
> [Fyodor Dostoyevsky, *The Brothers Karamazov*; 1879–80]

dot[1] /dot, dō/ *n* **1.** WRITTEN OR PRINTED POINT a small round written or printed mark that placed above the body of the lowercase letter "i" or one of a set of three replacing missing text **2.** SPOT OR SPECK a small round mark, spot, or speck ○ *The ship was just a dot on the horizon.* **3.** SMALL AMOUNT a very small amount, especially of butter used for basting ○ *a dot of butter* **4.** ONLINE INTERNET PUNCTUATION MARK a punctuation mark used to separate the various components of an Internet address **5.** COMMUNICATION MARK USED IN MORSE CODE the shorter of the two signaling elements used in Morse code, represented as a small round mark **6.** MUSIC SYMBOL PLACED AFTER NOTE IN MUSIC in written or printed music, a small round mark placed after a note or rest to increase its value by half **7.** LOGIC MARK INDICATING LOGICAL CONJUNCTION a small round mark used in logic to join compound sentences when both elements are true ■ *vt* (**dot·ted, dot·ting, dots**) **1.** PUT DOT OVER SOMETHING to mark something with a dot ○ *dot your i's* **2.** SPRINKLE SOMETHING WITH DOTS to scatter or sprinkle something with spots, specks, or small amounts of something ○ *Dot the fish with butter.* [Old English *dott* "head of a boil," probably < Germanic, "lump, plug"] —**dot·ter** *n* ◇ **on the dot (of)** exactly at the specified time ○ *arrived on the dot* ○ *was expected to get here on the dot of nine*

dot[2] /dot/ *n* in law, a woman's dowry [Mid-19C. Via French < Latin *dot-* "dowry"] —**do·tal** /dṓt'l/ *adj*

DOT *abbr* TRANSP, GOV Department of Transportation

dot ad·dress *n* the common notation for Internet addresses in the form A.B.C.D., each letter representing, in decimal notation, one byte of a four-byte address

dot·age /dṓtij/ *n* an offensive term for the lack of strength or concentration sometimes believed to be characteristic of old age [14C. < DOTE]

dot bomb *n* a failed Internet business (*humorous*)

dot-com /dot kóm/, **dot com** *n* a company that does business on the Internet or that provides Internet services [< the domain identification *.com* of company Internet addresses] —**dot-com** *adj*

dot-com·er /dot kómmər/, **dot·com·er** *n* **1.** somebody who works in a dot-com **2.** somebody who does business on the Internet or who consistently buys high-tech stocks

dote /dōt/ (**dot·ed, dot·ing, dotes**) *vi* to be very fond of somebody or something ○ *They dote on their grandchildren.* [12C Origin ?] —**dot·er** *n*

doth /duth/ 3rd person singular present of **do**[1] (*archaic*)

Do·than /dṓthən/ city in southeastern Alabama, southwest of Phenix City. Population: 58,998 (2002 estimate).

dot·ing /dṓting/ *adj* demonstrating great love and fondness for somebody or something ○ *doting parents of two new babies* —**dot·ing·ly** *adv*

dot ma·trix *n* a grid of dots selectively lit or colored to display or print letters, numbers, and other symbols

dot pitch *n* a measure of the clarity of a computer image, based on the amount of white space between the pixels or dots forming the image. The smaller the dot pitch, the greater the clarity.

dot prod·uct *n* MATH same as **scalar product**

dots per inch *n* full form of **dpi**

dot·ted /dóttəd/ *adj* **1.** WITH DOTS marked or patterned with dots **2.** COVERED WITH SPECKS scattered or sprinkled with small things or larger things seen from a distance ○ *a sky dotted with stars* **3.** RANDOMLY ARRAYED spread randomly over a wide area ○ *a lawn dotted with hoop-skirted belles* **4.** MUSIC INCREASED IN VALUE BY HALF describes a note or rest in written or printed music increased in value by half

dot·ted line *n* a printed line formed from dots or dashes, especially one on which somebody is to write something such as a signature

dot·ted swiss *n* a cotton fabric patterned with raised dots [Shortening of *Swiss muslin*]

dot·ter·el /dóttərəl/ (*plural* **-els** or *same*), **dot·trel** (*plural* **-trels** or *same*) *n* a reddish brown bird of the plover family with white markings on the head and neck. Native to: Europe, Asia. Latin name: *Eudromias morinellus*. [15C. < DOTE + *-rel* (< Old French *-erel*); because the plover is easy to catch]

dot·tle /dótt'l/ *n* the plug of tobacco that is left in a pipe after it has been smoked [15C. < DOT[1]]

dot·trel *n* another spelling of **dotterel**

dot·ty /dóttee/ (**-ti·er, -ti·est**) *adj* (*informal*) **1.** SILLY regarded as being irrational or impractical, often endearingly so **2.** UNCONVENTIONAL behaving in a manner that seems amusingly strange to others **3.** ABSURD illogical, impractical, or absurd **4.** INFATUATED very fond of or passionately interested in somebody or something [Late 19C. Origin ?] —**dot·ti·ly** *adv* —**dot·ti·ness** *n*

Dou·ai /doo áy/ city in Nord Department, Nord-Pas-de-Calais Region, northwestern France. A coal-mining and industrial center, it is situated south of Lille. Population: 42,796 (1999).

Dou·a·la /doo aálə/, **Du·a·la** chief port in Cameroon and chief city of Littoral Province, situated west of the capital Yaoundé. Population: 1,500,000 (1997).

Dou·ay Bi·ble /doó ay-/, **Dou·ay Ver·sion** *n* **1.** a Roman Catholic translation of the Latin Vulgate version of the Bible into English, written in the early 17th century **2.** a copy of the Douay Bible [Mid-19C. After *Douay* (modern DOUAI)]

dou·ble /dúbb'l/ *adj* **1.** BEING TWICE AS MUCH OR MANY being twice as much in size, number, or value **2.** HAVING TWO SIMILAR PARTS consisting of two identical, similar, or equal parts **3.** MEANT FOR TWO PEOPLE designed or intended for two people ○ *reserved a double room* **4.** FITTING DOUBLE BED describes bedding of a size that will fit onto a double bed **5.** TWO-LAYERED consisting of two layers **6.** FOLDED OVER ONCE folded in two, or bent over **7.** OF TWO ELEMENTS consisting of two different parts ○ *a phrase with a double meaning* **8.** ACTING IN CONTRASTING OR OPPOSING WAYS acting one way while feeling very differently, especially when this involves hypocrisy or deceit ○ *led a double life* **9.** BOT HAVING EXTRA PETALS describes flowers that have more petals than normal or plants that have flowers of this type **10.** MUSIC SOUNDING OCTAVE BELOW sounding an octave of a musical instrument lower than the written music indicates ■ *adv* **1.** TWICE AS MUCH twice as much as normal ○ *had to pay double to get in* **2.** IN TWO LAYERS so as to form two layers ■ *n* **1.** TWO TOGETHER two viewed or regarded together **2.** TWICE NORMAL AMOUNT twice the normal or standard amount ○ *He offered me double.* **3.** TWO MEASURES OF DRINK a drink containing two single measures, especially of spirits (*informal*) **4.** DUPLICATE IN APPEARANCE somebody or something that looks very like another, especially a living person bearing a strong resemblance to somebody else **5.** ROOM FOR TWO PEOPLE a hotel room for two people **6.** GHOST IDENTICAL TO LIVING PERSON an apparition that closely resembles a living person **7.** STAND-IN FOR MOVIE STAR a replacement for a movie actor, e.g., in scenes that involve danger, special skill, or nudity **8.** BET ON TWO RACES a bet on two races, in which any winnings from the first become the stake for the second (*informal*) **9.** SUCCESS IN TWO EVENTS success in two events or competitions in the same or successive years or series or against the same opponent **10.** ABRUPT DIRECTIONAL CHANGE a sharp change of direction **11.** CARDS CALL INCREASING SCORE in an auction at bridge, a call that increases the score for succeeding or failing in a contract **12.** TENNIS same as **double fault** (*informal*) **13.** BASEBALL BASEBALL HIT in baseball, a hit that enables a batter to reach second base **14.** MIL FAST MARCHING PACE a fast marching pace at twice the usual speed **15.** PRINTING same as **doublet** (sense 3) ■ *v* (**-bled, -bling, -bles**) **1.** *vti* INCREASE TWOFOLD to make something twice as large or numerous, or become twice as much or many ○ *We doubled our profits the following year.* **2.** *vt* FOLD SOMETHING IN TWO to fold or bend something in two **3.** *vi* HAVE SECOND FUNCTION to have a second or secondary function ○ *His felt hat doubled as a water pail.* **4.** *vi* ACT AS STAND-IN to replace a movie actor in scenes such as those that include danger, special skill, or nudity **5.** *vi* PLAY SECOND ROLE to play an additional part in the same performance **6.** *vt* MUSIC DUPLICATE MUSICAL PART to duplicate a musical part, either at the same pitch or an octave above or below **7.** *vi* MUSIC PLAY MORE THAN ONE MUSICAL INSTRUMENT to play one or more musical instruments, in addition to the principal one ○ *a violinist who doubles on cello* **8.** *vi* CARDS ANNOUNCE BRIDGE DOUBLE in an auction at bridge, to announce a double as a bid **9.** *vt* CHESS PLACE PIECES NEXT TO EACH OTHER to place two chess pieces of the same type and color together ○ *double your opponent's pawns* **10.** *vi* BASEBALL HIT DOUBLE in baseball, to make a hit that gives the batter time to run to second base **11.** *vt* BASEBALL ADVANCE TEAMMATE WITH HIT in baseball, to advance a teammate on the bases by hitting a double ○ *double a runner home* [12C. Via Old French *do(u)bler* < Latin *duplare* < *duplus* "twofold" < *duo* "two"] —**dou·ble·ness** *n* ◇ **on the double** right away and as quickly as possible ○ *told the children to form lines on the double*

double back *vi* to turn around and retrace your steps

double over *vi* to bend deeply from the waist, especially in response to pain or laughter

double up *vi* **1.** to share something with somebody else ○ *There weren't enough beds, so some of the children had to double up.* **2.** to bend the body over sharply from the waist, especially in response to pain or laughter

dou·ble-act·ing *adj* **1.** with one or more pistons that move in both directions, giving two strokes per cycle **2.** acting in opposite directions from a central point

dou·ble a·gent *n* a spy for one government who supplies secret information about that government to its rival

dou·ble bar *n* a symbol, ‖, that marks the end of a piece of music or the end of its principal sections

dou·ble-bar·reled *adj* **1.** describes a gun that has two barrels **2.** serving two purposes, or open to two possible interpretations

dou·ble bass *n* the largest and lowest in pitch of the instruments of the violin family, used in the modern symphony orchestra. It is also commonly found in jazz and dance bands, where it is usually plucked rather than bowed.

dou·ble-bass *adj* describes an instrument that is larger and lower in pitch than others of its group

dou·ble bas·soon *n* MUSIC same as **contrabassoon** (sense 1)

dou·ble bed *n* a bed intended for two people

dou·ble bill *n* a program of entertainment that has two main items, especially a consecutive presentation of two movies

dou·ble bind *n* **1.** an unresolvable situation from which there is no escape without undesirable consequences **2.** a situation in which conflicting demands make it impossible to do the right thing

dou·ble-blind *adj* describes an experiment in which neither the experimenters nor the subjects know which of two similar treatments is genuine and which is a control procedure

doub·le bluff *n* a deception in which somebody tells the truth while assuming that he or she will not be believed

dou·ble boil·er *n* a pair of cooking pots, one fitting on top of and partly inside the other. Food cooks gently in the upper pot while water simmers in the lower pot.

dou·ble bond *n* a chemical bond in which two atoms share two pairs of electrons

dou·ble-book *vti* to wrongly make the same reservation, especially for a hotel room or airplane seat, for two separate customers

dou·ble-breast·ed *adj* describes a coat or jacket that has a large overlap at the front, usually with two sets of buttons

dou·ble bri·dle *n* a bridle with four reins and a bit with two rings on each side

dou·ble-cell·ing *n* the housing of two prisoners in a space designed for only one

dou·ble check *n* **1.** a second examination to make sure of something **2.** a situation in chess in which a king is in check from two pieces at once

dou·ble-check *vti* to check something twice or for a second time ○ *I double-checked that the windows were locked.*

dou·ble chin *n* a fold of flesh or loose skin under the chin —**dou·ble-chinned** *adj*

dou·ble-click *vti* to press and release a mouse button twice in rapid succession in order to invoke a specific command

dou·ble-clutch *vi* to use the clutch twice when changing gear in a motor vehicle, first to put the gear lever into neutral and rev the engine, second to engage the new gear

dou·ble co·co·nut *n* PLANTS same as **coco-de-mer**

dou·ble con·cer·to *n* a concerto for two solo instruments

dou·ble cream *n UK* thick cream with a high fat content

dou·ble cross *n* the production of a new hybrid from parents, each of which is a first-generation hybrid of pure strains, or the hybrid produced

dou·ble-cross *vt* to betray or cheat somebody who believes that he or she is a partner or associate in the same, often criminal enterprise ■ *n* an act of double-crossing a partner or associate —**dou·ble-cross·er** *n* —**dou·ble-cross·ing** *adj*

dou·ble dag·ger *n* the printed character (‡), used to mark a cross-reference, especially to a footnote

dou·ble date *n* an arrangement for two couples to go out together socially as a foursome

dou·ble-date *vi* to go out socially as a couple with another couple

Dou·ble·day /dúbb'l dày/, **Abner** (1819–93) US army officer. He fought in the Mexican War (1846–48) and for the Union in the Civil War (1861–65). He is traditionally thought of as the creator of baseball, even though a similar game antedated his lifetime.

dou·ble-deal·ing *n* deliberately deceitful behavior, especially when involving the betrayal of a partner or associate —**dou·ble-deal·er** *n* —**dou·ble-deal·ing** *adj*

double-decker (sense 2)

dou·ble-deck·er /-dékər/ *n* **1.** something that has two layers, levels, or tiers ○ *a double-decker sandwich* **2.** a bus with an upper and a lower deck

dou·ble-de·clutch *vi UK* same as **double-clutch**

dou·ble de·com·po·si·tion *n* a chemical reaction in which two compounds exchange one or more of their components so that two new compounds are formed

dou·ble-den·si·ty *adj* describes a floppy or hard disk that can hold twice the amount of information as a standard disk

dou·ble de·scent *n* the use in some societies of sometimes the mother's and sometimes the father's ancestry in establishing specific features of social identity or status

dou·ble dig·ging *n* the process of digging a plot of ground to twice the normal depth and transferring soil from the lower level to the top in order to revitalize it before planting

dou·ble-dig·it *adj* being between 10 and 99 ○ *double-digit inflation*

doub·le dig·its *npl US* the numbers with two digits, from 10 to 99. Can term **double figures**

dou·ble-dip *n* an ice-cream cone containing two scoops of ice cream (*informal*)

dou·ble dip·ping *n* the fraudulent receipt of two incomes from the government, e.g., by holding a government job and collecting a government pension at the same time (*informal*) —**dou·ble dip·per** *n*

dou·ble doors *npl* two full-length doors that meet in the middle of the doorway when closed

dou·ble-dot·ted *adj* describes a musical note or rest that has two dots following it to indicate that its length is to be increased by three quarters

dou·ble drib·ble *n* in basketball, an illegal move in which the player dribbles the ball with both hands simultaneously or, having stopped, starts to dribble again

dou·ble Dutch *n* **1.** a skipping game in which players jump over two ropes that are swung crossing over each other by two turners **2.** *UK* speech or writing that cannot be understood at all (*informal*)

dou·ble-du·ty *adj* designed to do two different jobs

dou·ble ea·gle *n* **1.** a former US gold coin worth 20 dollars **2.** in golf, a score of three strokes under par for a hole

dou·ble-edged *adj* **1. HAVING TWO CUTTING EDGES** having a blade sharpened on both edges **2. AMBIGUOUS** having two possible meanings or interpretations, especially one that is apparently innocuous and another that is intentionally unkind or malicious **3. DOING TWO THINGS** achieving two purposes or having two effects

dou·ble-edged sword *n* a situation or event that has negative as well as positive consequences

dou·ble ef·fect *n* the ethical principle that intentionally doing wrong is impermissible, even if the action has good consequences, and that intentionally doing right is permissible, even if the action has bad consequences

dou·ble en·ten·dre /-aan taándrə, do͝ob'l aaN taáNdrə/ (*plural* **dou·ble en·ten·dres** /-aan taándrə, do͝o bb'l aaN taáNdrə/) *n* **1.** a remark that is ambiguous and sexually suggestive **2.** ambiguity in which one meaning is sexually suggestive [Late 17C. < obsolete French, "double understanding"]

dou·ble en·try *n* a bookkeeping system that records each transaction as a credit to one account and a debit from another

dou·ble ex·po·sure *n* **1.** the exposure of two separate images on a single piece of photographic film **2.** a photograph that contains one image superimposed on another

dou·ble-faced *adj* **1. FINISHED ON BOTH SIDES** describes fabrics that are finished on both sides **2. TWO-FACED** behaving insincerely or deceitfully **3. HAVING TWO USABLE SIDES** having two faces or sides that can be used ○ *a double-faced tape*

dou·ble fault *n* in tennis, two consecutive serves that land outside the service box or in the net, with the result that the server loses a point

dou·ble-fault *vi* in tennis, to make two consecutive faulty serves and lose a point as a result

dou·ble fea·ture *n* a program consisting of two full-length movies shown consecutively

dou·ble fig·ures *npl Can, UK* same as **double digits** —**dou·ble-fig·ure** *adj*

dou·ble flat *n* **1.** a symbol, 𝄫, placed in front of a musical note to indicate that the pitch of the note is to be lowered by two half tones **2.** a musical note marked with a double flat

dou·ble-glaze *vt* to fit a building with windows that have two layers of glass separated by a space, in order to improve insulation

dou·ble-head·er *n* **1.** two games played consecutively by the same teams, especially in baseball **2.** a train pulled by two locomotives coupled together

dou·ble he·lix *n* the molecular structure of DNA, consisting of a pair of polynucleotide strands connected by a series of hydrogen bonds and wound in opposing spirals

dou·ble-hung *adj* describes a window that has two sashes, each sliding vertically in its own track

dou·ble in·dem·ni·ty *n* the guaranteed payout of double the face value of a life insurance policy if the policyholder dies in an accident

dou·ble jeop·ard·y *n* the prosecution of somebody a second time for something that he or she has already been tried for. It is prohibited by the US Constitution.

dou·ble-joint·ed *adj* **1.** describes a joint or limb that has unusual flexibility and can bend in the direction opposite to the usual one **2.** describes somebody with double-jointed joints or limbs —**dou·ble-joint·ed·ness** *n*

dou·ble knit *n* a thick knitted fabric

dou·ble life *n* a situation in which somebody is simultaneously involved in two sets of circumstances or relationships and keeps each completely separate, and usually secret, from the other

dou·ble ne·ga·tion *n* in logic, the principle that a proposition and the negation of its negation mean one and the same thing

dou·ble neg·a·tive *n* a phrase containing two negatives

USAGE ***Double negatives*** of the type *I don't know nothing*, in which two negatives close together are intended to reinforce each other, are considered illiterate in current standard English, acceptable though they were in earlier usage. These are to be distinguished from the acceptable, if somewhat uncommon, construction *That's not a good idea, I don't think*, in which the reinforcing negatives appear in different clauses. The more usual type of acceptable double negative is seen in *It is not impossible* (= it is distinctly possible), in which the negatives are intended to cancel each other out. This is a figure of speech called *litotes*, a form of understatement.

---

dou·ble oc·cu·pan·cy *n* the use of a hotel room or other accommodations by two people (*hyphenated before a noun*)

dou·ble or noth·ing *n* a bet in gambling where a player who owes money has the debt doubled or canceled depending on the outcome of the next play

dou·ble-page spread *n* a feature or article that fills two facing pages of a newspaper or magazine

dou·ble-park *vti* to park a vehicle alongside another already parked and so cause an obstruction —**dou·ble-park·er** *n* —**dou·ble-park·ing** *n*

dou·ble play *n* in baseball, a play in which two players are put out

dou·ble pneu·mo·nia *n* pneumonia affecting both lungs

dou·ble quote *n* a quotation mark that consists of two marks ("), not one

dou·bler /dúbblər/ *n* an electronic device that doubles an input frequency or voltage

dou·ble reed *n* **1.** a reed in the oboe, English horn, or bassoon consisting of two halves that vibrate against each other when air passes through them **2.** a woodwind instrument that has a double reed

dou·ble re·frac·tion *n* OPTICS same as **birefringence**

dou·ble rhyme *n* a two-syllable rhyme e.g., "cooking" and "looking"

dou·bles /dúbb'lz/ (*plural same*) *n* **1.** a racket game played between two pairs of players **2.** *Carib* a popular and cheap fast food consisting of a sandwich of curried chickpeas in two fried seasoned batter patties (*informal*)

dou·ble salt *n* a salt that dissolves in solution as two substances, but crystallizes as one, e.g., alum

dou·ble sculls *n* a race between boats crewed by two rowers who sit one behind the other and pull two oars each

dou·ble sharp *n* **1.** a symbol, 𝄪 placed in front of a musical note to indicate that the pitch of the note is to be raised by two half tones **2.** a musical note marked with a double sharp

dou·ble-sid·ed *adj* used or usable on both sides

dou·ble-space *vt* to type or print text with a blank line between each typed or printed line

dou·ble·speak /dúbb'l speek/ *n* same as **double talk** (sense 1)

dou·ble stan·dard *n* a principle, rule, or expectation that is applied unfairly to different groups, one group usually being condemned for the slightest offense while the other is treated far more leniently

dou·ble star *n* ASTRON **1.** same as **binary star** **2.** same as **optical double star**

dou·ble-stop *vi* to draw the bow of a stringed instrument simultaneously across two strings, producing two tones ■ *n* a musical chord of two notes played on a stringed instrument —**dou·ble-stop·ping** *n*

dou·blet /dúbblət/ *n* **1.** CLOTHING **MAN'S JACKET** a man's close-fitting jacket, with or without sleeves, popular in Europe between the 15th and 17th centuries **2.** LING **WORD WITH SAME ROOT AS ANOTHER** either of two similar words in a language that have the same historical root but have arrived at their current forms via different languages, e.g., "mood" and "mode" **3.** PRINTING **REPEATED PRINTED LETTER, WORD, OR LINE** a letter, word, or line that is printed a second time in error **4.** OPTICS **PAIR OF LENSES USED TOGETHER** a pair of lenses designed to be used together so that one lens cancels out the distortions in the other **5.** MINERALS **FAKE GEM** a fake gem made by sticking a colored layer between two pieces of glass or by sticking a thin layer of a gem on a glass base [14C. < French, "something doubled"]

dou·ble tack·le *n* a pair of double pulleys for lifting or pulling

dou·ble take *n* a reaction of surprise or astonishment after an initial hesitation

dou·ble talk *n* **1.** intentionally ambiguous or confusing talk **2.** speech that includes a mixture of real words and nonsense syllables

dou·ble tax·a·tion *n* taxation applied in one country to foreign income received by a company when this income has already been taxed in the other country

dou·ble-team *vt* in various team games such as basketball or football, to use two players to guard an opponent —**dou·ble team** *n*

dou·ble·think /dúbb'l thingk/ *n* the conscious or unconscious holding of two opposing beliefs at the same time [Coined by George Orwell in *1984* (1949)]

dou·ble time *n* **1.** FIN **DOUBLE PAY** double the usual rate of pay **2.** MUSIC **DOUBLY FAST MUSICAL TEMPO** a tempo twice as fast as the basic tempo of a piece of music, or a passage played at that speed **3.** MIL **FAST MARCHING PACE** a fast marching pace of 180 steps per minute

dou·ble-time *vi* to march at the fast pace of 180 steps per minute

dou·ble·ton /dúbb'ltən/ *n* two cards of the same suit that are the only cards of that suit dealt to a player [Early 20C. After SINGLETON]

dou·ble-tongu·ing *n* the production of a rapid series of staccato notes on a wind or brass instrument by using rapid movements of the tongue —**dou·ble-tongue** *vti*

dou·ble·tree /dúbb'l tree/ *n* a bar used to harness two horses to a carriage or other vehicle [After SINGLETREE]

dou·blets /dúbbləts/ *npl* a pair of dice thrown simultaneously, each showing the same number of spots ■ *n* a word game in which one word is transformed into another by substituting letters, the object being to achieve this in the minimum number of substitutions (*takes a singular verb*)

dou·ble-u *n* the letter w

dou·ble vi·sion *n* a condition in which two images of the same object are seen simultaneously because the eyes are not focusing properly. Technical name **diplopia**

dou·ble wham·my *n* two setbacks or unpleasant experiences occurring very close together (*slang*)

dou·ble-wide /dúbb'l wīd/ *n* a manufactured or mobile home that is twice the width of a standard mobile home

dou·ble-ze·ro op·tion *n* an offer to limit the number of intermediate- and short-range nuclear missiles or remove them altogether if an opposing side agrees to do the same

dou·bloon /də blo͞on/ *n* a former Spanish gold coin [Early 17C. < Spanish *doblón* < *dobla* "double" < Latin *duplus*]

dou·blure /də blo͝or/ *n* a lining, especially one made of leather or highly decorated, inside the cover of a book [Late 19C. < French, "lining"]

dou·bly /dúbblee/ *adv* **1.** in two different ways **2.** to twice the usual degree or extent

doubt /dowt/ *vt* (**doubt·ed, doubt·ing, doubts**) **1. THINK SOMETHING UNLIKELY** to feel unconvinced or uncertain about something, or think that something is unlikely ○ *I doubt if he'll come.* **2. NOT TRUST SOMEBODY OR SOMETHING** to suspect that somebody is not sincere or trustworthy, or that something is not true, likely, or genuine ○ *no reason to doubt her* ■ *n* **1. UNCERTAINTY OR MISTRUST** a feeling or state of uncertainty, especially as to whether somebody is sincere or trustworthy, or as to whether something is true, likely, or genuine **2.** PHILOSOPHY **METHOD OF PHILOSOPHICAL QUESTIONING** a method of questioning claims to knowledge, especially in the philosophy of Descartes [13C. Via Old French *doter* < Latin *dubitare* "be uncertain" < *dubius* "uncertain"] —**doubt·a·ble** *adj* —**doubt·a·bly** *adv* —**doubt·er** *n* —**doubt·ing·ly** *adv* ◇ **beyond doubt** completely certain ◇ **no doubt** almost definitely ◇ **in doubt 1.** not feeling confident or sure about something **2.** unlikely or improbable ◇ **open to** *or* **in doubt** not certain, settled, foreseeable with confidence, or finally proved

SYNONYMS See *doubtful*.

doubt·ful /dówtfəl/ *adj* **1. HESITANT** not feeling sure about something **2. UNLIKELY** not likely to happen or be successful **3. INVITING SUSPICION** probably not true, honest, reputable, or genuine —**doubt·ful·ness** *n*

SYNONYMS ***doubtful, uncertain, unsure, in doubt, dubious, skeptical***

CORE MEANING: feeling doubt or uncertainty

doubtful not feeling sure about something ○ *The council was doubtful whether the public would want to pay the charges.* ○ *Oliver felt rather doubtful about having such a friend.* **uncertain** or **unsure** lacking clear knowledge or a definite opinion ○ *She seemed uncertain of her English, and asked for everything to be repeated.* ○ *Some of the biggest names in investment banking are unsure about the future.* **in doubt** not feeling confident or sure about something ○ *When in doubt, the jury often tends to acquit and not convict.* ○ *If the umpires are in any doubt about what to do, they consult with the referee.* **dubious** not sure about an outcome or conclusion ○ *The mayor was dubious about councils being asked to fund the alliance.* ○ *Agencies are dubious as to whether they should take action on behalf of a client.* **skeptical** tending not to believe or accept things but to question them ○ *Most people are fairly skeptical about the efficacy of this treatment.* ○ *In general, viewers tend to be highly skeptical of broadcasters' motives.*

doubt·ful·ly /dówtfəlee/ *adv* with or expressing doubt

doubt·ing Thom·as /dówting-/ *n* somebody who doubts something, especially until given proof [After Jesus Christ's apostle who doubted (John 20:24–9)]

doubt·less /dówtləss/ *adv* **1. CERTAINLY** certainly or almost certainly ○ *That was doubtless their intention, as these documents show.* **2. PROBABLY** probably or presumably ○ *You would doubtless have been informed in due course.* ■ *adj* (*formal*) **1. CERTAIN** impossible to doubt or deny **2. HAVING NO DOUBT** having no doubts or suspicions

douc /dook/ *n* a rare yellow-faced monkey of the langur family. Native to: Southeast Asia. Latin name: *Pygathrix nemaeus.* [Late 18C. < Vietnamese]

dou·ceur /doo súr/ *n* something given as a tip or a bribe (*used euphemistically*) [14C. < French, "sweetness, favor" < *douce* "sweet" < Latin *dulcis*]

douche /doosh/ *n* **1. CLEANING OF BODY BY SQUIRTING WATER** the cleaning of a part of the body or a body cavity with a jet of water or air **2. EQUIPMENT PRODUCING CLEANSING WATER JET** a piece of equipment that produces a jet of water or air for a douche ■ *vti* (**douched, douch·ing, douch·es**) **CLEAN BODY WITH WATER JET** to clean a part of the body or body cavity with a jet of water or air [Mid-18C. Via French < Italian *doccia* "water pipe" < Latin *duction-* "leading (through a pipe)"]

dou-dou /do͞o do͞o/, **doo-doo** *n Carib* used as a term of endearment [< French *doux* "sweet"]

dough /dō/ *n* **1.** a soft elastic mixture of flour and water, often with other ingredients such as yeast, oil, butter, salt, and sugar, that becomes bread or pastry when baked **2.** cash and other financial assets (*slang*) [Old English *dāg* < Indo-European, "to form"]

SPELLCHECK See *doe*.

dough boy, Dough Boy *n* a US infantryman in World War I

dough·boy /dṓ bòy/ *n* a ball of bread dough boiled, steamed, or fried as a dumpling (*slang*)

dough·face /dṓ fàyss/ *n* a Northerner who sided with the South during the Civil War, especially a Northern congressman who refused to condemn slavery

dough·nut /dṓ nùt/, **do·nut** *n* **1. ROUND CAKE WITH HOLE OR FILLING** a small sugar-coated cake of sweet dough, fried or baked, and either spherical with a filling of cream or jam, or ring-shaped with no filling **2.** MECH ENG **RING-SHAPED OBJECT** an object in the shape of an inflated ring, e.g., an accelerating tube in a nuclear reactor or an undersized spare tire **3. 360-DEGREE TURN IN VEHICLE** a tight 360-degree turn made in a motor vehicle or motor boat

~~**doughter**~~ incorrect spelling of **daughter**

dough·ty /dówtee/ (**-ti·er, -ti·est**) *adj* brave and determined (*archaic or humorous*) [Old English *dohtig, dyhtig* "worthy, virtuous" < Indo-European, "be fit, prosper"] —**dough·ti·ly** *adv* —**dough·ti·ness** *n*

dough·y /dṓ ee/ (**-i·er, -i·est**) *adj* **1.** soft, sticky, and elastic, like dough **2.** unhealthily pale and flabby —**dough·i·ness** *n*

Doug·las /dúggləss/ capital of the Isle of Man. It is a popular vacation resort. Population: 20,368 (1991).

Doug·las, Kirk (*b.* 1916) US movie actor. He has starred in over 70 Hollywood films, including *The Bad and the Beautiful* (1952). In 1995, he received a special Academy Award for his contribution to motion pictures. Born **Danielovitch, Issur**

Doug·las, Lord Alfred Bruce (1870–1945) British writer and poet. He was at the center of the scandal that led to the imprisonment of Oscar Wilde. He wrote *The City of the Soul* (1899) and a verse collection, *Sonnets and Lyrics* (1935). Full name **Douglas, Alfred Bruce, Lord**

> "I am the Love that dare not speak its name."
> [Lord Alfred Bruce Douglas, "Two Loves"; 1896]

Doug·las, Michael (*b.* 1944) US television and movie actor. He won an Academy Award for *Wall Street* (1987). His father is Kirk Douglas.

Doug·las, Stephen A. (1813–61) US politician. He lost the presidential election to Abraham Lincoln (1860), whom he then supported at the outbreak of the Civil War. Full name **Douglas, Stephen Arnold**

> "Slavery cannot exist a day or an hour anywhere unless it is supported by local police regulations."
> [Stephen A. Douglas, *Speech*; August 27, 1858]

Doug·las, Thomas Clement (1904–86) Scottish-born Canadian politician. He led the New Democratic Party from 1961 to 1971.

Doug·las, William O. (1898–1980) associate justice of the US Supreme Court (1939–75). Of strongly held liberal views, he championed individual rights, especially free speech. Full name **Douglas, William Orville**

> "The right to be let alone is indeed the beginning of all freedom."
> [William O. Douglas, *An Almanac of Liberty*; 1954]

Doug·las fir *n* **1.** a tall pine tree with distinctive rough bark and shaggy-looking cones. Use: timber, Christmas trees. Native to: northwestern North America. Latin name: *Pseudotsuga menziesii.* **2.** the strong durable wood of the Douglas fir tree [After David *Douglas* (1798–1834), Scottish botanist]

Doug·las-Home /dúggləss hyo͞om/, **Sir Alec, 14th Earl of Home** (1903–95) British prime minister. He was British foreign secretary (1960–63) and renounced his hereditary title to succeed Harold Macmillan as prime minister (1963–64). He was made a life peer in 1974. Full name **Douglas-Home, Alexander Frederick**. See table at **prime minister**

Doug·lass /dúggləss/, **Frederick** (1817–95) US abolitionist, orator, and writer. He escaped from slavery (1838) and campaigned against it and racism in the United States. He wrote *Narrative of the Life of Frederick Douglass, an American Slave* (1845).

> "If a slave has a bad master, his ambition is to get a better; when he gets a better, he aspires to have the best; and when he gets the best, he aspires to be his own master."
> [Frederick Douglass, *Speech, Moorfields, England*; May 12, 1846]

Doug·las spruce *n* TREES, INDUST same as **Douglas fir**

Dou·kho·bor /do͞okə bàwr/, **Du·kho·bor** *n* a member of an 18th-century Russian Christian group that rejected state and church authority and emigrated to western Canada at the end of the century to escape persecution [Late 19C. < Russian *Dukhobar* < *dukh* "spirit, Holy Ghost" + *-bor* "fighter"]

dou·la /do͞olə/ *n* a woman who is experienced in childbirth and who provides physical, emotional, and informational assistance and support to a mother before, during, or after childbirth [< Greek *doulē* "enslaved woman"]

doum /doom/, **doum palm, doom palm** *n* an Egyptian palm tree with egg-shaped fruits that have a gingery taste. Latin name: *Hyphaene thebaica.* [Early 18C. < Arabic *dūm*]

dour /dowr, door/ *adj* **1.** severe or gloomy, and unfriendly and unresponsive toward others **2.** grimly and stubbornly determined [14C. Probably via Gaelic *dūr* "obstinate" < Latin *durus* "hard"] —**dour·ly** *adv* —**dour·ness** *n*

dou·ra *n* PLANTS another spelling of **durra**

Dou·ro /dṓ ro͞o, dáw ro͞o/ river that rises in north central Spain and flows westward across Spain and northern Portugal, reaching the Atlantic Ocean near Porto. Length: 556 mi./895 km. Spanish name **Duero**

dou·rou·cou·li /do͞orə ko͞olee/ (*plural* **-lis**) *n* a fairly small, large-eyed, nocturnal monkey with an inflatable sac under its neck that amplifies its calls. Native to: South America. Genus: *Aotus.* [Mid-19C. Probably < language of a people of S Venezuela]

douse[1] /dowss/, **dowse** *vt* (**doused, dous·ing, dous·es; dowsed, dows·ing, dows·es**) **1. IMMERSE SOMEBODY OR SOMETHING IN WATER** to plunge or submerge somebody or something in water **2. PUT LIQUID ON SOMEBODY OR SOMETHING** to put a lot of water or other liquid on somebody or something **3. EXTINGUISH SOMETHING** to put out a light, fire, or flame, especially with water ■ *n* **DRENCHING** a thorough wetting or soaking [Early 17C. Origin ?] —**dous·er** *n*

douse[2] /dowss/ (**doused, dous·ing, dous·es**) *vt* to lower a sail, especially at speed [Mid-16C. Origin ?]

DOVAP /dṓ vàp/ *n* a system for measuring the speed and position of objects in flight that is based on the frequency of sound waves. Full form **Doppler velocity and position**

dove[1] /duv/ *n* **1. BIRD OF PIGEON FAMILY** a small bird of the pigeon family, with a cooing call. Family: Columbidae. **2.** SUPPORTER OF PEACE somebody who supports peace and the use of peaceful measures to avoid confrontation or war **3.** TERM OF ENDEARMENT used as an affectionate name for a loved one ■ *adj, n* COLORS same as **dove gray** [Assumed Old English *dūfe*, originally "dark-colored bird" < Indo-European, "darken"]

dove[2] /dōv/ past tense of **dive**

Dove *n* in Christianity, a manifestation or representation of the Holy Spirit

Dove /duv/, **Rita** (*b.* 1952) US poet and novelist. Her third collection of poetry, *Thomas and Beulah* (1986), won the 1987 Pulitzer Prize in poetry, and she served as poet laureate of the United States (1993–95).

> "He used to sleep like a glass of water / held up in the hand of a very young girl."
> [Rita Dove, "Straw Hat"; 1986]

> "A good poem is like a bouillon cube. It's concentrated and it nourishes you when you need it."
> [Rita Dove, *Time*; October 18, 1989]

dove·cote /dúv kòt/, **dove·cot** /-kòt/ *n* a structure with many separate entrances and compartments, used for housing domestic pigeons

dove gray *adj* of a mid-gray color with a tinge of pink or blue —**dove gray** *n*

dove·kie /dúvkee/ (*plural* **-kies**), **dove·key** (*plural* **-keys**) *n* a small squat seabird with a strong beak and, in winter, a white throat and breast. Native to: northern regions. Latin name: *Alle alle.* [Early 19C. Diminutive of DOVE[1]]

Do·ver /dṓvər/ **1.** city and state capital of Delaware, in the central part of the state, south of Wilmington. Population: 32,581 (2002 estimate). **2.** city in southeastern New Hampshire, situated on the Cocheco River, northwest of Portsmouth. It is an industrial center. Population: 27,784 (2002 estimate).

Do·ver, Strait of the narrowest part of the English Channel, between Dover, England, and Calais, France. Length: 21 mi./34 km.

Do·ver sole *n* **1.** a brownish mottled flat-bodied fish. Native to: Pacific coast of North America. Latin name: *Microstomus pacificus.* **2.** a flat-bodied fish. Native to: Europe. Latin name: *Solea solea.* [Early 20C. Probably after DOVER, England]

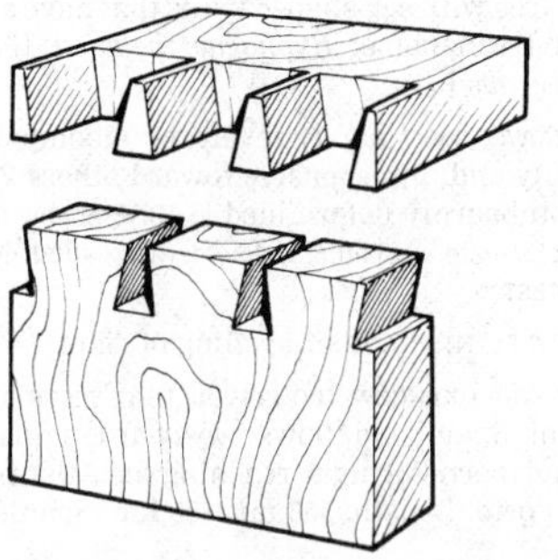

dovetail

dove·tail /dúv tàyl/ *v* (**-tailed, -tail·ing, -tails**) **1.** *vti* FIT TOGETHER to fit neatly together or combine smoothly and efficiently, or fit or combine things in this way **2.** *vt* JOIN PIECES OF WOOD to join wooden boards with interlocking V-shaped tenons ■ *n* **1.** V-SHAPED TENON a V-shaped projection on the end of a piece of wood that fits into a similarly shaped opening in another piece to form a strong joint **2.** *also* **dove·tail joint** JOINT WITH DOVETAILS a joint made using dovetails [< its shape]

dove·tail saw *n* a small saw with a reinforced back, slightly smaller than a tenon saw and used for fine woodworking

dov·ish /dúvvish/ *adj* advocating peaceful solutions and the avoidance of confrontation or war —**dov·ish·ness** *n*

Dow /dow/, **Herbert Henry** (1866–1930) Canadian-born US chemist. He discovered a way of extracting bromine from brine by electrolysis (1891) and founded a major chemical company in 1895.

dow·a·ger /dów əjər/ *n* **1.** a woman who has inherited a title or property from her deceased husband **2.** a rich-looking or respected woman of advanced years [Mid-16C. < Old French *douagere* < Latin *dos* "dowry"]

dow·a·ger's hump *n* a marked curving of the spine around the area of the shoulder blades, especially in women with osteoporosis

dow·dy /dówdee/ (**-di·er, -di·est**) *adj* **1.** unattractively plain and unfashionable **2.** wearing plain unfashionable clothes [Late 16C. < *dowd* "poorly dressed woman," origin ?] —**dow·di·ly** *adv* —**dow·di·ness** *n*

dow·el /dów əl/ *n* a short wooden or metal peg used to join two pieces of wood or metal by fitting tightly at each end into specially drilled holes in the two pieces to be joined ■ *vt* (**-eled, -el·ing, -els**) to join pieces of wood or metal using dowels [13C. Origin ?]

dow·er /dowr/ *n* **1.** WIDOW'S INHERITANCE a dead man's estate, or part of his estate, inherited by his widow **2.** CULTL ANTHROP same as **dowry** (sense 1) (*archaic*) **3.** NATURAL GIFT something, especially a skill or talent, with which somebody is endowed (*literary*) ■ *vt* (**-ered, -er·ing, -ers**) ENDOW SOMEBODY to endow somebody with something (*literary*) [13C. < Old French *douaire* < Latin *dotare* "endow" < *dos* "marriage portion"]

Dow Jones Av·er·ag·e *tdmk* a trademark for an index of the prices of selected industrial, transportation, and utilities stocks that is based on a formula developed and revised periodically by Dow Jones & Company, Inc.

down[1] /down/ (**downed, down·ing, downs,** *plural* **downs**) CORE MEANING: a grammatical word used to indicate movement or position toward a lower level or the ground ○ (prep) *He ran down the stairs and opened the door.* ○ (prep) *The sheep was caught in brambles 50 ft. down the hillside.* ○ (prep) *Tears were pouring down her cheeks.* ○ (adv) *I was numb from the waist down.* ○ (adv) *They all watched the sun go down.* ○ (adv) *She pressed a button and the window slid down.*

1. *prep* TO LOWER LEVEL IN SOMETHING toward or at a lower level in something ○ *I dropped my keys down a hole.* **2.** *prep* ALONG toward or at a position farther along the length of something and usually at a somewhat lower level ○ *halfway down the street* **3.** *adv* AT OR TO LOWER LEVEL at or to a physically lower level or position ○ *down in the basement* **4.** *adv* ONTO SURFACE out of the hand and onto a surface ○ *She calmly put her fork down.* **5.** *adv* AWAY FROM PRESENT LOCATION to another place away from the current location or base ○ *go down to the beach* **6.** *adv* TO MORE SOUTHERLY PLACE to a place in the south or to the south of the current location ○ *going down to Florida for the winter* **7.** *adv* TO OR AT LOWER AMOUNT to or at a lower amount or price ○ *to get interest rates down* **8.** *adv* SHORT BY PARTICULAR AMOUNT short of, having lost, or losing by a particular amount ○ *They were two goals down at halftime.* **9.** *adv* HAVING ONLY SO MUCH LEFT having only a particular amount left ○ *I'm down to my last dollar.* **10.** *adv* IN PART PAYMENT in part payment for something or as a deposit ○ *You put 5% down, and pay the rest in installments.* **11.** *adv* INCLUDING EVERYONE OR EVERYTHING including everyone or everything, from highest to lowest, within a group or hierarchy of people or things, or even including the person or thing mentioned ○ *everyone from the managing editor down* ○ *account for everything down to the last cent* **12.** *adv* TO LATER PERIOD from an earlier to a later time or person ○ *The piano had been handed down to him by his grandmother.* **13.** *adv* IN INFERIOR POSITION in or to an inferior, less free, or less privileged position or condition ○ *holding political opponents down* **14.** *adv* TO REDUCED CONDITION to a lower level of intensity or activity ○ *wind down after work* **15.** *adv* INTO LESS SOLID STATE into a different and less solid state ○ *The hot butter will melt down.* **16.** *adv* ON PAPER in writing on paper, as a record ○ *wrote it down* **17.** *adv* CHOSEN OR ARRANGED chosen or detailed for something, or arranged or scheduled for a particular time or date ○ *We're down for two sessions next month.* **18.** *adv* LEISURE VERTICALLY IN CROSSWORD PUZZLE in a vertical position in a crossword puzzle ○ *the solution to 10 down* **19.** *adv UK* EDUC AWAY FROM UNIVERSITY away from, or no longer at, a university ○ *down from Cambridge* **20.** *adv* NAUT TO WINDWARD having the rudder to windward **21.** *adj* UNHAPPY unhappy and gloomy **22.** *adj* COMPUT NOT IN OPERATION describes a computer system that is temporarily not in operation **23.** *adj* MADE IN PART PAYMENT made or given in part payment for something or as a deposit ○ *a down payment on the car* **24.** *adj* FOOTBALL NOT IN PLAY no longer in play **25.** *adj* BASEBALL PUT OUT eliminated from a game **26.** *adj* ON GROUND lying on the ground ○ *a down tree* **27.** *adj* AGREEABLE TO SOMETHING ready and willing to do something (*slang*) ○ *Great! I'm down for that.* **28.** *interj* INSTRUCTION TO DOG used as an instruction to a dog to stop jumping up or to lie or sit ○ *Down boy!* **29.** *vt* EAT OR DRINK SOMETHING to eat food or drink liquid, especially quickly or greedily **30.** *vt* BRING SOMEBODY OR SOMETHING TO GROUND to cause somebody or something to fall to the ground through being hurt or damaged **31.** *vt* FOOTBALL DECLARE BALL OUT OF PLAY in football, to declare a ball as no longer in play **32.** *n* FOOTBALL PLAY MADE IN FOOTBALL in football, one of four consecutive plays within which a team must either score or advance the ball at least ten yards [Old English *dūn(e)*, shortened < *adūn(e)* "from the hill" < *dūn* (see DOWN[3])] ◇ **be down on somebody** *or* **something** to show dislike or hostility toward somebody or something, often giving him, her, or it unfair treatment (*slang*) ◇ **be down to somebody** to be the responsibility of somebody ◇ **be down to something** to be the result of something ◇ **come down with something** to become sick with something ◇ **down at the heels** shabby and neglected ◇ **down under** to or in Australia or New Zealand (*informal*) ◇ **down with somebody** *or* **something!** used to express disapproval of, opposition to, or a desire to get rid of, somebody or something

down[2] /down/ *n* **1.** SOFT FLUFFY FEATHERS the soft fluffy feathers that are a young bird's first plumage **2.** BIRDS SOFT INNER FEATHERS the soft feathers that lie beneath the outer feathers in some adult birds **3.** FEATHERS AS STUFFING the soft breast feathers of a duck or goose, especially the female eider duck. Use: filling for pillows and quilts. **4.** COVERING OF SOFT HAIRS a covering of fine fluffy hairs, e.g., on a child's skin or on the skin of some fruits [14C. < Old Norse *dúnn*]

down[3] /down/ *n UK* a grassy treeless hill or ridge (*often used in place names*) ■ **downs** *npl* an area of gently rolling, treeless, grassy upland, used mainly as pasture [Old English *dūn*, origin ?]

Down /down/ *n* a sheep belonging to a southern English breed, e.g., the South Down or Dorset Down [Late 18C. < the DOWNS]

down-and-dirt·y *adj* crude and often unpleasant (*slang*) ○ *the down-and-dirty truth*

down-and-out *adj* **1.** JOBLESS AND POOR having no money or job, often no home, and little hope of things getting better (*informal*) **2.** UNABLE TO CARRY ON completely incapacitated and unable to carry on ■ *n* JOBLESS POOR PERSON somebody who lacks money, a job, and often a home (*informal*)

down-at-heel, down-at-the-heel *adj* **1.** worn-out or rundown from use or neglect **2.** shabbily dressed as a result of being poor

down·beat /dówn beet/ *adj* PESSIMISTIC showing or expressing pessimism and hopelessness ■ *n* **1.** FIRST BEAT IN BAR the first beat in a bar of music **2.** MUSIC CONDUCTOR'S DOWNWARD GESTURE the downward movement made by a conductor to indicate the downbeat of a bar of music **3.** MUSIC same as **downtempo**

down-bow *n* the action of drawing a bow from its heel toward its point across a stringed instrument

down·burst /dówn bùrst/ *n* a powerful downward wind, often part of a thunderstorm system, that creates strong horizontal winds in all directions when it strikes the ground and is a danger to aircraft

down·cast /dówn kàst/ *adj* **1.** sad and pessimistic **2.** looking or directed toward the ground ○ *with downcast eyes*

down·coun·try /dówn kùntree/ *US adj* coming from, associated with, or located in a low-lying, usually more populated region of a country as opposed to an upland area ■ *adv* in, to, or toward a low-lying region of a country

down·court /down káwrt/ *adj, adv* in, to, or toward the opposite end of a basketball or similar court

down·draft /dówn dràft/ *n* a downward movement of air, e.g., on the lee side of a mountain range or down a chimney

Down East, down East *n* New England, or more specifically, the US state of Maine (*informal*) —**Down East·er** *n* —**Down East·ern** *adj*

down·er /dównər/ *n* (*slang*) **1.** a gloomy person, situation, or experience **2.** a drug, especially a barbiturate, that induces calmness or sleepiness

Dow·ners Grove /dòwnərz-/ village in northeastern Illinois, southeast of Wheaton. It is a western suburb of Chicago. Population: 48,869 (2002 estimate).

Dow·ney /dównee/ city in southern California, southeast of Los Angeles. Population: 109,840 (2002 estimate).

down·fall /dówn fàwl/ *n* **1.** FAILURE OR RUIN the failure or ruin of a previously successful person, group, or organization **2.** CAUSE OF RUIN an action or situation responsible for the failure or ruin of a previously successful person, group, or organization **3.** METEOROL FALL OF RAIN OR SNOW a sudden heavy fall of rain or snow

down·fall·en /dówn fàwlən/ *adj* **1.** fallen from a position of fame, power, or wealth **2.** in a seriously neglected or ruined condition

down·field /dówn fèeld/ *adj, adv* in or toward the opponents' half of a field of play

down·force /dówn fàwrss/ *n* a force, produced by a combination of air resistance and gravity, that exerts a downward pressure on a moving vehicle and helps to counteract loss of control at high speeds

down·grade /dówn gràyd/ *vt* (**-grad·ed, -grad·ing, -grades**) **1.** LOWER STATUS OF SOMETHING to lower the status, value, or rating of something ○ *The hurricane was downgraded to a tropical storm.* **2.** MOVE SOMEBODY TO LESS IMPORTANT JOB to move somebody from one post or job to another with less responsibility, status, or pay **3.** DISPARAGE SOMEBODY OR SOMETHING to speak or write disparagingly about somebody or something ■ *n* DOWNWARD SLOPE a downward slope on a road

down·haul /dówn hàwl/ *n* a rope for pulling down or fixing down a sail, line, or boom to the deck ■ *vt* to pull a sail, line, or boom down and fix it to the deck

down·heart·ed /dòwn haártəd/ *adj* discouraged and unhappy —**down·heart·ed·ly** *adv* —**down·heart·ed·ness** *n*

down·hill *adv* /down híl/ TOWARD BOTTOM OF HILL toward the bottom of a hill or slope ■ *adj* /dówn hìl/ SLOPING DOWN sloping down or taking place on a downward slope ■ *n* /dówn hìl/ RACE DOWN MOUNTAINSIDE COURSE a skiing race against the clock down a long mountainside course with several hundred yards between marker flags ◇ **go downhill** to decline or deteriorate

down·hole /down hṓl/ *adj* describes equipment used inside an oil well

down·home /dówn hṓm/ *adj* appealingly simple, informal, and unpretentious, and therefore considered characteristic of ordinary people (*informal*) ○ *downhome cooking*

Down·ing Street /dówning-/ *n* **1.** the street off Whitehall in Westminster, central London, where the official residences of the British prime minister and chancellor of the exchequer are located **2.** the British prime minister or the British government ○ *Downing Street sources*

down·land /dówn lànd/ *n* undulating grass-covered hills in southern England, or similar, often flatter grassland in Australia and New Zealand

down·light /dówn lìt/ *n* a lamp or bulb whose light is directed straight downward

down·link /dówn lingk/ *n* a path for the transmission of signals and data between a vehicle or satellite in space and Earth —**down·link** *vti*

down·load /dówn lṓd/ *vti* (**-load·ed, -load·ing, -loads**) **1.** COMPUT TRANSFER DATA to transfer or copy data from one computer to another, or to a disk or peripheral device, or be transferred or copied in this way **2.** TRANSP UNLOAD to unload cargo or passengers ■ *n* COMPUT **1.** INSTANCE OF DOWNLOADING an instance or the process of downloading data **2.** DOWNLOADED DATA an amount of data downloaded in a single operation

Down Low, down low *n* among some young African American men who regard themselves as gay, a clandestine culture that involves secret gay relationships, but rejects the suggestion that the participants are themselves gay, effeminate, or bisexual (*slang*) [Late 20C. Originally popularized by the hip-hop singers TLC and R. Kelly, with the meaning "secret"]

down·mar·ket /dówn maàrkət/ *adj* cheap, appealing to mass taste, and regarded as being of low quality ■ *adv* toward the part of the market that deals in cheap, low-quality goods that appeal to mass taste

down pay·ment *n* a part of the full price of something paid at the time it is bought, with the remaining part to be paid later

down·pipe /dówn pìp/ *n UK* CONSTR same as **downspout**

down·play /dówn plày/ (**-played, -play·ing, -plays**) *vt* to make something seem less important, significant, or serious than it really is

down·pour /dówn pàwr/ *n* a heavy and sustained fall of rain

down quark *n* a quark with an electric charge of $-\frac{1}{3}$, zero strangeness, and zero charm

down·range /down ráynj/ *adj, adv* away from where a missile was fired

down·rig·ger /dówn riggər/ *n* a fishing line attached to a weighted cable so that the baited line trails at or near the bottom of the water

down·right /dówn rìt/ *adj* **1.** ABSOLUTE complete and utter ○ *a downright lie* **2.** STRAIGHTFORWARD frank in expressing opinions ■ *adv* ABSOLUTELY completely and utterly ○ *downright unfair* —**down·right·ly** *adv* —**down·right·ness** *n*

down·riv·er /down rívvər/ *adv, adj* toward or nearer the mouth of a river, or following the direction of its current ■ *n* COMPUT TRANSMISSION AWAY FROM CENTRAL NETWORK the transmission of data on a network away from a central distribution point

Downs /downz/ either of two chalk uplands in southern England, the North Downs in Surrey and Kent, and the South Downs in Hampshire and Sussex

down·scale /dówn skàyl/ *adj* same as **downmarket** ■ *vti* (**-scaled, -scal·ing, -scales**) to reduce the scale or extent of something, especially a business

down·shift /dówn shìft/ (**-shift·ed, -shift·ing, -shifts**) *vi* **1.** to change to a lower gear in a motor vehicle **2.** to move from a highly paid but stressful job to one that makes it possible to improve quality of life in other respects —**down·shift** *n*

down·side /dówn sìd/ *n* a negative side to something that also has positive aspects

down·size /dówn sìz/ (**-sized, -siz·ing, -siz·es**) *v* **1.** *vti* to reduce the size of a business or organization, especially by cutting the work force **2.** *vt* to make something physically smaller, or produce something in a smaller size

down·slide /dówn slìd/ *n* a downward trend or course

down·spin /dówn spìn/ *n* a very sudden and sharp reduction

down·spout /dówn spòwt/ *n* a pipe that carries rainwater from a roof gutter down to a drain or to the ground

Down's syn·drome *n* MED same as **Down syndrome**

down·stage /down stáyj/ *adv, adj* toward or at the front of a theater stage ■ *n* the front half of a theater stage

down·stairs /down stérz/ *adv* TO LOWER FLOOR down the stairs, or to a lower floor ■ *adj* ON LOWER FLOOR relating to or situated on a lower or the lowest floor ○ *a downstairs bathroom* ■ *n* LOWER FLOOR the lower floor of a building

down·state /down stáyt/ *adj, adv* **1.** in or to the southerly part of a state **2.** away from the big cities and in or into the more rural parts of a state whose major metropolitan area is to the north ○ *downstate Illinois* —**down·state** *n* —**down·stat·er** *n*

down·stream /down streém/ *adj* **1.** SITUATED TOWARD MOUTH OF RIVER situated toward or nearer the mouth of a river **2.** MANUF OF LATER PRODUCTION STAGES relating to or occurring in the later stages of production ■ *adv* **1.** GENETICS FURTHER FORWARD ON DNA MOLECULE further forward on a DNA molecule, in the direction in which the sequence is being read during replication **2.** GEOG TOWARD MOUTH OF RIVER toward or nearer the mouth of a river, or following the direction of the current ■ *n* COMPUT TRANSMISSION AWAY FROM CENTRAL NETWORK the transmission of data on a network away from a central distribution point

down·stroke /dówn stròk/ *n* a stroke moving or made in a downward direction

down·swing /dówn swìng/ *n* **1.** a downward trend or course **2.** the downward part of a golfer's swing

Down syn·drome /dówn-/, **Down's syn·drome** /dównz-/ *n* a genetic disorder characterized by a broad skull, blunt facial features, short stature, and learning difficulties. It is caused by the presence of an extra copy of a specific chromosome. [Mid-20C. After J. H. L. *Down* (1828–96), English physician]

down·tem·po /dówn tèmpō/ *n* electronic music that is for listening to instead of dancing to

down-the-line *adj* unwavering in support of or adherence to rules or policy

down·throw /dówn thrṑ/ *n* the relative vertical displacement of rocks on one side of a fault

down·tick /dówn tìk/ *n* **1.** a very small decrease or reduction **2.** a stock market transaction that is lower than the previous transaction in the same stock

down·time /dówn tìm/ *n* **1.** time during which work or production is stopped, e.g., because machinery is not working **2.** a period of relaxation or play between periods of work

down-to-earth *adj* practical and realistic

down·town /down tówn, dówn tòwn/ *adj, adv* IN OR TO TOWN'S CENTER in or to the center of a city, especially its business center ■ *n* **1.** CITY CENTER the center of a city, especially its business center **2.** LOWER MANHATTAN in New York City, the lower or southern end of Manhattan —**down·town·er** *n*

down·trend /dówn trènd/ *n* a downward trend or tendency

down·trod·den /dówn tròdd'n/ *adj* made submissive by constant harsh treatment

down·turn /dówn tùrn/ *n* a period or trend in which business or economic activity is reduced or is less successful

down·ward /dównwərd/ *adj* **1.** MOVING TO LOWER PLACE moving or directed to the ground or to a lower place ○ *a downward glance* **2.** MOVING TO LOWER LEVEL moving to a lower level or condition **3.** COMING FROM ORIGIN OR SOURCE descending from a source, origin, or beginning ■ *adv also* **down·wards** /-wərdz/ **1.** TOWARD LOWER PLACE toward the ground or a lower place **2.** TO LOWER LEVEL to a lower level or condition **3.** TO AND INCLUDING EVERYONE to and including all the members of an organization, even the most junior ○ *everyone from the general manager downward* **4.** TO LATER TIME to a later time or generation —**down·ward·ly** *adv* —**down·ward·ness** *n*

down·ward·ly mo·bile *adj* moving to a lower status, social class, or income bracket

down·ward mo·bil·i·ty *n* movement to a lower status, social class, or income bracket

down·wards *adv* same as **downward**

down·wash /dówn wòsh, -wàwsh/ *n* a downward wind, e.g., the wind created by an aircraft wing

down·wind /down wínd/ *adv, adj* **1.** in the direction that the wind is blowing **2.** in or into a position further along the line of the direction of the wind

down·y /dówneе/ (**-i·er, -i·est**) *adj* **1.** SOFT soft and fluffy **2.** COVERED WITH SOFT HAIRS covered with soft fine hairs **3.** FEATHER-FILLED filled with feathers [Mid-16C. < DOWN[2]] —**down·i·ness** *n*

down·y mil·dew *n* a disease of plants that produces gray velvety patches on lower leaf surfaces, caused by various fungi. Family: Peronosporaceae.

down·zone /dówn zṑn/ (**-zoned, -zon·ing, -zones**) *vti* to restrict or reduce the number of buildings in an area ○ *plans to downzone urban districts*

dow·ry /dówree/ (*plural* **-ries**) *n* **1.** BRIDE'S FAMILY'S GIFT TO BRIDEGROOM an amount of money or property given in some societies by a bride's family to her bridegroom or his family when she marries **2.** MAN'S GIFT TO BRIDE an amount of money or property transferred by a man to his bride when they marry **3.** CHR MONEY PAID TO ENTER NUNS' ORDER a sum of money required for a woman to enter some monastic orders **4. TALENT** a natural talent (*literary*) [14C. Via Anglo-Norman *dowarie* < Old French *douaire* (see DOWER)]

dowse[1] /dowz/ (**dowsed, dows·ing, dows·es**) *vi* to use a divining rod to search for underground water or minerals [Late 17C. Origin ?]

dowse[2] /dowss/ *vt, n* another spelling of **douse**[1]

dowse[3] /dowss/ *vt* SAILING another spelling of **douse**[2]

dows·er /dówzər/ *n* somebody who uses a divining rod to dowse

dows·ing rod /dówzing-, dówssing-/ *n* PARANORMAL same as **divining rod**

Dow·son /dówss'n/, **Ernest** (1867–1900) British poet. A friend of W. B. Yeats and Oscar Wilde, he published two collections of poems in 1896 and 1899 which include his most famous works, "Cynara" (1891) and "Vitae summa brevis" (1896). Full name **Dowson, Ernest Christopher**

> "They are not long, the days of wine and roses."
> [Ernest Dowson, "Vitae Summa Brevis Spem Nos Vetat Incohare Longam" ("The shortness of life prevents us from entertaining far-off hopes"); 1896]

Dow the·o·ry /dów-/ *n* a theory that states that stock market prices can be forecast on the basis of the movements of a selected group of stocks [After Charles *Dow* (1851–1902), US financial journalist and joint founder of Dow Jones and Company]

dox·as·tic /dok sástik/ *n* the branch of logic that deals with belief [Early 19C. < Greek *doxa* "opinion"] —**dox·as·tic** *adj*

dox·ie *n* RELIG another spelling of **doxy**

dox·ol·o·gy /dok sólləjee/ (*plural* **-gies**) *n* in Christian religious services, a hymn, prayer, or formula of worship in praise of God [Mid-17C. < medieval Latin *doxologia* "science of opinion" < Greek *doxa* "opinion"] —**dox·o·log·i·cal** /dòksə lójjik'l/ *adj*—**dox·o·log·i·cal·ly** *adv*

dox·o·ru·bi·cin /dòksə róobissin/ *n* an antibiotic obtained from a bacterium. Use: treatment of some tumors. [Late 20C. < *dioxo-* + Latin *rubus* "red" + -MYCIN]

dox·y /dóksee/ (*plural* **-ies**), **dox·ie** *n* a set of beliefs, especially religious beliefs (*informal*) [Mid-18C. Extracted < such words as ORTHODOXY, HETERODOXY]

dox·y·cy·cline /dòksi sí kleen, -klin/ *n* an antibiotic derived from tetracycline. Use: treatment of many diseases. [Mid-20C. Contraction of *deoxytetracycline*]

doy·en /dóy ən, doy én/ *n* a man who is the most experienced and respected member of a group or profession [15C. Via French < Latin *decanus* "person in charge of ten others" (see DEAN)]

doy·enne /doy én/ *n* a woman who is the most experienced and respected member of a group or profession [Mid-19C. < French, form of *doyen* (see DOYEN)]

Doyle /doyl/, **Sir Arthur Conan** (1859–1930) British writer and physician. He was author of the Sherlock Holmes detective novels, including *The Hound of the Baskervilles* (1902).

> "It is an old maxim of mine that when you have excluded the impossible, whatever remains, however improbable, must be the truth."
> [Sir Arthur Conan Doyle, *The Sign of Four*; 1889]

Doyle, Roddy (*b.* 1958) Irish novelist, playwright, and screenwriter. He won the British 1993 Booker Prize with *Paddy Clarke Ha Ha Ha*, building on the success of his first two novels *The Commitments* (1987) and *The Snapper* (1990), both made into movies.

> "Soul is the rhythm o' sex. It's the rhythm o' the factory too. The workin' man's rhythm. Sex an' factory. Not the factory I'm in, said Natalie. There isn't much rhythm guttin' fish."
> [Roddy Doyle, *The Commitments*; 1987]

D'Oy·ly Carte /dòylee kaárt/, **Richard** (1844–1901) British theatrical agent, manager, and producer. He founded an eponymous opera company in 1875 to perform the operettas of W. S. Gilbert and Arthur Sullivan. From 1881 these operettas were staged at his own Savoy Theater, London.

doz. *abbr* dozen

doze[1] /dōz/ (**dozed, doz·ing, doz·es**) *vi* **1.** to sleep lightly for a short time, especially during the day **2.** to spend time lazily or in a daydream [Mid-17C. Probably < N Germanic] —**doze** *n*

doze off *vi* to fall into a light sleep, especially unintentionally

doze[2] /dōz/ (**dozed, doz·ing, doz·es**) *vt* CONSTR same as **bulldoze** (sense 1) (*slang*) [Mid-20C. Back-formation < DOZER[1]]

doz·en /dúzz'n/ *n* (*plural same*) **GROUP OF 12** a group of 12 people or objects ■ *adj* **MANY** a large number of (*informal*) ○ *I've told you a dozen times already!* ■ **doz·ens** *npl* **A LARGE NUMBER** a large quantity or a great many (*informal*) ○ *has dozens of friends* ○ *gave away dozens more* [13C. Via Old French *dozeine* < Latin *duodecim* "twelve" < *duo* "two" + *decem* "ten"] —**doz·enth** *adj* ◇ **by the dozen** in large quantities

doz·er[1] /dṓzər/ *n* CONSTR same as **bulldozer** (*slang*) [Mid-20C. Shortening]

doz·er[2] /dṓzər/ *n* somebody sleeping lightly [Early 18C. < DOZE[1]]

do·zy /dṓzee/ (**-zi·er, -zi·est**) *adj* **1.** half asleep or tending to fall asleep or doze **2.** *US* rotten in the middle —**do·zi·ly** *adv*—**do·zi·ness** *n*

dp *abbr* **1.** COMPUT data processing **2.** PHYS dew point **3.** BASEBALL double play

DP *abbr* **1.** COMPUT data processing **2.** PHYS dew point **3.** *also* **D.P.** SOC WELFARE displaced person

D/P *abbr* COMM **1.** documents against payment **2.** documents against presentation

DPH *abbr* **1.** GOV Department of Public Health **2.** EDUC Doctor of Public Health

D.Phil. /dee fíl/, **D.Ph.** *abbr* EDUC Doctor of Philosophy

dpi *n* a measure of the density of the image produced by a computer screen or printer. Full form **dots per inch**

DPS *abbr* FIN dividends per share

DPT *abbr* IMMUNOL diphtheria, pertussis, tetanus (vaccine)

dpt. *abbr* **1.** department **2.** GRAM deponent

DPW *abbr* GOV Department of Public Works

dr *abbr* **1.** dining room (*used in advertisements*) **2.** MEASURE dram[1]

DR *abbr* **1.** NAVIG dead reckoning **2.** dining room (*used in advertisements*)

dr. *abbr* **1.** FIN debit **2.** MEASURE dram[1]

Dr. *abbr* **1.** Doctor **2.** Drive (*used in addresses*)

drab[1] /drab/ *adj* (**drab·ber, drab·best**) **1. LACKING COLOR OR BRIGHTNESS** uninteresting to look at because of a lack of color or brightness **2. BORING** lacking interest, enthusiasm, or excitement **3. OF PALE GRAYISH BROWN COLOR** of a dull pale grayish brown color ■ *n* **1. PALE GRAYISH BROWN COLOR** a dull pale grayish brown color **2.** TEXTILES **DULL-COLORED FABRIC** a gray or brown fabric [Early 16C. < Old French *drap* "cloth" (see DRAPE)] —**drab·ly** *adv* —**drab·ness** *n*

drab[2] /drab/ *n* **1. OFFENSIVE TERM** an offensive term that deliberately insults a woman's appearance or cleanliness (*archaic insult*) **2. OFFENSIVE TERM** an offensive term for a prostitute (*archaic*) ■ *vi* (**drabbed, drab·bing, drabs**) **USE PROSTITUTES** to have sex with prostitutes (*archaic*) [Early 16C. Origin ?]

drab·ble /drább'l/ (**-bled, -bling, -bles**) *vti* to become wet and dirty, or make something wet and dirty (*archaic*) [14C. < Low German *drabbeln* "splash in water"]

Drab·ble /drább'l/, **Margaret** (*b.* 1939) British novelist, editor, and critic. Her novels explore the dilemmas of women in contemporary society and include *The Needle's Eye* (1972) and *The Radiant Way* (1987). She edited *The Oxford Companion to English Literature* (1985).

> "When nothing is sure, everything is possible."
> [Margaret Drabble, *The Middle Ground*; 1980]

dra·cae·na /drə seénə/, **dra·ce·na** *n* **1.** a tropical evergreen plant with long, strap-shaped, often variegated leaves, popular as a house plant. Genus: *Dracaena*. **2.** a plant with long narrow leaves resembling a true dracaena. Genus: *Cordyline*. [Early 19C. Via modern Latin < Greek *drakaina*, feminine of *drakōn* "dragon"; from the supposed resemblance of the juice of one species to dragon's blood]

drachm /dram/ *n* **1.** MEASURE same as **dram**[1] (sense 2) **2.** *UK* same as **fluid dram 3.** MONEY, HIST same as **drachma** (sense 1) [14C. Via French < Greek *drakhmē* "number or amount one hand can hold" < assumed *drakh-* "grasp"]

drach·ma /drákmə/ (*plural* **-mas** or **-mae** /-mee/) *n* **1.** the main unit of the former Greek currency, before the euro **2.** MEASURE same as **dram**[1] (sense 2) **3.** an ancient Greek silver coin [Early 16C. Via Latin < Greek *drakhmē* (see DRACHM)]

Dra·co[1] /drákō/ *n* a large faint constellation of the northern hemisphere. See illustration at **constellation** [Late 17C. < Latin *draco, dracon-* (see DRAGON)]

Dra·co[2] /dráykō/ (*fl* 7th century B.C.) Athenian political leader and legislator. His legal code, established in Athens in 621 B.C., was considered to be unduly harsh and was later replaced by Solon's more moderate laws.

dra·co liz·ard /dràykō-/ *n* REPT same as **flying lizard** [< Latin *draco, dracon-* (see DRAGON)]

dra·co·ni·an /drə kṓnee ən/ *adj* **1.** unjustly harsh or severe **2.** relating to the Athenian legislator Draco or his wide-ranging and harsh code of laws [Late 19C. < Greek *Drakōn-* "Draco"] —**dra·co·ni·an·ism** *n*

dra·con·ic /drə kónnik/ *adj* **1.** relating to or like a dragon or dragons **2.** same as **draconian** [In sense 1 < Latin *draco, dracon-* (see DRAGON); in sense 2 < Greek *Drakō* "Draco"] —**dra·con·i·cal·ly** *adv*

Dra·cut /dráykət/ town in northeastern Massachusetts directly south of the New Hampshire border. It is a suburb of Lowell. Population: 28,828 (2002 estimate).

draff /draf/ *n* a residue left in brewing after the grain has been fermented. Use: cattle feed. [13C. Origin ?] —**draff·y** *adj*

draft /draft/ *n* **1. CURRENT OF COLD AIR** a current of uncomfortably cold air penetrating a room or other space **2. CURRENT OF AIR IN ENCLOSED SPACE** a current of air, especially one that is moving through an enclosed space such as a chimney or tunnel **3. PRELIMINARY VERSION** a preliminary version of a picture, document, or plan **4.** MIL **CONSCRIPTION** a system in which people are ordered to join the armed services in time of war **5. SYSTEM OF RECRUITING PLAYERS** a system of distributing the rights to unsigned players among professional sports teams **6.** FIN **CHECK** a written order to pay money from an account to a person or to another account **7.** ENG **REGULATING DEVICE** a valve that regulates the flow of air to or from a pipe such as a chimney **8.** BEVERAGES **BEER IN BARRELS** beer that is stored in and served from barrels or casks rather than bottles **9.** NAUT **DEPTH NEEDED BY SHIP TO FLOAT** the distance between the water line of a ship and the lowest part of its hull, which is the minimum depth of water it requires in order to float **10. PULLING ALONG OR DRAWING IN** the act of pulling something along, of drawing something in, or of breathing or drinking something **11. MOUTHFUL OF AIR, LIQUID, OR SMOKE** the amount of air, liquid, or smoke taken in in a single breath or swallow **12.** MED **DOSE OF LIQUID MEDICINE** a dose of medicine in liquid form (*dated*) ■ *v* (**draft·ed, draft·ing, drafts**) **1.** *vt* MIL **CALL SOMEBODY FOR MILITARY SERVICE** to select somebody for compulsory service in the armed forces **2.** *vt* **TRANSFER SOMEBODY SOMEWHERE FOR DUTY** to move or send somebody somewhere to carry out a particular task **3.** *vt* POL **CHOOSE SOMEBODY TO RUN FOR OFFICE** to choose somebody to run for elective office ○ *drafted her to run in the primary* **4.** *vt* **WRITE PRELIMINARY VERSION OF SOMETHING** to sketch or write a preliminary version of a picture, document, or plan **5.** *vi* TRANSP, SPORTS **FOLLOW PERSON OR VEHICLE CLOSELY** to follow closely behind another fast-moving competitor or vehicle, taking advantage of the reduced resistance to movement ■ *adj* **1.** BEVERAGES **SERVED FROM BARREL** stored in and served from a barrel rather than a bottle **2.** AGRIC **PULLING HEAVY LOADS** used to pull heavy loads ○ *a draft animal* [Mid-16C. Form of DRAUGHT] —**draft·er** *n* ◇ **on draft** available for serving from the barrel

draft board *n* a board of civilians responsible for registering, classifying, and selecting people for compulsory military service

draft dodg·er *n* somebody who seeks to avoid being drafted for military service

draft·ee /draf tée/ *n* somebody who has been drafted for military service

draft·er /dráftər/ *n* **1.** ARCHIT, ENG same as **draftsperson** **2.** a deviser and designer of something such as a document ○ *tried to understand the full intent of the drafters of the Constitution*

drafts·man /dráftsmən/ (*plural* **-men** /-mən/) *n* **1.** a man who makes detailed plans or drawings for buildings, ships, aircraft, or machines before they are built. This job is now done mainly by computer-aided design. **2.** a man who is skilled at drawing ○ *He's an excellent draftsman.* —**drafts·man·ship** *n*

drafts·per·son /dráfts pùrss'n/ (*plural* **-per·sons** or **-peo·ple** /-peep'l/) *n* **1.** a maker of detailed plans or drawings for buildings, ships, aircraft, or machines before they are built. This job is now done mainly by computer-aided design. **2.** somebody who is skilled at drawing

drafts·wom·an /dráfts wòommən/ (*plural* **-wom·en** /-wìmmin/) *n* **1.** a woman who makes detailed plans or drawings for buildings, ships, aircraft, or machines before they are built. This job is now done mainly by computer-aided design. **2.** a woman who is skilled at drawing

draft·y /dráftee/ (**-i·er, -i·est**) *adj* chilly and uncomfortable because of flowing currents of cold air —**draft·i·ly** *adv* —**draft·i·ness** *n*

drag /drag/ *v* (**dragged, drag·ging, drags**) **1.** *vt* **PULL SOMETHING ALONG WITH EFFORT** to move something, especially something that is too large, heavy, or cumbersome to carry, by pulling it along the ground or across a surface ○ *dragged the fallen tree out of the road* **2.** *vt* **PULL SOMEBODY OR SOMETHING BY FORCE** to move or remove somebody or something that resists, usually by pulling at the person or object with considerable force or violence **3.** *vt* **PERSUADE SOMEBODY TO COME AWAY** to cause, persuade, or force an unwilling person to stop doing something or to leave a place ○ *I'm sorry to drag you away from your work.* **4.** *vti* **TRAIL ALONG GROUND** to be in continuous contact with the ground while moving across it, or allow something to do this ○ *He dragged his feet as he walked.* **5.** *vti* **MOVE** to move, or move yourself or your feet, slowly and with difficulty or great reluctance ○ *I was so tired that I could scarcely drag myself up the stairs.* **6.** *vi* **PASS OR PROCEED SLOWLY** to pass or proceed at a very slow and boring pace ○ *The afternoon was beginning to drag.* **7.** *vt* COMPUT **MOVE ICON WITH MOUSE** to move an icon or other selected item on a computer screen by clicking on it with the mouse and pulling it to a new location **8.** *vt* **SEARCH UNDERWATER AREA** to search a river bed, pond, or other area of water using a net or hook in an attempt to find something or somebody **9.** *vi* **PUFF ON SMOKING MATERIAL** to put a cigarette, pipe, or cigar to the mouth and suck in the smoke (*informal*) **10.** *vi* **RACE IN CAR** to take part in a drag race ■ *n* **1. HINDRANCE** somebody or something that slows down physical movement or progress in an area or activity ○ *High interest rates have been a drag on the economy.* **2.** AVIAT, PHYS **RESISTANCE TO MOTION** the resistance experienced by a body moving through a fluid medium, especially by an aircraft when traveling through the air. Symbol **D** **3. SOMEBODY OR SOMETHING BORING** a person, task, duty, or event that is held to be extremely boring and irritating (*informal*) ○ *It was such a drag going alone.* **4. PUFF** a puff on a cigarette, pipe, or cigar (*informal*) **5. CLOTHING OF OPPOSITE SEX** clothing characteristic of one sex worn by a member of the other, especially women's clothing when worn by men (*slang*) **6. STREET** a street or road (*slang*) ○ *the main drag* **7. SLOW AND LABORIOUS MOVEMENT OR ACTION** an action or movement carried out slowly and with great effort or difficulty **8. DRAGGING MOVEMENT** a sound, movement, or act of dragging **9. LINE USED FOR DRAGGING RIVER** a line, chain, or hook that is used for searching or dredging the bottom of an area of water such as a river or pond **10.** VEHICLES **MACHINE OR VEHICLE THAT IS DRAGGED** a device or a vehicle such as a cart that is pulled along the surface of the ground **11.** MOTOR SPORTS same as **drag race** **12.** HUNTING **FOX SCENT** the scent left by a fox or other animal that is hunted by dogs **13.** HUNTING **ARTIFICIAL SCENT** an artificial scent put on the ground for hunting dogs to follow [14C. < either a form of DRAW or < related Old Norse *draga* < Germanic] ◇ **drag and drop** to click onto an item on a computer screen, move it with the mouse, and release it on an icon ◇ **drag your feet** *or* **heels** to be slow to act, usually because you would prefer to avoid doing anything ○ *dragging their feet on implementing the plan*

SYNONYMS See ***pull.***

drag down *vt* **1.** to reduce somebody or something to a lower level or an inferior status by force or pressure ○ *Stock indexes were dragged down by heavy selling today.* **2.** to make somebody feel listless, uninterested, or physically weak and tired ○ *Sitting home alone drags me down.*

drag in *vt* **1.** to insist on introducing an irrelevant topic into a conversation ○ *always drags in his own accomplishments* **2.** to involve an unwilling person in a particular situation ○ *Liz was going to the reunion and dragged me in.*

drag into *vt* **1.** to involve somebody in something dishonest, disreputable, or otherwise undesirable ○ *What are you trying to drag me into?* ○ *They were dragged into the scandal.* **2.** to insist on introducing an irrelevant topic or name into a conversation ○ *always drags his political opinions into our conversations*

drag on *vi* to continue for a very long time, especially past the expected or desired finishing time

drag out *vt* to make something last longer than is necessary or desirable

drag out of *vt* to force somebody to reveal or admit something ○ *Are you going to tell me, or do I have to drag it out of you?*

drag up *vt* to mention something that somebody does not want discussed or known, especially something unpleasant, upsetting, or embarrassing from that person's past

drag bunt *n* in baseball, a bunt made by a batter moving toward first base

drag chute *n* AUTOMOT, AEROSP same as **brake parachute**

dra·gée /dra zháy/ *n* **1. TINY CONFECTIONERY BALL** a tiny silver-coated ball used for decorating cakes **2. HARD-COATED CANDY** a candy consisting of a nut, piece of fruit, or other center covered in a hard sugar coating **3. SWEETENED PILL** a medicinal pill covered with a sugar coating to make it taste better [Late 17C. < French, modern form of Old French *dragie* (see DREDGE[2])]

drag·ger /drággər/ *n* a fishing boat that uses a trawl or dragnet

drag·gle /drágg'l/ (**-gled, -gling, -gles**) *v* **1.** *vti* to make something wet and dirty by trailing it along the ground, or become wet and dirty by being trailed along the ground **2.** *vi* to follow along behind somebody else in a slow and usually undisciplined or slovenly fashion [Early 16C. Probably < DRAG]

drag·gy /drággee/ (**-gi·er, -gi·est**) *adj* (*informal*) **1.** slow-moving ○ *a draggy musical* **2.** boring or otherwise annoying ○ *spent a draggy afternoon clearing the yard*

drag·hound /drág hòwnd/ *n* a hound used in a drag hunt to follow an artificial scent trail

drag hunt *n UK* a hunt in which a pack of hounds follows an artificial scent trail

drag·lift /drág lìft/ *n* a ski lift with metal bars or ropes that people hold onto as they are pulled up to the top of a slope on their skis

drag·line /drág lìn/ *n* **1.** a line that is used for dragging, e.g., when hauling a load or dragging a river or pond **2.** an excavating machine with a digging bucket attached by cables to a long jib and operated by being dragged back toward the machine by another cable

drag link *n* a link that conveys motion from the crank of one shaft to the crank of another. In motor vehicles, it is used to connect the steering gear to the steering arm.

drag·net /drág nèt/ *n* **1. POLICE HUNT FOR CRIMINAL** a systematic and coordinated search for a wanted person made by police **2. WEIGHTED NET USED UNDERWATER** a net with weights on it used when trawling for fish at sea or when searching for something at the bottom of a river or pond **3. NET FOR CATCHING GAME** a net that is drawn across the ground and used to trap small game

drag·o·man /drággəmən/ (*plural* **-mans** or **-men** /-mən/) *n* a guide or interpreter in some Arabic-, Turkish-, or Farsi-speaking countries (*archaic*) [16C. Via French, Italian, and medieval Greek < Arabic *targumān* < Aramaic *tūrgemānā* < Akkadian *targumānu* "interpreter"]

dragon

drag·on /drággən/ *n* **1. SCALY GREEN MONSTER** a mythical creature that has green scaly skin, wings, and a long tail, and breathes fire **2.** REPT **LARGE LIZARD** a large lizard, e.g., the Komodo dragon **3. OFFENSIVE TERM** an offensive term for a woman regarded as fierce and formidable (*insult*) [13C. Via French < Latin *dracon-* < Greek *drakōn* "snake"] ◇ **chase the dragon** to take heroin by heating it and breathing in the fumes (*slang*)

Drag·on *n* ASTRON same as **Draco**

drag·on ar·um *n* PLANTS same as **dragonroot** (sense 2)

drag·on boat *n* a long narrow boat decorated like a dragon, used especially by Chinese people when taking part in annual boat races celebrating the lunar year

drag·on·et /drággənət/ (*plural* **-ets** or *same*) *n* a small brightly colored spiny ocean fish with a flat head, narrow body, and large pectoral fins, living near the bottom of warm shallow waters. Family: Callionymidae. [14C. < DRAGON]

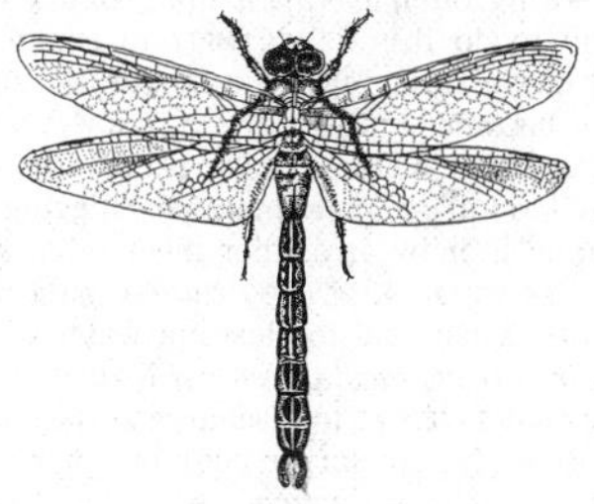

dragonfly

drag·on·fly /drággən flì/ (*plural* **-flies**) *n* an insect with a large head and eyes, a long thin body, and two pairs of iridescent often blue wings that usually remain outstretched when the insect is at rest. Suborder: Anisoptera.

drag·on·head /drággən hèd/ (*plural* **-heads** or *same*), **drag·on's head** (*plural* **drag·on's heads** or *same*) *n* a plant of the mint family grown for its spikes of double-lipped, white, pink, or purplish flowers. Genus: *Dracocephalum* or *Physostegia*.

drag·on·root /drággən ròot/ (*plural* **-roots** or *same*) *n* **1.** PLANTS same as **green dragon** **2.** a tuberous, foul-smelling, and poisonous perennial plant belonging to the arum family. Latin name: *Dracunculus vulgaris.*

drag·on's blood *n* a red resinous substance. Source: various trees including the dragon tree. Use: coloring varnishes, lacquers.

drag·on's teeth *npl* rows of short wedge-shaped concrete posts implanted in the ground as an antitank barrier, especially in World War II (*slang*) ◇ **sow dragon's teeth** to take action that is, either deliberately or accidentally, the cause of future quarreling and conflict (*literary*)

drag·on tree *n* an evergreen tree that has a trunk that grows very thick clusters of spiky leaves, orange fruit, and resin that is a source of dragon's blood. Native to: Canary Islands. Latin name: *Dracaena draco*.

dra·goon /drə go͞on/ *n* **1.** **MOUNTED INFANTRYMAN** in European armies of the 17th and 18th centuries, a mounted infantryman armed with a carbine **2.** **CAVALRYMAN** in armies of the late 18th and 19th centuries, a cavalryman, especially a heavily armed cavalryman. The word is retained in the names of some modern regiments that were originally cavalry regiments. ■ *vt* (**-gooned, -goon·ing, -goons**) **1.** **FORCE SOMEBODY** to involve somebody in an activity against his or her will, or force somebody to do something ○ *was dragooned into joining the chorus for the show* **2.** **SUBJUGATE SOMEBODY** to persecute or subjugate somebody using military troops [Early 17C. < French *dragon* "carbine, musket," literally "dragon"]

drag queen *n* a man who dresses as a woman, especially a performer who dresses in a flamboyant women's costume and traditionally affects feminine mannerisms for comic effect (*informal*)

drag race *n* a race between cars with specially modified bodies and engines on a straight track to discover which has the fastest acceleration —**drag rac·er** *n* —**drag rac·ing** *n*

drag·ster /drágstər/ *n* **1.** a car that is specially designed for and used in drag racing **2.** a driver who takes part in a drag race

drag strip *n* a short straight track, usually a quarter of a mile in length, used for drag racing

drain /drayn/ *n* **1.** **SEWAGE PIPE** a pipe or channel that carries water or sewage away from a place **2.** **SOMETHING THAT USES UP RESOURCES** something that diminishes or uses up resources or energy ○ *a serious drain on our cash reserves* **3.** **LOSS OR DIMINISHING** the gradual loss, withdrawal, or diminishing of something regarded as an important resource ○ *the drain of trained personnel from the industry* **4.** MED **DEVICE TO REMOVE FLUID FROM WOUND** a tube or other device placed in a wound or incision to draw off fluids such as blood, pus, or water **5.** AGRIC **ARTIFICIAL WATERWAY** an artificial waterway that allows for land drainage ■ *v* (**drained, drain·ing, drains**) **1.** *vti* **FLOW OUT** to flow out of something, often leaving it empty or dry, or allow a liquid to do this **2.** *vti* **EMPTY** to empty or dry something by allowing the water to flow out of or off it, or become empty or dry in this way ○ *drained and refilled the pool* **3.** *vt* AGRIC **DRY OUT LAND** to make marshy land drier by laying pipes, digging ditches or channels, or by any other means that removes the excess water **4.** *vt* GEOG **CHANNEL WATER AWAY FROM LAND** to be a channel for leading water off land ○ *The Loire drains most of central France.* **5.** *vi* GEOG **DISCHARGE INTO SOMETHING** to discharge surface water or flow into a river or larger body of water (*refers to geographic areas or watercourses*) ○ *The Mississippi River drains into the Gulf of Mexico.* **6.** *vt* **DRINK SOMETHING UP** to empty a cup, glass, or other container by drinking all its contents ○ *drained his coffee in one gulp* **7.** *vt* **USE SOMETHING UP** to use up or deplete something gradually, especially somebody's energy and resources, by making constant demands on it ○ *draining the company's financial resources* **8.** *vi* **WANE** to disappear gradually, or become less strong or intense ○ *The color drained from her cheeks.* **9.** *vt* **EXHAUST SOMEBODY** to leave somebody feeling physically or emotionally exhausted ○ *Working with toddlers really drains my energy.* [Old English *dreahnian* < Germanic] —**drain·a·ble** *adj* ◇ **down the drain** (*informal*) **1.** wasted or squandered with no hope of retrieval **2.** toward or in a state of total failure or ruin, especially financial failure

drain·age /dráynij/ *n* **1.** **DRAINING PROCESS** the process of draining liquid from something **2.** **SEWAGE SYSTEM** a system of pipes or channels that carries water or sewage away from a place **3.** MED **FLUID REMOVAL FROM BODY** the removal of fluid such as water, blood, or pus from a wound or part of the body, usually by means of a tube **4.** **FLUID REMOVED BY DRAINING** water, sewage, or another fluid removed by draining

drain·age ba·sin, drain·age ar·e·a *n* GEOG same as **catchment area** (sense 2)

drain·board /dráyn bàwrd/ *n* a slightly sloping metal or plastic surface with shallow grooves on it, next to a sink, that allows water to drain off wet dishes into the sink

drain·er /dráynər/ *n* a rack or container in which things are put so that liquid can drain off them

drain·ing board *n UK* same as **drainboard**

drain·pipe /dráyn pìp/ *n* a pipe that carries off rainwater, wastewater, or sewage to or through drains, especially a downspout attached to the side of a house

drake /drayk/ *n* a male duck [13C. Probably < Germanic]

Drake /drayk/, **Sir Francis** (1540?–96) English navigator and admiral. He was the first English person to circumnavigate the globe, and he later helped to defeat the Spanish Armada (1588).

> "The advantage of time and place in all practical actions is half a victory; which being lost is irrecoverable."
> [Sir Francis Drake, *Letter to Queen Elizabeth I*; 1588]

Dra·kens·berg /dra̋akənz bùrg/ mountain range extending through southeastern South Africa and Lesotho. The highest peaks include Thabana-Ntlenya, 11,424 ft./3,482 m.

Drake Pas·sage stretch of water between South America and the Antarctic Peninsula that separates the South Atlantic and South Pacific oceans. Length: 500 mi./800 km.

dram[1] /dram/ *n* **1.** **UNIT OF WEIGHT** a unit of mass in the avoirdupois system equal to 1/16 of an ounce (or approximately 1.77 grams) **2.** **UNIT OF WEIGHT** a unit of apothecaries' weight equal to $\frac{1}{8}$ of an ounce or 60 grains/3.89 grams **3.** **SMALL ALCOHOLIC DRINK** a small amount of an alcoholic drink, particularly whiskey or brandy (*dated*) **4.** **VERY SMALL AMOUNT** a very small amount of something ○ *not a dram of remorse* [15C. Via Old French *drame* or medieval Latin *drama* < Greek *drakhmē* (see DRACHM)]

dram[2] /dram/ *n* the main unit of Armenian currency. See table at **currency** [Via Armenian < Greek *drakhmē* (see DRACHM)]

DRAM /dée ràm/ *abbr* dynamic random access memory

dram. *abbr* dramatic

dra·ma /dra̋amə, drámmə/ *n* **1.** THEATER **PERFORMED PLAY** a serious play written for performance on stage, television, or radio **2.** ARTS **PLAYS AS GENRE** works written for performance on the stage, television, or radio considered as a literary genre ○ *17th-century French drama* **3.** THEATER **PRODUCING OR PERFORMING PLAYS** the performance, production, or writing of plays considered as a job, activity, or subject to be studied **4.** **EXCITING EVENT** a real-life event or situation that is particularly exciting or emotionally involving ○ *the drama of the trapped climbers* **5.** **DRAMATIC EVENTS OR QUALITY** exciting, tense, and gripping events and actions, or an exciting, tense, and gripping quality, either in a work of art or in a real-life situation ○ *an evening full of drama* [Early 16C. Via late Latin < Greek, "play, deed" < *dran* "do"]

Dram·a·mine /drámmə mèen/ *tdmk* a trademark for a motion-sickness medication

dra·mat·ic /drə máttik/ *adj* **1.** **SUDDEN AND MARKED** large in degree or scale, and often occurring with surprising suddenness ○ *a dramatic jump in prices* **2.** **STRIKING** bold, vivid, or strikingly impressive in appearance, color, or effect ○ *a dramatic view of the Alps* **3.** **EXCITING AND INTENSE** characterized, in real life or in art, by the kind of intense and gripping excitement, startling suddenness, or larger-than-life impressiveness associated with drama and the theater ○ *the dramatic rescue of the survivors at sea* **4.** **FOR THEATER** written for the theater, or relating to the theater, plays, or acting **5.** **HAVING POWERFUL EXPRESSIVE VOICE** having a powerful singing voice especially suited to the expression of intense emotion, e.g., in tragic or villainous roles in opera ○ *a dramatic tenor* [Late 16C. Via late Latin < Greek *drāmatikos* < *drama* (see DRAMA)]

dra·mat·i·cal·ly /drə máttikəlee/ *adv* **1.** in a way that grabs the attention and causes an excited, shocked, or startled reaction ○ *flung the papers dramatically to the floor* **2.** to a very noticeable degree and often with surprising suddenness ○ *The water quality has improved dramatically.*

dra·mat·ic i·ro·ny *n* a situation, or the irony arising from a situation, in which the audience has a fuller knowledge of what is happening in a drama than a character does

dra·mat·ic mon·o·logue *n* a poem or other literary work consisting of words supposedly spoken by a character, often in a specific situation, either directly to the reader or to a listener

dra·mat·ics /drə máttiks/ *n* the performance and production of plays for the theater, especially in a nonprofessional context (*takes a singular verb*) ■ *npl* theatrical and exaggerated behavior (*takes a plural verb*) ○ *Spare us the dramatics and just tell us what happened!*

dra·ma·tis per·so·nae /dràmətiss pər sṓnee, dra̋amətiss-, -nī/ *n* **LIST OF CHARACTERS** a list of the names of the characters who appear in a play, usually printed in the text of a play or in a theater program (*takes a singular verb*) ■ *npl* (*formal*; *takes a plural verb*) **1.** **CHARACTERS IN PLAY** the characters who appear in a play **2.** **PEOPLE IN SITUATION** the people involved in a specific situation [< Latin, "persons of the drama"]

dram·a·tist /drámmətist, dra̋amətist/ *n* a writer of plays for the stage, television, or radio

dram·a·tize /drámmə tìz, dra̋amə-/ (**-tized, -tiz·ing, -tiz·es**) *v* **1.** *vt* to turn a literary work or a real event into a drama for presentation on the stage, television, or radio **2.** *vti* to make something more dramatic, especially to exaggerate the importance or seriousness of a situation in an attention-seeking and theatrical way —**dram·a·ti·za·tion** /dràmməti záysh'n, dra̋amə-/ *n* —**dram·a·tiz·er** *n*

dram·a·turge /drámmə tùrj, dra̋amə tùrj/ *n* **1.** *also* **dra·mat·ur·gist** /-tùrjist/ a playwright, particularly one who works with a specific theater or company **2.** *also* **dra·ma·turg** a member of the staff of a theater with mainly literary responsibilities, e.g., choosing the plays for performance, editing and adapting texts, and writing program notes [Mid-19C. Via French < Greek *dramatourgos* "worker in drama" < *drama* (see DRAMA)]

dram·a·tur·gy /drámmə tùrjee, dra̋amə-/ *n* the art of the theater, especially with regard to the techniques involved in writing plays —**dram·a·tur·gic** /dràmmə túrjik, dra̋amə-/ *adj* —**dram·a·tur·gi·cal** *adj* —**dra·ma·tur·gi·cal·ly** *adv*

dram·e·dy /dra̋amədee, drámmədee/ (*plural* **-dies**) *n* a play, television show, or movie that mixes features of drama and comedy [Late 20C. Blend of DRAMA + COMEDY]

drank past tense of **drink**

drape /drayp/ *v* (**draped, drap·ing, drapes**) **1.** *vt* **PLACE FABRIC OVER SOMETHING** to hang a piece of fabric over something so that it falls in folds around it or covers it ○ *draped a scarf over her shoulders* **2.** *vt* **COVER SOMETHING WITH FABRIC** to cover something with a piece of fabric, usually so that the fabric hangs down around it in folds ○ *a chair draped in a dust sheet* **3.** *vi* **HANG IN FOLDS** to hang or be able to hang in loose folds on or over something ○ *a heavy fabric that will drape well* **4.** *vt* **REST PART OF BODY CASUALLY** to place part of the body on or over something such as the back of a chair, in a relaxed and casual way ○ *She draped herself elegantly over the sofa.* ■ *n* **1.** HOUSEHOLD same as **curtain** *n* (sense 1) (*usually used in the plural*) **2.** **PIECE OF DRAPING FABRIC** a piece of fabric used to drape over something **3.** MED **STERILE COVER** a piece of cloth placed over a patient's body during an examination or operation to provide a sterile area around the part of the body that is being treated **4.** **WAY FABRIC HANGS** the way in which fabric hangs and forms folds, especially when made into a garment ○ *adjusting the drape of the dress* [15C. < Old French *draper* < *drap* "cloth" < late Latin *drappus* < Celtic]

drap·er /dráypər/ *n UK* a dealer in fabric and sewing materials (*dated*) [14C. < Old French *drapier* < *drap* (see DRAPE)]

Dra·per /dráypər/ city in northern Utah on the the Jordan River. It is a southern suburb of Salt Lake City. Population: 29,268 (2002 estimate).

LANGUAGE HERITAGE ***Dravidian*** Much of English is made up of words from other languages, and Dravidian, a group of languages spoken in southern India and northeastern Sri Lanka, including Tamil, Telugu, Kannada, and Malayalam, is a small but significant contributor in this respect. From southern South Asia English has received especially names for foods, plants and materials from plants, and terms of music and dance.

From the cuisine of the region have come ***curry*** (late 16th century, from Tamil *kaṟi* "sauce"), ***dosa*** (a pancake, from Tamil), ***mango*** (late 16th, via Portuguese and Malay from Tamil), ***mulligatawny*** (late 18th, from Tamil *miḷaku-taṇṇi* "pepper-water"), ***poppadom*** (early 19th, from Tamil), and ***sambhar*** (a spiced vegetarian stew, mid-20th, via Tamil from Sanskrit *sambhāra* "collection"). Malayalam has given people the ***cachou*** to sweeten the breath (late 16th century, via French) and the ***jak*** fruit (late 16th, via Portuguese).

Names of plants and their products include ***areca*** (late 16th century, via Portuguese from Malayalam), ***betel*** (mid-16th, via Portuguese from Malayalam *veṟṟila*, itself from Tamil), ***coir*** (coconut fiber, late 16th, from Malayalam), ***copra*** (dried coconut, late 16th, from Malayalam via Portuguese), ***patchouli***, source of an aromatic oil (mid-19th, from Tamil), ***poon*** (late 17th, via Sinhalese from Malayalam or Tamil), ***teak*** (late 17th, via Portuguese from Tamil or Malayalam *tēkku*), and ***vetiver*** (mid-19th, via French from Tamil *veṭṭivēr*, from *vēr* "root"). Migrating animals include the ***bandicoot*** (late 18th, from Telugu *pandikokku*, literally "pig-rat") and the ***dhole*** (a wild dog, early 19th, probably from Kannada *tōḷa* "wolf").

In the arts have come ***Kathakali***, a form of drama combining dance and mime (from a Malayalam compound formed from Sanskrit *kathā* "story" + Malayalam *kaḷi* "play"), ***mridanga***, a kind of drum (from Tamil), and perhaps the ***tom-tom*** (from an imitative form in either Telugu or Hindi). A migrant with an unexpected musical connection is ***pariah***: hereditary drummers in southern India belonged to a low caste, and the word comes from Tamil *paṟaiyan* "drummer."

Some of the less obvious Dravidian migrants fall into no particular category: ***catamaran*** (early 17th century, from Tamil *kaṭṭumaram* "tied wood"), ***cheroot*** (late 17th, via French from Tamil), ***cot*** (mid-17th, from Hindi *khāṭ* "framework strung with rope and used as a bed," via Sanskrit from Tamil *kaṭṭu* "tie"), and ***godown*** ("warehouse," late 16th), which looks like a word formed from English elements but in fact came via Portuguese *guḍao* from Tamil *kiṭanku*, Kannada *gadangu* "store."

drap·er·y /dráypəree/ (*plural* **-ies**) *n* **1.** cloth or clothing that has been arranged to hang in elegant or decorative folds **2.** HOUSEHOLD same as **curtain** *n* (sense 1) (*usually used in the plural*) **3.** *UK* COMM same as **dry goods** [14C. < Old French *draperie* < *drap* (see DRAPE)]

dras·tic /drástik/ *adj* **1.** having a powerful effect or far-reaching consequences ○ *a crisis calling for drastic measures* **2.** very noticeable, significant, and usually worrying because of its amount or degree ○ *drastic budget cuts* [Late 17C. < Greek *drastikos* "effective, active" < *dran* "do"]

dras·ti·cal·ly /drástikəlee/ *adv* to a very great and usually very worrying degree

drat /drat/ *interj* used to express annoyance or frustration (*informal*) [Early 19C. Alteration of *od rot*, shortening of *God rot*]

draught *n, adj* UK spelling of **draft** ■ *n UK* BOARD GAMES same as **checker**[2] *n* (sense 2)

draught·board /dráft bàwrd/ *n UK* same as **checkerboard**

draughts /drafts/ *n UK* same as **checkers**

Dra·va /draávə/ tributary of the Danube River in south central Europe. It rises in the Italian Alps, flows through Austria and Slovenia, and then forms part of Croatia's frontier with Hungary. Length: 447 mi./719 km.

Dra·vid·i·an /drə víddee ən/ *n* a family of languages spoken in southern India and northeastern Sri Lanka. Native speakers: 200 million. [Mid-19C. < Sanskrit *Drāvida* "relating to the southern group (roughly the Tamils)"] —**Dra·vid·i·an** *adj*

draw /draw/ *v* (**drew** /droo/, **drawn** /drawn/, **draw·ing, draws**) **1.** *vti* MAKE PICTURE to make a line, picture, or plan on a surface using a pencil, pen, or crayon rather than paints ○ *She drew a picture of a flower.* **2.** *vt* DESCRIBE SOMETHING to depict or describe something in words ○ *He drew a vivid picture of life in 18th-century Philadelphia.* **3.** *vi* MOVE to move in a particular direction, often alongside, toward, or away from something else, and with a smooth steady motion ○ *Another car drew alongside ours.* **4.** *vi* APPROACH to approach through time, or move toward a point or stage in something, especially its end ○ *The meeting was drawing to a close.* **5.** *vt* PULL SOMEBODY OR SOMETHING to pull something, or lead or pull somebody, in a particular direction, especially toward or away from something ○ *She drew him toward the door.* **6.** *vt* TRANSP PULL VEHICLE to pull a vehicle along ○ *a carriage drawn by six horses* **7.** *vt* OPEN OR CLOSE CURTAIN to pull a curtain or blind across a window so that it covers or uncovers it **8.** *vt* PULL ON STRING to pull on a string, rope, or cord, usually in order to tighten it around something **9.** *vt* ARCHERY PULL BACK STRING OF BOW to pull back the string of a bow prior to shooting an arrow **10.** *vt* TAKE SOMETHING OUT to take or pull an object out of something in which it has been enclosed or embedded ○ *drew the letter out of the envelope* **11.** *vti* PULL WEAPON FROM SHEATH to pull a weapon from a holster or sheath in order to use it **12.** *vt* REMOVE LIQUID to remove liquid from a large container such as a barrel by means of a tap **13.** *vt* MED DRAIN WOUND to drain a liquid such as blood, pus, or water from a wound or incision **14.** *vt* HAUL UP WATER to haul up water from a well or other source using a bucket on a rope **15.** *vt* ELICIT RESPONSE to cause somebody or something to make a response or sound ○ *drew hoots of derision from the crowd* **16.** *vt* OBTAIN SOMETHING FROM SOURCE to obtain a physical or a moral resource from a place or thing ○ *drew courage from her example* **17.** *vt* OBTAIN INFORMATION FROM SOMEBODY to obtain information, a secret, or an opinion from somebody by questioning or persuasion (*often passive*) ○ *She refused to be drawn on the subject.* **18.** *vt* ATTRACT ATTENTION OR INTEREST to cause somebody's attention, eye, or interest to be directed toward somebody or something ○ *draw admiring glances* **19.** *vt* ATTRACT PEOPLE to attract a person or group to come to see something or somebody ○ *The performance always drew crowds.* **20.** *vt* SUCK SOMETHING IN to suck something in, especially air into the lungs ○ *I drew a long breath.* **21.** *vi* SMOKE CIGARETTE OR PIPE to suck smoke in from a cigarette or pipe **22.** *vi* ALLOW AIR THROUGH to allow a current of air to flow through, removing smoke or gases **23.** *vt* WITHDRAW MONEY to take money out of a bank, savings account, or similar source ○ *He drew $600 from the bank.* **24.** *vt* FIN RECEIVE MONEY to receive money regularly from a source ○ *draws a regular salary* **25.** *vt* WRITE CHECK to write a check, bill of exchange, or promissory note **26.** *vt* LAW WRITE OUT LEGAL DOCUMENT to compose or write out a legal document in the proper form **27.** *vt* ARRIVE AT CONCLUSION to arrive at a conclusion or inference by examining the evidence for something ○ *You'll have to draw your own conclusions.* **28.** *vt* FORMULATE SOMETHING to formulate or state a distinction, comparison, or parallel between two or more things ○ *drew a distinction between the causes of the two events* **29.** *vt* CHOOSE SOMETHING AT RANDOM to choose or be given something at random, usually in order to ensure that all participants are treated fairly ○ *They drew lots to see who would have to go.* **30.** *vt* CARDS TAKE PLAYING CARD in card games, to take a card from a stack, the deck, or the dealer **31.** *vt* CARDS MAKE PLAYERS PLAY PARTICULAR SUIT in card games, to make the other players play the cards they have in a specific suit by repeatedly leading that suit ○ *drew trumps and played twelve tricks* **32.** *vti* FINISH EQUAL to finish a game with the scores for the opposing sides the same or with neither side having won ○ *drew 1–1 in the semifinals* **33.** *vt* NAUT NEED PARTICULAR DEPTH OF WATER to need a particular depth of water in which to float **34.** *vt* MANUF MAKE WIRE to make wire by pulling a length of metal through a conical hole **35.** *vt* DISEMBOWEL SOMEBODY to disembowel a hanged person **36.** *vt* CUE GAMES GIVE BACKSPIN TO BALL in cue games, especially billiards, to give a backward spin to a ball when making a stroke **37.** *vt* GOLF MAKE BALL CURVE in golf, to hit a ball so that it curves in flight following the direction of the golfer's swing instead of traveling straight. The ball is drawn to the left by a right-handed player and to the right by a left-handed player. ■ *n* **1.** ACT OF DRAWING OR PULLING the act of pulling or sucking on something or otherwise drawing something **2.** GAMBLING LOTTERY a lottery, raffle, or other competition where the winner is decided by selecting a ticket at random **3.** GAMBLING CHOOSING LOTTERY WINNER the choosing of a winner in a lottery, raffle, or other competition by selecting a ticket at random **4.** SELECTION OF OPPONENTS the act of selecting at random which contestants are to play each other in a sports contest, or the resulting list of games to be played ○ *the draw for the third round of the competition* **5.** CARDS, GAMBLING SOMETHING CHOSEN AT RANDOM something chosen at random, e.g., a ticket in a lottery or a playing card or cards taken from a stack or the dealer **6.** ATTRACTION something or somebody that interests a lot of people and attracts them as spectators, visitors, or customers ○ *The rock band will be a huge draw for the local fair.* **7.** CONTEST THAT NEITHER SIDE WINS a contest that ends with both sides having the same score or with neither side having won **8.** DRAWING OF GUN the action of pulling a gun from its holster in order to fire it, especially in a gunfight **9.** GEOG SHALLOW GULLY a shallow natural channel into which rainwater drains **10.** MOVABLE PART OF DRAWBRIDGE the movable part of a drawbridge **11.** CARDS SECOND OR FURTHER DEAL in draw poker, the deal made to improve the players' hands after they have discarded [Old English *dragan* < Germanic, "carry"] —**draw·a·ble** *adj*

SYNONYMS See *pull*.

draw back *vi* **1.** pull back suddenly, e.g., in fear **2.** to decide not to continue with some contemplated, planned, or agreed action ○ *They drew back from the deal at the last moment.*

draw in *v* **1.** *vt* INVOLVE SOMEBODY to get somebody involved in something unwillingly (*often passive*) ○ *I got drawn in before I realized what the argument was really about.* **2.** *vt* SUCK SOMETHING IN to breathe or suck something in **3.** *vi UK* BEGIN EARLIER to begin earlier, so that darkness comes sooner (*refers to nights or evenings in fall*) **4.** *vi UK* BECOME SHORTER to become shorter, so that darkness comes sooner (*refers to days in fall*)

draw off *vt* to remove a small amount of liquid from a larger amount by means of a tube or pipe

draw on *v* **1.** *vt* USE SOMETHING to make use of a resource for personal benefit ○ *The novel draws on her experiences in Alaska.* **2.** *vi* ENTER LATER STAGE to enter a later stage, or move toward an end ○ *as the day drew on* **3.** *vt* TAKE IN SMOKE to inhale the smoke from a cigarette or pipe ○ *He drew on his pipe.* **4.** *vt* WITHDRAW MONEY FROM ACCOUNT to take money out of a bank or savings account

draw out *v* **1.** *vt* PROLONG SOMETHING to make something continue longer than is usual, necessary, or desirable ○ *I drew the conversation out as long as I could.* **2.** *vi* GROW LONGER to have more hours of daylight (*refers to days in spring*) **3.** *vt* GET SOMEBODY TO TALK to encourage a shy, hostile, or reserved person to talk at length or in detail, or to become more forthcoming in a social or legal situation ○ *drew the witness out during cross-examination* **4.** *vi* MOVE AWAY FROM SOMETHING to move away from a close or inner position ○ *The car drew out unexpectedly and hit the passing cyclist.*

draw up *v* **1.** *vt* WRITE SOMETHING OUT to prepare or write out a plan, list, or other document ○ *drawing up the terms of the contract* **2.** *vti* COME TO STOP to arrive at a point or place in a vehicle or on a horse and stop, or bring a vehicle or horse to a halt ○ *saw the bus draw up* **3.** *vt* BRING SOMETHING NEARER to place a chair or seat near something or somebody and sit down on it **4.** *vr* STRAIGHTEN UP to straighten the body in order to reach full height and look as imposing or dignified as possible ○ *drew herself up proudly before speaking*

draw·back /dráw bàk/ *n* **1.** something that causes problems or is a disadvantage or hindrance ○ *The only drawback is the size of the machine.* **2.** a refund of tax or import duty on goods that are later exported

draw·bar /dráw baar/ *n* a strong metal bar attached across the back of a tractor, locomotive, or other vehicle, with a coupling on it to which machinery or a trailer can be hitched

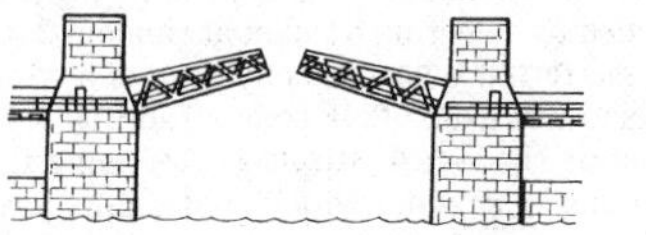

drawbridge

draw·bridge /dráw brìj/ *n* a bridge that is hinged at one end or in the middle and can be lifted up to cut off access to a place or allow something to pass beneath it

draw·down /dráw dòwn/ *n* **1.** the process of reducing or using up a supply or store of something **2.** a lowering of the level of the water in a reservoir

draw·ee /draw ée/ *n* the person or organization from whose account money is taken when a check or other order for payment is drawn

draw·er /(furniture) drawr, (other senses) dráw ər/ *n* **1.** STORAGE COMPARTMENT IN FURNITURE a storage compartment in a piece of furniture such as a desk, chest, or table that slides in and out and is usually shaped like a shallow rectangular box **2.** SOMEBODY WHO WRITES CHECK somebody who draws a check or money order **3.** SOMEBODY OR SOMETHING THAT DRAWS somebody or something that draws, especially somebody who draws pictures or plans ■ **draw·ers** *npl* UNDERPANTS large old-fashioned underpants with short legs, worn by men or women

draw·ing /dráw ing/ *n* **1.** a picture of something made with a pencil, pen, or crayon, usually consisting of lines, often with shading, but generally without color **2.** the art, activity, or practice of making pictures using a pencil, crayon, or pen ○ *I never was very good at drawing.* **3.** GAMBLING same as **draw** *n* (senses 2–3)

draw·ing ac·count *n* a company account from which a company employee may draw money for expenses or as an advance against a future salary payment

draw·ing board *n* a large flat board used for drawing and design work, usually attached to a frame with legs and adjustable to different heights and angles ◇ **back to the drawing board** back to the beginning or the planning stage of a failed operation or project, ready to start all over again (*informal*) ○ *Our proposal was rejected; we've got to go back to the drawing board.*

draw·ing card *n* ARTS same as **draw** *n* (sense 6)

draw·ing pin *n UK* same as **thumbtack**

draw·ing room *n* a large formal room in a house, in which guests are entertained [Mid-17C. Shortening of *withdrawing room*]

draw·knife /dráw nīf/ (*plural* **-knives** /-nīvz/) *n* a tool consisting of a narrow rectangular blade with a handle at either end set at right angles to it. Use: shaving the surface of wood.

drawl /drawl/ *n* a way of speaking in which the speaker draws out the vowel sounds and pronounces words slowly ■ *vti* (**drawled, drawl·ing, drawls**) to draw out the vowel sounds and pronounce words with a slow inflection when speaking [Late 16C. Probably < Middle Dutch *dralen* "linger, delay" < *dragan* "to draw"] —**drawl·er** *n* —**drawl·ing·ly** *adv*

drawn /drawn/ past tense of **draw** ■ *adj* appearing tired and careworn, usually as a result of anxiety, grief, or illness ○ *He looked pale and drawn.*

drawn but·ter *n* melted butter that has had the solids removed, served as a sauce, sometimes with herbs and seasoning

drawn-out *adj* continuing longer than is intended or desired

drawn-thread work, drawn work *n* embroidery in which some threads are pulled from the fabric and stitches are worked on the remaining threads to produce decorated open areas

draw·plate /dráw plàyt/ *n* a plate pierced by conical holes through which metal is drawn in wire making

draw pok·er *n* a form of poker in which each player is dealt five cards face down and after the first round of betting can draw replacements for any discards

draw·shave /dráw shàyv/ *n* WOODWORK same as **drawknife**

draw shot *n* in cue games, a shot in which the cue ball is hit below center so that the backspin makes it bounce back when it hits another ball

draw·string /dráw strìng/ *n* a cord threaded through a hem, piping, or eyelets around the opening in a bag or a garment so that it can be tightened or the opening can be closed

draw·tube /dráw toob/ *n* a tube that slides inside another tube, e.g., one of the extending tubes in a telescope

dray /dray/ *n* a large low horse-drawn cart with no fixed sides, designed for heavy loads [14C. < Old English *dragan* "to draw"]

dray·horse /dráy hàwrss/ *n* a large horse used for pulling a dray

dread /dred/ *vti* (**dread·ed, dread·ing, dreads**) **1.** FEEL EXTREMELY FRIGHTENED to feel extremely frightened or worried about something that may happen in the future **2.** BE RELUCTANT to be reluctant or frightened to do something because it is unpleasant, upsetting, or annoying ■ *n* **1.** TERROR a feeling of great fear or terror, especially at the thought of experiencing or encountering something unpleasant **2.** SOURCE OF DREAD something that is dreaded **3.** *also* **dred** RASTAFARIAN somebody who is considered a genuine Rastafarian (*slang; used in Black English*) ■ *adj* **1.** FEARED causing fear and extreme anxiety (*literary*) ○ *The dread day arrived.* **2.** AWE-INSPIRING inspiring fear and respect or awe in equal measure (*literary*) **3.** *also* **dred** GOOD good or excellent (*slang; used in Black English*) ■ *interj also* **dred** EXPRESSES APPROVAL used to express approval (*slang; used in Black English*) [12C. Shortened < Old English *adrǣdan, ondrǣdan* "counsel against" < *rǣdan* (see REDE)]

dread·ed /dréddəd/ *adj* inspiring great fear (*sometimes used humorously*)

dread·ful /drédfəl/ *adj* **1.** EXTREMELY BAD extremely unpleasant, harmful, or serious in its effects ○ *a dreadful mistake* **2.** EXTREME extreme in character or degree ○ *a dreadful waste of time* **3.** AWE-INSPIRING inspiring awe (*literary*) **4.** *also* **dread·full** WONDERFUL very good or pleasing (*slang; used in Black English*) —**dread·ful·ness** *n*

dread·ful·ly /drédfəlee/ *adv* **1.** in a very unsatisfactory or unpleasant way ○ *He behaved dreadfully.* **2.** *UK* to a very great extent

dreadlocks: Bob Marley

dread·locks /dréd lòks/, **dred·locks** *npl* long strands of hair that have been twisted closely from the scalp down to the tips in a style made popular by Rastafarians [Mid-20C. Because of a supposed fear of the power of faithful Rastafarians] —**dread·locked** *adj*

dread·nought /dréd nàwt/ *n* a heavily armed battleship whose main guns are all of the same caliber [Early 20C. After the British battleship *Dreadnought*]

dreads /dredz/, **dreds** *npl* HAIR same as **dreadlocks** [Late 20C. Contraction]

dream /dreem/ *n* **1.** SEQUENCE OF MENTAL IMAGES DURING SLEEP a sequence of images that appear involuntarily to the mind of somebody who is sleeping, often a mixture of real and imaginary characters, places, and events **2.** DAYDREAM a series of images, usually pleasant ones, that pass through the mind of somebody who is awake **3.** SOMETHING HOPED FOR something that somebody hopes, longs, or is ambitious for, usually something difficult to attain or far removed from present circumstances **4.** IDLE HOPE an idea or hope that is impractical or unlikely ever to be realized **5.** VAGUE STATE a state of inattention owing to preoccupation with thoughts or fantasies ○ *walks around in a dream* **6.** SOMETHING BEAUTIFUL somebody or something that seems particularly good-looking or wonderful ■ *v* (**dreamed** or **dreamt** /dremt/, **dream·ing, dreams**) **1.** *vti* HAVE DREAM WHILE SLEEPING to experience vivid mental images of something while sleeping **2.** *vi* DAYDREAM to let the mind dwell on pleasant scenes and images while awake, often resulting in inattention **3.** *vi* WISH to want something very much and imagine having or doing it, though it may be unlikely ○ *dreamed of living abroad* **4.** *vi* CONSIDER to think of or consider doing something regarded as wrong or inappropriate ○ *How could you even dream of doing such a thing?* ■ *adj* IDEAL perfect and wonderful in every way ○ *a dream vacation* [13C. Origin ?] —**dream·ful** *adj* ◇ **in your dreams** used to indicate that somebody's hope or expectation is completely unrealistic (*informal*)

dream up *vt* to devise or invent something, especially a complicated, ingenious, or ridiculous plan

dream·boat /dréem bōt/ *n* somebody considered to be very good-looking (*informal*)

dream·catch·er /dréem kàchər/ *n* a hoop-shaped hanging ornament of beads and feathers made by some Native North Americans, typically hung in the home, especially above a bed

dream·er /dréemər/ *n* **1.** somebody who is absorbed by fantasies or unrealistic plans **2.** somebody who dreams or is dreaming

dream·land /dréem lànd/ *n* **1.** a state of sleep or unconsciousness (*informal*) **2.** an imaginary, very pleasant, or perfect sphere of existence that exists only in dreams

dream·less /dréemləss/ *adj* deep, peaceful, and undisturbed by dreams ○ *a dreamless sleep* —**dream·less·ly** *adv* —**dream·less·ness** *n*

dream·like /dréem līk/ *adj* resembling a dream or the images in a dream, especially in seeming unreal or strange

dream·scape /dréem skàyp/ *n* a scene, setting, or picture that has the unreal or strange qualities usually associated with images in dreams

dream sheet *n* **1.** a form on which somebody serving in the military lists his or her preferences for postings and jobs (*slang*) **2.** a list of desirable postings made up by US military personnel, typical choices being bases close to home or the state of Hawaii **3.** same as **wish list** (*slang*)

dreamt past participle, past tense of **dream**

dream team *n* the best possible combination of people to perform a task (*informal*)

dream tick·et *n* a team of candidates running for associated political offices, especially those of president and vice president, who seem to have between them all the qualities needed for electoral success (*informal*)

dream world *n* a world that bears little resemblance to reality and exists only in the mind

dream·y /dréemee/ (**-i·er, -i·est**) *adj* **1.** VAGUE caused by dreaming or by thinking about something very pleasant and absorbing **2.** GIVEN TO DAYDREAMING having a tendency to spend time daydreaming or lost in thought **3.** UNREAL strange, vague, or ethereal, like an image in a dream **4.** SOOTHING gently soothing and relaxing **5.** GORGEOUS extremely good-looking or desirable (*informal*) —**dream·i·ly** *adv* —**dream·i·ness** *n*

drear /dreer/ *adj* dark, foreboding, and gloomy

(*literary*) ○ *a cold, drear day* [Mid-16C. Back-formation < DREARY]

drea·ry /dréeree/ (**-ri·er, -ri·est**) *adj* gloomy, unexciting, and certain to have a wearying and depressing influence ○ *a wet, dreary afternoon* [Old English *drēorig* "dripping with blood" < Germanic] —**drea·ri·ly** *adv* —**drea·ri·ness** *n*

dreck /drek/ *n* worthless trashy stuff, especially low-quality merchandise [Early 20C Via Yiddish *drek* "filth, dung" < Middle High German *drec*]

dredge[1] /drej/ *n* **1.** MACHINE FOR DIGGING UNDERWATER a machine equipped with a continuous revolving chain of buckets, a scoop, or a suction device for digging out and removing material from under water **2.** SHIPPING same as **dredger**[1] (sense 1) **3.** FISHERIES SHELLFISH NET a net on a frame dragged along the bottom of the sea or a river to gather shellfish ■ *v* (**dredged, dredg·ing, dredg·es**) **1.** *vti* USE DREDGE IN SEARCHING SOMETHING to search something, or search for something, using a dredge or a similar device **2.** *vt* DIG SOMETHING UP WITH DREDGE to remove or recover material from underwater by means of a dredge **3.** *vti* SHIPPING CLEAR CHANNEL to clear, deepen, or widen a waterway, especially one intended for shipping, using a dredge [Early 16C. Origin ?]
dredge up *vt* to bring something to light from an obscure source, e.g., to recall something bad that happened long ago or unearth some scandalous information

dredge[2] /drej/ (**dredged, dredg·ing, dredg·es**) *vt* to sprinkle or cover food with a coating of confectioner's sugar, flour, or sugar [Late 16C. Via Old French *dragie* "sugarplum, sugar almond" < Latin *tragemata* < Greek *tragēmata* "spices, sweets"]

dredg·er[1] /dréjjər/ *n* **1.** a boat or barge with a dredge on it, used mainly for clearing or deepening waterways **2.** CONSTR same as **dredge**[1] *n* (sense 1) [Early 16C. < DREDGE[1]]

dredg·er[2] /dréjjər/ *n* a container with small holes in the top used for sprinkling confectioner's sugar, flour, or sugar onto food [Mid-17C. < DREDGE[2]]

dred·locks *npl* another spelling of **dreadlocks**

dreds *npl* another spelling of **dreads**

dregs /dregz/ *npl* **1.** GRITTY PARTICLES IN LIQUID small solid particles found in liquids such as coffee or wine that sink to the bottom of a container and are most in evidence when the container is nearly empty **2.** LEAST VALUABLE PART the least valuable or most unpleasant part of something, especially a group of people ○ *the dregs of society* **3.** LAST REMAINING PART the last remaining, and often least attractive part of something (*literary*) ○ *sat through the dregs of a long boring evening* [14C. Probably < Old Norse *dregg* "sediment"]

D re·gion *n* **1.** the lowest part of the ionosphere above the Earth's surface **2.** a short sequence of various amino acids in an immunoglobulin that contributes to antibody diversity

drei·del /dráyd'l/, **drei·dl** *n* a toy that looks like a spinning top, used to play games during Hanukkah [Mid-20C. < Yiddish *dreydl* < Middle High German *dræhen* "turn"]

Drei·ser /drīssər, -zər/, **Theodore** (1871–1945) US novelist and journalist. He is known for his naturalist novels, including *An American Tragedy* (1925). Full name **Dreiser, Theodore Herman Albert**

> "Art is the stored honey of the human soul, gathered on wings of misery and travail."
> [Theodore Dreiser, *Life, Art and America*; 1917]

drench /drench/ *vt* (**drenched, drench·ing, drench·es**) **1.** SOAK SOMEBODY OR SOMETHING to make somebody or something completely wet ○ *got absolutely drenched in the storm* **2.** COVER WITH SOMETHING to cover or surround somebody or something with a large amount of something ○ *drenched in sunlight* **3.** VET GIVE LIQUID MEDICINE TO ANIMAL to give an animal a large dose of medicine in liquid form by mouth ■ *n* VET DOSE OF ANIMAL MEDICINE a large dose of medicine given to an animal in liquid form by mouth [Old English *drencan* "give to drink" < Germanic] —**drench·er** *n* —**drench·ing** *adj, n*

Dres·den /drézdən/ capital of the state of Saxony in east central Germany. Almost completely destroyed during World War II, it has been largely rebuilt and restored. Population: 474,443 (1997).

Dres·den chi·na *n Can, UK* fine and delicate porcelain as made in Meissen near Dresden in Germany since the early 18th century. US term **Meissen**[1]

dress /dress/ *v* (**dressed, dress·ing, dress·es**) **1.** *vti* PUT CLOTHES ON to put clothes on somebody or yourself, or put on clothes **2.** *vi* WEAR PARTICULAR CLOTHING to wear clothes of a particular type or in a particular way ○ *She usually dresses in black.* **3.** *vi* PUT ON APPROPRIATE CLOTHES to put on clothes appropriate to a particular occasion, especially formal clothes ○ *We need to dress for the theater.* **4.** *vt* DECORATE SOMETHING to make a place or object look festive by putting special decorations on it ○ *They dressed the big house for the holidays.* **5.** *vt* COMM ARRANGE GOODS IN WINDOW to arrange goods in a store window as an attractive display ○ *windows that were dressed for spring* **6.** *vt* MED COVER WOUND to put a bandage or other protective covering on a wound **7.** *vt* COOK PUT SAUCE ON SALAD to put mayonnaise, vinaigrette, or a similar sauce on a salad **8.** *vt* COOK, HUNTING CLEAN FISH AND GAME to clean and prepare fish, poultry, or meat for cooking or selling **9.** *vt* ARRANGE HAIR to arrange hair, e.g., by combing, clipping, or oiling it **10.** *vti* MIL COME OR BRING INTO ALIGNMENT to come, or bring troops, into a correct alignment with one another for a parade formation **11.** *vt* AGRIC SPREAD FERTILIZER ON SOIL to spread manure or fertilizer over the surface of an area of land **12.** *vt* FINISH MATERIAL to apply a finishing process to a material such as stone or lumber, usually in order to give it a smooth attractive surface ■ *n* **1.** WOMAN'S ONE-PIECE GARMENT a one-piece garment for women and girls combining a bodice, with or without sleeves, and a skirt, and covering most of the body **2.** PARTICULAR CLOTHES clothes of a particular type or style ○ *national dress* **3.** CLOTHES IN GENERAL clothes and clothing in general (*often used before nouns*) ○ *He has no interest in matters of dress.* ○ *a dress allowance* **4.** CLOTHES FOR PARTICULAR OCCASION the clothing required for a particular occasion ○ *casual dress* ○ *evening dress* **5.** *S Asia* SET OF CLOTHES an outfit or set of clothes for men or women **6.** OUTWARD APPEARANCE the outward appearance or covering of a thing, especially a living thing, or the way in which something is presented (*literary*) **7.** THEATER same as **dress rehearsal** (sense 1) (*informal*) ■ *adj* **1.** FORMAL describes clothes that are worn only on formal occasions ○ *dress uniform* **2.** REQUIRING FORMAL ATTIRE describes an event to which formal clothes must be worn ○ *a dress banquet* [14C. Via Old French *dresser* "arrange, prepare" < Vulgar Latin *directiare* < Latin *directus* "straight" (see DIRECT)] ◇ **dressed to kill** wearing very glamorous clothes, especially in order to impress somebody (*slang*)
dress down *v* (*informal*) **1.** *vi* to dress in a deliberately understated or casual way for an occasion **2.** *vt* to scold somebody severely
dress up *v* **1.** *vi* DRESS FORMALLY to put on formal or especially elegant clothes, usually for a special occasion such as a party **2.** *vi* PUT ON COSTUMES to put on a special costume or different clothes from those normally worn in order to look like or pretend to be somebody else **3.** *vt* DISGUISE SOMETHING to disguise something unpleasant and try to make it look more pleasant

dres·sage /drə saázh/ *n* **1.** the training of a horse to carry out a series of precise controlled movements in response to minimal signals from its rider **2.** a competitive event in which horse and rider are judged on the elegance, precision, and discipline of the horse's movements [Mid-20C. < French, "training" < *dresser* (see DRESS)]

dress cir·cle *n* a separate raised section of the auditorium in a theater, concert hall, or opera house, usually the first seating gallery above ground level

dress coat *n* a coat, forming part of a man's full evening dress, that is usually black with a cutaway skirt and tails

dress code *n* a set of requirements as to how people should dress, e.g., when at school or attending a function

dress-down day *n* a day, usually a Friday or during the summer months, on which office workers wear casual clothing to work

dress·er[1] /dréssər/ *n* **1.** a chest of drawers used in a bedroom for storing clothes, sometimes with a mirror on top **2.** a piece of furniture consisting of a set of shelves on top of a chest containing cupboards and drawers, often used for storing crockery and cutlery in traditional kitchens [Early 15C. < Old French *dresseur* < *dresser* (see DRESS)]

dress·er[2] /dréssər/ *n* **1.** SOMEBODY WHO DRESSES IN PARTICULAR WAY somebody who wears clothes in a particular way **2.** ACTOR'S ASSISTANT somebody who helps an actor to put on or change a costume before and during a performance **3.** PERSONAL GROOMING ASSISTANT somebody whose job it is to ensure that somebody else's wardrobe is in order [14C. < DRESS]

dress form *n* an adjustable dummy, used by tailors

dress·ing /dréssing/ *n* **1.** SALAD SAUCE a sauce used on salads, usually with an oil and vinegar or mayonnaise base **2.** MED WOUND COVERING a bandage or other sterile covering put on a wound to protect it from infection or further damage **3.** STUFFING a stuffing for poultry or meat **4.** AGRIC FERTILIZER a natural or artificial fertilizer for spreading on the soil

dress·ing-down *n* a scolding or severe reprimand, often in public (*informal*)

dress·ing gown *n* a coat made of soft light material that is worn over nightclothes or before or after a bath

dress·ing room *n* **1.** ROOM FOR TRYING ON CLOTHES a small room in a store for trying on clothes before making a decision about buying them **2.** ACTORS' ROOM TO PUT ON COSTUMES a room in a theater where actors can prepare for a performance by putting on their makeup and costumes **3.** ROOM TO CHANGE CLOTHES IN a small room in a house, hotel suite, or other place for people to change clothes

dress·ing ta·ble *n* a low table with drawers and a mirror attached to the top, usually placed in a bedroom so that somebody can sit at it while applying makeup

Dress·ler /drésslər/, **Marie** (1869–1934) Canadian-born US stage and movie actor. She won an Academy Award for her performance in *Min and Bill* (1930). Born **von Koerber, Leila**

dress·mak·er /dréss màykər/ *n* somebody who makes women's clothes, especially professionally —**dress·mak·ing** *n*

dress pa·rade *n* a military parade in which formal dress uniform is worn

dress re·hears·al *n* **1.** the final rehearsal of something such as a play, opera, or ballet in full costume and with lights, music, and effects, before it is given its first public performance **2.** a full-scale practice before any important event

dress sense *n* the ability to choose clothes well and coordinate colors and styles effectively

dress shield *n* a small fabric pad worn around the armpits of a piece of clothing to prevent sweat from showing or staining it

dress shirt *n* **1.** a shirt that is not casual and is suitable for wearing with a suit, e.g., at work **2.** a man's shirt worn with formal evening wear, usually white and with either a stiff collar or a ruffle down the front

dress suit *n* a man's suit worn as part of formal evening wear, especially with a tailcoat

dress u·ni·form *n* a ceremonial uniform worn by members of the armed forces for formal occasions

dress·y /dréssee/ (**-i·er, -i·est**) *adj* **1.** ELEGANT stylish and elegant **2.** WITH GUESTS DRESSED IN STYLE describes a social event at which stylish and elegant clothes are worn ○ *a very dressy buffet luncheon* **3.** OVERDRESSED dressed in an inappropriately elaborate or showy way —**dress·i·ly** *adv* —**dress·i·ness** *n*

drew past tense of **draw**

Drex·el /dréks'l/, **Anthony Joseph** (1826–93) US banker and philanthropist. He worked in investment banking and founded the Drexel Institute of Technology in Philadelphia (1891).

Drex·el Hill /dréks'l-/ town in southeastern

Pennsylvania, southwest of Philadelphia. Population: 29,744 (1996).

drey /dray/ *n* a squirrel's nest [Early 17C. Origin ?]

Drey·er /drī ər/, **Carl Theodor** (1889–1968) Danish movie director and screenwriter. His silent films include *The Passion of Joan of Arc* (1928).

drib /drib/ *n* a very small amount, usually a tiny drop of liquid or a fragment of material ○ *just a drib of paint on the porch floor* [Early 18C. Origin ?] ◇ **in dribs and drabs** in very small amounts or stages, and usually in a rather haphazard way ○ *People were beginning to arrive in dribs and drabs.*

drib·ble /dríbb'l/ *v* (**-bled, -bling, -bles**) **1.** *vi* **PRODUCE SALIVA** to let saliva spill out of the mouth **2.** *vti* **FLOW IN DROPS** to flow in drops or a small stream, or allow a liquid to flow or spill out in this way **3.** *vti* **MOVE BALL** to move a ball along using small repeated movements of the foot, the hand, or a stick **4.** *vti* BASKETBALL **BOUNCE BALL ON COURT** in basketball, to propel the ball in any direction on the court by bouncing it with the hands ■ *n* **1. TINY AMOUNT OF LIQUID** a small amount of liquid falling in drops or a thin stream **2. MOVEMENT WHILE DRIBBLING BALL** a movement or run made while dribbling a ball, especially in basketball or soccer ○ *a hard, fast dribble the length of the court* [Mid-16C. < *drib*, alteration of DRIP] —**drib·bler** *n* —**drib·bly** *adj*

drib·let /dríbblət/, **drib·blet** *n* a tiny amount of a liquid [Late 16C. < *drib*, alteration of DRIP]

dri·er[1] /drī ər/, **dry·er** *n* **1.** a machine or device for drying things **2.** a substance added to paint or ink to speed up the drying process

dri·er[2] /drī ər/ comparative of **dry**

dri·est superlative of **dry**

drift /drift/ *v* (**drift·ed, drift·ing, drifts**) **1.** *vi* **BE CARRIED ALONG** to be carried along by the flow of water or air **2.** *vi* **MOVE AIMLESSLY** to move in a slow, smooth, gentle, and unforced way, usually without any direction or purpose ○ *The crowd gradually drifted away.* **3.** *vi* **WANDER AIMLESSLY** to go from one place to another, never staying anywhere for very long and seeming to have little purpose **4.** *vi* NAVIG **WANDER FROM SET COURSE OR POSITION** to deviate from a set course or move gradually away from a fixed position **5.** *vi* **MOVE FROM ONE STATE TO ANOTHER** to move gradually from one state or situation to another in an unintentional, casual, or aimless way ○ *drifted into debt* **6.** *vi* **CHANGE GRADUALLY** to change or develop gradually, or move slowly from one point or position to another ○ *Prices have drifted downward in recent weeks.* **7.** *vti* **FORM HEAPS** to build up and form heaps as a result of the action of the wind or water currents, or cause something such as snow, sand, or leaves to do this ■ *n* **1. PILED-UP DEPOSITS** a heap, pile, or bank of something such as snow, sand, or leaves created by the action of the wind or water currents **2. DRIFTING MOVEMENT** a slow gentle movement in which something is carried along on a current of air or water **3. MATERIAL CARRIED ALONG** an amount of something carried along on a current of air or water ○ *drifts of smoke coming from the chimneys* **4. MOVEMENT OF PEOPLE** a gradual movement over a period of time of groups of people or animals toward or away from a place ○ *the drift of young people away from rural areas* **5. GRADUAL CHANGE** a broad and gradual change or development, e.g., in people's opinions or behavior ○ *a drift back to larger cars* ○ *a downward drift in prices* **6. GENERAL MEANING** the general meaning of an argument, opinion, or statement ○ *She used a lot of technical jargon but I managed to get the drift of her argument.* **7. INACTIVITY** a state of inactivity or indecision in which a person or group is carried along by events **8.** NAVIG **DEVIATION** the distance or extent to which a ship or aircraft deviates from its set course because of the action of wind or water currents **9.** GEOL **DEPOSIT OF GRAVEL** a loose deposit of sand, gravel, or rock left by a glacier or ice sheet **10.** GEOG **CURRENT** the motion of a river or broad ocean current **11.** MIN EXTRACT **HORIZONTAL MINESHAFT** a horizontal or almost horizontal mineshaft that follows a vein of ore **12.** MIN EXTRACT **CONNECTING PASSAGE IN MINE** a small passage in a mine connecting two main shafts or tunnels **13.** ELEC ENG **UNCONTROLLED CHANGE IN SETTING** a slow uncontrolled change in a previously adjusted setting, e.g., in the frequency to which an electronic device has been set **14.** MECH ENG **TAPERING STEEL TOOL** a tapering steel tool used to enlarge or align holes in pieces of metal before they are bolted or riveted **15. CONTROLLED SKID** a controlled slide used by racing drivers as a method of cornering at high speed **16.** *S Africa* **SHALLOWS OR FORD** a shallow part of a river, or a ford across it [14C. < Old Norse *drift* "snowdrift" < Germanic] —**drift·y** *adj*

drift·age /dríftij/ *n* **1.** material that has drifted along on and been deposited by air or water currents **2.** the distance by which a ship or aircraft has deviated from its set course owing to winds or currents

drift·er /dríftər/ *n* **1.** somebody who does not stay in the same place or job for long, but is always moving on, apparently without aim, from place to place **2.** a fishing vessel that fishes with a drift net

drift ice *n* large areas of ice floating in the open sea

drift net *n* a large fishing net supported by floats that is allowed to drift along with the current or is attached to a vessel

drift·wood /dríft wo͝od/ *n* broken pieces of wood that are found washed up on a beach or riverbank or floating in the sea or a river

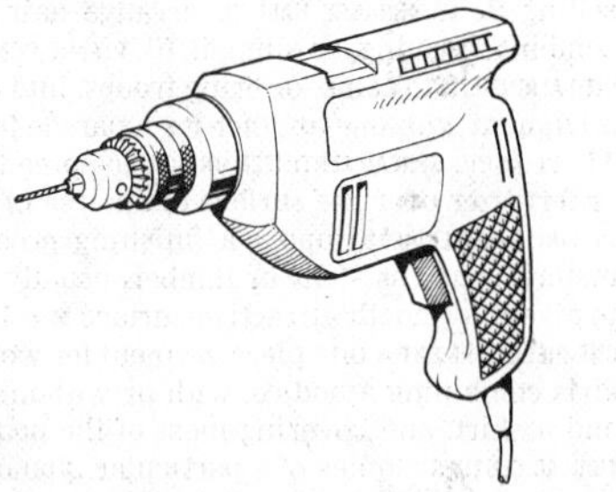

drill (sense 2)

drill[1] /dril/ *n* **1. PART OF TOOL THAT BORES HOLES** a long pointed piece of metal that is held in a machine and rotated at high speed to bore holes in hard substances such as wood, metal, masonry, or rock **2. BORING TOOL WITH DRILL** a tool or machine that holds, drives, and bores holes with a drill **3.** MIL **TRAINING BY REPETITION** a type of military training, particularly in marching maneuvers and weapons handling, that involves the constant repetition of a set pattern of movements or tasks **4.** EDUC **REPEATED EXERCISE** a sequence of tasks, exercises, or words repeated over and over until they can be performed faultlessly, as used in teaching military skills, languages, or basic arithmetic **5. SAFETY ROUTINE** a sequence of actions practiced repeatedly so that people know what to do in an emergency to ensure their safety **6. ROUTINE** a set procedure or routine for doing something (*informal*) **7.** MARINE BIOL **PREDATORY MOLLUSK** a invertebrate sea animal that preys on oysters by boring into their shells. Latin name: *Urosalpinx cinerea.* ■ *v* (**drilled, drill·ing, drills**) **1.** *vti* **MAKE HOLE WITH DRILL** to bore a hole in something with a drill **2.** *vti* MIL **PRACTICE MARCHING** to practice marching maneuvers repeatedly on a parade ground as a form of military training and discipline, or make troops do this **3.** *vt* EDUC **TEACH SOMEBODY BY ROTE** to make somebody repeat a sequence of exercises or procedures over and over again in order to learn it **4.** *vt* **SHOOT SOMEBODY OR SOMETHING** to shoot somebody with bullets, or shoot bullets into something (*informal*) **5.** *vt* **HIT BALL HARD** to hit a ball or shot with great force in a straight line toward somebody or something (*informal*) [Early 16C. < Middle Dutch *drillen* "make a hole, whirl"] —**drill·a·ble** *adj* —**drill·er** *n*

SYNONYMS See ***teach***.

drill down *vi* to access data or information organized in hierarchical form by starting from general information and moving through increasingly detailed data

drill[2] /dril/ AGRIC *n* **1. FURROW FOR SEEDS** a shallow furrow in which seeds are sown **2. SEED-PLANTING MACHINE** a machine for planting seeds in furrows **3. PLANTED ROW OF SEEDS** a row of seeds planted along a small furrow ■ *vt* (**drilled, drill·ing, drills**) **PLANT SEEDS WITH DRILL** to plant seeds with a drill [Early 18C. Origin ?]

drill[3] /dril/ *n* a tough cotton twill. Use: work clothes, uniforms. [Mid-18C. < German *Drillich* < Latin *trilix* "with three threads" < *licium* "thread"]

drill[4] /dril/ *n* a baboon with a black face and brown fur, similar to a mandrill, though smaller in size. Native to: West Africa. Latin name: *Papio leucophaeus.* [Mid-17C. < W African name]

drill·down /dríl dòwn/ *n* an act of accessing data or information organized in hierarchical form, starting from general information and moving through increasingly detailed data

drill·ing plat·form *n* a structure used in offshore oil drilling that supports drilling equipment and is either fixed to the seabed or floats independently

drill·ing rig *n* INDUST same as **rig**[1] *n* (sense 2)

drill in·struc·tor *n* a noncommissioned officer responsible for giving recruits their basic training

drill·mas·ter /dríl màstər/ *n* **1.** *UK* same as **drill instructor 2.** somebody who trains people in a very strict and militaristic way

drill pipe *n* INDUST same as **drill string**

drill press *n* a machine consisting of a powered drill on a vertical stand that is brought down onto the work automatically or by a hand lever

drill ser·geant *n* MIL same as **drill instructor**

drill·stock /dríl stòk/ *n* the part of a drilling tool or machine that holds the shank of the drill

drill string *n* a long metal pipe, progressively built up from lengths of steel tubing, that is attached above the drill when drilling for oil or gas and eventually forms the bore of the well

dri·ly /drīlee/, **dry·ly** *adv* with subtle irony or humor

drink /dringk/ *vti* (**drank** /drangk/, **drunk** /drungk/, **drink·ing, drinks**) **1. SWALLOW LIQUID** to take in liquid through the mouth **2. DRINK ALCOHOL** to drink an alcoholic beverage, especially habitually ○ *Don't drink and drive.* ■ *n* **1. DRINKABLE LIQUID** liquid that can be drunk, usually in a container ○ *There isn't much food or drink in the house.* **2. AMOUNT OF LIQUID** an amount of liquid that somebody drinks ○ *Could I have a drink of water?* **3. ALCOHOLIC BEVERAGE** alcoholic drink, especially an individual serving in a glass, bottle, or can **4. EXCESSIVE CONSUMPTION OF ALCOHOL** excessive consumption of alcohol **5. BODY OF WATER** the sea or a large body of water, e.g., a lake or swimming pool (*slang*) ○ *in the drink* ■ **drinks** *npl* **INFORMAL PARTY WITH DRINKS** an informal party at which alcoholic or other drinks are served, but no meal [Old English *drincan* < Germanic]

drink in *vt* **1.** to absorb as much liquid as is available ○ *The plants drank in the welcome rain.* **2.** to absorb eagerly every aspect of something with the mind and senses ○ *She stood silently on the beach, drinking in the beauty.*

drink to *vti* to wish somebody or something happiness, luck, success, or good health by raising a glass and then drinking from it ○ *Let's drink to the success of the venture.* ○ *We drank a toast to absent friends.*

drink up *vt* **1.** to drink all of something **2.** to absorb a liquid completely ○ *The dry earth drank up the rain.*

drink·a·ble /dríngkəb'l/ *adj* **1.** safe for humans or animals to drink **2.** pleasant or enjoyable to drink ○ *a very drinkable local fruit juice* —**drink·a·bil·i·ty** /drìngkə bíllətee/ *n*

drink-driv·ing *n UK* same as **drunk-driving** —**drink-driv·er** *n*

drink·er /dríngkər/ *n* **1.** somebody who drinks alcoholic beverages, especially to excess **2.** somebody who drinks a particular type of beverage (*used in combination*) ○ *I'm not a coffee drinker.*

drink·ing foun·tain *n* a device attached to a wall that produces a jet of water that people can drink

drink·ing song *n* a song, often rowdy or suggestive, sung by people drinking alcohol together

drink·ing wa·ter *n* water intended for people to drink, especially when free of harmful contents such as industrial waste, chemicals, or animal waste

drinks cab·i·net *n UK* same as **liquor cabinet**

drip /drip/ *v* (**dripped, drip·ping, drips**) **1.** *vti* **FALL OR LET**

FALL IN DROPS to fall as drops of liquid, or let liquid fall as drops ○ *The faucet is dripping.* **2.** *vt* LET SOMETHING OUT COPIOUSLY to let out something, particularly an emotion, in great quantity ○ *His voice positively dripped malice.* ■ *n* **1.** SMALL AMOUNT OF LIQUID a drop of liquid or moisture ○ *a bucket to catch the drips* **2.** DRIPPING OF LIQUID an instance or the process of a liquid falling in drops **3.** SOUND OF FALLING DROPS the sound of drops of liquid falling onto something ○ *the steady drip of a leaking faucet* **4.** *UK* MED same as **drip feed** (senses 1–2) **5.** *UK* MED same as **drip feed** (sense 3) (*informal*) **6.** OFFENSIVE TERM an offensive term for somebody regarded as socially inept, inadequate, or uninteresting (*slang insult*) **7.** ARCHIT PROTECTIVE GROOVE a protective groove cut in a sill or other overhang of a wall or building to cause water to drip freely **8.** FOOD CUP OF COFFEE a cup of ordinary coffee (*slang*) ○ *The guy in the corner wants a drip.* [Old English *dryppan* < Indo-European, "to drop"]

drip with *vt* **1.** HAVE DROPS FALLING CONTINUOUSLY to have liquid falling in a continuous stream of drops ○ *dripping with sweat* **2.** HAVE TOO MUCH OF SOMETHING to have too much of something, especially some kind of adornment, usually in a way that is considered to be bad taste ○ *a woman dripping with jewels* **3.** GIVE VENT TO EMOTION to give continuous expression to an emotion, especially a negative one such as spite, malice, or sarcasm ○ *Her voice dripped with sarcasm.*

drip cof·fee *n* coffee made by pouring hot water over ground coffee beans held in a filter above a pot so that it drips into the pot

drip-dry *adj* REQUIRING NO IRONING describes clothes or materials that do not wrinkle or crease as they dry, and so do not needing ironing ○ *a drip-dry shirt* ■ *vti* (**drip-dried, drip-dry·ing, drip-dries**) **1.** DRY WITHOUT CREASES to dry without creases when hung up wet, or cause something to dry in this way **2.** DRY HAIR NATURALLY to dry hair merely by exposing it to the air, without using a hair dryer, or become dry in this way

drip feed *n* **1.** MEDICAL PROCEDURE FOR INJECTING LIQUID injection of a therapeutic fluid such as blood, plasma, saline, or glucose directly into a vein at an adjustable rate from a plastic bag hung above a patient on a stand ○ *They put her on a drip feed* **2.** FLUID USED IN DRIP FEED the therapeutic fluid used in a drip feed ○ *Add antibiotic to the drip feed.* **3.** EQUIPMENT USED TO ADMINISTER DRIP FEED the equipment used to administer a drip feed (*informal*)

drip-feed *vt* **1.** to pass a liquid, especially a sugar solution, directly into somebody's vein using a drip feed **2.** to provide water or liquid nutrients to indoor plants or field crops continuously in small quantities

drip·less /drípplǝss/ *adj* designed or made not to drip ○ *This teapot has a dripless spout.*

drip pan *n* a shallow pan or cookie sheet used in the oven to catch the juices of roasting meat

drip·ping /drípping/ *adj* completely soaked ○ *She hurried in, cold and dripping from the storm.*

drip·ping pan *n* HOUSEHOLD same as **drip pan**

drip·pings /drípppingz/ *npl* the juices, including melted fat, produced by roasting or frying meat

drip·py /dríppee/ (**-pi·er, -pi·est**) *adj* **1.** TOO SENTIMENTAL silly and extremely sentimental (*slang*) ○ *a drippy love story* **2.** OFFENSIVE TERM an offensive term meaning socially inept, inadequate, or uninteresting (*slang insult*) **3.** WITH RAIN drizzly or tending to rain ○ *This is our fifth drippy day in a row.* —**drip·pi·ly** *adv* —**drip·pi·ness** *n*

drip·stone /dríp stōn/ *n* **1.** a protective stone drip in the overhang above a door or window **2.** calcium carbonate deposits in the form of stalactites or stalagmites

drive /drīv/ *v* (**drove** /drōv/, **driv·en** /drívvǝn/, **driv·ing, drives**) **1.** *vti* TRANSP CONTROL MOVEMENT OF VEHICLE to operate a vehicle, controlling its speed and direction, or be operated in this way ○ *He's learning to drive.* **2.** *vti* TRANSP TRAVEL OR CONVEY IN VEHICLE to travel somewhere in a vehicle, or take somebody somewhere in a vehicle ○ *I'll drive you to the airport.* **3.** *vt* ENG PROVIDE POWER FOR SOMETHING to supply the power that makes something work (*often passive*) ○ *The lawn mower is driven by a gasoline engine.* **4.** *vt* STEER PROGRESS OF SOMETHING to provide momentum toward the successful operation or functioning of something ○ *This company is driven by a concern for quality.* **5.** *vt* FORCE SOMEBODY OR SOMETHING INTO CONDITION to force somebody or something into a particular state or condition, often an extremely negative one ○ *Her son's behavior drove her to despair.* **6. drive your·self** *vr* FORCE YOURSELF TO WORK to force yourself to work too hard or for too long at something ○ *You drive yourself too hard.* **7.** *vt* MOVE PEOPLE OR ANIMALS to force a person or animal to go somewhere ○ *Rain drove them indoors.* **8.** *vt* FORCE SOMETHING IN OR OUT to push, knock, or hammer something forcefully into a particular position ○ *He drove the stakes into the ground.* **9.** *vti* MOVE OR PROPEL FORCEFULLY to move or be blown or thrown with great force against something, or provide the force that does this ○ *The wind drove the snow into huge drifts.* **10.** *vt* MAKE HOLE to make a hole or tunnel in something using great force **11.** *vt* SPORTS HIT BALL HARD in some sports, to kick or hit a ball or puck forcefully ○ *The clean-up batter drove the ball past the shortstop.* **12.** *vti* GOLF HIT LONG SHOT in golf, to hit a long shot from either a tee or a fairway when covering the principal distance between holes ○ *He drove into the rough.* **13.** *vti* BASKETBALL DRIBBLE THROUGH COURT AREA in basketball, to dribble the ball through a particular area of the court toward the basket ○ *She's unstoppable when she drives the baseline.* **14.** *vt* HUNTING CHASE GAME INTO OPEN to chase a hunted animal into the open where it can be killed ■ *n* **1.** TRANSP RIDE TAKEN IN VEHICLE a trip in a car or other vehicle ○ *go for a drive* **2.** *UK* ROADS same as **driveway** **3.** *also* **Drive** ROADS WIDE ROAD a street or road that can be used for vehicles, especially one that has more than two lanes or has pleasant views (*often used in place names*) **4.** ENG TRANSMISSION OF POWER the means of converting power into motion in a machine such as a motor vehicle ○ *a car with four-wheel drive* **5.** COMPUT same as **disk drive** **6.** HARD HIT OF BALL in some sports, a forceful shot or stroke in hitting a ball ○ *His drive to left field scored two runners.* **7.** GOLF LONG SHOT in golf, a long shot played from either a tee or fairway, when covering the principal distance between two holes **8.** BASKETBALL FAST MOVEMENT TOWARD BASKET in basketball, a fast direct run toward the basket while dribbling the ball ○ *Our players are having trouble scoring off drives.* **9.** FOOTBALL CONTINUOUS MOVEMENT TOWARD GOAL in football, steady movement toward a goal line, usually achieved in one or more series of downs ○ *They've been unable to manage a sustained drive in this quarter.* **10.** FOCUSED ENERGY energy and determination that helps somebody achieve what he or she wants to do ○ *Do you have the drive to achieve your ambitions?* **11.** PSYCHOL MOTIVATING NEED a powerful need or instinct that motivates behavior, e.g., hunger or sex **12.** MAJOR PLANNED EFFORT an organized effort made by a lot of people working together to achieve a goal ○ *a recruitment drive* **13.** MIL SUSTAINED MILITARY ATTACK a major sustained attack on an enemy, usually including armored vehicles and large guns **14.** AGRIC ROUNDUP OF LIVESTOCK a gathering and herding of cattle, sheep, or horses to a new pasture or to be sold for slaughter ○ *This will be my first cattle drive.* **15.** ELECTRONICS VOLTAGE voltage applied to the grid of a transmitting or amplifying valve or to the base of a transistor **16.** AUTOMOT FORWARD POSITION IN AUTOMATIC TRANSMISSION in an automatic transmission, the principal shift position that moves the vehicle forward [Old English *drīfan* < Indo-European] —**driv·a·ble** *adj* ◇ **drive somebody up the wall** to cause somebody to become extremely irritated or annoyed (*informal*)

drive at *vt* to be trying to say or intending to make understood (*informal*) ○ *It was hard to tell what she was driving at.*

drive-by (*informal*) *n* CRIME same as **drive-by shooting** ■ *adj* performed very quickly and with a lack of care or purpose ○ *a drive-by straightening up of the clutter*

drive-by shoot·ing *n* the illegal act of firing a firearm at somebody or something from a moving vehicle

drive chain *n* an endless chain that transmits power from one toothed wheel to another in a mechanical system

drive-in *n* a commercial establishment, e.g., a movie theater, that provides services or products to customers while they remain in their cars in a parking lot (*often used before a noun*)

driv·el /drívv'l/ *n* **1.** SILLY TALK silly and irrelevant or inaccurate talk ○ *They're talking drivel.* **2.** DROOLED SALIVA saliva dribbling from the mouth ■ *vi* (**-eled, -el·ing, -els**) **1.** TALK NONSENSE to talk silly and irrelevant or inaccurate nonsense **2.** DROOL to let saliva dribble from the mouth [Old English *dreflian*, origin ?] —**driv·el·er** *n* —**driv·el·ing** *n*

drive·line /drīv līn/ *n* MECH ENG same as **drive train**

driv·en /drívvǝn/ past participle of **drive** ■ *adj* **1.** striving to achieve personal goals because of a strong need or inner compulsion ○ *Driven people are often overachievers.* **2.** having a particular thing as a principal cause (*used in combination*) ○ *a demand-driven economy*

driv·er /drīvǝr/ *n* **1.** TRANSP SOMEBODY WHO CAN DRIVE somebody who operates a motor vehicle, or who is capable of operating one **2.** TRANSP CHAUFFEUR somebody who drives a car or limousine for other people **3.** GOLF CLUB WITH A WOODEN HEAD a golf club with a wide wooden head, deep face, and a long shaft, used to drive the ball from the tee down the fairway **4.** MECH ENG MACHINE PART THAT TRANSMITS MOVEMENT a part of a machine that causes another part to move **5.** TOOL THAT APPLIES PRESSURE a tool, e.g., a screwdriver or drill, that exerts heavy pressure on something else **6.** ELECTRONICS ELECTRONIC CIRCUIT an electronic circuit that produces an output used to control another circuit **7.** COMPUT CONTROLLING SOFTWARE a piece of computer software that controls the input and output of a device ○ *a printer driver* **8.** STRONG FORCE something that provides impetus or motivation, e.g., within an organization

driv·er ant *n* INSECTS same as **army ant**

driv·er·less /drīvǝrlǝss/ *adj* **1.** moving out of control without a driver **2.** capable of being operated without a driver ○ *driverless transit systems*

driv·er's li·cence *n* AUTOMOT Can spelling of **driver's license**

driv·er's li·cense *n US* a small card that somebody must carry whenever driving, obtained after a person has passed a test and demonstrated that he or she knows the laws that apply to good driving

driv·er's seat ◇ **in the driver's seat** in a position to determine the course or direction of something

driv·er's side *n* the side of a car on which the steering wheel is located, where the driver sits when operating a vehicle

dri·ver's test *n* a test of driving skills and knowledge, usually consisting of both a written and a road test that somebody must pass before driving without supervision on public roads

drive shaft *n* **1.** a rotating shaft that transmits the power from a motor or engine to another part of the machine, e.g., from the engine to the propeller of an aircraft **2.** the shaft that transmits power from the transmission to the differential in a rear-wheel drive automobile or truck

drive-through *n* a business such as a fast-food restaurant or bank that provides goods or services through a special window to customers who remain in their cars (*often used before a noun*)

drive time *n* **1.** a time during the morning or afternoon when commuters are driving to and from work in their cars and listening to the radio **2.** the amount of time that it takes to drive between two places

drive train *n* a mechanical part of a vehicle, including the drive shaft and universal joint, that connects the transmission with the axles and transmits power, torque, and motion

drive-up *n* a place in a commercial establishment such as a restaurant or bank where customers are served while remaining in their cars (*often used before a noun*)

drive·way /drīv wày/ *n* a private road that enables vehicles to travel from a public road to the entrance of a building such as a house or hotel

driv·ing /drīving/ *adj* **1.** FALLING HARD falling, blowing, or being blown very hard and forcefully ○ *driving rain* **2.** ABLE TO MAKE SOMETHING HAPPEN having the ability or influence to make something new or different happen ○ *She is the driving force behind the new development.* ○ *driving ambition* ■ *n* AUTOMOT PROCESS OF OPERATING VEHICLE the act or process of operating a motor vehicle, especially with regard to how skillful somebody is ○ *Your driving is even worse than usual today.* —**driv·ing·ly** *adv*

driv·ing chain *n UK* MECH ENG same as **drive chain**

driv·ing gloves *npl* gloves worn while driving a vehicle, often a sports car. They are usually made of leather or have leather palms and knitted fabric backs.

driv·ing i·ron *n* an iron golf club that can be used instead of a driver

driv·ing li·cence *n UK* same as **driver's license**

driv·ing range *n* a place or facility where golfers can practice their drive strokes, usually consisting of a row of small tees fronting an open area of ground

driv·ing while fe·male *n* a situation in which police officers use their authority, often in legitimate traffic stops, to harass or sexually assault women drivers

driz·zle /drízz'l/ *n* METEOROL **LIGHT RAIN** light steady rain ■ *v* (**-zled, -zling, -zles**) **1.** *vi* METEOROL **RAIN LIGHTLY** to rain lightly and steadily **2.** *vt* COOK **DRIBBLE LIQUID OVER FOOD** to pour very small quantities of a liquid in a thin stream over food ○ *Lightly drizzle the dressing over the vegetables.* [Mid-16C. Origin ?] —**driz·zly** *adj*

drogue /drōg/ *n* **1.** NAUT same as **sea anchor 2.** AEROSP same as **drogue parachute 3.** AIR FORCE a cylindrical target towed behind an aircraft, used for firing practice **4.** AVIAT a funnel-shaped receptacle attached to the refueling hose of a tanker aircraft that locates the probe of the receiving aircraft and fits over it, ensuring firm connection during refueling **5.** METEOROL same as **windsock** (*technical*) [Early 18C. Origin ?]

drogue par·a·chute *n* **1.** a small parachute, used on a spacecraft or satellite re-entering the atmosphere, that is released before a larger one to slow the object and stabilize it **2.** a small parachute used to release a larger one from its pack

droit /droyt, drwaa/ *n* a right or claim, either legal or moral, that is due to somebody and must be acknowledged [15C. Via French < late Latin *directum* "rule" < Latin *directus* "straight" (see DIRECT)]

droit de seign·eur /drwàa də say nyúr/, **droit du seign·eur** /-dyoo-/ *n* the supposed former legal right of a feudal lord to have sexual intercourse with the bride or daughter of an inferior, usually a serf, on the night of her wedding [< French, "lord's right"]

droll /drōl/ *adj* amusing in a wry or odd way ○ *a droll aside* [Early 17C. < French *drôle* "buffoon, comical"] —**droll·ness** *n* —**drol·ly** *adv*

SYNONYMS See ***funny.***

droll·er·y /drṓlaree/ (*plural* **-ies**) *n* **1. QUIRKY HUMOR** slightly wry or odd humor **2. TALKING OR BEHAVING AMUSINGLY** speech or behavior that is wryly or oddly amusing **3. SOMETHING FUNNY** an act or story that is wryly or oddly amusing

drom·ae·o·saur /drṓmee ə sàwr/ *n* a medium-sized fast-running dinosaur of the Cretaceous Period that had strong hind legs with a long sharp talon on each foot and long three-clawed hands [Late 20C. < modern Latin *Dromaeosaurus* < Greek *dromaios* "swift-running" + *sauros* "lizard"]

-drome *suffix* racecourse, field ○ *hippodrome* [Via Latin < Greek *dromos* "racecourse" < Indo-European, "walk, run"]

dromedary

drom·e·dar·y /drómmə dèrree, drúmmə-/ (*plural* **-ies**) *n* a camel with one hump. Raised for: working, racing. Native to: North Africa, Southwest Asia. Latin name: *Camelus dromedarius.* [13C. < Old French *dromedaire,* late Latin *dromedarius* < Latin *dromad-* "dromedary" < Greek *dromad-* "running"]

drom·ond /drómmənd, drúmm-/, **drom·on** /-mən/ *n* a sailing galley used in the Middle Ages [14C. Via Anglo-Norman *dromund* < late Latin *dromon-* < Greek *dromō* "swift ship" < *dromos* "running"]

-dromous *suffix* moving, migrating ○ *catadromous* [< modern Latin *-dromus* < Greek *dromos* "running"]

drone[1] /drōn/ *v* (**droned, dron·ing, drones**) **1.** *vi* **MAKE LOW HUMMING SOUND** to make a continuous low humming sound **2.** *vti* **TALK IN BORING VOICE** to talk or say something in a boring voice, usually for a long time ○ *I could hear his voice droning on in the background.* ■ *n* **1. LOW HUMMING SOUND** a continuous low humming sound **2.** MUSIC **UNCHANGING NOTE HELD DURING MELODY** a single note or chord that is held through a melodic part **3.** MUSIC **PIPE IN BAGPIPES PRODUCING CONTINUOUS NOTE** the pipe in a set of bagpipes that produces a single continuous note [Early 16C. < DRONE[2]] —**dron·ing·ly** *adv*

drone[2] /drōn/ *n* **1.** INSECTS **NONWORKER MALE BEE** a male bee that has no sting, does not gather pollen, and exists only to mate with the queen bee **2. LAZY PERSON** somebody who does not work or contribute anything, but relies on the work or energy of others (*insult*) **3.** AVIAT **AIRCRAFT WITH NO PILOT** an aircraft whose flight is controlled from the ground [Old English *drān* < Indo-European, "to buzz"] —**dron·ish** *adj*

dron·go /dróng gō/ (*plural* **-gos** or *same*), **dron·go shrike** *n* a bird that is usually black with a strong beak, glossy feathers, and a long forked tail. Native to: tropical Africa, Asia, Australia. Family: Dicruridae. [Mid-19C. < Malagasy]

drool /drool/ *v* (**drooled, drool·ing, drools**) **1.** *vi* **DRIBBLE SALIVA** to let saliva dribble from the mouth ○ *The dog lay drooling at his feet.* **2.** *vi* **SHOW EXAGGERATED APPRECIATION** to show excessive appreciation of somebody or something **3.** *vti* **TALK NONSENSE** to talk nonsense or foolishness ■ *n* **SALIVA DRIBBLING FROM MOUTH** saliva dribbling from the mouth [Early 19C. Origin ?] —**drool·ing·ly** *adv*

droop /droop/ *v* (**drooped, droop·ing, droops**) **1.** *vti* **HANG OR BEND DOWN LIMPLY** to move lower, hang down, or sag limply, or make something do this ○ *Her eyelids drooped with weariness.* **2.** *vi* **BE DISPIRITED** to become discouraged or dejected ○ *His spirits drooped at the prospect of the long and arduous journey.* ■ *n* **SAGGING** a lowered, sagging, or slumped position ○ *The droop of her shoulders suggested her disappointment.* [13C. < Old Norse *drūpa*] —**droop·i·ly** *adv* —**droop·i·ness** *n* —**droop·ing·ly** *adv* —**droop·y** *adj*

droop nose, **droop snoot** *n* an aircraft nose section that can be tilted downward to increase the pilot's range of vision during landing and takeoff

drop /drop/ *v* (**dropped, drop·ping, drops**) **1.** *vt* **LET GO OF SOMETHING** to let go of something and cause it to fall, either accidentally or intentionally ○ *He dropped the bowling ball on my foot.* ○ *Somebody had dropped a glove in the street.* **2.** *vi* **FALL** to fall from a higher place to a lower place **3.** *vti* **MOVE TO LOWER POSITION** to move into a lower position, or move the body or part of the body lower ○ *He dropped into a chair.* **4.** *vti* **FALL IN DROPS** to fall in drops of liquid, or make something do this ○ *We listened to the rain dropping on the roof.* **5.** *vti* **LESSEN** to decrease to a lower level, rate, or number, or make something do this ○ *The temperature dropped sharply overnight.* **6.** *vi* **SLOPE DOWNWARD** to slope downward, often in a particular way **7.** *vti* **LOWER VOICE** to lower the voice to a quieter level, or be lowered in this way ○ *She dropped her voice to a whisper.* **8.** *vt* **TAKE SOMEBODY OR SOMETHING SOMEWHERE** to take somebody or something to a place, usually by car, and leave the person or thing there ○ *Can you drop me at the bus station?* **9.** *vt* **WRITE SOMETHING TO SOMEBODY** to write and send an informal message or greeting to somebody ○ *Drop me a line when you get there.* **10.** *vt* **STOP DOING OR PLANNING SOMETHING** to abandon a plan or course of action ○ *We've dropped our plans to remodel the kitchen.* **11.** *vt* **STOP TALKING ABOUT SOMETHING** to stop talking about something, or stop being talked about ○ *Can we drop the subject please?* **12.** *vt* **END RELATIONSHIP WITH SOMEBODY** to end a close or intimate relationship with somebody (*informal*) **13.** *vt* **REMOVE SOMEBODY** to remove somebody from a group of which she or he was formerly a member ○ *She may be dropped from the team.* **14.** *vt* **OMIT LETTER OR WORD** to leave out a letter, word, or phrase ○ *You can drop the "Sir": just call me Max.* **15.** *vi* **COLLAPSE FROM EXHAUSTION** to collapse in a state of complete exhaustion ○ *I'm ready to drop.* **16.** *vi* **COLLAPSE** to lose consciousness or die, especially suddenly or unexpectedly (*informal*) ○ *People were dropping like flies from the extreme heat.* **17.** *vt* **LOSE MATCH OR GAME** to lose a match, game, or part of a game ○ *He got through to the finals without dropping a set.* **18.** *vt* **SAY SOMETHING CASUALLY** to say something with an air of pretended casualness ○ *She's dropping hints about what she wants for her birthday.* **19.** *vt* **HIT OR SHOOT SOMEBODY** to hit or shoot somebody so that he or she falls down (*informal*) **20.** *vt* **SPEND OR LOSE MONEY** to spend or lose a particular amount of money on something expensive or in gambling (*informal*) **21.** *vti* **HIT BALL INTO TARGET HOLE** to make the ball go into a target such as a hole or net, or go into a target hole or net **22.** *vt* VET **GIVE BIRTH TO OFFSPRING** to give birth to young, especially a foal **23.** *vt* DRUGS **TAKE ILLEGAL DRUGS** to take an illegal drug by mouth, especially in pill form (*slang*) **24.** *vt* HANDICRAFT **LOWER HEM OF SOMETHING** to lower the hem of something such as a garment or curtain **25.** *vt* AVIAT **DELIVER SOMEBODY OR SOMETHING BY PARACHUTE** to deliver somebody or something such as soldiers or supplies by parachute from an aircraft **26.** *vt* **UNLOAD SOMETHING** to unload something from a ship or vehicle ■ *n* **1. SMALL ROUND PORTION OF LIQUID** a very small amount of liquid that becomes a rounded or pear shape as it falls **2. SMALL AMOUNT OF LIQUID** a small amount of a liquid ○ *There's not a drop of milk in the house.* **3. TINIEST AMOUNT** a very small amount of a feeling or quality (*used in negative statements*) ○ *I swear there isn't a drop of sympathy in that man.* **4. DECREASE IN SOMETHING** a decrease in quantity or amount ○ *a drop in salary* **5. DISTANCE BETWEEN HIGH POINT AND GROUND** the distance between a higher level and a lower level or the ground **6. DESCENT** a slope or fall in ground level, usually sharp or sudden **7.** FOOD **SMALL ROUND PIECE OF CANDY** a small round or oval piece of candy (*used in combination*) ○ *cough drops* **8.** JEWELRY **ROUND EARRING OR PENDANT** an earring or pendant, usually round or pear-shaped **9.** MIL, AIR FORCE **DESCENT BY PARACHUTE** a descent from an aircraft by parachute **10. GOODS DELIVERED BY PARACHUTE** goods or equipment that an aircraft delivers by parachute, or people dropped by parachute (*often used in combination*) **11. DELIVERY** a delivery of goods ○ *make a drop every two weeks* **12. SECRET REPOSITORY FOR MESSAGES** a secret place where somebody leaves letters or messages to be picked up by somebody else **13. ACT OF LEAVING SECRET COMMUNICATION** the act of leaving a letter, message, or goods at a prearranged secret location ○ *It's too dangerous to make the drop tonight.* **14.** MAIL same as **maildrop 15.** THEATER same as **drop curtain** (sense 1) **16.** ELECTRONICS **CONNECTION ON LINE** a point on a transmission line where data can be put in or taken out **17. DELIVERY SLOT IN RECEPTACLE** a slot in something or a special outside container through which letters and borrowed or rented items such as videotapes and books can be inserted (*often used in combination*) ○ *Return the videotapes to the drop outside the store.* **18.** MEDIA **SHORT SPUR** a short line that feeds signals to an individual house or apartment from a cable television trunk line **19. TRAPDOOR UNDER GALLOWS** a trapdoor under a gallows on which somebody who is to be hanged stands **20.** HANDICRAFT **CURTAIN LENGTH** the measured length for a curtain, from the top of a window to its sill or to the floor ■ **drops** *npl* PHARM **LIQUID MEDICINE APPLIED IN SMALL QUANTITIES** liquid medicine delivered by a dropper to the ear, nose, or eye [< Old English *dropa* (noun), *droppian* (verb) < Indo-European] ◇ **a drop in the bucket** just a tiny part of the full quantity that is required, and thus insignificant ◇ **at the drop of a hat** without needing persuasion or prompting ◇ **get** *or* **have the drop on somebody** to catch somebody by surprise before he or she can surprise you (*informal*) ◇ **let something drop** to reveal information to somebody, often casually or accidentally

drop away *vi* **1.** same as **drop** *v* (sense 6) **2.** to leave a group or formation gradually, either on purpose or not ○ *One by one, each jet banked and dropped away from the formation.* **3.** to disappear gradually

drop back *or* **behind** *vi* to move more slowly than other people and gradually fall farther behind them

drop by *v* **1.** *vi* to visit somebody casually or without having agreed on a time **2.** *vt* to deliver somebody or something to a specific place ○ *Just drop the laundry by some time this afternoon.*

drop in *vi* to visit somebody casually or without having agreed on a time
drop into *vt* to go from a more active into a less active state of consciousness
drop off *v* **1.** *vi* to fall asleep (*informal*) **2.** *vi* to decline or fall to a lower level (*informal*) ○ *Sales tend to drop off during the summer.* **3.** *vt* same as **drop** *v* (sense 8)
drop out *vi* **1.** to abandon a project or activity without finishing it ○ *He dropped out of college in his final year.* **2.** to reject conventional society and live in an alternative way (*informal*)
drop over *or* **around** *vi* to visit somebody casually and without having agreed on a time ○ *Drop around any time.*

drop-box *n* a secure container attached to the outside of an office in which letters or packages may be deposited during periods when the office is closed

drop cloth *n* a large cloth used to cover surfaces such as floors and furniture to protect them from paint or dust

drop cur·tain *n* **1.** an unframed curtain that can be lowered to a theater stage from the flies, usually providing background scenery **2.** a theater curtain that is raised or lowered on stage, instead of being opened or closed by moving sideways

drop-dead *adv* in a way that is regarded as spectacular (*slang*) ○ *drop-dead gorgeous*

drop-down men·u *n* a vertical list of options that appears on clicking on an item in a computer screen. It remains visible until one of the options has been selected by clicking on it.

~~**droped**~~ incorrect spelling of **dropped**

drop forge *n* a machine used to shape or stamp molten metal by placing it between two dies and dropping a weight on it —**drop-forge** *vt*

drop front *n* a part of a writing desk that can be lowered to provide a writing surface and then raised to conceal the inner part of the desk (*hyphenated when used before a noun*) ○ *a drop-front desk*

drop goal *n* in rugby, a goal scored by dropping the ball and then kicking it

drop ham·mer *n* METALL same as **drop forge**

drop han·dle·bars *npl* on a racing bicycle, handlebars that curve downward, enabling the rider to adopt a more aerodynamic posture

drop-in *n* **1.** a casual visitor or client who has not made a previous arrangement to visit **2.** an informal party that does not require an invitation

drop-in cen·ter *n* a place that people can visit without an appointment to get advice or information, or to meet others

drop kick *n* **1.** in football, a way of kicking the ball by dropping it and kicking it just after it bounces **2.** in amateur wrestling, an illegal move in which one wrestler attacks another by leaping into the air and striking an opponent with both feet —**drop-kick** *vti*

drop leaf *n* an extension on the end of a table that can be folded down when not needed (*hyphenated when used before a noun*) ○ *a drop-leaf table*

drop·let /dróppləṭ/ *n* a very small drop of liquid

drop·light /dróp lìt/ *n* an electric light that can be raised or lowered by using a rope, cord, or pulley

drop lock *n* in international financial markets, a variable-rate bank loan that is automatically converted to a fixed-rate bond when long-term interest rates fall to a specific level

drop·mas·ter /dróp màstər/ *n* a noncommissioned officer in the US Air Force trained to prepare, load, tie down, and eject materials from a plane during an airdrop operation

drop-off *n* **1.** SLOPE IN GROUND a steep slope where the ground descends abruptly **2.** DECREASE a fall in the level of something **3.** PASSENGER STOP a point where people such as passengers are let out of motor vehicles

drop·out /dróp òwt/ *n* **1.** EDUC STUDENT WHO DOES NOT GRADUATE a student who leaves school or college without graduating **2.** UNCONVENTIONAL PERSON somebody who chooses an unconventional way of life (*informal*) **3.** COMPUT SECTION WITHOUT DATA a small section on a magnetic tape or disk that is missing data

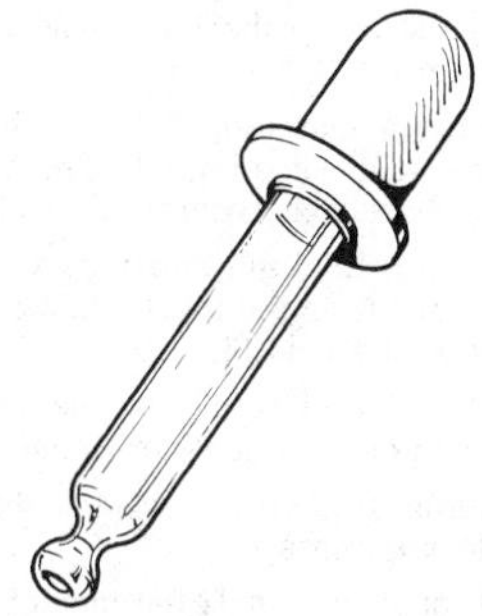

dropper

drop·per /dróppər/ *n* a small glass or plastic tube with a rubber bulb at one end that is used to suck up liquid and release it one drop at a time (*often used in combination*) ○ *an eye dropper*

drop·pings /dróppingz/ *npl* animal or bird excrement left on the ground or another surface

drop ship·ment *n* something sold by a retailer to a consumer that is shipped directly from the manufacturer or wholesaler to the consumer

drop shot *n* in racket games, a shot in which the ball drops abruptly to the ground just after passing over the net or hitting the wall

drop·sy /drópsee/ *n* MED same as **edema** (*dated*) [13C. Shortening of *hydropsy*, via Old French < medieval Latin *hydropsia* < Greek *hudrōps* "somebody with edema" < *hudōr* "water"] —**drop·si·cal** *adj* —**drop·sied** *adj*

drop tank *n* an extra tank of fuel on a fighter or bomber plane that enables the aircraft to fly longer and farther and can be jettisoned when empty

drop·wort /dróp wàwrt, -wùrt/ (*plural* **-worts** or *same*) *n* a plant with finely divided leaves. Flowers: small, white or red, in clusters. Native to: Europe, Asia. Latin name: *Filipendula vulgaris.* [< its tuberous root fibers]

drop zone *n* an area where troops or goods such as military equipment or medical supplies are to be landed, usually by parachute

drosh·ky /dróshkee/ (*plural* **-kies**), **dros·ky** /drŏskee/ *n* an open four-wheeled carriage drawn by horses, formerly used in Russia and Poland [Early 19C. < Russian *drozhki* "small wagon" < *drogi* "wagon"]

dro·som·e·ter /dro sómmətər/ *n* a device for measuring dew deposits [Early 19C. < Greek *drosos* "dew"]

dro·soph·i·la /drō sóffələ, drə-/ (*plural* **-las** or *same* or **-lae** /-lèe/) *n* a small two-winged fruit fly that is frequently used in genetic research. Genus: *Drosophila.* [Early 19C. < modern Latin < Greek *drosos* "dew" + *-philos* "loving"]

dross /dross, drawss/ *n* **1.** something that is worthless or of a low standard or quality ○ *I considered her early fiction to be pure dross.* **2.** the scum formed on molten metals, usually caused by oxidation [Old English *drōs* < Indo-European, "dark, muddy"] —**dross·y** *adj*

drought /drowt/ *n* **1.** a long period of extremely dry weather when there is not enough rain for the successful growing of crops or the replenishment of water supplies **2.** a lengthy and serious lack of something ○ *She experienced a period of creative drought.* [Old English *drūga* "dryness" < Germanic, "dry"] —**drought·y** *adj*

drouth /drowth/ *n* **1.** *Ireland, Scotland* METEOROL same as **drought** (sense 1) **2.** *UK regional* same as **thirst** *n* (sense 1)

drove[1] past tense of **drive**

drove[2] /drōv/ *n* **1.** GROUP OF ANIMALS MOVING a large number of animals, especially cattle, moving in the same direction, e.g., when being driven to a new grazing area **2.** TYPE OF STONE CHISEL a broad-edged chisel used for dressing stone ■ **droves** *npl* CROWDS OF PEOPLE very large numbers of people ○ *They came out of the football stadium in droves.* ■ *vti* (**droved, drov·ing, droves**) MOVE ANIMALS ALONG to move a herd or flock of animals from one place to another, usually over long distances, e.g., to new pastures or to market [Old English *drāf* < *drīfan* (see DRIVE)] —**drov·er** *n*

drown /drown/ (**drowned, drown·ing, drowns**) *v* **1.** *vti* to die by immersion and usually suffocation in water or other liquid, or kill a person or animal in this way. Death occurs either from lack of oxygen or as a result of cardiac arrest from the lowered body temperature. ○ *death by drowning* **2.** *vt* same as **drown out** (*often passive*) **3.** *vt* to cover or soak something, usually an item of food, with too much liquid ○ *He served us pancakes drowned in syrup.* [13C. Probably < N Germanic] —**drowned** *adj* —**drown·er** *n*
drown out *vt* to make so much noise that it is impossible to hear another sound (*often passive*)

drowse /drowz/ (**drowsed, drows·ing, drows·es**) *vi* to be in a state partway between sleeping and waking [Late 16C. Back-formation < DROWSY] —**drowse** *n*

drows·y /drówzee/ (**-i·er, -i·est**) *adj* **1.** ALMOST ASLEEP almost asleep or very lightly asleep **2.** CAUSING SLEEPINESS tending to make somebody feel sleepy ○ *a drowsy summer afternoon* **3.** SLUGGISH sluggish and dull [15C. < Old English *drūsian* "be sluggish" < Germanic] —**drows·i·ly** *adv* —**drows·i·ness** *n*

drub /drub/ *vt* (**drubbed, drub·bing, drubs**) **1.** DEFEAT SOMEBODY to defeat an opponent comprehensively **2.** BEAT SOMEBODY WITH STICK to beat somebody using a heavy stick or club **3.** STAMP YOUR FEET to stamp the feet hard on the ground ■ *n* BLOW WITH STICK a blow made using a heavy stick or club [Early 17C. Origin ?] —**drub·ber** *n* —**drub·bing** *n*

drudge /druj/ *n* a worker who performs dull and laborious tasks [15C. Origin ?] —**drudge** *vi* —**drudg·er** *n* —**drudg·ing·ly** *adv*

drudg·er·y /drújjəree/ *n* exhausting, boring, unpleasant work

SYNONYMS See *work*.

drudge·work /drúj wùrk/ *n* work that is boring and unpleasant ○ *We had to do hours of drudgework before we were happy with the yard.*

drudg·ing /drújjing/ *n S Atlantic US* on the coasts of especially Maryland and Virginia, the process of dredging for oysters as practiced by Chesapeake Bay watermen [Mid-18C. < variant of DREDGE[1]]

drug /drug/ *n* **1.** MEDICINAL SUBSTANCE a natural or artificial substance given to treat or prevent disease or to lessen pain **2.** ILLEGAL SUBSTANCE an often illegal and sometimes addictive substance that causes changes in behavior and perception and is taken for the effects **3.** PHARM MEDICAL SUBSTANCE a substance given to treat or prevent illness as defined in the US Food, Drug, and Cosmetic Act ■ *vt* (**drugged, drug·ging, drugs**) **1.** GIVE SOMEBODY DRUG to give a drug to somebody **2.** ADD DRUG TO SOMETHING to mix a drug with somebody's food or drink to make him or her fall asleep or become unconscious [14C. < French *drogue*]

drug a·buse *n* deliberate use of an illegal drug or of too much of a prescribed drug

drug bar·on *n* CRIME same as **drug lord**

drug czar *n* a senior official appointed to supervise the detection and suppression of illegal drug dealing (*informal*)

drugged /drugd/ *adj* **1.** heavily asleep, unconscious, or unable to function after being given drugs **2.** extremely tired and unable to concentrate ○ *drugged with sleep*

drug·get /drúggət/ *n* **1.** CARPETING FABRIC a thick heavy woolen or cotton and wool blend fabric. Use: floor coverings. **2.** RUG a coarse rug made of wool or cotton and wool **3.** WOOLEN FABRIC a woolen or wool-blend fabric. Use: formerly, clothing. [Mid-16C. < French *droguet*]

drug·gie /drúggee/, **drug·gy** (*plural* **-gies**) *n* a drug addict (*slang*)

drug·gist /drúggist/ *n* **1.** a pharmacist who runs a drugstore **2.** same as **pharmacist**

drug·gy /drúggee/ *adj* (**-gi·er, -gi·est**) characteristic of somebody who takes drugs regularly (*slang*) ○ *a druggy stupor* ■ *n* another spelling of **druggie**

drug hol·i·day *n UK* a period when somebody does not take medication normally given every day

drug lab *n* a room or building in which illegal raw drugs are processed for sale on the street

drug lord *n* a controller of an international network

for the production, processing, and sale of illegal drugs (*informal*)

drug mis·use *n* HEALTH same as **drug abuse**

drug of a·buse *n* any substance or medication that is misused as a recreational drug

drug·o·la /drug ṓlə/ *n* the use of illegal drugs as a bribe (*slang*) [Late 20C. After PAYOLA]

drug push·er *n* somebody who sells illegal drugs

drug run·ner *n* a smuggler of illegal drugs, usually by ship or airplane

drugs squad *n UK* the department of a police force that investigates the use and sale of illegal drugs

drug·store /drúg stàwr/ *n* a store where prescription and over-the-counter drugs are sold, as well as other goods

Dru·id /dróo id/, **dru·id** *n* **1.** a priest of an ancient religion practiced in Britain, Ireland, and Gaul until the people of those areas were converted to Christianity **2.** a man who worships and celebrates the forces of nature [Mid-16C. Directly or via French < Latin *druides* "Druids" < Celtic] —**dru·id·ic** /droo íddik/ *adj* —**dru·id·i·cal** *adj*

Dru·id·ess /dróo idəss/ *n* **1.** a woman priest of an ancient religion practiced in Britain, Ireland, and Gaul until the people of those areas were converted to Christianity **2.** a woman who worships and celebrates the forces of nature

Dru·id·ism /dróo i dìzzəm/ *n* an ancient Celtic religion in which the forces of nature were worshiped, and the priests were also prophets and poets, or the modern religion said to derive from it

drum /drum/ *n* **1.** PERCUSSION INSTRUMENT a musical instrument usually consisting of a membrane stretched across a hollow frame and played by striking the stretched membrane. Other hollow objects are also used as drums. **2.** TAPPING SOUND a regular tapping sound made by something striking a surface ○ *the drum of rain on the roof* **3.** CYLINDRICAL CONTAINER a large cylindrical container used for storing liquids such as oil or chemicals **4.** SPOOL a large spool around which wire, cable, or rope is wound for storage **5.** HOLLOW PART IN MACHINE a cylindrical hollow part in a machine such as a clothes drier **6.** ANAT same as **eardrum 7.** FISH THAT MAKES RHYTHMIC SOUND a large bony saltwater or freshwater fish that emits a repeated rhythmic sound. Family: Sciaenidae. **8.** CYLINDRICAL STONE BLOCK one of the cylindrical stone blocks used to make an architectural column **9.** SUPPORT FOR DOME a band or other structure around the bottom of a dome or circular ceiling that supports it ■ *vi* (**drummed, drum·ming, drums**) **1.** PLAY DRUM to play a drum or drums **2.** TAP SURFACE to tap repeatedly and rhythmically on a surface ○ *The rain was drumming on the roof.* **3.** MAKE SOUND WITH BEAK OR WINGS to produce a short burst of sound like a drum roll by rapidly beating with the beak or wings (*refers to birds*) [Mid-16C. Probably < Middle Dutch *tromme* "instrument making a loud noise," an imitation of the sound] ◇ **bang** *or* **beat the drum (for somebody** *or* **something)** to try to attract support and favorable attention for somebody or something (*informal*)

drum into *vt* to tell somebody something repeatedly and persistently until the person has learned it or will always remember it (*often passive*)

drum out *vt* to force somebody to leave a group or an organization, usually in disgrace (*usually passive*)

drum up *vt* **1.** to try actively to get more of something such as business or support **2.** to create or think up an explanation ○ *What excuse can I drum up this time?*

drum and bass, drum 'n' bass *n* popular music originating in the United Kingdom in the 1990s that has a fast rhythm, complex percussion, and very low bass lines

drum and bu·gle corps *n* a marching band consisting of percussion and bugle or fife players that performs precisely choreographed field drills

drum·beat /drúm bèet/ *n* **1.** SOUND OF DRUM a sound made by somebody beating a drum **2.** PASSIONATELY SUPPORTED CAUSE a cause that attracts passionate support **3.** INCESSANT CRITICISM heavy unending criticism, typically public criticism ○ *a steady drumbeat of accusations* —**drum·beat·er** *n* —**drum·beat·ing** *n*

drum brake *n* a brake on vehicles that operates by applying pressure to the inner part of the wheel (**brake drum**)

drum corps *n* a marching band, with percussion instruments and sometimes bugles or fifes, that performs precisely choreographed field drills

drum·ette /dru mét/ *n* the meaty part of a chicken wing separated from the rest of the wing [Because it resembles a small drumstick]

drum·fire /drúm fìr/ *n* **1.** continuous heavy gunfire **2.** a continuous intense sequence or round of something

drum·fish /drúm fish/ (*plural same* or **-fish·es**) *n* FISH same as **drum** *n* (sense 7)

drum·head /drúm hèd/ *n* **1.** the membrane, usually made of calfskin or plastic, that is stretched over the frame of a drum **2.** the round topmost part of a capstan that holds the capstan bars in position for turning

drum·head court-mar·tial *n* an informal brief trial held during military operations to hear charges of serious offenses committed by soldiers while in action [Because an upturned drum serves as the magistrate's bench]

drum kit *n Can, UK* same as **drum set**

drum·lin /drúmmlin/ *n* a long narrow ridge of gravel and rock deposited by a moving glacier, one end of which is blunt and the other end tapering [Mid-19C. < *drum* "ridge" < Irish *druim* "back, ridge"]

drum ma·chine *n* an electronic synthesizer that can reproduce drum and percussion sounds in various rhythms and combinations

drum ma·jor *n* a leader and conductor of a marching band who moves a baton up and down and twirls it rhythmically

drum ma·jor·ette *n* MUSIC same as **majorette**

drum·mer /drúmmər/ *n* **1.** DRUM PLAYER somebody who plays a drum **2.** TRAVELING SALESPERSON a traveling salesperson **3.** (*plural* **drum·mers** or *same*) AUSTRALIAN FISH a fish that frequents rocky shores. Native to: Australia. Family: Kyphosidae.

drum 'n' bass *n* MUSIC same as **drum and bass**

drum·roll /drúm rṑl/ *n* a very fast regular beating on a drum that sounds like one long sound

drum set, drum kit *n US* a set of percussion instruments used in bands, usually consisting of one or more snare drums, tom-toms, bass drums, and various cymbals. Can term **drum kit**

drum·stick /drúm stìk/ *n* **1.** the stick used to beat a drum **2.** the lower half of the leg of a bird such as a chicken when prepared for eating, so called because of its shape

drunk /drungk/ past participle of **drink** ■ *adj* **1.** INTOXICATED WITH ALCOHOL having drunk too much alcohol and lost control over behavior, movement, and speech **2.** EMOTIONALLY INTOXICATED overwhelmed with and judgmentally impaired by an intense emotion ○ *drunk with power* **3.** LONG-SOAKED describes a meat dish in Chinese cooking in which the meat, usually chicken, has been immersed in a liquid and boiled or marinated overnight ○ *drunk chicken* ■ *n* **1.** same as **drunkard 2.** DRINKING BOUT a bout of drinking too much alcohol (*slang*) ○ *One more drunk, and I divorce you.*

drunk·ard /drúngkərd/ *n* somebody who habitually drinks too much alcohol

drunk-driv·ing *n* the offense of driving a vehicle while having a higher blood alcohol content than the law allows ○ *Drunk-driving cost him his driver's license.* —**drunk-driv·er** *n*

drunk·en /drúngkən/ *adj* **1.** INTOXICATED overly excited by or as if by having consumed too much alcohol **2.** AFFECTED BY ALCOHOL drunk or frequently drunk **3.** INVOLVING EXCESS OF ALCOHOL involving too much alcohol, or occurring while people have had too much alcohol ○ *a drunken quarrel* [Old English, old past participle of DRINK] —**drunk·en·ly** *adv* —**drunk·en·ness** *n*

~~**drunkeness**~~ incorrect spelling of **drunkenness**

drunk tank *n* a special cell in a jail or police station where people who have been arrested for public drunkenness are kept (*slang*)

drupe /droop/ *n* a fruit with a thin outer skin, soft pulpy middle, and hard stony central part that encloses a seed. Apricots, plums, cherries, and almonds are drupes. [Mid-18C. Via modern Latin < Latin *drupa* "overripe olive" < Greek *druppa* "olive"]

drupe·let /dróoplət/, **dru·pel** /dróop'l/ *n* a small fruit enclosing a single seed that, with many other small sections, makes up a compound fruit such as a blackberry or raspberry

Druse *n* RELIG another spelling of **Druze**

druth·ers /drúthərz/ *npl* somebody's own free choice or preference (*informal*) ○ *If I had my druthers, I'd be lying on a beach somewhere.* [Late 19C. Alteration of *would rather*]

Druze /drooz/ (*plural same* or **Druz·es**), **Druse** (*plural same* or **Drus·es**) *n* a member of a religion similar to Islam that is found mainly in Israel, Lebanon, and Syria [Late 18C. Directly or via French < Arabic *durūz*, plural of *durzī*, after the religion's founder, Muḥammad ibn Ismā'īl *ad-Darazī* (d. 1019)] —**Dru·ze·an** *adj*

dry /drī/ *adj* (**dri·er** or **dry·er, dri·est** or **dry·est**) **1.** NOT WET not wet, or no longer wet **2.** LACKING MOISTURE IN AIR having little or no rain, or low humidity ○ *a dry climate* **3.** LACKING USUAL MOISTURE lacking natural oiliness or moistness ○ *dry skin* **4.** DRAINED OF WATER having no water because it has evaporated, drained away, or been depleted ○ *a dry riverbed* **5.** LACKING CUSTOMARY MOISTURE not producing or accompanied by associated moisture in the form of phlegm, tears, or vomit ○ *a dry cough* **6.** NOT REQUIRING LIQUID FOR USE made to be used without water ○ *dry shampoo* **7.** WITHOUT FLESH ATTACHED having no meat attached ○ *dry bones* **8.** THIRSTY thirsty and dehydrated **9.** BEVERAGES LACKING SWEETNESS describes wines that are not sweet because the sugar has been broken down during fermentation **10.** SERVED WITHOUT FAT OR LIQUID served without moist accompaniments such as butter, preserves, or gravy ○ *dry toast* **11.** STALE AND FLAVORLESS lacking appetizing moistness, e.g., because of being stale or overcooked **12.** SHREWDLY AMUSING witty in a shrewd, subtle, or sarcastic way **13.** BORING AND ACADEMIC dense and academic in style **14.** MATTER-OF-FACT plain and without unnecessary ornamentation ○ *a dry, matter-of-fact account of the incident* **15.** UNPRODUCTIVE unable to produce expected or creative results ○ *They've looked for him everywhere, and come up dry.* **16.** NOT ALLOWING ALCOHOL SALES not allowing legal sale of alcoholic beverages ○ *a dry county* **17.** ZOOL NO LONGER GIVING MILK describes a female animal that no longer produces milk **18.** CONTAINING NO MOISTURE from which the liquid or moisture has been removed ○ *Dry fruit has become popular as a snack.* ○ *dry weight* **19.** ELECTRONICS POORLY SOLDERED describes a solder joint on a circuit board that has not completely adhered to the surface and therefore will not conduct electricity ■ *v* (**dried, dry·ing, dries**) **1.** *vti* MAKE SOMETHING DRY to make something dry, or become dry ○ *It's your turn to dry the dishes.* **2.** *vt* FOOD INDUST PRESERVE FOOD BY EXTRACTING MOISTURE to preserve food, especially fruit, vegetables, and meat, by extracting most of the moisture from it ■ *n* (*plural* **drys** or **dries**) **1.** DRY PLACE a place that is dry or sheltered from the rain (*informal*) ○ *stay in the dry* **2.** POL PROHIBITIONIST a supporter of the legal prohibition of alcoholic beverages (*archaic*) [Old English *drȳge* < Germanic] —**dry·a·ble** *adj* —**dry·ness** *n*

SYNONYMS ***dry, dehydrated, desiccated, arid, parched, sere***

CORE MEANING: lacking moisture

dry not wet, or having little or no moisture ○ *prolonged periods of hot, dry weather* ○ *Use an exfoliating cream to remove patches of dry skin.* **dehydrated** lacking sufficient water, or having had water removed ○ *They were seriously dehydrated after five days without food or water.* ○ *instant foods such as dehydrated soups and canned meat* **desiccated** (used of products, especially food) free from moisture, or preserved by drying ○ *desiccated coconut* **arid** used of climate or a region that has a very low rainfall ○ *a plant that grows in hot, arid climates* ○ *the arid Red Sea coast* **parched** completely lacking in moisture because of hot conditions or lack of rainfall ○ *the recent floods in this usually parched region* **sere** (*literary*) dry and withered ○ *the sere grasses about the old well*

dry off *vti* to become drier, or make something drier

dry out *vti* **1.** to become completely dry, or make something completely dry ○ *It will take a while for the plaster to dry out.* **2.** to purge alcohol or other drugs from the body, or put somebody through such a process (*informal*)

dry up *v* **1.** *vti* **LOSE OR REMOVE MOISTURE** to lose water or moisture over a period, or make a river or pool lose its water over a period ○ *The river dried up centuries ago.* **2.** *vi* **STOP BEING AVAILABLE** to stop being available as a resource ○ *The project ended because our sources of funding dried up.* **3.** *vi* **RUN OUT OF IDEAS** to be unable to perform as usual or as expected ○ *His ideas have dried up.* **4.** *vi* **STOP TALKING** to stop talking, or forget lines during a performance or rehearsal (*informal; often used as a command*) ○ *Oh, just dry up, will you? I'm trying to think!* **5.** *vt UK* **DRY DISHES** to dry plates, dishes, pans, and cutlery with a cloth after they have been washed

dry·ad /drī əd, -àd/ (*plural* **-ads** or **-ad·es** /-ə dēez/) *n* in Greek mythology, a spiritual being believed to live in trees and forests [14C. Via Latin < Greek *Druad-* < *drus* "tree"] —**dry·ad·ic** /drī áddik/ *adj*

dry bat·ter·y *n* an electric battery that has more than one dry cell

dry-bone ore *n* a type of smithsonite that has many holes, found near the surface of the Earth's crust

dry cell *n* a current-generating electric cell that cannot be recharged and contains an electrolyte in the form of a paste or within a porous material to keep it from spilling

dry-clean *vt* to clean clothes or fabrics with a chemical solvent

dry clean·ing *n* **1.** the professional cleaning of clothes and fabrics using a chemical solvent **2.** clothes and other fabrics that require dry-cleaning or have just been dry-cleaned

dry cough *n* a cough that does not produce phlegm

Dry·den /drīd'n/, **John** (1631–1700) English poet, dramatist, and critic. His works include the play *Marriage à la Mode* (1672) and the verse satire *Absalom and Achitophel* (1681). He was made poet laureate by Charles II (1668), but having become a Catholic in 1685, was deprived of the office on the accession of William of Orange.

> "Happy the Man, and happy he alone, / He who can call today his own: / He who, secure within, can say, / Tomorrow do thy worst, for I have liv'd today."
> [John Dryden, *Translation of Horace's Odes*; 1685]

> "Reason to rule, but mercy to forgive: / The first is law, the last prerogative."
> [John Dryden, *The Hind and the Panther*; 1687]

dry dis·til·la·tion *n* CHEM same as **destructive distillation**

dry dock *n* an enclosed dock from which the water can be removed so that construction or repairs can be carried out below the water line of a boat or ship —**dry-dock** *vti*

dry·er[1] /drī ər/ comparative of **dry**

dry·er[2] another spelling of **drier**[1]

dry·est /drī ist/ superlative of **dry**

dry-eyed *adj* unable or unwilling to shed tears ○ *He remained dry-eyed throughout the trial.*

dry farm·ing *n* a method of growing crops in dry areas by selecting plants that are drought-resistant and using mulch to retain moisture in the soil, so making irrigation unnecessary —**dry farm·er** *n*

dry fly *n* an artificial lure used in fly-fishing that remains on the surface of the water instead of sinking

dry gin·ger *n* BEVERAGES same as **ginger ale**

dry goods *npl* goods such as fabrics, clothing, and notions, as distinct from hardware, food, and other products

dry hole *n* an oil well that has been drilled but that produces no oil, or not enough to make it economically profitable

dry ice *n* cold solid carbon dioxide at the temperature of −78.5°C/−110°F. Use: refrigeration, production of an artificial fog effect.

dry·ing oil *n* an organic oil, e.g., linseed or cottonseed oil, used as a base in paints and varnishes because it reduces drying time. Such oils form a tough thin film when exposed to air.

dry kiln *n* a large oven used to season cut lumber

dry land *n* the land as distinct from the ocean or a body of water

dry·land /drī lànd/ *n* areas prone to severe drought, e.g., deserts and savannas (*often used in the plural*) —**dry·land** *adj*

dry law *n* in some US states and counties, a law that forbids the sale of alcohol

dry·ly *adv* another spelling of **drily**

dry mar·ti·ni *n* a cocktail that contains a little dry vermouth mixed with gin or vodka

dry meas·ure *n* a system of units used to measure dry products such as grains and fruits by volume, or a unit in such a system

dry nurse *n* a nurse employed to look after somebody's young baby but not to breast-feed it (*archaic*) —**dry-nurse** *vt*

dry·o·pith·e·cine /drī ō píthə sēen/ (*plural* **-cines** or *same*) *n* an extinct ape of the Miocene and Pliocene epochs, believed by some scientists to be the ancestor of modern apes and humans. Genus: *Dryopithecus*. [Mid-20C. < modern Latin *Dryopithecus* < Greek *drus* "tree" + *pithēkos* "ape"]

dry point *n* **1.** **METHOD OF ENGRAVING** a technique of engraving in intaglio on a metal, usually copper, plate that produces a feathery effect in the lines of the print **2.** **STEEL NEEDLE** a hard steel needle used to engrave a metal plate **3.** **PRINT MADE BY DRY POINT** an engraving or print made by using dry point

dry-roast·ed *adj* describes shelled nuts that have been roasted without any oil

dry rot *n* **1.** **CRUMBLING DECAY IN WOOD** dry crumbling decay in wood caused by various fungi **2.** **PLANT DISEASE** a disease caused by various fungi that invade plant stems, bulbs, and fruits, causing them to dry out and decay **3.** **DESTRUCTIVE FUNGUS** a fungus that causes dry rot. Genus: *Merulius*.

dry run *n* a rehearsal of a planned action or activity (*informal*) ○ *Let's do a dry run to make sure it's going to work.*

dry-salt *vt* to use salt to dry and preserve food

dry salt meat *n regional* FOOD same as **fatback**

REGIONAL NOTE See ***fatback***.

dry sock·et *n* a painful condition caused when the blood left by an extracted tooth fails to clot or the clot is dislodged

dry·wall /drī wàwl/, **dry wall** *n* **1.** CONSTR **WALL MATERIAL** reinforced gypsum plaster sandwiched between two layers of strong paper in large sheets, used chiefly for interior walls **2.** **WALL MADE OF PLASTERBOARD** a wall constructed with sheets of plasterboard **3.** **WALL MADE WITHOUT MORTAR** a wall constructed of stone or masonry without mortar —**dry-wall** *vt*

dry wash *n* laundry that has been washed and dried but has not been ironed

d.s. *abbr* **1.** MUSIC dal segno **2.** BUSINESS days after sight **3.** document signed

D.Sc., **DSc** *abbr* Doctor of Science

D.S.C., **DSC** *abbr* NAVY Distinguished Service Cross

DSI *abbr* MED dysfunction of sensory integration

DSL *n* high-speed telephone line supplying telephony, television, and Internet access. Full form **digital subscriber line**

D.S.O., **DSO** *abbr* MIL Distinguished Service Order

DSS *abbr* **1.** GOV Department of Social Services **2.** Director of Social Services

DST *abbr* daylight-saving time

DT *abbr* daylight time

DTP *abbr* COMPUT desktop publishing

D.T.'s, **d.t.'s** *npl* MED same as **delirium tremens** (*informal*)

DTV *abbr* BROADCAST digital television

du /doo/, **Du** see also under surname

DU *abbr* MIL, PHYS depleted uranium

du·al /dōō əl/ *adj* **1.** **HAVING TWO SIMILAR ELEMENTS** having two parts, functions, aspects, or items of a similar kind ○ *dual citizenship* **2.** **HAVING TWO DISTINCT ASPECTS** made up of two distinct, often opposite, parts ○ *serve a dual purpose* **3.** **SPECIFYING TWO** in various languages, used to describe a grammatical number category, in addition to singular and plural, that specifies two people or things ■ *n* GRAM **DUAL NUMBER OR INFLECTED FORM** dual number, or, in various languages, the inflected form of a noun, pronoun, adjective, or verb that refers to dual number [Early 17C. < Latin *dualis* < *duo* "two"] —**du·al·ly** *adv*

SPELLCHECK dual or **duel**? Do not confuse the spelling of ***dual*** and ***duel***, which sound similar. ***Dual*** is chiefly used as an adjective, meaning "having two elements or aspects" or "double," as in *dual citizenship, a dual-purpose device*. ***Duel*** is chiefly used as a noun, denoting a fight between two people: *He took offense at this remark and challenged the man to a duel.*

Du·a·la[1] /doo ààlə/ (*plural same* or **-las**) *n* **1.** a member of an African people who live in Cameroon **2.** the language of the Duala people, belonging to the Bantu group of Niger-Congo languages —**Du·a·la** *adj*

Du·a·la[2] another spelling of **Douala**

du·al car·riage·way *n UK* same as **divided highway**

du·al e·con·o·my *n* an economy in which different sectors are growing at different rates. Manufacturing and service industries or rural and urban areas may show significant differences in economic performance.

du·al-hat·ted *adj* holding two military commands at the same time

du·al in-line pack·age *n* a rectangular housing for components such as integrated circuits or toggle switches that has a row of pins along the base of two opposite sides that can be plugged or soldered into a circuit board

du·al·ism /dōō ə lìzzəm/ *n* **1.** **STATE OF HAVING TWO PARTS** a state in which something has two distinct parts or aspects, which are often opposites **2.** **THEORY OF TWO OPPOSING CONCEPTS** a philosophical theory based on the idea of opposing concepts, especially the theory that human beings are made up of two independent constituents, the body and the mind or soul **3.** **DOCTRINE OF OPPOSING PRINCIPLES** the religious doctrine that two opposed and antagonistic forces of good and evil determine the course of events **4.** RELIG **DUAL NATURE OF PEOPLE** the religious idea that people are inherently dual in nature, both spiritual and physical —**du·al·ist** *n* —**du·al·is·tic** /dōō ə lístik/ *adj* —**du·al·is·ti·cal·ly** *adv*

du·al·i·ty /doo állətee/ (*plural* **-ties**) *n* **1.** **SOMETHING CONSISTING OF TWO PARTS** a situation or nature that has two states or parts that are complementary or opposed to each other **2.** **THEORY OF MATTER** in microphysics, the theory that both wave and particle theory account for the behavior of matter and energy under different conditions **3.** **MATHEMATICAL SYMMETRY OF OBJECTS OR OPERATIONS** a mathematical symmetry in which some objects or operations can be interchanged without invalidating a relationship, e.g., the interchange of points and lines in a plane in projective geometry

du·al-pur·pose *adj* capable of performing two functions satisfactorily ○ *a dual-purpose cleaner*

du·al sig·na·ture *n* E-COMMERCE the linking of two discrete parts of a single message allowing a cardholder to communicate with a merchant and a payment gateway simultaneously (*used in e-commerce*)

du·al trad·ing *n* the entering by somebody into a securities transaction both on a personal basis and for a customer, giving rise to a conflict of interest

Duar·te /dwààrtee/ city in southwestern California below the San Gabriel Mountains, east of Los Angeles. Population: 22,072 (2002 estimate).

Duar·te, José Napoleón (1925–90) Salvadorean politician. He was twice president of El Salvador (1980–82, 1984–89).

dub[1] /dub/ *vt* (**dubbed, dub·bing, dubs**) **1.** **GIVE SOMEBODY OR SOMETHING NICKNAME** to give a descriptive nickname to somebody or something ○ *The press dubbed him the King of Chess.* **2.** **HONOR SOMEBODY WITH RENAMING** to honor somebody by giving him or her a new name or description **3.** POL **CONFER KNIGHTHOOD ON SOMEBODY** to give somebody a knighthood by tapping the person on the shoulder with a sword as part of a formal ceremony **4.** INDUST **MAKE SOMETHING SMOOTH OR EVEN** to dress a material such as leather or timber to make it smooth or even **5.** FOOD **CLEAN MEAT** to clean meat, especially fish or poultry, in preparation for sale or eating **6.** SPORTS **PERFORM POORLY** to perform something such as a golf stroke ineptly ■ *n* **CLUMSY UNSKILLFUL PERSON** a clumsy, awkward, or unskillful person (*dated informal*) [Pre-12C. < Anglo-Norman *duber*, variant of Old French *adober* "equip with armor"] —**dub·ber** *n*

dub[2] /dub/ *vt* (**dubbed, dub·bing, dubs**) **1. ADD NEW SOUNDTRACK** to add a new soundtrack to a movie or television show with the dialogue in a different language but synchronized as closely as possible with the actors' lips ○ *The movie was dubbed into Italian.* **2. ADD SOUNDS TO MOVIE** to add sounds that have been recorded separately to a movie soundtrack **3. COPY SOMETHING ONTO NEW MEDIUM** to copy something already recorded onto a different recording medium **4. MAKE COPY** to make a copy of a record or tape ■ *n* **1. SOMETHING ADDED BY DUBBING** new sounds added by dubbing **2. COPY OF RECORDING** a copy made of a tape or recording **3. STYLE OF MUSIC** a style of popular music, originating in reggae in the 1970s, involving remixing records to bring some instruments into the foreground and causing others to echo [Early 20C. Shortening of DOUBLE] —**dub·ber** *n*

dub[3] /dub/ *v* (**dubbed, dub·bing, dubs**) **1.** *vt* **POKE AT SOMEBODY OR SOMETHING** to make a thrust at somebody or something **2.** *vti* MUSIC **DRUM** to beat drums or a drum ■ *n* **1. ACT OF THRUSTING** the act of poking at somebody or something **2.** MUSIC **DRUMMING** the sound of drumming or a drummer [Late 20C. Origin ?]

Du·bai /doo bī/, **Du·bayy** city in the northeastern United Arab Emirates, and the capital city of Dubai state. Population: 674,100 (1995).

Du Bar·ry /doo bárree/, **Marie Jeanne Bécu, Comtesse** (1743?–93) French courtier and mistress of Louis XV. A patron of the arts, she is reputed to have exercised considerable influence over Louis XV until his death in 1774. After the outbreak of the French Revolution (1792), she was tried and guillotined on charges of conspiracy.

Du·bayy another spelling of **Dubai**

dub·bing /dúbbing/ *n* **1. PROCESS OF ADDING NEW SOUNDTRACK** the process of providing a new soundtrack for a movie or television show with the dialogue in a different language but synchronized as closely as possible with the actors' lips **2. SOUNDTRACK** a soundtrack recorded for a movie or television show after the photography is finished **3. FINAL SOUNDTRACK** a final mix of all the soundtracks for a movie

Dub·ček /dóob chèk, dóop-/, **Alexander** (1921–92) Czech politician. His liberal reforms as leader of the Communist party led to Soviet invasion in 1968. Shortly afterward, he was ousted from power. He re-emerged as a popular figure in 1989.

> "Socialism with a human face must function again for a new generation. We have lived in the darkness for long enough."
> [Alexander Dubček, *Speech, Wenceslas Square, Prague*; November 4, 1989]

du·bi·e·ty /doo bī əteе/ (*plural* **-ties**) *n* (*formal*) **1.** a feeling of uncertainty about something **2.** something about which you are unsure [Mid-18C. < late Latin *dubietas* < Latin *dubius* "doubtful"]

Du·bin·sky /doo bínskee/, **David** (1892–1982) Russian-born US labor leader. He was president of the International Ladies' Garment Workers' Union (1932–66).

du·bi·ous /dóobee əss/ *adj* **1. UNSURE ABOUT OUTCOME** not sure about an outcome or conclusion ○ *I was a little dubious about whether or not to trust him.* **2. POSSIBLY DISHONEST OR IMMORAL** likely to be dishonest, untrustworthy, or morally worrisome in some way ○ *It's a dubious proposition.* **3. OF UNCERTAIN QUALITY** of uncertain quality, intention, or appropriateness ○ *The thesis is based on several dubious assumptions.* [Mid-16C. < Latin *dubius* "doubtful"] —**du·bi·ous·ly** *adv* —**du·bi·ous·ness** *n*

SYNONYMS See ***doubtful***.

du·bi·ta·ble /dóobitəb'l/ *adj* causing or leading to doubt or uncertainty (*formal*) [Early 17C. < Latin *dubitabilis* < *dubitare* "be uncertain"] —**du·bi·ta·bly** *adv*

Dub·lin /dúbblin/ **1.** city and capital of the Republic of Ireland. It is situated on the Liffey River in east central Ireland, at the head of Dublin Bay on the Irish Sea. Population: 481,854 (2002). Irish name **Baile Átha Cliath 2.** coastal county in Leinster Province in the Republic of Ireland. Population: 1,058,264 (2002). Area: 356 sq. mi./922 sq. km. **3.** city in western California east of San Francisco Bay and southeast of Oakland. Population: 34,345 (2002 estimate). —**Dub·lin·er** *n*

dub·ni·um /dúbnee əm/ *n* an extremely rare, unstable element. Source: high-energy bombardment of californium. Symbol **Db**. See table at **element**

Du Bois /doo bóyss/, **W. E. B.** (1868–1963) US historian, sociologist, and civil rights leader. He conducted the first research on the experience of African Americans in the United States and fought for racial equality, becoming the most influential African American intellectual of his time. Full name **Du Bois, William Edward Burghardt**

> "I believe that all men, black and brown and white, are brothers, varying through time and opportunity, in form and gift and feature, but differing in no essential particular, and alike in soul and the possibility of infinite development."
> [W. E. B. Du Bois, "Credo," *Darkwater: Voices from Within the Veil*; 1920]

Du·bos /doo báwss, -bőss/, **René** (1901–82) French-born US bacteriologist. He discovered tyrothricin (1939), the first commercially produced antibiotic. His writings on the environment include *So Human an Animal* (1968). Full name **Dubos, René Jules**

> "Epidemics have often been more influential than statesmen and soldiers in shaping the course of political history, and diseases may also color the moods of civilizations."
> [René Dubos, *The White Plague*; 1953]

Du·brov·nik /doo bráwvnik, dóo bràwvnik/ city, port, and vacation resort on the Dalmatian coast in southeastern Croatia. It suffered damage during ethnic conflict in the 1990s. Population: 49,728 (1991).

Du·buque /də byóok/ city and port in northeastern Iowa, on the Mississippi River. It forms the Iowa-Wisconsin border northeast of Cedar Rapids. Population: 57,031 (2002 estimate).

du·cal /dóok'l/ *adj* belonging to, relating to, or like a duke or dukedom ○ *a ducal palace* [15C. < French < *duc* (see DUKE)] —**du·cal·ly** *adv*

duc·at /dúkət/ *n* **1. OLD EUROPEAN COIN** a gold or silver coin formerly used in some European countries, e.g., Italy and the Netherlands **2. TICKET** a ticket for a performance (*dated informal*) ■ **duc·ats** *npl* **CASH** money or cash (*informal dated*) [14C. Via French < medieval Latin *ducatus* "duchy" (see DUCHY); because the word appeared on early coins]

Duc·ci·o di Buon·in·seg·na /dóochee ō di bwònnin sénnyə/ (1260–1320) Italian painter. A precursor of the Renaissance style, he endowed his subjects with humanity and emotion, most notably in his only signed work, the *Maestà* altarpiece (1308–11).

du·ce /dóo chày/ *n* an Italian term for "leader." The Italian Fascist leader Mussolini was called "Il Duce." [Early 20C. Via Italian < Latin *dux* "leader"]

Du·champ /doo shaáN/, **Marcel** (1887–1968) French-born US artist. He displayed everyday objects as works of art, and helped to introduce Cubism to the United States. He became a citizen of the United States in 1955, and later his work became an inspiration for the pop art movement.

> "Art may be bad, good or indifferent, but, whatever adjective is used, we must call it art, and bad art is still art in the same way as a bad emotion is still an emotion."
> [Marcel Duchamp, "The Creative Act," *Art News*; Summer 1957]

Du·chenne mus·cu·lar dys·tro·phy /doo shén-/, **Du·chenne's mus·cu·lar dys·tro·phy** /doo shénz-/, **Du·chenne dys·tro·phy, Du·chenne's dys·tro·phy** *n* a form of muscular dystrophy that attacks the muscles of the upper respiratory and pelvic areas, usually affecting boys and causing death before maturity [Late 19C. After G. B. A. *Duchenne* (1806–75), French neurologist]

duch·ess /dúchəss/ *n* **1.** a noblewoman of high rank. In the British Isles, this is the highest hereditary title of nobility. **2.** the wife or widow of a duke [14C. Via Old French *duchesse* < medieval Latin *ducissa*, feminine form of *dux* "leader"]

duch·esse sat·in /doo shéss-/ *n* a firm heavy satin with a glossy finish. Use: formal gowns.

duch·ess po·ta·toes /doo shèss-/ *npl* a mixture of mashed potatoes, eggs, and butter that is made into a patty and baked

duch·y /dúchee/ (*plural* **-ies**) *n* the territory over which a duke or duchess has jurisdiction [14C. Via Old French *duche* < medieval Latin *ducatus* < Latin *duc-*, stem of *dux* "leader"]

duck[1] /duk/ *n* **1.** (*plural* **ducks** or *same*) **COMMON WATER BIRD** a common water bird with webbed feet, short legs, and a broad flat beak. It is found all over the world, with the exception of Antarctica. Family: Anatidae. **2. FEMALE DUCK** a female duck **3. DUCK AS FOOD** the flesh of a duck when eaten as a food [Old English *dūce*, origin ?] ◇ **get** *or* **have your ducks all in a row** to have organized your life or a specific task so that it runs smoothly ◇ **take to something like a duck to water** to have a natural talent for something (*informal*)

duck[2] /duk/ *v* (**ducked, duck·ing, ducks**) **1.** *vti* **BEND QUICKLY** to bend or move the head down quickly, especially to avoid being hit by something **2.** *vi* **MOVE QUICKLY** to move somewhere very quickly, often to avoid being seen ○ *I ducked behind a desk and kept as still as possible.* **3.** *vti* **PLUNGE UNDER WATER** to push somebody under water, or move quickly so as to go below the surface of water **4.** *vt* **AVOID SOMETHING** to avoid dealing with something that ought to be dealt with ○ *The candidate ducked all the questions about her past.* **5.** *vi* CARDS **DELIBERATELY LOSE TRICK** to play a card lower than an opponent's on purpose in order to lose a trick ■ *n* **QUICK DOWNWARD MOVEMENT** a movement downward with the head, especially to avoid being hit by something [13C. Probably < assumed Old English *dūcan* < W Germanic, "dive, dip"] —**duck·er** *n* ◇ **duck and run** to avoid meeting somebody face to face

duck out *vi* to avoid or dodge doing something (*informal*) ○ *She's trying to duck out of paying her part of the bill.*

duck[3] /duk/ *n* strong, fairly stiff, closely woven cotton or canvas cloth. Use: protective clothing, furnishings. ■ **ducks** *npl* a pair of pants, usually white, or like those worn by sailors [Mid-17C. < Dutch *doek* "linen"]

duck-billed platypus

duck-billed plat·y·pus, duck·bill /dúk bìl/ *n* an egg-laying water mammal with a snout shaped like a duck's bill and webbed feet. Native to: Australia. Latin name: *Ornithorynchus anatinus.*

duck blind *n* a camouflaged shelter from which hunters shoot ducks

duck·board /dúk bàwrd/ *n* a temporary walkway made of wooden boards laid over a wet or muddy area to form a raised path

duck call *n* a device similar to a whistle that a duck hunter blows into in order to attract ducks

duck·ie *n, adj* another spelling of **ducky** (*dated informal*)

duck·ing stool *n* formerly, in Europe and New England, a chair or stool in which an offender was tied and then immersed in water as a punishment

duck·ling /dúkling/ *n* a duck that has not reached maturity

duck·pin /dúk pìn/ *n* a bowling pin smaller in size than a tenpin [Early 20C. < its shape]

duck·pins /dúk pìnz/ *n* a bowling game played with a small ball and pins smaller than tenpins (*takes a singular verb*)

ducks and drakes *n UK* a game in which flat stones are skipped across water by throwing them almost parallel to its surface (*takes a singular verb*) [Because suggestive of a waterfowl's movements] ◇ **play ducks and drakes with** to use something recklessly and wastefully

duck's ass *n* an offensive term for a man's hairstyle, popular in the 1950s, in which the hair is slicked back and drawn into a point at the back of the neck to look like a duck's tail

duck soup *n* something that is accomplished easily (*slang*)

duck·tail /dúk tàyl/ *n* HAIR same as **DA**[2]

duck·weed /dúk wèed/ *n* a free-floating water plant with small rounded leaves and without a stem that is found on still temperate waters. Genus: *Lemna.*

duck·y /dúkee/, **duck·ie** (*dated informal*) *adv* very good or excellent ○ *Everything's just ducky at the moment.* ■ *adj* charmingly pretty ○ *a ducky little cottage*

duct /dukt/ *n* **1.** CHANNEL a tube, pipe, or channel through which something can flow or be carried, e.g., in air-conditioning equipment **2.** TUBE IN BODY ORGAN a narrow tubular exit passageway in a gland or bladder through which fluid passes **3.** TUBE FOR CABLES a tube or channel containing electrical cables ■ *vt* (**duct·ed, duct·ing, ducts**) **1.** FIT SOMETHING WITH DUCTS to supply or equip something such as a building with a duct or a system of ducts **2.** ROUTE SOMETHING THROUGH CHANNEL to make a fluid or gas pass through a tube, pipe, or channel ○ *Exhaust fumes are ducted out of the workshop.* [Mid-17C. < Latin *ductus* < *ducere* "to lead"] —**duct·al** *adj* —**duct·less** *adj*

duc·tile /dúkt'l/ *adj* **1.** MALLEABLE ENOUGH TO BE WORKED able to be drawn out into wire or hammered into very thin sheets ○ *ductile metal* **2.** READILY SHAPED able to be molded or shaped without breaking **3.** READILY INFLUENCED easily persuaded or influenced [14C. Directly or via French < Latin *ductilis* "that may be led" < *ducere* "to lead"] —**duc·til·i·ty** /duk tíllətee/ *n*

SYNONYMS See ***pliable.***

duct·ing /dúkting/ *n* **1.** a duct or system of ducts **2.** materials, e.g., pipes and tubing, that can be used as ducts

duct·less gland *n* ANAT same as **endocrine gland**

duct tape *n* a very strong, wide, adhesive tape, typically silver in color, used especially in making temporary repairs to pipes

duct·work /dúkt wùrk/ *n* a system of ducts that has been constructed, or its design

dud /dud/ *n* **1.** somebody or something considered ineffective or a failure (*informal*) **2.** a munition that fails to fire or explode [Early 19C. Origin ?]

dude /dood/ *n* (*slang*) **1.** MAN a man or boy ○ *He's one cool dude.* ○ *Hey, dude, what's up?* **2.** CITY DWELLER VACATIONING OUT WEST a resident of the urban eastern seaboard who vacations on a dude ranch in the West **3.** FLASHILY DRESSED MAN a man who wears flashy, highly stylish clothes [Late 19C. Origin ?]
dude up *vi* to dress up, especially in very elaborate or stylish clothes (*slang*)

du·deen /doo dèen/ *n* a clay tobacco pipe with a short stem [Mid-19C. < Irish *dúidín* "small pipe" < *dúd* "pipe"]

dude ranch *n* a vacation resort offering outdoor activities that is or resembles a typical Western ranch

dude ranch·er *n* somebody who owns or runs a dude ranch —**dude ranch·ing** *n*

dudg·eon /dújjən/ *n* a fit of anger and irritation [Late 16C. Origin ?] ◇ **in high dudgeon** in a very angry or irritated mood

Dud·ley /dúddlee/ industrial city near Birmingham in the West Midlands, England. Population: 305,155 (2001).

Dud·ley, Robert ➧ **Leicester, Robert Dudley**

duds /dudz/ *npl* articles of clothing and accessories (*informal*) [15C. Origin ?]

due /doo/ *adj* **1.** EXPECTED TO ARRIVE expected to arrive imminently ○ *The baby is due in three weeks.* **2.** READY awaiting an event, as part of a normal chain or progression of other events ○ *due for a long-awaited promotion* **3.** CAUSED BY SOMEBODY OR SOMETHING caused by or attributable to somebody or something ○ *The delay was due to bad weather.* **4.** PAYABLE payable at once and on demand or at a stipulated time ○ *Payment is due in 30 days.* **5.** PROPER AND APPROPRIATE meeting all the necessary requirements and thus proper and appropriate to the situation ○ *after due consideration* **6.** OWED owed as a debt because of a right or an obligation ○ *Our deep gratitude is due to all those who have helped over the last few months.* ■ *n* SOMEBODY'S RIGHT something that somebody has deserved or is owed ○ *I'll give you your due – you were absolutely right.* ■ **dues** *npl* MEMBERSHIP FEES fees for membership in an organization ■ *adv* DIRECTLY AND EXACTLY in a direct exact way or course ○ *due west* [13C. Via Old French *deu* "owed" < Latin *debitus* < *debere* "owe"] ◇ **pay your dues** to gain a privilege or position through hard work or pain

SPELLCHECK See *dew.*

USAGE Some people object to the use of the phrase ***due to*** in sentences like these: *The concert has been canceled due to circumstances beyond our control* and *The flight was delayed due to bad weather.* Their objection is based on the fact that ***due*** is an adjective and should be used with a noun, as in *The delay was due to bad weather,* where *due* modifies *delay.* You can avoid using ***due to*** with a verb by replacing it with *owing to* or *because of*: *The concert has been canceled owing to circumstances beyond our control. The game was postponed because of bad weather.*

due bill *n* a document, exchangeable for merchandise or services, that acknowledges one party's indebtedness to another

due date *n* the date that something such as the payment of a bill or the birth of a baby is expected to occur

due dil·i·gence *n* **1.** the degree of care that a prudent person would exercise, which is a legally relevant standard for establishing liability **2.** the disclosure to potential buyers of all relevant information that applies to a security issue

du·el /dóo əl/ *n* **1.** a prearranged combat, especially in former times, between two people armed with lethal weapons, usually to settle a disagreement over a matter of honor **2.** a struggle or conflict between two people or groups [15C. < medieval Latin *duellum* "combat between two persons" < (influenced by Latin *duo* "two") Latin *duellum,* archaic form of *bellum* "war"] —**du·el** *vi* —**du·el·er** *n*

SPELLCHECK See *dual.*

du·el·ing pis·tol *n* a pistol specifically designed for fighting a duel, usually more finely manufactured than a normal pistol and often made in sets of two

du·el·ist /dóo əlist/ *n* **1.** a fighter of a duel **2.** a person or organization taking part in a dual-party conflict or competition ○ *corporate duelists struggling for market share*

~~**duely**~~ incorrect spelling of **duly**

du·en·na /doo énnə/ *n* a woman acting as a chaperon or governess to a younger woman, especially in Spain and Portugal in former times [Mid-17C. Via Spanish, "married lady" < Latin *domina* "lady"]

due-on-sale clause *n* a condition in a mortgage agreement stating that the outstanding amount will be repaid if the related property is sold, the borrower dies, or the property is refinanced

due proc·ess *n* **1.** fundamental principles of justice as opposed to a specific rule of law **2.** the entitlement of a citizen to proper legal procedures and natural justice

Due·ro /dwérō/ Spanish name for **Douro**

du·et /doo ét/ *n* **1.** an instrumental or vocal composition written for two performers of equal importance **2.** a pair of people, animals, or things [Mid-18C. < Italian *duetto,* literally "little duo" or German *Duett* < Latin *duo* "two"] —**du·et·tist** *n*

duff[1] /duf/ *vt* (**duffed, duff·ing, duffs**) to play a bad shot in golf by hitting the ground behind the ball (*informal*) ■ *adj UK* useless, broken, or of very low quality (*informal*) ■ *n N Am, Scotland* same as **litter** *n* (sense 6) [Mid-19C. Origin ?]

duff[2] /duf/ *n* an offensive term for the buttocks (*slang*) [Late 19C. Origin ?]

duf·fel /dúff'l/, **duf·fle** *n* **1.** woolen material with a nap on both sides **2.** gear, including clothing and equipment, used by campers and hikers [Late 17C. < Dutch, after *Duffel,* Belgium]

duf·fel bag *n* a cylindrical bag for personal belongings that is fastened with a drawstring

duf·fel coat *n* CLOTHING another spelling of **duffle coat**

duff·er /dúffər/ *n* **1.** UNINTELLIGENT PERSON somebody regarded as a slow learner or not competent at something (*informal dated insult*) **2.** SOMETHING WORTHLESS something worthless or useless (*dated informal*) **3.** *regional* PEDDLER a peddler of goods, especially cheap or worthless merchandise (*archaic*) [Mid-18C. Origin ?]

duf·fle *n* TEXTILES, CAMPING another spelling of **duffel**

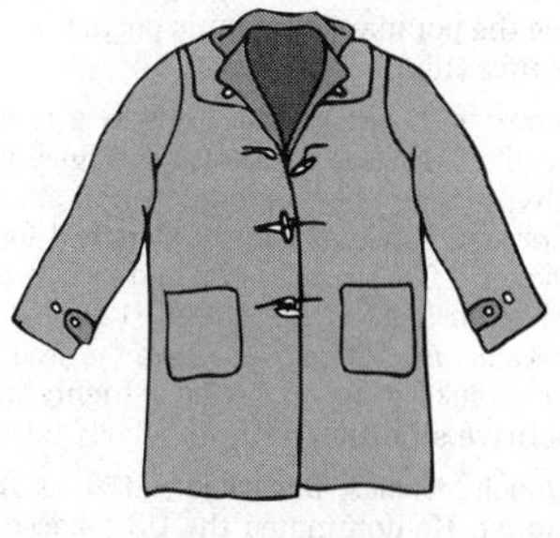

duffle coat

duf·fle coat, duf·fel coat *n* a heavy medium-length coat with a hood and toggles for fastening it that is made from duffel

Du·fy /doo fèe/, **Raoul** (1877–53) French painter, illustrator, and designer. Known for his paintings of the French Riviera in a popularized Fauvist style, he also designed textiles and pottery.

dug[1] past participle, past tense of **dig**

dug[2] /dug/ *n* an udder, teat, nipple, or breast of a female mammal [Mid-16C. Origin ?]

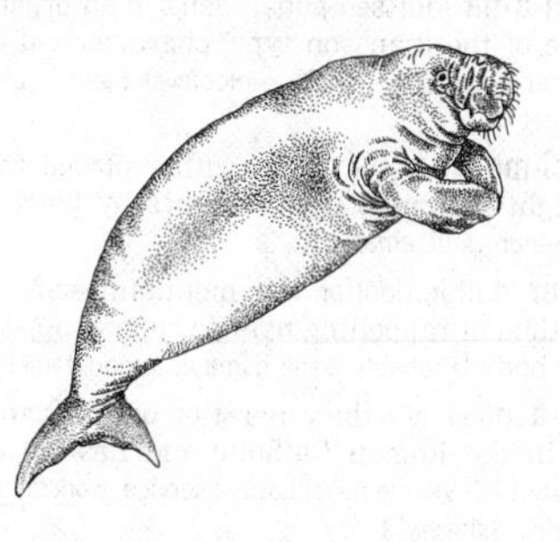

dugong

du·gong /dóo gàwng/ *n* a large plant-eating sea mammal, related to the manatee. It has a two-lobed tail, a cleft upper lip, forelimbs resembling flippers, and tusks in the male. Native to: shallow tropical coastal waters. Latin name: *Dugong dugon.* [Early 19C. < Malay *duyung*]

dug·out /dúg òwt/ *n* **1.** BASEBALL SHELTER either of two shelters, one for each team, on opposite sides of a baseball field where team members wait while not playing **2.** SOCCER SHELTER either of two shelters beside a sports field, especially a soccer field, for team officials such as the manager and trainer and team members who are not on the field **3.** CANOE MADE FROM HOLLOWED LOG a canoe or boat hollowed out from a log or tree trunk **4.** SOLDIERS' SHELTER a hole dug in the ground that is covered and used as a shelter, especially by soldiers

duh /də/ *interj* (*slang*) **1.** said as an ironic response to being told something obvious or well known ○ *"Billy asked me to the party, I think he really likes me!" –*

"Duh!" **2.** used in humorous acknowledgment of your own stupidity ○ *"What did you do with the keys?" – "Duh."*

DUI *abbr* driving under the influence

dui·ker /dīkər/, **duy·ker** *n* a small African antelope with short backward-pointing horns. Genera: *Cephalophus* or *Sylvicapra.* [Late 18C. < Afrikaans, literally "diver" < Middle Dutch *dūken* "dive"]

Duis·burg /do͝oss bùrg, do͞oz-/ city in North Rhine-Westphalia State, northwestern Germany, at the junction of the Rhine and Ruhr rivers. It is a major inland port. Population: 536,106 (1997).

du jour /doo zho͝or/ *adj* **1.** offered or served today ○ *the soup du jour* **2.** being the latest in a series, sequence, or trend [< French, "of the day"]

Du·ka·kis /doo kaákəss/, **Michael** (*b.* 1933) US politician. He was Democratic governor of Massachusetts (1974–79 and 1982–91) and ran for the US presidency in 1988. Full name **Dukakis, Michael Stanley**

Du·kas /doo kaáss, -kaá/, **Paul Abraham** (1865–1935) French composer and teacher. His few works include the popular symphonic poem *The Sorcerer's Apprentice* (1897).

duke /dook/ *n* **1. HIGH-RANKING NOBLEMAN** a nobleman of high rank **2. RULER OF PRINCIPALITY** a prince who rules a duchy, principality, or other small state **3. FIST** a hand or fist, especially a fist clenched for fighting or a boxer's fist raised as an indication of victory (*slang; often used in the plural*) [12C. Via Old French *duc* < Latin *dux* "leader" < *ducere* "to lead"] —**duke·dom** *n* ◇ **duke it out** to be in a highly aggressive competitive situation with somebody (*slang*)

Duke /dook/, **James Buchanan** (1856–1925) US industrialist. He dominated the US tobacco industry by 1889 and formed the American Tobacco Co. in 1890.

Du·kho·bor *n* CHR another spelling of **Doukhobor**

du·ku·na /do͞okoo naal/ *n Carib* a pudding made from cornmeal, coconut, grated sweet potatoes, raisins, and sugar, wrapped in leaves and steamed [Late 20C. < Akan]

du·la·hin /doo laá hin/ *n* a Hindu bride (*often used to address a new daughter-in-law*) [< Hindi]

dul·cet /dúlssət/ *adj* pleasant to hear, especially because of being soft or soothing [15C. < Old French *doucet* "sweet (thing)" < *doux* "sweet" < Latin *dulcis*]

dul·ci·a·na /dùlssee ánnə, -aánə/ *n* an organ stop or pipe of the diapason type, characterized by a soft sweet tone [Late 18C. < medieval Latin < Latin *dulcis* "sweet"]

dul·ci·mer /dúlssəmər/ *n* a zither played with lightweight hammers or sometimes by plucking [15C. < French *doulcemer*]

dul·fer /dúlfər, do͞olfər/ *n* in mountaineering, a classic method of rappelling using a rope wrapped around the body [Probably < the name of a mountaineer]

du·li·a /doo lī́ ə/ *n* the veneration of saints and angels, as in the Roman Catholic and Eastern churches [Early 17C. Via medieval Latin, "service, work done" < Greek *douleia* "slavery"]

dull /dul/ *adj* **1. BORING** arousing no interest or excitement **2. NOT VIVID** lacking vividness or brightness of hue **3. OVERCAST** not bright because of weather conditions such as thick clouds or mist **4. NOT INTENSELY FELT** not acutely or intensely felt or experienced, but prolonged ○ *a dull ache* **5. MUFFLED** muffled and not resonant ○ *a dull thud* **6. BLUNT** lacking sharpness or the ability to cut cleanly **7. UNINTELLIGENT** slow to understand or learn **8. SLOW TO RESPOND** lacking in alertness or speedy responsiveness ○ *dull reflexes* **9. LISTLESS** lacking in energy or enthusiasm ○ *dull, scattered applause* ■ *vti* (**dulled, dull·ing, dulls**) **1. REDUCE IN LOUDNESS** to become quieter, or cause something to become quieter **2. BECOME OR MAKE LESS ACUTE** to become less acute or intensely felt, or cause something to become less acute or intensely felt ○ *Sleepiness had dulled his hunger.* **3. BECOME OR MAKE BLUNT** to become less sharp, or cause something to become less sharp **4. BECOME OR MAKE LESS BRIGHT** to become less bright or intense, or cause something to become less bright or intense [Old English *dol* "slow-witted" < Germanic] —**dull·ish** *adj* —**dull·ness** *n* —**dul·ly** *adv*

SYNONYMS See *boring*[1].

dull·ard /dúllərd/ *n* somebody regarded as unintelligent or slow to comprehend (*literary*)

Dul·les /dúlliss/, **Allen Welsh** (1893–1969) US government official. The director of the Central Intelligence Agency (1953–61), he resigned after the disastrous Bay of Pigs landing in Cuba and the subsequent rout of the US invading force.

Dul·les, John Foster (1888–1959) US politician and diplomat. He was US secretary of state (1953–59), and delegate to the United Nations, which he helped to form.

> "The ability to get to the verge without getting into the war is the necessary art. If you cannot master it, you inevitably get into war. If you try to run away from it, if you are scared to go to the brink, you are lost."
> [John Foster Dulles, *Life*; January 16, 1956]

Dull Knife /dúl nī́f/ (1810?–83) Cheyenne leader. He opposed the removal of his people to a reservation in Oklahoma, and led two daring escape attempts.

dulls·ville /dúlz vìl/, **Dulls·ville** *n* (*slang*) **1.** a place, thing, or activity that is boring or unexciting ○ *This town is dullsville in the evening.* **2.** the condition of being bored or uninterested ○ *I sat there in dullsville during the entire eight-hour flight.* [Mid-20C. After place names]

dulse /dulss/ (*plural* **duls·es** or *same*) *n* a red alga with edible fronds that grows in the intertidal zone and near the low-water mark in northern temperate seas. Latin name: *Palmaria palmata.* [Early 17C. < Irish and Gaelic *duileasg*]

Du·luth /də lo͞oth/ major port and city in northeastern Minnesota, at the southern end of Lake Superior, northeast of Minneapolis. Population: 86,419 (2002 estimate).

du·ly /do͞olee/ *adv* **1.** in a proper, correct, or suitable way ○ *duly grateful* **2.** at the proper or expected time ○ *A signal was given and our bus duly departed.*

Du·ma /do͞omə, do͞o maá/ *n* **1.** the parliament of modern Russia, established in 1993 after the dissolution of the former Soviet Union **2.** a Russian council or parliament during the time of tsarist rule, set up around 1905 but quickly deprived of power [Late 19C. < Russian]

Du·mas[1] /doo maá, dyoo-/, **Alexandre** (1802–70) French novelist and dramatist. He wrote the celebrated novels *The Three Musketeers* (1844) and *The Count of Monte Cristo* (1844). Known as **Dumas père**. See Cultural note at **musketeer**

> "Business? It's quite simple: it's other people's money."
> [Alexandre Dumas, *The Money Question*; 1857]

Du·mas[2], **Alexandre** (1824–95) French playwright and novelist. He wrote *The Lady of the Camellias* (1848), on which Verdi based *La Traviata.* Known as **Dumas fils**

du Mau·ri·er /doo máwree àу/, **Dame Daphne** (1907–89) British novelist. Her books include *Jamaica Inn* (1936), *Rebecca* (1938), and *My Cousin Rachel* (1951).

> "Last night I dreamt I went to Manderley again."
> [Dame Daphne du Maurier, *Rebecca*; 1938]

dumb /dum/ *adj* **1. UNINTELLIGENT** regarded as having or showing a low level of intelligence (*informal insult*) **2. OFFENSIVE TERM** an offensive term meaning unable to speak **3. TEMPORARILY SPEECHLESS** temporarily unable to speak because of shock, fear, surprise, or anger **4. DONE WITHOUT SPEECH** performed or expressed without using speech **5. INTENTIONALLY SILENT** deliberately not speaking or refusing to speak **6. PRODUCING NO SOUND** designed or adapted to produce no sound **7. LACKING HUMAN SPEECH** lacking the power of speech because not human ■ *vt* (**dumbed, dumb·ing, dumbs**) **MAKE SOMEBODY TEMPORARILY SPEECHLESS** to make somebody temporarily unable to speak, especially by using shock or surprise (*literary*) [Old English < Indo-European, "sensory or mental impairment"] —**dumb·ly** *adv* —**dumb·ness** *n*

dumb down *vti* to make something less intellectually challenging (*informal*) ○ *Parents and teachers were adamantly opposed to dumbing down science courses.*

dumb-ass *adj* an offensive term meaning regarded as having or showing a low level of intelligence (*taboo*)

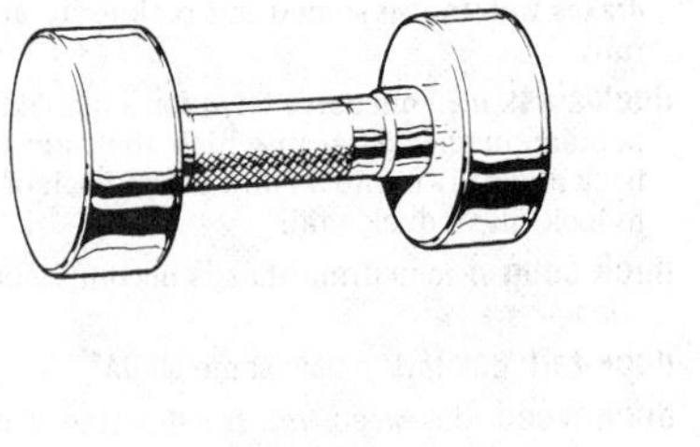

dumbbell

dumb·bell /dúm bèl/ *n* **1.** an exercise weight in the form of a metal bar with a metal disk or ball at each end **2.** an offensive term that deliberately insults somebody's intelligence or common sense (*slang insult*)

dumb blond, **dumb blonde** *n* an offensive term for a blond woman stereotyped as being good-looking but unintelligent

dumb bomb *n* a conventional bomb without guidance or targeting systems

dumb cane *n* a poisonous plant that if chewed can lead to loss of speech in adults or death in children and small animals. Native to: tropical America. Latin name: *Dieffenbachia seguine.*

~~dumbell~~ incorrect spelling of **dumbbell**

dumb·found /dùm fównd, dúm fòwnd/ (**-found·ed, -found·ing, -founds**), **dum·found** *vti* to make somebody temporarily speechless with astonishment [Mid-17C. < DUMB + CONFOUND]

dumb luck *n* good fortune that occurs unexpectedly (*informal*)

dum·bo /dúmbō/ (*plural* **-bos**) *n* an offensive term that deliberately insults somebody's intelligence or common sense (*slang insult*) [Mid-20C. After JUMBO]

DUMBO /dúmbō/ area of Brooklyn, New York, beneath and near the Brooklyn and Manhattan bridges. Its many warehouses were renovated into artists' lofts, homes, and stores in the late 20th century. [Acronym < *down under the Manhattan Bridge overpass*]

dumb show *n* **1.** communication without words by actors using gesture or facial expressions **2.** a play or part of a play presented in mime form

dumb·struck /dúm strùk/ *adj* made temporarily speechless by astonishment or shock

dumb ter·mi·nal *n* a terminal without an internal microprocessor and therefore without independent processing capability that can enter, transmit, and display alphanumeric data. Typically consisting of a keyboard and display screen, it responds to simple control codes from a computer to which it is connected.

dumb·wait·er /dúm wàytər/ *n* **1.** a small elevator used for moving food and tableware between the floors of a building **2.** a movable stand for food, often with revolving shelves, that is placed near a table

dum·dum bul·let /dúm dum-/, **dum·dum** *n* a bullet with a soft core or vertical cuts made in its point that expands on impact and inflicts a severe wound. The use of dumdum bullets is contrary to the Geneva Convention. [Late 19C. After *Dum Dum*, Calcutta, India]

dum·found *vti* another spelling of **dumbfound**

dumm·kopf /dúm kàwpf, -kàwf/ *n* somebody who is regarded as unintelligent and clumsy (*slang insult*) [Early 19C. < German < *dumm* "stupid" + *Kopf* "head"]

dum·my /dúmmee/ *n* (*plural* **-mies**) **1. MANNEQUIN IN STORE** a model of a human used for making or displaying clothes **2. MODEL USED BY VENTRILOQUIST** a large, sometimes stuffed, model of a human, as used by a ventriloquist **3. OFFENSIVE TERM** an offensive term that deliberately insults somebody's intelligence or credulity (*informal insult*) **4.** FOOTBALL **BAG USED IN TACKLING PRACTICE** in football, a stuffed bag, usually mounted on a frame, that represents an opposing player and is used in blocking and tackling practice **5. IMITATION** an imitation of something, especially one lacking a feature or function of the original and deceivingly substituted for it ○ *A lot of the system's switches are just dummies.* **6. FEIGNED PASS** in soccer, rugby, or a similar game, a feigned pass or other move intended to deceive an opponent, especially a tackler **7. PERSON OR ORGANIZATION ACTING AS FRONT** a person or organization serving as a front for another while pretending to be independent ○ *a dummy corporation* **8.** ARMS **NONEXPLOSIVE FORM OF MUNITION** a nonexplosive form of an explosive munition **9.** PUBL **MODEL BOOK** a set of model pages, often blank or containing only one group of printed pages (**signature**), that have been bound and jacketed to give an idea of the final book **10.** CARDS **SET OF CARDS SHOWN** an exposed hand of cards in bridge, consisting of the cards held by the player partnering the player who attempts to make the final contract, or the player who exposes his or her cards **11.** *Can, UK* same as **pacifier** (sense 2) **12.** PUBL **MODEL PAGE** a page that looks like the final product but is a computer-generated or pasted-up facsimile showing general design specifications ■ *vt* (**-mied, -my·ing, -mies**) PUBL **MAKE FACSIMILE OF PAGES** to make up a dummy of a page, or make up a set of pages into a dummy ○ *dummied several pages for the sales conference* [Late 16C. < DUMB + -Y[1]]

dummy up *vi* to remain or become silent (*slang*)

dum·my var·i·a·ble *n* a mathematical variable that can be replaced by another arbitrarily

Du·mont /doo máwnt/, **Gabriel** (1838–1906) Canadian military leader. He commanded rebels against government forces and settlers in Saskatchewan (1885).

du·mor·ti·er·ite /doo máwrtee ə rīt/ *n* a hard fibrous bright blue, bluish green, or pink aluminosilicate mineral containing boron [Late 19C. < French, after Eugène *Dumortier*, French paleontologist]

dump /dump/ *vt* (**dumped, dump·ing, dumps**) **1. DROP OR PUT DOWN SOMETHING CARELESSLY** to deposit something on a surface in a careless and usually noisy manner ○ *dumped the reports on my desk* **2. THROW SOMETHING OUT AS UNWANTED** to get rid of something that is unwanted, especially by taking it and leaving it somewhere **3. DISPOSE OF WASTE** to dispose of waste by moving it to a prearranged site **4. TERMINATE RELATIONSHIP WITH SOMEBODY** to end a romantic or sexual relationship with somebody, especially abruptly and hurtfully (*slang*) **5. REMOVE SOMEBODY UNDESIRABLE** to remove somebody deemed undesirable or a liability from a position such as leadership in a group, especially abruptly and unceremoniously (*slang*) **6. RELEGATE SOMEBODY TO CUSTODIAL CARE** to entrust somebody, e.g., a child or a person of advanced years, to custodial care (*slang disapproving*) **7.** PSYCHOL **CONFIDE NEGATIVE FEELINGS** to talk to somebody, especially a friend or therapist, about your negative feelings in order to relieve yourself of them (*slang*) ○ *I'm sorry to dump all this on you, but I've got no one else to talk to.* **8.** COMM **OFFLOAD CHEAP MERCHANDISE ON MARKET** to offer large quantities of cheaply priced merchandise for sale in a market often in order to maintain a higher price for the goods elsewhere **9.** FIN **GET RID OF STOCKS** to sell off large quantities of stock all at once, thereby driving the price down **10.** COMPUT **TRANSFER DATA WITHOUT PROCESSING** to transfer computer data from one site to another without processing it ■ *n* **1. WASTE DISPOSAL SITE** a place where waste materials can be left **2.** MIL **MUNITIONS AND SUPPLY AREA** a place for the temporary storage of munitions, food, water, fuel, and other supplies for distribution to troops **3. UNPLEASANT PLACE** an unpleasant or dirty place (*slang*) ○ *The hotel was a real dump.* **4.** COMPUT **TRANSFER OF UNPROCESSED DATA** a large-scale transfer of unprocessed data from one place to another **5. ACT OF THROWING SOMETHING AWAY** an act of discarding something **6. OFFENSIVE TERM** an offensive term for an act of evacuating the bowels (*slang*) [14C. Origin ?]

dump on *vt* to insult, criticize, or otherwise denigrate somebody else severely (*slang*)

dump·er /dúmpər/ *n* **1.** a person who or machine that disposes of waste by taking it to a prearranged site **2.** somebody who creates litter, especially by throwing out household items

dump·er truck *n UK* same as **dump truck**

dum·ping ground *n* **1.** a place where waste materials or unwanted items can be left **2.** a place or residential building regarded as housing people unwanted by the rest of society (*disapproving*)

dump·ling /dúmpling/ *n* **1. SMALL BALL OF DOUGH** a small dough ball cooked and served with a stew or soup **2. DESSERT** a baked dessert consisting of pastry wrapped around fruit **3. AFFECTIONATE TERM OF ADDRESS** used as an affectionate form of address (*informal*) **4. SOMEBODY PLUMP** somebody who is regarded as short and plump (*informal insult*) [Early 17C. Origin ?]

dump or·bit *n* an orbit that a communications satellite is moved into at the end of its useful life in which it will not collide with operational satellites

dumps /dumps/ *npl* a state of sadness and hopelessness (*informal*) ○ *feeling down in the dumps* [Early 16C. Plural of obsolete *dump*, origin ?]

Dump·ster /dúmpstər/ *tdmk* a trademark for large trash-and-garbage containers and hoisting units

dump truck *n* a heavy truck with an open bed that can be tilted up and back to unload cargo such as gravel, dirt, or refuse from construction sites

dump·y[1] /dúmpee/ (**-i·er, -i·est**) *adj* having a short and plump shape (*informal disapproving*) [Mid-18C. Origin ?] —**dump·i·ly** *adv* —**dump·i·ness** *n*

dump·y[2] /dúmpee/ (**-i·er, -i·est**) *adj* messy, cheap, and usually dirty (*informal*) ○ *a dumpy little airless apartment* [< DUMP]

dump·y lev·el *n* a surveying instrument for taking levels with a short fixed horizontal telescope

dun[1] /dun/ *n* **1.** COLORS **BROWNISH GRAY COLOR** a brownish gray color **2.** RIDING **BROWNISH GRAY HORSE** a horse with a brownish gray coat, black mane, tail, and legs, and usually a dark stripe on its back ■ *adj* (**dun·ner, dun·nest**) **1.** COLORS **BROWNISH GRAY** of a dun color **2. GLOOMY** darkly bleak and depressing (*literary*) ○ *a dun and bare prairie* [Old English *dunn* < Indo-European]

dun[2] /dun/ *vt* (**dunned, dun·ning, duns**) **HARASS SOMEBODY FOR DEBT REPAYMENT** to press or harass somebody persistently for the settlement of a debt ■ *n* **1. PAYMENT DEMAND** a pressing, usually written, demand for payment **2. DEBT COLLECTOR** somebody whose job is to collect debts owed to other people [Early 17C. Origin ?]

Du·nant /doo naáN/, **Jean Henri** (1828–1910) Swiss philanthropist. He founded the International Red Cross (1862–64) and shared the first Nobel Peace Prize (1901).

Dun·bar /dún baar/, **Paul Laurence** (1872–1906) US poet. The son of former slaves, he wrote poems in dialect about the experiences of African Americans.

> "But it's easy 'nough to titter w'en de stew is smokin' hot, / But hit's mighty ha'd to giggle w'en dey's nuffin' in de pot."
> [Paul Laurence Dunbar, "Philosophy," *The Complete Poems*; 1895]

Dun·can /dúngkən/ city in southern Oklahoma, south of Oklahoma City and southeast of Lawton. Population: 22,125 (2002 estimate).

AKG London

Isadora Duncan

Dun·can, Isadora (1877–1927) US dancer. She laid the foundation for modern dance, basing her ideas on the dances of the ancient Greeks. Full name **Duncan, Dora Angela**

> "I have sometimes been asked whether I consider love higher than art, and I have replied that I cannot separate them, for the artist is the only lover, he alone has the pure vision of beauty, and love is the vision of the soul when it is permitted to gaze upon immortal beauty."
> [Isadora Duncan, *My Life*; 1927]

Dun·can·ville /dúngkən vìl/ city in northeastern Texas, southeast of Mountain Creek Lake. It is a southwestern suburb of Dallas. Population: 36,203 (2002 estimate).

dunce /dunss/ *n* somebody who is regarded as slow to learn to learn or as generally unintelligent (*insult*) [Mid-16C. < *Duns* in John DUNS SCOTUS, whose writings were regarded by Renaissance thinkers as obscure and obtuse]

dunce cap, dunce's cap *n* a conical paper hat formerly worn as a punishment by a pupil who was considered to be slow to learn or lazy in school

dun·der·head /dúndər hèd/ *n* an offensive term that deliberately insults somebody's intelligence or capacity to learn (*informal insult*) [Early 17C. Origin ?] —**dun·der·head·ed** *adj* —**dun·der·head·ed·ness** *n*

dun·drear·ies /dun dreéreez/ *npl* long sideburns worn in conjunction with a clean-shaven chin [Mid-19C. After Lord *Dundreary* in Tom Taylor's comedy *Our American Cousin*, from the whiskers worn by actor E. A. Sothern]

dune /doon/ *n* a mound or ridge of sand formed by wind or water action, typically seen on coasts and in deserts [Late 18C. Via French < Middle Dutch *dūne*]

dune buggy

dune bug·gy *n* a motorized beach vehicle, usually without a top and with oversized tires to prevent it from getting stuck in sand

Dun·e·din /dun eéd'n/ city and port on the southeast coast of the South Island, New Zealand, situated on Otago Harbour. Population: 107,088 (2001).

Dun·ferm·line /dun fúrmlin/ manufacturing city in Fife, Scotland. Population: 55,083 (1991).

dung /dung/ *n* **1.** the solid excrement of animals, especially large animals such as cattle or horses **2.** AGRIC same as **manure** ■ *vt* (**dunged, dung·ing, dungs**) to cover land with dung or manure [Old English, origin ?] —**dung·y** *adj*

dun·ga·ree /dùng gə reé, dúng gə reè/ *n* a sturdy hard-wearing blue-denim fabric ■ **dun·ga·rees** *npl* pants made from strong material, usually blue denim [Late 17C. < Hindi *dungrī* "kind of coarse cloth," after a village near Mumbai (Bombay)]

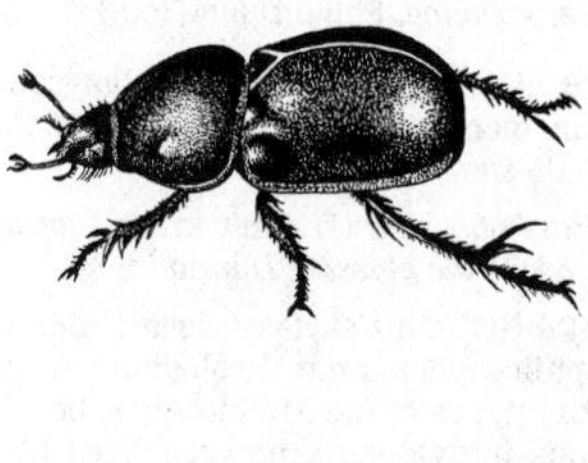

dung beetle

dung bee·tle *n* a scarab beetle that rolls large balls of dung into tunnels to feed the larvae that hatch from the eggs it lays there. Subfamily: Coprinae.

Dun·ge·ness crab /dùnjə néss-/ *n* a large edible crab. Native to: Pacific coast. Latin name: *Cancer magister*. [After *Dungeness*, Washington]

dun·geon /dúnjən/ *n* **1.** a prison cell, often underground, especially beneath a castle **2.** the secure main tower of a castle (*archaic*) [14C. Via Old French *donjon* "castle keep" (later "secure underground cell") < Latin *dominus* "lord"]

dun·geon-crawl *vi* in computer games, to engage in role-play that generally involves killing monsters and taking their treasure, frequently from underground lairs —**dun·geon crawl** *n*

dung·hill /dúng hìl/, **dung·heap** /dúng hèep/ *n* a pile of solid animal excrement

du·nite /dóo nìt, dú nìt/ *n* a coarse-grained dark igneous rock consisting mainly of a magnesium-rich olivine [Mid-19C. After Mt. *Dun*, New Zealand] —**du·nit·ic** /doo níttik, də níttik/ *adj*

dunk /dungk/ *v* (**dunked, dunk·ing, dunks**) **1.** *vt* DIP FOOD IN LIQUID to dip food into a liquid before eating it **2.** *vt* QUICKLY SUBMERGE IN LIQUID to submerge something in liquid, especially quickly and for a short time **3.** *vi* IMMERSE SELF IN WATER to immerse yourself in water for a short period (*informal*) ○ *a huge swimming pool to dunk in every morning* **4.** *vt* SHOVE SOMEBODY'S HEAD UNDER WATER to push somebody's head beneath the surface of water **5.** *vt* BASKETBALL PUT BASKETBALL INTO BASKET FROM ABOVE to put a basketball through the hoop from above by jumping and arcing the ball-carrying arm over the head ■ *n* BASKETBALL same as **dunk shot** [Early 20C. Via Pennsylvanian German *dunke* "dip" < Old High German *dunkōn*] —**dunk·er** *n*

Dunk·er /dúngkər/, **Dunk·ard** /dúngkərd/ *n* a member of a group of German-American Baptists, the German Baptist Brethren, who baptize by total immersion and oppose military service and official oath-taking. They also dress plainly and believe in living a simple life unencumbered by materialism. [Mid-18C. < Pennsylvanian German < *dunke* "dip"]

Dun·kirk /dún kùrk, dun kúrk/ port in northern France, in the Nord Department, Nord-Pas-de-Calais Region, near Calais. In World War II over 330,000 Allied troops were evacuated from the town by sea, under constant enemy fire. Population: 70,850 (1999).

dunk shot *n* in basketball, a basket made by putting the ball through the hoop from above

dun·lin /dúnnlin/ (*plural* **-lins** or *same*) *n* a small wading bird with a beak that curves downward. Native to: North America, Europe, Africa, Asia. Latin name: *Calidris alpina*. [Mid-16C. < DUN[1]]

Dun·lop /dún lòp/, **Weary** (1907–93) Australian surgeon and war hero. During World War II, he was taken prisoner in Java (1942). He kept a diary until the end of the war, revealing the appalling conditions that he and his companions endured on the Burma-Thailand Railway (1942–45). Full name **Dunlop, Sir Ernest Edward**

dun·nage /dúnnij/ *n* packing material used to cushion cargo on a ship [14C. Origin ?]

Dunne /dun/, **Finley Peter** (1867–1936) US journalist and humorist. He created the character of Mr. Dooley, an Irish barman and social commentator.

> "The further you get away from any period, the better you can write about it. You aren't subject to interruptions by people that were there."
> [Finley Peter Dunne. Quoted in *Mr. Dooley Remembers: the Informal Memoirs of Finley Peter Dunne*, Philip Dunne (ed.); 1963]

dun·nite /dú nìt/ *n* an explosive that contains ammonium picrate [Early 20C. After Col. B. W. *Dunn* (1860–1936), US army officer]

dun·no /də nṓ/ *contr* (I) don't know (*nonstandard*) ○ *"Who broke the glass?" "Dunno."*

Duns Sco·tus /dunz skṓtəss/, **John** (1266?–1308) Scottish philosopher and theologian. A deeply influential figure of the Middle Ages, he emphasized religious individuality and defended the doctrine of the Immaculate Conception. He founded the school of scholasticism known as Scotism.

Dun·sta·ble /dúnstəb'l/, **Dun·sta·ple** /dúnstəp'l/, **John** (1390?–1453) English composer. He wrote sacred and secular pieces that significantly advanced counterpoint and harmony. He was also a noted mathematician and astronomer.

Dun·wood·y /dun wŏŏdee/ town in northwestern Georgia, north of Atlanta. Population: 26,302 (1996).

du·o /dóo ō/ (*plural* **-os**) *n* **1.** PAIR OF CLOSELY ASSOCIATED PEOPLE two people who are considered to be closely connected in some way **2.** SET OF TWO CLOSELY RELATED THINGS a set of two items considered to be closely connected **3.** PLAYERS OF DUET a pair of musicians who play together **4.** DUET a duet, especially one for two instruments [Late 16C. Via Italian, "two" < Latin]

duo- *prefix* two ○ *duopoly* [< Latin < Indo-European]

du·o·dec·i·mal /dòo ə déssəm'l/ *adj* BASED ON 12 using units of 12 as a basis for counting or ordering. Although duodecimal systems are no longer commonly used, vestiges of them remain in such units as the foot, which is equal to 12 inches. ■ *n* **1.** DUODECIMAL NUMBER a number used to count or order in units of 12 **2.** 12TH a 12th part [Early 18C. < Latin *duodecimus* "twelfth"] —**du·o·dec·i·mal·ly** *adv*

du·o·dec·i·mo /dòo ə déssə mō/ (*plural* **-mos**) *n* a book size traditionally created by folding a single sheet of standard-sized printing paper to give 12 leaves or 24 pages [Mid-17C. < Latin *in duodecimo* "in twelfth"]

du·o·de·num /dòo ə dēenəm, doo ódd'nəm/ (*plural* **-na** /-ə dēenə, -ódd'nə/ or **-nums**) *n* the first short section of the small intestine immediately beyond the stomach [14C. < medieval Latin *intestinum duodenum digitorum* "intestine twelve finger-breadths long" < Latin *duodecim* "twelve"] —**du·o·de·nal** *adj*

du·o·logue /dóo ə lòg/ *n* **1.** a play or part of a play in which only two actors speak **2.** a dialogue between two actors, or a conversation between two people [Mid-18C. Blend of DUO + MONOLOGUE]

duo·mo /dwṓmō/ (*plural* **-mos**) *n* a cathedral in Italy [Mid-16C. Via Italian < Latin *domus* "house"]

du·op·o·ly /doo óppəlee/ (*plural* **-lies**) *n* an economic situation in which two powerful groups or organizations dominate commerce in one business market or commodity [Early 20C. After MONOPOLY] —**du·op·o·lis·tic** /doo òppə lístik/ *adj*

du·op·so·ny /doo ópsənee/ (*plural* **-nies**) *n* a situation in which two competing buyers exert controlling influence over many sellers [< DUO + *-opsony* < Greek *opsōnia* "purchasing of food"]

du·pat·ta /doo púttə/ *n S Asia* a scarf or covering for the head and upper body worn by women [< Hindi]

dupe /doop/ *vt* (**duped, dup·ing, dupes**) to persuade or induce somebody to do something by trickery or deception ○ *He was duped into thinking that they intended to pay.* ■ *n* an object of trickery or deceit [Late 17C. < French] —**dup·a·bil·i·ty** /dòopə bíllətee/ *n* —**dup·a·ble** *adj* —**dup·er** *n* —**dup·er·y** *n*

du·pi·on /dóopee òn/ *n* a rough silk fabric woven from threads of a double cocoon [Early 19C. Via French *doupion* < Italian *doppione* < *doppio* "double"]

du·ple /dóop'l/ *adj* in music, consisting of two beats to the bar or measure [Mid-16C. < Latin *duplus* "double"]

Du·ples·sis /dòo play sée/, **Maurice Le Noblet** (1890–1959) Canadian politician. He was premier of Quebec (1936–39 and 1944–59) as the leader of the Union Nationale Party.

du·plet /dóoplət/ *n* **1.** a group of two musical notes played in the time usually required by three **2.** a pair of electrons shared between two atoms that are joined in a chemical bond [Mid-17C. After DOUBLET]

du·ple time *n* a musical meter in which there are two beats to the measure, e.g., 2/4

du·plex /dóo plèks/ *n* **1.** BUILDINGS 2-FAMILY DWELLING a house that is divided into two halves and is inhabited by two separate families or tenants with separate entrances **2.** ELECTRONICS TRANSMISSION IN BOTH DIRECTIONS transmission of signals along a communications channel in both directions at the same time, e.g., over a telephone line **3.** ONLINE same as **full duplex** ■ *adj* **1.** TWOFOLD consisting of two parts, especially two identical or equivalent parts **2.** ENG HAVING TWO PARTS PERFORMING ONE OPERATION consisting of pairs of units or components that perform the same machine function but operate independently [Mid-16C. < Latin, "twofold" < *plicare* "to fold"] —**du·plex·i·ty** /doo pléksəte/ *n*

du·plex a·part·ment *n* an apartment that is on two floors with an inside stairway connecting the two levels

du·pli·cate *vt* /dóopli kàyt/ (**-cat·ed, -cat·ing, -cates**) **1.** COPY SOMETHING to make an identical version of something one or more times **2.** REPEAT SOMETHING to do something more than once, especially unknowingly or unnecessarily ■ *n* /dóoplikət/ **1.** COPY MADE an exact copy, especially of a document **2.** ANOTHER OF SAME a spare of the same kind **3.** REPEATED ACTION a repeat of an earlier action or achievement ■ *adj* /dóoplikət/ **1.** COPIED EXACTLY being an exact copy of something ○ *a duplicate key* **2.** HAVING TWO CORRESPONDING PARTS consisting of or existing in two corresponding parts [15C. < Latin *duplicat-*, past participle of *duplicare* "make twofold, double" < *duplus* "twofold"] —**du·pli·ca·ble** /dóoplikəb'l/ *adj* —**du·pli·cate·ly** /-kətlee/ *adv* —**du·pli·ca·tive** *adj* ◇ **in duplicate** so as to create or consist of two exact copies

SYNONYMS See *copy*.

du·pli·cate bridge *n* contract bridge in which the same hand is played by different consecutive players

du·pli·ca·tion /dòopli káysh'n/ *n* **1.** REPETITION OR COPYING the action or an act of duplicating something **2.** EXACT COPY an exact copy of something **3.** GENETICS REPETITION OF GENES a chromosome mutation in which a section of a chromosome, along with the genes it carries, occurs twice

du·pli·ca·tor /dóopli kàytər/ *n* something that makes copies, especially a machine for copying printed matter

du·plic·i·ty /doo plíssətee/ *n* **1.** the fact of being deceptive, dishonest, or misleading **2.** the state of being double or in a pair (*formal*) ○ *the duplicity of the stars of the constellation* [15C. Directly or via French < late Latin *duplicitas* < Latin *duplic-*, stem of *duplex* (see DUPLEX)] —**du·plic·i·tous** /doo plíssitəss/ *adj*

du Pont /doo pónt/, **Pierre S.** (1870–1954) US industrialist. As president of the family chemical firm from 1915, he oversaw its massive expansion during the first half of the 20th century. Full name **Du Pont, Pierre Samuel**

du Pont de Ne·mours /doo pònt də nə móor/, **Eleuthère Irénée** (1771–1834) US industrialist. He founded a gunpowder mill (1802) that became the largest factory of its kind in the United States.

du Pont de Ne·mours, Pierre Samuel (1739–1817) French economist. A friend and student of the French economist, François Quesnay, he was imprisoned for his royalist views and later immigrated to the United States, where he played an important role in the negotiations for the Louisiana Purchase.

dup·py /dúppee/ (*plural* **-pies**) *n Carib* a ghost of a dead person [Late 18C. Origin ?]

du Pré /doo práy/, **Jacqueline** (1945–87) British cellist and teacher. She is particularly famous for her interpretations of cello concertos. Her playing, though not her teaching, was halted in 1972 by multiple sclerosis.

du·ra·ble /dóorəb'l/ *adj* lasting for a long time, especially without sustaining damage or wear ○ *durable materials* ○ *a durable peace* [14C. Via French < Latin *durabilis* < *durare* "last, harden"] —**du·ra·bil·i·ty** /dòorə bíllətee/ *n* —**du·ra·ble·ness** *n* —**du·ra·bly** *adv*

du·ra·bles /dóorəb'lz/ *n* long-lasting products, e.g., motor vehicles and large appliances such as stoves and refrigerators

du·ra ma·ter /dóorə maàtər, dóorə máytər/ *n* the tough outermost membrane of the three that cover the brain and spinal cord [14C. < medieval Latin, literally "hard mother," translation of Arabic *al-'umm al-jāfiya* "coarse mother"] —**du·ral** /dóorəl/ *adj*

du·rance /dóorənss/ *n* forcible confinement or imprisonment (*archaic or literary*) [15C. < Old French < Latin *durare* "last, harden"]

Dur·ance /doo raàNss/ river in southeastern France, rising in the French Alps and flowing to its junction with the Rhône River, near Avignon. Length: 813 km/505 mi.

Du·rand /də ránd/, **Asher B.** (1796–1886) US engraver and painter. He was known for his engravings and for cofounding the Hudson River School of painting. Full name **Durand, Asher Brown**

"Learn first to perceive with truthfulness, and then aim to embody your perceptions; take no thought on the question of genius or of future fame; with these you have nothing to do. Seek not to rival or surpass a brother artist, and above all, let not the love of money overlap the love of art."
[Asher B. Durand, "The Crayon," *Letters on Landscape Painting*; 1855]

Du·ran·go /də ráng gō/ **1.** state in Northwestern Mexico. Capital: Durango. Population: 1,448,661 (2000). Area: 47,020 sq. mi./121,775 sq. km. **2.** capital of Durango State, in the Sierra Madre Mountains in the southern part of the state. Population: 491,436 (2000). Full name **Victoria de Durango**

Du·rant /də ránt/ city in southern Oklahoma on the Blue River, southeast of Oklahoma City and Ardmore. Population: 13,827 (2002 estimate).

Du·rant, Will (1885–1981) US historian. After publication of *The Story of Philosophy* (1926), he and his wife, Ariel, wrote *The Story of Civilization* (1935–75), an enormously popular series covering history from before Jesus Christ to the Napoleonic age. Full name **Durant, William James**

"Most history is guessing, and the rest is prejudice."
[Will Durant, *The Lessons of History*; 1968]

Du·ran·te /də ràntee/, **Jimmy** (1893–1980) US comic entertainer. Known for his prominent nose and raspy voice, he performed in cabaret, movies, and television. Full name **Durante, James Francis**

Du·ras /doo ra̅ass, doo ra̅a/, **Marguerite** (1914–96) Vietnamese-born French novelist, playwright, movie director, and screenwriter. Her works include the screenplay for *Hiroshima, mon amour* (1960) and the novel *The Lover* (1984).

du·ra·tion /də ráysh'n/ *n* the period of time that something lasts or exists ○ *an intermission of 15 minutes' duration* [14C. Via French < medieval Latin *duration-* < Latin *durare* "last, harden"] —**du·ra·tion·al** *adj* ◇ **for the duration 1.** for the entire period of time that something is going on or will continue to go on **2.** for the foreseeable future ○ *The house is yours for the duration; stay as long as you like.*

du·ra·tive /do͝orətiv/ *adj* describes a verb in a continuous tense or aspect or a verb indicating a continuous action

Dur·ban /dúrbən/ city, seaport, and tourist resort in KwaZulu-Natal Province in eastern South Africa. Population: 3,090,126 (1995).

dur·bar /dúr ba̅ar/ *n* formerly, an official reception or audience held by a local prince or British governor in colonial India, or by a local chief or British official in colonial Africa [Early 17C. < Urdu *darbār* < Persian *dar* "door" + *bār* "court"]

Dur·bin /dúrbin/, **Deanna** (*b.* 1921) Canadian-born US singer and actor. She became a teenage singing star in film musicals of the 1930s. Full name **Durbin, Edna Mae**

Dür·er /do͝orər, dyo͝orər/, **Albrecht** (1471–1528) German painter and engraver. The clarity of his paintings, e.g., in *Self Portrait* (1498), made him one of the most influential artists of the Reformation.

"The Creator fashioned men once and for all as they must be, and I hold that the perfection of form and beauty is contained in the sum of all men."
[Albrecht Dürer. Quoted in "Four Books on Human Proportion," *The Painter's Manual*, Walter L. Strauss (tr.); 1977]

du·ress /do͞o réss/ *n* **1.** the use of force or threats to make somebody do something **2.** illegal force or coercion, as used against a criminal suspect or a prisoner in lawful custody before trial [14C. Via Old French *duresse* < Latin *duritia* "hardness" < *durus* "hard"]

Du·rey /doo ráy/, **Louis Edmond** (1888–1979) French composer. He was a member of the Paris-based group of composers known as "Les Six," but left the group in 1921 to concentrate on more popular music that could express his communist ideals.

Dur·ga /dúrgə/ *n* in Hinduism, a goddess who is one of the most important deities, embodying for many the supreme manifest form of godhead

Dur·ga·pur /do͝orgə po͝or/, **Dur·gā·pur** city in Bangla State, eastern India. It is a major steel-producing center. Population: 425,836 (1991).

Dur·ham[1] /dúrrəm/ *n* a shorthorn beef or dairy cow belonging to a hardy breed originating in northeastern England [After *Durham*, N England]

Dur·ham[2] /dúrrəm/ **1.** county in northeastern England. The city of Durham is the administrative center. Population: 493,470 (2001). Area: 940 sq. mi./2,435 sq. km. **2.** city in central North Carolina, east of Greensboro, home to Duke University. Population: 195,914 (2002 estimate).

du·ri·an /do͝oree ən, -a̅an/ (*plural* **-ans** or *same*) *n* **1.** a foul-smelling but deliciously flavored fruit **2.** the tree that bears durians. Native to: tropical rain forests of Southeast Asia. Latin name: *Durio zibethinus.* [Late 16C. < Malay < *duri* "thorn, prickle"]

du·ri·crust /do͝ori krùst/ *n* a hard crust formed on the surface of the soil by the precipitation of soluble minerals from mineral waters, particularly during the dry season in semiarid climates [Early 20C. < Latin *durus* "hard"]

dur·ing /do͝oring/ *prep* **1.** throughout a period or event, either continuously or several times between the beginning and the end ○ *There was not even a whisper during the service.* **2.** at some point or moment within a period or event ○ *I can't remember the date, but it was during the winter.* [14C. Present participle of obsolete *dure* "last" < Old French *durer* < Latin *durus* "hard"]

dur·mast oak /dúr mast-/, **dur·mast** *n* an oak tree that has lobed leaves and yields a heavy flexible wood. Use: cabinet-making. Native to: Europe, Asia Minor. Latin name: *Quercus petraea.* [Late 18C. Origin ?]

durn /durn/ *interj, adj, adv, vt* (**durned, durn·ing, durns**) *Southern US* used to indicate frustration or mild anger (*informal*) ○ *Durn that cat, he just bit me!* [Variant of DARN[2]]

durned /durnd/ *adj Southern US* used to express mild frustration or anger (*informal*) ○ *Kids do the durnedest things!*

du·ro /do͝orō/ (*plural* **-ros**) *n* in some Latin American countries, a coin worth a peso or a dollar, or formerly in Spain, a coin worth five pesetas [Late 18C. < Spanish *peso duro* "hard or solid piastre"]

Du·ro·cher /də rṓshər/, **Leo** (1905–91) US baseball player. During his career in baseball he became manager of four national teams, retiring in 1973. Full name **Durocher, Leo Ernest.** Known as **Leo the Lip**

"All nice guys. They'll finish last. Nice guys. Finish last."
[Leo Durocher, *Nice Guys Finish Last*; 1975]

dur·ra /do͝orə/, **dou·ra** *n* a type of sorghum cultivated for its grain. Use: food grain, animal feed. Latin name: *Sorghum bicolor*. [Late 18C. < Arabic *dura*]

Dur·rell /dúr əl/, **Gerald** (1925–95) British naturalist and writer, brother of Lawrence Durrell. His books include the autobiographical *My Family and Other Animals* (1956) about his childhood on Corfu, as well as such books as *The Stationary Ark* (1976), which concerns his zoo and wildlife conservation trust on the island of Jersey.

"The sneeze in English is the harbinger of misery, even death. I sometimes think the only pleasure an Englishman has is in passing on his cold germs."
[Gerald Durrell, *My Family and Other Animals*; 1956]

Dür·ren·matt /do͝orrən ma̅at/, **Friedrich** (1921–90) Swiss writer. He wrote plays, including *The Physicists* (1961), existentialist detective novels, and critical essays.

"What was once thought can never be unthought."
[Friedrich Dürrenmatt, *The Physicists*; 1961]

Dur·rës /do͝orrəss/ city and seaport in western Albania, on the Adriatic Sea. The capital of Durrës District, it is situated about 20 mi./30 km west of the national capital Tirana. Population: 125,000 (1995).

dur·rie *n* TEXTILES another spelling of **dhurrie**

durst /durst/ past tense of **dare** (*archaic*)

du·rum wheat /dúrrəm-/, **du·rum** *n* a wheat that produces the type of flour used to make pasta and couscous. Latin name: *Triticum durum.* [Early 20C. < Latin, form of *durus* "hard"]

Dur·yea /do͝or yay, do͝or ee ày/, **Charles Edgar** (1861–1938) US automobile manufacturer and inventor. Together with his brother, James Frank Duryea, he built one of the first cars in the United States (1893).

Du·shan·be /doo shámbə, -sha̅am-/ capital city of Tajikistan, in the west of the country in the Gissar Valley. Population: 562,000 (2001).

dusk /dusk/ *n* **1.** PERIOD AFTER DAY BUT BEFORE NIGHT the period of the day after the sun has gone below the horizon but before the sky has become dark **2.** ABSENCE OF DAYLIGHT partial or almost complete darkness (*literary*) ■ *adj* DIM having little or insufficient light (*literary*) ■ *vti* (**dusked, dusk·ing, dusks**) DARKEN to become dark, or make something dark (*literary*) [Old English *dox* "dark in color" < Indo-European]

dusk·y /dúskee/ (**-i·er, -i·est**) *adj* **1.** DARK-COLORED somewhat dark in color **2.** DIM having little or insufficient light **3.** OFFENSIVE TERM an offensive term meaning having a somewhat dark skin or complexion (*dated*) —**dusk·i·ly** *adv* —**dusk·i·ness** *n*

Düs·sel·dorf /do͝oss'l dàwrf/ capital of North Rhine-Westphalia, west central Germany. Situated on the Rhine River, about 20 mi./32 km north of Cologne, it is the commercial and cultural center of the greater Ruhr area. Population: 572,638 (1997).

dust /dust/ *n* **1.** SMALL DRY PARTICLES very small dry particles of a substance such as sand or coal, either in the form of a deposit or a cloud **2.** HOUSEHOLD DIRT the small particles of dirt that settle on horizontal surfaces in buildings **3.** REMAINS FROM DECAY the small particles that something, especially a human body, is thought to be reduced to by decay after death **4.** EARTH AS BURIAL PLACE earth, particularly that of somebody's grave (*literary*) **5.** MED MINERS' DISEASE silicosis or another respiratory disease affecting miners (*informal*) ■ *v* (**dust·ed, dust·ing, dusts**) **1.** *vti* CLEAN DIRT PARTICLES OFF SOMETHING to remove small particles of dirt and lint from something, usually by wiping with a cloth **2.** *vt* SPRINKLE SOMETHING OVER SOMETHING to sprinkle a powdery substance over something ○ *dust the cake with powdered sugar* [Old English *dūst* < Germanic] —**dust·less** *adj* ◇ **(as) dry as dust** so scholarly and devoid of humor as to be arid in tone and content ◇ **bite the dust 1.** to die, especially in or as a result of a fight (*informal*) **2.** to suffer total failure (*slang*) ◇ **gather dust** to remain unused over a period of time ◇ **in the dust** a long way behind ○ *left the other challengers in the dust* ◇ **kick up** or **raise dust** to cause a controversy or loud disturbance (*slang*) ◇ **make the dust fly** to set about doing something energetically and aggressively (*slang*) ◇ **shake the dust (of something) from your feet** *UK* to leave somewhere forever, especially when glad to do so **dust up** *vt* to attack somebody verbally or physically (*slang*)

dust bath *n* a form of grooming behavior in animals, especially birds, that consists in rolling or making agitated movements in the dust on the ground in order to remove parasites

dust·bin /dúst bìn/ *n UK* same as **garbage can**

dust bowl *n* an area in a semiarid environment in which the topsoil is exposed and dust storms are likely to occur

Dust Bowl *n* a large area in the southern part of the central United States that suffered badly from wind erosion during the 1930s

dust·cart /dúst ka̅art/ *n UK* same as **garbage truck**

dust cloth *n US* a piece of cloth used for removing dust, especially from household objects and surfaces. Can term **duster**

dust cov·er *n* **1.** a cover, often made from transparent plastic, for protecting a piece of equipment **2.** PUBL same as **dust jacket**

dust dev·il *n* a rising or traveling funnel of dust, dirt, or sand that occurs on hot days, especially in desert or dry areas. Dust devils are smaller than tornadoes and are generally not dangerous.

dust·er /dústər/ *n* **1.** AGRIC **DEVICE FOR SPREADING AGROCHEMICALS** a machine or device for spreading powdered fungicide, insecticide, or fertilizer over crops or other plants **2.** CLOTHING **LONG LOOSE COAT** a long loose coat, sometimes one without buttons or lapels **3.** CLOTHING **HOUSECOAT** a woman's loose housecoat **4.** *Can, UK* same as **dust cloth** **5.** METEOROL same as **dust storm**

dust·i·ness /dústeenəss/ *n* the state of being covered with dust or containing dust

dust·ing /dústing/ *n* **1.** a thin, sometimes patchy covering of a powdery substance ○ *a dusting of snow on the ground* **2.** a defeat or setback (*slang*) ○ *a candidate who took a real dusting at the polls*

dust·ing pow·der *n* fine powder, e.g., talcum powder, especially for use on the skin

dust jack·et *n* a paper book cover that protects the hardbound binding and can be discarded

dust·man /dústmən/ (*plural* **-men** /-mən/) *n UK* same as **garbageman**

dust mite *n* a microscopic insect that lives in furnishings and bedding, feeding on dead skin particles shed by humans and other animals and that may cause allergies in some people

dust-off *adj* describes an aircraft such as a helicopter that is used to medevac wounded troops from a combat zone (*slang*) ○ *dust-off choppers*

dust·pan /dúst pàn/ *n* a container with a flat base and an open front into which dirt and dust can be swept

dust·sheet /dúst sheet/ *n UK* same as **drop cloth**

dust storm *n* a strong hot dry wind laden with dust

dust trap *n* a place where dust tends to accumulate

dust-up /dúst ùp/ *n* a violent argument or physical altercation, often one that starts and stops quickly (*slang*)

dust·y /dústee/ (**-i·er, -i·est**) *adj* **1.** **FULL OF DUST** covered with or containing dust **2.** COLORS **TINGED WITH GRAY** containing tinges of gray with other colors ○ *dusty pink* **3.** **BORING** uninteresting or uninspiring, especially through being outdated ○ *dusty political slogans* **4.** **LIKE DUST** resembling dust ○ *a dusty gold powder*

dust·y mill·er *n* a plant with gray or white leaves covered with a down resembling dust. Latin name: *Artemisia stelleriana.*

Dutch /duch/ *n* the official West Germanic language of the Netherlands and the Republic of Suriname. Native speakers: 20 million. ■ *npl* the people of the Netherlands collectively [14C. < Middle Dutch *dutsch* < Germanic, "people"] —**Dutch** *adj* ◇ **go Dutch** to pay for your own part of the cost of a meal or entertainment ◇ **in Dutch** in a state of disfavor, difficulty, or trouble (*informal*)

Dutch auc·tion *n* an auction in which the price is lowered gradually until somebody makes a bid

Dutch cap *n UK* a contraceptive diaphragm with triangular flaps, of a type no longer used (*informal*)

Dutch clo·ver *n* PLANTS same as **white clover**

Dutch cour·age *n* the temporary confidence supposedly obtained from drinking alcohol (*informal*)

Dutch door *n* a door that is divided into two horizontal sections above and below so that each section can be opened and closed independently

Dutch East In·dies /dùch-/ the islands of Indonesia during the period of Dutch colonial government from the late 18th century until independence in 1949

Dutch elm *n* a cultivated hybrid elm tree introduced to Great Britain from the Netherlands in the 17th century and now common in northeastern France and parts of western Great Britain and Ireland. Latin name: *Ulmus x hollandica.*

Dutch elm dis·ease *n* a disease of elm trees that eventually kills the tree, caused by a fungus, *Ceratocystis ulmi,* carried by a bark beetle [Because identified by Dutch scientists]

Dutch Gui·an·a /-gee ánnə, -gee aánə, -gī ánnə/ former name for **Suriname** (until 1948)

LANGUAGE HERITAGE ***Dutch*** Much of English is made up of words from other languages, and Dutch is a significant contributor in this respect, especially through seafaring and commerce and through colonies established in North America, southern Africa, and in what is now Indonesia.

Dutch maritime traditions introduced English to many nautical terms, from the command ***avast*** (an alteration of Dutch *hou'vast*, a shortening of *houd vast* "hold fast") to the ***yacht*** (from obsolete Dutch *jaghte*, a shortening of *jaghtschip* "chasing ship"), by way of ***boom*** ("beam at the bottom of a sail"), ***cruise***, ***marline***, ***skipper***, and ***taffrail***. Well-traveled Dutch-speakers described the ***dune*** (immediately from French, but ultimately from Middle Dutch), ***iceberg***, ***maelstrom***, and ***reef***. Individual fish are identified by Dutch names – ***lumpfish*** (from Middle Dutch *lumpe* "cod"), ***whiting*** – as is the collective ***school*** and the ***walrus***. Dutch transported words from the languages of far-off lands: from Malay, for example, ***bamboo***, ***cockatoo***, and ***gingham*** (from Malay *genggang* "striped"), and from Arabic ***monsoon*** (obsolete Dutch *monssoen*, via Portuguese *monção* from Arabic *mawsim* "season").

In the earliest period of borrowings, the source is often identified more generally as Low German, the group of West Germanic languages and dialects to which Dutch belongs (as indeed does English). Among early words specified as from Dutch are: (from the 13th century) ***booze*** and ***marten***; (from the 14th) ***bundle***, ***curl***, ***dam***, ***Dutch*** itself, ***groove***, ***rack***, ***scum***, and ***spout***; (from the 15th) ***bung***, ***croon***, ***mart***, ***prop***, ***snack***, and ***wagon***.

After the medieval period Dutch continued to penetrate all areas of English vocabulary, but one distinct strand relates to art: ***easel*** and ***landscape***, for example, recorded in the late 16th century; ***etch*** and ***sketch***, recorded in the mid-17th. Other areas include: cold-weather activities, for example, ***skate***, ***sled***, and ***sleigh***; food and drink, for example, ***advocaat***, ***brandy*** (originally *brandy-wine*, from Dutch *brandewijn* "burned (i.e. distilled) wine"), ***coleslaw***, and ***rijsttafel*** (a Dutch meal of Indonesian origin); arms and the military, for example, ***blunderbuss*** (an alteration of Dutch *donderbus* "thunder gun"), ***cashier*** ("dismiss somebody from the armed forces because of misconduct"), ***tattoo*** ("call to soldiers to return to quarters," from Dutch *taptoe* "shut the tap, i.e. of the beer barrel," a signal at closing time in taverns), and ***trigger***. One Dutch military term whose meaning and origin have been obscured by folk etymology is ***forlorn hope***; this came from Dutch *forloren hoop* "lost troop," originally "group of soldiers sent on a hopeless mission."

In North America the Dutch colony of New Amsterdam, later New York, had a distinct influence on American English. Though now in widespread use, ***boss*** was originally a North American term; the geographic feature the ***bluff*** is particularly North American, as is the ***stoop*** at the entrance to a house (the original Dutch ***stoep*** is similarly used in South Africa). Food terms of Dutch origin include ***cookie***, ***cruller***, and ***waffle***. ***Santa Claus*** visits children at Christmas because of the Dutch.

Settlers took Dutch to southern Africa in the 17th century. Their descendants were given the name ***Boer*** (from Dutch *boer* "farmer," the source also of ***boor***), and the form of Dutch spoken in southern Africa, known as Cape Dutch, developed into ***Afrikaans*** ("African"). Dutch or Afrikaans names were naturally given to unfamiliar animals, birds, and fish (***blesbok***, ***dassie***, ***eland***, ***snoek***), and to the land's characteristic geographic features (***veld***). Familiar outside South Africa are ***apartheid*** and, no longer particularly associated with the country, ***commandeer*** (via Afrikaans *kommandeer* from Dutch *kommanderen* "to command"), ***spoor*** ("visible trail of an animal"), and ***trek***.

Dutch hoe *n* a hoe used for weeding that is pushed instead of pulled

Dutch·man /dúchmən/ (*plural* **-men** /-mən/) *n* **1.** a man who comes from the Netherlands **2.** a piece of building material used to repair or conceal faulty construction

Dutch·man's breech·es *n* a woodland plant that has creamy white flowers with two spurs. Native to: eastern United States. Latin name: *Dicentra cucullaria.*

Dutch·man's pipe *n* a woody climbing vine that has mottled greenish brown flowers shaped like the bowl and stem of an old-fashioned tobacco pipe. Native to: eastern United States. Latin name: *Aristolochia sipho.*

Dutch ov·en *n* **1.** an iron or earthenware container with a lid, used for cooking stews or casseroles **2.** a metal box with an open front placed beside an open fire so that food can be cooked inside it

Dutch treat *n* an outing, e.g., to a restaurant or theater, where each person pays for himself or herself (*informal*)

Dutch un·cle *n* somebody, typically a mentor, who criticizes or advises in a frank, sometimes harsh manner (*informal*)

Dutch·wom·an /dúch wŏŏmmən/ (*plural* **-wom·en** /-wìmmin/) *n* a woman who comes from the Netherlands

du·te·ous /dŏŏtee əss/ *adj* obedient or showing a strong sense of duty (*archaic*) —**du·te·ous·ly** *adv* —**du·te·ous·ness** *n*

du·ti·a·ble /dŏŏtee əb'l/ *adj* subject to tax, especially as an import —**du·ti·a·bil·i·ty** /dŏŏtee ə bíllətee/ *n*

du·ti·ful /dŏŏtif'l/ *adj* **1.** done to fulfill obligations, often with little enthusiasm ○ *made a dutiful attempt at conversation* **2.** acting according to obligations ○ *a dutiful and hard-working employee* —**du·ti·ful·ly** *adv* —**du·ti·ful·ness** *n*

du·ty /dŏŏtee/ (*plural* **-ties**) *n* **1.** **OBLIGATION** something that somebody is obliged to do for moral, legal, or religious reasons ○ *your duties as a parent* **2.** **NEED TO MEET OBLIGATIONS** the urge to meet moral or religious obligations ○ *a strong sense of duty* **3.** **ALLOCATED TASK** a task or service allocated to somebody, especially in the course of work **4.** ECON **TAX** a tax on goods, especially imports and exports **5.** **QUALITY** suitability for a particular grade of use (*usually used in combination*) ○ *heavy-duty shoes* **6.** MECH ENG **MACHINE'S WORKLOAD** the amount of work that a machine is designed to do, or a measure of a machine's efficiency **7.** AGRIC **VOLUME OF WATER FOR IRRIGATION** the volume of water needed to irrigate an area of land in order to cultivate a crop from planting to harvest [13C. < Anglo-Norman *dueté* < Old French *deu* "owed" (see DUE)] ◇ **off duty** not at work (*hyphenated before nouns*) ○ *an off-duty police officer* ◇ **on duty** at work

SYNONYMS See ***job***.

du·ty-bound *adj* required to do something because it is morally or legally right

du·ty-free *adj* **EXEMPTED FROM EXCISE DUTIES** on or at which no customs or excise duties have to be paid ■ *adv* **WITHOUT CUSTOMS AND EXCISE DUTIES** without paying or charging customs or excise duties ■ *n* **STORE SELLING DUTY-FREE ITEMS** a store, especially at an airport or on board a ship, that sells duty-free goods (*informal*) ■ **du·ty-frees** *npl* **DUTY-FREE ITEMS** duty-free goods, especially the allowance of duty-free goods that a person is allowed to bring into his or her own country (*informal*)

du·ty of·fi·cer *n* an officer who is present in an office or headquarters and responsible for handling situations that may arise during a given period, especially a period when others are off duty

du·um·vir /doo úmvər/ (*plural* **-virs** or **-vi·ri** /-və reè/) *n* **1.** either of two people who share a position of authority equally between them **2.** a joint holder of a paired post in the ancient Roman government or judiciary [Early 17C. < Latin < *duo* "two" + *vir* "man"] —**du·um·vi·rate** *n*

Du·va·lier /dŏŏ vaal yáy/, **François** (1907–71) Haitian national leader and doctor. He was elected president in 1957 and declared himself president for life in 1964, instituting a dictatorial regime known for its violent purges and mass executions. Known as **Papa Doc**

> "My government has not been all that I had hoped for."
> [François Duvalier, *Papa Doc, Baby Doc,* James Ferguson; 1987]

Du·va·lier, Jean-Claude (*b.* 1951) Haitian national

leader. He succeeded his father François Duvalier as president (1971–86). Known as **Baby Doc**

du·vet /doo váy, dŏŏ vày/ *n* a bed quilt made up of broad channels stuffed with down or synthetic material, usually used inside a removable washable cover in place of or together with sheets and blankets [Mid-18C. < French, "(feather) down" < Old Norse *dūnn*]

du·vet day *n* any one of an agreed number of days that some employees can take as leave at short notice in addition to their official vacation entitlement [< the idea of wanting to remain under the duvet rather than go to work]

du·ve·tyn /dŏŏvə tèen/, **du·ve·tyne**, **du·ve·tine** *n* a soft velvety silk, cotton, wool, or rayon fabric with a nap [Early 20C. < French *duvetine* < *duvet* (see DUVET)]

du Vi·gneaud /doo vèenyō/, **Vincent** (1901–78) US biochemist. For his work on pituitary hormones, he won the Nobel Prize in Chemistry (1955).

Dux·bur·y /dúks bèrree, -bəree/ town in eastern Massachusetts, on the northwestern shore of Plymouth Bay, north of Plymouth and southeast of Boston. Population: 14,578 (2002 estimate).

dux·elles /dŏŏk sélz, duk-/ *n* a paste made from mushrooms sautéed with shallots and herbs in butter and used with stuffings, sauces, and soups, or as a garnish [Late 19C. After the Marquis *d'Uxelles*, 17C French nobleman]

D.V. *abbr* CHR Deo volente

DVD *n* an optical compact disk that can store a large quantity of video, audio, or other information. Full form **digital video disk**

DVD-A *n* an audio DVD

DVD-R, **DVD+R** *n* a DVD that can be used to record something but cannot be erased. Full form **digital video disk recordable**

DVD-ROM *n* a high-capacity optical disk on which data can be stored but not altered. Full form **digital video disk read only memory**

DVD-RW, **DVD+RW** *n* a DVD that can have its contents erased and something else recorded onto it many times. Full form **digital video disk rewritable**

DVI *abbr* COMPUT digital video imaging

Dvi·na /dvéenə/ river in northeastern Europe, comprising the Northern Dvina and the Western Dvina. Length: 634 mi./1,020 km.

D.V.M. *abbr* VET, EDUC Doctor of Veterinary Medicine

Dvo·řák /dváwr zhaak, -zhak/, **Antonín** (1841–1904) Bohemian Czech composer. An ardent nationalist, he based many of his musical themes on Czech folk songs. His ninth symphony, *From the New World* (1893), incorporates US folk music.

Dvo·rak key·board /dváwr zhàak-/ *n* a keyboard with frequently used keys placed near the center for quicker typing [After August *Dvorak*, 20C. US inventor]

DVR *abbr* MEDIA digital video recorder

DVT *abbr* MED deep vein thrombosis

DW *abbr* **1.** SHIPPING dead weight **2.** CHEM distilled water

dwarf /dwawrf/ *n* (*plural* **dwarves** /dwawrvz/ or **dwarfs**) **1. PERSON SMALL FOR MEDICAL REASONS** somebody of small stature due to medical reasons, usually somebody with an average-sized body but unusually short limbs, or somebody with growth hormone deficiency **2.** BIOL **SMALL PLANT OR ANIMAL** a plant or animal that is much smaller than others of its species, usually as a result of selective breeding (*often used before a noun*) ○ *a dwarf conifer* **3. SMALL IMAGINARY HUMANOID** a small stocky imaginary being resembling a human, associated with mountains, mines, and buried treasures. Fictional dwarves were often believed to have magic powers and to be sometimes malevolent. **4.** ASTRON same as **dwarf star** ■ *vt* (**dwarfed, dwarf·ing, dwarfs**) **1. MAKE SOMEBODY OR SOMETHING SEEM SMALL** to make somebody or something else seem very small or very unimportant by comparison ○ *The cathedral is dwarfed by the enormous tower blocks surrounding it.* **2. STUNT SOMEBODY'S OR SOMETHING'S GROWTH** to stunt the growth of somebody or something [Old English *dweorg* < Germanic] —**dwarf·ish** *adj* —**dwarf·ish·ly** *adv* —**dwarf·ish·ness** *n*

dwarf bean *n UK* same as **bush bean**

dwarf cor·nel *n* **1.** PLANTS same as **bunchberry 2.** a widely cultivated plant with scarlet berries that grows only about 8 in./20 cm high. Flowers: purple, surrounded by white bracts resembling petals. Native to: Arctic and alpine regions. Latin name: *Cornus suecica*.

dwarf gal·ax·y *n* a small galaxy that does not shine brightly and contains no more than a few million stars

dwarf·ism /dwáwr fìzzəm/ *n* the condition of being a dwarf

dwarf star *n* a star with relatively low mass, size, and luminosity. The Sun is a dwarf star.

dwarves plural of **dwarf**

dweeb /dweeb/ *n* somebody considered boring, silly, or socially inept (*slang insult*) [Late 20C. Origin ?]

dwell /dwel/ *vi* (**dwelt** /dwelt/ or **dwelled**, **dwell·ing**, **dwells**) to live and have a home in a particular place (*literary*) ■ *n* the portion of a cam's surface that permits a machine's operation to pause for a period of time at a given position [Old English *dwellan* "lead astray" < Indo-European, "rise in a cloud"] —**dwell·er** *n*

dwell on, **dwell upon** *vt* to think, write, or talk about something at considerable length

dwell·ing /dwélling/ *n* a house or other building or place in which somebody lives (*formal*) ■ *adj* living in a particular type of place or environment (*usually used in combination*) ○ *bottom-dwelling fishes*

dwelt past participle, past tense of **dwell**

DWEM /dwem/, **dwem** *abbr* full form **dead white European male**

DWF *abbr* driving while female

DWI *abbr* LAW driving while intoxicated

Dwight /dwīt/, **Timothy** (1752–1817) US cleric and educator. He left the Congregational ministry in 1795 to become president of Yale (1795–1817).

dwin·dle /dwínd'l/ (**-dled, -dling, -dles**) *vti* to decrease little by little in size, number, or intensity and approach zero, or make something decrease in this way ○ *Supplies were dwindling.* [Late 16C. < obsolete *dwine* "waste away" < Indo-European, "become exhausted"]

dwt. *abbr* MEASURE dead weight tonnage

Dy *symbol* CHEM ELEM dysprosium

dy. *abbr* **1.** delivery **2.** duty

dy·ad /dī àd/ *n* **1. COUPLE** two individual units, things, or people linked as a pair (*formal*) **2.** CHEM **ATOM WITH VALENCE OF TWO** an atom or chemical group with a valence of two **3.** MATH **VECTOR OPERATOR** a mathematical operator consisting of two vectors expressed without a multiplication sign between them **4.** MUSIC **TWO-NOTE CHORD** a musical chord consisting of two notes [Late 17C. Via late Latin < Greek *duad-* < *duo* "two"] —**dy·ad·ic** /dī áddik/ *adj* —**dy·ad·i·cal·ly** *adv*

Dy·ak (*plural same* or **-aks**) *n* PEOPLES same as **Dayak**

dy·ar·chy *n* POL another spelling of **diarchy**

dyb·buk /díbbək/ (*plural* **-buks** or **-buk·im** /díbbəkim/) *n* in Jewish folklore, a malevolent spirit of a dead person, believed able to take over a living person's body and control his or her behavior unless exorcised [Early 20C. Via Yiddish *dibek* < Hebrew *dibbūq* < *dābaq* "cling"]

Dyck /dīk/, **Sir Anthony van** (1599–1641) Flemish painter. He was active in Belgium, Italy, and England, and is noted for his sumptuous, large-scale portraits of English royalty and aristocrats.

dye /dī/ *v* (**dyed, dye·ing, dyes**) **1.** *vt* **COLOR SOMETHING BY SOAKING** to color or stain something, e.g., fabric or hair, by soaking it in a coloring solution so that it takes on the new color permanently or semipermanently **2.** *vi* **COLOR WELL OR BADLY** to respond to being treated with a coloring agent and take its color in a particular way ■ *n* **1. COLORING AGENT** a natural or synthetic substance that can be used to color something, e.g., a textile or hair, and is most often applied as a liquid **2. COLORING SOLUTION** a coloring solution containing a dye **3. COLOR PRODUCED** the color produced on something by a dye [Old English *dēah* "color, color that hides" < Germanic] —**dy·a·ble** *adj* —**dy·er** *n*

SPELLCHECK See *die*[1].

---

dyed-in-the-wool *adj* **1.** wholeheartedly and stubbornly attached to a set of beliefs, political party, or philosophy and totally convinced of its merits **2.** dyed before weaving into cloth

dye·line /dī lìn/ *n* PRINTING same as **diazo**

Dy·er /dī ər/, **Mary** (1610?–60) English-born American colonial Quaker martyr. Twice banished from Boston for her religious beliefs, she was finally hanged after defying the ruling for a second time.

dy·er's green·weed *n* a small bush, similar to broom, with flowers that were formerly used to produce a yellow dye. Native to: Europe, Asia. Latin name: *Genista tinctoria*.

dy·er's rock·et *n* a plant of the mignonette family with flowers that were formerly used to produce a yellow dye. Native to: Europe, Asia. Latin name: *Reseda luteola*.

dy·er's-weed *n* any plant that yields a dye, e.g., dyer's greenweed or dyer's rocket

dye·stuff /dī stùf/ *n* INDUST same as **dye** *n* (sense 1)

dye·wood /dī wŏŏd/ *n* any wood that can produce a dye

dy·ing /dī ing/ *adj* **1. ABOUT TO DIE** on the point of death **2. OCCURRING JUST BEFORE DEATH** carried out, spoken, or occurring at or just before the point of death **3. FINAL** occurring as something is about to reach its end ○ *in the dying seconds of the game*

dyke[1] /dīk/, **dike** *n* an offensive term for a lesbian (*slang*) [Mid-20C. Origin ?]

dyke[2] /dīk/ *n*, *vt* another spelling of **dike**[1]

Bob Dylan

Dy·lan /díllən/, **Bob** (*b.* 1941) US singer and songwriter. One of the most influential popular musicians of the 20th century, he first established his reputation with protest songs such as "Blowin' in the Wind" (1962) and "The Times They Are A-Changin'" (1964). Born **Zimmerman, Robert**

> "Money doesn't talk, it swears."
> [Bob Dylan, "It's Alright, Ma"; 1965]

> "Ah, but I was so much older then / I'm younger than that now."
> [Bob Dylan, "My Back Pages," *Another Side of Bob Dylan*; 1964]

dyn *symbol* PHYS dyne

dy·nam·ic /dī námmik/ *adj* **1. VIGOROUS AND PURPOSEFUL** full of energy, enthusiasm, and a sense of purpose and able both to get things going and to get things done **2. ACTIVE AND CHANGING** characterized by vigorous activity and producing or undergoing change and development ○ *a dynamic economy* **3.** PHYS **RELATING TO ENERGY AND MOTION** involving or relating to energy and forces that produce motion **4.** PHYS **RELATING TO DYNAMICS** involved in or connected with the study of dynamics **5.** MUSIC **RELATING TO LOUDNESS IN MUSIC** relating to or indicating variations in the loudness of musical sounds **6.** PHYS **CHANGING OVER TIME** describes any system that changes over time **7.** COMPUT **WHILE PROGRAM IS RUNNING** performed while a computer program is running ■ *n* **DRIVING FORCE** a driving or energizing force, especially one involved in a process of social or psychological change [Early 19C. Via French < Greek *dunamikos* < *dunamis* "force"] —**dy·nam·i·cal** *adj* —**dy·nam·i·cal·ly** *adv*

dy·nam·ic mark·ings, **dy·nam·ic marks** *npl* the symbols and words that indicate the degree of loudness or softness with which a piece, passage, or note of music should be played

dy·nam·ic range *n* **1.** the range of volume used within a single piece of music **2.** the range over which an electronic audio system can operate to a set standard of performance based on given limits for noise and distortion

dy·nam·ics /dī námmiks/ *n* PHYS **STUDY OF MOTION** the branch of mechanics that deals with motion and the way in which forces produce motion (*takes a singular verb*) ■ *npl* **1. CHANGE-PRODUCING FORCES** the forces that tend to produce activity and change in any situation or sphere of existence **2. PERSONAL RELATIONSHIPS** the relationships of power between the people in a group **3.** MUSIC **LOUDNESS AND SOFTNESS IN MUSICAL PIECE** the different levels of loudness and softness in a piece of music, and the way in which a performer reproduces them in performance **4.** MUSIC same as **dynamic markings**

dy·na·mism /dínə mìzzəm/ *n* **1.** a vigorously active, forceful, and energizing quality, especially as the hallmark of somebody's personality or approach to a task **2.** a philosophical or scientific theory stressing the role of dynamic forces in explaining phenomena, especially by interpreting events as an expression of forces residing within the object or person involved —**dy·na·mist** *n* —**dy·na·mis·tic** /dīnə místik/ *adj*

dy·na·mite /dínə mìt/ *n* **1. POWERFUL EXPLOSIVE** a powerful explosive consisting of a porous material such as wood pulp or sawdust, combined with ammonium or sodium nitrate, or nitroglycerin, and an antacid such as calcium carbonate. Use: blasting. **2. VERY EXCITING THING** something that or somebody who is exceptionally exciting or has an extremely powerful effect (*slang*) ○ *This music is absolute dynamite.* **3. VERY HARMFUL THING** something that or somebody who is potentially very dangerous or harmful (*slang*) ○ *news stories that were political dynamite* ■ *vt* (**-mit·ed, -mit·ing, -mites**) **BLOW SOMETHING UP WITH DYNAMITE** to blast or destroy something with dynamite [Mid-19C. < Greek *dunamis* "force"] —**dy·na·mit·er** *n*

dy·na·mo /dínəmō/ (*plural* **-mos**) *n* **1.** a machine that converts mechanical energy into electrical energy, usually in the form of direct current **2.** a hardworking, tirelessly energetic person [Late 19C. Shortening of *dynamo-electric machine*]

dynamo- *prefix* power, energy ○ *dynamometer* [< Greek *dunamis* "force"]

dy·na·mo·e·lec·tric /dìnəmō i léktrik/, **dy·na·mo·e·lec·tri·cal** /-k'l/ *adj* involved in or relating to the production of electrical from mechanical energy or of mechanical energy from electrical

dy·na·mom·e·ter /dìnə mómmətər/ *n* an instrument used to measure mechanical force or power such as the power output of an engine —**dy·na·mo·met·ric** /dìnəmō méttrik/ *adj* —**dy·na·mom·e·try** *n*

dy·na·mo·tor /dínə mōtər/ *n* an electrical device combining a motor and generator. Use: to convert alternating current to direct current, and vice versa. [Early 20C. < Greek *dunamis* "force"]

dy·nast /dí nàst, dínəst/ *n* **1.** a ruler, especially a hereditary monarch **2.** a member or founder of a dynasty [Mid-17C. Via Latin < Greek *dunastēs* "lord" < *dunasthai* "be able"]

dy·nas·ty /dínəstee/ (*plural* **-ties**) *n* **1.** a succession of rulers from the same family **2.** a prominent and powerful family or group of people whose members retain their power and influence through several generations [14C. Directly or via French < late Latin *dynastia* < Greek *dunastēs* "lord" (see DYNAST)] —**dy·nas·tic** /dī nástik, di-/ *adj* —**dy·nas·ti·cal·ly** *adv*

dyne /dīn/ *n* the centimeter-gram-second unit of force equal to the force that will accelerate a mass of one gram one centimeter per second per second. 1 dyne is equivalent to 10^{-5} newton. Symbol **dyn** [Late 19C. < Greek *dunamis* "force"]

dy·nein /dínin/ *n* a protein that uses chemical energy from ATP to create movement within microtubules such as cilia and flagella [Mid-20C. < DYNE]

dy·node /dí nōd/ *n* an electrode in an electron tube that produces electrons through secondary emission [Mid-20C. < Greek *dunamis* "force" (see DYNAMIC) + -ODE]

dys- *prefix* bad, impaired, pathological ○ *dysplasia* [Via Latin < Greek *dus-*]

dys·ar·thri·a /dis áarthree ə/ *n* difficulty in speech articulation caused by a lack of muscle control resulting from damage to the central nervous system [Late 19C. < modern Latin < Latin *dys-* "bad" + Greek *arthron* "joint"]

dys·cra·sia /dis kráyzhə/ *n* an unusual condition of the blood cells [14C. Via late Latin < Greek *duskrasia* "bad mixture" < *krasis* "mixing"]

dys·en·ter·y /díss'n tèrree/ *n* a disease of the lower intestine caused by infection with bacteria, protozoans, or parasites and marked by severe diarrhea, inflammation, and the passage of blood and mucus [14C. Directly or via French < Latin *dysenteria* < Greek *dusenteros* "having bad intestines" < *enteron* "intestine"] —**dys·en·ter·ic** /dìss'n térrik/ *adj*

~~dysentry~~ incorrect spelling of **dysentery**

dys·func·tion /diss fúngkshən/ *n* **1.** a disturbance in the usual pattern of activity or behavior ○ *a characteristic dysfunction of petty officialdom* **2.** an irregularity in the functioning of an organ or other part or system of the body

dys·func·tion·al /diss fúngkshən'l/ *adj* **1. RELATING BADLY** characterized by an inability to function emotionally or as a social unit ○ *a dysfunctional family* ○ *dysfunctional behavior* **2. NOT PERFORMING AS EXPECTED** failing to perform an expected function ○ *a dysfunctional bureaucracy* **3. AFFECTED BY DISEASE OR IMPAIRMENT** describes an organ or other part or system of the body that is unable to function regularly as a result of disease or impairment

dys·gen·ic /dis jénnik/ *adj* affecting later generations detrimentally by passing on undesirable characteristics

dys·gen·ics /dis jénniks/ *n* the study of factors relating to or causing a decrease in the survival of the genetically well-adapted members of a line of descent (*takes a singular verb*)

dys·graph·ia /dis gráffee ə/ *n* impairment of writing ability, arising from brain injury or disease [Mid-20C. < DYS- + Greek *graphia* "writing"]

dys·ki·ne·sia /dìss ki néezhə, dìss kī néezhə/ *n* impairment of control over ordinary muscle movement, often resulting in spasmodic movements or tics [Early 18C. Via modern Latin < Greek *duskinēsia* "difficulty in moving" < *kinēsis* "movement"]

dys·lex·i·a /diss léksee ə/ *n* a learning disorder marked by a severe difficulty in recognizing and understanding written language, leading to spelling and writing problems. It is not caused by low intelligence or brain damage. [Late 19C. < DYS- + Greek *lexis* "speech" < *legein* "speak"] —**dys·lex·ic** *adj, n*

dys·men·or·rhe·a /dìss mennə rée ə/, **dys·men·or·rhoe·a** *n* severe pain or cramps in the lower abdomen during menstruation —**dys·men·or·rhe·al** *adj* —**dys·men·or·rhe·ic** *adj*

dys·pa·reu·ni·a /dìspar yóonee ə/ *n* pain occurring during sexual intercourse [Late 19C. < DYS- + Greek *pareunos* "lying with somebody" < *para* "beside" + *eunē* "bed"]

dys·pep·sia /diss pépshə, -pépsee ə/ *n* acid indigestion (*technical*) [Early 18C. Via Latin < Greek *duspepsia* "difficult digestion" < *peptein* "cook, digest"]

dys·pep·tic /diss péptik/ *adj* **1.** having acid indigestion **2.** easily angered [Late 17C. < Greek *duspeptos* "difficult of digestion" < *peptein* "cook, digest"] —**dys·pep·tic** *n*

dys·pha·gia /dis fáyjə/ *n* difficulty in swallowing, with a variety of possible causes —**dys·phag·ic** /-fájjik/ *adj*

dys·pha·sia /diss fáyzhə, -fáyzee ə/ *n* difficulty in speaking and understanding spoken or written language, caused by brain injury or disease —**dys·pha·sic** /dis fáyzik/ *adj*

dys·phe·mism /dísfə mìzzəm/ *n* **1.** the deliberate substitution of an offensive expression for a neutral one **2.** an offensive expression deliberately substituted for a neutral one [Late 19C. < DYS- after *euphemism*] —**dys·phe·mis·tic** /dìsfə místik/ *adj*

dys·pho·ni·a /diss fónee ə/ *n* hoarseness or difficulty in speaking as a result of dysfunction of the vocal cords, caused by brain injury, brain disease, or chemical poisoning [Early 18C. Via modern Latin < Greek *dusphōnia* "roughness of sound" < *phōnē* "sound"] —**dys·phon·ic** /-fónnik/ *adj*

dys·pho·ri·a /diss fáwree ə/ *n* a state of feeling acutely hopeless, uncomfortable, and unhappy [Mid-19C. < Greek *dusphoria* "discomfort" < *pherein* "to bear"] —**dys·phor·ic** *adj*

dys·pla·sia /diss pláyzhə, -pláyzhee ə/ *n* unusual development or growth of a part of the body such as an organ, bone, or cell, including the total absence of such a part —**dys·plas·tic** /-plástik/ *adj*

dysp·ne·a /disp née ə, dísp née ə/ *n* difficulty in breathing, often caused by heart or lung disease [Mid-17C. Via Latin < Greek *duspnoia* "difficulty in breathing" < *pnein* "breathe"] —**dysp·ne·al** *adj* —**dysp·ne·ic** *adj*

dys·p·noe·a *n* MED UK spelling of **dyspnea**

dys·prax·i·a /dis práksee ə/ *n* **1.** poor coordination displayed by some children, diagnosed by illegible handwriting and inability to catch a ball and clap while the ball is in the air. It sometimes accompanies dyslexia. **2.** same as **apraxia** [< Greek *duspraxia* "ill success" < *praxis* "action"] —**dys·prax·ic** *adj*

dys·pro·si·um /diss prózee əm/ *n* a soft silvery element of the rare-earth group that is paramagnetic and highly reactive. Source: monazite, bastnaesite. Use: laser materials, nuclear research. Symbol **Dy**. See table at **element** [Late 19C. < Greek *dusprositos* "difficult to approach" < *ienai* "go"]

dys·rhyth·mi·a /dis ríthmee ə/ *n* an irregularity in a rhythm, especially of heartbeats or brain waves [Early 20C. < modern Latin, "bad rhythm" < Greek *rhuthmos* "rhythm"]

dys·to·ci·a /diss tóshə/ *n* unusually difficult childbirth [Early 18C. < Greek *dustokia* "difficult childbirth" < *tokos* "childbirth"] —**dys·to·ci·al** *adj*

dys·to·ni·a /di stónee ə/ *n* a neurological disorder that causes involuntary muscle spasms and twisting of the limbs

dys·to·pi·a /diss tópee ə/ *n* **1.** an imaginary place where everything is as bad as it possibly can be **2.** a vision or description of a dystopia [Mid-20C. < DYS- + UTOPIA] —**dys·to·pi·an** *adj*

dys·tro·phi·a *n* MED same as **dystrophy**

dys·troph·ic /diss tróffik/ *adj* **1.** relating to or affected by dystrophy **2.** describes a pond or lake containing unusually acidic brown water, lacking in oxygen, and unable to support much plant or animal life because of an excessive humus content

dys·tro·phin /dístrəfin/ *n* a protein found in muscle that is missing in people with muscular dystrophy

dys·tro·phy /dístrəfee/ (*plural* **-phies**), **dys·tro·phi·a** /də strófee ə/ *n* **1.** progressive degeneration of a body tissue such as muscle, caused by inadequate nourishment of the affected part, as a result of some unknown cause **2.** a condition in which pond or lake water is unable to support much plant or animal life because of an excessive humus content [Late 19C. < DYS- + -TROPHY]

dys·u·ri·a /diss yóoree ə, di shóoree ə/ *n* pain or difficulty in urinating —**dys·u·ric** *adj*

Dy·u·la /dee óola, dyóolə/ (*plural same* or **-las**) *n* **1.** a member of an African people who live mainly in the rain forests of the Ivory Coast **2.** a Mande language spoken in parts of the Ivory Coast, Burkina Faso, and Ghana. Native speakers: 1 million. —**Dy·u·la** *adj*

dz *abbr* Algeria (*used in Internet addresses*) See table at **domain name**

Dzer·zhinsk /dər zhínsk/ city in central European Russia on the Oka River. It is a chemical-manufacturing center. Population: 359,740 (1995).

dzig·ge·tai *n* ZOOL another spelling of **chigetai**

dzo /zō, dzō/ (*plural* **dzos** or *same*), **zo** /zō/ (*plural* **zos** or *same*), **zho** (*plural* **zhos** or *same*) *n* the offspring of a cow and a yak [Mid-19C. < Tibetan *mdso*]

Dzong·kha /zóngkə, dzóngkə/, **Dzong·ka** *n* a dialect of Tibetan that is the official language of Bhutan. Native speakers: 1 million. [Early 20C. < Tibetan, "language of the fortress"] —**Dzong·kha** *adj*

Dzun·gar·i·a /dzoong gérree ə, jùng-/ ◆ **Junggar Pendi**

Ee

e[1] /ee/ (*plural* **e's**), **E** (*plural* **E's** or **Es**) *n* **1.** the fifth letter of the English alphabet, representing a vowel sound **2.** a written representation of the letter "e"

e[2] *symbol* **1.** PHYS electron **2.** MATH used to refer to the transcendental number 2.718 282... **3.** CHESS used to refer to the fifth vertical row of squares from the left on a chessboard

e[3] *abbr* BASEBALL error

E[1] *symbol* **1.** *E* PHYS electric field strength **2.** *E* PHYS electromotive force **3.** MEASURE exa- **4.** PHYS internal energy **5.** LOGIC a negative categorical proposition

E[2] /ee/ (*plural* **E's** or **Es**) *n* **1. "E"-SHAPED OBJECT** something shaped like a letter "E" **2.** MUSIC **3RD NOTE IN C MAJOR** the third note of a scale in C major **3.** MUSIC **SOMETHING THAT PRODUCES E** a string, key, or pipe tuned to produce the note E **4.** MUSIC **SCALE BEGINNING ON E** a scale or key that starts on the note E **5.** MUSIC **WRITTEN SYMBOL OF E** a graphic representation of the tone of E **6.** DRUGS **ECSTASY** the drug ecstasy, or a tablet of the drug (*slang*)

E[3] *abbr* **1.** ELEC earth **2.** *also* **E.** east **3.** eastern **4.** TELECOM e-mail (*used to contrast with T, telephone number, and F, fax number*) **5.** TELECOM e-mail address (*used to contrast with T, telephone number and F, fax number*) **6.** LANG English **7.** BASEBALL error

e. *abbr* **1.** engineer **2.** engineering

e- *prefix* **1.** electronic ○ *e-mail* **2.** electronic data transfer via the Internet ○ *e-commerce* [Abbreviation of ELECTRONIC]

e-bank *n*
e-bank·ing *n*
e-bro·chure *n*
e-bul·le·tin *n*
e-bul·le·tin board *n*
e-cash *n*
e-cat·a·log *n*
e-com·merce *n*
e-con·fer·ence *n*
e-con·fer·enc·ing *n*
e-cop·y *n*
e-da·ta *n*
e-de·moc·ra·cy *n*
e-doc·u·ment *n*
e-fail·ure *n*
e-fraud *n*
e-fron·tier *n*
e-funds *npl*
e-gift *n*
e-jour·nal *n*
e-jour·nal·ism *n*
e-jour·nal·ist *n*
e-mag·a·zine *n*
e-mon·ey *n*
e-news *n*
e-news·pa·per *n*
e-news·room *n*
e-of·fice *n*
e-pay·ment *n*
e-pub·lish·ing *n*
e-purse *n*
e-shop *n*
e-shop·per *n*
e-shop·ping *n*
e-sig·na·ture *n*
e-sys·tem *n*
e-tag·ging *n*
e-text *n*
e-tick·et *n*
e-tick·et·ing *n*
e-toll *n*
e-toll·ing *n*
e-trad·er *n*
e-trad·ing *n*
e-trans·fer *n*
e-vot·ing *n*
e-war *n*
e-war·fare *n*

ea. *abbr* each

EAC *abbr* ECON East African Community

eace·worm /eess wùrm/ *n Northeast US* same as **earthworm** [< *eace* "earthworm" < Old English *æs* "bait, carrion"]

REGIONAL NOTE Often thought of as a typical Northern or New England term, ***eaceworm*** most clearly marks northern Rhode Island speech. Other forms are *easterworm* and *eastworm.*

each /eech/ *adj, pron, adv* used to refer to every member of a group of people or things, considered individually ○ *With each victory we get closer to the championship.* ○ *Is a VCR that can be connected to more than one TV better than buying one for each?* ○ *Environmental health officers were supervising an average of 40 cases each.* [Old English *ǣlc* < Germanic, "ever alike"]

USAGE each or **every**? In some contexts these two words are nearly interchangeable, as in *I examined each puppy in the litter* and *I examined every puppy in the litter.* Here the only difference is a slight shift in perspective from considering the animals individually, with ***each***, to considering them collectively, with ***every***. Either of the words, placed before the noun, requires the noun and the verb to be singular: *Each puppy is affectionate. Every puppy is affectionate.* ***Each***, though not ***every***, may also be placed after a plural noun, and then the plural governs the verb: *The puppies each have their own toys.* ***Each*** can also refer to two or more, whereas ***every*** must refer to three or more. ***Each*** can be an adjective (*each puppy*), a pronoun (*each of them*), and an adverb (*Give them a bowlful each*), whereas ***every*** is an adjective only (*every puppy*). The expression *each and every* relates to a singular noun only, and therefore takes a singular verb only: *Each and every passenger is required to present two photo IDs for identification.* Avoid use of this expression in formal writing, because it is objected to by some people as unnecessarily wordy.

each oth·er *pron* each one of two or more persons or things reciprocally

USAGE each other or **one another**? The traditional rule is that ***each other*** refers to two items and ***one another*** refers to more than two: *Joe and Lee respect each other deeply. All the people at the party knew one another already.* This distinction is not supported by the weight of usage, however. It has been used in the writings of Noah Webster, Samuel Johnson, and G. K. Chesterton, among others. There is no good reason to reject the alternatives *Joe and Lee respect one another deeply* and *All the people at the party already knew each other,* although the last example sounds somewhat less natural.

ea·ger /éegər/ *adj* **1.** enthusiastic and excited about something and impatiently waiting to do or get it ○ *eager to help* ○ *eager for praise* **2.** expressing enthusiastic interest and expectation or an impatient desire to do something ○ *an eager face* [13C. Via Anglo-Norman *egre* < Latin *acer* "sharp"] —**ea·ger·ly** *adv* —**ea·ger·ness** *n*

USAGE See ***anxious***.

ea·ger bea·ver *n* an enthusiastic worker or volunteer (*informal*) [< the perceived industriousness of beavers]

ea·gle /éeg'l/ *n* **1. LARGE BIRD OF PREY** a large bird of prey with a hooked beak and broad wingspan that hunts by day. Family: Accipitridae. **2. EAGLE AS SYMBOL OF POWER** the figure of an eagle used as a symbol of military or political power, e.g., on the standards carried by Roman legions **3.** GOLF **SCORE OF 2 UNDER PAR** in golf, a score of two under par for a single hole **4.** COINS **FORMER US GOLD COIN** a former US gold coin worth ten dollars ■ *vti* (**-gled, -gling, -gles**) GOLF **SCORE 2 UNDER PAR** in golf, to complete a hole in two strokes under par [14C. Via Anglo-Norman *egle* < Latin *aquila*]

ea·gle eye *n* **1.** extremely keen eyesight, especially over long distances **2.** the ability to notice what other people might miss —**ea·gle-eyed** *adj*

ea·gle owl *n* a large owl with brownish plumage and tufts of feathers on its head that look like horns. It is the largest species of owl in the world. Native to: Europe, Asia. Latin name: *Bubo bubo.*

ea·gle ray *n* a large fish with a projecting snout, massive jaws, and pectoral fins shaped like wings that propel it with a soaring motion. Native to: tropical and subtropical seas. Family: Myliobatidae.

Ea·gle Scout *n* a Boy Scout who has reached the highest level of attainment in the various tests of skill and endurance set by the Boy Scout organization

ea·glet /éeglət/ *n* a young eagle, especially before it leaves the nest

ea·gle·wood /éeg'l wòod/ (*plural* **-woods** or *same*) *n* **1.** a tree with fragrant resinous timber. Use: perfumes. Native to: Asia. Latin name: *Aquilaria agallocha.* **2.** INDUST same as **aloes** (sense 2)

ea·gre /éegər/ *n* GEOG same as **bore**[3] [Early 17C. Origin ?]

Ea·kins /áykinz/, **Thomas** (1844–1916) US artist. He is known for his realist paintings drawn from life such as *The Gross Clinic* (1875).

eal·dor·man /áwldərmən/ (*plural* **-men** /-mən/) *n* in Anglo-Saxon England, the principal magistrate and commander of the military forces of a shire [Old English *ealdormann*, early form of ALDERMAN]

Eal·ing /éeling/ borough in West London, England. Population: 300,9487 (2001).

Eames /eemz/ *tdmk* a trademark for chairs, especially and originally ones of molded plywood, whose seats and backs are shaped to accommodate human body contours

Eames /eemz/, **Charles** (1907–78) US designer. He is known for designing the prototype of the molded plywood chair that bears his name.

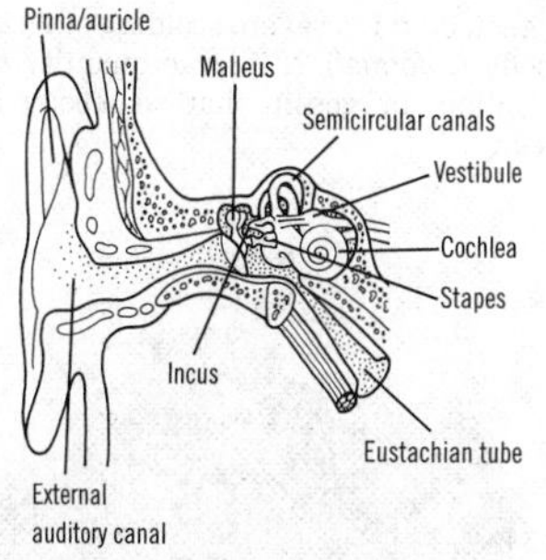

ear

ear[1] /eer/ *n* **1. ORGAN OF HEARING** the organ of hearing and balance in vertebrates. In mammals it is divided into three parts, the external, middle, and inner ear. The external ear collects sound, the middle ear contains small bones that amplify and transmit it, while the inner ear maintains balance and contains sensory nerve endings for detecting sound. **2. EXTERNAL PART OF HEARING ORGAN** the external part of an ear, visible in humans and most mammals on each side of the head as a flap of cartilage with skin surrounding or covering it **3. INVERTEBRATE SENSORY ORGAN** a sensory organ in invertebrates that is able to sense vibrations and perform a similar function to a vertebrate ear **4.** BIRDS same as **ear tuft** **5. EAR SHAPE** something shaped like an ear, especially a handle on a jug or jar **6.** ABILITY TO TELL SOUNDS APART the ability to distinguish accurately between different sounds, e.g., in speech or music ○ *She has a good ear for languages.* **7.** ATTENTION somebody's attention, especially when it is sympathetic or favorable ○ *lend an ear* **8.** MEDIA SECTION AT TOP CORNER OF NEWSPAPER a small section at the top corner of the front page of a newspaper for advertising or a weather forecast [Old English *ēare* < Indo-European, "ear"] —**ear·less** *adj* ◇ **all ears** listening, or ready to listen, attentively or enthusiastically to something (*informal*) ◇ **go in one ear and out the other** to be forgotten as soon as heard and so have absolutely no effect on somebody ◇ **have somebody's ear** to be a trusted adviser to somebody, especially somebody powerful or influential ◇ **have** *or* **keep your ear to the ground** to remain continuously alert to discover new developments or information ◇ **out on your ear** unceremoniously thrown out or dismissed from a place or position you previously occupied (*informal*) ○ *You'll be out on your ear if you're late again.* ◇ **prick up your ears** to begin listening or paying attention to something ◇ **set somebody on his** *or* **her ear, set something on its ear** to send somebody or something into a state of excited agitation, shock, or confusion ◇ **wet behind the ears** very inexperienced or naive

ear[2] /eer/ *n* the grain-bearing part at the top of the stalk of a cereal plant such as wheat, corn, or barley ■ *vi* (**eared, ear·ing, ears**) to form the part of a cereal plant that contains the grains [Old English *ēar* < Indo-European, "sharp"]

ear·ache /éer àyk/ *n* pain in the middle or inner ear. Technical name **otalgia**

ear bone *n* BIOL same as **otolith**

ear clip *n* **1.** a metal band or other ornament clipped to the upper part of the ear **2.** a clip-on earring

ear·drop /éer dròp/ *n* a pendant earring ■ **ear·drops** *npl* liquid medicine for the ear, usually inserted with a dropper

ear·drum /éer drùm/ *n* a membrane of thin skin and fibrous tissue that vibrates in response to sound waves, located between the external and the middle ear. Technical name **tympanic membrane**

eared /eerd/ *adj* with ears or with ears of a particular type (*usually used in combination*) ○ *long-eared*

eared seal /éerd-/ *n* a seal with conspicuous external ears and independent hind limbs or flippers that it uses to move on land. Sea lions and fur seals are eared seals. Family: Otariidae.

ear·flap /éer flàp/ *n* a piece of fabric or fur on a hat that can be let down to keep the ear warm (*often used in the plural*)

ear·ful /éer fòol/ *n* **1.** a severe scolding or lecture from somebody (*informal*) **2.** a large quantity of sound, conversation, or gossip that somebody hears or overhears

Barnaby's

Amelia Earhart

Ear·hart /ér haàrt/, **Amelia** (1898–1937) US aviator. She was the first woman to fly solo over both the Atlantic (1932) and part of the Pacific (1935). She disappeared over the Pacific in 1937 while attempting an around-the-world flight.

> "Courage is the price that Life exacts for granting peace."
> [Amelia Earhart, *Courage*; 1927]

ear·ing /éering/ *n* a small rope by which the upper corner of a sail is attached to a yard [Early 17C. Origin ?]

earl /url/ *n* a British nobleman of a rank above a viscount and below a marquess. The title corresponds to "count" in Europe, and Great Britain and Europe both use "countess" for a woman's equivalent rank. [Old English *eorl* "warrior, nobleman." Origin ?] —**earl·dom** *n*

ear·less seal *n* a seal that does not have conspicuous external ears and has short front and hind flippers that are adapted for swimming rather than moving on land. Family: Phocidae.

Earl Grey *n* a tea flavored with bergamot to produce a light-colored brew with a musky taste [Probably after Charles Grey, the second *Earl Grey* (1764–1845), British prime minister]

Earl Mar·shal *n* an officer of the English peerage who presides over the College of Heralds and organizes important ceremonial occasions

ear·lobe /éer lōb/ *n* the soft fleshy lower part of the outer ear

ear·ly /úrlee/ *adv* (**-li·er, -li·est**) **1.** BEFORE EXPECTED TIME before the expected or arranged time ○ *They arrived early.* **2.** NEAR BEGINNING OF SOMETHING at or near the beginning of a period of time, process, or sequence of events ○ *early in the interview* **3.** DURING FIRST STAGES at a time when something was not far advanced or developed or when somebody was at a comparatively young age ○ *She decided early that she wanted to become a teacher.* **4.** SOON without delay or before long ○ *Buy your tickets early, for seating is limited.* ■ *adj* (**-li·er, -li·est**) **1.** OCCURRING NEAR BEGINNING occurring at or near the beginning of a period of time, process, or sequence of events ○ *Early reports indicate a high level of interest.* **2.** OCCURRING BEFORE EXPECTED TIME occurring before the expected or arranged time ○ *early retirement* **3.** PRODUCED NEAR BEGINNING produced at, characteristic of, or representing a not very advanced stage in the development of somebody or something ○ *looking forward to an early end to the deadlock* **4.** IN NEAR FUTURE due, expected, or requested to happen in the very near future **5.** RIPENING BEFORE OTHERS flowering or ripening before other plant varieties of the same type ○ *an early bloomer* ○ *early peaches* [Old English *ǣrlīce* < Indo-European, "day"] —**ear·li·ness** *n* ◇ **early on** at the beginning or start of something such as a chain of events or a period of time ○ *We should have realized early on that financing would be a major problem.*

Ear·ly /úrlee/, **Jubal Anderson** (1816–94) US Confederate general. He interrupted his career as a lawyer to serve during the Mexican War (1846–48) and Civil War (1861–65).

ear·ly a·dopt·er *n* somebody who embraces a new product or technology as soon as it becomes available

ear·ly bird *n* (*informal*) **1.** an early riser **2.** somebody who arrives or acts earlier than the expected or arranged time [< the proverb *The early bird gets the worm*]

ear·ly col·lege *n* a high school administered jointly by a public school district and a college or university within the district, where the students study both high-school and college courses, receiving high-school diplomas and associate college degrees upon graduation [Early 21C.]

Ear·ly En·glish *adj* belonging to or typical of the style of early Gothic architecture used between the late 12th and late 13th centuries in England, characterized by sharply pointed arches and arched windows —**Ear·ly En·glish** *n*

ear·ly mod·ern *adj* relating to or typical of the period in European and world history from 1485 to the late 18th century

ear·ly mu·sic *n* music written during the medieval and Renaissance periods, sometimes also including the music of the baroque and early classical periods ■ *adj* typical of a way of performing early music that aims to be as authentic as possible, using period instruments, the contemporary performing style, and a carefully researched score

ear·ly re·tire·ment *n* retirement from work before the usual age, often offered, with special inducements, by employers as a way of reducing staff numbers

ear·ly ris·er *n* somebody who gets up early, especially on a regular basis

ear·ly warn·ing *n* advance notice that something, especially something dangerous or threatening, is going to happen

ear·ly warn·ing sys·tem *n* a network of radar, satellites, or other sensing devices designed to give advance warning of an enemy attack, especially in time to take countermeasures

ear·mark /éer maàrk/ *vt* (**-marked, -mark·ing, -marks**) **1.** DESIGNATE SOMETHING FOR PARTICULAR PURPOSE to select and reserve something to be used for a particular purpose ○ *That money's already been earmarked for upgrading the computer system.* **2.** PUT IDENTIFICATION MARK ON ANIMAL'S EAR to mark the ear of a farm animal with an identifying symbol, notch, or hole ■ *n* **1.** *US* IDENTIFYING CHARACTERISTIC a characteristic that makes it possible to recognize the nature or origins of something (*often used in the plural*) ○ *The crime seemed to have all the earmarks of an inside job.* **2.** IDENTIFICATION MARK ON ANIMAL'S EAR an identifying symbol, notch, or hole on or in the ear of a farm animal

ear·muffs /éer mùfs/ *npl* ear covers attached to an adjustable headband, worn in cold weather

earn /urn/ (**earned, earn·ing, earns**) *v* **1.** *vti* MAKE MONEY BY WORKING to receive money or payment of some other kind in return for work done ○ *earn enough to live on* **2.** *vt* DESERVE SOMETHING to acquire something as a result of personal actions or behavior ○ *earn praise* ○ *The remark earned him a stern rebuke.* **3.** *vt* FIN PRODUCE DIVIDENDS to produce interest or dividends from money invested [Old English *earnian* < Germanic, "harvest"]

earned in·come /ùrnd-/ *n* income from paid employment, not from investments

earned run *n* in baseball, a run scored without the benefit of an error or a wild pitch

earned run av·er·age *n* in baseball, the number of earned runs allowed by a pitcher every nine innings, used as a measure of the pitcher's performance

earn·er /úrnər/ *n* **1.** somebody who earns a particular level of income ○ *tax incentives for high earners* ○ *dual-earner families* **2.** an activity, job, product, or transaction that generates money ○ *Tourism is a major revenue earner.* ○ *a product that's one of the company's biggest earners*

ear·nest[1] /úrnəst/ *adj* **1.** intensely or excessively serious and grave in manner or attitude ○ *an earnest expression* ○ *earnest discussions about privacy and propriety* **2.** undertaken or made in a spirit of deep sincerity and conviction, or with deep feeling ○ *He interrupted me with an earnest assurance of help and support.* [Old English *eornost* < Germanic] —**ear·nest·ly** *adv* —**ear·nest·ness** *n* ◇ **in earnest 1.** serious and sincere in your actions, words, or intentions ○ *Is she in earnest?* **2.** in a determined and purposeful way ○ *Now the campaign would begin in earnest.*

ear·nest[2] /úrnəst/ *n* **1.** *also* **ear·nest mon·ey** a small advance payment that confirms a contract (*dated*) **2.** a sign, foretaste, or pledge of something to come (*literary*) [13C. Probably alteration of Old French *erres* "pledges" < Latin *arra* < Greek *arrabōn* "pledge" < Hebrew *'ērābhôn* < *'ārab* "to pledge"]

earn·ings /úrningz/ *npl* money earned through paid employment, as profit, or from investments

Earp /urp/, **Wyatt** (1848–1929) US frontiersman and law enforcement officer. He was based in Dodge City, Kansas, and later in Tombstone, Arizona, where he participated in the gunfight at the O.K. Corral (1881). Full name **Earp, Wyatt Berry Stapp**

ear·phone /éer fōn/ *n* a device that converts electrical signals into audible sound and is worn on or held close to the ear (*often used in the plural*)

ear·piece /éer peess/ *n* **1.** the part of a device such as a telephone, radio, or hearing aid that is held in, or close to, the ear **2.** the part of the frame of a pair of eyeglasses that fits over and around the ear

ear·pierc·ing *adj* extremely or painfully loud and shrill

ear·plug /éer plùg/ *n* a piece of something soft such as wax or foam rubber that is placed in the ear to keep out noise, water, or cold (*often used in the plural*)

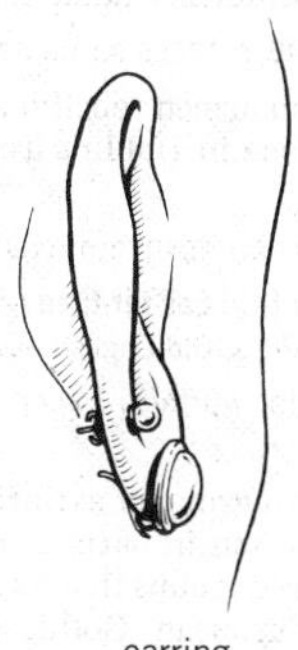

earring

ear·ring /éer rìng/ *n* a piece of jewelry worn on the ear, usually either clipped to the earlobe or attached through a hole pierced in it (*often used in the plural*)

ear·set /éer sèt/ *n* a piece of equipment attached to a computer or cell phone that enables the user to speak on the telephone without using the hands

ear shell *n* MARINE BIOL same as **abalone**

ear·shot /éer shòt/ *n* the distance within which sound is audible to somebody ○ *within earshot* [Early 17C. After words such as BOWSHOT]

ear·split·ting /éer splitting/ *adj* extremely loud or shrill —**ear·split·ting·ly** *adv*

ear stone *n* BIOL same as **otolith**

earth /urth/ *n* **1.** ASTRON another spelling of **Earth 2. LAND** the solid dry land surface of Earth, as opposed to the sea or sky **3. SOIL** the soft workable material in which plants grow **4. HUMAN INHABITANTS OF EARTH** all the human inhabitants of Earth (*formal*) **5. PURSUITS OF EVERYDAY LIFE** the pursuits of everyday human life, especially as opposed to matters of the spirit **6.** *UK* **BURROW** the hole or underground lair of a fox or other burrowing animal **7.** *UK* ELEC ENG same as **ground**[1] (sense 9) **8.** PHILOSOPHY, HIST **ONE OF FOUR ELEMENTS** in ancient and medieval philosophy, one of the four elements, earth, air, fire, and water, from which it was believed everything was made ■ *vt* (**earthed, earth·ing, earths**) *UK* ELEC ENG same as **ground**[1] *v* (sense 1) [Old English *eorþe* < Germanic] ◇ **come** *or* **be brought back (down) to earth** to return to reality after a period of happiness or unrealistic hopes ◇ **on earth** used to add intensity to a question, often indicating surprise or disbelief on the part of the questioner (*informal*) ○ *What on earth have you done to the computer now?*

Earth *n* the third planet in order from the Sun with an orbital period of 365.26 days, a diameter of 7,926 mi./12,756 km, and an average distance from the Sun of 93,000,000 mi./149,600,000 km. Surrounded by an atmosphere composed primarily of nitrogen and oxygen, it is the only planet in the universe known to support life.

earth·born /úrth bàwrn/ *adj* born on or originating from Earth, and therefore human, mortal, or earthly (*literary*)

earth·bound /úrth bòwnd/ *adj* **1. CONFINED TO EARTH** unable to leave Earth **2. MUNDANE AND UNIMAGINATIVE** exclusively concerned with or confined to ordinary everyday or worldly matters and lacking in imagination or spirituality **3. HEADING TOWARD EARTH** heading or moving toward Earth

earth col·or *n* a pigment obtained from earth, e.g., umber or ocher

earth·en /úrthən/ *adj* **1.** made of earth or baked clay **2.** from Earth and having human or mortal qualities

earth·en·ware /úrthən wèr/ *n* pottery made of fairly coarse-textured baked clay that is fired at a very low temperature

Earth Li·ber·a·tion Front *n* an environmental movement that stages demonstrations and takes direct action to defend forests and land from logging companies and developers

earth·light /úrth lìt/ *n* ASTRON same as **earthshine**

earth·ling /úrthling/ *n* **1.** especially in science fiction, a human being, as opposed to an extraterrestrial or supernatural being **2.** somebody who concentrates on everyday matters

earth·ly /úrthlee/ (**-li·er, -li·est**) *adj* **1.** belonging to or characteristic of the physical world, especially as opposed to a spiritual realm or heaven **2.** used to add intensity to a negative or question ○ *no earthly use*

earth·man /úrth màn/ (*plural* **-men** /-mèn/) *n* in science fiction, a resident of Earth, especially a man, as referred to by an extraterrestrial

earth moth·er *n* **1.** a woman who conveys a warm combination of sensuality and motherliness **2.** a goddess worshiped as a source of life and fertility

earth·mov·er /úrth mo͞ovər/ *n* a vehicle such as a bulldozer that is designed to move earth, especially in large quantities —**earth·mov·ing** *adj*

earth pil·lar *n* a pillar of soft material capped by a boulder of more resistant rock that protects it from erosion

earth·quake /úrth kwàyk/ *n* **1.** a violent shaking of the Earth's crust that may cause destruction to buildings and results from the sudden release of tectonic stress along a fault line or from volcanic activity **2.** an event that causes an upheaval in society, politics, or somebody's life

earth·rise /úrth rìz/ *n* the rising of Earth above the Moon's horizon, as seen from space or from the Moon itself

earth sci·ence *n* a science that deals with the Earth's physical properties, structure, or development, e.g., geology

earth·shak·ing /úrth shàyking/, **earth·shat·ter·ing** /-shàttəring/ *adj* extremely great or important, or having an extremely powerful effect —**earth·shak·ing·ly** *adv*

earth·shine /úrth shìn/ *n* sunlight reflected from Earth that illuminates the part of the Moon not receiving light directly from the Sun

earth sign *n* each of the three signs of the zodiac, Taurus, Virgo, and Capricorn, traditionally associated with stability and consistency

earth·star /úrth staar/ *n* a woodland fungus with a round outer surface that splits open in a star-shaped pattern to release spores. Genus: *Geastrum.*

earth sta·tion *n* a system for relaying radio signals between one or more satellites and other communications networks. Earth stations may be on the ground, at sea, or in aircraft.

earth tone *n* a color with an element of deep rich brown in it, e.g., gold or russet

earth·ward /úrthwərd/ *adj* directed or facing toward Earth or the ground ■ *adv also* **earth·wards** /-wərdz/ in the direction of the Earth or the ground

earth wax *n* INDUST, GEOL same as **ozocerite**

earth·wom·an /úrth wo͝ommən/ (*plural* **-wom·en** /-wìmmin/) *n* especially in science fiction, a woman resident of Earth as referred to by an extraterrestrial

earth·work /úrth wùrk/ *n* **1.** a fortification made of earth (*often used in the plural*) **2.** construction work involving excavating, earthmoving, and building embankments

earth·worm /úrth wùrm/ *n* a worm that burrows in the soil and helps to aerate and improve it. Family: Lumbricidae.

earth·y /úrthee/ (**-i·er, -i·est**) *adj* **1. LIKE SOIL** relating to or consisting of soil **2. NOT SQUEAMISH OR PRETENTIOUS** having or showing a hearty, cheerful, no-nonsense acceptance of the realities and facts of life **3. SOMEWHAT INDECENT** crude and coarse ○ *earthy humor* —**earth·i·ly** *adv* —**earth·i·ness** *n*

ear trum·pet *n* an early type of hearing aid consisting of a trumpet-shaped device that was held to the ear

ear tuft *n* a tuft of feathers above the eyes of some owls and other birds, causing the bird to look larger or blend in with foliage, but not used in hearing

ear·wax /éer wàks/ *n* a yellowish waxy substance secreted by glands in the external ear to protect the delicate lining of the outer ear. Technical name **cerumen**

ear·wig /éer wìg/ *n* a common insect with a slender shiny body, small forewings, antennae, and pincers at the end of its abdomen. Order: Dermaptera. ■ *vt* (**-wigged, -wig·ging, -wigs**) to try to influence somebody, e.g., a judge, privately or clandestinely [Old English *ēarwicga* < *ēare* "ear" + *wicga* "insect"]

ease /eez/ *n* **1. LACK OF DIFFICULTY** lack of difficulty in doing or achieving something ○ *defeated the challenger with ease* **2. LACK OF AWKWARDNESS** lack of awkwardness, stiffness, or self-consciousness in social situations ○ *He felt totally at ease with her.* **3. COMFORT AND AFFLUENCE** a comfortable and leisured state free from worries, problems, and restrictions, especially those affecting somebody's financial situation ○ *a life of ease* ■ *v* (**eased, eas·ing, eas·es**) **1.** *vt* **MAKE LESS UNPLEASANT** to make something less unpleasant, difficult, or restrictive **2.** *vti* **RELIEVE OR ABATE** to become, or to cause something to become, less strong or intense ○ *The rain eased.* ○ *The medication soon started to ease the pain.* **3.** *vti* **MANEUVER GENTLY** to maneuver gently and carefully, especially in a tight space, or to maneuver something in this way ○ *eased the truck into the space* **4.** *vt* **LOOSEN SOMETHING** to slacken something that is tied or fitted tightly **5.** *vt* **MAKE EASIER** to enable something to take place more easily ○ *This would certainly ease the measure's passage through Congress.* [12C. < French *aise* "comfort"]

ease off *v* **1.** *vi* to lessen in intensity ○ *The rain had begun to ease off.* **2.** *vt* to slacken a rope or cable

ease·ful /éezfəl/ *adj* giving relief from pain, suffering, or distress (*literary*) —**ease·ful·ly** *adv* —**ease·ful·ness** *n*

ea·sel /éez'l/ *n* a freestanding upright support for a painter's canvas or a blackboard, usually made of wood and having movable clamps [Late 16C. Via Dutch *ezel* "donkey" < Latin *asinus*]

ease·ment /éezmənt/ *n* a limited right to make use of a property owned by another, e.g., a right of way across the property [14C. < Old French *aisement* < *aise* "comfort"]

eas·i·ly /éezilee, éezlee/ *adv* **1. WITHOUT DIFFICULTY** without difficulty, effort, or strain ○ *We can easily be there by lunchtime.* **2. BY FAR** without doubt and by a large margin ○ *She's easily the best.* **3. AT LEAST** not less and probably far more than a particular number or amount ○ *There were easily 200 people at the meeting.*

east /eest/ *n* **1. DIRECTION IN WHICH SUN RISES** the direction that lies directly ahead of somebody facing the rising sun or that is located toward the right-hand side of a conventional map of the world **2. COMPASS POINT OPPOSITE WEST** the compass point that lies directly opposite west **3. AREA IN EAST** the part of an area, region, or country that is situated in or toward the east **4. POSITION EQUIVALENT TO EAST** the position equivalent to east in any diagram consisting of four points at 90 degree intervals **5.** another spelling of **East** ■ *adj* **1. SITUATED IN EAST** situated in, facing, or coming from the east of an area, region, or country **2. BLOWING FROM EAST** describes a wind that blows from the east ■ *adv* **TOWARD EAST** in or toward the east [Old English *ēast-* < Indo-European, "to shine"]

East /eest/ *n* **1. EASTERN REGION OF US** the region of the United States that includes the states east of the Mississippi River and north of the Mason-Dixon Line **2. ASIA** the countries of Asia, especially East Asia **3. FORMER COMMUNIST COUNTRIES** the Communist countries of Eastern Europe and Asia during the Cold War

East Af·ri·ca /éest-/ region in east central Africa, usually taken to comprise Burundi, Kenya, Rwanda, Somalia, Tanzania, and Uganda —**East Af·ri·can** *n, adj*

East An·gli·a /-áng glee ə/ mainly agricultural region in eastern England. It covers Norfolk, Suffolk, Cambridgeshire, and Essex, and includes the Norfolk Broads and the Fens. —**East An·gli·an** *n, adj*

East A·sia the countries, territories, and regions of China, Hong Kong, Japan, North Korea, South Korea, Macau, Mongolia, parts of Russia, and Taiwan. ◊ **Far East**

East Ben·gal former region created in 1905 when Bengal Province in northeastern British India was divided into Hindu West Bengal (now Bangla) and the mainly Muslim East Bengal. The division was reversed in 1912 and when British India was partitioned in 1947, East Bengal became East Pakistan. It became the People's Republic of Bangladesh in 1971. ◊ **West Bengal**

East Ber·lin capital of East Germany from 1949 until 1990, when both Berlin and Germany were reunified —**East Ber·lin·er** *n*

east·bound /ée̱st bòwnd/ *adj, adv* going or leading toward the east

East·bourne /ée̱st bàwrn/ seaside resort and conference center in East Sussex, southeastern England. Population: 89,667 (2001).

East Bruns·wick township in central New Jersey. Population: 48,082 (2002 estimate).

east by north *n* the direction or compass point midway between east and east-northeast —**east by north** *adj, adv*

east by south *n* the direction or compass point midway between east and east-southeast —**east by south** *adj, adv*

East·ches·ter /ée̱st chèstər/ town in southeastern New York, between Yonkers and New Rochelle. Population: 31,544 (2002 estimate).

East Chi·ca·go industrial city in northwestern Indiana, on the south shore of Lake Michigan. It is a suburb of Chicago. Population: 31,731 (2002 estimate).

East Chi·na Sea arm of the northwestern Pacific Ocean between the eastern coast of China and the Ryukyu Islands. It is bounded to the north by the Yellow Sea and to the south by Taiwan. Area: 482,300 sq. mi./1,249,200 sq. km.

East Coast easternmost part of the United States, consisting of the states along its eastern seaboard from Maine to Florida, especially the oldest, most urban part of this area: New England, New York, New Jersey, Pennsylvania, Maryland, Virginia, and Washington, D.C.

East End *n* an area in the east of London, England, traditionally inhabited by working-class people, now undergoing regeneration

Eas·ter /ée̱stər/ *n* **1.** CHRISTIAN FESTIVAL IN SPRING a Christian festival marking the resurrection of Jesus Christ. Date: the Sunday following the full moon on or after March 21. **2.** SUNDAY OF EASTER FESTIVAL the Sunday on which Easter is celebrated **3.** EASTER WEEKEND the period from the Friday before Easter to the Monday after [Old English *Ēastre* < Germanic dawn-goddess whose festival was celebrated at the vernal equinox < Indo-European, "to shine"]

Eas·ter bas·ket *n* a basket given to children on Easter morning that traditionally contains jelly beans and egg- and rabbit-shaped chocolates

Eas·ter bun·ny (*plural* **Eas·ter bun·nies**) *n* an imaginary rabbit that traditionally leaves Easter baskets for children on Easter morning and hides colored Easter eggs for them to find

Eas·ter cac·tus *n* a cactus with flattened branches, cultivated as an ornamental plant. Flowers: large, red, in clusters. Native to: South America. Latin name: *Rhipsalidopsis gaertneri*. [Because it blooms in the northern hemisphere's spring]

Eas·ter Day *n* CALENDAR same as **Easter** (sense 2)

Eas·ter egg *n* **1.** a hen's egg that has been dyed, painted, or decorated for Easter, often hidden for children to find in an Easter egg hunt **2.** a secret message, graphic, animation, or sound effect hidden in a computer program and activated by a specific undocumented sequence of keystrokes. An Easter egg is typically intended as a harmless joke or as a way to display the credits of the program's development team.

Eas·ter Is·land /ée̱stər-/ island in the South Pacific Ocean belonging to Chile. It is noted for its huge carved stone heads and hieroglyphic tablets. Population: 2,095 (1989). Area: 45 sq. mi./117 sq. km. —**Eas·ter Is·land·er** *n*

Barnaby's
Easter Island

Eas·ter lil·y *n* **1.** a cultivated spring-flowering lily. Flowers: large, white. **2.** *US regional, Can* a trillium, which has a flower with three petals

REGIONAL NOTE Although the term ***Easter lily*** is used of various US plants, including the Madonna lily, the "trillium" sense characterizes the speech of Washington State.

eas·ter·ly /ée̱stərlee/ *adj* **1.** IN EAST situated in or toward the east **2.** BLOWING FROM EAST describes a wind that blows from the east ■ *n* (*plural* **-lies**) WIND FROM EAST a wind that blows from the east —**east·er·ly** *adv*

Eas·ter Mon·day *n* the Monday at the end of the Christian festival of Easter

east·ern /ée̱stərn/ *adj* **1.** SITUATED IN EAST situated in the east of a region or country **2.** TOWARD EAST facing the east **3.** another spelling of **Eastern** (sense 1) **4.** BLOWING FROM EAST describes a wind that blows from the east

East·ern *adj* **1.** relating or belonging to the countries of Asia as viewed from Europe or North America **2.** relating or belonging to the Eastern Orthodox Church

East·ern brown pel·i·can *n* a pelican, formerly considered endangered, with a white head and silver gray feathers covering the rest of its body. Native to: Atlantic and Gulf coasts of the United States. Latin name: *Pelecanus occidentalis*.

East·ern Cape /ée̱stərn-/ province in South Africa, in the southeastern part of the country. Capital: Bisho. Population: 6,436,756 (2001). Area: 65,475 sq. mi./169,580 sq. km.

East·ern Church *n* the Christian churches of Southwest Asia, North Africa, and Eastern Europe seen as a group, including the Coptic Church and the Orthodox Church

East·ern Em·pire *n* HIST same as **Byzantine Empire**

east·ern·er /ée̱stərnər/, **East·ern·er** *n* somebody who comes from the eastern part of a geographic area, especially somebody from the eastern coast of the United States

East·ern Eu·rope region comprising the countries of east and central Europe that had close ties with the former Soviet Union, e.g., Poland, the Czech Republic, Slovakia, Hungary, Romania, Bulgaria, Albania, and the former Yugoslavia

East·ern Eu·ro·pe·an Time *n* the standard time in the time zone centered on longitude 30° E, which includes Finland and Greece. It is two hours later than Universal Time.

East·ern Ghats /-gaats/ mountain range in southeastern India, running parallel to the Coromandel Coast, with an average elevation of 2,000 ft./600 m

East·ern gold·finch *n* BIRDS same as **American goldfinch**

east·ern hem·i·sphere *n* the half of the Earth that lies east of the Greenwich meridian and contains Asia, Australasia, and most of Europe and Africa

east·ern·most /ée̱stərn mōst/ *adj* **1.** farthest to the east **2.** located at the most eastern extreme of an area, region, or country

East·ern Or·tho·dox Church *n* CHR same as **Orthodox Church** (sense 2)

East·ern Stan·dard Time, East·ern Time *n* the standard time in the time zone centered on longitude 75° W, which includes the eastern part of North America. It is five hours later than Universal Time.

East·ern Trans·vaal former name for **Mpumalanga**

East·ern white pine *n* TREES same as **white pine**

Eas·ter Ris·ing *n* an armed rebellion against British rule that took place in Dublin, Ireland, on Easter Day in 1916

Eas·ter Sun·day *n* CALENDAR same as **Easter** (sense 2)

Eas·ter·tide /ée̱stər tīd/, **Eas·ter·time** /-tīm/ *n* the period around Easter [12C. < Old English *eastertīd*]

eas·ter·worm /ée̱stər wùrm/ *n regional* same as **earthworm** [Origin ?]

East Ger·man·ic *n* a group of extinct languages that were formerly spoken in parts of Eastern Europe. It is one of the three groups that form the Germanic branch of Indo-European. Gothic is the only language in this group that has any known written form. —**East Ger·man·ic** *adj*

East Ger·ma·ny ◆ **German Democratic Republic** —**East Ger·man** *n, adj*

East Green·wich town and summer resort in central Rhode Island, southwest of Providence. Population: 13,347 (2002 estimate).

East·hamp·ton /eest hámptən/ town in west central Massachusetts, on the Manhan River, northwest of Springfield and southwest of Northampton. Population: 16,180 (2002 estimate).

East Hart·ford town in central Connecticut, on the eastern bank of the Connecticut River, opposite Hartford. Population: 49,650 (2002 estimate).

East Ha·ven /-háyv'n/ town and summer resort in southern Connecticut, on Long Island Sound. Population: 28,563 (2002 estimate).

East In·di·a Com·pa·ny *n* a trading company established in England in 1600 to trade with the East Indies, and later with India, which it effectively governed for many years. Similar companies were also founded in the Netherlands and France.

East In·dies /-índeez/ collective name formerly applied to India, Southeast Asia, and the Malay Archipelago, especially Indonesia —**East In·di·an** *adj, n*

east·ing /ée̱sting/ *n* **1.** DISTANCE TRAVELED EAST the net distance eastward that a boat travels when making for the east **2.** PART OF MAP REFERENCE the first part of a map reference that shows how far east a point lies from a reference line running from north to south **3.** NORTH-SOUTH GRID LINE ON MAP a grid line on a map running north to south

East Kil·bride /-kil brīd/ manufacturing city in south central Scotland near Glasgow. Population: 70,422 (1991).

East Lan·sing city on the Red Cedar River in southern Michigan. It is home to Michigan State University. Population: 46,272 (2002 estimate).

East Lon·don city in southeastern South Africa, a seaport and holiday resort. Population: 102,325 (1991).

East Los An·ge·les town in southwestern California, adjoining the city of Los Angeles. Population: 126,379 (1996).

East·man /ée̱stmən/, **George** (1854–1932) US inventor and philanthropist. He perfected the box camera (1888), the first camera designed specifically for roll film.

East·man, Max Forrester (1883–1969) US writer and editor. His work concentrated on radical politics and he edited the revolutionary magazine *The Masses* (1913–18).

East Mo·line city in northwestern Illinois, directly east of the Mississippi River on the Illinois-Iowa border. Population: 21,279 (2002 estimate).

east-north·east *n* the direction or compass point midway between east and northeast ■ *adj, adv* in, from, facing, or toward the east-northeast —**east-north·east·er·ly** *adj, adv*

Eas·ton /ée̱stən/ **1.** town in east central Maryland, on the Delmarva Peninsula, west of the Choptank River. It is southeast of Annapolis across the Chesapeake Bay. Population: 12,180 (2002 estimate). **2.** city in southeastern Massachusetts, directly southwest of Brockton and north of Taunton. Population: 22,698 (2002 estimate).

East Or·ange city in northeastern New Jersey, northwest of Newark. Population: 69,750 (2002 estimate).

East Pak·i·stan one of the two areas that made up Pakistan following the partition of British India in 1947. It became the independent People's Republic of Bangladesh in 1971.

East Pe·or·i·a city in central Illinois, on the eastern bank of the Illinois River, east of Peoria. Population: 22,434 (2002 estimate).

East Prov·i·dence city in eastern Rhode Island, a suburb of Providence. Population: 49,658 (2002 estimate).

East Prus·sia former German province on the Baltic Sea that was divided between Poland and Russia in 1945 —**East Prus·sian** *n, adj*

East Ren·frew·shire /-rén froo sheer, -rén frooshər/ council area in central Scotland. Area: 67 sq. mi./173 sq. km.

East Rid·ing of York·shire /-rīding-/ council area in northeastern England, established in 1996, covering largely the same area as the historic division. Population: 594,440 (1996). Area: 704 sq. mi./1,819 sq. km.

East Riv·er strait in southeastern New York State, separating Manhattan Island from Long Island. Length: 15 mi./24 km.

East Saint Lou·is city in southwestern Illinois, east of the Mississippi River, across from St. Louis, Missouri. Population: 30,995 (2002 estimate).

East Sea ➧ **Japan, Sea of**

east-south·east *n* the direction or compass point midway between east and southeast ■ *adj, adv* in, from, facing, or toward the east-southeast —**east-south·east·er·ly** *adj, adv*

East Sus·sex county in southeastern England. Its administrative center is Lewes. Area: 693 sq. mi./1,795 sq. km.

East Ti·mor former name for **Timor-Leste**

east·ward /éestwərd/ *adj* **IN EAST** toward or in the east ■ *n* **POINT IN EAST** a direction toward the east or a point in the east ■ *adv also* **east·wards** /-wərdz/ **TOWARD EAST** in an easterly direction —**east·ward·ly** *adj, adv*

East·wood /éest wŏŏd/, **Clint** (*b.* 1930) US movie actor and director. He is known for his westerns such as *The Good, the Bad and the Ugly* (1966) and *Unforgiven* (1992) and for his action movies such as *Dirty Harry* (1971). He was the mayor of Carmel, California (1986–88). Born **Eastwood, Clinton, Jr.**

> "Every actor should direct at least once. It gives you a tolerance, an understanding of the problems involved in making a film. In fact every director should act."
> [Clint Eastwood, *Playboy*, February 1974]

east·worm /éest wùrm/ *n regional* ZOOL same as **earthworm**

eas·y /éezee/ *adj* (**-i·er, -i·est**) **1. NOT DIFFICULT** not causing problems or difficulty, or not requiring much effort, work, or thought ○ *Answer the easy questions first.* ○ *It's easy to see why they chose him.* ○ *always taking the easy way out* **2. RELAXED AND INFORMAL** relaxed, informal, and without awkwardness or self-consciousness, especially in social situations ○ *had an easy manner* **3. GOOD-NATURED** good-natured and tolerant ○ *an easy disposition* **4. FINANCIALLY PROSPEROUS** characterized by financial prosperity and security and the comfort and peace of mind that goes with them ○ *dreams of selling her invention and living the easy life* **5. NOT HARSH** not severe or harsh ○ *She's always claiming that easy discipline makes people soft.* **6. GULLIBLE** not difficult to catch, acquire, take advantage of, or exploit ○ *unscrupulous sellers looking for easy targets* **7. LOOSE** not tight or close-fitting ○ *jeans that are an easy fit* **8. UNHURRIED** comfortable, unhurried, and not too fast ○ *took an easy pace up the trail* **9. NOT STEEP** not steep or difficult to climb up or down ○ *It's an easy slope to the top.* **10. NOT ANXIOUS** free from unpleasant feelings such as anxiety, guilt, or worry ○ *Rest easy; we'll be there soon.* **11. LACKING PREFERENCES** having no strong preferences (*slang*) ○ *We can do either: I'm easy.* **12. OFFENSIVE TERM** an offensive term meaning sexually promiscuous or too willing to become sexually involved (*slang*) **13.** ECON **READILY OBTAINABLE** readily obtainable, because demand is lower than usual ○ *easy credit* **14.** ECON **MARKED BY LOW DEMAND AND PRICES** characterized by low demand or overproduction and hence low prices ○ *an easy market* ■ *adv* **1. WITHOUT DIFFICULTY OR EFFORT** without difficulty or the need for hard work ○ *Everything comes easy to her.* **2. AT LEAST** certainly not less than a particular amount ○ *cost $400 easy* [12C. < Old French *aisié*, past participle of *aisier* "put at ease" < *aise* "comfort"] —**eas·i·ness** *n* ◇ **go easy on somebody** to treat or deal with somebody gently, leniently, or without harsh criticism or reproach (*informal*) ◇ **go** *or* **take it easy on something** to avoid using, eating, or drinking too much of something (*informal*) ◇ **take it easy 1.** to relax, avoid effort, or not work too hard **2.** to calm down and avoid becoming upset or angry

SYNONYMS ***easy, simple, straightforward, uncomplicated***

CORE MEANING: not difficult to do or achieve

easy not causing problems or difficulty, or not requiring much effort, work, or thought ○ *a computer designed to be easy to use* ○ *There is no easy way to answer this question.* **simple** able to be done or understood quickly or with very little effort ○ *Selecting different fonts is a simple process.* ○ *It's a basic concept, simple to grasp.* **straightforward** not difficult to understand or carry out ○ *It was a perfectly straightforward job.* **uncomplicated** readily understood, or easy to deal with ○ *We have made the process as clear and uncomplicated as possible to encourage you to invest.*

eas·y-care *adj* describes fabrics or clothes that are easy to wash and iron

eas·y chair *n* a comfortably upholstered chair, especially an armchair

~~easyer~~ incorrect spelling of **easier**

eas·y·go·ing /éezee gṓ ing/ *adj* **1.** having a relaxed, informal, and tolerant attitude and reluctant to make heavy demands or enforce strict discipline on people **2.** unhurried and comfortable

eas·y lis·ten·ing *n* popular music in an undemanding style, usually with a lyrical or romantic tune, gentle rhythms, and soft soothing orchestration

~~easyly~~ incorrect spelling of **easily**

eas·y mon·ey *n* money made with little effort, and often dishonestly (*informal*)

eas·y street *n* a situation in which somebody has no worries, especially no financial worries (*informal*) ○ *For three successful years we were living on easy street.*

eas·y vir·tue *n* lax sexual morals and promiscuous sexual habits (*dated*)

eat /eet/ (**ate** /ayt/, **eat·en** /éet'n/, **eat·ing, eats**) *v* **1.** *vti* **CONSUME AS SUSTENANCE** to take something into the mouth as food and swallow it ○ *They hadn't eaten for three days.* **2.** *vi* **DINE** to have a meal ○ *Are you ready to eat?* **3.** *vt* **CONSUME SOMETHING USUALLY** to include something as a usual or fundamental part of a diet ○ *Do dogs eat fish?* **4.** *vti* **PENETRATE** to penetrate the surface of something by corrosive or mechanical action ○ *Rust had eaten into the chrome.* **5.** *vt* **BOTHER SOMEBODY** to bother or annoy somebody (*slang*) ○ *What's eating her?* **6.** *vt* **USE LARGE QUANTITY OF SOMETHING** to use or consume something in large quantities (*slang*) ○ *a big car that eats gas* **7.** *vt US* **ABSORB COST OF SOMETHING** to absorb the cost of something (*slang*) ○ *You're going to have to eat that traffic fine.* **8.** *vt* **TABOO TERM** a highly offensive term meaning to perform oral sex on somebody (*taboo*) **9.** *vt US* **VANQUISH** to attack and subdue a person or group, e.g., in a competition (*slang*) ○ *ate us in the second half* [Old English *etan* < Indo-European] —**eat·er** *n*

eat away *vt* to consume or destroy something gradually ○ *The surface has been eaten away in parts by acid rain.*

eat away at *vt* **1.** to worry or be a continual source of distress to somebody ○ *Guilt had been eating away at him all day.* **2.** to deplete or use up something gradually by taking small amounts regularly ○ *medical expenses eating away at our income*

eat in *vi* to consume a meal at home ○ *Would you rather eat in or go to a restaurant?*

eat into *vt* to use up part of something, especially in a wasteful or nonproductive way ○ *ate into their savings*

eat out *vi* to consume a meal away from home, usually in a restaurant or similar establishment ○ *Let's eat out tonight.*

eat up *v* **1.** *vti* **EAT COMPLETELY** to consume food completely or with great appetite **2.** *vt* **OBSESS SOMEBODY** to absorb or obsess somebody (*usually passive*) ○ *hard to avoid being eaten up by envy* **3.** *vt* **RECEIVE SOMETHING ENTHUSIASTICALLY** to receive something with enthusiasm or pleasure (*informal*) ○ *The reading public eats up everything she writes.* **4.** *vt* **CONSUME SOMETHING QUICKLY** to consume or deal with something quickly (*informal*) ○ *Commuting eats up my time.*

eat·a·ble /éetəb'l/ *adj* fit, suitable, or pleasant to eat ■ *n* something that is fit, suitable, or pleasant to eat (*informal; usually used in the plural*) ○ *If you organize the drinks, we'll bring the eatables.*

eat·en past participle of **eat**

eat·er·y /éetəree/ (*plural* **-ies**) *n* a place where food is cooked and sold (*informal*)

eat·ing /éeting/ *adj* **1. SUITABLE AS FOOD** suitable for human consumption, especially uncooked ○ *eating apples* **2. INVOLVING FOOD** relating to or used for the consumption of food ○ *eating utensils* ■ *n* **FOOD** something that can be eaten, especially of a particular quality ○ *These apples are good eating.*

eat·ing dis·or·der *n* an emotional disorder that manifests itself in an irrational craving for, or avoidance of, food, e.g., bulimia

eats /eets/ *npl* same as **food** (sense 2) (*slang*) ○ *What do you do for eats around here?* [Late 19C. < EAT]

Eau Claire /ō klér/ **1.** river in west central Wisconsin that flows into the Chippewa River at the town of Eau Claire. Length: 70 mi./113 km. **2.** city in western Wisconsin, at the confluence of the Chippewa and Eau Claire rivers. Population: 62,361 (2002 estimate).

eau de co·logne /ō də kə lṓn/ *n* COSMETICS same as **cologne** [Early 19C. < French, "water of Cologne"]

eau de nil /ō də néel/ *adj* of a pale yellowish green color [Late 19C. < French, "water of the Nile"] —**eau de nil** *n*

eau de toi·lette /ō də twaa lét/ *n* COSMETICS same as **toilet water** [< French]

eau de vie /ō də vée/ *n* a strong alcoholic liquor, especially brandy [Mid-18C. < French, "water of life"]

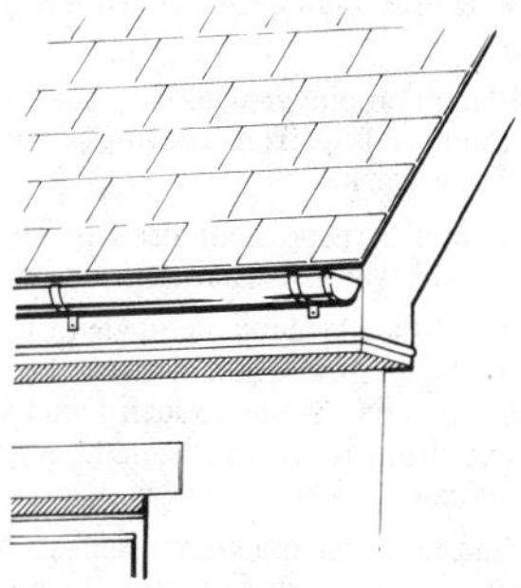

eaves

eaves /eevz/ *npl* the part of a roof that projects beyond the wall that supports it [Old English *efes* < Germanic]

eaves·drop /éevz dròp/ (**-dropped, -drop·ping, -drops**) *vi* to listen to a conversation without the speakers being aware of it [Early 17C. Probably back-formation < *eavesdropper* < obsolete *eavesdrop* "ground on which rainwater thrown off by eaves falls"; from standing in this area trying to hear private conversations] —**eaves·drop·per** *n*

eaves spout *n regional* a gutter, or the downspout of a gutter

REGIONAL NOTE See ***eaves trough.***

eaves trough *n US regional, Can* a gutter on a building

REGIONAL NOTE The Northern terms ***eaves trough*** and ***eaves spout*** extend from New England through the Midwest. In the earlier part of the 20th century, the

eaves trough form was general currency in New England and New York State, from Albany westward. At that time, ***eaves spout*** prevailed in the Western Reserve of Ohio. Indeed, that term was recorded for "rain gutter" as early as 1846 in Randolph County, North Carolina. Both terms have currency across the Western states to the Pacific coast, from Washington to California, where they survive as less common alternatives. Today they have been challenged or overtaken by the general currency terms *rain gutter* or *gutter* and *downspout*. In the Southern states, with the exception of the occasional occurrence of *trough*, the terms have been generally replaced by *gutter*.

E·ba·di /i baadee/, **Shirin** (*b.* 1947) Iranian lawyer, teacher, human rights activist, and one of the first woman judges in Iran. She is known for promoting peaceful, democratic solutions to social problems. She was awarded the Nobel Peace Prize (2003).

E·ban /éebən/, **Abba** (1915–2002) South African-born Israeli politician. He worked for the United Nations in Palestine (1946) and later held diplomatic and ministerial posts in Israel. These include being Israel's ambassador to the UN (1948–59) and to the United States (1950–59), and deputy prime minister (1963–66). Born **Solomon, Aubrey**

> "History teaches us that men and nations behave wisely once they have exhausted all other alternatives."
> [Abba Eban, *Speech, Times (London)*; December 17, 1970]

ebb /eb/ *vi* (**ebbed, ebb·ing, ebbs**) **1. RECEDE FROM SHORE** to recede from the land, as the tide falls (*refers to the sea or tide*) **2. DIMINISH** to diminish or lessen in intensity ○ *The pain gradually ebbed away.* ■ *n* **1. TIDAL MOVEMENT AWAY FROM LAND** the movement of a receding tide away from the land **2. DIMINUTION** a diminution or lessening in intensity ○ *the ebb and flow of the company's fortunes* [Old English *ebbian* < Germanic] ◇ **at a low ebb 1.** lacking hope and energy **2.** in a depleted condition

ebb tide *n* a receding tide, or the time when a tide recedes

EBCDIC /ébseedik/ *n* a binary computer character code, representing 256 standard letters, numbers, symbols, and control characters by means of eight binary digits. Full form **extended binary coded decimal interchange code**

e-beam *n* a stream of high-energy electrons. Use: food irradiation, sterilization, welding, imaging.

e-biz *n* BUSINESS same as **e-business** (sense 2) (*informal*)

e-block·er *n* an employer who uses special software to prevent employees from visiting particular websites while at work

E-boat *n* a fast torpedo boat used by the German navy in World War II [Abbreviation of ENEMY]

Eb·o·la /i bṓlə/, **Eb·o·la vi·rus** *n* a virus transmitted by blood and body fluids that causes the linings of bodily organs and vessels to leak blood and fluids, usually resulting in death [Late 20C. After the *Ebola* River, Democratic Republic of the Congo]

e-bomb, **E-bomb** *n* a weapon that creates a brief pulse of microwaves powerful enough to disable electronically operated systems, e.g., in computers, aircraft, and radar

eb·on /ébbən/ *n* COLORS same as **ebony** (sense 3) (*literary*) [14C. Via French < Greek *ebenos* < Semitic] —**eb·on** *adj*

E·bon·ics /i bónniks/ *n* LANG same as **African American Vernacular English** (*takes a singular verb*) [Late 20C. Blend of EBONY + PHONICS]

eb·on·ite /ébbə nīt/ *n* MANUF same as **vulcanite**

eb·on·ize /ébbə nīz/ (**-ized, -iz·ing, -iz·es**) *vt* to stain something black so that it resembles ebony

eb·on·y /ébbənee/ (*plural* **-ies**) *n* **1. DARK HARD WOOD** a hard blackish wood **2. ASIAN TREE** a tree that yields ebony. Native to: tropical Asia. Genus: *Diospyros.* **3. BROWNISH BLACK COLOR** black tinged with olive or brown [15C. < EBON, probably after IVORY] —**eb·on·y** *adj*

e-book *n* a battery-powered portable reading device displaying text on a high-resolution screen. E-books can be updated either from a book store or a website that sells digital texts.

E·bo·ra·cum /i báwrəkəm/ Roman name for the city of York, England

e·brac·te·ate /ee bráktee àyt/ *adj* describes plants that have no bracts [Mid-19C. < modern Latin *ebracteatus* "without bracts"]

Eb·ro /ébbrō/ river in northeastern Spain. It rises in the Cantabrian Mountains near Reinosa and flows to its delta on the Mediterranean coast, south of Tarragona. Length: 565 mi./910 km.

e·bul·lient /i búllyənt, i bóollyənt/ *adj* **1.** full of cheerful excitement or enthusiasm **2.** boiling or bubbling vigorously (*formal*) [Late 16C. < Latin *ebullient-*, present participle of *ebullire* "bubble out" < *bullire* "to bubble"] —**e·bul·lience** *n* —**e·bul·lient·ly** *adv*

e·bul·li·os·co·py /i bùllee óskəpee, i bóollee-/ *n* a process for determining the molecular weight of a substance by measuring the change it produces in the boiling point of a solution [Early 20C. < Latin *ebullire* (see EBULLIENT)] —**e·bul·li·o·s·cope** /i búllee ə skōp, i bóollee-/ *n*

eb·ul·li·tion /èbbə lísh'n/ *n* **1.** a state of bubbling up or boiling (*formal*) **2.** a sudden outbreak of violent emotion (*literary*) [14C. Via French < late Latin *ebullition-* < Latin *ebullire* (see EBULLIENT)]

e·bur·na·tion /èebər náysh'n, èbbər-/ *n* a hardening of the surfaces of bones in a joint as a result of the loss of their cartilage covering, occurring in such medical conditions as osteoarthritis [Mid-19C. < Latin *eburnus* "made of ivory" < *ebur* "ivory"]

e-busi·ness *n* **1.** a company that exists on the Internet, or the marketplace of such businesses collectively **2.** the conduct of business using Internet technology to create links between customers, suppliers, employees, and business partners (*used in e-commerce*)

EBV *abbr* MED Epstein-Barr virus

EB vi·rus *n* MED same as **Epstein-Barr virus**

EC *abbr* European Community

é·car·té[1] /ày kaar táy/ *n* a card game for two people played with 32 cards in which cards may be discarded in exchange for others [Early 19C. < French, literally "discarded"]

é·car·té[2] /ày kaar táy/ *n* a ballet position in which the arm and leg on one side of the body are extended [Early 20C. < French, literally "spread out"]

ECB *abbr* BANKING European Central Bank

ec·ce ho·mo /è chay hṓmō, èksee-, èkə-/ *n* a portrayal of Jesus Christ crowned with thorns [< Latin, literally "behold the man" (John 19:5)]

ec·cen·tric /ik séntrik, ek-/ *adj* **1. UNCONVENTIONAL** unconventional, especially in a whimsical way ○ *an eccentric mode of dress* **2.** TECH **AWAY FROM CENTER** away from the center or axis **3.** MATH **HAVING DIFFERENT CENTERS** describes circles with different centers **4.** ASTRON **ELLIPTICAL** describes an orbit that is elliptical rather than circular ■ *n* **1. UNCONVENTIONAL PERSON** an unconventional person who has unusual habits **2.** MECH ENG **MECHANICAL DEVICE** a mechanical device with an off-center axis of revolution that converts the rotary motion of one component of a mechanism to reciprocating motion in another [Mid-16C. < late Latin *eccentricus* < Greek *ekkentros* "out of center" < *kentron* (see CENTER)] —**ec·cen·tri·cal·ly** *adv*

ec·cen·tric·i·ty /èk sen tríssətee/ (*plural* **-ties**) *n* **1. ECCENTRIC QUALITY** a quality of being unconventional, especially in a whimsical way **2. ECCENTRIC ACT** an example or instance of unconventional whimsical behavior **3.** MECH ENG **DISTANCE BETWEEN MAIN AND SECONDARY AXIS** the distance between the axis about which an object rotates and a secondary axis on the object at which a device such as a rod could be attached **4.** ASTRON **DEVIATION** the deviation of the path of an orbiting body from a true circle **5.** MATH **GEOMETRIC CONSTANT** a constant that describes the shape of a conic section. It is equal to the ratio of the distance from a fixed point of any point on the curve to the distance of that point from the corresponding fixed straight line.

ec·chy·mo·sis /èki mṓssiss/ (*plural* **-mo·ses** /-mṓ seez/) *n* bleeding from broken blood vessels into surrounding tissue (*technical*) [Mid-16C. Via modern Latin < Greek *ekkhumōsis* < *ekkhumonothai* "pour out"]

eccl. *abbr* **1.** ecclesiastic **2.** ecclesiastical

Eccl. *abbr* BIBLE Ecclesiastes

eccles. *abbr* **1.** ecclesiastic **2.** ecclesiastical

Ec·cles /ék'lz/, **Sir John** (1903–97) Australian physiologist. He was joint winner of the Nobel Prize in physiology or medicine (1963) for his studies of the transmission of impulses between nerve cells. Full name **Eccles, Sir John Carew**

Eccles. *abbr* BIBLE Ecclesiastes

Ec·cle·si·as·tes /i kleezee áss teez/ *n* a book of the Bible that discusses the futility of life and how to be a God-fearing person. See table at **Bible**

ec·cle·si·as·tic /i kleezee ástik/ *n* a member of the clergy ■ *adj* CHR same as **ecclesiastical** [15C. Via French or ecclesiastical Latin < Greek *ekklēsiastikos* < *ekklēsiastēs* "member of an assembly" < *ekklēsia* "assembly, (later) church"]

ec·cle·si·as·ti·cal /i kleezee ástik'l/ *adj* belonging to or involving the Christian Church or clergy —**ec·cle·si·as·ti·cal·ly** *adv*

ec·cle·si·as·ti·cism /i kleezee ásti sìzzəm/ *n* **1.** excessive regard for the principles and customary practices of the Christian Church **2.** the principles or body of thought constituting organized Christianity

Ec·cle·si·as·ti·cus /i kleezee ástikəss/ *n* a book of teachings in the Roman Catholic Bible and the Protestant Apocrypha. See table at **Bible**

ec·cle·si·ol·o·gy /i kleezee óllәjee/ *n* **1.** the study of the history and theology of the Christian Church **2.** the study of the architecture and decoration of Christian churches

ec·crine /é krīn, ékrin/ *adj* describes sweat glands that are distributed all over the body, especially on the hands and feet, that do not secrete organic matter, and that are important in regulating body temperature [Mid-20C. < German *Ekkrin* < Greek *ekkrinein* "secrete"]

ec·dys·i·ast /ek dízzee àst/ *n* a performer of striptease (*humorous*) [Mid-20C. < ECDYSIS, after *gymnast*]

ec·dy·sis /ékdississ/ *n* the regular molting of an outer layer by arthropods such as insects and crustaceans, and by reptiles [Mid-19C. < Greek *ekdusis* < *ekduein* "put off, shed"]

ec·dy·sone /ékdi sṑn/ *n* a hormone that promotes metamorphosis and ecdysis in insects and crustaceans [Mid-20C. < ECDYSIS]

e·ce·sis /i seessiss/ *n* the successful establishment of a plant or animal species in a new environment [Early 20C. < Greek *oikēsis* "an inhabiting" < *oikos* "house"]

ECG *abbr* MED **1.** echocardiograph **2.** electrocardiogram **3.** electrocardiograph

E·che·ga·ray y Ei·za·guir·re /àychəgə rī ee àyssə geer ay, -gweer ay/, **José** (1832–1916) Spanish playwright and politician. As well as writing poetic dramas, which won him a shared Nobel Prize in 1904, he also held ministerial office (1868–74 and 1905).

ech·e·lon /éshə lòn/ *n* **1. LEVEL IN HIERARCHY** a level of authority or rank in an organization or system ○ *the lower echelons of society* **2. AIRCRAFT FORMATION WITH OFFSET POSITIONS** a group of aircraft flying in positions behind and to one side of the aircraft in front **3.** MIL **FORMATION WITH OFFSET POSITIONS** a formation in which individuals or units are positioned behind and to one side of those in front to give a stepped effect and allow each a clear view ahead **4.** PHYS **DEVICE FOR STUDYING SPECTRA** a series of glass plates of equal thickness arranged like steps, used in spectroscopy for studying the fine structure of spectral lines ■ *vti* (**-loned, -lon·ing, -lons**) **FORM ECHELON** to arrange something in or form an echelon [Late 18C. < French, "rung" < *échelle* "ladder" < Latin *scala* "stair"]

ORIGIN ***Echelon*** derives from French, and comes from the same Latin word as English *scale*[2].

ech·e·ve·ri·a /èchəvə ree ə/ *n* a low-growing cultivated plant with rosettes of fleshy leaves. Flowers: tubular, bell-shaped. Native to: tropical America. Genus: *Echeveria.* [Mid-19C. < modern Latin, after

Atanasio *Echeverría* (1766–1811), Mexican botanical illustrator]

e·chid·na /i kídnə/ *n* a spiny insect-eating mammal with a long snout and strong claws. Native to: Australia, New Guinea. Family: Tachyglossidae. [Mid-19C. Via modern Latin, "viper" < Greek *ekhidna* < *ekhis* "viper"]

echin- *prefix* same as **echino-** (*used before vowels*)

ech·i·na·ce·a /èkə náyssee ə/ *n* **1.** an herbal remedy prepared from the pulverized leaves and stems of purple coneflowers, thought to bolster the immune system **2.** PLANTS same as **coneflower** [< modern Latin < Greek *ekhinos* "hedgehog, sea urchin"]

ech·i·nate /ékə nàyt/, **ech·i·nat·ed** /-nàytəd/ *adj* describes plant and animal parts that have spines or similar outgrowths [Late 17C. < Latin *echinatus* < Greek *ekhinos* "hedgehog, sea urchin"]

e·chi·ni ARCHIT, MARINE BIOL plural of **echinus**

echino- *prefix* **1.** spiny ○ *echinoderm* **2.** echinoderm ○ *echinoid* [Via Latin < Greek *ekhinos* "hedgehog, sea urchin"]

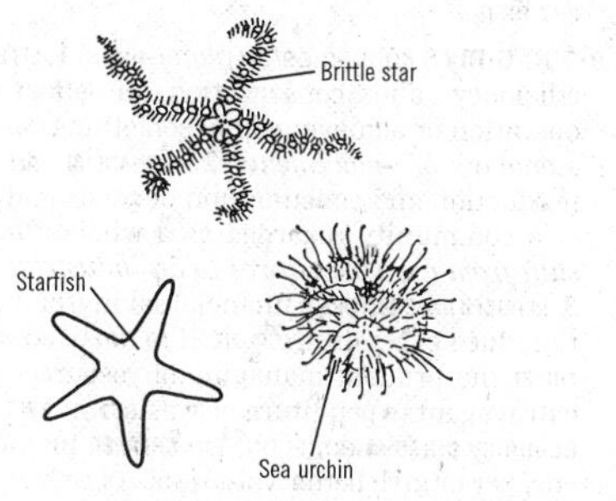

echinoderm

e·chi·no·derm /i kī́nə dùrm/ *n* an invertebrate ocean animal with a radially symmetrical body, tube feet, and a system of calcareous plates under the skin. Starfish, sea urchins, sea lilies, and sea cucumbers are echinoderms. Phylum: Echinodermata. [Mid-19C. < ECHINO- + Greek *derma* "skin"] —**e·chi·no·der·mal** /i kī̀nə dúrm'l/ *adj* —**e·chi·no·der·ma·tous** /-dúrmətəss/ *adj*

e·chi·noid /i kī́ nòyd, ékə nòyd/ *n* an invertebrate ocean animal with a hard ovoid body and movable spines. Sea urchins and sand dollars are echinoids. Class: Echinoidea. —**e·chi·noid** *adj*

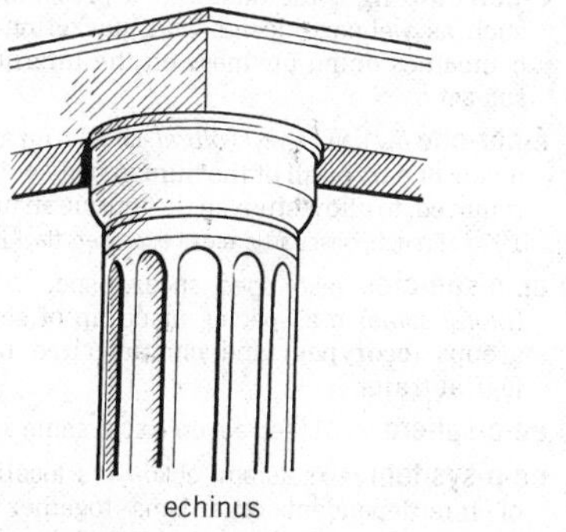
echinus

e·chi·nus /i kī́nəss/ (*plural* **-ni** /-nī/) *n* **1.** a rounded molding beneath the flat upper part (**abacus**) of a Doric or Tuscan column **2.** MARINE BIOL same as **sea urchin** [14C. < Latin (see ECHINO-)]

ech·o /ékō/ *n* (*plural* **-oes**) **1.** REPEATED SOUND the repetition of a sound caused by the reflection of sound waves from a surface **2.** SOMETHING SIMILAR something that repeats, imitates, or is reminiscent of something else ○ *Her songs found an echo in the hearts of thousands.* ○ *the current style with its echoes of the 1920s* **3.** PHYS RETURNED SIGNAL the signal reflected by an object struck by a radar transmission, or the image of this on a radar screen **4.** LITERAT REPETITION OF SOUNDS the repetition of sounds within a sequence of verse or prose **5.** MUSIC REPEATED MUSIC the repetition, usually more quietly, of a phrase or note in music **6.** MUSIC ELECTRONIC SOUND REPETITION the repetition of sound created electronically for effect or by accident **7.** MUSIC ORGAN CONTROL a device on some organs that gives the effect of an echo coming from a distance ■ *v* (**-oed, -o·ing, -oes**) **1.** *vt* REFLECT SOUND to make a sound repeat by the reflection of sound waves ○ *The surrounding peaks echoed the eagle's cry.* **2.** *vi* RESOUND to resound by the reflection of sound waves ○ *Their footsteps echoed down the tunnel.* **3.** *vi* BE FULL OF SOUND to be full of the repeated noise of a sound ○ *The auditorium echoed with cheering.* **4.** *vt* REPEAT SOMETHING SAID to repeat a statement or opinion, especially in agreement or imitation ○ *The completed report echoed the initial assessment.* **5.** *vt* IMITATE SOMETHING to imitate or be reminiscent of something else ○ *The building's design echoes the surrounding brownstone row houses.* **6.** *vt* COMPUT DISPLAY CHARACTER AS CHECK to return a character back to its source after a computer or communications device receives it, as an accuracy check. A common example is the display of a character on a computer monitor after it has been entered from a keyboard. [14C. Via French or Latin < Greek *ēkhō*] —**ech·o·ing·ly** *adv*

Ech·o *n* a code word for the letter "E," used in international radio communications

ech·o boom·er *n* SOC SCI same as **millennial** [After BABY BOOMER]

ech·o·car·di·o·gram /èkō kaárdee ə gràm/ *n* the visual record produced by an echocardiograph

ech·o·car·di·o·graph /èkō kaárdee ə gràf/ *n* an ultrasound device used to examine the working heart and display moving images of its action —**ech·o·car·di·o·graph·ic** /èkō kaardee ə gráffik/ *adj* —**ech·o·car·di·og·ra·phy** /èkō kaardee óggrəfee/ *n*

ech·o cham·ber *n* a room with sound-reflecting walls, used in making acoustic measurements or generating sound effects

ech·o·en·ceph·a·lo·gram /èkō en séffələ gràm/ *n* the visual record produced by an echoencephalograph

ech·o·en·ceph·a·lo·graph /èkō en séffələ gràf/ *n* an ultrasound device used to examine the structures of the brain —**ech·o·en·ceph·a·lo·graph·ic** /-sefələ gráffik/ *adj* —**ech·o·en·ceph·a·log·ra·phy** /èkō en sefə lóggrəfee/ *n*

ech·o·gram /ékō gràm/ *n* PHYS same as **sonogram**

e·chog·ra·phy /e kóggrəfee/ *n* PHYS same as **ultrasonography**

e·cho·ic /e kṓ ik/ *adj* **1.** resembling or relating to an echo **2.** LITERAT same as **onomatopoeic**

e·cho·ic mem·o·ry *n* the ability to remember and reproduce a sound in the two or three seconds after it is heard

ech·o·ism /ékō ìzzəm/ *n* **1.** a process by which the sound of a vowel changes to imitate the sound of a preceding vowel **2.** LITERAT same as **onomatopoeia**

ech·o·la·li·a /èkō láylee ə/ *n* the compulsive repetition of words spoken by somebody else, often a sign of a psychiatric disorder

ech·o·lo·ca·tion /èkō lō káysh'n/ *n* a means of locating an object based on an emitted sound and the reflection back from it, used naturally by some animals, e.g., bats, and electronically by humans

ech·o plate *n* an electromechanical device used in broadcasting or recording to create the effect of reverberation

ech·o·prax·i·a /èkō práksee ə/, **ech·o·prax·is** /-práksiss/ *n* the compulsive imitation of the actions of others, often a sign of a psychiatric disorder [Early 20C. < modern Latin < Greek *ēkhō* "echo" + *praxis* "action"]

ech·o quilt·ing *n* a quilting stitch that follows the outlines of an appliquéd design

ech·o sound·er *n* a device used to ascertain water depth or to locate underwater objects by measuring the time taken for emitted sound waves to return from either the bottom or the object

ech·o·vi·rus /ékō vī̀rəss/ *n* a virus found in the gastrointestinal tract, belonging to a group of retroviruses associated with intestinal and respiratory infections and meningitis [Mid-20C. Acronym < *enteric cytopathogenic human orphan*]

Eck·ert /ékərt/, **John Presper** (1919–95) US electronics engineer. He worked with John Mauchly on the ENIAC project (1943–46) that developed the first general-purpose electronic digital computer. They then set up a company (1946) that produced the first commercially available computer, UNIVAC.

Eck·hart /ék haart/, **Johannes** (1260?–1328?) German philosopher and Christian theologian. His writings set him among the founders of German philosophical mysticism. He was influenced both by the teachings of St. Thomas Aquinas and by the doctrines of neo-Platonism. Known as **Eckhart, Meister**

> "The greatest power available to man is not to use it."
> [Johannes Eckhart. Quoted in *The Jingle Bell Principle*, Miroslav Holub; 1992]

é·clair /ay klér, áy klèr/ *n* a long thin cream puff filled with whipped cream or custard and topped with chocolate frosting [Mid-19C. < French, literally "lightning"]

é·clair·cisse·ment /ay klèrseess maáN/ *n* a clearing up of something puzzling [Mid-17C. < French, "clearing up"]

e·clamp·si·a /i klámpsee ə/ *n* an illness that sometimes occurs during the later stages of pregnancy and involves high blood pressure and convulsions, sometimes followed by a coma [Mid-19C. Via modern Latin < French *éclampsie* < Greek *eklampsis* "sudden development" < *eklampein* "shine out"] —**e·clamp·tic** *adj*

é·clat /ay klaá, áy klaà/ *n* **1.** brilliant success ○ *The show came off with éclat.* **2.** ostentatious display (*literary*) [Late 17C. < French, literally "splinter, fragment"]

e·clec·tic /i kléktik/ *adj* **1.** made up of parts from various sources ○ *an eclectic collection of paintings* **2.** choosing what is best or preferred from a variety of sources or styles ○ *an eclectic taste in music* [Late 17C. < Greek *eklektikos* "picking out, selecting" < *eklegein* "pick out" < *legein* "choose"] —**e·clec·tic** *n* —**e·clec·ti·cal·ly** *adv*

e·clec·ti·cism /i klékti sìzzəm/ *n* the theory or use of an eclectic approach

e·clipse /i klíps/ *n* **1.** OBSCURING OF ASTRONOMICAL OBJECT the partial or complete hiding from view of an astronomical object, e.g., the Sun or Moon, when

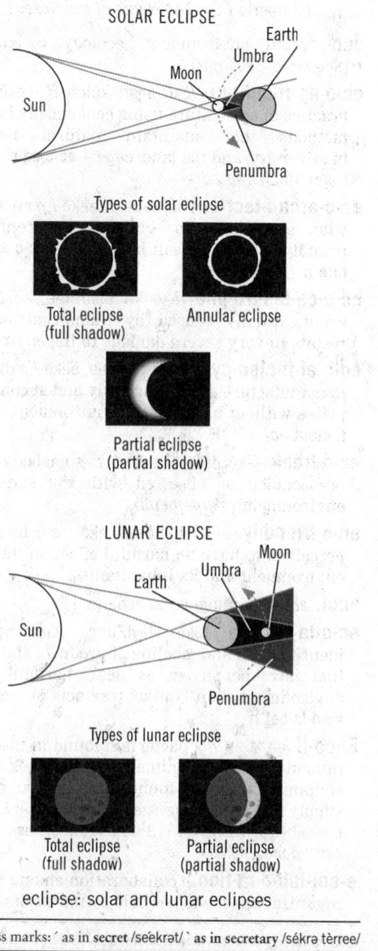

eclipse: solar and lunar eclipses

another astronomical object comes between it and the observer **2. LOSS OF LIGHT** a loss or blocking of light **3. DECLINE** a loss of status, power, or favor ○ *the eclipse of supply-side economics* ■ *vt* (**e·clipsed, e·clips·ing, e·clips·es**) **1. OUTDO SOMEBODY OR SOMETHING** to become more successful, powerful, or popular than something or somebody ○ *a performance that eclipsed all that went before* **2.** ASTRON **HIDE ASTRONOMICAL OBJECT** to cause a total or partial obscuring of another astronomical object **3. CAST SHADOW ON SOMETHING** to block the light falling on something, or cast a shadow on it [13C. Via French and Latin < Greek *ekleipsis* < *ekleipein* "no longer to appear or be present" < *leipein* "leave"]

e·clipse plum·age *n* dull feathers grown for a short period by some birds, especially male ducks, to replace the brightly colored breeding plumage

e·clips·ing bi·na·ry *n* a binary star whose orbit places it between its companion and the observer, resulting in an eclipse

e·clip·tic /i klíptik/ *n* the apparent path of the Sun's annual motion relative to the stars, shown as a circle passing through the center of the imaginary sphere (**celestial sphere**) containing all the astronomical objects. Eclipses of the Sun or Moon can occur only when the Moon crosses the ecliptic. ■ *adj* relating to, involving, or typical of an eclipse [14C. Via Latin < Greek *ekluptikos* < *ekleipein* (see ECLIPSE)]

ec·logue /ék làwg, -lòg/ *n* a pastoral poem, usually in the form of a dialogue between shepherds [15C. Via Latin < Greek *eklogē* "selection (of poems)" < *eklegein* (see ECLECTIC)]

e·clo·sion /i klṓzh'n/ *n* the emergence of an insect from its pupal case, or the hatching of a larva from an egg [Late 19C. < French *éclosion* < *éclore* "hatch, open" < Latin *excludere* "hatch"]

ECML *abbr* E-COMMERCE electronic commerce modeling language

Ec·o /ékō/, **Umberto** (*b.* 1932) Italian novelist and academic. His novels include *The Name of the Rose* (1981), *Foucault's Pendulum* (1988), and *The Island of the Day Before* (1995). He has written numerous critical works on literature and aesthetics.

> "The good of a book lies in being read."
> [Umberto Eco, *The Name of the Rose*; 1980]

eco- *prefix* environment, ecology ○ *ecofriendly* [Shortened < ECOLOGY]

ec·o·ag·ri·cul·ture /ékō ággri kùlchər/, ēēkō-/ *n* the practice of agriculture using ecologically beneficial methods that maintain natural resources, biodiversity, and the landscape —**ec·o·ag·ri·cul·tur·al** /-agri kúlchərəl/ *adj*

ec·o·arch·i·tect /ékō aárkə tekt, ēēkō-/ *n* an architect who specializes in building environmentally friendly energy-efficient buildings —**ec·o·arch·i·tec·ture** *n*

ec·o·ca·tas·tro·phe /ékō kə tástrəfee, ēēkō-/ *n* an event, usually caused by human actions, that results in very severe damage to the environment

ec·o·ef·fi·cien·cy /ékō i físh'n see, ēēkō-/ *n* the ability to manufacture goods efficiently and at competitive prices without harming the environment —**ec·o·ef·fi·cient** *adj*

ec·o·freak /ékō freēk, ēēkō-/ *n* somebody who is preoccupied or obsessed with the state of the environment (*slang insult*)

ec·o·friend·ly /ēēkō frèndlee, ékō-/ *adj* intended or perceived to have no harmful effect on the natural environment and its inhabitants

ecol. *abbr* **1.** ecological **2.** ecology

ec·o·la·bel·ing /ékō làyb'ling, ēēkō-/ *n* the identification and labeling of products and services that are perceived as less harmful to the environment than similar products or services —**ec·o·la·bel** *n*

E. co·li /ēē kṓ lī/ *n* a bacterium found in the colon of human beings and animals that becomes a serious contaminant when found in the food or water supply [Late 20C. Abbreviated < modern Latin *Escherichia coli*, after T. *Escherich* (1857–1911), German physician; *coli* "of the colon"]

e-col·lab·o·ra·tion *n* collaboration among people or organizations made possible by means of electronic technologies such as the Internet, video conferencing, and wireless devices

e·col·o·gy /i kólləjee/ *n* **1.** the study of the relationships between living organisms and their interactions with their natural or developed environment ○ *"A land ethic...should be as honest as Thoreau's Walden, and as comprehensive as the sensitive science of ecology."* (Stewart Udall, *The Quiet Crisis*; 1963) **2.** SOC SCI same as **human ecology** [Late 19C. < Greek *oikos* "house, habitation"] —**ec·o·log·i·cal** /èkə lṓjjik'l, ēēkə-/ *adj* —**ec·o·log·i·cal·ly** *adv* —**e·col·o·gist** *n*

econ. *abbr* **1.** economics **2.** economist **3.** economy

e·con·o·met·rics /i kònnə méttriks/ *n* the application of mathematical and statistical techniques to economic data and problems (*takes a singular verb*) —**e·con·o·met·ric** *adj* —**e·con·o·met·ri·cal·ly** *adv* —**e·con·o·me·tri·cian** /i kònnəmə trísh'n/ *n*

ec·o·nom·ic /èkə nómmik, ēēkə-/ *adj* **1. OF ECONOMY OR ECONOMICS** relating to economics, or the economy or business activities of a country ○ *economic policy* ○ *the economic outlook is bleak* **2. PROFITABLE** producing or capable of producing a satisfactory profit ○ *The planned expansion of the company is no longer an economic proposition.* **3. FINANCIAL** relating to or affecting material goods and financial resources ○ *There were economic benefits in delaying the sale.* **4.** same as **economical** (sense 4) [Late 16C. Directly or via French < Latin *oeconomicus* < Greek *oikonomikos* < *oikonomos* (see ECONOMY)]

USAGE **economic** or **economical**? The adjective ***economic*** denotes economics or the economy, and is concerned with aspects of the production, distribution, and consumption of goods and services: *a Nobel Laureate's economic theories.* The adjective ***economical***, on the other hand, has to do with the prudent management of resources and attempts to reduce expenditures: *It is much more economical to buy in bulk. Public transportation is economical, compared with hiring a limousine.* But the two adjectives can overlap in one sense, "efficient in terms of avoiding unnecessary expenditure": *an economical* [or *economic*] *use of electricity.*

---

ec·o·nom·i·cal /èkə nómmik'l, ēēkə-/ *adj* **1. RESOURCEFULLY FRUGAL** careful in making the best use of resources ○ *an economical cook* **2. INEXPENSIVE** costing relatively little in comparison with other things in the same class ○ *a home that's economical to run* **3. AVOIDING WASTE** efficient in terms of avoiding unnecessary waste ○ *provides an economic alternative to recycling* **4. EFFICIENT** efficient in terms of avoiding unnecessary expenditure of time or energy ○ *an economical gesture*

USAGE See ***economic.***

---

ec·o·nom·i·cal·ly /èkə nómmikəlee, ēēkə-/ *adv* **1. WITH REGARD TO ECONOMY OR ECONOMICS** with regard to economics, the economy of a country, or financial matters in general ○ *economically and socially developing societies* **2. PROFITABLY** in such a way as to produce a profit **3. FRUGALLY** in a thrifty or careful manner

ec·o·nom·ic de·ter·min·ism *n* the belief that the economic organization of a society determines the nature of all other aspects of its life

ec·o·nom·ic ge·og·ra·phy *n* a branch of geography that deals with the distribution and use of an area's economic resources

ec·o·nom·ic ge·ol·o·gy *n* the study of geologic deposits from the viewpoint of their value as resources

ec·o·nom·ic growth *n* growth in an economy as verified by recognized factors and indexes

ec·o·nom·ic in·di·ca·tor *n* a quantity expressed statistically and taken as a measure of an economic variable

ec·o·nom·ic mi·grant *n* a traveling worker who goes to an area where work or an easier life is available

ec·o·nom·ic pres·sure *n* the use of trade sanctions and other financial measures by one country or group of countries as a means of coercing another

ec·o·nom·ic rent *n* the payment received for a factor of production such as labor or machinery in excess of the amount needed to produce a good

ec·o·nom·ics /èkə nómmiks, ēēkə-/ *n* the study of the production, distribution, and consumption of goods and services (*takes a singular verb*) ■ *npl* the financial element of something (*takes a plural verb*) ○ *the economics of running a business* [Late 18C. Probably < French *économique*]

ec·o·nom·ic un·ion *n* a merging of the economies of two or more states to function as a unit that shares a common financial policy and currency

e·con·o·mism /i kónnə mìzzəm/ *n* **1.** the belief that economics is the most important element in a society **2.** the belief that bringing about an improvement in the living standards of its members is the chief goal of a political organization or labor union organization

e·con·o·mist /i kónnəmist/ *n* a student or expert in the field of economics

e·con·o·mize /i kónnə mīz/ (**-mized, -miz·ing, -miz·es**) *vi* to reduce expenditure, or use resources less wastefully ○ *We had to economize on fuel.* —**e·con·o·miz·er** *n*

e·con·o·my /i kónnəmee/ *n* (*plural* **-mies**) **1. EFFECTIVENESS** efficiency and conservation of effort in the operation or achievement of something ○ *a graceful economy of movement* **2. FINANCIAL AFFAIRS** the production and consumption of goods and services of a community regarded as a whole ○ *a gradual shift from an agricultural to an industrial economy* **3. REDUCED EXPENDITURE** a financial saving, or an attempt to reduce expenditure ○ *need to make economies* **4. THRIFT** the prudent managing of resources to avoid extravagant expenditure or waste **5.** TRAVEL same as **economy class** ■ *adj* ECON, FIN **CHEAPER** intended to be cheaper or give better value [15C. Directly or via French < Latin *oeconomia* < Greek *oikonomia* < *oikonomos* "steward of a household" < *oikos* "house" + *nemein* "manage"]

e·con·o·my class *n* a class of travel, especially on airlines, that is relatively low in price and carries the majority of passengers

e·con·o·my class syn·drome *n* thrombosis believed to be caused by a prolonged period of restricted movement and dehydration such as occurs during air travel

e·con·o·my drive *n* an organized attempt to reduce expenditure and waste

e·con·o·my of scale *n* a reduction in unit cost achieved by increasing the amount of production

e-con·sult·ing *n* the business of providing services such as webpage design and marketing advice to companies doing business on the Internet —**e-con·sult·ant** *n*

é·cor·ché /ày kawr sháy/ (*plural* **-chés**) *n* an anatomical model of part or all of the human body with the skin removed, to allow study of the muscle structure [Mid-19C. < French, past participle of *écorcher* "flay"]

ec·o·spe·cies /ékō speē sheez, -speē seez, ēēkō-/ (*plural same*) *n* a species made up of several subgroups (**ecotypes**) and characterized by its ecological traits

ec·o·sphere /ékō sfeēr, ēēkō-/ *n* ECOL same as **biosphere**

ec·o·sys·tem /ékō sìstəm, ēēkō-/ *n* a localized group of interdependent organisms together with the environment that they inhabit and depend on

ec·o·ter·ror·ism /ékō térrə rìzzəm, ēēkō-/ *n* **1.** the sabotage of the activities of people or corporations, e.g., industrial companies, considered to be polluting or destroying the natural environment **2.** deliberate destruction of the environment —**ec·o·ter·ror·ist** *n*

ec·o·tone /ékə tṑn, ēēkə-/ *n* a zone of transition between two different ecosystems, e.g., where the sea meets the land [Early 20C. < ECO- + Greek *tonos* "tension"]

ec·o·tour·ism /ékō toōr ìzzəm, ēēkō-/ *n* a form of tourism that strives to minimize ecological or other damage to areas visited for their natural or cultural interest

ec·o·tox·ic /ékō tóksik, ēēkō-/ *adj* causing severe damage to the environment —**ec·o·tox·ic·i·ty** /ékō tok síssətee, ēēkō-/ *n*

ec·o·tox·i·col·o·gy /ékō tòksi kóllәjee, éekō-/ *n* the study of how organisms are affected by chemicals released into the environment by human activities —**ec·o·tox·i·co·log·i·cal** /ékō toksikә lójjik'l, éekō-/ *adj*

ec·o·type /ékō tīp, éekō-/ *n* a subgroup of a species of organism whose members show genetically determined adaptations to some environmental conditions in their habitat

ec·o·war·ri·or /ékō wàwree әr, éekō-/ *n* an activist who takes direct, often unlawful, action on an environmental issue

ec·ru /é kroō, áy-/ *adj* of a pale brown color, like unbleached linen [Mid-19C. < French *écru* "raw, unbleached" < Latin *crudus* "raw"] —**ec·ru** *n*

~~**ecstacy**~~ incorrect spelling of **ecstasy**

ec·sta·sy /ékstәssee/ (*plural* **-sies**) *n* **1. INTENSE DELIGHT** a feeling of intense delight ○ *an evening of pure ecstasy* ○ *went into ecstasies over the photos* **2. INTENSE FEELING OR ACTIVITY** a feeling or activity characterized by its extreme intensity ○ *an ecstasy of remorse* **3.** *also* **Ec·sta·sy ILLEGAL RECREATIONAL DRUG** an illegal drug used as a stimulant and relaxer of inhibitions. Formula: $C_{11}H_{15}NO_2$. **4.** PSYCHOL **LOSS OF SELF-CONTROL** a mental state, usually caused by intense religious experience, sexual pleasure, or drugs, in which somebody is so dominated by an emotion that self-control and sometimes consciousness are lost [14C. Via French < Greek *ekstasis* < *existanai* "displace, drive out (of your mind)" < *histanai* "put"]

CULTURAL NOTE ***The Ecstasy of St. Theresa***, a sculpture (1645–52) by Italian artist Gianlorenzo Bernini. An altarpiece in the Cornaro Chapel in the church of Santa Maria Della Vittoria in Rome, it depicts a vision experienced by the Spanish saint Theresa during which an angel pierced her heart with a golden arrow, causing pain but also intense religious rapture.

ec·stat·ic /ik státtik, ek-/ *adj* **1. DELIGHTED** showing or feeling great pleasure or delight **2. DOMINATED BY EMOTION** completely dominated by an intense emotion ■ *n* **SOMEBODY SUBJECT TO TRANCES** somebody who experiences spells of intense emotion —**ec·stat·i·cal·ly** *adv*

ECT *abbr* MED electroconvulsive therapy

ec·ta·sia /ek táyzhә, -zhee ә/, **ec·ta·sis** /éktәssiss/ *n* a swelling or dilation of a part of the body (*technical*) [Late 19C. < modern Latin < Greek *ektasis* < *ekteinein* "stretch out"]

ecto- *prefix* external, outside ○ *ectotherm* [< Greek *ektos* < *ek* "out"]

ec·to·com·men·sal /éktә kә ménss'l/ *n* a plant or animal that lives on the outer surface or skin of another organism, causing its host no harm

ec·to·derm /éktә dùrm/ *n* the outermost of three cell layers of an embryo, from which the epidermis, nervous tissue, and sense organs develop

ec·to·gen·e·sis /èktō jénnәssiss/ *n* the development of an organism in an artificial environment, e.g., outside the body in which it would normally be found —**ec·tog·e·nous** /ek tójjәnәss/ *adj*

ec·to·mere /éktә meer/ *n* a cell (**blastomere**) produced during the division of a fertilized egg that develops with others into the outer cell layer (**ectoderm**) of an embryo

ec·to·morph /éktә màwrf/ *n* somebody who belongs to a physiological type that is tall with long lean limbs. ◊ **endomorph** (sense 1), **mesomorph** —**ec·to·mor·phic** /èktә máwrfik/ *adj*

-ectomy *suffix* surgical removal of a part of the body ○ *iridectomy* [< modern Latin *-ectomia* "cutting out" < Greek *ek-* "out" + *-tomia* (see -TOMY)]

ec·to·par·a·site /éktә párrә sīt/ *n* a parasite that lives on the outside of its host, e.g., on the skin or in the hair. Fleas are ectoparasites. —**ec·to·par·a·sit·ic** /-parә síttik/ *adj* —**ec·to·par·a·sit·ism** /-párrәsit ìzzәm/ *n*

ec·to·phyte /éktә fīt/ *n* a parasitic plant that lives on the outer surface of its host —**ec·to·phyt·ic** /èktә fíttik/ *adj*

ec·to·pi·a /ek tōpee ә/ *n* a change from the usual positioning of an organ or body part [Mid-19C. < modern Latin < Greek *ektopos* "out of place" < *topos* "place"]

ec·top·ic /ek tóppik/ *adj* describes an organ or body part occurring in an unusual position or form

ec·top·ic preg·nan·cy *n* the development of a fertilized egg outside the womb, e.g., in a fallopian tube

ec·to·plasm /éktә plàzzәm/ *n* **1.** the dense outer layer of the substance (**cytoplasm**) that surrounds the nucleus of a cell **2.** the substance believed by spiritualists to issue from a medium who is communicating with spirits —**ec·to·plas·mic** /èktә plázmik/ *adj*

ec·to·therm /éktә thùrm/ *n* an animal that maintains its body temperature by absorbing heat from its environment. All animals other than birds and mammals are ectotherms. ◊ **poikilotherm** [Mid-20C. < ECTO- + Greek *thermē* "heat"] —**ec·to·ther·mic** /èktә thúrmik/ *adj*

ec·to·troph·ic /èktә tróffik/ *adj* describes an association (**mycorrhiza**) between a fungus and the roots of a plant, in which the fungus obtains its nourishment by enveloping the roots in a sheath. ◊ **endotrophic**

é·cu /ay kyoō/ *n* a silver or gold coin of a number formerly used in France [Late 16C. < French, later form of Old French *escu* < Latin *scutum* "shield" (in their design)]

ECU /é koō/, **e·cu** *n* the official monetary unit of the European Union from 1979 to 1999. Full form **European Currency Unit**

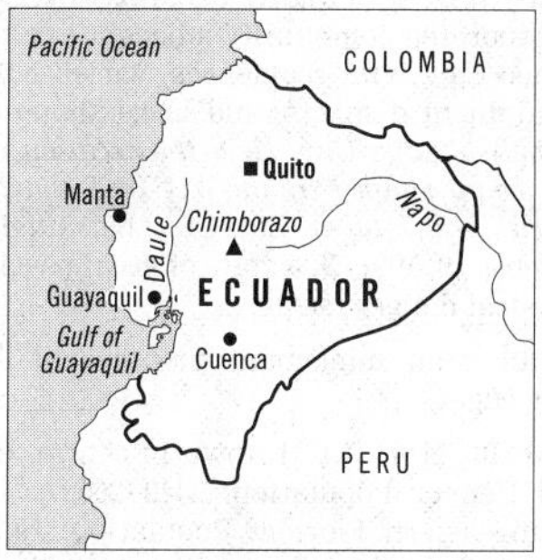

Ecuador

Ec·ua·dor /ékwә dàwr/ country in northwestern South America, bordered on the north by Colombia, on the south and east by Peru, and on the west by the Pacific Ocean. Language: Spanish. Currency: sucre. Capital: Quito. Population: 13,710,234 (2003). Area: 105,037 sq. mi./272,045 sq. km. Official name **Republic of Ecuador** —**Ec·ua·dor·i·an** /èkwә dáwree әn/ *n, adj*

ec·u·men·i·cal /èkyә ménnik'l/, **ec·u·men·ic** /-ménnik/ *adj* **1.** relating to, involving, or promoting the unity of different Christian churches and groups **2.** involving or promoting friendly relations between different religions [Late 16C. Via late Latin "general, universal" < Greek *oikoumenikos* < *oikoumenē* (*gē*) "inhabited (world)" < *oikos* "house"] —**ec·u·men·i·cal·ly** *adv*

ec·u·men·i·cal·ism *n* CHR same as **ecumenism**

ec·u·men·i·cal pa·tri·arch *n* the Archbishop of Constantinople, the most senior dignitary of the Eastern Church

ec·u·men·i·cism *n* CHR same as **ecumenism**

ec·u·men·ics /èkyә ménniks/ *n* the study of the goals and development of unity between different Christian churches and groups (*takes a singular verb*)

ec·u·me·nism /ékyәmә nìzzәm, i kyoōmә-/, **ec·u·men·i·cism** /èkyә ménni sìzzәm/, **ec·u·men·i·cal·ism** /èkyә ménnikә lìzzәm/ *n* a movement promoting unity between different Christian churches and groups

ec·ze·ma /éksәmә, égzәmә, ig zéemә/ *n* an inflammation of the skin characterized by reddening and itching and the formation of scaly or crusty patches that may leak fluid [Mid-18C. Via modern Latin < Greek *ekzema* "eruption" < *zein* "to boil" < Indo-European]

ed. *abbr* **1.** PUBL edited **2.** PUBL edition **3.** PUBL editor **4.** education

-ed[1] *suffix* **1.** used to form the past participle of regular verbs ○ *wasted* **2.** used to form the past tense of regular verbs ○ *nicked* ○ *landed* [Old English *-ed*, *-od* < Germanic]

-ed[2] *suffix* having, characterized by, like ○ *redheaded* ○ *bigoted* [Old English *-ede*, *-ode* < Germanic]

e·da·cious /i dáyshәss/ *adj* frequently consuming a great deal of food or drink (*formal*) [Early 19C. < Latin *edac-* "voracious, gluttonous" < *edere* "eat"] —**e·dac·i·ty** /i dássәtee/ *n*

E·dam[1] /éedәm, ée dàm/ *n* a mild Dutch cheese with a slightly rubbery texture, typically formed into balls covered with red wax [Early 19C. After EDAM[2]]

E·dam[2] /éedәm, ée dàm/ town in the western Netherlands, near Amsterdam, best known for the manufacture of the cheese to which it gives its name. Population: 7,153 (1994).

e·daph·ic /i dáffik/ *adj* describes the effect of soil characteristics, especially chemical or physical properties, on plants and animals [Late 19C. < Greek *edaphos* "floor, ground, soil"]

e·daph·ic cli·max *n* a stable ecological community that results from the content or properties of the soil rather than the climate

Ed·berg /éd bùrg/, **Stefan** (*b.* 1966) Swedish tennis player. He progressed from a junior grand slam in 1983 to winning Wimbledon and US Open singles championships (1988, 1990, 1991, and 1992).

ed·biz /éd bìz/ *n* the bureaucracies, textbook publishers, textbook authors, teachers, schools-of-education professors, teachers' unions, and lobbyists that, taken as whole, constitute the US public education sector (*slang*; *disapproving*) [20C. Combination of EDUCATION and *biz*, modeled on SHOWBIZ]

EDC *abbr* **1.** BUSINESS electronic data capture **2.** MIL European Defense Community

Ed·da /éddә/ *n* **1.** an early 13th-century collection of Old Norse poems **2.** a 13th-century collection compiled by Snorri Sturluson containing Norse myths, poems, and a treatise on poetry [Late 17C. Probably < Old Norse *óðr* "spirit, mind, passion, song, poetry"] —**Ed·dic** *adj*

Ed·ding·ton /éddingtәn/, **Sir Arthur** (1882–1944) British astronomer. He confirmed Einstein's general theory of relativity and wrote the popular *The Expanding Universe* (1933). Full name **Eddington, Sir Arthur Stanley**

> "We used to think that if we knew one, we knew two, because one and one are two. We are finding that we must learn a great deal more about 'and.'"
> [Sir Arthur Eddington. Quoted in *Mathematical Maxims and Minims*, N. Rose; 1988]

ed·do /éddō/ (*plural* **-does**) *n* PLANTS same as **taro** [Late 17C. Of W African origin]

ed·dy /éddee/ *n* (*plural* **-dies**) a movement in a flowing stream of liquid or gas in which the current doubles back to form a small whirl ■ *vi* (**-died, -dy·ing, -dies**) to flow contrary to the main current, or make something flow in this way ○ *He waded out, the stream eddying around his legs.* [15C. Origin ?]

Ed·dy /éddee/, **Mary Baker** (1821–1910) US religious leader. She founded the Church of Christ, Scientist, and the associated Christian Science movement, in Boston in 1879. Born **Baker, Mary**

> "Sin brought death, and death will disappear with the disappearance of sin."
> [Mary Baker Eddy, *Science and Health with Key to the Scriptures*; 1875]

ed·dy cur·rent *n* an electric current set up by an alternating magnetic field

Ed·dy·stone Rocks /éddistәn-/ dangerous rocks in the English Channel, near Plymouth, England. Four lighthouses have successively been built on or near the rocks since 1698.

edelweiss

e·del·weiss /áyd'l vìss, -wìss/ *n* a small plant with white woolly leaves. Flowers: small, yellow bracts surrounded by white modified leaves. Native to: Alps, mountains of Asia. Latin name: *Leontopodium alpinum*. [Mid-19C. < German, "noble white"]

e·de·ma /i deéma/ (*plural* **-mas** or **-ma·ta** /-mətə/), **oe·de·ma** *n* **1.** a buildup of excess serous fluid between tissue cells **2.** a swelling in a plant, chiefly caused by a buildup of excess water [15C. < Greek *oidēma* "swelling tumor" < *oidein* "swell"] —**e·dem·a·tous** /i démmətəss, i deémətəss/ *adj*

E·den /eéd'n/ *n* **1.** in the Bible, the garden where Adam and Eve first lived **2.** any place seen as being perfect, highly pleasing, or happy ○ *The first explorers saw America as an Eden.* —**E·den·ic** /ee dénnik/ *adj*

E·den /eéd'n/, **Anthony, 1st Earl of Avon** (1897–1977) British politician. He resigned as British foreign secretary in 1938 over his opposition to British appeasement of the Nazis, but served again as Winston Churchill's wartime foreign secretary (1940–45). He became prime minister in 1955 but resigned in 1957 after authorizing controversial military action against Egypt during the Suez Crisis of 1956. See table at **prime minister**

> "We must face the fact that the United Nations is not yet the international equivalent of our own legal system and the rule of law."
> [Anthony Eden, *Speech to the British Parliament, Hansard*; November 1, 1956]

E·den Prai·rie city on the Minnesota River in southeastern Minnesota. It is a suburb of Minneapolis. Population: 57,341 (2002 estimate).

e·den·tate /ee dén tàyt/ *n* a mammal with a placenta and few or no teeth, e.g., a sloth or armadillo. Native to: tropical America. Order: Edentata. ■ *adj* DENT same as **edentulous** (*technical*) [Early 19C. < Latin *edentatus* < *dent-* "tooth"]

e·den·tu·lous /ee dénchələss/, **e·den·tu·late** /-lət, -làyt/ *adj* with no teeth (*technical*) [Early 18C. < Latin *edentulus* < *dent-* "tooth"]

E·der·le /áydərlee/, **Gertrude Caroline** (1906–2003) US swimmer. She became the first woman to swim across the English Channel (1926).

Ed·gar /édgər/ *n* a small statuette awarded annually to authors for achievement in mystery fiction [Mid-20C. After *Edgar* Allan POE]

edge /ej/ *n* **1.** BORDER a line or area that is the outermost part or the part farthest away from the center of something ○ *a tablecloth with embroidered edges* **2.** PART ABOVE DROP the area where land suddenly falls away steeply ○ *the cliff edge* **3.** BRINK the point or moment just before a marked change or event ○ *on the edge of victory* **4.** MEETING SURFACES the line where two surfaces of something solid meet ○ *A cube has 6 faces and 12 edges.* **5.** SHARP SIDE the cutting side of a blade ○ *a razor's edge* **6.** SHARPNESS sharpness of a blade ○ *a knife with a fine edge* **7.** SHARP QUALITY a piercing, cutting, or wounding quality, e.g., of language or expression ○ *There was an unmistakable edge to her remarks.* **8.** VIGOR noticeable vigor and energy ○ *After the timeout there was a new edge to the team's play.* **9.** PROVOCATIVE RISKY MANNER an audacious, provocative, original quality or manner **10.** ADVANTAGE an advantage over somebody, e.g., a competitor (*informal*) ○ *Their strategy still has the edge over more recent approaches.* ■ *v* (**edged, edg·ing, edg·es**) **1.** *vt* ADD BORDER TO SOMETHING to add a border to something, especially a decorative one ○ *a handkerchief edged with lace* **2.** *vt* TRIM SOMETHING to cut, shape, or trim the border of something ○ *a tool for edging the lawn* **3.** *vt* SHARPEN SOMETHING to give a sharp edge to a blade **4.** *vi* MOVE GRADUALLY to move gradually sideways, or make something move in this direction by pushing it ○ *just room enough to edge through* **5.** *vt* SKIING LEAN ON PART OF SKI to put weight down on the outer or inner side of a ski so that its edge cuts into the snow ■ *adj* PROVOCATIVELY RISKY AND DARING operating or behaving in an intense, provocative, daring, and innovative fashion ○ *working in an edge business like cable television* [Old English *ecg* "corner, edge, sword" < Indo-European, "be sharp or pointed"] —**edg·er** *n* ◇ **live on the edge** to be habitually in highly stressful and demanding situations, often involving physical risk and danger ◇ **on edge** in an irritated or nervous state ◇ **take the edge off something 1.** to reduce the intensity or strength of something ○ *The snack took the edge off my hunger.* **2.** to do something that makes a situation or person less tense

edge in *vt US* to accommodate something with effort, e.g., because of lack of time, space, or opportunity ○ *usually manage to edge in a swim after work*

edge out *vt* **1.** to move somebody or something gradually out of position ○ *trying to edge him out of the presidency* **2.** to defeat a competitor by a narrow margin (*informal*) ○ *She was edged out of the championship.*

edge cit·y *n US* **1.** a highly urbanized, yet officially unincorporated community adjacent to a major established city, with residences, varied businesses, entertainment districts, and large shopping areas (*informal*) ○ *"Edge City ... is the creation of a new world, being shaped by the free in a constantly reinvented land."* (Joel Garreau, *Washington Post*; September 19, 1991) **2.** a state of great psychological or physical danger (*slang*)

edge tool *n* an implement that has at least one cutting edge

Edge·wa·ter /éj wàwtər/ **1.** town in central Colorado, west of Denver. Population: 5,449 (2002 estimate). **2.** town in eastern Florida. Population: 19,737 (2002 estimate). **3.** borough in northeastern New Jersey, situated on the Hudson River. Population: 7,906 (1998).

edge·wise /éj wìz/, **edge·ways** /-wàyz/ *adv, adj* with the edge or side leading or forward ○ *fit in edgewise* ○ *with an edgewise motion*

Edge·wood /éj wòod/ **1.** city in northern Kentucky. Population: 9,276 (2002 estimate). **2.** town in northeastern Maryland, northeast of Baltimore. Population: 23,903 (1990). **3.** borough in southwestern Pennsylvania, east of Pittsburgh. Population: 3,236 (2002 estimate).

Edge·worth /éj wùrth/, **Maria** (1767–1849) British novelist. Her best-known work, *Castle Rackrent* (1800), set in rural Ireland, influenced the development of the historical and regional novel in English.

edg·ing /éjjing/ *n* **1.** BORDER something used as a border or trim, usually for decoration or protection **2.** FORMING OF EDGE the formation of an edge ■ *adj* USED FOR EDGES used in forming an edge

edg·y /éjjee/ (**-i·er, -i·est**) *adj* **1.** ON EDGE nervous and irritable **2.** INTENSE having an intense or energetic quality or atmosphere ○ *an edgy neighborhood* **3.** TREND-SETTING stylish in an extreme or provocative way ○ *edgy clothes* —**edg·i·ly** *adv* —**edg·i·ness** *n*

edh /eth/, **eth** *n* a character (ð) used in the runic alphabet and in modern phonetics to represent the "th" sound that is found in the English words "this" and "other" [Mid-19C. < Danish]

EDI *abbr* E-COMMERCE electronic data interchange

ed·i·ble /éddəb'l/ *adj* suitable for eating by human beings [Early 17C. < Latin *edibilis* "eatable" < *edere* "eat"] —**ed·i·bil·i·ty** /éddə bíllətee/ *n* —**ed·i·ble·ness** *n*

ed·i·bles /éddəb'lz/ *npl* things to eat

e·dict /eé dìkt/ *n* **1.** a formal proclamation, especially one issued by a government, ruler, or other authority **2.** a formal or authoritative command [15C. < Latin *edictum* < past participle of *edicere* "proclaim" < *dicere* "say"]

ed·i·fi·ca·tion /èddəfi káysh'n/ *n* instruction or enlightenment, especially when it is morally or spiritually uplifting

ed·i·fice /éddəfiss/ *n* **1.** a building, especially a large or impressive one **2.** a large or complex structure or organization ○ *the edifice of government* [14C. Via French < Latin *aedificium* < *aedificare* "build" (see EDIFY)]

ed·i·fy /éddə fì/ (**-fied, -fy·ing, -fies**) *vt* to improve the morals or knowledge of somebody [14C. Via French *édifier* < Latin *aedificare* "build, construct, instruct" < *aedis* "building, temple" + *facere* "make"] —**ed·i·fi·er** *n*

ed·i·fy·ing /éddə fì ing/ *adj* providing morally useful knowledge or information

Ed·in·burgh /édd'nbərə, édd'n bùrrə/ capital city of Scotland, situated on the southern shore of the Firth of Forth. It is home to a cathedral, a castle, the royal Palace of Holyroodhouse, three universities, and the headquarters of the Scottish Parliament. Population: 418,748 (2001).

Ed·in·burgh, Duke of ➧ **Philip, Prince**

E·dir·ne /e deérnə/ city of northwestern Turkey, northwest of Istanbul. Population: 102,345 (1990).

Ed·i·son /éddiss'n/ township in central New Jersey, southwest of Elizabeth. Population: 99,925 (2002 estimate).

Library of Congress

Thomas Alva Edison

Ed·i·son, Thomas Alva (1847–1931) US inventor. He invented the light bulb (1879), the microphone (1877), the phonograph (1877), and many other devices.

> "Genius is one per cent inspiration and ninety-nine per cent perspiration."
> [Thomas Alva Edison. Quoted in *Harper's Magazine*; September 1932]

ed·it /éddit/ *vt* (**-it·ed, -it·ing, -its**) **1.** PREPARE TEXT FOR PUBLICATION to prepare a text for publication by correcting errors and ensuring clarity and accuracy **2.** DECIDE CONTENT OF PUBLICATION to be in overall charge of the publication of a newspaper, magazine, or broadcast program **3.** CUT MATERIAL to remove material from something such as a publication, broadcast item, recording, or movie, e.g., because it is lengthy or offensive ○ *was edited for bad language* ○ *has been edited down from 5 hours of live recording* ■ *n* TEXT PREPARATION the preparation of a text for publication or release, or a stage in this process ○ *Look out for any errors missed in the first edit.* [Late 18C. Back-formation < EDITOR] —**ed·it·ed** *adj*

edit out *vt* to delete an unwanted part of a text, movie, or recording ○ *Her walk-on part was eventually edited out.*

edit. *abbr* PUBL **1.** edited **2.** edition **3.** editor

e·di·tion /i dísh'n/ *n* **1.** PRINTED VERSION one version of a publication issued serially, periodically, or in multiple formats ○ *the morning edition of the newspaper* **2.** BROADCAST VERSION a version or installment of a broadcast for a particular time or purpose ○ *last week's edition of the show* **3.** PRINTED BATCH a batch of identical copies of a publication all printed at the same time **4.** BATCH OF ITEMS a batch or number of items all produced at the same time **5.** SIMILAR THING a version or copy of something ○ *a smaller edition of his father* [15C. < Latin *edition-* < *edit-*, past participle of *edere* "give out" < *dare* "give"]

e·di·ti·o prin·ceps /i dìshee ō prín sèps/ (*plural* **e·di-**

ti·o·nes prin·ci·pes /i dishee ōneez prínsə peez/) *n* the first printed edition of a piece of writing (*literary*) [< modern Latin, "first edition"]

ed·i·tor /édditər/ *n* **1.** PUBLISHING SUPERVISOR the overall supervisor of content for a book, newspaper, or magazine **2.** CHIEF JOURNALIST the supervisor of content in a part of a newspaper or magazine **3.** TEXT CORRECTOR somebody who prepares a text for publication **4.** CONTROLLER OF PROGRAM CONTENT somebody who supervises the content of a broadcast program **5.** MOVIE EDITOR somebody who prepares the final version of a movie, determining the length and the order of shots and scenes **6.** COMPUT same as **text editor** [Mid-17C. < late Latin, "producer, publisher" < Latin *edit-* (see EDITION)] —**ed·i·tor·ship** *n*

ed·i·to·ri·al /éddi táwree əl/ *adj* relating to, involving, or concerned with the editing of a text or broadcast ○ *editorial control* ○ *made editorial comments in the margins* ■ *n* an article in a newspaper or magazine that expresses the opinion of its editor or publisher —**ed·i·to·ri·al·ist** *n* —**ed·i·to·ri·al·ly** *adv*

ed·i·to·ri·al·ize /éddi táwree ə līz/ (**-ized, -iz·ing, -iz·es**) *vi* **1.** to express an opinion or view in an editorial in a publication **2.** to introduce personal opinions or views, especially inappropriately ○ *He couldn't resist the opportunity, when reporting on a burglary, to editorialize on security systems.*

ed·i·tor in chief (*plural* **ed·i·tors in chief**) *n* the overall editor of a publication, publishing house, or set of publications

e-di·vi·sion *n* a part of an organization set up to do business on the Internet

Ed.M. *abbr* EDUC Master of Education [Latin *Educationis Magister*]

Ed·monds /édməndz/ city in northwestern Washington State, north of Seattle. Population: 40,014 (2002 estimate).

Ed·mon·ton /édməntən/ capital city of Alberta, Canada, located in the center of the province, on the North Saskatchewan River. Population: 782,101 (2001).

Ed·mund /édmənd/, **St.** (841?–870) king of East Anglia. After defeat in battle by the Danes, he is said to have been martyred for refusing to deny Christianity.

Ed·mund I (921–946) king of the English. He made war on the Vikings, expelling them from England, and carried out legal reforms.

Ed·mund II (981?–1016) king of the English. He reigned for only a few months in 1016, until defeated in battle by Canute. He was allowed to keep control of the south of England, but died a month later. Known as **Edmund Ironside**

Ed·mund (of Ab·ing·don), St. (1175?–1240) English cleric and scholar. He was Archbishop of Canterbury from 1234 to 1240, and was canonized in about 1249.

Ed·munds·ton /édməndstən/ city in northwestern New Brunswick, Canada, across the US-Canadian border from Maine. Population: 14,867 (2001).

Ed·o /éddō/ (*plural same* or **-os**) *n* **1.** a member of a people living in the Benin region of Nigeria **2.** the language of the Edo people, belonging to the Kwa branch of the Niger-Congo family of languages. Native speakers: 1 million. [Late 19C. < Edo name for BENIN CITY] —**Ed·o** *adj*

E·dom /éedəm/ ancient kingdom situated south of the Dead Sea. According to the Bible, it was given to Esau.

E·dom·ite /éedə mīt/ *n* **1.** a member of an ancient people who lived in the kingdom of Edom in pre-Christian times **2.** an extinct language formerly spoken in the kingdom of Edom. It is one of the Semitic group of Afro-Asian languages, and is related to Hebrew. —**E·dom·it·ic** /éedə míttik/ *adj*

EDP *abbr* electronic data processing

e-dress *n* ONLINE same as **e-mail address**

EDT *abbr* **1.** TIME Eastern Daylight Time **2.** E-COMMERCE electronic depository transfer

EDTA *n* a colorless compound that reacts with metals. Use: food preservative, anticoagulant, treatment of lead poisoning. Formula: $C_{10}H_{16}N_2O_8$. Full form **ethylene diamine tetra-acetate**

edu *abbr* US educational organization (*used in Internet addresses*) See table at **domain name**

educ. *abbr* **1.** education **2.** educational

ed·u·cate /éjjə kàyt/ (**-cat·ed, -cat·ing, -cates**) *v* **1.** *vti* TEACH SOMEBODY to give knowledge to or develop the abilities of somebody by teaching ○ *had been educated at a public school* **2.** *vt* ARRANGE SCHOOLING FOR SOMEBODY to arrange or provide schooling for somebody ○ *They educated their daughters at home.* **3.** *vt* TRAIN SOMEBODY to train somebody, or improve somebody's awareness in a particular field ○ *need to educate people on environmentally safe procedures* **4.** *vt* DEVELOP SOMETHING to develop or improve a faculty or sense ○ *educate the palate* [15C. < Latin *educat-*, past participle of *educare* "bring up, rear," related to *educere* "lead out" < *ducere* "lead"] —**ed·u·ca·ble** /-kəb'l/ *adj* —**ed·u·ca·tive** *adj* —**ed·u·ca·tor·y** /éjjəkə tàwree/ *adj*

SYNONYMS See *teach*.

ed·u·cat·ed /éjjə kàytəd/ *adj* **1.** WELL TAUGHT having had a good education ○ *This is the writing of an educated person.* **2.** CULTURED showing good taste or refinement ○ *a quiet educated manner* **3.** KNOWLEDGEABLE having the benefit of experience or knowledge ○ *an educated opinion* ○ *cast an educated eye over the antiques*

ed·u·cat·ed guess *n* a guess that is based on a degree of experience, knowledge, or information

ed·u·ca·tion /èjjə káysh'n/ *n* **1.** EDUCATING the imparting and acquiring of knowledge through teaching and learning, especially at a school or similar institution ○ *"After all, what is education but a process by which a person begins to learn how to learn?"* (Peter Ustinov, *Dear Me*; 1977) **2.** KNOWLEDGE the knowledge or abilities gained through being educated **3.** INSTRUCTION training and instruction in a particular subject, e.g., health matters **4.** LEARNING EXPERIENCE an informative experience ○ *Spending a weekend in their house was a real education.* **5.** STUDY OF TEACHING the study of the theories and practices of teaching ○ *a degree in education* **6.** SYSTEM FOR EDUCATING PEOPLE the system of educating people in a community or society ○ *jobs in education*

ed·u·ca·tion·al /èjjə káyshən'l, -shnəl/ *adj* **1.** giving knowledge, instruction, or information **2.** relating to or concerned with education —**ed·u·ca·tion·al·ly** *adv*

ed·u·ca·tion·al·ist *n* EDUC same as **educationist**

ed·u·ca·tion·al psy·chol·o·gy *n* a branch of applied psychology that studies children in an educational setting and is concerned with the assessment of ability and aptitude and the evaluation of teaching and learning methods. Practitioners also deal with problems experienced by some children at school and in other learning situations. —**ed·u·ca·tion·al psy·chol·o·gist** *n*

ed·u·ca·tion·ist /èjjə káysh'nist/, **ed·u·ca·tion·al·ist** /-káyshən'list, -shnəlist/ *n* an expert in the theories or administration of education (*disapproving*)

ed·u·ca·tor /éjjə kàytər/ *n* **1.** a professional teacher **2.** an expert in the theories or administration of education

e·duce /i dooss/ (**e·duced, e·duc·ing, e·duc·es**) *vt* (*formal*) **1.** to elicit or derive something, e.g., a conclusion **2.** to make something latent develop or appear [15C. < Latin *educere* (see EDUCATE)]

e·duc·tion /i dúksh'n/ *n* **1.** the derivation or development of something, or something derived or developed (*formal*) **2.** the exhaust of an engine, especially an internal-combustion or steam engine (*technical*) [Mid-17C. < Latin *eduction-* < past participle of *educere* (see EDUCATE)]

e·dul·co·rate /i dúlkə ràyt/ (**-rat·ed, -rat·ing, -rates**) *vt* to remove soluble impurities from something by washing (*technical*) [Mid-17C. < medieval Latin *edulcorat-*, past participle of *edulcorare* "sweeten" < Latin *dulcis* "sweet"]

ed·u·tain·ment /èjjə táynmənt/ *n* television programs, computer software, or other media content intended both to entertain and educate users [Late 20C. Blend of EDUCATION + ENTERTAINMENT]

Ed·ward I /éddwərd/ (1239–1307) king of England. His reign (1272–1307) was marked by the development of parliamentary government and by conflicts with the Welsh, the Scots, and France. Known as **Edward Longshanks**

Ed·ward II (1284–1327) king of England. He was defeated by the Scots at the Battle of Bannockburn in 1314 and his reign (1307–27) ended in his forced abdication and murder. He was the first future king to be styled Prince of Wales (1301). Known as **Edward of Caernarvon**

Ed·ward III (1312–77) king of England. He ruled from 1327 until 1377. Through his mother, Isabella of France, he claimed the French throne, starting the Hundred Years' War.

Ed·ward IV (1442–83) king of England. As an outcome of the Wars of the Roses (1455–85), he became the first king of the House of York (1461–83). He was briefly deposed in 1470–71 by Lancastrian supporters of Henry VI.

Ed·ward V (1470–83?) king of England. On his accession in 1483, he was imprisoned by the future Richard III in the Tower of London and is thought to have been assassinated. With his brother he is often referred to as one of the "Princes in the Tower."

Ed·ward VI (1537–53) king of England. He was the son of Henry VIII and Jane Seymour. His reign (1547–53) saw a rapid advancement of Protestantism in England.

Ed·ward VII (1841–1910) king of the United Kingdom. Son of Queen Victoria, he was an avid sportsman and traveler, promoting good relations abroad. His reign (1901–10) is known as the Edwardian period.

Ed·ward VIII (1894–1972) king of the United Kingdom. His brief reign (January-December 1936) ended in abdication after the British Government refused to agree to his marrying US divorcée Wallis Simpson.

Ed·ward (the Black Prince) (1330–76) Prince of Wales. The eldest son of Edward III, he commanded English armies against France in the Hundred Years' War, distinguishing himself at Crécy (1346) and Poitiers (1356). He was the father of Richard II.

Ed·ward (the Con·fes·sor) (1002?–66) saint and king of the English (1042–66). He was canonized in 1161, but his reign was troubled by political conflict between Norman and English groups.

Ed·ward (the Mar·tyr) (963?–978) saint and king of the English (975–978). He was advised throughout his reign by the Archbishop of Canterbury, St. Dunstan. His assassination is thought to have been instigated by his stepmother Elfrida.

Ed·ward, Lake lake in the Great African Rift Valley straddling the border between the Democratic Republic of the Congo and Uganda. Area: 830 sq. mi./2,150 sq. km. Former name **Albert Edward Nyanza**

Ed·ward·i·an /ed wáwrdee ən, -waárdee-/ *adj* relating to, belonging to, or characteristic of British society during the reign of Edward VII in the first decade of the 20th century ■ *n* somebody who was alive or active during Edward VII's reign

Ed·wards /éddwərdz/, **Jonathan** (1703–58) American colonial theologian and cleric. A stern Calvinist, he was a leading figure in the religious revival known as the Great Awakening.

> "The soul of a natural man is the habitation of the devil."
> [Jonathan Edwards, "Sermon on Acts 16:29, 30" *The Works of President Edwards*; 1753]

ee *abbr* Estonia (*used in Internet addresses*) See table at **domain name**

-ee *suffix* **1.** somebody who receives or benefits from an action ○ *consignee* **2.** somebody who is the subject of a thing ○ *biographee* **3.** somebody who performs an action ○ *attendee* **4.** somebody connected with ○ *bargee* **5.** a kind of, especially a small one ○ *vestee* [Via Anglo-Norman < Latin *-atus*; sometimes Anglicization of French *-é*, or associated with -y[1]]

EEC *abbr* POL European Economic Community

EECA *abbr* E-COMMERCE end entity certificate authority

EEG *abbr* MED **1.** echoencephalograph **2.** electroencephalogram **3.** electroencephalograph

eel /eel/ (*plural* **eels** or *same*) *n* **1.** a fish with a long thin body resembling that of a snake, smooth skin without scales, and reduced fins. Freshwater eels typically migrate to the ocean to spawn. Order: Anguilliformes. **2.** any fish similar to a true eel in appearance, e.g., an electric eel [Old English *ǣl* < Germanic]

eel·grass /éel gràss/ *n* **1.** a perennial plant with long narrow dark green leaves that grows submerged in shallow seawater. Genus: *Zostera.* **2.** PLANTS same as **tape grass**

eel·pout /éel pòwt/ (*plural* **-pouts** or *same*) *n* **1.** an ocean fish with a long thin body like an eel. Family: Zoarcidae. **2.** FISH same as **burbot**

eel·worm /éel wùrm/ (*plural* **-worms** or *same*) *n* ZOOL same as **nematode**

e'en /een/ (*literary*) *n* evening ■ *adv* even

een·sy /éenssee/, **een·sy-ween·sy** /-wéenssee/ *adj* extremely small (*informal*) ○ *just an eensy bit more* [Alteration of TEENSY]

EENT *abbr* MED eye, ear, nose, and throat

EEO *abbr* SOC SCI, HR equal employment opportunity

EEOC *abbr US* GOV Equal Employment Opportunity Commission

e'er /er/ *adv* same as **ever** (*literary*) [Late 16C. Contraction]

-eer *suffix* **1.** a person engaged in or concerned with ○ *auctioneer* ○ *charioteer* **2.** a contemptible person or act ○ *profiteer* [Via French *-ier* < Latin *-arius*]

ee·rie /éeree/ (**-ri·er, -ri·est**) *adj* unnerving or unusual in a way that suggests a connection with the supernatural ○ *an eerie old house* [13C. Probably < Old English *earg* "cowardly"] —**ee·ri·ly** *adv* —**ee·ri·ness** *n*

~~**eery**~~ incorrect spelling of **eerie**

EET *abbr* TIME Eastern European Time

EFA *abbr* HEALTH essential fatty acid

ef·face /i fáyss/ (**-faced, -fac·ing, -fac·es**) *v* **1.** *vt* to remove or obliterate something by wearing away or rubbing out or some analogous process **2.** *vr* to act in an inconspicuous manner, especially because of shyness or modesty ○ *always effaces himself in company* [15C. < French *effacer* "wipe out, destroy" < *face* "face, appearance"] —**ef·face·a·ble** *adj* —**ef·face·ment** *n* —**ef·fac·er** *n*

ef·fect /i fékt/ *n* **1.** RESULT a change or changed state occurring as a direct result of action by somebody or something else ○ *showing the effects of prolonged malnutrition* **2.** POWER TO INFLUENCE success in bringing about a change in somebody or something, or the ability to achieve this ○ *I pleaded with them, but to no effect.* **3.** BEING IN FORCE OR OPERATION the state of being in force or operation, or of being the case, often from a particular point in time ○ *The new law doesn't come into effect until next month.* ○ *Much-needed changes were now being put into effect.* ○ *You have to wait for the medication to take effect.* **4.** IMPRESSION an impression produced in the mind of somebody who sees, hears, or reads something, especially one that is deliberately intended or engineered ○ *The overall effect of the new decor was light and spacious.* **5.** CAUSE OR PRODUCTION OF IMPRESSION something that produces an impression, or the process of causing a special feeling or impression ○ *a grand little speech made merely for effect* **6.** SPECIAL SOUND OR LIGHTING something done to produce a desired response or to add to the realism or theatricality of a movie, play, or broadcast (*often used in the plural*) **7.** SCIENTIFIC PHENOMENON a scientifically observed and described phenomenon ○ *the Doppler effect* ■ **ef·fects** *npl* BELONGINGS somebody's personal belongings, or the things that somebody is carrying about him or her (*formal*) ○ *Compensation will be paid for damage to or loss of personal effects.* ■ *vt* (**-fect·ed, -fect·ing, -fects**) DO OR MAKE SOMETHING to succeed in making or doing something ○ *They effected their escape through a rear window.* [14C. Directly or via French < Latin *effectus* "accomplish" < *facere* "make, do"] —**ef·fect·er** *n* —**ef·fect·i·ble** *adj* ◇ **in ef·fect** used to indicate that what is being said represents the truth of the matter, even though the words used may not be those that other people would choose ○ *In effect, this means that the program is shut down.* ◇ **to that ef·fect** having or indicating approximately the same meaning ○ *She objected and replied to that effect the next day.* ○ *The answer was "No" – or words to that effect.*

USAGE See *affect*[1].

ef·fec·tive /i féktiv/ *adj* **1.** PRODUCING RESULT causing a result, especially the desired or intended result ○ *an effective remedy for headaches* **2.** PRODUCING FAVORABLE IMPRESSION successful, especially in producing a strong or favorable impression on people ○ *effective use of imagery* **3.** ACTUAL actual or in practice, even if not officially or theoretically so ○ *was the effective leader during the premier's illness* **4.** OFFICIALLY IN FORCE officially in force, operative, or applicable ○ *a regulation effective as of next month* **5.** *US* TRUE AS RATE OF INTEREST describes the true or actual rate of interest that is paid on an interest-bearing account **6.** READY FOR ACTION fully equipped and ready for military action ■ *n* MILITARY PERSONNEL OR EQUIPMENT a soldier, military unit, or piece of military equipment that is ready for action —**ef·fec·tive·ness** *n* —**ef·fec·tiv·i·ty** /è fek tívvətee/ *n*

SYNONYMS ***effective, efficient, effectual, efficacious***

CORE MEANING: producing a result

effective causing a result, especially the desired or intended result ○ *an effective solution to the water supply problem* **efficient** capable of achieving the desired result with the minimum use of resources, time, and effort ○ *an efficient use of personnel* **effectual** (*formal*) potentially successful in producing a desired or intended result ○ *This idea exerts a direct and effectual influence on his thinking.* **efficacious** (*formal*) having the power to achieve a desired result, especially an improvement ○ *Diet may be as efficacious as medication in controlling the condition.*

ef·fec·tive·ly /i féktivlee/ *adv* **1.** in a way that produces a desired result **2.** in fact or in practical terms, though not usually directly or technically ○ *She was effectively barred from seeking another position with the firm.*

ef·fec·tor /i féktər/ *n* **1.** a body part, e.g., a muscle or organ, that is activated by a stimulus, particularly a nerve impulse **2.** a substance, procedure, or agent that produces an effect, e.g., a nerve ending activating a muscle or a molecule affecting enzyme activity

ef·fects-based *adj* describes a military operation or plan aimed at producing a specific outcome or event rather than destroying an enemy by attrition

ef·fec·tu·al /i fékchoo əl/ *adj* potentially successful in producing a desired or intended result (*formal*) [14C. < medieval Latin *effectualis* < Latin *effectus* (see EFFECT)] —**ef·fec·tu·al·i·ty** /i fèkchoo állətee/ *n* —**ef·fec·tu·al·ly** *adv* —**ef·fec·tu·al·ness** *n*

SYNONYMS See ***effective.***

ef·fec·tu·ate /i fékchoo àyt/ (**-at·ed, -at·ing, -ates**) *vt* to do, cause, or accomplish something (*formal*) [Late 16C. < medieval Latin *effectuat-*, past participle of *effectuare* < Latin *effectus* (see EFFECT)] —**ef·fec·tu·a·tion** /i fèkchoo áysh'n/ *n*

ef·fem·i·nate /i fémmənət/ *adj* **1.** an offensive term used to describe a man whose behavior, appearance, or speech is considered to be similar to that traditionally associated with women or girls **2.** weak through overrefinement or an absence of vigorous qualities (*disapproving*) [14C. < Latin *effeminatus*, past participle of *effeminare* "make feminine" < *femina* "woman"] —**ef·fem·i·na·cy** *n* —**ef·fem·i·nate·ly** *adv* —**ef·fem·i·nate·ness** *n*

ef·fen·di /i féndee/ (*plural* **-dis**) *n* **1.** in Southwest Asia and North Africa, an important or well-educated man **2.** a title of respect that is the Turkish equivalent of such English terms as "Mr." and "Sir" [Early 17C. Via Turkish *efendi* < modern Greek *aphentēs* < Greek *authentēs* "lord, master"]

ef·fer·ent /éffərənt/ *adj* describes nerves that carry impulses away from the brain or spinal cord, or blood vessels that carry blood away from an organ. ◊ **afferent** [Mid-19C. < Latin *efferent-*, present participle of *efferre* "bring out" < *ferre* "bring, carry"] —**ef·fer·ent** *n*

ef·fer·ent neu·ron *n* ANAT same as **motor neuron**

ef·fer·vesce /èffər véss/ (**-vesced, -vesc·ing, -vesc·es**) *vi* **1.** PRODUCE TINY GAS BUBBLES to give off gas in tiny bubbles, often producing foam and a hissing sound (*refers to liquids*) **2.** ESCAPE AS TINY BUBBLES to be given off by a liquid in the form of tiny bubbles (*refers to gases*) **3.** BE LIVELY to behave in a lively, high-spirited, or highly excited way [Early 18C. < Latin *effervescere* < *fervescere* "come to the boil" < *fervere* "be hot, boil"]

ef·fer·ves·cent /èffər véss'nt/ *adj* **1.** producing gas in the form of tiny bubbles **2.** behaving in a lively, high-spirited, or highly excited way —**ef·fer·ves·cence** *n* —**ef·fer·ves·cent·ly** *adv*

ef·fete /i féet/ *adj* **1.** characterized by decadence, overrefinement, or overindulgence **2.** lacking the strength or ability to get things done [Early 17C. < Latin *effetus* "worn out by bearing young" < *fetus* "breeding"] —**ef·fete·ly** *adv* —**ef·fete·ness** *n*

ef·fi·ca·cious /èffi káyshəss/ *adj* having the power to produce a desired result, especially an improvement (*formal*) [Early 16C. < Latin *efficac-* < *efficere* (see EFFECT)] —**ef·fi·ca·cious·ly** *adv* —**ef·fi·ca·cious·ness** *n*

SYNONYMS See ***effective.***

ef·fi·ca·cy /éffikəssee/, **ef·fi·cac·i·ty** /èffi kássətee/ *n* the ability to produce the desired result [Early 16C. < Latin *efficacia* < *efficac-* (see EFFICACIOUS)]

ef·fi·cien·cy /i físh'nsee/ (*plural* **-cies**) *n* **1.** COMPETENCE the ability to do something well or achieve a desired result without wasted energy or effort **2.** PRODUCTIVE USE OF RESOURCES the degree to which something is done well or without wasted energy **3.** MEASURE OF MACHINE'S ENERGY EFFECTIVENESS the ratio of the amount of energy used by a machine to the amount of work done by it. For example, the measurement of the amount of heat produced per unit of fuel when all of a fuel has been burned is a measure of a heating unit's efficiency. **4.** same as **efficiency apartment**

ef·fi·cien·cy a·part·ment *n* a small, usually furnished apartment consisting of one room that includes kitchen facilities and a separate bathroom

ef·fi·cient /i físh'nt/ *adj* **1.** performing tasks in an organized and capable way ○ *an efficient worker* **2.** capable of achieving the desired result with the minimum use of resources, time, and effort ○ *an efficient use of fuel* [14C. < Latin *efficient-*, present participle of *efficere* (see EFFECT)] —**ef·fi·cient·ly** *adv*

SYNONYMS See ***effective.***

ef·fi·cient cause *n* something that acts directly to initiate or produce changes in something else

ef·fi·gy /éffəjee/ (*plural* **-gies**) *n* **1.** a dummy, often roughly made and intentionally amusing or insulting, representing somebody disliked or despised **2.** a carved representation of a person, used as an architectural decoration or a monument [Mid-16C. < Latin *effigies* < *effingere* "portray, form" < *fingere* "fashion, shape"]

eff·ing /éffing/ *adj* an offensive term expressing strong feelings through its similarity in sound to other offensive terms (*slang*)

ef·flo·resce /èfflə réss/ (**-resced, -resc·ing, -resc·es**) *vi* **1.** BOT BLOOM to bloom or develop, like a flower coming into blossom (*literary*) **2.** CHEM LOSE WATER FROM CRYSTAL to lose water (**water of crystallization**) and become a powder (*refers to crystals*) **3.** CHEM BECOME ENCRUSTED WITH POWDERY DEPOSIT to become encrusted with a powdery deposit or crystals as a result of chemical change or the evaporation of a solution [Late 18C. < Latin *efflorescere* < *florescere* "come into flower" < *flos* "flower"]

ef·flo·res·cence /èfflə réss'nss/ *n* **1.** UNFOLDING AND FLOURISHING a process or time of development and unfolding (*literary*) **2.** CULMINATION the highest point of a process of development (*literary*) **3.** CHEM LOSS OF WATER FROM CRYSTAL the loss of water (**water of crystallization**) from a crystal **4.** GEOL POWDERY SUBSTANCE ON ROCK SURFACE a powdery substance that forms on the surface of rocks and brickwork —**ef·flo·res·cent** *adj*

ef·flu·ence /éffloo ənss/ *n* **1.** the act or process of flowing out **2.** something, often an immaterial substance or intangible influence, that flows out from a source (*literary*)

ef·flu·ent /éffloo ənt/ *n* **1.** liquid waste discharged from a sewage system, factory, nuclear power station, or other industrial plant **2.** a stream or river that flows out of a larger body of water such as a lake or a larger stream [15C. < Latin *effluent-*, present participle of *effluere* "flow out" < *fluere* "flow"]

ef·flu·vi·um /i flóovee əm, e-/ (*plural* **-vi·a** /-vee ə/) *n* an unpleasant smell or harmful fumes usually given off by waste or decaying matter (*often used in the plural*) [Mid-17C. < Latin < *effluere* (see EFFLUENT)] —**ef·flu·vi·al** *adj*

ef·flux /é flùks/ *n* **1.** INSTANCE OR ACT OF FLOWING OUT the act or process of flowing out **2.** SOMETHING THAT FLOWS OUT something that flows out of something else (*formal*) **3.** PASSING AWAY OF SOMETHING the passing away of something, e.g., time (*formal*) [Mid-16C. < medieval Latin *effluxus* < Latin *efflux-*, past participle of *effluere* (see EFFLUENT)] —**ef·flux·ion** /i flúksh'n, e-/ *n*

ef·fort /éffərt/ *n* **1.** ENERGY mental or physical energy that is exerted in order to achieve a purpose ○ *I wish they'd put a little more effort into it.* **2.** ACTIVITY DIRECTED TOWARD PARTICULAR END activities undertaken by a group of people in order to achieve a particular goal or overcome a particular difficulty ○ *the peacekeeping effort* **3.** ATTEMPT an attempt to do something, especially one that involves a considerable amount of exertion, work, or determination ○ *He made an effort to improve things.* **4.** RESULT OF ATTEMPT the result of a sincere attempt to do or make something ○ *It's not bad for a first effort.* **5.** PHYS APPLIED FORCE the force (**input force**) applied to a simple machine that produces an effect (**output force**) on the load [15C. < French < Old French *esforcier* "exert power" < Latin *fortis* "strong"] —**ef·fort·ful** *adj* —**ef·fort·ful·ly** *adv*

ef·fort·less /éffərtləss/ *adj* involving or appearing to involve little or no effort —**ef·fort·less·ly** *adv* —**ef·fort·less·ness** *n*

ef·front·er·y /ə frúntəree/ (*plural* **-ies**) *n* behavior or an attitude that is so bold or arrogant as to be insulting [Late 17C. < French *effronterie* < late Latin *effront-* "barefaced" < Latin *front-* "forehead"]

ef·ful·gence /i fóoljənss, -fúl-/ *n* brightness or a brilliant light radiating from something (*literary*) [Mid-17C. < late Latin *effulgentia* < Latin *effulgere* "shine brightly" < *fulgere* "shine"] —**ef·ful·gent** *adj*

ef·fuse (*formal*) *v* /i fyóoz/ (**-fused, -fus·ing, -fus·es**) **1.** *vti* POUR OUT to flow out, or make something such as a liquid, gas, or light flow out **2.** *vi* RADIATE to spread out or radiate from something ■ *adj* /i fyóoss/ BOT IRREGULARLY SPREAD tending to spread loosely or irregularly ○ *effuse lichens* [15C. < Latin *effus-*, past participle of *effundere* "pour out" < *fundere* "pour"]

ef·fu·sion /i fyóozh'n/ *n* **1.** UNRESTRAINED OUTPOURING OF FEELINGS an extravagant and sometimes excessive expression of feelings in speech or writing **2.** ACT OF POURING OUT the pouring out of something such as a liquid, gas, or light **3.** SOMETHING POURED OUT something such as a liquid, gas, or light that is poured out **4.** MED MOVEMENT OF BODY FLUIDS the oozing of fluids from blood or lymph vessels into body cavities or tissues as a result of inflammation **5.** MED FLUID IN BODY CAVITIES OR TISSUES lymph or blood present in body cavities or tissues as a result of inflammation **6.** PHYS FLOW OF GAS THROUGH SMALL OPENING the flow of a gas through a small aperture under pressure, particularly when the aperture is so small that the distance between molecules is significant

ef·fu·sive /i fyóossiv/ *adj* giving or involving an extravagant and sometimes excessive expression of feelings in speech or writing ○ *effusive thanks* —**ef·fu·sive·ly** *adv* —**ef·fu·sive·ness** *n*

~~eficient~~ incorrect spelling of **efficient**

Ef·ik /éffik/ (*plural same or* **-iks**) *n* **1.** a member of an Ibibio people who live in southeastern Nigeria **2.** a Niger-Congo language spoken in Nigeria. Native speakers: 4 million. [Mid-19C. < Efik] —**Ef·ik** *adj*

E-FIT /ée fit/ *tdmk* a trademark for software that creates a likeness of the face of a police suspect on the basis of a witness's description

EFL *abbr* EDUC English as a Foreign Language

EFM *abbr* MED electronic fetal monitor

EFRA /éffrə/ *abbr* E-COMMERCE electronic forms routing and approval

eft /eft/ *n* an immature newt in the terrestrial phase, usually reddish orange in color. Latin name: *Notophthalmus viridescens.* [Old English *efeta.* Origin ?]

EFT *abbr* E-COMMERCE electronic funds transfer

EFTA /éftə/ *abbr* ECON European Free Trade Association

EFTPOS /éft pòss/ *abbr* E-COMMERCE electronic funds transfer at point of sale

EFTS /efts/ *abbr* E-COMMERCE electronic funds transfer system

eg *abbr* Egypt (*used in Internet addresses*) See table at **domain name**

e.g. *abbr* for or as an example [Latin *exempli gratia*]

USAGE e.g. or **i.e.**? Do not confuse these two abbreviations, which mean different things and have different origins. The abbreviation ***e.g.***, meaning "for or as an example," comes from the Latin expression *exempli gratia* ("for example"). Use it when you want to list a few typical examples of the thing mentioned: *I have the laboratory equipment, e.g.,* [not *i.e.*] *beakers, thermometers, and test tubes, that we need.* Do not end a list that starts with ***e.g.*** with *etc.* The abbreviation ***i.e.***, meaning "that is, that is to say," comes from the Latin expression *id est* ("that is"). Use it when you want to give a more precise description of the thing mentioned: *The hearing, i.e.,* [not *e.g.*] *the preliminary hearing, is set for noon Friday.* Two periods punctuate ***e.g.*** and ***i.e.*** in US English, whereas they may be unpunctuated in British English. Surround these abbreviations with commas.

EGA *abbr* COMPUT enhanced graphics adapter

e·gad /i gád/ *interj* used to express surprise (*archaic*) [Late 17C. < alteration of AH + *gad*, euphemism for GOD]

e·gal·i·tar·i·an /i gàllə térree ən/ *adj* maintaining, relating to, or based on a belief that all people are, in principle, equal and should enjoy equal social, political, and economic rights and opportunities [Late 19C. < French *égalitaire* < *égal* "equal" < Latin *aequalis* (see EQUAL)] —**e·gal·i·tar·i·an** *n* —**e·gal·i·tar·i·an·ism** *n*

E·ge·ri·a /i jéeree ə/ *n* a woman who acts as a trusted adviser or loyal companion (*literary*) [Early 17C. After a Roman goddess and adviser to the early Roman king Numa Pompilius]

e·gest /i jést/ (**e·gest·ed, e·gest·ing, e·gests**) *vt* to excrete something from a cell or organism (*formal*) [15C. < Latin *egest-*, past participle of *egerere* "carry out" < *gerere* "carry"] —**e·ges·tion** *n* —**e·ges·tive** *adj*

e·ges·ta /i jéstə/ *npl* waste materials excreted from a cell or organism (*formal*) [Early 18C. < Latin, neuter plural of *egestus*, past participle of *egerere* "carry out" < *gerere* "carry"]

egg[1] /eg/ *n* **1.** ANIMAL REPRODUCTIVE STRUCTURE a large sex cell produced by birds, fish, insects, reptiles, and amphibians, enclosed in a protective covering that allows the fertilized embryo to continue developing outside the mother's body until it hatches **2.** HARD-SHELLED OBJECT LAID BY BIRD the hard-shelled oval object laid by hens and other birds **3.** BIRD'S EGG AS FOOD a bird's egg, especially a hen's egg, used as food ○ *scrambled eggs* **4.** SOMETHING SHAPED LIKE HEN'S EGG something that resembles a hen's egg in shape, e.g., a carved or molded ornament or an egg-shaped piece of candy **5.** REPRODUCTIVE CELL a female reproductive cell **6.** same as **person** (*informal dated*) ■ *vt US* THROW EGGS AT SOMEBODY to throw eggs at somebody or something, especially to express disapproval (*informal*) [14C. < Old Norse] —**egg·y** *adj* ◇ **have egg on your face** to be left in an embarrassing or humiliating situation, especially because of having made an obvious mistake ◇ **put all your eggs in one basket** to rely entirely on one person or thing, or on the outcome of one plan or course of action

egg[2] /eg/ (**egged, egg·ing, eggs**) *vt US* to incite somebody to do something ○ *was egged into making rash promises* [12C. < Old Norse *eggja* "urge" < Germanic]
egg on *vt* to encourage somebody to do something, especially something wrong, foolish, or dangerous ○ *She never would have done it herself, but the girls were egging her on.*

egg-and-dart *n* an ornamental pattern, commonly used in moldings on buildings or furniture, in which egg-shaped figures alternate with slightly tapered bars, arrows, or anchors

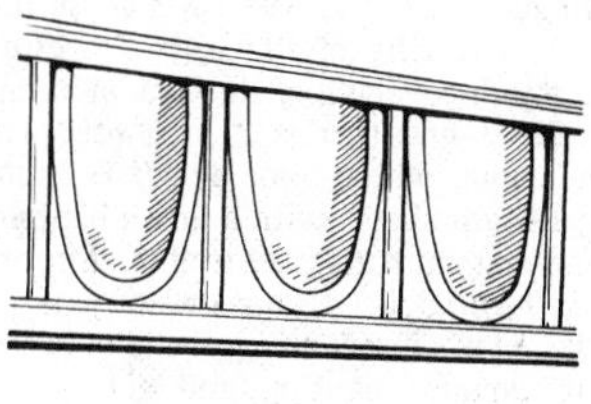

egg-and-dart

eg·gar /éggər/, **eg·ger** *n* a moth with a brown body and wings whose larvae spin egg-shaped cocoons in the branches of trees. Family: Lasiocampidae. [Early 18C. Probably because of its egg-shaped cocoon]

egg·beat·er /ég beètər/ *n* **1.** a kitchen utensil used for beating or blending ingredients such as raw eggs or cream, especially one with two sets of spaced vertical blades rotated by turning a handle **2.** a rotary-wing aircraft (*slang*)

egg bread *n regional* a soft cake made of cornmeal and eggs, baked in a pan

REGIONAL NOTE The term ***egg bread*** is used in the Carolinas and southern Maryland. Elsewhere in the South today, the term is frequently found in Upper and Lower Georgia, with its greatest use in Lower Alabama. See also ***batter bread.***

egg·case /ég kàyss/ *n* a protective covering containing eggs, especially one produced by organisms such as insects and mollusks

egg cream *n US* a carbonated drink made by mixing milk, chocolate syrup, and seltzer water

REGIONAL NOTE The soda-fountain drink ***egg cream*** is probably so called for its white froth, which resembles an egg white. This popular and inexpensive drink is associated with New York City residents, like the even more economical (and now dated) *two cents plain* (seltzer) and *chocolate phosphate* (seltzer and syrup). Of these, only the *chocolate phosphate* has much currency in other American cities.

egg·cup /ég kùp/ *n* a small bowl-shaped container, often with a short neck and wide base below the bowl, used for holding a boiled egg while it is being eaten

eg·ger *n* INSECTS another spelling of **eggar**

egg flip *n* a drink made by mixing beaten egg, sugar, and an alcoholic beverage, usually sherry, brandy, or port

egg foo yung /-foo yúng/ *n US* a Chinese dish that combines bean sprouts, onions, meat, and eggs. Can term **foo yung**

egg·head /ég hèd/ *n* an intellectual or bookish person (*informal*) [Early 20C. < the idea that a high forehead indicates brains] —**egg·head·ed** *adj*

egg·nog /ég nòg/ *n* a drink made of milk or cream, eggs, sugar, spice, and sometimes an alcoholic beverage such as brandy, bourbon, rye, or rum, traditionally served in the winter, especially at Christmas [Early 19C. < *nog*, a strong beer, origin ?]

egg·plant /ég plànt/ *n* **1.** FOOD VEGETABLE a large fruit with shiny purple skin, eaten cooked as a vegetable **2.** PLANT WITH LARGE EDIBLE FRUIT a plant of the nightshade family that produces eggplants. Native to: South and East Asia. Latin name: *Solanum melongena.* **3.** *US* COLORS BLACKISH PURPLE a very dark purple color. Can term **aubergine**

egg roll *n* a roughly cylindrical casing of thin egg dough enclosing a mixture of minced vegetables, common in Chinese-American cuisine

egg sac *n* the pouch or cocoon that a female spider spins to protect its eggs

eggs Ben·e·dict *n* ham and a poached egg in hollandaise sauce on a slice of toast or a split toasted

English muffin (*takes a singular or plural verb*) [Late 19C. Origin ?]

egg·shell /ég shèl/ *n* **1. HARD COVER OF EGG** the brittle protective covering of the egg of a bird, or the similar tough covering of the eggs of animals such as crocodiles and turtles **2. YELLOWISH WHITE COLOR** a pale yellowish white color ■ *adj* **1. SLIGHTLY GLOSSY** having a slight sheen, with a finish between that of gloss and mat paint **2. FRAGILE** fragile, thin, or delicate ○ *eggshell china* **3. YELLOWISH WHITE** pale yellowish white in color ◇ **walk on eggshells** to proceed with extreme wariness, caution, and tact

egg·shell blue *adj* having a delicate pale blue color —**egg·shell blue** *n*

egg tim·er *n* **1.** a small hourglass or clockwork device used to time the boiling of an egg **2.** COMPUT same as **hourglass** (sense 2)

egg tooth *n* a small projection on the beak of a baby bird or the upper jaw of a baby reptile, used to cut through the eggshell when hatching, and later shed

egg white *n* the clear viscous liquid found in an egg that turns solid and white when cooked

e·gis *n US* MYTHOL another spelling of **aegis**

e-giv·ing /ée gìvving/ *n* charitable giving carried out exclusively over the Internet by accessing a particular charity's website and using a credit card to make the donation (*informal*)

eg·lan·tine /égglən tīn, -teen/ (*plural* **-tines** or *same*) *n* PLANTS same as **sweetbriar** [14C. Via French *églantine* < Latin *aculentus* "spiny" < *acus* "needle"]

Eg·mont, Mount /ég mònt/ ➧ **Taranaki, Mount**

e·go /éegō, éggō/ (*plural* **e·gos**) *n* **1. SELF-ESTEEM** somebody's idea of his or her own importance or worth, usually of an appropriate level ○ *The climb left us with frostbite and bruised egos.* **2. INFLATED OPINION OF SELF** an exaggerated sense of self-importance and a feeling of superiority to other people **3. PSYCHOANAL PART OF MIND CONTAINING CONSCIOUSNESS** in Freudian psychology, one of three main divisions of the mind, containing consciousness and memory and involved with control, planning, and conforming to reality ○ *"The poor ego has a still harder time of it; it has to serve three harsh masters, and has to do its best to reconcile the claims and demands of all three."* (Sigmund Freud, *The Anatomy of the Mental Personality, Lecture 31*) ◊ **id**[1], **superego** **4. PHILOSOPHY SELF** the individual self, as distinct from the outside world and other selves [Early 19C. < Latin, "I"]

e·go·cen·tric /èegō séntrik, èggō-/ *adj* **1. SELFISH** interested only in personal needs and wants, and not caring about other people **2. LIMITED OR CONFINED IN OUTLOOK** limited in outlook or confined to things mainly relating to yourself **3. PHILOSOPHY CENTERED ON SELF** centered on the individual self, and considering it to be the hub of all experience —**e·go·cen·tric** *n* —**e·go·cen·tric·al·ly** *adv* —**e·go·cen·tric·i·ty** /èegō sen trìssətee, èggō-/ *n* —**e·go·cen·trism** *n*

e·go i·de·al *n* in Freudian psychoanalysis, a person's ideal image of what he or she could or should be, built up from observation of parents or other admired people

e·go·ism /éegō ìzzəm, éggō-/ *n* **1.** PHILOSOPHY the practice of making personal welfare and interests a primary or sole concern, sometimes at the expense of others **2.** ETHICS the ethical doctrine that the correct basis for morality is self-interest **3.** same as **egotism** (sense 1)

USAGE egoism or **egotism**? These two words, which are equally common, are often used interchangeably, though a distinction can be made. ***Egoism*** refers, in terms of philosophy, to theories in which self-interest is regarded as the principal motivating factor. And so an *egoist* believes an individual should seek as an end only his or her own welfare: *His conduct was characterized by ruthless egoism.* ***Egotism*** implies a vain self-absorption as a matter of behavior rather than an ethical principle, and an *egotist* is somebody who behaves in a selfish or self-centered way: *Her egotism makes her ignore other people's concerns.*

e·go·ist /éegō ist, éggō-/ *n* **1.** somebody who believes that the correct basis for morality is self-interest **2.** same as **egotist** (sense 1) —**e·go·is·tic** /èegō ístik, èggō-/ *adj* —**e·go·is·ti·cal** *adj* —**e·go·is·ti·cal·ly** *adv*

e·go·ma·ni·a /èegō máynee ə, èggō-/ *n* a dangerously obsessive preoccupation with the self —**e·go·ma·ni·ac** *n* —**e·go·ma·ni·a·cal** /-mə nī ək'l/ *adj* —**e·go·ma·ni·a·cal·ly** *adv*

e·go psy·chol·o·gy *n* a psychological theory based on the idea that the ego is an independent part of the personality that develops self-identity through conflict and its resolution over a lifetime

e·go surf (**e·go surfed, e·go surf·ing, e·go surfs**) *vi* to devote time looking for one's name or links to one's webpages, often to see who shares the same name —**e·go·surf·er** *n* —**e·go·surf·ing** *n*

e·go·tism /éegə tìzzəm, éggə-/ *n* **1. INFLATED SENSE OF SELF-IMPORTANCE** the possession of an exaggerated sense of self-importance and superiority to other people **2. PREOCCUPATION WITH SELF** the tendency to speak or write too much about yourself **3. SELFISHNESS** selfishness or self-centeredness [Early 18C. < EGO + *t* + -ISM]

USAGE See ***egoism***.

e·go·tist /éegətist, éggə-/ *n* **1.** somebody with an exaggerated sense of his or her own importance, especially somebody who tends to speak or write about himself or herself excessively **2.** somebody who is selfish or self-centered —**e·go·tis·tic** /èegə tístik, èggə-/ *adj* —**e·go·tis·ti·cal** *adj* —**e·go·tis·ti·cal·ly** *adv*

SYNONYMS See ***proud***.

e·go trip *n* a course of action or an experience that boosts somebody's sense of his or her own importance (*slang*) —**e·go-trip** *vi* —**e·go-trip·per** *n*

e·gre·gious /i gréejəss, -jee əss/ *adj* conspicuously bad or offensive (*formal*) ○ *an egregious violation of privacy* [Mid-16C. < Latin *egregius* "illustrious" < *greg-* "flock"] —**e·gre·gious·ly** *adv* —**e·gre·gious·ness** *n*

e·gress /ée grèss/ *n* **1. COMING OR GOING OUT** the act of coming or going out of a place (*formal*) **2. RIGHT TO LEAVE** the right to leave a place (*formal*) **3. EXIT** an exit from a place (*formal*) **4.** ASTRON same as **emersion** (sense 2) ■ *vt* (**e·gressed, e·gress·ing, e·gress·es**) *US* **LEAVE SOMEWHERE** to come or go out of a place (*formal*) [Mid-16C. < Latin *egressus* < *egredi* "go out" < *gradi* "proceed, step"]

e·gret /éegrət, éggrət/ *n* a small, mainly white heron that produces long drooping ornamental feathers on the lower part of the back at the start of the breeding season. Egrets' feathers were once popular as decorations for women's hats, so that the birds were hunted almost to extinction. Family: Ardeidae. [14C. Via Anglo-Norman *egrette* < Provençal *aigreta* < *aigron* "heron" < Germanic]

e·gu·si /e góossee/ *n* **1.** in West Africa, a mildly spiced stew that is thickened with blended melon seeds and contains fresh vegetable leaves and smoked fish **2.** the bean of a plant of the watermelon family, used in cooking. Latin name: *Citrullus lanatus.* [Early 20C. < Yoruba]

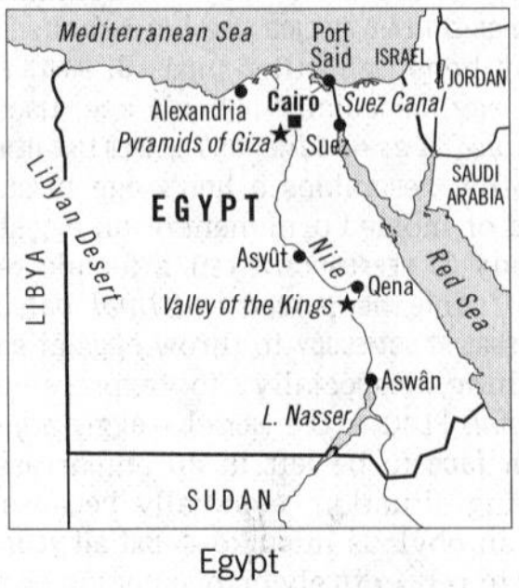

Egypt

E·gypt /éejipt/ country in northeastern Africa bordering the Mediterranean Sea and the Red Sea. It became a republic in 1952. Language: Arabic. Currency: Egyptian pound. Capital: Cairo. Population: 74,718,797 (2003). Area: 385,229 sq. mi./997,739 sq. km. Official name **Arab Republic of Egypt**

E·gyp·tian /i jípsh'n/ *n* **1. SOMEBODY FROM EGYPT** somebody who comes from Egypt **2. LANGUAGE OF ANCIENT EGYPT** the extinct Afro-Asiatic language of ancient Egypt that developed into Coptic around A.D. 200 **3. DIALECT OF ARABIC SPOKEN IN EGYPT** the dialect of Arabic spoken in modern Egypt. Native speakers: 65 million. —**E·gyp·tian** *adj*

E·gyp·tian plov·er *n* a black-and-gray bird with long legs that lives on sandy banks of rivers and lakes. Native to: Africa. Latin name: *Pluvianus aegyptius.*

E·gyp·tol·o·gy /èejip tóllajee/ *n* the study of the history, archaeology, culture, and language of ancient Egypt —**E·gyp·tol·o·gist** *n*

eh[1] /ay, e/ *interj* (*informal*) **1. PARDON ME?** used to ask somebody to repeat something **2. WHAT?** used to express surprise at something that has been said **3. ISN'T THAT SO?** used to invite somebody to respond to something that has been said, especially to agree with it or confirm that it is correct or accurately sums up a previous statement **4.** *Can* **ARE YOU WITH ME?** used to maintain or regain a listener's interest or to establish that what is being said is understood [Mid-16C. Natural exclamation]

eh[2] *abbr* Western Sahara (*used in Internet addresses*) See table at **domain name**

EHF *abbr* PHYS extremely high frequency

Ehr·lich /érlik, -likh/, **Paul** (1854–1915) German bacteriologist and immunologist. He shared a Nobel Prize in physiology or medicine (1908) for his work on immunology and also pioneered chemotherapy, developing a successful treatment for syphilis.

EHV *abbr* ELEC extra-high voltage

EIB *abbr* BANKING European Investment Bank

EIC *abbr US* ACCT earned income credit

Eich·en·dorff /īkən dàwrf, īkhən-/, **Joseph, Freiherr von** (1788–1857) German poet. His lyrical poems were set to music by Robert Schumann, Felix Mendelssohn, and others. He also wrote a popular novel, *Memoirs of a Good-for-Nothing* (1826). Full name **Eichendorff, Joseph Karl Benedikt von**

Eich·mann /īkmən, īkh maan/, **Adolf** (1906–62) German Nazi official and war criminal. Responsible for carrying out anti-Semitic policy during World War II, he was captured in Argentina in 1960 by Israeli agents, tried in Israel for crimes against humanity, and hanged two years later. Full name **Eichmann, Karl Adolf**

ei·co·sa·pen·taen·o·ic ac·id /īkō sə pèntənō ik-/ *n* BIOCHEM full form of **EPA**[1] [< Greek *eikosi* "twenty" + *penta-* "five"]

Eid /eed/, **Id** *n* **1.** ISLAM same as **Eid al-Adha** **2.** any Islamic religious festival [Late 17C. Via Arabic *'īd* "festival" < Aramaic]

Eid al-Ad·ha /èed al áadə/, **Eid ul-Ad·ha** /-ŏol-/ *n* an Islamic festival marking the sacrifice made by Abraham and the end of the annual pilgrimage to Mecca, traditionally celebrated by the sacrifice of sheep. Date: 10th-13th days of Dhu al-Hijjah. [< Arabic *'īd al-adha* "festival of the sacrifice"]

Eid al-Fitr /èed al féetər/, **Eid ul-Fitr** /-ŏol-/ *n* an Islamic festival marking the end of Ramadan. Date: 1st day of Shawwal. [< Arabic *'īd al-fitr* "festival of the breaking of the fast"]

ei·der /īdər/ (*plural* **-ders** or *same*), **ei·der duck** *n* a large sea duck, the male of which has distinctive black-and-white feathers. The female, the source of eiderdown, has mottled brown feathers. Native to: northern hemisphere. Genus: *Somateria.* [Late 17C. Via Icelandic *æður* < Old Norse *æðr*]

ei·der·down /īdər dòwn/ *n* **1.** the soft fluffy breast feathers of the female eider duck, used for stuffing pillows and bed coverings **2.** a warm bed covering in the form of a quilt or duvet stuffed with feathers

ei·der duck *n* BIRDS same as **eider**

ei·det·ic /ī déttik/ *adj* (*formal*) **1.** able to recall or reproduce things previously seen, with startling accuracy, clarity, and vividness ○ *an eidetic memory* **2.** recalled or reproduced with startling accuracy, clarity, and vividness ○ *eidetic images* [Early 20C. < Greek *eidētikos* < *eidos* "form"] —**ei·det·i·cal·ly** *adv*

ei·do·lon /ī dōlən/ (*plural* **-lons** or **-la** /-lə/) *n* (*literary*) **1.** a ghostly figure or image **2.** an idealized image of somebody or something [Mid-17C. < Greek *eidōlon* "idol" (see IDOL)]

Eid ul-Ad·ha *n* ISLAM same as **Eid al-Adha**

Eid ul-Fitr *n* ISLAM same as **Eid al-Fitr**

Eif·fel /ífʹl/, **Gustave** (1832–1923) French engineer. A specialist in metal structures, he is best known as the designer of the Eiffel Tower (1889) and architect of the inner structure of the Statue of Liberty (1885). Full name **Eiffel, Alexandre Gustave**

AKG London
Eiffel Tower, Paris, France

Eif·fel Tow·er *n* a 984-foot-/300-meter-high iron tower in central Paris, France. It was designed by Gustave Eiffel for the 1889 Paris Exposition.

ei·gen·val·ue /ígən vàllyoo/ *n* a value of a variable in an equation giving a solution that complies with the conditions that exist at a system's boundaries [Early 20C. < German *eigen* "own, particular" + VALUE, after German *Eigenwert*]

ei·gen·vec·tor /ígən vèktər/ *n* a vector whose value is not zero corresponding to a particular eigenvalue in the equation giving rise to the eigenvalue [Mid-20C. < German *Eigenvektor* < *eigen* "own, particular"]

Ei·ger /ígər/ mountain peak in the Bernese Alps, southeast of Bern, Switzerland. The north face of the mountain is notorious for the number of mountaineers who have died attempting to climb it. Height: 13,025 ft./3,970 m.

Eigg /eg/ island of the Inner Hebrides, northwestern Scotland. Population: 69 (1991). Area: 26 sq. mi./67 sq. km.

eight /ayt/ *n* **1. 8** the number 8 **2. SOMETHING WITH VALUE OF 8** something in a numbered series, e.g., a playing card, with a value of eight **3. GROUP OF 8** a group of eight objects or people **4. SOMETHING WITH 8 PARTS** something composed of eight parts or members, e.g., an eight-cylinder engine **5.** ROWING **CREW OF 8** a crew of eight rowers **6.** ROWING **RACING SHELL** a long narrow racing shell crewed by eight rowers ■ *symbol* **8 SYMBOL TO REPRESENT "ATE" OR "EAT"** a figure "8" used to replace "-ate-" or "-eat-" in words (*used in e-mails or text messages*) ○ *see U L8R* ○ *gr8* [Old English *e(a)hta* < Indo-European] —**eight** *adj, pron*

eight ball *n* **1.** in pool, the black ball, which has the number 8 on it **2.** a form of pool in which a player must pocket a given 7 of the 15 balls, and then pocket the eight ball, before his or her opponent does ◇ **behind the eight ball** in a difficult or awkward position (*slang*)

eight·een /ay téen/ *n* **1. 18** the number 18 **2. SOMETHING WITH VALUE OF 18** something in a numbered series with a value of 18 **3. GROUP OF 18** a group of 18 objects or people **4. 18** MOVIES, MEDIA **UK MOVIE RATING** in the United Kingdom, a rating given to movies and videos considered unsuitable for people under the age of 18 [Old English *e(a)hatēne* < Germanic] —**eight·een** *adj, pron*

eight·een·mo /ay téen mō/ (*plural* **-mos**) *n* PRINTING same as **octodecimo**

eight·eenth /ay téenth/ *n* **1.** one of 18 equal parts of something **2.** the birthday of somebody who has just reached 18 years of age —**eight·eenth** *adj, adv*

eight·een-wheel·er *n* a large truck, usually with 18 wheels, used to haul heavy loads. It consists of a cab and engine coupled to a large box-shaped container.

eight·fold /áyt fōld/ *adj* **1. MULTIPLYING BY 8** multiplying the original figure by eight **2. WITH 8 PARTS** consisting of eight parts ■ *adv* **BY 8** by eight, or to an amount eight times greater than the original

eight·fold path *n* in Buddhism, the means of achieving nirvana, emphasizing adherence to truth and moral values and comprising eight aspects. These are right understanding, right thought, right speech, right action, right livelihood, right effort, right mindfulness, and right concentration.

eighth /aytth, ayth/ *n* one of eight equal parts of something —**eighth** *adj, adv*

eighth note *n* a musical note with the time value of one-eighth of a whole note. It is written as a filled note-head with a stem and one tail.

eighth rest *n* in music, a rest equal in length to an eighth note

eight·i·eth /áytee əth/ *n* **1.** one of 80 equal parts of something **2.** the birthday of somebody who has just reached 80 years of age —**eight·i·eth** *adj, adv*

eight·pen·ny nail /áyt pènnee-/ *n* US a nail that is usually 2.5 in./6.4 cm in length

802.11 *n* a set of specifications for wireless local area networks

eight·vo /áyt vō/ (*plural* **-vos**) *n* PRINTING same as **octavo** (sense 2) [< *8vo*, written abbreviation of OCTAVO]

eight·y /áytee/ *n* (*plural* **-ies**) **1. 80** the number 80 **2. GROUP OF 80** a group of 80 objects or people ■ **eight·ies** *npl* **1. NUMBERS 80 TO 89** the numbers 80 to 89, especially as a range of Fahrenheit temperatures **2. YEARS FROM 80 TO 89** the years from 80 to 89 in a century **3. PERIOD FROM AGE 80 TO 89** the period of somebody's life from the age of 80 to 89 [13C. Shortening of Old English *hundeahtatig* < *hund-* "hundred" + *e(a)hta* "eight" + *-tig* "group of ten"] —**eight·y** *adj, pron*

eight·y-six (**eight·y-sixed, eight·y-six·ing, eight·y-six·es**), **86** (**86ed, 86ing, 86es**) *vt* (*slang*) **1.** to dispose of somebody or something **2.** US to refuse to serve somebody in a restaurant or bar [Mid-20C. Origin ?]

~~eigth~~ incorrect spelling of **eight**

Eijk·man /ík maan, áyk-/, **Christiaan** (1858–1930) Dutch physician. His research on diet-deficiency diseases, particularly beriberi, revealed the importance of vitamins in human physiology. He shared a Nobel Prize in physiology or medicine (1929).

EIL *abbr* English as an international language

Ei·lat /ay laat/, **E·lat** /ee laat/ seaport, tourist resort, and leading oil port in southern Israel, situated at the head of the Gulf of Aqaba. Population: 38,200 (1999).

-ein *suffix* a chemical compound related to one whose name ends in "-in" or "-ine" ○ *fluorescein* [Alteration of -IN]

Eind·ho·ven /índ hōv'n/ city and industrial center in the southern Netherlands. Population: 193,000 (1991).

Library of Congress
Albert Einstein

Ein·stein /ín stīn/, **Albert** (1879–1955) German-born US physicist. His theory of general relativity revolutionized scientific thought and served as the theoretical foundation for later exploitation of atomic energy. He won a Nobel Prize in physics in 1921 for his work explaining the photoelectric effect. He became a Swiss (1905) and later a US citizen (1940). In 1939 he joined other physicists in writing to President Franklin Roosevelt to warn him that Germany could possibly make an atomic bomb.

> "When you are courting a nice girl, an hour seems like a second. When you sit on a red-hot cinder a second seems like an hour. That's relativity."
> [Albert Einstein, *News Chronicle*; March 14, 1949]

> "Everything should be made as simple as possible, but not simpler."
> [Attributed to Albert Einstein]

ein·stein·i·um /ìn stínee əm/ *n* a synthetic radioactive element. Source: irradiated plutonium and other elements. Symbol **Es**. See table at **element** [After Albert EINSTEIN]

Eint·ho·ven /ínt hōv'n/, **Willem** (1860–1927) Dutch physiologist. His most important invention was the string galvanometer, which recorded precise measurements of electrical activity in the heart. He won a Nobel Prize in physiology or medicine (1924).

Ei·re /érrə, írə/ former name for **Ireland** (sense 2) (1937–49)

EISA *abbr* COMPUT extended industry standard architecture

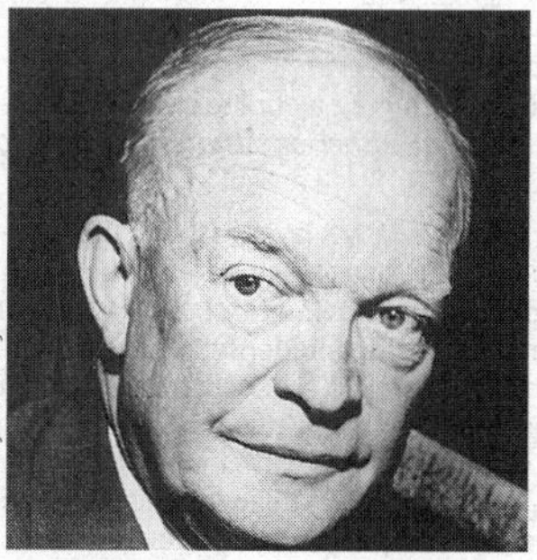
US Military Academy
Dwight D. Eisenhower

Ei·sen·how·er /íz'n hòwr/, **Dwight D.** (1890–1969) 34th president of the United States. He was supreme commander of Allied forces in Europe during World War II. As president, he adopted a policy of containing Communism throughout the world. Full name **Eisenhower, Dwight David**. Known as **Ike**

> "A people that values its privileges above its principles soon loses both."
> [Dwight D. Eisenhower, *Inaugural address, Washington, D.C.*; January 20, 1953]

Ei·sen·how·er, Mamie (1896–1979) US first lady (1953–61). She combined charity work with her keen interest in fashion. After her husband's death in 1969, she continued to live on the family farm in Pennsylvania. Full name **Eisenhower, Mamie Geneva Doud**

Ei·sen·stein /íz'n stīn/, **Sergey** (1898–1948) Soviet movie director. His innovative cinematographic techniques in movies such as *The Battleship Potemkin* (1925) made him a pioneering figure in the history of cinema.

eis·tedd·fod /ay stéth vòd, ī-/ (*plural* **-fods** or **-fod·au** /ày steth vód ī, ī-/) *n* a traditional Welsh festival at which competitions are held for performers and composers of music and poetry [Early 19C. < Welsh, "session, sitting"]

Eis·wein /íss wīn/ *n* a sweet white wine produced in Germany and Austria from grapes that have frozen on the vine, so that the sugar content is concentrated [Mid 20C. < German, "ice wine"]

ei·ther /éethər, íthər/ CORE MEANING: a grammatical word used to indicate or connect two situations, one of which may include or exclude the other ○ (adj) *It won't make much difference either way.* ○ (pron) *I refuse to meet either of them.* ○ (conj) *Either there's a problem or there isn't.* ○ (adv) *I don't want to go either.*

1. *adj, pron* **ONE OR OTHER** one or the other, when it does not matter which ○ (adj) *You can execute commands on either machine.* ○ (pron) *If either fell behind, the other would help him to catch up.* ○ (pron) *You can get this information from either of the two addressees.* ○ *either of them* **2.** *adj, pron* **INDICATES NEGATIVE** used to refer negatively to each of two situations, where the negative includes them both ○ (adj) *You cannot send e-mails to either address at the moment.* ○ (pron) *I'm not interested in either of them.* **3.** *adj* **BOTH** both of two things ○ *The red and yellow patches on either side of the Sun are radiation from the dust ring.* **4.** *conj* **INDICATES ALTERNATIVES** used preceding alternatives joined by "or" to indicate that there is a choice between two or more options

○ *Data sources may be either digital or analog.* **5.** *adv* **INDICATES CONNECTION** used in a negative statement that indicates a connection or a partial agreement with a previous statement (*at the end of a second statement*) ○ *You won't find the conditions exactly spartan, but don't expect luxury hotels either.* [Old English *ǣger,* contraction of *ǣg(e)hwæer* < Germanic, "always each of two"]

USAGE Singular or plural after **either**? ***Either*** is normally used with a singular verb: *Has either of you been to Paris? Either Lee or David is responsible.* Informally, however, the plural is used when the choices are regarded collectively rather than individually, and it is quite natural to say *Have either of you been to Paris?,* which permits the possibility that both the people addressed have done so. When ***either...or...*** occurs with a mixture of singular and plural subjects, the verb traditionally agrees with the subject that is closer to it: *Either Lee or his parents are at home.*

ei·ther-or *adj* offering a choice strictly limited to two options ○ *It's an either-or situation – either you accept or you refuse.*

e·jac·u·late *v* /i jákyə làyt/ (**-lat·ed, -lat·ing, -lates**) **1.** *vti* **EJECT SEMEN DURING ORGASM** to eject semen from the penis during orgasm **2.** *vt* **EXCLAIM SOMETHING SUDDENLY** to exclaim something suddenly and usually forcefully (*literary*) ■ *n* /i jákyələt/ **EJACULATED SEMEN** semen that has been ejected from the penis during orgasm [Late 16C. < Latin *ejaculat-,* past participle of *ejaculari* "throw out" < *jacere* "throw"] —**e·jac·u·la·tion** /i jàkyə láysh'n/ *n* —**e·jac·u·la·to·ry** /i jákyələ tàwree/ *adj*

e·ject /i jékt/ (**e·ject·ed, e·ject·ing, e·jects**) *v* **1.** *vt* **PUSH SOMETHING OUT WITH FORCE** to cause something to burst out from something else with considerable force **2.** *vt* **COMPEL SOMEBODY TO LEAVE** to force somebody to leave a place or give up a position, e.g., a job or membership ○ *They were forcibly ejected from the meeting.* **3.** *vi* AVIAT **LEAVE AIRCRAFT IN ESCAPE DEVICE** to escape from an aircraft in an emergency by means of an ejection seat or special capsule **4.** *vt* LAW **EVICT SOMEBODY** to remove somebody, especially a tenant, from a property by taking legal action **5.** *vt* SPORTS **DISMISS SOMEBODY FROM GAME** to dismiss a player from a game or competition for breaking the rules, e.g., in soccer, rugby, or hockey [15C. < Latin *eject-,* past participle of *e(j)icere* < *jacere* "throw"] —**e·ject·a·ble** *adj* —**e·jec·tion** /i jéksh'n/ *n* —**e·jec·tive** *adj*

e·jec·ta /i jéktə/ *n* substances ejected from something, especially the material thrown out by a volcanic eruption or from a star (*formal; takes a singular or plural verb*) [Late 19C. < Latin, neuter plural of past participle of *e(j)icere* (see EJECT)]

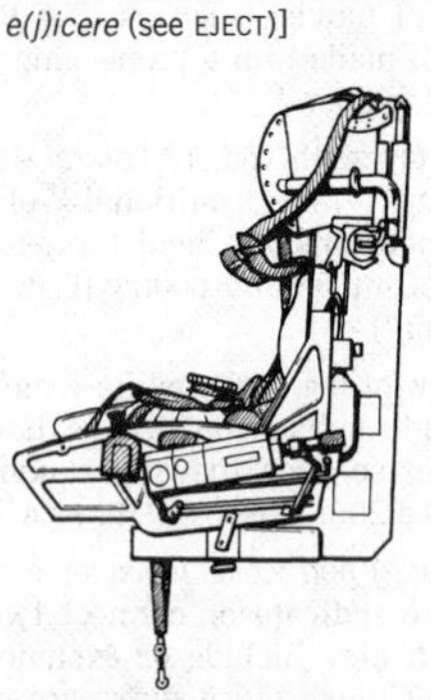

ejection seat

e·jec·tion seat *n* a seat in the cockpit of an aircraft that in an emergency propels the occupant clear of the craft by means of a rocket or explosive device

e·ject·ment /i jéktmənt/ *n* **1.** the act or process of ejecting somebody or something, or of being ejected from somewhere (*formal*) **2.** a legal action brought by somebody to recover possession of land that is being held by somebody else

e·jec·tor /i jéktər/ *n* **1.** a device for ejecting something from something else, especially a mechanism for ejecting an empty cartridge or shell from a gun **2.** a jet pump device that uses water, steam, or air to remove a gas, fluid, or powder from a space

e·jec·tor seat *n UK* AVIAT same as **ejection seat**

e·ji·do /e hée dō/ (*plural* **-dos**) *n Hispanic* in Mexico, an area of farmland held in communal ownership but divided into separate family plots [Late 19C. < Mexican Spanish, "common land" < Latin *exitus* (see EXIT); because located on the road leading out of a village]

eke /eek/ (**eked, ek·ing, ekes**) [Old English *ēacan, ēacian* "increase, add" < Germanic]

eke out *vt* **1. MAKE SOMETHING LAST WITH SPARING USE** to make a supply of something last by using it as slowly and economically as possible **2. SUPPLEMENT SOMETHING INSUFFICIENT OR INADEQUATE** to supplement something that is insufficient or inadequate, usually with difficulty and by hard work **3. GET SOMETHING ONLY WITH EFFORT** to manage to achieve something but only on a small scale and with a great deal of effort ○ *eked out a bare existence*

EKG *abbr* MED **1.** electrocardiogram **2.** electrocardiograph

e·kis·tics /i kístiks/ *n* the study of human settlements in all their aspects, including the origin and development of cities and city planning (*takes a singular verb*) [Mid-20C. < Greek *oikistikos* < *oikizein* "settle" < *oikos* "house"] —**e·kis·tic** *adj* —**ek·is·ti·cian** /èki stísh'n/ *n*

el /el/ *n US* an elevated railroad in a city (*informal*) [Early 20C. Shortening]

el. *abbr* GEOG elevation

e·lab·o·rate *adj* /i lábbərət/ **1. COMPLEX** having many different parts or a lot of detail, and organized in a complicated way ○ *an elaborate system* **2. FINELY OR RICHLY DECORATED** made with a lot of intricate detail or extravagant ornamentation ○ *an elaborate headdress* **3. DETAILED AND THOROUGH** thought out or organized with thoroughness and careful attention to detail ○ *elaborate preparations* ■ *v* /i lábbə ràyt/ (**-rat·ed, -rat·ing, -rates**) **1.** *vi* **GIVE MORE DETAIL ABOUT SOMETHING** to go into greater detail about something that has already been spoken about or described in broad terms ○ *Would you care to elaborate on that?* **2.** *vt* **WORK OUT SOMETHING IN DETAIL** to work out the details of something **3.** *vti* **MAKE OR BECOME MORE COMPLEX** to make something more complex or ornate, or become more complex or ornate [15C. < Latin *elaborat-,* past participle of *elaborare* "produce by effort or labor" < *labor* "labor"] —**e·lab·o·rate·ly** *adv* —**e·lab·o·rate·ness** *n* —**e·lab·o·ra·tion** /i làbbə ráysh'n/ *n* —**e·lab·o·ra·tor** *n*

El 'Al·a·mein /el àllə máyn, -àalə-/ coastal town in northern Egypt. It was the site of two important World War II battles in which British forces defeated German troops in 1942. Population: 980 (2001).

E·lam /éeləm/ ancient kingdom in southwestern Iran, east of the Tigris River. It was established before 4000 B.C. and corresponds to the present-day Khuzistan Province, Iran.

E·la·mite /éelə mìt/ *n* **1.** somebody from the ancient kingdom of Elam **2.** an extinct language formerly spoken in the ancient kingdom of Elam. Elamite has been attested by important discoveries of pictographic and cuneiform inscriptions dating from the third millennium B.C. through to the first millennium A.D. —**E·la·mite** *adj* —**E·la·mit·ic** /èelə míttik/ *adj*

é·lan /ay láan, -láaN/, **e·lan** *n* vigor and enthusiasm, often combined with self-confidence and style [Mid-19C. < French, < *élancer* "dart, throw" < *lance* (see LANCE)]

eland

e·land /éelənd/ (*plural* **e·lands** or *same*) *n* an antelope with humped shoulders, a dewlap, and tightly spiraling horns. It is the largest living antelope. Native to: central and southern Africa. Genus: *Taurotragus.* [Late 18C. Via Afrikaans < Dutch, "elk" < Lithuanian *élnis*]

é·lan vi·tal /ay láan vee táal, -láaN-/ *n* according to the philosophy of Henri Bergson, a creative life force present in all living things and responsible for evolution [< French, "vital ardor"]

el·a·pid /éllәpid/ *n* a venomous snake with short fangs at the front of the upper jaw, e.g., a cobra, coral snake, or mamba. Family: Elapidae. [Late 19C. < modern Latin *Elapidae* < Greek *elaps,* variant of *el(l)ops,* kind of fish and sea serpent] —**el·a·pid** *adj*

e·lapse /i láps/ *vi* (**e·lapsed, e·laps·ing, e·laps·es**) to pass or go by, especially in a gradual, slow, or imperceptible way ○ *Before we knew it, several hours had elapsed.* ■ *n* the passing of a period of time (*formal*) [Late 16C. < Latin *elaps-,* past participle of *elabi* "slip away" < *labi* "glide, fall"]

E·la·ra /éllərə/ *n* a small natural satellite of Jupiter, discovered in 1905. It is approximately 50 mi./80 km in diameter and occupies an intermediate orbit.

e·las·mo·branch /i lássmə bràngk, -lázmə-/ *n* a fish with a cartilaginous skeleton, e.g., a shark, ray, or skate. Subclass: Elasmobranchii. [Late 19C. < modern Latin *Elasmobranchii* < Greek *elasmos* "beaten metal" + *bragkhia* "gills"] —**e·las·mo·branch** *adj*

e·las·tic /i lástik/ *n* **1. STRETCHY MATERIAL** strips or threads of rubber or similar stretchable material, or fabric or tape with a stretchy material woven into it so that it can fit tightly around something **2.** same as **rubber band** ■ *adj* **1. MADE OF ELASTIC** made of or containing elastic **2. STRETCHY AND FLEXIBLE** describes an object or substance that can return quickly to its original shape and size after being bent, stretched, or squashed **3. EASILY CHANGED** able to incorporate changes or adapt to new circumstances easily **4. SPRINGY** light and springy, especially in movement ○ *an elastic gait* [Mid-17C. Via modern Latin < Greek *elastikos* "driving, propelling" < *elaunein* "drive"] —**e·las·ti·cal·ly** *adv*

SYNONYMS See ***pliable.***

e·las·tic band *n* same as **rubber band**

e·las·tic col·li·sion *n* a collision between two perfectly elastic bodies such that the final kinetic energy of the system is the same as the initial kinetic energy of the system

e·las·tic fi·ber *n* a smooth long thin fiber in connective tissue, composed mainly of the fibrous protein elastin

e·las·tic·i·ty /i là stíssətee, ee-/ *n* **1. ABILITY TO RETURN TO SHAPE** the ability of an object or substance to return quickly to its original shape and size after being bent, stretched, or squashed **2. FLEXIBILITY** the ability to incorporate changes or adapt to new circumstances easily **3.** ECON **RELATIVE CHANGE IN ECONOMIC VARIABLE** the relative change in an economic variable, e.g., demand, that occurs in reaction to changes in other variables, e.g., price or advertising input

e·las·ti·cize /i lásti sìz/ (**-cized, -ciz·ing, -ciz·es**) *vt* **1.** to put strips or threads of rubber or similar material into a fabric in order to make it stretchy **2.** to make something elastic or more elastic —**e·las·ti·cized** /i lásti sìzd/ *adj*

e·las·tic lim·it *n* the maximum stress that can be applied to a material without the material's becoming permanently deformed

e·las·tic wave *n* a wave propagated in a medium in which particles become temporarily displaced, transfer motion to other particles, and then return to their original state

e·las·tin /i lástin/ *n* a fibrous protein resembling collagen that is the main constituent of the elastic fibers of connective tissue [Late 19C. < ELASTIC]

e·las·to·mer /i lástəmər/ *n* a natural material such as rubber or a synthetic material such as polyvinyl that has elastic properties [Mid-20C. < ELASTIC] —**e·las·to·mer·ic** /i làstə mérrik/ *adj*

E·lat another spelling of **Eilat**

e·late /i láyt/ (**e·lat·ed, e·lat·ing, e·lates**) *vt* to make somebody very happy and excited [Late 16C. < Latin *elat-,* past participle of *efferre* "carry away" < *ferre* "carry"] —**e·late** *adj* —**e·lat·ed** *adj*

el·a·ter /éllətər/, **e·lat·er·id** /i láttərid/ *n* a beetle that belongs to the click beetle family. Family: Elateridae. [Mid-17C. < Greek *elatēr* "driver" < *elaunein* "drive"]

e·la·tion /i láysh'n/ *n* a feeling of great happiness and excitement

Elba

El·ba /élbə/ mountainous island off the western coast of Italy, the place of Napoleon's first period of exile (1814–15)

El·be /élbə, elb/ river in central Europe that rises in the northern Czech Republic and flows about 725 mi./1,167 km northwest to the North Sea

El·bert, Mount /élbərt/ mountain in central Colorado. It is the highest peak in the state and the highest of the Rocky Mountains. Height: 14,433 ft./4,399 m.

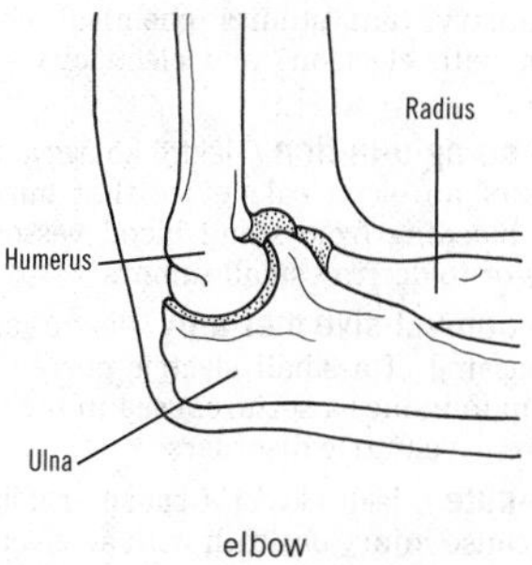

elbow

el·bow /élbō/ *n* **1. JOINT IN ARM** the joint between the upper and lower parts of the human arm **2. PART OF SLEEVE** the part of a sleeve that covers the elbow **3. JOINT IN ANIMAL LEG** the joint in an animal's forelimb corresponding to the elbow in a human **4. BEND** a bend in something such as a river, road, or pipe **5. SOMETHING BENT** something, especially a piece of pipe, made with a bend in it ■ *vti* (**-bowed, -bow·ing, -bows**) **1. PUSH SOMEBODY WITH ELBOW** to push or hit somebody or something with an elbow **2. MAKE WAY THROUGH CROWD** to progress through a crowd by pushing with the elbow or elbows [Old English *el(n)boga* "arm bend" < Germanic] ◇ **bend the** *or* **your elbow** to drink alcohol often (*informal*) ◇ **out at (the) elbows 1.** poorly dressed **2.** short of money

el·bow grease *n* hard physical effort or work, especially using the hands and arms (*informal*)

el·bow·room /élbō ro͝om, -ro͞om/ *n* (*informal*) **1.** space to move around in or work in comfortably **2.** freedom from restriction for a time, especially freedom to move or develop in a new area or direction

El·brus, Mount /el bro͝oss/, **El'brus** highest mountain in Europe, in the Caucasus Mountains in southern Russia, near the border with Georgia. Height: 18,510 ft./5,642 m.

El·burz Moun·tains /el bo͝orz-/ mountain range in northern Iran, near the southern shore of the Caspian Sea. The highest peak is Damavand, 18,386 ft./5,604 m.

El Ca·jon /èl kə hṓn/ city in southern California, a suburb of San Diego. Population: 95,555 (2002 estimate).

El Cen·tro /el séntrō/ city in southeastern California near the Mexican border. Population: 37,684 (2002 estimate).

El Cer·ri·to /èl sə reétō/ city in western California on the northeastern shore of San Francisco Bay, northwest of Oakland. Population: 23,513 (2002 estimate).

eld·er[1] /éldər/ *adj* **1. BORN EARLIER** born before another, especially within a family, or having more seniority **2. SUPERIOR** superior to others, either by rank or experience ■ *n* **1. SOMEBODY BORN EARLIER** somebody who was born before somebody else ○ *She is five years my elder.* **2. SOMEBODY WITH SENIORITY** somebody who is higher in rank **3. SENIOR MEMBER OF CHURCH** in some Christian churches, a senior lay member responsible for some aspects of church administration, the pastoral care of church members, and sometimes for teaching and preaching **4. SENIOR MEMBER OF COMMUNITY** a member of a family, tribal group, or village who is advanced in years and has influence and authority within the community [Old English *(i)eldra* < Germanic] —**eld·er·ship** *n* ◇ **the Elder** used after a person's name to indicate that he or she is the first-born person of a name shared by another ○ *Pitt the Elder*

USAGE elder or **older**? ***Elder*** and *eldest* are used only of people, and usually in the context of family relationships: *She is the elder of Ruth's daughters. Mark is my eldest son.* ***Older*** and *oldest* can apply to things as well as people, and can be used in a wider range of grammatical constructions: *I am older than David. It is the oldest church in Paris.* When ***eldest*** (or less commonly, ***elder***) is used after a verb (for example, *be*), it has to be preceded by *the*: *Who is the eldest?* not *Who is eldest?*

el·der[2] /éldər/ *n* a bush or tree with flat clusters of white flowers and purplish black berries. Latin name: *Sambucus nigra*. [Old English *ellærn*, origin ?]

el·der·ber·ry /éldər bèrree/ (*plural* **-ries**) *n* **1.** the fruit of the elder, especially the berry of any variety of elder that is used to make wine or jelly **2.** TREES same as **elder**[2]

eld·er·care /éldər kèr/ *n US* institutions and programs, both social and medical, focusing on the needs and care of senior citizens

El·der Ed·da *n* LITERAT same as **Edda** (sense 1)

eld·er·ly /éldərlee/ *adj* **1. PAST MIDDLE AGE** past middle age and approaching the later stages of life (*sometimes considered offensive*) **2. CHARACTERISTIC OF LIFE AFTER MIDDLE AGE** characteristic of or relating to life after middle age **3. OLD-FASHIONED** old and somewhat old-fashioned ■ *npl* **PEOPLE PAST MIDDLE AGE** older people considered as a group (*sometimes considered offensive*) —**el·der·li·ness** *n*

eld·er states·man *n* somebody advanced in years and experience, especially a politician or former politician, who is respected and whose advice is still valued and unofficially sought

eld·er states·wo·man *n* a woman advanced in years and experience, especially a politician or former politician, who is respected and whose advice is still valued and unofficially sought

eld·est /éldəst/ *adj* first, either in age or seniority [Old English *(i)eldest* < Germanic]

USAGE See ***elder***[1].

El Do·ra·do[1] /èl də raádō, -ráydō/ *n* **1.** a legendary place in South America where the streets were said to be paved with gold, and wealth and riches were to be had in abundance **2.** a place of great wealth or where great wealth can be acquired [Early 19C. < Spanish, literally "the gilded"]

El Do·ra·do[2] /èl də raádō, -ráydō/ city in southern Arkansas, southeast of Texarkana, directly north of the Louisiana border. Population: 21,119 (2002 estimate).

El·ea·nor of Aq·ui·taine /éllənər əv ákwi tàyn/ (1122?–1204) French-born queen of France (1137–52) and England (1154–89). After the annulment of her marriage to King Louis VII of France, she married the future King Henry II of England.

e-learn·ing *n* the acquisition of knowledge and skill using electronic technologies such as computer- and Internet-based courseware and local and wide-area networks

El·e·at·ic /èllee áttik/ *adj* relating to an ancient Greek school of philosophy that flourished in the 5th and 6th centuries B.C. It argued that philosophical reflection was more important than sensory observation. [Late 19C. < Latin *Eliaticus* < *Elea*, ancient Greek city in SW Italy] —**El·e·at·ic** *n* —**El·e·at·i·cism** /-sìzzəm/ *n*

elec. *abbr* **1.** electric **2.** electrical **3.** electricity

el·e·cam·pane /èlli kam páyn/ (*plural* **-panes** or *same*) *n* a tall perennial plant related to daisies and dandelions that has large toothed hairy leaves. Flowers: yellow. Use: herbal remedy made from roots for treating coughs and fevers. Latin name: *Inula helenium*. [14C. Contraction of medieval Latin *enula campana* "elecampane of the fields" < *enula* "elecampane," via Latin *inula* < Greek *helenion*]

e·lect /i lékt/ *v* (**e·lect·ed, e·lect·ing, e·lects**) **1.** *vt* **CHOOSE SOMEBODY BY VOTE** to choose somebody by a vote, e.g., for public office, an official role, or membership of a group ○ *She was elected leader of the commission.* **2.** *vt* **DECIDE TO DO SOMETHING** to make a decision to do something ○ *elected to stay* **3.** *vti US* **CHOOSE SOMETHING** to choose or select something, particularly a subject or course of study at college **4.** *vt* RELIG **CHOOSE SOMEBODY FOR SALVATION** especially in Christianity, to choose somebody by divine will for salvation ■ *adj* **1. CHOSEN BUT NOT YET IN OFFICE** chosen by a vote but not yet formally installed in office (*used in combination*) ○ *the president-elect* **2.** RELIG **CHOSEN BY GOD** chosen by God for special favor, salvation, or a task ○*"Samson has assumed that, as an elect instrument, he must be always actively engaged in God's service."* (John Spencer Hill, *John Milton: Poet, Priest, and Prophet*; 1979) ■ *npl* **1. SELECT GROUP** a specially privileged or gifted group (*literary*) ○ *World-class opera singers are among today's elect.* **2.** RELIG **PEOPLE CHOSEN BY GOD** people believed to be specially chosen or favored by God, e.g., those chosen by God for salvation [15C. < Latin *electus* < *eligere* "pick out" < *legere* "choose"] —**e·lect·a·ble** *adj*

e·lec·tion /i léksh'n/ *n* **1. EVENT AT WHICH PEOPLE VOTE** an organized event at which somebody is chosen by vote for something, especially a public office ○ *held an election* **2. CHOOSING OR BEING CHOSEN BY VOTE** the process of choosing somebody or of being chosen by vote ○ *He stood for election.* **3. SELECTION OF SOMETHING** the act or process of choosing something, e.g., a course of action or subject (*formal*) **4.** RELIG **SELECTION BY GOD FOR SOMETHING** especially in Christianity, the fact of being chosen by God, or God's act of choosing somebody, for special favor, salvation, or a task

E·lec·tion Day *n* a day designated by law for the election of people to public office. In the United States, Election Day for national elections is designated by law as the Tuesday after the first Monday in November in even-numbered years.

e·lec·tion·eer /i lèkshə neér/ (**-eered, -eer·ing, -eers**) *vi* **1.** to take an active part in an election campaign, especially as, or on behalf of, a candidate for political office **2.** to attempt to win votes in an election by being insincere and unscrupulous (*disapproving*) —**e·lec·tion·eer** *n* —**e·lec·tion·eer·ing** *n*

e·lec·tive /i léktiv/ *adj* **1. RELATING TO VOTING** relating to or involving voting ○ *elective office* **2. REQUIRING ELECTION** chosen by a vote, or held by somebody who is chosen by a vote ○ *The monarchy at that time was elective not hereditary.* **3.** EDUC **NOT COMPULSORY** describes a course of study that is optional, and not essential or compulsory ■ *n* EDUC **OPTIONAL SUBJECT OF STUDY** an optional course that a student may select from among several alternatives —**e·lec·tive·ly** *adv* —**e·lec·tive·ness** *n*

e·lec·tive mut·ism *n* PSYCHIAT same as **mutism**

e·lec·tor /i léktər/ *n* **1. MEMBER OF ELECTORAL COLLEGE** a member of an electoral college or the Electoral College **2. SOMEBODY WHO VOTES** a voter in an election **3.** *also* **E·lec·tor GERMAN RULER WHO ELECTED EMPEROR** a ruler of a German state within the Holy Roman Empire who was entitled to vote in the election of the emperor (*often used as a title*)

e·lec·tor·al /i léktərəl/ *adj* relating to or involving elections, electors, or voters —**e·lec·tor·al·ly** *adv*

e·lec·tor·al col·lege *n* a select body of people who elect somebody to an office on behalf of a larger group

E·lec·tor·al Col·lege *n* in the United States, the formal body elected by voters to choose the president and vice president. Although US voters in effect choose a president and vice president, they are formally voting for members of the Electoral College, who make the choice on their behalf.

e·lec·tor·ate /i léktərət/ *n* all the officially qualified voters within a particular country or area, or for a particular election

electr- *prefix* same as **electro-** (*used before vowels*)

E·lec·tra /i léktrə/ *n* in Greek mythology, the daughter of Agamemnon and Clytemnestra. She helped her brother Orestes to avenge their father's murder by killing their mother and Clytemnestra's lover. [< Greek *Ēlektra*, literally "bright, beaming" < *ēlektōr* "sun"]

E·lec·tra com·plex *n* in psychoanalysis, a daughter's unconscious unresolved sexual attraction to her father

E·lec·tra par·a·dox *n* a logical paradox arising from the possibility of somebody's knowing that something is true when it is described in one way but not when it is described in another [< a Greek myth in which Electra is said to recognize her brother Orestes from a description but not by sight]

e·lec·tret /i léktrət/ *n* a piece of insulating material that is permanently polarized and has a permanent electric field. Use: microphones and telephones. [Late 19C. Blend of ELECTRICITY + MAGNET]

e·lec·tric /i léktrik/ *adj* **1. INVOLVING OR CAUSED BY ELECTRICITY** relating to, involving, or caused by electricity ○ *electric power* **2. FOR ELECTRICITY** carrying or conveying electricity ○ *electric cables* **3. USING ELECTRICITY** powered or operated by electricity ○ *an electric guitar* ○ *electric vehicles* **4. TENSE OR EXCITED** full of tension or excitement and anticipation ○ *an electric atmosphere* **5. BRIGHT** extremely bright in color ○ *electric orange* ■ *n* **1. ELECTRICITY** electricity, or the electricity supply, e.g., to a house (*informal*) **2. SOMETHING OPERATED BY ELECTRICITY** a vehicle, machine, or other device that is powered by electricity [Mid-17C. < modern Latin *electricus* < *electrum* "amber" < Greek *ēlektron*]

USAGE electric or **electrical**? ***Electric*** is more commonly used than ***electrical*** to describe a device that works by electricity or is involved in producing or carrying electricity: *an electric oven; an electric socket.* ***Electrical*** is applied to more general things and to areas of study or activity that are concerned with electricity: *electrical appliances; electrical engineering.* ***Electric*** is the choice in the figurative meaning "tense or excited": *The atmosphere at the meeting was electric.*

e·lec·tri·cal /i léktrik'l/ *adj* **1.** same as **electric** *adj* (senses 1–2) **2. INVOLVING APPLICATION OF ELECTRICITY** involved in or involving the application of electricity in technology ○ *electrical energy* **3. RELATING TO ELECTRIC FUNCTIONING** involving or concerned with electric cables or circuits, or parts powered by electricity ○ *You'll need an electrician for the electrical work.* **4. CAUSED BY ELECTRICITY** caused by electricity or something that uses or conveys electricity —**e·lec·tri·cal·ly** *adv*

USAGE See *electric.*

e·lec·tri·cal en·gi·neer·ing *n* the branch of engineering that studies the practical applications of electricity in science and technology —**e·lec·tri·cal en·gi·neer** *n*

e·lec·tri·cal storm *n* a thunderstorm, especially one with a great deal of lightning

e·lec·tric blan·ket *n* a blanket containing an insulated electric heating element, used to warm a bed

e·lec·tric-blue *adj* of a bright metallic blue color —**e·lec·tric blue** *n*

e·lec·tric chair *n* **1.** a chair used to execute people sentenced to die by electrocution **2.** a sentence of death by electrocution in an electric chair

e·lec·tric con·stant *n* the absolute permittivity of free space, equal to 8.854 x 10^{-12} farad per meter. Symbol $\boldsymbol{\upsilon}_0$

e·lec·tric eel *n* a long air-breathing fish resembling a true eel that can release a strong discharge of electricity from specialized organs in the tail region. Native to: South American rivers. Latin name: *Electrophorus electricus.*

e·lec·tric eye *n* a device that converts light into electrical energy or uses it to regulate a flow of current, often incorporated into automatic control systems for doors and lighting

e·lec·tric fence *n* a wire fence carrying an electric current that gives a mild electric shock to any person or animal that touches it

e·lec·tric field *n* a field of force surrounding a charged body or associated with a fluctuating magnetic field, with which charged particles interact

e·lec·tric fire *n UK* a heater with an element that is made hot by an electric current passing through it, used to heat a room

e·lec·tric gui·tar *n* a guitar, often with a solid body, that has an electrical device for picking up sound fitted below the strings and connected to an amplifier and loudspeaker

e·lec·tri·cian /i lèk trísh'n, èe lek-/ *n* somebody licensed to install, maintain, repair, or approve electrical wiring or electrical goods

e·lec·tric·i·ty /i lèk tríssətee, èe lek-/ *n* **1.** PHYS **ENERGY CREATED BY MOVING CHARGED PARTICLES** a fundamental form of kinetic or potential energy created by the free or controlled movement of charged particles such as electrons, positrons, and ions **2. ELECTRIC CURRENT** electric current, especially when used as a source of power **3. ANTICIPATION OR TENSION** a feeling or atmosphere of excited anticipation or tension

e·lec·tric jazz *n* jazz produced using electronic instruments or other electronic devices

e·lec·tric light *n* **1.** a light operated by electricity, e.g., one with an electric bulb or a fluorescent tube **2.** the illumination produced by electricity

e·lec·tric mo·tor *n* a machine that converts energy from electricity into mechanical energy

e·lec·tric or·gan *n* **1.** a musical instrument that is a type of organ whose sound is produced or amplified by means of electricity **2.** in some fish, a specialized muscle tissue that creates an electric field used for finding enemies, obstacles, and food in murky water, and, in some species, for defense against attack

e·lec·tric pi·a·no *n* an electronic keyboard instrument that produces a sound similar to that of a piano

e·lec·tric po·ten·tial *n* the work required to bring a unit of positive electric charge from infinity to a specific point in an electric field. Symbol ***V***

e·lec·tric ray *n* a fish that can emit a strong electric discharge from organs in its enlarged pectoral fins. Native to: tropical or temperate seas. Family: Torpedinidae.

e·lec·tric ra·zor *n* a small electrically powered device used for shaving hair on the face or body

e·lec·tric shock *n* a sudden painful physical reaction consisting of nerve stimulation and muscle contraction, caused by an electric current flowing through the body

e·lec·tri·fy /i léktrə fī/ (**-fied, -fy·ing, -fies**) *vt* **1. CHARGE SOMETHING ELECTRICALLY** to charge something with electricity or pass an electric current through something **2. CONVERT SOMETHING TO USING ELECTRICITY** to convert something such as a railroad line or a piece of machinery so that it can operate on electric power **3.** MUSIC **AMPLIFY SOUNDS ELECTRICALLY** to amplify electrically the sounds produced by a musical instrument **4. THRILL SOMEBODY** to cause somebody to feel a sudden and surprising shock, thrill, or sense of excitement —**e·lec·tri·fi·a·ble** *adj* —**e·lec·tri·fi·ca·tion** /i lèktrəfi káysh'n/ *n* —**e·lec·tri·fied** *adj* —**e·lec·tri·fi·er** *n*

e·lec·tro /i léktrō/ *n* **1.** MUSIC same as **electronic music** **2.** *also* **e·lec·tro-funk** a style of electronic music with African American, urban, rap, and funk influences that became popular in the 1980s and itself influenced hip-hop and techno

electro- *prefix* **1.** electric, electricity, electronic ○ *electromyogram* **2.** electrolysis ○ *electrometallurgy* **3.** electron ○ *electropositive* [< modern Latin *electrum* (see ELECTRIC)]

e·lec·tro·a·cous·tic /i lèktrō ə ko͞ostik/ *adj* describes a device that converts sound into electrical signals or vice versa

e·lec·tro·a·cous·tics /i lèktrō ə ko͞ostiks/ *n* a branch of electronics that is concerned with the way in which electricity is converted into sound (*takes a singular verb*) —**e·lec·tro·a·cous·ti·cal·ly** *adv*

e·lec·tro·a·nal·y·sis /i lèktrō ə nálləssiss/ (*plural* **-y·ses** /-ə sèez/) *n* the use of electrolysis to perform chemical analysis —**e·lec·tro·an·a·lyt·ic** /i lèktrō an'l íttik/ *adj*—**e·lec·tro·an·a·lyt·i·cal** *adj*—**e·lec·tro·an·a·lyt·i·cal·ly** *adv*

e·lec·tro·car·di·o·gram /i lèktrō kaárdee ə gràm/ *n* a visual record of the heart's electrical activity made using an electrocardiograph

e·lec·tro·car·di·o·graph /i lèktrō kaárdee ə gràf/ *n* a device that records the electrical activity of the heart muscle via electrodes placed on the chest, and displays it as a visual record —**e·lec·tro·car·di·o·graph·ic** /-kaardee ə gráffik/ *adj* —**e·lec·tro·car·di·o·graph·i·cal·ly** *adv* —**e·lec·tro·car·di·og·ra·phy** /-kaardee óggrəfee/ *n*

e·lec·tro·cau·ter·y /i lèktrō káwtəree/ *n* the process of destroying unwanted tissue, e.g., warts and polyps, or sealing blood vessels, by means of an electrically heated needle

e·lec·tro·chem·i·cal /i lèktrō kémmik'l/ *adj* of or relating to electrochemistry —**e·lec·tro·chem·i·cal·ly** *adv*

e·lec·tro·chem·i·cal se·ries *n* a series in which the chemical elements are arranged in order of decreasing tendency to lose electrons

e·lec·tro·chem·is·try /i lèktrō kémmistree/ *n* a branch of chemistry that studies chemical change associated with electrons and electricity —**e·lec·tro·chem·ist** *n*

e·lec·tro·co·ag·u·la·tion /i lèktrō kō àggyə láysh'n/ *n* the use of an electrical device that burns tissue to stop bleeding from small blood vessels during surgery or to destroy small tumors

e·lec·tro·con·vul·sive ther·a·py /i lèktrō kən vùlssiv-/ *n* the passing of a small electric current through the brain to induce a seizure, used in the treatment of severe psychiatric disorders

e·lec·tro·cute /i léktrə kyo͞ot/ (**-cut·ed, -cut·ing, -cutes**) *vt* **1.** to cause injury or death with an electric shock **2.** to execute somebody by means of the electric chair [Late 19C. < ELECTRO- + EXECUTE] —**e·lec·tro·cu·tion** /i lèktrə kyo͞osh'n/ *n*

e·lec·trode /i lék trōd/ *n* a conductor through which electricity enters or leaves something such as a battery or a piece of electrical equipment

e·lec·tro·de·pos·it /i lèktrō di pózzit/ *vt* (**-it·ed, -it·ing, -its**) to deposit a substance, especially a metal, on an electrode by using electrolysis ■ *n* a substance deposited by using electrolysis —**e·lec·tro·dep·o·si·tion** /i lèktrō depə zísh'n, -deepə-/ *n*

e·lec·trode po·ten·tial *n* the potential difference produced between an electrode composed of a given chemical element and the solution in which it is immersed

e·lec·tro·di·al·y·sis /i lèktrō dī álləssiss/ (*plural* **-y·ses** /-ə sèez/) *n* a form of dialysis in which the separation of substances is accelerated by an electric current applied to the electrodes. The desalination of seawater is an example of a use of electrodialysis.

e·lec·tro·dy·nam·ics /i lèktrō dī námmiks/ *n* a branch of physics that studies how electric currents interact with magnetic and mechanical forces (*takes a singular verb*) —**e·lec·tro·dy·nam·ic** *adj*

e·lec·tro·dy·na·mom·e·ter /i lèktrō dìnə mómmətər/ *n* a device for measuring the strength of an electric current by the magnetic force it induces in a coil

e·lec·tro·en·ceph·a·lo·gram /i lèktrō en séffələ gràm/ *n* a record of the electrical activity of the brain that is produced by an electroencephalograph

e·lec·tro·en·ceph·a·lo·graph /i lèktrō en séffələ gràf/ *n* a machine that uses electrodes placed on the scalp to monitor the electrical activity of different parts of the brain, recording these as complex tracings. Irregularities recorded in the tracings may help in the diagnosis of organic brain disorders and in establishing clinical death. —**e·lec·tro·en·ceph·a·lo·graph·ic** /-sefələ gráffik/ *adj* —**e·lec·tro·en·ceph·a·log·ra·phy** /-sefə lóggrəfee/ *n*

e·lec·tro·fish·ing /i léktrō fishing/ *n* fishing that employs an electric current to attract or stun fish

e·lec·tro·form /i léktrə fàwrm/ (**-formed, -form·ing, -forms**) *vt* to form something, e.g., a medal, by using electrolysis to coat the surface of the mold or matrix with a metal

e·lec·tro-funk *n* MUSIC same as **electro** (sense 2)

e·lec·tro·graph /i léktrə gràf/ *n* **1.** ELECTRICAL ENGRAVING DEVICE an electrical device for engraving a design on a metal plate. Use: printing patterns on fabrics or wallpaper. **2.** ELECTRICAL PICTURE TRANSMISSION DEVICE an apparatus used to transmit pictures by electrical means, e.g., by fax **3.** TRANSMITTED PICTURE a picture transmitted and printed by an electrograph **4.** PHYS ELECTROMETER an electrometer that produces a graphic record of the measurements it makes **5.** PHYS GRAPH FROM ELECTROMETER the visual record produced by an electrometer

e·lec·tro·hy·drau·lic /i lèktrō hī dróllik/ *adj* using, or relating to the use of, electrical and hydraulic components —**e·lec·tro·hy·drau·li·cal·ly** *adv*

e·lec·tro·ki·net·ics /i lèktrō ki néttiks/ *n* a branch of physics that deals with the motion of electrically charged particles (*takes a singular verb*) —**e·lec·tro·ki·net·ic** *adj*

e·lec·trol·o·gist /i lèk tróllәjist, èe lek-/ *n* somebody who removes moles, warts, or body hair by electrolysis

e·lec·tro·lu·mi·nes·cence /i lèktrō loomə néss'nss/ *n* the emission of light by the application of an electric field to a substance —**e·lec·tro·lu·mi·nes·cent** *adj*

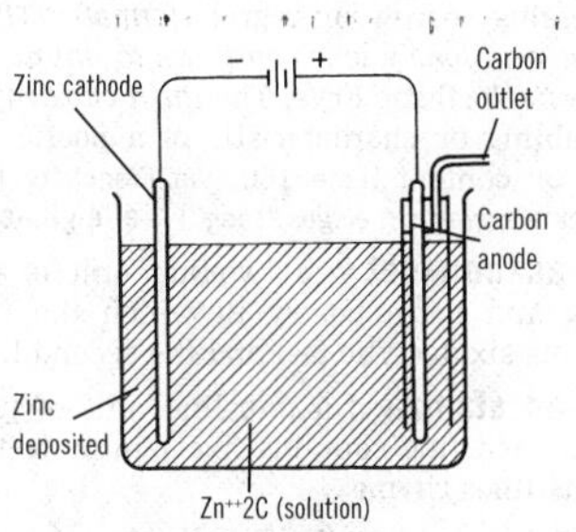

electrolysis: separation of zinc carbonate by electrolysis

e·lec·trol·y·sis /i lèk tróllisiss, èe lek-/ *n* **1.** the use of an electric current applied though a needle to remove body hair for cosmetic purposes, or to destroy warts, moles, or tumors for medical reasons **2.** the conduction of electricity through something melted or dissolved in order to induce decomposition of the melted or dissolved chemical into its components

e·lec·tro·lyte /i léktrə līt/ *n* **1.** CHEM COMPOUND SEPARABLE INTO IONS IN SOLUTION a chemical compound that separates into ions in a solution or when molten, and is able to conduct electricity **2.** CHEM ION IN ELECTROLYTE an ion in an electrolyte **3.** PHYSIOL ION IN CELL any ion in cells, blood, or other organic material. Electrolytes help to control fluid levels in the body, maintain normal pH levels, and ensure the correct electric potential between nerve cells that enables the transmission of nerve signals.

e·lec·tro·lyt·ic /i lèktrə líttik/ *adj* **1.** involved in or relating to electrolysis **2.** relating to, containing, or consisting of electrolytes —**e·lec·tro·lyt·i·cal·ly** *adv*

e·lec·tro·lyze /i léktrə līz/ (**-lyzed, -lyz·ing, -lyz·es**) *vt* to use electrolysis to decompose a chemical compound [Mid-19C. Blend of ELECTROLYSIS + ANALYZE]

e·lec·tro·mag·net /i lèktrō mágnət/ *n* a magnet consisting of a core, often made of soft iron, that is temporarily magnetized by an electric current flowing through a coil that surrounds it

e·lec·tro·mag·net·ic /i lèktrō mag néttik/ *adj* created by or relating to electromagnetism —**e·lec·tro·mag·net·i·cal·ly** *adv*

e·lec·tro·mag·net·ic field *n* a field of force associated with a moving electric charge and consisting of electric and magnetic fields that are generated at right angles to each other

e·lec·tro·mag·net·ic force *n* the force resulting from the interaction of charged particles and their electric and magnetic fields

e·lec·tro·mag·net·ic in·ter·fer·ence *n* interference in a circuit caused by the radiation of an electric or magnetic field or the operation of a nearby electric motor, e.g., disturbance on a television set

e·lec·tro·mag·net·ic ra·di·a·tion *n* radiation in the form of electromagnetic waves such as gamma rays, X-rays, ultraviolet light, visible light, infrared radiation, microwaves, and radio waves. The radiation has magnetic and electric fields that are perpendicular to each other and to the direction of propagation, and travels without a supporting medium.

e·lec·tro·mag·net·ic spec·trum *n* the complete range of electromagnetic radiation from the shortest waves (**gamma rays**) to the longest (**radio waves**)

e·lec·tro·mag·net·ic u·nit *n* any unit in the centimeter-gram-second system of units for measuring electricity and magnetism that gives a value of 1 to the magnetic constant, e.g., the abampere or the abvolt

e·lec·tro·mag·net·ic wave *n* a wave of energy with a frequency within the electromagnetic spectrum, generated by the periodic fluctuation of an electromagnetic field resulting from the acceleration or oscillation of an electric charge. Electromagnetic waves can be reflected, refracted, and polarized, and exhibit interference and diffraction effects.

e·lec·tro·mag·net·ism /i lèktrō mágnə tìzzəm/ *n* **1.** magnetism produced by an electric current **2.** the branch of physics concerned with the interaction of electric and magnetic fields

e·lec·tro·mech·an·i·cal /i lèktrō mə kánnik'l/ *adj* describes a mechanical device that is powered or controlled by electricity —**e·lec·tro·mech·an·i·cal·ly** *adv*

e·lec·tro·met·al·lur·gy /i lèktrō métt'l ùrjee/ *n* the range of metallurgical processes in which electricity has a key role, e.g., electroplating and the use of arc furnaces

e·lec·trom·e·ter /i lèk trómmətər, èelek-/ *n* a sensitive device for measuring extremely low voltages by means of the forces of attraction and repulsion between charged bodies on plates or wires

e·lec·tro·mo·tive /i lèktrō mṓtiv/ *adj* relating to or producing an electric current

e·lec·tro·mo·tive force *n* a force that causes the flow of electricity from one point to another

e·lec·tro·my·o·gram /i lèktrō mī ə gràm/ *n* a graphical tracing of the electrical activity in a muscle at rest or during contraction, used to diagnose nerve and muscle disorders

e·lec·tro·my·o·graph /i lèktrō mī ə gràf/ *n* a machine for producing a graphical tracing of the electrical activity picked up via electrodes inserted into muscle tissue. It consists of an amplifier, an electrically activated trace-drawing pen, and a moving strip of paper. —**e·lec·tro·my·o·graph·ic** /i lèktrō mī ə gráffik/ *adj* —**e·lec·tro·my·o·graph·i·cal·ly** *adv* —**e·lec·tro·my·og·ra·phy** /-mī óggrəfee/ *n*

e·lec·tron /i lék tròn/ *n* a stable negatively charged elementary particle with a small mass that is a fundamental constituent of matter and orbits the nucleus of an atom [Late 19C. < electric]

e·lec·tron af·fin·i·ty *n* the amount of energy needed to remove an electron from a negatively charged ion

e·lec·tron beam *n* PHYS same as **e-beam**

e·lec·tro·neg·a·tive /i lèktrō néggətiv/ *adj* **1.** with a negative electric charge, and so tending to move toward a positive electric pole **2.** tending to gain electrons to form a bond in a chemical reaction

e·lec·tro·neg·a·tiv·i·ty /i lèktrō negə tívvətee/ *n* a measure of the tendency of an atom in a molecule to attract the electrons in a chemical bond

e·lec·tron gun *n* a device that directs a steady stream of electrons in a desired direction, e.g., in a cathode-ray tube

e·lec·tron·ic /i lèk trónnik, èe lek-/ *adj* **1.** USING VALVES, TRANSISTORS, OR SILICON CHIPS relating to devices, systems, or circuits that employ components such as vacuum tubes, integrated circuits, or transistors in their design ○ *an electronic sensor* **2.** BY COMPUTER relating to, using, or accessed through a computer or computer network, e.g., the Internet ○ *electronic banking* **3.** PHYS OF ELECTRONS relating to electrons ○ *the electronic spectrum* **4.** PHYS OF CONTROLLED FLOW OF ELECTRONS relating to, or produced or operated by, the controlled flow of electrons through a semiconductor, a gas, or free space —**e·lec·tron·i·cal·ly** *adv*

e·lec·tron·i·ca /i lèk trónnikə, èe lek-/ *n* synthesized dance music that is written for home listening rather than purely for dancing to

e·lec·tron·ic church *n US* radio and television broadcasting devoted to religious services, especially Protestant ones, and their pastors and audience

e·lec·tron·ic con·fig·u·ra·tion *n* the three-dimensional arrangement within an atom or molecule of the atoms in their orbitals

e·lec·tron·ic da·ta proc·ess·ing *n* computer-based tasks involving the input and manipulation of data, usually using database programs

e·lec·tron·ic de·pos·i·to·ry trans·fer *n* the transfer of funds between bank accounts using the automated clearinghouse system

e·lec·tron·ic flash *n* a flash device used in high-speed photography that produces a very bright light by passing an electric charge through a gas-filled tube

e·lec·tron·ic funds trans·fer at point of sale *n* a system of paying for goods at the point of sale by the direct computerized transfer of money from the buyer's bank account to the seller's

e·lec·tron·ic jour·nal·ism *n* news coverage that is transmitted electronically, e.g., by television or over the Internet

e·lec·tron·ic mag·a·zine *n* a magazine that is distributed online over a computer network rather than being printed on paper

e·lec·tron·ic mail *n* ONLINE full form of **e-mail**

e·lec·tron·ic mall *n* a website that offers for sale the products and services of different vendors and handles all sales transactions for the vendors

e·lec·tron·ic mu·sic *n* music produced or modified by electronic means, often with the aid of a computer

e·lec·tron·ic news·gath·er·ing *n* television news coverage made at the time and place of the event or incident by means of video equipment

e·lec·tron·ic point of sale *n* a computerized checkout system in stores that records sales by scanning bar codes, automatically updates the retailer's stock lists, and provides a printout of the customer's purchases

e·lec·tron·ic pub·lish·ing *n* the production of documents in computer-readable form for distribution over a computer network or in other formats such as CD-ROMs

e·lec·tron·ic purse *n* a method of prepayment used in e-commerce, in which cash is stored electronically on a microchip

e·lec·tron·ics /i lèk trónniks, èe lek-/ *n* the branch of technology concerned with the design, manufacture, and maintenance of electronic devices (*takes a singular verb*) ■ *npl* the electronic parts of a piece of equipment, or electronic devices and equipment generally (*takes a plural verb*)

e·lec·tron·ic shop·ping *n* the ordering and purchase of goods and services over a computer network, especially over the Internet

e·lec·tron·ic sig·na·ture *n* an encoded attachment to an e-mail, verifying the identity of its sender

e·lec·tron·ic smog *n* nonionizing radiation produced in the atmosphere by sources such as radar and radio and television broadcasting, considered by some people to pose a general health risk

e·lec·tron·ic store·front *n* ONLINE same as **storefront** (sense 3)

e·lec·tron·ic su·per·high·way *n* ONLINE same as **information superhighway**

e·lec·tron·ic sur·veil·lance *n* the gathering of information using electronic devices such as video cameras and wiretaps, especially in crime detection and prevention or in espionage

e·lec·tron·ic town hall *n US* communication and discussion on television or over the Internet between members of the public and members of official bodies

e·lec·tron·ic trans·fer of funds *n* the transfer of money from one account to another by computer

e·lec·tron lens *n* a device that creates an electric or magnetic field around the path of an electron beam so that the beam may be focused

e·lec·tron mi·cro·graph *n* a photograph of a specimen taken using an electron microscope

e·lec·tron mi·cro·scope *n* a high-powered microscope that uses beams of electrons focused by an electron lens to create a magnified image on a fluorescent screen or photographic plate —**e·lec·tron mi·cros·co·py** *n*

e·lec·tron mul·ti·pli·er *n* a device for amplifying a very small current using the effects of secondary emission. Electrons from the original current strike an anode, producing secondary electrons that are directed to the next anode in a multistage process until the desired level of current is obtained.

e·lec·tron op·tics *n* the science that deals with the direction, deflection, or focusing of beams of electrons by electric and magnetic fields, e.g., in electron lenses (*takes a singular verb*)

e·lec·tron sea *n* a model for the electron state in metals in which a regular array of cations is surrounded by a group of loosely bound electrons

e·lec·tron shell *n* PHYS same as **shell** *n* (sense 19)

e·lec·tron trans·port *n* a process in which electrons are transferred from one compound to another with a release of energy occurring in the production of ATP

e·lec·tron tube *n* a device that consists of a sealed glass vessel containing a gas or a vacuum, within which electrons flow between electrodes

e·lec·tron volt *n* **1.** a unit of energy equal to the energy gained by an electron accelerated through a potential difference of one volt and equal to 1.602 x 10^{-19} joule. Symbol **eV 2.** the unit of mass of elementary particles, measured as a function of energy and usually expressed in terms of mega electron volts (**MeV**)

e·lec·tro-os·mo·sis *n* the movement of a liquid through a membrane under the effect of an electric field

e·lec·tro·paint /i léktrə pàynt/ (**-paint·ed, -paint·ing, -paints**) *vt* to apply paint to something by means of electrolysis

e·lec·tro·phile /i léktrə fìl/ *n* an atom, molecule, or chemical group that is attracted to electrons or accepts them —**e·lec·tro·phil·ic** /i lèktrə fíllik/ *adj*

e·lec·tro·phon·ic /i lèktrə fónnik/ *adj* producing sound by means of electronic equipment

e·lec·tro·pho·re·sis /i lèktrō fə réessiss/ *n* the movement of charged particles in a colloid or suspension when an electric field is applied to them [Early 20C. < ELECTRO- + Greek *phorēsis* "being carried" (see -PHORESIS)] —**e·lec·tro·pho·ret·ic** /-réttik/ *adj*

e·lec·troph·o·rus /i lèk tróffərəss, èe lek-/ (*plural* **-ri** /-rì/) *n* a device that produces electric charges from the friction between a disk and a metal plate [Late 18C. < ELECTRO- + *-phorus*, Latinization of -PHORE]

e·lec·tro·pho·tog·ra·phy /i lèktrō fə tóggrəfee/ *n* any form of photography that uses electricity to transfer an image onto paper, as in laser printing and photocopying —**e·lec·tro·pho·to·graph·ic** /i lèktrō fōtə gráffik/ *adj*

e·lec·tro·phys·i·ol·o·gy /i lèktrō fìzzee óllәjee/ *n* the branch of medicine or biology dealing with the study of electric activity in human or animal bodies —**e·lec·tro·phys·i·o·log·ic** /i lèktrō fìzzee ə lójjik/ *adj* —**e·lec·tro·phys·i·o·log·i·cal** *adj* —**e·lec·tro·phys·i·o·log·i·cal·ly** *adv* —**e·lec·tro·phys·i·ol·o·gist** *n*

e·lec·tro·plate /i léktrə plàyt/ *vt* (**-plat·ed, -plat·ing, -plates**) to use electrolysis to coat the surface of an object with metal ■ *n* objects coated with metal by means of electrolysis

e·lec·tro·po·ra·tion /i lèktrō paw ráysh'n/ *n* a method of introducing DNA from one organism into a protoplast of another using an electric pulse [< ELECTRO- + PORE[1]]

e·lec·tro·pos·i·tive /i lèktrō pózzətiv/ *adj* **1.** with a positive electric charge, and so tending to move toward a negative electric pole **2.** tending to release electrons to form a bond in a chemical reaction ◊ **electronegative**

e·lec·tro·re·cep·tor /i lèktrō ri séptər/ *n* an organ in fish such as sharks, electric eels, and catfish that detects electric charges

e·lec·tro·scope /i léktrə skōp/ *n* a device that detects and measures an electric charge, usually consisting of a rod holding two strips of gold foil that separate when the same charge is applied to each —**e·lec·tro·scop·ic** /i lèktrə skóppik/ *adj*

e·lec·tro·sen·si·tiv·i·ty /i lèktrō senssə tívvətee/ *n* the ability in an animal to detect naturally occurring electric currents and use them to navigate or locate objects

e·lec·tro·shock /i léktrō shòk/ *n also* **e·lec·tro·shock ther·a·py** PSYCHIAT same as **electroconvulsive therapy** ■ *vt* (**-shocked, -shock·ing, -shocks**) to administer electroconvulsive therapy to a patient

e·lec·tro·stat·ic /i lèktrō státtik/ *adj* **1.** produced by or relating to static electricity **2.** relating to electrostatics —**e·lec·tro·stat·i·cal·ly** *adv*

e·lec·tro·stat·ic gen·er·a·tor *n* PHYS same as **van de Graaff generator**

e·lec·tro·stat·ic pre·cip·i·ta·tor *n* a device that removes small particles of smoke, dust, or oil from air by electrostatically charging them and then attracting them to an oppositely charged collector plate or surface —**e·lec·tro·stat·ic pre·cip·i·ta·tion** *n*

e·lec·tro·stat·ic print·ing *n* a photocopying or printing process in which images are reproduced on a surface using electrostatic charges

e·lec·tro·stat·ics /i lèktrō státtiks/ *n* a branch of physics dealing with electric charges at rest (**static electricity**) (*takes a singular verb*)

e·lec·tro·stat·ic u·nit *n* a unit for measuring the magnitude of forces of repulsion between static electric charges in the centimeter-gram-second system, e.g., the statampere and the statvolt

e·lec·tro·sur·ger·y /i lèktrō súrjəree/ *n* the use of an electric device or current during surgery, e.g., to cut or cauterize tissue —**elec·tro·sur·gi·cal** *adj* —**e·lec·tro·sur·gi·cal·ly** *adv*

e·lec·tro·tech·nol·o·gy /i lèktrō tek nóllәjee/, **e·lec·tro·tech·nics** /-tékniks/ *n* the technological application of electrical and electronic engineering —**e·lec·tro·tech·nic** /-téknik/ *adj* —**e·lec·tro·tech·ni·cal** *adj*

e·lec·tro·ther·a·py /i lèktrō thérrəpee/ *n* any form of medical treatment that uses electricity as a cure or relief, e.g., to stimulate nerves and the muscles they are connected to —**e·lec·tro·ther·a·peu·tic** /-therə pyóotik/ *adj*

e·lec·tro·ther·mal /i lèktrō thúrm'l/ *adj* relating to electricity and heat, especially to the production of heat by electricity ○ *electrothermal energy conversion* —**e·lec·tro·ther·mal·ly** *adv*

e·lec·tro·type /i léktrō tìp/ *n* **1. DUPLICATE PRINTING PLATE MADE BY ELECTROPLATING** a duplicate of a block of type or engraving made by electroplating a wax, lead, or plastic mold of the original **2. SOMETHING PRINTED FROM ELECTROTYPE** an item that has been printed from an electrotype ■ *vt* (**-typed, -typ·ing, -types**) **PRINT SOMETHING USING ELECTROTYPE** to print something by a process that uses an electrotype —**e·lec·tro·typ·er** *n* —**e·lec·tro·typ·ic** /i lèktrō típpik/ *adj*

e·lec·tro·va·lence /i lèktrō váylənss/ *n* the combining power of an element, measured by the number of electrons one atom of it acquires from or transfers to another atom during the formation of a chemical compound —**e·lec·tro·va·lent** *adj*

e·lec·tro·va·lent bond *n* a chemical bond that is created during the formation of a compound by transfer of one or more electrons from one atom to another, the resulting oppositely charged ions being held together by attraction

e·lec·tro·weak /i léktrō wéek/ *adj* describes a type of fundamental interaction uniting electromagnetic forces with the weak interaction

e·lec·trum /i léktrəm/ *n* a pale-colored alloy of silver and gold. Use: jewelry and ornaments. [14C. < Latin (see ELECTRIC)]

e·lec·tu·ar·y /i lékchoo èrree/ (*plural* **-ies**) *n* a sweet-tasting paste made by mixing a drug with syrup or honey, administered by being applied to the teeth, tongue, or gums (*archaic*) [14C. < late Latin *electuarium*, probably < Greek *eleikton* < *eleikhein* "lick up"]

el·ee·mos·y·nar·y /èllə móss'n èrree, èllee ə-/ *adj* relating to, given as, or depending on charitable gifts (*formal*) [Late 16C. < medieval Latin *eleemosynarius* < *eleemosyna* "alms" < Greek *eleos* "mercy"]

el·e·gance /élləgənss/ *n* **1.** a combination of graceful stylishness, distinction, and good taste in appearance, behavior, or movement **2.** a satisfying or admirable neatness, ingenious simplicity, or precision in something ○ *the elegance of the solution* [Early 16C. Via French < Latin *elegantia* < *elegant-* (see ELEGANT)]

el·e·gant /élləgənt/ *adj* **1.** stylishly graceful, and showing sophistication and good taste in appearance and behavior **2.** pleasingly and often ingeniously neat, simple, or concise ○ *an equation elegant in its simplicity* [15C. Via French < Latin *elegant-* "choice, tasteful" < *eligire* (see ELECT)] —**el·e·gant·ly** *adv*

el·e·gi·ac /èllə jí ək/, **el·e·gi·a·cal** /-ək'l/ *adj* **1.** expressing sorrow or regret (*formal*) ○*"The same elegiac and lonely tone continues to haunt the later poetry."* (Northrop Frye, *The Bush Garden*; 1971) **2.** resembling or characteristic of a poetic elegy in form or content [Late 16C. Via French or late Latin < Greek *elegeiakos* < *elegos* "song"] —**el·e·gi·a·cal·ly** *adv*

el·e·gi·ac cou·plet *n* a two-line unit of classical Greek and Latin poetry in which the first line contains six dactylic feet and the second line five

el·e·gi·ac stan·za *n* a four-line unit of poetry in which each line contains five iambic feet and alternate lines rhyme

~~**elegible**~~ incorrect spelling of **eligible**

el·e·gist /éllәjist/ *n* a writer or speaker of an elegy

e·le·git /i léejit/ *n* a writ against a debtor's property that permits a creditor to keep it until the debt is paid [Early 16C. < medieval Latin, "he or she has chosen" (occurring in the writ), form of Latin *eligire* (see ELECT)]

el·e·gize /éllə jìz/ (**-gized, -giz·ing, -giz·es**) *v* **1.** *vti* to write or speak about somebody or something in a mournful sorrowful way ○ *He elegized his lost comrade.* **2.** *vi* to write, read, or recite an elegy

el·e·gy /éllәjee/ (*plural* **-gies**) *n* **1. MOURNFUL POEM** a mournful or reflective poem **2. POEM IN ELEGIAC COUPLETS OR STANZAS** a poem written in elegiac couplets or stanzas **3.** MUSIC **MUSICAL LAMENT FOR DEAD PERSON** an instrumental piece, or setting for a song, composed as a lament for somebody who has died [Early 16C. Directly or via French < Latin *elegia* < Greek *elegos* "song"]

CULTURAL NOTE ***Elegy Written in a Country Churchyard***, a poem (1750) by British writer Thomas Gray. Inspired by a churchyard at Stoke Poges, Buckinghamshire, England, it is a reflection on rural life, human ambitions, friendship, and mortality. It is considered the masterpiece of the "graveyard" school of literature, which was popular in the 1740s and 1750s.

el·e·ment /élləmənt/ *n* **1. SEPARATE PART OR GROUP** a separate identifiable part of something, or a distinct group within a larger group ○ *criminal elements in society* **2. SMALL QUANTITY** a small but significant trace of a quality or feeling ○ *There was an element of revenge in what she did.* **3. FACTOR** a cause or factor leading to something ○ *Surprise was the key element in insuring the success of the operation.* **4. HABITAT** a habitat or environment suited to an individual person ○ *She's in her element in the garden.* ○ *Parties*

CHEMICAL ELEMENTS

element	symbol	at.no.	at.wt.
actinium	Ac	89	[226]
aluminum	Al	13	26.98
americium	Am	95	[243]
antimony	Sb	51	121.75
argon	Ar	18	39.95
arsenic	As	33	74.92
astatine	At	85	[210]
barium	Ba	56	137.34
berkelium	Bk	97	[247]
beryllium	Be	4	9.01
bismuth	Bi	83	208.98
bohrium	Bh	107	[264]
boron	B	5	10.81
bromine	Br	35	79.9
cadmium	Cd	48	112.4
calcium	Ca	20	40.08
californium	Cf	98	[251]
carbon	C	6	12.01
cerium	Ce	58	140.12
cesium	Cs	55	132.91
chlorine	Cl	17	35.45
chromium	Cr	24	52
cobalt	Co	27	58.93
copper	Cu	29	63.55
curium	Cm	96	[247]
darmstadtium	Ds	110	[271]
dubnium	Db	105	[262]
dysprosium	Dy	66	162.5
einsteinium	Es	99	[254]
erbium	Er	68	167.26
europium	Eu	63	151.96
fermium	Fm	100	[257]
fluorine	F	9	19
francium	Fr	87	[223]
gadolinium	Gd	64	157.25
gallium	Ga	31	69.72
germanium	Ge	32	72.59
gold	Au	79	196.97
hafnium	Hf	72	178.49
hassium	Hs	108	[269]
helium	He	2	4
holmium	Ho	67	164.93
hydrogen	H	1	1.01
indium	In	49	114.82
iodine	I	53	126.9
iridium	Ir	77	192.22
iron	Fe	26	55.85
krypton	Kr	36	83.8
lanthanum	La	57	138.91
lawrencium	Lr	103	[256]
lead	Pb	82	207.2
lithium	Li	3	6.94
lutetium	Lu	71	174.97
magnesium	Mg	12	24.31
manganese	Mn	25	54.94
meitnerium	Mt	109	[268]
mendelevium	Md	101	[258]
mercury	Hg	80	200.59
molybdenum	Mo	42	95.94
neodymium	Nd	60	144.24
neon	Ne	10	20.18
neptunium	Np	93	237.05
nickel	Ni	28	58.71
niobium	Nb	41	92.91
nitrogen	N	7	14.01
nobelium	No	102	[255]
osmium	Os	76	190.2
oxygen	O	8	16
palladium	Pd	46	106.4
phosphorus	P	15	30.97
platinum	Pt	78	195.09
plutonium	Pu	94	[244]
polonium	Po	84	209
potassium	K	19	39.1
praseodymium	Pr	59	140.91
promethium	Pm	61	[145]
protactinium	Pa	91	231.04
radium	Ra	88	[226]
radon	Rn	86	[222]
rhenium	Re	75	186.2
rhodium	Rh	45	102.91
rubidium	Rb	37	85.47
ruthenium	Ru	44	101.07
rutherfordium	Rf	104	[261]
samarium	Sm	62	150.4
scandium	Sc	21	44.96
seaborgium	Sg	106	[266]
selenium	Se	34	78.96
silicon	Si	14	28.09
silver	Ag	47	107.87
sodium	Na	11	22.99
strontium	Sr	38	87.62
sulfur	S	16	32.06
tantalum	Ta	73	180.95
technetium	Tc	43	98.91
tellurium	Te	52	127.6
terbium	Tb	65	158.93
thallium	Tl	81	204.37
thorium	Th	90	232.04
thulium	Tm	69	168.93
tin	Sn	50	118.69
titanium	Ti	22	47.9
tungsten (wolfram)	W	74	183.85
ununbium	Uub	112	277
ununhexium	Uuh	116	289
ununquadium	Uuq	114	285
unununium	Uuu	111	272.15
ununtrium	Uut	113	284
ununpentium	Uup	115	288
uranium	U	92	283.04
vanadium	V	23	50.94
xenon	Xe	54	131.3
ytterbium	Yb	70	173.04
yttrium	Y	39	88.91
zinc	Zn	30	65.38
zirconium	Zr	40	91.22

Elements are listed with their symbol, atomic number (at.no.), and atomic weight (at.wt.). Atomic weights shown in square brackets are for the longest lived isotopes; those for neptunium, protactinium, and technetium are for the most technologically important isotopes.

are not their natural element. **5.** **HEATING PART OF APPLIANCE** a part of an electric heater, stove, or other appliance that heats up when an electric current is passed through it **6.** CHEM **CHEMICALLY INDIVISIBLE SUBSTANCE** any substance that cannot be broken down into a simpler one by a chemical reaction. Elements consist of atoms with the same number of protons in their nuclei, and 92 occur naturally on Earth. **7.** CHEM **SUPPOSED BASIC UNIT OF MATTER** any of the four primary substances, earth, air, fire, and water, that were formerly thought to be the materials from which all matter is constructed **8.** MATH **CONSTITUENT OF GEOMETRIC FIGURE** a point, line, plane, or other part of which a geometric figure is composed **9.** MATH **PART OF MATHEMATICAL QUANTITY** a part of a mathematical or geometric quantity, e.g., a number in an array or an angle in a triangle **10.** LOGIC, MATH **SET MEMBER** in mathematics and logic, a member of a set **11.** ELEC **COMPONENT OF ELECTRIC CIRCUIT** any component of an electric circuit **12.** OPTICS **COMPONENT OF OPTICAL SYSTEM** any lens or other component of an optical system **13.** ASTRON **PARAMETER-DEFINING ORBIT** any one of the parameters required to define the nature of an orbit and to determine the position of a planetary body within it [14C. Via French < Latin *elementum* "rudiment"]

el·e·men·tal /èllə mént'l/ *adj* **1.** **FUNDAMENTAL** basic and essential **2.** **RELATING TO NATURAL FORCES** relating to or caused by powerful natural forces ○ *elemental passions* **3.** **SIMPLIFIED OR SIMPLIFYING** reduced to, or reducing something to, a stark simplicity ○ *classic elemental sculptures* **4.** CHEM **OF CHEMICAL OR ANCIENT ELEMENTS** relating to the chemical elements, or to the elements of earth, air, fire, and water that were once thought to be the basic units of matter —**el·e·men·tal·ly** *adv*

el·e·men·ta·ry /èllə méntəree, -méntree/ *adj* **1.** **RUDIMENTARY** involving or encompassing only the most simple and basic facts or principles ○ *an elementary knowledge of computing* **2.** **SIMPLE TO DO OR UNDERSTAND** requiring little skill or knowledge **3.** **OF ELEMENTARY SCHOOL** relating to an elementary school or the education provided there —**el·e·men·ta·ri·ly** /-men térrəlee/ *adv* —**el·e·men·ta·ri·ness** *n*

el·e·men·ta·ry par·ti·cle *n* any one of the subatomic constituents of which matter and energy are composed, e.g., electrons, leptons, photons, or hadrons

el·e·men·ta·ry school *n* a school that provides the first four to eight years of basic education

el·e·ments /élləmənts/ *npl* **1.** **FORCES OF WEATHER** the forces of the weather, e.g., wind, cold, rain, or sunshine, especially when thought of as harsh and damaging ○ *We're pretty exposed to the elements up here on the hilltop.* **2.** **BASIC PRINCIPLES** the basic and most important things to be learned when studying a subject ○ *She was endeavoring to teach us the elements of a good prose style.* **3.** CHR **BREAD AND WINE IN COMMUNION** the bread and wine used in celebrating the Christian sacrament of Communion

el·e·mi /élləmee/ *n* a fragrant resin obtained from various tropical trees. Use: varnishes, inks, ointments, perfumes. [Mid-16C. Via modern Latin < Arabic *al-lāmī*]

e·len·chus /i léngkəss/ (*plural* **-chi** /-kī/) *n* an argument that refutes a proposition by proving the opposite of its conclusions [Mid-17C. Via Latin < Greek *elegkhos* "refutation"] —**e·lenc·tic** /i léngktik/ *adj*

el·e·phant /élləfənt/ (*plural* **-phants** or *same*) *n* **1.** **LARGE**

elephant

ANIMAL WITH LONG TRUNK a very large gray or grayish brown animal with a long flexible trunk, prominent ears, thick legs, and pointed tusks. Native to: Africa, South Asia. Latin name: *Loxodonta africana* or *Loxodonta cyclotis* or *Elephas maximus.* **2.** PALEONT **EXTINCT ANIMAL** an extinct animal to which modern elephants are related **3.** (*plural* **el·e·phants**) **SOMETHING VERY LARGE** somebody or something that is extremely large or much larger than average [13C. Via French < Latin *elephantus* < Greek *elephās* "elephant, ivory"]

El·e·phan·ta Is·land /èllə fántə-/ island in Mumbai harbor, western India, approximately 6 mi./10 km east of Mumbai. Area: 1.93 sq. mi./5 sq. km.

el·e·phant·bird *n* BIRDS same as **aepyornis**

el·e·phant fo·li·o *n* a book size from 24 to 25 in./61 to 63.5 cm in height

el·e·phant gar·lic *n* a mild-flavored variety of garlic with very large bulbs, often roasted as a vegetable. Latin name: *Allium ampeloprasum.*

el·e·phant grass *n* tall coarse grass or a similar plant. Native to: tropical Africa, South Asia. Genera: *Typha* or *Pennisetum.*

el·e·phant gun *n* a large-caliber gun, typically .410 or more, used in hunting big game.

el·e·phan·ti·a·sis /èlləfən tī́ əssiss/ *n* a chronic disease in which parasitic worms obstruct the lymphatic system, causing enlargement of parts of the body, e.g., the legs and scrotum, and hardening of the surrounding skin. It is transmitted by mosquitoes. [Mid-16C. Via Latin < Greek < *elephās* "elephant"]

el·e·phan·tine /èllə fán teen, -tīn, élləfən-/ *adj* **1. SLOW AND HEAVY** moving in a slow, heavy, and often clumsy or awkward way ○ *the heavy elephantine tread of his feet* **2. ENORMOUS** very large or very great **3. SIMILAR TO ELEPHANT** resembling an elephant [Early 16C. Via Latin < Greek *elephantinos* < *elephās* "elephant"]

el·e·phant seal *n* a large earless seal, the male of which has a long inflatable snout resembling an elephant's trunk. Native to: western North American coast, Antarctic islands. Latin name: *Mirounga angustirostris* or *Mirounga leonina.*

el·e·phant's ear *n* PLANTS same as **taro**

el·e·phant's foot (*plural* **el·e·phant's foots**) *n* an ornamental climbing or trailing plant of the yam family with a large above-ground tuber that is sometimes used for food. Native to: southern Africa. Latin name: *Dioscorea elephantipes.*

El·eu·sin·i·an /èllyə sínnee ən/ *adj* relating to Eleusis, a village near Athens where the Eleusinian mysteries were celebrated, or to the Eleusinian mysteries themselves ■ *n* somebody who was born in or was a citizen of Eleusis [Mid-17C. < Latin *Eleusinius* < Greek *Eleusinios* < *Eleusis*]

El·eu·sin·i·an mys·ter·ies *npl* in ancient Greece, the secret religious rites celebrated annually at Eleusis and Athens that honored Persephone, Demeter, and Dionysus

el·e·vate /éllə vàyt/ (**-vat·ed, -vat·ing, -vates**) *vt* **1. RAISE SOMETHING UP** to raise something to a higher level or position **2. INCREASE SOMETHING** to increase the amount or intensity of something ○ *This was one factor that elevated interest rates.* **3. RAISE SOMEBODY TO HIGHER RANK** to raise or promote somebody or something to a high or higher status, rank, or office **4. RAISE SOMEBODY'S MIND OR SPIRIT** to lift somebody's mind or spirit to a more enlightened or exalted level (*formal*) **5.** ARMS **MAKE GUN BARREL POINT HIGHER** to make the barrel of a field gun point at a higher angle [14C. < Latin *elevat-*, past participle of *elevare* < *levare* "lighten"]

SYNONYMS See ***raise.***

el·e·vat·ed /éllə vàytəd/ *adj* **1. AT HIGH LEVEL OR POSITION** raised above ground level or situated at a higher level than something else ○ *elevated track* **2. HIGH OR HIGHER IN RANK** high or higher in rank or status **3. INCREASED** increased in amount ○ *elevated levels of cholesterol* **4. AT A HIGH MORAL OR INTELLECTUAL LEVEL** set at a high moral or intellectual level ○ *Milton's elevated conception of the role of the poet*

el·e·vat·ed rail·road *n* a rail system operating on a raised structure, usually above a street

el·e·va·tion /èllə váysh'n/ *n* **1. HEIGHT ABOVE LOCATION** the height above a specific reference point, especially sea level ○ *at an elevation of 1,000 feet above sea level* **2. RAISING SOMETHING, OR BEING RAISED** the act of raising somebody or something in height or status, or the process of being raised in height or status ○ *They congratulated him on his elevation to the cardinalship.* **3. ABILITY TO JUMP, OR HEIGHT REACHED** especially in ballet or figure skating, the ability of somebody to jump high and hold the position briefly, or the height somebody can reach in jumping **4. INCREASE** an increase in something (*technical*) ○ *Among the effects was an elevation in the level of dopamine.* **5.** ARCHIT **ARCHITECTURAL DRAWING OF SIDE OF BUILDING** a scale drawing of any side of a building or other structure ○ *the front elevation of the proposed new wing* **6.** CIV ENG **ANGLE IN SURVEYING** the angle between a horizontal line and the line from a surveying instrument to a point above the horizontal, e.g., between eye level and a line to a nearby rooftop **7.** ARMS **ANGLE OF GUN BARREL ABOVE HORIZONTAL** the angle to which the barrel of a large gun is raised above the horizontal **8.** CHR **RAISING OF HOST AND CHALICE** the raising up and showing to the people of the Host or chalice by a priest immediately after their consecration during a Mass **9.** ASTRON same as **altitude** (sense 4) —**el·e·va·tion·al** *adj*

el·e·va·tor /éllə vàytər/ *n* **1. PLATFORM FOR TAKING UP OR DOWN** a platform, cage, or enclosed compartment that is raised or lowered mechanically and used to take people or things to a higher or lower level in a building **2. GRAIN STOREHOUSE** a storehouse for grain, equipped with a mechanism for taking in, lifting, and discharging the grain **3. HOISTING MACHINE** a machine with scoops or similar devices for hoisting something to a higher level **4. AIRCRAFT DEVICE CONTROLLING CLIMB AND DESCENT** a hinged flap, either of a pair on the rear portion of the horizontal stabilizing surface or tailplane of an aircraft, used to control the aircraft's up-and-down movement **5. AIRCRAFT PLATFORM ON CARRIER** on an aircraft carrier, a mechanized platform that transports aircraft from a below-the-deck hangar up to the flight deck and vice versa **6.** ANAT **MUSCLE THAT LIFTS PART OF BODY** a muscle that contracts to lift a part of the body

el·e·va·tor mu·sic *n* bland instrumental background music played over loudspeakers in elevators, stores, and other public places (*informal*)

el·e·va·tor shoe *n* a shoe designed to increase the height of the wearer

e·lev·en /i lévv'n/ *n* **1. 11** the number 11 **2. SOMETHING WITH VALUE OF 11** something in a numbered series with a value of 11 **3. GROUP OF 11** a group of 11 objects or people **4. TEAM OF 11** a team of 11 players, e.g., a football team or a field hockey team [Old English *endleofan* "one over (ten)" < Germanic] —**e·lev·en** *adj, pron*

e·lev·ens·es /i lévv'nzəz/ *n* a mid-morning snack (*takes a singular or plural verb*)

e·lev·enth /i lévv'nth/ *n* one of 11 equal parts of something —**e·lev·enth** *adj, adv*

e·lev·enth hour *n* the last moment before something happens ○ *"Time after time you'll find solutions are reached at the 59th minute of the eleventh hour."* (John Major, *Guardian Weekly;* April 3, 1994) —**e·lev·enth-hour** *adj*

el·e·von /éllə vòn/ *n* a hinged flap on an aircraft, especially one with a delta wing or no tail, that functions both as an elevator and an aileron [Mid-20C. Blend of ELEVATOR + AILERON]

elf /elf/ (*plural* **elves** /elvz/) *n* **1.** in folklore, a small lively imaginary being resembling a human with pointed ears, often considered to have a mischievous nature and magical powers **2.** any small person, especially a child, who plays pranks or tricks [Old English < Germanic] —**elf·like** *adj*

ELF *abbr* **1.** ENVIRON Earth Liberation Front **2.** English as a Lingua Franca **3.** MEDIA extremely low frequency

elf·in /élfin/ *adj* **1. OF OR LIKE ELVES** like, characteristic of, or associated with elves **2. BY ELVES** supposedly caused or made by elves **3. SMALL AND LIVELY** small, delicate, and charmingly sprightly, lively, or mischievous ○ *elfin features* **4. MAGICAL** having a magical charm or appeal

elf·ish /élfish/, **elv·ish** /élvish/ *adj* **1.** resembling or relating to an elf **2.** full of lively mischief —**elf·ish·ly** *adv*

elf·lock /élf lòk/ *n* a tangled coil of hair (*often used in the plural*)

Sir Edward Elgar

El·gar /él gaar, élgər/, **Sir Edward** (1857–1934) British composer. He was a major figure of late romanticism in music, writing both choral and orchestral works. His *Enigma Variations* (1899) and the patriotic *Pomp and Circumstance* marches (1901–07, 1930) are among his most popular pieces.

> "There is music in the air, music all round us: the world is full of it, and you simply take as much as you require."
> [Sir Edward Elgar. Quoted in *Sir Edward Elgar*, R. J. Buckley; 1905]

El·gin /élgin/ city in northeastern Illinois, on the Fox River, north of Aurora and west of Chicago. Population: 96,539 (2002 estimate).

El Gre·co ➧ **Greco, El**

el·hi /él hī/ *adj US* describes educational material relating to or designed for use in grades 1 to 12 ○ *elhi textbooks and software* [Mid-20C. < shortenings of ELEMENTARY + HIGH]

E·li·a /eélee ə/ ➧ **Lamb, Charles**

e·lic·it /i líssit/ (**-it·ed, -it·ing, -its**) *vt* **1.** to cause or produce something as a reaction or response to a stimulus of some kind ○ *His jokes failed to elicit even the faintest of smiles from her.* **2.** to bring something to light or cause something to be disclosed, especially by a process of questioning or research ○ *What were their chances of eliciting any worthwhile information from such an obstinately uncooperative witness?* [Mid-17C. < Latin *elicit-*, past participle of *elicere* "draw out (by trickery)" < *lacere* "deceive"] —**e·lic·i·ta·tion** /i lìssi táysh'n/ *n* —**e·lic·i·tor** *n*

SPELLCHECK elicit or **illicit**? Do not confuse the spelling of ***elicit*** and ***illicit***, which sound similar. ***Elicit*** is a verb meaning "produce as a response" or "bring to light," as in *to elicit information.* ***Illicit*** is an adjective meaning "illegal" or "socially unacceptable," as in *engaging in illicit activities.*

e·lide /i lī́d/ (**e·lid·ed, e·lid·ing, e·lides**) *vt* **1.** to omit a vowel, consonant, or syllable of a word, or leave out part of a sentence or phrase **2.** to omit, delete, or ignore something (*formal*) [Late 16C. < Latin *elidere* "strike out" < *laedere* "strike"]

el·i·gi·ble /éllijəb'l/ *adj* **1. QUALIFIED** entitled or qualified to do, be, or get something ○ *She is eligible to run for office.* **2. MARRIAGEABLE** considered a good candidate for marriage ○ *the most eligible bachelor in town* **3.** *US* **ALLOWED BY RULES TO CATCH FOOTBALL** in football, permitted by the rules to catch a forward pass during a play ■ *n* **SOMEBODY OR SOMETHING THAT MEETS REQUIREMENTS** somebody or something that matches up to a set of requirements ○ *We've separated the eligibles from the duds.* [15C. Via French, "fit to be chosen" < late Latin *eligibilis* "that may be chosen" < Latin *eligere* (see ELECT)] —**el·i·gi·bil·i·ty** /èllijə bíllətee/ *n* —**el·i·gi·bly** *adv*

E·li·jah /i líjə/ *n* in the Bible, a Hebrew prophet of the 9th century B.C. who fought against idolatry and paganism and maintained the worship of Jehovah

e·lim·i·nate /i límmə nàyt/ (**-nat·ed, -nat·ing, -nates**) *vt* **1. GET RID OF SOMETHING** to put an end to something, usually something undesirable ○ *They are pledged to eliminate poverty by the end of the century.* **2. REJECT SOMEBODY OR SOMETHING** to decide to exclude somebody or something from further consideration ○ *The police eliminated him from the list of suspects.* **3.** SPORTS **DEFEAT SOMEBODY IN COMPETITION** to defeat a player or team and put them out of a competition (*usually passive*) ○ *The local team was eliminated in the first round.* **4. MURDER SOMEBODY** to kill an opponent **5.** PHYSIOL **GET RID OF BODILY WASTE** to expel waste from the body (*technical*) **6.** MATH **REMOVE MATHEMATICAL VARIABLE** to remove variables from two or more simultaneous mathematical equations by combining the equations [Mid-16C. < Latin *eliminat-*, past participle of *eliminare* "turn out of doors" < *limen* "threshold"] —**e·lim·i·na·tion** /i lìmmə náysh'n/ *n* —**e·lim·i·na·tive** /-nàytiv/ *adj* —**e·lim·i·na·tor** *n* —**e·lim·i·na·to·ry** /-nə tàwree/ *adj*

ELINT /éllint/, **el·int** *n* the gathering of information by electronic means, e.g., from aircraft or ships, or the section of the military intelligence service involved in this [Mid-20C. < shortenings of ELECTRONIC + INTELLIGENCE]

El·i·on /éllee ən/, **Gertrude Belle** (1918–99) US chemist. She and fellow researcher George Hitchings pioneered research into drugs that kill harmful invading cells without damaging healthy body cells, which led to the development of AZT. They shared the 1988 Nobel Prize in physiology or medicine with James Black.

Barnaby's

George Eliot

El·i·ot /éllee ət/, **George** (1819–80) British novelist. Her naturalistic and humanistic books include *Adam Bede* (1859) and *Middlemarch* (1871–72). Pseudonym of **Evans, Mary Ann**

> "A woman dictates before marriage in order that she may have an appetite for submission afterwards."
> [George Eliot, *Middlemarch*; 1871–72]

El·i·ot, John (1604–90) English-born American colonial cleric. As a Christian missionary, he preached to the Native Americans in Massachusetts in their own language and published a Native American translation of the Bible (1661–63). Known as **Apostle to the Indians**

El·i·ot, T. S. (1888–1965) US-born British poet, critic, and dramatist. His poem *The Waste Land* (1922) represents a landmark in modern English poetry. He won the Nobel Prize in literature (1948). Later works include *Four Quartets* (1943) and the verse drama *Murder in the Cathedral* (1935). Full name **Eliot, Thomas Stearns**. See Cultural note at **hollow, wasteland**

> "Footfalls echo in the memory / Down the passage which we did not take / Towards the door we never opened / Into the rose garden. My words echo / Thus, in your mind."
> [T. S. Eliot, "Burnt Norton," *Four Quartets*; 1943]

> "Poetry is not a turning loose of emotion, but an escape from emotion; it is not the expression of personality, but an escape from personality."
> [T. S. Eliot, "Tradition and the Individual Talent"; 1920]

US Office of War Information

T. S. Eliot

ELISA /i lízə, i líssə/ *n* a widely used technique for determining the presence or amount of protein in a biological sample, using an enzyme that bonds to an antibody or antigen and causes a color change. Full form **enzyme-linked immunosorbent assay**

E·li·sha /i líshə/ *n* in the Bible, a Hebrew prophet of the 9th century B.C. who enjoyed political influence throughout the reigns of four kings of Israel. He was the disciple and successor of Elijah.

e·li·sion /i lízh'n/ (*plural* **-sions** or *same*) *n* **1.** the omission of a vowel, consonant, or syllable while pronouncing or writing something, sometimes as a natural shortening, as in "he's," sometimes for literary or poetic effect, as in "'tis" **2.** the suppression, omission, or deletion of something, or what has been suppressed, omitted, or deleted (*formal*) [Late 16C. < Latin *elision-* < *elidere* "strike out" (see ELIDE)]

e·lite /i léet, ay-/ *n* **1. PRIVILEGED MINORITY** a small group of people within a larger group who have more power, social standing, wealth, or talent than the rest of the group (*takes a singular or plural verb*) **2.** PRINTING **SIZE OF PRINTING TYPE** a 10-point type that has about 12 characters to the inch or just under 5 characters to the centimeter ■ *adj* **1. RICHEST, BEST, OR MOST POWERFUL** more talented, privileged, or highly trained than others ○ *elite troops* **2. FOR RICH OR PRIVILEGED PEOPLE** restricted to the rich or privileged ○ *an elite school* [Late 18C. < French < Latin *eligere* "pick out" (see ELECT)]

e·lit·ism /i lée tìzzəm, ay-/ *n* **1. BELIEF IN CONCEPT OF SUPERIORITY** the belief that some people or things are inherently superior to others and deserve preeminence, preferential treatment, or higher rewards because of their superiority **2. BELIEF IN CONTROL BY SMALL GROUP** the belief that government or control should be in the hands of a small group of privileged, wealthy, or intelligent people, or the active promotion of such a system **3. CONTROL BY SMALL GROUP** government or control by a small, specially qualified, or privileged group —**e·lit·ist** *n, adj*

e·lix·ir /i líksər/ *n* **1. CURE-ALL** a panacea or a quick or magical cure **2. SWEETENED DRUG** a sweetened solution of a drug in alcohol and water **3.** *also* **e·lix·ir of life MIRACULOUS SUBSTANCE** a substance once believed to prolong life indefinitely, or to transform base metals into gold [14C. Via medieval Latin < Arabic *al-iksir* < Greek *xērion* "dry powder for treating wounds" < *xēros* "dry"]

E·liz·a·beth /i lízzəbəth/ city in northeastern New Jersey, situated on Newark Bay. Population: 123,279 (2002 estimate).

E·liz·a·beth (1900–2002) queen consort of the United Kingdom. She married the second son of George V, who came to the throne as George VI in 1936, and was the mother of Queen Elizabeth II. Born **Bowes-Lyon, Lady Elizabeth**. Also known as **Queen Elizabeth, the Queen Mother**

> "Now we can look the East End in the face."
> [Elizabeth. Surveying the damage caused to Buckingham Palace by a bomb during the Blitz in World War II; 1940]

E·liz·a·beth I (1533–1603) queen of England and Ireland. The daughter of Henry VIII and Anne Boleyn, she established the Protestant Church in England and presided over a period of domestic political stability and global exploration.

> "I know I have the body of a weak and feeble woman, but I have the heart and stomach of a king, and of a king of England too."
> [Elizabeth I, *Speech to the troops at Tilbury on the approach of the Armada*; 1588]

E·liz·a·beth II (*b.* 1926) queen of the United Kingdom. Daughter of George VI and queen since 1952, she married Prince Philip in 1947 and has four children, Prince Charles, Princess Anne, Prince Andrew, and Prince Edward.

> "1992 is not a year I shall look back on with undiluted pleasure. In the words of one of my more sympathetic correspondents, it has turned out to be an 'annus horribilis.'"
> [Elizabeth II, *Speech*; December 25, 1992]

E·liz·a·be·than /i lìzzə béethən, -béthən/ *adj* relating to or characteristic of the life and times of Elizabeth I, queen of England and Ireland, who reigned from 1558 to 1603

E·liz·a·be·than son·net *n* LITERAT same as **Shakespearean sonnet**

E·liz·a·beth·town /i lízzəbəth tòwn/ city in north central Kentucky, northeast of Bowling Green and south of Louisville. Population: 23,080 (2002 estimate).

E·li·za·beth·ville /i lízzəbəth vìl/ former name for **Lubumbashi**

elk /elk/ (*plural same* or **elks**) *n* **1.** ZOOL same as **wapiti** **2.** *UK* same as **moose** [Old English *eolh*]

Elk /elk/ *n* a member of a men's social and charitable organization, the Benevolent and Protective Order of Elks

Elk Grove /élk-/ village in northern California, a southern suburb of Sacramento. Population: 75,175 (2002 estimate).

Elk Grove Vil·lage village in northeastern Illinois, southwest of Des Plaines. It is a suburb of Chicago. Population: 35,028 (2002 estimate).

Elk·hart /élk haart/ city in northern Indiana, at the confluence of the St. Joseph and Elkhart rivers, near the border with Michigan. Population: 51,782 (2002 estimate).

elk·hound /élk hòwnd/ *n UK* same as **Norwegian elkhound**

Elk Is·land Na·tion·al Park national park in central Alberta, Canada, 20 mi./48 km east of Edmonton, established in 1913. Area: 75 sq. mi./194 sq. km.

Elk·ton /élktən/ town in northeastern Maryland, on the Elk River at the northern end of Chesapeake Bay. Population: 13,094 (2002 estimate).

ell /el/ *n* **1.** *US* an extension of a building, usually at right angles to the main part **2.** something L-shaped or with a right-angled bend [Late 18C. Spelling of the letter *L*]

el·lag·ic ac·id /ə làjjik-/ *n* a yellow crystalline compound. Source: oak galls, tannins. Use: reduction of bleeding. Formula: $C_{14}H_6O_8$. [Early 19C. < French *ellagique* < anagram of *galle* "gallnut"]

El·lef Ring·nes Is·land /è lef ríng nayss-/ uninhabited island of the Canadian Sverdrup Island group, located in the Arctic Ocean, in the Northwest Territories. Area: 4,361 sq. mi./11,295 sq. km.

El·le·ry /élləree/, **William** (1727–1820) American politician. He was elected to the Second Continental Congress from Rhode Island (1776) and was a signatory to the Declaration of Independence.

Elles·mere Is·land /élz meer-/ uninhabited island in Nunavut Territory, northern Canada, in the Arctic

Ocean close to the northwestern coast of Greenland. Area: 75,767 sq. mi./196,236 sq. km.

Elles·mere Is·land Na·tion·al Park Re·serve former name for **Quttinirpaaq National Park**

Elles·mere Port city in Cheshire, northwestern England, situated on the Mersey River. Population: 64,504 (1991).

El·lice Is·lands /élliss-/ former name for **Tuvalu** (until 1975)

El·li·cott Cit·y /élli kot-/ town in central Maryland. Population: 41,396 (1996).

Duke Ellington

El·ling·ton /éllingtən/, **Duke** (1899–1974) US jazz pianist, composer, and bandleader. He came to fame in the early 1930s and is known for compositions such as "Sophisticated Lady" (1933). Born **Ellington, Edward Kennedy**

"Music to me is a sound sensation, assimilation, anticipation, adulation, and reputation."
[Duke Ellington, *Music is My Mistress*; 1973]

El·li·ott /éllee ət/, **Herb** (*b.* 1938) Australian athlete. He was the winner of the gold medal for the 1,500 meters at the 1960 Olympics. Between 1957 and 1961 he was never defeated at this distance. Full name **Elliott, Herbert James**

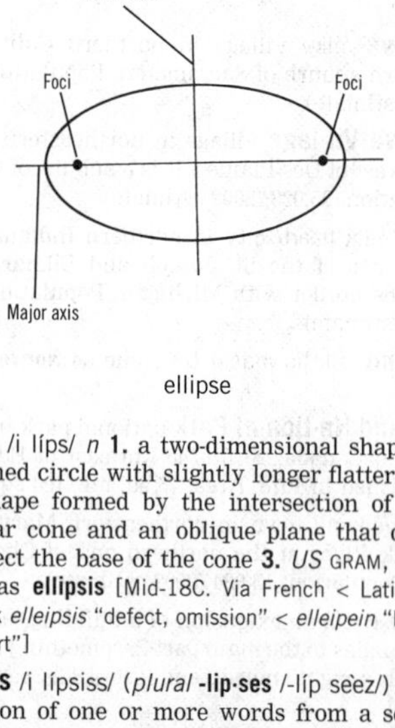

ellipse

el·lipse /i líps/ *n* **1.** a two-dimensional shape like a stretched circle with slightly longer flatter sides **2.** the shape formed by the intersection of a right circular cone and an oblique plane that does not intersect the base of the cone **3.** *US* GRAM, PRINTING same as **ellipsis** [Mid-18C. Via French < Latin *ellipsis* < Greek *elleipsis* "defect, omission" < *elleipein* "leave out, fall short"]

el·lip·sis /i lípsiss/ (*plural* **-lip·ses** /-líp seez/) *n* **1.** the omission of one or more words from a sentence, especially when what is omitted can be understood from the context. The omission of "go" at the end of "I went but my wife didn't" is an example of ellipsis. **2.** a printed mark, usually three dots (...), or, less often, asterisks (***), used to indicate that something has been omitted from a text [Early 17C. < Latin (see ELLIPSE)]

USAGE The ***ellipsis*** in the form of three dots is used when text is omitted from the beginning, middle, or end of a quotation: *Shakespeare wrote, "When sorrows come, they come…in battalions".* (The full quotation is *"When sorrows come, they come not single spies,/But in battalions"*). Any punctuation that precedes or follows the omitted text may or may not be shown before or after the ellipsis: *You can fool all the people some of the time…but you cannot fool all the people all of the time.* When the ellipsis comes at the end of a sentence, it is usually followed by a period. Dots are also used in direct speech to show that the speaker is hesitating or has left something unsaid: *"I don't know… I'll try… I can't promise anything."* In some styles of writing, asterisks are used when part of a word is omitted, usually part of a swearword.

el·lip·soid /i líp sòyd/ *n* a geometric surface or a solid figure shaped like an oval. Any section through an ellipsoid is either an ellipse or a circle. ■ *adj* in the shape of an ellipsoid —**el·lip·soid·al** /i lip sóyd'l/ *adj*

el·lip·ti·cal /i líptik'l/, **el·lip·tic** /i líptik/ *adj* **1.** MATH **LIKE ELLIPSE** in the shape or pattern of a geometric ellipse **2.** GRAM **RELATING TO ELLIPSIS** relating to ellipsis or containing an example of ellipsis **3.** **HIGHLY ECONOMICAL IN SPEECH OR WRITING** extremely concise in speech or writing, sometimes so concise as to be difficult or impossible to understand [Mid-17C. < Greek *elleiptikos* "defective" < *elleipein* "leave out, fall short"] —**el·lip·ti·cal·ly** *adv*

el·lip·ti·cal gal·ax·y *n* a galaxy with an overall elliptical or spherical shape and no arms or internal structure

el·lip·tic·i·ty /i lip tíssətee/ (*plural* **-ties**) *n* the deviation or degree of deviation of an ellipse or ellipsoid from a perfect circle or sphere. Ellipticity is measured as the ratio of the major axis to the minor axis of the ellipse or ellipsoid.

El·lis /élliss/, **Havelock** (1859–1939) British psychologist. His *Studies in the Psychology of Sex* (1897–1928) was a landmark in the analysis of sexual behavior. Full name **Ellis, Henry Havelock**

"Pain and death are a part of life. To reject them is to reject life itself."
[Havelock Ellis, *On Life and Sex: Essays of Love and Virtue*; 1922]

El·lis Is·land /élliss-/ complex of one natural and two artificial islands in upper New York Bay, eastern New Jersey, and southeastern New York State, near Manhattan. From 1892 to 1954 it served as a chief entry point for immigrants to the United States. Area: 0.04 sq. mi./0.11 sq. km.

El·li·son /élliss'n/, **Larry** (*b.* 1944) US entrepreneur. He founded (1977) and now runs one of the world's largest computer software companies. Full name **Ellison, Lawrence J.**

El·li·son, Ralph (1914–94) US writer. He is best known for his novel about US racial issues, *Invisible Man* (1952). Full name **Ellison, Ralph Waldo**

"I am an invisible man, I am a man of substance, of flesh and bone, fiber and liquids—and I might even be said to possess a mind. I am invisible, understand, simply because people refuse to see me."
[Ralph Ellison, *Invisible Man*; 1952]

Ells·worth /élz wùrth/, **Lincoln** (1880–1951) US explorer. He was the first person to fly over the Arctic (1926) and Antarctica (1935).

Ells·worth, Oliver (1745–1807) chief justice of the US Supreme Court. He helped to organize the US Congress and the federal court system, and was chief justice from 1796 to 1800.

Ells·worth Land high plateau in western Antarctica, south of the Antarctic Peninsula. It rises at the Vinson Massif, the highest point in Antarctica, to 16,863 ft./5,140 m.

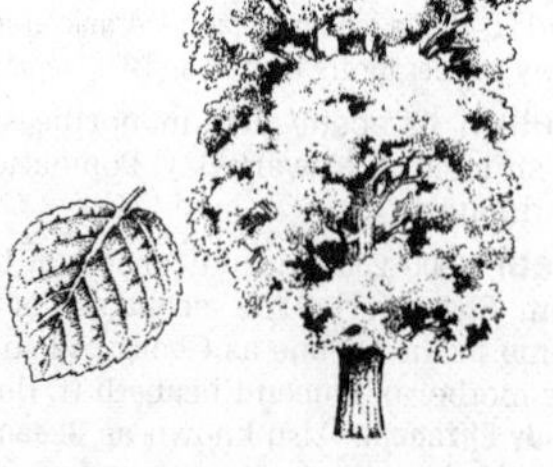

elm

elm /elm/ *n* **1.** a deciduous tree with serrated leaves and winged fruits. Native to: northern temperate regions. Genus: *Ulmus.* **2.** the hard dense wood of an elm tree. Use: furniture, boats, construction. [Old English < Indo-European]

elm bark bee·tle *n* the beetle that spreads the fungus causing Dutch elm disease. Family: Scolytidae.

Elm·hurst /élm hùrst/ city in northeastern Illinois, a residential and industrial suburb of Chicago. Population: 43,419 (2002 estimate).

El·mi·ra /el mírə/ city in southern New York on the Chemung River, west of Binghamton. Population: 30,417 (2002 estimate).

El Mis·ti ♦ **Misti**

El Mon·te /el móntee/ city in southern California, south of the San Gabriel Mountains, an eastern suburb of Los Angeles. Population: 119,918 (2002 estimate).

Elm·wood Park /élm wŏŏd-/ village in northeastern Illinois, west of Chicago. Population: 25,180 (2002 estimate).

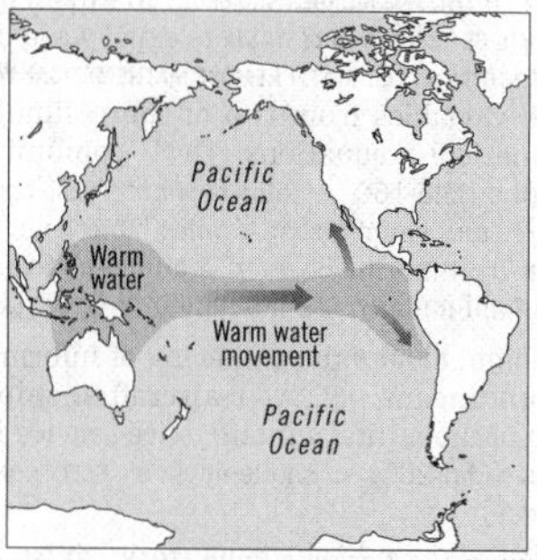

El Niño: map showing movement of warm water currents across the Pacific Ocean

El Ni·ño /el néenyō/ *n* a periodic change in the currents of the Pacific Ocean that occurs every five to eight years and brings unusually warm water to the coast of northern South America. It often leads to severe climate disruption to countries in and beside the Pacific. [< Spanish, shortening of *El Niño de Navidad* "the Christmas Child"; from the time of year when the currents change]

el·o·cu·tion /éllə kyóosh'n/ *n* the art of speaking clearly and well, with correct enunciation [15C. < Latin *elocution-* < *eloqui* (see ELOQUENT)] —**el·o·cu·tion·ar·y** *adj* —**el·o·cu·tion·ist** *n*

e·lo·de·a /i lódee ə/ *n* a plant that grows submerged in ponds and ditches. Use: oxygenating aquariums. Genus: *Elodea.* [Late 19C. < modern Latin < Greek *helōdēs* "marshy"]

E·lo·him /e ló hìm, èllō hím/ *n* in the Bible, a Hebrew word for God [Late 16C. < Hebrew *elōhīm*, plural of *elōah* "God"]

e·lon·gate /i láwng gàyt/ *vti* (**-gat·ed, -gat·ing, -gates**) **LENGTHEN** to make something longer, or become longer ■ *adj* **1.** **LONG** long and narrow or slender (*technical*) **2.** **MADE LONGER** lengthened or stretched out (*formal*) [Mid-16C. < late Latin *elongat-*, past participle of *elongare* "lengthen" < Latin *longus* "long"] —**e·lon·gat·ed** *adj*

e·lon·ga·tion /i làwng gáysh'n/ *n* **1.** **LENGTHENING** the act of lengthening something, or the condition of being lengthened **2.** **SOMETHING LENGTHENED** something that has become or been made longer **3.** ASTRON **ANGLE BETWEEN SUN AND ASTRONOMICAL OBJECT** the angle between the Sun and either the Moon or a planet, as seen from Earth or a point in space

e·lope /i lóp/ (**e·loped, e·lop·ing, e·lopes**) *vi* to go away suddenly without telling anyone, especially in order to marry or cohabit with a lover without the knowledge or consent of parents or guardians [Late 16C. < Anglo-Norman *aloper* "run away"] —**e·lope·ment** *n* —**e·lop·er** *n*

el·o·quence /élləkwənss/ *n* **1.** the ability to speak forcefully, expressively, and persuasively **2.** forceful, expressive, and persuasive language

el·o·quent /élləkwənt/ *adj* **1.** said or saying something in a forceful, expressive, and persuasive way **2.** expressing a feeling or thought clearly, memorably, or movingly [14C. Via French < Latin *eloquent-*, present participle of *eloqui* "speak out" < *loqui* "speak"] —**el·o·quent·ly** *adv* —**el·o·quent·ness** *n*

El Pas·o /el pássō/ city in western Texas on the Rio Grande, a port of entry from Mexico. Population: 577,415 (2002 estimate).

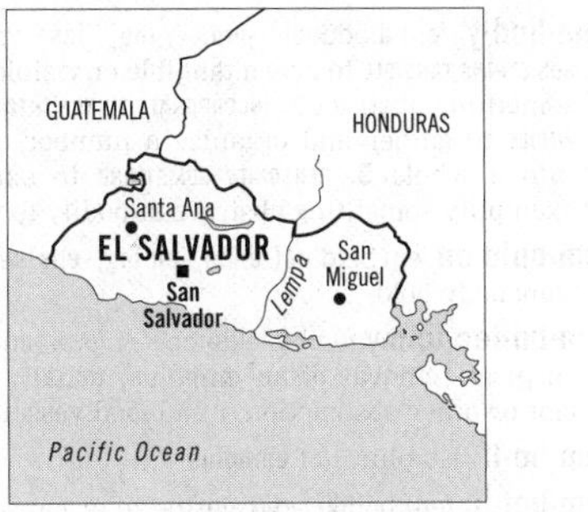

El Salvador

El Sal·va·dor /el sálvə dàwr/ country on the Pacific coast of Central America, bordered by Guatemala and Honduras. Language: Spanish. Currency: colón. Capital: San Salvador. Population: 6,470,379 (2003). Area: 8,124 sq. mi./21,041 sq. km. Official name **Republic of El Salvador.** ◊ **Salvadoran**

else /elss/ *adv* **1.** used to refer in a vague way to an additional person, place, or thing ○ *Something else I'd like to see is more jobs for skilled workers.* ○ *What else did she say?* ○ *I didn't go anywhere else.* **2.** used to refer in a vague way to somebody or something different or alternative ○ *Let's try something else.* ○ *He was unhappy and considered working somewhere else.* [Old English *elles* < Indo-European] ◇ **or else 1.** otherwise ○ *Go away, or else I'll call the police.* **2.** used to make a threat ○ *Have it ready by tomorrow, or else!*

El Se·gun·do /èl si go͝ondō/ city in southern California on the southeastern shore of Santa Monica Bay, south of Los Angeles. Population: 16,385 (2002 estimate).

else·where /éiss wèr, -hwèr/ *adv* at, in, or to another place ○ *If you're calling from elsewhere, please press 2 to speak to a representative.* ○ *They stock books that may be hard to find elsewhere.*

ELT *n* the teaching of English to nonnative speakers of English. Full form **English Language Teaching**

el·u·ant /éllyoo ənt/, **el·u·ent** *n* a solvent used to remove something from a substance [Mid-20C. < Latin *eluent-*, present participle of *eluere* (see ELUTE)]

Él·u·ard /élloo aàr, áyl waàr/, **Paul** (1895–1952) French poet. He is one of France's greatest 20th-century lyric poets and coauthor of the 1925 surrealist manifesto. He fought in the Communist Resistance in World War II. Pseudonym of **Grindel, Eugène**

"The earth is blue like an orange."
[Paul Éluard, *L'Amour, la poésie (Love and Poetry)*; 1929]

el·u·ate /élloo àyt, -ət/ *n* the liquid left after the process of elution, consisting of dissolved matter and the solvent used [Mid-20C. < Latin *eluere* (see ELUTE)]

e·lu·ci·date /i lo͞ossə dàyt/ (**-dat·ed, -dat·ing, -dates**) *vti* to explain or clarify something [Mid-16C. < late Latin *elucidat-*, past participle of *elucidare* "make clear" < Latin *lucidus* "clear"] —**e·lu·ci·da·tion** /i lo͞ossə dáysh'n/ *n* —**e·lu·ci·da·tive** *adj* —**e·lu·ci·da·tor** *n* —**e·lu·ci·da·to·ry** /i lo͞ossədə tàwree/ *adj*

e·lude /i lo͞od/ (**e·lud·ed, e·lud·ing, e·ludes**) *vt* **1.** to escape from or avoid somebody or something by cunning, skill, or resourcefulness **2.** to be beyond somebody's understanding or ability to be remembered ○ *Her name eludes me.* [Mid-16C. < Latin *eludere* "deceive, escape from, win from somebody at play" < *ludere* "play"]

SPELLCHECK See *allude.*

USAGE See *avoid.*

E·lul /é lùl/ *n* in the Jewish calendar, the sixth month of the religious year, lasting 29 days and falling at about the same time as August to September. See table at **calendar** [Mid-16C. < Hebrew *elūl*]

e·lu·sive /ə lo͞ossiv, i-/ *adj* **1.** HARD TO FIND difficult to find or catch **2.** HARD TO PIN DOWN difficult to understand, define, or identify **3.** HARD TO REMEMBER not easily called to mind or memory —**e·lu·sive·ly** *adv* —**e·lu·sive·ness** *n*

SPELLCHECK elusive, illusive, or **allusive**? Do not confuse the spelling of ***elusive, illusive,*** and ***allusive,*** which sound similar. ***Elusive,*** the most frequent of the three adjectives, means "difficult to catch, find, understand, or remember," as in *an elusive thief.* ***Illusive*** is another word for *illusory,* meaning "consisting of an illusion." ***Allusive*** means "making an allusion" or "characterized by allusions," as in *an allusive remark.*

e·lu·so·ry /ə lo͞ossəree, ə lo͞ozəree/ *adj* **1.** difficult to find or catch (*formal*) **2.** avoiding the issue in an evasive or deceitful way

e·lute /i lo͞ot/ (**e·lut·ed, e·lut·ing, e·lutes**) *vt* to remove one substance from another, usually an adsorbed material from an adsorbent surface, by washing it out with a solvent (*technical*) [Mid-18C. < Latin *elut-*, past participle of *eluere* "wash out" < *luere* "wash"] —**e·lu·tion** *n*

e·lu·tri·ate /ə lo͞otree àyt/ (**-at·ed, -at·ing, -ates**) *vt* to purify or separate something from a mixture by washing, decanting, or straining it (*technical*) [Mid-18C. < Latin *elutriat-*, past participle of *elutriare* "wash out" < *lutriare* "wash"] —**e·lu·tri·a·tion** /ə lo͞otree áysh'n/ *n*

e·lu·vi·a GEOL plural of **eluvium**

e·lu·vi·al /ə lo͞ovee əl/ *adj* of or relating to eluvium or eluviation

e·lu·vi·al de·pos·it *n* a concentration of an ore deposit formed as a result of the removal of less dense host material

e·lu·vi·a·tion /ə lo͞ovee áysh'n/ *n* a process by which material dissolved or suspended in water within soil moves down or sideways as rainwater moves through the soil

e·lu·vi·um /ə lo͞ovee əm/ (*plural* **-vi·a** /-vee ə/) *n* an accumulated mass of soil, sand, silt, or rock debris resulting from weathering or drifting [Late 19C. < Latin *eluere* (see ELUTE), after ALLUVIUM]

el·ver /élvər/ *n* a young freshwater eel, especially one that migrates from salt water [Mid-17C. < dialect *ellfare*, literally "eel-journey"]

elves plural of **elf**

elv·ish *adj* another spelling of **elfish**

E·ly /éelee/ cathedral city in Cambridgeshire, eastern England, situated on the Ouse River. It stands on a low hill in the fenland, known as the Isle of Ely. Population: 11,760 (1994).

E·ly·sian /i lízh'n/ *adj* **1.** relating to or typical of Elysium **2.** full of or giving great pleasure and delight (*literary*) [Mid-16C. < ELYSIUM[1]]

E·ly·sian Fields *npl* MYTHOL same as **Elysium**[1] (sense 1)

E·ly·si·um[1] /i lízhee əm, ə lízzee-/ *n* **1.** in Greek mythology, the home of the blessed after death **2.** any ideally delightful or blissful place or condition

E·ly·si·um[2] /i lízhee əm, ə lízzee-/ extensive low bulge on the surface of Mars in the northern hemisphere gently rising to a height of approximately 3 mi./5 km, supporting the volcanoes Hecates Tholus and Elysium Mons

el·y·tron /éllə tròn/ (*plural* **-tra** /-trə/), **el·y·trum** /-trəm/ (*plural* **-tra**) *n* a tough front wing, occurring in pairs on beetles and some other insects, that acts as a protective covering for the rear wings [Mid-18C. < Greek *elutron* "sheath"]

em /em/ *n* **1.** a unit of measurement of print size, equal to the point size of the typeface being used **2.** PRINTING same as **pica**[1] [Late 18C. Representing pronunciation of M[1]; because the letter is about this width]

'em /əm/ *contr* them (*informal*) [14C. Originally variant of Old English *hem* "them"; now regarded as a contraction]

EM *abbr* **1.** electromagnetic **2.** electron microscope **3.** enlisted man

E.M. *abbr* EDUC Engineer of Mines

em- *prefix* same as **en-** (*used before m, b, or p*) ○ *embark*

e·ma·ci·ate /i máyshee àyt/ (**-at·ed, -at·ing, -ates**) *vti* to become, or make somebody or something become, extremely thin [Early 17C. < Latin *emaciat-*, past participle of *emaciare* "make lean, waste away" < *macer* "lean"] —**e·ma·ci·a·tion** /i màyshee áysh'n/ *n*

e·ma·ci·at·ed /i máyshee àytəd/ *adj* extremely thin, especially because of starvation or illness

SYNONYMS See *thin.*

e-mail, **e·mail** /ée màyl/ *n* **1.** COMPUTER-TO-COMPUTER COMMUNICATION SYSTEM a system that allows text-based messages to be exchanged electronically, e.g., between computers or cell phones. Full form **electronic mail** **2.** E-MAIL MESSAGE a communication sent by e-mail ■ *vt* (**e-mailed, e-mail·ing, e-mails**) COMMUNICATE SOMETHING BY E-MAIL to send a message to somebody by e-mail

e-mail ad·dress *n* a URL that gives the origin or destination of an electronic message

e-mail short·hand *n* the set of acronyms and abbreviations for common phrases originally used in e-mail and subsequently in chat rooms, instant messaging, and newsgroup postings

em·a·lan·ge·ni MONEY plural of **lilangeni**

em·a·nate /émmə nàyt/ (**-nat·ed, -nat·ing, -nates**) *v* **1.** *vi* to come from or come out of somebody, something, or somewhere **2.** *vt* to emit, send out, or give out something such as rays or information (*formal*) [Mid-18C. < Latin *emanat-*, past participle of *emanare* "flow out, arise" < *manare* "flow"] —**em·a·na·tive** *adj*

em·a·na·tion /émmə náysh'n/ *n* **1.** ACT OF SENDING SOMETHING OUT the act of emitting, sending out, or giving out something **2.** SOMETHING SENT OUT something that issues or is sent out or given out from somebody, something, or somewhere **3.** PHYS RADIOACTIVE GAS any gas produced by radioactive decay, e.g., radon —**em·a·na·tion·al** *adj*

e·man·ci·pate /i mánssə pàyt/ (**-pat·ed, -pat·ing, -pates**) *vt* **1.** to free somebody from slavery, serfdom, or other such forms of bondage **2.** to free somebody from restrictions or conventions (*often passive*) [Early 17C. < Latin *emancipat-*, past participle of *emancipare* "to free from parental power" < *mancipium* "ownership"] —**e·man·ci·pa·tive** *adj* —**e·man·ci·pa·tor** *n* —**e·man·ci·pa·to·ry** *adj*

e·man·ci·pa·tion /i mànssə páysh'n/ *n* **1.** the act or process of setting somebody free or of freeing somebody from restrictions **2.** the condition or fact of being set free or freed from some restriction

E·man·ci·pa·tion Proc·la·ma·tion *n* a proclamation, effective on January 1, 1863, that was issued by President Abraham Lincoln and declared freedom for all slaves in states still in rebellion against the federal government

e·mar·gi·nate /i maárjə nàyt/ *adj* describes leaves or petals with a notch at the tip [Late 18C. < Latin *emarginatus*, past participle of *emarginare* "remove the edges of"] —**e·mar·gi·na·tion** /i maàrjə náysh'n/ *n*

EMAS /ée màss/ *n* a voluntary program of the European Union in which commercial and other organizations are encouraged to assess their approach to environmental matters against a given set of criteria. Full form **Eco-Management and Audit Scheme**

e·mas·cu·late /i máskyə làyt/ (**-lat·ed, -lat·ing, -lates**) *vt* **1.** CASTRATE SOMEBODY to remove the testicles of a male human being or animal (*literary*) **2.** WEAKEN SOMEBODY OR SOMETHING to deprive somebody or something of effectiveness, spirit, or force (*formal; sometimes considered offensive*) **3.** REMOVE STAMENS FROM FLOWER to remove the male reproductive organs (**stamens**) from a flower, e.g., to prevent self-pollination [Early 17C. < Latin *emasculat-*, past participle of *emasculare* "remove the male glands of, castrate" < *masculus* "male"] —**e·mas·cu·la·tion** /i màskyə láysh'n/ *n* —**e·mas·cu·la·tive** /i máskyə làytiv/ *adj* —**e·mas·cu·la·tor** *n* —**e·mas·cu·la·to·ry** /-lə tàwree/ *adj*

em·balm /em baàm/ (**-balmed, -balm·ing, -balms**) *vt* **1.** PRESERVE DEAD BODY to treat a dead body with a preservative substance in order to stop it decaying **2.** KEEP SOMETHING INTACT to protect something from change (*formal*) **3.** PERFUME SOMETHING to give a sweet scent to something (*literary*) [14C. < French *embaumer* < *baume* "balm"] —**em·balm·er** *n* —**em·balm·ment** *n*

em·bank /em bángk/ (**-banked, -bank·ing, -banks**) *vt* to surround or line a road, canal, or other area with an embankment

em·bank·ment /em bángkmənt/ *n* a ridge or raised platform built of earth or stone to confine a waterway or support a road or railroad line

~~embarass~~ incorrect spelling of **embarrass**

em·bar·ca·der·o /em baárkə dérrō/ (*plural* **-os**) *n Southwest US* a landing place on a waterway [Mid-19C. < Spanish < *embarcar* "embark"]

em·bar·go /em baárgō/ *n* (*plural* **-goes**) **1. RESTRICTION ON TRADE** a government order restricting or prohibiting commerce, especially trade in a given commodity or with a particular nation **2. OFFICIAL BAN** any official restraint or prohibition **3. ORDER HALTING MOVEMENT OF SHIPS** in the past, a government order that prohibited commercial ships from entering or leaving its ports, often as a measure during war ■ *vt* (**-goed, -go·ing, -goes**) **1. SEIZE SOMETHING** to confiscate or seize something for government use **2. PROHIBIT OR FORBID SOMETHING** in the past, to place an embargo on something [Late 16C. < Spanish < *embargar* "restrain, seize"]

em·bark /em baárk/ (**-barked, -bark·ing, -barks**) *vti* to go on board, or put or take somebody or something on board a ship or aircraft [Mid-16C. < French *embarquer* < *barque* "ship"] —**em·bar·ka·tion** /èm baar káysh'n/ *n* —**em·bark·ment** *n*

embark on, embark upon *vti* to start or engage in or involve somebody or something in an undertaking

~~embarras~~ incorrect spelling of **embarrass**

em·bar·ras de ri·chesses /aam baa raa də ree shéss/ *n* an overabundance of desirable things that makes choice among them difficult [< French, "embarrassment of wealth"]

em·bar·rass /em bárrəss/ (**-rassed, -rass·ing, -rass·es**) *v* **1.** *vti* to become or cause somebody to become painfully self-conscious, ill at ease, ashamed, or humiliated ○ *He's easily embarrassed.* **2.** *vt* to hinder or impede somebody or something (*archaic; often passive*) [Late 17C. Via French *embarrasser* "impede, disconcert" < Portuguese *embaraçar* < *baraço* "halter"]

USAGE Note the spelling with *-rr-* and *-ass*. ***Harass*** has only one *r*.

em·bar·rassed /em bárrəst/ *adj* **1.** painfully self-conscious, ill at ease, ashamed, or humiliated **2.** in financial difficulties because of a lack of money —**em·bar·rassed·ly** /em bárrəstlee, em bárrəssədlee/ *adv*

em·bar·rass·ing /em bárrəssing/ *adj* causing painful self-consciousness, uncomfortableness, shame, or humiliation —**em·bar·rass·ing·ly** *adv*

em·bar·rass·ment /em bárrəssmənt/ *n* **1. ACUTE SELF-CONSCIOUSNESS** a feeling of painful self-consciousness, uncomfortableness, shame, or humiliation ○ *blushed and fell silent in embarrassment* **2. SOMETHING THAT CAUSES SELF-CONSCIOUSNESS** something that causes a feeling of painful self-consciousness, uncomfortableness, shame, or humiliation **3. LACK OF MONEY** a state of financial difficulty ○ *financial embarrassment*

em·bas·sy /émbəssee/ (*plural* **-sies**) *n* **1. AMBASSADOR'S HEADQUARTERS** the residence and place of business of an ambassador **2. EMBASSY STAFF** an ambassador with his or her ambassadorial staff **3. AMBASSADOR'S POSITION AND RESPONSIBILITIES** the mission, rank, or function of an ambassador [Late 16C. < Old French *ambassé* < assumed Vulgar Latin *ambactiare* "go on a mission"]

em·bat·tle /em bátt'l/ (**-tled, -tling, -tles**) *vt* **1.** to arrange forces in readiness for battle **2.** to fortify something such as a building, village, or position in battle (*archaic; usually passive*) [14C. < Old French *embataillier* < *bataille* "battle"]

em·bat·tled /em bátt'ld/ *adj* **1. UNDER ASSAULT** under attack or subject to controversy **2.** MIL **FIGHTING OR READY TO FIGHT** ready for or engaged in battle **3.** CONSTR **WITH BATTLEMENTS** provided with battlements (*archaic*)

em·bat·tle·ments /em bátt'lmənts/ *npl* ARCHIT same as **battlements**

em·bay·ment /em báymənt/ *n* **1.** a bay in a coastline **2.** the process by which a bay is formed in a coastline

Emb·den-My·er·hof path·way /émdən mīər hof-/ *n* BIOCHEM same as **glycolysis** [After Gustav Georg *Embden* (1874–1933), German physiologist, and Otto Fritz *Meyerhof* (1884–1951), German-born US biochemist]

em·bed, im·bed *v* /em béd/ (**-bed·ded, -bed·ding, -beds**) **1.** *vti* **PLACE SOMETHING OR BE PLACED SOLIDLY** to fix something or become fixed in a surrounding mass **2.** *vti* **FIX SOMETHING IN MIND** to fix something deeply in the mind or memory (*often passive*) **3.** *vi* **BECOME LODGED** to become deeply and solidly lodged in something **4.** *vt* MEDIA **ASSIGN JOURNALIST TO MILITARY UNIT** to officially assign a journalist to travel with a military unit during war and report freely any information that does not jeopardize national security (*usually passive*) ○ *has been embedded with the 3rd Infantry Division since the war began* **5.** *vt* **SURROUND SOMETHING** to surround or cover something closely (*usually passive*) ■ *n* /ém bèd/ MEDIA **JOURNALIST TRAVELING WITH MILITARY UNIT** a journalist who has been officially assigned to travel with a military unit during war and report freely any information that does not jeopardize national security ○ *Embeds bring credibility to the war as independent truth-tellers.*

em·bel·lish /em béllish/ (**-lished, -lish·ing, -lish·es**) *vt* **1. BEAUTIFY SOMETHING** to increase the beauty of something by adding ornaments or decorations **2. ADD FALSE DETAILS TO SOMETHING** to make an account or description more interesting by inventing or exaggerating details **3.** MUSIC **ADD ORNAMENTATION TO MELODY** to add extra notes, accents, or trills to a melody to make it more beautiful or interesting [14C. < Old French *embelliss-*, stem of *embellir* "make beautiful" < *bel* "beautiful" < Latin *bellus*] —**em·bel·lish·ment** *n*

em·ber /émbər/ *n* **BURNING FRAGMENT** a small piece of glowing or smoldering material from a dying fire ■ **em·bers** *npl* **1. REMAINS OF FIRE** the glowing or smoldering remains of a dying fire **2. REMAINS OF PASSION** the dying but not yet extinguished remains of a great emotion, especially love (*literary*) [Old English *æmyrge* < Indo-European, "to burn"]

Em·ber Days /émbər-/, **em·ber days** *npl* days of prayer and fasting in Roman Catholic and Anglican Churches. Date: the Wednesday, Friday, and Saturday following Pentecost, the first Sunday after Lent, September 14, and December 13. [< Old English *ymbryne* "circuit" < *ryne* "course, running"; because they "come around" four times a year]

em·bez·zle /em bézz'l/ (**-zled, -zling, -zles**) *vti* to take for personal use money or property that has been given on trust by others, without their knowledge or permission [15C. < Anglo-Norman *embesiler* "steal" < Old French *besillier* "gouge, destroy"] —**em·bez·zle·ment** *n* —**em·bez·zler** *n*

SYNONYMS See ***steal***.

em·bit·ter /em bíttər/ (**-tered, -ter·ing, -ters**) *vt* **1.** to make somebody feel bitter or aggrieved **2.** to make something more bitter or acrimonious —**em·bit·tered** *adj* —**em·bit·ter·ment** *n*

em·blaze /em bláyz/ (**-blazed, -blaz·ing, -blaz·es**) *vt* (*archaic*) **1.** to light up or illuminate something **2.** to kindle something or set it on fire [15C. < BLAZE[1]]

em·bla·zon /em bláyz'n/ (**-zoned, -zon·ing, -zons**) *vt* **1. ADD DESIGN TO SOMETHING** to decorate or adorn something such as clothing with bright colors or a symbol or picture **2.** HERALDRY **DECORATE SHIELD OR FLAG** in heraldry, to decorate or adorn a shield or flag by depicting something, especially a coat of arms **3. MAKE SOMEBODY OR SOMETHING FAMOUS** to celebrate somebody or something, or make somebody or something famous (*literary; often passive*) —**em·bla·zon·er** *n* —**em·bla·zon·ment** *n*

em·bla·zon·ry /em bláyz'nree/ (*plural* **-ries**) *n* **1.** the act or process of putting heraldic decorations on something such as a shield or flag **2.** heraldic decorations on such things as shields or flags

em·blem /émbləm/ *n* **1. SYMBOL** something that visually symbolizes an object, idea, group, or quality **2. BADGE** a badge or sign that represents a person, group, or organization **3.** ART **ALLEGORICAL IMAGE** an allegorical picture, often with a motto, used to illustrate a moral lesson [15C. Via Latin, "inlaid design" < Greek *emblēma* "insertion" < *emballein* "to insert" < *ballein* "to throw"]

em·blem·at·ic /èmblə máttik/, **em·blem·at·i·cal** /-máttik'l/ *adj* relating to, consisting of, or acting as an emblem —**em·blem·at·i·cal·ly** *adv*

em·blem·a·tize /em blémmə tīz/ (**-tized, -tiz·ing, -tiz·es**) *vt* to serve as a symbol of something (*formal*)

em·bod·i·ment /em bóddimənt/ *n* **1.** a tangible or visible expression of an idea or quality **2.** the act or process by which something is made tangible or visible

em·bod·y /em bóddee/ (**-ied, -y·ing, -ies**) *vt* **1. MAKE SOMETHING TANGIBLE** to give a tangible or visible form to something abstract **2. INCORPORATE THINGS INTO ORGANIZED WHOLE** to gather and organize a number of things into a whole **3. PERSONIFY SOMETHING** to express or exemplify something abstract in bodily form

em·bold·en /em bṓld'n/ (**-ened, -en·ing, -ens**) *vt* to make somebody bold

em·bo·lec·to·my /èmbə léktəmee/ (*plural* **-mies**) *n* the surgical removal of an embolus, usually a blood clot or other obstruction, in a blood vessel

em·bo·li MED plural of **embolus**

em·bol·ic /em bóllik/ *adj* relating to or caused by an embolus or embolism

em·bo·lism /émbə lìzzəm/ *n* **1.** MED **BLOCKAGE OF ARTERY** a condition in which an artery is blocked by an embolus, usually a blood clot formed at one place in the circulation and then lodging in another **2.** MED same as **embolus** (*informal*) **3.** CALENDAR **INSERTION OF DAYS INTO CALENDAR** the insertion of a day or days into a calendar **4.** CHR **PRAYER DURING ROMAN CATHOLIC MASS** in the Roman Catholic Church, a prayer for deliverance from evil inserted in a Mass after the Lord's Prayer [14C. Via late Latin < Greek *embolismos* < *emballein* "to insert" (see EMBLEM)]

em·bo·li·za·tion /èmbəli záysh'n/ *n* the process or condition in which a blood vessel is blocked by a blood clot or other obstruction (**embolus**)

em·bo·lus /émbələss/ (*plural* **-li** /-lī/) *n* a mass, most commonly a blood clot, that becomes lodged in a blood vessel and obstructs it [Mid-17C. Via Latin < Greek *embolos* "peg, stopper, wedge" < *emballein* "to insert" (see EMBLEM)]

em·bon·point /aaN bawN pwáN/ *n* **1.** roundness of body shape caused by excess weight (*humorous*) ○ *"She was slightly inclined to embonpoint."* (J. M. Barrie, *Peter Pan*; 1904) **2.** a woman's breasts or chest [Late 17C. < French *en bon point* "in good condition"]

em·bos·om /em bŏŏzzəm/ (**-omed, -om·ing, -oms**) *vt* (*archaic*) **1.** to surround or envelop somebody or something, especially in a protective way **2.** to take somebody into your arms and hold him or her closely

em·boss /em báwss, -bóss/ (**-bossed, -boss·ing, -boss·es**) *vt* **1.** to decorate or mark a surface with a slightly raised design or lettering **2.** to give something the form of a raised pattern on a surface ○ *The title was embossed in gold lettering on the cover.* [14C. < Old French *embocer* < *boce* "protuberance"] —**em·boss·er** *n* —**em·boss·ment** *n*

em·bou·chure /aam bŏŏ shŏŏr/ *n* **1.** MUSIC **POSITION OF LIPS AND TONGUE** the adjustment of the lips and tongue in playing a wind instrument **2.** MUSIC **MOUTHPIECE** the mouthpiece of a wind instrument **3.** GEOG **RIVER MOUTH** the mouth of a river **4.** GEOG **VALLEY MOUTH** the mouth of a valley where it becomes a plain [Mid-18C. < French < *emboucher* "put to your mouth" < *bouche* "mouth"]

em·bour·geoise·ment /em bŏŏr zhwaázmənt, -zhwaaz maánt/ *n* the process by which a social group becomes middle-class in manners and attitudes [Mid-20C. < French, < *bourgeois* (see BOURGEOIS)]

em·bowed /em bṓd/ *adj* shaped like a vault or arch

em·bow·el /em bów əl/ (**-eled, -el·ing, -els**) *vt* same as **disembowel** (*archaic*)

em·bow·er /em bów ər/ (**-ered, -er·ing, -ers**) *vt* to shelter or enclose somebody or something in a bower or a place or structure resembling a bower (*literary*)

em·brace /em bráyss/ *v* (**-braced, -brac·ing, -brac·es**) **1.** *vti* **HUG SOMEBODY** to hug somebody in your arms affectionately or passionately, or hug each other affectionately or passionately **2.** *vt* **MAKE USE OF SOMETHING** to welcome and take advantage of something eagerly or willingly ○ *embrace an* *opportunity* **3.** *vt* ADOPT SOMETHING to adopt or take up something, especially a belief or way of life ○ *embraced free-market economics* **4.** *vt* COMPRISE SOMETHING to include something as part of a whole ○ *a new electoral district embracing both suburban and urban areas* **5.** *vt* SURROUND SOMETHING to surround or enclose something (*literary; often passive*) ■ *n* WARM HUG an affectionate or passionate hug [14C. < Old French *embracer* "take into your arms" < Latin *bracchium* "arm"] —**em·brace·able** *adj* —**em·brace·ment** *n* —**em·brac·er** *n*

em·brac·er·y /em bráyssəree/ *n* the offense of trying to influence a judge or jury, e.g., by bribery, threats, or promises

em·branch·ment /em bránchmənt/ *n* **1.** a branching out of a feature of the natural landscape, e.g., a river or mountain range **2.** a branch of something such as a river or mountain range [Mid-19C. < French *embranchement* < *branche* (see BRANCH)]

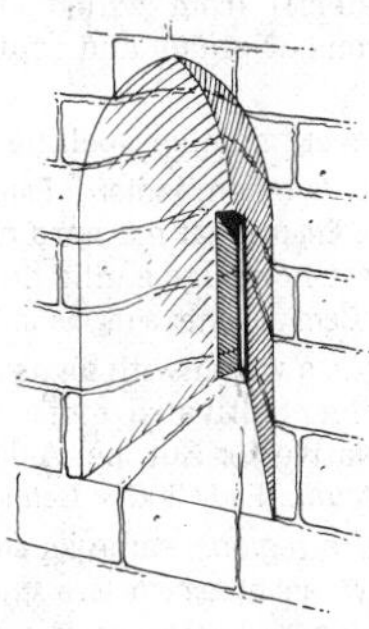

embrasure (sense 2)

em·bra·sure /em bráyzhər/ *n* **1.** an opening in the wall of a building for a door or window, tapered so as to be wider on the inside than on the outside **2.** a slanted opening in the wall or parapet of a fortification, designed so that a defender can fire through it on attackers [Early 17C. < French, < obsolete *embraser* "widen (a door or window)"]

em·brit·tle /em brítt'l/ (**-tled, -tling, -tles**) *vti* to become brittle, or make something become brittle

em·bro·cate /émbrə kàyt/ (**-cat·ed, -cat·ing, -cates**) *vt* to rub lotion or liniment onto a part of the body [Early 17C. < Latin *embrocat-*, past participle of *embrocare* "treat with healing liquid" < late Latin *embroc(h)a* < Greek *embrokhē* "lotion"]

em·bro·ca·tion /èmbrə káysh'n/ *n* a lotion or liniment that relieves muscle or joint pain

em·broi·der /em bróydər/ (**-dered, -der·ing, -ders**) *v* **1.** *vti* DO DECORATIVE NEEDLEWORK to do decorative needlework, or decorate fabric with needlework ○ *embroidering a tablecloth by hand* **2.** *vt* SEW DECORATION ONTO FABRIC to sew a particular pattern onto fabric ○ *embroidered their initials on the towels* **3.** *vti* EMBELLISH STORY to add exaggerated or fictitious details to an account of something to make it more interesting [14C. < Anglo-Norman *enbrouder* < Old French *brouder* "embroider" < Germanic] —**em·broi·der·er** *n*

embroidery

em·broi·der·y /em bróydəree/ (*plural* **-ies**) *n* **1.** ACT OF MAKING DECORATIVE NEEDLEWORK the craft of using needlework to make decorative designs **2.** SOMETHING WITH DECORATIVE NEEDLEWORK something produced by or ornamented with decorative needlework **3.** EMBELLISHMENT OF STORY elaboration or embellishment added to make an account of something more interesting

em·broil /em bróyl/ (**-broiled, -broil·ing, -broils**) *vt* **1.** to involve somebody or yourself in trouble, disagreement, or conflict **2.** to make something confused or overly complicated [Early 17C. < French *embrouiller* "confuse, confound" < *brouiller* "mix confusedly" < Germanic]

em·brue *vt* same as **imbrue**

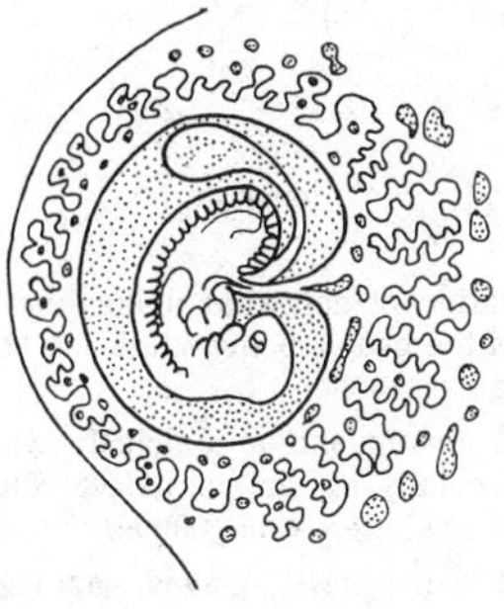

embryo: human embryo

em·bry·o /émbree ō/ (*plural* **-os**) *n* **1.** HUMAN OFFSPRING IN INITIAL DEVELOPMENTAL STAGE a human offspring in the early stages following conception up to the end of the eighth week, after which it is classified as a fetus **2.** ANIMAL IN INITIAL DEVELOPMENTAL STAGE the developing young of an animal from the earliest stages after conception up to birth or hatching **3.** PLANT IN INITIAL DEVELOPMENTAL STAGE a plant in its earliest stages of development. In seed-bearing plants, the embryo is contained within the seed. **4.** EARLY FORM OF SOMETHING an early form or rudimentary stage of something ○ *the embryo of an exciting new invention* [14C. Via Latin < Greek *embruon* < *bruein* "swell, grow"]

em·bry·o·gen·e·sis /èmbree ō jénnəssiss/, **em·bry·og·e·ny** /-ójjənee/ *n* the formation and growth of an embryo —**em·bry·o·ge·net·ic** /èmbree ō jə néttik/ *adj* —**em·bry·o·gen·ic** /-jénnik/ *adj*

em·bry·ol·o·gy /èmbree ólləjee/ *n* **1.** the scientific study of embryos and their development **2.** the study of the growth and development of the human embryo and fetus from conception to birth —**em·bry·o·log·ic** /-lójjik/ *adj* —**em·bry·o·log·i·cal** *adj* —**em·bry·o·log·i·cal·ly** *adv* —**em·bry·ol·o·gist** *n*

em·bry·on·ic /èmbree ónnik/ *adj* **1.** in an initial or rudimentary stage of development ○ *our embryonic city planning effort* **2.** relating to or characteristic of an embryo —**em·bry·on·al** /em brée ən'l, émbree-/ *adj* —**em·bry·on·ic·al·ly** *adv* —**em·bry·ot·ic** /èmbree óttik/ *adj*

em·bry·on·ic mem·brane *n* a membranous structure, e.g., the amnion, chorion, or yolk sac, that comes from a fertilized ovum but does not become part of the embryo

em·bry·o sac *n* a large oval cell found inside a female reproductive organ (**ovule**) of a flowering plant that contains the egg cell, which gives rise to the embryo and the endosperm nuclei

em·bry·ot·ic *adj* BIOL same as **embryonic** (sense 2)

em·bry·o trans·fer *n* the transplanting of an embryo from one female animal into the womb of a surrogate mother

em·bu·ti·do /em boo tée dō/ (*plural* **-dos**) *n Hispanic* a pork sausage, sometimes cooked in a broth [< Spanish < *embutir* "stuff, cram"]

em·cee /em sée/ (*informal*) *n* a person in charge of the proceedings at an event or entertainment ■ *vti* (**-ceed, -cee·ing, -cees**) to act as a master or mistress of ceremonies for an event [Mid-20C.< MC[2] "master of ceremonies"]

em dash *n* in printing, a dash that is one em long

-eme *suffix* a distinctive unit of linguistic structure ○ *lexeme* [< French *-ème* < *phonème* (see PHONEME)]

e·mend /i ménd/ (**e·mend·ed, e·mend·ing, e·mends**), **e·mend·ate** /éemən dàyt, i mén dàyt/ (**-at·ed, -at·ing, -ates**) *vt* to correct or alter a text in order to improve it [15C. < Latin *emendare* "take out a fault" < *menda* "fault, blemish"] —**e·men·da·tion** /èemən dáysh'n, èmmən-, i mèn-/ *n* —**e·mend·er** *n*

USAGE See ***amend***.

em·er·ald /émmərəld, émmrəld/ *n* a precious stone that is a form of beryl colored green by chromium. Use: gems. ■ *adj, n* COLORS same as **emerald green** [13C. Directly or via French *émeraude* < medieval Latin *esmeraldus*, alteration of Latin *smaragdus*, via Greek *smaragdos* "green gem" < Semitic, "to shine"]

em·er·ald cut *n* a rectangular multifaceted cut for gemstones, especially emeralds and diamonds

em·er·ald green *n* a bright green color, like that of an emerald —**em·er·ald-green** *adj*

Em·er·ald Isle /émmərəld-/ *n* Ireland, so called because of its vividly green countryside and because the wearing of green was associated with the struggle for national sovereignty

e·merge /i múrj/ (**e·merged, e·merg·ing, e·merg·es**) *v* **1.** *vi* COME OUT to appear out of or from behind something ○ *The butterfly emerges from the chrysalis.* **2.** *vi* SURVIVE to come out of an experience, condition, or situation, especially a difficult one ○ *emerged unscathed from the accident* **3.** *vti* BECOME KNOWN to become known or apparent ○ *It emerged that several officials had accepted bribes.* **4.** *vi* APPEAR OR HAPPEN to arise, appear, or occur ○ *They waited for a new leader to emerge.* [Late 16C. < Latin *emergere* "rise out or up" < *mergere* "dive, plunge"] —**e·mer·gence** *n*

e·mer·gen·cy /i múrjənssee/ *n* (*plural* **-cies**) SUDDEN CRISIS REQUIRING ACTION an unexpected and sudden event that must be dealt with urgently ■ *adj* **1.** USED IN EMERGENCY used or suitable for use in an emergency ○ *emergency funds* **2.** MED FOR IMMEDIATE TREATMENT requiring, providing, or given immediate medical attention ○ *an emergency appendectomy*

e·mer·gen·cy brake *n* **1.** a brake on a vehicle intended to be used when the main brakes have failed or when a sudden halt is required, or to prevent a parked vehicle from moving **2.** a mechanical device on a piece of machinery, used to bring the machinery to a halt when a dangerous condition arises

e·mer·gen·cy cord *n* a chain, cord, or handle in a railroad car that a passenger can pull in order to stop a train in an emergency

e·mer·gen·cy ex·it *n* an exit from a building or vehicle that is designed and designated as an escape route in an emergency such as a fire

e·mer·gen·cy med·i·cine *n* the branch of medicine dealing with the treatment of patients whose condition requires immediate action

e·mer·gen·cy pow·ers *npl* special powers given to a government or other authority to take extraordinary actions in order to cope with a crisis

e·mer·gen·cy room *n* a part of a hospital for patients who need immediate urgent attention, e.g., for heart attacks or traffic accidents

e·mer·gen·cy ser·vic·es *npl* the fire department, the police, and the ambulance services collectively, especially when mobilized to deal with emergencies

e·mer·gen·cy ve·hi·cle *n* an ambulance, fire engine, police car, or other vehicle used by the emergency services

e·mer·gent /i múrjənt/ *adj* **1.** NEW appearing, arising, occurring, or developing, especially for the first time **2.** *UK* POL same as **emerging** (sense 2) ■ *n* **1.** PLANT WITH UPPER PARTS ABOVE WATER a plant that has its roots under water but its upper part above the surface **2.** TALL TREE a forest tree that stands taller than surrounding trees

e·mer·gent ev·o·lu·tion *n* a theory of evolution that states that new organisms and characteristics appear at critical turning points and cannot be predicted from those already in existence

e·merg·ing /i múrjing/ *adj* **1.** starting to appear, arise, occur, or develop **2.** newly or recently independent as a nation

e·merg·ing tar·get *n* a target that is selected by military personnel during the course of combat, as opposed to one that has been selected prior to the start of fighting

e·mer·i·ta /i mérritə/ *adj* retired but retaining a professional title, especially as a woman professor (*used of women*) ○ *She's a professor emerita of biology.* ■ *n* (*plural* **-tae** /-tee/) a woman who has retired from a position but retains her former professional title, especially as a professor [Early 20C. < Latin, form of *emeritus* (see EMERITUS)]

e·mer·i·tus /i mérritəss/ *adj* retired but retaining a professional title, especially as a professor (*used of men*) ○ *He's a professor emeritus of chemistry.* ■ *n* (*plural* **-ti** /-tī/) a man who has retired from a position but retains his former professional title, especially as a professor [Early 17C. < Latin, past participle of *emerere* "serve out, earn, deserve" < *merere* "serve, earn"]

e·mersed /i múrst/ *adj* describes the stems, leaves, or other parts of a water plant that stand above the water surface [Late 17C. < Latin *emersus*, past participle of *emergere* (see EMERGE)]

e·mer·sion /i múrzh'n/ *n* **1.** the act or process of emerging **2.** the reappearance of an astronomical object after it has been eclipsed or occulted

Library of Congress

Ralph Waldo Emerson

Em·er·son /émmərss'n/, **Ralph Waldo** (1803–82) US essayist, lecturer, and poet. He was a major figure in the philosophical movement known as transcendentalism. His landmark works include *Nature* (1836). —**Em·er·so·ni·an** /èmmər sṓnee ən/ *adj*

> "Whoso would be a man must be a nonconformist."
> [Ralph Waldo Emerson, "Self-Reliance," *Essays*; 1841]

> "History is the action and reaction of these two, nature and thought—two boys pushing each other on the curbstone of the pavement."
> [Ralph Waldo Emerson, "Fate," *The Conduct of Life*; 1860]

Em·er·son, Roy (*b.* 1936) Australian tennis player. He holds the record for the most grand slam titles won by a male tennis player, with 12 singles titles and 16 doubles titles (1961–67). Full name **Emerson, Roy Stanley**

em·er·y /émməree/ *n* a variety of the mineral corundum. Use: abrasives. [15C. Via French *émeri* < Italian *smeriglio* < Greek *smuris* "abrasive powder"]

em·er·y board *n* a small strip of card or thin wood coated with powdered emery. Use: filing fingernails.

em·er·y pa·per *n* a strong paper coated with powdered emery. Use: abrasive for polishing.

em·er·y wheel *n* a wheel coated with powdered emery. Use: abrasive for polishing.

em·e·sis /émməssiss/ *n* vomiting (*technical*) [Late 19C. < Greek, < *emein* "to vomit"]

e·met·ic /i méttik/ *adj* causing a person or animal to vomit [Mid-17C. < Greek *emetikos* < *emein* "to vomit"] —**e·met·ic** *n* —**e·met·i·cal·ly** *adv*

em·e·tine /émmə teen/ *n* a chemical compound extracted from a South American plant (**ipecac**). Use: formerly, to induce vomiting. Formula: $C_{29}H_{40}O_4N_2$.

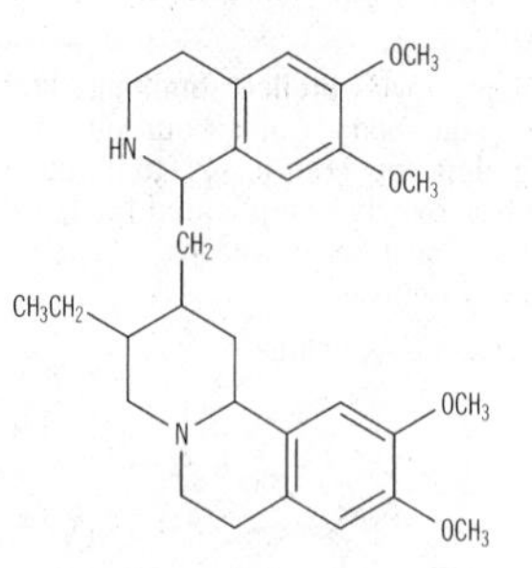

emetine

emf, **EMF** *abbr* PHYS electromotive force

EMG *abbr* MED **1.** electromyogram **2.** electromyograph

-emia, **-aemia**, **-hemia**, **-haemia** *suffix* referring to something in the blood [Via modern Latin < Greek *haima* "blood"]

e·mic /éemik/ *adj* **1.** relating to the analysis of structural and functional elements of language or behavior **2.** relating to the organization and interpretation of data that makes use of the categories of the people being studied. ◊ **etic** [Mid-20C. Shortening of PHONEMIC]

em·i·grant /émmigrənt/ *n* somebody who leaves a place, especially his or her native country, to go and live elsewhere —**em·i·grant** *adj*

em·i·grate /émmi gràyt/ (**-grat·ed, -grat·ing, -grates**) *vi* to leave a place, especially a native country, to go and live elsewhere [Late 18C. < Latin *emigrat-*, past participle of *emigrare* "move away from a place" < *migrare* "move from place to place"] —**em·i·gra·tion** /èmmi gráysh'n/ *n*

é·mi·gré /émmi gràv/ *n* somebody who has moved from their own to another country to live, usually for political reasons [Late 18C. < French, past participle of *émigrer* < Latin *emigrare* (see EMIGRATE)]

E·mil·ia-Ro·ma·gna /i meelee ə rō maányə/ region in Northern Italy, on the Adriatic Sea. Capital: Bologna. Population: 3,981,146 (2000). Area: 8,542 sq. mi./22,123 sq. km.

em·i·nence /émminənss/, **em·i·nen·cy** /-nənssee/ (*plural* **-cies**) *n* **1.** HIGH POSITION a position or rank of distinction or superiority **2.** HILL a high or raised area of ground (*formal*) **3.** ANAT BODY PROJECTION a projecting area of the body, especially a bone

Em·i·nence, **Em·i·nen·cy** (*plural* **-cies**) *n* in the Roman Catholic Church, a title and form of address for a cardinal

é·mi·nence grise /ày mee naaNss greéz/ (*plural* **é·mi·nences grises** /*pronunc. same*/) *n* somebody who exerts great power or influence secretly or unofficially [< French, "gray eminence," originally nickname of Père Joseph, secretary to Cardinal RICHELIEU]

em·i·nen·cy *n* same as **eminence**

Em·i·nen·cy *n* same as **Eminence**

em·i·nent /émminənt/ *adj* **1.** OF HIGH STANDING superior in position, fame, or achievement **2.** NOTICEABLE easy to see or notice **3.** HIGH in a high or raised position [15C. < Latin *eminent-*, present participle of *eminere* "stand out, project" < *minere* "stand, project"]

em·i·nent do·main *n* the power of a government to take private property for public use, usually with compensation paid to the owner

em·i·nent·ly /émminəntlee/ *adv* to a great degree ○ *He is eminently qualified to be a corporate officer.*

e·mir /ə meér/, **a·mir** *n* **1.** in some Islamic countries, an independent ruler, commander, or governor **2.** a title for a descendant of the prophet Muhammad [Early 17C. Via French < Arabic *amīr* "commander"]

e·mir·ate /émmi ràyt, -ət, i meérət/ *n* **1.** an area ruled by an emir **2.** the rank or office of an emir

em·is·sar·y /émmi sèrree/ (*plural* **-ies**) *n* **1.** an agent or representative sent on a particular mission **2.** a secret agent or spy (*dated*) [Early 17C. < Latin *emissarius* "somebody sent out" < *emiss-*, past participle of *emittere* (see EMIT)]

e·mis·sion /i mísh'n/ *n* **1.** LETTING SOMETHING OUT the act or process of letting something out or giving something out ○ *the emission of radiation* **2.** SOMETHING GIVEN OUT something that is produced or given out ○ *harmful exhaust emissions* **3.** PHYS RELEASED ENERGY energy released from a source, usually in the form of electromagnetic radiation **4.** PHYSIOL SOMETHING RELEASED FROM BODY a bodily discharge, especially of semen [15C. < Latin *emission-* < *emiss-*, past participle of *emittere* (see EMIT)]

e·mis·sion neb·u·la *n* a cloud of interstellar gas and dust that emits light when electrons recombine with protons to form hydrogen atoms

e·mis·sion stan·dards *npl* the maximum levels of pollutants permitted by a government to be discharged from motor vehicles

e·mis·siv·i·ty /èmmi sívvətee/ (*plural* **-ties**) *n* the ability of a surface to emit radiation, measured as the ratio of the energy radiated by a surface to that radiated by a blackbody at the same temperature. Symbol υ

e·mit /i mít/ (**e·mit·ted, e·mit·ting, e·mits**) *vt* **1.** PRODUCE SOMETHING to send or give out something ○ *an oil heater that emits smoke* **2.** UTTER SOMETHING to utter a sound ○ *emitted a giggle* **3.** PUT MONEY INTO CIRCULATION to put currency into circulation [Early 17C. < Latin *emittere* "send out" < *mittere* "send"]

e·mit·ter /i míttər/ *n* **1.** a person or thing that emits something **2.** in a transistor, a layer of semiconductor material from which charge carriers such as electrons originate and control the flow of current

Em·man·u·el *n* BIBLE another spelling of **Immanuel**

Em·men·tha·ler /émmən taàlər/, **Em·men·ta·ler**, **Em·men·thal** /-taàl/, **Em·men·tal** *n* a hard cheese of Swiss origin with large holes and a mild nutty flavor [Early 20C. < obsolete German, after a region in Switzerland]

em·mer /émmər/ *n* a wheat with awns and two grains in each spikelet, cultivated since ancient times. Use: fodder. Native to: Europe, Asia. Latin name: *Triticum dicoccum*. [Early 20C. < German]

em·met /émmət/ *n regional* same as **ant** (*archaic*) [Old English *ǣmete*, variant of *ǣmette* (see ANT)]

Em·met /émmət/, **Robert** (1778–1803) Irish patriot. He was a member of the nationalist United Irishmen. With French encouragement, he launched an abortive uprising in Ireland in 1803, and was tried and hanged.

> "Let no man write my epitaph...When my country takes her place among the nations of the earth, then and not till then let my epitaph be written."
> [Robert Emmet. Quoted in *This Most Distressful Country*, Robert Kee; 1972]

em·me·tro·pi·a /émmə trṓpee ə/ *n* the condition of the eye in which vision is accurate [Mid-19C. < Greek *emmetros* "in measure" + *ōps* "eye"] —**em·me·trop·ic** /-tróppik/ *adj*

Em·my /émmee/ (*plural* **-mys**) *n* a statuette awarded annually by the American Academy of Television Arts and Sciences for excellence in television programming, production, or performance [Mid-20C. Origin ?]

e·mo /i mṓ/ *adj* given to excessive displays of emotion (*informal*) ■ *n* a genre of punk rock music that began in the mid-1980s in Washington, D.C. and is noted for its thoughtful and emotional lyrics [Late 20C. Shortening of EMOTIONAL]

e·mol·lient /i móllyənt/ *adj* **1.** SOOTHING TO SKIN softening or soothing, especially to the skin **2.** CALMING trying to avoid anger and argument by using a calming manner (*formal*) ■ *n* SOOTHING SUBSTANCE a substance that softens or soothes something, especially the skin [Mid-17C. < Latin *emollient-*, present participle of *emollire* "soften" < *mollis* "soft"]

e·mol·u·ment /i móllyəmənt/ *n* a payment for work done (*formal*) [15C. < Latin *emolumentum* "profit, gain," literally "fee paid for grinding grain" < *emolere* "grind out"]

SYNONYMS See ***wage***.

e·mote /i mṓt/ (**e·mot·ed, e·mot·ing, e·motes**) *vi* to make an exaggerated show of emotions, e.g., in the playing of a dramatic part [Early 20C. Back-formation < EMOTION]

:-) Happy	:-(Sad	|-| Asleep	;-) Winking
:-)) Very happy	:-~) User has a cold	:-* Blowing a kiss	:-& Tongue tied
(:+(Scared	(-D Laughing	:-() Talking	:-O Shocked

emoticon

e·mo·ti·con /i mṓtə kòn/ *n* an arrangement of keyboard characters intended to convey an emotion, usually viewed sideways. See illustration on previous page [Late 20C. Blend of EMOTION + ICON]

e·mo·tion /i mṓsh'n/ *n* **1.** a strong feeling about somebody or something **2.** agitation or disturbance caused by strong feelings [Late 16C. < French, < *émouvoir* "stir up the feelings of" < Latin *emovere* "move out, remove" < *movere* "to move"]

e·mo·tion·al /i mṓshən'l, i mṓshnəl/ *adj* **1.** EXPRESSING EMOTION relating to or expressing emotion **2.** EASILY AFFECTED BY EMOTIONS being by nature easily affected by or quick to express emotions **3.** AFFECTED BY EMOTION affected or characterized by emotion, especially sadness ○ *an emotional tribute* **4.** STIRRING EMOTIONS arousing or affecting the emotions ○ *that emotional moment when the flag is raised* **5.** INSPIRED BY EMOTION inspired or governed by emotion, and not by reason or willpower ○ *made a hasty and emotional decision* —**e·mo·tion·al·i·ty** /i mṓsh'n állətee/ *n* —**e·mo·tion·al·ly** *adv*

e·mo·tion·al black·mail *n* the stirring up of uncomfortable feelings in somebody, especially sympathy or guilt, in order to persuade that person to do something

e·mo·tion·al crip·ple *n* an offensive term for somebody who has an emotional problem that prevents him or her from expressing feelings and having normal relationships with people

e·mo·tion·al in·tel·li·gence *n* the ability to understand your own feelings and those of other people, to take other people's feelings into account when reaching decisions, and to respond to people's feelings in a restrained and thoughtful way

e·mo·tion·al·ism /i mṓshən'l ìzzəm, i mṓshnə lìzzəm/ *n* **1.** a tendency to be easily swayed by the emotions **2.** an exaggerated or undue display of strong feelings

e·mo·tion·al·ist /i mṓshən'list, i mṓshnəlist/ *n* **1.** somebody whose thoughts or actions are greatly influenced by the emotions **2.** somebody who is overly demonstrative

e·mo·tion·al·ize /i mṓshən'l ìz, i mṓshnə lìz/ (**-ized, -iz·ing, -iz·es**) *vt* to present or treat something emotionally

e·mo·tion·less /i mṓsh'nləss/ *adj* not having or showing emotions —**e·mo·tion·less·ly** *adv* —**e·mo·tion·less·ness** *n*

e·mo·tive /i mṓtiv/ *adj* **1.** causing or intended to cause emotion ○ *a highly emotive issue* **2.** showing or characterized by emotion ○ *an emotive plea* [Mid-18C. < Latin *emotus*, past participle of *emovere* (see EMOTION)] —**e·mo·tive·ly** *adv* —**e·mo·tive·ness** *n*

e·mo·tiv·ism /i mṓti vìzzəm/ *n* the philosophical theory that ethical statements are not statements of fact but instead reflect the feelings of the speaker

EMP *abbr* PHYS electromagnetic pulse

Emp. *abbr* **1.** Emperor **2.** Empire **3.** Empress

em·pale /em páyl/ *vt* HERALDRY another spelling of **impale**

em·pa·na·da /èmpə naádə/ *n Hispanic* in Spanish, Filipino, or Latin American cuisine, a turnover with a spicy filling or in Mexican cuisine, one with a sweet filling [Mid-20C. < Spanish < past participle of *empanar* "bake or roll in pastry" < *pan* "bread"]

em·pan·el *vt* LAW same as **impanel**

em·pa·thize /émpə thìz/ (**-thized, -thiz·ing, -thiz·es**) *vi* to identify with and understand somebody else's feelings or difficulties ○ *empathized with them in their grief*

em·pa·thy /émpəthee/ *n* **1.** the ability to identify with and understand somebody else's feelings or difficulties **2.** the transfer of somebody's own feelings and emotions to an object such as a painting [Early 20C. < Greek *empatheia* "affection, passion"] —**em·pa·thet·ic** /èmpə théttik/ *adj* —**em·pa·thet·i·cal·ly** *adv* —**em·path·ic** /em páthik/ *adj* —**em·path·i·cal·ly** *adv*

em·pen·nage /aàmpə naázh, èmpə naázh, émpənij/ *n* the tail portion of an aircraft, including the stabilizer, elevator, vertical fin, and rudder [Early 20C. < French, literally "feathering (of an arrow)" < *empenner* "to feather" < *penne* "feather"]

~~**emperer**~~ incorrect spelling of **emperor**

em·per·or /émpərər, émprər/ *n* **1.** *also* **Em·per·or** a man who rules an empire **2.** INSECTS same as **emperor butterfly 3.** INSECTS same as **emperor moth** [12C. Via French < Latin *imperator* "commander" < *imperare* "to command" < *parare* "prepare"]

em·per·or but·ter·fly *n* a brightly colored butterfly that typically has mottled purple and brownish markings. Family: Nymphalidae. [< imperial associations of purple]

em·per·or moth *n* a large brightly colored moth with distinctive markings resembling eyes on its wings. Native to: Europe, Asia. Latin name: *Saturnia pyri.* [< its large size]

em·per·or pen·guin *n* the largest of the penguins, with bluish gray and black feathers, a white chest, and yellowish orange neck markings. It nurtures its young between its feet and a pouch-shaped fold in its abdomen. Native to: Antarctica. Latin name: *Aptenodytes forsteri.* [< its large size]

em·pha·sis /émfəsiss/ (*plural* **-pha·ses** /-fə seez/) *n* **1.** IMPORTANCE special importance, significance, or stress ○ *puts emphasis on exercise* **2.** FORCEFULNESS OF EXPRESSION forcefulness of expression to indicate the importance of something ○ *Your opening paragraph needs greater emphasis to grab the reader's attention.* **3.** EXTRA SPOKEN STRESS ON IMPORTANT WORD extra stress of voice put on a syllable, word, or phrase, usually to show its significance [Late 16C. Via Latin < Greek, "significance, appearance" < *emphainein* "to show, indicate" < *phainein* "to show"]

em·pha·size /émfə sìz/ (**-sized, -siz·ing, -siz·es**) *vt* to stress or give importance to something

em·phat·ic /em fáttik/ *adj* **1.** WITH EMPHASIS expressed, thought, or done with emphasis **2.** DEFINITE forcible and definite ○ *an emphatic refusal* **3.** GRAM SHOWING EMPHASIS GRAMMATICALLY describes a grammatical form that shows emphasis, e.g., the auxiliary "do" in the statement "I do like apples" [Early 18C. Via late Latin < Greek *emphatikos* < *emphasis* (see EMPHASIS)]

em·phat·i·cal·ly /em fáttikəlee/ *adv* **1.** with great force or definiteness **2.** used to reinforce the accuracy or appropriateness of a description ○ *It might be entertainment, but it is emphatically not education.*

em·phy·se·ma /èmfə seémə, -zeémə/ *n* **1.** a chronic medical disorder of the lungs in which the air sacs are dilated or enlarged and lack flexibility, so that breathing is impaired and infection sometimes occurs **2.** an unusual enlargement of an organ or body tissue caused by retention of air or other gas [Mid-17C. Via late Latin < Greek *emphusēma* "swelling" < *emphusan* "inflate" < *phusan* "blow"] —**em·phy·sem·a·tous** /èmfə sémmətəss, -zémmətəss/ *adj* —**em·phy·se·mic** *adj*

em·pire /ém pìr/ *n* **1.** LANDS RULED BY SINGLE AUTHORITY a group of nations, territories, or peoples ruled by a single authority, especially an emperor or empress **2.** MONARCHY HEADED BY EMPEROR OR EMPRESS a monarchy that has an emperor or empress as its ruler **3.** PERIOD OF EMPIRE'S EXISTENCE the period during which an empire exists **4.** LARGE FAR-FLUNG BUSINESS a very large, powerful, and extensive industrial or commercial organization **5.** PART OF ORGANIZATION SOMEBODY PERSONALLY CONTROLS a part of an organization controlled by a single person, especially somebody who is keenly protective of personal power **6.** ABSOLUTE POWER supreme or absolute power (*formal or literary*) [13C. Via French < Latin *imperium* "command" < *imperare* (see EMPEROR)]

Em·pire /ém pìr/ *adj* relating to a style of architecture, furniture, and clothing popular during the French First Empire (1804–15) during the reign of Napoleon I ○ *a dress with an Empire waist* ■ *n* a variety of red and yellow eating apple

em·pire-build·ing *n* the practice of attempting to acquire greater power and authority within an organization, especially by adding extra staff or subordinates —**em·pire-build·er** *n*

Em·pire Day *n* CALENDAR former name for **Commonwealth Day** (until 1958)

Em·pire gown *n* a woman's dress popular during the French First Empire, characterized by a low-cut neckline and a high waist from which the skirt hangs straight and loose

Em·pire State *n* a nickname for the state of New York (*informal*) [< its affluence and importance]

Em·pire State Build·ing *n* a skyscraper on Fifth Avenue in New York City built between 1930 and 1931. It has 102 stories and was the tallest building in the world for 40 years.

Em·pire State of the South *n* a nickname for the US state of Georgia

em·pir·ic /em pírrik/ *n* **1.** somebody who exclusively relies upon observation and experiment to determine the truth about something **2.** a charlatan or quack, especially in medicine (*archaic*) [Mid-16C. < Latin *empiricus* < Greek *empeirikos* "experienced" < *empeiros* "skilled" < *peira* "trial"]

em·pir·i·cal /em pírrik'l/ *adj* **1.** BASED ON OBSERVATION AND EXPERIMENT based on or characterized by observation and experiment instead of theory **2.** PHILOSOPHY DERIVED SOLELY FROM EXPERIENCE derived as knowledge from experience, particularly from sensory observation, and not derived from the application of logic **3.** MED BASED ON PRACTICAL MEDICAL EXPERIENCE based on practical experience in the medical treatment of real cases, and not on applied theory or scientific proof —**em·pir·i·cal·ly** *adv*

em·pir·i·cal for·mu·la *n* a chemical formula showing the relative proportion of elements in a compound instead of their structural arrangement or molecular weights, e.g., the formula H_2O

em·pir·i·cism /em pírri sìzzəm/ *n* **1.** APPLICATION OF OBSERVATION AND EXPERIMENT the application of observation and experiment, and not theory, in determining something **2.** PHILOSOPHY PHILOSOPHICAL BELIEF REGARDING SENSE-DERIVED KNOWLEDGE the philosophical belief that all knowledge is derived from the experience of the senses **3.** MED MEDICINE BASED SOLELY ON EXPERIENCE medicine that is based on practical experience, and not on theory or scientific proof —**em·pir·i·cist** *n*

em·place /em pláyss/ (**-placed, -plac·ing, -plac·es**) *vt* to put something into place or position [Mid-19C. Back-formation < EMPLACEMENT]

em·place·ment /em pláyssmənt/ *n* **1.** a position that is specially prepared for a large gun or group of guns **2.** the act of putting something into place or position, or the condition of being in place or position [Early 19C. < French, literally "placing in" < *place* "place"]

em·plane /em pláyn/ *vti Can, UK* TRANSP same as **enplane**

em·ploy /em plóy/ *vt* (**-ployed, -ploy·ing, -ploys**) **1.** GIVE PAID WORK TO SOMEBODY to hire somebody to work in exchange for money **2.** KEEP SOMEBODY BUSY to keep somebody occupied doing something **3.** USE SOMETHING to make use of something ■ *n* EMPLOYED STATE the condition of working for pay (*formal*) ○ *I was in his employ for several years.* [15C. Via French *emploier* "apply" < Latin *implicare* "involve, enfold" < *plicare* "to fold"] —**em·ploy·a·bil·i·ty** /em plòy ə bíllətee/ *n* —**em·ploy·a·ble** *adj*

SYNONYMS See *use.*

em·ploy·ee /em plóy ee, èm ploy eé/, **em·ploy·e** *n* a paid worker

em·ploy·er /em plóy ər/ *n* **1.** a person, business, or organization that hires and pays one or more workers **2.** somebody who uses something

em·ploy·ment /em plóymənt/ *n* **1.** WORKING FOR PAY the condition of working for pay **2.** WORK OR JOB DONE BY SOMEBODY the work, especially paid work, that somebody does **3.** NUMBER OF PAID WORKERS IN POPULATION the total number of people who work for pay in a particular population ○ *falling employment in manufacturing* **4.** USE OF SOMETHING the use of, or practice of doing, something ○ *their employment of ritual to promote a group identity* ○ *engaged in her usual employment of playing solitaire*

em·ploy·ment a·gen·cy, **em·ploy·ment bu·reau** *n* a commercial organization that finds jobs for people or people for jobs

Em·po·ri·a /em páwree ə/ city in eastern Kansas, on the Neosho River, northeast of Wichita and southwest of Topeka. Population: 26,739 (2002 estimate).

em·po·ri·um /em páwree əm/ (*plural* **-ri·ums** or **-ri·a**

/-ree əl/ *n* **1.** a store, usually a large one, that offers a wide selection of goods **2.** a marketplace or center of trade [Late 16C. Via Latin < Greek *emporion* < *emporos* "merchant, traveler" < *poros* "journey"]

em·pow·er /em pówr/ (**-ered, -er·ing, -ers**) *vt* **1.** to give somebody power or authority (*often passive*) **2.** to give somebody a greater sense of confidence or self-esteem —**em·pow·er·ment** *n*

em·press /émprəss/, **Em·press** *n* **1.** a woman who rules an empire **2.** the wife or widow of an emperor [12C. < Old French *empresse* < *emperor* (see EMPEROR)]

em·presse·ment /em préssmənt, aaN press maaN/ *n* great attentiveness or cordiality (*literary*) [Early 18C. < French, < *empresser* "urge, be eager" < *presser* (see PRESS[1])]

em·prise /em príz/ *n* (*formal*) **1.** a chivalrous, brave, or daring undertaking **2.** chivalrous skill or daring [13C. < Old French, < French *emprendre*, literally "seize into" < Latin *prendere* "seize"]

emp·ty /émptee, émtee/ *adj* (**-ti·er, -ti·est**) **1. CONTAINING NOTHING** not containing or holding anything ○ *a heap of empty bags* **2. UNFED** hungry or lacking food ○ *can't work on an empty stomach* **3. UNOCCUPIED** unoccupied or uninhabited ○ *There's an empty office next door.* **4. WITH NO PASSENGERS OR LOAD** without passengers, a load, or cargo ○ *The bus goes back to the depot empty.* **5. INSINCERE** lacking sincerity or truthfulness ○ *another empty promise* **6. MEANINGLESS** without value, meaning, or purpose ○ *contemplating his empty existence* **7. DULL** devoid of vitality ○ *an empty look* **8.** MATH, LOGIC **WITHOUT SET MEMBERS** describes a set that has no elements or members ■ *v* (**-tied, -ty·ing, -ties**) **1.** *vt* **REMOVE THE CONTENTS OF SOMETHING** to remove or pour out the contents of something ○ *emptied his pockets* **2.** *vti* **DISCHARGE OR TRANSFER** to discharge or transfer something, or be discharged and transferred ○ *The stream empties into the lake.* **3. emp·ty your·self** *vr* **UNBURDEN YOURSELF** to unburden or free yourself of something ○ *empty yourself of feeling* ■ *n* (*plural* **-ties**) **CONTAINER WITHOUT CONTENTS** a bottle or other container that has nothing in it [Old English *æmtig* "unoccupied, at leisure" < *æmetta* "rest, leisure." Origin ?] —**emp·ti·ly** *adv* —**emp·ti·ness** *n*

SYNONYMS See *vacant*.

emp·ty-hand·ed *adj* **1.** with nothing gained or achieved ○ *came back from the negotiations empty-handed* **2.** holding nothing in the hands

emp·ty-head·ed *adj* regarded as lacking in intelligence or seriousness

emp·ty nest·er *n* a parent whose children have grown up and moved away from home (*informal*)

emp·ty-nest syn·drome *n* distress, especially a lack of energy or an emotional letdown, experienced by a parent whose grown children have moved away from home

em·py·e·ma /èm pī éemə/ *n* an accumulation of pus in a body cavity such as the chest [Early 17C. Via late Latin < Greek *empuēma* < *empuein* "put pus in" < *puon* "pus"] —**em·py·e·mic** *adj*

em·py·re·al /èm pī rée əl, -pírree-/ *adj* **1.** relating to the sky, the celestial sphere, or heaven **2.** glorious and sublime (*literary*) [15C. < medieval Latin *empyreus* (see EMPYREAN)]

em·py·re·an /èm pī rée ən, -pírree-/ *n* **1.** the sky or celestial sphere (*literary*) **2.** the highest part of heaven, believed in ancient Greek and Roman times to contain pure fire or light and believed by some Christians to be the dwelling place of God (*archaic*) ■ *adj* same as **empyreal** (sense 2) [15C. < medieval Latin *empyreus* < Greek *empurios* "in fire" < *pur* "fire"]

EMS *abbr* **1.** MED electrical muscle stimulation **2.** E-COMMERCE electronics manufacturing services **3.** HEALTH SERVICES Emergency Medical Services **4.** FIN European Monetary System

EMT *abbr US* HEALTH SERVICES emergency medical technician

e·mu /ée myoo/ (*plural* **e·mus** *or* *same*) *n* a large flightless bird that is related to the ostrich and has three-toed feet and loose shaggy feathers. Native to: Australia. Latin name: *Dromaius novaehollandiae.* [Early 17C. < Portuguese *ema*]

emu

EMU *abbr* **1.** *also* **emu** *or* **e.m.u.** PHYS electromagnetic unit **2.** /ée em yoo, ée myoo/ ECON European Monetary Union

em·u·late /émmyə làyt/ (**-lat·ed, -lat·ing, -lates**) *vt* **1. TRY TO EQUAL SOMEBODY OR SOMETHING** to try to equal or surpass somebody or something that is successful or admired **2. COMPETE SUCCESSFULLY WITH SOMEBODY OR SOMETHING** to be successful in comparison with somebody or something else ○ *emulates the achievement of better-funded ventures* **3.** COMPUT **MODIFY TO IMITATE ANOTHER COMPUTER SYSTEM** to modify a computer system so that it appears to behave like another computer system, and can thereby accept data and run programs that are designed for the system being emulated [Late 16C. < Latin *aemulat-*, past participle of *aemulari* "to rival" < *aemulus* "rival"] —**em·u·la·tion** /èmmyə láysh'n/ *n* —**em·u·la·tive** *adj* —**em·u·la·tive·ly** *adv*

SYNONYMS See *imitate*.

em·u·la·tor /émmyə làytər/ *n* **1.** somebody or something that emulates another person or thing **2.** a piece of hardware or software that permits a computer system to run programs and process data designed for a different type of computer system. ◊ **simulator** (sense 1)

em·u·lous /émmyələss/ *adj* **1.** seeking to match or rival another's achievement or performance **2.** motivated or characterized by rivalry or imitation [14C. < Latin *aemulus* "rival"] —**em·u·lous·ly** *adv* —**em·u·lous·ness** *n*

e·mul·si·fi·er /i múlssə fī ər/ *n* a chemical agent that maintains or creates an emulsion. It is used especially as a food additive.

e·mul·si·fy /i múlssə fī/ (**-fied, -fy·ing, -fies**) *vti* to convert two or more liquids into an emulsion, or become an emulsion —**e·mul·si·fi·a·ble** *adj* —**e·mul·si·fi·ca·tion** /i mùlssəfi káysh'n/ *n*

e·mul·sion /i múlsh'n/ *n* **1. SUSPENSION OF LIQUID WITHIN ANOTHER LIQUID** a suspension of one liquid in another, e.g., oil in water or fat in milk **2. WATER-BASED PAINT WITH MAT FINISH** a water-based paint that usually has a mat finish. Use: interior decorating. **3.** PHOTOGRAPHY **LIGHT-SENSITIVE PHOTOGRAPHIC COATING** a thin light-sensitive coating of silver bromide or silver halide in a medium such as gelatin on a photographic plate, paper, or film [Early 17C. < Latin *emuls-*, past participle of *emulgere* "milk out" < *mulgere* "to milk"] —**e·mul·sive** *adj*

e·munc·to·ry /i múngktəree/ (*plural* **-ries**) *n* a body part or organ that removes waste products from the body, e.g., the kidneys, lungs, or skin [14C. < medieval Latin *emunctorius* < Latin *emungere* "blow the nose thoroughly" < *mungere* "blow the nose"]

en /en/ *n* a measure of printing width, half that of an em [Late 18C. Representing pronunciation of N[1]; because the letter is about this width]

en- *prefix* **1.** to put or go into, or cover with ○ *entomb* ○ *encamp* ○ *enfold* **2.** to provide with ○ *enlighten* **3.** to cause to be ○ *enlarge* **4.** thoroughly ○ *enmesh* **5.** in, within, into ○ *enzootic* [Via French < Latin *in* "in"]

-en *suffix* **1.** to cause to be or have ○ *brighten* ○ *strengthen* **2.** to come to be or have ○ *tauten* ○ *lengthen* **3.** made of or resembling ○ *wooden* [Old English < Germanic]

en·a·ble /in áyb'l, en-/ (**-bled, -bling, -bles**) *vt* **1. PROVIDE SOMEBODY WITH MEANS** to provide somebody with the resources, authority, or opportunity to do something **2. MAKE SOMETHING POSSIBLE** to make something possible or feasible ○ *enabling legislation* **3. GIVE SOMEBODY OR SOMETHING LEGAL AUTHORITY** to confer legal power or authority on somebody or something **4. CAUSE SOMETHING TO START TO OPERATE** to make a piece of equipment or computer system functional —**en·a·ble·ment** *n* —**e·na·bler** *n*

en·a·bling /in áybling, en-/ *adj* conferring new legal powers

en·act /in ákt, en-/ (**-act·ed, -act·ing, -acts**) *vt* **1.** to make proposed legislation into law **2.** to perform or relate something using acting —**en·act·a·ble** *adj* —**en·ac·tive** *adj* —**en·ac·tor** *n*

en·act·ment /in áktmənt, en-/ *n* **1.** the act or process of enacting something **2.** something that is enacted, especially a law

e·nal·a·pril /ə nálləpril/ *n* an ACE inhibitor drug. Use: temporary management of high blood pressure.

~~**enamal**~~ incorrect spelling of **enamel**

e·nam·el /i námm'l/ *n* **1. GLASSY DECORATIVE OR PROTECTIVE COATING** a glassy decorative or protective coating, usually colored and opaque, that is fused onto metal, glass, or ceramics **2. SOMETHING WITH ENAMEL COATING** something that is coated with enamel **3. PAINT WITH SHINY FINISH** a paint that gives a shiny smooth finish when dry **4.** DENT **HARD LAYER ON TOOTH** a hard thin calcium-containing layer that covers and protects the crown of a tooth ■ *vt* (**-eled, -el·ing, -els**) **1. COAT SOMETHING WITH ENAMEL** to decorate or coat all or part of an object with enamel **2. APPLY BRIGHT SHINY SURFACE TO SOMETHING** to apply a shiny brightly colored surface to something [14C. < Anglo-Norman *enamailler* "to enamel in" < Old French *esmail* "enamel" < Germanic, "melting"] —**e·nam·el·er** *n*

e·nam·el·ing /i námm'ling/ *n* **1.** the process of applying enamel to something **2.** the surface of something coated with enamel

e·nam·el·ware /i námm'l wèr/ *n* household utensils coated with enamel

e·nam·el·work /i námm'l wùrk/ *n* HANDICRAFT same as **enameling** (sense 2)

en·am·or /in ámmər, en-/ (**-ored, -or·ing, -ors**) *vt* (*formal or literary*) **1.** to inspire somebody with love or passion **2.** to charm, fascinate, or captivate somebody [13C. < Old French *enamourer* < *en-* "cause to" + *amour* "love"]

en·am·ored /in ámmərd, en-/ *adj* **1.** inspired with love or passion for somebody **2.** charmed, fascinated, or captivated by somebody or something ○ *I wasn't greatly enamored of her playing.*

USAGE The right preposition: Although **enamored** is quite similar in meaning to *in love* and *smitten,* it takes a different preposition. Compare: *He is enamored of her* with *She is in love with him* and *They are smitten with* [or *by*] *each other.*

en·am·our *vt* Can, UK spelling of **enamor**

en·an·ti·o·morph /i nántee ə màwrf/, **en·an·ti·o·mer** /i nántee əmər/ *n* either of a pair of molecules that are mirror images of each other in structure but cannot be superimposed [Late 19C. < Greek *enantios* "opposite"] —**en·an·ti·o·mor·phic** /i nàntee ə máwrfik/ *adj* —**en·an·ti·o·mor·phism** /-máwr fizzəm/ *n* —**en·an·ti·o·mor·phous** /-máwrfəss/ *adj*

en·an·ti·o·se·lec·tive /i nántee ō sə léktiv/ *adj* CHEM same as **stereoselective** [Late 20C. < Greek *enantios* "opposite"]

e·nate /ée nàyt/ *adj also* **e·nat·ic** /i náttik/ related through the mother ■ *n* somebody related on the mother's side [Mid-17C. < Latin *enatus*, past participle of *enasci* "issue out, be born"]

e·na·tion /i náysh'n/ *n* a small outgrowth on an organ, especially on a leaf, caused by a virus infection [Mid-19C. < Latin *enation-* < *enasci* "issue out, be born"]

enc, enc. *abbr* **1.** enclosed **2.** enclosure

en·cage /in káyj, en-/ (**-caged, -cag·ing, -cag·es**) *vt* to confine somebody or something in a cage or in something resembling a cage (*literary*)

en·camp /in kámp, en-/ (**-camped, -camp·ing, -camps**) *v*

1. *vi* to lodge in a camp 2. *vt* to provide somebody with lodging in a camp

en·camp·ment /in kámpmənt, en-/ *n* 1. CAMPSITE a place occupied by a camp 2. STAYING IN CAMP residence in a camp 3. MAKING CAMP the setting up of a camp

en·cap·su·late /in kápsə làyt, en-/ (**-lat·ed, -lat·ing, -lates**), **in·cap·su·late** *v* 1. *vt* to express something in concise form 2. *vti* to enclose something completely, or be enclosed completely —**en·cap·su·la·tion** /in kàpsə láysh'n, en-/ *n* —**en·cap·su·la·tor** *n*

en·cap·su·lat·ed /in kápsə làytəd, en-/ *adj* describes an organ or tumor covered by a thin protective membrane

en·case /in káyss, en-/ (**-cased, -cas·ing, -cas·es**) *vt* to surround something completely with a case or cover —**en·case·ment** *n*

en·caus·tic /en káwstik/ *adj* having pigments mixed with wax applied to a surface by heat ■ *n* an object or work of art whose colors are fused to a surface by the application of heat, especially an earthenware tile decorated with an inlaid design in the style of medieval floor tiles [Late 16C. Via Latin < Greek *egkaustikos* < *egkaiein* "burn in"]

en·ceinte[1] /en sáynt, aan sánt/ *adj* having a child developing in the womb (*used euphemistically*) [Early 17C. Via French < medieval Latin *incincta* "not girded" < Latin *cincta* "girded"]

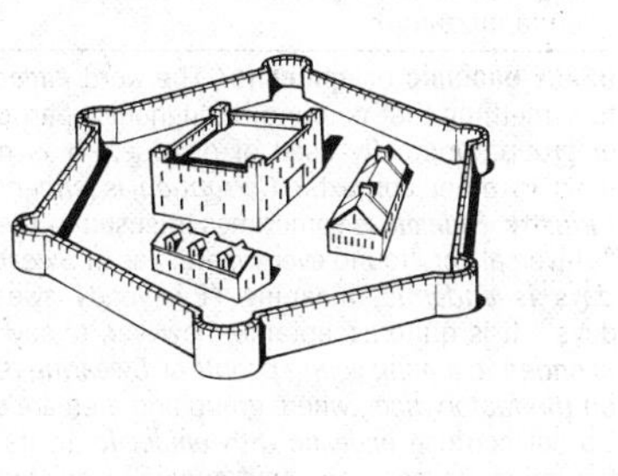

enceinte

en·ceinte[2] /en sáynt, aan sánt/ *n* 1. a defensive wall or enclosure 2. a place protected by a defensive wall or enclosure [Early 18C. Via French < Latin *incincta*, past participle of *incingere* "gird in"]

En·cel·a·dus /en sélladəss/ *n* a small natural satellite of Saturn, discovered in 1789. It is 309 mi./498 km in diameter and occupies an intermediate orbit.

encephal- *prefix* same as **encephalo-** (*used before vowels*)

en·ce·phal·ic /èn sə fállik/ *adj* related to the brain or its location within the cranium [Mid-19C. < Greek *egkephalos* "brain" (see ENCEPHALO-)]

en·ceph·a·li·tis /en sèffə lítiss/ *n* inflammation of the brain, usually caused by a viral infection —**en·ceph·a·lit·ic** /-líttik/ *adj*

en·ceph·a·li·tis le·thar·gi·ca /-lə thaárjikə/ *n* MED same as **sleeping sickness** (sense 2) (*technical*) [< modern Latin, "sleepy encephalitis"]

encephalo- *prefix* brain ○ *encephalogram* [Via modern Latin < Greek *egkephalos* "brain" < *en* "in" + *kephalē* "head"]

en·ceph·a·lo·gram /en séffələ gràm/ *n* 1. an X-ray photograph of the brain 2. MED same as **electroencephalogram**

en·ceph·a·lo·graph /en séffələ gràf/ *n* MED 1. same as **encephalogram** (sense 1) 2. same as **electroencephalograph** —**en·ceph·a·log·ra·phy** /en sèffə lóggrəfee/ *n*

en·ceph·a·lo·my·e·li·tis /en sèffəlō mī ə lítiss/ *n* inflammation of the brain and spinal cord —**en·ceph·a·lo·my·e·lit·ic** /-mī ə líttik/ *adj*

en·ceph·a·lon /en séffə lòn/ (*plural* **-la** /-lə/) *n* the brain of a vertebrate [Mid-18C. < Greek *egkephalon* "what is inside the head" < *kephalē* "head"] —**en·ceph·a·lous** *adj*

en·ceph·a·lop·a·thy /en sèffə lóppəthee/ *n* a disease of the brain —**en·ceph·a·lo·path·ic** /en sèffələ páthik/ *adj*

en·chain /in cháyn, en-/ (**-chained, -chain·ing, -chains**) *vt* 1. to bind somebody or something with chains (*formal or literary*) 2. to dominate somebody's attention or thoughts (*literary*) [14C. < French *enchaîner* < Latin *catenare* "to chain"] —**en·chain·ment** *n*

en·chant /in chánt, en-/ (**-chant·ed, -chant·ing, -chants**) *vt* 1. to charm, delight, or captivate somebody 2. to cast a spell on somebody or something [14C. Via French < Latin *incantare* "chant a magic formula upon" < *cantare* "sing"] —**en·chant·ed** *adj* —**en·chant·er** *n*

en·chant·ing /in chánting, en-/ *adj* captivating or delightful —**en·chant·ing·ly** *adv*

en·chant·ment /in chántmənt, en-/ *n* 1. STATE OF BEING ENCHANTED the act or condition of being enchanted 2. CHARM something that delights or captivates 3. SPELL a magic spell

en·chant·ress /in chántrəss, en-/ *n* 1. a woman who is charming or delightful 2. a woman who casts spells

en·chase /in cháyss, en-/ (**-chased, -chas·ing, -chas·es**) *vt* 1. to set jewelry or other decorative objects with gems 2. to emboss, engrave, or carve designs on metal [15C. < French *enchasser* "set (gems), encase" < *chasse* "case, box"]

en·chi·la·da /ènchi laádə/ *n* a fried tortilla rolled around a filling and served hot with a usually spicy sauce [Late 19C. < Mexican Spanish < past participle of *enchilar* "season with chili"]

en·chi·rid·i·on /èn kī ríddee ən/ (*plural* **-ons** or **-a** /-dee ə/) *n* a manual or handbook (*archaic*) [Mid-16C. Via late Latin < Greek *egkheiridion* "small thing in the hand" < *kheir* "hand"]

-enchyma *suffix* cellular tissue ○ *aerenchyma* [< PARENCHYMA]

en·ci·na /en seénə/ *n Southwest US* same as **live oak** [Early 20C. < Spanish, "holm oak" < late Latin *ilicina* < Latin *ilic-*]

En·ci·ni·tas /ènssi neétəss/ city in southern California on the Gulf of Santa Catalina, northwest of San Diego. Population: 59,796 (2002 estimate).

en·ci·pher /in sífər, en-/ (**-phered, -pher·ing, -phers**) *vt* to convert a text into code or cipher —**en·ci·pher·er** *n* —**en·ci·pher·ment** *n*

en·cir·cle /in súrk'l, en-/ (**-cled, -cling, -cles**) *vt* 1. to form a circle around somebody or something 2. to move in a circle around somebody or something —**en·cir·cle·ment** *n* —**en·cir·cling** *adj*

encl. *abbr* 1. enclosed 2. enclosure

en·clasp /in klásp, en-/ (**-clasped, -clasp·ing, -clasps**) *vt* to embrace or hold somebody or something tightly (*formal*)

en·clave /én klàyv, ón-/ *n* 1. a small country or territory that is culturally or ethnically different from a surrounding larger and distinct political unit. ◊ **exclave** 2. a distinct group that lives or operates together within a larger community [Mid-19C. < French < Old French *enclaver* "enclose" < Latin *in* "in" + *clavis* "key"]

en·clit·ic /en klíttik/ *adj* describes a word that depends on a preceding word for its formation or pronunciation [Mid-17C. Via late Latin < Greek *egklitikos* < *egklinein* "lean on"] —**en·clit·ic** *n*

en·close /in klṓz, en-/ (**-closed, -clos·ing, -clos·es**), **in·close** /in-/ *vt* 1. SURROUND SOMETHING to surround or shut in something 2. INSERT SOMETHING IN ENVELOPE OR PACKAGE to add something to the contents of an envelope or package 3. FENCE IN LAND OR BUILDING to surround land or a building with a fence, wall, or other boundary [14C. < Old French *enclos*, past participle of *enclore* < Latin *includere* "shut in" (see INCLUDE)] —**en·clos·a·ble** *adj* —**en·closed** *adj*

en·closed or·der *n* a Christian religious community whose members remain physically within it

en·clo·sure /in klṓzhər, en-/, **in·clo·sure** /in-/ *n* 1. SOMETHING INSIDE LETTER something extra enclosed in a letter or package 2. LAND SURROUNDED BY BOUNDARY an area of land surrounded by a fence, wall, or other boundary 3. BOUNDARY FENCE a fence, wall, or other boundary surrounding something 4. *UK* RESERVED AREA AT SPORTS EVENT an area of ground at a sports event set aside for specific spectators or competitors 5. ACT OF ENCLOSING LAND the act or process of enclosing land to prevent general use 6. CHR RESTRICTED PART OF CONVENT OR MONASTERY the part of a convent or monastery, especially the living quarters, that is restricted to members

en·code /in kṓd, en-/ (**-cod·ed, -cod·ing, -codes**) *vt* 1. CONVERT TEXT TO CODE to convert a message from plain text into code 2. COMPUT CONVERT COMPUTER CHARACTERS INTO DIGITAL FORM to convert input data such as analog signals, characters, and commands into a digital form recognizable by a computer 3. GENETICS PROVIDE GENETIC INFORMATION to carry the genetic information that enables a polypeptide, RNA molecule, or one of their constituent groups to be produced —**en·code·ment** *n*

en·co·mi·a plural of **encomium**

en·co·mi·ast /en kṓmee àst, -mee əst/ *n* a speaker or writer of an encomium (*formal*) [Early 17C. < Greek *egkōmiastēs* < *egkōmiazein* "to praise" < *egkōmion* (see ENCOMIUM)]

en·co·mi·um /en kṓmee əm/ (*plural* **-mi·ums** or **-mi·a** /-mee ə/) *n* (*formal*) 1. a formal text that expresses high praise for somebody 2. an expression of high praise [Mid-16C. Via Latin < Greek *egkōmion* "eulogy" < *kōmos* "revel"]

en·com·pass /in kúmpəss, en-/ (**-passed, -pass·ing, -pass·es**) *vt* 1. INCLUDE MUCH to include a wide or comprehensive range ○ *The ceremony will encompass contributions from many parts of the world.* 2. ENCIRCLE SOMETHING to surround, envelop, or encircle something 3. CAUSE SOMETHING TO OCCUR to cause or bring about something (*formal*) —**en·com·pass·ment** *n*

en·core /ón kàwr/ *n* EXTRA OR REPEATED PERFORMANCE an additional or repeated performance of something in response to a demand from an audience ■ *interj* USED TO DEMAND REPEAT PERFORMANCE used to demand an additional or repeated performance of something ■ *vt* (**-cored, -cor·ing, -cores**) ADD TO OR REPEAT PERFORMANCE to give an additional or repeated performance of something [Early 18C. < French, "still, again"]

en·coun·ter /in kówntər, en-/ *vt* (**-tered, -ter·ing, -ters**) 1. COME UP AGAINST SOMETHING to be faced with something difficult to deal with ○ *We don't expect to encounter any major problems.* 2. MEET SOMEBODY UNEXPECTEDLY to meet somebody or something, usually unexpectedly and briefly ○ *I encountered the girl for the first time in 1993.* 3. MEET SOMEBODY IN CONFLICT to confront somebody with hostility or aggression ■ *n* 1. UNEXPECTED MEETING a meeting with somebody or something, usually unexpected and brief 2. CONFRONTATION a hostile confrontation or difficult struggle [13C. < Old French *encontrer* "confront" < late Latin *incontra* "in front of" < Latin *in-* "in" + *contra* "against"]

en·coun·ter group *n* a small group of people, often guided by a leader, who meet in order to achieve personal growth, self-awareness, and social skills by means of emotional expression and interaction

en·cour·age /in kúr ij, en-/ (**-aged, -ag·ing, -ag·es**) *vt* 1. GIVE SOMEBODY HOPE OR CONFIDENCE to give somebody hope, confidence, or courage 2. URGE SOMEBODY TO DO SOMETHING to motivate somebody to take a course of action or continue doing something ○ *encouraged me to finish the course* 3. FOSTER SOMETHING to assist something to occur or increase ○ *encourage new solutions to traffic problems* [15C. < French *encoragier* < *en-* "cause" + *corage* "courage"] —**en·cour·ag·ing** *adj* —**en·cour·ag·ing·ly** *adv*

en·cour·age·ment /in kúr ijmənt, en-/ *n* 1. support of a kind that inspires confidence and a will to continue or develop 2. somebody who or something that gives somebody hope, confidence, or courage

en·croach /in krṓch, en-/ (**-croached, -croach·ing, -croach·es**) *vi* 1. to intrude gradually or stealthily, often taking away somebody's authority, rights, or property ○ *is encroaching on civil liberties* 2. to exceed the proper limits of something [14C. < Old French *encrochier* "seize" < *croc* "hook" < Old Norse *krōkr*] —**en·croach·er** *n* —**en·croach·ing·ly** *adv* —**en·croach·ment** *n*

en croute /aaN kroót/ *adj, adv* enclosed in a pastry crust ○ *salmon en croute* [Late 20C. < French *en croûte* "in a crust"]

en·crust /in krúst, en-/ (**-crust·ed, -crust·ing, -crusts**), **in·crust** /in-/ *vt* (*often passive*) 1. to cover something with a hard thick coating **2.** to embellish something richly, especially with jewels [Early 17C. Via French < Latin *incrustare* < *in-* "upon" + *crusta* "crust"]

en·crust·a·tion /in krust áysh'n, èn-/, **in·crust·a·tion** /in-/ *n* **1.** the act of encrusting something, or the state of being encrusted **2.** a hard thick coating or covering

en·crypt /in krípt, en-/ (**-crypt·ed, -crypt·ing, -crypts**) *vt* **1.** to convert a text into code or cipher **2.** to convert computer data and messages into something incomprehensible using a key, so that only a holder of the matching key can reconvert them —**en·cryp·tion** /en krípsh'n/ *n*

en·cul·tu·ra·tion /in kùlchə ráysh'n, en-/ *n* the gradual acceptance by a person or group of the standards and practices of another person or culture —**en·cul·tu·ra·tive** /in kúlchə ràytiv, en-/ *adj*

en·cum·ber /in kúmbər, en-/ (**-bered, -ber·ing, -bers**), **in·cum·ber** *vt* **1.** to hamper or impede somebody or something **2.** to burden or weigh down somebody or something (*often passive*) [14C. < Old French *encombrer* "obstruct" < *combre* "barrier"]

en·cum·brance /in kúmbrənss, en-/ *n* **1.** a hindrance or burden to somebody **2.** a charge or claim on property, especially a mortgage

en·cum·branc·er /in kúmbrənssər, en-/ *n* somebody who has a legal claim on property, especially a mortgage

en·cyc·li·cal /in síklik'l, en-/ *n* in the Roman Catholic Church, a formal statement issued by the pope to bishops, often on matters of doctrine [Mid-17C. < Greek *egkuklios* "circular, general" < *kuklos* "circle"]

en·cy·clo·pae·di·a, etc. another spelling of **encyclopedia, etc.**

en·cy·clo·pe·di·a /in sìklə peédee ə, en-/, **en·cy·clo·pae·di·a** *n* a reference work offering comprehensive information on all or specialized areas of knowledge [Mid-16C. < Greek *egkuklopaideia* "general education" < *egkuklios* (see ENCYCLICAL) + *paideia* "education" < *pais* "boy, child"]

en·cy·clo·pe·dic /in sìklə peédik, en-/, **en·cy·clo·pae·dic** *adj* covering or including a broad range of detailed knowledge such as is found in an encyclopedia —**en·cy·clo·pe·di·cal·ly** *adv*

en·cy·clo·pe·dism /in sìklə peé dìzzəm, en-/, **en·cy·clo·pae·dism** *n* comprehensive learning or knowledge

en·cy·clo·pe·dist /in sìklə peédist, en-/, **en·cy·clo·pae·dist** *n* a compiler of or contributor to an encyclopedia

En·cy·clo·pe·dist *n* a writer or editor of the *Encyclopédie* (1751–72), a French reference work in which the advanced secular, technical, and political ideas of the period were articulated

en·cyst /en síst/ (**-cyst·ed, -cyst·ing, -cysts**) *vti* to enclose or be enclosed in a cyst —**en·cys·ta·tion** /èn siss táysh'n/ *n* —**en·cyst·ed** *adj* —**en·cyst·ment** *n*

end /end/ *n* **1.** EXTREMITY OF OBJECT the tip or extremity of a long narrow object ○ *I'm surprised he knows which end of the mike to hold.* **2.** EXTREMITY OR LIMIT the limit, extent, or boundary of something ○ *They walked the valley from end to end.* ○ *at both ends of the political spectrum* **3.** FINAL PART the final part or finishing point of a period of time, of an event, or of a book, movie, or other work ○ *His address is at the end of the article.* ○ *the end of the lesson* **4.** TERMINATION the act or result of stopping something ○ *a scandal that brought his career to an abrupt end* **5.** GOAL a goal, object, or purpose ○ *for purely political ends* **6.** PART OF COMMUNICATIONS LINK either of the places connected by a communications link ○ *Pick up the phone and find out who's on the other end.* **7.** DEATH the experience of death ○ *met an untimely end* **8.** LEFTOVER PIECE a piece or part of something that is left over **9.** SHARE OF JOINT RESPONSIBILITY a part or portion of shared responsibility ○ *Are you sure they'll honor their end of the deal?* **10.** SPORTS AREA ON PLAYING FIELD the area at each end of a playing field **11.** FOOTBALL PLAYER POSITIONED AT END OF LINE in football, a player positioned at each end of the offensive or defensive line ■ *v* (**end·ed, end·ing, ends**) **1.** *vti* STOP to reach, or bring something to, a close or a final point ○ *She abruptly ended the meeting.* ○ *The meeting ended without an agreement being made.* **2.** *vi* STOP AT A PLACE to reach a particular place and stop there ○ *The road ends at a little village called Moneta.* [Old English *ende* < Indo-European, "front"] ◇ **an end in itself** something that is worth having or doing although it may not lead to anything ○ *A friendship should be satisfying; it is an end in itself and not a means to an end.* ◇ **at loose ends** having no purpose or occupation ○ *With all her work done she found herself at loose ends.* ◇ **come to** *or* **meet a sticky** *or* **bad end** to have an unpleasant or unfortunate outcome, especially a violent death (*informal*) ◇ **end for end** *US* reversed or inverted ○ *They turned the boxes end for end.* ◇ **end it all** to commit suicide ◇ **end on 1.** in such a way that an object's end piece or section is flush with a flat surface ○ *Set the desk end on to the wall.* **2.** *US* with the end facing or next to something ○ *The plane crash-landed on the runway, its tail section end on to the tarmac.* ◇ **end to end** in a row with the ends adjacent ○ *The beds of flowers were arranged end to end.* ◇ **in the end** when something has come to an end ○ *In the end, I had to admit he was right.* ◇ **make ends meet** to be able to afford to pay for the expenses of daily living ◇ **no end** very much indeed ◇ **no end of something** a great deal of something ○ *The old photocopier gave us no end of trouble.* ◇ **on end 1.** for an uninterrupted period ○ *The rain continued for weeks on end.* **2.** in a vertical position ○ *We left the table standing on end against the wall.* ◇ **the end of the line** *or* **road** the point beyond which somebody or something can no longer continue or survive ○ *The coming of the supermarkets was the end of the line for many small independent grocers.* ◇ **the...to end all...** something that is so impressive or important that nothing else of the same kind will ever rival it ○ *the war to end all wars* ○ *the movie to end all movies* ◇ **to no end** without success, or without achieving useful results (*formal*) ◇ **to the very end** for as long as is possible, however unpleasant the situation becomes ○ *The company's policy was to fight to the very end all consequent damage suits.* ◇ **until the end of time** forever

USAGE Avoid using the expression *to no end* (meaning "without success") when *no end* (meaning "very much indeed") is called for. Use *He annoyed her no end* [not *to no end*].

end in *vi* **1.** to have a particular kind of tip or extremity ○ *The dog's tail ends in a tuft of hair.* **2.** to have a particular outcome ○ *The relationship ended in an acrimonious split.*

end up *vi* **1.** to become something eventually **2.** to arrive at a destination at long last

end- *prefix* same as **endo-** (*used before vowels*)

-end *suffix* a person or thing to be treated in a particular way ○ *reverend* [< Latin *-endus, -endum*]

en·da·moe·ba /èndə meébə/ (*plural* **-bas** or **-bae** /-bee/), **en·da·me·ba** (*plural* **-bas** or **-bae**) *n* a parasitic protozoan found in the digestive tracts of some invertebrates, especially cockroaches and termites. Genus: *Endamoeba.*

en·dan·ger /in dáynjər, en-/ (**-gered, -ger·ing, -gers**) *vt* to expose somebody or something to danger —**en·dan·gered** *adj* —**en·dan·ger·ment** *n*

en·dan·gered spe·cies *n* a species whose numbers are so few, or are declining so quickly, that the animal, plant, or other organism may soon become extinct. Endangered species are sometimes protected under national or international law.

end-a·round *n* **1.** *also* **end-a·round play** in football, a play in which an end on one side carries the ball around the opposite side of the field **2.** *US* an indirect attack on a problem that avoids opponents instead of confronting them (*informal*)

end·ar·te·rec·to·my /èn daartə réktəmee/ (*plural* **-mies**) *n* the surgical removal of material that is wholly or partially obstructing blood flow in an artery [Mid-20C. < END- + ARTERY]

en dash *n* in printing, a dash that is one en in length

en·dear /in deér, en-/ (**-deared, -dear·ing, -dears**) *vt* to make somebody or something affectionately loved or greatly liked ○ *didn't endear herself to us*

en·dear·ing /in deéring, en-/ *adj* producing feelings of affection or fondness —**en·dear·ing·ly** *adv*

en·dear·ment /in deérmənt, en-/ *n* **1.** an expression of affection, especially a spoken one ○ *murmuring endearments* **2.** the showing of affection ○ *terms of endearment*

en·deav·or /in dévvər, en-/ *vt* (**-ored, -or·ing, -ors**) TRY HARD TO DO SOMETHING to make a serious and sincere effort to achieve something (*formal*) ■ *n* **1.** EFFORT an earnest attempt to achieve something **2.** ENTERPRISE an enterprise or directed activity ○ *offered help with my latest endeavor* [15C. < obsolete *put in dever,* partial translation of French *mettre en devoir* "put in duty"] —**en·deav·or·er** *n*

SYNONYMS See *try.*

en·deav·our *vt, n* Can, UK spelling of **endeavor**

En·de·cott /éndikət, -kòt/, **John** (1588?–1665) English-born American colonial administrator and Puritan leader, known for his intolerance of religious dissenters

en·dem·ic /en démmik/ *adj* **1.** MED RESTRICTED TO ONE PLACE describes a disease occurring within a particular area ○ *Typhoid fever used to be endemic in the Deep South.* **2.** ECOL LIVING IN DEFINED GEOGRAPHIC AREA describes a species of organism that is confined to a particular geographic region such as an island or river basin **3.** CHARACTERISTIC OF AREA characteristic of a particular place, or among a particular group, or area of interest or activity ■ *n* BIOL ORGANISM WITH LIMITED GEOGRAPHIC RANGE a species of organism that is confined to a particular geographic region [Mid-17C. < Greek *endēmos* "native" < *dēmos* "people"] —**en·dem·i·cal·ly** *adv* —**en·de·mic·i·ty** /èndə míssətee/ *n* —**en·dem·ism** /éndə mìzzəm/ *n*

USAGE endemic or **epidemic**? The word ***endemic*** refers to something that is found throughout a particular area or group. Originally used of diseases, it is now often used in other contexts: *Corruption is endemic in the industry.* ***Endemic*** is sometimes misused in the sense of "universal" or "found everywhere," as in *Swearing these days is endemic,* meaning "Everybody swears these days." It is quite acceptable, however, to say *Swearing is endemic among young people* or *Swearing is endemic on the factory floor,* where group and area are specified. Do not confuse ***endemic*** with ***epidemic***, in its literal or figurative senses: an ***epidemic*** spreads rapidly and usually lasts for a limited period.

end·er·gon·ic /èndər gónnik/ *adj* describes a chemical or biochemical reaction that requires energy [Mid-20C. < END- + Greek *ergon* "work"]

En·ders /éndərz/, **John Franklin** (1897–1985) US microbiologist. His research led to the development of vaccines against viral diseases such as poliomyelitis, mumps, and measles. He shared a Nobel Prize in physiology or medicine (1954).

~~**endevor**~~ incorrect spelling of **endeavor**

end·game /énd gàym/ *n* **1.** the final stage of a process or contest ○ *As the trial neared its close, reporters watched closely to see what the prosecutor's endgame would be.* **2.** in chess, the final stage of a game in which only a few pieces are left on the board

En·di·cott /éndikət, -kòt/ village in southern New York, on the Susquehanna River. Population: 12,886 (2002 estimate).

end·ing /énding/ *n* **1.** FINAL PART the final or concluding part of something ○ *nerve endings* ○ *a sad ending* **2.** WAY SOMETHING IS FINISHED the manner in which something is ended **3.** GRAM END PART OF WORD the terminating part of a word, e.g., an inflection or derivational suffix **4.** CHESS same as **endgame** (sense 2) **5.** PSYCHOANAL PROCESS OF CONCLUDING RELATIONSHIP the process of concluding a relationship with another person, especially a therapist. An ending may offer somebody an opportunity to explore feelings about separation and loss.

en·dive /én dìv, aaN deév/ *n* **1.** a plant grown for its tightly packed curly leaves. Use: in salads, as a garnish. Latin name: *Cichorium endivia.* **2.** *US* a plant grown for its mainly white, pointed, succulent leaves. Use: in salads. Latin name: *Cichorium intybus.* Can term **chicory** [14C. Via French < Latin *endivia* < medieval Greek *entubia*]

end·less /éndləss/ *adj* **1.** having no apparent end or limit ○ *endless patience* **2.** made continuous by joining the ends ○ *an endless belt* —**end·less·ly** *adv* —**end·less·ness** *n*

end line *n* in sports, a line at the end of a court or field that marks the boundary of a playing area

end man *n US* a man at the end of a line in a minstrel show

end mat·ter *n* PUBL same as **back matter**

end mo·raine *n* a ridge of rock, gravel, and soil at the terminal end of a glacier or ice field

end·most /énd mōst/ *adj* **1.** nearest or at the end **2.** last or most distant

end·note /énd nōt/ *n* a note of comment or reference placed at the end of an article, chapter, book, or essay instead of at the bottom of a page

endo- *prefix* in, within, inside ○ *endotracheal* [< Greek *endo* < Indo-European, "in"]

en·do·blast /éndō blàst/ *n* BIOL same as **endoderm** —**en·do·blas·tic** /éndō blástik/ *adj*

en·do·can·na·bi·noid /èndō kə nábbə nòyd/ *n* a chemical substance in the body belonging to a group resembling organic chemicals found in cannabis

en·do·car·di·a ANAT plural of **endocardium**

en·do·car·di·al /èndō kaárdee əl/ *adj* **1.** located within the heart **2.** concerned with the thin membranous lining (**endocardium**) of the heart's cavities

en·do·car·di·tis /èndō kaar dítiss/ *n* inflammation of the thin membranous lining (**endocardium**) of the heart's cavities —**en·do·car·dit·ic** /-díttik/ *adj*

en·do·car·di·um /èndō kaárdee əm/ (*plural* **-di·a** /-dee ə/) *n* the thin membranous lining of the heart's cavities

en·do·carp /éndə kaarp/ *n* the innermost of the three layers of the wall (**pericarp**) of a fruit. It may be toughened or hardened, as in a cherry stone or peach pit. (*technical*) —**en·do·car·pal** /éndə kaárp'l/ *adj*

en·do·cra·ni·um /èndō kráynee əm/ (*plural* **-ni·a** /-nee ə/) *n* ANAT same as **dura mater** —**en·do·cra·ni·al** *adj*

en·do·crine /éndəkrin, -kreen, -krīn/ *adj* relating to the endocrine glands or their secretions. ◊ **exocrine** [Early 20C. < ENDO- + Greek *krinein* "to separate"]

en·do·crine dis·rup·tor (*plural* **en·do·crine dis·rup·tors** or **en·do·crine dis·rup·ters**) *n* a substance that interferes with the endocrine system, sometimes causing reproductive or developmental problems, e.g., by mimicking a natural hormone

en·do·crine gland *n* any gland of the body that secretes hormones directly into the blood or lymph, e.g., the thyroid, pituitary, pineal, and adrenal glands

en·do·cri·nol·o·gy /èndəkrə nóllәjee/ *n* a branch of medicine that deals with disorders of the endocrine glands —**en·do·crin·o·log·ic** /èndə krinə lójjik/ *adj* —**en·do·crin·o·log·i·cal** *adj* —**en·do·cri·nol·o·gist** *n*

en·do·cy·to·sis /èndō sī tóssiss/ *n* the process by which a cell membrane folds inward to take in substances bound to its surface

en·do·derm /éndə dùrm/ *n* in an animal embryo, the innermost layer that develops into the lining of the respiratory and digestive tracts [Mid-19C. < ENDO- + Greek *derma* "skin"] —**en·do·der·mal** /èndə dúrm'l/ *adj*

en·do·der·mis /èndə dúrmiss/ *n* a layer of cells that marks the boundary between the inner core (**stele**) and outer surrounding tissue (**cortex**) of a plant root. It is also evident in the stems of some plants, notably ferns. [Late 19C. < ENDODERM, after *epidermis*]

en·do·don·tics /èndə dóntiks/, **en·do·don·tia** /-dónshə, -shee ə/ *n* the branch of dentistry that deals with diseases of the dental pulp (*takes a singular verb*) [Mid-20C. < ENDO- + ORTHODONTICS] —**en·do·don·tic** *adj* —**en·do·don·tist** *n*

en·do·en·zyme /èndō én zīm/ *n* an enzyme that is produced and functions inside cells

en·do·er·gic /èndō úrjik/ *adj* describes a chemical or nuclear reaction in which energy is absorbed. ◊ **exoergic** [Mid-20C. < ENDO- + Greek *ergon* "work"]

end-of-life *adj* relating to the needs of people who are dying or nearing the end of their lives ○ *a policy that provides end-of-life home care*

end of steel *n Can* **1.** the farthest point to which the rails of a railroad line have been laid **2.** the town at the end of a railroad line ○ *Dawson was the end of steel in the Yukon region.*

en·dog·a·my /en dóggəmee/ *n* **1.** the social practice of marrying another member of the same clan, people, or other kinship group **2.** pollination between the flowers of the same plant —**en·dog·a·mous** *adj*

en·do·gen·ic /èndō jénnik/ *adj* formed, located, or happening beneath the Earth's surface. ◊ **exogenic**

en·dog·e·nous /en dójjənəss/ *adj* **1.** having no apparent external cause ○ *endogenous depression* **2.** originating or growing within an organism or tissue ○ *endogenous secretions* ◊ **exogenous** —**en·dog·e·nous·ly** *adv* —**en·dog·e·ny** *n*

en·do·lymph /éndə limf/ *n* the fluid inside the membranous labyrinth of the ear —**en·do·lym·phat·ic** /èndə lim fáttik/ *adj*

en·do·me·tri·a ANAT plural of **endometrium**

en·do·me·tri·o·sis /èndō meetree óssiss/ *n* a medical condition in which the mucous membrane (**endometrium**) that normally lines only the womb is present and functioning in the ovaries or elsewhere in the body

en·do·me·tri·um /èndō meétree əm/ (*plural* **-tri·a** /-tree ə/) *n* the mucous membrane that lines the womb and increases in thickness in the later part of the menstrual cycle [Late 19C. < ENDO- + Greek *mētra* "womb"] —**en·do·me·tri·al** *adj*

en·do·mi·to·sis /èndō mī tóssiss/ *n* a process by which chromosomes divide within a cell but the nucleus does not, resulting in an increase in chromosome number —**en·do·mi·tot·ic** /-tóttik/ *adj*

en·do·morph /éndə màwrf/ *n* **1.** somebody whose body has a stocky build and a prominent abdomen. ◊ **ectomorph, mesomorph** **2.** a mineral surrounded by another. An example is tourmaline, often found enclosed in quartz. ◊ **perimorph** —**en·do·mor·phic** /èndə máwrfik/ *adj* —**en·do·mor·phy** *n*

en·do·nu·cle·ase /èndō nóoklee àyss, -àyz/ *n* an enzyme that splits DNA or RNA

en·do·par·a·site /èndō párrə sīt/ *n* a parasite that lives inside its host, e.g., a tapeworm —**en·do·par·a·sit·ic** /-parə síttik/ *adj* —**en·do·par·a·sit·ism** /-párrəssi tìzzəm, -sī tìzzəm/ *n*

en·do·pep·ti·dase /èndō pépti dàyss, -dàyz/ *n* an enzyme that splits proteins into peptides

en·do·phyte /éndə fīt/ *n* a plant or fungus that lives inside another plant. It may or may not be a parasite of its host plant. —**en·do·phyt·ic** /èndə fíttik/ *adj*

en·do·plasm /éndə plàzzəm/ *n* the inner, more fluid layer of cytoplasm in a cell —**en·do·plas·mic** /èndə plázmik/ *adj*

en·do·plas·mic re·tic·u·lum *n* an intricate system of tubular membranes in the cytoplasm of a cell. It is responsible for the synthesis and transport of materials to and from cells.

end or·gan *n* the specialized end of a sensory or motor nerve

en·dor·phin /en dáwrfin/ *n* a substance in the brain that attaches to the same cell receptors that morphine does. Endorphins are released when severe injury occurs, often abolishing all sensation of pain. [Late 20C. Blend of ENDOGENOUS + MORPHINE]

en·dorse /in dáwrss, en-/ (**-dorsed, -dors·ing, -dors·es**), **in·dorse** /in-/ *vt* **1. APPROVE SOMETHING FORMALLY** to give formal approval or permission for something ○ *This practice is not endorsed by headquarters.* **2. SUPPORT SOMEBODY OR SOMETHING** to give public support to somebody or something, especially during an election ○ *decided to endorse the mayor as a candidate for higher office* **3. PROMOTE PRODUCT** to give public approval of a product for advertising purposes ○ *a brand endorsed by a popular TV star* **4. SIGN BACK OF CHECK** to sign the back of a check, money order, or negotiable document in order to cash it or to make it payable to a specific payee **5. SIGN RECEIPT** to sign a document to acknowledge receipt of a payment **6. WRITE ON DOCUMENT** to write a comment on the back of a document ○ *a fitness report that had been endorsed on the back by its recipient* [15C. < medieval Latin *indorsare* < Latin *dorsum* "back"] —**en·dors·a·ble** *adj* —**en·dor·see** /èn dawr seé, in dàwr seé/ *n* —**en·dors·er** *n*

en·dorse·ment /in dáwrssmənt, en-/, **in·dorse·ment** /in-/ *n* **1. PUBLIC SUPPORT** public support for somebody or something **2. ADVERTISING TESTIMONIAL** an instance of public approval of a product for advertising purposes **3. OFFICIAL APPROVAL OR PERMISSION** official approval of or permission for something **4. SIGNATURE OR WRITTEN COMMENT** something, especially a signature, written on the back of a document to make it payable, to approve it, or to comment on it **5. ACT OF ENDORSING CHECK** an act or instance of endorsing a check or other financial document **6.** INSUR **POLICY ALTERATION** a clause added to an insurance policy that changes the coverage

en·do·scope /éndə skōp/ *n* a medical instrument consisting of a long tube inserted into the body, used for diagnostic examination and surgical procedures —**en·do·scop·ic** /èndə skóppik/ *adj* —**en·do·scop·ic·al·ly** *adv* —**en·dos·co·py** /en dóskəpee/ *n*

en·do·skel·e·ton /èndō skéllət'n/ *n* the internal skeleton of an animal, especially of a vertebrate —**en·do·skel·e·tal** *adj*

en·dos·mo·sis /èn doz mόssiss, -doss-/ *n* osmosis in which fluid is absorbed into a cell from a surrounding fluid —**en·dos·mot·ic** /-móttik/ *adj* —**en·dos·mot·i·cal·ly** *adv*

en·do·sperm /éndə spùrm/ *n* the tissue that surrounds the embryo inside a plant seed and provides nourishment for it —**en·do·sper·mic** /èndə spúrmik/ *adj*

en·do·spore /éndə spàwr/ *n* **1.** an asexual spore that is formed inside the cells of some bacteria and algae **2.** the inner layer of the wall of a spore —**en·do·spor·ous** /èndə spáwrəss, en dóspərəss/ *adj*

en·dos·te·um /en dóstee əm/ (*plural* **-te·a** /-tee ə/) *n* a layer of vascular tissue lining the inside of some bones, e.g., the femur [Late 19C. < END- + Greek *osteon* "bone"] —**en·dos·te·al** *adj*

en·do·sul·fan /èndō súlfən/ *n* a toxic organochlorine compound. Use: control of insects, mites, and ticks. Formula: $C_9H_6Cl_6O_3S$. [Mid-20C. < ENDO- + SULFUR]

en·do·sym·bi·o·sis /èndō sìm bī óssiss/ *n* **1.** symbiosis in which one organism lives inside the body of another and both function as a single organism **2.** a hypothetical evolutionary process by which some cellular structures may have developed as a result of the incorporation of free-living prokaryotes into the cytoplasm of eukaryotes —**en·do·sym·bi·o·tic** /-óttik/ *adj*

en·do·sym·bi·o·tic hy·poth·e·sis *n* a theory that the mitochondria and chloroplasts found within eukaryotic cells originated as free-living prokaryotic organisms

en·do·the·ci·um /èndō theéshee əm, -theéssee əm/ (*plural* **-ci·a** /-shee ə, -see ə/) *n* **1.** the inner tissue of the spore-producing capsule of a moss **2.** the tissue of the inner wall of an anther in a flower [Mid-19C. < ENDO- + Greek *thēkion* "little case" < *thēkē* "chest"]

en·do·the·li·a ANAT plural of **endothelium**

en·do·the·li·o·ma /èndō theelee ṓmə/ (*plural* **-mas** or **-ma·ta** /-mətə/) *n* a tumor of the cells that line internal body surfaces

en·do·the·li·um /èndə theélee əm/ (*plural* **-li·a** /-lee ə/) *n* a layer of cells that lines the inside of some body cavities, e.g., blood vessels [Late 19C. < modern Latin < Greek *endon* "within" + *thēlē* "nipple"] —**en·do·the·li·al** *adj* —**en·do·the·li·oid** *adj*

en·do·therm /éndə thùrm/ *n* an animal that is able to maintain a constant body temperature despite changes in the temperature of its environment [Mid-20C. < ENDO- + Greek *thermē* "heat"]

en·do·ther·mic /èndə thúrmik/, **en·do·ther·mal** /-thúrm'l/ *adj* **1.** maintaining a constant body temperature despite changes in the temperature of the environment **2.** describes a chemical reaction in which heat is absorbed. ◊ **exothermic** —**en·do·ther·my** /éndə thùrmee/ *n*

en·do·tox·in /éndə tòksin/ *n* a toxin produced within some bacteria that is released only when the bacteria disintegrate —**en·do·tox·ic** /èndə tóksik/ *adj*

en·do·tra·che·al /èndō tráykee əl/ *adj* located in or passed through the windpipe ○ *an endotracheal tube*

en·do·troph·ic /èndō tróffik/ *adj* describes an association (**mycorrhiza**) between a fungus and a plant in which the fungus obtains its nourishment from inside its plant host. ◊ **ectotrophic**

en·dow /in dów, en-/ (**-dowed, -dow·ing, -dows**) *vt* **1.** to provide a person or institution with income or property **2.** to provide somebody or something with desirable qualities, abilities, or characteristics (*usually passive*) ○ *The area is endowed with a perfect climate.* [14C. < Anglo-Norman *endouer* < Latin *dotare* "provide with a dowry" < *dot-* "dowry"]

en·dow·ment /in dówmənt, en-/ *n* **1.** NATURAL QUALITY a natural ability or quality ○ *A sharp mind was only one of her many endowments.* **2.** FUNDS OR PROPERTY an amount of income or property that has been provided to a person or institution, especially an educational institution **3.** GIVING OF ENDOWMENT the giving of an endowment, or an instance of this

en·do·zo·ic /èndə zṓ ik/ *adj* **1.** describes organisms that live inside an animal **2.** describes a method of seed dispersal in which the seeds are eaten by an animal and then passed out in the animal's feces

end·pa·per /énd pàypər/ *n* a sturdy sheet of paper pasted to the inside of a book's front or back cover and to the spine edge of the first or last page

end·pin /énd pìn/ *n* the adjustable spike-shaped leg at the bottom of a cello or double bass that the instrument rests on while being played

end·play /énd plày/ *n* in bridge, a play in which an opponent is forced to lead near the end of the hand and loses a trick that would otherwise have been won —**end·play** *vt*

end point *n* **1.** the point at which something is complete or comes to an end ○ *We'll try to reach a convenient end point by 4.30.* **2.** the point, marked by a color change or other indicator, at which a titration is complete

end·point /énd pòynt/ *n* **1.** the point located at each end of a line segment or at the end of a ray **2.** any computer on a network that can transmit or receive data

end prod·uct *n* the final result of a process or series of events or operations

end rhyme *n* the use of rhyme at the ends of lines of poetry, or an example of this

en·drin /éndrin/ *n* a white crystalline chlorinated hydrocarbon. Use: insecticide. Formula: $C_{12}H_8Cl_6O$. [Mid-20C. < END- + DIELDRIN]

end run *n* **1.** in football, a play in which the player with the ball attempts to run around the defensive line of the opposing team **2.** an attempt to get around an obstacle or difficulty, often by using deceitful methods (*informal*)

end-run (**end-ran, end-run, end-run·ning, end-runs**) *vt* to get around an obstacle or difficulty, often by using deceitful methods (*informal*)

end-stopped *adj* describes poetry containing a pause in meaning at the end of a line or couplet, as opposed to continuing into the next line or couplet

end ta·ble *n* a small table placed at the side of a couch or armchair, often with a lamp on top

en·due /in dṓō, en-/ (**-dued, -du·ing, -dues**), **in·due** /in dṓō/ *vt* to endow somebody or something with an ability or quality (*literary*) ○ *His successes have endued him with an aura of invincibility.* [14C. < French *enduire* < Latin *ducere* "to lead"]

en·dur·ance /in dóōrənss, en-/ *n* **1.** ABILITY TO BEAR PROLONGED HARDSHIP the ability or power to bear prolonged exertion, pain, or hardship ○ *an endurance test* ○ *legendary powers of endurance* **2.** TOLERATION OF HARDSHIP toleration of prolonged suffering or hardship ○ *Their quiet endurance of the situation earned them many friends.* **3.** PERSISTENCE OVER TIME the survival or persistence of something despite the ravages of time ○ *the endurance of ancient traditions* [15C. < French < *endurer* (see ENDURE)]

en·dure /in dóōr, en-/ (**-dured, -dur·ing, -dures**) *v* **1.** *vti* BEAR HARDSHIP to experience exertion, pain, or hardship without giving up ○ *The nation endured years of war to create a lasting peace.* **2.** *vt* TOLERATE DISAGREEABLE THINGS to tolerate or accept somebody or something that is extremely disagreeable (*formal*) ○ *I cannot endure that song.* **3.** *vi* SURVIVE to last or survive over a period of time, especially when faced with difficulties ○ *The philosophical ideas of the ancient Greeks endure to this day.* [14C. Via French *endurer* < Latin *indurare* "harden" < *durus* "hard"] —**en·dur·a·ble** *adj*

en·dur·ing /in dóōring, en-/ *adj* **1.** persisting or surviving in the face of difficulties **2.** patient or tolerant despite many difficulties —**en·dur·ing·ly** *adv* —**en·dur·ing·ness** *n*

en·du·ro /en dóōrō/ (*plural* **-os**) *n* a long race, especially one involving motorcycles or cars, in which the emphasis is on endurance rather than speed [Mid-20C. Alteration of ENDURANCE]

end us·er *n* a person or group that is one of the ultimate consumers or users that a product has been designed for ○ *a survey that is designed to assess what the end user really needs*

end·wise /énd wìz/, **end·ways** /-wàyz/ *adv* **1.** WITH END UP with an end up or forward **2.** TOWARD ENDS toward the ends **3.** WITH ENDS TOUCHING with one end next to another end

En·dym·i·on /en dímmee ən/ *n* in Greek mythology, a handsome man loved by the moon goddess Selene

end zone *n* either of the two areas at the ends of a football field between the goal line and the end line where a touchdown is scored

ENE *abbr* east-northeast

-ene *suffix* an unsaturated organic compound ○ *butene* [< Greek *-ēnē*, form of *-ēnos*, adjective suffix]

en·e·ma /énnəmə/ *n* **1.** the insertion of a liquid into the bowels via the rectum as a treatment, especially for constipation, or as an aid to diagnosis **2.** the liquid used when giving somebody an enema ○ *a barium enema* [Late 17C. Via late Latin < Greek < *enienai* "send or put in" < *hienai* "send"]

en·e·my /énnəmee/ (*plural* **-mies**) *n* **1.** UNFRIENDLY OPPONENT somebody who hates or seeks to harm somebody or something **2.** MILITARY OPPONENT a person or group, especially a military force, that fights against another in combat or battle **3.** HOSTILE POWER a hostile nation or power **4.** SOMETHING HARMFUL OR OBSTRUCTIVE something that harms or opposes something else ○ *In a case like this, time is the enemy.* [13C. Via French < Latin *inimicus* "enemy, unfriendly" < *amicus* "friend"]

en·er·get·ic /ènnər jéttik/ *adj* **1.** displaying great vigor or force **2.** requiring great vigor or stamina [Mid-17C. < Greek *energētikos* "active" < *ergon* "work"] —**en·er·get·i·cal·ly** *adv*

en·er·get·ics /ènnər jéttiks/ *n* the branch of physics that studies energy and its transformations (*takes a singular verb*)

en·er·gize /énnər jìz/ (**-gized, -giz·ing, -giz·es**) *v* **1.** *vt* GIVE SOMEBODY OR SOMETHING ENERGY to supply somebody or something with strength or power ○ *He felt energized by his nap.* **2.** *vti* MAKE OR BECOME ACTIVE to become, or cause something to become, vigorously active **3.** *vt* ELEC SUPPLY WITH ELECTRICAL POWER to supply something with a source of electrical power —**en·er·gi·za·tion** /ènnərji záysh'n/ *n* —**en·er·giz·er** *n*

en·er·gy /énnərjee/ (*plural* **-gies**) *n* **1.** ABILITY TO DO THINGS the ability or power to work or make an effort ○ *His illness left him feeling drained of energy.* **2.** VIGOR liveliness and forcefulness ○ *She gave a performance that was full of energy.* **3.** FORCEFUL EFFORT a vigorous effort or action ○ *We must concentrate our energies on the task in hand.* **4.** POWER SUPPLY OR SOURCE a supply or source of electrical, mechanical, or other form of power **5.** PHYS CAPACITY TO DO WORK the capacity of a body or system to do work. Symbol *E* [Mid-16C. Via French < Greek *energeia* < *ergon* "work." < Indo-European]

ORIGIN The Indo-European word from which ***energy*** is ultimately derived is also the ancestor of English *liturgy*, *organ*, *orgy*, *surgery*, and *work*, and perhaps also of *irk*.

---

en·er·gy au·dit *n* a survey of the use of energy in a building or organization, undertaken in order to make energy use as efficient as possible

en·er·gy bal·ance *n* a mathematical relationship, using the principle of the conservation of energy, that shows the energy inputs and outputs of a process or system

en·er·gy band *n* PHYS same as **band**[2] *n* (sense 7)

en·er·gy-band the·o·ry *n* PHYS same as **band theory**

e·ner·gy bar *n* a bar-shaped snack made of ingredients intended to boost somebody's physical energy

en·er·gy cri·sis *n* a situation in which available sources of energy are not sufficient to meet the demand

en·er·gy ef·fi·cient *adj* using electrical or other energy in an economical way (*hyphenated when used before a noun*)

en·er·gy lev·el *n* one of the discrete stable energy values that can be assumed by a physical system such as the electrons in an atom or an atomic nucleus

en·er·gy re·cov·er·y *n* the extraction of energy from synthetic materials, e.g., by using the heat from incineration of solid waste to generate electricity

en·er·gy tax *n* a tax on an energy source intended to discourage environmentally damaging sources and encourage energy conservation or use of alternative sources

en·er·gy ther·a·py *n* a holistic method of healing using energy supposedly contained in and surrounding the human body, mind, and spirit

en·er·vate /énnər vàyt/ (**-vat·ed, -vat·ing, -vates**) *vt* to weaken somebody's physical, mental, or moral vitality ○ *I was feeling quite enervated by the strain of moving.* [Early 17C. < Latin *enervat-*, past participle of *enervare* "extract the sinews of, weaken" < *nervus* "sinew"] —**en·er·va·tion** /ènnər váysh'n/ *n*

en·er·vat·ed /énnər vàytəd/ *adj* weakened or exhausted physically, mentally, or morally ○ *an enervated, dissolute age*

SYNONYMS See ***weak***.

---

en·er·vat·ing /énnər vàyting/ *adj* causing the physical, mental, or moral vitality to weaken

e-net·work *n* an Internet forum, usually of a professional nature and requiring a subscription to participate

En·e·we·tak /énnə wée tòk, ə née wə tòk/ circular atoll in the northwestern Marshall Islands in the Northern Pacific Ocean, a former testing ground for nuclear weapons. Population: 715 (1988). Area: 2 sq. mi./5 sq. km.

en·face /in fáyss, en-/ (**-faced, -fac·ing, -fac·es**) *vt* to mark something on the face of a document by writing, stamping, or printing —**en·face·ment** *n*

en fa·mille /aàN fa mée/ *adv* **1.** with family members, especially at home **2.** in an informal, relaxed, or casual way [Early 18C. < French, "in the family"]

en·fant ter·ri·ble /aaN faàN te réeblə/ (*plural* **en·fants ter·ri·bles** /*pronunc. same*/) *n* **1.** somebody whose unconventional behavior, attitudes, or remarks are shocking to others **2.** a young person, especially in the arts, who has become successful because of work that is radically innovative or extremely avant-garde [< French, "terrible child"]

en·fee·ble /in féeb'l, en-/ (**-bled, -bling, -bles**) *vt* to reduce the strength of somebody or something to the point of weakness [14C. < Old French *enfiblir* < *feble* (see FEEBLE)] —**en·fee·ble·ment** *n*

en·feoff /in féef, en-/ (**-feoffed, -feoff·ing, -feoffs**) *vt* formerly, to invest somebody with the freehold possession of a piece of land [14C. < Anglo-Norman *enfeoffer* < Old French *fief* (see FIEF)] —**en·feoff·ment** *n*

En·field[1] /én feeld/ town in northern Connecticut, situated on the eastern bank of the Connecticut River, near the Massachusetts border. Population: 45,379 (2002 estimate).

En·field[2] /én feeld/ *n* ARMS same as **Enfield rifle** [After a town in SE England]

En·field mus·ket *n* a muzzle-loading rifled musket used by British forces in the 19th century and by American troops in the Civil War [See ENFIELD[2]]

En·field ri·fle *n* **1.** a .30-caliber bolt-action breech-loading rifle used by US forces in World War I. **2.** a .303-caliber bolt-action breech-loading rifle, used by British forces in World War I and until the 1930s **3.** ARMS same as **Enfield musket** [See ENFIELD[2]]

en·fi·lade /énfə làyd, -laad/ *n* **1.** VULNERABLE POSITION a position in which troops are exposed to gunfire along the length of their formation. ◊ **defilade** **2.** RAKING FIRE gunfire that strikes a body of troops along its whole length ■ *vt* (**-lad·ed, -lad·ing, -lades**) **1. FIRE AT SOMETHING ALONG ITS LENGTH** to attack a position or body of troops with gunfire along its whole length **2. PLACE TROOPS OR GUNS FOR FIRING** to place guns or troops in a position from which they can fire on the whole length of an enemy position or body of troops [Early 18C. < French < *fil* "thread" < Latin *filum*]

en·fleu·rage /áaNflə ráazh/ *n* a process used in making perfume in which oils acquire fragrance by being exposed to the scent of flowers [Mid-19C. < French < *enfleurer* "saturate with the scent of flowers" < *fleur* "flower"]

~~**enflict**~~ incorrect spelling of **inflict**

en·fold /in fṓld, en-/ (**-fold·ed, -fold·ing, -folds**), **in·fold** /in-/ *vt* **1.** to surround or enclose somebody or something completely **2.** to hold somebody or something in an embrace —**en·fold·er** *n*

~~**enforcable**~~ incorrect spelling of **enforceable**

en·force /in fáwrss, en-/ (**-forced, -forc·ing, -forc·es**) *vt* **1. MAKE PEOPLE OBEY SOMETHING** to compel obedience to a law, regulation, or command **2. IMPOSE SOMETHING** to impose something by force **3. STRENGTHEN SOMETHING** to give strength or emphasis to something ○ *enforce an argument* [13C. < French *enforcir* < Latin *fortis* "strong"] —**en·force·a·bil·i·ty** /in fàwrssə bíllətee, en-/ *n* —**en·force·a·ble** *adj* —**en·force·ment** *n*

en·forc·er /in fáwrssər, en-/ *n* **1. SOMEBODY WHO ENFORCES LAW** somebody who enforces a rule, law, or order **2. CRIMINAL WHO INTIMIDATES** a member of a criminal gang who uses physical violence to intimidate and enforce compliance (*slang*) **3.** HOCKEY **INTIMIDATING PLAYER** in hockey, a player whose job is to intimidate opposing players or retaliate for rough play or violence

en·fran·chise /in frán chīz, en-/ (**-chised, -chis·ing, -chis·es**) *vt* **1. GIVE SOMEBODY RIGHT TO VOTE** to give somebody the right to vote in an election **2. SET SOMEBODY FREE** to set somebody free, especially from slavery **3. GIVE TOWN RIGHT OF REPRESENTATION** formerly, to grant political representation to a town or city [Early 16C. < Old French *enfranchir* < *franc* "free" < Latin *francus*] —**en·fran·chise·ment** *n*

ENG *abbr* electronic newsgathering

eng. *abbr* **1.** engine **2.** engineer **3.** engineering

Eng. *abbr* **1.** England **2.** English

en·gage /in gáyj, en-/ (**-gaged, -gag·ing, -gag·es**) *v* **1.** *vt* **HIRE SOMEBODY** to hire somebody for a job or to do some work **2.** *vt* **REQUIRE USE OF SOMETHING** to require the use or devotion of something ○ *Her writing engages most of her time.* **3.** *vti* **INVOLVE SOMEBODY, OR BECOME INVOLVED** to involve somebody in an activity, or become involved or take part in an activity ○ *engaged her in conversation for an hour* **4.** *vt* **ATTRACT SOMEBODY** to hold the attention of, or win the affection of somebody ○ *He was engaged by the child's open manner.* **5.** *vti* MIL **FIGHT SOMEBODY** to fight or begin a battle with an enemy **6.** *vt* **RESERVE SOMETHING** to reserve or rent something for personal use (*dated*) **7.** *vti* MECH ENG **INTERLOCK** to become interlocked, or bring something together and cause something to interlock ○ *engaged the gears* [Early 16C. < French *engager* < *gage* "pledge"] —**en·gag·er** *n*

en·ga·gé /àaN gaa zháy/ *adj* committed to a political cause or ideology, usually a left-wing one [Mid-20C. < French, past participle of *engager* (see ENGAGE)]

en·gaged /in gáyjd, en-/ *adj* **1. HAVING AGREED TO MARRY** having agreed to get married ○ *the newly engaged couple* **2. OCCUPIED** busy doing something ○ *The senator is otherwise engaged this afternoon.* **3.** MECH ENG **WITH PARTS INTERLOCKED** having teeth or other mechanical parts interlocked and often in operation **4.** *UK* TELECOM same as **busy** *adj* (sense 4) **5.** CONSTR **BUILT INTO OR ATTACHED TO WALL** describes a part of a building that is built into or attached to a wall

en·gaged tone *n UK* TELECOM same as **busy signal**

en·gage·ment /in gáyjmənt, en-/ *n* **1. AGREEMENT TO MARRY** an agreement to get married ○ *announce our engagement* **2. COMMITMENT TO ATTEND** an arrangement to be present at an event, especially a business or social appointment **3. SHORT JOB** a job that lasts for a short period of time, especially one for an entertainer in a club or theater ○ *a week-long engagement in Las Vegas* **4. BATTLE** a hostile encounter involving military forces ○ *a minor engagement on the frontier* **5.** MECH ENG **ACTIVE OR OPERATIONAL STATE** an act or condition of being activated or becoming operational

SYNONYMS See ***fight***.

en·gage·ment ring *n* a ring, often a diamond solitaire, given by a man to his fiancée to mark their engagement to marry. It is worn on the ring finger of the left hand.

en·gag·ing /in gáyjing, en-/ *adj* charming or pleasing in a way that attracts and holds the attention —**en·gag·ing·ly** *adv*

en garde /aaN gáard/ *interj* used to warn a fencer to assume the prescribed stance for the start of a match [< French, "on guard"]

Popperfoto

Friedrich Engels

En·gels /éng g'lz/, **Friedrich** (1820–95) German political thinker and revolutionary. He cowrote the *Communist Manifesto* (1848) with Karl Marx and supported Marx financially. He lived mainly in England.

> "The political authority of the state dies out. Man, at last the master of his own form of social organization, becomes at the same time the lord over Nature, his own master—free."
> [Friedrich Engels, *Socialism: Utopian and Scientific*; 1892]

en·gen·der /en jéndər/ (**-dered, -der·ing, -ders**) *v* **1.** *vti* to arise or come into existence, or cause something to do so ○ *Secrecy engenders suspicion.* **2.** *vt* to cause offspring to be conceived or born (*formal*) [14C. Via French < Latin *ingenerare* < *generare* "produce"] —**en·gen·der·er** *n*

en·gine /énjin/ *n* **1. MACHINE FOR POWERING EQUIPMENT** a machine that converts an energy source into mechanical power or motion ○ *a gasoline-powered engine* **2.** RAIL **RAILROAD LOCOMOTIVE** a railroad locomotive **3. DRIVING FORCE OR ENERGY SOURCE** something that supplies the driving force or energy to a movement, system, or trend ○ *a political movement that was seen as a great engine of social change* **4.** COMPUT **COMPUTER SOFTWARE** a computer program that performs a core or coordinating function for other programs, or has a special-purpose function **5.** MIL, HIST **BATTLEFIELD MACHINE** a battering ram, catapult, or other device used in warfare ○ *a siege engine* [14C. Via French < Latin *ingenium* "talent, clever device"] —**en·gined** *adj* —**en·gine·less** *adj*

en·gine block *n* the heavy metal casing that houses the cylinders in an internal-combustion engine

en·gine driv·er *n UK* RAIL same as **engineer** *n* (sense 2)

en·gi·neer /ènjə neér/ *n* **1.** ENG **ENGINEERING PROFESSIONAL** somebody who is trained as a professional engineer **2.** RAIL **LOCOMOTIVE DRIVER** somebody who operates a railroad locomotive **3.** MECH ENG **MECHANIC** somebody who operates or services machines **4.** NAUT, NAVY **SHIP'S OFFICER** an officer on a ship who is in charge of the engines **5.** MIL **CONSTRUCTION SOLDIER** a member of a unit of the armed forces that specializes in building and sometimes destroying bridges, fortifications, and other large structures **6. PLANNER** a planner, initiator, or supervisor of something, especially something that is achieved with ingenuity or secretiveness ○ *the engineer of the overthrow of the government* ■ *vt* (**-neered, -neer·ing, -neers**) **1. CONTRIVE SOMETHING** to plan something or bring it about, especially in an ingenious or secretive manner **2. USE ENGINEERING SKILL TO DESIGN SOMETHING** to use professional engineering skill to design or create something ○ *This car was engineered in Italy.* **3.** GENETICS **DEVELOP SOMETHING BY GENETIC MODIFICATION** to use the techniques of genetic modification to develop an organism or product [14C. < Old French *engigneor* "contriver" < Latin *ingenium* "talent, clever device"]

en·gi·neer·ing /ènjə neéring/ *n* **1. APPLICATION OF SCIENCE TO DESIGNING THINGS** the application of science in the design, planning, construction, and maintenance of buildings, machines, and other manufactured things ○ *leading the world in engineering* **2. PROFESSION INVOLVING TECHNICAL DESIGNING** a branch of engineering pursued as a profession, e.g., civil engineering or electronic engineering **3. CONTRIVANCE** the planning or bringing about of something, especially when done with ingenuity or secretiveness

en·gine room *n* the place on board a ship where the engines are housed

en·gir·dle /in gúrd'l, en-/ (**-dled, -dling, -dles**) *vt* to surround or encircle something (*literary*)

en·gla·cial /in gláysh'l, en-/ *adj* describes material or processes occurring within a glacier

Eng·land /íng glənd/ country forming the southern and largest part of the United Kingdom. Capital: London. Population: 49,138,831 (2001). Area: 50,352 sq. mi./130,410 sq. km.

En·gle·wood /éng g'l wòod/ **1.** city in north central Colorado, a suburb of Denver. Population: 32,963 (2002 estimate). **2.** city in northeastern New Jersey, near the Hudson River. Population: 26,159 (2002 estimate).

Eng·lish /íng glish/ *n* **1.** LANG **LANGUAGE OF UK, US, AND CANADA** a language of the United States, Canada, the United Kingdom of Great Britain and Northern Ireland, the Republic of Ireland, Australia, New Zealand, South Africa, and several other countries. Native speakers: 350 million. Other speakers: 375 million. See panel on next page **2.** EDUC **STUDY OF ENGLISH** the English language, together with literature written in it, as a subject of study **3. EASILY UNDERSTOOD ENGLISH** clear, understandable spoken or written English, as distinct from technical jargon, dialect, or nonstandard or incomprehensible speech or writing **4.** *US* **ENGLISH TRANSLATION** a translation of something from another language into English **5.** *also* **eng·lish** CUE GAMES **SPIN** spin applied to a billiard ball by striking it off-center ■ *npl* **PEOPLE FROM ENGLAND** people who come from England ■ *adj* **1. OF ENGLISH** relating to the language of English **2. OF THE ENGLISH** relating to the English or England [Old English *Englisc* < *Engle* "the Angles"] —**Eng·lish·ness** *n*

Eng·lish bond *n* an arrangement of bricks in a wall in which layers (**courses**) of bricks laid end to end (**stretchers**) alternate with layers of bricks laid side to side (**headers**). The stretchers of all layers are aligned vertically, and the headers are centered on the stretchers and the mortar joints between them.

Eng·lish break·fast *n* a breakfast usually consisting of cereal or fruit, followed by cooked bacon, eggs, sausages, and tomatoes, and then toast and marmalade or jam ○ *a choice of continental or full English breakfast*

Eng·lish bull·dog *n US* BREED same as **bulldog**

Eng·lish Can·a·da *n Can* the parts of Canada where English is the majority language

Eng·lish Ca·na·di·an *n Can* a Canadian whose first language is English or who is of English ancestry —**Eng·lish-Ca·na·di·an** *adj*

Eng·lish Chan·nel /ing glish-/ area of water linking the North Sea with the Atlantic Ocean. It lies between England and France. Length: 351 mi./565 km.

Eng·lish dai·sy *n US* PLANTS same as **daisy** (sense 1)

Eng·lish fox·hound *n* a medium-sized hunting dog, belonging to a breed originally developed in England, with a smooth, shorthaired coat that may be black, tan, or white or a mixture of these

Eng·lish horn *n US* a woodwind instrument that resembles an oboe but is larger, has a double reed, and is lower-pitched. Can term **cor anglais**

WORLD ENGLISH ***English***, a language originating in northwestern Europe, is the most widely used member of the Germanic language family. Anglo-Saxon settlers whose dialects were collectively known as "Englisc" arrived in Britain in the 5th century and in due course their language became identified as the main one of the kingdom of England. This early English was a homogeneous tongue, and the characteristic hybrid vocabulary of the present-day language is the result, successively, of Scandinavian, Norman-French, and Greco-Latin influence. For convenience, English is usually divided into four historical phases: Old English (around 500–1150), Middle English (around 1150–around 1450), Early Modern English (around 1450–1700), and Modern English (around 1700 onward). However, the distance and difference between Old and Modern English is as great as that between Latin and its descendant, French. After 1707, English became the primary language of first the United Kingdom and Ireland, then the British Empire at large, from which the United States broke away in the 1770s. The world's primary English-speaking countries today are the United States, the United Kingdom, Canada, Australia, Ireland, South Africa, New Zealand, and Singapore, and the many other nations and territories using English include Bangladesh, Ghana, Guyana, India, Hong Kong, Kenya, Jamaica, Malta, Malaysia, Nigeria, Pakistan, and the Philippines. All territories using the language tend to have distinctive pronunciations, grammatical features, and items of vocabulary, and, increasingly, varieties of the standard international language. English is a primary working language of the United Nations and the European Union and the sole working language of the Commonwealth, NATO, CARICOM, and ASEAN. It is also learned as a second language for purposes of education, employment, entertainment, electronic communication, and travel by a rapidly increasing number of people worldwide, approaching between one and two billion people. Since the 1960s the already immense literature of the language, primarily in the United States and United Kingdom, has been markedly extended throughout the English-speaking world, with English becoming overwhelmingly the primary language of global communication and the media. See also introductory essay on ***World English***.

Eng·lish i·vy *n US* PLANTS same as **ivy** (sense 1)

Eng·lish·man /íng glishmən/ (*plural* **-men** /-mən/) *n* a man who comes from England

Eng·lish muf·fin *n* a small flat round type of bread made with yeast dough and cooked on a griddle. It is split and toasted before serving.

Eng·lish sad·dle *n* a light hornless saddle with long side flaps and a low back and front

Eng·lish set·ter *n* a hunting dog with a silky white coat with brown or black markings, belonging to a medium-sized breed of setters

Eng·lish sheep·dog *n US* BREED same as **Old English sheepdog**

Eng·lish son·net *n US* LITERAT same as **Shakespearean sonnet**

Eng·lish spar·row *n US* BIRDS same as **house sparrow**

Eng·lish spring·er span·iel *n* a dog with a silky coat that may be a mixture of white, black, liver, or tan, belonging to a medium-sized breed of spaniels that was developed in England as a hunting dog

Eng·lish toy span·iel *n US* a toy dog with a thick wavy coat, belonging to a small breed of spaniels that originated in eastern Asia. King Charles and Blenheim are types of toy spaniels.

Eng·lish wal·nut *n US* **1.** a large wrinkled nut with a round shell in two halves **2.** a deciduous widely grown tree that produces English walnuts and lumber. Latin name: *Juglans regia.*

Eng·lish·wom·an /íng glish wŏŏmmən/ (*plural* **-wom·en** /-wìmmin/) *n* a woman who comes from England

en·gobe /én gōb/ *n* liquid clay used to decorate a ceramic piece before it has been fired and usually applied before the piece has dried [Mid-19C. < French]

en·gorge /in gáwrj, en-/ (**-gorged, -gorg·ing, -gorg·es**) *v* **1.** *vti* FILL WITH BLOOD to fill something with blood until it is congested, or become filled with blood **2.** *vt* DEVOUR SOMETHING to eat something greedily **3. en·gorge your·self** *vr* GORGE YOURSELF to gorge or fill yourself with food [15C. < French *engorger* < Old French *gorge* "throat" (see GORGE)] —**en·gorge·ment** *n*

engr. *abbr* **1.** *also* **engr** engineer **2.** engraved **3.** engraver **4.** engraving

en·graft /in gráft, en-/ (**-graft·ed, -graft·ing, -grafts**), **in·graft** /in-/ *vt* **1.** ATTACH SOMETHING PERMANENTLY to attach something permanently to something else by a process resembling grafting **2.** IMPLANT SOMETHING PERMANENTLY to implant something permanently or deeply in something else **3.** GRAFT PLANT PART to graft a bud or other plant part from one plant onto another (*technical*) **4.** GRAFT ANIMAL TISSUE to graft animal tissue from one part of the body onto another part or onto another animal (*technical*) —**en·graft·ment** *n*

en·grailed /in gráyld, en-/ *adj* **1.** edged with a series of concave indentations **2.** edged with a row of raised dots ○ *an engrailed gold coin* [14C. < Old French *engresler* "make thin" < *gresle* "thin" < Latin *gracilis*]

en·grain *vt* TEXTILES another spelling of **ingrain**

en·gram /én gràm/ *n* a hypothetical physical impression made in neural tissue by a mental stimulus, once regarded as an explanation of the persistence of memory [Early 20C. < German *Engramm* < Greek *gramma* "something written"]

en·grave /in gráyv, en-/ (**-graved, -grav·ing, -graves**) *vt* **1.** CARVE OR ETCH MATERIAL to carve or etch a hard surface with a design or lettering for decoration or printing ○ *engraved a silver cup* **2.** CARVE OR ETCH DESIGN to carve or etch a design or lettering into a hard surface for decoration or printing ○ *engraving a dedication on a watch* **3.** PRINT IMAGE to print an image, especially a raised image, from an engraved printing plate **4.** IMPRESS SOMETHING to impress something deeply, e.g., a memory on the mind —**en·grav·er** *n*

en·grav·ing /in gráyving, en-/ *n* **1.** PRINTING ENGRAVED PRINT a print of an image that was made using an engraved plate or block **2.** ART ENGRAVED DESIGN a design or lettering engraved into a hard surface for decoration or printing **3.** ART CUTTING OR ETCHING OF IMAGES the art or process of cutting or etching images into a hard surface **4.** PRINTING ENGRAVED SURFACE a plate, block, or other hard surface on which an image has been engraved for printing

en·gross[1] /in grṓss, en-/ (**-grossed, -gross·ing, -gross·es**) *vt* **1.** to take up somebody's whole attention ○ *The children were engrossed by the story.* **2.** to buy all of a commodity or enough of it to control its market [14C. < Old French *en gros*, medieval Latin *in grosso* "in bulk, wholesale" < late Latin *grossus* "bulky, coarse"] —**en·gross·er** *n*

en·gross[2] /in grṓss, en-/ (**-grossed, -gross·ing, -gross·es**) *vt* **1.** to write or print the final version of a legal document **2.** to copy a document in large clear handwriting (*dated*) [14C. < Anglo-Norman *engrosser*, medieval Latin *ingrossare* < late Latin *grossus* "bulky, coarse"] —**en·gross·er** *n*

en·gross·ing /in grṓssing, en-/ *adj* engaging somebody's whole attention —**en·gross·ing·ly** *adv*

en·gross·ment /in grṓssmənt, en-/ *n* **1.** COMPLETELY ABSORBED STATE the complete absorption of somebody's attention with something **2.** FIN CORNERING OF COMMODITY MARKET the purchasing of enough of a commodity to control the market in it **3.** LAW FINAL LEGAL COPY a formally prepared copy of a deed or other document for legal use **4.** LAW PREPARATION OF DOCUMENT the preparation of the final legal copy or a clean copy of a document (*dated*)

en·gulf /in gúlf, en-/ (**-gulfed, -gulf·ing, -gulfs**), **in·gulf** /in-/ *vt* **1.** to surround, cover over, and swallow up somebody or something, as floodwaters do **2.** to overwhelm somebody or something with a great amount or number of something (*often passive*) ○ *A deep grief engulfed the country after his death.* —**en·gulf·ment** *n*

en·hance /in hánss, en-/ (**-hanced, -hanc·ing, -hanc·es**) *vt* **1.** to improve or add to the strength, worth, beauty, or other desirable quality of something **2.** to increase the clarity, degree of detail, or another quality of an electronic image by using a computer program [13C. < Anglo-Norman *enhauncer* "raise up" < Latin *altus* "high"] —**en·hance·ment** *n* —**en·hanc·er** *n* —**en·hanc·ive** *adj*

en·har·mon·ic /in haar mónnik/ *adj* describes musical notes, e.g., A♯ and B♭, that appear differently in a score but have the same pitch in a tempered scale, e.g., on the piano. In other scales or on other instruments, enharmonic notes may actually have different pitches. —**en·har·mon·i·cal·ly** *adv*

e·nig·ma /i nígmə, e-/ *n* somebody or something that is not easily explained or understood [Mid-16C. Via Latin < Greek *ainigma* < *ainos* "fable"]

CULTURAL NOTE ***The Enigma Variations***, an orchestral work (1899) by British composer Edward Elgar. Elgar's most popular and widely performed work, it was originally entitled *Variations on an Original Theme.* Each of the variations is a musical portrait of a friend of Elgar, identified in the score only by his or her initials or nickname. The title of Elgar's piece influenced the Berlin engineer who built the now-famed German military cipher machine known as *Enigma*, a typewriter-like device capable of producing an infinite number of ciphers.

SYNONYMS See ***problem***.

en·ig·mat·ic /ènnig máttik/, **en·ig·mat·i·cal** /-máttik'l/ *adj* having a quality of mystery and ambiguity and so difficult to interpret, understand, or explain —**en·ig·mat·i·cal·ly** *adv*

SYNONYMS See ***obscure***.

en·isle /in íl, en-/ (**-isled, -isl·ing, -isles**) *vt* (*literary*) **1.** to isolate somebody or something from other people or things **2.** to make something into an island

en·jamb·ment /in jám mənt, en-, in jámb mənt, en-/, **en·jambe·ment** *n* the continuation of meaning, without pause or break, from one line of poetry to the next [Mid-19C. < French *enjambement* < *jambe* "leg" (see JAMB)] —**en·jambed** *adj*

en·join /in jóyn, en-/ (**-joined, -join·ing, -joins**) *vt* **1.** COMMAND SOMEBODY to command somebody to do something or behave in a particular way ○ *were enjoined to be silent* **2.** IMPOSE SOMETHING to impose a condition or course of action on others ○ *enjoined secrecy upon us* **3.** *US* FORBID SOMETHING to forbid or prohibit something forcefully ○ *The terms of the contract enjoin the disclosure of trade secrets.* **4.** LAW FORBID OR COMMAND LEGALLY to forbid or command somebody to do something by means of a legal injunction —**en·join·er** *n* —**en·join·ment** *n*

en·joy /in jóy, en-/ *v* (**-joyed, -joy·ing, -joys**) **1.** *vt* FIND SOMETHING PLEASING to take pleasure in something ○ *really enjoying the ballet* **2.** *vt* HAVE USE OF SOMETHING to have the full and satisfying use or benefit of something ○ *He will enjoy sole possession of the estate.* **3.** *vt* BENEFIT FROM CIRCUMSTANCES to benefit from a desirable condition or situation ○ *The resort enjoys months of uninterrupted sunshine.* **4. en·joy your·self** *vr* HAVE GOOD EXPERIENCE to have a pleasurable experience ○ *enjoyed themselves at the party* ■ *interj* HAVE A GOOD TIME used to express a wish for somebody to have a pleasurable experience [14C. < Old French *enjoïr* < Latin *gaudere* "rejoice"] —**en·joy·er** *n*

en·joy·a·ble /in jóy əb'l, en-/ *adj* providing or capable of providing pleasure ○ *The food is always enjoyable.* —**en·joy·a·ble·ness** *n* —**en·joy·a·bly** *adv*

en·joy·ment /in jóymənt, en-/ *n* **1.** PLEASURE pleasure that results from using or experiencing something ○ *eating with great enjoyment* **2.** EXPERIENCING OF SOMETHING PLEASURABLE the experiencing of something that provides pleasure ○ *his obvious enjoyment of the concert* **3.** SOURCE OF PLEASURE something that gives pleasure ○ *Fishing is one of her chief enjoyments.* **4.** USE OR BENEFIT the use or benefit of something, especially as a legal right ○ *the enjoyment of his property rights*

en·keph·a·lin /en kéffəlin/ *n* either of two chemicals with opiate qualities that are secreted in the brain and spinal cord and act to relieve pain [Mid-20C. < Greek *egkephalos* "brain" (see ENCEPHALO-)]

en·kin·dle /in kínd'l, en-/ (**-dled, -dling, -dles**) *v* **1.** *vt* to spark an emotional or intellectual response in somebody **2.** *vti* to set something on fire, or start burning —**en·kin·dler** *n*

enl. *abbr* 1. enlarged 2. enlisted

en·lace /in láyss, en-/ (**-laced, -lac·ing, -lac·es**), **in·lace** /in-/ *v* 1. *vt* to wrap something around with laces or something similar 2. *vti* to intertwine with something, or become intertwined —**en·lace·ment** *n*

en·large /in laárj, en-/ (**-larged, -larg·ing, -larg·es**) *v* 1. *vti* **MAKE OR BECOME LARGER** to increase the size, amount, or extent of something, or become larger 2. *vti* **BROADEN IN SCOPE** to broaden the scope of something, or become broader in scope ○ *the need for the investigation to be enlarged* 3. *vi* **GIVE MORE DETAIL** to speak or write at greater length or in more detail about something 4. *vt* PHOTOGRAPHY **MAKE LARGER VERSION OF PHOTOGRAPH** to make a photographic print or image that is larger than the original negative, print, or slide —**en·larg·er** *n*

SYNONYMS See *increase*.

en·large·ment /in laárjmənt, en-/ *n* 1. **PROCESS OF ENLARGING** the process of increasing, broadening, or enlarging something, or of being increased, broadened, or enlarged 2. **ADDITION TO SOMETHING** something added to something else to make it larger ○ *the enlargement of the transmission facilities* 3. **ENLARGED CONDITION** the increased, broadened, or enlarged state of something 4. PHOTOGRAPHY **ENLARGED PHOTOGRAPH** a photographic print or image that is larger than the negative, print, or slide from which it was made

en·light·en /in lít'n, en-/ (**-ened, -en·ing, -ens**) *vt* 1. **GIVE INFORMATION TO SOMEBODY** to give clarifying information to somebody ○ *Let me enlighten you about our problems.* 2. **FREE SOMEBODY FROM IGNORANCE** to free somebody from ignorance, prejudice, or superstition ○ *an article written to enlighten his critics* 3. **TEACH SOMEBODY RELIGION** to teach religious beliefs to an unbeliever —**en·light·en·er** *n* —**en·light·en·ing** *adj*

en·light·ened /in lít'nd, en-/ *adj* 1. **RATIONAL** free of ignorance, prejudice, or superstition ○ *an enlightened age* 2. **WELL INFORMED** having a sound and open-minded understanding of all the facts, or based on such an understanding ○ *an enlightened piece of legislation* 3. **HAVING ACHIEVED GREAT SPIRITUALITY** having achieved the realization of a spiritual or religious understanding

en·light·en·ment /in lít'nmənt, en-/ *n* 1. **ENLIGHTENING OF SOMEBODY** the enlightening of somebody, or something that enlightens somebody 2. **ENLIGHTENED STATE** the condition of somebody who has been enlightened 3. **ACHIEVEMENT OF SPIRITUAL STATE** the realization of spiritual or religious understanding, or, especially in Buddhism, the state attained when the cycle of reincarnation ends and human desire and suffering are transcended

En·light·en·ment *n* an 18th-century intellectual movement in western Europe that emphasized reason and science in philosophy and in the study of human culture and the natural world

en·list /in líst, en-/ (**-list·ed, -list·ing, -lists**) *vti* 1. to enroll somebody in a branch of the armed forces, or join the armed forces 2. to gain the cooperation or support of somebody or something, or become actively involved in an effort ○ *May I enlist your help in this?* —**en·list·ment** *n*

en·list·ed per·son *n US* a nonofficer member of the US armed forces, especially of a rank below noncommissioned officer

en·list·ee /en lìs teé/ *n US* somebody who has enlisted in the armed forces

en·liv·en /in lív'n, en-/ (**-ened, -en·ing, -ens**) *vt* 1. to make somebody or something more lively or interesting ○ *We felt enlivened after our walk in the fresh air.* 2. to make something brighter or more cheerful ○ *A few more pictures on the wall would enliven this room.* —**en·liv·en·er** *n* —**en·liv·en·ment** *n*

en masse /on máss, aaN maáss/ *adv* as a body, or in a group ○ *people arriving en masse to vote* [Late 18C. < French, "in a mass"]

en·mesh /in mésh, en-/ (**-meshed, -mesh·ing, -mesh·es**), **in·mesh** /in-/, **im·mesh** /i mésh/ *vt* 1. to entangle somebody or something in something from which it is difficult to be extricated or separated ○ *a government enmeshed in scandal* 2. to catch somebody or something in the mesh of a net —**en·mesh·ment** *n*

en·mi·ty /énmətee/ (*plural* **-ties**) *n* the extreme ill will or hatred that exists between enemies ○ *trying to resolve age-old enmities* [13C < Old French *enemistie* < Latin *inimicus* (see ENEMY)]

~~ennemy~~ incorrect spelling of **enemy**

En·ni·us /énnee əss/, **Quintus** (239–169? B.C.) Roman poet and dramatist, called the founding father of Roman poetry. He introduced the hexameter into Roman verse, invented the literary miscellany, and wrote an epic of Roman history, of which only fragments survive.

> "How like us is that ugly brute, the ape!" [Quintus Ennius, *De Divinatione*, Cicero; 1942 (tr. H. Rackham)]

en·no·ble /i nṓb'l, e-/ (**-bled, -bling, -bles**) *vt* 1. to confer a noble title on somebody 2. to make somebody or something noble or more dignified (*formal*) —**en·no·ble·ment** *n* —**en·no·bler** *n*

en·nui /on weé/ *n* weariness and dissatisfaction with life that results from a loss of interest or sense of excitement [Mid-18C. < French < Latin *in odio (est)* "(it is) hateful"]

e·no·ki /e nṓkee/, **e·no·ki mush·room** *n* a white edible mushroom with a small cap and long thin stem. Native to: eastern Asia, North America. Latin name: *Flammulina velutipes.* [Late 20C. < Japanese]

e·nol /eé nàwl/ *n* an organic compound that has a hydroxyl group bonded to a carbon atom that is attached to another carbon atom by a double bond [Mid-20C. < -ENE + -OL[1]] —**e·nol·ic** /ee nóllik/ *adj*

e·no·lase /eénō làyss, -làyz/ *n* an enzyme involved in the metabolism of carbohydrates

e·nol·o·gy /ee nólləjee/, **oe·nol·o·gy** *n* the scientific study of wine and the making of wine [Early 19C. < Greek *oinos* "wine"] —**e·no·log·i·cal** /eénə lójjik'l/ *adj* —**e·nol·o·gist** *n*

e·nor·mi·ty /ə náwrmətee/ (*plural* **-ties**) *n* 1. extreme evil or moral offensiveness ○ *the enormity of his crimes against humanity* 2. a very evil or morally offensive deed [15C. Via French < Latin *enormitas* < *enormis* "irregular" (see ENORMOUS)]

USAGE enormity or **enormousness**? ***Enormity*** is the older word, and after several changes in usage over several centuries it settled down in the 19th century in the meaning associated with evil. It is used in this way both as a concept or attribute and as a specific instance with a plural form: *We were shocked by the enormity of the crime. The regime committed many enormities to suppress opposition.* ***Enormousness*** is the only word in this pair that refers, in correct usage, to significant size: *We were daunted by the enormousness of the task.*

e·nor·mous /ə náwrməss/ *adj* unusually large or great in size, amount, or degree [Mid-16C. < Latin *enormis* "irregular" < *norma* "rule"] —**e·nor·mous·ly** *adv*

e·nor·mous·ness /ə náwrməssnəss/ *n* the quality of being huge in size, scope, or significance

USAGE See *enormity.*

e·nough /i núf/ *adj* 1. **ADEQUATE** as much as is needed ○ *enough time to go shopping* 2. **AS MUCH AS IS BEARABLE** as much or as many as can be tolerated ○ *in enough trouble already* ■ *adv* 1. **TO THE NECESSARY EXTENT** to an extent that is as much as is needed ○ *I couldn't run fast enough to catch the cat.* 2. **ADDS EMPHASIS** used to give emphasis to adverbs ○ *Oddly enough, we'd met before.* 3. **TO A TOLERABLE DEGREE** to an extent that is as much as can be tolerated ○ *She was arrogant enough before her promotion.* 4. **PASSABLY** to a moderate or satisfactory extent ○ *speaks the language well enough* ■ *pron* **NEEDED OR TOLERATED AMOUNT** the amount that is needed or that can be tolerated ○ *Bring more money; we never have enough.* ■ *interj* **STOP THAT!** used to tell somebody firmly to stop doing something (*informal*) ○ *Enough! There will be no more teasing in the car.* [Old English *genōg* < Germanic] ◇ **enough is enough** used by a speaker to indicate that he or she will tolerate no more of something

e·nounce /i nównss/ (**e·nounced, e·nounc·ing, e·nounc·es**) *vt* 1. to pronounce a word clearly and definitely 2. to state something in an official way (*formal*) [Early 19C. Via French *énoncer* < Latin *enuntiare* "tell" (see ENUNCIATE)] —**e·nounce·ment** *n*

en pap·il·lote ➧ **papillote**

en pas·sant /aaN paa saáN/ *adv* 1. in passing rather than as the full focus of somebody's attention (*formal*) ○ *He mentioned it en passant.* 2. in chess, used when a pawn that has moved two squares is captured by an enemy pawn as if it had only moved one square ○ *capture a pawn en passant* [Mid-17C. < French, "in passing"]

en·plane /in pláyn, en-/ (**-planed, -plan·ing, -planes**) *vti US* to board or allow somebody to board an aircraft. Can term **emplane**

en prise /aan preéz/ *adj* describes a chess piece positioned in such a way that it could be captured if it is not moved [Early 19C. < French, "in (position for) capture"]

en·quire, etc. another spelling of **inquire, etc.**

en·rage /in ráyj, en-/ (**-raged, -rag·ing, -rag·es**) *vt* to make somebody furiously angry —**en·rage·ment** *n*

en·rapt /in rápt, en-/ *adj* in a state of delight or ecstasy (*formal*)

en·rap·ture /in rápchər, en-/ (**-tured, -tur·ing, -tures**) *vt* to fill somebody with delight —**en·rap·ture·ment** *n*

en·rich /in rích, en-/ (**-riched, -rich·ing, -rich·es**) *vt* 1. **ENHANCE QUALITY OF SOMETHING** to improve the quality of something, usually by adding something else to it ○ *enriching the curriculum with multimedia resources* 2. FOOD INDUST **IMPROVE NUTRITIONAL CONTENT OF FOOD** to add substances such as vitamins or minerals to a food to improve its nutritional value ○ *calcium-enriched orange juice* 3. **MAKE SOMEBODY OR SOMETHING WEALTHIER** to increase the amount of wealth that somebody or something has ○ *economic systems that existed to enrich the settlers* 4. PHYS **ADD MORE OF CONSTITUENT TO SUBSTANCE** to boost the amount of an active substance in a mixture, e.g., in a fuel 5. AGRIC **IMPROVE SOIL** to improve the nutrient value of soil by adding natural or artificial fertilizers 6. **ADORN SOMETHING** to add to the beauty of something with decoration (*literary*) —**en·rich·er** *n* —**en·rich·ment** *n*

en·robe /in rṓb, en-/ (**-robed, -rob·ing, -robes**) *v* 1. *vti* to put ceremonial robes on somebody (*formal*) 2. *vt* to invest somebody with a grand or noble quality (*literary*)

en·roll /in rṓl, en-/ (**-rolled, -roll·ing, -rolls**), **en·rol** (**-rolled, -roll·ing, -rols**) *v* 1. *vti* **ADD NAME TO REGISTER** to enter your own or somebody else's name on an official register or list of members ○ *enroll the children in school* 2. *vt* **ENSURE AVAILABILITY OF RESOURCE** to make sure that something, especially somebody's help, will definitely be available 3. *vt* **ROLL SOMETHING UP** to form something into a roll 4. *vt* **WRITE OFFICIAL COPY OF SOMETHING** to produce the final version of something, usually a formal document or record [14C. < Old French *enroller* "put on a roll" < *rolle* (see ROLL)] —**en·roll·ee** /in rō leé, en-/ *n*

en·roll·ment /in rṓlmənt, en-/, **en·rol·ment** *n* 1. **SIGNING UP FORMALLY** the official act or process of entering your own or somebody else's name on a register or membership list ○ *a two-week open enrollment period* 2. **NUMBER OF PEOPLE REGISTERED** the number of people registered for something, e.g., a class ○ *a sharp increase in student enrollments* 3. **LIST OF PEOPLE REGISTERED** a list of people registered for or enrolled in something

en route /on róot/ *adv* during the trip to a destination [Late 18C. < French, "on (the) way"]

ens /enz/ (*plural* **en·tia** /énshə, éntee ə/) *n* an actual entity, as distinct from a quality or characteristic [Mid-16C. < late Latin, present participle (after Latin *absens* "absent") of Latin *esse* "be"]

ENS, Ens. *abbr* NAVY ensign

en·sal·a·dil·la /en sàllə deéyə/ *n Hispanic* potato salad with peas and bits of tomato [< American Spanish, "little salad"]

en·san·guine /in sáng gwin, en-/ (**-guined, -guin·ing, -guines**) *vt* to stain, smear, or cover something with blood (*archaic or literary; often passive*) ○ *"yet millions of men have supinely allowed the nerveless limbs of the posterity of such rapacious prowlers to rest quietly on their ensanguined thrones"* (Mary Wollstonecraft, *A Vindication of the Rights of Woman*; 1792)

en·sconce /in skónss, en-/ (**-sconced, -sconc·ing, -sconc·es**) *vt* to make somebody or yourself comfortably established, as though ready to stay a long while (*often passive*) ○ *were ensconced on the sofa*

en·sem·ble /on sómb'l/ *n* **1.** GROUP OF PERFORMERS a group of musicians, dancers, or actors who perform together with roughly equal contributions from all members **2.** OUTFIT OF CLOTHES a number of different items of clothing and accessories, put together to create an outfit **3.** SOMETHING FORMED BY SEVERAL ITEMS something created from a number of individual parts put together deliberately **4.** MUSIC MUSICAL SECTION INVOLVING ALL PERFORMERS a section of a larger musical work, e.g., a ballet or opera, that all the cast perform together ■ *adj* PERFORMED AS GROUP performed collaboratively, with no performer given prominence [Mid-18C. < French, "together" < Latin *insimul* "in at the same time" < *simul* "at the same time"]

En·se·na·da /ènssə naádə/ major deep-sea port city on the Pacific Ocean in Baja California, northwestern Mexico. Population: 370,730 (2000).

en·shrine /in shrīn, en-/ (**-shrined, -shrin·ing, -shrines**), **in·shrine** /in-/ *vt* **1.** to protect something from change, e.g., in a formal constitution ○ *principles enshrined in law* **2.** to keep or cherish something in a shrine or other special place —**en·shrine·ment** *n*

en·shroud /in shrówd, en-/ (**-shroud·ed, -shroud·ing, -shrouds**) *vt* **1.** to cover or obscure something (*usually passive*) ○ *mountains enshrouded in mist* **2.** to cover somebody in a shroud

en·si·form /énssə fàwrm/ *adj* describes leaves that are long and narrow with a pointed tip [Mid-16C. Via French < modern Latin *ensiformis* < Latin *ensi-* "sword" + *forma* "form, shape"]

en·sign *flag* /énssən, én sīn/; *rank* /énssən/ *n* **1.** FLAG INDICATING NATIONALITY a flag that shows the nationality of the ship or aircraft flying it or what military unit it belongs to **2.** NAVY US NAVY RANK an officer in the US Navy or Coast Guard of the lowest rank **3.** BADGE OF OFFICE an emblem or sign that indicates authority or command **4.** FLAG BEARER a bearer of a national emblem or a standard (*dated*) [14C. < Old French *enseigne* < Latin *insignia* (plural) "badges" < *signum* "mark"]

en·si·lage /énsəlij/ *n* **1.** the harvesting and preservation of green fodder crops for future use by fermentation in a silo **2.** AGRIC same as **silage** ■ *vt* (**-laged, -lag·ing, -lages**) AGRIC same as **ensile**

en·sile /in sīl, en-/ (**-siled, -sil·ing, -siles**) *vt* to preserve green fodder, e.g., grass, as silage by allowing it to ferment and become acidified in a silo [Late 19C. Via French < Spanish *ensilar* < *en* "in" + *silo* (see SILO)]

en·slave /in sláyv, en-/ (**-slaved, -slav·ing, -slaves**) *vt* **1.** to take somebody prisoner and claim legal ownership of that person and his or her labor **2.** to subject somebody to a dominating influence that takes away his or her freedom —**en·slav·er** *n*

en·slave·ment /in sláyvmənt, en sláyvmənt/ *n* the state or condition of being enslaved or otherwise bound into servitude

en·snare /in snér, en-/ (**-snared, -snar·ing, -snares**), **in·snare** /in-/ *vt* **1.** to lure somebody into a bad situation from which it is difficult to escape **2.** to catch an animal in a trap —**en·snare·ment** *n* —**en·snar·er** *n*

en·snarl /in snaárl, en-/ (**-snarled, -snarl·ing, -snarls**) *vt* to involve somebody or something in a situation that causes delay (*often passive*)

En·sor /én sàwr/, **James Sydney, Baron** (1860–1949) Belgian painter and engraver. He was a forerunner of expressionism. His works, notably *Christ's Entry into Brussels in 1889* (1888), often incorporated masked figures and macabre medieval imagery.

en·soul /in sōl, en-/ (**-souled, -soul·ing, -souls**), **in·soul** /in-/ *vt* (*literary*) **1.** to endow somebody with a soul **2.** to cherish deeply something such as a feeling or memory

en·sphere /in sféer, en-/ (**-sphered, -spher·ing, -spheres**), **in·sphere** /in-/ *vt* **1.** to make something sphere-shaped (*formal*) **2.** to enclose something in a sphere or in something like a sphere (*literary*)

en·sta·tite /énstə tīt/ *n* a brown, gray, or yellowish magnesium iron silicate mineral of the pyroxene group. Source: igneous rocks, meteorites. [Mid-19C. < German *Enstatit* < Greek *enstat-* "adversary"; from its refractoriness]

en·sue /in sóo, en-/ (**-sued, -su·ing, -sues**) *vi* **1.** to follow closely after something **2.** to be a consequence of something [14C. < Old French *ensu-*, stem of *ensuivre* < assumed Vulgar Latin *insequere* "follow in" < Latin *sequi* "follow"]

en·su·ing /in sóo ing, en-/ *adj* happening next or as a result

en suite /aaN swéet/ *adj, adv* **1.** forming part of a larger unit or set of rooms ○ *with a bathroom en suite* **2.** *US* forming part of a series or set (*formal*) [Late 18C. < French, "in succession"]

en·sure /in shóor, en-/ (**-sured, -sur·ing, -sures**), **in·sure** /in-/ *vt* to make sure that something will happen or be available ○ *ensure a supply of fresh food* ○ *We must ensure that the environment remains a central concern.* [14C. < Anglo-Norman *enseurer*, alteration of Old French *asseurer, assurer* (see ASSURE)]

USAGE See *assure*.

---

en·swathe /in swáyth, en-/ (**-swathed, -swath·ing, -swathes**) *vt* to wrap somebody or something in bandages or cloth (*literary*)

ENT *abbr* MED ear, nose, and throat

-ent *suffix* **1.** performing a particular action ○ *acquiescent* **2.** one that performs a particular action ○ *respondent* [< Latin *-ent-*, present participle ending] —**-ence** *suffix* —**-ency** *suffix*

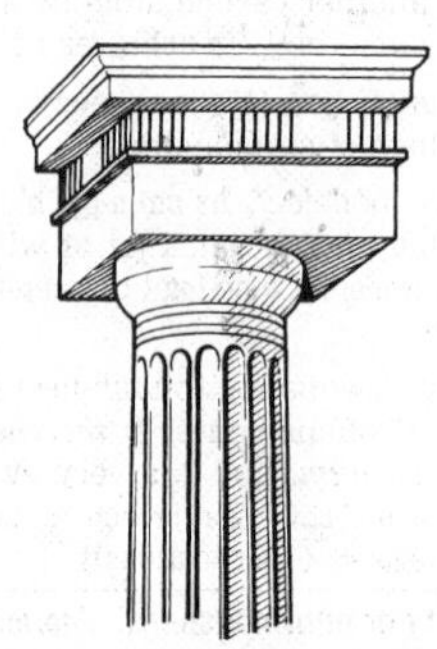

entablature

en·tab·la·ture /in tábblə chòor, en-/ *n* in classical architecture, the section of a structure that lies between the columns and the roof. It comprises, from bottom to top, the architrave, frieze, and cornice. [Early 17C. Via obsolete French < Italian *intavolatura* "boarding" < *intavolare* "board up, put on a table" < *tavola* "table"]

en·ta·ble·ment /in táyb'lmənt, en-/ *n* ARCHIT, SCULPTURE same as **plinth** (*technical*) [Mid-17C. < French < *table* "table"]

en·tail *vt* /in táyl, en-/ (**-tailed, -tail·ing, -tails**) **1.** HAVE SOMETHING AS CONSEQUENCE to involve or result in something inevitably **2.** RESTRICT OWNERSHIP OF BEQUEST to restrict the future ownership of real estate to particular descendants, through instructions written into a will ■ *n* /én tàyl/ LAW **1.** RESTRICTION OF FUTURE OWNERSHIP the limiting of the future ownership of bequeathed property to particular descendants **2.** ENTAILED PIECE OF REAL ESTATE a piece of real estate that has been entailed **3.** FUTURE OWNERS OF ENTAILED REAL ESTATE the line of descendants who own an entailed real estate [14C. < EN- + Old French *taille* "limitation" < *taillier* "to cut" (see TAILOR)] —**en·tail·ment** *n*

en·tan·gle /in táng g'l, en-/ (**-gled, -gling, -gles**) *vt* **1.** TANGLE SOMETHING UP to make something become twisted up in a mass of strands, e.g., netting or hair (*usually passive*) **2.** PUT SOMEBODY IN DIFFICULT SITUATION to involve somebody or something in a problem that will be difficult to escape from (*usually passive*) ○ *were entangled in corporate politics* **3.** COMPLICATE SOMETHING to make something more complicated or confusing ○ *The story entangles the facts with value judgments.* —**en·tan·gle·ment** *n*

en·ta·sis /éntəssiss/ *n* in architecture, a slight bulge in the shaft of a column, designed to counter the visual impression of concavity that a perfectly straight column would give [Mid-18C. < Greek, "straining" < *teinein* "to stretch"]

En·teb·be /en tébbə, -tébbee/ city on the northwestern shore of Lake Victoria near Kampala, southern Uganda. Its airport, one of the largest in East Africa, was the scene of a successful Israeli raid on a hijacked commercial aircraft in 1976 leading to the release of over 100 hostages. Population: 41,638 (1991 estimate).

en·tel·e·chy /en télləkee/ *n* **1.** the real existence of a thing, not merely its theoretical existence **2.** in some philosophies, a life-giving force believed to be responsible for the development of all living things [Early 17C. Via late Latin < Greek *entelekheia* "having completeness" < *entelēs* "complete" < *telos* "end"]

en·tente /aaN taáNt/ *n* **1.** a state of friendly agreement or understanding that exists or is declared between two or more countries **2.** the parties involved in an entente [Mid-19C. < French, "understanding" < *entendre* (see INTEND)]

en·tente cor·di·ale /aaN taáNt kàwrdee aál/ (*plural* **en·tentes cor·di·ales** /*pronunc. same*/) *n* amicable relations between countries or states, especially the agreement formed between France and Britain in 1904 [< French, "friendly understanding"]

en·ter /éntər/ *v* (**-tered, -ter·ing, -ters**) **1.** *vti* GO IN to go or come into a place **2.** *vt* COMPUT WRITE OR TYPE SOMETHING to write or type something in a book or on a computer ○ *The names and addresses are entered into a database.* **3.** *vt* SUBMIT SOMETHING FOR CONSIDERATION to submit something officially, e.g., a proposal, complaint, or bid, for formal consideration **4.** *vti* REGISTER AS COMPETITOR to register to take part in a competition ○ *enter the race for president* **5.** *vt* JOIN OR BECOME INVOLVED IN SOMETHING to join or become officially involved in something, especially a body such as a school or company ○ *more women entering the profession* **6.** *vi* THEATER WALK ON to come on stage during a play ○ *She enters stage right.* **7.** *vti* MAKE HOLE IN SOMETHING to force a way into something, or be pushed or inserted into something, especially the human body ○ *The bullet entered through the anterior abdominal wall.* **8.** *vt* LAW TAKE LEGAL OWNERSHIP OF LAND to go onto land and take legal possession of it ■ *n* COMPUT same as **return key** [13C. Via French < Latin *intrare* "go in, enter" < *intra* "inside, within"] —**en·ter·a·ble** *adj*

enter into *vt* **1.** TAKE PART IN SOMETHING ENTHUSIASTICALLY to get actively involved in something ○ *Enter into the spirit of things.* **2.** BE RELEVANT TO SOMETHING to be one of the factors that are relevant to something ○ *Money doesn't enter into it.* **3.** SIGN UP FOR SOMETHING to become one of the parties bound by a contract **4.** CONSIDER SOMETHING FORMALLY to go into a discussion or investigation about something ○ *I do not propose to enter into the issue of who is responsible.*

enter on, enter upon *vt* to start out on something, e.g., an important task or a significant period

enter- *prefix* same as **entero-** (*used before vowels*)

en·ter·al feed·ing /éntərəl-/ *n* direct infusion into the intestines of nutrients in liquid form [Partly < ENTERIC, partly back-formation < PARENTERAL]

en·ter·ic /en térrik/ *adj* relating to or situated in the intestine [Mid-19C. < Greek *enterikos* < *enteron* "intestine"]

en·ter·ic fe·ver *n* MED same as **typhoid**

en·ter·i·tis /éntə rītiss/ *n* inflammation of the intestine, most commonly of the small intestine

en·ter key *n* **1.** a key on a numeric keypad for entering calculations **2.** COMPUT same as **return key**

entero- *prefix* intestine ○ *enterotomy* [< Greek *enteron* < Indo-European, "in, inside"]

en·ter·o·bi·a·sis /èntərō bī əssiss/ *n* infestation of the large intestine with pinworms, especially in children

en·ter·o·coele /éntərō seèl/ *n* a body cavity (**coelom**) formed from an outgrowth in the wall of an embryonic intestine, especially in invertebrate ocean organisms such as starfish and sea urchins

en·ter·o·co·li·tis /èntərō kə lītiss/ *n* inflammation of the small and large intestine as a result of infection

en·ter·o·ki·nase /èntərō kī nàyss, -kí-/ *n* a duodenal enzyme that converts trypsinogen to trypsin

en·ter·on /éntə ròn/ *n* **1.** the alimentary canal, especially of an embryo **2.** the intestine of invertebrate ocean animals, e.g., sea anemones and jellyfish, that has one opening that serves as both mouth and anus [Mid-19C. < Greek, "intestine"]

en·ter·op·a·thy /éntə róppəthee/ (*plural* **-thies**) *n* any disease of the intestines

en·ter·os·to·my /éntə róstəmee/ (*plural* **-mies**) *n* the surgical creation of a permanent opening into the intestine through the abdominal wall —**en·ter·os·to·mal** *adj*

en·ter·ot·o·my /éntə róttəmee/ (*plural* **-mies**) *n* a surgical incision into the intestine

en·ter·o·tox·in /èntərō tóksin/ *n* any toxin produced by bacteria that causes the vomiting and diarrhea associated with food poisoning

en·ter·o·vi·rus /èntərō vírəss/ (*plural* **-rus·es**) *n* a virus that lives in the gastrointestinal tract but may multiply there and invade other parts of the body. Poliomyelitis is an enterovirus.

en·ter·prise /éntər prìz/ *n* **1.** COMMERCIAL BUSINESS a commercial company **2.** BUSINESS ACTIVITIES DIRECTED AT PROFIT organized business activities aimed specifically at growth and profit **3.** DARING NEW PROJECT a new, often risky, venture that involves confidence and initiative **4.** READINESS TO UNDERTAKE NEW VENTURES readiness to put effort into new, often risky, ventures or activities [15C. < Old French *entreprise* < past participle of *entreprendre* "undertake" < *prendre* "take" (see PRIZE[3])]

En·ter·prise /éntər prìz/ city in southeastern Alabama, southeast of Montgomery. Population: 21,370 (2002 estimate).

en·ter·prise cul·ture *n* a way of life that focuses on the importance of individual people creating their own businesses and wealth

en·ter·prise soft·ware *n* computer software designed to integrate and automate all of a company's functions

en·ter·prise zone *n* an economically depressed urban area where the government encourages new business ventures by offering financial incentives

en·ter·pris·ing /éntər prìzing/ *adj* showing initiative and a willingness to undertake new, often risky, projects —**en·ter·pris·ing·ly** *adv*

en·ter·tain /èntər táyn/ (**-tained, -tain·ing, -tains**) *v* **1.** *vti* AMUSE OR INTEREST AUDIENCE to engage a person or audience by providing amusing or interesting material **2.** *vti* OFFER HOSPITALITY to offer hospitality, especially by providing food and drink for guests at home **3.** *vt* CONSIDER SOMETHING to turn something over in the mind, looking at it from various points of view ○ *He would never entertain such an idea!* [15C. < Old French *entretenir* "hold together, support" < assumed Vulgar Latin *intertenere* "hold between" < Latin *tenere* "hold"]

en·ter·tain·er /èntər táynər/ *n* a provider of entertainment, especially a professional one

en·ter·tain·ing /èntər táyning/ *adj* enjoyable to watch, read, or listen to —**en·ter·tain·ing·ly** *adv*

en·ter·tain·ment /èntər táynmənt/ *n* **1.** ART OF KEEPING PEOPLE ENTERTAINED the various ways of amusing people, especially by performing for them **2.** ENJOYMENT the amount of pleasure or amusement somebody gets from something **3.** PERFORMANCE OR EXHIBITION something that is produced or performed for an audience ○ *chief among the evening's entertainments*

en·thal·py /én thàlpee, en thálpee/ *n* a thermodynamic property equal to the sum of the internal energy of a system and the product of its pressure and volume. Symbol **H** [Early 20C. < Greek *enthalpein* "to warm within" < *thalpein* "to heat"]

en·thral *vt* UK spelling of **enthrall**

en·thrall /in thráwl, en-/ (**-thralled, -thrall·ing, -thralls**), **in·thrall** /in-/ *vt* **1.** to delight or fascinate somebody thoroughly, engaging that person's attention completely **2.** to make somebody a prisoner and claim legal ownership of that person (*literary*) [Late 16C. < EN- + THRALL] —**en·thrall·ment** *n*

en·thralled /in thráwld/ *adj* fascinated and giving total attention to something

en·thrall·ing /in thráwling/ *adj* so interesting, delightful, or beautiful as to hold the attention completely

en·throne /in thrṓn, en-/ (**-throned, -thron·ing, -thrones**), **in·throne** /in-/ *vt* **1.** to install a monarch or bishop, especially in a ceremony that involves seating the person on a throne (*formal*) **2.** to regard somebody as being worthy of adoration (*literary*) —**en·throne·ment** *n*

en·thuse /in thóoz, en-/ (**-thused, -thus·ing, -thus·es**) *vti* **1.** ⚠ to have, or make somebody feel, great excitement or interest **2.** ⚠ to express enthusiasm about something or say something enthusiastically ○ *enthusing about the new restaurant* [Early 19C. Back-formation < ENTHUSIASM]

USAGE *"You've won a prize," the caller enthuses.* Unlike such other "back-formations" (words formed by removing the last part of another word) such as *diagnose, edit,* and *reminisce,* ***enthuse*** has yet to win universal acceptance, though it has been in use since the early 1800s.

---

en·thu·si·asm /in thóozee àzzəm, en-/ *n* **1.** passionate interest in or eagerness to do something **2.** something that arouses a consuming interest [Late 16C. Via late Latin < Greek *enthousiasmos* "possession by (a) god" < *enthous* "inspired" < *theos* "god"]

en·thu·si·ast /in thóozee àst, en-/ *n* somebody who is enthusiastic about something, especially a hobby [Early 17C. < Greek *enthousiastēs* "somebody inspired (by a god)" < *enthous* (see ENTHUSIASM)]

en·thu·si·as·tic /in thóozee ástik, en-/ *adj* showing passionate interest in something or eagerness about something —**en·thu·si·as·ti·cal·ly** *adv*

en·thy·meme /énthə meem/ *n* an argument that assumes the truth of one or more premises and therefore omits them from the logical sequence [Late 16C. Via Latin < Greek *enthumēma* "(something) in mind" < *thumos* "mind"]

en·tia PHILOSOPHY plural of **ens**

en·tice /in tíss, en-/ (**-ticed, -tic·ing, -tic·es**) *vt* to make a person or animal do something by offering something desirable [13C. Via Old French *enticier* < assumed Vulgar Latin *intitiare* "set on fire" < Latin *titio* "firebrand"] —**en·tice·ment** *n* —**en·tic·er** *n*

en·tic·ing /in tíssing, en-/ *adj* very desirable and hard to resist —**en·tic·ing·ly** *adv*

en·tire /in tír, en-/ *adj* **1.** WHOLE as a whole, from beginning to end, or including everything ○ *rained the entire night* **2.** ABSOLUTE in every way, without doubt or question ○ *The day was an entire fiasco.* **3.** VET UNGELDED describes a male animal, especially a stallion or dog, that has not been castrated **4.** BOT SMOOTH-EDGED describes leaves with smooth edges that are not lobed or indented **5.** IN ONE PIECE not damaged or broken up (*literary*) ○ *"with strength entire, and free Will arm'd"* (John Milton, *Paradise Lost*; 1667) ■ *n* same as **entirety** [14C. Via Old French *entier* < Latin *integrum*, form of *integer* "whole, intact"] —**en·tire·ness** *n*

en·tire·ly /in tírlee, en-/ *adv* **1.** in every sense ○ *an entirely different question* **2.** exclusively or individually ○ *I'm entirely at fault.*

en·tire·ty /in tírətee, en-/ *n* the whole extent of something

~~**entirly**~~ incorrect spelling of **entirely**

en·ti·tle /in tít'l, en-/ (**-tled, -tling, -tles**) *vt* **1.** GRANT SOMEBODY RIGHT to give somebody the right to have or to do something (*often passive*) **2.** GIVE TITLE TO SOMETHING to assign a title to something such as a book (*usually passive*) **3.** AWARD SOMEBODY HONOR to confer an official position or honor on somebody that brings a particular title with it [14C. Via French < late Latin *intitulare* < Latin *titulus* "inscription"] —**en·ti·tle·ment** *n*

en·ti·tle·ment pro·gram *n* a government program that targets a particular section of the population to receive specific social benefits

en·ti·ty /éntətee/ (*plural* **-ties**) *n* **1.** OBJECT something that exists as or is perceived as a single separate object **2.** PHILOSOPHY EXISTENCE the state of having existence **3.** PHILOSOPHY ESSENTIAL NATURE the essence or character of something [Late 16C. < medieval Latin *entitas* < late Latin *ent-*, stem of *ens* (see ENS)]

en·tomb /in tóom, en-/ (**-tombed, -tomb·ing, -tombs**) *vt* **1.** PUT CORPSE IN TOMB to put a corpse into a tomb **2.** PUT SOMETHING IN DEEP PLACE to put something in a place that is hidden or very deep ○ *the secret vaults where the treasures were entombed* **3.** BURY SOMEBODY OR SOMETHING to serve as a tomb for somebody or something ○ *the collapsed mine that entombed them* —**en·tomb·ment** *n*

entomo- *prefix* insect ○ *entomophilous* [Via French < Greek *entomon* < *entomos* "cut in two" < *temnein* "to cut"; because of insects' distinctly segmented bodies]

en·to·mol·o·gy /èntə móllәjee/ *n* the branch of zoology that deals with the study of insects [Mid-18C. < French *entomologie* or modern Latin *entomologia* "science of insects" < Greek *entomon* (see ENTOMO-)] —**en·to·mo·log·i·cal** /èntəmə lójjik'l/ *adj* —**en·to·mo·log·i·cal·ly** *adv* —**en·to·mol·o·gist** *n*

en·to·moph·a·gous /èntə móffəgəss/ *adj* feeding on insects

en·to·moph·i·lous /èntə móffələss/ *adj* describes flowering plants that are pollinated by insects —**en·to·moph·i·ly** *n*

en·tou·rage /óntə ràazh, óntə ráazh/ *n* **1.** a group of special employees who go with a high-ranking or famous person on visits and engagements **2.** the surroundings or environment (*literary*) [Mid-19C. < French < *entourer* "surround" < *tour* "circuit"]

en·tr'acte /ón tràkt, aan trákt/ (*plural* **-tr'actes**) *n* **1.** an interval between the acts of a play or opera **2.** an additional piece of entertainment during the break between the acts of a play or opera [Mid-18C. < obsolete French, "between the act(s)" < *acte* "act"]

en·trails /éntrəlz, én trayl/ *npl* **1.** INTERNAL ORGANS an animal's or person's internal organs **2.** INNER WORKINGS the various working parts inside something, especially something complex **3.** ANIMAL ORGANS USED FOR DIVINATION the internal organs of a sacrificial animal, used by the ancient Romans to try to determine the will of the gods [13C. Via Old French *entrailles* < medieval Latin *intralia*, alteration of Latin *interanea* "intestines" < *inter* "between"]

en·train[1] /in tráyn, en-/ (**-trained, -train·ing, -trains**) *vti* to board or to put somebody or something aboard a train [Late 19C. < EN] —**en·train·er** *n* —**en·train·ment** *n*

en·train[2] /in tráyn, en-/ (**-trained, -train·ing, -trains**) *vt* **1.** to cause something to happen as a consequence of an action **2.** to draw solid particles, air bubbles, or liquid drops into a moving fluid and carry them along in the flow [Mid-16C. < Old French *entraîner* "drag away" < *traîner* "drag"] —**en·train·ment** *n*

en·trance[1] /éntrənss/ *n* **1.** WAY IN a door or gate through which people enter **2.** ENTERING OF SITE the act or an instance of entering a place ○ *a highly theatrical entrance* **3.** RIGHT OF ENTRY the right to go into a place or to enter an institution [15C. < Old French < *entrer* (see ENTER)]

en·trance[2] /en tránss/ (**-tranced, -tranc·ing, -tranc·es**) *vt* **1.** to hold somebody's attention and produce a sense of wonder in that person **2.** to make somebody go into a trance [Late 16C. < EN[3]] —**en·tranc·ing** *adj* —**en·tranc·ing·ly** *adv*

en·trance·way /éntrənss wày/ *n* US same as **entryway**

en·trant /éntrənt/ *n* somebody who enters a competition or examination [Mid-17C. < French, present participle of *entrer* (see ENTER)]

SYNONYMS See ***candidate.***

---

en·trap /in tráp, en-/ (**-trapped, -trap·ping, -traps**) *vt* **1.** to be restrained or restricted by circumstances ○ *entrapped by poverty* **2.** to deceive somebody, especially to trick somebody into committing or admitting to a crime —**en·trap·ment** *n*

en·treat /in tréet, en-/ (**-treat·ed, -treat·ing, -treats**) *vti* to beg somebody for something, often repeatedly [14C. < Old French *entraitier* "treat in (a certain way)" < *traitier* (see TREAT)] —**en·treat·ing·ly** *adv*

en·treat·y /in tréetee, en-/ (*plural* **-ies**) *n* a serious and passionate request

en·tre·chat /óntrə shaa/ *n* in ballet, a leap in which the dancer's legs are crossed rapidly in the air and the heels are beaten together [Late 18C. Via French < Italian *(capriola) intrecciata* "intricate (caper)"]

en·tre·côte /óntrə kòt, áantrə-/, **en·tre·côte steak** *n* a piece of beef without any bone, cut from between the ribs [Mid-19C. < French, "between (the) rib(s)"]

en·trée /ón tràγ, on tráy/, **en·tree** *n* **1. MAIN COURSE** a dish served as the main part of a meal **2.** *UK* **DISH BEFORE MAIN COURSE** in a formal dinner, a light dish served before the main course **3. RIGHT OF ENTRY** something that permits entry into something, especially to an exclusive group or place [Late 18C. < French (see ENTRY)]

en·tre·mets /òntrə máy/ (*plural same / pronunc. same*) *n* **1.** in a formal dinner, a light dish served between the main course and the dessert **2.** a sweet dish, especially one served after cheese in a dinner of several courses [15C. < Old French, "between the course(s)" < *mes* "course"]

en·trench /in trénch, en-/ (**-trenched, -trench·ing, -trench·es**), **in·trench** /in-/ *v* **1.** *vt* **DIG DEFENSIVE DITCH AROUND SOMETHING** to defend something by surrounding it with trenches **2.** *vt* **PROTECT SOMETHING** to take action to protect an argument or position **3.** *vi* **TRESPASS** to encroach upon or trespass on somebody else's property or things (*archaic*) —**en·trench·ment** *n*

en·trenched /in trénch t, en-/ *adj* **1.** firmly held and hard to change ○ *deeply entrenched political views* **2.** firmly established and unlikely to change

en·tre nous /òntrə nóò/ *adv* in confidence [Late 17C. < French, "between ourselves"]

en·tre·pôt /óntrə pō/ *n* **1.** COMM same as **free port** (sense 2) **2.** a bonded warehouse [Early 18C. < French < *entreposer* "place in, store" < *poser* "to place"]

en·tre·pre·neur /òntrəprə núr, -nóòr/ *n* somebody who initiates or finances new commercial enterprises [Late 19C. < French, "somebody who undertakes" < *entreprendre* (see ENTERPRISE)] —**en·tre·pre·neu·ri·al** *adj* —**en·tre·pre·neur·i·al·ism** *n* —**en·tre·pre·neur·ism** *n* —**en·tre·pre·neur·ship** *n*

en·tre·sol /óntrə sàwl/ *n* BUILDINGS same as **mezzanine** *n* (sense 1) [Early 18C. Via French < Spanish *entresuelo* "between-level" < *suelo* "level" < Latin *solea* "sole, sandal"]

en·tro·py /éntrəpee/ *n* **1. MEASURE OF DISORDER** a measure of the disorder that exists in a system **2.** PHYS **MEASURE OF UNAVAILABLE ENERGY** a measure of the energy in a system or process that is unavailable to do work. In a reversible thermodynamic process, entropy is expressed as the heat absorbed or emitted divided by the absolute temperature. Symbol *S* **3.** COMMUNICATION **MEASURE OF EFFICIENCY** a measure of the random errors (**noise**) occurring in the transmission of signals, and from this a measure of the efficiency of transmission systems [Mid-19C. < Greek *en-* "in" + *tropē* "change," after ENERGY] —**en·tro·pic** /en tróppik/ *adj* —**en·tro·pi·cal·ly** *adv*

en·trust /in trúst, en-/ (**-trust·ed, -trust·ing, -trusts**), **in·trust** /in-/ *vt* to give something to another person to be responsible for —**en·trust·ment** *n*

en·try /éntree/ (*plural* **-tries**) *n* **1. GOING IN** an act or instance of somebody entering **2.** same as **entrance**[1] (sense 3) **3. PIECE OF WRITTEN INFORMATION** an item or piece of data included in a list or a book **4. INCLUDING OF ITEM ON LIST** the process of recording something in writing or on a computer ○ *data entry* **5. WAY IN** a way into a place **6. ENTRANT** a person, animal, or item entered in a contest ○ *the winning entry* **7.** CARDS **WINNING CARD** in some games, a card that can win a trick and thus gain the lead for a player [13C. Via French *entrée* < Latin *intrata* < past participle of *intrare* (see ENTER)]

en·try-lev·el *adj* at the lowest level and suitable for somebody who is new to a job, field, or subject

en·try·way /éntree wày/ *n* a way into a place, e.g., a doorway or passageway

en·twine /in twín, en-/ (**-twined, -twin·ing, -twines**), **in·twine** /in-/ *vti* to twist things together or to twist something around something else (*often passive*) —**en·twine·ment** *n*

en·twist /in twíst, en-/ (**-twist·ed, -twist·ing, -twists**), **in·twist** /in-/ *vti* same as **entwine**

e·nu·cle·ate /i nóoklee àyt/ *vt* (**-at·ed, -at·ing, -ates**) **1.** BIOL **TAKE OUT NUCLEUS** to remove the nucleus of a cell **2.** SURG **SURGICALLY REMOVE SOMETHING WHOLE** to remove something surgically, e.g., a tumor, from its capsule while keeping it intact ■ *adj* BIOL **LACKING A NUCLEUS** describes a cell without a nucleus [Mid-16C. < Latin *enucleat-*, past participle of *enucleare* "remove the pit from (olives, fruit)" < *nucleus* "kernel" (see NUCLEUS)] —**e·nu·cle·a·tion** /i nóoklee áysh'n/ *n*

e·nu·mer·ate /i nóomə ràyt/ (**-at·ed, -at·ing, -ates**) *vt* **1. LIST ITEMS INDIVIDUALLY** to name a number of things on a list one by one **2. COUNT THINGS** to count how many things there are in something **3.** *Can* POL **REGISTER A VOTER** to put a voter's name on an official list used in elections [Mid-17C. < Latin *enumerat-*, past participle of *enumerare* "count out" < *numerus* "number"] —**e·nu·mer·a·ble** *adj* —**e·nu·mer·a·tion** /i nóomə ráysh'n/ *n* —**e·nu·mer·a·tive** *adj* —**e·nu·mer·a·tor** *n*

e·nun·ci·ate /i núnssee àyt/ (**-at·ed, -at·ing, -ates**) *v* **1.** *vti* to pronounce something distinctly **2.** *vt* to give a speech or statement that explains something clearly [Early 17C. < Latin *enuntiat-*, past participle of *enuntiare* "announce" < *nuntius* "message, messenger"] —**e·nun·ci·a·tion** /i nùnssee áysh'n/ *n* —**e·nun·ci·a·tive** *adj* —**e·nun·ci·a·tive·ly** *adv* —**e·nun·ci·a·tor** *n*

en·ure *vt* LAW another spelling of **inure**

en·u·re·sis /ènnyə réessiss/ *n* involuntary discharge of urine, especially while asleep (*technical*) [Late 18C. < modern Latin < Greek *enourein* "urinate in" < *ouron* "urine"] —**en·u·ret·ic** /-réttik/ *adj*

en·vel·op /in vélləp, en-/ (**-oped, -op·ing, -ops**) *vt* **1. WRAP SOMETHING UP** to enclose somebody or something completely (*often passive*) **2. HIDE SOMETHING OR SOMEBODY** to conceal something or somebody (*often passive*) **3.** MIL **SURROUND ENEMY** to surround an enemy completely [14C. < Old French *envoluper* "wrap in"] —**en·vel·op·er** *n* —**en·vel·op·ment** *n*

SPELLCHECK envelope or **envelop**? Do not confuse the spelling of ***envelope*** and ***envelop***, which are spelled similarly but have different pronunciations. The verb ***envelop***, meaning "wrap," "hide," or "surround," is stressed on the middle syllable. The noun ***envelope*** has an "e" at each end and is stressed on the first and last syllables.

---

en·ve·lope /énvə lòp, ónvə-/ *n* **1. PAPER COVER FOR LETTER** a flat pocket of paper with a sealable flap for holding a letter **2. ENCLOSING CASE** something that surrounds or encloses something else ○ *seafood sauce in phyllo pastry envelopes* **3.** ZOOL **ENCLOSING STRUCTURE** a covering that encloses and protects an animal's body or a biological structure, e.g., a shell or membrane **4.** MATH **CURVE FORMING TANGENT** a curve or surface that forms a tangent to each of the members of a set of curves or surfaces, e.g., circles with a common center but different radii **5.** AVIAT **BALLOON** the bag of an airship or balloon that contains the gas **6.** AVIAT **PERFORMANCE LIMITS OF AIRCRAFT** the performance limits of a piece of equipment, particularly of an aircraft [Early 18C. < French *enveloppe* < *envelopper* "wrap in"] ◇ **push the envelope** to try to accomplish more than is theoretically possible (*informal*)

SPELLCHECK See ***envelop***.

---

en·ven·om /in vénnəm/ (**-omed, -om·ing, -oms**) *vt* **1.** to cause somebody to become malicious or hostile (*formal*) **2.** to make something poisonous (*technical*)

En·ver Pa·sha /énvər páashə, -páa shàa/, **General** (1881–1922) Turkish soldier and politician. He was elected leader of the revolutionary Young Turks in 1908 and became Turkey's minister of war in 1914. After World War I he fled to Russia, where he died in an anti-Bolshevik uprising.

en·vi·a·ble /énvee əb'l/ *adj* likely to evoke feelings of envy ○ *in the enviable position of having two job offers to choose from* —**en·vi·a·bly** *adv*

en·vi·ous /énvee əss/ *adj* wanting to have somebody else's success, good fortune, qualities, or possessions —**en·vi·ous·ly** *adv* —**en·vi·ous·ness** *n*

~~**enviroment**~~ incorrect spelling of **environment**

en·vi·ron /in vírən, -ví ərn/ (**-roned, -ron·ing, -rons**) *vt* same as **surround** *v* (sense 1) (*formal*) [14C. < Old French *environer* "make a circle around" < *viron* "circle" < *virer* "to turn"]

en·vi·ron·ment /in vírənmənt, -ví ərn-/ *n* **1. SURROUNDING INFLUENCES** all the external factors influencing the life and activities of people, plants, and animals **2. NATURAL WORLD** the natural world, especially when it is regarded as being at risk from the harmful influences of human activities **3. SET OF CONDITIONS** a set of external conditions, especially those affecting a particular activity (*usually in combination*) ○ *the home environment* ○ *a stimulating learning environment* **4.** COMPUT **COMPUTING FRAMEWORK** a framework within which a computer, program, or user operates

en·vi·ron·men·tal /in vìrən mént'l, -vì ərn-/ *adj* **1.** relating to the natural world, especially to its conservation ○ *environmental groups* **2.** relating to, or caused by, a person's or animal's surroundings ○ *environmental hazards*

en·vi·ron·men·tal ac·count·ing *n* the practice of including indirect costs and benefits of a product or activity such as its environmental effects on health and the economy along with its direct costs when making business decisions

en·vi·ron·men·tal art *n* creative art, usually on a grand scale, that is meant to invite the viewer to participate by interacting with the artwork

en·vi·ron·men·tal au·dit *n* an assessment of an organization's compliance with environmental laws and of the effectiveness of its environmental policies and practices

en·vi·ron·men·tal eq·ui·ty *n* the equal distribution of environmental risk among population groups regardless of race, income, gender, or age

en·vi·ron·men·tal health *n* the local government functions concerned with minimizing risks to public health and the local environment, including the monitoring of water and air quality, hygiene in restaurants and stores, and pest control

en·vi·ron·men·tal im·pact *n* the indirect and direct consequences of human actions on the natural environment

en·vi·ron·men·tal im·pact state·ment *n* a written statement of the likely environmental effects of a proposed development based on a scientific assessment or study ○ *"After the public comment period, the NRC will issue a final environmental impact statement by November."* (*Washington Post*; April 1999)

en·vi·ron·men·tal im·pact stud·y *n* an analysis carried out to determine the impact of a specific project, often a building project, on the environment

en·vi·ron·men·tal·ism /in vìrən mént'l ìzzəm, -vì ərn-/ *n* **1.** the movement, especially in politics and consumer affairs, that works toward protecting the natural world from harmful human activities **2.** a theory stating that somebody's environment is more influential than heredity in determining his or her development

en·vi·ron·men·tal·ist /in vìrən mént'list, -vì ərn-/ *n* **1.** somebody involved in issues relating to the protection of the natural world, especially a member of a political group campaigning against the perceived harmful effects of industrialized societies **2.** a supporter of the theory that somebody's environment is more influential than heredity in determining his or her development. ◊ **hereditarian**

en·vi·ron·men·tal la·bel·ing *n* ENVIRON same as **eco-labeling** —**en·vi·ron·men·tal la·bel** *n*

en·vi·ron·men·tal·ly /in vìrən mént'lee, -vì ərn-/ *adv* with regard to the natural world and its vulnerability to destructive influences ○ *the environmentally aware consumer*

en·vi·ron·men·tal·ly friend·ly, **en·vi·ron·ment-friend·ly** *adj* designed to minimize harm to the natural world, e.g., by using biodegradable ingredients

en·vi·ron·men·tal stud·ies *n* a course of academic study including a range of disciplines that relate to the environment (*takes a singular or plural verb*)

en·vi·ron·ment-friend·ly *adj* ENVIRON same as **environmentally friendly**

en·vi·rons /in vírənz, in ví ərnz/ *npl* the land or area surrounding a place [Mid-17C. < French, plural of *environ* "surroundings" < *viron* (see ENVIRON)]

en·vis·age /in vízzij, en-/ (**-aged, -ag·ing, -ag·es**) *vt* **1. FORESEE SOMETHING** to conceive of and contemplate a future possibility ○ *Do you envisage being able to avert a crisis?* **2. VISUALIZE SOMETHING** to form a mental picture of something or somebody **3. CONSIDER SOMETHING** to regard something in a particular way

[Early 19C. < French *envisager* < *visage* "face" (see VISAGE)]

en·vi·sion /in vízh'n, en-/ (**-sioned, -sion·ing, -sions**) *vt* to form a mental picture of something, typically something that may occur or be possible in the future

en·voi /én vòy/ *n* LITERAT another spelling of **envoy** (sense 3)

en·voy /én vòy/ *n* **1.** OFFICIAL REPRESENTATIVE somebody acting as a diplomat on behalf of a national government or sent as its official messenger **2.** *also* **en·voy ex·traor·di·nar·y** (*plural* **en·voys ex·traor·di·nar·y**) *UK* DIPLOMATIC MINISTER a minister in the UK Diplomatic Service of a rank above chargé d'affaires **3.** *also* **en·voi** LITERAT CONCLUSION OF LITERARY WORK the final section of a book or play, or a short stanza at the end of a poem, used for summing up or as a dedication [Mid-17C. < French *envoyé*, past participle of *envoyer* "send" < assumed Vulgar Latin *inviare* "put on the way" < Latin *via* "way"]

en·vy /énvee/ *n* the resentful or unhappy feeling of wanting somebody else's success, good fortune, qualities, or possessions ■ *vt* (**-vied, -vy·ing, -vies**) to desire something possessed by somebody else ○ *envy them their success* [13C. Via French *envie* < Latin *invidia* < *invidere* "look askance at" < *videre* "see"] —**en·vy·ing·ly** *adv* ◇ **be the envy of** to be the object of somebody's envy

en·wind /in wínd, en-/ (**-wound** /-wównd/, **-wound, -wind·ing, -winds**), **in·wind** /in-/ *vt* to wind or coil something around somebody or something (*literary*)

en·womb /in wóom, en-/ (**-wombed, -womb·ing, -wombs**) *vt* to hold something or somebody in a warm safe place (*literary*)

en·wound past participle, past tense of **enwind**

en·wrap /in ráp, en-/ (**-wrapped, -wrap·ping, -wraps**), **in·wrap** /in-/ *vt* **1.** to wrap something or somebody up **2.** to involve or engross somebody or something thoroughly (*formal; often passive*)

en·wreathe /in reéth, en-/ (**-wreathed, -wreath·ing, -wreathes**), **in·wreathe** /in-/ *vt* to encircle something, especially with decorations (*literary*)

en·zo·ot·ic /èn zō óttik/ *adj* describes an animal disease that occurs only within a specific geographic area ■ *n* a disease that affects animals in a specific area, locale, or region

en·zyme /én zīm/ *n* any complex chemical produced by living cells that is a biochemical catalyst [Late 19C. < German *Enzym* < modern Greek *enzumos* "leavened" < Greek *zumē* "leaven"] —**en·zy·mat·ic** /ènzə máttik/ *adj* —**en·zy·mic** /en zīmik, -zímmik/ *adj* —**en·zy·mi·cal·ly** *adv*

en·zy·mol·o·gy /ènzə mólləjee/ *n* the study of enzymes

EO *abbr US* LAW executive order (*followed by a number*)

e.o. *abbr* ex officio

eo- *prefix* oldest, earliest ○ *eolithic* [< Greek *ēōs* "dawn" < Indo-European]

E·o·cene /ée ə seen/ *n* the epoch of geologic time, 55 million to 38 million years ago, during which the ancestors of many modern animals appeared. See table at **geologic time** —**E·o·cene** *adj*

EOE *abbr* HR **1.** equal opportunity employer (*used in job advertisements*) **2.** equal opportunity employment

EOF *abbr* COMPUT end of file

e·o·hip·pus /ée ō híppəss/ (*plural* **-pus·es**) *n* a small prehistoric horse that lived in North America. It was dog-sized and had four toes on the front feet and three on the back feet. [Late 19C. < modern Latin < Greek *ēōs* "dawn" + *hippos* "horse"]

e·o·li·an /ee ōlee ən, -ōlyən/, **ae·o·li·an** *adj* carried or produced by the wind ○ *eolian deposits* [Early 20C. < AEOLUS]

E·o·li·an, etc. PEOPLES, LANG another spelling of **Aeolian, etc.**

e·o·lith /ée ə lìth/ *n* one of the oldest stone tools used by humans, believed by some scientists to have formed naturally

e·o·lith·ic /èe ə líthik/ *adj* relating to the earliest part of the Stone Age, during which time simple stone tools began to be used

e.o.m. *abbr* **1.** end of message (*used in e-mails or text messages*) **2.** COMM end of the month

e·on /ée òn, -ən/ *n* **1.** a length of time that is too long to measure **2.** a division of geologic time comprising two or more eras [Mid-17C. Via late Latin < Greek *aiōn* "age, lifetime"] —**e·o·ni·an** /ee ōnee ən/ *adj*

E·os /ée oss/ *n* in Greek mythology, the goddess of the dawn. Roman equivalent **Aurora**[1]

e·o·sin /ée əssin/ *n* a red crystalline solid. Use: biological stain, dye in cosmetics. Formula: $C_{20}H_6Br_4O_5K_2$. [Mid-19C. < Greek *ēōs* "dawn"; because of its color]

e·o·sin·o·phil /èe ə sínnə fil/ *n* a granular white blood cell that stains with the dye eosin and is thought to play a part in allergic reactions and the body's response to parasitic diseases —**e·o·sin·o·phil·ic** /-sinə fíllik/ *adj* —**e·o·si·noph·i·lous** /-si nóffələss/ *adj*

e·o·sin·o·phil·i·a /èe ə sinə fíllee ə/ *n* an increase in the number of granular white blood cells that stain with the dye eosin, occurring in some allergies and parasitic diseases

-eous *suffix* same as **-ous** [< Latin *-eus*]

EP[1] *n* a phonograph record that is the size of a single but contains a longer recording and is designed to be played at 33⅓ revolutions per minute rather than 45 [Mid-20C. Abbreviation of *extended play*]

EP[2] *abbr* TRAVEL European plan

Ep. *abbr* BIBLE **1.** Ephesians **2.** Epistle

ep- *prefix* same as **epi-** (*used before vowels or h*)

EPA[1] *n* a polyunsaturated essential fatty acid found in cold-water fish that has been linked to the reduction of cardiovascular disease and other health benefits. Full form **eicosapentaenoic acid**

EPA[2] *abbr* GOV Environmental Protection Agency

e·pact /ée pàkt/ *n* a period of about 11 days that represents the difference between the lunar year and the solar year [Mid-16C. Via French < late Latin *epacta* < Greek *epaktē (hēmera)* "added (day)" < *agein* "to lead"]

ep·an·a·lep·sis /èppənə lépsiss/ (*plural* **-lep·ses** /-lép seez/) *n* a phrase or set of words repeated later on in a speech or text as a rhetorical device [Late 16C. < Greek, "repetition" < *epana-* "again" + *lēpsis* "taking"] —**ep·an·a·lep·tic** *adj*

e·pan·or·tho·sis /èppə nawr thóssiss/ (*plural* **-tho·ses** /-thó seez/) *n* the immediate rephrasing of something said or written in order to emphasize or correct it [Late 16C. < Greek, "correction" < *epana-* "again" + *orthōsis* "making straight" < *orthos* "straight"] —**e·pan·or·thot·ic** /-thóttik/ *adj*

e-pa·per *n* a thin flexible sheet on which electronic information can be downloaded and read

ep·arch /ép aark/ *n* **1.** a bishop in the Greek Orthodox Church **2.** in modern Greece, the governor of a subdivision of a province [Mid-17C. < Greek *eparkhos*, literally "ruler over" < *arkhos* (see -ARCH)]

ep·ar·chy /ép aarkee/ (*plural* **-chies**) *n* **1.** a bishop's diocese in the Greek Orthodox Church **2.** in modern Greece, a subdivision of a province [Late 18C. < Greek *eparkhia* "prefecture, province" < *eparkhos* (see EPARCH)]

ep·au·let /éppə lèt, èppə lét/, **ep·au·lette** *n Can, UK* a decoration on the shoulder of a jacket or coat, especially on a military uniform. In officers' dress, epaulets are usually made of gold or silver braid. [Late 18C. < French *épaulette* < *épaule* "shoulder" < Latin *spatula* "broad piece, shoulder blade" (see SPATULA)]

é·pée /e páy/ (*plural* **é·pées**) *n* **1.** a fencing sword that has a narrow triangular blade with a blunted end and a large guard for the hand, heavier than a foil. It derives from the type of sword formerly used in dueling. **2.** the sport of fencing using épées [Late 19C. < French, "sword" < Latin *spatha* "broad double-edged sword" (see SPATHE)] —**é·pée·ist** *n*

ep·ei·rog·e·ny /è pī rójjənee/, **ep·ei·ro·gen·e·sis** /è pīrō jénnəssiss/ *n* the slow movements of the Earth's crust leading to the formation of features such as continents [Late 19C. < Greek *ēpeiros* "mainland, continent"] —**ep·ei·ro·gen·ic** /i pīrō jénnik/ *adj* —**ep·ei·ro·gen·i·cal·ly** *adv*

e·pen·the·sis /i pénthəssiss/ *n* insertion of an extra sound into a word, as happens in some dialect pronunciations or in a word's development over time. The "b" in "crumble" is an example of epenthesis. [Mid-17C. Via late Latin < Greek < *epentithenai* "insert" < *tithenai* "to place"] —**e·pen·thet·ic** /èppən théttik/ *adj*

e·pergne /i púrn, ày-/ *n* a large elaborate centerpiece for a table with containers for fruit or flowers [Mid-18C. Probably < French *épergne* "savings, treasury" < Old French *espargnier* < Germanic]

ep·ex·e·ge·sis /e pèksə jéessiss/ (*plural* **-ge·ses** /-jée seez/) *n* **1.** the addition of words or phrases to a text to clarify its meaning **2.** a word or phrase added to help explain the sense of a text [Early 17C. < Greek *epexēgēsis* < *epi* "in addition" + *exēgēsis* (see EXEGESIS)] —**ep·ex·e·get·ic** /-jéttik/ *adj* —**ep·ex·e·get·i·cal** *adj* —**ep·ex·e·get·i·cal·ly** *adv*

Eph. *abbr* BIBLE Ephesians

e·phah /éefə, éffə/, **e·pha** *n* an ancient Hebrew unit of dry measure, roughly equivalent to a bushel or 33 liters [14C. < Hebrew *ēpāh*]

e·phebe /é feeb, i féeb/, **e·phe·bus** /i féebəss/ (*plural* **-bi** /-bī/), **e·phe·bos** (*plural* **-bi**) *n* in ancient Greece, a young man aged between 18 and 20 who had just reached manhood or full citizenship and was undergoing military training [Mid-19C. Via Latin < Greek *ephēbos* "somebody approaching manhood" < *hēbē* "early manhood"] —**e·phe·bic** /i féebik/ *adj*

e·phe·dra /i féddrə, éffədrə/ (*plural* **-dras** or *same*) *n* **1.** a dietary supplement that is said to accelerate fat loss and increase energy, stamina, metabolic rate, and sex drive **2.** a bush with slender green jointed stems and whorls of small scaly leaves. Some species are a source of the drug ephedrine and the dietary supplement ephedra. Native to: warm temperate regions. Genus: *Ephedra*. [Early 20C. < modern Latin (see EPHEDRINE)]

e·phed·rine /i féddrin, éffə dreen/ *n* an alkaloid that dilates the air passages. Use: treatment of asthma and nasal congestion. [Late 19C. < modern Latin *Ephedra* < Latin *ephedra* "horsetail" < Greek, plant of a genus including some that contain this substance]

e·phem·er·a[1] /i fémmərə/ plural of **ephemeron**

e·phem·er·a[2] /i fémmərə/ (*plural* **-ae** /-ə rée/ or **-as**) *n* **1.** something that is transitory and without lasting significance **2.** INSECTS same as **mayfly** (sense 1) [14C. < medieval Latin < late Latin *ephemerus* "lasting only a day" < Greek *ephēmeros* < *hēmera* "day"]

e·phem·er·al /i fémmərəl/ *adj* lasting for only a short period of time ○ *the ephemeral nature of slang* ■ *n* a plant or insect that lives for only a short period of time. Groundsel and mayflies are ephemerals. —**e·phem·er·al·i·ty** /i fèmmə rállətee/ *n* —**e·phem·er·al·ly** *adv* —**e·phem·er·al·ness** *n*

SYNONYMS See ***temporary.***

e·phem·er·id /i fémmərid/ *n* an insect of the mayfly family that emerges in the summer from a long larval stage under water and lives only a matter of hours as an adult. Family: Ephemeridae. [Late 19C. < modern Latin *Ephemeridae* < Greek *ephēmeros* (see EPHEMERA[2])]

e·phem·er·is /i fémmərіss/ (*plural* **eph·e·mer·i·des** /èffə mérrə deez/) *n* a table listing the future positions of the Sun, Moon, and planets over a given period of time [Early 16C. Via Latin < Greek < *ephēmeros* (see EPHEMERA[2])]

e·phem·er·is time *n* a system of time measurement based on the Earth's orbit around the Sun and therefore independent of the irregularities of the Earth's rotation

e·phem·er·on /i fémmə ròn/ *n* (*plural* **-a** /-ərə/ or **-ons**) a short-lived thing (*usually used in the plural*) ■ **e·phem·er·a** *npl* collectible items that were originally designed to be short-lived ○ *He's a collector of ticket stubs, movie passes, and other ephemera.* [Late 16C. < Greek *ephēmeron*, form of *ephēmeros* (see EPHEMERA[2])]

Ephes. *abbr* BIBLE Ephesians

E·phe·sians /i féezh'nz/ *n* a book of the Bible, originally a letter to the church in Ephesus and traditionally attributed to St. Paul. (*takes a singular verb*) See table at **Bible** [15C. < Latin *ephesius* "of Ephesus" < Greek *ephesios* < *Ephesos* "Ephesus"]

Eph·e·sus /éffəssəss/ ancient Greek city on the western coast of Asia Minor, in present-day Turkey. An important center for early Christianity, it was also the site of the temple of Artemis, one of the Seven Wonders of the World.

eph·od /é fòd, ée-/ *n* an embroidered garment, believed to be like an apron with shoulder straps, worn by Hebrew priests in ancient Israel [14C. < Hebrew *ēpōd*]

eph·or /é fàwr, éffər/ (*plural* **-ors** or **-o·ri** /éffə rī/) *n* in ancient Greece, each of five magistrates elected in some Dorian states, especially Sparta, to supervise the king [Late 16C. Directly or via Latin < Greek *ephoros* "overseer" < *horan* "to see"] —**eph·or·al** *adj* —**eph·or·ate** *n*

E·phra·im·ite /éefree ə mìt/ *n* **1.** a member of the Hebrew tribe of Ephraim **2.** somebody who was born in the northern kingdom of Israel

epi- *prefix* **1.** on, over, above ○ *epiphyte* ○ *epipelagic* **2.** around, near ○ *epicalyx* **3.** after, in addition ○ *epiphenomenon* [< Greek *epi* "upon"]

ep·i·blast /éppi blàst/ *n* the outer layer of cells in an early embryo (**blastula**). It develops into ectoderm. —**ep·i·blast·ic** /èppi blástik/ *adj*

e·pib·o·ly /i píbbəlee/ *n* the growth of a layer of rapidly dividing cells over a layer of more slowly dividing cells during embryo development in the eggs of birds and reptiles [Late 19C. < Greek *epibolē* "throwing on" < *epiballein* < *ballein* "to throw"] —**ep·i·bol·ic** /èppi bóllik/ *adj*

ep·ic /éppik/ *n* **1.** LONG NARRATIVE POEM a lengthy narrative poem in elevated language celebrating the adventures and achievements of a legendary or traditional hero, e.g., Homer's *Odyssey* **2.** ELEVATED NARRATIVE POETRY the genre of poetic epics ○ *This term we'll cover epic, romance, and allegory.* **3.** LARGE-SCALE PRODUCTION a work of literature, cinema, television, or theater that is large-scale and expensively produced and often deals with a historical theme **4.** LONG SERIES OF EVENTS a long series of events characterized by adventures or struggle ○ *Our trek across town turned out to be an epic.* ■ *adj* **1.** OF EPIC POETRY celebrating the adventures and achievements of a legendary or traditional hero, in elevated language ○ *Milton's "Paradise Lost" is an epic poem.* **2.** IN STYLE OF EPIC POETRY having some of the characteristics of an epic ○ *an epic story of true love and adventure* **3.** VERY LARGE OR HEROIC impressive by virtue of greatness of size, scope, or heroism ○ *a scandal of epic proportions* [Late 16C. Via Latin < Greek *epikos* < *epos* "word, song," from *ep-*, stem of *eipein* "to say"] —**ep·i·cal** *adj* —**ep·i·cal·ly** *adv*

ep·i·ca·lyx /èppi káyliks, -kálliks/ (*plural* **-lyx·es** or **-ly·ces** /-li seez/) *n* a ring of modified leaves (**bracts**) that looks like an extra calyx at the base of a flower, e.g., in strawberries

ep·i·can·thic fold /èppi kanthik-/, **ep·i·can·thus** /-kánthəss/ (*plural* **-thi** /-thī/) *n* a fold of skin from the eyelid that partially covers the part of the eye nearest the nose

ep·i·carp /éppi kaarp/ *n* BOT same as **exocarp**

ep·i·cene /éppi seen/ *adj* **1.** HAVING CHARACTERISTICS OF BOTH GENDERS having both male and female characteristics **2.** NEITHER MALE NOR FEMALE of neither male nor female gender **3.** WEAK lacking vigor and strength **4.** WITH FEMALE CHARACTERISTICS describes a male having typically female characteristics (*literary*) **5.** GRAM SAME FOR MASCULINE AND FEMININE having only one grammatical form for both masculine and feminine in languages where nouns have genders ■ *n* **1.** SOMEBODY OF UNCLEAR GENDER a person of indeterminate gender (*literary*) **2.** GRAM EPICENE NOUN a noun with the same grammatical form for both masculine and feminine in languages where nouns have genders [15C. Via late Latin < Greek *epikoinos* "in common" < *koinos* "common"] —**ep·i·cen·ism** /éppissi nìzzəm/ *n*

ep·i·cen·ter /éppi sèntər/ *n* **1.** the exact location on the Earth's surface directly above the focus of an earthquake or underground nuclear explosion **2.** the very center or focal point ○ *Paris is the epicenter of the fashion world.* [Mid-19C. < Greek *epikentron* < *epikentros* "situated on a center" < *kentros* "center"] —**ep·i·cen·tral** /èppi séntrəl/ *adj*

ep·i·cot·yl /éppi kòtt'l/ *n* the tip of a plant embryo above the embryonic leaves (**cotyledons**) that gives rise to the stem of the new plant [Late 19C. < EPI- + Greek *kotulē* "cup, socket"]

ep·ic sim·i·le *n* a lengthy simile developed over a number of lines of verse in narrative poetry

Ep·ic·te·tus /èppik téetəss/ (A.D. 55–135) Greek philosopher. An advocate of Stoicism, he taught philosophy in Rome, preaching a doctrine of tolerance and calm acceptance of fate.

ep·i·cure /éppi kyoor/ *n* **1.** somebody who has developed a refined taste for food **2.** somebody who loves sensual pleasure and luxury [14C. < medieval Latin *epicurus*, after *Epicurus* "Epicurus"] —**ep·i·cur·ism** *n*

ep·i·cu·re·an /èppikyə rée ən, èppi kyóoree ən/ *adj* **1.** devoted to sensual pleasures and luxury, especially good food **2.** suitable for or pleasing to an epicure ○ *epicurean delicacies* ■ *n* same as **epicure** (sense 2) [14C. < French *épicurien* or Latin *epicureus*, after *Epicurus* "Epicurus"]

Ep·i·cu·re·an *adj* relating to the philosophy of Epicureanism ■ *n* a follower of Epicureanism

Ep·i·cu·re·an·ism /èppikyə rée ə nìzzəm, èppi kyóoree-/ *n* the school of philosophy founded by Epicurus, or its teachings

Ep·i·cu·rus /èppi kyóorəss/ (341–270 B.C.) Greek philosopher. His philosophy, Epicureanism, taught that the greatest good is freedom from pain and emotional disturbance.

> "If you fight against all your sensations, you will have no standard to which to refer, and thus no means of judging even those judgments which you pronounce false."
> [Epicurus, *The Principal Doctrines*; 4th century B.C.]

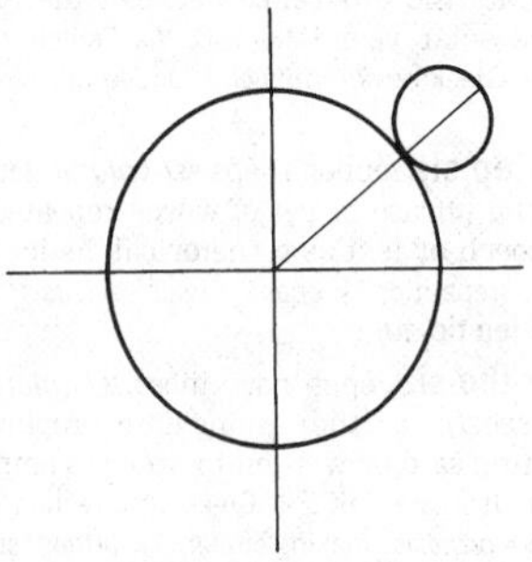

epicycle (sense 2)

ep·i·cy·cle /éppi sìk'l/ *n* **1.** in the Ptolemaic theory of the solar system, a circle that is followed by a planet, the circle itself being centered on a larger circle within which is the Earth. The epicycle accounts for irregularities of planetary motion in geocentric astronomy. **2.** a circle that rolls around the circumference of another circle, either inside or outside [14C. Via French or late Latin < Greek *epikuklos* < *kuklos* "circle"] —**ep·i·cy·clic** /èppi síklik, -síklik/ *adj* —**ep·i·cy·cli·cal** *adj*

ep·i·cy·clic train *n* a system of gears arranged such that one or more gears engage with and revolve around a fixed or moving part

ep·i·cy·cloid /èppi sī klòyd/ *n* a mathematical curve traced by a point on the circumference of a circle that rolls around the outside of the circumference of another circle —**ep·i·cy·cloid·al** /-sī klóyd'l/ *adj*

ep·i·dem·ic /èppi démmik/ *n* **1.** FAST-SPREADING DISEASE an outbreak of a disease that spreads more quickly and more extensively among a group of people than would normally be expected **2.** RAPID DEVELOPMENT a rapid and extensive development or growth, usually of something unpleasant ○ *an epidemic of civil unrest and rioting* ■ *adj* SPREADING UNUSUALLY QUICKLY AND EXTENSIVELY spreading more quickly and more extensively than would usually be expected ○ *Influenza was epidemic.* [Early 17C. < French *épidémique* < *épidémie* "an epidemic" < Greek *epidēmia* "disease prevalent among the people" < *dēmos* "people"] —**ep·i·dem·i·cal·ly** *adv* —**ep·i·de·mic·i·ty** /èppidə míssətee/ *n*

USAGE See *endemic*.

SYNONYMS See *widespread*.

ep·i·de·mi·ol·o·gy /èppi deemee óllәjee, -dèmmee-/ *n* **1.** the scientific and medical study of the causes and transmission of disease within a population **2.** the origin and development characteristics of a specific disease [Late 19C. < Greek *epidēmia* (see EPIDEMIC)] —**ep·i·de·mi·o·log·ic** /-deemee ə lójjik, -dèmmee-/ *adj* —**ep·i·de·mi·o·log·i·cal·ly** *adv* —**ep·i·de·mi·ol·o·gist** *n*

ep·i·der·mis /èppi dúrmiss/ *n* **1.** OUTER LAYER OF SKIN the thin outermost layer of the skin, itself made up of several layers, that covers and protects the underlying dermis **2.** ZOOL OUTER LAYER OF INVERTEBRATES' CELLS the outer layer of cells of invertebrates that secretes the protective waxy cuticle **3.** BOT OUTER CELL LAYER OF PLANT the outermost layer of cells of a plant. In woody plants the epidermis is usually replaced by corky protective tissue (**periderm**). [Early 17C. Via late Latin < Greek, "outer skin" < *derma* "skin"] —**ep·i·der·mal** *adj* —**ep·i·der·mic** *adj* —**ep·i·der·moid** *adj*

ep·i·di·a·scope /èppi dī ə skòp/ *n* a device for projecting an enlarged image of an opaque or transparent object onto a screen

ep·i·did·y·mis /èppi díddimiss/ (*plural* **-mi·des** /-mə deez/) *n* a coiled tube attached to the back and upper side of the testicle that stores sperm and is connected to the vas deferens [Early 17C. < Greek *epididumis* < *didumis* "testicle, twin" < *duo* "two"] —**ep·i·did·y·mal** *adj*

ep·i·dote /éppi dòt/ *n* a shiny green, yellow, or black hydrous aluminosilicate mineral containing calcium and iron. Source: metamorphic rocks. [Early 19C. < French *épidote* < Greek *epididonai* "give in addition" < *didonai* "give"; from its very long crystals] —**ep·i·dot·ic** /èppi dóttik/ *adj*

ep·i·du·ral /èppi dóorəl/ *n* a local anesthetic injected into the space between the outer membrane covering the spinal cord and the overlying bones of the spine. It is often used in childbirth. ■ *adj* located on or outside the outermost membrane covering the brain and spinal cord (**dura mater**) [Late 19C. < EPI- + *dura* < DURA MATER]

ep·i·fau·na /éppi fàwnə/ *npl* animals that live on the sea floor or attached to other animals or objects under water —**ep·i·fau·nal** /èppi fáwn'l/ *adj*

ep·i·fo·cal /èppi fók'l/ *adj* located or occurring at the point on the Earth's surface directly above the focus (**epicenter**) of an earthquake or underground nuclear explosion

ep·i·gam·ic /èppi gámmik/ *adj* describes a trait or behavior that attracts a mate, e.g., large antlers or bright colors [Late 19C. < EPI- + Greek *gamos* "marriage"]

ep·i·gas·tri·um /èppi gástree əm/ (*plural* **-tri·a** /-tree ə/) *n* the upper middle part of the abdomen [Late 17C. Via late Latin < Greek *epigastrion* < *epigastrios* "over the stomach" < *gaster* "stomach"]

ep·i·ge·al /èppi jée əl/ *adj* **1.** living or growing on, or right above the surface of the ground. ◊ **hypogeal** (sense 2) **2.** describes seed germination in which the embryo elongates so that the seed leaves (**cotyledons**) are carried above the soil to form the first leaves of the new plant [Mid-19C. < Greek *epigeios* "on the earth" < *gē* "earth"]

ep·i·gene /éppi jeen/ *adj* formed or occurring at the Earth's surface, especially with reference to weathering, erosion, and deposition [Early 19C. Via French < Greek *epigenēs* "born on or after" < *-genēs* "born"]

ep·i·gen·e·sis /èppi jénnəssiss/ *n* **1.** the theory that the development of tissues and organs during embryonic development proceeds by successive gradual change **2.** change in the mineral content or structure of a rock through external influences, e.g., the injection of a vein of ore into existing rock —**ep·i·gen·e·sist** *n* —**e·pig·e·nist** /i píjjənist/ *n*

ep·i·ge·net·ic /èppi jə néttik/ *adj* **1.** BIOL OF EXTERNAL ORIGIN having an external rather than a genetic origin **2.** BIOL DEVELOPING BY GRADUAL CHANGE relating to embryo development by gradual change **3.** GENETICS OF GENE CONTROL UNASSOCIATED WITH DNA relating to the control of changes in gene function that do not involve changes in DNA sequences **4.** GEOL CHANGING

AFTER FORMATION relating to changes in rock formations —**ep·i·ge·net·i·cal·ly** *adv*

ep·i·ge·net·ics /èppi jə néttiks/ *n* control of changes in gene function that do not involve changes in DNA sequences (*takes a singular verb*)

ep·i·ge·nome /èppi jée nõm/ *n* a subset of genes whose function is controlled by specific biochemical factors as well as by their DNA sequence —**ep·i·ge·nom·ic** /-jə nómmik, -jə nõmik/ *adj*

ep·i·ge·nom·ics /èppi jə nómmiks, -nõmiks/ *n* the study of the biochemical networks and linkages that control the function of genes within the epigenome (*takes a singular verb*)

e·pig·e·nous /i píjjənəss/ *adj* on or growing on the upper surface of something such as a leaf. ◊ **hypogenous**

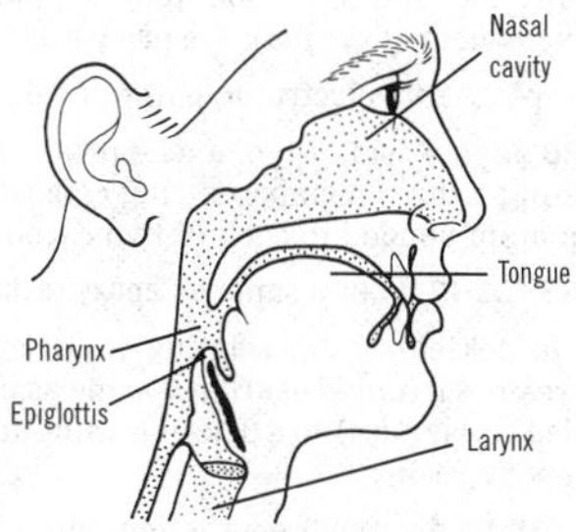

epiglottis

ep·i·glot·tis /èppi glóttiss/ (*plural* **-ti·ses** or **-tid·es** /-ti dèez/) *n* a flap of cartilage situated at the base of the tongue that covers the opening to the air passages when swallowing, preventing food or liquids from entering the windpipe (**trachea**) [15C. < Greek *epiglōttis*, literally "on the tongue" < *glōtta* (see GLOTTIS)] —**ep·i·glot·tal** *adj* —**ep·i·glot·tic** *adj*

ep·i·gone /éppi gõn/, **ep·i·gon** /-gòn/ *n* a mediocre imitator of somebody else, especially of an important artist or philosopher (*literary*) [Mid-18C. Via French < Greek *epigonos* "offspring" < *gignesthai* "be born"] —**ep·i·gon·ic** /èppi gónnik/ *adj* —**ep·i·gon·ism** /i píggə nìzzəm/ *n* —**ep·i·gon·ous** /i píggənəss/ *adj*

ep·i·gram /éppi gràm/ *n* **1.** WITTY SAYING a concise, witty, and often paradoxical remark or saying **2.** LITERAT SHORT POEM a short poem, often expressing a single idea, that is usually satirical and has a witty ending **3.** WITTY FORM OF EXPRESSION a witty or concise mode of expression, either written or spoken [15C. Directly or via French < Latin *epigramma* < Greek < *graphein* "write"] —**ep·i·gram·ma·tism** /èppi grámmə tìzzəm/ *n* —**ep·i·gram·ma·tist** /èppi grámmətist/ *n*

ep·i·gram·mat·ic /èppigrə máttik/, **ep·i·gram·mat·i·cal** /-máttik'l/ *adj* **1.** containing or in the form of an epigram **2.** tending to use epigrams —**ep·i·gram·mat·i·cal·ly** *adv*

ep·i·gram·ma·tize /èppi grámmə tìz/ (**-mat·ized, -ma·tiz·ing, -mat·iz·es**) *vti* to create a short and witty poem or saying about something

ep·i·graph /éppi gràf/ *n* **1.** a quotation at the beginning of a book, chapter, or section of a book, usually related to its theme **2.** an inscription on something such as a statue or building [Late 16C. < Greek *epigraphē* < *epigraphein* "write on" < *graphein* "write"] —**ep·i·graph·ic** /èppi gráffik/ *adj* —**ep·i·graph·i·cal** *adj* —**ep·i·graph·i·cal·ly** *adv*

e·pig·ra·phy /i píggrəfee/ *n* **1.** the study and deciphering of ancient inscriptions **2.** inscriptions or introductory quotations as a whole —**e·pig·ra·pher** *n* —**e·pig·ra·phist** *n*

e·pig·y·nous /i píjjənəss/ *adj* describes a flower in which the sepals, petals, and stamens arise from the enlarged tip of the flower axis (**receptacle**) above the ovary [Mid-19C. < modern Latin *epigynus* < Greek *gunē* "woman, pistil"] —**e·pig·y·ny** *n*

ep·i·la·tion /èppi láysh'n/ *n* COSMETICS same as **depilation** [Late 19C. < French *épilation* < *épiler* "remove hair" < Latin *pilus* "hair"]

ep·i·lep·sy /éppi lèpsee/ (*plural* **-sies**) *n* a medical disorder involving episodes of irregular electrical discharge in the brain and characterized by the periodic sudden loss or impairment of consciousness, often accompanied by convulsions [Mid-16C. Via French < Greek *epilēpsia* "seizure" < *epilambanein* "seize" < *lambanein* "grasp"]

ep·i·lep·tic /èppi léptik/ *adj* relating to or affected by epilepsy ■ *n* an offensive term for somebody who has epilepsy [Early 17C. Via French < Greek *epilēptikos* < *epilēpsia* (see EPILEPSY)] —**ep·i·lep·ti·cal·ly** *adv*

ep·i·lep·ti·form /èppi lépti fàwrm/ *adj* resembling epilepsy ○ *epileptiform convulsions*

ep·i·lep·to·gen·ic /èppi leptə jénnik/ *adj* causing or able to cause an epileptic episode

ep·i·lep·toid /èppi lép tòyd/ *adj* **1.** MED same as **epileptiform 2.** showing symptoms similar to those of epilepsy

ep·i·lim·ni·on /èppi límnee òn, -ən/ (*plural* **-ni·a** /-nee ə/) *n* the uppermost circulating layer of warm water in a lake with different temperatures at different levels in summer [Early 20C. < EPI- + Greek *limnion* "small lake" < *limnē* "lake"]

ep·i·logue /éppi lòg/, **ep·i·log** *n* **1.** LITERAT SHORT SECTION AT END OF BOOK a short chapter or section at the end of a literary work, sometimes detailing the fate of its characters **2.** THEATER CONCLUDING SPEECH a short speech, usually in verse, that an actor addresses directly to the audience at the end of a play **3.** THEATER ACTOR GIVING SHORT SPEECH the actor who addresses a short speech, usually in verse, directly to the audience at the end of a play [15C. Via French < Greek *epilogos* "additional speech" < *logos* "speech"]

ep·i·mys·i·um /èppi mízzee əm, -mízhee-/ (*plural* **-i·a** /-ee ə/) *n* the covering of connective tissue surrounding a muscle [Early 20C. < modern Latin < Greek *mus* (see MUSCLE)]

ep·i·nas·ty /éppi nàstee/ (*plural* **-ties**) *n* the outward and downward bending of a plant part resulting from different growth rates on the upper and lower sides [Late 19C. < EPI- + Greek *nastos* "pressed together"] —**ep·i·nas·tic** /èppi nástik/ *adj*

ep·i·neph·rine /èppi néffrin/, **ep·i·neph·rin** *n* **1.** a synthetic form of adrenaline. Use: to relax the airways and constrict blood vessels. **2.** the hormone adrenaline (*technical*) [Late 19C. < EPI- + Greek *nephros* "kidney"]

ep·i·neu·ri·um /èppi nóoree əm/ (*plural* **-ri·a** /-ree ə/) *n* a sheath of connective tissue around a nerve [Late 19C. < modern Latin < Greek *neuron* "nerve"] —**ep·i·neu·ri·al** /èppi nóoree əl/ *adj*

ep·i·pe·lag·ic /èppipə lájjik/ *adj* relating to or living in the upper zone of the ocean, from the surface to a depth of about 656 ft./200 m

Ep·i·Pen /éppee pèn/ *tdmk* a trademark for a portable disposable hypodermic syringe that has a spring-activated needle and contains epinephrine, for use in an emergency by somebody with severe allergic reactions or asthma

e·piph·a·ny /i píffənee/ (*plural* **-nies**) *n* **1.** a sudden intuitive leap of understanding, especially through an ordinary but striking occurrence ○ *It came to him in an epiphany what his life's work was to be.* **2.** the supposed manifestation of a divine being [Early 17C. See EPIPHANY] —**ep·i·phan·ic** /èppə fánnik/ *adj*

E·piph·a·ny /i píffənee/ *n* a Christian festival marking the visit of the Magi to celebrate Jesus Christ's birth or, in the Eastern Orthodox Church, the baptism of Jesus Christ. Date: January 6. [14C. Via French < Greek *epiphaneia* "manifestation" < *epiphanein* "to manifest" < *phanein* "to show"]

ep·i·phe·nom·e·nal·ism /èppifə nómmən'l ìzzəm/ *n* the view that consciousness is merely an aftereffect of physical processes in the brain and nervous system —**ep·i·phe·nom·e·nal·ist** *n*

ep·i·phe·nom·e·non /èppifə nómmə nòn/ (*plural* **-na** /-nə/) *n* **1.** a secondary phenomenon resulting from another **2.** a secondary incidental condition or symptom that appears during the course of an illness —**ep·i·phe·nom·e·nal** *adj* —**ep·i·phe·nom·e·nal·ly** *adv*

e·piph·y·sis /i píffissis/ (*plural* **-y·ses** /-i sèez/) *n* the end of a long bone that fuses with the shaft of the bone at the point where it was previously separated by cartilage to allow bone growth. Once the epiphyses fuse no further growth of long bones is possible. ◊ **diaphysis** [Mid-17C. Via modern Latin < Greek *epiphusis* "growing on" < *phusis* "growth"] —**ep·i·phys·e·al** /èppi fízzee əl/ *adj*

ep·i·phyte /éppi fìt/ *n* a plant that grows on top of or is supported by another plant but does not depend on it for nutrition. Mosses, tropical orchids, and many ferns are epiphytes. —**ep·i·phyt·ic** /èppi fíttik/ *adj* —**ep·i·phyt·i·cal·ly** *adv*

ep·i·phy·tot·ic /èppi fì tóttik/ *adj* describes an outbreak of disease that rapidly affects many plants in a specific area ■ *n* an outbreak of a plant disease that suddenly and rapidly affects many plants in a specific area

Epis. *abbr* **1.** *also* **Episc.** CHR Episcopal **2.** *also* **Episc.** CHR Episcopalian **3.** BIBLE Epistle

e·pi·sci·a /i píshə, i píshee ə/ *n* a plant with hairy leaves that is related to the African violet. Flowers: orange, pink, yellow. Native to: tropical America. Genus: *Episcia*. [Mid-19C. < modern Latin < Greek *episkios* "shaded" < *skia* "shadow"]

e·pis·co·pa·cy /i pískəpəssee/ *n* **1.** church government by bishops, as in the Roman Catholic, Eastern, and Episcopal Churches **2.** CHR same as **episcopate** (sense 3) [Mid-17C. < ecclesiastical Latin *episcopatus* (see EPISCOPATE)]

e·pis·co·pal /i pískəp'l/ *adj* **1.** relating to a bishop or bishops **2.** involving or recognizing church government by bishops [15C. < French *épiscopal* or ecclesiastical Latin *episcopalis* < *episcopus* (see BISHOP)] —**e·pis·co·pal·ly** *adv*

E·pis·co·pal *adj* relating to the Protestant Episcopal Church of North America or Scotland

E·pis·co·pal Church *n* an independent branch of the Anglican Church in North America and Scotland

e·pis·co·pa·lian /i pìskə páylee ən/ *adj* adhering to or practicing church government by bishops ■ *n* a supporter of church government by bishops —**e·pis·co·pa·lian·ism** *n*

E·pis·co·pa·lian *adj* relating to or belonging to the Episcopal Church of North America or Scotland ■ *n* a member of the Episcopal Church —**E·pis·co·pal·ian·ism** *n*

e·pis·co·pal·ism /i pískəp'l ìzzəm/ *n* the belief that authority in a church government should lie in a group of bishops

e·pis·co·pate /i pískəpət, -pàyt/ *n* **1.** OFFICE OR POSITION OF BISHOP the office, position, or term of office of a bishop **2.** DIOCESE a bishop's diocese or jurisdiction **3.** BISHOPS bishops as a group [Mid-17C. < ecclesiastical Latin *episcopatus* < *episcopus* (see BISHOP)]

e·pi·scope /éppi skõp/ *n UK* OPTICS same as **opaque projector**

e·pi·si·ot·o·my /i peezee óttəmee/ (*plural* **-mies**) *n* an incision sometimes made to enlarge the vaginal opening in the late stages of labor to prevent tearing and facilitate the birth [Late 19C. < Greek *epision* "pubic region"]

ep·i·sode /éppi sõd/ *n* **1.** SIGNIFICANT INCIDENT an event that is a part of but distinct from a greater whole and that often has specific significance ○ *Let's try to put this unfortunate episode behind us, OK?* **2.** LITERAT, MEDIA PART OF SERIALIZED WORK a part of a serialized story or program that is published or broadcast separately **3.** LITERAT EVENT IN NARRATIVE an incident, description, or series of events in a narrative that is part of the whole but may digress from the main plot ○ *The episode in the library reveals a lot about the main character.* **4.** MED OCCURRENCE OF ILLNESS an occurrence of a particular illness or symptom of an illness, usually one of a connected series, often repeated over a period of time ○ *episodes of breathlessness and chest pain* **5.** THEATER SECTION OF GREEK TRAGEDY a section of an ancient Greek tragedy between two choruses **6.** MUSIC DIGRESSIVE MUSICAL PASSAGE a digressive passage between two musical themes, e.g., in a rondo or fugue [Late 17C. < Greek *epeisodion* "addition," form of *epeisodios* "coming in besides" < *eisodos* "coming in" < *hodos* "road"]

ep·i·sod·ic /èppi sóddik/, **ep·i·sod·i·cal** /-sóddik'l/ *adj* **1.** OF EPISODE relating to or resembling an episode **2.** DIVIDED INTO EPISODES divided into or composed of closely connected but independent sections **3.**

SPORADIC happening at irregular intervals ○ *episodic pain in the lower back* **4.** TEMPORARY of a limited duration ○ *episodic wind squalls* —**ep·i·sod·i·cal·ly** *adv*

ep·i·some /éppi sōm/ *n* a genetic unit that can multiply independently in host cells or when integrated with a chromosome. Bacterial plasmids are examples of episomes. [Mid-20C. < EPI- + Greek *sōma* "body"] —**ep·i·so·mal** /èppi sṓm'l/ *adj* —**ep·i·so·mal·ly** *adv*

e·pis·ta·sis /i pístəssiss/ (*plural* **-ta·ses** /-tə seēz/) *n* the nonappearance of a characteristic determined by one gene because it has been suppressed or masked by the activity of another gene [Early 19C. < Greek, "stoppage" < *ephistanai* "to stop" < *histanai* "put"] —**ep·i·stat·ic** /èppi státtik/ *adj*

ep·i·stax·is /èppi stáksiss/ (*plural* **-stax·es** /-sták seēz/) *n* MED same as **nosebleed** (*technical*) [Late 18C. Via modern Latin < Greek < *epistazein* "to drip at (the nose)" < *stazein* "to drip"]

ep·i·ste·mic /èppi steēmik, -stémmik/ *adj* relating to knowledge [Early 20C. < Greek *epistēmē* "knowledge" < *epistasthai* "know" < *histasthai* "to stand"] —**ep·i·ste·mi·cal·ly** *adv*

ep·i·ste·mics /èppi steēmiks, -stémmiks/ *n* the use of logic, philosophy, psychology, and linguistics to study knowledge and the way it is processed by humans (*takes a singular verb*)

e·pis·te·mol·o·gy /i pìstə mólləjee/ *n* the branch of philosophy that studies the nature of knowledge, in particular its foundations, scope, and validity [Mid-19C. < Greek *epistēmē* (see EPISTEMIC)] —**e·pis·te·mo·log·i·cal** /i pìstəmə lójjik'l/ *adj* —**e·pis·te·mo·log·i·cal·ly** *adv* —**e·pis·te·mol·o·gist** *n*

e·pis·tle /i píss'l/ *n* **1.** a long formal letter, often intended to provide instruction (*formal*) **2.** a literary work in the form of a letter [12C. Directly or via French < Latin *epistola* < Greek *epistolē* "something sent" < *stellein* "send"]

E·pis·tle *n* **1.** a letter written by the apostle Paul or other early Christian writers and included as a book of the Bible **2.** an excerpt from one of the Epistles read as part of a service in a Christian church

e·pis·tle side, **E·pis·tle Side** *n* the right-hand side of a Christian church as somebody faces the altar [Because an excerpt from one of the Epistles is traditionally read from there as part of the Communion service]

e·pis·to·lar·y /i pístə lèrree/, **e·pis·to·la·to·ry** /i pístələ tàwree/ *adj* **1.** associated with, conducted by, or suitable for letters (*formal*) **2.** taking the form of a letter or a series of letters ○ *an epistolary novel* [Mid-17C. Directly or via French < Latin *epistolaris* < *epistola* (see EPISTLE)]

e·pis·tro·phe /i pístrəfee/ *n* repetition of a word or phrase at the end of consecutive clauses or sentences for rhetorical effect [Late 16C. < Greek < *epistrephein* "turn around" < *strephein* "to turn"]

ep·i·style /éppi stīl/ *n* ARCHIT same as **architrave** (sense 1) [Mid-16C. Directly or via French < Latin *epistylium* < Greek *epistulion* "on a column" < *stulos* "column"]

ep·i·taph /éppi tàf/ *n* **1.** an inscription on a tombstone or monument commemorating the person buried there **2.** a short speech or piece of writing celebrating the life of a recently deceased person [14C. Via French < Greek *epitaphion* "something above a tomb or burial" < *taphos* "funeral ceremonies, tomb"] —**ep·i·taph·ic** /èppi táffik/ *adj*

e·pit·a·sis /i píttəssiss/ (*plural* **-a·ses** /-ə seēz/) *n* in classical drama, the middle part of a play that develops the main action [Late 16C. Via modern Latin < Greek < *epiteinein* "intensify, stretch upon" < *teinein* "to stretch"]

ep·i·tax·y /éppi tàksee/ *n* growth of a layer of crystal on a single crystal of another substance [Mid-20C. < French *épitaxie* "growth on" < Greek *taxis* "growth"] —**ep·i·tax·i·al** /èppi táksee əl/ *adj*

ep·i·tha·la·mi·um /èppithə láymee əm/ (*plural* **-mi·a** /-mee ə/), **ep·i·tha·la·mi·on** /-mee ən, -mee òn/ *n* a poem or song written or performed in celebration of a wedding [Late 16C. < Greek *epithalamion* "(song sung) at the bridal chamber" < *thalamos* "bridal chamber"] —**ep·i·tha·la·mic** /-lámmik/ *adj*

ep·i·the·li·a ANAT plural of **epithelium**

ep·i·the·li·al /èppi theēlee əl/ *adj* describes tissue that forms a thin protective layer on exposed bodily surfaces and forms the lining of internal cavities, ducts, and organs

ep·i·the·li·al·ize /èppi theēlee ə līz/ (**-ized, -iz·ing, -iz·es**), **ep·i·the·lize** /-theē līz/ *vti* to become, or cause a part of the body to become, covered with epithelial tissue, as in the healing of a wound —**ep·i·the·li·al·i·za·tion** /epi theēlee əli záysh'n/ *n*

ep·i·the·li·um /èppi theēlee əm/ (*plural* **-li·a** /-lee ə/ or **-li·ums**) *n* a thin layer of tightly packed cells lining internal cavities, ducts, and organs of animals and covering exposed bodily surfaces, especially in wounds that are healing [Mid-18C. < modern Latin < Greek *thēlē* "teat, nipple"]

ep·i·the·lize *vti* MED same as **epithelialize** —**ep·i·the·li·za·tion** /èppi theeli záysh'n/ *n*

ep·i·ther·mal /èppi thúrm'l/ *adj* describes veins of gold or silver originally formed deep within the Earth's crust from ascending hot solutions

ep·i·thet /éppi thèt/ *n* **1.** INSULT an abusive insulting word or phrase **2.** DESCRIPTIVE WORD ADDED TO NAME a descriptive word or phrase added to or substituted for the name of somebody or something, highlighting a feature or quality ○ *easy to see how she earned herself the epithet "The All-Knowing"* **3.** BIOL PART OF TAXONOMIC NAME in biological classification, the species name that follows the genus name [Late 16C. Directly or via French *épithète* < Latin *epitheton* "something added" < Greek *epitheto*, past participle of *epitithenai* "put on" < *tithenai* "to place"] —**ep·i·thet·ic** /èppi théttik/ *adj* —**ep·i·thet·i·cal** *adj*

e·pit·o·me /i píttəmee/ *n* **1.** a highly representative example of a type, class, or characteristic ○ *Isn't she just the epitome of elegance?* **2.** a brief summary of a piece of writing (*formal*) [Early 16C. Via Latin < Greek < *epitemnein* "to cut short" < *temnein* "to cut"]

e·pit·o·mize /i píttə mīz/ (**-mized, -miz·ing, -miz·es**) *vt* **1.** to be a highly representative example of a type, class, or characteristic ○ *This incident epitomizes all that is wrong with modern society.* **2.** to write a brief summary of a piece of writing (*formal*) —**e·pit·o·mist** *n* —**e·pit·o·mi·za·tion** /i pìttəmi záysh'n/ *n*

~~epitomy~~ incorrect spelling of **epitome**

ep·i·zo·ic /èppi zṓ ik/ *adj* **1.** describes a nonparasitic animal or plant that lives on the external surface of a living animal **2.** describes plants whose seeds or spores are dispersed by being attached to the coats of animals —**ep·i·zo·ism** *n*

ep·i·zo·on /èppi zṓ òn/ (*plural* **-a** /-zṓ ə/), **ep·i·zo·ite** /-zṓ īt/ *n* an organism that lives on the external surface of a living animal [Mid-19C. < modern Latin, "on an animal" < Greek *zōion* "animal"] —**ep·i·zo·an** *adj*

ep·i·zo·ot·ic /èppi zō óttik/ *adj* describes an outbreak of disease that rapidly affects many animals in a specific area at the same time ■ *n* a disease that rapidly affects many animals in a specific area at the same time [Late 18C. < French *épizootique* "at animals" < Greek *zōion* "animal"] —**ep·i·zo·ot·i·cal·ly** *adv*

e plu·ri·bus u·num /ee plòori booss óonəm, -yóonəm/ one out of many (*used as the motto of the United States*) [Latin]

ep·och /éppək, eē pòk/ *n* **1.** SIGNIFICANT PERIOD a significant period in history or in somebody's life **2.** START OF HISTORICALLY SIGNIFICANT PERIOD the beginning of a long period of history considered particularly significant ○ *The invention of the telephone marked an epoch in the development of international communication.* **3.** GEOL UNIT OF GEOLOGIC TIME a unit of geologic time that is a division of a period and is characterized by rock formation ○ *the Holocene and Pleistocene epochs of the Quaternary period* **4.** ASTRON MOMENT IN TIME AS REFERENCE POINT a precise moment in time arbitrarily chosen as a reference point for defining the position of astronomical objects [Early 17C. Via modern Latin *epocha* < Greek *epokhē* "pause (in time)" < *ekhein* "to hold"] —**ep·och·al** /éppək'l, é pòk'l/ *adj*

ep·och-mak·ing *adj* having great historical importance or momentous significance ○ *Galileo's epoch-making discoveries*

ep·ode /ép ōd/ *n* **1.** in classical Greek drama, the part of a lyric ode that follows the strophe and the antistrophe **2.** a lyric ode characterized by couplets made up of a long line followed by a shorter one [Early 17C. Directly or via French < Latin *epodos* < Greek *epōidos* "sung after" < *ōidē* "song"]

ep·o·nym /éppə nìm/ *n* **1.** PERSON FOR WHOM SOMETHING IS NAMED a person or mythical character from whom something such as an invention, activity, or place takes its name **2.** NAME DERIVED FROM PERSON a name derived from the name of a person or mythical character. For example, "Rome" is an eponym coming from "Romulus." **3.** MED MEDICAL NAME FROM PERSON a medical name, e.g., that of a disease, derived from the name of a person [Mid-19C. < Greek *epōnumos* "given as a name" < *onuma* "name"] —**ep·o·nym·ic** /èppə nímmik/ *adj*

e·pon·y·mous /i pónnəməss/ *adj* having the name that is used as the title or name of something else, especially the title of a book, play, or movie ○ *the eponymous hero of the play* —**e·pon·y·mous·ly** *adv*

EPOS /eē pòss/ *abbr* electronic point of sale

ep·ox·ide /e pók sīd, i-/ *n* a chemical compound containing a three-membered ring consisting of an oxygen atom bonded to each of two carbon atoms

ep·ox·ide res·in *n* CHEM same as **epoxy resin**

ep·ox·y /e póksee, i-/ *adj* relating to an epoxide or epoxy resin ■ *n* (*plural* **-ies**) CHEM same as **epoxy resin** ■ *vt* (**-ied, -y·ing, -ies**) to stick one thing to another using epoxy resin

ep·ox·y res·in *n* a tough synthetic resin, containing epoxy groups, that sets after the application of heat or pressure. Use: adhesives, surface coatings.

Ep·ping For·est /épping-/ region of ancient woodland in Essex, southeastern England

EPROM /eē pròm/ *n* an integrated circuit that can be reprogrammed by a user to correct an error in the program or to add a function. Full form **erasable-programmable read-only memory**

eps *abbr* FIN earnings per share

ep·si·lon /épsi lòn, -lən/ *n* the fifth letter of the Greek alphabet, represented in the English alphabet as "e." See table at **alphabet** [Early 18C. < Greek *e psilon* "short e" (literally "bare e")]

Ep·som /épsəm/ city in Surrey, southeastern England. There is a racecourse on Epsom Downs, where the Derby horserace is run. Population: 90,437 (1991).

Ep·som salts *n* a bitter-tasting preparation of hydrated magnesium sulfate. Use: formerly, as a laxative and to reduce swelling. (*takes a singular verb*) [Because originally obtained from a mineral spring at EPSOM]

Ep·stein /ép stīn/, **Sir Jacob** (1880–1959) US-born British sculptor. His massively powerful, usually nude figures, including *Genesis* (1931), caused an uproar. His later portrait bronzes and monumental works were more immediately popular and less controversial.

Ep·stein-Barr vi·rus /èp stīn baár-/ *n* a virus believed to cause infectious mononucleosis and associated with burkitt's lymphoma and some carcinomas [Mid-20C. After M. A. *Epstein* (b. 1921) and Y. M. *Barr* (b. 1932), British virologists]

eq. *abbr* **1.** equal **2.** equation **3.** equivalent

E.Q. *n* the ratio of educational attainment to chronological age. Full form **educational quotient**

eq·ua·ble /ékwəb'l, eēk-/ *adj* **1.** calm and not easily disturbed ○ *She maintained the most equable of temperaments despite her financial problems.* **2.** free from variation and marked extremes [Mid-16C. < Latin *aequabilis* < *aequare* (see EQUATE)] —**eq·ua·bil·i·ty** /èkwə bíllətee, eēkwə-/ *n* —**eq·ua·ble·ness** *n* —**eq·ua·bly** *adv*

e·qual /eēkwəl/ *adj* **1.** IDENTICAL identical in size, quantity, value, or standard ○ *equal quantities of flour and sugar* **2.** WITH THE SAME RIGHTS having the same privileges, rights, status, and opportunities as others **3.** WITH EVEN BALANCE evenly balanced between opposing sides ○ *hoping for a more equal match in the second game* **4.** EQUIPPED WITH NECESSARY QUALITIES equipped with the necessary qualities or means to accomplish something ○ *didn't think he would be equal to the task* **5.** US IMPARTIAL treating or affecting all things impartially ○ *marked all the students' papers with an equal pen* **6. EQUIVALENT** having the same effect, application, or meaning as somebody or something else ■ *n* **SOMEBODY OR SOMETHING EQUAL** somebody or something equal in quality to another ○ *The computers are equals in speed, and this one costs less.* ■ *v* (**e·qualed, e·qual·ing, e·quals**) **1.** *vt* **DO SOMETHING EQUAL TO SOMETHING ELSE** to do, produce, or achieve something to the same standard or of the same value as something else ○ *And with that jump, she has equaled the world record.* **2.** *vi* **BECOME EQUAL** to become identical ○ *It will all equal out in the end.* **3.** *vt* MATH **HAVE SAME VALUE AS SOMETHING ELSE** to be equal to something else, usually in value ○ *Two plus two equals four.* [14C. < Latin *aequalis* < *aequus* "equal, even"] ◇ **first among equals** the most powerful or influential person in a group whose members are supposed to have equal status

e·qual-ar·e·a *adj* on a map projection, accurately representing the relative sizes of regions that are of equal area, although distorting shape and direction

e·qual·i·tar·i·an /i kwòlli térree ən/ *n, adj* POL same as **egalitarian** —**e·qual·i·tar·i·an·ism** *n*

e·qual·i·ty /i kwóllətee, ee-/ (*plural* **-ties**) *n* **1.** rights, treatment, quantity, or value equal to all others in a specific group ○ *full equality under the law* **2.** an equation in which the quantities on each side of an equal sign are the same

E·qual·i·ty State *n* a nickname for Wyoming

e·qual·ize /éekwə līz/ (**-ized, -iz·ing, -iz·es**) *v* **1.** *vt* **MAKE THINGS EQUAL** to make things uniform or equal ○ *You must equalize the liquid levels in each bottle.* **2.** *vt* *US* ELECTRONICS **ADJUST ELECTRONIC SIGNAL** to adjust the amplitude of an electronic signal **3.** *vi* *UK* **ACHIEVE SAME SCORE** to score a point or goal that brings a score level with that of an opponent ○ *They equalized just before halftime.* —**e·qual·i·za·tion** /èekwəli záysh'n/ *n*

e·qual·iz·er /éekwə līzər/ *n* **1. SOMEBODY OR SOMETHING THAT EQUALIZES THINGS** somebody or something that makes things uniform or equal **2.** ELECTRONICS **ELECTRONIC SOUND ADJUSTER** an electronic device used to reduce distortion in a sound system by internally adjusting the system's response to different audio frequencies **3.** *UK* SPORTS **GOAL OR POINT THAT LEVELS SCORES** a goal or point that brings a person's or team's score level with that of an opponent **4.** *regional* **PIVOTING BAR ON HORSE-DRAWN VEHICLE** a pivoting bar or set of bars on a horse-drawn carriage or other vehicle that equalizes the force of two or more whiffletrees

e·qual·ly /éekwəlee/ *adv* **1. IN SAME WAY** in an identical or uniform way ○ *treat people equally* **2. TO SAME EXTENT** to the same degree or extent ○ *This issue is equally important.* **3. IN SAME SIZED AMOUNTS** in parts or amounts of the same size ○ *Divide it equally between four people.* **4. AT SAME TIME** used to introduce a second statement that is of equal importance to the first but may contrast or balance it ○ *I want the business to succeed, but, equally, I don't want to be working all the time.*

USAGE ***Equally*** and ***as*** cannot be used together. You can say *She is a brilliant pianist, and her brother is equally talented* or *She is a brilliant pianist, and her brother is as talented,* but not *She is a brilliant pianist, and her brother is equally as talented.*

e·qual op·por·tu·ni·ty *n* the availability of the same rights, position, and status to all people, regardless of gender, sexual preference, age, race, ethnicity, or religion (*hyphenated before a noun*) ○ *a company providing equal opportunity* ○ *an equal-opportunity policy*

e·qual pay *n* the right of two people performing the same job to be paid the same amount of money regardless of differences of sex or race

e·qual sign *n* a mathematical symbol (=) used to indicate that two or more numbers, symbols, or terms have the same value as each other

e·qual tem·per·a·ment *n* the division of a musical octave into 12 equal half steps in the tuning of an instrument

e·qual time *n* *US* a broadcasting policy that gives opposing political candidates equal airtime for radio and television campaigning

e·qua·nim·i·ty /èekwə nímmətee, èkwə-/ *n* evenness of temper even under stress ○ *faced his critical constituents with equanimity* [Early 17C. < Latin *aequanimitas* < *aequus* "equal, even" + *animus* "mind"] —**e·quan·i·mous** /i kwónnəməss/ *adj*

e·quate /i kwáyt/ (**e·quat·ed, e·quat·ing, e·quates**) *v* **1.** *vt* **CONSIDER AS EQUIVALENT TO SOMETHING** to treat, show, or consider something as equivalent to something else ○ *equating money with happiness* **2.** *vt* *US* **REDUCE SOMETHING TO THE SAME LEVEL** to reduce something to the same level or value as something else **3.** *vt* MATH **FORM SOMETHING INTO EQUATION** to put something into the form of an equation involving an equality **4.** *vi* **APPEAR TO BE EQUAL** to be or appear to be the same (*formal*) ○ *Their two accounts of the incident seem to equate.* [15C. < Latin *aequat-*, past participle of *aequare* "make equal" < *aequus* "equal, even"] —**e·quat·a·bil·i·ty** /i kwàytə bíllətee/ *n* —**e·quat·a·ble** *adj*

e·qua·tion /i kwáyzh'n, i kwáysh'n/ *n* **1.** MATH **STATEMENT OF EQUALITY** a mathematical statement that two expressions, usually divided by an equal sign, are of the same value **2. SITUATION INVOLVING MANY VARIABLE FACTORS** a situation that has two or more variable aspects to be considered ○ *The selling option just does not enter into the equation.* **3. ACT OF REGARDING AS EQUAL** the act or process of making things equal or considering them to be equal **4. STATE OF BEING EQUAL** the state of being the same or equivalent ○ *bring the balance of power into equation* **5.** CHEM **REPRESENTATION OF CHEMICAL REACTION** a written representation of the reactants and products in a chemical reaction —**e·qua·tion·al** *adj* —**e·qua·tion·al·ly** *adv*

e·qua·tion of state *n* an equation that states the relationship between the pressure, temperature, and volume of a gas or liquid

e·qua·tion of time *n* the difference between apparent solar time and mean solar time, usually expressed as a correction to the apparent time. It varies in a complex annual pattern between maxima of about 15 minutes in February and November.

e·qua·tor /i kwáytər/ *n* **1.** GEOG **IMAGINARY CIRCLE AROUND EARTH** the imaginary great circle around Earth that is the same distance from the North and South Poles and divides Earth into the northern and southern hemispheres **2.** ASTRON **IMAGINARY CIRCLE AROUND ASTRONOMICAL OBJECT** the imaginary great circle around an astronomical object that is everywhere the same distance from the Poles **3.** ASTRON same as **celestial equator 4.** MATH **CIRCLE DIVIDING SPHERE INTO TWO** a circle that divides a sphere or other surface into two equal parts [14C. Directly or via French < medieval Latin *aequator*, in *aequator diei et noctis* "equalizer of day and night" < Latin *aequare* (see EQUATE)]

e·qua·to·ri·al /èekwə táwree əl, èkwə-/ *adj* **1.** relating to or present near the equator **2.** situated in the plane of an equator —**e·qua·to·ri·al·ly** *adv*

e·qua·to·ri·al cur·rent *n* a current that moves in a westerly direction near the surface of an ocean at the equator

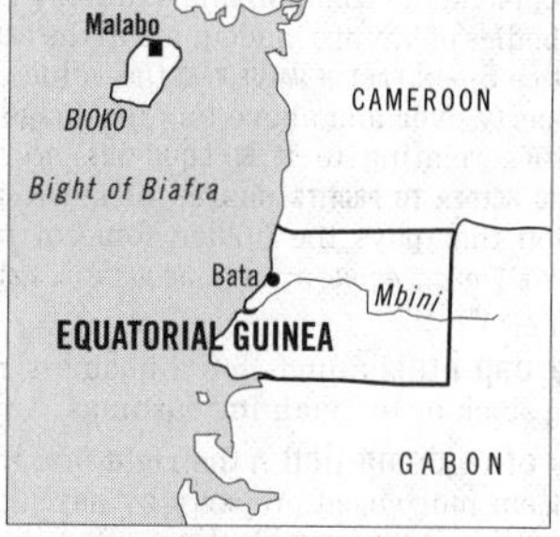

Equatorial Guinea

E·qua·to·ri·al Guin·ea /èekwə tawree əl-, èkwə-/ country in West Africa bordered by Cameroon, Gabon, and the Atlantic Ocean, and comprising a mainland section, Río Muni, and several islands. Language: Spanish. Currency: CFA franc. Capital: Malabo. Population: 510,473 (2003). Area: 10,831 sq. mi./28,051 sq. km. Official name **Republic of Equatorial Guinea**

e·qua·to·ri·al plate *n* the area midway between the poles of the spindle of a dividing cell, where chromosomes are aligned

e·qua·to·ri·al tel·e·scope *n* an astronomical telescope mounted so that it allows an astronomical object to be kept in view without adjustment as Earth rotates. This is accomplished by mounting it on two axes at right angles to each other, the one about which it rotates being parallel to Earth's axis.

eq·uer·ry /ékwəree/ (*plural* **-ries**) *n* **1.** an officer who is the personal attendant of the British monarch or a member of the royal family **2.** formerly, an officer in an aristocratic or royal household who was responsible for the supervision of the horses [Early 16C. Via obsolete French *escurie* < Old French *escuierie* "company of squires, prince's stables" < *escuier* (see ESQUIRE)]

e·ques·tri·an /i kwéstree ən/ *adj* **1. OF HORSES** relating to horses or horseback riding **2. DEPICTING SOMEBODY ON HORSEBACK** depicting somebody mounted on a horse ○ *an equestrian statue* **3. OF MOUNTED SOLDIERS** composed of soldiers on horseback ■ *n* **SKILLED RIDER** somebody who is skilled at riding horses or performing on horseback [Mid-17C. < Latin *equester* "of a horse-rider" < *eques* "horse-rider, knight" < *equus* "horse"] —**e·ques·tri·an·ism** *n*

e·ques·tri·enne /i kwèstree én/ *n* a woman who is skilled at riding horses or performing on horseback [Mid-19C. < EQUESTRIAN after French nouns ending in *-enne*]

equi- *prefix* equal ○ *equimolar* [< Latin *aequus*]

e·qui·an·gu·lar /èekwee áng gyələr, èkwee-/ *adj* describes a geometric figure in which all the angles are equal [Mid-17C. < late Latin *equiangulus* < Latin *angulus* "corner"]

e·qui·dis·tant /èekwi dístənt, èkwi-/ *adj* situated at the same distance from two or more places or points ○ *Baltimore is almost equidistant from Washington and Philadelphia.* [Late 16C. < French *équidistant* or medieval Latin *equidistant-* < Latin *distant-* (see DISTANT)] —**e·qui·dis·tance** *n* —**e·qui·dis·tant·ly** *adv*

e·qui·lat·er·al /èekwə láttərəl, èkwə-/ *adj* **WITH EQUAL SIDES** describes a geometric figure in which all the sides are of equal length ■ *n* **1. EQUAL-SIDED GEOMETRIC SHAPE** a geometric figure with all its sides of equal length **2. ANY SIDE OF EQUAL-SIDED GEOMETRIC SHAPE** any side of a geometric figure that is the same length as the other sides [Late 16C. Directly or via French *équilatéral* < late Latin *aequilateralis* < Latin *lateralis* (see LATERAL)] —**e·qui·lat·er·al·ly** *adv*

e·quil·i·brant /i kwíllibrənt/ *n* a force able to balance out another force and produce an equilibrium [Late 19C. < French *équilibrant* < *équilibre* "balance" < Latin *aequilibrium* (see EQUILIBRIUM)]

e·quil·i·brate /i kwíllə bràyt/ (**-brat·ed, -brat·ing, -brates**) *v* (*technical*) **1.** *vt* to counterbalance something, or bring something into a state of balance **2.** *vi* to be evenly balanced [Mid-17C. < late Latin *aequilibrat-*, past participle of *aequilibrare* < Latin *libra* "balance"] —**e·quil·i·bra·tion** /i kwìllə bráysh'n/ *n* —**e·quil·i·bra·tor** *n* —**e·quil·i·bra·to·ry** *adj*

e·quil·i·brist /i kwíllәbrist/ *n* a performer skilled in the art of balancing, especially tightrope walking (*archaic*)

e·qui·lib·ri·um /èekwə líbbree əm, èkwə líbb-/ (*plural* **-ri·ums** or **-ri·a** /-ree ə/) *n* **1. BODILY BALANCE** a physical state or sense of being able to maintain bodily balance **2. EMOTIONAL STABILITY** a mental state of calmness and composure **3. SITUATION OF BALANCE** a state or situation in which opposing forces or factors balance each other out and stability is attained **4.** PHYS **BALANCE BETWEEN FORCES** a static or dynamic state in which all forces or processes are in balance and there is no resultant change **5.** CHEM **STATE OF BALANCE IN CHEMICAL REACTION** the state in a reversible chemical reaction in which the reaction and its reverse reaction proceed at the same rate and balance each other so there is no further change [Early 17C. < Latin *aequilibrium* "equal balance" < *libra* "balance"]

e·qui·lib·ri·um con·stant *n* the constant value that expresses the relationship between the concentration of products and starting substances in a reversible chemical reaction at equilibrium. The equilibrium constant is strongly temperature dependent.

e·qui·mo·lar /èekwə mṓlər, èkwə-/ *adj* having an equal concentration of moles in one liter of solution

e·qui·mo·lec·u·lar /èekwəmə lékyələr, èkwə-/ *adj* describes a substance or mixture that has the same number of molecules as another

e·quine /ée kwīn, é-/ *adj* **1.** OF HORSES relating to, belonging to, or affecting horses **2.** RESEMBLING HORSE characteristic of or similar to a horse in appearance or behavior **3.** ZOOL BELONGING TO HORSE FAMILY belonging to or characteristic of the family of mammals that includes horses, zebras, and donkeys ■ *n* ZOOL HORSE OR HORSE'S RELATIVE a horse or other member of the horse family [Late 18C. < Latin *equinus* < *equus* "horse"]

e·qui·noc·tial /èekwə nókshəl, èkwə-/ *adj* **1.** TIME OCCURRING AT EQUINOX happening at or near either of the two equinoxes **2.** BOT WITH FLOWERS OPEN AT DEFINITE TIMES describes a plant whose flowers open and close at specific times of day **3.** ASTRON OF CELESTIAL EQUATOR relating to the celestial equator ■ *n* **1.** METEOROL STORM AT EQUINOX a storm or strong wind that occurs at an equinox **2.** ASTRON same as **celestial equator** [14C. < French *équinoctial* < Latin *aequinoctium* (see EQUINOX)]

e·qui·noc·tial cir·cle *n* ASTRON same as **celestial equator**

e·qui·noc·tial point *n* either of the two points on the celestial sphere where the Sun crosses the celestial equator. The points are called respectively the First Point of Aries and the First Point of Libra.

e·qui·noc·tial year *n* ASTRON same as **solar year**

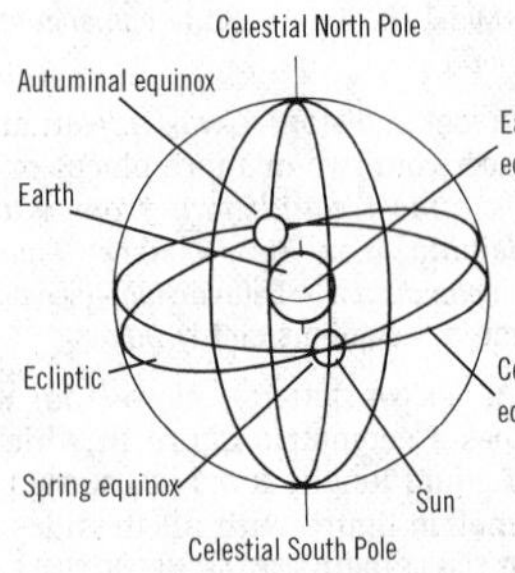

equinox: diagram showing the positions of the Sun and Earth at the spring and autumnal equinoxes

e·qui·nox /éekwə nòks, ékwə-/ *n* **1.** either of the two annual crossings of the equator by the Sun, once in each direction, when the length of day and night are approximately equal everywhere on Earth. The equinoxes occur around March 21 and September 23. **2.** ASTRON same as **equinoctial point** [14C. Directly or via French < Latin *aequinoctium* "equal night" < *nox* "night"]

e·quip /i kwíp/ (**e·quipped, e·quip·ping, e·quips**) *vt* **1.** to provide somebody or something with what is needed for a particular activity or purpose, e.g., with the appropriate tools, supplies, parts, or clothing ○ *a computer equipped with a modem and a CD-ROM drive* ○ *They equipped themselves with the most up-to-date camping gear.* **2.** to prepare somebody with the necessary education, training, or experience to succeed at a task or role in life (*often passive*) ○ *I'm sorry, but I don't feel equipped to answer that question.* [Early 16C. < French *équiper*, probably < Old Norse *skipa* "fit out a ship" < *skip* "ship"] —**e·quip·per** *n*

eq·ui·page /ékwəpij/ *n* **1.** a horse-drawn carriage, especially a luxurious one, or a carriage together with its horses and attendants **2.** the equipment and supplies needed for an undertaking, especially a military expedition or ship's journey

e·qui·par·ti·tion /èekwə paar tísh'n, èkwə-/ *n* the equal distribution of energy among the components of motion, e.g., linear movement and rotation, of the gas molecules in a system

~~equiped~~ incorrect spelling of **equipped**

e·quip·ment /i kwípmənt/ *n* **1.** NECESSARY ITEMS the tools, clothing, or other items needed for a particular activity or purpose ○ *camping equipment* **2.** PERSONAL RESOURCES FOR SUCCESS the intellectual and emotional resources that enable somebody to succeed at a task or role in life **3.** PROVIDING OF SOMEBODY WITH EQUIPMENT the equipping of somebody or something with what is necessary for a particular activity or purpose **4.** *US* TRANSPORTATION VEHICLES the rolling stock of a railroad necessary to carry passengers or goods

e·qui·poise /éekwə pòyz, ékwə-/ (*formal*) *n* **1.** a condition in which weights are in balance or there is a balance between different social, emotional, or intellectual influences **2.** something that creates a balanced state, usually by counterbalancing some other force or thing ■ *vt* (**-poised, -pois·ing, -pois·es**) same as **counterbalance**

e·qui·pol·lent /èekwə póllənt, èkwə-/ *adj* having the same weight, influence, validity, or effect as something else, or as each other (*formal*) [14C. < Old French *equipolent* < Latin *pollere* "be strong"] —**e·qui·pol·lence** *n* —**e·qui·pol·len·cy** *n* —**e·qui·pol·lent·ly** *adv*

e·qui·pon·der·ant /èekwə póndərənt, èkwə-/ *adj* equal, or evenly balanced, in weight, influence, or effect (*formal*) [Mid-17C. < medieval Latin *aequiponderant-*, present participle of *aequiponderare* "weigh the same" < Latin *ponderare* "weigh"] —**e·qui·pon·der·ance** *n* —**e·qui·pon·der·an·cy** *n*

e·qui·pon·der·ate /èekwə póndə ràyt, èkwə-/ (**-at·ed, -at·ing, -ates**) *vt* to equal the strength, power, or effect of something, creating a state of balance (*formal*) [Mid-17C. < medieval Latin *aequiponderat-*, past participle of *aequiponderare* (see EQUIPONDERANT), or alteration of PREPONDERATE]

e·qui·po·ten·tial /èekwəpə ténshəl, èkwə-/ *adj* describes a surface that has the same electric or gravitational potential at all points —**e·qui·po·ten·ti·al·i·ty** /-pə tenshee állətee/ *n*

e·qui·prob·a·ble /èekwə próbbəb'l, èkwə-/ *adj* equally likely to be true or to occur according to logic or mathematics

eq·ui·ta·ble /ékwitəb'l/ *adj* **1.** characterized by justice or fairness and impartiality toward those involved (*formal*) **2.** applicable under the law of equity as distinguished from common or statute law [Mid-16C. < French *équitable* < *équité* (see EQUITY)] —**eq·ui·ta·ble·ness** *n* —**eq·ui·ta·bly** *adv*

eq·ui·ta·tion /èkwi táysh'n/ *n* the skill and theory of riding horses (*formal*) [Mid-16C. Directly or via French < Latin *equitation-* < *equitare* "to ride on horseback" < *equus* "horse"]

eq·ui·tes /ékwi tàyss, -tàyz/ *npl* **1.** the cavalry of ancient Rome **2.** a privileged class of ancient Romans of a rank above the common people, whose members served as cavalry [Early 17C. < Latin, plural of *eques* (see EQUESTRIAN)]

eq·ui·ty /ékwətee/ *n* (*plural* **-ties**) **1.** FAIRNESS actions, treatment of others, or a general condition characterized by justice, fairness, and impartiality **2.** LAW JUSTICE TEMPERED BY ETHICS justice applied in conformity with the law, but influenced at the same time by principles of ethics and fair play **3.** LAW FAIR CLAIM a claim that is judged to be just and fair **4.** LAW MODIFICATION OF COMMON LAW the system of jurisprudence that supplements common and statutory law, when those bodies of law are inadequate in the attainment of justice **5.** FIN PART OF VALUE PAID the value of a piece of property over and above any mortgage or other liabilities relating to it ■ **eq·ui·ties** *npl* FIN STOCK ENTITLING HOLDER TO PROFITS shares of stock in a corporation that pays the holder some of its profits [14C. Via French *équité* < Latin *aequitas* < Latin *aequus* "equal, even"]

eq·ui·ty cap·i·tal *n* funds for a business raised by selling stock or by retaining earnings

eq·ui·ty of re·demp·tion *n* the right of a mortgagor to redeem mortgaged property by paying the sum owed within a reasonable time after the date on which payment was due

equiv. *abbr* equivalent

e·quiv·a·lence /i kwívvələnss/, **e·quiv·a·len·cy** /-lənssee/ *n* **1.** the fact of being the same, effectively the same, or interchangeable with something else **2.** the relationship between two statements, both of which are either true or false, and each of which can be proved from the other

e·quiv·a·lence re·la·tion *n* the relation between members of a set that is reflexive, symmetrical, and transitive, e.g., if "a" equals "b" and "b" equals "c," then "a" equals "c"

e·quiv·a·len·cy *n* same as **equivalence**

e·quiv·a·lent /i kwívvələnt/ *adj* **1.** EQUAL being the same, or effectively the same, in effect, value, or meaning as something and usually interchangeable with it ○ *That's equivalent to the amount of energy needed to power a single light bulb.* **2.** MATH OF SAME SIZE BUT DIFFERENT SHAPE describes geometric figures that have different shapes but equal areas, e.g., a circle and a square, or equal volumes, e.g., a cylinder and a cube **3.** MATH, LOGIC IN EQUIVALENCE RELATION describes members of a set that are in a reflexive, symmetrical, and transitive relation with each other **4.** MATH WITH SAME SOLUTION describes equations that share a common solution or solutions, e.g., for both $2x\text{-}3 = x\text{+}2$ and $x\text{-}5 = 0$ the solution is $x = 5$ ■ *n* **1.** SOMETHING CONSIDERED THE SAME something that is considered to be equal to or have the same effect, value, or meaning as something else ○ *He's the Italian equivalent of a district attorney.* **2.** CHEM same as **equivalent weight** [15C. < French *équivalent* < late Latin *aequivalere* "be of equal value" < Latin *valere* "to be strong"] —**e·quiv·a·lent·ly** *adv*

e·quiv·a·lent weight *n* the mass of a substance that will combine with or replace 8 parts by weight of oxygen or 1.008 parts of hydrogen

~~equivelent~~ incorrect spelling of **equivalent**

e·quiv·o·cal /i kwívvək'l/ *adj* **1.** AMBIGUOUS open to more than one interpretation, especially in being deliberately expressed in an ambiguous way in an attempt to mislead somebody ○ *an equivocal reply to a tough question* **2.** DIFFICULT TO INTERPRET difficult to interpret, understand, or respond to ○ *Their stance on this issue is equivocal and nobody knows how they are likely to react.* **3.** RAISING DOUBTS arousing doubts and suspicions, especially about somebody's honesty or sincerity ○ *To arrive at the peace talks with an armed guard was an equivocal gesture.* [Mid-16C. < late Latin *aequivocus* (see EQUIVOCATE)] —**e·quiv·o·cal·i·ty** /i kwìvvə kállətee/ *n* —**e·quiv·o·cal·ly** *adv* —**e·quiv·o·cal·ness** *n*

e·quiv·o·cate /i kwívvə kàyt/ (**-cat·ed, -cat·ing, -cates**) *vi* to speak vaguely or ambiguously, especially in order to mislead ○ *When pressed for a firm answer, she equivocated.* [15C. < late Latin *aequivocat-*, past participle of *aequivocare* < *aequivocus* "ambiguous" < Latin *vox* "voice"] —**e·quiv·o·cat·ing·ly** *adv* —**e·quiv·o·ca·tor** *n* —**e·quiv·o·ca·to·ry** /i kwívvəkə tàwree/ *adj*

e·quiv·o·ca·tion /i kwìvvə káysh'n/ *n* **1.** USE OF AMBIGUITY the use of vague or ambiguous and sometimes misleading language ○ *What we ask for is facts: what we get is equivocation or downright lies.* **2.** AMBIGUOUS STATEMENT an expression or statement that is vague or ambiguous and often deliberately misleading ○ *Their equivocations could not disguise the fact that corruption was rife in the committee.* **3.** LOGIC WRONG LOGICAL CONCLUSION an invalid conclusion based on statements in which one term has two different meanings

eq·ui·voque /ékwi vōk, éekwi-/, **eq·ui·voke** *n* (*formal*) **1.** PLAY ON WORDS an amusing use of an ambiguous word **2.** AMBIGUOUS WORD OR PHRASE a word or phrase with a double meaning **3.** AMBIGUITY ambiguity, double meaning, or misleading words and expressions [Early 17C. Directly or via French *équivoque* < late Latin *aequivocus* (see EQUIVOCATE)]

E·quu·le·us /i kwóolee əss/ *n* a constellation of the northern hemisphere, the second-smallest of the constellations. See illustration at **constellation**

er[1] /ur/ *interj* used to express hesitation [Mid-19C. Natural sound]

er[2] *abbr* Eritrea (*used in Internet addresses*) See table at **domain name**

Er *symbol* CHEM ELEM erbium

ER *abbr* **1.** BASEBALL earned runs **2.** HEALTH SERVICES emergency room

-er[1] *suffix* **1.** somebody or something that performs or undergoes a particular action ○ *adjuster* ○ *fryer* **2.** somebody connected with, often as an occupation ○ *trucker* **3.** somebody or something that has a particular characteristic, quality, or form ○ *fore-and-after* **4.** somebody from a particular place ○ *New Yorker* ○ *foreigner* [Partly Old English *-ere*

< Germanic; partly via Anglo-Norman < Latin *-arius*; partly < Old French *-eor* (see -OR[1])]

-er[2] *suffix* more ○ *greener* ○ *slower* [Old English *-re, -ra* < Germanic]

e·ra /éerə, érrə/ *n* **1.** TIME **DISTINCTIVE PERIOD OF HISTORY** a period of time made distinctive by a significant development, feature, event, or personality ○ *during the postwar era* **2.** TIME **PERIOD WITH ITS OWN CHRONOLOGICAL SYSTEM** a time period within which years are consecutively numbered from a particular significant event that provides its starting point ○ *the Christian era* **3.** TIME **DATE THAT BEGINS PERIOD** a significant date or event that is regarded as the beginning of a new period of time ○ *The agreement marked an era in US-Soviet relations.* **4.** GEOL **DIVISION OF EARTH'S HISTORY** a division of geologic time comprising several periods ○ *the Precambrian era* [Mid-17C. < late Latin *aera* "number used as a basis for counting"]

ERA *abbr* **1.** BASEBALL earned run average **2.** *US* LAW Equal Rights Amendment

e·rad·i·cate /i ráddi kàyt/ (**-cat·ed, -cat·ing, -cates**) *vt* to destroy or get rid of something completely, so that it can never recur or return [15C. < Latin *eradicat-*, past participle of *eradicare* "pull up by the roots" < *radix* "root"] —**e·rad·i·ca·ble** *adj* —**e·rad·i·ca·bly** *adv* —**e·rad·i·ca·tion** /i ràddi káysh'n/ *n* —**e·rad·i·ca·tive** *adj* —**e·rad·i·ca·tor** *n*

e·rase /i ráyss/ (**e·rased, e·ras·ing, e·ras·es**) *vt* **1. REMOVE WRITTEN MATERIAL** to remove written, typed, or printed material by rubbing it out, or obliterate it with something such as correction fluid **2. ELIMINATE SOMETHING** to remove or destroy something completely ○ *an ancient civilization, all traces of which had been erased over time* **3.** COMPUT **DELETE RECORDED DATA** to delete data or recorded material from a computer's memory, a magnetic tape, or other storage medium [Late 16C. < Latin *eras-*, past participle of *eradere* "scrape out" < *radere* "to scrape"] —**e·ras·a·bil·i·ty** /i ràyssə bíllətee/ *n* —**e·ras·a·ble** *adj*

e·ras·er /i ráyssər/ *n* something used to rub out written, typed, or printed material, e.g., a piece of rubber for pencil markings or a felt pad used on a chalkboard

E·ras·mus /i rázməss/, **Desiderius** (1466?–1536) Dutch scholar and writer. His works, combining a Christian outlook with Renaissance humanism, influenced both sides during the Reformation. Among his many other works was a new edition of the Greek New Testament (1516).

> "It is an unscrupulous intellect that does not pay to antiquity its due reverence...There are many kinds of genius; each age has its different gifts."
> [Desiderius Erasmus, *Works of Hilary*; 1523]

e·ra·sure /i ráyshər/ *n* **1.** the complete removal or destruction of something ○ *an erasure of data from a hard drive* **2.** the place where something has been rubbed out, or the mark left behind

Er·a·to /érrə tṑ/ *n* in Greek mythology, the Muse of lyric poetry, one of the nine Muses believed to inspire and nurture the arts

E·ra·tos·the·nes[1] /èrrə tósthə néez/ prominent deep crater on the Moon with a distinctive central peak, located at the southern edge of Mare Imbrium, 36 mi./58 km in diameter

E·ra·tos·the·nes[2] (276?–196? B.C.) Greek astronomer and mathematician. He is best known for his calculation of the Earth's circumference, which remained the most accurate one available until the 17th century.

er·bi·um /úrbee əm/ *n* a soft silvery metallic element of the rare-earth group. Source: monazite, bastnaesite. Use: alloys, pigment. Symbol **Er.** See table at **element** [Mid-19C. After *Ytterby*, town in Sweden]

Er·do·gan /ùrdō gaán/, **Recep Tayyip** (*b.* 1954) Turkish prime minister. A former mayor of Istanbul, he was convicted of inciting religious hatred in 1998, and on his release founded the Islamist-based Justice and Development Party (AK). Winning a prime ministerial election in 2002, he was nevertheless unable to take up the post until a constitutional amendment allowed a person with a criminal conviction to become a member of parliament, a prerequisite for holding the prime minister's office. He won a by-election and became prime minister in 2003.

ere /er/ *prep, conj* before or earlier in time than (*literary or archaic*) [Old English *ǣr* < Germanic]

SPELLCHECK See *air.*

Er·e·bus, Mount /érrəbəss/ active volcano on the eastern coast of Ross Island, Antarctica. Height: 12,448 ft./3,794 m.

e·rect /i rékt/ *adj* **1. STRAIGHT AND VERTICAL** in an upright position ○ *an erect plant stem* **2.** PHYSIOL **FIRM AND RIGID** stiff and swollen as a result of being filled with blood, e.g., when sexually aroused **3.** OPTICS **RIGHT SIDE UP** describes an optically produced image that is right side up and not inverted ■ *vt* (**e·rect·ed, e·rect·ing, e·rects**) **1. CONSTRUCT SOMETHING** to build a structure from basic parts and materials ○ *The building was erected in 1885.* ○ *erected a swing set* **2. SET SOMETHING UPRIGHT** to fix something in an upright position **3. ESTABLISH SYSTEM OR THEORY** to bring an organization, system, or theory into being ○ *The corporation erected a new legal department to deal with mergers and acquisitions.* **4.** MATH **DRAW FIGURE ON BASE** to draw or construct a line or figure on a given base [14C. < Latin *erect-*, past participle of *erigere* "set up" < *regere* "direct, rule"] —**e·rect·a·ble** *adj* —**e·rect·ly** *adv* —**e·rect·ness** *n*

e·rec·tile /i rékt'l, i rék tīl/ *adj* capable of filling with blood under pressure, swelling, and becoming stiff —**e·rec·til·i·ty** /i rèk tíllətee/ *n*

e·rec·tile dys·func·tion *n* a medical condition that prevents a man from achieving an erection or maintaining one throughout sexual intercourse

e·rec·tion /i réksh'n/ *n* **1. PUTTING SOMETHING UP** the construction or setting up of something **2. SWELLING OF TISSUE** the stiffened and swollen state of erectile tissue, especially that of the penis, usually as a result of sexual arousal **3. STRUCTURE** something that has been built or constructed (*formal*)

e·rec·tor /i réktər/ *n* **1.** a muscle that is capable of raising or holding up a body part **2.** somebody or something that erects things, generally things made elsewhere

E re·gion *n* the middle part of the ionosphere, lying approximately 50 to 70 mi./80 to 110 km above the Earth's surface, that reflects medium-length radio waves

ere·long /er láwng/ *adv* soon or in a short time (*literary or archaic*)

er·e·mite /érrə mīt/ *n* a hermit, especially one who lives alone for religious reasons (*literary*) [13C. Via French or late Latin < Greek *erēmitēs* (see HERMIT)] —**er·e·mit·ic** /èrrə míttik/ *adj* —**er·e·mit·i·cal** *adj* —**er·e·mit·ism** *n*

ere·now /er nów/ *adv* previously (*literary or archaic*)

er·e·thism /érrə thìzzəm/ *n* excessive sensitivity of a body part to stimuli (*technical*) [Early 19C. < French *éréthisme* < Greek *erethizein* "irritate"] —**er·e·this·mic** /èrrə thízmik/ *adj* —**er·e·this·tic** /-thístik/ *adj* —**er·e·thit·ic** /-thíttik/ *adj*

ere·while /er wīl, -hwīl/, **ere·whiles** /-wīlz, -hwīlz/ *adv* some time ago (*literary or archaic*)

erg[1] /urg/ *n* the centimeter-gram-second unit of energy or work equal to the work done by a force of one dyne acting through a distance of one centimeter. 1 erg is equivalent to 10^{-7} joule. [Late 19C. < Greek *ergon* "work"]

erg[2] /urg/ (*plural* **ergs** or **a·reg** /aá règ/) *n* a large, relatively flat area of desert covered with shifting windswept sand, especially in the Sahara [Late 19C. Via French < Arabic *'irḳ, 'erg*]

er·ga·tive /úrgətiv/ GRAM *adj* **1. ALLOWING OBJECT TO BE SUBJECT** describes a class of verbs in which the object of the transitive form can be used as the subject of the intransitive form with an equivalent meaning. "Open" is an example of an ergative verb in "I opened the door" and "The door opened." **2. INDICATING DOER OF ACTION AS OBJECT** describes a case of nouns in languages such as Inuit and Basque indicating that the object of the verb acts, while the subject is affected by the action ■ *n* **ERGATIVE WORD** an ergative verb, or a noun in the ergative case [Mid-20C. < Greek *ergatēs* "worker" < *ergon* "work"]

er·go /ér gō, úr gō/ *adv, conj* therefore [14C. < Latin]

er·go·cal·cif·er·ol /ùrgō kal síffə ràwl/ *n* BIOCHEM same as **vitamin D₂** [Mid-20C. < ERGOSTEROL]

er·gom·e·ter /ur gómmətər/ *n* an instrument for measuring muscle power or work done by muscles, e.g., when exercising [Late 19C. < Greek *ergon* "work"] —**er·go·met·ric** /ùrgə méttrik/ *adj*

er·go·nom·ic /ùrgə nómmik/ *adj* designed for maximum comfort, efficiency, safety, and ease of use, especially in the workplace —**er·go·nom·i·cal·ly** *adv*

er·go·nom·ics /ùrgə nómmiks/ *n* the study of how a workplace and the equipment used there can best be designed for comfort, efficiency, safety, and productivity (*takes a singular verb*) ■ *npl* those factors or qualities in the design of something, especially a workplace or equipment used by people at work, that contribute to comfort, efficiency, safety, and ease of use (*takes a plural verb*) [Mid-20C. < Greek *ergon* "work" after ECONOMICS] —**er·go·no·met·ric** /ùrgənə méttrik/ *adj* —**er·gon·o·mist** /ur gónnəmist/ *n*

er·gos·ter·ol /ur góstə ràwl/ *n* a sterol present in yeast and molds that is converted to vitamin D_2 by ultraviolet light [Early 20C. < ERGOT]

er·got /úrgət, úr gòt/ *n* **1.** a disease of cereals caused by the parasitic fungus *Claviceps purpurea* that grows in dense black masses (**sclerotia**) in the grains of the ear **2.** the dried sclerotia of an ergot fungus containing physiologically active substances. Use: treatment of migraines, initiation of labor in pregnancy. [Late 17C. < French, "rooster's spur"; from the appearance of the diseased grain] —**er·got·ic** /ur góttik/ *adj*

er·got·a·mine /ur góttə meen, -min/ *n* an alkaloid drug derived from ergot that causes constriction of blood vessels. Use: treatment of migraines. Formula: $C_{33}H_{35}N_5O_5$.

er·got·ism /úrgət ìzzəm/ *n* a severe toxic reaction to food containing ergot-contaminated grains, or excessive amounts of drugs containing ergot derivatives. The toxin produces neurological and gastrointestinal symptoms and, if not properly treated, gangrene.

Er·hard /er haard/, **Ludwig** (1897–1977) German politician. As finance minister, he achieved West Germany's postwar economic revival and was the Christian Democratic Chancellor from 1963 until 1966.

> "[Politics is] the art of dividing a cake in such a way that everyone believes he has the biggest piece."
> [Attributed to Ludwig Erhard]

er·i·ca /érrikə/ (*plural* **-cas** or *same*) *n* an evergreen bush or small tree of the heath family with small leathery leaves. Flowers: bell-shaped. Genus: *Erica.* [Early 17C. Via modern Latin < Greek *ereikē* "heath"]

er·i·ca·ceous /èrri káyshəss/ *adj* belonging or relating to the heath family, a group of evergreen bushes and small trees that includes the heath, heather, blueberry, rhododendron, azalea, and arbutus

Er·ic·son /érrikss'n/, **Leif** (975–1020) Icelandic explorer. He is traditionally believed to have been the first European to reach the North American mainland.

Er·ics·son /érrikssən/, **John** (1803–89) Swedish-born US inventor and engineer. After work on steam engines, he built the ironclad *Monitor*, which fought the Confederacy's ironclad *Merrimack* in the Civil War (1862).

Er·ic the Red /èrrik-/ (950?–1000?) Norwegian explorer. He was the father of Leif Ericson. Banished from Scandinavia for manslaughter, he explored Greenland (982–86), where he established the first European settlement. Born **Thorvaldson, Eric**

E·rid·a·nus /i ríddʼnəss/ *n* a large faint constellation of the southern hemisphere. See illustration at **constellation**

E·rie[1] /éeree/ *n* an extinct language formerly spoken in an area along the southern shores of Lake Erie. It was one of the Iroquoian group of the Hokan-Siouan family of North American languages. —**E·rie** *adj*

E·rie[2] /éeree/ city and port of entry on Lake Erie, northwestern Pennsylvania. It has been a major industrial center since the end of the 19th century. Population: 102,122 (2002 estimate).

E·rie, Lake lake in the United States and Canada. It is one of the five Great Lakes of North America. Area: 9,910 sq. mi./25,700 sq. km.

E·rie Ca·nal artificial inland waterway between Buffalo, on Lake Erie, and Albany, New York, where it links with the Hudson River. Length: 340 mi./547 km.

er·i·ger·on /i ríjjə ròn/ (*plural* **-ons** or *same*) *n* a plant of the daisy family, many species of which are cultivated as ornamentals. Fleabane is a type of erigeron. Genus: *Erigeron.* [Early 17C. Via Latin < Greek, "early old man"; from its former application to the groundsel, an early flowering plant with fluffy white seed heads]

Er·ik·son /érrikssən/, **Erik** (1902–94) German-born US psychoanalyst. He developed the concept of the identity crisis, as well as making major contributions to the field of child psychology. Full name **Erikson, Erik Homburger**

> "The identity crisis...occurs in that period of the life cycle when each youth must forge for himself some central perspective and direction, some working unity, out of the effective remnants of his childhood and the hopes of his anticipated adulthood."
> [Erik Erikson, *Young Man Luther*; 1958]

Er·in /érrin/ *n* the country of Ireland (*literary*)

Er·in go bragh /èrrin gō bráa/ *interj Ireland* an expression meaning "Ireland forever" [< ERIN + Irish *go brách, go bráth* "till doomsday"]

E·rin·y·es /i rínnee èez/ *npl* MYTHOL same as **Furies**

ERISA /i ríssə/ *abbr US* HR Employee Retirement Income Security Act

e·ris·tic /i rístik/ (*formal*) *adj also* **e·ris·ti·cal** /i rístik'l/ **ARGUMENTATIVE** fond of or characterized by argument or controversy ■ *n* **1. ART OF DISPUTING** the skill or practice of debating, especially in a manner involving subtle logic and specious argument **2. DEBATER** somebody who is an expert or delights in argument or controversy [Mid-17C. < Greek *eristikos* < *eris* "strife"] —**e·ris·ti·cal·ly** *adv*

Eritrea

Er·i·tre·a /èrri trée ə/ country on the Red Sea coast in northeastern Africa, bordered by Sudan and Ethiopia. A former Italian colony, it became part of Ethiopia in 1952 and fully independent in 1993. Language: Tigrinya, Tigre, Arabic. Currency: nakfa. Capital: Asmara. Population: 4,362,254 (2003). Area: 46,774 sq. mi./121,144 sq. km. Official name **State of Eritrea** —**Er·i·tre·an** *n, adj*

Er·lang·er /úr làngər/ city in northern Kentucky, northwest of Independence. It is a suburb of Cincinnati, Ohio. Population: 16,792 (2002 estimate).

Er·len·mey·er flask /úrlən mīr-, érlən-/ *n* a cone-shaped laboratory flask with a narrow neck and broad flat bottom [Late 19C. After Emil *Erlenmeyer* (1825–1909), German chemist]

er·mine /úrmin/ (*plural* **-mines** or *same*) *n* **1.** a small northern weasel with dark fur, whose silky winter coat is white except for a black-tipped tail. Latin name: *Mustela erminea.* **2.** the white fur of an ermine, once valued as a symbol of wealth, nobility,

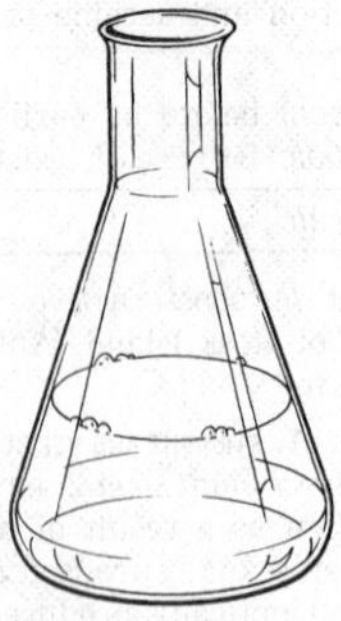
Erlenmeyer flask

ermine

or high rank [12C. < Old French *(h)ermine,* probably < medieval Latin *(mus) Armenius* "Armenian (mouse)"]

erne /urn/ (*plural* **ernes** or *same*), **ern** (*plural* **erns** or *same*) *n* a long-winged sea eagle. Native to: Europe. Latin name: *Haliaeetus albicilla.* [Old English *earn* < Indo-European]

Max Ernst

Ernst /ernst, urnst/, **Max** (1891–1976) German-born French artist. A cofounder of Dada and surrealism, he is known for the startling and violent imagery of his works.

> "The virtue of pride, which was once the beauty of mankind, has given place to that fount of all ugliness, Christian humility."
> [Attributed to Max Ernst]

e·rode /i rṓd/ (**e·rod·ed, e·rod·ing, e·rodes**) *v* **1.** *vti* **WEAR AWAY LAND** to wear away outer layers of rock or soil, or be gradually worn away by the action of wind or water **2.** *vt* GEOL **FORM LAND FEATURE BY WEATHERING** to form a land feature such as a valley or gully by the action of wind or water **3.** *vti* **DESTROY SOMETHING GRADUALLY** to diminish or destroy something gradually over time, or be gradually diminished or destroyed ○ *Higher inflation will erode our savings.* **4.** *vti* CHEM **EAT SUBSTANCE AWAY** to eat into or destroy something by corrosion or chemical action, or be damaged or destroyed in this way [Early 17C. Directly or via French < Latin *erodere* "gnaw off" < *rodere* "gnaw"] —**e·rod·i·bil·i·ty** /i rṓdə bíllətee/ *n* —**e·rod·i·ble** *adj*

e·rog·e·nous /i rójjənəss/, **er·o·gen·ic** /èrrə jénnik/, **e·rot·o·gen·ic** /i ròttə jénnik/ *adj* **1.** sensitive and arousing sexual feelings when touched or stroked **2.** stimulating sexual desire [Late 19C. < EROS]

e·rog·e·nous zone *n* an area of the body that is sensitive to sexual stimulation

Er·os /é ròss, éer òss/ *n* **1. GREEK GOD OF LOVE** in Greek mythology, the god of love. Roman equivalent **Cupid** **2.** *also* **er·os SEXUAL LOVE** sexual love or desire **3.** PSYCHOANAL **INSTINCT FOR SELF-PRESERVATION** in psychoanalytic theory, the instincts for self-preservation, pleasure, and procreation considered as a group [Late 17C. Via Latin < Greek, "sexual love"]

e·ro·sion /i rṓzh'n/ *n* **1.** the gradual destruction or reduction and weakening of something ○ *The erosion of profits was due to careless management.* **2.** the gradual wearing away of rock or soil by physical breakdown, chemical solution, and transportation of material, as caused, e.g., by water, wind, or ice [Mid-16C. < French *érosion* < Latin *eros-*, past participle of *erodere* (see ERODE)] —**e·ro·sion·al** *adj* —**e·ro·sion·al·ly** *adv*

e·ro·sive /i rṓssiv/ *adj* causing the gradual breaking down or wearing away of something, especially rock or soil —**e·ro·sive·ness** *n* —**e·ro·siv·i·ty** /i rō sívvətee/ *n*

e·rot·ic /i róttik/ *adj* **1.** arousing, or designed to arouse, feelings of sexual desire **2.** characterized by or arising out of sexual desire [Mid-17C. Via French < Greek *erōtikos* < *erōs* "sexual love"] —**e·rot·i·cal·ly** *adv*

e·rot·i·ca /i róttikə/ *n* art or literature intended to arouse sexual desire by portraying sex in an explicit way. ◊ **pornography** [Mid-19C. < Greek *erōtika,* neuter plural of *erōtikos* (see EROTIC)]

e·rot·i·cism /i rótti sìzzəm/, **er·o·tism** /érrə tìzzəm/ *n* **1. EROTIC QUALITY** an erotic quality in something, especially an erotic style or subject in literature or art ○ *the eroticism of her poetry* **2. SEXUAL DESIRE** feelings of sexual desire **3. EXCESSIVE SEXUAL EXCITEMENT** unusually persistent or frequent sexual interest or desire —**e·rot·i·cist** *n*

e·rot·i·cize /i rótti sīz/ (**-cized, -ciz·ing, -ciz·es**), **er·o·tize** /érrə tīz/ (**-tized, -tiz·ing, -tiz·es**) *vt* to make something erotic, especially by giving a sexual quality to something not usually regarded in that way ○ *The paintings were thought to eroticize flowers.* —**e·rot·i·ci·za·tion** /i ròttəsi záysh'n/ *n*

er·o·tism *n* same as **eroticism**

er·o·tize *vt* same as **eroticize**

eroto- *prefix* sexual desire ○ *erotogenic* [< Greek *erōt-*, stem of *erōs* "sexual love"]

e·ro·to·gen·ic *adj* same as **erogenous**

e·ro·to·ma·ni·a /i ròttə máynee ə/ *n* **1.** excessive and insatiable feelings of sexual desire **2.** the delusion of being loved by and romantically involved in a relationship with a person, especially somebody famous or of high social position —**e·ro·to·ma·ni·ac** *n*

err /ur, er/ (**erred, err·ing, errs**) *vi* **1.** to make a mistake or do an incorrect thing ○ *The committee erred in interpreting the contract.* **2.** to behave badly and do something that is morally wrong (*formal*) ○ *"To err is human, to forgive, divine."* (Alexander Pope, *Essay On Criticism*; 1711) [13C. Via French < Latin *errare* "to wander"]

SPELLCHECK See *air.*

er·ran·cy /érrənssee/ *n* (*formal*) **1.** incorrect or morally wrong behavior **2.** the propensity for making mistakes or acting improperly

er·rand /érrənd/ *n* **1.** a short trip somewhere to do something on behalf of somebody else, e.g., to buy something or deliver a message ○ *She sometimes runs errands for me if I'm not well enough to go out.* **2.** a task that somebody goes somewhere to carry out for somebody else [Old English *ǣrende* "message, mission" < ?]

er·rant /érrənt/ *adj* **1. BEHAVING BADLY** behaving in an unacceptable manner **2. TAKING WRONG ROUTE** wandering from an intended course, or not reaching an intended destination **3. LOOKING FOR ADVENTURE** wandering in search of adventure and romance (*literary*) [14C. < Latin *errant-*, present participle of *errare* "to wander"] —**er·rant·ly** *adv*

er·rant·ry /érrəntree/ *n* the wandering, romantic, and adventurous life of a knight errant

er·ra·ta PRINTING plural of **erratum**

er·rat·ic /i ráttik/ *adj* **1. INCONSISTENT** not predictable, regular, or consistent, especially in being likely to depart from expected standards at any time ○ *His driving tends to be rather erratic.* **2.** **OFTEN CHANGING DIRECTION** often changing direction and not following any definite course **3.** GEOL **CARRIED AND DEPOSITED BY ICE** describes a rock or boulder that was carried from its source by ice and deposited when the ice melted ■ *n* GEOL **ROCK MOVED BY ICE** a rock or boulder that was carried from its source by ice and deposited when the ice melted [14C. < Old French *erratique* < Latin *errare* "to wander"] —**er·rat·i·cal·ly** *adv* —**er·rat·i·cism** /i rátti sìzzəm/ *n*

er·ra·tum /e ráatəm, i-/ *n* (*plural* **-ta** /-tə/) a mistake in printing or writing, especially one noted on a list that is included with a printed book ■ **er·ra·ta** *npl* a list of mistakes noticed after a book was printed, often included as a separate sheet in the book [Mid-16C. < Latin, form of past participle of *errare* "to wander"]

er·ro·ne·ous /i rṓnee əss/ *adj* incorrect, based on an incorrect assumption, or containing something that is incorrect [14C. < Old French *erroneus* < Latin *erron-* "truant" < *errare* "to wander"] —**er·ro·ne·ous·ly** *adv* —**er·ro·ne·ous·ness** *n*

er·ror /érrər/ *n* **1.** **UNINTENTIONAL MISTAKE** something unintentionally done wrong, e.g., as a result of poor judgment or lack of care ○ *The report blames the crash on human error.* ○ *errors in his addition* **2.** **WRONG BELIEF** a belief or opinion that is contrary to fact or to established doctrine ○ *a serious error of judgment* **3.** **STATE OF BEING MISTAKEN** the state of holding incorrect beliefs or opinions, or the fact of acting wrongly or misguidedly ○ *caused by human error* **4.** **FACT OF BEING MISTAKE** the state or fact of being a mistake, or of being inappropriate or unacceptable ○ *He's seen the error of his ways.* **5.** BASEBALL **MISPLAY** in baseball, a fielding misplay, called when the official scorer judges that play should have either led to an out or prevented a runner from advancing **6.** COMPUT **PROBLEM IN COMPUTER PROGRAM** the failure of a computer program, subroutine, or system to produce an anticipated result **7.** MATH **MATHEMATICAL DIFFERENCE** a variation between the true value of a mathematical quantity and a calculated or measured value [13C. < Old French *err(o)ur* < Latin *errare* "to wander"] —**er·ror·less** *adj* ◇ **in error 1.** by mistake **2.** mistaken, or acting on the basis of a false assumption or belief

SYNONYMS See ***mistake***.

er·ror ac·count *n* an accounting convention for a stock market purchase or sale that was made in error. Companies either take immediate action to correct the error, or keep the position in the account to be rectified later.

er·ror code *n* a unique combination of characters printed or displayed by a computer that identifies a specific error or problem in its operation

er·ror mes·sage *n* a message indicating that a computer has encountered a problem, often suggesting alternative action. The message may take the form of a display on a monitor, text on a printer, a computer-generated voice, or a sequence of audio signals.

er·satz /ér zaats/ *adj* imitating or presented as a substitute for something of superior quality (*disapproving*) [Late 19C. < German, "replacement"]

Erse /urss/ *n* the Gaelic language, especially Irish Gaelic [14C. Early Scots variant of IRISH] —**Erse** *adj*

erst /urst/ *adv* in the past, or a long time ago (*archaic*) [Old English *ǣrest* "first" < Germanic]

erst·while /úrst wīl, -hwīl/ *adj* formerly holding a particular position or relationship ○ *Since leaving the bank, she has been ostracized by her erstwhile colleagues.* ■ *adv* at a time in the past (*archaic*)

ert /urt/ (**erted, ert·ing, erts**) *vi S Africa* to lose consciousness and fall to the ground as a result of taking illegal drugs (*slang*)

er·ub *n* JUDAISM same as **eruv**

e·ru·cic ac·id /i róossik-/ *n* a soft colorless solid fatty acid. Source: rapeseed. Use: manufacture of plastics. [< Latin *eruca* "rape plant"]

e·ruct /i rúkt/ (**e·ruct·ed, e·ruct·ing, e·ructs**), **e·ruc·tate** /i rúk tàyt/ (**-tat·ed, -tat·ing, -tates**) *vti* to expel stomach gases through the mouth (*technical*) [Mid-17C. < Latin *eruct-*, past participle of *eructare* "to belch or vomit up" < *ructare* "to belch"] —**e·ruc·ta·tion** /i rùk táysh'n, èe ruk-/ *n*

er·u·dite /érryə dīt, érrə-/ *adj* having or showing great knowledge gained from study and reading [15C. < Latin *erudit-*, past participle of *erudire* "instruct" < *rudis* "untrained"] —**er·u·dite·ly** *adv* —**er·u·dite·ness** *n*

er·u·di·tion /èrryə dísh'n, èrrə-/ *n* knowledge acquired through study and reading ○ *a work of great erudition*

SYNONYMS See ***knowledge***.

e·rupt /i rúpt/ (**e·rupt·ed, e·rupt·ing, e·rupts**) *v* **1.** *vi* **BURST OUT** to burst out suddenly or violently ○ *suddenly erupted into shouting* **2.** *vti* **VIOLENTLY RELEASE MATERIAL** to eject material such as gas, steam, ash, or lava, usually violently, from within ○ *The volcano last erupted in 1935.* **3.** *vi* **APPEAR ON SKIN** to appear as a rash or blemish on the skin or a mucous membrane **4.** *vi* **COME THROUGH GUM** to break through and emerge from a gum (*technical*; *refers to growing teeth*) [Mid-17C. < Latin *erupt-*, past participle of *erumpere* "to break out" < *rumpere* "to break"] —**e·rupt·i·ble** *adj* —**e·rup·tive** *adj* —**e·rup·tive·ly** *adv*

e·rup·tion /i rúpsh'n/ *n* **1.** **OUTBURST** a sudden outburst or occurrence of something **2.** **VIOLENT RELEASE OF MATERIAL** the violent ejection of material such as gas, steam, ash, or lava from a volcano **3.** MED **RASH OR BLEMISH ON SKIN** a rash or blemish, or the appearance of one, on the skin or a mucous membrane **4.** DENT **EMERGENCE OF TOOTH** an emergence of a growing tooth from a gum (*technical*)

er·uv /ay róov, áy rùv/ (*plural* **-u·vim** /-óovim/ or **-uvs**), **er·ub** /érróob/ (*plural* **-u·bim** or **-ubs**) *n* in some Jewish communities, a physical boundary within which some relaxations of the rules concerning the Jewish Sabbath are allowed. It may consist of the walls of a town, a natural barrier, or a special construction. [Early 18C. < Hebrew *'ērūbh* "mixture"]

Er·ving /úrving/, **Julius** (*b.* 1950) US basketball player. He is widely regarded as one of the greatest and most exciting scorers in basketball history. Full name **Erving II, Julius Winfield**. Known as **Dr. J**

-ery *suffix* **1.** place for ○ *brewery* **2.** activity or behavior ○ *trickery* **3.** collection of ○ *crockery* **4.** qualities or character of ○ *buffoonery* **5.** state or condition of ○ *drudgery* [< Old French *-erie* < *-er* "-er, -or" + *-ie* "-y"]

er·y·sip·e·las /èrri síppələss/ *n* a severe skin rash accompanied by fever and vomiting and caused by a streptococcal bacterium [14C. Via Latin < Greek *erusipelas* "red skin"] —**er·y·si·pel·a·tous** /èrrissi péllətəss/ *adj*

er·y·the·ma /èrri théemə/ *n* redness of the skin as a result of a widening of the small blood vessels near its surface. It has various causes, including fever and inflammation. [Late 18C. < Greek *eruthēma* < *eruthros* "red"] —**er·y·them·a·tous** /èrri thémmətəss, -théemə-/ *adj* —**er·y·the·mic** *adj*

erythr- *prefix* same as **erythro-** (*used before vowels*)

er·y·thrism /érrə thrìzzəm/ *n* unusual redness of plumage or hair, often with a ruddy complexion in humans [Late 19C. < Greek *eruthros* "red"] —**er·y·thris·mal** /èrrə thrízm'l/ *adj*

er·y·thrite /érrə thrīt/ *n* a pale red cobalt arsenate mineral. Use: glass colorant. [Mid-19C. < Greek *eruthros* "red"]

erythro- *prefix* **1.** red ○ *erythrocyte* **2.** red blood cell ○ *erythroblast* [< Greek *eruthros* "red" < Indo-European]

e·ryth·ro·blast /i ríthrə blàst/ *n* an immature red blood cell that is found in bone marrow and eventually develops into a mature red blood cell. Unlike a mature red blood cell, an erythroblast has a nucleus. —**e·ryth·ro·blas·tic** /i rìthrə blástik/ *adj*

e·ryth·ro·blas·to·sis /i rìthrō bla stṓssiss/ *n* the presence of immature red blood cells in the bloodstream that occurs especially in erythroblastosis fetalis

e·ryth·ro·blas·to·sis fe·tal·is /-fi tálliss/ *n* a serious blood disease of fetuses and newborn babies, in which the antibodies produced by an RH negative mother destroy the red blood cells of an RH positive fetus [*Fetalis* < modern Latin, "fetal"]

e·ryth·ro·cyte /i ríthrə sīt/ *n* a red blood cell (*technical*) —**e·ryth·ro·cyt·ic** /i rìthrə síttik/ *adj*

e·ryth·ro·my·cin /i rìthrə mīssin/ *n* a broad-spectrum antibiotic derived from the bacterium *Streptomyces erythreus*

e·ryth·ro·poi·e·sis /i rìthrō poy ee ssiss/ *n* the formation of red blood cells, a process that begins with stem cells in the bone marrow and ends with the release of mature red blood cells (**erythrocytes**) into circulation [Early 20C. < ERYTHROCYTE] —**e·ryth·ro·poi·et·ic** /-éttik/ *adj*

e·ryth·ro·poi·e·tin /i rìthrō poy éetin/ *n* a kidney hormone that stimulates the development of red blood cells in the bone marrow. The kidneys produce erythropoietin in response to lowered oxygen levels in body tissues. [Mid-20C. < ERYTHROPOIESIS]

es *abbr* Spain (*used in Internet addresses*) See table at **domain name** [Spanish *España*]

Es *symbol* CHEM ELEM einsteinium

E·sau /ée sàw/ *n* in the Bible, the son of Isaac and Rebekah, who sold his birthright to his brother, Jacob

Esc *abbr* COMPUT escape (key)

es·ca·drille /éskə drìl, èskə dréel/ *n* a squadron of usually six aircraft, especially a French air squadron of World War I [Early 20C. Via French < Spanish *escuadrilla* "little squadron" < *escuadra* "squadron"]

es·ca·lade /éskə làyd, -làad/ *n* an attack involving the use of ladders to scale the walls of a fortified place ■ *vt* (**-lad·ed, -lad·ing, -lades**) to scale the walls of a fortification using ladders [Late 16C. Directly or via French < Spanish *escalada*] —**es·ca·lad·er** *n*

es·ca·late /éskə làyt/ (**-lat·ed, -lat·ing, -lates**) *vti* to become or cause something to become greater, more serious, or more intense [Early 20C. Back-formation < ESCALATOR] —**es·ca·la·tion** /èskə láysh'n/ *n* —**es·ca·la·to·ry** *adj*

USAGE No one uses ***escalate*** now to mean "travel on an escalator," and the figurative meaning has taken over completely. Its earliest and still most common uses are in connection with military activity and conflicts: *Tourists were advised not to travel to the country as terrorist attacks continued to escalate.* It is used most effectively when it describes a development that proceeds in stages, rather than as a simple synonym for *increase* or *mount*.

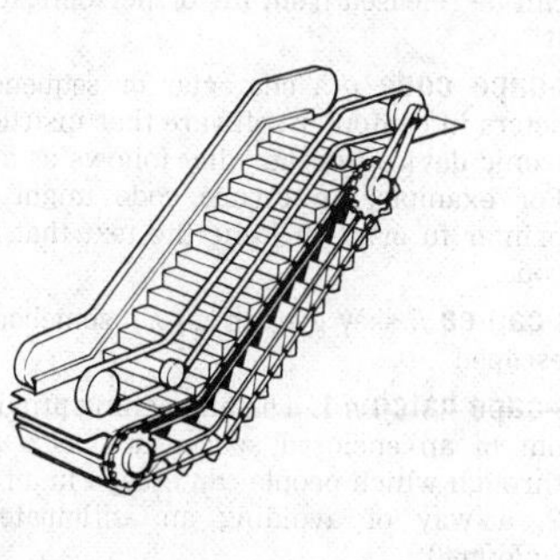

escalator

es·ca·la·tor /éskə làytər/ *n* **1.** a set of moving steps attached to a continuously circulating belt, that carries people up or down between levels in a building **2.** *also* **es·ca·la·tor clause** a stipulation in a contract that relates an increase or decrease in something to a change in something else, e.g., relating compensation to cost of living or prices to sales [Early 20C. < ESCALADE, after ELEVATOR]

es·cal·lop /i skólləp, i skálləp/ *n* HANDICRAFT same as **scallop** *n* (sense 5) [15C. < French *escalope* "shell"]

es·cal·ope /éskə lōp, èskə lṓp/ *n Can, UK* a slice of boneless lean meat, especially veal or poultry, that is beaten flat for cooking quickly or rolling around a stuffing. US term **scallop** [Early 19C. < French, "shell"; probably because it curls into a shell shape in cooking]

es·ca·pade /éskə pàyd/ *n* something exciting or adventurous that somebody does or is involved in, especially something showing recklessness or disregard for authority [Mid-17C. Via French < Spanish *escapada* "an escape" < assumed Vulgar Latin *excappare* (see ESCAPE)]

es·cape /i skáyp/ *v* (**-caped, -cap·ing, -capes**) **1.** *vti* **BREAK FREE FROM CAPTIVITY** to get free from captivity or confinement ○ *prisoners who attempted to escape* ○ *escaped their cage* **2.** *vt* **AVOID BAD SITUATION** to avoid danger, harm, or involvement in an unpleasant situation ○ *There's no escaping the fact that the house needs painting.* **3.** *vi* **LEAK OUT** to leak out from a container **4.** *vt* **BE TEMPORARILY UNKNOWN TO SOMEBODY** to fail to be noticed, remembered, or understood by somebody ○ *a little village whose name escapes me for the moment* **5.** *vti* **BE UTTERED** to be uttered by somebody unintentionally ○ *A muffled curse escaped his lips.* **6.** *vi* LEISURE **TAKE SHORT VACATION** to get away from work or responsibilities and take a trip or short vacation **7.** *vi* COMPUT **EXIT COMPUTER PROCEDURE** to exit from a computer program or file, cancel a command or operation, or return from the currently active menu to a previous one **8.** *vi* BOT **START GROWING IN WILD** to spread from a garden or other cultivated area and become established in the wild (*refers to cultivated plants*) ■ *n* **1. BREAKING FREE FROM CAPTIVITY** an act of getting free from captivity or confinement ○ *He made his escape while the guard was asleep.* **2. AVOIDANCE OF BAD SITUATION** the avoidance of a dangerous, harmful, or unpleasant situation ○ *had a narrow escape* **3. MEANS OF GETTING AWAY** a method, means, or route by which somebody can escape from a place or situation ○ *a fire escape* **4. DISTRACTION** something that takes the mind off routine or serious matters ○ *an escape from daily routine* **5. GAS OR LIQUID LEAK** a leak of gas or liquid from a container **6.** LEISURE **SHORT VACATION** a trip or short vacation taken to get away from work or responsibilities **7.** *also* **Es·cape** COMPUT **COMPUTER KEY** the key on a computer keyboard that allows a user to exit a program, cancel a command, or return to a previous menu ○ *Press escape to exit the program.* **8.** COMPUT same as **escape code 9.** BOT **WILD PLANT FORMERLY CULTIVATED** a plant that has spread from a garden or other cultivated area and is growing wild [13C. Via Old N French *escaper* < assumed Vulgar Latin *excappare* "throw off your cloak" < *cappa* "cloak"] —**es·cap·a·ble** *adj* —**es·cap·er** *n*

es·cape art·ist *n* **1.** a performer who is skilled at escaping from restraints or confinement **2.** somebody who is skilled at escaping from difficulty or danger

es·cape clause *n* a clause in a contract that sets out the conditions under which a party to the contract can be released from his or her obligations under it

es·cape code *n* a character or sequence of characters in computer software that instructs an electronic device to read what follows as a command. For example, an escape code might instruct a printer to print in italic the text that follows the code.

es·cap·ee /i skày peé, ès kay-/ *n* somebody who has escaped

es·cape hatch *n* **1.** a small opening providing a way out of an enclosed space such as a submarine, through which people can escape in an emergency **2.** a way of avoiding an anticipated problem (*informal*)

es·cape key *n* COMPUT same as **escape** *n* (sense 7)

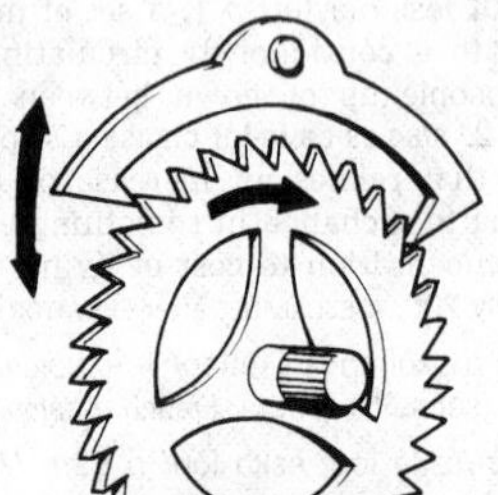

escapement: pallets on arm (top) engage teeth on wheel, driving gears in the movement

es·cape·ment /i skáypmənt/ *n* **1. CLOCK MECHANISM** in a clock or watch, a mechanism that permits motion in only one direction, allowing power from a spring or falling weight to turn gears connected to the hands **2.** MUSIC **PIANO MECHANISM** in a piano, a mechanism that allows the hammer to rebound from a string after striking it **3. TYPEWRITER MECHANISM** in a typewriter or printer, a mechanism that regulates the relative movement between the paper carrier and the typing or printing position on a line [Late 18C. < its allowing a cogwheel to "escape" or be released repeatedly]

es·cape ve·loc·i·ty *n* the minimum speed at which an object must travel to escape a planet's or moon's gravitational field in order to orbit around it or move off into space. At or near the Earth's surface, the escape velocity is about 25,000 mph/40,000 kph.

es·cape wheel *n* a toothed wheel in the mechanism of a clock or watch, designed to regulate the movement of the pendulum or balance wheel and so move the hands at regular intervals

es·cap·ism /i skáyp ìzzəm/ *n* **1.** something such as fantasy or entertainment that makes it possible to forget about the ordinary or unpleasant realities of life for a while **2.** the act of indulging in daydreams or fantasies to escape from everyday reality

es·cap·ist /i skáypist/ *adj* providing a means of forgetting about everyday or unpleasant realities for a while ■ *n* a daydreamer or fantasist who tries to avoid reality

es·cap·ol·o·gist /ès kay póllәjist/ *n* same as **escape artist** (sense 1)

es·cap·ol·o·gy /ès kay póllәjee/ *n* the skill of escaping from restraints or confinement as a form of entertainment

es·car·got /ès kaar gṓ/ *n* a snail that is cooked and served as food, especially presented in its shell with melted garlic butter [Late 19C. Via French < Old Provençal *escaragol*]

es·ca·role /éskə rōl/ *n* FOOD same as **endive** (sense 1) [Early 20C. Via French < Italian *scariola* < Latin *esca* "food" (see ESCULENT)]

es·carp /i skaárp/ *n* the inner side of a ditch dug as a fortification [Late 17C. Via French *escarpe* < Italian *scarpa* "slope"]

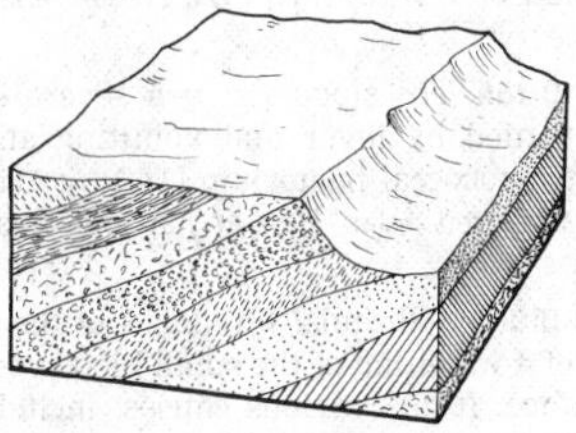

escarpment

es·carp·ment /i skaárpmənt/ *n* **1.** a steep slope or cliff that marks the boundary of a flat or gently sloping upland area such as a plateau, often formed by faulting or erosion **2.** a steep slope constructed in front of a fortification

-escent *suffix* **1.** beginning or inclined to be, becoming, slightly ○ *acquiescent* ○ *alkalescent* **2.** having a particular kind of luster ○ *iridescent* **3.** resembling, having ○ *arborescent* [Via French < Latin *-escent-*, present participle ending of verbs in *-escere*, expressing the beginning of action] —**-escence** *suffix*

es·char /és kaàr/ *n* a dry scab formed on skin that has been burned or cauterized [15C. Directly or via Old French *eschar(r)e* < late Latin *eschara* (see SCAR[1])]

es·cha·tol·o·gy /èskə tólləjee/ *n* the body of religious doctrines concerning the human soul in its relation to death, judgment, heaven, and hell [Mid-19C. < Greek *eskhatos* "last"] —**es·chat·o·log·i·cal** /èskətə lójjik'l, i skàttə-/ *adj* —**es·chat·o·log·i·cal·ly** *adv* —**es·cha·tol·o·gist** *n*

es·cheat /iss cheét/ *n* **1.** LAW **REVERSION OF PROPERTY TO STATE** the reversion of the property of a deceased person to the state when there are no legal heirs **2.** LAW, HIST **PROPERTY AFFECTED BY ESCHEAT** property that reverts by escheat **3.** HIST **REVERSION OF PROPERTY TO FEUDAL LORD** in medieval England, the reversion to a feudal overlord of the property of a deceased person when there was no legal heir or when a tenant was outlawed [13C. < Old French *eschete* and Anglo-Latin *escheta* < assumed Vulgar Latin *excadere* "fall away" < Latin *cadere* "fall"] —**es·cheat** *vti* —**es·cheat·a·ble** *adj*

Esch·er /éshər/, **M. C.** (1898–1972) Dutch graphic artist. He is known for his distinctive prints depicting intricate interlocking patterns and optical illusions based on mathematical concepts. Full name **Escher, Maurits Cornelius**

es·chew /ess chóò/ (**-chewed, -chew·ing, -chews**) *vt* to avoid doing or using something on principle or as a matter of course [14C. < Old French *eschiver*] —**es·chew·al** *n*

Es·cof·fier /es kóffee ày/, **Auguste** (1846–1935) French chef and cookbook author. Master of the haute cuisine style of French cooking, he gained an international reputation while working in London at the Savoy (1890–98) and Carlton (1899–1919) hotels. Full name **Escoffier, Georges Auguste**

es·co·lar /èskə laár/ *n* a fish with a slim bony body, jutting lower jaw, and sharp teeth. Native to: tropical and temperate deep seas. Family: Gempylidae. [Late 19C. Via Spanish, "student" (because of the rings around its eyes resembling spectacles) < late Latin *scholaris* (see SCHOLAR)]

Es·con·di·do /èskən deédō/ city in southwestern California, north of San Diego and east of Carlsbad. Population: 135,908 (2002 estimate).

es·cort *n* /éss kàwrt/ **1. PROTECTOR ON JOURNEY** one or more persons accompanying somebody or something as a guard or guide, or as a mark of honor **2. MALE SOCIAL PARTNER** a man accompanying a woman on a social occasion **3. HIRED SOCIAL PARTNER** a man or woman who is hired to accompany another person as a companion, especially to a social event or entertainment **4.** MIL **ACCOMPANYING MILITARY VESSEL OR AIRCRAFT** one or more warships or fighter aircraft accompanying a larger, more vulnerable ship or aircraft as protection **5. PROTECTION ON JOURNEY** protection or restraint provided by an escort ○ *proceed under escort* ■ *vt* /əss káwrt, éss kàwrt/ (**-cort·ed, -cort·ing, -corts**) **GO WITH SOMEBODY AS ESCORT** to accompany somebody or something as an escort ○ *The butler will escort you to the door.* [Late 16C. Via French *escorte* < Italian *scorta* < *scorgere* "to guide," via assumed Vulgar Latin *excorrigere* < Latin *corrigere* (see CORRECT)]

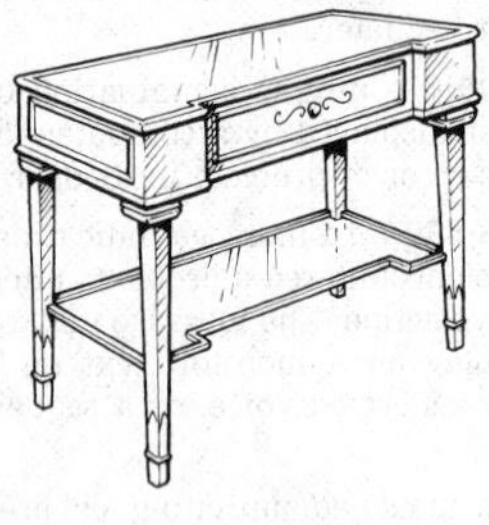

escritoire

es·cri·toire /èskri twaár/ *n* a writing desk, often with a hinged flap that conceals drawers and pigeonholes [Late 16C. Via Old French, "writing box" < medieval Latin *scriptorium* (see SCRIPTORIUM)]

es·crow /és krō, e skrṓ/ *n* an amount of money or property granted to somebody but held by a third party and only released after a specific condition has been met ■ *vt* (**-crowed, -crow·ing, -crows**) to place something in escrow [Mid-17C. < Anglo-Norman *escrowe* "scroll," variant of Old French *escroe* (see SCROLL)] ◇ **in escrow** kept for somebody until a specific condition has been met

es·cu·do /ə skoódō/ (*plural* **-dos**) *n* **1. CURRENCY UNIT OF CAPE VERDE** the main unit of currency of Cape Verde. See table at **currency 2. FORMER PORTUGUESE CURRENCY** the main unit of the former currency of Portugal **3. FORMER SPANISH AND S AMERICAN CURRENCY** a former unit of currency in Spain and several South American countries [Early 19C. Via Spanish and Portuguese < Latin *scutum* "shield"; because early coins resembled heraldic shields]

es·cu·lent /éskyələnt/ (*formal*) *adj* fit to be eaten ■ *n* something edible, especially a plant [Early 17C. < Latin *esculentus* < *esca* "food" < *edere* "eat"]

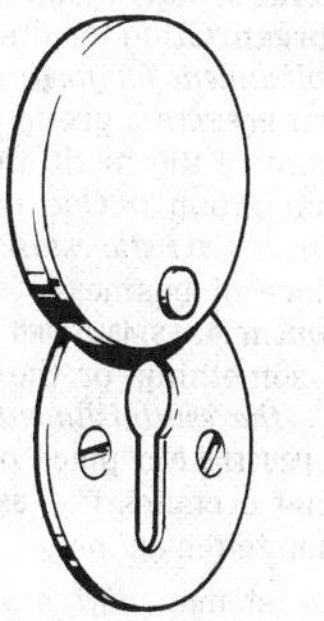

escutcheon (sense 2)

es·cutch·eon /ə skúchən/ *n* **1. HERALDIC SHIELD** a shield, especially one used in heraldry to display a coat of arms **2. PROTECTIVE SHIELD** a plate or shield fixed around something such as a light switch or keyhole, as an ornament or to protect the surrounding surface **3.** NAUT **NAMEPLATE ON VESSEL** a panel on the stern of a vessel on which the vessel's name is shown [15C. Via Anglo-Norman *escuchon* < Latin *scutum* "shield"] —**es·cutch·eoned** *adj*

Esd. *abbr* BIBLE Esdras

Es·dra·e·lon, Plain of /éss dray ée lon, èssdrə-/ plain in northern Israel between the Jordan River on the east and the Mediterranean Sea on the west. It is approximately 35 mi./60 km long and has an average width of 15 mi./24 km.

Es·dras /ézdrəss/ *n* **1.** either of two books of the Apocrypha **2.** either of two books of the Roman Catholic version of the Bible (**Douay Bible**), equivalent to the books of Ezra and Nehemiah in the Authorized Version

ESE *abbr* COMPASS east-southeast

-ese *suffix* **1.** from, of, native to, or inhabiting a particular place ○ *Taiwanese* **2.** the language of a particular place ○ *Chinese* **3.** the style of language of a particular group (*disapproving*) ○ *officialese* [Via Old French *-eis*, Italian *-ese* < Latin *-ensis* "originating in"]

SYNONYMS See ***language*** and ***jargon***[1].

~~**esential**~~ incorrect spelling of **essential**

es·er·ine /éssə reen/ *n* PHARM former name for **physostigmine** [Mid-19C. < French *ésérine* < Efik *esere* "Calabar bean"]

Es·fa·han /èsfə haán/, **Is·fa·han** /isfə-/ city in central Iran, capital of Esfahan Province. A former capital of Iran, it is renowned for its architecture. Population: 1,266,072 (1996).

Esh·kol /ésh kàwl, esh káwl/, **Levi** (1895–1969) Russian-born Israeli politician. He was prime minister of Israel from 1963 until his death in 1969. Born **Shkolnik, Levi**

es·ker /éskər/, **es·kar** *n* a long narrow winding ridge of sand or gravel, deposited by a stream flowing under a glacier [Mid-19C. < Irish *eiscir*]

Es·ki·mo /éskə mō/ (*plural* **-mos** or *same*) *n* **1.** a member of a people indigenous to northern Canada, Alaska, Greenland, and Siberia, comprising the Inuit and Yupik people (*sometimes considered offensive*) **2.** the language group comprising Inuit and Yupik [Late 16C. < French *Esquimaux* < Algonquian] —**Es·ki·mo** *adj*

USAGE See ***Inuit.***

Es·ki·mo-A·leut *n* a family of languages spoken in Greenland, Alaska, northern Canada, Siberia, and the Aleutian Islands

Es·ki·mo dog *n* a large powerful dog with a thick coat and erect ears that is used to pull sleds in Arctic regions

Es·ki·mo roll *n* a process or procedure by which a capsized kayak is rolled over underwater in order to come up righted

Es·ki·şe·hir /éskishə heér/ city in western Turkey, west of Ankara. Population: 470,981 (1997).

Eskimo dog

ESL *abbr* EDUC English as a second language

ESOL /ée sàwl/ *abbr* EDUC English for speakers of other languages

ESOP /ée sòp/ *n* an investment plan in which employees acquire stock of the company they work for by making tax-deductible contributions. Full form **employee stock ownership plan**

e·soph·a·gus /i sóffəgəss/ (*plural* **-guses** or **-gi** /-jī, -gī/), **oe·soph·a·gus** *n* the passage down which food moves between the throat and the stomach [14C. Via medieval Latin < Greek *oisophagos*] —**e·soph·a·ge·al** /i sòffə jée əl/ *adj*

es·o·ter·ic /èssə térrik/ *adj* **1. RESTRICTED TO INITIATES** intended for or understood by only an initiated few **2. ABSTRUSE** difficult to understand **3. SECRET** secret or highly confidential [Mid-17C. < Greek *esōterikos* "belonging to an inner circle" < *esōterō* "inner" < *esō* "within"] —**es·o·ter·i·cal·ly** *adv*

SYNONYMS See ***obscure.***

es·o·ter·i·ca /èssə térrikə/ *npl* things that are for initiates only or are difficult or secret [Early 20C. < Greek *esōterika*, form of *esōterikos* (see ESOTERIC)]

es·o·ter·i·cism /èssə térrə sìzzəm/ *n* **1.** beliefs or practices that are arcane, mysterious, or secret **2.** the condition or quality of being esoteric

ESP *abbr* **1.** EDUC English for special purposes **2.** PARAPSYCHOL extrasensory perception

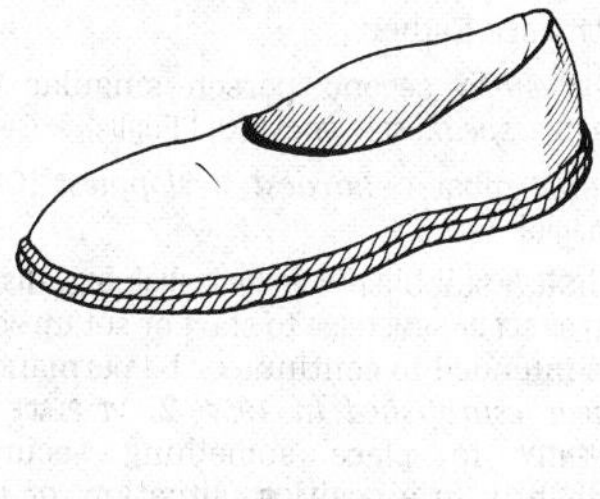

espadrille

es·pa·drille /éspə drìl/ *n* a light shoe with a fabric upper and a sole made of twisted cord [Late 19C. Via French < Provençal *espardilho* < *espart* "esparto (grass)" (from which originally made) < Latin *spartum* (see ESPARTO)]

es·pal·ier /əss pállyər, -pál yày/ *n* a plant, especially a fruit tree, trained to grow flat against a wall or other upright support [Mid-17C. Via French < Italian *spalliera* "shoulder support" < *spalla* "shoulder" < Latin *spatula* (see SPATULA)]

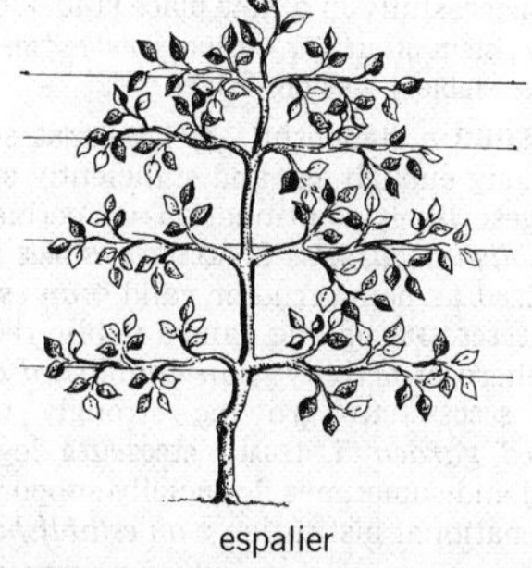

espalier

es·par·to /ə spaártō/ (*plural* **-tos**), **es·par·to grass** *n* a coarse grass. Use: paper, ropes, mats. Native to: southern Europe, northern Africa. Latin name: *Stipa tenacissima.* [Mid-19C. Via Spanish < Latin *spartum* < Greek *sparton* "rope"]

es·pe·cial /i spésh'l/ *adj* (*formal*) **1.** unusual or exceptional ○ *You'll need to take especial care.* **2.** mainly for somebody or something specific ○ *marked for my especial attention* [13C. Via Old French < Latin *specialis* "of a specific kind" < *species* (see SPECIES)]

es·pe·cial·ly /i spésh'lee/ *adv* **1. EXCEPTIONALLY** to an unusual or exceptional degree **2. PARTICULARLY** used to single out one among a range ○ *They're a helpful group, especially Mark.* **3. CHIEFLY** in most cases **4.** ⚠ **SPECIALLY** for a particular or specific purpose

USAGE especially or **specially**? Although traditionally there is a clear difference in meaning, both words are often used when the other is intended: *The hotel has specially designed ramps for the physically challenged.* (***Specially*** is wanted here because the ramps are designed "for a special purpose.") *The buildings are not especially large.* (***Especially*** is wanted here because the buildings are not "exceptionally" large.) In rapid conversation, the first syllable of ***especially*** tends to be slurred or omitted, and this practice can affect the correct choice when the words are written.

~~**especialy**~~ incorrect spelling of **especially**

Es·pe·ran·to /èspə rántō, -raán-/ *n* an artificial language invented in 1887, based on the root forms of some words common to the major European languages. In general, the word order is similar to that of English, although the grammar is more highly inflected. [Late 19C. After Doctor *Esperanto* "somebody who hopes," Esperanto pseudonym of Ludwik Zamenhof (1859–1917), Polish inventor of the language] —**Es·pe·ran·tist** *n*

es·pi·al /ə spí əl/ *n* (*archaic*) **1. SIGHTING SOMETHING** the act of sighting or discovering something **2. NOTICING SOMETHING** the act of noticing or detecting something **3. SPYING ON SOMEBODY OR SOMETHING** the act of secretly watching somebody or something [14C. < Old French *espialle* < *espier* (see SPY)]

es·pi·o·nage /éspee ə naazh/ *n* the use of spying or spies to gather secret information [Late 18C. < French *espionnage* < *espionner* "to spy" < *espion* "spy"]

es·pla·nade /ésplə naad, -nàyd/ *n* **1.** a long level area, especially by the sea, for walking or driving along **2.** a wide level area outside a fortification, where attackers will be exposed to fire from defenders [Late 17C. < French < Latin *explanare* "flatten out" (see EXPLAIN)]

Es·po·si·to /èspə zeétō/, **Phil** (*b.* 1942) Canadian ice hockey player. A center noted for his goal scoring, he played professionally between 1963 and his retirement in 1981. Full name **Esposito, Philip Anthony**

es·pous·al /i spówz'l/ *n* **1.** the adoption of something as a belief or cause **2.** a betrothal or wedding (*formal; often used in the plural*)

es·pouse /i spówz/ (**-poused, -pous·ing, -pous·es**) *vt* **1.** to adopt or support something as a belief or cause **2.** to marry somebody, or give somebody in marriage (*archaic*) [15C. Via Old French *espouser* < Latin *sponsare* < *spons-* (see SPONSOR)] —**es·pous·er** *n*

es·pres·si·vo /èsprə seévō/ *adv* played in an expressive way (*used as a musical direction*) [Late 19C. < Italian]

es·pres·so /e spréssō/, **ex·pres·so** /ik-/ *n* **1.** dark strong-tasting coffee made by using a special machine to pass steam under pressure or boiling water through finely ground coffee beans **2.** a serving of espresso coffee, usually in a small cup ○ *Two espressos and a cappuccino.* [Mid-20C. < Italian *(caffè) espresso* "pressed-out (coffee)" < past participle of *esprimere* "press out" < Latin *exprimere* (see EXPRESS)]

es·prit /e spreé/ *n* lively intelligence or wit [Late 16C. Via French < Latin *spiritus* (see SPIRIT)]

es·prit de corps /e spreé də káwr/ *n* a feeling of pride in belonging to a group and a sense of identification with it [< French, "group spirit"]

es·py /i spī/ (**-pied, -py·ing, -pies**) *vt* to catch sight of or detect something (*literary*) [14C. < Old French *espier* (see SPY)]

Esq. *abbr* Esquire (*used in correspondence*)

-esque *suffix* in the style or manner of ○ *Kafkaesque* ○ *statuesque* [Via French < assumed Vulgar Latin *-iscus* < Germanic]

Es·qui·malt /éskee màwlt/ seaport and naval station on southeastern Vancouver Island, British Columbia, Canada. It is a suburb of the city of Victoria. Population: 16,192 (1991).

es·quire /i skwīr/ *n* a youth serving as an attendant or shield bearer to a medieval knight, especially as a stage in his own training for knighthood [14C. Via Old French *escuier* < late Latin *scutarius* "shield bearer" < Latin *scutum* "shield"]

Es·quire *n* a courtesy title placed after a man's full name, especially the name of an attorney, in correspondence (*usually abbreviated*)

Es·qui·vel /éskee vél/, **Manuel** (*b.* 1940) Belizean prime minister. He was prime minister from 1984 to 1989 and again from 1993 to 1998.

ESR *abbr* **1.** PHYS electron spin resonance **2.** MED erythrocyte sedimentation rate

ess /ess/ *n* **1.** the letter s or S **2.** something shaped like an S [Mid-16C. < Latin *es*]

-ess *suffix* woman or girl ○ *heiress* [Via Old French and Latin < Greek *-issa*]

USAGE The suffix ***-ess*** is fast disappearing from the language, with the trend toward avoiding any unnecessary reference to gender. The suffixes *-er* and *-or* are not gender-specific in modern English: an *author* or *manager*, like a doctor or writer, may be male or female, so the words *authoress* and *manageress* are redundant. Some ***-ess*** words remain in use, for example, *heiress* and *actress*, although *actor* is increasingly used of both men and women. See also ***gender-neutral***.

es·say *n* /é sày, ə sáy/ **1.** SHORT NONFICTION PROSE PIECE a short analytic, descriptive, or interpretive piece of literary or journalistic prose dealing with a specific topic, especially from a personal and unsystematic viewpoint **2.** WORK RESEMBLING WRITTEN ESSAY an artistic or journalistic work resembling a written essay but in another medium ○ *not so much a short film as a cinematographic essay* **3.** ATTEMPT AT SOMETHING an attempt to accomplish something (*formal*) **4.** TEST OF SOMETHING a test or trial of something (*formal*) ■ *vt* /ə sáy, é sày/ (**-sayed, -say·ing, -says**) ATTEMPT TO DO SOMETHING to try out or attempt something (*formal*) ○ *Shall we essay a walk on the promenade?* [15C. < Old French *essaier* "to try" < assumed Vulgar Latin *exagiare* "weigh out" < Latin *agere* "do"]

es·say·ist /é sày ist/ *n* a writer of literary or journalistic essays

es·say·is·tic /è say ístik/ *adj* resembling or styled like a literary or journalistic essay

es·say ques·tion *n* a question in an examination that must be answered in a prose piece of a specific length

Es·sen /éss'n/ industrial city in the Ruhr valley, North Rhine-Westphalia State, west central Germany. Population: 617,955 (1997).

es·sence /éss'nss/ *n* **1.** IDENTIFYING NATURE the quality or nature of something that identifies it or makes it what it is ○ *You've described the city, but you haven't communicated its essence.* **2.** MOST IMPORTANT FEATURE the most important element or feature of something ○ *The essence of leadership is said to be the willingness of other people to follow.* **3.** PERFECT FORM the perfect or idealized form of something, especially when embodied in a person ○ *She's the essence of tact.* **4.** BIOCHEM CHEMICAL CONSTITUENT OF PLANT a purified plant extract **5.** COOK, COSMETICS CONCENTRATED PLANT EXTRACT a concentrated plant extract containing its unique flavor and fragrance ○ *vanilla essence* [14C. Via French < Latin *essentia* < *essent-*, present participle of *esse* "be"] ◇ **in essence** fundamentally or intrinsically ◇ **of the essence** of the highest importance for achieving something

es·sen·tial /i sénshəl/ *adj* **1.** NECESSARY of the highest importance for achieving something ○ *It's essential that we arrive on time.* ○ *an essential ingredient* **2.** BASIC being the most basic element or feature of something or somebody ○ *reinforcing the essential organizational framework* **3.** DEFINING constituting the property or characteristic of something that makes it what it is **4.** BIOCHEM REQUIRED IN DIET describes a nutrient that is not made by the body and is required in the diet for normal function ○ *essential vitamins and minerals* **5.** MED WITHOUT KNOWN CAUSE describes a disease that has no known cause ■ *n* (*usually used in the plural*) **1.** SOMETHING NECESSARY something that is absolutely necessary ○ *the essentials for survival* ○ *an essential for this kind of work* **2.** FUNDAMENTAL ASPECT a basic aspect of a particular subject ○ *You know the essentials of the case.* [14C. < late Latin *essentialis* < Latin *essentia* (see ESSENCE)] —**es·sen·ti·al·i·ty** /i sènshee állətee/ *n* —**es·sen·tial·ly** *adv* —**es·sen·tial·ness** *n*

SYNONYMS See ***necessary***.

es·sen·tial a·mi·no ac·id *n* any amino acid that the body cannot make and that must be obtained from food to maintain growth

es·sen·tial el·e·ment *n* a chemical element that is necessary to the healthy growth of an organism

es·sen·tial fat·ty ac·id *n* a natural fat or oil found in whole grains, seeds, nuts, and oily fish, required in the diet to make prostaglandins

es·sen·tial·ism /ə sénshəl ìzzəm/ *n* the doctrine that things have an essence or ideal nature that is independent of and prior to their existence —**es·sen·tial·ist** *n*

es·sen·tial oil *n* an oil extracted from plant material

Es·sex /éssiks/ **1.** town in central Maryland, east of Baltimore. Population: 40,872 (2002 estimate). **2.** county in eastern England. The administrative center is Chelmsford. Area: 1,419 sq. mi./3,674 sq. km.

Es·sex, Robert Devereux, 2nd Earl of (1566–1601) English soldier and courtier. His military successes in Europe against Spain were offset by diplomatic errors as lord lieutenant of Ireland (1599). Although he had been a favorite of Elizabeth I, he led an abortive insurrection in London and was beheaded.

es·so·nite /éssə nīt/ *n* a yellow to brown garnet [Early 19C. < Greek *hēssōn* "inferior" (because less hard than other garnets)]

EST *abbr* **1.** TIME Eastern Standard Time **2.** PSYCHIAT electric shock treatment

est. *abbr* **1.** established **2.** estimated **3.** estuary

Est. *abbr* BIBLE Esther

-est[1], **-st** *suffix* second person singular of verbs (*archaic*) ○ *speakest* ○ *goest* [Old English < Germanic]

-est[2] *suffix* most ○ *hardest* ○ *sloppiest* [Old English < Germanic]

es·tab·lish /i stábblish/ (**-lished, -lish·ing, -lish·es**) *v* **1.** *vt* START OR SET UP SOMETHING to start or set up something that is intended to continue or be permanent ○ *The firm was established in 1954.* **2.** *vt* PLACE SOMETHING PERMANENTLY to place something securely and permanently in a position, situation, or condition ○ *A settlement was established here two hundred years ago.* **3.** *vt* CONFIRM TRUTH OF SOMETHING to investigate something and prove or confirm its truth or validity ○ *We need to establish the cause of the accident.* **4.** *vt* CAUSE SOMETHING TO BE RECOGNIZED to cause something or somebody to become generally accepted or recognized ○ *established her reputation as a lead vocalist* **5.** *vt* MAKE CHURCH NATIONAL AND OFFICIAL to make a church an official national institution **6.** *vti* CAUSE PLANT TO GROW SUCCESSFULLY to grow, or cause a plant to grow, successfully in a new place [14C. < Old French *establiss-*, stem of *establir* < Latin *stabilire* "make stable" < *stabilis* "stable"] —**es·tab·lish·er** *n*

es·tab·lished /i stábblisht/ *adj* **1.** THRIVING started or set up long enough ago and sufficiently successful to suggest likely continuation or permanence ○ *an established business* **2.** ACCEPTED AS TRUE generally recognized as being true or valid ○ *an established fact* **3.** SUCCESSFUL having gained public recognition in a sphere of activity ○ *an established author* **4.** GROWING SUCCESSFULLY growing strongly ○ *an established garden* **5.** LEGALLY RECOGNIZED legally recognized and sometimes financially supported as an official national institution ○ *an established church*

es·tab·lish·ing shot /i stábblishing-/ *n* a shot in a movie that introduces a new scene

es·tab·lish·ment /i stábblishmənt/ *n* **1.** SOMETHING ESTABLISHED something that is established as a business, institution, organization, or undertaking ○ *worked for this establishment for forty years* **2.** *also* **Es·tab·lish·ment** PEOPLE IN POWER a group of people who hold power and control the institutions in a society or a professional group ○ *One period's avant-garde becomes the next's artistic establishment.* **3.** BUSINESS PREMISES a place of business ○ *banned them from the establishment* **4.** ESTABLISHING SOMETHING the act of establishing something, or the condition of being established ○ *the establishment of new guidelines for users* **5.** HOUSEHOLD a place of residence, or the household that occupies it —**es·tab·lish·men·tar·i·an** /i stàbblishmən térree ən/ *n*

es·ta·mi·net /e stàmmi náy/ *n* a small and simple café, bar, or bistro, especially in France [Early 19C. < French]

es·tan·cia /e staán syaá/ *n* a large landed estate, especially a cattle ranch, in South America [Mid-17C. Via Spanish, "station" < medieval Latin *stantia* < Latin *stant-*, present participle of *stare* "stand"]

es·tate /i stáyt/ *n* **1.** ALL OF SOMEBODY'S PROPERTY the whole of somebody's property, possessions, and capital, especially the property of somebody who is dead or bankrupt **2.** RURAL PROPERTY WITH RESIDENCE an area of rural, privately owned property that includes a large residence **3.** SOMEBODY'S OVERALL SITUATION the circumstances, period, or condition in which somebody lives **4.** POL, HIST SECTOR OF SOCIETY especially formerly in Europe, any of three traditional ranks or sectors of society with some political power, broadly, the clergy, the nobility, and the middle class [13C. < Old French *estat* (see STATE)]

es·tate-bot·tled *adj* describes wine bottled by the same vineyard at which it was made

es·tate car *n UK* same as **station wagon** [< its ability to hold the owner's possessions]

es·tate tax *n* a tax on the right to bequeath property, assessed on the value of the bequeather's property before it is passed on to the heirs

es·teem /i steém/ *vt* (**-teemed, -teem·ing, -teems**) **1.** VALUE SOMEBODY OR SOMETHING HIGHLY to have a high regard for somebody or something **2.** REGARD SOMETHING IN PARTICULAR WAY to consider something or somebody as having a particular quality (*formal*) ○ *esteem it a privilege* ■ *n* **1.** HIGH REGARD a high opinion and appreciation of somebody or something ○ *a relationship based on mutual esteem* **2.** VALUATION judgment or estimation of the worth of somebody or something [Early 16C. Via French *estimer* "to value" < Latin *aestimare* "estimate, assess"]

SYNONYMS See ***regard***.

Es·te·fan /éstə fàn/, **Gloria** (*b.* 1957) Cuban-born US singer and songwriter. She established herself first as a Spanish-language pop singer with the group Miami Sound Machine (1984–89) before gaining an international following as a solo artist. Born **Fajardo, Gloria Maria**

es·ter /éstər/ *n* an organic, often fragrant compound formed in a reaction between an acid and an alcohol with the elimination of water [Mid-19C. < German, contraction of *Essigäther* "acetic ether"]

es·ter·ase /éstə ràyss, -ràyz/ *n* any enzyme that catalyzes the hydrolysis of an ester

es·ter·i·fy /ə stérrə fī/ (**-fied, -fy·ing, -fies**) *vti* to change or make a substance change into an ester —**es·ter·i·fi·ca·tion** /ə stèrrəfi káysh'n/ *n*

Esth. *abbr* BIBLE Esther

Es·ther /éstər/ *n* **1.** in the Bible, the Jewish queen of Persia who is described as having rescued her Jewish subjects from massacre **2.** a book of the Bible that tells the story of Esther. See table at **Bible**

es·thete, etc. another spelling of **aesthete, etc.**

Es·ti·gar·ri·bi·a /èstigə ríbbee ə, -gaa-/, **José Félix** (1888–1940) Paraguayan general and president. He was president from 1939 until his death in an airplane crash.

es·ti·ma·ble /éstəməb'l/ *adj* **1.** deserving respect or admiration **2.** able to be estimated (*archaic*) [15C.

< French < Latin *aestimare* "estimate, assess"] —**es·ti·ma·ble·ness** *n* —**es·ti·ma·bly** *adv*

es·ti·mate *v* /éstə màyt/ (**-mat·ed, -mat·ing, -mates**) **1.** *vt* **CALCULATE SOMETHING ROUGHLY** to make an approximate calculation of something ○ *Can you estimate the time it will take?* **2.** *vi* **SUGGEST PRICE** to assess something such as an item to be bought or a job to be done, and to state a likely price for it ○ *Ask at least two contractors to estimate for the work.* **3.** *vt* **ASSESS SOMETHING** to form an opinion or judgment about somebody or something ○ *How would you estimate that performance?* ■ *n* /éstəmət/ **1. ROUGH CALCULATION** an approximate calculation ○ *At least a thousand people attended, by my estimate.* ○ *Here are the estimates for next month's sales figures.* **2. APPROXIMATE PRICE** an assessment of the likely price of something such as an item to be bought or a job to be done ○ *Their estimate is the lowest.* [Late 16C. < Latin *aestimare* "estimate, assess"] —**es·ti·ma·tive** *adj* —**es·ti·ma·tor** *n*

USAGE estimate or **estimation**? Broadly speaking, ***estimation*** refers to a thinking or valuing process and ***estimate*** to the result of such a process. *An estimate of the time needed* is the figure produced by working out how long something will take, whereas *an estimation of the time needed* is the calculation process that produces that figure. ***Estimation*** also has the meaning "judgment or opinion," which ***estimate*** does not have: *What, in your estimation, is the cause of the problem? She went down in their estimation when the truth came out.*

es·ti·ma·tion /éstə máysh'n/ *n* **1.** a judgment or opinion about somebody or something ○ *Her behavior bore out his estimation of her.* **2.** the act of estimating something, or the result of this

USAGE See ***estimate***.

es·ti·val /éstəv'l/, **aes·ti·val** *adj* relating to or happening during summer (*technical or literary*) [14C. Via French < Latin *aestivalis* < *aestivus* < *aestas* "summer"]

es·ti·vate /éstə vàyt/ (**-vat·ed, -vat·ing, -vates**), **aes·ti·vate** *vi* **1.** to be dormant during the summer or during months of drought (*refers to animals, especially some amphibians, reptiles, and insects*) **2.** to spend the summer in a particular place (*formal*) [Early 17C. < Latin *aestivat-*, past participle of *aestivare* < *aestivus* (see ESTIVAL)]

es·ti·va·tion /éstə váysh'n/, **aes·ti·va·tion** *n* **1.** ZOOL **SUMMER DORMANCY** dormancy in some animals during the summer or during months of drought **2.** BOT **ARRANGEMENT OF FLOWER BUD PARTS** the arrangement of the sepals and petals in a flower bud before it opens, especially in what way and to what extent the parts overlap **3. PASSING OF SUMMER** the act or fact of spending the summer in a particular place (*formal*)

Estonia

Es·to·ni·a /e stṓnee ə/ country on the Gulf of Finland in northeastern Europe, north of Latvia and west of Russia. The smallest of the Baltic States, it gained its independence from the former Soviet Union in 1991 and became a member of the European Union in 2004. Language: Estonian. Currency: kroon. Capital: Tallinn. Population: 1,408,556 (2003). Area: 17,462 sq. mi./45,227 sq. km. Official name **Republic of Estonia**

Es·to·ni·an /e stṓnee ən/ *n* **1.** somebody who comes from Estonia **2.** the official language of Estonia, belonging to the Finnic group of the Finno-Ugric branch of Uralic languages. Native speakers: 1.7 million. —**Es·to·ni·an** *adj*

es·top /e stóp/ (**-topped, -top·ping, -tops**) *vt* to use the legal rule of estoppel to prevent something [15C. < Anglo-Norman, Old French *estopper* "plug up" < Latin *stuppa* "tow, broken flax" (used for plugging gaps)] —**es·top·page** *n*

es·top·pel /e stópp'l/ *n* a legal rule that prevents somebody from stating a position inconsistent with one previously stated, especially when the earlier representation has been relied upon by others [Mid-16C. < Old French *estouppail* "stopper" < *estopper* (see ESTOP)]

es·tra·di·ol /èstrə dī̀ àwl/ *n* an estrogenic hormone present in the ovaries. Use: produced synthetically as a component of oral contraceptive products and for treatment of estrogen deficiency and breast cancer. Formula: $C_{18}H_{24}O_2$. [Mid-20C. < ESTRUS + DI-[1]]

es·tral *adj US* ZOOL same as **estrous**

es·trane /és tràyn/ *n* a steroid hormone derived from testosterone. Use: hormone replacement therapy.

es·trange /i stráynj/ (**-tranged, -trang·ing, -trang·es**) *vt* to cause somebody to stop feeling friendly or affectionate toward somebody else or sympathetic toward a tradition or belief (*usually passive*) ○ *He managed to become estranged from all of his friends.* [15C. Via Old French *estrangier* "alienate" < Latin *extraneare* "treat as a stranger" < *extraneus* (see STRANGE)] —**es·trange·ment** *n* —**es·trang·er** *n*

es·tranged /i stráynjd/ *adj* no longer living with a husband or wife

e-strat·e·gy *n* a strategy for conducting business on the Internet

es·tri·ol /éstree àwl/ *n* an estrogen produced in the ovaries and secreted in the urine during pregnancy [Early 20C. < ESTRUS + TRI-]

es·tro·gen /éstrəjən/, **oes·tro·gen** *n* a steroid hormone, produced mainly in the ovaries, that stimulates estrus and the development of female secondary sexual characteristics [Early 20C. < ESTRUS] —**es·tro·gen·ic** /èstrə jénnik/ *adj*

es·tro·gen-re·place·ment ther·a·py *n* treatment to maintain levels of the hormone estrogen in women after menopause to avoid bone fragility (**osteoporosis**) and protect against heart disease

es·trone /és trṑn/, **oes·trone** *n* an estrogenic hormone produced in the ovaries and synthesized for use in treating estrogen deficiency and breast cancer. Formula: $C_{18}H_{22}O_2$. [Early 20C. < ESTRUS]

es·trous /éstrəss/, **oes·trous, es·tral** /éstrəl/, **oes·tral** *adj* **1.** relating to or involving estrus **2.** describes a female mammal at the time of estrus [Early 20C. < ESTRUS]

es·trous cy·cle *n* a hormonally controlled reproductive cycle occurring in many female mammals, marked by a period of sexual activity, ovulation, and changes in the womb lining

es·trus /éstrəss/, **oes·trus** *n* a regular period of sexual excitement in many female mammals, during which the animal seeks to mate [Late 19C. Via Latin *oestrus* "frenzy" < Greek *oistros* "gadfly"]

es·tu·a·rine /éschoo ə rīn, -reen/ *adj* relating to, formed in, or found in an estuary

es·tu·ar·y /éschoo èrree/ (*plural* **-ies**) *n* the wide lower course of a river where the tide flows in, causing fresh and salt water to mix [Mid-16C. < Latin *aestuarium* < *aestus* "heat, surge, tide"] —**es·tu·ar·i·al** /èschoo érree əl/ *adj*

Es·tu·ar·y Eng·lish, Es·tu·ar·y *n* a variety of standard English influenced by Cockney, spoken by people in London and southeastern England along the Thames Estuary (*informal*)

esu, ESU *abbr* PHYS electrostatic unit

e·su·ri·ent /i sóoree ənt/ *adj* very hungry or greedy (*archaic or formal*) [Late 17C. < Latin *esurient-*, present participle of *esurire* "be hungry" < *edere* "eat"] —**e·su·ri·ence** *n* —**e·su·ri·en·cy** *n*

et *abbr* Ethiopia (*used in Internet addresses*) See table at **domain name**

ET *abbr* PARANORMAL extraterrestrial

-et *suffix* **1.** small one ○ *falconet* **2.** something worn on ○ *anklet* [< Old French]

e·ta[1] /áytə, éetə/ *n* the seventh letter of the Greek alphabet, represented in the English alphabet as "e" or "ē." See table at **alphabet** [15C. < Greek *ēta*]

e·ta[2] /áytə/ (*plural* **e·tas** or *same*) *n* in former times, a member of a Japanese class that was restricted to doing menial tasks [Late 19C. < Japanese]

ETA[1] *abbr* TIME estimated time of arrival

ETA[2] /éttə/, **Eta** *n* a Basque nationalist guerrilla group that seeks separation and independence from Spain for the Basque region [Mid-20C. < Basque, acronym < *Euzkadi ta Askatsuna* "Basque Nation and Liberty"]

é·ta·gère /áy taa zhér/, **e·ta·gere** *n* **1.** a piece of furniture made up of several open shelves, used to hold small objects **2.** a free-standing set of shelves, one set back above the other, used to display objects such as pots of plants [Mid-19C. < French, later form of Old French *estagiere* "scaffold" < *estage* (see STAGE)]

e-tail /ée tàyl/ *n* online retail operations, especially those conducted on the Internet [Late 20C. Contraction of *electronic retail*] —**e-tail·er** *n* —**e-tail·ing** *n*

et al.[1] /et ál/ *adv* and others (*used of joint authors of a book or article*) [Shortening of Latin *et alii*]

USAGE etc. or **et al.**? The abbreviation ***etc.*** (from the full form *et cetera/etcetera*) came into English from the Latin expression *et cetera* ("and the rest"). Do not use ***etc.*** as a substitute for the adverb ***et al.***, which came into English from another Latin expression, *et alii* ("and others"). Use ***etc.*** when you list some, or a few, of many items, as in *We will discuss the Plymouth Colony, the Puritans, the witchcraft trials, etc., in our early American literature seminar.* (Never write "and etc." or "& etc.", as these are redundant.) Use ***et al.*** when you mention one person or a few people out of several or many, as in bibliographies, footnotes, or textual references: *In the October issue of the medical journal, Smith, Jones, Roe, Doe, et al.,* [not etc.] *discuss correct insertion of artificial airways.*

et al.[2] /et ál/ *adv* and elsewhere [Shortening of Latin *et alibi*]

et·a·lon /áyt'l òn, étt'l òn/ *n* a spectroscopic device that has two flat parallel reflecting surfaces. Use: measuring wavelengths. [Early 20C. < French *étalon* "standard" < Old French *estal* "standing place"]

et·a·mine /éttə meen/ *n* a light, loosely woven cotton or worsted fabric [Early 18C. < French < Latin *stamineus* "made of threads" < *stamen* "thread in the warp of a loom"]

etc. *abbr* et cetera

USAGE See ***et al.***[1].

et cet·er·a /et séttərə, -séttrə/, **et·cet·er·a** *adv* used to indicate that a list contains other unspecified items ■ *n* one of several or many unspecified things or people [< Latin, "and the rest"]

PRONUNCIATION The correct pronunciations of ***et cetera*** are /et séttərə/, /et séttrə/, not /ek séttərə/.

etch /ech/ (**etched, etch·ing, etch·es**) *v* **1.** *vti* DESIGN **CUT DESIGN INTO SOMETHING WITH ACID** to create a design or drawing on the surface of something, especially a printing plate, by the action of an acid **2.** *vti* **CUT MARKS WITH SOMETHING SHARP** to cut a design or mark into the surface of something using a sharp point or laser beam **3.** *vt* **MAKE SOMETHING CLEARLY VISIBLE** to leave a clear and distinct impression of something (*usually passive*) ○ *His sorrow was etched on his face.* [Mid-17C. Via Dutch *etsen* < Old High German *ezzen* "eat away"] —**etch·er** *n*

etch·ing /éching/ *n* **1. PRINT FROM ETCHED PLATE** a print made from an etched plate **2. CREATION OF CUT DESIGNS** the art or process of creating etched designs or making prints from etched surfaces **3. PLATE FOR PRINTING ETCHED DESIGN** a printing plate with an etched design

ETD *abbr* TIME estimated time of departure

e·ter·nal /i túrn'l/ *adj* **1. EXISTING THROUGH ALL TIME** lasting for all time without beginning or end ○ *eternal life* **2. UNCHANGING** unaffected by the passage of time ○ *eternal truths* **3. SEEMINGLY EVERLASTING** seeming to go on forever or recur incessantly ○ *an eternal student* ■ *n* **SOMETHING EVERLASTING** something that lasts for all time without beginning or end [14C. Via French < late Latin *aeternal-* < Latin *aeternus* < *aevum* "age"] —**e·ter·nal·i·ty** /èetər nállətee/ *n* —**e·ter·nal·ly** *adv*

E·ter·nal *n* God as a universal spirit

E·ter·nal Cit·y *n* Rome, the capital of Italy

e·ter·nal·ize /ə túrn'l ìz/ (**-ized, -iz·ing, -iz·es**) *vt* **1.** to make something eternal **2.** to make something everlastingly famous

e·ter·nal tri·an·gle *n* a sexual or romantic relationship among three people that involves jealousy or other emotional conflicts [Because known throughout history]

e·ter·ni·ty /i túrnətee/ *n* **1.** INFINITE TIME time without beginning or end ○ *lost for all eternity* **2.** TIMELESSNESS the condition, quality, or fact of being without beginning or end **3.** RELIG TIMELESSNESS AFTER DEATH a timeless state conceived as being experienced after death **4.** VERY LONG TIME a very long or seemingly very long period of time ○ *It will take an eternity to put it together again.* ■ **e·ter·ni·ties** *npl* TRUTHS SAID TO BE ETERNAL beliefs or ideas about life that are conceived as being timeless [14C. Via French < Latin *aeternitas* < *aeternus* (see ETERNAL)]

CULTURAL NOTE ***From Here to Eternity***, a movie (1953) by director Fred Zinnemann. Based on James Jones's 1951 novel of the same name, it depicts the lives of US military personnel in Hawaii immediately prior to the attack on Pearl Harbor. It is perhaps best remembered for a scene in which Burt Lancaster and Deborah Kerr embrace in the surf.

e·ter·ni·ty ring *n* a ring with gemstones set around its whole circumference, intended to symbolize everlasting love

e·ter·nize /ə túr nìz/ (**-nized, -niz·ing, -niz·es**) *vt* same as **eternalize** (sense 1) [Mid-16C. < French *éterniser* < Latin *aeternus* (see ETERNAL)]

e·tē·sian wind /ə teézh'n-/ *n* an annual summer wind that blows from the northwest in the Aegean Sea and other parts of the eastern Mediterranean [Early 17C. < Latin *etesius* "annual" < Greek *etēsios* < *etos* "year"]

ETF *abbr* BANKING electronic transfer of funds

eth *n* LING another spelling of **edh**

-eth[1], **-th** *suffix* third person singular of verbs (*archaic*) ○ *goeth* ○ *speaketh* [Old English]

-eth[2] *suffix* another spelling of **-th**

eth·am·bu·tol /e thámbyə tàwl/ *n* a synthetically produced substance that acts against fungi and bacteria. Use: treatment of tuberculosis and other infections. [Mid-20C. < ETHYL + AMINE + BUTANOL]

eth·a·nal /éthə nàl/ *n* CHEM same as **acetaldehyde**

e·tha·na·mide /i thánnə mìd/ *n* CHEM same as **acetamide**

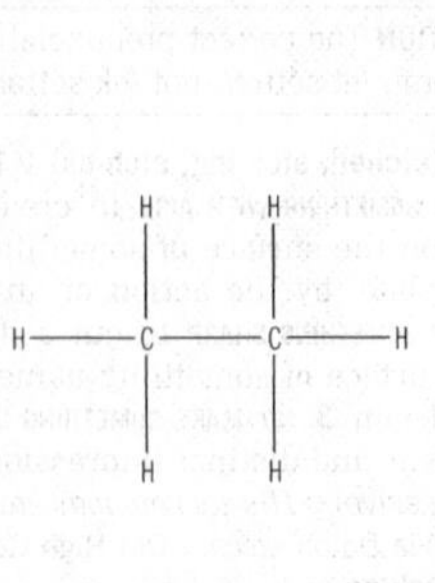

ethane

eth·ane /é thàyn/ *n* a colorless odorless gas that is highly flammable. Source: petroleum, natural gas. Use: fuel, refrigeration. Formula: C_2H_6. [Late 19C. < ETHYL]

eth·ane·di·o·ic ac·id /èth ayn dī ò ik-/ *n* CHEM same as **oxalic acid**

eth·a·no·ate /èthə nó àyt/ *n* CHEM same as **acetate**

eth·a·no·ic ac·id /èthə nò ik-/ *n* CHEM same as **acetic acid**

eth·a·no·ic an·hy·dride *n* CHEM same as **acetic anhydride**

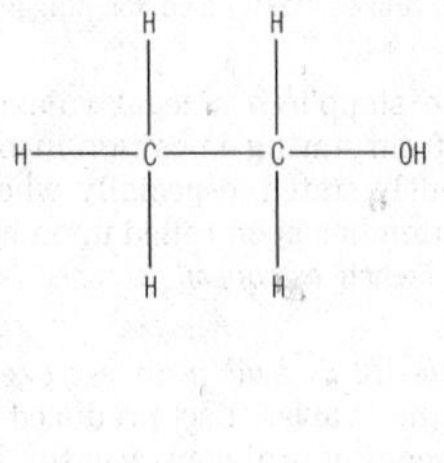

ethanol

eth·a·nol /éthə nàwl/ *n* a colorless liquid with a pleasant smell. Source: fermentation by yeasts and other microorganisms. Use: in alcoholic beverages, as solvent, in the manufacture of other chemicals. Formula: C_2H_5OH.

eth·a·nol·a·mine /èthə nóllə meén/ *n* a colorless viscous liquid. Use: manufacture of antibiotics, cosmetics, detergents, herbicides. Formula: C_2H_7NO.

Eth·el·bert /éth'l bùrt/, **king of Kent** (552?–616) He dominated southern England during his reign (560–616) and was the first Christian Anglo-Saxon monarch, being baptized in 597 by St. Augustine of Canterbury.

Eth·el·red I /éth'l rèd/, **Aeth·el·red I, king of Wessex and Kent** (830?–871). His reign (866–71) saw continual struggle with Danish invaders, whom he defeated at Ashdown in 871.

Eth·el·red II, Aeth·el·red II, king of the English (968–1016) His reign was marked by bitter military struggles. Known as **Ethelred the Unready**

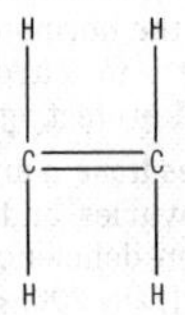

ethene

eth·ene /é theén/ *n* CHEM same as **ethylene** (*technical*) [Mid-19C. < ETHYL]

e·ther /eéthər/ *n* **1.** CHEM LIQUID SOLVENT a volatile colorless liquid with a pleasant smell. Use: solvent, formerly as an anesthetic. Formula: $C_2H_5OC_2H_5$. **2.** CHEM ORGANIC COMPOUND WITH LINKED HYDROCARBON GROUPS any organic compound containing two hydrocarbon groups linked by an oxygen atom **3.** SKY the sky, or the upper reaches of the atmosphere (*literary*) **4.** AIR Earth's atmosphere (*literary*) **5.** PHYS HYPOTHETICAL ELECTROMAGNETIC MEDIUM a medium formerly believed to fill the atmosphere and outer space and to carry electromagnetic waves ○ *send a message across the ether* [14C. Via Latin < Greek *aithēr* "upper air" < Indo-European, "to burn"] —**e·ther·ic** /i thérrik/ *adj*

e·the·re·al /i theéree əl/ *adj* **1.** EXQUISITE very delicate or highly refined ○ *ethereal beauty* **2.** AIRY very light, airy, or insubstantial ○ *Her fragrance lingered in the room, an ethereal reminder of her presence.* **3.** HEAVENLY belonging to the sky or the celestial sphere **4.** CHEM OF ETHER consisting of, containing, or relating to ether [Early 16C. < Latin *aetherius* < Greek *aithēr* (see ETHER)] —**e·the·re·al·i·ty** /i theéree állətee/ *n* —**e·the·re·al·ly** *adv* —**e·the·re·al·ness** *n*

e·the·re·al·ize /i theéree ə lìz/ (**-ized, -iz·ing, -iz·es**) *vt* to make something very delicate or highly refined —**e·the·re·al·i·za·tion** /i theéree əli záysh'n/ *n*

Eth·er·ege /éthərij/, **Sir George** (1635?–91) English playwright. His witty and mildly risqué plays such as *The Man of Mode* (1676), established the style for what is now called Restoration comedy.

e·ther·i·fy /i thérrə fì/ (**-fied, -fy·ing, -fies**) *vt* to convert a substance, especially an alcohol, into ether —**e·ther·i·fi·ca·tion** /i thèrrəfi káysh'n/ *n*

e·ther·ize /eéthə rìz/ (**-ized, -iz·ing, -iz·es**) *vt* **1.** CHEM same as **etherify 2.** formerly, to anesthetize a patient with ether —**e·ther·i·za·tion** /eèthəri záysh'n/ *n* —**e·ther·iz·er** *n*

Eth·er·net /eéthər nèt/ *tdmk* a trademark for a system for exchanging messages between computers on a local area network using coaxial, fiber optic, or twisted-pair cables

eth·ic /éthik/ *n* a system of moral standards or principles ○ *the Protestant work ethic* [Late 19C. Via French *éthique* < Greek *ēthikos* "ethical" < *ēthos* (see ETHOS)]

eth·i·cal /éthik'l/ *adj* **1.** CONFORMING TO ACCEPTED STANDARDS consistent with agreed principles of correct moral conduct ○ *While such activities are not strictly illegal, they are certainly not ethical.* **2.** OF ETHICS relating to or involving ethics **3.** PHARM AVAILABLE BY PRESCRIPTION ONLY describes a prescription drug —**eth·i·cal·i·ty** /èthi kállətee/ *n* —**eth·i·cal·ly** *adv* —**eth·i·cal·ness** *n*

eth·i·cist /éthissist/ *n* a student of ethics, or a devotee of ethical ideals

eth·ics /éthiks/ *n* the study of moral standards and how they affect conduct (*takes a singular verb*) ■ *npl* a system of moral principles governing the appropriate conduct for a person or group (*takes a plural verb*) [15C. Via Old French *ethiques* < Greek *ēthika* < *ēthikos* (see ETHIC)]

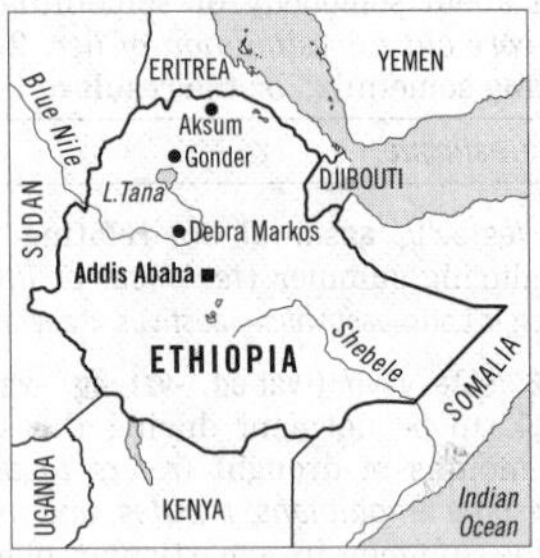

Ethiopia

E·thi·o·pi·a /eéthee ópee ə/ landlocked country in northeastern Africa, separated from the Red Sea by Eritrea and Djibouti, and from the Gulf of Aden by Somalia. It is the oldest independent country in Africa. Language: Amharic. Currency: birr. Capital: Addis Ababa. Population: 66,557,553 (2003). Area: 437,600 sq. mi./1,133,380 sq. km. Official name **Federal Democratic Republic of Ethiopia**. Former name **Abyssinia** —**E·thi·o·pi·an** *n, adj*

E·thi·op·ic /eéthee óppik, -ópik/ *n* LANG same as **Geez** [Mid-17C. Via Latin < Greek *aithiopikos* < *Aithiop-* "Ethiopian" < *aithein* "to burn" + *ōps* "face"]

eth·moid bone /èth moyd-/ *n* a perforated bone in the skull whose outer surfaces form part of the outer wall of the nasal cavity and the inner wall of the eye socket [Mid-18C. < Greek *ēthmoeidēs* "like a sieve" < *ēthmos* "sieve"] —**eth·moid·al** /eth móyd'l/ *adj*

eth·narch /éth naark/ *n* a ruler of a province or people, especially in the Roman Empire [Mid-17C. < Greek *ethnarkhēs* < *ethnos* "people, nation" + *-arkhēs* "ruler"] —**eth·nar·chy** *n*

eth·nic /éthnik/ *adj* **1.** SHARING CULTURAL CHARACTERISTICS sharing distinctive cultural traits as a group in society ○ *ethnic minorities* **2.** OF GROUP SHARING CULTURAL CHARACTERISTICS relating to a group or groups in society with distinctive cultural traits ○ *ethnic origins* **3.** OF PARTICULAR ORIGIN OR CULTURE relating to a person or to a large group of people who share a national, racial, linguistic, or religious heritage, whether or not they reside in their countries of origin ○ *ethnic Albanians* **4.** CULTURALLY TRADITIONAL belonging to or associated with the traditional culture of a social group ○ *ethnic clothing* ■ *n* MEMBER OF ETHNIC GROUP a member of an ethnic group within a society [14C. Via late Latin, "heathen" < Greek *ethnikos* < *ethnos* "people, nation" < Indo-European, "self"] —**eth·ni·cal·ly** *adv*

eth·nic cleans·ing *n* the violent elimination or removal of people from a country or area because of their ethnic backgrounds, by means of genocide or forced expulsion

eth·nic·i·ty /eth nı́ssətee/ (*plural* **-ties**) *n* ethnic affiliation or distinctiveness

eth·nic mi·nor·i·ty *n* an ethnic group that is a minority within a nation or society

ethno- *prefix* people, culture ○ *ethnohistory* [< Greek *ethnos* (see ETHNIC)]

eth·no·bot·a·ny /èthnō bótt'nee/ *n* the scientific study of the traditional classification and uses of plants in different human societies —**eth·no·bo·tan·i·cal** /èthnō bə tánnik'l/ *adj*—**eth·no·bo·tan·i·cal·ly** *adv*—**eth·no·bot·a·nist** *n*

eth·no·cen·trism /èthnō sén trìzzəm/ *n* a belief in or assumption of the superiority of the social or cultural group that a person belongs to (*disapproving*) —**eth·no·cen·tric** *adj* —**eth·no·cen·tri·cal·ly** *adv* —**eth·no·cen·tric·i·ty** /-sen trissə̀tee/ *n*

eth·no·gen·e·sis /èthnō jénnəssiss/ *n* the creation of a new ethnic group identity

eth·nog·ra·phy /eth nóggrəfee/ *n* a branch of anthropology concerned with the description of ethnic groups —**eth·nog·ra·pher** *n* —**eth·no·graph·ic** /èthnə gráffik/ *adj* —**eth·no·graph·i·cal·ly** *adv*

eth·no·his·to·ry /èthnō hístəree/ *n* the scientific study of how cultures have developed through history —**eth·no·his·to·ri·an** /èthnō hi stáwree ən/ *n* —**eth·no·his·to·ric** *adj*

eth·no·lin·guis·tics /èthnō ling gwístiks/ *n* the scientific study of the relationship between language and culture (*takes a singular verb*) —**eth·no·lin·guist** /èthnō líng gwist/ *n* —**eth·no·lin·guis·tic** *adj* —**eth·no·lin·guis·ti·cal·ly** *adv*

eth·nol·o·gy /eth nólləjee/ *n* **1.** the scientific comparison of different cultures **2.** ANTHROP same as **cultural anthropology**—**eth·no·log·ic** /èthnə lójjik/ *adj*—**eth·no·log·i·cal·ly** *adv* —**eth·nol·o·gist** *n*

eth·no·meth·od·ol·o·gy /èthnō methə dóllǝjee/ *n* the study of how people interact in ways that maintain the social structure of the situations in which they find themselves —**eth·no·meth·od·ol·o·gist** *n*

eth·no·mu·si·col·o·gy /èthnō myoozi kólləjee/ *n* the study of the music of non-Western cultures —**eth·no·mu·si·co·log·i·cal** /èthnō myoozikə lójjik'l/ *adj*—**eth·no·mu·si·col·o·gist** *n*

eth·no·na·tion·al·ist /èthnō náshən'l ist, -náshnəlist/ *adj* combining ethnic pride and cohesiveness with strong nationalism

e·thol·o·gy /ee thólləjee, i-/ *n* **1.** the study of the behavior of animals in their natural habitat, usually proposing evolutionary explanations **2.** PSYCHOL same as **human ethology** [Mid-17C. < Latin *ethologia* < Greek *ēthos* (see ETHOS)] —**eth·o·log·i·cal** /eethə lójjik'l, èthə-/ *adj* —**e·thol·o·gist** *n*

e·thos /ée thòss/ *n* the fundamental and distinctive character of a group, social context, or period of time, typically expressed in attitudes, habits, and beliefs [Mid-19C. < Greek *ēthos* "custom, disposition" < Indo-European, "self"]

eth·ox·y /i thóksee/, **eth·ox·yl** /i thóksəl/ *adj* forming or containing a chemical group composed of ethyl and oxygen. Formula: CH_3CH_2O. [Late 19C. < ETHYL + OXY-]

eth·ox·y·eth·ane /i thòksee ée thàyn/ *n* CHEM same as **ether** (sense 1) (*technical*)

eth·ox·yl *adj* CHEM same as **ethoxy**

eth·yl /éthəl/ *n* relating to the group of atoms derived from ethane after the loss of a hydrogen atom. Formula: $-C_2H_5$. [Mid-19C. < ETHER]

eth·yl ac·e·tate *n* a volatile colorless liquid with a pleasant fruity smell. Use: manufacture of perfumes, solvent. Formula: $C_4H_8O_2$.

eth·yl al·co·hol *n* CHEM same as **ethanol**

eth·yl·a·mine /éthələ meen, èthəl ámmin/ *n* a colorless volatile liquid. Use: petroleum refining, detergents. Formula: $C_2H_5NH_2$.

eth·yl·ate /éthə làyt/ (**-at·ed, -at·ing, -ates**) *vt* to attach an ethyl group to a molecule or to one of the molecules of a compound —**eth·yl·a·tion** /èthə láysh'n/ *n*

eth·yl car·ba·mate *n* CHEM same as **urethane** (sense 1)

eth·yl·ene /éthə leen/ *n* a colorless flammable gas. Source: petroleum, natural gas, ripening fruit. Use: manufacture of polymers and other chemicals, in metallurgy, to ripen and color harvested fruit. Formula: C_2H_4. —**eth·yl·e·nic** /èthə léenik/ *adj*

eth·yl·ene gly·col *n* a viscous colorless liquid with a sweet taste. Use: antifreeze, manufacture of polyester. Formula: $C_2H_6O_2$.

eth·yl·ene ox·ide *n* a soluble colorless gas. Use: synthesis of ethylene glycol and other chemicals, fumigant, sterilant. Formula: C_2H_4O.

eth·yl eth·a·no·ate *n* CHEM same as **ethyl acetate** (*technical*)

eth·yl mer·cap·tan *n* a strong-smelling colorless liquid. Use: added to odorless fuels to make leaks detectable. Formula: C_2H_5SH.

e·thyne /é thīn, e thīn/ *n* CHEM same as **acetylene**

et·ic /éttik/ *adj* making use of preestablished categories for organizing and interpreting anthropological data, rather than categories recognized within the culture being studied. ◊ **emic** (sense 2) [Mid-20C. < PHONETIC]

-etic *suffix* used to form adjectives from nouns ending in *-esis* ○ *geodetic* [Via Latin < Greek *-ētikos* < *-etos*]

e·ti·o·lat·ed /éetee ə làytəd/ *adj* **1.** describes a plant that is unusually tall and spindly and deficient in green pigment owing to lack of light **2.** feeble and without vigor or spirit [Late 18C. < French *étioler*] —**e·ti·o·la·tion** /èetee ə láysh'n/ *n*

e·ti·ol·o·gy /èetee óllǝjee/ (*plural* **-gies**), **ae·ti·ol·o·gy** *n* **1.** STUDY OF CAUSES the philosophical investigation of causes and origins **2.** MEDICAL SPECIALTY the branch of medicine that investigates the causes and origins of disease **3.** CAUSE OF DISEASE the set of factors that contributes to the occurrence of a disease [Mid-16C. Via Latin < Greek *aitiologia* "statement of the cause" < *aita* "cause"] —**e·ti·o·log·ic** /èetee ə lójjik/ *adj* —**e·ti·o·log·i·cal·ly** *adv* —**e·ti·ol·o·gist** *n*

et·i·quette /éttikət, étti kèt/ *n* the rules and conventions governing correct or polite behavior in society in general or in a specific social or professional group or situation ○ *Etiquette dictates that wedding invitations should be acknowledged in writing.* [Mid-18C. < French, literally "ticket"]

Et·na, Mount /étnə/ volcano in eastern Sicily. It is the highest active volcano in Europe and has had over 90 recorded eruptions. Height: 10,902 ft./3,323 m.

ETO *abbr* MIL European theater of operations

E·ton[1] /éet'n/ town in Buckinghamshire, England, on the Thames River opposite Windsor, site of Eton College. Population: 5,962 (1991).

E·ton[2] *n* EDUC same as **Eton College** —**E·to·ni·an** /ee tṓnee ən/ *n, adj*

E·ton col·lar *n* a broad stiff white collar turned down over the collar and lapels of a coat or jacket, especially one worn as part of the Eton College uniform

E·ton Col·lege *n* a prep school in the town of Eton, in southeastern England. It was founded in 1440 by Henry VI.

E·ton jack·et *n* a short black jacket with wide lapels and an open front, formerly worn by the pupils of Eton College

E·to·sha Na·tion·al Park /i tṓshə-/ national park in Namibia, southwestern Africa. Established in 1958, it contains the Etosha Pan, a salt desert that was once a lake. Area: 8,598 sq. mi./22,270 sq. km.

E·tru·ri·a /i trooree ə/ ancient region on the Northwestern coast of peninsular Italy, where the Etruscan civilization flourished between about 800 and 300 B.C. The region occupied roughly the same area as present-day Tuscany and part of Umbria, and at its greatest extent stretched from the Alps to the Tiber River. —**E·tru·ri·an** *n, adj*

Etruscan: gable end from Villa Giulia, Rome, Italy (4th century B.C.)

E·trus·can /i trúskən/ *n* **1.** a member of an ancient people who lived in Etruria and were overcome by the Romans during the 2nd century B.C. Their civilization flourished between about 800 and 300 B.C. **2.** an extinct language spoken in ancient Etruria that has no relation to Indo-European languages [Early 18C. < Latin *Etruscus* "of Etruria"] —**E·trus·can** *adj*

et seq., **et seqq.** *adv* and the others following, especially the next page or pages in a book ○ *p.20 et seq.* [Shortening of Latin *et sequens, et sequentia* "and the following one(s)"]

-ette *suffix* **1.** small ○ *diskette* **2.** female ○ *suffragette* ○ *usherette* **3.** imitation ○ *leatherette* [< Old French, form of *-et*]

é·tude /áy tood, ay tood/, **e·tude** *n* a short musical composition for a solo instrument intended to develop a point of technique or to display the performer's skill, but often played for its artistic merit [Mid-19C. < French, "study" < Latin *studium*]

é·tui /ay twée, e-/ *n* a small ornamental case for needles or other small items [Early 17C. < French, later form of Old French *estui* "prison" < *estuier* "to keep"]

ETV *abbr US* MEDIA Educational Television

ety., **etym.** *abbr* **1.** etymological **2.** etymology

et·y·ma LING plural of **etymon**

etymol. *abbr* LING **1.** etymological **2.** etymology

et·y·mol·o·gize /èttə móllə jīz/ (**-gized, -giz·ing, -giz·es**) *vti* to study, trace, or describe the origin and development of a word, or make a suggestion as to a word's possible origin and development

et·y·mol·o·gy /èttə mólləjee/ (*plural* **-gies**) *n* **1.** the study of the origins of words or parts of words and how they have arrived at their current form and meaning **2.** the origin of a word or part of a word, or a statement of this, and how it has arrived at its current form and meaning. An etymology often shows the different forms the word has taken in passing from one language to another, and sometimes shows related words in other languages. ○ *The words have the same spelling but different etymologies.* [14C. Via Old French < Greek *etumologia* < *etumon* (see ETYMON)] —**et·y·mo·log·i·cal** /èttəmə lójjik'l/ *adj*—**et·y·mo·log·i·cal·ly** *adv* —**et·y·mol·o·gist** *n*

et·y·mon /éttə mòn/ (*plural* **-ma** /-mə/ or **-mons**) *n* **1.** an earlier form of a word or part of a word, especially the first recorded form in any language **2.** a word or part of a word from which another word is derived [Late 16C. Via Latin < Greek *etumon* "true sense of a word" < *etumos* "true, original"]

Eu *symbol* CHEM ELEM europium

EU *abbr* POL European Union

eu- *prefix* good, well, true, easily ○ *euphonious* ○ *euplastic* [Via Latin < Greek *eus*]

eu·bac·te·ri·a /yoo bak téeree ə/ *npl* in modern biological classification, all those bacteria considered to be the true bacteria, characterized by their rigid cell walls

eu·ca·lyp·tol /yookə líp tàwl/, **eu·ca·lyp·tole** *n* a colorless oily liquid. Source: eucalyptus oil. Use: in pharmaceuticals, perfumes, flavorings. Formula: $C_{10}H_{18}O$.

eucalyptus

eu·ca·lyp·tus /yo͞okə líptəss/ (*plural* **-tus·es** or **-ti** /-tī/), **eu·ca·lypt** /yo͞okə lìpt/ *n* an evergreen tree that has aromatic leaves and produces timber, resin, and a medicinal oil. Native to: Australia. Genus: *Eucalyptus*. [Early 19C. < modern Latin < Greek *eu-* "well" + *kaluptos* "covered"; from the covering on the tree's buds]

eu·car·y·ote *n* BIOL another spelling of **eukaryote**

Eu·cha·rist /yo͞okərist/ *n* **1.** same as **Communion 2.** the symbolic or consecrated bread and wine eaten and drunk during the ceremony of the Eucharist [14C. < Old French < Greek *eukharistia* "giving of thanks" < *eukharistos* "grateful" < *kharizesthai* "show favor"] —**Eu·cha·ris·tic** /yo͞okə rístik/ *adj*

eu·chre /yo͞okər/ *n* **1.** CARD GAME OF WINNING TRICKS a card game played with the highest 32 cards in the deck in which each player receives five cards and must take at least three tricks to win **2.** THWARTING OF OPPONENT AT EUCHRE an instance of preventing another player from taking the three tricks needed to win a game of euchre ■ *vt* (**-chred, -chring, -chres**) **1.** THWART OPPONENT AT EUCHRE to prevent another player from taking the three tricks needed to win a game of euchre **2.** TRICK SOMEBODY to cheat, trick, or deceive somebody [Early 19C. Origin ?]

eu·chro·ma·tin /yoo krṓmətin/ *n* an expanded form of the material of which chromosomes are composed, occurring when DNA is being actively copied. It stains lightly only with basic dyes. ◊ **heterochromatin** —**eu·chro·mat·ic** /yo͝o krō máttik/ *adj*

Eu·clid /yo͞oklid/ (*fl* 300 B.C.) Greek mathematician. He taught in Alexandria and compiled the 13-volume *Elements* (300? B.C.), the standard text on geometry until the 19th century. —**Eu·clid·e·an** /yoo klíddee ən/ *adj*

Eu·clid·e·an ge·om·e·try *n* geometry according to the principles of Euclid, as described in his *Elements*, in which only one line parallel to another given line may pass through a given point

eu·de·mon /yoo de͞emən/, **eu·dae·mon** *n* a supposed benevolent supernatural being [Early 17C. < Greek *eudaimōn* "having a guardian spirit, fortunate, happy" < *eu-* "good" + *daimōn* "spiritual being, guardian"]

eu·de·mon·ism /yoo de͞emən ìzzəm/, **eu·dae·mon·ism** *n* an ethical doctrine that characterizes the value of life in terms of happiness —**eu·de·mo·nist** *n* —**eu·de·mon·is·tic** /yoo de͞emə nístik/ *adj*

eu·di·om·e·ter /yo͞odee ómmətər/ *n* an instrument used to measure the volume changes that take place in chemical gas reactions [Late 18C. < Greek *eudios* "fine (weather)" < *eu-* "good" + *dios* "heavenly"] —**eu·di·o·met·ric** /yo͞odee ə méttrik/ *adj* —**eu·di·o·met·ri·cal·ly** *adv* —**eu·di·om·e·try** *n*

Eu·dox·us of Cni·dus /yoo dòksəss əv nī́dəss/ (408–355 B.C.) Greek astronomer and mathematician. He developed a mathematical model for predicting planetary motion. His geometrical discoveries are thought to be behind much of Euclid's *Elements*.

Eu·gene /yoo je͞en/ city and county seat of Lane County in western Oregon, situated on the Willamette River, south of Salem and southwest of Portland. It is the state's second-largest city and is home to the University of Oregon. Population: 140,395 (2002 estimate).

eu·gen·i·cist /yoo jénnəssist/, **eu·gen·ist** /yo͞ojənist/ *n* a proposer of ways to improve human beings, especially by selective breeding, or somebody who advocates eugenics

eu·gen·ics /yoo jénniks/ *n* the proposed improvement of the human species by encouraging or permitting reproduction of only those people with genetic characteristics judged desirable. It has been regarded with disfavor since the Nazi period. (*takes a singular verb*) —**eu·gen·ic** *adj* —**eu·gen·i·cal·ly** *adv*

Eu·gé·nie /yoo je͞enee, ō zhay nee/ (1826–1920) Spanish-born empress of France (1853–71). After her marriage to Napoleon III (1853), she exerted considerable influence in political and military matters and served as regent in the emperor's absence. She and her husband fled to England after the fall of the Second Empire (1871). Born **Eugenia María de Montijo de Guzman**

eu·gen·ist *n* SOC SCI same as **eugenicist**

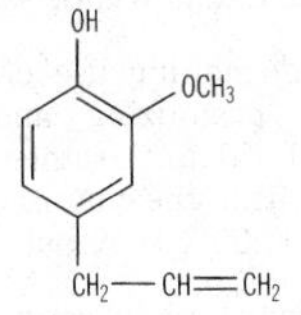

eugenol

eu·ge·nol /yo͞ojə nàwl/ *n* a colorless oily liquid. Source: cloves. Use: in dentistry to reduce pain, in perfumes. Formula: $C_{10}H_{12}O_2$. [Late 19C. < modern Latin *Eugenia*, former taxonomic name of the clove tree, after Prince *Eugène* of Savoy (1663–1736), Austrian general]

eu·gle·na /yoo gle͞enə/ *n* a single-celled freshwater organism that has appendages (**flagella**) for locomotion and produces its food by photosynthesis. Genus: *Euglena*. [Mid-19C. < modern Latin < Greek *eu-* "well" + *glēnē* "eyeball"] —**eu·gle·noid** *adj*

eu·he·mer·ism /yoo he͞emə rìzzəm, -hémmə-/ *n* the theory that mythology has its origins in history, the gods being deified heroes of the past [Mid-19C. < Latin *Euhemerus* < Greek *Euēmeros*, 4C B.C. Greek writer] —**eu·he·mer·ist** *n* —**eu·he·mer·is·tic** /yoo he͞emə rístik, -hèmmə-/ *adj* —**eu·he·mer·is·ti·cal·ly** *adv*

eu·he·mer·ize /yoo he͞emə rīz, -hémmə-/ (**-ized, -iz·ing, -iz·es**) *vti* to explain a myth or myths using the theory that the gods were originally historical heroes

eu·kar·y·ote /yoo kárree ōt/, **eu·car·y·ote** *n* any organism with one or more cells that have visible nuclei and organelles. The group contains all living and fossil cellular organisms except bacteria and cyanobacteria. [Mid-20C. < EU- + Greek *karuōtos* "having nuts" < *karuon* "nut"] —**eu·kar·y·ot·ic** /yoo kàrree óttik/ *adj*

eu·la·chon /yo͞olə kòn/ (*plural* **-chons** or *same*) *n* FISH same as **candlefish** [Mid-19C. < Lower Chinook *úłxan*]

Eu·ler /óylər/, **Leonhard** (1707–83) Swiss mathematician. He and Joseph Lagrange were the leading mathematicians of the 18th century. In some 800 publications he laid the foundations of modern analytic mathematics.

eu·lo·gi·a[1] /yoo lṓzhee ə, -lṓzhə/ *n* bread blessed and given after the liturgy in the Eastern Orthodox Church to those not present at Communion [Mid-18C. Via late Latin, "consecrated bread" < Greek (see EULOGIUM)]

eu·lo·gi·a[2] plural of **eulogium**

eu·lo·gis·tic /yo͞olə jístik/ *adj* full of praise for somebody or something —**eu·lo·gis·ti·cal·ly** *adv*

eu·lo·gi·um /yoo lṓjee əm/ (*plural* **-gi·a** /-jee ə/ or **-gi·ums**) *n* same as **eulogy** (sense 1) (*formal*) [Early 17C. < medieval Latin, probably blend of *eulogia* "praise" (< Greek, < *eu-* "well" + *-logia* "speaking") + Latin *elogium* "epitaph"]

eu·lo·gize /yo͞olə jīz/ (**-gized, -giz·ing, -giz·es**) *vti* to praise somebody or something very highly —**eu·lo·giz·er** *n*

eu·lo·gy /yo͞oləjee/ (*plural* **-gies**) *n* **1.** a speech or piece of writing that praises somebody or something very highly, especially a tribute to somebody who has recently died **2.** great praise (*formal*) [15C. < medieval Latin *eulogium* (see EULOGIUM)] —**eu·lo·gist** *n*

Eu·men·i·des /yoo ménni de͞ez/ *npl* in Greek mythology, three sister goddesses originally fertility goddesses, but later identified with the Furies [Late 17C. Via Latin < Greek < *eumenēs* "kindly, friendly" < *menos* "spirit"]

eu·nuch /yo͞onək/ *n* **1.** a man or boy whose testicles have been removed or do not function. Formerly, eunuchs were sometimes employed to guard the women of a harem or as court officials. **2.** a man who is regarded as lacking power or effectiveness (*informal insult*) [15C. Via Latin < Greek *eunoukhos* "attendant of a bedroom or harem" < *eunē* "bed" + *ekhein* "to keep"] —**eu·nuch·ism** *n*

eu·nuch·oid /yo͞onə kòyd/ *adj* lacking fully developed male sexual organs or characteristics

eu·on·y·mus /yoo ónnəməss/ *n* a tree or bush grown for its decorative evergreen foliage and clusters of orange or red fruits. Native to: northern temperate regions. Genus: *Euonymus*. [Mid-19C. Via modern Latin < Greek *euōnumos* "of good name, lucky"]

eu·pat·rid /yoo páttrid/ (*plural* **-ri·dae** /-ri de͞e/ or **-rids**) *n* somebody belonging to the hereditary class of nobles and landowners in ancient Athens [Mid-19C. < Greek *eupatridēs* "somebody of noble ancestry" < *patēr* "father"]

eu·pep·si·a /yoo pépsee ə, -pépshə/ *n* good or efficient digestion [Early 18C. < Greek, "digestibility" < *eupeptos* (see EUPEPTIC)]

eu·pep·tic /yoo péptik/ *adj* **1.** relating to or producing good digestion **2.** having a cheerful manner or disposition [Late 17C. < Greek *eupeptos* "easy to digest, having good digestion" < *eu-* "well" + *peptein* "digest"] —**eu·pep·ti·cal·ly** *adv*

eu·phe·mism /yo͞ofə mìzzəm/ *n* **1.** a word or phrase used in place of a term that might be considered too direct, harsh, unpleasant, or offensive **2.** the use of a word or phrase that is more neutral, vague, or indirect to replace a direct, harsh, unpleasant, or offensive term [Late 16C. < Greek *euphēmismos* < *euphēmizein* "speak with pleasing words" < *phēmē* "speech"] —**eu·phe·mist** *n* —**eu·phe·mis·tic** /yo͞ofə místik/ *adj* —**eu·phe·mis·ti·cal·ly** *adv*

USAGE ***Euphemisms*** make the unpalatable more palatable. People use euphemisms chiefly to conceal feared things, for example, death; to conceal the reality of unthinkable crimes; to conceal references to sex, body parts and fluids, and excrement; and to elevate otherwise lowly sounding or derogatory occupational titles and institutional names. For instance, there are hundreds of euphemisms used daily for *to die*, a few of which are *pass on/away, go to one's final rest*, and *depart/depart this life*. Similarly, *water landing* is often used by airlines in lieu of the terrifying *on-water ditching*. Two of the most notorious euphemisms for genocide are, of course, *the Final Solution* and *ethnic cleansing*. Euphemistic references to sex and physiology are legion: *sleep with* for *have sex with* and *break wind* for *fart* are typical, as is *social disease* for *sexually transmitted disease*. Euphemisms that elevate the language of occupational titles include, for example, *sanitation engineer* for *garbage collector*, and those that elevate rather harsh-sounding institutional names include *correctional facility* for *prison*. The capacity of a euphemism to conceal tends to diminish over the years, as it becomes more and more closely associated with its referent, and if the taboo against talking about the referent remains in force, a fresh euphemism needs to be found for it. For instance, *toilet* was once a euphemism (it had previously referred to a dressing room with washing facilities), but it has long since become a plainly understood term for "a place of urination and defecation," a term now needing its *own* euphemism: *rest room* and *powder room* for the room itself, and *commode* for the plumbing fixture.

eu·phe·mize /yo͞ofə mīz/ (**-mized, -miz·ing, -miz·es**) *vti* to avoid saying or writing something direct, harsh, unpleasant, or offensive by using milder or more indirect language —**eu·phe·miz·er** *n*

eu·pho·ni·ous /yoo fṓnee əss/ *adj* having a pleasant sound —**eu·pho·ni·ous·ly** *adv* —**eu·pho·ni·ous·ness** *n*

euphonium

eu·pho·ni·um /yoo fṓnee əm/ *n* a brass instrument similar to, but smaller than, a tuba, used mainly in military and brass bands [Mid-19C. < Greek *euphōnos* (see EUPHONY)]

eu·pho·nize /yŏŏfə nīz/ (**-nized, -niz·ing, -niz·es**) *vt* to make something sound pleasant

eu·pho·ny /yŏŏfənee/ (*plural* **-nies**) *n* a pleasant sound, especially in speech or pronunciation [15C. < French *euphonie* < Greek *euphōnos* "sweet-voiced" < *phōnē* "sound"] —**eu·phon·ic** /yoo fónnik/ *adj* —**eu·phon·i·cal·ly** *adv*

eu·phor·bi·a /yoo fáwrbee ə/ *n* a plant such as spurge or poinsettia with milky juice. Flowers: green. Genus: *Euphorbia*. [12C. < Latin *euphorbea* < *Euphorbus* (1C B.C.), physician to Juba, king of Mauritania]

eu·pho·ri·a /yoo fáwree ə/ *n* a feeling of great joy, excitement, or well-being ○ *She was in a state of euphoria after her win.* [Late 17C. Via modern Latin < Greek < *euphoros* "borne well, healthy"]

eu·pho·ri·ant /yoo fáwree ənt/ *n* a drug or other substance that induces euphoria —**eu·pho·ri·ant** *adj*

eu·phor·ic /yoo fáwrik/ *adj* extremely happy or excited ○ *She'll be euphoric when she hears these results.* —**eu·phor·i·cal·ly** *adv*

eu·phot·ic /yoo fóttik/ *adj* describes the upper layer of a body of water that allows the penetration of enough light to support photosynthetic, or green, plants

Eu·phra·tes /yoo fráyteez/ river in Southwest Asia, rising in Turkey and flowing through Syria and Iraq before joining the Tigris River near the Persian Gulf. Length: 1,700 mi./2,700 km.

Eu·phros·y·ne /yoo fróssənee/ *n* in Greek mythology, one of the three Graces who lived on Mount Olympus and tended the goddess Aphrodite

eu·phu·ism /yŏŏ fyoo ìzzəm/ *n* **1.** a literary style of the 16th and 17th centuries characterized by excessive use of devices such as alliteration, antithesis, and simile **2.** an affected or pompous expression or use of language (*formal*) [Late 16C. After *Euphues*, fictional character in the works of John Lyly (*c.* 1554–1606), English writer] —**eu·phu·ist** *n* —**eu·phu·is·tic** /yŏŏfyoo ístik/ *adj* —**eu·phu·is·ti·cal·ly** *adv*

eu·plas·tic /yoo plástik/ *adj* healing readily

eu·ploid /yŏŏ plòyd/ *adj* describes a cell or organism with a chromosome number that is an even multiple of the basic chromosome set for the species —**euploid** *n* —**eu·ploi·dy** *n*

Eur. *abbr* **1.** Europe **2.** European

Eur- *prefix* same as **Euro-** (*used before vowels*)

Eur·a·sia /yoo ráyzhə, -shə/ *n* the land mass consisting of the continents of Europe and Asia

Eur·a·sian /yoo ráyzh'n, -sh'n/ *n* SOMEBODY OF EUROPEAN AND ASIAN DESCENT somebody of both European and Asian descent ■ *adj* **1.** OF EUROPE AND ASIA relating to the land mass consisting of the continents of Europe and Asia **2.** OF EUROPEAN AND ASIAN DESCENT being of both European and Asian descent

Eur·at·om /yoor áttəm/ *n* an organization formed in 1957 to coordinate the development and use of atomic energy in Europe, later incorporated into the European Community [Mid-20C. Contraction of European Atomic Energy Commission]

eu·re·ka /yoo réekə/ *interj, n* used to express delight on finding, discovering, or solving something, or on finally succeeding in doing something ○ *I rolled back the rug and eureka – there it was!* [Early 17C. < Greek *heurēka* "I have found (it)" < *heuriskein* "to find," supposedly exclaimed by Archimedes when he discovered the principle of water displacement]

Eu·re·ka /yoo réekə/ city and port in northwestern California on Humboldt Bay, on the Pacific Ocean, northwest of Santa Rosa. Population: 25,866 (2002 estimate).

eu·rhyth·mic, etc. *adj* FITNESS, MUSIC another spelling of **eurythmic, etc.**

Eu·rip·i·des /yŏŏ ríppi dèez/ (480?–406? B.C.) Greek dramatist. After Aeschylus and Sophocles, he was the third of the great dramatists of the classical period in Athens. His works have been revived through the centuries and have influenced many writers, from Milton and Racine to those of the present day.

> "Bodies devoid of mind are as statues in the marketplace."
> [Euripides, *Electra*; 5th century B.C.]

eu·ro /yŏŏrō/ (*plural* **-ros** or *same*) *n* the main currency unit of the European Union, used since 2002 as local currency in most member states. See table at **currency.** ◊ **ECU** [Late 20C. Shortening of EUROPEAN]

Euro- *prefix* Europe, European ○ *Eurocurrency* [< EUROPE]

Eu·ro·beach /yŏŏrō bèech/ *n* a swimming beach in any of the countries of the European Union that meets the EU regulations for safe levels of bacteria in the water

Eu·ro·bond /yŏŏrō bònd/ *n* a bond measured in dollars or other currency and sold to investors from a country other than that whose currency is specified in the bond

Eu·ro·cen·tric /yŏŏrə séntrik/, **Eu·ro·po·cen·tric** /yoo rṓpə-/ *adj* focusing on Europe or its people, institutions, and cultures, often in a way that is arrogantly dismissive of others —**Eu·ro·cen·trism** *n*

Eu·ro·cheque /yŏŏrō chèk/ *n* a check that can be written in any European currency and the currency of some other countries, drawing on the writer's personal bank account in any of the participating countries

Eu·ro·crat /yŏŏrə kràt/, **eu·ro·crat** *n* an administrative official of the European Union, especially one in a senior post [Mid-20C. Blend of EURO- + BUREAUCRAT]

Eu·ro·cur·ren·cy /yŏŏrō kùr ənssee/ (*plural* **-cies**) *n* money deposited by companies and governments in banks outside the country in whose currency its value is stated [Mid-20C. Because originally dollars held in Europe]

Eu·ro·dol·lar /yŏŏrō dòllər/ *n* a US dollar on deposit in a bank outside the United States, especially a European bank (*usually used in the plural*)

Eu·ro·land /yŏŏrō lànd/, **eu·ro·land** *n* the countries in the European Union using the main currency unit of the European Union, the euro

Eu·ro·mar·ket /yŏŏrō maàrkət/ *n* **1.** the European Union considered as a single market **2.** the European financial markets collectively, especially when considered as a source of financing for international trade

Eu·ro-MP *n* a member of the European Parliament

Eu·ro·pa /yŏŏ rṓpə/ *n* **1.** in Greek mythology, a Phoenician princess who was abducted by Zeus and taken to the island of Crete. She was the mother of Minos. **2.** a large natural satellite of Jupiter, discovered in 1610 by Galileo. It is 1,940 mi./3,130 km in diameter and thought to have a thin icy crust.

Eu·rope /yŏŏrəp/ the second smallest continent after Australia, lying west of Asia, north of Africa, and east of the Atlantic Ocean. Population: 725,962,762 (2000). Area: 3,997,900 sq. mi./10,355,000 sq. km.

Eu·ro·pe·an /yŏŏrə pée ən/ *adj* **1.** OF EUROPE relating to Europe or its peoples, languages, or cultures **2.** OF EUROPEAN UNION relating to the European Union ■ *n* **1.** SOMEBODY FROM EUROPE somebody who comes from Europe or is of European descent **2.** ADVOCATE OF EUROPEAN UNION a supporter of the principles and ideals of the European Union

Eu·ro·pe·an Com·mis·sion *n* the executive arm of the European Union, which formulates policy and drafts most community legislation

Eu·ro·pe·an Com·mu·ni·ty *n* an economic and political union of 12 European countries that developed from the European Economic Community and was itself replaced in 1993 by the European Union

Eu·ro·pe·an Court of Jus·tice, Eu·ro·pe·an Court *n* an institution that ensures that the legislation of the European Union is interpreted and applied in the same way in each member state. There is one judge per member state, but the Court can sit as a panel of 13 judges instead of requiring all judges to be present.

Eu·ro·pe·an Cur·ren·cy U·nit *n* FIN full form of **ECU**

Eu·ro·pe·an E·co·nom·ic Com·mu·ni·ty *n* an alliance of six European countries begun in 1957 to promote free trade in Europe, and subsequently expanded in both membership and areas of interest, and called the European Community and then the European Union

Eu·ro·pe·an Free Trade As·so·ci·a·tion *n* a union of western European countries, established in 1960 to eliminate trade tariffs among member states. The original members were Austria, Denmark, the United Kingdom, Norway, Portugal, Sweden, and Switzerland.

Eu·ro·pe·an·ize /yŏŏrə pée ə nīz/ (**-ized, -iz·ing, -iz·es**) *vt* **1.** to make somebody or something part of European culture, or change somebody or something to fit in with European life, customs, or ideas **2.** to make a country part of the European Union, or make something conform to the regulations or specifications of the European Union —**Eu·ro·pe·an·i·za·tion** /yŏŏrə pee əni záysh'n/ *n*

Eu·ro·pe·an Mon·e·tar·y Sys·tem *n* formerly, a system for stabilizing currency exchange rates within the European Union, using the Exchange Rate Mechanism

Eu·ro·pe·an Par·li·a·ment *n* the primarily advisory legislature of the European Union. It consists of directly elected representatives from each member state.

Eu·ro·pe·an plan *n* a system of charging for hotel accommodations in which the cost of only the room and service is covered, not meals

Eu·ro·pe·an Un·ion *n* an economic and political alliance of 25 European nations. Its goals include a single economic community and social and political cooperation. See map on next page

eu·ro·pi·um /yoo rṓpee əm/ *n* a soft silvery white metallic element of the rare-earth group. Source: monazite, bastnaesite. Use: lasers. Symbol **Eu**. See table at **element** [Early 20C. < modern Latin < Latin *Europa* "Europe"]

Eu·ro·po·cen·tric *adj* same as **Eurocentric**

Eu·ro·zone /yŏŏrō zṑn/, **eu·ro·zone** *n* the geographic area comprising the European Union countries using the euro as a monetary unit

eury- *prefix* wide, broad ○ *euryphagous* [< Greek *eurus*]

eu·ry·bath·ic /yŏŏri báthik/ *adj* describes water organisms that tolerate a wide range of depths [Early 20C. < EURY- + Greek *bathos* "depth"] —**eu·ry·bath** /yŏŏri bàth/ *n*

Eu·ryd·i·ce /yoo ríddissee/ *n* in Greek mythology, the wife of Orpheus. When she died, Orpheus pursued her to Hades. His lyre-playing won her release, but his failure to observe conditions imposed resulted in her irrevocable loss.

eu·ry·ha·line /yŏŏri háy līn/ *adj* describes water organisms that tolerate a wide range of salinity [Late 19C. < EURY- + Greek *halinos* "of salt"]

eu·ryph·a·gous /yoo ríffəgəss/ *adj* describes organisms that consume a variety of different foods

eu·ryp·ter·id /yoo ríptərid/ *n* an extinct invertebrate animal that was common in fresh or brackish water during the Paleozoic era. Order: Eurypterida. [Late 19C. < modern Latin *Eurypterida* < Greek *eury-* "wide" + *pteron* "wing"]

eu·ry·ther·mal /yŏŏrə thúrm'l/, **eu·ry·ther·mic** /-thúrmik/, **eu·ry·ther·mous** /-thúrməss/ *adj* describes organisms that tolerate a wide range of temperatures —**eu·ry·therm** /yŏŏrə thùrm/ *n*

eu·ryth·mic /yoo rí<u>th</u>mik/, **eu·rhyth·mic, eu·ryth·mi·cal** /yoo rí<u>th</u>mik'l/, **eu·rhyth·mi·cal** *adj* **1.** having an aes-

European Union: map showing member states

thetically pleasing rhythm or structure **2.** relating to eurythmics or eurythmy

eu·ryth·mics /yoo ríthmiks/, **eu·rhyth·mics** *n* a system of physical exercise, therapy, and musical training in which the body moves rhythmically and gracefully in interpretation of a piece of music (*takes a singular or plural verb*)

eu·ryth·my /yoo ríthmee/, **eu·rhyth·my** *n* **1.** harmony of proportion or structure **2.** a system of rhythmic movement performed to verse or music for artistic or therapeutic purposes. It was invented by Rudolf Steiner. [Late 16C. Via Latin < Greek *euruthmia* "good proportion" < *rhuthmos* "proportion, rhythm"]

eu·ry·top·ic /yŏŏrə tóppik/ *adj* describes organisms that tolerate a wide range of environmental conditions [Mid-20C. < EURY- + Greek *topos* "place"] —**eu·ry·to·pic·i·ty** /yŏŏrə to píssətee/ *n*

Eu·se·bi·us (of Cae·sa·re·a) /yoo seébee əss-/ (260?–340?) bishop and Christian scholar, probably born in Palestine. He was bishop of Caesarea and worked on texts with his teacher, Pamphilus of Caesarea, as well as writing his *Ecclesiastical History*, a history of the Church until 324. Known as **Eusebius Pamphili**

Eu·se·bi·us (of Nic·o·me·di·a) (*d.* 342?) Syrian bishop and Christian theologian. He helped to spread Arianism, which denies Jesus Christ's divinity. He was patriarch of Constantinople (339–42).

eu·sta·chian tube /yoo stáysh'n-/, **Eu·sta·chian tube** *n* a bony passage extending from the middle ear to the nasopharynx that has a role in equalizing air pressure on both sides of the eardrum [Mid-18C. After Bartolomeo *Eustachio* (1520–74), Italian anatomist]

eu·sta·sy /yŏŏstəssee/ (*plural* **-sies**) *n* a worldwide change in sea level caused, e.g., by melting glaciers [Mid-20C. < EUSTATIC]

eu·stat·ic /yoo státtik/ *adj* relating to a global change in sea level [Mid-20C. < Greek *eu* "well" + *statikos* "static"]

eu·tec·tic /yoo téktik/ *adj* describes a mixture, especially an alloy, that has the lowest freezing point

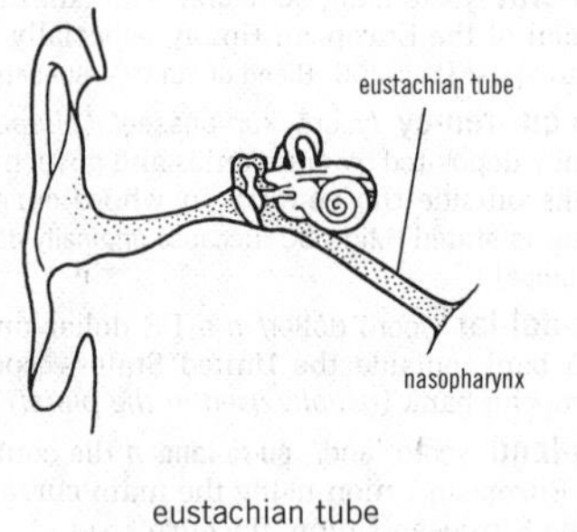

eustachian tube

of all combinations or constituents, or the temperature at which this occurs [Late 19C. < Greek *eutēktos* "easily melting" < *tēkein* "melt"] —**eu·tec·tic** *n*

Eu·ter·pe /yoo túrpee/ *n* in Greek mythology, the Muse of lyric poetry and music, one of the nine Muses believed to inspire and nurture the arts

eu·tha·na·sia /yŏŏthə náyzhə/ *n* the act or practice of killing somebody who has an incurable illness or injury, or of assisting that person to die. Euthanasia is illegal in most countries. [Early 17C. < Greek, "easy death" < *thanatos* "death"]

eu·tha·nize /yŏŏthə nīz/ (**-nized, -niz·ing, -niz·es**), **eu·than·a·tize** /yoo thánnə tīz/ (**-tized, -tiz·ing, -tiz·es**) *vt* to kill an incurably ill or injured person or animal to relieve suffering

eu·then·ics /yoo thénniks/ *n* the study of ways of enhancing people's environment and living standards in order to improve their health and well-being (*takes a singular verb*) [Early 20C. < Greek *euthenein* "thrive"] —**eu·then·ist** /yŏŏthənist/ *n*

eu·ther·i·an /yoo theéree ən/ *n* a mammal whose young develop within the womb surrounded by a placenta. Subclass: Eutheria. [Late 19C. < modern Latin *Eutheria* < Greek *thērion* "wild animal"] —**eu·ther·i·an** *adj*

eu·troph·ic /yoo tróffik, -trṓfik/ *adj* describes a body of water whose oxygen content is depleted by organic nutrients [Mid-20C. < Greek *eutrophia* "good nutrition" < *trephein* "nourish"] —**eu·tro·phy** /yŏŏtrəfee/ *n*

eu·troph·i·ca·tion /yoo tròffi káysh'n, -trṑfi-/ *n* the process by which a body of water becomes rich in dissolved nutrients from fertilizers or sewage, thereby encouraging the growth and decomposition of oxygen-depleting plant life and resulting in harm to other organisms

eV *symbol* ELEC electron volt

EVA *abbr* AEROSP extravehicular activity

e·vac·u·ant /i vákyoo ənt/ *adj* describes a drug that empties the bowels —**e·vac·u·ant** *n*

e·vac·u·ate /i vákyoo àyt/ (**-at·ed, -at·ing, -ates**) *v* **1.** *vt* MAKE EVERYONE LEAVE PLACE to empty a dangerous or potentially dangerous place of people ○ *Towns near the nuclear plant were evacuated as a precautionary measure.* **2.** *vti* MOVE TO SAFETY to leave or cause people to leave a place of danger and go somewhere safer ○ *The government has evacuated all its embassy officials from the city.* **3.** *vt* EMPTY SOMETHING to empty something by removing all its contents (*formal*) **4.** *vti* PHYSIOL EMPTY BOWELS OR BLADDER to discharge feces or urine from the body (*technical*) **5.** *vt* PHYS CREATE VACUUM IN SOMETHING to remove a gas from something, leaving a vacuum [14C. < Latin *evacuat-*, past participle of *evacuare* "empty (the bowels)" < *vacuus* "empty"] —**e·vac·u·a·tive** *adj* —**e·vac·u·a·tor** *n*

e·vac·u·a·tion /i vàkyoo áysh'n/ *n* **1.** CLEARING OF DANGEROUS PLACE an act or the process of emptying a dangerous or potentially dangerous place of people ○ *ordered the evacuation of the building* **2.** MOVING PEOPLE TO SAFETY a removal of people from a dangerous or potentially dangerous place to somewhere safe **3.** PHYSIOL DISCHARGE OF BODILY WASTE elimination of feces or urine from the body (*technical*) **4.** PHYSIOL BODILY WASTE feces or urine eliminated from the body (*technical*) **5.** PHYS CREATION OF VACUUM the process of creating a vacuum by the removal of a gas from something

e·vac·u·ee /i vàkyoo eé/ *n* somebody who is taken from a dangerous place and sent somewhere safer, especially during a war [Early 20C. < French *évacué*, past participle of *évacuer* "cease to occupy" < Latin *evacuare* (see EVACUATE)]

e·vade /i váyd/ (**e·vad·ed, e·vad·ing, e·vades**) *v* **1.** *vt* CLEVERLY ESCAPE SOMEBODY OR SOMETHING to escape or avoid somebody or something, usually by ingenuity or guile **2.** *vt* AVOID SOMETHING UNPLEASANT to avoid doing something unpleasant, especially something that is a moral or legal obligation **3.** *vti* GIVE INDIRECT RESPONSE to avoid dealing with or responding directly to something **4.** *vt* BE UNATTAINABLE TO SOMEBODY to be difficult or impossible for somebody to find, obtain, or achieve (*formal*) ○ *Success always evaded him.* [Early 16C. Via French < Latin *evadere* "to escape" < *vadere* "go, walk"] —**e·vad·a·ble** *adj* —**e·vad·er** *n*

USAGE See *avoid*.

e·vag·i·nate /i vájjə nàyt/ (**-nat·ed, -nat·ing, -nates**) *vt* to turn a hollow structure or bodily organ inside out [Mid-17C. < Latin *evaginat-*, past participle of *evaginare* "unsheathe" < *vagina* "sheath"] —**e·vag·i·na·tion** /i vàjjə náysh'n/ *n*

e·val·u·ate /i vállyoo àyt/ (**-at·ed, -at·ing, -ates**) *vt* **1.** EXAMINE AND JUDGE SOMETHING to consider or examine something in order to judge its value, quality, importance, extent, or condition ○ *We evaluated the situation carefully.* **2.** PUT VALUE ON SOMETHING to estimate the monetary value of something ○ *The appraiser evaluated the property at $100,000.* **3.** MATH FIND NUMERICAL VALUE OF SOMETHING to calculate a numerical value for a mathematical expression [Mid-19C. Back-formation < EVALUATION] —**e·val·u·a·tor** *n*

e·val·u·a·tion /i vàllyoo áysh'n/ *n* **1.** the act of considering or examining something in order to judge its value, quality, importance, extent, or condition **2.** a spoken or written statement of the value, quality, importance, extent, or condition of something [Mid-18C. < French *évaluation* < *évaluer* "find the value of" < Old French *value* (see VALUE)]

e·val·u·a·tive /i vállyoo àytiv, -ətiv/ *adj* **1.** relating to or based on examination and judgment of the value, quality, or importance of something **2.** expressing a judgment about something, or assigning a value to it, as opposed to describing a fact

evan. *abbr* CHR **1.** evangelical **2.** evangelist

ev·a·nesce /èvvə néss/ (**-nesced, -nesc·ing, -nesc·es**) *vi* to grow less until completely gone (*literary*) ○ *His cares evanesced.* [Mid-19C. < Latin *evanescere* "vanish" < *vanus* "empty"]

ev·a·nes·cent /èvvə néss'nt/ *adj* disappearing after only a short time —**ev·a·nes·cence** *n* —**ev·a·nes·cent·ly** *adv*

SYNONYMS See *temporary.*

evang. *abbr* CHR **1.** evangelical **2.** evangelist

e·van·gel /i vánjəl/ *n* CHR **1.** same as **evangelist** (sense 2) **2.** same as **Gospel** (senses 1–2) (*archaic*) **3.** *also* **E·van·gel** any of four Christian Gospels (*archaic*) [14C. < Old French *evangile* < Greek *euaggelion* "good news" < *euaggelos* "bringing good news" < *eu* "good" + *aggelein* "announce"]

e·van·gel·i·cal /èe van jéllik'l, èvvən-/ *adj* **1.** *also* **E·van·gel·i·cal** *or* **e·van·gel·ic** /-jéllik/ *or* **E·van·gel·ic** OF PROTESTANT CHURCHES EMPHASIZING PERSONAL SALVATION relating or belonging to any Protestant Christian church that emphasizes the authority of the Bible and salvation through the personal acceptance of Jesus Christ **2.** *also* **e·van·gel·ic** RELATING TO CHRISTIAN GOSPELS relating to or based on the Gospels of the Christian Bible **3.** *also* **e·van·gel·ic** WITH STRONG BELIEFS enthusiastic or zealous in support of a particular cause and very eager to make other people share its beliefs or ideals ■ *n also* **E·van·gel·i·cal** HOLDER OF EVANGELICAL BELIEFS somebody who has evangelical Christian beliefs —**e·van·gel·i·cal·ly** *adv*

e·van·gel·i·cal·ism /èe van jéllik'l ìzzəm, èvvən-/, **E·van·gel·i·cal·ism** *n* a Protestant movement of the Christian Church whose members believe in the authority of the Bible and salvation through the personal acceptance of Jesus Christ

e·van·gel·ism /i vánjə lìzzəm/ *n* **1.** the spreading of Christianity, especially through the activities of evangelists **2.** great enthusiasm, fervor, or zeal for a particular cause

e·van·gel·ist /i vánjəlist/ *n* **1.** *also* **E·van·gel·ist** a writer of any of the four books of the Christian Bible known as a Gospel **2.** a Christian who tries to persuade other people to become Christian, especially at public gatherings or in broadcasts —**e·van·gel·is·tic** /i vànjə lístik/ *adj* —**e·van·gel·is·ti·cal·ly** *adv*

e·van·gel·ize /i vánjə lìz/ (**-ized, -iz·ing, -iz·es**) *vti* **1.** to convert somebody or the people of an area to Christianity, especially by preaching or missionary work **2.** to try to persuade other people to share enthusiasm for specific beliefs and ideals —**e·van·gel·i·za·tion** /i vànjəli záysh'n/ *n* —**e·van·gel·iz·er** *n*

Ev·ans, Mount /évv'nz/ mountain in north central Colorado, site of a high-altitude laboratory. Height: 14,264 ft./4,348 m.

Ev·ans, Dame Edith (1888–1976) British actor. She is remembered for her Shakespearean roles and also for her performance as Lady Bracknell in the 1951 movie of *The Importance of Being Earnest.* Full name **Evans, Dame Edith Mary**

Ev·ans, Maurice (1901–89) British-born US actor and producer. He began his career playing Shakespearean roles on stage and later became a character actor in movies and television productions.

Ev·ans, Walker (1903–75) US photographer. He is known for his records of everyday life in the United States from the Great Depression onward.

Ev·ans-Prit·chard /-prìchərd/, **Sir E. E.** (1902–73) British anthropologist. Often living with the peoples he studied, he pioneered the view that sees culturally distinct beliefs as forming a coherent functional system. Full name **Evans-Pritchard, Sir Edward Evan**

Ev·ans·ton /évvənstən/ city in northeastern Illinois on Lake Michigan. It is a suburb of Chicago. Population: 73,421 (2002 estimate).

Ev·ans·ville /évvənz vìl/ city in southwestern Indiana, on the northern bank of the Ohio River, southwest of Bloomington. Population: 119,081 (2002 estimate).

e·vap·o·rate /i váppə ràyt/ (**-rat·ed, -rat·ing, -rates**) *v* **1.** *vti* CHANGE LIQUID TO VAPOR to change a liquid into a vapor, usually by heating to below its boiling point, or change from a liquid to vapor in this way ○ *The water evaporates, increasing the moisture in the air.* **2.** *vt* REMOVE LIQUID FROM SOMETHING to remove liquid from something, usually by heating, to produce a more concentrated or solid substance **3.** *vi* VANISH to disappear gradually, or fade away to nothing **4.** *vt* PHYS DEPOSIT FILM to deposit something such as a metal film on a surface through the condensation of a vaporized substance [15C. < Latin *evaporat-*, past participle of *evaporare* "go out in vapor" < *vapor* "steam, heat"] —**e·vap·o·ra·ble** *adj* —**e·vap·o·ra·tive** *adj*

e·vap·o·rat·ed milk /i váppə raytəd-/ *n* milk that has been thickened by removing some of the water by evaporation

e·vap·o·ra·tion /i vàppə ráysh'n/ *n* a process in which something is changed from a liquid to a vapor without its temperature reaching boiling point

e·vap·o·ra·tor /i váppə ràytər/ *n* **1.** the vaporization portion of a refrigeration system **2.** a vaporizing device that removes water or other solvents to obtain the dried or concentrated residue, e.g., in the preparation of powdered milk from milk

e·vap·o·rite /i váppə rìt/ *n* a sedimentary rock or deposit that results from the evaporation of salt water in lagoons and saline lakes. Gypsum and rock salt are evaporites. [Early 20C. < EVAPORATION] —**e·vap·o·rit·ic** /i vàppə ríttik/ *adj*

e·vap·o·tran·spi·ra·tion /i vàppō transpi ráysh'n/ *n* the return of moisture to the air through both evaporation from the soil and transpiration by plants [Mid-20C. < EVAPORATION]

e·va·sion /i váyzh'n/ *n* **1.** AVOIDANCE OF SOMETHING avoidance of something unpleasant, especially a moral or legal obligation **2.** MEANS OF AVOIDANCE a means of escaping or avoiding something, especially one that involves cunning or deceit **3.** AVOIDING OF ISSUE failure to give a direct answer to a direct question, usually in order to conceal the truth [15C. Via French < Latin *evasion-* < *evadere* (see EVADE)]

USAGE See *avoidance.*

e·va·sive /i váyssiv/ *adj* **1.** not giving a direct answer to a direct question, usually in order to conceal the truth **2.** intended to avoid something unpleasant, e.g., trouble or an attack ○ *took evasive action* —**e·va·sive·ly** *adv* —**e·va·sive·ness** *n*

Ev·att /évvət/, **Herbert Vere** (1894–1965) Australian judge and politician. He was deputy prime minister of Australia (1946–49) and leader of the Australian Labor Party (1951–60). He was also first president of the general assembly of the United Nations (1948–49).

eve /eev/ *n* **1.** the day or days immediately before an important event or special occasion ○ *He died on the eve of his 100th birthday.* **2.** *also* **Eve** the day, evening, or night before a religious festival or public holiday **3.** same as **evening** *n* (senses 1–2) (*literary*) ○ *on a cold winter's eve* [12C. Variant of EVEN²]

Eve /eev/ *n* in the Bible, the first woman created by God, and Adam's companion in the Garden of Eden

e·vec·tion /i véksh'n/ *n* a periodic irregularity in the motion of the Moon caused by the variation in the gravitational attraction of the Sun as the Moon orbits Earth [Mid-17C. < Latin *evection-* < *evect-*, past participle of *evehere* "carry out, elevate" < *vehere* "carry"] —**e·vec·tion·al** *adj*

e·ven¹ /éev'n/ *adj* **1.** NOT SLOPING, ROUGH, OR IRREGULAR having no slope, roughness, or irregularities **2.** AT SAME HEIGHT at the same distance above the ground or other point of reference **3.** ALIGNED lining up along the same horizontal or vertical line and usually with equal spaces between **4.** NOT CHANGING OR FLUCTUATING not changing or fluctuating in level or strength **5.** SIMILAR THROUGHOUT the same all over or throughout ○ *an even consistency* **6.** EQUAL IN AMOUNT equal in amount, number, or extent ○ *At the end of the first round, the score was even.* **7.** WELL-BALANCED between competitors of equal strength or skill, and therefore fair or well-balanced **8.** EXACT IN AMOUNT exact in amount, number, or extent ○ *an even dozen* **9.** NOT OWING ANYTHING not or no longer owing anything to each other (*informal*) ○ *Give me five dollars, and we'll call it even.* **10.** CALM AND STEADY calm and controlled **11.** MATH EXACTLY DIVISIBLE BY TWO describes a number or quantity that can be exactly divided by two with nothing left over, e.g., 2, 6, 30, or 518. ◊ **odd** *adj* (sense 2) **12.** WITH EVEN NUMBER having a number that can be exactly divided by two ○ *on the even pages* ■ *vti* (**e·vened, e·ven·ing, e·vens**) LEVEL OR EQUALIZE to make something more level or equal, or become more level or equal ○ *Atlanta scored three quick runs to even the score.* [Old English *efen* < Germanic] —**e·ven·er** *n* —**e·ven·ly** *adv* —**e·ven·ness** *n* ◇ **get even (with somebody)** to take revenge on somebody ○ *They took advantage of me, and I was determined to get even.*

even out *vti* **1.** to become or make something more flat, smooth, or level **2.** to make two or more different things more equal, or become more equal

even up *vti* to become or make something more equal, fair, or well-balanced

e·ven² /éev'n/ *n* same as **evening** *n* (senses 1–2) (*literary*) ○ *at even, when the sun was set* [Old English *æfen* (see EVENING)]

e·ven³ /éev'n/ CORE MEANING: used for emphasis to indicate something surprising, unlikely, or extreme ○ *Even I know how to repair a flat!*

adv **1.** SO MUCH AS used after a negative for emphasis to indicate something unexpected and usually annoying or disappointing ○ *She couldn't even remember my name.* **2.** TO GREATER EXTENT used for emphasis in comparisons to indicate the degree to which something exists ○ *His writing is even messier than hers, and hers is barely legible.* ○ *I never liked him much, but after today I like him even less.* **3.** OR MORE EXACTLY used to indicate that the description that follows applies in addition to and more strongly or precisely than the preceding one ○ *She is careful with her money, even miserly.* **4.** TO UNEXPECTED EXTENT used to emphasize that something is surprisingly true (*archaic*) ○ *I will follow thee even unto the ends of the earth.* [Old English *efne* < Germanic] ◇ **even so** regardless of anything else ○ *It sounds unlikely; even so, it could be true.*

e·ven break *n* an equal opportunity for winning or losing

e·ven chance *n* an equal likelihood that something will or will not happen

e·ven·hand·ed /éev'n hándəd/ *adj* treating everyone fairly, without favoritism or discrimination ○ *an evenhanded distribution of the profits* —**e·ven·hand·ed·ly** *adv* —**e·ven·hand·ed·ness** *n*

eve·ning /éevning/ *n* **1.** LATE PART OF DAY the part of the day between afternoon and night, as daylight begins to fade **2.** TIME BEFORE BEDTIME the part of the day between sunset or the last main meal of the day and bedtime ○ *We went out for the evening.* **3.** ACTIVITY HELD DURING EVENING a social gathering, meeting, or entertainment held in the evening ○ *Thank you for an enjoyable evening.* **4.** PERIOD AT END the final part of a period of time, e.g., somebody's life or a historical era (*literary*) ○ *the evening of the British Empire* **5.** *Southern US* AFTERNOON the afternoon, especially middle to late afternoon ■ *interj* same as **good evening** (*informal*) [Old English *æfnung* < *æfen* < Indo-European, "lateness"]

eve·ning bag *n* a pocketbook designed for elegant or otherwise special occasions, often made from more expensive materials and smaller and less sturdy than a daytime bag

eve·ning dress *n* **1.** clothing worn by men or women for formal social events held in the evening. A man in evening dress usually wears a dinner jacket and black tie, and a woman usually wears a full-length dress of elegant design. **2.** *UK* same as **evening gown**

eve·ning gown *n* a woman's dress suitable for formal social events held in the evening, usually a full-length dress of elegant design

eve·ning prayer, Eve·ning Prayer *n* CHR same as **evensong** (sense 1)

eve·ning prim·rose *n* a biennial plant with hairy leaves and seeds that yield an oil used especially in treatments for menstrual problems. Genus: *Oenothera.* See illustration on next page [Because its yellow flowers open in the evening]

eve·nings /éevningz/ *adv* in the evening, especially regularly

eve·ning star *n* a bright planet that can be seen in the western sky around sunset, usually Venus but occasionally Mercury

evening primrose

E·ven·ki /i véngkee, i wéngkee/ (*plural same or* **-kis**), **E·wen·ki** /i wéngkee/ *n* **1.** a member of an ethnic group that lives mainly in eastern parts of Asia of the former Soviet Union and northwestern China **2.** a Tungusic language spoken in eastern parts of Asia of the former Soviet Union and northwestern China. It belongs to the Mongolian branch of Altaic. Native speakers: 30,000. [Via Russian, "Evenki people" < Evenki] —**E·ven·ki** *adj*

e·ven mon·ey *n* a betting situation in which the odds of winning or losing are equal and the winnings equal the stake ■ *adj* equally likely or unlikely ○ *It's even money she'll forget.*

e·ven·song /eev'n sàwng/ *n* **1.** the daily evening worship service of the Anglican Church **2.** vespers (*archaic*)

e·ven-ste·ven, **e·ven Ste·ven** *adj* (*informal*) **1.** with all debts or grievances mutually settled **2.** with equal scores or chances of winning ○ *At the end of the first round the two teams were even-steven.* [Probably arbitrary]

e·vent /i vént/ *n* **1.** IMPORTANT INCIDENT an occurrence, especially one that is particularly significant, interesting, exciting, or unusual ○ *the events leading up to the strike* **2.** ORGANIZED OCCASION an organized occasion such as a social function or sports competition ○ *She has competed in many international events.* **3.** INDIVIDUAL SPORTS CONTEST a race or other competition that forms part of a larger sports occasion such as the Olympic Games ○ *The 100 meters is his best event.* **4.** PHILOSOPHY SOMETHING THAT HAPPENS a happening or occurrence **5.** PHYS SINGLE POINT IN SPACE-TIME an occurrence defined in the theory of relativity as a single point in space-time **6.** COMPUT OCCURRENCE AFFECTING COMPUTER PROGRAM an occurrence or happening of significance to a computer program, e.g., the clicking of a mouse button or the completion of a write operation to a disk [Late 16C. < Latin *eventus* < past participle of *evenire* "happen" < *venire* "come"] ◇ **be wise after the event** to know with hindsight what should have been done or said in a situation ◇ **in the event of something** if something should happen

e·vent-driv·en *adj* describes a computer program with a main loop that waits for an event and then passes the details along

e·ven-tem·pered *adj* not easily angered or upset

e·vent·er /i véntər/ *n* a horse or rider that regularly competes at eventing

e·vent·ful /i véntfəl/ *adj* **1.** full of important, interesting, or exciting occurrences **2.** having a major effect on somebody's life —**e·vent·ful·ly** *adv* —**e·vent·ful·ness** *n*

e·vent ho·ri·zon *n* the theoretical boundary surrounding a black hole, within which gravitational attraction is so great that nothing, not even radiation, can escape because the escape velocity is greater than the speed of light

e·ven·tide /eev'n tìd/ *n* same as **evening** *n* (senses 1–2) (*literary*)

e·vent·ing /i vénting/ *n* an equestrian competition that includes dressage, cross-country riding, and stadium jumping, usually over three days

e·vent·less /i véntləss/ *adj* having no significant events

e·vent mar·ket·ing *n* promotional activities involving an event such as a sporting or social event, designed to bring a product to the attention of the public

e·ven·tu·al /i vénchoo əl, i vénchəl/ *adj* happening in the course of time or events, usually much later ○ *her eventual fall from power* [Early 17C. < French *éventuel* < Latin *eventus* (see EVENT)]

e·ven·tu·al·i·ty /i vènchoo állətee/ (*plural* **-ties**) *n* a possible occurrence or result, especially something undesirable or unexpected ○ *We must be prepared for all eventualities.*

e·ven·tu·al·ly /i vénchoo alee, i vénchəlee/ *adv* **1.** after a long time, especially after many problems or setbacks ○ *We eventually managed to open the door.* **2.** at some later time after a series of events ○ *She hopes eventually to study art.*

e·ven·tu·ate /i vénchoo àyt/ (**-at·ed, -at·ing, -ates**) *vi* to happen as a final result (*formal*) **eventuate in** *vt* to cause or result in something, especially after an extended period of time (*formal*) ○ *The oil spill eventuated in the destruction of wildlife habitats along the coast.*

e·ven·weave /eevən weev/ *n* a fabric with warp and weft threads that are equally thick and tense and in equal numbers in any square measurement

ev·er /évvər/ *adv* **1.** ⚠ AT ANY TIME used for emphasis in indicating any time in the past or future ○ *This is the most fascinating book I've ever read.* ○ *Will I ever see you again?* ○ *It's his biggest blunder ever.* **2.** USED TO INDICATE SURPRISE used for emphasis to indicate surprise, shock, or incomprehension at something ○ *Where ever can it be?* **3.** INCREASINGLY to an increasing degree (*formal*) ○ *The questions were becoming ever more technical.* **4.** USED AS INTENSIFIER used to emphasize a particular quality, especially to express enthusiasm (*informal*) ○ *Was I ever glad to get home!* **5.** ALWAYS showing at all times a particular quality ○ *He is ever anxious to please.* [Old English *ǣfre* < Indo-European, "eternity"]

USAGE The best book **ever**: Some people object to this use of ***ever*** because they maintain that ***ever*** should include the future as well as the past. However, the future can rarely be accounted for, and the idiom is well established in conversational use, although it would not normally be used in more formal spoken or written English.

Barnaby's

Mount Everest: western shoulder of the mountain

Ev·er·est, Mount /évvərist/ mountain in the Himalaya range on the border between Nepal and the Tibet Autonomous Region of China. It is the highest mountain in the world. Height: 29,035 ft./8,850 m.

Ev·er·ett /évvərət/ **1.** city in eastern Massachusetts on the Mystic River, near Boston. Population: 37,772 (2002 estimate). **2.** city and seaport in northwestern Washington, near Seattle. Population: 97,088 (2002 estimate).

Ev·er·ett, Edward (1794–1865) US diplomat, educator, and orator. He delivered the oration at Gettysburg prior to Lincoln's address.

> "When I am dead, no pageant train / Shall waste their sorrows at my bier, / Nor worthless pomp of homage vain / Stain it with hypocritic tear."
> [Edward Everett, "Dirge of Alaric the Visigoth," *Best Loved Story Poems*; 1941]

ev·er·glade /évvər glàyd/ *n* US a stretch of marshy grassland usually covered with water for at least part of the year

Ev·er·glade kite *n* BIRDS same as **snail kite**

Ev·er·glades /évvər glàydz/ subtropical swamp covering much of southern Florida. Area: 5,000 sq. mi./12,950 sq. km.

Barnaby's

Everglades National Park

Ev·er·glades Na·tion·al Park national park in southern Florida, established in 1947. It contains the largest subtropical wilderness in the United States. Area: 2,357 sq. mi./6,105 sq. km.

ev·er·green /évvər green/ *adj* **1.** WITH LEAVES THROUGHOUT YEAR describes a tree or bush that retains its foliage throughout the year **2.** REMAINING FRESH OR POPULAR describes people or things that always seem fresh, lively, or interesting, and that remain popular despite their age ■ *n* **1.** EVERGREEN TREE a tree or bush that retains its foliage throughout the year **2.** SOMEBODY OR SOMETHING STAYING LIVELY AND INTERESTING somebody or something that remains fresh, lively, interesting, or popular ■ **ev·er·greens** *npl* US DECORATIVE BRANCHES twigs or branches cut from evergreen trees or bushes and used for decoration

Ev·er·green Park /évvər green-/ village in northeastern Illinois that is a residential suburb of Chicago. Population: 20,665 (2002 estimate).

Ev·er·green State *n* a nickname for the US state of Washington

ev·er·last·ing /évvər lásting/ *adj* **1.** LASTING FOR EVER never failing or coming to an end **2.** LASTING LONG TIME continuing indefinitely or for a long time **3.** INCESSANT going on for too long and becoming tedious or annoying ○ *everlasting grumbling* ■ *n* **1.** INFINITY infinite time **2.** PLANTS FLOWER THAT LOOKS FRESH WHEN DRIED a plant with flowers that keep their shape and color when dried, e.g., helichrysum —**ev·er·last·ing·ly** *adv* —**ev·er·last·ing·ness** *n*

Ev·er·last·ing *n* same as **God**

ev·er·last·ing flow·er *n* PLANTS same as **everlasting** *n* (sense 2)

ev·er·more /èvvər máwr, évvər màwr/ *adv* from now until the end of time or the end of somebody's life (*literary*) ○ *I will be evermore in your debt.*

Ev·ers /évvərz/, **Medgar** (1925–63) US civil rights leader. He was a major figure in the National Association for the Advancement of Colored People (NAACP) until his murder in 1963.

> "Freedom has never been free."
> [Medgar Evers, *Speech*; June 7, 1963]

e·ver·sion /i vúrzh'n, i vúrsh'n/ *n* **1.** the process or condition of being turned inside out ○ *eversion of the bladder* **2.** a condition of being turned outward ○ *an eversion of the feet* [Mid-18C. Directly or via French < Latin *eversion-* < *evers-*, past participle of *evertere* (see EVERT)] —**e·ver·si·ble** *adj*

e·vert /i vúrt/ (**e·vert·ed, e·vert·ing, e·verts**) *vt* to turn an organ or other body part outward or inside out [Mid-16C. < Latin *evertere* "turn out" < *vertere* "to turn"]

Popperfoto

Chris Evert

Ev·ert /évvərt/, **Chris** (*b.* 1954) US tennis player. She won 16 grand slam singles championships during her career (1972–89). See illustration on previous page. Full name **Evert, Christine Marie**

"That's my whole game, playing steady and letting them make errors. I win more games that way than by hitting winners." [Chris Evert, *Times (London)*; August 1, 1972]

ev·er·where /évvər wèr, èvvər wér, -hwàir, -hwáir/ *adv Southern US* **1.** same as **everywhere** **2.** same as **wherever**

ev·er·which /évvər wìch, èvvər wích, -hwìch, -hwích/ *pron Southern US* same as **whichever**

eve·ry /évvree/ CORE MEANING: used to indicate each member of a group without exception ○ *Every life has value.*
adj **1.** EACH EXCLUDING NONE each member of a group, without exception ○ *Every life is precious.* **2.** TO GREATEST EXTENT used to emphasize that there is all there could be of a particular quality ○ *The committee has every intention of exploring this issue.* **3.** RECURRING AT PARTICULAR INTERVAL used to indicate each occurrence in recurrent or intermittent groups of things, or to indicate a ratio ○ *We intend to meet every two weeks.* ○ *Take this medicine every three hours.* [13C. < Old English *ǣfre ǣlc* "ever each"] ◇ **every now and then, every now and again** occasionally ◇ **every other** each alternate thing, person, or occasion

USAGE See *each.*

eve·ry·bod·y *pron* same as **everyone**

eve·ry·day /évvree dày/ *adj* **1.** ORDINARY AND UNREMARKABLE having no remarkable feature to set it apart ○ *an everyday story of city life* **2.** OCCURRING EACH DAY happening or done each day ○ *an everyday occurrence* **3.** USED ON ORDINARY OCCASIONS suitable for use on ordinary days or for routine tasks, rather than on special occasions ■ *n* ORDINARY OCCASIONS routine or daily life —**eve·ry·day·ness** *n*

USAGE everyday or **every day**? When you intend to use either of these words as an adjective or a noun meaning "ordinary occasions," as in *everyday life* or *part of the everyday*, the one-word version is correct. Adverbial uses, as in *We should eat fruit every day*, and the noun use meaning "each day," as in *Every day is different*, call for the two-word version. Thus *everyday in every way* means "ordinary in all respects," whereas *every day in every way* means "daily and completely."

Eve·ry·man /évvree màn/ *n* **1.** *also* **eve·ry·man** somebody, usually a man, considered to be typical or representative of all human beings **2.** the hero of a medieval morality play who represents the whole of the human race

eve·ry·one /évvree wùn/, **eve·ry·bod·y** /-bòddee/ *pron* every person, whether of a defined group or in general ○ *Everyone is going to come to the office party.* ○ *This is not just for one area; it will affect everyone around the country.*

eve·ry·place /évvree plàyss/ *adv US* same as **everywhere** (*informal*) ○ *I've looked everyplace.*

eve·ry·thing /évvree thìng/ *pron* **1.** all the items, actions, or facts in a given situation ○ *Everything I do is for my family.* ○ *Is everything all right?* **2.** used to emphasize that somebody or something is the most important person or thing there is ○ *To them, family is everything.*

eve·ry·where /évvree wèr, -hwèr/ *adv* in or to all conceivable places ○ *Children everywhere play these games.* ○ *Her cat followed her everywhere she went.*

Eve·ry·wom·an /évvree wòommən/, **eve·ry·wom·an** *n* a woman considered to be typical or representative of women generally

e·vict /i víkt/ (**e·vict·ed, e·vict·ing, e·victs**) *vt* **1.** EJECT SOMEBODY FROM PROPERTY to force a tenant to leave a property, especially the tenant's residence, usually because he or she has failed to comply with the terms of the lease **2.** THROW SOMEBODY OUT to force somebody to leave a place, usually because of bad behavior ○ *She was evicted from the game for insulting the referee.* **3.** GET BACK PROPERTY to recover property or title to property from somebody by legal means [15C. < Latin *evict-*, past participle of *evincere* (see EVINCE)] —**e·vict·ee** /i vìk tée/ *n* —**e·vic·tion** *n* —**e·vic·tor** *n*

ev·i·dence /évvid'nss/ *n* **1.** SIGN OR PROOF something that gives a sign or proof of the existence or truth of something, or that helps somebody to come to a particular conclusion ○ *There is no evidence that the disease is related to diet.* **2.** PROOF OF GUILT the objects or information used to prove or suggest the guilt of somebody accused of a crime ○ *The police have no evidence.* **3.** STATEMENTS OF WITNESSES the oral or written statements of witnesses and other people involved in a trial or official inquiry ■ *vt* (**-denced, -denc·ing, -denc·es**) DEMONSTRATE OR PROVE to demonstrate or prove something (*usually passive*) ○ *Their unwillingness to participate is evidenced by their failure to contact us.*

ev·i·dence-based med·i·cine *n* the use of clinical methods and decision-making that have been thoroughly tested by properly controlled, peer-reviewed medical research

ev·i·dent /évvid'nt/ *adj* easy or clear to see or understand ○ *The full extent of her injuries did not become evident until they tried to move her.* [14C. Via Old French < Latin *evident-* "clear" < *videre* "see"]

ev·i·den·tial /èvvi dénshəl/ *adj Can, UK* LAW same as **evidentiary** —**ev·i·den·tial·ly** *adv*

ev·i·den·tia·ry /èvvi dénshəree, -dénshee èrree/ *adj US* relating to, consisting of, or based on evidence ○ *statements with no evidentiary value* Can term **evidential**

ev·i·dent·ly /évvidəntlee/ *adv* **1.** used to indicate that something is undoubtedly true, often because it is there to be seen ○ *Evidently, you have not grasped all the ramifications of this proposal.* **2.** used to indicate that something may be true based on available evidence ○ *He then completely ignored her, evidently intent on hurting her feelings even more.*

e·vil /éev'l/ *adj* **1.** MORALLY BAD profoundly immoral or wrong **2.** HARMFUL deliberately causing great harm, pain, or upset ○ *This evil act is clearly the work of terrorists.* **3.** CAUSING MISFORTUNE characterized by, bringing, or signifying bad luck ○ *an evil omen* **4.** MALICIOUS characterized by a desire to cause hurt or harm ○ *an evil mood* **5.** DEVILISH connected with the devil or other powerful destructive forces ○ *evil spirits* **6.** DISAGREEABLE very unpleasant ○ *What an evil smell!* ■ *n* **1.** WICKEDNESS the quality of being profoundly immoral or wrong **2.** *also* **E·vil** FORCE CAUSING HARMFUL EFFECTS the force believed to bring about harmful, painful, or unpleasant events ○ *a struggle between good and evil* **3.** SOMETHING EVIL a situation or thing that is very unpleasant, harmful, or morally wrong ○ *the social evil of alcoholism* [Old English *yfel* < Indo-European, "exceeding due limits"] —**e·vil·ly** *adv* —**e·vil·ness** *n*

e·vil·do·er /éev'l dòo ər, èev'l dóo ər/ *n* somebody who does evil acts —**e·vil·do·ing** *n*

e·vil eye *n* **1.** a piercing look that conveys strong feelings of hatred, disapproval, jealousy, or malice, or that supposedly can cause harm **2.** a supernatural or magical power that some people believe can bring harm or cause bad luck ○ *an amulet to protect children from the evil eye*

E·vil One *n* RELIG same as **devil**

e·vince /i vínss/ (**e·vinced, e·vinc·ing, e·vinc·es**) *vt* **1.** to show a feeling or a quality clearly ○ *She evinced her disapproval of the production by leaving the auditorium.* **2.** to indicate something by action or implication [Late 16C. < Latin *evincere* "win out" < *vincere* "conquer"] —**e·vinc·i·ble** *adj*

e·vis·cer·ate /i víssə ràyt/ (**-at·ed, -at·ing, -ates**) *vt* **1.** DISEMBOWEL SOMEBODY to remove the internal organs or entrails of a person or an animal **2.** REMOVE IMPORTANT PART OF SOMETHING to remove an essential part of something and so weaken it **3.** SURG REMOVE CONTENTS OF ORGAN to remove the contents of the eyeball or another organ or body cavity [Late 16C. < Latin *eviscerat-*, past participle of *eviscerare* < *viscera* "internal organs, entrails"] —**e·vis·cer·a·tion** /i vìssə ráysh'n/ *n* —**e·vis·cer·a·tor** *n*

E·vi·ta /e véetə/ ➧ **Perón, Eva**

ev·o·ca·tion /èvvə káysh'n, èe vō-/ *n* **1.** a re-creation of something not present, especially an event or feeling from the past ○ *an accurate evocation of that period* **2.** the transfer of a case from a lower to a higher court for review

e·voc·a·tive /i vókətiv/ *adj* prompting vivid memories or images of things not present, especially things from the past ○ *an outfit evocative of the 1960s* —**e·voc·a·tive·ly** *adv* —**e·voc·a·tive·ness** *n*

e·voke /i vṓk/ (**e·voked, e·vok·ing, e·vokes**) *vt* **1.** STIMULATE MEMORIES FROM PAST to bring to mind a memory or feeling, especially from the past ○ *evoke childhood memories* **2.** CAUSE REACTION OR FEELING to provoke a particular reaction or feeling ○ *Her question evoked a bitter retort.* **3.** CAUSE SOMETHING TO APPEAR to make beings appear who are normally invisible ○ *evoke a spirit* [Early 17C. < Latin *evocare* "call out" < *vocare* "to call"] —**ev·o·ca·ble** /évvəkəb'l, i vṓkəb'l/ *adj* —**ev·o·ca·tor** /évvə kàytər/ *n* —**e·vo·ker** *n*

ev·o·lute /évvə lòot/ *n* the curve formed by the set of points that are the centers of curvature of another geometric curve (**involute**) [Mid-18C. < Latin *evolut-*, past participle of *evolvere* (see EVOLVE)]

ev·o·lu·tion /èvvə lóosh'n, èevə-/ *n* **1.** BIOL THEORY OF DEVELOPMENT FROM EARLIER FORMS the theoretical process by which all species develop from earlier forms of life. According to this theory, natural variation in the genetic material of a population favors reproduction by some individuals more than others, so that over the generations all members of the population come to possess the favorable traits. **2.** BIOL DEVELOPMENTAL PROCESS the natural or artificially induced process by which new and different organisms develop as a result of changes in genetic material **3.** GRADUAL DEVELOPMENT the gradual development of something into a more complex or better form ○ *the evolution of democracy in Western Europe* **4.** PATTERN CAUSED BY MOVEMENT a pattern formed by a series of movements **5.** PHYS GIVING OFF HEAT OR GAS the emission of heat, gas, or vapor **6.** MATH FINDING ROOT OF NUMBER an algebraic operation in which the root, e.g., the square root or cube root, of a number is found. ◊ **involution** (sense 6) **7.** MIL MILITARY EXERCISE a military exercise or maneuver carried out according to a plan [Early 17C. < Latin *evolut-*, past participle of *evolvere* (see EVOLVE)] —**ev·o·lu·tion·al** *adj* —**ev·o·lu·tion·al·ly** *adv*

ev·o·lu·tion·ar·y /èvvə lóosh'n èrree, èevə-/ *adj* **1.** OF EVOLUTION relating to the theory of biological evolution **2.** FROM EVOLUTION resulting from or conferred by evolution ○ *evolutionary advantage* **3.** GRADUAL developing in small increments that accumulate to bring about significant change ○ *an evolutionary process* —**ev·o·lu·tion·ar·i·ly** *adv*

ev·o·lu·tion·ism /èvvə lóosh'n ìzzəm, èevə-/ *n* **1.** the theory of biological evolution **2.** belief in the theory of biological evolution —**ev·o·lu·tion·ist** *n*

e·volve /i vólv/ (**e·volved, e·volv·ing, e·volves**) *v* **1.** *vti* DEVELOP GRADUALLY to develop something gradually, often into something more complex or advanced, or undergo such development **2.** *vti* BIOL DEVELOP VIA EVOLUTIONARY CHANGE in evolutionary theory, to develop from an earlier biological form **3.** *vt* PHYS EMIT HEAT OR GAS to give off heat, gas, or vapor [Early 17C. < Latin *evolvere* "roll out" < *volvere* "to roll"] —**e·volv·a·ble** *adj* —**e·volve·ment** *n*

~~evry~~ incorrect spelling of **every**

EW *abbr* MIL enlisted woman

E·wa Beach /áy vaà-, -waà-/ town on Oahu Island, Hawaii, west of Honolulu. Population: 14,255 (2002 estimate).

ewe /yoo/ *n* a female sheep, especially when fully grown [Old English *ēowu* < Indo-European]

E·we /áy wày, áy vày/ (*plural same* or **E·wes**) *n* **1.** a member of a West African people living in coastal regions of Ghana, Togo, and Benin **2.** the language of the Ewe people, belonging to the Kwa branch of the Niger-Congo family. Native speakers: 3 million. [Mid-19C. < Ewe] —**E·we** *adj*

Ew·ell /yóo əl/, **Richard Stoddert** (1817–72) US soldier. He led the Confederate army after Stonewall Jackson's death.

ewe-neck *n* a thin concave neck in a horse or dog, considered to be a disadvantage —**ewe-necked** *adj*

E·wen·ki *n, adj* PEOPLES, LANG another spelling of **Evenki**

ewer

ew·er /yoŏ ər/ *n* a large jug or pitcher with a wide spout [15C. < Anglo-Norman < Old French *aiguière* < Latin *aquarius* "of water" < *aqua* "water"]

Ew·ing's sar·co·ma /yoŏ ingz-/, **Ew·ing's tu·mor** *n* a highly malignant cancerous tumor that develops in the long bones, pelvis, or ribs, usually in children and adolescents [Early 20C. After James *Ewing* (1866–1943), US pathologist]

ex[1] /eks/ *n* the letter X [Late 19C. < the pronunciation]

ex[2] /eks/ *n* a former spouse, boyfriend, or girlfriend (*informal*) [Early 19C. < EX-[1]]

ex[3] /eks/ *prep* **1.** not including or participating in ○ *ex dividend* **2.** sold directly from the place of production with no charge before collection ○ *ex works* [Mid-19C. < Latin (see EX-[1])]

ex. *abbr* **1.** examination **2.** example **3.** except **4.** exchange **5.** executive **6.** express **7.** extra

Ex. *abbr* BIBLE Exodus

ex-[1] *prefix* **1.** out, outside, away ○ *exclave* ○ *explant* **2.** not, without **3.** former ○ *ex-convict* [< Latin, "out of" < Indo-European, "out"]

ex-[2] *prefix* same as **exo-** (*used before vowels*)

exa- *prefix* one million million million (10^{18}). Symbol **E** [< HEXA-]

ex·ac·er·bate /ig zássər bàyt/ (**-bat·ed, -bat·ing, -bates**) *vt* to make an already bad or problematic situation worse ○ *Her silence merely exacerbated the problem.* [Mid-17C. < Latin *exacerbat-*, past participle of *exacerbare* "make thoroughly harsh" < *acerbus* "harsh, bitter"] —**ex·ac·er·ba·tion** /ig zàssər báysh'n/ *n*

ex·act /ig zákt/ *adj* **1.** CORRECT accurate and correct in all important details ○ *an exact account* **2.** PRECISE precise and not allowing for any variation ○ *a check for the exact amount* **3.** THIS AND NO OTHER used to emphasize that what is being referred to is one precise and often significant thing and not any other ○ *on this exact spot* **4.** STRICT rigorous and thorough ○ *an exact argument* **5.** FUNCTIONING ACCURATELY characterized by precise measurements ○ *exact instruments* ■ *vt* (**-act·ed, -act·ing, -acts**) **1.** OBTAIN SOMETHING to demand and obtain something, especially payment ○ *exacted a heavy tribute from their defeated enemies* **2.** INFLICT SOMETHING AS SUFFERING to make somebody endure something unpleasant (*formal*) ○ *I was already thinking how I could exact revenge for what he had done.* **3.** REQUIRE SOMETHING to call for something as a matter of necessity or urgency [15C. < Latin *exact-*, past participle of *exigere* "to demand" < *agere* "to drive"] —**ex·act·a·ble** *adj* —**ex·act·ness** *n* —**ex·ac·tor** *n*

ex·act·a /ig záktə/ *n US* a type of bet, especially on dogs or horses, that pays if the two entries chosen come in first and second in the order predicted. Can term **exactor** [Mid-20C. < American Spanish *quiniela exacta* "exact quinella," game of chance]

ex·act·ing /ig zákting/ *adj* **1.** requiring concentration and strict attention to detail ○ *an exacting task* **2.** demanding hard work and great effort ○ *an exacting boss* —**ex·act·ing·ly** *adv* —**ex·act·ing·ness** *n*

ex·ac·tion /ig záksh'n/ *n* **1.** ACT OF DEMANDING AND OBTAINING SOMETHING the act of forcing somebody to give something, especially payment **2.** UNFAIR DEMAND an unfair or excessive demand for something, especially money (*formal*) **3.** PAYMENT OBTAINED BY FORCE a sum of money that has been forcibly demanded and obtained (*formal*)

ex·ac·ti·tude /ig zákti toŏd/ *n* the quality or state of being exact, precise, or accurate ○ *"The children were drilled in their parts with a military exactitude; obedience and punctuality became cardinal virtues."* (Frank Norris, *McTeague – A Story of San Francisco*; 1899)

ex·act·ly /ig záktlee/ *adv* **1.** PRECISELY used to emphasize that a particular quality or quantity is stated precisely ○ *One lap around the park is exactly two miles.* **2.** FULLY used to emphasize that what is stated is true in all details or to the fullest extent ○ *He did exactly what I said he would.* **3.** SHOWING AGREEMENT used to indicate agreement that what has just been said is true or correct ○ *"We need to give this more thought." "Exactly."* **4.** SHOWING DISAPPROVAL used in questions to ask for precise information, often implying suspicion or disapproval ○ *So exactly what are you doing?*

ex·ac·tor /ig záktə/ *n Can* GAMBLING same as **exacta**

ex·act sci·ence *n* a science such as physics that deals with precise quantifiable measurements

~~exagerate~~ incorrect spelling of **exaggerate**

ex·ag·ger·ate /ig zájjə ràyt/ (**-at·ed, -at·ing, -ates**) *v* **1.** *vti* to state that something is better, worse, larger, more common, or more important than is true or usual **2.** *vt* to make something appear more noticeable or prominent than is usual or desirable [Mid-16C. < Latin *exaggerat-*, past participle of *exaggerare* "heap up" < *agger* "heap" < *gerere* "carry"] —**ex·ag·ger·at·ing·ly** *adv* —**ex·ag·ger·a·tion** /ig zàjjə ráysh'n/ *n* —**ex·ag·ger·a·tive** *adj* —**ex·ag·ger·a·tor** *n*

ex·ag·ger·at·ed /ig zájjə ràytəd/ *adj* made to seem better, worse, larger, or more important than is true or usual ○ *greatly exaggerated reports of widespread looting* —**ex·ag·ger·at·ed·ly** *adv*

ex·alt /ig záwlt/ (**-alt·ed, -alt·ing, -alts**) *vt* **1.** PRAISE SOMEBODY OR SOMETHING to praise or worship somebody or something (*formal*) **2.** PROMOTE SOMEBODY OR SOMETHING to raise somebody or something in rank, position, or esteem (*formal*) ○ *exalted to the rank of major* **3.** INTENSIFY SOMETHING to increase the intensity or effect of something (*formal*) **4.** STIMULATE SOMETHING to stimulate a mental quality or faculty (*archaic*) ○ *"Of Lorna, of my lifelong darling, of my more and more loved wife, I will not talk; for it is not seemly that a man should exalt his pride."* (R. D. Blackmore, *Lorna Doone, A Romance of Exmoor*; 1869) [15C. < Latin *exaltare* "put up high" < *altus* "high"] —**ex·alt·er** *n*

ex·al·ta·tion /ĕg zawl táysh'n/ *n* **1.** FEELING OF EXTREME HAPPINESS a feeling of intense or excessive happiness or exhilaration (*formal*) ○ *the miseries and exaltations of romance* **2.** RAISING UP the act of raising or holding something up (*formal*) **3.** FLOCK a flock of larks (*literary*)

ex·alt·ed /ig záwltəd/ *adj* (*formal*) **1.** ELEVATED high in rank, position, or esteem **2.** NOBLE grand or noble in character **3.** HIGH-SPIRITED in very high spirits —**ex·alt·ed·ly** *adv* —**ex·alt·ed·ness** *n*

ex·am /ig zám/ *n* **1.** a test designed to assess somebody's ability or knowledge in a particular subject or field ○ *a chemistry exam* **2.** *US* a medical inspection of a particular kind carried out on a patient ○ *my annual physical exam* Can term **examination** (sense 3) [Mid-19C. Shortening of EXAMINATION]

ex·a·men /ig záymən/ *n* in the Roman Catholic Church, an examination of conscience [Early 17C. < Latin (see EXAMINE)]

ex·am·i·na·tion /ig zàmmə náysh'n/ *n* **1.** the process of looking at and considering something carefully with the idea of learning something ○ *Their applications are currently under examination.* **2.** EDUC full form of **exam** (sense 1) **3.** *Can, UK* MED same as **exam** (sense 2) **4.** LAW an interrogation of a witness or other party to a case in a court of law

ex·am·ine /ig zámmin/ (**-ined, -in·ing, -ines**) *vt* **1.** STUDY SOMETHING to inspect or study somebody or something in detail ○ *examine the scene for fingerprints* **2.** INVESTIGATE SOMETHING to analyze something in order to understand or expose it ○ *examine your conscience* **3.** EDUC TEST SOMEBODY to test the knowledge or ability of somebody by giving written, oral, or practical examinations **4.** MED INSPECT CONDITION OF PATIENT to inspect a patient in order to determine his or her condition or health ○ *examined by a qualified physician* **5.** LAW INTERROGATE WITNESS to ask questions of a witness or other party to a case in a court of law [14C. Via French < Latin *examinare* "weigh" < *examen* "weighing out" < *exigere* (see EXACT)] —**ex·am·in·a·ble** *adj* —**ex·am·in·ee** /ig zàmmə née/ *n* —**ex·am·in·er** *n*

ex·am pa·per *n UK* the printed set of questions used to test somebody's knowledge in an exam

ex·am·ple /ig zámp'l/ *n* **1.** SAMPLE something that is representative by virtue of having typical features of the thing it represents ○ *a fine example of Baroque carving* **2.** MODEL a person, action, or thing taken as a model to be copied or avoided by others ○ *Her achievement is an example to us all.* **3.** ILLUSTRATION SUPPORTING SOMETHING an illustration that supports or provides more information on an opinion, theory, or principle ○ *The prosecutor then listed several examples of the accused's mismanagement of funds.* **4.** LEARNING AID an exercise or description that illustrates a principle, method, or problem ○ *Each chapter contains easy-to-follow examples.* ■ *vt* (**-pled, -pling, -ples**) EXEMPLIFY SOMETHING to be an example of something (*archaic; usually passive*) [14C. < Old French < Latin *exemplum* "take out" < *eximere* "take out" < *emere* "take"] ◇ **for example** used to introduce a typical instance of somebody or something ◇ **make an example of somebody** to punish somebody as a warning to others who might be inclined to offend in the same way

ex·an·the·ma /ĕg zan théemə/ (*plural* **-ma·ta** /-mətə/ or **-mas**), **ex·an·them** /eg zánthəm/ *n* **1.** a skin rash appearing as a sign of some infectious diseases such as measles **2.** a disease characterized by the appearance of a skin rash, e.g., measles or scarlet fever [Mid-17C. Via late Latin < Greek *exanthēma* "eruption" < *anthein* "to blossom" < *anthos* "flower"] —**ex·an·the·mat·ic** /eg zànthə máttik/ *adj* —**ex·an·them·a·tous** /ĕg zan thémmətəss/ *adj*

ex·arch /éks aark/ *n* **1.** a bishop in the Eastern Orthodox Church of a rank above a metropolitan **2.** the ruler of a province in the Byzantine Empire [Late 16C. Via ecclesiastical Latin *exarchus* < Greek *exarkhos* "leader" < *exarkhein* "to lead" < *arkhein* "to rule"] —**ex·arch·al** /ek saark'l/ *adj*

ex·ar·chate /éks aar kayt/, **ex·ar·chy** /-kee/ (*plural* **-chies**) *n* the office, domain, or term of an exarch

ex·as·per·ate /ig záspə ràyt/ (**-at·ed, -at·ing, -ates**) *vt* **1.** to make somebody very angry or frustrated, often by repeatedly doing something annoying (*usually passive*) ○ *Guests were exasperated by their hosts' constant bickering.* See Synonyms at **annoy 2.** to make an unpleasant condition or feeling worse (*literary*) [Mid-16C. < Latin *exasperat-*, past participle of *exasperare* "irritate, roughen" < *asper* "rough"] —**ex·as·per·at·ed·ly** *adv* —**ex·as·per·at·ing** *adj* —**ex·as·per·at·ing·ly** *adv* —**ex·as·per·a·tion** /ig zàspə ráysh'n/ *n*

SYNONYMS See *annoy.*

~~exaust~~ incorrect spelling of **exhaust**

Ex·cal·i·bur /ek skállәbәr/ *n* in Arthurian legend, King Arthur's magic sword that was given to him by the mysterious Lady of the Lake [15C. Alteration of medieval Latin *Caliburnus* < Middle Welsh *Caletuwlch* or Middle Irish *Caladbolg*, sword of Irish legend]

ex ca·the·dra /èks kə théedrə/ *adj, adv* with the authority of status or rank ○ *imposed the decisions ex cathedra* [< Latin, "from the (teacher's) chair"]

ex·ca·vate /ékskə vàyt/ (**-vat·ed, -vat·ing, -vates**) *v* **1.** *vti* REMOVE EARTH to remove earth or soil by digging or scooping out ○ *Several feet of soil were excavated from the building site.* **2.** *vti* HOLLOW SOMETHING OUT to make a hole or cavity in something by removing the material inside ○ *excavate a tooth* **3.** *vti* UNCOVER SOMETHING WITH DIFFICULTY to discover or uncover something valuable by effort **4.** *vt* FORM SOMETHING BY HOLLOWING to form a shape or cavity by hollowing ○ *excavates a hollow in the sand as its nest* **5.** *vti* ARCHAEOL DIG FOR ARTIFACTS to dig in a place carefully and methodically, taking notes about procedures, conditions, and finds, with a view to uncovering objects of archaeological interest [Late 16C. < Latin *excavat-*, past participle of *excavare* "hollow out" < *cavus* "hollow"]

ex·ca·va·tion /èkskə váysh'n/ *n* **1.** the act or process of digging out ○ *recent excavations in Sumatra* **2.** a hole that has been made by digging or hollowing something out, or part of an archaeological site that has been excavated

ex·ca·va·tor /ékskə vàytər/ *n* **1.** a large machine with a hinged metal bucket attached to a hydraulic arm, used to move large quantities of earth or soil or for lifting **2.** a person or animal that digs or hollows something out, especially somebody engaged in archaeological excavation

~~**excede**~~ incorrect spelling of **exceed**

ex·ceed /ik séed/ (**-ceed·ed, -ceed·ing, -ceeds**) *vt* **1.** BE GREATER THAN SOMETHING to be greater than something in quantity, degree, or scope ○ *The cost of the movie is reported to have exceeded 20 million dollars.* **2.** GO BEYOND LIMITS to go beyond the limits of something in quantity, degree, or scope ○ *He was fined for exceeding the speed limit.* ○ *You've exceeded your authority.* **3.** OUTDO SOMETHING OR SOMEBODY to be better than something or somebody ○ *descriptions of nature that far exceed anything else we've heard* [14C. Via Old French *excéder* < Latin *excedere* "go beyond, depart" < *cedere* "go"]

SPELLCHECK See *accede.*

ex·ceed·ance /ik séed'nss/ *n* **1.** *US* GOING BEYOND an instance of going beyond a limit ○ *fined $50 for each exceedance* **2.** *US* EXCESSIVE AMOUNT the amount by which something exceeds a limit ○ *an exceedance of 50 parts per million* **3.** EXCESSIVE POLLUTION a situation in which the concentration of a pollutant exceeds a standard or permissible limit

ex·ceed·ing /ik séeding/ *adj* very great (*literary*) ○ *exceeding joy* ■ *adv* to an unusually high degree (*archaic*)

ex·ceed·ing·ly /ik séedinglee/ *adv* to an unusually high degree ○ *You've been exceedingly generous.*

ex·cel /ik sél/ (**-celled, -cel·ling, -cels**) *v* **1.** *vi* to be outstanding or have a particular talent in something ○ *excels in marketing* **2.** *vt* to do better than all others, than a given standard, or than previous personal achievement [15C. < Latin *excellere* "rise above" < assumed *cellere* "rise"]

ex·cel·lence /éksələnss/ *n* **1.** the quality or state of being outstanding and superior ○ *an award for excellence in photography* **2.** a feature or respect in which somebody or something is superior and outstanding

Ex·cel·len·cy /éksələnssee/ (*plural* **-cies**), **Ex·cel·lence** /-lənss/ *n* a title and form of address for some high officials such as governors, ambassadors, and high-ranking Roman Catholic clergy

ex·cel·lent /éksələnt/ *adj* of a very high quality or standard ■ *interj* used to show wholehearted approval or agreement [14C. Via French < Latin *excellent-* present participle of *excellere* (see EXCEL)] —**ex·cel·lent·ly** *adv*

ex·cel·si·or /ik sélssee ər/ *n US* packing material made from wood shavings [Mid-19C. Originally proprietary name < Latin, "higher"]

ex·cept /ik sépt/ (**-cept·ed, -cept·ing, -cepts**) CORE MEANING: a grammatical word indicating the only person or thing that does not apply to a statement just made, or a fact that modifies the truth of that statement ○ (prep) *Every house in the street except ours is painted white.* ○ (prep) *I like all vegetables except cabbage.* ○ (conj) *The fires that annually sweep over the prairies prevent the growth of timber, except along the river courses.* ○ (conj) *He dislikes the game except when he wins.*
1. *prep* other than ○ *every house except ours* **2.** *conj* same as **unless** (*archaic*) **3.** *vt* to leave out or exclude somebody or something (*formal; usually passive*) [14C. < Latin *except-*, past participle of *excipere* "take out" < *capere* "take"] ◇ **except for** apart from ○ *He had always been healthy except for an irregular heartbeat.* ◇ **except that** with the exception of the fact that, or if it were not for the fact that ○ *The twins looked identical, except that one had dyed his hair.* ○ *I would come, except that I have another engagement.*

USAGE except, except for, or **excepting:** Often the question of whether to use ***except*** or ***except for*** is a matter of indifference: *We'd all seen the play except* [or *except for*] *Joe.* Where the exception is closely paired with what it is an exception to, ***except*** is more usual: *All of us except Joe had seen the play.* ***Except for*** is used where the connection to what is being excepted is indirect, and is also more common at the beginning of a sentence: *Except for that, we were in agreement.* ***Excepting*** is the correct choice after *not*: *She was the most important person in his life, not excepting his mother.*

USAGE See *accept.*

ex·cept·ed /ik séptəd/ *adj* with the exception of a particular person or thing ○ *present company excepted* ○ *"Hazel eyes excepted, two years more might make her all that he wished."* (Jane Austen, *Emma*; 1816)

ex·cept·ing /ik sépting/ *prep, conj* used to indicate the only person or thing excluded from a statement just made (*formal*)

USAGE See *except.*

ex·cep·tion /ik sépsh'n/ *n* **1.** SOMEBODY OR SOMETHING EXCLUDED somebody or something that is not included in or does not fit into a general rule, pattern, or judgment ○ *make an exception for family members* **2.** EXCLUSION the act or condition of being excluded **3.** CRITICISM a criticism, usually a negative one (*formal*) **4.** LAW LEGAL CLAUSE a clause in a legal document that limits the effect of a part or the whole of it ○ *has read through and approved all the exceptions* **5.** LAW FORMAL OBJECTION USED IN COURT a formal objection formerly used in court proceedings ◇ **take exception (to something)** to be annoyed or offended by something ◇ **the exception that proves the rule** something that, by being an exception, shows that a general rule exists

ex·cep·tion·a·ble /ik sépshənəb'l/ *adj* causing or liable to cause objection or offense (*formal*)

USAGE See *exceptional.*

ex·cep·tion·al /ik sépshən'l, ik sépshnəl/ *adj* **1.** having or showing intelligence or ability well above average ○ *an exceptional talent* **2.** not conforming to a general rule or pattern ○ *exceptional circumstances* —**ex·cep·tion·al·i·ty** /ik sèpshə nállətee/ *n* —**ex·cep·tion·al·ly** *adv* —**ex·cep·tion·al·ness** *n*

USAGE exceptional or **exceptionable**? ***Exceptional*** is the more common word and refers, often favorably, to a person or thing unusual in some way: *She has exceptional powers of concentration.* However, ***exceptional*** is also used in a factual or neutral way: *Expenses can be reimbursed only in exceptional cases.* ***Exceptionable***, despite its similar sound, has a very different meaning, referring to something that arouses disapproval or offense: *There was something in his manner that we found exceptionable.* More often, it is used in the negative form *unexceptionable*, meaning "good enough to provide no reason for criticism or objection."

ex·cep·tive /ik séptiv/ *adj* relating to or of the nature of an exception

ex·cerpt *n* /ék sùrpt/ a section or passage taken from a longer work such as a book, movie, musical composition, or document ■ *vt* /ik súrpt/ (**-cerpt·ed, -cerpt·ing, -cerpts**) to select a section or passage from a longer work (*usually passive*) [Mid-16C. < Latin *excerpt-*, past participle of *excerpere* "pluck out" < *carpere* "pluck"] —**ex·cerpt·i·ble** /ik súrptəb'l/ *adj* —**ex·cerp·tion** *n* —**ex·cerp·tor** *n*

ex·cess *n* /ik séss, ék sèss/ **1.** SURPLUS an amount or quantity beyond what is considered proper, usual, or sufficient ○ *leaped up in an excess of enthusiasm* **2.** EXTRA the amount by which one quantity exceeds another **3.** UNRESTRAINED BEHAVIOR behavior or activity that goes beyond what is socially or morally acceptable, or beyond what is good for somebody's health or well-being ○ *led a life of excess* **4.** *UK, Carib* INSUR same as **deductible** ■ *adj* /ék sèss, ik séss/ **1.** MORE THAN ENOUGH more than is usual, required, or allowed ○ *excess capacity* **2.** REQUIRED IN ADDITION constituting or being required as an additional payment ○ *excess postage* ■ *vt* /ik séss, ék sèss/ (**-cessed, -cess·ing, -cess·es**) *US* DISMISS FROM EMPLOYMENT to dismiss an employee as part of a program of layoffs ○ *was excessed in the most recent downsizing* [14C. Via French *excès* < Latin *excessus* < past participle of *excedere* (see EXCEED)] ◇ **to excess** beyond what is considered normal, sufficient, or healthy

SPELLCHECK See *access.*

ex·cess bag·gage *n* **1.** luggage that is heavier than the amount a passenger is allowed to take on a flight without an extra charge **2.** *US* something somebody would rather not have (*informal*)

ex·cess de·mand *n* demand for a product or service that outstrips the supply and so pushes the price up

ex·ces·sive /ik séssiv/ *adj* beyond what is considered acceptable, proper, usual, or necessary ○ *excessive hilarity* —**ex·ces·sive·ly** *adv* —**ex·ces·sive·ness** *n*

ex·cess sup·ply *n* supply of a product or service that outstrips the demand and so pushes the price down

exch. *abbr* **1.** exchange **2.** POL exchequer

Exch. *abbr* POL exchequer

ex·change /iks cháynj/ *v* (**-changed, -chang·ing, -chang·es**) **1.** *vt* GIVE SOMETHING AND GET SOMETHING to give something and receive something different in return ○ *exchange land for peace* ○ *exchange tokens for cash* **2.** *vti* SWAP to give something and receive another of the same or an equivalent in return ○ *exchange glances* **3.** *vt* REPLACE SOMETHING to hand something over and receive as a replacement something more suitable or more satisfactory ○ *exchanged her coat for one a size smaller* **4.** *vt* CHESS TAKE PIECE OF SIMILAR VALUE in chess, to take a piece in return for one, usually of similar value, that an opponent has just taken or will soon take ■ *n* **1.** FIN BUILDING USED FOR COMMERCIAL ACTIVITIES a building used as a center for the trading of commodities, securities, or other assets, or the market operating there **2.** GIVING AND RECEIVING the action or process or an instance of exchanging something for something else or for something the same ○ *an exchange of compliments* **3.** ARGUMENT a short conversation, often between two people or groups who are angry ○ *a bitter exchange* **4.** SOMETHING GIVEN OR RECEIVED something given or received in place of another **5.** FIN SYSTEM OF PAYMENTS a system of payments in which commercial documents such as bills of exchange, are used instead of money **6.** FIN MONEY TRANSFER BETWEEN TWO CURRENCIES the transferring or a transfer of equal amounts of money between two currencies **7.** FIN FEE FOR PAYMENT the percentage or fee that is charged when paying in commercial documents instead of money **8.** TELECOM same as **telephone exchange** **9.** CHESS TAKING OF CHESS PIECES the taking of chess pieces of similar value by each player in consecutive or nearly consecutive moves **10.** PHYS TRANSFER OF PARTICLE the transfer of an elementary particle of one type between two others of a different type, creating a force [14C. < Old French < assumed Vulgar Latin *excambiare* < late Latin *cambiare* "barter" (see CHANGE)] —**ex·change·a·bil·i·ty** /iks chàynjə bíllətee/ *n* —**ex·change·a·ble** *adj* —**ex·chang·er** *n*

ex·change force *n* a force existing between particles due to the transfer of another particle

ex·change par·ti·cle *n* a virtual particle that travels between elementary particles undergoing one of the four fundamental interactions, strong, weak, electromagnetic, and gravitational

ex·change rate *n* the rate at which a unit of the currency of one country can be exchanged for a unit of the currency of another country

Ex·change Rate Mech·a·nism *n* a system of controlling the exchange rate between some countries in the European Union that sets an agreed limit on the extent to which rates can fluctuate in relation to one another

ex·change stu·dent *n* a student who studies in another country as part of a program in which students trade places

ex·cheq·uer /iks chékər/ *n* **1.** formerly in the United Kingdom and some other countries, the government department responsible for collecting taxes and managing public spending **2.** a national treasury or account, especially the UK government's account at the Bank of England, or the assets in it [13C. < Old French *eschequier* "counting table, chessboard" < *eschec* "check"; from the custom of counting royal revenue on a checked tablecloth]

ex·ci·mer /éksəmər/ *n* a stable atomic pair (**dimer**) in which one of the two bound atoms is in a higher energy state [Mid-20C. Contraction of *excited dimer*]

ex·cip·i·ent /ik síppee ənt/ *n* an inert substance combined with a drug [Early 18C. < Latin *excipient-*, present participle of *excipere* "take out" (see EXCEPT)]

ex·cise[1] *n* /ék sīz/ **1.** TAX ON GOODS FOR DOMESTIC MARKET taxation of or a tax imposed on goods for a domestic market only **2.** LICENSING CHARGE a tax paid for a license, such as one required to use a vehicle on public roads or to engage in some commercial activities ■ *vt* /ik sīz/ **(-cised, -cis·ing, -cis·es)** TAX SOMEBODY OR SOMETHING to impose an excise on somebody or something [15C. Via Middle Dutch < Old French *acceis* "tax, toll"] —**ex·cis·a·ble** /ik sīzəb'l/ *adj*

ex·cise[2] /ik sīz/ **(-cised, -cis·ing, -cis·es)** *vt* **1.** to delete a part of something such as a text (*formal*) **2.** to remove something by cutting, especially in surgery [Late 16C. < Latin *excis-*, past participle of *excidere* "to cut out" < *caedere* "to cut"] —**ex·ci·sion** /ik sízh'n/ *n*

ex·cit·a·ble /ik sítəb'l/ *adj* **1.** nervous and liable to become quickly excited **2.** describes a nerve or tissue that is able to respond to a stimulus —**ex·cit·a·bil·i·ty** /ik sītə bíllətee/ *n* —**ex·cit·a·ble·ness** *n* —**ex·cit·a·bly** *adv*

ex·ci·tant /ik sít'nt/ *n* a drug that stimulates or augments a response ■ *adj* tending to excite or stimulate something

ex·ci·ta·tion /èk sī táysh'n, èksi-/ *n* **1.** EXCITING the act or process of exciting something (*formal*) **2.** BEING EXCITED the state of being excited **3.** PHYSIOL ACTIVITY CAUSED BY STIMULATION the activity or altered condition produced in a cell, tissue, or organ as a result of stimulation **4.** ELEC ENG PRODUCTION OF MAGNETIC FIELD the production of a magnetic field in a generator or motor by passing electricity through the coil **5.** PHYS RAISING ENERGY OF ATOM the addition of sufficient energy to an electron, atom, atomic nucleus, or molecule to raise it from its lowest energy level **(ground state)** to a higher energy level **6.** ELECTRONICS APPLICATION OF SIGNAL MAKING TRANSISTOR OPERATE the application of an electrical signal to a device such as a transistor, causing it to operate —**ex·ci·ta·to·ry** /ik sítə tàwree/ *adj*

ex·cite /ik sít/ **(-cit·ed, -cit·ing, -cites)** *v* **1.** *vti* STIMULATE FAVORABLY to cause somebody to feel enjoyment or pleasurable anticipation ○ *a book with an opening that fails to excite* **2.** *vt* STIMULATE SOMEBODY UNFAVORABLY to make a person or animal feel nervous apprehension or an unpleasant state of heightened emotion ○ *Don't excite the dog or he'll bite.* **3.** *vt* AROUSE SOMEBODY PHYSICALLY to cause somebody to feel physical desire **4.** *vt* AROUSE EMOTION to cause somebody to feel a particular emotion or reaction ○ *excite suspicion* **5.** *vt* EVOKE SOMETHING IN MIND to cause a memory, thought, or other response to form in the mind ○ *an image that excited a memory* **6.** *vt* PHYS RAISE PARTICLE TO HIGHER ENERGY LEVEL to raise an electron, atom, atomic nucleus, or molecule above its lowest energy level **(ground state)** to a higher energy level **7.** *vt* PHYSIOL MAKE SOMETHING MORE ACTIVE to stimulate or increase the rate of activity of an organ, tissue, or other body part **8.** *vt* ELEC ENG PRODUCE MAGNETIC FIELD IN ELECTRIC MACHINE to produce a magnetic field in a generator or motor by supplying electricity to the coil **9.** *vt* ELECTRONICS APPLY SIGNAL CAUSING DEVICE TO OPERATE to apply an electrical signal that will cause a device such as a transistor to operate [14C. Directly or via French < Latin *excitare* "rouse" < *ciere* "summon, set in motion"] —**ex·cit·ed** *adj* —**ex·cit·ed·ly** *adv*

ex·cit·ed state *n* the condition of a physical system, especially of atoms and atomic nuclei, that has an energy level higher than the lowest possible level **(ground state)**

ex·cite·ment /ik sítmənt/ *n* **1.** BEING EXCITED the feeling or condition of lively enjoyment or pleasant anticipation ○ *finding it difficult to contain her excitement* **2.** EXCITING SOMETHING the act or process of stimulating something ○ *excitement of electrons* **3.** EXCITING EVENT something that engages people's attention or emotions in a lively and compelling way ○ *Going in a helicopter was a great excitement for the children.*

ex·cit·er /ik sítər/ *n* **1.** CAUSE OF EXCITEMENT somebody or something that causes excitement **2.** ELEC ENG SMALL AUXILIARY GENERATOR a small generator or transmitter that provides the necessary energy to run a larger device or amplifier **3.** ELEC ENG ELECTRICAL OSCILLATOR an oscillator for supplying a radio transmitter with the basic wave that is modified to carry a radio signal

ex·cit·ing /ik síting/ *adj* causing feelings of happiness and enthusiasm or nervousness and tension —**ex·cit·ing·ly** *adv*

ex·ci·ton /éksi tòn/ *n* a mobile neutral combination of an electron in an excited state and a hole in a crystal. Exciton activity is important in semiconductors. [Mid-20C. < EXCITATION + -ON[1]]

ex·ci·to·tox·i·ci·ty /èksitō tok síssətee/ *n* the degree to which a substance is believed to be toxic to nerve cells through excessive stimulation [Mid-20C. < EXCITER] —**ex·ci·to·tox·ic** /èksitō tóksik/ *adj* —**ex·ci·to·tox·i·cal·ly** *adv*

ex·cit·o·tox·in /èksitō tóksin/ *n* a substance that is believed to kill or damage nerve cells through excessive stimulation [Late 20C. < EXCITER]

excl. *abbr* **1.** exclamation **2.** exclusive

ex·claim /ik skláym/ **(-claimed, -claim·ing, -claims)** *vti* to speak or cry out loudly and suddenly, often through surprise, anger, or excitement [Late 16C. Directly or via French < Latin *exclamare* "call out" < *clamare* "call"] —**ex·claim·er** *n*

~~**exclaimation**~~ incorrect spelling of **exclamation**

ex·cla·ma·tion /èksklə máysh'n/ *n* **1.** a word, phrase, or sentence that is shouted out suddenly, often through surprise, anger, or excitement ○ *an exclamation of horror* **2.** the act of crying out suddenly —**ex·cla·ma·tion·al** *adj*

ex·cla·ma·tion point *n* **1.** a punctuation mark (!) used after an exclamation or interjection, and sometimes after a command **2.** a mark (!) used to indicate a road hazard or a mistake or point of note in a text, or as a mathematical or logical symbol

USAGE The ***exclamation point*** follows an expression of surprise, anger, admiration, pain, etc., which may or may not be a full sentence: *I couldn't believe my eyes! What a pity! Ouch!* It sometimes marks the end of a command or warning, especially in direct speech: *Come here! Look out!* The exclamation point may be used for effect in creative writing or informal letters, but should not be overused. It is not normally used at all in formal writing. It should never be immediately preceded or followed by a period, but it may occasionally be used with a question mark in informal letters or e-mails to indicate exasperation or disbelief, especially in posing a rhetorical question: *How many times do I have to tell you?!*

ex·clam·a·to·ry /ik sklámmə tàwree/ *adj* marked by or involving an exclamation or exclamations —**ex·clam·a·to·ri·ly** *adv*

ex·clave /ék sklàyv/ *n* a part of a country that is isolated from the main body of the country, being surrounded by foreign territory [Late 19C. < EX-[1] + ENCLAVE]

ex·clo·sure /ik sklṓzhər/ *n* an area fenced in to keep out animals or intruders

ex·clude /ik sklóod/ **(-clud·ed, -clud·ing, -cludes)** *vt* **1.** KEEP SOMEBODY OR SOMETHING OUT to prevent somebody or something from entering or participating ○ *I felt excluded from the family celebrations.* **2.** REJECT SOMEBODY OR SOMETHING to prevent somebody or something from being considered or accepted ○ *cannot exclude the possibility of treason* **3.** OMIT SOMETHING OR SOMEBODY to fail to include something or somebody ○ *Three names were inadvertently excluded from the list.* [14C. < Latin *excludere* "to shut out" < *claudere* "to shut"] —**ex·clud·a·bil·i·ty** /ik sklòodə bíllətee/ *n* —**ex·clud·a·ble** *adj* —**ex·clud·er** *n*

ex·clud·ing /ik sklóoding/ *prep* used to mention items that are not being included or considered ○ *a annual income of $2 million, excluding the profits from overseas investments*

ex·clu·sion /ik sklóozh'n/ *n* **1.** EXCLUDING the act of excluding something or somebody **2.** BEING EXCLUDED the state of being excluded, especially from mainstream society and its advantages ○ *addressing the issue of social exclusion* **3.** EXCLUDED PERSON OR THING somebody or something that has been excluded [15C. < Latin *exclusion-* < *exclus-*, past participle of *excludere* (see EXCLUDE)] —**ex·clu·sion·ar·y** *adj*

ex·clu·sion·ar·y rule *n* a law that prevents illegally obtained evidence from being used in a criminal trial

ex·clu·sion·ist /ik sklóozh'nist/ *US adj* **1.** DISCRIMINATORY describes a policy that excludes individual people or groups from areas or rights and privileges **2.** PROTECTIONIST describes a policy that excludes specific imports or forms of commerce ■ *n* EXCLUSION ADVOCATE a supporter of exclusionist policies —**ex·clu·sion·ism** *n* —**ex·clu·sion·is·tic** /ik sklóozh'n ístik/ *adj*

ex·clu·sion prin·ci·ple *n* QUANTUM PHYS same as **Pauli exclusion principle**

ex·clu·sion zone *n* **1.** an area where an authority has banned a particular activity **2.** an area that is off-limits to people because a hazardous substance has been released ○ *the Chernobyl exclusion zone*

ex·clu·sive /ik sklóossiv/ *adj* **1.** HIGH-CLASS limited to a group of people, especially one considered fashionable or wealthy ○ *an exclusive club* **2.** SELECTIVE excluding or intending to exclude many from participation or consideration **3.** RESTRICTED IN USE only available to or used by one person, group, or organization ○ *Members have exclusive use of the pool.* **4.** APPEARING IN ONE PLACE published or broadcast in only one place ○ *exclusive coverage* **5.** SOLE being the only one ○ *Bicycles are the exclusive means of transport in the city center.* **6.** EXCLUDING OTHER THINGS focused or targeted on one thing only ○ *exclusive attention* **7.** NOT INCLUDING STATED NUMBERS not including the numbers, dates, or other series members mentioned immediately before ○ *from July 8 to July 17 exclusive* ◊ **inclusive** (sense 1) **8.** COMM RESTRICTING TRADE restricting trade in some goods or services only to those who have signed the contract or agreement **9.** LOGIC WHERE BOTH CANNOT BE TRUE describes a proposition **(disjunction)** where one alternative rules out the other, e.g., being an odd number rules out the possibility of being an even number. ◊ **inclusive** (sense 6) ■ *n* REPORT IN ONE PUBLICATION OR PROGRAM a news report or article that is printed in only one publication or broadcast on only one channel ○ *an exclusive on the wedding* [15C. < medieval Latin *exclusivus* < Latin *exclus-*, past participle of *excludere* (see EXCLUDE)] —**ex·clu·sive·ly** *adv* —**ex·clu·sive·ness** *n* —**ex·clu·siv·i·ty** /èk skloo sívvətee/ *n* ◇ **exclusive of** not including ○ *The price covers all your vacation costs, exclusive of travel insurance.*

ex·clu·siv·ism /ik sklóossi vìzzəm/ *n* the practice or policy of being exclusive or excluding others —**ex·clu·siv·ist** *n, adj*

ex·cog·i·tate /eks kójji tàyt/ **(-tat·ed, -tat·ing, -tates)** *vt* to consider or think about something carefully and thoroughly (*formal*) [Early 16C. < Latin *excogitat-*, past participle of *excogitare* "think out" < *cogitare* "think" (see COGITATE)] —**ex·cog·i·ta·ble** *adj*

ex·com·mu·ni·cate *vt* /èkskə myóoni kàyt/ **(-cat·ed, -cat·ing, -cates)** EXCLUDE SOMEBODY FROM CHRISTIAN COMMUNITY to exclude a baptized Christian from taking part in Communion because of doctrine or moral behavior that is adjudged to offend against God or the Christian community ■ *adj* /-kət, -kàyt/ EXCOMMUNICATED having been officially excluded from taking part in Communion ■ *n* /-kət/ EXCOMMUNICATED PERSON somebody who has been formally excluded from taking part in Communion [15C. < late Latin *excommunicat-*, past participle of *excommunicare* "put out of the community" < Latin *communis* "common"] —**ex·com·mu·ni·ca·ble** *adj* —**ex·com·mu·ni·ca·tion** /èkskə myooni káysh'n/ *n* —**ex·com·mu·ni·ca·tive** *adj* —**ex·com·mu·ni·ca·tor** *n*

ex·con *n* same as **ex-convict** (*informal*) [Early 20C. Shortening]

ex·con·vict *n* somebody who has served time in prison

ex·co·ri·ate /ik skáwree àyt/ **(-at·ed, -at·ing, -ates)** *vt* **1.** to severely criticize somebody or something (*formal*) ○ *The paper excoriated the governor's conduct in this case.* **2.** MED to remove skin from a person or animal [15C. < Latin *excoriat-*, past participle of *excoriare* "strip off the hide" < *corium* "hide, skin"] —**ex·co·ri·a·tion** /ik skàwree áysh'n/ *n* —**ex·co·ri·a·tor** *n*

ex·cre·ment /ékskrəmənt/ *n* waste material, particularly feces, discharged from the body (*technical*) [Mid-16C. < Latin *excrementum* < *excretus*, past participle of *excernere* (see EXCRETE)] —**ex·cre·ment·al** /èkskrə mént'l/ *adj* —**ex·cre·men·ti·tious** /èkskrəmən tíshəss/ *adj*

ex·cres·cence /ik skréss'nss/ *n* **1.** a growth that sticks out from the body of a human, animal, or plant **2.**

an ugly addition or extension to something such as a building

ex·cres·cent /ik skréss'nt/ *adj* **1.** SUPERFLUOUS added or growing out unnecessarily (*formal*) **2.** BIOL RELATING TO OUTGROWTH relating to or like an outgrowth on an organism **3.** LING ADDED IN SPEAKING describes a speech sound that occurs in a word to allow ease of pronunciation [15C. < Latin *excrescent-*, present participle of *excrescere* "grow out" < *crescere* "grow"] —**ex·cres·cent·ly** *adv*

ex·cre·ta /ik skréetə/ *npl* any waste matter discharged from the body, e.g., feces or urine (*technical*) [Mid-19C. < Latin, "things excreted" < form of past participle of *excernere* (see EXCRETE)] —**ex·cre·tal** *adj*

ex·crete /ik skréet/ (**-cret·ed, -cret·ing, -cretes**) *vt* **1.** to isolate and discharge waste matter generated during metabolism, e.g., through urinating or defecating (*formal*) **2.** to eliminate waste matter from leaves and roots [Early 17C. < Latin *excret-*, past participle of *excernere* "separate out, discharge" < *cernere* "to separate"] —**ex·cre·to·ry** /ékskrə tàwree/ *adj*

ex·cre·tion /ik skréesh'n/ *n* **1.** the act or process of discharging waste matter from the tissues or organs **2.** waste matter that has been discharged from an animal or a plant

ex·cru·ci·ate /ik skróoshee àyt/ (**-at·ed, -at·ing, -ates**) *vt* (*formal*) **1.** to inflict severe mental and emotional distress on somebody **2.** to inflict physical pain on somebody [Late 16C. < Latin *excruciat-*, past participle of *excruciare* "torture thoroughly" < *cruciare* "torture, crucify" < *cruc-* "cross"] —**ex·cru·ci·a·tion** /ik skróoshee áysh'n/ *n*

ex·cru·ci·at·ing /ik skróoshee àyting/ *adj* **1.** extremely painful, physically or emotionally **2.** intolerably embarrassing, tedious, or irritating ○ *The first act was bad enough, but the second was just excruciating.* —**ex·cru·ci·at·ing·ly** *adv*

ex·cul·pate /ékskəl pàyt, ik skúl-/ (**-pat·ed, -pat·ing, -pates**) *vt* to free somebody from blame or accusation of guilt (*formal*) [Mid-17C. < medieval Latin *exculpat-*, past participle of *exculpare* "remove from blame" < Latin *culpa* "blame"] —**ex·cul·pa·ble** /ik skúlpəb'l/ *adj* —**ex·cul·pa·tion** /ékskəl páysh'n/ *n*

ex·cul·pa·to·ry /ik skúlpə tàwree/ *adj* tending to prove that somebody is free from guilt or blame (*formal*) ○ *exculpatory evidence*

ex·cur·sion /ik skúrzh'n/ *n* **1.** SHORT TRIP a short trip to a place and back, for pleasure or a purpose **2.** GROUP ON SHORT TRIP a group of people who are taking a short trip **3.** DIGRESSION a temporary deviation from a regular course or pattern ○ *After an unsuccessful excursion into banking, he returned to public life.* **4.** PHYS ALTERNATING MOTION an oscillating or alternating motion away from a point of equilibrium and back **5.** PHYS DISTANCE COVERED a distance that an oscillating body moves away from the point of equilibrium **6.** PHYSIOL MOVEMENT OF BODY PART the movement of a part or organ of the body, e.g., the lungs, from the resting position to another position [Late 16C. < Latin *excursion-* < *excurs-*, past participle of *excurrere* "run out" < *currere* "to run"]

ex·cur·sion fare *n* a reduced fare, usually carrying various restrictions, that is offered by a passenger carrier

ex·cur·sion·ist /ik skúrzhənist/ *n* somebody who goes on an excursion, especially for pleasure (*dated*)

ex·cur·sive /ik skúrssiv/ *adj* tending to digress from the main topic, often in a rambling and wordy manner (*formal*) [Late 17C. < obsolete *excurse* "digress" < Latin *excurs-* (see EXCURSION)] —**ex·cur·sive·ly** *adv* —**ex·cur·sive·ness** *n*

ex·cur·sus /ik skúrssəss/ (*plural* **-sus·es** or *same*) *n* a lengthy digression from the main topic (*formal*) [Early 19C. < Latin, "excursion" < *excurs-* (see EXCURSION)]

ex·cu·sa·do /es kōo sáa dō/ (*plural* **-dos**) *n Hispanic* same as **toilet** (senses 1–2) [< American Spanish < Spanish *excusar* "to excuse"]

ex·cus·a·to·ry /ik skyóozə tàwree/ *adj* tending or serving to excuse somebody or something (*formal*)

ex·cuse *v* /ik skyóoz/ (**-cused, -cus·ing, -cus·es**) **1.** *vt* FORGIVE SOMETHING to release somebody from blame or criticism for a mistake or wrongdoing ○ *excuse their tardiness* **2.** *vt* OVERLOOK SOMETHING to make allowances for somebody or something ○ *Please excuse my spelling.* **3.** *vt* RELEASE SOMEBODY FROM OBLIGATION to release somebody from an obligation or responsibility ○ *was excused from gym class because of a sprained ankle* **4.** *vt* JUSTIFY SOMETHING to provide a reason or explanation for somebody's behavior that makes it appear more acceptable or less offensive ○ *That doesn't excuse the way he acted last night.* **5.** *vt* ALLOW SOMEBODY TO LEAVE to allow somebody to leave, or say politely that somebody should leave ○ *asked if he could be excused* **6. ex·cuse your·self** *vr* APOLOGIZE FOR LEAVING to leave with a polite apology or explanation ○ *excused herself and left the room* ■ *n* /ik skyóoss/ **1.** JUSTIFICATION a reason or explanation, not necessarily true, given in order to make something appear more acceptable or less offensive ○ *There can be no excuse for laziness.* **2.** FALSE REASON a false reason that enables somebody to do something he or she wants to do or avoid something he or she does not want to do ○ *the perfect excuse to do nothing* **3.** BAD EXAMPLE an inept performer of a particular action or task (*informal*) ○ *a poor excuse for a cook* **4.** NOTE JUSTIFYING ABSENCE a note from a doctor or parent confirming that somebody is not well enough to go to work or attend school [15C. Via French < Latin *excusare* "remove from accusation" < *causa* "accusation"] —**ex·cus·a·ble** *adj* —**ex·cus·a·ble·ness** *n* —**ex·cus·a·bly** *adv* —**ex·cus·er** *n* ◇ **excuse me 1.** used to attract attention politely, e.g., when asking somebody to move aside or when interrupting somebody **2.** used to apologize for doing something rude or embarrassing, e.g., belching **3.** used to indicate politely that you disagree with something or think that it is incorrect **4.** used to ask somebody to repeat what he or she has just said because you did not hear it properly or did not understand it

ex-di·rec·to·ry *adj UK* same as **unlisted**

ex div·i·dend *adv, adj* without the right to the current dividend on purchase

exe /éksə/ *abbr* a file extension for a program file. Full form **executable**

ex·ec /ig zék/ *n* an executive or executive officer (*informal*) [Late 19C. Shortening]

exec. *abbr* LAW executor

ex·e·cra·ble /éksəkrəb'l/ *adj* **1.** extremely bad, or of very low quality ○ *has execrable taste* **2.** deserving to be detested ○ *execrable behavior* [14C. Via French < Latin *execrabilis* < *execrari* (see EXECRATE)] —**ex·e·cra·ble·ness** *n* —**ex·e·cra·bly** *adv*

ex·e·crate /éksə kràyt/ (**-crat·ed, -crat·ing, -crates**) *v* (*literary or formal*) **1.** *vt* DETEST SOMEBODY OR SOMETHING to feel loathing for somebody or something **2.** *vt* DENOUNCE SOMEBODY OR SOMETHING to declare somebody or something to be loathsome **3.** *vti* CURSE SOMEBODY OR SOMETHING to curse or put a curse on somebody or something [Mid-16C. < Latin *execrari* "undo consecration" < *sacrare* (see SACRED)] —**ex·e·cra·tive** *adj* —**ex·e·cra·tor** *n*

ex·e·cra·tion /éksə kráysh'n/ *n* (*literary or formal*) **1.** CURSE a curse or swearword ○*"With an execration the thoroughly terrified robber threw down the pocketbook, and the relieved owner hastened forward to pick it up."* (Horatio Alger, Jr., *Struggling Upward*; 1868) **2.** SOMETHING CURSED something that is cursed or detested **3.** EXECRATING the act of execrating somebody or something, or the state of being execrated

ex·e·cut·a·ble /éksə kyóotəb'l/ *adj* describes a computer file, often carrying the extension .exe, that can be run as a program —**ex·e·cut·a·ble** *n*

ex·ec·u·tant /ig zékyət'nt/ *n* a usually skilled performer of a musical, dance, or theater piece (*formal*)

ex·e·cute /éksə kyòot/ (**-cut·ed, -cut·ing, -cutes**) *v* **1.** *vt* PUT TO DEATH to kill somebody as part of a legal or extralegal process **2.** *vt* PERFORM ACTION to complete or perform an action or movement, especially one requiring skill **3.** *vt* CARRY OUT INTENTION to put an instruction or plan into effect **4.** *vti* COMPUT RUN ON COMPUTER to run a computer file or program in response to a command or instruction **5.** *vt* CREATE ART to produce or create something, usually a work of art, to a specific design ○ *execute a drawing* **6.** *vt* LAW CARRY OUT TERMS OF LEGAL DOCUMENT to carry out the terms laid out in a will, legal document, or legal decision ○ *execute a sentence* **7.** *vt* LAW SIGN LEGAL DOCUMENT BEFORE WITNESSES to sign a will or other legal document in the presence of witnesses in order to make it binding [14C. < Latin *execut-*, past participle of *exsequi* "follow out" < *sequi* "follow"]

SYNONYMS See ***kill***[1] and ***perform***.

ex·e·cut·er *n US* LAW another spelling of **executor** (sense 1)

ex·e·cu·tion /éksə kyóosh'n/ *n* **1.** KILLING the killing of somebody as part of a legal or extralegal process **2.** PERFORMING OF SOMETHING the carrying out of an action, instruction, command, or movement ○ *a plan that failed in execution* **3.** MANNER OF PERFORMANCE the style or manner in which something is carried out or accomplished **4.** LAW CARRYING OUT OF LEGAL PROVISIONS the carrying out of the provisions of a legal document such as a will or contract **5.** LAW SIGNING OF A DOCUMENT the formal signing of a legal document in the presence of witnesses in order to make it binding (*formal*) **6.** LAW ENFORCEMENT OF COURT JUDGMENT the carrying out or enforcing of a judgment made in court **7.** LAW WRIT a legal writ that orders the carrying out of a judgment or decision

ex·e·cu·tion·er /éksə kyóosh'nər/ *n* **1.** an official who puts to death somebody who has been sentenced to capital punishment **2.** a hired assassin

ex·e·cu·tion time *n* the amount of time needed for a complete run of a computer program routine

ex·ec·u·tive /ig zékyətiv/ *n* **1.** SENIOR MANAGER a senior manager in a company or organization, whose job it is to make and implement major decisions **2.** GOVERNMENT SECTION RESPONSIBLE FOR DECISIONS the section of a country's government that is responsible for implementing legislative decisions **3.** COMMITTEE THAT MAKES DECISIONS a committee or group in a political organization that makes decisions and has the authority to implement them ■ *adj* **1.** OF POLICYMAKING responsible for or relating to the making and implementing of general decisions in a company, organization, or government ○ *a meeting of the executive committee* **2.** FOR BUSINESSPEOPLE restricted to or designed to be used by business executives ○ *the executive suite* **3.** VERY EXPENSIVE very expensive and so only affordable by those who earn high salaries ○ *executive homes* [15C. < Old French *executif* < *executer* "carry out" < Latin *execut-* (see EXECUTE)] —**ex·ec·u·tive·ly** *adv*

ex·ec·u·tive a·gree·ment *n* an agreement between a US president and a foreign head of state that has not been given approval by the Senate

Ex·ec·u·tive Coun·cil *n* in Canada, the cabinet of a provincial government

ex·ec·u·tive di·rec·tor *n* a director of a company who is employed by the company in a senior management position

ex·ec·u·tive jet *n* a small jet aircraft designed for private use, especially one used to transport corporate executives

ex·ec·u·tive lounge *n* a lounge in an airport or hotel for the use of people who are traveling first-class

Ex·ec·u·tive Man·sion *n* POL same as **White House** (sense 1)

ex·ec·u·tive of·fi·cer *n* **1.** somebody in a senior management position in an organization **2.** a military or naval officer who is second in command of a unit

ex·ec·u·tive or·der *n* a rule or order that is issued by the executive branch of the government and has the status of a law

ex·ec·u·tive priv·i·lege *n* the right of the president and other government officials in the executive branch to refuse to reveal confidential material if this would interfere with the administration's ability to govern

ex·ec·u·tive pro·duc·er *n* **1.** the head producer in charge of other producers at a movie or television studio **2.** the producer who handles the finances for a movie

ex·ec·u·tive sec·re·tar·y *n* **1.** a secretary who reports to a senior manager or executive in a company **2.** a senior official who handles an organization's business operations

ex·ec·u·tive ses·sion *n* a meeting of the US Senate, closed to the public, to discuss confidential government business such as judicial appointments or the ratification of treaties

ex·ec·u·tive toy *n* a small but usually sophisticated and expensive toy marketed as suitable for an executive's desk and used to aid concentration or relieve stress

ex·ec·u·tor /ig zékyətər, éksə kyōōtər/ *n* **1.** *also* **ex·ec·u·ter** somebody named in a will or appointed by a court to carry out the instructions contained in a will **2.** somebody who performs an action or task [13C. Via Anglo-Norman < Latin < *execut-* (see EXECUTE)] —**ex·ec·u·to·ri·al** /ig zèkyə táwree əl/ *adj* —**ex·ec·u·tor·ship** *n*

ex·ec·u·to·ry /ig zékyə tàwree/ *adj* **1.** coming into effect at a future time or in accordance with circumstances **2.** relating to the task or process of carrying out laws, policies, or instructions [15C. < late Latin *executorius* < Latin *executor* (see EXECUTOR)]

ex·e·dra /éksədrə, ek sēedrə/ *n* **1.** FURNITURE **LONG CURVED OUTDOOR BENCH** a long curved or semicircular outdoor bench, usually with a high back **2.** ANCIENT HIST **CONVERSATION ROOM** in ancient Greece and Rome, a room for relaxation or conversation, especially a semicircular recess in a larger hall with a continuous bench along the wall **3.** ARCHIT **RECESS** a recess or niche (*technical*) [Early 18C. Via Latin < Greek, "outside seat" < *hedra* "seat"]

ex·e·ge·sis /èksə jéessiss/ (*plural* **-ses** /-jée seez/) *n* **1.** the explanation or interpretation of texts, especially religious writings **2.** an explanation or interpretation of a specific text, especially a religious one [Early 17C. < Greek *exēgēsis* < *exēgeisthai* "interpret" < *hēgeisthai* "to guide"]

ex·e·gete /éksə jeet/ *n* a student and interpreter of texts, especially religious writings [Mid-18C. < Greek *exēgētes* < *exēgeisthai* (see EXEGESIS)]

ex·e·get·ic /èksə jéttik/, **ex·e·get·i·cal** /-jéttik'l/ *adj* **1.** relating to the study and interpretation of texts, especially religious writings **2.** intended to explain or interpret something, especially a written text (*formal*) [Early 17C. < Greek *exēgetikos* < *exēgeisthai* (see EXEGESIS)] —**ex·e·get·i·cal·ly** *adv*

ex·e·get·ics /èksə jéttiks/ *n* the branch of theology dealing with the study and interpretation of religious writings (*takes a singular verb*)

ex·e·ge·tist /èksə jéttist/ *n* RELIG same as **exegete**

exellent incorrect spelling of **excellent**

ex·em·pla plural of **exemplum**

ex·em·plar /ig zém plaar, ig zémplər/ *n* **1.** **IDEAL** an ideal example of something, worthy of being copied or imitated (*literary*) ○ *Michelangelo's "David" is an exemplar of Renaissance sculpture.* **2.** **TYPICAL EXAMPLE** a typical example or instance of something (*literary*) **3.** **COPY OF BOOK** a copy of a book or text, especially one from which further copies have originated [15C. Directly or via French < late Latin *exemplarium* < Latin *exemplum* (see EXAMPLE)]

ex·em·pla·ry /ig zémpləree/ *adj* **1.** **SETTING EXAMPLE** so good or admirable that others would do well to copy it ○ *the child's exemplary conduct* **2.** **SERVING AS EXAMPLE** designed to serve as a warning to others ○ *exemplary punishment* **3.** **GIVING EXAMPLE** serving as an illustration or example of something (*formal*) [Late 16C. < late Latin *exemplaris* < Latin *exemplum* (see EXAMPLE)] —**ex·em·plar·i·ly** *adv* —**ex·em·pla·ri·ness** *n* —**ex·em·plar·i·ty** /ègzəm plárrətee/ *n*

ex·em·pli·fy /ig zémplə fī/ (**-fied, -fy·ing, -fies**) *vt* **1.** **BE EXAMPLE OF SOMETHING** to show or illustrate something by being a typical or model example of it ○ *He exemplified all the qualities of a natural leader.* **2.** **GIVE EXAMPLE OF SOMETHING** to give an example or examples in order to make something clearer or more convincing ○ *Perhaps you could exemplify your point with a few statistics.* **3.** LAW **MAKE COPY OF DOCUMENT** to make an official copy of a legal document [15C. < medieval Latin *exemplificare* < Latin *exemplum* (see EXAMPLE)] —**ex·em·pli·fi·a·ble** /ig zèmplə fī əb'l/ *adj* —**ex·em·pli·fi·ca·tion** /ig zèmpləfi káysh'n/ *n* —**ex·em·pli·fi·er** *n*

ex·em·pli gra·ti·a /ig zèmpli gráyshee ə, ik sèmpli graatee aa/ *adv* full form of **e.g.** [Mid-17C. < Latin, "for example's sake"]

ex·em·plum /ig zémpləm/ (*plural* **-pla** /-plə/) *n* **1.** a brief story told to illustrate a moral point or support an argument **2.** an example or illustration (*literary*) [Late 19C. < Latin (see EXAMPLE)]

ex·empt /ig zémpt/ *adj* **NOT SUBJECT TO SOMETHING** freed from or not subject to something such as a duty, tax, or military service that is required of others ○ *tax-exempt savings accounts* ○ *Students were exempt from service in the armed forces.* ■ *vt* (**-empt·ed, -empt·ing, -empts**) **1.** **FREE SOMEBODY FROM OBLIGATION** to allow or entitle somebody not to do something that others are obliged to do **2.** **RELEASE SOMETHING FROM RULE** to release something from a rule that applies to others ○ *a law that exempts certain capital gains from taxes* ■ *n* **EXEMPTED PERSON OR THING** somebody or something that is exempt from something [14C. Directly or via French < Latin *exempt-*, past participle of *eximere* (see EXAMPLE)] —**ex·empt·i·ble** *adj*

ex·emp·tion /ig zémpshən/ *n* **1.** permission or entitlement not to do something that others are obliged to do ○ *an exemption from jury duty* **2.** somebody or something that is exempt, e.g., income that is not taxed ○ *a range of tax exemptions*

ex·en·ter·ate /ig zéntə ràyt/ (**-at·ed, -at·ing, -ates**) *vt* to remove surgically all the organs and other contents of a body cavity, usually to minimize the spread of cancer [Early 17C. < Latin *exenterat-*, past participle of *exenterare*, alteration of Greek *exenterizein* "remove the intestine" < *enteron* "intestine"] —**ex·en·ter·a·tion** /ig zèntə ráysh'n/ *n*

exept incorrect spelling of **except**

ex·er·cise /éksər sīz/ *n* **1.** **PHYSICAL ACTIVITY** physical activity and movement, especially when intended to keep a person or animal fit and healthy ○ *Regular exercise is important.* **2.** **PHYSICAL MOVEMENT** a physical movement or action, or a series of movements or actions, designed to make the body stronger and fitter or to show off gymnastic skill (*often used in the plural*) ○ *warm-up exercises* **3.** **PRACTICE OF SKILL OR PROCEDURE** a series of actions, movements, or tasks performed repeatedly or regularly as a way of practicing and improving a skill or procedure (*often used in the plural*) ○ *voice exercises for singers* **4.** EDUC **PIECE OF WORK** a piece of work intended to test somebody's knowledge or skill ○ *Test yourself by doing the exercises at the back of the book.* **5.** MIL **MILITARY TRAINING OPERATIONS OR MANEUVERS** a set of extensive operations or maneuvers, usually under simulated combat conditions, intended to train military personnel, test their equipment, and assess their capabilities **6.** **ACTIVITY INTENDED TO ACHIEVE PURPOSE** an action, activity, or undertaking intended to achieve a specific purpose ○ *The object of the exercise is to make money fast.* **7.** **CARRYING OUT OR USING SOMETHING** the carrying out or making use of something such as a choice, duty, responsibility, or right (*formal*) ○ *We urge the exercise of patience and restraint.* ■ *npl* **ex·er·ci·ses** **TRADITIONAL CEREMONIES** ceremonies and speeches constituting a formal event ○ *graduation exercises* ■ *v* (**-cised, -cis·ing, -cis·es**) **1.** *vi* **GET EXERCISE** to undertake physical exercise in order to keep fit and healthy **2.** *vt* **SUBJECT BODY TO PHYSICAL EXERTION** to subject the body, or part of it, to repetitive physical exertion or energetic movement in order to strengthen it or improve its condition ○ *a routine designed to exercise your back and thigh muscles* **3.** *vt* **EXERT ANIMAL PHYSICALLY** to make an animal exert itself physically in order to keep it healthy and fit **4.** *vt* **PRACTICE AND DEVELOP SKILL** to develop a particular faculty or skill by carrying out specific tasks or procedures repeatedly or systematically **5.** *vt* **PUT SOMETHING TO PRACTICAL USE** to make use of a right or responsibility ○ *They have the power to prevent the merger, if they choose to exercise it.* **6.** *vt* **SHOW TYPE OF BEHAVIOR** to adopt a type of behavior or a quality of character when dealing with a situation ○ *Exercise extreme care in your dealings with them.* **7.** *vt* **OCCUPY OR WORRY SOMEBODY** to be a cause for serious thought, worry, or anxiety (*formal*) ○ *It is not a question that has exercised me greatly in the past.* **8.** *vti* MIL **TAKE PART IN MILITARY TRAINING OPERATIONS** to take part in, or make troops take part in, large-scale operations or maneuvers as part of combat training [14C. Via French < Latin *exercitium* < *exercere* "keep busy" < *arcere* "restrain"] —**ex·er·cis·a·ble** *adj*

ex·er·cise ball *n* a large inflated ball used in exercises to strengthen muscles and improve flexibility and balance

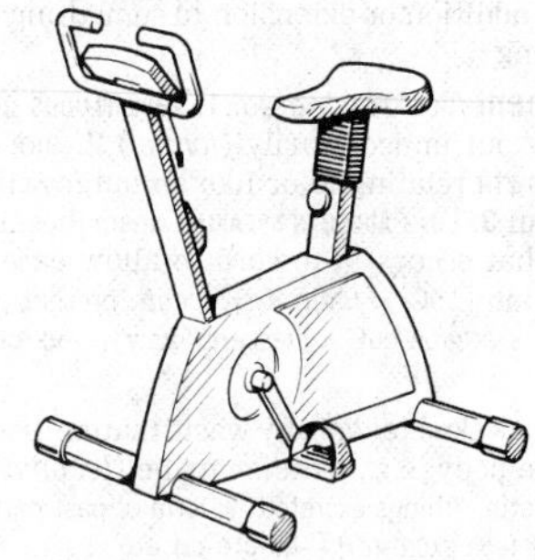

exercise bike

ex·er·cise bike, ex·er·cise bi·cy·cle *n* an exercise machine in the form of a stationary bicycle that is pedaled vigorously for exercise

ex·er·cise book *n* a book containing exercises in a subject for students to complete

ex·er·cise price *n* the price at which the holder of stock options or warrants has the right to buy or sell

ex·er·cis·er /éksər sīzər/ *n* **1.** a piece of equipment used to exercise all or part of the body **2.** somebody who performs physical exercises or who exercises something, especially somebody hired to exercise racehorses

exercize incorrect spelling of **exercise**

ex·er·gon·ic /èksər gónnik/ *adj* describes a spontaneous biochemical reaction that releases energy [Mid-20C. < EX-[1] + Greek *ergon* "work"]

ex·ergue /ék sùrg, ég zùrg/ *n* the part of a coin or medal that carries secondary details such as the date and place of minting [Late 17C. Via French < medieval Latin *exergum* < Greek *ex-* "outside" + *ergon* "work"]

exerpt incorrect spelling of **excerpt**

ex·ert /ig zúrt/ (**-ert·ed, -ert·ing, -erts**) *v* **1.** *vt* to apply influence, pressure, or authority in an attempt to have a powerful effect on a situation **2.** **ex·ert your·self** *vr* to make a strenuous physical or mental effort ○ *The doctor has told him not to exert himself in any way.* [Mid-17C. < Latin *ex(s)ert-*, past participle of *ex(s)erere* "thrust out, put forth" < *serere* "join, braid, entwine"]

ex·er·tion /ig zúrsh'n/ *n* **1.** **STRENUOUS EFFORT** strenuous exercise or effort **2.** **STRENUOUS ACTION** an action that involves strenuous effort (*often used in the plural*) ○ *After his exertions in the garden, he felt he deserved a rest.* **3.** **BRINGING OF SOMETHING TO BEAR** the application of pressure or influence ○ *the exertion of pressure on unsuspecting clients*

Ex·e·ter /éksətər/ **1.** town in southeastern New Hampshire, settled in 1638. Population: 14,326 (2002 estimate). **2.** historic cathedral city on the Exe River in Devon, southwestern England. Population: 111,076 (2001).

ex·e·unt /éksee ənt/ *vi* used as a stage direction in a text in place of "exit" when more than one actor is to leave the stage. ◊ **exit** *n* (sense 6), *v* (sense 4) [15C. < Latin, "they go out," form of *exire* (see EXIT)]

ex·fo·li·ant /eks fōlee ənt/ *n* a cosmetic cream or lotion designed to remove dead skin

ex·fo·li·ate /eks fōlee àyt/ (**-at·ed, -at·ing, -ates**) *vti* **1.** to scrub skin with a gritty substance to remove the dead surface layer **2.** to remove or shed a thin outer layer from something such as a mineral or a bone during surgery [Mid-17C. < late Latin *exfoliat-*, past participle of *exfoliare* "take leaves from" < Latin *folium* "leaf"] —**ex·fo·li·a·tion** /eks fōlee áysh'n/ *n* —**ex·fo·li·a·tive** *adj* —**ex·fo·li·a·tor** *n*

ex gra·tia /eks gráyshə, -graatee aa/ *adj, adv* given as a gift, favor, or gesture of goodwill, rather than because it is owed ○ *an ex gratia payment* [Mid-18C. < Latin, "out of kindness"]

ex·ha·la·tion /èkshə láysh'n, èksə-/ *n* **1.** **BREATH FROM LUNGS** a breath exhaled from the lungs **2.** **BREATHING OUT** the act of breathing out **3.** **SCENT OR VAPOR GIVEN OFF** a scent, a vapor, or fumes given off by something (*literary*)

ex·hale /eks háyl/ (**-haled, -hal·ing, -hales**) *v* **1.** *vti* to breathe out, or breathe something out **2.** *vt* to give off something such as a smell or a vapor (*literary*) [14C. Via French < Latin *exhalare* < *halare* "breathe"]

ex·haust /ig záwst/ *v* (**-haust·ed, -haust·ing, -hausts**) **1.** *vt* **TIRE SOMEBODY OUT** to make somebody feel very tired or weak **2.** *vt* **USE SOMETHING UP** to use up all that is available of something ○ *Our supplies of fuel were now exhausted.* **3.** *vt* **TRY OUT ALL POSSIBILITIES** to try out or consider every one of a number of possibilities **4.** *vt* **SAY EVERYTHING ABOUT SOMETHING** to say or write everything about something, so that nothing is left to be discussed **5.** *vt* **DRAIN SOMETHING OF ITS RESOURCES** to draw off or use up all the resources contained within something ○ *overgrazing that has exhausted the pasture* **6.** *vti* INDUST **LET OUT WASTE GASES** to escape, or allow steam or waste gases to escape, at the end of an industrial process ○ *Waste gases are exhausted through the flue.* **7.** *vt* PHYS **REMOVE GAS TO CREATE VACUUM** to remove all of the air or gas from a container in order to create a vacuum inside it ■ *n* **1. DISCHARGE OF WASTE GASES** the discharge of waste gases, vapor, and fumes created by and released at the end of a process, especially from the working of an internal-combustion engine **2. ESCAPE SYSTEM FOR WASTE GASES** a pipe or other piece of apparatus through which waste gases escape [Mid-16C. < Latin *exhaust-*, past participle of *exhaurire* "draw out" < *haurire* "draw (water) out or up, drain"] —**ex·haust·ed** *adj* —**ex·haust·er** *n* —**ex·haust·i·bil·i·ty** /ig zàwstə bíllətee/ *n* —**ex·haust·i·ble** *adj*

ex·haus·tion /ig záwsch'n/ *n* **1.** a state of extreme physical or mental tiredness or collapse ○ *After five hours' walking in the heat, he was close to exhaustion.* **2.** the process of using up the entire stock or contents of something (*formal*) ○ *The aid agency fears the imminent exhaustion of food reserves.* [Early 17C. < Latin *exhaustion-* < *exhaust-* (see EXHAUST)]

ex·haus·tive /ig záwstiv/ *adj* involving or dealing with everything relevant to the matter in hand ○ *an exhaustive account of the author's life* —**ex·haus·tive·ly** *adv* —**ex·haus·tive·ness** *n*

ex·haust pipe *n* UK same as **tailpipe**

ex·hib·it /ig zíbbit/ *v* (**-it·ed, -it·ing, -its**) **1.** *vti* **DISPLAY ART** to display something, especially a work of art, in a public place such as a museum or gallery **2.** *vt* **SHOW SOMETHING TO OTHERS** to show something off for others to look at or admire ○ *She decided it was a good time to exhibit her skills as a negotiator.* **3.** *vt* **REVEAL QUALITY** to show the outward signs of something, especially an emotion or a physical or mental condition ○ *The wings exhibited signs of metal fatigue.* **4.** *vt* LAW **GIVE SOMETHING AS EVIDENCE** to present something to be used as evidence in a court of law ■ *n* **1. OBJECT ON DISPLAY** an object displayed in public, especially in a museum or gallery or for a show or competition **2. ACT OF EXHIBITING** the act of displaying something ○ *an impressive exhibit of strength* **3.** ARTS same as **exhibition** (sense 1) **4.** LAW **PIECE OF EVIDENCE** an object or document presented or identified as evidence in a court of law [15C. Partly < Latin *exhibere* "hold out, display" < *habere* "hold"; partly back-formation < EXHIBITION] —**ex·hib·i·to·ry** *adj*

ex·hi·bi·tion /èksə bísh'n/ *n* **1. PUBLIC DISPLAY OF WORKS OF ART** a public display, usually for a limited period, of a collection of works of art or objects of special interest **2. DISPLAYING OF SOMETHING** the displaying of something in public ○ *one or two of the works on exhibition* **3. DEMONSTRATION OF SKILL** a demonstration of a particular skill or craft ○ *a karate exhibition* **4. DISPLAY OF BEHAVIOR** a display of a particular type of behavior, usually bad behavior ○ *an embarrassing exhibition of greed* [14C. Directly or via French < late Latin *exhibition-* "handing over, display" < Latin *exhibere* (see EXHIBIT)]

CULTURAL NOTE ***Pictures at an Exhibition***, a suite (1874) of piano pieces by the Russian composer Modest Mussorgsky. The compositions were written in memory of the architect and painter Victor Alexandrovich Hartmann and inspired by paintings and drawings displayed at a memorial exhibition of the artist's work. They were later orchestrated by Maurice Ravel.

ex·hi·bi·tion game *n* a sports contest played purely as a display of skill and an entertainment for spectators, having no bearing on team or individual standings

ex·hi·bi·tion·ism /èksə bísh'n ìzzəm/ *n* **1.** loud, exaggerated, or boastful behavior designed to attract attention **2.** a psychological disorder causing a compulsion to show the genitals in public —**ex·hi·bi·tion·ist** *n* —**ex·hi·bi·tion·is·tic** /èksə bìsh'n ístik/ *adj*

ex·hi·bi·tion match *n* SPORTS same as **exhibition game**

ex·hib·i·tive /ig zíbbitiv/ *adj* displaying or demonstrating something (*formal*) ○ *an agreement exhibitive of the goodwill of both parties* —**ex·hib·i·tive·ly** *adv*

ex·hib·i·tor /ig zíbbitər/, **ex·hib·it·er** *n* somebody who exhibits something, especially somebody whose artistic work is exhibited

ex·hil·a·rate /ig zíllə ràyt/ (**-rat·ed, -rat·ing, -rates**) *vt* to make somebody feel happy, excited, and more than usually vigorous and alive [Mid-16C. < Latin *exhilarat-*, past participle of *exhilarare* "gladden thoroughly" < *hilarare* "gladden" < Greek *hilaros* "cheerful, glad"] —**ex·hil·a·rat·ing·ly** *adv* —**ex·hil·a·ra·tion** /ig zìllə ráysh'n/ *n* —**ex·hil·a·ra·tive** *adj* —**ex·hil·a·ra·tor** *n*

~~**exhilerating**~~ incorrect spelling of **exhilarating**

~~**exhileration**~~ incorrect spelling of **exhilaration**

ex·hort /ig záwrt/ (**-hort·ed, -hort·ing, -horts**) *v* (*formal*) **1.** *vt* to urge somebody strongly and earnestly to do something **2.** *vi* to give somebody urgent or earnest advice [14C. Directly or via French < Latin *exhortari* "encourage thoroughly" < *hortari* "encourage, urge"] —**ex·hor·ta·tive** /ig záwrtətiv/ *adj* —**ex·hort·er** *n*

ex·hor·ta·tion /èg zawr táysh'n/ *n* (*formal*) **1.** something said or written in order to urge somebody strongly to do something **2.** the giving of earnest advice or encouragement

ex·hume /ig zóom, -zyóom, ik syóom/ (**-humed, -hum·ing, -humes**) *vt* **1.** to dig up a corpse from a grave **2.** to reveal, reestablish, or refer again to something long forgotten or neglected ○ *Cultures are reinvented and dead traditions exhumed for the tourists.* [15C. < medieval Latin *exhumare* < *humare* "bury" < Latin *humus* "ground, earth"] —**ex·hu·ma·tion** /èksyoo máysh'n, èksoo-, ègzoo-, ègzyoo-/ *n* —**ex·hum·er** *n*

~~**exibition**~~ incorrect spelling of **exhibition**

ex·i·gen·cy /éksəjənssee, égzə-, ig zíjj-/ (*plural* **-cies**), **ex·i·gence** /éksəjənss, égzə-/ *n* (*formal*) **1.** something that a situation demands or makes urgently necessary and that puts pressure on the people involved (*often used in the plural*) ○ *unable to cope with the exigencies of political life* **2.** a difficult situation requiring urgent action [Late 16C. < late Latin *exigentia* < Latin *exigent-*, present participle of *exigere* (see EXACT)]

ex·i·gent /éksəjənt, égzə-/ *adj* (*formal*) **1.** needing immediate action **2.** making heavy demands on somebody ○ *an exigent boss* [Early 17C. < Latin *exigent-* (see EXIGENCY)] —**ex·i·gent·ly** *adv*

ex·ig·u·ous /ig zíggyoo əss, ik sígg-/ *adj* scanty or meager (*formal*) ○ *barely surviving on their exiguous supplies* [Mid-17C. < Latin *exiguus* < *exigere* "weigh precisely, measure" (see EXACT)] —**ex·i·gu·i·ty** /ègzi gyóo ətee, èksi-/ *n* —**ex·ig·u·ous·ly** *adv* —**ex·ig·u·ous·ness** *n*

ex·ile /ég zìl, ék sìl/ *n* **1. ABSENCE FROM OWN COUNTRY** unwilling absence from a home country or place of residence, whether enforced by a government or court as a punishment, or self-imposed for political or religious reasons ○ *living in exile* **2. SOMEBODY LIVING OUTSIDE OWN COUNTRY** a citizen of one country who is forced or chooses to live in another **3. BANISHMENT** official expulsion from a home, country, or area, sometimes to a particular place, as a punishment ○ *exile to Siberia* ■ *vt* (**-iled, -il·ing, -iles**) **BANISH SOMEBODY FROM HOME OR COUNTRY** to order somebody to leave and stay away from his or her own country or home [14C. Via French < Latin *exilium* "banishment" < *exul* "banished person"] —**ex·il·ic** /ig zíllik, ik síllik/ *adj*

Ex·ile *n* BIBLE same as **Babylonian captivity**

ex·ine /ék sèen, -sìn/ *n* the outer layer of a pollen grain or other spore. The surface patterns vary among different plant groups, allowing the makeup of former plant populations to be deduced from preserved pollen samples. [Late 19C. Origin ?]

ex·ist /ig zíst/ (**-ist·ed, -ist·ing, -ists**) *vi* **1. BE** to be, especially to be a real, actual, or current thing, not merely something imagined or written about ○ *Does life exist on other planets?* **2. LIVE** to be alive, or continue to live ○ *Humans need water and food to exist.* **3. OCCUR** to be present or found in a particular place or situation ○ *Shortages exist on products in high demand.* **4. SURVIVE** to manage to survive or stay alive ○ *The lost hikers existed for two days on berries.* **5. LIVE AN UNSATISFACTORY LIFE** to live an unsatisfactory, joyless, or humdrum life, as opposed to an exciting or meaningful one ○ *simply existing from day to day* [Early 17C. Probably back-formation < EXISTENCE]

~~**existance**~~ incorrect spelling of **existence**

ex·is·tence /ig zíst'nss/ *n* **1. BEING REAL** the state of being real, actual, or current, rather than imagined, invented, or obsolete ○ *evidence for the existence of other worlds* **2. PRESENCE IN PLACE OR SITUATION** the presence or occurrence of something in a particular place or situation ○ *discovered the existence of the bacterium in sheep* **3. WAY OF LIVING** a way of living, especially a life of severe hardship ○ *scratch out a pitiable existence* **4. EVERYTHING** all living things ○ *hymns that celebrate the wonder of existence* **5. SINGLE LIVING THING** something that lives or exists (*literary* or *archaic*) [14C. Directly or via French < late Latin *existentia* < Latin *ex(s)istere* "emerge, come into being" < *sistere* "cause to stand firm"]

ex·is·tent /ig zíst'nt/ (*formal*) *adj* **1. REAL** real or actual, not imagined or invented **2. CURRENT** currently existing or in operation ■ *n* **REAL THING** a real or living thing

ex·is·ten·tial /ègzi sténshəl, èksi-/ *adj* **1. RELATING TO HUMAN EXISTENCE** concerned with or relating to existence, especially human existence **2.** PHILOSOPHY **CRUCIAL IN SHAPING INDIVIDUAL DESTINY** in the context of existentialism, involved in or vital to the shaping of a person's self-chosen mode of existence and moral stance with respect to the rest of the world **3.** LOGIC **ASSERTING EXISTENCE** governed by the existential quantifier and thus asserting the existence of something by saying that there is at least one object that possesses the properties specified ■ *n* LOGIC **EXISTENTIAL PROPOSITION** a proposition governed by the existential quantifier —**ex·is·ten·tial·ly** *adv*

ex·is·ten·tial·ism /ègzi sténsh'l ìzzəm, èksi-/ *n* a philosophical movement begun in the 19th century that denies that the universe has any intrinsic meaning or purpose. It requires people to take responsibility for their own actions and shape their own destinies. [Mid-20C. < German *Existentialismus*, translation of Danish *existents-forhold* "condition of existence"] —**ex·is·ten·tial·ist** *n, adj*

ex·is·ten·tial quan·ti·fi·er *n* the logical constant, frequently symbolized as "Ex," that is a prefix to another clause and that is read as saying "there is at least one object such that." ◊ **universal quantifier**

ex·ist·ing /ig zísting/ *adj* currently present, in operation, or available ○ *Existing legislation is inadequate to cover these cases.*

ex·it /égzit, éksit/ *n* **1. MEANS OF LEAVING PLACE** a door or other means of leaving a room or building **2. DEPARTURE** an act of leaving a room, building, or gathering **3. PLACE FOR LEAVING EXPRESSWAY** a ramp by which a vehicle can leave an expressway or other main road with limited access **4. DEATH** departure from life (*literary*) **5.** COMPUT **TERMINATION OF COMPUTER OPERATION** an act of terminating a computer operation **6.** THEATER **ACTOR'S LEAVING OF STAGE** an actor's departure from the stage ■ *v* (**-it·ed, -it·ing, -its**) **1.** *vti* **LEAVE** to leave something such as a room, building, or gathering ○ *In the event of a fire, exit the building at the rear.* **2.** *vi* **DIE** to cease to live (*literary*) **3.** *vti* COMPUT **TERMINATE COMPUTER PROGRAM** to terminate the running of a computer operating system, program, or routine in a program **4.** *vi* THEATER **GO OFFSTAGE** to leave the stage as part of a performance of a play (*refers to actors*) ◊ **exeunt** [Mid-16C. < Latin *exitus* "departure" < past participle of *exire* "go out" < *ire* "go"]

ex·it poll *n* a poll conducted by asking people how they voted as they leave the voting place, designed to give an early indication of the result of an election

ex·it vi·sa *n* a visa that gives somebody official permission to leave a country, e.g., in time of war

ex li·bris /eks léebriss/ *adv* from the library of the person whose name follows (*used on bookplates*) [< Latin, "from the books (of)"]

Ex·moor Na·tion·al Park /éks moor-, -mawr-/ national park in a moorland region of Somerset and northern Devon, southwestern England. Area: 267 sq. mi./692 sq. km.

ex ni·hi·lo /eks nee ə lō, -neehi-/ *adv, adj* from or out of nothing (*formal*) [Late 16C. < Latin]

exo- *prefix* outside, external ○ *exothermic* [< Greek *exō* < *ex* "out" < Indo-European]

ex·o·bi·ol·o·gy /èksō bī óllәjee/ *n* a branch of biology concerned with the possibility that life forms exist on other planets and with the problems of adapting the Earth's life forms to alien environments —**ex·o·bi·o·log·i·cal** /-bī ә lójjik'l/ *adj* —**ex·o·bi·ol·o·gist** *n*

ex·o·carp /éksō kaarp/ *n* the outer layer of the fruit wall (**pericarp**), e.g., the skin of some fruits

ex·o·crine /éksәkrin, -kreen, -krīn/ *adj* relating to exocrine glands or their secretions. ◊ **endocrine** [Early 20C. < EXO- + Greek *krinein* "to separate"]

ex·o·crine gland *n* a gland that releases a secretion through a duct to the surface of an organ, e.g., the sweat and salivary glands

ex·o·cy·clic /èksō síklik, -síklik/ *adj* situated outside a chemical ring structure ○ *an exocyclic bond*

ex·o·cy·to·sis /èksō sī tṓssiss/ *n* the release to a cell surface of substances such as waste or secretions through vesicles. It occurs following the fusion of the membrane surrounding the vesicles with the membrane forming the outer wall of the cell. —**ex·o·cy·tot·ic** /-sī tóttik/ *adj*

Exod. *abbr* BIBLE Exodus

ex·o·don·tics /èksә dóntiks/, **ex·o·don·tia** /-dónshә/ *n* the branch of dentistry concerned with extracting teeth (*takes a singular verb*) [Early 20C. < EXO- + Greek *odont-* "tooth"] —**ex·o·don·tist** *n*

ex·o·dus /éksәdәss/ *n* a departure or going out or away from a place that involves large numbers of people [Pre-12C. Via ecclesiastical Latin, "(biblical Book of) Exodus" < Greek, "way out" < *hodos* "way, road"]

Ex·o·dus *n* **1.** a book of the Bible which describes the flight of the Israelites from Egypt and Moses receiving the Ten Commandments on Mount Sinai. It is the second book of the Pentateuch. See table at **Bible 2.** in the Bible, the flight of Moses and the Israelites from Egypt

ex·o·en·zyme /èksō én zīm/ *n* an enzyme that acts outside the cell that secretes it

ex·o·er·gic /èksō úrjik/ *adj* describes a nuclear or chemical reaction that produces energy. ◊ **endoergic** [Mid-20C. < EXO- + Greek *ergon* "work"]

ex of·fi·ci·o /èks ә físhee ō/ *adv, adj* as a result of the official position somebody holds ○ *Heads of state are often ex officio heads of the armed forces.* [Mid-16C. < Latin, "out of duty, on account of office"]

ex·og·a·my /ek sóggәmee/ *n* **1.** the custom in some societies of marrying outside their people's own social group **2.** the fusion of sex cells (**gametes**) of organisms not closely related, as occurs in cross-pollination and outbreeding —**ex·og·a·mous** *adj*

ex·o·gen·ic /èksō jénnik/ *adj* formed, located, or happening on the Earth's surface. ◊ **endogenic**

ex·og·e·nous /ek sójjәnәss/ *adj* originating outside an organism or system [Mid-19C. < modern Latin *exogena* "growing on the outside" < Greek *genēs* "born"] —**ex·og·e·nous·ly** *adv*

ex·on /ék sòn/ *n* a discontinuous sequence of DNA that codes for protein synthesis and carries the genetic code for the final messenger RNA molecule. ◊ **intron** [Late 20C. < shortening of *expressed* + -ON[1]]

ex·on·er·ate /ig zónnә ràyt/ (**-at·ed, -at·ing, -ates**) *vt* **1.** to declare officially that somebody is not to blame or is not guilty of wrongdoing **2.** to relieve somebody from an obligation or responsibility [15C. < Latin *exonerat-*, past participle of *exonerare* "take off a burden" < *onus* "burden"] —**ex·on·er·a·tion** /ig zònnә ráysh'n/ *n* —**ex·on·er·a·tive** *adj*

ex·oph·thal·mos /èks әf thálmәss/, **ex·oph·thal·mus** *n* unusual protrusion of the eyeball, sometimes resulting from an aneurysm [Early 17C. Directly or via modern Latin < Greek *exophthalmos* "(condition of) the eye being outside" < *ophthalmos* "eye"] —**ex·oph·thal·mic** *adj*

ex·or·bi·tant /ig záwrbit'nt/ *adj* **1.** far greater or higher than is reasonable ○ *exorbitant prices* **2.** going beyond what is usual, proper, or manageable [15C. < ecclesiastical Latin *exorbitant-*, present participle of *exorbitare* "go out of the track" < Latin *orbita* "track" < *orbis* "circle"] —**ex·or·bi·tant·ly** *adv*

ex·or·cise /ék sawr sīz, éksәr-/ (**-cised, -cis·ing, -cis·es**), **ex·or·cize** (**-cized, -ciz·ing, -ciz·es**) *vt* **1.** FREE PERSON OR PLACE FROM EVIL to use prayers and religious rituals with the intention of ridding a person or place of the supposed presence or influence of evil spirits **2.** SEND EVIL AWAY to use prayers and religious rituals with the intention of driving away an evil spirit believed to be possessing a person or place **3.** GET RID OF OPPRESSIVE FEELING to clear the mind of a painful or oppressive feeling or memory [15C. Directly or via French < ecclesiastical Latin *exorcizare* < Greek *exorkizein* "swear out (an evil spirit)" < *orkos* "oath"] —**ex·or·cis·er** *n*

ex·or·cism /ék sawr sìzzәm, éksәr-/ *n* **1.** DRIVING OUT OF EVIL SPIRITS the use of prayers or religious rituals to drive out evil spirits believed to be possessing a person or place **2.** CEREMONY TO DRIVE OUT EVIL SPIRITS a religious ceremony in which somebody attempts to drive out an evil spirit believed to be possessing a person or place **3.** THING DONE TO EXPEL EVIL a special ritual or spoken formula used with the intention of driving out evil spirits **4.** CLEARING MIND OF OPPRESSIVE FEELINGS the act of ridding the mind of oppressive feelings or memories [14C Via ecclesiastical Latin < ecclesiastical Greek *exorkismos* < *exorkizein* (see EXORCISE)] —**ex·or·cist** *n*

ex·or·cize *vt* RELIG another spelling of **exorcise**

ex·or·di·um /eg záwrdee әm/ (*plural* **-di·ums** or **-di·a** /-dee ә/) *n* an opening section, especially of a lecture or a piece of scholarly writing (*formal*) [Late 16C. < Latin < *exordiri* "begin"] —**ex·or·di·al** *adj*

ex·o·skel·e·ton /èksō skéllәt'n/ *n* a hard covering on the outside of organisms such as crustaceans, insects, turtles, and armadillos that provides support and protection —**ex·o·skel·e·tal** *adj*

ex·os·mo·sis /èks oz mṓssiss, -oss-/ *n* movement of fluid toward a solution of lower concentration, as is the case when water percolates through a cell membrane into the medium surrounding the cell [Mid-19C. < French *exosmose* < Greek *ōsmos* "act of pushing"] —**ex·os·mot·ic** /-móttik/ *adj*

ex·o·sphere /éksō sfeer/ *n* the outermost region of the atmosphere of Earth or another planet —**ex·o·spher·ic** /èksō sféerik, -sférrik/ *adj*

ex·o·spore /éksә spàwr/ *n* **1.** a spore that is formed outside a parent cell, or outside a spore-bearing organ, especially by extrusion **2.** the outermost layer of a spore

ex·os·to·sis /èkso stṓssiss/ (*plural* **-to·ses** /-tṓ seez/) *n* a benign bony growth on the surface of a bone or a tooth root, caused by inflammation or repeated trauma [Late 16C. < Greek, "bony outgrowth" < *osteon* "bone"]

ex·o·ter·ic /èksә térrik/ *adj* capable of being understood by most people, not just an informed or select minority (*formal*) [Mid-17C. Via Latin < Greek *exōterikos* < *exōterō* "outer" < *exō* "outside"] —**ex·o·ter·i·cal·ly** *adv*

ex·o·ther·mic /èksō thúrmik/, **ex·o·ther·mal** /-thúrm'l/ *adj* describes a chemical reaction that produces heat. ◊ **endothermic** [Late 19C. < French *exothermique* < Greek *thermē* "heat"] —**ex·o·ther·mi·cal·ly** *adv*

ex·ot·ic /ig zóttik/ *adj* **1.** STRIKINGLY DIFFERENT strikingly unusual and often very colorful and exciting or suggesting distant countries and unfamiliar cultures **2.** ECOL FROM ELSEWHERE introduced from another place or region ○ *an exotic species* ■ *n* SOMEBODY OR SOMETHING UNUSUAL AND STRIKING a person or thing that is foreign and unusual, especially a plant or animal [Late 16C. Via Latin *exoticus* < Greek *exōtikos* < *exō* "out, outside"] —**ex·ot·i·cal·ly** *adv* —**ex·ot·i·cism** /ig zótti sìzzәm/ *n* —**ex·ot·ic·ness** *n*

ex·ot·i·ca /ig zóttikә/ *npl* exotic or extraordinary things, especially when forming a collection [Late 19C. < Latin, form of *exoticus* (see EXOTIC)]

ex·ot·ic danc·er *n* a striptease performer

ex·o·tox·in /èksō tóksin/ *n* a highly potent soluble toxin produced by a bacterium and released into its infected host, often affecting the central nervous system. Exotoxins are produced in diphtheria, botulism, and tetanus, and are among the most potent known toxins.

exp. *abbr* **1.** experiment **2.** experimental **3.** expiration **4.** expired **5.** expires **6.** MATH exponential function **7.** export **8.** exported **9.** express

ex·pand /ik spánd/ (**-pand·ed, -pand·ing, -pands**) *v* **1.** *vti* MAKE OR BECOME LARGER to become or make something become larger in size, scope, or extent, or greater in number or amount ○ *We need to expand our client base.* **2.** *vti* DESCRIBE SOMETHING MORE FULLY to explain or describe something more fully, usually by giving more detail ○ *The film expands on themes familiar from her earlier work.* **3.** *vti* OPEN OUT to open out or open something out wider after being kept folded in **4.** *vt* GIVE FULL FORM OF SOMETHING to give the full form of something such as the abbreviation of a word **5.** *vi* RELAX to relax and become friendlier and more talkative **6.** *vti* PHYS INCREASE IN SIZE OR VOLUME to increase or cause something to increase in size or volume as a result of a rise in temperature or decrease in pressure **7.** *vti* MATH REWRITE MATHEMATICAL EXPRESSION to rewrite a mathematical expression as the sum or product of its terms, or be rewritten in this way. For example, $(x+1)(x-1)+2x$ expands to x^2+2x-1. [15C. Directly or via Anglo-Norman < Latin *expandere* "spread out" < *pandere* "spread"] —**ex·pand·a·bil·i·ty** /ik spàndә bíllәtee/ *n* —**ex·pand·a·ble** *adj* —**ex·pand·er** *n* —**ex·pan·si·ble** /ik spánssәb'l/ *adj*

SYNONYMS See ***increase***.

ex·pand·ed /ik spándәd/ *adj* **1.** MADE LARGER extended, unfolded, or outstretched **2.** INDUST MADE INTO FOAM describes plastics made into a lightweight solid foam by the introduction of gas during the manufacturing process ○ *expanded polyurethane* **3.** PRINTING WIDER THAN USUAL describes typefaces or printed characters that are wider than usual in relation to their height

ex·pand·ed met·al *n* strong metal mesh made by cutting slits in sheet metal and stretching it out of shape. Use: reinforcing material in construction.

ex·panse /ik spánss/ *n* a wide area or surface, especially of sea, land, or sky [Mid-17C. < modern Latin *expansum* "firmament" < Latin *expans-*, past participle of *expandere* (see EXPAND)]

ex·pan·sile /ik spánssәl/ *adj* **1.** relating to expansion or the ability to expand **2.** able to expand or be expanded

ex·pan·sion /ik spánsh'n/ *n* **1.** PROCESS OF ENLARGEMENT the process of increasing, or increasing something, in size, extent, scope, or number ○ *This site does not give us enough room for expansion.* **2.** INCREASE an increase, or the amount by which something increases, in size, extent, or scope ○ *Geologists measured the expansion of the volcanic island.* **3.** GROWTH BY LAND ACQUISITION the increase of a country's size by the acquisition of new territory ○ *westward expansion* **4.** ACT OF EXPANDING the act or state of expanding, opening, or spreading out **5.** FULLER TREATMENT a fuller or more detailed treatment or version of something ○ *The expansion of "Dr." is "Doctor."* **6.** PHYS INCREASE IN DIMENSIONS an increase in the dimensions of something as a result of a rise in temperature or decrease in pressure **7.** MECH ENG COMBUSTION STAGE IN ENGINE a stage in an engine cycle during which the fuel and air mixture explodes, thereby increasing in volume and providing power **8.** MATH EXPANDED MATHEMATICAL EXPRESSION the result of expanding a mathematical expression [Early 17C. < late Latin *expansion-* < Latin *expans-* (see EXPANSE)]

ex·pan·sion·ar·y /ik spánsh'n èrree/ *adj* bringing about expansion, especially economic or territorial expansion

ex·pan·sion board *n* COMPUT same as **expansion card**

ex·pan·sion bolt *n* a bolt with an attachment on the screw end that expands as the bolt is tightened, thereby securing it. See illustration on next page

ex·pan·sion card *n* a printed circuit board adding features or capability to a computer

ex·pan·sion·ism /ik spánsh'n ìzzәm/ *n* a policy of expanding a country's economy or territory —**ex·pan·sion·ist** *n, adj* —**ex·pan·sion·is·tic** /ik spànshә nístik/ *adj*

ex·pan·sion joint *n* a gap left between adjacent parts

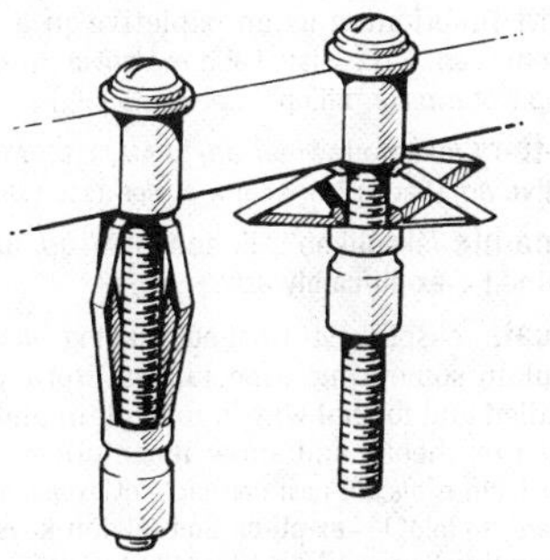
expansion bolt

or surfaces, e.g., between the concrete sections that form the road surface of a bridge, to prevent buckling when they expand under heat

ex·pan·sion slot *n* a receptacle for an expansion card that interfaces with a computer's internal circuitry

ex·pan·sive /ik spánssiv/ *adj* **1.** EXTENSIVE covering a wide area or broad in scope ○ *a large house with expansive grounds* **2.** EXPANDING capable of, having a tendency to, or typically undergoing expansion ○ *polymers with expansive capability* **3.** WITH OUTSTRETCHED ARMS with the arms stretched out and open wide ○ *an expansive gesture* **4.** LAVISH generous, lavish, or extravagant in scale ○ *an expansive lifestyle* **5.** COMMUNICATIVE willing to talk openly and at some length, usually in a relaxed and jovial way ○ *He gradually became more expansive once he got to know us.* **6.** PSYCHIAT HAVING EXAGGERATED FEELINGS OF SELF-WORTH having or characterized by extreme feelings of euphoria and delusions of grandeur or self-importance —**ex·pan·sive·ly** *adv* —**ex·pan·sive·ness** *n* —**ex·pan·siv·i·ty** /èk span sívvətee/ *n*

ex par·te /eks paártee/ *adj, adv* made or undertaken on behalf of only one of the parties involved in a court case [Early 17C. < Latin, "from a (or the) side"]

ex·pat /èks pát/ *n* same as **expatriate** *n* (sense 1) (*informal*) [Mid-20C. Shortening]

ex·pa·ti·ate /ek spáyshee àyt/ (**-at·ed, -at·ing, -ates**) *vi* **1.** to speak or write about something at length ○ *We had to listen to him expatiating on the shortcomings of our system.* **2.** to wander or roam at will (*archaic*) [Mid-16C. < Latin *ex(s)patiat-*, past participle of *ex(s)patiari* "walk out" < *spatiari* "walk" < *spatium* "space"] —**ex·pa·ti·a·tion** /ek spàyshee áysh'n/ *n*

ex·pa·tri·ate *n* /eks páytree ət, -àyt/ **1.** SOMEBODY WHO HAS MOVED ABROAD a citizen who has left his or her own country to live in another, usually for a prolonged period **2.** SOMEBODY WITHOUT CITIZENSHIP a citizen who has renounced his or her citizenship or whose citizenship has been revoked ■ *adj* /eks páytree ət, -àyt/ OF EXPATRIATES relating to people who live outside their own country ■ *v* /eks páytree àyt/ (**-at·ed, -at·ing, -ates**) **1.** *vi* SETTLE ABROAD to settle in another country **2.** *vti* TAKE AWAY SOMEBODY'S CITIZENSHIP to deprive somebody of native citizenship, or renounce native citizenship voluntarily **3.** *vt* EXILE SOMEBODY to send somebody away from his or her own country as a punishment [Mid-18C. < Latin *expatriat-*, past participle of *expatriare* "leave your native land" < *patria* "native land" < *pater* "father"] —**ex·pa·tri·a·tion** /eks pàytree áysh'n/ *n*

~~expatriot~~ incorrect spelling of **expatriate**

ex·pect /ik spékt/ (**-pect·ed, -pect·ing, -pects**) *v* **1.** *vt* CONFIDENTLY BELIEVE SOMETHING to believe with confidence, or think it likely, that an event will happen in the future ○ *A few setbacks along the way were only to be expected.* **2.** *vt* WAIT FOR ANTICIPATED THING to wait for, or look forward to, something that is believed to be going to happen or arrive ○ *I'm expecting a visit from them any day now.* **3.** *vt* DEMAND SOMETHING AS RIGHT OR DUTY to demand or anticipate receiving something because of a perceived right to it or because it is due or appropriate ○ *They expect you to abide by their rules.* **4.** *vti* BE GOING TO HAVE BABY to be pregnant with or look forward to the birth of a child (*informal; used only in progressive tenses*) ○ *She is expecting her third in July.* [Mid-16C. < Latin *ex(s)pectare* "look out for" < *spectare* "look at" < *specere* "to look"] —**ex·pect·a·ble** *adj* —**ex·pect·a·bly** *adv* —**ex·pect·ed·ly** *adv* —**ex·pect·ed·ness** *n*

ex·pec·tan·cy /ik spéktənssee/ (*plural* **-cies**), **ex·pec·tance** /ik spéktənss/ *n* **1.** excited awareness that something is about to happen ○ *An air of expectancy hung over the crowd.* **2.** something expected, especially an amount or length of time expected on the basis of statistical calculations

ex·pec·tant /ik spéktənt/ *adj* **1.** EXCITEDLY ANTICIPATING SOMETHING excitedly aware that something is about to happen **2.** EXPECTING BABY expecting the birth of a baby **3.** EXPECTING SOMETHING FAVORABLE expecting something, especially something that will bring success or wealth (*formal*) [14C. Directly or via French < Latin *ex(s)pectant-*, present participle of *ex(s)pectare* (see EXPECT)]

ex·pec·tant·ly /ik spéktəntlee/ *adv* in the expectation that something interesting, exciting, or pleasurable will happen

ex·pec·ta·tion /èk spek táysh'n/ *n* **1.** ANTICIPATION OF SOMETHING HAPPENING a confident belief or strong hope that a particular event will happen **2.** NOTION OF SOMETHING a mental image of something expected, often compared to its reality (*often used in the plural*) ○ *All our expectations of a quiet evening at home were dashed by the arrival of guests.* **3.** EXPECTED STANDARD a standard of conduct or performance expected by or of somebody (*often used in the plural*) ○ *Her work wasn't up to expectations.* **4.** same as **expectancy** (sense 1) ■ **ex·pec·ta·tions** *npl* PROSPECTS FOR FUTURE somebody's likely prospects of wealth or success in the future, especially of inheriting money under somebody's will

CULTURAL NOTE ***Great Expectations***, a novel (1861) by British writer Charles Dickens. It is the story of the orphan Pip, his early encounter with the convict Magwitch, and his love for the beautiful Estella, who lives with her eccentric guardian Miss Havisham. Pip subsequently receives a fortune from an unknown benefactor and moves to London, but is forced to return penniless to the humble blacksmith's home where he grew up. It is here that he ultimately reaches maturity and finds happiness.

ex·pect·ed val·ue *n* the value of a random variable that is most likely to occur, calculated by multiplying the sum of every possible value by a factor representing the probability of its occurrence

ex·pec·to·rant /ik spéktərənt/ *adj* causing phlegm to be coughed up ■ *n* a medicine that stimulates the production of phlegm. Use: treatment of coughs.

ex·pec·to·rate /ik spéktə ràyt/ (**-rat·ed, -rat·ing, -rates**) *vti* to cough up and spit out phlegm, thus clearing the bronchial passages [Early 17C. < Latin *expectorat-*, past participle of *expectorare* "get out of the chest" < *pectus* "chest, breast"] —**ex·pec·to·ra·tion** /ik spèktə ráysh'n/ *n*

ex·pe·di·en·cy /ik speédee ənssee/ (*plural* **-cies**), **ex·pe·di·ence** /-ənss/ *n* **1.** the use of methods that bring the most immediate benefits, based on practical rather than moral considerations **2.** the usefulness, appropriateness, or advisability of something, especially of a particular action or type of behavior in a particular situation ○ *doubts about the expediency of such a course in the present crisis* **3.** same as **expedient** *n*

ex·pe·di·ent /ik speédee ənt/ *adj* **1.** APPROPRIATE appropriate, advisable, or useful in a situation that requires action **2.** ADVANTAGEOUS advantageous for practical rather than moral reasons ○ *She changed her vote because it was expedient for her to do so.* ■ *n* SOMETHING ACHIEVING OBJECTIVES QUICKLY something done or a method used to achieve an objective quickly, regardless of whether it is fair, right, or wise in the long term [14C. Directly or via French < Latin *expedient-*, present participle of *expedire* (see EXPEDITE)] —**ex·pe·di·ent·ly** *adv*

ex·pe·dite /ékspə dìt/ (**-dit·ed, -dit·ing, -dites**) *vt* (*formal*) **1.** to ensure that something takes place or is dealt with more quickly than usual **2.** to deal with something, especially a business transaction, swiftly and efficiently [15C. < Latin *expedit-*, past participle of *expedire* "set free" < *pes* "foot"] —**ex·pe·dit·er** *n*

ex·pe·di·tion /èkspə dísh'n/ *n* **1.** ORGANIZED TRIP BY GROUP a trip made by a group of people for a particular purpose, e.g., to explore unknown territory, to do scientific study, or to achieve a military objective ○ *a scientific expedition to the ocean floor* **2.** GROUP TAKING PART IN EXPEDITION a group of people who go on an expedition together ○ *The expedition returned at the end of the month.* **3.** OUTING a short outing, usually for a pleasurable purpose **4.** PROMPTNESS speed, promptness, or efficiency in doing something ○ *carried out our errand with expedition* [15C. Directly or via French < Latin *expedition-* < *expedire* (see EXPEDITE)]

ex·pe·di·tion·ar·y /èkspə dísh'n èrree/ *adj* sent to fight or do military service in another country ○ *an expeditionary force*

ex·pe·di·tious /èkspə díshəss/ *adj* speedy, or carried out promptly and efficiently —**ex·pe·di·tious·ly** *adv* —**ex·pe·di·tious·ness** *n*

ex·pel /ik spél/ (**-pelled, -pel·ling, -pels**) *vt* **1.** to compel somebody to leave or give up membership in an institution such as a school, political party, or club ○ *expel a child from school* **2.** to push or drive something out with force ○ *Air is expelled under pressure from outlets under the hovercraft's apron.* [14C. < Latin *expellere* "drive out" < *pellere* "beat, drive"] —**ex·pel·la·ble** *adj* —**ex·pel·lee** /èk spe leé, ik spè-/ *n* —**ex·pel·ler** *n*

ex·pel·lant /ik spéllənt/, **ex·pel·lent** *adj* capable of expelling something, especially from the body ■ *n* a medicine that causes the body to get rid of something undesirable, especially intestinal worms

~~expence~~ incorrect spelling of **expense**

ex·pend /ik spénd/ (**-pend·ed, -pend·ing, -pends**) *vt* **1.** to use up time, energy, effort, or some other resource **2.** to spend money or an amount of money (*formal*) [15C. < Latin *expendere* "weigh out (money in payment)" < *pendere* "weigh"] —**ex·pen·der** *n*

ex·pend·a·ble /ik spéndəb'l/ *adj* **1.** NOT WORTH PRESERVING not worth preserving or saving for reuse **2.** DISPENSABLE easily sacrificed or dispensed with if the need arises or in order to achieve an aim ■ *n* EXPENDABLE ITEM an expendable person or thing —**ex·pend·a·bil·i·ty** /ik spèndə bíllətee/ *n*

ex·pen·di·ture /ik spéndəchər/ *n* **1.** an amount of money spent, as a whole or on a particular thing ○ *when income exceeds expenditure* **2.** the consuming or using up of something ○ *the huge expenditure of time and human resources on this project* [Mid-18C. After *expenditor* "somebody in charge of expenditure"]

ex·pense /ik spénss/ *n* **1.** MONEY SPENT ON SOMETHING the amount of money spent in order to buy or do something **2.** SOMETHING EXPENSIVE TO BUY something that costs money, usually a lot of money, to buy, keep, or run **3.** USING UP OF SOMETHING the using up or loss of something ○ *preserved his integrity at the expense of his job* **4.** ACCT VALUE OF RESOURCE USED the value of a resource that has been used during the current accounting period and can be charged against revenues for that period ■ **ex·pens·es** *npl* BUSINESS EXPENDITURES an amount of money that somebody spends for business purposes that is reimbursable by an employer or deductible from income tax ■ *vt* (**-pensed, -pens·ing, -pens·es**) **1.** TREAT SOMETHING AS CHARGEABLE OR DEDUCTIBLE to identify something as an expense for tax, accounting, or expense-account purposes ○ *expensed our moving costs* **2.** CHARGE SOMEBODY FOR EXPENSES to charge personal expenses to somebody else [14C. Via Anglo-Norman < late Latin *expensa* < Latin *expendere* (see EXPEND)]

ex·pense ac·count *n* **1.** a benefit given by an employer that entitles an employee to be repaid for some or all of the expenses incurred in the course of his or her employment **2.** the amount of an employee's expenses during a particular period, or a record of this

~~expensiv~~ incorrect spelling of **expensive**

ex·pen·sive /ik spénssiv/ *adj* **1.** COSTING A LOT costing a large amount of money **2.** CHARGING A LOT charging high prices **3.** VERY DISADVANTAGEOUS involving serious losses or disadvantage to a particular person or group ○ *an expensive first quarter for the home team* —**ex·pen·sive·ly** *adv* —**ex·pen·sive·ness** *n*

~~experiance~~ incorrect spelling of **experience**

ex·pe·ri·ence /ik speéree ənss/ *n* **1.** INVOLVEMENT IN SOMETHING OVER TIME active involvement in an activity or exposure to events or people over a period of time that leads to an increase in knowledge or skill ○ *Experience is the best teacher.* **2.** KNOWLEDGE OR SKILL ACQUIRED knowledge or skill gained through being involved in or exposed to something over a period of time ○ *Paper qualifications are no substitute for real-life experience.* **3. SUM TOTAL OF SOMEBODY'S EXPERIENCES** the sum total of the things that have happened to a person and of his or her past thoughts and feelings ○ *Nothing quite like this has ever been done before, at least not in my experience.* **4. SOMETHING THAT HAPPENS TO SOMEBODY** something that happens to somebody or an event that somebody is involved in ○ *an experience that changed his life* **5.** PHILOSOPHY **KNOWLEDGE FROM OBSERVATION** knowledge acquired through the senses, and not through abstract reasoning ■ *vt* (**-enced, -enc·ing, -enc·es**) **1. HAVE PERSONAL KNOWLEDGE OF SOMETHING** to be exposed to, involved in, or affected by something ○ *the most thrilling ride I've ever experienced* **2. FEEL SOMETHING** to feel a particular sensation or emotion ○ *experience a tingling sensation* [14C. Via French < Latin *experientia* < *experiri* "try out"]

CULTURAL NOTE ***Songs of Experience***, a collection of poems (1794) by the British writer William Blake. Blake's *Songs of Innocence* (1789) described the world from the optimistic viewpoint of an innocent child. In this, its adult counterpart, he portrays a world of disease, poverty, and irredeemable corruption. The collection includes perhaps his best-known poem, "The Tyger".

ex·pe·ri·enced /ik spéeree ənst/ *adj* possessing knowledge and skill acquired through involvement in or exposure to something over a period of time ○ *an experienced pilot*

ex·pe·ri·en·tial /ik spèeree énshəl/ *adj* derived from or relating to experience as opposed to other methods of acquiring knowledge [Mid-17C. After a word such as *inferential*] —**ex·pe·ri·en·tial·ly** *adv*

ex·per·i·ment *n* /ik spérrəmənt/ **1. SCIENTIFIC TEST** a test, especially a scientific one, carried out in order to discover whether a theory is correct or what the results of a particular course of action would be ○ *a chemistry experiment* **2. DOING SOMETHING NEW** an attempt to do something new or to see what will happen ○ *switching to decaf as an experiment* **3. USE OF REPEATED TESTS AND TRIALS** the use of tests and trials in order to make discoveries ○ *developed the protocol by experiment* ■ *vi* /ik spérrə mènt/ (**-ment·ed, -ment·ing, -ments**) **1. TRY NEW THINGS** to try out new methods of doing or using things ○ *a reluctance to experiment with new ingredients* **2.** SCI **CARRY OUT SCIENTIFIC TEST** to carry out a scientific test of a theory or process [14C. Directly or via Old French < Latin *experimentum* "trial, test" < *experiri* "try out"] —**ex·per·i·men·ta·tion** /ik spèrrəmən táysh'n/ *n* —**ex·per·i·ment·er** *n*

ex·per·i·men·tal /ik spèrrə mént'l/ *adj* **1. RELATING TO SOMETHING NEW AND UNTRIED** employing ideas, methods, or materials that have not been tried before ○ *a new, experimental form of treatment* **2.** SCI **RELATING TO SCIENTIFIC EXPERIMENTS** relating to, involving, or based on scientific experiments **3. BASED ON EXPERIENCE AND EVIDENCE** based on experience and practical evidence, and not on ideas —**ex·per·i·men·tal·ly** *adv*

ex·per·i·men·tal·ism /ik spèrrə mént'l ìzzəm/ *n* the use of new techniques in artistic, literary, or musical works —**ex·per·i·men·tal·ist** *n*

ex·per·i·men·tal psy·chol·o·gy *n* the branch of psychology that studies the basic mechanisms of the mind, e.g., perception, thinking, learning, and memory, often using experiments with individuals in controlled situations

ex·pert *n* /ék spùrt/ **1. SOMEBODY SKILLED OR KNOWLEDGEABLE** somebody with a great deal of knowledge about, or skill, training, or experience in, a particular field or activity ○ *a medical expert* **2.** *US* **HIGHEST RANK OF MARKSMANSHIP** in shooting, the highest grade of marksmanship **3.** *US* **HIGHEST-RANKED SHOOTER** in shooting, somebody who has achieved the grade of expert ■ *adj* /ék spùrt, ik spúrt/ **1. SKILLFUL OR KNOWLEDGEABLE** having a great deal of knowledge about, or skill, training, or experience in, a particular field or activity ○ *an expert pizza maker* **2. DONE BY SOMEBODY WITH SPECIALIST KNOWLEDGE** given or done by somebody who is skilled, trained, or experienced in the relevant subject area ○ *expert advice* [14C. Via French < Latin *expert-*, past participle of *experiri* "try out"] —**ex·pert·ly** *adv* —**ex·pert·ness** *n*

ex·per·tise /èkspər téez/ *n* the skill, knowledge, or opinion possessed by an expert [Mid-19C. < French < *expert-* (see EXPERT)]

ex·pert sys·tem *n* a computer program that applies artificial-intelligence methods to problem-solving

ex·pert wit·ness *n* somebody called to answer questions on the stand in a court of law in order to provide specialized information relevant to the case being tried

ex·pi·ate /ékspee àyt/ (**-at·ed, -at·ing, -ates**) *vt* to make amends, show remorse, or suffer punishment for wrongdoing [Late 16C. < Latin *expiat-*, past participle of *expiare* "atone completely" < *pius* "dutiful"] —**ex·pi·a·tion** /èkspee áysh'n/ *n* —**ex·pi·a·tor** *n* —**ex·pi·a·to·ry** /ékspee ə tàwree/ *adj*

~~expidition~~ incorrect spelling of **expedition**

ex·pi·ra·tion date *n* **1.** a date printed on the packaging of food and drug products that indicates the time after which they should not be used **2.** the date after which something such as a credit card or rain check is no longer valid

ex·pi·ra·to·ry /ik spīrə tàwree/ *adj* relating to the process of breathing out, or used in breathing out

ex·pire /ik spīr/ (**-pired, -pir·ing, -pires**) *vi* **1. END OR BE NO LONGER VALID** to come to an end or be no longer valid or in operation ○ *My visa has expired.* **2. DIE** to die or release a last breath (*formal or literary*) **3.** same as **exhale** (*technical*) [14C. Via French < Latin *exspirare* "breathe out" < *spirare* "breathe"] —**ex·pi·ra·tion** /èkspə ráysh'n/ *n*

ex·pi·ry /ik spīree/ *n* **1.** the fact of coming to an end and being no longer valid after a particular period of time ○ *two weeks before the date of expiry* **2.** death, especially the death of a person (*formal or literary*)

ex·pi·ry date *n UK* same as **expiration date**

ex·plain /ik spláyn/ (**-plained, -plain·ing, -plains**) *v* **1.** *vti* **GIVE DETAILS ABOUT SOMETHING** to give an account of something with enough clarity and detail to be understood by somebody else ○ *I explained to him that we had no option.* **2.** *vt* **CLARIFY MEANING OF SOMETHING** to make the meaning of something clear to somebody ○ *Can you explain this sentence to me?* **3.** *vti* **GIVE REASON FOR SOMETHING** to give the reason for something that has happened, often as justification for it ○ *Let me explain why I'm late.* **4. ex·plain your·self** *vr* **JUSTIFY BEHAVIOR** to give reasons to justify personal behavior or actions ○ *You'll have to explain yourself to the principal.* **5. ex·plain your·self** *vr* **MAKE SELF UNDERSTOOD** to express ideas or thoughts in a way that is easily understood ○ *I'm not explaining myself very well.* [Early 16C. < Latin *explanare* "flatten out, unfold" < *planus* "flat, clear"] —**ex·plain·a·ble** *adj* —**ex·plain·er** *n*

explain away *vt* to give excuses, reasons, or explanations for something in an attempt to show that it is less serious, important, or problematic than it seems

~~explaination~~ incorrect spelling of **explanation**

ex·pla·na·tion /èksplə náysh'n/ *n* **1.** a statement giving reasons for something or details of something ○ *an explanation of how the machine works* **2.** the act of giving details about something or reasons for something ○ *The explanation of what had happened took some time.* [14C. < Latin *explanation-* < *explanare* (see EXPLAIN)]

ex·plan·a·to·ry /ik splánnə tàwree/ *adj* giving reasons or details that explain something ○ *an explanatory leaflet* [Early 17C. < late Latin *explanatorius* < Latin *explanare* (see EXPLAIN)] —**ex·plan·a·to·ri·ly** *adv*

ex·plant /ek splánt/ *vt* (**-plant·ed, -plant·ing, -plants**) to remove living tissue from an organism and place it in a culture medium ■ *n* a piece of tissue removed from an organism and placed in a culture medium [Early 20C. After IMPLANT] —**ex·plan·ta·tion** /èk splan táysh'n/ *n*

ex·ple·tive /éksplətiv/ *n* **1.** LING **SWEARWORD** an exclamation, especially a swearword **2.** GRAM **WORD WITH NO MEANING** a word that carries no meaning but has a grammatical function in a sentence. In the sentence "There are three books on the table," "there" is an expletive. **3.** LITERAT **MEANINGLESS WORD IN LINE OF POETRY** a word added to a line of verse in order to fill it out, usually for the sake of the meter. In the line "When and that I was a little tiny lad," the words "and that" are expletives. ■ *adj* GRAM, LITERAT **USED AS EXPLETIVE** functioning as an expletive in a sentence or poem [Early 17C. < late Latin *expletivus* < *explet-*, past participle of *explere* "fill up" < *plere* "to fill"]

ex·ple·to·ry /éksplə tàwree/ *adj* GRAM, LITERAT same as **expletive** *adj* [Late 17C. < Latin *explet-* (see EXPLETIVE)]

ex·pli·ca·ble /éksplikəb'l, ik splíkəb'l/ *adj* able to be explained —**ex·pli·ca·bly** *adv*

ex·pli·cate /ékspli kàyt/ (**-cat·ed, -cat·ing, -cates**) *vt* **1.** to explain something, especially a literary text, in a detailed and formal way **2.** to explain and develop an idea or theory and show its implications [Early 16C. < Latin *explicat-*, past participle of *explicare* "unfold" < *plicare* "to fold"] —**ex·pli·ca·tion** /èkspli káysh'n/ *n* —**ex·pli·ca·tive** /ékspli kàytiv, ik splíkətiv/ *adj* —**ex·pli·ca·tor** *n*

ex·plic·it /ik splíssit/ *adj* **1. CLEAR AND OBVIOUS** expressing all details in a clear and obvious way, leaving no doubt as to the intended meaning ○ *Could you be more explicit about what the report needs to cover?* **2. DEFINITE** definite and unqualified, and not implied or guessed at ○ *I didn't have explicit knowledge of what was going on, but I knew something was up.* **3. SHOWING OR DESCRIBING SEX OPENLY** portraying nudity or sexual activity in an open and direct way **4.** MATH **WITH ONLY INDEPENDENT VARIABLES** describes a mathematical function that contains only variables whose value is independent of the value of the other variables in the function [Early 17C. Directly or via French < Latin *explicit-*, irregular past participle of *explicare* (see EXPLICATE)] —**ex·plic·it·ly** *adv* —**ex·plic·it·ness** *n*

USAGE explicit or **implicit**? ***Explicit*** means "clear, obvious, and definite": *explicit directions; had explicit knowledge of the plot because of being one of the conspirators.* ***Implicit*** means "implied or unstated but understood," "absolute," and "present as a necessary component": *nodding and smiling that signified implicit agreement with our position; implicit faith; the implicit confidentiality between physician and patient.*

ex·plode /ik splṓd/ (**-plod·ed, -plod·ing, -plodes**) *v* **1.** *vti* **BLOW UP OR BURST** to blow up or burst with a sudden release of chemical or nuclear energy and a loud noise, or cause something to blow up or burst in this way **2.** *vti* **BURST OR SHATTER** to burst like a bomb or shatter into many pieces, or cause something to do this **3.** *vi* **EXPRESS EMOTION** to give vent to an emotion, suddenly or violently ○ *He exploded into roars of laughter.* **4.** *vi* **INCREASE DRAMATICALLY** to increase suddenly in extent or severity in an uncontrolled way ○ *The growth rate in home ownership exploded.* **5.** *vi* **PRODUCE VIVID DISPLAY** to produce a vivid, often sudden display of light or color ○ *Her late paintings explode with intense reds and oranges.* **6.** *vi* **APPEAR SUDDENLY** to appear, start, or move suddenly and forcefully ○ *The band exploded onto the pop scene late last year.* **7.** *vt* **DISPROVE THEORY** to show that a belief or theory is completely wrong [Mid-16C. < Latin *explodere* "drive off the stage by clapping" < *plaudere* "to clap"] —**ex·plod·er** *n*

ex·plod·ed /ik splṓdəd/ *adj* showing the parts of something as separate items in a diagram, but with their relative positions maintained ○ *an exploded drawing*

ex·ploit *vt* /ik splóyt/ (**-ploit·ed, -ploit·ing, -ploits**) **1. TAKE ADVANTAGE OF SOMEBODY** to take selfish or unfair advantage of a person or situation, usually for personal gain **2. USE SOMETHING FOR BENEFIT** to use or develop something in order to gain a benefit ○ *fully exploit natural gas reserves* ■ *n* /ék splòyt, ik splóyt/ **EXCITING ACT** an interesting or daring action or achievement [Mid-16C. Via Old French, "accomplishment" < Latin *explicit-*, past participle of *explicare* (see EXPLICATE)] —**ex·ploit·a·ble** *adj* —**ex·ploit·a·tive** *adj* —**ex·ploit·er** *n* —**ex·ploit·ive** *adj*

ex·ploi·ta·tion /èk sploy táysh'n/ *n* **1.** the practice of taking selfish or unfair advantage of a person or situation, usually for personal gain **2.** the use or development of something in order to gain a benefit

ex·plo·ra·tion /èksplə ráysh'n/ *n* **1. TRAVEL FOR DISCOVERY** travel undertaken to discover what a place is like or where it is ○ *polar exploration* **2. INVESTIGATION OF SOMETHING** a careful investigation or study of something such as data, a particular subject, or possible courses of action **3. SEARCHING FOR NATURAL RESOURCES** the testing of a number of places for natural resources, e.g., drilling or boring for samples that will be examined for possible mineral deposits **4.** MED **EXAMINATION FOR DIAGNOSIS** the examination of a part of the body in order to make a diagnosis

ex·plor·a·to·ry /ik splάwrə tàwree/ *adj* involving exploration ○ *an exploratory mission* ○ *exploratory surgery*

ex·plore /ik splάwr/ (**-plored, -plor·ing, -plores**) *v* **1.** *vti* **TRAVEL FOR DISCOVERY** to travel to or in a place in order to discover what it is like or what is there **2.** *vti* **INVESTIGATE OR STUDY SOMETHING** to make a careful investigation or study of something ○ *exploring all possible avenues of research* **3.** *vti* **SEARCH PLACE FOR NATURAL RESOURCES** to make a search of an area for natural resources such as mineral deposits **4.** *vt* MED **EXAMINE SOMETHING TO MAKE DIAGNOSIS** to examine a part of the body in order to make a diagnosis [Mid-16C. Via French < Latin *explorare* "search out" < *plorare* "cry out"]

ex·plor·er /ik splάwrər/ *n* somebody who travels to distant or unfamiliar places to find out more about them ○ *polar explorers of the early 20th century*

Ex·plor·er *n* a Scout aged between 14 and 21 taking part in a program run by the Boy Scouts of America that enables young people to gain work experience in a career in which they are interested

ex·plo·sion /ik splṓzh'n/ *n* **1. SUDDEN NOISY RELEASE OF ENERGY** the sudden loud release of energy and a rapidly expanding volume of gas that occurs when a bomb detonates or gas explodes **2. BURSTING OR SHATTERING OF SOMETHING** a bursting with a loud noise, or a shattering of something into many pieces **3. SUDDEN LOUD NOISE** a loud noise that occurs suddenly **4. SUDDEN BURST OF EMOTION** a sudden release of intense feeling such as anger ○ *an explosion of rage* **5. DRAMATIC INCREASE** a sudden and dramatic increase in something such as a population or an activity ○ *the explosion in e-mail subscriptions* **6. INTENSE DISPLAY** a vivid, often sudden display of light or color **7.** PHON same as **plosion** [Early 17C. < Latin *explosion-* < *explos-*, past participle of *explodere* (see EXPLODE)]

ex·plo·sive /ik splṓssiv, -splṓz-/ *adj* **1. LIKELY TO EXPLODE** able or serving to explode ○ *an explosive mixture of oxygen and methane* **2. OPERATED BY EXPLODING** designed to explode or operated by means of something that explodes ○ *an explosive device* **3. LIKELY TO GENERATE VIOLENT ANGER** likely to cause or erupt suddenly into angry disagreement or violence ○ *an explosive temperament* **4. SUDDEN AND DRAMATIC** happening or appearing suddenly and dramatically ○ *Tourism experienced explosive growth in the 1990s.* **5.** PHON same as **plosive** ■ *n* **1. SOMETHING THAT EXPLODES** a substance or device that suddenly produces a volume of rapidly expanding gas **2.** PHON same as **plosive** —**ex·plo·sive·ly** *adv* —**ex·plo·sive·ness** *n*

ex·po /ék spṑ/ *n* a large exhibition or trade fair [Mid-20C. Shortening of EXPOSITION]

ex·po·nent /ik spṓnənt, ék spṑnənt/ *n* **1. ADVOCATE OF CAUSE** a supporter or promoter of a cause **2. EXPLAINER OF SOMETHING** somebody who explains or interprets something ○ *an exponent of Kant's philosophy* **3. PRACTITIONER OF ART OR SKILL** a performer or practitioner of an art or skill, especially somebody who is regarded as an excellent example of how something should be done ○ *an exponent of the rococo style* **4.** MATH **NUMBER INDICATING MULTIPLICATION** a number or variable placed to the upper right of a number or mathematical expression that indicates the number of times the number or expression is to be multiplied by itself, as in 2^3, which equals 8 [Late 16C. < Latin *exponent-*, present participle of *exponere* (see EXPOUND)]

ex·po·nen·tial /èkspə nénshəl/ *adj* **1. RAPIDLY GROWING** rapidly becoming greater in size ○ *an exponential increase in sales* **2.** MATH **INVOLVING MATHEMATICAL EXPONENT** describes a mathematical entity such as a curve, function, equation, or series that contains, is expressed as, or involves numbers or quantities raised to an exponent **3.** MATH **USING BASE OF NATURAL LOGARITHMS** describes a mathematical entity that involves the transcendental number *e*, the base of natural logarithms, raised to an exponent —**ex·po·nen·tial·ly** *adv*

ex·po·nen·tial func·tion *n* a mathematical expression with the formula e^x, in which *e* is the base of natural logarithms. Symbol **exp**

ex·po·nen·ti·a·tion /èkspə nenshee áysh'n/ *n* the multiplication of a number or quantity by itself a given number of times, the number of times being the power to which the number or quantity is to be raised

ex·port *v* /ik spάwrt, ék spàwrt/ (**-port·ed, -port·ing, -ports**) **1.** *vti* COMM **SEND GOODS ABROAD** to send goods for sale or exchange to other countries **2.** *vt* SOC SCI **SPREAD ONE SOCIETY'S CULTURE TO ANOTHER** to cause the spread of ideas, values, or a way of life from one society, culture, or nation to another **3.** *vt* COMPUT **ALTER FORMAT OF COMPUTER DATA** to convert data from a computer program into a form suitable for a different program or environment ■ *n* /ék spàwrt/ COMM **1. SELLING OF GOODS ABROAD** the selling of goods to other countries **2. PRODUCT SOLD ABROAD** a product sold and transported to another country [15C. < Latin *exportare* "carry away" < *portare* "carry"] —**ex·port·a·bil·i·ty** /ik spàwrtə bíllətee/ *n* —**ex·port·a·ble** *adj* —**ex·por·ta·tion** /èk spawr táysh'n/ *n* —**ex·port·er** *n*

ex·pose /ik spṓz/ (**-posed, -pos·ing, -pos·es**) *v* **1.** *vt* **PUT SOMEBODY IN UNPROTECTED SITUATION** to put somebody or something in a vulnerable or potentially dangerous situation ○ *financially exposed* **2.** *vt* **MAKE SOMEBODY EXPERIENCE SOMETHING** to cause somebody to have a personal and often enlightening experience of something ○ *exposing the children to theater* **3.** *vt* **ALLOW SOMETHING TO BE SEEN** to uncover something or turn it over with the result that it can be seen ○ *expose the wound to the air* **4.** *vt* **REVEAL SOMEBODY'S WRONGDOINGS** to reveal that somebody has done something wrong, especially by publishing or broadcasting the information **5. ex·pose your·self** *vr* **REVEAL PART OF BODY INDECENTLY** to uncover a part of the body, especially the genitals, in public in an indecent way **6.** *vt* PHOTOGRAPHY **ALLOW LIGHT ONTO FILM** to allow light to fall on light-sensitive material such as photographic film, usually by opening a camera shutter [15C. < French *exposer* < (after *poser* "place") < Latin *exponere* "set out" (see EXPOUND)] —**ex·pos·al** *n* —**ex·pos·er** *n*

ex·po·sé /èks pō záy/ (*plural* **-sés**) *n* **1.** a book or article that reveals details of a scandal or crime **2.** a formal and systematic statement giving facts about something [Early 19C. < French, past participle of *exposer* (see EXPOSE)]

ex·posed /ik spṓzd/ *adj* **1. VISIBLE OR UNPROTECTED** uncovered and therefore visible or without protection ○ *Cover any exposed areas of skin liberally with sunscreen.* **2. WITH NO SHELTER** unprotected from wind and weather by shelter from trees or higher ground **3. UNPROTECTED FROM HARM** vulnerable to danger or harm **4.** CLIMBING **CARRIED OUT ON ROCK FACE** describes a mountain ascent carried out on a high, sheer, and open rock face —**ex·posed·ness** *n*

ex·po·si·tion /èkspə zísh'n/ *n* **1. EXHIBITION OR FAIR** a large exhibition, e.g., of industrial achievements, sometimes international in scope **2. DETAILED DESCRIPTION OR DISCUSSION** a detailed description of a theory, problem, or proposal discussing the issues involved, or a commentary on a written text discussing its meaning and implications **3. ACT OF DESCRIBING OR DISCUSSING SOMETHING** the act of describing and discussing a theory, problem, or proposal, or of commenting on a written text **4.** MUSIC **OPENING SECTION OF MUSICAL COMPOSITION** the opening section of a piece of music, especially of a sonata or fugue, in which the principal themes are introduced **5.** LITERAT, THEATER **REVELATION OF STORY'S BACKGROUND** the part of a literary or dramatic work in which the basic facts of setting and character are made known [14C. Directly or via French < Latin *exposition-* < *exposit-*, past participle of *exponere* (see EXPOUND)] —**ex·pos·i·tive** /ik spózzətiv/ *adj* —**ex·pos·i·tor** *n* —**ex·pos·i·to·ry** /-tàwree/ *adj*

ex post fac·to /èks pōst fák tō/ *adj, adv* applying to events that have already occurred as well as to subsequent events [Mid-17C. < Latin *ex postfacto*, literally "from what is done afterward"]

ex·pos·tu·late /ik spóschə làyt/ (**-lat·ed, -lat·ing, -lates**) *vi* to express disagreement or disapproval, especially when attempting to dissuade somebody from doing something [Late 16C. < Latin *expostulat-*, past participle of *expostulare* "demand from" < *postulare* "to demand"] —**ex·pos·tu·la·tion** /ik spòschə láysh'n/ *n* —**ex·pos·tu·la·to·ry** *adj*

SYNONYMS See ***object***.

ex·po·sure /ik spṓzhər/ *n* **1. CONTACT WITH SOMETHING** the experience of coming into contact with an environmental condition or social influence that has a harmful or beneficial effect ○ *exposure to the classics* ○ *exposure to second-hand smoke* **2.** BROADCAST, MEDIA **PUBLICITY** the reporting of events by the broadcast or print media **3. REVELATION OF SCANDAL OR IDENTITY** the revelation of a scandal or of somebody's secrets or private information **4.** MED **HARMFUL EFFECTS OF WEATHER** the harmful effects of cold or other extreme weather conditions **5.** PHOTOGRAPHY **TIME THAT LIGHT FALLS ON FILM** an amount of light permitted to fall on light-sensitive material such as film or paper coated with emulsion **6.** PHOTOGRAPHY **TAKING OF PHOTOGRAPH** the act or process of taking a photograph **7.** PHOTOGRAPHY **FILM OR PLATE EXPOSED FOR PHOTOGRAPH** a section of film or a photographic plate exposed to light in taking a photograph **8.** ARCHIT **DIRECTION ROOM OR BUILDING FACES** the direction something faces or the way it is sited relative to sunlight or wind direction ○ *This room has a southern exposure.* **9.** FIN **RISK OF FINANCIAL LOSS** the state of being at risk of financial loss, or the amount of possible financial loss involved

ex·po·sure me·ter *n* a device for measuring the intensity of light for photography, often giving the value as a combination of shutter speed and lens aperture

ex·pound /ik spównd/ (**-pound·ed, -pound·ing, -pounds**) *vti* to give a detailed description and explanation of a theory or viewpoint or an explanation of the meaning and implications of a written text [13C. Via Old French < Latin *exponere* "explain, set out" < *ponere* "to place"] —**ex·pound·er** *n*

ex·press /ik spréss/ *v* (**-pressed, -press·ing, -press·es**) **1.** *vt* **SAY SOMETHING** to state thoughts or feelings in words ○ *I'd like to express my gratitude.* **2.** *vt* **SHOW MEANING SYMBOLICALLY** to convey meaning by gesture, behavior, representation in art or drama, or in some other symbolic way ○ *Casual handholding can express profound love between two people.* **3. ex·press your·self** *vr* **REVEAL YOUR THOUGHTS** to make your thoughts and feelings known to other people ○ *able to express herself through her music* **4.** *vt* **REPRESENT SOMETHING AS SYMBOL** to use a symbol, figure, or formula to represent something such as a quantity in a different way ○ *Express the fractions as decimal numbers.* **5.** *vt* MAIL **SEND SOMETHING BY SPECIAL FAST DELIVERY** to send a package or message using a special rapid-delivery service **6.** *vt* **SQUEEZE SOMETHING OUT** to force a liquid out of something by squeezing or pressing **7.** *vt* GENETICS **PRODUCE INHERITED CHARACTERISTIC** to produce an observable inherited characteristic ○ *Some genes are only expressed in adults.* ■ *adj* **1.** TRANSP, MAIL **DONE OR TRAVELING VERY QUICKLY** traveling, moving, or delivered quickly and directly to the destination ○ *Take the express train.* **2.** COMM **FOR BRIEF TRANSACTIONS** relating to purchases or other transactions that can be completed quickly and easily, e.g., because only one or a few items are involved ○ *We can use the express checkout.* **3. STATED CLEARLY** stated in a clear unambiguous way ○ *his express wish* **4. SPECIFIC** definitely, and usually exclusively, intended or specified ○ *was formed for the express purpose of building affordable housing* ■ *adv* **BY RAPID TRANSFER OR TRANSPORTATION SYSTEM** by a special rapid-delivery service or an express train, bus, or similar mode of transportation ■ *n* **1.** TRANSP **FAST TRAIN OR BUS** a fast train or bus that travels direct to its destination, making few or no stops on the way **2. FAST DELIVERY SERVICE** a special rapid-delivery service, or the organization providing it [14C. < medieval Latin *expressare* "press out" and Latin *expressus* "clearly evident" < Latin *exprimere* "press out" < *premere* "press"] —**ex·press·er** *n* —**ex·press·i·ble** *adj*

ex·pres·sion /ik sprésh'n/ *n* **1. LOOK ON SOMEBODY'S FACE** a look on somebody's face, conveying a thought or feeling ○ *listened with a puzzled expression* **2.** LANGUAGE **WORD OR PHRASE** a word or phrase that communicates an idea ○ *It's a common expression in this part of the country.* **3. CONVEYING OF THOUGHTS OR FEELINGS** the communication of thoughts or feelings, e.g., directly to another person or through a work of art ○ *a heart-rending expression of sorrow* **4. WAY OF COMMUNICATING SOMETHING** something done or given as a means of communicating a feeling or thought to somebody else ○ *As an expression of my gratitude, I'd like you to accept this vase.* **5. INFLECTION IN VOICE** somebody's intonation or tone of voice **6.** MUSIC **INTERPRETIVE ELEMENT OF MUSIC** the interpretive element of music, including tempo, dynamics, articulation, and phrasing, by which a player or singer evokes emotions **7.** MATH **MATHEMATICAL REPRESENTATION** a combination of constants, operators, and variables representing numbers or quantities ○ *an algebraic expression* —**ex·pres·sion·al** *adj*

ex·pres·sion·ism /ik spréshʼn ìzzəm/ *n* **1.** an artistic movement that flourished in Germany between 1905 and 1925 whose adherents sought to represent feelings and moods rather than objective reality, often distorting color and form. The term is also used more loosely to apply to the work of Matisse and the Fauves. **2.** THEATER, LITERAT a literary movement of the early 20th century, especially in the theater, that represented external reality in a highly stylized and subjective manner, attempting to convey a psychological or spiritual reality rather than a record of actual events. The expressionists include the playwrights August Strindberg, Georg Wedekind, and Eugene O'Neill. —**ex·pres·sion·ist** *n, adj* —**ex·pres·sion·is·tic** /ik sprèshʼn ístik/ *adj* —**ex·pres·sion·is·ti·cal·ly** *adv*

ex·pres·sion·less /ik spréshʼnləss/ *adj* showing no emotion or interest by the tone of voice or facial movements —**ex·pres·sion·less·ly** *adv* —**ex·pres·sion·less·ness** *n*

ex·pres·sion mark *n* a symbol or written direction, often in Italian, that indicates the expression to be used in performing a piece of music

ex·pres·sive /ik spréssiv/ *adj* **1. FULL OF EXPRESSION** expressing a great deal of feeling and meaning ○ *an expressive face* **2. CONVEYING SOMETHING** communicating a particular meaning ○ *a gesture expressive of the utmost contempt* **3.** MED **RELATING TO SPEAKING AND WRITING DISORDERS** relating to disorders involving the expression of ideas in speech and writing as opposed to the interpretation of what is heard or read —**ex·pres·sive·ly** *adv* —**ex·pres·sive·ness** *n*

ex·pres·siv·i·ty /èk spre sívvətee/ (*plural* **-ties**) *n* **1.** the ability or the extent to which somebody has the ability to communicate emotion or meaning **2.** the extent to which a gene affects the observable characteristics (**phenotype**) of an organism

ex·press lane *n US* the lane on a multilane limited-access highway designated for fast-traveling vehicles, located on the left. Can term **fast lane**

ex·press·ly /ik spréslee/ *adv* **1.** in a clear and unambiguous way ○ *He expressly rejected my offer.* **2.** in a way that shows a deliberate intention or choice ○ *He told me the present was meant expressly for me.*

Ex·press Mail *tdmk* a trademark for the overnight delivery service of the United States Postal Service

ex·pres·so *n* BEVERAGES another spelling of **espresso**

ex·press·way /ik spréss wày/ *n* a limited-access road with several lanes in each direction, designed for fast direct travel especially through or around a city

ex·pro·pri·ate /ik sprṓpree àyt/ (**-at·ed, -at·ing, -ates**) *vt* to take property or money from somebody, either legally for the public good or illegally by theft or fraud [Late 16C. < medieval Latin *expropriat-*, past participle of *expropriare* "take away and make your own" < Latin *proprius* "your own"] —**ex·pro·pri·a·tion** /ik sprṑpree áyshʼn/ *n* —**ex·pro·pri·a·tor** *n* —**ex·pro·pri·a·to·ry** *adj*

ex·pul·sion /ik spúlshən/ *n* **1.** the act of compelling somebody to leave or give up membership in an institution such as a school, political party, or club, usually as a punishment **2.** the forcing out of somebody or something from something ○ *expulsion of air from the lungs* [15C. < Latin *expulsion-* < *expuls-*, past participle of *expellere* (see EXPEL)] —**ex·pul·sive** *adj*

ex·punge /ik spúnj/ (**-punged, -pung·ing, -pung·es**) *vt* **1.** to delete or blot out something unwanted **2.** to destroy or put an end to something [Early 17C. < Latin *expungere* "prick out" < *pungere* "mark with a point"; from the placing of points next to text to be deleted] —**ex·punc·tion** /ik spúngkshʼn/ *n* —**ex·pung·er** *n*

ex·pur·gate /ékspər gàyt/ (**-gat·ed, -gat·ing, -gates**) *vt* to remove words or passages considered offensive or unsuitable from a book before publication [Late 17C. < Latin *expurgat-*, past participle of *expurgare* "cleanse out" < *purgare* "purify"] —**ex·pur·ga·tion** /èkspər gáyshʼn/ *n* —**ex·pur·ga·tor** *n* —**ex·pur·ga·to·ri·al** /ik spùrgə táwree əl/ *adj* —**ex·pur·ga·to·ry** /ik spúrgə tàwree/ *adj*

expwy, **expy** *abbr US* expressway

ex·qui·site /ik skwízzit, ékskwizit/ *adj* **1. FINELY BEAUTIFUL** very beautiful and delicate or intricate ○ *exquisite workmanship* **2. EXCELLENT** perfect and delightful ○ *an exquisite translation of Ovid* **3. SENSITIVE AND DISCRIMINATING** sensitive and capable of detecting subtle differences ○ *exquisite taste in dress* **4. INTENSE** felt with a sharp intensity ○ *exquisite pain* [Mid-16C. < Latin *exquisit-*, past participle of *exquirere* "seek out" < *quaerere* "seek, ask"] —**ex·qui·site·ly** *adv* —**ex·qui·site·ness** *n*

ex·sert /ik súrt/ *vt* (**-sert·ed, -sert·ing, -serts**) to thrust out or project something ○ *A bee exserts its sting.* ■ *adj also* **ex·sert·ed** projecting beyond an enclosing or adjoining part ○ *an exsert stamen* [Early 19C. < Latin *ex(s)ert-*, past participle of *ex(s)erere* (see EXERT)] —**ex·ser·tion** *n*

ext. *abbr* **1.** extension **2.** exterior **3.** external **4.** PHARM extract

ex·tant /ékstənt, ek stánt/ *adj* still in existence ○ *Three copies of the document are extant.* [Mid-16C. < Latin *exstant-*, present participle of *exstare* "exist" < *stare* "to stand"]

~~**extasy**~~ incorrect spelling of **ecstasy**

ex·tem·po·ra·ne·ous /ik stèmpə ráynee əss/, **ex·tem·po·rar·y** /ik stémpə rèrree/, **ex·tem·po·ral** /ik stémpərəl/ *adj* **1. DONE UNREHEARSED** performed without any preparation **2. PREPARED BUT SAID WITHOUT NOTES** prepared in advance but delivered without notes **3. SKILLED AT SPEAKING UNREHEARSED** skilled at speaking without preparation or notes **4. MAKESHIFT** done as a temporary measure [Mid-17C. < late Latin *extemporaneus* < *ex tempore*, literally "out of the moment"] —**ex·tem·po·ra·ne·i·ty** /ik stèmpərə nee ətee/ *n* —**ex·tem·po·ra·ne·ous·ly** *adv* —**ex·tem·po·ra·ne·ous·ness** *n*

ex·tem·po·re /ik stémpəree/ *adj, adv* with little or no preparation [Mid-16C. < Latin *ex tempore*, literally "out of the moment"]

ex·tem·po·rize /ik stémpə rìz/ (**-rized, -riz·ing, -riz·es**) *vti* **1. PERFORM SOMETHING WITHOUT PREPARATION** to perform or say something without having made any preparation **2.** MUSIC **IMPROVISE MUSIC** to compose or perform a piece of music by improvising **3. HANDLE IN MAKESHIFT WAY** to do or devise something in a makeshift fashion [Mid-17C. < EXTEMPORE] —**ex·tem·po·ri·za·tion** /ik stèmpəri záyshʼn/ *n* —**ex·tem·po·riz·er** *n*

ex·tend /ik sténd/ (**-tend·ed, -tend·ing, -tends**) *v* **1.** *vti* **OPEN OUT INTO SPACE** to stretch out into space, or stretch something out into space ○ *fully extended the robot's arm* **2.** *vt* **INCREASE SIZE OF SOMETHING** to make something larger, longer, or broader in scope ○ *extend the driveway* ○ *extending the scope of the law* **3.** *vi* **OCCUPY DISTANCE OR SPACE** to continue for a distance or occupy a space, often within a particular range ○ *The city extends for another mile in both directions.* **4.** *vi* **CONTINUE FOR TIME** to last or continue for a period of time, usually a particular one ○ *talks extending over the weekend* **5.** *vt* **INCREASE TIME SPAN** to increase the length of time something lasts or the length of time before something applies or ceases to apply **6.** *vti* **BE APPLICABLE TO SOMEBODY OR SOMETHING** to affect or apply to somebody or something, or make something do this ○ *The offer extends to new readers too.* **7.** *vt* **INCREASE AMOUNT BY ADDING SOMETHING** to increase the amount of something by adding something else to it ○ *There's not much stew left, but we could always extend it by adding more potatoes and vegetables.* **8.** *vt* **OFFER OR GIVE SOMETHING** to offer or provide something to somebody ○ *extended the hand of friendship* **9.** *vt* **MAKE EXTRA EFFORT** to work, or make somebody or something work, as hard as possible to achieve the best possible result ○ *need to extend themselves to finish on time* **10.** *vt* ACCT **CALCULATE LINE TOTAL ON INVOICE** to calculate the total on the line of an invoice by multiplying quantity by price [14C. < Latin *extendere* "stretch out" < *tendere* "hold out, stretch"] —**ex·tend·a·bil·i·ty** /ik stèndə bíllətee/ *n* —**ex·tend·a·ble** *adj* —**ex·ten·si·ble** /ik sténssəbʼl/ *adj*

SYNONYMS See *increase.*

ex·tend·ed /ik sténdəd/ *adj* **1. MADE LONGER OR LARGER** stretched or pulled out, lengthened, enlarged, or expanded **2. LASTING LONGER THAN USUAL** lasting longer than is normal or typical **3. HAVING WIDER RANGE** having wider influence, effect, or application **4.** CLOTHING **EXTRA LARGE OR SMALL** larger or smaller than other items in the range ○ *suits in extended sizes* —**ex·tend·ed·ly** *adv*

Ex·tend·ed Bi·na·ry Cod·ed Dec·i·mal In·ter·change Code *n* COMPUT full form of **EBCDIC**

ex·tend·ed fam·i·ly *n* the family as a unit embracing parents and children together with grandparents, aunts, uncles, cousins, and sometimes more distant relatives

ex·tend·ed-play *adj* (*not hyphenated when used after a verb*) **1.** describes a videotape format that can record four or six hours of material on a two-hour tape **2.** describes a vinyl record of the same size as a single but with two tracks on each side instead of one

ex·tend·ed school *n US* a program of care, education, and recreational activities beyond regular school hours, designed especially for school-age children who have no home supervision after school

ex·tend·er /ik sténdər/ *n* **1.** a substance that is added to a product to dilute it, add body to it, or modify it in other ways **2.** the part of a lowercase letter such as "p" or "h" that projects above or below the body of the letter

ex·ten·si·ble /ik sténsəbʼl/ *adj* having the capability of being extended [Early 17C. Directly or via French < medieval Latin *extensibilis* < Latin *extens-* (see EXTENSION)] —**ex·ten·si·bil·i·ty** /ik stènsə bíllətee/ *n* —**ex·ten·si·bly** *adv*

Ex·ten·si·ble Mark·up Lan·guage *n* COMPUT full form of **XML**

ex·ten·sim·e·ter *n* ENG same as **extensometer**

ex·ten·sion /ik sténshʼn/ *n* **1. EXTENDING OR BEING EXTENDED** the act or process of increasing the size, scope, range, or application of something, or the fact of being increased in size, scope, range, or application ○ *the extension of parental leave to fathers* ○ *the extension of the waterway network* **2. ADDITIONAL PERIOD OF TIME** an additional period of time allowed for completion of work or payment of a debt ○ *You'll never finish that paper on time: why don't you ask for an extension?* **3. RANGE** the range or sphere over which something extends **4.** TELECOM **ADDITIONAL TELEPHONE LINE** an additional telephone line or telephone connected to the main line in a building or organization, often having its own number **5.** TELECOM **TELEPHONE NUMBER OF EXTENSION** the number used to contact a telephone extension within a building or organization **6. ADDITIONAL PIECE** a piece that has been or can be added, or that can be pulled out, to enlarge or lengthen something **7.** BUILDINGS **ADDITION TO BUILDING** a room or area added to an existing building ○ *We're having an extension built onto the kitchen.* **8. OFF-CAMPUS COLLEGE PROGRAM** courses or facilities provided by a college or university for people who are unable to attend classes on the campus or during scheduled class periods **9.** ELEC same as **extension cord** **10.** ANAT **STRAIGHTENING OF LIMB** the stretching out of a limb after it has been bent, or the position attained by a limb after stretching it **11.** LOGIC **BROADER SENSE OF EXPRESSION** the broad range of meaning of an expression, as opposed to its precise meaning. The extension of the term "man" is the set comprising all men, whereas the meaning of the word "man" is "an adult male human being." **12.** MATH **SET INCLUDING TWO SIMILAR SETS** a mathematical set that includes as subsets all the members of a given set and of another similar set **13.** COMPUT same as **file extension** ■ **ex·ten·sions** *npl* **EXTRA HAIR ATTACHED TO YOUR OWN** lengths of real or synthetic hair attached to the hair to create a longer hairstyle [Early 16C. < late Latin *extension-* < Latin *extens-*, past participle of *extendere* (see EXTEND)] —**ex·ten·sion·al** *adj* —**ex·ten·sion·al·ly** *adv*

ex·ten·sion a·gent *n* somebody employed by a federal or state government to provide information to the public about agriculture, health, or home economics

ex·ten·sion cord *n* a length of electrical cord with a plug at one end and a socket at the other, used to connect an appliance when the electrical supply is some distance away

ex·ten·sive /ik sténssiv/ *adj* **1. LARGE IN AMOUNT** great in amount or number ○ *extensive water damage from the flooding* **2. BROAD IN SCOPE** great in extent, range, or application ○ *extensive research into the origins of language* **3. VAST** covering a large area ○ *a hotel set in extensive grounds* **4.** AGRIC **USING LOW TECHNOLOGICAL INPUT** relating to a farming practice in which a large area of land is cultivated using little labor and expense, resulting in a relatively small crop. ◊ **intensive** [Early 17C. Directly or via French < late Latin *extensivus* < Latin *extens-* (see EXTENSION)] —**ex·ten·sive·ly** *adv* —**ex·ten·sive·ness** *n*

ex·ten·som·e·ter /èk sten sómmətər/, **ex·ten·sim·e·ter** /-símmətər/ *n* a device for measuring small changes of length in a sample, especially those caused by stress or thermal expansion in a metal [Late 19C. < Latin *extens-* (see EXTENSION)]

ex·ten·sor /ik sténssər/ *n* a muscle that straightens or extends a part of the body, e.g., an arm or leg [Early 18C. < modern Latin < Latin *extens-* (see EXTENSION)]

ex·tent /ik stént/ *n* **1. RANGE OR SCOPE** the area or range covered or affected by something ○ *the location and extent of the damage* **2. DEGREE** the degree to which something applies ○ *To what extent should we allow newspaper reporters into people's private lives?* **3. REGION** an area of land or water **4.** LAW **WRIT ALLOWING SEIZURE OF PROPERTY** a writ that authorizes somebody to take possession of the property of a person who owes him or her money [Late 16C. Via Anglo-Norman, "valuation of land" < medieval Latin *extenta* < Latin *extendere* (see EXTEND)]

ex·ten·u·ate /ik sténnyoo àyt/ (**-at·ed, -at·ing, -ates**) *vt* to make a mistake or wrongdoing seem less serious than it first appeared, e.g., by providing a mitigating excuse for it [Early 16C. < Latin *extenuat-*, past participle of *extenuare* "thin out" < *tenuis* "thin"] —**ex·ten·u·at·ing** *adj* —**ex·ten·u·at·ing·ly** *adv* —**ex·ten·u·a·tion** /ik stènnyoo áysh'n/ *n* —**ex·ten·u·a·tive** *adj* —**ex·ten·u·a·tor** *n* —**ex·ten·u·a·to·ry** *adj*

ex·ten·u·at·ing cir·cum·stan·ces *npl* factors that make somebody's actions excusable or less blameworthy

ex·te·ri·or /ik stéeree ər/ *adj* **1. ON OUTSIDE** on or for the outside of something ○ *the exterior walls of the building* **2. COMING FROM OUTSIDE** coming from outside or beyond somebody or something ○ *There must be some exterior cause for this.* **3.** ARTS **OUTDOOR** describes an image depicting an outdoor setting or a photograph or movie scene taken out of doors ○ *an exterior shot* ■ *n* **1. OUTSIDE** the outside surface, appearance, or coating of something **2. OUTWARD APPEARANCE** somebody's outward appearance as distinct from his or her inner thoughts ○ *her calm exterior* **3.** ARTS **SCENE SET OUT OF DOORS** an outdoor scene, especially as represented in the visual arts [Early 16C. < Latin, "more outward" < *exter* "outward, on the outside"] —**ex·te·ri·or·i·ty** /ik stèeree áwrətee/ *n*

ex·te·ri·or an·gle *n* **1.** an angle on the outside of a polygon, formed between a side and an extension of an adjacent side **2.** any of four angles formed on the outside of a pair of lines that are crossed by a third line

ex·te·ri·or·ize /ik stéeree ə rìz/ (**-ized, -iz·ing, -iz·es**) *vt* **1.** same as **externalize 2.** to remove an internal organ from the body, e.g., in order to perform surgery on it —**ex·te·ri·or·i·za·tion** /ik stèeree əri záysh'n/ *n*

ex·ter·mi·nate /ik stúrmə nàyt/ (**-nat·ed, -nat·ing, -nates**) *vt* to kill or destroy somebody or something completely ○ *a species nearly exterminated by hunting* [Late 16C. < Latin *exterminat-*, past participle of *exterminare* "drive beyond the boundaries" < *terminus* "boundary"] —**ex·ter·mi·na·tion** /ik stùrmə náysh'n/ *n* —**ex·ter·mi·na·to·ry** /ik stúrmənə tàwree/ *adj*

ex·ter·mi·na·tor /ik stúrmə nàytər/ *n* **1.** somebody whose job is to kill unwanted insects and other animals **2.** somebody or something that kills or destroys somebody or something else completely

ex·tern /ék stùrn/, **ex·terne** *n US* a nonresident doctor or other staff member attached to a hospital [Early 17C. Via French < Latin *externus* (see EXTERNAL)] —**ex·tern·ship** *n*

ex·ter·nal /ik stúrn'l/ *adj* **1. OUTSIDE** situated on, happening on, or coming from the outside ○ *external forces* **2. FOR USE ON OUTSIDE** suitable or designed for use only on the outside or surface of something, especially the body ○ *This medication is for external use only.* **3. OUTSIDE SCOPE OF SOMETHING** existing outside the body or mind, or the limits of something ○ *the external world* **4. VISIBLE FROM OUTWARD APPEARANCE** conveyed by somebody's or something's outward appearance, as opposed to what is inside or underneath **5. OUTSIDE ORGANIZATION** relating to, forming, or from a separate or independent organization ○ *external auditors* **6.** POL **RELATING TO FOREIGN COUNTRIES** dealing with or involving relations with foreign countries ■ *n* **EXTERIOR OF SOMETHING** the outer surface of something ■ **ex·ter·nals** *npl* **1. OUTWARD APPEARANCES** the outward appearance of somebody or something, especially when it is not considered to be a true indication of the person's or thing's real nature **2. SURROUNDINGS** somebody's or something's circumstances or environment [Late 16C. Partly < French *externe*, partly < Latin *externus* < *exter* "outward, on the outside"] —**ex·ter·nal·ly** *adv*

ex·ter·nal-com·bus·tion en·gine *n* an engine that converts into power heat generated from fuel consumed outside the engine, e.g., a steam engine. ◊ **internal-combustion engine**

ex·ter·nal de·gree *n* a university degree awarded to a candidate who, instead of taking traditional courses to fulfill degree requirements, works and studies off campus

ex·ter·nal ear *n* the outside part of the ear, consisting of the auricle and auditory canal

ex·ter·nal·ism /ik stúrn'l ìzzəm/ *n* **1.** excessive concern about outward forms and appearances, especially in religious matters **2.** the view that the content of thoughts depends at least partly on relationships with objects outside the mind —**ex·ter·nal·ist** *n*

ex·ter·nal·i·ty /èkstər nállətee/ (*plural* **-ties**) *n* **1. QUALITY OF BEING EXTERNAL** the fact or quality of being external **2. SOMETHING OUTSIDE OR EXTERNAL** an outward form or appearance, or anything that is outside or external to somebody or something **3.** ECON **CONSEQUENCE OF PRODUCTION IGNORED IN PRICING** a factor such as environmental damage, that results from the way something is produced but is not taken into account in establishing the market price of the goods or materials concerned

ex·ter·nal·ize /ik stúrn'l ìz/ (**-ized, -iz·ing, -iz·es**) *vt* **1. GIVE OUTWARD EXPRESSION TO SOMETHING** to express ideas or feelings in some visible or perceptible way in order to communicate them to somebody else **2. PERCEIVE SOMETHING AS EXTERNAL** to attribute something to causes in the outside world **3.** PSYCHOL **ATTRIBUTE FEELINGS TO OUTSIDE CAUSES** to attribute emotions or inner conflicts to outside causes, sources, or surroundings —**ex·ter·nal·i·za·tion** /ik stùrn'li záysh'n/ *n*

ex·ter·nal res·pi·ra·tion *n* the exchange of gases between an organism's respiratory system, e.g., the lungs in vertebrates, and the outside environment

ex·terne *n* HEALTH SERVICES another spelling of **extern**

ex·ter·o·cep·tor /ékstərō séptər/ *n* a body part or sensory organ that is able to receive outside stimuli, e.g., the eye, ear, or any of the nerve endings in the skin [Early 20C. < Latin *exter* "outward, on the outside" + RECEPTOR] —**ex·ter·o·cep·tive** *adj*

ex·ter·ri·to·ri·al *adj* POL, LAW same as **extraterritorial**

ex·tinct /ik stíngkt/ *adj* **1. HAVING NO LIVING MEMBERS** having no members of the species or family in existence, as is the case with many organisms known only from fossils **2. NO LONGER IN EXISTENCE** having died out or ceased to exist ○ *relics of extinct and forgotten civilizations* **3.** GEOL **NO LONGER ERUPTING** describes a volcano that is no longer active or likely to erupt **4.** SOC SCI, LAW **NOT NOW VALID** no longer valid or practiced ○ *This custom has for many years been almost extinct.* **5. EXTINGUISHED** extinguished, quenched, or no longer burning [15C. < Latin *exstinct-*, past participle of *exstinguere* (see EXTINGUISH)]

SYNONYMS See ***dead.***

ex·tinc·tion /ik stíngksh'n/ *n* **1. FACT OF BECOMING EXTINCT** the gradual process by which a group of related organisms dies out **2. OBSOLESCENCE** the process or fact of disappearing completely from use ○ *"Dominant languages and dialects spread widely, and lead to the gradual extinction of other tongues."* (Charles Darwin, *The Descent of Man;* 1871) **3.** GEOL **PROCESS OF BECOMING INACTIVE** the permanent ceasing of eruptions in a volcano **4.** SOC SCI, LAW **STATE OF BEING NO LONGER VALID** the state of no longer being valid or practiced, or the process of ceasing to be valid or practiced **5. DESTRUCTION OF SOMEBODY OR SOMETHING** the destruction or killing off of somebody or something ○ *the extinction of self and ego through meditation* **6.** PHYS, ASTRON **LOWERING OF RADIATION INTENSITY** the reduction of radiation intensity because of absorption or scattering as it passes through matter. This effect is observed in the reduction in the intensity of electromagnetic radiation reaching Earth from astronomical objects because of the interference of interstellar gas and dust. **7.** PSYCHOL **REDUCTION IN RESPONSE** the decreasing or dying out of a behavioral response created by conditioning because of a lack of reinforcement —**ex·tinc·tive** *adj*

ex·tin·guish /ik stíng gwish/ (**-guished, -guish·ing, -guish·es**) *vt* **1. PUT OUT FIRE OR LIGHT** to put out something that is burning or giving off light ○ *The last of the oil-well fires was finally extinguished.* **2. END SOMETHING** to take away or bring to an end something such as a hope, feeling, custom, or practice ○ *As the days went by, hope for more survivors was extinguished.* **3. DESTROY SOMEBODY OR SOMETHING** to kill or destroy somebody or something completely ○ *They intended to extinguish the enemy by force of numbers.* **4. OUTSHINE** to outshine or eclipse somebody or something by having greater brilliance ○ *beauty that extinguishes all others by comparison* **5.** LAW **PAY DEBT** to pay off a debt **6.** LAW **MAKE SOMETHING INVALID** to make something no longer valid or applicable **7.** PSYCHOL **DECREASE RESPONSE** to cause a decrease in a behavioral response created by conditioning because of a lack of reinforcement [Early 16C. < Latin *exstinguere* "quench completely" < *stinguere* "quench, prick"] —**ex·tin·guish·a·ble** *adj* —**ex·tin·guish·ment** *n*

ex·tin·guish·er /ik stíng gwishər/ *n* **1.** EMERGENCIES same as **fire extinguisher 2.** somebody or something that puts an end to something else or eliminates its effects

ex·tir·pate /ékstər pàyt/ (**-pat·ed, -pat·ing, -pates**) *vt* **1.** to completely get rid of, kill off, or destroy somebody or something considered undesirable (*formal*) **2.** to remove something surgically [Mid-16C. < Latin *ex(s)tirpat-*, past participle of *ex(s)tirpare* "root out" < *stirps* "stem, root"] —**ex·tir·pa·tion** /èkstər páysh'n/ *n* —**ex·tir·pa·tive** /ékstər pàytiv/ *adj* —**ex·tir·pa·tor** *n*

ex·tol /ik stṓl/ (**-tolled, -tol·ling, -tols**), **ex·toll** (**-tolled, -tol·ling, -tolls**) *vt* to praise somebody or something with great enthusiasm and admiration [Early 16C. < Latin *extollere* "raise up" < *tollere* "raise"] —**ex·tol·ler** *n* —**ex·tol·ment** *n*

ex·tort /ik stáwrt/ (**-tort·ed, -tort·ing, -torts**) *vt* to obtain something such as money or information from somebody by using force, threats, or other unacceptable methods [15C. < Latin *extort-*, past participle of *extorquere* "twist out" < *torquere* "to twist"] —**ex·tort·er** *n* —**ex·tor·tive** *adj*

ex·tor·tion /ik stáwrsh'n/ *n* **1.** LAW **OBTAINING SOMETHING BY ILLEGAL THREATS** the crime of obtaining something such as money or information from somebody by using force, threats, or other unacceptable methods **2. CHARGING OF UNFAIRLY HIGH PRICES** the charging of an excessive amount of money for something (*informal*) **3. GETTING SOMETHING BY FORCE** the acquisition of something through the use of force or threats —**ex·tor·tion·ar·y** *adj* —**ex·tor·tion·er** *n* —**ex·tor·tion·ist** *n*

ex·tor·tion·ate /ik stáwrsh'nət/ *adj* **1.** highly excessive, especially in price **2.** involving or using extortion —**ex·tor·tion·ate·ly** *adv*

ex·tra /ékstrə/ *adj* **1. MORE THAN USUAL** added to, or over and above, the usual, original, or necessary amount ○ *Take extra precautions when traveling in bad weather.* **2. MORE AND BETTER** greater in degree and of better quality than is normal **3. CHARGED FOR IN ADDITION** charged for in addition to the basic cost ○ *You get one free drink with the meal; further drinks are extra.* ■ *adv* **EXCEPTIONALLY** to a greater extent than is usual or expected ○ *Be extra careful at that crossing.* ■ *pron* **MORE** more than the usual amount or price ○ *The hotel charges extra for cable TV.* ■ *n* **1. SOMETHING CHARGED FOR IN ADDITION** something for which an additional charge is made, or the additional charge itself ○ *Make sure there are no hidden extras.* **2. SOMETHING ADDITIONAL** something additional or unexpected ○ *The remaining items are optional extras.* **3.** MOVIES **NONSPEAKING MOVIE ACTOR** somebody employed in a minor, usually nonspeaking, part in a movie, e.g., in a crowd scene **4.** MEDIA **SPECIAL EDITION OF NEWS-**

PAPER a special edition of a newspaper or magazine, often reporting later news or concentrating on a particular subject ○ *a sports extra* **5.** *US* EXCELLENT THING something of exceptionally high quality [Mid-17C. Probably shortening of EXTRAORDINARY]

extra-, extro- *prefix* beyond or outside something ○ *extraterrestrial* ○ *extracurricular* [< Latin *extra* "outside, beyond" < *exter* "outer"]

ex·tra-base hit *n* in baseball, a hit that allows the batter to take more than one base, scoring a double, triple, or home run

ex·tra·cel·lu·lar /èkstrə séllyələr/ *adj* situated or happening outside a cell or cells —**ex·tra·cel·lu·lar·ly** *adv*

ex·tra·chro·mo·so·mal /èkstrə krōmə sṓm'l/ *adj* describes an inheritance of characteristics that is controlled by factors not carried on chromosomes

ex·tra·cor·po·re·al /èkstrə kawr páwree əl/ *adj* situated or happening outside the body —**ex·tra·cor·po·re·al·ly** *adv*

ex·tra·cra·ni·al /èkstrə kráynee əl/ *adj* situated or happening outside the skull

ex·tract *vt* /ik strákt/ (**-tract·ed, -tract·ing, -tracts**) **1.** PULL SOMETHING OUT to pull something out, often using force ○ *have a tooth extracted* **2.** OBTAIN SOMETHING FROM SOURCE to obtain something from a source, usually by separating it out from other material ○ *a few snippets of information that I managed to extract from the conversation* **3.** GET SOMETHING BY FORCE to obtain something from somebody who is unwilling to give it, often by using force or threats ○ *extracted a confession from him* **4.** COPY PASSAGE OF TEXT to copy or remove a passage from a text ○ *This scene is extracted from the author's memoirs.* **5.** DERIVE PLEASURE FROM SOMETHING to obtain pleasure or enjoyment from something **6.** CHEM, INDUST TAKE SOMETHING OUT OF COMPOUND to obtain a substance from a compound, in solid, liquid, or gas form, by using an industrial or chemical process **7.** MATH FIND ROOT OF NUMBER to calculate the value of the root, e.g., the square root or cube root, of a number ■ *n* /ék stràkt/ **1.** PASSAGE FROM TEXT OR MOVIE a passage taken from a publication, movie, or play ○ *an extract from her forthcoming book* **2.** PURIFIED SUBSTANCE a concentrated or purified substance obtained by first using a solvent to dissolve this substance when present in a mixture and then evaporating the solvent ○ *vanilla extract* **3.** CHEM, INDUST SUBSTANCE SEPARATED FROM COMPOUND a substance obtained from a compound by an industrial or chemical process ○ *mineral extracts* **4.** PHARM CONCENTRATED SOLUTION an alcohol solution of the pharmaceutically active agents in a natural product [15C. < Latin *extract-*, past participle of *extrahere* "pull out" < *trahere* "pull"] —**ex·tract·a·ble** *adj*

ex·trac·tion /ik strákshʼn/ *n* **1.** TAKING OUT OF SOMETHING the process of extracting something or of being extracted **2.** SOMETHING EXTRACTED something that has been extracted **3.** DENT REMOVAL OF TOOTH the removal of a tooth or teeth **4.** CHEM SEPARATION OF SUBSTANCES the separation of a substance from a mixture by dissolving one or more of the components in a solvent **5.** ETHNIC ORIGIN the original nationality of somebody's ancestors ○ *of Spanish extraction*

ex·trac·tive /ik stráktiv/ *adj* **1.** EXTRACTABLE capable of being extracted **2.** USED IN EXTRACTING used in the process of extraction **3.** OBTAINED BY EXTRACTION obtained as a result of extraction ■ *n* **1.** SOMETHING EXTRACTABLE something that can be extracted **2.** CHEM PART OF CHEMICAL EXTRACT the insoluble part of a chemical extract —**ex·trac·tive·ly** *adv*

ex·tract·or /ik stráktər/ *n* **1.** a device that removes a liquid from a solid, e.g., the juice out of a fruit **2.** the part of a firearm that removes spent cartridges from the chamber

ex·tra·cur·ric·u·lar /èkstrə kə ríkyələr/ *adj* **1.** EDUC OUTSIDE NORMAL CURRICULUM done or happening outside the normal curriculum of a school, college, or university **2.** OUTSIDE SOMEBODY'S NORMAL DUTIES not part of the normal duties of a job or profession **3.** WITH SOMEBODY OTHER THAN PARTNER involving somebody other than a spouse or partner (*informal*)

ex·tra·dit·a·ble /ékstrə dītəb'l/ *adj* **1.** describes a crime for which somebody may be extradited **2.** liable to be extradited for a crime

ex·tra·dite /ékstrə dīt/ (**-dit·ed, -dit·ing, -dites**) *vt* to return somebody accused of a crime by a different legal authority to that authority for trial or punishment [Mid-19C. Back-formation < EXTRADITION]

ex·tra·di·tion /èkstrə dísh'n/ *n* the process of returning somebody accused of a crime by a different legal authority to that authority for trial or punishment [Mid-19C. < French < Latin *ex-* "out" + *tradition-* "deliverance" (see TRADITION)]

ex·tra·dos /ékstrə dòss, -dòss/ (*plural* **-dos** /-dōz/ or **-dos·es**) *n* the outer curve of an arch [Late 18C. < French < Latin *extra* "outside" + French *dos* "back"]

ex·tra·em·bry·o·nic mem·brane /èkstrə èmbree onik-/ *n* a membrane derived from embryonic tissue that lies outside the embryo, e.g., the yolk sac, amnion, and chorion

ex·tra·ga·lac·tic /èkstrə gə láktik/ *adj* existing, originating, or happening outside the Milky Way, the galaxy that contains our solar system

ex·tra·ju·di·cial /èkstrə joo dísh'l/ *adj* **1.** happening or originating outside the normal course of legal proceedings **2.** outside the jurisdiction of a court —**ex·tra·ju·di·cial·ly** *adv*

ex·tra·le·gal /èkstrə leég'l/ *adj* not permitted by or subject to the law —**ex·tra·le·gal·ly** *adv*

ex·tra·lim·i·tal /èkstrə límmit'l/ *adj* describes a species or group of organisms found outside a given area, e.g., a population of bears outside a national park

ex·tra·mar·i·tal /èkstrə márrit'l/ *adj* involving sexual relations with somebody other than a marriage partner

ex·tra·mun·dane /èkstrə mun dáyn, -mún dàyn/ *adj* not belonging to the physical world [Mid-17C. < late Latin *extramundanus* < *extra mundum* "outside the world or universe"]

ex·tra·mu·ral /èkstrə myóorəl/ *adj* **1.** outside or additional to the usual courses of study at a university, college, or other educational institution, though usually connected with them **2.** outside the walls or boundaries of something such as a castle, town, or organization [Mid-19C. < Latin *extra muros* "outside the walls"]

ex·tra·ne·ous /ik stráynee əss/ *adj* **1.** NOT RELEVANT not relevant or applicable **2.** NOT ESSENTIAL not essential or important **3.** COMING FROM OUTSIDE existing or coming from outside [Mid-17C. < Latin *extraneus* "foreign, strange" < *extra* (see EXTRA-)] —**ex·tra·ne·ous·ly** *adv* —**ex·tra·ne·ous·ness** *n*

ex·tra·net /ékstrə nèt/ *n* an extension of the intranet of a company or organization, giving authorized outsiders controlled access to the intranet

ex·tra·nu·cle·ar /èkstrə nóoklee ər/ *adj* **1.** existing in or affecting parts of a cell outside the nucleus **2.** existing, happening, or originating outside the nucleus of an atom

ex·tra·or·di·naire /èkstrə awrd'n ér, ik stràwd'n-/ *adj* excellent or outstanding (*used after nouns*) ○ *a piano player extraordinaire* [Mid-20C. Via French < Latin *extraordinarius* (see EXTRAORDINARY)]

ex·traor·di·nar·y /ik stráwrd'n èrree, èkstrə áwrd'n-/ *adj* **1.** UNUSUALLY EXCELLENT OR STRANGE very unusual and deserving attention and comment because of being wonderful, excellent, strange, or shocking ○ *Her mathematical abilities are extraordinary for a ten-year-old.* **2.** ADDITIONAL additional and having a special purpose ○ *an extraordinary meeting* **3.** EMPLOYED FOR SPECIAL PURPOSE employed for a special purpose or to do additional work (*used after nouns*) ○ *ambassador extraordinary* **4.** ADDITIONAL AND GREATER additional to and going beyond the ordinary or established scope of something ○ *The president used his extraordinary powers to introduce major economic reform.* [15C. < Latin *extraordinarius* < *extra ordinem* "out of order, exceptionally"] —**ex·traor·di·nar·i·ly** /ik stràwrd'n érrəlee, èkstrə awrd'n-/ *adv* —**ex·traor·di·nar·i·ness** *n*

ex·traor·di·nar·y gen·er·al meet·ing *n* a meeting of a company or a formally constituted association, specially called by the board or a group of stockholders or members, to discuss a particular, and usually important, piece of business

ex·tra point *n* in football, a point scored by kicking the field goal awarded after a touchdown

ex·trap·o·late /ik stráppə làyt/ (**-lat·ed, -lat·ing, -lates**) *v* **1.** *vti* to use known facts as the starting point from which to draw inferences or conclusions about something unknown ○ *We try to avoid extrapolating a flu epidemic from mere anecdotal evidence.* **2.** *vt* to estimate a value that falls outside a range of known values, e.g., by extending a curve on a graph [Mid-19C. < EXTRA- + INTERPOLATE] —**ex·trap·o·la·tion** /ik stràppə láysh'n/ *n* —**ex·trap·o·la·tive** /-làytiv/ *adj* —**ex·trap·o·la·tor** *n*

ex·tra·sen·so·ry /èkstrə sénssəree/ *adj* relating to or involving powers of perception other than the normal five senses

ex·tra·sen·so·ry per·cep·tion *n* the apparent ability of some people to become aware of things by means other than the normal senses, e.g., through clairvoyance or telepathy

ex·tra·so·lar /èkstrə sṓlər/ *adj* existing in or relating to space outside our solar system

ex·tra·ter·res·tri·al /èkstrə tə réstree əl/ *adj* existing or coming from somewhere outside Earth and its atmosphere ■ *n* a living being that comes from outside Earth, especially in science fiction

ex·tra·ter·ri·to·ri·al /èkstrə teri táwree əl/, **ex·ter·ri·to·ri·al** /èks teri-/ *adj* **1.** situated or coming from outside a country's territorial boundary **2.** LAW, POL relating to or involving exemption from the legal jurisdiction of a country of residence —**ex·tra·ter·ri·to·ri·al·ly** *adv*

ex·tra·ter·ri·to·ri·al·i·ty /èkstrə tèrrə tawree állətee/ *n* exemption from the legal jurisdiction of a country of residence, granted to people such as foreign diplomats

ex·tra time *n UK* SPORTS same as **overtime** *n* (sense 3)

ex·tra·u·ter·ine /èkstrə yóotərin, -rīn/ *adj* occurring or situated outside the womb ○ *an extrauterine pregnancy*

ex·trav·a·gance /ik strávvəgənss/, **ex·trav·a·gan·cy** /-gənssee/ (*plural* **-cies**) *n* **1.** IMMODERATE SPENDING excessive or wasteful spending of money ○ *was condemned to poverty by their father's extravagance* **2.** EXPENSIVE THING something that is expensive or wasteful ○ *A car like that is an extravagance in today's economic climate.* **3.** EXCESSIVENESS the exaggerated, excessive, or extremely flamboyant nature of something, e.g., a wild unreasonableness in somebody's speech or behavior

ex·trav·a·gant /ik strávvəgənt/ *adj* **1.** SPENDING TOO MUCH characterized by excessive or wasteful spending ○ *was criticized for her extravagant lifestyle* **2.** UNREASONABLY HIGH IN PRICE unreasonably high in price or cost **3.** BEYOND WHAT IS REASONABLE exaggerated or unreasonable ○ *an extravagant claim* **4.** FLAMBOYANT profusely or exaggeratedly decorated, decorative, or showy **5.** ABUNDANT existing or produced in quantity ○ *extravagant praise* [14C. < medieval Latin < Latin *extra* "outside" + *vagari* "wander"] —**ex·trav·a·gant·ly** *adv*

ex·trav·a·gan·za /ik stràvvə gánzə/ *n* **1.** a lavish and spectacular entertainment **2.** any spectacular or elaborate display [Mid-18C. < Italian *estravaganza* "peculiar behavior" < *estravagante* "extravagant"]

~~extravagent~~ incorrect spelling of **extravagant**

ex·trav·a·sate /ik strávvə sàyt/ (**-sat·ed, -sat·ing, -sates**) *vti* to leak, or cause blood or other fluid to leak, from a vessel into surrounding tissue as a result of injury, burns, or inflammation [Mid-17C. < EXTRA- + Latin *vas* "vessel"] —**ex·trav·a·sa·tion** /ik stràvvə sáysh'n/ *n*

ex·tra·vas·cu·lar /èkstrə váskyələr/ *adj* not contained in the body's blood or lymph vessels

ex·tra·ve·hic·u·lar ac·tiv·i·ty /èkstrə vi híkyələr-/ *n* activity undertaken by an astronaut outside the spacecraft during a mission, e.g., a repair to the craft, or an experiment on the surface of the Moon

ex·tra·ver·sion *n* PSYCHOL, MED same as **extroversion**

ex·tra·vert *n*, *adj* PSYCHOL same as **extrovert**

ex·tra-vir·gin ol·ive oil *n* the highest quality of olive oil, made from the first cold pressing of ripe olives

ex·treme /ik streém/ *adj* **1.** GREAT OR INTENSE highest in intensity or degree ○ *will withstand extreme pressure* **2.** NOT REASONABLE going far beyond what is reasonable, moderate, or normal ○ *an extreme reaction* ○ *the extreme right wing of the party* **3.** FARTHEST OUT farthest out, especially from the center ○ *the extreme north of the country* **4.** SEVERE very strict or severe ○ *extreme and costly security measures* **5.** LEISURE,

SPORTS **SENSATION-SEEKING** describes sports or leisure activities in which participants actively seek out dangerous or even life-threatening experiences ○ *extreme skiing* ■ *n* **1. FURTHEST LIMIT** the furthest limit or highest degree of something ○ *the extreme of bad taste* **2. END OF SCALE** something or somebody that represents each of the two ends of a scale or range, e.g., the highest or lowest degree of something, or a quality and its polar opposite ○ *alternated between the extremes of hope and despair* **3. FIRST OR LAST TERM** the first or last term in a mathematical proportion or series ■ **ex·tremes** *npl* **DRASTIC MEASURES** drastic or unreasonable measures ○ *The authorities have been driven to extremes by the widespread popular unrest.* [15C. Via French < Latin *extremus* "farthest, last" < *ex* "out"] —**ex·treme·ness** *n*

ex·treme·ly /ik stréemlee/ *adv* to a very high degree ○ *She plays the violin extremely well.*

ex·treme·ly high fre·quen·cy *n* a radio frequency in the range between 30,000 and 300,000 megahertz

ex·treme·ly low fre·quen·cy *n* a radio frequency below 30 hertz

ex·treme unc·tion *n* the Roman Catholic sacrament of anointing the sick (*dated*)

ex·trem·ism /ik stréem ìzzəm/ *n* the holding of extreme political or religious views or the taking of extreme actions on the basis of those views —**ex·trem·ist** *n, adj*

ex·trem·i·ty /ik strémmətee/ *n* (*plural* **-ties**) **1. HAND OR FOOT** a limb of a person or animal, or the part of a limb that is farthest from the body, especially somebody's hand or foot (*often used in the plural*) **2. FARTHEST POINT** a point that is the farthest out, especially from the center ○ *the southernmost extremity of the continent* **3. HIGHEST DEGREE** the highest degree or greatest intensity of something ○ *in the extremity of her grief* **4. DANGER** a situation or state of great danger or distress ○ *They prayed for help in their extremity.* ■ **ex·trem·i·ties** *npl* **DRASTIC MEASURES** drastic or unreasonable measures (*formal*)

~~**extremly**~~ incorrect spelling of **extremely**

ex·trem·o·phile /ik stréem ə fìl/ *n* an organism, especially a microorganism, that thrives in climatic or environmental extremes such as the intense heat of a boiling sulfur pool or the intense cold of Arctic permafrost

ex·tri·cate /ékstri kàyt/ (**-cat·ed, -cat·ing, -cates**) *vt* to release somebody or something with difficulty from a physical constraint or an unpleasant or complicated situation ○ *was unable to extricate himself from the contract* [Early 17C. < Latin *extricat-*, past participle of *extricare* "remove from perplexities" < *tricae* "perplexities"] —**ex·tri·ca·ble** /ékstrikəb'l, ik stríkəb'l/ *adj* —**ex·tri·ca·tion** /ékstri káysh'n/ *n*

ex·trin·sic /ik strínssik, -zik/ *adj* **1.** not an essential part of something ○ *It's a good point, but extrinsic to the argument.* **2.** coming or operating from outside something ○ *extrinsic influences* [Mid-16C. < late Latin *extrinsecus* "outer" < Latin *exter* "external" + adverb-forming ending *-im* + *secus* "alongside of"] —**ex·trin·si·cal·ly** *adv*

extro- *prefix* same as **extra-** [Alteration, after INTRO-]

~~**extrordinary**~~ incorrect spelling of **extraordinary**

ex·trorse /ék stràwrss, ik stráwrss/ *adj* used to describe a plant part that faces or turns outward or away from a center [Mid-19C. < late Latin *extrorsus* "in an outward direction" < Latin *extra* "outside" + *versus* "toward," past participle of *vertere* "to turn"]

ex·tro·ver·sion /ékstrə vùrzh'n, èkstrə vúrzh'n/, **ex·tra·ver·sion** *n* **1.** interest in and involvement with people and things outside the self **2.** the turning inside out of an organ or other body part, especially the womb [Mid-17C. < EXTRO- + Latin *version-* "turning" < *vertere* "to turn"] —**ex·tro·ver·sive** *adj* —**ex·tro·ver·sive·ly** *adv*

ex·tro·vert /ékstrə vùrt/, **ex·tra·vert** *n* **1.** somebody who is sociable and self-confident **2.** somebody whose interests are directed outside the self [Early 20C. < EXTRO- + Latin *vertere* "to turn"] —**ex·tro·vert** *adj* —**ex·tro·vert·ed** *adj*

ex·trude /ik stróod/ (**-trud·ed, -trud·ing, -trudes**) *vt* **1.** to force or squeeze something out **2.** to make something by forcing a semisoft material such as plastic or molten metal through a specially shaped mold or nozzle [Mid-16C. < Latin *extrudere* "thrust out" < *trudere* "to thrust"] —**ex·trud·a·ble** *adj*

ex·tru·sion /ik stróozh'n/ *n* **1.** INDUST **SOMETHING FORMED BY BEING EXTRUDED** something formed by forcing semisoft material through a specially shaped mold or nozzle **2.** INDUST **PROCESS OF EXTRUDING** the process or an instance of making something by forcing semisoft material through a specially shaped mold or nozzle **3.** GEOL **IGNEOUS ROCK** an igneous rock formed by the emission of molten material (**magma**) through cracks in the Earth's surface where it forms a lava flow **4.** GEOL **MOVEMENT OF MOLTEN ROCK** the movement of molten material (**magma**) from a volcano or through cracks in the Earth's surface to form solidified igneous rock [Mid-16C. < medieval Latin *extrusion-* < Latin *extrudere* (see EXTRUDE)]

ex·tru·sive /ik stróossiv/ *adj* describes rock formed from molten material (**magma**) that has flowed out of cracks in the Earth's surface

ex·u·ber·ant /ig zóobərənt/ *adj* **1. FULL OF ENTHUSIASM** full of happy high spirits and vitality **2. ABUNDANT** growing in great abundance or profusion **3. LAVISH** lavish or elaborate, often to the point of being excessive [15C. Via French < Latin *exuberant-*, present participle of *exuberare* "be very fruitful" < *uberare* "be fruitful" < *uber* "fertile"] —**ex·u·ber·ance** *n* —**ex·u·ber·ant·ly** *adv*

ex·u·date /éksyə dàyt/ *n* a substance such as sweat or a cellular waste product that is exuded from a cell or organ

ex·u·da·tion /èksyə dáysh'n/ *n* **1.** the release of a substance through pores or a surface cut, e.g., the release of sweat from the body or resin from a tree **2.** BIOL same as **exudate** —**ex·u·da·tive** /éksyə dàytiv/ *adj*

ex·ude /ig zóod/ (**-ud·ed, -ud·ing, -udes**) *v* **1.** *vt* to communicate a particular quality or feeling in abundance and very clearly, usually through general behavior and body language ○ *a voice that exuded confidence* **2.** *vti* to release something such as a liquid or an odor slowly from a gland, pore, membrane, or cut, or ooze out slowly [Late 16C. < Latin *ex(s)udare* "ooze out like sweat" < *sudare* "to sweat"]

ex·ult /ig zúlt/ (**-ult·ed, -ult·ing, -ults**) *vi* **1.** to be extremely happy or joyful about something ○ *exulted in his newfound freedom* **2.** to be very happy or triumphant about something unpleasant that happens to somebody else ○ *The victors exulted over their enemies' annihilation.* [Late 16C. Via French *exulter* < Latin *exsultare* "keep leaping up" < *exsalire* "leap out" < *salire* "leap"] —**ex·ul·ta·tion** /èksəl táysh'n, ègzəl-/ *n* —**ex·ult·ing·ly** *adv*

ex·ul·tant /ig zúltənt/ *adj* extremely happy, joyful, or triumphant ○ *an exultant roar from the crowd* —**ex·ul·tant·ly** *adv*

ex·urb /ék sùrb/ *n* a prosperous residential area outside a city, beyond the suburbs [Mid-20C. Back-formation < *exurban* (< Latin *ex* "out of" + *urbs* "city"), after SUBURB] —**ex·ur·ban** /ek súrbən/ *adj* —**ex·ur·ban·ite** *n*

ex·ur·bi·a /ek súrbee ə, eg zúr-/ *n* the prosperous residential area beyond the suburbs of a city [Mid-20C. After SUBURBIA]

ex·u·vi·ae /ig zóovee èe/ *npl* skins, shells, or other body coverings cast off by animals [Mid-17C. < Latin, "things cast off" < *exuere* "divest yourself of"] —**ex·u·vi·al** *adj*

-ey *suffix* same as **-y**[1] [Variant]

ey·as /ī əss/ (*plural* **-as·es** or **-as·ses**), **ey·ass** *n* a young hawk or falcon, especially one bred for falconry [15C. Alteration of obsolete *nias* < French *niais* "bird taken from the nest" < Latin *nidus* "nest"]

Eyck /īk/, **Jan van** (1390?–1441) Flemish painter. He painted in vivid oil colors in a naturalistic style and is regarded as the greatest Flemish artist of the 15th century.

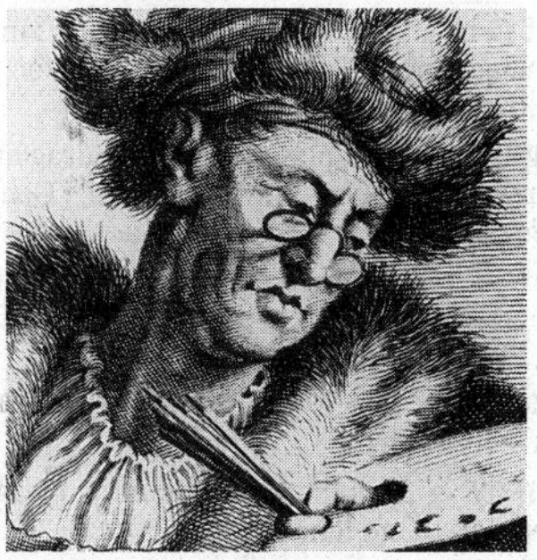

Jan van Eyck: portrait engraving by Joachim von Sandrart

eye /ī/ *n* **1. ORGAN OF VISION** the organ of sight or light sensitivity in vertebrates, usually occurring in pairs. The eye is an approximately spherical organ with light-sensitive rod and cone cells in the retina, which is responsible for converting light into impulses that are transmitted to the brain for interpretation. **2. VISIBLE AREA OF EYE** the externally visible part of the eye and the area of face around it, including the orbit, eyelid, and eyelashes **3. POWER OF SIGHT** the ability to see (*often used in the plural*) ○

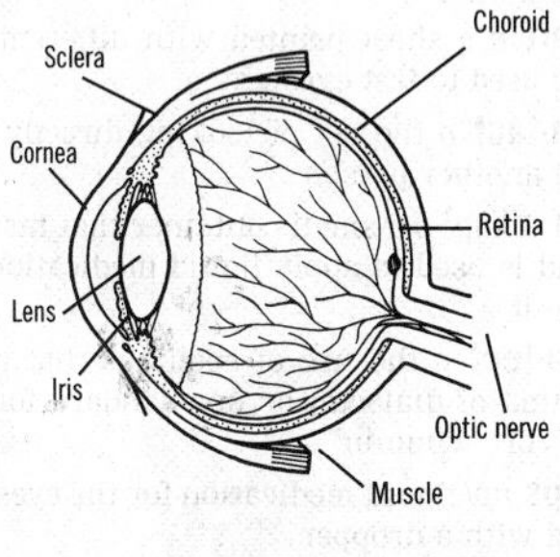

eye

If my eyes get any worse I'll have to wear glasses. **4. ATTENTION** somebody's attention or gaze ○ *He took his eye off the prisoners at the wrong moment.* **5. EXPRESSION** a look, or the particular facial expression of somebody who is looking at something ○ *She looked me over with a cold eye.* **6. APPRECIATION OF SOMETHING** an ability to recognize and appreciate something ○ *He's got a good eye for talent.* **7. OPINION** a point of view or way of thinking ○ *He can do no wrong in her eyes.* **8. NEW SHOOT ON POTATO** a dark round patch on a potato tuber, from which a new shoot grows **9. HOLE IN NEEDLE** a hole in the top of a needle for passing a thread through **10.** METEOROL **CENTER OF STORM** a calm area at the center of a storm **11.** CLOTHING **LOOP PART OF FASTENER** a loop into which a small hook fits, used as a means of fastening two parts of a garment together **12.** ZOOL same as **eyespot** (sense 2) **13.** FOOD **TASTY CUT OF MEAT** a choice central cut of meat ■ *vt* (**eyed, eye·ing** or **ey·ing, eyes**) **LOOK AT SOMETHING** to look at something or somebody inquisitively ○ *She quickly eyed the building up and down.* [Old English *ēage* < Indo-European] —**eyed** *adj* —**eye·less** *adj* ◇ **close** *or* **shut your eyes to something** to ignore or overlook something obvious ◇ **cry your eyes out** to cry bitterly ◇ **easy on the eye** pleasant to look at (*informal*) ◇ **give somebody the eye** to look at somebody in a way that signals sexual interest ◇ **have eyes in the back of your head** to be aware of what is happening when unable to see it (*informal; usually used in negative statements*) ◇ **keep an eye on somebody** *or* **something 1.** to watch somebody or something closely **2.** to take care of somebody or something, especially for a short time ◇ **keep your eye on the ball** to pay close attention to the matter in hand ◇ **see eye to eye (with somebody)** to have a similar outlook or viewpoint to somebody else ◇ **turn a blind eye (to something)** to pretend not to be aware of something ◇ **with an eye to something** having something as a purpose or objective ◇ **with your eyes (wide) open** fully aware of the implications of what you are doing

eye·ball /ī bàwl/ *n* **ROUND MASS OF EYE** the round mass of the eye within its bony socket ■ **eye·balls** *npl* **WEBSITE VISITORS** users of the Internet who visit a particular website or use a particular product (*slang*) ○ *sites competing for eyeballs* ■ *vt* (**-balled, -ball·ing, -balls**) **STARE AT SOMEBODY** to stare at somebody or something intently (*informal*)

eye bank *n* a place where human corneas taken from people who have recently died are stored for use in corneal transplants

eye·bath /ī bàth/ *n UK* MED same as **eyecup**

eye·bolt /ī bòlt/ *n* a bolt with an eye or ring at the end instead of the usual head, used for pulling, lifting, or fastening

eye·bright /ī brīt/ *n* a plant of the snapdragon family. Flowers: white and purple, small. Genus: *Euphrasia.* [Because formerly used for treating eye diseases]

eye·brow /ī bròw/ *n* **1.** the arched line of hair above each eye socket **2.** the upper bony ridge of the eye socket. Technical name **supraorbital ridge**

eye·brow pen·cil *n* a soft cosmetic pencil used to darken the eyebrows

eye can·dy *n* **1.** something visually pleasing but intellectually undemanding (*slang*) **2.** ONLINE, COMPUT ornamental visual features on a computer monitor or a webpage

eye-catch·ing *adj* striking or unusual and so attracting people's attention easily —**eye-catch·er** *n* —**eye-catch·ing·ly** *adv*

eye chart *n* a sheet printed with different sizes of letters, used to test eyesight

eye con·tact *n* the act of looking directly into the eyes of another person

eye·cup /ī kùp/ *n* a small container that fits over the eye and is used to apply liquid medication to it or cleanse it

eye di·a·lect *n* the use of spellings that represent the sound of dialectal or nonstandard forms, e.g., "enuff" or "wimmin"

eye drops *npl* liquid medication for the eyes, usually applied with a dropper

eye·ful /ī fo͝ol/ *n* **1.** a long steady look at something or somebody (*informal*) ○ *Get an eyeful of this!* **2.** an offensive term for somebody or something that is very beautiful, especially a woman who has a pleasing appearance (*slang*)

eye·glass /ī glàss/ *n* **1.** a single framed lens for correcting defective vision, e.g., a monocle **2.** OPTICS same as **eyepiece** ■ **eye·glass·es** *npl* a pair of glasses (*formal*)

eye·hole /ī hòl/ *n* BUILDINGS same as **peephole** (sense 2)

eye·hook /ī ho͝ok/ *n* a hook that is fixed to a ring at the end of a rope or chain

eye·lash /ī làsh/ *n* a short stiff hair that grows in a row from the edge of the eyelid (*often used in the plural*)

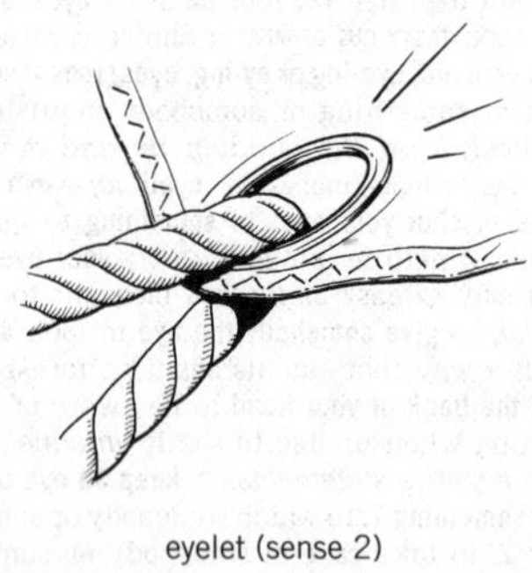

eyelet (sense 2)

eye·let /īlət/ *n* **1.** HOLE FOR CORD a small hole, especially one made in clothing, for a lace or cord to be passed through **2.** METAL REINFORCEMENT FOR HOLE a small ring of metal or stiff fabric fixed to a hole, especially one made in clothing, to strengthen its edges **3.** ORNAMENTED HOLE IN EMBROIDERY a small hole with ornamental stitched edges in embroidered fabric **4.** BUILDINGS same as **peephole** (sense 2) [14C. Anglicization of Old French *oillet* "little eye" < *oil* "eye" < Latin *oculus*]

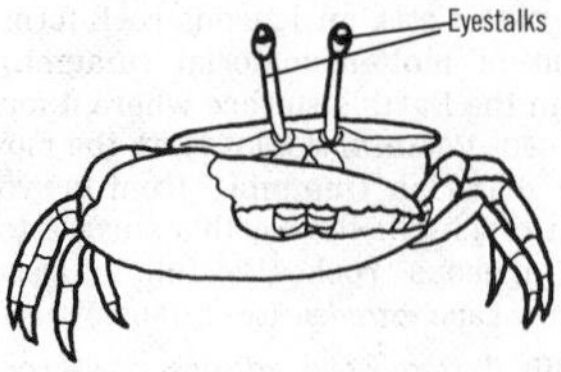

eyestalk

eye lens *n* a lens in the eyepiece of an optical instrument such as a microscope or pair of binoculars

eye·lid /ī lìd/ *n* a protective fold of skin and muscle that can be closed to cover the front of the eyeball ◇ **not bat an eyelid** to show no sign of emotion, especially of surprise or distress

eye·lift /ī lìft/ *n* a surgical operation to improve the appearance of the area around the eyes, e.g., by removing wrinkles

eye·line /ī līn/ *n* the level of somebody's gaze when he or she is looking at something

eye·lin·er /ī līnər/ *n* a cosmetic worn along the edges of the eyelids to emphasize the eyes

eye-o·pen·er *n* (*informal*) **1.** a surprising or revealing experience or piece of information **2.** an alcoholic drink that is believed to help somebody to wake up, especially first thing in the morning —**eye-o·pen·ing** *adj*

eye patch *n* a covering worn over one eye to protect it or conceal it

eye·piece /ī peèss/ *n* the part of an optical instrument that holds the lens on the side the user looks through

eye-pop·ping *adj* so striking or unusual as to cause amazement (*informal*) ○ *eye-popping entertainment* —**eye-pop·per** *n*

eye rhyme *n* the use of words that, because they are similarly spelled, look as if they rhyme but are in fact pronounced differently, e.g., "bough" and "enough"

eye·shade /ī shàyd/ *n* a tinted or opaque visor worn around the head to protect the eyes from glare

eye shad·ow *n* a colored cosmetic for the area around the eyes, especially the eyelids

eye·shot /ī shòt/ *n* the range over which the eye can see

eye·sight /ī sīt/ *n* the power of sight

eye sock·et *n* either of the two bony recesses in the skull that contain the eyeballs

eyes-on·ly *adj* intended to be seen only by the person to whom it is addressed ○ *an eyes-only memo*

eye·sore /ī sàwr/ *n* an offensively ugly building or place

eye·spot /ī spòt/ *n* **1.** a small pigmented area or organelle that is sensitive to light, found in some algae and simple multicellular organisms, including some flatworms, and jellyfish **2.** a marking shaped like an eye, e.g., on the wings of some butterflies or on a peacock's tail

eye·stalk /ī stàwk/ *n* a flexible stalk with a compound eye at the tip, found in crustaceans and some mollusks

eye·strain /ī stràyn/ *n* tiredness or irritation in the eyes caused, e.g., by an uncorrected visual defect or by prolonged close work. It is not recognized as a medical condition by ophthalmologists.

eye·tooth /ī to͞oth/ (*plural* **-teeth** /-teèth/) *n* a canine tooth found on each side of the upper jaw [Because directly below the eye] ◇ **give your eyeteeth for something** to be prepared to do anything to be able to do or have something

eye·wash /ī wòsh, ī wàwsh/ *n* **1.** a liquid used to cleanse or soothe the eyes **2.** pretentious nonsense that is intended to flatter or deceive (*informal*) ○ *The official version is just so much eyewash.*

eye·wear /ī wèr/ *n* something worn over the eyes to protect them or correct sight, e.g., glasses, goggles, or contact lenses

eye·wit·ness /ī wìtnəss/ *n* somebody who saw and can give evidence about an event

ey·ra /érrə, áyrə/ *n* a jaguarundi in its reddish brown seasonal color phase [Early 17C. Via Spanish < Tupi-Guarani *(e)irára*]

Eyre, Lake /er/ largest salt lake in Australia, located in central South Australia. Area: 3,600 sq. mi./9,300 sq. km.

Eyre, Edward John (1815–1901) British explorer and colonial official. He completed the first overland trip from Sydney to Adelaide and led further expeditions into central and southwestern Australia.

Eyre Pen·in·su·la peninsula in southern South Australia that separates the Great Australian Bight from the Spencer Gulf. Area: 21,236 sq. mi./55,000 sq. km.

ey·rie /érree, eéree/ *n* BIRDS another spelling of **aerie**

ey·rir /áy reèr/ (*plural* **au·rar** /ō raàr/) *n* a subunit of Icelandic currency. See table at **currency** [Early 20C. < Icelandic, probably < Latin *aureus* "gold coin"]

Eys·enck /ī zèngk/, **H. J.** (1916–97) German-born British psychologist. He was an authority on personality studies and contributed to the controversial area of the links between genetics and intelligence. Full name **Eysenck, Hans Jürgen**

EZ /eézee/, **E-Z** *abbr* easy

Ez. *abbr* BIBLE Ezra

Ezek. *abbr* BIBLE Ezekiel

E·ze·ki·el /i zeékee əl/ *n* **1.** in the Bible, a Hebrew priest and prophet who lived in the 6th century B.C. As the Jews' spiritual leader during the Babylonian captivity, he foretold the creation of a Jewish nation. **2.** a book of the Bible that describes the Jews' exile in Babylon in the 6th century B.C., traditionally attributed to Ezekiel. It contains prophecies of the destruction and subsequent rebuilding of Jerusalem and Judah. See table at **Bible**

e-zine /eé zeèn/ *n* a website with contents and layout modeled on a print magazine [< *e(lectronic)* *(maga)zine*]

Ezr. *abbr* BIBLE Ezra

Ez·ra /ézzrə/ *n* **1.** in the Bible, a Hebrew high priest who lived in the 5th century B.C. He led the Jews back to Jerusalem from their exile in Babylon and founded a Jewish nation. **2.** a book of the Bible that describes the rebuilding of the Jewish state in Judah after the Babylonian captivity, traditionally attributed to Ezra. See table at **Bible**

Ff

f[1] /ef/ (*plural* **f's**), **F** (*plural* **F's** or **Fs**) *n* **1.** the sixth letter of the English alphabet, representing a consonant sound **2.** a written representation of the letter "f"

f[2] *symbol* **1.** MEASURE femto- **2.** OPTICS f-number **3.** PHYS focal length **4.** PHYS frequency (sense 4) **5.** MATH function **6.** used to refer to the sixth vertical row of squares from the left on a chessboard

F[1] *symbol* **1.** MEASURE farad **2.** MEASURE faraday (*usually italicized*) **3.** CHEM ELEM fluorine **4.** PHYS force (sense 9)

F[2] *abbr* **1.** MEASURE Fahrenheit **2.** false **3.** ELEC farad **4.** fathom **5.** COMMUNICATION fax (number) **6.** February **7.** EDUC Fellow **8.** female **9.** GRAM feminine **10.** METALL fine[1] *adj* (sense 12) **11.** PUBL folio **12.** MUSIC forte[2] *adv* (*used as a musical direction*) **13.** Friday

F[3] /ef/ (*plural* **F's** or **Fs**) *n* **1. "F"-SHAPED OBJECT** something shaped like a letter "F" **2. 4TH NOTE IN C MAJOR** the fourth note of a scale in C major **3. SOMETHING THAT PRODUCES F** a string, key, or pipe tuned to produce the note F **4. SCALE BEGINNING ON F** a scale or key that starts on the note F **5. WRITTEN SYMBOL FOR F** a graphic representation of the tone of F **6.** EDUC **"FAIL" GRADE** the sixth lowest grade in a series used to indicate a "fail" in grading a student's work

f. *abbr* **1.** MEASURE Fahrenheit **2.** folio **3.** following (page) **4.** SPORTS foul

F. *abbr* **1.** MEASURE Fahrenheit **2.** fathom **3.** February **4.** female **5.** GRAM feminine **6.** METALL fine[1] *adj* (sense 12) **7.** folio **8.** Friday

f/ *symbol* PHOTOGRAPHY f-number

F2F *abbr* face-to-face (*used in e-mails or text messages*)

F2T *abbr* free to talk (*used in e-mails or text messages*)

fa /faa/ *n* a syllable that represents the fourth note in a scale when singing solfeggio. In fixed solfeggio it represents the note F.

FA *abbr* **1.** MIL field artillery **2.** FIN financial adviser **3.** ARTS fine art **4.** SOCCER Football Association **5.** SHIPPING freight agent

F.A. *abbr* fine art

FAA *abbr* AVIAT Federal Aviation Administration

fab /fab/ *adj* same as **fabulous** (sense 3) (*informal*) ○ *It was a fab party!* [Mid-20C. Shortening]

AKG London

Peter Carl Fabergé: decorative jeweled egg (1901)

Fa·ber·gé /fàbbər zhāy/, **Peter Carl** (1846–1920) Russian goldsmith and jeweler. He designed and produced highly decorative gifts, notably gold and enamel Easter eggs, for European royalty. Born **Fabergé, Karl Gustavovich**

Fa·bi·an /fáybee ən/ *adj* **1. OF FABIAN SOCIETY** relating to, belonging to, or associated with the Fabian Society **2. CAUTIOUS** using delaying tactics and avoiding direct confrontation ■ *n* **MEMBER OF FABIAN SOCIETY** a member or supporter of the Fabian Society [Late 16C. < Latin *Fabianus* "of Fabius" (see Quintus FABIUS MAXIMUS)]

Fa·bi·an So·ci·e·ty *n* a political organization founded in Britain in 1884 with the objective of bringing about socialism by gradual and lawful means rather than by revolution

Fa·bi·us Max·i·mus /fáybee əss máksiməss/, **Quintus** (275?–203 B.C.) Roman general. As a result of his delaying tactics, Rome successfully countered the invasion of Hannibal during the Second Punic War. Full name **Fabius Maximus Verrucosus, Quintus.** Known as **Fabius Cunctator (the "Delayer")**

fa·ble /fáyb'l/ *n* **1. STORY THAT TEACHES LESSON** a short story with a moral, especially one in which the characters are animals **2. LEGEND** a story about supernatural, mythological, or legendary characters and events **3. FALSE ACCOUNT** a false or improbable account of something ○ *His version of events turned out to be a complete fable.* **4. MYTHS AND LEGENDS** myths and legends collectively ○ *a character out of fable* ■ *vt* (**-bled, -bling, -bles**) **TELL STORY** to tell a story or describe something in a fable (*archaic; usually passive*) [13C. Via Old French < Latin *fabula* "story" < *fari* "speak"] —**fa·bler** *n*

CULTURAL NOTE ***Fables***, a collection of stories attributed to the Greek writer Aesop (620?–560? B.C.). Many of the tales feature animals as characters and each one illustrates a specific moral. Traditionally said to be the origin of the literary fable (although earlier examples have been found), they were used by the ancient Greeks for both educational and rhetorical purposes.

fa·bled /fáyb'ld/ *adj* **1.** famous because of being described or recounted in legends ○ *Eldorado, the fabled city of gold* **2.** made-up or fictitious

fab·li·au /fáblee ō/ (*plural* **-aux** /-ōz/) *n* a comic and often bawdy story in verse, especially of a kind popular in 12th- and 13th-century France [Early 19C. < French < plural of Old French *fablel* "little story" < *fable* (see FABLE)]

Fab·ri·a·no ➧ **Gentile da Fabriano**

fab·ric /fábbrik/ *n* **1. CLOTH** any type of cloth made from woven, knitted, or felted thread or fibers **2. TEXTURE** the particular texture or quality of a kind of cloth **3. SUBSTANCE** the fundamental structure or makeup of something ○ *the fabric of her being* **4.** INDUST **STRUCTURAL MATERIAL** the material from which something is constructed, especially a building, or the physical structure of something ○ *damage to the fabric of the church* [15C. Via Old French < Latin *fabrica* "trade, manufactured object" < *faber* "worker in metal or stone, artisan"]

fab·ri·cate /fábbri kàyt/ (**-cat·ed, -cat·ing, -cates**) *vt* **1. INVENT FALSE STORY** to make up something that is not true ○ *accused the police of fabricating evidence* **2. CONSTRUCT SOMETHING** to make or construct something from different parts **3. FORGE SOMETHING** to falsify something such as a signature or document [15C. < Latin *fabricat-*, past participle of *fabricare* "make" < *fabrica* (see FABRIC)] —**fab·ri·ca·tor** *n*

fab·ri·ca·tion /fàbbri káysh'n/ *n* **1. DELIBERATELY UNTRUE ACCOUNT** an invented statement, story, or account devised with intent to deceive ○ *The story is a complete fabrication.* **2. CONCOCTING LIES** the act of making up or falsifying something ○ *his fabrication of documents* **3. ACT OF MAKING SOMETHING** the construction of something, or something that has been constructed or made

SYNONYMS See *lie*[2].

fab·ric soft·en·er, **fab·ric con·di·tion·er** *n* a substance added to laundry in a washing machine or drier to keep fabric soft

fab·u·late /fábbyə làyt/ (**-lated, -lat·ing, -lates**) *vt* to make a fictional account or representation of something [Early 17C. < Latin *fabulat-*, past participle of *fabulari* "talk" < *fabula* (see FABLE)]

fa·bu·lism /fábbyə lìzzəm/ *n* a lie (*formal*) ○ *"Perhaps the most consequential of [the reporter's] fabulisms came in a story last October..."* (Hendrik Hertzberg *The New Yorker*; May 26, 2003)

fab·u·list /fábbyəlist/ *n* **1.** a writer or reciter of fables **2.** a teller of fanciful stories

fab·u·lous /fábbyələss/ *adj* **1. AMAZING** amazingly or almost unbelievably great or impressive ○ *paid out fabulous sums of money* **2. TYPICAL OF FABLES** described in or typical of myths and legends **3. EXCELLENT** extremely good, pleasant, or enjoyable (*informal*) ○ *You look fabulous in that outfit!* [15C. Directly or via French < Latin *fabulosus* "celebrated in fable" < *fabula* (see FABLE)] —**fab·u·lous·ly** *adv* —**fab·u·lous·ness** *n*

fa·cade /fə saád/, **fa·çade** *n* **1.** the face of a building, especially the principal or front face showing its most prominent architectural features **2.** the way something or somebody appears on the surface, especially when that appearance is false or meant to deceive ○ *Her geniality is just a facade.* [Mid-17C. < French < *face* (see FACE), after Italian *facciata*]

face /fayss/ *n* **1. FRONT OF HEAD** the front of the human head, where the eyes, nose, mouth, chin, cheeks, and forehead are **2. PERSON** somebody who is being looked at (*informal*) ○ *It's nice to see so many familiar faces here today.* **3. COUNTENANCE** a facial expression or look of a particular kind ○ *an unhappy face* **4. UNPLEASANT FACIAL EXPRESSION** an expression in which the face is distorted, e.g., to show distaste or as a way of being rude to somebody ○ *The children made faces behind his back.* **5. WAY SOMETHING LOOKS** the general or outward appearance of something ○ *The arrival of the automobile changed the face of the modern city.* **6. FALSE APPEARANCE** an outward appearance that does not show the true nature of somebody's feelings or is intended to deceive ○ *Even after a third defeat he was still putting on a brave face.* **7. REPUTATION** personal prestige or reputation ○ *a way of enabling her to back down without losing face* **8. BOLDNESS** impudence or self-assurance (*informal*) ○ *How can he have the face to come back here after what he said?* **9. FACE MAKEUP** makeup applied to the face (*informal*) ○ *didn't even have time to put on my face* **10. SURFACE OF OBJECT** a plane surface or side of a three-dimensional object such as a geometric figure or gem ○ *A cube has six faces.* **11. OUTSIDE OF BUILDING** the exterior of the front or side of a large building ○ *the evening sun shining on the west face* **12. SIDE OF CLIFF** the steep exposed side of a cliff **13. SIDE OF MOUNTAIN** a steep mountainside, often named for the direction it faces ○ *the north face of Mt. Rainier* **14. WORKING AREA IN MINE** an area in a mine from which a mineral such as coal is being extracted **15. TYPEFACE** a typeface, or the area of a printing character that actually prints **16.** DIAL ON CLOCK OR INSTRUMENT the surface of a timepiece or similar instrument that displays the time or other data **17.** SIDE OF CARD SHOWING VALUE the side of a playing card that is marked with numbers and symbols **18.** WORKING SURFACE OF IMPLEMENT the functional side of something such as a tool or golf club **19.** SIDE OF COIN either surface of a coin, especially one with somebody's head on it ■ *v* (**faced, fac·ing, fac·es**) **1.** *vti* TURN TOWARD PARTICULAR DIRECTION to be positioned or turn so that the face or front side is directed a particular way or toward something or somebody ○ *The largest bedroom faces south.* **2.** *vt* BE OPPOSITE SOMEBODY OR SOMETHING to be in a position opposite somebody or something ○ *The boys faced each other.* **3.** *vt* COME UP AGAINST SOMEBODY OR SOMETHING to meet or confront somebody or something directly and bravely ○ *Their retreat was cut off and they had no choice but to stand and face the enemy.* **4.** *vt* ACCEPT FACTS to accept the reality of a difficult or unpleasant situation ○ *Let's face it, our chances of being on time are slim.* **5.** *vt* HAVE TO BE DEALT WITH to require to be dealt with by somebody ○ *She was faced with the task of breaking the news to her family.* ○ *the problems facing them* **6.** *vt* EXPECT SOMETHING BAD to have the prospect of experiencing something unpleasant, usually within a short period of time ○ *They face ruin if the bank calls in the loan.* ○ *could face a jail sentence* **7.** *vt* LINE OR DECORATE SOMETHING to line or trim the edge of something with a contrasting material ○ *The cuffs were faced with velvet.* **8.** *vt* SMOOTH STONE to put a smooth surface on a piece of stone **9.** *vti* ORDER TROOPS TO TURN to order troops to turn in a particular direction, or turn in a particular direction when ordered to do so ○ *The captain ordered her troops to face left.* [13C. Via French < Latin *facies* "appearance, aspect, form, face"] —**face·a·ble** *adj* ◇ **be staring somebody in the face** to be obvious but unnoticed ○ *Why call in a management consultant, when the cause of the problem is staring you in the face?* ◇ **be staring something in the face** to be facing something undesirable but inevitable ○ *We were staring bankruptcy in the face.* ◇ **face down** *or* **downward** with the face or front placed downward ◇ **face to face 1.** in the actual presence of another person **2.** in direct contact with, or having first-hand knowledge of, an unpleasant fact or situation ◇ **face up** *or* **upward** with the face or front placed upward ◇ **fly in the face of something** to defy something deliberately or recklessly ◇ **get in somebody's face** to annoy somebody (*informal*) ◇ **get out of my face** used for impolitely telling somebody to stop annoying you (*informal*) ◇ **have a long face** to look miserable or disappointed ◇ **in (the) face of something** when confronted by or in spite of something ○ *remained united in the face of strong opposition* ◇ **in your face** so frank or direct as to be unnerving or intimidating (*informal; hyphenated when used before a noun*) ○ *an in-your-face style of documentary moviemaking* ◇ **not just a pretty face** having more to offer than an attractive appearance ◇ **on the face of it** judging by appearances only ◇ **set your face against something** to oppose something with determination ◇ **show your face (somewhere** *or* **at something)** to put in an appearance somewhere ○ *He won't dare show his face at her house again.* ◇ **written all over somebody's face** obvious from somebody's expression (*informal*) ○ *She was standing by the broken window with guilt written all over her face.*

ORIGIN The Latin word *facies* "appearance, face" from which ***face*** is derived is also the source of English *facade, facet, superficial,* and *surface.*

face down *vt* to prevail against somebody in a direct confrontation

face off *vi* **1.** in hockey, lacrosse, and other sports, to start or restart play by dropping the puck or ball between two opposing players **2.** to confront each other or somebody else (*informal*)

face up to *vt* **1.** to accept having to deal with something unpleasant **2.** to confront somebody or something bravely

face an·gle *n* an angle between two flat surfaces on a polyhedron

face card *n* a king, queen, or jack in a deck of cards

face-cen·tered *adj* describes a crystal lattice with an atom in the center of each unit cell face as well as at the corners

face·cloth /fáyss klòth/ *n Can, UK* a small cloth used in washing the face and hands. US term **washcloth**

-faced *suffix* **1.** having a particular number of faces **2.** having a face of a particular kind

face·down /fáyss dòwn/ *n* a determined confrontation between two adversaries

face·less /fáyssləss/ *adj* **1.** anonymous and impersonal ○ *infuriating replies from faceless officials* **2.** lacking character or distinctive features ○ *a faceless waiting room* —**face·less·ly** *adv* —**face·less·ness** *n*

face·lift /fáyss lìft/ *n* **1.** a surgical operation in which the skin of the face is pulled back and up to tighten it and remove wrinkles. Technical name **rhytidectomy 2.** a renovation or refurbishment of something such as an area or a building ○ *The whole harbor area could use a facelift.*

face mask *n* a covering for the whole head or the face alone, used either to protect or to disguise the face

face-off *n* **1.** in hockey, lacrosse, and other sports, a start or restart of play in which the referee drops the puck or ball between two opposing players **2.** a direct confrontation

face pack *n* a cosmetic preparation that cleanses the pores of the face and removes dead layers of skin

face paint *n* any of various paints used to decorate the face and be easily washed off ○ *She got a set of face paints for her birthday.*

face peel *n* same as **chemical peel**

face·plate /fáyss plàyt/ *n* **1.** PART OF LATHE a perforated metal disk at the end of the spindle or headstock of a lathe for holding a workpiece in place **2.** SEE-THROUGH PART OF HEADGEAR the transparent part of a piece of protective headgear that protects the face while allowing the wearer to see **3.** FRONT OF CATHODE-RAY TUBE the front of a cathode-ray tube, on which an image is seen

face pow·der *n* a flesh-colored cosmetic powder applied to the face to make it look smoother or less shiny

fac·er /fáyssər/ *n* a lathe tool used to smooth a surface

face-sav·ing *adj* intended to preserve somebody's reputation and dignity ○ *find a face-saving compromise* —**face-sav·er** *n*

fac·et /fássət/ *n* **1.** ASPECT OF SOMETHING a part or possible aspect of something ○ *an important facet of our work* **2.** FACE OF GEMSTONE any surface of a cut gemstone **3.** ZOOL PART OF INSECT EYE a lens segment in the compound eye of an insect or other arthropod **4.** ANAT FLAT AREA a smooth flat area on a hard surface such as a bone or a tooth ■ *vt* (**fac·et·ed** *or* **fac·et·ted, fa·cet·ing** *or* **fa·cet·ting, fac·ets**) CUT FACETS IN SOMETHING to cut facets in something, especially a gemstone [Early 17C. < French *facette* "little face" < *face* (see FACE)]

fa·ce·ti·ae /fə séeshee èe/ *npl* witty or humorous remarks (*archaic*) [Early 16C. < Latin, "jokes," plural of *facetia* (see FACETIOUS)]

face time *n* **1.** TIME SPENT FACE-TO-FACE time spent dealing face to face with other people (*informal*) ○ *The schedule calls for weekly e-mail reports as well as some actual face time between team members.* **2.** TIME SPENT ON TELEVISION the amount of time that somebody spends appearing on television ○ *We need more face time to sway public opinion on this issue.* **3.** EXTRA TIME AT PLACE OF EMPLOYMENT the amount of time somebody spends at his or her place of employment, especially beyond normal working hours ○ *What is she trying to prove with all this face time?*

fa·ce·tious /fə séeshəss/ *adj* intended to be humorous but often silly or inappropriate [Late 16C. < French *facétieux* < *facétie* "joke" < Latin *facetia* < *facetus* "graceful, witty"] —**fa·ce·tious·ly** *adv* —**fa·ce·tious·ness** *n*

SYNONYMS See *funny.*

face-to-face *adj, adv* (*not hyphenated when used after a verb*) **1.** in the physical presence of somebody else ○ *a face-to-face encounter* **2.** in direct contact or confrontation ○ *We came face to face with the situation.*

face val·ue *n* **1.** the value that is shown on something, especially a bill, coin, or stamp **2.** the apparent worth or meaning of something, which may be better than its true worth or meaning ○ *We'd be unwise to take his promises at face value.*

fa·cial /fáysh'l/ *adj* relating to the face ○ *an unhappy facial expression* ■ *n* a beauty treatment for the face, usually consisting of a facial massage followed by cleansing and makeup —**fa·cial·ly** *adv*

fa·cial·ist *n* a beautician who specializes in beauty treatments for the face

fa·cial nerve *n* a nerve of the seventh cranial pair that controls the muscles of the face and jaw, and the sensory abilities of the palate, front of the tongue, and nose

fa·cial scrub *n* a slightly abrasive cream or lotion used on the face to remove a layer of dead skin and improve the complexion

-facient *suffix* causing, making ○ *febrifacient* [< Latin *facient-*, present participle of *facere* "do, make"]

fa·ci·es /fáyshee èez, fáysheez/ (*plural same*) *n* **1.** BIOL GENERAL APPEARANCE the general characteristic appearance of something such as a plant or animal species **2.** GEOL ROCK FEATURES INDICATING FORMATION the combined physical and chemical features of a rock that indicate the manner of its formation or deposition **3.** MED FACIAL APPEARANCE LINKED TO DISEASE the appearance of somebody's face as a characteristic of a particular disease or condition [Early 18C. < Latin (see FACE)]

fac·ile /fáss'l/ *adj* **1.** EASY TO DO requiring little effort **2.** FLUENT BUT INSINCERE produced, spoken, or speaking so fluently and easily as to seem insincere or superficial **3.** SUPERFICIAL made or arrived at without any serious thought or depth of feeling and therefore of little value or significance **4.** WORKING EASILY working, acting, or done smoothly and easily [15C. Via French, "easy" < Latin *facilis* "easy to do, pliant, courteous" < *facere* "do, make"] —**fac·ile·ly** *adv* —**fac·ile·ness** *n*

fa·cil·i·tate /fə sílli tàyt/ (**-tat·ed, -tat·ing, -tates**) *vt* to make something easy or easier to do [Early 17C. Via French < Italian *facilitare* "make easy" < *facile* "easy" < Latin *facilis* (see FACILE)] —**fa·cil·i·ta·tive** *adj*

fa·cil·i·ta·tion /fə sìlli táysh'n/ *n* **1.** the process of making something easy or easier **2.** a decrease in the resistance to a nerve impulse in a neural pathway, brought about by prior or repeated stimulation

fa·cil·i·ta·tor /fə sílli tàytər/ *n* **1.** somebody who enables a process to happen, especially somebody who encourages people to find their own solutions to problems or tasks **2.** an organizer and provider of services for a meeting, seminar, or other event

fa·cil·i·ty /fə síllətee/ *n* (*plural* **-ties**) **1.** SOMETHING WITH PARTICULAR FUNCTION something designed or created to provide a service or fulfill a need (*often used in the plural*) ○ *A wide range of facilities is available at the sports center, including a weight room and saunas.* ○ *a health-care facility* **2.** SKILL an ability to do something easily **3.** EFFORTLESSNESS ease in doing something or in being done ■ **fa·cil·i·ties** *npl* same as **toilet** (sense 2)

fac·ing /fáyssing/ *n* **1.** LINING THAT FINISHES EDGE a lining sewn inside a garment to neaten the edges, or to decorate them when a part of it such as a collar is turned back **2.** LINING MATERIAL fabric used for facing **3.** CONSTR WALL SURFACE a layer of material that covers the outer surface of a wall to decorate or protect it ■ **fac·ings** *npl* CUFFS AND COLLAR OF JACKET contrasting coverings on the cuffs and collar of a jacket, especially a military jacket

-facing *suffix* pointing in a particular direction

~~**facism**~~ incorrect spelling of **fascism**

fack /fak/ (**facked, fack·ing, facks**) *vi* to speak truthfully about something (*slang*) [Alteration of FACT]

FACP, F.A.C.P. *abbr* Fellow of the American College of Physicians

FACS, F.A.C.S. *abbr* Fellow of the American College of Surgeons

fac·sim·i·le /fak símməlee/ *n* **1.** an exact copy or reproduction of something such as a document, a coin, or somebody's handwriting **2.** same as **fax** *n* (sense 1) (*dated*) ■ *vt* (**-led, -le·ing, -les**) to make an exact copy or reproduction of something [Late 16C.

< modern Latin, < Latin *facere* "do, make" + *simile* "similar"]

fac·sim·i·le e·di·tion *n* a book or print that is reprinted in exactly the same style as an earlier edition, often being a photographic reproduction of the original

fact /fakt/ *n* **1.** SOMETHING KNOWN TO BE TRUE something that can be shown to be true, to exist, or to have happened **2.** TRUTH OR REALITY OF SOMETHING the truth or actual existence of something, as opposed to the supposition of something or a belief about something ○ *based on fact* **3.** PIECE OF INFORMATION a piece of information, e.g., a statistic or a statement of the truth **4.** LAW ACTUAL COURSE OF EVENTS the circumstances of an event or state of affairs, rather than an interpretation of its significance ○ *Matters of fact are issues for a jury, while matters of law are issues for the court.* **5.** LAW SOMETHING BASED ON EVIDENCE something that is based on or concerned with the evidence presented in a legal case [15C. < Latin *factum* "deed" < *fact-*, past participle of *facere* "do, make"] ◇ **after the fact** after something, especially a criminal act, has been done ◇ **before the fact** before something, especially a criminal act, has been done ◇ **in fact, in actual fact** used to correct a previous misunderstanding or to reinforce a previous statement

USAGE The phrase ***in fact***, as in *She is, in fact, correct*, is spelled as two words, never as *infact*.

ORIGIN The Latin word *facere* "to do, make," from which ***fact*** is derived, is also the source of English *difficult, effect, facile, faction*[1], *factor, fashion, feasible, feat, feature*, and *fetish*.

fact-find·ing *adj* FOR GATHERING INFORMATION intended to find out information about something ○ *on a fact-finding mission* ■ *n* **1.** GATHERING INFORMATION activity that is intended to find out information about something **2.** LAW FAMILY-COURT TRIAL a trial in a family court —**fact-find·er** *n*

fac·tion[1] /fákshən/ *n* **1.** a group that is a minority within a larger group and has interests or beliefs that are not always in harmony with the larger group **2.** conflict or dissension within a group [15C. Via French < Latin *faction-* "act of making" < *fact-* (see FACT)] —**fac·tion·al** *adj* —**fac·tion·al·ly** *adv*

fac·tion[2] /fákshən/ *n* **1.** writing or filmmaking that portrays real people or events by dramatizing the facts using the techniques of fiction **2.** a piece of writing, a movie, or a television program that portrays real people or events in a dramatized way [Mid-20C. Blend of FACT + FICTION] —**fac·tion·al** *adj*

-faction *suffix* the making or production of something ○ *liquefaction* [Via French < Latin *-faction-* < *fact-* (see FACT)]

fac·tion·al·ism /fákshənə lìzzəm/ *n* the existence of or conflict between groups within a larger group —**fac·tion·al·ist** *n*

fac·tion·al·ize /fákshənə lìz/ (**-ized, -iz·ing, -iz·es**) *vti* to split into factions, or cause a group to split into factions

fac·tious /fákshəss/ *adj* liable to cause, taking part in, or characteristic of conflict within a group [Mid-16C. Directly or via French < Latin *factiosus* < *factio, faction-* (see FACTION[1])] —**fac·tious·ly** *adv* —**fac·tious·ness** *n*

fac·ti·tious /fak tíshəss/ *adj* **1.** contrived and insincere rather than genuine **2.** not real or natural but artificial or invented (*formal*) [Mid-17C. < Latin *factitius* < *fact-* (see FACT)] —**fac·ti·tious·ly** *adv* —**fac·ti·tious·ness** *n*

fac·ti·tive /fáktitiv/ *adj* describes a verb that takes a direct object and a complement. An example is "appoint" in "They appointed her Head of Department" where "her" is the direct object and "Head of Department" is a noun complement. [Mid-19C. < modern Latin *factitivus* < Latin *factitare* "do again" < *fact-* (see FACT)] —**fac·ti·tive·ly** *adv*

fact of life *n* an unavoidable truth, especially an unpleasant one ■ **facts of life** *npl* basic information on sexual matters and reproduction

fac·toid /fák tòyd/ *n* **1.** something that may not be true but is widely accepted as true because it is repeatedly quoted, especially in the media **2.** ⚠ a small and often unimportant bit of information

USAGE The popular meaning of ***factoid***, "a small, unimportant piece of information," is regarded by some people as incorrect.

fac·tor /fáktər/ *n* **1.** INFLUENCE something that contributes to or has an influence on the outcome of something ○ *Access to emergency exits is an important factor when planning the layout of a public building.* **2.** LEVEL a quantity or level of something ○ *sunblock with a protection factor of 30* **3.** MATH QUANTITY MULTIPLIED WITH OTHERS one of two or more numbers or quantities that can be multiplied together to give a particular number or quantity ○ *3 and 5 are factors of 15.* **4.** AMOUNT BY WHICH SOMETHING IS MULTIPLIED a particular amount by which something is multiplied ○ *The number of visitors to the museum has increased by a factor of three.* **5.** BUSINESS SOMEBODY TRADING FOR COMMISSION a person or organization that buys and sells goods for a commission **6.** BUSINESS BUSINESS AGENT an agent or transactor of business for somebody else **7.** FIN FINANCING COMPANY a business that makes loans to other businesses on the security of their accounts receivable or that buys their accounts receivable at a discounted price **8.** BIOCHEM BIOLOGICAL SUBSTANCE a biological substance that has a physiological effect ■ *v* (**-tored, -tor·ing, -tors**) **1.** *vi* BUSINESS ACT AS FACTOR to work as a factor **2.** *vt* MATH WORK OUT FACTORS to calculate the factors of a number or expression [15C. Via French < Latin, < *fact-* (see FACT)] —**fac·tor·a·bil·i·ty** /fàktərə bìllətee/ *n* —**fac·tor·a·ble** *adj*

factor in *vt* to include or consider something as contributing to or influencing something else, e.g., when making a decision

fac·tor·age /fáktərij/ *n* **1.** the fees or commission charged by a factor **2.** the business of working as a factor

fac·tor a·nal·y·sis *n* a statistical technique used to determine the relative strength of various influences on an outcome

fac·to·ri·al /fak táwree əl/ *n* MATH PRODUCT OF MULTIPLICATION the number resulting from multiplying a whole number by every whole number between itself and 1 inclusive. 6 factorial, or 6!, is 6 x 5 x 4 x 3 x 2 x 1 = 720. Symbol ! ■ *adj* **1.** MATH OF FACTORIAL relating to or involving a factorial **2.** BUSINESS INVOLVING FACTOR involving or characteristic of a commercial factor or the work of such a factor —**fac·to·ri·al·ly** *adv*

fac·tor·ing /fáktəring/ *n* the business of buying debts at a discount so as to make a profit from collecting them

fac·tor·ize /fáktə rìz/ (**-ized, -iz·ing, -iz·es**) *vti UK* MATH same as **factor** *v* (sense 2) —**fac·tor·i·za·tion** /fàktəri záysh'n/ *n*

fac·tor·ship /fáktər shìp/ *n* the position or business of being a factor for another person or business

fac·tor VIII *n* a protein substance that promotes the clotting of blood. Its inherited absence causes hemophilia.

fac·to·ry /fáktəree/ (*plural* **-ries**) *n* **1.** BUILDING WHERE GOODS ARE MANUFACTURED a building or complex of buildings where goods are manufactured on a large scale using machinery or automation, e.g., an automobile assembly plant (*often used before a noun*) ○ *a factory worker* **2.** PRODUCTIVE PLACE a place or organization that produces a particular thing regularly and in some quantity (*informal*) ○ *As far as popular music was concerned, it was a hit factory.* **3.** COMM PLACE ABROAD WHERE AGENTS DID BUSINESS formerly, a place where business was carried out abroad by commercial agents (**factors**), especially a trading station

fac·to·ry farm *n* a farm where animals are raised on a large scale using intensive methods and modern equipment —**fac·to·ry farm·ing** *n*

fac·to·ry floor *n* the area of a factory where the manufacturing process is carried out, as opposed to the administration areas

fac·to·ry ship *n* a large fishing vessel equipped to process and freeze its own catch, or a whole fleet's catch, of fish or whales

fac·to·tum /fak tṓtəm/ *n* somebody employed to do a variety of jobs for somebody else [Mid-16C. < Latin, "do everything!" < *fac*, imperative of *facere* "do, make" + *totum* "all"]

fact sheet *n* **1.** a collection of information about a product, given to people who will write advertisements or broadcast favorable statements about the product **2.** *UK* a printed sheet or booklet giving information about something, especially a subject covered in a broadcast program

fac·tu·al /fákchoo əl, fákchəl/ *adj* **1.** involving, containing, or based on facts **2.** consisting of the truth or including only those things that are actual [Mid-19C. After ACTUAL] —**fac·tu·al·i·ty** /fàk choo állətee/ *n* —**fac·tu·al·ly** *adv* —**fac·tu·al·ness** *n*

fac·tu·al·ism /fákchoo ə lìzzəm, fákchə-/ *n* a strict devotion to or adherence to facts —**fac·tu·al·ist** *n*

fac·u·la /fákyələ/ (*plural* **-lae** /-lee/) *n* a large, bright, extremely hot region on the Sun's surface, usually occurring near a sunspot [Early 18C. < Latin, "little torch"] —**fac·u·lar** *adj*

fac·ul·ta·tive /fák'l tàytiv/ *adj* **1.** ALLOWING SOMETHING TO HAPPEN enabling or capable of permitting something to happen or be done, but not able to force its occurrence **2.** NOT REQUIRED optional, not obligatory **3.** BIOL ASSOCIATED WITH VARIETY OF CONDITIONS able to live or take place under a range of external conditions ○ *a facultative parasite* —**fac·ul·ta·tive·ly** *adv*

fac·ul·ty /fák'ltee/ (*plural* **-ties**) *n* **1.** ABILITY a capacity or ability that somebody is born with or learns ○ *a great faculty for learning languages* **2.** MENTAL POWER a mental power or ability such as reason or memory **3.** EDUC ENTIRE TEACHING STAFF the entire teaching staff of a university, college, or school, including any administrators holding academic rank **4.** EDUC TEACHING STAFF FOR PARTICULAR UNIVERSITY DIVISION the teaching staff of a particular faculty in a university or college **5.** EDUC DIVISION OF UNIVERSITY a department or group of departments dealing with a particular subject in a university or college **6.** ALL MEMBERS OF PROFESSION all of the people who practice a particular profession, especially medicine **7.** POWER GRANTED BY AUTHORITY a power or right given by an authority [14C. Via French < Latin *facultas* < *facilis* "easy"]

fad /fad/ *n* something that is embraced very enthusiastically for a short time, especially by many people [Mid-19C. Origin ?] —**fad·dism** *n* —**fad·dist** *n*

Fad·den /fádd'n/, **Sir Arthur William** (1895–1973) Australian politician. He was leader of the Country Party (1941–58) and was briefly prime minister of Australia in 1941. See table at **prime minister**

fad·dish /fáddish/ *adj* **1.** very popular but only for a short time **2.** tending to have strongly held, but brief, enthusiasms —**fad·dish·ly** *adv* —**fad·dish·ness** *n*

fad·dy /fáddee/ *adj UK* **1.** tending to have strongly held likes and dislikes about food ○ *a faddy eater* **2.** same as **faddish** (sense 2)

fade /fayd/ *v* (**fad·ed, fad·ing, fades**) **1.** *vti* GRADUALLY BECOME LESS BRIGHT OR LOUD to lose brightness, color, or loudness gradually, or make something do this ○ *The clothes had faded from months of washing.* **2.** *vi* BECOME TIRED to lose strength, freshness, and vigor ○ *His concentration faded after about an hour.* **3.** *vi* DISAPPEAR SLOWLY to die away or vanish gradually ○ *The movie ends with a close-up that gradually fades to black.* **4.** *vi* LOSE EFFECTIVENESS to become less effective temporarily ○ *the engine faded* **5.** *vi US* LEAVE to leave or depart (*slang*) ○ *They faded sometime after midnight.* **6.** *vi US* FOOTBALL DROP BACK TO PASS in football, to drop back from the line of scrimmage before passing the ball (*refers to the quarterback*) **7.** *vti* SPORTS CURVE OR CAUSE TO CURVE to curve from a straight path, or cause a ball to curve from a straight path **8.** *vt* GAMBLING MATCH BET IN DICE GAME in dice, to match the bet of an opponent (*slang*) ■ *n* **1.** GRADUAL LESSENING IN BRIGHTNESS OR LOUDNESS a gradual decrease in brightness, distinctness, or loudness **2.** GRADUAL DISAPPEARANCE OF IMAGE a gradual disappearance of an image in a film or television show **3.** SPORTS CURVING PATH OF BALL the curve of a ball, especially a golf ball, away from a straight path or flight **4.** *US* OFFENSIVE TERM an offensive term for a Black person who has adopted predominantly white friends and attitudes (*slang*) [14C. < French *fade* "weak, pale"] —**fad·a·ble** *adj* —**fad·ed·ness** *n* —**fad·er** *n*

fade away *vi* **1.** to become gradually fainter or weaker and finally disappear **2.** to become thin and unhealthy

fade in *vti* to make a sound gradually audible or an image gradually visible, or become gradually audible or visible

fade out *vti* to make an image or sound gradually fainter until it disappears, or become gradually fainter before disappearing

fade·a·way /fáydə wày/ *n US* **1.** GRADUAL DISAPPEARANCE a gradual decrease in the brightness, color, or loudness of something until it disappears completely **2.** DODGE BY BASEBALL RUNNER in baseball, a base runner's slide to one side to avoid being tagged out **3.** SCREWBALL in baseball, a screwball (*dated*)

fade-in *n* the gradual introduction of a sound until it is audible or of an image until it is visible

fade·less /fáydləss/ *adj* not fading in sunlight or after washing —**fade·less·ly** *adv*

fade-out *n* **1.** a gradual decrease in brightness or loudness as an image or sound becomes fainter, until it disappears **2.** a gradual reduction in the strength of a television or radio broadcast signal, especially with temporary loss of reception, often because of transmission interference

fa·do /faa thoo/ (*plural* **-dos**) *n* a sad Portuguese folk song with guitar accompaniment [Early 20C. < Portuguese, "fate"]

fae·ces *npl* PHYSIOL UK spelling of **feces**

fa·e·na /faa áynə/ *n* a series of maneuvers in the final stages of a bullfight, leading up to the killing of the bull by the matador [Early 20C. < Spanish, "task"]

fa·er·ie /fáy əree, férree/, **fa·er·y** (*plural* **-ies**) *n* (*literary*) **1.** another spelling of **fairy** *n* (sense 1) **2.** the world of the fairies, or fairyland [Late 16C. Mock-medieval alteration of FAIRY]

Faer·oe Is·lands /férrō-/ another spelling of **Faroe Islands**

Faer·o·ese *n, adj* LANG, PEOPLES another spelling of **Faroese**

fa·er·y *n* another spelling of **faerie** (*literary*)

FAF *abbr* financial aid form

FAFSA /fáfsə/ *abbr* EDUC Free Application for Federal Student Aid

fag[1] /fag/ *n* SCHOOLBOY'S HELPER at a private British school, a schoolboy who has to do menial jobs and run errands for an older schoolboy (*dated*) ■ *v* (**fagged, fag·ging, fags**) **1.** *vti US* EXHAUST THROUGH WORK to exhaust somebody through drudgery or hard labor, or become exhausted in this way **2.** *vi UK* ACT AS SCHOOLBOY'S HELPER at a private British school, to do menial jobs and run errands for an older schoolboy (*dated*) [Mid-16C. Origin ?]

fag[2] /fag/ *n UK* same as **cigarette** (*informal*) [Late 19C. Shortening of FAG END]

fag[3] /fag/ *n* an offensive term for a gay man (*slang*) [Early 20C. Shortening of FAGGOT[1]] —**fag·gy** *adj*

fag end *n* **1.** the last part of something after the best of it has been used ○ *the fag end of the day* **2.** the remaining part of a piece of cloth, most of which has been used

fag·got[1] /fággət/ *n* an offensive term for a gay man (*slang*) [Early 20C. < FAGOT as an offensive term for a woman] —**fag·got·ry** *n* —**fag·got·y** *adj*

fag·got[2] /fággət/ *n, vt* INDUST another spelling of **fagot**

fag·got·ing *n US* HANDICRAFT another spelling of **fagoting**

fag·ot /fággət/, **fag·got** *n* **1.** BUNDLE OF STICKS FOR FIREWOOD a bundle of sticks or twigs, especially wood to be burned as fuel **2.** BUNDLE OF PIECES OF METAL a bundle of pieces of metal, especially pieces of iron or steel for welding ■ *vt* (**-ot·ed, -ot·ing, -ots**) **1.** COLLECT SOMETHING AND TIE INTO BUNDLE to collect things, especially sticks, and tie them into a bundle or bundles **2.** HANDICRAFT STITCH WITH FAGOTING to sew something using fagoting [13C. Via Old French < Italian *faggotto* < Greek *phakelos* "bundle"]

fag·ot·ing /fággəting/, **fag·got·ing** *n* **1.** a decorative way of sewing two hemmed pieces of fabric together, filling the gap between them with an insertion stitch **2.** an embroidery technique in which lengthwise threads are pulled out and the cross threads tied into bundles, producing a decorative openwork effect

fah *n* MUSIC UK spelling of **fa**

Fahd /faad/ (*b.* 1923) king of Saudi Arabia (1982–). He held several ministerial posts from 1953 before succeeding his half-brother, Khalid, to the throne. Amid calls for democratic reform, he established the Consultative Council (1992) of 60 ministerial advisers.

fahl·band /faal bànd, -baant/ *n* a thin bed of rock that contains metal sulfide minerals, although not in sufficient quantity to be used as an ore [Late 19C. < German, "pale (ash-colored) band"]

Fah·ren·heit /fárrən hīt/ *adj* using or measured on a temperature scale on which water freezes at 32° and boils at 212° under normal atmospheric conditions. In scientific and technical contexts temperatures are now usually measured in degrees Celsius instead of Fahrenheit. ◊ **Celsius.** Symbol **F** [Mid-18C. After Gabriel *Fahrenheit* (1686–1736) German physicist]

FAIA, F.A.I.A. *abbr* Fellow of the American Institute of Architects

FAIC, F.A.I.C. *abbr* Fellow of the American Institute of Chemists

fa·ience /fī aanss, fay-/, **fa·ïence** *n* earthenware decorated with colored opaque metallic glazes ○ *a faience bowl* [Late 17C. < French, after *Faïence* "Faenza," town in N Italy]

fail /fayl/ *v* (**failed, fail·ing, fails**) **1.** *vi* BE UNSUCCESSFUL to be unsuccessful in trying to do something ○ *This plan can't fail.* **2.** *vi* BE UNABLE TO DO SOMETHING to be incapable of doing something or unwilling to do it ○ *She failed to see what the problem was.* **3.** *vti* EDUC NOT PASS EXAM OR COURSE to fall short of the standard required to pass an examination, course, or piece of academic work ○ *He failed English.* **4.** *vt* EDUC JUDGE STUDENT NOT GOOD ENOUGH to judge a student not good enough to pass an examination, course, or piece of academic work **5.** *vi* STOP FUNCTIONING OR GROWING to stop working or not perform or grow as expected ○ *The brakes on the car failed.* **6.** *vi* COMM COLLAPSE FINANCIALLY to collapse financially, becoming insolvent or bankrupt ○ *The business failed after six years.* **7.** *vt* LET SOMEBODY DOWN to abandon, forsake, or let somebody down by not doing what is expected or needed ○ *My courage failed me.* **8.** *vi* BECOME WEAKER to lose strength, loudness, or brightness ○ *The light began to fail.* ■ *n* FIN STOCKBROKER'S DEFAULT the failure by a stockbroker to deliver stock to a purchaser within the normal delivery period [13C. Via Old French *faillir* < Latin *fallere* "deceive somebody's hopes, disappoint"] ◇ **without fail** without exception

failed /fayld/ *adj* unsuccessful, or not having done what is expected or needed ○ *a failed attempt to circumnavigate the world in a balloon*

fail·ing /fáyling/ *n* **1.** SHORTCOMING a fault or weakness **2.** FAILURE a failure to do something such as pass a course or work properly ■ *prep* WITHOUT if something does not happen ○ *Failing a resolution of the dispute by this afternoon, we will suspend negotiations.*

SYNONYMS See *flaw*[1].

---

faille /fīl/ *n* a closely woven, slightly ribbed silk, cotton, or rayon fabric [Mid-16C. < French]

fail-safe *adj* **1.** SWITCHING TO SAFE CONDITION designed to switch equipment or a system to a safe condition if there is a fault or failure **2.** WITH SAFETY DEVICE protected by or using a fail-safe mechanism **3.** SURE TO SUCCEED incapable of failing ■ *v* (**fail-safed, fail-saf·ing, fail-safes**) **1.** *vt* SAFEGUARD SOMETHING FROM FAILURE to make something safe in the event of failure through use of a fail-safe device or procedure **2.** *vi US* SWITCH TO SAFE CONDITION to switch automatically to a safe condition in the event of a failure in the supply, control, or structural system of something ■ *n* SOMETHING THAT SAFEGUARDS a fail-safe device or procedure

fail-soft *adj US* describes electronic equipment that can operate at a reduced level after the failure of a component or power supply

fail·ure /fáylyər/ *n* **1.** LACK OF SUCCESS a lack of success in or at something **2.** SOMETHING LESS THAN THAT REQUIRED something that falls short of what is required or expected ○ *Failure will not be tolerated.* **3.** SOMEBODY OR SOMETHING THAT FAILS somebody or something that is unsuccessful ○ *She made him feel like a failure.* **4.** BREAKDOWN OF SOMETHING a breakdown or decline in the performance of something, or an occasion when something stops working or stops working adequately ○ *engine failure* **5.** LACK OF DEVELOPMENT OR PRODUCTION inadequate growth, development, or production of something ○ *crop failure* **6.** BUSINESS BANKRUPTCY a financial collapse, usually leading to bankruptcy

fail·ure to thrive *n* a pronounced lack of growth in a child because of inadequate absorption of nutrients or a serious heart or kidney condition, resulting in below-average height and weight

fain /fayn/ (*archaic*) *adv* HAPPILY with gladness or eagerness ■ *adj* **1.** EAGER willing or eager to do something **2.** COMPELLED forced by an obligation or circumstances to do something [Old English *faegen* "glad" < Germanic]

fai·né·ant /fáynee ənt/ (*literary*) *adj* unwilling to do anything ■ *n* somebody who is regarded as lazy [Early 17C. < French, alteration of *fait-nient* "does nothing" < *faignant* "shirker"]

faint /faynt/ *adj* **1.** DIM not bright, clear, or loud **2.** UNENTHUSIASTIC done feebly and without conviction ○ *damned the new book with faint praise* **3.** DIZZY dizzy or weak, as if about to become unconscious ○ *All of a sudden he felt faint.* **4.** SLIGHT remote or slight ○ *a faint chance* ■ *vi* (**faint·ed, faint·ing, faints**) **1.** LOSE CONSCIOUSNESS BRIEFLY to become unconscious, especially for a short time, because of a reduction in the flow of blood to the brain **2.** WEAKEN to become weak or lose courage (*archaic*) ■ *n* SUDDEN LOSS OF CONSCIOUSNESS a sudden, usually brief, loss of consciousness, caused by a reduction in the flow of blood to the brain. Technical name **syncope** (sense 1) [13C. < Old French < *faindre* "pretend, shirk"] —**faint·er** *n* —**faint·ly** *adv* —**faint·ness** *n*

SPELLCHECK faint or **feint**? Do not confuse the spelling of ***faint*** and ***feint***, which sound similar. ***Faint***, the more frequent of the two words, can be used as an adjective meaning "dizzy," "weak," or "slight" (as in *to feel faint, a faint smell, a faint chance*), or as a noun or verb referring to a sudden loss of consciousness. ***Feint*** is a noun or verb referring to a deceptive action in sport or combat.

---

faint-heart·ed *adj* lacking resolve, boldness, or enthusiasm —**faint-heart·ed·ly** *adv* —**faint-heart·ed·ness** *n*

SYNONYMS See *cowardly*.

---

fair[1] /fer/ *adj* **1.** REASONABLE OR UNBIASED not exhibiting any bias, and therefore reasonable or impartial ○ *a fair decision* **2.** DONE PROPERLY done according to the rules ○ *fair and free elections* **3.** NOT STORMY OR CLOUDY sunny or clear, and without much wind ○ *fair weather* **4.** NAUT GOOD FOR SAILING describes conditions that are favorable for sailing or travel by boat ○ *a fair wind* **5.** PLEASING TO LOOK AT beautiful or pleasing to the eye (*literary*) ○ *a fair maiden* **6.** NOT BLOCKED clear and unobstructed ○ *a fair view of the enemy's forces* **7.** LIGHT-COLORED with light-colored hair or skin **8.** SIZEABLE reasonably large in size or quantity ○ *They had a fair number of responses to the advertisement.* **9.** ACCEPTABLE no more than acceptable or average ○ *Your performance this year has been only fair.* **10.** BETTER THAN ACCEPTABLE moderately good or reasonable ○ *a fair understanding* **11.** UNSULLIED not marred by any blemish or stain ○ *to preserve your fair name* **12.** FALSE DESPITE APPEARANCES seemingly good or true, but actually false or insincere ○ *fair words* **13.** BASEBALL IN FAIR TERRITORY constituting a fair ball according to the rules of baseball ○ *The ball's not going to stay fair.* ■ *adv* **1.** PROPERLY in accordance with the rules or what is expected ○ *She's always played fair with me.* **2.** BASEBALL IN FAIR TERRITORY in or into fair territory on a baseball field **3.** DIRECTLY in a direct or straight way, and squarely ○ *hit fair in the center of the board* ■ *v* (**faired, fair·ing, fairs**) **1.** *vi Scotland* IMPROVE to become bright after cloud or rain (*refers to the weather or sky*) **2.** *vt* MAKE SMOOTH AND EVEN to smooth or streamline the surface of something such as an aircraft wing or tabletop [Old English *faeger* "beautiful" < Germanic, "suitable"] ◇ **fair and square** justly, fairly, or according to the rules ◇ **fair enough** acceptable and understandable, but not ideal ◇ **fair's fair** used to urge or appeal for just or even treatment (*informal*) ◇ **fair to middling** reasonably good or reasonably well (*informal; hyphenated when used before a noun*) ◇ **for fair** *US* utterly or completely (*informal*) ◇ **no fair** used to indicate that something is unfair or against the rules (*informal*)

SPELLCHECK fair or **fare**? Do not confuse the spelling of ***fair*** and ***fare***, which sound similar. ***Fair*** is chiefly used as an adjective and has many meanings, including "reasonable and just," "light in color," and "moderately good," as in *fair treatment, fair hair, fair weather.* ***Fair*** is also used as a noun, denoting an outdoor entertainment or a commercial exhibition. The noun ***fare***, on the other hand, means "cost of travel," "food," or "entertainment," as in *fare-paying passengers, good wholesome fare, dull fare for viewers.* ***Fare*** is also used as a verb, meaning "get on in a particular way": *How did she fare in the exam?*

fair off, fair up *vi Southern US* to become bright after cloudiness or rain (*refers to the weather or sky*)

REGIONAL NOTE An essentially Southern term concerning clearing of the weather, ***fair off*** is used alongside the less frequent ***fair up*** and ***fair***. Today, ***fair off*** is found most frequently in the Lower South, especially in Georgia, Alabama, Mississippi, and Louisiana, beyond the New Orleans focal area. Taken together, the use of ***fair off*** and ***fair up*** surpasses that of all other synonyms except *break, break off,* and the general currency term *clear up.*

fair[2] /fer/ *n* **1. EVENT WITH FARM COMPETITIONS AND AMUSEMENTS** an annual outdoor event, held especially in a state or county, with competitions for the best livestock, produce, and prepared foods and with entertainment, rides, and other amusements **2.** *UK* same as **carnival** (sense 2) **3. COMMERCIAL EXHIBITION** an exhibition, often held annually, at which companies show their products to potential buyers or inform people of business and job opportunities ○ *a book fair* ○ *a trade fair* **4. SALE TO RAISE MONEY** a sale of goods to raise money for something, especially a charity [13C. Via Old French < late Latin *feria* "holiday" < Latin *feriae* (plural)]

fair ball *n* a baseball batted into the portion of the field within the foul lines, unless it subsequently crosses the foul line between home and first or third base before being fielded

Fair·banks /fér bàngks/ city in eastern Alaska, on the northern bank of the Tanana River, northeast of Anchorage. Population: 30,780 (2002 estimate).

Fair·banks /fáir bàngks/, **Charles** (1852–1918) US politician. He was a US senator (1897–1905) before serving as vice president under Theodore Roosevelt (1905–09). Full name **Fairbanks, Charles Warren**

Fair·banks, Douglas (1883–1939) US silent movie actor. He is best known for his swashbuckling performances in movies such as *The Mark of Zorro* (1920). Born **Ullman, Douglas Elton**

fair catch *n* in football, a catch of a kicked ball by the receiver who has signaled that he or she will not run

fair cop·y *n* an unmarked version of a document that has been corrected and retyped or printed out again

Fair Cred·it Re·port·ing Act *n* a law requiring lenders and credit reporting agencies to communicate credit information held by them to the people it relates to and to correct wrong information

Fair·field /fér feeld/ **1.** town in northern Alabama, a western suburb of Birmingham. Population: 12,068 (2002 estimate). **2.** city in western California, northeast of San Francisco and southwest of Sacramento. Population: 101,935 (2002 estimate). **3.** city in southwestern Connecticut, situated on Long Island Sound. Population: 57,715 (2002 estimate).

fair game *n* a permissible object of pursuit, ridicule, or attack

fair·ground /fér gròwnd/ *n* a large open outdoor space where fairs or exhibitions may be held

fair-haired *adj* with light-colored hair

fair-haired boy *n* somebody who is the favorite of a person or a group (*informal*)

fair·ing /férring/ *n* a streamlined structure added to an aircraft, car, or other vehicle to reduce drag

Fair Isle[1] /fér ìl/ *n* a traditional Shetland Islands knitting design, used especially for sweaters, that incorporates bands of repeated multicolored geometric motifs [Mid-19C. After FAIR ISLE[2]]

Fair Isle[2] /fér ìl/ southernmost of the Shetland Islands, off the northern coast of Scotland. It is situated approximately midway between the main Shetland Islands and the Orkney Islands. Population: 70. Area: 8 sq. mi./15 sq. km.

Fair Lawn /-làwn/ borough in Northeastern New Jersey, Northeast of Paterson. Population: 7,333 (2002 estimate).

fair·lead /fér leed/, **fair·lead·er** /-leedər/ *n* a ring, hole, or other device through which a rope is guided in order to reduce friction and prevent chafing, or to keep it in place

fair·ly /férlee/ *adv* **1. HONESTLY** in a just, honest, proper, or legitimate way **2. MODERATELY** to a reasonable or moderate degree ○ *a fairly easy decision* **3. CONSIDERABLY** to a considerable degree ○ *The ground fairly shook with the impact.*

fair-mind·ed *adj* able to make impartial and just judgments, or resulting from such a judgment — **fair-mind·ed·ly** *adv* —**fair-mind·ed·ness** *n*

Fair·mont /fér mònt/ city in northern West Virginia on the Monongahela River, southwest of Morgantown and northeast of Parkersburg. Population: 19,026 (2002 estimate).

fair·ness /férnəss/ *n* **1.** the condition of being just or impartial **2.** the condition of being pleasing to look at ◇ **in (all) fairness** so as to be just and impartial ○ *In all fairness, I don't see how this is important.*

fair·ness doc·trine *n* the principle that licensed broadcasters should give equal air time to opposing views on controversial issues

Fair Oaks /-ōks/ district in northeastern Virginia, directly east of Richmond. It was the site of the Battle of Seven Pines (1862) during the US Civil War.

fair play *n* conduct that adheres to the rules or is just and equitable

fair sex *n* women and girls collectively (*literary; sometimes offensive*)

fair shake *n* (*informal*) **1.** just or reasonable treatment **2.** a reasonable chance to attempt something

fair-spo·ken *adj* speaking in a pleasant and polite way (*archaic*) —**fair-spo·ken·ness** *n*

fair ter·ri·to·ry *n* the area of a baseball field within the foul lines, including home plate, the foul poles, and the foul lines themselves

fair-trade *vt* to sell something in compliance with a fair-trade agreement

fair-trade a·gree·ment *n US* an agreement between a manufacturer of a product and distributors or retailers that the product will not be sold for less than a price set by the manufacturer

fair·way /fér wày/ *n* **1.** the closely mown area on a golf hole that forms the main avenue between a tee and a green **2.** a navigable channel or the usual course followed by boats in a river, harbor, or other body of water

Fair·weath·er, Mount /fér wèthər/ mountain in the St. Elias Mountains on the border between Alaska and British Columbia, Canada. Part of Glacier Bay National Park and Preserve, it is the highest peak in southern Alaska. Height: 15,299 ft./4,663 m.

fair-weath·er *adj* **1.** able to be relied upon only when things are going well **2.** suitable, done, or taking part only when the weather is fine

Fair·weath·er Cape /fèr wèthər-/ cape on the southeastern coast of Alaska, approximately 35 mi./55 km south of Mount Fairweather

fair·y /férree/ *n* (*plural* **-ies**) **1. SMALL SUPERNATURAL CREATURE** an imaginary supernatural being, usually resembling a small person, with magic powers. In folklore, fairies may be kindly or malicious. **2. OFFENSIVE TERM** an offensive term for a gay man (*slang*) ■ *adj* **OF FAIRIES** relating to, belonging to, or characteristic of fairies ○ *a fairy princess* [14C. < Old French *faerie* "enchantment" < *fae* "fairy" < Latin *fata* "the Fates," plural of *fatum* "fate"] —**fair·y·like** *adj*

fair·y god·moth·er *n* **1.** in some fairy stories, a kind fairy in the form of a woman who gives vital help to somebody, especially to the hero or heroine. Perhaps the most famous fairy godmother is the one who appears to Cinderella and enables her to attend the prince's ball. **2.** somebody, especially a woman, who gives generous help, often anonymously

fair·y·land /férree lànd/ *n* **1.** the imaginary country where fairies live **2.** an enchanting place, e.g., a fantasy world existing in somebody's imagination

fair·y pen·guin (*plural* **fair·y pen·guins** or *same*) *n* a penguin with a bluish back that grows to only 15.5 in./40 cm tall. Native to: coastal waters of South Australia and the South Island, New Zealand. Latin name: *Eudyptula minor.*

fair·y ring *n* a ring of mushrooms or grass darker than the surrounding grass, traditionally thought to be associated with dancing fairies but actually marking the outer edge of growth of various underground perennial fungi

fair·y shrimp *n* a tiny soft-bodied crustacean found in fresh or brackish water that has an elongated body and eleven pairs of appendages. Order: Anostraca.

fair·y tale *n* **1.** a story for children about fairies or other imaginary beings and events, often containing a moral message **2.** an improbable invented account of something, often a false excuse

CULTURAL NOTE *Grimm's Fairy Tales*, a collection of folk tales (1812–15) compiled and edited by German scholars Jacob and Wilhelm Grimm. Based on written sources dating back to the 16th century and on German folk tales, it includes many stories now famous worldwide, including "Cinderella," "Hansel and Gretel," and "Rumpelstiltskin." With their universal themes the tales were seen by the Grimms as repositories of the hopes, passions, and fears of humankind.

fair·y-tale *adj* **1.** derived from or typical of a fairy tale **2.** like something from a fairy tale, especially in being fortunate, happy, or extravagantly beautiful

Fai·sal /físs'l/ (1905–75) king of Saudi Arabia (1964–75). He was made foreign secretary of the newly formed Saudi Arabia in 1932 and became premier in 1953. After serving as regent, he forced his brother Saud to abdicate the throne and instituted extensive economic and social reforms during his reign. Full name **Faisal ibn Abdul Aziz**

> "We feel that the Arabs and the Jews are cousins in race, having suffered similar oppression at the hands of powers stronger than ourselves."
> [Faisal. Quoted in *Dawn of the Promised Land*, Ben Wicks; 1997]

Fai·sal I (1885–1933) king of Iraq (1921–33). An Arab nationalist leader, he was the first king of Iraq and the son of the founder of the Hashemite dynasty.

Fai·sal II (1935–58) king of Iraq (1939–58). A minor during most of his reign, he was assassinated during a military coup.

Fai·sal·a·bad /físsələ bàd, -baad/, **Fai·sal·ā·bād** city situated in the Punjab, northeastern Pakistan, 75 mi./121 km west of Lahore. Population: 1,977,246 (1998).

fait ac·com·pli /fèt ə kom plée, fàyt ə koN plée/ (*plural* **faits ac·com·plis** /*pronunc. same*/) *n* something that is already done or decided and seems unalterable [Mid-19C. < French, "accomplished fact"]

faith /fayth/ *n* **1. BELIEF OR TRUST** belief in, devotion to, or trust in somebody or something, especially without logical proof ○ *I wouldn't put my faith in him to straighten things out.* **2. RELIGION OR RELIGIOUS GROUP** a system of religious belief, or the group of people who adhere to it **3. TRUST IN GOD** belief in and devotion to God ○ *Her faith is unwavering.* **4. SET OF BELIEFS** a strongly held set of beliefs or principles ○ *people of different political faiths* **5. LOYALTY** allegiance or loyalty to somebody or something [13C. Via Old French *feid* < Latin *fides* "trust, belief"] ◇ **keep faith with somebody** *or* **something** to be loyal or true to a person or promise ◇ **keep the faith** do not despair regardless of what may happen ○ *Keep the faith; we'll get through this.* ◇ **on faith** without demanding proof

faith·ful /fáythfəl/ *adj* **1. UNWAVERING IN BELIEF** believing firmly in something or somebody, especially a religion or a political doctrine **2.** CONSISTENTLY LOYAL consistently trustworthy and loyal, especially to a person, promise, or duty **3.** NOT ADULTEROUS OR PROMISCUOUS not having sexual relations with somebody other than a spouse or partner **4.** CONSCIENTIOUS displaying or resulting from a sense of responsibility or devotion to duty ○ *faithful performance of his duties* **5.** CORRECT accurate and true ○ *a faithful account of the events* ■ *n* SOMEBODY OR SOMETHING RELIABLE a person or thing that can be trusted and relied upon ○ *The meeting was attended by all the long-term party faithful.* ■ *npl* **1.** *also* **Faith·ful** RELIGIOUS BELIEVERS the believers in a religion considered as a group, especially Muslims or Christians **2.** LOYAL SUPPORTERS people who are committed to something or somebody, especially the loyal members of a political party ○ *the party faithful* —**faith·ful·ly** *adv* —**faith·ful·ness** *n*

faith heal·er *n* a healer who attempts to treat illness or disorders through prayer, sometimes also by touching the affected person —**faith heal·ing** *n*

faith·less /fáythləss/ *adj* **1.** DISHONEST disloyal to somebody or something, e.g., in not keeping a promise or performing a duty **2.** UNTRUSTWORTHY not to be trusted or relied on **3.** NOT RELIGIOUS not believing in a religious faith —**faith·less·ly** *adv* —**faith·less·ness** *n*

fa·ji·tas /fə heétəss/ *npl Hispanic* a dish consisting of beef or other meat, especially chicken, that has been marinated, grilled, cut into strips, and served in a soft tortilla [Late 20C. < Mexican Spanish, literally "little strips, belts"]

fake[1] /fayk/ *n* **1.** SOMEBODY OR SOMETHING NOT GENUINE a person or thing that appears or is presented as being genuine but is not **2.** SPORTS MOVE TO DECEIVE OPPONENT a move made by a player in an attempt to mislead a sports opponent about the player's intended play ○ *He made a fake to the right, and then charged to the hoop.* ■ *adj* NOT GENUINE not genuine, but meant to be taken for genuine ■ *v* (**faked, fak·ing, fakes**) **1.** *vt* FALSELY PRESENT SOMETHING AS GENUINE to make or produce something and claim it is genuine when it is not **2.** *vti* PRETEND FEELING OR KNOWLEDGE to pretend to have, feel, or know something ○ *faked a knowledge of Italian* **3.** *vti US* SPORTS PERFORM MOVE TO DECEIVE OPPONENT to perform a move in an attempt to mislead a sports opponent ○ *The pitcher faked a throw to first base.* **4.** *vt* ARTS IMPROVISE WHILE PERFORMING to improvise or ad-lib a piece of music or lines in a play during a performance [Late 18C. < *feague*, 16C criminal slang for "rob, tamper with," origin ?] —**fak·er** *n*

fake out *vt* to deceive or surprise somebody, especially by bluffing (*informal*)

fake[2] /fayk/ NAUT *vt* (**faked, fak·ing, fakes**) same as **flake**[3] ■ *n* (*plural* **fakes** or **flakes**) same as **flake**[3] [15C. Origin ?]

fak·ie /fáykee/ *adv* in skateboarding, moving backward on the board (*slang*) —**fak·ie** *adj*

fa·kir /fə keér/, **fa·keer, fa·qir** *n* **1.** a religious Muslim, especially a Sufi, who lives by begging **2.** a Hindu ascetic who lives by begging and whose religious practice often includes the performance of extraordinary feats of physical endurance [Early 17C. Directly or via French < Arabic, "poor man"]

~~**falacy**~~ incorrect spelling of **fallacy**

fa·la·fel /fə laáf'l/, **fe·la·fel** *n* a deep-fried ball of ground chickpeas seasoned with onions and spices, originating in Southwest Asia [Mid-20C. Via Egyptian Arabic *falāfil* < Arabic *fulful* "pepper"]

Fa·lange /fə lánj/ *n* a Spanish fascist movement founded in 1933 and dissolved in 1977. It was the official ruling party of Spain under General Francisco Franco. [Mid-20C. < Spanish, "phalanx"] —**Fa·lan·gist** *n*

Fa·la·sha /fə laáshə/ (*plural* **-shas** or *same*) *n* a member of an Ethiopian Jewish religious group, most of whom now live in Israel (*often offensive*) [Early 18C. < Amharic, "exile"]

fal·chion /fáwlchən/ *n* a short sword with a broad, slightly curved blade, used in medieval times [14C. Via Old French *fauchon* < Latin *falc-*, "sickle"]

falchion

fal·con /fálkən, fáwl-/ *n* **1.** a fast powerful bird of prey related to the hawk that often catches birds in flight. Family: Falconidae. **2.** a female hawk that is trained to hunt small birds and animals [13C. Via Old French < late Latin *falcon-*]

CULTURAL NOTE ***The Maltese Falcon***, a movie (1941) by John Huston. Based on Dashiell Hammett's 1930 detective novel, it is regarded as one of the finest examples of film noir. Private investigator Sam Spade's attempts to track down the murderer of his partner lead to a group of people who share a common interest in a priceless statuette of a falcon.

fal·con·et /fálkə nèt/ *n* **1.** a small falcon found in forests. Native to: Asia. Genus: *Microhierax*. **2.** a small falcon found in open woodland. Native to: South America. Latin name: *Spiziapteryx*.

fal·co·nine /fálkə nīn/ *adj* relating to or typical of a falcon

fal·con·ry /fálkənree, fáwl-/ *n* the breeding, training, and use of falcons or other hawks to hunt small prey and return from flight at their handler's direction —**fal·con·er** *n*

fal·de·ral *n* another spelling of **folderol**

Fal·do /fáldō/, **Nick** (*b.* 1957) British golfer. A British Ryder Cup team member, he has won the British Open three times (1987, 1990, and 1992) and is a three-time US Masters champion (1989, 1990, and 1996). Full name **Faldo, Nicholas Alexander**

> "I didn't like team sports because it annoyed me that if you do your bit you could still go home a loser."
> [Nick Faldo, *The Times (London)*; April 11, 1989]

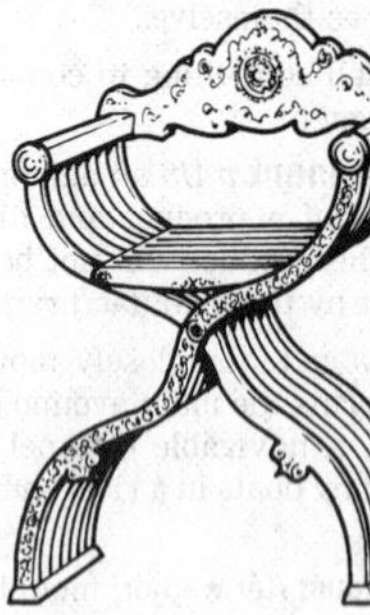

faldstool

fald·stool /fáwld stōōl/ *n* **1.** FOLDING SEAT FOR BISHOP a folding seat, especially one used by a bishop when officiating away from the throne or at another church **2.** FOLDING STOOL FOR WORSHIPER a small folding stool with a raised attachment like a desk at which a worshiper kneels to pray **3.** DESK IN CHURCH a desk from which the liturgy is read during a church service [Old English *fældstōl* < FOLD[1] + STOOL; partly < medieval Latin *faldistolium* < Germanic]

Fa·lis·can /fə lískən/ *n* an ancient language spoken in Italy, related to the Latin language that replaced it [Late 17C. < Latin *Faliscus* "of Falerii," important city of Etruria] —**Fa·lis·can** *adj*

Falk·land Is·lands /fáwklənd-/, **Falk·lands** /fáwkləndz/ group of islands and British dependency in the South Atlantic Ocean, 300 mi./483 km east of the Strait of Magellan. After a brief war in 1982 with the United Kingdom, the government of Argentina maintains its claim to these islands.

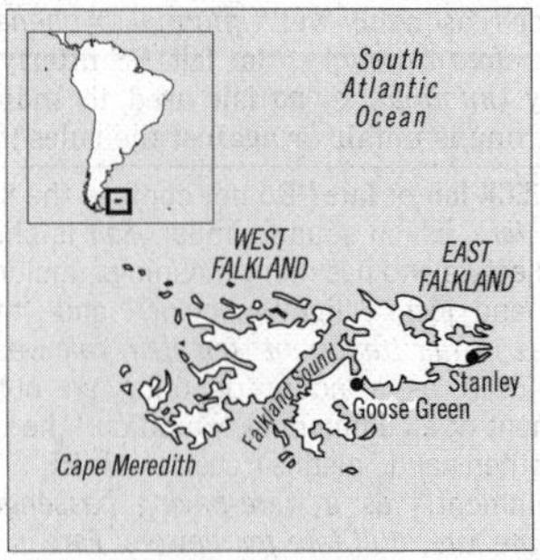

Falkland Islands

Population: 2,317 (1995). Area: 4,700 sq. mi./12,173 sq. km. Spanish name **Islas Malvinas**

fall /fawl/ *vi* (**fell** /fel/, **fall·en** /fáwlən/, **fall·ing, falls**) **1.** MOVE DOWNWARD to come down freely from a higher to a lower position, moved by the force of gravity ○ *The vase fell to the floor and shattered.* **2.** DROP OR BE LOWERED to drop or be dropped or lowered ○ *The curtain fell at the end of the performance.* **3.** COME DOWN SUDDENLY FROM UPRIGHT POSITION to drop or come down suddenly from an upright position, especially by accident ○ *The horse fell at the first fence.* **4.** BECOME LESS to become lower or be reduced in amount, value, or quality ○ *Prices have fallen in the last year.* **5.** ACOUSTICS BECOME LOWER IN PITCH to become lower in pitch or volume **6.** MIL BE TAKEN BY FORCE to be conquered or captured by a military force ○ *The city fell despite the best efforts of the army.* **7.** MIL DROP TO GROUND IN BATTLE to drop to the ground in battle after being wounded or having died ○ *He fell at the Battle of the Alamo.* **8.** POL COLLAPSE POLITICALLY to lose political power or be defeated ○ *The administration fell after only six months in office.* **9.** BE DRAPED to hang down ○ *When her hair is down it falls across her shoulders.* **10.** TAKE PLACE to happen or occur as if falling on something and enveloping it ○ *Night fell suddenly.* **11.** DISPLAY DISAPPOINTMENT to show an expression of disappointment ○ *Their faces fell when they heard the result.* **12.** GROW SAD to become sad and gloomy or to lose hope ○ *Our hearts fell.* **13.** STOP TO LOOK to settle or come to rest ○ *His gaze fell on an open book.* **14.** BE AVERTED to look away or downward ○ *Her eyes fell.* **15.** BEGIN TO BE IN PARTICULAR STATE to begin to be in, or enter into, a particular state or condition ○ *The class eventually fell silent.* ○ *fall to work* **16.** CHR SIN to sin or give in to temptation (*archaic*) **17.** GEOG SLOPE to slope downward and away ○ *The land falls gradually to the lake.* ■ *n* **1.** ACT OF MOVING DOWN FREELY an act of falling or moving down freely or suddenly ○ *She broke her arm in a fall.* **2.** SOMETHING FALLEN something that falls or has fallen, or the amount that has fallen ○ *a heavy fall of snow* **3.** DISTANCE DOWN the distance that something drops or could fall ○ *a ten-foot fall* **4.** LOWERING OF SOMETHING a decrease in the amount, size, quantity, or quality of something ○ *Even a slight fall in prices is welcome.* **5.** SEASON BETWEEN SUMMER AND WINTER the season between summer and winter when leaves change color and fall to the ground. Can term **autumn** **6.** GEOG SLOPE a slope that leads downward and away **7.** GEOG WATERFALL a waterfall or steep rapids (*often used in the plural, often used in place names*) ○ *Niagara Falls* **8.** MIL MILITARY LOSS a military defeat or the loss of something to an enemy ○ *the fall of Berlin in 1945* **9.** POL POLITICAL COLLAPSE a loss of political power or control ○ *the fall of the government* **10.** RELIG COMMISSION OF SIN a giving in to temptation or committing of a sin **11.** END OF HOISTING ROPE the end of a rope or chain to which power is applied when hoisting something **12.** WRESTLING MOVE FORCING OPPOSING WRESTLER TO FLOOR in wrestling, a scoring move in which a wrestler forces the opponent's shoulders to the floor for a specific period **13.** HAIRPIECE a hairpiece of long hair, usually attached to the top of the head with the join covered by the wearer's own hair **14.** CLOTHING ORNAMENTAL DECORATION OF LACE an ornamental piece of lace, veiling, or other light fabric that hangs draped from a collar or hat **15.** CLOTHING same as **falling band** **16.** BOT DOWNWARD FACING PART OF IRIS BLOSSOM the outer part of an iris flower, resembling a petal, that hangs down in front ■ *adj* FOR OR OF AUTUMN appropriate for or associated with autumn [Old English *feallan* < Germanic] ◇ **fall flat** to fail to have the intended effect

◇ **fall foul** *or* **afoul of 1.** to come into conflict with somebody or something **2.** NAUT to collide with something ◇ **fall short** to be less than is needed ◇ **fall short of something** to fail to meet a desired standard ◇ **break a fall** *Carib* to fall, especially heavily
fall among *vt* to become associated unwittingly with a group of people
fall apart *vi* **1.** to collapse, fail, or break into pieces **2.** to be in a state of great emotional distress (*informal*)
fall away *vi* **1.** DECREASE to become smaller in number, quantity, or size ○ *Attendance fell away after the third week of the course.* **2.** SLOPE to slope downward **3.** STOP ASSOCIATING WITH SOMEBODY to withdraw friendship, devotion, or support
fall back *vi* **1.** to retreat or move back, e.g., during a battle **2.** to be overtaken by others in a race or contest
fall back on, fall back upon *vt* to resort to something, especially something familiar, if other plans fail
fall behind *v* **1.** *vti* to fail to keep up with somebody or something **2.** *vi* to be late in doing something such as making a regular payment or completing a task ○ *He fell behind with the car payments.*
fall down *vi* **1.** to collapse or drop to the ground **2.** to be invalid or unsuccessful
fall down on *vt* to be unsuccessful or negligent in something
fall for *vt* **1.** to become infatuated or in love with somebody or something **2.** to be deceived by something (*informal*)
fall in *vi* **1.** to join or form an organized rank ○ *The whistle blew and the soldiers fell in.* **2.** to collapse inward
fall in with *vt* **1.** to meet and start associating with somebody or a group **2.** to agree or comply with somebody or something
fall off *v* **1.** *vi* to decrease in size, number, or quality ○ *Stock prices have fallen off in the last couple of days.* **2.** *vti* to deviate from a course to sail downwind, or make a boat sail downwind
fall on, fall upon *vt* **1.** ATTACK to attack somebody vigorously, especially by surprise (*literary*) **2.** BE RESPONSIBILITY OF to be borne by somebody as a responsibility or liability ○ *It fell on the surgeon to tell the patient's family that the operation was unsuccessful.* **3.** *UK* BEGIN SOMETHING EAGERLY to begin eating or doing something eagerly
fall out *v* **1.** *vi* to have a quarrel with somebody, especially one that leads to strained relations **2.** *vti* to leave organized ranks or positions, or break up organized ranks or positions
fall over *vti* to drop accidentally to the ground, especially by tumbling from an upright position or tripping over something ○ *I fell over a pile of books that had been left on the floor.* ○ *Be careful that you don't fall over!* ◇ **fall (all) over yourself** to be very eager or enthusiastic in doing something ○ *He was falling over himself to make everybody feel at home.*
fall through *vi* to fail to happen in the expected way
fall to *v* **1.** *vt* BE DUTY OF SOMEBODY to be the responsibility, obligation, or duty of somebody or a group ○ *It falls to the council to decide the matter.* **2.** *vti* START to begin doing something **3.** *vt* BE GIVEN to be given by right or inheritance to somebody
fall upon *vt* same as **fall on**

Fall *n* in Judaism and Christianity, the lapse of humankind into a sinful state as a result of Adam and Eve's failure to obey God

Fall /fawl/, **Albert Bacon** (1861–1944) US politician. He was secretary of the interior (1921–23), and was convicted (1931) of accepting a bribe in connection with the leasing of naval oil reserves during his administration, known as the "Teapot Dome" scandal.

fal·la·cious /fə láyshəss/ *adj* **1.** containing or involving a mistaken belief or idea **2.** deceptive or misleading [Early 16C. Via Old French < Latin *fallaciosus* < *fallacia* (see FALLACY)] —**fal·la·cious·ly** *adv* —**fal·la·cious·ness** *n*

fal·la·cy /fálləssee/ (*plural* **-cies**) *n* **1.** MISTAKEN BELIEF OR IDEA something that is believed to be true but is erroneous **2.** LOGIC INVALID ARGUMENT an argument or reasoning in which the conclusion does not follow from the premises **3.** LOGIC LOGICAL ERROR IN ARGUMENT a mistake made in a line of reasoning that invalidates it **4.** DECEPTIVENESS the condition of being misleading or deceptive [15C. Via Old French < Latin *fallacia* "deception" < *fallere* "deceive"]

fal·lal /fa lál, fa laal, fá làl/ *n* a fancy ornament or piece of clothing [Early 18C. Origin ?] —**fal·lal·er·y** /fa lálləree/ *n*

fall·a·way /fáwlə wày/ *adj* in basketball, performed by a player as the player moves away from the basket

fall·back /fáwl bàk/ *n* **1.** something that can be used as a replacement or substitute if something else does not work **2.** a retreat or withdrawal

fall·board /fáwl bàwrd/ *n US* the hinged cover that protects a piano keyboard when the instrument is not being played

fall·en /fáwlən/ past participle of **fall** ■ *npl* those people killed in war or battle, especially while fighting

fall·en an·gel *n* **1.** in Christian, Jewish, and Muslim tradition, a rebellious angel who was punished by God by being banished from heaven **2.** a bond that was investment grade when it was issued, but that has subsequently been downgraded

fall·en arch *n* a flattening of the arch of the foot (*usually used in the plural*)

fall·en wom·an *n* a woman who is regarded as sinful or disgraced because she has had sexual relations outside marriage (*literary*)

fall·er /fáwlər/ *n* **1.** a person, animal, or thing that falls **2.** FORESTRY same as **feller**[1] (sense 1)

fall·fish /fáwl fìsh/ (*plural same or* **-fish·es**) *n* a large minnow that makes a substantial nest by piling up small pebbles. Native to: eastern North America. Latin name: *Semotilus corporalis*.

fall guy *n* (*slang*) **1.** somebody who takes the blame for somebody else's mistake or wrongdoing **2.** somebody who is easily tricked or deceived

fal·li·ble /fálləb'l/ *adj* **1.** liable to make mistakes **2.** liable to be wrong or misleading [15C. < medieval Latin *fallibilis* < Latin *fallere* "deceive"] —**fal·li·bil·i·ty** /fàllə bíllətee/ *n* —**fal·li·ble·ness** *n* —**fal·li·bly** *adv*

fall·ing ac·tion *n US* in a work of fiction or in a drama, the events that follow the climax and lead to the denouement

fall·ing band *n* a large collar, often trimmed with lace, turned down flat onto the shoulders, worn by men in the 17th century

fall·ing-off *n* a decrease in size, number, or quality

fall·ing-out (*plural* **fall·ings-out** *or* **fall·ing-outs**) *n* a disagreement, especially one that leads to strained relations with somebody

fall·ing rhythm *n US* poetic meter in which the stress falls consistently on the first syllable of a foot

fall·ing star *n* ASTRON same as **meteor** (sense 2)

fall line *n* **1.** GEOG IMAGINARY LINE ALONG TOP OF SLOPE an imaginary line along the edge of higher land, marked by rapids and waterfalls, that indicates where rivers begin to descend more steeply from a highland region to a lowland one **2.** SKIING NATURAL ROUTE OF DESCENT OF HILL the natural route of descent on a hill between two given points **3.** CLIMBING LINE CONNECTING HIGH AND LOW POINT vertical line connecting a high and low point on a mountain or cliff

fall·off /fáwl àwf, -òf/ *n* a decrease or decline, especially in the price of or demand for something

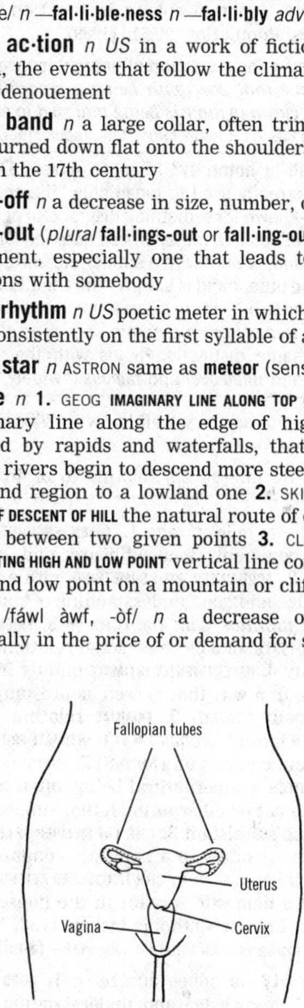

fallopian tube

fal·lo·pi·an tube /fə lōpee ən-/, **Fal·lo·pi·an tube** *n* either of two narrow tubes through which a female mammal's eggs pass from either of the ovaries to the womb [Early 18C. After Gabriello *Fallopio* (1523–62), Italian anatomist]

fall·out /fáwl òwt/ *n* **1.** RADIOACTIVE PARTICLES a cloud of radioactive dust that is created by a nuclear explosion and settles back down to the ground **2.** DESCENT OF RADIOACTIVE DUST the descent from the atmosphere of particles from a cloud of radioactive dust **3.** INCIDENTAL CONSEQUENCES consequences, especially undesirable ones, that result incidentally from a situation or event

fall·out shel·ter *n* a place of refuge built to protect people from the effects of a nuclear weapon

fal·low[1] /fállō/ *adj* **1.** AGRIC LEFT UNSEEDED AFTER PLOWING left unseeded after plowing for a period of time in order to recover natural fertility **2.** CURRENTLY INACTIVE currently inactive but with the possibility of activity or use in the future ■ *n* AGRIC LAND WITHOUT CROPS land that has not been planted or sown with crops [13C. < Old English *fealh* < *fealgian* "break up land by plowing"] —**fal·low·ness** *n*

fal·low[2] /fállō/ *adj* of a light yellowish brown color [Old English *fealu* < Indo-European] —**fal·low** *n*

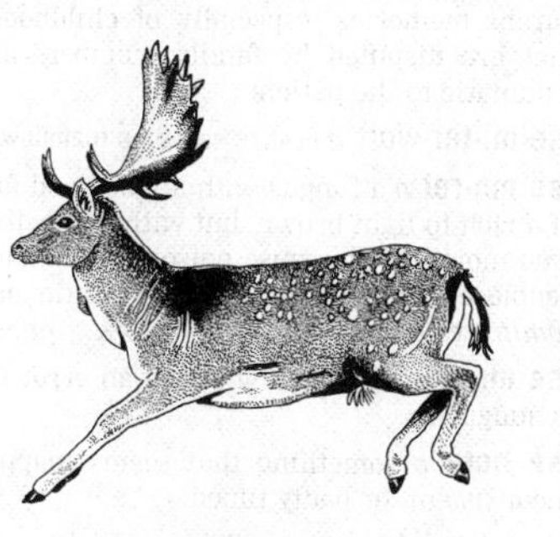
fallow deer

fal·low deer *n* a deer, the male of which has broad flattened antlers and a brown coat spotted with white in summer. Native to: Europe, Asia. Latin name: *Dama dama*.

Fall Riv·er /fàwl-/ city in southeastern Massachusetts, 12 mi./19 km northwest of New Bedford. Population: 92,660 (2002 estimate).

Fal·mouth /fálməth/ town on Cape Cod, in southeastern Massachusetts between Buzzards Bay and Vineyard Sound. Population: 33,628 (2002 estimate).

false /fawlss/ *adj* (**fals·er, fals·est**) **1.** INCORRECT not conforming to facts or truth ○ *was given false information* **2.** MISTAKEN resulting from a mistaken belief or a misunderstanding ○ *have a false impression of the situation* **3.** ARTIFICIAL imitating, copying, or having the same function as a particular thing and replacing or used alongside it ○ *false eyelashes* **4.** DELIBERATELY DECEPTIVE done with or having the intention of deceiving somebody ○ *false promises* **5.** NOT GENUINE intentionally made or adopted to deceive somebody ○ *false papers* **6.** TREACHEROUS disloyal and untrustworthy **7.** BIOL CONFUSABLE WITH PARTICULAR PLANT OR ANIMAL superficially resembling and often mistaken for a particular plant or animal ○ *false acacia* ■ *adv* DISHONESTLY in a dishonest and disloyal way (*literary*) [Pre-12C. Directly or via Old French < Latin *falsus* < *fallere* "deceive"] —**false·ly** *adv* —**false·ness** *n*

false a·ca·cia *n UK* same as **locust** (sense 3)

false a·larm *n* **1.** a situation in which an alarm goes off unnecessarily **2.** something that appears to be a problem but is not ○ *The company's impending bankruptcy proved to be a false alarm.*

false ar·rest *n US* an arrest made without legal authority

false bed·ding *n* GEOL same as **cross-bedding**

false-card (**false-card·ed, false-card·ing, false-cards**) *vi* to play a card in bridge to mislead an opponent about the cards held in the suit led

false dawn *n* **1.** light that appears in the east just before dawn **2.** a sign that promises but does not deliver good results

false e·con·o·my *n* an apparent short-term saving

that eventually results in extra expense that could have been avoided

false friend *n* **1.** a word in a second language that closely resembles a word in somebody's first language but means something different **2.** a friend proven to be disloyal and untrustworthy

false fruit *n* BOT same as **pseudocarp**

false·hood /fáwlss hòod/ *n* **1. LIE** an intentionally untrue statement **2. TELLING OF LIES** the act of spreading lies ○ *a defendant noted for falsehood* **3. SOMETHING NOT CONSISTENT WITH FACT** something that does not correspond with the known or observable facts ○ *I can't answer for the truth or falsehood of his story as I've never been to China.*

SYNONYMS See *lie*[2].

false im·pris·on·ment *n* the unlawful confinement of somebody

false keel *n* an extension to a vessel's keel, added to protect the main keel or to increase stability

false mem·o·ry syn·drome *n* a situation in which examination, therapy, or hypnosis has elicited apparent memories, especially of childhood abuse, that are disputed by family members and often traumatic to the patient

false mi·ter·wort *n* PLANTS same as **foamflower**

false mo·rel *n* a fungus with a lobed and folded cap of a rich to light brown, but without cavities like a true morel. It can cause poisoning, although some people eat it with no problems. Latin name: *Gyromitra esculenta*.

false move *n* an action showing an error of timing or judgment

false note *n* something that seems inappropriate, inconsistent, or badly timed

false po·si·tion *n* a situation in which somebody is forced to act in an inconsistent or uncharacteristic way

false pos·i·tive *n* **1.** MED, SCI the result of a medical, chemical, or biological test that appears to be positive but is in fact erroneous **2.** a situation in which data about somebody produces an incorrect match against a checklist, e.g., when a passenger profile is matched against a list of suspected terrorists [Late 20C]

false preg·nan·cy *n* a condition in which a woman has the mistaken belief that she is pregnant and displays symptoms and signs of pregnancy. Technical name **pseudocyesis**

false pre·ten·ses *npl* deception or misrepresentation in order to gain something from somebody ○ *He gained her trust under false pretenses.*

false rib *n* a rib connected to the lowest true rib rather than directly to the breastbone. In humans the three lower ribs on each side are false ribs.

false start *n* **1.** a situation in which a competitor in a race breaks a regulation governing the starting procedure and the race has to be restarted **2.** a failed attempt to begin something

false step *n* **1.** an action showing an error of judgment **2.** an act of stumbling

false to·paz *n* CRYSTALS same as **citrine** *n* (sense 1)

fal·set·to /fawl séttō/ *n* (*plural* **-tos**) **1. HIGH SINGING METHOD** a method used by male singers to sing at a very high pitch by using more air and a combination of vocal chord vibration and head resonance. It is used by countertenors in classical music. **2. FALSETTO SINGER** a male singer who sings in a very high voice **3. FALSETTO VOICE** a very high voice used by a male singer ■ *adv* **IN FALSETTO VOICE** in an artificially or unusually high voice [Late 18C. < Italian, "little false (one)" < *falso* "false" < Latin *falsus* (see FALSE)]

false·work /fáwlss wùrk/ *n* a structure or frame that supports something that is being built

fals·ies /fáwlsseez/ *npl* two pads worn inside a bra to make the breasts look larger or more shapely (*informal*)

fal·si·fy /fáwlssə fī/ (**-fied, -fy·ing, -fies**) *vt* **1. ALTER FRAUDULENTLY** to alter something in order to deceive **2. DISPROVE** to prove that something is incorrect **3. MISREPRESENT** to misrepresent the facts in order to mislead ○ *They falsified every detail of their story.* [15C. Directly or via French *falsifier* < medieval Latin *falsificare* "act dishonestly" < Latin *falsus* (see FALSE) + *facere* "do, make"] —**fal·si·fi·a·bil·i·ty** /fàwlssə fī ə bíllətee/ *n* —**fal·si·fi·a·ble** *adj* —**fal·si·fi·ca·tion** /fàwlssəfi káysh'n/ *n* —**fal·si·fi·er** *n*

fal·si·ty /fáwlssətee/ (*plural* **-ties**) *n* **1.** the fact or condition of being untrue **2.** something that is untrue [13C. Directly or via French < Latin *falsitas* < *falsus* (see FALSE)]

Fal·staff·i·an /fawl stáffee ən/ *adj* characteristic of the Shakespearean character Sir John Falstaff in being bawdy, pleasure-loving, given to outlandish bragging, and of great size

falt·boat /fólt bōt, fáwlt-/ *n UK* same as **foldboat** [See FOLDBOAT]

fal·ter /fáwltər/ (**-tered, -ter·ing, -ters**) *v* **1.** *vi* **LOSE CONFIDENCE** to become unsure and hesitant **2.** *vi* **BEGIN TO FAIL** to lose strength, power, or vitality **3.** *vi* **STUMBLE** to move unsteadily **4.** *vti* **SPEAK OR ACT HESITANTLY** to show a loss of confidence, especially to speak or act with hesitation ○ *Trembling with shame, she faltered an apology.* [14C. Origin ?] —**fal·ter·er** *n* —**fal·ter·ing·ly** *adv*

SYNONYMS See *hesitate*.

Fal·un Gong /faa lòon góng/ *n* a spiritual philosophy or movement, with roots in traditional Chinese belief, teaching cultivation of an orb of energy in the lower abdomen through breathing exercises. This is believed to lead to improved physical and spiritual health and even to the acquisition of supernatural powers. [Late 20C. < Chinese, "law wheel"]

fam. *abbr* **1.** familiar **2.** family

F.A.M. *abbr* Free and Accepted Masons

Fa·ma·gus·ta /fàmmə gòostə/ seaport and resort on the eastern coast of Cyprus, near Nicosia. It was a wealthy Venetian colony in the 15th and 16th centuries. Population: 20,516 (1989).

fame /faym/ *n* the condition of being very well known ○ *the fame that goes with being a recording star* ○ *His only claim to fame is being married to a socialite.* [12C. Via French < Latin *fama* "talk, report, reputation"]

USAGE fame or **notoriety**? In contemporary English ***notoriety*** is correctly used to mean only "the condition of being well-known for something disgraceful or otherwise undesirable," as in *a mayor whose notoriety stems from election fraud.* A word with a similar meaning is *infamy.* ***Fame*** on the other hand is simply "the condition of being very well known," as in *a governor whose fame* [not *notoriety*] *stems from his heroic service in the Korean War.* The same distinction holds with the adjectives ***notorious*** (and ***infamous***) and ***famous*** ("widely known").

famed /faymd/ *adj* very well known ○ *The restaurant was famed for its steaks.*

fa·mil·ial /fə míllyəl/ *adj* relating to or involving a family

fa·mil·iar /fə míllyər/ *adj* **1. OFTEN ENCOUNTERED** well known, commonly seen or heard, and easily recognized **2. ACQUAINTED WITH SOMETHING** with a thorough knowledge and good understanding of something ○ *Are you familiar with the theory?* **3. FRIENDLY** in or characteristic of a close personal relationship with somebody **4. IMPERTINENTLY INTIMATE** unduly friendly or intimate in a way that is seen as presumptuous or impertinent (*dated*) **5. FAMILIAL** relating to or involving a family (*archaic*) ■ *n* **1. INTIMATE FRIEND** a close friend and companion (*formal*) **2.** PARANORMAL **SPIRIT HELPING WITCH** a supernatural being, often taking the form of a cat or other animal, that supposedly acts as a witch's assistant **3.** CHR **LAY MEMBER OF MONASTERY** a residential worker in a monastic community who has not taken a vow **4.** CHR **HOUSEHOLD ATTENDANT OF POPE OR BISHOP** a domestic servant in the household of a pope or Roman Catholic bishop [13C. Via French < Latin *familiaris* < *familia* (see FAMILY)] —**fa·mil·iar·ly** *adv*

fa·mil·iar·i·ty /fə millee árrətee/ *n* **1. GOOD KNOWLEDGE** thorough knowledge and understanding of something ○ *Familiarity with database systems would be an advantage.* **2. INTIMACY** closeness and friendliness in a personal relationship **3. FAMILIAR QUALITY** the quality of being known ○ *The place had a strange familiarity about it.* **4.** (*plural* **fa·mil·iar·i·ties**) **UNWELCOME INTIMACY** an intimacy that is improper and presumptuous (*dated*)

fa·mil·iar·ize /fə míllyə rīz/ (**-ized, -iz·ing, -iz·es**) *vt* to acquire or provide somebody with information or experience necessary for understanding or doing something ○ *You should familiarize yourself with the emergency procedure.* —**fa·mil·iar·i·za·tion** /fə mìllyəri záysh'n/ *n* —**fa·mil·iar·iz·er** *n*

fa·mil·iar spir·it *n* PARANORMAL same as **familiar** *n* (sense 2)

~~**familier**~~ incorrect spelling of **familiar**

fam·i·ly /fámməlee/ *n* (*plural* **-lies**) **1. GROUP OF RELATIVES** a group of people who are closely related by birth, marriage, or adoption **2. PEOPLE LIVING TOGETHER** a group of people living together and functioning as a single household, usually consisting of parents and their children **3. LINEAGE** all the people who are descended from a common ancestor **4. OFFSPRING** a child or set of children born to somebody ○ *They're not ready to start a family.* **5. GROUP WITH SOMETHING IN COMMON** a group whose members are related in origin, characteristics, or occupation **6.** LING **RELATED LANGUAGES** a group of languages that have a common origin **7.** BIOL **SET OF RELATED ORGANISMS** in taxonomic classification, a category of related organisms, comprising one or more genera **8.** MATH **RELATED MATHEMATICAL SHAPES OR EXPRESSIONS** a set of related mathematical curves, surfaces, or functions, usually expressed as a single equation containing one or more parameters or arbitrary constants ○ *a family of concentric circles* **9.** CHEM same as **series** (sense 6) **10.** *US* CRIME **BRANCH OF MAFIA** a branch of the Mafia or of a similar large criminal group (*informal*) **11.** *S Asia* same as **wife** ■ *adj* **1. USED BY FAMILY** used, owned, or employed by a family, or suitable for one ○ *the family car* **2. APPROPRIATE FOR CHILDREN** suitable to be experienced by families with children ○ *family viewing* **3. SERVING FAMILIES** serving families and not just businesses or institutions ○ *a family butcher* [15C. < Latin *familia* "servants of a household, household, family" < *famulus* "servant"] ◇ **in the family way** pregnant (*informal dated*)

fam·i·ly al·low·ance *n Can, UK* an allowance formerly paid by the government in the United Kingdom and Canada to parents or guardians of children below a specific age

fam·i·ly Bi·ble *n* a large Bible handed down in a family from one generation to another, usually containing records of births, marriages, and deaths

fam·i·ly cir·cle *n* **1.** the members of a family who are closely related and usually live together **2.** *US* an area or tier in a theater where the seats are less expensive

fam·i·ly court *n* a court that rules on domestic disputes, especially those involving the care and custody of children

fam·i·ly doc·tor *n* a doctor who treats patients' general medical problems

fam·i·ly leave *n US* a temporary leave of absence for an employee, usually unpaid, so that he or she can take care of family concerns such as emergency child care or a serious illness

fam·i·ly man *n* **1.** a married man with children **2.** a married man who enjoys family life and spends a lot of time with his wife and children

fam·i·ly·moon /fámməlee mòon/ *n* an after-wedding vacation trip on which the bride and groom's children by prior marriages accompany their respective parents [Early 21C. Modeled on HONEYMOON]

fam·i·ly name *n* same as **surname** *n* (sense 1)

fam·i·ly plan·ning *n* the use of birth control methods to choose the number and timing of children born into a family

fam·i·ly room *n* **1.** a room in a family home used for relaxation, entertainment, or children's play **2.** a hotel room that can accommodate adults and their children

fam·i·ly style *adj, adv US* providing food in serving dishes on the table, so that people can serve themselves (*hyphenated when used before a noun*)

fam·i·ly tree *n* a chart that shows the relationships of members of a family over time, including dates of marriages, births, and deaths

fam·i·ly wom·an *n* **1.** a married woman with children **2.** a married woman who enjoys family life and spends a lot of time with her husband and children

fam·ine /fámmin/ *n* **1.** EXTREME FOOD SCARCITY a severe shortage of food resulting in widespread hunger **2.** DEFICIENCY OF SOMETHING a severe shortage of something **3.** EXTREME HUNGER extreme hunger and starvation [14C. < French < *faim* "hunger" < Latin *fames*]

fam·ish /fámmish/ (**-ished, -ish·ing, -ish·es**) *vti* to be extremely hungry, or make somebody extremely hungry (*often passive*) [14C. < obsolete *fame* < Old French *afamer* < Latin *fames* "hunger"] —**fam·ish·ment** *n*

fa·mous /fáyməss/ *adj* **1.** known and recognized by many people **2.** excellent and satisfying (*dated*) [14C. Via Old French < Latin *famosus* < *fama* "talk, report, reputation"] —**fa·mous·ly** *adv* —**fa·mous·ness** *n*

USAGE See ***fame***.

fam·u·lus /fámmyələss/ (*plural* **-li** /-lī/) *n* a personal secretary or attendant, especially to a scholar or magician (*literary*) [Mid-19C. < Latin, "servant"]

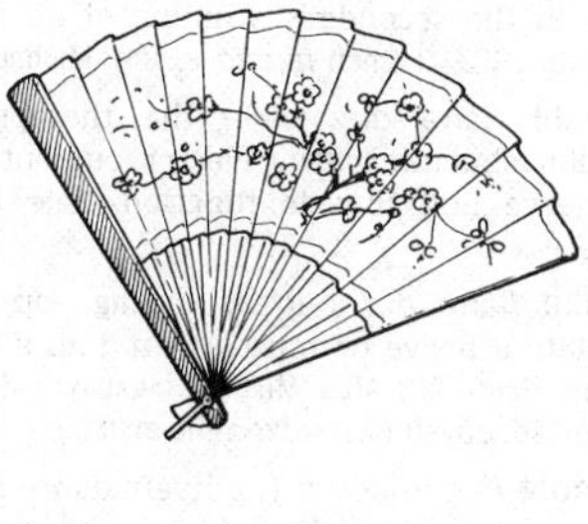

fan (sense 2)

fan[1] /fan/ *n* **1.** DEVICE FOR MOVING AIR a device to circulate currents of air, especially one with rotating blades **2.** PERSONAL COOLING DEVICE a flat disk on a handle or a folding semicircular device for waving back and forth in order to cool the face **3.** SOMETHING FAN-SHAPED something in the shape of an open hand-held fan, e.g., the tail of a peacock **4.** AGRIC WINNOWING MACHINE a machine with a series of revolving blades used to winnow or clean grain ■ *v* (**fanned, fan·ning, fans**) **1.** *vt* BLOW ON SOMETHING to blow a current of air steadily and lightly across or around something, either cooling or agitating it ○ *A cool breeze fanned the shore.* **2.** *vt* MOVE AIR USING FAN to move air around using a fan **3.** *vt* MAKE SITUATION TENSE to cause emotions to become more intense or a situation to become more volatile **4.** *vt* AGRIC SEPARATE GRAIN FROM CHAFF to winnow grain by blowing away the chaff **5.** *vt* ARMS FIRE GUN WITH REPEATED CHOPPING MOVEMENT to fire a gun repeatedly by holding the trigger back and chopping at the hammer with the open hand **6.** *vti* SPREAD ACROSS SOMETHING to spread out in the shape of an open hand-held fan, or spread something out in this way **7.** *vt* US BASEBALL, HOCKEY STRIKE OUT in baseball and hockey, to strike at the ball or puck unsuccessfully (*slang*) [Pre-12C. < Latin *vannus* "device for winnowing grain"] —**fan·ner** *n*

fan out *vti* to spread out in the shape of an open hand-held fan, or spread something out in this way

fan[2] /fan/ *n* **1.** an enthusiastic admirer of a celebrity or public performer **2.** same as **fanatic** *n* (sense 2) [Late 19C. Shortening of FANATIC]

fa·nat·ic /fə náttik/ *n* **1.** a holder of extreme or irrational enthusiasms or beliefs, especially in religion or politics **2.** somebody who is very enthusiastic about a pastime or hobby ■ *adj* same as **fanatical** [Mid-16C. Directly or via French < Latin *fanaticus* "inspired by a god, frenzied" < *fanum* "temple"] —**fa·nat·i·cism** /fə nátti sìzzəm/ *n*

fa·nat·i·cal /fə náttik'l/ *adj* excessively enthusiastic about a particular belief, cause, or activity —**fa·nat·i·cal·ly** *adv* —**fa·nat·i·cal·ness** *n*

fa·nat·i·cize /fə nátti sīz/ (**-cized, -ciz·ing, -ciz·es**) *vti* to make somebody fanatical about something, or become fanatical about something

fan belt *n* a continuous belt that turns a fan, especially one turning the cooling fan in the engine of a motor vehicle

fan·ci·er /fánsee ər/ *n* **1.** somebody who is especially interested in or enthusiastic about something **2.** somebody with a special interest in the breeding of a particular animal or plant ○ *a pigeon fancier*

fan·ci·ful /fánsif'l/ *adj* **1.** IMAGINARY based on imagination or dreams **2.** IMAGINATIVE AND IMPRACTICAL led by imagination rather than realism and practicality **3.** CURIOUSLY MADE strangely and imaginatively designed or made —**fan·ci·ful·ly** *adv* —**fan·ci·ful·ness** *n*

fan club *n* an organization whose members are devoted to a celebrity or public performer, providing information and sometimes organizing special events

fan·cy /fánsee/ *adj* (**-ci·er, -ci·est**) **1.** NOT PLAIN elaborately or ornately decorated **2.** INTRICATE intricately and skillfully performed ○ *fancy footwork* **3.** *US* HIGH QUALITY describes food items of superior quality **4.** EXPENSIVE expensively priced or highly valued ○ *fancy prices* ○ *fancy restaurants charging high prices* **5.** SELECTIVELY BRED describes animals that have been bred for specific features and qualities ■ *vt* (**-cied, -cy·ing, -cies**) **1.** *UK* WISH FOR SOMETHING to want to do or have something ○ *I fancy a walk this afternoon.* ○ *Do you fancy a coffee?* **2.** *UK* DESIRE SOMEBODY to find somebody sexually desirable (*informal*) ○ *I'm sure he fancies you!* **3.** *UK* IDENTIFY SOMEBODY AS POTENTIAL WINNER to think that somebody will succeed ○ *Who do you fancy for the title?* **4.** SUPPOSE SOMETHING to be inclined to think that something is the case ○ *I fancy that it will be bright and sunny tomorrow.* **5.** IMAGINE SOMETHING to form the idea of something in the imagination ■ *interj UK* EXPRESSING SURPRISE used to express surprise or incredulity (*informal*) ○ *Fancy! All that money!* ○ *Fancy that! I would never have believed it!* ■ *n* (*plural* **-cies**) **1.** SUDDEN LIKING an impulsive liking for somebody or desire for something ○ *The hat caught my fancy.* ○ *She seems to have taken quite a fancy to him.* **2.** NOTION an unfounded belief about something **3.** SOMETHING IMAGINARY something created by the imagination, especially something of a playful or superficial nature **4.** LIKELY WINNER something or somebody thought likely to succeed or win **5.** PLAYFUL IMAGINATIVENESS the faculty of using the imagination playfully or inventively **6.** GOOD TASTE good critical taste and judgment (*formal*) **7.** BOXING ENTHUSIASTS enthusiasts of a sport or pastime, especially boxing (*archaic*) [15C. Contraction of FANTASY] —**fan·ci·ly** *adv* —**fan·ci·ness** *n*

fancy up *vt US* to decorate something

fan·cy dress *n* unusual clothing worn to a social gathering, often depicting a famous person, fictional character, or historical period [Because according to the wearer's fancy]

fan·cy-free *adj* free to go anywhere and do anything ○ *footloose and fancy-free*

fan·cy man *n* **1.** the lover or boyfriend of a woman, especially a married woman (*dated informal*) **2.** same as **pimp** (*archaic*)

fan·cy wom·an *n* **1.** the lover or girlfriend of a man, especially a married man (*dated informal*) **2.** a prostitute (*archaic*)

fan·cy·work /fánsee wùrk/ *n* embroidery and other decorative needlework

fan dance *n* an erotic dance in which large fans are used to mask and reveal parts of the dancer's nude body

fan·dan·go /fan dáng gō/ (*plural* **-gos**) *n* **1.** a vigorous Spanish or Latin American dance in triple time, traditionally performed by a man and woman as a courtship ritual **2.** the music for a fandango [Mid-18C. < Spanish]

fan·dom /fándəm/ *n* fans collectively, especially of a public entertainer such as a movie or TV star

fan·fare /fán fàir/ *n* **1.** a short dramatic series of notes played on trumpets or other brass instruments, especially to mark the arrival of somebody important **2.** any dramatic and ostentatious event, especially an announcement or publicity stunt [Mid-18C. < French]

fan·fold /fán fòld/ *adj* folded into pleats by making alternate folds in opposite directions ○ *fanfold computer paper*

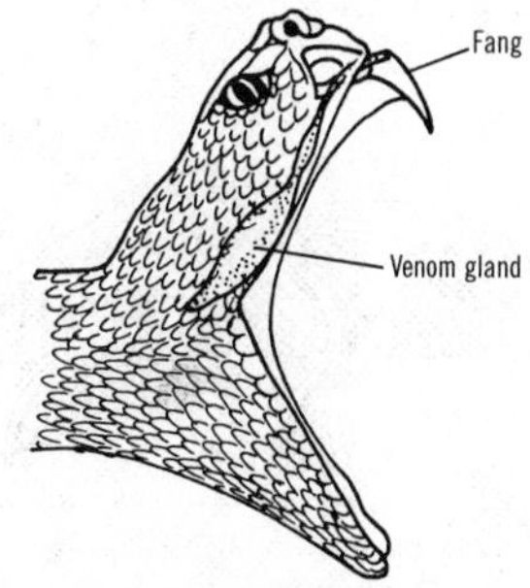

fang (sense 2)

fang /fang/ *n* **1.** CANINE TOOTH a long pointed tooth of an animal on each side of the mouth toward the front **2.** SNAKE'S TOOTH a tooth of a venomous snake, with a hollow or grooves through which venom is emitted **3.** SPIDER'S MOUTHPART either of the pair of mouthparts of a spider, from which poison is emitted [Pre-12C. < Old Norse, "capture, grasp"] —**fanged** *adj*

Fang /fang, faang/ (*plural same* or **Fangs**) *n* **1.** a member of a people who live mainly in the rain forests of Gabon, Equatorial Guinea, and Cameroon **2.** the Bantu language spoken by the Fang people, belonging to the Benue-Congo branch of the Niger-Congo family of languages. Native speakers: 2 million. [Mid-19C. < French *Fan*, probably < Fang *Pangwe*] —**Fang** *adj*

fan heat·er *n UK* an electric heater that blows out a current of warm air using a fan

fan·ion /fánnyən/ *n* a small marking flag used by surveyors and soldiers [Early 18C. < French, "small maniple"]

fan·jet /fán jèt/ *n US* **1.** a jet engine with a large turbine-driven fan located in a forward duct that increases thrust and reduces noise by forcing air back around the exhaust **2.** an aircraft powered by one or more fanjets ▶ Can term **turbofan**

Fan Kuan /faàn kwaán/ (*fl* 990–1030) Chinese artist. He is noted for his landscapes of mountains and streams, which he painted while living alone in the mountains.

fan let·ter *n* a letter written to a celebrity by a fan

fan·light /fán līt/ *n* **1.** a semicircular window above a door or another window, often with struts forming the shape of an open hand-held fan **2.** *UK* ARCHIT same as **transom** (sense 4)

fan mail *n* letters sent to celebrities by their fans

Fan·nie Mae /fànnee máy/ *n US* the Federal National Mortgage Association, a private corporation sponsored by the government that supplies funds for mortgages, or a publicly traded security backed by it

fan·ny /fánnee/ (*plural* **-nies**) *n* **1.** the buttocks (*slang*) **2.** *UK* a highly offensive term for the female genitals (*taboo slang*) [Early 20C. Origin ?]

fan·ny pack *n* a pouch for valuables, strapped around the waist

fan palm *n* a palm tree with divided fan-shaped leaves

fan·tab·u·lous /fan tábbyələss/ *adj* extremely good (*humorous*) [Mid-20C. Blend of FANTASTIC + FABULOUS]

fan·tail /fán tàyl/ *n* **1.** FAN-SHAPED TAIL OR END a tail or the end of something shaped like an open hand-held fan **2.** BIRDS PIGEON WITH FAN-SHAPED TAIL a breed of domestic pigeon with a broad fan-shaped tail **3.** BIRDS BIRD WITH BROAD TAIL a small bird with a fan-shaped tail. Native to: Australia, New Zealand, Asia. Genus: *Rhipidura*. **4.** FISH GOLDFISH WITH BROAD TAIL a goldfish with a broad double tail fin. See illustration on next page **5.** *US* NAUT ROUNDED PART OF STERN a rounded overhanging part of a ship's stern **6.** WINDMILL SAIL a secondary sail on a windmill that keeps the main sails facing into the wind

fan-tan /fán tàn/ *n* **1.** a Chinese gambling game in which players bet on how many items that have been concealed under a bowl remain after being counted off in fours **2.** a card game in which players seek to discard all their cards in a sequence based on the same suit as a seven that has been led [Late 19C. < Chinese < *fān* "turn, chance" + *tān* "to spread out"]

fantail (sense 4)

fan·ta·sia /fan táyzhə, fan táyzhee ə/ *n* an instrumental composition in a free and improvisatory style, sometimes based on well-known melodies [Early 18C. < Italian, literally "fantasy, imagination," via Latin < Greek *phantasia* (see FANTASY)]

CULTURAL NOTE ***Fantasia***, a movie (1940) produced by Walt Disney. This ambitious attempt to popularize classical music consists of cartoon animation matched to eight famous musical compositions. Its best-known sequences include hippos dancing to Ponchielli's "Dance of the Hours" and Mickey Mouse as the protagonist of Dukas' "The Sorcerer's Apprentice."

fan·ta·size /fántə sīz/ (**-sized, -si·zing, -siz·es**) *vti* to indulge in fantasies of the imagination, or imagine something as a fantasy —**fan·ta·sist** *n*

fan·tast /fán tàst/, **phan·tast** *n* somebody who has impractical daydreams [Late 16C. Via medieval Latin *phantasta* and German *Phantast* < Greek *phantastēs* "boaster" < *phantazein* (see FANTASY)]

fan·tas·tic /fan tástik/, **fan·tas·ti·cal** /-ik'l/ *adj* **1. EXCELLENT** extraordinarily good **2. INCREDIBLE** apparently impossible but real or true ○ *the fantastic story of his journey home* **3. IMAGINARY** existing only in the imagination **4. ENORMOUS** much larger than is usual, expected, or desirable **5. BIZARRE** extremely strange in appearance ○ *a rich fabric in a fantastic pattern of greens and blues* **6. UNLIKELY** unusual and unlikely to be successful ○ *a fantastic scheme to get rich quickly* ■ *interj* **EXPRESSING PLEASURE** used to express surprise, pleasure, or approval (*informal*) ○ *You won the game? Fantastic!* [14C. Via French < Greek *phantastikos* < *phantazein* (see FANTASY)] —**fan·tas·ti·cal·i·ty** /fan tàsti kállətee/ *n* —**fan·tas·ti·cal·ness** *n*

fan·tas·ti·cal·ly /fan tástikəlee/ *adv* **1. VERY** extremely **2. VERY WELL** in a superb way **3. STRANGELY** in a weird and strange way

fan·ta·sy /fántəssee/ *n* (*plural* **-sies**) **1. IMAGINATIVE POWER** the creative power of the imagination **2. MENTAL IMAGE OR DREAM** an image or dream created by the imagination **3. IMPRACTICAL IDEA** an unrealistic and impractical idea ○ *She has this fantasy that someday she'll write a novel.* **4.** PSYCHOL **CREATION OF MENTAL IMAGES** in psychology, the creation of exaggerated mental images in response to an ungratified need **5.** LITERAT **GENRE OF FICTION** a type of fiction featuring imaginary worlds and magical or supernatural events **6.** MUSIC same as **fantasia** ■ *vti* (**-sied, -sy·ing, -sies**) same as **fantasize** [14C. Via Old French < Greek *phantasia* "appearance, imagination" < *phantazein* "make visible" < *phainein* "to show"]

Fan·ti /fántee, fáantee/ (*plural same* or **-tis**), **Fan·te** (*plural same* or **-tes**) *n* **1.** a member of an African people living in the rain forests of Ghana and the Côte d'Ivoire **2.** a dialect of Akan spoken in parts of Ghana and the Côte d'Ivoire [Early 19C. < Fanti] —**Fan·ti** *adj*

fan·tod /fán tòd/ *n* nervous anxiety (*informal*) ○ *He had a fit of the fantods.* [Mid-19C. Origin ?]

fan vault·ing *n* a form of vaulting in which ribs fan out from the four corners of a bay, like a fan

fan·wort /fán wùrt, -wàwrt/ *n* a water plant of the lily family with fan-shaped submerged and floating leaves. Genus: *Cabomba.*

fan·zine /fán zeèn/ *n* an amateur magazine produced for fans of a pastime or celebrity [Mid-20C. < FAN² + MAGAZINE]

FAO *abbr* Food and Agriculture Organization (of the UN)

FAQ /fak, èf ay kyóo/ *abbr* **1.** SHIPPING free alongside quay **2.** frequently asked questions

fa·qir *n* HINDUISM another spelling of **fakir**

FAQs /faks, èf ay kyóoz/ *abbr* frequently asked questions

far /faar/ (**far·ther** /fáarthər/ or **fur·ther** /fúrthər/, **far·thest** /fáarthəst/ or **fur·thest** /fúrthəst/) CORE MEANING: an adverb and adjective indicating that something is a long way away in distance or time ○ (adv) *How far did you have to drive?* ○ (adj) *In the far distance were the lights of a settlement.*

1. *adv* **NOT NEARBY** at, to, or from a great distance ○ *We saw the first outline of the shore far ahead.* **2.** *adv* **NOT CLOSE IN TIME** at or to a long time from the point of reference ○ *Sadly the time for completion falls far in the future.* **3.** *adv* **TO SPECIFIC EXTENT** to the extent that is desirable or necessary ○ *How far will you take your complaint?* **4.** *adv* **MUCH OR MANY** to or by a considerable degree ○ *Keeping a dog healthy is far more complicated than it seems.* ○ *There are far fewer factory jobs available these days.* **5.** *adj* **DISTANT** remote in space or time ○ *He stood there, gazing out to the far horizon.* ○ *He had lived there once in the far past.* **6.** *adj* **MORE DISTANT** more distant from somebody or something ○ *on the far side of the room* **7.** *adj* **EXTREME** having an extreme position in a particular direction ○ *His politics are far left of center.* [Old English *feor(r)*, via Germanic, "farther beyond" < Indo-European] ◇ **as far as 1.** to the greatest distance possible ○ *moved away as far as he could without seeming rude* **2.** to the extent that ○ *She's happier as far as I can tell.* ◇ **far and away** without a doubt and by a large margin ○ *She is far and away the best player that we have.* ◇ **far and near** everywhere ○ *Doctors from far and near flocked to his bedside.* ◇ **far and wide** covering a great distance ○ *The church bells will be heard far and wide.* ◇ **far from** not at all ○ *I'm far from satisfied with the outcome.* ◇ **far from it** on the contrary ○ *He was not the tallest boy in the class – far from it.* ◇ **far gone 1.** in a state of deterioration and unable to function ○ *These shoes can't be repaired – they're too far gone.* **2.** very intoxicated (*informal*) ○ *She was too far gone to drive home.* ◇ **far out** used to express amazement and approval (*dated slang*) ◇ **go far 1.** to be very successful ○ *He is very talented and I am sure he will go far in his chosen career.* **2.** to last or be sufficient ○ *Three loaves of bread won't go far once my family gets going.* ◇ **go too far, take something too far** to do or say something that is unacceptable or that exceeds reasonable limits ○ *Harriet paused, and realized that she had gone too far.* ◇ **in so far as** to the extent that ◇ **so far 1.** up to this moment ○ *So far, 150 people have shown an interest in the product.* **2.** up to a certain point, extent, or degree ○ *Freedom of information can only go so far.* ◇ **so far so good** indicates satisfaction with progress made up to this point ○ *So far so good, but the last part of the climb is the hardest.*

Fa·ra·bi /fə ráabee/, **al-** (A.D. 873?–950?) Arabian philosopher. He influenced Islamic philosophy with his studies of Plato and Aristotle.

far·ad /fárrəd, fá ràd/ *n* the SI unit of capacitance equal to that of a capacitor carrying one coulomb of charge when a potential difference of one volt is applied. Symbol **F** [Mid-19C. After Michael FARADAY]

far·a·da·ic *adj* ELEC same as **faradic**

far·a·day /fárrə dày/ *n* a unit of electric charge equal to that needed to deposit a unit amount of singly charged substance during electrolysis, equivalent to 96,485 coulombs. Symbol ***F*** [Early 20C. After Michael FARADAY]

Far·a·day /fárrə dày/, **Michael** (1791–1867) British physicist and chemist. He is best known for his discoveries of electromagnetic induction and of the laws of electrolysis. He also showed how electromagnetic induction could be used in generators and transformers.

Michael Faraday

> "I express a wish that you may, in your generation, be fit to compare to a candle; that you may, like it, shine as lights to those about you; that, in all your actions, you may justify the beauty of the taper by making your deeds honorable and effectual in the discharge of your duty to your fellow men."
> [Michael Faraday, *A Course of Six Lectures on the Chemical History of a Candle*; 1861]

fa·rad·ic /fə ráddik/, **far·a·da·ic** /fàrrə dáy ik/ *adj* relating to an intermittent alternating current produced in the secondary winding of an induction coil [Late 19C. < French *faradique*, after Michael FARADAY]

far·a·dism /fárrə dìzzəm/ *n* the therapeutic application of an alternating electric current to stimulate nerve and muscle function [Late 19C. After Michael FARADAY]

far·a·dize /fárrə dīz/ (**-dized, -diz·ing, -diz·es**) *vt* to stimulate a nerve or muscle using an alternating current [Mid-19C. After Michael FARADAY] —**far·a·di·za·tion** /fèrrədi záysh'n/ *n* —**far·a·diz·er** *n*

far·an·dole /fárrən dōl/ *n* **1.** a lively dance from Provence in 6/8 or 4/4 time in which dancers link hands to form a weaving line following the leader **2.** the music for a farandole [Mid-19C. Via French < modern Provençal *farandoulo*]

far·a·way /fáarə wày/ *adj* **1. REMOTE** a great distance away **2. SOUNDING DISTANT** heard from a distance **3. DREAMY** having a dreamy absent-minded expression or appearance —**far·a·way·ness** *n*

FARC /faark/ *abbr* Revolutionary Armed Forces of Colombia. Spanish name **Fuerzas Armadas Revolucionarias de Colombia**

farce /faarss/ *n* **1. ABSURD SITUATION** a ridiculous situation in which everything goes wrong or becomes a sham ○ *It was a complete farce – the bride changed her mind at the last minute and the two families had a public shouting match.* **2. COMIC PLAY** a comic play in which authority, order, and morality are at risk and ordinary people are caught up in extraordinary events **3. STYLE OF COMIC DRAMA** the style of comic drama in which authority, order, and morality are at risk and ordinary people are caught up in extraordinary events **4.** FOOD same as **forcemeat** [Early 16C. < French, "stuffing" < Latin *farcire* "to stuff"]

far·ceur /faar súr/ *n* **1.** an actor in or writer of farces **2.** somebody who is intentionally comical (*literary*) [Late 17C. < French < *farce* (see FARCE)]

far·ci·cal /fáarsik'l/ *adj* **1.** resembling a farce in being ridiculous and confused **2.** performed or written in the style of a farce —**far·ci·cal·i·ty** /fàarsi kállətee/ *n* —**far·ci·cal·ly** *adv*

far cry *n* a long way in distance or character

far·cy /fáarsee/ *n* a form of the infectious horse disease glanders [14C. < French *farcin* < Latin *farcire* "to stuff"]

far·del /fáard'l/ *n* a bundle or pack of something tied up for carrying (*archaic*) [14C. < Old French, "bundle, load" < *farde* "bundle"]

fare /fair/ *n* **1. COST OF TRAVEL** the amount charged for a journey **2. PASSENGER** a paying passenger in a taxi **3. FOOD** food that is provided, especially when simple and substantial **4. ENTERTAINMENT** the particular type of material provided by a magazine, television show, or other form of entertainment ○ *a channel offering the usual fare of makeover programs and celebrity interviews* ■ *vi* (**fared, far·ing, fares**) **1. MANAGE IN DOING SOMETHING** to get on in a particular way in doing or experiencing something ○ *How did she fare in the exam?* **2. HAPPEN** to turn out in a particular way for somebody **3. EAT** to dine or be given food **4.**

TRAVEL to go on a journey (*literary*) [Old English *fær, faru* "journey" < Germanic]

SPELLCHECK See *fair*[1].

Far East /faar éest/ a former term for the countries of East Asia, sometimes extended to include those of Southeast Asia (*dated*) —**Far-East·ern** *adj*

Fare·ham /fáirəm/ city situated between Portsmouth and Southampton in Hampshire, southern England. Population: 107,977 (2001).

~~Farenheit~~ incorrect spelling of **Fahrenheit**

fare·well /fair wél/ *n* **1.** EXPRESSION OF PARTING GOOD WISHES an act of leaving or an activity marking somebody's departure **2.** GOOD WISHES ON PARTING an expression of good wishes on parting ○ *came too late to bid her farewell* ■ *adj* SAYING GOODBYE marking an end, conclusion, or leave-taking ■ *interj* GOODBYE used to express good wishes at parting (*literary*) ○ *Farewell, my friend!* [14C. < *Fare well*, said to somebody setting out on a journey]

Fare·well, Cape /fair wél, fáir wèl/ cape on the northern coast of the South Island, New Zealand. It is the northernmost point of the South Island.

far·fal·le /faar fáalay/ *npl* pasta made in the shape of bows [Early 17C. < Italian *farfalla* "candle-fly, moth"]

far·fel /fáarf'l/, **far·fal** *n* pasta in the shape of small grains [Late 19C. < Yiddish *farfl* < Middle High German *varveln* "noodles, noodle soup"]

far-fetched *adj* exaggerated and unconvincing

far-flung *adj* **1.** distributed over a wide area **2.** at a great distance

Farge ♦ **La Farge, John**

Far·go /fáargō/ city in southeastern North Dakota, on the Minnesota border, south of Grand Forks. Population: 91,204 (2002 estimate).

Far·go, William George (1818–81) US entrepreneur. With Henry Wells, he organized a transcontinental express delivery company (1852) that shipped goods by stagecoach.

Fa·ri·da·bad /fə réedə bàd, -baàd/, **Fa·rī·dā·bād** industrial city in Haryana State, northern India. Population: 1,054,981 (2001).

fa·ri·na /fə réenə/ *n* **1.** flour or meal made from wheat, nuts, or vegetables, often used in pastries and soups **2.** *UK* starch, especially that made from potatoes [14C. < Latin, "ground corn, flour, meal" < *far* "spelt, grain"]

far·i·na·ceous /fàrrə náyshəss/ *adj* containing or consisting of starch [Mid-17C. < late Latin *farinaceus* < Latin *farina* (see FARINA)]

far·i·nose /férrə nòss/ *adj* **1.** consisting of or yielding food starch **2.** describes plant leaves or stems that have a powdery or floury appearance, especially because of a covering of fine whitish hairs [Early 18C. < late Latin *farinosus* < Latin *farina* (see FARINA)]

far·kle·ber·ry /fáark'l bèrree/ (*plural* **-ries**) *n* a bush of the heath family that has leathery leaves and hard black berries with stony seeds. Native to: southeastern United States. Latin name: *Vaccinium arboreum*. [Mid-18C. Origin ?]

farm /faarm/ *n* **1.** AGRICULTURAL LAND AND BUILDINGS an area of land where crops are grown or animals are reared for commercial purposes, together with appropriate buildings **2.** PLACE PRODUCING PARTICULAR ANIMALS OR CROPS an area of land or water where particular animals, birds, fish, or crops are raised for commercial purposes (*usually used in combination*) ○ *a trout farm* **3.** FARM BUILDINGS a farmhouse or group of farm buildings **4.** LAND USED BY INDUSTRY a piece of land on which something is stored, produced, or processed, especially on an industrial scale (*usually used in combination*) ○ *an antenna farm* ■ *v* (**farmed, farm·ing, farms**) **1.** *vti* USE LAND FOR AGRICULTURE to use land for growing crops and rearing animals for sale **2.** *vt* REAR SOMETHING COMMERCIALLY to rear animals, birds, or fish commercially **3.** *vt* same as **farm out** (sense 1) [14C. Via French, "lease" < medieval Latin *firma* "fixed payment" < Latin *firmare* "fix, settle, confirm" < *firmus* "firm"] —**farm·a·ble** *adj* —**farm·ing** *n*

CULTURAL NOTE ***Animal Farm***, a novel (1945) by British writer George Orwell. A satirical allegory of Stalinist Russia, it describes how a group of farm animals, led by pigs, overthrow their human owner and try to run the farm on egalitarian principles. Corrupted by power, the pigs distort their ideology to support their increasingly brutal tyranny, justifying their actions with slogans such as "All animals are equal, but some are more equal than others."

farm out *vt* **1.** SEND WORK OUT to send work out to be done by somebody else **2.** SEND ELSEWHERE FOR CARE to send children or animals to be looked after by somebody else **3.** *US* REASSIGN PLAYER to assign a major league player to a minor league team

farm·er /fáarmər/ *n* somebody who owns or operates a farm

Far·mer /fáarmər/, **Fannie** (1857–1915) US home economist. She edited *The Boston Cooking-School Cook Book* (1896), out of which grew the classic *Fannie Farmer Cookbook*. Full name **Farmer, Fannie Merritt**

> "I certainly feel that the time is not far distant when a knowledge of the principles of diet will be an essential part of one's education. Then mankind will eat to live, be able to do better mental and physical work, and disease will be less frequent."
> [Fannie Farmer, *The Boston Cooking-School Cookbook*; 1896]

Far·mer, James (1920–99) US civil rights leader. He founded the nonviolent Congress of Racial Equality (CORE) (1942) and served as its national director (1961–66). Full name **Farmer, James Leonard**

> "Evil societies always kill their consciences."
> [James Farmer, *Lay Bare The Heart: An Autobiography of the Civil Rights Movement*; 1985]

farm·er cheese *n US* a mild cheese made from pressing together milk curds

Far·mer Mac *n* the US Federal Agricultural Mortgage Agency (*informal*) [Alteration]

farm·er's lung *n* inflammation of the lungs marked by chronic shortness of breath and caused by an allergic reaction to fungal spores from moldy hay

farm·ers' mar·ket *n* a market, usually held outdoors, where farmers sell fresh produce direct to the public

farm·er's match *n Midwest* a match that ignites on any surface, as opposed to a safety match

REGIONAL NOTE The term ***farmer's match*** is found in the Upper Midwest, especially South Dakota.

farm hand *n* somebody hired to work on a farm

farm·house /fáarm hòwss/ *n* (*plural* **-hous·es** /-hòwzəz/) a house on a farm, especially the main dwelling place of the farmer ■ *adj* produced on a farm or of a similar style or quality as that produced on a farm

Far·ming·ton /fáarmingtən/ city in northwestern New Mexico, northeast of Gallup and northwest of Santa Fe. Population: 40,563 (2002 estimate).

farm·land /fáarm lànd/ *n* land that is suitable for farming or used by farmers

farm·stead /fáarm stèd/ *n* a farm and all its buildings, regarded as a unit

farm team *n* a sports team in a minor league that is owned by or affiliated with a major league team

farm·wom·an /fáarm wòommən/ (*plural* **-wom·en** /-wìmmin/) *n US* a woman who lives or works on a farm

farm·work·er /fáarm wùrkər/ *n* same as **farm hand**

farm·yard /fáarm yaàrd/ *n* an enclosed or surfaced area beside farm buildings

Farn·ham /fáarnəm/, **John Peter** (*b.* 1949) British-born Australian recording artist. His *Whispering Jack* (1986) was the bestselling Australian album of the 1980s.

Far North *n Can* the part of Canada to the north of 60° in latitude

far·o /fáirō/ *n* a card game in which players bet against the dealer on the order in which cards are turned up [Mid-18C. Probably alteration of PHARAOH, after Italian *faraone*]

Far·o /faá rō/ seaport on the southern coast of Portugal and capital of the Algarve District. It is the country's southernmost city. Population: 31,966 (1991).

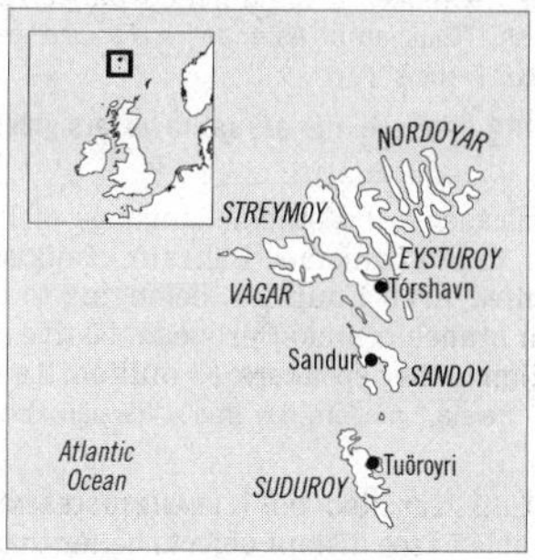

Faroe Islands

Far·oe Is·lands /fáirō-/, **Faer·oe Is·lands** group of islands in the North Atlantic Ocean, almost midway between Iceland and the Shetland Islands. The islands have been Danish territory since 1814. Capital: Tórshavn. Population: 45,661 (2001). Area: 540 sq. mi./1,399 sq. km.

Far·o·ese /fàirō éez, fàirō éess/ (*plural same*), **Faer·o·ese** *n* **1.** the North Germanic language spoken in the Faroe Islands. Native speakers: 45,000. **2.** somebody who comes from the Faroe Islands —**Far·o·ese** *adj*

far-off *adj* distant in location or time

fa·rouche /fə róosh/ *adj* **1.** unsociable and lacking grace because of fierceness, sullenness, or shyness **2.** menacing in appearance or behavior [Mid-18C. Via French < medieval Latin *forasticus* < Latin *foras* "out of doors, outside"]

Fa·rouk I /fə róok/ (1920–65) king of Egypt. He was the last king of Egypt (1936–52), and after a coup lived in exile in Monaco.

> "Soon there will be only five kings left—the Kings of England, Diamonds, Hearts, Spades, and Clubs."
> [Farouk I, *As I Recall*, Lord Boyd-Orr; 1966]

far-out *adj* (*dated slang*) **1.** strange and unconventional **2.** extremely good or enjoyable —**far-out·ness** *n*

far·ra·go /fə raá gō, -ráy-/ (*plural* **-gos** or **-goes**) *n* a confused mixture of things [Mid-17C. < Latin, "mixed fodder for cattle, medley" < *far* "spelt, grain"]

Far·ra·gut /fárrəgət/, **David** (1801–70) US naval officer. He commanded Union ships during the Civil War and became a national hero after the Battle of Mobile Bay (1864). Full name **Farragut, David Glasgow**

> "Damn the torpedoes—full speed ahead."
> [David Farragut, *Remark*; August 5, 1864]

Far·ra·khan /fárrə kaàn/, **Louis Abdul** (*b.* 1933) US religious leader. Having long been a member of the Nation of Islam, he led the organization after 1978 and broadened its base with calls for African American self-reliance. He organized the Million Man March in Washington, D.C., in 1995. Born **Walcott, Louis Eugene**

far-reach·ing *adj* having widespread implications, influences, or effects

Far·rell /fárrəl/, **James T.** (1904–79) US novelist. He is best known for his *Studs Lonigan* trilogy (1932–35). Full name **Farrell, James Thomas**

Far·rel·ly /fárrəlee/, **Midget** (*b.* 1944) Australian surfer. He was the winner of the first official surfing world championship, held in Sydney, Australia, in 1964. Born **Farrelly, Bernard**

Far·rer /fárrər/, **William James** (1845–1906) British-born Australian agricultural scientist, who was a pioneer of wheat breeding in Australia. He developed domestic strains of wheat that produced greater yields than overseas strains.

far·ri·er /fárree ər/ *n* a maker and fitter of horseshoes [Mid-16C. Via French < Latin *ferrarius* < *ferrum* "horseshoe, iron"] —**far·ri·er·y** *n*

far·row[1] /fárrō/ *vi* (**-rowed, -row·ing, -rows**) to give birth to a litter of piglets ■ *n* a litter of young pigs [Old English *fearh* "young pig" < Indo-European]

far·row² /fárrō/ *adj* not pregnant with a calf [15C. Probably < Flemish *verwe-*, *varwe-*, in *verwekoe*, *varwekoe* "cow that has become barren"]

far·ru·ca /fə ro͝okə/ *n* a flamenco dance [Early 20C. < Spanish, "Galician or Asturian" < *Farruco*, pet form of *Francisco* "Francis"]

far·see·ing /faar seé ing/ *adj* same as **farsighted** (senses 2–3)

Far·si /fáarsee/ *n* the official language of Iran, also spoken in Afghanistan, Bahrain, Tajikistan, and the United Arab Emirates, belonging to the Indo-Iranian branch of Indo-European. Native speakers: 30 million. Other speakers: 55 million. [Late 19C. Via Arabic, "Persia," modern-day Iran < Persian *Pars*] —**Far·si** *adj*

far·sight·ed /faar sītəd/ *adj* **1.** UNABLE TO SEE NEARBY OBJECTS CLEARLY able to see distant objects better than nearby ones **2.** HAVING SOUND JUDGMENT wise and able to anticipate the future **3.** SEEING FAR able to see a long way ○ *farsighted birds of prey* —**far·sight·ed·ly** *adv* —**far·sight·ed·ness** *n*

fart /faart/ *vi* (**fart·ed, fart·ing, farts**) an offensive term meaning to release intestinal gases through the anus, usually with an accompanying sound (*slang*) ■ *n* **1.** an offensive term for a release of intestinal gases through the anus (*slang*) **2.** an offensive term for somebody who is regarded as unpleasant, boring, or irritating (*slang insult*) [Old English *feortan* < Indo-European]

fart around *vi* an offensive term meaning to waste time by behaving foolishly (*slang*)

far·ther /fáarthər/ *adv* **1.** TO GREATER DISTANCE to or at a point that is more distant in space or time **2.** TO GREATER EXTENT to a greater degree or extent ◊ **further** ■ *adj* **1.** MORE DISTANT more distant in space or time **2.** ADDITIONAL adding to the quantity or extent of something (*archaic*) [13C. Variant of FURTHER] —**far·ther·most** *adj*

USAGE See *further*.

far·thest /fáarthəst/ *adv* **1.** TO GREATEST DISTANCE to a more distant point in space or time than anything else **2.** TO GREATEST EXTENT to a greater degree or extent than anything else ■ *adj* MOST DISTANT more distant in space or time than anything else

USAGE See *further*.

far·thing /fáarthing/ *n* **1.** the lowest value or smallest amount **2.** a former British coin worth a quarter of an old penny [Old English *fēorthung* "quarter of a penny" < *fēortha* "fourth" + *-ing* "fractional part"]

far·thin·gale /fáarthing gàyl/ *n* a structure worn under the skirt by women in the late 16th and early 17th centuries to give it the shape of a cone, bell, or drum [Early 16C. Via Old French *verdugale* < Spanish *verdugado* < *verdugo* "rod, stick"]

fart·lek /fáartlək/ *n* SPORTS same as **interval training** [Mid-20C. < Swedish < *fart* "speed" + *lek* "play"]

Far West *n US* the area of the continental United States west of the Great Plains

FAS *abbr* **1.** MED fetal alcohol syndrome **2.** SHIPPING free alongside ship

f.a.s. *abbr* SHIPPING free alongside ship

FASA *abbr* Fellow of the American Society of Appraisers

fas·ces /fá seéz/ *npl* in ancient Rome, a bundle of rods containing an ax with a projecting blade, carried in front of magistrates [Late 16C. < Latin, plural of *fascis* "bundle"]

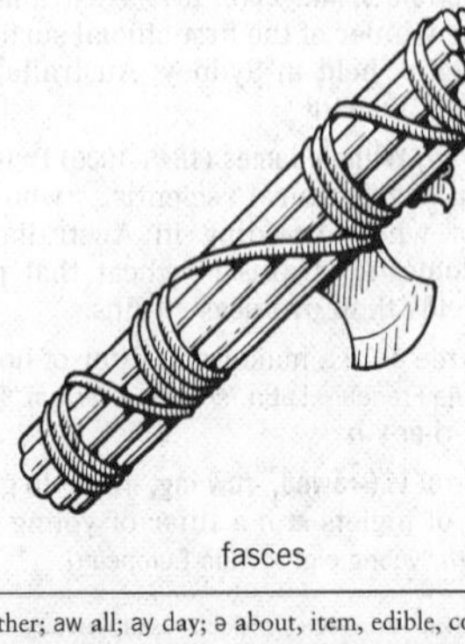

fasces

fas·ci·a *architecture* /fáshee ə, fáyshee ə/; *anatomy* /fáshee ə/ (*plural* **-ci·ae** *architecture* /fáshee ee, fáyshee ee/; *anatomy* /fáshee ee/ or **-cias**) *n* **1.** ARCHIT FLAT SURFACE ON BUILDING the flat horizontal surface immediately below the edge of a roof **2.** ANAT CONNECTIVE TISSUE a sheet or band of connective tissue covering or binding together parts of the body such as muscles or organs **3.** BIOL BAND OF COLOR a broad band of color, e.g., on an insect [Mid-16C. < Latin, "band, fillet, casing of a door"] —**fas·cial** /fásh'l/ *adj*

fas·ci·ate /fáshee àyt/, **fas·ci·at·ed** /-àytəd/ *adj* describes plant stems or branches that have grown together and become unusually flattened [Mid-17C. < Latin *fasciare* "swathe" < *fascia* "band, fillet"] —**fas·ci·ate·ly** *adv*

fas·ci·a·tion /fàshee áysh'n/ *n* uncharacteristic fusion and flattening of several plant stems

fas·ci·cle /fássik'l/ *n* **1.** BUNDLE a small bunch or bundle of something **2.** BOT PLANT PARTS BUNCHED TOGETHER a cluster of plant parts such as branches, leaves, or stems **3.** ANAT BUNDLE OF FIBERS a bundle of nerve, muscle, or tendon fibers **4.** PUBL PART OF BOOK PUBLISHED AS INSTALLMENT a section of a book published in installments as a volume or pamphlet [15C. < Latin *fasciculus* "small bundle" < *fascis* "bundle"] —**fas·ci·cled** *adj* —**fas·cic·u·lar** /fə síkyələr/ *adj* —**fas·cic·u·late** /fə síkyələt, -làyt/ *adj*

fas·ci·cule /fássi kyo͞ol/ *n* PUBL same as **fascicle** (sense 4) [Late 19C. < Latin *fasciculus* (see FASCICLE)]

fas·ci·it·is /fàshee ítiss/ *n* inflammation of the bands of connective tissue (**fascia**) between muscles or around organs, from infection or unknown causes [Late 19C. < FASCIA]

fas·ci·nate /fássə nàyt/ (**-nat·ed, -nat·ing, -nates**) *v* **1.** *vti* to hold somebody's attention completely or irresistibly **2.** *vt* to make somebody or something unable to move, especially out of fear [Late 16C. < Latin *fascinat-*, past participle of *fascinare* "bewitch" < *fascinum* "spell, witchcraft"] —**fas·ci·nat·ed·ly** *adv* —**fas·ci·na·tor** *n*

fas·ci·nat·ing /fássə nàyting/ *adj* inspiring a great interest or attraction —**fas·ci·nat·ing·ly** *adv*

fas·ci·na·tion /fàssə náysh'n/ *n* **1.** POWER TO CAPTURE ATTENTION the power to hold somebody's attention completely or irresistibly **2.** SOMETHING FASCINATING something that inspires great interest **3.** INTEREST IN SOMETHING complete absorption in something interesting ○ *I can't understand his fascination with tarantulas.*

fas·cine /fə seén/ *n* a long piece or bundle of wood used for engineering purposes to line or fill a trench [Late 17C. Via French < Latin *fascina* < *fascis* "bundle"]

fas·ci·o·li·a·sis /fə see ə lī əssiss, fə sī ə-/ *n* a disease caused by an infestation of parasitic liver flukes [Late 19C. < modern Latin *Fasciola hepatica* "liver fluke" < Latin *fasciola* "small bandage" < *fascia* "band, fillet"]

fas·cism /fá shìzzəm/, **Fas·cism** *n* any movement, ideology, or attitude that favors dictatorial government, centralized control of private enterprise, repression of all opposition, and extreme nationalism —**fas·cist** /fáshist/ *n, adj* —**fas·cis·tic** /fə shístik/ *adj*

fash /fash/ *US* (*slang*) *n* same as **fashion** *n* (senses 1–3) ■ *adj* same as **fashionable** [Late 19C. Shortening]

fash·ion /fásh'n/ *n* **1.** CLOTHING STYLES style in clothing, hair, and personal appearance generally ○ *the latest in men's fashions* **2.** BUSINESS OF STYLES the business of creating, promoting, or studying the latest styles in clothing and hair **3.** CURRENT STYLE the style of dress, behavior, way of living, or other expression that is popular at present ○ *a way of speaking that is no longer in fashion* **4.** MANNER a particular way of behaving or doing something **5.** SHAPE the form or shape of something **6.** TYPE a type or variety ■ *vt* (**-ioned, -ion·ing, -ions**) **1.** MAKE SOMETHING to give shape or form to something ○ *fashion a chair from some leftover pieces of wood* **2.** INFLUENCE SOMETHING to change somebody's character or beliefs by influence or training ○ *attitudes fashioned by his grandparents* **3.** ADAPT SOMETHING to adapt something or make something suitable ○ *fashion it to fit over the bump in the middle* [14C. Via French *façon* "shape" < Latin *faction-* (see FACTION¹)] —**fash·ion·er** *n* ◇ **after a fashion** in some way but not very well

SYNONYMS See *make*.

-fashion *suffix* in the manner of

fash·ion·a·ble /fásh'nəb'l/ *adj* **1.** following a style that is currently popular ○ *fashionable ideas* **2.** popular with rich, famous, or otherwise glamorous people ○ *a fashionable nightspot* —**fash·ion·a·bil·i·ty** /fàsh'nə bíllətee/ *n* —**fash·ion·a·ble·ness** *n* —**fash·ion·a·bly** *adv*

fash·ion house *n* a business that designs, makes, and sells fashionable clothes, typically associated with an important designer

fash·ion·is·ta /fàsh'n eéstə/ *n* somebody involved in the fashion industry (*informal*) [< FASHION + Spanish *-ista* < Latin *-ista* (see -IST)]

fash·ion mod·el *n* somebody whose job is to model clothes

fash·ion pho·tog·ra·phy *n* the art or practice of taking photographs of models wearing clothes or clothing accessories, especially for fashion magazines

fash·ion plate *n* **1.** a wearer of the latest fashions **2.** an illustration showing a style of clothing, especially a current or new fashion

fash·ion shoot *n* a session for photographing or filming models wearing fashionable clothing or accessories

fash·ion state·ment *n* an item of clothing or set of clothes that expresses something about the attitude, point of view, or lifestyle of the wearer

~~**fashon**~~ incorrect spelling of **fashion**

~~**fasinating**~~ incorrect spelling of **fascinating**

Fass·bind·er /fáass bìndər/, **Rainer Werner** (1946–82) German movie director. He is renowned for politically controversial plays and films such as *The Marriage of Maria Braun* (1979) that often criticize social institutions.

> "I hope to build a house with my films. Some of them are the cellar, some are the walls, and some are the windows. But I hope in time there will be a house."
> [Rainer Werner Fassbinder. Quoted in *Halliwell's Filmgoer's Companion*, Leslie Halliwell; 1993]

fast¹ /fast/ *adj* **1.** ACTING OR MOVING RAPIDLY acting, functioning, or moving quickly, or capable of doing this ○ *a fast car* **2.** DONE QUICKLY lasting or taking a relatively short time ○ *a fast trip* **3.** RUNNING AHEAD OF TIME indicating a time that is later than the correct time ○ *My watch is ten minutes fast.* **4.** CONDUCIVE TO RAPID SPEED adapted to or allowing rapid movement ○ *driving in the fast lane* **5.** REQUIRING SPEEDY MOVEMENT requiring agility and quickness of movement and reaction **6.** PHOTOGRAPHY WITH SHORT EXPOSURE describes photographic equipment that requires or permits a relatively short exposure time **7.** DEBAUCHED energetically pursuing excitement and enjoyment (*informal*) ○ *in with a fast crowd* **8.** PROMISCUOUS wanting or tending to start sexual relationships with people very soon after meeting them (*informal*) **9.** TRICKY using quick-wittedness to trick or cheat people (*informal*) ○ *a fast bargainer* **10.** MADE EASILY acquired very easily and sometimes dishonestly (*informal*) ○ *fast money* **11.** UNFADING not liable to fade or change color **12.** STRONG AND CLOSE strong, close, and steadfast, e.g., in a relationship (*literary*) ○ *fast friends* **13.** FASTENED firmly attached, fastened, or fixed **14.** SHUT firmly closed ■ *adv* **1.** RAPIDLY at great speed ○ *You drive too fast.* **2.** IMMEDIATELY in quick succession **3.** AT INCORRECT TIME ahead of the correct time ○ *The clock is running a little fast.* **4.** SOUNDLY in a deep and peaceful way ○ *fast asleep* **5.** FIRMLY allowing no movement or no chance of slipping or escaping ○ *held fast by ice* **6.** RECKLESSLY without regard to consequences (*informal*) ○ *live fast and die young* [Old English *fæst* "firm" < Germanic] ◇ **pull a fast one** to trick or cheat somebody (*slang*)

fast² /fast/ *v* (**fast·ed, fast·ing, fasts**) **1.** *vi* ABSTAIN FROM FOOD to abstain from food, or some types of food, especially as an act of religious observance **2.** *vt* DEPRIVE SOMEBODY OF FOOD to deprive a person or animal of food ■ *n* PERIOD OF FASTING a period of time spent abstaining from food [Old English *fæstan* < Germanic] —**fast·er** *n*

fast-act·ing *adj* beginning to take effect soon after being used ○ *a fast-acting analgesic*

fast·back /fást bàk/ *n* **1.** a back of a car that forms a continuous curve downward from the rear edge of the roof **2.** a car with a fastback

fast·ball /fást bàwl/ *n* a baseball pitch at top speed

fast break *n* in team sports, a swift counterattack made in an attempt to score before the opposing players have the chance to recover their defensive positions —**fast-break** *vi*

fast-breed·er re·ac·tor *n* a nuclear reactor in which the chain reaction is maintained mainly by fast neutrons. It is capable of producing more fissionable material than it consumes.

fas·ten /fáss'n/ (**-tened, -ten·ing, -tens**) *v* **1.** *vti* SECURE SOMETHING to attach something firmly, usually using parts or devices made to achieve this, or become firmly attached in this way ○ *These snaps won't fasten.* **2.** *vti* SHUT TIGHTLY to close something firmly or securely, or become firmly or securely closed ○ *fasten the door shut* **3.** *vt* HOLD SOMETHING FIRMLY to use a tool, device, or body part to hold somebody or something firmly **4.** *vti* CONCENTRATE ATTENTION to focus the mind or eyes concentratedly on something, or become focused in this way ○ *His suspicions fastened upon the woman sitting opposite him.* **5.** *vi* BECOME NUISANCE to single somebody out for attention in a persistent and usually unwelcome manner ○ *just some guy who fastened onto me in the street* [Old English *fæstnian* < Germanic, "firm"]

fas·ten·er /fáss'nər/ *n* a device, e.g., a button, hook, or zipper, used to close something, especially a piece of clothing

fas·ten·ing /fáss'ning/ *n* a device that fastens something, e.g., a clasp, hook, or lock

fast food *n* highly processed restaurant foods that are prepared quickly or are available on demand (*hyphenated when used before a noun*) ○ *a fast-food diet of burgers and fries*

fast-for·ward *n* **1.** FUNCTION FOR WINDING TAPE FORWARD a function on an electronic recording device such as a tape or videocassette recorder that causes the tape to wind forward quickly **2.** BUTTON FOR FAST-FORWARD FUNCTION a mechanism used to control the fast-forward function on an electronic recording device, e.g., a button or switch ■ *vti* (**fast-for·ward·ed, fast-for·ward·ing, fast-for·wards**) **1.** ADVANCE TAPE RAPIDLY to wind a tape forward quickly on an electronic recording device **2.** ADVANCE QUICKLY to advance rapidly, or move something forward rapidly, e.g., in time or in rate of progress (*informal*) ○ *decided to fast-forward negotiations so as to avoid a strike*

fas·tid·i·ous /fa stíddee əss/ *adj* **1.** concerned that even the smallest details should be just right ○ *fastidious about his appearance* **2.** easily disgusted by things that are not perfectly clean [15C. < Latin *fastidiosus* < *fastidium* "disgust"] —**fas·tid·i·ous·ly** *adv* —**fas·tid·i·ous·ness** *n*

fas·tig·i·a MED plural of **fastigium**

fas·tig·i·ate /fa stíjjee ət/, **fas·tig·i·at·ed** /-àytəd/ *adj* describes a tree or other plant with upright clustering branches that taper toward the top —**fas·tig·i·ate·ly** *adv*

fas·tig·i·um /fa stíjjee əm/ (*plural* **-i·ums** or **-i·a** /-ee ə/) *n* a period during which an illness, often a fever, is at its most severe [Late 17C. < Latin]

fast·ing /fásting/ *n* abstention from food, or some types of food, especially as an act of religious observance

fast lane *n* **1.** *Can, UK* the lane of an expressway or divided highway that is used by vehicles traveling at high speed or passing slower traffic. US term **express lane 2.** HECTIC LIFESTYLE the kind of lifestyle that is busy, exciting, often highly stressful, and sometimes devoted to pleasure (*informal*) ○ *living life in the fast lane* **3.** ROUTE TO SUCCESS a rapid but extremely competitive route to progress, promotion, or success —**fast-lane** *adj*

fast mo·tion *n* filmed action that is faster than is naturally possible, achieved by shooting the film at a rate slower than that projected. It is often used for comic effect. (*hyphenated when used before a noun*) ○ *a fast-motion sequence*

fast·ness /fástnəss/ *n* **1.** FIXEDNESS the state or quality of being firm, fixed, or secure ○ *deceived about the fastness of their friendship* **2.** UNFADING QUALITY the ability of a dye to retain its color and not to fade **3.** FORTRESS a fortress, stronghold, or other secure place (*archaic or literary*)

fast neu·tron *n* a neutron that has energy in excess of 1.5 MeV, sufficient to produce fission in uranium 238

fast-talk *vt* to influence or deceive somebody with false but appealing arguments (*informal*) ○ *fast-talked them into parting with the car keys* —**fast-talk·er** *n* —**fast-talk·ing** *adj*

fast track *n* **1.** a railroad track for fast trains alongside one for slower trains **2.** a rapid and sometimes highly competitive route to progress or advancement that exists alongside the slower conventional one (*informal*) ○ *a fast track to promotion for the brightest recruits*

fast-track *v* **1.** *vti* GO QUICKLY to advance, develop, or process something rapidly, or be handled rapidly ○ *fast-tracking the best of the new recruits* **2.** *vt* DEAL WITH SOMETHING FIRST to give priority to somebody or something ○ *fast-track an application* ■ *adj* ADVANCING RAPIDLY progressing rapidly or encouraging rapid progress —**fast-track·er** *n*

fat /fat/ *n* **1.** NUTRITIONAL COMPONENT OF FOOD a water-soluble substance, solid at room temperature, that belongs to a group of chemicals that are main constituents of food derived from, e.g., animal tissue, nuts, and seeds. Fats are esters of glycerol and fatty acids. ○ *a diet that is lower in fat* **2.** ANAT TISSUE CONTAINING FAT animal or vegetable tissue made up of cells that contain fat, especially the layer of cells under the skin that in excess make somebody overweight **3.** COOK COOKING MEDIUM a solid or liquid substance that is derived from animals or plants and is used as a cooking medium or ingredient, e.g., butter or sunflower oil ○ *rub the fat into the flour* **4.** EXCESS amounts that are surplus to what is needed or wanted (*informal*) ○ *a budget with little fat* ■ *adj* (**fat·ter, fat·test**) **1.** OVERWEIGHT having a body weight greater than is considered desirable or advisable **2.** CONTAINING FAT containing a lot of fat or too much fat ○ *pork that was rather fat* **3.** THICK very wide or large ○ *a fat book* **4.** PROFITABLE bringing large profits or financial rewards ○ *a fat construction contract* **5.** REWARDING providing good opportunities or rewards ○ *offered a fat part in a movie* **6.** RICH owning great wealth ○ *grown fat on the profits* **7.** PLENTIFUL with abundant contents, stocks, or supplies ○ *a fat savings account* **8.** AGRIC FERTILE land that is very productive for agricultural purposes ■ *vti* (**fat·ted, fat·ting, fats**) AGRIC same as **fatten** (sense 1) [Old English *fat(t)* < Indo-European] —**fat·ly** *adv* —**fat·ness** *n* ◇ **chew the fat** to have a leisurely conversation (*slang*) ◇ **live off the fat of the land** to live easily by having essential things provided with little or no effort ◇ **the fat is in the fire** something irreversible has happened that will cause trouble

FAT /fat/ *n* in the MS-DOS disk-operating system, an internal store of information about the structure of files on a disk (*often used before a noun*) Full form **file allocation table**

Fa·tah, Al *n* POL ➧ **Al Fatah**

fa·tal /fáyt'l/ *adj* **1.** LEADING TO DEATH causing or capable of causing death ○ *a fatal car crash* **2.** RUINOUS causing destruction, disaster, or ruin ○ *a fatal mistake in calculations* **3.** DECISIVE marking an important or decisive stage in a process or series of events ○ *everything that's happened since that fatal day* **4.** PREDESTINED arranged or controlled by fate (*archaic*) ■ *n US* INSTANCE OF DEATH an instance of death, especially one caused by an auto, plane, train, or bus crash (*informal*) ○ *a fatal on the turnpike during rush hour* [14C. Directly or via French < Latin *fatalis* < *fatum* (see FATE)] —**fa·tal·ly** *adv*

SYNONYMS See ***deadly.***

fa·tal·ism /fáyt'l izzəm/ *n* **1.** DOCTRINE OF FATE the philosophical doctrine according to which all events are fated to happen, so that human beings cannot change their destinies **2.** BELIEF IN ALL-POWERFUL FATE the belief that people are powerless against fate **3.** FEELING OF POWERLESSNESS AGAINST FATE an attitude of resignation and passivity that results from the belief that people are powerless against fate —**fa·tal·ist** *n* —**fa·tal·is·tic** /fàyt'l ístik/ *adj* —**fa·tal·is·ti·cal·ly** *adv*

fa·tal·i·ty /fay tállətee, fə-/ (*plural* **-ties**) *n* **1.** UNEXPECTED DEATH a death resulting from accident or disaster ○ *The traffic accident resulted in three fatalities.* **2.** DEADLINESS the ability to cause death, disaster, or destruction ○ *fatality associated with toxic waste exposure* **3.** PREDETERMINATION BY FATE the quality or state of being predetermined by fate **4.** EVENTS BELIEVED TO BE FATED an event or train of events thought to be determined by fate

fa·tal·i·ty rate *n* SOC SCI same as **death rate**

fa·ta mor·ga·na /faàtə mawr gaànə/, **Fa·ta Mor·ga·na** *n* a mirage or an illusion [< Italian, "Morgan le Fay"; from the belief that a fairy caused the mirage frequently seen near the Strait of Messina]

fat·back /fát bàk/ *n* fatty meat from the upper part of a side of pork, usually dried and cured by salt

REGIONAL NOTE Fatty meat from the upper part of a side of pork, usually without lean, is also called *fat meat, fat pork, boiling meat, dry salt meat, salt bacon, salt meat, seasoning meat, side meat, sowbelly,* and *white bacon.* The meat is used in the South and West primarily to season boiled and steamed vegetables. Because the substance so closely approximates ordinary bacon, in both its location on the hog and its applications in cooking, ***fatback*** often merges with *middling meat, streak of lean,* and other bacon synonyms, all of which invariably include lean.

fat bod·y *n* **1.** in the bodies of insects, especially larvae, a fatty tissue used as a source of energy during metamorphosis and hibernation **2.** in some amphibians and reptiles, a fatty tissue found near the genital glands

fat camp *n US* a residential camp that helps children to lose undesired weight (*slang*)

fat cat *n* (*slang*) **1.** somebody who is extremely wealthy and privileged (*hyphenated when used before a noun*) **2.** *US* somebody wealthy who contributes a substantial amount of money to a political campaign

fat cell *n* a cell that synthesizes and stores fat

Fat Cit·y, fat cit·y *n* prosperous circumstances (*slang*)

fate /fayt/ *n* **1.** FORCE PREDETERMINING EVENTS the force or principle believed to predetermine events ○ *little knew what fate had in store for him* **2.** OUTCOME a consequence or final result ○ *What was the fate of the mission?* **3.** DESTINY something with decisive or far-reaching consequences that inevitably happens to somebody or something ○ *felt it was her fate to marry him* **4.** DISASTROUS CONSEQUENCE a disastrous or ruinous outcome ■ *vt* (**fat·ed, fat·ing, fates**) MAKE SOMETHING INEVITABLE to predetermine something, usually with negative results (*usually passive*) [14C. < Latin *fatum* "something spoken (by the gods)" < past participle of *fari* "speak"] —**fat·ed** *adj* ◇ **tempt fate** to do something risky that depends too much on luck for success and might end in misfortune or disaster

fate·ful /fáytfəl/ *adj* **1.** WITH HIGHLY SIGNIFICANT CONSEQUENCES certain to have very important, often dire consequences ○ *a fateful decision* **2.** DECIDED BY FATE predetermined or controlled by fate **3.** OMINOUS prefiguring what is to come, especially something disastrous ○ *a fateful sign* —**fate·ful·ly** *adv* —**fate·ful·ness** *n*

Fates /fayts/ *npl* in Greek mythology, the three goddesses Clotho, Lachesis, and Atropos, often depicted as women of advanced years spinning a thread, who were believed to decree the events and duration of somebody's life. The Greeks believed that Clotho spun the thread that represented somebody's life, Lachesis decided the extent of it, and Atropos was responsible for cutting it. Greek equivalent **Moirai.** Roman equivalent **Parcae**

fat face *n* a typeface with wide main strokes and prominent serifs that produces a relatively heavy dark image when set as text

fat farm *n* a health spa dedicated to helping people lose weight (*slang*)

fat-free *adj* describes foods that contain no animal or vegetable fat

fath, **fath.** *abbr* fathom

fat·head /fát hèd/ *n* an offensive term for somebody who is considered foolish or stupid (*slang insult*) —**fat·head·ed** *adj* —**fat·head·ed·ly** *adv* —**fat·head·ed·ness** *n*

fa·ther /fáa*th*ər/ *n* **1.** MAN WHO IS PARENT a man who is the parent of a human being, or a male animal that has produced offspring ○ *been like a father to me* **2.** MAN ACTING AS PARENT a man who brings up and looks after a child as if he were its father **3.** MAN WHO IS ANCESTOR a man who is an ancestor, especially the founder of a family or people ○ *the land of our fathers and mothers* **4.** MAN WHO IS FOUNDER a man who establishes, founds, or originates something ○ *the father of modern linguistics* **5.** PROTOTYPE something that is a prototype or original version of something else **6.** MAN WHO IS LEADER a man who is a community or civic leader ○ *the town fathers* ■ *v* (**-thered, -ther·ing, -thers**) **1.** *vt* BECOME FATHER OF OFFSPRING to cause a woman or female animal to produce offspring **2.** *vti* BE LIKE FATHER TO SOMEBODY to act as a father to somebody, especially by giving advice, comfort, and protection **3.** *vt* FOUND SOMETHING to establish, found, or originate something ○ *father a plan* [Old English *fæder* < Indo-European] —**fa·ther·hood** *n*

CULTURAL NOTE ***Fathers and Sons***, a novel (1862) by Russian writer Ivan Turgenev. It deals with the conflicting attitudes toward social change (particularly the emancipation of serfs) among Russia's younger radical intelligentsia, represented by the novel's nihilistic protagonist, Bazarov, and the older liberal gentry, to which Turgenev himself belonged. The novel was seen as Turgenev's acknowledgment that Russia's future was now in the hands of a new generation.

Fa·ther *n* **1.** GOD in Christianity, God, especially when considered as the first person of the Trinity **2.** CHR same as **church father** **3.** TITLE FOR CHRISTIAN CLERIC a title and form of address used for a Christian cleric, especially in the Roman Catholic, Orthodox, and Episcopal Churches **4.** RESPECTFUL TITLE FOR MAN a respectful term of address for a man who is past middle age **5.** PERSONIFICATION something personified as a man of advanced years

Fa·ther Christ·mas *n UK* same as **Santa Claus**

fa·ther con·fes·sor *n* a Roman Catholic priest who hears confessions and gives advice

fa·ther fig·ure *n* a man whom other people look up to for advice, inspiration, or protection

fa·ther-in-law (*plural* **fa·thers-in-law**) *n* the father of somebody's husband or wife

fa·ther·land /fáa*th*ər lànd/ *n* **1.** somebody's native land or country **2.** the native land of somebody's ancestors

fa·ther·less /fáa*th*ərləss/ *adj* having no father or no one identified as a father —**fa·ther·less·ness** *n*

fa·ther·ly /fáa*th*ərlee/ *adj* having or showing the qualities traditionally associated with a father such as love, support, and protection ○ *fatherly affection* —**fa·ther·li·ness** *n*

Fa·ther's Day *n* a day observed as a celebration of fatherhood in the United States, the United Kingdom, Canada, Australia, and some other Commonwealth countries. Date: third Sunday in June, or, in Australia and New Zealand, first Sunday in September.

Fa·ther Time *n* the personification of time as a bearded man of advanced years, usually wearing a robe and carrying a scythe and an hourglass

fath·om /fá*th*əm/ *n* MEASURE OF WATER DEPTH a unit of length equal to 6 ft./1.83 m, used mainly in nautical contexts for measuring the depth of water ■ *vt* (**-omed, -om·ing, -oms**) **1.** COMPREHEND SOMETHING to understand something, usually something profound or mystifying ○ *couldn't fathom why he came back* **2.** MEASURE WATER DEPTH to measure the depth of water, especially using a sounding line [Old English *fæþm*, origin ?] —**fath·om·a·ble** *adj*

fath·om·less /fá*th*əmləss/ *adj* **1.** too deep to be measured **2.** impossible to understand —**fath·om·less·ly** *adv* —**fath·om·less·ness** *n*

fa·tigue /fə tée̱g/ *n* **1.** MENTAL OR PHYSICAL EXHAUSTION extreme tiredness or weariness resulting from physical or mental activity ○ *weak with fatigue after the long march* **2.** INABILITY TO RESPOND TO SITUATION the temporary inability of somebody to respond to a situation as a result of overexposure or excessive activity (*often used in combination*) ○ *compassion fatigue* **3.** PHYSIOL INABILITY TO RESPOND TO STIMULUS the temporary inability of an organ or body part such as a muscle or nerve cell to respond to a stimulus and function normally after continuous activity or stimulation **4.** ENG WEAKENING OF MATERIAL UNDER STRESS the weakening or breakdown of a material subjected to prolonged or repeated stress ○ *metal fatigue* **5.** MIL NONMILITARY WORK DONE BY SOLDIERS manual or menial work done by soldiers, often as a punishment (*often used before a noun*) ■ **fa·tigues** *npl* MIL INFORMAL MILITARY UNIFORMS informal military uniforms worn every day and in battle, as distinct from formal uniforms ■ *vti* (**-tigued, -tigu·ing, -tigues**) **1.** MAKE OR BECOME TIRED to tire somebody out as a result of physical or mental activity, or become tired out in this way **2.** WEAKEN UNDER STRESS to weaken or break something, or become weakened or broken, when subjected to prolonged or repeated stress [Mid-17C. Via French, "to tire" < Latin *fatigare*] —**fat·i·ga·ble** /fáttigəb'l/ *adj* —**fa·tigued** *adj*

Fat·i·ma /fáttəmə/ (A.D. 606?–632) Arabian religious figure. The youngest daughter of the prophet Muhammad, she is revered especially by Shiite Muslims.

Fá·ti·ma /fáttəmə/ village in west central Portugal, northeast of Lisbon. It is a place of pilgrimage for Roman Catholics and has been a shrine since 1917. Population: 5,445 (1991).

Fat·i·mid /fáttə mìd/, **Fat·i·mite** /-mìt/ *n* **1.** a member of a Muslim dynasty, descended from Muhammad's daughter Fatima and her husband Ali, that ruled North Africa and parts of Egypt and Syria from A.D. 909 to 1171 **2.** a descendant of Muhammad's daughter Fatima and her husband Ali [Mid-19C. < Arabic *Fāṭima* "Fatima"]

fat lip *n* a lip swollen from having been hit in a fist fight (*slang*)

fat meat, **fat pork** *n regional* FOOD same as **fatback**

REGIONAL NOTE See ***fatback***.

fat·so /fátsō/ (*plural* **-soes**) *n* an offensive term for somebody who is overweight (*slang insult*) [Mid-20C. Probably < *fats*, offensive term for an overweight person]

fat·ten /fátt'n/ (**-tened, -ten·ing, -tens**) *v* **1.** *vti* FEED ANIMAL to make an animal fat by feeding it plentifully, usually for slaughter, or be made fat for this purpose **2.** *vti* MAKE OR BECOME FAT to become fat or fatter, or make somebody fat or fatter **3.** *vt* ENLARGE SOMETHING to make something larger, richer, or fuller ○ *fatten your wallet* **4.** *vt* FERTILIZE LAND to make land or soil more fertile —**fat·ten·er** *n*

fat·ten·ing /fátt'ning/ *adj* **1.** high in fat or calorie content, and so likely to make some people gain weight **2.** becoming fat and therefore suitable for slaughter —**fat·ten·ing·ly** *adv*

fat·ty /fáttee/ *adj* (**-ti·er, -ti·est**) **1.** CONTAINING FAT containing fat or grease, especially in large or distasteful amounts **2.** DERIVED FROM FAT derived from or chemically related to fat ○ *fatty alcohol* **3.** WITH ACCUMULATED FAT containing accumulated fat, sometimes in undesirable amounts ○ *fatty tissue* ■ *n* (*plural* **-ties**) OFFENSIVE TERM an offensive term for somebody who is overweight (*slang insult*) —**fat·ti·ness** *n*

fat·ty ac·id *n* an organic acid belonging to a group that may occur naturally as waxes, fats, and essential oils and consisting of a straight chain of carbon atoms linked by single bonds and ending in a carboxyl group. Source: animal and plant materials. Formula: $C_nH_{n+1}COOH$.

fat·ty de·gen·er·a·tion *n* deterioration in the function of an organ such as the liver or heart, caused by the accumulation of unusually high levels of fats in its cells

fat·ty oil *n* CHEM same as **fixed oil**

fa·tu·i·ty /fə tóo ətee/ (*plural* **-ties**) *n* (*formal*) **1.** a lack of intelligence or thought combined with complacency **2.** an action or remark that shows a lack of intelligence or thought combined with complacency —**fa·tu·i·tous** *adj*

fat·u·ous /fáchoo əss/ *adj* showing a lack of intelligence or thought combined with complacency ○ *a fatuous joke* [Early 17C. < Latin *fatuus*] —**fat·u·ous·ly** *adv* —**fat·u·ous·ness** *n*

fat·wa /fáttwə/, **fat·wah** *n* a formal legal opinion or religious decree issued by an Islamic leader [Early 17C. < Arabic *fatwā* < *aftā* "decide a point of law"]

fat·ware /fát wèr/ *n* COMPUT same as **bloatware**

fau·bourg /fṓ bùrg, fō bŏŏr/ *n* **1.** *Southern US* a suburb or quarter situated just outside New Orleans **2.** an inner suburb or quarter of a city, especially in France [15C. < French, alteration (after *faux* "false") of Old French *forsborc* < Latin *foris* "outside" + late Latin *burgus* "fat" (< Germanic)]

Fau·bus /fṓbəss/, **Orval E.** (1910–94) US politician. While governor of Arkansas, he used the National Guard to try to prevent the racial integration of Little Rock High School (1957). Full name **Faubus, Orval Eugene**

fau·ces /fáw sèez/ *npl* the passage between the back of the mouth and the pharynx [15C. < Latin, "throat"] —**fau·cal** /fáwk'l/ *adj* —**fau·cial** /fáwsh'l/ *adj*

fau·cet /fáwssit/ *n* a valve operated by a handle that controls the flow of a liquid, especially from pipes supplying water [14C. Via Old French *fausset* or Provençal *falset* < *falser* "bore in" < late Latin *falsare* "to corrupt" < Latin *falsus* "false"]

REGIONAL NOTE See ***spigot***.

Library of Congress

William Faulkner

Faulk·ner /fáwknər/, **William** (1897–1962) US writer. He is regarded as one of the greatest American novelists for his stream-of-consciousness works about Southern life, including *The Sound and the Fury* (1929). He won the Nobel Prize in literature (1949). Full name **Faulkner, William Cuthbert**. See Cultural note at **fury** —**Faulk·ner·i·an** /fawk nèeree ən/ *adj*

> "Time is dead as long as it is being clicked off little wheels; only when the clock stops does time come to life."
> [William Faulkner, "June Second 1910," *The Sound and the Fury*; 1929]

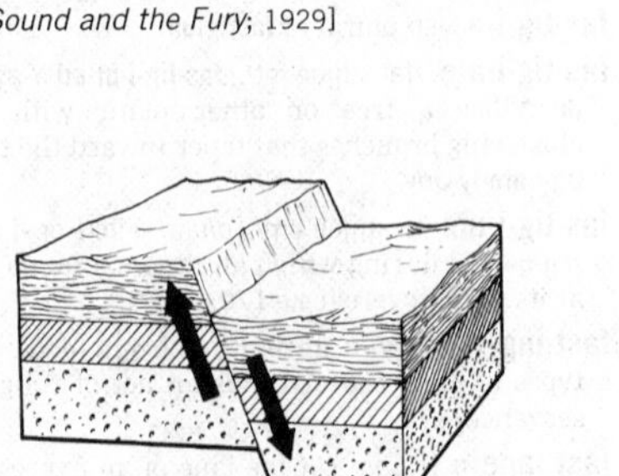

fault: displacement of rock layers in Earth's crust

fault /fawlt/ *n* **1.** RESPONSIBILITY FOR MISTAKE responsibility for a mistake, failure, or act of wrongdoing ○ *It's his fault we're late.* **2.** PERSONAL SHORTCOMING a failing or character weakness in somebody ○ *My main fault is laziness.* **3.** DEFECT something that detracts from the integrity, functioning, or perfection of something else ○ *an electrical fault* **4. MISTAKE** an error, especially in calculation **5. MISDEMEANOR** a wrongful action **6.** GEOL **DISPLACEMENT IN EARTH'S CRUST** a displacement of rock layers in the Earth's crust in response to stress, accompanied by a break in the continuity of the rocks on each side of the fault line **7.** RACKET GAMES **INVALID SERVE IN RACKET GAMES** in racket games such as tennis, a serve that is invalid because it fails to land within a prescribed area **8.** SHOW JUMPING **PENALTY MARK IN SHOW JUMPING** a penalty mark awarded in show jumping for various errors such as a failure or refusal to clear a fence ■ *v* (**fault·ed, fault·ing, faults**) **1.** *vt* **BLAME SOMEBODY OR SOMETHING** to blame, criticize, or find a flaw in somebody or something ○ *You can't fault his results.* **2.** *vi* **MAKE MISTAKE** to commit a fault or make a mistake (*archaic*) **3.** *vi* GEOL **DISPLACE** to respond to stress by becoming displaced and developing as a geologic fault (*refers to rock layers*) [13C. Via Old French *faut(e)* "lack" < assumed Vulgar Latin *fallitum* "failing" < Latin *fallere* "fail"] ◇ **find fault with somebody** *or* **something** to criticize somebody or something, often unfairly ○ *She's always finding fault with the children's work.* ◇ **to a fault** excessively ○ *naive and generous to a fault*

SYNONYMS See ***flaw***[1].

fault·find·ing /fáwlt fìnding/ *n* constant and often petty complaining or criticism —**fault·find·er** *n* —**fault·find·ing** *adj*

fault·less /fáwltləss/ *adj* having no faults or flaws ○ *a faultless performance* —**fault·less·ly** *adv* —**fault·less·ness** *n*

fault line *n* a linear feature on the Earth's surface, occurring where displaced rock layers have broken through the Earth's surface

fault plane *n* the surface along which displacement of rock layers has taken place in a geologic fault

fault tol·er·ance *n* the ability of a computer or network to preserve the integrity of data during a malfunction

fault·y /fáwltee/ (**-i·er, -i·est**) *adj* containing flaws, especially ones that cause malfunctions ○ *faulty wiring* ○ *faulty logic* —**fault·i·ly** *adv* —**fault·i·ness** *n*

faun /fawn/ *n* in Roman mythology, a rural god, often depicted as a creature with the body of a man and the legs and horns of a goat. Greek equivalent **satyr** (sense 1) [14C. Directly or via French < Latin *Faunus* "Faunus"]

SPELLCHECK faun or **fawn**? Do not confuse the spelling of ***faun*** and ***fawn***, which sound similar. A ***faun*** is a mythological being depicted as part man and part goat; a ***fawn*** is a young deer. ***Fawn*** is also an adjective and noun referring to a pale yellowish brown color, as in *a fawn jacket*, or a verb meaning "try to win favor" or "attempt to please somebody," as in *fawning over the celebrities he interviews.*

fau·na /fáwnə/ (*plural* **-nas** or **-nae** /-nee/) *n* **1.** the animal life of a particular region or period, considered as a whole **2.** a catalog or list describing the animals of a particular region or period [Late 18C. Via modern Latin < late Latin *Fauna* "Fauna," an ancient Italian rural goddess, sister of FAUNUS] —**fau·nal** *adj* —**fau·nal·ly** *adv* —**fau·nis·tic** /faw nístik/ *adv* —**fau·nis·ti·cal·ly** *adv*

Fau·nus /fáwnəss/ *n* in Roman mythology, the god of nature, farming, and fertility. He was the grandson of Saturn. Greek equivalent **Pan**

Fau·ré /faw ráy/, **Gabriel** (1845–1924) French composer and organist. His best-known work is the *Requiem* (1887) for solo voices, choir, and orchestra. Full name **Fauré, Gabriel Urbain**

Faust /fowst/ (*b.* 1480?) German fortune teller and magician. Reputed to have sold his soul to the devil, he is most noted for the legends concerning him that formed the basis for numerous literary and musical works. —**Faust·i·an** *adj*

faute de mieux /fōt də myö/ *adv* in the absence of something better ○ *the feeling that she had married him faute de mieux* [< French, "lack of better"]

fau·teuil /fō töy/ *n* an upholstered armchair, usually with open sides (*technical*) [Mid-18C. Via French < Old French *faudestuel* "folding chair" < Germanic]

fauve /fōv/, **Fauve** *n* an artist belonging to an early 20th-century movement in French painting (**fauvism**) characterized by the use of simple forms and bright colors (*often used before a noun*) [Early 20C. < French, "wild, wild animal," via Old French *falve* "tawny" < Germanic]

fau·vism /fō vìzzəm/, **Fau·vism** *n* an early 20th-century movement in painting, begun in about 1905 by a group of French artists, including Matisse, and characterized by the use of simple forms and bright colors

fau·vist /fōvist/ *n* ART same as **fauve** —**fauv·ist** *adj*

faux /fō/ *adj* made in imitation of a natural material such as leather or fur ○ *faux marble* [Late 20C. Via French < Latin *falsus* (see FALSE)]

faux a·mi /fō za meé/ (*plural* **faux a·mis** /*pronunc. same*/) *n* LING same as **false friend** (sense 1) [< French]

faux-na·ïf /fō naa eéf/ *adj* pretending to be simple or without sophistication (*literary*) [< French, "falsely naive"] —**faux-na·ïf** *n*

faux pas /fō paá/ (*plural* **faux pas** /fō paáz/) *n* an embarrassing mistake that breaks a social convention [< French, "false step"]

SYNONYMS See ***mistake.***

fa·va bean /faávə-/ *n* PLANTS, FOOD same as **broad bean** [Via Italian < Latin *faba*]

fave /fayv/ *n, adj* same as **favorite** (*slang*) [Mid-20C. Shortening]

fa·ve·la /fə véllə/ *n* a shantytown or slum area, especially in Brazil [Mid-20C. < Brazilian Portuguese]

fa·vism /faá vìzzəm/ *n* acute anemia caused by an allergic reaction to broad beans or the plant's pollen, usually as a result of a hereditary enzyme deficiency [Early 20C. < Italian *favismo* < *fava* "broad bean" (see FAVA BEAN)]

fa·vo·ni·an /fə vōnee ən/ *adj* (*literary*) **1.** relating to the west or the west wind **2.** benign or kind [Mid-17C. < Latin *favonianus* < *Favonius* "west wind"]

fa·vor /fáyvər/ *n* **1. KIND ACT** an act of kindness performed or granted out of goodwill ○ *lent me the car as a favor* **2. APPROVING ATTITUDE** an approving, friendly, or supportive attitude ○ *They seem to be out of favor with the judges.* **3. PREFERENCE** preferential treatment shown to somebody **4. TOKEN OF LOYALTY** something given or worn as a token of love, allegiance, or goodwill **5. SMALL GIFT** a small gift given to each guest at a party ■ **fa·vors** *npl* SEX sexual intimacy, especially when consented to by a woman (*dated*) ■ *vt* (**-vored, -vor·ing, -vors**) **1. PREFER SOMEBODY OR SOMETHING** to show a preference for somebody or something ○ *He favored loud suits and colorful ties.* **2. SUPPORT SOMEBODY OR SOMETHING** to express support for somebody or something ○ *voters who favored reform* **3. ASSIST SOMEBODY OR SOMETHING** to be advantageous to somebody or something ○ *tax measures that favor the rich* **4. SHOW SOMEBODY PREFERENTIAL TREATMENT** to distinguish somebody by giving him or her something valuable ○ *favored him with the best seat* **5. BE CAREFUL WITH SOMETHING** to treat or use something gently ○ *favoring a bad knee* **6. TREAT SOMEBODY OR SOMETHING WITH KINDNESS** to treat somebody or something with particular approval or kindness **7. RESEMBLE SOMEBODY** to resemble somebody, usually a parent, in appearance ○ *favors her mother* [14C. Via Old French, "friendly regard" < Latin, < *favere* "be well disposed toward"] —**fa·vor·er** *n* ◇ **curry favor with somebody** to try to gain favor with a superior by flattery and obsequiousness ○ *They put more energy into currying favor with the principal than they ever put into their work.*

SYNONYMS See ***regard.***

fa·vor·a·ble /fáyvərəb'l/ *adj* **1. APPROVING** expressing approval or admiration ○ *a favorable reaction* **2. GAINING APPROVAL** winning approval or favor ○ *make a favorable impression* **3. PROMISING** suggesting future improvement or good results ○ *a favorable outlook* **4. ADVANTAGEOUS** acting in a beneficial way ○ *favorable winds* **5. CONSENTING** expressing agreement or consent ○ *a favorable response* —**fa·vor·a·ble·ness** *n* —**fa·vor·a·bly** *adv*

fa·vored /fáyvərd/ *adj* **1. CHOSEN** preferred to any other ○ *The favored plan is unfortunately the costliest.* **2. DISTINGUISHED** enjoying the advantages of a particular thing ○ *a child favored with his father's good nature* **3. PRIVILEGED** enjoying advantages or privileges denied to others —**fa·vored·ness** *n*

fa·vor·ite /fáyvərit, -vrit/ *adj* **MOST LIKED** preferred or most liked ■ *n* **1. PERSON OR THING LIKED MOST** somebody or something that is liked most of all or preferred to all others ○ *Which author is your favorite?* **2. COMPETITOR MOST LIKELY TO WIN** a competitor considered to be the most likely to win, especially in a horserace **3. SOMEBODY FAVORED BY SUPERIOR** somebody who is treated with special favor by a superior [Late 16C. Via obsolete French *favorit* < Italian *favorito*, past participle of *favorire* "to favor" < *favore* "favor" < Latin *favor* (see FAVOR)]

fa·vor·ite son *n* **1.** a successful man who is admired by the people of his hometown or home state **2.** *US* a politician preferred for nomination as a presidential candidate by delegates from his own state at a national convention

fa·vor·it·ism /fáyvəri tìzzəm, fáyvri-/ *n* **1.** the practice of giving special treatment or unfair advantages to a person or group ○ *accused of showing favoritism toward certain students* **2.** the state of being a favorite person or group

fa·vour *n, vt* Can, UK spelling of **favor**

fav·our·ite *adj, n* Can, UK spelling of **favorite**

fa·vus /fáyvəss/ *n* an infectious skin disease that affects people, especially on the scalp, and some domestic animals, causing the formation of dry yellowish encrustations. It is caused by a fungus, *Trichophyton schoenleinii.* [Mid-16C. < Latin, "honeycomb"]

Fawkes /fawks/, **Guy** (1570–1606) English conspirator. He was executed for his role in the Gunpowder Plot against James I on November 5, 1605.

> "A desperate disease requires a dangerous remedy."
> [Guy Fawkes. Quoted in *Dictionary of National Biography*, 1917]

fawn[1] /fawn/ *n* **1. YOUNG DEER** a young deer, especially one that is unweaned or less than a year old **2. YELLOWISH BROWN COLOR** a pale yellowish brown color ■ *vi* (**fawned, fawn·ing, fawns**) **PRODUCE FAWN** to give birth to a fawn [14C. Via French *faon* "young animal" < assumed Vulgar Latin *feton-* < Latin *fetus* "offspring"] —**fawn** *adj*

SPELLCHECK See ***faun.***

fawn[2] /fawn/ (**fawned, fawn·ing, fawns**) *vi* **1.** to seek attention or try to win favor by flattery and obsequious behavior ○ *admirers fawning at his feet* **2.** to attempt to please somebody by showing enthusiastic affection ○ *started fawning all over me as soon as I walked in* [Old English *fagnian* "rejoice" < *fægen* "glad" < Germanic] —**fawn·er** *n* —**fawn·ing·ly** *adv* —**fawn·ing·ness** *n*

fawn lil·y *n* a flowering plant with mottled leaves. Flowers: cream, yellow. Native to: North America. Genus: *Erythronium.* [< its mottled leaves]

fax /faks/ *n* **1. MESSAGE SENT ELECTRONICALLY** a document or image that is transmitted in digitized electronic form over telephone lines and reproduced in its original form on the receiving end **2. SYSTEM FOR TRANSMITTING DOCUMENTS** a system of transmitting documents and images electronically over telephone lines (*often used before a noun*) ○ *sent by fax* **3.** *also* **fax ma·chine TRANSMITTING MACHINE** a machine incorporating a telephone that sends and receives documents or images via fax ■ *vt* (**faxed, fax·ing, fax·es**) **SEND BY FAX** to send a document or image electronically using a fax machine [Mid-20C. Shortening of FACSIMILE]

fax·back /fáks bàk/ *n* **1.** an automated system of responding by fax, used especially for requesting and receiving documents, e.g., by using a touch-tone phone, or by downloading a document from a website to a fax machine **2.** a document received in response to a request using a faxback system

fax·mo·dem *n* a modem that enables a computer to send and receive faxes

fax-on-de·mand *n* technology that sends a fax automatically to somebody who telephones a particular number for information

fay[1] /fay/ *n* a fairy, elf, or other small supernatural being from folklore (*literary*) ○"*You are, upon the whole, a sort of fay, or sprite – not a woman!*" (Thomas Hardy, *Jude the Obscure*; 1895) [14C. Via Old French *fa(i)e* "fairy" < Latin *Fata*, goddess of fate < *fatum* (see FATE)]

fay[2] /fay/ (**fayed, fay·ing, fays**) *vti* to join pieces of wood together tightly, or fit tightly inside another piece of wood [Old English *fēgan* < Indo-European, "fasten"]

fay[3] /fay/ *n US* same as **ofay** (*slang insult*) [Early 20C. Shortening]

Fa·yette ➧ **La Fayette, Marie Madeleine**

Fay·ette·ville /fáy ət vìl/ city in northwestern Arkansas, northeast of Fort Smith and west of the White River. It is home to the University of Arkansas. Population: 60,732 (2002 estimate).

faze /fayz/ (**fazed, faz·ing, faz·es**) *vt* to disconcert or disturb somebody ○ *Bad news doesn't seem to faze her.* [Mid-19C. Variant of dialectal *feeze* "frighten" < Old English *fēsian* "drive away" < Germanic]

SPELLCHECK faze or **phase**? Do not confuse the spelling of ***faze*** and ***phase***, which sound similar. ***Faze*** is a verb meaning "disconcert": *Don't be fazed by the size of the instruction manual.* ***Phase***, the more common word, can be used as a noun meaning "a stage of development," "an aspect," or as a verb meaning "do something in stages": *It's just a phase he's going through. The old system is being phased out.*

fa·zen·da /fə zéndə/ *n* a large estate, farm, plantation, or cattle ranch, especially in Brazil or Portugal [Early 19C. Via Portuguese, originally "place with things to be done" < Latin *facienda* "things to be done" < *facere* "do, make"]

fb, f.b. *abbr* SPORTS fullback

FBI, F.B.I. *n* a bureau of the US Department of Justice that deals with matters of national security, interstate crime, and crimes against the government. Full form **Federal Bureau of Investigation**

FCA *abbr* ACCT full cost accounting

FCC, F.C.C. *n* the federal agency that oversees radio, television, and telecommunications in the United States. Full form **Federal Communications Commission**

F clef *n* MUSIC same as **bass clef**

FD, F.D. *abbr* **1.** MED fatal dose **2.** HIST, CHR Fidei Defensor **3.** Fire Department **4.** BUSINESS free delivery

FDA, F.D.A. *n* the federal agency that oversees trade in and the safety of food and drugs in the United States. Full form **Food and Drug Administration**

FDIC, F.D.I.C. *n* the federally chartered organization that insures deposits in US banks. Full form **Federal Deposit Insurance Corporation**

F dis·tri·bu·tion *n* a statistical measure of the spread or scattering of members of two observed random samples as a test of whether the samples have the same variability. The F distribution is obtained by taking the ratio of the chi-square distributions of the samples divided by the number of their degrees of freedom. [Mid-20C. After Sir Ronald *Fisher* (d. 1962), British statistician]

FDNY *abbr* Fire Department of New York

FDR *abbr* Franklin Delano Roosevelt

Fe *symbol* CHEM ELEM iron [< Latin *ferrum*]

fe·al·ty /fée əltee/ (*plural* **-ties**) *n* **1.** the loyalty sworn to a feudal lord by a vassal or tenant **2.** loyalty or allegiance shown to anyone (*archaic or literary*) [13C. Via Old French *feau(l)te* < Latin *fidelitas* (see FIDELITY)]

fear /feer/ *n* **1.** FEELING OF ANXIETY an unpleasant feeling of anxiety or apprehension caused by the presence or anticipation of danger ○ *showed no signs of fear* **2.** FRIGHTENING THOUGHT an idea, thought, or other entity that causes feelings of fear ○ *irrational fears* **3.** REVERENCE respect or awe for somebody or something ○ *the fear of God* **4.** WORRY a concern about something that threatens to bring bad news or results (*often used in the plural*) ○ *fears for their safe return* ■ *v* (**feared, fear·ing, fears**) **1.** *vti* BE AFRAID to be frightened of somebody or something or about taking action ○ *She fears going to the dentist.* **2.** *vt* FEEL REVERENCE FOR SOMEBODY OR SOMETHING to show respect for or be in awe of somebody or something ○ *fear God* **3.** *vt* EXPRESS REGRETFULLY to be sorry to say something (*formal*) ○ *I fear that you have not been successful on this occasion.* [Old English *fǣr* "calamity, danger," *fǣran* "frighten" < Indo-European, "to try"]

fear for *vt* to be worried or apprehensive about somebody or something that appears to be at risk or in danger

fear·ful /féerf'l/ *adj* **1.** WORRIED feeling anxiety or apprehension ○ *fearful for the safety of her investment* **2.** FRIGHTENING causing or likely to cause fear ○ *a fearful storm* **3.** TIMID nervous and easily frightened ○ *a fearful kitten* **4.** SCARED arising from or expressing fear ○ *a fearful expression* **5.** FEELING REVERENCE feeling respect or awe for somebody or something ○ *gazed in fearful wonder* **6.** VERY BAD extreme in degree, intensity, or badness (*informal*) ○ *had a fearful headache* —**fear·ful·ly** *adv* —**fear·ful·ness** *n*

fear·less /féerləss/ *adj* resolute in the face of dangers or challenges —**fear·less·ly** *adv* —**fear·less·ness** *n*

SYNONYMS See ***courage***.

fear·some /féerssəm/ *adj* **1.** FRIGHTENING inspiring fear ○ *a fearsome howling* **2.** IMPRESSIVE evoking awe and respect **3.** TIMID easily frightened —**fear·some·ly** *adv*— **fear·some·ness** *n*

~~**feasable**~~ incorrect spelling of **feasible**

fea·si·bil·i·ty /feezə bíllətee/ (*plural* **-ties**) *n* **1.** the degree to which something can be achieved or put into effect (*often used before a noun*) ○ *examining the feasibility of the proposed merger* **2.** something that can be carried out or achieved ○ *That idea isn't even a remote feasibility.*

fea·si·bil·i·ty stud·y *n* a preliminary study undertaken to assess whether a planned project is likely to be practical and successful and to estimate its cost

fea·si·ble /feezəb'l/ *adj* **1.** capable of being achieved or put into effect **2.** reasonable enough to be believed or accepted ○ *a feasible plan* [15C. < French *faisable* < *fais-*, stem of *faire* "do" < Latin *facere* "do, make"] —**fea·si·ble·ness** *n* —**fea·si·bly** *adv*

feast /feest/ *n* **1.** LARGE MEAL a large and elaborate meal **2.** CELEBRATORY MEAL an elaborate meal for many people that celebrates an occasion ○ *a wedding feast* **3.** SOMETHING VERY AGREEABLE something that provides a great deal of pleasure ○ *a feast for the eyes* **4.** RELIG RELIGIOUS CELEBRATION a periodic religious celebration, often marked by a special meal ■ *vi* (**feast·ed, feast·ing, feasts**) **1.** ATTEND CELEBRATORY MEAL to be present at a celebratory meal **2.** ENJOY EATING to eat heartily or with enjoyment ○ *feasting on strawberries and cream* **3.** TAKE DELIGHT to derive great or prolonged pleasure from something ○ *feast on the magnificent scenery* [12C. Via French < Latin *festa*, form of *festus* "joyous"] —**feast·er** *n*

feast day *n* **1.** a day on which a religious festival takes place **2.** a day on which an elaborate celebratory meal is enjoyed

Feast of Ded·i·ca·tion, Feast of Lights *n* JUDAISM same as **Hanukkah**

Feast of Lots *n* JUDAISM same as **Purim**

Feast of St. Mi·chael and All An·gels *n* CHR same as **Michaelmas**

Feast of Tab·er·na·cles *n* JUDAISM same as **Sukkoth**

Feast of the As·sump·tion *n* CHR same as **Assumption** (sense 2)

Feast of the Ho·ly In·no·cents *n* CHR same as **Holy Innocents' Day**

Feast of Weeks *n* JUDAISM same as **Shavuoth**

feat /feet/ *n* a remarkable act or achievement involving courage, skill, or strength ○ *achieved the impressive feat of winning three gold medals* [14C. Via Old French *fait* "deed" < Latin *factum* (see FACT)]

feath·er /féthər/ *n* **1.** PART OF BIRD'S PLUMAGE a part of a bird's plumage, consisting of a hollow central shaft with numerous interlocking fine strands on either side **2.** SOMETHING RESEMBLING FEATHER something with light or wispy strands that give it a superficial resemblance to a bird's feather, e.g., the leaf of a plant **3.** SOMETHING UNIMPORTANT something small, trivial, or of minimal value **4.** MINERALS FLAW IN PRECIOUS STONE a feather-shaped flaw in a precious stone **5.** ARCHERY ARROW ATTACHMENT a piece of a feather attached to the end of an arrow or dart to make it fly straight **6.** ARCHERY BLUNT END OF ARROW the end of an arrow that has a feather fitted on it **7.** CONSTR PART OF WOOD JOINT a projecting strip of wood fitted into a groove in the edge of a board to form a joint **8.** ROWING HORIZONTAL OAR POSITION the horizontal position in which an oar is held in order to reduce wind resistance when it is raised from the water between strokes ■ **feath·ers** *npl* **1.** ZOOL LONG HAIR ON ANIMALS fringes of hair on the legs or tails of some dogs and horses **2.** ATTIRE the clothes that somebody is wearing (*dated*) ■ *v* (**-ered, -er·ing, -ers**) **1.** *vt* FIT SOMETHING WITH FEATHERS to fit something such as an arrow with a feather or feathers **2.** *vt* COVER SOMETHING WITH FEATHERS to cover or decorate somebody or something with feathers **3.** *vti* FRAY to fray a surface or end by cutting it or wearing it away, or become frayed in this way **4.** *vt* CUT HAIR TO FORM LAYERS to style hair by cutting and thinning in order to give a layered texture **5.** *vi* SPREAD to grow or move out at an angle from a central line in a pattern resembling the structure of a feather **6.** *vti* ROWING TURN OAR BLADE HORIZONTAL to turn an oar so that the blade face is parallel to the water in order to reduce wind resistance when it is raised from the water between strokes **7.** *vt* AVIAT ALTER POSITION OF PROPELLER BLADES to change the angle of an aircraft's propeller so that the line of the blades is roughly parallel to the line of flight and air resistance is minimized **8.** *vt* CONSTR CONNECT BOARDS WITH TONGUE-AND-GROOVE JOINT to join two boards or pieces of wood by using a tongue-and-groove joint [Old English *feþer* < Indo-European, "to fly"] —**feath·ered** *adj*— **feath·er·like** *adj* ◇ **a feather in somebody's cap** an act or achievement that gives somebody cause to be proud ○ *Getting the award is a real feather in my cap.*

feath·er·bed /féthər bèd/ (**-bed·ded, -bed·ding, -beds**) *vi* to overstaff or limit production, especially in compliance with a union contract, in order to save or create jobs

feath·er·bed·ding /féthər bèdding/ *n* the practice of overstaffing or limiting production, especially in compliance with a union contract, in order to save or create jobs

feath·er·brain /féthər bràyn/ *n* somebody who is regarded as forgetful, thoughtless, or inattentive (*informal insult*) —**feath·er·brained** *adj*

feath·er dust·er *n* a brush used for dusting, made of long feathers attached to a stick

feath·er·edge /féthər èj/ *n* **1.** TAPERED BOARD a board or plank with a thin tapering edge **2.** TAPERING EDGE OF BOARD the thinner tapering edge of a wedge-shaped board or plank **3.** PAPER same as **deckle edge** ■ *vt* (**-edged, -edg·ing, -edges**) HONE TO EDGE to taper a side or end of a board or plank to a very thin edge

feath·er grass *n* a perennial grass plant that has feathery clusters of spikelets. Genus: *Stipa*.

feath·er·head /féthər hèd/ *n* same as **featherbrain** (*informal insult*) —**feath·er·head·ed** *adj*

feath·er·ing /féthəring/ *n* **1.** PLUMAGE the feathers on a bird **2.** FEATHERS ATTACHED TO ARROW the feathers attached to an arrow or dart, or their arrangement **3.** ZOOL LONG HAIR ON ANIMAL'S LEGS fringes of hair on the legs or tails of some dogs and horses **4.** PRINTING PATTERN OF INK SOAKING INTO PAPER the spreading of ink in lines like veins through printed paper that is too absorbent

feath·er palm *n* a palm tree with feathery leaves

feath·er star *n* a free-swimming invertebrate ocean animal with between five and ten feathery arms radiating from a central disk. Order: Comatulida.

feath·er·stitch /féthər stìch/ *n* ornamental embroidery stitching with a zigzag pattern ■ *vt* (**-stitched, -stitch·ing, -stitch·es**) to sew or decorate something with featherstitch

feath·er·weight /féthər wàyt/ *n* **1.** PROFESSIONAL WEIGHT CATEGORY in professional boxing, a weight category for competitors whose weight does not exceed 126 pounds/57.1 kg **2.** AMATEUR WEIGHT CATEGORY in amateur boxing, a weight category for competitors whose weight does not exceed 125 pounds/57 kg **3.** FEATHERWEIGHT BOXER a professional boxer who competes at featherweight level **4.** LIGHTWEIGHT ATHLETE in sports such as wrestling, a competitor at lightweight level **5.** SOMEBODY OR SOMETHING LIGHT OR INSIGNIFICANT somebody or something that is very light, small, or insignificant

feath·er·y /féthəree/ *adj* 1. similar to a feather or feathers, especially in lightness or softness 2. made of or covered in feathers —**feath·er·i·ness** *n*

fea·ture /féechər/ *n* 1. DISTINCTIVE PART a part of something that distinguishes it ○ *a geographic feature* 2. PART OF FACE a part of a face that contributes to its distinct character, especially the eyes, nose, or mouth 3. MOVIES FULL-LENGTH MOVIE a full-length motion picture 4. MOVIES MAIN MOVIE IN PROGRAM formerly, the main motion picture in a movie program 5. PUBL REGULAR ARTICLE a regular item in a newspaper or magazine or on a broadcast 6. PUBL MAIN ARTICLE an article that is given particular prominence in a newspaper or magazine 7. BROADCAST MAIN TELEVISION OR RADIO PROGRAM a television or radio program that is considered especially important or popular 8. ATTRACTIVE ASPECT OF SOMETHING something offered as a special attraction, e.g., a particular aspect of something ○ *a refrigerator with several energy-saving features* 9. LING PROPERTY OF A LINGUISTIC UNIT a distinctive property of a linguistic unit. Voicing is a feature of the consonants *b*, *d*, and *g*. ■ *v* (-tured, -tur·ing, -tures) 1. *vt* CONTAIN SOMETHING AS IMPORTANT ELEMENT to have or present somebody or something as an important element of something ○ *This week's activities will feature horseback riding and golf.* 2. *vti* GIVE OR HAVE PROMINENCE IN PERFORMANCE to give prominence to somebody taking part in a performance or to something performed or portrayed in a performance, or be given prominence in this way ○ *a movie featuring two of today's most popular actors* 3. *vt US* IMAGINE OR VISUALIZE SOMETHING to imagine or visualize something mentally (*informal*) ○ *I can't feature her coming back.* 4. *vi* FIGURE IN SOMETHING to figure in or be a part of something ○ *Marriage doesn't feature in their plans.* [14C. Via Old French *faiture* "form" < Latin *factura* "something made" < *fact-* (see FACT)] —**fea·tured** *adj*

fea·ture crea·ture *n* somebody who adds excessive features to a design, software program, or website, often at the expense of coherence or utility (*slang*)

fea·ture film *n* a full-length motion picture

fea·ture-length *adj* being as long as a feature film ○ *a feature-length episode*

fea·ture·less /féechərləss/ *adj* lacking any distinctive characteristics or properties

Feb. *abbr* CALENDAR February

feb·ri·fa·cient /fèbbrə fáysh'nt/ *adj* causing, producing, or promoting fever [Early 19C. < Latin *febris* "fever"]

fe·brif·ic /fə bríffik/ *adj* 1. capable of causing somebody to have a fever 2. affected by a fever [Early 18C. < obsolete French *fébrifique* < Latin *febris* "fever"]

feb·ri·fuge /fébbrə fyooj/ *n* a drug that reduces fever [Late 17C. < French *fébrifuge* < Latin *febris* "fever"] —**feb·ri·fug·al** /fə bríffyəg'l, fébbrə fyoóg'l/ *adj* —**feb·ri·fuge** *adj*

fe·brile /fébbrəl, féebrəl/ *adj* relating to, involving, or typical of fever [Mid-17C. < French *fébrile* or medieval Latin *febrilis* < Latin *febris* "fever"]

Feb·ru·ar·y /fébbroo èrree, fébbyoo-/ (*plural* -ies) *n* in the Gregorian calendar, the second month of the year, lasting 28 days or, in leap years, 29 days. See table at **calendar** [14C. Via Old French *feverier* < Latin *februarius (mensis)* "(month) of purification"; from an annual Roman festival]

PRONUNCIATION The generally preferred pronunciation of ***February*** is /fébbroo èrree/, in which the first *r* is sounded. The variant pronunciation, to which some people object, is /fébbyoo èrree/, in which the first *r* is dropped. This dropping of *r* is an example of a normal process that happens when some speakers are confronted with the repeated occurrence of the same sound within a word. Finding it difficult to articulate both sounds, especially when trying to say a word fast, some speakers will simply drop one of the two sounds. It is also possible that the variant pronunciation of ***February*** was influenced by the pronunciation /jánnyoo èrree/ for *January*.

~~Febuary~~ incorrect spelling of **February**

FEC *abbr* Federal Election Commission

fec. *abbr* he or she made it [Latin *fecit*]

fe·ces /féesseez/ *npl* the body's solid waste matter, composed of undigested food, bacteria, water, and bile pigments and discharged from the bowel through the anus [14C. < Latin *faeces*, plural of *faex* "sediment, dregs"] —**fe·cal** /féek'l/ *adj*

feck·less /fékləss/ *adj* 1. unable or unwilling to do anything useful 2. lacking the thought or organization necessary to succeed ○ *feckless attempts at starting a business* [Late 16C. < obsolete *feck* "value, efficacy," shortening of EFFECT] —**feck·less·ly** *adv* —**feck·less·ness** *n*

fec·u·la /fékyələ/ (*plural* -lae /-lee/) *n* 1. a starch extracted as sediment from a mixture of water and crushed plants 2. a piece of excrement, especially an insect dropping [Late 17C. < Latin *faecula* "crust of wine" < *faex* "dregs, sediment"]

fec·u·lent /fékyələnt/ *adj* very dirty or foul, especially polluted by excrement (*formal*) [15C. Directly or via French < Latin *faeculentus* < *faeces* (see FECES)] —**fec·u·lence** *n*

fe·cund /féekənd, fék-/ *adj* 1. capable of producing much vegetation or many offspring 2. able to produce many different and original ideas ○ *a fecund liar* [14C. Directly or via French < Latin *fecundus*]

fe·cun·date /féekən dàyt, fék-/ (-dat·ed, -dat·ing, -dates) *vt* 1. MAKE SOMEBODY OR SOMETHING PRODUCTIVE to make somebody or something fruitful or productive (*literary*) 2. FERTILIZE SOMETHING to fertilize a plant (*archaic*) 3. IMPREGNATE WOMAN OR FEMALE ANIMAL to make a woman or female animal pregnant (*archaic*) —**fe·cun·da·tion** /fèekən dáysh'n, fèk-/ *n*

fe·cun·di·ty /fi kúndətee/ *n* 1. the ability to produce offspring, especially in large numbers 2. the ability to produce many different and original ideas (*formal*)

fed past participle, past tense of **feed**

Fed /fed/, **fed** *n US* (*informal*) 1. FEDERAL RESERVE BOARD the Federal Reserve Board 2. FEDERAL RESERVE SYSTEM the Federal Reserve System 3. FEDERAL AGENT a Federal agent or official, especially an agent of the FBI or the EPA

fed. *abbr* POL 1. federal 2. federated 3. federation

Fed. *abbr* 1. Federal 2. Federated

fe·da·yee /fe daà yée, -dà-/ (*plural* -yeen /-yéen/), **fi·da·yee** *n* an Arab commando or guerrilla, especially one who fights against Israel [Mid-20C. < Arabic, Persian *fidā'ī* "somebody who sacrifices himself or herself"]

fed·er·al /féddərəl, féddrəl/ *adj* 1. MADE UP OF ALLIES relating to a form of government in which several states or regions defer some powers, e.g., in foreign affairs, to a central government while retaining a limited measure of self-government 2. CENTRAL relating to a political unit established on a federal basis, especially its central government 3. ASSOCIATED relating to or characteristic of a unified body with constituent parts that retain a measure of autonomy 4. *US* OF US ARCHITECTURAL STYLE relating to, involving, or typical of a classical style of architecture, decoration, and furniture popular in the United States in the late 18th and early 19th centuries ■ *n* SUPPORTER OF ALLIANCE a supporter of joining an alliance [Mid-17C. < Latin *foeder-*, stem of *foedus* "treaty"] —**fed·er·al·ly** *adv*

Fed·er·al *adj* involving or supporting the Union during the Civil War ■ *n* 1. a soldier or supporter of the Union during the Civil War 2. HIST same as **Federalist**

Fed·er·al Bu·reau of In·ves·ti·ga·tion *n* full form of **FBI**

fed·er·al case *n* a matter in law that comes under the jurisdiction of a federal court ◇ **make a federal case out of something** to make a fuss about something trivial ○ *Why do you have to make a federal case out of everything?*

Fed·er·al Com·mu·ni·ca·tions Com·mis·sion *n* full form of **FCC**

Fed·er·al De·pos·it In·sur·ance Cor·po·ra·tion *n* full form of **FDIC**

fed·eral dis·trict *n* an area in which the seat of the national government of a federation such as the United States is located

Fed·er·al E·lec·tion Com·mis·sion *n* a federal agency that oversees the financing of federal elections

fed·er·al funds *npl* money lent overnight from one Federal Reserve Bank to another. The rate of interest charged on such loans is a key economic indicator.

fed·er·al gov·ern·ment *n* the central government of a federation

fed·er·al·ism /féddərə lìzzəm, féddrə-/ *n* 1. POLITICAL SYSTEM a political system in which several states or regions defer some powers, e.g., in foreign affairs, to a central government while retaining a limited measure of self-government 2. PRINCIPLE OF FEDERAL POLITICAL SYSTEM the principle of a federal system of government 3. SUPPORT FOR FEDERAL POLITICAL SYSTEM support for a federal system of government

Fed·er·al·ism *n* the political doctrine of the former Federalist Party

fed·er·al·ist /féddərəlist, féddrə-/ *n* 1. a supporter of a federal system of government 2. *Can* somebody who supports the federation of the Canadian provinces and opposes separatism

Fed·er·al·ist *n* a supporter of the former Federalist Party

Fed·er·al·ist Par·ty *n* a former political party of the United States advocating a strong centralized government within the federal system. Founded in 1787, it declined in influence after 1800.

fed·er·al·ize /féddərə lìz/ (-ized, -iz·ing, -iz·es) *vt* 1. to bring various states together in a federal union 2. to place something under the control of a federal government —**fed·er·al·i·za·tion** /fèddərəli záysh'n/ *n*

Fed·er·al Re·pub·lic of Ger·ma·ny /fèddərəl-/ the former West Germany

Fed·er·al Re·serve Bank *n* one of the 12 US reserve banks responsible for regulating the affiliated banks in its own district

Fed·er·al Re·serve Board *n US* the group responsible for supervising the Federal Reserve System

Fed·er·al Re·serve note *n* a bank note or certificate, sometimes used as money, issued by a Federal Reserve Bank

Fed·er·al Re·serve Sys·tem *n* the US banking system that regulates money supply and interest rates, consisting of 12 Federal Reserve Banks that regulate the activities of affiliated banks in their own districts

Fed·er·al Trade Com·mis·sion *n* a federal agency that enforces several federal antitrust and consumer-protection laws

fed·er·ate /féddə ràyt/ (-at·ed, -at·ing, -ates) *vti* to join together in a federation, or cause various bodies to join together in a federation [Late 17C. < Latin *foederat-*, past participle of *foederare* < *foedus* "treaty"]

Fed·er·at·ed States of Mic·ro·nes·i·a ➧ **Micronesia** (sense 2)

fed·er·a·tion /féddə ráysh'n/ *n* 1. POLITICAL UNIT a political unit formed from smaller units on a federal basis 2. ALLIANCE a group of various bodies or parties that have united to achieve a common goal 3. JOINING IN FEDERAL UNION an act of joining in a federal union or a federal system of government [Early 18C. Via French < Latin *foederation-* < *foederat-* (see FEDERATE)]

fed·er·a·tive /féddə ràytiv, -rətiv/ *adj* relating to, characteristic of, or forming a federation [Late 17C. < Latin *foederat-* (see FEDERATE)]

fe·do·ra /fə dáwrə/ *n* a soft felt hat with a brim and a crease along the length of its crown [Late 19C. < *Fédora*, drama by Victorien Sardou (1831–1908), French playwright]

fed up *adj* having reached the limits of tolerance or patience with somebody or something (*informal*) ○ *got fed up with working all the time*

fee /fee/ *n* 1. PAYMENT FOR SERVICES a payment for professional services 2. CHARGE MADE BY INSTITUTION a charge made by an institution, e.g., for membership, entrance, or the administering of an examination 3.

RIGHT TO OWNERSHIP OF LAND a right to land that can be passed on by inheritance **4.** HIST same as **fief** (sense 1) [14C. Via Anglo-Norman variant of Old French *feu* < medieval Latin *feudum* (see FEUD[2])]

ORIGIN ***Fee*** and its close relatives *feudal* and *fief* take us back to the beginnings of European feudal society, when the ownership of cattle symbolized wealth. The Indo-European source of ***fee***, denoting "livestock," is also the source of the German word *Vieh* "cattle."

SYNONYMS See ***wage***.

Feeb /feeb/, **Fee·bie** /fée bee/ *n US* an agent of the FBI (*slang*) [Alteration of FBI]

fee·ble /féeb'l/ (**-bler, -blest**) *adj* **1.** lacking physical or mental strength or health **2.** unlikely to convince ○ *a feeble excuse* [12C. Via Old French *fe(i)ble* < Latin *flebilis* "lamentable, weak" < *flere* "weep"] —**fee·ble·ness** *n* —**fee·bly** *adv*

SYNONYMS See ***weak***.

fee·ble-mind·ed *adj* **1.** OFFENSIVE TERM an offensive term meaning foolish or thoughtless **2.** NOT WELL THOUGHT-OUT done without forethought or planning ○ *a feeble-minded plan* **3.** OFFENSIVE TERM an offensive term meaning below average in intelligence (*dated*) —**fee·ble-mind·ed·ly** *adv* —**fee·ble-mind·ed·ness** *n*

feed /feed/ *v* (**fed** /fed/, **feed·ing, feeds**) **1.** *vt* GIVE FOOD TO SOMEBODY to give food to a person or an animal **2.** *vt* GIVE SOMETHING AS FOOD to give something as food to a person or an animal ○ *fed the horse carrots* **3.** *vt* SERVE AS FOOD FOR SOMEBODY to serve as or be enough food for a person or an animal ○ *This loaf won't feed us all.* **4.** *vi* EAT to eat food, or take regular nourishment ○ *Most whales feed on plankton.* **5.** *vt* SUPPORT SOMETHING to sustain or encourage a belief or behavior ○ *Compliments merely feed vanity.* **6.** *vt* PROVIDE SOMETHING WITH NECESSARY MATERIAL to provide something with the necessary materials for operation **7.** *vti* MOVE GRADUALLY to move something gradually into, through, or out of something, or be moved in this way **8.** *vt* THEATER GIVE PERFORMER CUE to deliver a line or cue to another performer **9.** *vti* PASS BALL TO PLAYER to pass a ball to a teammate (*informal*) **10.** *vt* UTIL SUPPLY WITH POWER to supply power or an electrical signal to a system, component, or station **11.** *vti* BROADCAST SEND BROADCAST to provide a local television or radio broadcast to a larger audience by using a satellite or network ■ *n* **1.** ACT OF FEEDING an act or occasion of feeding **2.** FOOD food for animals, especially livestock **3.** LARGE MEAL a meal, especially a large and satisfying one (*informal*) **4.** PROVIDER OF MATERIAL FOR MACHINE a device that supplies material to a machine, e.g., the paper tray on a printer **5.** BROADCAST NETWORK SIGNAL the signal a network sends to local radio or television stations for broadcast ○ *The local television station lost the network's feed for a few minutes.* **6.** THEATER SOMEBODY WHO PROVIDES CUES somebody who delivers a line or cue to a performer [Old English *fēdan* < Germanic]

feed into *vt* **1.** to add weight and impetus to something **2.** to connect with and contribute to something larger, e.g., a road or river

feed·back /féed bàk/ *n* **1.** RETURN OF OUTPUT the return of part of the output of a machine, system, or circuit to the input in a way that affects its performance **2.** NOISE IN LOUDSPEAKER the high whistling or howling noise caused by feedback in a loudspeaker **3.** RESPONSE comments in the form of opinions about and reactions to something, intended to provide useful information for future decisions and development

feed·back cir·cuit *n* a circuit in which a portion of the output signal is returned to the input, often in order to control or stabilize the circuit

feed·back con·trol loop *n* the connection or path that forms an electrical loop from the output to the input of a feedback circuit

feed·back fac·tor *n* the fraction of an output signal that is returned to and combined with the input signal

feed·back in·hi·bi·tion *n* an internal control on a hormone or enzyme that causes a reduction in activity once the end product reaches a specific concentration

feed·back loop *n* a cycle of behavior in which two people each act to reinforce the other's action

feed·bag /féed bàg/ *n* **1.** a bag placed over the muzzle of a horse from which it can eat **2.** *UK* a bag or sack containing food for livestock

feed·er /féedər/ *n* **1.** EATER a person or animal that eats, especially a particular food or in a particular way **2.** CONTAINER FOR ANIMAL'S FOOD a device that supplies food for birds or other animals ○ *a bird feeder in the garden* **3.** SUPPLIER OF FOOD somebody who provides food **4.** MACHINE PART a part of a machine that accepts or controls the input of material to be processed ○ *a document feeder* **5.** AGRIC LIVESTOCK an animal that is fattened for sale or slaughter **6.** GEOG TRIBUTARY a stream or river that joins the flow of a larger one **7.** TRANSP CONNECTING CARRIER a road, railroad, or airline that carries traffic from a relatively small place to a city in order to connect with a larger carrier **8.** UTIL POWER LINE a power line that carries power from a generating station to a substation or network **9.** BROADCAST CONNECTION a line that connects an antenna to a receiver or transmitter **10.** EDUC PRIMARY SCHOOL a primary or middle school whose graduates go on to a particular secondary school

feed·ing fren·zy *n* **1.** an instance of frantic activity centered on a person or organization that occurs when other people, especially journalists, sense an opportunity they can exploit (*informal*) **2.** an intense violent period of eating that occurs when a large number of animals of the same or related species such as sharks or piranhas converge on a food source

feed·ing ground *n* an area where wildlife regularly comes to feed

feed·lot /féed lòt/ *n* an area or building in which livestock are kept while being fattened for slaughter

feed·stock /féed stòk/ *n* a raw material used in the industrial manufacture of a product

feed·stuff /féed stùf/ *n* feed for livestock, especially consisting of processed and balanced ingredients

feed·through /féed thro͞o/ *n* an electrical conductor that connects two sides of a circuit board

feel /feel/ *v* (**felt** /felt/, **feel·ing, feels**) **1.** *vi* SEEM TO YOURSELF to seem to yourself to be in a particular physical or emotional state ○ *Don't feel sad.* **2.** *vi* CAUSE PARTICULAR SENSATION to cause a particular physical or emotional sensation ○ *The water feels cold.* **3.** *vt* EXPERIENCE SOMETHING to experience an emotion or physical sensation ○ *felt no regret* **4.** *vt* HAVE SENSATION IN BODY PART to have physical sensation in a part of the body **5.** *vt* BE AFFECTED BY SOMETHING to be deeply affected emotionally by something painful **6.** *vt* TOUCH SOMETHING to perceive something using the sense of touch **7.** *vt* EXAMINE SOMETHING to test or examine something by touching it **8.** *vt* ADVANCE HESITANTLY to make your way forward slowly, guided by the sense of touch, or tentatively, because what is ahead is hard to see or uncertain **9.** *vi* USE TOUCH IN SEARCHING to use the sense of touch to try to find something ○ *feel around for my keys* **10.** *vt* THINK SOMETHING IS TRUE to be convinced about something by instinct or intuition rather than concrete evidence ○ *I feel you're lying to me.* **11.** *vt* BE AWARE OF SOMETHING to be instinctively aware of something, usually an emotion, that is not visible or apparent **12.** *vt* BELIEVE SOMETHING to have the opinion or belief that something is the case ○ *She felt she could no longer carry on.* ■ *n* **1.** ACT OF TOUCHING an act of touching something **2.** IMPRESSION GAINED FROM TOUCH an impression of something gained through touching or being touched by it ○ *the feel of wool against the skin* **3.** SENSE OF TOUCH the sensation felt on touching something ○ *hot to the feel* **4.** IMPRESSION SENSED FROM SOMETHING an impression, appearance, effect, or atmosphere sensed from something ○ *a hotel with a more traditional feel* **5.** INSTINCT FOR SOMETHING an instinctive understanding of, or talent for, something ○ *He has a feel for these things.* **6.** GROPE a sexual touch, usually uninvited (*informal*) [Old English *fēlan* < Indo-European] ◇ **feel like 1.** to have an inclination or desire for something ○ *I don't feel like eating at present.* **2.** to have or acknowledge a physical or emotional condition that is considered comparable to something else ○ *They made me feel like a criminal.*

feel for *vt* to experience sympathy or compassion for somebody

feel out *vt* to try to establish, often in an indirect way, the nature of a situation or somebody's attitude or opinion about something

feel up *vt* to touch somebody sexually, especially without permission (*informal*)

feel up to *vt* to consider yourself ready for something or able to do something

feel·er /féelər/ *n* **1.** SOMEBODY WHO FEELS somebody who or something that feels something **2.** ATTEMPT TO TEST OTHERS' REACTION something said or done to test the reaction of others to an idea, plan, or project **3.** ZOOL TOUCHING ORGAN an organ of touch in various animals, e.g., an insect's antenna

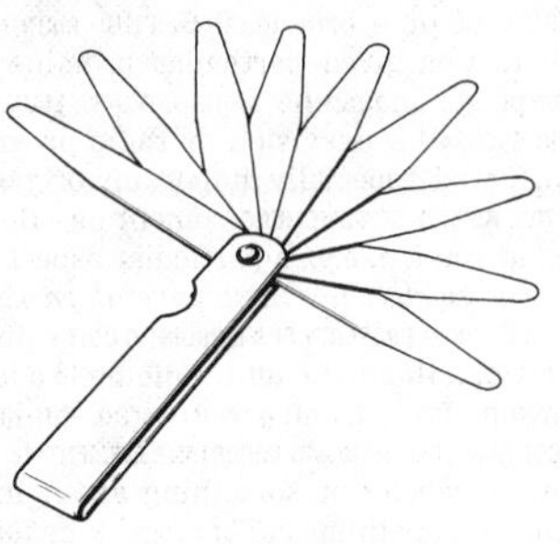

feeler gauge

feel·er gauge *n* a thin strip of metal of a specific size used to measure or set a gap between parts of a mechanism

feel-good *adj* causing, involving, or typical of a sense of well-being or satisfaction

feel-good fac·tor *n* something that causes or demonstrates a sense of well-being or satisfaction (*informal*) ○ *The government can show reduced unemployment figures and lower inflation but the all-important feel-good factor remains elusive in the public's mind.*

feel·ing /féeling/ *n* **1.** SENSE OF TOUCH the sensation felt on touching something **2.** ABILITY TO HAVE PHYSICAL SENSATION the ability to perceive physical sensation in a part of the body ○ *Slowly the feeling returned to his fingers.* **3.** SOMETHING EXPERIENCED PHYSICALLY OR MENTALLY a perceived physical or mental sensation **4.** SOMETHING FELT EMOTIONALLY a perceived emotional state **5.** AFFECTION the emotional response of love, sympathy, or tenderness toward somebody **6.** ABILITY TO EXPRESS EMOTION the capacity to experience strong emotions **7.** IMPRESSION SENSED a particular impression, appearance, effect, or atmosphere sensed from something ○ *There was a feeling of abandonment about the old house.* **8.** INSTINCTIVE AWARENESS an instinctive awareness or presentiment of something ○ *I have a feeling you're going to be disappointed.* **9.** INSTINCTIVE UNDERSTANDING OR TALENT an instinctive understanding of or talent for something ○ *has a real feeling for this kind of work* **10.** EXPRESSIVE ABILITY the ability to express strong emotion, especially in performance ○ *Play the piece again with more feeling.* ■ **feel·ings** *npl* SENSIBILITIES somebody's emotional susceptibilities ○ *I didn't want to hurt their feelings.* ■ *adj* **1.** SENSITIVE TO TOUCH able to experience the sensation of touch **2.** EXPRESSIVE expressing or full of strong emotion **3.** HAVING STRONG EMOTIONS easily or strongly affected by emotion —**feel·ing·ly** *adv*

fee sim·ple (*plural* **fees sim·ple**) *n* a form of property ownership in which the owner has outright and unconditional disposal rights ○ *The deed transferred ownership in fee simple.*

fee split·ting *n US* the practice in which part of a client's fee is paid by one professional to another for having referred the client

feet plural of **foot**

fee tail (*plural* **fees tail**) *n* a form of property ownership in which the property may be inherited only by a specific line of heirs

Feh·ling's so·lu·tion /fáylingz-/ *n* a solution of copper sulfate, sodium potassium tartrate, and sodium hydroxide. Use: detection of aldehydes, including sugars. [Late 19C. After Hermann von *Fehling* (1812–85), German chemist]

Feh·ling's test, **Fehlings test** *n* the use of Fehling's solution to detect the presence of aldehydes and sugars [See FEHLING'S SOLUTION]

feign /fayn/ (**feigned, feign·ing, feigns**) *vt* **1.** PRETEND SOMETHING to make a show or pretense of something ○ *She feigned ignorance.* **2.** INVENT SOMETHING to make up or fabricate something **3.** COPY SOMEBODY OR SOMETHING to imitate or copy somebody or something [13C. < French *feign-*, present stem of *feindre* "pretend, shirk" < Latin *fingere* "fabricate, form"]

fei·jo·a /fay yṓ ə, -hṓ ə/ *n* **1.** a green fruit that tastes like pineapple and is eaten raw or cooked. Use: jellies, preserves. **2.** a tree that produces feijoas. Native to: South America. Latin name: *Acca sellowiana.* [Late 19C. < modern Latin, after J. da Silva Feijó (1760–1824), Brazilian naturalist]

fei·jo·a·da /fàyzhṑo aá daá, fàyzhə waádə/ *n* a Brazilian party dish of meat with rice, black beans, green vegetables, and hot pepper sauce [Mid-20C. < Portuguese < *feijão* "edible bean" < Latin *phaseolus*]

~~**feind**~~ incorrect spelling of **fiend**

Fei·ning·er /fíningər/, **Lyonel Charles Adrian** (1871–1956) US artist. His work showed a strong cubist influence in its geometric style and translucent colors.

feint /faynt/ *n* **1.** DECEPTIVE ACTION a deceptive action made to disguise what is really intended **2.** DECEPTIVE MOVE a deceptive move in a competitive sport **3.** MIL MOCK ATTACK a mock attack by a military force, intended to draw the enemy's attention away from the true attack ■ *vti* (**feint·ed, feint·ing, feints**) MAKE DECEPTIVE MOVE to make a movement intended to deceive somebody [Late 17C. < French *feinte* "sham, pretense" < past participle of *feindre* (see FEIGN)]

SPELLCHECK See *faint.*

feist /fīst/ *n regional* a small dog [Late 18C. Variant of *fist,* shortening of *fisting cur* < obsolete *fisten* "break wind" < Germanic]

feist·y /fístee/ (**-i·er, -i·est**) *adj* (*informal*) **1.** characterized by spirited, sometimes aggressive, behavior **2.** likely to respond in an irritable or touchy way —**feist·i·ly** *adv* —**feist·i·ness** *n*

Feke /feek/, **Robert** (1705?–50?) American artist, noted for his colorful portraits of prominent colonial families. His first and largest portrait was *Family of Isaac Royall* (1741).

fe·la·fel *n* FOOD another spelling of **falafel**

feld·spar /féld spaár/, **fel·spar** /fél-/ *n* an extremely common aluminosilicate mineral containing varying proportions of calcium, sodium, potassium, and other elements. Feldspar minerals are subdivided into two groups, orthoclase feldspars and plagioclase feldspars. [Late 18C. Alteration of German *Feldspath*, literally "field mineral"]

feld·spath·ic /feld spáthik/ *adj* consisting of, containing, or typical of feldspar [Mid-19C. < German *Feldspath* "feldspar"]

feld·spath·oid /féld spath òyd/ *n* a mineral of a group similar to the feldspars but lower in silica [Late 19C. < German *Feldspath* "feldspar"]

fe·lic·i·tate /fə líssi tàyt/ (**-tat·ed, -tat·ing, -tates**) *vt* to congratulate somebody, or wish somebody happiness (*formal*) [Early 17C. < late Latin *felicitat-*, past participle of *felicitare* "make happy" < Latin *felix* "fruitful, happy"] —**fe·lic·i·ta·tor** *n*

fe·lic·i·ta·tion /fə lìssi táysh'n/ (*formal*) *n* an act of congratulating somebody or wishing somebody happiness ■ **fe·lic·i·ta·tions** *npl* used as a greeting or to wish somebody happiness

fe·lic·i·tous /fə líssitəss/ *adj* **1.** APPROPRIATE appropriate or highly suitable ○ *a felicitous choice of words* **2.** PLEASANT pleasing or agreeable **3.** FORTUNATE happy or fortunate [Mid-16C. < FELICITY] —**fe·lic·i·tous·ly** *adv* —**fe·lic·i·tous·ness** *n*

fe·lic·i·ty /fə líssətee/ (*plural* **-ties**) *n* **1.** HAPPINESS happiness or contentment **2.** SOMETHING PRODUCING HAPPINESS something that creates happiness **3.** APPROPRIATENESS an appropriate or pleasing manner **4.** SOMETHING APPROPRIATE something appropriate or pleasing [14C. Via French < Latin *felicitas* < *felix* "fruitful, happy"]

fe·lid /féelid/ (*plural* **-lids** or *same*) *n* ZOOL same as **feline** (*technical*) [Late 19C. < modern Latin *Felidae* < Latin *feles* "cat"]

fe·line /fée līn/ *adj* **1.** OF CAT FAMILY belonging to or typical of animals of the cat family, including lions, tigers, and domestic cats **2.** RESEMBLING CAT similar to a cat, especially in graceful movement or stealthiness ○ *feline suppleness* ■ *n* MEMBER OF CAT FAMILY an animal belonging to the cat family. Domestic cats, lions, and tigers are felines. Family: Felidae. [Late 17C. < Latin *felinus* < *feles* "cat"] —**fe·line·ly** *adv* —**fe·line·ness** *n* —**fe·lin·i·ty** /fi línnətee/ *n*

fe·line dis·tem·per *n* an infectious viral disease of cats that causes vomiting and diarrhea and is often fatal

fell[1] /fel/ past tense of **fall**

fell[2] /fel/ *vt* (**felled, fell·ing, fells**) **1.** CHOP TREE DOWN to cut down a tree **2.** KNOCK SOMEBODY DOWN to knock somebody down, or cause somebody to fall **3.** HANDICRAFT SEW SEAM FLAT to sew a seam by turning an edge over and sewing it down on the inside ■ *n* **1.** NUMBER OF TREES CUT DOWN an amount of timber cut down at one time or over one period **2.** HANDICRAFT SEWN SEAM a seam sewn by turning an edge over and sewing it down on the inside [Old English *fellan* "cause to fall" < Germanic] —**fell·a·ble** *adj*

fell[3] /fel/ *adj* (*archaic or literary*) **1.** having an extremely cruel or vicious character **2.** capable of killing somebody or destroying something [13C. < Old French *fel*, form of *felon* (see FELON[1])]

fell[4] /fel/ *n* **1.** the hide of an animal **2.** the thin membrane between an animal's hide and its flesh [Old English < Indo-European]

fel·la /féllə/ *n* a man or boy (*informal*) [Mid-19C. Representing nonstandard pronunciation of FELLOW]

fel·lah /féllə, fə laá/ (*plural* **-la·hin** /-heén/ or **-la·heen**) *n* in an Arab country, a member of the laboring class who lives off the land [Mid-18C. < Arabic *fallah* "tiller of the soil" < *falahah* "split, till the soil"]

fel·late /fə láyt/ (**-lat·ed, -lat·ing, -lates**) *vti* to stimulate a man's genitals using the tongue and lips [Late 19C. < Latin *fellat-* (see FELLATIO)] —**fel·la·tor** *n*

fel·la·ti·o /fə láyshee ṑ/, **fel·la·tion** /fə láysh'n/ *n* the sexual stimulation of a man's genitals using the tongue and lips [Late 19C. < modern Latin < Latin *fellat-*, past participle of *fellare* "suck"]

fell·er[1] /féllər/ *n* **1.** somebody who fells trees **2.** a person who or a machine attachment that fells seams [14C. < FELL[2]]

fel·ler[2] /féllər/ *n* a man or boy (*informal*) [Early 19C. Representing nonstandard pronunciation of FELLOW]

Fel·ler /féllər/, **Bob** (*b.* 1918) US baseball player. A pitcher noted for his fastball, he pitched three no-hitters and struck out 2,581 batters in 18 seasons with the Cleveland Indians (1936–56). Full name **Feller, Robert William Andrew**

Federico Fellini: directing his *Satyricon* (1969)

Fel·li·ni /fə leénee/, **Federico** (1920–93) Italian movie director. He was known for his use of fantasy and satire, and won Academy Awards for *La Strada* (1954), *Nights of Cabiria* (1957), *8½* (1963), and *Amarcord* (1974).

> "The visionary is the only true realist."
> [Federico Fellini. Recalled on his death, *USA Today*; November 1, 1993]

Fel·li·ni·esque /fə leénee ésk/ *adj* blending reality and fantasy as Federico Fellini does in his movies

fel·loe *n* same as **felly**

fel·low /féllō/ *n* **1.** MALE a man or boy **2.** COMPANION a companion or colleague (*dated*) **3.** ONE OF PAIR either of a pair of objects (*dated*) **4.** EQUAL somebody or something of the same rank or quality (*dated*) **5.** BOYFRIEND somebody's boyfriend (*dated informal*) **6.** EDUC GRADUATE STUDENT a graduate student who is supported by a university department to teach or do research ○ *a research fellow* ■ *adj* BEING IN SAME GROUP belonging to the same group, occupation, rank, or location [Pre-12C. < Old Norse *félagi* "partner" < *fé* "money"]

Fel·low *n* a member of a learned or scientific society ○ *Fellow of the American College of Surgeons*

fel·low ser·vant *n* an employee whose employer is not legally responsible for harm or injury done to him or her by another employee

fel·low·ship /féllō shìp/ *n* **1.** SHARING OF EXPERIENCES a sharing of common interests, goals, experiences, or views **2.** GROUP OF LIKE-MINDED PEOPLE a group of people who share common interests, goals, experiences, or views **3.** COMPANIONSHIP companionship or friendly association **4.** SIMILARITY membership in a group, or the sharing of characteristics with others **5.** EDUC GRADUATE POST a university post awarded to a graduate student who is supported by a university department to teach or undertake research **6.** EDUC FINANCIAL ENDOWMENT a financial endowment set up to support graduate students **7.** EDUC MEMBERSHIP OF UNIVERSITY STAFF membership on the governing board of a university or college, usually also involving teaching duties

fel·low trav·el·er *n* **1.** a sympathizer with the cause of an organized group, especially the Communist Party, without joining it **2.** somebody who takes the same journey as another at the same time

fel·ly /féllee/ (*plural* **-lies**), **fel·loe** /féllō/ *n* an outer rim of a wooden wheel, or a segment of this, with a metal tire shrunk around it [Old English *felg* < Indo-European, "turn"]

fe·lo-de-se /fe lṑdə sáy/ (*plural* **fe·lo·nes-de-se** /fe lōneez-/ or **fe·los-de-se**) *n* **1.** somebody who commits suicide **2.** an act of committing suicide [Early 17C. < Anglo-Latin, "crime against yourself"]

fel·on[1] /féllən/ *n* somebody who is guilty of a felony ■ *adj* characterized by evil or depravity (*archaic*) [13C. Via French < medieval Latin *fellon-* "evildoer"]

fel·on[2] /féllən/ *n* MED same as **whitlow** [14C. Origin ?]

fe·lo·ni·ous /fə lṓnee əss/ *adj* relating to felonies or a felony —**fe·lo·ni·ous·ly** *adv* —**fe·lo·ni·ous·ness** *n*

fel·o·ny /féllənee/ (*plural* **-nies**) *n* a serious crime such as murder that is punished more severely than a misdemeanor [13C. < Old French *felonie* < *felon* (see FELON[1])]

fel·sic /félssik/ *adj* describes igneous rocks or minerals that are light in color, indicating relatively high levels of quartz and feldspars [Early 20C. Blend of FELDSPAR + SILICA]

fel·site /fél sīt/ *n* a light-colored igneous rock that consists chiefly of feldspar and quartz and can only be precisely classified by microscopic examination [Late 18C. < FELDSPAR] —**fel·sit·ic** /fel síttik/ *adj*

fel·spar *n* MINERALS another spelling of **feldspar**

felt[1] /felt/ past participle, past tense of **feel**

felt[2] /felt/ *n* **1.** WOOL OR ANIMAL-HAIR FABRIC a fabric made from wool or animal hair by compressing, heating, or treating the fibers with chemicals **2.** SYNTHETIC FABRIC a synthetic fabric made by the process of matting, especially a heavy paper permeated with asphalt, used as a roof sealant ○ *roofing felt* ■ *v* (**felt·ed, felt·ing, felts**) **1.** *vt* MAKE FELT OUT OF SOMETHING to make wool or hair into felt fabric **2.** *vt* PUT FELT ON ROOF to cover a roof with roofing felt **3.** *vi* BECOME MATTED to become matted, or come to resemble felt [Old English < Indo-European, "strike, beat, pound"] —**felt·y** *adj*

felt·ing /félting/ *n* **1.** felt fabric **2.** the process of making felt

felt pen *n* same as **felt-tipped pen**

felt tip *n* **1.** a pen point made from felt or a similar compressed fiber **2.** same as **felt-tipped pen**

felt-tipped pen *n* a pen with a point made from felt or a similar compressed fiber

felucca

fe·luc·ca /fə lóokə, -lúkə/ *n* a small sailboat with curving triangular sails **(lateen-rigged)**, used in the Mediterranean Sea and on the Nile River [Early 17C. Via Italian < Mediterranean Arabic *fluka*]

fel·wort /fél wùrt, -wàwrt/ *n* a plant of the gentian family. Flowers: purple. Native to: Europe, China. Latin name: *Gentianella amarella.* [Old English *feldwyrt* "field plant"]

fem *n, adj* another spelling of **femme** (*slang*)

fem. *abbr* **1.** BIOL female **2.** GRAM feminine

FEMA /féemə/ *abbr US* Federal Emergency Management Agency

fe·male /fée màyl/ *adj* **1.** OF WOMEN relating or belonging to women or girls **2.** BIOL OF THE SEX THAT PRODUCES OFFSPRING relating or belonging to the sex that produces sex cells **(gametes)** that fuse with male sex cells during sexual reproduction **3.** BOT PRODUCING SEEDS describes the part of a plant that produces the female sex cells, e.g., a carpel **4.** BOT HAVING CARPELS describes flowers that have carpels but no stamens **5.** ENG MADE WITH RECESS describes a component or part of a component such as an electric socket that has a recess designed to receive a corresponding projecting part ■ *n* **1.** BIOL FEMALE ORGANISM a female person or animal **2.** OFFENSIVE TERM an offensive term for a girl or woman **3.** BOT PLANT WITH FEMALE FLOWERS a plant that has only female flowers [14C. Alteration (after MALE) of Old French *femelle* < Latin *femella* < *femina* (see FEMININE)] —**fe·male·ness** *n*

fe·male cir·cum·ci·sion, fe·male gen·i·tal mu·ti·la·tion *n* the practice of circumcision of adolescent women in some cultures that generally involves the surgical removal of the clitoris or the sewing up of the vaginal opening

fe·male im·per·son·a·tor *n* a man, often appearing as a solo theatrical performer, who dresses as and imitates a woman

fe·male suf·frage *n US* LAW same as **women's suffrage**

feme /fem/ *n* a woman or wife [Mid-16C. Via Anglo-Norman < Latin *femina* (see FEMININE)]

feme cov·ert /fem kúvvərt/ (*plural* **femes cov·ert** /femz kúvvərt/) *n* a married woman [< Anglo-Norman, "covered woman"]

feme sole /fem sṓl/ (*plural* **femes sole** /femz sṓl/) *n* a single woman, taken to include unmarried women, widows, divorcées, and married women living independently and separately from their husbands [< Anglo-Norman, "single woman"]

fem·i·ne·i·ty /fèmmə née ətee/ *n* same as **femininity** (sense 1) [Early 19C. < Latin *femineus* "womanish" < *femina* (see FEMININE)]

fem·i·nine /fémmənin/ *adj* **1.** CONVENTIONALLY ASSOCIATED WITH WOMEN conventionally thought to be appropriate for a woman or girl **2.** ATTRIBUTED TO WOMEN considered to be characteristic of women **3.** EFFEMINATE relating to qualities, actions, or types of behavior in a man or boy that are conventionally associated with women or girls **4.** GRAM LINGUISTICALLY FEMALE IN GENDER describes a class of words or forms in various languages that includes the majority of words referring to females ■ *n* GRAM FEMININE WORD OR FORM a word or form that in a specific language is classified grammatically as feminine [14C. Via French < Latin *femininus* < *femina* "woman" < Indo-European, "suck"] —**fem·i·nine·ly** *adv* —**fem·i·nine·ness** *n*

fem·i·nine cae·su·ra *n* a pause in a line of scanned verse that does not come immediately after a stressed syllable

fem·i·nine end·ing *n* **1.** an inflectional morpheme attached to the end of a word that marks it as belonging to the feminine gender **2.** an ending of a line of verse that finishes with an extra unstressed syllable

fem·i·nine rhyme *n* a rhyme scheme in which the lines containing rhyming words end in unstressed syllables

~~femininity~~ incorrect spelling of **femininity**

fem·i·nin·i·ty /fèmmə nínnətee/ *n* **1.** CONVENTIONALLY FEMININE QUALITY the quality of looking and behaving in ways conventionally thought to be appropriate for a woman or girl **2.** CONVENTIONAL IDEA ABOUT WOMEN a manner or feature commonly attributed to women **3.** EFFEMINACY the qualities, actions, or types of behavior in a man or boy that are conventionally associated with women or girls **4.** WOMEN women as a group (*dated*)

fem·i·nism /fémmə nìzzəm/ *n* **1.** belief in the need to secure rights and opportunities for women equal to those of men, or a commitment to securing these **2.** the movement committed to securing and defending rights and opportunities for women that are equal to those of men [Mid-19C. < French *féminisme*] —**fem·i·nist** *n, adj*

fem·i·nize /fémmə nìz/ (**-nized, -niz·ing, -niz·es**) *vt* **1.** MAKE SOMETHING SUITABLE FOR WOMEN to give somebody or something characteristics considered suitable for women ○ *seeking to feminize the profession* **2.** MAKE SOMEBODY CONVENTIONALLY LIKE WOMAN to make somebody behave in ways conventionally associated with women (*often passive*) **3.** MED MAKE MALE DEVELOP FEMALE SEXUAL CHARACTERISTICS to cause a man to develop secondary female sexual characteristics as a result of a hormone imbalance —**fem·i·ni·za·tion** /fèmməni záysh'n/ *n*

femme /fem/, **fem** (*slang*) *n* **1.** WOMAN a woman or girl **2.** SOMEBODY BEHAVING FEMININELY somebody who behaves in a conventionally feminine way ■ *adj* BEHAVING IN FEMININE WAY describes somebody, originally usually a lesbian, who behaves in a conventionally feminine way [Early 19C. < French < Latin *femina* (see FEMININE)]

femme fa·tale /fém fə tàl, -taál, fám-/ (*plural* **femmes fa·tales** /*pronunc. same*/) *n* a woman who is considered to be highly attractive and to have a destructive effect on those who succumb to her charms (*disapproving*) [< French, "deadly woman"]

fem·o·ra ANAT plural of **femur**

fem·o·ral /fémmərəl/ *adj* relating to, in, or involving the thigh or femur [Late 18C. < Latin *femor-*, stem of *femur* "thigh"]

femto- *prefix* one quadrillionth, or millionth of a billionth (10^{-15}) ○ *femtometer* Symbol **f** [< Danish or Norwegian *femten* "fifteen"]

fe·mur /féemər/ (*plural* **fe·murs** *or* **fem·o·ra** /fémmərə/) *n* **1.** ANAT MAIN BONE IN HUMAN THIGH the main bone in the human thigh, the strongest bone in the body **2.** ZOOL LARGE BONE IN VERTEBRATE LEG a bone equivalent to the human thighbone in other vertebrates **3.** INSECTS INSECT LEG PART the third and largest segment of an insect's leg, between the trochanter and the tibia [Mid-16C. < Latin, "thigh"]

fen /fen/ *n* an inland area of low-lying marshy land, now often drained and cultivated because of its nutrient-rich soil [Old English *fen(n)* < Germanic]

fence /fenss/ *n* **1.** ENCLOSING STRUCTURE a structure erected to enclose an area and act as a barrier, especially one made of wood or with posts and wire **2.** OBSTACLE a specially constructed obstacle that horses must jump over in a race or as part of a show jumping circuit **3.** BUYER OF STOLEN GOODS somebody who buys stolen goods from thieves and then sells the goods (*slang*) **4.** same as **fencing** (sense 1) (*archaic*) ■ *v* (**fenced, fenc·ing, fenc·es**) **1.** *vt* ENCLOSE AREA WITH FENCE to enclose an area or close a gap by erecting a fence **2.** *vti* DEAL IN STOLEN GOODS to buy or sell stolen goods (*slang*) **3.** *vi* FIGHT WITH SWORD to fight using a slender sword, formerly in combat, now as a competitive sport **4.** *vi* EVADE QUESTIONING to avoid answering a question ○ *a candidate fencing with the press* **5.** *vi* ARGUE to engage in repartee or witty argument with somebody [14C. Shortening of DEFENSE] —**fence·less** *adj* —**fenc·er** *n* ◇ **mend fences** to restore good relations with a friend or neighbor after a dispute or quarrel ◇ **sit** *or* **be on the fence** to refuse to make a choice between sides in a dispute or contest

fence in *vt* **1.** to enclose somebody or something inside a fence **2.** to prevent somebody from moving or acting freely

fence off *vt* to enclose or separate something with a fence

fence·row /fénss rṑ/ *n* the uncultivated strip of land on which a fence stands, including a narrow area on each side of it

fence sit·ter *n* somebody who is unwilling or unable to choose between sides (*informal*)

fencing: as one fencer lunges forward the other prepares to parry

fenc·ing /fénssing/ *n* **1.** SWORD FIGHTING the art or practice of fighting with slender swords, formerly in combat, now as a competitive sport **2.** FENCE MATERIALS materials used in making fences, e.g., posts and wire **3.** FENCES fences considered collectively **4.** EVASIVENESS evasiveness in responding to questioning **5.** REPARTEE repartee or witty argument **6.** DEALING IN STOLEN GOODS the business of buying and selling stolen goods (*slang*)

fend /fend/ (**fend·ed, fend·ing, fends**) *vt* to defend somebody or something from harm (*archaic*) [13C. Shortening of DEFEND]

fend for *vt* to support or provide for somebody, especially yourself ○ *He's used to fending for himself.*

fend off *vt* **1.** to push somebody or something away, or turn somebody or something aside **2.** to push against an approaching vessel or object in order to prevent a collision

fend·er /féndər/ *n* **1.** CORNER OF CAR any of the corner parts of the body of a motor vehicle, that surround each wheel **2.** BICYCLE WHEEL COVERING a curved piece of metal or plastic fixed above the front and back wheels of a bicycle to protect the cyclist from being splashed with mud **3.** *US* RAIL METAL GUARD AT FRONT OF LOCOMOTIVE a metal guard built onto the front of a locomotive to push away any obstruction and lessen injury to people or animals struck by the locomotive **4.** FIREGUARD a metal guard built onto the front of an open fire to prevent coals from falling out **5.** PROTECTIVE CUSHION an inflatable cylinder, rubber tire, or something similar, hung over the side of a vessel to protect it from rubbing against a pier or another ship

fend·er-bend·er *n* a collision between vehicles in which only minor damage occurs (*informal*)

fend·er pile *n* a pile driven into the bottom of a body of water near a berth to protect the pier or wharf against damage by incoming vessels

fen·es·tel·la /fènnə stéllə/ (*plural* **-lae** /-lee/) *n* **1.** PART OF ALTAR a small opening for holding relics at the south side of an altar in a Roman Catholic church **2.** NICHE IN CHANCEL WALL a niche in the wall of a chancel that houses the piscina and credence table **3.** ARCHIT WINDOW a small window or similar opening in a wall [Late 18C. < Latin, diminutive of *fenestra* "window"]

fe·nes·tra /fə néstrə/ (*plural* **-trae** /-tree/) *n* **1.** ANAT SMALL ANATOMICAL OPENING a small anatomical opening covered by a membrane, e.g., either of two cavities **(fenestra rotunda, fenestra ovalis)** inside the ear **2.** INSECTS TRANSPARENT MARKING a transparent marking on a moth's wing **3.** ARCHIT WINDOW a window or similar opening on the outer wall of a building [Early 19C. < Latin, "window"] —**fe·nes·tral** *adj*

fen·es·trat·ed /fénnə stràytəd/, **fen·es·trate** /fénnə stràyt, fə nés tràyt/ *adj* **1.** ARCHIT **HAVING WINDOWS** made with windows or similar openings **2.** BIOL **WITH OPENINGS** having openings or perforations **3.** INSECTS **WITH TRANSPARENT MARKINGS** describes a moth's wing that has transparent markings

fen·es·tra·tion /fènnə stráysh'n/ *n* **1.** the design and placing of windows in a building **2.** the surgical cutting of an opening in the labyrinth of the inner ear to restore somebody's hearing

feng shui /fəng shwáy/ *n* a Chinese system that studies people's relationships to their environment, especially their home or workspace, in order to achieve maximum harmony with the spiritual forces believed to influence all places [Late 18C. < Chinese, "wind water"]

Fe·ni·an /féenee ən/ *n* **1.** a member of an Irish revolutionary republican organization founded in the United States in 1857 to fight for Irish independence **2.** in Irish legend, a member of the warriors, the Fianna [Early 19C. < Old Irish *féne*, the ancient population of Ireland] —**Fe·ni·an·ism** *n*

fen·land /fén lànd, fénnlənd/ *n* a wide inland area of low-lying marshy land, especially in East Anglia in eastern England

fen·nec /fénnik/ *n* a small large-eared desert fox with light tan fur. Native to: North Africa. Latin name: *Vulpes zerda* or *Fennecus zerda*. [Late 18C. Via Arabic *fanak* < Persian]

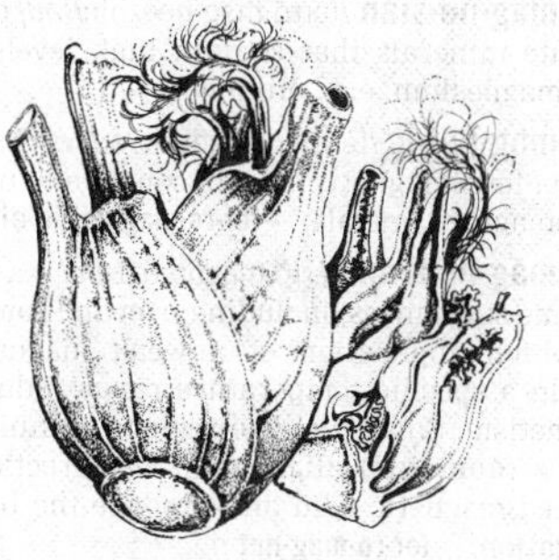

fennel

fen·nel /fénn'l/ *n* **1.** an aromatic plant, the seeds and feathery leaves of which have a light aniseed flavor. Use: cooking. Native to: Europe. Latin name: *Foeniculum vulgare* var. *dulce*. **2.** a plant that produces a clump of short edible stalks resembling celery but with an aniseed flavor. Latin name: *Foeniculum vulgare* var. *azoricum*. [Old English *finugle* < Latin *faeniculum*, diminutive of *faenum* "hay"]

Fens /fenz/ region of reclaimed marshland in eastern England surrounding the Wash and covering parts of Cambridgeshire, Lincolnshire, and Norfolk. Area: 695 sq. mi./1,800 sq. km.

fen·ta·nyl /féntənil/ *n* a narcotic drug. Use: painkiller. [Alteration of the drug's chemical name]

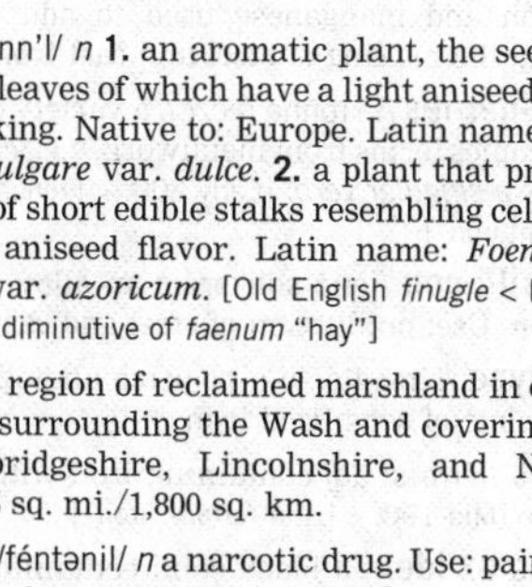

fenugreek

fen·u·greek /fénnyə greek, fénnə-/ *n* **1.** the aromatic seeds of a leguminous plant. Use: in medicine, food flavoring. **2.** the leguminous plant whose seeds are fenugreek. Native to: Europe, Asia. Latin name: *Trigonella foenum-graecum*. [Old English *fenogrecum* and Old French *fenugrec* < Latin *faenugraecum* "Greek hay," dried and used by the Romans for fodder]

fen·u·ron /fénnyə ròn/ *n* a white crystalline compound. Use: herbicide. Formula: $C_9H_{12}N_2O$. [< alteration of PHEN- + UREA]

feoff /feef/ *n* HIST same as **fief** (sense 1) [13C. < Anglo-Norman *feoffer* < Old French *feu*, *fieu* "fee" < medieval Latin *feudum* (see FEUD[2])] —**feoff** *vt* —**feoff·ment** /féfmənt, féef-/ *n*

feoff·ee /fe fée, fi-/ *n* a vassal holding land granted by a feudal lord

feoff·ment /féfmənt, féef-/ *n* a grant of freehold property by a feudal lord

FEP *abbr* COMPUT front-end processor

FEPA *abbr* Fair Employment Practices Act

FEPC *abbr* Fair Employment Practices Commission

-fer *suffix* a person or thing that bears ○ *conifer* [< Latin < *ferre* "carry"]

fe·ral /féerəl, férrəl/, **fe·rine** /féer ìn/ *adj* **1.** describes animals or plants that live or grow in the wild after having been domestically reared or cultivated ○ *feral cats* **2.** similar to or typical of a wild animal, or living wild [Early 17C. < Latin *fera* "wild animal"]

Fer·ber /fúrbər/, **Edna** (1885–1968) US writer. A prolific novelist, many of her most famous works, including *Showboat* (1926), *Giant* (1952), and the Pulitzer Prize winning *So Big* (1924) were later adapted for stage or screen.

> "Life can't ever really defeat a writer who's in love with writing."
> [Edna Ferber, *A Kind of Magic*; 1963]

fer-de-lance /fèr də lánss/ (*plural same* or **fer-de-lances**) *n* a large, highly venomous snake of the pit viper family. Native to: tropical America. Latin name: *Bothops atrox*. [Late 19C. < French, "spearhead"]

Fer·di·nand I /fúrd'n ànd/ (1005?–65) king of Castile (1035–65) and León (1037–65). He reconquered much of Portugal from the Moors. Known as **Ferdinand the Great**

Fer·di·nand I (1503–64) Holy Roman Emperor (1558–64), king of Bohemia (1526–64), and king of Germany (1531–64). He negotiated the treaties of Passau (1552) and Augsburg (1555), which ended the religious wars in Germany by allowing territorial princes to determine the religion of their subjects.

> "Let justice be done, though the world perish."
> [Motto of Ferdinand I]

Fer·di·nand III (1608–57) king of Hungary. As king of Bohemia (1627–57) and Holy Roman Emperor (1637–57), he commanded the imperial armies fighting the Thirty Years' War

Fer·di·nand V (1452–1516) king of Castile (1474–1504); as Ferdinand II, king of Sicily (1468–1516) and of Aragón (1479–1516); as Ferdinand III, king of Naples (1503–16). His marriage to Isabella I of Castile (1469) united the two most powerful kingdoms of Spain. His reign saw the completion of the reconquest of Spain from the Moors (1492), the four voyages of Columbus to the Americas (1492–1504), and the establishment of the Spanish Inquisition (1478). Known as **Ferdinand the Catholic**

fer·e·to·ry /férrə tàwree/ (*plural* **-ries**) *n* a container or an area in a church where relics are kept [14C. < Old French *fiertre* < Greek *pheretron* "bier" < *pherein* "carry"]

Fer·ga·na /fər gáanə/ city in eastern Uzbekistan, about 260 mi./420 km east of the capital, Tashkent. Population: 191,000 (1994). Former name **Skobelev** (1907–24)

fe·ri·a /féeree ə, férree ə/ (*plural* **-ri·as** or **-ri·ae** /-ree èe/) *n* in the Roman Catholic Church, any weekday that is not a feast day [14C. < Latin, "holiday"] —**fe·ri·al** *adj*

fe·rine *adj* ZOOL same as **feral** (sense 1)

Fe·rin·ghee /fə ríng gee/, **Fe·rin·ghi** *n* in South and Southwest Asia and parts of East Asia, an offensive term for a foreigner, especially one with white skin (*offensive*) [Early 17C. Via Urdu < Persian *firangi* "Frankish, western"]

Fer·man·agh /fər mánnə/ county in southwestern Northern Ireland. The main town is Enniskillen.

Fer·mat /fer máa/, **Pierre de** (1601–65) French mathematician. One of the greatest 17th-century mathematical theorists, he was a pioneer in the fields of probability theory, analytic geometry, and differential calculus.

fer·ma·ta /fer máatə/ *n* **1.** an act of holding a musical note, chord, or pause longer than the indicated time value **2.** MUSIC same as **pause** *n* (sense 5) [Late 19C. < Italian]

Fer·mat's last the·o·rem *n* hypothesis about whole numbers proven about 330 years after Fermat conjectured it in the mid-17th century. The theorem holds that of whole numbers raised to the same whole-numbered powers greater than two, no two of them add to a third; that is, $a^n+b^n=c^n$ has no solution in whole numbers if $n > 2$.

fer·ment *vti* /fər mént/ (**-ment·ed, -ment·ing, -ments**) **1.** **SUBJECT TO OR UNDERGO FERMENTATION** to subject something to fermentation, or be subjected to fermentation **2.** **STIR OR BE STIRRED UP** to stir up somebody or something, or be stirred up **3.** **DEVELOP** to cause, develop, or evolve something, or be developed or evolved ○ *Her brain was continually fermenting new schemes.* ■ *n* /fúr mènt/ **1.** **COMMOTION** a state or situation of extreme agitation or commotion about something **2.** **SUBSTANCE CAUSING FERMENTATION** an agent, enzyme, or cell that causes fermentation [14C. < Old French *fermenter* < Latin *fermentum* "yeast"] —**fer·ment·a·bil·i·ty** /fər mèntə bíllətee/ *n* —**fer·ment·a·ble** *adj* —**fer·men·ta·tive** *adj*

SPELLCHECK Do not confuse the spelling of ***ferment*** and ***foment*** ("cause trouble"), which sound similar. The verb ***ferment*** means "subject to the chemical process of fermentation," "stir up," or "develop," as in *ferment new ideas*. It is this last sense that perhaps most causes confusion with ***foment***, which means "stir up trouble or rebellion."

fer·men·ta·tion /fùrmən táysh'n, -men-/ *n* the breakdown of carbohydrates by microorganisms. Many pharmaceuticals are produced by fermentation.

fer·men·ta·tion lock *n* a valve used in winemaking to seal a container of fermenting wine, allowing gas to escape but no air to enter

fer·ment·er /fər méntər/ *n* **1.** BIOCHEM same as **ferment** *n* (sense 2) **2.** *also* **fer·men·tor** an apparatus that maintains the ideal conditions for fermentation, e.g., the growing of microorganisms

fer·mi /fúrmee, fér-/ *n* a unit of length used mainly for nuclear distances, equivalent to 10^{-15} m [Early 20C. After Enrico FERMI]

Fer·mi /férmee/, **Enrico** (1901–54) Italian-born US physicist. He received the Nobel Prize in physics (1938) for his work on particle physics and nuclear fission. He constructed the first atomic pile at the University of Chicago (1942).

> "Whatever Nature has in store for mankind, unpleasant as it may be, men must accept, for ignorance is never better than knowledge."
> [Enrico Fermi, *Atoms in the Family: My Life with Enrico Fermi*, Laura Fermi; 1955]

Fer·mi-Di·rac sta·tis·tics *n* statistical mechanics used to find the energy distribution of particles that obey the Pauli exclusion principle (*takes a singular or plural verb*) [After Enrico FERMI and Paul DIRAC]

fer·mi·on /fúrmee òn, fér-/ *n* an elementary particle with a half-integral spin that obeys the Pauli exclusion principle. Electrons, protons, and neutrons are types of fermions. [After Enrico FERMI]

fer·mi·um /fúrmee əm, fér-/ *n* an artificially produced radioactive element. Source: bombardment of plutonium with neutrons. Use: tracer. Symbol **Fm**. See table at **element** [After Enrico FERMI]

fern /furn/ (*plural* **ferns** or *same*) *n* a plant that has roots, stems, and fronds, but no flowers, and reproduces by means of spores. Order: Filicales. See illustration on next page [Old English *fearn* < Indo-European] —**fern·y** *adj*

Fer·nan·do de No·ro·nha /fər nàndō də nə rṓnyə/

fern

island group in the Atlantic Ocean off the coast of Brazil, approximately 250 mi./400 km northeast of Cape São Roque. Population: 1,266 (1980). Area: 10 sq. mi./26 sq. km.

Fer·nan·do Póo /fər nàndō pṓ, -naàndō-/ former name for **Bioko**

fern bar *n* a fashionable bar or restaurant with ferns or other plants for decoration

fern·er·y /fúrnəree/ (*plural* **-ies**) *n* **1.** a container or cultivated area in which ferns are grown **2.** a collection of growing ferns

fern seed *n* a tiny spore by which a fern reproduces. Because their smallness makes them difficult to see, at one time it was believed that carrying fern seeds made somebody invisible. ○*"We have the receipt of fern seed, we walk invisible"* (William Shakespeare, *Henry IV Pt I*; 1597)

fe·ro·cious /fə rṓshəss/ *adj* **1.** very fierce or savage **2.** very intense [Mid-17C. < Latin *feroc-* "wild-looking"] —**fe·ro·cious·ly** *adv* —**fe·ro·cious·ness** *n* —**fe·roc·i·ty** /fə róssətee/ *n*

-ferous *suffix* bearing, containing, producing ○ *diamondiferous* [< French *-fère* or Latin *-fer* "carrying, bearing"]

ferr- *prefix* same as **ferro-**

Fer·ra·ra /fə raárə/ city on the Po River near Bologna in Emilia-Romagna Region, northern Italy. Population: 130,992 (2001).

Fer·ra·ri /fə raáree/, **Enzo** (1898–1988) Italian race car driver and automobile manufacturer. From the 1950s, he designed and produced racing cars that achieved success in Grand Prix competitions.

Fer·ra·ro /fə raárō/, **Geraldine** (*b.* 1935) US politician. A lawyer and Democratic member of the US Congress from New York (1978–85), she was the first woman vice-presidential candidate of a major political party (1984). Full name **Ferraro, Geraldine Anne**

> "Vice president – it has such a nice ring to it!"
> [Geraldine Ferraro, Quoted in *New York Times*; July 13, 1984]

fer·re·dox·in /fèrrə dóksin/ *n* an iron-containing protein found in plants that is active in photosynthesis [Mid-20C. < Latin *ferrum* "iron" + REDOX]

fer·ret[1] /férrət/ *n* (*plural* **-rets** or *same*) **1.** DOMESTICATED POLECAT a typically albino polecat bred for use in hunting rabbits or rats and kept as a pet. Latin name: *Mustela eversmanni.* **2.** *US* ZOOL same as **black-footed ferret 3.** PERSISTENT SEARCHER a persistent searcher or investigator ■ *vti* (**-ret·ed, -ret·ing, -rets**) HUNT WITH FERRET to hunt rabbits or rats using a ferret [14C. Via Old French *furet* < assumed Vulgar Latin *furittus* "little thief" < Latin *fur* "thief"] —**fer·ret·er** *n* —**fer·ret·y** *adj*

ferret about, ferret around *vi* to search in an area persistently ○ *ferreting about in a drawer*

ferret out *vt* **1.** to force somebody or something out of a hiding place by persistent searching **2.** to discover something hidden by persistent searching

fer·ret[2] /férrət/ *n* a narrow silk tape. Use: edging or binding fabric. [Mid-17C. Probably alteration of Italian *fioretti* "floss silk" < *fiore* "flower"]

fer·ret·ing[1] /férrəting/ *n* the practice of hunting rabbits or rats with ferrets

fer·ret·ing[2] /férrəting/ *n* HANDICRAFT same as **ferret**[2]

ferri- *prefix* **1.** same as **ferro- 2.** ferric iron ○ *ferricyanide* [< Latin *ferrum* "iron"]

fer·ri·age /férree ij/ *n* **1.** the action or business of transporting passengers or cargo by ferry **2.** the fee charged for carrying somebody or something by ferry

fer·ric /férrik/ *adj* containing iron, especially with a valence of three [Late 18C. < Latin *ferrum* "iron"]

fer·ric am·mo·ni·um cit·rate *n* a nontoxic iron salt. Use: treatment of anemia. Formula: $Fe(NH_4)_3(C_6H_5O_7)_2$.

fer·ric chlo·ride *n* a dark red iron-containing salt. Use: in medicine as an astringent, in industry as a coagulating agent. Formula: $FeCl_3$.

fer·ric ox·ide *n* a reddish brown solid containing iron and oxygen. Source: rust, hematite. Use: pigment, in jeweler's rouge for polishing, on magnetic recording tape. Formula: Fe_2O_3.

fer·ric sul·fate *n* a pale yellow solid chemical containing iron, oxygen, and sulfur. Use: pigments, water purification, dyeing, medicine. Formula: $Fe_2(SO_4)_3$.

fer·ri·cy·a·nide /fèrri sī́ ə nīd/ *n* any salt containing iron and six cyanide groups. Use: manufacture of pigments.

fer·rif·er·ous /fə ríffərəss/ *adj* describes a rock or mineral deposit that contains iron, often at a level high enough to make extraction economically worthwhile [Early 19C. < Latin *ferrum* "iron"]

fer·ri·mag·ne·tism /fèrri mágnə tìzzəm/ *n* a property of some substances such as ferrites in which two different types of iron having unequal magnetic moments occur aligned in antiparallel, giving an appreciable bulk magnetization —**fer·ri·mag·net** *n* —**fer·ri·mag·net·ic** /fèrri mag néttik/ *adj* —**fer·ri·mag·net·i·cal·ly** *adv*

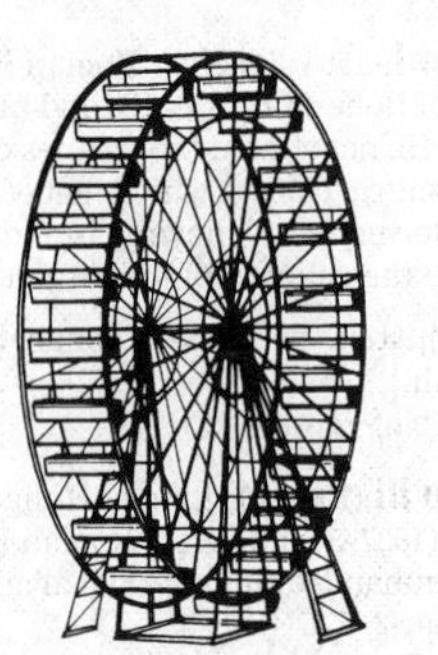
Ferris wheel

Fer·ris wheel /férriss-, férrəss-/, **fer·ris wheel** *n* an amusement park ride consisting of a giant revolving wheel with seats that hang down from its rim and stay horizontal as the wheel rotates [Late 19C. After G. W. G. *Ferris* (1859–96), US engineer]

fer·rite /fé rīt/ *n* **1.** MAGNETIC IRON OXIDE a mixed oxide of iron and another metal such as cobalt or nickel. Use: in electronics, in magnets. **2.** FORM OF IRON OCCURRING IN STEEL a form of iron occurring in steel, cast iron, and pig iron **3.** IRON MINERAL a mineral containing iron oxide, e.g., magnetite, occurring as small grains in various rocks [Mid-19C. < Latin *ferrum* "iron"]

fer·ri·tin /férrət'n/ *n* an iron-binding protein found in the liver, that stores iron in the body. When required, iron is released and used in the production of hemoglobin in red blood cells. [Mid-20C. < FERRI- + *-t-* + -IN]

ferro- *prefix* **1.** iron ○ *ferroalloy* **2.** ferrous iron ○ *ferrocyanide* [< Latin *ferrum* "iron"]

fer·ro·al·loy /fèrrō á lòy/ *n* an iron alloy, containing a large proportion of one or more other elements, that is added to molten metal during iron and steel production to give the required composition

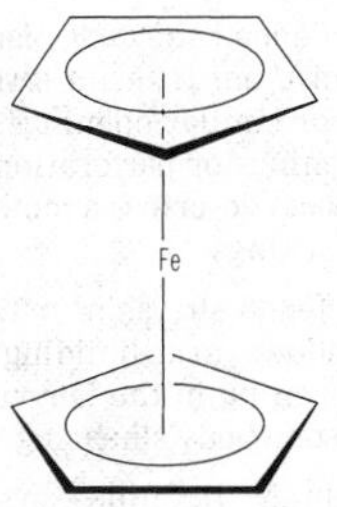

ferrocene

fer·ro·cene /férrō seen/ *n* an orange-red crystalline solid in which an atom of iron is situated between two rings that are composed of five carbon and five hydrogen atoms. Formula: $Fe(C_5H_5)_2$. [Mid-20C. < FERRO- + contraction of *cyclopentadiene*, a hydrocarbon]

fer·ro·con·crete /fèrrō kóng kreet/ *n* CONSTR same as **reinforced concrete**

fer·ro·cy·a·nide /fèrrō sī́ ə nīd/ *n* any salt containing iron and six cyanide groups. Use: in blue pigments.

fer·ro·e·lec·tric /fèrrō i léktrik/ *adj* describes a crystalline compound that has a natural spontaneous electric polarization that can be reversed by the application of an electric field ■ *n* a substance that is ferroelectric —**fer·ro·e·lec·tri·cal·ly** *adv* —**fer·ro·e·lec·tric·i·ty** /fèrrō i lek tríssətee, fèrrō ee-/ *n*

fer·ro·mag·ne·sian /fèrrō mag neézh'n/ *adj* describes silicate minerals that contain high levels of iron and magnesium, e.g., olivine

fer·ro·mag·net·ic /fèrrō mag néttik/ *adj* with the property of ferromagnetism. Iron, cobalt, and nickel are ferromagnetic metals. —**fer·ro·mag·net·ic·al·ly** *adv*

fer·ro·mag·ne·tism /fèrrō mágnə tìzzəm/ *n* a property of some substances, including iron and some alloys, in which application of a weak magnetic field within a specific temperature range induces high magnetism. Small discrete regions within the substance (**domains**) align with the direction of an applied magnetic field and produce the bulk magnetization. —**fer·ro·mag·net** *n*

fer·ro·man·ga·nese /fèrrō máng gə neez/ *n* an alloy of iron and manganese used to add manganese during the making of steel and cast iron

fer·ron·ner·ies /fe rónnə reez/ *n* a variety of ceramics that copies forms from metalwork, e.g., candlesticks (*takes a singular verb*) [Early 20C. < French, "iron work, wrought iron"]

fer·ro·sil·i·con /fèrrō síllikən/ *n* an alloy of iron and silicon. Use: production of steel and cast iron.

fer·ro·type /férrō tīp/ *n* a positive photograph made on a plate of sensitized iron

fer·rous /férrəss/ *adj* containing iron with a valence of two [Mid-19C. < Latin *ferrum* "iron"]

fer·rous ox·ide *n* a black solid containing iron and oxygen. Use: manufacture of steel and enamels. Formula: FeO.

fer·rous sul·fate *n* a white or pale green iron salt. Use: in inks, tanning, treatment of iron-deficient anemia. Formula: $FeSO_4.7H_2O$.

fer·rous sul·fide *n* a black solid containing iron and sulfur. Source: pyrite, marcasite. Use: making hydrogen sulfide. Formula: FeS.

fer·ru·gi·nous /fə roójənəss/ *adj* **1.** containing or resembling iron **2.** of a reddish brown color, like rust [Mid-17C. < Latin *ferrugin-* "iron rust" < *ferrum* "iron"]

fer·rule /férrəl/, **fer·ule** *n* **1.** PROTECTIVE CAP ON SHAFT a usually metal cap or ring attached to the end of something long and thin such as a walking stick in order to strengthen it **2.** CYLINDRICAL JOINT a metal cylinder used to make a pipe joint **3.** CONNECTION FOR FISHING ROD PIECES a connection that joins the pieces of a fishing rod, consisting of male and female couplings that fit together ■ *vt* FIT SOMETHING WITH FERRULE to provide something with a ferrule [Early 17C. Alteration (after Latin *ferrum* "iron") of *virolle* < Latin *viriae* "bracelets"]

fer·ry /férree/ *n* (*plural* **-ries**) **1. BOAT MAKING REGULAR SHORT CROSSINGS** a boat used to transport passengers, vehicles, or goods across water, especially one operating regularly across a river or narrow channel **2. COMMERCIAL TRANSPORT SERVICE** a commercial service transporting passengers, vehicles, or goods across water **3. PLACE WHERE FERRY BERTHS** a place where passengers, vehicles, or goods are transported across water by ferry **4. RIGHT TO OPERATE FERRY** a legal right to operate and charge for a ferry service ■ *v* (**-ried, -ry·ing, -ries**) **1.** *vt* **TRANSPORT SOMEBODY OR SOMETHING BY FERRY** to transport somebody or something across water by ferry **2.** *vi* **GO BY FERRY** to travel by ferry **3.** *vt* **TRANSPORT PASSENGERS** to transport passengers or goods back and forth by any vehicle ○ *He had to ferry his children to school every morning.* **4.** *vt* **DELIVER AIRCRAFT** to deliver an aircraft by flying it to its operator [14C. < Old Norse *ferja*, or stem of *ferjuskip* "ferryboat," *ferjukarl* "ferryman" < Germanic]

fer·ry·boat /férree bōt/ *n* same as **ferry** *n* (sense 1)

fer·ry·man /férree màn, -mən/ (*plural* **-men** /-mèn, -mən/) *n* an owner, operator, or worker of a ferry

fer·tile /fúrt'l/ *adj* **1. ABLE TO PRODUCE OFFSPRING** capable of breeding or reproducing **2. ABLE TO DEVELOP** describes an egg or seed that has the capacity to grow and develop **3. REPRODUCING OFTEN** producing many offspring **4. PRODUCING GOOD CROPS** describes an area that produces many plants, fruit, or crops **5. RICH IN PLANT NUTRIENTS** describes soil or land that is rich in the nutrients needed to sustain the growth of healthy plants **6. CREATIVE** readily able to produce new ideas ○ *a fertile imagination* **7.** PHYS **CAPABLE OF BECOMING FISSILE** capable of being converted into fissile or fissionable material, typically in a nuclear reactor [15C. Directly or via French < Latin *fertilis* < *ferre* "bear, carry"] —**fer·tile·ly** *adv* —**fer·tile·ness** *n*

Fer·tile Cres·cent /fúrt'l-/ area of fertile land in Southwest Asia reaching from Israel to the Persian Gulf and incorporating the Tigris and Euphrates rivers in Iraq. The ancient Babylonian, Sumerian, Assyrian, Phoenician, and Hebrew civilizations arose here.

fer·til·i·ty /fur tíllətee/ *n* **1.** the quality or condition of being fertile **2.** the birthrate of a population [15C. Via French < Latin *fertilitas* < *fertilis* (see FERTILE)]

fer·til·i·ty cult *n* a form of religion using ceremonies meant to ensure the fertility of the people and agriculture of a community

fer·til·i·ty drug *n* a drug that stimulates ovulation. Use: in in vitro fertilization.

fer·til·i·ty fac·tor *n* GENETICS same as **sex factor**

fer·til·i·za·tion /fùrt'lə záysh'n/ *n* **1. STARTING REPRODUCTION** the act or process of enabling reproduction by insemination or pollination **2. UNION OF MALE AND FEMALE CELLS** the union of male and female reproductive cells (**gametes**) to produce a fertilized reproductive cell (**zygote**). Fertilization can take place inside the female's body, as in humans, or outside the body, as in fish. **3. APPLICATION OF FERTILIZER** the act or process of applying fertilizer to soil or plants

fer·ti·lize /fúrt'l ìz/ (**-lized, -liz·ing, -liz·es**) *vt* **1.** to cause a female gamete to develop a new individual by uniting it with a male gamete **2.** to apply fertilizer to soil or plants [Mid-17C. < FERTILE] —**fer·ti·liz·a·ble** *adj*

fer·til·iz·er /fúrt'l ìzər/ *n* an organic or synthetic substance usually added to or spread onto soil to increase its ability to support plant growth

fer·ule[1] /férrəl/ *n* a cane, rod, or flat piece of wood used to punish children by striking them, usually on the hand [15C. < Latin *ferula* "fennel stalk, rod"]

fer·ule[2] /férrəl/ *n*, *vt* CONSTR another spelling of **ferrule**

fe·rul·ic ac·id /fə ròolik-/ *n* an aromatic chemical found in some plants that is similar to vanillin. Ferulic acid is a component of asafetida, a bitter resin derived from a plant of the parsley family. Formula: $C_{10}H_{10}O_4$. [< Latin *ferula* "fennel stalk, rod"]

fer·vent /fúrvənt/ *adj* **1.** showing ardent or extremely passionate enthusiasm **2.** glowing as a result of intense heat (*archaic or literary*) [14C. Via Old French < Latin *fervent-*, present participle of *fervere* "to boil"] —**fer·ven·cy** *n* —**fer·vent·ly** *adv* —**fer·vent·ness** *n*

fer·vid *adj* same as **fervent** [Late 16C. < Latin *fervidus* < *fervere* "to boil"] —**fer·vid·ly** *adv* —**fer·vid·ness** *n*

fer·vor /fúrvər/ *n* **1.** ardent or extremely passionate enthusiasm **2.** intense heat (*archaic or literary*) [14C. Via Old French < Latin, < *fervere* "to boil"]

fer·vour *n* Can, UK spelling of **fervor**

Fès ➧ **Fez**

fes·cen·nine /féssə nìn, -neen/, **Fes·cen·nine** *adj* indecent, especially using coarse or vulgar language (*archaic or literary*) [Early 17C. < Latin *Fescenninus* "of Fescennia," town in Etruria known for scurrilous verse]

fes·cue /féskyoo/ *n* **1.** a perennial grass that has narrow spiky leaves. Use: lawns, pasture. Genus: *Festuca*. **2.** a pointer, e.g., a stick or piece of straw, used to point out letters for children learning to read [14C. Alteration of *festu* < Old French, "straw" < Latin *festuca*]

fess[1] /fess/, **fesse** *n* a broad horizontal band crossing the middle section of a heraldic shield [15C. Via Old French *fesse* < Latin *fascia* "band, sash"]

fess[2] /fess/ (**fessed, fess·ing, fess·es**) [Early 19C. Shortening of CONFESS]

fess up *vi* to admit to something (*informal*) ○ *Come on, fess up! Was it you?*

fesse *n* another spelling of **fess**[1]

fess point *n* the central point of a heraldic shield

-fest *suffix* **1.** a gathering or festival of a particular type ○ *love-fest* ○ *talk-fest* **2.** a movie filled with horrific gory detail ○ *"Night of the Living Dead" is a real gore-fest.* [Mid-19C. Via German *Fest* < Latin *festum* "feast, festival"]

fes·tal /fést'l/ *adj* same as **festive** (*archaic*) [15C. Via Old French < Latin *festum* "feast, festival"] —**fes·tal·ly** *adv*

fes·ter /féstər/ *v* (**-tered, -ter·ing, -ters**) **1.** *vi* **PRODUCE PUS** to produce pus because of an infection or ulceration, usually of the skin **2.** *vi* **BECOME ROTTEN** to decay **3.** *vi* **DETERIORATE** to be in or enter a state of decline ○ *neighborhoods allowed to fester* **4. GET MORE INTENSE** to become increasingly intense or worse ○ *Hatred and tension continue to fester in the war-torn city.* ○ *festering discontent* ■ *n* MED **SORE DISCHARGING PUS** a small sore or ulcer containing or discharging pus [14C. Via Old French *festre* "pipe-like ulcer" < Latin *fistula*]

fes·ti·na·tion /fèstə náysh'n/ *n* a style of tottering walk that is characteristic of people with Parkinson's disease [Mid-16C. < Latin *festination-* < *festinare* "to hurry"]

fes·ti·val /féstəv'l/ *n* **1. TIME OF CELEBRATION** a day or period of celebration, often one of religious significance **2. PROGRAM OF CULTURAL EVENTS** a program or series of performances or other cultural events, usually held at regular intervals, often in one place ■ *adj* **APPROPRIATE TO FESTIVAL** typical of or appropriate to a festival [14C. Via Old French < medieval Latin *festivalis* < Latin *festivus* (see FESTIVE)]

fes·ti·val·go·er /féstəv'l gō ər/ *n* an attender of a festival

fes·tive /féstiv/ *adj* **1.** relating to, suitable for, or typical of a feast, festival, or holiday **2.** marked by cheerfulness and joy ○ *in a festive mood* [Mid-17C. < Latin *festivus* "festive" < *festum* "feast, festival"] —**fes·tive·ly** *adv* —**fes·tive·ness** *n*

fes·tiv·i·ty /fe stívvətee/ *n* (*plural* **-ties**) **1. CELEBRATION** a celebration, feast, or party **2. ENJOYMENT** the enjoyment or merrymaking typical of a celebration ■ **fes·tiv·i·ties** *npl* **CELEBRATIONS** celebrations or merrymaking [14C. Directly or via French < Latin *festivitas* < *festivus* (see FESTIVE)]

festoon

fes·toon /fe stòon/ *n* **1. GARLAND** an ornamental chain of flowers, leaves, or ribbons hanging in a loop or curve between two points **2. ARTISTIC REPRESENTATION OF FESTOON** a carved or painted representation of a festoon, e.g., on a building, in a painting, or on pottery ■ *vt* (**-tooned, -toon·ing, -toons**) **1. HANG FESTOONS ON SOMETHING** to decorate something with festoons **2. JOIN WITH FESTOONS** to join things together with festoons **3. SHAPE INTO FESTOONS** to make something into festoons [Mid-17C. Via French *feston* < Italian *festone* "ornament for festivities" < assumed Vulgar Latin *festa* "festivities" < Latin *festum* "feast, festival"] —**fes·tooned** *adj*

fes·toon blind *n* a blind for a window, made of cloth gathered into rows that can be drawn up to hang in curves

fest·schrift /fést shrìft/, **Fest·schrift** (*plural* **-schrifts** or **-schrif·ten** /-shrìftən/) *n* a volume of writings by various people collected in honor of somebody such as a writer or scholar [Early 20C. < German, "celebration-writing"]

FET, F.E.T. *abbr* **1.** FIN federal excise tax **2.** ELECTRONICS field-effect transistor

fet·a /féttə/ *n* a firm crumbly salty cheese made from sheep's or goat's milk and preserved in brine, originally from Greece. It is now produced in other countries, though still most often used as an ingredient in Greek dishes. [Mid-20C. < modern Greek *pheta*]

fe·tal /feet'l/, **foe·tal** *adj* relating to or characteristic of a fetus [Early 19C. < FETUS]

fe·tal al·co·hol syn·drome *n* a condition affecting babies born to women who drank excessive amounts of alcohol during pregnancy, characterized by a range of effects including malformed facial features and learning difficulties

fe·tal he·mo·glo·bin *n* a hemoglobin common in the fetus and newborn, but normally present only in small amounts in adults, except in some forms of anemia

fe·tal mem·brane *n* BIOL same as **extraembryonic membrane**

fe·tal po·si·tion *n* a body position in which the body lies curled up on one side with the head bowed and the legs and arms drawn in toward the chest. As well as being a comfortable position for relaxation, the fetal position is often assumed by people during intense emotional trauma.

fetch[1] /fech/ *v* (**fetched, fetch·ing, fetch·es**) **1.** *vt* **GO AND GET SOMEBODY OR SOMETHING** to go after and bring back somebody or something ○ *She went upstairs to fetch her car keys.* **2.** *vt* **CAUSE SOMEBODY'S OR SOMETHING'S APPEARANCE** to make somebody or something appear or come **3.** *vt* **SELL SOMETHING AT PARTICULAR PRICE** to sell something for a particular amount of money ○ *The painting fetched $600 at an auction.* **4.** *vti* **RETRIEVE SOMETHING** to retrieve animals that have been shot or something that has been thrown such as a stick or ball ○ *The boy threw the ball and told the dog to fetch it.* **5.** *vt* **UTTER DEEP SIGH OR GROAN** to utter a sigh or groan with a deep breath **6.** *vt* **HIT SOMEBODY WITH BLOW** to inflict a blow on somebody or on a part of somebody's body (*informal*) ○ *fetched his opponent a kick on the shins* **7.** *vt* **DRAW IN BREATH** to draw a breath or gasp of air into the lungs **8.** *vt* **PLEASE SOMEBODY** to attract or charm somebody (*often passive*) ○ *was fetched by the notion of going to New York* **9.** *vt* **ARRIVE SOMEWHERE BY BOAT** to reach or arrive at a place by sailing ○ *fetched port at nightfall* **10.** *vt* *Malaysia* **TAKE SOMEWHERE** to take somebody somewhere ○ *My neighbor fetches me to the office every morning.* ■ *n* **1. ACT OF FETCHING** the act or an instance of fetching somebody or something **2. STRATAGEM** a dodge, trick, or stratagem ○ *They used cunning fetches to swindle money out of the gullible.* **3.** METEOROL **DISTANCE WIND TRAVELS UNOBSTRUCTED** the distance wind or waves can travel without obstruction [Old English *feccean*, origin ?] —**fetch·er** *n* ◇ **fetch and carry (for somebody)** to do menial tasks for somebody

fetch up *v* **1.** *vi* **ARRIVE** to arrive or come to a halt somewhere (*informal*) ○ *After a week on the road, we fetched up at a small coastal town.* **2.** *vi* NAUT **HALT SUDDENLY** to come to a sudden halt ○ *The boat fetched up on a sandbar.* **3.** *vt* **CAUSE SOMEBODY OR SOMETHING TO STOP** to make somebody or something come to a stop ○ *His abrupt tone fetched me up short.*

fetch[2] /fech/ *n* a vision, apparition, or ghost appearing as the doppelgänger of a living person [Late 17C. Origin ?]

fetch·ing /féching/ *adj* **1.** pleasant, stylish, or becoming in appearance **2.** having a charming or captivating quality ○ *a fetching hat* —**fetch·ing·ly** *adv*

fete /fayt, fet/, **fête** *n* **1.** PARTY a large elaborate party, often outdoors **2.** HOLIDAY a holiday or day of celebration **3.** RELIGIOUS FESTIVAL a religious festival, e.g., a saint's day ■ *vt* (**fet·ed, fet·ing, fetes; fêt·ed, fêt·ing, fêtes**) ARRANGE CELEBRATIONS FOR SOMEBODY to entertain or honor somebody with an elaborate party (*usually passive*) [Mid-18C. Via French *fête* < Latin *festum* "feast, festival"]

fête cham·pê·tre /fàyt shaaN péttrə/ (*plural* **fêtes cham·pê·tres** /*pronunc. same*/) *n* an outdoor party or festival [< French, "rural festival"]

fet·ich *n* another spelling of **fetish** (*archaic*)

fe·ti·cide /féetə sīd/, **foe·ti·cide** *n* **1.** the act of destroying a fetus **2.** an agent or drug used to destroy a fetus —**fe·ti·cid·al** /féetə sīd'l/ *adj*

fet·id /féttid/, **foe·tid** *adj* having a rotten or offensive smell ○ *fetid odor of rotten meat* [15C. < Latin *fetidus* < *fetere* "to stink"] —**fet·id·ly** *adv* —**fet·id·ness** *n*

fe·ti·pa·rous /fi típpərəss/, **foe·ti·pa·rous** *adj* used to describe animals that give birth to incompletely developed young, e.g., marsupials [Late 19C. < FETUS]

fet·ish /féttish/ *n* **1.** MAGICAL OBJECT something, especially an inanimate object, that is revered or worshiped because it is believed to have magical powers or be animated by a spirit **2.** OBJECT OF OBSESSION an object, idea, or activity that somebody is irrationally obsessed with or attached to ○ *make a fetish of neatness* **3.** OBJECT AROUSING SEXUAL DESIRE something that arouses sexual excitement in somebody, e.g., an inanimate object or nonsexual part of the body [Early 17C. Via French *fétiche* "charm, sorcery" < Latin *factitius* "made by art, artificial" (see FACTITIOUS)]

fet·ish·ism /fétti shìzzəm/ *n* **1.** BELIEF IN FETISH the belief in, use of, or worship of a magical fetish **2.** OBSESSION WITH SOMETHING an irrational obsession with or attachment to something **3.** SEXUAL AROUSAL WITH FETISH the use of a fetish to produce sexual arousal —**fet·ish·ist** *n*

fet·ish·ize /fétti shīz/ (**-ized, -iz·ing, -iz·es**) *vt* to make a fetish of something

fet·lock /fét lòk/ *n* **1.** PROJECTION ON HORSE'S LEG the part of the lower leg of a horse or related animal situated above and behind the hoof and projecting down from the associated joint **2.** HAIR ON FETLOCK the tuft of hair growing on a fetlock **3.** *also* **fet·lock joint** LEG JOINT the joint at the fetlock [14C. Probably < form of FOOT + LOCK[2] "hair"]

fe·tol·o·gy /fee tóllәjee/, **foe·tol·o·gy** *n* a branch of medicine concerned with the study and treatment of the fetus [Mid-20C. < FETUS] —**fe·tol·o·gist** *n*

fe·to·pro·tein /féetō prṓ teen/ *n* a protein found in healthy fetuses that is also found in adults with some malignant conditions [Mid-20C. < FETUS]

fe·tor /féetər/, **foe·tor** *n* a strong offensive smell [15C. < Latin < *fetere* "to stink"]

fe·to·scope /féetə skōp/, **foe·to·scope** *n* a fiber optic device for viewing a fetus in the uterus [Late 20C. < FETUS + *-scope*] —**fe·tos·co·py** /fee tóskəpee/ *n*

fet·ter /féttər/ *n* (*often used in the plural*) **1.** SHACKLE FOR ANKLES a chain or shackle fastened to somebody's ankles or feet **2.** RESTRAINT a means of confinement, restriction, or restraint ○ *These harsh rules keep us in fetters.* ■ *vt* (**-tered, -ter·ing, -ters**) **1.** PUT FETTERS ON SOMEBODY to shackle somebody with fetters **2.** RESTRAIN SOMEBODY OR SOMETHING to confine, restrict, or restrain somebody or something ○ *fettered by her own inhibitions* [Old English *feter* < Germanic]

fet·tle /fétt'l/ *n* METALL same as **fettling** ■ *vt* (**-tled, -tling, -tles**) **1.** MANUF TRIM CASTING to remove molding or excess material from a ceramic or metal casting **2.** METALL LINE FURNACE to line the hearth of a furnace with fettling **3.** METALL REPAIR FURNACE to repair the lining of a furnace [Old English *fetel* "girdle, strap" < Germanic, "hold"] —**fet·tler** *n* ◇ **in fine** *or* **good fettle** in good health, condition, or spirits

fet·tling /fétt'ling/ *n* loose material that is resistant to heat, typically sand or ore, used to line the hearths of some types of furnaces before the molten metal is introduced

fet·tuc·ci·ne /fèttə chéenee/, **fet·tuc·ci·ni** *n* **1.** pasta made in narrow flat strips, slightly narrower and thicker than tagliatelle (*takes a singular or plural verb*) **2.** a pasta dish made with fettuccine [Early 20C. < Italian, "little ribbons"]

fet·tuc·ci·ne Al·fre·do /-al fráydō/ *n* a pasta dish of fettuccine in a cream sauce [After *Alfredo* all'Augusteo, restaurant in Rome]

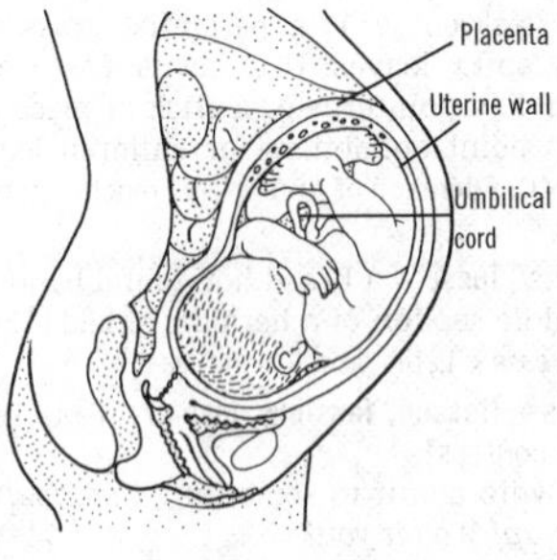

fetus: human fetus

fe·tus /féetəss/, **foe·tus** *n* an unborn vertebrate at a stage when all the structural features of the adult are recognizable, especially an unborn human offspring after eight weeks of development [14C. < Latin, "offspring"]

feud[1] /fyood/ *n* **1.** LONG VIOLENT DISPUTE a bitter prolonged violent quarrel or state of hostility between families, clans, or other groups **2.** PROLONGED DISAGREEMENT a prolonged disagreement, dispute, or quarrel ■ *vi* (**feud·ed, feud·ing, feuds**) PARTICIPATE IN FEUD to take part in or perpetuate a feud [13C. < Old French *fe(i)de* "vendetta, hostility" < Germanic]

feud[2] /fyood/ *n* HIST same as **fief** (sense 1) [Early 17C. < medieval Latin *feudum* "land or other property used as a reward for service" < Indo-European, "wealth, cattle"]

feu·dal /fyóod'l/ *adj* **1.** relating to, typical of, or resembling feudalism **2.** relating to a fief [Early 17C. < medieval Latin *feudalis* < *feudum* (see FEUD[2])] —**feu·dal·ly** *adv*

feu·dal·ism /fyóod'l ìzzəm/ *n* **1.** the legal and social system that existed in medieval Europe, in which vassals held land from lords in exchange for military service **2.** a system of economic, political, or social organization resembling European feudalism, e.g., in medieval Japan —**feu·dal·ist** *n* —**feu·dal·is·tic** /fyóod'l ístik/ *adj*

feu·dal·i·ty /fyoo dállətee/ (*plural* **-ties**) *n* **1.** the quality or condition of being feudal **2.** a feudal holding or system

feu·dal·ize /fyóod'l īz/ (**-ized, -iz·ing, -iz·es**) *vt* to make something feudal in nature —**feu·dal·i·za·tion** /fyóod'li záysh'n/ *n*

feu·da·to·ry /fyóodə tàwree/ *n* (*plural* **-ries**) TENANT OF FEUDAL LAND somebody holding land by feudal tenure ■ *adj* **1.** INVOLVING FEUDAL RELATIONSHIP relating to or characteristic of the relationship between a feudal lord and a vassal **2.** SUBJECT TO OVERLORDSHIP owing feudal allegiance to an overlord or another state [Late 16C. < medieval Latin *feudatorius* < past participle of *feudare* "invest with feudal property" < *feudum* (see FEUD[2])]

feuil·le·ton /fṓyə taaN/ *n* **1.** a section of a European newspaper containing reviews, serial fiction, and articles of general interest **2.** an article, review, or other piece published in a feuilleton [Mid-19C. < French *feuillet* "little leaf" < *feuille* "leaf" < Latin *folium* "leaf, page"]

fe·ver /féevər/ *n* **1.** UNUSUALLY HIGH BODY TEMPERATURE a body temperature that is unusually high, usually caused by bacterial or viral infections and commonly accompanied by shivering, headache, and an increased pulse rate. Technical name **pyrexia 2.** DISEASE WITH FEVER a disease in which somebody typically has an unusually high body temperature, e.g., typhoid fever, yellow fever, or scarlet fever **3.** CRAZE an intense and often brief enthusiasm or craze **4.** STATE OF EXCITEMENT a state of intense agitation, excitement, or emotion (*often used in combination*) ■ *v* (**-vered, -ver·ing, -vers**) **1.** *vi* MED HAVE A FEVER to get or show the symptoms of a fever ○ *She fevered intermittently throughout the night.* **2.** *vt* AGITATE SOMEBODY to throw somebody into a state of intense agitation, excitement, or emotion [Pre-12C < Latin *febris*]

fe·ver blis·ter *n* MED same as **cold sore**

fe·vered /féevərd/ *adj* **1.** affected by fever **2.** showing great agitation, excitement, or emotion

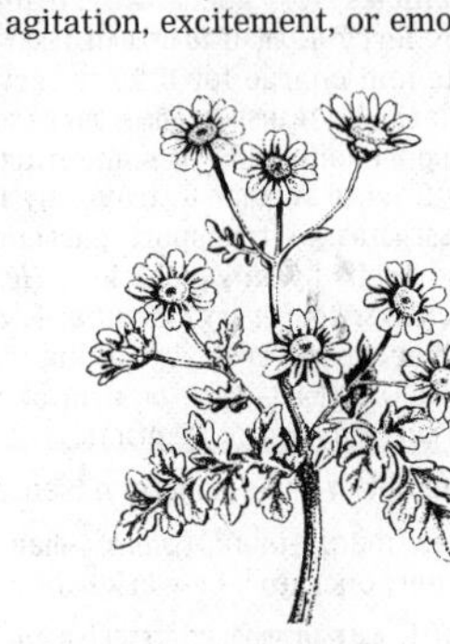

feverfew

fe·ver·few /féevər fyoo/ *n* a perennial plant whose leaves are a popular remedy for headaches and migraine. Native to: Europe. Latin name: *Tanacetum parthenium.* [Pre-12C. < Latin *febris* "fever" + -FUGE]

fe·ver·ish /féevərish/ *adj* **1.** HAVING FEVER affected by a fever **2.** RELATING TO FEVER relating to, causing, or caused by a fever ○ *a feverish cold* **3.** AGITATED showing intense agitation, excitement, or emotion —**fe·ver·ish·ly** *adv* —**fe·ver·ish·ness** *n*

fe·ver pitch *n* a state of intense agitation, excitement, or emotion ○ *His grand slam brought the crowd to a fever pitch.*

fe·ver tree *n* a tree whose bark was used to treat malaria. Native to: southeastern United States. Latin name: *Pinckneya pubens.*

fe·ver·wort /féevər wùrt, -wàwrt/ *n US* a plant such as horse gentian or boneset used medicinally

few /fyoo/ (**few·er, few·est**) CORE MEANING: a grammatical word used to indicate that there are not many or hardly any people or things ○ (adj) *There were few books on the shelves.* ○ (adj) *spending her few free hours relaxing in front of the television* ○ (pron) *Many people have entered the contest, but few will win prizes.* ○ (pron) *Few of the gardens had been cared for.*

1. *npl, pron, adj* a limited or exclusive number, e.g., an elite or minority of people ○ (npl) *the fortunate few who managed to escape sickness this winter* ○ (npl) *The needs of the many outweigh the needs of the few.* ○ (pron) *Few would have thought it.* **2.** *adj, pron* **a few** not very many people or things, but more than two, and sometimes more than might be expected ○ (adj) *We had a few meetings before signing the contract.* ○ (pron) *Only a few ever achieve real artistic success.* ○ (pron) *A few of the kids wanted to watch a video.* [Old English *fēawa* < Indo-European] —**few·ness** *n* ◇ **few and far between** scarce or infrequent (*informal*) ◇ **quite a few** a fairly large number (*informal*)

USAGE fewer or **less**? As a general rule, ***fewer*** is used with things you can count (*fewer meetings, fewer people*), whereas ***less*** is used with things you cannot count (*less time, less money*). The same difference applies to the use of ***fewer than*** and ***less than***: *fewer than twenty people, less than an hour.* Designations of price, age, and measurement are normally regarded as singular, the idea being that, for example, *It cost less than ten dollars* has to do with an amount of money rather than a number of individual dollars. The use of ***less*** where the sense of countable number is strong (*You may use the express lane if you have less than eight items*) is relatively common, though many object to it.

fey /fay/ *adj* **1.** IRRATIONAL behaving or talking in very unusual, uninhibited ways that suggest possible psychiatric disorder ○ *Everyone was convinced he was fey because he rehearsed his lines in the park.* **2.** SUPERNATURAL relating to or typical of magic or the supernatural **3.** CLAIRVOYANT supposedly able to see into the future **4.** *Scotland* DOOMED TO DIE believed to be doomed or destined to die, especially as indicated by peculiar, usually elated behavior [Old English *fǣge* "fated to die" < Germanic] —**fey·ly** *adv* —**fey·ness** *n*

Feyn·man /fīnmən/, **Richard** (1918–88) US physicist. He shared the Nobel Prize in physics (1965) for work on quantum electrodynamics. Full name **Feynman, Richard Phillips**

> "For a successful technology, reality must take precedence over public relations, for nature cannot be fooled."
> [Richard Feynman, *Rogers Commission Report on the Space Shuttle Challenger Accident*; June 6, 1986]

Feyn·man di·a·gram *n* a diagrammatic representation of interactions between elementary particles [After Richard FEYNMAN]

fez /fez/ (*plural* **fez·zes**) *n* a brimless felt hat shaped like a cone with a flat top, usually red with a black tassel, worn by men in eastern Mediterranean and North African countries. In the past it was the national headdress of Turkish men. [Early 19C. Via French < Turkish *fes*]

Fez /fez/, **Fès** /fess/ city in northern Morocco, northeast of Casablanca. The oldest of the country's four imperial cities, it is about 100 mi./161 km east of Rabat. Population: 774,754 (1994).

Fez·zan /fə zán/ desert region and former province in southwestern Libya. It was part of the Ottoman Empire between the 16th and 19th centuries.

ff *abbr* MUSIC fortissimo

ff. *abbr* **1.** PUBL folios **2.** following (*used of lines or pages*)

FFDO *n* a commercial pilot trained, qualified, and authorized to carry a firearm in the cockpit for use in protecting the aircraft, its passengers, and the crew from terrorist hijacking. Full form **federal flight deck officer** [Early 21C.]

FG *abbr* **1.** FOOTBALL, BASKETBALL field goal **2.** fine grain

FHA *abbr* **1.** GOV Federal Housing Administration **2.** POL Future Homemakers of America

FHLB *abbr US* BANKING Federal Home Loan Bank

fi·a·cre /fee ákrə/ *n* a small horse-drawn carriage with four wheels, formerly used for hire like a taxi [Late 17C. < French, after the Hôtel de St. *Fiacre*]

fi·an·cé /fèe on sáy, fee ón sày/ *n* the man to whom a woman is engaged to be married [Mid-19C. < French, past participle of *fiancer* "betroth" < Old French *fiance* "a promise"]

fi·an·cée /fèe on sáy, fee ón sày/ *n* the woman to whom a man is engaged to be married [Mid-19C. < French, form of *fiancé* (see FIANCÉ)]

fi·an·chet·to /fèe ən chéttō, -kéttō/ *n* (*plural* **-tos** or **-ti** /-tee/) in chess, the initial movement (**development**) of a bishop from its original position to the second square of the adjacent knight's file ■ *vt* (**-toed, -to·ing, -tos**) to move a bishop using a fianchetto [Mid-19C. < Italian, "little flank" < *fianco* "flank"]

Fi·an·na /fée ənə/ *npl* in Irish legend, a band of warriors celebrated for feats of heroism [Late 18C. < Irish, "band of warriors and hunters"]

Fi·an·na Fáil /fèe ənə fáal/ *n* one of the two main Irish political parties, founded in 1926 [< Irish, "warriors of Ireland"]

fi·as·co /fee áskō/ (*plural* **-cos**) *n* **1.** a total failure, especially a humiliating or ludicrous one **2.** a wine bottle having a round bottom and often in a straw covering resembling a basket [Mid-19C. Via Italian, "bottle" < medieval Latin *flasco* "flask"; sense "failure" from theatrical slang]

fi·at /fée ət, -aat/ *n* **1.** a formal or official authorization of something **2.** an authoritative and often arbitrary command [14C. < Latin, "let it be done"]

fi·at mon·ey *n* paper money that a government declares to be legal tender although it is not based on or convertible into coins and therefore depends on government decree to determine its value

fib /fib/ (*informal*) *n* an insignificant or harmless lie ■ *vi* (**fibbed, fib·bing, fibs**) to tell an insignificant or harmless lie [Early 17C. Origin ?] —**fib·ber** *n*

SYNONYMS See *lie*[2].

fi·ber /fībər/, **fi·bre** *n* **1.** THIN THREAD a long slender thread or filament **2.** TEXTILES THREAD FOR YARN a fine thread of a natural or synthetic material that can be spun into yarn **3.** TEXTILES CLOTH cloth or material made of fibers **4.** TEXTILES FIBROUS STRUCTURE the texture or structure of a material made of fibers **5.** HEALTH COARSE FIBROUS SUBSTANCES IN FOOD the coarse fibrous substances, largely composed of cellulose, that are found in grains, fruits, and vegetables, and aid digestion. This largely indigestible plant matter is considered to play a role in the prevention of many diseases of the digestive tract. **6.** STRENGTH OF CHARACTER somebody's strength of character or sense of right and wrong ○ *the moral fiber of the nation* **7.** ESSENTIAL CHARACTER the fundamental character, quality, or makeup of something **8.** BOT LONG THICK-WALLED PLANT CELL a long narrow plant cell with walls thickened with lignin that is a major component of the plant's supporting tissue. Fiber cells are frequently found in the outer walls of plant stems. **9.** BOT PLANT STRANDS FOR MAKING ROPE AND TEXTILES strands of fiber cells removed from the stems or leaves of plants such as flax or hemp, that can be separated and woven **10.** BOT THIN ROOT a thin narrow root of a plant **11.** ANAT THREAD-SHAPED BODY STRUCTURE a long thin structure of the body tissues, e.g., muscle cells and nerve cells [Mid-16C. Via French < Latin *fibra* "filament"] —**fi·bered** *adj*

fi·ber·board /fībər bàwrd/ *n* building material made by compressing wood fibers into sheets

fi·ber bun·dle *n* a flexible group of parallel optical fibers held in a fixed arrangement with respect to one another

fi·ber·fill /fībər fil/ *n* synthetic stuffing or insulating material. Use: cushions, comforters, clothing.

Fi·ber·glas /fībər glàss/ *tdmk* a trademark for a material made of glass fibers and plastic

fi·ber·glass /fībər glàss/ *n* **1.** compressed glass fibers. Use: insulation. **2.** a material made from fiberglass. Use: boat hulls, car bodies.

fi·ber op·tics *n* the technology of transferring information, e.g., in communications or computer technology, through thin flexible glass or plastic tubes (**optical fibers**) using modulated light waves. Information is transmitted in the form of coded pulses. (*takes a singular or plural verb*) —**fi·ber-op·tic** *adj*

fi·ber·scope /fībər skōp/ *n* an instrument that uses fiber optics to transmit images from inaccessible places such as the interior of the body. Use: microsurgery, diagnosis.

Fi·bo·nac·ci num·ber /fèebə naáchee-/ *n* a number in an unending Fibonacci sequence [See FIBONACCI SEQUENCE]

Fi·bo·nac·ci se·quence *n* an unending series of numbers in which each number except for the first two is the sum of the preceding two, e.g., 0,1,1,2,3,5,8.... Such sequences frequently have applications in botany, psychology, and astronomy. [After Leonardo *Fibonacci*, 13C Italian mathematician]

fibr- *prefix* same as **fibro-** (*used before vowels*)

fi·bre *n* another spelling of **fiber**

fibri- *prefix* same as **fibro-**

fi·bri·form /fíbbrə fàwrm/ *adj* having the form of a fiber or fibers

fi·bril /fībrəl, fíbbrəl/ *n* a small or delicate fiber or part of a fiber (*technical*) [Mid-17C. < modern Latin *fibrilla* "little fiber" < Latin *fibra* "fiber"] —**fi·bril·lar** /fíbbrələr/ *adj* —**fi·bril·lar·y** *adj* —**fi·bril·li·form** *adj* —**fi·bril·lose** *adj* —**fib·ril·lous** *adj*

fi·bril·late /fíbbrə làyt/ (**-lat·ed, -lat·ing, -lates**) *vti* to undergo rapid irregular beating or uncontrolled contraction, or make the heart or muscles undergo this [Mid-19C. < modern Latin *fibrilla* (see FIBRIL)] —**fib·ril·la·tive** *adj*

fib·ril·la·tion /fìbbrə láysh'n/ *n* **1.** RAPID IRREGULAR HEARTBEAT rapid chaotic beating of the heart muscles in which the affected part of the heart may stop pumping blood **2.** RAPID CONTRACTION OF MUSCLE FIBERS rapid uncontrolled contraction of individual muscle fibers with little or no movement of the muscle as a whole **3.** FORMATION OF FIBERS the formation of fibers or fibrils

fi·brin /fíbrin/ *n* an insoluble fibrous protein that is produced in the liver from the soluble protein fibrinogen and helps in blood clotting. It forms a network of fibers in which blood cells become trapped, thus producing a clot. [Early 19C. < FIBER] —**fi·bri·noid** /fībrə nòyd/ *adj* —**fi·bri·nous** /fībrənəss/ *adj*

fi·brin·o·gen /fī brínnəjən/ *n* a soluble protein present in the blood that is activated by thrombin to form fibrin. Fibrinogen is a clotting factor and is required to prevent major blood loss. —**fi·brin·o·gen·ic** /fìbrənō jénnik/ *adj* —**fi·brin·o·gen·i·cal·ly** *adv* —**fi·bri·nog·e·nous** /fìbrə nójjənəss/ *adj*

fi·bri·nol·y·sin /fìbrə nólləsin/ *n* an enzyme in blood that breaks down fibrin and disperses blood clots

fi·bri·nol·y·sis /fìbrə nólləssiss/ *n* the destruction of fibrin and blood clots —**fi·bri·no·lyt·ic** /fìbrənō líttik/ *adj*

fibro- *prefix* **1.** fiber ○ *fibroin* **2.** fibrous tissue ○ *fibroma* [< Latin *fibra* "fiber"]

fi·bro·blast /fībrō blàst/ *n* a large flat cell in connective tissue that secretes collagen and elastic fibers

fi·bro·car·ti·lage /fìbrō kaárt'lij/ *n* strong, relatively inelastic cartilage containing bundles of collagen fibers

fi·bro·cys·tic /fìbrō sístik/ *adj* describes an unusual growth of fibrous tissue that contains cystic spaces, occurring particularly in glandular tissue such as the breast. Fibrocystic disease of the pancreas is called cystic fibrosis.

fi·broid /fī bròyd/ *adj* resembling or consisting of fibers or fibrous tissue ■ *n* a benign growth composed of fibrous and muscle tissue, especially one that develops in the wall of the womb and is associated with painful and excessive menstrual flow. Fibroids can be removed surgically and are not life-threatening, but fibroids in the womb reduce the chance of pregnancy.

fi·bro·in /fī brō in/ *n* a tough white protein secreted by spiders and silkworms that quickly solidifies into the thread used to form webs and cocoons

fi·bro·ma /fī brṓmə/ (*plural* **-mas** or **-ma·ta** /-mətə/) *n* a nonmalignant tumor of fibrous connective tissue such as cartilage —**fi·brom·a·tous** /fī brómmətəss/ *adj*

fi·bro·my·al·gi·a /fìbrō mī áljee ə/ *n* a disorder causing aching muscles, sleep disorders, and fatigue, associated with raised levels of the brain chemicals that transmit nerve signals (**neurotransmitters**)

fi·brose[1] /fībrōss/ (**-brosed, -bros·ing, -bros·es**) *vi* to form tissue consisting of or resembling fibers [Late 19C. Back-formation < FIBROSIS]

fi·brose[2] /fībrōss/ *adj* containing or resembling fibers (*technical*) [Late 17C. < modern Latin *fibrosus* < Latin *fibra* "filament"]

fi·bro·sis /fī brṓssiss/ *n* a thickening and scarring of connective tissue most often following injury, infection, lack of oxygen, or surgery [Late 19C. < Latin *fibra* "fiber"] —**fi·brot·ic** /fī bróttik/ *adj*

fi·bro·si·tis /fìbrə sītiss/ *n* pain and stiffness, especially in the back muscles

fi·brous /fībrəss/ *adj* **1.** consisting of or resembling fibers **2.** describes a mineral that crystallizes in thin elongated threads, e.g., asbestos —**fi·brous·ly** *adv* —**fi·brous·ness** *n*

fi·brous root *n* a root system in some plants such as grasses that consists of numerous very fine branches of approximately the same length

fi·bro·vas·cu·lar /fìbrō váskyələr/ *adj* describes plant tissue that provides structural support and conducts sap

fi·bro·vas·cu·lar bun·dle *n* BOT same as **vascular bundle**

fib·u·la /fíbbyələ/ (*plural* **-lae** /-lee/ or **-las**) *n* **1.** HUMAN LEG BONE the outer and narrower of the two bones in the human lower leg between the knee and ankle **2.** ANIMAL LEG BONE the thinner outer bone of the two bones in the lower leg or hind leg of terrestrial vertebrates between the knee and ankle **3.** CLASP in ancient Greece and Rome, a brooch or clasp shaped like a modern safety pin used to fasten cloaks [Late 16C. < Latin, "brooch, clasp"] —**fib·u·lar** *adj*

-fic *suffix* making, causing ○ *sudorific* [< Latin *-ficus* < *facere* "make, do"]

FICA /fīkə/ *abbr US* FIN Federal Insurance Contributions Act

-fication *suffix* production, process ○ *versification* ○ *unification* [< Latin *-fication-* < *-ficatus*, past participle of verbs ending in *-ficare* "make" < *facere* "make, do"]

fice /fīss/ *n regional* VERTEB same as **feist** [Mid-19C. Variant]

fiche /feesh/ *n* (*informal*) **1.** same as **microfiche 2.** same as **ultrafiche** [Mid-20C. Shortening]

Fich·te /fíktə, fíkhtə/, **Johann Gottlieb** (1762–1814) German philosopher. An important figure in the German philosophical school of idealism, he was a pupil of Kant, and his work, in particular *The Vocation of Man* (1800), was an important influence on Hegel and later philosophers.

fich·u /físhoo, fee shoó/ *n* a woman's triangular scarf made of a lightweight material such as muslin or lace, worn around the neck and shoulders, especially in the 18th and early 19th centuries [Mid-18C. < French, "knotted," past participle of *ficher* "stick in" < Latin *figere* "to fix"]

fick·le /fík'l/ (**-ler, -lest**) *adj* likely to change, especially in affections, intentions, loyalties, or preferences [Old English *ficol* "deceitful" < Indo-European, "hostile"] —**fick·le·ness** *n*

~~**ficticious**~~ incorrect spelling of **fictitious**

fic·tile /fíkt'l/ *adj* **1.** MALLEABLE molded or capable of being molded, as clay can be for making pottery **2.** MADE OF CLAY molded in earth or clay by a potter **3.** RELATING TO POTTERY MAKING relating to the making of earthenware or pottery [Early 17C. < Latin *fictilis* < *fingere* "to make, shape"]

fic·tion /fíksh'n/ *n* **1.** LITERARY WORKS OF IMAGINATION novels and stories that describe imaginary people and events **2.** WORK OF FICTION a novel, story, or other work of fiction **3.** UNTRUE STATEMENT something that is untrue and has been made up to deceive people ○ *The account she gave was pure fiction.* **4.** PRETENSE the act of pretending or inventing something ○ *the fiction that their marriage had become* **5.** LAW SOMETHING ASSUMED TO BE TRUE something that is assumed in law to be true regardless of whether or not it is true [14C. Via Old French < Latin *fiction-* < *fingere* "to make, shape"] —**fic·tion·al** *adj*

ORIGIN The Latin word *fingere* "to make, shape," from which ***fiction*** is derived, is also the source of English *effigy, feign, figment,* and *figure.*

fic·tion·al·ize /fíkshən'l īz/ (**-ized, -iz·ing, -iz·es**) *vt* to make something into fiction, or make a fictional version of something ○ *a fictionalized life of Shakespeare* —**fic·tion·al·i·za·tion** /fìkshən'li záysh'n/ *n*

fic·ti·tious /fik tíshəss/ *adj* **1.** FALSE not true or genuine, and intended to deceive ○ *He gave a fictitious name when confronted.* **2.** FICTIONAL invented by somebody's imagination, especially as part of a work of fiction **3.** LAW ASSUMED TO BE TRUE assumed to be true for legal purposes, regardless of whether or not it is true [Early 17C. < Latin *ficticius* < *fingere* "to make, shape"] —**fic·ti·tious·ly** *adv* —**fic·ti·tious·ness** *n*

fic·tive /fíktiv/ *adj* **1.** relating to fiction or imaginative invention **2.** not genuine or true [Late 15C. Directly or via French < medieval Latin *fictivus* < *fingere* "to make, shape"] —**fic·tive·ly** *adv*

fi·cus /fíkəss/ (*plural same* or **-cus·es**) *n* a tree, bush, or plant that belongs to the genus that includes the fig and many familiar garden or houseplants such as the rubber plant. Genus: *Ficus.* [15C. < Latin, "fig tree, fig"]

fid /fid/ *n* **1.** a bar used to support a topmast on a boat **2.** a tapered wooden implement used to separate the strands of a rope in splicing [Early 17C. Origin ?]

-fid *suffix* divided in parts ○ *multifid* [< Latin *-fidus* < *fid-*, stem of *findere* "to split"]

fid·a·yee *n* another spelling of **fedayee**

fid·dle /fídd'l/ *n* **1.** VIOLIN a musical instrument of the viol or violin family, especially the violin. Violins are often called fiddles in folk, bluegrass, or country music, but in classical music the term is sometimes disparaging. **2.** FRAUDULENT ACTIVITY a fraudulent or illegal way of getting money (*informal*) **3.** TRIVIAL MATTERS nonsensical or trivial matters or behavior **4.** NAUT GUARDRAIL ON SHIP'S TABLE a small guardrail on top of a table or stove on a ship, used to prevent things from sliding off ■ *v* (**-dled, -dling, -dles**) **1.** *vi* TINKER to tinker with something to try to make it work properly ○ *She fiddled with the controls on the video recorder.* **2.** *vi* TAMPER to interfere, meddle, or tamper with something (*informal*) ○ *Who's been fiddling with my computer?* **3.** *vi* MOVE HANDS NERVOUSLY to move the hands or fingers nervously or restlessly, or play with something in the hands in this way ○ *The schoolboy fiddled nervously with his pencil.* **4.** *vi* PLAY VIOLIN to play the fiddle **5.** *vt* SWINDLE SOMEBODY to cheat a person or organization (*informal*) **6.** *vti* WASTE TIME to waste time doing unimportant things ○ *fiddle the day away* **7.** *vt* FALSIFY RECORDS to falsify something such as financial accounts, especially for dishonest personal gain (*informal*) [Pre-12C. < medieval Latin *vitula* "instrument played at festivals" < Latin *vitulari* "hold celebrations"]

fiddle around *vi* to waste time doing unimportant things (*informal*)

fid·dle·back /fídd'l bàk/, **fid·dle·back chair** *n* a chair with a back shaped like the body of a violin

fid·dle-de-dee /fídd'l dee deé/ *interj* used to express mild annoyance, disagreement, or impatience (*dated informal*) [Ending nonsensical]

fid·dle-fad·dle /fídd'l fàdd'l/ *n* NONSENSE nonsense or trifling matters (*informal*) ■ *interj* NONSENSE used to express the view that something is nonsense (*dated informal*) ■ *vi* (**fid·dle-fad·dled, fid·dle-fad·dling, fid·dle-fad·dles**) WASTE TIME to waste time with unimportant matters (*informal*) [Late 16C. < FIDDLE + *faddle* "nonsense"] —**fid·dle-fad·dler** *n*

fid·dle-foot·ed *adj US* **1.** showing excitability or nervousness **2.** having a tendency to roam

fiddlehead

fid·dle·head /fídd'l hèd/, **fid·dle·neck** /-nèk/ *n* **1.** the coiled frond of a young fern, often cooked and eaten as a delicacy **2.** an ornamental carving on a ship's bow, shaped like the scroll at the end of the fingerboard of a violin

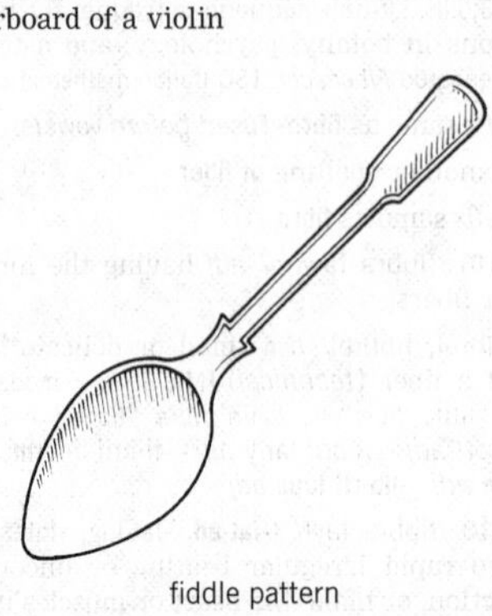

fiddle pattern

fid·dle pat·tern *n* the design of a fork or spoon with a handle that has a tapering wide end —**fid·dle-pat·tern** *adj*

fid·dler /fíddlər/ *n* **1.** VIOLIN PLAYER a player of the violin, especially in folk music **2.** TIME WASTER somebody who wastes time **3.** SOMEBODY WHO TOYS WITH SOMETHING somebody who aimlessly plays or fidgets with something **4.** SWINDLER a cheat or swindler (*informal*) **5.** MARINE BIOL same as **fiddler crab**

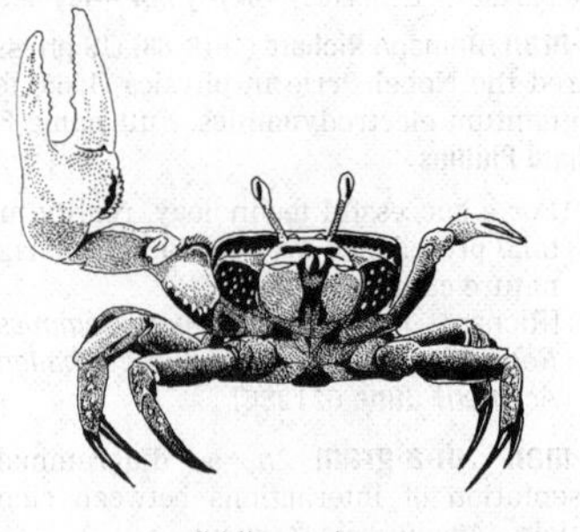

fiddler crab

fid·dler crab *n* a small burrowing sea crab. Males have one enlarged claw that they move like a violinist's arm as a signal during courtship. Genus: *Uca.*

fid·dle·stick /fídd'l stìk/ *n* (*informal*) **1.** a bow for playing a violin **2.** something that is unimportant or worthless ○ *I don't care a fiddlestick what you think.*

fid·dle·sticks /fídd'l stìks/ *interj* used to express mild annoyance, disagreement, or impatience (*dated informal*)

fid·dle·wood /fídd'l wòod/ *n* **1.** the hard wood of a tropical American tree **2.** a tree that yields fiddlewood. Native to: tropical America. Genus: *Citharexylum.*

fid·dling /fíddling/ *adj* petty or unimportant

fid·dly /fíddlee/ (**-dli·er, -dli·est**) *adj UK* difficult to do, handle, or use, usually because intricate work with the hands or small objects are involved (*informal*) ○ *Changing the battery in this type of watch can be quite a fiddly job.*

FIDE *abbr* CHESS World Chess Federation [French acronym < *Fédération Internationale des Échecs*]

Fi·dei De·fen·sor /fee dày ee də fén sàwr/ *n* HIST, CHR same as **Defender of the Faith** [< Latin]

fi·de·ism /fee day ìzzəm/ *n* the view that religious knowledge depends on faith and revelation [Late 19C. < Latin *fides* "faith"] —**fi·de·ist** *n* —**fi·de·is·tic** /fee day ístik/ *adj*

Fi·del·ism /fi dél ìzzəm/ *n* the practice or policies of Castroism [Mid-20C. After Fidel CASTRO]

fi·del·i·ty /fi déllətee/ *n* **1.** LOYALTY loyalty to an allegiance, promise, or vow **2.** SEXUAL FAITHFULNESS faithfulness to a sexual partner, especially a husband or wife **3.** FACTUAL ACCURACY accuracy in reporting facts or details **4.** ELECTRONICS PRECISION OF REPRODUCTION the extent to which an electronic device such as a stereo system or television accurately reproduces sound or images [15C. Directly or via French < Latin *fidelitas* "faithfulness" < *fides* "faith"]

fi·del·i·ty card *n US* a card issued by a business to customers or clients that rewards them for regular patronage with special benefits such as discounts and free gifts. Can term **loyalty card**

fidg·et /fíjjət/ *vi* (**-et·ed, -et·ing, -ets**) **1.** MOVE AROUND NERVOUSLY to move around in a restless, absent-minded, or uneasy manner **2.** FIDDLE NERVOUSLY to fiddle or play with something in a restless, absent-minded, or uneasy manner ○ *He kept fidgeting with his glasses as he spoke to her.* ■ *n* SOMEBODY WHO FIDGETS somebody who behaves in a restless, absent-minded, or uneasy manner ■ **fidg·ets** *npl* UNEASINESS a state of restlessness, absent-mindedness, or unease expressed by continual nervous movements ○ *He seems to have a case of the fidgets.* [Late 17C. < *fidge* "twitch, fidget," origin ?] —**fid·get·ing·ly** *adv*

fidg·et·y /fíjjətee/ *adj* **1.** tending to fidget **2.** restless or ill at ease —**fidg·et·i·ness** *n*

fi·do /fídō/ (*plural* **-dos**) *n US* a coin with a minting error [Mid-20C. Acronym < *freaks, irregulars, defects, and oddities*]

fi·du·cial /fi dóosh'l/ *adj* **1.** relating to or founded on trust or faith (*formal*) **2.** accepted or used as a standard of comparison, measurement, or reference

3\. LAW same as **fiduciary** *adj* (sense 2) [Late 16C. < late Latin *fiducialis* < Latin *fidere* "to trust"] —**fi·du·cial·ly** *adv*

fi·du·ci·ar·y /fi dóoshee èrree, fi dóoshəree/ *adj* **1.** RELATING TO RELATIONSHIP INVOLVING TRUSTEE relating to the relationship between a trustee and the person or body for whom the trustee acts **2.** RELATING TO TRUST relating to or based on a trust **3.** TRUSTING GOVERNMENT TO STAND BEHIND MONEY relating to or depending on confidence in a government for the value of fiat money ■ *n* (*plural* **-ies**) TRUSTEE a manager entrusted to control property or to act on behalf of and for the benefit of another [Late 16C. < Latin *fiduciarius* "(holding) in a trust" < *fidere* "to trust"] —**fi·du·ci·ar·i·ly** *adv*

fie /fī/ *interj* used to express disapproval of, or annoyance or disgust with, somebody or something (*archaic*) [14C. Via French *fi* < Latin, expressing disgust at a stench]

Library of Congress

Arthur Fiedler

Fied·ler /féedlər/, **Arthur** (1894–1979) US conductor. As director of the Boston Pops Orchestra (1930–79), he arranged programs that were a mixture of light classical music and popular tunes.

fief /feef/ *n* **1.** a piece of land formerly granted by a feudal lord to somebody in return for service **2.** POL same as **fiefdom** [Early 17C. Via French < Old French *feu* < medieval Latin *feudum* (see FEUD²)]

fief·dom /féefdəm/ *n* **1.** something, e.g., territory or a sphere of activity, that is controlled or dominated by a particular person or group **2.** the lands controlled by a feudal lord

field /feeld/ *n* **1.** AGRIC AREA OF AGRICULTURAL LAND an area of open ground, especially an area used to grow crops or graze livestock **2.** PLAYING AREA an open expanse of ground kept or marked off as a playing area for a particular sport **3.** GEOL AREA RICH IN RESOURCES an area of land or seabed that is rich in an exploitable natural resource ○ *a gas field* **4.** GEOG BROAD AREA OF SOMETHING an expanse of something such as ice, snow, or lava ○ *an ice field* **5.** AREA OF ACTIVITY an activity or subject, especially one that is somebody's particular responsibility, specialty, or interest **6.** PLACE OUTSIDE INSTITUTION the environment outside a workplace, office, school, or laboratory in which somebody has direct contact with clients, the public, or the phenomena being studied ○ *out in the field* **7.** MIL AREA OF MILITARY OPERATIONS the location of military operations **8.** MIL same as **battlefield** (sense 1) **9.** MIL same as **battle** *n* (sense 1) (*literary or archaic*) **10.** GROUP OF CONTESTANTS all the participants in a race or other competitive event **11.** ALL PARTICIPANTS EXCEPT LEADER all the participants in a race or competitive event except the leader, winner, or favorite ○ *five lengths ahead of the field* **12.** MATH SET OF MATHEMATICAL ELEMENTS a set of mathematical elements with two properties that are like addition and multiplication for ordinary numbers **13.** PHYS AREA OF FORCE an area or region within which a force exerts an influence at every point **14.** OPTICS same as **field of view** **15.** COMPUT STORAGE AREA FOR INFORMATION an area in a computer memory or program, or on a monitor screen, where information such as characters or numbers can be entered and manipulated **16.** HERALDRY BACKGROUND FOR DESIGN the background surface or color on which a design is displayed, e.g., on a flag, coin, or coat of arms ■ *v* (**field·ed, field·ing, fields**) **1.** *vt* SPORTS RETRIEVE BALL in baseball or cricket, to retrieve, pick up, or catch a ball in play, usually after it has been struck by the person batting **2.** *vi* SPORTS BE FIELDER in baseball or cricket, to act as a fielder **3.** *vt* SELECT SOMEBODY FOR COMPETITION to select a person, group, or team to participate in an event, especially a competitive event ○ *We did not have enough players to field a team.* **4.** *vt* DEPLOY GROUP to send out a large number of people or things to accomplish a task, especially to deploy military forces for action **5.** *vt* DEAL WITH QUESTION OR COMPLAINT to respond to something such as a question or complaint [Old English *feld* < Indo-European, "flat"] ◇ **play the field 1.** to be unwilling to commit to a sexual or romantic relationship with one person and prefer to date a number of people **2.**

Field /feeld/, **Cyrus West** (1819–92) US entrepreneur. He was responsible for the laying of the first successful transatlantic telephone cable (1866).

Field, David Dudley (1805–94) US lawyer and legal reformer. His code of US civil procedure was enacted in 1848.

> "The greatest achievement ever made in the cause of human progress is the total and final separation of church and state."
> [David Dudley Field, *Jurisprudence*; 1893]

Field, Eugene (1850–95) US writer. He is best known for his witty newspaper columns and poetry for children such as "Little Boy Blue" (1892).

Field, Marshall (1834–1906) US entrepreneur. From 1867 he headed the Chicago department store that was later to bear his name and that was noted for its innovative merchandising practices.

> "Give the lady what she wants!"
> [Attributed to Marshall Field]

Field, Stephen J. (1816–99) associate justice of the US Supreme Court (1863–97). His decisions were usually conservative. Full name **Field, Stephen Johnson**

field ar·til·ler·y *n* large guns that are mobile enough to be brought close to the front line

field burning *n* the agricultural practice of burning off large fields and range pasture in the late summer and early fall in the southwestern, Midwestern, western, and Pacific Northwest areas of the United States in order to stimulate grass regrowth or clear the ground

field coil *n* the coil of wire that, when carrying current, produces the magnetization inside an electrical motor or generator needed for it to operate

field corn *n* corn that is grown as feed for livestock

field day *n* **1.** TIME OF UNRESTRAINED ACTIVITY an opportunity for unrestrained activity ○ *If the slightest hint of this gets out, the press will have a field day.* ○ *had a field day shopping for new clothes* **2.** DAY FOR AMATEUR COMPETITIONS a day devoted to amateur outdoor sports and competitions, especially at a school **3.** DAY FOR OUTDOOR ACTIVITIES a day spent in outdoor activities **4.** *US* DAY FOR MILITARY SHOW a day devoted to military exercises and display, usually performed in front of spectators

field-ef·fect tran·sis·tor *n* a transistor, with three or more electrodes, in which the output current is controlled by a variable electric field

field e·mis·sion *n* the liberation of electrons from the surface of a metallic conductor subjected to a strong electric field

field·er /féeldər/ *n* in baseball or cricket, a player who is positioned on the field of play to catch or retrieve the ball when it is struck by the person batting

field·er's choice *n* in baseball, an attempt by a fielder to put out a base runner when the ball is hit, allowing the batter to reach first base safely

field e·vent *n* an athletic event in a track-and-field meet that takes place on an open area not on a track, e.g., the discus, javelin, long jump, or high jump

field·fare /féeld fèr/ (*plural* **-fares** or *same*) *n* a migratory thrush with reddish brown feathers, a gray head and rump, and a noisy call. Native to: Europe, Asia. Latin name: *Turdus pilaris.* [Assumed Old English *feldefare* "field dweller"]

field glass·es *npl* same as **binoculars**

field goal *n* **1.** in football, a score worth three points, made by kicking the ball over the crossbar from a point about ten yards behind the line of scrimmage **2.** in basketball, a goal made during normal play by throwing the ball through the basket. It is worth two points, or three points if scored from beyond a specific distance.

field-grade of·fi·cer *n* MIL same as **field officer**

field guide *n* an illustrated manual that is used to identify plants, animals, or birds in their natural habitats

field hand *n US regional, Can* a laborer on a farm

REGIONAL NOTE See ***hand.***

field hock·ey *n* a game played outdoors in which two teams of 11 players each use curved sticks to direct a ball into each other's netted goal

field hos·pi·tal *n* a center for medical treatment on a battlefield or in an isolated place

field house *n* **1.** a building equipped with storage facilities and dressing rooms for the use of sports teams **2.** a building containing a large space for athletic events, often with seating for spectators

Field·ing /féelding/, **Henry** (1707–54) British novelist and dramatist. He is considered to be a founder of the English novel, with *Joseph Andrews* (1742) and *Tom Jones* (1749).

> "It hath been often said, that it is not death, but dying, which is terrible."
> [Henry Fielding, *Amelia*; 1751]

field lens *n* the lens that is farthest from the eye in the compound eyepiece of an optical instrument

field mag·net *n* an electromagnet or permanent magnet that supplies the magnetic field in an electric machine

field mar·shal *n* an officer in the British Army and in some other armies of the highest rank

field mouse (sense 2)

field mouse *n* **1.** the most common North American vole. Genus: *Microtus.* **2.** *UK* a small mouse with large eyes and ears and a long tail that lives in fields and gardens. Native to: Europe, Asia. Genus: *Apodemus.*

field mush·room *n* a common edible mushroom. Latin name: *Agaricus campestris.*

field of·fi·cer *n* a military officer of middle rank, e.g., a major or colonel

field of fire *n UK* an area exposed to fire from a weapon or group of weapons

field of hon·or *n* a battlefield, or the site of a duel

field of view *n* the area in the eyepiece of an optical instrument in which the image is visible

field of vi·sion *n* the whole area that can be seen by the eyes when they are kept fixed in one direction

field pop·py *n* PLANTS same as **corn poppy**

W. C. Fields

Fields /feeldz/, **W. C.** (1880–1946) US actor and comedian. He is best known for his portrayal of irascible irresponsible characters struggling to keep one step ahead of the law. One of his most popular films is *My Little Chickadee* (1940). Born **Dukenfield, William Claude**

"It's a funny old world—a man's lucky to get out of it alive."
[W. C. Fields, *You're Telling Me*; 1934]

field sports *npl UK* outdoor country sports that involve killing or capturing animals, especially hunting, shooting, and fishing

field·stone /féeld stòn/ *n* a stone found in fields and used, often in unfinished form, for building

field·strip /féeld strìp/ (**-stripped, -strip·ping, -strips**) *vt US* to take apart a weapon for inspection or for cleaning, lubrication, or repair

field test *n* a test carried out on a product under normal conditions of use

field tri·al *n* **1.** INDUST same as **field test 2.** a competition to determine how well hunting dogs perform

field trip *n* a trip made by students or researchers to study something firsthand

field wind·ing *n* ELEC same as **field coil**

field·work /féeld wùrk/ *n* **1. WORK DONE OUTSIDE NORMAL PLACE** work undertaken outside the school, office, or laboratory in order to gain knowledge through direct contact and observation **2. SOCIAL RESEARCH AMONG POPULATION** social or anthropological research carried out among the subjects of the research, done by observing and interviewing them **3.** MIL **TEMPORARY FORTIFICATION** a temporary defensive earthwork or fortification —**field·work·er** *n*

fiend /feend/ *n* **1. DEVIL** an evil supernatural being, especially a devil from hell **2. SOMEBODY EVIL** somebody regarded as wicked or cruel **3.** *US* **TROUBLEMAKER** a mischievous or annoying person, especially a child ○ *Those little fiends ate all the cake!* **4. SOMEBODY WITH STRONG INTEREST** an ardent enthusiast of a subject or activity **5.** *US* **SOMEBODY PROFICIENT** somebody with a specialized skill or talent (*informal*) ○ *She's a real math fiend.* [Old English *fēond* "hated person, enemy" (hence "the enemy of everyone," the devil) < *fēogan* "to hate" < Germanic]

fiend·ish /féendish/ *adj* **1. DIABOLICAL** resembling a devil or demon **2. CUNNING AND MALICIOUS** characterized by devilish cunning, ingenuity, and malice **3. PERPLEXING** extremely difficult to solve or analyze **4. DISAGREEABLE** extremely bad or unpleasant (*informal*) ○ *fiendish weather* —**fiend·ish·ly** *adv* —**fiend·ish·ness** *n*

~~**fient**~~ incorrect spelling of **feint**

fierce /feerss/ (**fierc·er, fierc·est**) *adj* **1. AGGRESSIVE** characterized by or showing aggression or anger ○ *a fierce guard dog* **2. VIOLENT OR INTENSE** characterized by the violence or intensity of the forces, activity, or participants involved ○ *It was a fierce battle.* ○ *a fierce storm* **3. PROFOUND** deeply and intensely felt and often aggressively expressed ○ *He felt a fierce loyalty to his family.* [13C. Via Anglo-Norman *fers* "brave, proud, hostile" < Latin *ferus* "wild, untamed"] —**fierce·ly** *adv* —**fierce·ness** *n*

fi·er·i fa·ci·as /fì ə rī fáyshee əss/ *n* a legal document that authorizes a sheriff to sell enough of a debtor's property to settle the claim of a creditor [< Latin, "you should cause to be done"]

fier·y /fí əree, fíree/ (**-i·er, -i·est**) *adj* **1. GLOWING HOT** burning or full of fire **2. RED** bright red in color **3. SHOWING INTENSE EMOTION** full of or prone to sudden extremes of emotions **4. SPICY** extremely hot or spicy to the taste **5. INFLAMED** red and inflamed —**fier·i·ly** *adv* —**fier·i·ness** *n*

fier·y cross *n* **1.** formerly, in the Scottish Highlands, a burning wooden cross, carried by runners to call men to arms **2.** in the United States, a burning wooden cross adopted as a symbol of the Ku Klux Klan

fi·es·ta /fee éstə/ *n* **1.** a celebration or festival linked to a religious holiday, especially in a Spanish-speaking country **2.** an event in celebration of something [Mid-19C. Via Spanish < Latin *festum* "feast, festival"]

FIFA /féefə/ *n* the governing organization of international soccer [French acronym < *Fédération Internationale de Football Association*]

fife /fīf/ *n* a small high-pitched flute without keys, often used in military and marching bands [Mid-16C. Via German *Pfeife* or French *fifre* "fife, fife player" < assumed Vulgar Latin *pipa* < Latin *pipare* "to peep, chirp"] —**fif·er** *n*

Fife /fīf/ council area in east central Scotland. Area: 511 sq. mi./1,323 sq. km.

fife rail *n* a low rail around the lower part of the mast of a sailing ship, with belaying pins to which running rigging is attached [Origin ?]

FIFO /fí fò/ *abbr* ACCT first in, first out

fif·teen /fif téen/ *n* **1. 15** the number 15 **2. SOMETHING WITH VALUE OF 15** something in a numbered series with a value of 15 **3. GROUP OF 15** a group of 15 objects or people **4. 15** MOVIES, MEDIA **UK MOVIE RATING** in the United Kingdom, a rating given to movies and videos considered unsuitable for those under the age of fifteen [Old English *fīftēne* < *fīf* "five" + *-tēne* (< Germanic, "ten")] —**fif·teen** *adj, pron*

fif·teenth /fif téenth/ *n* one of 15 equal parts of something —**fif·teenth** *adj, adv*

fifth /fifth/ *n* **1. ONE OF 5 PARTS OF SOMETHING** one of five equal parts of something **2. 5 IN SERIES** item number five in a series **3. MEASURE OF LIQUOR** a fifth part of a gallon of alcoholic liquor **4.** MUSIC **5-NOTE INTERVAL** in a diatonic scale, an interval stretching from one note to another five notes higher, or the sound made when both these notes are played simultaneously **5.** MUSIC same as **dominant** *n* (sense 1) **6.** AUTOMOT **5TH GEAR** in some cars or motor vehicles, the fifth gear **7.** BALLET same as **fifth position** [Old English *fīfta* < *fīf* (see FIVE)] —**fifth** *adj, adv*

Fifth *n US* same as **Fifth Amendment** (*informal*) ◇ **take the Fifth** to refuse to answer an awkward or self-incriminating question

Fifth A·mend·ment *n* an amendment to the US Constitution stating, among other things, that defendants or witnesses in criminal trials need not testify against themselves and may not be subjected to double jeopardy

fifth col·umn *n* a secret or subversive group that seeks to undermine the efforts of others and promote its own ends [Originally, a group of supporters that General Mola claimed to have inside Madrid during the Spanish Civil War, in addition to the four columns of his army besieging the city] —**fifth col·um·nist** *n*

fifth-gen·er·a·tion *adj* describes a highly advanced and as yet undeveloped level of computer technology, incorporating artificial intelligence

fifth·ly /fífthlee/ *adv* used to introduce the fifth point in an argument or discussion

fifth po·si·tion *n* in ballet, a position in which the feet are turned outward with the heel of the front foot level with and touching the base of the big toe of the back foot

fifth wheel *n* **1.** somebody or something whose presence is superfluous or unwanted **2.** same as **spare tire** (sense 1) **3.** a horizontal bearing that allows a vehicle's front axle to swivel left or right relative to its body, or that allows a trailer attached to a tractor vehicle to pivot

fif·ti·eth /fiftee əth/ *n* **1. ONE OF 50 PARTS** one of 50 equal parts of something **2. 50 IN SERIES** item number 50 in a series **3. 50TH BIRTHDAY** somebody's 50th birthday —**fif·ti·eth** *adj, adv*

fif·ty /fíftee/ *n* (*plural* **-ties**) **1. 50** the number 50 **2. GROUP OF 50** a group of 50 objects or people ■ **fif·ties** *npl* **1. NUMBERS 50 TO 59** the numbers 50 to 59, particularly as a range of Fahrenheit temperatures ○ *in the low fifties* **2. YEARS FROM 50 TO 59** the years from 50 to 59 in a century **3. PERIOD FROM AGE 50 TO 59** the period of somebody's life from the age of 50 to 59 [Old English *fīftig* < FIVE + *-tig* "ten"] —**fif·ty** *adj, pron*

fif·ty-fif·ty *adv* in two equally divided parts or shares ○ *We'll split the profits fifty-fifty.* ■ *adj* equally likely that either of two possibilities may come about ○ *a fifty-fifty chance*

fig

fig[1] /fig/ *n* **1.** a pear-shaped fruit with sweet flesh and many seeds, often preserved or dried **2.** a tree that produces figs. Native to: tropical and subtropical regions. Latin name: *Ficus carica.* [13C. Via Old French *figue* < Latin *ficus*] ◇ **not give** *or* **care a fig for somebody** *or* **something** not to care about somebody or something at all

fig[2] /fig/ *n* the way somebody is dressed, usually in particularly grand or formal clothing (*archaic*) [Mid-19C. < variant of archaic *feague* "beat, work at briskly," origin ?]

fig. *abbr* **1.** figurative **2.** figure

fig·gy duff /fíggee-/ *n Can* in Newfoundland, a boiled pudding containing raisins [< FIG[1] in dialect sense "raisin"]

fight /fīt/ *v* (**fought** /fawt/, **fought, fight·ing, fights**) **1.** *vti* **USE VIOLENCE** to use violent physical means such as blows with fists or a weapon to try to overpower somebody **2.** *vti* **GO TO WAR** to go to war, or engage in armed conflict with another country, force, or group **3.** *vi* **TAKE PART IN WAR** to take part in a war or battle, e.g., as a member or unit of the armed forces involved in it **4.** *vt* **CARRY ON BATTLE OR CONTEST** to enter into or carry on a battle or other contest such as an election or court case **5.** *vi* **STRUGGLE DETERMINEDLY** to make a strenuous effort to do, obtain, achieve, or defend something **6.** *vti* **OPPOSE SOMETHING** to make vigorous efforts to oppose, resist, or overcome something or somebody ○ *fight injustice* **7.** *vi* **ARGUE** to quarrel with somebody or with each other **8.** *vti* **BOX AGAINST SOMEBODY** to take part in a boxing match against somebody ■ *n* **1. VIOLENT ENCOUNTER** a conflict between individual people or groups in which each tries to do physical harm to, or defeat, the other **2. MAJOR EFFORT** a determined attempt to achieve something or resist something or somebody **3. VERBAL CONFRONTATION** a verbal dispute or quarrel **4. PROPENSITY TO FIGHT** the ability or willingness to continue a battle or struggle ○ *We've still got a lot of fight left in us.* **5. BOXING MATCH** a boxing match or similar contest [Old English *feohtan* "to fight" < W Germanic] —**fight·a·ble** *adj* ◇ **fight it out** to fight or argue until a decisive result is obtained ◇ **fight shy of something** to try to avoid something

SYNONYMS ***fight, battle, war, conflict, engagement, skirmish, clash***

CORE MEANING: a struggle between opposing armed forces

fight a physical struggle between individual people or groups such as battalions or armies ○ *During the fight, the soldier overpowered the guard and captured his rifle.* ○ *The fight for the village was part of an operation against rebel resistance.* **battle** a large-scale fight between armed forces involving combat between armies, warships, or aircraft ○ *killed in the Battle of the Bulge* ○ *Her brother was one of the casualties of the land battle.* **war** a period of hostile relations between countries, states, or factions that leads to fighting between armed forces, especially in land, air, or sea battles ○ *at the outbreak of war* ○ *a long-running civil war* ○ *the war years* ○ *the post-war period* **conflict** warfare between opposing forces, especially a prolonged and bitter but sporadic struggle ○ *an end to bloody conflict in the region* ○ *a border conflict with sporadic troop clashes* ○ *armed conflict* **engagement** a hostile encounter involving military forces ○ *Planes attacked artillery and command sites in the largest military engagement of the war to date.* **skirmish** an incident where fighting breaks out briefly between two small groups, sometimes as part of a larger battle ○ *a skirmish with guerrillas in which several men were killed* ○ *The last skirmish in the three-day battle came just after midnight.* **clash** a short fierce encounter with another person or group, often involving physical combat ○ *tried to avoid a clash of arms* ○ *The meeting was marred by a clash between the demonstrators and security guards.*

fight back *v* **1.** *vi* GET BACK AT SOMEBODY to resist or retaliate when attacked **2.** *vi* COUNTERATTACK to counterattack or make a determined effort to recover after initial defeat or difficulty ○ *They fought back from being down 15 points to win the game.* **3.** *vt* RESTRAIN TEARS OR EMOTION to suppress something such as tears or the outward expression of an emotion or impulse

fight off *vt* **1.** to drive away or resist an attacker **2.** to make an effort not to succumb to something such as an illness or an unpleasant feeling

fight·er /fítər/ *n* **1.** ATTACKING AIRCRAFT a fast armed military aircraft designed principally to attack enemy aircraft **2.** VERY DETERMINED PERSON a determined person who struggles to achieve or resist something **3.** SOLDIER somebody who fights, especially as a soldier **4.** BOXER a competitor in a boxing match

fight·er-bomb·er *n* an aircraft designed to combine the roles of fighter and bomber

fight·ing chair /fíting-/ *n US* a chair attached to the deck of an oceangoing fishing boat for an angler to sit in while struggling to bring large game fish to the boat

fight·ing chance *n* a possibility of success, but only with sustained effort

fight·ing cock *n UK* same as **gamecock**

fighting fish

fight·ing fish *n* a small brightly colored, highly aggressive freshwater fish with long flowing fins, often kept in aquariums. Native to: Southeast Asia. Genus: *Betta*.

fight-or-flight re·ac·tion *n* a set of physiological changes, including an increase in heart rate, blood pressure, and the flow of adrenaline, that constitutes the body's instinctive response to impending danger or other stress

fig leaf *n* **1.** a stylized representation of a leaf of the fig tree, formerly used as a covering for the genitals in painting or sculpture **2.** an unconvincing or inadequate attempt to conceal something considered shameful or wrong

fig·ment /fígmənt/ *n* something produced by or only existing in somebody's imagination [15C. < Latin *figmentum* "formation, figure, creation" < *fingere* "to form, shape"]

Fi·gue·res Ol·sen /fi gáyrəss ólss'n/, **José María** (*b.* 1954) president of Costa Rica (1994–98). The son of former president José María Figueres Ferrer, he became the youngest leader in Latin America when he won the 1994 election.

fig·ur·al /fíggyərəl/ *adj* ARTS same as **figurative** (sense 2)

fig·u·rant /fíggyərənt/ *n* a male ballet dancer who does not perform solo [Late 18C. < French, present participle of *figurer* "represent" < Latin *figura* (see FIGURE)]

fig·u·rante /fíggyə raánt, fíggyə raántee/ *n* a female ballet dancer who does not perform solo [Late 18C. < French, form of *figurant* (see FIGURANT)]

fig·u·ra·tion /fíggyə ráysh'n/ *n* **1.** FIGURATIVE REPRESENTATION OF SOMETHING a depiction of something in emblematic or allegorical form **2.** MUSIC USE OF MUSICAL FIGURES AS EMBELLISHMENT the use of musical figures or other ornaments to embellish or vary a theme **3.** ARTS GIVING SOMETHING FIGURATIVE FORM the process of giving allegorical or emblematic form to something abstract, especially by representing it using human or animal figures

fig·u·ra·tive /fíggyərətiv/ *adj* **1.** NOT LITERAL using or containing a nonliteral sense of a word or words **2.** REPRESENTATIONAL relating to or representing form in art by means of human or animal figures **3.** REPRESENTING BY ALLEGORICAL FIGURES using an allegorical or emblematic human or animal figure to represent an abstract idea or quality —**fig·u·ra·tive·ly** *adv* —**fig·u·ra·tive·ness** *n*

fig·ure /fíggyər/ *n* **1.** SYMBOL REPRESENTING NUMBER a symbol representing something other than a letter of the alphabet, especially a number **2.** AMOUNT EXPRESSED NUMERICALLY an amount or value expressed as a number **3.** SOMEBODY'S BODY SHAPE the shape of an individual human body, especially with regard to its slimness or attractiveness **4.** ARTS REPRESENTATION a representation of a human being in a picture or sculpture **5.** HUMAN SHAPE SEEN INDISTINCTLY a human shape seen in outline or indistinctly or that is unidentified **6.** SOMEBODY WITHIN PARTICULAR CONTEXT a person, especially with regard to status within a context, e.g., in history or in a community or profession ○ *She was a prominent figure in her community.* **7.** SOMEBODY SERVING AS EXAMPLE somebody regarded as having qualities that exemplify a particular role in life (*usually used in combination*) ○ *a father figure* **8.** WAY SOMEBODY APPEARS TO OTHERS the general impression somebody makes on other people **9.** PUBL ILLUSTRATIVE DRAWING OR DIAGRAM an illustrative drawing or diagram in a book or article **10.** SHAPE OR OUTLINE OF SOMETHING something represented by a shape or outline **11.** MATH GEOMETRIC FORM any two- or three-dimensional geometric form consisting of points, lines, curves, or planes **12.** HANDICRAFT PATTERN OR DESIGN a pattern or design, especially on cloth or wood **13.** DANCE, ICE SKATING DANCE OR SKATING ROUTINE a sequence of movements performed by dancers or ice-skaters in a routine **14.** MUSIC GROUP OF MUSICAL NOTES a short progression of musical notes that produces a single distinct impression **15.** LOGIC FORM OF SYLLOGISM the form of a syllogism in Aristotelian logic as determined by the position of the middle term ■ **figures** *npl* MATHEMATICAL CALCULATIONS calculations involving numbers (*informal*) ■ *v* (**-ured, -ur·ing, -ures**) **1.** *vi* BE INCLUDED IN SOMETHING to appear, take part, or be included in something ○ *did not figure in the outcome* **2.** *vt US* BELIEVE OR CONCLUDE to believe or come to the conclusion that something is the case (*informal*) ○ *She figured he must have been telling the truth.* **3.** *vt US* BELIEVE SOMEBODY TO BE SOMETHING to believe somebody or something to be a particular type ○ *I had him figured for a lawyer.* **4.** *vt* IMAGINE SOMETHING to form an idea about or envision something ○ *The way I figure it, she must have seen the guy somewhere before.* **5.** *vti US* BE UNSURPRISING to be or happen as expected ○ *It just figures they'd show up late.* **6.** *vti US* MATH CALCULATE to use mathematical calculations to work out an amount or value [13C. Via French < Latin *figura* "form, shape, figure" < *fingere* "make, shape"] ◇ **cut a fine** *or* **sorry figure** to look impressive *or* unimpressive ◇ **go figure** used to indicate that you think a situation you have described is odd or hard to comprehend (*slang*)

figure in *vt US* to take something into account ○ *She failed to figure in all the consequences.*

figure on *vt* to plan or assume that something should or will happen ○ *We can figure on running a loss this year.*

figure out *vt* **1.** to find a solution or explanation for something **2.** to reach a decision or conclusion about something

SYNONYMS See ***deduce***.

fig·ured /fíggyərd/ *adj* decorated with a design or pattern

fig·ured bass *n* a bass part of a musical composition, typically baroque or classical, in which the notes have numbers written above them to indicate which chords to play

fig·ure eight, fig·ure of eight *n* **1.** an outline of the number eight formed with two loops and one continuous line, e.g., in figure skating or aerobatics **2.** a knot formed by passing one end of a cord or rope through a loop formed on another part of it, forming the shape of the number eight

fig·ure·head /fíggyər hèd/ *n* **1.** a carving, usually of a full- or half-length human figure, built into the bow of a sailing ship **2.** the apparent head of an organization or institution who has no real responsibility or authority

fi·gure of eight *n* same as **figure eight**

fig·ure of mer·it *n* a parameter or characteristic of a machine, component, or instrument that is used as a measure of its performance

fig·ure of speech *n* an expression or use of language in a nonliteral sense in order to achieve a particular effect. Metaphors, similes, and hyperbole are all common figures of speech.

fig·ure skat·ing *n* a form of competitive skating in which skaters trace patterns on the ice and perform spins, jumps, and other maneuvers —**fig·ure skat·er** *n*

fig·u·rine /fíggyə reén/ *n* a small ornamental figure, often of ceramic or metal [Mid-19C. Via French < Italian *figurina* "small figure" < Latin *figura* (see FIGURE)]

fig wasp *n* a wasp that breeds in caprifigs and pollinates the flowers of wild fig trees. Native to: Europe. Genus: *Blastophaga*.

fig·wort /fíg wùrt, -wàwrt/ (*plural* **-worts** *or same*) *n* a tall woodland plant of the snapdragon family. Flowers: small, greenish, in clusters. Genus: *Scrophularia*. [Mid-16C. < FIG[1] as dialect term for hemorrhoids, which it was used to treat]

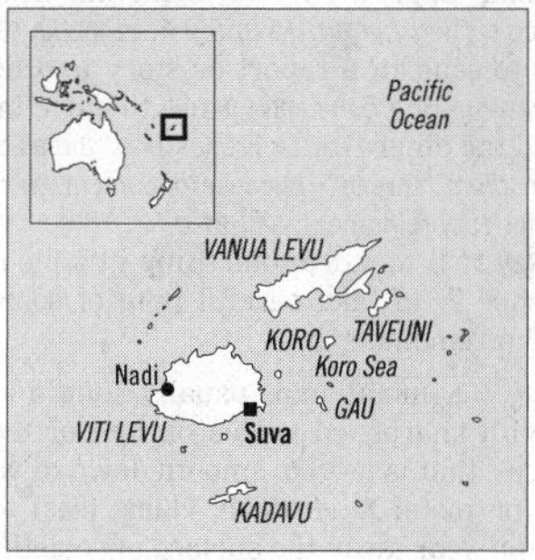

Fiji

Fi·ji /feéjee/ island nation in the southern Pacific Ocean north of New Zealand and east of northern Australia. A British colony from 1874, it gained its independence in 1970. Having left the British Commonwealth in 1987, it rejoined in 1997. Language: English. Currency: Fijian dollar. Capital: Suva. Population: 868,531 (2003). Area: 7,095 sq. mi./18,376 sq. km. Official name **Republic of Fiji**

Fi·ji·an /feéjee ən, fi jeé ən/ *n* **1.** a language spoken on the islands of Fiji, belonging to the eastern branch of the Austronesian family of languages. Native speakers: 400,000. **2.** somebody who comes from Fiji —**Fi·ji·an** *adj*

filagree incorrect spelling of **filigree**

fil·a·ment /fílləmənt/ *n* **1.** SLENDER STRAND OR FIBER a slender strand or fiber of a material **2.** ELEC ENG WIRE CONDUCTOR IN LIGHT BULB a thin wire that produces light in an incandescent bulb or emits electrons in a vacuum tube when electricity passes through it **3.** BOT FLOWER PART the stalk that supports the pollen-bearing anther in the male reproductive organ (**stamen**) of a flower **4.** MICROBIOL LONG STRAND OF CELLS a long strand of similar cells joined end to end, as found in some bacteria and algae [Late 16C. < French, or modern Latin *filamentum* < Latin *filum* "thread"] —**fil·a·men·ta·ry** /fìllə méntəree/ *adj*—**fil·a·men·tous** /-təss/ *adj*

fil·a·ree /fìllə ree, fìllə reé/ *n US* PLANTS same as **alfilaria**

fi·lar·i·a /fi lérree ə/ (*plural* **-ae** /fi lérree eè/ or *same*) *n* a parasitic worm that is carried as a larva by biting insects and lives as an adult in the blood or tissues of vertebrates, causing filariasis. Family: Filaridae. [Mid-19C. < modern Latin *Filaria* < Latin *filum* "thread"] —**fi·lar·i·al** *adj* —**fi·lar·i·an** *adj*

fil·a·ri·a·sis /fìllə rī́ əssiss/ *n* a disease caused by parasitic worms (**filaria**) that inflames and obstructs the lymphatic glands, sometimes resulting in elephantiasis

fil·a·ture /fíllə chòor, fílləchər/ *n* **1. REELING OF SILK FROM COCOONS** the process of reeling silk fibers from cocoons **2. SILK REEL** a spool used in filature **3. SILK FACTORY** a factory that reels silk fibers [Mid-18C. Via French < Italian *filatura* < Latin *filum* "thread"]

fil·bert /fílbərt/ (*plural* **-berts** or *same*) *n* **1.** FOOD same as **hazelnut 2.** TREES same as **hazel** (sense 2) [14C. < Anglo-Norman *philbert*, after St. *Philibert*, whose feast day falls in August, when hazelnuts begin to ripen]

filch /filch/ (**filched, filch·ing, filch·es**) *vt* to steal something opportunistically, usually a small item or amount of little value (*informal*) [13C. Origin ?] —**filch·er** *n*

SYNONYMS See ***steal***.

file[1] /fīl/ *n* **1. STORAGE FOR PAPERS** a folder, cabinet, or other container that holds papers for convenient storage and reference **2. ORDERED COLLECTION** a collection of related documents or papers arranged so that they can be consulted easily **3.** COMPUT **COMPUTER INFORMATION** a uniquely named collection of program instructions or data stored on a hard drive, disk, or other storage medium and treated as a single entity **4. LINE** a line of people or things standing or moving one behind the other ■ *v* (**filed, fil·ing, files**) **1.** *vt* **STORE SOMETHING IN ORDER** to arrange and store something in a file for future reference **2.** *vt* LAW **SUBMIT SOMETHING** to submit something such as a claim or complaint to the appropriate authority so that it can be put on record **3.** *vi* LAW **BRING LAWSUIT** to make a formal application for something such as a divorce ○ *filed for bankruptcy* **4.** *vt* MEDIA **SEND IN NEWS REPORT** to send in a report or story to a newspaper or news agency **5.** *vi* **MOVE IN LINE** to move in line one behind the other [15C. < French *filer* "thread on a string" < Latin *filum* "thread"; because documents were hung on string for easy reference] —**fil·er** *n*

file away *vt* **1.** to store something in a file for future reference **2.** to take careful note of something in order to remember it

file[2] /fīl/ *n* a metal tool, usually long and narrow and with sharpened ridges on one or more of its surfaces, that is used to smooth down or wear away wood or metal ■ *vti* (**filed, fil·ing, files**) to smooth down or wear away the surface of something using a file [Old English *fēol* < Indo-European, "cut, carve"]

fi·lé /feé lày, fi láy/ *n* a powder made from the ground leaves of the sassafras tree that is used in Cajun cooking to thicken and flavor soups, gumbos, and other dishes [Mid-19C. < French, past participle of *filer* "twist" < Latin *filum* "thread"]

file al·lo·ca·tion ta·ble *n* COMPUT full form of **FAT**

file cab·i·net *n* COMM same as **filing cabinet**

file clerk *n* an employee in an office who stores and retrieves documents and other records

file ex·ten·sion *n* a set of characters following the period after the name of a DOS file, identifying the file type

file·fish /fíl fish/ (*plural same* or **-fish·es**) *n* a long bony fish with rough-edged scales, a tiny mouth, and a sharp dorsal spine over the eye. Native to: tropics. Family: Balistidae.

file for·mat *n* the pattern and convention by which a computer program stores information in a file

File·gate /fíl gàyt/ *n* a scandal in the Clinton White House involving the alleged improper acquisition and use by Clinton staffers of FBI background files of people with access to the White House property (*slang*)

file man·ag·er *n* a computer program that arranges and manipulates files and directories

file·name /fíl nàym/ *n* a set of characters, sometimes restricted in number, serving as an identifying title for a computer file and often including a file extension

file serv·er *n* a computer in a network that stores application programs and data files accessed by other computers

fi·let FOOD *n* another spelling of **fillet** *n* (sense 1) ■ *vt* another spelling of **fillet** *v* (sense 1)

fi·let cro·chet /fi láy, feè lày/ *n* crochet in the form of a square mesh stitched with a double crochet stitch, in which the combination of holes and filled-in squares creates the pattern [< French]

fi·let mi·gnon /fi lày meen yáwN, feè lày-/ *n* a small round boneless beefsteak cut from the inside of the loin and usually grilled, fried, or broiled [< French, "dainty fillet"]

fil·i·al /fíllee əl/ *adj* **1.** relating or appropriate to a child's relationship with, or feelings toward, his or her parents ○ *filial duty* **2.** GENETICS describes the first generation that results from crossing two parental lines [15C. Directly or via Old French < late Latin *filialis* "of a son or daughter" < Latin *filius* "son," *filia* "daughter"] —**fil·i·al·ly** *adv* —**fil·ial·ness** *n*

fil·i·ate /fíllee àyt/ (**-at·ed, -at·ing, -ates**) *vt* to determine the paternity of a child in a court of law, especially an illegitimate child [Late 18C. < medieval Latin *filiat-*, past participle of *filiare* "acknowledge as your child" < *filius* "son," *filia* "daughter"]

fil·i·a·tion /fíllee áysh'n/ *n* **1.** the process of determining legally who is the father of a child whose paternity is in dispute **2.** the condition of being the child of particular parents (*formal*) [15C. Via Old French < medieval Latin *filiation-* "relationship as a child" < Latin *filius* "son," *filia* "daughter"]

fil·i·bus·ter /fílli bùstər/ *n* **1. POLITICAL DELAYING TACTIC** a tactic used to delay or prevent the passage of legislation, e.g., a long irrelevant speech **2.** POL **LEGISLATIVE OBSTRUCTOR** an obstructor of the passage of legislation **3.** *US* MIL **MILITARY ADVENTURER** a mercenary or irregular in a revolutionary army of a foreign country ■ *v* (**-tered, -ter·ing, -ters**) **1.** *vti* **TRY TO BLOCK LEGISLATION WITH FILIBUSTER** to try to stop legislation being passed by making long speeches **2.** *vi US* MIL **BE A MILITARY ADVENTURER ABROAD** to serve as a mercenary or irregular in a revolutionary army of a foreign country [Mid-19C. Via Spanish *filibustero* < Dutch *vrijbuiter* "pirate"] —**fil·i·bus·ter·er** *n* —**fil·i·bus·ter·ism** *n* —**fil·i·bus·ter·ous** *adj*

fil·i·cide /fílli sīd/ *n* (*formal*) **1.** the killing by a parent of a son or daughter **2.** a parent who kills his or her own son or daughter [Mid-17C. < Latin *filius* "son," *filia* "daughter"] —**fil·i·cid·al** /fílli sīd'l/ *adj*

fil·i·form /fílli fàwrm, fíli-/ *adj* long, thin, and fine like a thread [Mid-18C. < Latin *filum* "thread"]

filigree: detail of decorative filigree and jeweled medieval book cover (1225–30)

fil·i·gree /fílli greè/ *n* **1. LACY METAL ORNAMENTATION** delicate decorative openwork made from thin twisted wire in silver, gold, or another metal **2. DELICATE WORK** a delicate ornamental tracery ■ *vt* (**-greed, -gree·ing, -grees**) **FORM SOMETHING INTO DELICATE PATTERN** to form something into a delicate ornamental openwork design [Late 17C. Alteration of French *filigrane* < Italian *filigrana* < Latin *filum* "thread" + *granum* "grain"] —**fil·i·gree** *adj*

fil·ing[1] /fíling/ *n* the activity of storing files in their proper place

fil·ing[2] /fíling/ *n* a tiny particle or shaving of metal, e.g., one removed with a file (*often used in the plural*) ○ *iron filings*

fil·ing cab·i·net *n* a piece of office furniture containing drawers for storing files

fil·ing clerk *n UK* same as **file clerk**

fil·ing sys·tem *n* a method of organizing office files, especially one that identifies and organizes the major headings under which documents are to be filed

fil·i·o·pi·e·tis·tic /fìllee ō pī ə tístik/ *adj* having great reverence for ancestors (*formal*) [Late 19C. < Latin *filius* "son," *filia* "daughter"]

Fil·i·pi·no /fìllə peénō/, **Pil·i·pi·no** /pìllə-/ *adj* **OF THE PHILIPPINES** relating to the Philippines, or their languages, peoples, or cultures ■ *n* (*plural* **-nos**) **1.** LANG **OFFICIAL LANGUAGE OF THE PHILIPPINES** the official language of the Philippines, an Austronesian language based on Tagalog. Native speakers: 15 million. **2.** PEOPLES **SOMEBODY FROM THE PHILIPPINES** somebody who comes from the Philippines [Late 19C. < Spanish < (*las islas*) *Filipinas* "the Philippines"]

fill /fil/ *v* (**filled, fill·ing, fills**) **1.** *vti* **MAKE SOMETHING FULL OR BECOME FULL** to make a container full, or become full ○ *The bathtub filled rapidly.* **2.** *vt* **TAKE UP ALL THE SPACE** to take up the space inside or cover the surface area of something ○ *The room was filled with light.* **3.** *vt* **COVER BLANK AREA** to cover a page or a blank space on a page with writing or drawing **4.** *vt* **BECOME ABUNDANT** to become present and very noticeable throughout something ○ *The scent of spring filled the air.* **5.** *vti* **MAKE SOMEBODY FEEL POWERFUL EMOTION** to cause somebody to experience a strong emotion, usually to the exclusion of all others, or be taken over by a strong emotion ○ *The news filled me with dread.* **6.** *vt* **CLOSE UP HOLE** to plug a hole, crack, or cavity in something **7.** *vt* **MEET NEED** to satisfy a need or requirement ○ *The retreat filled her need for solitude.* **8.** *vt* **OCCUPY FREE TIME** to occupy a period of time with an activity ○ *They filled their days with busywork until she returned.* **9.** *vt* **PROVIDE SOMETHING** to carry out somebody's instructions to supply something ○ *fill a prescription* **10.** *vt* **HOLD OFFICE** to hold a job or office and carry out the duties associated with it **11.** *vt* **CHOOSE SOMEBODY** to elect or appoint somebody to a vacant job or position **12.** *vt* COOK **PUT FILLING INTO SOMETHING** to put a type of food into something such as a cake or sandwich as its filling **13.** *vt* CONSTR **ADD SOMETHING TO RAISE SURFACE LEVEL** to build up the surface of something with earth, stones, or other materials until it reaches a desired level **14.** *vti* **POWER SAIL WITH WIND** to stretch a sail and make it bulge, or bulge under the pressure of the wind ■ *n* **1. PLENTY OF SOMETHING** a sufficient or excessive quantity of something ○ *I've had my fill of his complaints.* **2. ENOUGH TO MAKE CONTAINER FULL** enough of something to fill a container, or the act of filling a container **3. MATERIAL TO RAISE SURFACE** material used to build up the surface of something to a desired level, e.g., earth or stones **4.** MUSIC **IMPROVISED MUSIC** music improvised to fill designated spaces in a jazz or other musical score [Old English *fyllan* < Germanic]

fill in *v* **1.** *vt* **COLOR BLANK SPACE ON SOMETHING** to cover a blank space on something with coloring or shading **2.** *vt* **PLUG CAVITY AND MAKE SURFACE LEVEL** to put material into a cavity in a surface to make the surface level **3.** *vt* **OCCUPY TIME** to spend a period of time that would otherwise be unoccupied in an activity **4.** *vi* **BE SUBSTITUTE FOR SOMEBODY** to act as a substitute for somebody **5.** *vt* **GIVE SOMEBODY INFORMATION** to supply somebody with new or necessary information about something

fill out *v* **1.** *vt* to write information into the blank spaces on a form or document **2.** *vti* to become larger and more substantial, or make something larger and more substantial

fill up *v* **1.** *vti* **BECOME OR MAKE SOMETHING FULL** to become full, or make something full **2.** *vt* **SATISFY SOMEBODY'S HUNGER** to give somebody the feeling of having eaten enough **3.** *vi* AUTOMOT **MAKE FUEL TANK FULL** to fill a vehicle's tank with fuel

fille de joie /feè də zhwaá/ (*plural* **filles de joie** /feè də zhwaá, feèz də zhwaá/) *n* a woman prostitute (*euphemistic*) [< French, "girl of pleasure"]

filled gold *n US* a thin layer of gold bonded to a backing layer of brass or other base metal. Can term **rolled gold**

fill·er /fíllər/ *n* **1.** SOMETHING THAT FILLS somebody who or something that fills something **2.** PLUGGING OR COATING SUBSTANCE a substance used to plug a crack or cavity or smooth a surface **3.** SUBSTANCE ADDED FOR BULK a substance that is used to fill spaces or add bulk or strength to a material, e.g., sizing **4.** MEDIA, BROADCAST LESS IMPORTANT MATERIAL something, often relatively unimportant, added to fill space or time, e.g., in a newspaper or broadcast **5.** TOBACCO FILLING the tobacco inside a cigar or cigarette **6.** INDUST PADDING a material that is used to stuff something such as a quilt or toy, e.g., cotton or down

fil·lér /fí lèr/ *n* a subunit of Hungarian currency. See table at **currency** [Early 20C. < Hungarian]

fil·let /fíllit/; *of food* /fi láy/ *n* **1.** *also* **fi·let** FOOD BONELESS PORTION OF FISH OR MEAT a boneless portion cut from a fish, a poultry breast, or the rib area of beef, lamb, or pork **2.** CLOTHING RIBBON WORN AROUND THE HEAD a ribbon worn across the forehead, as an ornament or to hold back the hair **3.** ARCHIT FLAT NARROW MOLDING a raised or sunken ornamental surface set between larger surfaces **4.** PRINTING DECORATIVE LINE ON THE COVER OF BOOK a thin decorative line impressed onto the cover of a book, or the tool used to make it ■ *vt* **(-let·ed, -let·ing, -lets) 1.** *also* **fi·let** FOOD PREPARE BONELESS PORTION to cut and prepare boneless portions of fish, poultry, or meat **2.** USE BINDING OR DECORATION to bind hair or decorate a surface with a fillet [14C. < Old French *filet* < Latin *filum* "thread"]

fill-in *n* a temporary replacement or substitute for somebody

fill·ing /fílling/ *n* **1.** DENT PLUG FOR DECAYED TOOTH a plug made of metal or composite material used to fill a tooth cavity **2.** GETTING SOMETHING FILLED the process or an instance of having something such as a cavity in a tooth filled **3.** SUBSTANCE USED TO FILL SOMETHING a substance used to fill the space inside something, pad it, or add bulk to it **4.** FOOD MIXTURE PUT INSIDE FOOD a food mixture that is put inside something else such as a pie, pastry case, or sandwich **5.** TEXTILES THREADS GOING ACROSS FABRIC the horizontal threads or yarn in a woven fabric ■ *adj* SATISFYING HUNGER leaving somebody with the feeling of having eaten enough

fill·ing sta·tion *n* TRANSP same as **gas station**

fil·lip /fíllip/ *n* **1.** FEELING OF ENCOURAGEMENT something that provides a stimulus or encouragement to somebody or something **2.** SNAPPING MOVEMENT OF FINGERS a snapping of the tip of one of the fingers against the ball of the thumb in order to make a sound or to propel a small object ■ *vt* **(-liped, -lip·ing, -lips) 1.** PROPEL SOMETHING WITH FILLIP to strike or propel something by snapping the fingertip against the ball of the thumb **2.** GIVE SOMEBODY OR SOMETHING INCENTIVE to provide a stimulus or encouragement to somebody or something [15C. An imitation of the sound of flicking or snapping the fingers]

fill light *n* in photography and filmmaking, a secondary source of light used to eliminate, reduce, or soften shadows

Millard Fillmore

Fill·more /fíl màwr/, **Millard** (1800–74) 13th president of the United States. A member of the Whig Party, he served as vice president (1849–50) before assuming the presidency (1850–53) upon the death of Zachary Taylor. See table at **president**

"An honorable defeat is better than a dishonorable victory."
[Millard Fillmore, *Address*; September 13, 1844]

fill-up *n* a filling of something, especially a vehicle's fuel tank

fil·ly /fíllee/ (*plural* **-lies**) *n* **1.** a female horse under four years of age **2.** an offensive term for a young woman or girl (*dated informal*) [15C. < Old Norse *fylja*]

film /film/ *n* **1.** PHOTOGRAPHY COATED STRIP FOR TAKING PICTURES a thin translucent strip or sheet of cellulose coated with a light-sensitive emulsion, used in a camera to take still or moving pictures **2.** *UK* MOVIES same as **movie 3.** MOVIES MOTION PICTURES COLLECTIVELY movies collectively, considered as a medium for recording events, a form of entertainment, or an art form **4.** INDUST VERY THIN SHEET OF SOMETHING material, especially a plastic, in the form of a very thin, flexible, translucent, or transparent sheet. Use: wrapping. **5.** THIN LAYER a thin coating of a substance such as dust, liquid, or ice covering the surface of something **6.** SOMETHING MAKING VIEW HAZY a thin haze or mist or something similar that blurs somebody's view ■ **films** *npl UK* MOVIE INDUSTRY the industry of moviemaking (*informal*) ■ *v* **(filmed, film·ing, films) 1.** *vt* TAKE PICTURES OF SOMETHING to record somebody or something on film **2.** *vti* MAKE MOTION PICTURE to make or be involved in the making of a motion picture **3.** *vt* MAKE MOVIE OF SOMETHING to make a motion picture of a book, story, or event **4.** *vi* BE GOOD FOR FILMING to be a suitable subject for cinematic treatment ○ *a story that would film well* [Old English *filmen* "membrane, skin" < Indo-European]
film over *vi* to become covered with a thin or misty layer of something

film badge *n* a piece of photographic film incorporated into a badge and used to register the wearer's exposure to nuclear radiation

film·go·er /fílm gō ər/ *n UK* MOVIES same as **moviegoer**

film·i /fílmee/ *S Asia adj* **1.** OF INDIAN MOVIE INDUSTRY relating to the Indian motion picture industry **2.** SENSATIONAL melodramatic or exaggerated ■ *n* MOVIE STAR a star of the Indian motion picture industry [Late 20C. < FILM + Hindi *-i*, adjective suffix]

film·ic /fílmik/ *adj* characteristic or reminiscent of a movie, especially in the techniques used to tell a story or describe a scene —**film·i·cal·ly** *adv*

film li·brar·y *n* a large collection of motion pictures or newsreels used as an archive

film·mak·er /fílm màykər/ *n* a producer or director of movies —**film·mak·ing** *n*

film noir /fílm nwaár/ (*plural* **films noirs** /*pronunc. same*/) *n* a cinematic genre popular in the 1940s and 1950s, often filmed in urban settings with extensive use of shadows, cynical in outlook, and featuring antiheroes [Mid-20C. < French, "black film"]

film·og·ra·phy /fil móggrəfee/ (*plural* **-phies**) *n* **1.** a list of the motion pictures made by an actor or director or on a topic **2.** writing about motion pictures [Mid-20C. Blend of FILM + BIBLIOGRAPHY]

film·set·ting /fílm sètting/ *n UK* same as **photo-composition** —**film·set** *vt* —**film·set·ter** *n*

film star *n UK* MOVIES same as **movie star**

film·strip /fílm strìp/ *n* a length of developed photographic film containing a series of still images to be projected onto a screen

film·y /fílmee/ **(-i·er, -i·est)** *adj* **1.** consisting or made of very thin translucent material **2.** covered or misted over with a thin layer of something —**film·i·ly** *adv* —**film·i·ness** *n*

fi·lo /fée lō/, **fi·lo pas·try** *n UK* FOOD same as **phyllo** [Variant]

Fi·lo·fax /fílō fàks/ *tdmk* a trademark for a compact loose-leaf binder containing sheets of paper in different colors, used as a personal portable filing system and address book

fils[1] /fils/ (*plural* **filses** or *same*) *n* a subunit of currency in several Middle-Eastern countries. See table at **currency** [Late 19C. < Arabic *fals*, small copper coin]

fils[2] /feess/ *n* in France and French-speaking countries, a word used after a man's or boy's surname to distinguish him from his father of the same name ○ *Henri Dupont fils* [Late 19C. < French, "son"]

fil·ter /fíltər/ *n* **1.** STRAINING DEVICE a device made of or containing a porous material used to collect particles from a liquid or gas passing through it **2.** POROUS MATERIAL USED FOR STRAINING any porous layer or material such as sand, paper, or cloth, used in or as a filter **3.** PHOTOGRAPHY TINTED SCREEN a tinted glass or dyed gelatin screen placed on a camera lens to control light or color or distort an image **4.** COMPUT DEVICE RESTRICTING THE PASSAGE OF FREQUENCIES a device or computer program that allows the passage of some frequencies or digital elements and blocks others **5.** same as **filter tip** (sense 1) ■ *v* **(-tered, -ter·ing, -ters) 1.** *vti* PASS SOMETHING THROUGH FILTER to put something such as fluid, light, or electrical impulses through a filter to remove or recover something, or be passed through a filter to do this **2.** *vi* PASS THROUGH SOMETHING to seep or pass through a filter or something that is intended to act as a barrier ○ *The sunlight filtered in through the shutters.* **3.** *vi* TRICKLE to move or pass slowly and gradually ○ *People filtered into the auditorium.* [14C. Via Old French *filtre* "felt" (used for filtering liquids) < medieval Latin *filtrum* < Germanic] —**fil·ter·a·ble** *adj* —**fil·ter·er** *n* —**fil·ter·less** *adj* —**fil·tra·ble** *adj*

fil·ter bed *n* a thick layer of gravel, charcoal, or other filtering material in a tank, used to remove sewage or other impurities from liquids

fil·ter cof·fee *n UK* same as **drip coffee**

fil·ter feed·er *n* an ocean animal that feeds on organic particles or small organisms that it filters from the water, e.g., a clam, sponge, or baleen whale —**fil·ter-feed·ing** *adj*

fil·ter pa·per *n* porous paper used as or in a filter

fil·ter tip *n* **1.** a small cylindrical mouthpiece made of a dense porous material attached to the end of a cigarette to remove tar and other impurities from the smoke **2.** a cigarette with a filter tip —**fil·ter-tipped** *adj*

filth /filth/ *n* **1.** dirt or refuse that is disgusting or excessive **2.** something considered extremely morally objectionable or obscene, e.g., coarse language or explicit descriptions, or depictions of sexual activity [Old English *fȳlð* < Germanic]

filth·y /fílthee/ *adj* **(-i·er, -i·est) 1.** EXTREMELY DIRTY extremely or disgustingly dirty ○ *Your hands are filthy!* **2.** MORALLY OBJECTIONABLE considered extremely morally objectionable or obscene **3.** DESPICABLE used to express contempt or strong disapproval (*informal*) ○ *a filthy liar* ■ *adv* VERY to an extreme degree (*informal*) ○ *filthy rich* —**filth·i·ly** *adv* —**filth·i·ness** *n*

SYNONYMS See *dirty.*

fil·trate /fíl tràyt/ *n* the material that emerges from a filtering process, usually a liquid or gas from which impurities have been removed ■ *vti* **(-trat·ed, -trat·ing, -trates)** to pass through a filter, or put something through a filter [Early 17C. < modern Latin *filtrat-*, past participle of *filtrare* "filter" < medieval Latin *filtrum* (see FILTER)]

fil·tra·tion /fil tráysh'n/ *n* the process of passing or putting something through a filter

fi·lum /fíləm/ (*plural* **-la** /-lə/) *n* a fine part or structure of a living organism that is long and thin like a thread [Mid-19C. < Latin, "thread, filament, fiber"]

fim·bri·a /fímbree ə/ (*plural* **-bri·ae** /-bree èe/) *n* a fringed border or part in the body, e.g., that found at the entrance to the fallopian tubes [Mid-18C. < Latin, "border, fringe"] —**fim·bri·al** *adj*

fim·bri·ate /fímbree ət/, **fim·bri·at·ed** /-àytəd/ *adj* describes parts of organisms that have a fringed border [15C. < Latin *fimbriatus* "fringed" < *fimbria* "border, fringe"] —**fim·bri·a·tion** /fìmbree áysh'n/ *n*

fin[1] /fin/ *n* **1.** ZOOL PART OF FISH USED FOR MOTION a flexible organ, sometimes paddle-shaped or fan-shaped, extending from the body of a fish or other water animal and helping in balance and propulsion **2.** NAUT PART ATTACHED TO HULL OF SUBMARINE a wing-shaped often movable blade attached low on the hull of a vessel such as a submarine that helps to control and stabilize it **3.** AVIAT UPRIGHT PART OF AIRCRAFT'S TAIL a fixed vertical surface at the tail of an aircraft that gives stability and to which the rudder is attached **4.** AVIAT, AEROSP **STABILIZING STRUCTURE ON ROCKET OR MISSILE** any small flat fixed structure extending from the body of a rocket, missile, or aircraft that gives stability in flight **5. RIB ON HEATING DEVICE** a flat metal part projecting from a heating mechanism such as a radiator that helps to increase the transfer of heat to the surrounding air **6.** SWIMMING same as **flipper** (sense 2) **7.** AUTOMOT **DECORATIVE EXTENSION ON AUTOMOBILE BODY** an ornamental extension on the body of a motor vehicle, especially on the rear fender ■ *vi* (**finned, fin·ning, fins**) **SWIM USING FINS** to swim or beat the water with fins, or show a fin above water [Old English *fin(n)* < Germanic] —**finned** *adj*

fin[2] /fin/ *n US* a five-dollar bill (*informal*) [Mid-19C. Shortening of Yiddish *finef* "five"]

fin. *abbr* **1.** finance **2.** financial **3.** finish

Fin. *abbr* **1.** Finland **2.** Finnish

fi·na·gle /fi náyg'l/ (**-gled, -gling, -gles**) *vti* to trick, cheat, or manipulate somebody in order to obtain or achieve something (*informal*) ○ *He finagled his way out of the difficulty.* [Early 20C. Origin ?] —**fi·na·gler** *n*

fi·nal /fīn'l/ *adj* **1. LAST** last of a number or series of similar things ○ *a final reminder* **2. ALLOWING NO CHANGE** conclusive and allowing no further discussion ○ *The editor's decision is final.* **3. ENDING** occurring at the end of something ○ *the final curtain* ■ *n* **END OF SERIES** the last and most important in a series of sports or other contests that decides the winner of a tournament or competition ■ **fi·nals** *npl* **1. LAST DECISIVE ROUNDS OF TOURNAMENT** the last decisive rounds of a tournament or competition during which the winners of previous rounds play each other **2. LAST UNIVERSITY EXAMINATIONS** the examinations that take place at the end of a course of study or studies for a professional qualification [14C. Directly or via French < Latin *finalis* "last" < *finis* "final moment, end"]

fi·nal ap·proach *n* the last stage of an aircraft's descent before landing, from its turning into line with the runway to the procedures immediately preceding touchdown

fi·nal cut *n* the approved and edited version of a movie prior to its being released for viewing by the public

fi·nal·e /fi nállee, -naalee/ *n* **1. FINAL THEATRICAL SCENE** a scene or musical number that brings a stage performance or an act of a performance to an end **2. FINAL SECTION OF MUSIC** a final movement or section of a musical composition **3. FINAL EVENT IN SERIES** an event that is the last or climactic event in a series [Mid-18C. Via Italian < Latin *finalis* (see FINAL)]

fi·nal·ist /fīn'list/ *n* a competitor who has qualified to take part in the finals of a contest

fi·nal·i·ty /fī nállətee, fi-/ (*plural* **-ties**) *n* **1.** the quality, state, or condition of being concluded or decided, permitting no further progress or development ○ *He spoke with an air of finality.* **2.** an act, belief, or statement that is final

fi·nal·ize /fīn'l īz/ (**-ized, -iz·ing, -iz·es**) *vt* **1.** to bring something to a point at which everything has been agreed upon and arranged **2.** to complete an agreement, sale, or other transaction —**fi·nal·i·za·tion** /fīn'li záysh'n/ *n* —**fi·nal·iz·er** *n*

USAGE finalize or **make final**? Though **finalize** has been in use for many years, even increasing in currency by the end of the 20th century, it is still disapproved of by many people in spite of its obvious utility in being a more concise way of saying "make final." You may wish to substitute *finish, complete,* or *make final.*

fi·nal·ly /fīn'lee/ *adv* **1. AT LAST** after a long period of time or a long delay and often after previous unsuccessful attempts ○ *So you've finally decided to ask her out, right?* **2. DEFINITIVELY** in a way that rules out further continuance, change, or discussion ○ *The venue won't be finally decided until the next meeting.* **3. AS LAST IN THE SERIES** as the last in a series of things or actions ○ *We visited Belgium, Holland, Germany, and finally Switzerland.* **4. AS THE LAST WORD** used to introduce the last in a series of things said by somebody ○ *Finally, I'd like to thank all of you for coming here tonight.*

Fi·nal So·lu·tion, fi·nal so·lu·tion *n* the plan to murder systematically all the Jews of Europe, conceived and put into action by the Nazis during World War II [Translation of German *Endlösung*]

~~finaly~~ incorrect spelling of **finally**

fi·nance /fī nànss, fi nánss/ *n* **1. CONTROL OF MONEY** the business or art of managing the monetary resources of an organization, country, or person ○ *high finance* **2. MONEY REQUIRED** the money necessary to do something, especially to fund a project ■ **fi·nanc·es** *npl* **THE MONEY SOMEBODY HAS** the money at the disposal of an organization, country, or person ○ *It'll depend on the state of my finances at the end of the month.* ■ *vt* (**-nanced, -nanc·ing, -nanc·es**) **PROVIDE MONEY FOR SOMETHING** to raise or provide the money required for something or by somebody [14C. < French < *finer* "to end, settle" < Latin *finis* "end"] —**fi·nance·a·ble** *adj*

fi·nance bill *n* an act passed by a legislature to raise or provide money for public expenditure

Fi·nance Can·a·da *n* GOV same as **Department of Finance Canada**

fi·nance com·pa·ny *n* a business enterprise that loans money to individual people or to companies against collateral, especially to buy homes or items on an installment plan

fi·nan·cial /fi nánshəl, fī-/ *adj* relating to or involving money or finance —**fi·nan·cial·ly** *adv*

fi·nan·cial an·a·lyst *n* somebody working for a financial institution whose job involves studying the performance of particular companies and making recommendations to buy or sell their shares

fi·nan·cial dis·tress *n* the violation of loan covenants, the inability to pay current bills, or other difficulties relating to bankruptcy that a business may experience

fi·nan·cial in·sti·tu·tion *n* an organization, e.g., a bank or brokerage, that offers financial services such as deposit taking, checking accounts, loans, or various investment services

Fi·nan·cial Times In·dus·tri·al Or·di·nar·y Share In·dex *n* an index of prices on the London Stock Exchange based on the average price of 30 shares. It is produced by the *Financial Times.*

Fi·nan·cial Times Stock Ex·change 100 In·dex *n* FIN full form of **FTSE 100 Index**

fi·nan·cial year *n UK* ACCT same as **fiscal year**

fin·an·cier /fìnnən seér, fínnən seér/ *n* a wealthy investor who is skilled in financial matters [Early 17C. < French < *finance* (see FINANCE)]

~~finantial~~ incorrect spelling of **financial**

fin·back /fín bàk/ *n* a large baleen whale that has a prominent dorsal fin. Latin name: *Balaenoptera physalus.* ◊ **rorqual**

finch

finch /finch/ *n* a small songbird with a short broad beak for cracking seeds and colorful plumage, especially in males. Family: Fringillidae. [Old English *finc* < Germanic]

Finch /finch/, **Peter** (1916–77) British-born Australian actor. A stage and screen performer, he received a posthumous Academy Award for his role in *Network* (1976). Born **Mitchell, William**

find /fīnd/ *v* (**found** /fownd/, **find·ing, finds**) **1.** *vt* **DISCOVER SOMETHING AFTER SEARCHING** to discover something or somebody after a search ○ *He was found wandering a mile from his home.* **2.** *vt* **GET SOMETHING BACK** to recover something after losing it ○ *I can't find my car keys.* **3.** *vt* **DISCOVER SOMETHING FOR FIRST TIME** to realize, understand, or locate something for the first time, especially by studying or observing ○ *We have to find answers to the problem of global warming.* **4.** *vt* **DISCOVER SOMETHING ACCIDENTALLY** to notice or come across somebody or something by chance ○ *I found my glasses under the table.* **5.** *vt* **EXPERIENCE SOMETHING** to notice or experience something personally ○ *They found great comfort in their work.* ○ *I think you'll find them easy to get along with.* **6.** *vt* **MANAGE TO GET SOMETHING** to make a special effort to gather something together or summon something up ○ *I don't know where we'll find the money.* **7.** *vt* **REACH GOAL** to succeed in reaching something aimed for ○ *He has finally found his place as a world-class tennis player.* **8.** *vt* SCI **RECORD SOMETHING AS OCCURRING** to observe something such as a natural species as existing or occurring (*often passive*) ○ *This species is found all across the continent.* **9.** *vti* LAW **REACH VERDICT** to decide about something or somebody at the end of a legal procedure, or announce the decision reached ○ *The jury found for the plaintiff.* **10.** *vt* **SUPPLY NEED** to bring or provide something that is necessary for a process to occur ○ *You will need to find your own transportation and equipment for the job.* **11.** *vr* **BECOME CONSCIOUS OF YOUR OWN CONDITION** to become aware of being in a particular place or state ○ *He found himself in an empty street.* **12. find your·self** *vr* **MAKE DECISIONS ABOUT YOUR OWN LIFE** to become more self-aware and self-motivated (*informal*) ○ *She finally found herself and became a successful artist.* ■ *n* **DISCOVERY** something noteworthy or valuable that has been found, or somebody who is talented and is brought to public attention ○ *a real find* [Old English *findan* < Indo-European, "to tread, go"] —**find·a·ble** *adj*

find out *v* **1.** *vti* to get to know something, especially by asking somebody or searching in an appropriate source, or just by chance ○ *I don't know how they found out about the proposed merger.* **2.** *vt* to detect and expose an offense ○ *He was quickly found out and his lies exposed.*

find·er /fīndər/ *n* **1.** a locator of something **2.** a small wide-angle telescope attached parallel to the optical axis of a larger telescope to help locate astronomical objects

fin de siè·cle /fàN də syéklə/ *n* the final years of the 19th century, characterized as being a time of decadence and self-doubt [< French, "end of the century"]

find·ing /fīnding/ *n* **1. RESEARCH RESULT** a piece of information obtained from an investigation, especially scientific research **2.** LAW **VERDICT** a conclusion that is reached and recorded at the end of a judicial or other formal inquiry ■ **find·ings** *npl US* **MATERIALS FOR CRAFTWORK** small articles or tools used in making craftwork, e.g., metal clips used on earrings

fine[1] /fīn/ *adj* (**fin·er, fin·est**) **1. VERY WELL OR SATISFACTORY** in a good, acceptable, or comfortable condition (*informal*) ○ *Everything's fine, thank you.* **2. NOT COARSE** made up of tiny particles ○ *fine sand* **3. SUNNY** with sunny and clear skies ○ *a fine morning* **4. THIN** very thin, sharp, or delicate ○ *fine features* ○ *fine hair* **5. GOOD-LOOKING** very good to look at ○ *a fine view of the valley* **6. OUTSTANDING** far better than the average ○ *a fine wine* **7. DELICATELY FORMED** showing special skill, detail, or intricacy, especially in artistic work ○ *fine detail* **8. SMALL AND DELICATE** set very closely and carefully together ○ *fine stitching* **9. UNPLEASANT** extremely unsuitable or undesirable (*informal; used ironically*) ○ *This is a fine mess!* **10. VERY SUBTLE** so particular or small that it may hardly be noticeable ○ *a maze of fine legal detail* ○ *a fine distinction* **11. SPURIOUSLY IMPRESSIVE** sounding or looking good, but probably just for show (*used ironically*) ○ *nothing but fine gestures* **12. EXTREMELY PURE** with any or most impurities removed, especially in a precious metal ■ *adv* **1. WELL** very well (*informal*) ○ *It works just fine.* ○ *The patient is doing fine.* **2. INTO SMALL PIECES** into tiny or delicate bits ○ *Chop the onions very fine.* ■ *v* (**fined, fin·ing, fines**) **1.** *vt* **SHARPEN SOMETHING** to make something thinner or sharper (*technical*) **2.** *vti* **PURIFY** to purify beer or wine, or be purified [13C. < French *fin* < Latin *finire* "to finish" (see FINISH)] —**fine·ness** *n*

ORIGIN The Latin word *finire* "to finish" from which **fine** is derived and the related nouns *finis* are also sources of English *affinity, confine, define, final, finance, finesse, finish, finite, paraffin,* and *refine.*

fine[2] /fīn/ *n* a sum of money that somebody is ordered to pay for breaking a law or rule ■ *vt* (**fined, fin·ing, fines**) to take a fixed amount of money from somebody who has broken a law or a rule [13C. Via French *fin* < Latin *finis* "end," in medieval Latin a sum to be paid on completion of legal proceedings] —**fin·a·ble** *adj*

fine[3] /feen/ *n* WINE same as **fine champagne** [Shortening]

fi·ne[4] /féé nàү/ *n* the place on a music score that shows where the piece finishes after a repeated section, or the symbol that marks this place [Late 18C. < Italian < Latin *finis* "end"]

fine art *n* **1.** ARTS **CREATION OF BEAUTIFUL OBJECTS** artistic work that is meant to be appreciated for its own sake, rather than to serve some useful function **2.** EDUC **COLLEGE COURSE IN ART** a course of study designed to teach students practical artistic skills as well as the theory and history of art **3.** ARTS **PURE ART** any art form that is considered to have purely aesthetic value, e.g., painting, sculpture, architecture, drawing, or engraving (*often used in the plural*) **4.** **IMPRESSIVELY DETAILED TECHNIQUE** something that requires great skill, talent, or precision (*informal*) ○ *the fine art of public speaking*

fine cham·pagne /feen sham pàyn/ *n* a brandy made from grapes grown in the Grande and Petite Champagne areas of the Charente region of western France. At least half the grapes must come from the Grande Champagne area. [Mid-19C. < French < *fine* "fine" + *champagne* "open space" < late Latin *campania* "level country" < Latin *Campania*, province in Italy]

fine chem·i·cal *n* a chemical product that is made in relatively small quantities and is typically high in cost, e.g., a flavoring or vitamin

Fi·ne Gael /feenə gáyl/ *n* one of the major political parties in the Republic of Ireland, founded in 1933 [< Irish, literally "end"]

fine-grained, **fine-grain** *adj* formed with a smooth, even, or closely patterned grain ○ *fine-grained wood*

fine·ly /fīnlee/ *adv* **1.** into small, thin, or delicate pieces **2.** in a careful, delicate, or sensitive way ○ *an actor finely tuned to her audience's reactions* ○ *finely wrought*

fine print *n* the detailed part of a document that is printed in small characters, often regarded with suspicion as containing unattractive conditions the author hopes the signer will not notice

fin·er·y /fīnəree/ *n* clothing, jewelry, or accessories that are especially dressy and stylish, usually worn on special occasions [Late 17C. < FINE[1], after BRAVERY in the archaic sense "ostentation, show"]

fines herbes /feenz érb/ *npl* a mixture of finely chopped herbs used to flavor a dish [< French, "fine herbs"]

fine·spun /fīn spùn/ *adj* spun or stretched out thinly ○ *finespun yarn*

fi·nesse /fi néss/ *n* **1.** **PHYSICAL SKILL** elegant ability and dexterity ○ *using a combination of power and finesse* **2.** **TACTFUL TREATMENT** a delicate and skillful approach in dealing with a troublesome situation ○ *shows great tact and finesse* **3.** CARDS **TACTIC IN BRIDGE** in bridge, an attempt to win a trick with a lower-value card while holding a higher card not in sequence, hoping that the opponent to the left will not play a card of intervening value ■ *v* (**-nessed, -ness·ing, -ness·es**) **1.** *vti* CARDS **TRY WINNING TRICK IN BRIDGE** in bridge, to attempt to win a trick with a finesse **2.** *vt US* **CONTROL IN A DEVIOUS WAY** to use subtle tricks or deception to manipulate something or somebody ○ *find some way of finessing the negotiations* [Mid-16C. < French, "fineness" < *fin* (see FINE[1])]

fine struc·ture *n* the separation of light of particular wavelengths produced by atoms or molecules into two or more very similar wavelengths, caused by the interaction of particular quantum mechanical properties

fine-tooth comb, **fine-toothed comb** *n* **1.** a thorough approach to an investigation or search, in which every detail is examined ○ *poring over the statements with a fine-tooth comb* **2.** a comb with very narrow tightly set teeth

fine-tune (**fine-tuned, fine-tun·ing, fine-tunes**) *v* **1.** *vt* to adjust the engine of a motor vehicle in order to improve its performance **2.** *vti* to make tiny adjustments to something in order to achieve the best possible performance or appearance —**fine-tun·ing** *n*

fin·fish /fín fìsh/ *n* an ocean fish, as opposed to a shellfish, jellyfish, or other so-called fish

fin·foot /fín fòòt/ (*plural* **-foots** or *same*) *n* a diving bird that lives along rivers and lakes. Native to: Africa, Asia. Family: Heliornithidae.

fin·ger /fíng gər/ *n* **1.** ANAT **DIGIT OF HAND** a digit of the hand, sometimes excluding the thumb (*often used before a noun*) **2.** CLOTHING **PART OF GLOVE** a long narrow part of a glove that fits over a finger **3.** **NARROW STRIP** something that resembles a finger in shape ○ *a finger of sand* **4.** FOOD **LONG NARROW PIECE OF FOOD** a small portion of food about as long and thick as a finger **5.** BEVERAGES **APPROXIMATE QUANTITY OF ALCOHOL** an approximate measure of alcoholic beverage in a glass, equal in depth to the width of a finger **6.** MEASURE **APPROXIMATE UNIT OF LENGTH** an approximate unit of measurement, equal to the width or length of a finger ■ *v* (**-gered, -ger·ing, -gers**) **1.** *vt* **TOUCH SOMETHING** to feel or move the fingers across something, often in a gentle, affectionate, or thoughtful way ○ *fingered the fabric lovingly* **2.** *vt* **GIVE SOMEBODY UP TO THE POLICE** to inform the police of the whereabouts or illegal activities of somebody (*slang*) **3.** *vti* MUSIC **PLAY MUSICAL INSTRUMENT** to handle the strings or keys of a musical instrument with the fingers **4.** *vt* MUSIC **MARK MUSICAL SCORE FOR FINGERING** to show on a musical score which fingers the musician should use **5.** *vt* ONLINE **LOCATE COMPUTER USERS** to obtain and display information about other users of the same computer or on other computers connected through a network or the Internet [Old English, < Indo-European, "five"] —**fin·ger·er** *n* —**fin·ger·less** *adj* ◇ **cross your fingers** used to express a hope that things will turn out well ◇ **give (somebody) the finger** to make an aggressively obscene gesture with the middle finger extended upward and held toward somebody (*slang*) ◇ **have a finger in every pie** to be involved in many advantageous or lucrative projects ◇ **have a finger in the pie** to be involved in a particular project, especially in a way that other people find annoying ◇ **let something slip through your fingers** to fail to take advantage of something that would have been of benefit to you ◇ **put your finger on something** to identify something, especially something difficult or elusive ◇ **twist somebody around your little finger** to succeed in getting somebody to do exactly as you wish

fin·ger·board /fíng gər bàwrd/ *n* **1.** a long strip of wood fixed on the neck of a stringed instrument against which strings are pressed in order to vary the pitch **2.** in skateboarding, a miniature board used to demonstrate or mimic stunts using the fingers

fin·ger bowl *n* a small bowl of water put beside a place setting at a table so that fingers can be cleaned, e.g., after picking up food with the hands

fin·ger food *n* small items of food made to be eaten with the fingers

fin·ger·fuck /fíng gər fùk/ (**-fucked, -fuck·ing, -fucks**) *vt* a highly offensive term meaning to use the fingers to stimulate a woman's genitals (*taboo*)

fin·ger hole *n* one of a series of holes on a woodwind instrument that a player covers with the fingers in order to register a pitch

fin·ger·ing /fíng gəring/ *n* **1.** the action or technique of using the fingers to play a musical instrument **2.** the markings on a musical score that show a musician which fingers to use

Fin·ger Lakes /fíng gər-/ group of eleven glacial lakes in western New York, the center of the state's wine region

fin·ger·ling /fíng gərling/ *n* a small fish less than one year old, especially a salmon or trout

fin·ger·mark /fíng gər maark/ *n* a smear or greasy mark left after somebody has touched something with a finger

fin·ger mil·let *n* a short-stemmed millet with an ear divided into five parts, cultivated widely in southern India, Sri Lanka, and parts of Africa. Latin name: *Eleusine coracana*. [Because its ears resemble the fingers of a hand]

fin·ger·nail /fíng gər nàyl/ *n* a flat protective layer of keratin that covers the end part of a finger's upper surface

fin·ger-paint *vti* to put paint directly onto a surface with the fingers —**fin·ger-paint·ing** *n*

fin·ger·pick /fíng gər pìk/ *n* a musician's pick with a curved part for attaching it to the finger —**fin·ger·pick** *vti*

fin·ger·print /fíng gər prìnt/ *n* **1.** **PATTERN ON FINGERTIP** an impression of the curved lines of skin at the end of a finger that is left on a surface or made by pressing an inked finger onto paper **2.** **DISTINGUISHING CHARACTERISTIC** a unique characteristic, mark, or pattern that can be used to identify somebody or something ■ *vt* (**-print·ed, -print·ing, -prints**) **RECORD FINGERPRINTS OF SOMEBODY** to press each of somebody's fingertips in ink and then onto paper in order to make a set of marks that can be used to identify that person

fing·er pup·pet *n* a very small puppet that is put over and operated by one finger

fin·ger·spell·ing /fíng gər spèlling/ *n* a form of sign language communication using the fingers to gesture the spelling of words

fin·ger·stall /fíng gər stàwl/ *n* a sheath-shaped protective covering worn over an injured finger

fin·ger·tip /fíng gər tìp/ *n* the tip of a finger ■ *adj* involving the use of the fingertips and so very sensitive or delicate ○ *fingertip controls* ◇ **have something at your fingertips** **1.** to know all the details of something thoroughly **2.** to have something available and nearby

fin·ger wave *n* a wave in the hair made by shaping damp hair with the fingers and a comb

Fin·go /fíng gō/ (*plural same* or **-gos**) *n* a member of an African people who live among the Xhosa in the Eastern Cape province of South Africa [Early 19C. < Xhosa *mfengu* "destitute wanderer"]

fin·i·al /fínnee əl/ *n* **1.** ARCHIT **ARCHITECTURAL DECORATION** a carved decoration at the top of a gable, spire, or arched structure **2.** FURNITURE **FURNITURE DECORATION** an ornamental feature on the top or end of an object such as a piece of furniture, stair post, or curtain rail, e.g., a carved knob **3.** PRINTING **CURVE IN TYPEFACE** a curve that ends a main stroke in some italic typefaces [15C. < assumed Anglo-Norman or Anglo-Latin word, "final" < Latin *finis* "end"]

fin·ick·y /fínnikee/ (**-i·er, -i·est**), **fin·ick·ing** /-king/, **fin·i·cal** /-k'l/ *adj* **1.** difficult to please, and tending to concentrate on small or unimportant details **2.** complicated by trivial details [Late 16C. Probably altered < FINE[1] + *-ical*] —**fin·ick·i·ness** *n*

SYNONYMS See *careful*.

fin·ing /fīning/ *n* **1.** the process of clarifying a liquid, especially wine or beer **2.** the process of removing undissolved gas from molten glass

fin·is /fínniss, fi née/ *interj* used to indicate that something has or must come to an end completely [14C. < Latin, "end"]

fin·ish /fínnish/ *v* (**-ished, -ish·ing, -ish·es**) **1.** *vti* **STOP** to come to an end, or bring something to an end ○ *We've finished eating.* ○ *Can we finish work for tonight?* **2.** *vt* **CONSUME** to eat, drink, or use all of something ○ *Who finished the cake?* **3.** *vt* **DESTROY SOMEBODY OR SOMETHING** to kill, ruin, or exhaust somebody or something (*informal*) ○ *finished his career in business* **4.** *vt* **COMPLETE SURFACE EFFECT OF SOMETHING** to treat something, especially wood or metal, in order to achieve a desired surface effect **5.** *vt* **GIVE SOMETHING OR SOMEBODY FINAL ENHANCEMENTS** to give something or somebody the final touches, qualities, or skills that are required to create a desired effect ■ *n* **1.** **END PART** the terminating part of something **2.** **SPECIAL TOP LAYER** a surface texture or final coat applied to something, especially wood or metal ○ *a mirror with a gilt finish* **3.** SPORTS **END OF RACE** the final part of a race, especially a sprint, acceleration, or challenge, near the finish line **4.** CONSTR, MANUF **QUALITY OF WORKMANSHIP** the degree of care with which a product has been manufactured or a job of work has been carried out, judged by its final appearance ○ *The finish on the woodwork is poor.* [14C. < Old French *feniss-*, stem of *fenir* < Latin *finire* < *finis* "end"] —**fin·ish·er** *n*

finish off *vt* **1.** **COMPLETE SOMETHING** to bring something to an end, e.g., by making it as complete as is wished or needed **2.** USE SOMETHING UP to eat, drink, or use up all of something **3.** DESTROY SOMEBODY OR SOMETHING to kill, ruin, or exhaust somebody or something (*informal*)

finish up *v* **1.** *vt* same as **finish off** (sense 2) **2.** *vi UK* to be in a particular place or condition in the end, often not the planned one

finish up with *vt* to be left with something ○ *finished up with three identical pieces*

finish with *vt* **1.** to end a relationship or partnership with somebody (*informal*) **2.** to stop using, wanting, or being interested in something

fin·ished /fínnisht/ *adj* **1.** produced and completed with skill and professionalism **2.** having no further prospect of success or development

fin·ish·ing /fínnishing/ *n* the tasks that complete the production process of a garment, fabric, or material

fin·ish·ing line *n UK* same as **finish line**

fin·ish·ing nail *n* a slender nail with a small head that is used in carpentry

fin·ish·ing school *n* a private school for girls close to college age in which social skills, the arts, and academic courses are taught

fin·ish·ing touch *n* a final small change or addition made to something

fin·ish line *n* a real or imaginary line that marks the end of a race

Fin·is·terre, Cape /fínni stér, féenee stérrə/ headland in the autonomous region of Galicia, northwestern Spain, extending into the Atlantic Ocean and forming the westernmost part of the mainland

fi·nite /fī́ nīt/ *adj* **1.** LIMITED having an end or limit ○ *We have only a finite amount of resources.* **2.** MATH COUNTABLE having a countable number of elements **3.** GRAM USING VERB THAT CREATES LIMITS appearing in a verb form that limits person, number, and tense [14C. < Latin *finitus*, past participle of *finire* (see FINISH)] —**fi·nite·ly** *adv* —**fi·nite·ness** *n*

fin·i·tude /fínni tòod/ *n* the condition of being finite (*formal*)

fink /fingk/ *n* **1.** SOMEBODY STRONGLY DISLIKED somebody regarded as contemptible (*dated slang insult*) **2.** INFORMER an informant who gives an authority such as the police information that incriminates somebody (*dated slang*) **3.** STRIKEBREAKER a worker who continues to work although colleagues are on strike (*dated slang disapproving*) ■ *vi* (**finked, fink·ing, finks**) **1.** INFORM ON OTHERS to give an authority information about somebody's criminal or bad behavior (*dated slang*) **2.** BE STRIKEBREAKER to continue to work in defiance of a strike (*dated slang disapproving*) [Late 19C. Origin ?]

fink out *vi* to fail to do something after previously agreeing or volunteering to do it (*slang*)

Fink /fingk/, **Mike** (1770?–1823?) US folk hero. His adventurous life as a scout and trapper on the frontier gave rise to many legends, and he became a popular hero.

fin keel *n* a fin-shaped part that extends downward from the underside of a sailboat to give extra stability

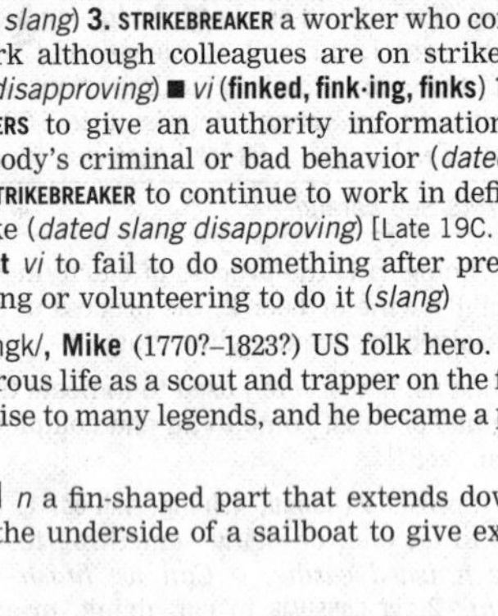

Finland

Fin·land /fínnlənd/ country in northern Europe on the Baltic Sea. Approximately a third of the country lies within the Arctic Circle. Language: Finnish, Swedish. Currency: markka. Capital: Helsinki. Population: 5,190,785 (2003). Area: 130,559 sq. mi./338,145 sq. km. Official name **Republic of Finland**. Finnish name **Suomi**

Fin·land, Gulf of arm of the Baltic Sea, extending about 250 mi./400 km east between Finland and Estonia. Area: 11,600 sq. mi./30,044 sq. km.

Fin·land·ize /fínnlən dīz/ (**-ized, -iz·ing, -iz·es**) *vt* to make a small country or power act in an accommodating way toward a superpower [Mid-20C. From the behavior of Finland toward the Soviet Union after World War II] —**Fin·land·i·za·tion** /fìnnləndi zāysh'n/ *n*

Fin·lay /fínlee/ river in north central British Columbia, Canada, that flows southeast into Williston Lake. Length: 250 mi./400 km.

Finn /fin/ *n* **1.** somebody who comes from Finland **2.** somebody who speaks a Finnic language [Old English *Finnas* (plural)]

fin·nan had·dock /fínnən-/, **fin·nan had·die** /-háddee/ *n* a haddock split and smoked on the bone over oak or peat so that the flesh takes on a pale yellow color [< *Findon*, fishing village near Aberdeen in Scotland]

Fin·nic /fínnik/ *n* a group of languages in northeastern Europe belonging to the Finno-Ugric branch of Uralic. Native speakers: 7 million. ■ *adj* **1.** relating to the Finnic group of languages or its speakers **2.** PEOPLES same as **Finnish**

~~finnish~~ incorrect spelling of **finish**

Finn·ish /fínnish/ *n* the Finnic official language of Finland, also spoken in Estonia and European Russia. Native speakers: 6 million. ■ *adj* relating to Finnish or the Finns

Fin·no-U·gric /fìnnō óogrik, -yóogrik/, **Fin·no-U·gri·an** /-óogree ən, -yóogree-/ *n* a group of northeastern European languages that is one of two major branches of Uralic. Native speakers: 22 million. —**Fin·no-U·gric** *adj*

fi·no /féenō/ *n* a very pale dry sherry [Mid-19C. < Spanish, "fine" < Latin *finire* (see FINISH)]

fi·noc·chi·o /fi nókee ō/ (*plural same or* **-os**) *n* PLANTS same as **fennel** (sense 2) [Early 18C. Via Italian < Latin *faeniculum* (see FENNEL)]

fin whale *n* MARINE BIOL same as **finback**

fiord *n* GEOG another spelling of **fjord**

Fiord·land Na·tion·al Park /fyàwrdlənd-/ national park on the southwestern coast of the South Island, New Zealand, established in 1952. It was designated a World Heritage Site in 1986. Area: 4,678 sq. mi./12,116 sq. km.

Fio·ren·ti·no /fyòrrən téenō/, **Rosso** (1494–1540) Italian painter. His most famous work, *Descent from the Cross* (1521), features the bold use of color and dramatic contrast that characterizes the mannerist school of painting. Born **di Guasparre, Giovanni Battista di Jacopo**

fio·ri·tu·ra /fyàwrə tóorə/ (*plural* **-re** /-ray/) *n* an embellished vocal figure in opera of the 17th and 18th centuries, similar to a cadenza and often improvised. It was later applied to keyboard and violin music. [Mid-19C. < Italian < *fiorire* "to flower" < Latin *florere* (see FLOURISH)]

fip·ple /físp'l/ *n* a small wooden plug in a woodwind instrument or organ pipe that redirects air and creates vibrations [Early 17C. Origin ?]

fip·ple flute *n* an end-blown flute containing a fipple

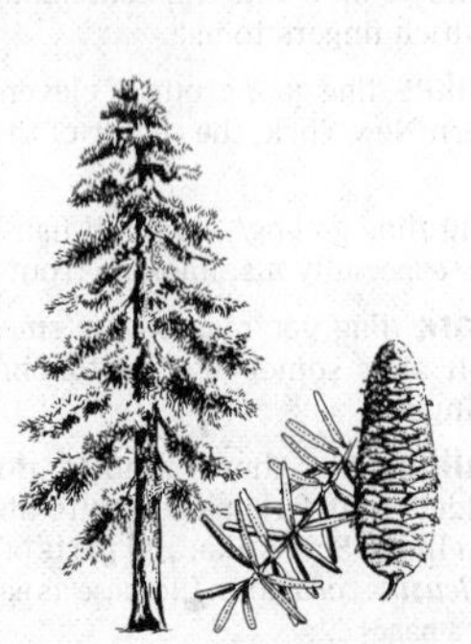

fir

fir /fur/ (*plural* **firs** or *same*) *n* **1.** EVERGREEN TREE WITH NEEDLE-SHAPED LEAVES an evergreen tree with needle-shaped leaves and erect female cones. Genus: *Abies.* **2.** EVERGREEN LIKE FIR an evergreen tree that resembles a true fir, e.g., a Douglas fir **3.** WOOD OF FIR the wood of the fir or a related tree [14C. Origin ?]

Fir·daw·si /feer dówssee/ (940?–1020?) Persian poet. He is best known for the epic *The Book of Kings* (1010), which traces the history of the Persian empire. Full name **Abdul Qasim Mansur**

fire /fīr/ *n* **1.** DESTRUCTIVE BURNING OF SOMETHING a situation in which something such as a building or an area of land is destroyed or damaged by burning (*often used before a noun*) ○ *destroyed by fire* ○ *fire damage* **2.** PILE OF BURNING FUEL a collection of material such as logs or coal that is set alight and used as fuel for heating, cooking, or burning something **3.** BLAZE the light, heat, and flames caused by something that is burning **4.** PROCESS OF BURNING the rapid production of light, heat, and flames from something that is burning, e.g., in the combustion of wood, coal, or petroleum **5.** ARMS DISCHARGE FROM GUNS a discharge of ammunition from one or more guns ○ *The troops advanced under heavy fire.* **6.** ARMS LAUNCH OF PROJECTILE the process or timing of sending off a missile or rocket **7.** CONTINUOUS ATTACK a series of things that follow each other quickly and relentlessly, especially if hostile or intimidating ○ *She took heavy fire from her political opponents.* **8.** GEM'S BRILLIANCE the shine and sparkle of a gemstone **9.** PASSION energy, spirit, or intensity of feeling ○ *the composer's creative fire* ■ *v* (**fired, fir·ing, fires**) **1.** *vti* ARMS DISCHARGE BULLET OR GUN to discharge ammunition or a projectile, or cause a weapon to do this **2.** *vi* ARMS BE DISCHARGED be activated and discharge ammunition or a projectile **3.** *vti* LAUNCH SOMETHING FORCEFULLY to launch something powerfully through the air, or be launched in this way **4.** *vt* DISMISS SOMEBODY FROM WORK to dismiss somebody from employment (*informal*) **5.** *vi* START UP to begin to burn fuel and start working ○ *The engine fired and the racecar took off.* **6.** *vt* STOKE OR FILL WITH FUEL to keep supplying fuel to something such as a furnace, engine, or oven **7.** *vt* CERAMICS BAKE POTTERY IN KILN to put pottery into a kiln to be baked hard **8.** *vt* STRIKE SOMETHING WITH FORCE to hit or throw something forcefully **9.** *vt* EXCITE SOMEBODY to arouse strong emotion in somebody (*often passive*) ○ *She was fired with enthusiasm.* **10.** *vt* DESTROY SOMETHING WITH FIRE to cause something to burn, especially in order to destroy it (*formal or dated*) **11.** *vt Malaysia, Singapore* TELL SOMEBODY OFF to criticize or reprimand somebody (*informal*) ○ *The boss fired me twice last week.* ■ *interj* **1.** WARNING CRY used to tell others that a dangerous fire has started **2.** COMMAND TO SHOOT used to command the discharge of guns or other weapons, missiles, or projectiles ○ *Ready, aim, fire!* [Old English *fȳr* < Indo-European] —**fired** *adj* —**fir·er** *n* ◇ **on fire 1.** in a condition of combustion in which flames, heat, and usually smoke are being produced **2.** full of eagerness or passion ◇ **open fire (on somebody** *or* **something)** to begin attacking somebody or something ◇ **play with fire** to do something dangerous or risky ◇ **set fire to something** to make something start burning ◇ **set the world on fire** to do something remarkable or very successful ◇ **under fire 1.** MIL shot at by weapons **2.** subject to severe criticism

CULTURAL NOTE ***Pale Fire***, a novel (1962) by Russian-born Vladimir Nabokov. Partly an attack on parasitic critics, it is presented as a long poem by John Shade, with introduction, notes, and index by Charles Kinbote. Kinbote's commentary gradually reveals him to be an unscrupulous critic, ready to use the work of others to further his own career.

SYNONYMS ***fire, blaze, conflagration, inferno***

CORE MEANING: burning and flames

fire the light, heat, and flames caused by something burning, whether deliberately or accidentally produced ○ *the crackling fire in the hearth* ○ *a fire that gutted the building* **blaze** a brightly or intensely burning fire, or a large fire ○ *The blaze threatened to engulf a nearby house.* ○ *A 7,500-acre blaze closed the main road through the forest over the weekend.* **conflagration** a large fire that causes a great deal of damage ○ *The explosion of the fuel tanks consumed the plane in a terrifying conflagration.* **inferno** a very large fire burning fiercely and uncontrollably, or a place being consumed by a large uncontrollable fire ○ *The* *store rapidly became a roaring inferno of smoke and fire.*

fire away *vi* **1.** to begin or keep on shooting **2.** to begin doing something, especially asking questions (*informal*)

fire off *vt* **1.** to say or ask something quickly and aggressively, especially a question or demand ○ *firing off an angry e-mail* **2.** to discharge a bullet, missile or projectile

fire up *v* **1.** *vti* MAKE SOMEBODY ENTHUSIASTIC to cause somebody to become enthusiastic, or become enthusiastic **2.** *vt* GET SOMETHING GOING to initiate the operation of something **3.** *vti* START TO BURN to begin to burn, or set something burning

fire a·larm *n* a bell or siren that is sounded if a fire starts

fire and brim·stone *n* in the Christian religion, eternal punishment in hell [See (Genesis 19:24, Revelation 19:20)]

fire ant *n* a predatory ant that inflicts a painful sting. Native to: tropical and temperate regions. Genus: *Solenopsis.* [< the burning sensation its sting causes]

fire·arm /fír aàrm/ *n* a portable weapon that fires ammunition, e.g., a pistol or rifle

fire·back /fír bàk/ *n* **1.** a metal lining placed behind a fireplace **2.** the area of wall where a fireback is placed

fire·ball /fír bàwl/ *n* **1.** PHYS CENTER OF NUCLEAR EXPLOSION the highly ionized spherical region of bright hot gas and dust at the center of a nuclear explosion **2.** DYNAMIC PERSON an extremely energetic and dynamic person (*informal*) Same as **ball of fire 3.** ASTRON BRIGHT METEOR an exceptionally bright meteor **4.** BALL LIGHTNING a discharge of ball lightning

fire·bird /fír burd/ *n* a songbird with bright red or orange feathers

fire blight *n* an infectious disease of apples, pears, and other fruit trees that blackens leaves and kills branches and is caused by the bacterium *Erwinia amylovora*

fire·board /fír bàwrd/ *n Southern US* a mantel over a fireplace

REGIONAL NOTE The term ***fireboard*** is largely restricted to the highlands of Appalachia in West Virginia, Kentucky, Tennessee, the Carolinas, Georgia, Alabama, and the Ozarks of Arkansas. In these places, ***fireboard*** contrasts with the general currency word *mantel*, with Southern *mantelpiece*, and, in the interior lower plains of Georgia and Alabama, with the blend *mantelboard*.

fire·boat /fír bōt/ *n* a vessel equipped with high-pressure hoses and pumps that take in and shoot seawater, river water, or lake water onto burning vessels. Fireboats are also used to spray water in the air in a port as an official welcoming gesture to an important visiting vessel.

fire·bomb /fír bòm/ *n* a bomb designed to start a fire —**fire·bomb** *vti* —**fire·bomb·er** *n* —**fire·bomb·ing** *n*

fire·box /fír bòks/ *n* an enclosure for a fire in a stove, furnace, or the engine of a steam locomotive

fire·brand /fír brànd/ *n* **1.** somebody with a strong or aggressive personality who encourages unrest **2.** a burning stick carried by somebody as a torch or a weapon

fire·brat /fír bràt/ *n* a small wingless insect related to the silverfish, found in warm moist places. Latin name: *Thermobia domestica.*

fire·break /fír bràyk/ *n* a strip of land that has been cleared of trees, bushes, and any other combustible material in order to prevent a fire from spreading

fire·brick /fír brìk/ *n* a brick that can withstand very high temperatures. Use: fireplaces, furnaces.

fire bri·gade *n UK* EMERGENCIES same as **fire department**

fire·bug /fír bùg/ *n* somebody who starts fires causing damage or destruction, especially repeatedly and for pleasure (*slang*)

fire chief *n* a leader of a fire company or department

fire·clay /fír klày/ *n* a durable clay that can withstand great heat. Use: firebricks, crucibles, furnace linings.

fire com·pa·ny *n* a group of firefighters stationed in one location, along with their vehicles and equipment

fire con·trol *n* the control of naval or artillery fire directed at a target

fire·crack·er /fír kràkər/ *n* a firework consisting of a small paper or cardboard cylinder filled with an explosive that makes one or several loud bangs when lit

fire·damp /fír dàmp/ *n* a mixture of methane and other hydrocarbon gases that forms in coalmines and is explosive when mixed with air [< DAMP "noxious gas"]

fire de·part·ment *n* an organization of people trained to prevent, control, and extinguish fires and to rescue people from fires and other dangerous situations

fire·dog /fír dàwg, fír dòg/ *n Southern US* HOUSEHOLD same as **andiron**

fire door *n* **1.** a fireproof door that is normally kept closed or locked in order to ensure that any fire is confined to one area **2.** an emergency exit opened from inside

fire·drake /fír dràyk/, **fire·drag·on** /-dràggən/ *n* a dragon that breathes fire (*archaic or literary*) [Old English *draca* "dragon" < Greek *drakōn* "serpent"]

fire drill *n* a rehearsal for evacuating a building quickly and safely in the event of a fire or other emergency

fire-eat·er *n* **1.** an entertainer who appears to swallow flames from a burning stick **2.** an aggressive, angry, or argumentative person (*informal*) —**fire-eat·ing** *n*

fire en·gine *n* a large road vehicle equipped with ladders, hoses, and other equipment for fighting fires and rescuing people

fire es·cape *n* a specially designed means of getting out of a building if it catches fire, especially an exterior metal stairway attached to the building

fire ex·tin·guish·er *n* a cylindrical metal container holding a substance such as foam or vaporizing liquid that can be sprayed onto a fire in order to put it out

fire·fight /fír fìt/ *n* a fierce battle involving a heavy exchange of gunfire

fire·fight·er /fír fìtər/ *n* somebody who attempts to control or extinguish fires, and to rescue people or animals from danger —**fire·fight·ing** *n*

fire·fly /fír flì/ (*plural* **-flies**) *n* a winged nocturnal beetle that, during courtship, produces an intermittent light from luminescent chemicals in its abdominal organs. Family: Lampyridae.

fire·guard /fír gaàrd/ *n* **1.** a metal, usually meshed screen that is put around the front of an open fire, mainly to stop sparks from flying out and to prevent people from going too close **2.** same as **firebreak**

fire·house /fír hòwss/ *n US* EMERGENCIES same as **fire station**

fire hy·drant *n* an upright pipe, usually in a street, connected to a water main with a valve to which a hose can be attached, e.g., by firefighters

fire in·sur·ance *n* insurance that offers coverage against damage or loss caused by fire

fire i·rons *npl* a set of implements used for tending a fire in a fireplace, especially a shovel, tongs, poker, and brush

Fire Is·land Na·tion·al Sea·shore /fír-/ national park incorporating a sand barrier island off Long Island, southeastern New York. It is a popular tourist area. Area: 31 sq. mi./79 sq. km.

fire·light /fír lìt/ *n* the flickering light given off by an open fire

fire·lock /fír lòk/ *n* in early firearms, a mechanism that struck a spark from flint or steel and caused a charge to explode

fire·man /fírmən/ (*plural* **-men** /-mən/) *n* **1.** MAN WHO IS FIREFIGHTER a man who is a firefighter, especially one who works for a fire company **2.** *US* NAVY SHIP'S ENGINEER an enlisted man in the US Navy who operates and services engines and similar machinery **3.** *US* BASEBALL RELIEVER in baseball, a relief pitcher (*slang*) **4.** RAIL, BOATING STOKER a man who stokes a furnace, especially on a steam locomotive or steamboat

fire management *n* the science and practice of intentionally burning in a controlled and selective way grasses, brush, undergrowth, and trees in an area so as to maintain an ecological balance of species and prevent uncontrolled forest or prairie fires

fire mar·shal *n* **1.** a state or local official whose job is to investigate suspicious fires and work in the areas of fire prevention and building inspection **2.** an employee of a plant or other industrial site who is responsible for firefighting equipment and fire safety procedures

Fi·ren·ze /fi rént say/ ➧ **Florence**

fire o·pal *n* a translucent reddish opal

fire pink *n* a wild plant of the pink family. Flowers: bright scarlet. Native to: North America. Latin name: *Silene virginica.*

fire·place /fír plàyss/ *n* a recess, usually with a mantelpiece above it, built into the wall of a room as a place to light an open fire

fire·plug /fír plùg/ *n US* EMERGENCIES same as **fire hydrant**

fire·pow·er /fír pòwr/ *n* **1.** the capability of a military unit or weapon to direct effective fire at an enemy **2.** the capability or potential of a person, team, or organization for effective action ○ *the team's lack of firepower this season*

fire·proof /fír proòf/ *adj* treated or manufactured so as to be impossible or very difficult to burn and therefore destroy by fire —**fire·proof** *vt*

fire-re·sis·tant *adj* treated or made so as to be very slow to catch fire and burn

fire-re·tar·dant *adj* tending not to catch fire easily and therefore checking the spread of fire

fire sale *n* **1.** a sale of goods or property damaged in a fire **2.** a sale of goods or property at very low prices (*informal; hyphenated when used before a noun*) ○ *fire-sale prices*

fire screen *n* HOUSEHOLD same as **fireguard** (sense 1)

fire ship *n* formerly, a ship loaded with explosives or combustibles that was set on fire and allowed to drift as a weapon among enemy ships

fire·side /fír sìd/ *n* the space around a fireplace or hearth ■ *adj* cozy, familiar, or homey ○ *a fireside chat*

fire·side chat *n* an informal talk made to the nation on radio or television by the president of the United States. During the Great Depression Franklin D. Roosevelt gave fireside chats over the radio as a way of raising national morale and explaining his policies.

fire sign *n* each of the three signs of the zodiac, Aries, Leo, and Sagittarius, traditionally associated with a fiery, assertive, and dynamic temperament

fire sta·tion *n* a building where professional firefighters are stationed and their vehicles and equipment are kept

fire·stone /fír stōn/ *n* a form of sandstone that can withstand great heat. Use: to line kilns and furnaces.

Fire·stone /fír stōn/, **Harvey Samuel** (1868–1938) US entrepreneur. He became president of his own tire and rubber company (1900) and established large-scale rubber plantations in Liberia (1926).

fire·storm /fír stàwrm/ *n* **1.** a large extremely intense fire sustained by strong inwardly rushing winds that feed a rising column of hot air **2.** *US* a strong, sometimes violent, upheaval or outburst ○ *a firestorm of protest*

fire·thorn /fír thàwrn/ *n US* a thorny evergreen bush cultivated for its bright orange or red fruits. Native to: Europe, Asia. Genus: *Pyracantha.* Can term **pyracantha**

fire·trap /fír tràp/ *n* a building or structure regarded as a fire hazard, because it is either built of combustible materials or lacks adequate means of escape

fire·truck /fír trùk/ *n* EMERGENCIES same as **fire engine**

fire·walk·ing /fír wàwking/ *n* the rite or practice of walking barefoot over hot coals, ashes, or stones —**fire·walk·er** *n*

fire·wall /fír wàwl/ *n* **1. WALL PREVENTING THE SPREAD OF FIRE** a fireproof wall put in place to ensure that if a fire occurs it is confined to one area **2.** COMPUT **SECURITY SOFTWARE** a piece of computer software intended to prevent unauthorized access to system software or data **3.** COMM **BARRIER WITHIN COMPANY** a legal barrier set up between sections of a corporation to prevent them from sharing inside information when this might lead to a conflict of interest ■ *vt* (**-walled, -wall·ing, -walls**) *US* **ACCELERATE TO TOP SPEED** to accelerate something to the maximum speed (*slang*)

fire·wa·ter /fír wàwtər/ *n* strong and harsh-tasting alcoholic liquor (*dated slang*)

fire·weed /fír wèed/ *n* a perennial plant of the evening primrose family that grows on recently cleared land. It has spike-shaped clusters of purplish red flowers. Genus: *Epilobium*. [Because often the first to grow on land that has been burned]

fire·wom·an /fír wòommən/ (*plural* **-wom·en** /-wìmmin/) *n* a woman who is a firefighter, especially one who works for a fire company

fire·wood /fír wòod/ *n* wood that is burned as fuel

fire·work /fír wùrk/ *n* **BRIGHT EXPLODING OBJECT** a package of manufactured chemicals designed to make a loud and brilliant explosion when lit ■ **fire·works** *npl* **1. SHOW USING FIREWORKS** a display of many brilliant fireworks **2. ANGRY OUTBURST** a display of violent temper (*informal*) **3. SPECTACULAR DISPLAY** an impressive display of talent (*informal*)

~~**firey**~~ incorrect spelling of **fiery**

fir·ing /fíring/ *n* the application of great heat to a ceramic object in a kiln, in order to harden it or to fix an applied substance such as a glaze

fir·ing line *n* **1.** the forefront of a movement, operation, or activity, especially one that is controversial **2.** an exposed position from which guns are fired at an enemy, or the troops who occupy it

fir·ing or·der *n* the sequence of ignition of the cylinders in an internal-combustion engine

fir·ing pin *n* the pin behind the barrel of a firearm that strikes the container of explosive (**primer**) to make the cartridge fire

fir·ing squad *n* a group of soldiers who carry out an execution by gunfire or deliver a ceremonial volley over a grave

fir·kin /fúrkin/ *n* **1.** a British unit of capacity used especially in the brewing industry, equal to nine UK gallons **2.** a small wooden tub used, especially in the past, for storing food or liquids [14C. Probably < assumed Middle Dutch *verdelkijn* "small fourth" < *veerde* "fourth"]

firm[1] /furm/ *adj* **1. NOT YIELDING TO TOUCH** compact and solid when pressed ○ *a firm mattress* **2. SECURE** fixed securely and unlikely to give way ○ *a firm hold* **3. DETERMINED** showing certainty or determination ○ *You need to be more firm with them.* **4. TRUSTWORTHY** reliable and able to be trusted ○ *firm evidence* **5. STEADY** showing no or few fluctuations ○ *a firm price* ■ *adv* **UNYIELDINGLY** in a determined and unshakable way ○ *standing firm despite a wave of criticism* ■ *vti* (**firmed, firm·ing, firms**) **MAKE OR BECOME FIRM** to become firm or firmer, or make something firm or firmer [14C. Via Old French < Latin *firmus*] —**firm·ly** *adv* —**firm·ness** *n*
firm up *vt* to make something more definite, clear, or less liable to change ○ *Let's firm up the date of the meeting.*

firm[2] /furm/ *n* a group of people who form a commercial organization selling goods or services [14C. < Italian *firma* < late Latin *firmare* "confirm by signing" < Latin, "strengthen" < *firmus* "strong"]

fir·ma·ment /fúrməmənt/ *n* **1.** the sky, considered as an arch (*literary*) **2.** the world occupied by all the celebrities in a particular field such as the theater or sports ○ *a big name in the yachting firmament* [13C. Via French < Latin *firmamentum* < *firmus* "strong"]

firm·ware /fúrm wèr/ *n* software stored on a memory chip in a computer or computer device instead of being part of a program [Because the instructions will not be lost when power is shut off]

firn /furn/ *n* GEOG same as **névé** (sense 1) [Mid-19C. Via German, "of last year" < Old High German *firni* "old"]

firn·i /fúrnee/ *n* in South Asian cuisine, a dessert made of noodles, rice, or wheat simmered in milk, and nuts and raisins [Via Hindi *firnī* < Persian]

firn wind *n* a summer wind that blows downhill off a glacier during the day

first /furst/ *adj* **1. BEFORE REST IN ORDER** preceding or ahead of any others in order **2. EARLIER THAN REST** occurring before any others in a series **3. MOST IMPORTANT** having a higher rank, significance, or authority than others in the same category **4. FUNDAMENTAL** forming a basis or foundation for something **5. BEST** best in quality or achievement **6.** MUSIC **PLAYING OR SINGING CHIEF PART** playing or singing the most important or highest of two or more parts for instruments or voices of the same type ○ *the first violins* ○ *the first sopranos* ■ *n* **1. NEW THING** something that has not been done before or has not occurred before **2. 1 IN SERIES** the ordinal number assigned to item number one in a series **3. ONE AHEAD OF ANY OTHER** the one positioned before any other in achievement, rank, quality, or time **4.** AUTOMOT **FIRST GEAR** the lowest gear in a motor vehicle **5.** BALLET same as **first position 6.** BASEBALL same as **first base** ○ *grounded out to first* **7.** MUSIC **INSTRUMENT OR VOICE TAKING CHIEF PART** the instrument or voice that plays or sings the most important or highest of two or more parts for instruments or voices of the same type ■ *adv* **1. BEFORE OTHERS IN TIME** earlier than somebody or something else ○ *arriving first, as usual* **2. ORIGINALLY** for the first time ○ *first tried it on a dare* **3. INITIALLY** at the start ○ *seemed nervous at first* **4. MORE WILLINGLY** used to indicate a preference [Old English *fyr(e)st* < Indo-European]

first aid *n* emergency medical treatment for somebody who is ill or injured, given before more thorough medical attention can be obtained

First A·mend·ment *n* an amendment to the US Constitution that forbids Congress from interfering with a citizen's freedom of religion, speech, assembly, or petition

first base *n* **1.** in baseball, the initial base that a player attempts to reach **2.** in baseball, the position played by the infielder defending first base ◇ **get to first base** to succeed in the initial phase of an activity, especially in making advances to a prospective romantic or sexual partner (*informal*)

first base·man *n* in baseball, a fielder responsible for the area near first base

first-born *n* the first offspring to be born to a set of parents ■ *adj* born first of all

First Cause *n* in Christianity, God as the originator of everything

first class *n* **1. BEST ACCOMMODATIONS** the best accommodations offered on an airplane, ship, or train **2. PRIORITY MAIL SERVICE** a mail service that guarantees priority in delivery in return for a higher charge **3. BEST CLASS** the highest rank, standard, or quality

first-class *adj* **1. BEST** of the highest standard of excellence **2. MOST LUXURIOUS** most exclusive and expensive **3.** MAIL **GIVEN PRIORITY IN MAIL SERVICE** costing more to mail and given priority in delivery —**first-class** *adv*

first class·man *n* *US* a fourth-year student at a military college

first course *n* a dish or selection of dishes served at the beginning of a meal

first cous·in *n* same as **cousin** (sense 1)

first-day cov·er *n* an envelope, often specially designed, that bears a newly issued stamp and a postmark for the day on which it was first issued

first-de·gree burn *n* a burn marked by pain and reddening of the skin but without blistering or charring of tissue

first-de·gree mur·der *n* murder that is carried out with the planned and deliberate intention of killing somebody

first down *n* **1.** in football, the first of four consecutive plays, or three plays in Canadian football, by which the offensive team has to move the ball ten yards to retain possession **2.** in football, ten or more yards gained by an offensive team during a series of plays, entitling it to keep the ball for another series of plays

first e·di·tion *n* **1. ORIGINAL COPY OF BOOK** a copy of a book in its original printed and published format **2. ORIGINAL PRINTING OF PUBLICATION** the total number of copies of a book issued by the original publisher in the first instance **3. FIRST NEWSPAPER OF DAY** the first batch or copy of a newspaper on a day of publication

first es·tate *n* in societies that date from feudal times, the social and political class that consists of senior members of the clergy

first fam·i·ly *n* *US* a family with great social prestige, especially one with a long history and residence in a place

First Fam·i·ly *n* *US* the president of the United States and the president's spouse and children

first fin·ger *n* ANAT same as **index finger**

first floor *n* **1.** same as **ground floor 2.** *UK* the floor of a building immediately above the floor at ground level

first-foot *Scotland n also* **first-foot·er** the first person to visit a household in the New Year, especially one going first-footing ■ *vti* to be the first visitor to a household in the New Year, especially in the practice of first-footing

first-foot·ing *n Scotland* the traditional practice of going to the house of a friend or neighbor soon after midnight on December 31, with good wishes and gifts of food, drink, and fuel

first fruits *npl* **1.** the first harvest of the season or year **2.** the first results of an activity

first-gen·er·a·tion *adj* **1.** relating to or being the children of parents who have left one country to settle in another **2.** describes the earliest computers, which were based on vacuum tubes

first·hand /fùrst hánd/ *adj, adv* obtained directly from an original source, and not via somebody else

first in, first out *n* COMPUT same as **pushup** (sense 2)

first la·dy *n* **1.** *also* **First La·dy** *US* **US LEADER'S SPOUSE OR HOSTESS** the wife of the president of the United States or of a US state governor, or the woman appointed by him to act as his official hostess **2. GOVERNMENT LEADER'S PARTNER** the wife or hostess of a high government official, especially of a country's leader **3. WOMAN NOTABLE IN HER PROFESSION** the most important or respected woman member of a profession or field of activity

first lan·guage *n* **1.** the language that somebody learned in infancy **2.** the principal language in a neighborhood, district, region, or country

first lieu·ten·ant *n* **1.** *US* an officer in the US Army, Air Force, or Marine Corps of a rank above second lieutenant **2.** a naval officer in charge of the upkeep and maintenance of a ship

first light *n* the earliest time of the day, when the sun begins to rise

first·ling /fúrstling/ *n* the first offspring, product, or result (*archaic or literary*)

first love *n* **1. FIRST RECIPIENT OF SOMEBODY'S LOVE** the first object of somebody's love or interest **2. FAVORITE** the object of somebody's greatest interest or affection ○ *Sailing was always his first love.* **3. FIRST EXPERIENCE OF LOVE** the experience of being in love for the first time

first·ly /fúrstlee/ *adv* used to introduce the first point in an argument or discussion

first mate *n* an officer on a merchant ship or any nonnaval vessel of a rank above second mate

first min·is·ter *n* the title of the leader of the National Assembly of Northern Ireland, Scotland, or Wales

first name *n* a personal name that accompanies a family name to identify somebody fully

First Na·tion *n* in Canada, any of the communities of indigenous people who are descended from the peoples that inhabited Canada before the arrival of European settlers

first night *n* **1. FIRST PERFORMANCE OF A NEW SHOW** the first public performance of a new production of a play or show **2. NIGHT OF THE FIRST PERFORMANCE** the night on which the first performance of a new play or show takes place **3.** *also* **First Night NEW YEAR'S EVE ENTERTAINMENT** a celebration when a city sponsors a public program of cultural events and family-oriented entertainment. Date: New Year's Eve. —**first night·er** *n*

first of·fend·er *n* somebody with no previous criminal record who breaks the law and is convicted for the first time

first of·fi·cer *n* **1.** NAUT same as **first mate 2.** the officer who is second-in-command on an aircraft after the captain

first-past-the-post *adj Can, UK* describes a voting system in which the winner needs to receive more votes than anyone else but does not need an absolute majority of the votes cast

First Peo·ple *npl Can* same as **First Nation**

first per·son *n* **1. VERB OR PRONOUN FORM** the form of a verb or pronoun used to refer to the speaker or writer. In English, the first-person singular pronoun is "I," and the plural is "we." **2. SET OF GRAMMATICAL FORMS** the grammatical set containing the forms indicating the first person **3. WRITING IN FIRST PERSON** a style of writing using first-person forms ○ *Write your account in the first person.*

first-per·son shoot·er *n* a computer game primarily involving the shooting of opponents that uses first-person view

first-per·son view *n* in a computer game, a computer screen view corresponding to what the character being enacted by the player would see

first po·si·tion *n* in ballet, a position in which the feet are turned outward with the heels touching

first prin·ci·ple *n* a fundamental rule underlying a theory, faith, or procedure

first prin·ci·ples *npl* the basic ideas that underpin something, or the basic rules that govern it

first quar·ter *n* one of four phases of the Moon, during which one-half of the Moon's visible surface is illuminated by the Sun

first-rate *adj* of the best quality or the highest standard

first read·ing *n* the introduction of a bill in a legislature prior to debate and a vote

first re·fus·al *n* the right to decide whether or not to buy something before it is offered to other potential buyers

first re·spond·er /-ri spóndər/ *n* the first person, e.g., an emergency medical technician or a police officer, who arrives at the scene of a disaster, accident, or life-threatening medical situation. The first responder's duties include providing medical assistance and calling other emergency caregivers to the scene.

first ser·geant *n US* a noncommissioned officer who holds a senior position administering a unit of the US Army, Air Force, or Marine Corps

First State *n* a nickname for the US state of Delaware

first strike *n* the use of nuclear weapons against an enemy state that is similarly armed, intended to destroy its military capacity and prevent it from attacking first (*hyphenated when used before a noun*) ○ *first-strike capability*

first thing *adv* **1.** very early in the morning **2.** before doing anything else

first wa·ter *n* the highest grade in gemstones

First World *n* the principal industrialized countries of the world, including the United States, the United Kingdom, the nations of western Europe, Japan, Canada, Australia, and New Zealand

First World War *n* HIST same as **World War I**

firth /furth/ *n Scotland* (*often used in place names*) **1.** a river estuary **2.** a wide inlet of the sea [14C. < Old Norse *fjörðr*]

FISA /físsə/ *abbr* LAW Foreign Intelligence Surveillance Act

FISA court *n* a US court composed of a rotating panel of federal judges that sits in secrecy to review prosecutors' requests to wiretap telephones of suspected spies and terrorists and to conduct searches

fisc /fisk/ *n US* a public treasury [Late 16C. Directly or via French < Latin *fiscus* "rush basket, purse, treasury"]

fis·cal /físk'l/ *adj* **1.** relating to public revenues, especially the revenue from taxation ○ *fiscal prudence* **2.** relating to financial matters in general [Mid-16C. Directly or via French < Latin *fiscalis* < *fiscus* "rush basket, purse, treasury"] —**fis·cal·ly** *adv*

fis·cal year *n* a 12-month period at the end of which all accounts are completed in order to provide a statement of a company's, organization's, or government's financial condition, or for tax purposes. A fiscal year does not necessarily correspond to a calendar year.

Fi·scher /físhər/, **Bobby** (*b.* 1943) US chess player. In 1972, he became the first chess player from the United States to win the world championship, and he held the title until 1975. Full name **Fischer, Robert James**

> "I like the moment when I break a man's ego."
> [Bobby Fischer, *Newsweek*; July 31, 1972]

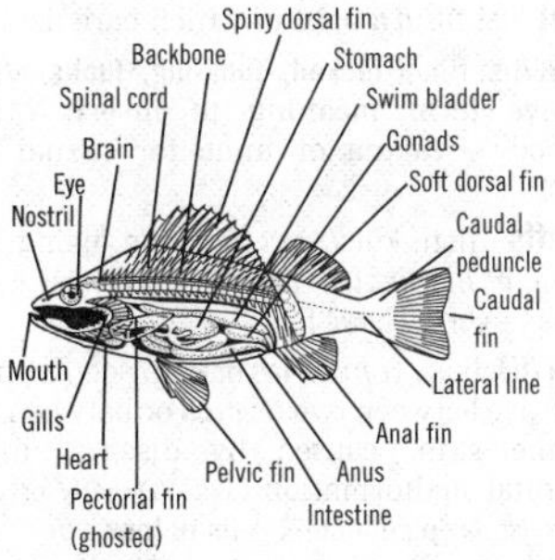

fish: anatomy of a fish

fish /fish/ *n* (*plural same* or **fish·es**) **1. WATER VERTEBRATE WITH GILLS** a cold-blooded vertebrate animal that lives in water. It typically has jaws, fins, scales, a slender body, a two-chambered heart, and gills for providing oxygen to the blood. (*often used before a noun*) ○ *a fish tank* **2. FISH CONSUMED AS FOOD** the flesh of any edible fish eaten as food, either cooked or raw (*often used before a noun*) ○ *fish soup* **3. SOMEBODY UNUSUAL** an odd or unusual person (*informal*) ○ *an odd fish* ■ *v* (**fished, fish·ing, fish·es**) **1.** *vi* **CATCH FISH** to use a rod, net, or other method to bring fish out of the water **2.** *vt* **CATCH FISH IN PLACE** to try to get fish from a particular river, lake, or stream **3.** *vi* **SEARCH** to feel around with the hands in order to find something (*informal*) [Old English *fisc* < Indo-European] ◇ **drink like a fish** to habitually drink a lot of alcoholic liquor (*informal*) ◇ **have other fish to fry** to have something else to do, usually something more interesting (*informal*) ◇ **like a fish out of water** ill at ease in a situation

fish for *vt* to try to obtain something, especially in an indirect way or in difficult circumstances ○ *fish for compliments*

fish out *vt* to find something or take something out, especially after searching with the hands (*informal*) ○ *fishing out a coin from his pocket*

Fish *n* ZODIAC same as **Pisces** (sense 2)

Fish /fish/, **Hamilton** (1808–93) US politician. He served as a member of the US House of Representatives (1843–45), governor of New York (1849–50), US senator (1851–57), and US secretary of state (1869–77).

fish and brew·is *n Can* a dish made from salt cod with stewed hardtack and fried salt pork

fish and chips *n* a fillet of fish deep-fried in batter, served with French fries (*takes a singular or plural verb*)

fish·bowl /físh bōl/ *n* **1.** a round clear open-topped container of water in which a pet goldfish is kept **2.** a place or condition of high public visibility and little or no personal privacy

fish cake *n* a round flat individual cake made from cooked fish and potato, coated with breadcrumbs, and usually fried

fish crow *n* a small crow that feeds on fish and mollusks. Native to: the Gulf and Atlantic coasts of North America. Latin name: *Corvus ossifragus.*

fish duck *n* BIRDS same as **merganser**

fish ea·gle *n* an eagle, especially one with white feathers, that feeds on fish. Genus: *Haliaeetus.*

fish·er /físhər/ *n* a species of marten with dense dark brown fur. Native to: northern North America. Latin name: *Martes pennanti.*

fish·er·man /físhərmən/ (*plural* **-men** /-mən/) *n* a man who catches fish as a sport or occupation

fish·er·man's bend *n* a knot used to tie the end of a line to a ring or spar

fish·er·man's knot *n* a knot for joining the ends of two ropes, consisting of one or two overhand knots that tighten with tension on the line

fish·er·per·son /físhər pùrss'n/ (*plural* **-peo·ple** /-peep'l/ or **-per·sons**) *n* somebody who catches fish as a sport or occupation

fish·er·wom·an /físhər wŏŏmmən/ (*plural* **-wom·en** /-wìmmin/) *n* a woman who catches fish as a sport or occupation

fish·er·y /físhəree/ (*plural* **-ies**) *n* **1. PLACE FOR REARING FISH** a region of water or a tank in which fish are reared **2. REGION OF WATER FOR FISHING** a region of water where industrial fishing is practiced **3. FISH BUSINESS** a business that harvests, processes, or sells fish **4. FISHING INDUSTRY** the catching, processing, or selling of fish, including the industries and occupations involved in these activities **5.** LAW **RIGHT TO FISH** the right to fish in an area

Fish·es /físhəz/ *n* ZODIAC same as **Pisces** (sense 2)

fisheye lens: view from a fisheye lens of Wall Street, New York City

fish·eye lens /fish ī-/ *n* a wide-angle lens that gives an extremely wide field of view, up to 180 degrees. Straight lines are curved and distorted by this type of lens.

fish farm *n* a place with facilities for rearing fish commercially —**fish farm·er** *n* —**fish farm·ing** *n*

fish fin·ger *n UK* same as **fish stick**

fish fry *n* a meal with deep-fried fish as the main course

fish·gig /fish gìg/ *n* a pole with barbs, used for spearing fish [Mid-16C. Alteration of *fizgig* < FIZZ + *gig* "giddy girl," after FISH]

fish hawk *n* BIRDS same as **osprey**

fish·hook /físh hŏŏk/ *n* **1.** a sharp metal hook used for catching fish **2.** a symbol used in logic to represent an "if-then" proposition

fish·ing /físhing/ *n* **1.** the sport, industry, or occupation of catching fish **2.** a place for fishing

fish·ing ex·pe·di·tion *n* an investigation or line of questioning that strays from its ostensible purpose (*informal*)

fish·ing rod *n* a long flexible pole to which a line and usually a reel are attached for catching fish

fish joint *n* a connection in which two rails or beams are joined together by one or more fishplates

fish ket·tle *n* an oblong pan, often with a rack inside, for cooking a whole fish

fish knife *n* a broad-bladed knife with blunt edges, used for eating fish

fish lad·der *n* a series of pools on an incline, separated by short increments so as to enable fish to swim up past a dam or other obstruction

fish louse *n* a small flat rounded crustacean with

sucking mouth parts that lives as a parasite on fish. Class: Branchiura.

fish·meal /físh mēel/ *n* a substance prepared from ground dried fish. Use: animal feed, fertilizer.

fish·mon·ger /físh mùng gər, -mòng-/ *n* somebody whose job is to sell fish to people for food

fish·net /físh nèt/ *n* **1.** a net used to catch fish **2.** open mesh fabric. Use: stockings, pantyhose.

fish·plate /físh plàyt/ *n* a flat piece of metal bolted between two abutting rails or beams to join them, especially on railroad track [Mid-19C. Origin ?]

fish·pond /físh pònd/ *n* a pond where fish are found or kept

fish pro·tein con·cen·trate *n* a food supplement that contains high concentrations of protein and is prepared from fish

fish·skin dis·ease /físhskin-/ *n* same as **ichthyosis** (*informal*)

fish stick *n* a rectangular piece of filleted or ground fish that is covered in breadcrumbs or batter

fish sto·ry *n* an implausible story boasting about something that was nearly accomplished (*informal*) [< traditional exaggeration of the size of fish almost caught]

fish·tail /físh tàyl/ *vi* (**-tailed, -tail·ing, -tails**) **1.** AUTOMOT **SWING FROM SIDE TO SIDE** to swing from side to side, especially uncontrollably, while moving forward in a motor vehicle **2. SWING AN AIRPLANE'S TAIL** to move the tail of an airplane from side to side in order to reduce speed ■ *adj* **GATHERED AND FLARED** describes the back of a skirt or dress that has a section that is closely gathered or pleated and then flares out

fish·way /físh wày/ *n* FISHERIES same as **fish ladder**

fish·wife /físh wīf/ *n* **1.** an offensive term for a woman who is regarded as loud-voiced and lacking in manners (*insult*) **2.** a woman selling fish (*archaic*)

fish·worm /físh wùrm/ *n regional* same as **earthworm**

REGIONAL NOTE The dialect term ***fishworm*** is found in most parts of the country, with the highest incidence in New England and the North Central states. In the South, *earthworm*, a general-currency word elsewhere, is frequent in all types of speech and especially in folk speech.

fish·y /físhee/ (**-i·er, -i·est**) *adj* **1. LIKE FISH** like fish, especially in taste, smell, or coldness or sliminess to the touch **2. DUBIOUS** arousing suspicion (*informal*) **3. EXPRESSIONLESS** cold and expressionless, like the eye of a fish ○ *He gave me a fishy look.* —**fish·i·ly** *adv* —**fish·i·ness** *n*

Fisk /fisk/, **James** (1834–72) US financier. A stock market speculator, he and his partners caused Black Friday (1869) when they tried to corner the gold market.

fissi- *prefix* **1.** cleft, separated ○ *fissipedal* **2.** biological fission ○ *fissiparous* [< Latin *fiss-*, past participle of *findere* "split" < Indo-European]

fis·sile /físs'l/ *adj* **1.** PHYS same as **fissionable 2.** describes a rock that can be split along a grain or a plane of cleavage, e.g., slate or schist [Mid-17C. < Latin *fiss-* (see FISSI-)] —**fis·sil·i·ty** /fi síllətee/ *n*

fis·sion /físh'n/ *n* **1.** PHYS **SPLITTING OF ATOMIC NUCLEUS RELEASING ENERGY** the spontaneous or induced splitting of an atomic nucleus into smaller parts, usually accompanied by a significant release of energy **2. BREAKING UP** the act or process of separating into parts **3.** GENETICS **DIVISION OF AN ORGANISM** the division of a single-celled organism into two equal parts, each part growing into a complete organism [Early 17C. < Latin *fission-* < *fiss-* (see FISSI-)]

fis·sion·a·ble /físh'nəb'l/ *adj* able to undergo nuclear fission —**fis·sion·a·bil·i·ty** /físh'nə bíllətee/ *n*

fis·sion bomb *n* same as **atomic bomb** (*technical*)

fis·sion-track dat·ing *n* a way to determine the age of a mineral from the tracks made by fission products of the uranium it contains

fis·sip·a·rous /fi síppərəss/ *adj* describes an organism that reproduces by dividing into two equal parts, each of which grows into a complete organism —**fis·sip·a·rous·ly** *adv*

fis·si·ped /físsə pèd/ *adj* describes animals that have toes separated from each other, e.g., dogs and cats ■ *n* an animal with separated toes. Suborder: Fissipedia. [Mid-17C. < late Latin *fissiped-* < Latin *fiss-* (see FISSI-) + *ped-* "foot"]

fis·sure /físhər/ *n* **1. CRACK** a long narrow crack or opening, especially in rock **2. PROCESS OF SPLITTING** the process of dividing along a line **3. SCHISM IN GROUP** a division into factions of a group or political party **4.** ANAT **SPLIT IN BODY PART** a natural or pathological division in a body part ■ *vti* (**-sured, -sur·ing, -sures**) **SPLIT, OR CAUSE TO SPLIT** to split something along fairly regular lines, or undergo this process [14C. Directly or via French < Latin *fissura* < *fiss-* (see FISSI-)]

fist /fist/ *n* **1. CLENCHED HAND** a hand with the fingers closed in the palm **2.** same as **hand** *n* (sense 2) (*informal*) **3.** same as **handful** (sense 1) (*informal*) **4.** PRINTING same as **index** *n* (sense 8) ■ *v* (**fist·ed, fist·ing, fists**) **1.** *vt* **STRIKE SOMEBODY WITH FIST** to hit somebody or something with a fist **2.** *vt US* **HANDLE** to handle something roughly or carelessly (*informal*) **3.** *vti* same as **fistfuck** (*taboo*) [Old English *fȳst* < Germanic] —**fist·ful** *n*

fist·fight /físt fīt/ *n* a fight in which bare fists are used

fist·fuck /físt fùk/ (**-fucked, -fuck·ing, -fucks**) *vti* a highly offensive term meaning to insert a fist into somebody's vagina or anus for sexual pleasure (*taboo*)

fist·i·cuffs /físti kùfs/ *npl* fighting using the fists (*archaic or humorous*) [Early 17C. Probably < *fisty* "with the fists" + CUFF[2] "blow"]

fis·tu·la /físchələ/ (*plural* **-las** or **-lae** /-lee/) *n* an opening or passage between two organs or between an organ and the skin, caused by disease, injury, or congenital malformation [14C. Directly or via French < Latin *fistula* "pipe, flute"] —**fis·tu·lous** *adj*

fit[1] /fit/ *v* (**fit·ted** or **fit, fit·ting, fits**) **1.** *vti* **BE THE RIGHT SIZE OR SHAPE** to be of a suitable size or shape for something or somebody ○ *See if this jacket fits.* **2.** *vti* **BE APPROPRIATE** to be appropriate or suitable for something ○ *make the punishment fit the crime* **3.** *vti* **BE COMPATIBLE** to agree or be in accordance with something ○ *no one fitting that description* **4.** *vt* **TRY CLOTHING ON SOMEBODY** to try clothing on somebody to determine if changes are necessary **5.** *vt* **EQUIP SOMEBODY OR SOMETHING** to provide somebody or something with equipment of a particular kind ○ *fitted with extra security features* **6.** *vt* **MAKE SOMEBODY OR SOMETHING READY** to make somebody or something ready or suitable for a task, function, or purpose ○ *an education that will fit her for a career in business* **7.** *vt* **INSTALL SOMETHING** to install something, or put something in place ■ *adj* (**fit·ter, fit·test**) **1. APPROPRIATE** suitable, acceptable, or appropriate for a purpose ○ *dishes fit for everyday use* **2. WORTHY** worthy or deserving of something ○ *not fit to serve as an officer* **3. WELL IN HEALTH** in good health **4. STRONG AND HEALTHY** physically strong and healthy, especially because of taking regular exercise **5. APPEARING LIKELY TO DO SOMETHING** appearing likely to do something because of being in an extreme condition (*informal*) ○ *looked fit to drop* ■ *n* **1. WAY THAT SOMETHING FITS** the way in which something conforms to standards of proper length, tightness, and shape ○ *These shoes are a better fit than the other pair.* **2. RELATIONSHIP FOR BEST FUNCTION** a relationship between corresponding parts or related things that enables proper functioning ○ *check the replacement chassis for fit* [14C. Origin ?] ◇ **fit to be tied** very angry and exasperated (*informal*) ◇ **fit to kill** to an extreme degree that captures attention

fit in *v* **1.** *vi* to conform harmoniously to other members of a group or other things in a setting ○ *She's been able to fit in well at her new school.* **2.** *vt* to find a time or place for somebody or something that does not conflict with other arrangements ○ *The dentist can fit you in at three.* ○ *I love the theater but can't fit it into my schedule.*

fit out *vt* to equip or provide something or somebody with required items such as supplies or clothes

fit[2] /fit/ *n* **1.** a sudden occurrence of a physical activity or an emotional mood ○ *a fit of laughing* ○ *a coughing fit* **2.** sudden violent convulsions, e.g., in a child with a high fever or somebody experiencing a seizure [Old English *fitt*, origin ?] ◇ **in** *or* **by fits and starts** starting and stopping repeatedly ◇ **throw a fit** to show strong emotion, especially anger (*informal*)

fitch /fich/, **fitch·et** /fíchət/ *n* ZOOL same as **polecat** (sense 1) [15C. < Middle Dutch *fisse*]

Fitch /fich/, **John** (1743–98) US inventor who built the first successful steamboat (1787). His boats operated on the Delaware River (1787–90).

Fitch·burg /fích bùrg/ city in northern Massachusetts, south of the border with New Hampshire and northwest of Leominster. Population: 39,727 (2002 estimate).

fit·chet *n* ZOOL same as **fitch**

fit·ful /fítfəl/ *adj* starting and stopping irregularly ○ *a fitful sleep* —**fit·ful·ly** *adv* —**fit·ful·ness** *n*

fit·ness /fítnəss/ *n* **1. BEING PHYSICALLY FIT** the state of being physically fit **2. SUITABILITY** suitability of somebody or something for a particular purpose **3.** GENETICS **ABILITY TO REPRODUCE SUCCESSFULLY** the ability of an organism to produce offspring that survive and reproduce

fit·ness cen·ter *n* a place with facilities and equipment for people to maintain or improve their physical fitness

fit·ted /fíttəd/ *adj* **1.** tailored to fit closely to the body ○ *a fitted jacket* **2.** *UK* built or fixed to fill or cover a specific space ○ *a fitted wardrobe* ○ *fitted carpets*

fit·ted sheet *n* a sheet with elastic at the corners that makes it fit snugly over a mattress

fit·ter /fíttər/ *n* **1.** a maintainer, repairer, or assembler of mechanical equipment **2.** somebody who alters clothes to make them fit

fit·ting /fítting/ *adj* **SUITABLE** appropriate for the circumstances ○ *a fitting end to her career* ■ *n* **1. TRYING ON OF CLOTHES** the trying on of a piece of clothing to see if it requires alteration **2. DETACHABLE PART** a detachable part, especially for a device or machine **3. WORK OF FITTER** the work performed by a fitter ■ **fit·tings** *npl* **ASSOCIATED PARTS** decorations, furniture, and accessories that belong to a building, vehicle, or machine —**fit·ting·ly** *adv* —**fit·ting·ness** *n*

fit·ting room *n* a room for trying on or fitting clothes in a store

Fitz·ger·ald /fits jérrəld/, **Edward** (1809–83) British poet and translator. He is best known for his translation (1859) into rhymed verse of the *Rubáiyát* by the Persian poet, Omar Khayyam.

AKG London

Ella Fitzgerald

Fitz·ger·ald, Ella (1917–96) US jazz singer. She was known for her scat singing and extensive song repertoire.

> "I always thought my music was pretty much hollering."
> [Ella Fitzgerald, *Ella Fitzgerald*, Bud Kliment; 1988]

Library of Congress

F. Scott Fitzgerald

Fitz·ger·ald, F. Scott (1896–1940) US writer. He wrote novels and short stories that chronicled the mood and manners of the 1920s. Among his works is *The Great Gatsby* (1925). Full name **Fitzgerald, Francis Scott Key**. See Cultural note at **great, tender**[1]

"Show me a hero and I will write you a tragedy."
[F. Scott Fitzgerald, "Notebooks E", *The Crack-Up: with Other Uncollected Pieces, Note-Books and Unpublished Letters*; 1945]

Fitz·Ger·ald /fits jérrald/, **G. F.** (1851–1901) Irish physicist. He suggested a way of producing electromagnetic waves that led to wireless telegraphy. He helped devise the Lorenz-FitzGerald contraction that was used by Einstein in his theory of relativity. Full name **FitzGerald, George Francis**

five /fīv/ *n* **1.** 5 the number 5 **2.** GROUP OF 5 a group of five objects or people **3.** SOMETHING WITH VALUE OF 5 something in a numbered series with a value of 5, e.g., a playing card ○ *the five of clubs* ○ *to throw a five* **4.** MONEY $5 BILL a bill worth five dollars [Old English *fīf* < Indo-European] —**five** *adj, pron* ◇ **take five** to take a few minutes' break from work or other activity (*informal*)

five-and-dime *n* a variety store of a type, now obsolete, that sold housewares, toys, candy, small pets, and other assorted items at reasonable prices

five-and-ten, five-and-ten-cent store *n* COMM same as **five-and-dime**

Five Civ·i·lized Na·tions, Five Civ·i·lized Tribes *npl* five Native North American peoples, the Choctaw, Cherokee, Chickasaw, Creek, and Seminole, who were briefly self-governing in the Indian Territory after being displaced from their land in the southeastern United States

five-fin·ger *n* PLANTS same as **cinquefoil**

five-fin·ger dis·count *n* an act of shoplifting (*slang*)

five·fold /fīv fōld/ *adj* **1.** TIMES 5 with or equal to five times as much or as many **2.** WITH 5 PARTS composed of five parts or sections ■ *adv* BY FIVE TIMES AS MUCH by five times as much or as many

five hun·dred *n* euchre or rummy in which the winner is the first to reach 500 points

Five Na·tions *n* **1.** *UK* an international rugby championship held annually between teams representing England, France, Ireland, Scotland, and Wales, replaced in 2000 by a championship also involving Italy (*takes a singular verb*) **2.** the original Iroquois Confederacy of five Native North American peoples, the Mohawk, Onondaga, Cayuga, Oneida, and Seneca, founded in the 16th century and lasting until 1722

five nines *npl* a very high measure or degree of product reliability, used especially in information technology

five o'clock shad·ow *n* beard growth noticeable later in the day on a man who shaved in the morning

five of a kind *n* a poker hand consisting of four cards of the same denomination plus a wild card

five·pen·ny /fīv pènnee/ *adj* costing or worth five pence

Five Pil·lars of Is·lam *npl* the basic tenets of Islam, which are a belief in Allah and in Muhammad as his prophet, in prayer, in charity, in fasting, and in making a pilgrimage to Mecca

five·pins /fīv pìnz/ *n* a bowling game played in Canada in which five pins are used (*takes a singular verb*)

fiv·er /fívər/ *n* (*informal*) **1.** a banknote worth five dollars **2.** *UK* in the United Kingdom, a banknote worth five pounds

five-spice pow·der *n* a Chinese mixed spice consisting of star anise, Sichuan pepper, cinnamon, fennel, and cloves

five-spot, five·spot /fīv spòt/ *n* a banknote worth five dollars (*informal*)

five-star *adj* having the highest quality

five-star gen·er·al *n* a general of the highest rank, with an insignia of five stars

527 com·mi·tee *n* a political fundraising group that can accept state funding legally for party candidates via corporations, unions, and the wealthy in excess of the campaign-finance contribution limits established by Congress in 2002 [After the section of the US federal tax code that permits such practices]

fix /fiks/ *v* (**fixed, fix·ing, fix·es**) **1.** *vt* MEND OR CORRECT SOMETHING to repair, mend, or correct something **2.** *vt* PREPARE SOMETHING AS FOOD to prepare something, especially a meal or a drink **3.** *vt* ARRANGE OR ORDER SOMETHING to arrange or put something in order **4.** *vt* AGREE SOMETHING to agree, arrange, or settle something, especially a time or a price **5.** *vt* INFLUENCE SOMETHING DISHONESTLY to influence a person or outcome dishonestly (*informal*) ○ *The trial was fixed.* **6.** *vt* TAKE REVENGE ON SOMEBODY to take revenge on or punish somebody (*informal*) **7.** *vt* ATTRIBUTE SOMETHING to attribute something, especially blame ○ *to fix the blame on other people* **8.** *vt* DIRECT SOMETHING to direct or concentrate the eyes, attention, or mind ○ *She fixed her eyes on the path ahead.* **9.** *vti* MAKE OR BECOME SECURE to make something stable, firm, or secure, or become so **10.** *vt* VET STERILIZE ANIMAL to spay or castrate an animal (*informal*) **11.** *vt* HOLD SOMEBODY'S ATTENTION to hold or capture the attention or interest of somebody ○ *fixed us with a baleful smile* **12.** *vt* FASTEN SOMETHING to fasten something in place ○ *She fixed the notice to the door with a thumbtack.* **13.** *vt* BIOCHEM CONVERT NITROGEN TO A STABLE FORM to convert atmospheric nitrogen to a stable or biologically available form, as soil bacteria do **14.** *vt* PHOTOGRAPHY, ART MAKE IMAGE PERMANENT to treat something such as a photographic film or plate with chemicals in order to make a permanent image **15.** *vti* CHEM MAKE OR BECOME STABLE to make a chemical or compound stable and nonvolatile, or undergo this process **16.** *vt* BIOL PRESERVE SOMETHING FOR EXAMINATION to preserve a specimen in a chemical solution for study under a microscope **17.** *vi* DRUGS INJECT A DRUG to inject an illegal drug (*slang*) ■ *n* **1.** PREDICAMENT a predicament or difficult situation ○ *in a fix* **2.** SUPERFICIAL SOLUTION an immediate and often temporary solution (*informal*) ○ *a quick fix* **3.** INFLUENCING DISHONESTLY an instance of influencing an outcome or person dishonestly **4.** DRUGS ILLEGAL DRUG INJECTION an injection of an illegal drug (*slang*) **5.** STIMULATING DOSE a dose of or exposure to something pleasurable and stimulating (*humorous*) ○ *a chocolate fix* **6.** NAVIG CALCULATION OF POSITION a calculation of the position of an object using radar or other forms of observation **7.** UNDERSTANDING an understanding or identification of something (*informal*) ○ *Do you have a fix on what the problem is?* [15C. < Latin *fix-*, past participle of *figere* "to fix"] —**fix·a·ble** *adj* ◇ **be fixing to do something** *regional* to be on the verge of doing something ○ *They're fixing to get married.* ◇ **the fix is in** the case or other matter has already been dishonestly decided, e.g., by the use of bribes (*slang*)
fix on *vt* to select something
fix up *vt* **1.** ARRANGE A CONTACT FOR SOMEBODY to arrange a business or social contact, or a romantic or sexual partner, for somebody **2.** REPAIR SOMETHING to restore something to working order or proper order **3.** GET SOMETHING FOR SOMEBODY to provide something for somebody ○ *He said he could fix me up with a good used car.* **4.** ARRANGE SOMETHING to arrange something such as a meeting or a date

fix·ate /fík sàyt/ (**-at·ed, -at·ing, -ates**) *v* **1.** *vi* FOCUS ON SOMETHING to focus exclusively on something **2.** *vt* OBSESS SOMEBODY to obsess or preoccupy somebody or something totally **3.** *vti* PSYCHOL FORM A FIXATION to form or have a psychological fixation with a person or object **4.** *vti* BECOME OR MAKE FIXED to make something stable or secure, or become so [Late 19C. < Latin *fix-* (see FIX)]

fix·a·tion /fik sáysh'n/ *n* **1.** OBSESSION an obsession or preoccupation **2.** PSYCHOL, PSYCHOANAL IMMATURE PSYCHOSEXUAL BEHAVIOR a theoretical strong libidinal attachment to a person or object, formed during early childhood, that results in neurotic or arrested psychosexual behavior in adulthood **3.** BIOCHEM CONVERSION OF NITROGEN the conversion by soil bacteria of atmospheric nitrogen to a stable biologically available form **4.** CHEM STABILIZATION OF CHEMICAL the process of stabilizing a chemical or compound **5.** BIOL PRESERVING FOR EXAMINATION the preservation of biological specimens with chemicals

fix·a·tive /fíksətiv/ *n* (*plural same* or **-tives**) **1.** LIQUID SPRAYED FOR PROTECTION a liquid sprayed onto a drawing, photograph, or other surface to protect it **2.** GLUE a substance used to hold something in place **3.** COSMETICS PERFUME ADDITIVE a substance added to a perfume to make it evaporate less rapidly **4.** BIOL CHEMICAL PRESERVATIVE a chemical solution that preserves a biological specimen for microscopic study **5.** TEXTILES FABRIC ADDITIVE a substance applied to dyed fabrics to make the dye colorfast ■ *adj* TENDING TO FIX acting or tending to protect, preserve, or stabilize something

fixed /fikst/ *adj* **1.** SECURE immovable or securely in position **2.** NOT SUBJECT TO CHANGE not subject to change in amount or time **3.** NOT CHANGING unchanging in expression **4.** AGREED ON arranged or agreed upon **5.** HELD IN MIND firmly or dogmatically held in the mind **6.** PROVIDED WITH SOMETHING in the position of having something available for use ○ *How are you fixed for money?* **7.** DISHONESTLY ARRANGED unfairly or illegally arranged (*slang*) **8.** CHEM CHEMICALLY STABLE combined in stable form ○ *fixed nitrogen* **9.** ASTROL STABLE IN ZODIACAL TERMS describes Taurus, Leo, Scorpio, and Aquarius, signs of the zodiac associated with stability —**fix·ed·ly** /-ədlee/ *adv* —**fix·ed·ness** /-ədnəss/ *n*

fixed ac·tion pat·tern *n* a pattern of behavior in an organism that appears to be developed completely when first stimulated

fixed as·set *n* an asset of a business that is central to its operation and is not traded (*usually used in the plural*)

fixed cost *n* a business expense that does not vary according to the amount of business (*usually used in the plural*)

fixed i·de·a *n* PSYCHOL same as **idée fixe**

fixed in·come *n* income from securities such as bonds that are the same for each period

fixed line *adj* describes a telephone that is connected to a network via underground or aboveground lines

fixed oil *n* a nonvolatile oil composed of fatty acids, usually of animal or vegetable origin

fixed pen·al·ty *n* a fine of a specific amount given for an offense, especially a traffic violation

fixed point *n* a temperature that has a fixed value under specific conditions and can be used to calibrate instruments, e.g., the boiling or freezing point

fixed-point *adj* describes numbers in which the decimal place is always in a fixed position

fixed-wing *adj* describes an aircraft that has stationary wings, especially as distinct from rotor blades

fix·er /fíksər/ *n* **1.** SOMEBODY WHO ARRANGES SOMETHING DISHONEST somebody who arranges something, especially by dishonest or illegal means (*slang*) **2.** PHOTOGRAPHY CHEMICAL IN PHOTOGRAPHY a chemical that halts the development of a photographic image on film or paper **3.** SOMEBODY OR SOMETHING THAT FIXES a person who or an object that fixes something

fix·ing /fíksing/ *n UK* HOLDING DEVICE a means of holding an item in place ■ **fix·ings** *npl* (*informal*) **1.** INGREDIENTS the ingredients required for a particular dish **2.** FOOD ACCOMPANIMENTS the typical accompaniments for a particular dish

fix·i·ty /fíksətee/ (*plural* **-ties**) *n* **1.** the quality or state of being fixed and unchanging **2.** something that is unchanging (*formal*)

fix·ture /fíkschər/ *n* **1.** an object with a fixed position and function **2.** somebody considered to be permanently established in a place or position [Late 16C. Probably alteration, after MIXTURE, of *fixure* < late Latin *fixura* < Latin *fix-* (see FIX)]

fizz /fiz/ *vi* (**fizzed, fizz·ing, fizz·es**) **1.** PRODUCE GAS BUBBLES to produce bubbles of gas **2.** HISS to make a hissing or continuous soft crackling sound ■ *n* **1.** EFFERVESCENCE the sparkling quality of a drink caused by bubbles of gas **2.** HISSING SOUND a hissing or continuous soft crackling sound **3.** LIVELINESS a quality of liveliness or excitement ○ *All the fizz has gone out of the election campaign.* **4.** SPARKLING DRINK a sparkling drink, especially champagne [Mid-17C. An imitation of the sound]

fiz·zle /fízz'l/ *vi* (**-zled, -zling, -zles**) **1.** FAIL AFTER GOOD START to fail or peter out, especially after a good start (*informal*) **2.** MAKE HISSING SOUND to make a gentle hissing sound ■ *n* **1.** FAILURE a fiasco or total failure (*informal*) 2. **HISSING SOUND** a gentle hissing sound [Mid-16C. Probably < obsolete *fist* "break wind" < Germanic]

fiz·zler /fízzlər/ *n US* (*informal*) 1. a firecracker that sputters and hisses but does not explode 2. an event that is not as lively or exciting as expected

fizz·y /fízzee/ (**-i·er, -i·est**) *adj* producing or containing gas bubbles —**fizz·i·ly** *adv* —**fizz·i·ness** *n*

fj *abbr* Fiji (*used in Internet addresses*) See table at **domain name**

fjord: Geiranger fjord, Norway

fjord /fyawrd/, **fiord** *n* a long narrow coastal inlet with steep sides, often formed by glacial action, especially along the western coast of Norway [Late 17C. Via Norwegian < Old Norse *fjǫrðr*]

Fkr *abbr* MONEY krona[2]

FL *abbr* 1. LANGUAGE foreign languages 2. *UK* AIR FORCE Flight Lieutenant 3. Florida

fl. *abbr* 1. floor 2. MONEY florin 3. floruit 4. MUSIC flute

Fl. *abbr* 1. Flanders 2. SPORTS flanker 3. Flemish

Fla. *abbr* Florida

flab /flab/ *n* excess or unwanted fat on somebody's body (*informal*) [Early 20C. Back-formation < FLABBY]

flab·ber·gast /flábbər gàst/ (**-gast·ed, -gast·ing, -gasts**) *vt* to amaze or astonish somebody completely (*informal; usually passive*) [Late 18C. Origin ?]

flab·by /flábbee/ (**-bi·er, -bi·est**) *adj* (*informal*) 1. having excess body fat or sagging flesh 2. done without vitality or force [Late 17C. Alteration of *flappy*] —**flab·bi·ly** *adv* —**flab·bi·ness** *n*

fla·bel·la BIOL, CHR plural of **flabellum**

fla·bel·late /flə béllət, flábbə làyt/, **fla·bel·li·form** /flə béllə fàwrm/ *adj* describes an organism or body part that is shaped like an open handheld fan [Late 18C. < Latin *flabellum* (see FLABELLUM)]

fla·bel·lum /flə béllәm/ (*plural* **-la** /-lə/) *n* 1. a fan-shaped organ or body part 2. a fan with a long handle, formerly used in the Roman Catholic Church to keep away insects during the Mass [Mid-19C. < Latin, "fan" < *flabrum* "gust" < *flare* "to blow"]

flac·cid /flássid, fláksid/ *adj* 1. soft, limp, or lacking firmness 2. lacking energy, enthusiasm, or competence [Early 17C. Directly or via French < Latin *flaccidus* < *flaccus* "flabby"] —**flac·cid·i·ty** /fla síddətee, flak-/ *n* —**flac·cid·ly** *adv*

~~**flacid**~~ incorrect spelling of **flaccid**

flack[1] /flak/ (*slang*) *n* a press agent or publicist ■ *vti* (**flacked, flack·ing, flacks**) to act as a press agent or publicity agent for somebody [Mid-20C. Origin ?] —**flack·er** *n* —**flack·er·y** *n*

flack[2] *n* ARMS another spelling of **flak**

flac·on /flákən, flá kòn/ *n* a small, often decorated, stoppered bottle used especially for perfume [Early 19C. < French (see FLAGON)]

flag[1] /flag/ *n* 1. **CLOTH FLOWN AS EMBLEM** a piece of cloth, often rectangular and flown from a pole, carrying a distinctive design and used as an emblem or for signaling 2. **DECORATION** a small ornament, emblem, or pin showing the colors and design of a flag 3. **IDENTITY SYMBOLIZED BY FLAG** a national or group identity symbolized by a flag 4. **MARKING DEVICE** a marking device, e.g., a tab, that is attached to something to make it easier to identify or more conspicuous 5. COMPUT **COMPUTER PROGRAM MARKER** an indicator generated by a computer program to denote a condition such as an error 6. TRANSP **MARKER SHOWING A TAXI FOR HIRE** formerly, a small marker on a taximeter, raised to show a taxi's availability for hire 7. FOOTBALL **PENALTY MARKER** a colored cloth thrown to the ground by a football official to indicate illegal play 8. MUSIC **NOTE MARKER** an angled line on the stem of a musical note, indicating its value 9. NAVY same as **flagship** (sense 2) 10. MEDIA same as **masthead** (sense 1) 11. VERTEB **HAIR FRINGE BENEATH DOG'S TAIL** a fringe of hair that grows on the lower part of the tail in some dog breeds such as setters 12. ZOOL **DEER'S TAIL** the tail of a deer ■ *vt* (**flagged, flag·ging, flags**) 1. FOOTBALL **INDICATE PENALTY** in football, to indicate a penalty by throwing down a flag 2. **MARK SOMETHING** to mark something such as a page or a place, in order to draw attention to it ○ *I've flagged the passages that need rewriting.* 3. **INDICATE SOMETHING** to draw somebody's attention to something ○ *The report flagged items for concern.* 4. **SEND SOMEBODY MESSAGE BY FLAG** to signal somebody or send somebody information using a flag 5. *US* **CUT SOMEBODY OFF FROM DRINK** to refuse to serve somebody more alcoholic beverages because of apparent drunkenness (*slang*) 6. **DECORATE SOMETHING WITH FLAGS** to decorate something with flags 7. HUNTING **ATTRACT ANIMAL'S ATTENTION** to attract the attention or curiosity of wild game by waving something [Mid-16C. Origin ?] —**flag·ger** *n*

CULTURAL NOTE ***Flag***, a painting by Jasper Johns (1945). The first of many such variations that Johns created on this theme, it consists of a US flag painted on canvas using encaustic. Its apparent banality infuriated many commentators; others responded positively to its playful ambiguity (is it a flag or a painting?) and saw it as Johns' reaction to the emotionalism of Abstract Expressionism.

flag down *vt* to stop a vehicle or its driver by making signs to the driver

flag[2] /flag/ (**flagged, flag·ging, flags**) *vi* 1. to become weak, tired, or less attentive 2. to hang down limply, or droop [Mid-16C. Origin ?]

flag[3] /flag/ *n* CONSTR, GEOL same as **flagstone** (sense 1) ■ *vt* (**flagged, flag·ging, flags**) CONSTR, ROADS to pave a surface with flagstones [15C. Probably < N Germanic] —**flagged** *adj*

flag[4] /flag/ *n* 1. a plant of the iris family, usually one with large flowers and leaves 2. a long narrow leaf of a plant such as an iris [14C. Origin ?]

flag cap·tain *n* the captain of the flagship of a fleet

flag con·ser·va·tive *n* a zealous neoconservative who believes that the United States is duty-bound to engage in global policing for the good of the civilized world and to engage in combat if necessary, in order to ensure the furtherance of the national interest, national security, and the security of US allies ○*"Flag conservatives truly believe America is not only fit to run the world but that it must."* (Norman Mailer, "Only in America," *New York Review of Books*; March 27, 2003) [Early 21C]

flag day *n UK* same as **tag day**

Flag Day *n* a holiday marking the official adoption of the design of the US flag in 1777. Date: June 14.

fla·gel·la BIOL plural of **flagellum**

flag·el·lant /flájjələnt/ *n* 1. a penitent who whips himself or herself as a means of repentance 2. somebody who uses whipping to achieve pleasure [Late 16C. < Latin *flagellant-*, present participle of *flagellare* "to whip" < *flagellum* (see FLAGELLUM)] —**flag·el·lant·ism** *n*

fla·gel·lar /flə jéllər/ *adj* relating to a flagellum

flag·el·late[1] /flájjəlàt, -làyt, flə jéllət/ (**-lat·ed, -lat·ing, -lates**) *vt* to whip somebody, especially for sexual or religious purposes [Early 17C. < Latin *flagellat-*, past participle of *flagellare* "to whip" < *flagellum* (see FLAGELLUM)]

flag·el·late[2] /flájjələt, -làyt, flə jéllət/ *n* **MICROORGANISM WITH FLAGELLA** a microorganism with long thin cellular appendages (**flagella**). Some flagellates are pathogenic parasites that cause diseases such as giardiasis in humans. ■ *adj also* **flag·el·lat·ed** BIOL 1. **RESEMBLING A THREAD** similar to a long thin cellular appendage (**flagellum**) 2. **WITH APPENDAGES RESEMBLING THREADS** describes an organism or cell that has long thin cellular appendages (**flagella**) [Mid-19C. < FLAGELLUM]

flag·el·la·tion[1] /flàjjə láysh'n/ *n* the act of whipping yourself or somebody else, especially for sexual or religious purposes

flag·el·la·tion[2] /flàjjə láysh'n/ *n* the formation or arrangement of flagella on an organism

fla·gel·li·form /flə jéllə fàwrm/ *adj* describes an organism or body part that is long, tapering, and very narrow [Early 19C. < FLAGELLUM]

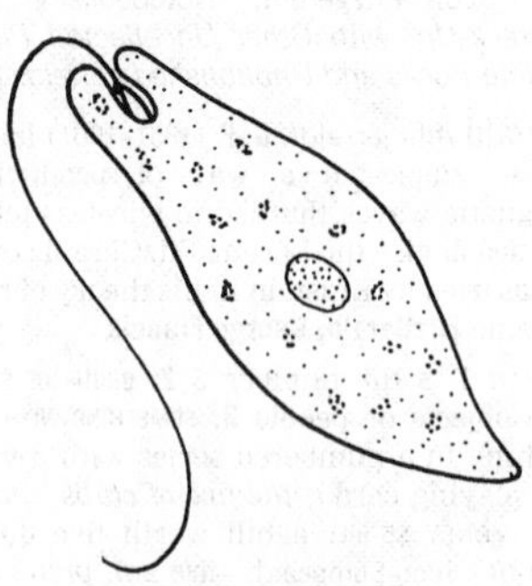
flagellum

fla·gel·lum /flə jélləm/ (*plural* **-la** /-lə/ or **-lums**) *n* 1. a long thin tapering outgrowth of the cells of many microorganisms such as protozoans, that is a means of locomotion 2. the very thin terminal part of an insect's antenna [Early 19C. < Latin, "little scourge" < *flagrum* "scourge"]

flag·eo·let[1] /flàjjə lét, flày-/ *n* a slender-podded variety of green bean that can be eaten either fresh or dried [Late 19C. Via French < Latin *phaseolus* "bean"]

flag·eo·let[2] /flàjjə lét, flày-/ *n* a musical instrument of the 16th and 17th centuries resembling the flute [Mid-17C. < French, "little flute" < Old French *flageol* "flute"]

flag foot·ball *n* a form of football in which play is stopped by the removal of a flag from the waist of the player with the ball, rather than by tackling

Flagg /flag/, **James Montgomery** (1877–1960) US writer and illustrator. He created the Uncle Sam "I Want You" poster (1917) to recruit soldiers during World War I.

flag·ging[1] /flágging/ *adj* 1. decreasing in strength, power, or ability 2. hanging down limply or drooping (*archaic*) —**flag·ging·ly** *adv*

flag·ging[2] /flágging/ *n* an area paved with flagstones

fla·gi·tious /flə jíshəss/ *adj* (*formal*) 1. extremely cruel, wicked, or vicious 2. notorious or infamous [14C. < Latin *flagitiosus* < *flagitium* "shameful crime" < *flagitare* "demand vehemently"] —**fla·gi·tious·ly** *adv* —**fla·gi·tious·ness** *n*

flag·man /flágmən/ (*plural* **-men** /-mən/) *n* a man who holds a flag, usually to make signals, e.g., to control traffic

flag of con·ven·ience *n* a flag of a country under which a ship is registered because of its favorable regulations, not for any real connection with the ship's owners or business

flag of·fi·cer *n* an officer in the US Navy or Coast Guard of a rank above captain who is entitled to display a flag indicating personal rank

flag of truce *n* a white flag flown to indicate surrender, a request or offer of conference, or other peaceful intent

flag·on /flággən/ *n* 1. **CONTAINER FOR BEVERAGES** a container for beverages with a handle, narrow neck, spout, and sometimes a lid 2. **LARGE BOTTLE FOR ALCOHOLIC DRINK** a large bottle with a short or narrow neck for an alcoholic drink 3. **AMOUNT HELD IN FLAGON** the amount that a flagon contains [14C. Via French *flacon* < late Latin *flascon-* "flask"]

flag·per·son /flág pùrss'n/ (*plural* **-per·sons** or **-peo·ple** /-pèep'l/) *n* somebody who holds a flag, usually to make signals, e.g., to control traffic

flag·pole /flág pōl/ *n* a pole on which a flag is flown ◇ **run something up the flagpole** to put forward an idea or suggestion in order to gauge general reaction to it (*informal*)

flag rank *n* a rank of admiral in the US Navy or Coast Guard

fla·grant /fláygrənt/ *adj* very obvious and contrary to standards of conduct or morality ○ *a flagrant violation of the suspect's civil rights* [15C. Directly or via French < Latin *flagrant-*, present participle of *flagrare* "to burn"] —**fla·grance** *n* —**fla·gran·cy** *n* —**fla·grant·ly** *adv*

USAGE See *blatant*.

flag·ship /flág shìp/ *n* **1. MOST IMPORTANT OF GROUP** the most important or prestigious among a group of similar and related things ○ *the flagship of the hotel spa chain* ○ *the company's flagship hotel* **2.** NAVY **COMMANDING SHIP** the ship from which the admiral or unit commander controls the operation of a fleet **3.** SHIPPING **MAIN COMMERCIAL SHIP** the main ship in a commercial fleet

flag·staff /flág stàf/ *n* same as **flagpole**

Flag·staff /flág stàf/ city in northern Arizona, northeast of Phoenix and southwest of the Painted Desert. Population: 55,173 (2002 estimate).

flag·stick /flág stìk/ *n* the flag pole that marks the position of the hole on a putting green

flag·stone /flág stōn/ (*plural same* or **-stones**) *n* **1.** a slab of stone or concrete used for making floors or paving **2.** fine-textured rock that can be split into slabs suitable for use in paving

flag stop *n* a station or place where a bus or train stops only when signaled by somebody waiting to board

flag-wav·ing *n* an excessive and emotional display of patriotism —**flag-wav·er** *n*

flag·wom·an /flág wŏŏmmən/ (*plural* **-wom·en** /-wìmmin/) *n* a woman who holds a flag, usually to make signals, e.g., to control traffic

Fla·her·ty /flá ərtee/, **Robert Joseph** (1884–1951) US documentary filmmaker. He is known for his ethnographic documentary about Inuit life, *Nanook of the North* (1922).

flail /flayl/ *v* (**flailed, flail·ing, flails**) **1.** *vti* **THRASH AROUND** to thrash or swing something around violently or uncontrollably, or move in this way **2.** *vt* **HIT SOMETHING** to strike or hit something ■ *n* **1.** AGRIC **MANUAL THRESHING IMPLEMENT** a manual threshing implement consisting of a wooden handle attached to a free-swinging wooden or metal bar **2.** ARMS **WEAPON LIKE FLAIL** a weapon shaped like a threshing flail, used especially in the Middle Ages [Pre-12C. Probably via an assumed Old English word (influenced by Old French *flaiel*) < Latin *flagellum* (see FLAGELLUM)]

flair /fler/ *n* **1.** a natural ability to do something well, especially creative or artistic ability **2.** obvious elegance or stylishness [Late 19C. < French, "sense of smell" < Old French *flairer* "to smell" < late Latin *flagrare*, alteration of Latin *fragrare* "emit an odor"]

SPELLCHECK See *flare*.

SYNONYMS See *talent*.

flak /flak/, **flack** *n* **1.** antiaircraft fire directed from the ground **2.** strong adverse criticism (*informal*) [Mid-20C. < German, acronym < *Flieger Abwehr Kanone* "airplane defense canon"]

flake[1] /flayk/ *n* **1. SMALL FLAT PIECE** a small flat piece or small part of a layer broken or detached from a larger object ○ *flakes of paint* **2. SMALL MANUFACTURED ITEM** a small thin flat object that is manufactured, sold, and used or consumed in quantity ○ *soap flakes* **3.** *US* same as **snowflake** (sense 1) **4. OFFENSIVE TERM** an offensive term for somebody regarded as eccentric or irrational (*informal insult*) **5.** *US* DRUGS same as **cocaine** (*slang*) ■ *v* (**flaked, flak·ing, flakes**) **1.** *vi* **FALL OFF IN FLAKES** to form into flakes and fall or peel off **2.** *vt* **BREAK SOMETHING INTO FLAKES** to break something into flakes, or break flakes from something ○ *flaked stones to fashion arrowheads* **3.** *vt* **COVER SOMETHING WITH FLAKES** to cover or coat something with flakes [14C. Probably < N Germanic] —**flak·er** *n*

flake out *vi* (*slang*) **1.** to collapse or fall asleep because of exhaustion **2.** *US* to behave in an irrational way that prevents normal functioning

flake[2] /flayk/ *n* a platform or frame for drying fish or other food [14C. Origin ?]

flake[3] /flayk/ *vt* (**flaked, flak·ing, flakes**) to coil or loop a rope so that it will not tangle when used ■ *n* a single loop of a rope that has been neatly coiled [Early 17C. Origin ?]

flake white *n* a pigment made from flakes of white lead

flak·ey *adj* another spelling of **flaky**

flak jack·et *n* a reinforced vest or jacket for protection against gunfire or shrapnel

flak·y /fláykee/ (**-i·er, -i·est**), **flak·ey** *adj* **1. AN OFFENSIVE TERM** an offensive term describing somebody regarded as eccentric or irrational (*informal insult*) **2. MADE OF FLAKES** made of or separating easily into small pieces ○ *with a flaky texture* **3. BREAKING INTO FLAKES** forming or tending to break off in flakes ○ *flaky skin* —**flak·i·ly** *adv* —**flak·i·ness** *n*

flak·y pas·try *n UK* a crust made from layers of pastry dough dotted with fat that puffs up and forms light layers when baked

flam /flam/ *n* a drumbeat of two nearly simultaneous strokes [Late 18C. Probably an imitation of the sound]

flam·bé /flaam báy/ *adj* served in liquor, usually brandy, that has been burned off or is still burning ○ *bananas flambé* ■ *vt* (**-béed, -bé·ing, -bés**) to pour liquor over food and light it in order to burn off the alcohol and impart the flavor of the liquor to the food [Late 19C. < French, past participle of *flamber* "singe, pass through flame" < Latin *flamma* "flame"]

flam·beau /flám bō/ (*plural* **-beaux** /-bōz/ or **-beaus**) *n* **1. TORCH** a lighted torch made of wicks dipped in wax **2. CANDLESTICK** a large decorative candlestick **3.** *Carib* **TORCH LIT WITH KEROSENE** a torch made by stuffing cloth into a bottle or sometimes a bamboo joint containing kerosene [Mid-17C. < French, "torch, flame" < *flambe* (see FLAMBOYANT)]

flam·boy·ant /flam bóy ənt/ *adj* **1. SHOWY** showy and dashing in a self-satisfied way **2. BRIGHTLY COLORED** brightly colored and striking **3. HIGHLY DECORATED** elaborate or richly decorated **4. AUDACIOUS** unrestrained by prevailing standards of propriety **5.** ARCHIT **OF FRENCH GOTHIC ARCHITECTURE** relating to or characteristic of 14th- to 16th-century French Gothic architecture, which is noted for its fine detailing and pointed decoration ■ *n* TREES same as **royal poinciana** [Mid-19C. < French, present participle of *flamboyer* "blaze" < *flambe* "flame" < Latin *flamma* "flame"] —**flam·boy·ance** *n* —**flam·boy·ant·ly** *adv*

flame /flaym/ *n* **1. HOT GLOWING BODY OF BURNING GAS** a hot glowing mass of burning gas, often carrying fine incandescent particles **2. STRONG FEELING** an intense feeling or emotion **3. ANGRY E-MAIL MESSAGE** a rude, abusive, or threatening e-mail message or newsgroup posting **4. REDDISH-ORANGE COLOR** a brilliant reddish orange color **5. LOVER** a sweetheart or lover (*informal*) ○ *an old flame* ■ *v* (**flamed, flam·ing, flames**) **1.** *vi* **PRODUCE FLAME** to burn producing flame **2.** *vti* **SEND JUDGMENTAL E-MAIL** to criticize somebody with offensive and disparaging e-mail **3.** *vi* **HAVE FIERY GLOW** to have or develop a fiery glow, especially suddenly ○ *Her cheeks flamed as she spoke.* **4.** *vt* **SUBJECT SOMETHING TO FIRE** to treat something with or subject something to flames **5.** *vi* **FEEL STRONG EMOTION** to display or feel intense emotion **6.** *vt* **MAKE SOMETHING BURN** to make something burn (*archaic*) [14C. Via Anglo-Norman and French < Latin *flamma* "flame"] —**flame** *adj* —**flam·er** *n* —**flam·y** *adj* ◇ **fan the flames** to make a tense or difficult situation worse ◇ **shoot somebody** *or* **something down in flames** to reject or refute an idea or suggestion emphatically

flame-arc lamp *n* a lamp that uses an electric arc maintained between carbon electrodes that are infused with metallic salts to provide color to the flame

flame bait *n* an inflammatory statement intentionally posted in an online discussion group to elicit a strong response or start a flame war (*informal*)

flame car·bon *n* a carbon electrode containing metallic salts that, with other similar carbon electrodes, has the effect of coloring the arc produced between the electrodes

flame cell *n* in some invertebrates such as flatworms, a hollow excretory cell that has a tuft of projections **(cilia)** resembling hairs whose movement serves to force out waste products [Because the movement of the cilia suggests tongues of flame]

fla·men /fláymən/ (*plural* **fla·mens** or **flam·i·nes** /flámmə neez/) *n* in ancient Roman religion, a priest belonging to a group of 15, each of whom oversaw the rituals connected with a particular deity [14C. < Latin]

Barnaby's

flamenco

fla·men·co /flə méngkō/ (*plural* **-cos**) *n* **1.** a dance of Spanish origin with hand clapping and stamping of feet **2.** the strongly rhythmic music that accompanies flamenco dancing [Late 19C. Via Spanish, "Flemish person" < Middle Dutch *Vlaming*]

flame net·tle (*plural same*) *n US* PLANTS same as **coleus**

flame·out /fláym òwt/ *n* the unintentional extinguishing of the flame of a jet engine in flight, e.g., through a failure of combustion or the fuel supply

flame·proof /fláym proof/ *adj* **1. RESISTANT TO FIRE** resistant to catching fire (*often used of textiles and clothing*) **2.** ELEC ENG **NOT EXPLOSIVE** describes electrical apparatus designed so that an explosion of inflammable gas inside will not ignite inflammable gas outside **3.** COOK **FOR COOKING WITH DIRECT HEAT** describes containers that can be used when cooking on a stove top or under a grill ■ *vt* (**-proofed, -proof·ing, -proofs**) **MAKE SOMETHING FLAME RESISTANT** to make something resistant to flames or combustion —**flame·proof·er** *n*

flame-re·tard·ant, flame-re·sist·ant *adj* made or chemically treated to resist catching fire

flame test *n* a test for the presence of various metals in a substance by noting the colors produced when a small amount is placed in a flame and vaporized

flame·throw·er /fláym thrō ər/ *n* a weapon that projects a stream of burning liquid

flame tree *n* **1.** a tropical tree cultivated for its bright orange, yellow, or red flowers, e.g., royal poinciana **2.** a tree with bright red flowers that bloom in spring before its leaves emerge. Native to: Australia. Latin name: *Brachychiton acerifolius*.

flame war *n* a period of repeated exchanges of abusive and insulting e-mail between people or groups

flam·i·nes RELIG plural of **flamen**

flam·ing /fláyming/ *adj* **1. PRODUCING FLAMES** burning and producing flames **2. INTENSE** very angry, intense, or passionate ○ *flaming indignation* **3. GLOWING** brightly glowing ○ *flaming cheeks* **4. VIVID IN COLOR** vivid in color ■ *n* ONLINE **DELUGE OF CRITICAL E-MAIL** a large volume of abusive and insulting e-mail directed at somebody

flamingo

fla·min·go /flə míng gō/ (*plural* **-gos** or **-goes** or *same*) *n* **1.** a large long-necked wading bird with a downward-curving beak, webbed feet, and pinkish white plumage with black wing feathers. Native to: tropical brackish waters. Family: Phoenicopteridae. **2.** a deep pink color tinged with orange [Mid-16C. Via Portuguese < obsolete Spanish *flamengo*] —**fla·min·go** *adj*

ORIGIN Whether its ultimate source is Dutch or Latin, the motivation behind the bird's name is its bright appearance. The Latin derivation would make it the "flame"-colored bird; the Dutch derivation would depend on the reputation the people of Flanders had in the Middle Ages for bright flamboyant dress (whence the Spanish dance, the *flamenco*).

flam·ing sword *n* a cultivated bromeliad with long inflorescences. Flowers: yellow with reddish bracts. Native to: French Guiana. Latin name: *Vriesea splendens.*

flam·ma·ble /flámməb'l/ *adj* readily capable of catching fire —**flam·ma·bil·i·ty** /flàmmə bíllətee/ *n*

USAGE flammable or **inflammable**? Although ***inflammable*** looks like the opposite of ***flammable***, the two words actually have the same meaning, both describing something that is easily set on fire. The *in-* prefix of ***inflammable*** means "into," rather than "not," and the adjective is ultimately derived from the same Latin word as the verb *inflame*. In view of the potentially disastrous consequences of such misinterpretation, ***flammable*** has become the word of choice, especially in the labeling of commercial and industrial products. The word most frequently used to convey the opposite meaning is ***nonflammable***.

flan /flan/ *n* **1.** *US* FOOD **CUSTARD DESSERT** a custard dessert topped with caramel syrup **2. TART** a tart with a fruit, custard, or other filling **3. METAL DISK FOR STAMPING AS COIN** a circular metal blank ready to be stamped as a coin [Mid-19C. Via French < medieval Latin *fladon-* < Germanic]

Flan·ders /flándərz/ region of Northwestern Europe that was a powerful independent state between the 11th and 14th centuries. It is equivalent to the present-day provinces of Flanders in Belgium, Nord Department in France, and part of Zeeland Province in the Netherlands.

flâ·ne·rie /flaan rée, flaanə rée/ *n* aimless idling or strolling [Late 19C. < French < *flâner* "stroll, lounge around"]

flâ·neur /flaa núr/ *n* an idler or loafer [Mid-19C. < French < *flâner* "stroll, lounge around"]

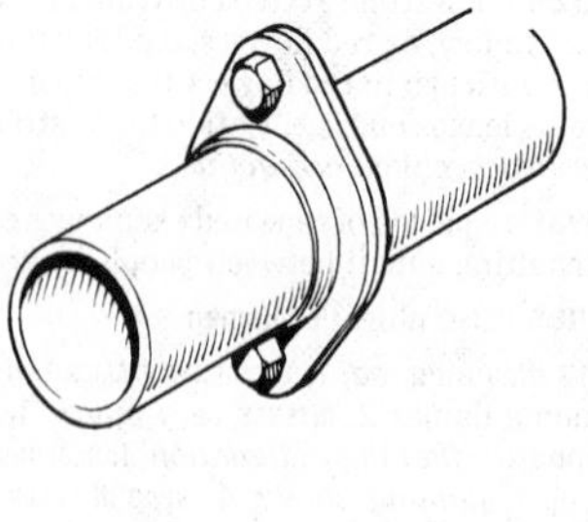

flange

flange /flanj/ *n* a projecting collar, rim, or rib on an object for fixing it to another object, holding it in place, or strengthening it. Flanges are often found on pipes and shafts. [Late 17C. Origin ?] —**flanged** /flanjd/ *adj*

flanged rail *n* an early form of rail with a raised edge (**flange**) on one side to stabilize wheels traveling on it. On modern trains the flange is on the wheel.

flank /flangk/ *n* **1.** MIL **SIDE OF MILITARY FORMATION** the left or right side of a military formation **2.** ANAT **SIDE OF LOWER TORSO** each side of the body of a person or an animal between the last rib and the hip **3. CUT OF BEEF** a cut of meat, especially beef, from an animal's flank **4. SIDE OF SOMETHING** the side of any object **5. SIDE OF SPORTS FIELD** either of the sides of a sports field inside the playing area ○ *not used to playing on the left flank* ■ *vt* (**flanked, flank·ing, flanks**) **BE BY SIDE OF SOMETHING** to be on or at the side of something or somebody ○ *He was flanked by secret service officers.* [Pre-12C. < French *flanc*]

flan·ken /flaángkən/ *n US* a cut of meat taken from the short ribs of beef [Mid-20C. Via Yiddish < German *Flanken*, plural of *Flank* "flank, side" < French *flanc*]

flank·er /flángkər/ *n* **1.** FOOTBALL same as **split end** (sense 1) **2.** FOOTBALL same as **flankerback 3.** MIL a soldier in a unit that protects the flank of a military column on the march

flank·er·back /flángkər bàk/ *n* in football, an offensive back positioned outside the play formation

flan·nel /flánn'l/ *n* **1. SOFT COTTON CLOTH** a soft cotton cloth with a nap on one side. Use: clothing, sleepwear, sheets. **2. SOFT WOOLEN CLOTH** a soft closely woven woolen or wool-blend cloth. Use: clothing. ■ **flan·nels** *npl* **1. PANTS MADE OF FLANNEL** clothing, especially slacks, made from flannel **2. FLANNEL UNDERWEAR** woolen underwear of thick flannel [14C. Origin ?] —**flan·nel·ly** *adj*

flan·nel cake *n regional* FOOD same as **pancake** *n* (sense 1)

flan·nel·ette /flànn'l ét/ *n* a light cotton cloth with a soft brushed surface on one side

flan·nel·flow·er /flánn'l flòwr/ *n* a wild plant with leaves covered in soft white hairs. Flowers: creamy white. Native to: eastern Australia. Latin name: *Actinotus helianthi.*

flan·nel leaf *n* PLANTS same as **mullein** [Because it resembles the material]

flan·nel-mouthed *adj* **1.** *US* garbled and indistinct **2.** speaking obsequiously and deceptively

Flan·ne·ry /flánnəree/, **Tim** (*b.* 1956) Australian biologist. He is the author of *The Future Eaters* (1994) and *The Eternal Frontier* (2001). Full name **Flannery, Timothy**

flap /flap/ *v* (**flapped, flap·ping, flaps**) **1.** *vti* **MOVE WINGS UP AND DOWN** to move something up and down, especially wings or arms during or as if in flight, or be moved up and down in this way **2.** *vi* **FLY BY MOVING WINGS** to fly by moving the wings repeatedly **3.** *vti* **MOVE OR SWAY REPEATEDLY** to cause something to move or sway in one direction and then another repeatedly and often noisily, or move in this way ○ *flags flapping in the breeze* **4.** *vt* **HIT WITH BROAD OBJECT** to hit somebody or something with a broad flat object ○ *He flapped his hand on the table.* **5.** *vt* **TOSS SOMETHING** to fling down or toss something (*informal*) ○ *flapped the report on the table* **6.** *vi* **BE PANICKY** to be flustered or panicky (*informal*) **7.** *vt* PHON **MAKE "R" SOUND** to make an "r" sound by briefly striking the roof of the mouth with the tongue, as in "parrot" ■ *n* **1. FLAT THIN PIECE USED AS COVER** a flat thin piece attached along one edge, usually used as a cover for an opening ○ *the flap of an envelope* **2. BLOW FROM BROAD OBJECT** a blow or slap from a broad object **3. DUST JACKET PART** either of the two parts of a dust jacket that fold inside a book's cover and are usually printed with information about the book or author **4. COMMOTION** a commotion or state of upset, especially a disordered argument (*informal*) ○ *Don't get into a flap about it.* **5. ACT OR SOUND OF FLAPPING** an act of or the sound made by flapping ○ *The bird disappeared with a flap of its wings.* **6.** AVIAT **AIRCRAFT WING CONTROL SURFACE** a narrow movable surface attached to the rear edge of an aircraft wing that is used to create lift or drag **7.** SURG **MASS OF TISSUE FOR GRAFTING** a mass of tissue, used for surgical grafting, that remains partially attached and retains its blood supply **8.** PHON **"R" SOUND** an "r" sound made by briefly striking the roof of the mouth with the tongue, as in "parrot" [14C. Origin ?] —**flap·py** *adj*

flap·doo·dle /fláp dòod'l/ *n* silly talk or nonsense (*slang*) [Mid-19C. Origin ?]

flap·jack /fláp jàk/ *n* **1.** FOOD same as **pancake** *n* (sense 1) **2.** *UK* a cake made of oats, syrup, and butter and cut into squares before eating

flap·per /fláppər/ *n* **1. YOUNG UNCONVENTIONAL WOMAN OF 1920S** a young woman of the 1920s who disdained conventions of decorum and established fashion. Flappers were associated with the Charleston dance, bobbed hair, and very short dresses. **2. SOMETHING FLAPPING AROUND** an object that flaps around **3. BROAD FLAT OBJECT** a broad flat object used for striking something

flare /fler/ *v* (**flared, flar·ing, flares**) **1.** *vti* **BURN SUDDENLY AND BRIGHTLY** to burn suddenly and brightly, or cause something to burn in this way **2.** *vi* **START UP AGAIN** to recur, worsen, or intensify suddenly ○ *His gout flared up again.* **3.** *vi* **ANGER SUDDENLY** to become suddenly angry **4.** *vti* **WIDEN** to widen or spread outward, or cause something to widen or spread outward ○ *Her nostrils flared.* **5.** *vt* **SIGNAL SOMEBODY FOR HELP** to signal somebody for help by means of a device used to produce a light signal **6.** *vt* INDUST **BURN OFF GAS** to ignite and burn off unwanted waste gas in open air ■ *n* **1. SUDDEN BLAZE OF LIGHT** a sudden blaze of light or fire used to signal distress or location or for illumination ○ *the flare of naval signal lights* **2. DEVICE FOR PRODUCING FLARE** a device used to produce a light signal calling for help ○ *a distress flare* **3. FLAME** a sudden or unsteady flame ○ *the flare of distant oil wells* **4. WIDENING SHAPE** a shape that widens or spreads outward ○ *a long skirt with a flare* **5. OUTBURST OF EMOTION** a sudden outburst, especially of a negative emotion ○ *a flare of anger* **6.** INDUST **FLAME FOR BURNING OFF WASTE GAS** a flame that burns off unwanted waste gas in the open air **7.** FOOTBALL **SHORT AND WIDE PASS** in football, a pass to a back running laterally **8.** OPTICS, PHOTOGRAPHY **UNWANTED LIGHT IN OPTICAL DEVICE** unwanted light reaching a photographic image, especially when reflected from an internal lens **9.** MED **INFLAMMATION** an area of inflammation on the skin ■ **flares** *npl* **PANTS WITH WIDE LEGS BELOW KNEE** pants with legs that widen significantly below the knee, first popular in the late 1960s [Mid-16C. Origin ?] —**flared** *adj*

SPELLCHECK flare or **flair**? Do not confuse the spelling of ***flare*** and ***flair***, which sound similar. ***Flare*** can be used as a noun or verb referring to a sudden blaze of light or fire, an outburst of emotion, or a widening out: *The gasoline made the fire flare up. The crew set off distress flares. Tempers flared as the meeting progressed. She wore a flared skirt.* ***Flair*** is only used as a noun, meaning "talent" or "stylishness," as in *a flair for public speaking, to dress with flair.*

flare·back /flér bàk/ *n* **1.** a flame inside a gun's breech caused by the ignition of gases remaining after the weapon has been fired **2.** a reaction or effect directed back toward a point of origin

flare stack *n* a large open-air burner used to dispose of excess flammable gas at an oil refinery, well, or platform

flare-up *n* **1. RECURRENCE OF SOMETHING** a recurrence of something, especially a disease **2. SUDDEN OCCURRENCE OF FIRE OR LIGHT** a sudden occurrence or increase of fire or light **3. SUDDEN OUTBURST OF AGGRESSION** a sudden occurrence of emotion or violence (*informal*)

flar·ing /flérring/ *adj* **1. BURNING DIMLY** burning dimly or unsteadily **2. SHOWY** bright and showy **3. BECOMING WIDER** widening out —**flar·ing·ly** *adv*

flash /flash/ *v* (**flashed, flash·ing, flash·es**) **1.** *vti* **EMIT LIGHT SUDDENLY** to cause light to appear suddenly or in brief bursts from something, or appear in this way ○ *We could see the lights of police cars flashing in the distance.* **2.** *vti* **REFLECT LIGHT FROM ANOTHER SOURCE** to reflect light suddenly or briefly, or make a source of light reflect from a surface ○ *sunlight flashing on the water* **3.** *vti* **CATCH FIRE SUDDENLY** to burst into flame suddenly, or cause something to burst into flame **4.** *vti* COMMUNICATION **SIGNAL TO SOMEBODY WITH LIGHTS** to signal to somebody or communicate something by quickly turning lights on and off **5.** *vi* **MOVE QUICKLY** to move or pass very quickly in a particular direction **6.** *vti* **APPEAR MOMENTARILY** to appear briefly, or cause something to appear briefly ○ *flash a message onto the screen* **7.** *vt* **DISPLAY SOMETHING OSTENTATIOUSLY** to show off or display something in order to impress people ○ *flashed her vulgar jewelry* **8.** *vt* **FILL SOMETHING WITH RUSH OF WATER** to fill something suddenly with a great flow of water **9.** *vt* **COAT SURFACE FOR PROTECTION** to cover the surface of an object with a thin coating, usually for protection or as a stage in processing **10.** *vi* **EXPOSE BODY INDECENTLY IN PUBLIC** to expose the genitals briefly and intentionally in public (*slang*) **11.** *vt* CONSTR **PROTECT ROOF FROM LEAKING** to install pieces of sheet metal (**flashing**) on a roof joint or window joint to make it waterproof ■ *n* **1. SUDDEN BURST OF LIGHT** a sudden bright display of light, fire, or something bright ○ *flashes of lightning* **2. SUDDEN BURST OF MOOD OR THOUGHT** a sudden occurrence of an emotional mood or intellectual activity ○ *a flash of inspiration* **3. BRIEF MOMENT** a brief moment or instant ○ *I'll be there in a flash.* **4. LIGHT PATCH** a patch of light or bright color on a dark background, e.g., on an animal's coat **5.** **BRIGHT LIGHTING USED IN PHOTOGRAPHY** the brief illumination of a subject for photographic purposes **6.** **DEVICE USED TO LIGHT PHOTOGRAPHIC SUBJECT** a device used in flash photography to produce a short bright light **7.** *US* same as **flashlight** (*informal*) **8.** **RUSH OF WATER** a sudden rush of water down a watercourse, or a device that produces this **9.** **SHORT NEWS BROADCAST** a sudden important news story requiring immediate broadcast **10.** *US* **RUSH** the sudden effects felt when taking a mind-altering recreational drug (*slang*) **11.** *US* MED same as **hot flash** **12.** **LANGUAGE USED IN UNDERWORLD** the language used by criminals, thieves, and their associates (*archaic slang*) [13C. Probably an imitation of the sound of splashing] —**flash·ness** *n* ◇ **a flash in the pan** a sudden brief success that is not, or not likely to be, repeated ◇ **in a flash 1.** very rapidly **2.** suddenly

flash back *vi* **1.** to recall an intensely vivid memory of a traumatic experience **2.** to go back to a scene at an earlier point in a narrative, out of chronological order, to fill in information or explain something in the present

flash forward *vi* to jump forward in time to a scene at a later point in a narrative, out of chronological order, usually for dramatic effect or irony

flash on *vt US* to remember or think of something suddenly (*informal*) ○ *I just flashed on my first day in school.*

flash·back /flásh bàk/ *n* **1.** **PAINFUL MEMORY** an intensely vivid memory of a traumatic experience that returns repeatedly **2.** **EARLIER EVENT OR SCENE** a scene or event from the past that appears in a narrative out of chronological order, to fill in information or explain something in the present ○ *Much of the film's exposition is handled through flashbacks.* **3.** **DRUG AFTEREFFECT** the later experiencing of the effects of a hallucinogenic drug such as LSD long after discontinuing use of the drug

flash blind·ness *n* temporary blindness after the flash of a gun discharge or other explosion, particularly at night

flash·board /flásh bàwrd/ *n* a structure made of boards fitted at the top of a dam to add to its height and increase the amount of water that can be held back

flash·bulb /flásh bùlb/ *n* a small glass bulb filled with shredded metallic foil that produces a brief intense flash of light for taking photographs

flash burn *n* a burn caused by brief exposure to a source of intense heat

flash·card /flásh kaàrd/ *n* a card with words or numbers printed on it that is briefly displayed as a learning device

flash·er /fláshər/ *n* **1.** **FLASHING LIGHT** a light that flashes as a signal, especially on a vehicle **2.** **DEVICE MAKING LIGHT FLASH** a device that switches a light on and off automatically to make it flash **3.** **SOMEBODY WHO EXPOSES PRIVATE PARTS** a person, especially a man, who gains pleasure from publicly exposing the genitals (*slang*)

flash flood *n* a sudden and often destructive surge of water down a narrow channel or sloping ground, usually caused by heavy rainfall

flash-for·ward *n* a scene or event from the future that appears in a narrative out of chronological order, usually for dramatic effect or irony

flash·gun /flásh gùn/ *n* a device that holds a flashtube or flashbulb and automatically discharges it as the attached camera's shutter opens

flash·ing /fláshing/ *n* pieces of sheet metal attached around the joints and angles of a roof to protect against leakage

flash·light /flásh lìt/ *n* **1.** **PORTABLE LIGHT SOURCE** a small hand-held lamp usually powered by batteries **2.** **BURST OF BRIGHT LIGHT FOR PHOTOGRAPHY** a brief intense flash of light produced by a photographic lamp **3.** **BRIGHT FLASHING LIGHT** any bright light that flashes, e.g., a beacon

flash mem·o·ry *n* a programmable read-only computer memory chip that can be erased and reprogrammed in blocks rather than single bytes

flash-mob·bing *n* the practice of people appearing in groups in public places and performing harmless attention-seeking activities. They are mobilized by somebody on the Internet who tells them when and where to gather and what to do. (*informal*) —**flash-mob·ber** *n*

flash·o·ver /flásh òvər/ *n* an unintended electric arc around or over the surface of an insulator

flash pho·tog·ra·phy *n* photography that illuminates its subject with a brief flash of artificial light

flash pho·tol·y·sis *n* a method of studying photochemical reactions in gases in which the gas is exposed to very brief intense flashes of light and the results are analyzed with a spectroscope

flash·point /flásh pòynt/ *n* **1.** **CRITICAL STAGE** the critical stage in some process, event, or situation at which action, change, or violence occurs **2.** **TROUBLE SPOT** a place where violence is likely to break out suddenly, usually as a result of social or political tension **3.** CHEM **TEMPERATURE OF VAPOR IGNITION** the lowest temperature at which a flammable liquid will give off enough vapor to ignite briefly when exposed to a flame

flash·tube /flásh tòob/ *n* a glass or quartz tube filled with xenon gas that emits a short intense burst of light for flash photography when electric current is passed through it

flash u·nit *n* **1.** a flashtube and its power supply in a single compact unit **2.** a flashgun, or a unit comprising a flashgun and reflector

flash·y /fláshee/ (**-i·er, -i·est**) *adj* **1.** stylish and expensive-looking in an obvious or ostentatious way **2.** showing momentary or superficial brilliance —**flash·i·ly** *adv* —**flash·i·ness** *n*

flask /flask/ *n* **1.** **SMALL BOTTLE** a small glass bottle, often with a long neck, of the type used in laboratory work **2.** **SMALL FLAT CONTAINER FOR ALCOHOL** a small thin flat container with a narrow neck, carried in a pocket and usually used to hold liquor **3.** *Carib* **HALF A BOTTLE OF RUM** in Trinidad, half a bottle of rum (*informal*) **4.** ARMS, HIST same as **powder flask** **5.** METALL **MOLD USED IN FOUNDRY** a frame packed full of sand, used in a foundry to make a mold **6.** INDUST **CONTAINER FOR SPENT NUCLEAR FUEL** a very strong container in which irradiated nuclear fuel is transported [14C. < medieval Latin *flasca*, late Latin *flascon-*]

flat[1] /flat/ *adj* (**flat·ter, flat·test**) **1.** **LEVEL AND HORIZONTAL** level and horizontal, without any slope ○ *The flat plains stretch for miles.* **2.** **EVEN AND SMOOTH** even and smooth, without any bumps or hollows ○ *back on the flat road* **3.** **NOT CURVED** not curved inward or outward ○ *a boat with a flat bottom* **4.** **WITH LITTLE CURVATURE** with relatively little depth or curvature ○ *a vase with flat sides* **5.** **LYING HORIZONTAL** in a horizontal position, parallel with or stretched out on the ground ○ *plants lying flat after the heavy rain* **6.** **TOUCHING SOMETHING ELSE** with the whole extent touching another surface at all points ○ *Stand it flat against the wall.* **7.** **NO LONGER BUBBLY** having lost effervescence ○ *flat champagne* **8.** **NOT FULL OF AIR** no longer full of air ○ *a flat tire* **9.** **BELOW CORRECT PITCH** sounded or sounding a little lower than the intended pitch level ○ *Your E string is flat.* **10.** **ONE HALF-STEP BELOW NATURAL** pitched one half-step below a particular note ○ *in the key of B flat* **11.** **LACKING EXCITEMENT** without any interest or excitement ○ *Some days life just seems flat.* **12.** **WITHOUT FLAVOR** lacking flavor or seasoning ○ *This soup tastes flat.* **13.** **MONOTONOUS IN SOUND** with no variation in pitch or intonation ○ *expressed her displeasure in a flat voice* **14.** **COMMERCIALLY INACTIVE** not commercially active ○ *The market is fairly flat at the moment.* **15.** **NOT VARYING** not varying in amount or level ○ *They charge a flat fee of $50.* **16.** **EMPHATICALLY ABSOLUTE** categorical and without any qualification ○ *a flat denial of the charges* **17.** **LOW-HEELED** with low heels or no heels at all ○ *flat shoes* **18.** **NOT SHINY** not shiny or glossy ○ *a flat white paint* **19.** **WITH LOW ARCHES** describes feet with arches so low that all the sole makes contact with the ground **20.** MED **INDICATING CESSATION OF PHYSIOLOGICAL ACTIVITY** showing no variation on a monitoring machine, and thereby indicating that physiological activity has stopped ○ *a flat EKG* **21.** PHON **RESEMBLING VOWEL SOUND IN "FAT"** describes the vowel "a" as it is pronounced in "fat" or "badge" **22.** NAUT **TAUT** describes a sail that is stretched so as to be taut ■ *adv* (**flat·ter, flat·test**) **1.** **BELOW PITCH** below the intended pitch ○ *She tends to sing flat.* **2.** **EXACTLY** no more and no less ○ *He ran the mile in four minutes flat.* **3.** **VERY** used to add emphasis (*informal*) ○ *flat broke* **4.** FIN **WITHOUT INTEREST** not accruing any interest ○ *The bonds were trading flat.* ■ *n* **1.** **LEVEL SURFACE** a flat part or surface ○ *the flat of a knife blade* **2.** **DEFLATED TIRE** a tire that has become deflated (*informal*) **3.** MUSIC **NOTE LOWERED BY HALF-STEP** a sign (♭) placed next to a note to show that it is to be lowered by a half-step, or a note that is lowered a half-step ○ *a key with four flats* **4.** GEOG **LARGE STRETCH OF LEVEL GROUND** a large stretch of level ground, e.g., of mud exposed at low tide or of salt deposits (*usually used in the plural*) ○ *the great salt flats* **5.** GARDENING **SHALLOW BOX FOR SEEDLINGS** a shallow lidless box or frame for seedlings **6.** THEATER **MOVABLE SCENERY** theatrical scenery mounted on a movable wooden frame **7.** *US* RAIL same as **flatcar** **8.** NAUT same as **flatboat** **9.** MAIL **BIG FLAT ENVELOPE** a large flat piece of mail ■ **flats** *npl* CLOTHING **LOW-HEELED SHOES** shoes with low heels ■ *v* (**flat·ted, flat·ting, flats**) **1.** *vti US* **FLATTEN** to make something flat or become flat ○*"in the winter the fur grew thick and flatted out along her sides"* (Henry David Thoreau, *Walden*; 1854) **2.** *vt* **MAKE NOTE FLAT** to lower a note a half step **3.** *vt* **SING OR PLAY SOMETHING FLAT** to sing or play a note below the intended pitch [14C. < Old Norse *flatr* < Indo-European] —**flat·ness** *n*

flat[2] /flat/ *n UK* same as **apartment** (sense 1) [Early 19C. Alteration, after FLAT[1], of Scots *flet* "interior of a house" < Old English *flet(t)* "house, floor" < Germanic]

flat back four *n* in soccer, a formation of four defenders deployed in a straight line across the field and generally maintaining this straight-line arrangement during play

flat·bed /flát bèd/ *n* TRANSP **1.** same as **flatbed trailer** **2.** same as **flatbed truck**

flat·bed press *n* PRINTING same as **cylinder press**

flat·bed scan·ner *n* a device connected to a computer on which documents are laid flat and an optical sensor passes over them converting text and images into digital form for storage, retrieval, and transmission by the computer

flat·bed trail·er *n* a trailer consisting of a completely open platform with no sides or railings

flat·bed truck *n* a truck that has a completely open platform at the rear with no sides or railings

flat·boat /flát bòt/ *n* a large boat with a flat bottom used for transporting goods on shallow waterways

flat·bot·tom /flát bòttəm/, **flat·bot·tomed** /-bóttəmd/ *adj* made with a flat bottom ○ *a flatbottom boat*

flat·bread /flát brèd/ *n* bread baked in round flat loaves and usually made with unleavened dough, e.g., pitta, nan, chapatis, and tortillas

flat·car /flát kaàr/ *n* a railroad freight car that has no roof or sides

flat-chest·ed /flàt chéstəd/ *adj* having small breasts

flat-coat·ed re·triev·er *n* a large dog with a thick, smooth, black or reddish brown coat, belonging to a breed originally developed in England for retrieving game

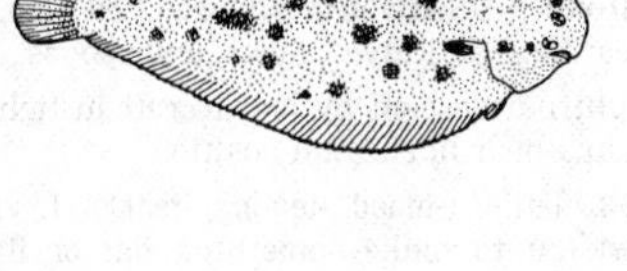

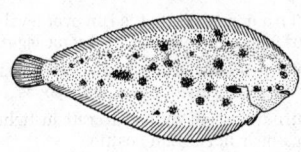

flatfish

flat·fish /flát fìsh/ (*plural same* or **-fish·es**) *n* any fish with a flat body and both eyes on the upper side, including the flounder, sole, and halibut. Order: Pleuronectiformes.

flat·foot /flát fòot/ *n* **1.** a condition of the feet in which the arches are so low that all of the sole makes contact with the ground **2.** (*plural* **flat·foots** or **flat·feet** /-fèet/) an offensive term for a police officer, typically one on foot patrol (*dated slang*)

flat-foot·ed, **flat·foot·ed** /flàt fŏŏtəd/ *adj* **1.** HAVING FLAT FEET having feet with arches so low that all the sole makes contact with the ground **2.** *US* FIRMLY ON THE GROUND with both feet on the ground **3.** UNPREPARED unable to react or respond quickly ○ *Her question caught me flat-footed.* ■ *adv* UNEQUIVOCALLY in a firm and direct way (*informal*) ○*"a good many come out flat-footed and said it was scandalous"* (Mark Twain, *The Adventures of Huckleberry Finn*; 1884) —**flat-foot·ed·ly** *adv* —**flat-foot·ed·ness** *n*

Flat·head[1] /flát hèd/ (*plural same* or **-heads**) *n* a member of a Native North American people who originally lived in western Montana and northern Idaho

Flat·head[2] /flát hèd/ river in North America, rising in southeastern British Columbia, Canada, and flowing south into Montana, where it joins the Clark Fork River after passing through Flathead Lake. Length: 245 mi./394 km.

flat·head cat·fish /flàt hed-/ *n* a large catfish with a yellowish body and brown markings. Native to: Mississippi Valley, southeastern United States. Latin name: *Pylodictis olivaris.*

flat·i·ron /flát ìrn/ *n* an iron used to press clothes, especially one that has to be heated on a hearth or stove

flat·land /flát lànd/ *n* an expanse of land that does not vary in height above sea level

flat·land·er /flát làndər/ *n Western US* in California, a person formerly from a city who relocates to the hill country and who is regarded by the long-term local residents as having little or no knowledge of local ecological needs (*disapproving*) ○*"The ... wildfires ... have renewed debate about the rush of flatlanders who are lured by a Western lifestyle seemingly removed from traffic, crime, and smog."* (Associated Press *Roanoke Times*; November 9, 2003)

flat·line /flát lìn/ *n* a monitor readout on an EEG or EKG indicating total cessation of brain or cardiac activity, respectively ■ *vi* (**-lined, -lin·ing, -lines**) to show none of the electrical currents associated with heart or brain activity on a monitor (*slang*) —**flat·lin·er** *n*

flat·ly /fláttlee/ *adv* **1.** firmly and without qualification ○ *They flatly rejected our offer.* **2.** in a voice that shows no emotion

flat out *adv* (*informal*) **1.** at top speed **2.** in a blunt manner ○ *told me flat out he didn't trust me*

flat-out, **flat·out** /flàt ówt/ *adj US* being an extreme or thorough example of something (*informal*) ○ *a flat-out lie*

flat·pack /flát pàk/ *n UK* an item of furniture that is sold as a set of pieces packed flat, for ease of storage and transportation, and assembled by the buyer

flat pan·el *n* a very thin computer screen with a flat viewing surface that employs liquid-crystal display technology, commonly used in portable personal computers —**flat-pan·el** *adj*

flat·pick /flát pìk/ *n* a flat thin piece of plastic or metal, usually triangular, used to pluck and strum a stringed instrument such as a guitar or banjo

flat race *n* a horserace that is run over level ground, without fences to be jumped —**flat rac·ing** *n*

flat sil·ver *n US* silver or silver-plated utensils used for eating, e.g., knives, forks, and spoons

flat spin *n* a descent by an aircraft in tight circles and in a near horizontal position

flat·ten /flátt'n/ (**-tened, -ten·ing, -tens**) *v* **1.** *vti* MAKE OR BECOME FLAT to make something flat or flatter, or become flat or flatter **2.** *vr* STAND FLAT AGAINST SOMETHING to press the body against a flat surface **3.** *vt* CRUSH OR HUMILIATE SOMEBODY to make somebody feel crushed or humiliated **4.** *vt* DEFEAT SOMEBODY to defeat somebody convincingly (*informal*) **5.** *vt UK* MUSIC same as **flat**[1] (senses 2–3) —**flat·ten·er** *n*

flatten out *v* **1.** *vi* to become lower and relatively stable ○ *Stock prices have flattened out over the year.* **2.** *vti* to spread out over an area, or spread something out

flat·ter[1] /fláttər/ (**-tered, -ter·ing, -ters**) *v* **1.** *vt* COMPLIMENT SOMEBODY TO WIN FAVOR to compliment somebody too much, often without sincerity, especially in order to gain an advantage **2.** *vt* APPEAL TO SOMEBODY'S VANITY to please somebody by paying him or her particular attention, especially with a request to take some prominent role ○ *I was flattered to be asked to judge the competition.* **3.** *vt* MAKE SOMEBODY OR SOMETHING LOOK GOOD to show somebody or something to advantage, or make somebody or something seem better looking than in reality ○ *a studio portrait that really flatters her* **4. flat·ter your·self** *vr* CONGRATULATE YOURSELF EXCESSIVELY to feel satisfied with some aspect of yourself or with something you have done, especially when the perception is false ○ *He flatters himself on being a good judge of character.* [12C. Origin ?] —**flat·ter·er** *n* —**flat·ter·ing** *adj* —**flat·ter·ing·ly** *adv*

flat·ter[2] /fláttər/ *n* any tool used to make something flat [< Old Norse *flatr* (see FLAT[1])]

flat·ter·y /fláttəree/ *n* **1.** an act or instance of complimenting somebody, often excessively or insincerely, especially in order to gain an advantage **2.** complimentary remarks, especially when excessive or insincere [14C. < Old French *flaterie* < *flater* "flatter"]

flat·tish /fláttish/ *adj* somewhat or relatively flat ○ *a flattish hairdo*

flat·top /flát tòp/ *n* **1.** a hairstyle in which the hair is brushed up and then cut short and flat across the top **2.** *US* same as **aircraft carrier** (*informal*)

flat tun·ing *n* the tuning of a musical instrument, or of instruments playing together, so that the pitch of the notes is lower than normal. This is sometimes done by early-music groups.

flat·u·lent /fláchələnt/ *adj* **1.** CAUSING GAS IN DIGESTIVE SYSTEM causing excessive gas (**flatus**) to be created in the stomach and intestines **2.** FULL OF DIGESTIVE GAS having excessive gas (**flatus**) in the digestive system **3.** POMPOUS OR SELF-IMPORTANT having or showing excessive self-importance (*literary*) [Late 16C. Via French < modern Latin *flatulentus* < Latin *flatus* "blowing, blast" < *flare* "to blow"] —**flat·u·lence** *n* —**flat·u·lent·ly** *adv*

fla·tus /fláytəss/ *n* gas produced in the digestive system by bacterial fermentation and containing high amounts of hydrogen sulfide and methane, usually expelled from the body through the anus (*technical*) [Mid-17C. < Latin (see FLATULENT)]

flat·ware /flát wèr/ *n* **1.** knives, forks, and spoons used for eating **2.** dishes used for eating that are flat or relatively shallow, e.g., plates and saucers, as opposed to deeper pieces (**hollowware**)

flat-wa·ter *adj* done on a calm or slow-moving body of water

flat·weave /flát wēev/ *adj* woven without a pile ○ *a flatweave carpet*

flat·wise /flát wìz/, **flat·ways** /-wàyz/ *adv* with the flat side down or foremost

flat·work /flát wùrk/ *n* large pieces of laundry that are easier to iron in a mangle than by hand, e.g., sheets and tablecloths

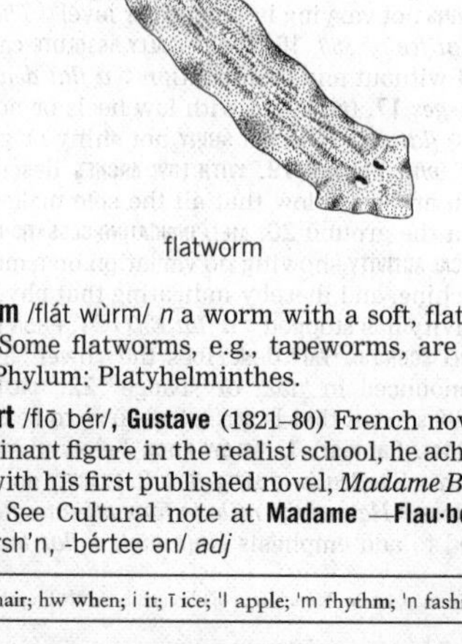

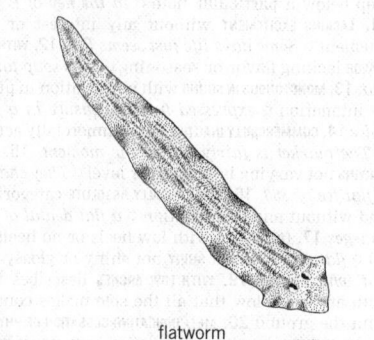

flatworm

flat·worm /flát wùrm/ *n* a worm with a soft, flattened body. Some flatworms, e.g., tapeworms, are parasites. Phylum: Platyhelminthes.

Flau·bert /flō bér/, **Gustave** (1821–80) French novelist. A dominant figure in the realist school, he achieved fame with his first published novel, *Madame Bovary* (1857). See Cultural note at **Madame** —**Flau·ber·tian** /flō bérsh'n, -bértee ən/ *adj*

"We shouldn't touch our idols: the gilt comes off on our hands."
[Gustave Flaubert, *Madame Bovary*; 1857]

flaunt /flawnt/ *v* (**flaunt·ed, flaunt·ing, flaunts**) **1.** *vt* SHOW SOMETHING OFF to display something ostentatiously ○ *She flaunts her wealth every chance she gets.* **2. flaunt your·self** *vr* PARADE YOURSELF to parade yourself without shame or modesty **3.** *vti* WAVE to wave or flutter in the wind, or make something wave or flutter by moving it around (*dated*) ■ *n* DISPLAY an ostentatious display [Mid-16C. Origin ?] —**flaunt·er** *n* —**flaunt·ing·ly** *adv*

USAGE flaunt or **flout**? When expressing the idea of shameless or ostentatious display, the correct choice is ***flaunt***: *He flaunted his ill-gotten riches by purchasing a huge mansion and seven luxury cars.* In terms of openly disobeying or defying a law or convention, only ***flout*** is the correct choice: *The driver flouted the law when he double-parked.*

flaunt·y /fláwntee/ (**-i·er, -i·est**) *adj US* inclined to show off —**flaunt·i·ly** *adv* —**flaunt·i·ness** *n*

flau·ta /flów taa/ *n Hispanic* a tortilla rolled around a savory filling, usually beef or chicken, and fried [< Spanish, "flute," probably < Provençal *flaüt*]

flau·tist /fláwtist, flów-/ *n* MUSIC same as **flutist** [Mid-19C. < Italian *flautisto* < *flauto* "flute" < Provençal *flaüt*]

flav- *prefix* same as **flavo-** (*used before vowels*)

fla·va·none /fláyvə nōn, flávvə-/ *n* a substance derived from flavone [Mid-20C. < FLAVO- + -ANE + -ONE]

fla·vin /fláyvin/ *n* a yellowish pigment belonging to a group present in plants and animals [Mid-19C. < Latin *flavus* "yellow"]

flavo- *prefix* **1.** yellow ○ *flavone* **2.** flavin ○ *flavoprotein* [< Latin *flavus* "yellow" < Indo-European]

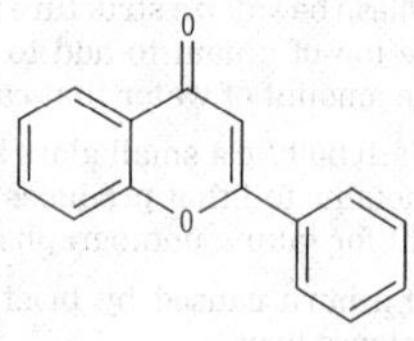

flavone

fla·vone /fláy vōn/ *n* a crystalline compound from which yellow pigments are derived. Formula: $C_{15}H_{10}O_2$.

fla·vo·noid /fláyvə nòyd/ *n* a naturally occurring phenolic compound belonging to a large group that includes many plant pigments. Flavonoids have beneficial effects in the human diet as antioxidants, neutralizing free radicals which damage body tissue and lead to heart disease, strokes, and cancer.

fla·vo·pro·tein /flàyvō prō tēen/ *n* an enzyme that is involved in cell respiration

fla·vor /fláyvər/ *n* **1.** CHARACTERISTIC TASTE an identifiable or distinctive quality of food or drink perceived with the combined senses of taste and smell ○ *The soup didn't have much flavor.* **2.** SOMETHING ADDING FLAVOR TO FOOD a substance used to give food or drink an identifiable or distinctive taste **3.** UNIQUE CHARACTERISTIC the unique individual characteristic of an artistic work, especially a work of literature ○*"borrowing its flavor from the works of William Gibson and Austin sci-fi author Bruce Sterling"* (John Perry Barlow, *Crime and Puzzlement*; 1990) **4.** TYPE a type or kind of something (*slang*) ○ *Each flavor of the operating system provides its own unique commands or features.* **5.** PHYS PROPERTY OF ELEMENTARY PARTICLES a physical property that distinguishes types of quarks and some types of leptons ■ *vt* (**-vored, -vor·ing, -vors**) **1.** GIVE FLAVOR TO FOOD to give food or drink an identifiable or distinctive taste, usually by adding something ○ *Flavor the stew with rosemary.* **2.** GIVE SOMETHING UNIQUENESS to give a unique characteristic to an artistic work, especially a work of literature

○ *A certain terseness flavors her prose.* [14C. Alteration, after SAVOR, of Old French *flaor* "aroma" < blend of Latin *flatus* "blowing" + *foetor* "stench"] —**fla·vor·er** *n* —**fla·vor·ful** *adj* —**fla·vor·ful·ly** *adv* —**fla·vor·ful·ness** *n* —**fla·vor·less** *adj* —**fla·vor·less·ly** *adv* —**fla·vor·less·ness** *n* —**fla·vor·some** *adj* —**fla·vor·y** *adj*

fla·vor en·hanc·er *n* a substance added to processed food or drink to improve or intensify its flavor

fla·vor·ing /fláyvəring/ *n* a natural or artificial substance added to food or drink to give it an identifiable taste

fla·vor·ist /fláyvərist/ *n US* somebody trained to isolate and blend chemicals in order to create artificially the taste and smell of a specific food

fla·vour *n, vt* Can, UK spelling of **flavor**

flaw[1] /flaw/ *n* **1.** PHYSICAL BLEMISH a physical disfigurement that prevents something from being totally perfect and detracts from its value **2.** DETRACTING FEATURE a feature that is regarded as unfavorable ○ *There's a flaw in your argument.* **3.** LAW INVALIDATING MISTAKE IN DOCUMENT in a legal document, an error that can make it invalid [14C. Origin ?] —**flawed** *adj*

SYNONYMS ***flaw, imperfection, fault, defect, blemish, failing, shortcoming, weakness***

CORE MEANING: something that detracts from perfection

flaw a physical disfigurement that prevents something from being totally perfect and detracts from its value, or a feature that is regarded as unfavorable ○ *a tiny flaw in the glass* ○ *a fatal flaw in their strategy* **imperfection** something that makes somebody or something less than perfect ○ *a minor imperfection on the shiny surface* ○ *They accepted us, with all our imperfections, as co-workers.* **fault** something that detracts from the integrity, functioning, or perfection of something, or a feature of somebody's character that is regarded as unfavorable ○ *a design fault* ○ *regarded it as a serious fault of the education system* ○ *His worst fault is his unreliability.* **defect** a physical error in a machine or system, especially one that prevents it from functioning correctly, or a feature of something that is regarded as inadequate ○ *A house may show a hidden defect several years after construction.* ○ *a metabolic defect* ○ *regarded his disinclination to stand up for himself as a character defect* **failing** a deficiency in the way that something takes place or operates, or a feature of somebody's character regarded with disapproval ○ *The management acknowledged this failing in the system.* ○ *At least unpunctuality isn't one of my failings.* **blemish** a mark that detracts from the appearance of something, or a feature that detracts from somebody's personal reputation or good record ○ *a small blemish that only an expert would have noticed* ○ *the only blemish on an otherwise perfect record* **shortcoming** a failure in a system or organization, or a feature of somebody's character regarded with disapproval ○ *The omission of this test is a serious shortcoming in the service offered.* ○ *The team's main shortcoming has been letting advantages slip away.* **weakness** a weak point in the structure or arrangement of something, or a feature of somebody's character regarded with disapproval ○ *The intermittent supply of electricity is a definite weakness.* ○ *They were asked to analyze their team's strengths and weaknesses.* ○ *Indecision was always one of his weaknesses.*

flaw[2] /flaw/ *n* **1.** a brief gust of wind **2.** a short storm or spell of bad weather [Early 16C. Probably < Middle Low German *vlāge*, or < N Germanic] —**flaw·y** *adj*

flaw·less /fláwləss/ *adj* without any blemish or imperfection ○ *a flawless performance* —**flaw·less·ly** *adv* —**flaw·less·ness** *n*

flax /flaks/ *n* **1.** FIBER USED TO MAKE LINEN a fine light-colored plant fiber. Use: linen textiles. **2.** PLANT YIELDING FIBER AND OIL a plant that yields oil from its seeds and flax from its stems. Latin name: *Linum usitatissimum*. **3.** PALE YELLOW a pale yellow color [Old English *flæx* < Indo-European, "braid"] —**flax·y** *adj*

flax·en /fláksən/ *adj* **1.** of the pale grayish yellow color of flax **2.** made from flax fibers

Flax·man /fláksmən/, **John** (1755–1826) British sculptor and illustrator. He was appointed the first professor of sculpture at the Royal Academy in 1810. His

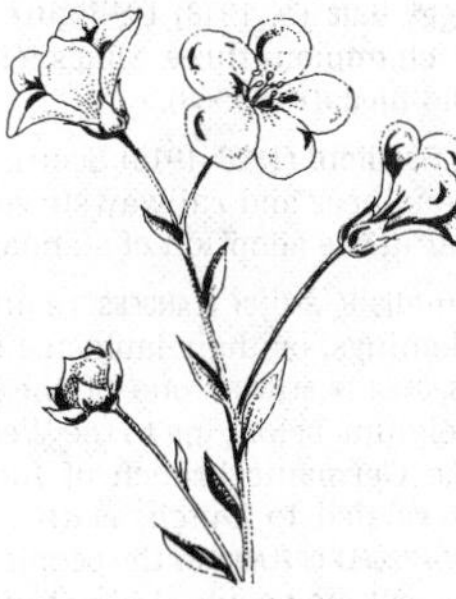

flax (sense 2)

simple illustrations of classical texts are characterized by clean neoclassical lines.

flax·seed /fláks sēed/ *n* the seed of the flax plant, especially when used as the source of flaxseed oil. ◊ **linseed**

flax·seed oil *n* oil obtained from the seeds of the flax plant, especially as used in products to promote human and animal health

flay /flay/ (**flayed, flay·ing, flays**) *vt* **1.** LASH OR FLOG SOMEBODY to whip or beat a person or animal severely **2.** STRIP SKIN OFF SOMEBODY to remove the skin or outer covering from somebody or something **3.** CRITICIZE SOMEBODY HARSHLY to criticize somebody or something harshly and severely, and sometimes unfairly **4.** STRIP SOMEBODY OF BELONGINGS to take all the money or valuables from somebody, especially by the use of deceit, intimidation, or similar means (*dated*) [Old English *flēan* < Indo-European, "to strike"] —**flay·er** *n*

F lay·er *n* the transition zone between the solid inner core of Earth and its more fluid outer layer, at a depth of approximately 3,200 mi./5,100 km

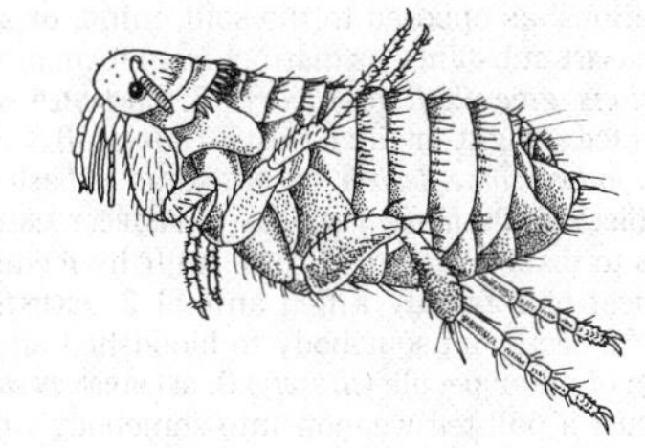

flea

flea /flee/ *n* **1.** a small wingless insect with legs adapted for jumping that sucks blood and lives as a parasite on warm-blooded animals. Order: Siphonaptera. **2.** a small beetle or crustacean that resembles or jumps like a flea, e.g., a water flea, flea beetle, or sand flea [Old English *flēa(h)* < Indo-European]

SPELLCHECK flea or **flee**? Do not confuse the spelling of ***flea*** and ***flee***, which sound similar. ***Flea*** is a noun denoting a small parasitic insect: *The dog has fleas.* ***Flee*** is a verb meaning "run away" or "pass quickly": *We were forced to flee for our lives.*

flea·bag /flée bàg/ *n* (*informal*) **1.** a cheap shabby hotel or rooming house **2.** a dirty or scruffy living being, especially one that is infested with fleas

flea·bane /flée bàyn/ *n* a wild plant of the daisy family with yellow flowers. Genus: *Erigeron*. [Because of its supposed ability to repel fleas]

flea bee·tle *n* a very small beetle with large hind legs adapted for jumping. The beetle and its larvae are pests of vegetable crops. Subfamily: Halticinae.

flea·bite /flée bìt/ *n* **1.** the bite of a flea, or the small red mark caused by this **2.** a small loss or petty annoyance (*informal*)

flea-bit·ten *adj* **1.** COVERED WITH FLEAS OR FLEABITES covered with fleabites or infested with fleas **2.** WITH PALE FLECKED COAT describes a horse that has a pale coat with reddish brown flecks **3.** CHEAP AND SHABBY cheap, shabby, or run-down (*informal*)

flea col·lar *n* a collar, usually for dogs or cats, containing a chemical that repels or kills fleas

flea-flick·er *n* in football, a play in which the ball is quickly passed laterally from one player to another to confuse the defense

fleam /fleem/ *n* **1.** a beveled cutting edge on a sawtooth **2.** a surgical knife formerly used to open a vein in bloodletting [15C. Via Old French *flieme* < Greek *phlebotomon* "vein-cutter" < *phlebos* "vein"]

flea mar·ket *n* a market, usually outdoors, with individual stalls selling various types of merchandise such as antiques, used household items, and cut-rate goods

flèche

flèche /flesh, flaysh/, **fleche** *n* **1.** ARCHIT SLENDER CHURCH SPIRE a slender spire, especially one that emerges from the roof of a church at the point where the ridges intersect **2.** ARCHIT BUTTRESS FEATURE a joint at the top of a buttress, designed to add weight and assist in transferring load from roof to ground **3.** MIL POINTED FORTIFICATION a fortification with two faces that form a jutting angle [Early 18C. < French, "arrow"]

flé·chette /flay shét, fle-/, **fle·chette** *n* a small arrow or dart used in various types of missiles or projectiles intended to kill or injure people [Early 20C. < French, "little arrow" < *flèche* "arrow"]

fleck /flek/ *n* any one of a number of very small marks, streaks, or pieces scattered on a surface or throughout a block of something ○ *flecks of mica in granite* ■ *vt* (**flecked, fleck·ing, flecks**) to mark something with small streaks or spots ○ *Sunlight flecked the path ahead.* [14C. Origin ?]

Fleck·er /flékər/, **James Elroy** (1884–1915) British poet. He was the author of the collection *The Golden Journey to Samarkand* (1913) and the verse drama *Hassan*, produced posthumously in 1922. Full name **Flecker, James Herman Elroy**

> "It was so old a ship—who knows, who knows?/And yet so beautiful, I watched in vain/To see the mast burst open with a rose,/And the whole deck put on its leaves again."
> [James Elroy Flecker, "The Old Ships"; 1915]

flec·tion *n* ANAT another spelling of **flexion**

fled past participle, past tense of **flee**

fledge /flej/ (**fledged, fledg·ing, fledg·es**) *v* **1.** *vi* BECOME CAPABLE OF FLIGHT to become capable of flight and leave the nest (*refers to young birds*) **2.** *vt* RAISE YOUNG BIRD to raise a young bird until it is capable of flight **3.** *vt* ARCHERY EQUIP ARROW WITH FEATHERS to put feathers on an arrow **4.** *vt* PROVIDE SOMETHING WITH FEATHERS to provide or cover something with feathers or something similar [Mid-16C. < obsolete *fledge* "fledged, ready to fly" < Germanic]

fledg·ling /fléjjling/, **fledge·ling** *n* **1.** YOUNG BIRD a young bird that has recently become capable of flight **2.** SOMEBODY INEXPERIENCED a young or inexperienced person ■ *adj* INEXPERIENCED inexperienced because still learning or just starting to do something ○ *a fledgling business*

flee /flee/ (**fled** /fled/, **flee·ing, flees**) *v* **1.** *vti* to run away from something ○ *fled the burning building* **2.** *vi* to pass or disappear quickly (*literary*) [Old English *flēon* < Indo-European] —**fle·er** *n*

SPELLCHECK See ***flea***.

fleece /fleess/ *n* **1.** WOOLLY COAT OF SHEEP the coat of wool on a sheep or similar animal **2.** WOOL SHORN FROM SHEEP the wool shorn at one time from a sheep or similar animal **3.** SOFT COVERING a soft woolly covering or mass ○ *rocks with a fleece of moss* **4.** SOFT FABRIC WITH NAP OR PILE a soft warm fabric with a brushed nap or woolly pile. Use: outer garments, lining. **5.** WARM JACKET a soft warm jacket ■ *vt* (**fleeced, fleec·ing, fleec·es**) **1.** SWINDLE SOMEBODY OUT OF MONEY to take too much money from somebody by cheating or overcharging (*informal*) ○ *They make their living by fleecing tourists.* **2.** GIVE SOFT WOOLLY COVER TO SOMETHING to cover something with something that is soft and woolly in texture or appearance (*literary*) ○ *Clouds fleeced the summer sky.* **3.** AGRIC SHEAR SHEEP to shear wool from a sheep [Old English *flēos* < W Germanic] —**fleec·er** *n*

fleec·y /fléessee/ (**-i·er, -i·est**) *adj* **1.** consisting of fleece or something similar **2.** soft and woolly in appearance or texture —**fleec·i·ly** *adv* —**fleec·i·ness** *n*

fleer /fleer/ (*formal*) *vi* (**fleered, fleer·ing, fleers**) to smile or laugh with contempt ■ *n* a taunting or derisive look, smile, or comment [14C. Probably < N Germanic] —**fleer·ing·ly** *adv*

fleet[1] /fleet/ *n* **1.** a number of warships functioning as a single unit under one command, or all the ships of a nation's navy **2.** a number of road vehicles, boats, or aircraft owned, working, or managed as a unit, usually by a commercial enterprise ○ *The company has a large fleet of service vehicles.* [Old English *flēot* "ships" < *flēotan* "to float, swim" < Germanic]

fleet[2] /fleet/ (*literary*) *adj* **1.** MOVING QUICKLY moving quickly or nimbly **2.** QUICKLY PASSING passing or fading quickly ■ *v* (**fleet·ed, fleet·ing, fleets**) **1.** *vi* MOVE QUICKLY to move quickly or nimbly **2.** *vti* PASS QUICKLY to pass or fade quickly, or cause something to pass or fade quickly [Early 16C. Probably < Old Norse *fljótr* < Germanic] —**fleet·ly** *adv* —**fleet·ness** *n*

Fleet ♦ **Van Fleet, James A.**

fleet ad·mi·ral, Fleet Ad·mi·ral *n* an officer in the US Navy of the highest rank, having an insignia of five stars, this rank and title used only in wartime

fleet·ing /fleéting/ *adj* passing or fading quickly [Old English < *flēotan* (see FLEET[1])] —**fleet·ing·ly** *adv* —**fleet·ing·ness** *n*

SYNONYMS See *temporary.*

Fleet Street /fleét street/ *n* the people and practices involved in the British newspaper industry [After a street in central London where most British national newspapers were formerly produced]

flei·shig /fláyshik, flī-/ *adj* under Jewish dietary laws, relating to, containing, or used only for meat or meat products. ◊ **pareve** [Mid-20C. < Yiddish *fleyshik* < *fleysh* "meat"]

Flem·ing /flémming/ *n* **1.** somebody who comes from Flanders **2.** a Belgian who speaks Flemish [Pre-12C. Directly or via Old Norse < Middle Dutch *Vlaminc*]

Flem·ing /flémming/, **Sir Alexander** (1881–1955) British microbiologist. He was the codeveloper of the world's first antibiotic, penicillin. He shared the Nobel Prize in physiology or medicine (1945) with Howard Walter Florey and Ernst Boris Chain for this discovery.

> "It was astonishing that for some considerable distance around the mould growth the staphococcal colonies were undergoing lysis. What had formerly been a well-grown colony was now a faint shadow of its former self...I was sufficiently interested to pursue the subject."
> [Sir Alexander Fleming. Quoted in *Portraits of Nobel Laureates in Medicine and Physiology,* Sarah R. Riedman and Elton T. Gustafson; 1963]

Flem·ing, Ian (1908–64) British writer. His fictional hero James Bond, secret agent 007, appeared in 12 novels and 7 short stories, beginning with *Casino Royale* (1953).

> "Most marriages don't add two people together. They subtract one from the other."
> [Ian Fleming, *Diamonds Are Forever;* 1956]

Flem·ing, Peggy Gale (*b.* 1948) US figure skater. She was world champion three times (1966–68) and Olympic gold medalist (1968).

Flem·ing, Sir Sandford (1827–1915) Scottish-born Canadian civil engineer and railway surveyor. He was instrumental in the adoption of standard time.

Flem·ish /flémmish/ *adj* OF FLANDERS relating to Flanders, the Flemings, or their language or culture ■ *n* LANGUAGE SPOKEN IN BELGIUM one of the official languages of Belgium, belonging to the West Germanic group of the Germanic branch of Indo-European and closely related to Dutch. Native speakers: 5 million. ■ *npl* PEOPLE OF FLANDERS the people of Flanders, or Flemish-speaking people [14C. < Middle Dutch *Vlamisch* < *Vlāmland* "Flanders"]

Flem·ish bond *n* a style of brickwork in which bricks laid with the end facing out (**headers**) alternate with those laid lengthwise (**stretchers**), horizontally and vertically

Flem·ish school *n* art and artists of the 15th and 16th centuries in the Netherlands. Artists of the Flemish school, e.g., Van Eyck and Rogier van der Weyden, combined carefully observed subjects with complex religious iconography.

flense /flenss/ (**flensed, flens·ing, flens·es**), **flench** /flench/ (**flenched, flench·ing, flench·es**) *vt* to strip the skin or blubber from a whale or seal [Early 19C. < Danish *flensa*] —**flens·er** *n*

flesh /flesh/ *n* **1.** SOFT TISSUE OF BODY the soft tissues, primarily muscle and fat, that cover the bones of people and other animals **2.** HUMAN SKIN AS OUTER SURFACE the outer surface of the human body **3.** MEAT OF ANIMALS the flesh of animals, including birds and fish, regarded as food **4.** PULP OF FRUITS AND VEGETABLES the soft pulpy edible parts of fruits and vegetables, as opposed to the skin, core, pit, and other parts that are not usually eaten **5.** PEOPLE people in general (*literary*) ○ *the way of all flesh* **6.** PHYSICAL ASPECT OF HUMANITY the physical body along with its needs and limitations, as opposed to the soul, mind, or spirit **7.** SUBSTANCE substance as distinct from form or style ○ *Actions give flesh to theory.* **8.** UNWANTED WEIGHT unwanted weight or fatty tissue (*informal*) ○ *could afford to lose some flesh* **9.** COLORS same as **flesh color** ■ *vt* (**fleshed, flesh·ing, flesh·es**) **1.** INSTRUCT ANIMAL BY FEEDING to teach a dog or bird to hunt by feeding it the meat of a freshly killed animal **2.** ACCUSTOM TO KILLING to accustom somebody to bloodshed and the killing of other people (*literary*) **3.** GET BLOOD ON WEAPON to thrust a pointed weapon into somebody's flesh, especially when using it for the first time (*literary*) **4.** MANUF CLEAN INSIDE OF ANIMAL SKIN in tanning, to scrape away the soft tissue adhering to a hide [Old English *flǣsc* "soft tissue, meat" < Germanic] ◇ **in the flesh** in person ◇ **press the flesh** to greet and shake the hands of many people in public, as a political or promotional exercise (*informal*)

flesh out *v* **1.** *vt* to add substance and detail to something ○ *flesh out a business proposal* **2.** *vi* to put on weight, or become overweight (*informal*)

flesh and blood *n* **1.** people, or a person, related to somebody by birth **2.** RELIG same as **flesh** *n* (sense 6)

flesh-and-blood *adj* representing life, people, and events in a way perceived as believable or realistic

flesh col·or *n* a pink color with tinges of yellow or gray, like that of a white person's skin —**flesh-col·ored** *adj*

flesh·er /fléshər/ *n* in tanning, a person who or a device that removes any flesh adhering to the inside of an animal hide

flesh fly *n* a fly whose larvae feed on the flesh of living or dead animals. Family: Sarcophagidae.

flesh·ings /fléshingz/ *npl* **1.** flesh-colored tights formerly worn by actors **2.** flesh scraped from an animal's hide

flesh·ly /fléshlee/ (**-li·er, -li·est**) *adj* **1.** BODILY relating to the human body ○ *the fleshly concerns of daily living* **2.** RELATING TO PHYSICAL PLEASURE enjoying or concerned with the pleasures of the body **3.** NOT SPIRITUAL not focused on spiritual matters **4.** PLUMP plump or fat (*archaic*) —**flesh·li·ness** *n*

flesh·pot /flésh pòt/ *n* a place known to provide sexual or sensual entertainment (*usually used in the plural*) ○ *Police keep an eye on the local fleshpots.* [Mid-16C. See Exodus 16:3]

flesh wound *n* a wound that penetrates the flesh but does not damage bones or vital organs

flesh·y /fléshee/ (**-i·er, -i·est**) *adj* **1.** PLUMP having a noticeable amount of flesh on the body **2.** WITH MORE FLESH with thicker or softer flesh than other parts of the body ○ *the fleshy part of the hand at the base of the thumb* **3.** SOFT AND JUICY with thick soft juicy pulp ○ *the fleshiest peaches of the season* —**flesh·i·ness** *n*

fletch /flech/ (**fletched, fletch·ing, fletch·es**) *vt* ARCHERY same as **fledge** (sense 3) [Mid-17C. Alteration of FLEDGE, influenced by FLETCHER]

fletch·er /fléchər/ *n* a maker of arrows [13C. < Old French *flech(i)er* < *flèche* "arrow"]

fletch·ings /fléchingz/ *npl* the feathered part of an arrow

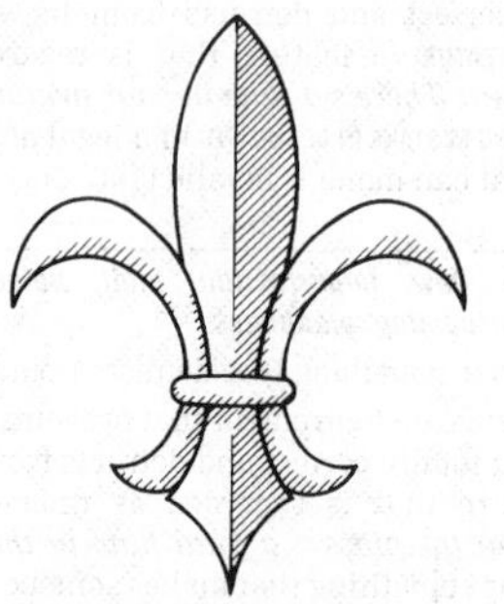

fleur-de-lis

fleur-de-lis /flùr də leé/ (*plural* **fleurs-de-lis** /-leéz/), **fleur-de-lys** (*plural* **fleurs-de-lys**) *n* **1.** a heraldic symbol or design in the form of three tapering petals tied by a surrounding band, formerly used by the kings of France **2.** PLANTS same as **iris** (sense 2) **3.** the flag of Quebec, which has four white fleurs-de-lis on a blue background [< Old French *flour de lys* "flower of the lily"]

fleur·et /flur ét, flŏŏ rét/, **fleur·ette** *n* a decorative motif in the form of a small flower [Early 19C. < French, "little flower" < *fleur* "flower" < Old French *flour* (see FLOWER)]

flew past tense of **fly**[1]

SPELLCHECK See *flu.*

flex /fleks/ *v* (**flexed, flex·ing, flex·es**) **1.** *vti* BEND to bend something, or be able to be bent ○ *The board flexes as you step on it.* **2.** *vt* BEND BODY PART to bend something, especially a joint of the body **3.** *vti* PRODUCE MUSCULAR CONTRACTION to move or tense a muscle, or become tense or contracted ■ *n* BENDING ABILITY bending, or the ability to bend [Early 16C. < Latin *flex-* (see FLEXIBLE)]

~~**flexable**~~ incorrect spelling of **flexible**

flex·a·tone /fléksə tōn/ *n* a percussion instrument consisting of a handle with a narrow metal sheet attached that is struck to produce a tunable sound

flex·i·ble /fléksəb'l/ *adj* **1.** ABLE TO BEND WITHOUT BREAKING able to bend or be bent repeatedly without damage or injury **2.** ABLE TO ADAPT TO NEW SITUATION able to change or be changed according to circumstances **3.** SUBJECT TO INFLUENCE able to be persuaded or influenced [15C. Directly or via French < Latin *flexibilis* < *flex-*, past participle of *flectere* "bend"] —**flex·i·bil·i·ty** /flèksə bíllətee/ *n* —**flex·i·ble·ness** *n* —**flex·i·bly** *adv*

flex·i·ble ben·e·fits *n* a benefits program for employees that offers them a range of types and levels of benefit from which to choose

flex·i·ble time *n US* HR same as **flextime**

flex·ile /fléksəl, -sīl/ *adj* same as **flexible** (sense 1) [Mid-17C. < Latin *flexilis* < *flex-* (see FLEXIBLE)]

flex·ion /flékshən/, **flec·tion** *n* **1.** BENDING OF LIMB the bending of a limb or joint **2.** POSITION OF BENT PART the position of a bent limb or joint **3.** BENDING OF SOMETHING the bending of something, or its bent state [Early 17C. < Latin *flexion-* < *flex-* (see FLEXIBLE)] —**flex·ion·al** *adj*

flex·i·time *n* HR same as **flextime**

flex·og·ra·phy /flek sóggrəfee/ *n* a relief printing technique that uses a rotary press, a flexible plate, and a water-based ink [Mid-20C. < Latin *flex-* (see

FLEXIBLE)] —**flex·o·g·ra·pher** *n* —**flex·o·graph·ic** /flèksə gráffik/ *adj* —**flex·o·graph·i·cal·ly** *adv*

flex·or /fléksər/ *n* a muscle that bends a joint or limb when it is contracted [Early 17C. < modern Latin < Latin *flex-* (see FLEXIBLE)]

flex·time /fléks tīm/, **flex·i·time** /flékseе-/ *n* a system that allows employees to set their own daily times of starting and finishing work, within specific limits [Late 20C. Blend of FLEXIBLE + TIME]

flex·u·ous /flékshoo əss/, **flex·u·ose** /-ōss/ *adj* curving, winding, or turning (*formal*) [Early 17C. < Latin *flexuosus* < *flex-* (see FLEXIBLE)] —**flex·u·os·i·ty** /flèkshoo óssətee/ *n* —**flex·u·ous·ly** *adv*

flex·ure /flékshər/ *n* **1.** an act of bending or being flexed **2.** a bend or curve, e.g., in a body part or organ [Late 16C. < Latin *flexura* < *flex-* (see FLEXIBLE)] —**flex·ur·al** *adj*

flib·ber·ti·gib·bet /flìbbərtee jíbbit/ *n* somebody who is regarded as silly, irresponsible, or scatterbrained, especially one who chatters or gossips (*dated*) [15C. Probably an imitation of the sound of meaningless chatter]

flic /flik/ *n* a member of the French police (*slang*) [Late 19C. < French]

flick[1] /flik/ *n* **1.** QUICK MOVEMENT a quick jerking movement **2.** QUICK BLOW a sharp light blow made with a quick jerking movement, usually of the finger **3.** SPLASH OF COLOR a light splash or streak ○ *flicks of paint left on the floor* ■ *v* (**flicked, flick·ing, flicks**) **1.** *vt* HIT SOMETHING WITH QUICK BLOW to hit something or somebody sharply or lightly with the end of something, usually with a quick jerking movement ○ *He flicked me with his towel.* **2.** *vti* MOVE JERKILY to move with a quick sharp jerk, or make something move with a quick sharp jerk ○ *The cow's tail flicked back and forth.* **3.** *vt* MOVE SOMETHING WITH QUICK BLOW to move, propel, or remove something with a sharp light blow or a quick movement of the finger or hand ○ *Would you flick that bug off me?* ○ *flick a switch* [15C. An imitation of the sound of a light blow]

flick through *vt* to turn the pages of a book or magazine quickly ○ *flicked through a couple of magazines while I waited*

flick[2] /flik/ (*dated informal*) *n* MOVIES same as **movie** (*often used in combination*) ■ **flicks** *npl* the movies in general [Early 20C. Shortening of FLICKER[1]; from the flickering of early films]

flick[3] /flik/ *n S England, Wales* animal fat found around kidneys and other organs (*informal*) [Late 16C. Probably variant of FLITCH]

flick·er[1] /flíkər/ *vi* (**-ered, -er·ing, -ers**) **1.** SHINE UNSTEADILY to burn or shine unsteadily **2.** FLUTTER OR MOVE JERKILY to move with a fluttering or fast jerky motion **3.** APPEAR BRIEFLY to appear or exist only briefly ○ *A smile flickered across her face.* ■ *n* **1.** FLUCTUATING LIGHT an unsteady or wavering light ○ *the flicker of candles in the dark* **2.** QUICK MOVEMENT a quick fluttering movement **3.** TRANSIENT FEELING OR EXPRESSION a brief feeling that quickly passes, or an indication of this on somebody's face ○ *a flicker of anxiety* [Old English *flicorian* "to flutter," suggestive of the movement] —**flick·er·ing·ly** *adv*

flick·er[2] /flíkər/ *n* a woodpecker that has wings that show yellow or red in flight. Native to: deciduous woods of North America. Latin name: *Colaptes auratus.* [Early 19C. Probably an imitation of its call]

flick·er·tail squir·rel /flìkər tàyl-/, **flick·er·tail go·pher** *n regional* same as **ground squirrel** (sense 1)

flick knife *n UK* same as **switchblade**

flick-on *n* in soccer and field hockey, a light touch on a moving ball with the foot, head, or stick intended to guide it toward a teammate

fli·er /flī ər/, **fly·er** *n* **1.** AVIAT AIRCRAFT PILOT the pilot of an aircraft **2.** AVIAT AIRCRAFT PASSENGER a passenger on an aircraft ○ *frequent fliers* **3.** MEDIA PRINTED SHEET WIDELY DISTRIBUTED a short piece of printed matter, usually an advertisement, that is widely distributed **4.** BUILDINGS STEP IN STRAIGHT STAIRCASE a rectangular step in a straight flight of stairs **5.** RISKY UNDERTAKING a daring or risky financial undertaking (*informal*) **6.** TRACK AND FIELD, SWIMMING same as **flying start**

flight[1] /flīt/ *n* **1.** PROCESS OR ACT OF FLYING the process or act of moving through the air or through space **2.** AIR TRIP a trip through air or space in a form of transportation ○ *daily flights of a thousand miles or more* **3.** TRAVEL SCHEDULED FLIGHT a scheduled flight with a commercial airline, usually designated by letters and numbers ○ *flight TC546 to Vancouver* **4.** ABILITY TO FLY the ability to travel through the air with wings ○ *an experimental ultralight tested for flight* ○ *an ancient bird incapable of flight* **5.** BUILDINGS SERIES OF STEPS BETWEEN FLOORS a group of stairs that go from one level of a building to another ○ *We live three flights up.* **6.** GROUP FLYING TOGETHER a group of aircraft or birds flying together, sometimes in a set pattern **7.** AIR FORCE GROUP OF MILITARY AIRCRAFT a group of aircraft in the US Air Force that forms a subdivision of a squadron **8.** RAPID MOVEMENT swift passage, progress, or motion, especially through the air **9.** EXTRAORDINARY MENTAL FEAT an act or the process of imagining extraordinary things ○ *a flight of the imagination* **10.** ARCHERY, LEISURE TAIL OF ARROW OR DART the feathers on an arrow or dart ■ *v* (**flight·ed, flight·ing, flights**) **1.** *vi* FLY TOGETHER to fly or migrate together **2.** *vt* HUNTING SHOOT FLYING BIRD in hunting, to shoot a bird as it flies **3.** *vt* ARCHERY, LEISURE PUT TAIL ON ARROW OR DART to put feathers on an arrow or dart **4.** *vt* LAUNCH OBJECT ON FLOATING COURSE to make a ball or dart seem to float inexorably toward its target [Old English *flyht* < Germanic]

flight[2] /flīt/ *n* the act of running away from something or somebody [12C. < assumed Old English, < Germanic]

flight ar·row *n* a light arrow used for long-distance shooting

flight at·ten·dant *n* somebody employed by an airline to attend to the needs, comfort, and safety of passengers during flights

flight bag *n* a soft suitcase of a size that can be carried on an aircraft

flight cou·pon *n* a portion of an airline ticket that indicates the departure and arrival points of a passenger for a single journey or each leg of a journey

flight da·ta re·cord·er *n* same as **flight recorder**

flight deck *n* **1.** the upper deck of an aircraft carrier that is used as a runway **2.** the compartment at the front of an airplane where the pilot, copilot, and flight engineer sit

flight en·gi·neer *n* the crew member of an airplane who monitors the performance of its systems, including the engines

flight en·ve·lope *n* a set of limits to performance that exist in the design of an aircraft, e.g., altitude, range, payload, and maneuverability

flight feath·er *n* any feather in a bird's wing or tail that is necessary for flight, usually a large stiff one

flight·less /flītləss/ *adj* describes birds that are incapable of flight. Ostriches, penguins, and kiwis are flightless birds.

flight lev·el *n* the height at which a particular aircraft is allowed to fly at a particular time

flight lieu·ten·ant *n* an officer in the British Royal Air Force of a rank above flying officer

flight line *n* the area of an airfield, especially a military airfield, where airplanes are parked, serviced, and loaded or unloaded

flight of fan·cy *n* an idea or thought that is very imaginative but completely impractical or even ridiculous

flight path *n* the course taken by an aircraft, spacecraft, or projectile

flight pay *n* pay in addition to the regular salary that the members of a US military aircrew get when they take part in authorized flights

flight plan *n* a record outlining the details of a proposed flight

flight re·cord·er *n* an electronic instrument installed on an aircraft that records details of its performance in flight. The details recorded can be used to discover the cause of a crash.

flight·see·ing /flīt seeing/ *n* the practice of transporting tourists to otherwise inaccessible wilderness areas by helicopter, for viewing the areas by air or for organized hikes —**flight·seer** *n*

flight sim·u·la·tor *n* **1.** a computerized device that exactly reproduces the conditions that occur on the flight deck of an aircraft and that can be used to train pilots **2.** **flight sim·u·la·tor, flight sim** a computer game that involves simulated flight control

flight suit *n US* a one-piece flame-retardant suit worn by military aircrews when flying

flight sur·geon *n* a medical officer in the US Air Force who practices aviation medicine and looks after the health of flight crews

flight-test (**flight-test·ed, flight-test·ing, flight-tests**) *vt* to test the performance of an aircraft, spacecraft, missile, or component in flight —**flight test** *n*

flight·wor·thy /flīt wùrthee/ *adj* in good enough condition to fly —**flight·wor·thi·ness** *n*

flight·y /flītee/ (**-i·er, -i·est**) *adj* constantly changing plans, emotions, or opinions —**flight·i·ly** *adv* —**flight·i·ness** *n*

flim·flam /flím flàm/ (*slang*) *n* **1.** TRICK OR SWINDLE an attempt to cheat somebody **2.** DECEPTIVE TALK talk that confuses or deceives ■ *vt* (**-flammed, -flam·ming, -flams**) CHEAT SOMEBODY to cheat somebody [Mid-16C. Origin ?] —**flim·flam·mer** *n* —**flim·flam·mer·y** *n*

flim·sy /flímzee/ (**-si·er, -si·est**) *adj* **1.** NOT STRONG weak and too easily broken ○ *flimsy furniture* **2.** EASILY TORN light, thin, and easily torn ○ *a flimsy cotton blouse* **3.** UNCONVINCING difficult to believe or accept ○ *The grounds for an appeal are flimsy at best.* ○ *a flimsy excuse* [Early 18C. Probably < alteration of FILM after CLUMSY] —**flim·si·ly** *adv* —**flim·si·ness** *n*

SYNONYMS See *fragile*.

flinch /flinch/ (**flinched, flinch·ing, flinch·es**) *vi* **1.** to make an involuntary small backward movement in response to pain or something frightening or shocking **2.** to avoid thinking about something, confronting something, or doing something ○ *We will not flinch from danger.* [Mid-16C. < Old French *flenchir* "turn aside" < Germanic, "to bend"] —**flinch·er** *n* —**flinch·ing·ly** *adv*

SYNONYMS See *recoil*.

flin·ders /flíndərz/ *npl* tiny fragments of something [15C. Origin ?]

Flin·ders /flíndərz/ river in northern Queensland, Australia that rises in the Great Dividing Range and flows northwest to the Gulf of Carpentaria. Length: 520 mi./840 km.

Flin·ders, Matthew (1774–1814) British explorer. He was the first sailor to circumnavigate Tasmania (1798) and Australia (1802–03).

Flin·ders bar /flíndərz-/ *n* a bar of soft iron mounted under a compass to compensate for local magnetism and prevent it affecting the reading of the compass [After Matthew FLINDERS]

Flin·ders Is·land island off the coast of northeastern Tasmania, Australia. Local industries include fishing, farming, and tourism. Population: 868 (2002 estimate). Area: 807 sq. mi./2,089 sq. km.

Flin·ders Ranges mountain chain in eastern South Australia. More than 310 mi./500 km long, its highest peak is St. Mary's Peak, 3,825 ft./1,166 m.

fling /fling/ *v* (**flung** /flung/, **fling·ing, flings**) **1.** *vt* THROW SOMETHING VIOLENTLY to throw something or somebody carelessly or forcefully **2.** *vr* MOVE FORCEFULLY to move forcefully in a way that seems impressive or dramatic ○ *She flung herself onto the chair and began to sob.* **3.** *vt* MOVE YOUR HEAD OR ARMS to move your head or arms in a particular direction suddenly and dramatically **4.** *vr* WORK ENTHUSIASTICALLY AND ENERGETICALLY to start doing something with great enthusiasm and energy ○ *She flings herself into every project she undertakes.* ■ *n* (*informal*) **1.** SHORT AFFAIR a brief sexual relationship **2.** TIME FOR PLEASURE a short period of carefree enjoyment, especially before a time that is expected to be less exciting or enjoyable ○ *one last fling before settling down to a full-time job* [13C. < N Germanic < Indo-European, "to strike"] —**fling·er** *n*

SYNONYMS See *throw*.

fling off *vt* to take off a piece of clothing quickly, or remove forcefully something that is covering you

flint /flint/ (*plural same* or **flints**) *n* **1.** GEOL VERY HARD QUARTZ THAT MAKES SPARKS a very hard grayish black fine-grained form of quartz that produces a spark when struck with steel. It occurs as nodules and bands in chalk. Flint was used in prehistoric times to make tools. **2.** PREHIST **TOOL MADE OF FINE-GRAINED QUARTZ** a piece of fine-grained quartz shaped into a tool by prehistoric people **3. SPARK-MAKING ROCK** a piece of flint used to make a spark **4. PART OF CIGARETTE LIGHTER** the part of a cigarette lighter, consisting of a small iron alloy cylinder, that makes a spark [Old English, < Germanic, "to split"]

Flint /flint/ city in southeastern Michigan, a major centre for assembling motor vehicles. Population: 121,763 (2002 estimate).

Flint, F. S. (1885–1960) British poet and translator. His *Cadences* (1915) features the sparse verse characteristic of the Imagist movement. His later work is written in a more romantic style. Full name **Flint, Frank Stewart**

flint corn *n* corn with kernels that contain hard starch, e.g., popcorn. Latin name: *Zea mays*.

flint glass *n* high-quality glass containing lead oxide that has a high index of refraction. Use: lenses, cut glass, costume jewelry.

flint·knap·ping *n* the method, mainly used by prehistoric people, of chipping and splitting flint to make tools —**flint·knap·per** *n*

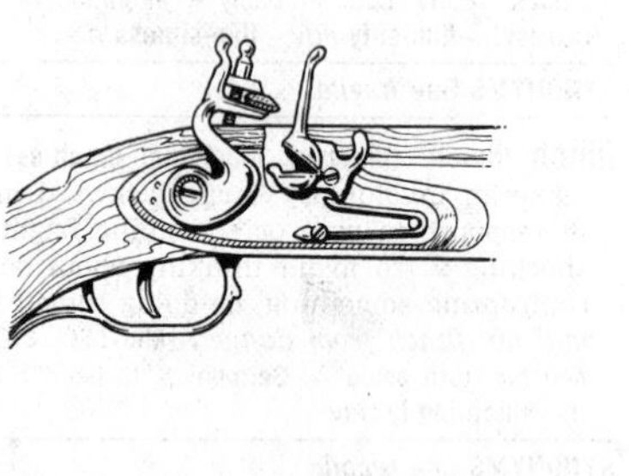

flintlock

flint·lock /flínt lòk/ *n* **1.** a firearm with a firing mechanism **(gunlock)** where a flint embedded in the hammer ignites a gunpowder charge **2.** a firing mechanism **(gunlock)** that has a flint embedded in the hammer to produce the spark

Flint·shire /flínt sheèr, -shər/ county in northeastern Wales, on the border with England. Population: 148,594 (2001). Area: 169 sq. mi./437 sq. km.

flint·y /flíntee/ (**-i·er, -i·est**) *adj* **1.** hard, inflexible, and showing no emotion **2.** containing or related to flint —**flint·i·ly** *adv* —**flint·i·ness** *n*

flip /flip/ *v* (**flipped, flip·ping, flips**) **1.** *vti* **TURN SOMETHING OVER** to turn something over from one side to the other with a quick movement of the wrist, hand, or fingers **2.** *vt* **MOVE SOMETHING WITH QUICK LIGHT MOTION** to move something with a small sharp quick motion ○ *She flipped the light on and walked in.* **3.** *vt* **TOSS SOMETHING CARELESSLY** to throw or toss something carelessly and lightly ○ *flip a pen across the table* **4.** *vti* **TURN PAGES OF READING MATERIAL** to turn the pages of a magazine or book quickly **5.** *vti* **SPIN COIN** to flick the edge of a coin with your thumb so that it spins in the air before landing **6.** *vi* **GET SUDDENLY ANGRY** to become very angry or upset suddenly (*slang*) ○ *When I told her I wouldn't help her, she just flipped.* **7.** *vi* **GET EXCITED AT SOMETHING NICE** to become excited over something that is pleasurable or attractive (*slang*) ■ *adj* (**flip·per, flip·pest**) **FLIPPANT** showing a lack of seriousness that is considered inappropriate (*informal*) ○ *a flip remark* ■ *n* **1. COIN'S SPIN** the spin of a coin or other object as it is tossed or thrown **2.** SPORTS **TURNING OF BODY** a turning of the body through 360 degrees by springing from the ground or while diving **3.** BEVERAGES **ALCOHOL AND EGG DRINK** an alcoholic drink containing beaten egg [Mid-16C. Probably an imitation of the sound]

flip·book /flíp bòòk/ *n* a small book containing a series of images of the same thing in different positions that create the illusion of movement when the pages are turned quickly

flip chart *n* a visual aid consisting of a large pad of paper mounted on an easel, used to present information

flip-flop *n* **1.** CLOTHING **BACKLESS SANDAL** a backless foam-rubber sandal with a V-shaped strap secured between the toes and at the sides of the foot (*informal*) **2. CHANGE OF MIND** a change of opinion, especially by a politician (*informal*) **3.** GYMNASTICS **BACKWARD SOMERSAULT** a backward flip of the body **4.** ELECTRONICS **CIRCUIT WITH TWO STABLE STATES** an electronic circuit or mechanical device that has two stable states and can be switched between the two. Early computers used flip-flops as their memory storage units. ■ *vi* (**flip-flop·ped, flip-flop·ping, flip-flops**) **CHANGE OPINION** to have a change of opinion, especially when this leads to a change of policy (*informal*) ○ *flip-flopped on the issue of employer responsibility*

flip·pant /flíppənt/ *adj* showing a lack of seriousness that is thought inappropriate [Early 17C. < FLIP, after heraldic adjectives such as RAMPANT] —**flip·pan·cy** *n* —**flip·pant·ly** *adv*

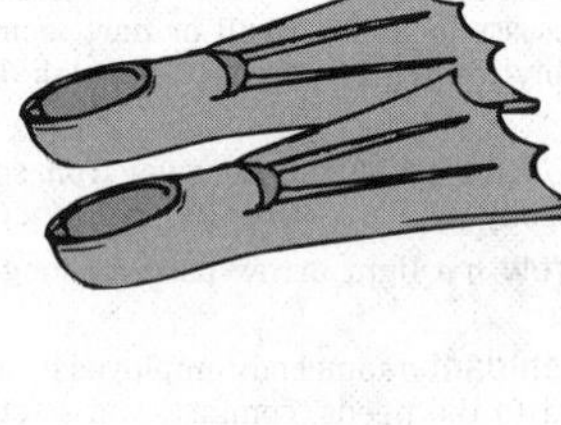

flipper (sense 2)

flip·per /flíppər/ *n* **1. WATER ANIMAL'S LIMB** a broad flat limb that an animal such as a penguin, seal, or whale uses for swimming **2. DIVER'S FOOTWEAR** a broad flat rubber extension worn on each of the feet to aid in swimming **3. PINBALL FEATURE** a small button-operated bat in a pinball machine that is used to keep the ball in play

flip phone *n* a cell phone with one hinged section that opens up for use and folds up when not in use

flip·ping /flípping/ *adj, adv* used to emphasize annoyance or displeasure with something (*slang*) ○ *Will you turn that flipping music down?*

flip side *n* **1.** the disadvantages involved in doing something as opposed to the advantages that have previously been mentioned (*slang*) **2.** the song on a single record that the record company thinks will be less popular with record buyers, or the side of the record with that song on it (*dated*)

flip-top *n* a type of lid on a package that is hinged so that it moves up and down for opening and closing

flirt /flurt/ *v* (**flirt·ed, flirt·ing, flirts**) **1.** *vi* **BEHAVE ALLURINGLY** to behave in a playfully alluring way **2.** *vt* **FLICK SOMETHING** to flick or jerk something ■ *n* **SOMEBODY BEHAVING IN PLAYFULLY ALLURING WAY** somebody who behaves in a playfully alluring way [Mid-16C. Origin ?] —**flirt·er** *n* —**flirt·ing·ly** *adv*

flirt with *vt* **1.** to consider an idea without doing anything serious about it or letting it have an effect ○ *flirted with the idea of going to college, but decided not to* **2.** to act in a way that may bring serious trouble or damage ○ *You're flirting with disaster when you drive that fast.*

flir·ta·tion /flur táysh'n/ *n* **1.** a short playful interaction based on lighthearted feeling, especially one that suggests sexual interest **2.** a period of considering or participating in something in a superficial way ○ *a flirtation with vegetarianism*

flir·ta·tious /flur táyshəss/ *adj* behaving playfully and in a way that gives the impression of sexual interest —**flir·ta·tious·ly** *adv* —**flir·ta·tious·ness** *n*

flirt·y /flúrtee/ (**-i·er, -i·est**) *adj* **1.** same as **flirtatious** (*informal*) **2.** suitable for a flirtatious person or a person in a flirtatious mood —**flirt·i·ly** *adv* —**flirt·i·ness** *n*

flit /flit/ (**flit·ted, flit·ting, flits**) *vi* **1.** to move quickly from one place to another without stopping for long **2.** to be briefly present or visible [12C. < Old Norse *flytja* "carry about" < Germanic, "to float"] —**flit·ter** *n*

flitch /flich/ *n* **1.** a log cut lengthwise from a tree, ready for further processing at a mill **2.** a side of bacon or one side of a pork carcass without the leg or shoulder [Old English *flicce* < Germanic, "to tear"]

flit·ter[1] /flíttər/ *vi* (**-tered, -ter·ing, -ters**) to move around in a restless or nervous way ■ *n* a rapid, repetitive, or back-and-forth movement in something small [14C. < FLIT]

flit·ter[2] /flíttər/ *n regional* a small cake [Alteration of FRITTER[1]]

REGIONAL NOTE In the Appalachian Highlands, ***flitter*** identifies a pancake or flapjack; especially in the Piedmont South, it signals a fritter cake, often containing fruit or meat, fried in deep fat.

fliv·ver /flívvər/ *n* a small, cheap, and usually old car (*dated informal*) [Early 20C. Origin ?]

float /flōt/ *v* (**float·ed, float·ing, floats**) **1.** *vi* **REST ON SURFACE OF LIQUID** to move or rest on the surface of a liquid without sinking **2.** *vt* **PLACE OR MOVE SOMETHING ON LIQUID** to place something or make something move on the surface of a liquid **3.** *vi* **STAY UP IN AIR** to move slowly and lightly through the air **4.** *vi* **BE HEARD OR SMELLED FAINTLY** to carry across a distance, especially as a sound or smell ○ *The sound of laughter floated across the water.* **5.** *vi* **LIVE AIMLESSLY** to live without a fixed purpose or plan ○ *He floated from job to job.* **6.** *vt* **PROPOSE PLAN** to propose a plan for consideration in order to see what response it receives (*informal*) **7.** *vi* **MOVE GRACEFULLY** to move lightly and gracefully ○ *They floated across the dance floor.* **8.** *vt* FIN **SELL SHARES IN COMPANY** to finance a company by selling stock in it to the public **9.** *vt* FIN **SELL STOCKS OR BONDS** to offer stocks or bonds for sale on a stock exchange **10.** *vti* ECON **ALLOW CURRENCY VALUE TO CHANGE** to allow the exchange rate value of a currency to fluctuate freely in an open market, or fluctuate in this way **11.** *vt* AGRIC **IRRIGATE LAND** to flood or irrigate land ■ *n* **1. FLOATING OBJECT** an object or device that floats or is used to keep another object buoyant **2. VEHICLE IN PARADE** a truck or other large vehicle that has been elaborately decorated for a parade **3.** FISHING same as **bobber 4.** BEVERAGES **SOFT DRINK WITH ICE CREAM** a soft drink with a scoop of ice cream floating in it **5.** BANKING **PERIOD BETWEEN DEPOSIT AND WITHDRAWAL** the period between the deposit of funds by a customer and the availability of the funds for withdrawal **6.** CONSTR **PLASTERER'S TROWEL** a tool with a handle and flat rectangular blade for applying plaster to a wall **7.** MECH ENG **BALL IN FLOW-REGULATING DEVICE** the hollow ball that rests on the water level in a tank as part of the device (**ball cock**) that regulates the flow of water into the tank **8.** *UK* SWIMMING same as **kickboard 9.** NAUT **PADDLE WHEEL BLADE** a blade in a paddle wheel **10.** BIOL same as **air bladder** [Old English *flotian* < Germanic] —**float·a·bil·i·ty** /flṑtə bíllətee/ *n* —**float·a·ble** *adj*

float around *vi* to be the subject of frequent discussion or attention ○ *a rumor floating around about a pending engagement*

float cham·ber *n* a chamber in a carburetor that has a floating valve to control the entry and level of gasoline

float·er /flṓtər/ *n* **1. SOMETHING FLOATING** somebody or something that is floating **2. CASUAL WORKER** a casual worker who goes from job to job (*informal*) **3. WORKER SHIFTING TO VARIOUS TASKS** an employee who is switched from job to job as needed **4. DEAD BODY** a dead body found floating in water (*slang*) **5.** *US* **ILLEGAL VOTER** a voter who illegally goes to polling stations using a false registration or the name of somebody who has not voted (*informal*) **6. INSURANCE POLICY** an insurance policy that covers articles lost anywhere **7.** OPHTHALMOL **SPOT INTERFERING WITH VISION** a shadow of opaque debris in the vitreous humor of the eye seen as a moving dark spot, or as a group of them, by the person affected. Technical name **muscae volitantes**

REGIONAL NOTE See *trashmover.*

float glass *n* flat polished transparent glass made by solidifying molten glass as it floats on liquid of higher density such as tin

float·ing /flṓting/ *adj* **1. NOT FIXED INTO POSITION** not fixed but moving around **2.** MED **OUT OF NORMAL POSITION** not in the normal place in the body, having moved out of position ○ *a floating kidney* **3.** FIN **FLUCTUATING IN MONETARY VALUE** free to fluctuate in exchange rate value in relation to other currencies ○ *the floating* *euro* **4.** MECH ENG **OPERATING SMOOTHLY** operating smoothly and without vibration

float·ing dock *n* **1.** a large structure that can be submerged to let a ship enter and then raised with the ship inside to be used as a dry dock **2.** a small dock supported by piles on which it can move up and down with any change in water level

float·ing is·land *n* a dessert consisting of custard on which are placed pieces of meringue or jelly that appear to float

float·ing-point *adj* describes numbers in which the digits and the location of the decimal place are treated separately

float·ing pol·i·cy *n* an insurance policy that covers loss of or damage to goods being transported by sea, regardless of the ship carrying them

float·ing rib *n* a rib attached only to the spine and not to the breastbone. In humans the two lower ribs on each side are floating ribs.

float·ing vot·er *n* *UK* POL same as **swing voter**

float·plane /flṓt plàyn/ *n* a seaplane that has one or more floats that enable it to land on water

float tank *n* ALTERN MED same as **flotation tank**

float·y /flṓtee/ (**-i·er, -i·est**) *adj* **1.** seeming to move slowly through the air **2.** capable of floating easily

floc /flok/ *n* a woolly (**flocculent**) mass that forms in a liquid as a result of precipitation or the aggregation of suspended particles [Early 20C. Shortening of FLOCCULUS]

floc·cil·la·tion /flòksi láysh'n/ *n* aimless plucking at bedclothes, a sign that a person is approaching death [Mid-19C. < modern Latin *floccillus* "little tuft of wool" < Latin *floccus* "tuft of wool"]

floc·cose /fló kòss/ *adj* describes plant parts that are covered with tufts of soft hair [Mid-18C. < late Latin *floccosus* < Latin *floccus* "tuft of wool"]

floc·cu·late /flókyə làyt/ (**-lat·ed, -lat·ing, -lates**) *vti* **1.** to cause particles suspended in water to aggregate into clumps or masses that then sink or can be removed by filtering, or aggregate in this way **2.** to form fluffy masses, or cause clouds to form fluffy masses —**floc·cu·la·tion** /flòkyə láysh'n/ *n*

floc·cule /fló kyoòl/ *n* a small mass of woolly or cloudy particles [Mid-19C. < modern Latin *flocculus* (see FLOCCULUS)]

floc·cu·lent /flókyələnt/ *adj* **1.** having a fluffy or woolly appearance **2.** describes the woolly mass of solids (**precipitate**) produced in a liquid by a chemical reaction [Early 19C. < Latin *floccus* "tuft of wool"] —**floc·cu·lence** *n* —**floc·cu·len·cy** *n* —**floc·cu·lent·ly** *adv*

floc·cu·lus /flókyələss/ (*plural* **-li** /-lī/) *n* a mass of gas that appears as either a dark or a bright spot on the surface of the Sun, often near to a sunspot [Late 18C. < modern Latin, "small tuft of wool" < Latin *floccus* "tuft of wool"]

floc·cus /flókəss/ (*plural* **-ci** /fló kī, -kee, flók sī, -see/) *n* a tuft of woolly hair, or a fluffy or downy covering [Mid-19C. < Latin, "tuft of wool"]

flock /flok/ *n* **1. GROUP OF ANIMALS** a group of birds, sheep, or goats that travel, live, or feed together **2. CROWD OF PEOPLE** a large group of people of the same type **3.** CHR **CONGREGATION** the members of a church congregation under the leadership of a priest or pastor ■ *vi* (**flocked, flock·ing, flocks**) **GO IN LARGE NUMBERS** to go to a place or event in large numbers [Old English *flocc*, origin ?]

flock pa·per *n* wallpaper with a raised pattern that is velvety to the touch [*Flock* "powdered wool" (with which originally made) < Latin *floccus* "tuft of wool"]

Flod·den Field /flódd'n-/ plain in Northumberland, northern England, near the Scottish border. It was the site of a battle in 1513 in which England beat Scotland, and in which King James IV of Scotland was killed.

floe /flō/ *n* GEOG same as **ice floe** [Early 19C. Probably < Norwegian *flo* "layer"]

SPELLCHECK floe or **flow**? Do not confuse the spelling of ***floe*** and ***flow***, which sound similar. ***Floe*** is only used as a noun, denoting a sheet of floating ice. The word ***flow*** is much more frequent in general usage and can be used as a verb or a noun, referring to free or smooth movement, for example, of water or traffic: *Blood flows through the veins. There has been a steady flow of refugees across the border.*

flog /flog/ (**flogged, flog·ging, flogs**) *vt* **1. BEAT SOMEBODY VERY HARD** to hit a person or animal very hard using something such as a whip, strap, or stick **2.** MEDIA **PUBLICIZE AGGRESSIVELY** to publicize or advertise something aggressively (*informal*) **3. CRITICIZE SOMEBODY** to criticize somebody very severely ○ *flogged in the press for his continual policy flip-flops* **4.** *UK* COMM same as **sell** (*informal*) [Late 17C. Origin ?] —**flog·ging** *n*

flog·ger /flóggər/ *n* somebody who approves of flogging as a punishment

flo·ka·ti /flō kaátee/ (*plural* **-tis**) *n* a handwoven woolen Greek rug with a shaggy pile [Mid-20C. < modern Greek *phlokatē* < Latin *floccus* "tuft of wool"]

flong /flawng/ *n* a sheet of papier-mâché used to make a mold for a metal plate for printing a page of newspaper [Late 19C. < French *flan* "mold" (see FLAN)]

flood /flud/ *n* **1. WATER COVERING PREVIOUSLY DRY AREA** a very large amount of water that has overflowed from a source such as a river or a broken pipe onto a previously dry area **2. HUGE NUMBER** a very large number of people or things ○ *a flood of complaints* **3. HIGH TIDE** the flowing in to land of water, associated with a rising tide **4.** ELEC same as **floodlight** *n* (sense 1) ■ *v* (**flood·ed, flood·ing, floods**) **1.** *vti* **COVER AREA WITH WATER** to cover a previously dry area with large amounts of water, or be covered with large amounts of water **2.** *vi* **OVERFLOW** to undergo conditions in which water overflows banks or barriers **3.** *vi* **ARRIVE IN LARGE NUMBERS** to arrive somewhere in very large numbers ○ *Messages of support are still flooding in.* **4.** *vt* **SEND SOMEBODY MANY CALLS OR LETTERS** to send a very large number of calls, letters, or complaints to an organization (*usually used in the passive*) ○ *We have been flooded with offers of help.* **5.** *vi* **FEEL EMOTION SUDDENLY AND INTENSELY** to feel a particular emotion, sensation, or memory suddenly and intensely **6.** *vti* **FILL WITH LIGHT** to shine strongly so that a place becomes filled with a bright or glowing light (*literary*) **7.** *vt* ECON **SUPPLY OR PRODUCE SOMETHING TO EXCESS** to supply too much of a product to a market, pushing prices down and keeping them low **8.** *vti* AUTOMOT **SUPPLY TOO MUCH GAS TO CARBURETOR** to send too much gas to a carburetor in a car engine, or be supplied with too much, so that the car fails to start [Old English *flōd* < Germanic] —**flood·a·ble** *adj* —**flood·ed** *adj* —**flood·er** *n* ◇ **be in flood** to be so full of water that banks or barriers are overflowed

flood out *vt* to force somebody to leave a place or stop using something because flooding makes it impossible to stay or continue

Flood *n* in the Bible (Genesis 7–8), a devastating flood, taken as a sign of God's anger at people's wickedness. The Flood was survived only by Noah, his family, and pairs of all the animal species that took refuge in the ship (**ark**) that Noah was told to build by God.

flood·gate /flúd gàyt/ *n* a gate in a watercourse that is used to control the flow

flood·ing /flúdding/ *n* the situation that results when land that is usually dry is covered with water as a result of a river overflowing or heavy rain

flood·light /flúd līt/ *n* **1. POWERFUL LAMP USED AT NIGHT** a large powerful lamp that produces a strong broad beam of light and is used to illuminate the outside of public buildings or sports events at night **2. POWERFUL BEAM OF LIGHT** a broad powerful beam of intense bright light produced artificially ■ *vt* (**-light·ed** or **-lit** /-lìt/, **-light·ing, -lights**) **LIGHT SOMETHING WITH FLOODLIGHTS** to illuminate something with floodlights

flood·lit /flúd lìt/ *adj* illuminated by floodlights ○ *a floodlit match*

flood·mark /flúd maàrk/ *n* the highest level reached by a tide or flood water, or a mark that indicates this level

flood·plain /flúd plàyn/, **flood plain** *n* an area of low-lying land across which a river flows that is covered with sediment as a result of frequent flooding

flood tide *n* **1.** the incoming tide, or the period of time between low water and the following high water **2.** an irresistible or overwhelming force of feeling such as strong public outrage or enthusiasm

flood·wall /flúd wàwl/ *n* a wall built along the seashore or the bank of a river to prevent flooding of adjacent land

flood·wa·ter /flúd wàwtər/ *n* the water of a flood that is carried over river and stream banks and inundates previously dry land

floo·ey /floò ee/ *adj US* in a disordered state, or out of order (*dated slang*) [Early 20C. Origin ?]

floor /flawr/ *n* **1. PART OF ROOM TO WALK ON** the flat horizontal part of a room on which people walk **2. STORY** all the rooms on one level of a building ○ *an office on the fourth floor* **3. LEVEL AREA** a flat open space for an activity or for seating ○ *Are your seats in the stands or on the floor?* **4.** GEOG **NATURAL GROUND LEVEL** the ground at the bottom of an ocean, lake, cave, valley, or forest **5.** POL **PART OF LEGISLATURE WHERE MEMBERS SIT** the part of the building housing a legislative body where the members sit and where official debates and discussions take place **6.** FIN **PLACE WHERE SECURITIES ARE TRADED** the part of a stock exchange where securities, futures, or options contracts are traded **7.** MANUF **WORKING AREA OF FACTORY** the area of a factory where workers manufacture or assemble products **8.** COMM **PART OF STORE FOR MERCHANDISE DISPLAY** the part of a retail store where merchandise is displayed and sold **9.** DANCE same as **dance floor** (*informal*) **10. PEOPLE PRESENT AT MEETING** all the people present in the audience at a meeting, as opposed to the main speakers ○ *I'll take questions from the floor later.* **11.** FIN **LOWEST LIMIT** a lower limit, e.g., on an interest rate or the value of an asset **12.** *UK* AUTOMOT same as **floorboard** (sense 2) ■ *vt* (**floored, floor·ing, floors**) **1. ASTONISH SOMEBODY** to make somebody feel astonished and unable to react ○ *He was floored by the announcement of the changes.* **2.** BOXING **KNOCK DOWN** to knock somebody down with a punch **3.** AUTOMOT **PRESS ACCELERATOR DOWN HARD** to depress a motor vehicle's accelerator as far as it will go in order to increase speed to the maximum (*slang*) [Old English *flōr* < Indo-European, "flat"] —**floor·er** *n* ◇ **have the floor** to address a meeting, or have the right to address a meeting ◇ **take the floor 1.** to rise to speak to a group of people **2.** to begin to dance, e.g., in a ballroom or nightclub ◇ **wipe** *or* **mop (up) the floor with somebody** to defeat somebody completely and decisively (*informal*)

floor·age /fláwrij/ *n* the floor area of a building

floor·board /fláwr bàwrd/ *n* **1.** one of the strips of wood that are used to make a wood floor **2.** the flat, lower part of a motor vehicle's interior where the accelerator, clutch, and brake pedals are found and where the driver and passengers put their feet

floor·cov·er·ing /fláwr kùvvəring/ *n* material for covering floor surfaces, e.g., carpeting, or a carpet or mat made from such a material

floor ex·er·cise *n* an event in a gymnastics competition that consists of a series of tumbling exercises in a timed routine performed on a mat

floor hock·ey *n* a version of hockey played using hockey sticks and a plastic puck or ball in a gymnasium. It is occasionally played with sticks without blades and a rubber ring.

floor·ing /fláwring/ *n* the materials from which a floor is made

floor lamp *n* a tall lamp with a base that stands on the floor

floor lead·er *n* a member of a legislative body chosen by fellow party members to organize their activities and strategy on the floor of the legislature

floor-length *adj* describes a garment such as a dress that extends to the floor or the ankles

floor man·ag·er *n* **1.** an employee of a department store or large store who is in charge of one floor or department, supervising staff and dealing with customers' complaints **2.** *US* a chooser of speakers and controller of debate on the floor of a political convention

floor plan *n* a plan of a room or floor of a building drawn to scale as if viewed from above

floor sam·ple *n* a piece of merchandise that is sold

at a reduced price because it has been used in store displays or as a demonstration model

floor·show /fláwr shō/ *n* a series of shows featuring dancers, singers, comedians, or magicians at a nightclub

floor·walk·er /fláwr wàwkər/ *n* an employee in a department store who supervises sales staff and assists customers

floo·zy /flóozee/, **floo·zie** (*plural* **-zies**) *n* an offensive term that deliberately insults a woman as being vulgar and promiscuous (*slang insult*) [Early 20C. Origin ?]

flop /flop/ *vi* (**flopped, flop·ping, flops**) **1. SIT OR LIE DOWN HEAVILY** to sit or lie down heavily by relaxing the muscles and letting the body fall **2. MOVE LIMPLY** to move limply or heavily **3. FAIL COMPLETELY** to be completely unsuccessful (*informal*) ■ *n* **1. TOTAL FAILURE** a complete failure (*informal*) **2. HEAVY DULL SOUND** the sound made by something falling heavily [Early 17C. Alteration of FLAP] —**flop·per** *n*

flop·house /flóp hòwss/ (*plural* **-houses** /-hòwzəz/) *n* a cheap hotel or rooming house (*informal*) [Early 20C. < FLOP "lie down, sleep"]

flop·py /flóppee/ *adj* (**-pi·er, -pi·est**) soft and tending to hang down limply or loosely ■ *n* (*plural* **-pies**) COMPUT same as **floppy disk** (*informal*) —**flop·pi·ly** *adv* —**flop·pi·ness** *n*

flop·py ba·by syn·drome *n* MED same as **floppy infant syndrome**

flop·py disk *n* a small flexible magnetically coated disk in a rigid plastic case on which data can be stored or retrieved by a computer [Late 20C. < its flexibility, as opposed to a HARD DISK]

flop·py in·fant syn·drome *n* a condition of marked muscle relaxation in a baby so that when supported face down the baby droops over the hand like an inverted "U"

flops /flops/, **FLOPS** *abbr* floating-point operations per second (*used to indicate the speed of a computer*)

flop·ti·cal /flóptik'l/ *adj* relating to a system for storing computer data on a disk that combines magnetic and optical technology [Late 20C. Blend of FLOPPY + OPTICAL]

flo·ra /fláwrə/ (*plural* **-ras** or **-rae** /-ree/) *n* **1. PLANTS** plant life, especially all the plants found in a particular country, region, or time regarded as a group (*formal*) ○ *the flora of Australia* **2. DESCRIPTION OF PLANTS** a systematic set of descriptions of all the plants of a particular place or time **3.** MICROBIOL **BACTERIA THAT INHABIT BODY ORGANS** all the usually harmless bacteria inhabiting a part of the body, regarded as a group or population [Early 16C. < Latin *Flora*, Roman goddess of flowers < *flor-* "flower"]

flo·ral /fláwrəl/ *adj* relating to, containing, or suggestive of flowers [Mid-17C. < Latin *Floralis* "of Flora" or *flor-* (see FLORA)] —**flo·ral·ly** *adv*

flo·ral en·ve·lope *n* BOT same as **perianth**

Flo·ral Park /fláwrəl-/ town in Nassau County, Long Island, east of New York City. Population: 15,974 (2002 estimate).

Flor·ence /fláwrənss/ **1.** capital of Florence Province and Tuscany Region, central Italy. Situated on the Arno River, about 145 mi./233 km northwest of Rome, it is one of the world's leading artistic and cultural centers. Population: 356,118 (2001). Italian name **Firenze 2.** city in northwestern Alabama on the northern bank of the Tennessee River, near Wilson Dam. Population: 35,814 (2002 estimate). **3.** city in northeastern South Carolina, northwest of Myrtle Beach and northeast of Columbia. Population: 30,019 (2002 estimate).

Flor·ence fen·nel *n* PLANTS same as **fennel** (sense 2)

Flor·en·tine /fláwrən teen/ *adj* **1. OF FLORENCE** relating to the Italian city of Florence, or its people or culture **2.** ARTS, ARCHIT **TYPICAL OF ART OF RENAISSANCE FLORENCE** relating to the style of art or architecture in Florence during the Renaissance **3.** COOK **WITH SPINACH** cooked or served with spinach ○ *eggs Florentine* ■ *n* PEOPLES **SOMEBODY FROM FLORENCE** somebody who comes from the Italian city of Florence [13C. < Latin *Florentinus* < *Florentia* "Florence"]

Flor·en·tine stitch *n* HANDICRAFT same as **bargello**

Flo·res /fláwrəss/ mountainous island in southeastern Indonesia, one of the Lesser Sunda Islands. The chief towns are Ende and Ruteng. Population: 272,750 (1989). Area: 5,480 sq. mi./14,200 sq. km.

flo·res·cence /flaw réssənss/ *n* flowering [Late 18C. < modern Latin *florescentia* < Latin *florescent-*, present participle of *florescere* "begin to flower" < *florere* (see FLOURISH)] —**flo·res·cent** *adj*

~~**florescent**~~ incorrect spelling of **fluorescent**

Flo·res Sea sea situated between the eastern end of Java and the western end of the Banda Sea in Indonesia

flo·ret /fláwrət/ *n* **1.** a small flower, especially one in a flower head consisting of many flowers **2.** a small part into which the edible flower head of cauliflower or broccoli can be separated [Late 17C. < Latin *flor-* "flower"]

Flo·rey /fláwree/, **Sir Howard Walter, Baron Florey of Adelaide and Marston** (1898–1968) Australian scientist. He was the codeveloper of the world's first antibiotic, penicillin. He shared the Nobel Prize in physiology or medicine (1945) with Alexander Fleming and Ernst Boris Chain for this discovery.

Flo·ri·a·nó·po·lis /flàwree ə nóppəliss/ city and capital of Santa Catarina State, southern Brazil, situated on Santa Catarina Island. Population: 271,281 (1996).

flo·ri·at·ed /fláwree àytəd/ *adj* decorated with designs based on flowers and leaves [Mid-19C. < Latin *flor-* "flower"]

flo·ri·bun·da /flàwrə búndə/ *n* a hybrid cultivated rose. Flowers: small, in large sprays. [Late 19C. < modern Latin, form of *floribundus* "flowering profusely" < Latin *flor-* "flower"]

flor·i·cane /fláwri kàyn/ *n* a plant stem that flowers and bears fruit in its second year, e.g., in raspberries [< Latin *flor-* "flower"]

flo·ri·cul·ture /fláwri kùlchər/ *n* the growing of flowers as a crop [Early 19C. < Latin *flor-* "flower," after HORTICULTURE] —**flo·ri·cul·tur·al** /flàwri kúlchərəl/ *adj* —**flo·ri·cul·tur·al·ly** *adv* —**flo·ri·cul·tur·ist** /fláwri kùlchərist, flàwri kúlchərist/ *n*

flor·id /fláwrid/ *adj* **1.** having an unhealthily glowing pink or red complexion **2.** ornate and overly complicated in wording and general style [Mid-17C. Via French < Latin *floridus* "flowery" < *flor-* "flower"] —**flo·rid·i·ty** /flə ríddətee/ *n* —**flor·id·ly** *adv* —**flor·id·ness** *n*

Florida

Flor·i·da /fláwridə, flór-/ state in the southeastern United States bordered by Alabama, Georgia, the Atlantic Ocean, and the Gulf of Mexico. Capital: Tallahassee. Population: 16,713,149 (2002 estimate). Area: 59,928 sq. mi./155,213 sq. km. —**Flor·id·i·an** /flə ríddee ən/ *adj, n*

Flor·i·da, Straits of channel between the southern tip of Florida and the island of Cuba, connecting the Gulf of Mexico to the Atlantic Ocean. Length: 300 mi./485 km. Width: 50 to 150 mi./80 to 240 km.

Flor·i·da ar·row·root *n US* PLANTS same as **coontie** (sense 2)

Flor·i·da Keys /-keez/ chain of islands and reefs in southern Florida, extending southwestward in an arc from the southern end of Biscayne Bay into the Gulf of Mexico. The islands, which include Key Largo and Key West, are connected by bridges and causeways and are a popular vacation destination. Length: 192 mi./309 km.

flo·rif·er·ous /flaw ríffərəss/ *adj* bearing or able to bear many flowers [Mid-17C. < Latin *florifer* < *flor-* "flower"] —**flo·rif·er·ous·ly** *adv* —**flo·rif·er·ous·ness** *n*

flo·ri·le·gi·um /flàwrə leejee əm/ (*plural* **-gi·a** /-jee ə/) *n* an anthology of literary extracts (*archaic*) [Early 17C. < modern Latin, "gathering of flowers"]

flor·in /fláwrin/ *n* **1. OLD BRITISH COIN** a unit of currency used in Britain between 1849 and 1968, equivalent to two shillings **2. GOLD OR SILVER COIN** a gold or silver coin, especially a Dutch guilder **3. FLORENTINE COIN** a gold coin first minted in Florence in 1252, or any similar coin used elsewhere in Europe [14C. Via Old French < Italian *fiorino* < *fiore* "flower" (because originally a coin bearing a lily) < Latin *flor-*]

flo·rist /fláwrist/ *n* **1.** a dealer in flowers and ornamental plants **2.** a shop that sells flowers and other ornamental plants [Early 17C. < Latin *flor-* "flower"]

flo·rist·ics /flaw rístiks/ *n* a branch of botany dealing with the types, numbers, distribution, and relationships of plant species in a particular area or areas (*takes a singular verb*) [Late 19C. < FLORA]

-florous *suffix* bearing flowers ○ *multiflorous* [< Latin *flor-* "flower"]

flo·ru·it /fláwryoo it/ *v* used, especially abbreviated as "fl," before the name or numerical designator of the period in the past when a particular person or movement was most active (*formal*) [Mid-19C. < Latin, "flourished"]

flo·ry /fláwree/ *adj* containing a fleur-de-lis [14C. < Old French *flo(u)ré* < *flour* (see FLOWER)]

Flo·ry /fláwree/, **Paul John** (1910–85) US chemist. He was awarded the Nobel Prize in chemistry (1974) for his work on polymers.

floss /flawss/ *vti* (**flossed, floss·ing, floss·es**) DENT **CLEAN BETWEEN TEETH** to clean between individual teeth using dental floss ■ *n* **1.** DENT same as **dental floss 2.** TEXTILES **SILKWORM FIBERS** short or waste fibers prepared from the outside of a silkworm's cocoon **3.** PLANTS **PLANT FIBERS** the mass of fine silken fibers that covers the seeds of the silk-cotton tree or of a cotton plant **4.** HANDICRAFT **EMBROIDERY THREAD** an embroidery thread made up of six strands loosely twisted together that can be separated for fine work [Mid-18C. Origin ?] —**floss·er** *n*

floss·y /fláwssee/ (**-i·er, -i·est**) *adj* **1.** *US* ornate or showy in a flashy, often almost vulgar way **2.** consisting of or looking like floss —**floss·i·ly** *adv* —**floss·i·ness** *n*

flo·tage /flṓtij/ *n* **1.** same as **flotation** (senses 1–2) **2.** NAUT same as **flotsam** (sense 1)

flo·ta·tion /flō táysh'n/ *n* **1. FLOATING** the act, process, or condition of floating **2. CAPABILITY OF FLOATING** the ability to float on a liquid or remain on top of a soft surface (*technical*) **3.** FIN **SELLING OF STOCK IN COMPANY** the financing of a company by selling stock in it or a new debt issue or the offering of stock and bonds for sale on the stock exchange **4.** TRANSP **ADHERENCE OF TIRE TO SURFACE** the ability of a tire tread to adhere to and remain on top of a soft surface such as wet ground or snow **5.** CHEM **SEPARATION PROCESS** a process for separating materials such as a mixture of minerals in an ore according to their different abilities to float in a given liquid [Early 19C. < FLOAT]

flo·ta·tion bags *npl* large bags that inflate when a helicopter or spacecraft lands in the sea and keep it afloat and upright

flo·ta·tion de·vice *n* something that enables somebody to stay afloat in the sea, e.g., a life jacket or seat cushion (*technical*)

flo·ta·tion tank *n* a sealed tank filled with salt water and minerals that somebody can float in to relieve stress

flo·ta·tion ther·a·py *n* a method of relieving stress that involves floating in salt water in a sealed tank while listening to music

flo·tel /flō tél/ *n* a moored boat or an oil rig that provides lodging for offshore workers [Late 20C. Contraction of *floating hotel*]

flo·til·la /flō tíllə/ *n* **1. FLEET OF BOATS** a fleet of usually small boats **2.** NAVY **US NAVAL UNIT** a US naval unit consisting of two squadrons of small warships **3. GROUP OF THINGS** a group of things operating or moving together [Early 18C < Spanish, "small fleet" < *flota* "fleet," via Old French < Old Norse *floti*]

flot·sam /flótsəm/ *n* **1.** wreckage, debris, or refuse from a ship, found floating in the water. In maritime law, flotsam is what is found floating after a ship has sunk and jetsam is what was thrown from a ship while it was in trouble. **2.** people who live on the margins of society, e.g., homeless people (*sometimes offensive*) [Early 17C. < Anglo-Norman *floteson* < *floter* "float" < Germanic] ◇ **flotsam and jetsam** discarded objects or odds and ends

flounce[1] /flownss/ (**flounced, flounc·ing, flounc·es**) *vi* to move with exaggerated angry swaggering motions showing displeasure or indignation [Mid-16C. Origin ?] —**flounce** *n*

flounce[2] /flownss/ *n* a strip of cloth that has been gathered into pleats on one side and then stitched onto a garment or curtain as a decoration [Early 18C. Alteration of Old French *fronce* "pleat" (probably after FLOUNCE[1]) < Germanic]

flounc·ing /flównssing/ *n* material used to make flounces

floun·der[1] /flówndər/ (**-dered, -der·ing, -ders**) *vi* **1.** MAKE UNCONTROLLED MOVEMENTS to make clumsy uncontrolled movements while trying to regain balance or move forwards **2.** HESITATE IN CONFUSION to act in a way that shows confusion or a lack of purpose **3.** BE IN SERIOUS DIFFICULTY to have serious problems and be close to failing [Late 16C. Origin ?]

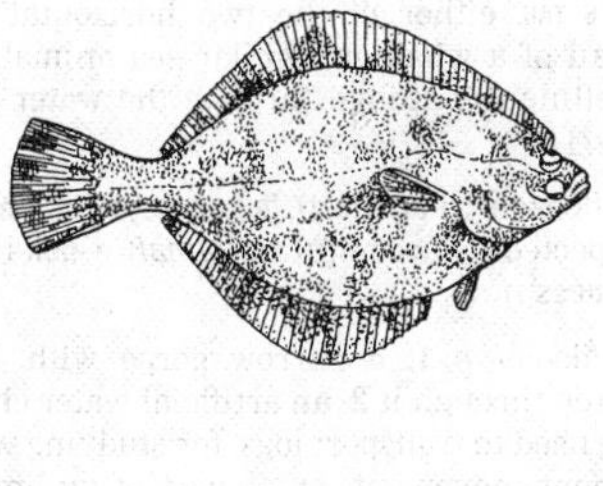

flounder

floun·der[2] /flówndər/ (*plural same* or **-ders**) *n* **1.** EDIBLE FLATFISH an edible flatfish of shallow coastal waters. Families: Pleuronectidae or Bothidae. **2.** EDIBLE EUROPEAN FLATFISH an edible flatfish that has grayish brown mottled skin with orange spots and prickly scales. Native to: Europe. Latin name: *Platichthys flesus*. **3.** FLOUNDER AS FOOD the flesh of a flounder used as food [15C. Via Anglo-Norman *floundre* < N Germanic]

flour /flowr/ *n* **1.** FINELY GROUND CEREAL GRAINS a powder made by grinding the edible parts of cereal grains. Use: bread, cakes, pastry, sauce thickener. **2.** GROUND FOODSTUFF a finely ground powder made from any dried plant such as chickpea, banana, cassava, or potato ■ *vt* (**floured, flour·ing, flours**) COVER SOMETHING WITH FLOUR to cover or coat food, food preparation utensils, or a work surface with flour [13C. Variant of FLOWER "the best (ground meal)"]

SPELLCHECK **flour** or **flower**? Do not confuse the spelling of ***flour*** and ***flower***, which sound similar. ***Flour*** is a powder used to make bread, pastry, etc.; the word is also used as a verb, meaning "cover with flour." The word ***flower*** is chiefly used as a noun, denoting the colorful part of a plant (as in *a bunch of flowers, roses coming into flower*); as a verb it means "produce flowers" or "develop to maturity."

~~**flourescent**~~ incorrect spelling of **fluorescent**

~~**flouride**~~ incorrect spelling of **fluoride**

~~**flourine**~~ incorrect spelling of **fluorine**

flour·ish /flúrrish/ *v* (**-ished, -ish·ing, -ish·es**) **1.** *vi* BE HEALTHY OR GROW WELL to be strong and healthy or grow well, especially because conditions are right **2.** *vi* DO WELL to sustain continuous steady strong growth ○ *The economy is flourishing.* **3.** *vt* BRANDISH SOMETHING to wave something in a dramatic way that draws attention to it ■ *n* **1.** HAND MOVEMENT a dramatic body movement that attracts attention, e.g., a sweep of the hand **2.** LOOP OR CURL an embellishment to something handwritten, e.g., a loop or curly line **3.** MUSIC ORNAMENTAL TRUMPET CALL a fanfare heralding the arrival of an important person **4.** MUSIC SHORT PRELUDE OR POSTLUDE a short, often improvised, passage at the beginning or end of a piece of music **5.** MUSIC SHOWY MUSICAL INTERLUDE a brief, often showy, technical passage within a piece of music [13C. < Old French *floriss-*, stem of *florir* "to bloom" < Latin *florere* < *flor-* "flower"] —**flour·ish·er** *n*

flour·y /flówree/ (**-i·er, -i·est**) *adj* covered or coated with flour, or tasting of flour

flout /flowt/ (**flout·ed, flout·ing, flouts**) *vt* to show contempt for a law or convention by openly disobeying or defying it [Mid-16C. Origin ?] —**flout·er** *n* —**flout·ing·ly** *adv*

USAGE See *flaunt*.

flow /flō/ *vi* (**flowed, flow·ing, flows**) **1.** MOVE FREELY FROM PLACE TO PLACE to move freely from one place to another in large numbers or amounts in a steady unbroken stream ○ *measures to allow traffic to flow freely* **2.** PHYS MOVE IN ONE MASS to move freely in one continuous mass (*refers to fluids*) **3.** PHYSIOL CIRCULATE IN BODY to move through the veins and arteries of the body (*refers especially to blood*) **4.** BE SAID FLUENTLY to be expressed uninhibitedly and eloquently ○ *The conversation began to flow.* **5.** BE AVAILABLE IN QUANTITY to be readily available and consumed in large amounts (*refers to alcoholic drinks*) **6.** BE EXPERIENCED INTENSELY to be experienced very intensely, often in a way that is visible to other people ○ *A wave of love flowed across her face.* **7.** EMANATE AS RESULT to derive from something as a result or series of results ○ *The consequences that flowed from the decision were distressing.* **8.** HANG LOOSELY to fall or hang loosely and gracefully (*refers to clothes or hair*) ○ *Her long hair flowed over her shoulders.* **9.** OCEANOG MOVE TOWARD LAND to move toward the land as the tide rises (*refers to the ocean or tidal water*) **10.** GEOL CHANGE SHAPE UNDER PRESSURE to change shape gradually in response to pressure without the development of cracks or fissures ■ *n* **1.** UNHINDERED STEADY MOVEMENT a steady unbroken stream of people, goods, vehicles, money, or information from one place to another ○ *the unending flow of refugees* **2.** MASS OR QUANTITY FLOWING a mass or quantity of material that is flowing or has flowed ○ *a giant lava flow pouring down into the valley* **3.** MED MENSTRUAL BLOOD the quantity of blood during menstruation **4.** MOVEMENT OF FLUID OR ELECTRICAL CHARGE the movement of liquid, gas, or electrical charge **5.** OCEANOG TIDAL MOVEMENT TOWARD LAND the movement of a rising tide toward the land **6.** COMMUNICATION ELOQUENT EXPRESSION OF THOUGHTS the continuous eloquent expression of thoughts or ideas in speech or writing **7.** *US* PSYCHOL EXPERIENCE OF HEIGHTENED AWARENESS psychological and physical experience in which challenges presented are perfectly matched by the participants' skills, often resulting in heightened states of awareness, confidence, and performance [Old English *flōwan* < Indo-European] —**flow·ing·ly** *adv* ◇ **go with the flow 1.** to follow the lead of other people and react to their opinions or actions passively **2.** to adapt to the prevailing mood or situation in a relaxed way

SPELLCHECK See *floe*.

flow·age /flṓ ij/ *n* **1.** FLOWING the act of flowing or overflowing **2.** OVERFLOWING WATER the water resulting from overflow **3.** PHYS GRADUAL DEFORMATION the gradual change in shape that occurs in solids such as asphalt that can flow without breaking when heat is applied

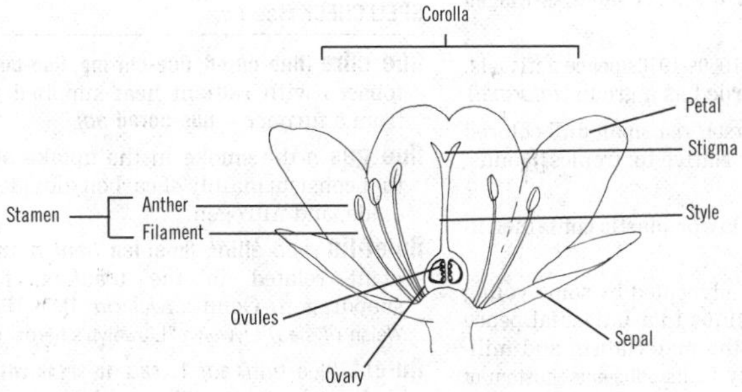

flower: cross section of a flower

flow chart, flow·chart /flṓ chaart/ *n* a diagram that represents the sequence of operations in a process

flow-chart·ing *n* the designing of a flow chart or charts

flow cy·tom·e·try *n* a diagnostic test revealing the arrangement and amount of DNA in a cell, used to distinguish benign cells from malignant ones and to monitor the effect of anticancer treatment

flow di·a·gram *n* MANAGEMT same as **flow chart**

flow·er /flówr/ *n* **1.** COLORED PART OF PLANT a colored, sometimes scented, part of a plant that contains its reproductive organs. It consists of a leafy shoot with modified leaves, petals, and sepals surrounding male or female organs, stamens, and pistils. **2.** STEM WITH FLOWER a plant stem with one or more flowers that has been picked from the plant on which it grew **3.** PLANT WITH FLOWERS a small plant grown for the attractiveness of its flowers **4.** BOT FLOWERING STATE the state or period during which a plant has open blooms on it ○ *The roses are just coming into flower.* **5.** BEST the best part of or most perfect example of something ○ *the flower of the nation's youth* ■ *vi* (**-ered, -er·ing, -ers**) **1.** BOT PRODUCE BLOOMS to begin to produce blooms **2.** DEVELOP TO MATURITY to develop and reach maturity [12C. < Anglo-Norman *flur*, Old French *flour* < Latin *flor-* "flower"] —**flow·ered** *adj* —**flow·er·less** *adj*

SPELLCHECK See *flour*.

flow·er·bed /flówr bèd/ *n* a clearly delineated area of a garden or park planted with flowering plants

flow·er bug *n* an insect that feeds on other small insects found in flowers. Family: Anthorcoridae.

flow·er child *n* a young person in the 1960s and 1970s who rejected materialism and war, especially the Vietnam War, and preached universal peace and love as the solution to the world's problems (*informal*) [< their custom of wearing or carrying flowers as a symbol of peace]

flow·er·er /flówrər/ *n* a plant that flowers, usually at a particular time or in a particular manner ○ *a late flowerer*

flow·er·et /flówrət/ *n* FOOD same as **floret** (sense 2)

flow·er girl *n* a young girl who carries flowers in the procession preceding a bride at a wedding

flow·er head *n* **1.** a cluster of small flowers on a single stem **2.** a dense arrangement of flower buds, e.g., in cauliflower or broccoli

flow·er·ing /flówring/ *adj* capable of producing noticeable flowers ■ *n* the moment in the development of an idea, style, or movement when it gains recognition and becomes successful

flow·er·ing dog·wood *n* a deciduous tree with inconspicuous flowers surrounded by showy white or pink bracts, and leaves that turn red or purple in the fall. Latin name: *Cornus florida*.

flow·er·ing ma·ple *n* a tropical plant that has lobed leaves like the maple. Flowers: brightly colored. Genus: *Abutilon*.

flow·er·ing plant *n* any plant that is capable of producing noticeable flowers

flow·er·ing quince *n* a spiny deciduous plant that is grown for its attractive red or pink flowers and fragrant yellow fruit. Native to: Asia. Genus: *Chaenomeles*.

flow·er·ing win·ter·green *n* PLANTS same as **fringed polygala**

flow·er peo·ple *npl* young 1960s-1970s peace activists, the flower children, regarded as a group (*informal*)

flow·er·pierc·er /flówr pèersər/ *n* a small dull-colored bird that feeds on nectar. Native to: tropics. Genus: *Diglossa.*

flow·er·pot /flówr pòt/ *n* a clay or plastic container in which plants are grown

flow·er pow·er *n* the idea advocated by some young people in the 1960s and 1970s that universal peace and love should replace the materialism and militarism of Western society [< its adherents' custom of wearing or carrying flowers as a symbol of peace and love]

flow·er press·ing *n* the process of preserving cut flowers by laying them on a flat surface and pressing them with a heavy object

flow·ers /flówrz/ *n* a fine powder produced by sublimation or condensation (*takes a singular verb*)

flow·er·y /flówree/ (**-i·er, -i·est**) *adj* **1.** **POMPOUSLY LITERARY** full of ornate, overly elaborate expressions **2.** **ORNAMENTED WITH FLOWERS** decorated or patterned with flowers **3.** **LIKE FLOWERS** relating to flowers —**flow·er·i·ness** *n*

flow·me·ter /flṓ meetər/ *n* an instrument for measuring the rate of flow of liquids or gases, especially in a pipe

flown past participle of **fly**[1]

flow sheet *n* **1.** MANAGEMT same as **flow chart** **2.** a schematic diagram showing the equipment and connecting pipes that make up a process plant and sometimes showing flow rates and quantities of material

flow·stone /flṓ stṑn/ *n* a layered deposit of calcium carbonate (**calcite**) on rock where water has flowed or dripped, e.g., on the walls or floor of a cave

fl oz, fl. oz. *abbr* MEASURE fluid ounces

FLQ *n* a terrorist organization seeking the secession of Quebec from Canada. It was particularly active during the 1960s and 1970s. Full form **Front de Libération du Québec**

FLRA *abbr* Federal Labor Relations Authority

FLSA *abbr* Fair Labor Standards Act

flu /floo/ *n* a viral illness producing a high temperature, sore throat, running nose, headache, dry cough, and muscle pain. The illness is widespread, especially during winter months, and can sometimes be fatal. [Mid-19C. Shortening of INFLUENZA] —**flu·like** *adj*

SPELLCHECK flu, flue, or **flew**? Do not confuse the spelling of ***flu, flue,*** and ***flew,*** which sound similar. The nouns ***flu*** and ***flue*** are probably the most likely to be confused: ***Flu*** is an illness, whereas a ***flue*** is a smoke or heat outlet or a type of organ pipe. ***Flew*** is the past tense of the verb *fly*: *Time flew past.*

---

flub /flub/ (*informal*) *vti* (**flubbed, flub·bing, flubs**) **MESS UP SOMETHING** to blunder or make a mess of something ○ *He flubbed his lines and the audience booed.* ■ *n* **1.** **BLUNDER OR GAFFE** an embarrassing clumsy mistake **2.** **BLUNDERER** somebody who makes embarrassing blunders [Early 20C. Probably suggestive of clumsiness] —**flub·ber** *n*

flu·clox·a·cil·lin /floo klòksə síllin/ *n* a penicillin drug. Use: treatment of streptococcal infections and pneumonia.

flu·con·a·zole /floo kónnə zṑl/ *n* an antifungal drug

fluc·tu·ate /flúkchoo àyt/ (**-at·ed, -at·ing, -ates**) *vi* to change often from high to low levels or from one thing to another in an unpredictable way [Mid-17C. < Latin *fluctuat-*, past participle of *fluctuare* < *fluere* "to flow"] —**fluc·tu·ant** *adj* —**fluc·tu·a·tion** /flùkchoo áysh'n/ *n*

flue /floo/ *n* **1.** **SMOKE OR HEAT OUTLET** a shaft, tube, or pipe used as an outlet to carry smoke, gas, or heat, e.g., from a fireplace or furnace **2.** MUSIC **TYPE OF ORGAN PIPE** an organ pipe in which the sound is produced by passing air across an opening with a lip **3.** MUSIC **OPENING ON ORGAN PIPE** the lipped opening on an organ pipe that initiates vibrations and sound when air passes across it [15C. Origin ?]

SPELLCHECK See *flu.*

---

flue-cure (**flue-cured, flue-cur·ing, flue-cures**) *vt* to cure tobacco with radiant heat supplied through flues from a furnace —**flue-cured** *adj*

flue gas *n* the smoke in the uptake of a boiler fire that consists mainly of carbon dioxide, carbon monoxide, and nitrogen

flu·el·lin /floo éllin/, **flu·el·len** /-ən/ *n* an annual wild plant related to the toadflax, foxglove, and snapdragon. Genus: *Kickxia.* [Mid-16C. Alteration of Welsh *(llysiau) Llywelyn* "Llewelyn's herbs"]

flu·ent /flóo ənt/ *adj* **1.** **ABLE TO SPEAK WITH EASE** able to speak a language effortlessly and correctly **2.** **EFFORTLESSLY EXPRESSED** spoken or expressed effortlessly and correctly **3.** **SMOOTHLY FLOWING** flowing in a smooth graceful way (*literary*) [Late 16C. < Latin *fluent-*, present participle of *fluere* "flow"] —**flu·en·cy** *n* —**flu·ent·ly** *adv*

ORIGIN The Latin word *fluere* "to flow," from which ***fluent*** is derived, is also the source of English *affluent, effluent, fluctuate, fluid, fluvial, flux, influence, mellifluous,* and *superfluous.*

---

flue pipe *n* MUSIC same as **flue** (sense 2)

flue stop *n* an organ stop that controls a set of flues

fluff /fluf/ *n* **1.** **LIGHT BALLS OF FIBER** soft light balls of thread or fiber that collect together on material such as wool or cotton **2.** **DOWNY FUZZ** the soft downy fuzz found on young birds or some seeds **3.** **NONSENSE** something of no importance or consequence (*slang*) ■ *vt* (**fluffed, fluff·ing, fluffs**) **1.** **DO SOMETHING BADLY** to do something badly, especially because of loss of concentration or forgetfulness (*informal*) **2.** **SHAKE SOMETHING TO INSERT AIR** to shake, pat, or brush something in order to get air into it **3.** BIRDS **RAISE FEATHERS** to raise the feathers in a way that makes the body appear bigger [Late 18C. Origin ?]

fluff·y /flúffee/ (**-i·er, -i·est**) *adj* **1.** **SOFT AND LIGHT** consisting of something soft and light to the touch such as wool or feathers **2.** **DOWNY OR FEATHERY** covered in something soft and light to the touch such as down or feathers **3.** COOK **SOFT AND LIGHT IN TEXTURE** soft and light in texture because air has been beaten or whisked in —**fluff·i·ly** *adv* —**fluff·i·ness** *n*

flü·gel·horn /flóog'l hàwrn/, **flu·gel·horn** *n* a brass instrument with valves, similar to a cornet but with a larger bell [Mid-19C. < German *Flügelhorn* "wing horn"; from its use to signal to beaters on the flanks in a shoot] —**flü·gel·horn·ist** *n*

flu·id /flóo id/ *n* **1.** **LIQUID** a liquid substance (*not in technical use*) **2.** PHYS, CHEM **LIQUID OR GAS** a substance whose molecules flow freely, so that it has no fixed shape and little resistance to outside stress, e.g., a liquid or gas ■ *adj* **1.** PHYS **FLOWING** capable of flowing like a liquid or gas (*technical*) **2.** **MOVING OR SMOOTHLY CARRIED OUT** smooth and graceful in a way that seems relaxed ○ *a series of fluid arm movements* **3.** **UNSTABLE** likely to change ○ *The situation in the western sector is fluid.* [15C. Via Old French < Latin *fluidus* "flowing" < *fluere* "flow"] —**flu·id·al** *adj* —**flu·id·al·ly** *adv* —**flu·id·i·ty** /floo íddətee/ *n* —**flu·id·ly** *adv* —**flu·id·ness** *n*

flu·id clutch *n* AUTOMOT same as **fluid drive**

flu·id dram *n* a unit of liquid capacity in the apothecary system, equal to $\frac{1}{8}$ of a fluid ounce

flu·id drive *n* a device for transmitting rotation between two shafts by means of the acceleration and deceleration of a hydraulic fluid by turbines with blades, used in automatic transmissions in motor vehicles

flu·id dy·nam·ics *n* the scientific study of the forces acting on liquids and gases and the resulting movements of these fluids (*takes a singular verb*)

flu·id·ex·tract /flóo id ék stràkt/ *n* a concentrated solution in alcohol of a drug derived from a plant

flu·id·ic /floo íddik/ *adj* **1.** relating to fluids **2.** relating to or operated by fluidics

flu·id·ics /floo íddiks/ *n* the use of systems based on the movements and pressure of fluids to control operations, instruments, and industrial processes (*takes a singular verb*)

flu·id·ize /flóo i dìz/ (**-ized, -iz·ing, -iz·es**) *vt* **1.** to make something fluid **2.** to make a solid move as a fluid, e.g., by pulverizing it into fine powder and passing a gas through it in order to induce flow —**flu·id·i·za·tion** /flòo idi záysh'n/ *n* —**flu·id·iz·er** *n*

flu·id·iz·ed bed *n* a powder or other solid particulate material suspended in an upward flow of air or other gas that behaves like a fluid. It is an effective way of transferring heat or moisture between a gas and a solid or of producing some chemical reactions.

flu·id me·chan·ics *n* the branch of mechanics that deals with the properties of gases and liquids and their application in practical engineering (*takes a singular verb*)

flu·id ounce *n* **1.** a unit of volume measurement in the US customary system equal to $\frac{1}{16}$ of a US pint or 29.57 ml **2.** a unit of liquid measurement in the British imperial system equal to $\frac{1}{20}$ of an imperial pint or 28.41 ml

fluke[1] /flook/ *n* **1.** **ACCIDENTAL SUCCESS** something surprising or unexpected that happens by accident (*informal*) **2.** CUE GAMES **SHOT IN BILLIARDS** a successful shot in pool, billiards, or snooker that happens by accident ■ *vt* (**fluked, fluk·ing, flukes**) **POT BALL BY ACCIDENT** to make a successful shot by accident, especially in pool, billiards, or snooker [Mid-19C. Origin ?]

fluke[2] /flook/ *n* **1.** ZOOL same as **trematode** **2.** *UK regional* a flatfish, especially a flounder [Old English *flōc* < Indo-European, "be flat"]

fluke[3] /flook/ *n* **1.** **PART OF ANCHOR** either of the triangular blades at the end of each arm of an anchor **2.** **BARB ON HARPOON OR ARROW** a barb on the head of a harpoon or an arrow, or the barbed head itself **3.** **PART OF WHALE'S TAIL** either of the two horizontal lobes of the tail of a whale or similar sea animal, used in propelling the animal through the water [Mid-16C. Origin ?]

fluk·y /flóokee/ (**-i·er, -i·est**), **fluk·ey** *adj* accidentally and unexpectedly successful (*informal*) —**fluk·i·ly** *adv* —**fluk·i·ness** *n*

flume /floom/ *n* **1.** a narrow gorge with a stream running through it **2.** an artificial water channel or chute used to transport logs, for studying water and sediment movement, or as part of an amusement park ride [12C. Via Old French *flum* < Latin *flumen* "river" < *fluere* "flow"]

flum·mer·y /flúmməree/ *n* **1.** meaningless words, statements, or language, especially when intended as flattery (*literary*) **2.** a cream, milk, or custard dessert set with gelatin and sometimes flavored with Madeira and lemon [Early 17C. < Welsh *llymru*]

flum·mox /flúmməks/ (**-moxed, -mox·ing, -mox·es**) *vt* to make somebody confused or perplexed and unable to react (*informal*) [Mid-19C. Origin ?]

flung past participle, past tense of **fling**

flu·ni·tra·ze·pam /flòonī trázzə pam/ *n* an illegal drug developed to treat insomnia that is sometimes used as a date-rape drug because it causes semiconsciousness [Late 20C. < FLUORO- + NITRO- + *-azepam*, INN stem]

flunk /flungk/ (**flunked, flunk·ing, flunks**) *v* (*informal*) **1.** *vti* to fail an exam or course **2.** *vt* to give a student a failing grade [Early 19C. Origin ?] —**flunk·er** *n*

flunk out *vi* to be expelled from a school, college, or course because of failing grades (*informal*)

flun·key *n* HR another spelling of **flunky**

flunk·out /flúngk òwt/ *n* *US* a student who fails in school or college and has to leave because of it (*disapproving*)

flun·ky /flúngkee/ (*plural* **-kies**), **flun·key** (*plural* **-keys**) *n* **1.** an assistant who carries out unimportant jobs for somebody and who behaves obsequiously to that person (*informal*) **2.** a man who is a servant in livery, e.g., a footman [Mid-18C. < Scots, Origin ?] —**flun·ky·ism** *n*

flu·or /flóo àwr, flóo ər/ *n* MINERALS same as **fluorite** [Early 17C. < modern Latin (see FLUORIC)]

fluor- *prefix* CHEM same as **fluoro-** (*used before vowels*)

fluo·ra·pa·tite /flòo ráppə tìt/ *n* a common form of the mineral apatite, containing fluorine

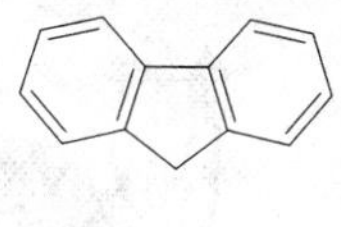

fluorene

flu·o·rene /flŏŏr ēen, fláwr-/ *n* a white insoluble crystalline solid. Source: coal tar. Use: manufacture of dyes. Formula: $C_{13}H_{10}$. [Late 19C. < FLUORO- (because it fluoresces)]

fluo·resce /flŏŏ réss, flaw-/ (**-resced, -resc·ing, -resc·es**) *vi* to exhibit or undergo the phenomenon of fluorescence [Late 19C. Back-formation < FLUORESCENT] —**fluo·resc·er** *n*

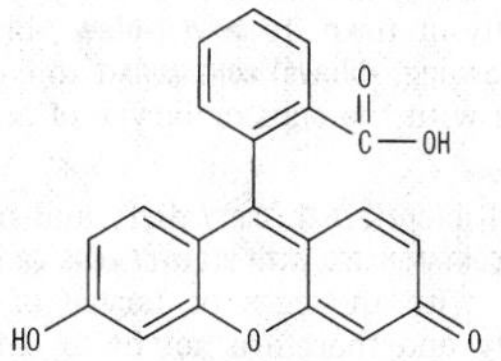

fluorescein

fluo·res·ce·in /flŏŏ réssee in, flaw-/ *n* an orange-red crystalline compound that fluoresces green in blue light. Use: to reveal features of the cornea. [Late 19C. < FLUORESCE + -EIN]

fluo·res·cence /flŏŏ réss'nss, flaw-/ *n* **1.** the emission of electromagnetic radiation, especially light, by an object or substance exposed to radiation or bombarding particles **2.** the radiation emitted as a result of fluorescence

fluo·res·cent /flŏŏ réss'nt, flaw-/ *adj* **1.** PHYS **CAPABLE OF FLUORESCING** exhibiting or able to undergo fluorescence ○ *a fluorescent dye* **2. CONTAINING FLUORESCENT TUBES** containing or produced by fluorescent tubes ○ *fluorescent lighting* **3. DAZZLING IN COLOR** very bright and dazzling in color ○ *fluorescent pink* [Mid-19C. < FLUORSPAR (which has this property)]

fluo·res·cent lamp, fluo·res·cent light *n* an electric lamp containing a low pressure vapor, usually mercury, in a glass tube. Passing an electric current through it produces ultraviolet radiation that is converted into visible light by a coating inside the tube.

fluo·res·cent tube *n* the tube of a fluorescent lamp

fluo·ric /floo áwrik/ *adj* relating to or produced from fluorine or fluorite [Late 18C. < obsolete French *fluorique* < modern Latin *fluor* "mineral used as a flux" < Latin *fluere* "flow"]

fluor·i·date /flŏŏri dàyt/ (**-dat·ed, -dat·ing, -dates**) *vt* to add small quantities of fluoride salts to a water supply —**fluor·i·da·tion** /flŏŏri dáysh'n/ *n*

fluor·ide /flŏŏr ìd, fláwr-/ *n* a chemical compound consisting of fluorine and another element or group [Early 19C. < FLUORINE]

fluo·rim·e·ter /flŏŏ rímmətər/ *n* PHYS same as **fluorometer**

fluor·i·nate /flŏŏri nàyt, fláwri-/ (**-nat·ed, -nat·ing, -nates**) *vt* to treat something, or cause something to combine, with fluorine or a fluorine compound —**fluor·i·na·tion** /flŏŏri náysh'n, flàwri-/ *n*

fluor·ine /flŏŏr ēen, fláwr-/ *n* a toxic pale yellow gaseous element of the halogen group that is the most reactive and oxidizing agent known. Source: fluorite, cryolite. Use: water treatment, making fluorides and fluorocarbons. Symbol **F**. See table at **element** [Early 19C. < modern Latin *fluor* (see FLUORIC)]

fluor·ite /flŏŏr ìt, fláwr-/ *n* a variously colored crystalline mineral consisting of calcium fluoride. Use: flux. [Mid-19C. < modern Latin *fluor* (see FLUORIC)]

fluoro- *prefix* **1.** fluorine ○ *fluorocarbon* **2.** fluorescence ○ *fluoroscope* [< FLUORINE, FLUOR]

fluor·o·car·bon /flŏŏrō kaárbən, flàwrō-/ *n* a chemically inert compound containing carbon and fluorine. Use: nonstick coatings, lubricants, refrigerants, solvents.

fluor·o·chem·i·cal /flŏŏrō kémmik'l, flàwrō-/ *n* a chemical compound containing fluorine

fluor·o·chrome /flŏŏrō krōm, fláwrō-/ *n* a molecule or part of a molecule that exhibits fluorescence. Use: marker in biological specimens.

fluo·rog·ra·phy /flŏŏ róggrəfee, flaw-/ *n* MED same as **photofluorography**

fluo·rom·e·ter /flŏŏ rómmətər, flaw-/, **fluo·rim·e·ter** /flŏŏ rímmətər/ *n* an instrument used to detect and measure fluorescence —**fluo·ro·met·ric** /flŏŏrō méttrik, flàwrō-/ *adj* —**fluo·rom·e·try** *n*

fluor·o·scope /flŏŏrə skōp, fláwrə-/ *n* an instrument with which X-ray images of the body can be viewed directly on a screen —**fluor·o·scop·ic** /flŏŏrə skóppik, flàwrə-/ *adj* —**fluor·o·scop·i·cal·ly** *adv* —**fluo·ros·co·py** /flŏŏ róskəpi/ *n*

fluo·ro·sis /flŏŏ rṓssiss, flaw-/ *n* a condition caused by excessive exposure to fluorine and marked by mottling of the teeth and damage to the bones —**fluo·rot·ic** /-róttik/ *adj*

fluor·o·u·ra·cil /flŏŏrō yŏŏrə sìl, flàw-/ *n* a fluorine-containing drug. Use: treatment of some cancers.

flu·or·spar /flŏŏr spaàr, flŏŏ ər-, fláwr-/ *n* MINERALS same as **fluorite** [Late 18C. < modern Latin *fluor* (see FLUORIC)]

flu·ox·e·tine /floo óksə tēen/ *n* a drug that raises serotonin levels. Use: treatment of anxiety and depression. [Late 20C. < FLUORINE + OXY- + *-etine*]

flu·phen·a·zine /floo fénnə zēen/ *n* a tranquilizing antipsychotic drug. Use: treatment of schizophrenia. [Mid-20C. Contraction of *fluorophenothiazine*, its chemical name]

flur·ry /flúr ee, flúrree/ *n* (*plural* **-ries**) **1. BURST OF ACTIVITY** a short period when a lot of things happen **2. SHORT WEATHER PATTERN** a sudden short period of snowfall ■ *v* (**-ried, -ry·ing, -ries**) **1.** *vt* **MAKE UNCERTAIN** to make somebody feel agitated and confused **2.** *vi* **SNOW LIGHTLY** to snow lightly and intermittently [Late 17C. Probably blend of obsolete *flurr* "flutter" + HURRY]

flush[1] /flush/ *v* (**flushed, flush·ing, flush·es**) **1.** *vti* **TURN RED** to become red in the face or on the skin, or make somebody become red **2.** *vti* **HAVE ROSY COLOR** to glow with a reddish color, or make something glow in this way **3.** *vti* **MAKE WATER FLOW THROUGH TOILET** to clean a toilet by making water flow through the bowl, or undergo this process **4.** *vt* **DISPOSE OF SOMETHING IN TOILET** to put something into the toilet and flush it **5.** *vt* **CLEAN WITH WATER** to clean or clear something by liberally pouring water or another liquid into, on, or through it ■ *n* **1. REDDISHNESS** a reddish color or glow in the face or on the skin **2. SUDDEN FEELING** a sudden intense feeling ○ *a faint flush of hope* **3. BEGINNING OF GOOD TIME** the beginning of an exciting or pleasurable period ○ *in the first flush of youth* **4. SUDDEN RUSH OF THINGS** a sudden increased number of things ○ *a flush of new applications* **5. SURGE OF WATER** a liberal flow of water, e.g., to clean something such as a toilet **6. SURGE OF HEAT** a sudden surge of heat **7. NEW GROWTH** a burst of new growth appearing rapidly on a plant [13C. Origin ?] —**flush·a·ble** *adj* —**flush·er** *n*

flush[2] /flush/ *adj* **1. LEVEL** completely level so as to form an even surface **2. BESIDE OR AGAINST SOMETHING** directly next to or closely against something ○ *The chairs were flush against the wall.* **3. TEMPORARILY RICH** having plenty of money temporarily (*informal*) **4. ABUNDANT** abundant or overflowing ○ *a party flush with celebrities* **5.** PRINTING **WITH EVEN MARGIN** having an even margin on a printed page, without any indentations ■ *adv* **1. COMPLETELY LEVEL** so as to be completely level and form an even surface without sticking out **2. DIRECTLY** directly or squarely ○ *was hit flush on the jaw* ■ *vt* (**flushed, flush·ing, flush·es**) **FIT THINGS COMPLETELY LEVEL** to fit two things so that they are completely level and form an even surface [Mid-16C. Probably < FLUSH[1]] —**flush·ness** *n*

flush[3] /flush/ *vt* (**flushed, flush·ing, flush·es**) to force a person or animal out of hiding ■ *n* a bird or birds frightened out of hiding [13C. Origin ?] —**flush·er** *n*

flush[4] /flush/ *n* in poker and other games, a hand consisting of cards all in the same suit [Early 16C. Via obsolete French *flus* < Latin *fluxus* (see FLUX)]

flushed /flusht/ *adj* **1.** red in the face **2.** feeling excited or happy

flus·ter /flústər/ *vti* (**-tered, -ter·ing, -ters**) to become nervous or agitated, or make somebody become nervous or agitated ■ *n* a nervous or agitated state [Early 17C. Origin ?] —**flus·tered** *adj*

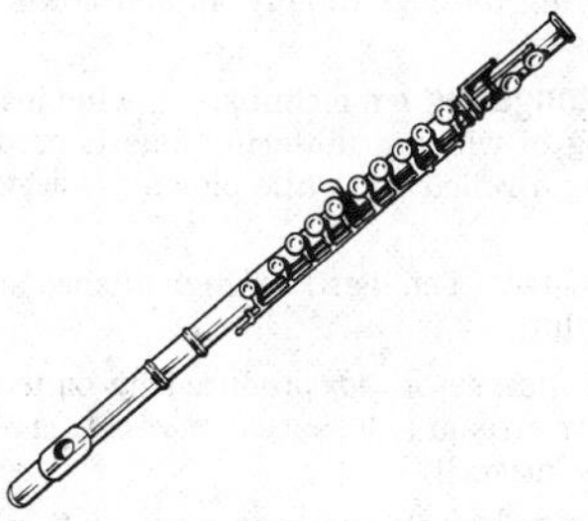

flute

flute /floot/ *n* **1. WIND INSTRUMENT WITH HIGH SOUND** a woodwind instrument with a cylindrical narrow body, usually held out to the right of the player, who blows across a hole in the mouthpiece to generate a high-pitched sound. The flute family includes the piccolo, the alto flute, and the bass flute. **2. INSTRUMENT WITHOUT REED** a wind instrument without a reed **3. ORGAN STOP** an organ stop with a tone like a flute **4.** ARCHIT **GROOVE IN COLUMN** a rounded groove running down an architectural column **5. DECORATIVE GROOVE** a decorative groove or pleat **6.** HOUSEHOLD **TALL GLASS FOR SPARKLING WINE** a tall narrow glass used for sparkling wines ■ *v* (**flut·ed, flut·ing, flutes**) **1.** *vi* **MAKE SOUND LIKE FLUTE** to whistle, sing, or speak in a way that suggests the sound of a flute **2.** *vt* **MAKE FURROWS IN SOMETHING** to make rounded grooves in something [14C. Via Old French *flaute*, Middle Dutch *flute* < Old Provençal *flaut*] —**flut·ed** *adj*

flut·er /flŏŏtər/ *n* MUSIC same as **flutist**

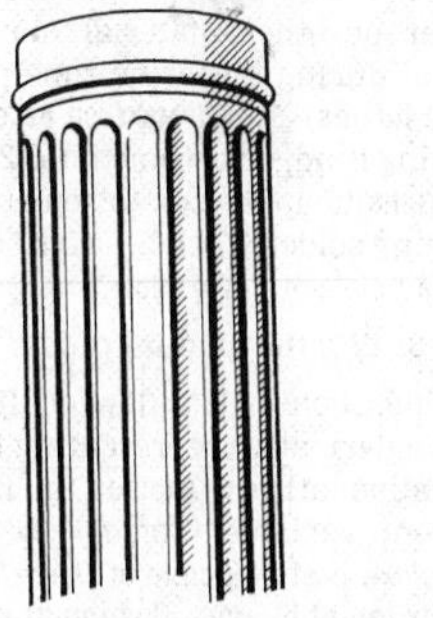

fluting

flut·ing /flŏŏting/ *n* **1. DECORATIVE FURROWS** decoration with parallel grooves **2. MAKING OF DECORATIVE FURROWS** the forming of decorative grooves in something **3. MAKING OF FLUTE SOUND** the act of playing a flute or of making sounds like those of a flute

flut·ist /flŏŏtist/ *n* somebody who plays the flute

flut·ter /flúttər/ *v* (**-tered, -ter·ing, -ters**) **1.** *vi* **WAVE GENTLY** to move gently but with quick changes in direction or with a wavy motion ○ *A tissue fluttered to the ground.* **2.** *vti* **MOVE SOMETHING LIGHT BACK AND FORTH** to move something light or small in quick back-and-forth motions, or be moved in this way ○ *Her eyelids fluttered.* **3.** *vti* **FLAP WINGS** to flap the wings rapidly (*refers to birds*) **4.** *vi* **FLY** to move by flapping the wings rapidly (*refers to birds*) **5.** *vi* **BEAT RAPIDLY** to beat rapidly because of a medical disorder or because of nervousness or excitement (*refers to the heart*) **6.**

vi **QUIVER** to have a quivering feeling because of nervousness or excitement **7.** *vt* **MAKE NERVOUS** to make somebody feel agitated or nervous (*usually used in the passive*) **8.** *vi* **MOVE RESTLESSLY** to move around in a restless or nervous way ■ *n* **1. QUICK MOVEMENT** a rapid, repetitive, or back-and-forth movement in something small **2. AGITATION** a state of nervous excitement or agitation **3.** MED **RAPID HEARTBEAT** a condition marked by rapid, but regular heartbeat **4.** RECORDING **SOUND DISTORTION** a high frequency distortion in the pitch of recorded sound **5.** *UK* GAMBLING **SMALL BET** a small bet on something (*informal*) [Old English *floterian* < Germanic] —**flut·ter·er** *n* —**flut·ter·ing·ly** *adv* —**flut·ter·y** *adj*

flut·ter·board /flúttər bàwrd/ *n* SWIMMING same as **kickboard** [Mid-20C. < FLUTTER KICK]

flut·ter kick *n* a swimming technique that consists of moving the legs rapidly up and down in short strokes

flut·ter-tongu·ing *n* a technique in wind-instrument playing in which a fluttering tone is produced by making a rolled "r" while blowing —**flut·ter-tongue** *vti*

flut·y /flóotee/ (**-i·er, -i·est**) *adj* high-pitched and clear, like a flute

flu·vi·al /flóovee əl/ *adj* produced by or found in a river or stream [14C. < Latin *fluvialis* < *fluvius* "river" < *fluere* "to flow"]

flu·vi·o·ma·rine /flóovee ō mə réen/ *adj* **1.** relating to water and sediment deposits of rivers in a sea or ocean **2.** BIOL same as **diadromous** [Mid-19C. < Latin *fluvius* "river" (see FLUVIAL)]

flux /fluks/ *n* **1. CONSTANT CHANGE** constant change and instability **2.** METALL **SOLDERING AID** a substance that promotes the fusion of two substances or surfaces. Use: soldering, welding. **3.** PHYS **RATE OF FLOW ACROSS AREA** the rate of flow of something such as energy, particles, or fluid volume across or onto a given area **4.** PHYS **STRENGTH OF FIELD IN PARTICULAR AREA** the strength of a field such as a magnetic or electric field acting on a particular area, equal to the area size multiplied by the component of the field acting at right angles to the area **5.** MED **EXCESSIVE BODILY DISCHARGE** an excessive discharge or flow from the body, especially the bowels (*dated*) **6.** METALL **SMELTING AID** a substance added to molten ore that combines with impurities to form slag for extraction **7.** CERAMICS **GLAZE COMPONENT** a substance added to a ceramic glaze to make it flow more readily **8.** PHILOSOPHY **THEORY OF CHANGE** the notion that change is the fundamental nature of reality, as described by Heraclitus **9.** OCEANOG **QUANTITY OF MOVEMENT** the quantity of water or other material moved in a specific direction during a specific time period ■ *v* (**fluxed, flux·ing, flux·es**) **1.** *vti* **MAKE OR BECOME FLUID** to make something fluid, or become fluid **2.** *vt* METALL **PUT FLUX ON SOMETHING** to apply flux to something, especially a joint being soldered [14C. Via Old French < Latin *fluxus*, < past participle of *fluere* "flow"]

flux den·si·ty *n* the amount of flux per unit area

flux·ion /flúkshən/ *n* **1.** a flow or discharge of liquid **2.** MATH a derivative representing the rate of change of a mathematical function in relation to an independent variable (*dated*) [Mid-16C. < French, or < Latin *flux-*, past participle of *fluere* "flow"] —**flux·ion·al** *adj* —**flux·ion·al·ly** *adv* —**flux·ion·ar·y** *adj*

fly[1] /flī/ *v* (**flew** /floo/, **flown** /flōn/, **fly·ing, flies**) **1.** *vi* **MOVE THROUGH AIR** to travel through the air using wings or an engine **2.** *vi* **TRAVEL IN AIRCRAFT** to travel in an aircraft **3.** *vt* **TAKE SOMEBODY OR SOMETHING BY AIR** to take or send things or passengers in an aircraft **4.** *vti* **BE PILOT** to pilot an aircraft or spacecraft **5.** *vt* **TRAVEL OVER AREA BY AIR** to travel over a particular area in an aircraft **6.** *vi* **TRAVEL WITH AIRLINE OR IN CLASS** to travel with a particular airline or in a particular class in an aircraft **7.** *vi* **CARRY OUT MISSION BY AIR** to carry out a mission or operation in an aircraft **8.** *vti* **FLOAT THROUGH AIR** to make something such as a kite move through the air, or move through the air **9.** *vti* **DISPLAY FLAG ON POLE** to display a flag by attaching it to a pole, building, or mast, or be displayed in this way **10.** *vt* SHIPPING **SHOW COUNTRY OF REGISTRATION** to display a flag that indicates a particular country of registration (*refers to a ship*) ○ *flying the Spanish flag* **11.** *vi* **MOVE FREELY IN AIR** to move freely because of the speed of the air ○ *She ran down the street, her hair flying.* **12.** *vi* **GO VERY FAST** to go to or from a place at top speed ○ *I must fly!* **13.** *vi* **MOVE QUICKLY AND FORCEFULLY** to move with speed through the air by force of impact ○ *sent debris flying everywhere* **14.** *vi* **PASS QUICKLY** to pass very fast ○ *The weekend had simply flown.* **15.** *vi* **BE DISCUSSED INCREASINGLY** to be passed on or gossiped about by a swiftly increasing number of people ○ *Bad news flies.* **16.** *vi* **BE QUICK TO DO SOMETHING** to rush to do something quickly ○ *He flew to our aid.* **17.** *vi* **BE ACCEPTABLE** to be acceptable, successful, or useful (*informal*) ○ *come up with a proposal that will fly* **18.** *vi* **DISAPPEAR** to disappear or be used up quickly ○ *Money just flies out of her hands.* **19.** *vt* THEATER **HANG SOMETHING ABOVE STAGE** to suspend lights or set components above a stage **20.** *vt* HUNTING **MAKE HAWK CHASE PREY** to cause a hawk to fly after prey **21.** (*past and past participle* **flied**) *vi* BASEBALL **HIT FLY** in baseball, to hit a fly ball ○ *She flied twice in the second inning.* ■ *n* (*plural* **flies**) **1.** CLOTHING **FRONT OPENING OF PANTS** a covered zipper or row of buttons, especially one at the front of a pair of pants **2. ENTRANCE FLAP OF TENT** a flap at the entrance of a tent **3. OUTER ROOF OF TENT** a light tarpaulin secured over the top of a tent **4.** BASEBALL **BALL HIT HIGH** in baseball, a hit that goes high but usually not very far **5. WIDTH OF FLAG** the distance between the outer edge of a flag and the staff it is attached to **6. EDGE OF FLAG** the outer edge of a flag **7.** MECH ENG same as **flywheel 8.** *UK* TRANSP **HORSE-DRAWN CARRIAGE** in former times, a carriage for hire, drawn by one horse ■ **flies** *npl* THEATER **AREA ABOVE STAGE** the space above a stage in a theater, where lights and scenery are hung [Old English *flēogan* < Indo-European] —**fly·able** *adj* ◇ **fly high** to enjoy a period of great success or happiness ◇ **let fly (at somebody) 1.** to speak angrily to somebody **2.** to throw something at somebody ◇ **on the fly 1.** while in a hurry ○ *caught me on the fly* **2.** *US* while something is flying ○ *caught the ball on the fly* **3.** *US* without preparation, in the present moment ○ *answered all their questions on the fly* **4.** COMPUT while a computer program is running (*informal*)

fly at *vt Can, UK* same as **fly into** (sense 2)

fly in *vi* to arrive by aircraft

fly into *vt* **1.** to suddenly start feeling and expressing a strong emotion ○ *fly into a rage* **2.** *US* to attack somebody by rushing toward that person, hitting him or her or speaking angrily. Can term **fly at**

fly out *vi* **1.** to travel by plane to a particular destination or from a particular airport **2.** in baseball, to be put out when the ball you hit is caught by a fielder

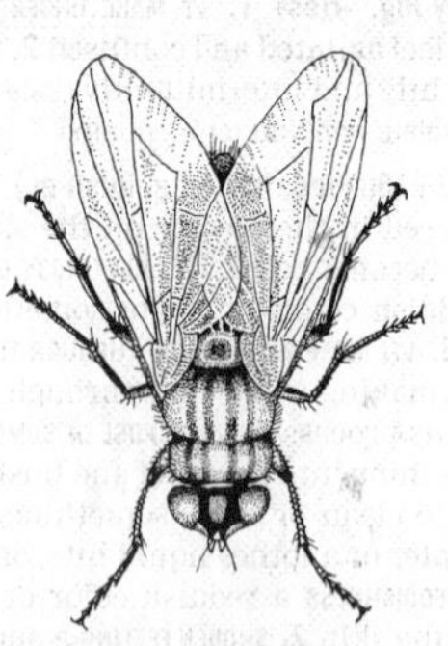

fly

fly[2] /flī/ (*plural* **flies**) *n* **1. SMALL TWO-WINGED INSECT** a two-winged insect, many of which are of an order that includes pests. Order: Diptera. **2. FLYING INSECT** a flying insect, e.g., a caddis fly or dragonfly (*usually used in combination*) **3.** FISHING **FLY-FISHING LURE** a fishhook with feathers or other attachments to make it resemble a flying insect. Use: fly-fishing. [Old English *flēoge* < Germanic] ◇ **a fly in the ointment** a problem that spoils a good situation ◇ **there are no flies on somebody** used to say that somebody is intelligent and not easily tricked

fly[3] /flī/ *adj* stylish and fashionable (*slang*) [Early 19C. Origin ?]

Fly /flī/ river in south-western Papua New Guinea, forming part of the border with Indonesia. Length: 650 mi./1,050 km.

fly ag·a·ric *n* a poisonous mushroom with a bright red or orange cap and white spots. Latin name: *Amanita muscaria.* [< its former use as an insecticide]

fly agaric

fly ash *n* fine particles of ash resulting from the combustion of a solid fuel

fly·a·way /flī ə wày/ *adj* easily made airborne or affected by a breeze ○ *flyaway hair*

fly·back /flī bàk/ *n* in a television tube, the rapid return of the electron beam in the direction opposite to scanning

fly ball *n* BASEBALL same as **fly**[1] *n* (sense 4)

fly·blow /flī blō/ *n* **1. BLOWFLY EGG OR LARVA** the egg or larva of a blowfly or flesh fly **2. INFESTATION WITH BLOWFLY EGGS OR LARVAE** an infestation with the eggs or larvae of a blowfly or flesh fly ■ *vt* (**-blew** /-bloo/, **-blown** /-blōn/, **-blow·ing, -blows**) **CONTAMINATE** to contaminate something with the eggs or larvae of a blowfly or flesh fly

fly·blown /flī blōn/ *adj* **1. DIRTY** dirty and in bad condition **2. CONTAMINATED WITH BLOWFLY EGGS OR LARVAE** contaminated with the eggs or larvae of a blowfly or flesh fly and therefore not fit to eat **3. TAINTED** contaminated with something undesirable

fly·boat /flī bōt/ *n* a small fast boat [Late 16C. < Dutch *vlieboot* < *Vlie*, channel off the N coast of the Netherlands]

fly·boy /flī bòy/ *n* a man who is a pilot in the Air Force (*informal*)

fly bridge *n* NAUT same as **flying bridge**

fly·by /flī bī/ *n* a flight close to a particular position or object, especially a flight by a space vehicle close to a planet, usually for observation purposes

fly-by-night *adj* **1. UNSCRUPULOUS IN BUSINESS** unscrupulous or not creditworthy in business or commerce **2. EPHEMERAL** not lasting long ■ *n also* **fly-by-night·er 1. ABSCONDING DEBTOR** somebody who leaves without paying debts **2. DUBIOUS OR SHAKY BUSINESS** a business with financial problems or a bad reputation

fly-by-wire *n* an aircraft flight control system that has electronic rather than mechanical controls

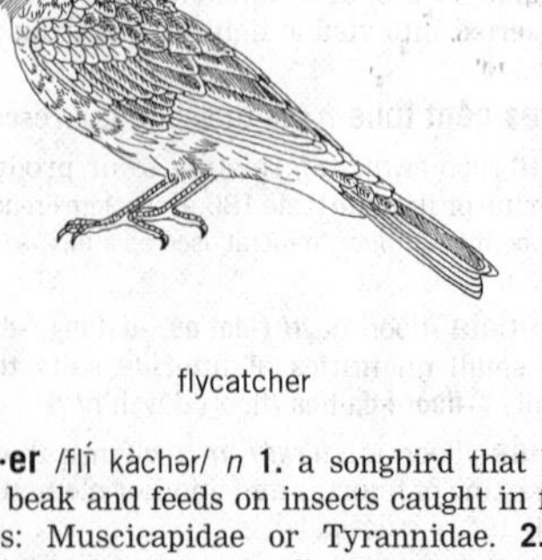

flycatcher

fly·catch·er /flī kàchər/ *n* **1.** a songbird that has a slender beak and feeds on insects caught in flight. Families: Muscicapidae or Tyrannidae. **2.** any similar bird of the same family. Native to: America. Family: Tyrannidae.

fly-drive *adj* describes a vacation or travel option that includes a flight and a rental car at the destination

fly·er *n* another spelling of **flier**

fly-fish *vi* to fish using a rod, reel, and line, and a lure resembling a fly —**fly-fish·er** *n* —**fly-fish·ing** *n*

fly·fish·er·man /flī fishərmən/ (*plural* **-men** /-mən/) *n* a fisherman who uses a rod, reel, and line, and a lure resembling a fly

fly front *n* a covered zipper or row of buttons at the front of a garment

fly gal·ler·y *n* a hidden platform above a stage from where objects suspended from the flies are controlled

fly half *n* RUGBY same as **stand-off half**

fly·ing /flī ing/ *adj* **1.** **CAPABLE OF OR IN FLIGHT** capable of flight, or in flight **2.** **MOVING FAST** moving very quickly **3.** **HAPPENING QUICKLY** happening or passing very quickly **4.** SAILING **NOT HELD AT EDGE** describes a sail held at the corners only, not the edge ■ *n* **1.** **AIR TRAVEL** travel by aircraft **2.** **PILOTING** the piloting of aircraft

CULTURAL NOTE ***The Flying Dutchman***, an opera (1843) by German composer Richard Wagner. The protagonist is a Dutch seaman who, as a result of an act of blasphemy, has been condemned to roam the oceans until he is saved by the love of a woman. In Norway, he meets Senta, who commits a desperate act of faith that results in his redemption.

fly·ing boat *n* a seaplane with a fuselage that acts like a boat's hull and provides buoyancy on water

fly·ing bomb *n* an explosive robot plane, guided missile, or rocket bomb (*informal*)

fly·ing bridge *n* an open deck of a ship with a secondary set of navigational devices

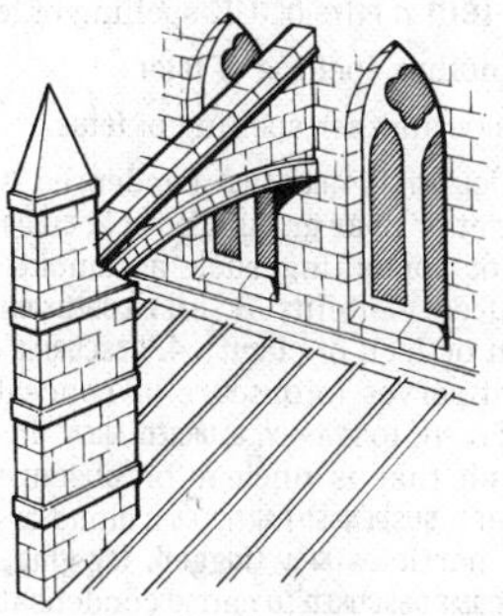

flying buttress

fly·ing but·tress *n* an exterior support for a wall (**buttress**) that sticks out from the wall and is typically arch-shaped, often used in Gothic cathedrals to withstand the outward thrust of the very high walls

fly·ing drag·on *n* ZOOL same as **flying lizard**

fly·ing field *n* a small airfield from which aircraft, usually light aircraft, can operate

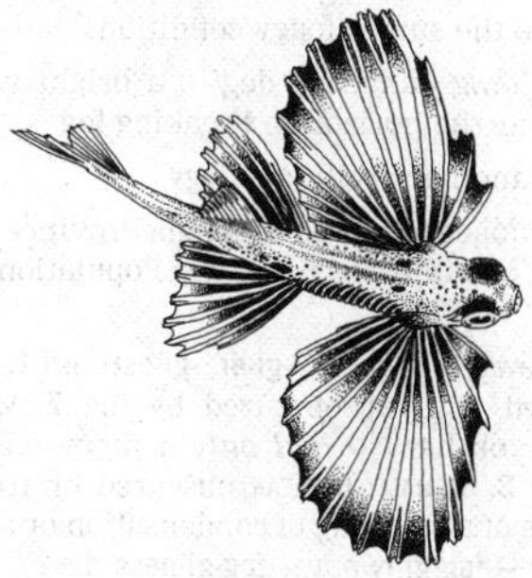

flying fish

fly·ing fish *n* a fish with fins that can be held out like wings, enabling it to glide short distances above the water. Native to: warm or tropical seas. Family: Exocoetidae.

fly·ing fox *n* a large fruit bat with a wingspan up to 5 ft./152 cm. Native to: Australasia. Genus: *Pteropus*.

fly·ing frog *n* a frog with webbed feet that it uses to glide between the trees in which it lives. Native to: Asia. Latin name: *Racophorus reinwardii*.

fly·ing gur·nard *n* an ocean fish that resembles the gurnard but has large fins enabling it to glide short distances above the water. Native to: tropics. Family: Dactylopteridae.

flying fox

fly·ing jib *n* on a ship with more than one sail at the front, the foremost triangular sail projecting from the vessel

fly·ing leap *n* a jump or leap taken while running

fly·ing le·mur *n* a mammal with a flap of skin between its front and back limbs that it uses to glide between the trees in which it lives. Native to: Southeast Asia. Family: Dermoptera.

fly·ing liz·ard *n* a small lizard with a flap of skin between its front and back limbs that it uses to glide through the air. Native to: tropics. Genus: *Draco*.

fly·ing ma·chine *n* an aircraft, especially a very early one

fly·ing mare *n* a wrestling maneuver in which the attacker grasps the opponent's arm and then turns to throw the opponent over the shoulder

fly·ing mouse *n* a computer mouse that can be lifted and used as a pointer in a three-dimensional environment

fly·ing pha·lan·ger *n* a small marsupial with a flap of skin between its front and back limbs that it uses to glide between trees. Native to: Australasia. Family: Phalangeridae.

fly·ing sail·boat *n* a racing sailboat to which carbon-fiber foils are welded beneath the outriggers, thereby providing lift of 15 ft. above the ocean surface, reducing drag, and generating high speeds once the vessel has already reached 15 knots or more

fly·ing sau·cer *n* a disk-shaped flying object believed to be an extraterrestrial spacecraft

fly·ing squad *n* a group of troops or police officers who can be quickly deployed

fly·ing squir·rel *n* a nocturnal squirrel with a flap of skin between its front and back limbs that it uses to glide between trees. Native to: northern Europe, North America, Asia. Family: Petauristinae.

fly·ing start *n* a start of a race in which competitors cross the starting line at racing speed ◇ **off to a flying start** begun or beginning very successfully

fly·ing wedge *n* a group of law-enforcement officers in a wedge-shaped formation who are thus able to move into crowds effectively

fly·ing wing *n* in Canadian football, the 12th player, who has a variable position behind the scrimmage line

fly-kick *n* in some martial arts, a kick executed in mid-air with one leg straight and the other flexed at the knee and hip

fly·leaf /flī lēef/ (*plural* **-leaves** /-lēevz/) *n* the first page in a hardbound book, which forms a continuous sheet with the page stuck inside the front cover [< FLY[1]]

fly·man /flīmən/ (*plural* **-men** /-mən/) *n* somebody, especially a man, whose job is to operate parts of the scenery from the flies in a theater

fly net *n* a net or sheet of netting used to keep flying insects out of or away from something

Errol Flynn: as the Earl of Essex in *The Private Lives of Elizabeth and Essex* (1939)

Flynn /flin/, **Errol** (1909–59) Australian-born US actor. He played the swashbuckling hero in romantic costume drama films such as *Captain Blood* (1935) and *The Adventures of Robin Hood* (1938). Born **Flynn, Errol Leslie Thomas**

fly or·chid *n* an orchid in which the lower part of the flower resembles an insect. Native to: Europe. Latin name: *Ophrys insectifera*.

fly·o·ver /flī ōvər/ *n* **1.** the flight of an aircraft or formation of aircraft over a place as a spectacle for people on the ground **2.** *UK* ROADS same as **overpass**

fly·pa·per /flī pàypər/ *n* paper coated with a sticky poisonous substance that attracts and kills flies

fly-past *n UK* same as **flyover** (sense 1)

fly·per·son /flī pùrss'n/ *n* somebody whose job is to operate parts of the scenery from the flies in a theater

fly rod *n* a long flexible fishing rod for use in fly-fishing

flysch /flish/, **Flysch** *n* a thick deposit of sedimentary rock formed in salt water by erosion of adjacent steep mountains [Early 19C. < Swiss German]

fly sheet *n UK* CAMPING same as **fly**[1] *n* (sense 3)

fly·sheet /flī shēet/ *n* a sheet or pamphlet containing printed information or advertising

fly·speck /flī spèk/ *n* **1.** **FLY'S FECES** a tiny mark made by a fly's feces **2.** **TINY MARK** a tiny mark or stain ■ *vt* (**-specked, -speck·ing, -specks**) **MARK WITH FLYSPECKS** to mark something with the tiny spots of flies' feces or similar stains (*usually used in the passive*)

fly swat·ter *n* a tool used to strike and kill insects, consisting of a long flexible handle with a flat piece of plastic net attached

fly·trap /flī tràp/ *n* **1.** PLANTS same as **Venus's flytrap** **2.** a device for catching flies

fly-ty·ing *n* the making of artificial flies that can be used to catch fish —**fly-ti·er** *n*

fly·way /flī wày/ *n* a traditional route taken by migrating birds

fly·weight /flī wàyt/ *n* **1.** **WEIGHT CATEGORY IN PROFESSIONAL BOXING** in professional boxing, a weight category for competitors whose weight does not exceed 112 lb./51 kg **2.** **WEIGHT CATEGORY IN AMATEUR BOXING** in amateur boxing, a weight category for competitors whose weight does not exceed 112 lb./51 kg **3.** **BOXER COMPETING AT FLYWEIGHT** a professional or amateur boxer who competes at flyweight level

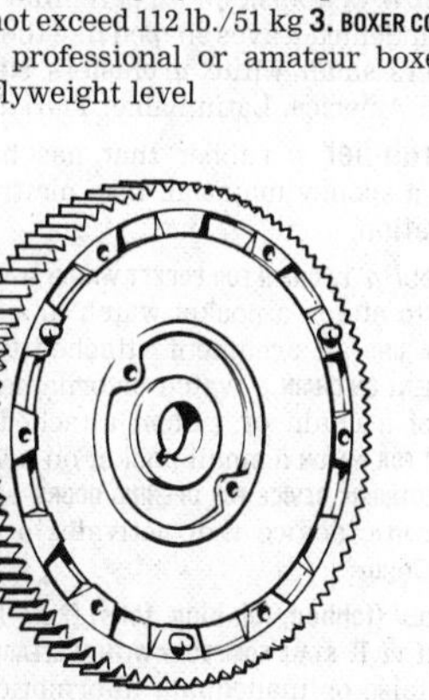

flywheel

fly·wheel /flī weel, -hweel/ *n* a heavy wheel or disk that helps because of its inertia to maintain a constant speed of rotation in a machine or to store energy. See illustration on previous page

fm *abbr* ONLINE Micronesia (*used in Internet addresses*) See table at **domain name**

Fm *symbol* CHEM ELEM fermium

FM *abbr* **1.** (*plural* **FMs**) ARMY field manual **2.** ENG figure of merit **3.** MEDIA frequency modulation **4.** Micronesia

fm. *abbr* **1.** MEASURE fathom **2.** MEDIA frequency modulation

FMB *abbr* SHIPPING Federal Maritime Board

FMCS *abbr* HR Federal Mediation and Conciliation Service

FMS *abbr* **1.** PSYCHOL false memory syndrome **2.** AVIAT flight management system

FMVSS *abbr* TRANSP Federal Motor Vehicle Safety Standards

FN *abbr* POL foreign national

fn. *abbr* PUBL footnote

FNMA *abbr* FIN Federal National Mortgage Association

f-num·ber *n* the ratio of the focal length to the effective diameter of a camera lens. Symbol **f** [Abbreviation of FOCAL]

fo *abbr* Faroe Islands (*used in Internet addresses*) See table at **domain name**

FO, **F.O.** *abbr* **1.** ARMY field-grade officer **2.** ARMY field order **3.** FIN finance officer **4.** MIL flight officer **5.** MIL flying officer

fo. *abbr* PUBL folio

F/O. *abbr* MIL flight officer

foal /fōl/ *n* an unweaned horse or related animal ■ *vi* (**foaled, foal·ing, foals**) to give birth to a foal [Old English *fola* < Indo-European, "small"]

foam /fōm/ *n* **1. MASS OF BUBBLES** a mass of bubbles of gas or air on the surface of a liquid **2. THICK FROTHY SUBSTANCE** a thick but light mixture that contains a lot of tiny bubbles ○ *Beat the egg whites into a foam.* ○ *shaving foam* **3. FIRE-EXTINGUISHING SUBSTANCE** a thick chemical froth used to extinguish flames **4. MATERIAL CONTAINING BUBBLES** rubber, plastic, or other material filled with many small bubbles of air to make it soft or light **5. FROTHY SALIVA** frothy saliva produced as a result of exertion or disease **6.** same as **sea** (sense 1) (*literary*) ■ *v* (**foamed, foam·ing, foams**) **1.** *vi* **PRODUCE BUBBLES** to produce a mass of bubbles **2.** *vi* **PRODUCE FROTHY SALIVA** to produce foam from the mouth **3.** *vi* **BE ANGRY** to express great anger (*informal*) **4.** *vi US* **TEEM** to be packed with people (*informal*) **5.** *vt* **FILL WITH BUBBLES** to transform a material into foam by aerating it in liquid form and then solidifying it [Old English *fām* < Indo-European] —**foam·y** *adj*

foamed slag *n* slag from a blast furnace that is aerated while it is still molten. Use: building or insulation material.

foam·er /fōmər/ *n* **1.** a device used to make liquid frothy by incorporating air **2.** somebody who is very devoted to a hobby, especially a model railroad enthusiast

foam·flow·er /fōm flòwr/ *n* a perennial woodland plant with indented leaves shaped like those of the maple. Flowers: small, white, in clusters. Native to: eastern North America. Latin name: *Tiarella cordifolia.*

foam rub·ber *n* rubber that has been aerated to form a spongy material. Use: mattresses, padding, insulation.

fob[1] /fob/ *n* **1. CHAIN FOR POCKET WATCH** a chain or ribbon used to attach a pocket watch to a vest **2. ORNAMENT ON KEY RING** an ornament attached to a key ring **3. ORNAMENT ON CHAIN** a watch or ornament worn on the end of a chain or ribbon attached to clothing **4. POCKET FOR WATCH** a small pocket on a vest for a watch **5. ELECTRONIC DEVICE FOR OPENING DOORS** a small portable electronic device that activates a door lock [Mid-17C. Origin ?]

fob[2] /fob/ (**fobbed, fob·bing, fobs**) [Late 16C. Origin ?]
fob off *vt* **1. STALL SOMEBODY WITH MISLEADING INFORMATION** to give false or inadequate information to somebody in order to stop further questions **2. GIVE SOMETHING INFERIOR TO SOMEBODY** to provide somebody with something different from and inferior to what he or she wanted **3. GIVE SOMETHING UNWANTED TO SOMEBODY** to pass something unwanted to somebody else, using deceitful persuasion

FOB, **F.O.B.** *abbr* COMM free on board

f.o.b., **fob** *abbr* COMM free on board

fob watch *n* a round watch kept in a special pocket on a vest

fo·cac·cia /fə kaachə, fō-/ *n* flat Italian bread, often sprinkled with a topping before baking, and served hot or cold [Mid-20C. Via Italian < assumed Vulgar Latin *focacia* < Latin *focus* "hearth, fireplace"]

fo·cal /fōk'l/ *adj* **1. PRINCIPAL** main and most important **2. FOCUSING IMAGE** relating to bringing an image into focus **3. AT OR FROM FOCAL POINT** located at, passing through, or measured from a focal point —**fo·cal·ly** *adv*

fo·cal dis·tance *n* OPTICS same as **focal length**

fo·cal in·fec·tion *n* a bacterial infection in one part of the body that may cause symptoms elsewhere in the body

fo·cal·ize /fōk'l īz/ (**-ized, -iz·ing, -iz·es**) *v* **1.** *vti* to focus something, or be brought into focus **2.** *vt* to limit something to a local area —**fo·cal·i·za·tion** /fōk'li zāysh'n/ *n*

fo·cal length *n* the distance from the center of a lens or the surface of a mirror to the point at which light passing through the lens or reflected from the mirror is focused. Symbol **f**

fo·cal-plane shut·ter *n* a camera shutter positioned just in front of the film, instead of being built into the lens

fo·cal point *n* **1.** the point at which parallel rays meeting a lens, curved mirror, or other optical system converge or appear to diverge **2.** an object of concentrated or immediate attention

fo·cal ra·tio *n* OPTICS same as **f-number**

Foch /fosh/, **Ferdinand** (1851–1929) French general. He was appointed supreme military commander of the Allied forces on the Western Front in the final year of World War I (1918).

> "My center is giving way, my right is retreating; situation excellent. I shall attack."
> [Ferdinand Foch, "Ferdinand Foch," *Reputations Ten Years After*, B. H. Liddell Hart; 1928]

fo·ci plural of **focus**

fo'c's'le *n* NAUT same as **forecastle**

fo·cus /fōkəss/ *n* (*plural* **-cus·es** or **-ci** /-sī/) **1. MAIN EMPHASIS** concentrated effort or attention on a particular thing ○ *The committee's focus must be on finding solutions to the problem.* **2. AREA OF CONCERN** an area of concern, responsibility, or investigation ○ *an inquiry with a narrow focus* **3. CONCENTRATED QUALITY** a concentrated and unified quality ○ *to bring focus to the problem* **4. SHARPNESS OF IMAGE** the quality that makes an image sharply defined with clear edges and contrast **5. SHARPNESS OF VISION** the condition of seeing images sharply and clearly **6.** (*plural* **fo·ci**) OPTICS same as **focal point** (sense 1) **7.** PHOTOGRAPHY **DEVICE FOR ADJUSTING CAMERA LENS** a device on a camera for adjusting the lens **8.** (*plural* **fo·ci**) MED **DISEASE ORIGIN** the point from which a disease spreads or where it localizes **9.** (*plural* **fo·ci**) GEOG **CENTER OF EARTHQUAKE OR EXPLOSION** the point of origin of an earthquake or underground nuclear explosion **10.** (*plural* **fo·ci**) MATH **POINT ON CONE** a fixed point in a plane that in combination with a particular straight line specifies a conic section ■ *vti* (**-cused** or **-cussed, -cus·ing** or **-cus·sing, -cus·es** or **-cus·ses**) **1. CONCENTRATE MAINLY ON SOMETHING** to concentrate effort or attention on a particular thing or a particular aspect of a thing **2. ADJUST VISION TO SEE CLEARLY** to adjust your vision so that you see clearly and sharply, or become adjusted for clear vision **3.** OPTICS **ADJUST LENS** to adjust a lens so that the image viewed is clear and sharp **4.** OPTICS **MEET AT SINGLE POINT** to make rays of light meet at a single point, or meet at a single point [Mid-17C. < Latin, "hearth, fireplace"] —**fo·cus·a·ble** *adj* —**fo·cus·er** *n*

fo·cused /fōkəst/, **fo·cussed** *adj* **1.** concentrated on a particular thing **2.** single-minded and determined

fo·cus group *n* a small group of representative people who are questioned about their opinions as part of political or market research

fo·cussed *adj* another spelling of **focused**

fod·der /fóddər/ *n* **1. ANIMAL FOOD** hay, straw, or similar food for livestock **2. MATERIAL FOR STIMULATING RESPONSE** people, ideas, or images that are useful in stimulating a creative or critical response **3. EXPENDABLE PEOPLE OR THINGS** people or things regarded as the necessary but expendable ingredient that makes a system or scheme work (*usually used in combination*) ○ *case studies seized upon as thesis fodder* ■ *vt* (**-dered, -der·ing, -ders**) **FEED LIVESTOCK** to give food to livestock [Old English *fōdor* < Indo-European, "to feed"] —**fod·der·er** *n*

foe /fō/ *n* an enemy or opponent of somebody or something (*formal*) [Old English *gefā* < Indo-European, "hostile"]

FOE, **FoE** *abbr* Fraternal Order of Eagles

foehn /fayn, fōn/, **föhn** *n* a warm dry wind that blows down the lee slope of a mountain range, originally and especially the Alps [Mid-19C. Via German < Latin *favonius* "west wind" < *favere* "favor, be well disposed toward"]

foe·tal, **etc.** BIOL another spelling of **fetal, etc.**

foe·tid *adj* another spelling of **fetid**

foe·to·pro·tein *n* PHYSIOL UK spelling of **fetoprotein**

foe·tor *n* another spelling of **fetor**

foe·tus *n* BIOL another spelling of **fetus**

fog /fawg, fog/ *n* **1. THICK MIST** condensed water vapor in the air at or near ground level **2. CLOUD OF SOMETHING** a cloud of something such as smoke in the air that reduces visibility **3. HAZY CONFUSION** a state of confusion or lack of clarity **4. OBSCURING AGENT** something that serves to obscure or conceal ○ *a fog of excuses* **5.** PHOTOGRAPHY **BLURRED AREA** an area on a photograph that is unclear or obscured by stray light **6.** CHEM **SUSPENDED PARTICLES** a cloud or suspension of liquid particles ■ *v* (**fogged, fog·ging, fogs**) **1.** *vti* **MAKE OR BECOME OBSCURED** to cause condensation to form on a transparent surface, or become covered with condensation **2.** *vt* **MAKE SOMETHING UNCLEAR** to make something unclear or confused **3.** *vti* PHOTOGRAPHY **EXPOSE FILM TO LIGHT** to contaminate film or a developing image with light, usually accidentally, or undergo this process [Mid-16C. Origin ?] —**fogged** *adj*

fog bank *n* a mass of thick fog, especially at sea

fog·bound /fáwg bòwnd, fóg-/ *adj* **1.** unable to move or operate because visibility is diminished by fog **2.** enveloped in fog

fog·bow /fáwg bō, fóg-/ *n* a faint arc of light seen opposite the sun in foggy conditions

fog·dog /fáwg dàwg, fóg dòg/ *n* a bright white spot seen near the horizon in breaking fog

fo·gey *n* another spelling of **fogy**

Fog·gi·a /fójjee ə/ capital of Foggia Province in Apulia Region, southeastern Italy. Population: 155,203 (2001).

fog·gy /fáwgee, fóggee/ (**-gi·er, -gi·est**) *adj* **1. FILLED WITH FOG** filled with or obscured by fog **2. VAGUE** very unclear or hazy ○ *had only a foggy idea of who he was* **3. VISUALLY UNCLEAR** obscured or translucent because of a covering of condensation or something similar —**fog·gi·ly** *adv* —**fog·gi·ness** *n*

Fog·gy Bot·tom *n US* the US Department of State in Washington, D.C. (*informal*) [After a low-lying area near the Potomac River in Washington, D.C.]

fog·horn /fáwg hàwrn, fóg-/ *n* a horn sounded on a ship or boat when fog reduces visibility, as a warning to other vessels

fog light, **fog·lamp** /fáwg làmp, fóg-/ *n* a front or rear light on a car with a beam designed to penetrate fog

fo·gy /fōgee/ (*plural* **-gies**), **fo·gey** (*plural* **-geys**) *n* an old-fashioned person who resists change or novelty [Late 18C. < Scots, origin ?] —**fo·gy·ish** *adj* —**fo·gy·ism** *n*

föhn *n* METEOROL another spelling of **foehn**

foi·ble /fóyb'l/ *n* **1.** an idiosyncrasy or small weakness (*usually used in the plural*) **2.** the weakest part of a sword blade from the middle to the point [Mid-17C. Via obsolete French < Old French *feble* (see FEEBLE)]

foie gras /fwaa graa/ *n* goose liver swollen as a result of force-feeding the bird on corn, usually eaten as a pâté [Early 19C. < French, "fatted liver"]

foil[1] /foyl/ *n* **1.** METAL IN THIN SHEETS metal in a very thin flexible sheet **2.** GOOD CONTRAST TO SOMETHING a useful or interesting contrast to something **3.** METAL COATING ON MIRROR the thin reflective metal coating on the back of a mirror **4.** NAUT same as **hydrofoil** (sense 2) **5.** AVIAT same as **airfoil** **6.** ARCHIT ARC IN GOTHIC WINDOW an arc at the top of a Gothic window ■ *vt* (**foiled, foil·ing, foils**) COVER SOMETHING WITH FOIL to cover or coat something with metal foil [14C. Via Old French < Latin *folium* "leaf," *folia* "leaves"]

foil[2] /foyl/ (**foiled, foil·ing, foils**) *vt* **1.** to prevent somebody from succeeding in something **2.** to obscure the trail in order to hinder pursuers (*refers to a hunted animal*) [14C. Origin ?]

foil[3] /foyl/ *n* a long thin sword with a small disk on the end, used in fencing [Late 16C. Origin ?]

foils /foylz/ *n* the art or sport of fencing with foils (*takes a singular verb*) —**foils·man** /fóylzmən/ *n*

foist /foyst/ (**foist·ed, foist·ing, foists**) *vt* **1.** IMPOSE SOMETHING ON SOMEBODY to force somebody to accept something undesirable ○ *always foists the dirty jobs on me* **2.** GIVE SOMEBODY SOMETHING INFERIOR to give somebody something inferior on the pretense that it is genuine, valuable, or desirable ○ *tried to foist it off on us as an antique* **3.** INSERT SOMETHING SURREPTITIOUSLY to introduce or insert something surreptitiously [Mid-16C. Probably < Dutch dialect *vuisten* "hold in your hand" (as when hiding dice) < Middle Dutch *vuist* "fist"]

Fo·kine /faw kéen, fō-/, **Michel** (1880–1942) Russian-born US dancer and choreographer. His work revitalized traditional classical ballet by introducing increased expression into the predominantly technical dance form. Born **Fokine, Mikhail Mikhailovich**

fol. *abbr* **1.** PUBL folio **2.** followed **3.** following

fol·a·cin /fóllәsin/ *n* BIOCHEM same as **folic acid** [Mid-20C. < FOLIC ACID]

fo·late /fō làyt/ *n* **1.** BIOCHEM same as **folic acid** **2.** a salt or ester of folic acid [Mid-20C. < FOLIC ACID]

fold[1] /fōld/ *v* (**fold·ed, fold·ing, folds**) **1.** *vt* BEND SOMETHING FLAT to bend something thin and flat over on itself **2.** *vt* MAKE SOMETHING SMALLER BY FOLDING to bend something over on itself more than once **3.** *vti* BEND SOMETHING TO MAKE IT COMPACT to bend part of something so as to make it more streamlined or more compact, or undergo this process ○ *This can be folded for easy storage.* **4.** *vt* COVER SOMETHING to wrap or cover something ○ *folded the note inside a magazine* **5.** *vi* GO OUT OF BUSINESS to fail and stop operating as a business **6.** *vi* ACCEPT DEFEAT to give in and accept defeat ○ *folded in the final minutes of the game* **7.** *vi* CARDS GIVE UP HAND in poker and other card games, to stop playing a hand in the belief that it cannot win **8.** *vt* PUT ARMS AROUND SOMEBODY to put your arms around somebody **9.** *vt* DRAW LIMBS TOWARD BODY to draw in the arms, legs, or hands toward the body, or place them together with the joints bent **10.** *vt* BRING WINGS TOGETHER to bring the wings together or next to the body **11.** *vti* GEOL DISTORT ROCK LAYER to cause a layer of rock to bend, or undergo this process **12.** *vi* BIOCHEM DEVELOP UNIQUE STRUCTURE to develop a specific three-dimensional structure that is unique to each different protein, in order to function properly (*refers to a protein chain*) ■ *n* **1.** BENT PART a part of something folded **2.** CREASE a line, crease, or raised part made when something has been folded **3.** HANGING FOLDED PART a part of something that hangs in a folded shape ○ *the heavy folds of the curtains* **4.** COIL a single coil in a rope, or a snake lying in coils **5.** GEOL DISTORTION IN ROCK LAYER a bend formed in a rock layer in response to forces in the rock **6.** *UK* SMALL VALLEY a small valley in a hilly area [Old English *fealdan* < Indo-European, "to fold"] —**fold·a·ble** *adj*

fold in *vt* to add a food ingredient to a mixture carefully and lightly

fold up *v* **1.** *vti* to fold something completely, or become folded completely **2.** *vi* to collapse from laughter, pain, or strong emotion

fold[2] /fōld/ *n* **1.** ENCLOSED AREA FOR SHEEP an enclosed area where sheep or other livestock can be kept **2.** GROUP WITH THINGS IN COMMON a group to which something or somebody naturally belongs because of shared interests or traits **3.** ENCLOSED ANIMALS sheep or other livestock in a fold **4.** FLOCK a flock of sheep ■ *vt* (**fold·ed, fold·ing, folds**) ENCLOSE LIVESTOCK to put or keep livestock in an enclosed area [Old English *fald*, origin ?]

-fold *suffix* **1.** divided into parts ○ *manifold* **2.** times ○ *tenfold* [Old English *-feald*; related to *fealdan* (see FOLD[1])]

fold·a·way /fóldә wày/ *adj* designed to be folded for compact storage

fold·boat /fóld bōt/ *n* a boat like a kayak consisting of waterproof fabric over a collapsible frame [Early 20C. Translation of German *Faltboot* "folding boat" < *falten* "to fold" + *Boot* "boat"]

fold·er /fóldәr/ *n* **1.** FOLDED CARDBOARD TO HOLD PAPERS a piece of cardboard folded to make a file in which papers can be held **2.** COMPUT FILE CONTAINER a conceptual container for computer files in some operating systems, corresponding to a directory or subdirectory **3.** FOLDED PAMPHLET a circular printed on folded paper

fol·de·rol /fóldә ràwl/, **fal·de·ral** /faaldә raal/ *n* **1.** an attractive but valueless object or trinket **2.** silly nonsense (*dated*) [Early 19C. < *fol de rol*, nonsense refrain in songs]

fold·ing /fólding/ *adj* designed to be folded for compact storage

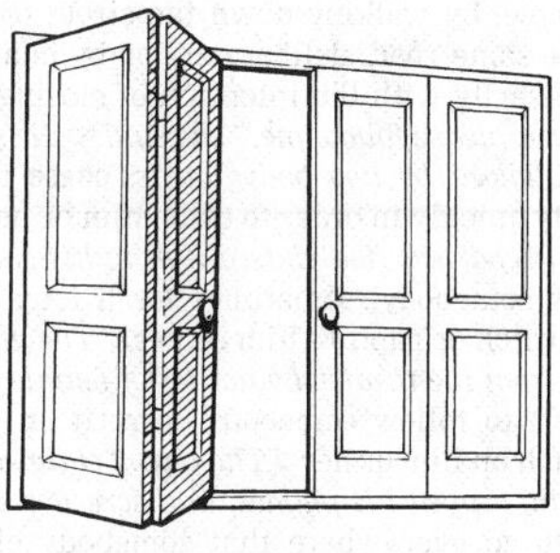

folding door

fold·ing door *n* a door consisting of hinged panels that fold against each other

fold·ing mon·ey *n* money in the form of bills rather than coins (*informal*)

fold·ing press *n* a wrestling maneuver in which the opponent is pressed into a fetal position and held down

fold·out /fóld òwt/ *n* **1.** PUBL same as **gatefold** **2.** a piece of furniture, or part of it, that unfolds and opens out of its stored position for use —**fold·out** *adj*

fold·up /fóld up/ *adj* designed to be folded for compact storage ■ *n* *US* a failure of a business ○ *foldups brought on by adverse economic conditions*

Fo·ley /fólee/, **Thomas** (*b.* 1929) US politician. He served as a member of the US House of Representatives from Washington State (1965–95) and was Speaker of the House (1989–95). Full name **Foley, Thomas Stephen**

fo·ley art·ist *n US* somebody who adds sound effects to a filmed performance [After Jack *Foley*, US sound engineer]

fo·li·a·ceous /fòlee áyshәss/ *adj* **1.** BOT relating to or resembling a leaf **2.** GEOL consisting of thin sheets [Mid-17C. < Latin *foliaceus* < *folium* "leaf"]

fo·li·age /fólee ij, fólij/ *n* **1.** the leaves of a plant or tree **2.** architectural ornamentation based on leaves and stems [Mid-15C. Alteration (after Latin *folium*) of Old French *foillage* < *foille* "leaf" < Latin *folium*] —**fo·li·aged** *adj*

fo·li·age plant *n* a plant cultivated for its attractive leaves

fo·li·ar /fólee әr/ *adj* relating to, producing, or being the leaves of a plant [Late 19C. < modern Latin *foliaris* < Latin *folium* "leaf"]

fo·li·ate *adj* /fólee әt, -àyt/ **1.** RELATING TO LEAVES relating to or resembling leaves **2.** GEOL same as **foliated** (sense 1) **3.** LEAF-SHAPED in the shape of a leaf ■ *v* /fólee àyt/ (**-at·ed, -at·ing, -ates**) **1.** *vt* DECORATE SOMETHING WITH LEAVES to decorate something with leaves or very thin layers **2.** *vt* MAKE METAL INTO FOIL to form metal into a thin sheet or foil **3.** *vt* PUBL NUMBER PAGES OF BOOK to number the leaves of a book or manuscript **4.** *vi* DEVELOP LEAVES to develop foliage **5.** *vti* LAYER to separate something into very thin layers, or undergo this process [Early 17C. Adjective < Latin *foliatus* < *folium* "leaf"; verb < Latin *folium*]

-foliate *suffix* having leaves ○ *bifoliate* [< Latin *foliatus* (see FOLIATE)]

fo·li·at·ed /fólee àytәd/ *adj* **1.** GEOL formed in or composed of separable layers **2.** ARCHIT decorated with stylized architectural leaves or foliage

fo·li·a·tion /fòlee áysh'n/ *n* **1.** LEAF FORMATION the formation of leaves **2.** BEARING OF LEAVES the state of being in leaf **3.** ARCHIT ORNAMENTATION architectural ornamentation consisting of stylized foliage **4.** ARCHIT GOTHIC WINDOW DECORATION architectural decoration consisting of carving between two arches (**cusps**) and arcs (**foils**) at the top of Gothic windows **5.** PUBL NUMBERING OF PAGES the numbering of consecutive pages in a book or manuscript **6.** GEOL LAYERED TEXTURE OF ROCK a characteristic of metamorphosed rocks in which minerals are aligned in one direction so that the rock can readily be split into thin layers

fo·lic ac·id *n* an important B complex vitamin, found in green vegetables and liver [< Latin *folium* "leaf"; because found in leafy green vegetables]

fo·lie à deux /fòllee a dő/ (*plural* **fo·lies à deux** /*pronunc. same*/) *n* a psychiatric disorder with symptoms common to two people who are very close. Often only one person actually has a disorder, the other choosing to share the symptoms or delusions of the first. [Late 19C. < French, "dual delusion"]

fo·li·o /fólee ō/ *n* (*plural* **-os**) **1.** LARGE BOOK OR MANUSCRIPT a book or manuscript in the largest size usual for books, traditionally created by folding a single sheet of standard-sized printing paper once, giving two leaves or four pages **2.** LARGE SHEET FOR BOOK a standard-sized sheet of printing paper folded once to give two leaves or four pages **3.** PAGE NUMBERED ON FRONT a paper or parchment page that is numbered on the front but not the back **4.** PAGE NUMBER a page number (*technical*) **5.** LAW MEASUREMENT FOR LEGAL DOCUMENTS a unit for measuring the length of legal documents, usually 100 words in the United States and 72 or 90 in the United Kingdom **6.** ACCT LEDGER PAGE a page, or two facing pages, of a ledger ■ *vt* (**-oed, -o·ing, -os**) NUMBER PAGES to number the pages in a book ■ *adj* LARGE-FORMAT printed in folio size [Mid-15C. < late Latin *folio* "at the page" < Latin *folium* "leaf, page"]

fo·li·ose /fólee òss/ *adj* describes the body (**thallus**) of a lichen or similar plant that is thin, flattened, and lobed like a leaf [Early 18C. < Latin *foliosus* < *folium* "leaf"]

folk /fōk/ *npl* PEOPLE IN GENERAL people, especially people of the same type (*takes a plural verb*) ■ *n* MUSIC same as **folk music** (*takes a singular verb*) ■ *adj* **1.** TRADITIONAL IN COMMUNITY relating to the traditional culture passed down in a community or country ○ *folk customs* **2.** FROM IDEAS OF ORDINARY PEOPLE relating to the traditional beliefs or ideas of ordinary people [Old English *folc* < Indo-European, "fill"]

folk art *n* paintings and decorative objects made in a naive style

folk dance *n* **1.** a dance that is traditional to a culture, community, or country **2.** the music for a folk dance

folk et·y·mol·o·gy *n* **1.** the replacement of an unfamiliar word or form by a more familiar one. An example is the replacement of *girasole* with *Jerusalem* in *Jerusalem artichoke*. **2.** an idea about the origin of a word that is generally believed but is incorrect. The idea that the origin of the word "posh" is "port out, starboard home," referring to the more expensive side of ships traveling between the UK and India, is a folk etymology.

folk he·ro *n* somebody who is renowned for activities that appear to the public but which may be fictional or exaggerated

folk·ie /fṓkee/ *n* (*informal*) **1.** a folk singer or musician **2.** a fan of folk music

folk·lore /fṓk làwr/ *n* **1.** TRADITIONAL LOCAL STORIES traditional stories and explanations passed down in a community or country **2.** LOCAL LEGENDS stories and gossip that become traditional within a group of people **3.** CULTL ANTHROP STUDY OF TRADITIONS the study of traditional stories, music, and customs —**folk·lor·ic** *adj*

folk·lor·ist /fṓk làwrist/ *n* a student of the traditional stories, music, and customs of a culture or community —**folk·lor·is·tic** /fṓk law rístik/ *adj*

folk mass *n* a Christian mass in which folk music replaces some or all of the traditional music

folk med·i·cine *n* medicine based on traditional customs and belief, often using herbal remedies

folk mem·o·ry *n* a memory kept alive by a community and passed from one generation to the next

folk mu·sic *n* **1.** traditional songs and music, passed from one generation to the next **2.** modern music composed in imitation of traditional music

folk-rock *n* popular music that combines the melodies of folk music with the rhythms of rock music

folks /fōks/ *npl* **1.** same as **folk 2.** used to address a group of people (*informal*) ○ *Folks, we're ready to start now.* **3.** parents or close family

folk sing·er *n* a singer of folk songs —**folk sing·ing** *n*

folk song *n* **1.** a traditional song that has been passed down orally **2.** a modern song composed in the style of traditional folk music, often performed by a solo singer —**folk sing·er** *n*

folk·sy /fṓksee/ (**-si·er, -si·est**) *adj* **1.** *US* friendly and informal **2.** simple and unsophisticated in the tradition of folk crafts or folklore —**folk·si·ly** *adv* —**folk·si·ness** *n*

folk·tale /fṓk tàyl/, **folk tale** *n* a story or legend that is passed down orally from one generation to the next and becomes part of a community's tradition

folk·way /fṓk wày/ *n* a custom that is recognized as being old or traditional (*usually used in the plural*)

Fol·lette ♦ **La Follette, Robert Marion**

fol·li·cle /fóllik'l/ *n* **1.** a small anatomical sac, cavity, or gland involved in secretion or excretion **2.** a dry case formed from a single fruit that splits along one side to release seeds [Early 15C. < Latin *folliculus* "small sack" < *follis* "bellows"] —**fol·lic·u·lar** /fə líkyələr/ *adj*

fol·li·cle-stim·u·lat·ing hor·mone *n* a hormone that stimulates the growth of egg follicles in the ovaries and the making of sperm in the testes

fol·lic·u·li·tis /fə likyə lítəss/ *n* inflammation of one or more follicles, especially of the hair, producing small boils

fol·lies /fólleez/, **Fol·lies** *n* a theatrical revue with elaborate costumes, music, and dancing (*dated; takes a singular or plural verb*)

fol·low /fóllō/ *v* (**-lowed, -low·ing, -lows**) **1.** *vti* COME AFTER SOMEBODY OR SOMETHING to come after somebody or something in position, time, or sequence ○ *the main course followed by dessert* **2.** *vt* ADD TO SOMETHING ALREADY DONE to add to something already done by doing something else, usually a related thing ○ *She'll follow her lecture with a demonstration.* **3.** *vti* GO AFTER SOMEBODY OR SOMETHING to take the same route behind another person, e.g., by walking down the street or driving along the same road, deliberately or by chance ○ *followed them home* **4.** *vt* KEEP SOMEBODY UNDER SURVEILLANCE to have somebody's movements under constant surveillance ○ *ordering the suspect to be followed* **5.** *vt* WATCH SOMEBODY OR SOMETHING CLOSELY to watch, observe, or pay close attention to somebody or something ○ *eyes seemed to follow me around the room* **6.** *vt* GO ALONG ROUTE to go along something such as a road or path ○ *following the path* **7.** *vt* TAKE SAME DIRECTION AS SOMETHING to take the same course or go in the same direction as something else ○ *The road follows the river along the valley.* **8.** *vt* GO AS DIRECTED BY SOMETHING to go in the direction indicated by something such as a signpost ○ *Follow that sign ahead.* **9.** *vt* OBEY SOMETHING to act in accordance with something, especially with instructions or directions given by somebody else ○ *only if you follow my instructions* **10.** *vt* DEVELOP IN ACCORDANCE WITH SOMETHING to be or develop in accordance with something, usually something already known about or established ○ *following the same pattern of behavior* **11.** *vti* DO SAME AS SOMEBODY OR SOMETHING to imitate or do the same as somebody or something ○ *She followed her father into medicine.* **12.** *vti* UNDERSTAND SOMETHING to understand something such as an explanation or narrative ○ *can't follow her explanation* **13.** *vt* ENGAGE IN ACTIVITY to engage in or practice something such as a career, occupation, or lifestyle ○ *I decided to follow a career in law.* **14.** *vt* KEEP ABREAST OF SOMETHING to keep informed about or up to date with the progress of something ○ *Are you following the television series about twins?* **15.** *vt* BE ABOUT SOMETHING to be about somebody or something, especially to describe or depict what happens to somebody or something over a period of time ○ *The story follows a typical American family.* **16.** *vi* RESULT FROM SOMETHING to happen after and as a result of something else ○ *Issue too many instructions and confusion invariably follows.* **17.** *vti* BE LOGICAL RESULT to be a logical consequence of something ○ *follows from their loss of sponsorship* **18.** *vt* READ WORDS OR MUSIC to read the words or music of something while listening to it **19.** *vt Malaysia* ACCOMPANY SOMEBODY to go with somebody ○ *Can I follow you to the market?* ■ *n* CUE GAMES same as **follow shot** (sense 1) [Old English *folgian, fylgan*, origin ?] —**fol·low·a·ble** *adj* ◇ **as follows** as listed or described next

SYNONYMS ***follow, chase, pursue, tail, shadow, stalk, trail***

CORE MEANING: to go after or behind

follow to take the same route behind another person, for example, by walking down the street or driving along the same road, deliberately or by chance, and not necessarily with the intention of closing the gap ○ *"Will you please follow me," she said.* ○ *He's usually closely followed by two bodyguards.* **chase** to follow somebody quickly in order to catch him or her ○ *Once a pack of reporters had chased him to his car.* **pursue** to follow somebody, sometimes for a long time, in order to catch or capture him or her ○ *The group was pursued from the theater by hordes of female fans.* **tail** (*informal*) to follow somebody secretly in order to keep watch on him or her ○ *The report claimed officers tailed him, tapped his phones, and screened his mail.* **shadow** to go everywhere that somebody else goes, especially secretly, in order to watch what he or she is doing. ○ *Until he saw the photographs, he had had no idea he was being shadowed.* **stalk** to follow or try to get close to a person or hunted animal unobtrusively, or harass a person criminally by following or contacting them obsessively. ○ *watched their cat patiently stalking a bird* ○ *an abusive man who stalked his former partner* **trail** to follow tracks or traces left by a person or animal that is no longer in sight ○ *The police trailed the missing couple all over Europe by their hotel registrations and bank withdrawals.* ○ *We could smell the pungent scent of fox as we trailed dog-like paw marks.*

follow on *vi* to continue or resume something such as a course of action or a narrative ○ *I'll follow on from where you left off.*

follow out *vt* to carry something out in full or to the end

follow through *v* **1.** *vti* to take further action as a consequence or extension of a previous action, especially to continue something through to completion **2.** *vi* in a sport, to continue the movement of an arm or leg past the point of contact or of release after hitting, throwing, or kicking a ball or other object

follow up *vt* **1.** to act or make further investigations on the basis of information received ○ *Police are following up a new lead.* **2.** to continue or add to something already done by doing some related thing ○ *I followed up my phone call with a letter of confirmation.*

fol·low·er /fóllō ər/ *n* **1.** SUPPORTER a supporter or admirer of a person, cause, or activity ○ *a follower of Martin Luther King* ○ *a follower of the Yankees* **2.** SOMEBODY COMING AFTER somebody who comes or travels after somebody or something else **3.** MEMBER OF ENTOURAGE a servant, attendant, or subordinate, usually one of a number of people accompanying an important person **4.** IMITATOR somebody or something that copies or imitates something else

fol·low·er·ship /fóllō ər shìp/ *n US* **1.** the fact of being a follower, supporter, or disciple of somebody or something **2.** same as **following** *n* (sense 1)

fol·low·ing /fóllō ing/ *adj* **1.** NEXT coming after in time or sequence **2.** ABOUT TO BE MENTIONED about to be mentioned or listed ○ *He has visited the following countries: Canada, France, and Australia.* **3.** MOVING SAME WAY blowing or flowing in the same direction as somebody or something, especially a boat or aircraft, is traveling ○ *a following wind* ■ *n* **1.** GROUP OF FOLLOWERS a group of people who admire or support somebody or something over a period of time ○ *The band has a large following in this country.* **2.** SOMETHING TO BE SPECIFIED the people or things about to be mentioned or listed (*takes a plural verb*) ○ *You will need the following: a piece of wood, a saw, a hammer, and some nails.* ■ *prep* AFTER after something, or after something and as a result of it ○ *Following the accident it was months before he felt safe in a car.*

fol·low-my-lead·er *n UK* same as **follow-the-leader**

fol·low-on *adj* coming after as a continuation or consequence —**fol·low-on** *n*

fol·low shot *n* **1.** in billiards and similar games, a shot that makes the cue ball continue to move in the same direction as the target ball after striking it **2.** a camera shot in which the camera moves with the subject following alongside or behind

fol·low-the-lead·er *n* a game in which the players, usually children, move along in a line, all copying the actions of the person at the front

fol·low-through *n* **1.** further action continuing or completing something previously done or begun ○ *Your follow-through on the project was inadequate.* **2.** in a sport, the continuation of the movement of an arm or leg past the point of contact or of release after hitting, throwing, or kicking a ball or other object

fol·low-up *n* **1.** further action or investigation or a subsequent event that results from and is intended to supplement something done before ○ *intended as a follow-up to the summit meeting in Vienna* **2.** a book, film, article, or report that continues a story or provides further information —**fol·low-up** *adj*

fol·ly /fóllee/ (*plural* **-lies**) *n* **1.** UNREASON thoughtlessness, recklessness, or thoughtless or reckless behavior ○ *She realized, too late, the folly of her course of action.* ○ *It would be folly to continue.* **2.** IRRATIONAL THING a thoughtless or reckless act or idea (*often used in the plural*) **3.** ARCHIT ECCENTRIC BUILDING a building of eccentric or overelaborate design, usually built for decorative rather than practical purposes **4.** *US* MISGUIDED UNDERTAKING an undertaking that is excessively costly or extravagant, especially one that leads to financial loss or ruin [13C. < Old French *folie* < *fol* "foolish" (see FOOL)]

Fol·som[1] /fólssəm/ *adj* relating to a prehistoric culture of the southern plains of North America that made leaf-shaped flint projectile points with a concave base [Early 20C. Village in NE New Mexico]

Fol·som[2] /fólssəm/ town on Folsom Lake in north central California, northeast of Sacramento. It is home to Folsom State Prison, built in 1880, and California's first hydroelectric plant, dating from 1895. Population: 61,256 (2002 estimate).

fo·ment /fō mént/ (**-ment·ed, -ment·ing, -ments**) *vt* to cause or stir up trouble or rebellion [14C. < late Latin *fomentare* < Latin *fomentum* "warm soothing application" < *fovere* "warm, keep warm"] —**fo·men·ta·tion** /fōmən táysh'n, -men-/ *n*

SPELLCHECK See ***ferment***.

fo·mites /fṓ mìts/ *npl* inanimate objects capable of carrying germs from an infected person to another person, e.g., clothes or bedding [Mid-19C. < Latin, plural of *fomes* "kindling wood"]

fond[1] /fond/ *adj* **1.** FEELING AFFECTION feeling love, affection, or preference for somebody or something ○ *I've grown fond of this old house.* **2.** AFFECTIONATE showing or characterized by affection, love, or pleasant feelings ○ *fond memories of the time we spent there* **3.** EXPERIENCING PLEASURE liking or finding enjoyment in something ○ *fond of classical music* ○

His dog is fond of chasing rabbits. **4. OVERLY DOTING** feeling or showing excessive affection, often to the point of being overindulgent with somebody ○ *Her fond parents could deny her nothing.* **5. TOO OPTIMISTIC** foolishly unrealistic ○ *fond hopes* [14C. Probably < past participle of obsolete *fon* "be foolish" < *fon* "fool," origin ?] —**fond·ly** *adv* —**fond·ness** *n*

SYNONYMS See *love.*

fond[2] /fond/ *n* a background, especially of a piece of decorated lace [Mid-17C. Via French < Latin *fundus* "bottom"]

fon·da /fóndə/ *n Hispanic* a small, simple restaurant with tables and chairs and a lunch counter, where simple meals are served [Early 19C. Via Spanish < Arabic *funduq*]

Fon·da /fóndə/, **Henry** (1905–82) US movie and stage actor. He is best known for films such as *The Grapes of Wrath* (1940) and *On Golden Pond* (1981), for which he won an Academy Award.

Fon·da, Jane (*b.* 1937) US movie actor and political activist. The daughter of Henry Fonda, she won Academy Awards for *Klute* (1971) and *Coming Home* (1978). She has also written and produced popular exercise books and videotapes.

> "A man has every season, while a woman has only the right to spring."
> [Jane Fonda, *Daily Mail*; September 13, 1989]

Fon·da, Peter (*b.* 1939) US movie actor and director. The son of Henry Fonda, he is best known for the biker film *Easy Rider* (1969). Full name **Fonda, Peter Seymour**

fon·dant /fóndənt/ *n* **1.** a smooth paste made from boiled sugar syrup, often colored or flavored, used as a filling for chocolates or a coating for cakes, nuts, or fruit **2.** a candy made from or filled with fondant [Late 19C. < French, present participle of *fondre* (see FONDUE)]

Fond du Lac /fòn də lák/ industrial city in eastern Wisconsin, situated at the southern end of Lake Winnebago. Population: 42,295 (2002 estimate).

fon·dle /fónd'l/ (**-dled, -dling, -dles**) *v* **1.** *vt* to stroke, handle, or touch something or somebody gently, in a loving or affectionate way ○ *idly fondling the cat's ears* **2.** to touch or caress somebody in an aggressive or unwelcome way [Late 17C. Back-formation < obsolete *fondling* "foolish person" < FOND[1]] —**fon·dler** *n*

fon·due /fon dóo, -dyóo/, **fon·du** *n* a dish eaten by dipping small pieces of food into the contents of a pot, usually melted cheese, hot oil, or a sauce, placed on the table [Late 19C. < French, form of past participle of *fondre* "melt" < Latin *fundere*]

Fon·se·ca, Gulf of /fawn sáykə/ large inlet of the Pacific Ocean on the western coast of Central America, south of El Salvador, west of Honduras, and north of Nicaragua. Area: 749 sq. mi./1,940 sq. km.

font[1] /font/ *n* **1. RECEPTACLE FOR BAPTISMAL WATER** a large container in a Christian church that holds the water sprinkled in baptisms **2. RECEPTACLE FOR HOLY WATER** a container for holy water, usually found at the entrance to a Roman Catholic church **3. ABUNDANT SOURCE OF SOMETHING** somebody or something seen as a source or inexhaustible supply of something (*literary*) **4. FOUNTAIN** a fountain, spring, or well (*literary*) [Pre-12C. < Latin *font-*, stem of *fons* "spring"] —**font·al** *adj*

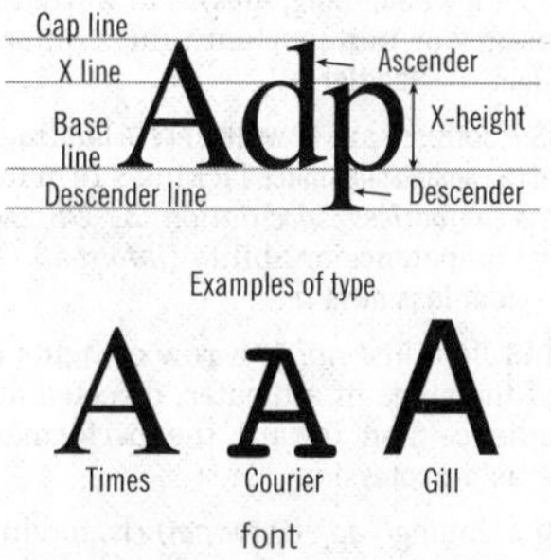

font

font[2] /font/ *n* a full set of printing type or of printed or screen characters of the same design and size [Late 16C. < Old French *fonte* "casting" < *fondre* (see FONDUE)]

Fon·taine /fon táyn/, **Pierre-François-Léonard** (1762–1853) French architect. With his partner Charles Percier, he introduced the Empire style of architecture, designing monumental projects such as the *Champs Elysées* (1806).

Fon·taine·bleau /fóntin blṑ, fàwN ten blṑ/ town in the Ile-de-France Region on the Seine River in France, about 40 mi./64 km southeast of Paris, the site of a magnificent 16th-century chateau. Population: 15,942 (1999).

Fon·tan·a /fon tánnə/ city in southern California, directly southeast of the San Gabriel Mountain and west of San Bernardino. Population: 143,607 (2002 estimate).

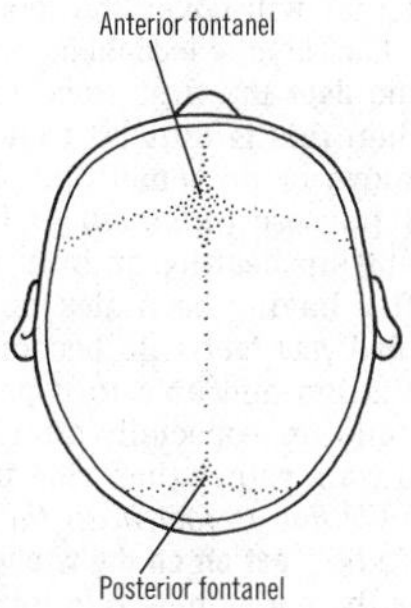

fontanel

fon·ta·nel /fòntə nél/, **fon·ta·nelle** *n* a soft, membrane-covered space between the bones at the front and the back of a young baby's skull [15C. < Old French *fontenel* "little spring" < *fontaine* (see FOUNTAIN)]

Fon·tanne /fon tán/, **Lynn** (1887?–1983) British-born US stage actress. She often worked with her husband, Alfred Lunt, on Broadway and in touring productions.

Dame Margot Fonteyn

Fon·teyn /fon táyn/, **Dame Margot** (1919–91) British ballet dancer. She was known for her role as Aurora in *The Sleeping Beauty* and her partnership with Rudolf Nureyev during the 1960s and 1970s. Born **Hookham, Margaret**

> "I'm sure if everyone knew how physically cruel dancing really is, nobody would watch—only those people who enjoy bull-fights!"
> [Dame Margot Fonteyn. Quoted in *The Art of Margot Fonteyn*, Keith Money; 1965]

fon·ti·na /fon téénə/ *n* a semihard mild Italian cheese made from cows' milk [Mid-20C. < Italian dialect]

foo /foo/ *n US* a term used as a universal substitute for something real, especially when discussing technological ideas and problems (*slang*) ○ *I don't know what's wrong, maybe the computer has bad foo.* ○ *Can her foo be trusted with this software?*

food /food/ *n* **1. SOURCE OF NUTRIENTS** material that provides living things with the nutrients they need for energy and growth **2. SOLID NOURISHMENT** substances, or a particular substance, providing nourishment for people or animals, especially in solid as opposed to liquid form ○ *gave them food and water* **3. MENTAL STIMULUS** something that sustains or stimulates the mind or soul ○ *food for thought* [Old English *fōda* < Indo-European]

food ad·di·tive *n* a natural or artificial substance that is added to food during processing to make it look or taste better or last longer

Food and Drug Ad·min·is·tra·tion *n* full form of **FDA**

food bank *n* a place where food is collected before being distributed to people without the money to buy food

food chain *n* a hierarchy of different living things, each of which feeds on the one below

food court *n* the part of a shopping mall where snacks and light meals can be bought from a number of different outlets, often with a communal eating area

food fish *n* any fish that people eat

food hall *n* the part of a department store where food is sold

food·ie /fóodee/, **food·y** (*plural* **-ies**) *n* an enthusiast of cooking, eating, or shopping for good food (*informal*)

food poi·son·ing *n* acute inflammation of the mucous membrane of the stomach and intestines caused by eating food contaminated with toxic substances or with microorganisms that generate toxins

food pro·ces·sor *n* an electrical kitchen appliance consisting of a container in which food can be cut, sliced, shredded, grated, blended, beaten, or liquidized automatically by a variety of removable revolving blades

food stamp *n* a coupon that can be used to buy food, given by the government to people without the money to buy food

food·stuff /fóod stùf/ *n* something that can be eaten, especially one of the basic components of the human diet (*usually used in the plural*)

food sup·ple·ment *n* PHARM same as **supplement** *n* (sense 4)

food web *n* the interlocking food chains within an ecological community

food·y *n* another spelling of **foodie**

foo·fa·raw /fóofə ràw/ *n* **1.** ornate or excessive ornamentation or finery **2.** a great fuss over something trivial [Mid-20C. Origin ?]

fool /fool/ *n* **1. UNINTELLIGENT PERSON** somebody considered to lack good sense or judgment ○ *Only a fool would invest in this scheme.* **2. RIDICULOUS PERSON** somebody considered to be or made to appear ridiculous ○ *I feel like such a fool dressed this way.* **3.** FOOD **CREAMY FRUIT DESSERT** a cold dessert made from puréed fruit mixed with cream or custard **4. COURT ENTERTAINER** formerly, somebody employed to amuse a monarch or noble, usually by telling jokes, singing comical songs, or performing tricks **5.** *US* **ENTHUSIAST** somebody who is talented at, interested in, or fond of a particular thing ○ *a dancing fool* **6. OFFENSIVE TERM** an offensive term for somebody with below-average intelligence or a psychiatric disorder (*archaic*) ■ *adj* **UNINTELLIGENT AND NOT SENSIBLE** showing a lack of good sense or judgment (*informal*) ○ *That fool salesperson said it would fit.* ■ *v* (**fooled, fool·ing, fools**) **1.** *vt* **TRICK SOMEBODY** to trick or deceive somebody ○ *Don't be fooled by her promises.* **2.** *vi* **SPEAK IN JEST** to say something jokingly or not seriously, or pretend, jokingly, that something false is true ○ *I was only fooling – of course you can come.* **3.** *vi* **BEHAVE COMICALLY** to behave in a comical, playful, or silly way [13C. Via Old French *fol* "fool, foolish" < Latin *follis* "bellows, windbag"] ◇ **be nobody's fool** to be wise enough not to be easily deceived ◇ **make a fool (out) of somebody** to deceive or trick somebody, or make somebody look ridiculous ◇ **make a fool of yourself** to act in a foolish, ridiculous, or embarrassing way

fool around *vi* **1. BEHAVE IRRESPONSIBLY** to behave in a thoughtless or irresponsible way ○ *Don't fool around with those tools.* **2. CLOWN AROUND** to behave in a silly or comical way **3. WASTE TIME** to waste time by doing silly or unimportant things **4. HAVE CASUAL SEX** to participate in casual or illicit sexual relationships

fool away *vt US* to waste time or money in an aimless manner or on foolish things ○ *fooled away the summer playing computer games*

fool with *vt* to treat or handle somebody or something

without due care or respect ○ *Who's been fooling with the TV?*

fool·er·y /fo͞oləree/ (*plural* **-ies**) *n* (*dated*) **1.** irresponsible or playful behavior **2.** an irresponsible or playful act

fool·har·dy /fo͞ol haardee/ *adj* showing boldness or courage but not wisdom or good sense —**fool·har·di·ly** *adv* —**fool·har·di·ness** *n*

fool·ish /fo͞olish/ *adj* **1.** NOT SENSIBLE showing, or resulting from, a lack of good sense or judgment ○ *foolish behavior* **2.** SEEMING RIDICULOUS feeling or appearing ridiculous ○ *Wipe that foolish grin off your face!* **3.** *US* EMBARRASSED unsure about the appropriateness of one's actions or speech ○ *I felt foolish with everyone watching.* **4.** UNIMPORTANT lacking importance or substance ○ *a foolish little worry* —**fool·ish·ly** *adv* —**fool·ish·ness** *n*

fool·proof /fo͞ol pro͞of/ *adj* **1.** designed to continue working properly in the face of any kind of human error, incompetence, or misuse **2.** so well thought out that failure is thought to be impossible

fool's cap *n* **1.** a brightly colored cap with points ending in bells or tassels, worn by court jesters **2.** *US* EDUC same as **dunce cap**

fools·cap /fo͞olz kàp/ *n* **1.** a large size of paper, approximately 13.5 in./34.3 cm by 17 in./43.2 cm, mostly used for writing and printing **2.** *US* CLOTHING same as **fool's cap** [Late 17C. In sense 1 < the watermark of a fool's cap originally on the paper]

fool's er·rand *n* a task that is performed for no good reason or that fails to accomplish anything useful

fool's gold *n* a sulfide mineral with a golden luster, especially pyrite

fool's mate *n* in chess, the quickest checkmate, achieved on the second move by the player with the black pieces

fool's par·a·dise *n* a state of happiness that is temporary and insubstantial because it is based on illusions or unrealistic hopes ○ *living in a fool's paradise*

fool's-pars·ley *n* a poisonous weed with finely divided leaves that resemble parsley and white flowers. Native to: Europe, naturalized in North America. Latin name: *Aethusa cynapium.*

foos·ball /fo͞oz bàwl/ *n* a game based on soccer that is played on a table with rows of small model players. The models are attached to metal poles that pass through the sides of the table and are spun and moved from side to side in order to hit the ball.

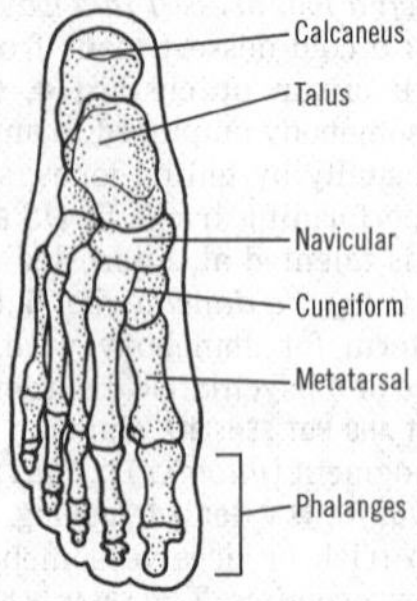

foot: bone structure of a human foot

foot /fo͝ot/ *n* (*plural* **feet** /feet/) **1.** END OF LEG the part of the leg of a vertebrate below the ankle joint that supports the rest of the body and maintains balance when standing and walking ○ *The wave knocked me off my feet.* **2.** ORGAN OF ATTACHMENT an organ or muscle surface that an invertebrate such as a mollusk uses to grip or move itself along **3.** UNIT OF LENGTH a unit of length in the US customary and British imperial systems equal to 12 in./30.48 cm ○ *The aircraft is cruising at 30,000 feet.* Symbol ' **4.** LOWEST PART the bottom or lowest part of something ○ *scribbled at the foot of the page* **5.** PART OF SOCK OR BOOT the part of a sock, stocking, or boot that is shaped to cover the foot **6.** PART LIKE FOOT something that is shaped like or acts like a human or animal foot, e.g., a shaped part at the end of the leg of a chair **7.** WAY OF WALKING a particular way of walking (*literary*) **8.** BOT LOWER PART OF PLANT the lower part of the stem of a plant, or the base of the spore-producing body (**sporophyte**) of mosses and liverworts **9.** HANDICRAFT PART OF SEWING MACHINE the part of a sewing machine, close to the needle, that is lowered onto the material to hold it in position. Most sewing machines have detachable and interchangeable feet for different functions. **10.** MIL SOLDIERS WHO FIGHT ON FOOT soldiers who fight principally on foot, rather than on horses or in vehicles (*takes a plural verb*) ○ *commanding a company of foot* **11.** LITERAT UNIT OF POETIC METER a basic unit of rhythm in poetry, made up of a fixed combination of stressed and unstressed or long and short syllables ■ **foots** /fo͝ots/ *npl* FOOD INDUST SEDIMENT the solid material that gradually falls to the bottom of various liquids such as vegetable oil ■ *vt* (**foot·ed, foot·ing, foots**) **1.** PAY FULL COST OF SOMETHING to pay the full amount of something ○ *We had to foot the bill for the party.* **2.** ADD UP NUMBERS to add up the figures in a column ○ *footed up the columns of the budget* **3.** MAKE FOOT OF SOCK in knitting or sewing, to add the part that will cover the foot to a sock or stocking [Old English *fōt* < Indo-European] —**foot·ed** *adj* ◇ **a foot in the door** the first stage toward a goal, especially when this is difficult to achieve ◇ **drag your feet** to move or do something slowly and reluctantly on purpose (*informal*) ◇ **fall** *or* **land on your feet** to end up healthy or in a good position, especially after having been sick or in a difficult situation ◇ **find your feet 1.** to become accustomed to a new situation and able to cope with it **2.** to manage to stand up, especially after having fallen ◇ **foot it 1.** to walk rather than ride in a vehicle or on a horse ○ *We had to foot it all the way home.* **2.** to dance (*dated*) ◇ **get off on the wrong foot** to begin something badly, e.g., a new relationship or job ◇ **get on** *or* **to your feet 1.** to rise from a reclining or sitting position **2.** to return to a healthy or financially stable condition after a period of illness or financial difficulty ◇ **have somebody** *or* **something at your feet** to be the object of enormous admiration and devotion from somebody or something ◇ **have feet of clay** to have a weakness or flaw that is not obvious at first ◇ **have** *or* **keep both** *or* **your feet on the ground** to act and think sensibly and realistically ◇ **land on your feet** same as **fall** *or* **land on your feet** ◇ **on foot** walking, as opposed to riding on horseback or in a vehicle ◇ **put your best foot forward** to try as hard as you can to impress or please somebody ◇ **put your feet up** to stop working and relax ◇ **put your foot down 1.** to be firm about something and make sure your wishes are obeyed or respected **2.** to make a motor vehicle travel faster by pressing the accelerator ◇ **put your foot in it, put your foot in your mouth** to make an embarrassing mistake, especially by being tactless (*informal*) ◇ **set foot in** *or* **on something** to go to or into a place ○ *I'll never set foot in that place again.* ◇ **shoot yourself in the foot** to do something that unexpectedly turns out to be disadvantageous or harmful to your own interests ◇ **sweep somebody off his** *or* **her feet** to charm somebody completely or make him or her fall in love with you in a very short time

ORIGIN The Indo-European word from which ***foot*** is ultimately derived is also the ancestor of English *antipodes, impede, octopus, pawn*², *pedal*¹, *pedestal, pedestrian, pedigree, pioneer, podium, tripod,* and *vamp*².

foot·age /fo͝ottij/ *n* **1.** a shot or sequence of shots on film or videotape, usually of a particular scene or event, or the length of film or videotape that contains these shots ○ *They had some good footage of the president's visit to the island.* **2.** the size or amount of something measured in feet

foot-and-mouth dis·ease *n* a highly contagious viral disease affecting animals with divided hooves, especially cattle, sheep, and pigs, in which the animal develops ulcers in the mouth and near the hooves

foot·ball /fo͝ot bàwl/ *n* **1.** *US* GAME PLAYED WITH OVAL BALL a game in which 2 teams of 11 players score points by carrying an oval ball across their opponents' goal line or by kicking the ball through the opponents' goal posts. Can term **American football 2.** *UK* same as **soccer 3.** *Can* CANADIAN FOOTBALL a game that is similar to US football but takes place on a larger field, has 12 players on each team, and uses 3 rather than 4 plays to advance at least 10 yards or score **4.** BALL GAME any game in which two teams kick or carry a ball into a goal or over a line, e.g., rugby, Australian Rules, or Gaelic football **5.** BALL USED IN FOOTBALL the large oval ball used in the game of football **6.** PROBLEM PASSED AROUND a point or problem that is used as an excuse for argument by opposing groups, without any real attempt at finding a solution ○ *a political football* **7.** *US* BRIEFCASE WITH NUCLEAR CODES the briefcase that holds the nuclear codes available to the president of the United States (*informal*) —**foot·ball·er** *n*

foot·bath /fo͝ot bàth/ (*plural* **-baths** /-bàths, -bàthz/) *n* **1.** a bowl used when bathing the feet, or a shallow pool where people can disinfect their feet before entering a swimming pool **2.** the action of bathing the feet

foot·board /fo͝ot bàwrd/ *n* **1.** a vertical part across the bottom end of a bedstead **2.** a board or small platform used to support the feet in a vehicle

foot·boy /fo͝ot bòy/ *n* a boy employed as a servant or page

foot brake *n* a brake operated by pressing a pedal with the foot, especially in a motor vehicle

foot·bridge /fo͝ot brìj/ *n* a narrow bridge suitable for people walking and not for vehicles

foot-drag·ger *n* somebody who is slow or reluctant to do what is required (*informal*) —**foot-drag·ging** *n*

foot·er /fo͝ottər/ *n* **1.** a piece of text, e.g., a title or date, below the main text on a page, especially one that is automatically inserted on each page by word-processing software **2.** somebody or something of a particular height or length in feet (*usually used in combination*) ○ *Both of her sons were six-footers.* **3.** ARCHIT, CONSTR same as **footing** (sense 5) [Early 17C. < FOOT]

foot·fall /fo͝ot fàwl/ *n* **1.** the sound made by somebody's foot coming into contact with the ground as he or she walks **2.** the number of potential customers who visit a store or business in a given period

foot fault *n* in tennis, a fault committed by a server whose foot touches any part of the baseline or court before the ball has been hit —**foot-fault** *vi*

foot·gear /fo͝ot geer/ *n* coverings worn on the feet, especially shoes and boots

foot·hill /fo͝ot hìl/ *n* a hill at the bottom of a higher mountain or mountain range and forming part of the approaches to it (*often used in the plural*)

foot·hold /fo͝ot hōld/ *n* **1.** a secure starting position from which further advances can be made ○ *The company has gained a foothold in the multimedia industry.* **2.** a place or thing that will support the foot of a climber, especially a crack, hollow, or ledge in a rock face

foot·ing /fo͝otting/ *n* **1.** STABILITY OF FEET a stable secure position for or placement of the feet when standing or walking ○ *He lost his footing on the icy slope.* **2.** BASE FOR PROGRESS a foundation or basis for further advancement or development ○ *gives the organization a firm footing* **3.** STATUS the status or condition of something, often in relation to something else ○ *The government moved swiftly to place the armed forces on a war footing.* ○ *put the discussion on a more scientific footing* **4.** RELATIONSHIP the position or status of people in relation to one another ○ *back on a friendly footing* **5.** ARCHIT, CONSTR FOUNDATION the foundation or base of a structure such as a wall or column **6.** *US* CONDITION OF SURFACE the condition of a surface for walking or running such as a racetrack **7.** *US* TOTAL the total of a column of figures

foo·tle /fo͞ot'l/ (**-tled, -tling, -tles**) *vi* to waste time doing unnecessary or unimportant things (*informal*) [Late 19C. Origin ?] —**foo·tler** *n*

foot·less /fo͝otləss/ *adj* **1.** WITHOUT FEET lacking a foot or feet **2.** *US* LACKING SUBSTANCE lacking a firm foundation or basis ○ *footless speculation* **3.** *US* LACKING SKILL lacking competence or ability (*informal*) —**foot·less·ly** *adv* —**foot·less·ness** *n*

foot·lights /fo͝ot lìts/ *npl* **1.** a row of lights along the front of the stage in a theater, directed away from the audience and toward the performers **2.** the theater as a profession

foo·tling /fo͞otling/ *adj* (*informal*) **1.** having no importance or serious usefulness **2.** lacking skill or competence

foot·lock·er /fŏŏt lòkər/ *n* a strong case or box for personal belongings kept at the foot of somebody's bed, especially in a barracks or dormitory

foot·loose /fŏŏt lŏŏss/ *adj* free to go anywhere and do anything because not limited by personal ties or responsibilities

foot·man /fŏŏtmən/ (*plural* **-men** /-mən/) *n* a man employed as a servant, especially a servant in uniform in a mansion or palace

foot·mark /fŏŏt maark/ *n* same as **footprint** (sense 1)

foot·note /fŏŏt nōt/ *n* **1.** INFORMATION AT FOOT OF PAGE a note at the bottom of a page, giving further information about something mentioned in the text above. A reference number or symbol is usually printed after the relevant word in the text and before the corresponding footnote. **2.** ADDITIONAL DETAIL an extra comment or information added to what has just been said ○ *As a footnote, let me say that I only found this out yesterday.* **3.** MINOR DETAIL a relatively unimportant part of a larger issue or event ○ *His career is now just a footnote in history.* ■ *vt* (**-not·ed, -not·ing, -notes**) SUPPLY TEXT WITH FOOTNOTES to provide a text with footnotes, or provide a footnote for a particular reference within the text

foot·pad[1] /fŏŏt pàd/ *n* a flat structure at the bottom of a leg of a spacecraft, designed to prevent the craft sinking into the surface it has landed on [< PAD[1]]

foot·pad[2] /fŏŏt pàd/ *n* somebody who robs people who are traveling on foot (*archaic*) [Late 17C. < obsolete *pad* "path, highwayman" < Dutch]

foot pas·sen·ger *n* a passenger on a car ferry who is not traveling with a motor vehicle

foot·path /fŏŏt pàth/ (*plural* **-paths** /-pàthz, -pàths/) *n* a narrow path for people on foot

foot-pound *n* in physics, a unit of work equal to the work done by lifting a mass of one pound vertically against gravity through a distance of one foot

foot-pound-sec·ond *adj* relating or belonging to a system of measurements based on the foot, pound, and second as base units of length, mass, and time

foot-pound-sec·ond u·nits, foot-pound-sec·ond sys·tem of u·nits *n* MEASURE, PHYS same as **fps units**

foot·print /fŏŏt prìnt/ *n* **1.** OUTLINE OF FOOT a mark made by the foot of a person or animal or a shoe, especially an indentation on something soft like snow or a dirty mark on a floor ○ *footprints in the ground below the window* **2.** AREA OF SURFACE an area of a surface, especially the amount of space a piece of computer hardware occupies on a desk, or a spacecraft's target landing area on the moon or a planet **3.** AREA WHERE SOMETHING IS EFFECTIVE the area over which something occurs or is effective, e.g., the area where a signal from a communications satellite can be received **4.** TROOP PRESENCE IN AREA the presence, quantity, type, and defined mission of armed troops deployed to a region, nation, or area, e.g., for combat or peacekeeping duties ○ *The administration has not yet decided the size of the US Army's footprint in that region.*

foot·race /fŏŏt ràyss/, **foot race** *n* a race run by people on foot

foot·rest /fŏŏt rèst/ *n* a support for both feet when sitting down, e.g., beneath a desk, or for one foot while standing, e.g., a low rail at a bar

foot·rope /fŏŏt rōp/ *n* **1.** a rope to which the lower edge of a sail is stitched **2.** a rope fixed beneath a ship's yard for sailors to stand on as they furl a sail

foot rot, foot·rot /fŏŏt ròt/ *n* **1.** VET, AGRIC a bacterial infection of sheep and cattle that causes inflammation of the hooves **2.** a fungal disease that causes the roots and base of a plant to rot

foot rule *n* a strip of wood, metal, or plastic, used for measuring and drawing straight lines, that is one foot long or is marked in feet

foot·sie /fŏŏtsee/ *n* a form of flirtation in which people use their feet to touch the feet and legs of somebody else, especially done secretly while sitting at a table (*informal*) ◇ **play footsie** (*informal*) **1.** to engage in footsie **2.** *US* to collaborate with another person or organization, often in an underhand way

foot·slog /fŏŏt slòg/ (**-slogged, -slog·ging, -slogs**) *vi* to march, tramp, or trudge on foot, especially over difficult ground such as thick mud —**foot·slog·ger** *n* —**foot·slog·ging** *n*

foot sol·dier *n* **1.** a soldier who fights principally on foot, not on horseback or in a vehicle **2.** somebody who does routine but essential work

foot·sore /fŏŏt sàwr/ *adj* with feet that are painful or tired, usually from too much walking —**foot·sore·ness** *n*

foot·stall /fŏŏt stàwl/ *n* the pedestal or base of a structure, especially a pillar or statue

foot·step /fŏŏt stèp/ *n* **1.** SOUND OF SOMEBODY WALKING the sound made when somebody's foot hits the ground in walking ○ *I heard footsteps on the stairs.* **2.** MOVEMENT OF FOOT WHEN WALKING the action of raising a foot and putting it down somewhere else while walking **3.** DISTANCE COVERED BY STEP the distance covered by a single step in walking **4.** MARK MADE BY FOOT a mark left by the sole of a foot or shoe **5.** STEP OR STAIR a single step or stair on which to put a foot while moving up or down ◇ **follow in somebody's footsteps** to take the same course in life or work as another person in the past

foot·stone /fŏŏt stōn/ *n* a memorial stone at the foot of a grave

foot·stool /fŏŏt stŏŏl/ *n* a low stool, often with a padded top, on which to rest the feet while sitting down

foot·wall /fŏŏt wàwl/ *n* the rock layer that lies immediately beneath a vein of ore or other mineral deposit or a fault plane

foot·way /fŏŏt wày/ *n* a narrow path or walk for people on foot, e.g., beside a road or railroad

foot·wear /fŏŏt wèr/ *n* coverings worn on the feet, especially shoes, boots, sandals, or slippers, but often including socks or stockings

foot·well /fŏŏt wèl/ *n* the hollow space below a motor vehicle's dashboard where people in the front seats can put their feet

foot·work /fŏŏt wùrk/ *n* **1.** MOTION OF FEET the movement of the feet in sports or dancing, especially when skillfully done **2.** SKILLFUL MANEUVERING skillful or devious maneuvering in order to achieve or avoid something (*informal*) ○ *It took some fancy footwork to make it all happen.* **3.** *US* WORK THAT INVOLVES WALKING work that involves a lot of moving around, especially on foot

foot·worn /fŏŏt wàwrn/ *adj* **1.** worn down or made thin by being walked on by many people for a long time **2.** same as **footsore**

foo yung /foo yáwng, -yúng, -yŏŏng/, **foo young, fu yung** *n Can, UK* FOOD a Chinese-style dish, similar to an omelet, in which the eggs are combined with bean sprouts, onions, and meat or seafood. US term **egg foo yung** [Mid-20C. < Cantonese *foō yung* "hibiscus"]

foo·zle /fŏŏz'l/ *vti* (**-zled, -zling, -zles**) to do something badly or clumsily, especially to bungle a shot in golf ■ *n* something done badly or clumsily, especially a bungled shot in golf [Mid-19C. Origin ?] —**foo·zler** *n*

fop /fop/ *n* a man who is so obsessed by fashion and vain about his own appearance that he becomes ridiculous [15C. Origin ?] —**fop·per·y** *n* —**fop·pish** *adj* —**fop·pish·ly** *adv* —**fop·pish·ness** *n*

for *stressed* /fawr/; *unstressed* /fər/ CORE MEANING: a preposition indicating that something is directed at somebody, done to benefit somebody, or done on somebody's behalf ○ *Look – there's a letter for you.* ○ *I'd do anything for you.* ○ *The lawyer acted for some of the heirs.*

1. *prep* AIMED AT intended to be received or used by somebody, or aimed at somebody ○ *It's for you – it's a present.* ○ *advice for first-time buyers* **2.** *prep* TO BENEFIT OF intending or intended to benefit somebody or something ○ *She would make any sacrifice for the cause.* **3.** *prep* ON BEHALF OF on behalf of somebody or something ○ *Don't make excuses for him.* **4.** *prep* INSTEAD OF instead of or in place of somebody or something, sometimes mistakenly ○ *You'll have to find a stand-in for him while he's away.* ○ *I took her for the boss.* **5.** *prep* IN SERVICE OF in the service or employment of somebody or something ○ *She works for a large company.* **6.** *prep* TOWARD in the direction of ○ *The following day, we headed for Paris.* **7.** *prep* LASTING indicating how long something lasts, continues, or extends ○ *The interview only lasted for a few minutes.* ○ *There was fog for the next mile or so.* **8.** *prep* BECAUSE OF indicating a reason why something happens or is done ○ *I did it for love.* **9.** *prep* DESIGNED TO DO indicating the purpose of an object, action, or activity ○ *That towel is for drying your hands.* **10.** *prep* LINKS CONCEPTS used to link two concepts, one of which is the object of the other ○ *a cause for concern* ○ *a passion for opera* **11.** *prep* IN EXCHANGE FOR at a cost of, or giving or receiving something in exchange ○ *got it for a few dollars* **12.** *prep* AS TRIBUTE TO in honor of ○ *named for its inventor* **13.** *prep* GIVEN WHAT IS USUAL with reference to the normal characteristics of something ○ *It's very warm for April.* **14.** *prep* INDICATING OCCASION at, or planned to be at, a particular time, or on a particular occasion ○ *The meeting was scheduled for four o'clock.* ○ *Will you be home for Christmas?* **15.** *prep* INDICATES COMPARISON indicating a comparison or equivalence between two things ○ *Pound for pound, the elephant's energy consumption is the lowest of all land animals.* **16.** *prep* IN ORDER TO GET in order to get, achieve, have, keep, or become something ○ *Lee's hoping for promotion.* ○ *He was searching for a place to sit.* **17.** *prep* DESPITE in spite of or notwithstanding something ○ *He enjoyed himself very much, for all his complaining.* **18.** *prep* INDICATES RESPONSIBILITY indicating that somebody has the right or responsibility to do something ○ *I can't help you – it's for you to decide.* **19.** *prep* HAVING SAME MEANING AS having the same meaning as another word or phrase ○ *The everyday term for rubella is German measles.* **20.** *prep* INDICATES CROSS-REFERENCE indicating that information can be found elsewhere ○ *For further details, consult the owner's manual.* **21.** *adv, prep* IN SUPPORT OF SOMETHING in favor of or in support of something ○ (prep) *Who's for the motion and who's against it?* ○ (adv) *Ten voted for, and eleven against.* **22.** *conj* BECAUSE for the reason or seeing that (*formal*) ○ *I left in haste, for I was already late for the appointment.* [Old English < Indo-European, "forward"]

USAGE See ***because***.

for. *abbr* **1.** foreign **2.** forestry

for- *prefix* **1.** away, down, falsely ○ *forfend* ○ *forswear* **2.** completely, extremely ○ *forgather* [Old English; related to FOR]

fo·ra plural of **forum**

for·age /fáwrij/ *n* **1.** FOOD FOR ANIMALS food for animals, especially crops grown to feed horses, cattle, and other livestock **2.** SEARCH a search or the process of searching for something, especially a search for food and supplies or a search among a varied collection of things **3.** RAID BY SOLDIERS a raid carried out by soldiers, especially to seize food or supplies ■ *v* (**-aged, -ag·ing, -ag·es**) **1.** *vi* WANDER AROUND SEARCHING to go from place to place looking for food and supplies **2.** *vti* RAID FOR FOOD to raid a place, especially for food or supplies **3.** *vi* SEARCH to engage in a search ○ *He foraged around in the drawer and pulled out a faded photograph.* **4.** *vt* FIND BY SEARCHING to obtain something, especially food, from a place by searching or rummaging ○ *She foraged a half-eaten cake from the trash can.* **5.** *vt* FEED ANIMALS to give forage to horses, cattle, or other animals [14C. < Old French *fourrage* < *fuerre* "fodder, straw" < Germanic] —**for·ag·er** *n*

for·age cap *n Can, UK* MIL same as **service cap**

For·a·ker /fáwrəkər/ mountain in the Alaska Range in Denali National Park and Preserve, southern Alaska. Height: 17,400 ft./5,304 m.

for·am /fáwrəm/ *n* MARINE BIOL same as **foraminifer** [Early 20C. Shortening]

fo·ra·men /fə ráymən/ (*plural* **-ram·i·na** /-rámmənə/ or **-ra·mens**) *n* a natural opening or cavity in a human or animal body, usually one through which blood vessels and nerves pass through bone [Late 17C. < Latin < *forare* "bore a hole"] —**fo·ram·i·nal** /fə rámmən'l/ *adj* —**fo·ram·i·nous** /-fə rámmənəss/ *adj*

fo·ra·men mag·num /fə ràymən mágnəm/ *n* the opening at the base of the skull through which the spinal cord passes to become the medulla oblongata of the brain [Late 19C. < Latin, "large opening"]

fo·ra·men o·val·e /fə ràymən ō vállee, -váylee, -vaálee/ *n* an opening in the wall between the two sides of the fetal heart that allows blood to pass from right to left. Sometimes it fails to close after birth and persists into adulthood. [Mid-19C. < Latin, "oval opening"]

fo·ram·i·na ANAT plural of **foramen**

for·a·min·i·fer /fàwrə mínnəfər/ (*plural* **-fer·a** /-fərə/ or **-fers**) *n* a large protozoan found mainly in seawater that has a shell perforated with many small holes through which temporary cytoplasmic protrusions (**pseudopodia**) project. The calcium-containing shells of foraminifera are the main component of chalk and some limestone deposits. Order: Foraminifera. [Mid-19C. < modern Latin *Foraminifera* (plural) < Latin *foramen* (see FORAMEN) + *-fer* "bearing"] —**fo·ram·i·nif·er·al** /fəràmmə níffərəl/ *adj* —**fo·ram·i·nif·er·ous** /fə ràmmə níffərəss/ *adj*

for·as·much as /fàwrəz múch əz/ *conj* since or in view of the fact that (*archaic*)

for·ay /fáw rày/ *n* **1.** SUDDEN RAID a sudden attack or raid by a military force **2.** EXPLORATION OF SOMETHING UNFAMILIAR an attempt at some new occupation or activity ○ *the ex-salesman's first foray into management* **3.** BRIEF JOURNEY a short trip or visit to a place, usually for a specific purpose ■ *v* (**-ayed, -ay·ing, -ays**) **1.** *vi* MAKE INCURSION to make a sudden attack or raid **2.** *vt* MAKE RAID ON to raid or loot a place [14C. Back-formation < *forayer* < Old French *fourrier* < *fuerre* (see FORAGE)] —**for·ay·er** *n*

forb /fawrb/ *n* any broad-leaved herbaceous plant that is not a grass, especially one that grows in a prairie or meadow [Early 20C. < Greek *phorbē* "food" < *pherbein* "to feed"]

for·bade, **for·bad** past tense of **forbid**

for·bear[1] /fawr bér, fər-/ (**-bore** /-báwr/, **-borne** /-báwrn/, **-bear·ing, -bears**) *v* (*formal*) **1.** *vi* to not do or say something that you could do or say, especially when this shows self-control or consideration for the feelings of others ○ *I forbore to criticize their efforts, though criticism was well deserved.* **2.** *vti* to tolerate something with patience or endurance ○ *willing to forbear their failures* [Old English *forberan*, literally "bear against"] —**for·bear·er** *n* —**for·bear·ing** *adj* —**for·bear·ing·ly** *adv*

USAGE forbear or **forebear**? Either spelling may be used for the noun, meaning "ancestor," but ***forebear*** is the more frequent of the two: *The walls were lined with portraits of his illustrious forebears* [or *forbears*]. ***Forbear*** is the only acceptable spelling for the verb, meaning "hold back" or "tolerate": *We must forbear* [not *forebear*] *from judging people on first impressions.*

for·bear[2] *n* another spelling of **forebear**

for·bear·ance /fawr bérrənss, fər-/ *n* **1.** PATIENCE patience, tolerance, or self-control, especially in not responding to provocation (*formal*) **2.** REFRAINING FROM ACTION the fact of deliberately not doing or saying something when you could do or say it (*formal*) **3.** LAW REFRAINING FROM LEGAL RIGHT the fact of not exercising a legal right, especially of not insisting on payment of a debt at the due date and giving the debtor more time to pay

Forbes /fawrbz/, **B. C.** (1880–1954) US publisher. He was the founder and editor (1916–54) of *Forbes* magazine. Full name **Forbes, Bertie Charles**

Forbes 500 /fàwrbz fīv húndrəd/ *n* the top 500 companies in the United States, as listed by *Forbes* magazine

for·bid /fər bíd, fawr-/ (**-bade** /-bád, -báyd/ or **-bad** /-bád/, **-bid·den** /-bídd'n/ or **-bid, -bid·ding, -bids**) *vt* **1.** ORDER SOMEBODY NOT TO DO SOMETHING to tell somebody, especially forcefully, not to do or have something ○ *I forbid you to mention his name.* **2.** NOT ALLOW SOMETHING to state authoritatively that something must not be done ○ *The rules of the game strictly forbid the use of a dictionary.* **3.** MAKE SOMETHING IMPOSSIBLE to make something impossible, or prevent something from happening (*formal*) ○ *Discretion forbids me to mention any names.* [Old English *forbēodan*, literally "command against"] —**for·bid·dance** *n* —**for·bid·der** *n* ◇ **God** *or* **heaven forbid** used to express the hope that something will not happen or be done

for·bid·den /fər bídd'n, fawr-/ *adj* **1.** NOT PERMITTED not allowed by order of somebody or by law ○ *That's a forbidden subject in this company.* **2.** OUT OF BOUNDS to which entry is not allowed, or allowed only to a specific person or group of people ○ *This part of the temple was forbidden to everybody except the high priest.* **3.** PHYS IMPROBABLE OR DISALLOWED AS ENERGY LEVEL describes an energy level or transition in a quantum mechanical system that is either highly improbable or disobeys selection rules and is therefore not allowed

Barnaby's

Forbidden City: Hall of Supreme Harmony

For·bid·den Cit·y *n* a walled complex of buildings (1421–1911) in Beijing, China, that includes the former Imperial Palace. It was closed to ordinary citizens until 1912 and is now a museum.

for·bid·den fruit (*plural* **for·bid·den fruits** or *same*) *n* something desired or pleasurable that somebody is not allowed to have or do, especially some form of sexual indulgence that is illegal or considered immoral [< the fruit, forbidden to Adam and Eve, of the tree of knowledge of good and evil (Genesis 2:17)]

for·bid·ding /fər bídding, fàwr-/ *adj* **1.** HOSTILE presenting an appearance that seems hostile or stern ○ *The mountains looked distant and forbidding.* **2.** UNINVITING appearing to involve a great deal of unpleasantness or difficulty ○ *the forbidding prospect of further difficulties ahead* **3.** DANGEROUS OR THREATENING appearing to present a danger or threat ○ *a rocky and forbidding shore* —**for·bid·ding·ly** *adv* —**for·bid·ding·ness** *n*

~~**forboding**~~ incorrect spelling of **foreboding**

for·bore past tense of **forbear**[1]

for·borne past participle of **forbear**[1]

force /fawrss/ *n* **1.** NATURAL STRENGTH the power, strength, or energy that somebody or something possesses ○ *Trees were blown down by the force of the storm.* **2.** PHYSICAL POWER physical power, effort, or violence used against somebody or something that resists ○ *The use of force should be a last resort.* **3.** EFFECTIVENESS the condition of being effective, valid, or applicable ○ *The new regulations come into force next week.* **4.** NONPHYSICAL POWER power or strength that is intellectual or moral rather than physical ○ *swayed by the force of your argument* **5.** SOMEBODY OR SOMETHING WITH GREAT INFLUENCE somebody or something that has great power or influence, especially in a particular field ○ *She remained a force in local politics until her death.* **6.** GROUP ORGANIZED TO FIGHT a body of military personnel, ships, or aircraft brought together to fight in a battle or a war ○ *A naval task force has been sent to the area.* **7.** POLICE OFFICERS a professional body of police officers ○ *He left the force in 1985.* **8.** PEOPLE WORKING TOGETHER a group of people who work together for a particular purpose ○ *a sales force* **9.** PHYS INFLUENCE THAT MOVES SOMETHING a physical influence that tends to change the position of an object with mass, equal to the rate of change in momentum of the object. Symbol ***F*** **10.** METEOROL WIND STRENGTH the strength of the wind, especially as measured on the Beaufort scale, from 0 to 12 (*often used in combination*) ○ *a force nine gale* ■ **forc·es** *npl* ORGANIZED MILITARY SERVICE the professional military organizations belonging to a country ○ *Were you in the forces?* ■ *vt* (**forced, forc·ing, forc·es**) **1.** COMPEL SOMEBODY to use superior physical or mental power to make somebody or yourself do something that is not agreeable ○ *The weather forced us to turn back.* ○ *She forced herself to be polite to him.* **2.** MOVE SOMETHING WITH STRENGTH to use physical strength or violence to move something or somebody that puts up resistance ○ *If the key won't turn easily, don't force it.* ○ *I had to force the last bit of toothpaste out of the tube.* ○ *She forced the dog back into the house.* **3.** CREATE PASSAGE BY STRENGTH to create a way or passage through something using physical strength or another kind of power ○ *They forced a path through the jungle.* **4.** OBTAIN SOMETHING BY PRESSURE to obtain something or make something happen by using physical or mental pressure ○ *She's been trying to force a confrontation all week.* **5.** BREAK SOMETHING OPEN to open something that is locked or jammed by using power or effort, often breaking or damaging it in the process ○ *This door has been forced.* **6.** STRAIN TO DO SOMETHING to produce or use something in a strained or unnatural way ○ *Just agree with whatever she says and try to force a smile.* **7.** MAKE PLANT MATURE to cause a plant to flower or mature before its normal time **8.** RAPE SOMEBODY to subject somebody to rape (*dated*) **9.** BASEBALL PUT RUNNER OUT in baseball, to put out a runner on a force play **10.** BASEBALL CREATE RUN in baseball, to create a run by walking a batter when the bases are full **11.** CARDS MAKE PLAYER PLAY SPECIFIC WAY in a card game, to give a player no choice but to play a specific card or make a specific bid or move [13C. < Old French < Latin *fortis* "strong"] —**force·a·ble** *adj* —**force·less** *adj* —**forc·er** *n* ◇ **in force 1.** in a large or strong group **2.** effective or valid ◇ **join forces** to combine together, or combine with somebody else, for a joint effort

force down *vt* **1.** to eat or drink something very reluctantly, often because pressured to do so or to avoid offending somebody **2.** to compel an aircraft to land, usually because of lack of fuel, damage, or bad weather

force on, force up·on *vt* to make somebody or a group of people accept something unwillingly ○ *This method was forced on us by headquarters.*

~~**forceably**~~ incorrect spelling of **forcibly**

forced /fawrst/ *adj* **1.** NOT NATURAL not natural or spontaneous, but produced by an act of will ○ *The courtiers greeted the king's witticism with forced laughter.* **2.** NECESSARY not done voluntarily but out of necessity ○ *a forced error* **3.** COMPELLED done because somebody who has power requires it —**forc·ed·ly** /-sədlee/ *adv* —**forc·ed·ness** /-sədnəss/ *n*

forced la·bor *n* work that somebody is made to do against his or her will, often as a punishment or to repay a debt

forced land·ing *n* an unscheduled landing that a pilot of an aircraft is compelled to make, usually because of an emergency

forced march *n* a march of troops or prisoners made as quickly as possible and without the normal amounts of rest

force-feed *vt* **1.** to make people or animals swallow food against their will, e.g., by putting it directly down their throat through a funnel or tube. Animals may be force-fed to fatten them up, and people who refuse to eat may be force-fed to keep them alive. **2.** to make people learn or assimilate things, often without fully understanding them, that they might reject if given the choice

force field *n* in science fiction, an invisible protective barrier around something

force flow *n* the movement and number of troops and their logistics by land, sea, and air into or out of a theater of operations or a deployment zone

force·ful /fáwrssfəl/ *adj* **1.** possessing or characterized by strength and power **2.** tending to make a powerful impression on people or to persuade people ○ *a forceful argument for merging our businesses* —**force·ful·ly** *adv* —**force·ful·ness** *n*

force-land *vti* to land an aircraft before it gets to its destination because of an emergency, or land in these circumstances ○ *The pilot had to force-land in a field.*

force ma·jeure /fàwrss maa zhúr/ *n* **1.** an unexpected event that crucially affects somebody's ability to do something and can be used in law as an excuse for not having carried out the terms of an agreement (*formal*) **2.** a force that is superior in power or impossible to resist [Late 19C. < French, "superior force"]

force-march *vti* to make soldiers or prisoners march somewhere in the shortest possible time and without the normal amounts of rest, or march somewhere in this way ○ *The captured personnel were force-marched north.*

force·meat /fáwrss meet/ *n* finely chopped meat, fish, or vegetables mixed with other ingredients and used as a stuffing or garnish [Late 17C. < variant of FARCE]

force of hab·it *n* the ability of a behavior pattern that has become habitual to reassert itself automatically even in situations where it is no longer appropriate ○ *Even after she retired, she woke at six every morning by force of habit.*

force-out *n* in baseball, an act of putting a base runner out by a force play

force play *n* a baseball play in which a runner, forced to run to the next base because the batter hits the ball, is put out by a fielder at that base

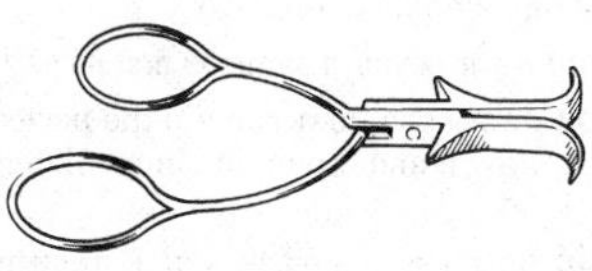

forceps

for·ceps /fáwrssəps, fáwr sèps/ *npl* **1.** a specialized surgical instrument of different designs but always with two parts that move together to hold something such as dressings, tissues, or organs **2.** a body part that is shaped or works like pincers, e.g., the grasping parts of some insects [Mid-16C. < Latin, "pincers"]

force pump *n* a pump that uses pressure to move a liquid

force-ripe *adj* **1.** describes fruit picked before it is ripe, then ripened by squeezing it or storing it in a warm place **2.** *Carib* precocious, especially in sexual matters —**force-rip·en** *vt*

forc·i·ble /fáwrssəb'l/ *adj* **1.** using physical power against somebody or something that resists ○ *the forcible removal of the lock* **2.** having enough power or force to persuade people ○ *It was a forcible reminder that we must be on our guard.* —**forc·i·bil·i·ty** /fàwrssə bíllətee/ *n* —**forc·i·ble·ness** *n* —**forc·i·bly** *adv*

ford /fawrd/ *n* a shallow part of a river or stream where people, animals, or vehicles can cross it ■ *vt* (**ford·ed, ford·ing, fords**) to walk, ride, or drive across a river or stream at a place where the water is shallow [Old English < Germanic] —**ford·a·ble** *adj*

Ford /fawrd/, **Elizabeth Bloomer** (*b.* 1918) US First Lady (1974–77). She helped establish the Betty Ford Center for the treatment of alcohol and drug abuse. Known as **Betty**

Ford, Ford Madox (1873–1939) British novelist. His masterpiece was *The Good Soldier* (1915). He founded the *English Review* (1908). Born **Hueffer, Ford Hermann**. See Cultural note at **soldier**

> "Only two classes of books are of universal appeal. The very best and the very worst."
> [Ford Madox Ford, *Joseph Conrad*; 1924]

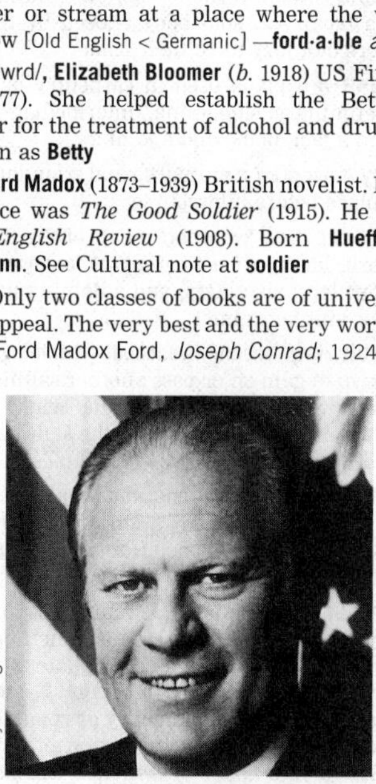

Library of Congress

Gerald R. Ford

Ford, Gerald R. (*b.* 1913) 38th president of the United States. A Republican, he was the only president (1974–77) elected neither president nor vice president, having attained those posts following the resignations of Richard Nixon and Spiro Agnew, respectively. Full name **Ford, Gerald Rudolph**. See table at **president**

> "Our long national nightmare is over. Our constitution works..."
> [Gerald R. Ford, *Gerald R. Ford*, J. G. Lankevich; 1977]

Ford, Glenn (*b.* 1916) Canadian-born US movie actor. His movies include *The Big Heat* (1953) and *Blackboard Jungle* (1955). Born **Newton Ford, Gwyllyn Samuel**

Ford, Harrison (*b.* 1942) US movie actor. He is best known for his roles as Han Solo in the *Star Wars* trilogy (1977–83) and as Indiana Jones in the *Raiders of the Lost Ark* trilogy (1981–89).

> "Los Angeles is where you've got to be an actor. You have no choice. You go there or New York. I flipped a coin...It came up New York. So I flipped it again."
> [Harrison Ford, *Cinema*; 1981]

Library of Congress

Henry Ford

Ford, Henry (1863–1947) US industrialist, best known for his pioneering achievements in the automobile industry. In 1903 he founded a major motor company, introducing assembly-line production on a massive scale.

> "The whole secret of a successful life is to find out what it is one's destiny to do, and then do it."
> [Henry Ford, "Success," *Forum*; October 1928]

> "History is more or less bunk."
> [Henry Ford. Interview with Charles N. Wheeler, *Chicago Tribune*; May 25, 1916]

Ford, John (1895–1973) US movie director. Winner of six Academy Awards, he is best known for his work on classic Westerns, including *Stagecoach* (1939). Born **O'Fearna, Sean Aloysius**

> "It is easier to get an actor to be a cowboy than to get a cowboy to be an actor."
> [Attributed to John Ford]

Forde /fawrd/, **Frank** (1890–1983) Australian politician. He was briefly a caretaker prime minister of Australia in July 1945 after the death of John Curtin. Full name **Forde, Francis Michael**. See table at **prime minister**

fore /fawr/ *adj* AT FRONT having a position at or near the front of something, especially a ship, an aircraft, or an animal ■ *adv* TOWARD FRONT at or toward the front, especially of a ship or aircraft ■ *n* FRONT the front of something, or something at the front (*literary*) ■ *interj* GOLF WARNING ABOUT GOLF BALL used to warn people that you are hitting a golf ball in their direction [Old English, "before, previously" < Germanic] ◇ **to the fore** to a position of prominence or importance

fore- *prefix* **1.** before, earlier ○ *forejudge* **2.** front, in front ○ *forebrain* [Old English < *fore* (see FORE)]

fore-and-aft *adj* parallel to or running along the length of something, especially a ship

fore-and-af·ter *n* a boat with a fore-and-aft rig

fore-and-aft rig *n* an arrangement of a ship's sails such that, when set, they are parallel to the length of the vessel

fore-and-aft sail *n* a quadrilateral sail that extends behind the mast rather than across the boat. The upper edge is supported by a pole (**gaff**) attached to the mast. Bermuda rigs are fore-and-aft sails.

fore·arm[1] /fáwr aàrm/ *n* the part of the human arm between the elbow and the wrist, or the corresponding part of an animal's foreleg

fore·arm[2] /fawr aárm/ (**-armed, -arm·ing, -arms**) *vt* to prepare or arm somebody in advance

fore·arm smash *n* a blow struck with the forearm in wrestling

fore·bear /fáwr bèr/, **for·bear** *n* an ancestor, especially one who died a long time ago (*often used in the plural*) [15C. < FORE- + variant of obsolete *beer* "somebody who is" < BE[1]]

USAGE See *forbear*[1].

fore·bode /fawr bṓd/ (**-bod·ed, -bod·ing, -bodes**) *vti* (*formal*) **1.** to be or give an advance warning of something that may happen, especially something undesirable ○ *The gathering clouds foreboded a terrible storm.* **2.** to have a feeling that something bad is going to happen before it does —**fore·bod·er** *n*

fore·bod·ing /fawr bṓding/ *n* **1.** PREMONITION a feeling that something bad is going to happen **2.** BAD OMEN a sign or warning that something bad is going to happen ■ *adj* OMINOUS indicating, warning, or suggesting that something undesirable is likely to happen —**fore·bod·ing·ly** *adv* —**fore·bod·ing·ness** *n*

fore·brain /fáwr bràyn/ *n* the front section of the brain in adults, or the part farthest forward of the three parts of the brain in an embryo

fore·cad·die /fáwr kàddee/ *n* in golf, a caddie who watches from the fairway to see where the balls land

fore·cast /fáwr kàst/ *vt* (**-cast·ed, -cast** or **-cast·ed, -cast·ing, -casts**) **1.** SUGGEST WHAT WILL HAPPEN to predict or work out something that is likely to happen such as the weather conditions for the days ahead **2.** BE EARLY SIGN OF SOMETHING to be an advance indication of something that is likely or certain to happen ■ *n* **1.** WEATHER PREDICTION a prediction of weather conditions for the near future, usually broadcast on television or radio or printed in a newspaper ○ *Have you heard the forecast for tomorrow?* **2.** PREDICTION OF FUTURE DEVELOPMENTS an estimation or calculation of what is likely to happen in the future, especially in business or finance —**fore·cast·a·ble** *adj* —**fore·cast·er** *n*

fore·cas·tle /fṓks'l, fáwr kàss'l/, **fo'c's'le** /fṓks'l/ *n* **1.** the space at the front end of a ship below the main deck, traditionally where the crew's quarters were located **2.** a raised section of deck at the bow of a ship

fore-check *vi* in hockey, to check a player of an opposing team in the opposition's defensive zone —**fore-check·er** *n*

fore·close /fawr klṓz/ (**-closed, -clos·ing, -clos·es**) *v* **1.** *vti* END MORTGAGE to take away a mortgagee's right to redeem a mortgage, usually because payments have not been made ○ *The bank foreclosed on the property.* **2.** *vt* SHUT SOMEBODY OR SOMETHING OUT to bar or exclude somebody or something (*formal*) **3.** *vt* SETTLE SOMETHING BEFOREHAND to settle or resolve something in advance (*formal*) **4.** *vt* PREVENT SOMETHING to prevent or hinder something (*formal*) **5.** *vt* HOLD SOMETHING EXCLUSIVELY to have an exclusive right or claim to something (*formal*) [13C. < Old French *forclos*, past participle of *forclore* < Latin *foris* "outside" + *claudere* "shut, close"] —**fore·clos·a·ble** *adj*

fore·clo·sure /fawr klṓzhər/ *n* a legal process by which a mortgagee's right to redeem a mortgage is taken away, usually because of failing to make payments

fore·course /fáwr kàwrss/ *n* a foresail, especially the lowest of a ship's foresails

fore·court /fáwr kàwrt/ *n* **1.** an open area at the front of a building, especially one in front of a service station, hotel, or railroad station **2.** the part of the court nearest the net or front wall in games such as tennis, badminton, and handball

fore·deck /fáwr dèk/ *n* the part of a ship's deck between the bridge and the forecastle

fore·doom /fawr do͞om/ (**-doomed, -doom·ing, -dooms**) *vt* to condemn something or somebody in advance to failure or destruction (*formal; usually passive*)

fore-edge *n* the outer edge of a printed page

fore·fa·ther /fáwr faa̲th̲ər/ *n* (*often used in the plural*) **1.** a male ancestor, usually one who died long ago (*literary*) ○ *in the proud tradition of our forefathers* **2.** a member of an earlier generation from whom traditions, values, or ideas have been inherited

fore·feet ZOOL, NAUT plural of **forefoot**

fore·fend *vt* another spelling of **forfend** (*archaic*)

fore·fin·ger /fáwr fìng gər/ *n* ANAT same as **index finger**

fore·foot /fáwr fo͝ot/ (*plural* **-feet** /-fe̅et/) *n* **1.** either of the front feet of a four-legged animal **2.** the front end of a ship's keel

fore·front /fáwr frùnt/ *n* **1.** the most prominent, important, active, or responsible position in something **2.** the part at or nearest the front of something

fore·gath·er *vi* another spelling of **forgather** (*formal*)

fore·go[1] /fawr gṓ/ (**-went** /-wént/, **-gone** /-gáwn, -gón/, **-go·ing, -goes**) *vti* to go or come before something in position, time, or sequence (*archaic*) —**fore·go·er** *n*

fore·go[2] *vt* another spelling of **forgo**

fore·go·ing /fawr gṓ ing, fáwr gṑ ing/ (*formal*) *adj* going or coming before something, especially in speech or writing ■ *n* in speech or writing, the thing or things just mentioned (*takes a singular or plural verb*) ○ *As is evident from the foregoing, much remains to be done.*

fore·gone /fáwr gàwn, -gòn/ *adj* previously completed or determined

fore·gone con·clu·sion *n* something that will inevitably happen as a result of something else

fore·ground /fáwr gròwnd/ *n* **1.** PART THAT APPEARS NEAREST the part of a picture or scene that appears nearest the viewer **2.** same as **forefront** (sense 1) ■ *adj* COMPUT CURRENTLY RECEIVING COMMANDS currently receiving commands, usually through the keyboard, while other programs are operating independently ○ *foreground processing* ■ *vt* (**-ground·ed, -ground·ing, -grounds**) HIGHLIGHT SOMETHING to put something in an important position and so draw attention to it

fore·gut /fáwr gùt/ *n* the front end of the embryonic gut in animals. In vertebrates it develops into the pharynx, esophagus, stomach, and top part of the intestines.

fore·hand /fáwr hànd/ *n* **1.** STROKE IN RACKET GAMES in racket games, a basic stroke played with the palm of the racket hand facing forward **2.** RIDING FRONT PART OF HORSE the part of a horse in front of the rider and saddle ■ *adj* PLAYED AS FOREHAND in racket games, played with the palm of the racket hand facing forward, or relating to a stroke played in this way ■ *adv* RACKET GAMES WITH FOREHAND STROKE in racket games, with a forehand stroke or action ■ *vt* (**-hand·ed, -hand·ing, -hands**) PLAY BALL WITH FOREHAND STROKE in racket games, to hit the ball with a forehand stroke

fore·hand·ed /fawr hándəd/ *adj, adv* RACKET GAMES same as **forehand** ■ *adj US* (*literary*) **1.** prudent about saving money **2.** financially well-off —**fore·hand·ed·ly** *adv* —**fore·hand·ed·ness** *n*

fore·head /fáwrəd, fáwr hèd/ *n* the part of the face above the eyebrows, below the hairline and between the temples

fore·hoof /fáwr ho͝of/ (*plural* **-hooves** /-ho͝ovz/ or **-hoofs**) *n* the hoof of either of the two front legs of a four-legged animal (**quadruped**)

for·eign /fáwrən/ *adj* **1.** OF ANOTHER COUNTRY relating to, from, or located in a country or countries other than your own ○ *She speaks three foreign languages.* **2.** DEALING WITH ANOTHER COUNTRY dealing with or involved with a country or countries other than your own ○ *foreign policy* **3.** COMING FROM OUTSIDE introduced from outside into a place where it does not belong, often in the human body **4.** UNCHARACTERISTIC not usually associated with a particular person or thing ○ *Such outbursts are quite foreign to her nature.* **5.** IRRELEVANT not related or relevant (*formal*) ○ *observations that are foreign to the matter in hand* **6.** LAW BEYOND JURISDICTION being beyond the jurisdiction of an area or a country ○ *foreign waters* [13C. < Old French *forein* < Latin *foras, foris* "out of doors, abroad" < *fores* "door"] —**for·eign·ly** *adv* —**for·eign·ness** *n*

for·eign bill *n* a bill of exchange that is issued in one country but payable in another

for·eign bo·dy *n* an unwanted substance or object that is in a place where it does not belong, especially in somebody's body, often introduced from an external location and causing irritation or contamination

for·eign cor·re·spon·dent *n* a journalist who sends news reports from other countries for broadcast or publication in his or her own country

for·eign draft *n* FIN same as **foreign bill**

for·eign·er /fáwrənər/ *n* **1.** somebody who comes from a country other than your own **2.** somebody who does not feel, or is not deemed to be, part of a group

for·eign ex·change *n* **1.** the conversion of one currency into another, or the buying and selling of different currencies **2.** the currencies of countries other than your own, or international currencies generally

for·eign·ism /fáwrə nìzzəm/ *n* something that is characteristically foreign, especially a custom or idiom

for·eign le·gion *n* a section of an army consisting of foreign volunteers, especially that of the French army

for·eign min·is·ter *n* in many countries, a minister in a government who is responsible for relations with other countries

for·eign min·is·try *n* in many countries, the department of government responsible for relations with other countries

for·eign mis·sion *n* **1.** diplomatic personnel sent to represent their country abroad **2.** missionaries who try to convert the inhabitants of another country to Christianity or another religion

For·eign Of·fice *n* in the United Kingdom and some other countries, the department of the government that is responsible for relations with other countries

for·eign-re·turned *adj S Asia* having lived abroad, especially for education or training, and now back living in South Asia

For·eign Sec·re·tar·y *n* the cabinet minister in the UK government responsible for relations with other countries

for·eign ser·vice *n* a country's diplomatic and consular staff

fore·judge /fawr júj/ (**-judged, -judg·ing, -judg·es**) *vti* to judge a matter before knowing all the facts or evidence (*formal*) —**fore·judg·ment** *n*

fore·knowl·edge /fawr nóllij/ *n* knowledge or awareness that something is going to happen, either from information that has been acquired, or by paranormal means

fore·la·dy /fáwr làydee/ (*plural* **-dies**) *n US* HR same as **forewoman** (sense 1)

fore·land /fáwrlənd/ *n* **1.** HEADLAND a stretch of land that juts out into the sea or an estuary **2.** LAND IN FRONT land described in relation to what lies behind it, especially a plain in front of mountains **3.** ROCK IN FRONT OF MOUNTAINS a stable mass of rock that juts out in front of a mountain belt

fore·leg /fáwr lèg/ *n* either of the two front legs of a four-legged animal (**quadruped**)

fore·limb /fáwr lìm/ *n* either of the two front limbs of a four-limbed vertebrate, e.g., a flipper, arm, wing, or fin

fore·lock[1] /fáwr lòk/ *n* **1.** a lock of hair that grows or falls over the forehead **2.** the part of a horse's mane that falls forward between its ears

fore·lock[2] /fáwr lòk/ *n* a pin or wedge inserted through the end of a bolt to stop it being removed

fore·man /fáwrmən/ (*plural* **-men** /-mən/) *n* **1.** a man who is in charge of a group of other workers, e.g., on a construction site or in a factory **2.** somebody, especially a man, chosen by the other members of a jury to be their leader —**fore·man·ship** *n*

Fore·man /fáwrmən/, **George** (*b.* 1949) US professional boxer. Winner of the world heavyweight championship title (1973–74), he made a comeback to regain the title in 1994 at the age of 45.

> "I have the body of a man half my age. Unfortunately, he's in terrible shape."
> [George Foreman, *Guardian (London)*; December 28, 1996]

fore·mast /fáwr màst/; *nautical usage* /fáwrməst/ *n* the mast nearest the front or bow of a vessel with two or more masts

fore·milk /fáwr mìlk/ *n* the relatively low-fat milk with a high sugar content that is produced by a woman's breast at the beginning of a breast feed

fore·most /fáwr mōst/ *adj* **1.** CHIEF most important or notable **2.** FARTHEST FORWARD nearest to the front ○ *the foremost section of the aircraft* ■ *adv* **1.** IN FIRST POSITION most importantly, or in the most important position ○ *a partner who will put your interests foremost* **2.** TO FRONT at or toward the front [Old English *formest* < *forma* "first" + -EST[2], later interpreted as < FORE + -MOST]

fore·moth·er /fáwr mùth̲ər/ *n* a woman ancestor, usually one who died long ago

fore·name /fáwr nàym/ *n* same as **first name**

fore·noon /fáwr no͞on, fawr no͞on/ *n* the period of time between dawn and noon or immediately before noon

fo·ren·sic /fə rénssik, -rénzik/ *adj* **1.** relating to the application of science to decide questions arising from crime or litigation ○ *forensic evidence* **2.** relating to debate and formal argumentation ○ *forensic oratory* [Mid-17C. < Latin *forensis* "of legal proceedings" < *forum* "forum" (as a place for discussion)] —**fo·ren·si·cal·i·ty** /fə rènssi kállətee, -rènzi-/ *n* —**fo·ren·si·cal·ly** *adv*

fo·ren·sic med·i·cine *n* the branch of medicine that has a specifically legal purpose, e.g., in establishing the cause of a death

fo·ren·sics /fə rénssiks, -rénziks/ *n* the practice or study of formal debate (*takes a singular or plural verb*)

fore·or·dain /fàwr awr dáyn/ (**-dained, -dain·ing, -dains**) *vt* to arrange or determine an event in advance of its happening —**fore·or·dain·ment** *n* —**fore·or·di·na·tion** /fàwr awrd'n áysh'n/ *n*

fore·part /fáwr paart/ *n* **1.** the front part of something, or the part of something in front **2.** the first or early part of a given period of time

fore·paw /fáwr pàw/ *n* either of the two front feet of a land mammal that does not have hooves

fore·peak /fáwr pe̅ek/ *n* the interior part of a boat or ship nearest the bow

fore·per·son /fáwr pùrss'n/ (*plural* **-per·sons** or **-peo·ple** /-pe̅ep'l/) *n* **1.** a skilled worker who is in charge of a group of other workers, e.g., on a building site or in a factory **2.** somebody chosen by the other members of a jury to be their leader

fore plane *n* a plane used in carpentry or joinery for preliminary smoothing, intermediate in size between a jack plane and a jointer

fore·play /fáwr plày/ *n* mutual sexual stimulation that takes place before intercourse

fore·quar·ter /fáwr kwàwrtər/ *n* half of the front half of a pork, lamb, or beef carcass ■ **fore·quar·ters** *npl* the front legs, shoulders, and adjoining parts of a horse or similar animal

fore·reach /fawr re̅ech/ (**-reached, -reach·ing, -reach·es**) *v* **1.** *vti* to gain on or pass another sailing vessel, especially when sailing into the wind **2.** *vi* to continue moving in a ship after the sails have been taken down or the engine switched off

fore·run /fawr rún/ (**-ran** /-rán/, **-run, -run·ning, -runs**) *vt* **1.** to serve as an indication of or anticipate something that is to happen (*formal*) **2.** to go before something (*archaic*)

fore·run·ner /fáwr rùnnər/ *n* **1.** PREDECESSOR an earlier person or thing that had a role or function similar to somebody or something coming later ○ *the forerunner of the modern food processor* **2.** SOMEBODY OR SOMETHING SHOWING FUTURE somebody or something that brings news of or is an indication of what is to happen ○ *a forerunner of unsettled weather* **3.** ONE AHEAD OF OTHERS somebody or something that goes ahead of others, e.g., a skier who skis down a course just before the beginning of a race

fore·sail /fáwr sàyl/; *nautical usage* /fáwrs'l/ *n* **1.** the main square sail on the front mast of a square-rigged boat **2.** the main or lowest triangular sail on a fore-and-aft-rigged vessel

fore·see /fawr seé/ (**-saw** /-sáw/, **-seen** /-seén/, **-see·ing, -sees**) *vti* to know or expect that something is going to happen before it does ○ *He couldn't have foreseen the consequences of his actions.* —**fore·see·a·ble** *adj* —**fore·see·a·bly** *adv* —**fore·se·er** *n*

fore·shad·ow /fawr sháddō/ (**-owed, -ow·ing, -ows**) *vt* to indicate or suggest something, usually something unpleasant, that is going to happen —**fore·shad·ow·er** *n*

fore·shank /fáwr shàngk/ *n* **1.** the upper part of either of the two front legs of a four-legged animal **(quadruped) 2.** a cut of meat taken from the foreshank of a lamb or sheep

fore·sheet /fáwr sheèt/ *n* a rope used to keep a corner of a foresail in place ■ **fore·sheets** *npl* the part of an open boat that lies forward of the structural member used as the foremost rower's seat

fore·shock /fáwr shòk/ *n* a slight tremor or minor earthquake, often one of many and usually preceding a larger earthquake or volcanic eruption

fore·shore /fáwr shàwr/ *n* **1.** the part of a shore that lies between the highest and lowest watermarks **2.** the part of a shore between the high watermark and cultivated or economically exploited land

fore·short·en /fawr sháwrt'n/ (**-ened, -en·ing, -ens**) *vt* **1.** in visual arts, to make something appear shorter than it actually is in order to create a three-dimensional effect on the basis of the laws of perspective **2.** to make a text shorter (*formal*)

fore·sight /fáwr sīt/ *n* **1.** ABILITY TO THINK AHEAD the ability to envision possible future problems or obstacles **2.** PREMONITION an act or instance of knowing something beforehand **3.** LOOKING FORWARD the act of looking forward **4.** READING TAKEN IN SURVEYING in surveying, an observation or measurement made looking forward **5.** FRONT GUNSIGHT the front sight on a gun —**fore·sight·ed** *adj*

fore·skin /fáwr skìn/ *n* a fold of skin that covers the end of the penis

for·est /fáwrəst/ *n* **1.** LARGE DENSE GROWTH OF TREES a large area of land covered in trees and other plants growing close together, or the trees growing on it **2.** WOODLAND FOR HUNTING especially in former times, an area of woodland owned by a monarch and set aside for hunting **3.** LARGE NUMBER OF UPRIGHT OBJECTS a collection of often tall upright objects, densely packed and so resembling a forest of trees ○ *a forest of microphones* ■ *vt* (**-est·ed, -est·ing, -ests**) CREATE FOREST ON LAND to plant an area with a large number of trees [13C. Via French < late Latin *forestis (silva)* "outside (woods)" < *foris* "out of doors" (see FOREIGN)] —**for·est·al** *adj* —**for·est·ed** *adj* —**fo·res·tial** /fə réschəl/ *adj* ◇ **not see the forest for the trees** used to indicate that somebody is too concerned with the details to appreciate the general nature of a situation or problem

For·est ▸ De Forest, Lee

fore·stall /fawr stáwl/ (**-stalled, -stall·ing, -stalls**) *vt* **1.** to prevent or hinder somebody from doing something, or something from happening, by acting in advance **2.** to stop or slow down sales of a product in a market by buying that product in large quantities beforehand [14C. < Old English *foresteall* "ambush" < *steall* "standing place" < Germanic] —**fore·stall·er** *n* —**fore·stall·ment** *n*

for·es·ta·tion /fàwrə stáysh'n/ *n* the planting or incidence of trees over a large area

fore·stay /fáwr stày/ *n* a rope or cable **(stay)** extending from the head of the foremast to the deck of a ship and used for supporting the mast

for·est·er /fáwrəstər/ *n* **1.** MANAGER OF FOREST somebody engaged in forest management and conservation **2.** FOREST DWELLER a person or animal living in a forest (*archaic*) **3.** INSECTS WOODLAND MOTH a woodland moth that flies by day. Family: Zyglaenidae.

for·est floor *n* the layer of organic matter on the ground in a forest

for·est green *adj* of a dark green color, like the foliage on a pine tree ○ *forest-green uniforms* —**for·est green** *n*

For·est Hills /fáwrəst-/ residential area in the borough of Queens, New York City, at the western end of Long Island. The US Open tennis championship was held there until 1978.

for·est·land /fáwrəst lànd/ *n* a piece of land covered with trees or set aside for the cultivation of trees

for·est rang·er *n* FORESTRY same as **ranger** (sense 1)

for·est·ry /fáwrəstree/ *n* **1.** PLANTING AND GROWING OF TREES the science or skill of planting and growing trees or managing forests **2.** FOREST MANAGEMENT the management of forests for profitable ends such as timber production **3.** COMMERCIAL FORESTLAND forestland, especially that planted and commercially managed rather than growing naturally

fore·taste *n* /fáwr tàyst/ a sample or indication of what is to come ■ *vt* /fawr táyst, fáwr tàyst/ (**-tast·ed, -tast·ing, -tastes**) to have a sample or indication of what is to come

fore·tell /fawr tél/ (**-told** /-tṓld/, **-tell·ing, -tells**) *vt* to predict what is going to happen, especially by means of supposed magic or supernatural powers (*literary*) —**fore·tell·er** *n*

fore·thought /fáwr thàwt/ *n* careful thought in order to be prepared for the future —**fore·thought·ful** *adj* —**fore·thought·ful·ly** *adv* —**fore·thought·ful·ness** *n*

fore·to·ken (*literary*) *n* /fáwr tṑkən/ a warning sign of what is to come ■ *vt* /fawr tṓkən/ (**-kened, -ken·ing, -kens**) to be or give a warning sign of what is to come

fore·told past participle, past tense of **foretell**

fore·top /fáwr tòp/; *nautical usage* /fáwtəp/ *n* a platform at the top of a ship's foremast

fore·top·gal·lant /fàwr top gállənt/; *nautical usage* /fàwtəp gállənt/ *adj* relating to the section of a mast directly above the foremast

fore·top·mast /fawr tóp màst/; *nautical usage* /fawr tópməst/ *n* the mast above the platform at the top of a ship's foremast

fore·top·sail /fawr tóp sàyl/; *nautical usage* /fawr tóps'l/ *n* a sail attached to the mast above the platform at the top of a ship's foremast

for·ev·er /faw révvər, fə-/ *adv* **1.** FOR ALL TIME for all future time **2.** FOR VERY LONG TIME for a very long or seemingly endless time (*informal*) ○ *If we wait for him, we'll be here forever.* **3.** CONSTANTLY regularly or constantly, and often annoyingly (*informal*) ○ *chattered forever* **4.** AT ALL TIMES at all times or on every occasion (*literary*) ○ *From that moment on, she was forever careful.*

for·ev·er·more /faw rèvvər máwr, fə-/ *adv* from now on and for all time (*literary*)

~~**foreward**~~ incorrect spelling of **forward**

fore·warn /fawr wáwrn/ (**-warned, -warn·ing, -warns**) *vt* to warn somebody about something that is going to happen (*often passive*) —**fore·warn·er** *n* —**fore·warn·ing·ly** *adv*

fore·went past tense of **forego**[1]

fore·wing /fáwr wìng/ *n* either of the pair of front wings on a four-winged insect

fore·wom·an /fáwr wŏŏmmən/ (*plural* **-wom·en** /-wìmmin/) *n* **1.** a woman who is in charge of a group of workers, e.g., on a construction site or in a factory **2.** a woman chosen by the other members of a jury to be their leader

fore·word /fáwr wùrd, fáwrwərd/ *n* an introductory note, essay, or chapter in a book, often written by somebody other than the author

forex *abbr* FIN foreign exchange

fore·yard /fáwr yaàrd/ *n* the lowest spar for supporting a sail on a foremast

for·feit /fáwrfət/ *n* **1.** GIVING SOMETHING UP the act or an instance of giving something up or being deprived of something as a punishment **2.** PENALTY FOR WRONGDOING something that is taken away as a punishment or has to be given up to make up for a mistake or wrongdoing **3.** PENALTY FOR BREAKING LAW something that is taken away as a penalty for breaking a law or contract **4.** PENALTY IN GAME an object that a player must give up or a task that a player must perform as a penalty in a game ■ *adj* TAKEN AWAY AS PUNISHMENT taken away or given up as a punishment for a mistake or wrongdoing ■ *vt* (**-feit·ed, -feit·ing, -feits**) **1.** BE DEPRIVED OF SOMETHING to lose something or have something taken away as punishment for a mistake or wrongdoing ○ *forfeit the right to your inheritance* **2.** GIVE SOMETHING UP to give something up willingly in order to pursue or obtain something else ○ *forfeited her inheritance and married outside her parents' faith* **3.** TAKE SOMETHING AWAY AS PENALTY to take something away as a penalty for breaking a law or contract [13C. < Old French *forfet*, past participle of *forfaire* "commit a crime," literally "do beyond" < *fors* "beyond" < Latin *foris* (see FOREIGN)] —**for·feit·a·ble** *adj* —**for·feit·er** *n*

for·feits *n* a game in which a player must give something up or perform a task each time he or she commits a fault or loses a round (*takes a singular verb*)

for·fei·ture /fáwrfə chŏŏr, fáwrfəchər/ *n* **1.** something that has been taken away or has had to be given up as a penalty for breaking a law or contract **2.** the act of forfeiting something

for·fend /fawr fénd/ (**-fend·ed, -fend·ing, -fends**), **fore·fend** *vti* to protect or secure against something happening (*archaic*) ○ *Heaven forfend that I should end up like that!*

~~**forfiet**~~ incorrect spelling of **forfeit**

for·gath·er /fawr gáthər/ (**-ered, -er·ing, -ers**), **fore·gath·er** *vi* (*formal*) **1.** ASSEMBLE AS GROUP to come together as a group **2.** MEET BY CHANCE to meet, usually by chance **3.** ASSOCIATE to spend time socially with somebody [15C. < Dutch *vorgaderen* "meet, assemble," altered after GATHER]

for·gave past tense of **forgive**

forge[1] /fawrj/ *n* **1.** METAL WORKSHOP a workshop where metal is heated and shaped into objects by hammering **2.** FURNACE FOR HEATING METAL a furnace used to heat metal to a very high temperature **3.** MACHINE FOR HAMMERING METAL a machine with two tool faces that are brought together to hammer pieces of metal into specific shapes ■ *v* (**forged, forg·ing, forg·es**) **1.** *vti* MAKE ILLEGAL COPY OF SOMETHING to make or produce an illegal copy of something so that it looks genuine, usually for financial gain **2.** *vt* ESTABLISH SOMETHING WITH EFFORT to establish and strive to develop something with great effort ○ *forge a durable relationship with the community* **3.** *vt* SHAPE METAL to shape or form metal by heating and hammering it [13C. < French *forger* "make" < Latin *fabricare* (see FABRICATE)] —**forge·a·bil·i·ty** /fàwrjə bíllətee/ *n* —**forge·a·ble** *adj* —**forg·er** *n*

forge[2] /fawrj/ (**forged, forg·ing, forg·es**) *vi* **1.** to move forward with a sudden increase of speed ○ *forging past the runner on the inside* **2.** to move slowly and steadily ○ *"We were forging through a narrow passage, rock-lined, and tube-like."* (Edgar Rice Burroughs, *The Gods of Mars*; 1913) [Mid-18C. Origin ?]

forge ahead *vi* to move forward rapidly or steadily and persistently

for·ger·y /fáwrjəree/ (*plural* **-ies**) *n* **1.** the act of making or producing an illegal copy of something so that it looks genuine, usually for financial gain **2.** an illegal copy of something such as a document or painting that has been made to look genuine

for·get /fər gét/ (**-got** /-gót/, **-got·ten** /-gótt'n/, **-get·ting, -gets**) *v* **1.** *vti* NOT REMEMBER to fail or be unable to remember something ○ *I'll never forget my first day in school.* **2.** *vt* LEAVE SOMETHING BEHIND to leave something behind accidentally ○ *I've forgotten my keys.* **3.** *vti* NEGLECT SOMEBODY OR SOMETHING to fail to give due attention to somebody or something ○ *Don't just disappear and forget about us all.* **4.** *vt* STOP WORRYING ABOUT SOMETHING to stop thinking or worrying about somebody or something ○ *I'd just forget about it if I were you.* **5.** *vti* NOT MENTION SOMEBODY OR SOMETHING to fail to mention somebody or something **6. for·get your·self** *vr* LOSE CONTROL to lose control of manners, emotions, or behavior ○ *Oh dear, I'm forgetting myself! Let me take your coat.* [Old English *forgietan* "miss your hold on" < Germanic] —**for·get·ter** *n* ◇ **forget it** (*informal*) **1.** used to let somebody know that something is not really very important and so not worth worrying about **2.** used to tell somebody that you are definitely not going to do something that has been suggested, proposed, or asked of you

SYNONYMS See ***overlook.***

for·get·ful /fər gétfəl/ *adj* **1.** tending to forget things **2.** not giving due attention to somebody or something (*formal*) ○ *forgetful of his contractual obligations* —**for·get·ful·ly** *adv* —**for·get·ful·ness** *n*

forget-me-not

for·get-me-not *n* a small plant of the borage family. Flowers: small, delicate, pale blue. Genus: *Myosotis*. [Because worn by lovers]

for·get·ta·ble /fər géttəb'l/ *adj* not easily remembered, or not worthy of being remembered

for·give /fər gív/ (**-gave** /-gáyv/, **-giv·en** /fər gívvən/, **-giv·ing**, **-gives**) *v* **1.** *vti* STOP BEING ANGRY ABOUT SOMETHING to stop being angry about or resenting somebody or somebody's behavior **2.** *vt* PARDON SOMEBODY to excuse somebody for a mistake, misunderstanding, wrongdoing, or inappropriate behavior **3.** *vt* CANCEL OBLIGATION to cancel an obligation such as a debt [Old English *forgiefan*, literally "abstain from giving"] —**for·giv·a·ble** *adj* —**for·giv·a·bly** *adv* —**for·giv·er** *n*

for·give·ness /fər gívnəss/ *n* **1.** the act of pardoning somebody for a mistake or wrongdoing **2.** the tendency to forgive offenses readily and easily ○ *She had little forgiveness in her nature.* [Old English *forgiefenes*, literally "forgiven-ness"]

for·giv·ing /fər gívving/ *adj* **1.** willing to forgive, especially in most circumstances **2.** allowing for or coping well with a degree of imprecision, lack of skill, or other imperfection —**for·giv·ing·ly** *adv* —**for·giv·ing·ness** *n*

for·go /fawr gṓ/ (**-went** /-wént/, **-gone** /-gáwn, -gón/, **-going**, **-goes**), **fore·go** *vt* to do without something, especially voluntarily ○ *forgo the comforts of home while traveling*

for·got past tense of **forget**

for·got·ten past participle of **forget**

for·got·ten man *n* **1.** a once prominent man no longer in the news or the public's awareness **2.** *US* during the Great Depression, an average worker considered by some to be deprived and ignored by the federal government

~~**forhead**~~ incorrect spelling of **forehead**

~~**foriegn**~~ incorrect spelling of **foreign**

Fo·ril·lon Na·tion·al Park /fawree yàwN-/ national park and wildlife sanctuary on the Gaspé Peninsula, Quebec, Canada, in the Gulf of St. Lawrence. Area: 93 sq. mi./240 sq. km.

for in·stance *n* an example of something (*informal*) ○ *Give me a for instance.*

fo·rint /fáwrint/ *n* the main unit of Hungarian currency. See table at **currency** [Mid-20C. < Hungarian < Italian *fiorino* (see FLORIN)]

fork /fawrk/ *n* **1.** UTENSIL FOR EATING a small, usually metal utensil with a handle and two, three, or four prongs, used for eating or for preparing food **2.** GARDEN OR AGRICULTURAL TOOL a garden or agricultural tool with a handle and usually three or four prongs, used for digging, lifting, and turning over **3.** DIVIDING POINT IN ROAD OR RIVER the point where a road or river divides into two or more parts **4.** BRANCH OF ROAD OR RIVER one of the branches that a road or river divides into **5.** ENG PART OF MACHINE a part of a machine or device that has prongs or is fork-shaped **6.** CHESS CHESS POSITION a chess position in which two pieces are under attack from one of the opponent's pieces, usually the knight **7.** METEOROL FLASH OF LIGHTNING a branch or flash of the type of lightning that splits into two branches ■ *v* (**forked, fork·ing, forks**) **1.** *vti* MOVE SOMETHING WITH FORK to carry, pick up, dig, or turn something over using a fork **2.** *vi* DIVIDE INTO TWO to split into two or more branches (*refers to roads and rivers*) **3.** *vi* GO ALONG FORK to take one of the branches that a road or river has divided into **4.** *vt* CAUSE SOMETHING TO BRANCH to make something into a shape that branches in two **5.** *vt* CHESS MOVE PIECE IN CHESS to position a chess piece so that it is threatening two of the opponent's pieces at the same time [Old English *forca*, via Germanic < Latin *furca* "pitchfork"] —**forked** *adj* —**fork·er** *n* —**fork·ful** /fáwrk fo͝ol/ *n*

fork over, fork out, fork up *vti* to pay the money required for something, or spend a lot of money, often grudgingly (*informal*)

fork·ball /fáwrk bàwl/ *n* in baseball, a pitch in which the ball is held between the spread index and middle finger. It usually dips sharply before reaching the batter. —**fork·ball·er** *n*

forked light·ning *n Can, UK* same as **chain lightning**

forked tongue *n* a tongue that speaks lies or words that are insincere or misleading (*literary or humorous*)

fork·lift /fáwrk lìft/ *n* **1.** a lifting device with two long rigid steel bars that can be raised and lowered, used especially to move pallets loaded with boxes or other goods **2.** VEHICLES same as **forklift truck** ■ *vt* (**-lift·ed, -lift·ing, -lifts**) to lift or move heavy loads using a forklift

forklift truck

fork·lift truck *n* a small motor-driven vehicle equipped with a forklift, used especially in factories for moving goods on pallets

fork·lift up·grade *n* a major upgrade of a computer system or network necessitating a significant investment in new hardware and software

for·lorn /fər láwrn, fawr-/ *adj* **1.** LONELY AND MISERABLE lonely and miserable, as though deserted or abandoned **2.** DESOLATE deserted or abandoned and showing signs of neglect **3.** HOPELESS desperate and doomed to failure (*literary*) **4.** DEPRIVED deprived of something (*literary or archaic*) ○ *"My only strength and stay: forlorn of thee, Whither shall I betake me, where subsist?"* (John Milton, *Paradise Lost*; 1667) [Old English *forloren*, past participle of *forlēosan* "lose completely"] —**for·lorn·ly** *adv* —**for·lorn·ness** *n*

for·lorn hope *n* **1.** a desperate or futile hope **2.** a desperate or doomed undertaking [By folk etymology < Dutch *forloren hoop* "lost troop"; originally "a group of soldiers sent on a hopeless mission"]

form /fawrm/ *n* **1.** VARIETY OF SOMETHING a type of something that has various different types ○ *a rare form of cancer* **2.** MANIFESTATION the particular way that something is or appears to be ○ *bonuses in the form of extra vacation days* **3.** BASIC STRUCTURE the shape or structure of a thing that gives it its distinctive character, considered apart from its content, color, texture, or composition **4.** SHAPE OF SOMETHING the shape or appearance of a thing that makes it identifiable ○ *a constellation in the form of a diamond* **5.** INDISTINCT SHAPE a shape like a person or other living thing that cannot be clearly made out ○ *a shadowy form in the distance* **6.** DOCUMENT a document, usually with blank spaces for answers or information to be supplied ○ *fill out the form* **7.** CONDITION OF SOMEBODY OR SOMETHING the condition of an organization, team, performer, athlete, or animal, with regard to fitness, health, and ability to perform well ○ *a violinist at the top of her form* **8.** TRACK RECORD the previous record of a horse, athlete, or team **9.** BEHAVIOR behavior or manners with reference to propriety ○ *It's considered bad form to cheat at games.* **10.** FORMULA a fixed set or order of words or procedures, e.g., in a religious ceremony or a legal document **11.** BIOL SUBDIVISION OF SPECIES a subdivision of a species, ranking below variety, usually indicating a minor difference among members, e.g., in color **12.** ARTS OUTLINE STRUCTURE the structure, design, or arrangement of a work of art or piece of writing, as opposed to its content **13.** ARTS MODE OF EXPRESSION a fixed mode of literary or musical expression ○ *a strict adherence to sonata form* **14.** ARTS, INDUST MOLD OR FRAME a mold, frame, or model within which or around which something can be shaped ○ *concrete forms* **15.** CLOTHING HUMAN SHAPE a model of a human body or torso, used for fitting or displaying clothes **16.** FURNITURE BENCH a long low wooden seat or bench with no back rest **17.** *US* PRINTING PRINTING TEMPLATE a body of typographical elements assembled in a chase in preparation for printing. Can, UK spelling **forme** **18.** LING WORD IN RELATION TO ITS ROOT a word considered in relation to its root or the word it is derived from **19.** LING LOOK OR SOUND OF WORD the way a word is written or how it sounds, as opposed to its meaning **20.** *UK* EDUC BRITISH SCHOOL GRADE in the United Kingdom, a class or grade in school ■ *v* (**formed, form·ing, forms**) **1.** *vti* GIVE SHAPE TO SOMETHING to give a shape or arrangement to something, or take shape ○ *A circle of onlookers formed around the injured man.* **2.** *vti* START TO EXIST to cause something to develop or exist, or begin to develop or exist, especially as part of a natural process ○ *Crystals began to form at the bottom of the jar.* **3.** *vt* SET SOMETHING UP to establish or organize something ○ *form a task force to monitor the impact of deregulation* **4.** *vt* MAKE SOMETHING to make or construct something, often by arranging or combining component parts ○ *The plural is formed by adding an "s."* **5.** *vt* CONCEIVE OF SOMETHING to develop an opinion, impression, or idea in the mind ○ *not enough information to form an opinion* **6.** *vt* CAUSE SOMETHING TO DEVELOP to influence somebody strongly through teaching, discipline, or example, and cause a particular personal development ○ *an early life in the country that formed his quiet nature* **7.** *vt* CREATE SOMETHING to acquire or establish and develop something intangible such as a habit or relationship ○ *form an alliance with other family members* **8.** *vt* SERVE AS SOMETHING to constitute or be a basic element or characteristic of something ○ *a mountain range forming a natural boundary between the two countries* [13C. Via French < Latin *forma* "mold, shape, beauty"] —**form·a·ble** *adj* ◇ **take form** to become visible, distinct, or discernible ○ *A plan started to take form in his mind.* ◇ **true to form** as could be expected judging from somebody's past behavior ○ *True to form, they were exactly twenty minutes late.*

-form *suffix* having a particular form ○ *fibriform* [< Latin *forma* "mold, shape, beauty"]

for·mal /fáwrm'l/ *adj* **1.** OFFICIAL done or carried out in accordance with established or prescribed rules ○ *We made a formal protest.* **2.** CONVENTIONALLY CORRECT characterized by or organized in accordance with conventions governing correctness, behavior, or dress ○ *He's terribly formal and always calls me Mr. Day.* **3.** METHODICAL done in an organized and precise manner ○ *formal research in artificial intelligence* **4.** NOT FAMILIAR IN STYLE used in serious, official, or public communication but not appropriate in everyday contexts ○ *a formal word* **5.** CLOTHING ELEGANT TO WEAR suitable to wear for an important occasion, e.g., a tuxedo for men and a full-length dress for women ○ *formal dress required* **6.** EDUC ACQUIRED IN SCHOOL OR COLLEGE undertaken or acquired by study in an educational institution ○ *no formal training as a journalist* **7.** ORDERED arranged or laid out in a regular, ordered, or symmetrical way ○ *a formal garden* **8.** OF FORM OR STRUCTURE relating to the form or structure of something **9.** OFFICIALLY CONSTITUTED officially constituted or organized as opposed to spontaneously developed ○ *a formal organization* **10.** LOGIC, MATH SYMBOLIC relating to or using symbols and abstract structures rather than natural language **11.** PHILOSOPHY OF ESSENCE RATHER THAN CONTENT relating to the structure or essence of something rather than its content ■ *n* **1.** IMPORTANT OCCASION an important social or ceremonial occasion **2.** SPECIAL CLOTHES an outfit of clothing for an important social occasion, especially a woman's full-length dress ○ *a new formal for the prom* [14C. < Latin *formalis* < *forma* "mold, shape, beauty"] —**for·mal·ly** *adv* —**for·mal·ness** *n*

for·mal·de·hyde /fawr máldə hīd/ *n* a colorless gas with a distinctive smell. Use: manufacture of resins and fertilizers, preservation of organic specimens. Formula: HCHO. [Late 19C. < FORMIC]

for·ma·lin /fáwrməlin/ *n* a solution of formaldehyde in water. Use: disinfectant, preservation of organic specimens. [Late 19C. < FORMALDEHYDE]

for·mal·ism /fáwrm'l ìzzəm/ *n* **1.** **EMPHASIS ON OUTWARD APPEARANCE** a strong or excessive emphasis on outward appearance or form instead of content or meaning **2.** PHILOSOPHY, MATH **THEORY OF SYMBOLS** the view that mathematical symbols are meaningless, though mathematical concepts and structures can be valuable **3.** THEATER **STYLIZATION** stylization and emphasis on symbolism in theatrical productions —**for·mal·ist** *n* —**for·mal·is·tic** /fàwrm'l ístik/ *adj* —**for·mal·is·ti·cal·ly** *adv*

for·mal·i·ty /fawr mállətee/ (*plural* **-ties**) *n* **1.** **FORMALNESS** the quality or condition of being formal, or the degree to which something is formal ○ *dress to suit the formality of the occasion* **2.** **OFFICIAL PROCEDURE** an official procedure that must be followed as part of a longer procedure or event (*often used in the plural*) ○ *several formalities to complete at customs* **3.** **NECESSARY BUT INSIGNIFICANT PROCEDURE** a procedure that must be followed because it is a rule or custom, but has little significance or effect in itself ○ *just a formality* **4.** **ATTENTION TO PROPRIETY** strict or excessive attention to propriety or ceremony

for·mal·ize /fáwrm'l īz/ (**-ized, -iz·ing, -iz·es**) *vt* **1.** **MAKE SOMETHING OFFICIAL** to make something official or valid, e.g., by signing a document **2.** **GIVE SHAPE TO SOMETHING** to give a specific shape or form to something **3.** **MAKE SOMETHING FORMAL** to make something formal or more formal ○ *a formalized version of his earlier account* —**for·mal·iz·a·ble** *adj* —**for·mal·i·za·tion** /fàwrm'li záysh'n/ *n* —**for·mal·iz·er** *n*

for·mal log·ic *n* the branch of logic concerned with the formal methods of deducing conclusions from propositions

for·mal meth·ods *npl* methods of specifying and evaluating computer systems using techniques from mathematics and logic

for·mal·wear /fáwrm'l wèr/ *n* clothes suitable for an important occasion, e.g., a tuxedo for men and a full-length dress for women

for·mant /fáwrmənt/ *n* a frequency range where vowel sounds are at their most distinctive and characteristic pitch [Early 20C. Via German < Latin *formant-*, present participle of *formare* < *forma* "mold, shape, beauty"]

for·mat /fáwr màt/ *n* **1.** **STRUCTURE** the way in which something is presented, organized, or arranged ○ *change the format of the conference to accommodate more speakers* **2.** PUBL **LAYOUT** the layout and presentation of a publication, including its size and the paper and type used ○ *a small-format reference work* **3.** COMPUT **DATA ORGANIZATION** the structure or organization of digital data for storing, printing, or displaying ○ *files in ASCII format* ■ *vt* (**-mat·ted, -mat·ting, -mats**) **1.** **ARRANGE LAYOUT OF SOMETHING** to arrange the layout or organization of something **2.** COMPUT **ORGANIZE DISK FOR DATA STORAGE** to organize a disk in such a way that data can be stored on it [Mid-19C. Via French and German < Latin *formatus (liber)* "(book) shaped (in a special way)" < *formare* (see FORMANT)]

for·mate /fáwr màyt/ *n* any salt or ester of formic acid [Early 19C. < FORMIC]

for·ma·tion /fawr máysh'n/ *n* **1.** **DEVELOPMENT** the process by which something develops or takes a particular shape ○ *a strong influence on the formation of her character* **2.** **CREATION** the process of creating something or coming into existence ○ *the formation of a bipartisan legislative committee* **3.** **SHAPE OF SOMETHING** the shape or structure that something develops into ○ *interesting cloud formations* **4.** **FORMAL PATTERN** the pattern into which a number of people or things is arranged ○ *Twelve planes flew past in formation.* **5.** GEOL **ROCK UNIT** a unit of rock consisting of a succession of strata or an igneous intrusion —**for·ma·tion·al** *adj*

form·a·tive /fáwrmətiv/ *adj* **1.** **INFLUENTIAL** important and influential, particularly in the shaping or development of character ○ *during their formative years* **2.** LING **USED TO FORM WORDS** relating to or used in the formation of derived words or inflected forms of words ■ *n* LING **WORD-FORMING ELEMENT** an element used in the formation of derived words or inflected forms of words, e.g., a suffix or prefix —**form·a·tive·ly** *adv*

form·a·tive as·sess·ment *n* the assessment at regular intervals of a student's progress with accompanying feedback in order to help to improve the student's performance

form class *n* **1.** GRAM same as **part of speech** **2.** a group of words with one or more grammatical characteristics in common

form crit·i·cism *n* **1.** textual criticism that examines the literary conventions used in order to discover the origin and history of a text or its creators **2.** a method of analyzing the Bible to determine the presumed original oral form of the written text by removing known historical conventions that emerged at a later period —**form crit·ic** *n* —**form crit·i·cal** *adj*

forme *n* PRINTING Can, UK spelling of **form** *n* (sense 17)

For·men·te·ra /fàwr men táy raà/ fourth largest of the Spanish Balearic Islands in the western Mediterranean Sea. Population: 5,435 (1998). Area: 31 sq. mi./81 sq. km.

for·mer[1] /fáwrmər/ *adj* **1.** **HAVING BEEN SOMETHING** having had a particular name or status during an earlier period ○ *the former Soviet Union* **2.** **PREVIOUS** occurring at or existing in an earlier time or period ○ *met her on a former occasion* **3.** **FIRST OF TWO** being the first of two things or people mentioned **4.** **PRECEDING** earlier or near the beginning of a text or list ○ *a conclusion inconsistent with the argument in the former part of the paper* ■ *n* **THE FIRST OF TWO** the first of two things or people mentioned ○ *Smith and Brown both work here, the former is an accountant and the latter is an engineer.* [12C. < Old English *forma* "first" < Germanic + ER]

for·mer[2] /fáwrmər/ *n* **1.** **SHAPER OF SOMETHING** somebody or something that forms, creates, or shapes something (*usually in combination*) **2.** *UK* **SCHOOL STUDENT** in the UK, a member of a particular form or class in a school (*always used in combination*) ○ *a sixth former* **3.** ELEC ENG **SHAPING TOOL** a tool used for giving the correct shape to an electrical coil or winding [14C. < FORM]

for·mer·ly /fáwrmərlee/ *adv* during or at an earlier period, but no longer

For·mer Yu·go·slav Re·pub·lic of Mac·e·do·ni·a ♦ **Macedonia** (sense 1)

for·mes·tane /fawr méss táyn/ *n* an estrogen-blocking drug. Use: treatment of some breast cancers.

form·fit·ting /fáwrm fitting/ *adj* fitting tightly around the contours of the body ○ *formfitting sportswear*

form ge·nus *n* an artificial taxonomic category based on similarities that may be superficial. Imperfect fungi and fragmented plant fossils are grouped in form genera.

for·mic /fáwrmik/ *adj* **1.** relating to ants **2.** relating to or containing formic acid [Late 18C. < Latin *formica* "ant"]

For·mi·ca /fawr mīkə/ *tdmk* a trademark for a strong plastic laminate sheeting that is durable and easy to clean, and is often used to cover work surfaces

for·mic ac·id *n* a colorless corrosive liquid that occurs naturally in ants and some plants. Use: paper, textiles, insecticides, refrigerants. Formula: HCOOH.

for·mi·car·y /fáwrmi kèrree/ (*plural* **-ies**), **for·mi·car·i·um** /fàwrmi kérree əm/ (*plural* **-car·i·a** /-kèrree ə/) *n* an ant hill, including its subterranean passages (*technical*) [Early 19C. < medieval Latin *formicarium* < Latin *formica* "ant"]

for·mi·ca·tion /fàwrmi káysh'n/ *n* a neurologically based hallucination in which somebody feels as if insects are crawling on his or her skin. It is found in some cases of chemical toxicity and among drug and alcohol abusers. [Early 18C. < Latin *formication-* < *formicare* "crawl like an ant" < *formica* "ant"]

for·mi·da·ble /fáwrmədəb'l, fər míddəb'l, fàwr míddəb'l/ *adj* **1.** **DIFFICULT TO DEAL WITH** difficult to deal with or overcome ○ *a formidable task* **2.** **AWE-INSPIRING** inspiring respect or wonder because of size, strength, or ability ○ *a formidable display of skill* **3.** **FRIGHTENING** causing fear, dread, or alarm [14C. Directly or via French < Latin *formidabilis* < *formidare* "to fear" < *formido* "terror"] —**for·mi·da·bil·i·ty** /fàwrmədə bíllətee, fər mìddə-, fawr mìddə-/ *n* —**for·mi·da·ble·ness** *n* —**for·mi·da·bly** *adv*

USAGE The traditional pronunciation of ***formidable*** has the stress on the first syllable, but the alternative variant pronunciation, with the stress on the second syllable, is also heard.

form·less /fáwrmləss/ *adj* **1.** **SHAPELESS** lacking a clear shape or structure ○ *a formless figure in the mist* **2.** **DISORGANIZED** lacking apparent organization or structure ○ *formless prose* **3.** **NOT MATERIAL** existing without a physical form ○ *formless beings* —**form·less·ly** *adv* —**form·less·ness** *n*

form let·ter *n* a printed letter that is sent out to a large number of people, e.g., one dealing with a frequently arising complaint, or one used in advertising

for·mu·la /fáwrmyələ/ (*plural* **-las** or **-lae** /-lèe/) *n* **1.** **PLAN** a plan for or method of doing something ○ *agree on a peace formula to end fighting* **2.** **METHOD OF DOING SOMETHING** a prescribed and more or less invariable way of doing something to achieve a particular end **3.** **ESTABLISHED FORM OF WORDS** an established and recognized form of words, e.g., in a ceremony or legal document **4.** CHEM **SET OF SYMBOLS REPRESENTING CHEMICAL COMPOSITION** a representation of the composition of a chemical compound using symbols for the atoms of which it is composed **5.** MATH, PHYS **RULE EXPRESSED IN SYMBOLS** a rule or principle represented in symbols, numbers, or letters, often in the form of an equation ○ *a formula for calculating the distance between planets* **6.** FOOD **MILK FOR BABIES** a preparation used as an alternative to human breast milk and intended to provide all the nutrients an infant requires **7.** **for·mu·la** (*plural* **-las**), **For·mu·la** **CATEGORY OF RACING CAR** a category of racecar according to technical specifications such as engine capacity, size, and weight, used as a basis for professional competition (*usually used in combination*) ○ *formula one racing* [Early 17C. < Latin, "little form" < *forma* "mold, shape, beauty"]

for·mu·la·ic /fàwrmyə láy ik/ *adj* **1.** having the nature of or expressed in terms of a formula **2.** unoriginal and reliant on previous models or ideas ○ *His writing is stilted and formulaic.* —**for·mu·la·i·cal·ly** *adv*

for·mu·la·rize /fáwrmyələ rīz/ (**-rized, -riz·ing, -riz·es**) *vt* MATH same as **formulate** (sense 3) —**for·mu·la·ri·za·tion** /fàwrmyələri záysh'n/ *n* —**for·mu·la·riz·er** *n*

for·mu·lar·y /fáwrmyə lèrree/ *n* (*plural* **-ies**) **1.** **PHARMACEUTICAL REFERENCE BOOK** a reference book containing a list of pharmaceutical products with details of their use, preparation, properties, and formulas **2.** **RELIGIOUS WRITINGS** a book or collection of writings or procedures, especially ones connected with a church **3.** **FIXED FORMULA** a fixed formula for doing something or dealing with something (*archaic or technical*) ■ *adj* **OF FORMULA** relating to or having the nature of a formula

for·mu·late /fáwrmyə làyt/ (**-lat·ed, -lat·ing, -lates**) *vt* **1.** **DEVISE SOMETHING** to draw something up carefully and in detail ○ *formulated his plan* **2.** **EXPRESS SOMETHING WITH CARE** to express or communicate something carefully or in specific words ○ *formulate an opinion* **3.** MATH, PHYS **EXPRESS SOMETHING IN FORMULA** to express something by means of or as a formula —**for·mu·la·tion** /fàwrmyə láysh'n/ *n* —**for·mu·la·tor** *n*

for·mu·la weight *n* CHEM same as **molecular weight**

for·mu·lism /fáwrmyə lìzzəm/ *n* a belief in or reliance on formulas, especially inadequate or obsolete ones —**for·mu·list** *n, adj* —**for·mu·lis·tic** /fàwrmyə lístik/ *adj*

for·mu·lize /fáwrmyə līz/ (**-lized, -liz·ing, -liz·es**) *vt* MATH same as **formulate** (sense 3) —**for·mu·li·za·tion** /fàwrmyəli záysh'n/ *n*

form word *n* GRAM same as **function word**

form·work /fáwrm wùrk/ *n* a structure generally made of timber in which liquid concrete is placed, compacted, and allowed to harden

for·myl /fáwr mil/ *n* a chemical group containing carbon, hydrogen, and oxygen. Formula: HCO. [Mid-19C. < FORMIC]

For·nax /fáwr naks/ *n* a small constellation of the southern hemisphere. See illustration at **constellation**

for·ni·cate[1] /fáwrni kàyt/ (**-cat·ed, -cat·ing, -cates**) *vi* to have sexual intercourse outside marriage (*formal*) [Mid-16C. < ecclesiastical Latin *fornicat-*, past participle of *fornicari* < Latin *fornic-* "arch, brothel" (because prostitutes in Rome solicited under building arches)] —**for·ni·ca·tor** *n*

for·ni·cate[2] /fáwrnikət, fáwrni kàyt/, **for·ni·cat·ed** /fáwrni kàytəd/ *adj* with an arched, vaulted, or bending form [Early 19C. < Latin *fornicatus* < *fornic-* "arch, vault"]

for·ni·ca·tion /fàwrni káysh'n/ *n* **1.** sexual intercourse between two consenting adults who are not married to each other **2.** in the Bible, sexual intercourse between a man and woman who are not married, or any form of sexual behavior considered to be immoral

for·nix /fáwrniks/ (*plural* **-ni·ces** /-ni seez/) *n* a structure or fold in the shape of an arch, especially either of two bands of white fibers in the brain [Late 17C. < Latin (stem *fornic-*), "arch, vault"]

for-prof·it *adj* established or designed to make a profit ○ *a for-profit clinic*

For·rest /fáwrəst/, **Edwin** (1806–72) US stage actor, known for his powerful tragedy acting. He encouraged drama writing in the United States by offering prize money for plays.

For·rest, Nathan Bedford (1821–77) US general. He was one of the Confederacy's most daring cavalry commanders during the Civil War.

"Ah, colonel, all's fair in love and war, you know."
[Nathan Bedford Forrest, *A Civil War Treasury of Tales, Legends and Folklore*, Benjamin Albert Botkin (ed.); 1960]

For·res·tal /fáwrəstal, -stàwl/, **James Vincent** (1892–1949) US banker and government official. He was secretary of the navy (1944–47) and the first secretary of defense (1947–49).

for·sake /fər sáyk, fawr-/ (**-sook** /-sŏŏk/, **-sak·en** /-sáykən/, **-sak·ing, -sakes**) *vt* **1.** to withdraw companionship, protection, or support from somebody **2.** to give up, renounce, or sacrifice something that gives pleasure [Old English *forsacan* "abstain from disputing"] —**for·sak·en** *adj* —**for·sak·en·ly** *adv* —**for·sak·en·ness** *n* —**for·sak·er** *n*

~~**forseeable**~~ incorrect spelling of **foreseeable**

for·sooth /fər sŏŏth, fawr-/ *adv* in truth (*archaic*) [Old English *forsoþ* "for the truth"]

For·ster /fáwrstər/, **E. M.** (1879–1970) British novelist. He was the author of *A Room with a View* (1908), *Howards End* (1910), and *A Passage to India* (1924). Full name **Forster, Edward Morgan.** See Cultural note at **passage**[1], **view**

"The very poor are unthinkable and only to be approached by the statistician and the poet."
[E. M. Forster, *Howards End*; 1910]

for·ster·ite /fáwrstə rìt/ *n* a magnesium silicate mineral of the olivine group [Early 19C. After J. R. *Forster* (1729–98), German naturalist]

for·swear /fawr swáir/ (**-swore** /-swáwr/, **-sworn** /-swáwrn/, **-swear·ing, -swears**) *v* (*archaic or literary*) **1.** *vt* to vow to stop doing, having, or using something ○ *forswear political violence* **2.** *vi* to be guilty of giving false evidence under oath [Old English *forswerian* "renounce by swearing"]

for·syth·i·a /fər síthee ə, fawr-, fawr sī́thi ə/ *n* a bush that flowers in early spring before its leaves emerge. Flowers: yellow. Genus: *Forsythia.* [Mid-19C. After William *Forsyth* (1737–1804), Scottish horticulturist]

PRONUNCIATION The word *forsythia* can be pronounced three ways and all three are correct: /fər síthee ə, fawr síthee ə, fawr sī́ thee ə/. In the first two the *i* is pronounced like the *i* in *it*, and in the third it is pronounced like the *i* in *ice*. In some regions of the United States, the last pronunciation is prevalent.

fort /fawrt/ *n* **1.** a building or group of buildings with strong defenses, usually strategically located and guarded by troops **2.** a permanent military post consisting of several buildings ○ *Fort Bragg* [15C. Directly or via French < Italian *forte* "strong (place)" < Latin *fortis* "strong"] ◇ **hold the fort** to take charge of something in the absence of the person usually responsible (*informal*)

ORIGIN The Latin word *fortis* "strong" from which ***fort*** is derived is also the source of English *forte*[1], *fortitude*, *fortress*, and *pianoforte*.

For·ta·le·za /fàwrtə láyzə/ port and capital city of Ceará State, northeastern Brazil, situated at the mouth of the Paeju River on the Atlantic Ocean. Population: 1,965,513 (1996).

for·ta·lice /fáwrtəliss/ *n* a small fort or part of the fortifications of a larger fort [15C. < medieval Latin *fortalitia* < Latin *fortis* "strong"]

For·tas /fáwrtəss/, **Abe** (1910–82) associate justice of the US Supreme Court (1965–69). He was forced to resign for alleged financial improprieties. Full name **Fortas, Abraham**

Fort Bragg /fawrt brág/ US military post in central North Carolina, Northwest of Fayetteville. Area: 200 sq. mi./520 sq. km.

Fort Col·lins /-kóllinz/ city and county seat of Larimer County, northern Colorado, northeast of Boulder. Population: 124,665 (2002 estimate).

Fort Dodge /-dój/ city in north central Iowa, on the eastern bank of the Des Moines River, northwest of Des Moines. Population: 24,897 (2002 estimate).

for·te[1] /fawrt, fáwr tày/ *n* **1.** something that somebody is particularly good at ○ *Cooking is not really my forte.* **2.** the strongest section of a sword's blade, between the middle and the hilt [Mid-17C. Via French *fort* "strong" < Latin *fortis*; later influenced by FORTE[2]]

for·te[2] /fáwr tày, fáwrtee/ *adv* to be played or sung loudly (*used as a musical direction*) ■ *n* a note or passage of music played or sung, or to be played or sung, loudly [Early 18C. Via Italian, "strong, loud" < Latin *fortis*] —**for·te** *adj*

~~**forteen**~~ incorrect spelling of **fourteen**

for·te·pi·an·o /fáwr tay pyánnō, -pyaánō/ (*plural* **-os**) *n* an early form of piano, especially a piano of the 18th century [Mid-18C. < Italian < *forte* "loud" + *piano* "soft"]

for·te·pi·an·o *adv* to be played or sung loudly and then suddenly softly (*used as a musical direction*) [Late 19C. < FORTE[2] + PIANO[2]] —**for·te·pi·a·no** *adj*

forth /fawrth/ *adv* **1.** ONWARD forward in time, place, degree, or order (*formal*) ○ *from this day forth* **2.** INTO VIEW out into view (*formal*) ○ *brought forth the prisoner* **3.** ABROAD away from a particular place such as a country or region (*archaic*) [Old English *forþ* < Indo-European] ◇ **and so forth** used to indicate that there are more things of the kind just mentioned, without having to name them ○ *bottles, cans, jars, and so forth*

SPELLCHECK forth or **fourth**? Do not confuse the spelling of ***forth*** and ***fourth***, which sound similar. ***Forth*** is an adverb meaning "forward," "onward," or "out," as in *go forth, from that day forth, bring forth.* ***Fourth*** is a noun, adjective, and adverb referring to one of four parts or a position corresponding to the number four, as in *cut the pie into fourths, the fourth month of the year, come fourth in the race.*

Forth /fawrth/ river in southern Scotland that flows eastward from Aberfoyle, Perth, and Kinross, to Alloa, where it widens to form the Firth of Forth. Length: 117 mi./188 km.

Forth, Firth of estuary of the Forth River in southeastern Scotland. It extends about 48 mi./77 km eastward from Alloa to the North Sea.

FORTH /fawrth/ *n* a high-level computer programming language used in scientific and industrial control applications [Late 20C. After the corporation that developed it]

forth·com·ing /fawrth kúmming, fáwrth kùmming/ *adj* **1.** FUTURE about to appear or happen ○ *plans for the forthcoming celebration* **2.** READY WHEN WANTED available when required or requested ○ *We were assured that the money would be forthcoming.* **3.** INFORMATIVE willing to talk or give information ○ *not very forthcoming about his personal life*

forth·right /fáwrth rìt/ *adj* **1.** OUTSPOKEN direct in speech or manner and very honest **2.** SIMPLE plain and simple in style ■ *adv* OUTSPOKENLY in a direct and very honest way ○ *answered the question forthright* —**forth·right·ly** *adv* —**forth·right·ness** *n*

forth·with /fawrth wíth/ *adv* without delay

for·ti·eth /fáwrtee əth/ *n* **1.** one of 40 equal parts of something **2.** somebody's 40th birthday —**for·ti·eth** *adj, adv*

for·ti·fi·ca·tion /fàwrtəfi káysh'n/ *n* **1.** STRUCTURE FOR DEFENSE a structure built in order to strengthen a place's defenses, e.g., a wall, ditch, or rampart (*often used in the plural*) **2.** BUILDING OF DEFENSES the art or practice of strengthening or creating defenses, e.g., by building walls or digging ditches **3.** PLACE THAT CAN BE DEFENDED a position or place that can be defended

for·ti·fied wine *n* a drink that is made from wine to which a strong alcohol such as grape brandy has been added, e.g., sherry, port, or Marsala. Fortified wines are usually drunk as aperitifs, digestifs, or liqueurs.

for·ti·fy /fáwrtə fì/ (**-fied, -fy·ing, -fies**) *vt* **1.** MAKE PLACE SAFER to make a place less susceptible to attack by building or creating defensive structures such as walls, ditches, or ramparts **2.** MAKE SOMETHING STRONGER to strengthen or reinforce the structure of something ○ *fortify a sea wall* **3.** ADD INGREDIENTS TO SOMETHING to add further ingredients to food or drink in order to improve its flavor or add nutrients (*usually passive*) ○ *breakfast cereal fortified with vitamins* **4.** ENCOURAGE SOMEBODY to give somebody physical, mental, or moral strength or encouragement **5.** MAKE SOMETHING MORE POWERFUL to make something more powerful or persuasive ○ *fortify an argument* [15C. Via French *fortifier* < late Latin *fortificare* "make strong" < Latin *fortis* "strong"] —**for·ti·fi·a·ble** *adj* —**for·ti·fi·er** *n* —**for·ti·fy·ing·ly** *adv*

for·tis /fáwrtiss/ *adj* describes a consonant that is produced with great muscular tension and pressure of breath, e.g., "p" or "t" ■ *n* (*plural* **-tes** /-teez/) a fortis consonant, e.g., "p" or "t" [Early 20C. < Latin, "strong"]

for·tis·si·mo /fawr tíssə mò/ *adv* extremely loudly (*used as a musical direction*) ■ *n* (*plural* **-mos** or **-mi** /-mee/) a passage of music, or an individual note or chord, played fortissimo [Early 18C. < Italian, "loudest" < *forte* (see FORTE[2])] —**for·tis·si·mo** *adj*

for·ti·tude /fáwrtə tŏŏd/ *n* strength and endurance in a difficult or painful situation [14C. Via French < Latin *fortitudo* "strength, courage" < *fortis* "strong"] —**for·ti·tu·di·nous** /fàwrtə tŏŏd'nəss/ *adj*

Fort Knox /-nóks/ US military post and reservation in northern Hardin County, central Kentucky. It has been the location of the US Gold Depository since 1936. Area: 5,155 sq. mi./13,350 sq. km.

Fort Lau·der·dale /-láwdər dàyl/ city and county seat of Broward County, southeastern Florida, situated on the Atlantic Ocean 25 mi./40 km north of Miami. Population: 138,194 (2002 estimate).

Fort Leav·en·worth /-lévv'n wùrth/ US military base directly north of the city of Leavenworth, northeastern Kansas. It is home to the US Army Command and General Staff College and a military prison.

Fort Lee /-leé/ borough in northeastern New Jersey, situated on the Palisades along the Hudson River, northeast of Jersey City. Population: 36,963 (2002 estimate).

Fort Mc·Mur·ray /-mək múr ee/ town on the Athabaska River in northeastern Alberta, western Canada. Population: 41,466 (2001).

Fort Meade /-meéd/ **1.** city in central Florida, south of Lakeland. Population: 5,693 (2002 estimate). **2.** US military base in central Maryland, southwest of Baltimore

Fort My·ers /-mī́rz/ city and county seat of Lee

County, southwestern Florida, south of Charlotte Harbor. Population: 49,960 (2002 estimate).

fort·night /fáwrt nìt/ *n UK* a period of 14 days [Old English *feowertine niht* "fourteen nights"]

fort·night·ly /fáwrt nìtlee/ *UK adj, adv* occurring once every 14 days ■ *n* (*plural* **-lies**) a publication that appears once every two weeks

Fort Pierce /-pe'erss/ city and county seat of St. Lucie County, eastern Florida, northeast of Lake Okeechobee. Population: 37,989 (2002 estimate).

FORTRAN /fáwr tràn/ *n* the earliest high-level computer programming language [Mid-20C. Contraction of FORMULA + TRANSLATION]

for·tress /fáwrtrəss/ *n* **1.** a fortified place with a long-term military presence, often including a town **2.** something that is impenetrable or acts as protection [14C. < Old French *forteresse* "strong place" < Latin *fortis* "strong"]

Fort Saint John /-saynt jón/ town on the Peace River in northeastern British Columbia, Canada. Population: 16,034 (2001).

Fort Sas·katch·e·wan /-sa skáchəwən/ town in Alberta, Canada, northeast of Edmonton. Population: 13,121 (2001).

Fort Smith /-smíth/ city at the confluence of the Arkansas and Poteau rivers in western Arkansas on the border with Oklahoma. It is the second largest city in the state. Population: 81,519 (2002 estimate).

Fort Stan·wix Nat·ion·al Mon·u·ment /-stànwiks-/ national monument on the site of a reconstructed 18th-century fort in Rome, New York. Area: 16 acres./6.3 hectares.

Fort Sum·ter Na·tion·al Mon·u·ment /-sùmtər-/ national monument on the site of a historic fort situated on the southern side of the entrance to Charleston Harbor, South Carolina. It was the site of the first battle of the Civil War in 1861.

Fort Thom·as /-tómməss/ city in northern Kentucky, north of Independence and southeast of Covington. It is a suburb of Cincinnati, Ohio. Population: 16,238 (2002 estimate).

for·tu·i·tous /fawr to͝o itəss/ *adj* **1.** happening by chance, especially giving rise to a fortunate outcome **2.** ⚠ bringing or indicating good fortune [Mid-17C. < Latin *fortuitus* < *fors* "chance, luck"] —**for·tu·i·tous·ly** *adv* —**for·tu·i·tous·ness** *n*

USAGE fortuitous or **fortunate**? The word ***fortuitous*** means "accidental or unplanned," as in *a fortuitous encounter with my old roommate of 30 years ago, whom I hadn't seen since graduation.* Nowadays, it is frequently used in contexts where the chance event described has a fortunate outcome. An extended meaning, "lucky," used in English at least since the 1920s, is controversial. Substitute ***fortunate*** for ***fortuitous*** when the meaning is *lucky*: *In a fortunate* [not *fortuitous*] *turn of events, the lost package was found and handed in by a passer-by.*

for·tu·i·ty /fawr to͝o ətee/ (*plural* **-ties**) *n* **1.** something that happens by chance or accident **2.** lucky chance or accident

for·tu·nate /fáwrchənət/ *adj* **1.** LUCKY enjoying good luck **2.** RESULTING FROM LUCK happening as a result of good luck **3.** BRINGING LUCK bringing good luck [14C. < Latin *fortunatus* < *fortuna* "fate, luck"] —**for·tu·nate·ness** *n*

USAGE See ***fortuitous***.

for·tu·nate·ly /fáwrchənətlee/ *adv* **1.** by lucky chance **2.** used to show that the speaker or writer is happy to be able to report something ○ *Fortunately, we've been given more time to finish the job.*

~~**fortunatly**~~ incorrect spelling of **fortunately**

for·tune /fáwrchən/ *n* **1.** GREAT WEALTH OR PROPERTY a large amount of financial wealth or material possessions ○ *inherited the family fortune* **2.** LARGE SUM OF MONEY an extremely large amount of money (*informal*) ○ *That must have cost you a fortune.* **3.** *also* **For·tune** FATE chance, or the personification of chance, regarded as affecting human activities **4.** LUCK luck, especially good luck **5.** DESTINY somebody's personal destiny ○ *went to seek their fortune in other countries* ■ **for·tunes** *npl* LIFE'S UPS AND DOWNS chance happenings throughout life that may turn out well or badly ○ *the fortunes of war* [13C. Via French < Latin *fortuna* "fate, (good) luck"]

For·tune 500 /-fìv húndrəd/ *n* the top 500 companies in the US, as listed by Fortune magazine

for·tune cook·ie *n* a Chinese cookie folded and baked around a piece of paper on which a saying or a prediction of somebody's fortune is written. Fortune cookies are served in Chinese restaurants.

for·tune hunt·er *n* somebody who seeks riches, especially by attempting to marry a wealthy partner (*disapproving*) —**for·tune hunt·ing** *n* —**for·tune-hunt·ing** *adj*

for·tune tell·er *n* somebody who predicts the future, e.g., by reading palms or using tarot cards —**for·tune tell·ing** *n* —**for·tune-tell·ing** *adj*

Fort Wal·ton Beach /-wàwlt'n-/ city on the Gulf of Mexico in Oskaloosa County, northwestern Florida, east of Pensacola. Population: 20,098 (2002 estimate).

Fort Wayne /-wáyn/ city in northeastern Indiana, southeast of Elkhart. The St. Joseph, St. Marys, and Maumee rivers run through the city. Population: 210,070 (2002 estimate).

Fort Worth /-wúrth/ city and county seat of Tarrant County in northeastern Texas, situated on the Trinity River, west of Dallas. Historically known for its stockyards, it is a major industrial center. Population: 567,516 (2002 estimate).

for·ty /fáwrtee/ *n* (*plural* **-ties**) **1.** 40 the number 40 **2.** GROUP OF 40 a group of forty objects or people **3.** TENNIS POINT in a game of tennis, the score awarded to a player with a score of thirty on winning a further point ■ **for·ties** *npl* **1.** NUMBERS 40 TO 49 the numbers 40 to 49, particularly as a range of temperature **2.** YEARS FROM 40 TO 49 the years from 40 to 49 in a century **3.** PERIOD FROM AGE 40 TO 49 the period of somebody's life from the age of 40 to 49 [Old English *feowertig* < FOUR + *-tig* "ten"] —**for·ty** *adj, pron*

for·ty-five *n* **1.** *also* **.45** a pistol with a .45 caliber. **2.** a record smaller than an LP that is played at 45 revolutions per minute

for·ty·ish /fáwrtee ish/ *adj* **1.** approximately 40 in number **2.** around the age of 40

for·ty-nin·er *n* a prospector in the gold rush of 1849 in California

for·ty-ninth par·al·lel *n* the border between the United States and Canada, that runs at 49° latitude along most of its length

for·ty·some·thing /fáwrtee sùmthing/ *n* somebody between 40 and 49 years of age (*informal*) ■ *adj* between 40 and 49 years of age

for·ty winks *n* a short sleep (*informal; takes a singular or plural verb*)

fo·rum /fáwrəm/ (*plural* **-rums** or **-ra** /-rə/) *n* **1.** PLACE TO EXPRESS YOURSELF a medium in which the public may debate an issue or express opinions, e.g., a magazine or newspaper **2.** MEETING FOR DISCUSSION a meeting to discuss matters of general interest **3.** INTERNET DISCUSSION GROUP an Internet discussion group for participants with common interests **4.** LAW COURT a law court or tribunal **5.** PUBLIC SQUARE IN ROMAN CITIES in ancient Rome, a public square or marketplace in a city where business was conducted and the law courts were situated [15C. < Latin, "enclosed space around a house, marketplace" < *foris* "out of doors"]

for·ward /fáwrwərd/ (**-ward·ed, -ward·ing, -wards**) CORE MEANING: to or toward a front position or direction ○ (adv) *Conover pushed his cup forward, but Johnny ignored it.* ○ (adj) *Most of the energy in gasoline makes engines hot; less than half gets converted to forward motion.*

1. *adv also* **for·wards** /-wərdz/ AHEAD to or toward what is ahead in space or time ○ *He sprang forward and embraced his grandmother.* **2.** *adv also* **for·wards** PROGRESSING towards a goal ○ *The company has taken a step forward in employee safety.* **3.** *adv also* **for·wards** INDICATES IMPROVEMENT indicates that something progresses or improves ○ *The EU is moving forward on monetary union.* **4.** *adv also* **for·wards** NAUT TO FRONT OF VESSEL toward the front of a boat or ship ○ *I was ordered forward to swab the deck.* **5.** *adv also* **for·wards** TOWARD FRONT toward the front of something such as an aircraft or a building ○ *I'd like to be seated further forward.* **6.** *adv also* **for·wards** TO PUBLIC ATTENTION from obscurity into public view ○ *The unknown actor came forward and accepted the lead role.* **7.** *adj* AHEAD directed toward what is ahead in space and time ○ *The magnetic field exerts a forward force on charged particles.* **8.** *adj* RELATING TO FUTURE directed toward a future goal ○ *forward planning* **9.** *adj* NAUT AT FRONT OF VESSEL situated at or near the front of a boat or ship ○ *the forward deck* **10.** *adj* AT FRONT situated at or near the front of something such as an aircraft or a building ○ *The forward seats are the most popular.* **11.** *adj* UNRESTRAINED IN BEHAVIOR behaving boldly in defiance of moral or social restraints ○ *I'm not sure I approve of her behavior; she's very forward.* **12.** *n* SPORTS ATTACKING PLAYER in some team sports such as basketball, hockey, or soccer, a principal offensive player **13.** *vt* REDIRECT MAIL to send on mail from the address to which it was originally sent ○ *She was anxious to know if any letters might have come that had not been forwarded to her.* **14.** *vt* ADVANCE OR PROMOTE SOMETHING to assist the progress of something ○ *I will do anything you like if it means we can forward your cause.* [Old English *forweard* "in the direction of the front" < *fore* (see FORE)] —**for·ward·ly** *adv* —**for·ward·ness** *n*

USAGE See ***toward***.

for·ward bi·as *n* a voltage applied to a semiconductor or a junction in a semiconductor, in a direction to cause a higher current to flow

for·ward·er /fáwrwərdər/ *n* a person or company whose business is the collection, shipment, and delivery of goods

for·ward·ing /fáwrwərding/ *n* the collection, shipment, and delivery of goods

for·ward·ing ad·dress *n* a new address to which mail is to be redirected

for·ward-look·ing *adj* planning for or looking ahead to the future

for·ward pass *n* in football, a pass thrown from a position behind the line of scrimmage in the direction of the opposing team's goal

for·ward roll *n* in gymnastics, a movement in which the body is rolled over in a forward direction, placing the head on the ground and bringing the feet over the head

for·wards *adv* same as **forward**

for·ward slash *n* COMPUT, PRINTING same as **slash** *n* (sense 5)

for·ward-stepped *adj* describes a mast positioned in the front of the boat

for·ward volt·age *n* ELEC ENG same as **forward bias**

Fos·bur·y flop /fòzbəree-/ *n* in the high jump, a technique in which the contestant clears the bar with the back of the shoulders followed by the arched body [Mid-20C. After Richard (Dick) *Fosbury* (b. 1947), US athlete]

fos·car·net /foss kaárnət/ *n* an antiviral drug. Use: treatment of a type of herpes.

fos·sa[1] /fóssə/ (*plural* **-sae** /-se'e/) *n* a hollow, pit, or groove in a part of the body such as in a bone [Mid-17C. < Latin, "ditch" (see FOSSE)]

fos·sa[2] /fóssə/ (*plural* **-sas** or **-sa** /-se'e/) *n* a slender reddish brown carnivorous animal that resembles a cat, has sharp retractile claws, and feeds on small animals, birds, and insects. Native to: Madagascar. Latin name: *Cryptoprocta ferox.* [Mid-19C. < Malagasy *fosa*]

fosse /fawss/ *n* a wide ditch, usually filled with water and used for defense [Pre-12C. Via French < Latin *fossa* < *fodere* "dig"]

Fos·se /fóssee/, **Bob** (1927–87) US dancer, choreographer, and director. He won his first Tony Awards for his imaginative dance sequences in the Broadway musicals *Pajama Game* (1953) and *Damn Yankees* (1955), and he directed the Academy Award-winning films *Cabaret* (1972) and *All That Jazz* (1980). Full name **Fosse, Robert Louis**

"I've been accused of editing too much. But audiences get bored so quickly."
[Bob Fosse, *Cue*; February 1, 1980]

Barnaby's
fossil: a trilobite

fos·sil /fóss'l/ *n* **1.** PRESERVED REMAINS OF ANIMAL OR PLANT the remains of an animal or plant preserved from an earlier era inside a rock or other geologic deposit, often as an impression or in a petrified state **2.** SOMEBODY WHO WILL NOT CHANGE somebody regarded as old-fashioned and unwilling to change (*informal insult*) **3.** SOMETHING OUTDATED something that has outlived its usefulness, e.g., a discredited theory **4.** LING OLD WORD NOW USED SPECIFICALLY a word or part of a word that was once used generally but now survives only in a few contexts, e.g., *couth* in *uncouth* [Mid-16C. Via French *fossile* < Latin *fossilis* "dug up" < *fodere* "dig"]

fos·sil fu·el *n* any carbon-containing fuel derived from the decomposed remains of prehistoric plants and animals, e.g., coal, peat, petroleum, and natural gas

fos·sil·if·er·ous /fòssə líffərəss/ *adj* describes a rock or other geologic deposit that has fossils within it

fos·sil·ize /fóss'l ìz/ (**-ized, -iz·ing, -iz·es**) *vti* **1.** to convert something into a fossil, preserve something as a fossil, or become a fossil **2.** to become outdated, fixed, or unchanging, or make somebody or something incapable of change —**fos·sil·iz·a·ble** *adj*—**fos·sil·i·za·tion** /fòss'li záysh'n/ *n*—**fos·sil·ized** *adj*

fos·sil wa·ter *n* water in underground strata that has accumulated over millions of years and is therefore not a renewable resource, unlike other ground water

fos·so·ri·al /fo sáwree əl/ *adj* describes animals that have large forelimbs or other adaptations for digging and burrowing, or to describe the parts of the body used for this purpose [Mid-19C. < medieval Latin *fossorius* < Latin *fossor* "digger" < *fodere* "dig"]

fos·ter /fáwstər, fóstər/ *vt* (**-tered, -ter·ing, -ters**) **1.** NURTURE CHILD to provide a child with care and upbringing **2.** DEVELOP SOMETHING to encourage the development of something **3.** KEEP ALIVE FEELING OR THOUGHT to keep a feeling or thought alive ■ *adj* PROVIDING OR RECEIVING PARENTAL CARE giving or receiving a home and parental care and upbringing, usually on a short-term basis, although unrelated by blood or adoption. Foster care is provided for children whose natural parents are dead, absent, or unfit or unable to look after them. ○ *a foster child* [Old English *fostrian* "nourish, raise a child" < *foster* "food" < Germanic] —**fos·ter·er** *n*

Fos·ter /fáwstər, fóstər/, **Jodie** (*b.* 1962) US movie actor and director. She won Academy Awards for best actress for her work in *The Accused* (1988) and *The Silence of the Lambs* (1991). Born **Foster, Alicia Christian**

Andrew Ward
Sir Norman Foster

Fos·ter, Norman, Baron Foster of Thames Bank (*b.* 1935) British architect. His designs such as the terminal building (1991) for Stansted Airport, Essex, England, combine elegant forms with complex engineering and technologically advanced materials. He won the Pritzker Architecture Prize in 1999. Full name **Foster, Norman Robert**

Fos·ter, Stephen Collins (1826–64) US songwriter. His songs include "My Old Kentucky Home" (1853) and "Beautiful Dreamer" (1862).

fos·ter·age /fáwstərij, fóstərij/ *n* **1.** CARING FOR ANOTHER'S CHILD the act of looking after or bringing up a child who is unrelated by blood or adoption, often on a short-term basis and in exchange for payment by a local authority **2.** BEING FOSTER CHILD the process of being looked after or brought up in a home by parents who are unrelated by blood or adoption **3.** ENCOURAGING DEVELOPMENT the process of encouraging the development of something beneficial

Fos·ter Cit·y /fáwstər-, fóstər-/ city in California on the San Mateo Peninsula. It is a suburb of San Francisco. Population: 29,194 (2002 estimate).

FOT, f.o.t. *abbr* free on truck

~~fotograph~~ incorrect spelling of **photograph**

Fou·cault /foo kṓ/, **Jean-Bernard Léon** (1819–68) French physicist. He helped devise a way of calculating the speed of light and proved that it traveled more slowly through water than through air. He demonstrated the Earth's rotation by suspending a pendulum from the ceiling of the Panthéon dome, Paris (1851).

Fou·cault, Michel (1926–84) French philosopher. He showed how ideas of truth about human nature change in the course of history. His chief works were *Madness and Civilization* (1960), *The Order of Things* (1966), and *Discipline and Punish* (1975).

> "Psychology can never tell the truth about madness because it is madness that holds the truth of psychology."
> [Michel Foucault, *Mental Illness and Psychology*; 1976]

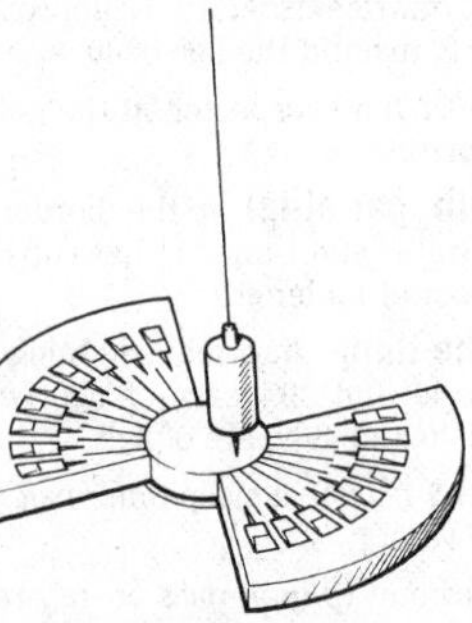
Foucault pendulum

Fou·cault pen·du·lum *n* a heavy free-swinging pendulum suspended by a long thin wire, whose plane of motion appears to change as Earth rotates [Mid-19C. After Jean-Bernard Léon FOUCAULT]

fouet·té /fwe táy, fòo ə táy/ *n* a ballet step in which the dancer stands on one foot and moves the other leg quickly out and in again, often while doing a pirouette [Mid-19C. < French, past participle of *fouetter* "whip"]

fought past participle, past tense of **fight**

foul /fowl/ *adj* **1.** DISGUSTING disgusting to the senses ○ *brackish, foul-tasting water* ○ *a foul smell* **2.** FILLED WITH DIRT clogged with dirt or so obstructed as to be unusable ○ *a foul pipe* **3.** DIRTY covered in dirt **4.** CONTAMINATED contaminated by impurities ○ *foul city air* **5.** UNPLEASANT extremely unpleasant or disagreeable in nature (*informal*) ○ *in a foul mood* **6.** VULGAR obscene or otherwise offensive in expression or behavior ○ *foul language* **7.** ILLEGAL IN SPORT contrary to the rules of a sport **8.** BASEBALL OUTSIDE FOUL LINE in baseball, outside a foul line **9.** DISHONEST behaving in an unfair and unacceptable way ○ *suspected of having gotten rich by foul means* **10.** INCLEMENT stormy or wet and unpleasant for outdoor activities **11.** ROTTEN decaying and rotten **12.** EVIL spiritually or morally vicious **13.** ENSNARLED entangled with something and unable to move ○ *a foul anchor line* ■ *n* **1.** ILLEGAL ACTION IN SPORT an illegal action against an opposing player, or an action that breaks the rules of a sport **2.** BASEBALL FOUL BALL in baseball, a foul ball **3.** ENTANGLEMENT PREVENTING MOVEMENT an entanglement or collision that prevents movement ■ *v* (**fouled, foul·ing, fouls**) **1.** *vti* ACT ILLEGALLY IN SPORT to act illegally against an opposing player, or violate a rule of a sport **2.** *vti* BASEBALL HIT BALL FROM FAIR TERRITORY in baseball, to hit a ball outside a foul line **3.** *vti* ENSNARL AND PREVENT MOVEMENT to entangle or catch something so that it cannot move, or become entangled or caught and unable to move ○ *careful not to foul her fishing line* **4.** *vti* OBSTRUCT OR BECOME OBSTRUCTED to clog or block something, or become clogged or blocked **5.** *vt* MAKE SOMETHING DIRTY to make something dirty, especially by defecation **6.** *vt* BRING SHAME ON SOMEBODY to bring disgrace to a person or to somebody's reputation [Old English *ful* "filthy, decaying" < Germanic] —**foul·er** *n*—**foul·ly** *adv*—**foul·ness** *n*

SPELLCHECK foul or **fowl**? Do not confuse the spelling of ***foul*** and ***fowl***, which sound similar. ***Foul*** is used as an adjective meaning "unpleasant" or "vulgar" (as in *foul weather, foul language*) or as an adjective, verb, or noun referring to dirtiness, illegal action in sport, or entanglement preventing movement. ***Fowl*** is only used as a noun, denoting an edible bird or game bird.

foul out *vi* to be forced to leave a game after committing more than the permitted number of fouls

foul up *vti* **1.** to do something badly or incompetently, or be bungled or mismanaged (*informal*) **2.** to clog or entangle something, or become clogged or entangled

fou·lard /foo laárd/ *n* **1.** a soft silk or rayon fabric, usually patterned **2.** something made of foulard, especially a scarf or handkerchief [Mid-19C. < French]

foul ball *n* in baseball, a struck ball that lands outside a foul line

foul line *n* **1.** BASEBALL LINE SHOWING FAIR OR FOUL BALL in baseball, either of the lines extending from home plate through first and third bases to the end of the playing field **2.** BASKETBALL LINE FOR FREE THROWS in basketball, either of two lines on a court from which players get unobstructed chances to make a basket after they have been fouled **3.** DESIGNATED LIMIT OF PLAY in some sports, a boundary beyond which a ball or player is not permitted, e.g., the line in bowling where the player must stop before releasing the ball

foul-mouthed *adj* using obscene or otherwise offensive language, especially habitually

foul play *n* **1.** UNFAIRNESS unfair action or behavior **2.** CRIME treachery or criminal violence **3.** ACTION AGAINST RULES action that is contrary to the rules of a sport

foul shot *n* BASKETBALL same as **free throw**

foul tip *n* in baseball, a pitched ball that glances off a bat and is deflected into foul territory, usually back toward the catcher

foul-up *n* a blunder, or the confusion or failure that results from a blunder (*informal*)

found[1] /fownd/ (**found·ed, found·ing, founds**) *vt* **1.** to establish and organize something for the future such as an institution or business **2.** to support something such as a conclusion with evidence or reasoning [13C. Via French *fonder* < Latin *fundare* < *fundus* "bottom, base"]

found[2] /fownd/ (**found·ed, found·ing, founds**) *vt* **1.** to cast something, especially metal or glass, by melting it and pouring it into a mold **2.** to produce objects such as machine parts by melting metal or glass and pouring it into molds [14C. Via French *fondre* "dissolve and blend" < Latin *fundere* "pour, melt"]

found[3] past participle, past tense of **find**

foun·da·tion /fown dáysh'n/ *n* **1.** SUPPORT FOR BUILDING a part of a building, usually below the ground, that transfers and distributes the weight of the building onto the ground (*often used in the plural*) **2.** SUPPORT FOR IDEA the basis of something such as a theory or an idea **3.** COSMETICS BASE LAYER OF MAKEUP a cosmetic in liquid, cream, or cake form, usually colored, that is applied as a base for makeup **4.** ESTABLISHMENT OF INSTITUTION OR ORGANIZATION the setting up of an institution or organization **5.** CHARITABLE OR EDUCATIONAL ORGANIZATION an institution that has been formally set up with an endowment fund, e.g., a school, research establishment, charitable trust, or hospital **6. FUND SUPPORTING INSTITUTION** an endowment fund that supports an institution **7.** CLOTHING same as **foundation garment 8. BASE FABRIC FOR PATCHWORK** a fabric to which other pieces of fabric are sewn in patchwork or appliqué —**foun·da·tion·al** *adj* —**foun·da·tion·al·ly** *adv*

foun·da·tion gar·ment *n* a piece of women's underwear intended to control and shape her figure, e.g., a corset

foun·da·tion stone *n* **1.** a stone laid during a ceremony to mark the start of construction of a building or institution **2.** the basis on which something is founded

foun·da·tion stop *n* an organ stop with a strong fundamental tone

found·er[1] /fówndər/ *n* somebody who establishes an institution, business, or organization [14C. < FOUND[1]]

foun·der[2] /fówndər/ *v* (**-dered, -der·ing, -ders**) **1.** *vi* **BREAK DOWN** to fail (*refers to an undertaking*) ○ *Negotiations foundered on a single issue.* **2.** *vi* **SINK** to become filled with water and sink (*refers to a ship*) **3.** *vi* **CRUMPLE** to give way and fall to the ground **4.** *vi* **FALL** to stumble and fall (*refers to a horse and its rider*) **5.** *vti* **MAKE OR BECOME ILL BY OVERFEEDING** to make livestock ill by overfeeding, or become ill by overfeeding ■ *n* VET same as **laminitis** [14C. < Old French *fondrer* "send or sink to the bottom, fall in ruins" < Latin *fundus* "bottom"]

found·ing fa·ther /fòwnding-/ *n* a founder of an institution, movement, or organization

Found·ing Fa·ther *n* one of the members of the convention that drafted the US Constitution

found·ling /fówndling/ *n* an abandoned baby of unknown parentage [13C. < past participle of FIND]

found ob·ject *n* ARTS same as **objet trouvé**

found·ry /fówndree/ (*plural* **-ries**) *n* **1.** a building equipped for the casting of metal or glass **2.** the skill or practice of casting metal or glass

fount[1] /fownt/ *n* (*literary*) **1.** a source of something **2.** a fountain or spring of water [16C. Shortening of FOUNTAIN]

fount[2] /font, fownt/ *n UK* another spelling of **font**[2]

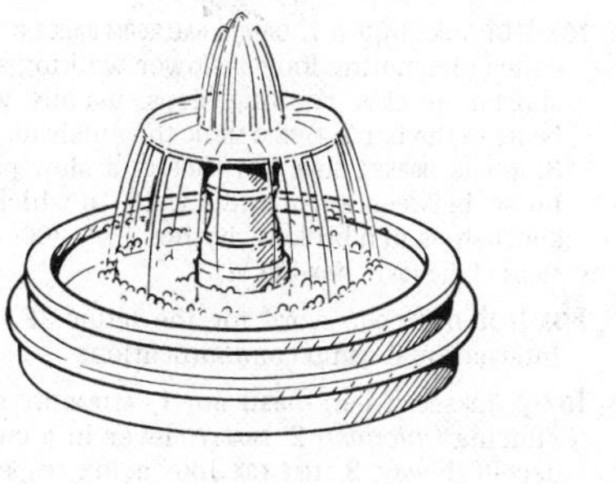

fountain

foun·tain /fównt'n/ *n* **1. ORNAMENTAL WATER FEATURE** an ornamental structure featuring a jet or jets of water, often emerging from a statue into a pool **2. NATURAL SPRING** a natural source of water **3.** same as **drinking fountain 4. SPRAY OF LIQUID** a jet of water or some other liquid **5. SPRAY OF SUBSTANCE** a sudden discharge of something into the air such as sparks, lava, or steam **6. SOURCE** the source of something abstract **7. RESERVOIR OF LIQUID** a reservoir of liquid for use as needed, e.g., in an oil lamp or for printing ink [14C. < French *fontaine* < Latin *fontanus* "of a spring" < *fons* "spring"]

foun·tain·head /fównt'n hèd/ *n* **1.** a spring that is the source of a stream **2.** the primary source of something abstract

foun·tain pen *n* a pen with a pointed metal tip (**nib**) that is supplied with ink from a refillable reservoir in the body of the pen or from an inserted cartridge

Foun·tain Val·ley /fównt'n-/ city on the Santa Ana River, southwestern California. It is a suburb of Los Angeles. Population: 55,553 (2002 estimate).

four /fawr/ *n* **1.** 4 the number 4 **2. SOMETHING WITH VALUE OF 4** something in a numbered series with a value of four, e.g., a playing card ○ *the four of spades* ○ *throw a four* **3. GROUP OF 4** a group of four objects or people ○ *a four for bridge* **4.** ROWING **4-OARED RACING BOAT** a light narrow racing boat with four oars **5.** ROWING **4-MEMBER ROWING CREW** a rowing crew with four members **6.** LAWN BOWLING **BOWLING TEAM** a team of four lawn bowling players ■ **fours** *npl* ROWING **BOAT RACES** races for boats with a crew of four ■ *prep* **4 FOR** the number 4 used to replace the word "for" (*used in e-mails or text messages*) ○ *just 4 U* ■ *symbol* **4 FORE** the number 4 used to replace "fore" within words (*used in e-mails or text messages*) ○ *B4 U go* [Old English *fēower* < Indo-European] —**four** *adj, pron*

four-bag·ger *n US* BASEBALL same as **home run** (*informal*)

four-by-four, 4x4 *n* a four-wheel-drive motor vehicle

four-by-two *n UK* CONSTR same as **two-by-four**

four·chette /foor shét/ *n* a small band that joins the folds of skin at the back of the opening to the vagina, sometimes torn in childbirth [Mid-18C. < French, "small fork" < *fourche* < Latin *furca* "pitchfork, forked stick"]

four-col·or *adj* describes the process of full-color printing by superimposing images in cyan, magenta, yellow, and black

Four Cor·ners /fáwr kàwrnerz/ region in the southwestern United States, at the point where the borders of Colorado, New Mexico, Arizona, and Utah come together

four-cy·cle *adj US* describes an internal-combustion engine in which the piston makes four strokes to complete a cycle. Can term **four-stroke**

four-di·men·sion·al *adj* having or determined by four dimensions, especially as in some formulations of relativity theory that use three spatial dimensions and a mathematically modified form of time as the fourth

four·drin·i·er /foor drínnee ər, -ày/, **Four·drin·i·er** *n* a paper-making machine that produces a continuous web or roll of paper [Mid-19C. After Henry and Sealy *Fourdrinier*, British paper makers]

411 /fàwr wun wún/, **four-one-one** *n* information, especially inside information or gossip, typically passed orally (*informal*) ○ *They heard the 411 on a possible buyout and sold their stock.* [After a telephone number for directory information]

four-eyed fish *n* a fish whose eyes are divided into two lobes so that the upper part can see above the water and the lower part can see below. Native to: Central America. Latin name: *Anableps anableps.*

four-eyes *n* an offensive term for somebody who wears eyeglasses (*informal insult*)

4-F *n* the lowest rating given to somebody who registers for military service, indicating that the person is unfit for service

four flush *n* in poker, a bad hand containing four cards of the same suit and one odd card

four-flush (**four-flushed, four-flush·ing, four-flush·es**) *vi* **1.** in poker, to bet coolly and boldly despite holding a bad hand such as a four flush **2.** to try to mislead somebody in a bold way (*informal*) —**four-flush·er** *n*

four·fold /fáwr fòld/ *adj, adv* **MULTIPLIED BY 4** four times as great in size or amount ■ *adj* **1. WITH 4 ELEMENTS** with four parts or members **2. CONSISTING OF 4 PARTS** consisting of four parts or made up of four parts

404 /fàwr ō fáwr/ *n* an offensive term for somebody regarded as ignorant or stupid (*slang insult*) ■ *adj* completely confused and unable to deal with a problem or situation (*slang*) [< an error message displayed on a web browser when the page requested cannot be located]

four-four-two *n* in soccer, one of the most common outfield team formations comprising four defenders, four midfielders, and two attackers

4GL *abbr* COMPUT fourth-generation language

4-H, Four-H *n* a national youth organization sponsored by the Department of Agriculture in rural areas, with programs for young people in home economics, agriculture, community service, and personal development [Because the aim is to improve the head, heart, hands, and health] —**4-H'er** *n*

four-hand·ed *adj* **1.** describes a game, especially a card game, played by four people **2.** composed or arranged for two people to play at the piano

Four Hun·dred *npl US* the wealthiest or most exclusive group of people in a community

Fou·rier /fóoree ày/, **Charles** (1772–1837) French social scientist. His *Theory of Four Movements and of General Destinies* (1808) advocated a socialist reorganization of society. Full name **Fourier, François Marie Charles**

> "The extension of women's rights is the basic principle of all social progress."
> [Charles Fourier, *Theory of Four Movements and of General Destinies*; 1808]

Fou·rier /fóorree ày/, **Jean-Baptiste Joseph, Baron** (1768–1830) French mathematician. He used a trigonometric series, now called the Fourier series, to describe heat conduction in *The Analytical Theory of Heat* (1822). This method continues to be widely used in mathematical physics.

Fou·ri·er a·nal·y·sis *n* the analysis of a periodic function using the terms of a Fourier series as an approximation [Early 20C. See FOURIER SERIES]

Fou·ri·er se·ries *n* an infinite trigonometric series of terms consisting of constants multiplied by sines or cosines, used in the approximation of periodic functions [Late 19C. After Jean-Baptiste Joseph FOURIER]

four-in-hand *n* **1. 4-HORSE CARRIAGE** a carriage drawn by four horses with one driver **2. 4 HORSES DRAWING CARRIAGE** a team of four horses drawing a carriage **3. WAY OF TYING NECKTIE** a necktie tied in a slipknot at the collar with the ends left hanging

four-leaf clo·ver *n* a clover leaf divided into four leaflets instead of the usual three, believed to bring good luck to the person who finds it

four-let·ter word *n* a short English word relating to sex or excretion that is often used as a swearword and is generally regarded as offensive or taboo. They are sometimes written with some letters replaced by asterisks or a dash.

four-o'clock (*plural same or* **four-o'clocks**) *n* an ornamental plant. Flowers: tubular red, white, or yellow, opening in the late afternoon. Native to: tropical America. Latin name: *Mirabilis jalapa.*

401(k) /fàwr ō wun káy/ *n* a retirement plan for employed people that allows them to invest part of their income without paying any tax until the money is withdrawn after retirement [After the section of the federal tax code that allows it]

four·pen·ny nail /fáwrpənee-, fáwr pènnee-/ *n US* a nail 1.5 in./3.8 cm long [< the medieval price, four pennies per hundred]

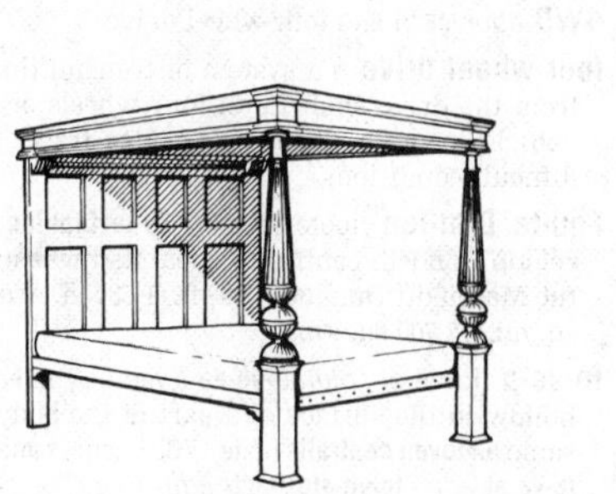

four-poster

four-post·er, four-post·er bed *n* a bed with a tall post at each corner, from which a canopy and drapes are sometimes hung

four·ra·gère /fòorə zhér/ *n* a braided cord awarded as a military decoration to a unit or person and usually worn on the left shoulder of a uniform [Early 20C. < French < *fourrage* (see FORAGE)]

four·score /fawr skáwr/ *adj* the number 80, or a quantity of 80 (*archaic*) ○ *fourscore years and ten*

four·some /fáwrssəm/ *n* **1.** a group of four people, usually taking part in some activity together **2.** a game of golf between two pairs of players, especially when each pair has one ball that the partners hit alternately

four·square /fawr skwér/ *adv, adj* showing certainty and determination (*literary*)

four-stroke *adj Can, UK* AUTOMOT describes an internal-combustion engine in which the piston makes four strokes to complete a cycle. US term **four-cycle**

four·teen /fàwr teen/ *n* **1.** 14 the number 14 **2. SOMETHING WITH VALUE OF 14** something in a numbered series with a value of 14 **3. GROUP OF 14** a group of 14 objects or people —**four·teen** *adj, pron*

four·teenth /fàwr teenth/ *n* one of 14 equal parts of something —**four·teenth** *adj*

fourth /fawrth/ *n* **1. ONE OF 4 PARTS OF SOMETHING** one of four equal parts of something **2. 4 IN SERIES** the ordinal number assigned to item number four in a series **3.** MUSIC **INTERVAL OF 4 NOTES** in a standard musical scale, the interval between one note and another that lies three notes above or below it. In the scale of C major, C and F form a fourth. **4.** MUSIC **NOTE 4TH AWAY FROM ANOTHER** in a standard musical scale, a note that is a fourth away from another note **5.** BALLET same as **fourth position** —**fourth** *adj, adv*

SPELLCHECK See *forth.*

fourth di·men·sion *n* time in relativity theory modified mathematically and used in combination with the usual three spatial dimensions to specify the location in space and time of events —**fourth-di·men·sion·al** *adj*

fourth es·tate, Fourth Es·tate *n* journalists, the press, or the media in general [In addition to the three estates (the Lords Spiritual, the Lords Temporal, and the House of Commons)]

fourth-gen·er·a·tion lan·guage *n* an advanced computer programming language that is more like human language than are the standard high-level programming languages

fourth·ly /fáwrthlee/ *adv* used to introduce the fourth point in an argument or discussion

Fourth of Ju·ly *n* same as **Independence Day**

fourth po·si·tion *n* in ballet, a position in which the feet are turned outward with the right leg extended so that the right foot is one step in front of the left foot

Fourth World *n* the very poorest or least developed countries of the world

four-twen·ty *n S Asia* a swindler who deceives by persuasive speech (*slang*) [< the number of a section of the Indian Penal Code (popularized by the title of a Hindi film)]

~~**fourty**~~ incorrect spelling of **forty**

4WD *abbr* MECH ENG four-wheel drive

four-wheel drive *n* a system of transmitting power from the drive shaft to all four wheels of a motor vehicle in order to provide better traction under difficult conditions

Fou·ta Djal·lon /fòotə jə lón/, **Fu·ta Djal·lon** plateau region in north central Guinea. Its highest point is the Massif du Tamgué, 5,043 ft./1,537 m. Area: 30,000 sq. mi./77,700 sq. km.

fo·ve·a /fóvee ə/ (*plural* **-ve·ae** /-vee ee/) *n* **1.** a small hollow in the surface of a part of the body **2.** ANAT same as **fovea centralis** [Late 17C. < Latin, "small pit"] —**fo·ve·al** *adj* —**fo·ve·ate** /-àyt/ *adj*

fo·ve·a cen·tra·lis /-sen tráalis/ *n* a shallow pit in the center of the retina that is free of blood vessels and has the highest concentration of cells sensitive to color and bright light (**cones**). The fovea centralis is the area of most acute vision. [< Latin, "central fovea"]

fo·ve·o·la /fō vée ələ/ (*plural* **-lae** /-lee/) *n* a small fovea [Mid-19C. < Latin < *fovea* "small pit"] —**fo·ve·o·lar** *adj* —**fo·ve·o·late** *adj* —**fo·ve·o·lat·ed** /fóvee ə làytəd/ *adj*

fowl /fowl/ (*plural same* or **fowls**) *n* **1. CHICKEN** a bird kept for its meat and eggs, especially a chicken **2. EDIBLE OR GAME BIRD** a bird that is used as food or hunted for sport, e.g., a goose or pheasant **3. BIRD'S FLESH** the flesh of any edible bird **4.** same as **bird** (sense 2) (*archaic*) [Old English *fugol* "bird" < Germanic]

SPELLCHECK See *foul.*

fowl·er /fówlər/ *n* a shooter or trapper of wild birds

Fow·ler /fówlər/, **Daniel** (1810–94) British-born Canadian artist. His watercolors depict scenes of Lake Ontario's Amherst Island, where he lived.

Fowles /fowlz/, **John** (*b.* 1926) British novelist. His works include *The Collector* (1963), *The Magus* (1965), and *The French Lieutenant's Woman* (1969). Full name **Fowles, John Robert**. See Cultural note at **magus**

> "We all write poems; it is simply that poets are the ones who write in words."
> [John Fowles, *The French Lieutenant's Woman*; 1969]

fowl·ing /fówling/ *n* the shooting or trapping of wild birds as a livelihood or for sport

fowl·ing piece *n* a light gun that fires small shot, used in hunting game birds

fowl pest *n* a disease of domesticated poultry caused by an influenza virus that reduces the growth rate or egg production

fox

fox /foks/ *n* **1. WILD ANIMAL WITH BUSHY TAIL** a carnivorous animal of the dog family that has a pointed muzzle, large ears, a long bushy tail, and usually reddish brown or gray fur. Foxes are found throughout most of the world and hunt alone, mainly at night, relying on cunning and an acute sense of hearing and smell. Genus: *Vulpes*. **2. FOX FUR** the fur of the fox **3. TRICKSTER** a sly and cunning person (*informal*) **4. GOOD-LOOKING PERSON** a good-looking young person (*slang*) ■ *vt* (**foxed, fox·ing, fox·es**) **1. DECEIVE OR OUTWIT SOMEBODY** to deceive or outwit somebody by means of sly trickery **2. BAFFLE SOMEBODY** to confuse or baffle somebody (*often passive*) [Old English, < Indo-European]

Fox[1] /foks/ (*plural same*) *n* **1.** a member of a Native North American people who lived in Michigan, Wisconsin, Illinois, and Iowa, and now live mainly in Oklahoma and Iowa. Following US attempts under a spurious treaty to move the Fox from their lands in Illinois, they joined with the Sauk in the Black Hawk War of 1832. **2.** a language spoken in parts of Iowa and Oklahoma, belonging to the Algonquian group of Algonquian-Wakashan. Native speakers: 2,000. [Translation of French *Renards*, translation of Iroquoian *Skenchiohronon* "people of the red fox"] —**Fox** *adj*

Fox[2] /foks/ river of eastern Wisconsin, rising in Columbia County and flowing southwestward before emptying into Lake Michigan at Green Bay. Length: 175 mi./282 km.

Fox, Charles James (1749–1806) British politician. He was twice foreign secretary (1782, 1806) and one of the principal leaders of the Whig Party in the period of the American and French Revolutions.

> "Kings govern by means of popular assemblies only when they cannot do without them."
> [Charles James Fox, *Speech to the British Parliament*; October 31, 1776]

Fox, Vicente (*b.* 1942) Mexican politician. He was elected president of Mexico in 2000. Full name **Fox Quesada, Vicente**

Foxe Ba·sin /fóks-/ bay in Nunavut, northeastern Canada, surrounded by Baffin Island, Melville Peninsula, and Hudson Bay. Depth: 295 ft./90 m.

foxed /fokst/ *adj* describes books or paper stained with yellowish brown spots from having been kept in damp conditions

fox·fire /fóks fìr/ *n* a luminescent glow produced by some fungi when in contact with rotting wood

foxglove

fox·glove /fóks glùv/ (*plural same* or **-gloves**) *n* a tall plant that is the source of the drug digitalis. Flowers: purple or white, thimble-shaped. Latin name: *Digitalis purpurea.*

fox grape *n* a wild grape that has purplish fruits and is the source of many cultivated grape varieties. Native to: eastern United States. Latin name: *Vitis labrusca.*

fox·hole /fóks hōl/ *n* a small hole dug in the ground to protect a sniper or other soldier from enemy fire

fox·hound /fóks hòwnd/ *n* a small shorthaired dog that has great speed and stamina, belonging to either of two breeds that are used to hunt foxes

fox hunt·er *n* **1.** a hunter of foxes for sport **2.** a horse used for foxhunting

fox·hunt·ing /fóks hùnting/ *n* a sport in which mounted hunters pursue a fox through open countryside with a pack of foxhounds —**fox·hunt** *n, vi*

fox·tail /fóks tàyl/, **fox·tail grass** *n* a grass with soft cylindrical spikes resembling the tail of a fox. Genera: *Alopecurus* or *Setaria* or *Hordeum.*

fox ter·ri·er *n* a small dog that is either wirehaired or has a smooth coat, belonging to a breed that is white with dark markings

fox·trot /fóks tròt/ *n* **1.** DANCE **BALLROOM DANCE** a ballroom dance alternating longer slower walking steps and shorter quicker running steps, usually with four beats to the bar **2.** MUSIC **MUSIC** the music for a foxtrot **3.** RIDING **HORSE'S SLOW TROTTING PACE** a slow pace for a horse, between a trot and a walk, in which it takes short steps in a broken rhythm [Early 20C. < the short steps of the fox] —**fox·trot** *vi*

Fox·trot *n* a code word for the letter "F," used in international radio communications

fox·y /fóksee/ (**-i·er, -i·est**) *adj* **1. ATTRACTIVE** sensually alluring (*informal*) **2. CRAFTY** clever in a cunning or deceitful way **3. LIKE FOX** like a fox, especially in appearance or through having a strong pungent smell **4.** COLORS **REDDISH BROWN** of a reddish brown color, like fox fur **5.** WINE **SHARP OR MUSKY** having the rather sharp, pungent, or musky flavor of fox grapes —**fox·i·ness** *n*

foy·er /fóy ər, fwaá yày/ *n* **1.** *US* the entrance hall or vestibule in a private house **2.** the lobby in a public building such as a hotel or theater [Mid-19C. Via French < medieval Latin *focarius* < Latin *focus* "fireplace, hearth"]

FPC *abbr* **1.** Federal Power Commission **2.** FOOD INDUST fish protein concentrate

fpl *abbr* fireplace

fpm *abbr* MEASURE feet per minute

FPO *abbr* NAVY fleet post office

fps *abbr* **1.** MEASURE feet per second **2.** *also* **f.p.s.** MEASURE foot-pound-second **3.** PHOTOGRAPHY frames per second (*a measure of camera shutter speed*)

FPS[1] *n* a measure of the rate of screen refreshment in a real-time computer game. Full form **frames per second**

FPS[2] *abbr* COMPUT GAMES first-person shooter

fps u·nits, fps sys·tem of u·nits *n* a system of units based on the foot, second, and pound mass that is now almost wholly superseded by SI units

fr *abbr* France (*used in Internet addresses*) See table at **domain name**

Fr *symbol* CHEM ELEM francium

FR *abbr* BUILDINGS family room

fr. *abbr* from

Fr. *abbr* **1.** CHR Father **2.** France **3.** Frau **4.** French **5.** CHR Friar **6.** CALENDAR Friday

Fra /fraa/, **fra** *n* used as a title for an Italian monk or friar, the equivalent of the English title "Brother" [Late 19C. < Italian, shortening of *frate* "brother, friar" < Latin *frater*]

fra·cas /fráykəss, frákəss/ (*plural same*) *n* a noisy quarrel or fight [Early 18C. < French, "crash, roar" < Italian *fracassare* "cause an uproar"]

frac·tal /frákt'l/ *n* an irregular or fragmented geometric shape that can be repeatedly subdivided into parts, each of which is a smaller copy of the whole. Fractals are used in computer modeling of natural structures that do not have simple geometric shapes such as clouds, mountainous landscapes, and coastlines. [Late 20C. < French < Latin *fract-* (see FRACTION)] —**frac·tal** *adj*

frac·tion /frákshən/ *n* **1.** MATH **NUMBER THAT IS NOT WHOLE NUMBER** a number that is not a whole number, e.g., $\frac{1}{2}$ (**simple fraction**) or 0.5 (**decimal fraction**), formed by dividing one quantity into another **2. SMALL AMOUNT** a small part, amount, or proportion of something ○ *a fraction of the cost* **3. PART** a part or element of a larger whole or group ○ *spent a sizable fraction of his time working on this project* **4.** CHR **BREAKING OF BREAD BY PRIEST** during Communion in the Roman Catholic tradition, the breaking off of a piece of bread by the priest who places it in the chalice **5.** CHEM **SEPARATED COMPONENT** an individual component or portion of a mixture, separated by differences in chemical or physical properties [14C. Via Old French < late Latin *fraction-* < Latin *fract-*, past participle of *frangere* "break"] ◇ **a fraction** by a very small amount or distance ○ *Move it just a fraction to the right.*

ORIGIN The Latin word *frangere* "to break," from which ***fraction*** is derived, and forms related to it, are also sources of English *fracture, fragile, fragment, frail*, and *saxifrage*.

frac·tion·al /frákshən'l/ *adj* **1. SLIGHT** very small or slight ○ *a fractional increase in temperature* **2.** MATH **OF FRACTIONS** relating to or involving fractions **3.** TRAVEL **OF SHARES IN PASSENGER AIRCRAFT** relating to ownership of travel space in a passenger jet, whereby the owners purchase shares under contracts stipulating, e.g., monthly management fees and in-air fuel charges **4.** CHEM **OF SEPARATION OF COMPONENTS** relating to the process of separating individual components from a mixture on the basis of the chemical or physical properties that make them different from other components

frac·tion·al dis·til·la·tion *n* the process of using a volatile liquid to separate components that have different boiling points, by first heating the liquid and then condensing and collecting the components as they vaporize

frac·tion·al·ize /frákshən'l ìz/ (**-ized, -iz·ing, -iz·es**) *vt* to divide something into parts or sections —**frac·tion·al·i·za·tion** /fràkshən'li záysh'n/ *n*

frac·tion·al·ly /frákshən'lee/ *adv* very slightly, or to a very slight degree

frac·tion·ate /frákshə nàyt/ (**-at·ed, -at·ing, -ates**) *v* **1.** *vti* to divide or break something into parts, or be divided or broken into parts (*formal*) **2.** *vt* CHEM to separate a mixture into its components, e.g., by crystallization or distillation —**frac·tion·a·tion** /fràkshə náysh'n/ *n* —**frac·tion·a·tor** *n*

frac·tious /frákshəss/ *adj* irritable and likely to complain or misbehave [Late 17C. < FRACTION] —**frac·tious·ly** *adv* —**frac·tious·ness** *n*

frac·ture /frákchər/ *n* **1. BONE BREAK** a break in a bone **2. ACT OF BREAKING SOMETHING** the act of breaking something, especially a bone **3. BREAK OR CRACK** a break, split, or crack in an object or a material **4. SPLIT IN SYSTEM** a split or division in something such as a system, organization, or agreement ○ *the fractures that are already starting to appear in the peace treaty* **5.** GEOL **ROCK BREAK** a break in a rock or mineral, across which there is a separation ■ *vti* (**-tured, -tur·ing, -tures**) **1. BREAK** to break or crack something, especially a particular bone or a bone in a particular part of the body, or be broken or cracked **2. CAUSE OR UNDERGO DAMAGE** to cause damage or disruption to something or destroy it, or be damaged, disrupted, or destroyed [Mid-16C. Directly or via French < Latin *fractura* < *fract-* (see FRACTION)] —**frac·tur·a·ble** *adj*

frae /fray/ *prep Scotland* same as **from** (*nonstandard*) [13C. Variant of FRO]

frag /frag/ *n* **GRENADE** a fragmentation grenade (*slang*) ■ *vt* (**fragged, frag·ging, frags**) **1. KILL SOMEBODY WITH EXPLOSIVE** to kill or wound a soldier of your own or your allies' forces with a fragmentation grenade or other explosive device (*slang*) **2. KILL VIRTUAL OPPONENT** in a computer game, to kill an opponent [Mid-20C. Shortening of FRAGMENTATION] —**frag·ger** *n* —**frag·ging** *n*

frag·fest /frág fèst/ *n* a computer game that involves killing many opponents

frag·ile /frájjəl/ *adj* **1. EASILY BROKEN** not having a strong structure or not made of robust materials, and therefore easily broken or damaged ○ *too fragile to be used as toys* **2. NOT SECURE** unlikely to withstand any severe stresses and strains ○ *a fragile peace* **3. PHYSICALLY WEAK** in a weak bodily condition, usually as a result of illness ○ *in fragile health* [15C. Directly or via French < Latin *fragilis* < source of *frangere* "break"] —**frag·ile·ly** *adv* —**fra·gil·i·ty** /frə jíllətee/ *n*

SYNONYMS ***fragile, delicate, frail, flimsy***

CORE MEANING: easily broken or damaged

fragile not having a strong structure or not made of robust materials, and therefore easily broken or damaged ○ *protected by a fragile wooden structure* ○ *an ecologically fragile area* **delicate** having a fine, often beautiful, structure that is easily damaged or broken. ○ *a delicate lace fabric* ○ *delicate foliage* **frail** made of weak or delicate materials and easy to break or damage, or not secure, or physically weak and vulnerable to injury ○ *separated by a frail wooden barrier* ○ *a frail economy* ○ *a frail elderly relative* **flimsy** weak and too easily broken, or thin and easily torn ○ *huddled under flimsy shelters* ○ *a flimsy coat*

frag·ile-X syn·drome *n* a genetic condition, caused by a damaged X chromosome with an apparently almost detached part near the end of the long arm, that causes learning difficulties in boys and men

frag·ment *n* /frágmənt/ **1. BROKEN PIECE** a piece, usually a small piece, broken off something or left when something is shattered **2. INCOMPLETE PIECE** an incomplete or isolated piece of something ○ *only heard fragments of the conversation* ■ *vti* /frag mént/ (**-ment·ed, -ment·ing, -ments**) **1. BREAK INTO SMALL PIECES** to break something into small pieces, or be broken in this way ○ *The metal is designed to fragment on impact.* **2. BREAK UP** to lose a sense of unity or cohesion, with the result that something splits into isolated and often conflicting elements, or cause something to do this ○ *Civil war had fragmented the nation and hindered development.* [Mid-16C. Directly or via French < Latin *fragmentum* < source of *frangere* "break"] —**frag·ment·ed** /frag méntəd/ *adj*

frag·men·tal /frag mént'l/ *adj* **1.** same as **fragmentary** **2.** describes rocks that are made up of fragments of preexisting rocks

frag·men·tar·y /frágmən tèrree/ *adj* consisting of the physical fragments or small disconnected items of something —**frag·men·tar·i·ly** /fràgmən térrəlee/ *adv*

frag·men·ta·tion /fràgmən táysh'n/ *n* **1. BREAKING UP OF SOMETHING** the process of shattering or breaking up into fragments **2. LOSS OF UNITY AND COHESION** the loss of unity and cohesion and the splitting of something into isolated and often conflicting parts ○ *The result, inevitably, would be social fragmentation.* **3. SHATTERING OF EXPLOSIVE DEVICE** the scattering of the shattered parts of a grenade or other explosive device **4.** COMPUT **BREAKING UP OF DATA PACKET** the breaking up of computer data into smaller nonconsecutive pieces for more efficient storage and transmission. The danger inherent in this process is that the relationship between the pieces may be lost.

frag·men·ta·tion bomb *n* a bomb or shell with a thick casing that is designed to shatter on detonation into many destructive fragments in order to cause maximum damage or injury

frag·men·ta·tion gre·nade *n* a grenade with a thick casing that is designed to shatter on detonation into many destructive fragments in order to cause maximum damage or injury

frag·men·tize /frágmən tìz/ (**-tized, -tiz·ing, -tiz·es**) *vti US* same as **fragment** *v*

Fra·go·nard /fràggə naár/, **Jean Honoré** (1732–1806) French painter and engraver. He is known for his rococo paintings such as *The Swing* (1766) and *The Progress of Love* (1771–73) that depict romantic scenes of contemporary life. His main source of income, commissions from the aristocracy, dried up at the start of the French Revolution.

fra·grance /fráygrənss/ *n* **1. SWEET SMELL** a pleasant sweet smell ○ *a plant with an exotic heady fragrance* **2. SWEETNESS OF SMELL** the characteristic of being sweet-smelling **3. PERFUME** something that has a distinctive smell, e.g., a perfume or cologne ○ *a great new fragrance for men* ○ *fragrance-free cosmetics* —**fra·granced** *adj*

SYNONYMS See ***smell***.

fra·grance strip *n* a sealed strip of card or paper included with something such as a magazine advertisement and impregnated with a fragrance that is released when the cover is peeled off

fra·gran·cy /fráygrənssee/ *n* same as **fragrance** (sense 2)

fra·grant /fráygrənt/ *adj* having a pleasant sweet smell [15C. Directly or via French < Latin *fragrant-*, present participle of *fragrare* "emit a (good or bad) odor"] —**fra·grant·ly** *adv*

fraid·y-cat /fráydee-/ *n US* somebody who is scared or who lacks courage (*informal; usually used by or to children*) Can term **scaredy-cat** [< shortening of AFRAID]

frail /frayl/ (**frail·er, frail·est**) *adj* **1. PHYSICALLY WEAK** in a physically weakened state and vulnerable to injury ○ *a frail elderly relative* **2. EASY TO BREAK OR DAMAGE** made of weak or delicate materials and easy to break or damage ○ *It didn't look as if such a frail chair would support her weight.* **3. NOT SECURE** lacking any secure foundation in fact or reality and unlikely to be realized or be successful ○ *frail hopes of success* **4. MORALLY WEAK** easily tempted and persuaded to do something morally bad or wrong [14C. Via Old French *fraile* < Latin *fragilis* (see FRAGILE)] —**frail·ly** *adv* —**frail·ness** *n*

SYNONYMS See ***fragile*** and ***weak***.

frail·ty /fráyltee/ (*plural* **-ties**) *n* **1. WEAKNESS** physical weakness, or weakness of materials and construction **2. MORAL WEAKNESS** inherent moral weakness in humanity or in a person leading to difficulty in resisting temptation or avoiding wrongdoing **3. CHARACTER FLAW** a character flaw arising out of moral weakness (*often used in the plural*) ○ *ordinary human frailties*

fraise /frayz/ *n* a cone-shaped grooved drill bit used for enlarging a previously drilled hole [Early 17C. < French, "lining of a calf's abdomen"; from its numerous folds]

Frak·tur /frak to͝or/, **frak·tur** *n* a thick ornate style of printed letter, the standard typeface for all printing in German until the mid-20th century. It was used in the calligraphy and artwork of the Pennsylvania Dutch. [Late 19C. Via German < Latin *fractura* (see FRACTURE)]

Fra Mau·ro /fraà máwrō/ eroded crater on the Moon north of Mare Nubium, approximately 59 mi./95 km in diameter. Apollo 14 landed close to Fra Mauro in 1971.

fram·be·sia /fram beézhə/ *n* MED same as **yaws** [Early 19C. < modern Latin < French *framboise* "raspberry" (suggested by the sores produced by the disease)]

frame /fraym/ *n* **1. SUPPORTING STRUCTURE** an underlying or supporting structure that consists of solid parts such as beams or struts with spaces between them and has something built around or on top of it ○ *a bike with a steel frame* **2. SURROUNDING STRUCTURE** a structure that surrounds or encloses a particular space ○ *a picture frame* ○ *a door frame* **3.** OPHTHALMOL **LENS-HOLDING PART OF EYEGLASSES** the part of a pair of eyeglasses that holds the lenses and fits around the wearer's face **4. HOLLOW SHAPE FOR NEEDLECRAFT AND PAINTING**

an open structure across which a piece of material can be stretched to be painted or embroidered, or across which threads can be stretched for weaving **5. CONTEXT** the general background or context against or within which something takes place ○ *the story's historical frame* **6. HUMAN BODY** somebody's body, especially with reference to its size and shape ○ *He eased his enormous frame into the chair.* **7.** MOVIES, PHOTOGRAPHY **PICTURE ON STRIP OF FILM** one of the individual pictures that make up a strip of movie film, or a single exposure on a strip of photographic negative or slide images **8.** MOVIES, MEDIA **VISIBLE PART OF FILMED ACTION** in film, video, or TV, the particular area of action that is captured by the camera and forms the rectangular image that appears on the screen ○ *characters moving out of the frame to the left* **9.** PHOTOGRAPHY **IMAGE BORDER** the border or set of borders of a projected image **10.** PUBL **SINGLE PICTURE IN COMIC STRIP** one of the individual pictures that make up a comic strip **11.** GARDENING same as **cold frame** **12.** LAWN BOWLING **ROUND OF BOWLING** one of the ten rounds in a bowling game **13.** *UK* CUE GAMES same as **rack**[1] *n* (senses 7–9) **14.** ONLINE **AREA OF COMPUTER SCREEN** a rectangular area on a computer screen, containing all or a portion of a webpage. More than one frame can be displayed concurrently. **15.** COMPUT **SINGLE CYCLE OF PULSES** a single cycle of pulses in a string of repeated pulses **16.** COMPUT **DATA PACKET** a variable-length data packet preceded and followed by addressing and control information that is transmitted between network points as a unit. Some control frames contain no data. **17.** CRIME same as **frame-up** (sense 1) (*slang*) ■ **frames** *npl* **1.** OPHTHALMOL same as **frame** (sense 3) **2.** ONLINE **WEB BROWSER FEATURE** a web browser feature that segments the window being displayed, allowing the concurrent display of two or more pages on the same screen ■ *vt* (**framed, fram·ing, frames**) **1. PUT SOMETHING IN FRAME** to mount a picture in a frame **2. FORM SURROUNDING FRAMEWORK FOR SOMETHING** to form a surrounding border or framework, especially a decorative or contrasting one, around something (*often passive*) ○ *a delicate face framed by abundant black hair* **3. CONSTRUCT IDEA OR STATEMENT** to construct or compose something that is to be written or spoken ○ *She framed her words carefully.* **4. EXPRESS SOMETHING IN PARTICULAR WAY** to express something in a particular type of language ○ *framed the argument in legal terms* **5. MOUTH WORDS** to mouth words silently **6. CAUSE SOMEBODY TO APPEAR GUILTY** to make an innocent person appear guilty, e.g., by forging incriminating evidence (*slang*) **7. ARRANGE RESULT OF SOMETHING IN ADVANCE** to use dishonest or illegal methods to arrange the result of a contest in advance, e.g., by paying a player to lose deliberately (*slang*) ■ *adj* CONSTR, ARCHIT **WITH WOODEN FRAMEWORK** constructed on a framework of wooden beams, then covered with boards or shingles ○ *a white frame house with black shutters* [Old English *framian* "make progress, be helpful, prepare, shape" < *fram* (see FROM)] —**frame·a·ble** *adj*

frame of mind *n* somebody's psychological state, attitude, or mood at a specific time

frame of ref·er·ence *n* **1.** the set of norms, values, or ideas that affect the way somebody interacts with others, either in everyday life or in a particular situation **2.** MATH a set of geometric axes used to determine the location of a point in space

fram·er /fráymər/ *n* **1.** somebody who makes and fits frames for pictures **2.** *also* **Fram·er** *US* any one of the delegates who drew up the Constitution of the United States

frame rate *n* the refresh rate of what is shown on the screen in a real-time computer game

frame sto·ry *n* a narrative that provides the framework within which a number of different stories, which may or may not be connected, can be told. An example of a frame story is the pilgrims' ride to Canterbury that provides the starting point for Chaucer's *Canterbury Tales.*

frame-up *n* (*slang*) **1.** a conspiracy to make an innocent person appear guilty, e.g., by forging incriminating evidence **2.** a situation in which the result of a contest is dishonestly or illegally arranged in advance

frame·work /fráym wùrk/ *n* **1. UNDERLYING SET OF IDEAS** a set of ideas, principles, agreements, or rules that provides the basis or outline for something intended to be more fully developed at a later stage ○ *providing a framework for next week's discussions* **2. CONTEXT** the general background to, or context for, a particular action or event ○ *within the framework of Jewish religious tradition* **3. SYSTEM OF INTERCONNECTING BARS** a structure of connected horizontal and vertical bars with spaces between them, especially one that forms the skeleton of another structure **4.** HANDICRAFT **ARTICLES WOVEN OR EMBROIDERED ON FRAME** articles produced by weaving or embroidering cloth on a frame

fram·ing /fráyming/ *n* **1. WAY SOMETHING IS FRAMED** the way that something is framed **2.** MOVIES **ADJUSTMENT OF FILM PROJECTOR SETTINGS** the adjustment of the settings on a film projector so that the image is in the correct position on the screen **3.** MOVIES **COMPOSITION OF FILM SCENE** the composition of a scene within the visual field of the camera for shooting in a film

Fra·ming·ham /fráyming hàm/ town in eastern Massachusetts. It is a suburb of Boston. Population: 66,827 (2002 estimate).

franc /frangk/ *n* **1.** the main unit of currency in several French-speaking countries. See table at **currency** **2.** the main unit of the former currency in France, Belgium, and Luxembourg [14C. < French]

France

France /franss/ largest country in western Europe. Its present constitution was established in 1958 with the proclamation of the Fifth Republic. Language: French. Currency: Euro. Capital: Paris. Population: 60,182,529 (2003). Area: 210,026 sq. mi./543,965 sq. km. Official name **French Republic**

France, Anatole (1844–1924) French writer. He produced a large body of writings, including novels, drama, verse, critical and philosophical essays, and historical works. He won the Nobel Prize in literature (1921). Pseudonym of **Jacques Anatole François Thibault**

> "To die for an idea is to place a pretty high price upon conjectures."
> [Anatole France, *The Revolt of the Angels*; 1933]

fran·chise /frán chīz/ *n* **1.** COMM **LICENSE TO SELL COMPANY'S PRODUCTS** an agreement or license to sell a company's products exclusively in a particular area or to operate a business that carries that company's name **2. BUSINESS OPERATED UNDER LICENSE** a business licensed to sell a company's products exclusively in a particular area or to operate a business that carries that company's name **3.** COMM **AREA OF COMMERCIAL OPERATION** the area in which somebody has a commercial franchise **4. PRIVILEGE GRANTED BY AUTHORITY** a right or privilege, or an exemption from a duty or obligation, granted by a government or other authority **5. RIGHT TO VOTE** the right to vote, especially to elect representatives to a national legislature or a parliament **6. PROFESSIONAL SPORTS TEAM** a professional sports team that is a member of an organized league (*informal*) **7.** SPORTS **LICENSE FOR SPORTS TEAM** an agreement or license to own a sports team **8.** *also* **fran·chise play·er** *US* **VALUABLE SPORTS TEAM MEMBER** a player who is valuable and important to a team (*informal*) [14C. < French < *franc* "free" (see FRANK[1])] —**fran·chise** *vt* —**fran·chis·ee** /fràn chī zeé/ *n* —**fran·chise·ment** /frán chīzmənt, fránchiz-/ *n* —**fran·chis·er** *n*

Fran·cis I /frànssiss/ (1494–1547) king of France. His reign (1515–47) was dominated by conflict with Charles V, Holy Roman Emperor.

> "Of all I had, only honor and life have been spared."
> [Francis I, *Letter to his mother, Louise of Savoy*; February 24, 1525]

Fran·cis II (1768–1835) last Holy Roman Emperor (1792–1806) and, as Francis I, first emperor of Austria (1804–35). He dissolved the Holy Roman Empire in 1806 and united with Great Britain and Russia to defeat Napoleon (1815). In the subsequent Congress of Vienna (1815), he regained most of the territory Austria had lost in the Napoleonic wars.

Fran·cis (of As·si·si), St. (1182–1226) Italian mystic and preacher. He founded the Franciscan and Poor Clare orders of the Roman Catholic Church. Born **Bernardone, Giovanni Francesco**

> "Grant me the treasure of sublime poverty."
> [Francis (of Assisi). Quoted in *A History of Medieval Europe*, Maurice Keen; 1967]

Fran·cis·can /fran sískən/ *n* a member of an order of friars and nuns, founded by St. Francis of Assisi, that now has three separate branches and is largely devoted to missionary and charitable work. [Late 16C. Via French < modern Latin *Franciscanus* < *Franciscus* "Francis"] —**Fran·cis·can** *adj*

Fran·cis Fer·di·nand ➧ **Franz Ferdinand**

Fran·cis Jo·seph I ➧ **Franz Josef**

Fran·cis of Sales /-saál/, **St.** (1567–1622) French cleric and writer. A leader of the Counter-Reformation, he became bishop of Geneva (1602).

> "Big fires flare up in a wind, but little ones are blown out unless they are carried in under cover."
> [Francis of Sales, *Introduction to The Devout Life*; 1609]

fran·ci·um /frànssee əm/ *n* an unstable radioactive element of the alkali-metal group. Source: uranium ore, or made artificially from actinium and thorium. Symbol **Fr.** See table at **element** [Mid-20C. After FRANCE, home of its discoverer]

fran·cize /frán sīz/ (**-cized, -ciz·ing, -ciz·es**) *vt Can* to make a person, business, or group adopt French as a working language, especially in Quebec, Canada [Late 20C. < French *franciser* < *français* "French"] —**fran·ci·za·tion** /fràn si záysh'n/ *n*

Franck /frangk, fraaNk/, **César Auguste** (1822–90) Belgian-born French composer and organist. He combined classical form with romantic content in his best-known work, the Symphony in D minor (1886–88), which has served as a model for subsequent French composers.

AKG London
Francisco Franco

Fran·co /frángkō/, **Francisco** (1892–1975) Spanish general and national leader. He defeated the Republican army during the Spanish Civil War (1936–39) and established a dictatorship in Spain in 1939, ruling until his death in 1975.

Franco- *prefix* France, French ○ *Francophile* [< late Latin *Francus* "Frank" < Germanic]

Fran·co·ni·an /frang kōnee ən/ *n* a group of medieval dialects of German spoken in an area extending from present-day Bavaria and Alsace, and up the Rhine valley —**Fran·co·ni·an** *adj*

Fran·co·phile /frángkə fīl/, **Fran·co·phil** /-fil/ *n* somebody who likes France, the French people, or the French way of life ■ *adj* liking or admiring France, the French people, or the French way of life —**Fran·co·phil·i·a** /fràngkə fíllee ə/ *n*

Fran·co·phobe /frángkə fōb/ *n* somebody who intensely dislikes France, the French people, or the French way of life —**Fran·co·pho·bi·a** /fràngkə fṓbee ə/ *n*

Fran·co·pho·bic /fràngkə fṓbik/ *adj* having an intense dislike of France, the French people, or the French way of life

fran·co·phone /frángkə fōn/ *n* SPEAKER OF FRENCH somebody who speaks French, especially as a first language ■ *adj* **1.** FRENCH-SPEAKING speaking French as a first or main language **2.** OF FRENCH-SPEAKING AREA relating to a place where French is used as the main language, the official language, or a lingua franca ○ *Francophone Africa* —**Fran·co·phon·ic** /fràngkə fónnik/ *adj*

fran·gi·ble /fránjəb'l/ *adj* brittle, or designed to be easily broken (*formal or technical*) ○ *glass and other frangible products* ○ *frangible aluminum masts* [15C. Directly or via Old French < medieval Latin *frangibilis* < *frangere* "break"] —**fran·gi·bil·i·ty** /frànjə bíllətee/ *n*

fran·gi·pane /fránjə pàyn/ *n* an almond-flavored cream or custard used in pastries, cakes, and other sweet foods [Mid-19C. < French, "frangipani" (perfume made with bitter almonds)]

fran·gi·pan·i /frànjə pánnee, -paánee/ (*plural* **-is**) *n* **1.** TREES a deciduous tree with strongly perfumed, white, yellow, or pink flowers. Native to: tropical America. Genus: *Plumeria*. **2.** a perfume derived from frangipani flowers or imitating their scent **3.** FOOD same as **frangipane 4.** TREES same as **native frangipani** [Mid-19C. After Muzio *Frangipani*, 16C Italian creator of a perfume for gloves]

Fran·glais /frong gláy, fróng glày/, **fran·glais** *n* an informal form of French that includes many English loanwords and phrases. For French traditionalists, it is seen as evidence of the extent to which American and British cultural imperialism has permeated French and French-Canadian life. [Mid-20C. < French, blend of *français* "French" + *anglais* "English"] —**Franglais** *adj*

frank[1] /frangk/ *adj* **1.** EXPRESSING TRUE OPINION open, honest, and sometimes forceful in expressing true feelings and opinions ○ *Let me be frank with you.* **2.** SHOWING OPENNESS AND BLUNTNESS allowing people's true feelings and opinions to be openly and often bluntly stated ○ *a frank discussion of our differences* **3.** PLEASINGLY HONEST having or showing an appealingly open and honest nature ○ *has a frank manner that won her many friends* **4.** UNDISGUISED openly expressed, without concealment or disguise ○ *regarded him with frank loathing* ■ *vt* (**franked, franking, franks**) MAIL **1.** PRINT MARK OVER STAMP to print an official mark over the stamp on a letter or package to show that payment has been formally accepted **2.** PRINT MARK SHOWING POSTAGE PAID to print a mark on a piece of mail, instead of using a postage stamp, to show that postage has been paid or that there is no postage charge ■ *n* **1.** OFFICIAL MARK ON MAIL an official mark printed on a piece of mail to show that postage has been paid or that postage is free of charge **2.** MAIL RIGHT TO FREE MAIL DELIVERY the right to have mailed items delivered free of charge [14C. Via French, "free, generous, candid" < medieval Latin *francus* "Frank, free"; from the granting of full political freedom in Gaul only to the Franks] —**frank·ness** *n*

frank[2] /frangk/ *n US* same as **frankfurter** (*informal*) [Mid-20C. Shortening]

Frank /frangk/ *n* a member of a Germanic people who lived along the Rhine valley and spread westward during the decline of the Roman Empire in the 4th century A.D. They conquered vast areas of western Europe, taking over Gaul and becoming the dominant people in an area covering much of present-day western Germany. [Old English *Franca* < Germanic] —**Frank·ish** *adj*

Frank /frangk/, **Anne** (1929–45) German-born Jewish writer. She kept a diary during her years in hiding during the German occupation of the Netherlands (1942–44). She and her family were captured in 1944, and she died in a concentration camp.

> "I want to go on living even after death!"
> [Anne Frank, *Diary*; April 4, 1944]

frank·en·food /frángkən fōōd/ *n* food or a food product produced using genetic engineering (*slang disapproving*) [Late 20C. < shortening of FRANKENSTEIN]

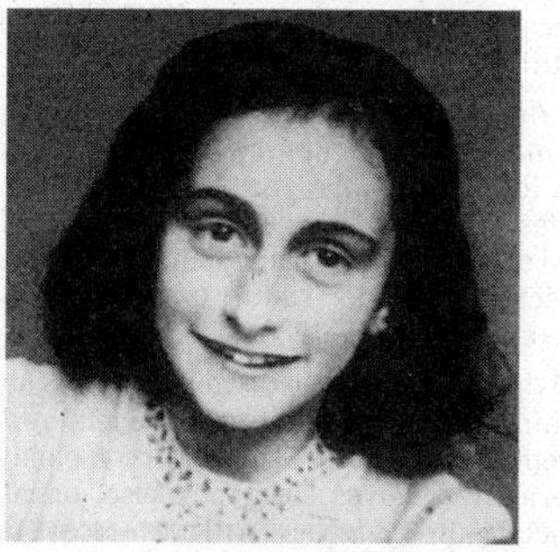
AKG London

Anne Frank

Popperfoto

Aretha Franklin

Frank·en·stein /frángkən stīn/ *n* **1.** CREATOR OF SOMETHING DESTRUCTIVE a creator of something that causes ruin or destruction, or brings about a personal downfall **2.** MONSTER a monster typically represented as a very large coarse-featured person, often with features such as bolts in the neck and a shambling walk **3.** *also* **Frank·en·stein's mon·ster** OUT-OF-CONTROL INVENTION a creation or invention that gets beyond its maker's control and threatens harm or destruction [Early 19C. < novel by Mary Shelley (1818), in which the main character, Baron *Frankenstein*, creates a living man]

Frank·en·thal·er /frángkən thàwlər, -thòllər/, **Helen** (*b.* 1928) US artist. She is known for her abstract expressionism and innovative techniques for applying color to canvas.

> "Just as in relations with people, as in art, if you always stick to style, manners, and what will work, and you're never caught off guard, then some beautiful experiences never happen."
> [Helen Frankenthaler, *Interview, Arts magazine*, Cindy Nemser; November 1971]

Frank·fort /fránkfərt/ **1.** city in central Indiana, southeast of Lafayette and northwest of Indianapolis. Population: 16,593 (2002 estimate). **2.** capital of Kentucky, in the north central part of the state, on the Kentucky River, northwest of Lexington and east of Louisville. Population: 27,660 (2002 estimate).

Frank·furt /frángkfərt, -foort/ **1.** *also* **Frank·furt am Main** /-aam mīn/ city in west central Germany, in the state of Hessen. Situated on the Main River, it is a major commercial and financial center. Population: 652,412 (1997). **2.** *also* **Frank·furt an der O·der** /-aan der ṓdər/ city in northeastern Germany, in the state of Brandenburg. It is situated east of Berlin on the Oder River. Population: 87,863 (1989).

frank·furt·er /frángkfərtər/, **frank·furt** /-fərt/ *n* a thin-skinned sausage, originally from Germany, made of finely minced smoked pork or beef and grilled, fried, or boiled [Late 19C. < German *Frankfurter Wurst*, smoked sausage first produced in Frankfurt am Main]

Frank·furt·er /frángkfərtər/, **Felix** (1882–1965) Austrian-born associate justice of the US Supreme Court (1939–62). He advocated judicial restraint.

> "There is no inevitability in history except as men make it."
> [Attributed to Felix Frankfurter. Quoted in *Saturday Review*; October 30, 1954]

frank·in·cense /frángkən sènss/ *n* an aromatic gum or resin used as incense, especially in religious ceremonies, and in perfumes. It is obtained from trees of the genus *Boswellia*, native to Africa. [14C. < Old French *franc encens* "superior-quality incense"]

frank·ing ma·chine *n UK* MAIL same as **postage meter**

Frank·ish /frángkish/ *n* EXTINCT GERMANIC LANGUAGE an extinct Germanic language spoken by the Franks. The French vocabulary shows a heavy Frankish influence. ■ *adj* **1.** OF FRANKS relating to the Franks **2.** OF FRANKISH relating to Frankish

Frank·lin /frángklin/ city in Williamson County on the Harpeth River, Tennessee. Population: 45,175 (2002 estimate).

Frank·lin, Aretha (*b.* 1942) US soul singer. Known as "The Queen of Soul," she began her recording career in 1960. Her most famous recordings include "Respect" (1967) and "I Never" (1967). Full name **Franklin, Aretha Louise**

> "Now there's a plain bare fact...Soul came up from gospel and blues."
> [Aretha Franklin. Quoted in *Nowhere to Run*, Gerri Hirshey; 1984]

Frank·lin, Benjamin (1706–90) American diplomat, printer, author, and scientist. He helped draft, then signed, the Declaration of Independence (1776) and was a US diplomat to France (1776–85). His famous autobiography was published posthumously. Also renowned as a scientist, he invented the Franklin stove (1740s), lightning rod (1752), and bifocal lens (1760).

> "In this world nothing can be said to be certain but death and taxes."
> [Benjamin Franklin, *Letter to Jean-Baptiste Le Roy*; November 13, 1789]

Frank·lin, Sir John (1786–1847) British naval officer and explorer. He died on his fourth Arctic expedition, during which the Northwest Passage was discovered (1845).

Frank·lin, Rosalind Elsie (1920–58) British biophysicist. Her research contributed to the discovery of the double-helix structure of DNA.

Frank·lin, William (1731–1813) American colonial administrator. The illegitimate son of Benjamin Franklin, he was a Loyalist governor of New Jersey (1763–76) during the Revolution. After 1782 he lived in England.

frank·lin·ite /frángkli nīt/ *n* a black weakly magnetic mineral of the spinel group, containing iron, manganese, and zinc [Early 19C. After *Franklin*, New Jersey]

Frank·lin Square residential town in Nassau County, southeastern Long Island, New York. Population: 28,205 (2002 estimate).

Frank·lin stove *n* a cast-iron heating stove with doors, whose interior is like an open fireplace [Late 18C. After Benjamin FRANKLIN, who invented it]

Frank·lin Strait body of water in Nunavut, north central Canada, between Prince of Wales Island and Boothia Peninsula

frank·ly /frángklee/ *adv* **1.** used to indicate that you are expressing an honest personal opinion, often a negative one ○ *Most of what she said was, frankly, a pack of lies.* **2.** in an honest, sincere, and often blunt or forthright way ○ *was asked personal questions that he answered remarkably frankly*

fran·tic /frántik/ *adj* **1.** in a state in which it is impossible to keep feelings or behavior under control, usually through fear, worry, or frustration **2.** characterized by great haste and excitement and a great deal of usually disorganized activity [Early 16C. < French *frénétique* (see FRENETIC)] —**fran·ti·cal·ly** *adv*

~~**franticly**~~ incorrect spelling of **frantically**

Franz Fer·di·nand /frànz fúrd'n ànd/ (1863–1914) Archduke of Austria. His assassination and that of his wife, the Duchess of Hohenburg, while on an official visit to Sarajevo in 1914, led to the outbreak of World War I.

Franz Jo·sef /frànz jṓzəf/ (1830–1916) emperor of Austria (1848–1916) and king of Hungary (1867–1916). He divided his Austrian empire into the dual

Austro-Hungarian monarchy in 1867, during a reign that was characterized by nationalist strife culminating in the outbreak of World War I (1914).

Franz Jo·sef Land archipelago of about 100 small ice-covered islands in the Arctic Ocean, northwestern Russia, including Alexandra Land, George Land, Wilczek Land, and Graham Bell Island. Area: 7,990 sq. mi./20,700 sq. km.

frap /frap/ (**frapped, frap·ping, fraps**) *vt* to tie something down, or tie things together, with ropes [Mid-16C. < Old French *fraper* "hit"]

frap·pé /fra páy, frap/ *n* **1.** FOOD **COLD DESSERT** a dish consisting of fruit-flavored water ice, served before a meal or as a dessert **2.** BEVERAGES **ICED ALCOHOLIC DRINK** an alcoholic drink, especially a liqueur, served poured over crushed ice **3.** *also* **frap·pe** /frap/ *New England* BEVERAGES **MILK SHAKE** a milk shake ■ *adj* BEVERAGES **CHILLED** chilled or poured over crushed ice ○ *a café frappé* [Mid-19C. < French, past participle of *frapper* "hit, chill"]

Frap·puc·ci·no /fràppə cheénō/ *tdmk* a trademark for a drink made of coffee blended with milk, crushed ice, and flavorings

Fra·ser /fráyzər, fráyzhər/ river in south central British Columbia, Canada. It rises in the Rocky Mountains and empties into the Strait of Georgia, near Vancouver. Length: 850 mi./1,370 km.

Fra·ser /fráyzər/, **Dawn** (*b.* 1937) Australian swimmer. She was the first woman to swim the 100 meters freestyle in under one minute and the first swimmer to win three consecutive Olympic gold medals in that event (1956, 1960, and 1964). Full name **Fraser, Dawn Lorraine**

Fra·ser, Peter (1884–1950) Scottish-born New Zealand politician. A Labor Party politician, he served as prime minister of New Zealand from 1940 to 1949. See table at **prime minister**

Fra·ser, Simon (1776–1862) US-born Canadian fur trader and explorer. He founded settlements in British Columbia (1805–08) and explored the Fraser River.

Fra·ser Is·land island off the coast of southern Queensland, Australia. It is the largest sand island in the world. Population: 100. Area: 642 sq. mi./1,662 sq. km.

frass /frass/ *n* excrement or debris left behind by an insect or insect larva [Mid-19C. < German < *fressen* "eat, devour"]

frat /frat/ *n* a fraternity at a college or university (*informal*) [Late 19C. Shortening]

fra·ter·nal /frə túrn'l/ *adj* **1.** **OF BROTHERS** existing between brothers or felt by one brother for another **2.** **SHOWING FRIENDSHIP AND MUTUAL SUPPORT** showing friendship and mutual support between people or groups with the same interests or aims ○ *fraternal greetings* **3.** **OF FRATERNITIES** relating to or organized as a fraternity **4.** BIOL **FROM TWO OVA** describes twins that have developed from two ova, instead of from a single ovum [15C. < medieval Latin *fraternalis* < Latin *frater* "brother"] —**fra·ter·nal·ism** *n* —**fra·ter·nal·ly** *adv*

fra·ter·ni·ty /frə túrnətee/ (*plural* **-ties**) *n* **1.** **SOCIETY FOR COLLEGE MEN** a social society for men who are students at a college or university, with a name consisting of individually pronounced Greek letters **2.** **PEOPLE WITH SOMETHING IN COMMON** a group of people with something such as being in the same profession or sharing the same pastime in common ○ *the banking fraternity* **3.** **BROTHERLY LOVE** feelings of friendship and mutual support between people ○ *liberty, equality, and fraternity* **4.** **SOCIETY FORMED FOR COMMON PURPOSE** a group or society formed by people who share the same interests [14C. Via French < Latin *fraternitas* < *frater* "brother"]

frat·er·nize /fráttər nīz/ (**-nized, -niz·ing, -niz·es**) *v* **1.** *vi* to spend time socially with other people, especially people with whom it is not regarded as acceptable to be friendly ○ *fraternizing with the enemy* **2.** *vti* to enter into a sexual relationship with a person of a different rank against military regulations [Early 17C. Via French < medieval Latin *fraternizare* < Latin *frater* "brother"] —**frat·er·ni·za·tion** /fràttərni záysh'n/ *n* —**frat·er·niz·er** *n*

frat·ri·cide /fráttri sīd/ *n* **1.** the crime of killing a brother **2.** somebody who kills a brother [15C. Via French < Latin *fratricida* "brother-killer"] —**frat·ri·cid·al** /fràttri sīd'l/ *adj*

Frau /frow/ (*plural* **Frau·en** /fróws ən/ or **Fraus**) *n* in German-speaking countries, used as a title equivalent to English "Mrs." or "Ms." before the name or professional title of a married woman. It is also used as a courtesy title for some unmarried women, especially of senior status. ○ *Frau Koch* [Early 19C. < German, "woman, wife"]

fraud /frawd/ *n* **1.** **CRIME OF CHEATING SOMEBODY** the crime of obtaining money or some other benefit by deliberate deception **2.** **SOMEBODY WHO DECEIVES** somebody who deliberately deceives somebody else, usually for financial gain **3.** **SOMETHING INTENDED TO DECEIVE** something that is intended to deceive people ○ *a story that was subsequently exposed as a fraud* [14C. Via Old French < Latin *fraud-* "cheating, fraud"]

fraud·ster /fráwdstər/ *n* a criminal who obtains money or some other benefit by deliberate deception

fraud·u·lent /fráwjələnt/ *adj* not honest, true, or fair, and intended to deceive people —**fraud·u·lence** *n* —**fraud·u·lent·ly** *adv*

fraud·u·lent pref·er·ence *n Can* the improper preferential treatment of one creditor over another in bankruptcy proceedings

fraught /frawt/ *adj* **1.** full of or accompanied by problems, dangers, or difficulties ○ *an evening fraught with embarrassment* **2.** full of or expressing nervous tension and anxiety ○ *looking fraught and close to tears* [14C. < past participle of obsolete *fraught* "load with cargo" < Middle Dutch or Middle Low German *vrachten*]

Fräu·lein /fróy līn, frów-/ (*plural same* or **-leins**) *n* in German-speaking countries, used as a title equivalent to English "Miss" before the name or professional title of a girl or unmarried woman. It is also used as a form of address. ○ *Fräulein Bauer* [Late 17C. < German, "little woman" < *Frau* "woman, wife"]

Fraun·ho·fer lines /frówn hōfər-/ *npl* narrow dark lines in the Sun's spectrum, caused mainly by absorption in the cooler outer layers of the Sun's atmosphere [Mid-19C. After Joseph von *Fraunhofer* (1787–1826), German scientist]

frax·i·nel·la /fràksə néllə/ *n* PLANTS same as **gas plant** [Mid-17C. < modern Latin < Latin *fraxinus* "ash tree"; from the shape of the leaves]

fray[1] /fray/ *vti* (**frayed, fray·ing, frays**) **1.** **WEAR AWAY AND HANG IN THREADS** to wear away the edge or surface of cloth or rope by friction, causing threads to hang loose, or be worn away in this way ○ *frayed at the cuffs* **2.** **MAKE OR BECOME STRAINED** to become strained, causing irritability or anger, or cause somebody's nerves, temper, or patience to become strained ○ *Tempers were already fraying.* ■ *n* **WORN PART WITH LOOSE THREADS** a worn area on cloth or rope, with loose threads showing [15C. Via French *frayer* < Latin *fricare* "rub"]

fray[2] /fray/ *n* **1.** an argument, quarrel, or rowdy fight ○ *The local newspaper immediately joined the fray.* **2.** an exciting, energetic, or stressful activity or situation ○ *back into the fray* [14C. Shortening of AFFRAY]

Fra·zer /fráyzər/, **Sir James George** (1854–1941) British anthropologist. In his most famous work, *The Golden Bough* (1890), he examines the relationship between myth and religion. See Cultural note at **bough**

fra·zil /fráyz'l, frázz'l/ *n* ice that forms as small plates drifting in rapidly flowing water when it is too turbulent for pack ice to form [Late 19C. < Canadian French *frasil*]

fraz·zle /frázz'l/ *n* **1.** **EXHAUSTED STATE** a state of complete emotional and physical exhaustion ○ *was wearing herself to a frazzle* **2.** **FRAYED CONDITION** a frayed or worn condition ■ *v* (**-zled, -zling, -zles**) **1.** *vt* **EXHAUST SOMEBODY** to completely exhaust somebody emotionally and physically **2.** *vi* **BE FRAYED** to fray or become worn ○ *Shred the strips of fabric so they frazzle and blend together.* [Early 19C. Probably blend of FRAY[1] + FRIZZLE[1] or obsolete *fazle* "ravel"]

fraz·zled /frázz'ld/ *adj* **1.** exhausted and in a very confused or irritable state (*informal*) **2.** frayed and in a generally worn, tangled, or otherwise unsatisfactory state

FRB *abbr* BANKING Federal Reserve Board

FRCPC *abbr* MED Fellow of the Royal College of Physicians, Canada

FRCSC *abbr* SURG Fellow of the Royal College of Surgeons, Canada

freak[1] /freek/ *n* **1.** **STRIKINGLY UNUSUAL PERSON, ANIMAL, OR PLANT** a person, animal, or plant that is strikingly unusual and appears to be unique or occurs very rarely (*sometimes considered offensive*) **2.** **UNUSUAL OCCURRENCE** a highly unusual or unlikely occurrence, often brought about by a unique or very rare combination of circumstances **3.** **IMPULSE** something somebody suddenly does or decides for no real reason **4.** **FANATIC** somebody who is fanatical about something (*informal*) ○ *a club for fitness freaks* **5.** **OFFENSIVE TERM** an offensive term for somebody who is thought to behave unconventionally or have unusual tastes or habits (*informal insult*) **6.** **DRUG USER** an addict or user of a particular drug (*slang*) **7.** same as **hippie** (*dated slang*) ■ *adj* **HIGHLY UNUSUAL OR UNLIKELY** highly unusual or unlikely, and often brought about by a unique or very rare combination of circumstances ■ *vti* (**freaked, freak·ing, freaks**) (*slang*) **1.** **BECOME OR MAKE OVEREMOTIONAL** to become very nervous, upset, or angry, or make somebody become so ○ *a loud explosion that freaked the cattle* **2.** **BEHAVE STRANGELY** to behave wildly or irrationally, or make somebody behave wildly or irrationally, sometimes under the effects of hallucinations or feelings of paranoia, often as a result of taking drugs [Mid-16C. Origin ?]

freak out *vti* to become extremely upset or agitated, or make somebody become so (*slang*)

freak[2] /freek/ (**freaked, freak·ing, freaks**) *vt* to streak or spot something with color (*archaic*) [Mid-17C. Origin ?]

freak·ing /freéking/ *adj* an offensive term expressing strong feelings by its similarity in sound to other offensive terms (*slang*)

freak·ish /freékish/ *adj* **1.** extremely, disconcertingly, or ridiculously unusual (*offensive in some contexts*) ○ *a freakish accident* **2.** tending to change suddenly and unpredictably ○ *freakish weather* —**freak·ish·ly** *adv* —**freak·ish·ness** *n*

freak-out, freak·out /freék owt/ *n* (*slang*) **1.** an outburst of emotion or agitated behavior **2.** a drug-induced bout of hallucination or paranoia, especially a frightening one

freak·y /freékee/ (**-i·er, -i·est**) *adj* unusual, strange, or bizarre (*slang*) —**freak·i·ly** *adv* —**freak·i·ness** *n*

Fré·chette /fray shét/, **Louis Honoré** (1839–1908) French-Canadian poet and politician. He is known for his epic cycle of historical poems *Story of a People* (1887).

freck·le /frék'l/ *n* a harmless small brownish patch on somebody's skin, usually one of a cluster, that becomes larger and deeper in color when the skin is exposed to the sun. Freckles are caused by the presence of larger melanin-containing cells in the basal layer of the skin. ■ *vti* (**-led, -ling, -les**) to become marked with freckles, or mark something with freckles [15C. Alteration of obsolete *frecken* "freckle" < Old Norse *freknur* "freckles"] —**freck·ly** *adj*

Fred·die Mac /fréddee màk/ *n* the Federal Home Loan Mortgage Corporation, a private corporation created by Congress that supplies funds for mortgages, or a publicly traded security backed by it

Fred·er·ick /fréddrik/ city in north central Maryland, west of the Monocacy River. It is a trade and shipping center in an agricultural region. Population: 56,063 (2002 estimate).

Fred·er·ick I (1123?–90) Holy Roman Emperor and king of Germany (1152–90), and king of Italy (1155–90). His campaigns against the papacy and the allied northern Italian cities known as the Lombard League ended in defeat at the battle of Legnano (1176). He died while on campaign in the Third Crusade. Known as **Frederick Barbarossa**

Fred·er·ick II[1] (1194–1250) Holy Roman Emperor (1215–50) and, as Frederick I, king of Sicily (1198–1250). He captured Jerusalem (1228) during the Fifth Crusade and established peace in Sicily. He struggled throughout his rule with the papacy and the allied northern Italian cities of the Lombard League, and was excommunicated three times (1227, 1239, and 1245).

Fred·er·ick II[2] (1712–86) king of Prussia. Under his political and military leadership (1740–86), Prussia doubled in size and became a major European power. He gathered a circle of writers and musicians around him at his palace of Sans Souci. Known as **Frederick the Great**

Fred·er·icks·burg /fréddriks bùrg/ city of northeast Virginia north of Richmond. It was the site of one of the bloodiest battles of the Civil War in December 1862, when Robert E. Lee's smaller Confederate force defeated Ambrose Burnside's Union forces. Population: 20,076 (2002 estimate).

Fred·er·ic·ton /fréddriktən/ capital of New Brunswick Province, eastern Canada, situated in the south central part of the province, on the St. John River. Population: 54,068 (2001).

free /free/ *adj* (**fre·er, fre·est**) 1. COSTING NOTHING requiring no money to be paid ○ *Win a free meal for two.* 2. NOT KEPT PRISONER not, or no longer, physically bound or restrained, e.g., as a prisoner or in slavery ○ *Once outside the prison walls he would be a free man.* ○ *They hoped to be set free within the week.* 3. NOT RESTRICTED IN RIGHTS not subject to censorship or control by a ruler, government, or other authority, and enjoying civil liberties ○ *It's a free country.* 4. SELF-RULING not ruled by a foreign country or power 5. NOT REGULATED not controlled, restricted, or regulated by any external thing ○ *You are free to choose.* 6. NOT BUSY not busy or occupied with work ○ *had virtually no free time* ○ *She'll be free in a moment.* 7. NOT BEING USED not being used, reserved, or taken by somebody else ○ *no free seats left* 8. NOT ATTACHED not tied or attached to something ○ *grabbed the free end of the rope* 9. NOT AFFECTED BY PARTICULAR THING not subject to or affected by a particular thing, especially something undesirable (*often used in combination*) ○ *drinking water that is free of contamination* ○ *a trouble-free trip* 10. NOT CONTAINING SOMETHING not containing a particular thing (*often used in combination*) ○ *a salt-free diet* 11. DISREGARDING TRADITIONAL LIMITATIONS performed or written without being subjected to traditional conventions or restraints ○ *free verse* 12. NOT BLOCKED not blocked or obstructed by anything ○ *allowing the free flow of electricity* 13. NOT PHYSICALLY RESTRICTED not restricted by something such as tight clothing, stiffness, or lack of space ○ *interfering with its free movement* 14. GIVING SOMETHING READILY giving or expending something generously or readily ○ *They're very free with their advice.* 15. NOT EXACT not following the original version of something word for word or very precisely ○ *a free translation* 16. OPEN AND HONEST spontaneous, open, and without awkwardness or reserve in speaking to or dealing with other people ○ *an appealingly free and open manner* 17. CHEM NOT CHEMICALLY COMBINED not chemically combined with another substance 18. PHYS NOT INCORPORATED IN LARGER BODY not permanently incorporated in a larger body such as an atom, molecule, or compound 19. NAUT FAVORABLE favorable to sailing ○ *a free wind* 20. LING ABLE TO BE USED ALONE describes a unit of meaning (**morpheme**) that can be used on its own as a word, without needing to be part of another word ■ *adv* 1. WITHOUT COST without paying any money ○ *They let you in free if you show your student card.* 2. OUT OF RESTRICTED POSITION out of a position in which somebody or something is tied, fixed, restricted, or restrained ○ *managed to wriggle free from his grasp* ■ *vt* (**freed, free·ing, frees**) 1. RELEASE SOMEBODY FROM CAPTIVITY to release somebody from physical bonds or restrictions, captivity, or slavery ○ *The defendants were freed after their acquittal.* 2. RID SOMEBODY OR SOMETHING OF SOMETHING to remove a restriction, a burden, or an unwanted or undesirable thing from somebody or something ○ *freed from the cares of high public office* 3. MAKE SOMEBODY OR SOMETHING AVAILABLE to make somebody or something available for use or able to do something ○ *This should free you to do more of your own research.* 4. UNCLOG SOMETHING OBSTRUCTED to clear something of an obstruction [Old English *freo* < Indo-European, "dear, beloved"] ◇ **for free** without paying ◇ **free and easy** relaxed, friendly, and informal ◇ **make free with somebody** to behave in too familiar and informal a way toward somebody ◇ **make free with something** to use something in an overfamiliar or overindulgent way, without showing respect or restraint

USAGE See *gift*.

free up *vt* 1. to make available for use something that is currently occupied, otherwise employed, or subject to a restriction ○ *frees up some space on my hard disk* 2. to enable something that is tightly fastened, jammed, or blocked to move freely (*informal*) ○ *freed up a key intersection*

free a·gent *n* 1. somebody who does not depend on, or is not answerable to or for, somebody else 2. a professional athlete who is in a position to sign a contract to play for any team

free a·long·side ship *adj, adv* with the cost of delivery to the dockside included, but not the cost of loading onto a ship

free as·so·ci·a·tion *n* 1. the spontaneous and uncensored expression of thoughts or ideas, in which each one is allowed to lead to or suggest the next 2. in psychoanalysis, a technique for exploring a patient's unconscious by stimulating the spontaneous and uncensored expression of thoughts or feelings through the use of stimuli such as key words —**free-as·so·ci·ate** *vi*

free·base /free bàyss/ *n* CONCENTRATED COCAINE cocaine that has been concentrated using water and a volatile liquid such as ether ■ *v* (**-based, -based, -bas·ing**) 1. *vt* PREPARE COCAINE FOR SMOKING to prepare cocaine for smoking by heating it with water and a volatile liquid such as ether in order to concentrate it 2. *vti* SMOKE COCAINE to smoke or inhale freebased cocaine [< the "freeing" of the concentrated cocaine base]

free·bie /freebee/ *n* something given or obtained free of charge, especially a promotional gift (*informal*)

free·board /free bàwrd/ *n* the distance between the deck of a ship and the level of the water

free·boot·er /free bootər/ *n* a plunderer, especially a pirate [Late 16C. < Dutch *vrijbuiter* "somebody who takes booty freely"] —**free·boot** *vi*

free·born /free bàwrn/ *adj* 1. born as a free citizen, and therefore not a slave or serf 2. relating to or intended for people who are freeborn

free·carv·ing *n* a style of snowboarding that focuses on carving deep tracks in the snow with tight cornering rather than on doing stunts

free climb·ing *n* mountain or rock climbing without aids such as spikes and ladders, though usually with ropes and other safety equipment

free·div·ing /free dìving/ *n* the extreme sport of submerging into deep water for as long as possible without the aid of oxygen tanks —**free·div·er** *n*

freed·man /freedmən, -màn/ (*plural* **-men** /-mən, -mèn/) *n* a man who has been freed from slavery

free·dom /freedəm/ *n* 1. ABILITY TO ACT FREELY a state in which somebody is able to act and live as he or she chooses, without being subject to any undue restraints or restrictions ○ *live in freedom* ○ *religious freedom* 2. RELEASE FROM CAPTIVITY OR SLAVERY release or rescue from being physically bound, or from being confined, enslaved, captured, or imprisoned 3. COUNTRY'S RIGHT TO SELF-RULE a country's right to rule itself, without interference from, or domination by, another country or power 4. RIGHT TO ACT OR SPEAK FREELY the right to speak or act without restriction, interference, or fear ○ *gave them the freedom to enter without passports* 5. ABSENCE OF SOMETHING UNPLEASANT the state of being unaffected by, or not subject to, something unpleasant or unwanted ○ *freedom from fear* 6. EASE OF MOVEMENT the ability to move easily without being limited by something such as tight clothing or lack of space ○ *loose clothing allowing complete freedom of movement* 7. RIGHT TO OCCUPY PLACE the right to use or occupy a place and treat it as your own ○ *Off-season, we had the freedom of the whole house and the beach.* 8. HONORARY CITIZENSHIP citizenship of a town or city, together with special privileges, formally awarded to somebody as an honor ○ *was given the freedom of the city* 9. FRANKNESS openness and friendliness in speech or behavior 10. EXCESSIVE CONFIDENCE OR FAMILIARITY overconfidence, overfamiliarity, or a lack of proper restraint or decorum 11. PHILOSOPHY FREE WILL the ability to exercise free will and make choices independently of any external determining force

free·dom fight·er *n* a participant in an armed revolution against a government or political system regarded as unjust

free·dom march *n* an organized march by people campaigning for civil rights, e.g., any of the marches that took place in the United States in the 1960s with the aim of ending racial segregation —**free·dom march·er** *n*

free·dom rid·er *n* a civil rights activist who, during the early 1960s, joined one of the interracial groups riding buses through parts of the southern United States to protest against racial segregation —**free·dom ride** *n*

freed·wom·an /freed wòommən/ (*plural* **-wom·en** /-wimmin/) *n* a woman who has been freed from slavery

free e·lec·tron *n* an electron that is not bonded to an atom or molecule and so is free to move under external electric or magnetic fields

free en·er·gy *n* a measure of the capacity of a system to do work, such as the likelihood of a particular chemical reaction to form products. Symbol ***G***

free en·ter·prise *n* the doctrine or practice of giving companies the freedom to trade and make a profit without government control

free fall, free-fall *n* 1. RAPID DECLINE a sudden sharp uncontrollable drop in something such as value, popularity, or credibility ○ *The value of the currency has gone into free fall.* 2. DESCENT WITH UNOPENED PARACHUTE a descent through the air with an unopened parachute as the first part of a parachute jump 3. PHYS UNRESTRICTED MOVEMENT IN EARTH'S GRAVITATIONAL FIELD an ideal state in which the only force to which something is subjected is the Earth's gravitational attraction. As an example, a craft in space is subject only to a diminished gravitational force and is not restricted by buoyancy or air resistance.

free-fall (**free-fell, free-fall·en, free-fall·ing, free-falls**) *vi* 1. to undergo a sudden sharp uncontrollable drop in something such as value, popularity, or credibility 2. to descend through the air with an unopened parachute during the first part of a parachute jump

free-fire zone *n* an area in a conflict zone where troops may fire on targets at will without requesting permission from a superior

free flight *n* the movement of a rocket or missile through the air after its engine has stopped

free-float·ing *adj* not committed or dedicated to one specific thing, especially a political party or cause

free-float·ing anx·i·e·ty *n* a state of anxiety that is not associated with any specific event or external condition

free-for-all *n* a disorganized argument, contest, or fight in which everyone present participates (*informal*)

free form *n* a shape, especially a piece of sculpture, that is asymmetric and irregular, though usually with a flowing outline

free·form /free fàwrm/ *adj* 1. unconventional in shape or design, especially in being asymmetric and irregular, but with a flowing outline 2. spontaneously or individually created, and not produced in accordance with accepted or prescribed standards

free hand *n* complete freedom to take action or make decisions ○ *gave him a free hand in designing the house*

free·hand /free hànd/ *adj, adv* done by hand and without using drawing instruments such as rulers or compasses

free·hand·ed /free hándəd/ *adj* giving generously, or always ready to give ○ *children of freehanded parents* —**free·hand·ed·ly** *adv* —**free·hand·ed·ness** *n*

free-heel ski·ing *n* the sport of downhill skiing in ski bindings similar to those used in cross-country that leave the heels free

free·hold /free hòld/ *n* 1. legal ownership of a property giving the owner unconditional rights, including the right to grant leases and take out mortgages 2. a property that has freehold status —**free·hold·er** *n*

free jazz *n* a style of jazz, developed in the 1960s, that has no set harmonies or melodic patterns

free kick *n* in soccer, a kick of a stationary ball awarded for an infringement by a member of the opposing team, who must stand at least ten yards from where the kick is made

free·lance /freé lànss/ *n* **1. SOMEBODY WORKING FOR DIFFERENT COMPANIES** a self-employed person working, or available to work, for a number of employers, and usually hired for a limited period **2. MAVERICK** somebody, especially a politician, who is not committed to any group and takes action or forms alliances independently **3.** *also* **free lance** HIST **MEDIEVAL MERCENARY** a mercenary soldier in medieval Europe ■ *adj* **WORKING FREELANCE** working or earning a living as a freelance ■ *adv* **AS FREELANCE** independently, as a freelance ○ *worked freelance as a journalist* ■ *vi* **(-lanced, -lanc·ing, -lanc·es) WORK AS FREELANCE** to work independently as a freelance [Early 19C. < the idea of a medieval knight with a lance offering his services to whoever was willing to pay]

free·lanc·er /freé lànssər/ *n* HR same as **freelance** *n* (sense 1)

free-liv·ing *adj* able to live or move independently, and not parasitic, symbiotic, or sessile ○ *free-living organisms*

free·load·er /freé lòdər/ *n* an exploiter of somebody else's generosity or hospitality (*informal*) —**free·load** *vi*

free love *n* sexual relationships without marriage or commitment to a single partner, especially as practiced by the 19th- and early-20th-century avant-garde and in the 1960s

free lunch *n* something given free and with nothing expected in return (*informal*)

free·ly /freélee/ *adv* **1. WITHOUT RESTRICTIONS** without restrictions, controls, or limits ○ *able to move freely from country to country* **2. IN LARGE AMOUNTS** in large or generous quantities ○ *gave freely to a number of well-known charities* **3. OPENLY** honestly and openly ○ *felt able to speak freely about his ordeal for the first time* **4. WITHOUT TIGHTNESS OR STIFFNESS** without being restricted by something such as tight clothing, stiffness, or lack of space ○ *clothes that allowed him to move more freely* **5. USED TO EMPHASIZE HONESTY** used to persuade somebody that you are being open and honest by accepting criticism ○ *I freely admit that mistakes were made.*

free·man /freémən/ (*plural* **-men** /-mən/) *n* **1.** a man who has been formally given citizenship of a place, together with various special privileges, as an honor ○ *a freeman of the city* **2.** a man who is not a slave or serf

Free·man /freémən/, **Cathy** (*b.* 1973) Australian sprinter. The first Aboriginal sprinter to win a gold medal at the Commonwealth Games (1994), she went on to win a gold medal in the 400 meters at the 2000 Olympic Games. Full name **Freeman, Catherine Astrid Salome**

Free·man, Morgan (*b.* 1937) US stage, television, and movie actor, best known for his critically acclaimed character roles. Among his movie credits are *Driving Miss Daisy* (1989) and *The Shawshank Redemption* (1994).

free mar·ket *n* an economic system in which businesses operate without government control in matters such as pricing and wage levels —**free-mar·ket** *adj* —**free-mar·ket·eer** *n*

free·mar·tin /freé maàrt'n/ *n* a sterile female twin born with a male calf [Late 17C. Origin ?]

free·ma·son /freé màyss'n/ *n* a member of an organization of skilled stonemasons traveling from place to place in medieval Europe [14C. Origin ?]

Free·ma·son *n* a member of a worldwide society, the Free and Accepted Masons, that is known particularly for its charitable work and its secret rites

Free·ma·son·ry /freé màyss'nree/ *n* **1.** the institutions, beliefs, and practices of the Freemasons **2.** *also* **free·ma·son·ry** an instinctive understanding and comradeship among people with something in common

freeness *n* the quality or state of being free

free·net /freé nèt/ *n* an online computer information network that charges no access fees, often run by volunteers as a public service

free on board *adj, adv* with the cost of delivery to a port and loading onto a ship included

free on rail *adj, adv* with the cost of delivery to a railroad station and loading onto a train included

free port *n* **1.** a port open to commercial ships from all countries on equal terms **2.** a zone at a port or airport that allows the duty-free import of goods that are to be reexported

Free·port /freé pàwrt/ **1.** town and tourist resort situated on the southwestern coast of Grand Bahama Island, the Bahamas. Population: 26,574 (1990). **2.** city in northern Illinois, east of Dubuque and west of Rockford. Population: 25,929 (2002 estimate). **3.** village in southeastern New York, on the southern coast of Long Island. Population: 43,978 (2002 estimate).

free rad·i·cal *n* a highly reactive atom or group of atoms with an unpaired electron

free-range *adj* **1.** free to move about and feed at will, and not confined in a battery or pen ○ *free-range chickens* **2.** produced by free-range poultry or livestock ○ *free-range eggs*

free rein *n* complete freedom to make decisions and take action without consulting anyone else

free ride *n* something obtained at no cost or with no effort (*slang*)

free rid·er *n* **1.** somebody who benefits from a system without contributing to it **2.** a consumer who refuses to pay for a good or service, but who cannot be prevented from using it

free·rid·ing /freé rìding/ *n* a basic style of snowboarding that involves traveling over the snow without performing stunts —**free·ride** *adj*

freesia

free·sia /freézhə, -zee ə/ *n* a plant grown from a corm, popular as a cut flower. Flowers: fragrant, tubular, brightly colored. Native to: southern Africa. Genus: *Freesia*. [Late 19C. After Friedrich H. T. *Freese* (1795–1896), German physician]

free size *adj* CLOTHING made in one size only, a size large enough to fit most people ○ *All the T-shirts are free size.*

free skat·ing *n* competitive ice skating in which the skater makes up his or her own program from a list of approved moves

free·ski·ing /freé skeè ing/ *n* the sport of skiing on downhill skis that have curved tips front and back, permitting the skier to execute moves similar to those of snowboarders on slopes and in halfpipes [Late 20C.] —**free·ski·er** *n*

free soil *n US* those states in the United States in which slavery was prohibited before the Civil War —**free-soil** *adj*

free-so·lo·ing *n* the sport of climbing boulders and rock faces without a safety line or a partner to catch or break a fall

free space *n* a region in which there is no matter and no gravitational or electromagnetic fields

free speech *n* the right to express any opinion publicly

free spir·it *n* somebody who lives without regard to what convention dictates or what others expect —**free-spir·it·ed** *adj* —**free-spir·it·ed·ness** *n*

free-spo·ken *adj* expressing opinions frankly, without worrying about embarrassing or offending others (*archaic or literary*)

free·stand·ing /free stánding/ *adj* **1. NOT ATTACHED TO SUPPORT** standing alone, and not attached to a wall, floor, or other structure for support **2. INDEPENDENT** existing or operating as an independent unit or entity ○ *a freestanding hospital not associated with the nearby university medical school* **3.** GRAM **GRAMMATICALLY INDEPENDENT** grammatically independent and able to function as a main clause

Free State[1] *n* **1.** a US state in which slavery was not tolerated before the Civil War **2.** a nickname for Maryland

Free State[2] /freé stàyt/ province in South Africa, in the central part of the country. Capital: Bloemfontein. Population: 2,706,754 (2001). Area: 49,980 sq. mi./129,480 sq. km.

free·stone /freé stòn/ *n* **1.** a variety of masonry stone that has a uniform texture and can be chiseled without breaking or splitting, e.g., limestone or fine sandstone **2.** a pit to which the flesh of a fruit does not cling, or a fruit that has such a pit

free·style /freé stìl/ *adj* **1.** SWIMMING **USING FRONT CRAWL** describes a swimming contest in which the competitors can use any swimming stroke and usually use the front crawl **2.** WRESTLING **NO-HOLDS-BARRED** describes a wrestling style in which all legal holds and tactics are allowed ■ *n* **1.** SPORTS **FREESTYLE CONTEST** a freestyle race, event, or contest **2.** EXTREME SPORTS **SNOWBOARDING STYLE FOCUSING ON STUNTS** a style of snowboarding that focuses on performing stunts and special maneuvers —**free·styl·er** *n*

free·style ski·ing *n* the sport of downhill skiing, involving the performance of acrobatic moves such as high jumps and somersaults

free-swim·ming *adj* able to swim about freely, and not living attached to something or in one position ○ *free-swimming larvae*

free-swing·ing *adj US* bold and blunt in speech, style, or approach (*informal*)

free·think·er /free thíngkər/ *n* an independent thinker who refuses to accept established views or teachings, especially on religion —**free·think·ing** *adj, n*

free thought *n* thinking that refuses to accept established views or teachings, especially on religion

free throw *n* in basketball, an opportunity to shoot at the basket unhindered by the opposing players, awarded to a player who has been fouled

free-throw line *n* BASKETBALL same as **foul line** (sense 2)

Free·town /freé tòwn/ capital, largest city, and chief port of Sierra Leone, on the coast of West Africa. Founded in 1787 as a settlement for free slaves, it became the capital when Sierra Leone gained independence in 1961. Population: 699,000 (1995).

free trade *n* international trade that is not subject to protective regulations or tariffs intended to restrict foreign imports —**free-trad·er** *n*

free verse *n* verse without a fixed metrical pattern, usually having unrhymed lines of varying length

free·ware /freé wèr/ *n* any computer program or application that is available at no cost to the user

free·way /freé wày/ *n* **1.** ROADS same as **expressway 2.** a highway that can be used without paying a toll

free-weight *n* a weight that is used for lifting exercises and is not attached to any other piece of apparatus, e.g., a dumbbell or barbell

free·wheel /free weél, -hweél/ *vi* **(-wheeled, -wheel·ing, -wheels) 1. TRAVEL WITHOUT USING POWER** to continue moving on a bicycle or in a vehicle without using power to drive the wheels ○ *Once you get to the top, you can freewheel all the way down the other side.* **2. LIVE IN CAREFREE WAY** to live or act without conventional constraints, purpose, or regard for responsibilities ■ *n* **1. DEVICE ON BICYCLE** a mechanism in the hub of the rear wheel of a bicycle that enables the rear wheel to continue to rotate when the rider stops pedaling **2. DEVICE IN MOTOR VEHICLE TRANSMISSION** a mechanism in the transmission of a motor vehicle that disengages the drive shaft and allows it to rotate freely when revolving at a higher speed than the engine shaft

free·wheel·ing /free weéling, -hweél-/ *adj* **1. TRAVELING WITHOUT POWER** continuing to move without the use of power **2. CAREFREE** without conventional constraints, purpose, or regard for responsibilities ○ *led a freewheeling life of travel and adventure* **3. UNSTRUCTURED** not restricted by rules, formal structure, or established procedures ○ *a freewheeling discussion that touched on many topics* **4. WITH FREEWHEEL** relating to, having, or using a freewheel mechanism on a bicycle or in a motor vehicle

free will *n* the ability to act or make choices as a free and autonomous being and not solely as a result of compulsion or predestination ◇ **of your own free will** without being forced by somebody or something else

free·will /fréé wìl/ *adj* done willingly rather than by compulsion

free·wom·an /fréé wòommən/ (*plural* **-wom·en** /-wìmmin/) *n* a woman who is not a slave or serf

free world *n* the countries of the world with democratic governments and capitalist or moderately socialist economic systems, as opposed to those with totalitarian or communist governments or economic systems

freeze /freez/ *v* (**froze** /frōz/, **fro·zen** /frṓz'n/, **freez·ing, freez·es**) **1.** *vti* TURN LIQUID TO SOLID THROUGH COLD to change into a solid by the loss of heat, or cause liquid to do this, especially to change into ice ○ *Salt water freezes at a lower temperature than fresh water.* **2.** *vti* BECOME COVERED WITH ICE to become covered with ice, or cause the surface of something to be covered with ice ○ *The lake froze for only the second time in living memory.* **3.** *vti* BECOME BLOCKED WITH ICE to become blocked with ice, or cause something to become blocked with ice ○ *Do you think it's cold enough to freeze the pipes in the attic?* **4.** *vti* BECOME HARD THROUGH COLD to harden through the effects of cold or frost, or cause something to harden ○ *We couldn't play because the ground was frozen solid.* **5.** *vti* BECOME STUCK THROUGH COLD to become fixed or stuck to something else as a result of cold, or cause something to become fixed in this way ○ *The wipers were frozen to the windshield.* **6.** *vt* PRESERVE SOMETHING WITH EXTREME COLD to preserve something, especially food, by subjecting it to and storing it at a temperature well below freezing point ○ *Store airtight up to two weeks or freeze.* **7.** *vti* FEEL VERY COLD to feel extremely cold, or cause somebody to feel extremely cold ○ *They left us to freeze outside, while they went into the house.* **8.** *vti* BE HARMED OR KILLED BY COLD to be harmed or killed, or harm or kill somebody or something, with cold or frost **9.** *vi* DROP TO FREEZING POINT to be at or fall to a temperature at or below freezing point ○ *The forecast says it's likely to freeze again tonight.* **10.** *vti* STOP MOVING to stop, or cause somebody to stop and remain still, e.g., as a result of fear or surprise or as part of a game ○ *A loose floorboard creaked in the hallway; Jenny froze.* **11.** *vi* COME TO STANDSTILL THROUGH SHOCK to become unable to act, react, or speak in a normal way, usually through fear or shock ○ *I was OK in rehearsals, but in front of an audience, I simply froze.* **12.** *vi* STOP RESPONDING to stop responding to instructions (*refers to computers*) ○ *The screen freezes whenever I attempt to save a document.* **13.** *vt* TREAT SOMEBODY ICILY to discourage or intimidate somebody by behaving in an unfriendly or hostile way ○ *She froze him with an icy glare.* **14.** *vt* HALT SOMETHING BEFORE COMPLETION to halt or limit the development or production of something ○ *The talks remain frozen at the procedural stage.* **15.** *vt* KEEP SOMETHING AT PRESENT LEVEL to fix something such as prices, rents, or wages at a specific level, usually by government action to prevent an increase ○ *Interest rates were frozen at their 1996 level.* **16.** *vt* KEEP ASSET FROM DISAPPEARING to prevent a financial asset from being sold or liquidated ○ *They froze her bank account immediately.* **17.** *vt* PROHIBIT SOMETHING to stop the manufacture, sale, or use of something **18.** *vi* BECOME UNFRIENDLY to become suddenly unfriendly and uncommunicative ○ *When I asked him about campaign contributions, he simply froze up.* **19.** *vt* ANESTHETIZE PART OF BODY to anesthetize part of somebody's body with a local anesthetic **20.** *vt* STOP FILM AT FRAME to stop a moving film at a specific frame and show that frame as a still image **21.** *vt* CAPTURE INSTANT OF MOVEMENT to produce a still photographic image of somebody or something in movement or action ○ *He pressed the Pause button, freezing her delighted expression.* **22.** *vt* KEEP POSSESSION OF PUCK OR BALL in sports, to keep possession of the puck or ball and prevent the other team from attempting to score ■ *n* **1.** VERY COLD WEATHER a period when the temperature drops and stays below freezing point, especially for a long time **2.** RESTRICTION ON SOMETHING a restrictive measure that prevents something such as prices, wages, or production from rising above a specific level ○ *a temporary freeze on imports* [Old English *frēosan* < Indo-European, "freeze, burn"]

SPELLCHECK freeze or **frieze**? Do not confuse the spelling of ***freeze*** and ***frieze***, which sound similar. ***Freeze*** is chiefly used as a verb, meaning "make or become hard through cold," "stop moving," or "fix at a specific level." It is sometimes used as a noun, as in *the big freeze of last winter, a price freeze.* ***Frieze*** is only used as a noun, denoting a decorative band on a wall.

freeze out *vt* to exclude somebody from participation in something by cold or unfriendly treatment (*informal*) ○ *We feel we are being frozen out of the negotiations.*

freeze-dry *vt* to preserve something, especially food, by first freezing it, then placing it in a vacuum to remove moisture before returning it to room temperature. The low processing temperature and absence of liquid water help to retain color, flavor, and texture. —**freeze-dried** *adj* —**freeze-dry·ing** *n*

freeze-etch·ing *n* the preparation of a biological specimen for examination with an electron microscope by freezing and splitting it to reveal its internal structure and allow a replica to be made —**freeze-etch** *vt* —**freeze-etched** *adj*

freeze-frame *n* a single frame of a film or video recording viewed as a static image

freeze-out *n* an excluding of somebody from participation by cold or unfriendly treatment (*informal*)

freez·er /fréézər/ *n* a storage cabinet, compartment, or room where food or other perishable goods can be frozen and preserved at a very low temperature

freez·er burn *n* the pale dry spots that form when moisture evaporates from frozen food that is inadequately wrapped

freeze-up *n* a period of extremely cold weather

freez·ing /fréézing/ *adj* **1.** VERY COLD extremely cold (*informal*) **2.** FORMING ICE forming ice crystals on contact with a surface ○ *freezing fog* ■ *adv* VERY to an extreme degree (*informal*) ○ *freezing cold* ■ *n* FREEZING POINT the point at which water freezes

freez·ing point *n* the temperature at which a liquid solidifies, e.g., the temperature at which water turns to ice

free zone *n* an area at a port or in a city where goods may be received or stored without payment of customs duties

Fre·ge /fráygə/, **Gottlob** (1848–1925) German mathematician and logician. He devised the first complete system of symbolic logic in his 1879 work *Begriffsschrift* and is considered the founder of modern mathematical logic.

F re·gion *n* the highest part of the ionosphere that reflects high-frequency radio waves. It is divided into two layers, the F_1, which extends upward from 112 mi./180 km and is present only during the day, and the F_2, extending upward from 186 mi./300 km.

Frei·burg /frí bùrg/ city in Baden-Württemberg State, southwestern Germany. It is the cultural and economic center of the Black Forest. Population: 198,496 (1997).

Frei·del-Crafts re·ac·tion /fríd'l kráfts-/ *n* a chemical reaction using metallic halides such as aluminum chloride, or acids such as catalysts. Use: chemical manufacture. [After Charles *Friedel* (1832–99), French chemist, and James M. *Crafts* (1839–1917), US chemist]

freight /frayt/ *n* **1.** GOODS FOR TRANSPORTATION goods or cargo carried by a commercial means of transportation **2.** COMMON CLASS OF TRANSPORTATION the ordinary method or class of commercial transportation for goods, slower and cheaper than express **3.** CHARGE FOR CARRYING GOODS a charge paid for the transportation of goods **4.** *US* RAIL same as **freight train 5.** BURDEN a load or burden (*literary*) ■ *vt* (**freight·ed, freight·ing, freights**) **1.** TRANSPORT GOODS to send or transport goods or cargo by commercial carrier **2.** LOAD VEHICLE WITH CARGO to load a ship, train, aircraft, or vehicle with goods or cargo to be transported **3.** BURDEN SOMETHING OR SOMEBODY to load something or somebody with something such as feeling, significance, or emotion (*literary; usually passive*) [15C. < Middle Low German or Middle Dutch *vrecht*]

freight·age /fráytij/ *n* **1.** TRANSPORTATION CHARGE a charge paid for the transportation of goods or cargo **2.** COMMERCIAL CARRIAGE OF GOODS the commercial transportation of goods or cargo **3.** GOODS CARRIED the goods that are carried by a ship or vehicle

freight car *n* a railroad car that carries freight, usually one that is enclosed

freight·er /fráytər/ *n* **1.** a ship or aircraft designed to carry freight **2.** an employee who sends, forwards, or receives freight, or who charters something to carry freight

freight ton *n* a unit used in measuring and pricing freight in maritime shipping, varying according to the type of goods carried but usually corresponding to 1,000 kg or 40 cubic ft

freight train *n* a railroad train that carries only freight

~~**freind**~~ incorrect spelling of **friend**

Frei Ru·iz-Ta·gle /fràу roo èess taá glay/, **Eduardo** (*b.* 1942) president of Chile. During his presidency (1994–2000), he attempted to curb military power by constitutional reform.

~~**freize**~~ incorrect spelling of **frieze**

Fre·man·tle /fréé mànt'l/ city and port in southwestern Western Australia, now part of the metropolitan area of Perth. Population: 26,126 (2002 estimate).

frem·i·tus /frémmitəss/ (*plural same*) *n* a vibration or tremor, resulting from a physical action such as speaking or coughing, felt by hand and used to assess whether the chest is affected by disease [Early 19C. < Latin, "roaring" < *fremere* "to roar"]

Fre·mont /fréé mònt/ city on San Francisco Bay in western California, southeast of San Francisco. Population: 206,856 (2002 estimate).

Fré·mont /fréé mònt/, **John Charles** (1813–90) US army officer, explorer, and politician. He charted and mapped much of the Far West, including most of the Oregon Trail (1842).

fre·na ANAT plural of **frenum**

French /french/ *n* the official language of France and some other countries, belonging to the Romance group of Indo-European that developed from Latin. Native speakers: 70 million. Other speakers: 220 million. See panel on next page ■ *npl* the people of France collectively [Old English *frencisc* < Germanic] —**French** *adj*

CULTURAL NOTE ***The French Connection***, a movie (1971) by William Friedkin. Set in New York, it depicts the attempts of an uncompromising policeman, Popeye Doyle, to break up an international drug ring originating in Marseille, France. It is memorable for Gene Hackman's intense performance and a dramatic chase along elevated railroad tracks. "*French Connection*-style drug enforcement operations" and other such expressions soon came to be used regularly in the United States as a result of the movie's fame.

French /french/, **Daniel Chester** (1850–1931) US artist. The most popular US sculptor of his day, he is known for the *Minute Man* in Concord, Massachusetts (1875) and his monumental sculpture of Abraham Lincoln (1919) in the Lincoln Memorial, Washington, D.C.

French and In·di·an Wars *npl* a series of four North American wars (1689–1763) between French and British forces and their Native American allies

French bean *n UK* FOOD same as **string bean** (sense 1)

French bread *n* white bread in the form of a long slim cylindrical loaf with a crisp crust and soft inside

French Cam·e·roons /frènch kàmmə ro͞onz/ former region in west central Africa, administered by France from 1919 to 1960, and now part of Cameroon

French Can·a·da *n* the parts of Canada where French is spoken

French Ca·na·di·an *n* **1.** somebody who comes from a French-speaking part of Canada **2.** the form of the French language spoken in Canada —**French-Ca·na·di·an** *adj*

French chalk *n* a soft white variety of talc. Use: to make tailoring marks on cloth, to remove grease stains from clothes.

French Cre·ole *n* somebody of European and African

LANGUAGE HERITAGE ***French*** Much of English is made up of words from other languages, and it has such a long history and such deep assimilation of migrants from French that many words of French origin are unrecognized as such. Within a century of the Norman Conquest of England in 1066, Old English had adopted, for example, ***castle***, ***justice***, ***place***, ***service***, and ***war***. During the medieval period French, while remaining the usual language of the court and the law, also penetrated all areas of English life, giving such diverse vocabulary as ***language*** itself, ***adventure***, ***cage***, ***force***, ***pain***, and ***tavern***, and later also, for example, ***agree***, ***army***, ***card***, ***famine***, and ***library***. Migration continued with words such as ***passport***, ***amuse***, and ***aristocracy*** (15th century), ***bomb***, ***career***, ***favorite***, ***improve***, and ***society*** (16th), ***attitude***, ***cosmetic***, ***develop***, ***group***, and ***vest*** (17th). From the 18th century words tend to be more identifiably of French origin: ***amateur***, ***bouquet***, ***foyer***, ***souvenir***, and ***vaudeville*** (18th); ***cigarette***, ***mirage***, and ***questionnaire*** (19th); ***discotheque***, ***saboteur***, and ***voyeur*** (20th).

In modern English particular mention might be made of the contribution of French in the areas of food and cooking, fashion, the arts (especially dance and music), automobiles, and aviation.

It has long been noted that words for the flesh of animals as food tend to derive from French while those for the animals themselves remain of English (Germanic) origin: thus ***cow*** (English) but ***beef*** (French); ***sheep*** (English) but ***mutton*** (French); ***deer*** (English) but ***venison*** (French). From the 18th century, however, such basic terms are supplemented by more sophisticated French émigrés: ***cuisine*** itself in the late 18th century, closely followed by ***chef***, ***gastronomy***, and ***gourmet***; the 18th century also saw the arrival of terms ranging from ***batterie de cuisine*** ("a set of cooking utensils, pots, and pans") to ***casserole***, ***meringue***, and ***terrine***; 19th-century culinary terms include ***croissant***, ***crouton***, ***marmite***, and ***sauté***, some of which could be encountered in a ***restaurant*** or ***café***; the 20th century acquired ***haute cuisine*** at its beginning and ***nouvelle cuisine*** toward its end, as well as ***coulis***, ***gratinee***, and also a new sense ("long thin loaf") of ***baguette***.

The world of ***fashion*** (itself a word adopted from French in the 14th century), clothing, and textiles is also inhabited by French migrants, from the basic ***jacket*** (15th century) and ***beret*** (early 19th) to ***haute couture*** (early 20th); the superficially modern ***denim*** dates from the late 17th century – the word derives from French *(serge) de Nîmes* "(serge) of Nîmes" (a city in southwestern France). Fashionable migrants continue to be welcomed: the ***bustier*** and ***faux*** ("imitation," as in *faux fur*) both came into English toward the end of the 20th century.

The arts are also heavily indebted to French, which provides the language with many terms of music and dance, and practically all the standard terms of ballet (***ballerina***, from Italian, being the most notable exception): for example, ***arabesque***, ***entrechat***, ***pas de deux***, the ***tutu*** (from a baby-talk alteration of *cucu*, from *cul* "buttocks"), and ***ballet*** itself. More general terms include ***bass***, ***clef***, ***concert***, ***harmony***, ***lyric***, ***octave***, and ***tambourine***; a relatively recent and more exotic migrant is ***zouk***, a style of dance music originating in Guadeloupe and Martinique. In the visual arts, French provided the ***artist*** and his or her ***palette***, and especially the names of schools such as ***impressionism*** (with its ***plein-air*** painting) and ***pointillism***. Other important "isms" also came from French, including ***chauvinism*** and ***feminism***.

Science and technology also have their fair share of French words, represented here by the ***automobile*** and the ***airplane*** (French *aéroplane*), housed respectively in a ***garage*** and ***hangar***. ***Helicopter*** also arrived from French, as did the less successful ***ornithopter***, an early flying machine that operated using flapping wings, and the ***limousine***. Other migrants into the vocabulary of ***aviation*** (formed in French from Latin *avis* "bird") include ***aeronautical***, ***aileron***, ***fuselage***, ***monocoque***, and ***parachute***.

A separate wave of migration of French words took place in North America, where French settlements in Canada introduced English to terms such as ***coureur de bois*** ("fur trapper," literally "woods runner"), ***mush*** (a command to sled dogs, originally in *mush on!* and probably from French *marchons* "let us march"), ***shanty*** ("shack," thought to be from Canadian French *chantier* "lumberjack's hut"), and ***voyageur*** ("transporter of furs and supplies"). A French Canadian has been a ***Canadien*** or ***Canadienne*** since the mid-19th century, and the people of Quebec have been ***Québécois*** in English (late 19th century) almost as long as they have been *Quebecers* (mid-19th). Until 1803 parts of the United States (the "Louisiana Purchase") were French territory: ***Mardi Gras*** (literally "fat Tuesday"), the carnival around Shrove Tuesday, known especially from New Orleans, is one linguistic relic of this earlier time, as is the ***bayou*** ("area of slow-moving water"), via Louisiana French from Choctaw *bayuk* "small river forming part of a delta."

descent whose ancestors were French immigrants to Trinidad

French cuff *n* a wide cuff, usually for a shirtsleeve, designed to be folded back upon itself and fastened with a cuff link

French curve *n* a thin piece of plastic or other material with curved edges and a number of curved shapes cut out of it, designed to help designers and engineers draw curves

French door *n* ARCHIT same as **French window** (*usually used in the plural*)

French dress·ing *n* **1.** a salad dressing made of oil and vinegar with seasoning, whisked or shaken until emulsified or mixed **2.** a creamy salad dressing, usually made commercially, consisting of mayonnaise with tomato flavoring

French E·qua·to·ri·al Af·ri·ca /-ekwə tàwree əl-/ former French territory in west central Africa between 1910 and 1958. It consisted of the present-day countries of the Central African Republic, Chad, the Republic of Congo, and Gabon.

French fact *n Can* the existence of French-speaking areas of Canada, or their culture, as a constituent but distinct part of the country

French For·eign Le·gion *n* a section of the French army consisting of foreign volunteers

French fries, French fried po·ta·toes *npl* thin strips of potato fried in deep fat

French Gui·an·a /-gee ánnə, -aánə, -gī-/ overseas region of France, situated on the northeastern coast of South America and bordered by Brazil, Suriname, and the Atlantic Ocean. It is France's oldest overseas territory and the only French territory on the American mainland. Capital: Cayenne. Population: 114,808 (1990). Area: 35,135 sq. mi./91,000 sq. km. —**French Gui·an·an** *adj, n* —**French Gui·an·ese** /-gee ə néez, -gī-/ *adj, n*

French Guin·ea former name for **Guinea**

French harp *n regional* a harmonica

REGIONAL NOTE The term ***French harp*** is most commonly found in the west midland region, from Kentucky to Texas, including Missouri, Arkansas, Louisiana, and Mississippi. In the Gulf States, it helps delimit the south midland region, as far east as Tennessee, Georgia, and Alabama.

French heel *n* a curved heel of medium height for women's shoes

French horn

French horn *n* a brass musical instrument with a long looped pipe ending in a wide round bell, with other pipes and valves attached to it within the loop. French horns have a mellow, brassy tone, and are usually played with one hand in the bell of the instrument to control its volume.

French·i·fy /frénchə fī/ (**-fied, -fy·ing, -fies**), **french·i·fy** *vt* to give a French appearance or character to something or somebody —**French·i·fi·ca·tion** /frènchəfi káysh'n/ *n*

French In·di·a former territory comprising four French colonies in southeastern India, including the city of Pondicherry. It was ceded to India in 1956.

French kiss *n* a kiss in which one partner's tongue is inserted in the other partner's mouth

French knot *n* an embroidery stitch made by looping the thread around the needle before pushing it through the fabric

French leave *n* a quick departure or absence, without explanation or permission (*dated informal*) [< a supposed French custom of leaving a party without saying goodbye]

French·man /frénchmən/ (*plural* **-men**) *n* a man who comes from France

French mar·i·gold *n* a widely cultivated ornamental flower. Flowers: yellowish orange heads with red petals. Latin name: *Tagetes patula*.

French pleat *n UK* same as **French roll**

French pol·ish *n* shellac dissolved in alcohol. Use: wood varnish. —**French-pol·ish** *vt*

French Pol·y·ne·sia overseas territory of France, consisting of several groups of small islands in the eastern South Pacific Ocean. Language: French. Currency: CFP franc. Capital: Papeete. Population: 188,814 (1988). Area: 1,359 sq. mi./3,521 sq. km.

French press *n* a coffeepot fitted with a plunger that is used to push the floating coffee grounds to the bottom of the pot when the coffee is ready to drink

French pro·vin·cial *n* a contemporary style of architecture or furnishings based on those of the French provinces in the 17th and 18th centuries

French Re·pub·li·can Cal·en·dar, French Rev·o·lu·tion·ar·y Cal·en·dar *n* the calendar adopted by the French during and briefly after the French Revolution. It had 12 months of 30 days, each made up of three ten-day weeks. The months were given names alluding to nature and seasonal weather.

French roll *n* a woman's hairstyle in which the hair is formed into a vertical roll at the back of the head

French seam *n* a seam stitched twice, completely enclosing the raw edges of the fabric

French Su·dan former name for **Mali** (1898–1959)

French toast *n* sliced bread dipped in egg beaten with milk, lightly fried or grilled, and served with maple syrup

French twist *n* HAIR same as **French roll**

French West Af·ri·ca former French colonial territory in western Africa between 1895 and 1958. It consisted of the present countries of Benin, Burkina Faso, Côte d'Ivoire, Guinea, Mali, Mauritania, Niger, and Senegal.

French win·dow *n* either of a pair of doors in an outside wall made of glass panels and opening in the middle (*usually used in the plural*)

French·wom·an /frénch wŏŏmmən/ (*plural* **-wom·en** /-wìmmin/) *n* a woman who comes from France

Fre·neau /fri nṓ/, **Philip Morin** (1752–1832) US journalist and poet. He is known for his patriotic verse, written during and after the American Revolution.

> "Hills sink to plains, and man returns to dust, / That dust supports a reptile or a flower; / Each changeful atom by some other nursed / Takes some new form, to perish in an hour."
> [Philip Morin Freneau, *The House of Night*; 1777–78]

fre·net·ic /frə néttik/ *adj* characterized by feverish activity, confusion, and hurry ○ *frenetic gestures* [14C. Via French and Latin < Greek *phrenētikos* < *phrenitis* "delirium" < *phrēn* "mind"] —**fre·net·i·cal·ly** *adv* —**fre·net·i·cism** /-nétti sìzzəm/ *n*

fren·u·lum /frénnyələm/ (*plural* **-la** /-lə/) *n* **1.** a small stiff bristle on the hind wing of moths that keeps the forewings and hind wings together during flight **2.** a small fold of skin or membrane that limits the movement of an organ, typically smaller than a frenum [Early 18C. < modern Latin, "small frenum" < Latin *frenum* (see FRENUM)]

fre·num /freénəm/ (*plural* **-nums** or **-na** /-nə/) *n* a small fold of skin or membrane that limits the movement of an organ, especially the band of tissue connecting the tongue to the floor of the mouth [Mid-18C. < Latin *frenum* "bridle" < *frendere* "grind"]

fren·zied /frénzeed/ *adj* characterized by uncontrolled activity, agitation, or emotion —**fren·zied·ly** *adv* —**fren·zied·ness** *n*

fren·zy /frénzee/ *n* **1.** OUT-OF-CONTROL BEHAVIOR a state of uncontrolled activity, agitation, or emotion **2.** BURST OF ACTIVITY a burst of energetic activity **3.** MENTAL ILLNESS a temporary period of symptoms of a psychiatric disorder (*often offensive*) [14C. Via French < medieval Latin *phrenesia* < Greek *phrenitis* (see FRENETIC)]

Fre·on /freé òn/ *tdmk* a trademark for any of a number of chemical compounds containing fluorine, and often chlorine or bromine. Use: as solvents, as aerosol propellants, in refrigeration.

freq. *abbr* **1.** PHYS, BROADCAST, STATS frequency **2.** GRAM frequentative **3.** frequently

fre·quen·cy /freékwənssee/ (*plural* **-cies**) *n* **1.** *also* **fre·quence** /freékwənss/ FREQUENT OCCURRENCE the fact of happening often or regularly at short intervals ○ *quite good friends, judging by the frequency of his visits* **2.** RATE OF OCCURRENCE the number of times that something happens during a period of time ○ *We're trying to establish the frequency of his visits. Did he come once a month?* **3.** BROADCAST WAVELENGTH FOR BROADCASTING a wavelength on which a radio or television signal is broadcast and to which a receiving set can be tuned **4.** PHYS RATE OF RECURRENCE the number of times that something such as an oscillation, a waveform, or a cycle is repeated within a specific length of time, usually one second. Symbol *ν*, *f* **5.** STATS NUMBER OF OCCURRENCES OF STATISTICAL RESULT the number of times a particular result occurs in a statistical survey (**absolute frequency**), or the ratio of that number to the total results obtained in the survey (**relative frequency**)

fre·quen·cy dis·tri·bu·tion *n* a way of classifying statistical data that allows comparisons of the results in each category

fre·quen·cy mod·u·la·tion *n* a method of radio transmission in which the frequency of the wave carrying the signal is varied in accordance with the particularities of the sound being broadcast

fre·quent *adj* /freékwənt/ **1.** OCCURRING OFTEN happening often or regularly at short intervals ○ *her frequent appearances on television* **2.** HABITUAL doing something often ○ *a frequent visitor to the museum* ■ *vt* /fri kwént, freékwənt/ (**-quent·ed, -quent·ing, -quents**) GO SOMEWHERE OFTEN to go to or be in a place often [15C. Via French < Latin *frequent-* "crowded, numerous"] —**fre·quen·ta·tion** /freékwən táysh'n/ *n* —**fre·quent·er** /fri kwéntər, freékwəntər/ *n* —**fre·quent·ness** *n*

fre·quen·ta·tive /fri kwéntətiv/ *adj* describes a verb, verb form, or affix that expresses repeated action —**fre·quen·ta·tive** *n*

fre·quent fli·er, **fre·quent fly·er** *n* an air passenger who travels frequently, especially somebody registered to receive benefits for accumulated mileage ○ *a frequent-flier discount*

fre·quent guest *n* somebody who often stays at the same hotel or hotel chain, especially while traveling on business, and is therefore offered free overnight stays and other benefits

fre·quent·ly /freékwəntlee/ *adv* on many occasions with little time between them ○ *They change their address so frequently, it's difficult to know where to send the letter.*

fres·co /fréskō/ *n* (*plural* **-coes** or **-cos**) **1.** PAINTING DONE ON FRESH PLASTER a painting on a wall or ceiling done by rapidly brushing watercolors onto fresh damp or partly dry plaster **2.** TECHNIQUE OF PAINTING ON FRESH PLASTER the technique or method of painting on fresh plaster ■ *vt* (**-coed, -co·ing, -coes**) PAINT WALL OR CEILING WITH FRESCO to paint a fresco on a wall or ceiling [Late 16C. < Italian, "fresh" (referring to plaster)] —**fres·co·er** *n* —**fres·co·ist** *n*

fresh /fresh/ *adj* **1.** NOT STALE recently harvested or made and showing no sign of staleness or decay ○ *peas fresh from the pod* **2.** NOT PRESERVED not having been preserved, aged, or processed, e.g., by canning

Barnaby's

fresco: detail of 16th-century wall painting at Sigirya, Sri Lanka

or freezing ○ *fresh fruits and vegetables* **3.** ADDITIONAL OR AS REPLACEMENT additional to or replacing something that existed, was used before, or is past its best ○ *I took out the old ink cartridge and put in a fresh one.* **4.** NEW new or clean and showing no signs of previous use ○ *The hotel provides fresh towels.* **5.** NOT AFFECTED BY TIME not changed, diminished, or spoiled by the passage of time ○ *Write it down while it's still fresh in your memory.* **6.** WHOLESOME natural, pure, and wholesome, especially in smell ○ *the fresh smell of clean linen* **7.** EXCITINGLY DIFFERENT excitingly or refreshingly different from what somebody is used to or what has been done previously ○ *fresh ideas* **8.** NOT TIRED alert and full of energy ○ *I'd better get this done while my mind is still fresh.* **9.** NOT SALTY describes water that is not salty **10.** BLOWING STRONGLY describes a breeze or wind that is blowing quite strongly ○ *a fresh wind from the west* **11.** COOL cool or colder than usual ○ *It's rather fresh today.* **12.** BRIGHT pleasantly bright, light, and pure or clear **13.** HEALTHY healthy-looking and clear in appearance ○ *a fresh complexion* **14.** RECENTLY ARRIVED having recently come from a place, activity, or event ○ *Fresh from his trip to the Antarctic, Sir Ronald is in the studio to tell us about his experiences.* **15.** WITHOUT EXPERIENCE lacking experience **16.** MAKING UNWANTED SEXUAL ADVANCES making inappropriate sexual overtures to somebody (*informal*) **17.** OVERFAMILIAR bold and overfamiliar toward somebody, especially somebody considered a superior (*informal*) ○ *Don't you get fresh with me, young man.* **18.** AGRIC HAVING RECENTLY CALVED having recently calved and therefore able to give milk **19.** *Carib* BAD SMELLING especially of fish or meat, smelling slightly rotten ■ *adv* RECENTLY very recently or newly ○ *fresh-cooked salmon* ■ *n* COOL PERIOD the cool early part of the day [Old English *fersc* "pure, not salty," and partly < Old French *freis* "new, recent" < Germanic] —**fresh·ness** *n*

SYNONYMS See ***new***.

fresh air *n* the air outside a building or any other enclosed place, thought of as being healthy and reviving ○ *What you need is fresh air and exercise.*

fresh breeze *n* a wind of between 19 and 24 mi./30 and 38 km per hour, classified as force five on the Beaufort scale

fresh·en /frésh'n/ (**-ened, -en·ing, -ens**) *v* **1.** *vti* MAKE OR BECOME FRESH to make something fresh or fresher, or become fresh or fresher **2.** *vi* INCREASE IN STRENGTH to blow more strongly (*refers to winds*) ○ *wind force three, freshening from the southwest* **3.** *vt* REFILL DRINK to refill somebody's glass or drink **4.** *vi* CALVE AND LACTATE to calve and begin to produce milk —**fresh·en·er** *n*

freshen up *v* **1.** *vi* to make yourself clean and neat by washing or changing clothes **2.** *vt* same as **freshen** (sense 3)

fresh·er /fréshər/ *n UK* EDUC same as **freshman** (sense 1) [Late 19C. < shortening of FRESHMAN]

fresh·et /fréshət/ *n* **1.** a small sudden flood or rise in the level of a river, caused by heavy rainfall or a rapid thaw, especially after a period of dry weather **2.** a stream of fresh water emptying into a body of salt water [Late 16C. Probably < Old French *freschete* < *freis* (see FRESH)]

fresh-faced *adj* young and healthy-looking

fresh gale *n* a wind of between 39 and 46 mi./62 and 74 km per hour, classified as force eight on the Beaufort scale

fresh·ly /fréshlee/ *adv* very recently or newly

fresh·man /fréshmən/ (*plural* **-men** /-mən/), **fresh·per·son** /frésh pùrss'n/ (*plural* **-per·sons** or **-peo·ple** /-peèp'l/) *n* **1.** a student in the first year of high school or college **2.** *US* a beginner, or a newcomer to a job or position ○ *freshmen in the Senate*

fresh·wa·ter /frésh wàwtər/ *adj* **1.** NOT MARINE relating to, consisting of, or living in fresh water **2.** INLAND used on or accustomed only to inland waters, not the sea **3.** *US* PROVINCIAL located inland and considered provincial and unsophisticated (*informal*)

fresh·wa·ter Yan·kee *n Carib* an offensive term for somebody who returns to the Caribbean after a visit abroad, usually to the United States, behaving and speaking like somebody from the place visited (*slang*)

fresh·wom·an /frésh wŏŏmmən/ (*plural* **-wom·en** /-wìmmin/) *n* a woman student in the first year of high school or college

Fres·nel lens /frə nél-/ *n* a thin lens of short focal length with a surface consisting of concentric rings, each having a curvature corresponding to a similar ring of a plain convex lens [Mid-19C. After Augustin-Jean *Fresnel* (1788–1827), French physicist]

Fres·no /frézno/ city and county seat of Fresno County, central California, 155 mi./249 km southeast of San Francisco. Population: 445,227 (2002 estimate).

fret[1] /fret/ *v* (**fret·ted, fret·ting, frets**) **1.** *vti* WORRY to be worried, irritated, or agitated about something, or cause somebody to be so **2.** *vti* WEAR AWAY to wear away or corrode the surface of something, or become worn away or corroded **3.** *vt* MAKE HOLE BY CONSTANT RUBBING to create a hole or groove in something by constant wear or rubbing **4.** *vti* FLOW IN RIPPLES OR SMALL WAVES to flow with a constant busy rippling motion or with small choppy waves, or cause water to flow in this way (*literary*) ○ *"I love the brooks that down their channels fret"* (Wordsworth, *Ode on Intimations of Immortality*; 1807) ■ *n* HOLE MADE BY FRETTING a hole, groove, or mark made by constant wear or rubbing [Old English *fretan* "devour" < Germanic, "eat up"]

fret[2] /fret/ *n* a small ridge of a set placed across the fingerboard of a stringed instrument such as a guitar or sitar, indicating the position in which to place the fingers to produce a desired note [Early 16C. Origin ?] —**fret·less** *adj* —**fret·ted** *adj*

fret[3] /fret/ *n* a pattern of repeated geometric figures, usually consisting of straight lines, used as an ornament or in an ornamental border [14C. < Old French *frete* "trellis"] —**fret** *vt*

fret·ful /frétfəl/ *adj* easily worried, irritated, or agitated [Late 16C. < FRET[1]] —**fret·ful·ly** *adv* —**fret·ful·ness** *n*

fret·man /frétmən/ (*plural* **-men** /-mən/) *n* a musician who plays guitar, especially in jazz or pop music (*slang*) [Late 20C. < FRET[2]]

fret·saw /frét sàw/ *n* a saw with a thin narrow fine-toothed blade usually mounted across a U-shaped frame. Use: cutting curved shapes in wood. [Mid-19C. < FRET[3]]

fret·work /frét wùrk/ *n* **1.** ornamental woodwork made by cutting holes in a piece of wood with a fretsaw to create an intricate pattern of wood and spaces **2.** decorative designs consisting of frets [Early 17C. < FRET[3]]

Freud /froyd/, **Anna** (1895–1982) Austrian-born British psychoanalyst. The daughter of Sigmund Freud, she worked closely with her father in the development of psychoanalytical theory. She later specialized in child psychoanalysis, founding the Hampstead Child Therapy Course and Clinic in London in 1947 and establishing a journal, *Psychoanalytic Study of the Child*, in 1945.

Freud, Sigmund (1856–1939) Austrian physician and founder of psychoanalysis. He developed many theories central to psychoanalysis, the psychology of human sexuality, and dream interpretation. His works include *The Interpretation of Dreams* (1900) and *Totem and Taboo* (1913).

> "The conscious mind may be compared to a fountain playing in the sun and falling back into the great subterranean pool of

AKG London

Sigmund Freud

subconscious from which it rises."
[Sigmund Freud. Quoted in *Bartlett's Unfamiliar Quotations*, Leonard Louis Levinson (ed.); 1972]

Freu·di·an /fróydee ən/ *adj* **1.** RELATING TO FREUD relating to Sigmund Freud, his writings, or his psychoanalytical theories and methods **2.** CONCERNING ROLE OF SEXUALITY IN BEHAVIOR demonstrating or understandable in terms of Freud's theories, especially with regard to sexuality and its role in human relations ■ *n* FOLLOWER OF FREUD somebody who follows Freud or is influenced by Freud's theories or methods of psychoanalysis —**Freu·di·an·ism** *n*

Freu·di·an slip *n* an accidental mistake, usually the use of the wrong word in a sentence, thought to betray somebody's subconscious preoccupations

Frey·a /fráy ə/ *n* in Norse mythology, the goddess of love, fertility, and beauty

F.R.G., FRG *abbr* Federal Republic of Germany

Fri. *abbr* CALENDAR Friday

fri·a·ble /frī́ əb'l/ *adj* easily reduced to tiny particles ○ *sand incorporated to make the soil more friable* [Mid-16C. Directly or via French < Latin *friabilis* < *friare* "crumble"] —**fri·a·bil·i·ty** /frī̀ ə bíllətee/ *n* —**fri·a·ble·ness** *n*

SYNONYMS See *fragile*.

fri·ar /frī́r/ *n* a man belonging to a Roman Catholic religious order, especially a mendicant one. The four main orders of friar are the Augustinians, Carmelites, Dominicans, and Franciscans. [13C. Via French *frère* < Latin *frater* "brother"] —**fri·ar·ly** *adj*

fri·ar's lan·tern *n* same as **will-o'-the-wisp** (sense 1)

fri·ar·y /frī́ree/ (*plural* **-ies**) *n* **1.** a community of friars **2.** a building housing a community of friars

frib·ble /fríbb'l/ (*archaic*) *vti* (**-bled, -bling, -bles**) to waste or fritter something away ■ *n* an idle or frivolous person [Early 17C. An imitation of the sound of stammering or mumbling]

fric·as·see /fríkə sée, fríkə sée/ *n* meat, usually chicken or veal, cooked in its own stock, or a wine and stock mixture, then thickened with cream [Mid-16C. < French *fricassée*, form of past participle of *fricasser* "cut up and cook in sauce"] —**fric·as·see** *vt*

fric·a·tive /fríkətiv/ *adj* describes a consonantal speech sound made by forcing the breath through a narrow opening [Mid-19C. < modern Latin *fricativus* < Latin *fricare* "rub"] —**fric·a·tive** *n*

Frick /frik/, **Henry Clay** (1849–1919) US industrialist and philanthropist. He amassed a fortune in the steel industry and bequeathed his Manhattan townhouse, with its notable collection of paintings, to the city of New York.

fric·tion /fríkshən/ *n* **1.** RUBBING the rubbing of two objects against each other when one or both are moving **2.** PHYS RESISTANCE ENCOUNTERED BY MOVING OBJECT the resistance encountered by an object moving relative to another object with which it is in contact **3.** MED THERAPEUTIC RUBBING deliberate rubbing of a body part as a way of stimulating blood circulation, warming, or relieving pain **4.** DISAGREEMENT disagreement or conflict, stopping short of violence, between people, groups, or nations with differing objectives or views [Mid-16C. Via French < Latin *friction-* < *fricare* "rub"] —**fric·tion·al** *adj*

fric·tion clutch *n* a clutch in a vehicle or machine that transmits power through surface friction between two plates covered with a layer of a fibrous material such as asbestos

fric·tion match *n* a match that lights when rubbed against an abrasive surface

fric·tion tape *n* US waterproof adhesive tape made of cloth or plastic and used to insulate electrical conductors. Can term **insulating tape**

Fri·day /frī́ dày, -dee/ *n* the fifth day of the traditional working week, coming after Thursday and before Saturday [Old English *Frīgedæg* "day of the goddess Frigg"]

Fri·days /frī́ dàyz/ *adv* **1.** every Friday **2.** on every Friday

fridge /frij/ *n* HOUSEHOLD same as **refrigerator** (*informal*) [Early 20C. Shortening]

fried /frīd/ *adj* **1.** COOKED BY FRYING having been cooked by frying **2.** US INTOXICATED incapacitated by alcohol or drugs (*slang*) **3.** EXHAUSTED incoherent from fatigue (*slang*)

Popperfoto

Betty Friedan

Frie·dan /free dán/, **Betty** (*b.* 1921) US feminist author and founder in 1966 of the National Organization for Women (NOW). Her landmark book *The Feminine Mystique* (1963) challenged the idealization of women's traditional roles. Born **Goldstein, Betty Naomi**

"Today the problem that has no name is how to juggle work, love, home, and children."
[Betty Friedan, *The Second Stage*; 1987]

Fried·man /fréedmən/, **Milton** (*b.* 1912) US economist. He is considered a leading protagonist of the theory that a free market, rather than government intervention, can best produce a balanced rate of economic growth. He received the Nobel Prize in economics (1976).

"Inflation is a form of taxation that can be imposed without legislation."
[Milton Friedman, *The Times (London)*; 1981]

Fried·rich /fréedrik/, **Caspar David** (1774–1840) German painter. In his meticulously observed landscape paintings such as *Monk on the Seashore* (1809–10), the human figure is often depicted as solitary and insignificant.

Fried·rich·stras·se /fréedreekh shtraàsə/ *n* a fashionable street in Berlin, Germany, on which the border crossing Checkpoint Charlie was located during the Cold War

~~**frieght**~~ incorrect spelling of **freight**

friend /frend/ *n* **1.** SOMEBODY EMOTIONALLY CLOSE somebody who trusts and is fond of another ○ *I know her, in fact she's a friend of mine.* **2.** ACQUAINTANCE somebody who thinks well of or is on good terms with somebody else ○ *I have a friend at the office who might be able to help out.* **3.** ALLY an ally, or somebody who is not an enemy ○ *You can say what you like about the principal; you're among friends here.* **4.** ADVOCATE OF CAUSE a defender or supporter of a cause, group, or principle ○ *She's no friend of tax-and-spend policies.* **5.** PATRON a patron of a charity or institution. Friends of cultural institutions often receive privileges such as invitations to special events and the opportunity to order tickets before the general public. ○ *a friend of the New York City Ballet* ■ *v* (**friend·ed, friend·ing, friends**) **1.** *vt Malaysia, Singapore* BE SOMEBODY'S FRIEND to be friends with somebody (*informal*) ○ *I don't want to friend you any more!* **2.** *vi Carib* BE LOVERS to have a sexual relationship with somebody ○ *They friending long time.* [Old English *frēond* < Germanic, "to love"] ◇ **be friends (with somebody)** to be a friend of or on friendly terms with somebody ◇ **make friends (with somebody)** to begin a friendship or become friendly with somebody

Friend *n* a member of the Religious Society of Friends, called Quakers

friend·less /fréndləss/ *adj* without a friend —**friend·less·ness** *n*

friend·ly /fréndlee/ *adj* (**-li·er, -li·est**) **1.** AFFECTIONATE AND TRUSTING characteristic of or suitable to a relationship between friends ○ *She's been friendly to us since we moved in.* **2.** HELPFUL tending to be beneficial or favorable toward somebody or something (*sometimes used in combination*) ○ *She was only offering some friendly advice.* ○ *We support the campaign for wildlife-friendly farming.* **3.** ON SAME SIDE not antagonistic toward or in conflict with another ○ *encountered only friendly aircraft* **4.** PLEASANT AND WELCOMING having a pleasant welcoming atmosphere **5.** NOT FIERCELY COMPETITIVE not played or undertaken in a fiercely competitive mood **6.** EASY TO USE safe or easy to use or operate, or easy to understand (*usually used in combination*) ○ *made of child-friendly materials* ■ *n* (*plural* **-lies**) UK GAME NOT FORMING PART OF COMPETITION a game that is played mainly for practice or entertainment and not as a scheduled event in a competition or league ○ *a series of friendlies* ■ *adv* (**-li·er, -li·est**) LIKE FRIEND in a manner that befits friends —**friend·li·ly** *adv* —**friend·li·ness** *n* ◇ **be friendly with somebody** to be a friend of or on friendly terms with somebody

friend·ly fire *n* gunfire or artillery fire coming from your own or your allies' forces, sometimes causing accidental death or injury

Friend·ly Is·lands /frèndlee-/ ➧ **Tonga**[2]

friend of the court *n* LAW same as **amicus curiae**

friend·ship /frénd shìp/ *n* **1.** RELATIONSHIP BETWEEN FRIENDS a relationship between two or more people who are friends ○ *a friendship that has lasted more than 40 years* **2.** MUTUALLY FRIENDLY FEELINGS the mutual feelings of trust and affection and the behavior that typify relationships between friends ○ *Any feeling of friendship toward him had long since disappeared.* **3.** FRIENDLY RELATIONS a relationship between people, organizations, or countries that is characterized by mutual assistance, approval, and support ○ *Anglo-American friendship*

Friends of the Earth *n* an international organization that lobbies and campaigns on environmental matters (*takes a singular or plural verb*)

fri·er *n* COOK another spelling of **fryer**

fries /frīz/ *npl* FOOD same as **French fries**

Frie·sian /fréezh'n/ *n* UK BREED same as **Holstein** ■ *n, adj* LANG, PEOPLES same as **Frisian** [Early 20C. Variant of FRISIAN]

Fries·land /fréezlənd/ coastal province in northern Netherlands, that includes four of the West Frisian Islands. Population: 624,435 (2000). Area: 1,298 sq. mi./3,361 sq. km.

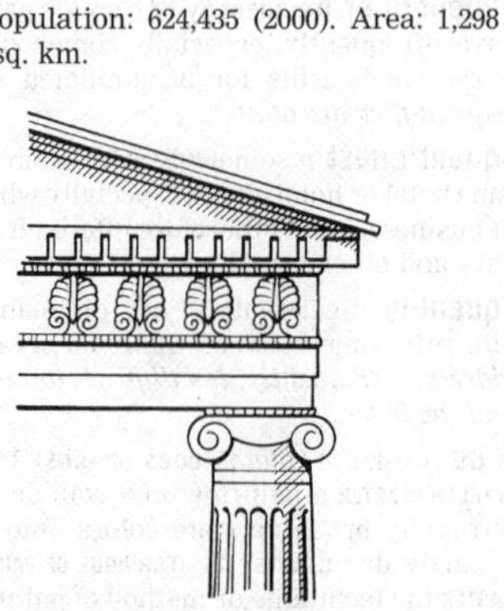

frieze

frieze[1] /freez/ *n* **1.** a band of decoration running along the wall of a room, usually just below the ceiling **2.** a horizontal band forming part of the entablature of a classical building, situated between the architrave and the cornice, and often decorated with sculpted ornaments or figures [Mid-16C. Via French < medieval

Latin *frisium* < Latin *Phrygium (opus)* "Phrygian (work)" (the Phrygians being famous for their crafts)]

SPELLCHECK See *freeze*.

frieze[2] /freez/ *n* **1.** coarse shaggy woolen cloth **2.** *US* a long shaggy carpet pile [15C. Via French *frise* < medieval Latin *frisia* "Frisian (cloth)"]

frig /frig/ (**frigged, frig·ging, frigs**) *vti* (*taboo*) **1.** a highly offensive term meaning to have sexual intercourse with somebody **2.** a highly offensive term meaning to masturbate, or masturbate somebody [Late 16C. Origin ?]

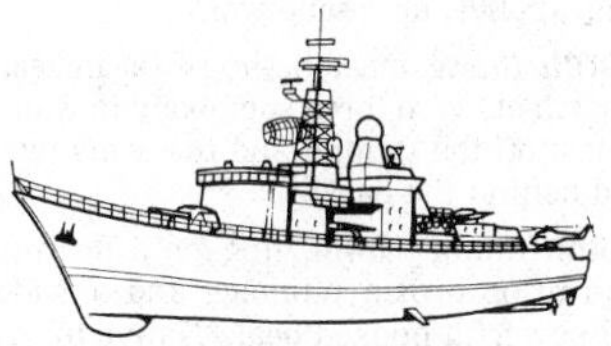

frigate

frig·ate /fríggət/ *n* **1.** *US* **MEDIUM-SIZED WARSHIP** a US warship of medium size, larger than a destroyer but smaller than a cruiser, and used mainly for escort duty **2. WARSHIP SMALLER THAN DESTROYER** a British warship next in size below a destroyer and with a similar armament and function **3. SAILING SHIP EQUIPPED FOR WAR** in the 18th and early 19th centuries, a fast square-rigged fighting ship [Late 16C. Via French *frégate* < Italian *fregata*]

frig·ate·bird /fríggət bùrd/ *n* a large black seabird with powerful wings, a forked tail, and a long hooked beak. Frigate birds often take food from other birds in flight. Native to: tropical waters. Family: Fregatidae. [Probably < its swift flight]

frig·ging /frígging/ *adj, adv* a highly offensive term expressing annoyance or disgust (*taboo*)

fright /frīt/ *n* **1. SUDDEN FEAR** a sudden intense feeling of being threatened or in danger **2. EXPERIENCE OF BEING AFRAID** an experience of sudden fear ○ *You gave me a terrible fright sneaking up that way.* **3. SOMETHING VERY UNPLEASANT LOOKING** somebody or something that looks grotesque, ludicrous, or extremely unattractive (*informal*) ○ *My hair's a fright this morning.* ○ *What a fright Sam looked in that outfit.* [Old English *fryhto* < Germanic]

fright·en /frít'n/ (**-ened, -en·ing, -ens**) *v* **1.** *vti* to make somebody feel fear, or be made to feel fear **2.** *vt* to force or drive somebody or something away through fear ○ *had frightened off all the competition* —**fright·ened** *adj*

~~frightend~~ incorrect spelling of **frightened**

fright·en·er /frít'nər/ *n* somebody or something that is frightening

fright·en·ing /frítning/ *adj* causing fear or alarm —**fright·en·ing·ly** *adv*

fright·ful /frítfəl/ *adj* **1. VERY SERIOUS** used to indicate the seriousness or severity of something ○ *now faced the frightful prospect of losing their farm* **2. FOUL** extremely bad or unpleasant ○ *a frightful smell* **3. VERY GREAT** used to indicate that somebody or something is an extreme example of a particular thing ○ *The speaker turned out to be a frightful bore.* **4. TERRIFYING** capable of causing fear, shock, or dread ○ *looked down from a frightful height* —**fright·ful·ness** *n*

fright·ful·ly /frítfəlee/ *adv* extremely or excessively (*dated or humorous*)

fright wig *n* a wig that is intended to be amusing, with long hair sticking out in all directions

frig·id /fríjjid/ *adj* **1. VERY COLD** having a very cold temperature ○ *I was kept waiting in a frigid little room.* **2. SEXUALLY UNRESPONSIVE** unable or unwilling to respond sexually, to enjoy sexual intercourse, or to experience orgasm during intercourse **3. LACKING EMOTIONAL WARMTH** lacking warmth, friendliness, or enthusiasm ○ *a frigid reply* [15C. < Latin *frigidus* < *frigus* "cold"] —**fri·gid·i·ty** /fri jíddətee/ *n* —**frig·id·ly** *adv* —**frig·id·ness** *n*

Frig·id Zone *n* either of two areas of the Earth's surface, one lying between the Arctic Circle and the North Pole, the other lying between the Antarctic Circle and the South Pole

fri·jo·le /free hṓlay/, **fri·jol** /free hṓl, freé hṓl/ (*plural* **-jo·les** /-hṓleez, -hṓleez/) *n Hispanic* in the cooking of Mexico and the southwestern United States, a bean such as a pinto, kidney, or black bean [Late 16C. Via Spanish, Catalan *fesol*, and Latin *phaseolus* < Greek *phasēlos* "legume"]

REGIONAL NOTE The use of the term ***frijole*** marks the Mexican American territory of south and west Texas, New Mexico, Arizona, and southern California. *Frijoles* are sometimes called *Mexican beans*.

fri·jo·les re·fri·tos /free hṓleez ri freétōs/ *n Hispanic* FOOD same as **refried beans** [< American Spanish]

frill /fril/ *n* **1.** CLOTHING **DECORATIVE BAND WITH MANY FOLDS** a decorative strip of material gathered into many tight folds and sewn along one edge **2.** COOK **PAPER BAND WITH FRINGED EDGE** a paper band with one edge cut into a fringe, placed on bone ends as decoration and to allow the meat to be picked up by the bone end **3.** ZOOL **RUFF OF FEATHERS, FUR, OR SKIN** a ring of fur or feathers or a fold of skin around the neck of a bird or animal, looking like a frill **4. UNNECESSARY ADDITION** an addition to something that is unnecessary, although it may enhance its appearance, interest, or value (*usually used in the plural*) ○ *No frills, thank you, just give me the basic model.* ■ *vt* (**frilled, frill·ing, frills**) **1.** HANDICRAFT **MAKE STRIP OF MATERIAL INTO FRILL** to make a strip of fabric or paper into a frill **2. ADD FRILL TO SOMETHING** to decorate something with a frill [Late 16C. Origin ?] —**frilled** *adj* —**frill·i·ness** *n* —**frill·y** *adj*

frilled liz·ard /frìld-/ *n* a large lizard with a broad membrane of skin around its neck that it can spread out like a ruff. Native to: Australia. Latin name: *Chlamydosaurus kingii*.

Friml /frímm'l/, **Rudolf** (1879–1972) Czech-born US composer. He wrote operettas such as *Rose Marie* (1923) and songs, including "Indian Love Call." Full name **Friml, Charles Rudolf**

fringe /frinj/ *n* **1. DECORATIVE EDGING OF STRANDS** a decorative border of short parallel strands or raveled threads held closely together at one end by stitching and hanging loosely at the other end **2. ANY BORDER OR EDGING** something that serves as or resembles a border ○ *a fringe of reeds circling the pond* **3. OUTER LIMIT** the outer edge, or something considered to be on the outer edge and not central to an activity, interest, or issue (*often used in the plural*) ○ *outposts on the fringes of civilization* **4. LESS IMPORTANT AREA** an area of action that is far away from the center of activity or interest in a specific field (*usually used in the plural*) ○ *on the fringes of political life* **5.** *UK* same as **bangs**[1] (*see* **bang**) **6. FACTION** members of a group or organization who hold views not representative of the group and usually more extreme ○ *the radical fringe of a political party* **7.** GOLF **AREA BORDERING PUTTING GREEN** the area surrounding a putting green on a golf course where the grass is allowed to grow slightly longer than on the green itself **8.** OPTICS **BAND PRODUCED BY DIFFRACTION OF LIGHT** a light, dark, or colored band of light produced by diffraction or interference **9.** *US* FIN same as **fringe benefit** (*informal*) ■ *adj* **1. OUTLYING** situated on the edge or away from the center of something **2. MINOR** playing a minor role in a play or story **3. UNCONVENTIONAL** not part of the established or conventional mainstream of something such as the movie industry, theater, or medicine **4. NOT IN MAIN PART** not in the main part of something such as a conference or organization, especially if putting forward or discussing radical or unconventional ideas ■ *vt* (**fringed, fring·ing, fring·es**) **1. FORM FRINGE AROUND SOMETHING** to form a fringe or border around something ○ *A thin mustache and beard fringed his lips.* **2. PUT DECORATIVE FRINGE ON SOMETHING** to decorate something with a fringe or border [14C. Via French < Latin *fimbriae* "threads"] —**fringed** *adj* —**fring·y** *adj*

fringe ar·e·a *n* an area at or just beyond the edge of a radio or television transmitter's range, where signals are likely to be weak or distorted

fringe ben·e·fit *n* **1.** an additional benefit provided to an employee, e.g., a company car or health insurance **2.** any additional or incidental advantage derived from an activity

fringed gen·tian *n* an annual or biennial plant. Flowers: blue, bell-shaped with fringed petals. Native to: North America. Latin name: *Gentianopsis crinita*.

fringed or·chis, **fringed or·chid** *n* an orchid with a fringed lip. Flowers: yellow, white, purple, greenish. Native to: North America. Genus: *Habenaria*.

fringed po·lyg·a·la /-pə líggələ/ *n* a small herb cultivated as a wildflower. Flowers: fringed reddish purple. Native to: eastern North America. Latin name: *Polygala paucifolia*.

fringe tree *n* an ornamental tree. Flowers: white, in hanging clusters. Native to: eastern United States, China. Genus: *Chionanthus*.

fring·ing reef *n* a coral reef that borders or is directly attached to the shore of an island or a continent

frip·per·y /fríppəree/ (*plural* **-ies**) *n* **1. ARTICLE WORN FOR SHOW** a showy item of clothing or an adornment worn for display or effect **2. OSTENTATION** pretentious display or showiness **3. SOMETHING TRIFLING** something of little value or importance [Mid-16C. < French *friperie* < Old French *frepe* "rag, old clothes"]

Fris·bee /frízbee/ *tdmk* a trademark for a plastic disk thrown from person to person in a game

Frisch /frish/, **Max** (1911–91) Swiss dramatist and novelist. His plays include *The Firebugs* (1958) and *Andorra* (1961). Among his novels are *I'm Not Stiller* (1954), *Homo Faber* (1957), and *Man in the Holocene* (1979). Full name **Frisch, Max Rudolf**

> "Joking is the third best method of hoodwinking people. The second best is sentimentality...But the best and safest method...is to tell the plain unvarnished truth."
>
> [Max Frisch, *The Firebugs*; 1958; tr. 1962]

fri·sé /free záy/ *n* a fabric with a long nap, usually of uncut loops. Use: upholstery, rugs. [Late 19C. < French < past participle of *friser* "curl"]

Fri·sian /frí<u>zh</u>'n, freé<u>zh</u>'n/ *n* **1.** a West Germanic language spoken in the Netherlands and Germany. Native speakers: 350,000. **2.** somebody who comes from Friesland or the Frisian Islands [Late 16C. < Latin *Frisii* "the Frisians" < Old Frisian *Frīsa*] —**Fri·sian** *adj*

Fri·sian Is·lands /frí<u>zh</u>'n-, freé<u>zh</u>'n-/ group of islands in the North Sea off the coasts of the Netherlands, northwestern Germany, and southwestern Denmark. They include the Dutch West Frisian Islands, the German East Frisian Islands, and the North Frisian Islands, divided between Germany and Denmark.

frisk /frisk/ *v* (**frisked, frisk·ing, frisks**) **1.** *vi* **LEAP PLAYFULLY** to leap, skip, or dance around in a carefree way **2.** *vt* **SEARCH SOMEBODY QUICKLY** to search somebody by quickly passing the hands over clothes and into pockets ■ *n* **1. PLAYFUL LEAP** a playful leap, skip, or dance **2. QUICK SEARCH** a quick search of somebody's clothes and pockets [Early 16C. < Old French *frisque* "lively"] —**frisk·er** *n* —**frisk·ing** *n*

fris·ket /frískət/ *n* a thin frame that keeps a sheet of paper in position and masks any portions not to be printed while the sheet is being printed on a hand-operated press [Late 17C. < French *frisquette* < Old French *frisque* "lively"]

frisk·y /fTrískee/ (**-i·er, -i·est**) *adj* behaving or tending to behave in a lively, playful way —**frisk·i·ly** *adv* —**frisk·i·ness** *n*

fris·son /fri sóN/ *n* a brief intense reaction, usually a feeling of excitement, recognition, or terror, accompanied by a physical shudder or thrill [Late 18C. Via French, "shiver" < assumed Vulgar Latin *friction-* < Latin *frigere* "be cold"]

frit /frit/ *n* **1. BASIC MATERIALS FOR GLASS** the basic materials from which glass, pottery glazes, or enamels are made, when they are in a partially bonded state at the beginning of the manufacturing process **2. GROUND FLUX** a flux that is stabilized by melting it with silica and regrinding it into a fine powder ■ *vt* (**frit·ted, frit·ting, frits**) **MAKE SOMETHING INTO FRIT** to fuse or partially fuse materials in order to make frit [Mid-

17C. < Italian *fritta*, past participle of *friggere* "fry" < Latin *frigere*]

frit fly *n* a small black fly whose larvae are destructive to cereal crops. Latin name: *Oscinella frit*. [< Latin *frit* "speck on an ear of grain"]

frit·il·lar·y /fríttʼl èrree/ (*plural* **-ies**) *n* **1.** a plant of the lily family with long narrow leaves. Flowers: bell-shaped with spotted or checkered petals. Genus: *Fritillaria*. **2.** a brownish butterfly with black spots or narrow bands on its wings and usually silver spots on the underside of its hind wings. Family: Nymphalidae. [Mid-17C. < modern Latin *Fritillaria* < Latin *fritillus* "dice box"]

frit·ta·ta /fri taátə, free-/ *n* a firm thick Italian omelet that may contain any of a variety of chopped ingredients, including meat or vegetables [Mid-20C. < Italian < *fritto*, past participle of *friggere* (see FRIT)]

frit·ter[1] /fríttər/ *n* a cake formed by frying a small amount of a soft batter and often containing chopped fruit, vegetables, or meat [14C. < French *friture* < Latin *frict-*, past participle of *frigere* "fry"]

frit·ter[2] /fríttər/ (**-tered, -ter·ing, -ters**) *vt* to break, cut, or tear something into small pieces or shreds [Early 18C. < obsolete *fritters* "fragments, scraps," origin ?]
fritter away *vt* to waste something by expending it in small quantities over a period of time on things that are not worthwhile

frit·to mis·to /fríttō místō/ (*plural* **frit·to mis·tos** or **frit·ti mis·ti** /fríttee místee/) *n* an Italian dish consisting of a mixture of bite-sized pieces of various foods such as seafood, meat, or vegetables, and sometimes sweet things such as cake, deep-fried in light batter [< Italian, "mixed fry"]

fritz /frits/ [Early 20C. Origin ?] ◇ **on the fritz** out of order or not working properly (*informal*)

Fri·u·lan *n* LANG, PEOPLES same as **Friulian**

Fri·u·li /free óolee/ historical region of southeastern Europe comprising parts of present-day northeastern Italy and Slovenia

Fri·u·lian /free óolee ən/, **Fri·u·lan** /free óolən/ *n* **1.** a dialect of Rhaetian spoken in northwestern Italy **2.** somebody who comes from the region of Friuli or who speaks Friulian —**Fri·u·lian** *adj*

friv·ol /frívvəl/ (**-oled, -ol·ing, -ols**) *v* **1.** *vi* to behave or spend time in a frivolous way **2.** *vt* to spend or waste something such as time or money foolishly or frivolously [Mid-19C. Back-formation < FRIVOLOUS] —**friv·ol·er** *n*

fri·vol·i·ty /fri vóllətee/ (*plural* **-ties**) *n* **1.** FRIVOLOUS BEHAVIOR silly and trivial behavior or activities **2.** SOMETHING FRIVOLOUS a frivolous action or thing **3.** TRIVIALITY the state of being trivial and unimportant [Late 18C. < French *frivolité* < Latin *frivolus* "silly, unimportant"]

friv·o·lous /frívvələss/ *adj* **1.** lacking in intellectual substance and not worth serious consideration **2.** silly and trivial [15C. < Latin *frivolus* "silly, unimportant"] —**friv·o·lous·ly** *adv* —**friv·o·lous·ness** *n*

frizz[1] /friz/ *vti* (**frizzed, frizz·ing, frizz·es**) to form a mass of tight curls or tufts, or be curled in this way (*refers to hair*) ■ *n* a mass of tightly curled or tufted hair [Late 16C. < French *friser* "to curl"]

frizz[2] /friz/ (**frizzed, frizz·ing, frizz·es**) *vti US* to sizzle while frying or cooking, or fry or cook something so that it sizzles [Mid-19C. Shortening of FRIZZLE[1]]

friz·zle[1] /frízzʼl/ (**-zled, -zling, -zles**) *vti* **1.** to burn or shrivel, or cause something to burn or shrivel, especially while cooking **2.** to sizzle while frying or cooking, or fry or cook something so that it sizzles [Mid-18C. Probably blend of FRY[1] + FIZZLE or SIZZLE]

friz·zle[2] /frízzʼl/ *vti* (**-zled, -zling, -zles**) to frizz hair, or become frizzed ■ *n* a short tight curl [Mid-16C. Probably < FRIZZ[1]]

friz·zle fowl *n Carib* a chicken of a type that has very curly feathers, often considered to have magical qualities

friz·zy /frízzee/ (**-zi·er, -zi·est**), **friz·zly** /frízzlee/ (**-zli·er, -zli·est**) *adj* forming or styled in tight curls —**friz·zi·ly** *adv* —**friz·zi·ness** *n* —**friz·zli·ness** *n*

Frl. *abbr* Fräulein

fro[1] /frō/ *adv* ▸ **to and fro** [13C. < Old Norse *frá* "from"]

fro[2] /frō/ *n US* an Afro hairstyle (*informal*) [Mid-20C. Shortening]

frock /frok/ *n* **1.** DRESS a woman's or girl's dress (*dated*) **2.** LOOSE OUTER GARMENT a loose baggy outer garment with sleeves that covers the top half of the body to below the waist, traditionally worn by artists and farm workers **3.** MONK'S GOWN a loose full-length gown with wide sleeves worn by the monks, friars, or clerics of some religious orders **4.** same as **frock coat** ■ *vt* (**frocked, frock·ing, frocks**) CHR INDUCT AS MEMBER OF CLERGY to invest somebody as a member of the clergy [14C. < French *froc* < Germanic]

frock coat

frock coat *n* in the 19th century, a man's knee-length coat for formal day wear

froe /frō/, **frow** *n* a cutting tool with one end of its blade fastened at right angles to a short handle. Use: to split wood along the grain to make shingles or barrel staves. [Late 16C. Origin ?]

Froe·bel /frṓbʼl/, **Friedrich Wilhelm August** (1782–1852) German educator. He established the first kindergarten, and was an advocate of play, practical activities, and songs in the education of young children. —**Froe·bel·i·an** /frə beélee ən, frō-/ *adj*

frog

frog[1] /frawg, frog/ *n* **1.** AMPHIB SMALL WEB-FOOTED WATER ANIMAL a small tailless amphibious animal with smooth moist skin, webbed feet, and long back legs used for jumping. Family: Ranidae. **2.** HANDICRAFT SUPPORT FOR FLOWERS IN ARRANGEMENT an object, usually with spikes or perforations, used to support the stems of flowers when making a flower arrangement **3.** MUSIC NUT ON BOW a nut used to secure and tighten the strings of a violin bow and hold them away from the bow stick **4.** another spelling of **Frog** (*slang offensive*) [Old English *frogga* < Germanic] ◇ **have a frog in your throat** to be hoarse and unable to speak clearly

frog[2] /frawg, frog/ *n* a decorative fastening for the front of a garment, consisting of a loop of braid or cord and a button, knot, or toggle that fits into the loop [Early 18C. Origin ?] —**frogged** *adj*

frog[3] /frawg, frog/ *n* a tough flexible pad in the middle of the sole of a horse's hoof [Early 17C. Origin ?]

frog[4] /frawg, frog/ *n* a steel plate used to guide the wheels of a train over a place where two rails cross [Mid-19C. Origin ?]

Frog /frawg, frog/ *n* an offensive term for a French person (*slang*) [Late 18C. < frogs' legs as a French dish]

frog·eye /fráwg ī, fróg-/ *n* a fungal disease of plants that causes rounded spots to appear on the leaves

frog·fish /fráwg fish, fróg-/ (*plural same* or **-fish·es**) *n* an ocean fish that lives near the seabed and has a globe-shaped warty or prickly body with fins adapted for catching prey. Family: Antennariidae.

frog·hop·per /fráwg hòppər, fróg-/ *n* **1.** INSECTS same as **spittlebug 2.** *Carib* an insect that sucks the juice from growing sugar cane, considered a major agricultural pest. Genus: *Aeneolamia*. [Early 18C. < their shape and leap]

frog kick *n* a kick used especially in swimming the breaststroke, in which the legs are first simultaneously bent, then straightened, to push the swimmer along

frog·man /fráwgmən, fróg-/ (*plural* **-men** /-mən/) *n* an underwater swimmer equipped with breathing apparatus, a wet suit, flippers, and other underwater gear, especially somebody engaged in military, police, or rescue work

frog·march /fráwg maàrch, fróg-/ (**-marched, -march·ing, -march·es**) *vt* to force somebody to walk, feet off or almost off the ground and the arms twisted and pinned behind the back

frog·mouth /fráwg mòwth, fróg-/ *n* a nocturnal bird with gray or brown plumage and a wide mouth with a powerful hooked beak. Native to: Australia, Asia. Family: Podargidae.

frog spit *n* **1.** a foamy green mass of small plants or algae floating on the surface of a pond **2.** INSECTS same as **cuckoo spit**

frog stran·gle *n regional* a heavy downpour

REGIONAL NOTE See ***trashmover***.

Frois·sart /frwaa saár, fróy saárt/, **Jean** (1333?–1410?) French historian and poet. His *Chronique de France, d'Angleterre, d'Ecosse et d'Espagne* (1372–1410?) is an important record of the major events of The Hundred Years' War (1337–1453) between England and France and of chivalric life in the late 14th century.

frol·ic /fróllik/ *vi* (**-icked, -ick·ing, -ics**) PLAY LIGHTHEARTEDLY to frisk around, behave, or play in a carefree, uninhibited way ○ *children frolicking at the beach* ■ *n* **1.** SOMETHING LIVELY AND CAREFREE a lively carefree game, action, or amusement **2.** CAREFREE PLAY lively carefree play or behavior ○ *"As a result, Anne had the golden summer of her life as far as freedom and frolic went."* (Lucy Maud Montgomery, *Anne of Green Gables*; 1908) [Early 16C. < Dutch *vrolijk* "glad, joyous" < *vro* "happy"] —**frol·ick·er** *n*

frol·ic·some /frólliksəm/ *adj* frisky and full of fun and high spirits

from *stressed* /frum, from/; *unstressed* /frəm/ CORE MEANING: a preposition used to indicate the source or beginning of something, in terms of location, context, or time ○ *The condition can manifest itself anytime from adolescence onward.* ○ *Most funding comes from the government.* ○ *highlights from her latest novel* ○ *You can connect to our computer network from home.*
prep **1.** RANGE used to indicate a range, either of time, amount, or things ○ *We are open from 2 to 4:30.* ○ *They sell everything, from washing machines to magazines.* **2.** DISTANCE used to indicate the distance between two things or places ○ *The nearest town is not far from here.* **3.** USING used to indicate the materials or substances something is made of ○ *built from native pine* **4.** CAUSE used to indicate the cause of or reason for something ○ *low morale resulting from staff cuts* **5.** RESTRAINT used to indicate that an action does not happen or should not happen ○ *prevented from seeing her* [Old English *fram, from* < Indo-European, "forward, toward"]

fro·mage frais /frə maázh fráy/ *n UK* a fresh cheese with a light creamy taste, a texture like thick cream or yogurt, and a variable fat content [< French, "fresh cheese"]

Fromm /from/, **Erich** (1900–80) German-born US psychoanalyst. He emphasized the link between human personalities and socioeconomic patterns. His books include *Escape from Freedom* (1941) and *The Sane Society* (1955).

> "The deepest need of man is the need to overcome his separateness, to leave the prison of his aloneness."
> [Erich Fromm, *The Art of Loving*; 1956]

frond /frond/ *n* **1.** a large leaf divided into many thin sections that is found on many flowerless plants, especially ferns and palms **2.** a growth that resembles the leaf of a fern or palm tree, especially a growth of seaweed that resembles leaves [Late 18C. < Latin *frond-*, stem of *frons* "leaf"] —**frond·ed** *adj*

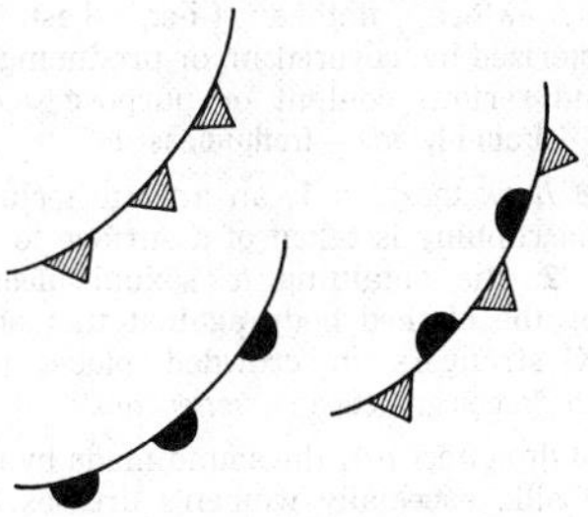

front: meteorological symbols indicating warm and cold weather fronts

front /frunt/ *n* **1.** PART OR SURFACE FACING FORWARD the part or surface that faces forward, is intended to be seen first, has the main entrance, or is facing the direction of motion or the direction people face ○ *You can only see the front of the house from here.* **2.** FORWARD AREA the area, section, or position just ahead of, close to, or at the forward part of something ○ *You sit in the front and I'll ride in the back.* **3.** FRONT DOOR the door at the front or the area beyond it ○ *I'll go out the front, and you go out the back.* **4.** FIRST PAGES the beginning or first pages of a book or magazine **5.** FACADE OF BUILDING a facade of a building, especially the one that faces the street, or a part of it ○ *Bring the car around to the front.* **6.** SIDE OF PROPERTY ADJOINING SOMETHING the side of a property that borders something else, e.g., a street, lake, or river **7.** FORWARD DIRECTION the direction straight ahead ○ *Face the front.* **8.** POSITION AHEAD a place or position approximately ahead of somebody ○ *To our front was a clump of trees.* **9.** LEADING POSITION a prominent or leading position in any field of activity ○ *companies at the front of genetic research* **10.** NOTICEABLE POSITION a conspicuous position ○ *a disturbing aspect that came to the front* **11.** ASPECT a way of viewing a situation ○ *Things looked desperate on all fronts.* **12.** *UK* SEASIDE PROMENADE a street, area of land, or promenade running alongside the beach or shore at a seaside or lakeside resort **13.** DELIBERATELY ASSUMED BEHAVIOR a manner or type of behavior adopted by somebody in order to deal with a situation or disguise the person's true feelings ○ *put on a brave front* **14.** COVER FOR ILLEGAL ACTIVITIES an apparently respectable person, organization, or business acting as a cover for illegal or secret activities ○ *The grocery store was a front for drug deals.* **15.** FIGUREHEAD a nominal leader or head who has no real authority **16.** MIL BATTLE ZONE an area where armies are facing one another, or where fighting between armies is taking place ○ *soldiers returning from the front* **17.** MIL SPACE DEFENDED BY ARMY UNIT the width of territory occupied or defended by an army or a military unit facing an enemy ○ *Each section was defending a front of some two miles.* **18.** MIL DIRECTION IN WHICH TROOPS ARE FACING the direction in which troops are facing when formed in line **19.** PARTICULAR AREA OF ACTIVITY a particular area of activity or operations ○ *There have been a lot of changes on the domestic front.* **20.** METEOROL INTERFACE BETWEEN AIR MASSES a line along which one mass of air meets another that is different in temperature or density **21.** POL GROUP WITH COMMON PURPOSE a group of people or organizations with a common purpose, especially a broad political coalition ○ *a national liberation front* **22.** CLOTHING PART OF GARMENT the part of a garment or the clothing that covers the front part of the body, especially the chest ○ *You've got gravy all down your front.* **23.** CLOTHING DETACHABLE FRONT FOR SHIRT a detachable shirt front, especially part of a man's formal dress shirt **24.** *UK* IMPERTINENCE cheek or cockiness ○ *That took a bit of front!* **25.** FACE the face or forehead (*archaic*) ■ *adj* **1.** AT FRONT situated at, on, or near the front of something, or placed farther forward than others **2.** PHON PRODUCED WITH TONGUE FORWARD describes a vowel sound that is produced with the back of the tongue close to the forward part of the roof of the mouth ■ *v* (**front·ed, front·ing, fronts**) **1.** *vt* FACE TOWARD SOMETHING to have a front that faces toward something ○ *a hotel fronting the ocean* **2.** *vt* GIVE COVERING OR APPEARANCE TO SOMETHING to give something a front or visible surface of a particular kind ○ *The building is fronted with red brick.* **3.** *vi* ACT AS COVER FOR ILLEGAL ACTIVITY to act as a respectable cover for something secret or illegal or for somebody doing something secret or illegal **4.** *vt US* PROVIDE SOMETHING BEFORE PAYMENT to provide something such as money or to provide a service in advance of payment (*informal*) ○ *If you can front me the money, I'll rent some movies for the weekend.* **5.** *vt* BE HEAD OF GROUP to be the head, leader, or spokesperson of a group or organization such as a band ○ *a group fronted by a young lawyer from Chicago* **6.** *vt* HOST PROGRAM to act as the emcee of a television or radio program **7.** *vt* CONFRONT SOMEBODY OR SOMETHING to face up to somebody or something confidently (*archaic*) [13C. Via French < Latin *front-* "forehead, front"] ◇ **in front 1.** leading or ahead of somebody or something else **2.** close to or in the front of something, or farther forward than somebody else **3.** in the lead in a race or competition ○ *Polls show the current mayor far in front as the election nears.* ◇ **in front of 1.** ahead of somebody or in the direction in which somebody is facing **2.** close to the front of something **3.** in the presence, sight, or hearing of somebody ◇ **out front 1.** THEATER in front of the curtain or in the auditorium, as opposed to on the stage **2.** at or to the front of a building ○ *I'll go out front and talk to them.* ◇ **up front 1.** close or closer to the front of something **2.** in advance, e.g., before any work is done or any goods are delivered **3.** direct and honest (*informal*) ○ *He was very up front about having no money.*

CULTURAL NOTE ***All Quiet on the Western Front***, a novel (1929) by German writer Erich Maria Remarque. This classic antiwar novel, which was based on the author's own experiences as an 18-year-old soldier in the German army during World War I, is a grimly realistic account of trench warfare. It was made into a movie by Lewis Milestone in 1930.

front·age /frúntij/ *n* **1.** FRONT OF BUILDING the front side of a building or piece of property **2.** LAND BETWEEN BUILDING AND STREET the land between a building and a street or road **3.** LENGTH OF FRONT the length of the front of a building or piece of land next to a street, river, or lake **4.** PIECE OF LAND ADJOINING SOMETHING a piece of land situated next to a street, river, or lake **5.** EXPOSURE the direction in which a building faces

front·age road *n* ROADS same as **service road**

fron·tal[1] /frúnt'l/ *adj* **1.** AT OR IN FRONT situated at or in the front of something **2.** SHOWING FRONT OF SOMETHING showing the front of somebody or of something, especially a naked body ○ *full frontal nudity* **3.** MIL TOWARD ENEMY FRONT directed against an enemy's front, usually across open ground ○ *a frontal attack* **4.** DIRECT AND FORCEFUL direct, forceful, and intended to be overwhelming ○ *made a frontal attack on her political opponent* **5.** ANAT RELATING TO FOREHEAD relating to the forehead or the front part of the skull **6.** METEOROL RELATING TO WEATHER FRONTS involving or relating to weather fronts [Mid-17C. < modern Latin *frontalis* < Latin *front-* "forehead, front"] —**fron·tal·ly** *adv*

fron·tal[2] /frúnt'l/ *n* **1.** a cloth covering for the front of an altar in a Christian Church **2.** the facade of a building or tomb [14C. Via Old French *frontel* "ornament for the forehead" < Latin *frontale* < *front-* (see FRONT)]

fron·tal bone *n* the bone forming the front part of the skull that shapes the forehead and part of the eye sockets and nasal cavity

fron·tal lobe *n* the front part of each hemisphere of the brain

fron·tal lo·bot·o·my *n* SURG same as **prefrontal lobotomy**

front bench *n* in a parliament, the bench on each side nearest the floor of the chamber, reserved for government ministers on one side and their opposition-party counterparts on the other

front burn·er *n* a position of importance or priority (*informal*) ○ *a plan which seems to be no longer on the front burner*

front·court /frúnt kàwrt/, **front court** *n* **1.** in basketball, the half of a court containing the basket in which a team attempts to score **2.** the forward and center players of a basketball team

front desk *n* a reception desk or information desk near the main entrance of a building

front door *n* **1.** the main entrance to a house or other building, closed by a door **2.** the usual and unsuspicious way of achieving a position

Fron·te·nac /fróntə nàk, froNt naák/, **Louis de Buade, Comte de Palluau et de** (1620–98) French soldier and colonial governor of New France (now Canada) (1672–82, 1689–98). During his governorship, he extended the boundaries of the French territory in North America and repulsed an attack on Quebec by the British (1689).

front end *n* **1.** the user interface of a computer system **2.** COMPUT same as **front-end processor**

front-end *adj* **1.** AUTOMOT OF FRONT OF MOTOR VEHICLE relating to or located on or in the forward part of a motor vehicle ○ *sustained front-end damage when running into a huge pothole* **2.** OF START OF PROCESS relating to the start of a process or project, especially a commercial or financial one ○ *heavy front-end costs* **3.** OF USER INTERFACE relating to the user interface of a computer system

front-end load *n* an amount, making up a large part of the initial payments, paid by an investor in a mutual fund or other long-term investment, intended to cover commissions and other expenses

front-end load·er *n* an excavating machine with a hydraulically operated shovel on the front

front-end pro·ces·sor *n* a computer that carries out preliminary processing on data before passing it to another computer for further processing

fron·ten·is /frun ténniss, frón tènniss/ *n Hispanic* a Latin American form of tennis played on a court that has three walls [Late 20C. < American Spanish, blend of *frontón* "jai-alai court" + *tenis* "tennis"]

fron·tier /frun teér/ *n* **1.** INTERNATIONAL BORDER a border between two countries, or the land immediately adjacent to this ○ *cross the frontier into Spain* **2.** EDGE OF SETTLEMENT the part of a country with expanding settlement that is being opened up by hunters, herders, and other pioneers in advance of full urban settlement **3.** LIMIT OF KNOWLEDGE the furthest limit of knowledge in a specific field ○ *pushing back the frontiers of science* [14C. < Anglo-Norman *frounter*, French *frontière* "front part (of an army)" < *front* (see FRONT)]

fron·tiers·man /frun teérzmən/ (*plural* **-men** /-mən/) *n* a man living in a frontier area, especially an area newly opened up for settlement

fron·tiers·wom·an /frun teérz wòommən/ (*plural* **-wom·en** /-wìmmin/) *n* a woman living in a frontier area, especially an area newly opened up for settlement

fron·tis·piece /frúntiss peess/ *n* **1.** PUBL BOOK ILLUSTRATION an illustration at the beginning of a book, usually facing the title page **2.** ARCHIT BUILDING FACADE the principal facade of a building, treated as a separate element **3.** ARCHIT PEDIMENT a pediment, usually ornamental, above a window or door [Late 16C. Via French *frontispice* (altered after PIECE) < late Latin *frontispicium* "facade" < Latin *frons* "forehead" + *specere* "look at"]

front·let /frúntlət/ *n* **1.** DECORATIVE BAND a decorative band worn on the forehead **2.** ZOOL ANIMAL'S FOREHEAD an animal's forehead, especially a bird's when it has a different color from the rest of the head **3.** CHR ALTAR-CLOTH BORDER a decorated border on the frontal of an altar in a Christian Church [15C. < Old French *frontelet* "little forehead band" < *frontel* (see FRONTAL[2])]

front·line /frúnt lìn/ *n also* **front line 1.** MIL FORWARD LINE the forward line of a battle, position, or formation **2.** ADVANCED POSITION the most advanced, important, or conspicuous position in any situation ○ *on the front lines of the battle for equality* **3.** BASKETBALL same as **frontcourt** (sense 2) ■ *adj* **1.** AT LIMITS OF ATTAINMENT that is the most advanced or important of its kind ○ *frontline research* **2.** BORDERING TROUBLE SPOT relating to countries that border another country in which an armed conflict is taking place **3.** *US* REGULAR belonging among or relating to regular members of a team ○ *a frontline pitcher* **4.** DEALING DIRECTLY WITH CUSTOMERS describes employees dealing directly with customers, or a job that requires them to do so

front·line state *n* a nation situated on the border of a war-torn or war-threatened area

front-load *vt* to assign the bulk of the costs of something such as a mutual fund investment, to an early stage

front load·er *n* a washing machine or dryer in which clothes are loaded through a door at the front rather than the top

front·load·ing /frùnt lṓding/ *n* the practice, by minors, of consuming large quantities of alcohol as quickly as possible in order to become intoxicated before going out to clubs or parties where they are not permitted lawfully to drink (*slang*)

front·man /frúntmən/ (*plural* **-men** /-mən/) *n* (*informal*) **1.** *also* **front man** an apparent leader of an organization or activity in which somebody else has the real power, secretly or illegally concealed **2.** a man who is lead singer of a band or other musical group

front mat·ter *n* the material that appears in a book before the main text, e.g., the title page, copyright information, the table of contents, and the preface

front mon·ey *n US* payment made in advance for services or goods

front of·fice *n* the management or executives of an organization who decide on policy

fron·to·gen·e·sis /frùntō jénnəssiss/ *n* the formation or development of a weather front

fron·tol·y·sis /frun tólləssiss/ *n* the weakening or disappearance of a weather front [Mid-20C. < FRONT + -LYSIS]

fron·ton /frón tòn/ *n* a court used for the game of jai alai [Late 19C. < Spanish < *fronte* "forehead" < Latin *front-* (see FRONT)]

front-page *adj* important or interesting enough to appear on the front page of a newspaper ■ *vt* (**front-paged, front-pag·ing, front-pag·es**) *US* to print something on the front page of a newspaper

front room *n* a living room in the front of a house

front-run·ner, front·run·ner /frúnt rùnnər/ *n* somebody in a leading position in a race or contest (*informal*) ○ *the new front-runner in the senatorial race*

front·side 1080 /frùntsīd ten áytee/ *n* in snowboarding, three full revolutions 10 feet above a pipe, the most difficult move in the sport

front·ward /frúntwərd/ *adj* toward or at the front ■ *adv also* **front·wards** /-wərdz/ toward or in the direction of the front

front-wheel drive *n* a system of powering motor vehicles that uses the engine to drive the front wheels only

front·wom·an /frúnt wŏŏmmən/ (*plural* **-wom·en** /-wìmmin/) *n* a woman who is lead singer of a band or other musical group (*informal*)

frosh /frawsh/ (*plural same*) *n* same as **freshman** (sense 1) (*informal*) [Early 20C. Alteration of FRESHMAN]

frost /frawst/ *n* **1.** FROZEN WATER crystals of frozen water deposited on a cold surface **2.** FREEZING TEMPERATURE an outdoor temperature below freezing point, resulting in the deposit of ice crystals ○ *had a hard frost as late as May* **3.** CHILLY MANNER a coldness of manner **4.** FREEZING the act or process of freezing **5.** FAILURE something that meets with an unenthusiastic reception, e.g., an artistic performance or a new book (*informal*) ○ *The opening night was a true frost.* ■ *v* (**frost·ed, frost·ing, frosts**) **1.** *vti* METEOROL COVER OR BECOME COVERED WITH FROST to cover something with frost, especially hoar frost, or become covered with frost **2.** *vt* MAKE SURFACE OPAQUE to make something, especially glass or a window, unable to be seen through by giving its surface a rough or fine-grained texture **3.** *vt* PUT FROSTING ON SOMETHING to cover a cake or other pastry with icing or frosting ○ *a frosted sponge cake* **4.** *vt* HAIR TINT HAIR STRANDS to change the color of isolated strands of hair by pulling the strands through a rubber or plastic cap with holes in it and then dyeing or peroxiding the hair **5.** *vt* KILL PLANTS BY FREEZING to damage or kill crops or garden plants by freezing temperatures [Old English *forst, frost* < Germanic]

frost up *vi* to become covered in frost or ice, especially in a way that hinders a function ○ *The freezer has frosted up so much that the door won't close.*

Library of Congress

Robert Frost

Frost /frawst/, **Robert** (1874–1963) US poet. He is best known for his spare poems about New England life, including "Stopping by Woods on a Snowy Evening" and "The Road Not Taken." He was poetry consultant to the Library of Congress (1958–59) and he won the Pulitzer Prize four times (1924, 1931, 1937, and 1943). Full name **Frost, Robert Lee**. See Cultural note at **wood**

> "The woods are lovely, dark and deep. / But I have promises to keep, / And miles to go before I sleep. / And miles to go before I sleep."
> [Robert Frost, "Stopping by Woods on a Snowy Evening"; 1923]

frost·bite /fráwst bīt/ *n* INJURY BY FREEZING damage to body extremities caused by prolonged exposure to freezing conditions, characterized by numbness, tissue death, and gangrene ■ *vt* (**-bit** /-bit/, **-bit·ten** /-bìtt'n/, **-bit·ing, -bites**) INJURE BY FREEZING to damage something by prolonged exposure to freezing conditions (*usually passive*) ■ *adj* OF WINTER SPORTS relating to or involving sports pursued in extremely cold winter weather, e.g., racing small boats or riding sailboards equipped with blades on frozen lakes ○ *a frostbite derby*

frost-free *adj* describes an appliance such as a refrigerator or freezer that does not need to be defrosted

frost heave, frost heav·ing *n* the cracking of the surface of a road or piece of ground by the freezing and upward expansion of subsurface water, or a damaged surface resulting from this

frost·ing /fráwsting/ *n* **1.** SOFT ICING a variety of soft icing for cakes made by whisking egg whites and sugar over hot water or incorporating hot syrup into whisked egg whites **2.** RICH ICING icing that is typically thick and rich and made with sugar, milk, eggs, butter, or cream **3.** ROUGH SURFACE a roughened or dull surface produced on something, especially glass or metal

frost line *n* **1.** the point below the surface of the ground beyond which frost will not penetrate **2.** a line on a map joining places subject to the same number of frosts a year or to the same degree of frost

frost weath·er·ing *n* the shattering of rock caused by the freezing of water in surface cracks and hollows, and in the pore spaces

frost·work /fráwst wùrk/ *n* **1.** the patterns made by frost on various surfaces, especially windows, that often resemble tracery or the fronds of ferns **2.** decoration on metal or glass imitating the patterns made naturally by frost

frost·y /fráwstee/ (**-i·er, -i·est**) *adj* **1.** VERY COLD cold enough for the formation of frost **2.** COVERED IN FROST covered in frost, especially hoar frost **3.** COLD TO TASTE cold to the touch or taste ○ *a frosty beer* **4.** COLD IN MANNER cold and unwelcoming in manner **5.** WHITE LIKE FROST looking like hoar frost, especially in whiteness ○ *a shock of matted frosty hair* —**frost·i·ly** *adv* —**frost·i·ness** *n*

froth /frawth, froth/ *n* **1.** FOAM a mass of bubbles in or on the surface of a liquid **2.** FOAMY SALIVA a foamy mixture of saliva and air bubbles produced at the mouth in some diseases or by exhaustion **3.** TRIVIA anything seen as being insubstantial or trivial ○ *The conversation at the party was mostly froth and posturing.* ■ *v* (**frothed, froth·ing, froths**) **1.** *vt* CAUSE SOMETHING TO FOAM to make something produce foam, or cover something with foam **2.** *vi* CREATE FOAM to produce foam or emerge as foam ○ *froth at the mouth* [14C. < Old Norse *froða* or *frauð*]

froth flo·ta·tion *n* MIN EXTRACT same as **flotation** (sense 5)

froth·y /fráwthee, fróthee/ (**-i·er, -i·est**) *adj* **1.** characterized by, covered in, or producing foam **2.** with no serious content or purpose ○ *a frothy sitcom* —**froth·i·ly** *adv* —**froth·i·ness** *n*

frot·tage /fraw taázh/ *n* **1.** an artistic technique in which a rubbing is taken of a surface to create a design **2.** the obtaining of sexual pleasure by rubbing the clothed body against that of others, usually strangers in crowded places [Mid-20C. < French, "rubbing, friction" < *frotter* "rub"]

frou·frou /froō froō/ *n* **1.** the sound made by the rustling of silk, especially women's dresses **2.** fancy trimmings or elaborate decoration, especially on women's clothes [Late 19C. < French, an imitation of the sound]

frow *n* another spelling of **froe**

fro·ward /frṓ ərd/ *adj* stubbornly disobedient or contrary (*archaic*) [Old English *fráward* "in a direction leading away from" < Old Norse *frá* "from"] —**fro·ward·ly** *adv* —**fro·ward·ness** *n*

Fro·ward, Cape /frṓ ərd/ cape in southern Chile, the southernmost tip of mainland South America. Spanish name **Cabo Froward**

frown /frown/ (**frowned, frown·ing, frowns**) *v* **1.** *vi* to show a facial expression of displeasure or concentration by wrinkling the brow **2.** *vt* to communicate something by frowning [14C. < Old French *froignier* "to frown, snort" < *froigne* "scowl"] —**frown** *n* —**frown·er** *n* —**frown·ing·ly** *adv*

frown on, frown upon *vt* to dislike or disapprove of something

SYNONYMS See ***disapprove***.

frowst·y /frówstee/ (**-i·er, -i·est**) *adj UK* same as **frowzy** (sense 2) [Mid-19C. Origin ?] —**frowst·i·ness** *n*

frow·zy /frówzee/ (**-zi·er, -zi·est**) *adj* **1.** messy or shabby in personal appearance or manner of dress ○ *a frowzy loafer* **2.** unpleasant to be in because of mustiness, staleness, or a bad smell [Late 17C. Origin ?] —**frowz·i·ness** *n*

fro-yo /frṓ yṑ/ *n US* frozen yogurt (*slang*) [Shortening]

froze past tense of **freeze**

fro·zen /frṓz'n/ past participle of **freeze** ■ *adj* **1.** WITH ICE covered by or made into ice ○ *a frozen lake* **2.** AFFECTED BY ICE made inoperable, damaged, or obstructed by ice or freezing temperatures ○ *All trains are delayed because of frozen signals.* ○ *no running water in the house because of frozen pipes* **3.** EXTREMELY COLD characterized by extreme cold ○ *the frozen north* **4.** PRESERVED BY FREEZING preserved by freezing for eating at a later time ○ *frozen pizza* **5.** IMMOBILE immobile or unable to move ○ *She stood there, frozen in terror.* **6.** FIN FIXED deliberately fixed at a given level to avoid undesirable economic or social consequences **7.** FIN NOT AVAILABLE TO BE SOLD describes assets that cannot be sold or otherwise liquidated —**fro·zen·ly** *adv* —**fro·zen·ness** *n*

fro·zen smoke *n* TECH same as **solid smoke**

FRS *abbr* GOV Federal Reserve System

F.R.S. *abbr* Fellow of the Royal Society

FRSC *abbr Can* Fellow of the Royal Society of Canada

frt. *abbr* TRANSP freight

fruc·tan /frúktan/ *n* a natural polymer, composed of units of fructose arranged in a chain, that is an important source of stored energy for some plants [Mid-20C. < FRUCTOSE]

fruc·tif·er·ous /fruk tíffərəss, frŏŏk-/ *adj* describes a tree or other plant that bears fruit [Mid-17C. < Latin *fructifer* "fruit-bearing" < *fructus* "fruit" (see FRUIT)]

fruc·ti·fi·ca·tion /frùktəfi káysh'n, frŏŏk-/ *n* **1.** PRODUCTION OF FRUIT the production of fruit or fruits by a tree or other plant **2.** FRUIT OF SEED-BEARING PLANT the fruit produced by a seed-bearing plant **3.** SEED-BEARING PART a seed-bearing or spore-bearing part of a plant, alga, or fungus

fruc·ti·fy /frúktə fī, frŏŏk-/ (**-fied, -fy·ing, -fies**) *vti* to become productive or fruitful, or cause to become productive or fruitful (*formal or technical*) [14C. Via French *fructifier* < Latin *fructificare* < *fructus* "fruit" (see FRUIT)]

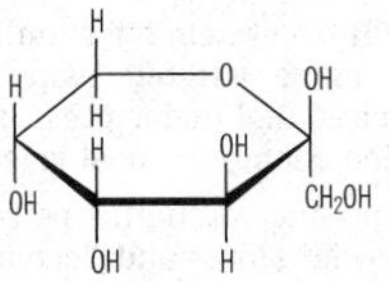

fructose

fruc·tose /frúk tōz, -tōss, frŏŏk-/ *n* a simple sugar found in fruits and honey. Formula: $C_6H_{12}O_6$. [Mid-19C. < Latin *fructus* "fruit" (see FRUIT)]

fruc·tu·ous /frúkchoo əss, frŏŏk-/ *adj* productive of much fruit, or full of fruit (*formal*) [14C. Directly or via Old French < Latin *fructuosus* < *fructus* "fruit" (see FRUIT)]

fru·gal /frŏŏg'l/ *adj* **1.** characterized by thriftiness and avoidance of waste **2.** involving very little expense [Early 16C. Directly or via French < Latin *frugalis* < *frugi* "economical, useful" < *frug*, stem of *frux* "fruit, value"] —**fru·gal·i·ty** /froo gállətee/ *n* —**fru·gal·ly** *adv* —**fru·gal·ness** *n*

fru·giv·o·rous /froo jívvərəss/ *adj* describes an animal that eats mainly fruit [Early 18C. < Latin *frug-* "fruit"] —**fru·gi·vore** /frŏŏjə vàwr/ *n*

fruit /froot/ *n* **1.** EDIBLE PART OF PLANT an edible part of a plant, usually fleshy and containing seeds **2.** OVARY OF PLANT the ripened seed-bearing ovary of a plant. It is usually considered to be sweet and fleshy, as in plums, but may be dry, as in poppies, or be a simple edible supporting structure, as in strawberries. **3.** PRODUCE the produce of any plant grown or harvested by humans ○ *the fruits of the field* **4.** PRODUCT OF SOMETHING the product or consequence of something done ○ *We are now seeing the fruits of our efforts.* **5.** OFFSPRING the offspring of humans or animals (*dated*) **6.** SPORE-PRODUCING PART a spore-producing part of a plant **7.** WINE FRUITY TASTE a fruity taste in wine ○ *a big red with lots of fruit* **8.** OFFENSIVE TERM an offensive term for a gay man (*slang*) ■ *vti* (**fruit·ed, fruit·ing, fruits**) PRODUCE FRUIT to bear fruit, or cause a plant or tree to bear fruit ○ *This variety fruits in August.* [12C. Via French < Latin *fructus* "enjoyment, produce, fruit" < past participle of *frui* "enjoy, have the use of"] ◇ **bear fruit** to be successful in the end, typically after planning and effort have been expended

fruit·age /frŏŏtij/ *n* **1.** FRUIT PRODUCTION the production of fruit, the condition of a plant or tree when bearing fruit, or the time when this happens **2.** FRUITS fruits as a group **3.** RESULT OR EFFECT the results or cumulative set of effects deriving from a usually long-term process (*formal*)

frui·tar·i·an /froo térree ən/ *n* somebody who only eats fruit [Late 19C. After VEGETARIAN]

fruit bat *n* a large bat of a group including mostly fruit-eaters but some pollen- or nectar-eaters. Native to: Europe, Asia, Africa. Suborder: Megachiroptera.

fruit·cake /frŏŏt kàyk/ *n* **1.** a dense cake containing dried fruit such as raisins, currants, and sultanas **2.** an offensive term for somebody considered to be irrational or out of touch with reality (*insult*)

fruit cock·tail *n* a mixture of small or diced fruits such as pears, peaches, and pineapple, typically sold canned in syrup

fruit cup *n* same as **fruit cocktail**

fruit drop *n* the falling from the tree of fruit that is not fully ripe

fruit fly *n* **1.** a small insect that eats decaying fruit. Genus: *Drosophila*. **2.** a small insect that eats plant tissue. Order: Trypetidae.

fruit·ful /frŏŏtfəl/ *adj* **1.** BEARING MUCH FRUIT bearing fruit, especially in abundance **2.** PROLIFIC producing many offspring ○ *a fruitful marriage* **3.** CAUSING FERTILITY causing or promoting fertility or productivity ○ *fruitful soil* **4.** CREATIVE highly productive or creative ○ *a fruitful imagination* **5.** SUCCESSFUL OR BENEFICIAL producing useful results or benefits ○ *a fruitful investigation* —**fruit·ful·ly** *adv* —**fruit·ful·ness** *n*

fruit·ing bod·y *n* a part of some fungi from which spores are released

fru·i·tion /froo ísh'n/ *n* **1.** COMPLETION a state or point in which something has come to maturity or had a desired outcome ○ *Our plans have come to fruition.* **2.** ENJOYMENT OF INTENDED OUTCOME the enjoyment of a desired outcome when it happens ○ *a sense of fruition* **3.** BOT PLANT'S FRUIT PRODUCTION the production of fruit by a tree or other plant [15C. Via French < late Latin *fruition-* < Latin *frui* "enjoy, have the use of"]

fruit·less /frŏŏtləss/ *adj* **1.** producing nothing, or nothing worthwhile ○ *a fruitless discussion* **2.** producing no fruit —**fruit·less·ly** *adv* —**fruit·less·ness** *n*

fruit·let /frŏŏtlət/ *n* **1.** a fruit of smaller than usual size **2.** a part of a multiple fruit

fruit ma·chine *n UK* GAMBLING same as **slot machine** (sense 1)

fruit sal·ad *n* **1.** a dish of various pieces of fresh or canned fruit, often served with lettuce and dressing **2.** *US* the rows of small narrow colorful campaign, service, and combat decorations worn by US military personnel on the left chest area of their uniforms (*slang*)

fruit sug·ar *n* BIOCHEM same as **fructose**

fruit tree *n* a tree cultivated for its fruit

fruit·wood /frŏŏt wŏŏd/ *n* the wood of a fruit tree, especially when used in cabinetmaking

fruit·y /frootee/ (**-i·er, -i·est**) *adj* **1.** OF FRUIT relating to, resembling, or reminiscent of fruit **2.** RICH IN TONE rich and resonant in voice tone **3.** *US* FOOLISH considered foolish or irrational (*informal*) ○ *fruity Victorian love poems* **4.** OFFENSIVE TERM an offensive term for a man considered to be excessively or inappropriately effeminate (*slang*) —**fruit·i·ly** *adv* —**fruit·i·ness** *n*

fru·men·ta·ceous /frŏŏmən táyshəss/ *adj* made from, containing, or like wheat or any similar grain [Mid-17C. < late Latin *frumentaceus* < *frumentum* "corn, grain"]

fru·men·ty /frŏŏməntee/, **fur·mi·ty** /fúrmətee/ *n* a dish made from wheat cooked in water to a thick consistency with added flavoring [14C. < Old French *frumentee, fourmentee* < *frument, fourment* "grain" < Latin *frumentum*]

frump /frump/ *n* (*informal insult*) **1.** an offensive term for a woman considered not to be good-looking or not to dress well **2.** an offensive term for somebody considered to be drab, dull, or old-fashioned [Mid-16C. Probably shortening of *frumple* "wrinkle" < Middle Dutch *verrompelen* "rumple completely"] —**frump·ish** *adj* —**frump·y** *adj*

frus·trate /frú stràyt/ (**-trat·ed, -trat·ing, -trates**) *vt* **1.** to prevent somebody or something from succeeding or something from coming to fruition ○ *All attempts to put to sea were frustrated by high winds.* **2.** to make somebody feel disappointed, exasperated, or weary because of thwarted goals or unsatisfied desires [15C. < Latin *frustrat-*, past participle of *frustrari* "deceive, frustrate, render useless" < *frustra* "in vain, without effect"] —**frus·trat·er** *n* —**frus·trat·ing** *adj* —**frus·trat·ing·ly** *adv*

frus·trat·ed /frú stràytəd/ *adj* feeling exasperated, discouraged, or unsatisfied

frus·tra·tion /fru stráysh'n/ *n* **1.** DISSATISFACTION a feeling of disappointment, exasperation, or weariness caused by goals being thwarted or desires unsatisfied **2.** FRUSTRATING OF SOMEBODY OR SOMETHING an act or instance of causing somebody or something to be dissatisfied or unfulfilled **3.** SOMETHING THAT THWARTS something that blocks, thwarts, and upsets somebody all at the same time ○ *His lack of ambition was a frustration to his father.*

frus·tule /frús chool/ *n* the hard cell wall of a microscopic organism (**diatom**) [Mid-19C. < Latin *frustulum* "small piece" < *frustum* "bit (cut off), piece (of a whole)"]

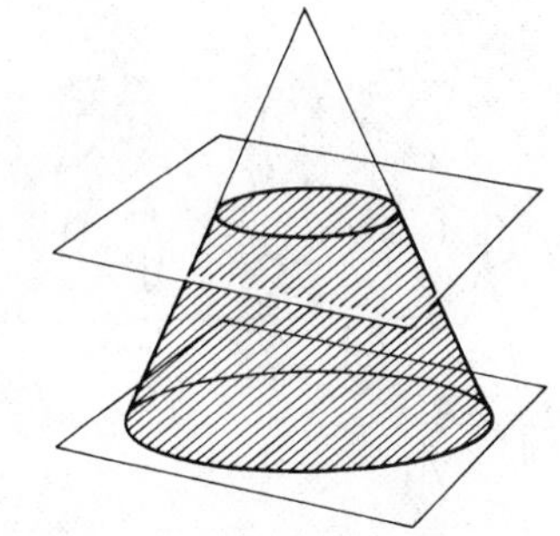

frustum

frus·tum /frústəm/ *n* the part of a solid between its base and a plane that cuts it parallel to the base [Mid-17C. < Latin, "bit (cut off), piece (of a whole)"]

fru·tes·cent /froo téss'nt/ *adj* looking or growing like a shrub [Early 18C. < Latin *frutex* "shrub"] —**fru·tes·cence** *n*

fry[1] /frī/ *v* (**fried, fry·ing, fries**) **1.** *vti* COOK QUICKLY IN FAT to cook something in fat over high heat, or be cooked in this way **2.** *vi* BECOME HOT OR OVERHEATED to become extremely hot as a result of the surrounding temperature (*informal*) ○ *We'll fry in this heat!* **3.** *vt* BURN CIRCUIT OUT to burn out an electrical component or circuit by passing too much current through it (*slang*) ○ *Turn it down before you fry the speakers.* **4.** *vti US* EXECUTE SOMEBODY, OR BE EXECUTED to execute somebody in an electric chair, or be executed in this way (*slang*) ■ *n* (*plural* **fries**) **1.** *US* FRIED DISH a fried dish, sometimes of various items mixed together ○ *a mixed fry of various shellfish, served with a light salad* **2.** OCCASION WITH FRIED FOOD a social occasion at which the food is fried ○ *a fish fry on the beach* [13C. Via French *frire* < Latin *frigere* "roast, fry"]

fry[2] /frī/ *npl* **1.** YOUNG FISHES the young of various fish **2.** YOUNG ANIMALS the young of various animals that breed or hatch in large numbers **3.** CHILDREN small offspring of human parents (*humorous*) [13C. Probably < Anglo-Norman *frei*, Old French *frai* "spawn" < *froier* "to spawn" < Latin *fricare* "rub"]

Frye /frī/, **Northrop** (1912–91) Canadian literary critic. He is best known as a proponent of archetypal criticism. His most important work is his *Anatomy of Criticism* (1957). Full name **Frye, Herman Northrop**

> "Value judgments are founded on the study of literature; the study of literature can never be founded on value judgments."
> [Northrop Frye, *Anatomy of Criticism*; 1957]

fry·er /frī́r/, **fri·er** *n* **1.** a container in which food is fried (*usually used in combination*) **2.** a young chicken suitable for frying

fry·ing pan, **fry pan** *n* a shallow metal pan with a long handle, used for frying food ◇ **out of the frying pan (and) into the fire** from one difficult or dangerous situation to an even worse one

FS *abbr* **1.** POL Foreign Service **2.** FORESTRY Forest Service

FSH *abbr* BIOCHEM follicle-stimulating hormone

FSLIC *abbr* BANKING Federal Savings and Loan Insurance Corporation

f-stop *n* a setting for a lens aperture that corresponds with an f-number

ft., **ft** *abbr* **1.** MEASURE foot *or* feet **2.** MIL fort

FTC *abbr* COMM Federal Trade Commission

fth. *abbr* MEASURE fathom

FTP *n* a standard procedure that allows one computer to transfer files to and from another over a network such as the Internet. Full form **file transfer protocol** ■ *vt* (**FTPed, FT·Ping, FTPs**) to transfer data using FTP

FTSE 100 In·dex /fŏŏtsee wun húndrəd-/, **FTSE** *n* an average of the London stock exchange prices of the stocks of the 100 largest British companies, published daily. Full form **Financial Times Stock Exchange 100 Index**

fuchsia

fuch·sia /fyoóshə/ *n* **1.** a widely-cultivated tropical plant or bush. Flowers: purplish, reddish, or white, drooping. Genus: *Fuchsia.* **2.** a brilliant deep purplish pink color [Late 18C. < modern Latin, after Leonhard *Fuchs*] —**fuch·sia** *adj*

fuch·sin /fyoóksin/, **fuch·sine** /fyoók seen, -sin/ *n* a dark green crystalline solid that when dissolved in water makes a bluish red solution. Use: textile dye, bacteria stain, disinfectant. Formula: $C_{20}H_{19}N_3.HCl$. [Mid-19C. < French *fuchsine*, or directly < German *Fuchs* "fox" (translation of French *Renard*, the company that first produced the dye)]

fu·ci MARINE BIOL plural of **fucus**

fuck /fuk/ (*taboo*) *v* (**fucked, fuck·ing, fucks**) **1.** *vti* a highly offensive term meaning to have sexual intercourse with somebody **2.** *vt* a highly offensive term used like a command, often followed by another word, to express anger, contempt, or rejection **3.** *vt* a highly offensive term meaning to ruin, botch, or destroy something **4.** *vt* a highly offensive term meaning to treat somebody unjustly or harshly ■ *n* **1.** a highly offensive term for an act of sexual intercourse **2.** a highly offensive term for somebody considered as a sexual partner of a particular quality **3.** *US* a highly offensive term for a person, usually highlighting a particular characteristic **4.** a highly offensive term for something of little or no value ■ *interj* a highly offensive term used without a following word to express exasperation, fear, or surprise or to add emphasis [Early 16C. Origin ?]

fuck around *vt* (*taboo*) **1.** a highly offensive term meaning to behave stupidly or carelessly **2.** a highly offensive term meaning to treat somebody in a careless, insincere, or inconsiderate way

fuck off *vi* (*taboo*) **1.** a highly offensive term used as a command dismissing somebody in an angry or contemptuous way **2.** a highly offensive term meaning to go away

fuck over *vt US* a highly offensive term meaning to treat people unjustly or take advantage of them (*taboo*)

fuck up *v* (*taboo*) **1.** *vt* a highly offensive term meaning to damage or botch something **2.** *vt* a highly offensive term meaning to make somebody confused or inflict emotional or mental damage on somebody **3.** *vi* a highly offensive term meaning to make a bad mistake or bungle something

fuck with *vt* a highly offensive term meaning to treat another person in a careless or disrespectful way (*taboo*)

fuck all *pron* (*taboo*) **1.** a highly offensive term meaning nothing at all **2.** a highly offensive term meaning not any

fucked *adj* (*taboo*) **1.** a highly offensive term meaning broken or destroyed **2.** a highly offensive term meaning in a situation in which trouble or failure is imminent

fucked up *adj* (*taboo*) **1.** a highly offensive term meaning affected by or displaying symptoms of psychological or emotional disorder **2.** a highly offensive term meaning mismanaged or very clumsily or badly done **3.** a highly offensive term meaning injured, broken, or destroyed **4.** a highly offensive term meaning completely intoxicated, especially as a result of taking drugs

fuck·er /fúkər/ *n* **1.** a highly offensive term expressing extreme dislike for somebody (*taboo insult*) **2.** a highly offensive term for any unnamed person, an obscene equivalent of "guy" or "fellow" (*taboo*)

fuck·face /fúk fàyss/ *n* a highly offensive term expressing extreme contempt for somebody (*taboo insult*)

fuck·ing /fúking/ *adj* a highly offensive term intensifying or emphasizing a word or statement (*taboo*)

fuck·up /fúk ùp/ *n* **1.** a highly offensive term meaning a bad mistake or something bungled (*taboo*) **2.** a highly offensive term meaning somebody regarded as incompetent (*taboo insult*)

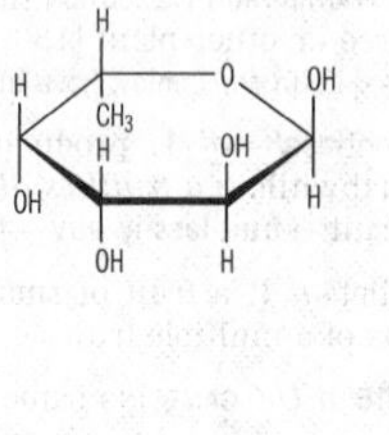

fucose

fu·cose /fyoó kòss/ *n* a six-carbon monosaccharide produced in plant polysaccharides [Early 20C. < FUCUS; from its presence in brown algae]

fu·co·xan·thin /fyoókō zánthin/ *n* a brown carotenoid pigment found in some algae [Late 19C. < FUCUS; from its presence in brown algae]

fu·cus /fyoókəss/ (*plural* **-ci** /-sì/ or **-cus·es**) *n* a greenish brown seaweed. Genus: *Fucus.* [Early 17C. Via modern Latin < Latin, "rock lichen, red or purple color" < Greek *phukos* "seaweed"] —**fu·coid** /fyoó kòyd/ *adj*

fud·dle /fúdd'l/ *v* (**-dled, -dling, -dles**) **1.** *vt* CONFUSE SOMEBODY AS IF WITH DRINK to make a person or mental faculty confused, often through intoxication **2.** *vi* DRINK TOO MUCH to drink too much alcohol regularly (*archaic*) ■ *n* FUDDLED STATE a state of confusion or drunkenness [Late 16C. Origin ?]

fud·dy-dud·dy /fúddee dùddee/ (*plural* **fud·dy-dud·dies**) *n* an old-fashioned or dull person, especially one past middle age (*informal; offensive in some contexts*) ○ *This is for kids, not fuddy-duddies like us.* [Early 20C. Origin ?]

FUD fac·tor *n* a sales technique employed to cause a buyer to hesitate in purchasing a competitive product. Asking the prospective customer if the competitive item meets all applicable government or industry standards, warranties, and service contracts is an example. (*slang*) [Acronym < *fear, uncertainty, and doubt*]

fudge /fuj/ *n* **1.** CONFECTION soft candy made by boiling milk and sugar and then beating the liquid until it crystallizes and becomes slightly grainy in texture. Many flavorings and other ingredients can be added. **2.** CHOCOLATE CAKE FILLING rich chocolate filling or topping, or squares of rich chocolate cake **3.** NONSENSE nonsensical talk (*informal*) ■ *vti* (**fudged, fudg·ing, fudg·es**) ALTER SOMETHING TO DECEIVE to fiddle with or otherwise alter something in order to deceive or remain noncommittal (*informal*) ○ *fudged the figures to make the bottom line look better* [Early 17C. Origin ?]

Fu·e·gi·an /fyoo éejee ən, fwáy-/ *adj* relating to Tierra del Fuego, or its people or culture ■ *n* somebody, especially a Native South American, who comes from any of the islands of Tierra del Fuego

fueh·rer *n* another spelling of **führer**

fu·el /fyoó əl/ *n* **1.** SOURCE OF ENERGY something that is burned to provide power or heat **2.** SOURCE OF NUCLEAR ENERGY the fissionable material used to create power in a nuclear generator **3.** SOURCE OF STIMULATION something that stimulates or maintains something else, especially an emotion ○ *Her refusal to answer questions added fuel to his curiosity.* ■ *v* (**-eled, -el·ing, -els**) **1.** *vt* SUPPLY SOMETHING WITH FUEL to supply something with material to burn for power or heat **2.** *vt* STIMULATE SOMETHING to stimulate or maintain something, especially an emotion ○ *fueled her passion* **3.** *vi* OBTAIN FUEL to take on supplies of fuel for running a vehicle [12C. Via Anglo-Norman *fuaille*, Old French *fouaille* < assumed Vulgar Latin *focalia* "(things) for the fire" < Latin *focus* "fireplace, hearth"] —**fu·el·er** *n*

fu·el-air bomb *n* a thermobaric bomb

fu·el cell *n* a device that generates electricity by converting the chemical energy of a fuel and an oxidant to electric energy

fu·el ef·fi·cien·cy *n* the ability to make the best use of the fuel being used —**fu·el-ef·fi·cient** *adj*

fu·el in·jec·tion *n* a system for running an internal-combustion engine without using a carburetor, forcing vaporized fuel under pressure directly into the combustion chamber —**fu·el-in·ject·ed** *adj*

fu·el oil *n* a product of liquid petroleum, burned chiefly to power ships and locomotives and to provide domestic heating

fu·el rod *n* a metal tube containing nuclear fuel that is used in some types of nuclear reactors

Fu·en·tes /foo én tàyss, fwén-/, **Carlos** (*b.* 1928) Mexican writer. He is known for his metaphysical novel *The Death of Artemio Cruz* (1962).

> "Every storyteller is a child of Scheherazade, in a hurry to tell the tale so that death may be postponed one more time."
> [Carlos Fuentes, "The Storyteller," *The Picador Book of Latin American Stories*; 1998]

fu·fu /foó foò/ *n Carib, W Africa* a dish made from mashed plantain, yams, or cassava, eaten rolled into balls as the starchy accompaniment to soups or stews [Mid-18C. < Twi *fufuu*]

fug /fug/ *n* a stale or airless atmosphere (*informal*) [Late 19C. Probably alteration of FOG]

fu·ga·cious /fyoo gáyshəss/ *adj* **1.** fleeting or passing away quickly (*formal*) **2.** describes a plant or flower that lasts only briefly before withering or dropping [Early 17C. < Latin *fugac-* "fleeing swiftly" < *fugere* "flee"] —**fu·ga·cious·ly** *adv* —**fu·ga·cious·ness** *n* —**fu·gac·i·ty** /fyoo gássətee/ *n*

fu·ga·to /foo gaátō/ *adv, adj* in the style of a fugue ■ *n* (*plural* **-tos**) a piece of music in the style of a fugue [Mid-19C. < Italian < past participle of *fugare* "compose as a fugue" < *fuga* (see FUGUE)]

-fuge *suffix* something that drives out ○ *febrifuge* [Via French < Latin *fugere* "flee," *fugare* "drive out" < *fuga* "flight"]

fu·gi·tive /fyoójətiv/ *n* **1.** SOMEBODY WHO RUNS AWAY somebody who flees, e.g., from justice, enemies, or brutal treatment **2.** SOMETHING ELUSIVE an elusive or ephemeral thing ■ *adj* **1.** RUNNING AWAY fleeing, especially fleeing arrest or punishment **2.** BRIEF lasting only briefly ○ *the fugitive hours* **3.** ITINERANT moving around from place to place **4.** HARD TO UNDERSTAND difficult to understand or retain ○ *the fugitive nature of higher mathematics* **5.** FOR SPECIFIC OCCASION written or composed for a specific occasion or on a subject of only passing interest (*literary*) ○ *a collection of essays, letters, and fugitive pieces* [14C. Directly or via French < Latin *fugitivus* < *fugit-*, past participle of *fugere* "flee"] —**fu·gi·tive·ly** *adv* —**fu·gi·tive·ness** *n*

fu·gle /fyoóg'l/ (**-gled, -gling, -gles**) *vi* to act as or like a fugleman in training or leading others [Mid-19C. Back-formation < FUGLEMAN]

fu·gle·man /fyoóg'l màn, -mən/ *n* **1.** somebody acting as a leader or example to others **2.** formerly, a soldier used to teach drill movements by performing them in front of trainees [Early 19C. Alteration of German *Flügelmann* "wing man, man on the flank"]

fu·gu /foó goò/ *n* a poisonous pufferfish that is eaten, especially in Japan, after the poisonous parts are removed [Mid-20C. < Japanese]

fugue /fyoog/ *n* **1.** a musical form in which a theme is first stated, then repeated and varied with accompanying contrapuntal lines **2.** *also* **fugue state** a disordered state of mind in which somebody typically wanders from home and experiences a loss of memory relating only to the previous, rejected, environment [Late 16C. Directly or via French < Italian *fuga* < Latin, "flight"] —**fu·gal** *adj*

füh·rer /fyoórər/, **fueh·rer** *n* a leader who is regarded as autocratic (*offensive in some contexts*) [Mid-20C. < German *Führer* "leader," a title (in full *Führer und Reichs-*

kanzler "Leader and Chancellor of the Empire") adopted by Adolf Hitler, leader of the German National Socialist Party before and during World War II]

Mount Fuji

Fu·ji, Mount /fo͝ojee/, **Fu·ji·ya·ma** /fo͝ojee yaámə, -maa/ highest mountain in Japan, on central Honshu Island, southwest of Tokyo. A dormant volcano in the shape of an almost perfect cone, it is considered to be sacred by many Japanese people. Height: 12,387 ft./3,776 m.

Fu·jian /foo jyaán/, **Fu·kien** /-kyén/ province in southeastern China, on the coast opposite the island of Taiwan. Capital: Fuzhou. Population: 32,610,000 (1997). Area: 46,000 sq. mi./120,000 sq. km.

Fu·ji·mo·ri /fo͝ojee máwree/, **Alberto** (*b.* 1938) Peruvian politician. He served as president of Peru (1990–2000) becoming the first person of Japanese descent to lead a Latin American country.

Fu·ji·sa·wa /fo͝ojee saáwə, -waa/ city southwest of Yokohama in Kanagawa Prefecture, southeastern Honshu, Japan. Population: 382,038 (2002).

Fu·ji·ta scale /foo jeétə-/ *n* a scale used to rank tornadoes by the amount of damage they do to human-made structures and natural objects. The scale runs from F-0 to F-5, with F-0 indicating light damage caused by winds of 40–72 mph/64–116 kph and F-5 indicating the devastation caused by winds of 261–318 mph/415–512 kph. [Late 20C. After Tetsuya Theodore *Fujita* (1920–98), Japanese-born US chemist]

Fu·ji·ya·ma /fo͝ojee yaámə, -maa/ same as **Fuji, Mount**

Fu·kien another spelling of **Fujian**

Fu·ku·i /foo ko͝o ee/ capital city of Fukui Prefecture, west central Honshu, Japan. Population: 249,656 (2002).

Fu·ku·o·ka /fo͝okoo ṓkə, -kaa/ port and capital city of Fukuoka Prefecture on northern Kyushu, southwestern Japan. Kyushu University was founded there in 1911. Population: 1,302,454 (2002).

Fu·ku·shi·ma /fo͝okə sheémə, fo͝okoo sheé maa/ capital city of Fukushima Prefecture, on the Abukuma River in north central Honshu, Japan. Population: 288,926 (2002).

Fu·ku·ya·ma /fo͝okə yaámə, fo͝okoo yaá maa/ city on the Inland Sea in Hiroshima Prefecture, Honshu Island, Japan. Population: 381,098 (2002).

-ful *suffix* **1.** full of ○ *hateful* **2.** having the nature of ○ *rightful* **3.** tending to ○ *forgetful* **4.** an amount that fills ○ *capful* **5.** full to ○ *brimful* [Old English, < *full* (see FULL[1])]

Fu·la /fo͝olə/ (*plural same* or **-las**), **Fu·lah** (*plural same* or **-lahs**) *n* **1.** a member of an ethnically diverse nomadic people living in western and central Africa **2.** LANG same as **Fulani** (sense 1) [Late 18C. < Fulani *pulo* "person"] —**Fu·la** *adj*

Fu·la·ni /fo͞o laánee, foo laánee/ (*plural same* or **-nis**) *n* **1.** a Niger-Congo language spoken over a large area of West Africa, especially in Nigeria, Guinea-Bissau, Burkina-Faso, Gambia, Benin, Guinea, and Senegal. Native speakers: 15 million. **2.** PEOPLES same as **Fula** (sense 1) [Mid-19C. < Hausa] —**Fu·la·ni** *adj*

Ful·bright /fo͝ol brīt/, **J. William** (1905–95) US educator and politician. While a US Democratic senator from Arkansas (1945–74) and chair of the influential Senate Foreign Relations Committee (1959–74), he was a leading critic of the Vietnam War. He sponsored the Fulbright Act (1946), which enacted a major US program of international educational exchanges. Full name **Fulbright, James William**

> "We must dare to think about 'unthinkable things' because when things become unthinkable, thinking stops and action becomes mindless."
> [J. William Fulbright, *Speech to Senate*; March 27, 1964]

> "We are inclined to confuse freedom and democracy, which we regard as moral principles, with the way in which these are practiced in America—with capitalism, federalism and the two-party system, which are not moral principles, but simply the accepted practices of the American people."
> [J. William Fulbright, *Speech to Senate*; March 27, 1964]

ful·crum /fo͝olkrəm, fúlkrəm/ (*plural* **-crums** or **-cra** /-krə/) *n* **1.** PIVOT the point or support about which a lever turns **2.** PROP something that supports something else revolving about it or depending on it ○ *The fulcrum of the building plan is the major retail tenant.* **3.** ZOOL SUPPORT IN ANIMAL part of an animal that acts as a hinge or support, especially scales on the fins of some fish [Late 17C. < Latin, "post or foot of a couch, bedpost" < *fulcire* "prop up, support"]

ful·fill /fo͝ol fíl/ (**-filled, -fill·ing, -fills**), **ful·fil** (**-filled, -fill·ing, -fils**) *v* **1.** *vt* ACHIEVE SOMETHING to do what is necessary to bring about or achieve something expected, desired, or promised ○ *went on to fulfill her early promise of greatness* **2.** *vt* CARRY OUT ORDER to do what is necessary to carry out a request or command ○ *The instructions have been fulfilled to the letter.* **3.** *vt* SATISFY SOMETHING to be good enough or of the type necessary to meet a standard or requirement **4.** *vt* COMPLETE SOMETHING to do what is necessary to complete or bring something to an end **5.** *vt* SUPPLY SOMETHING to supply the full amount of something ordered ○ *fulfill an order for new cars* **6.** **ful·fill your·self** *vr* REALIZE AMBITIONS to feel satisfied with what you are doing or realize your expectations or ambitions [Old English *fullfyllan* "fill up, make full" < FULL[1] + FILL] —**ful·fill·er** *n* —**ful·fill·ment** *n*

SYNONYMS See *perform*.

ful·filled /fo͝ol fíld/ *adj* satisfied with what you are doing or that you have realized your expectations or ambitions ○ *a fulfilled person who had enjoyed a long successful career*

ful·fill·ing /fo͝ol fílling/ *adj* giving satisfaction to somebody as an activity or goal in life ○ *a fulfilling job opportunity*

ful·gent /fo͝oljənt, fúl-/ *adj* gleaming brilliantly (*literary*) [15C. < Latin *fulgent-*, present participle of *fulgere* "flash, shine"] —**ful·gen·cy** *n* —**ful·gent·ly** *adv*

ful·gu·rate /fo͝olgə ràyt, fúl-/ (**-rat·ed, -rat·ing, -rates**) *v* **1.** *vi* to flash with or like lightning (*formal*) **2.** *vt* MED to destroy unwanted tissue such as a wart using a high-frequency electric current [Mid-17C. < Latin *fulgurat-*, past participle of *fulgurare* "lighten, flash" < *fulgere* "flash, shine"] —**ful·gu·rant** *adj* —**ful·gu·ra·tion** /fo͝olgə ráysh'n, fùlgə-/ *n*

ful·gu·rite /fo͝olgə rīt, fúl-/ *n* a tube of hard, glassy material formed by lightning striking sand [Mid-19C. < Latin *fulgur* "lightning"]

fu·lig·i·nous /fyoo líjjənəss/ *adj* (*formal*) **1.** having the color or consistency of soot or smoke **2.** like soot in cloudiness or obscurity [Late 16C. Directly or via French *fuligineux* < late Latin *fuliginosus* < Latin *fuligin-*, stem of *fuligo* "soot"] —**fu·lig·i·nous·ly** *adv*

full[1] /fo͝ol/ *adj* **1.** FILLED TO CAPACITY holding as much or as many as is possible **2.** WITH MUCH OR MANY having a large amount or number of something ○ *full of mischief* **3.** GREATEST IN EXTENT being at the highest degree or largest extent ○ *at full speed* ○ *I like my coffee full strength.* **4.** WITH NOTHING MISSING with nothing or nobody left out or missing, or with no part uncompleted or used ○ *the full complement of staff* **5.** COMPLETELY DEVELOPED at the end or peak of development ○ *roses in full bloom* **6.** COMPLETELY SO having reached or fulfilled all requirements for a position, rank, or description ○ *a full colonel* **7.** HAVING EATEN ENOUGH satisfied by an amount eaten or drunk **8.** BUSY filled with activity or achievement ○ *live a full life* **9.** PLUMP fleshy and with a rounded shape ○ *a full figure* **10.** WITH SAME PARENTS sharing both natural parents ○ *my full brother* **11.** CHARGED WITH EMOTION affected by strong deep emotion ○ *We left the place with full hearts and shining eyes.* **12.** PREOCCUPIED deeply preoccupied with something ○ *She's always full of her troubles.* **13.** SONOROUS with depth or power, e.g., of sound ○ *chanted in full voice* **14.** BEVERAGES RICHLY FLAVORED with a rich strong flavor and substantial quality ○ *a full-flavored coffee* **15.** CLOTHING WITH MUCH FABRIC made with a lot of fabric and not close-fitting **16.** BASEBALL WITH THREE RUNNERS in baseball, with a runner at first, second, and third base ○ *bases are full* ■ *adv* **1.** COMPLETELY to the greatest or complete extent ○ *turned full around* **2.** EXACTLY in a precise or exact position ○ *He took a punch full on the mouth.* **3.** VERY to a high degree ○ *What happened next we know full well.* ■ *n* FULLEST STATE the greatest extent or highest degree ○ *We enjoyed ourselves to the full.* ■ *v* (**fulled, full·ing, fulls**) **1.** *vt* HANDICRAFT SEW GATHERS AND TUCKS to make a garment full by sewing gathers in it **2.** *vi* BECOME FULL to wax and become full (*refers to the moon*) [Old English, < Indo-European] —**full·ness** *n* —**full·y** *adv* ◇ **be full of yourself** to be very conceited and arrogant ◇ **full up** completely full (*informal*) ◇ **in full** to the complete amount or extent, omitting nothing ○ *The opera has never been performed in full.*

full[2] /fo͝ol/ (**fulled, full·ing, fulls**) *vti* to make cloth bulkier by dampening and beating it, or become bulkier by being dampened and beaten [14C. Probably back-formation < FULLER[1]]

full·back /fo͝ol bàk/ *n* **1.** FOOTBALL OFFENSIVE PLAYER in football, a player in the offensive backfield who lines up behind the quarterback and is used mainly for blocking **2.** DEFENDER in sports such as soccer, rugby, or field hockey, a player in a defensive position **3.** FULLBACK POSITION the position played by a fullback

full beam *n UK* AUTOMOT same as **high beam**

full-blood·ed *adj* **1.** of unmixed breed **2.** healthily vigorous or forceful —**full-blood·ed·ly** *adv* —**full-blood·ed·ness** *n*

full-blown *adj* **1.** in its most complete, extreme, strongest, or developed form ○ *full-blown malaria* **2.** in bloom and fully open

full board *n UK* same as **American plan**

full-bod·ied *adj* **1.** with a rich strong flavor and substantial quality **2.** rich in tone and strong in volume

full-bore *adj* of a caliber larger than .22 in.

full-bot·tomed *adj* describes a wig that is long and full at the back

full cir·cle *adv* back to the starting point, usually after passing through various stages

full cost ac·count·ing *n* BUSINESS, ENVIRON the practice of including indirect costs and benefits of a product or activity, e.g., its social and environmental effects on health and the economy, along with its direct costs when making business decisions

full count *n* in baseball, the situation in which the batter has three balls and two strikes

full-court press *n* **1.** in basketball, the practice of putting pressure on opposing players in all parts of the court as opposed to merely defending the backcourt **2.** any major effort involving several people (*informal*) ○ *The DA wants a full-court press on this case.*

full cous·in *n* same as **cousin** (sense 1)

full dress *n* clothes suitable or prescribed for a ceremony or formal occasion (*hyphenated when used before a noun*)

full-dress *adj* of considerable importance and often exhaustively complete ○ *a full-dress investigation*

full du·plex *n* a communications channel that supports the simultaneous transmission of data in two directions

full em·ploy·ment *n* the state of a country's economy in which everyone available for work has a job

full·er[1] /fo͝ollər/ *n* somebody who makes cloth bulkier by dampening and beating it [Pre-12C. < Latin *fullo*]

full·er[2] /fŏŏllər/ *n* a hammer used by a blacksmith for forging grooves and spreading hot iron [Early 19C. Origin ?]

Ful·ler /fŏŏllər/, **Margaret** (1810–50) US writer and critic. She was the founding editor of the transcendentalist journal *The Dial* (1840–42) and author of the classic feminist work *Woman in the Nineteenth Century* (1845). Full name **Fuller, Sarah Margaret**

> "Let Ulysses drive the beeves home, while Penelope there piles up the fragrant loaves; they are both employed well if these be done in thought and love, willingly. But Penelope is no more meant for a baker or weaver solely, than Ulysses for a cattle-herd."
> [Margaret Fuller, *Woman in the Nineteenth Century*; 1845]

Ful·ler, Melville W. (1833–1910) chief justice of the US Supreme Court (1888–1910). Nominated by President Grover Cleveland, he broadened the power of the federal courts during his tenure. Full name **Fuller, Melville Weston**

Ful·ler, R. Buckminster (1895–1983) US engineer, designer, architect, and writer. He used innovative technology to address the global problems facing humanity in the second half of the 20th century. He championed the geodesic dome as a versatile, sturdy, and cost-effective building structure. Full name **Fuller, Richard Buckminster**

> "Now there is one outstandingly important fact regarding Spaceship Earth, and that is that no instruction book came with it."
> [R. Buckminster Fuller, *Operating Manual for Spaceship Earth*; June 10, 1969]

ful·ler·ene /fŏŏllə reen/ *n* a form of carbon made up of up to 500 carbon atoms arranged in a sphere or tube [Late 20C. Shortening of BUCKMINSTERFULLERENE]

ful·ler's earth *n* an absorbent clay used in fulling cloth and in filtering liquids

ful·ler's tea·sel *n* a plant with large prickly flower heads, formerly used to raise the nap on cloth. Native to: Europe, Asia. Latin name: *Dipsacus sativus*.

Ful·ler·ton /fŏŏllərt'n/ city in southwestern California, northeast of Long Beach. Population: 128,842 (2002 estimate).

full-face *adj* with the whole of the face visible, facing the viewer ○ *a full-face portrait*

full-fash·ioned *adj US* shaped to fit the lines of the body ○ *full-fashioned stockings* Can term **fully-fashioned**

full-fea·tured *adj* describes an electronic device or piece of software that has all the features that a user would hope for or expect

full-fig·ured *adj* having a fleshy rounded body, or designed to be worn by somebody, especially a woman, with a fleshy rounded body

~~fullfill~~ incorrect spelling of **fulfill**

full-fledged *adj* **1. COMPLETELY DEVELOPED** at a point of complete development or maturity ○ *a full-fledged microelectronics industry* **2. FULLY QUALIFIED** with full status or rank ○ *a full-fledged helicopter pilot* **3.** BIRDS **ABLE TO FLY** describes a young bird that is able to fly and leave the nest

full-fron·tal *adj* **1.** showing the whole front of the body including the genitals **2.** whole-hearted and uninhibited (*informal*) ○ *She made a full-frontal attack on her opponents.*

full-grown *adj* having developed to maturity or adulthood

full house *n* a poker hand containing three cards of the same value and a pair of a different value

full-length *adj* **1. REACHING TO ANKLES** describes a garment such as a coat or skirt that extends to the ankles or floor **2. SHOWING WHOLE BODY** describes a mirror or portrait showing the whole length of the body **3. NOT SHORTENED** consisting of the whole or usual amount or duration of something

full marks *npl UK* **1.** a perfect score in an assessment or on an examination **2.** high praise or commendation (*informal*) ○ *Full marks to the driver for managing to find the place.*

full mon·ty /-móntee/ *n* **1.** *UK* everything that is needed or appropriate or makes up a full set or the whole of something (*slang*) **2.** a striptease routine that ends with the performer completely naked [Origin ?]

ORIGIN There are various unsubstantiated theories about the origin of the ***full monty***. One refers it to Montague Burton, an early 20th-century British tailor and retailer of made-to-measure clothes: *the full Montague Burton* is said to have meant "a three-piece suit for Sunday best." Another explanation refers it to the full cooked English breakfast reputedly demanded by Field Marshal Bernard Montgomery. However the expression was not recorded until much later than the peak of fame of either of these men. The sense "striptease routine" derives from a popular British movie *The Full Monty* (1997), in which unemployed Sheffield steelworkers develop a striptease act to earn money and restore self-esteem.

full moon *n* **1.** the phase of the Moon when its surface as seen from Earth is fully illuminated by the Sun **2.** the period of time during which the Moon appears fully illuminated as a circle

full-mo·tion vi·de·o *n* a movie sequence shown on a computer screen, e.g., within a computer game

full-mouthed *adj* **1.** having the complete set of adult teeth **2.** said loudly or vigorously

full nel·son *n* a wrestling hold in which one wrestler puts both arms beneath an opponent's arms from behind and then exerts pressure by clasping the hands at the back of the opponent's neck

full-on *adj UK* possessing a particular quality to the fullest extent ○ *He's turned into a full-on computer nerd.*

full-page *adj* taking up the whole of the page on which it is printed ○ *a full-page illustration* ○ *a full-page story*

full pro·fes·sor *n* a university professor of the highest grade

full-rigged *adj* describes a sailing ship that has at least three square-rigged masts

full-scale *adj* **1.** having exactly the same dimensions and proportions as the original **2.** done with total commitment of effort and resources ○ *a full-scale manhunt*

full-ser·vice *adj* providing a complete range of services ○ *a full-service gas station*

full-size, full-sized *adj* **1.** being the normal size for its kind **2.** *US* measuring 54 by 75 in./137 by 190 cm or suitable as linen for a bed of this size

full stop *n* **1.** *UK* same as **period** *n* (sense 5) **2.** a complete halt or an end ○ *This delay has brought production to a full stop.*

full time *adv* during all of the time considered standard or appropriate for the activity in question ○ *worked full time* ■ *n* in soccer and other sports, the end of a match

full-time *adj* **1.** involving or using all of the time considered standard or appropriate for an activity, especially work ○ *a full-time student* **2.** occurring at or indicating the end of a soccer or other match ○ *the full-time score* —**full-tim·er** *n*

full-wave rec·ti·fi·er *n* a circuit, used in the design of electronic equipment such as radios, computers, and televisions, that operates on both the positive and negative cycles of an alternating current

ful·ly /fŏŏllee/ *adv* **1.** to the greatest extent possible or required ○ *The flight is fully booked.* **2.** to the full extent of a particular time, quantity, or number ○ *We waited fully 40 minutes.*

ful·ly-fash·ioned *adj Can, UK* CLOTHING same as **full-fashioned**

ful·ly-fledged *adj UK* BIRDS same as **full-fledged**

ful·ly-grown *adj UK* same as **full-grown**

ful·mar /fŏŏlmər, -maar/ *n* a seabird of the petrel family that resembles a gull in appearance and nesting habits. Native to: Arctic. Genus: *Fulmarus*. [Late 17C. < Old Norse *fúll* "foul" (because it regurgitates its stomach's contents when disturbed) + *már* "gull"]

ful·mi·nant /fŏŏlmənənt, fúl-/ *adj* **1.** exploding violently **2.** describes illness coming on suddenly and with severe symptoms of short duration [Early 17C. Directly or via French < Latin *fulminant-*, present participle of *fulminare* (see FULMINATE)]

ful·mi·nate /fŏŏlmə nàyt, fúl-/ *vti* (**-nat·ed, -nat·ing, -nates**) **1. SPEAK SCATHINGLY** to express forceful criticism of somebody or something ○ *an article fulminating against the arms trade* ○ *fulminated that it was unacceptable* **2. EXPLODE** to detonate or explode violently, or cause something to detonate or explode violently ■ *n* CHEM **EXPLOSIVE SALT OR ESTER** an explosive salt or ester of fulminic acid, especially fulminate of mercury [15C. < Latin *fulminat-*, past participle of *fulminare* "lighten, strike with lightning" < *fulmen* "lightning"] —**ful·mi·na·tion** /fŏŏlmə náysh'n, fùl-/ *n* —**ful·mi·na·tor** *n* —**ful·mi·na·to·ry** /-nə tàwree/ *adj*

ful·mi·nate of mer·cu·ry *n* the mercury salt of fulminic acid. Use: in explosives and detonators. Formula: $HgC_2N_2O_2$.

ful·mi·nat·ing /fŏŏlmə nàyting, fúl-/ *adj* **1.** able or likely to explode or detonate **2.** MED same as **fulminant** (sense 2)

ful·min·ic ac·id /fŏŏl mínnik-, ful-/ *n* an unstable compound that smells of bitter almonds. Use: manufacture of explosives. Formula: HONC. [< Latin *fulmin-*, stem of *fulmen* "lightning"]

ful·some /fŏŏlssəm/ *adj* **1.** effusive or fawning to the point of being offensive ○ *embarrassed by their fulsome compliments* **2.** great in amount or intensity [13C. < FULL[1] + -SOME[1]] —**ful·some·ly** *adv* —**ful·some·ness** *n*

USAGE ***Fulsome*** has overlapping meanings that are quite different in effect; when you use it, be sure that your surrounding context makes your intended meaning crystal clear. ***Fulsome*** is traditionally used to mean "effusive or fawning to the point of being offensive," as in *a fulsome display of marital affection inappropriate in public* and *an interview laden with fulsome compliments for a notorious criminal*. In the first example, you can substitute *excessive* and in the second you can substitute *effusive* or *unctuous*. The meaning "great in amount or intensity," from an original sense of ***fulsome*** that fell into disuse, has been revived. It has been used so much in recent years that it has all but obscured the other meaning. This usage most commonly occurs in *fulsome praise* and *a fulsome apology*, as in *He is a true national hero, deserving of fulsome praise*, where *abundant* would be a better, more precise choice. Instead of *a fulsome apology*, it is best to use *a full apology*, so that everyone will understand exactly what is meant.

Ful·ton /fŏŏlt'n/ town in central New York, north of Syracuse. Population: 11,681 (2002 estimate).

Ful·ton, Robert (1765–1815) US inventor and engineer. He built the first efficient steamboat, the *Clermont* (1807), thus inaugurating a new era of power-driven navigation.

ful·vous /fŏŏlvəss/ *adj* of an orange-brown color (*literary*) [Mid-17C. < Latin *fulvus* "reddish-yellow"]

Fu Man·chu mus·tache /foo mán chōō-, fōō man chōō-/ *n* a mustache with long drooping ends [After a character in the novels of Sax Rohmer (British writer Arthur Sarsfield Ward (1886–1959))]

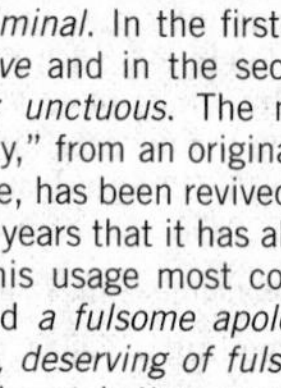

fumaric acid

fu·mar·ic ac·id /fyoo márrik-/ *n* a colorless crystalline solid. Source: some plants and molds, or synthesized from benzene. Use: manufacture of resins. Formula:

$C_4H_4O_4$. [< modern Latin *Fumaria* < late Latin *fumaria* "fumatory" < Latin *fumus* "smoke"]

fu·ma·role /fyo͞omə rōl/ *n* a vent in a volcanic area from which steam and hot gases such as sulfur dioxide are emitted [Early 19C. Via Italian *fumaruolo* < late Latin *fumariolum* "vent, smoke-hole" < Latin *fumus* "smoke"] —**fu·ma·rol·ic** /fyo͞omə róllik/ *adj*

fu·ma·to·ry /fyo͞omə tàwree/ *adj* relating to, involving, or typical of fumigation or smoking [Mid-19C. < Latin *fumat-*, past participle of *fumare* "smoke"]

fum·ble /fúmb'l/ *v* (**-bled, -bling, -bles**) **1.** *vti* **GROPE CLUMSILY** to grope clumsily in search of something ○ *fumbled in his pockets for his keys* ○ *fumbled her way along the passage* **2.** *vi* **HESITATE** to act clumsily, hesitantly, or unsuccessfully ○ *She fumbled through the introductions.* **3.** *vt* **BUNGLE SOMETHING** to do something clumsily or inefficiently ○ *This is your last chance, so don't fumble it.* **4.** *vti* **DROP OR MISHANDLE BALL** in sports, to drop or fail to catch a ball ■ *n* **1. FUMBLED ACTION** an act or instance of fumbling **2. FUMBLED BALL** in sports, a ball that is dropped or mishandled [Mid-16C. Origin ?] —**fum·bler** *n* —**fum·blingl·y** *adv*

fume /fyoom/ *v* (**fumed, fum·ing, fumes**) **1.** *vi* **BE ANGRY** to feel great anger, especially anger that is not fully expressed **2.** *vi* **EMIT GAS** to emit gas, smoke, or vapor, or be emitted in this form **3.** *vt* **FUMIGATE** to treat something with a gas, smoke, or other fumigant ■ *n* **1. SMOKE** smoke, gas, or vapor, especially when unpleasant or harmful (*often used in the plural*) ○ *a chemical that emits noxious fumes when exposed to air* **2. ACRID SMELL** an acrid or nauseating smell (*often used in the plural*) **3. FIT OF ANGER** a state of great anger [14C. Via French < Latin *fumus* "smoke"] —**fum·ing·ly** *adv* —**fum·y** *adj*

fu·met /fyo͞omət/ *n* a strongly-flavored stock obtained from cooking fish, meat, or vegetables [Early 18C. < French < *fumer* "to smoke" < Latin *fumus* "smoke"]

fu·mi·gant /fyo͞omigənt/ *n* a substance that gives off fumes, especially one used as a disinfectant or to kill pests [Late 19C. < Latin *fumigant-*, present participle of *fumigare* (see FUMIGATE)]

fu·mi·gate /fyo͞omi gàyt/ (**-gat·ed, -gat·ing, -gates**) *vti* to treat something with fumes, or be treated with fumes, especially to kill microorganisms or pests [Mid-16C. < Latin *fumigat-*, past participle of *fumigare* "to smoke" < *fumus* "smoke"] —**fu·mi·ga·tion** /fyo͞omi gáysh'n/ *n* —**fu·mi·ga·tor** *n*

fum·ing sul·fu·ric ac·id *n* a very concentrated solution of sulfuric acid that gives off fumes

fun /fun/ *n* **1. AMUSEMENT** a time or feeling of enjoyment or amusement ○ *Just for fun, we wore silly hats.* **2. SOMETHING AMUSING** something that provides enjoyment or amusement ○ *Skiing can be family fun.* **3. MOCKERY** playful joking, often at the expense of another ○ *What's said in fun can still hurt.* ■ *adj* (*informal*) **1. AMUSING** providing enjoyment or amusement ○ *We'll have a fun time tonight.* **2. CHEAP AND FLAMBOYANT** flamboyant in style and often made of cheap synthetic materials, designed to be used or worn for fun ○ *fun jewelry* ■ *vi* (**funned, fun·ning, funs**) **BEHAVE PLAYFULLY** to behave in a playful or joking way (*informal*) ○ *Don't pay any attention to him; he's just funning.* [Late 17C. < obsolete *fon* "fool," origin ?] ◇ **fun and games** (*informal*) **1.** difficulty or trouble (*used ironically*) ○ *A broken sprinkler in the stockroom overnight gave us some fun and games in the morning.* **2.** carefree amusement ○ *life isn't all fun and games* ◇ **like fun** (*informal*) **1.** with great speed or effort ○ *We'll have to work like fun to finish this order on time.* **2.** *US* certainly not ○ *Like fun I am!* ◇ **make fun of somebody** *or* **something** to make somebody or something appear ridiculous ◇ **poke fun at somebody** *or* **something** to mock or ridicule somebody or something

Fu·na·ba·shi /fo͞onə ba͞ashee/ city in Chiba Prefecture on the northeastern coast of Tokyo Bay, Honshu Island, Japan. Population: 551,916 (2002).

Fu·na·fu·ti /fo͞onə fo͞otee/ atoll and capital of Tuvalu, located in the western Pacific Ocean. The atoll's main town is Fongafale. Population: 3,432 (1990). Area: 1 sq. mi./2.6 sq. km.

fu·nam·bu·list /fyoo námbyəlist/ *n* an acrobat who walks while balancing on a suspended rope [Late 18C. < French *funambule* or Latin *funambulus* < *funis* "rope" + *ambulare* "to walk"] —**fu·nam·bu·late** /-làyt/ *vi* —**fu·nam·bu·lism** *n*

Fun·chal /fo͞on sha͞al/ capital of the Madeira Islands, an autonomous region of Portugal, in the North Atlantic Ocean. Situated on the southern coast of Madeira, it is a major resort. Population: 115,950 (1995).

func·tion /fúngkshən/ *n* **1. PURPOSE** an action or use for which something is suited or designed ○ *Its function is to collect water.* ○ *a watch with an alarm function* **2. ROLE** an activity or role assigned to somebody or something **3. EVENT** a social gathering or ceremony, especially a formal or official occasion ○ *a black-tie function* **4. DEPENDENT FACTOR** a quality or characteristic that depends upon and varies with another ○ *Success is a function of determination and ability.* **5.** MATH **VARIABLE QUANTITY** a variable quantity whose value depends upon the varying values of other quantities **6.** MATH **CORRESPONDENCE BETWEEN MEMBERS OF DIFFERENT SETS** a relationship between two mathematical sets, in which each member of one set corresponds uniquely to a member of the other set. Symbol **f** **7.** COMPUT **SINGLE COMPUTER OPERATION** a named and stored basic operation of a computer yielding a single result when invoked **8.** COMPUT **COMPUTER PROGRAM'S MAIN PURPOSE** the purpose of a computer program or piece of computer equipment, e.g., database management or printing **9.** GRAM **ROLE OF WORD OR PHRASE** a grammatical role performed by a word or phrase in a specific construction ○ *Noun phrases can fulfill many functions.* ■ *vi* (**-tioned, -tion·ing, -tions**) **1. SERVE PURPOSE** to serve a particular purpose, or perform a particular role ○ *hats functioning both as fashion statements and as protection against the sun* **2. BE IN WORKING ORDER** to operate normally, fulfilling a purpose or role ○ *When the heart ceases to function, the patient is clinically dead.* [Mid-16C. < Latin *function-* < *funct-*, past participle of *fungi* "perform"] —**func·tion·less** *adj*

func·tion·al /fúngkshən'l/ *adj* **1. PRACTICAL** having a practical application, or serving a useful purpose ○ *designs that are functional yet fun* **2. OPERATIONAL** in good working order, or working at the moment ○ *The elevator will not be functional for several hours.* **3.** MED **HAVING NO ORGANIC CAUSE** without apparent organic or structural cause ○ *a functional disorder* **4.** LING **RELATING TO LANGUAGE AS COMMUNICATION** relating to the function of language as a communicating tool, rather than to its form ○ *functional linguistics* —**func·tion·al·i·ty** /fùngkshə nállətee/ *n* —**func·tion·al·ly** *adv*

func·tion·al food *n* food containing nutritional additives that is promoted as being beneficial to health and able to prevent or reduce diseases such as tooth decay and cancer ○ *"the first spread formulated to act against cholesterol in a market for so-called functional foods"* (*The Guardian*; April 1999)

func·tion·al ge·nom·ics *n* the study of the relationships between gene structure and biological function in organisms (*takes a singular verb*)

func·tion·al group *n* a group of atoms that reacts as a single unit and determines the properties and structure of a class of compounds, e.g., a hydroxyl group in alcohols

func·tion·al il·lit·er·ate *n* somebody whose reading and writing abilities are inadequately developed to meet everyday needs —**func·tion·al·ly il·lit·er·ate** *adj*

func·tion·al·ism /fúngkshən'l ìzzəm/ *n* **1. BELIEF IN FUNCTION OVER FORM** belief that the intended function of something should determine its design, construction, and choice of materials, or a 20th-century design movement based on this belief **2.** PHILOSOPHY **PHILOSOPHY EMPHASIZING PRACTICAL** a philosophy or system that gives practical and utilitarian concerns priority over aesthetic concerns **3.** SOC SCI **ASSESSMENT OF SOCIAL INSTITUTIONS BY ROLE** the analysis and explanation of social institutions according to the function they perform in society, e.g., the family seen as an institution for social stability and cohesion —**func·tion·al·ist** *n, adj* —**func·tion·al·is·tic** /fùngkshən'l ístik/ *adj*

func·tion·al lit·er·a·cy *n* the level of skill in reading and writing that a person needs to cope with everyday adult life

func·tion·al shift *n* a change in the grammatical function of a word, e.g., from noun to verb

USAGE ***Functional shift*** is a process in which a word shifts from one grammatical function to another. For example,

1. a noun can be used as a verb: *to access a computer file*

2. a verb as a noun: *having a laugh*

3. a noun as an adjective: *a prestige apartment complex*

4. an interjection as a verb: *Audiences were wowed by his new musical.*

5. an adverb as a noun: *the ins and outs*, or as a verb: *upping the limit.*

Functional shift is sometimes controversial, but it has been a well-established phenomenon in English since the 16th century. Shakespeare used it enthusiastically: *"Be he ne'er so vile, this day shall gentle his condition"* (Henry V).

func·tion·ar·y /fúngkshə nèrree/ (*plural* **-ies**) *n* an official, especially somebody with trivial duties

func·tion key *n* a button on a computer keyboard or terminal that instructs the computer to perform a specific task. The same key may be programmed to perform different tasks in different programs.

func·tion word *n* a word that has little meaning on its own but serves a specific syntactic function in a phrase or sentence

func·tor /fúngktər/ *n* **1.** somebody or something that performs a function (*formal*) **2.** GRAM same as **function word** [Mid-20C. < FUNCTION]

fund /fund/ *n* **1. SUPPLY** a source or stock of something ○ *a vast fund of knowledge* **2. RESERVE OF MONEY** a sum of money saved or invested for a particular purpose ○ *We've started an education fund for our children.* **3. ORGANIZATION ADMINISTERING RESERVE OF MONEY** an organization that manages a sum of money for a particular purpose ○ *a mutual fund* ■ **funds** *npl* **1. MONEY** money, especially money that is available to spend ○ *I'm a little short of funds at the moment.* **2. UK GOVERNMENT SECURITIES** British government securities that finance the national debt and pay a fixed rate of interest ■ *vt* (**fund·ed, fund·ing, funds**) **1. PROVIDE MONEY FOR SOMETHING** to provide money needed to finance a project or keep it running (*often passive*) ○ *environmental projects that are funded by local government* **2.** FIN **PROVIDE MONEY TO PAY DEBT** to provide a sum of money to pay off a debt or its interest **3.** FIN **MAKE DEBT LONG-TERM** to convert a short-term debt into a long-term debt with a fixed rate of interest [Mid-17C. < Latin *fundus* "bottom"] —**fund·er** *n*

fun·da·ment /fúndəmənt/ *n* **1. FOUNDING PRINCIPLE** an underlying principle or theory on which something is founded (*formal; often used in the plural*) **2. BUTTOCKS** the buttocks or the anus (*archaic or humorous*) **3.** GEOG **NATURAL LANDFORM** a natural land surface that has not been altered by people [13C. Via French < Latin *fundamentum* < *fundus* "bottom"]

fun·da·men·tal /fùndə mént'l/ *adj* **1. BASIC** relating to or affecting the underlying principles or structure of something ○ *We need to make fundamental changes in our business.* **2. CENTRAL** serving as an essential part of something ○ *Free speech is one of the fundamental rights guaranteed by the Constitution.* **3.** MUSIC **OF CHORD'S LOWEST NOTE** relating to the lowest note of a chord in root position, the note that gives the chord its basic harmony **4.** PHYS **OF LOWEST FREQUENCY** relating to or produced by the lowest frequency component in a complex vibration ■ *n* **1. BASIC PRINCIPLE OR ELEMENT** a basic and necessary component of something, especially an underlying rule or principle (*often used in the plural*) ○ *The class teaches the fundamentals of karate.* **2.** MUSIC **PRINCIPAL TONE** the principal tone in a chord, from which other harmonics are generated **3.** PHYS **LOWEST FREQUENCY** the lowest frequency in a vibration or periodic wave —**fun·da·men·tal·ly** *adv*

fun·da·men·tal in·ter·ac·tion *n* PHYS same as **interaction** (sense 3)

fun·da·men·tal·ism /fùndə mént'l ìzzəm/ *n* **1.** a religious or political movement based on a literal interpretation of and strict adherence to doctrine, especially as a return to former principles **2.** the belief that religious or political doctrine should be implemented literally, not interpreted or adapted —**fun·da·men·tal·ist** *n, adj* —**fun·da·men·tal·is·tic** /fùndə ment'l ístik/ *adj*

fun·da·men·tal law *n* the founding rules and principles or constitution on which a government is based, as distinct from its legislative acts

fun·da·men·tal par·ti·cle *n* PHYS same as **elementary particle**

-funded *suffix* with money provided by a particular institution or person ○ *government-funded*

~~**fundemental**~~ incorrect spelling of **fundamental**

fun·di ANAT plural of **fundus**

fund·ing /fúnding/ *n* financial support

fund·rais·er /fúnd ràyzər/ *n* **1.** somebody who generates money for a nonprofit or political organization, especially an organizer of campaigns to raise money **2.** an activity or event that is intended to generate money to support a nonprofit or political organization

fund·rais·ing /fúnd ràyzing/ *n* the organized activity of soliciting and collecting money for a nonprofit or political organization

fun·dus /fúndəss/ (*plural* **-di** /-dī/) *n* the part of a hollow organ of the body farthest from its opening, e.g., the part of the eye's retina opposite the pupil [Mid-18C. < Latin, "bottom"] —**fun·dic** *adj*

Fun·dy, Bay of /fúndee/ inlet of the Atlantic Ocean off Canada, separating New Brunswick and Nova Scotia, Canada. Its rapid tides are among the highest in the world, reaching 60 ft./18 m. Depth: 650 ft./200 m. Length: 171 mi./275 km.

Fun·dy Na·tion·al Park national park and wildlife reserve along the Bay of Fundy, southwestern New Brunswick, Canada. Area: 80 sq. mi./206 sq. km.

fu·ner·al /fyóonərəl/ *n* **1.** CEREMONY FOR SOMEBODY WHO HAS DIED a rite held to mark the burial or cremation of a corpse, especially a ceremony held immediately before burial or cremation **2.** FUNERAL PROCESSION a procession of mourners following a body to its place of burial or cremation **3.** END an end to something's existence ○ *We have witnessed the funeral of the amateur game.* [14C. Via Old French *funerailles* "funeral rites" < medieval Latin *funeralia* < late Latin *funeralis* "of death rituals" < Latin *funer-*, stem of *funus* "death ritual"] ◇ **be somebody's funeral** to be something disapproved of that somebody else chooses to do (*informal*) ○ *If he wants to work extra hours, that's his funeral.*

fu·ner·al di·rec·tor *n* US somebody, especially the proprietor of a funeral home, whose job is to manage funerals and often also to prepare corpses for burial or cremation. Can term **undertaker**

fu·ner·al home, fu·ner·al par·lor *n* a business establishment where corpses are prepared for burial or cremation and where a funeral service may also be held and the body viewed by mourners

fu·ner·ar·y /fyóonə rèrree/ *adj* relating to or suitable for a burial or funeral [Late 17C. < late Latin *funerarius* < Latin *funer-* (see FUNERAL)]

fu·ne·re·al /fyə néeree əl/ *adj* **1.** relating to or suitable for a funeral **2.** very slow, solemn, mournful, or dismal [Early 18C. < Latin *funereus* < *funer-* (see FUNERAL)] —**fu·ne·re·al·ly** *adv*

fun·fest /fún fèst/ *n* a party, especially one at which amusing activities are organized (*informal*)

fun fur *n* synthetic fur fabric ○ *Orange fun fur was all the rage at the winter fashion shows that year.*

fun·gal /fúng g'l/, **fun·gous** /fúng gəss/ *adj* **1.** describes a condition caused by a fungus ○ *a fungal infection* **2.** relating to a fungus, or resembling a fungus in appearance or texture

fun·gi BIOL plural of **fungus**

fun·gi·ble /fúnjəb'l/ *adj* describes commodities that can be traded or substituted for an equal amount of a like commodity, usually to satisfy a contract ■ *n* a commodity that is fungible (*often used in the plural*) [Late 17C. < medieval Latin *fungibilis* < Latin *fungi* "perform"] —**fun·gi·bil·i·ty** /fùnjə bílləteé/ *n*

fun·gi·cide /fúnjə sīd, fúng gə-/ *n* a substance used to destroy or inhibit the growth of fungi —**fun·gi·cid·al** /fùnjə sīd'l, fùng gə-/ *adj* —**fun·gi·cid·al·ly** *adv*

fun·gi·form /fúnjə fàwrm, fúng gə-/ *adj* shaped like a mushroom

fun·gi·stat /fúnjə stàt, fúng gə-/ *n* a substance that inhibits the growth of fungi without killing them —**fun·gi·stat·ic** /fùnjə státtik, fùng gə-/ *adj*

fun·go /fúng gō/ (*plural* **-goes**) *n* **1.** in baseball, an act of hitting the ball high into the air, usually to give fielders catching practice **2.** BASEBALL same as **fungo bat** [Mid-19C. Origin ?]

fun·go bat *n* a lightweight bat used in baseball practice to hit fungoes

fun·goid /fúng gòyd/ *adj* resembling, characteristic of, or caused by a fungus ○ *a fungoid growth* ■ *n* a fungus, or a growth resembling a fungus

fun·gous *adj* FUNGI same as **fungal**

fun·gus /fúng gəss/ (*plural* **-gi** /fún jī, fúng gī/ or **-gus·es**) *n* a single-celled or multicellular organism without chlorophyll that reproduces by spores and lives by absorbing nutrients from organic matter. Fungi include mildews, molds, mushrooms, rusts, smuts, and yeasts. [Early 16C. < Latin]

fun house *n* a building at an amusement park that customers walk or ride through past objects and devices designed to amuse or startle them

fu·ni·cle /fyóonik'l/ *n* ANAT, BOT same as **funiculus** [Mid-17C. Anglicization]

fu·nic·u·lar /fyoo níkyələr/ *adj* **1.** OF ROPE'S TENSION relating to a rope, especially its tension **2.** MECH ENG ROPE-OPERATED operated by a rope or cable, especially one wound or pulled by a machine **3.** ANAT, BOT OF FUNICULUS relating to a funiculus ■ *n* RAIL FUNICULAR RAILWAY a funicular railway or railway car [Mid-17C. < Latin *funiculus* (see FUNICULUS)]

funicular railway

fu·nic·u·lar rail·way *n* a railway used on short steep inclines in which cars that counterbalance each other run on parallel tracks linked to a cable

fu·nic·u·lus /fyoo níkyələss/ (*plural* **-li** /-lī/) *n* **1.** a cord-shaped part of the body, e.g., the umbilical cord or a bundle of nerve fibers in the spinal cord **2.** a stalk of a plant ovule that connects it or a seed to the placenta [Mid-17C. < Latin, "little rope" < *funis* "rope"]

funk[1] /fungk/ *n* **1.** MUSICAL STYLE popular music that derives from jazz, blues, and soul and is characterized by a heavy rhythmic bass and backbeat **2.** EARTHY MUSICAL QUALITY a rhythmic earthy quality in music (*slang*) **3.** US LACK OF WORLDLINESS lack of sophistication, especially the kind of simplicity or naiveté thought by some to be characteristic of rural or provincial areas (*slang*) [Mid-20C. Back-formation < FUNKY]

funk[2] /fungk/ *n* a state of melancholy or hopeless sadness (*informal*) ○ *He's been in a funk since the divorce.* [Mid-18C. Origin ?] ◇ **be in a blue funk** to be in a melancholy state (*dated informal*)

funk[3] /fungk/ *n* a strong unpleasant odor (*slang*) [Early 17C. Origin ?]

funked-up *adj* exhilarated by, fond of, or featuring funk music (*slang*)

funk·y /fúngkee/ (**-i·er, -i·est**) *adj* **1.** SMELLY with a strong unpleasant odor (*slang*) **2.** CASUAL down-to-earth and informal, sometimes in ways seen as lacking style or as tasteless (*slang*) ○ *These clothes are too funky to wear to work.* **3.** FASHION UNCONVENTIONAL offbeat, creative, and novel (*informal*) ○ *a return to the funky styles of the 1970s* **4.** MUSIC LIKE BLUES resembling blues music (*slang*) **5.** MUSIC LIKE FUNK MUSIC with the backbeat and rhythmic bass typical of funk music **6.** US UNCOMFORTABLE causing discomfort or unease (*slang*) ○ *Since we grounded him, any conversation has been pretty funky.* [Mid-20C. < FUNK[3]] —**funk·i·ly** *adv* —**funk·i·ness** *n*

fun-lov·ing *adj* relating to somebody who seeks and enjoys life's pleasures

fun·nel /fúnn'l/ *n* **1.** UTENSIL USED IN POURING LIQUIDS a cone-shaped utensil with a large opening at the top and a small opening or tube at the bottom. Use: to guide liquids and other substances into containers. **2.** CHIMNEY a vertical pipe from which smoke and exhaust gases escape, especially one on a steamship or steam engine ■ *v* (**-neled, -nel·ing, -nels**) **1.** *vti* MOVE INTO NARROW SPACE to move into and through a narrow space, or direct something into and through a narrow space ○ *an efficient system for funneling crowds through the turnstiles* **2.** *vt* CONCENTRATE RESOURCES SOMEWHERE to direct or channel all of something from one place or use to another ○ *Funds were funneled away from other projects.* **3.** *vt* MAKE FUNNEL-SHAPED to form something into the shape of a funnel [15C. Via Provençal *fonilh* < Latin *infundibulum* < *infundere* "pour in" < *fundere* "pour"]

fun·nel cloud *n* a funnel-shaped cloud that projects from the base of a thundercloud and often develops into a tornado

fun·nel·form /fúnn'l fàwrm/ *adj* describes a flower or other plant part that is shaped like a funnel or cone

fun·nel·neck /fúnn'l nèk/ *n* a straight high collar resembling a turtleneck that has not been folded over, extending from the collarbone to the chin or jawline —**fun·nel·neck** *adj*

funnel-web spider

fun·nel-web spi·der, fun·nel-web *n* a large black spider that is highly venomous and makes funnel-shaped webs. Native to: Australia. Family: Dipluridae.

fun·ni·ly /fúnnəlee/ *adv* **1.** INTRODUCING COMMENT ON SOMETHING STRANGE used to introduce a comment on something considered strange or odd ○ *Funnily enough, nobody seemed to notice.* **2.** STRANGELY in a way that seems strange or odd ○ *The dog has been acting*

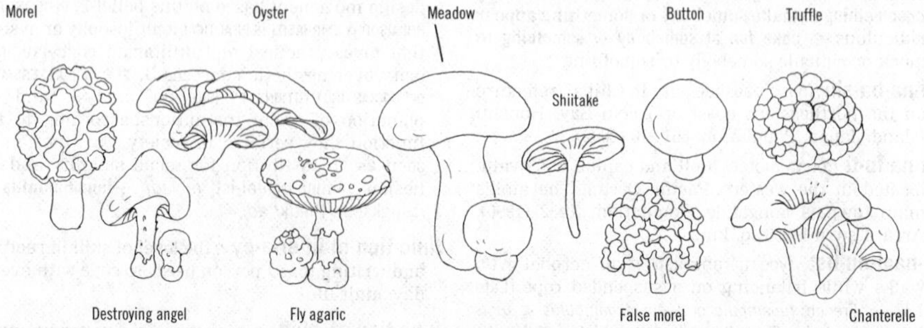

types of fungi

funnily ever since surgery. 3. COMICALLY in an amusing or humorous way

fun·ny /fúnnee/ *adj* (**-ni·er, -ni·est**) **1.** COMICAL causing amusement, especially enough to provoke laughter **2.** STRANGE odd or perplexing ○ *That's funny, I can't find my keys.* **3.** UNCONVENTIONAL out of the ordinary in a quaint or comical way ○ *a funny little doorway through an arch* **4.** UNWELL nauseated, faint, or otherwise slightly ill (*informal*) **5.** TRICKY slyly deceitful and dishonest (*informal*) ○ *Don't try anything funny, or I'll call the police.* ■ *n* (*plural* **-nies**) JOKE an amusing remark or joke (*informal*) ■ **fun·nies** *npl* NEWSPAPER COMIC STRIPS the section of a newspaper containing the comic strips [Mid-18C. < FUN] —**fun·ni·ness** *n*

SYNONYMS ***funny, amusing, comic, comical, droll, facetious, humorous, witty, hilarious***

CORE MEANING: causing or intended to cause amusement

funny causing amusement, especially enough to provoke laughter ○ *funny spontaneous banter* ○ *He realized the ad was trying to be funny, but it went beyond good taste.* **amusing** causing somebody to smile or laugh or be amused, often in a subdued way ○ *an amusing story about his early life* ○ *An amusing situation arose when she mistook me for my brother.* **comic** capable of inducing amusement, smiles, or laughter ○ *a company with a reputation for work that is moving and comic* ○ *a comic novel about the difficulties of being different* **comical** funny to the extent of being absurd, especially if unintentional ○ *Their dismay was almost comical.* ○ *a comical rolling walk* **droll** amusing in a wry or odd way ○ *a droll description of a new recruit who had arrived that day* **facetious** intended to be humorous but often silly or inappropriate. ○ *a facetious remark* **humorous** intended to be amusing and make people laugh ○ *He could keep people entertained with a seemingly endless fund of jokes and humorous anecdotes.* **witty** using words in an inventive, clever, and amusing way ○ *a witty parody of the Orpheus story* ○ *If the magazine's readers believe that they are buying it because it's witty or urbane, they are just kidding themselves.* **hilarious** extremely funny ○ *Just when you think you're in for a standard ending, the play surprises you with a hilarious twist.*

fun·ny bone *n* (*informal*) **1.** the point at the outside of the elbow where a nerve is so close to the longer arm bone that a blow often causes a tingling sensation **2.** a person's sense of humor ○ *a story that tickled my funny bone* [< the tingling feeling when the nerve is hit]

fun·ny book *n US* same as **comic book** (*dated informal*)

fun·ny busi·ness *n* dealings or goings-on that involve trickery, deceit, or dishonesty (*informal*)

fun·ny farm *n* an offensive term for a mental health facility (*dated slang*)

fun·ny ha-ha *adj* funny in a humorous way, as distinct from funny in a strange way. ◊ **funny peculiar**

fun·ny-look·ing *adj* having a strange or unexpected appearance

fun·ny·man /fúnnee màn/ *n* a man who is a comedian, clown, or humorist (*dated informal*)

fun·ny mon·ey *n* (*informal*) **1.** COUNTERFEIT MONEY counterfeit or forged currency **2.** ILLICITLY GAINED MONEY money obtained from a legally or morally suspect source **3.** CURRENCY WITH LITTLE VALUE currency, especially an unfamiliar one, with an inflated value

fun·ny pa·per *n* a section of a newspaper that contains comic strips (*dated informal*; *often used in the plural*)

fun·ny pe·cu·liar *adj* funny in a strange way, as distinct from funny in a humorous way. ◊ **funny ha-ha**

fun park *n* an area with amusement facilities, especially water slides and rides

fun·plex /fún plèks/ *n* an entertainment complex that features games, sports, and eating facilities [Late 20C.]

fun run *n* a noncompetitive run over a moderately long course, organized to promote health and fitness or to raise money for charity

fun·ster /fúnstər/ *n* somebody who likes to have fun or who enjoys telling or playing jokes (*dated informal*)

fur /fur/ *n* **1.** MAMMAL'S COAT the soft dense coat of hair on a hairy animal **2.** ANIMAL HAIR hairs from an animal's coat **3.** DRESSED PELT a dressed pelt from an animal such as a mink or seal that includes the animal's soft coat of hair. Use: garments, decoration. **4.** FUR COAT a garment made from fur pelts, especially a coat, jacket, or stole **5.** SOMETHING HAIRY something with a fuzzy or hairy texture or appearance **6.** COATING ON TONGUE a whitish coating of dead cells on the tongue that sometimes accompanies an illness (*informal*) **7.** HERALDRY PELT ON COAT OF ARMS a representation of an animal skin on a coat of arms [14C. < obsolete *fur* "to line" < Old French *forrer* < *forre* "lining"] —**fur·less** *adj* —**furred** *adj* ◇ **make the fur fly** to cause trouble or a disturbance (*informal*)

fur. *abbr* MEASURE furlong

fu·ran /fyŏŏr àn, fyoor án/ *n* a colorless flammable liquid. Use: solvent, manufacture of polymers. [Late 19C. Contraction of FURFURAN]

fu·ra·nose /fyŏŏrə nòss/ *n* a sugar made up of a ring of four carbon atoms and one oxygen atom

fur·bear·er /fúr bèrrər/ *n* an animal with fur, especially fur with high commercial value, e.g., a fox or mink —**fur·bear·ing** *adj*

fur·be·low /fúrbə lō/ *n* **1.** RUFFLE a gathered or pleated piece of material, especially as an ornament on a woman's garment **2.** FLAMBOYANT BEHAVIOR a showy or pretentious way of behaving (*literary*; *often used in the plural*) ■ *vt* (**-lowed, -low·ing, -lows**) DECORATE CLOTHING WITH RUFFLE to add a furbelow to a garment for ornamentation [Late 17C. Origin ?]

fur·bish /fúrbish/ (**-bished, -bish·ing, -bish·es**) *vt* **1.** to brighten something by polishing **2.** CONSTR same as **refurbish** (*literary*) [14C. < Old French *fourbiss-* < Germanic] —**fur·bish·er** *n*

fur·cate /fúr kàyt/ *vi* (**-cat·ed, -cat·ing, -cates**) to divide into two separate strands or branches ■ *adj* divided into separate strands or branches ○ *furcate leaves* [Early 19C. < late Latin *furcatus* "forked" < Latin *furca* "fork"] —**fur·cate·ly** *adv* —**fur·ca·tion** /fur káysh'n/ *n*

fur·cu·la /fúrkyələ/ (*plural* **-lae** /-lee/) *n* the V-shaped bone that is formed from two fused collarbones, found between the breasts of a bird (*technical*) [Mid-19C. < Latin, "small fork" < *furca* "fork"] —**fur·cu·lar** *adj*

fur·fur /fúr fùr/ (*plural* **-fur·es** /-fyə reez/) *n* a tiny piece of scaly or flaky skin, e.g., a particle of dandruff (*technical*) [15C. < Latin, "bran, scales"]

fur·fu·ra·ceous /fùrfə ráyshəss, fùrfyə-/ *adj* **1.** covered with or resembling particles of dandruff **2.** relating to or resembling bran

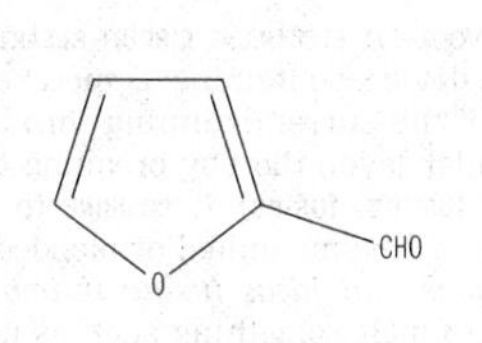

furfural

fur·fu·ral /fúrfəral, fúrfyə-/ *n* a colorless liquid with a distinctive smell. Source: plants. Use: manufacture of plastics, in oil refining, in agriculture. Formula: $C_5H_4O_2$.

fur·fu·ran /fúrfə ràn, fúrfyə-/ *n* CHEM same as **furan**

Fu·ries /fyŏŏreez/ *npl* in Greek mythology, three terrifying snake-haired winged goddesses, named Alecto, Megaera, and Tisiphone, who mercilessly punished wrongdoing, especially when committed within families. They were later identified with the Eumenides.

fu·ri·o·so /fyŏŏree ṓssō/ *adv* to be played with vigor and passion (*used as a musical direction*) [Mid-17C. Via Italian < Latin *furiosus* (see FURIOUS)] —**fu·ri·o·so** *adj*

fu·ri·ous /fyŏŏree əss/ *adj* **1.** extremely or violently angry ○ *I was furious with him for spreading such lies.* **2.** involving a great deal of energy, violence, or speed ○ *the pianist's furious assault on the keys* [14C. Via French < Latin *furiosus* < *furia* "rage" (see FURY)] —**fu·ri·ous·ly** *adv* —**fu·ri·ous·ness** *n*

furl /furl/ *vti* (**furled, furl·ing, furls**) to roll up and secure something made of fabric, or be rolled up and secured ■ *n* a rolled-up section of something such as a flag or sail [Late 16C. < French *ferler* < *ferm* "firm, firmly" + *lier* "to tie"]

fur·long /fúr làwng/ *n* a measure of distance equal to 220 yd. (approximately 201 m), now used mainly on racetracks [Old English *furlang* < *furh* (see FURROW) + *lang* (see LONG[1])]

fur·lough /fúr lō/ *n* **1.** LEAVE FROM DUTY leave of absence from duty, especially military duty **2.** GRANT OF LEAVE an official paper authorizing leave of absence **3.** *US* LEAVE FROM PRISON a period of leave granted to a prisoner, usually as a reward for good behavior and to reduce incarceration costs **4.** *US* WORK LAYOFF a layoff of workers, especially one that is temporary ■ *vt* (**-loughed, -lough·ing, -loughs**) **1.** GIVE LEAVE TO to grant leave of absence or other leave to somebody, especially a member of the armed services or a prisoner **2.** *US* LAY WORKERS OFF to lay workers off from work, especially temporarily ○ *Sixty workers were furloughed after the Christmas rush.* [Early 17C. < Dutch *verlo* "leave"]

fur·nace /fúrnəss/ *n* **1.** a device in which heat is produced by burning fuel either to warm a building or to undertake an industrial process such as smelting metal ○ *an oil furnace* **2.** an extremely hot place (*informal*) ○ *This kitchen is a furnace!* [13C. Via Old French *fornais* < Latin *fornax*]

Fur·neaux Group /fúrnō-/ group of islands situated off the coast of northeastern Tasmania, Australia. The largest islands are Flinders and Cape Barren Island. Population: 1,010. Area: 900 sq. mi./2,330 sq. km.

fur·nish /fúrnish/ (**-nished, -nish·ing, -nish·es**) *vt* **1.** to provide and install furniture and other fittings such as carpets and curtains in a place ○ *The lobby is furnished in an Art Deco style.* **2.** to supply something, or provide somebody with something (*formal*) ○ *Could you furnish us with the names and addresses of your clients?* [15C. < Old French *furniss-*, stem of *furnir* < Germanic] —**fur·nish·er** *n*

fur·nished /fúrnisht/ *adj* containing or supplied with furniture ○ *a furnished apartment*

fur·nish·ings /fúrnishingz/ *npl* **1.** articles of furniture and other useful or decorative items for a room, e.g., carpets and curtains **2.** *US* clothes and clothing accessories, e.g., belts and scarves ○ *men's furnishings*

fur·ni·ture /fúrnichər/ *n* **1.** TABLES AND CHAIRS the movable items in a room or patio, e.g., chairs, desks, or cabinets, **2.** PRINTING TYPE SEPARATORS in traditional hot-metal printing, strips of wood, metal, or plastic that are placed between type in order to make spaces and hold the type in place **3.** EQUIPMENT the equipment or accessories used for an activity, e.g., a ship's tackle or a horse's saddle and harnesses (*archaic*) [Early 16C. < Old French *fourniture* < *furnir* (see FURNISH)]

fu·ror /fyŏŏr àwr/ *n* **1.** an angry or indignant public reaction to something ○ *The verdict of not guilty created a furor in the courtroom.* **2.** a state of intense excitement or activity ○ *the furor surrounding the release of their latest album* [15C. < Latin < *furere* "to rage"]

fu·ro·re /fyŏŏ ráwree/ *n UK* same as **furor** [Late 18C. Via Italian < Latin *furor* (see FUROR)]

fu·ro·se·mide /fyoo rṓssə mīd/ *n* a drug that induces urination. Use: treatment of edema. [Mid-20C. < 1st syllable of *furyl* "chemical derived from furan" + *-sem-*, origin ?]

fur·ri·er /fúrree ər/ *n* **1.** a dealer in furs **2.** a person or establishment that makes or sells clothes and accessories of animal fur [14C. Alteration (after CLOTHIER) of *furrer* < Old French *forreor* < *forrer* (see FUR)]

fur·ring /fúr ing/ *n* **1.** CLOTHING FUR PART OF CLOTHING fur trim or lining for a garment **2.** MED WHITE COVERING a whitish coating of dead cells on the tongue of somebody who is sick **3.** CONSTR MAKING OF SURFACE OF STRIPS the placing of strips of wood, metal, or brick across the studs or joists in a building to create a firm and level foundation for plaster, flooring, or another surface (*often used before a noun*) ○ *furring strips* **4.** CONSTR **STRIPS USED UNDER SURFACE** strips used in a building for furring

fur·row /fúrrō/ *n* **1. TRENCH IN PLOWED FIELD** a narrow trench in soil made by a plow **2. GROOVE** a rut or groove in a surface **3. WRINKLE ON FOREHEAD** a wrinkle on the skin of the forehead, as a result of frowning or age ■ *vti* (**-rowed, -row·ing, -rows**) **MAKE FURROWS IN SOMETHING** to make furrows in something, or become marked with furrows ○ *He furrowed his brow.* [Old English *furh* < Indo-European] —**fur·rowed** *adj*

fur·ry /fúr ee/ (**-ri·er, -ri·est**) *adj* **1. COVERED IN FUR** covered in fur, or with a coat that is covered in fur ○ *furry animals* **2. LOOKING OR FEELING LIKE FUR** resembling fur in texture or appearance **3.** *US* **BLURRED** not clear or distinct, especially not seen or heard clearly ○ *the last few words of a pretty furry radio message* **4.** MED **COVERED IN WHITISH COATING** describes a tongue covered with a whitish coating of dead cells

fur seal *n* a seal with a double coat of fur, including a dense soft underfur that is highly valued for making garments. Many fur seal populations have been severely decreased by commercial hunting. Genera: *Arctocephalus* or *Callorhinus*.

Fur Seal Is·lands /fur seel-/ ◆ **Pribilof Islands**

Fürth /fürt/ city in the state of Bavaria, southern Germany, situated just northwest of Nuremberg. Population: 107,799 (1997).

fur·ther /fúrthər/ *adj* **ADDITIONAL** that is more than or adds to the quantity or extent of something ○ *until further notice* ○ *Do you have anything further to add?* ■ *adv* **1. TO GREATER DISTANCE** to or at a point that is more distant in place or time ○ *further into the future* **2. TO GREATER EXTENT** to a greater degree or extent ○ *Let's not pursue the matter any further.* **3. IN ADDITION** used to introduce an additional statement or point ○ *She said further that she would not accept any excuses.* ■ *vt* (**-thered, -ther·ing, -thers**) **ADVANCE SOMETHING** to help or give a boost to the progress of something ○ *All this media attention will further our cause.* [Old English *furþor, furþur* "more forward" < Germanic] —**fur·ther·er** *n* —**fur·ther·most** *adj* ◇ **further to** following on from something that has been written or discussed (*formal*) ○ *Further to our phone conversation, I would like to confirm the order.*

USAGE further or **farther**? Strictly speaking ***farther*** is the preferred spelling when referring to physical distance, as in *Have we much farther to go?* Now ***further*** is commonly used in this context, although its use is traditionally reserved for figurative contexts, as in *I have nothing further to add*, or *It took a further two phone calls before I got through.* ***Furthest*** and ***farthest*** behave similarly.

fur·ther·ance /fúrthərənss/ *n* advancement of an objective or interest ○ *In the furtherance of equal opportunity, such discrimination is prohibited by law.*

fur·ther·more /fúrthər màwr, fùrthər máwr/ *adv* used to introduce an additional statement or point ○ *She claimed furthermore that he did not own the business but only worked there.*

fur·thest /fúrthəst/ *adj* **MOST DISTANT** more distant in place or time than anything else ○ *the furthest planet from the Sun* ■ *adv* **1. TO GREATEST DISTANCE** to or at a more distant point in space or time than anything else ○ *Whoever gets the furthest wins the prize.* **2. TO GREATEST EXTENT** to a greater degree or extent than anything else ○ *The dollar has fallen furthest against the pound in the last year.*

USAGE See ***further.***

fur·tive /fúrtiv/ *adj* **1.** done in a way that is intended to escape notice ○ *conspirators exchanging furtive glances* **2.** presenting the appearance, or giving the impression, of somebody who has something to hide [Early 17C. Via French < Latin *furtivus* "hidden, stolen" < *furtum* "theft" < *fur* "thief" < Indo-European, "carry"] —**fur·tive·ly** *adv* —**fur·tive·ness** *n*

SYNONYMS See ***secret.***

fu·run·cle /fyoȯr ùngk'l/ *n* a boil on the skin (*technical*) [Late 17C. < Latin *furunculus* "knob on a vine" < *fur* "thief" (because it "steals" the sap)] —**fu·run·cu·lar** /fyə rúngkyələr/ *adj*

fu·run·cu·lo·sis /fyə rùngkyə lṓssiss/ *n* **1.** a medical condition in which large areas of the skin are covered in persistent boils **2.** a virulent bacterial disease that affects salmon and trout and can be devastating in the densely populated waters of fish farms

fu·ry /fyoȯree/ (*plural* **-ries**) *n* **1. RAGE** violent anger ○ *She could not contain her fury any longer.* **2. BURST OF ANGER** an outburst of violent anger ○ *He stormed off in a fury.* **3. WILD FORCE** a state of excited or frenetic activity ○ *debris scattered in the wake of the tornado's fury* **4. OFFENSIVE TERM** an offensive term for a woman who is regarded as malevolent and spiteful (*dated*) [14C. Via French < Latin *furia* < *furere* "to rage"] ◇ **like fury** with great speed or energy

CULTURAL NOTE *The Sound and the Fury,* a novel (1929) by William Faulkner. Set in the South, it recounts the financial and moral decline of a wealthy family. The story, which centers on the daughter Caddy, is told in four parts, three of which are narrated by family members.

SYNONYMS See ***anger.***

Fu·ry *n* in Greek mythology, one of the Furies

furze /furz/ *n UK* PLANTS same as **gorse** [Old English *fyrs*, origin ?]

fu·sain /fyoo záyn, fyoȯ zàyn/ *n* **1.** ART **CHARCOAL STICK** a fine stick of charcoal for drawing, made from wood from the spindle tree **2.** ART **CHARCOAL DRAWING** a drawing or sketch done with fusain charcoal **3.** MINERALS **GRAY COAL** dark gray bituminous carbon found in some kinds of coal [Late 19C. Via French, "spindle tree, charcoal made from its wood" < Latin *fusus* "spindle"]

~~**fuschia**~~ incorrect spelling of **fuchsia**

fus·cous /fúskəss/ *adj* of a dark grayish-brown color (*literary or technical*) [Mid-17C. < Latin *fuscus* "dusky"]

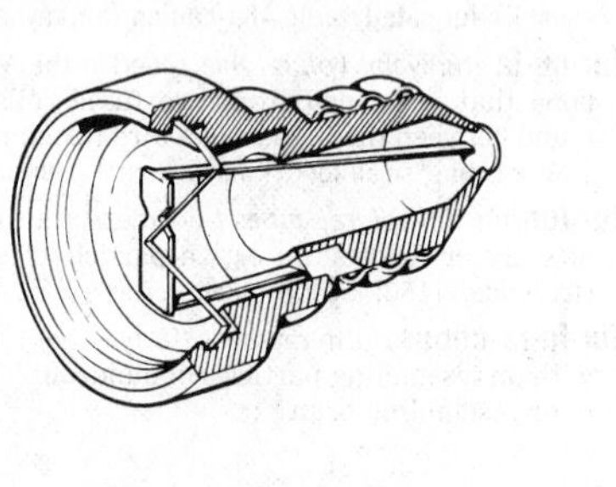

fuse

fuse[1] /fyooz/ *n* **ELECTRICAL CIRCUIT BREAKER** an electrical safety device containing a piece of a metal that melts if the current running through it exceeds a particular level, thereby breaking the circuit ■ *vti* (**fused, fus·ing, fus·es**) **1. COMBINE** to unite or blend things, or become united or blended into a whole ○ *sensations and ideas fusing intimately together* **2. LIQUEFY** to melt something such as metal or plastic, or become melted at a very high temperature [Late 16C. < Latin *fus-*, past participle of *fundere* "melt, pour"]

fuse[2] /fyooz/, **fuze** ARMS *n* **1. EXPLOSIVE LEAD** a cord or trail of a combustible substance that is ignited at one end to carry a flame to an explosive device farther away **2. DETONATOR** a mechanical or electrical detonator that triggers an exploding device such as a bomb or grenade ■ *vt* (**fused, fus·ing, fus·es; fuzed, fuz·ing, fuz·es**) **EQUIP DEVICE WITH DETONATOR** to equip an exploding device such as a bomb or grenade with a mechanical or electrical detonator [Mid-17C. Via Italian *fuso* "spindle" < Latin *fusus*]

fuse box *n* a box, often attached to a wall, that contains the fuses that protect all the electrical circuits in a building or part of a building

fused quartz, fused sil·i·ca *n* GLASS same as **quartz glass**

fu·see /fyoo zee/, **fu·zee** *n* **1. FLARE** a red flare used as a warning device on railroads or roads **2. WINDPROOF MATCH** a large-headed match that is not easily extinguished in the wind **3. CLOCK PULLEY** a conical pulley with a spiral groove, used in clock and watch mechanisms **4.** *US* ARMS **EXPLOSIVES FUSE** a combustible fuse leading to an explosive device [Late 16C. Via French *fusée* "spindle, fuse, flare" < Latin *fusus* "spindle"]

fu·se·lage /fyoȯssə laazh, fyoȯzə-/ *n* the body of an airplane, containing the cockpit, passenger seating, and cargo hold but excluding the wings [Early 20C. < French < Latin *fusus* "spindle"]

fu·sel oil /fyoȯz'l-/ *n* an oily liquid mixture. Source: insufficiently distilled alcoholic liquors. Use: solvent, in chemical manufacturing. [Mid-19C. < German *Fusel* "bad liquor"]

Fu·shun /foȯ shoȯn/ city and industrial center in Liaoning Province, northeastern China. Population: 1,530,000 (1995).

fu·si·ble /fyoȯzəb'l/ *adj* describes metals and other materials that are easily melted or liquefied ○ *fusible alloys* —**fu·si·bil·i·ty** /fyoȯzə bílləte̅e/ *n*

fu·si·form /fyoȯzə fàwrm/ *adj* tapering at both ends, like a spindle ○ *fusiform bacteria* [Mid-18C. < Latin *fusus* "spindle"]

fu·sil /fyoȯz'l/ *n* a lightweight musket with a flintlock firing mechanism [Late 16C. < French, "steel in a flintlock, musket" < late Latin *focus* "fire"]

fu·sil·ier /fyoȯzə leer/, **fu·sil·eer** *n* formerly, a soldier armed with a lightweight musket (**fusil**) [Late 17C. < French < *fusil* "musket" (see FUSIL)]

fu·sil·lade /fyoȯssə laad, -làyd, fyoȯzə-/ *n* **1. BLAST OF GUNFIRE** the firing of several guns at once or in quick succession **2. ONSLAUGHT** a sustained attack or barrage, e.g., of missiles or words ■ *vt* (**-lad·ed, -lad·ing, -lades**) **FIRE AT ENEMY** to subject an enemy to a sustained burst of gunfire [Early 19C. < French < *fusiller* "shoot" < *fusil* "musket" (see FUSIL)]

fu·sil·li /fyoo zíllee/ *npl* pasta in the form of short spiral shapes [Late 20C. < Italian, "little spindles" < Latin *fusus* "spindle"]

fu·sion /fyoȯzh'n/ *n* **1. BLENDING** the merger or a blending of two or more things such as materials or ideas ○ *a fusion of vegetarianism and pacifism* **2. HEATING AND LIQUEFYING SOMETHING** the molten state of a substance, or the change it undergoes to become molten **3.** PHYS same as **nuclear fusion 4.** MUSIC **COMBINATION OF MUSICAL STYLES** the merger, or the resulting blend, of musical styles or elements from more than one tradition, e.g., jazz and rock [Mid-16C. Directly or via French < Latin *fusion-* < *fundere* "melt, pour"]

SYNONYMS See ***mixture.***

fu·sion bomb *n* a nuclear bomb, especially a hydrogen bomb, whose explosion is caused by the energy released by a nuclear fusion reaction

fu·sion food, fu·sion cui·sine *n* a style of cooking that uses ingredients and techniques from around the world, especially one that combines Eastern and Western influences

fu·sion in·hib·i·tor *n* a drug that prevents a virus such as HIV from binding to and entering a human cell

fu·sion·ism /fyoȯzh'n ìzzəm/ *n* the formation of political coalitions, support for their formation, or belief in their effectiveness —**fu·sion·ist** *n, adj*

fuss /fuss/ *n* **1. COMMOTION** activity that is needlessly or excessively busy or excited **2. NEEDLESS WORRY** excessive concern over details or trivial matters **3. PROTEST** a complaint or protestation, often over something insignificant ○ *The kids made a fuss about going to bed early.* **4. ARGUMENT** a noisy disagreement or dispute ○ *There'll be a fuss if he gets home late again.* **5. DISPLAY OF AFFECTION OR CONCERN** an excited or abundant display of affection or affectionate concern ○ *She was irritated by the fuss they made over her sprained ankle.* ■ *vi* (**fussed, fuss·ing, fuss·es**) **1. WORRY TOO MUCH** to be too concerned about details or trivial matters **2. FIDDLE WITH SOMETHING** to keep moving or touching something busily, nervously, or aimlessly ○ *He fussed with the dials, hoping he'd look like he knew what he was doing.* [Early 18C. Origin ?] —**fuss·er** *n*

fuss·budg·et /fúss bùjjət/ *n* somebody who typically worries about trivial things (*informal*) [Early 20C. < BUDGET "bundle"]

fuss·y /fússee/ (**-i·er, -i·est**) *adj* **1. CONCERNED WITH MINOR THINGS** tending to worry over details or trivial things **2. CHOOSY** very dogmatic about likes and dislikes ○ *a very fussy eater* **3.** *US* **EASILY UPSET** frequently or easily irritated 4. ELABORATE made or decorated with excessive detail ○ *a dress with a fussy lace collar* 5. *US* DEMANDING AND DETAILED requiring or accomplished with care and attention to details ○ *I'd better open that window for you — the lock is a bit fussy.* —**fuss·i·ly** *adv* —**fuss·i·ness** *n*

SYNONYMS See *careful*.

fus·tian /fúschən/ *adj* BOMBASTIC written or spoken with pretentiousness or pomposity (*formal*) ○ *delivered a fustian speech on the floor of the Senate* ■ *n* 1. BOMBAST pompous or pretentious speech or writing (*formal*) 2. COTTON-LINEN CLOTH a coarse sturdy cloth that is a blend of cotton and linen 3. COTTON FABRIC WITH NAP a durable cotton fabric, e.g., corduroy or moleskin [13C. Via French < medieval Latin *fustaneum*]

fus·tic /fústik/ *n* 1. YELLOW DYE a yellow dye obtained from the wood of some trees 2. WOOD YIELDING YELLOW DYE the wood from which the dye fustic is obtained 3. DYE-YIELDING TROPICAL TREE a tree whose wood yields the dye fustic. Native to: tropical America. Latin name: *Chlorophora tinctoria*. 4. DYE-YIELDING EUROPEAN TREE a tree whose wood yields the dye fustic. Native to: Europe. Latin name: *Cotinus coggyria*. [15C. Via Old French *fustoc* < Arabic *fustuk* < Greek *pistakē* "pistachio tree"]

fus·ty /fústee/ (-ti·er, -ti·est) *adj* 1. smelling of damp, dust, mildew, or age 2. old-fashioned and conservative in style, appearance, habits, or attitudes ○ *needed to transform a rather fusty image* [Late 15C. < obsolete *fust* "wine cask," via French < Latin *fustis* "wood, club"] —**fus·ti·ly** *adv* —**fus·ti·ness** *n*

fut. *abbr* 1. future 2. FIN futures

Fu·ta Djal·lon ♦ **Fouta Djallon**

fu·thark /fóo thaark/, **fu·thorc** /-thàwrk/, **fu·thork** *n* the runic alphabet of 24 letters, used in northwestern Europe between the 3rd and 17th centuries [Mid-19C < the first six letters: *f, u, þ, a* or *o, r,* and *k*]

fu·tile /fyóot'l/ *adj* 1. having no practical effect or useful result 2. lacking serious value, substance, or a sense of responsibility [Mid-16C. < Latin *futilis* "leaky, worthless"] —**fu·tile·ly** *adv* —**fu·tile·ness** *n*

fu·til·i·tar·i·an /fyoo tìllə térree ən/ *n* a believer that human efforts are wasted and futile [Early 19C. < FUTILITY, after UTILITARIAN] —**fu·til·i·tar·i·an** *adj* —**fu·til·i·tar·i·an·ism** *n*

fu·til·i·ty /fyoo tíllətee/ (*plural* -ties) *n* 1. POINTLESSNESS lack of usefulness or effectiveness 2. POINTLESS ACTION an action that has no use, purpose, or effect 3. *US* FRIVOLITY lack of importance, seriousness, or sensibleness

fu·ton /fóo tòn/ *n* 1. a firm Japanese-style cotton-covered mattress used as a seat or bed, either on the floor or on a wooden frame 2. a futon together with the wooden frame it sits on, especially a frame designed to convert from a sofa to a bed [Late 19C. < Japanese < *fu* "quilt" (< Middle Chinese *phu*) + *ton* "round" (< Middle Chinese *thuan*)]

fut·tock /fúttək/ *n* a curved middle timber forming the frame of a traditional wooden boat or ship [13C. Origin ?]

fut·tock plate *n* a circular metal plate attached to the top of a ship's shorter masts. Ropes or rods supporting a taller mast are secured to futtock plates.

fut·tock shroud *n* a rope or rod stretching from the top of a taller mast to the top of a lower mast, to support the taller mast

fu·ture /fyóochər/ *n* 1. TIME TO COME time that has yet to come ○ *saving money for the future* 2. HAPPENINGS TO COME events that have not yet happened ○ *The future will be shaped by our advancing technology.* 3. EXPECTED FORTHCOMING CONDITION an expected or projected state ○ *Her future is bleak.* 4. GRAM TENSE REFERRING TO THINGS TO COME the tense or form of a verb used to refer to events that are going to happen or have not yet happened ■ **fu·tures** *npl* FIN COMMODITIES TRADED FOR LATER DELIVERY goods or stocks sold for future delivery, or the contracts for them ■ *adj* 1. YET TO OCCUR expected to be or happen at a time still to come ○ *my future sister-in-law* 2. GRAM OF TENSE EXPRESSING FUTURE describes a verb form or tense that expresses actions or states that are going to happen or have not yet happened [14C. Via French < Latin *futurus* "going to be"]

fu·ture·less /fyóochərləss/ *adj* seeming to have no chance of developing or being successful ○ *poured money into futureless projects* —**fu·ture·less·ness** *n*

fu·ture per·fect *n* the form of a verb expressing a completed action in the future, as "will have finished" does in the sentence "They will have finished by tomorrow"

fu·ture shock *n* difficulty in, and stress from, coping with rapid changes in society, especially technological changes

fu·ture tense *n* GRAM same as **future** (sense 4)

fu·tur·ism /fyóochə rìzzəm/ *n* 1. *also* **Fu·tur·ism** an early 20th-century artistic movement that attempted to express the dynamic nature of the modern age using technology as its subject 2. belief in the need to look to the future rather than reflect on the past, coupled with an optimism that personal and social fulfillment lies in the future —**fu·tur·ist** *n, adj*

fu·tur·is·tic /fyóochə rístik/ *adj* 1. suggesting the future in design or technology 2. depicting life in a future time —**fu·tur·is·ti·cal·ly** *adv*

fu·tu·ri·ty /fyoo tóorətee, -chóorətee/ (*plural* -ties) *n* 1. the future as a concept or state ○ *a grammatical construction expressing futurity* 2. an event that is going to happen or has not happened yet (*formal*) 3. HORSERACING same as **futurity race**

futurity race *n US* a horse race in which horses are entered well in advance, often before they are born. The race is usually run when the horses are two years old.

fu·tur·ol·o·gy /fyóochə róllәjee/ *n* the study and forecasting of the future, with predictions based on the likely outcomes of current trends —**fu·tur·o·log·i·cal** /fyóochərə lójjik'l/ *adj* —**fu·tu·rol·o·gist** *n*

futz /futs/ (**futzed, futz·ing, futz·es**) *vi* to spend time frivolously, lazily, or aimlessly (*informal*) ○ *spends hours futzing with that computer* [Early 20C. Probably alteration of Yiddish *arumfartzen* "fool around"]

Fu·xin /fóo shín/ city in Liaoning Province, northeastern China, west of Shenyang. Population: 879,477 (1991).

fuze *n, vt* ARMS another spelling of **fuse**[2]

fu·zee *n* MECH ENG, ARMS, RAIL another spelling of **fusee**

Fu·zhou /fóo jṓ/ city and capital of Fujian Province, southeastern China, near the mouth of the Min River, northeast of Taiwan. Population: 1,590,000 (1995).

fuzz[1] /fuz/ *n* FLUFF a mass of short fine hairs or fibers ■ *vti* (**fuzzed, fuzz·ing, fuzz·es**) 1. COVER SOMETHING WITH FUZZ to become covered with fuzz, or cover something with fuzz ○ *sweaters that fuzz after the first wash* 2. BLUR to make something such as an image or explanation blurred or unclear, or become blurred or unclear ○ *All this talk has fuzzed my brain.* [Late 16C. Probably < Dutch or Low German]

fuzz[2] /fuz/ *n* an offensive term for the police (*dated slang*) [Early 20C. Origin ?]

fuzz·box /fúz bòks/ *n* an electrical device that distorts the sound that passes through it, especially a pedal-operated device wired to an electric guitar

fuzz·y /fúzzee/ (-i·er, -i·est) *adj* 1. COVERED WITH FUZZ covered with a mass of short fine hairs or fibers 2. CONSISTING OF FUZZ in the form of a mass of short fine hairs or fibers 3. FRIZZY describes hair growing in a very tight curly mass 4. BLURRED not sharp enough to be seen or heard clearly ○ *a fuzzy picture* 5. INCOHERENT not clearly thought out or set out ○ *The initial plan was fairly fuzzy.* 6. COMPUT FOR FUZZY LOGIC using or designed to use fuzzy logic ○ *fuzzy computing* [Early 17C. Origin ?] —**fuzz·i·ly** *adv* —**fuzz·i·ness** *n*

fuzz·y·head·ed /fùzzee héddəd/ *adj* not thinking or communicating clearly (*informal*) ○ *a fuzzyheaded notion* —**fuzz·y·head·ed·ness** *n*

fuzz·y log·ic *n* logic that allows for imprecise or ambiguous answers to questions, forming the basis of computer programming designed to mimic human intelligence

fuzz·y search *n* a computer search that returns not only exact matches to the search request, but also close matches that include possibilities and allow for such things as spelling errors

FWD *abbr* AUTOMOT 1. four-wheel drive 2. front-wheel drive

fwd. *abbr* forward

f-word, F-word *n* a euphemism for the highly offensive word "fuck"

fwy. *abbr* ROADS freeway

fx *abbr* France, Metropolitan (*used in Internet addresses*) See table at **domain name**

FX *abbr* 1. FIN foreign exchange 2. MOVIES (special) effects

fy *abbr* fiscal year

-fy *suffix* (*usually used after -i-*) 1. to make or produce ○ *satisfy* ○ *speechify* 2. to cause to become or to resemble ○ *gasify* ○ *ladify* ○ *solidify* [Via Old French *-fier* < Latin *facere* "do, make"]

FYI *abbr* ONLINE for your information (*used in e-mails, text messages, or office memos*)

fyke /fīk/ *n* a bag-shaped fishing net, held open by hoops [Mid-19C. < Dutch *fuik*]

fyl·fot /fíl fòt/ *n* a decorative or religious symbol in the form of a swastika [15C. Origin ?]

Fyn /fin, fün/ the second-largest island in Denmark, between southern Jutland and the island of Sjælland. Population: 470,528 (1996). Area: 1,150 sq. mi./2,978 sq. km.

F.Y.R.O.M. *abbr* Former Yugoslav Republic of Macedonia

fz. *abbr* MUSIC sforzando

Gg

g[1] /jee/ (*plural* **g's**), **G** (*plural* **G's** or **Gs**) *n* **1.** the seventh letter of the English alphabet, representing a consonant sound **2.** a written representation of the letter "g"

g[2] *symbol* **1.** PHYS acceleration of free fall as a result of gravity **2.** used to refer to the seventh vertical row of squares from the left on a chessboard

G[1] /jee/ (*plural* **G's** or **Gs**) *n* **1.** **"G"-SHAPED OBJECT** something shaped like a letter "G" **2.** MUSIC **5TH NOTE IN C MAJOR** the fifth note of a scale in C major **3.** MUSIC **SOMETHING THAT PRODUCES G** a string, key, or pipe tuned to produce the note G **4.** MUSIC **SCALE BEGINNING ON G** a scale or key that starts on the note G **5.** MUSIC **WRITTEN SYMBOL OF G** a graphic representation of the tone of G **6.** MOVIES **GENERAL-AUDIENCE MOVIE RATING** a movie rating meaning that a movie or video is appropriate for anyone to watch **7.** MONEY **$1,000** one thousand dollars (*slang*)

G[2] *symbol* **1.** ELEC conductance **2.** PHYS gauss **3.** PHYS gravitational constant **4.** BIOCHEM guanine

G[3] *abbr* **1.** SOC SCI gay (*in personal ads*) **2.** giga- **3.** EDUC good (*used as a grade*) **4.** MONEY guilder **5.** MONEY guinea **6.** Gulf (*used in placenames*)

g. *abbr* **1.** gauge **2.** GRAM gender **3.** GRAM genitive **4.** MEASURE gram **5.** MONEY guilder **6.** MONEY guinea

G. *abbr* **1.** MONEY guilder **2.** MONEY guinea **3.** Gulf (*used in place names*)

G7 /jee sévv'n/ *n* the group of the seven most industrialized nations in the world that met to discuss and draw up global economic policies before they were joined by Russia to form G8. The seven were Canada, France, (West) Germany, Italy, Japan, the United Kingdom, and the United States. Full form **Group of Seven**

G8 /jee áyt/ *n* the group of the eight most industrialized nations in the world, comprising Canada, France, Germany, Italy, Japan, Russia, the United Kingdom, and the United States. Representatives from these countries meet regularly to discuss and draw up global economic policies. Full form **Group of Eight**

ga *abbr* Gabon (*used in Internet addresses*) See table at **domain name**

Ga *symbol* CHEM ELEM gallium

GA *abbr* **1.** LAW general agent **2.** Georgia **3.** ONLINE go ahead (*used in e-mails or text messages*)

G.A. *abbr* **1.** General Assembly (of the United Nations) **2.** SHIPPING, INSUR general average

GAAP *abbr* ACCT generally accepted accounting principles

gab /gab/ (**gabbed, gab·bing, gabs**) *vi* to talk at length about trivial matters (*informal*) ○ *We just sat there gabbing all afternoon.* [Early 18C. Origin ?] —**gab** *n* —**gab·ber** *n*

GABA *abbr* BIOCHEM gamma-aminobutyric acid

gab·ar·dine /gábbər deen/ *n* **1.** a smooth durable cotton, wool, or synthetic fabric woven with a pattern of parallel diagonal ridges (**twill**) ○ *a gabardine jacket* **2.** a garment made of gabardine **3.** CLOTHING same as **gaberdine** (sense 1) [Early 20C. Alteration of GABERDINE]

gab·ble /gább'l/ (**-bled, -bling, -bles**) *v* **1.** *vti* to speak or say something rapidly and incoherently **2.** *vi* to make the high throaty sounds that geese and some other birds make [Late 16C. Origin ?] —**gab·ble** *n* —**gab·bler** *n*

gab·bro /gá brō/ *n* a dark coarse-grained basic igneous rock containing calcium-rich plagioclase feldspar and pyroxene [Mid-19C. < Italian dialect, probably < Latin *glaber* "smooth, bald"] —**gab·bro·ic** /ga brṓ ik/ *adj*

gab·by /gábbee/ (**-bi·er, -bi·est**) *adj* talking or inclined to talk to an excessive and irritating degree (*informal*)

ga·belle /gə bél/ *n* **1.** a French tax on salt imposed until 1790 **2.** any tax, especially a tax imposed in a foreign country (*literary*) [15C. Via Old French *gabel* < Arabic *ḳabāla* "tax, duty"]

gab·er·dine /gábbər deen/ *n* **1.** a long loose coat or smock made of coarse cloth, worn by men, especially Jewish men, during the Middle Ages **2.** TEXTILES, CLOTHING same as **gabardine** (senses 1–2) [Early 16C. < Old French *gauvardine*]

gab·fest /gáb fèst/ *n* (*informal*) **1.** an informal gathering where idle chat or gossip is exchanged **2.** a long informal chat or discussion ○ *The student's simple question started a gabfest among the pundits.*

Ga·bin /ga báN/, **Jean** (1904–76) French actor. His portrayal of a tragic hero in *Maria Chapdelaine* (1934) brought him instant fame. He is best known for his roles in Marcel Carné's film noir classics *Quai des brumes* (1938) and *Le Jour se lève* (1939). Born **Moncorgé, Jean-Alexis**

ga·bi·on /gáybee ən/ *n* **1.** a wickerwork basket filled with rocks, used as a temporary fortification **2.** a cylindrical metal container filled with earth and stones, used in the construction and rerouting of waterways and in flood control [Mid-16C. Via French < Italian *gabbione* "large cage" < *gabbia* "cage" < Latin *cavea*]

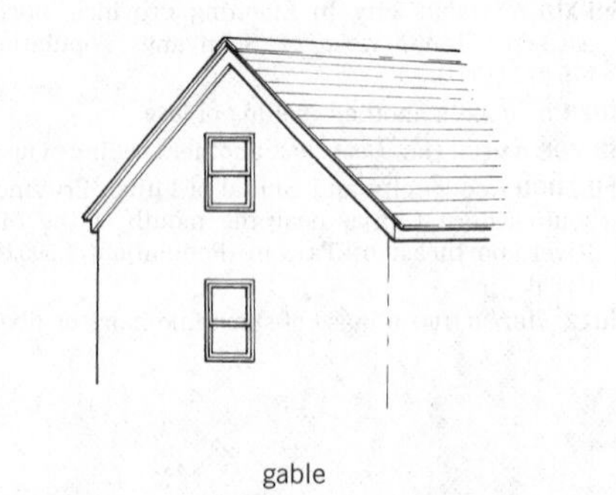

gable

ga·ble /gáyb'l/ *n* **1.** the triangular top section of a side wall on a building with a pitched roof that fills the space beneath where the roof slopes meet **2.** ARCHIT same as **gable end** **3.** a triangular structure added to a building for decoration, e.g., a canopy over a door or window [14C. Directly or via Old French < Old Norse *gafl*] —**ga·bled** *adj*

CULTURAL NOTE ***Anne of Green Gables***, a children's story (1908) by Canadian writer Lucy Maud Montgomery. Set on Prince Edward Island in Canada, it is the story of a vivacious 11-year-old orphan, Anne Shirley, who is sent to live with farmers Matthew and Marilla Cuthbert. Having expected a boy, the Cuthberts cannot hide their disappointment, but Anne's courage, spirit, and vivid imagination soon win them over.

Clark Gable

Ga·ble /gáyb'l/, **Clark** (1901–60) US movie actor. He won an Academy Award for his performance in the romantic comedy *It Happened One Night* (1934), but he is best known for his role as Rhett Butler in *Gone With the Wind* (1939). Full name **Gable, William Clark**

ga·ble end *n* a side wall that comes to a peak where the slopes of a pitched roof meet

ga·ble roof *n* a roof with two slopes and a gable at each end

Ga·bo /gaábō/, **Naum** (1890–1977) Russian-born US sculptor, one of the founders of the constructivist school. His work drew on cubism, and he experimented with kinetic art. Born **Pevsner, Naum Neemia**

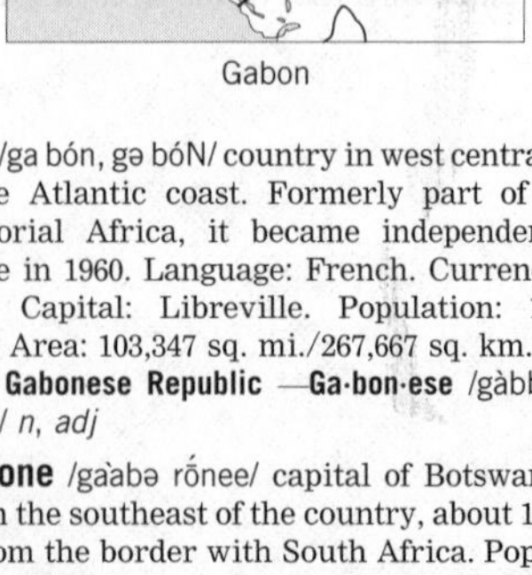

Gabon

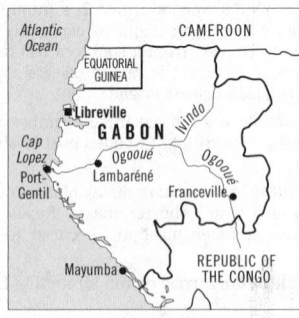

Ga·bon /ga bón, gə bóN/ country in west central Africa on the Atlantic coast. Formerly part of French Equatorial Africa, it became independent from France in 1960. Language: French. Currency: CFA franc. Capital: Libreville. Population: 1,321,560 (2003). Area: 103,347 sq. mi./267,667 sq. km. Official name **Gabonese Republic** —**Ga·bon·ese** /gàbbə neez, -neess/ *n, adj*

Ga·bo·rone /gaábə ronee/ capital of Botswana, situated in the southeast of the country, about 12 mi./19 km from the border with South Africa. Population: 185,891 (2001).

Ga·bri·el /gáybree əl/ *n* in Christian, Islamic, and Jewish tradition, an archangel who acts as God's messenger. In Christian and Jewish tradition, he appeared to Mary, Zacharias, and Daniel, and in Islamic tradition, he revealed the Koran to Muhammad.

gad[1] /gad/ *vi* (**gad·ded, gad·ding, gads**) to go around having fun in a carefree and aimless manner (*humorous*) ○ *gadding about* ■ *n* carefree or aimless wandering (*archaic*) [15C. Probably back-formation < obsolete *gadling* "wanderer" < Old English *gædeling* "companion" < Germanic] —**gad·der** *n*

gad[2] /gad/ *n* **1.** MIN EXTRACT **HEAVY TOOL** in mining, a heavy steel or iron wedge with a pointed or chisel-shaped edge, used to break coal, rock, or ore from the rock face **2.** AGRIC **CATTLE PROD** a sharp pointed tool used to drive cattle ■ *vt* (**gad·ded, gad·ding, gads**) MIN EXTRACT **SEPARATE MINERALS FROM ROCK** to break up coal or ore using a gad [13C. < Old Norse *gaddr* "goad, spike" < Germanic, "pointed stick"]

gad·a·bout /gáddə bòwt/ *n* a restless and aimless seeker of pleasure (*humorous*)

Ga·daf·fi another spelling of **Qaddafi**

gad·a·rene /gáddə reèn/ *adj* rushing headlong en masse (*literary*) [Early 19C. Via Latin < Greek *Gadarēnos* "inhabitant of Gadara," town in the Bible where a herd of swine rushed into the sea (Matthew 8:28)]

Gad·da·fi another spelling of **Qaddafi**

Gad·dis /gáddiss/, **William** (1922–98) US writer. He is known for darkly humorous novels such as *The Recognitions* (1955) and *Carpenter's Gothic* (1985).

> "Justice? You get justice in the next world, in this world you have the law."
> [William Gaddis, *A Frolic of His Own*; 1994]

gad·fly /gád flī/ (*plural* **-flies**) *n* **1.** a fly that irritates livestock by biting them and sucking their blood. Horseflies are a type of gadfly. Family: Tabanidae. **2.** somebody regarded as persistently annoying or irritating [< GAD[1]]

gadg·et /gájjət/ *n* **1.** a small device that performs or aids a simple task **2.** a small device that appears useful but is often unnecessary or superfluous [Late 19C. Origin ?] —**gadg·et·y** *adj*

gadg·e·teer /gàjjə teér/ *n* an inventor or enthusiastic user of gadgets

gadg·et·ry /gájjətree/ *n* gadgets collectively, especially when perceived as impressively complicated

ga·did /gáddid, gáydid/, **ga·doid** /gáy dòyd, gá dòyd/ *n* an ocean fish of the family that includes cod, haddock, and hake. Family: Gadidae. ■ *adj* belonging to the family of ocean fish that includes cod, haddock, and hake [Mid-19C. < modern Latin *gadus* "cod" < Greek *gados*]

gad·o·lin·ite /gádd'lə nìt/ *n* a black or brown silicate mineral containing beryllium, iron, and yttrium. Source: pegmatites. [Early 19C. After Johan *Gadolin* (1760–1852), Finnish mineralogist]

gad·o·lin·i·um /gàdd'l ínnee əm/ *n* a rare silvery white metallic element. Source: monazite, bastnaesite. Use: high-temperature alloys, neutron absorber in nuclear reactors and fuels. Symbol **Gd**. See table at **element** [Late 19C. < GADOLINITE]

ga·droon /gə droón/, **go·droon** /gō droón/ *n* an ornamental feature that consists of a series of convex curves or inverted fluting. It is often applied as an edging to a curved surface, especially on silver. [Late 17C. < French *godron* "pucker, crease"] —**ga·drooned** *adj* —**ga·droon·ing** *n*

Gads·den /gádzdən/ industrial city on the northern bank of the Coosa River, in northeastern Alabama. Population: 42,158 (1998).

gad·wall /gád wàwl/ *n* a common freshwater duck with gray and brown feathers. Native to: Europe, North America. Latin name: *Anas strepera*. [Mid-17C. Origin ?]

gad·zooks /gad zoóks/ *interj* used to express surprise or as a mild oath (*archaic or humorous*) [Late 17C. < *Gad* "God" + *zooks*, origin ?]

Gae·a *n* MYTHOL **Gaia**

Gael /gayl/ *n* **1.** somebody from Scotland, Ireland, or the Isle of Man who speaks Gaelic **2.** somebody from the Scottish Highlands [Mid-18C. < Scottish Gaelic *Gael*, *Gàidheal* < Old Irish *Goídel*, plural of *Gáidl*]

Gael·ic /gáylik/ *n* **CELTIC LANGUAGE OF BRITISH ISLES** any of the forms of the Celtic language used in Scotland, Ireland, or the Isle of Man ■ *adj* **1.** **OF GAELIC** relating to any of the forms of the Celtic language of Scotland, Ireland, or the Isle of Man **2.** **OF GAELIC-SPEAKING PEOPLE** relating to Gaelic-speaking people or their culture

LANGUAGE HERITAGE See ***Celtic.***

gaff[1] /gaf/ *n* **1.** **HOOKED FISH POLE** a pole with a large hook on the end that is used to hold and land a large fish **2.** **POLE AT TOP OF SAIL** a pole attached to a mast and used to support the upper edge of a fore-and-aft sail **3.** **HOOK FOR SOMEBODY MAINTAINING OVERHEAD LINE** a climbing hook used by somebody erecting or repairing a telephone or power line **4.** **METAL SPUR ON FIGHTING COCK** a metal spur that is fixed to the leg of a fighting cock **5.** **GIMMICK USED IN HOAX** a gimmick or trick, often used in a hoax or attempt at fraud ■ *vt* (**gaffed, gaff·fing, gaffs**) **1.** **CATCH FISH WITH HOOKED POLE** to catch and hold a fish with a gaff **2.** **ARM SOMETHING WITH GAFF** to provide or arm something such as a fighting cock with a gaff **3.** **CHEAT OR SWINDLE** to cheat or swindle somebody (*slang*) [14C. < Old French *gaffe* "boat hook" (see GAFFE)]

gaff[2] /gaf/ *n* **1.** *UK* worthless nonsense (*informal*) **2.** *Carib* relaxed informal conversation or chat [Early 19C. Origin ?] ◇ **blow the gaff** to reveal a secret (*slang*)

gaffe /gaf/, **gaff** *n* a clumsy social mistake or breach of etiquette, e.g., an insensitive remark [Early 20C. < French, originally "boat hook," via Old French < Old Provençal *gaf*]

gaf·fer /gáffər/ *n* the chief electrician in charge of lighting on a movie or television set (*informal*) [Late 16C. Probably contraction of GODFATHER]

gaff-rig *n* a sailing vessel rigged with fore-and-aft sails supported by a gaff —**gaff-rigged** *adj*

gaff-top·sail *n* a small, usually triangular, sail set above a gaff

gag /gag/ *n* **1.** **SOMETHING PUT OVER MOUTH** something such as a piece of cloth that is forcibly put over or into somebody's mouth to prevent the person from speaking or crying out **2.** **RESTRAINT OF SPEECH** a restraint on free speech ○ *put a gag on a newspaper* **3.** **COMIC WORDS OR ACTION** a comic story, action, or incident told or performed by an actor or comedian **4.** **TRICK** a trick, hoax, or practical joke (*informal*) **5.** **MOUTH PROP** a device that is placed in a patient's mouth to keep it open during surgical work on the mouth or throat **6.** **CHOKING** an instance or the action of choking or retching (*informal*) ■ *v* (**gagged, gag·ging, gags**) **1.** *vt* **PUT SOMETHING OVER SOMEBODY'S MOUTH** to put something over or into somebody's mouth to prevent the person from speaking or crying out **2.** *vt* **RESTRAIN SPEECH** to prevent or restrain the free speech of somebody or something **3.** *vti* **CHOKE OR RETCH** to make somebody nearly choke or retch, or choke or retch because of something stuck in the throat or because of a very unpleasant sight or smell **4.** *vi* **TELL JOKES** to tell jokes or perform as a comedian **5.** *vt* **PROP SOMEBODY'S MOUTH OPEN** to hold somebody's mouth open during surgery by means of a gag **6.** *vt* **PUT BIT ON HORSE** to put a strong bit (**gag-bit**) on a horse **7.** *vt* **OBSTRUCT PIPE OR VALVE** to block or obstruct something such as a pipe or valve [15C. Probably an imitation of the sound of choking]

ga·ga /gaá gaá/ *adj* (*informal*) **1.** an offensive term that insults somebody's mental abilities, especially those of a senior citizen **2.** completely infatuated or very enthusiastic ○ *totally gaga over his girlfriend* [Early 20C. < French, an imitation of the sound of mumbling]

ga·ga·ku /gaa gaá koo/ *n* an ancient form of Japanese classical music played at the imperial court and on ceremonial occasions [Early 20C. < Japanese]

Ga·ga·rin /gə gaárin/, **Yuri** (1934–68) Soviet cosmonaut. He became the first person to be launched into space when he orbited Earth in *Vostok I* on April 12, 1961. Full name **Gagarin, Yuri Alekseyevich**

> "I don't see any God up here."
> [Yuri Gagarin, *speaking from orbit*; 1961]

Ga·gauz /gə gáwz/ (*plural same* or **-gau·zi** /-zeè/) *n* **1.** a Turkic language spoken in an area north of the

AKG London

Yuri Gagarin

Black Sea, especially in southern Moldova, Ukraine, and Romania. Native speakers: 150,000. **2.** *also* **Ga·gau·zi·an** /gə gáwzee ən/ a member of a Turkic people who live in southwestern Moldova —**Ga·gauz** *adj*

gag-bit *n* a strong bit sometimes used to help control an unruly horse

gage[1] /gayj/ (*archaic*) *n* **1.** **PLEDGE** something that is given or left as security until a debt is paid or an obligation is fulfilled **2.** **TOKEN OF CHALLENGE** a glove or other object that is thrown down or offered as a challenge to fight **3.** **CHALLENGE** a challenge to fight ■ *vt* (**gaged, gag·ing, gag·es**) **1.** **OFFER SOMETHING AS SECURITY** to offer something as security against a debt or other obligation **2.** **OFFER SOMETHING AS STAKE** to offer something as a stake in a bet [13C. < Old French < Germanic]

gage[2] /gayj/ *n, vt* another spelling of **gauge**

Gage /gayj/, **Thomas** (1721–87) British-born army general and colonial administrator. He commanded British forces in North America (1763–72), and his actions as governor of Massachusetts colony (1774–76) helped precipitate the American Revolution.

gag·er *n* COMM another spelling of **gauger**

gag·ger /gággər/ *n* a piece of metal used to wedge the core of a casting mold in position

gag·ging or·der *n* UK LAW same as **gag order**

gag·gle /gágg'l/ *n* **1.** a flock of geese **2.** a group of people, especially a noisy or disorderly group ○ *a gaggle of children* [14C. Origin ?]

gag·man /gág màn/ (*plural* **-men** /-mèn/) *n* ARTS same as **gagster** (sense 1) (*informal*)

gag or·der /gágging-/ *n* a court order that forbids any public commentary or media reporting on a case that is currently being heard in court

gag rule *n* a rule in a legislative body that limits or prevents discussion or debate on a particular issue

gag·ster /gágstər/ *n* (*informal*) **1.** a writer or teller of jokes **2.** a trickster or practical joker

gahn·ite /gaá nìt/ *n* a dark green mineral consisting of zinc aluminum oxide [Early 19C. After J. G. *Gahn* (1745–1818), Swedish chemist]

GAI *abbr* FIN guaranteed annual income

Gai·a /gí ə/, **Gae·a** /jeé ə/ *n* in Greek mythology, the personification of the Earth

gai·e·ty /gáy ətee/ (*plural* **gai·e·ties** or **gay·e·ties**) *n* **1.** **JOYFULNESS** a lighthearted and lively feeling or way of behaving **2.** **SPIRITED ACTIVITY** joyful and lively activity or festivity **3.** **BRIGHT APPEARANCE** the showiness or bright colorful appearance of something such as clothing (*dated*) [Mid-17C. < Old French *gaieté* < *gai* "happy"]

gai·jin /gí jin/ (*plural same*) *n* a foreigner in Japan or among Japanese people [Mid-20C. < Japanese]

gai·ly /gáylee/ *adv* **1.** in a happy, cheerful, or carefree manner **2.** brightly or colorfully (*dated*)

gain[1] /gayn/ *v* (**gained, gain·ing, gains**) **1.** *vt* **ACQUIRE SOMETHING** to obtain something or the benefit of something through effort, skill, or merit ○ *gain recognition as an actor* ○ *gained access to heads of state* **2.** *vti* **BECOME GREATER** to grow or increase or acquire more of something ○ *She was steadily gaining in confidence.* **3.** *vi* **PROFIT** to derive personal advantage from something ○ *No one stands to gain from the deal.* **4.** *vt* **EARN SOMETHING** to earn money or other compensation for work ○ *gain a living* ○ *apply for an internship to help gain credits toward a degree* **5.** *vi* **GET CLOSER OR FARTHER AWAY** to come closer to somebody or something pursued, or increase the distance from a pursuer ○ *They are behind but they're gaining on us.* **6.** *vt* **WIN SOMETHING BY COMPETING** to win something in competition or conflict ○ *gained second place in the dash* ○ *gain a decisive victory* **7.** *vti* **INCREASE IN OR BY SOMETHING** to come to have more of something, or increase by a particular amount ○ *The dollar had gained two points.* ○ *gain weight* **8.** *vti* TIME **RUN AHEAD OF CORRECT TIME** to run fast, or run a particular amount of time ahead of the correct time (*refers to clocks or watches*) ○ *My watch gains at least ten minutes every day.* **9.** *vt* **REACH PLACE** to arrive at a place that it was hoped to reach (*literary*) ○ *once we had finally gained the shore* ■ *n* **1. ACHIEVEMENT** an advantage or improvement that has been earned or acquired through effort ○ *despite the political gains of recent years* **2. AMOUNT INCREASED** an increase or profit of a particular amount ○ *saw a 12 point gain in the market* **3. BENEFIT** financial profit or personal advantage ○ *abused power for personal gain* **4.** ELEC ENG **MEASURE OF INCREASE IN SIGNAL STRENGTH** a ratio of the output power to the input power of an amplifier that is more than one and indicates an increase in signal strength ■ **gains** *npl* **ACQUISITIONS** something acquired, earned, or won, especially money [15C. < Old French *gaignier* < Germanic, "graze, hunt"] —**gain·a·ble** *adj*

SYNONYMS See ***get***[1].

gain[2] /gayn/ *n* **NOTCH** a notch or groove cut into a board so that another part can be fitted into it ■ *vt* (**gained, gain·ing, gains**) **1. CUT NOTCH** to cut a notch or groove into a board so that another part can be fitted into it **2. FIT PART IN NOTCH** to fit a part into a gain or connect parts using a gain [Mid-19C. Origin ?]

gain·er /gáynər/ *n* **1. SOMEBODY GAINING** somebody who or something that gains **2.** FIN **RISING STOCK** a stock that increases in value during a trading period **3. DIVE** a dive in which the diver jumps forward, does a back somersault in the air, and enters the water feet first, facing away from the board

Gaines·ville /gáynz vìl, -vəl/ **1.** city and county seat of Alachua County, northern Florida, southwest of Jacksonville. Population: 95,177 (2002 estimate). **2.** city and county seat of Hall County, north central Georgia, northeast of Atlanta. Population: 27,968 (2002 estimate).

gain·ful /gáynf'l/ *adj* bringing profit or advantage ○ *gainful employment* —**gain·ful·ly** *adv* —**gain·ful·ness** *n*

gain·say /gayn sáy, gáyn sày/ (**gain·said** /gayn sáyd, gáyn sàyd, gayn séd/, **gain·say·ing, gain·says** /gayn sáyz, gáyn sàyz, gayn séz/) *vt* (*formal*) **1.** to say that something is false **2.** to oppose or contradict somebody ○ *I won't gainsay you.* [14C. < Old English *gegn* "against" < Germanic] —**gain·say·er** *n*

Gains·bor·ough /gáynz bùr ō, -bərə/, **Thomas** (1727–88) British painter. He painted society portraits and English landscapes including *The Watering Place* (1777).

'gainst /gaynst/, **gainst** *prep* against (*literary*) [Late 16C. Shortening]

Gaird·ner, Lake /gérdnər/ dry salt lake in south central South Australia, about 240 mi./385 km northwest of Adelaide. Area: 1,900 sq. mi./4,800 sq. km.

gait /gayt/ *n* **1. MANNER OF WALKING** a way of walking, running, or moving along on foot ○ *his familiar unsteady gait* **2. PATTERN OF HORSE'S STEPS** any of the four paces of a horse, namely walk, trot, canter, and gallop, each having a specific pattern of leg movements **3. SPEED OF PROGRESS** the speed at which something moves or progresses ○ *Work proceeded at a steady gait.* [15C. Variant of GATE "way, street"]

SPELLCHECK gait or **gate**? Do not confuse the spelling of ***gait*** and ***gate***, which sound similar. ***Gait*** is only used as a noun, denoting a manner of moving on foot, as in *a horse's gait.* ***Gate*** is chiefly used as a noun, denoting a movable barrier (as in *close the gate*), an arrival or departure point at an airport, etc., but it can also be a verb, meaning "control with a gate" or "install a gate in."

-gaited *suffix* with a particular way of walking ○ *slow-gaited*

gai·ter /gáytər/ *n* (*usually used in the plural*) **1. LEG COVERING** a strip of fabric, leather, or waterproof material covering the leg from the instep to either the ankle or the knee. Modern gaiters are usually made of waterproof fabric and are worn by climbers, walkers, and skiers. **2. ELASTICIZED SHOE** an ankle-high shoe with elastic at the sides and no laces **3. OVERSHOE** an overshoe with a fabric top [Early 18C. < French *guêtre*] —**gai·tered** *adj*

Gai·thers·burg /gáythərz bùrg/ city in central Maryland, northwest of Rockville and Washington, D.C. Population: 56,300 (2002 estimate).

gal[1] /gal/ *n* a girl or woman (*informal; sometimes considered offensive*) [Late 18C. Reproducing a pronunciation of GIRL]

gal[2] /gal/ *n* a unit of acceleration in the centimeter-gram-second system equal to 1 cm per second per second. It is primarily used in gravitational field and geodetic measurements. [Early 20C. Shortening of GALILEO]

GAL *abbr* ONLINE get a life (*used in e-mails or text messages*)

gal. *abbr* MEASURE gallon

Gal. *abbr* BIBLE Galatians

ga·la /gáylə, gáalə/ *n* **1.** a special festive occasion that typically includes food and entertainment **2.** *UK* a sporting event, especially a swimming contest, with a variety of different races and competitions ○ *a swimming gala* [Early 17C. Via Old French *gale* "merrymaking" < Arabic *khil'a* "fine garment given as a present, festive attire, festive occasion"]

galact- *prefix* same as **galacto-** (*used before vowels*)

ga·lac·ta·gogue /gə láktə gòg/ *adj* causing the production and secretion of milk ■ *n* an agent that stimulates the production and flow of breast milk [< GALACT- + Greek *agōgos* "leading" < *agein* "to lead"]

ga·lac·tic /gə láktik/ *adj* **1.** relating or belonging to a galaxy, especially the Milky Way **2.** of immense or enormous size or quantity (*informal*) [Mid-19C. < Greek *galakt-* (see GALAXY)] —**ga·lac·ti·cal·ly** *adv*

ga·lac·tic e·qua·tor, ga·lac·tic cir·cle *n* the imaginary circle on the sky formed by extending the plane that passes through the center of the Milky Way. It is inclined at approximately 62° to the celestial equator.

ga·lac·tic ha·lo *n* the large region of space surrounding the Milky Way, enclosing the main spiral arms, older fainter stars and globular clusters, and the outer regions of the galactic magnetic field

galacto- *prefix* milk ○ *galactosemia* [< Greek *galakt-* (see GALAXY)]

ga·lac·to·poi·e·sis /gə làktō póy əssiss/ *n* the production of milk by the cells of the glandular structure of the breast

ga·lac·to·poi·et·ic /gə làktə poy éttik/ *adj* stimulating lactation

ga·lac·tor·rhe·a /gə làktə rée ə/ *n* excessive milk flow during lactation, or spontaneous milk flow in the absence of childbirth and nursing

ga·lac·tor·rhoe·a *n* MED UK spelling of **galactorrhea**

gal·ac·tos·am·ine /gə làk tóssə meen, gàllək-/ *n* an amino derivative of galactose, found in cartilage

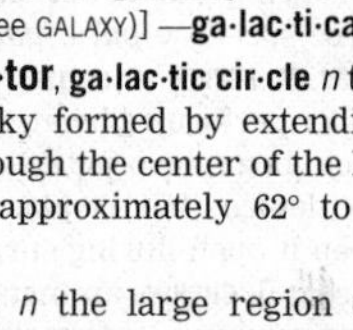

galactose

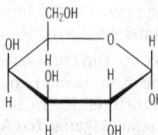

ga·lac·tose /gə lák tòss, -tòz/ *n* a six-carbon sugar that is a constituent of lactose Formula: $C_6H_{12}O_6$.

ga·lac·to·se·mi·a /gə làk tō séemee ə/ *n* a genetic disorder causing the absence of an enzyme necessary for the breakdown of galactose in milk to glucose

ga·lac·to·si·dase /gə làktə sī dàyss, -dàyz/ *n* an enzyme that breaks down lactose

ga·lac·to·side /gə láktə sīd/ *n* a compound made up of galactose combined with another sugar or a nonsugar

ga·la·go /gə láy gō/ (*plural* **-gos**) *n* ZOOL same as **bush baby** [Mid-19C. < modern Latin]

ga·lah /gə laá/ *n* a common cockatoo with a gray back and wings, a pink breast and head, and a pale pink crest. Native to: Australia. Latin name: *Eulophus roseicapillus.* [Mid-19C. < an Aboriginal language]

Gal·a·had /gállə hàd/ *n* **1.** in Arthurian legend, the noblest knight of the Round Table, who succeeded in his quest for the Holy Grail **2.** a man considered to be chivalrous, noble, or pure in actions or attitudes

ga·lan·gal /gə láng g'l/ *n* **1.** the pungent underground stem of a ginger plant, sold fresh or dried and ground. Use: cookery, medicine. **2.** a plant of the ginger family grown for its edible underground stem. Native to: eastern Asia. Latin name: *Alpinia officinarum.* **3.** PLANTS same as **galingale** [Pre-12C. Via Old French *galingal* < Arabic *kalanjān*]

gal·an·tine /gállən téen/ *n* a dish of boned and cooked white meat, poultry, or fish, usually stuffed, molded into shape, and served cold in its own jelly [14C. Via Old French < medieval Latin *galatina*]

ga·lan·ty show /gə lántee-/ *n* a play performed by manipulating paper figures and casting their shadows on a screen [Origin ?]

Ga·la·pa·gos gi·ant tor·toise /gə laápə gòss-, -laápəgəss-/, **Ga·la·pa·gos tor·toise** *n* a giant tortoise that is native to the Galápagos Islands. It grows up to 4 ft./1.2 m long and weighs up to 500 lb./225 kg. Latin name: *Geochelone elephantopus.*

Galapagos Islands

Ga·la·pa·gos Is·lands /gə laápə gòss-, -laápəgəss-/, **Ga·lá·pa·gos Is·lands** group of islands in the Pacific Ocean approximately 650 mi./1,050 km west of Ecuador. They are known for harboring unique species of wildlife, especially the giant tortoise. Population: 9,785 (1990). Area: 3,075 sq. mi./7,964 sq. km.

Ga·la·pa·gos tor·toise *n* REPT same as **Galapagos giant tortoise**

gal·a·te·a /gàllə tée ə/ *n* a strong cotton fabric with a twill weave that is often striped. Use: clothes. [Late 19C. After HMS *Galatea*; originally used for children's sailor suits]

Gal·a·te·a /gàllə tée ə/ *n* a small inner natural satellite of Neptune, discovered in 1989 by the spacecraft Voyager 2. It is approximately 95 mi./150 km in diameter.

Ga·la·ţi /gaa laáts, -laátsee/ inland port in Romania, situated on the Danube River, northeast of Bucharest. Population: 641,647 (1997).

Ga·la·tians /gə láysh'nz/ *n* a book of the Bible, originally a letter addressed to the people of Galatia and traditionally attributed to St. Paul. (*takes a* *singular verb*) See table at **Bible** [Early 17C. < *Galatia*, ancient country of central Asia Minor]

ga·lax /gáy làks/ *n* an evergreen plant of the southeastern United States with glossy leaves and white berries. Genus: *Galax*.

gal·ax·y /gálləksee/ (*plural* **-ies**) *n* **1.** a group of billions of stars and their planets, gas, and dust that extends over many thousands of light-years and forms a unit within the universe. Held together by gravitational forces, most of the estimated 50 billion galaxies are shaped as spirals and ellipses, with the remainder being asymmetric. **2.** a gathering of famous, brilliant, or distinguished people or things [14C. Via Old French < Greek *galaxias (kuklos)* "milky (circle)" < *galakt-*, stem of *gala* "milk"]

Gal·ax·y /gálləksee/ *n* ASTRON same as **Milky Way**

gal·ba·num /gálbənəm/ *n* a yellowish to green or brown aromatic bitter gum resin derived from several related Asian plants. Use: incense, medicinally as a counterirritant. Genus: *Ferula*. [12C. Via Latin < Greek *khalbanē* < Semitic]

Gal·braith /gál bràyth/, **John Kenneth** (*b.* 1908) Canadian-born US economist. Long a professor at Harvard, he published numerous scholarly and popular works such as *The Affluent Society* (1958) that examined the political ramifications of economics. See Cultural note at **affluent**

> "Politics is not the art of the possible. It consists in choosing between the disastrous and the unpalatable."
> [John Kenneth Galbraith, *Ambassador's Journal*; 1969]

> "The salary of the chief executive of the large corporation is not a market reward for achievement. It is frequently in the nature of a warm personal gesture by the individual to himself."
> [John Kenneth Galbraith, *Annals of an Abiding Liberal*; 1979]

gale /gayl/ *n* **1.** an extremely strong wind that measures 8 or 9 on the Beaufort scale and has a speed of between 39 mi./63 km and 54 mi./87 km per hour **2.** a very strong wind [Mid-16C. Origin ?]

ga·le·a /gáylee ə/ (*plural* **-ae** /-ee/) *n* a part or organ shaped like a helmet, e.g., the upper petal of some flowers or one of the mouthparts of an insect [Mid-19C. < Latin, "helmet"] —**ga·le·ate** *adj*

gale-force *adj* describes air currents that measure between 7 and 10 on the Beaufort scale and have a speed of between 32 and 63 mi./51 and 102 km per hour ○ *a gale-force wind*

Ga·len /gáylən/ (129–99?) Greek physician and scholar. His anatomical studies formed the basis of European medical practice for 1,400 years.

> "That physician will hardly be thought very careful of the health of others who neglects his own."
> [Galen, *Of Protecting the Health*; 2nd century]

ga·le·na /gə leénə/ *n* a lustrous blue-gray crystalline mineral consisting of lead sulfide. Use: source of lead and silver. [Late 17C. < Latin, "lead at a certain stage of smelting"]

ga·len·i·cal /gə leénik'l/ *n* any medicinal preparation made from plant or animal tissue ■ *adj* made from plant or animal tissue rather than synthesized [Mid-17C. < GALEN]

ga·len·ite /gə leé nīt/ *n* MINERALS same as **galena**

ga·lère /gə lér/ *n* **1.** a group of people with a particular attribute or interest, especially something undesirable, in common **2.** an unpleasant predicament [Mid-18C. Via French, "galley" < Catalan *galera* < Middle Greek *galea*]

Gales·burg /gáylz bùrg/ city in northwestern Illinois, south of Moline and northwest of Peoria. Population: 33,237 (2002 estimate).

Ga·li·bi /gə leébee/ (*plural same* or **-bis** /-beez/) *n* **1.** a member of an indigenous South American people who live in French Guiana **2.** a Carib language spoken in French Guiana. Galibi is spoken by fewer than a thousand people. [Late 19C. < Carib, "strong man"] —**Ga·li·bi** *adj*

Ga·li·cia /gə líshə, -líshee ə/ **1.** autonomous region and former kingdom in northwestern Spain. It contains the provinces of La Coruña, Lugo, Orense, and Pontevedra. Capital: Santiago de Compostela. Population: 2,731,669 (1991). Area: 9,464 sq. mi./29,434 sq. km. **2.** historic region in eastern Europe. A former principality, it has belonged to Poland and Austria, and is now divided between southeastern Poland and western Ukraine. —**Ga·li·cian** *adj*

Gal·i·le·an[1] /gàllə leé ən/, **Gal·i·lae·an** *n* **1.** somebody who comes from Galilee **2.** same as **Christian** (*archaic*) [Mid-16C. < Latin *Galilea* "Galilee"] —**Gal·i·le·an** *adj*

Gal·i·le·an[2] /gàllə leé ən/ *adj* relating to the Italian scientist Galileo, his theories, or his inventions [Early 18C. < GALILEO]

gal·i·lee /gállə leè/ *n* a small porch or chapel found at the western end of some medieval churches or cathedrals [15C. Via Old French < medieval Latin *galilea*, after Latin *Galilea* "Galilee"]

Gal·i·lee /gállə leè/ region of ancient Palestine, Now part of northern Israel, situated between the Jordan River and the Sea of Galilee. It was the scene of Jesus Christ's ministry.

Gal·i·lee, Sea of freshwater lake on the Jordan River in northeastern Israel. It is 686 ft./209 m below sea level. Area: 64 sq. mi./166 sq. km.

Galileo: portrait drawing by Guido Reni

Ga·li·le·o /gàllə leé ō, -láy ō/ (1564–1642) Italian physicist and astronomer. One of the founders of Europe's scientific revolution, his main contributions include the application of the telescope to astronomy and the discovery of the laws of falling bodies and the motions of projectiles. Born **Galilei, Galileo**

> "In my studies of astronomy and philosophy I hold this opinion about the universe, that the Sun remains fixed in the center of the circle of heavenly bodies, without changing its place; and the Earth, turning upon itself, moves around the Sun."
> [Galileo, *Letter to Cristina di Lorena, Grandduchess of Tuscany*; 1615]

gal·in·gale /gállin gàyl/ *n* a plant of the sedge family with aromatic roots. Flowers: reddish, growing in a cluster directly from the stem. Latin name: *Cyperus longus*. [Variant of GALANGAL]

gal·i·ot /gállee ət, -òt/, **gal·li·ot** *n* **1.** formerly, a light fast ship propelled by sails and oars used in the Mediterranean **2.** formerly, a light shallow single-masted Dutch merchant ship [15C. < Old French, "little galley" < medieval Latin *galea* "galley"]

gal·i·pot /gálli pòt/ *n* crude turpentine in resin form. Source: several southern European pine species. [Late 18C. Via French < Provençal *garapot* "pine resin"]

gall[1] /gawl/ *n* **1.** impudent boldness ○ *And then he had the gall to tell us to leave!* **2.** a feeling of bitterness or resentment (*literary*) **3.** BIOL same as **bile** (sense 1) (*archaic*) [12C. < Old Norse *gall* "bile" < Germanic, "yellow"]

gall[2] /gawl/ *n* **1.** SORE CAUSED BY RUBBING a sore on the skin of an animal that is caused by friction **2.** CAUSE OF ANGER something that angers or irritates somebody (*dated*) **3.** ANGER a feeling of annoyance or anger (*dated*) ■ *vt* (**galled, gall·ing, galls**) **1.** MAKE SOMEBODY ANGRY to make somebody extremely angry **2.** VET CAUSE FRICTION SORE ON to cause a sore on the skin by rubbing [14C. < Middle Low German *galle* "sore"]

gall[3] /gawl/ *n* a swelling on a tree or plant caused by insects, fungi, bacteria, or external damage [14C. Via Old French < Latin *galla* "oak gall"]

Gall /gawl/ (1840?–94) Hunkpapa Sioux leader. He led many attacks against US forces, but after surrendering in 1881, he encouraged his people to accept assimilation.

Gal·la /gállə/ *n, adj* LANG, PEOPLES same as **Oromo** [Late 19C. Origin ?]

gal·la·mine /gállə meèn/ *n* a short-acting but powerful muscle relaxant. Use: general anesthesia. [Late 19C. < *Gallic* (< GALLIUM) + AMINE]

gal·lant *adj* /gə lánt, -laánt/ **1.** COURTEOUS courteous and thoughtful, especially toward women **2.** BRAVE brave, spirited, and honorable (*literary*) **3.** MAJESTIC grand and majestic (*archaic*) ■ *n* /gə lánt, -laánt, gállənt/ **1.** MAN COURTEOUS TO WOMEN a man who is courteous and thoughtful in his behavior toward women (*dated*) **2.** MALE LOVER a man who is a woman's lover (*archaic*) **3.** DANDY a fashionable young man (*archaic*) ■ *vti* /gə lánt, -laánt/ (**-lant·ed, -lant·ing, -lants**) WOO to court a woman (*archaic*) [14C. < Old French, present participle of *galer* "make merry"] —**gal·lant·ly** *adv*

Gal·lant /gə lánt/, **Mavis** (*b.* 1922) Canadian writer. She is known for her incisively written short stories, collected in volumes such as *Home Truths* (1981). Born **Young, Mavis**

gal·lant·ry /gálləntree/ (*plural* **-ries**) *n* **1.** COURAGE bravery, especially in war or in a situation of great danger **2.** COURTESY courteous and thoughtful behavior, especially toward women **3.** SOMETHING GALLANT SAID OR DONE a courageous or chivalrous action or remark (*dated*)

Gal·la·tin /gállət'n/ river that rises in northwestern Wyoming and flows northward into Montana, where it joins the Jefferson and Madison rivers to form the Missouri River. Length: 125 mi./201 km.

Gal·la·tin /gállətin/, **Albert** (1761–1849) Swiss-born US politician. As secretary of the treasury (1801–14) he reduced the public debt and oversaw the Louisiana Purchase (1803). Full name **Gallatin, Abraham Alfonse Albert**

Gal·lau·det /gàllə dét/, **Thomas** (1787–1851) US educator. He founded the first free school for hearing-impaired people in the United States, in Hartford, Connecticut (1817). Full name **Gallaudet, Thomas Hopkins**

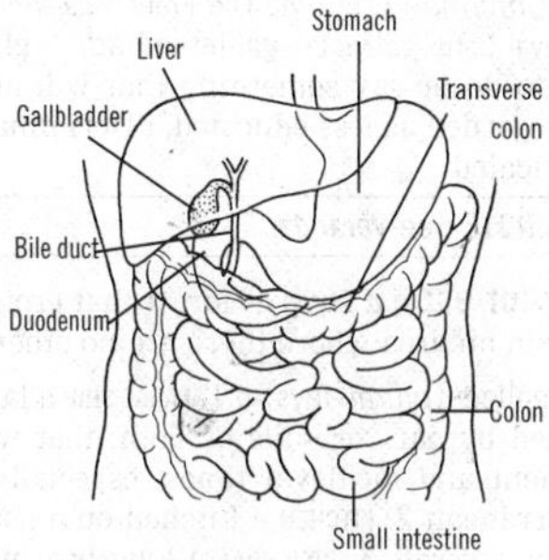

gallbladder

gall·blad·der /gáwl blàddər/ *n* a small muscular sac on the right underside of the liver, in which bile secreted by the liver is stored and concentrated until needed for the digestive process

Gal·le /gaálə/ port on the southwestern coast of Sri Lanka. Population: 84,000 (1990 estimate).

gal·le·ass /gállee əss/, **gal·li·ass** *n* a large fast warship with three masts, used in the Mediterranean in the 16th and 17th centuries [Mid-16C. Via Old French < Old Italian *galeaza* "large galley"]

gal·le·on /gállee ən/ *n* a large three-masted sailing ship used especially by the Spanish between the 15th and 18th centuries. See illustration on next page [Early 16C. Either via Middle Dutch *galjoen* < Old French *galion* "large galley," or < Spanish *galeón*]

gal·le·ri·a /gàllə rée ə/ *n* a roofed court with shops or businesses opening onto it, usually at several levels [Late 19C. < Italian]

galleon

gal·ler·y /gálləree/ *n* (*plural* **-ies**) **1.** PLACE FOR ART EXHIBITIONS a place where artwork is exhibited and sometimes sold **2.** STUDIO a photographer's studio **3.** BALCONY a balcony or passage running along the wall of a large building **4.** ENCLOSED WALKWAY a corridor, hall, or other enclosed passageway inside a building **5.** LONG NARROW ROOM a long narrow space or room used for a particular purpose **6.** COVERED WALKWAY a long covered passageway that is open on one or both sides **7.** *Can, Southern US* VERANDA an open-roofed porch or veranda that runs along the side of a house **8.** *Carib* FRONT PORCH a porch on the front of a house **9.** UNDERGROUND PASSAGE an underground tunnel or passage, especially one made by an animal or one that is part of a mine or a military site **10.** PART OF THEATER a seating area projecting from the back and sides out over the main floor of a theater or auditorium, especially the highest section of this area containing the cheapest seats **11.** SEATS IN GALLERY the seats located in the gallery of a theater or auditorium **12.** AUDIENCE IN CHEAPEST SEATS the people who sit in the gallery of a theater **13.** OFFENSIVE TERM an offensive term applied to the general public, viewed as having no discrimination or sophistication **14.** SPECTATORS a group of spectators, especially at a tennis or golf match **15.** STAGE RIG a narrow platform above a stage from which technicians can adjust lights, move props, or operate machinery **16.** ASSORTED COLLECTION a varied collection of people or things ○ *a gallery of famous names* **17.** SHIP'S BALCONY a platform or balcony at the rear of a ship **18.** DECORATIVE RAIL a decorative metal or wooden rail on a table top, shelf, or tray ■ *vi Carib* SHOW OFF OR BOAST to show off or flaunt possessions or status (*informal*) [15C. Via Old French *galerie* "portico" < medieval Latin *galeria*] —**gal·ler·ied** *adj* ◇ **play to the gallery** to do or say something that will appeal to those regarded as less educated, discriminating, or sophisticated

REGIONAL NOTE See *veranda*.

gal·ler·y for·est *n* a strip of forest that grows along a river in an area where there are no other trees

gal·ley /gállee/ (*plural* **-leys**) *n* **1.** LARGE SHIP a large ship propelled by oars or sails or both, that was used in ancient and medieval times, especially in the Mediterranean **2.** KITCHEN a kitchen on a boat, ship, train, or aircraft **3.** ROW BOAT a long boat propelled by oars, especially in England **4.** PRINT TRAY a long metal tray used for holding type that is ready for printing **5.** PRINTING same as **galley proof** [13C. Via Old French and medieval Latin < medieval Greek *galea*]

gal·ley proof *n* a first test copy of printed material, usually not divided into pages, on which corrections are marked

gal·ley slave *n* **1.** formerly, one of a team of convicts or slaves forced to row a galley **2.** somebody who is given menial tasks to do (*dated humorous*)

gal·ley-west *adv* into a state of disorder, confusion, or destruction (*archaic slang*) ○ *"Then she grabbed up the basket and slammed it across the house and knocked the cat galley-west"* (Mark Twain, *The Adventures of Huckleberry Finn*; 1884) [Late 19C. Alteration of *Colly-west* "awry" < *Collyweston*, village in Northamptonshire, England]

gall·fly /gáwl flī/ (*plural* **-flies**) *n* an insect that causes swellings (**galls**) on plants when it deposits its eggs on them, e.g., the gall midge or gall wasp

gal·liard /gállyərd/ *n* **1.** a lively European dance in triple time, popular in the 16th and 17th centuries **2.** the music for a galliard, written in triple time, part of the baroque dance suite [14C. < Old French]

gal·li·ass /gállee əss/ *n* another spelling of **galleass**

Gal·lic /gállik/ *adj* **1.** relating to France, or its language, people, or culture **2.** relating to ancient Gaul or the Gauls [Late 17C. < Latin *Gallia* "Gaul"]

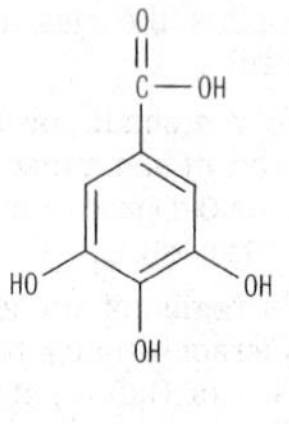

gallic acid

gal·lic ac·id /gàllik-/ *n* a colorless crystalline solid. Source: plants, tannin. Use: tanning agent, manufacture of inks and paper, in photography. Formula: $C_7H_6O_5$. [< Latin *galla* "oak apple" (used in making the acid)]

Gal·li·can·ism /gállikə nìzzəm/ *n* a French movement in favor of giving more autonomy to the Roman Catholic Church in individual countries and reducing the authority of the pope —**Gal·li·can** *adj, n*

Gal·li·cism /gálli sìzzəm/ *n* **1.** a word or phrase of French origin used in another language **2.** a characteristic of the French

Gal·li·cize /gálli sīz/ (**-cized, -ciz·ing, -ciz·es**) *vti* to become French or like something French, or make something such as a word, custom, or characteristic French —**Gal·li·ci·za·tion** /gàllissi záysh'n/ *n*

Gal·lienne ♦ **Le Gallienne, Eva**

gal·li·gas·kins /gàlli gáskinz/ *npl* loose-fitting breeches or stockings that were worn by men in the 16th and 17th centuries [Late 16C. Origin ?]

gal·li·mau·fry /gàlli máwffree/ (*plural* **-fries**) *n* a jumble of various things or people [Mid-16C. < French *galimafrée*]

gall·ing /gáwling/ *adj* having the effect of frustrating and annoying somebody —**gall·ing·ly** *adv*

gal·li·nip·per /gállə nìppər/ *n regional* a large mosquito or fly that bites people or animals (*humorous*) [Late 17C. Origin ?]

gal·li·nule /gállə no͞ol/ *n* a bird that both wades and swims and typically has dark feathers and a yellow-tipped red beak with a red shield above it. Native to: swampy regions. Family: Rallidae. [Late 18C. < modern Latin *gallinula* "little hen"]

gal·li·ot *n* another spelling of **galiot**

Gal·lip·o·li /gə líppəlee/ peninsula in European Turkey, extending into the Dardanelles, and including an important seaport of the same name. It has historically been of great strategic importance to Istanbul. The peninsula was the site of a major World War I campaign in 1915, when Allied troops, including many from Australia and New Zealand, failed to take control of the Dardanelles.

gal·li·pot /gállə pòt/ *n* a small pot used by pharmacists as a container for medications [15C. Probably < GALLEY, because galleys brought such goods from the Mediterranean]

gal·li·um /gállee əm/ *n* a rare metallic element, blue-gray when solid and silver when liquid. Source: coal, bauxite. Use: high-temperature thermometers, semiconductors, alloys. Symbol **Ga**. See table at **element** [Late 19C. < Latin *Gallia* "France"]

gal·li·um ar·se·nide *n* a dark gray crystalline solid containing gallium and arsenic. Use: manufacture of semiconductors, solar cells, lasers. Formula: GaAs.

gal·li·vant /gállə vànt/ (**-vant·ed, -vant·ing, -vants**) *vi* (*informal*) **1.** to travel around with no purpose except enjoyment **2.** to flirt or play romantically [Early 19C. Origin ?]

gal·li·wasp /gállə wàwsp/ *n* a lizard with a long body that is related to the slowworm. Native to: marshes of Central America and the Caribbean. Family: Anguidae. [Late 17C. Origin ?]

gall midge *n* a small fly resembling a mosquito whose larvae cause swellings (**galls**) on plants. Family: Cecidomyidae.

gall mite *n* a mite that causes swellings (**galls**) on the fruits, leaves, or buds of plants. Family: Phytoptidae.

gall·nut /gáwl nùt/ *n* a small round swelling (**gall**) on a plant

gal·lo·glass /gállō glàss/, **gal·low·glass** *n* a medieval mercenary soldier or armed servant of a Celtic chieftain, especially in Ireland [15C. < Irish *gallóglach* "young foreign servant, warrior"]

gal·lon /gállən/ *n* **1.** US UNIT OF VOLUME a unit of capacity in the US customary system equal to eight US pints (approximately 3.79 liters) **2.** *UK* BRITISH UNIT OF VOLUME a unit of capacity in the British imperial system equal to eight British imperial pints (approximately 4.55 liters) ■ *adj* HOLDING GALLON with a capacity of one gallon ○ *a gallon jar* [13C. < Anglo-Norman *galon* < medieval Latin *galleta* "jug"]

gal·lon·age /gállənij/ *n* **1.** a capacity or amount measured in gallons **2.** the rate at which a liquid is used, pumped, or transmitted, measured in gallons per second, minute, or hour

gal·loon /gə lo͞on/ *n* a narrow band of embroidery, lace, braid, or silver or gold thread, used as a trimming on clothes or upholstery [Early 17C. < French *galon* < *galonner* "trim with braid"] —**gal·looned** *adj*

gal·loot *n* another spelling of **galoot** (*slang insult*)

gal·lop /gálləp/ *n* **1.** FASTEST PACE OF HORSE the fastest pace of a horse, in which all four feet are off the ground at the same time **2.** FAST PACE OF FOUR-LEGGED ANIMAL a fast movement similar to a horse's gallop made by any four-legged animal **3.** FAST RIDE ON HORSE a ride on a horse at a gallop ■ *v* (**-loped, -lop·ing, -lops**) **1.** *vti* RIDE HORSE FAST to ride a horse at a gallop **2.** *vi* DO SOMETHING VERY FAST to do something in a great hurry ○ *gallop through lunch* **3.** *vt* MOVE SOMETHING QUICKLY to move or transport something at a gallop or at a very fast pace [Early 16C. < Old French *galoper*, variant of *waloper* < Germanic] —**gal·lop·er** *n*

gal·lo·pade /gállə pàyd, -pàad, gàllə pàad/ *n* DANCE, MUSIC same as **galop** [Mid-18C. < French *galopade* < *galoper* (see GALLOP)]

gal·lop·ing /gáləping/ *adj* **1.** proceeding or developing at a very fast rate ○ *galloping pneumonia* **2.** resembling a gallop in speed or rhythm

Gal·lo-Ro·mance /gàllō-/, **Gal·lo-Ro·man** *n* a group of dialects spoken in France between the 7th and the 10th centuries. It constitutes an intermediate developmental stage between the end of Vulgar Latin and the appearance of Old French. —**Gal·lo-Ro·mance** *adj*

Gal·lo·way /gállə wày/ region on the Solway Firth in southwestern Scotland —**Gal·lo·vid·i·an** /gàllə víddee ən/ *adj, n*

gal·low·glass *n* HIST another spelling of **galloglass**

gal·lows /gállōz/ (*plural same*) *n* **1.** FRAME FOR HANGING CRIMINALS a wooden frame, usually made of two upright posts and a crossbeam with a noose attached, used to execute people by hanging **2.** STRUCTURE LIKE GALLOWS a structure that resembles a gallows, e.g., one used to suspend slaughtered animals **3.** EXECUTION BY HANGING death by hanging as capital punishment for a criminal offense [13C. < Old Norse *gálgi* < Germanic, "pole"]

gal·lows bird *n* somebody who is regarded as deserving to be hanged (*archaic informal*)

gal·lows hu·mor *n* macabre humor that finds irony or comedy in serious matters such as death

gal·lows tree *n* CRIME same as **gallows** (sense 1)

gall·stone /gáwl stōn/ *n* a small hard mass that forms in the gallbladder, sometimes as a result of infection or blockage. Gallstones consist mainly of cholesterol, bile pigments, and calcium salts.

Gal·lup /gálləp/ city in northwestern New Mexico, near the Arizona border. It is located in a coal and uranium mining region, and is an important Navajo and Zuñi trading center. Population: 20,177 (2002 estimate).

Gal·lup, George (1901–84) US public opinion analyst and statistician. A pioneer in the use of statistical methods for determining public opinion on social, economic, and political issues, he is best known for founding the Gallup Poll (1935). Full name **Gallup, George Horace**

> "I could prove God statistically."
> [Attributed to George Gallup]

Gal·lup Poll *n* a survey in which a sample of people taken as a representative cross section of society are asked their opinions on a specific subject

gal·lus·es /gáləssəz/ *npl N Am, Scotland* suspenders for pants [Mid-19C. Plural of *gallus*, alteration of GALLOWS; from the two supports]

gall wasp *n* a wasp that lays its eggs in plant tissue, causing swellings (**galls**). Family: Cynipidae.

ga·loot /gə lóot/, **gal·loot** *n* somebody regarded as clumsy or thoughtless (*slang insult*) [Early 19C. Origin ?]

gal·op /gálləp/ *n* **1.** a lively dance in double time that was popular in the 19th century **2.** the music for a galop, in double time [Mid-19C. < French]

ga·lore /gə láwr/ *adj* in large quantities or numbers (*used after a noun*) ○ *There'll be food galore at the party.* [Early 17C. < Irish *go leor* "sufficiency"]

ga·losh·es /gə lóshəz/ *npl* a pair of waterproof shoes, often made of rubber, worn over other shoes as protection against rain or snow [14C. Via Old French *galoche* "little sandal" < Latin *gallicula* < *Gallica (solea)* "sandal (from Gaul)"]

Gals·wor·thy /gáwlz wùrthee/, **John** (1867–1933) British novelist and playwright. His most famous work, a collection of five novels about the Edwardian and Victorian upper-middle classes entitled *The Forsyte Saga* (1922), was made into a television series in 1967 and again in 2002. See Cultural note at **saga**

> "There is just one rule for politicians all over the world. Don't say in Power what you say in Opposition: if you do you only have to carry out what the other fellows have found impossible."
> [John Galsworthy, *Maid in Waiting*; 1931]

Galt /gawlt/, **Sir Alexander Tilloch** (1817–93) British-born Canadian politician. He was a Liberal legislator and cabinet minister who helped negotiate US access to Canadian fisheries.

ga·lumph /gə lúmf/ (**-lumphed, -lumph·ing, -lumphs**) *vi* (*informal*) **1.** to walk or run in a boisterous or clumsy way **2.** to stride or march in a prancing triumphant way [Late 19C. Blend of GALLOP + TRIUMPH]

ga·luth /gaa lóot, -lóoth/ *n* the Jewish Diaspora [Late 20C. < Hebrew *gālūth* "exile"]

galv. *abbr* **1.** galvanic **2.** galvanized

Gal·va·ni /gal vaánee/, **Luigi** (1737–98) Italian physiologist. A professor of anatomy, he studied the effects of electricity on animal nerves and muscles.

gal·van·ic /gal vánnik/ *adj* **1.** relating to or involving the direct-current electricity that is chemically generated between dissimilar metals, e.g., in a battery **2.** sudden, startling, or convulsive, like an electric shock or its effects [Late 18C. < French *galvanique*, after Luigi GALVANI] —**gal·van·i·cal·ly** *adv*

gal·van·ic cell *n* ELEC ENG same as **primary cell**

gal·van·ic skin re·sponse *n* a change in the electrical conductivity of the skin caused by sweating and increased blood flow and linked to a strong emotion such as fear. Lie detector tests use this change as a way of measuring whether somebody is telling the truth.

gal·va·nism /gálvə nìzzəm/ *n* **1.** the production of direct-current electricity from a chemical reaction, e.g., between dissimilar metals in a battery **2.** the application of electricity to the human body to stimulate nerves and muscles as part of a medical treatment [Late 18C. < French *galvanisme*, after Luigi GALVANI]

gal·va·nize /gálvə nìz/ (**-nized, -niz·ing, -niz·es**) *vt* **1.** STIMULATE SOMEBODY TO ACT to stimulate somebody or something into great activity **2.** COAT METAL WITH ZINC to coat a metal, usually iron or steel, with zinc to prevent corrosion **3.** STIMULATE BODY ELECTRICALLY to stimulate the nerves or muscles of somebody's body using an electric current [Early 19C. < French *galvaniser*, after Luigi GALVANI] —**gal·va·ni·za·tion** /gàlvəni záysh'n/ *n* —**gal·va·niz·er** *n*

gal·va·nom·e·ter /gàlvə nómmətər/ *n* an instrument used to detect or measure the strength and direction of small electric currents by means of a coil in a magnetic field that moves a pointer or light —**gal·va·no·met·ric** /gàlvənə méttrik/ *adj* —**gal·va·nom·e·try** *n*

Gal·ves·ton /gálvist'n/ port and county seat of Galveston County in southeastern Texas, situated southeast of Houston on Galveston Island in Galveston Bay, an arm of the Gulf of Mexico. Population: 56,685 (2002 estimate).

Gal·way /gáwl wày/ **1.** seaport on Galway Bay and capital of Galway County, on the western coast of the Republic of Ireland. Population: 57,241 (2002). **2.** county in Connacht Province, western Republic of Ireland. Area: 2,293 sq. mi./5,939 sq. km. —**Gal·we·gian** /gal wéejən/ *adj, n*

Gal·way Bay inlet of the Atlantic Ocean on the western coast of the Republic of Ireland

gam[1] /gam/ *n* **1.** MIGRATING WHALES a group of migrating whales **2.** SOCIAL VISIT BETWEEN WHALERS a social visit between whalers or other sailors, especially while at sea (*informal*) ■ *v* (**gammed, gam·ming, gams**) (*informal*) **1.** *vi* MEET UP to meet socially, especially at sea **2.** *vt* TO CHAT WITH SOMEBODY to visit with somebody socially [Mid-19C. Origin ?]

gam[2] /gam/ *n* somebody's leg, especially a woman's (*dated slang or considered offensive*) [Late 18C. Probably alteration of *gamb* "heraldic device resembling an animal's leg" < northern form of Old French *jambe* "leg"]

Ga·ma /gámmə, gaámə/, **Vasco da** (1469?–1524) Portuguese navigator and explorer. He led the first European expedition to reach India by sailing around Africa (1497–99).

ga·ma grass /gámmə-/ *n* a tall coarse grass that is grown for fodder. Native to: North America. Latin name: *Tripsacum dactyloides*. [Mid-19C. Origin ?]

ga·may /gá mày/ *n* **1.** a fruity red wine made from a variety of black grape grown mainly in Burgundy, east central France **2.** the black grape variety used to make gamay [Mid-19C. After *Gamay*, village in Burgundy, France]

gam·ba /gámbə/ *n* MUSIC same as **viola da gamba**

gam·bade /gam báyd, -baád/ *n* RIDING same as **gambado**[2] [Early 16C. < French, probably < Italian *gambata* < *gamba* "leg"]

gam·ba·do[1] /gam báy dō, -baá-/ (*plural* **-does** or **-dos**) *n* **1.** either of a pair of protective leather holders for a rider's feet, attached to a horse's saddle **2.** either of a pair of rider's leggings [Mid-17C. < Italian *gamba* "leg" + *-ado*]

gam·ba·do[2] /gam báy dō, -baá-/ (*plural* **-does** or **-dos**) *n* **1.** LOW JUMP BY HORSE in dressage, a low leap in which the horse has all four feet off the ground **2.** LEAP a leap or caper **3.** PRANK a prank or escapade [Early 19C. < Spanish *gambada* < *gamba* "leg"]

gam·beer *n* INDUST another spelling of **gambier**

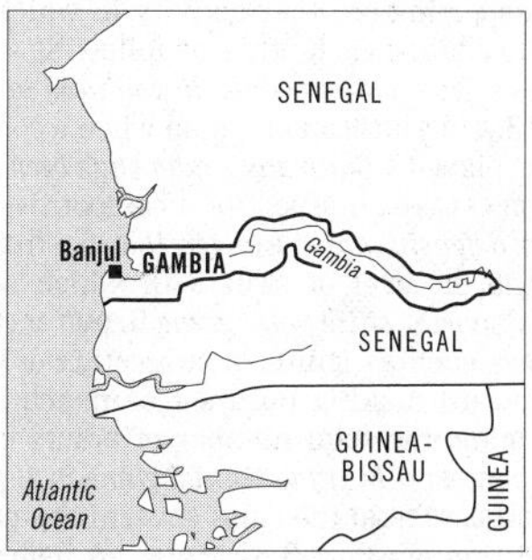

Gambia

Gam·bi·a /gámbee ə/ **1.** country on the coast of West Africa, bordered on the north, east, and south by Senegal. It became an independent member of the British Commonwealth in 1965. Language: English. Currency: dalasi. Capital: Banjul. Population: 1,501,050 (2003). Area: 4,361 sq. mi./11,295 sq. km. Official name **Republic of the Gambia 2.** river in western Africa that rises in Guinea, flows westward through the Gambia, and empties into the Atlantic Ocean near Banjul. Length: 700 mi./1,100 km. —**Gam·bi·an** *n, adj*

gam·bier /gám beer/, **gam·bir, gam·beer** *n* a resinous astringent substance. Source: leaves of a tropical Asian woody vine. Use: medicinally as an astringent or tonic, in tanning and dyeing. [Early 19C. < Malay *gambir*, the plant]

gam·bit /gámbit/ *n* **1.** STRATAGEM a maneuver or stratagem used to secure an advantage **2.** CONVERSATIONAL OPENER a remark used to open a conversation **3.** CHESS OPENING MOVE IN CHESS in chess, an opening move in which a player sacrifices a pawn or other minor piece in order to gain a strategic advantage [Mid-17C. < Italian *gambetto* "act of tripping somebody up (in wrestling)" (after French *gambit*) < *gamba* "leg"]

gam·ble /gámb'l/ *v* (**-bled, -bling, -bles**) **1.** *vi* PLAY GAMES OF CHANCE to play games such as poker or roulette that involve risking money, or bet on horse races or other events, in the hope of winning money **2.** *vt* BET MONEY to bet a sum of money on the outcome of an event or competition **3.** *vi* TAKE CHANCE ON SOMETHING to take a risk in the hope and expectation of a desired result ○ *gambling on nice weather* **4.** *vi* ENDANGER SOMETHING to behave in a way that risks harming somebody or something ○ *gambled with the success of the show* **5.** *vt* LOSE OR RISK LOSING SOMETHING to lose or risk losing something, especially money, by betting or doing something dangerous or rash ○ *She gambled her inheritance away.* ■ *n* **1.** BET a bet made in the hope of winning money **2.** RISKY ACTION an action whose outcome is uncertain and very possibly undesirable ○ *I took a gamble on them being away from home.* [Early 18C. < GAME[1] + *-le*, literally "keep on playing"] —**gam·bler** *n*

gam·bling /gámbling/ *n* the practice of playing games of chance or betting in the hope of winning money

gam·boge /gam bṓj/ *n* **1.** RESIN a gum resin obtained from various Asian trees that produces a yellow pigment **2.** YELLOW PIGMENT a yellow pigment made from gamboge resin **3.** YELLOW COLOR a strong yellow color [Mid-17C. < modern Latin *gambaugium* < *Cambodia*]

gam·bol /gámb'l/ *vi* (**-boled, -bol·ing, -bols**) to leap or skip around playfully ■ *n* an instance of leaping around playfully [Mid-16C. Alteration of GAMBADE]

gam·brel /gámbrəl/ *n* **1.** the joint of a leg of an animal, especially a horse, that corresponds to the human ankle **2.** a frame in the shape of a horse's hind leg used by butchers for hanging animal carcasses **3.** ARCHIT same as **gambrel roof** [Mid-16C. < Old N French *gamberel* < *gambier* "forked stick" < *gambe*, variant of *jambe* "leg"]

gam·brel roof *n* **1.** a two-sided roof that has two slopes on each side, the lower slope being steeper than the upper **2.** *UK* a roof with sloping ends and sides and a small gable at both ends

game[1] /gaym/ *n* **1.** SOMETHING PLAYED FOR FUN an activity that people participate in, together or on their own, for fun ○ *It's only a game!* **2.** COMPETITIVE ACTIVITY WITH

RULES a sporting or other activity in which players compete against each other by following a fixed set of rules ○ *How many people do you need to play this game?* **3.** COMPETITION an occasion when a competitive game is played ○ *Saturday's game has been canceled.* **4.** ASPECT OF GAME an aspect of a competitive activity ○ *Their defensive game was terrible.* **5.** STYLE OF PLAYING the style or level of skill with which somebody plays a sport ○ *raise your game* **6.** PART OF COMPETITION in sports such as tennis, a subsection of play that goes toward making up a set or match **7.** NUMBER NEEDED TO WIN the total number of points needed to win a contest ○ *In table tennis, game is 21 points.* **8.** RULES GOVERNING SPORT the rules governing a particular competition or sport **9.** EQUIPMENT an item or set of items that is needed to play a particular game, e.g., a board, dice, counters, a deck of cards, or a piece of computer software ○ *a compendium of games* **10.** ACTIVITY LIKE GAME an activity that resembles a game, e.g., one that involves intense interest and competitiveness and is carried out by its own specific and often unspoken rules **11.** STRATAGEM a way of behaving that is aimed at manipulating people or trying to deceive them ○ *So that's your game?* **12.** ILLEGAL ACTIVITY a strategy, activity, or behavior that is questionable, and often illegal (*informal*) **13.** OCCUPATION a business or occupation (*informal*) ○ *the advertising game* **14.** SOMETHING NOT TAKEN SERIOUSLY an activity or situation that somebody does not treat seriously ○ *Life's a game as far as he's concerned.* **15.** HUNTING ANIMALS FOR HUNTING wild animals, birds, or fish that are hunted for sport **16.** MEAT OF HUNTED ANIMALS the meat of wild animals, birds, or fish that have been killed for sport **17.** RIDICULE the act of ridiculing, criticizing, or tricking somebody for fun, or the target of such ridicule, criticism, or trickery ○ *She's easy game for a trickster like him.* **18.** MATH MATHEMATICAL MODEL a mathematical model describing a contest played under specific rules in which each participant has only partial control ■ **games** *npl* EVENT WITH MANY SPORTING CONTESTS an event that consists of many different sporting activities and usually lasts for several days ■ *adj* **1.** READY AND WILLING ready and willing to do something, especially something new or unusual **2.** BRAVE brave in spirit or character ■ *v* (**gamed, gam·ing, games**) **1.** *vi* GAMBLE to play games of chance for money **2.** *vi* COMPUT GAMES PLAY COMPUTER GAMES to play computer or video games **3.** *vt* MANIPULATE SOMETHING CUNNINGLY to manipulate something cunningly in order to advance yourself or attain your goals in an underhanded manner (*slang*) ○ *gaming his way to the top of his profession* [Old English *gamen* < Germanic, "people participating together"] —**game·ly** *adv* —**game·ness** *n* ◇ **ahead of the game** anticipating and reacting more promptly than others to new developments ◇ **give the game away** to reveal a secret, usually without intending to ◇ **play the game** to follow the rules of a given situation, even if they are unspoken ◇ **the game's up** the plan or trick has failed or been discovered (*informal*) ◇ **the only game in town** the only possibility ◇ **game the system** to manipulate and take unfair advantage of loopholes in rules and regulations in order to make that system of rules and regulations work to your own advantage in risky, typically illegal, schemes

game[2] /gaym/ *adj* an offensive term meaning injured or with impaired mobility (*dated*) [Late 18C. Origin ?]

game ball *n* a ball from a game awarded to one or more of the players of the winning team in recognition of an outstanding contribution to the victory

game bird *n* a bird that is hunted for sport, e.g., a pheasant or grouse

game·cock /gáym kòk/ *n* a rooster that has been bred and trained for fighting

game con·trol·ler *n* a handheld control mechanism for a computer game

game fish *n* **1.** a fish, particularly an ocean fish, that is caught for sport. Sharks are popular game fish. **2.** a fish that is reserved by law or other regulation for anglers and that cannot be caught and sold commercially —**game fish·ing** *n*

game fowl *n* a domestic fowl bred and trained for fighting

game·keep·er /gáym keepər/ *n* somebody employed to take care of birds or animals hunted for sport, especially on an estate or game preserve —**game·keep·ing** *n*

gam·e·lan /gámmə làn/ *n* an Indonesian orchestra that consists mainly of percussion instruments such as chimes, gongs, and wooden xylophones [Early 19C. < Javanese]

game of chance *n* a game, usually played for money, in which the outcome depends to some degree on chance, e.g., on the throw of dice

game of skill *n* a game in which the outcome depends entirely or principally on the skill of the players, e.g., chess or bridge

game·pad /gáym pàd/ *n* a handheld control mechanism for a computer game

game plan *n* **1.** a strategy that somebody devises to achieve a goal **2.** the strategy that a team or player devises for use during a game

game·play /gáym plày/ *n* the entertainment value of a computer game, including aspects such as user interface and game design

game-play·ing *n* manipulative or deceitful behavior ○ *I've had enough of this endless game-playing.*

game point *n* **1.** in sports such as tennis and badminton, a situation in which one player or side has only to win the next point to win the game **2.** in sports such as tennis and badminton, the point that will decide the final outcome of a game

game pre·serve *n* a large area of land where birds or animals are kept in protected conditions in the wild, either for conservation purposes or to be hunted for sport

gam·er /gáymər/ *n* somebody who regularly plays computer or video games or role-play games

game room *n* a room in a house or public building that is set aside and equipped for games such as pool or table tennis

games con·sole *n* COMPUT GAMES same as **console**[2] (sense 7)

game show *n* a television program in which people compete for money or prizes

games·man·ship /gáymzmən shìp/ *n* **1.** the use of tactics or stratagems to gain an advantage in business, politics, or life ○ *political gamesmanship* **2.** the use of unconventional but not strictly illegal tactics to gain an advantage in a competitive game —**games·man** *n*

games room *n* UK LEISURE same as **game room**

game·ster /gáymstər/ *n* somebody who plays gambling games (*archaic*)

gamet- *prefix* same as **gameto-**

gam·e·tan·gi·um /gàmmə tánjee əm/ (*plural* **-gi·a** /-jee ə/) *n* the part of a plant, especially an organ or cell in algae and fungi, where gametes are produced [Late 19C. < modern Latin *gameta* (see GAMETE) + Greek *aggeion* "vessel"] —**gam·e·tan·gi·al** *adj*

gam·ete /gá meet/ *n* a specialized male or female cell with half the normal number of chromosomes that unites with a cell of the opposite sex in the process of sexual reproduction. Ova and spermatozoa are gametes that unite to produce a cell (**zygote**) that may develop into an embryo. [Late 19C. < modern Latin *gameta* < Greek *gamos* "marriage"] —**ga·met·ic** /gə méttik/ *adj*

game the·o·ry *n* a mathematical theory primarily concerned with determining an optimal strategy for situations in which there is competition or conflict, e.g., in business activities or military operations —**game the·o·ret·ic** *adj* —**game the·o·rist** *n*

gameto- *prefix* relating to a gamete ○ *gametophore* [< GAMETE]

ga·me·to·cyte /gə meetə sìt/ *n* **1.** a cell that divides to produce two specialized male or female cells (**gametes**) **2.** the malaria organism in the stage in its life cycle during which it reproduces in the blood of a mosquito

ga·me·to·gen·e·sis /gə meetə jénnəssis/ *n* the production of gametes from gametocytes by cell division (**meiosis**) —**ga·me·to·gen·ic** *adj* —**gam·e·tog·e·nous** /gàmmə tójjənəss/ *adj*

ga·me·to·phore /gə meetə fàwr/ *n* an upright branch in plants such as mosses that bears the reproductive organs —**ga·me·to·phor·ic** /gə meetə fáwrik/ *adj*

ga·me·to·phyte /gə meetə fìt/ *n* in the life cycle of organisms such as mosses, fungi, and algae which have two distinct alternating forms, the form in which sex organs and gametes are produced —**ga·me·to·phyt·ic** /gə meetə fíttik/ *adj*

gam·ey *adj* another spelling of **gamy**

gam·in /gámmin/ *n* a young child, usually a boy, often homeless, who roams the streets (*archaic*) [Mid-19C. < French]

ga·mine /gá meen/ *n* **1.** BOYISH GIRL a girl or young woman who is boyish in appearance **2.** GIRL STREET URCHIN a young girl, often homeless, who roams the streets ■ *adj* APPEALINGLY BOYISH describes girls or young women who are charmingly boyish in appearance [Late 19C. < French, form of *gamin* "child on the streets"]

gam·ing /gáyming/ *n* **1.** the practice of playing games such as poker or roulette for money **2.** the practice of playing computer games or role-play games —**gam·ing** *adj*

gam·ma /gámmə/ *n* **1.** 3RD LETTER OF GREEK ALPHABET the third letter of the Greek alphabet, represented in the English alphabet as "g." See table at **alphabet** **2.** THIRD ITEM the third item in a list or classification system **3.** PHYS UNIT OF MASS a unit of mass equal to 10^{-6} gram **4.** PHOTOGRAPHY MEASURE OF CONTRAST OF IMAGE a measure of the degree of contrast in a developed photograph or a television image **5.** CHEM 3RD POSITION IN CARBON CHAIN the third position in a carbon chain or ring, starting from a specific group or atom. Symbol γ ■ *adj* CHEM 3RD NEAREST TO DESIGNATED ATOM describes the third nearest atom to a particular atom or group of atoms in an organic molecule [15C. Via Latin < Greek]

Gam·ma *n* the third brightest star in a constellation (*followed by the Latin genitive*)

gam·ma-a·mi·no bu·ty·ric a·cid *n* an amino acid that prevents onward transmission of nerve impulses in cells

gam·ma cam·er·a *n* a diagnostic instrument used in medicine to produce images of internal organs after the injection of a radioactive drug that releases gamma rays into the body

gam·ma de·cay *n* a radioactive decay process between two energy levels within a nucleus in which a gamma ray is emitted

gam·ma·di·on /gə máydee òn, -ən/ *n* a pattern consisting of four capital Greek gammas, especially when joined at the center to form a swastika [Mid-19C. < late Greek, < Greek *gamma* "gamma"]

gam·ma glob·u·lin *n* a protein component of blood serum that contains the antibodies, the body's main defense against infection. It is also produced commercially from human plasma and used in the treatment and prevention of diseases such as measles, hepatitis, and poliomyelitis.

gam·ma·hy·drox·y·bu·ty·rate /gàmmə hì dròksee byootə ràyt/ *n* a colorless chemical compound with anesthetic properties that occurs naturally in animals. Use: treating anxiety, as an anesthetic. Formula: $C_4H_8O_3$.

gam·ma ra·di·a·tion *n* electromagnetic waves of higher frequency and shorter wavelength than X-rays that are emitted by some radioactive isotopes and in some nuclear reactions

gam·ma ray *n* a high-energy photon emitted after nuclear reactions or spontaneously from the nucleus of a radioactive atom that lowers the energy level of the nucleus. Gamma rays do not carry any electric charge or mass and share the high-frequency end of the electromagnetic spectrum with X-rays, which have similar properties.

gam·mon[1] /gámmən/ *n* **1.** the lower part of a side of bacon, cooked whole or cut into slices **2.** cured or smoked ham [15C. < Old N French *gambon* "ham" < *gambe* "leg"]

gam·mon[2] /gámmən/ *n* a win in backgammon when the losing player has not succeeded in removing any pieces from the board [Mid-18C. < early form of GAME[1]] —**gam·mon** *vt*

gam·mon[3] /gámmən/ *UK* (*dated informal*) *n* false or meaningless talk that is intended to deceive somebody ■ *vti* (**-moned, -mon·ing, -mons**) to trick or deceive somebody, especially by talking nonsense [Early 18C. Origin ?]

gam·mon[4] /gámmən/ (**-moned, -mon·ing, -mons**) *vt* to fasten a bowsprit to the front of a ship [Late 17C. < GAMMON[1], probably with reference to the tying up of a ham]

gamo- *prefix* **1.** joined together ○ *gamosepalous* **2.** sexual ○ *gamogenesis* [< Greek *gamos* "marriage"]

gam·o·gen·e·sis /gàmmō jénnəssiss/ *n* sexual reproduction (*technical*) —**gam·o·ge·net·ic** /gàmmō jə néttik/ *adj* —**gam·o·ge·net·i·cal·ly** *adv*

gam·o·sep·al·ous /gàmmə sépp'ləss/ *adj* describes plants with sepals that are joined or partially joined together

Gam·ow /gámmov/, **George** (1904–68) Russian-born US theoretical physicist. He made important contributions in a variety of fields, including molecular biology and radioactivity. A proponent of the big bang theory that the universe was created in a gigantic explosion, he was also a prolific author of science books for the general public.

gamp /gamp/ *n UK* an umbrella, especially a large old one (*archaic informal*) [Mid-19C. After Sarah Gamp, character in Dickens's novel *Martin Chuzzlewit*, who carries an umbrella]

gam·ut /gámmət/ *n* **1.** the entire range of something **2.** the whole series of recognized musical notes, from lowest to highest [15C. Contraction of medieval Latin *gamma ut* < Greek *gamma*, letter representing the musical note one below the top note in the medieval scale, + *ut*, the lowest note]

gam·y /gáymee/ (**-i·er, -i·est**), **gam·ey** (**-i·er, -i·est**) *adj* **1.** TASTING OF OR LIKE GAME having a strong flavor like that of a wild bird or animal that is hunted for food **2.** RANK-SMELLING having a strong bad smell **3.** LEWD sexually suggestive or obscene —**gam·i·ly** *adv* —**gam·i·ness** *n*

-gamy *suffix* **1.** marriage ○ *polygamy* **2.** reproductive union ○ *syngamy* **3.** reproductive organs, method of fertilization ○ *karyogamy* [< Greek *gamos* "marriage"] —**-gamic** *suffix* —**-gamous** *suffix*

ga·nache /gaa naásh, gə-/ *n* a sweet creamy chocolate filling or frosting for cakes and pastries, made from cream and melted chocolate [Late 20C. Via French, "jaw," and Italian *ganascia* < Greek *gnathos*]

Ga·na·pa·ti /gaánə páttee/ *n* HINDUISM same as **Ganesha**

Gan·da /gándə/ *n* a Bantu language spoken in Uganda. Native speakers: 4 million. [Mid-20C. < Bantu] —**Gan·da** *adj*

gan·der /gándər/ *n* **1.** MALE GOOSE an adult male goose **2.** LOOK a look or glance at somebody or something (*informal*) **3.** OFFENSIVE TERM an offensive term for somebody who is thought to be unserious and frivolous (*informal insult*) [Old English *gandra* < Indo-European, "goose"]

Gan·der /gándər/ town in northeastern Newfoundland, Canada that is home to the region's air traffic control center. Population: 9,391 (2001).

Gan·dhi /gaándee/, **Indira** (1917–84) prime minister of India. The daughter of Jawaharlal Nehru, she was twice prime minister (1966–77, 1980–84), and was assassinated by members of her Sikh bodyguard. Born **Nehru, Indira Priyadarshini**

> "I don't mind if my life goes in the service of the nation. If I die today every drop of my blood will invigorate the nation."
> [Indira Gandhi, *Sunday Times (London)*; December 3, 1989]

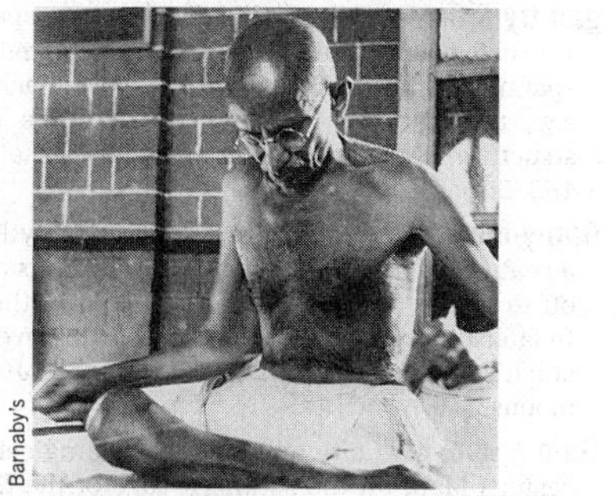

Mohandas Karamchand Gandhi

Gan·dhi, Mohandas Karamchand (1869–1948) Indian nationalist leader. His campaign of nonviolent civil resistance to British rule led to India's independence (1947). He was assassinated by a Hindu extremist as a protest against his pluralistic policies. Known as **Gandhi, Mahatma**

> "Complete independence through truth and nonviolence means the independence of every unit, be it the humblest of the nation, without distinction of race, color or creed."
> [Mohandas Karamchand Gandhi. Quoted in *Questions in the Philosophy of Restraint*, Indira Rothermund; 1963]

Gan·dhi, Rajiv (1944–91) prime minister of India (1984–89). The son of Indira Gandhi, he entered politics in 1981 after the death of his brother Sanjay and was killed in a bomb explosion in 1991.

Gan·dhi, Sonia (1946–) Italian-born Indian politician. The widow of Rajiv Gandhi, she became leader of the Congress Party in 1998 and was elected to Parliament in 1999. In 2004 her party won the general election, but she declined to be prime minister. Born **Maino, Sonia**

Gan·dhi·na·gar /gàndee núggər/ capital city of Gujarat State in western India, on the outskirts of Ahmedabad. It is India's second planned city, designed and built in the 1960s. Population: 225,000 (1995).

gan·dy danc·er /gándee-/ *n* a laborer in a railroad section gang who lays or maintains tracks (*slang*) [Origin ?]

ga·nef /gaánəf/, **ga·nev** /gaánəv/, **ga·nof** /gaánəf/, **go·nif, gon·of** *n* somebody regarded as unscrupulous, thieving, or cheating (*informal insult*) [Early 20C. Via Yiddish < Hebrew *gannāḇ*]

Ga·nesh Cha·tur·thi /-chə tóorthee/ *n* a Hindu festival honoring the god Ganesh. Date: early Bhadrapada

Ga·ne·sh /gə néesh/, **Ga·ne·sha** /gə néeshə/, **Ga·ne·sa** /gə néessə/ *n* in Hinduism, the god of wisdom and problem solving who is the son of Shiva and Parvati and is represented as a pot-bellied man with an elephant's head

ga·nev *n* CRIME same as **ganef**

gang[1] /gang/ *n* **1.** GROUP OF TROUBLEMAKING YOUNG PEOPLE a group of young people who spend time together for social reasons and may engage in delinquent behavior **2.** GROUP OF CRIMINALS a group of people who work together for some criminal or antisocial purpose **3.** PEOPLE WHO ENJOY EACH OTHER'S COMPANY a group of people with similar interests who like to spend time together **4.** GROUP OF WORKERS a group of people working together, especially a group of laborers **5.** SET OF TOOLS a set of tools or devices arranged to be used or operated together ■ *v* (**ganged, gang·ing, gangs**) **1.** *vi* FORM GROUP to form, act, or move in a gang ○ *The kids ganged together to clean the park.* **2.** *vt* ATTACK SOMEBODY TOGETHER to attack somebody as a group **3.** *vt* PUT OBJECTS IN GROUP to group similar objects in a set **4.** *vt* ELECTRONICS COMBINE SWITCHES to combine several switches or devices on a single shaft so as to switch multiple connections at one time [12C. < Old Norse *gangr* "journey"]

gang up *vi* to join together in a group, especially for the purpose of attack, intimidation, or opposition

gang up on *vt* to join together in a group in order to attack, intimidate, or oppose somebody

gang[2] /gang/ *n* MIN EXTRACT another spelling of **gangue**

Gan·ga /gúng gə/ *n S Asia* Hindi name for **Ganges**

gang·bang /gáng bàng/ (*slang; considered offensive by some people*) *n* **1.** SERIAL INTERCOURSE WITH ONE PERSON sexual intercourse between one consenting person and several others in succession **2.** ORGY a group sex session in which participants have sex with a succession of partners **3.** GANG RAPE a multiple rape by a gang of people ■ *v* (**-banged, -bang·ing, -bangs**) **1.** *vti* HAVE MULTIPLE INTERCOURSE WITH ONE PERSON to have sexual intercourse with somebody on the same occasion as others do **2.** *vti* GANG-RAPE to gang-rape somebody **3.** *vi* BE MEMBER OF VIOLENT GANG to participate in the activities of a criminal or violent gang —**gang·bang·er** *n*

gang·bus·ter /gáng bùstər/ *n* a law-enforcement officer charged with breaking up criminal gangs (*dated slang*) ■ *adj* unusually successful or effective (*slang*) ○ *a gangbuster sale* ◇ **like gangbusters** with a lot of energy or enthusiasm or to great effect (*slang*) ○ *The movie takes off like gangbusters and never lets up.*

Ganges

Gan·ges /gán jeez/ river in northern India, regarded as sacred by Hindus. It rises in the Himalaya range, flows southeastward through Bangladesh, and empties into the Bay of Bengal, forming one of the world's largest deltas. Length: 1,560 mi./2,510 km. Hindi name **Ganga**

gang·land /gáng lànd, -lənd/ *n* the world of organized crime —**gang·land** *adj*

gan·gli·a ANAT plural of **ganglion**

gan·gling /gáng gling/, **gan·gly** /-glee/ (**-gli·er, -gli·est**) *adj* tall and thin, with a loose awkward gait [Early 19C. Origin ?]

gan·gli·on /gáng glee ən/ (*plural* **-gli·a** /-glee ə/ or **-gli·ons**) *n* **1.** a structure that contains a dense cluster of nerve cells **2.** a harmless swelling similar to a cyst that forms on a joint or tendon [Late 17C. < Greek *gagglion* "tumor, nerve bundle"] —**gan·gli·on·ic** /gàng glee ónnik/ *adj*

gan·gly *adj* same as **gangling**

gang·plank /gáng plàngk/ *n* a movable walkway such as a bridge or plank, used when boarding or disembarking from a ship

gang rape *n* the rape of one person by several people in succession —**gang-rape** *vti*

gan·grene /gáng green, gang green/ *n* local death and decay of soft tissues of the body as a result of lack of blood to the area ■ *vti* (**-grened, -gren·ing, -grenes**) to affect body tissue with gangrene, or become affected with gangrene [Mid-16C. Via French < Greek *gaggraina*] —**gan·gre·nous** /gáng grənəss/ *adj*

gang·sta /gángstə/ *n* **1.** GANG MEMBER a member of an urban street gang **2.** MUSIC RAP PERFORMER somebody who performs gangsta rap ■ *adj* OF GANGS AND GANGSTA RAP relating to or characteristic of urban street gangs, their activities, or gangsta rap

gang·sta rap /gángstə-/ *n* rap music in which the lyrics tend to deal with gangs and killings [Alteration of GANGSTER]

gang·ster /gángstər/ *n* a member of an organized gang of criminals, especially a racketeer —**gang·ster·ish** *adj* —**gang·ster·ism** *n*

Gang·tok /gang tók/ capital city of Sikkim State in northeastern India. Population: 25,024 (1991).

gangue /gang/, **gang** *n* worthless rock or other matter occurring in a vein or deposit within or alongside a valuable mineral. ◊ **matrix** (sense 5) [Early 19C. Via French < German *Gang* "way, lode"]

gang·way /gáng wày/ *n* 1. **NARROW WALKWAY** a narrow passageway, especially a temporary walkway 2. **ENTRANCE IN SHIP'S SIDE** an opening in the side of a ship through which it is boarded by means of a gangplank 3. NAUT same as **gangplank** ■ *interj* **MAKE WAY** used to indicate to people in a crowd that they should make way because somebody is coming through

gan·is·ter /gánnistər/ *n* a hard rock containing silica that can endure high temperatures and is used to line furnaces [Early 19C. Origin ?]

gan·ja /gáanjə, gán-/ *n* a potent form of marijuana used for smoking [Early 19C. < Hindi *gājā*]

gannet

gan·net /gánnət/ *n* a large fish-eating seabird, usually white with black-tipped wings, that lives in offshore colonies. Genera: *Sula* or *Morus.* [Old English *ganot* < Indo-European, "goose"]

Gan·nett Peak /gànnət-/ mountain in the Central Rocky Mountains, western Wyoming. It forms part of the Wind River Range and is the highest peak in the state. Height: 13,804 ft./4,207 m.

ga·nof *n* CRIME another spelling of **ganef**

gan·oid /gá nòyd/ *adj* describes a type of scale found on gar and other primitive fish, consisting of dentine-covered bone with a thick outer layer of a substance (**ganoine**) similar to enamel ■ *n* a primitive fish that has ganoid scales [Mid-19C. < French *ganoïde* < Greek *ganos* "brightness"]

Gan·su /gáan sóo/ agricultural province in northern China dominated by semiarid plateaus and basins. Capital: Lanzhou. Population: 24,670,000 (1997). Area: 175,290 sq. mi./454,000 sq. km.

gant·let[1] /gáwntlət, gáant-/ *n* a section of railroad track where two parallel lines are arranged so that one rail of each line is between the rails of the other line ■ *vt* (**-let·ed, -let·ing, -lets**) to construct or merge two railroad tracks to form a gantlet [Variant of GAUNTLET[2]]

gant·let[2] /gáwntlət, gáant-/ *n* MIL, CLOTHING another spelling of **gauntlet**[1], **gauntlet**[2]

gant·line /gánt lìn/ *n* a rope run through a pulley on a mast and used to hoist people or things [Mid-18C. Origin ?]

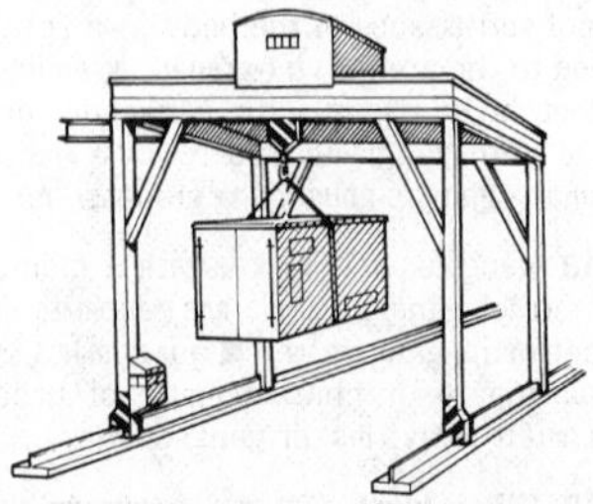

gantry (sense 2)

gan·try /gántree/ (*plural* **-tries**) *n* 1. a frame spanning railroad tracks and used to display signals 2. a spanning framework used to support machinery, e.g., the platform that supports a crane or the structure used to erect and service rockets [Late 16C. Origin ?]

Gan·y·mede /gánnə meed/ *n* 1. in Greek mythology, a beautiful young Trojan prince whom Zeus carried off to Mount Olympus to be cupbearer to the gods. In later times he symbolized homosexual love or the spirit's ascent to heaven. 2. the largest of Jupiter's moons

Ga·o /gáa ō, gow/ city and ancient trading center in eastern Mali, on the southern edge of the Sahara. It is situated on the Niger River. Population: 63,000 (1998).

GAO *abbr* GOV General Accounting Office

Gao Ke·gong /gòw kə góng/ (1248–1310?) Chinese artist. He is noted for his paintings of the mountain landscapes of southern China.

gaol /jayl/ *n, vt UK* CRIME another spelling of **jail**

CULTURAL NOTE ***The Ballad of Reading Gaol***, a poem (1898) by British writer Oscar Wilde. Wilde's last work, written while he was imprisoned for "homosexual activities," it is the story of the trial and execution of murderer Charles Thomas Wooldridge, a fellow inmate at the jail. It deals with the harshness of prison conditions and the idea of forgiveness.

gap /gap/ *n* 1. **BREAK IN STRUCTURE** a break or opening in a structure or arrangement such as a fence or military defense line 2. **SOMETHING MISSING** an area where there is a complete or partial absence of something such as data ○ *gaps in his employment record* 3. **INTERVAL OF TIME** an interval of time during which an action or event stops occurring ○ *after a gap of three years* 4. **DISPARITY** a significant difference between two situations, attitudes, or perceptions ○ *the gap between rich and poor* 5. **PROBLEM CAUSED BY DISPARITY** a problem caused by a difference between two situations, attitudes, or perceptions ○ *technology gap* ○ *generation gap* 6. GEOG **OPENING BETWEEN MOUNTAINS** a ravine or pass in a mountain range 7. ELEC ENG same as **spark gap** ■ *v* (**gapped, gap·ping, gaps**) 1. *vti* **PRODUCE OR DEVELOP GAP** to create a gap or opening in a barrier, or become open or separated by a gap 2. *vt* ELEC ENG **ADJUST SPARK PLUG GAP** to adjust the gap between the electrodes of a spark plug [14C. < Old Norse, "chasm"] —**gap·py** *adj*

gape /gayp/ *vi* (**gaped, gap·ing, gapes**) 1. **STARE WITH MOUTH OPEN** to look at somebody or something in surprise or wonder, usually with an open mouth ○ *He stood gaping at us in disbelief.* 2. **OPEN MOUTH** to open the mouth wide 3. **OPEN INTO GAP** to open or split apart with a gap ○ *His wound was gaping open and he was losing blood.* ■ *n* 1. **OPEN-MOUTHED STARE** a stare of surprise or wonder in which the mouth is wide open 2. **OPENING OF MOUTH** an opening of the mouth wide, e.g., in surprise or wonder 3. **BIG GAP** a wide opening in something 4. ZOOL **WIDTH OF OPEN MOUTH** the width of the open mouth of an animal [13C. < Old Norse *gapa* "open the mouth"]

SYNONYMS See ***gaze***.

gap·ing /gáyping/ *adj* wide open and deep ○ *gaping holes in the roof*

gap-toothed *adj* having wide spaces between the teeth

gap year *n UK* a period of time taken off by a student after the completion of secondary education and before starting higher or further education

gar /gaar/ (*plural same* or **gars**) *n* 1. a large primitive freshwater fish with a heavy armor of bony scales and a long toothy jaw. Native to: North and Central America. Family: Lepisosteidae. 2. a fish that is similar in appearance to or related to a gar, e.g., a needlefish [Mid-18C. Shortening of GARFISH]

GAR, G.A.R. *abbr* ARMY, HIST Grand Army of the Republic

ga·rage /gə ráazh, -ráaj/ *n* 1. **BUILDING FOR MOTOR VEHICLES** a building for parking or storing one or more motor vehicles 2. **ESTABLISHMENT REPAIRING MOTOR VEHICLES** an establishment that repairs and often sells motor vehicles, and sometimes sells gasoline, diesel, and oil 3. *also* **ga·rage mu·sic** MUSIC **SOULFUL DANCE MUSIC** a style of dance music inspired by disco and combining 4/4 rhythms with vocals, associated with soul music of the 1990s ■ *vt* (**-raged, -rag·ing, -rag·es**) **PUT VEHICLE IN GARAGE** to park or store a motor vehicle in a garage [Early 20C. < French < *garer* "to shelter"]

ga·rage sale *n* a sale of unwanted or unused household items that is held in the garage or driveway of the seller's home

Ga·ra·gum Des·ert /gàrrə gum-/ desert occupying a large proportion of Turkmenistan. Area: 140,000 sq. mi./350,000 sq. km.

ga·ram ma·sa·la /gaa ráam mə sáalə/ *n* a mixture of spices used in South Asian cooking to give a hot pungent flavor to a dish [Mid-20C. < Hindi *garam masālā* "hot spices"]

Gar·a·mond /gárrə mònd, gaa raa móN/, **Gar·a·mond type** *n* a Roman typeface often used in books [Mid-19C. After Claude *Garamond* (1499–1561), French type founder]

~~garantee~~ incorrect spelling of **guarantee**

garb /gaarb/ *n* 1. **TYPICAL OUTFIT** a particular type of clothing, especially the uniform or typical outfit worn by members of a profession ○ *military garb* 2. **APPEARANCE** the outward appearance that somebody or something has ○ *short-term economic gain in the garb of science* ■ *vt* (**garbed, garb·ing, garbs**) 1. **DRESS SOMEBODY** to clothe somebody or yourself in a particular type of clothing 2. **DISGUISE SOMETHING** to cover or disguise something as something else ○ *garbed his philanthropic activities in anonymity* [Late 16C. Via obsolete French *garbe* "elegance" < Italian *garbo*]

gar·bage /gáarbij/ *n* 1. **DISCARDED WASTE** discarded food waste or any other unwanted or useless material 2. **NONSENSE** talk or writing that is worthless nonsense or lies 3. **SOMEBODY OR SOMETHING WORTHLESS** somebody or something regarded as totally worthless 4. COMPUT **WORTHLESS DATA** inaccurate, useless, or meaningless data in a computer [15C. < Anglo-Norman] —**gar·bag·y** *adj*

gar·bage can *n* a container for waste matter, especially one for food waste or one that is kept outside for collection by a waste-disposal service

gar·bage col·lec·tor *n* same as **garbageman**

gar·bage dis·pos·al *n* an electrical device, installed beneath a kitchen sink, that grinds up food so that it can go into the waste pipe

gar·bage·man /gáarbij màn/ (*plural* **-men** /-mèn/) *n* somebody employed to haul away trash

gar·bage truck *n* a large motor vehicle used to collect and compact waste materials left bagged or in containers outside buildings

gar·ban·zo /gaar báanzō/ (*plural* **-zos**), **gar·ban·zo bean** *n* FOOD same as **chickpea** (sense 1) [Mid-18C. < Spanish]

gar·ble /gáarb'l/ *vt* (**-bled, -bling, -bles**) 1. **JUMBLE MEANING OF SOMETHING** to confuse a message or information so that it is misleading or unintelligible ○ *He garbled the details, but the outline of the story is clear.* 2. COMMUNICATION **SCRAMBLE TRANSMISSION OF SOMETHING** to cause the corruption of a transmitted message or signal ○ *The announcement was completely garbled.* ■ *n* COMMUNICATION 1. **CONFUSED MESSAGE** a confused or corrupted message, piece of information, or signal that is misleading or unintelligible 2. **CONFUSING OF MESSAGE** the act of confusing or corrupting a message, piece of information, or signal so that it is misleading or unintelligible [15C. Via Italian *garbellare* "sift" and Arabic *ġarbala* < late Latin *cribellum* "small sieve" < Latin *cribrum* "sieve"] —**gar·bled** *adj*

Gar·bo /gáarbō/, **Greta** (1905–90) Swedish-born US movie actor, noted for her beauty and reticence. Her movies include *Anna Christie* (1930), *Grand Hotel* (1932), *Camille* (1937), and *Ninotchka* (1939). After her retirement in 1941, she lived as a recluse. Born **Gustaffson, Greta**

> "I never said, 'I want to be alone.' I only said, 'I want to be *left* alone.' There is all the difference."
> [Greta Garbo. Quoted in *Garbo*, John Bainbridge; 1955]

gar·board /gaár bàwrd/ *n* the continuous band of planking on a ship's hull next to its keel [Early 17C. < obsolete Dutch *gaarboord*]

gar·bol·o·gy /gaar bóllǝjee/ *n* the study of a cultural group by an examination of what it discards [Late 20C. < GARBAGE] —**gar·bol·o·gist** *n*

Gar·cí·a /gaar seé ǝ/, **Carlos Poléstico** (1896–1971) president of the Philippines. He was vice president (1954–57) before serving as president (1957–61).

Gar·cí·a Lor·ca /gaar seè ǝ-/ ◆ **Lorca, Federico García**

Gar·cí·a Már·quez /-maár kèz/, **Gabriel** (*b.* 1928) Colombian writer. In novels such as *100 Years of Solitude* (1967) and *Love in the Time of Cholera* (1985), he developed a distinctive style of fantasy blended with realism. He won the Nobel Prize in literature (1982). See Cultural note at **solitude**

Gar·cí·a Rob·les /-róblǝss/, **Alfonso** (1911–91) Mexican diplomat. He helped draft the international Nuclear Nonproliferation Treaty (1968), and shared the Nobel Peace Prize (1982) for his long campaign against nuclear weapons.

gar·çon /gaar sõN, -sóN/ *n* a waiter in a French restaurant or café [Early 17C. < French]

gar·da /gaárdǝ/ (*plural* **-daí** /-deè/) *n* a police officer in the Republic of Ireland [See GARDA]

Gar·da /gaárdǝ/ *n* the police force of the Republic of Ireland [Early 20C. < Irish, shortening of *Garda Síochána* "civic guard"]

Gar·da, Lake /gaárdǝ/ largest lake in Italy and the center of a major resort region. It is situated in northern Italy, between Brescia and Verona. Area: 143 sq. mi./370 sq. km.

gar·daí POLICE plural of **garda**

gar·dant *adj* HERALDRY another spelling of **guardant**

gar·den /gaárd'n/ *n* **1. PLANTED AREA OF GROUND** a plot of ground where plants such as fruits, vegetables, or flowers are grown **2. PARK** a park or recreational area for the public, generally planted with flowers, bushes, and trees (*often used in the plural*) ○ *the botanical gardens* **3. FARMING REGION** a fertile well-cultivated region **4. OUTDOOR EATING AND DRINKING ESTABLISHMENT** an eating or drinking establishment that serves its patrons outdoors ○ *a beer garden* **5. ARENA OR STADIUM** a large public arena or stadium **6.** *UK* same as **yard**[2] *n* (sense 1) ■ *adj* **1. RELATING TO GARDEN** relating to, produced in, frequenting, or used in a garden **2.** *UK* ZOOL same as **garden-variety** ■ *vi* **(-dened, -den·ing, -dens) TAKE CARE OF GARDEN** to plan or tend a garden [14C. Via Old N French *gardin* < Vulgar Latin *(hortus) gardinus* "enclosed (garden)"] —**gar·den·er** *n*

CULTURAL NOTE ***The Secret Garden***, a children's story (1911) by British writer Frances Hodgson Burnett. It is the tale of a lonely orphan, Mary Lennox, who is sent to live with her uncle Archibald, a widower whose wife died as a result of a fall from a tree in her beloved garden. In restoring the garden, Mary finds happiness and helps the family recover from its misfortune.

Gar·de·na /gaar deénǝ/ city in southwestern California. It is a suburb of Los Angeles. Population: 59,657 (2002 estimate).

gar·den a·part·ment *n* **1.** an apartment on the ground floor or in the basement of a building with access to a lawn or garden **2.** an apartment building that has a garden or lawn

gar·den cen·ter *n* a retail establishment that sells plants and gardening equipment

Gar·den Cit·y /gaárd'n-/ **1.** city in southeastern Michigan, near Detroit. Population: 39,880 (2002 estimate). **2.** town in southeastern New York State, on Long Island, east of Queens. It is the home of Adelphi University. Population: 21,700 (2002 estimate).

gar·den flat *n UK* same as **garden apartment** (sense 1)

Gar·den Grove city in southwestern California, south of Anaheim. Population: 167,429 (2002 estimate).

gar·den he·lio·trope *n* a tall variety of valerian with a root from which the drug valerian was formerly extracted for use in medicine. Flowers: tiny, fragrant, purple, pink, or white, in clusters. Latin name: *Valeriana officinalis.*

gar·de·nia /gaar deényǝ/ *n* an evergreen tree or bush with shiny leaves. Flowers: white, fragrant. Native to: Africa, Asia. Genus: *Gardenia.* [Mid-18C. < modern Latin, after Alexander *Garden* (1730–91), Scottish-American naturalist]

gar·den·ing /gaárd'ning/ *n* the activity of tending a garden, especially as a profession, chore, or hobby

Gar·den of E·den *n* BIBLE same as **Eden**

Garden of Geth·sem·a·ne *n* same as **Gethsemane**

gar·den par·ty *n* a party held in a garden or yard

Gar·den State *n* a nickname for New Jersey

gar·den-va·ri·e·ty *adj* common or ordinary ○ *a garden-variety murder mystery*

garde·robe /gaárd ròb/ *n* **1.** formerly, a closet, wardrobe, or room where clothes were kept **2.** formerly, a small toilet consisting of a bench with holes made above a pit, usually built into a wall or projecting from it [14C. < Old French < *garder* "keep" + *robe* "robe"]

~~gardian~~ incorrect spelling of **guardian**

Gar·di·ners Is·land /gaárd'nǝrz-/, **Gar·di·ner's Is·land** island in SE New York, in Gardiners Bay, off the tip of E Long Island. In 1639 it became the first English settlement in present-day New York State. Area: 5 sq. mi./13 sq. km.

Gard·ner /gaárdnǝr/, **Erle Stanley** (1889–1970) US writer and lawyer. A practicing lawyer for about 20 years, he is best known for his fictional lawyer Perry Mason, who appeared in more than 80 of his detective novels.

Gar·field /gaár feéld/ city in northeastern New Jersey, situated on the Passaic River, southeast of Paterson. Population: 29,765 (2002 estimate).

Library of Congress

James A. Garfield

Gar·field, James A. (1831–81) 20th president of the United States. A Republican member of the US House of Representatives (1863–80), he was president for only four months (1881) before he was assassinated. Full name **Garfield, James Abram.** See table at **president**

> "The world's history is a divine poem, of which the history of every nation is a canto, and every man a word."
> [Attributed to James A. Garfield, *The Meaning of History*, N. Gordon and Joyce Carper; 1991]

gar·fish /gaár fìsh/ (*plural* **-fish·es** or *same*) *n* FISH same as **gar** [15C. < Old English *gār* "spear"; from the shape of its jaw]

gar·gan·tu·an /gaar gánchoo ǝn/ *adj* tremendously large in amount, number, or size [Late 16C. < *Gargantua*, giant hero of *Gargantua* (1534) by François Rabelais]

gar·gle /gaárg'l/ *v* **(-gled, -gling, -gles) 1.** *vti* **CLEANSE MOUTH AND THROAT** to rinse or disinfect the mouth and throat by holding liquid in the back of the mouth and stirring it up with air breathed out from the lungs **2.** *vi* **MAKE GUTTURAL SOUND** to make a sound like that made when rinsing the mouth and throat with liquid ■ *n* **1. MOUTHWASH** a liquid used to rinse the mouth and throat **2. GUTTURAL SOUND** a sound like that made when rinsing the mouth and throat with liquid [Early 16C. < French *gargouiller* < Old French *gargouille* "throat" < Latin *gurgulio* "gullet"]

gargoyle

gar·goyle /gaár gòyl/ *n* **1. GROTESQUE DRAINAGE SPOUT** a spout in the form of a grotesque animal or human figure that projects from the gutter of a building and is designed to cast rainwater clear of the building **2. STATUE OF GROTESQUE FIGURE** a grotesque carved figure **3. SOMEBODY LIKE CARVED FIGURE** somebody thought to resemble a carved gargoyle (*insult*) [15C. < Old French *gargouille* (see GARGLE)]

gar·i·bal·di /gàrrǝ báwldee/ *n* a woman's loose-fitting blouse that imitates the red shirt worn by Giuseppe Garibaldi [Mid-19C. After GARIBALDI]

Gar·i·bal·di /gàrrǝ báwldee/, **Giuseppe** (1807–82) French-born Italian patriot. He played a leading role in the unification of Italy (1859–61), defeating the rulers of Sicily and Naples at the head of his army, the so-called Red Shirts.

> "Men, I am getting out of Rome. Anyone who wants to carry on the war against the outsiders, come with me. I can't offer you either honors or wages; I offer you hunger, thirst, forced marches, battles and death. Anyone who loves his country, follow me."
> [Giuseppe Garibaldi, *Garibaldi*, G. Guerzoni; 1929]

Gar·i·fu·na /gàrrǝ foónǝ/ (*plural same* or **-nas**) *n* an Afro-Latino people of West African, Carib, and Arawak ancestry who now live on the Caribbean coasts of Guatemala, Belize, Honduras, and Nicaragua. They were passengers on a slave ship that wrecked on St. Vincent, but after being evicted by the British in 1797, resettled on the Central American coast. [Late 20C. < Arawakan]

gar·ish /gérrish/ *adj* **1. GAUDY** crudely showy ○ *a garish outfit* **2. OVERLY ORNAMENTED** excessively ornate or elaborate ○ *a garish balcony and staircase* **3. DRESSED TOO BRIGHTLY** wearing clothing or makeup that is extremely brightly colored **4. TOO BRIGHT** excessively bright ○ *a hideous garish yellow* [Mid-16C. Origin ?] —**gar·ish·ly** *adv* —**gar·ish·ness** *n*

gar·land /gaárlǝnd/ *n* **1. FLOWER WREATH** a wreath of intertwined flowers or leaves worn as an ornament or as a sign of honor **2. HANGING FLOWER DECORATION** a festoon of flowers or paper hung as decoration **3.** LITERAT **ANTHOLOGY** a collection of short pieces of literature ■ *vt* **(-land·ed, -land·ing, -lands) PUT GARLAND ON SOMEBODY OR SOMETHING** to decorate or adorn somebody or something with garlands [14C. < Old French *garlande*]

Gar·land /gaárlǝnd/, **Hamlin** (1860–1940) US writer. A writer of harshly realistic social novels, he is remembered for his autobiographical *Son of the Middle Border* (1917), and the Pulitzer Prize-winning *Daughter of the Middle Border* (1921). Full name **Garland, Hannibal Hamlin**

> "It is blind fetishism, timid provincialism, or commercial greed which puts the works of 'the masters' above the living, breathing artist."
> [Hamlin Garland, *Crumbling Idols: Twelve Essays on Art and Literature*; 1894]

Gar·land, Judy (1922–69) US movie actor and singer. She starred in movies including *The Wizard of Oz* (1939), *Meet Me in St. Louis* (1944), and *A Star is Born* (1954), and from the 1950s performed primarily as a singer. Born **Gumm, Frances**

"We cast away priceless time in dreams, born of imagination, fed upon illusion, and put to death by reality."
[Judy Garland. Quoted in *Judy Garland*, Anne Edwards; 1974]

garlic

gar·lic /gáarlik/ (*plural same* or **-lics**) *n* **1. BULB WITH STRONG ODOR** a bulb or clove with a pungent odor and flavor that is commonly used in cooking **2. STRONG-TASTING PLANT** a plant that is the source of garlic. Latin name: *Allium sativum.* **3. PLANT LIKE GARLIC** a plant related to or resembling true garlic [Old English *gārlēac* < *gār* "spear" + LEEK] —**gar·lick·y** *adj*

gar·lic bread *n* bread seasoned with butter and garlic and baked or toasted

gar·lic press *n* a small kitchen tool, usually made of metal or plastic, that minces a clove of garlic by squeezing it through small holes

gar·lic salt *n* a preparation of salt and powdered garlic used as a food seasoning

gar·ment /gáarmənt/ *n* a piece of clothing ■ *vt* (**-ment·ed, -ment·ing, -ments**) to put clothing on somebody (*literary; often passive*) [14C. < French *garnement* "equipment" < *garnir* (see GARNISH)]

gar·ment bag *n* a piece of soft-sided luggage shaped for carrying dresses, suits, or other clothing on hangers

Gar·mo Peak /gaármō-/ former name for **Ismail Samani Peak**

Gar·neau /gaar nṓ/, **François Xavier** (1809–66) Canadian historian. Considered the first historian of French Canada, he wrote the *History of Canada* (1845–48).

gar·ner /gáarnər/ (**-nered, -ner·ing, -ners**) *vt* **1. WIN OR GAIN SOMETHING** to earn or acquire something by effort **2. GATHER INFORMATION** to collect or accumulate something such as information or facts **3. GATHER IN SOMETHING** to gather something into storage or into a granary [12C. Via Anglo-Norman *gerner* "storehouse" < Latin *granarium* (see GRANARY)]

Gar·ner /gáarnər/, **John N.** (1868–1967) vice president of the United States. A Democrat from Texas, he was a US representative (1903–33) and Speaker of the House (1931–33) before serving as vice president during Franklin D. Roosevelt's first two terms (1933–41). Full name **Garner, John Nance**

gar·net /gáarnət/ *n* **1.** a variously colored crystalline silicate mineral. Source: metamorphic and igneous rocks. Use: gems. **2.** a dark red color [13C. Probably via Middle Dutch *garnate* < Old French *grenat* "dark red" < *pome grenate* "pomegranate," because of its color] —**gar·net** *adj*

gar·ni·er·ite /gáarnee ə rìt/ *n* a soft green form of the mineral serpentine consisting of hydrated nickel magnesium silicate. Use: source of nickel. [Late 19C. After Jules *Garnier* (1839?–1904), French geologist]

gar·nish /gáarnish/ *vt* (**-nished, -nish·ing, -nish·es**) **1. ENHANCE FOOD OR DRINK** to add something as an accompaniment to food or drink that enhances its flavor or appearance **2. EMBELLISH SOMETHING** to decorate something with an ornament **3.** LAW same as **garnishee** ○ *garnish wages for child support* ■ *n* **1. ENHANCEMENT FOR FOOD OR DRINK** something added as an accompaniment to food or drink to enhance its flavor or appearance **2. SOMETHING DECORATIVE** an ornament or decoration for something [14C. < French *garniss-*, stem of *garnir* "equip, adorn, warn" < Germanic] —**gar·nish·ing** *n*

gar·nish·ee /gaàrni sheé/ *vt* (**-eed, -ee·ing, -ees**) **1. CONFISCATE DEBTOR'S MONEY** to take the money or property of a debtor by legal authority **2. SUMMONS DEBTOR** to serve somebody with a legal summons concerning the taking of wages or property to satisfy a debt ■ *n* **SUMMONSED DEBTOR** somebody who is served with a legal summons stating that wages or property may be taken to satisfy a debt

gar·nish·ment /gáarnishmənt/ *n* **1.** a legal summons or warning concerning the taking of a debtor's property or wages to satisfy a debt **2.** an ornamentation or embellishment on or of something

gar·ni·ture /gáarnichər, -choor/ *n* something that decorates or embellishes something [15C. < French < *garnir* (see GARNISH)]

Ga·ronne /gaa ráwn/ river in southwestern France. Rising in the Spanish Pyrenees, it flows through Toulouse and Bordeaux before joining the Dordogne at the Gironde estuary. Length: 357 mi./575 km.

gar·pike /gáar pìk/ (*plural* **-pikes** or *same*) *n* FISH same as **gar** (sense 1)

gar·ret /gárrət/ *n* a room at the top of a house, immediately below the roof [15C. < Old French *garite* "watchtower" < *garir* "defend" < Germanic, "protect"]

Gar·rick /gárrik/, **David** (1717–79) British actor, theatrical manager, and playwright. He brought a new naturalism to the stage in legendary performances, and managed London's Drury Lane Theatre (1747–76).

"Prologues precede the piece—in mournful verse; / As undertakers—walk before the hearse."
[David Garrick, *Apprentice*, Arthur Murphy; 1756]

gar·ri·son /gárriss'n/ *n* **1. STATIONED TROOPS** a body of troops stationed at a military post **2. PLACE FOR STATIONING TROOPS** a military post where troops are stationed ■ *vt* (**-soned, -son·ing, -sons**) **1. SUPPLY PLACE WITH TROOPS** to provide a fort or town with a military post and troops **2. STATION TROOPS AT PLACE** to station troops at a military post [13C. < Old French, "fortification" < *garir* (see GARRET)]

Gar·ri·son /gárriss'n/, **William Lloyd** (1805–79) US abolitionist and reformer. The founding editor of the abolitionist journal *The Liberator* (1831–65), he was an uncompromising and eloquent opponent of slavery. He later campaigned for the rights of women and Native Americans.

"I am in earnest—I will not equivocate—I will not excuse—I will not retreat a single inch; and I will be heard!"
[William Lloyd Garrison, "Salutory Address," *The Liberator*; January 1, 1831]

gar·ri·son cap *n* MIL same as **overseas cap**

gar·ri·son house *n* a style of house common in New England in which the second floor projects over the first floor at the front [< its resemblance to early forts]

gar·rote /gə rót, -rốt/, **gar·rotte** *n* **1. WEAPON FOR STRANGULATION** a weapon consisting of a wire or cord with handles at each end, used in strangulation **2. METAL BAND USED IN EXECUTIONS** an iron band placed around the neck and tightened in order to execute somebody **3. EXECUTION BY STRANGULATION** a method of execution in which an iron band is tightened around somebody's neck until death occurs ■ *vt* (**-rot·ed, -rot·ing, -rotes; -rot·ted, -rot·ting, -rottes**) **KILL SOMEBODY WITH GARROTE** to execute or kill somebody by means of a garrote [Early 17C. < Spanish *garrote* "cudgel, stick for tightening a cord"]

gar·ru·li·ty /gə róoləteе/ *n* excessive or pointless talkativeness

gar·ru·lous /gárrələss/ *adj* **1.** excessively or pointlessly talkative **2.** using many or too many words [Early 17C. < Latin *garrulus* < *garrire* "to chatter"] —**gar·ru·lous·ly** *adv* —**gar·ru·lous·ness** *n*

SYNONYMS See ***talkative.***

Gar·son /gáarss'n/, **Greer** (1908?–96) Irish-born US actor, known for her matriarchal movie roles in the 1940s and 1950s. She won an Academy Award for *Mrs. Miniver* (1942).

gar·ter /gáartər/ *n* **1.** an elastic band used to hold up a stocking, sock, or shirt sleeve **2.** a clip device, attached to a band, girdle, or belt, that fastens to the top of socks or stockings to hold them up [14C. < Old French *gartier* < *garet* "bend of the knee" < Celtic] —**gar·ter** *vt*

gar·ter belt *n* a woman's undergarment in the form of a belt to which two or more garters are attached to hold up stockings

gar·ter snake *n* a small nonpoisonous snake whose back is typically marked with yellow or red stripes running the length of the body. Native to: Central and North America. Genus: *Thamnophis.*

gar·ter stitch *n* knitting done in the same stitch, whether knit or purl, for every row [< its use in making garters]

garth /gaarth/ *n* a small courtyard or enclosed space [14C. < Old Norse *garðr*]

Popperfoto

Marcus Garvey

Gar·vey /gáarvee/, **Marcus** (1887–1940) Jamaican-born US civil rights advocate. He founded the Universal Negro Improvement Association (1914) and created a "Back to Africa" movement in the United States. Full name **Garvey, Marcus Moziah**

"I asked, 'Where is the Black man's Government?' 'Where is his King and his kingdom?' 'Where is his President, his country, and his ambassador, his army, his navy, his men of big affairs?' I could not find them, and then I declared, 'I will help to make them.'"
[Marcus Garvey, "The Negro's Greatest Enemy"; 1923]

Gar·y /gárree/ steel-producing city in northwestern Indiana, on the southern shore of Lake Michigan, west of Portage. Population: 100,945 (2002 estimate).

Gar·y, Elbert Henry (1846–1927) US business executive. He led the United States Steel Corporation (1901–27). Gary, Indiana, is named for him.

gas /gass/ *n* (*plural* **gas·es** or **gas·ses**) **1.** CHEM **SUBSTANCE SUCH AS AIR** a substance that is neither a solid nor a liquid at ordinary temperatures and has the ability to expand infinitely, e.g., air **2.** AUTOMOT **GASOLINE** gasoline for internal-combustion engines **3.** INDUST, GEOL **FOSSIL FUEL** a combustible gaseous substance used as a fuel, e.g., natural gas or propane **4.** AUTOMOT **ACCELERATOR** the pedal used for accelerating a motor vehicle (*informal*) ○ *step on the gas* **5.** MIL, CRIME **GAS FOR POISONING OR ASPHYXIATING** a gaseous mixture used as a poison, irritant, or asphyxiating agent **6.** PHARM **ANESTHETIC** a gaseous substance used as an anesthetic **7.** PHYSIOL **FLATULENCE** the gaseous product of digestion (*informal*) **8. SOMEBODY OR SOMETHING ENTERTAINING** somebody or something that is very thrilling or entertaining (*slang*) **9. NONSENSE** meaningless empty talk (*slang*) ■ *v* (**gassed, gas·sing, gas·es** or **gas·ses**) **1.** *vt* **HARM SOMEBODY WITH GAS** to attack, injure, or kill a person or animal with a poisonous, irritating, or asphyxiating gas **2.** *vi* **RELEASE GAS** to give off gas or a gas **3.** *vi* **TALK IDLY** to talk too much, especially about unimportant matters (*informal*) [Mid-17C. < Dutch, alteration of Greek *khaos* "empty space"] —**gas·sing** *n*

gas up *vti* to fill the fuel tank of a motor vehicle with gasoline

gas·bag /gáss bàg/ *n* somebody who talks too much, especially about trivial subjects (*dated informal*)

gas burn·er *n* a nozzle or opening from which gas issues and burns, e.g., on a stove

gas cham·ber *n* a room in which people are killed by means of poisonous gas

gas chro·ma·tog·ra·phy *n* a method of separating the volatile constituents of a substance by means of gas for the purpose of analysis —**gas chro·mat·o·graph** *n*

gas·con /gáskən/ *n* a boastful person (*archaic*) [Late 18C. < Gascons' legendary boastfulness]

Gas·con *n* **1.** somebody who lives in or was born or raised in Gascony, formerly a province in southwestern France **2.** a dialect of French spoken in Gascony [14C. Via French < Latin *Vascon-*] —**Gas·con** *adj*

gas con·stant *n* the constant in an equation that describes the relation of the pressure and volume of a gas to its absolute temperature. It equals 8.314 joules per kelvin. Symbol **R**

gas-cooled re·ac·tor *n* a nuclear reactor that uses carbon dioxide or helium as a coolant

Gas·coyne /gáss kòyn/ river in northern Western Australia that rises between the Collier and Robinson ranges and empties into the Indian Ocean at Shark Bay. Length: 470 mi./760 km.

Gas·coyne-Cec·il /gàss koyn séss'l/, **Robert Arthur Talbot** ➧ **Salisbury, Robert Arthur Talbot Gascoyne-Cecil**

gas-dis·charge tube *n* a tube containing gas from which light is emitted when an electric current is passed through the gas atoms and excites them

gas·e·ous /gássee əss, gáshəss/ *adj* **1. RESEMBLING GAS** neither solid nor liquid and with a tendency to expand infinitely, as does air **2. CONTAINING GAS** full of or containing gas **3. VERBOSE** having or using too many words, especially in a meaningless way (*informal*) [Late 18C. After AQUEOUS] —**gas·e·ous·ness** *n*

gas ex·change *n* the transfer of gases between an organism and its environment, e.g., the process by which oxygen enters the body and carbon dioxide is expelled from it via the lungs

gas fit·ter *n* a worker who fits and repairs gas pipes, gas fittings, and gas appliances

gas gan·grene *n* a form of gangrene, caused by aerobic clostridia bacteria, in which gas forms in injured body tissue

gas-guz·zler *n* a motor vehicle that burns comparatively large amounts of fuel (*informal*)

gash /gash/ *n* a long deep narrow slash or cut [Mid-16C. Alteration of Old N French *garser* "to cut," via late Latin *charaxare* "sharpen" < Greek *kharassein*] —**gash** *vt*

gas·hold·er /gáss hòldər/ *n* a very large tank used for storing gas that is used as combustible fuel

gas·house /gáss hòwss/ (*plural* **-hous·es** /-hòwzəz/) *n* INDUST same as **gasworks**

gas·i·form /gássə fàwrm/ *adj* CHEM same as **gaseous** (sense 1)

gas·i·fy /gássə fī/ (**-fied, -fy·ing, -fies**) *vti* to convert a solid or liquid into a gas, or become a gas —**gas·i·fi·ca·tion** /gàssəfi káysh'n/ *n*

gas jet *n* **1.** UTIL same as **gas burner 2.** a flame of burning gas

Gas·kell /gásk'l/, **Elizabeth** (1810–65) British novelist. Her novels document social conditions in newly industrialized Britain, and include *Mary Barton* (1848), *Cranford* (1851–53), and *North and South* (1855). Born **Stevenson, Elizabeth Cleghorn**. Known as **Gaskell, Mrs.**

> "I'll not listen to reason...Reason always means what someone else has got to say."
> [Elizabeth Gaskell, *Cranford*; 1853]

gas·ket /gáskət/ *n* **1.** a piece of material such as rubber, used to render a joint impermeable to gas or liquid **2.** a light line for securing a furled sail [Early 17C. Origin ?]

gas·kin /gáskin/ *n* the part of the back leg of a four-legged hoofed animal, especially a horse, that is equivalent to the lower thigh in humans [Late 16C. Origin ?]

gas law *n* a law governing the physical behavior of gases, e.g., Boyle's law or Charles's law

gas·light /gáss lìt/ *n* **1. ILLUMINATION FROM BURNING GAS** light produced by burning coal gas or natural gas **2. LAMP FUELED BY GAS** a lamp or fixture that produces light by burning gas ■ *vt* (**-lit** /-lìt/ or **-light·ed, -light·ing, -lights**) **TERRIFY SOMEBODY ELSE** to terrify and confuse somebody else to the extent that the victim questions his or her own sanity

gas-liq·uid chro·ma·tog·ra·phy *n* SCI same as **gas chromatography**

gas·lit /gáss lìt/ *adj* **1.** illuminated by light from lamps or fixtures that burn gas **2.** strangely and menacingly eerie in atmosphere or tone

gas·man /gáss màn/ (*plural* **-men** /-mèn/) *n* a worker who checks gas meters in order to note the amount of gas used in a specific period

gas mark *n UK* a mark on the temperature regulator of the oven of a gas stove, indicating a gradation of heat

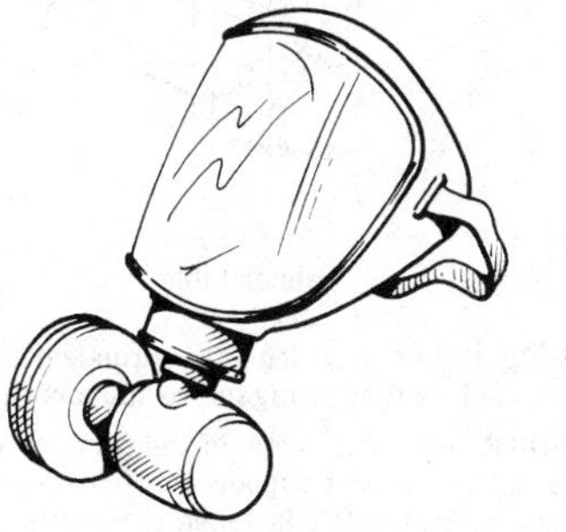

gas mask

gas mask *n* a mask provided with a filter and worn to protect the wearer's face and lungs from harmful gases

gas me·ter *n* a device installed inside or outside a residential or commercial building to measure the amount of gas consumed in a specific period

gas·o·hol /gássə hàwl/ *n* a fuel used in motor vehicles that consists of 90 percent gasoline blended with 10 percent alcohol. The alcohol is produced by the fermentation of an agricultural product high in sugar, e.g., corn. [Late 20C. Blend of GASOLINE + ALCOHOL]

gas oil *n* a light petroleum distillate with a viscosity and boiling point between that of kerosene and lubricating oil. Gas oils include diesel fuel, heating oil, and light fuel oils.

gas·o·line /gássə lèen, gàssə lèen/ *n* a volatile flammable liquid made from petroleum and used as fuel in internal-combustion engines

gas·om·e·ter /ga sómmətər/ *n* **1.** an apparatus for measuring and storing gas in a laboratory **2.** UTIL same as **gasholder**

gasp /gasp/ *v* (**gasped, gasp·ing, gasps**) **1.** *vi* **BREATHE IN SHARPLY** to draw in breath with a sudden short audible intake **2.** *vi* **LABOR TO BREATHE** to breathe with laborious effort **3.** *vt* **SAY SOMETHING WITH GASP** to say something with a sudden short audible intake of breath ■ *n* **1. SUDDEN INTAKE OF BREATH** a sudden short audible intake of breath, e.g., in surprise or pain **2. INSTANCE OF DIFFICULT BREATHING** a laborious effort to breathe [14C. < Old Norse *geispa* "yawn"] ◇ **the last gasp** somebody's final attempt or action, or the final phase of something

Gas·pé /gass páy/ city in southeastern Quebec Province, Canada, near Forillon National Park. Population: 3,277 (2001).

Gas·pé Pen·in·su·la peninsula in southeastern Quebec Province, Canada, bordered by the St. Lawrence River, Chaleur Bay, and New Brunswick. Area: 11,400 sq. mi./29,500 sq. km.

gas-per·me·a·ble *adj* describes a type of contact lens that allows air to pass through it to the eye for added comfort

gas plant *n* a perennial plant of the rue family with strong-smelling leaves that give off a flammable gas. Flowers: white. Native to: Europe, Asia. Latin name: *Dictamnus albus*.

gas·ser /gássər/ *n* **1.** a well that produces natural gas **2.** something, e.g., a joke, that is very thrilling or entertaining (*dated slang*)

gas sta·tion *n* a place at which drivers can buy fuel, oil, and other motoring supplies, and sometimes also have car repairs done

gas·sy /gássee/ (**-si·er, -si·est**) *adj* **1. FULL OF GAS** full of or containing gas such as carbon dioxide **2. LIKE GAS** resembling gas in being neither a solid nor a liquid at ordinary temperatures and able to expand infinitely **3. VERBOSE** having or using too many words, especially in a meaningless way (*informal*) —**gas·si·ness** *n*

gas·tight /gáss tìt/ *adj* preventing any gas from passing through

gastr- *prefix* same as **gastro-** (*used before vowels*)

gas·trec·to·my /ga stréktəmee/ (*plural* **-mies**) *n* the surgical removal of all or part of the stomach. It is usually performed in the treatment of stomach cancer or severe stomach ulcers.

gas·tric /gástrik/ *adj* relating to, involving, or near the stomach [Mid-17C. < modern Latin *gastricus* < Greek *gastēr* "stomach"]

gas·tric juice *n* the acidic digestive fluid secreted by glands in the stomach

gas·tric ul·cer *n* an erosion in the stomach wall caused by gastric acid, digestive enzymes, or other factors that may include bacterial infection

gas·trin /gástrin/ *n* a hormone produced in the stomach that increases the release of gastric juice

gas·tri·tis /ga strítəss/ *n* inflammation of the mucous membrane that lines the stomach

gastro- *prefix* stomach, belly ○ *gastrectomy* [< Greek *gastr-*, stem of *gastēr* "stomach" (see GASTRIC)]

gas·troc·ne·mi·us /gàss trok nèemee əss/ (*plural* **-mi·i** /-mee ī/) *n* the largest muscle in the calf of the leg, extending from the thigh bone to the Achilles tendon. When it contracts, it causes the foot to point downward. [Late 17C. Via modern Latin < Greek *gastroknēmia* "calf of the leg" < *gastēr* "stomach"; from its bulging form]

gas·tro·en·ter·i·tis /gàstrō entə rítəss/ *n* inflammation of the stomach and the intestines, with vomiting and diarrhea, usually as a result of bacterial or viral infection

gas·tro·en·ter·ol·o·gy /gàstrō entə róllәjee/ *n* the branch of medicine concerned with the study and treatment of diseases of the stomach and intestines and their associated organs —**gas·tro·en·ter·o·log·ic** /gàstrō entərə lójjik/ *adj* —**gas·tro·en·ter·ol·o·gist** *n*

gas·tro·e·soph·a·ge·al re·flux dis·ease /gàstrō i sòffə jèe əl-/ *n* the chronic reflux of stomach contents into the esophagus, resulting in heartburn

gas·tro·in·tes·ti·nal /gàstrō in téstən'l/ *adj* relating to the stomach and intestines

gas·tro·lith /gástrə lìth/ *n* **1.** a stone swallowed by an animal such as a bird or dinosaur as an aid to the digestion of food **2.** a stone that has formed in the stomach

gas·trol·o·gy /ga stróllәjee/ *n* the study of the stomach and its diseases —**gas·tro·log·i·cal** *adj* —**gas·trol·o·gist** *n*

gas·tro·nome /gástrə nòm/, **gas·tron·o·mist** /ga strónnəmist/ *n* a connoisseur of good food [Early 19C. < French, back-formation < *gastronomie* (see GASTRONOMY)]

gas·tron·o·my /ga strónnəmee/ (*plural* **-mies**) *n* **1.** the art and appreciation of preparing and eating good food **2.** a particular style of cooking or dining, e.g., one that is characteristic of a particular country or region [Early 19C. Via French *gastronomie* < Greek *gastronomia*, alteration of *gastrologia* "study of the stomach"] —**gas·tro·nom·ic** /gàstrə nómmik/ *adj* —**gas·tro·nom·i·cal·ly** *adv*

gas·tro·plas·ty /gástrə plàstee/ (*plural* **-ties**) *n* a surgical operation to repair a malformation of the stomach

gas·tro·pod /gástrə pòd/ *n* a mollusk that has a head with eyes, a large flattened foot, and often a single shell, e.g., a limpet, snail, or slug. Class: Gastropoda. [Early 19C. < modern Latin *Gastropoda* "stomach-foot"] —**gas·tro·pod** *adj*

gas·tro·scope /gástrə skòp/ *n* an instrument passed through the mouth and used to examine the stomach, consisting of a flexible tube that contains optical fibers coupled to an eyepiece and light source —**gas·tro·scop·ic** /gàstrə skóppik/ *adj* —**gas·tros·co·py** /ga stróskəpee/ *n*

gas·tros·to·my /ga stróstəmee/ (*plural* **-mies**) *n* a surgical operation in which an opening for a tube is made through the wall of the stomach and joined to an opening in the adjacent abdominal wall. It allows food and liquids to be placed directly into the stomach via a tube when the esophagus is affected by disease or recovering from surgery.

gas·trot·o·my /ga stróttəmee/ (*plural* **-mies**) *n* a surgical incision into the stomach for examination of the cavity or to remove a foreign object

gas·tro·vas·cu·lar /gàstrō váskyələr/ *adj* describes a part of the body involved in both digestion and circulation, e.g., the central body cavity of some jellyfish

gas·tru·la /gástrələ/ (*plural* **-las** or **-lae** /-lee̅/) *n* the stage in embryonic development after the blastula during which the embryo develops two layers [Late 19C. < modern Latin, "little stomach" < Greek *gastēr* "stomach"] —**gas·tru·lar** *adj*

gas·tru·la·tion /gàstrə láysh'n/ *n* the process of cell movements by which a developing embryo forms distinct layers that later grow into different organs —**gas·tru·late** /gástrə làyt/ *vi*

gas tur·bine *n* an internal-combustion engine in which a turbine is turned by hot gases consisting of compressed air and the products of the fuel's combustion

gas·works /gáss wùrks/ (*plural same*) *n* a factory where gas for heating and illuminating is produced, especially from coal

gat[1] /gat/ *n* a passage or channel of water that extends inland from a shore [Late 16C. Probably < Old Norse *gat* "hole"]

gat[2] /gat/ *n* same as **handgun** (*dated slang*) [Early 20C. Shortening of GATLING GUN]

gat[3] past tense of **get**[1] (*archaic*)

gate /gayt/ *n* **1. BARRIER ACROSS GAP** a movable barrier, usually on hinges, that closes a gap in a fence or wall **2. OPENING IN WALL** an opening in a wall or fence **3. OPENING IN DEFENSIVE STRUCTURE** an opening in a castle or city wall or other defensive structure **4. POINT OF ACCESS** a means of access or entrance **5. ARRIVAL OR DEPARTURE POINT** the area at an airport or a railroad or bus station where passengers arrive and depart **6. BARRIER AT TOLLBOOTH** a movable barrier restricting access, e.g., at a tollbooth **7.** same as **starting gate** (sense 1) (*informal*) **8. BARRIER FOR FLUID** a sliding barrier, valve, or other mechanism for regulating the passage of a fluid **9. SPECTATORS** the total number of people who pay for admission to an entertainment or sports event **10. MONEY FROM TICKETS** the total amount of money paid for tickets for an entertainment or sporting event **11.** SKIING **PATH BETWEEN POLES** the space between two markers through which a skier passes in a slalom race **12.** COMPUT **LOGIC CIRCUIT** a logical device in a computer, with one output channel and one or more input channels, that emits a signal only when specific input conditions are met **13.** ELECTRONICS **REGULATING SWITCH** an electronic switch that regulates the flow of current or the passage of a signal in a circuit **14.** ROWING **FASTENING FOR OAR** a fastening with a hinge that serves to keep an oar in its oarlock **15.** *N England, Scotland* **WAY** a path or road ■ *vt* (**gat·ed, gat·ing, gates**) **1. CONTROL SOMETHING USING GATE** to control or regulate somebody or something with a gate **2. PUT GATE IN SOMETHING** to install a gate in something, e.g., in a fence [Old English *geat* < Germanic, "opening in a wall." Partly < Old Norse *gata* "path"]

SPELLCHECK See *gait*.

-gate *suffix* political scandal [< WATERGATE]

ga·teau /ga tṓ, gaa-/ (*plural* **-teaux** /-tṓz/ or **-teaus**), **gâ·teau** (*plural* **-teaux** /-tṓ/) *n* **1.** a rich cake, usually consisting of several layers held together with a cream filling **2.** food baked and served in a form resembling a cake [Mid-19C. < French, "cake"]

gate·crash·er /gáyt kràshər/ *n* somebody who attends a party or other event without an invitation or ticket —**gate·crash** *vti*

gate·fold /gáyt fṑld/ *n* a page in a publication that is larger than the other pages and is folded to fit

gate·house /gáyt hòwss/ (*plural* **-hous·es** /-hòwzəz/) *n* a building or house above or beside a gate

gate·keep·er /gáyt keepər/ *n* **1.** a supervisor or guard who tends a gate **2.** a person or group that controls access to somebody or something —**gate·keep·ing** *n*

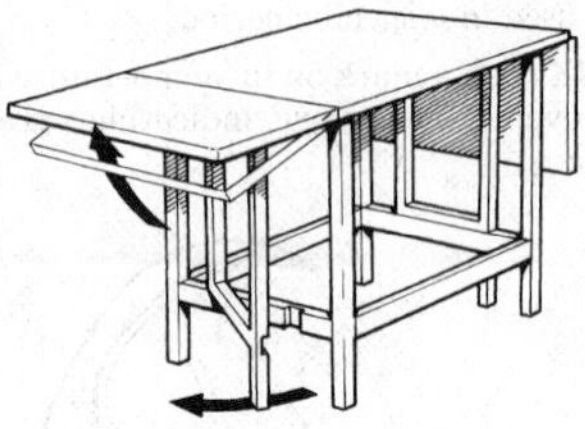

gateleg table

gate·leg ta·ble /gàyt leg-/ *n* a drop-leaf table with movable legs that swing out to support the leaves

gate·post /gáyt pṑst/ *n* one of the posts on each side of a gate. One post supports the gate and the gate closes against and is fastened to the other.

ga·ter, **'ga·ter** *n* REPT another spelling of **gator** (*informal*)

Gates /gayts/, **Henry Louis, Jr.** (*b.* 1950) US educator, scholar, and critic. One of the most prominent academics in the United States, he has been chair of Harvard's Afro-American Studies program since 1991.

Gates, Horatio (1728?–1806) British-born US army officer. A general in the Continental Army, he was credited with the American victory at Saratoga in 1777.

Gates, William Henry III (*b.* 1955) US business executive. He is chief software architect and chairman of Microsoft Corporation, a leading software company, which he cofounded in 1975. He is also the author of *The Road Ahead* (1995) and *Business @ the Speed of Thought* (1999). Known as **Bill**

> "Technology is just a tool. In terms of getting the kids working together and motivating them, the teacher is the most important."
> [William Henry Gates III, "For the Record," *Independent on Sunday (London)*; October 12, 1997]

Gates·head /gáyts hèd/ industrial city in County Durham, northeastern England. Population: 191,151 (2001).

Gates of the Arc·tic Na·tion·al Park and Pre·serve national park consisting mainly of tundra in northern Alaska, north of the Arctic Circle. Area: 13,238 sq. mi./34,287 sq. km.

gate·way /gáyt wày/ *n* **1. OPENING WITH GATE** an opening that may be closed by a gate **2. ACCESS POINT** a means of access to something ○ *the gateway to educational success* **3.** COMPUT **COMPUTER-NETWORK CONNECTION** software or hardware that links two computer networks **4.** COMPUT **NETWORK ENTRY POINT** an entry point to a computer network

gate·way drug *n* a drug that does not cause physical dependence but may lead to the use of addictive drugs

gate·way page *n* the initial webpage that a visitor to a website sees and that contains key words and phrases that enable a search engine to find it

gath·er /gáthər/ *v* (**-ered, -er·ing, -ers**) **1.** *vti* **FORM INTO GROUP** to bring people or things together to form a group, or come together to form a group **2.** *vt* **HARVEST SOMETHING** to pick or harvest a crop **3.** *vt* **COLLECT DATA** to compile something such as information or ideas from various sources **4.** *vt* **ATTRACT FOLLOWING** to attract a group of people as supporters, followers, or an audience ○ *The street players have gathered quite a crowd.* **5.** *vti* **ACCUMULATE SOMETHING** to accumulate a gradually increasing mass or quantity of something, or be accumulated gradually ○ *Clouds gathered on the horizon.* **6.** *vt* **FIND INNER STRENGTH** to summon up energies, courage, or strength from within **7.** *vt* **SURMISE SOMETHING** to conclude something from intuition or observation **8.** *vt* **BRING SOMEBODY OR SOMETHING CLOSE** to draw somebody or something close **9.** *vt* **LIFT SOMEBODY OR SOMETHING UP** to pick or scoop somebody or something up **10.** *vti* **WRINKLE BROW** to draw the brow into wrinkles, or be drawn into wrinkles **11.** *vt* **PULL FABRIC TOGETHER** to draw fabric together in a series of folds along a line of stitching **12.** *vt* PRINTING **PUT PAGES IN ORDER** to assemble the printed sections of a book in the correct order for binding **13.** *vt* GLASS **PREPARE MOLTEN GLASS FOR BLOWING** to collect molten glass at the end of a tube for blowing and shaping **14.** *vi* MED **FORM PUS-FILLED HEAD** to form and fill with pus ■ *n* **1. FOLD IN FABRIC** one in a series of folds in fabric **2.** GLASS **MOLTEN GLASS BALL** a ball of molten glass collected on a tube for blowing and shaping [Old English *gaderian* < Indo-European, "bring together"] —**gath·er·er** *n*

SYNONYMS See *collect*[1].

gath·er·ing /gáthəring/ *n* **1. ASSEMBLY** a meeting or crowd of people **2. CLUSTER OF THINGS** a collection of objects **3. COLLECTING OF SOMETHING** the collecting of people or objects into a group **4. FOLDS IN CLOTH** a series of folds in fabric **5.** MED **BOIL** a pus-filled swelling

Gat·ling gun /gáttling-/ *n* an early machine gun with multiple barrels firing in rotation [Mid-19C. After Richard Jordan *Gatling* (1818–1903), US inventor]

ga·tor /gáytər/, **'ga·tor, ga·ter, 'ga·ter** *n* same as **alligator** *n* (sense 1) (*informal*) [Mid-19C. Shortening]

GATT /gat/, **Gatt** *abbr* General Agreement on Tariffs and Trade

Ga·tún, Lake /gə tóon/ artificial lake on the Chagres River in Panama. It is an important part of the Panama Canal system. Area: 170 sq. mi./430 sq. km.

Gat·wick /gáttwik/ London's second largest international airport, located to the south of the city on the border between the counties of Surrey and Sussex, England

gauche /gōsh/ *adj* lacking grace or tact in social situations [Mid-18C. < French, "left-handed"] —**gauche·ly** *adv* —**gauche·ness** *n*

Gau·cher dis·ease /gō sháy-/ *n* a genetic metabolic disorder in which a fatty substance accumulates in the body, especially the spleen, liver, lungs, and bone marrow. The disorder is characterized by bruising, fatigue, anemia, low blood platelets, and enlargement of the liver and spleen. [Mid-20C. After P. C. E. *Gaucher* (1854–1918), French physician]

gau·che·rie /gṑshə rée/ *n* **1.** a lack of grace or tact in social situations **2.** an act that is graceless or tactless [Late 18C. < French, < *gauche* "left-handed"]

gau·cho /gówchō/ *n* (*plural* **-chos**) *Hispanic* a cowboy of the South American pampas or prairie ■ **gau·chos** *npl* women's culottes adapted from the wide-bottomed mid-calf leather pants worn by South American cowboys and first popular in the late 1960s [Early 19C. < American Spanish]

gau·cho pants *npl* a pair of gauchos

gaud /gawd/ *n* a showy trinket or ornament (*archaic*) [14C. Origin ?]

gaud·er·y /gáwdəree/ (*plural* **-ies**) *n* showy and ostentatious clothing or jewelry, or its display

Gau·dí /gow dée, gówdee/, **Antoni** (1852–1926) Spanish architect. His individual and unconventional style of architecture is typified in the unfinished Church of the Sagrada Família (1883) in Barcelona. He was a leading exponent of the Catalan branch of art nouveau, "modernisme." Full name **Gaudí i Cornet, Antoni Plàcid**

gaud·y /gáwdee/ (**-i·er, -i·est**) *adj* brightly colored or showily decorated to an unpleasant or vulgar degree [15C. < GAUD] —**gaud·i·ly** *adv* —**gaud·i·ness** *n*

gauge /gayj/, **gage** *vt* (**gauged, gaug·ing, gaug·es; gaged, gag·ing, gag·es**) **1. CALCULATE SOMETHING** to determine the amount, quantity, size, or extent of something

○ *It's quite difficult to gauge the distance accurately.* **2. EVALUATE SOMETHING** to form a judgment of something uncertain or variable, especially somebody's behavior, feelings, or abilities ○ *Try to gauge his mood before raising the proposal.* **3. ENSURE CONFORMITY TO STANDARD** to ensure that something conforms to a standard of measurement ■ *n* **1. MEASURING DEVICE** a device or instrument for measuring an amount or quantity or for testing accuracy **2. MEASUREMENT** a standard measurement or scale of measurement **3. CRITERION** a standard or system of measurement for assessing somebody or something ○ *a gauge of the applicant's ability* **4. DISTANCE BETWEEN RAILS** the distance between the two rails of a railroad track **5. DISTANCE BETWEEN WHEELS** the distance between two wheels on an axle of a vehicle **6. THICKNESS OF WIRE** the diameter of something, especially of wire or a needle **7. THICKNESS OF MATERIAL** the thickness of a thin material such as sheet metal or plastic film **8.** NAUT **RELATIVE POSITION** the position of a ship in relation to another vessel and the wind **9.** TEXTILES **FINENESS OF KNIT** the fineness of knitted fabric expressed in terms of the number of loops for each unit of width **10.** CONSTR **ADDED PROPORTION OF PLASTER OF PARIS** the proportion of plaster of Paris that is added to mortar to speed up the setting of the mixture [14C. < Old N French, variant of French *jauge*] —**gauge·a·ble** *adj*

gaug·er /gáyjər/, **gag·er** *n* a person who or instrument that gauges something

gauge the·o·ry *n* a theory describing the interactions between elementary particles by considering particles to be quantized fields

Gau·guin /gō gáN/, **Paul** (1848–1903) French painter. One of the most influential postimpressionist painters, he is known for his use of flat fields of deep color. After 1891 he lived mostly in Polynesia, the inspiration for many of his most powerful works. Full name **Gauguin, Eugène Henri Paul**

Gau·ha·ti /gow haátee/ industrial city and port on the Brahmaputra River in Assam State, northeastern India. Population: 814,575 (2001).

Gaul /gawl/ *n* **1. ANCIENT FRANCE** an ancient region of western Europe that included large portions of France, Belgium, and neighboring parts of Italy, the Netherlands, and Germany. It was invaded and conquered by the Romans before 100 B.C. and again in the Gallic Wars of 58–51 B.C. under Julius Caesar. **2. SOMEBODY FROM GAUL** somebody who came from ancient Gaul **3. FRENCH PERSON** somebody who is French [15C. < Latin *Gallus*]

Gaul·ish /gáwlish/ *n* an extinct Celtic language spoken in Gaul before the Roman conquest ■ *adj* relating to ancient Gaul, or its people, language, or culture

Gaulle ♦ **de Gaulle, Charles**

Gaull·ism /gáw lìzzəm/ *n* **1.** the nationalist and conservative principles and policies of General Charles de Gaulle, leader of France after World War II, and his followers **2.** the political movement founded on the principles of Charles de Gaulle —**Gaull·ist** *n, adj*

gaunt /gawnt/ *adj* **1.** extremely thin and bony in appearance **2.** stark in outline or appearance [15C. Origin ?] —**gaunt·ly** *adv* —**gaunt·ness** *n*

gaunt·let[1] /gáwntlət/, **gant·let** /gáwntlət, gaánt-/ *n* a glove with a long wide cuff that covers and protects part of the forearm [15C. < French *gantelet* "little glove" < *gant* "glove" < Germanic] ◇ **throw down the gauntlet** to issue a challenge

gaunt·let[2] /gáwntlət/, **gant·let** /gáwntlət, gaánt-/ *n* a punishment formerly used in the military in which somebody was forced to run between two lines of men armed with weapons who beat him as he passed [Mid-17C. Alteration, influenced by GAUNTLET[1], of *gantlop* < Swedish *gatlopp* "passageway"] ◇ **run the gauntlet** to endure attack or criticism from all sides

gaur /gowr/ *n* a large wild ox with a dark coat. Native to: mountains of southeastern Asia. Latin name: *Bos gaurus.* [Early 19C. < Sanskrit *gaura* < Indo-European]

~~**gaurd**~~ incorrect spelling of **guard**

Gause's prin·ci·ple /gòwzəz-/, **Gause prin·ci·ple** /gòwz-/ *n* ECOL same as **competitive exclusion** [After G. F. *Gause* (1910–), Russian biologist]

gauss /gowss/ (*plural same* or **gauss·es**) *n* the centimeter-gram-second unit of magnetic flux density, equivalent to 10^{-4} tesla. Symbol **G** [Late 19C. After Karl Friedrich *Gauss* (1777–1855), German mathematician]

Gauss·i·an /gówssee ən/ *adj* relating to or formulated by Karl Friedrich Gauss, especially statistically normal [Late 19C. After Karl Friedrich *Gauss* (see GAUSS)]

Gauss·i·an curve *n* STATS same as **normal curve**

Gauss·i·an dis·tri·bu·tion *n* STATS same as **normal distribution**

Gau·teng /khow téng/ province in South Africa, in the north central part of the country. Capital: Johannesburg. Population: 8,837,157 (2001). Area: 6,568 sq. mi./17,010 sq. km.

Gau·tier /gō tyáy/, **Théophile** (1811–72) French writer. His works include the novel *Mademoiselle de Maupin* (1835) and the verse collection *Émaux et camées* (1852).

> "Everything passes. Robust art alone is eternal, the bust survives the city."
> [Théophile Gautier, "L'Art"; 1857]

gauze /gawz/ *n* **1. FINELY WOVEN FABRIC** a thin, almost transparent, loosely woven cotton or silk cloth. Use: curtains, clothes. **2. SURGICAL DRESSING** a dressing for wounds made of loosely woven material such as cotton **3. WIRE MESH** a thin mesh made of wire or other material **4. HAZE** a fine haze or mist [Mid-16C. < French *gaze*] —**gauz·i·ly** *adv* —**gauz·y** *adj*

ga·vage /gə vaázh/ *n* the feeding of an animal or a person through a tube passed into the stomach [Late 19C. < French < *gaver* "stuff down the throat"]

gave past tense of **give**

gav·el /gávv'l/ *n* a small hammer used by a judge, chair of a meeting, or auctioneer to draw people's attention or to mark the conclusion of a transaction ■ *vti* **(-eled, -el·ing, -els)** to use a gavel to bring an end to something or to stop discussion [Early 19C. Origin ?]

gav·el-to-gav·el *adj* extending from the beginning to the end of a political meeting or similar event (*informal*)

ga·vi·al /gáyvee əl/ *n US* a large reptile resembling a crocodile that has a very long narrow snout and feeds on fish and frogs. Native to: India, Borneo, Sumatra. Latin name: *Gavialis gangeticus.* Can term **gharial** [Early 19C. Via French < Hindi *ghariyāl*]

Ga·vi·ri·a /gaávə reé ə/, **César** (*b.* 1947) Colombian secretary general of the Organization of American States. A former president of Colombia (1990–94), he was first elected OAS secretary general in 1994 and re-elected in 1999.

Gäv·le /yévvlə/ port and capital of the county of Gävleborg, eastern Sweden, north of Stockholm. Population: 90,308 (1998).

ga·votte /gə vót/ *n* **1.** a French country dance in 4/4 time, popular in the 18th century **2.** the music for a gavotte [Late 19C. Via French < Provençal *Gavot* "inhabitant of the Alps"]

GAW *abbr* FIN guaranteed annual wage

Ga·wain /gə wáyn/ *n* in Arthurian legend, a knight who was the enemy of Sir Lancelot and who fought a mysterious green knight

Gawd /gawd/, **gawd** *interj, n* God, used to suggest irony or rustic pronunciation in oaths (*slang*)

gawk /gawk/ *vi* **(gawked, gawk·ing, gawks)** to stare stupidly or rudely (*informal*) ■ *n* somebody regarded as awkward or clumsy (*dated insult*) [Late 17C. Origin ?]

SYNONYMS See ***gaze.***

gawk·y /gáwkee/ **(-i·er, -i·est)** *adj* awkward and clumsy, often because of being tall and not well coordinated (*informal*) —**gawk·i·ly** *adv* —**gaw·ki·ness** *n*

gawp /gawp/ **(gawped, gawp·ing, gawps)** *vi* to stare stupidly or rudely (*informal*) ○ *Don't just stand there gawping, help her!* [Late 17C. Origin ?]

SYNONYMS See ***gaze.***

gay /gay/ *adj* **1. ATTRACTED TO SAME SEX** relating to sexual attraction or activity among members of the same sex **2. MERRY** full of light-heartedness and merriment (*dated*) **3. BRIGHT IN COLOR** brightly colored (*dated*) **4. CAREFREE** having or showing a carefree spirit (*dated*) **5. DEBAUCHED** leading a debauched or dissolute life (*dated*) ■ *n* **GAY MAN OR LESBIAN** somebody, especially a man, who is attracted to other members of the same sex [13C. < Old French *gai* "happy"] —**gay·ness** *n*

USAGE ***Gay*** is preferred to *homosexual*. The adjective ***gay*** encompasses both men and women, but when there is a need to specify both genders, as in *gay and lesbian alliances*, ***gay*** describes men. Avoid using ***gay*** as a noun, as in *He's a gay* and *Four gays walked in*, because it can be taken to be offensive. Preferred substitutes are *He is gay* and *Four gay people/men/women walked in.*

ga·yal /gə yaál/ (*plural same* or **-yals**) *n* a wild or semidomesticated ox with a dark coat and white leg markings. Native to: South Asia, Myanmar. Latin name: *Bos frontalis.* [Late 18C. < Bengali]

gay·dar /gáy daàr/ *n* the supposed instinctive ability of gay people to identify others who are also gay (*informal*) [Blend of GAY + RADAR]

Marvin Gaye

Gaye /gay/, **Marvin** (1939–84) US singer and songwriter. He was one of the most successful soul singers from the 1960s and had an international bestselling hit with "I Heard It Through the Grapevine" (1968).

Gay-Lus·sac's law /gày lə sáks-/ *n* the principle that when gases combine in a chemical reaction they do so in simple ratios of their volumes, and that any gaseous product is also produced in a simple ratio [Early 19C. After Joseph-Louis *Gay-Lussac* (1778–1850), French physicist]

gay pride *n* a movement that encourages gay people to be open and proud about their homosexuality (*informal*)

gay rights *npl* civil rights for gay people, particularly the right to be treated without discrimination both legally and socially (*informal*)

gaz. *abbr* **1.** MEDIA gazette **2.** PUBL gazetteer

Ga·za /gaázə/ seaport and principal city of the Gaza Strip, on the Mediterranean coast. An important city in biblical times, it has both historic and current political significance. Population: 353,632 (1997).

ga·zar /gə zaár/ *n* a stiff loosely woven silk [Mid-20C. Origin ?]

Ga·za Strip region on the eastern Mediterranean coast bordered on the south by Egypt and on the east and north by Israel. Administered by Egypt from 1949 and Israel from 1967, it became an autonomous zone under the control of the Palestinian National Authority in 1994. The city of Gaza is the region's administrative center. Population: 1,274,868 (2003). Area: 146 sq. mi./378 sq. km.

gaze /gayz/ *vi* **(gazed, gaz·ing, gaz·es)** to look for a long time with unwavering attention ○ *He gazed longingly at the yacht.* ■ *n* a long steady look or stare [14C. Origin ?] —**gaz·er** *n*

SYNONYMS ***gaze, gape, gawk, ogle, rubberneck, stare***

CORE MEANING: to look at somebody or something steadily or at length

gaze to look for a long time with unwavering attention ○ *He gazed into her eyes.* ○ *People stood around gazing up at the departure and arrival boards.* **gape** to look at somebody or something in surprise or wonder, usually with an open mouth ○ *The boys of sixteen and seventeen gaped at Lily as if she were a goddess.* ○ *Francis gaped – he just couldn't comprehend what he* *was seeing.* **gawk** (*informal*) to stare stupidly or rudely ○ *Hundreds of people crowded around, gawking at the sculpture.* **ogle** to look at somebody for sexual enjoyment or as a way of showing sexual interest ○ *lines of eyes, peeping and ogling* ○ *ogled the girls' legs* **rubberneck** (*informal*) to stare at somebody or something in an excessively inquisitive or insensitive way ○ *One passer-by crashed his motorcycle rubbernecking while driving by.* ○ *Rubbernecking drivers slowed to gape at the wreckage.* **stare** to look at somebody or something directly and intently without moving the eyes away, often as a result of curiosity or surprise, or to express rudeness or defiance ○ *He halted on the threshold and stared in astonishment at the collection of memorabilia that littered every surface.* ○ *He stared coldly at his father for a moment and then left the room.*

ga·ze·bo /gə zeébō/ (*plural* **-bos** or **-boes**) *n* **1.** a small, usually open-sided and slightly elevated building, situated in a spot that commands a pleasant view **2.** a lightweight freestanding open-sided canopy for use in a garden, usually as a sunshade [Mid-18C. Origin ?]

gaze·hound /gáyz hòwnd/ *n* a dog that hunts by sight rather than by smell, e.g., a greyhound or Afghan hound

gazelle

ga·zelle /gə zél/ (*plural* **-zelles** or *same*) *n* a small graceful swift antelope with long ringed horns and black face markings. Native to: plains of Africa and Asia. Genera: *Gazella* or *Procapra*. [Early 17C. < Old French *gazel*]

ga·zette /gə zét/ *n* **1. NEWSPAPER** a newspaper, especially a local newspaper or the official paper of an organization ○ *the Medical Union Gazette* **2.** *UK* **PUBLICATION WITH OFFICIAL NEWS** an official publication in which government appointments, public notices, lists of bankruptcies, and other items appear ■ *vt* (**-zet·ted, -zet·ting, -zettes**) *UK* **PUBLISH SOMETHING IN GAZETTE** to publish or announce something or name somebody in a gazette (*often passive*) [Early 17C. Directly or via French < Italian *gazzetta* < Venetian dialect *gazeta de la novità* "pennyworth of news"]

gaz·et·teer /gàzzə teér/ *n* a dictionary or index of places, usually with descriptive or statistical information

ga·zil·li·on /gə zíllyən/ *n* an extremely large number or quantity (*slang*) [Late 20C. < *Gaz-*, origin ? + MILLION or BILLION]

gaz·pa·cho /gə spaáchō, gəz paáchō/ *n* a chilled soup based on stock or tomato juice and containing chopped raw vegetables and seasoning [Early 19C. < Spanish]

G.B. *abbr* **1.** PHYS gilbert **2.** Great Britain

GBLT *abbr* gay, bisexual, lesbian, transgender

Gbyte *abbr* COMPUT gigabyte

Gc *abbr* PHYS gigacycle

GCA *abbr* AVIAT ground-controlled approach

G.C.D. *abbr* MATH greatest common divisor

G.C.F., g.c.f. *abbr* MATH greatest common factor

G clef *n* MUSIC same as **treble clef**

GCS *abbr* MED Glasgow Coma Scale

gd *abbr* Grenada (*used in Internet addresses*) See table at **domain name**

Gd *symbol* CHEM ELEM gadolinium

gd. *abbr* good

G·dansk /gə daánsk, -dánsk/ city, seaport, and shipbuilding center in northern Poland. It is situated at the mouth of the Vistula River, on the Baltic Sea. Population: 461,300 (1997). German name **Danzig**

GDI *abbr* COMPUT graphics device interface

GDP *abbr* COMM gross domestic product

GDR, G.D.R. *abbr* HIST German Democratic Republic

G·dy·nia /gə dínnee ə, -dínnyə/ seaport and city on the Gulf of Gdansk, northern Poland. Population: 251,600 (1997).

ge *abbr* Georgia (*used in Internet addresses*) See table at **domain name**

Ge *symbol* CHEM ELEM germanium

ge- *prefix* same as **geo-** (*used before vowels*)

gean /geen/ *n* same as **sweet cherry** [Mid-16C. < Old French *guine*]

ge·an·ti·cline /jee ánti klīn/ *n* a large region of rock raised up from the Earth's surface [Late 19C. < Greek *gē* "earth"] —**ge·an·ti·cli·nal** /jee ànti klīn'l/ *adj*

gear /geer/ *n* **1. FIXED TRANSMISSION SETTING** one of several fixed transmission settings in a vehicle that determine power or direction **2. TOOTHED PART THAT TRANSMITS MOTION** a toothed mechanical part, e.g., a wheel or cylinder, that engages with a similar toothed part to transmit motion from one rotating body to another **3. SET OF PARTS TO TRANSMIT MOTION** a unit of a mechanism that transmits motion from one part to another part for performing a particular function ○ *steering gear* **4. ENGAGED STATE** the state of a vehicle when one of its gears is engaged ○ *The car won't start when it's in gear.* **5. LEVEL OF EFFICIENCY** the particular speed or efficiency with which somebody works (*informal*) ○ *I feel as if I'm still in first gear.* **6. MACHINERY** a piece or system of machinery with a particular function **7. EQUIPMENT** the equipment that is needed for a particular activity (*informal*) ○ *hiking gear* **8. CLOTHES** clothes and accessories of a particular kind (*informal*) ○ *You have to have the right gear.* **9.** NAUT **SAILING EQUIPMENT** the equipment, rigging, and other objects that belong to a particular boat or sailor **10.** RIDING **HARNESS** a horse's harness ■ *vt* (**geared, gear·ing, gears**) **1. PUT GEARS IN SOMETHING** to equip something with gears **2. ENGAGE GEAR OF VEHICLE** to put a vehicle into gear [13C < Old Norse *gervi* "make ready"]

gear to, gear to·ward *vt* to adapt or adjust something so that it fits in or works effectively with something else (*usually passive*) ○ *We've tried to gear ourselves to the younger market.*

gear up *vti* to prepare somebody or something to do something, take action in preparation for something (*usually passive or continuous*) ○ *We're all geared up for the next round of talks.*

gear·box /geér bòks/ *n UK* same as **transmission** (sense 5)

gear·ing /geéring/ *n* **1.** a set of mechanical gears, or the power that it provides ○ *complaints about the gearing on the older model* **2.** the process or act of providing a system with gears **3.** *UK* FIN same as **leverage** *n* (sense 5)

gear lev·er *n UK* MECH ENG same as **gearshift**

gear·shift /geér shìft/ *n* a lever or mechanism in a car or other vehicle or machine that is used to shift or engage gears

gear stick *n UK* MECH ENG same as **gearshift**

gear tooth *n* one of the many small projections on a gearwheel that fits in the space between two other projections on another gearwheel, thus engaging the gear

gear train *n* a collection of gears used to transmit power

gear·wheel /geér weèl, -hweèl/ *n* MECH ENG same as **gear** *n* (sense 2)

ge·bel *n* GEOG another spelling of **jebel**

gecko

geck·o /gékō/ (*plural* **-os** or **-oes** /-ōz/) *n* a small tropical or subtropical nocturnal insect-eating lizard with hooked ridges on the pads of its feet that permit it to climb smooth vertical surfaces. Family: Gekkonidae. [Late 18C. < Malay dialect *geko(k)*]

GED *n* a diploma for adults equivalent to a high-school diploma. Full form **General Equivalency Diploma**

ge·dank·en ex·per·i·ment /gə daángkən-/ *n* a test of a hypothesis that can be performed only in the mind [Mid-20C. < German]

gee[1] /jee/ *interj* **1. EXPRESSING ENTHUSIASM** used to express surprise or to register a reaction to something, especially enthusiasm or ironic enthusiasm **2. HURRY UP!** used to urge a horse, cow, or similar animal to move faster, to go straight ahead, or to turn right ■ *vt* (**geed, gee·ing, gees**) **HURRY ANIMAL UP** to urge a horse, cow, or similar animal to move faster, to go straight ahead, or to turn right [Mid-18C. Origin ?]

gee[2] /jee/ (*plural* **gees** or *same*) *n* one thousand dollars (*informal*) [Mid-20C. Representing the pronunciation of G[1] (sense 7)]

Gee·chee /geéchee/ *n S Atlantic US* LANG, PEOPLES same as **Gullah** [After the Ogeechee River plantations of Georgia, where Black English was spoken]

geek /geek/ *n* **1. AWKWARD PERSON** somebody regarded as unattractive and socially awkward (*insult*) **2.** COMPUT **OBSESSIVE COMPUTER USER** somebody who is a proud or enthusiastic user of computers or other technology, sometimes to an excessive degree (*informal*) **3.** ARTS **OUTRAGEOUS CARNIVAL PERFORMER** a carnival performer whose act consists of outrageous feats such as biting the heads off live animals [Late 19C. Probably variant of English dialect *geck* "fool" < Low Dutch] —**geek·y** *adj*

Gee·long /jə láwng/ industrial city and seaport in Victoria, southeastern Australia. Population: 153,100 (1997).

geese BIRDS plural of **goose**

gee whiz *interj* same as **gee**[1] *interj* (sense 1)

gee-whiz *adj* causing or characterized by wonderment (*informal*) ○ *a gee-whiz new electronic gadget*

Ge·ez /gee éz, gay-/, **Ge'ez** *n* an ancient language formerly spoken in Ethiopia and still the liturgical language in the Ethiopian Christian Church [Late 18C. < Ethiopic] —**Geez** *adj*

gee·zer /geézər/ *n* **1.** a senior citizen, especially a man who is eccentric or irritable (*informal; sometimes considered offensive*) **2.** *UK* same as **man** *n* (sense 1) (*slang*) [Late 19C. Representing dialect pronunciation of *guiser* (< GUISE)]

ge·fil·te fish /gə filtə-/ *n* a Jewish dish consisting of finely chopped fish mixed with crumbs, eggs, and seasoning and served as balls or cakes. Gefilte fish was originally a dish of finely chopped or minced fish stuffed in a fish's body cavity before boiling or poaching. [Late 19C. < Yiddish, "stuffed fish"]

ge·gen·schein /gáygən shīn/ *n* a faint elliptical glow in the night sky opposite the setting sun, caused by the reflection of sunlight by dust in space [Late 19C. < German, "opposite glow"]

Geh·rig /gérrig/, **Lou** (1903–41) US baseball player. A star first baseman for the Yankees (1923–39), he played in 2,130 consecutive games, retiring with a lifetime batting average of .340. He died of amyotrophic lateral sclerosis, which came to be known as Lou Gehrig's disease. Full name **Gehrig, Henry Louis**. Known as **the Iron Horse**

Gei·ger count·er /gígər-/ *n* an instrument used to measure the intensity of ionizing radiation by detecting particles from a radioactive substance [Early 20C. After Hans *Geiger* (1882–1945), German physicist]

gei·sha /gáyshə, géé-/ (*plural same* or **-shas**), **gei·sha girl** *n* **1.** a Japanese woman educated to accompany men as a hostess, with skills such as dancing, conversation, and music **2.** a Japanese prostitute [Late 19C. < Japanese < *gei* "art" (< Middle Chinese *nejh*) + *sha* "person" (< Middle Chinese *tšia?*)]

gel /jel/ *n* **1. HAIR STYLING PRODUCT** a substance with the consistency of jelly that is used for styling hair **2.** CHEM **SEMISOLID** a semisolid mixture of small particles of a solid in a liquid **(colloid) 3. LIGHT FILTER** a sheet of colored acetate used in theater, television, and film lighting to create different lighting effects ■ *vi* **(gelled, gel·ling, gels) 1. BECOME GEL** to become semisolid, having been in a liquid state **2. TAKE FORM** to take on a definite form (*informal*) ○ *The idea didn't begin to gel until I'd gotten home.* **3. GET ALONG** to get along well together (*informal*) [Late 19C. Shortening of GELATIN] —**gel·a·ble** *adj*

ge·la·da /jélləda, jə laáda/ (*plural* **-das** or *same*), **ge·la·da ba·boon** *n* a large baboon with brown hair and a bare red patch on its chest. Native to: northeastern Africa. Latin name: *Theropithecus gelada*. [Mid-19C. < Amharic *č'ällada*]

gel·ate /jé làyt/ (**-at·ed, -at·ing, -ates**) *vi* to become or form a gel [Early 20C. Back-formation < GELATION²]

ge·la·ti FOOD plural of **gelato**

gel·a·tin /jéllət'n/, **gel·a·tine** *n* **1.** a transparent protein material made from boiling animal hides, bone, and cartilage that forms a firm gel when mixed with water. Use: foods, medicine, glue, photography. **2.** THEATER, MOVIES, MEDIA same as **gel** *n* (sense 3) [Early 19C. Via French *gélatine* < Italian *gelatina* < Latin *gelata* "frozen"]

gel·a·tin dy·na·mite *n* ARMS, CHEM same as **gelignite**

ge·lat·i·nize /jə látt'n ìz, jéllət'n-/ (**-nized, -niz·ing, -niz·es**) *v* **1.** *vti* to make something gelatinous, or become gelatinous **2.** *vt* to coat a photographic medium with gelatin —**ge·lat·i·ni·za·tion** /jə làtt'ni záysh'n/ *n* —**ge·lat·i·niz·er** *n*

ge·lat·i·nous /jə látt'nəss/ *adj* **1.** having a semisolid form resembling gelatin **2.** relating to or containing gelatin —**ge·lat·i·nous·ly** *adv* —**ge·lat·i·nous·ness** *n*

ge·la·tion¹ /jə láysh'n/ *n* the solidification of a liquid by freezing (*technical*) [Mid-19C. < Latin *gelation-* < *gelare* "freeze"]

ge·la·tion² /jə láysh'n/ *n* the process of becoming a gel [Early 20C. < GEL]

ge·la·to /jə laátō/ (*plural* **-ti** /-tee/) *n* an Italian ice cream made from milk, gelatin, sugar, and fruit [Early 20C. < Italian, "frozen" < Latin *gelare* "freeze"]

geld¹ /geld/ (**geld·ed** or **gelt** /gelt/, **geld·ing, gelds**) *vt* **1.** to castrate an animal, especially a horse **2.** to take away the strength or virility of somebody or something [13C. < Old Norse *gelda* < *geldr* "barren"]

geld² /geld/ *n* a land tax paid by landholders to the crown in late Anglo-Saxon and Norman times [15C. Via medieval Latin *geldum* < Old English *gield* "payment"]

geld·ing /gélding/ *n* a castrated horse or other animal [14C. < GELD¹]

Gel·dof /gél dawf/, **Sir Bob** (*b.* 1954) Irish musician and philanthropist. He was the leader of the rock group the Boomtown Rats (1975–86), founded the charity Band Aid for famine relief (1984), and received an honorary knighthood (1986). Full name **Geldof, Robert Frederick Zenon**

> "Most people get into bands for three very simple rock-and-roll reasons: to get laid, to get fame, and to get rich."
> [Sir Bob Geldof, *Melody Maker*; August 27, 1977]

gel·id /jéllid/ *adj* exceedingly cold (*literary*) [Early 17C. < Latin *gelidus* < *gelu* "frost, intense cold"] —**ge·lid·i·ty** /jə líddətee/ *n* —**gel·id·ly** *adv*

gel·ig·nite /jéllig nìt/ *n* dynamite consisting of gelled nitroglycerin, potassium nitrate, and wood pulp or guncotton. It is often used under water. [Late 19C. < GELATIN + Latin *ignis* "fire"]

UPI/Corbis-Bettmann

Martha Gellhorn

Gell·horn /géll hàwrn/, **Martha** (1908–98) US journalist and novelist. She became a war correspondent in 1937 and reported on the Spanish Civil War (1936–39) and World War II. Her novels include *A Stricken Field* (1940) and *Liana* (1948).

> "Never believe governments, not any of them, not a word they say; keep an untrusting eye on all they do."
> [Martha Gellhorn, recalled on her death, *Daily Telegraph (London)*; February 17,1998]

Gell-Mann /gèl mán/, **Murray** (*b.* 1929) US physicist. He proposed the existence of quarks and won the Nobel Prize in physics (1969).

> "Both biological and cultural diversity are now severely threatened and working for their preservation is a critical task."
> [Murray Gell-Mann, *The Quark and the Jaguar*; 1994]

gelt¹ *n* same as **money** (*slang*) [Early 16C. < German *Geld*, Yiddish *gelt* < Germanic]

gelt² VET past participle, past tense of **geld¹**

gem /jem/ *n* **1. JEWEL** a precious stone that has been cut and polished for use as jewelry or decoration **2. SOMEBODY OR SOMETHING EXCELLENT** somebody or something considered to be valuable, useful, or beautiful (*informal*) ○ *Our baby-sitter is such a gem!* ■ *vt* **(gemmed, gem·ming, gems) DECORATE SOMETHING WITH GEMS** to decorate something with gems or with something resembling gems (*literary*; *usually passive*) [Pre-12C. < Latin *gemma* "bud, jewel"]

GEM *abbr* ground-effect machine

Ge·ma·ra /gə maárə/ *n* the second part of the Talmud, forming a set of commentaries on the first part of the Talmud, the Mishnah [Early 17C. < Aramaic *gĕmārâ* "completion"] —**ge·ma·ric** *adj* —**Ge·ma·rist** *n*

gem·i·nate *adj* /jémminət, -nàyt/ *also* **gem·i·nat·ed** growing or arranged in pairs ○ *a geminate leaf* ■ *vti* /jémmi nàyt/ (**-nat·ed, -nat·ing, -nates**) to make something paired, or become paired or doubled [Late 16C. < Latin *geminat-*, past participle of *geminare* < *geminus* "twin"] —**gem·i·na·tion** /jèmmi náysh'n/ *n*

Gem·i·ni /jémmə nì, -nee/ *n* **1. CONSTELLATION IN NORTHERN HEMISPHERE** a zodiacal constellation of the northern hemisphere, also known as the Twins or Castor and Pollux, after its two brightest stars. See illustration at **constellation 2. 3RD ZODIAC SIGN** the third sign of the zodiac, represented by twins and lasting from approximately May 21 to June 20. Gemini is classified as an air sign. **3.** *also* **Gem·i·ni·an SOMEBODY BORN UNDER GEMINI** somebody whose birthday falls between May 21 and June 20 [Pre-12C. < Latin, plural of *geminus* "twin"] —**Gem·i·ni** *adj*

gem·ma /jémmə/ (*plural* **-mae** /-mee/) *n* an asexual bud-shaped structure that can detach from the parent and form a plant. Liverworts and mosses produce gemmae. [Late 18C. < Latin, "bud, jewel"] —**gem·ma·ceous** /je máyshəss/ *adj*

gem·mate /jé màyt/ *adj* **REPRODUCING BY GEMMAE** forming gemmae or reproducing by means of gemmae ■ *vi* **(-mat·ed, -mat·ing, -mates) REPRODUCE BY GEMMAE** to form gemmae or reproduce by means of gemmae [Early 17C. < Latin *gemmat-*, past participle of *gemmare* "produce buds" < *gemma* "bud, jewel"] —**gem·ma·tion** /je máysh'n/ *n*

gem·mif·er·ous /je míffərəss/ *adj* **1.** producing precious stones **2.** producing gemmae

gem·mip·a·rous /je míppərəss/ *adj* BIOL same as **gemmate** —**gem·mip·a·rous·ly** *adv*

gem·mol·o·gy *n* GEOL same as **gemology**

gem·mule /jémmyool/ *n* a reproductive structure produced by asexual reproduction in freshwater and ocean sponges —**gem·mu·la·tion** /jèmmyə láysh'n/ *n*

gem·ol·o·gy /je mólləjee/, **gem·mol·o·gy** *n* the study of gems and gemstones —**gem·o·log·i·cal** /jèmmə lójjik'l/ *adj* —**gem·ol·o·gist** *n*

ge·mot /gə mṓt/, **ge·mote** *n* an assembly for judicial or legislative purposes in pre-Norman England [Old English *gemōt* < *mōt* (see MOOT)]

gems·bok /gémz bòk/ (*plural* **-boks** or *same*) *n* a large antelope with long straight horns and broad black markings on its head and upper legs. Native to: southwestern and eastern Africa. Latin name: *Oryx gazella*. [Late 18C. Via Afrikaans < Dutch, "wild antelope buck"]

Gem State *n* a nickname for Idaho

gem·stone /jém stṑn/ *n* a mineral or stone suitable for use in jewelry after cutting and polishing

ge·müt·lich /gə mo͝otlik, -mǘtli*kh*/ *adj* warm and friendly [Mid-19C. < German < *Gemüt* "heart, spirit"]

ge·müt·lich·keit /gə mo͝otlik kìt, -mǘtli*kh*-/ *n* warmth and friendliness [Mid-19C. < German < *gemütlich* (see GEMÜTLICH)]

gen. *abbr* **1.** BIOL, GRAM gender **2.** MIL general **3.** GRAM genitive **4.** BIOL genus

Gen. *abbr* **1.** *also* **GEN** MIL General **2.** BIBLE Genesis

-gen, **-gene** *suffix* **1.** something that produces ○ *hallucinogen* **2.** something that is produced ○ *phosgene* [Via French *-gène* < Greek *-genēs* "born" < Indo-European, "beget"] —**-genic** *suffix* —**-geny** *suffix*

gen·darme /*zh*ón daàrm/ *n* a police officer in France and French-speaking countries. In France, gendarmes are part of the armed forces, their responsibility being that of general law enforcement. [Mid-16C. < French, singular < *gens d'armes* "men of arms"]

gen·dar·me·rie /*zh*on daàrməree/ *n* **1.** gendarmes considered as a body **2.** in France and French-speaking countries, a police station or police barracks [Mid-16C. < French < *gendarme* (see GENDARME)]

gen·der /jéndər/ *n* **1.** ⚠ **SOMEBODY'S SEX** the sex of a person or organism, or of a whole category of people or organisms (*often euphemistic to avoid the word "sex"*) **2.** GRAM **CATEGORIZATION OF NOUNS** the classification of nouns and pronouns in some languages according to the forms taken by adjectives, modifiers, and other grammatical items associated syntactically with them **3.** GRAM **CATEGORY OF NOUN** any one of the categories into which nouns and pronouns are divided in languages that have gender, e.g., masculine, feminine, neuter, or common [14C. < Old French *gendre* < Latin *gener-*, stem of *genus* "birth, kind"] —**gen·der·less** *adj*

USAGE gender or **sex**? Traditionally, ***gender*** has referred to grammatical classifications in languages, and ***sex*** has referred to the biological classifications to which gender is analogous. For some time, however, anthropologists have used ***gender*** to distinguish cultural categories from biological ones: *Gender roles are indistinct among the young of this society; the two sexes play together frequently.* Cultural and biological categories are interrelated, of course, and thus at times it can be difficult to decide which word is more appropriate. ***Gender*** has become the preferred form in the 21st century, as in *Gender is an important factor to consider when hiring new employees* and in idiomatic expressions such as *gender gap.*

gen·der aware·ness *n* sensitivity to the perceived differences between men and women or boys and girls in environments such as the workplace and the classroom

gen·der bend·er *n* **1.** an offensive term for somebody who dresses or acts in a way that is intended to blur the traditional distinctions between men and women (*slang*) **2.** a device that converts a male plug or connector to female or vice versa —**gen·der ben·ding** *n*

gen·der bi·as *n* unfair difference in the treatment of men or women because of their sex

gen·der dys·pho·ri·a *n* PSYCHOL same as **gender identity disorder**

gen·dered /jéndərd/ *adj* relating to or appropriate to one gender rather than the other ○ *gendered clothing*

gen·der gap *n* a noticeable difference in behavior or attitudes between men and women or boys and girls

gen·der i·den·ti·ty dis·or·der *n* a condition in which somebody identifies strongly with the opposite sex and experiences discomfort with his or her birth gender

gen·der-neu·tral *adj* avoiding references to masculinity and femininity and their cultural associations

USAGE It is increasingly regarded as good practice to avoid unnecessary reference to gender. Wherever possible, choose a gender-neutral alternative, for example, *camera operator* or *police officer* for words like *cameraman* or *policewoman*. Do not use *he/him/his/etc.* or *she/her/etc.*, to refer to people of unspecified gender, as in *A child of his age should be able to dress himself.* In this example, the best solution is to recast the sentence in the plural: *Children of that age should be able to dress themselves.* In other cases, *they/them/their* may be used as gender-neutral singular forms, though many people object to constructions such as *Each student should proofread their essay.* A less controversial but more cumbersome option is *he or she/him or her/his or her*, as in *Each student should proofread his or her essay.* See also ***-ess***, ***-person***, and ***they***.

gen·der re·as·sign·ment *n* MED a surgical operation, usually with accompanying hormone treatment, that changes somebody's physical characteristics to approximate those of the opposite sex

gen·der-spe·cif·ic *adj* affecting or involving only men or only women, or only boys or only girls

gene /jeen/ *n* the basic unit capable of transmitting characteristics from one generation to the next. It consists of a specific sequence of DNA or RNA that occupies a fixed position (**locus**) on a chromosome. [Early 20C. Via German *Gen* < Greek *genos* "birth, race"]

ORIGIN The Indo-European word from which ***gene*** is ultimately derived is also the ancestor of English *gender, genealogy, general, generate, generous, genesis, genie, genital, genius, genocide, genre, gentle, genus, gonad, indigenous, ingenuous, innate, jaunty, kin, kind*[1], *nation*, and *nature*.

-gene *suffix* same as **-gen**

ge·ne·al·o·gy /jeènee óllәjee/ (*plural* **-gies**) *n* **1. STUDY OF HISTORY OF FAMILIES** the study of the history of families and the line of descent from their ancestors **2. FAMILY HISTORY** a pedigree or line of descent that can be traced directly from an ancestor or earlier form, especially that of a specific person or family **3. FAMILY TREE** a chart or table that shows the line of descent from an ancestor or earlier form, especially that of a specific person or family [14C. Via French *généalogie* < Greek *genealogia* < *genea* "race, generation"] —**ge·ne·a·log·i·cal** /jeènee ә lójjik'l/ *adj* —**ge·ne·a·log·i·cal·ly** *adv* —**ge·ne·al·o·gist** *n*

gene am·pli·fi·ca·tion *n* GENETICS same as **amplification** (sense 6)

gene chip *n* a small piece of material (**substrate**) containing minute samples of DNA. Use: in genetic testing.

gene clon·ing *n* the process of producing any number of identical copies of a gene. Gene cloning is now carried out using a machine that automatically performs the polymerase chain reaction (**PCR**).

gene ex·pres·sion *n* the process by which a gene's coded information is converted into the structures operating in a cell

gene flow *n* the natural transfer of genes from one population into the genetic makeup of another population through hybridization and interbreeding

gene fre·quen·cy *n* the ratio of a specific form of a gene (**allele**) to the total number of forms in a specific population

gene gun *n* a device for injecting tiny particles coated with DNA into cells or tissue as a method of genetic modification

gene mu·ta·tion *n* GENETICS same as **point mutation**

~~**geneology**~~ incorrect spelling of **genealogy**

gene pool *n* the total of all genes carried by all individuals in an interbreeding population

gene probe *n* a fragment of DNA or RNA marked by a chemical or radioactive substance that will bind to a given gene, used as a tag in order to identify or isolate that gene

gen·er·a BIOL, LOGIC plural of **genus**

gen·er·al /jénnәrәl/ *adj* **1. OVERALL** relating to or including all or nearly all of the members of a category, group, or whole ○ *a general increase in demand* **2. USUAL** applying or happening in most cases ○ *as a general rule* **3. WIDESPREAD** shared or participated in by many ○ *a general sense that something ought to be done* **4. MISCELLANEOUS** having a varied content or wide scope ○ *a general store* **5. NOT SPECIALIZED** unspecialized or lacking specialized knowledge ○ *a book that was intended for the general reader* **6. NOT SPECIFIC** not specific, detailed, or clearly defined ○ *She spoke in the most general terms.* **7. HIGH-RANKING** with overall authority, or of superior rank ○ *a general manager* ■ *n* **1.** *also* **Gen·er·al HIGH RANKING OFFICER** an officer in the US Army, Air Force, or Marine Corps of a rank above lieutenant general, or a Canadian Army or Air Force officer of equivalent rank **2.** MIL same as **general officer 3.** MED same as **general anesthetic** (*informal*) **4.** HEALTH SERVICES same as **general hospital** (*informal*) **5. THE PUBLIC** the public as a whole (*archaic*) [12C. Via French < Latin *generalis* "of the whole class" < *genus* "race, kind"] —**gen·er·al·ness** *n* ◇ **in general 1.** as a whole **2.** in most cases or circumstances

CULTURAL NOTE ***The General***, a movie (1926) starring actor Buster Keaton. Regarded as one of the greatest silent comedies, it is set during the Civil War and is based on a historical incident: the hijack of a Confederate train by Union soldiers. Keaton plays railroad man Johnnie Gray, whose attempts to recapture the train involve superb visual gags, gripping drama, and brilliantly timed stunts.

gen·er·al ad·mis·sion *n* the price for a seat in an unreserved area at a spectator event

gen·er·al an·es·thet·ic *n* an anesthetic that produces loss of sensation in the whole body together with unconsciousness

gen·er·al as·sem·bly, Gen·er·al As·sem·bly *n* **1.** a legislature, especially in one of the US states **2.** the highest governing body of various Presbyterian churches, or the meeting of such a body

Gen·er·al As·sem·bly *n* the assembly of the United Nations

gen·er·al av·er·age *n* liability for loss or damage to an insured ship or its cargo that is shared among all those with an interest in the venture

Gen·er·al Court *n* **1.** a state legislative body in Massachusetts or New Hampshire **2.** a legislative body in colonial New England

gen·er·al·cy /jénnәrәlsee, jénnrәlsee/ *n* **1.** the office of general, or the period during which this office is held **2.** generals considered collectively

gen·er·al de·liv·er·y *n* **1.** a service of the post office that holds mail for people without an address or post office box **2.** an address on an item of mail indicating that it should be held at a post office until collection by the addressee

gen·er·al e·lec·tion *n* an election in which the citizens of a country or state vote to elect representatives of most or all constituencies to a legislative body

Gen·er·al Head·quar·ters *n* MIL full form of **GHQ**

gen·er·al hos·pi·tal *n* a hospital that does not specialize in any one type of medical treatment

gen·er·al·is·si·mo /jènnәrә líssәmō/ (*plural* **-mos**) *n* in some countries, the supreme commander of a combined military force consisting of the army, navy, and air force [Early 17C. < Italian, "great general" < Latin *generalis* (see GENERAL)]

gen·er·al·ist /jénnәrәlist/ *n* somebody with knowledge, skills, or interests in many areas but with no specialty

gen·er·al·i·ty /jènnә rállәtee/ (*plural* **-ties**) *n* **1. GENERAL STATEMENT** a statement or remark that concerns the main aspects of something rather than the details **2. STATE OF BEING GENERAL** the quality or state of being general **3. GENERAL PRINCIPLE** a statement or principle that is true in most cases **4. UNIMPORTANT REMARK** a remark about something that is not important in itself but is useful to open or keep up a conversation **5.** same as **majority** (sense 1)

gen·er·al·i·za·tion /jènnәrәli záysh'n/ *n* **1. SWEEPING STATEMENT** a statement presented as a general truth but based on limited or incomplete evidence **2. GENERAL STATEMENT** a statement or conclusion that is derived from and applies equally to a number of cases ○ *not enough data to permit a generalization* **3. MAKING OF GENERALIZATIONS** the making of general or sweeping statements **4.** LOGIC **INFERENCE FROM INSTANCE** the application of the rules of inference that go from an instance to a universal or to an existential statement **5.** PSYCHOL **USE OF LEARNED RESPONSE** the act of responding to a new stimulus in the same way as to a conditioned stimulus

gen·er·al·ize /jénnәrә līz/ (**-ized, -iz·ing, -iz·es**) *v* **1.** *vi* **MAKE SWEEPING STATEMENT** to state a supposed general truth about something on the basis of limited or incomplete evidence **2.** *vti* **EXPRESS SOMETHING GENERAL** to express something general on the basis of particulars **3.** *vti* **GIVE WIDER USE TO SOMETHING** to use something in a wider or different range of circumstances, or be used in this way **4.** *vt* **MAKE SOMETHING GENERALLY KNOWN** to bring something into general use or to general knowledge (*usually passive*) **5.** *vi* MED **SPREAD** to spread to other parts of the body **6.** *vti* LOGIC **MAKE INFERENCE** to infer a general conclusion from particulars or a universal statement from an instance —**gen·er·al·iz·a·ble** *adj*

gen·eral knowl·edge *n* knowledge of a broad range of facts or subjects

gen·er·al·ly /jénnәrәlee/ *adv* **1. USUALLY** in most cases or circumstances **2. AS WHOLE** as a whole or without exception ○ *not meant for the public generally* **3. VAGUELY** without being specific, detailed, or clearly defined ○ *spoke generally about his life* **4. WIDESPREAD** so as to be widespread ○ *become generally known*

gen·er·al meet·ing *n* a meeting to which all members of a group or organization are invited

gen·er·al ob·li·ga·tion *adj* describes a bond supported by all the resources and revenue-raising powers of a municipality or other issuer

gen·er·al of·fi·cer *n* an Army, Navy, Air Force, or Marine Corps officer of a rank above colonel, or the equivalent in other nations' armed forces

Gen·er·al of the Air Force *n* an officer in the US Air Force of the highest rank, having an insignia of five stars, this rank and title used only in wartime

Gen·er·al of the Ar·mies *n* formerly, an officer in the US Army of the highest rank, above a General of the Army

Gen·er·al of the Ar·my *n* an officer in the US Army of the highest rank, having an insignia of five stars, this rank and title used only in wartime

gen·er·al prac·tice *n* the work of a doctor who treats patients' general medical problems, referring them to specialists or hospitals for more specialized care

gen·er·al prac·ti·tion·er *n* a doctor who treats patients' general medical problems, either at an office or, sometimes, at patients' homes (*dated*)

gen·er·al pub·lic *n* the people of a country considered as a whole ○ *Members of the general public are welcome to attend.*

gen·er·al pur·pose *adj* useful for a wide variety of purposes

gen·er·al rel·a·tiv·i·ty *n* PHYS same as **relativity** (sense 2)

Gen·er·al Ser·vic·es Ad·min·is·tra·tion *n* a management agency of the federal government, concerned mainly with managing federal buildings and sites and providing equipment and supplies to federal employees

gen·er·al·ship /jénnərəl shìp/ *n* **1.** MILITARY COMMAND the art or practice of exercising military leadership in a war **2.** GENERAL'S RANK the rank or tenure of a general **3.** LEADERSHIP skillful leadership or management of people or an organization

gen·er·al staff *n* a group of military officers whose job is to assist senior officers in the planning and coordination of military operations

gen·er·al store *n* a store that sells a wide variety of goods such as groceries and household supplies, most often found in small communities where there are no department stores or supermarkets

gen·er·al strike *n* a strike involving all or a majority of workers in a country

gen·er·al the·o·ry of rel·a·tiv·i·ty *n* PHYS same as **relativity** (sense 2)

gen·er·ate /jénnə ràyt/ (**-at·ed, -at·ing, -ates**) *vt* **1.** CREATE SOMETHING to bring something into existence or effect ○ *measures to generate more income* **2.** PRODUCE ENERGY to produce or originate a form of energy through a chemical or physical process **3.** MATH, LING PRODUCE SET to produce a set or sequence by the application of defined rules or the performance of defined operations **4.** MATH PRODUCE FORM to create a curve with a moving point or a surface with a moving curve [Early 16C. < Latin *generat-*, past participle of *generare* "beget" < *genus* "race, birth"] —**gen·er·a·ble** *adj*

gen·er·a·tion /jènnə ráysh'n/ *n* **1.** GROUP OF CONTEMPORARIES all of the people who were born at approximately the same time, considered as a group, and especially when considered as having shared interests and attitudes ○ *the younger generation* **2.** STAGE IN DESCENT a single stage in the descent of a family or a group of people, animals, or plants, or the individual members of that stage ○ *three generations down the line* **3.** TIME TAKEN TO PRODUCE NEW GENERATION the period of time that it takes for people, animals, or plants to grow up and produce their own offspring, in humans held to be between 30 and 35 years ○ *after three generations of war and conflict* **4.** PARTICULAR GENERATION IN SEQUENCE a particular numbered stage in the sequence of generations of a person being identified with a particular characteristic (*usually used in combination*) ○ *a first-generation immigrant* ○ *a third-generation graduate* **5.** NEW TYPE a particular stage in the development of a product or technology, especially one marking a significant advance ○ *one of the new generation of computers* **6.** PHASE IN LIFE CYCLE one of the successive phases that make up the life cycle of some organisms ○ *the gametophyte generation* **7.** PRODUCTION OF POWER the production of electricity, heat, or some other form of energy **8.** PRODUCTION OF YOUNG the act or process of bringing offspring into being **9.** MATH GENERATING OF GROUP OR SHAPE the act or process of generating a set, sequence, curve, or surface **10.** PHYS NUCLEI IN CHAIN REACTION in a chain reaction, a group of nuclei that come from a previous group —**gen·er·a·tion·al** *adj*

gen·er·a·tion gap *n* the difference in attitudes, behavior, and interests between people of different generations, especially between parents and their children

gen·er·a·tion X, Gen·er·a·tion X *n* the generation of people born roughly during the years 1965 to 1980 in Western countries, especially the United States, often regarded as disillusioned, cynical, or apathetic [< *Generation X: Tales for an Accelerated Culture*, novel by Douglas Coupland] —**gen·er·a·tion X·er** *n*

gen·er·a·tion Y, Gen·er·a·tion Y *n* **1.** the generation of people born approximately in or after 1980 in Western countries, especially the United States (*informal*) **2.** SOCIOL same as **millennial** [After GENERATION X]

gen·er·a·tive /jénnə ràytiv, -rətiv/ *adj* **1.** relating to the production of young **2.** involving the ability to produce or originate something ○ *generative linguistic theory* —**gen·er·a·tive·ly** *adv* —**gen·er·a·tive·ness** *n*

gen·er·a·tive cell *n* BIOL same as **gamete**

gen·er·a·tive gram·mar *n* the rules from which all the grammatical sentences, and only the grammatical sentences, of a language can be generated

gen·er·a·tor /jénnə ràytər/ *n* **1.** DEVICE FOR PRODUCING ELECTRICITY a machine or device that is used to convert mechanical energy, such as that provided by the combustion of fuel or by wind or water, into electricity **2.** DEVICE FOR PRODUCING GAS a device in which a gas is formed **3.** ORIGINATOR somebody or something responsible for generating something such as an idea, plan, or strategy

gen·er·a·trix /jènnə ráytriks/ (*plural* **-tri·ces** /-tri sèez, jènnərə trī-/) *n* an element such as a point or line that is used in the production of a geometric figure such as a curve or surface

ge·ner·ic /jə nérrik/ *adj* **1.** APPLYING GENERALLY applying to any member of a group or class ○ *a generic weakness in design* **2.** SUITABLE FOR BROAD RANGE usable or suitable in a variety of contexts ○ *generic software that can run on a variety of machines* **3.** BIOL OF GENUS relating to or characteristic of a genus **4.** PHARM WITH GENERAL NAME describes a pharmaceutical product that does not have a brand name or trademark ■ *n* PHARM same as **generic drug** [Late 17C. < French *générique* < Latin *genus* "race, kind"] —**ge·ner·i·cal·ly** *adv*

ge·ner·ic drug *n* a drug sold or dispensed under a name that is not a trademark

gen·er·os·i·ty /jènnə róssətee/ (*plural* **-ties**) *n* **1.** KINDNESS willingness to give money, help, or time freely **2.** NOBILITY nobility of character **3.** SUBSTANTIAL SIZE pleasingly large size or quantity ○ *He ate everything, despite the generosity of the portions.* **4.** GENEROUS ACT a generous, kind, or noble act [15C. < Latin *generositas* < *generosus* (see GENEROUS)]

gen·er·ous /jénnərəss/ *adj* **1.** KIND willing to give money, help, or time freely ○ *a very generous offer* **2.** NOBLE having or showing nobility of character ○ *a generous gesture of forgiveness* **3.** SUBSTANTIAL pleasingly large in size or quantity ○ *a generous slice of cake* **4.** WINE FULL-FLAVORED describes wine that is rich and full-flavored [Late 16C. Via French *généreux* < Latin *generosus* "of noble birth" < *genus* "race, birth"] —**gen·er·ous·ly** *adv* —**gen·er·ous·ness** *n*

SYNONYMS ***generous, liberal, magnanimous, munificent, bountiful***

CORE MEANING: giving readily to others

generous willing to give money, help, or time freely ○ *I was deeply touched by her generous gift.* ○ *I've seen how generous he is with his time and what an inspiration he is to young writers.* **liberal** freely giving money, time, or other assets ○ *During her lifetime, she was a liberal benefactor to public institutions.* ○ *a liberal attitude toward government spending* **magnanimous** very generous, kind, or forgiving ○ *a magnanimous gesture of fair play* ○ *It is easy to be magnanimous, when you have been as fortunate in life as I have been.* **munificent** very generous in giving a lot of money ○ *received a munificent sum for books written and yet to be written* **bountiful** (*literary*) giving generously, particularly to less fortunate people ○ *Society has become more selfish and the rich are no longer so bountiful to the poor.*

Gen·e·see /jènnə sèe/ river in the northeastern United States, rising in Pennsylvania and flowing northward past Rochester, New York, before emptying into Lake Ontario. Length: 144 mi./232 km.

gene se·quence *n* the order of nucleotides in a gene

gene se·quenc·ing *n* the process of determining the individual arrangement of nucleotides that compose a specific gene

gen·e·sis /jénnəssiss/ (*plural* **-e·ses** /-i sèez/) *n* the time or circumstances of something's coming into being ○ *the genesis of this new project* [Early 17C. < GENESIS]

Gen·e·sis /jénnəssiss/ *n* a book of the Bible, in which the creation of the world is described. It is the first book of the Pentateuch. See table at **Bible** [Pre-12C. Via Latin < Greek, "birth"]

-genesis *suffix* production, origin ○ *sporogenesis* [Via Latin < Greek, "birth"]

gene splic·ing *n* a technique in which segments of DNA or RNA, often from different organisms, are combined, in order to be introduced into an organism

gen·et[1] /jénnit/ *n* **1.** a small carnivorous mammal related to the civet that has a ringed tail, spotted sides, and retractable claws. Native to: wooded regions of southern Europe and Africa. Genus: *Genetta.* **2.** the fur of the genet [14C. < Old French *genette*]

gen·et[2] /jénnit/ *n* ZOOL another spelling of **jennet**

Ge·net /zhə náy/, **Jean** (1910–86) French writer. He is best known for existentialist dramas such as *The Maids* (1947) and *The Balcony* (1957).

> "To achieve harmony in bad taste is the height of elegance."
>
> [Jean Genet, *The Thief's Journal*; 1949]

gene ther·a·py *n* the treatment of a genetic disease through the insertion of normal or genetically altered genes into cells in order to replace or make up for the nonfunctional or missing genes

ge·net·ic /jə néttik/, **ge·net·i·cal** /-ik'l/ *adj* involving, resulting from, or relating to genes or genetics [Mid-19C. < GENESIS, after pairs such as *antithesis, antithetic*] —**ge·net·i·cal·ly** *adv*

ge·net·i·cal·ly mod·i·fied *adj* describes an organism that has received genetic material from another, resulting in a permanent change in one or more of its characteristics

ge·net·ic code *n* the order of the nucleotide sequences in DNA or RNA that form the basis of heredity through their role in protein synthesis

ge·net·ic coun·sel·ing *n* counseling that concerns the risks, treatments, and management of inherited genetic disorders for people with some likelihood of being affected by them, either personally or as parents —**ge·net·ic coun·sel·or** *n*

ge·net·ic drift *n* the random changes that occur in the gene frequency of small isolated populations, resulting in the loss or preservation of genes over the generations

ge·net·ic en·gi·neer·ing *n* GENETICS same as **genetic modification** —**ge·net·ic en·gi·neer** *n*

ge·net·ic fin·ger·print·ing *n* GENETICS same as **DNA fingerprinting** —**ge·net·ic fin·ger·print** *n*

ge·net·i·cist /jə néttəssist/ *n* a student of or specialist in genetics

ge·net·ic load *n* the average number of unfavorable recessive gene mutations per individual in a population

ge·net·ic ma·ni·pul·ation *n* GENETICS same as **genetic modification**

ge·net·ic map *n* a graphic representation of the arrangement of genes on a chromosome

ge·net·ic map·ping *n* the technique or process of identifying genes on a chromosome

ge·net·ic mark·er *n* a known, usually dominant, gene that is used to identify genes, chromosomes, and traits known to be associated with that gene

ge·ne·tic mo·di·fi·ca·tion *n* the alteration and recombination of genetic material by technological means, resulting in transgenic organisms

ge·net·ic probe *n* GENETICS same as **gene probe**

ge·net·ic pro·fil·ing *n* GENETICS same as **DNA fingerprinting** —**ge·net·ic pro·file** *n*

ge·net·ics /jə néttiks/ *n* the branch of biology that deals with heredity and genetic variations (*takes a singular verb*) ■ *npl* the genetic makeup of an organism or group of organisms (*takes a plural verb*)

ge·net·ic screen·ing *n* the analysis of DNA samples of a group of people, carried out in order to find out whether they carry the genes associated with specific inherited diseases or disorders

ge·net·ic se·quenc·ing *n* GENETICS same as **gene sequencing**

gene trans·fer *n* the insertion of genetic material from one organism into another in a laboratory procedure, to produce an effect such as resistance to disease

gen·e·trix /jénnətriks/ (*plural* **-tri·ces** /-trī seèz/) *n* a biological mother (*technical*) [15C. Directly or via French < Latin < *gignere* "beget"]

ge·ne·va *n* BEVERAGES same as **genever**

Ge·ne·va /jə neévə/ city in western Switzerland, capital of Geneva Canton, situated at the western end of Lake Geneva. It is the headquarters of many international organizations, including the International Red Cross and the World Health Organization. Population: 175,800 (2001). French name **Genève** —**Ge·ne·van** *adj, n* —**Gen·e·vese** /jènnə veéz, -veéss/ *adj, n*

Ge·ne·va, Lake largest lake in central Europe. It straddles the border between Switzerland and the Haute-Savoie department in southeastern France. Area: 224 sq. mi./580 sq. km.

Ge·ne·va Con·ven·tion *n* an international agreement that establishes standards for the treatment of those who are sick, wounded, or killed in battle and those who are prisoners of war

ge·ne·ver /jə neévər/, **ge·ne·va** *literary* /-və/ *n* Dutch gin [Early 18C. Via Dutch < Old French *genevre* < Latin *juniperus* "juniper"]

Gen·ghis Khan /jèng giss kaán/ (1167?–1227) Mongol conqueror. His conquests extended the Mongolian empire throughout Asia from the Pacific to the Black Sea. Born **Temujin**

> "It is forbidden ever to make peace with a monarch, a prince or a people who have not submitted."
> [Genghis Khan, *Laws*; 1206?]

gen·ial /jeényəl/ *adj* **1.** having a kind and good-natured disposition or manner **2.** pleasantly mild and warm so as to be conducive to life and growth ○ *a genial climate* [Mid-16C. < Latin *genialis* "nuptial" < *genius* (see GENIUS)] —**ge·ni·al·i·ty** /jeènee állətee/ *n* —**gen·ial·ly** *adv* —**gen·ial·ness** *n*

gen·ic /jeénik, jénnik/ *adj* relating to or produced by a gene or genes —**gen·i·cal·ly** *adv*

ge·nic·u·late /jə níkyələt/ *adj* **1.** bent at an angle like a knee ○ *geniculate antennae* **2.** with a joint or joints that can be bent like a knee [Early 17C. < Latin *geniculatus* "knotted" < *genu* "knee"] —**ge·nic·u·late·ly** *adv* —**ge·nic·u·la·tion** /jə nìkyə láysh'n/ *n*

ge·nie /jeénee/ *n* in Arabian folklore, a magical spirit that has supernatural powers and will obey the commands of the person who summons it [Mid-17C. Via French *génie* < Latin *genius* (see GENIUS)]

ge·ni·i plural of **genius** (senses 4–6)

gen·i·pap /jénnə pàp/ *n* **1.** a reddish brown fruit resembling an orange. Use: preserves, drinks. **2.** an evergreen tree that produces genipaps. Native to: tropical America. Latin name: *Genipa americana*. [Early 17C. Via Portuguese *jenipapo* < Tupi *ianipaba*]

ge·nis·tein /jə nístin/ *n* an isoflavone found in soy products that is a possible natural cancer preventive [Early 20C. < Latin *genista* "broom (the plant)"]

gen·i·tal /jénnit'l/ *adj* relating to the external sexual organs or to reproduction [14C. Directly or via French < Latin *genitalis* < *gignere* "beget"] —**gen·i·tal·ly** *adv*

gen·i·tal her·pes *n* a sexually transmitted disease caused by the herpes simplex virus and affecting the genital and anal regions with painful blisters

gen·i·tals /jénnit'lz/, **gen·i·ta·li·a** /jènni táylee ə/ *npl* the reproductive organs, especially the external sex organs

gen·i·tal wart *n* a wart of the genital or anal area caused by a sexually transmitted virus

gen·i·tive /jénnitiv/ *n* **1.** a grammatical case that affects nouns, pronouns, and adjectives and that usually indicates possession **2.** a word or phrase in the genitive [14C. Directly or via French < Latin *genitivus* < *gignere* "beget"] —**gen·i·tive** *adj*

gen·i·tor /jénnitər/ *n* a biological parent (*technical*) [15C. Directly or via French < Latin < *gignere* "beget"]

gen·i·to·u·ri·nar·y /jènnitō yoórə nèrree/ *adj* relating to or affecting the genital and urinary organs [Mid-19C. < Latin *genitalis* (see GENITAL)]

gen·i·ture /jénni choòr, -chər/ *n* somebody's birth (*archaic*) [Mid-16C. Directly or via French < Latin *genitura* < *gignere* "beget"]

gen·ius /jeényəss, jeénee əss/ *n* **1.** SOMEBODY WITH OUTSTANDING TALENT somebody with exceptional ability, especially somebody whose intellectual or creative achievements gain worldwide recognition **2.** OUTSTANDING TALENT exceptional intellectual or creative ability **3.** SOMEBODY WITH SPECIFIC SKILL a person with great specialized skill ○ *a genius with computers* **4.** (*plural* **ge·ni·i** /-nee ī/) QUALITY a special quality that characterizes a place, period, or people **5.** (*plural* **ge·ni·i**) GUARDIAN SPIRIT in Roman mythology, a guardian spirit of a person, place, or institution **6.** (*plural* **ge·ni·i**) DEMON a supposed demon or supernatural being **7.** INFLUENCE somebody who or something that exerts a strong influence ○ *an evil genius* [14C. < Latin, "guardian spirit" < *gignere* "beget"]

SYNONYMS See *talent*.

ge·ni·us lo·ci /jeénee əss lṓ sī/ *n* **1.** the atmosphere that characterizes a place **2.** the supposed guardian spirit of a place [< Latin, "spirit of the place"]

gen·o·a /jénnō ə/, **gen·o·a jib** *n* a very large triangular front sail on a sailboat, especially a racing yacht [Mid-20C. After GENOA]

Gen·o·a /jénnō ə/ seaport and industrial city on the Gulf of Genoa, northwestern Italy, the capital of Genoa Province, Liguria Region. Population: 610,307 (2001). —**Gen·o·ese** /jènnō eéz, -eéss/ *n, adj*

gen·o·a jib *n* SAILING same as **genoa**

gen·o·cide /jénnə sīd/ *n* the systematic killing of all the people from a national, ethnic, or religious group, or an attempt to do this [Mid-20C. < Greek *genos* "race"] —**gen·o·cid·al** /jènnə sīd'l/ *adj* —**gen·o·cid·al·ly** *adv*

ge·nome /jeé nōm/ *n* the full complement of genetic information that an organism inherits from its parents, especially the set of chromosomes and the genes they carry [Mid-20C. < Greek *genos* "offspring, race" + CHROMOSOME] —**ge·nom·ic** /jee nómmik/ *adj*

ge·nom·ics /jee nómmiks, -nṓmiks/ *n* the identification and study of gene sequences in the DNA of organisms (*takes a singular verb*)

ge·no·tox·ic·i·ty /jènnō tok sissətee/ *n* the degree to which something causes damage to or mutation of DNA [Late 20C. < GENE] —**ge·no·tox·ic** /jènnō tóksik/ *adj* —**ge·no·tox·ic·al·ly** *adv*

ge·no·tox·in /jènnō tóksin/ *n* a substance that can cause damage to or mutation in DNA [Late 20C. < GENE]

gen·o·type /jénnə tīp/ *n* **1.** the genetic makeup of an organism, as opposed to its physical characteristics (**phenotype**) **2.** a group of organisms that share a similar genetic makeup [Early 20C. < German *Genotypus* < Greek *genos* "offspring, race" + Latin *typus* (see TYPE)] —**gen·o·typ·ic** /jènnə típpik/ *adj* —**gen·o·typ·i·cal·ly** *adv*

-genous *suffix* used to form adjectives from nouns ending in "-gen" and "-geny" ○ *homogenous*

~~**genrally**~~ incorrect spelling of **generally**

~~**genration**~~ incorrect spelling of **generation**

gen·re /zhaánrə, zhaáN-/ *n* **1.** one of the categories, based on form, style, or subject matter, into which artistic works of all kinds can be divided. For example, the detective novel is a genre of fiction. **2.** painting depicting household scenes [Early 19C. Via French, "type" < Latin *genus* "birth, kind"]

SYNONYMS See *type*.

gen·ro /gèn rṓ/ (*plural same*) *n* **1.** in Japan in the 19th and early 20th centuries, a group of elder statesmen who advised the emperor (*takes a singular or plural verb*) **2.** a member of the genro advising the Japanese emperor [Late 19C. < Japanese, "first elders"]

gens /jenz/ (*plural* **gen·tes** /jénteèz/) *n* **1.** in ancient Rome, a group of aristocratic families with the same name, descended from a common ancestor on the male side **2.** a clan, especially one that traces its descent on the male side (*dated*) [Mid-19C. < Latin, "race, clan"]

gent /jent/ *n* same as **gentleman** (*informal humorous*) [Mid-16C. Shortening]

gen·ta·mi·cin /jèntə mīss'n/ *n* a broad-spectrum antibiotic, usually administered by injection. It can cause serious side effects. [Mid-20C. < *genta-*, origin ? + alteration of -MYCIN]

gen·teel /jen teél/ *adj* **1.** WELL-MANNERED having or displaying refinement and good manners, especially manners that suggest an upper-class background **2.** PRETENTIOUS overdoing the refinement, delicacy of behavior, or snobbishness thought characteristic of the upper classes in order to create an impression of higher social status **3.** RELATING TO UPPER CLASSES relating to the upper classes (*dated*) [Late 16C. < French *gentil* (see GENTLE)] —**gen·teel·ly** *adv* —**gen·teel·ness** *n*

gen·teel·ism /jen teé lìzzəm/ *n* a word or phrase used in place of another one considered vulgar

gen·tes ANCIENT HIST, ANTHROP plural of **gens**

gen·tian /jénshən/ *n* **1.** SHOWY FLOWERING PLANT a plant belonging to a large family of annual or perennial species, several of which are cultivated as ornamental alpines. Flowers: typically bright blue or violet, trumpet-shaped. Native to: northern temperate regions and extending south to the Andes. Family: Gentianaceae. **2.** MEDICINAL ROOT the dried roots and rhizome of a European plant. Use: digestive stimulant in herbal medicine. **3.** PLANT PRODUCING DIGESTIVE AID the plant that produces the digestive stimulant gentian [14C. < Latin *gentiana*, after *Gentius*, 2C B.C. king of Illyria]

gen·tian blue *adj* of a purplish blue color —**gen·tian blue** *n*

gen·tian vi·o·let *n* a green dye derived from rosaniline that forms a violet solution in water. Use: biological stain, formerly, in antiseptic lotions.

gen·tile /jén tīl/ *n* **1.** NON-JEWISH PERSON somebody who is not Jewish **2.** SOMEBODY CHRISTIAN a Christian, as distinguished from somebody who is Jewish **3.** NON-MORMON in the Church of Jesus Christ of Latter-Day Saints, somebody who is not a member of this Church **4.** HEATHEN a disbeliever in God (*disapproving*) ■ *adj* **1.** NOT JEWISH not belonging to the Jewish people or faith **2.** CHRISTIAN Christian, as distinguished from Jewish **3.** GRAM DENOTING PLACE OR PEOPLE describes a noun such as "Welsh" or "Texan" that gives the name of a place or a people [14C. < Latin *gentilis* "of the same clan" (see GENTLE)]

Gen·ti·le da Fab·ri·a·no /jen teé lay daa faábree aánō/ (1370?–1427) Italian painter. Although much of his work has been lost, he is considered one of the greatest exponents of the International Gothic style. His most famous surviving work is the *Adoration of the Magi* (1423), an altarpiece painted in Florence. Born **di Massio, Gentile di Niccolò di Giovanni**

Gen·ti·les·chi /jèntə léskee/, **Artemisia** (1593?–1651?) Italian painter. One of the first women to receive recognition as an artist, she used the technique of chiaroscuro to great effect, as seen in *Judith Slaying Holofernes* (1620?).

gen·til·i·ty /jen tíllətee/ *n* **1.** REFINEMENT courteous and well-mannered behavior, especially when it suggests an upper-class background **2.** UPPER-CLASS STATUS the status or way of life of somebody from the upper classes **3.** PRETENTIOUSNESS exaggeratedly refined, delicate, or snobbish behavior, affected in order to create an impression of higher social status **4.** MEMBERS OF UPPER CLASS people from the upper classes [14C. < French *gentilité* < *gentil* (see GENTLE)]

gen·tle /jént'l/ *adj* (**-tler, -tlest**) **1.** KIND having a mild and kind nature or manner **2.** MILD being moderate in force or degree so that the effects are not severe ○ *a gentle reprimand* **3.** USING LITTLE FORCE using little force or violence ○ *a gentle tap on the shoulder* **4.** NOT STEEP not rising very steeply ○ *a gentle slope* **5.** UPPER-CLASS relating to or having a high social status or class **6.** CHIVALROUS having a gracious and honorable manner (*archaic*) ■ *vt* (**-tled, -tling, -tles**) **1.** SOOTHE SOMEBODY to cause somebody to become less agitated by means of words or actions (*literary*) **2.** TAME ANIMAL to calm an animal and make it domesticated (*formal*) [Pre-12C. Via French *gentil* "well-born" < Latin *gentilis* "of the same clan" < *gens* "race, clan"] —**gen·tle·ness** *n* —**gent·ly** *adv*

gen·tle breeze *n* a wind of between 8 and 12 mi./13 and 19 km per hour on the Beaufort scale

gen·tle·folk /jént'l fòk/, **gen·tle·folks** *npl* people from a high social class, especially those with an independent income (*archaic*)

gen·tle·man /jént'lmən/ (*plural* **-men** /-mən/) *n* **1. POLITE AND CULTURED MAN** a cultured man who behaves with courtesy and thoughtfulness **2. MAN** used as a polite term to refer to a man, regardless of his social position or behavior ○ *Good morning, ladies and gentlemen.* **3. UPPER-CLASS MAN** a man from a high social class, especially a man with an independent income **4.** HIST **MAN WITH COAT OF ARMS** in English history, a man who was not strictly of noble birth but was entitled to a coat of arms. He ranked above a yeoman in the social order. —**gen·tle·man·li·ness** *n* —**gen·tle·man·ly** *adj*

gen·tle·man-at-arms *n* a member of a troop of forty men who act as a ceremonial guard for the British sovereign on state occasions

gen·tle·man farm·er *n* **1.** a farmer with an independent source of income who farms for pleasure rather than for money **2.** a man who owns a farm but employs a manager and staff to work it

gen·tle·man's a·gree·ment *n* an agreement based on trust, not written down, and not enforceable by law

gen·tle·man's gen·tle·man *n* the manservant of an upper-class man (*dated*)

gen·tle·men's a·gree·ment *n* same as **gentleman's agreement**

gen·tle·wom·an /jént'l wòomən/ (*plural* **-wom·en** /-wìmmin/) *n* **1. POLITE AND CULTURED WOMAN** a cultured woman who behaves with courtesy and thoughtfulness **2. UPPER-CLASS WOMAN** a woman from a high social class, especially a woman with an independent income **3.** HIST **LADY'S PERSONAL ATTENDANT** a woman acting as a personal attendant to a lady of high social rank

gen·tri·fy /jéntrə fī/ (**-fied, -fy·ing, -fies**) *vt* to transform a run-down or aging neighborhood into a more prosperous one, e.g., through investment in remodeling buildings or houses —**gen·tri·fi·ca·tion** /jèntrəfi káysh'n/ *n*

gen·try /jéntree/ *n* **1. UPPER CLASSES** the group of people who make up the upper social classes **2. ENGLISH SOCIAL CLASS** the English social class that ranks just below the aristocracy and consists of families who are not of noble birth but are entitled to have a coat of arms **3. PEOPLE** people of a particular kind ○ *the fur-clad gentry who live there* [14C. < Old French *genterie* "nobility" < *gentil* (see GENTLE)]

gents /jents/ *n UK* same as **men's room** (*takes a singular or plural verb*)

gen·u·flect /jénnyə flèkt/ (**-flect·ed, -flect·ing, -flects**) *vi* **1.** to bend the right knee to the floor and rise again as a gesture of religious respect, especially in a Roman Catholic or Anglican church **2.** to show undeserved or unnecessarily deferential respect for somebody or something [Mid-19C. < ecclesiastical Latin *genuflectere* "bend the knee" < Latin *genu* "knee" + *flectere* "bend"] —**gen·u·flec·tion** /jènnyə fléksh'n/ *n*

gen·u·ine /jénnyoo in/ *adj* **1. REAL** having the qualities or value claimed ○ *a genuine Cézanne* **2. SINCERELY FELT** not affected or pretended ○ *a look of genuine surprise* **3. CANDID** honest and open in relationships with others ○ *a very genuine person* **4. PURE BRED** being of unmixed breeding ○ *of genuine stock* [Late 16C. < Latin *genuinus*] —**gen·u·ine·ly** *adv* —**gen·u·ine·ness** *n*

ge·nus /jéenəss/ (*plural* **gen·e·ra** /jénnərə/) *n* **1.** BIOL **SET OF CLOSELY RELATED SPECIES** a category in the taxonomic classification of related organisms, comprising one or more species. Similar genera are grouped into families. **2.** LOGIC **BROADER TERM FOR SOMETHING** the more general class or kind in which something is included, e.g., the species "dog" is included in the genus "animal" **3. GROUP** a class or group of any kind [Mid-16C. < Latin, "birth, race, kind"]

geo- *prefix* **1.** earth, soil ○ *geomagnetic* ○ *geophyte* **2.** geography, global ○ *geostrategy* [< Greek *gē* "Earth"]

ge·o·ar·chae·ol·o·gy /jèe ō aarkee óllәjee/ *n* a branch of geology dealing with archaeological sites, especially their formation, including dating, mineral identification, and soil analysis —**ge·o·ar·chae·ol·o·gic** /-aarkee ə lójjik/ *adj* —**ge·o·ar·chae·ol·o·gi·cal** *adj* —**ge·o·ar·chae·ol·o·gist** *n*

ge·o·bot·a·ny /jèe ō bótt'nee/ *n* BOT same as **phytogeography** —**ge·o·bo·tan·i·cal** /jèe ō bə tánnik'l/ *adj* —**ge·o·bot·a·nist** *n*

ge·o·cen·tric /jèe ō séntrik/ *adj* **1. HAVING EARTH AT ITS CENTER** describes the solar system when it is regarded as having the Earth as its center **2. CONSIDERED FROM EARTH'S CENTER** measured from, or considered as if viewed from, the center of the Earth **3. WITH EARTH AS CENTER OF FOCUS** having the Earth and its inhabitants as the center of a theory or belief —**ge·o·cen·tri·cal·ly** *adv*

ge·o·chem·is·try /jèe ō kémmistree/ *n* the study of the chemical composition of the Earth's solid matter, and of the solid matter of other planets, meteors, and asteroids —**ge·o·chem·i·cal** *adj* —**ge·o·chem·i·cal·ly** *adv* —**ge·o·chem·ist** *n*

ge·o·chro·nol·o·gy /jèe ō krə nóllәjee/ *n* the study of the ages and relative ages of geologic events and rock formations —**ge·o·chron·o·log·i·cal** /jèe ō kronə lójjik'l/ *adj* —**ge·o·chron·o·log·i·cal·ly** *adv* —**ge·o·chro·nol·o·gist** *n*

ge·o·chro·nom·e·try /jèe ō krə nómmətree/ *n* the measurement of the age of a rock, mineral, or sequence of rocks, or of an event such as a volcanic eruption —**ge·o·chron·o·met·ric** /jèe ō kronə méttrik/ *adj*

ge·o·co·ro·na /jèe ō kə rṓnə/ *n* the outermost region of the Earth's atmosphere, reaching to a height approximately 15 times the radius of the Earth and consisting mainly of hydrogen

ge·ode /jèe ōd/ *n* **1.** a roughly spherical rock mass containing a cavity lined or filled with crystals that have grown unimpeded and so are frequently perfectly formed **2.** the crystal-lined cavity within a geode [Late 17C. Via Latin *geodes* < Greek *geōdēs* "earthy" < *gē* "Earth"]

ge·o·des·ic /jèe ə déssik/ *adj* **1.** MATH relating to the geometry of curved surfaces **2.** GEOG same as **geodetic** ■ *n* MATH the shortest line between two points on a curved or flat surface

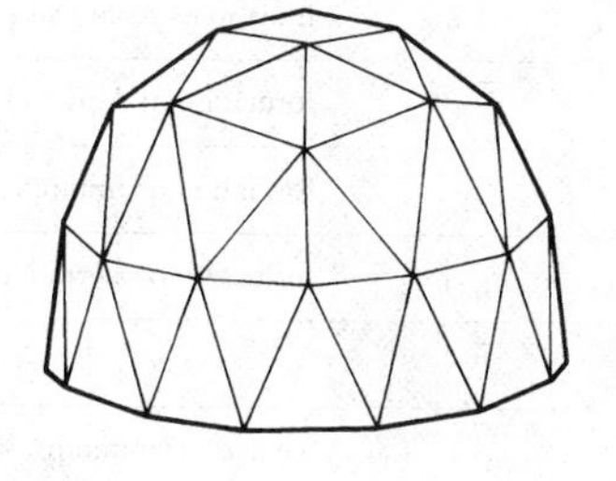

geodesic dome

ge·o·des·ic dome *n* a dome that has many flat straight-sided faces formed by a framework of bars that intersect to form equilateral triangles or polygons

ge·o·des·ic line *n* MATH same as **geodesic**

ge·od·e·sy /jee óddəssee/ *n* the branch of science that deals with the precise measurement of the size and shape of the Earth, the mapping of points on its surface, and the study of its gravitational field [Late 16C. Via modern Latin < Greek *geōdaisia* < *daiein* "to divide"] —**ge·od·e·sist** *n*

ge·o·det·ic /jèe ə déttik/, **ge·o·det·i·cal** /-ik'l/ *adj* relating to the precise measurement of the Earth's surface or of points on its surface [Late 17C. < Greek *geōdaitēs* "land surveyor" < *daiein* "to divide"] —**ge·o·det·i·cal·ly** *adv*

ge·o·det·ic sur·vey *n* a survey of a very large area of land, with the curvature of the Earth's surface taken into account

geo·duck /gòo ee dùk/, **gwe·duc** *n* a very large clam. Native to: northwestern Pacific coast of North America. Latin name: *Panope generosa.* [Late 19C. < Salish *gʷídeq*]

ge·o·dy·nam·ics /jèe ō dī námmiks/ *n* a branch of geology concerned with the study of processes within the Earth's interior and their causative forces (*takes a singular verb*) —**ge·o·dy·nam·ic** *adj*

ge·o·dy·na·mo /jèe ō dī́nəmō/ *n* the process whereby the rotational movement of the Earth's molten iron core sustains the planet's magnetic field

ge·o·ec·o·nom·ics /jèe ō ekə nómmiks, -eekə-/ *n* the study of how the economies of the world's nations relate to and affect each other (*takes a singular verb*) —**ge·o·ec·o·nom·ic** *adj* —**ge·o·ec·o·nom·i·cal·ly** *adv* —**ge·o·e·con·o·mist** /-i kónnəmist/ *n*

Geof·frey of Mon·mouth /jèffree əv mónməth/ (1100?–54) English historian and cleric. His 12-volume *Historia Regum Britanniae* (*The History of the Kings of Britain*) (1139?) is a mixture of history and myth, parts of which later formed the basis of the legend of King Arthur.

geog. *abbr* **1.** geographic **2.** geographical **3.** geography

ge·o·graph·ic /jèe ə gráffik/, **ge·o·graph·i·cal** /-gráffik'l/ *adj* relating to geography or to the geography of a specific region [Mid-16C. Via French or late Latin < Greek *geōgraphikos* < *geōgraphos* "writer about the Earth"] —**ge·o·graph·i·cal·ly** *adv*

ge·o·graph·ic mile *n* MEASURE same as **nautical mile**

geo·graph·ic pro·fil·ing *n* the science of predicting where a criminal lives, based on the locations and frequencies of the crimes committed and following the principle that most offenders carry out crimes relatively locally

ge·og·ra·phy /jee óggrəfee/ (*plural* **-phies**) *n* **1. STUDY OF EARTH'S PHYSICAL FEATURES** the study of all the physical features of the Earth's surface, including its climate and the distribution of plant, animal, and human life **2. PHYSICAL FEATURES** the physical features of a place or region, e.g., mountains and rivers **3. BOOK ON GEOGRAPHY** a book on geography **4. LAYOUT OF PLACE** the arrangement of the different parts of a building, city, or other place **5. ARRANGEMENT** the way that something is arranged and the relationships between its different parts ○ *the geography of the criminal mind* [15C. Via Latin < Greek *geōgraphia* "writing about the Earth"] —**ge·og·ra·pher** *n*

ge·o·hy·drol·o·gy /jèe ō hī dróllәjee/ *n* GEOL same as **hydrogeology** —**ge·o·hy·dro·log·ic** /jèe ō hīdrə lójjik/ *adj* —**ge·o·hy·drol·o·gist** *n*

ge·oid /jèe òyd/ *n* **1.** the slightly flattened sphere that is the shape of the Earth, used in calculating the precise measurements of points on the Earth's surface **2.** a hypothetical surface of the Earth that would exist if a cross section were taken at sea level [Late 19C. < Greek *geoeidēs* (see GEODE)] —**ge·oi·dal** *adj*

geol. *abbr* **1.** geologic **2.** geological **3.** geology

ge·o·log·ic time *n* the period of time that extends from the beginning of the world to the present day. See table on next page

ge·ol·o·gize /jee óllə jīz/ (**-gized, -giz·ing, -giz·es**) *vti* to study geology in general, or the geology of a specific place

ge·ol·o·gy /jee óllәjee/ *n* **1. STUDY OF ROCKS AND MINERALS** the study of the structure of the Earth or another planet, especially its rocks, soil, and minerals, and its history and origins **2. STRUCTURE OF AREA** the rocks, minerals, and physical structure of a specific area **3. BOOK ON GEOLOGY** a book on geology [Mid-18C. < modern Latin *geologia* "description of the Earth"] —**ge·o·log·ic** /jèe ə lójjik/ *adj* —**ge·o·log·i·cal** *adj* —**ge·o·log·i·cal·ly** *adv* —**ge·ol·o·gist** *n*

geom. *abbr* **1.** geometric **2.** geometrical **3.** geometry

ge·o·mag·ne·tic /jèe ō mag néttik/ *adj* relating to the magnetic properties of the Earth, or the study of them —**ge·o·mag·net·i·cal·ly** *adv*

ge·o·mag·net·ic pole *n* GEOG same as **magnetic pole** (sense 2)

ge·o·mag·net·ic storm *n* METEOROL same as **magnetic storm**

MAIN DIVISIONS OF GEOLOGIC TIME

Million years ago	Division	Significant events
4,500+	pre-Archean Eon	formation of the Earth
4,000	Archean Eon	formation of land masses, oceans, atmosphere first single-celled organisms, blue-green algae
2,500	Proterozoic Eon	formation of mountains, glaciers, ozone layer; first invertebrates
570	Phanerozoic Eon	
	Paleozoic Era	
	Cambrian Period	formation of S continent Gondwanaland; first shellfish, sponges
500	Ordovician Period	N America collides with Europe; primitive fish in shallow seas, first coral
435	Silurian Period	Europe separates from N America; first airbreathing animal (scorpion), land plants
410	Devonian Period	Eurasia, Gondwanaland, and America collide; first amphibians, insects
360	Carboniferous Period	
	Mississippian Period	first fern forests, swamps, winged insects, sharks
	Pennsylvanian Period	formation of coal, oil, gas deposits; first reptiles
290	Permian Period	continents combine to form Pangaea; first conifers, mass extinction of invertebrates
248	Mesozoic Era	
	Triassic Period	Pangaea breaks up; first dinosaurs, evergreen forests
206	Jurassic Period	N and S America move west; first mammals, birds
144	Cretaceous Period	Africa and India drift north; extinction of dinosaurs
65	Cenozoic Era	
	Tertiary Period	
	Paleocene Epoch	Antarctica and Australia split; first marsupials, hoofed mammals
55	Eocene Epoch	India joins Asia; first primates, bats, sea mammals
38	Oligocene Epoch	formation of Alps and Himalayas; first elephants, monkeys, great apes
24	Miocene Epoch	formation of Antarctic ice sheet, N prairies; first humanlike apes
5	Pliocene Epoch	formation of Sierra Nevada range; primate ancestors of *Homo sapiens*
1.6	Quaternary Period	
	Pleistocene Epoch	ice ages; mammoths, saber-toothed tigers, early humans
0.01	Holocene Epoch	melting ice sheets; extinctions caused by human activity, global warming

ge·o·mag·ne·tism /jèe ō mágnə tìzzəm/ *n* **1.** the magnetic properties of the Earth **2.** the study of the magnetic properties of the Earth

ge·o·man·cy /jée ə mànssee/ *n* the art or practice of making predictions based on patterns made by a handful of earth thrown on the ground or by lines connecting randomly placed dots [14C. Via medieval Latin < Greek *geōmanteia* "divination from the Earth" < *manteia* "divination"] —**ge·o·man·cer** *n* —**ge·o·man·tic** /jèe ə mántik/ *adj*

ge·om·e·ter /jee ómmətər/ *n* a student of or an expert in geometry [15C. Via late Latin < Greek *geōmetrēs* "land measurer" < *gē* "Earth" + *metrēs* "measurer"]

ge·o·met·ric /jèe ə méttrik/, **ge·o·met·ri·cal** /-ik'l/ *adj* **1.** RELATING TO GEOMETRY conforming to the laws and methods of geometry **2.** USING SIMPLE LINES using straight lines and simple shapes such as circles or squares **3.** INCREASING FAST increasing or decreasing very rapidly ○ *geometric growth* [Mid-17C. Via French *géométrique* < Greek *geōmetrikos* < *geōmetrēs* (see GEOMETER)] —**ge·o·met·ri·cal·ly** *adv*

Ge·o·met·ric *adj* relating to a period of ancient Greek culture, between 900 and 700 B.C., noted for its decorative use of simple lines and shapes, especially on pottery

ge·o·met·ri·cal *adj* same as **geometric**

ge·o·met·ric mean *n* the average of a set of *n* values, described mathematically as the *nth* root of their product

ge·o·met·ric pro·gres·sion *n* a series of numbers in which each number is separated by the same numerical step

ge·o·met·rics /jèe ə méttriks/ *npl* straight lines and simple shapes, e.g., circles or squares, used in design and decoration

ge·o·met·ric se·ries *n* a series of numbers (**geometric progression**) separated by a constant numerical step expressed as a sum, e.g., 1+4+16+64

ge·om·e·trid /jee ómmətrid/ *n* a moth with a slender body and broad wings and larvae that crawl with a characteristic looping movement. Family: Geometridae. [Late 19C. < modern Latin *Geometridae* "land measurers"] —**ge·om·e·trid** *adj*

ge·om·e·trize /jee ómmə trīz/ (**-trized, -triz·ing, -triz·es**) *v* **1.** *vt* to represent something in geometric form **2.** *vti* to apply the principles of geometry to something —**ge·om·e·tri·za·tion** /jee òmmətri záysh'n/ *n*

ge·om·e·try /jee ómmətree/ *n* **1.** MATHEMATICS OF SHAPES the branch of mathematics that is concerned with the properties and relationships of points, lines, angles, curves, surfaces, and solids. See illustration on next page **2.** KIND OF GEOMETRY a particular system or class of geometry, e.g., a set of distinct theories or its application to a particular type of problem or object ○ *Euclidean geometry* ○ *solid geometry* **3.** BOOK ON GEOMETRY a book on geometry **4.** ARRANGEMENT OF SOMETHING the way the different parts of something

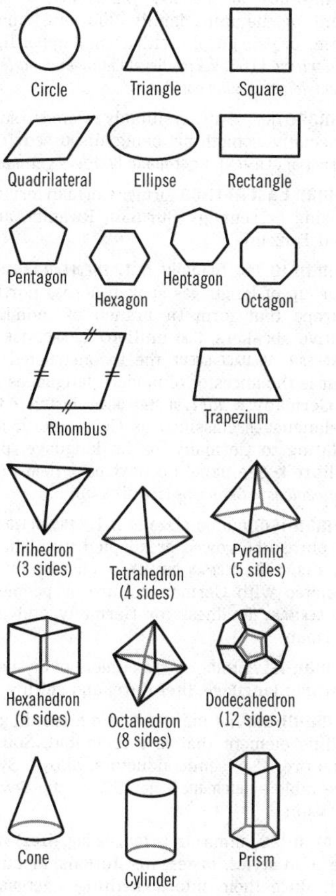

geometry: shapes and solids

fit together in relation to each other [14C. Via French *géométrie* < Greek *geōmetria* "measuring of the Earth" < *gē* "Earth" + *metron* "measure"] —**ge·om·e·tri·cian** /jèe əmə trísh'n, jee òmmə-/ *n*

ge·o·mor·phic /jèe ə máwrfik/ *adj* relating to the surface features of the Earth or another planet

ge·o·mor·phol·o·gy /jèe ə mawr fóllәjee/ *n* the branch of geology that examines the formation and structure of the features of the surface of the Earth or of another planet —**ge·o·mor·pho·log·ic** /jèe ə mawrfə lójjik/ *adj* —**ge·o·mor·pho·log·i·cal** *adj* —**ge·o·mor·pho·log·i·cal·ly** *adv* —**ge·o·mor·phol·o·gist** *n*

ge·oph·a·gy /jee óffəjee/ *n* the eating of soil, clay, or chalk

ge·o·phone /jèe ə fōn/ *n* an electronic instrument that picks up vibrations in the Earth

ge·o·phys·ics /jèe ə fízziks/ *n* the branch of earth science that deals with the physics and physical processes of the Earth, especially using noninvasive techniques such as acoustic surveys of the structure of rocks (*takes a singular verb*) —**ge·o·phys·i·cal** *adj* —**ge·o·phys·i·cal·ly** *adv* —**ge·o·phys·i·cist** /-fízzəssist/ *n*

ge·o·phyte /jèe ə fīt/ *n* a perennial plant that propagates from organs such as bulbs, tubers, or rhizomes that are below ground

ge·o·pol·i·tics /jèe ō póllətiks/ *n* **1.** the relationships that exist between a country's politics and its geography, or the influences that geography has on political relations between countries (*takes a plural verb*) **2.** the study of the interrelationship between politics, geography, and population distribution in or between countries (*takes a singular verb*) —**ge·o·po·lit·i·cal** /jèe ō pə líttik'l/ *adj* —**ge·o·po·lit·i·cal·ly** *adv* —**ge·o·pol·i·ti·cian** /jèe ō polə tísh'n/ *n*

ge·o·pon·ics /jèe ə pónniks/ *n* the scientific study of agriculture (*takes a singular verb*) [Early 17C. < Greek *geōponikos* "of farming" < *geōponos* "farmer"] —**ge·o·pon·ic** *adj*

geo·pro·fil·ing /jèeō prṓfīling/ *n* CRIME same as **geographic profiling**

Geor·die /jáwrdee/ *n* the dialect of English spoken in Tyneside in northeastern England [Mid-19C. < local pronunciation of *Georgie*, diminutive of the name *George*] —**Geor·die** *adj*

George I /jawrj (1660–1727) king of Great Britain and Ireland. German-born, he was the great-grandson of James I and the first of Britain's Hanoverian kings (1714–27).

George II (1683–1760) king of Great Britain and Ireland. German-born British monarch who as king (1727–60) was a field commander in the War of the Austrian Succession (1740–48).

George III (1738–1820) king of Great Britain and Ireland. He was the first British-born Hanoverian king. His reign (1760–1820) was marked by the American Revolution. In later years, he was increasingly affected by a psychiatric disorder that led finally to the establishment of a regency (1811) under his son, later George IV.

> "Born and educated in this country I glory in the name of Briton."
> [George III, *Speech from the throne*; 1760]

George IV (1762–1830) king of Great Britain and Ireland. Notorious for his extravagant habits, he was regent for George III (1811–20) and king (1820–30).

George V (1865–1936) king of Great Britain and Northern Ireland. His reign (1910–36) saw the partition of Ireland (1922). Notable for his naval career, he renounced the family's German titles during World War I.

> "How is the Empire?"
> [George V, *Attributed last words*; January 21, 1936]

George VI (1895–1952) king of Great Britain and Northern Ireland. He succeeded to the throne after the abdication of his brother Edward VIII (1936). He was greatly admired for his national leadership during World War II.

> "It is not the walls that make the city, but the people who live within them. The walls of London may be battered, but the spirit of the Londoner stands resolute and undismayed."
> [George VI, *Radio broadcast*; September 23, 1940]

George, Henry (1839–97) US economist and social philosopher. An influential writer and lecturer, he proposed to abolish poverty by means of a "single-tax" on land, in works such as *Progress and Poverty* (1879).

> "We cannot safely leave politics to politicians, or political economy to college professors. The people themselves must think, because the people alone can act."
> [Henry George, *Social Problems*; 1883]

George, Lake lake in the foothills of the Adirondack Mountains, eastern New York State. Noted for its beauty, it has long been a resort center and was of military importance during the French and Indian War and the Revolution. Area: 44 sq. mi./114 sq. km.

George, St. (*d.* A.D. 303?) patron saint of England. According to legend, he killed a dragon that was terrorizing a village and then converted the inhabitants to Christianity. He was made patron saint of England in the 14th century.

Geor·ges Bank /jàwrjəz-/ underwater plateau in the northern Atlantic Ocean, off the coast of Cape Cod, Massachusetts, and Nova Scotia. It is one of the world's most productive fishing areas. Length: 175 mi./280 km.

George·town /jáwrj tòwn/ **1.** port and capital city of Guyana. It is on the Atlantic coast at the mouth of the Demerara River. Population: 275,000 (1999). **2.** affluent residential and commercial district of northwestern Washington, D.C. and the home of Georgetown University. Originally a separate port on the Potomac River, it was incorporated into the District of Columbia in 1871.

George Town 1. town and capital of the Cayman Islands, situated on Grand Cayman Island in the northwestern Caribbean. Population: 19,000 (1996). **2.** town in northern Tasmania, Australia. It is one of Australia's oldest settlements. Population: 6,483 (2002 estimate). **3.** seaport and capital city of Penang State, Malaysia. It was the site of the first British settlement in Malaysia. Population: 219,380 (1991).

georg·ette /jawr jét/ *n* a thin lightweight silk or cotton fabric with a matte finish (*often used before a noun*) [Early 20C. After Madame *Georgette* de la Plante, late 19C. Parisian dressmaker]

Georgia

Geor·gia /jáwrjə/ **1.** state in the southeastern United States, bordered by South Carolina, the Atlantic Ocean, Florida, Alabama, North Carolina, and Tennessee. Capital: Atlanta. Population: 8,560,310 (2002 estimate). Area: 58,977 sq. mi./152,750 sq. km. **2.** country on the eastern coast of the Black Sea bordered on the north by Russia and on the south by Turkey, Armenia, and Azerbaijan. The country is dominated by the Greater Caucasus to the north and the Lesser Caucasus to the south. Language: Georgian. Currency: lari. Capital: Tbilisi. Population: 4,934,413 (2003). Area: 26,900 sq. mi./69,700 sq. km. Official name **Republic of Georgia**

Geor·gia, Strait of channel between Vancouver Island and the mainland of the northwestern United States and southwestern Canada, connected to the Pacific Ocean by waterways to the southwest and northwest. It forms a section of the Inside Passage between Washington and Alaska. Length: 150 mi./240 km. Width: 30 mi./48 km.

Geor·gian[1] /jáwrjən/ *adj* **1.** HIST **OF 1714 TO 1830 IN BRITAIN** relating to the time of the British kings George I, II, III, and IV, who reigned consecutively from 1714 to 1830 **2.** ARCHIT **OF 18C ARCHITECTURAL STYLE** built in or imitating a neoclassical style of architecture or furniture that flourished in Great Britain and the United States in the 18th and early 19th centuries **3.** LITERAT **OF 20C LITERARY MOVEMENT** relating to a movement in early 20th-century poetry that favored traditional styles, especially pastoral ■ *n* LITERAT **GEORGIAN WRITER** a writer whose works belong to the Georgian literary movement [Late 18C. < the man's name *George*]

Geor·gian[2] /jáwrjən/ *n* **1. SOMEBODY FROM US STATE OF GEORGIA** somebody who comes from the state of Georgia **2. SOMEBODY FROM GEORGIA** somebody who comes from the Republic of Georgia **3. LANGUAGE OF GEORGIA** the official language of the Republic of Georgia, belonging to the Kartvelian language family. Native speakers: 3.5 million. [15C. < GEORGIA] —**Geor·gian** *adj*

Geor·gian Bay /jàwrjən-/ northeastern arm of Lake Huron, in southeastern Ontario, Canada. Area: 5,800 sq. mi./15,000 sq. km.

Geor·gian Bay Is·lands Na·tion·al Park national park incorporating 59 islands on the eastern side of Georgian Bay in southeastern Ontario, Canada. Area: 9.7 sq. mi./25 sq. km.

geor·gic /jáwrjik/ *adj* **RURAL** relating to or depicting rural life (*literary*) ■ *n* **POEM ABOUT RURAL LIFE** a poem about rural life ■ *adj* AGRIC **OF AGRICULTURE** relating to agriculture [Early 16C. Via Latin < Greek *geōrgikos* < *geōrgos* "farmer" < *gē* "Earth"]

ge·o·sci·ence /jèe ō sī ənss/ *n* a science that deals with the Earth, e.g., geology or geophysics —**ge·o·sci·en·tist** *n*

ge·o·sphere /jèe ō sfeer/ *n* the solid matter of the Earth, as distinct from the seas, plants, animals, and surrounding atmosphere —**ge·o·spher·ic** /jèe ō sfírrik, -sférrik/ *adj*

ge·o·sta·tion·ar·y /jèe ō stáysh'n èrree/ *adj* describes the orbit of a satellite that circles the Earth above the equator at a speed matching the Earth's rotation, thus appearing to remain stationary, or a satellite in such an orbit. Most communications satellites are in geostationary orbit.

ge·o·strat·e·gy /jèe ō stráttəjee/ (*plural* **-gies**) *n* **1.** the study of strategy in relation to the geopolitical situation of a country or region **2.** the policy of a nation based on a combination of geographic and political factors —**ge·o·stra·te·gic** /-strə tèejik/ *adj* —**ge·o·strat·e·gist** *n*

ge·o·stroph·ic /jèe ə stróffik/ *adj* arising from the rotation of the Earth —**ge·o·stroph·i·cal·ly** *adv*

ge·o·syn·chro·nous /jèe ō síng krənəss/ *adj* AEROSP same as **geostationary**

ge·o·syn·cline /jèe ō síng klīn/ *n* a long broad depression in the Earth's crust where it has sunk over time as it has accumulated a thick layer of sedimentary deposits —**ge·o·syn·cli·nal** /jèe ō sing klīn'l/ *adj*

ge·o·tax·is /jèe ō tákssiss/ *n* movement by an organism or cell in response to the force of gravity —**ge·o·tac·tic** *adj* —**ge·o·tac·ti·cal·ly** *adv*

ge·o·tec·ton·ic /jèe ō tek tónnik/ *adj* relating to the large-scale structure of the Earth's crust —**ge·o·tec·ton·i·cal·ly** *adv*

ge·o·ther·mal /jèe ō thúrməl/, **ge·o·ther·mic** /-thúrmik/ *adj* relating to or produced by the heat in the interior of the Earth —**ge·o·ther·mal·ly** *adv*

ge·o·ther·mal en·er·gy *n* energy in the form of heat obtained from hot circulating ground water

ge·o·ther·mal gra·di·ent *n* the change in temperature encountered with depth within the Earth

ge·ot·ro·pism /jee óttrə pìzzəm/ *n* plant growth or movement in response to gravity. Upward growth of plant parts, against gravity, is called negative geotropism, and downward growth of roots is called positive geotropism. —**ge·o·tro·pic** /jèe ə trṓpik, -tróppik/ *adj* —**ge·o·tro·pi·cal·ly** *adv*

ger. *abbr* GRAM gerund

Ger. *abbr* **1.** CULTL ANTHROP, LANG German **2.** Germany

ge·rah /gèerə/ *n* an ancient Hebrew coin worth one twentieth of a shekel [Mid-16C. < Hebrew *gērāh*]

ge·ra·ni·ol /jə ráynee àwl/ *n* a pale yellow or colorless alcohol that smells like geraniums. Source: essential oils. Use: in perfumes, flavorings. Formula: $C_{10}H_{18}O$. [Late 19C. < GERANIUM]

geranium

ge·ra·ni·um /jə ráynee əm/ *n* **1.** PLANTS **PLANT WITH BRIGHTLY COLORED FLOWERS** a popular garden plant with large rounded leaves. Flowers: bright red, pink, white, on tall stalks. Genus: *Pelargonium.* **2.** PLANTS **PLANT WITH SAUCER-SHAPED FLOWERS** a plant with divided leaves, e.g., cranesbill and herb Robert. Flowers: pink, blue, white, red, saucer-shaped. Genus: *Geranium.* **3.** COLORS **BRIGHT RED COLOR** a red color tinged with orange, like that of a scarlet geranium [Mid-16C. Via Latin < Greek *geranion* < *geranos* "crane"; from the resemblance of the spur on some species' fruit to a crane's bill] —**ge·ra·ni·um** *adj*

gerbil

ger·bil /júrb'l/ *n* a small rodent resembling a mouse with long back legs. Native to: hot dry parts of Africa, Asia. [Mid-19C. Via French *gerbille* < modern Latin *gerbillus,* diminutive of *gerboa* (see JERBOA)]

GERD *abbr* MED gastroesophageal reflux disease

ge·re·nuk /gérrə nòok, gə rénnək/ (*plural* **-nuks** or *same*) *n* a slender antelope, the male of which has long horns that curve backward. Native to: eastern Africa. Latin name: *Litocranius walleri.* [Late 19C. < Somali]

ger·fal·con *n* BIRDS another spelling of **gyrfalcon**

ger·i·at·ric /jèrree áttrik/ *adj* **1.** MED **RELATING TO SENIOR CITIZENS** relating to the diagnosis, treatment, and prevention of illness in senior citizens **2.** **OFFENSIVE TERM** an offensive term meaning showing the effects of age ■ *n* MED **SENIOR CITIZEN** a senior citizen (*technical; used in medical contexts*) [Early 20C. < Greek *gēras* "old age"]

ger·i·at·rics /jèrree áttriks/ *n* the branch of medicine that deals with the illnesses and medical care of senior citizens (*takes a singular verb*) —**ger·i·a·tri·cian** /jèrree ə trísh'n/ *n*

Gé·ri·cault /zhayri kṓ/, **Théodore** (1791–1824) French painter. The leading romantic painter of his time, he developed a colorful dramatic style exemplified in his best-known work *Raft of the Medusa* (1818–19).

Ge·rin-La·joie /zhay ràN lə zhwàa/, **Antoine** (1824–82) Canadian writer. He wrote poems, plays, and novels, including *Jean Rivard: le défricheur* translated into English (1862) as *Jean Rivard: the Settler* and founded two magazines.

germ /jurm/ *n* **1.** MICROBIOL **MICROORGANISM** a microorganism, especially one that can cause disease **2.** MICROBIOL **CELL** the smallest element in an organism such as a spore or a fertilized egg that is capable of growing into a complete adult or part **3.** **BEGINNING** the first sign of something that will develop ○ *the germ of an idea* [Mid-15C. Via French *germe* < Latin *germen* "seed, sprout" < *gignere* "beget"]

ger·man /júrmən/ *adj* having the same parents, or closely related (*formal*) ○ *brothers-german* [Via French *germain* < Latin *germanus* "having the same parents" < *germen* (see GERM)]

Ger·man /júrmən/ *n* **1.** **SOMEBODY FROM GERMANY** somebody who comes from Germany **2.** **LANGUAGE OF GERMANY** the official language of Germany, Austria, and Liechtenstein and one of the official languages of Switzerland, also spoken elsewhere in the world, belonging to the Germanic branch of Indo-European. Native speakers: 100 million. Other speakers: 100 million. **3.** **SOMEBODY WHO SPEAKS GERMAN** somebody whose first language is German [14C. < Latin *Germanus,* applied to a group of related peoples of northern and central Europe] —**Ger·man** *adj*

germ·a·nate /júrmə nàyt/ *n* a salt containing an anionic grouping of germanium and oxygen

Ger·man cock·roach *n* a small brown cockroach that is a common pest throughout the world. Latin name: *Blattella germanica.*

Ger·man De·mo·cra·tic Re·pub·lic /jùrmən-/ former republic of central Europe, reunited with the rest of Germany in 1990. It was founded under the influence of the former Soviet Union in 1949 and recognized as an independent state in 1955. Area: 41,768 sq. mi./108,178 sq. km.

ger·man·der /jər mándər/ (*plural* **-ders** or *same*) *n* a plant of the mint family. Flowers: small, pink, white, or pale purple, with a small upper lip. Genus: *Teucrium.* [15C. Via medieval Latin *germandr(e)a* < Greek *khamaidrus* "ground oak"]

ger·mane /jər máyn/ *adj* suitably related to something, especially something being discussed [Early 17C. Variant of GERMAN] —**ger·mane·ly** *adv* —**ger·mane·ness** *n*

Ger·man East Af·ri·ca former German territory comprising present-day Burundi, Rwanda, and mainland Tanzania

Ger·man·ic /jər mánnik/ *n* **1.** **EUROPEAN LANGUAGE GROUP** a group of languages spoken across northwestern Europe that forms a branch of Indo-European. Native speakers: 500 million. **2.** **ANCESTOR OF MODERN EUROPEAN LANGUAGE GROUP** the reconstructed language that is the ancestor of modern languages classified as Germanic ■ *adj* **1.** **OF GERMANIC** relating to the group of languages classified as Germanic **2.** **OF GERMANY** relating to Germany, or its language, people, or culture ► See panel on next page [Mid-17C. < Latin *Germanicus* < *Germanus* (see GERMAN)]

Ger·man·ism /júrmə nìzzəm/ *n* **1.** **GERMAN WORD** a word or phrase borrowed or adapted from the German language **2.** **GERMAN QUALITY** a custom or trait associated with German culture or people **3.** **LIKING FOR GERMANY** fondness for Germany and all things German

Ger·man·ist /júrmənist/ *n* a student of or specialist in German language, literature, and culture

ger·ma·ni·um /jər máynee əm/ *n* a brittle gray crystalline element that is a metalloid. Source: coal, zinc ore. Use: semiconductors, alloys. Symbol **Ge.** See table at **element** [Late 19C. < Latin *Germanus* (see GERMAN)]

ger·man·ize /júrmə nīz/ (**-ized, -iz·ing, -izes**) *vti* to adopt German styles, tastes, institutions, or customs, or introduce them into something —**ger·man·i·za·tion** /jùrməni záysh'n/ *n*

Ger·man mea·sles *n UK* MED same as **rubella**

Ger·man·o·phile /jər mánnə fīl/ *n* an admirer of Germany and the German people

Ger·man·o·phobe /jər mánnə fṓb/ *n* a hater of Germany or the German people

Ger·man shep·herd *n* a large working dog with medium-length hair, pointed ears, and a muscular build, belonging to a breed originally developed in Germany that is often used as a guard dog or police dog

Ger·man sil·ver *n* METALL same as **nickel silver**

Ger·man·town /júrmən tòwn/ district of Philadelphia, Pennsylvania. It was the site of an unsuccessful attack on the British camp by George Washington's troops in the Revolution in 1777.

Germany

Ger·ma·ny /júrmənee/ country in central Europe. Divided into East and West Germany following World War II, it became a unified country again in 1990. Language: German. Currency: euro. Capital: Berlin. Population: 82,398,326 (2003). Area: 137,827 sq. mi./356,970 sq. km. Official name **Federal Republic of Germany**

germ cell *n* MICROBIOL same as **germ** (sense 2)

ger·mi·cide /júrmə sīd/ *n* a substance that kills germs —**ger·mi·ci·dal** /jùrmə sīd'l/ *adj*

LANGUAGE HERITAGE ***German*** Much of English is made up of words from other languages, and German is an important contributor, especially to the vocabulary of medicine and other sciences. For example, ***aspirin***, first recorded in English in the 19th century, comes directly from German: it is a contraction of *acetylierte Spirsäure* "acetylated spiraeic acid," an old name for *salicylic acid*. Other such German émigrés are ***cobalt*** (late 17th century, from German *Kobalt*, a variant of *Kobold* "harmful goblin," from miners' belief that cobalt ore was harmful to neighboring silver ore), ***heroin*** (late 19th, from German *Heroin*, originally a trademark), and ***peptide*** (early 20th).

German scientific vocabulary has also used words whose ultimate ancestries lie in other lands and languages. Examples are ***allergy***, which arrived in English in the early 20th century from German *Allergie* but is formed from Greek *allos* "other"; ***botulism***, which came from German *Botulismus* "sausage poisoning," from Latin *botulus* "sausage"; and ***neuron***, which came from German *Neuron* from a Greek word meaning "sinew, cord, nerve." Occasionally German has combined with other languages to create what might be called "international portmanteau words" combining the sound and meaning of two words. A good example is ***lumpenproletariat***, a mix of German *Lumpen*, the plural of *Lump* "ragamuffin," and French *prolétariat* "the working class."

Many direct borrowings from German are easily recognizable because they have gone through little or no structural alterations in transit. These words encompass many subject categories. A few examples are, by category: psychology ***angst***, ***gestalt***; politics ***bund***, ***realpolitik***; zoology ***dachshund***, ***schnauzer***; literature ***festschrift***, ***bildungsroman***; literature and sociology ***Sturm und Drang***; music ***leitmotif***; mythology ***Götterdämmerung***; food ***hasenpfeffer***, ***kaffeeklatsch***, ***pretzel***, ***sauerbraten***, ***sauerkraut***, ***stollen***, ***strudel***, ***zwieback***; education ***kindergarten***; warfare ***blitzkrieg*** (from which we get ***blitz***), ***stalag*** (a contraction of *Stammlager* "main camp"); and general terms such as ***ersatz***, ***gesundheit***, ***kitsch***, ***schadenfreude***, ***spiel***, ***wunderkind***, and ***zeitgeist***. Some English words come from German place names. Among them are ***frankfurter***, ***hamburger***, ***hock***, and ***rottweiler*** from *Frankfurt am Main*, *Hamburg*, *Hocheim*, and *Rottweil*, respectively.

Some German borrowings into English have undergone structural alterations to such an extent that they no longer overtly resemble their ancestral roots. One is ***poodle***, first recorded in English in the early 19th century, coming from German *Pudel*, a shortening of *Pudelhund*, from a Low German word *pudeln* "to splash in water" plus *Hund* "dog." A few English words are direct loan translations from German. Among them are: ***thing-in-itself***, a translation of *Ding an sich*, ***Brown Shirt***, a translation of *Braunhemd*, ***superman***, from *Übermensch* (itself an 1883 coinage by Nietzsche and a direct borrowing into English as well), ***world view***, a translation of *Weltanschauung* (also a direct borrowing into English), the expression ***out of sight***, a translation of *ausgezeichnet*, and the infamous ***Final Solution***, a translation of *Endlösung*. In another, rather quirky, migratory pattern, the English word ***boxer*** "fighter" transited the English Channel to Germany, there to be applied to the dog because of its wide, flattened nose, and then returned to English in the early 20th century in this new sense.

ger·mi·nal /júrmən'l/ *adj* **1.** relating to reproductive cells **2.** relating or belonging to the earliest stage in the development of something (*formal*) [Early 19C. < Latin *germen* (see GERM)] —**ger·mi·nal·ly** *adv*

ger·mi·nal disk *n* BIOL same as **blastodisk**

ger·mi·nal ves·i·cle *n* the enlarged nucleus of an egg before it develops into an ovum

ger·mi·nate /júrmə nàyt/ (**-nat·ed, -nat·ing, -nates**) *v* **1.** *vti* to start to grow from a seed or spore into a new individual, or cause a seed or spore to do this **2.** *vi* to be created and start to develop ○ *seeds of doubt germinating in his mind* [Late 16C. < Latin *germinat-*, past participle of *germinare* < *germen* (see GERM)] —**ger·mi·na·tion** /jùrmə náysh'n/ *n* —**ger·mi·na·tive** *adj* —**ger·mi·na·tor** *n*

germ lay·er *n* any of the three distinct layers of cells formed during an embryo's early stages of development (**gastrulation**)

germ line *n* a group of cells in a developing embryo from which reproductive cells (**gametes**) develop, regarded as the line of descent from one generation to another

germ·plasm /júrm plàzzəm/ *n* the hereditary material that is transmitted from one generation to another

germ the·o·ry *n* **1.** the theory that all infectious and contagious diseases are caused by microorganisms **2.** the theory that organisms develop from previous generations through the growth of germ cells

germ tube *n* a hollow tube that grows from a germinating spore

germ war·fare *n* MIL same as **biological warfare**

germ·y /júrmee/ (**-i·er, -i·est**) *adj* full of harmful microorganisms (*informal*) —**germ·i·ness** *n*

ger·o·don·tics /jèrrə dóntiks/ *n* the branch of dentistry focusing on the needs of senior citizens (*takes a singular verb*) [Late 20C. < Greek *gēras* "old age"] —**ger·o·don·tic** *adj*

Ge·ro·na /je rṓnə, hə-/ city and capital of Gerona Province, Catalonia, northeastern Spain. It is situated about 55 mi./90 km northeast of Barcelona. Population: 77,475 (2002).

Ge·ron·i·mo /jə rónnəmō/ (1829–1909) Chiricahua Apache leader. A warrior of legendary courage, he began in 1876 to lead his people in raids on white settlers to oppose the forcible dispossession of Native Americans from their land in New Mexico. He was captured by government troops in 1886. He later became a farmer in Oklahoma. Born **Goyathlay**

"It [Arizona] is my land, my home, my father's land, to which I now ask to be allowed to return. I want to spend my last days there, and be buried among those mountains."
[Geronimo, *Letter to President Ulysses S. Grant*; 1877]

geront- *prefix* aging, old age ○ *gerontology* [Via French < Greek *geront-*, stem of *gerōn* "old man"]

geronto- same as **geront-** [Via French < Greek *gerōn* "old man"]

ger·on·toc·ra·cy /jèrrən tókrəssee/ (*plural* **-cies**) *n* **1.** a system of government in which the elders are chosen as rulers **2.** a group of elders who make up a government —**ge·ron·to·crat** /jə róntə kràt/ *n* —**ge·ron·to·crat·ic** /jə ròntə kráttik/ *adj*

ger·on·tol·o·gy /jèrrən tóllәjee/ *n* the scientific study of aging and its effects —**ge·ron·to·log·ic** /jə ròntə lójjik/ *adj* —**ge·ron·to·log·i·cal** *adj* —**ger·on·tol·o·gist** *n*

Ger·ry /gérree/, **Elbridge** (1744–1814) vice president of the United States. He signed the Declaration of Independence and the Articles of Confederation, and as governor of Massachusetts (1810–12) reorganized electoral districts in a process that came to be called "gerrymandering." He was James Madison's vice president (1813–14).

ger·ry·man·der /jérree màndər/ *vti* (**-dered, -der·ing, -ders**) TRY TO GET EXTRA VOTES UNFAIRLY to manipulate an electoral area, usually by altering its boundaries, in order to gain an unfair political advantage in an election ■ *n* **1.** ACT OF GERRYMANDERING an unfair manipulation of an electoral area for political advantage **2.** MANIPULATED ELECTORAL AREA an electoral area manipulated in such a way as to give one political party an unfair advantage in an election [Early 19C. Blend of Elbridge GERRY + SALAMANDER, from the shape of an electoral district he created to favor his own party]

Gersh·win /gúrshwin/, **George** (1898–1937) US composer. Jazz, classical, and popular influences combined in his outstandingly inventive works, many of which became American classics. He wrote *Rhapsody in Blue* (1924), and, with his brother Ira Gershwin, the opera *Porgy and Bess* (1935), and songs including "Someone to Watch Over Me." Born **Gershvin, Jacob**

"It ain't necessarily so— / The things that you're liable / To read in the Bible— / It ain't necessarily so."

AKG London
George Gershwin

[George Gershwin, "It Ain't Necessarily So," *Porgy and Bess*; 1935]

Gersh·win, Ira (1896–1983) US lyricist and dramatist. A collaborator with his brother George Gershwin and other leading composers, he wrote lyrics for 20 Broadway musicals, and shared a Pulitzer Prize for *Of Thee I Sing* (1931). Born **Gershvin, Israel**

"I got rhythm, / I got music, / I got my man— / Who could ask for anything more?"
[Ira Gershwin, "I Got Rhythm," *Girl Crazy*; 1930]

ger·und /jérrənd/ *n* a noun formed from a verb, describing an action, state, or process. In English, it is formed from the verb's *-ing* form, e.g., "smoking" in "No smoking." In Latin it is a noun ending in "-ndum." [Early 16C. < late Latin *gerundium* < Latin *gerere* "carry on"] —**ge·run·di·al** /jə rúndee əl/ *adj*

ge·run·dive /jə rúndiv/ *n* a Latin adjective ending in "-ndus," formed from a verb and meaning "that must or ought to be done" [15C. < late Latin *gerundivus modus* "gerundive mood" < *gerundium* (see GERUND)] —**ge·run·di·val** /jèrrən dív'l/ *adj*

Ge·sell /gi zél/, **Arnold** (1880–1961) US psychologist. He pioneered research into child development using movie cameras and one-way mirrors. Full name **Gesell, Arnold Lucius**

Ges·ner /géssnər/, **Abraham** (1797–1864) Canadian inventor and geologist. He is known as the founder of the modern petroleum industry because of his patents for distilling bituminous material.

ges·so /jéssō/ *n* **1.** a mixture of plaster and glue or size. Use: in sculpture, as a background for paintings. **2.** (*plural* **ges·soes**) a painting done on gesso, or a sculpture made from it [Late 16C. Via Italian < Latin *gypsum* (see GYPSUM)] —**ges·soed** *adj*

ge·stalt /gə shtáalt/ (*plural* **-stalts** or **-stalt·en** /-shtáalt'n/), **Ge·stalt** *n* a set of things such as a person's thoughts and experiences considered as a whole and regarded as amounting to more than the sum of its parts [Early 20C. < German, "shape"] —**ge·stalt·ist** *n*

ge·stalt psy·chol·o·gy *n* a branch of psychology that treats behavior and perception as an integrated whole and not simply the sum of individual stimuli and responses

ge·stalt ther·a·py *n* a form of psychotherapy in which emphasis is placed on feelings and on the influence on personality development of unresolved personal issues from the past

Ge·sta·po /gə stáa pō, -shtáa-/ *n* the secret state police under the Nazi regime in Germany, noted for its brutality [Mid-20C. German acronym < *Geheime Staatspolizei* "Secret State Police"]

ges·tate /jéss tàyt/ (**-tat·ed, -tat·ing, -tates**) *vti* **1.** to carry offspring in the womb, or develop as offspring in the womb **2.** to develop in the mind, or allow an idea or plan to develop in the mind [Mid-19C. < Latin *gestat-* (see GESTATION)] —**ges·ta·to·ry** /jéstə tàwree/ *adj*

ges·ta·tion /je stáysh'n/ *n* **1.** BIOL CARRYING OF OFFSPRING IN WOMB the process of carrying offspring in the womb during pregnancy **2.** BIOL PERIOD OF DEVELOPMENT OF FETUS the period of development of the offspring during pregnancy **3.** DEVELOPMENT the development of an idea or plan in the mind, or the time it takes to develop

[Mid-16C. < Latin *gestation-* < *gestat-*, past participle of *gestare* "carry in the womb" < *gerere* "carry"] —**ges·ta·tion·al** *adj*

ges·tic·u·late /je stíkyə làyt/ (**-lat·ed, -lat·ing, -lates**) *vti* to move the arms or hands when speaking, or express something with movements of the arms or hands [Early 17C. < Latin *gesticulat-*, past participle of *gesticulari* < *gestus* "action, gesture" < *gerere* "carry, act"] —**ges·tic·u·la·tion** /je stìkyə láysh'n/ *n* —**ges·tic·u·la·tive** *adj* —**ges·tic·u·la·tor** *n* —**ges·tic·u·la·to·ry** /je stíkyələ tàwree/ *adj*

ges·ture /jéschər/ *n* **1.** BODY MOVEMENT a movement made with a part of the body in order to express meaning or emotion or to communicate an instruction **2.** ACTION COMMUNICATING SOMETHING an action intended to communicate feelings or intentions **3.** USE OF GESTURES the use of body movements to communicate ■ *vti* (**-tured, -tur·ing, -tures**) MAKE BODY MOVEMENT to make a movement with a part of the body in order to express meaning or emotion or to communicate an instruction [15C. < medieval Latin *gestura* "deportment" < Latin *gerere* "carry, act"] —**ges·tur·al** *adj* —**ges·tur·al·ly** *adv*

ORIGIN The Latin word *gerere* "to carry, act" from which ***gesture*** is derived, is also the source of English *congest, digest, gestation, gesticulate, ingest, jest,* and *suggestion.*

ge·sund·heit /gə zŏŏnt hīt/ *interj* used to wish good health to somebody who has just sneezed [Early 20C. < German, "health"]

get[1] /get/ (**got** /got/, **got·ten** /gótt'n/, **get·ting, gets**) CORE MEANING: a verb indicating that somebody obtains, receives, earns, or is given something. It is often used instead of more formal terms such as "obtain" or "acquire." ○ *We're trying to ensure that our child gets a good education.* ○ *Where will they get the money to buy the land?*

1. *vi* BECOME to become or begin to have a particular quality ○ *When I get nervous, I get scared.* **2.** *vt* CAUSE SOMETHING TO BE DONE to cause something to happen or be done ○ *I must get the car cleaned.* **3.** *vt* BRING SOMETHING to fetch or bring something ○ *I'm going back to my apartment to get my watch.* ○ *I'll get your coat for you.* **4.** *vt* CATCH ILLNESS to be affected by an illness or medical condition ○ *He got chicken pox last year.* **5.** *vi* BE IN PARTICULAR STATE to enter or leave a particular state or condition ○ *Get ready to leave in five minutes.* **6.** *vi* MOVE SOMEWHERE to succeed in moving or arriving somewhere ○ *It was already midnight when we got home.* **7.** *aux v* FORMS PASSIVES used instead of "be" as an auxiliary verb to form passives ○ *If you play with matches you will get burned.* **8.** *vt* PREPARE FOOD to prepare a meal ○ *I'll get dinner tonight.* **9.** *vt* PERSUADE SOMEBODY to persuade somebody to do something ○ *Colleagues had tried to get her to take a vacation.* **10.** *vt* USE FORM OF TRANSPORTATION to take a particular form of transportation ○ *I don't want to drive – I'd rather get a plane.* **11.** *vt* OBTAIN RESULT to obtain a result, e.g., by experiment or calculation ○ *What's the answer? I get nine.* **12.** *vt* RECEIVE SIGNAL to receive a broadcast signal such as a radio or television broadcast ○ *I can't get Channel 5 with that antenna.* **13.** *vt* HAVE TIME to have the time or opportunity to do something ○ *I'll fix it as soon as I get the time.* **14.** *vt* HAVE IDEA to have or receive an idea, impression, feeling, or benefit ○ *You've got the wrong impression – I'm not like that at all.* ○ *I get a lot of pleasure from his stories.* **15.** *vt* MANAGE TO SEE SOMETHING to succeed in seeing something ○ *get a close-up look* **16.** *vt* BEGIN SOMETHING to begin doing something (*informal*) ○ *Let's get going – we have to be there by eight.* **17.** *vt* MANAGE SOMETHING to manage or contrive something (*informal*) ○ *How did she get to be so famous?* **18.** *vt* UNDERSTAND SOMETHING to hear or understand something, e.g., a joke or somebody's point (*informal*) ○ *What's that? I didn't get what you said.* **19.** *vt* IRRITATE SOMEBODY to annoy or irritate somebody (*informal*) ○ *That high whining noise really gets me.* **20.** *vt* ARREST SOMEBODY to arrest or capture somebody (*informal*) ○ *They got him just as he was running out of the bank.* **21.** *vt* HIT SOMEBODY to hit somebody on the body (*informal*) ○ *The blow got him in the face.* **22.** *vt* HAVE REVENGE ON SOMEBODY to have revenge on somebody, especially by killing the person (*informal*) ○ *The heroes get Dracula in the end.* **23.** *vi* GAIN ACCESS to gain access to somebody with intent to bribe him or her (*informal*) ○ *I thought he was incorruptible, but they finally got to him.* **24.** *vi* LEAVE to go away from a place or person (*informal; often used in commands*) ○ *Now get!* **25.** *vt* CONCEIVE SOMEBODY to beget or conceive somebody (*archaic*) [13C. < Old Norse *geta* < Indo-European, "seize"] —**get·a·ble** *adj* ◇ **get with it** to become fashionable and responsive to new styles and ideas (*informal*)

USAGE got or **gotten**? ***Get*** is an overworked verb. It is better to use a more specific term in formal writing whenever you can. The past participles ***got*** and ***gotten*** convey slightly different ideas. *They have gotten an apartment in Boston* means they have recently taken the apartment, whereas *They have got an apartment in Boston* simply indicates that they have it. (There are those who would argue, with reason, that in a sentence like this one ***got*** is redundant, and that *have* alone would do the job.) In informal usage, *have got* can also be followed by an infinitive to denote obligation (*I've got to go to the party* means "I must"), whereas *have gotten* with an infinitive denotes opportunity (*I've gotten to go to the party* means "I've been given the chance to attend").

USAGE The use of ***get*** instead of *be* to form the passive is more acceptable in some contexts than others: *The house is* [or *gets*] *cleaned once a week. The exposition was* [not *got*] *opened by the mayor.* ***Get*** is usually more informal than *be*: an interviewer might ask an interviewee *If you are offered the job, will you accept it?* whereas the interviewee might tell a friend, *If I get offered the job, I'll take it.* ***Get*** is probably most acceptable when it is used to imply that the subject of the sentence bears at least some responsibility for an event or action, as in *If you play with matches, you may get burned* as opposed to *The driver of the vehicle was badly burned in the crash.*

SYNONYMS ***get, acquire, obtain, gain, procure, secure***

CORE MEANING: to come into possession of something

get to obtain, receive, earn, or be given something ○ *He managed to get a job on a building site.* ○ *"The public will get a worse railroad for more money," he claimed.* **acquire** to get possession of something, sometimes suggesting that time or effort was involved ○ *the knowledge, skills, and understanding that students are expected to acquire* ○ *He inherited some property and acquired more through marriage.* **obtain** to get something, especially by making an effort or having the necessary qualifications ○ *The best results are obtained from watercolors.* ○ *Schools and colleges can obtain the documents from the relevant agencies.* **gain** to get something through effort, skill, or merit ○ *The candidate was steadily gaining more support.* ○ *Students are encouraged to become an intern to gain experience of the world of work.* **procure** to get something, especially with effort or special care ○ *He procured a copy of the book from the local library.* **secure** to get something, especially after using considerable effort to persuade somebody to grant or allow it ○ *Having just secured world rights for her first book, she's leading a life of leisure.* ○ *The team has secured lucrative support from two local firms.*

get about *vi* **1.** to be able to move around while affected by or recovering from a medical condition **2.** same as **get around** (sense 1)

get across *vti* to make something understood, or communicate clearly ○ *I don't seem to be getting across to you.*

get after *vt* to keep telling somebody to do something in an annoying way (*informal*) ○ *You'll have to get after him if you want it finished by the weekend.*

get ahead *vi* to become successful, especially when compared to others ○ *He's a good worker, but he hasn't got what it takes to get ahead in this line of business.*

get along *vi* **1.** BE FRIENDLY WITH SOMEBODY to be on good terms with somebody socially **2.** MANAGE to make progress in a situation ○ *How's he getting along in the new job?* **3.** LEAVE to leave a place (*often used in commands*)

get around *v* **1.** *vi* HAVE SOCIAL LIFE to be socially active and aware of what is happening ○ *I have the feeling you don't get around much.* **2.** *vi* BECOME KNOWN to become widely known ○ *If news of this gets around, I may have to change my plans.* **3.** *vt* DEAL SUCCESSFULLY WITH OBSTRUCTION to manage to operate in spite of a regulation, prohibition, or difficulty **4.** *vt* PERSUADE SOMEBODY to talk or charm somebody into doing what you want **5.** *vi* SAY OR DO SOMETHING AT LAST finally to say or do something after delay, hesitation, or being involved with other things ○ *I wondered when you'd get around to telling me that.*

get at *vt* **1.** REACH SOMEBODY OR SOMETHING to succeed in reaching, finding, or making contact with somebody or something ○ *There's no way he'll get at the data without the password.* **2.** MEAN SOMETHING to imply, suggest, or be trying to say something ○ *What exactly are you getting at?* **3.** CRITICIZE SOMEBODY REPEATEDLY to criticize somebody continually and unreasonably ○ *You're always getting at me, and I'm sick of it.* **4.** FIND SOMETHING OUT to discover or find out something ○ *We were determined to get at the source of the rumors.*

get away *vi* **1.** to escape from somebody or something ○ *They caught one man, but the rest got away.* **2.** to succeed in leaving or spending time away from a place ○ *We hope to get away for a few days next month.*

get away with *vt* to manage to do something without being blamed or penalized or experiencing an expected bad result ○ *You could get away with a phone call, but it would be better to write.*

get back *vt* to recover something that has been given away, lent to somebody, or lost

get back at *vt* to take revenge on somebody

get back to *vt* **1.** to return to a place, topic, or activity ○ *Let's get back to what Steve was saying earlier.* **2.** to give somebody an answer or continue a discussion, especially by letter, e-mail, or telephone ○ *Leave it with me, and I'll get back to you as soon as possible.*

get by *v* **1.** *vi* JUST MANAGE TO KEEP GOING to manage to survive or just make ends meet ○ *It's hard to get by on $100 a week.* **2.** *vi* SUCCEED WITH MINIMAL EFFORT to get through something by doing as little work as possible **3.** *vt* CLOSELY PASS SOMEBODY OR SOMETHING to pass or move behind somebody or something closely ○ *We got by that parked truck with only an inch to spare.* **4.** *vt* PASS INSPECTION to pass somebody's inspection or receive somebody's approval, with the implication that this should not have happened ○ *How on earth did those errors get by the proofreader?*

get down *v* **1.** *vt* DEMORALIZE SOMEBODY to make somebody demoralized or discouraged ○ *This job is beginning to get me down.* **2.** *vt* WRITE SOMETHING to write something down, especially immediately **3.** *vt* SWALLOW SOMETHING to swallow something, especially unwillingly or with difficulty ○ *The medicine smelled so bad I just couldn't get it down.* **4.** *vi* HAVE FUN to relax and enjoy yourself in an unrestrained way (*informal*) ○ *It's time to get down and party.* **5.** *vi Malaysia* LEAVE VEHICLE to get out of a vehicle ○ *Where do you have to get down?*

get down to *vt* to start concentrating seriously on something or on getting something done

get in *v* **1.** *vi* ARRIVE to arrive somewhere, especially home ○ *When does your plane get in?* **2.** *vi* BE CHOSEN to succeed in being admitted to a group or organization, e.g., by election or interview ○ *You know if they get in they'll change some of the old laws.* **3.** *vti* GET INVOLVED WITH SOMEBODY OR SOMETHING to become involved with a group or in an activity, or let somebody become involved ○ *got in with the wrong crowd* **4.** *vt* MANAGE TO DO SOMETHING to succeed in finding or making an opportunity to do something ○ *I don't think we can get four interviews in before lunch.*

get into *vt* **1.** to begin to experience difficulties, or make somebody experience difficulties ○ *You'll get into all kinds of trouble if you do that.* **2.** to become involved or absorbed in something ○ *She's starting to get into programming.*

get off *v* **1.** *vi* LEAVE to set out from a place or position ○ *We have to get off at the crack of dawn tomorrow.* **2.** *vti* BE ABLE TO LEAVE WORK to be allowed to leave work, especially at the end of the working day ○ *What time do you get off this afternoon?* **3.** *vt* SEND COMMUNICATION OR PACKAGE to send a written communication or package ○ *I need to get these letters off tonight.* **4.** *vi* HAVE LUCKY ESCAPE to experience only minor consequences of a mistake, misguided action, or accident ○ *Considering what might have happened, I think you got off very lightly.* **5.** *vti* GAIN ACQUITTAL to be acquitted in a court of law, or successfully defend somebody in a court of law (*informal*) ○ *A good lawyer could get him off with no trouble.* **6.** *vi* BE SO BOLD to be bold enough to say or do something (*informal; usually disapproving*) ○ *Where does he get off thinking he can speak to me that way?* **7.** *vi* BE AROUSED OR EXCITED to experience excitement, physical arousal, or the effects of a drug (*slang*) **8.** *vi* TABOO TERM a highly offensive term meaning to have an orgasm (*taboo*)

get on *vi* **1.** DEAL WITH SITUATION to deal with a situation and make reasonable progress of a particular kind ○ *How's Ben getting on in school?* **2.** BE FRIENDLY to have a reasonably friendly social relationship with somebody ○ *She gets on well with the neighbors.* **3.** KEEP GOING to continue doing something **4.** BECOME OLDER to become more advanced in years

get out *v* **1.** *vti* LEAVE OR MAKE SOMEBODY LEAVE to leave a place or situation, or enable somebody to leave one **2.** *vi* BECOME KNOWN to become widely known, especially contrary to somebody's wishes ○ *If this ever gets out, I'll be so embarrassed!* **3.** *vt* PRODUCE OR PUBLISH SOMETHING to produce or publish something, especially a newspaper or magazine **4.** MAKE SOUND to make a sound or say something (*informal*) ○ *too choked up to get anything out* ■ *interj* EXPRESSION OF DISBELIEF used as an expression of disbelief (*informal*) ○ *Get out! You actually said that?*

get out of *vt* to avoid doing or having to experience something, or enable somebody to avoid something ○ *He got out of paying for the meal.*

get over *vt* **1.** RECOVER FROM SOMETHING to recover from an illness or bad experience ○ *He's upset, but he'll get over it.* **2.** DEAL WITH DIFFICULTY to overcome or cope with a difficulty ○ *Once she'd gotten over her lack of confidence, she enjoyed the meeting.* **3.** MAKE PEOPLE UNDERSTAND OR ACCEPT SOMETHING to succeed in making something clear or persuasive ○ *He's very good at getting his ideas over to an audience.* **4.** GET SOMETHING FINISHED to finish dealing with something boring, annoying, or unpleasant ○ *I just want to get the whole thing over with as soon as possible.*

get through *v* **1.** *vt* SURVIVE DIFFICULT TIME to endure to the end of a difficult time or situation ○ *How I got through those weeks I just don't know.* **2.** *vt* FINISH to finish something ○ *Did you ever get through that novel?* **3.** *vt* USE OR SPEND SOMETHING to use, eat, or spend something, especially a large amount in a short time ○ *We seem to be getting through the copier paper at an alarming rate.* **4.** *vti* MAKE SOMEBODY UNDERSTAND to make somebody understand something that is being communicated ○ *How can I get it through to you that this is our only hope?* **5.** *vi* SUCCEED IN CONTACTING SOMEBODY to contact somebody, especially by telephone ○ *I finally got through to her.*

get to *vt* **1.** START DEALING WITH SOMETHING to start dealing with something ○ *Leave it with me; I'll get to it later today.* **2.** START DOING SOMETHING to start to do something ○ *If they get to arguing, we'll never stop them.* **3.** EVOKE EMOTIONS to have an emotional impact on somebody ○ *Goodbyes always get to me.* **4.** ANNOY SOMEBODY to start to annoy somebody ○ *His whining was beginning to get to me.*

get together *v* **1.** *vi* MEET to meet for social or business purposes ○ *The project team needs to get together once a week or so.* **2.** *vi* FORM ALLIANCE to form an alliance or relationship ○ *They may be getting together to corner the market.* **3.** *vi* REACH AGREEMENT to reach agreement with somebody ○ *get together on the major issues* **4.** *vt* GATHER SOMETHING to bring together or accumulate something, especially money ○ *They managed to get together enough capital to open a business.* **5.** *vt* GET SOMETHING ORGANIZED to organize your personal affairs or focus your approach to an activity (*informal*) ○ *took some time off to get her life together* ◇ **get it together** to become organized and calm so as to perform efficiently (*slang*) ○ *had better get it together before his boss loses patience*

get up *v* **1.** *vti* GET OUT OF BED to get out of bed, or make somebody get out of bed **2.** *vti* CLIMB to ascend or climb something **3.** *vi* STAND UP to rise to your feet from a seated position **4.** *vt* ROUSE ENERGY to raise your energy, strength, courage, or similar qualities ○ *I'm trying to get up the enthusiasm to go back to work.* **5.** *vt* ORGANIZE SOMETHING to organize something by persuading other people to take part ○ *She got up a collection to help homeless people.* **6.** *vt* DRESS SOMEBODY to dress somebody in a particular way (*informal*) ○ *She was got up as Cleopatra.* **7.** *vi* GET STRONGER to become stronger or more turbulent (*refers to winds or the sea*)

get up to *vt* to do something bad or annoying (*informal*) ○ *I have no idea what they've been getting up to while we've been away.*

get[2] /get/ *n* **1.** RACKET GAMES DIFFICULT TENNIS RETURN in tennis and some other racket games, a shot that makes a return difficult **2.** AGRIC, HORSERACING MALE ANIMAL'S OFFSPRING the progeny sired by an animal, especially a racehorse **3.** *N England, Scotland* BRAT an unpleasant child (*often an insult, implying illegitimacy*) [14C. < GET[1]]

ge·ta /gé taa/ (*plural same* or **-tas**) *n* a Japanese shoe with a wooden sole [Late 19C. < Japanese]

get·a·way /géttə wày/ *n* **1.** ACT OF LEAVING an act of leaving a place, especially a quick exit made by somebody who has just committed a crime **2.** START OF MOVEMENT an act of starting to move, e.g., in a race **3.** SHORT VACATION a short vacation or break ○ *a weekend getaway* **4.** PLACE TO ESCAPE TO a place remote from everyday life to use for a vacation ○ *It's only a rough cabin that we use as a getaway.*

get-go, **get·go** /gét gò/ *n* the very beginning of something (*informal*) ○ *I knew from the get-go this thing wasn't going to work.*

Geth·sem·a·ne /geth sémmənee/ *n* in the Bible, the olive grove just outside Jerusalem where Jesus Christ was betrayed after the Last Supper (Matthew 26:36)

get-out *n UK* a means of avoiding or escaping from something such as an obligation or commitment (*often used before a noun*) ○ *The contract had a get-out clause.* ◇ **as...as all get-out** to the greatest possible extent (*slang*) ○ *The ground was as flat as all get-out.*

get·ter /géttər/ *n* a substance added to absorb the unwanted product of a chemical process, e.g., the excess gas in a light bulb

get-to·geth·er *n* a meeting or social gathering (*informal*)

get-tough *adj* taking a firm and decisive approach to social or political problems

Get·ty /géttee/, **J. Paul** (1892–1976) US oil executive. He became a multimillionaire at the head of his own oil company, and he founded the J. Paul Getty Museum in Malibu, to display his collection of art. Full name **Getty, Jean Paul**

> "The meek shall inherit the earth but not the mineral rights."
> [J. Paul Getty. Quoted in *The Great Getty Crown*, Robert Lenzer; 1985]

Get·tys·burg /gétteez bùrg/ borough and county seat of Adams County in southern Pennsylvania, southwest of Harrisburg. It was the site of a decisive Northern victory during the Civil War on July 1–3 1863, when George Meade's troops halted the northward advance of Robert E. Lee. Abraham Lincoln's Gettysburg Address was delivered there on November 19, 1863, dedicating the Gettysburg National Cemetery. Population: 7,653 (2002 estimate).

get·up /gét ùp/, **get-up** *n* the costume or clothes that somebody is wearing (*informal*)

get-up-and-go *n* energy and enthusiasm (*informal*)

get-well *adj* expressing the hope that somebody will soon recover from an illness ○ *a get-well card*

ge·ul·lah /gə ŏŏ laa/ *n* a Jewish prayer of thanks to God for the deliverance of the Jews from Egypt

GeV *abbr* MEASURE, PHYS giga-electron volt

ge·valt /gə vaalt/, **ge·vald** *interj* an expression of alarm, shock, or dismay [Via Yiddish < German *Gewalt* "power"]

gew·gaw /gyoo gàw/ *n* a showy but inexpensive object, especially an ornament [12C. Origin ?]

Ge·würz·tra·mi·ner /gə voorts trə meenər/ *n* **1.** a medium-dry, slightly spicy white wine made from a white grape grown mainly in Alsace and Germany **2.** a white grape variety. Use: to make Gewürztraminer. [Mid-20C. < German < *Gewürz* "spice" + *Traminer*, type of grape < *Termeno* village in N Italy]

geyser: Rotorua, New Zealand

gey·ser /gízər/ *n* a spring that throws a jet of hot water or steam into the air at intervals [Late 18C. After *Geysir*, hot spring in Iceland < Old Norse *geysa* "gush"]

gey·ser·ite /gízə rìt/ *n* a gray or white mineral form of hydrated silica. Source: hot spring deposits.

gf *abbr* French Guiana (*used in Internet addresses*) See table at **domain name**

GF *abbr* ONLINE girlfriend (*used in e-mails or text messages*)

GFN *abbr* ONLINE gone for now (*used in e-mails or text messages*)

G-force *n* the force of gravity

gg *abbr* Guernsey (*used in Internet addresses*) See table at **domain name**

GG *abbr* **1.** ONLINE gotta go (*used in e-mails or text messages*) **2.** *Can, UK* Governor General

gh *abbr* Ghana (*used in Internet addresses*) See table at **domain name**

GH *abbr* PHYSIOL growth hormone

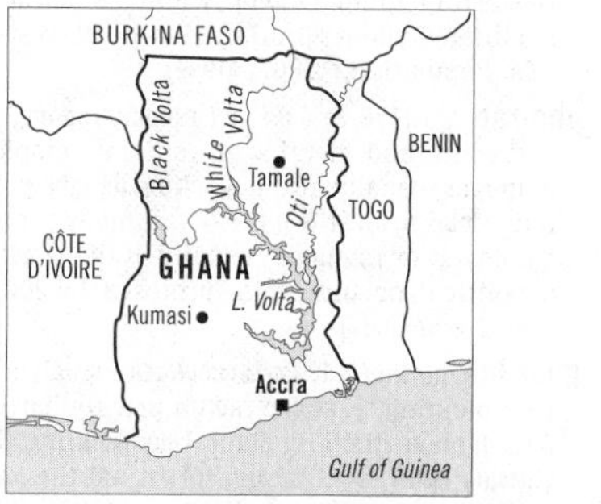

Ghana

Gha·na /gaanə/ country on the northern coast of the Gulf of Guinea in West Africa, bordered by Burkina Faso, Togo, and Côte d'Ivoire. It became an independent member of the British Commonwealth in 1957. Language: English. Currency: cedi. Capital: Accra. Population: 20,467,707 (2003). Area: 92,090 sq.

WORLD ENGLISH ***Ghanaian English*** is the English language as used in Ghana (population 20 million), the largest English-speaking nation in West Africa after Nigeria. Local contact with the language dates from 1631. Standard English is the official language, West African Pidgin English is widespread, and indigenous languages include Ashanti, Ewe, Fanti, and Ga, all of which have an influence on English usage, especially in vocabulary. Ghanaians strongly resist the idea of a distinctive Ghanaian English, and although standard and pidgin shade into one another, many seek to maintain a sharp line between them. In local usage "r" is not pronounced in such words as *art, door, worker.* Usage includes expressions adopted from local languages, often as the first element in compounds, as in the terms *bodom beads, kente cloth,* and in localisms such as an *airtight* "a metal box," an *outdooring* "a christening ceremony," and to *enskin* "to enthrone a chief by draping him in an animal skin."

mi./238,500 sq. km. Official name **Republic of Ghana**. Former name **Gold Coast** (sense 2) (1874–1957) —**Gha·na·ian** /gaa náy ən/ *n, adj*

Ghan·ai·an Eng·lish *n* a variety of English spoken in Ghana. See panel on previous page

~~Ghandi~~ incorrect spelling of **Gandhi**

gha·ra·ra /gə ra̋arə/ *n* loose trousers pleated below the knee, worn by women in or from South Asia, usually with a long tunic (**kameez**) [< Persian *garāra*]

gha·ri·al /gérree əl/ *n Can, UK* a large reptile resembling a crocodile that has a very long narrow snout and feeds on fish and frogs. Native to: India, Borneo, Sumatra. Latin name: *Gavialis gangeticus*. US term **gavial** [Early 19C < Hindi *ghariyāl*]

ghar·ry /gárree/ (*plural* **-ries**) *n S Asia* a horse-drawn carriage, especially one for hire [Early 19C. < Hindi *gāṛī*]

ghast·ly /gástlee/ *adj* (**-li·er, -li·est**) **1.** HORRIFYING horrifying, shocking, or very upsetting ○ *She had a ghastly experience with the last dentist she went to.* **2.** TERRIBLE very bad or unpleasant ○ *There's a ghastly smell coming from somewhere in this room.* ○ *It was all a ghastly mistake.* **3.** NOT WELL feeling unwell (*informal*) **4.** VERY PALE very pale or white in a way that is reminiscent of a ghost or a corpse (*literary*) ■ *adv* EXTREMELY used to emphasize paleness or whiteness ○ *"Her eyes grew large, her face ghastly pale."* (Charlotte Gilman, *Herland*; 1915) [14C. < obsolete *gast* "frighten" < Germanic] —**ghast·li·ness** *n*

ghat /gaat/ *n* in South Asia, a place on a river bank with steps down to the water, especially one where people bathe as a sacred rite or one near which the dead are cremated [Early 17C. < Hindi *ghāṭ*]

Ghats ♦ **Eastern Ghats, Western Ghats**

Gha·za·li /gə za̋alee/, **al-** (1058–1111) Islamic theologian and philosopher. His *The Revival of the Religious Sciences* is a classic work of Islam. Full name **Ghazali, Abu Hamid Muhammad ibn Muhammad al-Tusi al-**

gha·zi /ga̋azee/ *n* a warrior who has fought for Islam against non-Muslims [Mid-18C. < Arabic *al-gāzī*, form of *gazā* "invade"]

GHB *abbr* DRUGS gammahydroxybutyrate

ghee /gee/, **ghi** *n* clarified butter, especially as used in South Asian cooking [Mid-17C. Via Hindi *ghī* < Sanskrit *ghṛtam*]

Ghent /gent/ capital of East Flanders Province, northwestern Belgium. One of Belgium's oldest cities, it is situated about 35 mi./56 km northwest of Brussels. Population: 224,074 (1999).

ghe·rao /gə rów/ *S Asia vt* (**-raoed, -rao·ing, -raos**) to surround and detain an official, employer, or manager, usually at the workplace, as a political or industrial protest ■ *n* the detainment of an official, employer, or manager, usually at the workplace, as a political or industrial protest [Mid-20C. < Hindi *ghernā* "surround"]

gher·kin /gúrkin/ *n* **1.** SMALL CUCUMBER a small cucumber. Use: pickling. **2.** PRICKLY FRUIT a prickly hard-skinned fruit from a climbing plant. Use: pickling. **3.** TROPICAL CLIMBING PLANT a climbing plant of the cucumber family that produces gherkins. Native to: Caribbean. Latin name: *Cucumis anguria*. [Early 17C. < assumed obsolete Dutch *gurkkijn* "small cucumber" < *gurk* "cucumber"]

ghet·to /géttō/ (*plural* **-tos** or **-toes**) *n* **1.** AREA OF CITY INHABITED BY MINORITY an area of a city lived in by a minority group, especially a run-down and densely populated area lived in by a group that experiences discrimination **2.** JEWISH QUARTER in former times, an area in European towns in which the Jewish population was required to live **3.** ENVIRONMENT OF ISOLATION an environment where a group of people live or work in isolation, whether by choice or circumstance ○ *the teenage employment ghetto of fast food and retailing* [Early 17C. < Italian]

ghet·to blast·er *n* a large radio and cassette or CD player with a built-in speaker at each end, carried by a handle at the top (*informal; often considered offensive*)

ghet·to cred·i·bil·i·ty *n* popularity and acceptability among Black people, especially young urban Black people (*slang; offensive in some contexts*)

ghet·to·ize /géttō ìz/ (**-ized, -iz·ing, -iz·es**) *vt* **1.** to restrict a minority group to a specific area of a city **2.** to isolate, pigeonhole, or limit the scope or opportunities for somebody or something (*sometimes considered offensive*) —**ghet·to·i·za·tion** /gèttō i záysh'n/ *n*

ghi *n* FOOD another spelling of **ghee**

Ghib·el·line /gíbbə lèen, gíbbəlin/ *n* a member of a political party in medieval Italy that supported the claims of the Holy Roman Emperors to rule Italy and opposed the Guelphs, who supported the popes [Late 16C. < Italian *Ghibellino*, probably < Middle High German *Waiblingen*, estate belonging to family whose members included rulers of the Holy Roman Empire and kings of Germany and Sicily]

ghil·lie *n* CLOTHING another spelling of **gillie**

gho·ma·sio *n* FOOD another spelling of **gomasio**

ghost /gōst/ *n* **1.** SUPPOSED SPIRIT REMAINING AFTER DEATH the supposed spirit of somebody who has died, believed to appear as a shadowy form or to cause sounds, the movement of objects, or a frightening atmosphere in a place **2.** TRACE a faint, weak, or greatly reduced appearance, trace, or possibility of something ○ *the ghost of a smile* **3.** SECONDARY IMAGE a faint duplicate image of something seen on a screen or photograph or through a telescope, and caused by the reception of a double signal or by a mechanical defect **4.** NONEXISTENT PERSON OR THING an entity that seems to exist but does not, e.g., a name entered on a list by mistake or a fictitious employee on a company payroll **5.** LITERAT same as **ghostwriter 6.** RELIG SOUL somebody's soul or spirit (*archaic*) ■ *v* (**ghost·ed, ghost·ing, ghosts**) **1.** *vt* LITERAT WRITE SOMETHING UNDER ANOTHER'S NAME to be the ghostwriter of a work **2.** GLIDE to glide silently like a ghost [Old English *gāst* < W Germanic] —**ghost·like** *adj* —**ghost·y** *adj* ◇ **give up the ghost 1.** to stop working or functioning for good (*informal*) **2.** to die (*literary*)

ghost·bust·er /gōst bùstər/ *n* somebody supposedly able to drive away ghosts, poltergeists, and other apparitions (*informal*)

ghost crab *n* a white burrowing crab. Native to: sandy shorelines in many parts of the world. Genus: *Ocypoda*.

ghost dance *n* **1.** a religious dance of Native North Americans, performed with the supposed participation of the spirits of all the Native North Americans murdered by the European immigrants **2.** *also* **Ghost Dance** a religious movement, widely spread among Plains Native American peoples in North America in the late 19th century, that promised the revival of traditional Native North American culture

ghost·ing /gṓsting/ *n* the appearance of faint duplicate images on a screen, monitor, or photograph, or through a telescope

ghost·ly /gṓstlee/ (**-li·er, -li·est**) *adj* **1.** like a ghost in being insubstantial, pale, or apparently not of this world **2.** having an atmosphere or quality that suggests ghosts or the presence of ghosts ○ *the ghostly music that opens the symphony* —**ghost·li·ness** *n*

ghost site *n* a website that is obsolete and no longer updated, but still available for viewing

ghost sto·ry *n* a story about a ghost or ghosts, or a haunted place or person, intended to frighten the reader or hearer

ghost town *n* **1.** a town with few or no inhabitants, especially one that was formerly a busy prosperous place, e.g., an abandoned mining town **2.** a formerly or usually inhabited place that is deserted (*informal*) ○ *The business district is a ghost town on weekends.*

ghost word *n* a word created through a mistake that may be copied afterward into other texts and eventually enter a language

ghost·writ·er /gōst rìtər/ *n* somebody who writes something for or with somebody else, the other person receiving sole credit as the author —**ghost·write** *vti*

ghoul /gool/ *n* **1.** SOMEBODY MORBIDLY INTERESTED IN REPULSIVE THINGS somebody who is morbidly fascinated with death, disaster, or repulsive things **2.** PARANORMAL EVIL SPIRIT a supposed evil and terrifying spirit **3.** ISLAM BODY-SNATCHING DEMON in Islamic folklore, an evil demon that eats freshly buried bodies, and often abducts children or attacks unwary travelers [Late 18C. < Arabic *gūl*]

ghoul·ish /go͝olish/ *adj* **1.** showing a morbid fascination with death, disaster, or repulsive things **2.** terrifyingly hideous or cruel —**ghoul·ish·ly** *adv* —**ghoul·ish·ness** *n*

GHQ *n* the headquarters of an organization, especially a military headquarters commanded by a general. Full form **General Headquarters**

GHz *symbol* MEASURE, ELEC gigahertz

gi[1] *abbr* MEASURE gill[2]

gi[2] /gee/, **gie** *n* an outfit worn for karate or judo [< Japanese]

gi[3] *abbr* Gibraltar (*used in Internet addresses*) See table at **domain name**

GI[1] /jèe ì/ *n* US SOLDIER a soldier in the US armed forces ■ *adj* **1.** FOR SOLDIERS provided or issued by the armed forces for the use of its members ○ *a GI hat* **2.** FOR VETERANS provided or intended for veterans of the armed forces ○ *GI benefits* [Mid-20C. Abbreviation of *government issue*, reinterpretation of *GI* "galvanized iron" on various items of US Army equipment]

GI[2] *abbr* **1.** INDUST galvanized iron **2.** ANAT gastrointestinal

Gia·co·met·ti /jàkə méttee/, **Alberto** (1901–66) Swiss sculptor and painter. He is best known for his bronze sculptures of elongated human figures such as *Stehende III* (1962).

gi·ant /jí ənt/ *n* **1.** VERY TALL IMAGINARY CREATURE in fairy tales and legends, an imaginary being who resembles a human but is much taller, larger, and stronger **2.** SOMEBODY EXTRAORDINARILY ACCOMPLISHED somebody whose talents or achievements are particularly outstanding ○ *one of the giants of the silent-movie era* **3.** SOMEBODY OR SOMETHING LARGER THAN USUAL a person, animal, plant, or organization that is much larger than is usual **4.** MYTHOLOGICAL BEING in Greek mythology, a being of immense size and strength who fought against Zeus and the other gods of Mount Olympus ■ *adj* VERY BIG taller, larger, or more powerful than is usual ○ *a giant tidal wave* [13C. Via Old French *geant* < Greek *gigant-*]

gi·ant ant·eat·er *n* a large bushy-tailed anteater, now rare. Native to: pampas regions of South America. Latin name: *Myrmecophaga tridactyla*.

gi·ant clam *n* an extremely large clam, weighing as much as 500 lb./230kg. Native to: Pacific and Indian oceans. Latin name: *Tridacna gigas*.

gi·ant·ess /jí əntəss/ *n* in fairy tales and legends, an imaginary being similar to a woman in shape but much taller, larger, and stronger

gi·ant·ism /jí ənt ìzzəm/ *n* **1.** MED same as **gigantism 2.** the quality or condition of being much taller, larger, or stronger than is usual

gi·ant-kill·er *n* somebody or something that defeats a superior or better-known opponent, especially in sports, business, or politics

gi·ant pan·da *n* ZOOL same as **panda** (sense 1)

gi·ant plan·et *n* one of the four largest planets in the solar system, Jupiter, Saturn, Uranus, and Neptune

gi·ant red·wood *n* TREES same as **giant sequoia**

Gi·ant's Cause·way /jí ənts-/ headland on the northern coast of Northern Ireland, consisting of thousands of polygonal columns of basalt, thought to be ancient lava formations

gi·ant se·quoi·a *n* a coniferous evergreen tree that grows up to 260 ft./80 m high. Native to: California. Latin name: *Sequoiadendron giganteum*.

gi·ant-sized *adj* much larger than others of the same type or class

gi·ant sla·lom *n* a downhill ski race on a course that is longer and steeper than that used for a slalom

gi·ant star *n* a low-density star with a diameter up to 100 times greater than that of the Sun

gi·ant tor·toise *n* a very large tortoise with a shell that can grow to be 4 ft./1.2 m long. Native to: Galápagos and Seychelles islands. Genus: *Geochelone.*

giaour /jowr/ *n* a non-Muslim, especially a Christian (*archaic insult*) [Mid-16C. Via Turkish *gâvur* < Arabic *kāfir* "unbeliever"]

gi·ar·di·a /jee áardee ə, jáardee ə/ *n* **1.** a single-celled protozoan, some forms of which live as parasites in the gut of humans and other vertebrates, causing an infection (**giardiasis**). Genus: *Giardia.* **2.** MED same as **giardiasis** [Early 20C. < modern Latin, after A. *Giard* (1846–1908), French biologist]

gi·ar·di·a·sis /jèe aar dī́ əssiss, jee ər-, jaar-/ *n* an infection of the gut with the waterborne microscopic protozoan giardia. It is usually caused by drinking contaminated water and results in severe diarrhea and vomiting.

gib /gib/ *n* something that is made of metal and holds another piece of metal or a machine part in place, e.g., a wedge, pin, bolt, or plate ■ *vt* (**gibbed, gib·bing, gibs**) to hold something in place with a gib [Late 18C. Origin ?]

gib·ber /jíbbər/ (**-bered, -ber·ing, -bers**) *vi* to make sounds or speak words unintelligibly ○ *Stop gibbering and tell me what's wrong.* [Early 17C. Probably an imitation of the sound] —**gib·ber** *n*

gib·ber·el·lic ac·id /jibbə rèllik-/ *n* a plant growth hormone involved in stem elongation. Formula: $C_{19}H_{22}O_6$.

gib·ber·el·lin /jìbbə réllin/ *n* a plant hormone that promotes growth and seed germination [Mid-20C. < modern Latin *Gibbera*, genus of fungi < Latin *gibbus* "hump"]

gib·ber·ing /jíbbəring/ *adj* unable to make sounds or speak words intelligibly

gib·ber·ish /jíbbərish/ *n* spoken or written language perceived as unintelligible or devoid of sense [Early 16C. Probably < GIBBER after SPANISH, POLISH, etc.]

gib·bet /jíbbit/ *n* **1.** HANGING POST an upright post with a beam projecting horizontally from its top, from which the bodies of executed criminals were hung on public display **2.** CRIME same as **gallows** (sense 1) ■ *vt* (**-bet·ed, -bet·ing, -bets**) **1.** DISPLAY BODY AFTER EXECUTION to display the body of a criminal on a gibbet after execution **2.** HANG SOMEBODY to execute somebody by hanging (*archaic*) **3.** ATTACK SOMEBODY'S REPUTATION to expose somebody to ridicule or contempt, especially in popular publications (*archaic*) [12C. < Old French *gibet* "staff, gallows" < *gibe* "staff"]

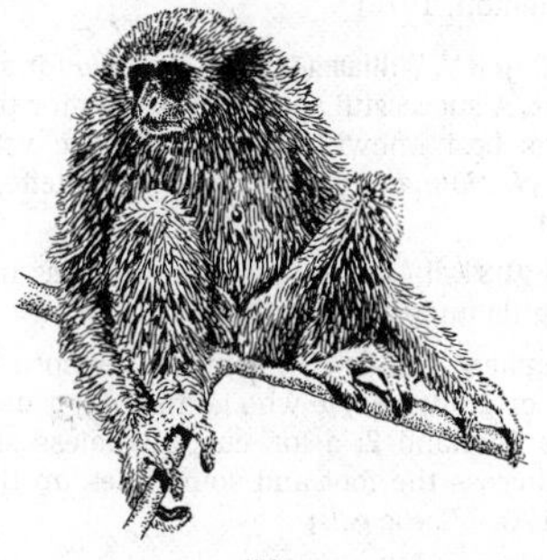

gibbon

gib·bon /gíbbən/ *n* a small tree-dwelling ape with a slender body and long arms that allow it to swing rapidly and agilely from branch to branch. Native to: Southeast Asia. Genus: *Hylobates.* [Late 18C. < French]

Gib·bon /gíbbən/, **Edward** (1737–94) British historian. His major work, *The History of the Decline and Fall of the Roman Empire* (1776–88), is a classic of British historiography.

> "History...is, indeed, little more than the register of the crimes, follies, and misfortunes of mankind."
> [Edward Gibbon, *The History of the Decline and Fall of the Roman Empire*; 1776–88]

gib·bous /gíbbəss/ *adj* **1.** describes the Moon or a planet before and after it is full, when it has more than half its disk illuminated **2.** bulging outward or swollen [14C. < late Latin *gibbosus* "hunchbacked" < Latin *gibbus* "hump"] —**gib·bos·i·ty** /gi bóssətee/ *n* —**gib·bous·ly** *adv* —**gib·bous·ness** *n*

Gibbs /gibz/, **J. Willard** (1839–1903) US mathematical physicist. He laid the foundation for the science of physical chemistry in *On the Equilibrium of Heterogeneous Substances* (1876–78). Full name **Gibbs, Josiah Willard**

Gibbs free en·er·gy *n* PHYS same as **free energy** [After J. Willard GIBBS]

gibb·site /gíb zīt/ *n* a gray-white mineral consisting of hydrated aluminum oxide. Source: laterite, bauxite. Use: source of aluminum. [Early 19C. After George *Gibbs* (1776–1833), US mineralogist]

gibe /jīb/, **jibe** *n* a comment that is intended to hurt or provoke somebody or to show derision or contempt ■ *vti* (**gibed, gib·ing, gibes; jibed, jib·ing, jibes**) to make a comment that is intended to hurt or provoke somebody or to show derision or contempt [Mid-16C. Origin ?] —**gib·ing·ly** *adv*

gib·lets /jíbbləts/ *n* the liver, heart, gizzard, and neck of a bird that has been prepared for cooking. Giblets are often boiled to make stock for gravy. [14C. < Old French *gibelet* "game stew"]

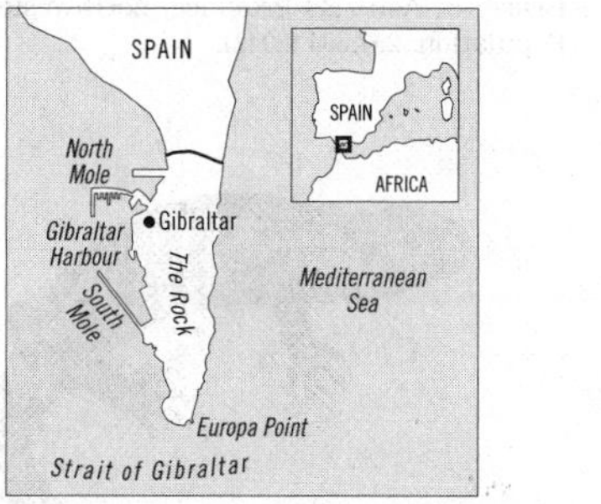

Gibraltar

Gib·ral·tar /ji bráwltər/ British dependency on a narrow promontory that is near the southernmost point of the Iberian Peninsula. It occupies a strategic position at the western entrance to the Mediterranean Sea. Population: 27,000 (2001). Area: 2.3 sq. mi./5.8 sq. km. —**Gi·bral·tar·i·an** /ji brawl térree ən/ *n, adj*

Gib·ral·tar, Rock of limestone and shale ridge near the southern tip of the Iberian Peninsula, overlooking the Strait of Gibraltar. Height: 1,398 ft./426 m.

Gib·ral·tar, Strait of channel connecting the Mediterranean Sea to the Atlantic Ocean and separating North Africa from the Rock of Gibraltar. Length: 40 mi./60 km.

Gib·ran /ji braán/, **Khalil** (1883–1931) Lebanese-born US mystic, painter, and poet. His mystical works inspired a new school of Arab-American poetry, and *The Prophet* (1923) reached a wide popular audience.

> "Everyone has experienced that truth: that love, like a running brook, is disregarded, taken for granted; but when the brook freezes over, then people begin to remember how it was when it ran, and they want it to run again."
> [Khalil Gibran. Quoted in *Beloved Prophet*, Virginia Hilu (ed.); 1972]

Gib·son /gíbss'n/, **Althea** (1927–2003) US tennis player and golfer. She won Wimbledon and the US Open tennis championships in 1957 and 1958, and became a professional golfer in 1963.

> "If I made it, it's half because I was game enough to take a wicked amount of punishment along the way and half because there were an awful lot of people who cared enough to help me."
> [Althea Gibson, *I Always Wanted to Be Somebody*; 1958]

Gib·son, Charles Dana (1867–1944) US illustrator. He is known for his sketches of the "Gibson girl."

Gib·son Des·ert desert in central Western Australia, consisting mainly of sand ridges and plains. Area: 60,200 sq. mi./156,000 sq. km.

Gib·son girl *n* an idealized fashionable young woman of the late 1890s and early 1900s, as depicted in the drawings of illustrator Charles Dana Gibson. Gibson's wife, Irene Langhorne, inspired the drawings, which show clothes with a high neck, full sleeves, and a narrow waist.

gid /gid/ *n* a disease affecting primarily sheep, that makes them walk and stand unsteadily, caused by a tapeworm larva [Early 17C. Back-formation < GIDDY]

gid·dap /gi dáp, -dúp/ *interj* same as **giddyup**

gid·dy /gíddee/ (**-di·er, -di·est**) *adj* **1.** DIZZY feeling dizzy or unsteady and as if about to fall down **2.** CAUSING DIZZINESS causing dizziness or a feeling of unsteadiness ○ *climbed to a giddy height* **3.** ELATED extremely happy and excited ○ *giddy with anticipation* **4.** NOT SENSIBLE not level-headed and sensible, but likely to act impulsively or behave foolishly (*dated*) [Old English *gidig* "severely mentally challenged" < Germanic] —**gid·di·ly** *adv* —**gid·di·ness** *n*

gid·dy·up /giddee úp/ *interj* used to make a horse go faster [Early 20C. Alteration of GET UP]

Gide /zheed/, **André** (1869–1951) French writer. His many works of fiction and nonfiction frequently explore the theme of moral responsibility, and include his celebrated *Journal* (1939–51). He won the Nobel Prize in literature (1947). Full name **Gide, André Paul Guillaume**

> "One does not discover new lands without consenting to lose sight of the shore for a very long time."
> [André Gide, *The Counterfeiters*; 1925]

gie *n* MARTIAL ARTS another spelling of **gi**[2]

Giel·gud /géel go͝od/, **Sir John** (1904–2000) British actor. He was one of the leading Shakespearean interpreters of his generation. Full name **Gielgud, Sir Arthur John**

gif /jif/ *abbr* a file extension for a GIF file. Full form **Graphic Interchange Format**

GIF /gif/ a service mark for a format for graphics files, widely used on the World Wide Web. Full form **Graphic Interchange Format**

gift /gift/ *n* **1.** SOMETHING GIVEN something that is given to somebody, usually on order to provide pleasure or to show gratitude ○ *a birthday gift* **2.** SPECIAL TALENT a natural ability that somebody appears to have been born with ○ *a gift for making people feel at ease* **3.** ACT OF GIVING the act of giving something to somebody ○ *her gift of $500,000 to help to build a new school* **4.** SOMETHING EASILY GAINED something that is obtained or achieved easily (*informal*) ○ *The last run was a gift; that should have been an easy catch.* ■ *vt* (**gift·ed, gift·ing, gifts**) GIVE SOMETHING to give or concede something to somebody as a gift [13C. < Old Norse *gipt* < Germanic]

USAGE Marketers are fond of the expression *free gift*, but because any ***gift*** worthy of its name is free, the result of using the two words together is unnecessary and should be avoided.

SYNONYMS See ***talent***.

GIFT /gift/ *n* a method designed to aid conception in which eggs are removed from a woman's ovary, mixed with sperm, and placed in one of her fallopian tubes. Full form **gamete intrafallopian transfer**

gift cer·tif·i·cate *n* a slip of paper issued by a commercial establishment that can be exchanged for goods or services worth its purchase price, usually bought as a gift

gift·ed /gíftəd/ *adj* **1.** TALENTED having great natural talent or intelligence **2.** SHOWING SOMEBODY'S TALENT showing that somebody has great natural talent or intelligence ○ *a gifted performance* **3.** EXCEPTIONAL requiring special education because of great natural talent or intelligence ○ *a gifted student* **4.** FOR GIFTED STUDENTS relating to special education for gifted students ○ *the talented and gifted program* —**gift·ed·ly** *adv* —**gift·ed·ness** *n*

SYNONYMS See ***intelligent.***

gift of gab *n* a natural ability to talk fluently, eloquently, or persuasively (*informal*)

gift of tongues *n* the ability to produce utterances in a state of religious ecstasy or trance that are usually unintelligible and thought by some to manifest the influence of the Holy Spirit

gift to·ken, gift vouch·er *n UK* same as **gift certificate**

gift·ware /gíft wèr/ *n* goods that are marketed for buying as gifts for other people, e.g., china and crystal

gift·wrap /gíft ràp/ *n also* **gift·wrap·ping** /-ràpping/ specially decorated paper used to wrap gifts ■ *vt* (**-wrapped, -wrap·ping, -wraps**) to wrap something in specially decorated paper

Gi·fu /gée fòo/ city and capital of Gifu Prefecture, central Honshu, Japan, 65 mi./105 km northwest of Nagoya. Population: 401,269 (2002).

gig[1] /gig/ *n* **1. ONE-HORSE CARRIAGE** a light open two-wheeled carriage pulled by a single horse. It was a popular form of private transportation in 19th-century Europe and the United States. **2. ROWBOAT** a small light rowboat carried on board a sailing ship **3. RACING BOAT** a light rowboat used for racing [Late 18C. Origin ?]

gig[2] /gig/ (*informal*) *n* **1. MUSICAL PERFORMANCE** a performance by a musician or group of musicians at a place where they are booked to play but do not regularly perform **2. TEMPORARY JOB** a temporary or short-term job ○ *landed a gig as a radio news announcer* ■ *vi* (**gigged, gig·ging, gigs**) **PERFORM MUSIC FOR AUDIENCE** to give a musical performance to an audience in exchange for payment [Early 20C. Origin ?]

gig[3] /gig/ *n* **1.** a spear with a prong on one end used to catch fish or frogs **2.** a system of hooks without barbs that is dragged through schools of fish in order to catch them [Early 18C. Shortening of *fishgig*, probably < Spanish *fisga* "harpoon" after FISH] —**gig** *vti*

gig[4] /gig/ (*slang*) *n* a military demerit ■ *vt* (**gigged, gig·ging, gigs**) to give a soldier a demerit [Mid-20C. Origin ?]

gig[5] /gig/ *n* COMPUT same as **gigabyte** (*informal*) [Shortening]

giga- *prefix* **1.** a billion (10^9) ○ *gigaton* Symbol **G 2.** in the binary system, a billion (2^{30}) ○ *gigabyte* [< Greek *gigas* "giant"]

gig·a·bit /gíggə bìt/ *n* a unit of capacity of a computer local area network, equal to one megabyte of computer information, or 1,073,741,824 bits

gi·ga·byte /gíggə bìt/ *n* **1.** a unit of computer data or storage space equivalent to 1,024 megabytes. Symbol **Gbyte 2.** one million bytes

gig·a·cy·cle /gíggə sìk'l/ *n* a unit of electric oscillation equal to one billion cycles

gig·a·flop /gíggə flòp/ *n* a unit of computer processing speed equal to one billion floating-point operations per second [Late 20C. < GIGA- + acronym < *floating-point operations per second*]

gig·a·hertz /gíggə hùrts/ (*plural same*) *n* a unit of frequency equal to one billion hertz, or cycles, per second. Symbol **GHz**

gi·gan·tic /jī gántik/ *adj* **1.** very large, tall, or bulky ○ *a gigantic cargo plane* **2.** very great ○ *a gigantic task* [Early 17C. < Latin *gigant-* "giant" < Greek *gigas*] —**gi·gan·ti·cal·ly** *adv*

gi·gan·tism /jī gán tìzzəm, jí gàn-/ *n* **1.** excessive growth due to overproduction of growth hormone by the pituitary gland before the end of adolescence **2.** the quality or condition of being very large, tall, or bulky

gi·gan·tom·a·chy /jì gan tómәkee/ (*plural* **-chies**) *n* in Greek mythology, the battle between the gods of Olympus and the rebellious giants who were children of the older gods (*literary*) [Late 16C. < Greek *gigantomachia* "giant war"]

gig·a·ton /gíggə tùn/ *n* a unit of explosive force equal to one billion tons of TNT

gig·a·watt /gíggə wàat/ *n* a unit of electric power equal to one billion watts. Symbol **GW**

gig·gle /gígg'l/ *vti* (**-gled, -gling, -gles**) **LAUGH LIGHTLY** to laugh audibly but not loudly, sometimes without meaning to, in a way that is characteristic of children ■ *n* **QUICK LAUGH** a quiet laugh that is sometimes involuntary in a way that is characteristic of children ■ **gig·gles** *npl* **FIT OF LAUGHTER** an uncontrollable and recurring urge to laugh (*informal*) [Early 16C. An imitation of the sound] —**gig·gler** *n* —**gig·gling** *adj* —**gig·gly** *adj*

GIGO /gí gṑ/ *n* the principle that a computer program or process is only as good as the ideas or data put into it. Full form **garbage in, garbage out**

gig·o·lo /jíggə lṑ/ (*plural* **-los**) *n* **1.** a man who receives payments or gifts from a woman in exchange for being her sexual or social partner **2.** a man whose job is to be a dancing partner or escort for a woman [Early 20C. < French < *gigole* "woman who is a professional dance partner"]

gig·ot /jíggət, zhee gṓ/ *n* a leg of lamb or mutton [Early 16C. < French, "small leg" < French dialect *gigue* "leg" < *giguer* "hop"]

gig·ot sleeve *n* a sleeve that is close-fitting on the lower arm and full and loose on the upper arm [< its shape]

Gi·jón /gee háwn, hee hṓn/ seaport on the Bay of Biscay in Asturias Province, northwestern Spain. Population: 257,694 (2002).

Gila monster

Gi·la mon·ster /héelə-/ *n* a large brightly colored venomous lizard that feeds on eggs and small animals. Native to: desert areas of the southwestern United States and Mexico. Latin name: *Heloderma suspectum.* [Late 19C. After the Gila River]

Gi·la Riv·er /héelə-, géelə-/ river that rises in southwestern New Mexico and flows westward, crossing Arizona to join the Colorado River near Yuma. It is an important source of irrigation water. Length: 649 mi./1,044 km.

gil·bert /gílbərt/ *n* a unit of magnetomotive force in the centimeter-gram-second system, equal to 0.7958 ampere-turns in the SI system [Late 19C. After William *Gilbert* (1544–1603), English physician and scientist]

Gil·bert /gílbərt/ town in central Arizona, part of the greater Phoenix metropolitan area. Population: 135,055 (2002 estimate).

Gil·bert, Cass (1858–1934) US architect. He designed the 60-story Gothic Revival Woolworth Building in New York City (1909–13) and the US Supreme Court Building, Washington, D.C. (1924–35).

Gil·bert, Sir Humphrey (1539?–83) English navigator. The half-brother of Sir Walter Raleigh, he claimed Newfoundland for England in 1583 and founded the first English colony in North America there, near present-day St. John's.

> "We are as near to heaven by sea as by land."
> [Sir Humphrey Gilbert. Quoted in *Third and Last Voyages of the English Nation*, Richard Hakluyt; 1600]

Gil·bert, Sir W. S. (1836–1911) British librettist and dramatist. He is best known for his long collaboration with Sir Arthur Sullivan, writing light operas including *The Pirates of Penzance* (1879). Full name **Gilbert, Sir William Schwenck**

Gil·bert and El·lice Is·lands /-élliss-/ former British colony situated in the western Pacific Ocean. The group consisted of the Gilbert Islands, now part of Kiribati, and the Ellice Islands, now Tuvalu.

gild /gild/ (**gild·ed, gild·ing, gilds**) *vt* **1. COVER SOMETHING WITH GOLD** to cover something with a thin layer of gold leaf or a substance that looks like gold **2. MAKE SOMETHING SEEM BETTER** to make something seem better than it really is **3. COLOR SOMETHING GOLD** to give a golden color or tinge to something (*literary*) [Old English *gyldan* < Germanic] —**gild·er** *n*

SPELLCHECK See ***guild.***

gild·ed /gíldəd/ *adj* **1.** ARTS same as **gilt**[1] **2.** wealthy and privileged ○ *gilded youth*

gild·ing /gílding/ *n* **1.** the process of applying a thin layer of gold leaf or a substance that looks like gold to a surface **2.** ARTS same as **gilt**[1] *n* (sense 1)

Gil·e·ad, Mount /gíllee ad/ mountain in northwestern Jordan that also gives its name to an area east of the Jordan River, the Dead Sea, and the Sea of Galilee. Height: 3,597 ft./1,096 m.

gill[1] /gil/ *n* **1.** the organ that fish and some other water animals use to breathe, consisting of a membrane containing many blood vessels through which oxygen passes. They are internal in most fish and external in tadpoles and some mollusks. **2.** a thin radiating plate on the underside of the cap of a mushroom or other fungus where its spores are produced [14C. < Old Norse] —**gilled** *adj* ◇ **green around the gills, white around the gills** appearing nauseated (*informal*) ◇ **to the gills** to the fullest possible extent

gill[2] /jil/ *n* a unit of liquid measure equal to a quarter of a pint (118 ml in the United States and 142 ml in the United Kingdom) [14C. Via Old French *gille* < late Latin *gillo* "water pot"]

gill[3] /jil/, **jill** *n* a young woman (*archaic; sometimes considered offensive*) [15C. Shortening of the given name *Gillian*]

gill arch /gíl-/ *n* the bony or cartilaginous arch supporting the filaments that make up the gill of a fish

Gilles de la Tour·ette syn·drome /zheel də laa tòo rét-/ *n* MED full form of **Tourette syndrome**

Gil·les·pie /gi léspee/, **Dizzy** (1917–93) US jazz musician. A trumpeter with both large and small bands, he was a leading exponent of bebop and pioneered Afro-Cuban jazz in the United States. Full name **Gillespie, John Birks**

> "It's taken me all my life to learn what not to play."
> [Dizzy Gillespie. Quoted in *Jazz Is*, Nat Hentoff; 1976]

Gil·lette /ji lét/, **William** (1855–1937) US actor and playwright. A successful adapter of works for the stage, he was best known for his dramatic version of *Sherlock Holmes* (1899). Full name **Gillette, William Hooker**

gill fun·gus /gíl-/ *n* a fungus that produces its spores from gills underneath a cap

gil·lie /gíllee/, **ghil·lie** *n* **1.** somebody whose job is to assist or guide people who go fishing or deer-stalking in Scotland **2.** a low-cut tongueless shoe that laces across the foot and sometimes up the ankle [Late 17C. < Gaelic *gille*]

Gil·ling·ham /jíllingəm/ city in southeastern England, on the Medway River. Population: 96,200 (1994).

gill net /gíl-/ *n* a net that is suspended vertically in the water like a curtain in order to catch fish by their gills —**gill·net·ter** *n*

gill slit /gíl-/ *n* one of the openings on either side of the head of a fish or amphibian that contain its gills

gil·ly·flow·er /jíllee flòwr/ *n* **1.** a clove-scented pink or carnation **2.** a scented flower, e.g., a stock or wallflower (*archaic*) [14C. < Alteration (after FLOWER) of French *girofle*, via medieval Latin *caryophyllum* "clove" < Greek *karuophullon* "nut leaf"]

Gil·man /gílmən/, **Charlotte Perkins** (1860–1935) US social reformer and writer. She promoted feminism in public lectures and in writings including *Women* *and Economics* (1898). Her best-known work is *The Yellow Wallpaper* (1892), a fictionalized account of her own depression. Born **Perkins, Charlotte Anna**

> "Where young boys plan for what they will achieve and attain, young girls plan for whom they will achieve and attain."
> [Charlotte Perkins Gilman, *Women and Economics*; 1898]

Gil·roy /gíl ròy/ city in western California, southeast of San Jose. Population: 43,145 (2002 estimate).

gilt[1] /gilt/ *adj* **COVERED WITH GILT** covered with a thin layer of gold or a substance that looks like gold ■ *n* **1. THIN LAYER OF GOLD** a thin layer of gold or of a substance that looks like gold applied to a surface **2. GOVERNMENT BOND** a bond issued by the government in the United Kingdom (*often used in the plural*) [15C. < past participle of GILD]

SPELLCHECK See ***guilt***.

gilt[2] /gilt/ *n* a young female pig, especially one that has not yet had a litter [14C. < Old Norse *gyltr*]

gilt-edged *adj* **1.** very safe as an investment ○ *gilt-edged securities* **2.** having a gilded edge

gimbal

gim·bal /gímb'l, jím-/ *n* **1.** NAVIG **RING FOR HOLDING COMPASS STEADY** a pivoted ring mounted at right angles to one or two others to ensure that something such as a ship's compass always remains horizontal **2.** MECH ENG **CONNECTION OF REVOLVING PARTS** an interconnection that allows one part of a mechanism such as a clock's works to revolve independently of another revolving part that contains it ■ *vt* **(-baled, -bal·ing, -bals) PUT SOMETHING ON GIMBALS** to support something on gimbals [Late 16C. Variant of GIMMAL]

gim·crack /jím kràk/ *adj* showy or superficially appealing, but badly made and worthless [14C. Origin ?] —**gim·crack** *n* —**gim·crack·er·y** *n*

gim·el /gímm'l/ *n* the third letter of the Hebrew alphabet, represented in the English alphabet as "g" or "gh." See table at **alphabet** [< Hebrew *gīmel*]

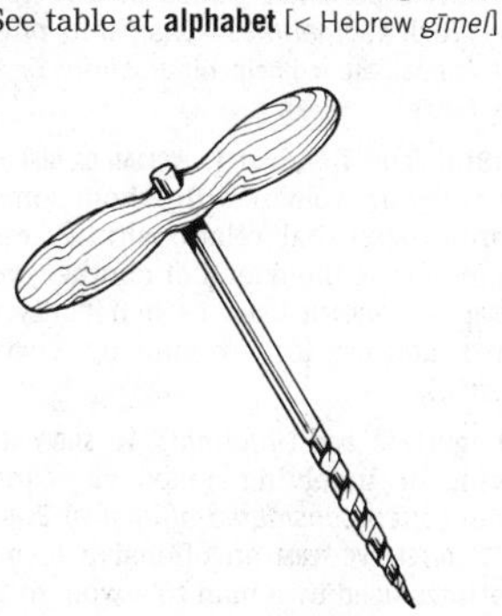

gimlet

gim·let /gímmlət/ *n* **1. TOOL FOR BORING HOLES IN WOOD** a small tool for boring holes in wood consisting of a slim metal rod with a sharp corkscrew end, fitted in a handle at a right angle **2. COCKTAIL WITH LIME JUICE** a cocktail made of vodka or gin with lime juice ■ *vt* **(-let·ed, -let·ing, -lets) BORE INTO SOMETHING** to pierce or penetrate something ■ *adj* **PIERCING** seeming to penetrate or pierce somebody or something ○*"to meet anew the gimlet glances"* (Thomas Hardy, *Jude the Obscure*; 1895) [14C. < Old French *guimbelet* "small auger" < *guimble* "auger" < Germanic]

gim·let-eyed *adj* having eyes that seem to penetrate or pierce, or to notice everything

gim·mal /gímm'l, jímm'l/ *n* MECH ENG, NAVIG same as **gimbal** [Late 16C. Alteration of obsolete *gemel* "double ring," via Old French < Latin *gemellus* < *geminus* "twin"]

gim·me /gímmee/ *contr* give me (*nonstandard*) ■ *n* (*informal*) **1.** *also* **gim·mie SOMETHING EASILY GOTTEN** something easily gained or accomplished ○ *The women's draw is shaping up as a gimme for the defending champion.* **2.** GOLF **SHORT PUTT TAKEN AS SUCCESSFUL** in an informal game of golf, a short easy putt for which the golfer can record a single stroke without actually having to hit the ball **3. GREED** greed or acquisitiveness

gim·mick /gímmik/ *n* **1. DISHONEST TRICK** a piece of trickery or manipulation intended to achieve a result dishonestly ○ *It's not a genuine offer, just a sales gimmick.* **2. HIDDEN DISADVANTAGE** a piece of concealed information that, if known, would make an offer or opportunity less attractive ○ *It sounds great, but what's the gimmick?* **3. SOMETHING GRABBING ATTENTION** something that attracts attention or publicity, e.g., a new technique or device **4. GADGET** an ingenious device, mechanism, or ploy, especially one that works in a concealed way [Early 20C. Origin ?] —**gim·mick·y** *adj*

gim·mick·ry /gímmikree/ *n* **1.** gimmicks in general **2.** the use of a gimmick or gimmicks to deceive somebody or attract attention

gim·mie *n* another spelling of **gimme** *n* (sense 1) (*informal*)

gimp[1] /gimp/, **guimpe** /gamp/ *n* a silk or cotton trimming that has a wire or cord running through it [Mid-17C. < Dutch]

gimp[2] /gimp/ *n* **1. DIFFICULTY IN WALKING** difficulty in walking, caused by injury or stiffness (*informal*) **2. OFFENSIVE TERM** an offensive term for somebody with a physical challenge, especially somebody who has difficulty walking or who uses a wheelchair (*slang*) **3. CLUMSY PERSON** somebody regarded as clumsy or ineffectual (*slang insult; often considered offensive*) ■ *vi* **(gimped, gimp·ing, gimps) WALK WITH DIFFICULTY** walk with difficulty (*informal*) [Early 20C. Origin ?] —**gimp·y** *adj*

gin[1] /jin/ *n* **1.** a strong colorless alcoholic drink distilled from grain and flavored with juniper berries **2.** CARDS same as **gin rummy** (*informal*) [Early 18C. Shortening of GENEVER]

gin[2] /jin/ *n* **1.** MECH ENG **HOIST** a simple hoist operated by hand **2.** HUNTING **TRAP** a snare or trap, usually one consisting of a noose made of wire for catching small animals ■ *vt* **(ginned, gin·ning, gins) 1.** HUNTING **CATCH ANIMAL IN GIN** to trap an animal with a gin **2.** INDUST **CLEAN RAW COTTON** to separate cotton from its seeds using a cotton gin [13C. Shortening of Old French *engin* "engine"]

gin up *vt regional* to concoct or invent something, or exaggerate its importance (*informal*) ○ *a story ginned up by the public relations people*

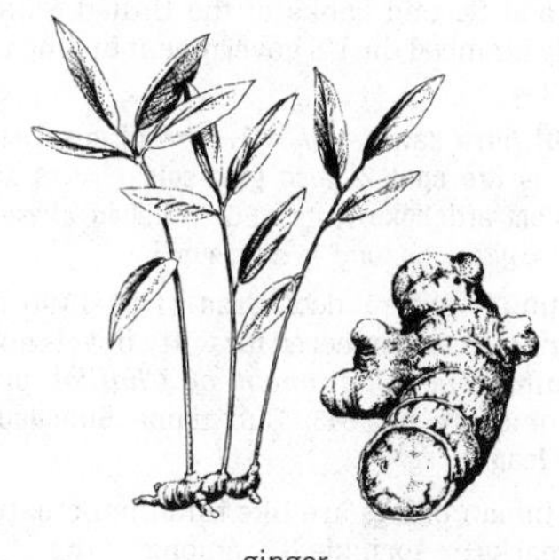

ginger

gin·ger /jínjər/ *n* **1. HOT-TASTING SPICE** the hot-tasting edible underground stem (**rhizome**) of an Asian plant, eaten fresh, pickled, candied, or in powdered form as a spice, especially in Asian cooking **2. PLANT YIELDING GINGER** a widely cultivated plant that yields ginger. Native to: Asia. Latin name: *Zingiber officinale*. **3. BROWNISH YELLOW COLOR** a yellow color with an orange or brownish tinge **4. VIGOR** excitement, liveliness, or animation (*informal*) ■ *adj* **1. MADE WITH GINGER** flavored with fresh or powdered ginger **2. OF BROWNISH YELLOW COLOR** of a yellow color with an orange or brownish tinge ■ *vt* **(-gered, -ger·ing, -gers) ADD GINGER TO SOMETHING** to add ginger as a spice to something [Pre-12C. < Old French *gingi(m)bre*, via Latin and Greek < Pali *singivera*] —**gin·ger·y** *adj*

ORIGIN The source of the Pali word from which ***ginger*** derives was a Sanskrit compound meaning literally "horn-body" – a reference to the shape of the edible ginger root. By the time it had passed through Greek *ziggiberis* into Latin, it had become *zinziberi*. After classical times this developed to *gingiber* or *gingiver*, which Old English borrowed as *gingifer*. English acquired the word again in the 13th century from Old French, and this combined with the descendant of the Old English form to produce Middle English *gingivere*, from which modern English ***ginger*** is derived.

ginger up *vt* to make something more lively, active, or interesting [< inserting a piece of ginger into the anus of a slothful horse]

gin·ger ale *n* an effervescent nonalcoholic drink flavored with ginger

gin·ger beer *n* a nonalcoholic beverage strongly flavored with fermented ginger and sometimes carbonated

gin·ger·bread /jínjər brèd/ *n* **1. GINGER-FLAVORED CAKE** a moist dark cake made with molasses and flavored with ginger **2. GINGER-FLAVORED COOKIE** a ginger-flavored cookie, often cut into the stylized shape of a person, animal, or Christmas tree **3.** ARCHIT **ELABORATE DECORATION** showy and elaborate decoration, especially on the outside of a building (*often used before a noun*) ○ *a Victorian gingerbread cottage* [13C. By folk etymology (by association with BREAD) < Old French *gingembrat* "preserved ginger" < medieval Latin *gingiber* "ginger"]

gin·ger·bread man *n* a cookie in the stylized shape of a person, made from gingerbread and often decorated

gin·ger group *n Can, UK* a group, often within a party or association, whose objective is to stimulate debate and press for more radical or decisive action on something

gin·ger·ly /jínjərlee/ *adv* in a very cautious, wary, or tentative way ○ *He gingerly unscrewed the radiator cap.* ■ *adj* very cautious, wary, or tentative ○ *made a gingerly approach to the sick animal* [Early 16C. Origin ?]

gin·ger·root /jínjər ro͝ot/ *n* fresh ginger in the form of whole rhizomes

gin·ger snap *n* a thin crisp cookie flavored with ginger

ging·ham /gíngəm/ *n* a light plain-weave cotton fabric with checks in white and another color (*often used before a noun*) ○ *a gingham dress* [Early 17C. Via Dutch *gingang* < Malay *genggang* "striped"]

gin·gil·i /jín jillee/ *n S Asia* in Indian cuisine, sesame seeds or oil [Early 18C. < Hindi and Marathi *jiñjalī*]

gin·gi·va /jínjəvə, jin jívə/ (*plural* **-vae** /-vee/) *n* the gum around the roots of the teeth (*technical*) [Late 19C. < Latin] —**gin·gi·val** *adj*

gin·gi·vec·to·my /jìnjə véktəmee/ (*plural* **-mies**) *n* a surgical operation to remove tissue from the gums

gin·gi·vi·tis /jìnji vítiss/ *n* inflammation of the gums around the roots of the teeth

ging·ko *n* TREES another spelling of **ginkgo**

gin·gly·mus /jíng gləməss/ (*plural* **-mi** /-mī/) *n* a hinge joint of the human body (*technical*) [Late 16C. Via modern Latin < Greek *ginglumos* "hinge"]

Gin·grich /gíng grich/, **Newt** (*b.* 1943) US Speaker of the House of Representatives (1995–98). A Georgia Republican, he sat in the US House of Representatives for 20 years. He was the first Republican Speaker of the House since 1954. Full name **Gingrich, Newton Leroy**

gink /gingk/ *n* somebody, especially a man, who is considered strange, unintelligent, or clumsy (*informal insult*) [Early 20C. Origin ?]

ginkgo

gink·go /gíng kō/ (*plural* **-goes**), **ging·ko** (*plural* **-koes**) *n* a widely cultivated deciduous tree of primitive origin, with fan-shaped leaves. Native to: China. Latin name: *Ginkgo biloba*. [Late 18C. Via Japanese < Chinese *yínxìng* "silver apricot"]

gink·go bi·lo·ba /-bī lṓbə/ *n* an herbal preparation made from the pulverized leaves of the ginkgo tree [< modern Latin genus name]

gin mill *n* a low-class bar or saloon (*dated slang*)

Gin·nie Mae /jìnnee máy/ *n* the Government National Mortgage Association, a US government agency that provides liquidity to the mortgage market

gi·nor·mous /jī náwrməss/ *adj UK* extraordinarily large in size (*informal*) [Mid-20C. Blend of GIGANTIC + ENORMOUS]

gin rum·my *n* a card game similar to rummy in which two players collect sets and sequences of cards. A hand can be won if cards totaling ten or fewer points are uncombined. [< GIN[1]; pun on RUMMY[1], as if < RUM[1]]

Gins·berg /gínzbərg/, **Allen** (1926–97) US poet. His *Howl* (1956) launched the Beat movement.

> "What if someone gave a war and Nobody came? Life would ring the bells of Ecstasy and Forever be Itself again."
> [Allen Ginsberg, "Graffiti"; 1972]

Gins·burg /gínzbərg/, **Ruth Bader** (*b.* 1933) associate justice of the US Supreme Court. A legal activist on behalf of women's rights, she was appointed an associate justice in 1993.

> "In commercial law, the person duped was too often a woman. In a section on land tenure, one 1968 textbook explains that 'land, like women, was meant to be possessed.'"
> [Ruth Bader Ginsburg, "Portia Faces Life–The Trials of Law School," *Ms.*; April 1974]

ginseng

gin·seng /jín sèng/ (*plural* **-sengs** or *same*) *n* **1.** a forked aromatic root used in traditional Chinese medicine and more widely as a tonic **2.** the plant that produces the ginseng root. Native to: South Asia, North America. Genus: *Panax*. [Mid-17C. < Chinese *rénshēn* < *rén* "man" + *shēn*, type of herb]

gin·zo /gínzō/ (*plural* **-zoes**) *n* an offensive term for somebody of Italian ancestry (*dated insult*) [Mid-20C. Origin ?]

Gior·gio·ne /jàwr jṓnee/ (1478?–1510) Italian painter. Although none of his signed works has survived, the works that have been assigned to him, e.g., *The Tempest* (1507), give a new prominence to atmosphere at the expense of storytelling. Born **Barbarelli, Giorgio**

Giot·to /jáwtō, jee óttō/ (1267?–1337) Italian painter. One of the first European painters to portray human forms naturalistically, he exerted a profound influence on artists of the Renaissance. Full name **Giotto di Bondone**

Gip·sy *n, adj* PEOPLES another spelling of **Gypsy**

giraffe

gi·raffe /jə ráf/ (*plural* **-raffes** or *same*) *n* a large animal with an extremely long neck, long legs, and a yellowish coat mottled with brown patches. Giraffes are ruminants. Native to: open grassland in Africa. Latin name: *Giraffa camelopardalis*. [Late 16C. Via French *girafe* or Italian *giraffa* < Arabic *zarāfa*]

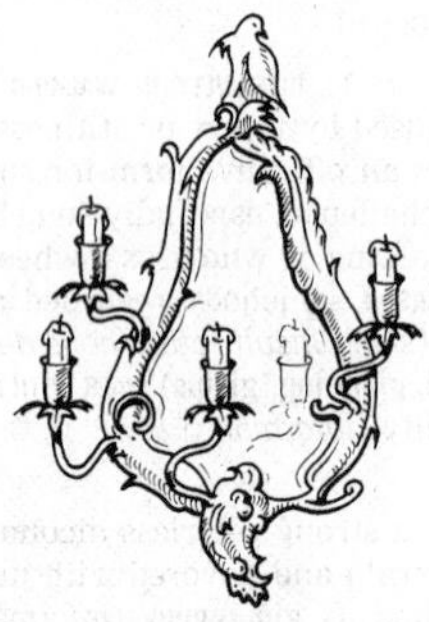

girandole

gir·an·dole /jírrən dṑl/, **gir·an·do·la** /ji rándʼlə/ *n* **1.** WALL-MOUNTED CANDLEHOLDER a wall-mounted branched candleholder that often incorporates a mirror between the candlestick branches **2.** STARBURST JEWELRY an earring or pendant with a large central stone surrounded by several smaller ones **3.** ROTATING FIREWORK an elaborate rotating firework **4.** WATER JET a revolving water jet [Mid-17C. Via French < Italian *girandola* < late Latin *gyrare* "gyrate"]

Gi·rard /jə raárd/, **Stephen** (1750–1831) French-born US banker. He was a principal stockholder in both the First and Second banks of the United States, and largely financed the US government during the War of 1812.

gir·a·sol /jírrə sàwl, -sṑl/ *n* **1.** *also* **gir·o·sol** MINERALS same as **fire opal 2.** *also* **gir·a·sole** PLANTS same as **Jerusalem artichoke** [Late 16C. < Italian *girasole* "sunflower" < *girare* "to turn" + *sole* "sun"]

Gi·rau·doux /zheerō dóō/, **Jean** (1882–1944) French writer. He is remembered for witty novels and plays including *The Madwoman of Chaillot* produced posthumously in 1945. Full name **Giraudoux, Hyppolyte Jean**

> "Human beings are like timid punctuation marks sprinkled among the incomprehensible sentences of life."
> [Jean Giraudoux, *Siegfried*; 1922]

gird /gurd/ (**gird·ed** or **girt** /gurt/, **gird·ing, girds**) *v* **1. gird your·self** *vr* GET SELF READY to prepare yourself for conflict or vigorous activity **2.** *vt* PUT BELT AROUND SOMEBODY to put a girdle or belt around yourself or another person (*literary*) **3.** *vt* FASTEN SOMETHING ON to secure something to yourself with a belt, straps, or a girdle (*literary*) **4.** *vt* SURROUND SOMETHING to surround or encompass something (*literary*) ○ *a castle girded with a moat* [Old English *gyrdan* < Germanic]

gird·er /gúrdər/ *n* a large strong beam, often of steel, forming a main spanning and supporting part in a framework

gir·dle /gúrdʼl/ *n* **1.** WOMAN'S FOUNDATION GARMENT a woman's elasticized foundation garment or corset extending from the waist to the thigh **2.** NARROW BELT a cord worn around the waist to hold in a large loose-fitting garment such as a kaftan or a monk's habit **3.** SOMETHING THAT SURROUNDS something that surrounds or encircles something else (*literary*) **4.** ANAT RING OF BONE a ring-shaped structure of bone, especially the pelvic girdle or pectoral girdle, which support the upper and lower limbs respectively **5.** FORESTRY RING AROUND TREE TRUNK a ring around a tree trunk made by removing the bark and underlying tissue in order to kill the tree **6.** PART OF CUT GEMSTONE the outer edge of a gem, by which it is held in its setting ■ *vt* (**-dled, -dling, -dles**) **1.** SURROUND SOMETHING to surround or encircle something (*literary*) **2.** FORESTRY CUT RING OF BARK FROM TREE to remove a ring of bark and underlying tissue from a tree trunk in order to kill the tree [Old English *gyrdel* < Germanic]

gird·ler /gúrdlər/ *n* an insect that makes a groove around a branch or twig in which to lay its eggs, thereby killing the branch

gir·i /gírree/ *n* a social obligation or debt (*informal*) [< Japanese]

girl /gurl/ *n* **1.** FEMALE CHILD a human female from birth until the age at which she is considered an adult **2.** ⚠ YOUNG WOMAN a young woman between childhood and adulthood (*often considered offensive*) **3.** ⚠ WOMAN OF ANY AGE a woman of any age, especially one who is a friend or contemporary, or who is younger than the speaker (*informal; often considered offensive*) ○ *a night out with the girls* **4.** DAUGHTER somebody's daughter, especially when a child (*informal*) **5.** GIRLFRIEND somebody's girlfriend **6.** WAY OF ADDRESSING WOMAN used as a friendly, intimate, or patronizing form of address to a woman (*sometimes considered offensive*) **7.** OFFENSIVE TERM an offensive term for a young woman servant or employee (*dated*) **8.** FEMALE ANIMAL a female animal, especially a young one (*informal; often used before a noun*) ○ *a girl kitten* [13C. Origin ?] —**girl·hood** *n*

USAGE girl or **woman**? ***Girl*** is used more often as an alternative for ***woman***, especially in reference to a young woman, than *boy* is for *man*. (*Boy* in reference to an adult is normally found only in the plural or in meanings such as *boyfriend*.) However, the use of ***girl*** for a teenager or an adult is often regarded as patronizing or disrespectful, especially when it comes from a man.

---

girl Fri·day *n* a young woman whose job is to be somebody's personal assistant and to do general office work (*sometimes considered offensive*) [After *Man Friday*, all-around helper in *Robinson Crusoe* (1719) by Daniel Defoe]

girl·friend /gúrl frènd/ *n* **1.** WOMAN OR GIRL SWEETHEART OR LOVER a girl or woman with whom somebody has a romantic or sexual relationship **2.** WOMAN FRIEND a woman who is the friend of another woman **3.** WAY OF ADDRESSING WOMAN used as a friendly or intimate form of address to a woman by a woman friend (*informal*)

girl·ie /gúrlee/ *adj* (*informal*) **1.** SHOWING NUDE WOMEN showing or involving naked or scantily dressed women (*often considered offensive*) **2.** same as **girly** ■ *n* **1.** OFFENSIVE TERM an offensive term of address sometimes used by a man to a woman **2.** LITTLE GIRL a young girl (*dated informal*)

girl·ish /gúrlish/ *adj* **1.** characteristic of girls **2.** more suitable for a girl than for an adult woman —**girl·ish·ly** *adv* —**girl·ish·ness** *n*

girl pow·er *n* the ability of or opportunity for teenage girls and young women to make decisions for themselves and shape their own lives

Girl Scout *n* a member of the Girl Scouts, an organization that aims to enable girls to socialize and learn skills in a wholesome environment

girl·y /gúrlee/ (**-i·er, -i·est**) *adj* extremely or deliberately feminine (*informal*) ○ *a girly lace collar*

girn /gurn/ (**girned, girn·ing, girns**), **gurn** (**gurned, gurn·ing, gurns**) *vi N England, Scotland* **1.** to complain, whine, or grumble **2.** to make a bad-tempered or discontented face [14C. Alteration of GRIN]

gi·ro /jírō/ (*plural* **-ros**) *n* **1.** in European countries and the United Kingdom, a system that enables money to be transferred quickly and cheaply between accounts or between the financial institutions of a country **2.** *UK* a check, cashable at a post office in European countries, for the payment of a government benefit such as unemployment benefit (*informal*) [Late 19C. Via German < Italian, "circulation (of money)"]

gi·ron *n* HERALDRY another spelling of **gyron**

Gi·ronde /jə rónd, zhee róNd/ navigable river estuary in southwestern France, formed where the Dordogne and Garonne rivers meet. Length: 45 mi./72 km.

gir·o·sol *n* MINERALS another spelling of **girasol** (sense 1)

girt past participle, past tense of **gird**

girth /gurth/ *n* **1.** DISTANCE AROUND SOMETHING the distance around something thick and cylindrical such as a tree trunk or somebody's waist ○ *a man of ample girth* **2.** SADDLE BAND a broad band fastened around the belly of a horse to keep a saddle in place ■ *vt* (**girthed, girth·ing, girths**) **1.** FASTEN SADDLE ON HORSE to put or fasten a girth on a horse **2.** SURROUND SOMETHING to surround or encircle something (*literary*) [14C. < Old Norse *gjörð* "girdle"]

GISA *n* a strain of a common infection-causing bacterium that shows resistance to treatment by some of the commonly used glycopeptide antibiotics. Full form **glycopeptide intermediate Staphylococcus aureus**

gi·sarme /gi za̋arm, ji-/ *n* a medieval foot soldier's weapon that had a long shaft and a head with an ax blade on one side and a sharp point on the other [13C. < Old French *guisarme*]

Gis·card d'Es·taing /zhiss ka̋ar de stáng/, **Valéry** (*b.* 1926) French president (1974–81). He served as minister of finance twice (1962–66 and 1969–74) before succeeding Georges Pompidou to the presidency on an independent republican ticket.

Gish /gish/, **Dorothy** (1898–1968) US actor. The sister of Lillian Gish, she was a star of silent movies and later of the stage. Born **de Guiche, Dorothy**

Gish, Lillian (1893–1993) US actor. Perhaps the greatest of all silent-movie actors, she continued a long career on both stage and screen, appearing on film for the last time in 1987. Born **de Guiche, Lillian**

> "You can't teach acting. You learn that from the human race."
> [Lillian Gish, *PBS TV*, July 11, 1988]

gis·mo *n* another spelling of **gizmo**

gist /jist/ *n* **1.** the essential point or meaning of something **2.** the essential grounds for a legal action [Early 18C. < Old French *cest action gist* "this action lies"]

git[1] /git/ (**got·ten** /gótt'n/, **git·ting, gits**) *vti regional* same as **get**[1] (*nonstandard*) [19C. Variant]

git[2] /git/ *n UK* an offensive term for somebody regarded as annoying, troublesome, unpleasant, or thoughtless (*informal insult*) [Mid-20C. Variant of GET[2]]

gite /zheet/ *n* a country cottage or small house in France offering fairly simple accommodations that can be rented for a vacation [Late 18C. < French *gîte* "stopping place"]

git-go *n* another spelling of **get-go**

git·tern /gíttərn/ *n* a medieval stringed instrument that was a forerunner of the guitar [14C. Via Old French *guiterne* < Latin *cithara* (see CITHARA)]

Giu·li·a·ni /jo͞olee a̋anee/, **Rudolph W.** (*b.* 1944) US mayor of New York City (1993–2001) known for his tough stance against crime, and for his leadership after the terrorist attack on the World Trade Center (September 11, 2001)

Giu·li·o Ro·ma·no /jo͞oli ō rō ma̋anō/ (1499?–1546) Italian painter and architect in the mannerist style. He was the chief pupil of Raphael and assisted him in many of his works. His own paintings include the *Martyrdom of St. Stephen*. He also designed the drainage system, cathedral, street plan, and several prominent buildings in Mantua.

~~**giutar**~~ incorrect spelling of **guitar**

give /giv/ (**gave** /gayv/, **giv·en** /gívvən/, **giv·ing, gives**) CORE MEANING: a verb used to indicate that somebody presents or delivers something that he or she owns to another person to keep or use ○ *He gave Brian $800 with the understanding he would pay the rest at a later date.* ○ *The program would give education grants to people who do community service.* ○ *My mother gave me this cardigan for Christmas.* ○ *What will you give me for the car?* ○ *When we arrived they gave us badges with our names on them.*

1. *vt* PASS SOMETHING TO SOMEBODY to place something that you are holding in the temporary possession of another person ○ *Could you give me the phone?* ○ *He gave her the umbrella while he searched in his pockets for change.* **2.** *vt* GRANT SOMETHING TO SOMEBODY to allow somebody to have something such as power or a right ○ *Opponents of the bill claimed it gave too much power to the mine owners.* **3.** *vt* COMMUNICATE SOMETHING to impart or convey something such as information, advice, or opinions to somebody ○ *Give them my love.* **4.** *vt* CONVEY SOMETHING to cause somebody to have an idea or impression ○ *Whatever gave you that idea?* **5.** *vt* IMPART SOMETHING to make somebody experience a particular physical or emotional feeling ○ *She said the steady paycheck gave her a sense of security.* **6.** *vt* PERFORM SOMETHING to carry out or perform something in public ○ *Not one of these actors gave a performance that was worthy of the prize.* **7.** *vt* MAKE OR DO SOMETHING used with nouns referring to physical actions to indicate that the action is being made or done ○ *She gave Paul a quick, accusing glance.* **8.** *vt* PROVIDE SERVICE to perform an action or service for somebody ○ *He gave her a foot massage to relax her.* ○ *The guide gave us a tour of the ruins.* **9.** *vt* DEVOTE SOMETHING to devote or sacrifice something such as time or effort ○ *He gave his whole life to helping children in need.* **10.** *vt* ORGANIZE SOMETHING to organize a social event ○ *They gave a party in her honor when she returned from the expedition.* **11.** *vt* CAUSE TO BELIEVE SOMETHING to lead somebody to have a particular understanding about something ○ *I was given to understand that they had left.* **12.** *vt* VALUE SOMETHING to estimate something at a particular amount or value ○ *What do you give for his chances of getting her back?* **13.** *vi* YIELD to collapse or break under pressure ○ *The wheel gave under the heavy load.* ○ *When people are under constant pressure from work and home, something has to give.* **14.** *vt* CONCEDE SOMETHING to yield to somebody's opinion, or admit that somebody has an advantage or a specific characteristic or ability ○ *You're not a coward, I'll give you that.* **15.** *vt* TOAST SOMEBODY to propose a toast to somebody ○ *I give you the bride and groom!* **16.** *vt* INTRODUCE SOMEBODY to present or introduce somebody such as a performer or speaker to an audience ○ *Ladies and gentlemen, I give you the Grand Panjandrum!* **17.** *n* RESILIENCE the ability or tendency to yield under pressure [Old English *giefan* < Indo-European] —**giv·er** *n* ◇ **give me...** I'd rather do or have... (*informal*) ○ *Give me a quiet evening with a book any time.* ◇ **give or take** used to indicate that a figure given is fairly accurate, within the stated range ○ *worth about half a million, give or take a few thousand dollars*

SYNONYMS *give, present, confer, bestow, donate, grant*

CORE MEANING: to hand over something to somebody

give to place something that you are holding in the temporary possession of another person ○ *I gave her my key.* **present** to give something in a formal or ceremonial way ○ *He was presented with a consolation prize.* **confer** (*formal*) to give something such as a title, honor, or favor to somebody ○ *Several other honorary degrees were conferred at the ceremony.* **bestow** (*formal*) to present something, especially something valuable or undeserved, to somebody ○ *The award for lifetime achievement was bestowed on her not long before she died.* **donate** to give a contribution to a charitable organization or other good cause, or, in a medical context, to give blood for blood transfusions or organs for transplant ○ *The painting was donated to the gallery by the artist's widow.* **grant** to agree to allow a request, favor, or privilege, or formally or officially to give money or property ○ *We were granted the right to appeal.*

give away *vt* **1.** GIVE SOMETHING AS PRESENT to give or offer something without charging for it **2.** DISCLOSE SOMETHING BY MISTAKE to reveal information or a secret, often without meaning to **3.** BETRAY SOMEBODY to betray somebody by providing information **4.** PRESENT BRIDE TO HUSBAND AT WEDDING to accompany a bride to her future husband's side and formally present her to him just before the words of the wedding ceremony are spoken **5.** LET OPPONENT SCORE POINT to allow an opponent to get an advantage, especially inadvertently, through poor or illegal play

give back *vt* to return something, especially to its rightful or original owner

give in *vi* **1.** LOSE to admit defeat **2.** BREAK to collapse or break under pressure **3.** ACCEPT CONDITIONS to accept demands or conditions

give of *vr* **give of your·self** to devote or dedicate your time or energy to something

give off *vt* to send out or emit something

give on to *vt UK* to overlook or lead to something ○ *The French windows give on to a small paved area.*

give out *v* **1.** *vt* HAND SOMETHING OVER to hand over or distribute something **2.** *vt* MAKE SOMETHING KNOWN to declare something or make something known, especially publicly ○ *She gave out the exam grades in reverse order.* **3.** *vt* EMIT SOMETHING to send out or emit something **4.** *vi* BE USED UP to run out or be finished ○ *My courage gave out, and I couldn't face her after all.* **5.** *vi* STOP WORKING to fail or stop working

give over *vt* to hand somebody or something over to somebody or something else

give over to *v* **1.** *vt* to dedicate or assign something to a particular purpose or use ○ *This area will be given over to a children's playground.* **2. give yourself over to** *vr* to abandon yourself to an emotion or experience (*literary*) ○ *She gave herself over to despair.*

give up *v* **1.** *vi* SURRENDER to surrender or admit defeat **2.** *vt* HAND OVER SOMEBODY OR SOMETHING to hand over or part with somebody or something ○ *She gave up her seat to the man with a baby.* **3.** *vt* LOSE HOPE FOR SOMEBODY OR SOMETHING to stop hoping for a good outcome with regard to somebody or something ○ *Where have you been? We'd given you up as lost.* **4.** *vt* STOP USING OR DOING SOMETHING to stop or renounce using or doing something ○ *give up chocolate for a week* **5.** *vt* STOP TRYING to abandon a pursuit that has a goal ○ *Darkness fell, but they didn't give up looking for the missing children.* **6.** *vt* DEVOTE YOURSELF TO SOMETHING to devote or dedicate yourself to an emotion, experience, or activity, especially exclusively ○ *He gave himself up to working for the cause.* **7.** *vt* REVEAL INFORMATION to reveal information or a secret **8.** *vt* BASEBALL ALLOW OPPONENT SOMETHING IN BASEBALL in baseball, to allow an opposing player something while pitching ◇ **give it up for somebody** *or* **something** to applaud somebody or something enthusiastically (*slang*)

give up on *vt* **1.** to abandon something, especially a plan **2.** to lose hope about somebody or something

give-and-take *n* (*informal*) **1.** mutual cooperation and understanding between people or groups, often involving concessions on all sides **2.** a useful exchange of ideas or information in which everyone involved benefits

give·a·way /gívvə wày/ *n* **1.** SOMETHING THAT REVEALS something that serves to reveal, betray, or expose something ○ *Her accent's a dead giveaway.* **2.** GIFT something that is offered free of charge or at very little cost, often as a publicity gimmick or incentive to buy (*informal*) **3.** GAME SHOW a radio or TV game show that offers contestants the chance to win prizes, especially cash prizes (*informal*) ■ *adj* (*informal*) **1.** VERY INEXPENSIVE extremely low in price **2.** FREE free of charge ○ *a giveaway sample of a new shampoo*

give·back /gív bàk/ *n* **1.** a concession over wages or other gesture of goodwill made by employees, often in return for later benefits from the employer or management **2.** something that is or has been returned (*informal*)

giv·en /gívvən/ past participle of **give** ■ *adj* **1.** PARTICULAR relating to a particular person, thing, or concept

○ *from any given starting point* **2. ARRANGED EARLIER** previously arranged or specified ○ *If I can't make it at the given time, I'll phone you.* **3. VALIDATED** validated or executed on the date mentioned (*formal*) ○ *this last will and testament given by my hand this 13th day of February 1898* ■ *prep* **1. GRANTED** assuming that somebody has the opportunity or ability to do or have something ○ *Given time, I'm sure we can find a solution.* **2. IN VIEW OF** taking into consideration ○ *given the uncertainty of the situation* ■ *n* **ACCEPTED FACT** a fact or event that is accepted as true or definite at the outset and that affects subsequent reasoning ◇ **given to** inclined to something or likely to do or be something

giv·en name *n* the name or names that somebody is given at birth or baptism in addition to the family name

Gi·za /geézə/ city in northern Egypt on the western bank of the Nile River, southwest of Cairo. It is the site of the Sphinx and Egypt's three most famous pyramids. Population: 4,779,000 (1998).

giz·mo /gízmō/ (*plural* **-mos**), **gis·mo** *n* a gadget, especially a mechanical or electrical device considered to be more complicated than necessary (*informal*) [Mid-20C. Origin ?]

giz·zard /gízzərd/ *n* **1. PART OF BIRD'S DIGESTIVE TRACT** a thick-walled muscular sac in the alimentary tract of birds where food is broken down by muscular action and by small stones ingested for that purpose **2. DIGESTIVE STRUCTURE** a structure in invertebrates and fish where digestion takes place **3. STOMACH** the stomach or alimentary canal generally (*informal*) [14C. Via Old French *giser* < Latin *gigeria* "cooked poultry entrails"]

GLA *n* an essential fatty acid required to form prostaglandins, found in high concentrations in evening primrose oil and borage oil. It can be taken as a dietary supplement for menstrual disorders and for the pain of arthritis. Full form **gamma linolenic acid**

gla·bel·la /glə béllə/ (*plural* **-lae** /-lee/) *n* the part of the human forehead that lies just above the nose and between the eyebrows. It is one of the crucial points used in measuring and classifying skull types in physical anthropology and craniometry. [Early 19C. < modern Latin < Latin *glaber* "hairless"] —**gla·bel·lar** *adj*

gla·brate /gláy bràyt, -brət/ *adj* BIOL same as **glabrous** [Mid-19C. < Latin *glabrare* "make hairless" < *glaber* "hairless"]

gla·bres·cent /glay bréss'nt/ *adj* becoming hairless over time [Mid-19C. < Latin *glabescere* "become smooth" < *glaber* "hairless"]

gla·brous /gláybrəss/ *adj* smooth and lacking hairs or bristles ○ *glabrous leaves* [Mid-17C. < Latin *glaber* "hairless"] —**gla·brous·ness** *n*

gla·cé /gla sáy/ *adj* **1. GLAZED WITH SUGAR SOLUTION** coated with a sugar solution that results in a glazed finish ○ *glacé cherries* **2. MADE FROM POWDERED SUGAR AND LIQUID** made by mixing powdered sugar and a liquid, usually water **3. SMOOTHLY GLOSSY** having a smooth glossy finish [Mid-19C. < French, past participle of *glacer* "glaze" < *glace* (see GLACIER)]

Glace Bay /gláyss-/ town on the Atlantic coast in Cape Breton County, northeastern Nova Scotia, Canada, situated on the Atlantic Ocean 12 mi./19 km east of Sydney. Population: 21,187 (2001).

gla·cial /gláysh'l/ *adj* **1. RELATING TO GLACIER** relating to or caused by a glacier or glaciers ○ *glacial movements and deposits* **2. CONTAINING EXPANSES OF ICE** characterized by the presence of ice masses **3. ICE-AGE** describes any geologic time when a large part of the Earth was covered in ice **4. EXTREMELY COLD** icily or bitingly cold ○ *a glacial wind* **5. COLDLY HOSTILE** unfriendly or hostile ○ *a glacial look* **6. DETACHED** characterized by detachment and an absence of emotion ○ *glacial determination* **7. SLOW** moving or advancing extremely slowly ○ *the glacial pace of the negotiations* ■ *n also* **Gla·cial** GEOL same as **glacial period** [Mid-17C. Via Old French < Latin *glacialis* "icy" < *glacies* "ice"] —**gla·cial·ly** *adv*

gla·cial a·ce·tic ac·id *n* acetic acid that is 99.8% or more pure [Because it forms crystals resembling ice]

gla·cial pe·ri·od *n* any period of geologic time when most of the Earth was covered in ice

gla·ci·ate /gláyshee àyt/ (**-at·ed, -at·ing, -ates**) *v* **1.** *vti* to cover something with a glacier, or become covered with a glacier **2.** *vt* to affect something by the action of a glacier, especially by erosion [Early 17C. < Latin *glaciat-*, past participle of *glaciare* "freeze" < *glacies* "ice"] —**gla·ci·a·tion** /glàyshee áysh'n/ *n*

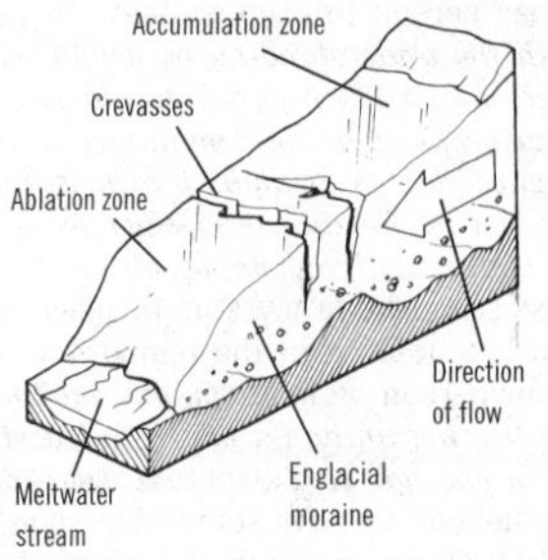

glacier: composition of a glacier

gla·cier /gláyshər/ *n* a large body of continuously accumulating ice and compacted snow, formed in mountain valleys or at the poles, that deforms under its own weight and slowly moves [Mid-18C. < French < *glace* "ice" < Latin *glacies*] —**gla·ciered** *adj*

Gla·cier Bay /gláyshər-/ inlet of the Pacific Ocean in southeastern Alaska. It was opened by retreating glaciers in the 19th century.

Gla·cier Bay Na·tion·al Park and Pre·serve national park in southeastern Alaska, established as a national monument in 1925 and a national park in 1980. It is noted for its glaciers and wide variety of plant and animal life. Area: 5,130 sq. mi./13,286 sq. km.

gla·cier meal *n* GEOL same as **rock flour**

gla·cier milk *n* water cloudy with particles of rock that flows from a melting glacier

Gla·cier Na·tion·al Park 1. national park in Northwestern Montana, with about 50 glaciers and over 200 lakes, established in 1910. Area: 1,584 sq. mi./4,102 sq. km. **2.** national park in the Selkirk and Purcell mountains in southeastern British Columbia, Canada, established in 1886. Area: 521 sq. mi./1,349 sq. km.

gla·ci·ol·o·gy /glàyshee óllajee/ *n* the branch of scientific study concerned with the formation, movement, and effects of glaciers and ice in general —**gla·ci·o·log·ic** /glàyshee ə lójjik/ *adj* —**gla·ci·o·log·i·cal** *adj* —**gla·ci·ol·o·gist** *n*

gla·cis /gla seé, glássee, gláyssiss/ (*plural same*) *n* **1. GENTLE INCLINE** a slope, especially one that is not very long or steep **2. DEFENSIVE SLOPE** a slope in front of a fortification designed to make it easier to fire on attacking forces **3. NEUTRAL TERRITORY** a stretch of neutral ground between two opposing or warring forces **4.** MIL same as **glacis plate** [Late 17C. < French < Old French *glacier* (see GLANCE)]

gla·cis plate *n* the armored plate at the front of a military tank [< its slant]

Glack·ens /glákənz/, **William** (1870–1938) US artist. Known for his impressionist paintings, he was a member of the group called The Eight. Full name **Glackens, William James**

glad[1] /glad/ *adj* (**glad·der, glad·dest**) **1. DELIGHTED** happy and pleased ○ *I'm so glad you came.* **2. CHEERFULLY WILLING** willing or ready to do something ○ *always glad to help* **3. GRATEFUL** appreciative of or grateful for something ○ *glad of the chance to relax* **4. PLEASING** giving pleasure, delight, or happiness ○ *on this glad occasion* **5. BRIGHT** bright and cheerful (*literary*) ○ *this glad June day* ■ *vti* (**glad·ded, glad·ding, glads**) **GLADDEN** to gladden somebody, or become glad (*archaic*) [Old English *glæd* < Germanic] —**glad·ly** *adv* —**glad·ness** *n*

glad[2] /glad/ *n* PLANTS same as **gladiolus** (*informal*) [Early 20C. Shortening]

glad·den /gládd'n/ (**-dened, -den·ing, -dens**) *vti* to feel cheerful and hopeful, or cause somebody to feel cheerful and hopeful ○ *It gladdens my heart to hear that.*

glade /glayd/ *n* **1.** an area in a wood or forest without trees or bushes **2.** same as **everglade** [Early 16C. Origin ?] —**glad·y** *adj*

glad hand *n* **1.** a hand extended in welcome or greeting, especially one offered insincerely or for motives of self-advancement **2.** a friendly welcome

glad-hand *vti* to offer somebody a friendly greeting or handshake, often insincerely or for motives of self-advancement —**glad-hand·er** *n*

glad·i·ate /gláddee àyt, -ət/ *adj* shaped like the blade of a sword ○ *the gladiate leaves of an iris* [Late 18C. < Latin *gladius* "sword"]

glad·i·a·tor /gláddee àytər/ *n* **1. FIGHTER IN ROMAN ARENA** in ancient Rome, a professional fighter who fought another combatant or a wild animal in public entertainments set in an arena. Often gladiators were criminals or slaves who were equipped with nets, nooses, swords, or other weapons. **2. AVID SUPPORTER OR CAMPAIGNER** a vigorous fighter or campaigner for or against a cause or person **3. BOXER** a professional boxer (*informal*) [Mid-16C. < Latin < *gladius* "sword"] —**glad·i·a·to·ri·al** /glàddee ə táwree əl/ *adj*

glad·i·o·lus /glàddee óləss/ (*plural same* or **-li** /-lī/ or **-lus·es**), **glad·i·o·la** /-lə/ (*plural* **-las** or *same*) *n* **1.** a widely grown plant with long sword-shaped leaves. Flowers: large, funnel-shaped, growing in tall spikes. Native to: tropics, southern Africa. Genus: *Gladiolus*. **2.** the large central part of the breastbone (**sternum**) [16C. < Latin, "little sword" < *gladius* "sword"]

glad rags *npl* somebody's best clothes, reserved for special occasions (*informal*)

glad·some /gládssəm/ *adj* feeling, showing, or bringing happiness (*literary*) ○ *gladsome tidings* —**glad·some·ly** *adv* —**glad·some·ness** *n*

Glad·stone[1] /glád stŏn, -stən/ *n* **1.** a small four-wheeled horse-drawn carriage with a collapsible roof **2.** HOUSEHOLD same as **Gladstone bag** [Mid-19C. See GLADSTONE BAG]

Glad·stone[2] /gládstən/ coastal city in southeastern Queensland, Australia, an industrial center and tourist resort. It is the gateway to the southern Great Barrier Reef. Population: 27,099 (2002 estimate).

W. E. Gladstone

Glad·stone /glád stŏn, -stən/, **W. E.** (1809–98) British politician. The leader of the Liberal Party after 1867, he was four times prime minister between 1868 and 1894 (1868–74, 1880–85, 1886, and 1892–94). He introduced national education in Britain (1870). Full name **Gladstone, William Ewart**

> "National injustice is the surest road to national downfall."
> [W. E. Gladstone, *Speech at Plumstead, London*; 1878]

Glad·stone bag *n* a small suitcase or portmanteau consisting of a rigid frame on which two compartments of the same size are hinged together [Late 19C. After W. E. GLADSTONE, noted for the amount of traveling he undertook in his public life]

Glag·o·lit·ic /glàggə líttik/ *adj* **1.** belonging or relating to an ancient Slavonic alphabet that was replaced by the Cyrillic alphabet **2.** belonging or relating to a Roman Catholic community of southwestern Croatia, whose liturgical books are still written in the Glagolitic alphabet [Early 19C. < modern Latin *glagoliticus* < Serbo-Croatian *glagǒljica* < Old Church Slavonic *glagolŭ* "word"]

glair /gler/, **glaire** *n* **1.** EGG WHITE a sizing, glazing, or adhesive substance made from egg white and used especially in bookbinding **2.** SUBSTANCE SIMILAR TO EGG-WHITE SIZING a substance that resembles glair in appearance or function ■ *vt* (**glaired, glair·ing, glairs; glaired, glair·ing, glaires**) PUT GLAIR ON SOMETHING to apply glair to something [14C. Via French < Latin *clarus* "clear"]

glam /glam/ (*slang*) *n* EXTREME GLAMOUR glamour, especially when it is overstated or ironic ■ *adj* EXTREMELY GLAMOROUS glamorous, especially in an overstated or ironic way ○ *a really glam dress* ■ *vt* (**glammed, glam·ming, glams**) *also* **glam up** GLAMORIZE EXCESSIVELY to make somebody or something glamorous, especially in an overstated or ironic way [Mid-20C. Shortening]

glam·or *n, adj* another spelling of **glamour**

glam·or·ize /glámmə rīz/ (**-ized, -iz·ing, -iz·es**), **glam·our·ize** *vt* **1.** to make somebody or something glamorous **2.** to make something seem more interesting, romantic, or glamorous than it really is —**glam·or·i·za·tion** /glàmməri záysh'n/ *n* —**glam·or·iz·er** *n*

glam·or·ous /glámmərəss/, **glam·our·ous** *adj* **1.** dressed or made up to be good-looking, especially in a high-fashion manner ○ *glamorous models strutting down the runway* **2.** desirable, especially in an exciting, stylish, or opulent way ○ *a glamorous lifestyle* —**glam·or·ous·ly** *adv* —**glam·or·ous·ness** *n*

glam·our /glámmər/, **glam·or** *n* **1.** EXCITING ALLURE an irresistible alluring quality that somebody or something possesses by virtue of seeming much more exciting, romantic, or fashionable than ordinary people or things ○ *the glamour of a career in the movies* **2.** EXPENSIVE GOOD LOOKS striking physical good looks or sexual impact, especially when it is enhanced with highly fashionable clothes or makeup **3.** SPELL a magical spell or charm (*archaic*) [Early 18C. Alteration of GRAMMAR "enchantment, spell"] —**glam·our** *adj*

glam·our·ize *vt* another spelling of **glamorize**

glam·our·ous *adj* another spelling of **glamorous**

glance /glanss/ *v* (**glanced, glanc·ing, glanc·es**) **1.** *vi* LOOK QUICKLY to look at something quickly, especially for only a second or two ○ *He glanced in our direction.* **2.** *vi* MAKE CURSORY EXAMINATION to look over or through something without really studying it **3.** *vi* TOUCH ON SOMETHING BRIEFLY to make a brief or passing allusion to something ○ *an introductory course that merely glances at the wider historical issues* **4.** *vi* GLINT to reflect or shine, especially intermittently or for only a short time ○ *green feathers glancing in the sunlight* **5.** *vt* STRIKE SOMETHING AT ANGLE to strike something briefly or lightly at an angle ○ *The stone glanced his shoulder.* ■ *n* **1.** QUICK LOOK a quick look at somebody or something ○ *a glance in our direction* **2.** PASSING MENTION a brief mention of something ○ *The book takes only a brief glance at contemporary music.* **3.** CURSORY EXAMINATION a cursory quick examination of something ○ *I haven't even had a glance at the report yet.* **4.** OBLIQUE STRIKE an act or instance of something striking another thing briefly or lightly at an angle **5.** GLINT OF LIGHT a sudden or quick flash or gleam of light ○ *glances of sunlight through the trees* [15C. Alteration (influenced by *glent* "to shine") of *glace* < Old French *glacier* "to slide" < *glace* (see GLACIER)] ◇ **at a glance** immediately and without having to make a close study ◇ **at first glance** initially or on first examination

glance off *vt* to come into quick light contact with something and then deflect at an angle ○ *The stone glanced off the windshield.*

glanc·ing /glánssing/ *adj* **1.** STRIKING OBLIQUELY coming into contact with another object and then deflecting at an angle ○ *a glancing blow* **2.** FLICKERING OR FLASHING giving off light in a flickering or flashing manner **3.** TEMPORARY lasting only a short time —**glanc·ing·ly** *adv*

gland[1] /gland/ *n* **1.** SECRETING CELL MASS in animals, a cell or group of cells that secretes a specific substance. Endocrine glands secrete directly into the bloodstream, while exocrine glands secrete through ducts into a cavity or to the surface of the body. **2.** ORGAN LIKE GLAND an anatomical structure that resembles a gland, especially a lymph node (*not in technical usage*) **3.** PLANT ORGAN in plants, a cell or group of cells that secrete substances, e.g., a nectary gland [Late 17C. Via French < Latin *glandula* "tonsil" < *glans* "acorn"] —**gland·less** *adj*

gland[2] /gland/ *n* a metal sleeve put around a rotating shaft or rod to prevent leakage, e.g., around a shaft emerging from a ship's hull [Early 19C. Probably < Old Norse *glam* "noise"]

glan·ders /glándərz/ *n* an infectious, often fatal, disease of horses, characterized by ulcers of the skin, lungs, or upper respiratory tract and heavy discharge of mucus from the nose. It is caused by the bacterium *Pseudomonas mallei.* (*takes a singular verb*) [15C. < Old French *glandres* "swelling of the glands" < Latin *glandula* (see GLAND[1])] —**glan·dered** *adj* —**glan·der·ous** *adj*

glan·des ANAT plural of **glans**

glan·du·lar /glánjələr/ *adj* **1.** RELATING TO GLANDS relating to, functioning as, or affecting a gland or glands **2.** RESULTING FROM GLAND DYSFUNCTION describes a medical condition caused by a malfunctioning gland or glands **3.** HAVING GLAND characterized by the presence of a gland or glands **4.** BODILY natural to the body, especially hormonally or sexually (*informal*) [Mid-18C. Via French *glandulaire* < Latin *glandula* (see GLAND[1])]

glan·du·lar fe·ver *n* MED same as **infectious mononucleosis**

glan·dule /glán dool/ *n* a small gland or a part resembling a small gland [14C. Directly or via French < Latin *glandula* (see GLAND[1])]

glan·du·lous /glánjələss/ *adj* ANAT, MED same as **glandular** —**glan·du·lous·ly** *adv*

glans /glanz/ (*plural* **glan·des** /glándeez/) *n* **1.** *also* **glans pe·nis** the rounded tip of a penis **2.** *also* **glans cli·tor·i·dis** /-kli táwri diss/ the erectile tissue at the tip of a clitoris [Mid-17C. < Latin, "acorn"]

glare[1] /gler/ *v* (**glared, glar·ing, glares**) **1.** *vi* STARE STONILY to stare intently and angrily **2.** *vt* EXPRESS SOMETHING WITH STARE to express or signal anger, disapproval, contempt, or another negative emotion by giving a steady stare ○ *He glared his disapproval at the youngsters.* **3.** *vi* BE UNPLEASANTLY BRIGHT to shine brightly and intensely, often dazzlingly **4.** *vi* STAND OUT OBTRUSIVELY to be very conspicuous, blatant, or obtrusive ○ *Mistakes glared from every page of the report.* **5.** *vi* BE UNPLEASANTLY AND OVERLY ORNATE to be excessively decorated or garish ■ *n* **1.** ANGRY LOOK a prolonged stare expressing anger, disapproval, contempt, or another negative emotion **2.** EXCESSIVE BRIGHTNESS dazzling or uncomfortable brightness ○ *a screen on the monitor to reduce glare* **3.** MEDIA SPOTLIGHT excessive attention from the media **4.** GAUDY ORNAMENTATION gaudy coloration or decoration [13C. < Middle Low German *glaren* "gleam"]

glare[2] /gler/ *n* METEOROL same as **black ice** ■ *adj* having a smooth and slippery surface [Mid-16C. Origin ?]

glare ice *n* METEOROL same as **black ice**

glar·ing /glérring/ *adj* **1.** OBVIOUS easily perceived or detected ○ *a report full of glaring mistakes* **2.** ANGRY expressing anger, disapproval, contempt, or another negative emotion ○ *a glaring look of sheer contempt* **3.** UNPLEASANTLY BRIGHT intensely or dazzlingly bright **4.** GARISH gaudy or brash, especially in a tasteless way ○ *painted in glaring oranges and greens* —**glar·ing·ly** *adv* —**glar·ing·ness** *n*

glar·y /glérree/ (**-i·er, -i·est**) *adj* **1.** staring steadily and often angrily ○ *glary eyes* **2.** dazzlingly or uncomfortably bright ○ *a glary computer screen*

Glas·gow /glásskō, glássgō, gláz-/ **1.** city on the Clyde River, southwestern Scotland. An industrial and commercial center, it has a cathedral and three universities. Population: 606,651 (2001). **2.** city in southern Kentucky, northeast of Barren River Lake, east of Bowling Green and near Mammoth Cave National Park. Population: 13,434 (2002 estimate).

Glas·gow /gláskō/, **Ellen** (1873–1945) US writer. Her novels critically examined the problems of the South. She won a Pulitzer Prize for *In This Our Life* (1941). Full name **Glasgow, Ellen Anderson Gholson**

> "The war wasn't the worst thing...The worst thing is this sense of having lost our way in the universe. The worst thing is that the war has made peace seem so futile. It is just as if the bottom had dropped out of idealism."
>
> [Ellen Glasgow, *They Stooped to Folly*; 1929]

Glas·gow co·ma scale *n* a system for assessing the severity of brain impairment in somebody with a brain injury using the sum of scores given for eye opening, verbal, and motor responses. A high score of 15 indicates no impairment and a score of eight or less indicates severe impairment.

glas·nost /glaáz nōst, -nòst/ *n* a policy that commits a government or organization to greater accountability, openness, discussion, and freer disclosure of information than previously, especially that of Mikhail Gorbachev in the former Soviet Union [Late 20C. < Russian, "publicness"]

glass /glass/ *n* **1.** TRANSPARENT SOLID SUBSTANCE a hard, usually transparent substance that shatters easily. Source: sand melted in combination with other oxides such as lime or soda. Use: windows, bottles, lenses. **2.** UNCRYSTALLIZED SUBSTANCE LIKE GLASS a solid substance similar to glass formed by melting and cooling without crystallizing **3.** GLASS CONTAINER a container without a handle made from glass, for drinking from **4.** QUANTITY IN GLASS the amount a drinking glass holds **5.** GARDENING PROTECTING COVER a glass cover, greenhouse window, or insulating material used to protect germinating plants ○ *Keep the seedlings under glass for the first four weeks.* **6.** HOUSEHOLD same as **glassware** **7.** HOUSEHOLD same as **looking glass** **8.** OPTICS same as **magnifying glass** **9.** GEOL same as **volcanic glass** **10.** DRUGS ILLEGAL DRUG a smokable form of methamphetamine used as an illegal drug **11.** METEOROL same as **barometer** (*dated*) ■ **glass·es** *npl* **1.** OUTER EYEWEAR a pair of sight-correcting or protective lenses set in frames that fit over the ears and sit on the bridge of the nose **2.** same as **binoculars** ■ *vt* (**glassed, glass·ing, glass·es**) **1.** PUT GLASS OVER SOMETHING to cover or fit something with glass ○ *glassed the porch* **2.** INSERT INTO GLASS CONTAINER to put something into a glass container or one made of a material resembling glass ○ *glassed the specimens in formalin* [Old English *glæs* < Germanic] —**glass** *adj* —**glass·ful** *n* —**glass·like** *adj*

AKG London

Philip Glass

Glass /glass/, **Philip** (*b.* 1937) US composer. He is known for his minimalist compositions, including the opera *Einstein on the Beach* (1976).

glass blow·ing *n* the forming or shaping of a glass object by blowing air through a tube into a mass of semimolten glass —**glass blow·er** *n*

glass ceil·ing *n* an unofficial but real impediment to somebody's advancement into upper-level management positions because of discrimination based on the person's gender, age, race, ethnicity, or sexual preference

glass chin *n* BOXING same as **glass jaw** (*informal*)

glass cloth *n* a polishing cloth with fine particles of glass in it

glass cut·ter *n* **1.** a tool used to cut glass or to etch designs into glass **2.** somebody whose job is to cut glass or to make cut glass

glassed-in /glást-/ *adj* made using glass panes ○ *a glassed-in Florida room*

glass eel *n* a larval form of the American or European eel with a flattened transparent body. Native to: Atlantic Ocean.

glass eye *n* an artificial eye made from glass, or material similar to glass, so as to resemble a natural eye

glass fi·ber *n* INDUST same as **fiberglass** (sense 2)

glass·fish /gláss fish/ (*plural same* or **-fish·es**) *n* **1.** a small, almost transparent tropical fish often kept in aquariums. Genus: *Chanda.* **2.** a slender, almost transparent ocean fish eaten as a delicacy in Japan. Native to: northwestern Pacific. Latin name: *Salangichthys microdon.*

glass har·mon·i·ca *n* a set of drinking glasses or glass bowls, filled to graduated levels with water, that produce sounds of different pitches when their rims are rubbed with a moist finger. It was popular as a musical instrument in the 18th century, when various mechanical versions also existed.

glass·house /gláss hòwss/ (*plural* **-hous·es** /-hòwzəz/) *n* **1.** a public position that brings somebody a high level of media attention and scrutiny **2.** INDUST same as **glassworks 3.** *UK* GARDENING same as **greenhouse** (sense 1)

glass·ine /gla séen/ *n* a transparent paper treated with a glaze to make it greaseproof and resistant to the passage of air. Use: book jackets, food packaging.

glass jaw *n* in boxing, a jaw that is highly vulnerable to an opponent's punches (*informal*)

glass·mak·er /gláss màykər/ *n* somebody whose job is to make glass —**glass·mak·ing** *n*

glass snake *n* a limbless lizard, or one with vestigial limbs, that can snap off its tail as a defense mechanism to confuse predators. Native to: Europe, Asia, North America. Genus: *Ophisaurus.* [< its brittle tail]

glass·ware /gláss wèr/ *n* objects made of glass considered as a group

glass wool *n* fine-spun glass fibers formed into a woolly mass. Use: insulation, in air filters, in the manufacture of fiberglass.

glass·work /gláss wùrk/ *n* **1.** the technique or result of cutting and fitting glass, especially glass panes for windows and doors **2.** the production or manufacture of glass or glass objects **3.** HOUSEHOLD same as **glassware** —**glass·work·er** *n*

glass·works /gláss wùrks/ (*plural same*) *n* a factory for the manufacture of glass or glass objects

glass·wort /gláss wùrt, -wàwrt/ (*plural same* or **-worts**) *n* a plant with fleshy stems and small leaves that was formerly a source of the soda used in making glass. Native to: salt marshes. Genus: *Salicornia.*

glass·y /glássee/ (**-i·er, -i·est**) *adj* **1.** SMOOTH AND SLIPPERY having a highly smooth, slippery, and often reflective surface **2.** LIKE GLASS resembling glass in being smooth, reflective, or transparent **3.** BLANKLY EXPRESSIONLESS lacking expression or animation ○ *a blank glassy look* —**glass·i·ly** *adv* —**glass·i·ness** *n*

glass·y-eyed *adj* having a blank staring expression

Glas·ton·bur·y /glástən bèrree/ historic market town in Somerset, southwestern England. The site of a 10th-century abbey and an Iron Age lake village, it also hosts an annual music festival. Population: 8,100 (1993 estimate).

Glas·we·gian /glass wéejən, glaz-/ *n* somebody who comes from Glasgow, Scotland [Early 19C. < GLASGOW, after NORWEGIAN] —**Glas·we·gian** *adj*

Glau·ber's salt /glówbərz-, gláw-/, **Glau·ber salt** /glówbər-, gláw-/ *n* a colorless crystalline sodium sulfate. Use: in solar energy systems, manufacture of dyes, glass, and paper, laxative. [Mid-18C. After Johann Rudolf *Glauber* (1604–68), German chemist]

glau·co·ma /glaw kṓmə/ *n* an eye disorder marked by unusually high pressure within the eyeball that leads to damage of the optic disk [Mid-17C. Directly or via Latin < Greek *glaukōma* < *glaukos* "blue-gray, green"] —**glau·co·ma·tous** *adj*

glau·co·nite /gláwkə nìt/ *n* a green clay mineral containing iron and potassium. Use: fertilizer. [Mid-19C. < German *Glaukonit* < Greek *glaukos* "blue-gray, green"] —**glau·co·nit·ic** /glàwkə níttik/ *adj*

glau·cous /gláwkəss/ *adj* **1.** describes plants or fruit that are covered in a grayish, whitish, or bluish waxy or powdery substance **2.** of a dull grayish green or blue color [Late 17C. < Latin *glaucus* "blue-gray, green" < Greek *glaukos*]

glaze /glayz/ *v* (**glazed, glaz·ing, glaz·es**) **1.** *vt* CERAMICS COVER POTTERY WITH FINISH LIKE GLASS to put a clear or colored coating on a ceramic object and fire it in a kiln, in order to fix the coloration, make it watertight, or give it a shiny appearance **2.** *vt* COOK COAT FOOD WITH MILK OR EGG to brush food with milk, egg, or sugar before baking in order to produce a shiny brown finish **3.** *vt* ART COAT OIL PAINTING to give something, especially an oil painting, a transparent or semitransparent coating in order to enhance or slightly alter the color tones **4.** *vt* COVERINGS GIVE PROTECTIVE COVERING TO SOMETHING to place a protective or decorative coating on something, especially a natural material such as leather, cotton, or paper **5.** *vti* MAKE OR BECOME GLASSY to become unfocused and expressionless as a result of loss of interest, distraction, or tiredness, or cause the eyes to become like this **6.** *vt* METEOROL COVER SOMETHING WITH ICE to cause a thin layer of ice to form on something **7.** *vt* CONSTR FIT SOMETHING WITH GLASS to fit glass into or over something, especially a window, door, or picture ■ *n* **1.** CERAMICS COVERING RESEMBLING GLASS a shiny, smooth, transparent, or colored glassy coating on a ceramic object, produced by firing the treated object in a kiln, or the substance or process employed to achieve this **2.** COOK COATING FOR FOOD a shiny brown finish on food or the substance used for achieving this effect **3.** ART COATING FOR OIL PAINTING a transparent or semitransparent coating on something, especially an oil painting, used to enhance or slightly alter the color tones, or the substance used to achieve this effect **4.** COVERINGS PROTECTIVE COVERING a protective or decorative coating on something, especially a natural material such as leather, cotton, or paper, or the substance used for making this kind of coating **5.** METEOROL LAYER OF ICE a thin coating of ice formed when rain or moisture in the air comes into contact with a surface that is cold enough to cause it to freeze [14C. < GLASS, after GRAZE[1], GRASS] —**glaz·er** *n*

glaze over *vi* to become unfocused and expressionless as a result of loss of interest, distraction, or tiredness (*refers to eyes*) ○ *Her eyes glazed over as the sedative began to take effect.*

glazed /glayzd/ *adj* **1.** APPEARING UNINTERESTED OR DISTRACTED showing that you are not at all interested or that you are distracted or tired ○ *sat with a glazed expression trying to stay awake* **2.** WITH SHINY COATING covered with a clear shiny protective or decorative coating **3.** FITTED WITH GLASS fitted with or covered with glass

glaze ice, glazed frost *n UK* METEOROL same as **glaze** *n* (sense 5)

gla·zier /gláyzhər/ *n* somebody whose job is to install glass, especially in windows and doors

glaz·ing /gláyzing/ *n* **1.** HARD SHINY COATING the glaze coating on an object **2.** COVERING OF SOMETHING WITH GLAZE an act or the process of putting a glaze on something **3.** GLASS FOR WINDOW glass in general, especially the type of glass used in doors or windows or glass that has been installed in windows or doors **4.** INSTALLATION OF GLASS an act or the process of installing glass

GLBT *abbr* gay, lesbian, bisexual, or transgender

gleam /gleem/ *vi* (**gleamed, gleam·ing, gleams**) **1.** SHINE BRIGHTLY to shine brightly and continuously **2.** FLASH FOR SHORT TIME to flash, flicker, or appear briefly or indistinctly ■ *n* **1.** BRIGHT SHINE a steady bright shine **2.** FLASH OF LIGHT a beam of light, especially one that is reflected, dim, or coming from an indistinct source **3.** BRIEF SHOW a slight or momentary indication of something ○ *a gleam of interest* [Old English *glǣm* < Germanic] —**gleam·er** *n* ◇ **a gleam in somebody's eye** something at the very earliest stage of planning or development

gleam·ing /gléeming/ *adj* shining, especially with health, cleanliness, or newness ○ *gleaming black hair* —**gleam·ing·ly** *adv*

glean /gleen/ (**gleaned, glean·ing, gleans**) *v* **1.** *vt* to obtain information in small amounts over a period of time **2.** *vti* to go over a field or area that has just been harvested and gather by hand any usable parts of the crop that remain [14C. Via Old French *glener* < late Latin *glennare* < Celtic] —**glean·er** *n*

glean·ings /gléeningz/ *npl* **1.** objects or ideas that have been gathered or amassed over a period of time, especially when they form a collection or comprehensive whole **2.** the usable parts of a crop that are left behind in a harvested field or area and can be gathered in by hand

gle·ba /gléebə/ (*plural* **-bae** /glée bee/) *n* a mass of tissue in which spores are formed in the fruiting bodies of fungi such as truffles and puffballs [Mid-19C. < Latin, "clod"]

glebe /gleeb/ *n* **1.** *UK* in the United Kingdom, a piece of land belonging to a church and lent temporarily to a member of the clergy to provide additional income **2.** land or soil, especially when considered as a source of abundant natural produce (*literary*) [14C. < Latin *gleba* "clod"]

glee /glee/ *n* **1.** GREAT DELIGHT joyful or animated delight **2.** GLOATINGLY JUBILANT FEELING jubilant and often smug pleasure, especially as a result of somebody else's bad luck or failure **3.** MUSIC SONG FOR UNACCOMPANIED VOICES a part song for three or more unaccompanied voices, usually men's, of a type that first became popular in England in the 18th century [Old English *glēo* < Germanic, "merriment"] —**glee·ful** *adj*

glee club *n* a group of people who get together to sing, especially short part songs

~~**gleeming**~~ incorrect spelling of **gleaming**

gleet /gleet/ *n* **1.** inflammation of the urethra, accompanied by a discharge of pus and mucus, and characteristic of a late stage in the development of gonorrhea **2.** a discharge of pus and mucus in a late stage of gonorrhea [14C. < Old French *glette* "slime" < Latin *glittus* "sticky"]

glei *n* GEOL another spelling of **gley**

Gleich·schal·tung /glík shaal tung/ *n* the forced standardization and complete suppression of all opposition in the political, social, and economic life and institutions of a country by an oppressive government or regime [Mid-20C. < German]

Gleizes /glez/, **Albert Leon** (1881–1953) French artist. He cowrote an influential defense of cubism with Jean Metzinger, *Du Cubisme* (1912). He was an important figure in the cubist movement and founded an artists' community in southeastern France in 1927.

glen /glen/ *n* a long narrow valley [15C. < Scottish Gaelic *gleann*]

Glen·coe /glèn kṓ/ mountain pass in the Scottish Highlands where, in 1692, Campbell soldiers massacred 38 men of the MacDonald clan. Length: 5 mi./8 km.

Glen Cove /glèn kṓv/ city on the northern shore of Long Island, southeastern New York State. Population: 26,886 (2002 estimate).

Glen·dale /glén dàyl/ **1.** city in Los Angeles County, southwestern California, directly north of Los Angeles. Population: 199,430 (2002 estimate). **2.** city in central Arizona, a western suburb of Phoenix. Population: 230,564 (2002 estimate).

Glen·dale Heights village in northeastern Illinois, north of Wheaton, a western suburb of Chicago. Population: 32,953 (2002 estimate).

Glen·do·ra /glen dáwrə/ city in Los Angeles County, southwestern California, 17 mi./27 km northeast of Los Angeles. Population: 50,567 (2002 estimate).

Glen El·lyn /glèn éllin/ village in northeastern Illinois, a western suburb of Chicago. Population: 27,187 (2002 estimate).

glen·gar·ry /glen gárree/ (*plural* **-ries**) *n* a small brimless hat with a crown creased from front to back and usually a pair of ribbons hanging from the back, sometimes worn as part of Scottish highland dress. It also forms part of the uniform of some Scottish regiments. See illustration on next page [Mid-19C. After *Glengarry*, a valley in northern Scotland]

Glenn /glen/, **John** (*b.* 1921) US astronaut and senator. He was the first US astronaut to orbit Earth (1962), and the oldest astronaut ever to go into space (1998).

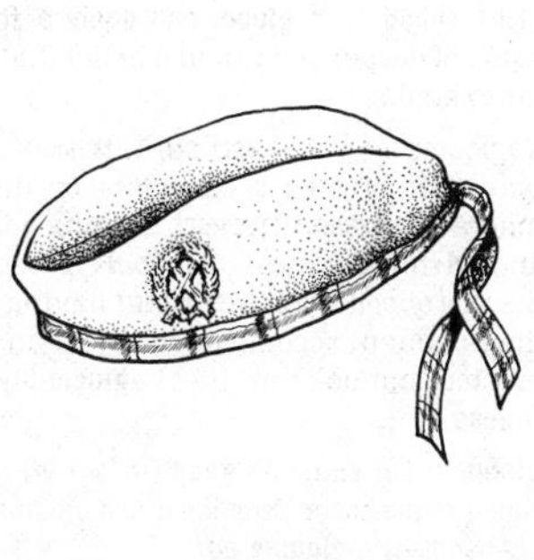

glengarry

John Glenn

He was a Democratic US senator from Ohio (1974–99). Full name **Glenn, John Herschel, Jr.**

gle·noid /glé nòyd, glée-/ *adj* **1.** shaped like a small shallow cup or socket **2.** relating to the cup-shaped socket in the shoulder that holds the head of the humerus [Early 18C. < French *glénoïde* < Greek *glēnē* "eyeball, socket"]

Glens Falls /glènz-/ city in Warren County, eastern New York, situated at a waterfall on the Hudson River, 38 mi./61 km northeast of Amsterdam. Population: 14,194 (2002 estimate).

Glen·view /glen vyoō, glén vyoō/ village on the Chicago River in northeastern Illinois, northwest of Skokie. It is a northern suburb of Chicago. Population: 44,042 (2002 estimate).

gley /glay/, **glei** *n* a sticky bluish gray clay soil or soil layer that forms in heavily waterlogged areas [Early 20C. < Ukrainian *glei*]

gli·a /glī́ ə, glée ə/ *n Can, UK* ANAT the network of supporting tissue and fibers that nourishes nerve cells within the brain and spinal cord. It comprises several layers of cells and makes up about 40 percent of the total volume of nerve tissue. US term **neuroglia** [Late 19C. < Greek, "glue"] —**gli·al** *adj*

gli·a·din /glī́ ə din/, **gli·a·dine** /-deen, -din/ *n* a simple cereal protein, e.g., from wheat or rye [Mid-19C. < French *gliadine* < Greek *glia* "glue"]

glib /glib/ *adj* **1. SLICK** fluent in a superficial or insincere way ○ *a glib talker* **2. SUPERFICIAL** shallow and lacking thought or preparation ○ *a glib generalization* **3. CASUAL AND RELAXED** easy, unconcerned, and informal in attitude ○ *a glib smile* [Late 16C. Origin ?] —**glib·ly** *adv* —**glib·ness** *n*

gli·ben·cla·mide /gli bénklə mīd/ *n UK* PHARM same as **glyburide**

glide /glīd/ *v* (**glid·ed, glid·ing, glides**) **1.** *vti* **MOVE SMOOTHLY** to move in a smooth, effortless, and often graceful way, or cause something to move in this way ○ *seals gliding through the water* **2.** *vi* **CHANGE STATE SMOOTHLY** to pass smoothly, slowly, or gradually into a particular state ○ *gliding in and out of consciousness* **3.** *vti* AVIAT **LAND WITHOUT USING ENGINE** to bring an aircraft in to land without using engine power, or land without using the engine **4.** *vi* MUSIC **USE PORTAMENTO** in music, to slide from one note to another **5.** *vi* PHON **MAKE INTERMEDIATE SPEECH SOUND** to produce an intrusive speech sound when moving from one point of articulation to the next ■ *n* **1. SMOOTH MOVEMENT** a smooth, effortless, and often graceful movement **2.** DANCE **SMOOTH FLOWING DANCE** a dance with a smooth flowing movement **3.** DANCE **DANCE STEP** a smoothly flowing dance step **4.** AVIAT **LANDING WITHOUT USING ENGINE** a controlled aircraft descent using no engine power **5.** GEOG **SLOW-MOVING WATER** a stretch of calm, slowly flowing water in a river or large stream **6.** MUSIC same as **portamento 7.** MUSIC **EXTENSION FOR TROMBONE** a piece of metal tubing used to extend the length of a trombone so that lower notes can be produced **8.** PHON **INTERMEDIATE SPEECH SOUND** an intrusive speech sound produced when a speaker is moving from one point of articulation to the next, e.g., the "w" sound in the middle of "going" **9.** PHON same as **semivowel 10.** FURNITURE **METAL DISK ON FURNITURE** a metal or plastic disk affixed to the bottom of the leg of a piece of furniture, to facilitate moving it across the floor **11.** FURNITURE **TRACK FOR DRAWER** a track along which a drawer can be slid in or out easily [Old English *glīdan* < Germanic]

glide path *n* the prescribed descent of an aircraft coming in to land that is shown to the pilot by means of a radio beam and acts as an aid to navigation

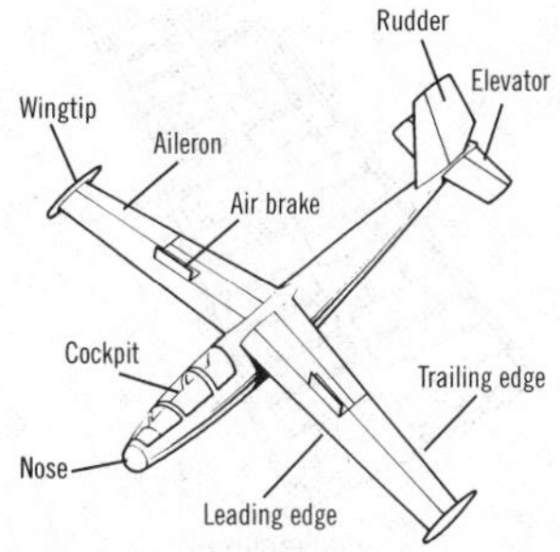

glider

glid·er /glī́dər/ *n* **1.** AVIAT **AIRCRAFT WITH NO ENGINE** an aircraft without an engine that flies by riding air currents. It becomes airborne by being towed up by an airplane or by being catapulted into the air from the ground. **2.** FURNITURE **TYPE OF ROCKING CHAIR** a type of rocking chair in which the rockers move on a stationary base beneath the chair **3. PORCH SWING** a porch swing hung from an upright framework instead of from the ceiling

glide slope *n* AVIAT same as **glide path**

glid·ing *n* the activity of flying a glider

glim·mer /glímmər/ *vi* (**-mered, -mer·ing, -mers**) **1. EMIT DIM GLOW** to emit a faint or intermittent light **2. BE PRESENT TO SMALL EXTENT** to be present faintly or in only a small amount ○ *Hope still glimmered in their hearts.* ■ *n* **1. FAINT FLASHING LIGHT** a faint or intermittent glowing light ○ *a glimmer of campfires in the distance* **2. SMALL AMOUNT OF SOMETHING** a faint sign or small amount of something ○ *a glimmer of interest* [15C. Probably < N Germanic]

glim·mer·ing /glímməring/ *n* same as **glimmer** *n* (sense 2) ■ *adj* emitting a faint or intermittent light

glimpse /glimps/ *n* **1. BRIEF LOOK** a quick or incomplete look or sighting of somebody or something ○ *I just caught a glimpse of her face in the crowd.* **2. SMALL INDICATION** a small, brief, or indistinct indication or appearance of something ■ *v* (**glimpsed, glimps·ing, glimps·es**) **1.** *vt* **SEE SOMETHING OR SOMEBODY BRIEFLY** to catch sight of somebody or something briefly or incompletely **2.** *vi* **TAKE BRIEF LOOK** to have a quick or incomplete look at or through something [14C. Ultimately < Germanic]

glint /glint/ *vi* (**glint·ed, glint·ing, glints**) **FLASH BRIEFLY** to gleam or flash, especially brightly or momentarily ○ *Anger glinted in her eyes.* ■ *n* **1. BRIEF FLASH** a slight or momentary gleam or flash ○ *a glint of daylight through the curtains* **2. SLIGHT INDICATION** a slight indication of something ○ *a glint of humor in his eyes* **3. SHININESS** a shiny or glossy appearance [15C. Probably alteration of *glent* "to gleam" < N Germanic]

gli·o·ma /glī ṓmə/ (*plural* **-mas** or **-ma·ta** /-mətə/) *n* a tumor composed of connective tissue (**neuroglia**) of the nervous system and affecting the brain or spinal cord [Late 19C. < Greek *glia* "glue"] —**gli·o·ma·tous** *adj*

glis·sade /gli saád/ *n* **1.** a gliding ballet step in which one foot slides forward, backward, or to one side **2.** a controlled slide down a snowy slope made without skis by somebody in a standing or crouching position [Mid-19C. < French < Old French *glisser* "to slide" < Old Dutch *glissen*] —**glis·sade** *vi* —**glis·sad·er** *n*

glis·san·do /gli sándō/ (*plural* **-di** /-dee/ or **-dos**) *n* **1.** an act of sliding a finger or thumb up or down a keyboard or harp strings from one note to another **2.** an act of sliding a finger along a stringed instrument's fingerboard or slowly moving a trombone's slide in and out to create a smooth change in pitch between two notes [Late 19C. < Italian < Old French *glisser* (see GLISSADE)]

glis·ten /glíss'n/ (**-tened, -ten·ing, -tens**) *vi* **1.** to shine brightly or reflect light from a wet surface ○ *leaves glistening after the rain* **2.** to have a glossy sheen (*refers to hair or an animal's pelt*) [Old English *glisnian* < Germanic] —**glis·ten** *n*

glis·ter /glístər/ (**-tered, -ter·ing, -ters**) *vi* to glitter brightly (*archaic*) [14C. Probably < Middle Low German *glistern*]

glitch /glich/ *n* **1.** a minor hitch or technical problem ○ *glitches in the software* **2.** a sudden unwanted electronic signal, e.g., from a power surge or a temporary irregular supply of power [Mid-20C. Probably < Yiddish *glitsh* "slip" < Old High German *glītan* "to glide"] —**glitch·y** *adj*

glit·ter /glíttər/ *vi* (**-tered, -ter·ing, -ters**) **1. SPARKLE** to sparkle or shimmer brightly ○ *an evening gown glittering with sequins* **2. SHINE WITH EMOTION** to look bright or expressive with an emotion such as anger or love (*refers to eyes*) **3. BE VIVACIOUS** to exhibit liveliness and charm ○ *a radiant personality who glittered at every event she attended* **4. BE FULL OF GLAMOR** to be characterized by the presence of somebody or something glamorous ○ *The event glittered with Hollywood stars.* ■ *n* **1. SPARKLY DECORATION** small pieces of reflective material, e.g., on a greeting card or in eye makeup **2. SPARKLING LIGHT** bright sparkling light **3. GLAMOUR** dazzling glamour ○ *the glitter of a command performance at the opera* **4.** *Can* METEOROL same as **glaze** *n* (sense 5) [14C. < Old Norse *glitra*] —**glit·ter·ing·ly** *adj* —**glit·ter·y** *adj*

glit·te·ra·ti /glìttə raátee/ *npl* famous, rich, or fashionable people thought of as a group, especially those who are frequently photographed by the media (*informal*) [Mid-20C. Blend of GLITTER + LITERATI]

glit·ter·ing *adj* **1. SPARKLING** reflecting light in bright sparkling flashes ○ *glittering diamonds* **2. GLAMOROUS** attended by many people who are glamorous or famous ○ *a glittering event* **3. SUCCESSFUL** involving outstanding successes or achievements ○ *a glittering career*

glitz /glits/ *n* **1.** glamour, especially that associated with show business or celebrities **2.** extravagant and often tasteless display, especially of wealth [Late 20C. Back-formation < GLITZY]

glitz·y /glítsee/ (**-i·er, -i·est**) *adj* **1.** glamorous, especially in relation to show business or celebrities **2.** extravagant and often tasteless, especially in the display of wealth [Mid-20C. Probably < German *glitzern* "to glitter"] —**glitz·i·ly** *adv* —**glitz·i·ness** *n*

Gli·wi·ce /gli veétsə, glee-/ industrial city in Katowice Province, southern Poland, west of the city of Katowice. Population: 212,800 (1997).

gloam·ing /glṓming/ *n* the period of fading light after sunset but before dark (*literary*) [Old English *glōmung* < *glōm* "twilight" < Germanic]

gloat /glōt/ (**gloat·ed, gloat·ing, gloats**) *vi* to feel or express smug self-satisfaction about something such as an achievement, a possession, or somebody else's misfortune [Late 16C. Origin ?] —**gloat** *n* —**gloat·er** *n* —**gloat·ing·ly** *adv*

glob /glob/ *n* a small amount of a soft or semiliquid substance (*informal*) [14C. Origin ?] —**glob·by** *adj*

glob·al /glṓb'l/ *adj* **1. WORLDWIDE** relating to or happening throughout the whole world **2. OVERALL** taking all the different aspects of a situation into account **3. SPHERICAL** shaped like a globe or sphere **4.** COMPUT **RELATING TO WHOLE OF SYSTEM** covering or affecting the whole of a computer system, program, or file — **glob·al·ly** *adv*

glob·al e·con·o·my *n* the interdependent economies of the world's nations, regarded as a single economic system ○ *Decisions taken at the meeting were significant not only for the region but for the global economy.*

glob·al·ism /glṓb'l ìzzəm/ *n* the belief or advocacy that political policies should take worldwide issues into account before focusing on national or state concerns —**glob·al·ist** *n*

glob·al·ize /glṓb'l ìz/ (**-ized, -iz·ing, -iz·es**) *vti* **1.** to become adopted on a global scale, or cause something, especially social institutions, to become adopted on a global scale **2.** to become international or start operating at the international level, or cause something, especially a business or company, to become international —**glob·al·i·za·tion** /glṓb'li záysh'n/ *n* —**glob·al·iz·er** *n*

glob·al vil·lage *n* the whole world considered as a single community served by electronic media and information technology

glob·al warm·ing *n* an increase in the world's temperatures, believed to be caused in part by the greenhouse effect

globe /glōb/ *n* **1.** MAP OF EARTH ON SPHERE a hollow sphere representing the Earth and illustrated with the continents, seas, and islands, especially one showing and labeling the countries **2.** EARTH the planet Earth **3.** HOLLOW SPHERICAL OBJECT a rounded hollow object, especially one made of glass, e.g., a cover for a lamp, or a goldfish bowl **4.** PART OF MONARCH'S REGALIA a hollow sphere, usually made of gold or another precious metal, that forms part of a monarch's regalia and symbolizes the power or sovereignty of the ruler **5.** *Can, S Africa* same as **light bulb** ■ *vti* (**globed, glob·ing, globes**) FORM INTO GLOBE to form a globe, or cause something to form a globe [Mid-16C. Directly or via Old French < Latin *globus* "ball, sphere"] —**glo·boid** *adj, n*

globe am·a·ranth *n* an ornamental garden plant with colorful whorls of leaves and flower heads made up of several distinct blossoms. Latin name: *Gomphrena globosa.*

globe ar·ti·choke *n* PLANTS, FOOD same as **artichoke** (senses 1–2)

globe·fish /glṓb fish/ (*plural same* or **-fish·es**) *n* FISH **1.** same as **puffer** (sense 2) **2.** same as **porcupine fish** [< its shape when inflated]

globe·flow·er /glṓb flòwr/ *n* a poisonous plant with ball-shaped flowers, consisting of large white, pale yellow, or orange sepals that almost entirely enclose the smaller petals. Genus: *Trollius.*

globe this·tle *n* a plant with jagged-edged leaves. Flowers: large white, bluish, ball-shaped. Native to: Asia, Mediterranean. Genus: *Echinops.*

globe·trot /glṓb tròt/ (**-trot·ted, -trot·ting, -trots**) *vi* to travel frequently and to a great variety of distant destinations —**globe·trot·ter** *n*

glo·big·er·i·na /glō bìjjə rī́nə, -reénə/ (*plural* **-nas** or **-nae** /-neé/) *n* a marine protozoan with a spiny rounded spiral shell. Genus: *Globigerina.* [Mid-19C. < modern Latin < Latin *globus* "ball, sphere" + *gerere* "carry"] —**glo·big·er·i·nal** *adj*

glo·big·er·i·na ooze *n* a deposit on the ocean floor that consists of globigerina shells and is found almost worldwide

glo·bin /glṓbin/ *n* the protein component of hemoglobin [Late 19C. Shortening of HEMOGLOBIN]

glo·boid /glṓ bòyd/ *adj* shaped like a ball ■ *n* a ball-shaped part, especially one found in plant granules

glo·bose /glṓbōss/, **glo·bous** /glṓbəss/ *adj* BIOL same as **globoid** [15C. < Latin *globosus* < *globus* "ball, sphere"] — **glo·bose·ly** *adv* —**glo·bos·i·ty** /glō bóssətee/ *n*

glob·u·lar /glóbbyələr/ *adj* **1.** having the shape of a ball **2.** containing or consisting of globules [Mid-17C. < Latin *globolus* (see GLOBULE)] —**glob·u·lar·i·ty** /glòbbyə lérrətee/ *n* —**glob·u·lar·ly** *adv*

glob·u·lar clus·ter *n* an approximately spherical cluster of densely packed stars, located within a spherical halo around the Milky Way galaxy

glob·ule /glóbbyool/ *n* a small ball-shaped object, especially one that is liquid or semiliquid [Mid-17C. Via French < Latin *globulus* "little globe" < *globus* "ball, sphere"]

glob·u·lif·er·ous /glòbbyə líffərəss/ *adj* composed of, containing, or producing globules

glob·u·lin /glóbbyəlin/ *n* a protein found in blood serum

glo·cal·iz·a·tion /glṑkə lī záyshən/ *n* the process of adapting an internationally sold product or service to different local cultures and markets [Late 20C. Blend of GLOBAL and LOCALIZATION]

glo·chid·i·um /glō kíddee əm/ (*plural* **-i·a** /-ee ə/) *n* **1.** *also* **glo·chid** /glṓkid/ a barbed hair or bristle that grows on plants such as the prickly pear or among the spores on ferns **2.** a parasitic larva of some mussels that has hooks or suckers used to attach itself to the fins or gills of fish. Family: Unionidae. [Late 19C. < modern Latin < Greek *glōkhis* "arrowhead"] — **glo·chid·i·al** *adj* —**glo·chid·i·ate** /glō kíddee ət/ *adj*

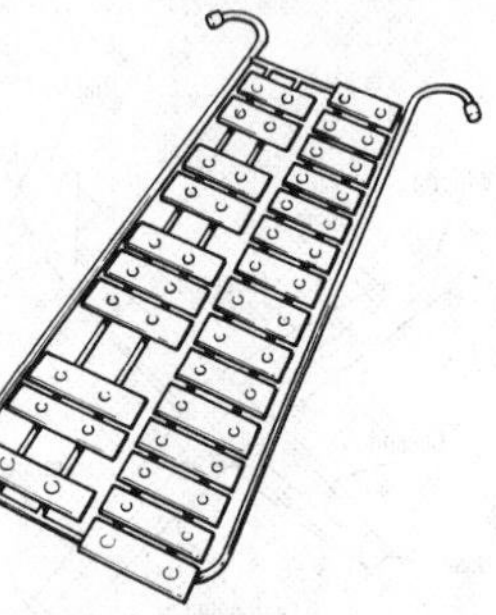

glockenspiel

glock·en·spiel /glókən speél, -shpeél/ *n* a percussion instrument consisting of a set of tuned metallic bars, played by striking the individual bars with small light hammers [Early 19C. < German, "bell-play"]

glogg /glog/ *n* a hot punch consisting of brandy, red wine, and sherry, and flavored with sugar, spices, fruit pieces, and blanched almonds. It was originally served in Scandinavia at Christmas. [Early 20C. < Swedish *glögg*]

glom /glom/ (**glommed, glom·ming, gloms**) *vi* (*slang*) **1.** to grab or seize hold of something ○ *businesspeople who glom any idea that has been floated by a management guru* **2.** to begin to understand or realize something ○ *Kids soon glom onto what's considered to be cool.* [Early 20C. Probably variant of Scottish English *glaum* "snatch at," origin ?]

glom·er·ate /glómmərət, -ràyt/ *adj* **1.** formed into a tight ball or cluster **2.** tightly wound together, like a ball of string [Late 18C. < Latin *glomerat-*, past participle of *glomerare* "make into a ball" < *glomus* "ball of thread"]

glom·er·ule /glómmə rool/ *n* **1.** a flat-topped flower head formed by a compact cluster of short-stalked flowers **2.** a cluster of spores formed into a ball shape [Late 18C. Via French < modern Latin *glomerulus* (see GLOMERULUS)] —**glo·mer·u·late** /glo mérrələt, glə-/ *adj*

glo·mer·u·li ANAT plural of **glomerulus**

glo·mer·ul·o·ne·phri·tis /glo mèrrəlō nə frī́təss, glə-/ *n* an inflammatory disease affecting the clusters of capillaries (**glomeruli**) in the cortex of a kidney

glo·mer·u·lus /glo mérryələss, glə-/ (*plural* **-li** /-lī/) *n* **1.** a tightly packed cluster of blood vessels, nerve fibers, or other cells **2.** a round cluster of interconnected capillaries found in the cortex of a kidney, which remove body waste to be excreted as urine —**glo·mer·u·lar** *adj* [Mid-19C. < modern Latin, "little ball" < Latin *glomus* "ball of thread"]

gloom /gloom/ *n* **1.** MURKY DARKNESS a state of darkness or partial darkness, especially one in which shadows or poor visibility create a cheerless or dispiriting atmosphere **2.** DESPONDENCY a feeling or atmosphere of despair, despondency, or misery ■ *v* (**gloomed, gloom·ing, glooms**) **1.** *vi* BE DESPONDENT to feel or look despondent or miserable **2.** *vti* MAKE OR BECOME DARK to become dark, or cause something to become dark [13C. Origin ?] ◇ **gloom and doom** a feeling or expression of despondency and a belief that disaster is about to strike

gloom·y /glóomee/ (**-i·er, -i·est**) *adj* **1.** MURKILY DARK dark in a way that creates a cheerless or dispiriting atmosphere **2.** OFFERING LITTLE HOPE causing a feeling of despair and hopelessness ○ *gloomy prospects* ○ *a gloomy scene of poverty* **3.** DESPONDENT having a feeling of sadness, often accompanied by a morbid or uninterested outlook on life —**gloom·i·ly** *adv* — **gloom·i·ness** *n*

gloop /gloop/ *n UK* same as **goop** (*informal*) [Late 20C. An imitation of the sound semiliquid material makes when poured or handled] —**gloop·y** *adj*

glop /glop/ *n* (*informal*) **1.** a soft lump or mixture of something, especially unappetizing food ○ *a glop of cold mashed potatoes* **2.** something that is considered to be overly sentimental or of little value, e.g., a piece of music or writing [Early 20C. An imitation of the sound semiliquid material makes when poured or handled] —**glop·py** *adj*

Glo·ri·a /gláwree ə/ *n* **1.** a hymn or set of words in Latin that begins with the word "Gloria" and is used in the Christian liturgy to praise God **2.** the words of the Gloria set to music [15C. < Latin, "glory"]

Glo·ri·a in Ex·cel·sis /-ek sélsiss, -eks chélsiss/ *n* **1.** a hymn or set of words in Latin that begins with the words "Gloria in Excelsis" and is used in the Christian liturgy to praise God **2.** the words of Gloria in Excelsis set to music [< Latin, "glory in the high places"]

Glo·ri·a Pa·tri /-paátree/ *n* **1.** a short hymn or set of words in Latin that begins with the words "Gloria Patri" and is used in the Christian liturgy to praise God **2.** the words of Gloria Patri set to music [< Latin, "glory to the father"]

glo·ri·fied /gláwrə fīd/ *adj* described in much more grandiose or fanciful terms than are warranted ○ *They call it an antique auction, but it's really just a glorified garage sale.*

glo·ri·fy /gláwrə fī/ (**-fied, -fy·ing, -fies**) *vt* **1.** MAKE SOMETHING APPEAR SUPERIOR to cause something to seem more pleasant, important, or desirable than is actually the case **2.** EXTOL SOMEBODY OR SOMETHING to praise somebody or something highly **3.** RELIG PRAISE DEITY to worship or offer praise to a deity —**glo·ri·fi·ca·tion** /glàwrəfi káysh'n/ *n* —**glo·ri·fi·er** *n*

glo·ri·ole /gláwree ōl/ *n* a halo around somebody's head [Mid-19C. Via French < Latin *gloriola* "little glory" < *gloria* "glory"]

glo·ri·o·sa /glàwree ṓssə/ (*plural* **-sas** or *same*) *n* a tropical climbing plant of the lily family, popular as a greenhouse plant. Flowers: large, yellow, orange, red. Genus: *Gloriosa.* [< modern Latin < Latin *gloriosus* (see GLORIOUS)]

glo·ri·ous /gláwree əss/ *adj* **1.** EXCEPTIONALLY LOVELY beautiful in a way that inspires wonder or joy ○ *glorious summer weather* **2.** OUTSTANDING so good or distinguished as to merit praise and lasting fame ○ *a glorious career* **3.** ENJOYABLE highly enjoyable [14C. Via Anglo-Norman, Old French < Latin *gloriosus* < *gloria* "glory"] —**glo·ri·ous·ly** *adv* —**glo·ri·ous·ness** *n*

Glo·ri·ous Rev·o·lu·tion *n* in England, the overthrow of King James II in 1688 that established the power of Parliament over the monarch

glo·ry /gláwree/ *n* (*plural* **-ries**) **1.** EXALTATION the fame, admiration, and honor that is given to somebody who does something important **2.** ACHIEVEMENT something that brings or confers admiration, praise, honor, or fame **3.** PRAISE OF DEITY praise and thanksgiving offered as an act of worship to a deity ○ *Glory to God in the highest.* **4.** AWESOME SPLENDOR majesty or splendor **5.** ASTOUNDING BEAUTY beauty that inspires feelings of wonder or joy ○ *the glory of a bright spring morning* **6.** HEAVEN the idealized beauty and bliss of heaven **7.** HALO a halo around somebody's head ■ *interj* EXPRESSING SURPRISE used to express great surprise, shock, dismay, or pleasure (*dated*) [13C. Via Anglo-Norman, Old French < Latin *gloria*] ◇ **glory be** used to express great surprise, shock, dismay, or pleasure (*dated*) ◇ **go to glory** to die (*dated*) ◇ **in your glory** in a state of great happiness, satisfaction, or triumph

glory in *vt* to derive great pride, pleasure, amusement, or satisfaction from something

glo·ry days *npl* the period of somebody's greatest achievement or happiness

glo·ry hole *n* **1.** a cupboard or small room used for storage, especially of rarely used objects, where they are often kept in a messy or disorganized way (*dated*) ○ *There's a box of old photographs somewhere in the glory hole.* **2.** a storage space below deck near the stern of a ship [Origin ?]

glo·ry-of-the-snow (*plural same* or **glo·ry-of-the-snows**) *n* a widely-cultivated, small bulbous plant of the lily family. Flowers: blue, early-blooming. Native to: eastern Mediterranean, western Asia. Latin name: *Chionodoxa luciliae*.

gloss[1] /glawss, gloss/ *n* **1.** SHININESS a shiny quality, especially on a smooth surface **2.** DECEPTIVE AND SUPERFICIAL ATTRACTIVENESS an attractive appearance that often conceals something unattractive or inferior **3.** CONSTR same as **gloss paint** ■ *vt* (**glossed, gloss·ing, gloss·es**) MAKE SOMETHING SHINY to apply a coating or gloss to a surface to make it shine [Mid-16C. Origin ?]

gloss over *vt* to intentionally leave out negative information, or treat something superficially, in order to make it appear more attractive or acceptable

gloss[2] /glawss, gloss/ *n* **1.** EXPLANATORY PHRASE a short definition, explanation, or translation of a word or phrase that may be unfamiliar to the reader, often located in a margin or collected in an appendix or glossary **2.** INTERPRETATION an interpretation or explanation of something ○ *Her account provides an interesting gloss on the theme of widowhood.* ■ *vt* (**glossed, gloss·ing, gloss·es**) **1.** EXPLAIN SOMETHING to give a short definition, explanation, or translation of a word or phrase that may be unfamiliar to the reader **2.** INSERT EXPLANATIONS IN TEXT to add or enter the necessary glosses in a manuscript or piece of writing **3.** GIVE MISLEADING EXPLANATION OF SOMETHING to interpret or explain something in a deliberately misleading or negative way [Mid-16C. Via French < Latin *glossa* "obscure word" < Greek *glōssa* "tongue, language, obscure word"]

glos·sa /gláwssə, glóssə/ (*plural* **-sae** /-ssee/ or **-sas**) *n* **1.** ANAT same as **tongue** (sense 1) (*technical*) **2.** a structure in the mouth of an insect that resembles a tongue [Late 19C. Via modern Latin < Greek *glōssa* "tongue, language, obscure word"] —**glos·sal** *adj*

glos·sa·ry /gláwssəree, glóss-/ (*plural* **-ries**) *n* an alphabetical collection of specialist terms and their meanings, usually in the form of an appendix to a book [14C. < Latin *glossarium* < *glossa* (see GLOSS[2])] —**glos·sar·i·al** /glaw sérree əl, glo-/ *adj* —**glos·sar·i·al·ly** *adv* —**glos·sa·rist** *n*

glos·sec·to·my /glaw séktəmee, glo-/ (*plural* **-mies**) *n* partial or total removal of the tongue by surgery [< Greek *glōssa* "tongue"]

glos·seme /gláw seem, gló-/ *n* the smallest meaningful unit of a language [Early 20C. < Greek *glōssema* "word requiring explanation" < *glōssa* "tongue, language, obscure word"]

glos·si·tis /glaw sítiss, glo-/ *n* inflammation of the tongue [Early 19C. < Greek *glōssa* "tongue"] —**glos·sit·ic** /glaw síttik, glo-/ *adj*

glos·so·la·li·a /glàwssō láylee ə, glòssō-/ *n* **1.** RELIG same as **speaking in tongues** **2.** nonsensical or invented speech, especially resulting from a trance or schizophrenia [Late 19C. < Greek *glōssa* "tongue, language, obscure word"]

glos·so·pha·ryn·ge·al /glàwssō fə rínjəl, -fàrrin jée əl, glòssō-/ *adj* relating to the tongue and pharynx [Early 19C. < Greek *glōssa* "tongue"]

glos·so·pha·ryn·ge·al nerve *n* either of the ninth pair of cranial nerves, which activate the muscles of the tongue, pharynx, and parotid gland

gloss paint *n* a paint that produces a smooth shiny durable surface

gloss·y /gláwssee, glóssee/ *adj* (**-i·er, -i·est**) **1.** SHINY AND SMOOTH having a smooth shiny surface or texture ○ *A glossy coat is the sign of a healthy animal.* **2.** SUPERFICIALLY STYLISH creating a superficial impression of wealth, beauty, or fashionable elegance (*informal*) ○ *a glossy lifestyle that conceals years of financial struggle* ■ *n* (*plural* **-ies**) PHOTO WITH SHINY FINISH a photograph printed on shiny smooth paper ○ *Please provide an 8 x 10 glossy.* —**gloss·i·ly** *adv* —**gloss·i·ness** *n*

gloss·y mag·a·zine *n UK* PUBL same as **slick** *n* (sense 3)

glot·tal /glótt'l/ *adj* **1.** relating to the glottis **2.** describes a speech sound that is produced by wholly or partially closing the glottis

glot·tal stop *n* a consonantal speech sound created by closing and then opening the glottis before a vowel, which produces a sudden audible release of air as in "uh oh!" between "uh" and "oh." In languages such as Arabic, glottal stops are part of the standard consonant system.

glot·tis /glóttiss/ (*plural* **-tis·es** or **-ti·des** /-ti deez/) *n* **1.** the long opening between the vocal cords at the upper part of a vertebrate's windpipe (**larynx**). The glottis is open during breathing but is closed by the epiglottis during swallowing. **2.** all of the anatomy of the larynx that is involved in producing the voice in a human or vertebrate animal [Late 16C. Via modern Latin < Greek < *glōtta*, variant of *glōssa* "tongue"]

Glouces·ter /glóstər/ **1.** cathedral city on the Severn River in Gloucestershire, west central England. Population: 109,885 (2001). **2.** resort city and port in northeastern Massachusetts, on the southeastern side of Cape Ann, on the Atlantic Ocean. Population: 30,664 (2002 estimate).

Glouces·ter·shire /glóstər sheer, -shər/ largely rural county in west central England, on the border with Wales. Area: 1,024 sq. mi./2,642 sq. km.

glove /gluv/ *n* **1.** SHAPED COVERING FOR HAND a shaped covering for the hand that includes five separated sections for the thumb and fingers, and extends to the wrist or the elbow **2.** SPORTS PROTECTION FOR HAND a padded protective covering for the hand worn in some sports **3.** CLOTHING same as **gauntlet**[1] ■ *vt* (**gloved, glov·ing, gloves**) PUT GLOVE ON SOMETHING to cover the hand with a glove, or cover an object with something that is like a glove ○ *Gloved and hatted, the children ventured out into the snow.* [Old English *glōf* < Germanic, "hand"] —**glove·less** *adj* ◇ **the gloves are off** used to indicate that a course of action is about to be pursued in a ruthless and uncompromisingly aggressive way ○ *The gloves are off in the political debate.*

glove box *n* **1.** AUTOMOT same as **glove compartment** **2.** a sealed container that allows radioactive or toxic substances to be handled safely using a pair of gloves attached to openings in its sides

glove com·part·ment *n* a small enclosed storage space in the dashboard of a vehicle

glove pup·pet *n Can, UK* a puppet that fits over the hand like a glove and is operated by the user's thumb and fingers. US term **hand puppet**

glow /glō/ *n* **1.** LIGHT FROM SOMETHING HOT a light produced by something that has been heated to a high temperature but is not in flames ○ *the glow of the embers in the grate* **2.** SOFT STEADY LIGHT a soft steady light, especially one without heat or flames ○ *the glow of the neon lights* **3.** SOFT REFLECTED LIGHT a soft warm reflected light ○ *the golden glow of the tapestries on the far wall* **4.** ROSINESS OF COMPLEXION a brightness or redness in somebody's complexion, e.g., because of exercise or good health ○ *the healthy glow that exercise gives you* **5.** REDNESS OF EMBARRASSMENT a redness of the face or complexion, especially one caused by embarrassment ○ *face suffused with a glow of shame* **6.** HAPPY FEELING a sense of happiness or well-being ○ *a warm glow of satisfaction* ■ *vi* (**glowed, glow·ing, glows**) **1.** EMIT LIGHT AND HEAT to emit light as a result of being extremely hot ○ *The embers of the fire still glowed in the grate.* **2.** EMIT SOFT STEADY LIGHT to emit a soft steady light without heat or flames ○ *the neon signs glowing red and blue* **3.** REFLECT LIGHT SOFTLY to emit a soft warm reflected light ○ *the walls glowing orange and gold in the afternoon sun* **4.** SHINE WITH HEALTH to show the bright eyes and smooth skin that are a sign of good health **5.** BE FLUSHED WITH EMBARRASSMENT to have blood rush to the face, especially because of embarrassment **6.** FEEL WARM AND CONTENTED to feel a pleasant warm sensation owing to happiness, satisfaction, or love ○ *The winners glowed with pride.* [Old English *glōwan* < Germanic]

glow·er /glówr/ *vi* (**-ered, -er·ing, -ers**) to look at somebody or something with sullen anger or strong resentment ■ *n* a sullen or resentful stare [15C. Origin ?] —**glow·er·ing** *adj* —**glow·er·ing·ly** *adv*

glow·ing /glṓ ing/ *adj* **1.** SHINING SOFTLY AND STEADILY emitting a soft steady light **2.** REDDISH GOLD rich, strong, or bright in color, especially when reddish or gold ○ *the glowing colors of autumn* **3.** FULL OF PRAISE praising somebody or something in very warm appreciative terms ○ *glowing reports of the performance* **4.** ROSY red or rosy as a result of excitement, well-being, or good health —**glow·ing·ly** *adv*

glow plug *n* a plug attached to a diesel engine that makes it easier to start in cold weather by warming it up

glow stick /glṓ stìk/ *n* LEISURE, SAFETY same as **lightstick**

glow·worm /glṓ wùrm/ *n* a larva of some types of firefly, or a beetle of a closely related family, that emits greenish light from organs in its abdomen. Families: Lampyridae or Phengodidae.

glox·in·i·a /glok sínnee ə/ *n* a popular house plant with large colorful bell-shaped flowers. Native to: tropical America. Genus: *Sinningia*. [Early 19C. After Benjamin P. *Gloxin*, 18C German botanist]

gloze /glōz/ (**glozed, gloz·ing, gloz·es**) *vt* to attempt to underplay or minimize something unpleasant or embarrassing ○ *tried to gloze over the scandalous story* [13C. < French *gloser* < *glose* "comment, gloss" < Latin *glossa* (see GLOSS[2])]

gluc- *prefix* same as **gluco-** (*used before vowels*)

glu·ca·gon /glóokə gòn/ *n* a pancreatic hormone that raises blood sugar by promoting conversion of glycogen to glucose in the liver [Early 20C. < GLUCO- + Greek *agōn*, present participle of *agein* "lead"]

gluco- *prefix* glucose ○ *glucocorticoid* [< GLUCOSE]

glu·co·cor·ti·coid /glòokō káwrti kòyd/ *n* a steroid hormone (**corticoid**) that influences carbohydrate metabolism. Use: treatment of inflammatory conditions.

glu·co·ne·o·gen·e·sis /glòokō nee ə jénnəssiss/ *n* the production of glucose, especially in the liver, from amino acids, fats, and other substances that are not carbohydrates —**glu·co·ne·o·ge·net·ic** /-nee əjə néttik/ *adj*

glu·co·sa·mine /gloo kóssəmin/ *n* **1.** an amino derivative of glucose that occurs naturally in supportive tissues and plant cell walls **2.** ALTERN MED, BIOCHEM same as **glucosamine sulfate** [Late 19C. < GLUCOSE]

glu·co·sa·mine sul·fate *n* a substance derived from the chitin of shellfish. Use: as a food supplement, as a treatment for arthritis and other joint disorders.

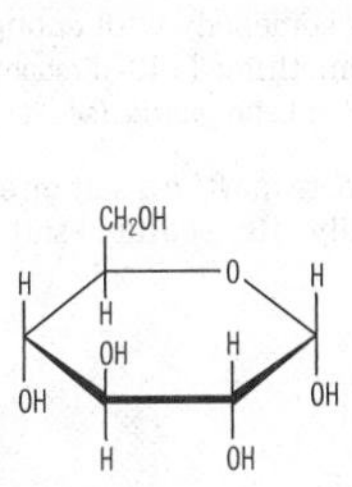

glucose

glu·cose /glóo kòss/ *n* **1.** a six-carbon monosaccharide produced in plants by photosynthesis and in animals by the metabolism of carbohydrates. The commonest form, dextrose, is used by all living organisms. Formula: $C_6H_{12}O_6$. **2.** a syrup containing dextrose, maltose, dextrin, and water that is obtained from starch. Use: food manufacture, alcoholic fermentation. [Mid-19C. Via French < Greek *gleukos* "sweet wine"] —**glu·co·sic** /gloo kóssik/ *adj*

glu·co·si·dase /gloo kóssi dàyss, -dàyz/ *n* an enzyme that splits glucose off glucosides

glu·co·side /glóokə sīd/ *n* a glycoside that yields glucose on hydrolysis —**glu·co·si·dal** /glóokə sīd'l/ *adj*—**glu·co·sid·ic** /-síddik/ *adj*—**glu·co·sid·i·cal·ly** *adv*

glu·co·su·ri·a /glòokō shóoree ə, -sóoree ə/ *n* MED same as **glycosuria** —**glu·co·su·ric** *adj*

glu·cu·ron·ic ac·id /glòokyoǒ rònnik-/ *n* an acid derived from glucose that is present in cartilage and detoxifies poisons [Early 20C. < GLUCO- + Greek *ouron* "urine"]

glue /gloo/ *n* **1. ANIMAL-BASED ADHESIVE** an adhesive substance obtained by boiling animal parts such as bones, hides, horns, and hooves **2. ADHESIVE** a natural or synthetic substance used as an adhesive **3. SOMETHING THAT UNITES PEOPLE** a unifying factor or influence ○ *Mutual love and understanding is the glue that holds this family together.* ■ *vt* (**glued, glu·ing, glues**) **1. STICK THINGS TOGETHER** to stick things together or reconstitute something using an adhesive substance ○ *It took hours to glue the vase back together.* **2. KEEP SOMEBODY STILL** to cause somebody to remain still, or cause somebody to give all his or her attention (*informal; usually passive*) ○ *eyes glued to the TV* [13C. Via French *glu* < Latin *gluten*] —**glue·like** *adj*—**glu·ey** *adj*—**glu·i·ly** *adv*—**glu·i·ness** *n*

glue-sniff·ing *n* the practice of inhaling the fumes from glues and volatile solvents in order to become intoxicated —**glue-sniff·er** *n*

glug /glug/ *n* **1.** a gurgling sound of a quantity of liquid being poured from a bottle or similar vessel **2.** a quantity of liquid, especially of an alcoholic drink, drunk or poured from a bottle or similar vessel ○ *Here, have a glug of champagne.* [Late 17C. An imitation of the sound] —**glug** *vti*

glum /glum/ (**glum·mer, glum·mest**) *adj* quietly melancholic or miserable [Mid-16C. < variant of GLOOM "feel or look despondent"] —**glum·ly** *adv*—**glum·ness** *n*

glume /gloom/ *n* either of a pair of dry leaves at the base of the spikelet in an ear of a grass or cereal plant [Late 18C. < Latin *gluma* "husk"] —**glu·ma·ceous** /gloo máyshəss/ *adj*

glu·on /glóo òn/ *n* a theoretical elementary particle without mass, thought to be involved in binding the subatomic particles (**quarks**) together [Late 20C. < GLUE]

glut /glut/ *n* **EXCESS SUPPLY** a larger supply of something than is needed, especially of a crop or product ○ *There is usually a glut of fresh vegetables in August.* ■ *vt* (**glut·ted, glut·ting, gluts**) **1. SUPPLY MARKET WITH TOO MUCH** to supply a market with an excess of something, especially a product, leading to a fall in price ○ *Cheaper products from abroad glutted the market, lowering profits.* **2. GIVE SOMEBODY ENOUGH OR TOO MUCH** to feed or supply somebody with enough or more than enough of something [14C. Probably via Old French *gloutir* "swallow" < Latin *gluttire* (see GLUTTON)]

glu·ta·mate /glóotə màyt/ *n* a salt or ester of glutamic acid, especially its sodium salt (**monosodium glutamate**)

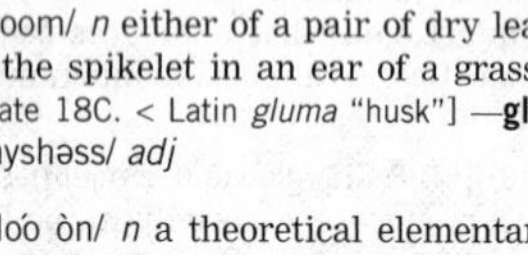

glutamic acid

glu·tam·ic ac·id /gloo tàmmik-/ *n* an amino acid found in plant and animal proteins that triggers nerve impulses in cells Formula: $C_5H_9NO_4$. [< GLUTEN + AMINE]

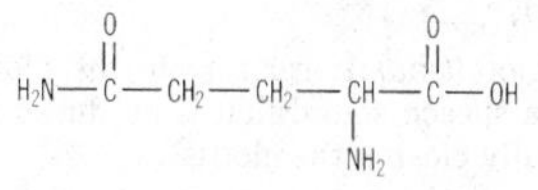

glutamine

glu·ta·mine /glóotə meen/ *n* an amino acid found in proteins and synthesized by humans and animals Formula: $C_5H_{10}N_2O_3$. [Late 19C. Blend of *glutamic* (see GLUTAMIC ACID) + AMINE]

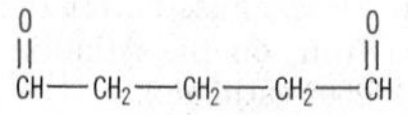

glutaraldehyde

glu·tar·al·de·hyde /glòotə ráldə hīd/ *n* an oily water-soluble liquid. Use: disinfectant, tanning agent, biological fixative. Formula: $C_5H_8O_2$. [Mid-19C. < *glutaric* < GLUTEN]

glu·ta·thi·one /glòotə thī ōn/ *n* a peptide consisting of glutamic acid, cysteine, and glycine that is an important antioxidant [Early 20C. < *glutamic* (see GLUTAMIC ACID)]

glu·te·i ANAT plural of **gluteus**

glu·ten /glóot'n/ *n* a mixture of two proteins found in some cereal grains, especially wheat. People who have celiac disease are allergic to gluten. [Late 16C. Via French < Latin, "glue"]

glutes /gloots/ *npl* the gluteus muscles (*informal*) [< GLUTEUS]

glu·te·us /glóotee əss/ (*plural* **-te·i** /-tee ī/) *n* a large muscle in the buttocks in a group of three that move the thigh in humans, especially the gluteus maximus [Late 17C. Via Modern Latin < Greek *gloutos* "buttock"] —**glu·te·al** *adj*

glu·te·us max·i·mus /-máksiməss/ (*plural* **glu·te·i max·i·mi** /-máksi mī/) *n* the outermost of the three large gluteus muscles that form each buttock in humans [< modern Latin, "largest gluteus"]

glu·ti·nous /glóot'nəss/ *adj* having a sticky consistency ○ *glutinous rice*

glut·ton /glútt'n/ *n* **1.** somebody who habitually eats or drinks too much **2.** ZOOL same as **wolverine** [13C. Via Old French < Latin *glutton-* < *gluttire* "to swallow" < *gula* "throat"] —**glut·ton·ous** *adj* —**glut·ton·ous·ly** *adv* ◇ **a glutton for punishment** somebody who appears to need or enjoy difficulty, discomfort, or stress

glut·ton·y /glútt'nee/ *n* the act or practice of eating and drinking to excess. Gluttony is one of the seven deadly sins in Christian tradition.

gly·bu·ride /glī byóor īd/ *n* a sulfonylurea drug. Use: treatment of non-insulin-dependent diabetes.

glyc- *prefix* same as **glyco-** (*used before vowels*)

glyc·er·ide /glíssə rīd/ *n* an ester formed by the combination of glycerol with an acid. Source: animal and vegetable fats and oils. [Mid-19C. < GLYCERIN]

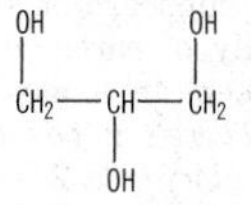

glycerin

glyc·er·in /glíssərin/, **glyc·er·ine** /glíssərin, -reen/ *n* a thick, sweet, odorless, colorless, or pale yellow liquid. Source: fats and oils as a byproduct of soap manufacture. Use: solvent, antifreeze, plasticizer, manufacture of soaps, cosmetics, lubricants, and dynamite. Formula: $C_3H_8O_3$. [Mid-19C. < French < Greek *glukeros*, alteration of *glukus* "sweet"]

glyc·er·ol /glíssə ràwl/ *n* CHEM same as **glycerin** (*technical*) [Late 19C. < GLYCERIN]

glyc·er·yl /glíssəril/ *n* a chemical group derived from glycerol by removing or replacing hydroxide, especially a trivalent group CH_2CHCH_2 [Mid-19C. < GLYCERIN]

glyc·er·yl tri·ni·trate *n* CHEM same as **nitroglycerin**

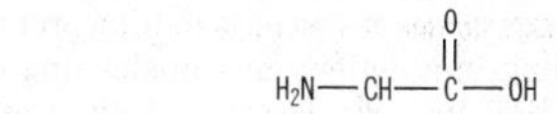

glycine

gly·cine /glī seen/ *n* an amino acid found in most proteins that inhibits the transmission of nerve impulses in cells Formula: $C_2H_5NO_2$. [Mid-19C. < Greek *glukus* "sweet"]

gly·ci·tein /glíssi teen/ *n* an isoflavone derivative found in soy products that is a possible natural cancer preventative

glyco- *prefix* **1.** sugar ○ *glycosuria* **2.** glycogen ○ *glycolysis* [< Greek *glukus* "sweet" < Indo-European]

gly·co·gen /glīkəjən/ *n* a polysaccharide found in the liver and muscles that is easily converted to glucose for energy —**gly·co·gen·ic** /glīkə jénnik/ *adj*

gly·co·gen·e·sis /glīkə jénnəssiss/ *n* the formation of glycogen from glucose —**gly·co·ge·net·ic** /glīkəjə néttik/ *adj*

gly·co·gen·ol·y·sis /glīkəjə nólləssiss/ *n* the breakdown of glycogen to glucose —**gly·co·gen·o·lyt·ic** /glīkə jen'l íttik/ *adj*

gly·col /glī kōl/ *n* CHEM **1.** same as **ethylene glycol 2.** same as **diol** [Mid-19C. < GLYCERIN] —**gly·col·ic** /glī kóllik/ *adj*

gly·col·ic ac·id *n* a compound found in unripe fruit. Use: tanning, pesticides, pharmaceuticals, adhesives, plasticizers.

gly·co·lip·id /glīkə líppid/ *n* a sugar-containing lipid present in cell membranes

gly·col·y·sis /glī kólləssiss/ *n* the breakdown of glucose to pyruvate, with the release of usable energy. This metabolic process takes place in nearly all living cells. —**gly·co·lyt·ic** /glīkə líttik/ *adj*

gly·co·pep·tide /glīkə pép tīd/ *n* a peptide that contains carbohydrate

gly·co·pep·tide in·ter·med·i·ate Staph·y·lo·coc·

cus au·re·us /-áwree əss/ *n* MED, MICROBIOL full form of **GISA**

gly·co·pro·tein /glīkə prṓ teen/ *n* a protein that contains carbohydrate

gly·co·side /glīkə sīd/ *n* a compound belonging to a group that reacts with water to form a sugar and a nonsugar. Some glycosides are used medicinally. [Mid-20C. < *glycose*, variant of GLUCOSE] —**gly·co·sid·ic** /glīkə síddik/ *adj*

gly·co·su·ri·a /glīkō shóoree ə, -sóor-/ *n* the presence of sugar in the urine, usually a sign of diabetes [Mid-19C. < *glycose*, variant of GLUCOSE] —**gly·co·su·ric** *adj*

gly·co·sy·la·tion /glīkō sī láysh'n/ *n* the addition of a saccharide unit to a protein [Mid-20C. < *glycose*, variant of GLUCOSE]

glyph /glif/ *n* **1.** ARCHIT **CARVED GROOVE IN ANCIENT GREEK ARCHITECTURE** an ornamental carved channel or groove, especially a vertical one like those on a Doric frieze **2.** ANCIENT HIST **CARVED SYMBOL OR CHARACTER** a symbol or character, especially one that has been incised or carved out in a stone surface like the characters of the ancient Maya writing system **3.** **MODERN SYMBOLIC CHARACTER** a nonverbal symbol, e.g., one used on a road sign **4.** COMPUT **CHARACTER IN FONT** the symbol or symbols that form a single character in a font [Late 18C. Via French *glyphe* < Greek *gluphē* "carving" < *gluphein* "carve"] —**glyph·ic** *adj*

glyph·o·sate /glīfə sàyt/ *n* a herbicide that is taken into the system of a plant, affecting its growth. Use: control of perennial grasses and many weeds, especially in arable fields.

glyp·tic /glíptik/ *adj* relating to the art of engraving or carving, especially on precious stones [Early 19C. Directly or via French *glyptique* < Greek *gluptikos* < *gluptēs* "carver" < *gluphein* "carve"]

glyp·tog·ra·phy /glip tóggrəfee/, **glyp·tics** /glíptiks/ *n* the art or process of engraving or carving on precious stones —**glyp·to·graph** /glíptə gràf/ *n* —**glyp·tog·ra·pher** *n* —**glyp·to·graph·ic** /glìptə gráffik/ *adj* —**glyp·to·graph·i·cal** *adj*

gm *abbr* Gambia (*used in Internet addresses*) See table at **domain name**

GM *abbr* **1.** BUSINESS general manager **2.** GENETICS genetic modification **3.** GENETICS genetically modified **4.** CHESS grand master **5.** ARMS guided missile

gm. *abbr* gram[1]

G-man *n* an agent of the Federal Bureau of Investigation (*dated slang*) [< abbreviation of GOVERNMENT]

GMAT[1] *tdmk* a trademark for a standardized test taken by applicants to business schools in the United States. Full form **Graduate Management Admission Test**

GMAT[2] *abbr* Greenwich Mean Astronomical Time

GMO *abbr* GENETICS genetically modified organism

GMP *abbr* BIOL guanosine monophosphate

GMT *abbr* Greenwich Mean Time

GMTA *abbr* great minds think alike (*used in e-mails or text messages*)

gn *abbr* Guinea (*used in Internet addresses*) See table at **domain name**

gn. *abbr* MONEY guinea (sense 1)

gnarl[1] /naarl/ *n* a hard lump, knot, or swelling on a tree trunk or branch [Early 19C. Back-formation < GNARLED]

gnarl

gnarl[2] /naarl/ *vi* to snarl or growl (*archaic*) [Late 16C. < *gnar* "to snarl, growl," an imitation of the sound]

gnarled /naarld/ *adj* **1.** twisted and full of knots ○ *an ancient gnarled tree* **2.** twisted, misshapen, or weather-beaten because of age, hard work, or illness ○ *gnarled hands* [Early 17C. Alteration of *knurled*]

gnarl·y /naarlee/ (**-i·er, -i·est**) *adj* **1.** extremely difficult, risky, and challenging (*slang*) ○ *gnarly surf off Santa Monica beach* **2.** extraordinarily good or pleasurable (*dated slang*) ○ *bought a gnarly skateboard* [< GNARL[1], perhaps from the way rough water appeared to surfers]

gnash /nash/ (**gnashed, gnash·ing, gnash·es**) *vt* to grind your teeth together, especially in pain, anger, or frustration [15C. Origin ?]

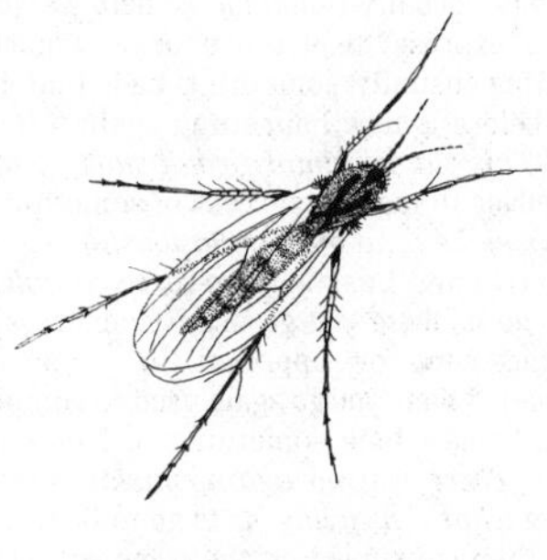

gnat

gnat /nat/ *n* a small two-winged biting fly, e.g., a black fly or a midge [Old English *gnætt* < Indo-European]

gnat·catch·er /nát kàchər/ *n* a small songbird with a long tail and slender beak that feeds on insects. Native to: North America. Genus: *Polioptila*.

gnath·ic /náthik/, **gna·thal** /náyth'l, náth'l/ *adj* relating to the jaw [Late 19C. < Greek *gnathos* "jaw"]

gna·thi·on /náythee òn/ *n* the lowest point on the midline of the lower jaw [Late 19C. < Greek *gnathos* "jaw"]

gna·thos·tome /náythə stōm, náth-/ *n* a vertebrate that has a mouth with jaws, as do all vertebrates except agnathans. Lampreys and hagfish are gnathostomes. Superclass: Gnathostomata. [Early 20C. < Greek *gnathos* "jaw" + *stoma* "mouth"]

-gnathous *suffix* having a particular kind of jaw ○ *prognathous* [< Greek *gnathos* "jaw" < Indo-European]

gnaw /naw/ (**gnawed, gnaw·ing, gnaws**) *v* **1.** *vti* **CHEW AT SOMETHING** to chew or bite on something persistently, often reducing it gradually to a particular state ○ *a terrier gnawing away at a huge bone* **2.** *vt* **MAKE SOMETHING BY CHEWING** to make something by grinding with the teeth and chewing ○ *The hamster escaped by gnawing a hole in its cage.* **3.** *vi* **CAUSE WORRY** to cause somebody constant anxiety or distress ○ *That question still gnaws at me after all these years.* **4.** *vi* **GRADUALLY REDUCE** to reduce the effectiveness or influence of something bit by bit ○ *a profound sense of unease that gnaws at our sense of well-being* **5.** *vt* **ERODE SOMETHING** to wear something away often until it reaches a particular shape or size ○ *The wind and waves had gnawed the rocks into fantastic shapes.* [Old English *gnagen* < Germanic] —**gnaw** *n* —**gnaw·a·ble** *adj* —**gnaw·er** *n*

gnaw·ing /náw ing/ *adj* persistent and troubling or uncomfortable ○ *gnawing doubts* —**gnaw·ing·ly** *adv*

gnawn past participle of **gnaw** (*archaic*)

gneiss /nīss/ *n* a coarse-grained high-grade metamorphic rock formed at high pressures and temperatures, in which light and dark mineral constituents are segregated into visible bands [Mid-18C. < German] —**gneiss·ic** *adj* —**gneiss·ose** *adj*

gnoc·chi /nókee, nyókee/ *npl* in Italian cooking, dumplings made of potato, semolina, or flour, usually boiled and served with soup or a sauce [Late 19C. < Italian]

gnome[1] /nōm/ *n* **1.** **TINY SUPERNATURAL BEING** in folklore and fairy tales, a small imaginary being usually portrayed as a hunchbacked man with a long white beard who lives underground guarding treasure **2.** **STATUE OF GNOME** a small figure or statue representing a gnome, used as a decoration **3.** **OFFENSIVE TERM** an offensive term that deliberately insults somebody's relatively small size and appearance [Mid-17C. Via French < modern Latin *gnomus*] —**gnome·like** *adj* —**gnom·ish** *adj* ◇ **the gnomes of Zurich** international bankers and financiers, especially those based in Switzerland (*dated humorous*)

gnome[2] /nōm/ *n* a short saying or proverb that expresses a general idea or principle [Late 16C. < Greek *gnōmē* "opinion, judgment" < *gignōskein* "know"]

gno·mic /nṓmik/ *adj* **1.** resembling or containing proverbs or other short pithy sayings that express basic truths ○ *His gnomic utterances were widely quoted by journalists.* **2.** opaque or difficult to understand [Early 19C. Directly or via French < Greek *gnōmikos* < *gnōmē* (see GNOME[2])] —**gnom·i·cal·ly** *adv*

gno·mon /nṓ mòn, nṓmən/ *n* **1.** the arm of a sundial, used to show the time of day by the position of its shadow **2.** the part of a parallelogram that is left when a smaller similar parallelogram has been taken from its corner [Mid-16C. Directly or via French or Latin < Greek *gnōmōn* "indicator" < *gignōskein* "know"] —**gno·mon·ic** /nō mónnik/ *adj* —**gno·mon·i·cal·ly** *adv*

gno·sis /nṓssiss/ *n* knowledge of spiritual truths reputedly possessed by the ancient Gnostics, who believed them to be essential to salvation [Late 16C. < Greek *gnōsis* "investigation, knowledge" < *gignōskein* "know"]

gnos·tic /nóstik/ *adj* relating to knowledge, especially knowledge of spiritual truths [Mid-17C. See GNOSTIC]

Gnos·tic /nóstik/ *n* somebody who believes in Gnosticism [Late 16C. Via ecclesiastical Latin < Greek *gnōstikos* < *gignōskein* "know"] —**Gnos·tic** *adj*

Gnos·ti·cism /nósti sìzzəm/ *n* a pre-Christian and early Christian religious movement teaching that salvation comes by learning esoteric spiritual truths that free humanity from the material world, believed in this movement to be evil

gno·to·bi·ot·ics /nṑtō bī óttiks/ *n* the scientific study of organisms living either in a germ-free or a controlled environment, as when a known contaminant has been introduced (*takes a singular verb*) [Mid-20C. < Greek *gnōtos* "known"] —**gno·to·bi·ot·ic** *adj* —**gno·to·bi·ot·i·cal·ly** *adv*

GNP *abbr* ECON gross national product

gnu

gnu /noo/ (*plural same or* **gnus**) *n* a large antelope with a head resembling that of an ox, a short mane, a beard, downward curving horns, and a tufted tail. Native to: Africa. Latin name: *Connochaetes gnou* or *Connochaetes taurinus*. [Late 18C. Probably via Dutch *gnoe* < Khoisan]

go[1] /gō/ (**went** /went/, **gone** /gawn, gon/, **go·ing, goes** /gōz/, *plural* **gos**) CORE MEANING: a basic intransitive verb of motion expressing movement from an unspecified point of departure or from a place that is already known or assumed ○ *Do you have any idea where he went?* ○ *She never went anywhere without her glasses.* ○ *Johnny went back inside for another cup of coffee.* ○ *I've always wanted to go to Paris.*

1. *vi* **DEPART** to leave a place ○ *Please don't go.* ○ *He's going tomorrow.* **2.** *vi* **MOVE TO ACT** to move toward a person or place with the intention of doing something specific ○ *We had to go and pick up our little boy who was playing at a friend's house.* ○ *After the* *wedding they went to live in Spain.* **3.** *vi* PROCEED TO ACTIVITY to leave a place and proceed toward an activity, often a recreational activity ○ *They go for a jog every morning.* **4.** *vi* ATTEND to attend a place regularly ○ *She went to Rutgers University at night to earn her teaching degree.* **5.** *vi* TAKE PART to take part in a television or radio program ○ *The President went on television to defend the White House's decision.* **6.** *vi* LEAD to lead to, or begin or end at, a particular place (*refers to a route or travel service*) ○ *Take the road that goes into the center of town.* ○ *The new bus service will go from New York to Buffalo.* **7.** *vi* ELAPSE to elapse or pass (*refers to time*) ○ *The year went pleasantly.* **8.** *vi* BE ALLOTTED to be allotted to a particular recipient or used for a particular purpose (*refers to money or other resources*) ○ *The house will go to his surviving children.* ○ *Much of her income went toward household bills.* **9.** *vi* BE GIVEN to be given to somebody as a quality or attribute ○ *The credit should go to the one who tries hardest.* **10.** *vi* BE DISCARDED to be eliminated, given up, or got rid of ○ *This old sweater has just got to go!* ○ *Thousands of jobs will have to go.* **11.** *vi* BE SPENT to be spent or used up ○ *Those sandwiches went pretty fast!* **12.** *vi* LEAVE JOB to leave a job or organization ○ *He was costing the company thousands and had to go.* **13.** *vi* BLEND IN to blend, harmonize, or be appropriate with something else ○ *They wanted to find a carpet that would go with the existing decor.* ○ *Those pants just don't go.* **14.** *vi* FIT IN to fit in a place because of being the right shape or size ○ *I tried to push the package through the mail slot but it wouldn't go.* **15.** *vi* BELONG to have somewhere as a usual or proper place ○ *The towels go in the cupboard in the bathroom.* **16.** *vi* BE PUT to be put into something as one of the parts that form it ○ *all the elements that go to make a successful musical* **17.** *vi* FUNCTION to function or operate ○ *Can you get my car going again?* ○ *Without capital to make it go, our business plan was merely hopes written out on paper.* **18.** *vi* FAIL to get weaker and begin to fail or give way ○ *My eyesight is starting to go.* **19.** *vi* BREAK DOWN to stop working properly and start to break down ○ *I think the battery may be going.* **20.** *vi* same as **die**[1] (sense 1) (*euphemistic*) ○ *She went peacefully in her sleep.* **21.** *vi* BECOME to change so as to come to be in a particular state or condition ○ *The crowd went wild.* **22.** *vi* BE DRESSED OR EQUIPPED to be in a particular state with regard to dress or equipment ○ *They went barefoot on the beach.* **23.** *vi* PROCEED to proceed or happen in a particular way ○ *How did it go at work today?* ○ *We were trying to figure out what really went wrong.* ○ *The intruder went unchallenged.* **24.** *vi* UK MAKE NOISE AS SIGNAL to make a noise such as a ring or a knock to attract attention ○ *She had just closed the front door when the phone went.* **25.** *vi* MAKE NOISE to make a particular noise ○ *The horn went beep.* ○ *Cows go "moo."* **26.** *vi* REACH POINT to proceed to or reach a particular position or level ○ *"The freedom she experienced, the indulgence with which she was treated, went beyond her expectations."* (Thomas Hardy, *The Mayor of Casterbridge*; 1886) **27.** *vi* SERVE to be of such a nature or quality as to do something ○ *It just goes to show how careful you have to be.* **28.** *vi* COMPARE to compare with other people or things of the same kind ○ *As vacations abroad go, it was probably the best we've ever had.* **29.** *vi* SOUND to proceed in terms of sound or words (*refers to a piece of music or writing*) ○ *How does that tune go again?* **30.** *vi* ACCOMPANY EACH OTHER to occur with or be present at the same time as something else ○ *It's not necessarily the case that intelligence and common sense go together.* **31.** *vi* CIRCULATE to circulate as information around a place or among people ○ *It soon went around the whole village that she had inherited a fortune.* **32.** *vi* HAVE RECOURSE to turn to a procedure as a result of unresolved problems ○ *They couldn't agree, so they went to arbitration.* **33.** *vi* BE AUTHORITY to be necessarily accepted as what will be the case in a given situation ○ *Whatever she says goes in our home.* **34.** *vi* ENDURE to continue surviving or succeeding in a difficult situation ○ *Human beings can go for much longer without food than without water.* **35.** *vt* BET SOMETHING IN CARDS to bet or bid a particular set of cards in a card game ○ *I go three clubs.* **36.** *vt* SAY SOMETHING to say something quoted (*nonstandard*) ○ *So she goes, "If you want it done then do it yourself."* **37.** *vi* EXPRESSING FUTURE ACTION used to express future action or intent (*used in progressive tenses*) ○ *What are we going to do?* **38.** *n* UK ATTEMPT MADE an attempt or chance to do something ○ *She passed the exam on the second go.* **39.** *n* TURN TAKEN a move or turn in a game ○ *It's your go.* **40.** *n* ENERGY energy and vibrancy (*informal*) ○ *I've had so much more go since changing my diet.* **41.** *adj* FUNCTIONING ready and operating properly (*informal*) ○ *All systems are go.* [Old English *gān* < Indo-European] ◇ **anything goes** used to indicate that anything is to be tolerated or accepted as the norm ○ *In this place almost anything goes!* ◇ **don't even go there** don't mention that particular subject, or don't even think about it (*informal*) ◇ **have a go (at something)** to make an attempt at something (*informal*) ○ *He said that he had never skied before but he was willing to have a go at it.* ◇ **have a go at somebody** *UK* to attack somebody verbally (*informal*) ◇ **here we go (again)!** used to express displeasure or resignation that something, usually something bad, that has happened before is now happening again ○ *Here we go again! This old car simply won't start.* ◇ **make a go of something** to make a success of something ○ *They couldn't make a go of the relationship.* ◇ **on the go** very active and busy ○ *a two-career couple, always on the go* ◇ **there you go** used to express general encouragement or approval to somebody else (*informal*) ◇ **there you go again** used to complain that somebody has done something bad or wrong yet again ○ *There you go again, misinterpreting and twisting what I'm saying.* ◇ **to go** to be taken home rather than consumed on the premises ○ *one pizza to go* ◇ **go quail** *Southwest US* to scatter in all directions, as some groups of illegal immigrants to the US do when pursued along the US-Mexican border (*slang*)

go about *vt* to deal with a problem, assignment, or task

go after *vt* **1.** to make a deliberate effort to get or find something seen as desirable or advantageous ○ *I decided to go after a teaching job I saw in the paper.* **2.** to try to catch somebody who is running away

go ahead *vi* **1.** to start or continue with something, especially after a period of uncertainty or delay ○ *Let's go ahead and start our meal without her.* **2.** used to indicate that somebody is welcome to do something (*informal*) ○ *"Would you mind if I used your phone?" "Sure, go ahead."*

go along *vi* **1.** ACCOMPANY SOMEBODY to accompany somebody on a trip ○ *I went along just to keep her company.* **2.** FOLLOW ANOTHER'S LEAD to follow the lead of somebody else ○ *When she suggested that they study Chinese before the trip, he went right along.* **3.** DEVELOP IN PARTICULAR MANNER to develop or progress in a particular manner, especially favorably (*informal*) ○ *Things were going along reasonably well until she lost her job again.*

go along with *vt* to accept something or obey somebody, especially reluctantly or to the surprise of others ○ *You can't go along with it – it's breaking the law.*

go around *v* **1.** *vi* KEEP COMPANY to spend a lot of time with a particular person or as a member of a particular group (*informal*) ○ *We went around together all the time.* **2.** *vi* TRAVEL FROM PLACE TO PLACE to travel from one place to another ○ *We tend to go around by taxi.* **3.** *vti* BE WIDELY KNOWN OR CURRENT to be experienced or known by a lot of people, often in a particular place **4.** *vti* BE ENOUGH FOR EVERYONE to be able to be distributed to everyone ○ *There aren't enough pens to go around, so you'll have to share.* ◇ **what goes around comes around** used to say that whatever happens now will have an effect in the future (*informal*)

go at *vt* to attempt something enthusiastically or energetically ○ *He went at the snow shoveling as if it were a race.*

go away *vi* **1.** to leave the place where you live, especially in order to take a vacation (*informal*) ○ *Are you going away this summer?* **2.** used to tell somebody to leave because he or she is annoying you ○ *Go away! I'm busy.*

go back *vi* **1.** to originate from a particular date, period, or time ○ *a tradition that goes back to the time of George Washington* **2.** *Malaysia* to return to your home

go back on *vt* to have a change of mind about something previously agreed or promised ○ *You can't go back on your word – a deal's a deal.*

go by *v* **1.** *vi* PASS IN TIME to move onward in terms of time ○ *As the years go by, he gets more and more mellow.* **2.** *vt* REGARD SOMETHING AS TRUE to treat advice or information as reliable or true **3.** *vt* USE PARTICULAR SOURCE OF INFORMATION to use a particular way of doing something or finding something out ○ *All we had to go by was a soggy map.* **4.** *vi* MAKE BRIEF VISIT to pay a brief, often unannounced or informal, visit to somebody ○ *I'll go by Hannah's house and give her the books.*

go down *vi* **1.** SINK to sink beneath the surface of a body of water ○ *An oil tanker went down off the coast of Alaska.* **2.** CRASH to fall from the air and crash ○ *The plane went down somewhere in the mountains.* **3.** GO BELOW HORIZON to sink below the horizon ○ *The sun had already gone down by the time we got back.* **4.** BE RECEIVED to be received in a particular way ○ *an idea that didn't go down at all well with the stockholders* **5.** COMPUT MALFUNCTION to break down or stop working ○ *Since the airline's computers have gone down, we can't get flight information yet.* **6.** BE REMEMBERED to be remembered in a particular way ○ *She will surely go down as one of the greatest athletes of all time.* **7.** TAKE PLACE to happen or be happening (*slang*) ○ *Hey, what's going down?* ○ *When the robbery went down, the cops rushed to the scene.* **8.** SUFFER DISGRACE to be disgraced or ruined (*informal*) ○ *If he goes down, he'll take the whole department with him.* **9.** BE EATABLE OR DRINKABLE to be able to be eaten or drunk, especially easily or enjoyably (*informal*) ○ *With sick children, soup tends to go down more easily than solid foods.* **10.** *UK* EDUC LEAVE UNIVERSITY AT END OF TERM to leave college or a university at the end of term or the end of the academic year **11.** CARDS FAIL TO ACHIEVE BRIDGE TRICKS in the game of bridge, to fail to attain the number of tricks that has been contracted for

go down on *vt* a highly offensive term meaning to perform oral sex on somebody (*taboo*)

go for *vt* **1.** TRY TO OBTAIN SOMETHING YOU WANT to make an effort to obtain something because it is suitable for you or important to you (*informal*) ○ *I really think you should go for that sales job.* **2.** LIKE SOMEBODY OR SOMETHING LOT to prefer, like, or be interested in something or somebody (*informal*) ○ *I don't really go for science fiction.* **3.** CHOOSE SOMETHING to choose one thing rather than another (*informal*) ○ *I think I'll go for the chocolate cheesecake – how about you?* **4.** ATTACK SOMEBODY to attack somebody physically or verbally **5.** COMMAND PRICE to be worth or sold for a particular amount ○ *In the end the house went for far less than its market value.* **6.** BE RELEVANT TO SOMEBODY to apply or be relevant to somebody ○ *She needs to be more careful in her work – and that goes for you, too!* ◇ **go for it** not to stop or relax until you aggressively reach your goal (*slang; often used as a command*) ○ *The coach told the team to get out there and go for it.* ◇ **have something going for you** to be in a situation where something is useful or helpful to you to a particular extent (*informal*) ○ *She has a lot going for her in the tennis championship, given her season's record.*

go in *vi* **1.** to become hidden by clouds ○ *Once the sun went in, it got really cold.* **2.** to launch an attack, or begin another maneuver ○ *After the police went in, things rapidly got out of hand.*

go in for *vt* **1.** to enjoy a particular activity ○ *I don't really go in for team sports myself.* **2.** to substitute for another player on a team such as an injured or ejected teammate ○ *Number 8 went in for the injured first-string quarterback.*

go into *vt* **1.** ENTER SPACE to enter a place or building ○ *Let's go into the house – it's freezing out here.* **2.** BEGIN CAREER to begin a job or career in a particular area of activity ○ *She went into advertising and made lots of money.* **3.** LOOK INTO SOMETHING to examine or look into something in detail and with thoroughness **4.** BE FACTOR OF NUMBER to be a factor of a number or amount ○ *15 won't go into 125.* **5.** CONTRIBUTE TOWARD SOMETHING to contribute toward something, or be one of the parts that form something ○ *all the elements that go into making a successful musical* **6.** BE SPENT

on something to be used or spent for a purpose ○ *Millions have gone into finding a cure.*

go in with *vt* to begin participating in a project or venture with other people ○ *I went in with four friends to start a restaurant.*

go off *vi* **1. DETONATE** to explode or be fired **2. BEGIN SOUNDING** to start to ring, sound, or vibrate ○ *The smoke alarm goes off whenever we make toast.* **3. BE CARRIED OUT** to be carried out or conducted in a particular manner ○ *I think the conference went off as well as could be expected.* **4. DEPART** to set out in a particular manner or for a particular place or purpose ○ *We decided to go off early.* ○ *endless TV images of soldiers going off to war*

go on *v* **1.** *vi* **CONTINUE RIGHT ALONG** to continue to happen ○ *The dispute went on for another nine months before it was resolved.* **2.** *vi* **ELAPSE** to elapse or move forward, bringing change (*refers to time*) ○ *As time went on, I thought about it less.* **3.** *vi* **OCCUR** to happen or take place ○ *I asked him what was going on.* **4.** *vti* **MAKE PUBLIC ENTRANCE** to make an entrance onto a stage or other public place ○ *She went on every night to rapturous applause.* **5.** *vi* **TALK TOO MUCH** to talk too much and much too long ○ *She's always going on about her yacht.* **6.** *vi* **CONTINUE SPEAKING** to continue speaking, especially after a pause ○ *She then went on about the latest international incident.* **7.** *vi* **DO SOMETHING AFTERWARD** to do something after the time or period you are referring to ○ *She finished fourth, but went on to win the championship the following year.* **8.** *vt* **USE AS RELIABLE INFORMATION** to use something as reliable information ○ *The police have very little to go on at this stage.* **9.** *vi* **EXPRESSING ENCOURAGEMENT** used to encourage somebody to do something, usually something the person is reluctant to do (*informal*) ○ *Go on, you'll have a great time!* **10.** *vt* **APPROXIMATE SOMETHING** to be close to a particular age, time, or number (*used in progressive tenses*) ○ *He must be going on 50.*

go out *vi* **1. SOCIALIZE** to socialize and enjoy yourself away from home ○ *She loves going out, but he prefers to stay at home.* **2. FLOW OUTWARD FROM SHORE** to flow away from the shoreline ○ *The tide had gone out.* **3. BECOME UNFASHIONABLE** to stop being fashionable ○ *Muttonchops went out in the late 1800s.* **4. DATE SOMEBODY** to go on a date with somebody ○ *They've been going out for six months.* **5. BE EXTINGUISHED** to stop burning or functioning ○ *The fire has gone out.*

go out to *vt* to be offered or extended to a person or group ○ *Our thoughts go out tonight to the friends and relatives of the victims.*

go over *v* **1.** *vi* **CHANGE ALLEGIANCE** to change allegiance and start supporting somebody or something else ○ *In a surprise move, the Senator went over to the opposition party.* **2.** *vt* **EXAMINE SOMETHING CAREFULLY** to examine or check something carefully ○ *The police went over the car looking for fingerprints.* **3.** *vt* **REHEARSE AND MEMORIZE SOMETHING** to practice or repeat something in order to learn it ○ *The actors were all busy going over their lines.* **4.** *vi* **BE RECEIVED** to be received in a particular way ○ *The campaign platform went over well with the convention delegates.*

go stern *vi Malaysia, Singapore* to move backward in a vehicle (*informal*) ○ *You'll need to go stern a few more meters.*

go through *v* **1.** *vt* **UNDERGO UNPLEASANTNESS** to undergo hardship or difficulties, usually in stages and over a period of time ○ *They're going through a series of business setbacks.* **2.** *vt* **EXAMINE SOMETHING THOROUGHLY** to examine or inspect something very carefully ○ *The police went through his luggage but found nothing suspicious.* **3.** *vi* **GAIN OFFICIAL APPROVAL** to be accepted or approved officially, after having gone through channels or set procedural stages **4.** *vt* **CONSUME SOMETHING IN QUANTITY** to use, eat, or spend something, especially a large amount in a short time ○ *They go through hundreds of dollars of groceries a week.*

go under *vi* **1. SINK IN WATER** to sink below the surface of the water ○ *I managed to grab him as he went under for the third time.* **2. FAIL** to close down or fail **3. LOSE CONSCIOUSNESS** to lose consciousness, especially after being given an anesthetic ○ *They began the operation as soon as she'd gone under.*

go up *vi* **1. BE BUILT** to be constructed ○ *A new supermarket went up where the theater used to be.* **2. BE DISPLAYED** to be put on display ○ *A notice has gone up saying how we can be contacted.* **3. DETONATE OR IGNITE** to explode or burst into flames ○ *The whole place went up in a matter of seconds.* **4.** *UK* **GO TO A UNIVERSITY** to go to or return to a college or university at the beginning of a term or academic year

go with *vt* **1. DATE SOMEBODY** to spend time romantically and socially with somebody (*informal*) ○ *Anna's been going with Alex for a month now.* **2. BE PART OF SOMETHING** to be a normal or usual part of something ○ *The long hours go with the job.* **3. ADOPT OR FOLLOW AN IDEA** to adopt or follow a particular approach or point of view ○ *Just go with the plan as it stands for the time being and we'll see what happens.*

go without *vt* to be deprived of something such as money or food ○ *You'll have to go without breakfast if you want to catch the early train.* ○ *Children from rich families had new clothes, while poor children had to go without.*

go[2] /gō/ *n* a Japanese board game played with black and white stones on a surface marked with 19 lines intersecting each other to create 367 crossing points. The object of the game is to capture the larger part of the board and the opponent's stones. [Late 19C. < Japanese]

GO *abbr* MIL general order

go·a /gṓ ə/ *n* a gazelle with a brownish gray coat, the male of which has backward curving horns. Native to: Tibet. Latin name: *Procapra picticaudata.* [Mid-19C. < Tibetan *dgoba*]

Go·a /gṓ ə/ state on the western coast of India. Formerly a Portuguese territory, it was incorporated into India in 1961 and became a separate Indian state in 1987. Capital: Panaji. Population: 1,343,998 (2001). Area: 1,429 sq. mi./3,702 sq. km.

goad /gōd/ *vt* (**goad·ed, goad·ing, goads**) **1. CAUSE SOMEBODY TO ACT** to provoke or incite somebody into action (*often passive*) **2. PROD ANIMAL WITH STICK** to prod an animal with a long pointed stick ■ *n* **1. POINTED ANIMAL PROD** a long pointed stick used for prodding cattle and other animals **2. STIMULUS** something that encourages an activity or process to begin, increase, or develop [Old English *gād* < Germanic]

SYNONYMS See *motive.*

go-a·head *n* permission or approval to proceed with something (*informal*) ○ *Once we get the go-ahead from the bank, we can get things moving.*

goal /gōl/ *n* **1. TARGET AREA** in a game such as soccer or hockey, the space or opening into which a ball or puck must go to score points, usually a pair of posts with a crossbar and often a net ○ *The kick landed just to the left of the goal.* **2. AIM** something that somebody wants to achieve ○ *One of my goals for this year is to learn Spanish.* **3. SCORE** the score gained by getting the ball or puck into the goal ○ *leading by three goals to two* **4. SUCCESSFUL SHOT** a successful attempt at hitting, kicking, or throwing a ball or hitting a puck into a goal ○ *one of the greatest goals of all time* **5. RACE'S END** the end of a race ○ *The runners are still several minutes from the goal.* [14C. Origin ?]

goal-di·rect·ed *adj* strongly motivated and highly organized in achieving tasks that are specified in advance

goal·ie /gṓlee/ *n* same as **goalkeeper**

goal·keep·er /gṓl keepər/ *n* in games such as soccer and field hockey, a defensive player positioned in or near a goal whose main task is to keep the ball or puck from crossing the goal line into the goal

goal kick *n* **1.** in soccer, a free kick taken from the six-yard-line by a defensive player when the ball has been driven out of play over the end line (**goal line**) by an opposing player **2.** in rugby, a free kick by a member of the attacking team, aimed at clearing the defenders' crossbar and designed to convert a five-point try into a seven-point score

goal·less /gṓlləss/ *adj* having no goals to aim for in life or work

goal line *n* in games such as football and field hockey, the line where goalposts are positioned and over which the ball must pass or be carried to make a score. A touchdown can be scored anywhere along the line, but to score in soccer and field hockey circumstances the ball also has to pass between the posts.

goal·mouth /gṓl mòwth/ (*plural* **-mouths** /-mòwthz/) *n* in games such as soccer and hockey, the area directly in front of the goal

goal-o·ri·ent·ed *adj* same as **goal-directed**

goal·post /gṓl pōst/ *n* in games such as football and field hockey, either of two posts, usually supporting a crossbar between them, that together mark the boundary of the goal ◇ **move the goalposts** *UK* to change the rules or conditions after a project has started or a course of action has been embarked on ○ *We'll never finish the software if Marketing keeps moving the goalposts.*

goal·tend·er /gṓl tèndər/ *n* SPORTS same as **goalkeeper**

goal·tend·ing /gṓl tènding/ *n* **1.** the act of trying to keep a puck or ball from entering a goal, especially in hockey **2.** in basketball, illegal interference with a ball that is in its downward arc toward the basket or that is in or on the rim of the basket

goanna

go·an·na /gō ánnə/ *n* a large monitor lizard of which there are several varieties. Native to: Australia. Genus: *Varanus.* [Mid-19C. Alteration of IGUANA]

go-a·round *n* (*informal*) **1. ONE INSTANCE** an instance of something ○ *The question was settled during the first go-around of talks.* **2.** same as **runaround** (sense 1) **3. CIRCLING OF SOMETHING** the act or occurrence of going around something ○ *The plane made one more go-around of the airport and landed.* **4. VOCAL ARGUMENT** an argument, often a loud one ○ *A noisy go-around in the foyer was heard by all in the restaurant.*

goat /gōt/ *n* **1.** (*plural* **goats** or *same*) an agile animal that is related to sheep and has backward curving horns, straight hair, and a short tail. Goats are ruminants. Raised for: wool, meat, milk. Genus: *Capra.* **2.** a man who is regarded as lecherous (*insult*) **3.** same as **scapegoat** [Old English *gāt* < Indo-European] —**goat·ish** *adj* ◇ **get somebody's goat** to annoy or irritate somebody (*informal*) ○ *Their constant carping over trivia really gets my goat.*

Goat *n* ZODIAC same as **Capricorn** (sense 1)

goat an·te·lope (*plural* **goat an·te·lopes** or *same*) *n* a mammal related to goats that also has features characteristic of antelopes. Chamois, goral, and mountain goat are goat antelopes. Subfamily: Caprinae.

goat cheese *n* cheese made from goat's milk

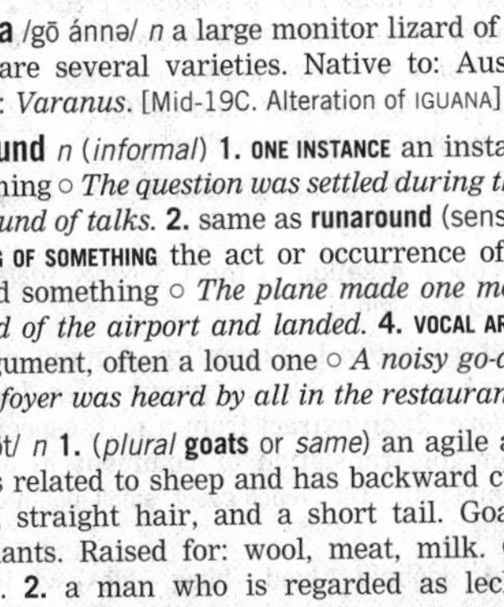

goatee: actor Tom Hanks wearing a goatee

goat·ee /gō tée/ *n* a short pointed beard on the chin but not the cheeks [< its resemblance to a goat's beard]

goat·fish /gṓt fìsh/ (*plural same* or **-fish·es**) *n US* a distinctively colored fish with two thin flexible appendages **(barbels)** beneath the mouth that are probably used as feelers. Native to: seabed in warm seas. Family: Mullidae. Can term **red mullet** [< barbels beneath its mouth]

goat·herd /gṓt hùrd/ *n* somebody who tends and herds goats

goat moth *n* a large pale-gray European moth with wood-boring larvae that give off an odor like that of goats. Latin name: *Cossus cossus.*

goats·beard /gṓts bèerd/ *n* **1.** a plant with woolly stems. Flowers: large, yellow, resembling the dandelion. Native to: Europe, Asia, now also growing in the United States. Latin name: *Tragopogon pratensis.* **2.** a tall perennial plant. Flowers: small, white, in long spikes. Native to: eastern North America. Latin name: *Aruncus dioicus.* [< the down on the seeds]

goat's cheese *n* FOOD same as **goat cheese**

goat·skin /gṓt skìn/ *n* **1.** LEATHER leather made from the skin of a goat **2.** LEATHER WINE FLASK a wine container made from the skin of a goat **3.** SKIN OF GOAT the skin or hide of a goat

goat's milk *n* milk from a goat, used for drinking and for making cheese

goat's rue *n* a leguminous plant used for feeding livestock. Flowers: pink, yellow. Native to: North America. Latin name: *Teprosia virginiana.*

goat·suck·er /gṓt sùkər/ *n* BIRDS same as **nightjar** [< a belief that it sucked milk from goats]

goat-water *n Carib* a lightly thickened stew made with goat meat and vegetables, often served at weddings and parties

gob[1] /gob/ *n* **1.** a lump of a soft or wet substance (*slang*) ○ *a huge gob of whipped cream* **2.** a large quantity or amount (*slang humorous; often used in the plural*) ○ *She wears gobs of makeup.* ○ *They made a gob of dough on that land deal.* [14C. < Old French *gobe* "mouthful" < *gober* "swallow"]

gob[2] /gob/ *n UK* the human mouth (*slang disapproving*) [Mid-16C. Origin ?]

gob[3] /gob/ *n* a sailor in the US Navy (*dated slang*) [Early 20C. Origin ?]

gob·bet /góbbət/ *n* **1.** a quantity of liquid, often in a sticky blotch ○ *Gobbets of grease covered the top of the stove.* **2.** an extract from a text, especially one chosen for translation or comment in an examination [13C. < Old French *gobet* "small mouthful" < *gobe* (see GOB[1])]

gob·ble[1] /góbb'l/ (**-bled, -bling, -bles**) *vt* **1.** to eat something quickly and greedily ○ *He gobbled up all the pizza.* **2.** to use something up quickly or in large amounts (*informal humorous*) ○ *watching the pay phone gobble her money* [Early 17C. Probably < GOB[1]]

gob·ble[2] /góbb'l/ *vi* (**-bled, -bling, -bles**) to make the characteristic gurgling sound of a male turkey or a sound resembling this ■ *n, interj* the gurgling sound made by a male turkey [Late 17C. An imitation of the sound]

gob·ble·dy·gook /góbb'ldee gòòk/, **gob·ble·de·gook** *n* language that is difficult or impossible to understand, especially nonsense or technical jargon (*informal*) ○ *This manual is full of gobbledygook.* [Mid-20C. An imitation of a turkey's gobble]

gob·bler /góbblər/ *n* a male turkey (*informal*)

Go·be·lin /góbəlin/ *n* a tapestry produced by the Gobelin factory in Paris, characterized by vivid pictorial scenes

go-be·tween *n* somebody who communicates or mediates between people during a negotiation, transaction, or secret operation

go·bi /góbee/ *n S Asia* in Indian cuisine, cauliflower or cabbage [< Punjabi]

Go·bi Des·ert /góbee-/ desert in northern China and southern Mongolia, the coldest and one of the largest deserts in the world. Area: 500,000 sq. mi./1,300,000 sq. km.

gob·let /góbblət/ *n* **1.** a drinking vessel with a stem and base, especially one of metal or glass **2.** a large bowl-shaped cup used formerly for drinking (*archaic*) [14C. < Old French *gobelet* "small cup" < *gobel* "cup"]

gob·let cell *n* a cell shaped like a goblet that secretes mucus. Goblet cells are found in the intestines and respiratory system of mammals and the epidermis of fish.

gob·lin /góbblin/ *n* an imaginary being resembling a small man of unpleasant appearance, usually evil or mischievous [14C. Probably via Anglo-Norman < medieval Latin *gobelinus*, a supposed spirit]

go·bo[1] /gṓbō/ (*plural* **go·bos** or **gob·oes**) *n* **1.** a shield that is placed around a microphone to keep out unwanted sounds **2.** a black screen placed around the lens of a camera or video camera to keep out unwanted light [Mid-20C. Origin ?]

go·bo[2] /gṓbō/ *n* in Japanese and Hawaiian cuisine, the slender root of the burdock, having a sweet, earthy flavor. It is cooked thinly sliced or shredded and added to soup and stews. [< Japanese]

gob·smacked /góbsmàkt/, **gob·struck** /gób strùk/ *adj UK* extremely surprised or shocked (*slang*) [< GOB[2]]

gob·stop·per /gób stòppər/ *n Can, UK* a large hard sweet that changes colour as it is sucked. US term **jawbreaker** [Early 20C. < GOB[2]]

go·by /gṓbee/ (*plural* **-bies** or *same*) *n* a small long-bodied spiny-finned freshwater or ocean fish whose pelvic fins form a sucker. Gobies are usually found in burrows or crevices. Family: Gobiidae. [Mid-18C. Via Latin *gobius* < Greek *kōbios*, a small fish]

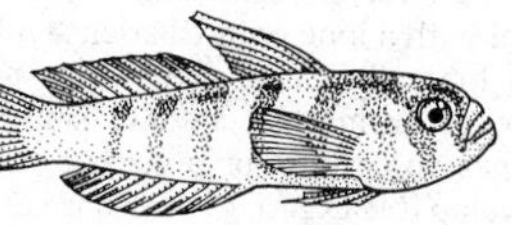

goby

go-cart *n* **1.** a light open-framed car large enough for a child or young teenager to sit in, containing a small engine and used for racing **2.** MOTOR SPORTS same as **kart** [Late 17C. < GO[1] "walk"; originally a device for helping a baby to walk]

god /god/ *n* **1.** SUPERNATURAL BEING one of a group of supernatural male beings in some religions, each of which is worshiped as the personification or controller of some aspect of the universe ○ *Thor, the Norse god of thunder* **2.** FIGURE OR IMAGE a representation of a god, used as an object of worship ○ *the little bronze god standing in a niche above the altar* **3.** SOMETHING THAT DOMINATES something that is so important that it takes over somebody's life (*informal*) ○ *worshiping the false god of fame* **4.** SOMEBODY ADMIRED a man who is widely admired or imitated (*informal*) ○ *He was one of the rock music gods of the early Seventies.* ■ **gods** *npl* FATE the entire group of supernatural beings viewed as deciding human fate [Old English, < Indo-European, "that which is invoked"] —**god·less·ly** *adv* —**god·less·ness** *n*

God *n* the being believed in monotheistic religions such as Judaism, Islam, and Christianity to be the all-powerful all-knowing creator of the universe, worshiped as the only god ■ *interj* used to express or emphasize feelings such as anger, helplessness, and frustration (*sometimes considered offensive*)

Go·dard /gō daár/, **Jean-Luc** (*b.* 1930) French movie director. A director of the French new wave, he became influential in the 1960s with movies such as *Breathless* (1960) and *Weekend* (1967).

> "I like a film to have a beginning, a middle, and an end, but not necessarily in that order."
> [Attributed to Jean-Luc Godard, *Time*; September 14, 1981]

Go·da·va·ri /gō daávəree/ river in central India that is sacred to Hindus. It rises in the Western Ghats and empties into the Bay of Bengal. Length: 900 mi./1,400 km.

god-aw·ful, God-aw·ful *adj* extremely bad or unpleasant (*slang; sometimes considered offensive*)

god·child /gód chìld/ (*plural* **-chil·dren** /-chìldrən/) *n* somebody whose spiritual upbringing is made the responsibility of one or more godparents. This arrangement is usually declared at the person's baptism or christening.

god·damn /gód dàm/ (*slang*) *adj, adv also* **god·dam** *or* **god·damned** /gód dàmd/ used to emphasize a word or idea, or to express anger, frustration, or some other strong emotion (*sometimes considered offensive*) ■ *interj* an offensive term used to express anger, frustration, or some other strong emotion

God·dard /góddərd/, **Robert** (1882–1945) US physicist. His innovations in rocket design included the development of liquid-fuel rockets (1926), instrument-carrying rockets (1929), and the first rocket to exceed the speed of sound (1935). Full name **Goddard, Robert Hutchings**

> "God pity a one-dream man."
> [Robert Goddard. Quoted in *Broca's Brain*, Carl Sagan; 1980]

god·daugh·ter /gód dàwtər/ *n* a girl or woman who is somebody's godchild

god·dess /góddəss/ *n* **1.** SUPERNATURAL BEING one of the group of supernatural female beings in some religions, worshiped as the personification or controller of some aspect of the universe ○ *Athena, the Greek goddess of wisdom* **2.** FIGURE OR IMAGE a representation of a goddess, used as an object of worship ○ *the statue of the goddess, standing in the temple's first niche* **3.** SOMEBODY ADMIRED a woman who is widely admired or imitated, especially for her beauty (*informal*) ○ *a screen goddess*

Gö·del /gṓd'l/, **Kurt** (1906–78) Austrian-born US mathematician. He is noted for his theories about the completeness of logic and the consistencies of arithmetic. Full name **Gödel, Kurt Friedrich**

godess incorrect spelling of **goddess**

Go·dey /gṓdee/, **Louis Antoine** (1804–78) US publisher. He published *Godey's Lady's Book* (1830–77), the leading US women's magazine of its time.

god·fa·ther /gód faàthər/ *n* **1.** MAN GODPARENT a man who is somebody's godparent **2.** ORGANIZED-CRIME BOSS a man who heads a criminal organization, especially a Mafia leader (*informal*) **3.** PATRON OR FOUNDER a man who provides inspiration or support, especially financial help, for a person or cause (*informal*) ○ *the godfather of the joint venture*

CULTURAL NOTE ***The Godfather***, a movie (1972) by Francis Ford Coppola. Based on the novel (1969) by Mario Puzo, it describes the attempts of the Sicilian Corleone family to maintain its control of the New York Mafia when a group of renegade families set up a drug-smuggling ring. Together with its two sequels, *The Godfather Part II* (1974) and *The Godfather Part III* (1990), it brought new meaning to terms such as "godfather" and "consigliere."

God-fear·ing /-fèering/ *adj* devout or deeply religious

god·for·sak·en /gódfər sàykən, gòdfər sáykən/ *adj* depressing, deserted, or empty ○ *The soldiers couldn't wait to get out of that godforsaken desert.*

God-giv·en *adj* existing or applying as part of the natural order of the universe rather than arranged by humanity ○ *God-given abilities*

god·head /gód hèd/ *n* the nature or essence of being divine

God·head *n* the Christian God, especially when considered as the Holy Trinity

god·hood /gód hòòd/ *n* RELIG same as **godhead**

Go·di·va /gə dívə/, **Lady** (1040?–80?) English noblewoman. According to legend, she obtained a remission of heavy local taxes levied by her husband, Leofric, Earl of Chester, by riding naked through the marketplace in Coventry, England on a horse.

god·less /góddləss/ *adj* **1.** not believing in or worshiping God or any god (*disapproving*) **2.** having an evil or immoral nature (*formal*) —**god·less·ly** *adv* —**god·less·ness** *n*

god·like /gód līk/ *adj* fit for God or a god, or having the qualities of God or a god, e.g., superhuman power, beauty, or imagination

god·ly /góddlee/ (**-li·er, -li·est**) *adj* **1.** devoted to or worshiping God (*formal*) **2.** fit for or having the divine qualities of God or a god —**god·li·ness** *n*

god·moth·er /gód mùthər/ *n* a woman who is somebody's godparent

go·down /gō̄ dòwn/ *n* a warehouse, especially in South and Southeast Asia [Late 16C. Via Portuguese *gudao* < Tamil *kitanku*, Kannada *gadangu* "store"]

god·par·ent /gód pèrrənt/ *n* a sponsor of a baptized child who promises to take a personal interest in him or her. Godparents often maintain close, almost familial relationships with a godchild.

go·droon *n* HANDICRAFT another spelling of **gadroon**

God's A·cre /gòdz áykər/ *n* a churchyard or cemetery (*archaic*) [< German *Gottesacker*]

God's coun·try *n* a nation or piece of land that is dearly loved

god·send /gód sènd/ *n* **1.** something good that happens unexpectedly **2.** something received that proves extremely useful, or somebody who arrives and gives much-needed help [Early 19C. < *God's send* < SEND[1] "thing sent"]

god's eye *n* a small object in the form of a circle within a rectangle, used as a decoration and symbol of good fortune. A god's eye is usually made with colored yarns or thread wound around a framework of sticks.

God's gift *n* an extremely admirable, valued, or talented person (*often used ironically*) ○ *He thought he was God's gift to the movie industry.*

god sim *n* a computer simulation game in which a player is managing a large imaginary territory such as a world or an ecosystem but does not represent a person

god·son /gód sùn/ *n* a man or boy who is somebody's godchild

God·speed /gód spéed/ *interj* used to wish somebody a safe trip or successful endeavor (*dated*) [15C. < *God speed you* "may God speed you"]

Godt·håb /gód hàwb, gót hàwp/ former name for **Nuuk**

Go·du·nov /gŏŏd'n àwf, gódd'n-, gə dŏŏ náwf/, **Boris Fyodorovich** (1551?–1605) tsar of Russia (1598–1605). During his rule as regent to Tsar Fyodor I Ivanovich (1584–98) and as tsar, he strengthened the monarchy and the church, imposed a system of serfdom, and was the first Russian ruler to banish political exiles to Serbia.

God·win Aus·ten, Mount /gòddwin áwstən/ ♦ **K2**

god·wit /gód wìt/ *n* a large wading bird that has a long, slightly upturned beak and long legs and is related to curlews and sandpipers. Native to: found worldwide. Genus: *Limosa*. [Mid-16C. Origin ?]

Goeb·bels /gŏ́bbl'z/, **Joseph** (1897–1945) German Nazi politician. He was Adolf Hitler's minister of propaganda (1933–45). Full name **Goebbels, Paul Joseph**

> "Should the German people lay down arms, the Soviets...would occupy all eastern and south-eastern Europe together with the greater part of the Reich. Over all this territory, which with the Soviet Union included, would be of enormous extent, an iron curtain would at once descend."
> [Joseph Goebbels, *Das Reich (The Reich)*; February 23, 1945]

go·er /gṓ ər/ *n* **1.** somebody who regularly attends something (*usually used in combination*) ○ *festival-goers* **2.** a spirited or fast-moving person or animal (*informal*)

Goe·ring /gérring, gúr ing/, **Gö·ring** /gŏ́ring/, **Hermann** (1893–1946) German Nazi leader. Adolf Hitler's second in command, he organized and commanded Nazi Germany's air force, directed its economy, and planned much of Germany's military strategy in World War II. Convicted of war crimes and sentenced to death at the Nuremberg trials (1946), he committed suicide before execution. Full name **Goering, Hermann Wilhelm**

Goe·thals /gṓth'lz/, **George Washington** (1858–1928) US engineer and army officer. He was chief engineer of the Panama Canal (1907–14).

AKG London

Johann Wolfgang von Goethe: portrait (1826) by Heinrich Christoph Kolbe

Goe·the /gṓtə/, **Johann Wolfgang von** (1749–1832) German writer and scientist. A seminal figure of European literature, he was a prolific writer of poems, novels, plays, criticism, and letters. His masterwork is the dramatic poem *Faust* (published in two parts 1808, 1832). He was also author of the novel *The Sorrows of Young Werther* (1774).

> "Besides, civilization, which now licks / Us all so smooth, has taught even the Devil tricks; / The northern fiend's becoming a lost cause— / Where are his horns these days, his tail, his claws?"
> [Johann Wolfgang von Goethe, *Faust*; 1808]

> "Talent develops in quiet places, character in the full current of human life."
> [Johann Wolfgang von Goethe, *Torquato Tasso*; 1790]

goe·thite /gṓ thìt, gṓ tìt/ *n* an earthy rust-colored hydrated iron oxide mineral formed by the alteration of iron minerals [Early 19C. After GOETHE]

go·fer /gṓfər/ *n* somebody who runs errands or performs other menial tasks (*informal; sometimes offensive*) [Mid-20C. < reduced pronunciation of *go for*]

Gog and Ma·gog /gòg ənd máy gòg/ *npl* in parts of the Bible, the names given to the enemies of God's people. In the book of Ezekiel, Gog is named as the ruler of a land named Magog, while Revelations names Gog and Magog as nations that were under Satan's rule.

go-get·ter *n* an enterprising and aggressive person (*informal*) —**go-get·ting** *adj, n*

gog·gle /gógg'l/ *v* (**-gled, -gling, -gles**) **1.** *vi* STARE WIDE-EYED to stare with eyes wide open, usually in astonishment **2.** *vti* ROLL EYES to roll the eyes, or roll about in the eye socket ■ *adj* BULGING bulging from the eye socket ○ *goggle eyes* ■ *n* WIDE-EYED STARE a staring or leering look at somebody with eyes wide open [14C. Probably < a verb imitative of moving backward and forward] —**gog·gly** *adj*

gog·gle-eyed *adj* with staring eyes

gog·gles /gógg'lz/ *npl* protective eyeglasses, usually made of plastic or glass and fitting tight to the face

Gogh ♦ **van Gogh, Vincent**

go-go *adj* **1.** ENERGETIC characterized by energy and forcefulness **2.** FIN SPECULATIVE bringing or expected to bring quick or high returns on any investment ○ *These go-go stocks carry risk and are not for the timid investor.* **3.** DISCO relating to or seen in discotheques or music clubs (*dated*) ■ *n* STYLE OF MUSIC a style of US popular music from the 1980s, an amalgamation of disco, funk, and Latin sounds [Doubling of GO[1], probably after French *à gogo* "galore"]

go-go danc·er *n* an energetic, usually scantily dressed dancer, who entertains in a nightclub (*dated*)

Go·gol /gṓgəl, -gàwl/, **Nikolay Vasilyevich** (1809–52) Russian writer. One of the greatest exponents of Russian literary realism, he is best known for his satirical play *The Government Inspector* (1836) and the novel *Dead Souls* (1842).

Goh Chok Tong /gṓ chok tóng/ (*b.* 1941) prime minister of Singapore (1990–). A member of the People's Action Party, he was elected to parliament in 1976 and held several ministerial portfolios before becoming deputy prime minister in 1985.

Goi·â·ni·a /goy áanee ə, goy ánnyə/ capital city of Goiás State in south central Brazil. Population: 1,004,098 (1996).

Goi·del /góyd'l/ *n* a Celt who speaks a Goidelic language [Late 19C. < Old Irish (see GAEL)]

Goi·del·ic /goy déllik/ *n* the northern branch of the Celtic family of languages, comprising Irish Gaelic, Scottish Gaelic, and Manx. Native speakers: 300,000. —**Goi·del·ic** *adj*

go·ing /gṓ ing/ *n* **1.** ACT OF LEAVING an act of leaving somewhere **2.** CONDITIONS FOR PROGRESS conditions for making progress ○ *The going gets tough when you reach the rocky terrain.* **3.** CONDITIONS UNDER FOOT the state of the ground as it affects ease and speed of movement, especially for horses in a race ○ *The going is good on the track.* ■ *adj* **1.** SUCCESSFUL currently operating successfully ○ *a going business* **2.** ACCEPTED AS STANDARD currently accepted as standard or valid ○ *the going rate for platinum* **3.** EXISTING currently in existence or available ○ *the best thing going*

go·ing-o·ver (*plural* **go·ings-o·ver**) *n* (*informal*) **1.** THOROUGH EXAMINATION a thorough examination or check ○ *They gave the results a thorough going-over before making their report.* **2.** ACT OF OVERHAULING an action by which something is thoroughly improved or restored to a previous condition, e.g., an act of cleaning, polishing, or dusting something ○ *The house got a complete going-over before the arrival of the in-laws.* **3.** SCOLDING OR BEATING a verbal scolding or physical beating

go·ings-on *npl* events or activities, especially of a noteworthy or suspicious nature (*informal*)

goi·ter /góytər/ *n* enlargement of the thyroid gland appearing as a swelling of the front of the neck. Iodine deficiency is one of several causes. [Early 17C. Via French < Latin *guttur* "throat"] —**goi·trous** *adj*

goi·tre *n* MED Can, UK spelling of **goiter**

Go·lan Heights /gṓ laan-/ disputed upland region on the border between Israel and Syria, northeast of the Sea of Galilee. Administered by Syria until 1967, it was first occupied and then, in 1981, annexed by Israel. Area: 483 sq. mi./1,250 sq. km.

gold /gōld/ *n* **1.** YELLOW METALLIC ELEMENT a soft, heavy corrosion-resistant, yellow metallic element that is highly valued, found in underground veins and alluvial deposits. Use: jewelry, alloys. Symbol **Au**. See table at **element** **2.** RICH YELLOW HUE a deep rich yellow color that resembles that of the metal gold **3.** THINGS MADE OF GOLD things made of gold, e.g., coins or pieces of jewelry **4.** WEALTH much money or wealth **5.** same as **gold medal** (*informal*) **6.** ARCHERY BULL'S EYE the bull's eye of a target, which is usually gilt [Old English < Indo-European] —**gold** *adj*

Gold·berg /gṓldbərg/, **Arthur Joseph** (1908–90) US politician and associate justice of the US Supreme Court. He sat on the Supreme Court (1962–65), and was US ambassador to the United Nations (1965–68).

Gold·berg, Rube (1883–1970) US cartoonist. He is known for his comic diagrams of complex contraptions that performed ridiculously simple actions. Full name **Goldberg, Reuben Lucius**

Gold·berg, Whoopi (*b.* 1949) US actor. Her movies include *The Color Purple* (1985), and she won an Academy Award for her performance in *Ghost* (1990). Born **Johnson, Caryn**. See illustration on next page

gold brick *n* **1.** a brick or other thing that appears to be made of gold but is not actually valuable **2.** an offensive term for a person regarded as a loafer or shirker (*informal; insult*)

Popperfoto

Whoopi Goldberg

gold·brick /gṓld brìk/ (**-bricked, -brick·ing, -bricks**) *vi* to avoid work by making excuses (*informal; disapproving*) —**gold·brick·er** *n*

gold bug *n* a supporter of a single gold standard (*dated informal*)

gold card *n* a credit card issued to people with incomes higher than a specific amount, that allows the holder to have a special credit limit and other extra facilities

gold cer·tif·i·cate *n* a security representing ownership of a quantity of gold, with the actual bullion held in a designated repository

gold coast, Gold Coast *n* **1.** the most exclusive residential area of a place **2.** the floor or area in an office building where the top management of a company has its offices (*slang*)

Gold Coast /gṓld-/ **1.** city on the Pacific coast, southeastern Queensland, Australia. It straddles the border between Queensland and New South Wales. Population: 438,473 (2002 estimate). **2.** former name for **Ghana**

gold dig·ger *n* **1.** an offensive term for a person who is regarded as seeking intimate relationships for material gain (*insult*) **2.** a miner looking for gold deposits —**gold-dig·ging** *n*

gold disk *n* **1.** the master disk from which a CD-ROM is made **2.** *UK* same as **gold record**

gold·en /gṓldən/ *adj* **1.** COLORED LIKE GOLD with the color of gold ○ *golden hair* **2.** MADE OF GOLD made largely or wholly of gold ○ *a golden crown* **3.** EXCELLENT especially good **4.** IDYLLIC describes a period when there is general or individual success, happiness, or prosperity ○ *the golden years of their lives* **5.** FAVORED popular or successful, or likely to become so ○ *the golden boys and girls of the downhill ski circuit* —**gold·en·ly** *adv* —**gold·en·ness** *n*

Gold·en /gṓld'n/ town in the foothills of the Rocky Mountains in Jefferson County, north central Colorado, 10 mi./16 km west of Denver. Population: 17,366 (2002 estimate).

gold·en age *n* **1.** a period of great prosperity or achievement, especially in the arts **2.** in classical mythology, the first age of the world characterized by idyllic happiness and innocence

gold·en ag·er *n* somebody over retirement age

gold·en Al·ex·an·ders (*plural same*) *n* a perennial plant of the carrot family. Flowers: small, yellow. Native to: woods and meadows of North America. Latin name: *Zizia aurea*. [Origin ?]

gold·en an·ni·ver·sa·ry *n* a 50th anniversary, e.g., of a wedding, or its celebration

gold·en as·ter *n* a perennial plant. Flowers: yellow, resembling daisies. Native to: North America. Genus: *Chrysopsis*.

Gold·en Bay /gṑld'n-/ bay on the northern coast of the South Island, New Zealand. It extends 25 mi./40 km from Farewell Spit in the west to Separation Point in the east.

gold·en brown *n* a yellowish brown color —**gold·en-brown** *adj*

gold·en-brown al·ga *n* a freshwater or marine alga that is yellow to golden brown in color. Division: *Chrysophyta*. (*often used in the plural*)

gold·en calf *n* an unworthy object that is esteemed or worshiped, especially money [< that worshiped by the Israelites (Exodus 32)]

gold·en club *n* a water plant with floating leaves and a yellow club-shaped flower sheath. Native to: eastern North America. Latin name: *Orontium aquaticum*.

Gold·en De·li·cious *n* a variety of eating apples with greenish or yellowish skin and a soft sweet flesh

gold·en ea·gle *n* a large dark brown eagle with golden brown feathers on its head and neck. Native to: mountainous regions of northern hemisphere. Latin name: *Aquila chrysaetos*.

gol·den·eye /gṓld'n ì/ *n* **1.** a black-and-white diving duck with yellow eyes. Native to: northern regions. Latin name: *Bucephala clangula* or *Bucephala islandica*. **2.** an insect with yellow eyes and delicate lacy wings. Family: Chrysopidae.

Gold·en Fleece *n* in Greek mythology, the fleece of the winged ram Chrysomallus, kept in a sacred grove by King Aeëtes, from where it was stolen by Jason

Barnaby's

Golden Gate Bridge

Gol·den Gate Bridge *n* a long suspension bridge across the entrance to San Francisco Bay, California. It was opened in 1937 and links San Francisco with Marin County.

gold·en glow *n* a tall garden plant. Flowers: double yellow, resembling daisies. Latin name: *Rudbeckia laciniata*.

gold·en ham·ster *n* a small animal with tan fur, a short tail, and large cheek pouches for storing food, which is often kept as a pet or used as a laboratory animal. The widespread domestic population came from a single female and 12 young caught in Syria in 1930. Latin name: *Mesocricetus auratus*.

gold·en hand·cuffs *npl* generous benefits promised to an employee on joining a company to discourage him or her from leaving to work elsewhere (*informal*)

gold·en hand·shake *n* a large sum of money given to an employee to compensate for the loss of a job or compulsory early retirement (*informal*)

gold·en hel·lo *n* a large sum of money given after an employment contract has been signed, offered as an inducement to somebody to accept the new job or join the hiring organization (*informal*)

Gold·en Horde *n* the Mongol army that invaded and dominated large parts of eastern Europe in the 13th century

Gold·en Horn inlet of the Bosporus in the European part of Turkey. It forms the harbor of Istanbul. Length: 5 mi./8 km.

Gold·en Horse·shoe /-háwrss shōō/ *n Can* the prosperous region of southern Ontario running around the western end of Lake Ontario, including Toronto and Hamilton

gold·en li·on tam·a·rin *n* a small monkey with brilliant golden fur and mane. Native to: coastal forests of Brazil. Latin name: *Leontopithecus rosalia*.

gold·en mean *n* **1.** the middle course that avoids extremes in either direction **2.** ARTS same as **golden section**

gold·en nem·a·tode *n* a small worm that can infest potato fields, causing severe damage to crops and loss of productive farm land. Latin name: *Heterodera rostochiensis*.

gold·en old·ie *n* a song that was popular in the past and has remained popular or become popular again (*informal*)

golden op·por·tu·ni·ty *n* an especially good chance

gold·en par·a·chute *n* an employment agreement that gives generous benefits to a senior executive who is forced to leave a company (*informal*)

gold·en re·triev·er *n* a medium-sized dog belonging to a breed with cream to golden hair. Its companionable nature makes it a popular family pet.

gold·en rob·in *n* BIRDS same as **Baltimore oriole**

gold·en·rod /gṓld'n ròd/ (*plural* **-rods** or *same*) *n* a tall-stemmed plant that blooms in late summer. Flowers: small, yellow, in clusters. Native to: Europe, North America. Genus: *Solidago*.

gold·en rule *n* **1.** a basic rule that must be followed **2.** the rule of conduct that advises people to treat others in the same manner as they wish to be treated themselves

gold·en·seal /gṓld'n sèel/ *n* a small perennial woodland plant of the buttercup family that has a thick yellow rootstock used in herbal medicine for its healing and antiseptic properties. Flowers: small, greenish. Native to: eastern North America. Latin name: *Hydrastis canadensis*.

gold·en sec·tion *n* the proportion arising from the division of a straight line into two so that the ratio of the whole line to the larger part is exactly the same as the ratio of the larger part to the smaller part [Because considered to be the most aesthetically pleasing proportion]

gold·en shin·er *n* a common freshwater fish of the minnow family, with a deep body and a golden color. Native to: eastern North America. Latin name: *Notemigonus crysoleucas*.

Gold·en State *n* a nickname for California

gold·en tri·an·gle *n* the part of Southeast Asia where Laos, Thailand, and Myanmar meet and where much opium is grown

gold·field /gṓld fèeld/ *n* an area with gold mines

gold-filled *adj* made of metal covered with a layer of gold

gold·finch /gṓld fìnch/ *n* a small finch with yellow and black markings. Native to: North America, Europe, Asia. Genus: *Carduelis*.

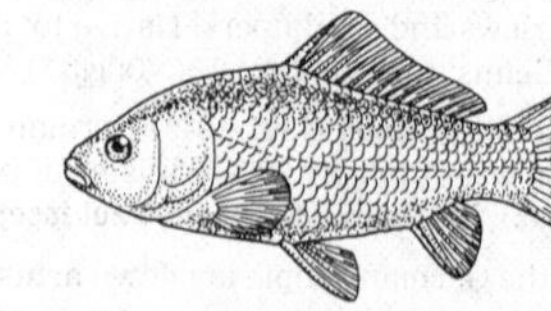

goldfish

gold·fish /gṓld fìsh/ (*plural same* or **-fish·es**) *n* an orange-red freshwater aquarium and pond fish related to carps and minnows. Native to: East Asia. Latin name: *Carassius auratus*.

gold·fish bowl *n* **1.** a clear glass or plastic bowl in which to raise and keep goldfish **2.** a situation or place that is always open to public view or scrutiny

gold leaf *n* gold that is beaten out into very thin sheets and used for gilding and lettering

UPI/Corbis-Bettmann

Emma Goldman

Gold·man /gṓldmən/, **Emma** (1869–1940) Russian-born US anarchist. A fiery writer and lecturer, she was imprisoned and deported (1919) for her radical political activities in the United States, and wrote the autobiographical *Living My Life* (1931).

"If the production of any commodity necessitates the sacrifice of human life, society should do without that commodity, but it cannot do without that life."
[Emma Goldman, *Anarchism and Other Essays*; 1917]

gold med·al *n* a medal that is made of gold or something representing gold, given as a first prize for excellence or winning a competition —**gold med·al·ist** *n*

gold mine *n* a rich source of something valuable, especially easily obtained wealth ○ *Some of the smaller shops are little gold mines.*

gold plate *n* **1.** bowls, goblets, and other utensils made of gold **2.** a thin coating of gold on another metal, usually produced by electroplating

gold-plat·ed *adj* having a thin coating of gold, usually produced by electroplating —**gold-plate** *vt*

gold record *n* MUSIC, RECORDING a golden replica of a recording that has achieved a particular exceptionally high number of sales. Sales of an album must exceed 500,000, and those of a single one million.

gold re·serve *n* a fund of gold in coins or bullion held by a central bank and regarded as providing a foundation for a paper currency and security for borrowing

gold-rimmed *adj* **1.** decorated with a thin gold-colored band at the edge ○ *a gold-rimmed mug* **2.** having a thin frame that is gold-colored or made of gold ○ *gold-rimmed eyeglasses*

gold rush *n* **1.** a sudden wave of migration to new territory because gold has been discovered there. One of the most famous gold rushes was to the Klondike in Yukon, Canada, from 1896. **2.** a sudden rush to make money from a new source or by a new means

CULTURAL NOTE ***The Gold Rush***, a movie (1925) by director and actor Charles Chaplin. Set during the California gold rush of 1849, it places Chaplin's gentle and sensitive Tramp character in the materialistic, amoral environment of a mining town to great comic effect. In one famous scene, Chaplin is reduced to eating his shoes, but eventually he strikes it rich and returns home a wealthy man.

gold·smith /gṓld smìth/ *n* a maker of or dealer in gold objects

Gold·smith /gṓld smìth/, **Sir James** (1933–97) French-born British business executive. He had extensive business interests, and used his fortune to fund conservative political causes such as the Referendum Party (1994). Full name **Goldsmith, Sir James Michael**

"Brussels is a madness. I will fight it from within."
[James Goldsmith. Referring to the European Union, *Times (London)*; June 10, 1994]

Gold·smith, Oliver (1730–74) Irish-born British writer. He is best remembered for his novel *The Vicar of Wakefield* (1766) and his comedy *She Stoops to Conquer* (1773).

"Such is the patriot's boast, where'er we roam, / His first, best country ever is, at home."
[Oliver Goldsmith, *The Traveler*; 1764]

"The true use of speech is not so much to express our wants as to conceal them."
[Oliver Goldsmith, "On the Use of Language," *The Bee, no. 3*; October 20, 1759]

gold·smith bee·tle *n* a beetle of the scarab family that has a metallic gold color. Latin name: *Cotalpa lanigera.*

gold stan·dard *n* **1.** a system of defining monetary units in terms of their value in gold, usually accompanied by the free circulation of gold and free exchange of currency into it **2.** the very best example of its kind

gold·stone /gṓld stṑn/ *n* MINERALS same as **aventurine** (sense 2)

gold·thread /gṓld thrèd/ *n* a low-growing evergreen plant found in mossy woods or swamps. Native to: North America, northern Asia, and Europe. Genus: *Coptis.*

Gold·wa·ter /gṓld wàwtər/, **Barry M.** (1909–98) US politician. He served as Republican US senator from Arizona (1953–65, 1969–87). He was defeated by Lyndon B. Johnson for the presidency (1964). Full name **Goldwater, Barry Morris**

"I would remind you that extremism in the defense of liberty is no vice! And let me remind you also that moderation in the pursuit of justice is no virtue!"
[Barry Goldwater, *presidential nomination acceptance speech*, Republican National Convention; July 16, 1964]

Gold·wyn /gṓldwin/, **Samuel** (1882–1974) Russian-born US movie producer. He was one of Hollywood's most influential producers. His movies include *The Best Years of Our Lives* (1946) and *Porgy and Bess* (1959). Born **Gelbfisz, Schmuel**

"A verbal contract isn't worth the paper it is written on."
[Samuel Goldwyn. Quoted in *The Great Goldwyn*, Alva Johnston; 1937]

go·lem /gṓləm/ *n* in Jewish legend, an imaginary being made of clay and brought to life by magical incantations. The most famous was made by Rabbi Loew in the 16th century to defend the Jews of Prague from a pogrom. [Late 19C. Via Yiddish < Hebrew *golem* "shape, mass"]

golf /gawlf/ *n* an outdoor game in which an array of special clubs with long shafts are used to hit a small ball from a prescribed starting point into a series of holes. The object of the game is to complete the course in as few strokes as possible. ■ *vi* (**golfed, golf·ing, golfs**) to play the game of golf [15C. Origin ?] —**golf·er** *n*

Golf *n* a code word for the letter "G," used in international radio communications

golf ball *n* a small hard ball used for playing golf

golf cart *n* a motorized vehicle used to drive around on a golf course during play

golf club *n* **1.** STICK FOR HITTING GOLF BALLS a specially designed club with a long shaft and a metal or wooden head, used in golf to strike the ball **2.** GOLFERS' ASSOCIATION an association of people who play golf, usually on the same course **3.** PREMISES OF GOLFERS' ASSOCIATION the premises or facilities used by a golf club

golf course *n* an area of land designed for playing golf on

golf·ing /gáwlfing/ *n* the activity of playing golf (*often used before a noun*) ○ *a golfing umbrella*

golf links *npl* GOLF same as **golf course**

golf wid·ow *n* a woman whose husband or partner spends many hours playing golf (*informal; humorous*)

gol·gap·pa /gol gúppə/ *n S Asia* in Indian cuisine, a ball of mashed potato with spices and tamarind juice, wrapped in puff pastry and fried [< Hindi]

Gol·gi ap·pa·ra·tus /gáwljee-/, **Gol·gi bod·y**, **Gol·gi com·plex** *n* a membranous structure in the cytoplasm of cells consisting of layers of flattened sacs and functioning in the processing and transporting of proteins [Early 20C. After Camillo *Golgi* (1844–1926), Italian histologist]

Gol·go·tha /gólgəthə/ *n* same as **Calvary** [Via late Latin < Greek, alteration of Aramaic *gōgoltā* "skull"]

go·li·ath /gə lī́ əth/ *n* a gigantic or overpowering opponent or competitor ○ *a corporation regarded as the goliath of the oil industry* [Late 16C. After GOLIATH]

Go·li·ath /gə lī́ əth/ *n* in the Bible, a giant Philistine who was slain by David using a sling and a stone

Go·li·ath bee·tle *n* a very large scarab beetle that can measure up to 6 in./15 cm in length and has bold black, white, and brown markings. Native to: tropical Africa. Latin name: *Goliathus giganteus.*

Go·li·ath frog *n* a very large frog that can measure up to 12 in./30 cm. Native to: central Africa. Latin name: *Rana goliath.*

go·li·ath grou·per *n* a large dark spotted ocean fish of the grouper family with rough scales. Native to: warm and tropical waters. Latin name: *Epinephelus itajara.*

gol·li·wog /góllee wòg/, **gol·li·wogg** *n* an offensively grotesque cloth doll with a black face and hair and brightly colored clothes. Now rarely made, the dolls are offensive to Black people, as is the term itself. (*offensive*) [Late 19C. After a character in books by US writer Bertha Upton (d. 1912)]

gol·ly /góllee/ *interj* used to express surprise, amazement, or anxiety, or for emphasis (*dated informal*) ○ *Golly, we're in real trouble now!* [Late 18C. Alteration of GOD]

go·ma·si·o /gō maássee ō/, **gho·ma·si·o** *n* a seasoning mixture made of ground sesame seeds and salt, used especially in Japanese cooking [< Japanese]

gom·broon /góm broon/ *n* pottery made in Iran and elsewhere in imitation of white Chinese porcelain [Late 17C. After *Gombroon* (now Bandar Abbas), port in Iran]

Go·mor·rah /gə máwrə/ *n* a place or society marked by evil, depravity, and promiscuousness (*disapproving*) [Early 20C. After an ancient city destroyed by God because of its wickedness (Genesis 19)]

Gom·pers /gómpərz/, **Samuel** (1850–1924) British-born US labor leader. As the first president of the American Federation of Labor (AFL) (1886–95, 1896–1924), he was the dominant figure in the US labor movement.

"To protect workers in their inalienable rights to a higher and better life; to protect them, not only as equals before the law, but also in...their liberties as men, as workers, and as citizens; to overcome and conquer prejudices and antagonism...the glorious mission of the trade unions."
[Samuel Gompers, *Speech*; 1898]

gon- *prefix* same as **gono-** (*used before vowels*)

-gon *suffix* a figure having a particular number of angles ○ *undecagon* ○ *polygon* [< Greek *-gōnon* < *gōnia* "angle, corner" < Indo-European, "knee, bend"]

go·nad /gṓ nàd/ *n* an organ that produces reproductive cells (**gametes**), e.g., a testis or an ovary [Late 19C. < modern Latin *gonad-*, stem of *gonas* < Greek *gonos* "seed, generation"] —**go·nad·al** /gō nádd'l/ *adj* —**go·nad·ic** /gō náddik/ *adj*

go·nad·o·troph·ic *adj* another spelling of **gonadotropic**

go·nad·o·tro·phin *n* another spelling of **gonadotropin**

go·nad·o·trop·ic /gō nàddə tróppik, gònnədō-/, **go·nad·o·troph·ic** /-trófik/ *adj* stimulating or acting on the gonads

go·nad·o·trop·ic-re·leas·ing hor·mone *n* a hormone released by the hypothalamus that causes the secretion of luteinizing hormone and follicle-stimulating hormone by the pituitary gland

go·nad·o·tro·pin /gō nàddə trṓpin, gónnədə-/, **go·nad·o·tro·phin** /-trṓfin/ *n* a hormone secreted by the pituitary gland, and in some mammals by the placenta during pregnancy, that influences gonadal activity, including the onset of sexual maturity and regulation of reproductive activity

Go·na·ïves /gṑnə éev/ city in western Haiti, situated northwest of Port-au-Prince. Population: 63,291 (1995).

Gon·court /gawN kŏŏr/, **Edmond de** (1822–96) French novelist and diarist. He collaborated with his brother Jules de Goncourt (1830–70) on works including a 40-year journal of French social and literary life. Full name **Goncourt, Edmond Louis Antoine de**

> "Antiquity was perhaps created to provide professors with their bread and butter."
> [Edmond de Goncourt, *Le Journal des Goncourts (The Goncourt Journals)*; 1887–96]

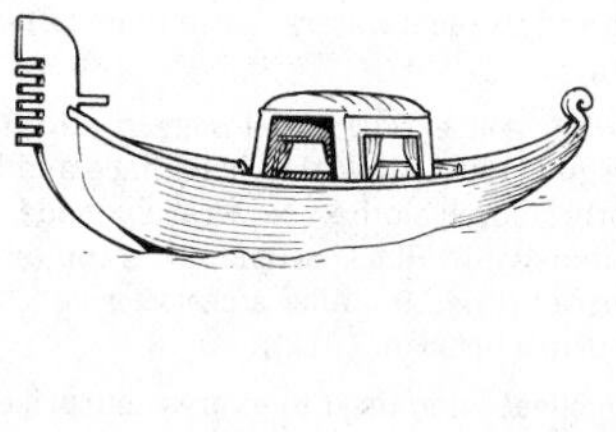

gondola

gon·do·la /góndʼlə, gən dṓlə/ *n* **1.** VENETIAN CANAL BOAT a narrow flat-bottomed boat, used on the canals of Venice, that has a curved prow and stern and is moved along with a long pole **2.** CABLE CAR a car or cabin suspended from cables, especially one attached to a ski lift **3.** CAR BELOW BALLOON a basket or cabin suspended from a balloon or airship, for carrying people or equipment **4.** FLAT-BOTTOMED RIVERBOAT a large flat-bottomed riverboat **5.** RAIL same as **gondola car 6.** WIDE-MOUTHED CONTAINER a wide-mouthed vase or bowl, usually broader than it is high [Mid-16C. Via Venetian Italian < Rhaeto-Romance *gondolà* "to roll, rock"]

gon·do·la car *n* a long, open, low-sided rail car

gon·do·lier /gònd'l éer, gónd'l éer/ *n* somebody who guides a gondola through water, especially on the canals of Venice

Gond·wa·na·land /gon dwáanə lànd/ ancient landmass, consisting of the southern part of the supercontinent of Pangea. Comprising South America, Africa, peninsular South Asia, Australia, and Antarctica, it began to break up approximately 200 million years ago.

gone /gawn, gon/ past participle of **go**[1] ■ *adj* **1.** ABSENT absent after leaving somewhere ○ *She has been gone for hours.* **2.** IRRECOVERABLE beyond hope of recovery ○ *All hopes for a truce are gone.* **3.** USED UP having been completely used up ○ *If the milk is all gone, we'll drink our coffee black.* **4.** PREGNANT having been pregnant for a particular number of months ○ *She's eight months gone.* **5.** DEAD no longer living (*informal*) **6.** UNEASY giving a sensation of giddiness or mild nausea **7.** EXHILARATED excited or exhilarated, e.g., while listening to music (*slang*) **8.** INFATUATED affected by a strong feeling of attraction toward somebody (*dated slang*) ○ *He's gone on your sister.*

gon·er /gáwnər, gónnər/ *n* somebody or something beyond hope of recovery, especially somebody who is dead or about to die (*slang*) ○ *It looks like he's a goner.*

gon·fa·lon /gónfə lṑn/ *n* a banner suspended from a crossbar, often with an edge cut like streamers, used as the standard of some medieval Italian republics or carried in church processions [Late 16C. Via Italian *gonfalone* < Old French *gonfanon* < Germanic, "war banner"]

gon·fa·lon·ier /gònfələ néer/ *n* **1.** a bearer of a gonfalon **2.** the chief magistrate of some medieval Italian republics, who carried the republic's gonfalon

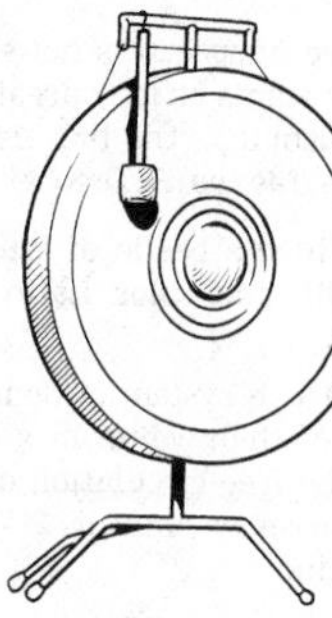

gong

gong /gawng/ *n* **1.** RESONANT BRONZE PLATE a circular bronze plate that makes a resonant sound when struck with a mallet, used as an orchestral percussion instrument or to summon people to meals **2.** WARNING BELL a round metal bell that is struck by a mechanically operated hammer, used as an alarm ■ *v* (**gonged, gong·ing, gongs**) **1.** *vi* SOUND LIKE GONG to sound resonantly like a gong **2.** *vt* SUMMON SOMEBODY to summon somebody with a gong [Early 17C. < Malay, an imitation of the sound made]

Gon·gor·ism /gáwng gə rìzzəm/ *n* a style in Spanish literature characterized by ornate devices, classical allusions, and deliberate obscurity [Early 19C. After Góngora y Argote (1561–1627), Spanish poet] —**Gon·gor·is·tic** *adj*

go·nid·i·um /gō níddee əm/ (*plural* **-i·a** /-ee ə/) *n* **1.** an asexual reproductive cell in some algae, e.g., a zoospore **2.** a chlorophyll-containing algal cell in the body (**thallus**) of a lichen [Mid-19C. < modern Latin < Greek *gonos* "offspring"] —**go·nid·i·al** *adj*

gon·if *n* CRIME same as **ganef**

go·ni·om·e·ter /gṑnee ómmətər/ *n* **1.** an instrument for measuring angles, especially those between crystal faces **2.** a device for establishing the bearing of an incoming radio signal [Mid-18C. < French *goniomètre* < Greek *gonia* "angle"] —**go·ni·o·met·ric** /-ə méttrik/ *adj* —**go·ni·o·met·ri·cal** *adj* —**go·ni·om·e·try** *n*

go·ni·on /gṓnee òn/ *n* the point on either side of the lower jaw where it turns upward [Late 19C. < French < Greek *gonia* "angle"]

go·ni·ot·o·my /gṑnee óttəmee/ (*plural* **-mies**) *n* an operation to treat glaucoma by cutting into the narrow angle between the back of the cornea and the root of the iris to allow drainage of aqueous humor

gonk /gawngk/ (**gonked, gonk·ing, gonks**) *vti* to tell a lie to somebody about something or embellish the truth, especially in an online conversation in a chat room (*slang*) ○ *Are you gonking me?* [Mid-20C. Invention] —**gonk** *n*

gon·na /gónnə/ *contr* going to (*nonstandard*)

gono- *prefix* sexual, generative, semen, seed ○ *gonopore* [< Greek *gonos* "offspring, procreation" < Indo-European, "beget"]

gon·o·coc·cus /gònnə kókəss/ (*plural* **-coc·ci** /-kók sī, -kó kī/) *n* a spherical bacterium that causes gonorrhea. Latin name: *Neisseria gonorrhoeae*. [Late 19C. < GONORRHEA] —**gon·o·coc·cal** *adj* —**gon·o·coc·cic** *adj*

gon·of *n* CRIME same as **ganef**

go-no-go *adj* requiring or involving a definitive decision either to proceed with a course of action or to abandon it

gon·o·pore /gónnə pàwr/ *n* an external reproductive pore in some insects and worms through which reproductive cells are secreted

gon·or·rhe·a /gònnə rée ə/, **gon·or·rhoe·a** *n* a sexually transmitted bacterial disease that causes inflammation of the genital mucous membrane, burning pain when urinating, and a discharge. It is caused by a gonococcus bacterium. [16C. Via modern Latin < Greek *gonorrhoia* "flowing of semen" < *gonos* "semen"] —**gon·or·rhe·al** *adj*

-gony *suffix* **1.** origin ○ *cosmogony* **2.** method of reproduction ○ *schizogony* [< Greek *gonos* (see GONO-)]

Gon·za·les /gən záaləss/, **Pancho** (1928–95) US tennis player. He dominated men's tennis in the 1950s, and in 1969 played the longest ever match at Wimbledon, defeating Charlie Pasarell after 112 games. Full name **Gonzales, Richard Alonzo**

gon·zo /gónzō/ *adj* (*slang*) **1.** unusual or strange **2.** characterized by subjective interpretation and exaggeration ○ *Gonzo journalism is unlike the work of the impartial observer.* [Late 20C. Origin ?]

goo /goo/ *n* (*informal*) **1.** a sticky substance, typically something unpleasant **2.** cloying emotionalism [Early 20C. Origin ?]

goo·ber /gŏŏbər/, **goo·ber pea** *n Can, Southern US* same as **peanut** (sense 1) [Mid-19C. < Mbundu *nguba*, Kongo, and other W African languages]

good /gŏŏd/ *adj* (**bet·ter** /béttər/, **best** /best/) **1.** OF HIGH QUALITY of a high quality or standard, either on an absolute scale or in relation to another or others ○ *The meal wasn't good.* ○ *He'll make a very good doctor.* ○ *I smashed one of my good plates.* **2.** SUITABLE having the appropriate qualities to be something or to fit a purpose ○ *Futons make good chairs as well as beds.* ○ *The bicycle is good for short trips.* **3.** SKILLED possessing the necessary skill or talent to do something ○ *I'm not a very good driver.* ○ *She's good at science.* **4.** VIRTUOUS having or showing an upright and virtuous character ○ *You're a good man, Joe.* **5.** KIND having or showing a kind and generous disposition ○ *She was always very good to me.* **6.** AFFORDING PLEASURE affording pleasure or comfort ○ *He's a man who insists on the finer things in life: good food, good books, and the theater.* **7.** UNDAMAGED having undergone no deterioration or damage ○ *I smelled the meat and found it was still good.* **8.** AMPLE sufficiently large, or providing more than enough of something ○ *Between them they have a good income.* **9.** HONORABLE worthy of honor or high esteem ○ *They come from a good family.* **10.** VALID acceptable as true or genuine and sufficient for the purpose ○ *There had better be a good explanation for this mess.* ○ *Don't travel unless your insurance is good.* **11.** HELPFUL helping somebody to organize thoughts or make decisions ○ *She gave me some good advice.* **12.** PLEASANT pleasant to look at ○ *Don't let her good looks distract you from her intelligence.* **13.** BENEFICIAL beneficial to health or well-being ○ *Eating lots of fruit is good for you.* ○ *It's good to talk.* **14.** FAVORABLE suitable and likely to produce the right results or conditions ○ *a good time to take a vacation* **15.** METICULOUS careful and thorough ○ *Take a good look around.* **16.** FINANCIALLY ADVANTAGEOUS financially or commercially advantageous or reliable ○ *I made a few good investments last year.* **17.** GENUINE that is what it appears to be ○ *a good dollar bill* **18.** OBEDIENT well behaved and obedient ○ *The children are always good when we take them out.* **19.** WELL-MANNERED socially correct ○ *very good behavior* **20.** ABLE TO DO MORE remaining in operation or effect, or able to continue doing something ○ *The car will be good for another 6,000 miles.* **21.** ABLE TO PAY able to pay or contribute something or to allow a sum to be drawn ○ *He's good for at least a thousand dollars.* **22.** GUARANTEED TO BE PAID describes a debt that will be paid in full ○ *a good debt* **23.** PRODUCING RESULT able to produce a particular result ○ *John is always good for a laugh.* **24.** SIZABLE considerable in extent or size ○ *a good selection of books on computers* **25.** FULL at least a particular time or length ○ *It's a good 30 years since we met.* **26.** WITHIN BOUNDS inside the required area for a shot, throw, or pass to be allowed ○ *The umpire said that the catch was good.* **27.** USED IN EXCLAMATIONS used in exclamations of surprise, dismay, or other strong feelings (*informal*) ○ *Good heavens! I've won first prize!* **28.** HEALTHY well in health (*informal*) ○ *"How are you?" "I'm good, thanks."* ■ *interj* EXPRESSING SATISFACTION used to express satisfaction or pleasure in something that has just been said or to confirm it ○ *"They've just arrived." "Good."* ■ *n* 1. **BENEFICIAL EFFECT** something resulting in a beneficial effect or state ○ *the common good* ○ *What good will complaining do?* 2. **GOODNESS** the quality of being good 3. **POSITIVE PART** the positive part or aspect of something ○ *You have to take the good with the bad in this agreement.* 4. **SOMETHING WORTH HAVING** something worth having or achieving ○ *the future good of the nation* 5. **ITEM OF MERCHANDISE** an item for sale or use, often one produced for later consumption [Old English *gōd* < Germanic, "unite"] ◇ **be (all) to the good** to be to somebody's benefit ◇ **for good** permanently from the time in question ○ *They've gone for good.* ◇ **give as good as you get** to contend as effectively as your opponent ◇ **good and** completely and entirely (*informal*) ○ *I'll get up in the morning when I'm good and ready, and not before.* ◇ **make good** to become successful, often after an unpromising start ◇ **make good (on) something** 1. to perform something successfully ○ *We must make good our attempt to win the trophy.* 2. to carry out something intended or promised ○ *She made good on her promise to repay the money on time.* 3. to compensate for something, especially for damage or loss 4. to demonstrate the truth or correctness of something ○ *If you cannot make good on these charges, the defendant will not stand trial.* ◇ **never had it so good** to have not possessed so many benefits before ◇ **to the good** richer by a particular amount of money ○ *By the end of the day, we were 50 dollars to the good.* ◇ **be up to no good** to be in the process of doing or planning something wrong or illegal (*informal*)

USAGE good or **well**? ***Good*** is the correct choice as an adjective after the linking verbs *be*, *appear*, and *seem*, and so-called sensory verbs such as *smell* and *taste*: *The jacket looks good. This steak tastes good.* ***Well*** is the correct choice as an adverb when it appears after other verbs that neither link nor designate sensory functions: *The jacket looks good and fits you well. Cook the steak well if you expect it to taste good.*

good af·ter·noon *interj* used when people meet or part, or begin or end a telephone conversation, during the afternoon

Good Book *n* the Christian Bible (*informal*)

good·bye /gŏŏd bī́/, **good-bye** *interj* used when people part or end a telephone conversation ○ *Goodbye! I'll see you next year.* ■ *n* an act of making a farewell ○ *It's time to say our goodbyes and catch the plane.* [Late 16C. < *God be with you*]

good cause *n* 1. something or somebody deserving help, especially a charity 2. a sufficient legal standard or reason

good eve·ning *interj* used when people meet or part, or begin or end a telephone conversation, during the evening

good faith *n* honesty of intention ○ *an effort to fulfill the contract in good faith*

good-for-noth·ing *n* an offensive term for a person who is regarded as lazy and irresponsible (*insult*) —**good-for-noth·ing** *adj*

Good Fri·day *n* a Christian holy day marking the death of Jesus Christ. Date: Friday before Easter Day.

Good Fri·day plant *n* PLANTS same as **moschatel**

good guy *n* a worthy or law-abiding person, especially in a novel or movie (*informal*)

good·heart·ed /gŏŏd haártəd/ *adj* having or showing a kind and generous nature —**good·heart·ed·ly** *adv* —**good·heart·ed·ness** *n*

Good Hope, Cape of /gŏŏd hṓp/ tip of the Cape Peninsula, South Africa. It is situated about 30 mi./48 km south of Cape Town and was rounded by the Portuguese navigator Bartolomeu Dias in 1488.

good-hu·mored *adj* disposed to be cheerful and friendly, or reflecting such an attitude —**good-hu·mored·ly** *adv*

good·ie *n* another spelling of **goody**

good·ies *npl* (*informal*) 1. foods such as cakes and chocolates that are regarded as tasty treats 2. objects that are nice to own or receive, especially small luxuries

Good·ing /gŏŏdding/, **Cuba, Jr.** (*b.* 1968) US actor. He came to prominence in *Boyz N the Hood* (1991) and won an Academy Award for best supporting actor for *Jerry Maguire* (1996).

good·ish /gŏŏddish/ *adj* 1. moderately good in quality 2. moderately large in quantity or extent ○ *a goodish helping*

good life *n* a life of carefree comfort and luxury ○ *living the good life in Palm Springs*

good-look·ing *adj* having a pleasant personal, especially facial, appearance —**good-look·er** *n*

SYNONYMS ***good-looking, attractive, beautiful, handsome, lovely, pretty***

CORE MEANING: having a pleasing appearance

good-looking having a pleasant personal, especially facial, appearance ○ *She was strikingly good-looking, with dark hair and eyes.* ○ *a good-looking young man* **attractive** pleasing in appearance or manner, or sexually desirable ○ *an attractive young couple* ○ *an attractive smile and appealing manner* **beautiful** very pleasing and impressive to look at (more often used of women than of men) ○ *beautiful eyes* ○ *a beautiful child* **handsome** with good facial features or a pleasing general appearance (generally used of men, but also of women who have strong but pleasant features) ○ *They make a handsome couple.* **lovely** pleasing to look at (most often used of women) ○ *You are looking lovely tonight.* **pretty** with a pleasant face that is appealing, rather than outstandingly beautiful (most often used of girls and women) ○ *a pretty young girl, aged eight*

good looks *npl* a pleasant personal appearance, especially facial appearance

good-luck bone *n regional* same as **wishbone** (sense 1)

REGIONAL NOTE See ***pulley bone***.

good·ly /gŏŏddlee/ (**-li·er, -li·est**) *adj* 1. **SOMEWHAT LARGE** moderately large in quantity or extent 2. **ATTRACTIVE** having a fine appearance (*archaic*) 3. **PLEASANT** of a pleasing quality (*archaic*) —**good·li·ness** *n*

Good·man /gŏŏdmən/, **Benny** (1909–86) US jazz musician. A virtuoso clarinettist, he popularized swing music during the 1930s and 1940s leading his own band. Full name **Goodman, Benjamin David**. Known as **the King of Swing**

> "Something happens when you find out that what you're doing is no longer music—that it's become entertainment. It's a subtle thing and affects what you're playing."
> [Benny Goodman, *Interview, Hear Me Talkin' to Ya*; 1955]

good morn·ing *interj* used when people meet or part, or begin or end a telephone conversation, during the morning

good name *n* somebody's reputation for honesty and integrity

good na·ture *n* a pleasant and obliging disposition

good-na·tured *adj* having or showing a pleasant and obliging disposition —**good-na·tured·ly** *adv* —**good-na·tured·ness** *n*

good·ness /gŏŏdnəss/ *n* 1. **GOOD QUALITY** the quality of being good 2. **VIRTUOUSNESS** personal virtue or kindness 3. **GOOD PART** the nutrition or other benefit to be derived from something ○ *Vegetables lose a lot of their goodness if you overcook them.* ■ *interj* **EXPRESSING SURPRISE** used to express surprise or amazement, or for emphasis ○ *Goodness! What was that?* ◇ **for goodness sake** used to express surprise, exasperation, or extreme anxiety, or for emphasis ◇ **goodness knows** used to indicate bafflement or lack of knowledge about something ○ *Goodness knows what they're doing out there at midnight.*

good night *interj* used to convey good wishes when people part or end a telephone conversation at night, especially at bedtime

good of·fic·es *npl* help or support, especially help in resolving a dispute

good old boy /gŏŏd ōl bóy/, **good ol' boy, good ole boy** *n* a stereotype of a man who is part of a peer group and conforms to the behavior characteristic of the group, especially a white man in parts of the rural southern United States (*often offensive*)

goods /gŏŏdz/ *n* **MERCHANDISE** articles for sale or use, often those produced for later consumption, as opposed to services (*takes a singular or plural verb*) ■ *npl* 1. **COMMERCIAL FABRICS** commercial textile fabrics (*takes a singular or plural verb*) 2. **PORTABLE PROPERTY** portable personal property (*takes a plural verb*) 3. *UK* **MERCHANDISE MOVED BY RAIL** merchandise that is transported, especially by rail (*takes a plural verb; often used before a noun*) ○ *a goods train* 4. **SOMETHING PROMISED** something promised or expected (*informal; takes a plural verb*) ○ *You can rely on her to come up with the goods.* 5. **INCRIMINATING EVIDENCE** information or evidence that will incriminate somebody (*slang; takes a plural verb*)

Good Sa·mar·i·tan *n* a helper of those who are in trouble [< the parable of the Good Samaritan (Luke 10:30–37), who helps a stranger beaten by robbers]

goods and chat·tels *npl* items of movable property, as distinct from buildings and land (*formal; often humorous*)

goods and serv·ic·es tax *n* in Canada, Australia, and New Zealand, a value-added tax charged on all goods and services

good-sized *adj* rather large in size ○ *The recipe called for a good-sized piece of chocolate.*

good-tem·pered *adj* having or showing a placid disposition —**good-tem·pered·ly** *adv* —**good-tem·pered·ness** *n*

good-time girl *n* a young woman whose chief objective is thought to be the pursuit of pleasure (*informal; often offensive*)

good turn *n* a friendly act that helps or benefits somebody else ○ *One good turn deserves another.*

good·will /gŏŏd wíl, gŏŏdwil/ *n* 1. **FRIENDLY DISPOSITION** friendly disposition toward somebody or something (*often used before a noun*) ○ *a goodwill gesture* 2. **WILLINGNESS** cheerful willingness to do something 3. ACCT **NONTANGIBLE VALUE OF BUSINESS** the value of a business over and above its tangible assets 4. **CHARITY SHOP** a shop that sells donated goods in order to raise money for charity

good word *n* 1. a comment recommending somebody or made in favor or defense of somebody ○ *He promised to put in a good word for me.* 2. the information or answer to a question that somebody would wish to have (*informal*) ○ *What's the good word? Will the plane take off?*

good works *npl* activities that are charitable or helpful to others

good·y /gŏŏddee/ *n* (*plural* **-ies**) *also* **good·ie** something desirable, especially something sweet to eat (*often used in the plural*) ■ *interj* used to express great pleasure (*informal*) ○ *Oh goody, ice cream!*

Good·year /gŏŏd yeer/, **Charles** (1800–60) US inventor. He discovered the vulcanization process for rubber (1839).

good·y-good·y (*informal*) *n* (*plural* **good·y-good·ies**) same as **goody two-shoes** ■ *adj* irritatingly well-behaved or smugly virtuous [Mid-19C. Reduplication]

good·y two-shoes *n* somebody smugly well-behaved, irritatingly virtuous, or sanctimonious (*informal*) [Mid-20C. < a character in a children's book]

goo·ey /gōō ee/ (**-i·er, -i·est**) *adj* 1. sticky and soft ○ *gooey chocolate frosting* 2. cloyingly sentimental (*informal*) ○ *a gooey romantic novel* —**goo·ey·ness** *n*

goof /gōōf/ *n* 1. **MISTAKE** a mistake or blunder (*informal*) 2. **OFFENSIVE TERM** an offensive term for somebody regarded as unintelligent or incompetent (*informal insult*) ■ *v* (**goofed, goof·ing, goofs**) (*informal*) 1. *vi* **MAKE MISTAKE** to make a thoughtless or unintelligent mistake 2. *vt* **BOTCH SOMETHING** to spoil something through incompetence or lack of intelligence [Early 20C. Probably < dialect *goff* "somebody considered unintelligent," via French and Italian < medieval Latin *gufus* "awkward, unintelligent"]

goof around *vi* to behave in a playful or silly way (*informal*) ○ *Once the pressure of exams was off, the students just goofed around.*

goof off *v* to waste time instead of working (*informal*) ○ *The crew goofed off when the boss left early.*

goof·ball /go͝of bàwl/ *n* **1.** an offensive term for somebody regarded as thoughtless or unintelligent (*slang insult*) **2.** a barbiturate or other drug in the form of a pill (*slang*)

goof-off *n* a lazy or irresponsible person (*insult*)

goof·proof /go͝of pro͞of/ *adj* same as **foolproof** (*informal*)

goof-up *n* a silly mistake (*informal*)

goof·y /go͝ofee/ (**-i·er, -i·est**) *adj* **1.** an offensive term for somebody regarded as silly or unintelligent (*informal insult*) **2.** in skateboarding and similar sports, used to describe a stance on the board in which the rider's right foot is nearer the front end (*slang*) —**goof·i·ly** *adv* —**goof·i·ness** *n* —**goof·y** *adv*

goof·y-foot·er *n* in skateboarding and similar sports, somebody who rides on the board with his or her right foot nearest to the front end —**goof·y-foot** *adj* —**goof·y-foot·ed** *adj*

goo·gol /go͞og'l, go͞o gàwl/ *n* the number equal to the numeral 1 followed by 100 zeros or 10^{100} [Mid-20C. Invention]

goo·gol·plex /go͞og'l plèks, go͞o gawl plèks/ *n* the number equal to the numeral 1 followed by 10^{100} zeros [Mid-20C. < GOOGOL + Latin *plexus* "intricate, braided"]

goo-goo *adj* expressing affection or sentimental attachment (*informal; disapproving*) ○ *goo-goo eyes* [Early 20C. Origin ?]

gook[1] /gook/ *n* a highly offensive term for an East Asian or Southeast Asian person or somebody of East Asian or Southeast Asian descent (*slang; insult*) [Mid-20C. Origin ?]

gook[2] *n* same as **guck**

goom·bah /go͞om baa/ *n* a close friend or associate, especially an older person acting as somebody's mentor (*slang*) [Mid-20C. Probably < Italian dialect, alteration of Italian *compàre* "godfather, accomplice, friend"]

goon /goon/ *n* **1.** a professional gangster whose work is beating up or terrorizing people (*informal*) **2.** somebody regarded as clumsy or uncouth (*informal insult*) [Mid-19C. Origin ?]

goon·da /go͞on daa/ *n S Asia* a ruffian or hooligan [Early 20C. < Hindi *gunḍā* "rascal"] —**goon·da·ism** *n*

goo·ney /go͞onee/ (*plural* **-neys**), **goo·ny** (*plural* **-nies**), **goo·ney bird, goo·ny bird** *n* an albatross, especially a black-footed albatross [Late 16C. Origin ?]

goop /goop/ *n* a semiliquid sticky or messy substance (*informal*) [Early 20C. Alteration] —**goop·y** *adj*

goos·an·der /goo sándər/ *n* a waterfowl with a narrow serrated beak, the male of which has a dark head and white body. Native to: Europe, North America. Latin name: *Mergus merganser*. [Early 17C. Probably < GOOSE + Old Norse *andar-*, stem of *ond* "duck"]

goose

goose /gooss/ *n* (*plural* **geese** /geess/) **1. LONG-NECKED WATER BIRD** a large waterfowl with a long neck and webbed feet, noted for its seasonal migrations and distinctive honking sound. Geese resemble swans but have shorter necks. Subfamily: Anserinae. **2. FEMALE BIRD** a female goose **3. FLESH OF GOOSE** the flesh of the goose, cooked and eaten as food **4. OFFENSIVE TERM** an offensive term for a person who is regarded as silly **5.** (*plural* **goos·es**) **TAILOR'S IRON** an iron with a long curved handle, used by tailors for pressing and smoothing cloth **6.** (*plural* **goos·es**) **PROD IN BUTTOCKS** a poke between or pinch on the buttocks (*slang*) ■ *vt* (**goosed, goos·ing, goos·es**) (*slang*) **1. PROD SOMEBODY IN BUTTOCKS** to poke or pinch somebody on the buttocks **2. ENCOURAGE SOMEBODY** to spur somebody on to action [Old English *gōs* < Indo-European] ◇ **kill the goose that laid the golden egg** to destroy something that is or has been a regular, dependable source of profit or benefit

goose bar·na·cle *n* a barnacle with a flattened shell, feathery appendages, and a fleshy stalk used to attach itself to surfaces, especially floating wood. Genus: *Lepas.*

gooseberry

goose·ber·ry /go͞oss bèrree/ (*plural* **-ries**) *n* **1. ACID FRUIT** an acid-tasting green or sometimes red fruit of a spiny plant, usually eaten cooked and sweetened (*often used before a noun*) ○ *gooseberry pie* **2. SPINY FRUIT BUSH** a spiny fruit bush that produces gooseberries. Native to: Europe, Asia. Latin name: *Ribes uva-crispa*. **3. PLANT WITH BERRIES LIKE GOOSEBERRIES** a plant bearing berries similar to gooseberries, e.g., the currant [Mid-16C. Origin ?]

goose·ber·ry gourd *n* FOOD same as **gherkin** (sense 2)

goose bumps *npl* temporary pimples on the skin brought on by cold or fear or by sudden excitement, and caused by the contraction of connective tissues (**papillae**) at the base of hairs

Goose Creek /go͞oss-/ town in southeastern South Carolina, directly northwest of Charleston and southeast of Columbia. Population: 30,179 (2002 estimate).

goose egg *n* a zero, especially one or a set of them indicating no score in a game or contest (*slang*)

goose·fish /go͞oss fish/ (*plural same* or **-fish·es**) *n* FISH same as **monkfish** (sense 1) [Early 19C. < GOOSE + FISH]

goose·flesh /go͞oss flèsh/ *n* skin affected by goose bumps

goose·foot /go͞oss fo͝ot/ *n* a weed with small greenish flowers and berries and leaves that resemble a goose's foot. Genus: *Chenopodium.*

goose·grass /go͞oss gràss/ *n* **1.** *UK* same as **cleavers 2.** PLANTS same as **yard grass**

goose·neck /go͞oss nèk/ *n* something curved like a goose's neck or U-shaped, e.g., a pipe joint or a flexible neck on a lamp (*often used before a noun*) ○ *a gooseneck lamp*

goose·neck bar·na·cle *n* ZOOL same as **goose barnacle**

goose pim·ples *npl* same as **goose bumps**

goose step *n* a military marching step performed with straight legs swung high in a forward movement —**goose-step** *vi*

goos·y /go͞ossee/ (**-i·er, -i·est**), **goos·ey** *adj* **1. RESEMBLING GOOSE** similar to a goose **2. HAVING GOOSE BUMPS** affected by goose bumps or the nervousness or fear that can cause them (*informal*) **3. SILLY** behaving in what is regarded as a silly or scatterbrained way (*disapproving*)

GOP *n* the Republican Party. Full form **Grand Old Party**

go·pher /gṓfər/ *n* **1.** a small short-tailed rodent that has fur-lined cheek pouches and short legs and digs sizable burrows. Native to: North and Central America. Family: Geomyidae. **2.** ZOOL same as **ground squirrel 3.** an Internet system that organizes files into menus containing links to text files, graphic images, databases, and additional menus (*often used before a noun*) ○ *a gopher site* **4.** *Southern US* same as **gopher tortoise** [Late 18C. Origin ?]

go·pher ball *n* in baseball, a pitched ball that is hit for a home run (*informal*)

go·pher snake *n* REPT same as **bull snake**

Go·pher State *n* a nickname for Minnesota

go·pher tor·toise *n* a burrowing tortoise. Native to: southeastern United States. Latin name: *Gopherus polyphemus.*

go·pher·wood /gṓfər wo͝od/ *n* in the Bible, the wood from which Noah's ark was supposed to have been made, or the tree from which it came [Early 17C. < Hebrew *gōpher*]

Go·rakh·pur /gáwrək po͝or/ industrial city in Uttar Pradesh State, northern India. It is a major railroad hub and trading center. Population: 505,566 (1991).

gor·al /gṓrəl/ *n* a small short-horned antelope. Native to: Himalaya region and adjacent Southeast Asia. Genus: *Nemorhaedus.* [Mid-19C. < a Himalayan language]

Go·raz·de /gə ráaz dáy/ town in eastern Bosnia and Herzegovina. A predominantly Muslim town, it was one of six "safe areas" designated by the UN Security Council during the Bosnian-Croatian-Serbian War. Population: 37,500 (1991).

Barnaby's

Mikhail Gorbachev

Gor·ba·chev /gáwrbə chàwf/, **Mikhail** (*b.* 1931) Soviet politician. As general secretary of the Soviet Communist Party (1985–91) and president (1988–91), he initiated democratic reforms that precipitated the disintegration of the Soviet Union and the end of the Cold War. He won the Nobel Peace Prize (1990). Full name **Gorbachev, Mikhail Sergeyevich**

> "Democracy is the wholesome and pure air without which a socialist public organization cannot live a full-blooded life."
> [Mikhail Gorbachev, *Report to the 27th Party Congress of the Communist Party of the USSR*; February 25, 1986]

Gor·di·an knot /gáwrdee ən-/ *n* a problem for which it is very difficult to find a solution [Late 16C. < the knot of *Gordius*, king of Gordium, which was to be loosened only by the future ruler of Asia: Alexander the Great sliced through it]

Sophie Bassouls

Nadine Gordimer

Gor·di·mer /gáwrdəmər/, **Nadine** (*b.* 1923) South African novelist. Her works examine the tensions of apartheid in South Africa. She won the Nobel Prize in literature (1991).

"When one says one writes for 'anyone who reads me' one must be aware that 'anyone' excludes a vast number of readers who cannot 'read' you or me because of givens they do not share with us in unequal societies."
[Nadine Gordimer, *Living in Hope and History*; 1999]

Gor·don /gáwrd'n/, **Charles William** (1860–1937) Canadian missionary and novelist. He ministered to the workers in the mines and forests of northwestern Canada and wrote, among other novels, *Black Rock* (1898). Pseudonym **Connor, Ralph**

Gor·don Riv·er the longest river in Tasmania, Australia, rising in the center of the island and flowing west into the southern Indian Ocean. Length: 112 mi./181 km.

Gor·don set·ter *n* a gun dog with a long black-and-tan coat, belonging to a breed developed in Scotland [Mid-19C. After Alexander *Gordon*, 4th Duke of Gordon (1743–1827)]

gore¹ /gawr/ (**gored, gor·ing, gores**) *vt* to pierce the flesh of a person or animal with horns or tusks [14C. Origin ?]

gore² /gawr/ *n* thick coagulating blood, especially blood shed as a result of violence [Old English *gor* "dirt, dung" < Germanic]

gore³ /gawr/ *n* a triangular piece of cloth that is sewn to others to form loose skirt [Old English *gāra*, origin ?] —**gored** *adj*

Gore /gawr/, **Al** (*b.* 1948) vice president of the United States (1993–2001). A Democrat from Tennessee, he was a US representative (1977–85) and senator (1985–93) before becoming Bill Clinton's vice president. Full name **Gore, Albert Arnold, Jr.**

"If we allow the information superhighway to bypass the less fortunate sectors of our society—even for an interim period—we will find that the information rich will get richer while the information poor get poorer..."
[Al Gore, *Speech to the National Press Club*; December 21,1993]

Gó·rec·ki /gaw rétskee/, **Henryk Mikolaj** (*b.* 1933) Polish composer. A leading figure of musical post-modernism, he wrote avant-garde pieces in the 1950s and 1960s such as *Scontri* (1960) but his later works, including *Symphony No. 3* (1976), are influenced by Polish folk and religious music.

Go·ren /gáw ràyn/, **Charles** (1901–91) US bridge player. He invented point-count bidding and wrote a popular newspaper column and many books about contract bridge. Full name **Goren, Charles Henry**. Known as **Mr. Bridge**

Gor·gas /gáwrgəss/, **William Crawford** (1854–1920) US physician and army officer. He rid Havana (1898) and the Panama Canal Zone (1904–10) of yellow-fever-carrying mosquitoes, and was the army surgeon general during World War I.

gorge /gawrj/ *n* **1. NARROW VALLEY** a deep narrow, usually rocky, valley **2. CONTENTS OF STOMACH** the contents of the stomach, especially when they are perceived as rising in the throat out of disgust or anger **3.** BIRDS **HAWK'S FOOD POUCH** a food storage pouch in the throat of a hawk **4. GREEDY EATING** an act of eating greedily and to excess **5. OBSTRUCTION IN PASSAGE** a mass of something obstructing a passage, especially a mass of ice obstructing a river **6.** MIL **ENTRANCE TO OUTWORK** a narrow entrance at the rear of an outwork in a fortification ■ *v* (**gorged, gorg·ing, gorg·es**) **1.** *vti* **EAT GREEDILY** to eat something greedily and to excess ○ *They gorged on chocolates.* ○ *They sat at the counter gorging meat and potatoes.* **2.** *vt* PHYSIOL same as **engorge** (sense 1) [14C. Via French, "throat" < Latin *gurge* "abyss, whirlpool"] —**gorg·er** *n*

gor·geous /gáwrjəss/ *adj* **1.** outstandingly beautiful or richly colored ○ *dressed in gorgeous silks* **2.** very pleasant (*informal*) ○ *a gorgeous spring morning* [15C. < Old French *gorgias* "stylish, elegant"] —**gor·geous·ly** *adv* —**gor·geous·ness** *n*

Gor·ges /gáwrjəz/, **Sir Ferdinando** (1566?–1647) English soldier and colonizer. He founded two companies (1606–19 and 1620–35) for colonizing lands in present-day Maine.

gor·get /gáwrjət/ *n* **1.** MIL **ARMOR FOR THROAT** a crescent-shaped piece of armor for protecting the throat **2.** CLOTHING **PART OF NUN'S HEADDRESS** the part of a nun's headdress that covers the neck and shoulders **3.** JEWELRY **NECKLACE** a circular or crescent-shaped ornament worn around the neck **4.** ZOOL **COLORED BAND ON THROAT** a band or patch of distinctive color on the throat of a bird or other animal [15C. < Old French *gorgete* < *gorge* "throat" (see GORGE)]

Gor·gon /gáwrgən/ *n* **1.** in Greek mythology, a monstrous woman with snakes for hair who turned those who looked at her into stone **2.** *also* **gor·gon** an offensive term for a woman regarded as very frightening or ugly (*insult*) [14C. < Latin *Gorgon-*, stem of *Gorgo* < Greek *Gorgō* < *gorgos* "terrible"] —**Gor·go·ni·an** /gawr gṓnee ən/ *adj*

gor·go·ni·an /gawr gṓnee ən/ *n* a coral with a flexible horny branched skeleton. Family: Gorgonacea. [Mid-19C. < modern Latin *Gorgonia* < Latin *Gorgon-* (see GORGON)] —**gor·go·ni·an** *adj*

Gor·gon·zo·la /gàwrgən zṓlə/, **gor·gon·zo·la** *n* a moist Italian blue cheese with a strong flavor [Late 19C. After a Milanese village]

Gor·ham /gáwrəm/ town in southwestern Maine, north of Saco and west of Portland. Population: 14,620 (2002 estimate).

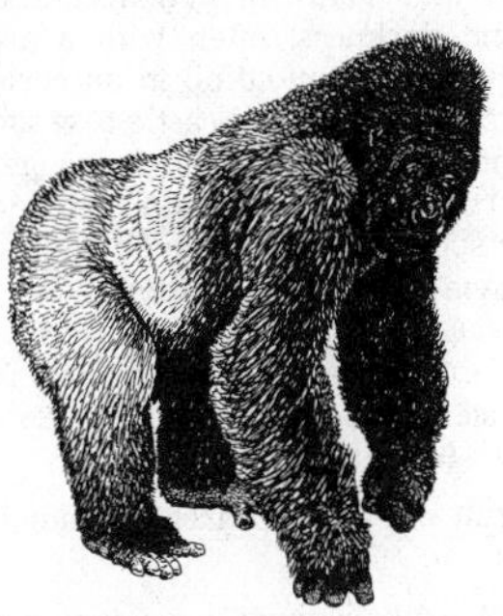

gorilla

go·ril·la /gə rílla/ *n* **1.** the largest ape, with a relatively short but very powerful body and coarse dark hair. Native to: central Africa. Latin name: *Gorilla gorilla.* **2.** somebody who is regarded as large or brutal, especially a hired thug (*informal*) [Mid-19C. Via modern Latin < Greek *gorillas*]

SPELLCHECK Do not confuse the spelling of ***gorilla*** and ***guerrilla*** ("a paramilitary soldier"), which sound similar.

Gö·ring another spelling of **Goering**

Gor·ky /gáwrkee/, **Gor·ki** former name for **Nizhniy Novgorod**

Gor·ky, Arshile (1904–48) Armenian-born US painter. His work helped introduce European surrealism into American art and influenced the abstract expressionists. Born **Adoian, Vosdanig Manoog**

Gör·litz /gúrlits, gőr-/ industrial city in Saxony State, east central Germany, on the border with Poland. Population: 67,755 (1997).

Gor·lov·ka ➧ **Horlivka**

gor·mand·ize /gáwrmən dīz/ (**-ized, -iz·ing, -iz·es**) *vti* to eat food gluttonously [Mid-16C. < GOURMANDISE "gluttony"] —**gor·mand·iz·er** *n*

gorm·less /gáwrmləss/ *adj UK* lacking intelligence, common sense, or initiative (*informal*) [Mid-19C. Variant of *gaumless* < *gaum* "understanding, heed" < Old Norse *gaumr*]

go-round *n* same as **go-around** (sense 1) (*informal*)

gorp /gawrp/ *n* a snack mixture used especially by hikers and campers, often made of nuts, seeds, dried fruits, and chocolate chips [Mid-20C. Origin ?]

~~**gorrilla**~~ incorrect spelling of **gorilla**

gorse

gorse /gawrss/ *n* a spiny bush with yellow flowers and black pods. Genus: *Ulex.* [Old English *gors* < Indo-European, "be prickly or rough"]

go·ry /gáwree/ (**-ri·er, -ri·est**) *adj* **1. BLOODY** covered with blood or gore **2. INVOLVING BLOODSHED** involving much bloodshed **3. HORRIBLE** arousing horror or terror ○ *the gory details* —**gor·i·ly** *adv* —**gor·i·ness** *n*

Gos·ford /góssfərd/ coastal city in eastern New South Wales, Australia, situated 53 mi./85 km north of Sydney. Population: 162,184 (2002 estimate).

gosh /gosh/ *interj* used to express surprise, amazement, or pleasure (*informal*) [Mid-18C. Substitution for GOD]

goshawk

gos·hawk /góss hàwk/ *n* a large hawk with broad rounded wings and a long tail. Native to: Europe, North America. Latin name: *Accipiter gentilis.* [12C. < Old English *goshafoc* < forms of GOOSE + HAWK¹]

Go·shen /gósh'n/ city in northern Indiana, on the Elkhart River, northwest of Fort Wayne and southeast of Elkhart. Population: 29,683 (2002 estimate).

gosht /gosht/ *n S Asia* red meat such as lamb or beef [< Hindi]

gos·ling /gózzling/ *n* a young goose [15C. < Old Norse *gøslingr* < *gas* "goose"]

go-slow *n UK* same as **slowdown**

gos·pel /góspəl/ *n* **1.** a set of beliefs held strongly by a group or person **2.** something believed to be absolutely and unquestionably true **3.** MUSIC same as **gospel music** [13C. < GOSPEL]

Gos·pel /góspəl/ *n* **1. TEACHINGS OF JESUS CHRIST** the teachings of Jesus Christ and the story of his life **2. BOOK OF BIBLE** a book of the Bible belonging to a set of four, Matthew, Mark, Luke, and John, that tell the story of the life of Jesus Christ **3. BIBLE EXTRACT** an extract from one of the Gospels read as part of a Christian religious service [Old English *gōdspel* "good news" < forms of GOOD + SPELL²]

gos·pel·er /góspələr/, **gos·pel·ler** *n* **1.** a reader of the Gospel in a Christian religious service **2.** a preacher of the Gospel (*disapproving*)

gos·pel mu·sic *n* highly emotional evangelical vocal music that originated among African American Christians in the southern United States and was a strong influence in the development of soul music

gos·pel side *n* in a Christian church, the left side of the altar as faced by the congregation. ◊ **epistle side**

gos·pel truth *n* same as **gospel** (sense 2)

Gos·port /góss pàwrt/ city in Hampshire, southern England, on Portsmouth harbor. Population: 76,415 (2001).

gos·sa·mer /góssəmər/ *n* **1. FINE COBWEBS** a fine film of cobwebs, often seen floating in the air or covered with dew on the ground **2. DELICATE FABRIC** a delicate, sheer fabric or gauze **3. SOMETHING SHEER AND DELICATE** something delicate, sheer, and filmy [14C. Probably < GOOSE + SUMMER[1], period of mild autumn weather when goose was in season and such webs were often seen in the air] —**gos·sa·mer·y** *adj*

gos·san /góss'n/ *n* a yellow or red layer on the surface of minerals rich in iron oxide, produced by alteration and leaching of sulfide ores [Late 18C. Probably < Cornish < *gōs* "blood"]

Gos·sett /góssət/, **Louis, Jr.** (*b.* 1936) US actor. He won an Academy Award for his performance in *An Officer and a Gentleman* (1982).

gos·sip /góssip/ *n* **1. CONVERSATION ABOUT PERSONAL MATTERS** conversation about the personal details of others' lives, whether rumor or fact, especially when malicious **2. CASUAL CONVERSATION** informal conversation or writing about recent and often personal events **3. HABITUAL TALKER** somebody who habitually discusses the personal details of others' lives ■ *vi* (**-siped, -sip·ing, -sips**) **TALK ABOUT OTHER PEOPLE** to spread rumors or tell people the personal details of others' lives, especially maliciously [Old English *godsibb* "godparent, close friend" < GOD + SIB "relative"] —**gos·sip·er** *n* —**gos·sip·ry** *n* —**gos·sip·y** *adj*

SYNONYMS See *talkative*.

gos·sip col·umn *n* a regular feature in a magazine or newspaper where rumors and personal or intimate facts about celebrities are exposed —**gos·sip col·um·nist** *n*

gos·sip·mong·er /góssip mùng gər, -mòng-/ *n* somebody who spreads gossip

gos·sy·pol /góssə pàwl/ *n* a substance that inhibits sperm production. Source: cotton seeds. [Late 19C. < modern Latin *Gossypium* < Latin *gossypion* "cotton tree"]

got past participle, past tense of **get**[1]

Gö·ta Ca·nal /yùrtə-, yǒtə-/ waterway in southwestern Sweden, linking Gothenburg on the western coast with Stockholm on the Baltic coast. Length: 240 mi./386 km.

got·cha /gótchə/ (*informal*) *interj* **EXPRESSING TRIUMPH OVER ANOTHER** used to indicate that somebody has been successfully tricked or caught out in some way or to indicate comprehension of something ■ *n* **1. UNEXPECTED PROBLEM** an unexpected problem or drawback **2. UNFORESEEN SOFTWARE PROBLEM** a surprise or unforeseen problem in the way a piece of software works [Mid-20C. < a pronunciation of *got you*]

Göt·e·borg ♦ **Gothenburg**

goth /goth/ *n* **1. SOMEBODY UNCIVILIZED** an uncivilized or barbaric person **2. MUSICAL STYLE** a style of popular music that combines features of heavy metal with punk **3. STYLE OF CLOTHES AND MAKE-UP** a style of fashion, popular among men and women in the 1980s, characterized by black clothes, heavy silver jewelry, black eye makeup and lipstick, and often pale face makeup **4. FOLLOWER OF GOTH MUSIC AND FASHION** a fan of goth music and fashion [Mid-17C. < GOTH]

Goth /goth/ *n* **1.** a member of an ancient Germanic people who settled south of the Baltic and founded kingdoms in many parts of the Roman Empire between the 3rd and the 5th centuries **2.** MUSIC, FASHION another spelling of **goth** (senses 2–4) [Old English *gotan* "Goths" < late Latin *Gothi* < Germanic]

Goth·am /góthəm/ *n* a nickname for New York City [Originally used by Washington Irvine, after *The Wise Men of Gotham*, folk tale; popularized by the Batman stories]

Goth·en·burg /góthən bùrg/ seaport and industrial city on the Göta River estuary in southwestern Sweden. It is the second largest city and principal port of Sweden. Population: 459,593 (1998). Swedish name **Göteborg**

goth·ic /góthik/ *adj* **1. UNCIVILIZED** barbarous or uncivilized **2.** LITERAT another spelling of **Gothic** *adj* (sense 4) ■ *n* **1.** MUSIC, FASHION same as **goth** (senses 2–3) **2. SIMPLE TYPEFACE** a simple sans serif typeface with strokes of uniform width **3. HEAVY ANGULAR TYPEFACE** a heavy bold angular early typeface [Late 17C. < GOTHIC] —**goth·i·cal·ly** *adv*

Gothic: interior of Cologne Cathedral, Germany (begun 1248)

Goth·ic /góthik/ *adj* **1. OF MEDIEVAL ARCHITECTURAL STYLE** belonging to a style of architecture used in Western Europe between the 12th and 15th centuries, and characterized by pointed arches, flying buttresses, and high curved ceilings **2. OF MEDIEVAL ARTISTIC STYLE** belonging to a style of music, painting, or sculpture practiced in parts of Europe between the 12th and 15th centuries **3. OF MIDDLE AGES** relating to or characteristic of the Middle Ages **4. OF EERIE FICTION STYLE** belonging to a genre of fiction characterized by gloom and darkness, often with a grotesque or supernatural plot unfolding in an eerie or lonely location such as a ruined castle **5. OF GOTHS** relating to the ancient Goths, or their language or culture ■ *n* **EXTINCT LANGUAGE OF ANCIENT GOTHS** an extinct language formerly spoken by the ancient Goths in parts of Scandinavia and around the Baltic Sea. It belongs to the East Germanic group of the Germanic branch of Indo-European languages. [Late 16C. Directly or via French < late Latin *Gothicus* < *Gothi* (see GOTH)] —**Goth·i·cal·ly** *adv* —**Goth·i·ciz·er** *n*

Goth·ic arch *n* a pointed arch, as found in Gothic churches

goth·i·cism /góthi sìzzəm/ *n* crudeness of style or manner, or an example of such crudeness

Goth·i·cism *n* use of the Gothic style of architecture, art, or literature —**Goth·i·cist** *n*

Goth·ic Re·viv·al *n* a style of architecture based on a reintroduction of the Gothic style, popular in the 18th and 19th centuries

Got·land /góttlənd/, **Gott·land** island and county of Sweden, situated in the Baltic Sea about 50 mi./80 km from the mainland. Population: 58,120 (1995). Area: 1,212 sq. mi./3,140 sq. km.

got·ta /góttə/ *vi* got to (*informal*) [Representing a pronunciation]

got·ten past participle of **get**[1]

USAGE See *get*[1].

Göt·ter·däm·mer·ung /gòttər dámmə rŏŏng, gòttər démmə-/, **göt·ter·däm·mer·ung** *n* **1.** in Germanic mythology, the destruction of the gods after battle with the forces of doom **2.** the overthrow or violent ending of a regime or institution [Early 20C. < German, "twilight of the gods"]

Göt·tin·gen /gŏtingən/ university city in Lower Saxony, central Germany. It is situated about 55 mi./89 km south of Hanover. Population: 127,519 (1997).

Gott·land ♦ **Gotland**

Gott·schalk /góch àwk/, **Louis Moreau** (1829–69) US composer and pianist. He was the first US pianist to achieve international recognition. His own works incorporated Caribbean rhythms and melodic styles.

gouache /gwaash, goo áash/ *n* **1. PAINTING TECHNIQUE** a method of painting in which opaque watercolors are mixed with gum **2. PAINT USED IN GOUACHE** the paint used in the gouache technique **3. GOUACHE PAINTING** a painting done with gouache [Late 19C. Via French < Italian *guazzo* "puddle"]

Gou·da[1] /góodə, gówdə/ *n* a mild Dutch cheese, typically sold in a flat sphere covered in wax [Mid-19C. After GOUDA[2]]

Gou·da[2] /góodə, gówdə/ city in South Holland Province, western Netherlands. Famous for its cheese, it is situated about 13 mi./21 km northeast of Rotterdam. Population: 71,827 (2000).

Gou·dy /gówdee/, **Frederic William** (1865–1947) US typographer. He created over 100 different typefaces and wrote a number of books, including *A Half Century of Type Design and Typography* (1946).

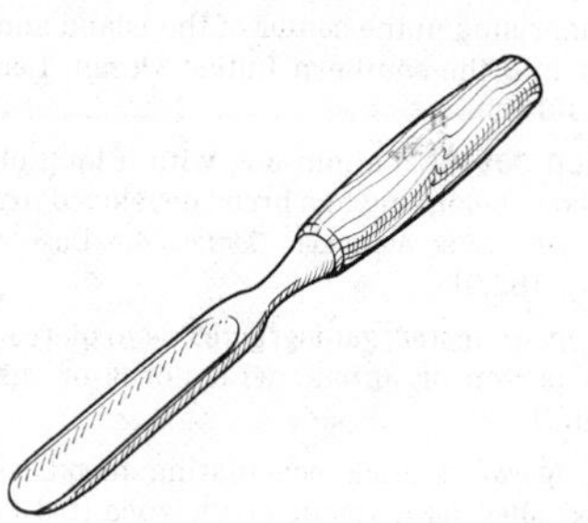
gouge *n* (sense 1)

gouge /gowj/ *vt* (**gouged, goug·ing, goug·es**) **1. CARVE OUT HOLE** to cut or scoop a hole or groove in something, usually using a sharp tool **2. FORM ROUGHLY BY CUTTING** to form something by roughly cutting it out of surrounding material **3. INJURE SOMEBODY'S EYE** to attack somebody's eye with the thumb **4. OVERCHARGE SOMEBODY** to cheat somebody or act dishonestly by demanding an unreasonably high price for goods or services (*informal*) ■ *n* **1. CHISEL WITH CONCAVE BLADE** a chisel with a concave blade. Use: cutting grooves and holes in wood. **2. SMALL HOLE** a mark, groove, or hole, usually made with a pointed tool **3. OVERCHARGING** an instance of paying too much or being charged exorbitantly for goods or services (*informal*) **4.** GEOL **ROCK FRAGMENTS** clay material produced by the grinding together of rock surfaces in a fault or within a mineral vein [Late 15C. Via French < late Latin *gubia*, *gulbia* < Celtic] —**goug·er** *n*

gou·lash /góo laash, -làsh/ *n* **1. HUNGARIAN STEW** a stew of Hungarian origin, made with beef, veal, lamb, or pork and seasoned with paprika **2. MIXTURE** an eclectic and uncoordinated mixture of something **3. DEALING OF CARDS** a way of dealing cards that have already been arranged in a specific order, without shuffling them first [Mid-19C. < Hungarian *gulyás*, shortening of *gulyás hús* "herdsman's meat"]

Gould /goold/, **Jay** (1836–92) US financier and speculator. He gained a reputation as a ruthless businessman through his hostile takeover of Erie Railroad. His scheme to corner the gold market led to a stock market crash (1869), known as Black Friday. Born **Gould, Jason**

> "Science is an integral part of culture. It's not this foreign thing, done by an arcane priesthood. It's one of the glories of human intellectual tradition."
> [Jay Gould, *Independent (London)*; January 24, 1990]

Gould, Morton (1913–96) US composer and conductor. He used folk and jazz themes in works such as *Fall River Legend* (1948) and the Pulitzer Prize-winning *String Music* (1994).

Gould, Stephen Jay (1941–2002) US paleontologist. He helped to originate the "punctuated equilibrium" theory of evolution, and reached a popular audience with his *Natural History* magazine column (from 1974).

> "Nature is amoral, not immoral...It existed for eons before we arrived, didn't know we were coming, and doesn't give a damn about us."
> [Stephen Jay Gould, *Rocks of Ages: Science and Religion in the Fullness of Life*; 1999]

Gou·nod /góonō, goo nṓ/, **Charles François** (1818–93) French composer. As well as sacred choral music, he wrote several operas including his best known work, *Faust* (1859), based on the poem by Goethe.

gou·ra·mi /goo raámee/ (*plural same* or **-mis**) *n* a freshwater fish, many species of which are capable of breathing air and are often kept in aquariums. Native to: Southeast Asia. Family: Anabantidae. [Late 19C. Via Malay *gurami* "freshwater carp" < Javanese *graméh*]

gourd

gourd /gawrd/ *n* **1.** a hard-skinned fleshy fruit produced by several different plants related to cucumbers and squash. Use: dried decorations, hollowed out for bowls, cups. **2.** a plant that produces gourds. Native to: tropical regions, cultivated worldwide. Genera: *Curcurbita* or *Lagenaria*. [14C. Via Anglo-Norman *gurde* < Latin *cucurbita*] ◇ **off** *or* **out of your gourd** not thinking clearly or rationally (*slang*)

gourde /goord/ *n* the main unit of currency in Haiti. See table at **currency** [Mid-19C. Via Haitian Creole < French *gourd* "dull, heavy" < Latin *gurdus* "unintelligent person"]

gour·mand /góor maánd, góormənd/ *n* a lover of food who often eats excessively or greedily [15C. < French, "glutton"]

gour·man·dise /góormən deéz/ *n* an appreciation of good food and drink [15C. < French < *gourmand* "glutton"]

gour·met /goor máy, góor mày/ *n* somebody who enjoys and knows a lot about good food and drink ■ *adj* relating to high-quality food that is sophisticated, expensive, rare, or meticulously prepared [Early 19C. < French, alteration (influenced by *gourmand* "glutton") of Middle French *groumet* "servant, vintner's assistant" < English GROOM]

gout /gowt/ *n* **1.** a metabolic disorder mainly affecting men in which excess uric acid is produced and deposited in the joints, causing painful swelling, especially in the toes and feet **2.** a large blob or clot of something, usually of blood [13C. Via French < Latin *gutta* "drop of liquid"; from the belief that gout was caused by drops of a morbid fluid in the blood]

gout·weed /gówt weèd/ *n* a plant that causes problems as a weed in gardens. Flowers: small, white, in clusters. Native to: Europe, North America. Latin name: *Aegopodium podagraria*. [< its use in treating gout]

gout·y /gówtee/ (**-i·er, -i·est**) *adj* **1.** affected by or tending to contract gout **2.** resulting from or causing gout —**gout·i·ness** *n*

gov *abbr* government organization (*used in Internet addresses*) See table at **domain name**

gov. /guv/ *abbr* **1.** government **2.** governor

~~**govenor**~~ incorrect spelling of **governor**

~~**goverment**~~ incorrect spelling of **government**

gov·ern /gúvvərn/ (**-erned, -ern·ing, -erns**) *v* **1.** *vti* HAVE POLITICAL AUTHORITY to be responsible officially for directing the affairs, policies, and economy of a state, country, or organization **2.** *vt* CONTROL SOMETHING to control, regulate, or direct something **3.** *vt* HAVE INFLUENCE OVER SOMETHING to have or exercise an influence over something ○ *issues that govern the final settlement* **4.** *vt* RESTRAIN SOMETHING to control something by restraint (*formal*) ○ *unable to govern her emotions* **5.** *vt* MECH ENG CONTROL SPEED OF ENGINE to maintain the speed of an engine or keep it from going above a specific level by controlling the fuel or steam supply **6.** *vt* LAW BE LAW FOR SOMETHING to be the defining rule for something **7.** *vt* GRAM DETERMINE FORM OF WORD to dictate the inflection, mood, or case of another word [13C. Via Old French *governer* and Latin *gubernare* < Greek *kubernan* "steer"] —**gov·ern·a·ble** *adj*

gov·er·nance /gúvvərnənss/ *n* **1.** MANNER OF GOVERNMENT the system or manner of government **2.** STATE OF GOVERNING A PLACE the act or state of governing a place **3.** AUTHORITY control or authority (*formal*)

gov·ern·ess /gúvvərnəss/ *n* especially formerly, a woman employed to teach children in their own homes, and sometimes also to care for the children [15C. < Old French *governeresse*, form of *governeour* "governor"]

gov·ern·ment /gúvvərnmənt/ *n* **1.** POLITICAL AUTHORITY a group of people who have the power to make and enforce laws for a country or area **2.** STYLE OF GOVERNMENT a type of political system **3.** THE STATE VIEWED AS RULER the state and its administration viewed as the ruling political power **4.** BRANCH OF GOVERNMENT a branch or agency of a government, taken as the whole (*informal*) **5.** CONTROL OF SOMETHING the management or control of something **6.** EDUC POLITICAL SCIENCE political science as a subject of study **7.** GRAM DETERMINATION OF INFLECTION the determination of the inflection, mood, or case of a word by another word —**gov·ern·ment** *adj* —**gov·ern·ment·al** /gùvvərn mént'l/ *adj* —**gov·ern·ment·al·ly** *adv*

gov·ern·ment·al·ize /gùvvərn mént'l ìz/ (**-ized, -iz·ing, -iz·es**) *vt* to put a sphere of activity under the power of the government

gov·ern·ment·ese /gùvvərnmən teéz, -teéss/ *n* language that is full of difficult jargon, thought to be characteristic of language used by governments

Gov·ern·ment House *n Can* in Canada, the official residence of the governor-general or, in some provinces, the lieutenant governor

gov·er·nor /gúvvərnər/ *n* **1.** US STATE EXECUTIVE the elected executive of state government in the United States **2.** GOVERNING OFFICIAL an appointed or elected official who governs a state, colony, or province for a specific term **3.** GOVERNING BODY MEMBER a member of a governing body of an institution **4.** *UK* same as **warden** (sense 1) **5.** AUTHORITY FIGURE an authority figure, e.g., an employer or boss (*informal*) **6.** MECH ENG REGULATING DEVICE a device for regulating the speed of an engine —**gov·er·nor·ship** *n*

gov·er·no·rate /gúvvərnərət/ *n* **1.** an administrative district of a country controlled by a governor ○ *Al Qayrawan Governorate* **2.** the condition of being a governor, or the term of office of a governor

gov·er·nor-gen·er·al (*plural* **gov·er·nors-gen·er·al** or **gov·er·nor-gen·er·als**) *n* **1.** a governor who has authority over deputy governors **2.** the representative of the British Crown in some countries of the Commonwealth of Nations —**gov·er·nor-gen·er·al·ship** *n*

Gov·er·nors Is·land /gúvvərnərz-/ island in New York Bay, just south of the tip of Manhattan Island, that was used as a military post until the 19th century. Area: 173 acres/70 hectares.

govt. *abbr* government

Gow·er Pen·in·su·la /gòw ər-/ rocky peninsula on the coast of Swansea district, southern Wales. Length: 15 mi./24 km.

gown /gown/ *n* **1.** ELEGANT DRESS a woman's full-length elegant or formal dress for special occasions **2.** LONG ROBE a long robe, often dark in color, worn on official occasions by people such as judges, professors, and university graduates **3.** LOOSE OUTER GARMENT a loose cloak or robe worn, e.g., by surgeons, to protect clothes ■ *vt* (**gowned, gown·ing, gowns**) PUT GOWN ON SOMEBODY to dress somebody in a loose robe [14C. Via Old French *goune* < late Latin *gunna* "fur or leather garment"]

gowns·man /gównzmən/ (*plural* **-men** /-mən/) *n* a man, e.g., an academic, who wears a gown for professional reasons (*dated*)

goy /goy/ (*plural* **goy·im** /góy im/ or **goys**) *n* an offensive term for somebody who is not Jewish [Mid-19C. Via Yiddish < Hebrew *gōy* "(non-Jewish) nation or people"] —**goy·ish** *adj*

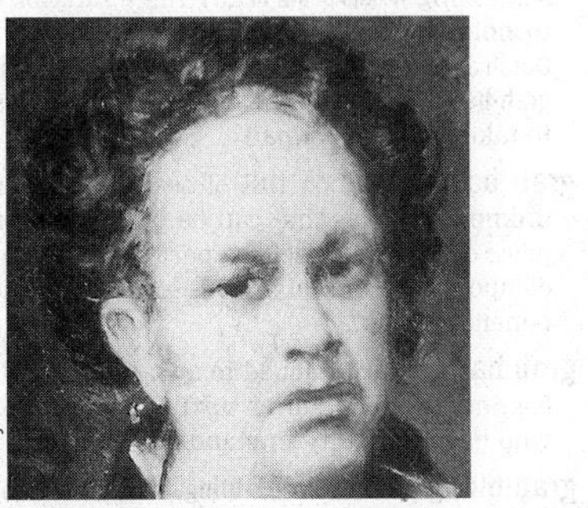

Barnaby's

Francisco de Goya: self-portrait

Go·ya /góy ə/, **Francisco de** (1746–1828) Spanish painter. One of the greatest Spanish masters, he was known for his naturalistic tapestry designs, portraits, and several series of satirical etchings, including *The Caprices* (1797–99). Full name **Goya y Lucientes, Francisco José de**

goy·im JUDAISM plural of **goy** (*offensive*)

gp *abbr* Guadeloupe (*used in Internet addresses*) See table at **domain name**

GP *abbr* **1.** MUSIC general pause **2.** HEALTH SERVICES general practice **3.** HEALTH SERVICES general practitioner **4.** SPORTS Grand Prix

GPA *abbr* EDUC grade point average

g.p.d. *abbr* MEASURE gallons per day

g.p.h. *abbr* MEASURE gallons per hour

g.p.m. *abbr* MEASURE gallons per minute

GPO *abbr* Government Printing Office

GPRS *n* a system that provides immediate and continuous access to the Internet from wireless devices such as cell phones. Full form **general packet radio service**

GPS *n* a worldwide navigation system that uses information received from orbiting satellites. Full form **Global Positioning System**

USAGE See *ATM*.

---

g.p.s. *abbr* MEASURE gallons per second

GPU *n* the Soviet secret police, from 1922 to 1923 [< Russian *Gosudarstvennoe politicheskoe upravlenie* "State Political Directorate"]

gq *abbr* Equatorial Guinea (*used in Internet addresses*) See table at **domain name**

GQ *abbr* MIL General Quarters

gr *abbr* Greece (*used in Internet addresses*) See table at **domain name**

gr. *abbr* **1.** grade **2.** MEASURE grain **3.** MEASURE gram[1] **4.** MEASURE gross

Gr. *abbr* **1.** Greece **2.** PEOPLES, LANG Greek

GR8 *abbr* ONLINE great (*used in e-mails or text messages*)

Graaf·i·an fol·li·cle /graáfee ən-, gràffee ən-/ *n* a small fluid-filled sac (**vesicle**) containing a maturing ovum. Graafian follicles are found in the ovaries of mammals. [Mid-19C. After Regnier de *Graaf* (1641–73), Dutch anatomist]

grab /grab/ *v* (**grabbed, grab·bing, grabs**) **1.** *vt* GRASP SOMETHING to take hold of something quickly, suddenly, or forcefully ○ *Grab a pen and sit down.* **2.** *vti* TRY TO GRASP to try to grasp something that is hard to reach or in short supply ○ *Stop grabbing or I won't give you any.* **3.** *vt* SEIZE SOMETHING to take something violently or dishonestly ○ *grab the money and run* **4.** *vt* HAVE EMOTIONAL IMPACT ON SOMEBODY to appeal to, attract, impress, or affect somebody emotionally (*informal*) ○ *The movie didn't really grab me.* **5.** *vt* HURRIEDLY GET SOMETHING to obtain something quickly and without difficulty (*informal*) ○ *I'll just grab a bite to eat.* **6.** *vi* TAKE HOLD SUDDENLY to take hold suddenly or intermittently ○ *The brakes grabbed and the car went into a skid.* ■ *n* **1.** GRABBING the act of grabbing something ○ *He made a grab at my arm.* **2.** SOMETHING

GRABBED something that is grabbed **3.** DEVICE FOR GRABBING an apparatus or device used for grasping hold of something **4.** GRABBING ABILITY the ability or capacity to hold something fast [Late 16C. Probably < Middle Dutch or Middle Low German *grabben*] —**grab·ba·ble** *adj* —**grab·ber** *n* ◇ **up for grabs** available for the first comer to take or use (*informal*)

grab bag *n* **1.** a box full of sealed bags containing unknown objects that can be purchased for a fixed price or are the prize in a party game **2.** something composed of miscellaneous or mismatched components (*informal*)

grab bar *n* a bar attached to a wall to provide a grip, e.g., near a bath tub or next to a toilet, for people who have difficulty in standing up

grab·ble /grább'l/ (**-bled, -bling, -bles**) *vi* **1.** to scratch or search around with the hands **2.** to tumble or fall to the ground on all fours [Late 16C. Probably < Dutch *grabbelen* < *grabben* "grab"] —**grab·bler** *n*

grab·by /grábbee/ (**-bi·er, -bi·est**) *adj* **1.** GRASPING pushy and grasping (*informal disapproving*) **2.** ADHERING capable of holding fast or adhering (*informal*) **3.** DRAWING ATTENTION drawing people's attention (*informal*) ○ *a grabby headline* **4.** OVERTLY SEXUAL prone to making overt sexual advances (*informal disapproving*) —**grab·bi·ness** *n*

gra·ben /graabən/ *n* a broad valley, especially a rift valley [Late 19C. < German *Graben* "ditch"]

Gra·ble /gráyb'l/, **Betty** (1916–73) US actor, dancer, and singer. She was a star of musical films in the 1940s. Full name **Grable, Elizabeth Ruth**

> "There are two reasons why I am successful in show business and I am standing on both of them."
> [Attributed to Betty Grable]

Grac·chus /grákəss/, **Gaius Sempronius** (153–121 B.C.) Roman politician and social reformer. During his two terms as tribune (123 and 122 B.C.), he sought to enforce the land reforms championed by his brother, Tiberius. He failed to get reelected a third time and was found dead shortly afterward.

Grac·chus, Tiberius Sempronius (163–133 B.C.) Roman politician and social reformer. Popular with farmers and poorer members of society, he served as tribune (133 B.C.) and introduced a bill for land reform. He was murdered during a riot following the senate's opposition to his standing for a second term as tribune.

grace /grayss/ *n* **1.** ELEGANCE elegance, beauty, and smoothness of form or movement **2.** POLITENESS dignified, polite, and decent behavior ○ *She fended off queries with her usual grace.* **3.** GENEROSITY OF SPIRIT a capacity to tolerate, accommodate, or forgive people **4.** PRAYER AT MEALTIMES a short prayer of thanks to God said before, or sometimes after, a meal **5.** FIN same as **grace period** **6.** PLEASING QUALITY a pleasing and admirable quality or characteristic (*usually used in the plural*) **7.** GIFT OF GOD TO HUMANKIND in Christianity, the infinite love, mercy, favor, and goodwill shown to humankind by God **8.** FREEDOM FROM SIN in Christianity, the condition of being free of sin, e.g., through repentance to God **9.** MUSIC same as **grace note** ■ *vt* (**graced, grac·ing, grac·es**) **1.** CONTRIBUTE PLEASINGLY TO SOMETHING to make a pleasing contribution to an event, often by attending it (*often ironic*) ○ *So good of you to grace us with your presence.* **2.** ADD ELEGANCE TO SOMETHING to add elegance, beauty, or charm to something **3.** ORNAMENT MUSIC to add ornamental or decorative notes to a piece of music [12C. Via French < Latin *gratia* < *gratus* "pleasing"] ◇ **fall from grace** to lose a favored or privileged position ◇ **with (a) bad grace** in a rude and bad-tempered way ◇ **with (a) good grace** in a polite and willing way

Grace *n* used as a title when addressing a duke, duchess, or archbishop

grace cup *n* a cup of wine or liquor passed around at the end of a meal for a final toast

grace·ful /gráyssf'l/ *adj* **1.** showing elegance, beauty, and smoothness of form or movement **2.** marked by poise, dignity, and politeness —**grace·ful·ly** *adv* —**grace·ful·ness** *n*

grace·less /gráyssləss/ *adj* **1.** lacking elegance in form or movement **2.** bad-mannered and undignified —**grace·less·ly** *adv* —**grace·less·ness** *n*

grace note *n* a note added to a piece of music as an embellishment, usually played quickly before a principal note and written smaller than a normal note on the page

grace pe·ri·od *n* the extra time allowed before having to pay a debt or complete a transaction

Grac·es /gráyssəz/ *n* in Greek mythology, three sister goddesses, Aglaia, Euphrosyne, and Thalia, who had the power to grant charm, happiness, and beauty

grac·ile /gráss'l/ *adj* gracefully slender and slight (*literary*) [Early 17C. < Latin *gracilis*] —**grac·ile·ness** *n* —**gra·cil·i·ty** /grə síllətee/ *n*

gra·cious /gráyshəss/ *adj* **1.** KIND AND POLITE full of tact, kindness, and politeness ○ *a gracious refusal* **2.** CONDESCENDINGLY POLITE condescendingly indulgent and generous to perceived inferiors **3.** ELEGANT luxurious and elegant ○ *gracious living* **4.** HAVING DIVINE GRACE displaying divine grace, mercy, or compassion ■ *interj* EXPRESSES SURPRISE used to express surprise, dismay, or indignation [13C. Via French < Latin *gratiosus* "agreeable" < *gratia* (see GRACE)] —**gra·cious·ly** *adv* —**gra·cious·ness** *n*

grack·le /grák'l/ *n* **1.** a noisy blackbird with metallic black feathers and a long keel-shaped tail. Native to: North America. Genus: *Quiscalus*. **2.** a starling with mostly black feathers. Native to: Europe, Asia. Genera: *Gracula* or *Onychognathus*. [Late 18C. Via modern Latin *Gracula* < Latin *graculus* "jackdaw"]

grad /grad/ *n* EDUC same as **graduate** *n* (sense 1) (*informal*) [Shortening of GRADUATE]

grad. *abbr* **1.** MATH, BIOL, PHYS gradient **2.** EDUC graduated

grad·a·ble /gráydəb'l/ *adj* **1.** capable of being graded **2.** describes an adjective or adverb capable of having a comparative and superlative form —**grad·a·bil·i·ty** /gràydə bíllətee/ *n*

gra·date /gráy dàyt/ (**-dat·ed, -dat·ing, -dates**) *v* **1.** *vti* to pass imperceptibly from one shade or degree of intensity to another, or cause something to do this **2.** *vt* to arrange something in steps, grades, or ranks [Mid-18C. Back-formation < GRADATION]

gra·da·tion /gray dáysh'n/ *n* **1.** SERIES OF DEGREES a series of gradual and progressive degrees, steps, or stages **2.** SINGLE DEGREE a degree, step, or stage in a gradual progression **3.** DISCRETE ARRANGEMENT the arrangement of something according to size, rank, or quality **4.** COLOR CHANGE the gradual and progressive change from one color or tone to another **5.** PHON VOWEL CHANGE a change in the length or quality of a vowel within a word, signifying a change in function such as tense or number **6.** GEOG LEVELING OF LAND the process of leveling land by erosion or deposition of sediment [Late 16C. Directly or via French < Latin *gradation-* "making steps" < *gradus* "step, stage"] —**gra·da·tion·al** *adj* —**gra·da·tion·al·ly** *adv*

grade /grayd/ *n* **1.** YEAR IN SCHOOL a class or year in a school, especially in the US and Canadian school systems ○ *She'll be in the tenth grade this year.* **2.** MARK FOR QUALITY OF WORK a mark given for work in school or college, usually using the descending scale of A, B, C, D, and F **3.** LEVEL IN SCALE OF PROGRESSION a level, step, or stage in a scale of progression, quality, or size (*often used in combination*) ○ *low-grade gasoline* **4.** MARK SHOWING A LEVEL a mark that indicates a level, step, or stage in a process **5.** RANK a rank or class, e.g., in the military **6.** PEOPLE IN RANK a group of people of the same rank **7.** FOOD CLASSIFICATION a category indicating the relative quality of food as determined by the US Department of Agriculture ○ *grade A eggs* **8.** GRADIENT a gradient or slope, especially on a road or railroad **9.** CONSTR GROUND LEVEL the level at which the ground meets a building ○ *below-grade wiring* **10.** AGRIC MIXED OFFSPRING an animal with one purebred parent and one of unknown breeding **11.** PHON VOWEL FORM a form of vowel morpheme when a vowel varies owing to gradation ■ *vt* (**grad·ed, grad·ing, grades**) **1.** ARRANGE THINGS BY DEGREES to arrange or classify things or people according to rank, quality, or level **2.** ASSIGN GRADE TO SOMETHING to assign a mark or rating to something such as a student's work **3.** MAKE ROAD LEVEL to level a road or railroad by adjusting its gradients **4.** AGRIC IMPROVE A BREED to improve a breed by crossing with a purebred animal [Early 16C. Via French < Latin *gradus* "step, stage"] ◇ **make the grade** to meet the required standard

---

ORIGIN The Latin word *gradus* "step," from which ***grade*** is derived, and its related verb *gradi* "to walk, go," are also the sources of English *aggression, congress, degrade, degree, digress, gradient, gradual, ingredient, progress, retrograde,* and *transgress.*

---

grade cross·ing *n* a place where a road crosses a railroad or two rail lines cross at the same level

grad·ed sed·i·ment *n* a sediment deposited on land or the seabed in which there is an upward gradation of the grains from coarse to fine

grade in·fla·tion *n* the assignment of higher than deserved grades to students' work in order to compensate for diminishing expectations and falling educational standards

grade point av·er·age *n* the average of a student's grades over a fixed period, calculated by assigning a value of 4 to A, 3 to B, 2 to C, 1 to D, and 0 to F

grad·er /gráydər/ *n* **1.** STUDENT a student in a particular grade in school ○ *first graders* **2.** SOMEBODY OR SOMETHING THAT GRADES a person who or machine that grades something **3.** EARTH LEVELER a machine with a wide blade that levels the ground, used in road construction

grade school *n* an elementary or primary school —**grade-school·er** *n*

grade sep·a·ra·tion *n* a crossing of roads or railroads requiring an overpass or underpass

gra·di·ent /gráydee ənt/ *n* **1.** SLOPE an upward or downward slope, e.g., in a road or railroad **2.** STEEPNESS the rate at which the steepness of a slope increases **3.** PHYS MEASURE OF CHANGE a measure of change in a physical quantity such as temperature or pressure over a particular distance **4.** BIOL RATE OF GROWTH a change in a series of alterations in the rate of growth or metabolism of an organism, cell, or organ **5.** MATH SLOPE ON CURVE the slope of a line or a tangent at any point on a curve ■ *adj* SLOPING sloping evenly and uniformly [Mid-17C. Partly < Latin *gradient-*, present participle of *gradi* "walk" (< *gradus* "step"), partly < GRADE after QUOTIENT]

gra·di·ent post *n* a small post with arms to represent gradients that is used beside a railroad line to indicate where the gradient changes

gra·din /gráyd'n/, **gra·dine** /gráy deen, grə deen/ *n* **1.** a raised step above or behind an altar in a church **2.** one of a set of steps arranged on a slope [Mid-19C. Via French < Italian *gradino* "small step" < *grado* "step" < Latin *gradus*]

grad·u·al /grájjoo əl/ *adj* **1.** HAPPENING SLOWLY proceeding or developing slowly by steps or degrees ○ *a gradual improvement* **2.** CHANGING SLOWLY changing slowly ○ *a gradual incline* ■ *n* CHR **1.** SUNG VERSES in some Christian services, a set of scriptural verses sung after the epistle at Communion **2.** RELIGIOUS MUSIC BOOK a book of music for the sung parts of the Communion service [15C. < medieval Latin *gradualis* < Latin *gradus* "step, stage"] —**grad·u·al·ly** *adv* —**grad·u·al·ness** *n*

grad·u·al·ism /grájjoo ə lìzzəm/ *n* **1.** the principle, theory, or policy of allowing change, especially political change, to take place gradually rather than suddenly or drastically **2.** the theory that change in rocks and fossils happens by a gradual historical process —**grad·u·al·ist** *n, adj* —**grad·u·al·is·tic** /gràjjoo ə lístik/ *adj*

grad·u·ate *n* /grájjoo ət/ **1.** SOMEBODY WHO HAS COMPLETED STUDIES somebody who has obtained a diploma or degree, e.g., from a high school or college **2.** HOLDER OF DEGREE somebody who has obtained a bachelor's degree from a college, university, or other higher education institution **3.** SCI CONTAINER WITH MARKINGS a container, e.g., a flask or tube, with graduated markings that is used for measuring liquids ■ *v* /grájjoo àyt/ (**-at·ed, -at·ing, -ates**) **1.** *vi* EDUC FINISH

SCHOOL OR COLLEGE to receive a diploma or degree after completing a course of study in a school, college, or university ○ *We both graduated from high school in 1996.* **2.** *vt* EDUC **GIVE A CERTIFICATE** to give a diploma or degree to a student completing a course of study **3.** *vi* **MOVE UP** to move upward from one level or activity to another ○ *I've graduated from skiing to snowboarding.* **4.** *vt* **MARK SOMETHING WITH DEGREES OR LEVELS** to mark something with units of measurement **5.** *vt* **SORT THINGS BY DIFFERENCES** to sort things into groups according to quality, size, or type ■ *adj* /grájjoo ət/ EDUC **PAST BACHELOR'S DEGREE** relating to education for students who have acquired a bachelor's degree [15C. < medieval Latin *graduat-*, past participle of *graduare* "confer a degree on" < Latin *gradus* "step, stage"] —**grad·u·a·tor** *n*

USAGE Avoid using the verb ***graduate*** transitively to mean "to receive a diploma or degree from," as in *She graduated Duke in 1999.* Say instead *She graduated from Duke in 1999* or *She was graduated from Duke in 1999.* It is correct, however, to use ***graduate*** transitively to mean "to confer a diploma or degree on," as in *Harvard Law School graduated 200 new attorneys last year.*

grad·u·at·ed /grájjoo àytəd/ *adj* **1. IN STAGES** divided into regular steps or stages **2. MARKED WITH LINES** marked with lines to enable measurement **3.** FIN **BASED ON INCOME** describes a system of taxation under which those with the greatest income or assets pay the highest percentage of tax

grad·u·ate school *n* a university or university division for advanced students who have obtained a bachelor's degree

grad·u·a·tion /gràjjoo áysh'n/ *n* **1. COMPLETION OF STUDIES** the completion of a course of academic study ○ *the number of credits required for graduation* **2. DEGREE CEREMONY** a ceremony in which degrees or diplomas are awarded to students who have successfully completed their studies ○ *attended her grandson's graduation* **3. MARK ON INSTRUMENT** a unit of measurement or division marked on an instrument **4. DIVIDING PROCESS** the process of marking or dividing something according to quantity or quality

Graec·ism, etc. UK spelling of **Grecism, etc.**

Graeco- *prefix* another spelling of **Greco-**

Graf /graaf/, **Steffi** (*b.* 1969) German tennis player. She turned professional at age 13, and went on to win 22 grand slam titles, including seven Wimbledon trophies. She retired from tennis in 1999.

graf·fi·ti /grə feétee/ *n* drawings or words that are scratched, painted, or sprayed on walls or other surfaces in public places [Mid-19C. < Italian, plural of *graffito* (see GRAFFITO)]

USAGE graffito or **graffiti**? ***Graffito*** is an Italian borrowing into English, and its plural in Italian is ***graffiti***. It is acceptable, however, to use ***graffiti*** as a singular when the meaning is "inscriptions in general": *Graffiti has marred the walls on this block for far too long,* though *Graffiti have marred the walls...* is the more technically appropriate. ***Graffiti*** is also regularly used as a singular to mean "an inscription": *It's just another gang-related graffiti,* though ***graffito*** is the more technically correct term.

graf·fi·to /grə feétō/ (*plural* **-ti** /-tee/) *n* **1.** an instance of graffiti scratched, painted, or sprayed on a surface (*formal*) **2.** an ancient drawing or inscription on a wall or rock surface [Mid-19C. < Italian, "scribbling" < *graffio* "scratching," via Latin *graphium* "stylus" < Greek *grapheion* < *graphein* "write"]

USAGE See ***graffiti***.

~~**grafitti**~~ incorrect spelling of **graffiti**

graft[1] /graft/ *n* **1. TRANSPLANTED TISSUE** a piece of living tissue or an organ that is transplanted to a patient's body, either from a donor or from another part of the patient's body. Grafts are used to replace damaged or diseased tissue or organs. **2. PLANT TISSUE JOINED TO ANOTHER PLANT** a piece of living tissue from the shoot of a plant that is joined to the stem and root system of another plant, resulting in the growth of a single plant **3. GRAFT LOCATION** the place where tissue is implanted by means of a graft **4. GRAFTED PLANT** a plant that is the product of a graft **5. JOINING PROCESS** the process of joining one thing to another ■ *vt* (**graft·ed, graft·ing, grafts**) **1. TRANSPLANT TISSUE** to transplant a piece of living tissue or an organ to a part of a patient's body. The tissue or organ may be either from a donor or from another part of the patient's body. **2. UNITE PLANT TISSUE** to join a piece of tissue from a part of one plant to the stem and root system of another plant to produce desirable characteristics such as vigor or resistance to disease in the new plant **3. JOIN DISSIMILAR THINGS** to join two things that do not share a natural relationship or affinity for each other [15C. Via Old French *grafe* "pencil" (from a similarity with the shoot of a plant) < late Latin *graphium* (see GRAFFITO)] —**graft·er** *n*

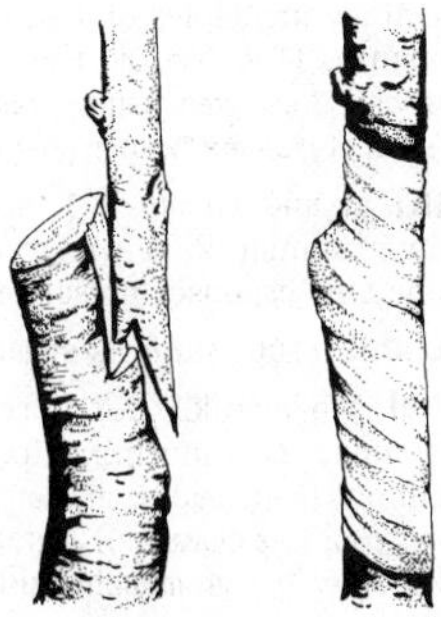

graft[1] (sense 2)

graft[2] /graft/ *n* **1. CORRUPT ACTIONS OF OFFICIAL** the use of dishonest or illegal means to gain money or property by somebody in a position of power or in elected office **2. MONEY OBTAINED CORRUPTLY** something obtained illegally by taking advantage of high position or office ■ *vti* (**graft·ed, graft·ing, grafts**) **GET BY DECEIT** to obtain money or property by deceit (*informal*) [Mid-19C. Origin ?] —**graft·er** *n*

Gra·ham /gráy əm/, **Billy** (*b.* 1918) US evangelist. A charismatic preacher, he has held large-scale evangelistic rallies throughout the United States and Europe since 1949. Full name **Graham, William Franklin**

> "Heaven is full of answers to prayers for which no one ever bothered to ask."
> [Billy Graham, *Encounter Weekly*; 1996]

Popperfoto

Katharine Graham

Gra·ham, Katharine (1917–2001) US newspaper executive. She was publisher of *The Washington Post* (1969–79). Born **Meyer, Katharine**

> "If we had failed to pursue the facts as far as they led, we would have denied the public any knowledge of an unprecedented scheme of political surveillance and sabotage."
> [Katharine Graham. On the *Washington Post*'s investigative reportage of the Watergate scandal, *Washington Post*; March 5, 1973]

Gra·ham, Martha (1893–1991) US dancer, choreographer, and teacher. The most influential figure in modern dance, she created a dance language using flexible movements intended to express emotional power.

AKG London

Martha Graham: performing in *Judith* (1957)

> "Every dance is a kind of fever chart of the heart...it makes visible the interior landscape."
> [Martha Graham, recalled on her death; April 1, 1991]

gra·ham crack·er /gráy əm-/ *n* a flat dry sweetened cracker, light brown in color and made from graham flour [see GRAHAM FLOUR]

gra·ham flour *n* unsifted whole-wheat flour [After Dr. Sylvester *Graham* (1794–1851), N American dietary reformer]

Gra·ham Land northern section of the Antarctic Peninsula, part of the British Antarctic Territory

Gra·ham's law *n* a law in chemistry relating the diffusion rate of a gas to the inverse square root of its density [After Thomas *Graham* (1805–69), Scottish chemist]

Gra·hams·town /gráy əmz tòwn/ city in Eastern Cape Province, southern South Africa, situated about 60 mi./100 km northeast of Port Elizabeth. Population: 19,783 (1991).

grail /grayl/ *n* something that is eagerly sought [Late 19C. < GRAIL]

Grail /grayl/ *n* according to medieval legend, the cup said to have been used by Jesus Christ at the Last Supper, and by Joseph of Arimathea to collect his blood and sweat at the Crucifixion. It was sought by medieval knights. [14C. Via Old French *grael* < medieval Latin *gradalis* "dish"]

grain /grayn/ *n* **1. CEREALS** cereal crops **2. SMALL SEED** a small hard seed **3. TINY SINGLE PIECE** a tiny individual piece of something such as sand or salt **4. SMALL AMOUNT** a tiny amount of something ○ *He doesn't have one grain of common sense!* **5. PATTERN IN MATERIAL** the arrangement, direction, or pattern of the fibers in wood, leather, stone, or paper, typically aligned along a single axis ○ *When painting, follow the grain of the wood.* **6. PHOTOGRAPHIC PARTICLE** a particle forming part of a photographic emulsion on whose size the extent of possible enlargement depends **7.** TEXTILES **DIRECTION OF THREADS** the line of the threads in a fabric **8. SIDE OF LEATHER** the side of leather from which hair has been removed **9. BASIC QUALITY** the basic quality or characteristic of something or somebody ○ *firmly set in the grain* **10.** MEASURE **UNIT OF WEIGHT** the smallest unit of weight in the avoirdupois (1/7000 pound) and apothecaries' systems (1/5760 pound), equal to approximately 0.065 grams **11.** CHEM **SMALL CRYSTAL** a small crystal, especially one forming part of a crystalline solid **12. PROPELLANT FOR ROCKET** a mass of solid propellant for a rocket or missile **13. DYE** red or purple dye made from cochineal insects (*archaic*) ■ *v* (**grained, grain·ing, grains**) **1.** *vti* **GRANULATE** to break down into small particles or grains, or make something break down into small particles **2.** *vt* **MIMIC PATTERN OF WOOD** to paint or stain a material with a pattern similar to wood or leather **3.** *vt* **TREAT LEATHER** to soften or raise the pattern of leather **4.** *vt* **REMOVE HAIR FROM LEATHER** to remove the hair from leather **5.** *vt* **GIVE SOMETHING GRAINY APPEARANCE** to give something a rough or granular appearance **6.** *vt* **GIVE GRAIN TO ANIMAL** to feed grain to an animal [13C. Via French < Latin *granum* "seed"] —**grained** *adj* —**grain·er** *n* —**grain·less** *adj* ◇ **go against the grain** to be contrary to somebody's natural inclinations, wishes, or feelings

ORIGIN The Latin word *granum* "seed," from which **grain** is derived, is also the source of English *filigree, garner, granary, grange, granite, gravy, ingrain,* and *pomegranate.* Its Indo-European ancestor in turn gave rise to English *corn*[1].

grain al·co·hol *n* alcohol made from a fermented cereal

grain el·e·va·tor *n* AGRIC same as **elevator** (sense 2)

Grain·ger /gráynjər/, **Percy** (1882–1961) Australian-born US pianist and composer. His 400 compositions, many based on folk music, include *Green Bushes* (1905–21) and *Shepherds Hey* (1908–22). Born **Grainger, George Percy**. Full name **Grainger, Percy Aldridge**

grains of par·a·dise *npl* the peppery brown seeds of a western African plant. Use: to add piquancy to mulled wine and other drinks, formerly, in veterinary medicine.

grain sor·ghum *n* a variety of sorghum that is grown for grain or forage

grain·y /gráynee/ (**-i·er, -i·est**) *adj* **1. NOT CLEAR** describes a photograph that is unclear and poorly defined because of a large grain size or overenlargement **2. RESEMBLING GRAINS** resembling or composed of grains **3. NOT SMOOTH** having a granular rather than a smooth texture **4. LIKE WOOD GRAIN** resembling the grain of wood, leather, stone, or paper —**grain·i·ness** *n*

gram[1] /gram/ *n* a metric unit of mass, equal to 0.001 kg or equivalent to approximately 0.035 oz. Symbol **g** [Late 18C. Via French *gramme* and late Latin *gramma* < Greek *gramma* "small weight"]

gram[2] /gram/ *n* an edible legume, e.g., chickpea, lentil, or mung bean [Early 18C. Via obsolete Portuguese < Latin *granum* "seed"]

gram. *abbr* GRAM **1.** grammar **2.** grammatical

-gram *suffix* **1.** something written, drawn, or recorded ○ *trigram* ○ *oscillogram* **2.** a message delivered by a third party ○ *telegram* ○ *kissagram* [< Greek *gramma* "something written"]

gra·ma /grámmə/, **gram·ma, gra·ma grass, gram·ma grass** *n* a pasture grass that grows in western North America and South America. Genus: *Bouteloua.* [Mid-19C. Via American Spanish < Latin *gramen* "grass"]

gram at·om *n* a quantity of a chemical element whose mass in grams is the same as its atomic weight

gram cal·o·rie *n* MEASURE same as **calorie** (sense 1)

gram e·quiv·a·lent *n* the quantity of a substance whose mass in grams is the same as its chemical equivalent weight

gra·mer·cy /grə múrssee/ *interj* (*archaic*) **1.** used as an expression of thanks **2.** used as an expression of surprise or wonder [14C. < Old French *grant merci* "(God give you) great reward"]

gram flour *n* a gluten-free flour, used in South Asian cooking, that is usually made from ground chickpeas and is pale yellow in color [< GRAM[2]]

gram·i·ci·din /gràmmi sīd'n/, **gram·i·ci·din D** /gràmmi sīd'n dee/ *n* a toxic antibiotic applied externally in creams and drops [Mid-20C. < GRAM-POSITIVE + -CIDE]

gra·min·e·ous /grə mínnee əss/, **gram·i·na·ceous** /gràmmə náyshəss/ *adj* **1.** belonging to the grass family **2.** resembling grass (*technical*) [Mid-17C. < Latin *gramineus* < *gramin-*, stem of *gramen* "grass"] —**gra·min·e·ous·ness** *n*

gram·i·niv·o·rous /gràmmi nívvərəss/ *adj* feeding on grass (*technical*) [Mid-18C. < Latin *gramin-* (see GRAMINEOUS)]

gram·ma, gram·ma grass *n* PLANTS, BOT same as **grama**

gram·mar /grámmər/ *n* **1. RULES FOR LANGUAGE** the system of rules by which words are formed and put together to make sentences **2. PARTICULAR SET OF LANGUAGE RULES** the rules for speaking or writing a particular language, or an analysis of the rules of a particular aspect of language ○ *Spanish grammar* ○ *case grammar* **3. QUALITY OF LANGUAGE** the spoken or written form of language that somebody uses with regard to accepted standards of correctness ○ *bad grammar* **4. GRAMMAR BOOK** a book dealing with the grammar of a language **5. ANALYTIC SYSTEM** a systematic treatment of the elementary principles of a subject and their interrelationships [14C. Via Old French *gramaire* and Latin *grammatica* < Greek *grammatikos* "relating to letters" < *grammat-*, stem of *gramma* "written character, letter"]

gram·mar·i·an /grə mérree ən/ *n* **1.** somebody who is skilled in grammar **2.** a writer on grammar, especially one who espouses prescriptive rules

gram·mar school *n* EDUC same as **elementary school**

gram·mat·i·cal /grə máttik'l/ *adj* **1.** relating to the rules of grammar **2.** conforming to the accepted rules of grammar [Early 16C. < late Latin *grammaticalis* < Greek *grammatikos* (see GRAMMAR)] —**gram·mat·i·cal·i·ty** /grə màtti kállətee/ *n* —**gram·mat·i·cal·ly** *adv* —**gram·mat·i·cal·ness** *n*

gram·ma·tol·o·gy /gràmmə tólləjee/ *n* the study of writing systems [Mid-20C. < Greek *grammat-* "written character" (see GRAMMAR)] —**gram·ma·to·log·ic** /gràmmətə lójjik/ *adj*—**gram·ma·to·log·i·cal** *adj*—**gram·ma·tol·o·gist** *n*

~~grammer~~ incorrect spelling of **grammar**

gram mol·e·cule *n* a quantity of a molecular chemical compound whose mass in grams is the same as its molecular weight —**gram-mo·lec·u·lar** *adj*

gram·my /grámmee/ (*plural* **-mies**) *n* same as **grandmother** (*informal; usually used by or to children*) [Shortening]

Gram·my /grámmee/ *tdmk* a trademark for an award given annually for achievement in the recorded music industry

Gram-neg·a·tive, gram-neg·a·tive *adj* describes bacteria that lose the color of a gentian violet stain when subjected to Gram's method of classifying bacteria

gram·o·phone /grámmə fōn/ *n* RECORDING same as **record player** (*dated*) [Late 19C. Alteration of PHONOGRAM]

gram·pa /grámpə/ *n* same as **grandfather** (*informal; usually used by or to children*) [Contraction of GRANDPA]

Gram·pi·an Moun·tains /gràmpee ən-/ mountain range in central Scotland that forms a natural division between the Highlands and Lowlands. The highest peak is Ben Nevis, 4,406 ft./1,343 m.

Gram·pi·an Re·gion former region in northeastern Scotland that included the present-day council areas of Aberdeenshire and Moray

Gram-pos·i·tive, gram-pos·i·tive *adj* describes bacteria that retain the color of a gentian violet stain when subjected to Gram's method of classifying bacteria

gramps /gramps/ *n* (*informal*) **1.** same as **grandfather** (*usually used by or to children*) **2.** a disrespectful term of address for a man of advanced years [< contraction of GRANDPA]

gram·pus /grámpəss/ (*plural same* or **-pus·es**) *n* a large gray dolphin with a blunt snout, short flippers, and a tall dark gray fin. Native to: warm seas. Latin name: *Grampus griseus.* [Early 16C. Alteration of Old French *graspeis* < medieval Latin *crassus piscis* "fat fish"]

Gram's meth·od /grámz-/, **Gram's stain** *n* a technique used to classify bacteria according to their ability to lose or retain the color of a gentian violet stain, applied within the framework of an established test procedure. The retention or loss of stain indicates a particular cell-wall structure and distinguishes two types of bacteria. [Late 19C. After H. C. J. Gram (1853–1938), Danish physician]

gran /gran/ *n* same as **grandmother** (*informal; usually used by or to children*) [Mid-19C. Shortening]

gra·na BIOL plural of **granum**

Gra·na·da /grə naádə/ city and capital of Granada Province in the autonomous region of Andalusia, southern Spain. It is the site of the Alhambra, a Moorish palace and citadel. Population: 240,522 (2002).

gran·a·dil·la /grànnə díllə, -deé yə/ *n* **1.** a purple egg-shaped passion fruit **2.** a passionflower that produces granadillas. Native to: tropical regions. Latin name: *Passiflora quadrangularis.* [Early 17C. < Spanish, "little pomegranate" < *granada* "pomegranate"]

gran·a·ry /gránəree, gráy-/ (*plural* **-ries**) *n* **1.** a warehouse or storeroom for grain **2.** a region where grain is abundant [Late 16C. < Latin *granarium* < *granum* "seed"]

Gran Cha·co /graán chaákō/ thinly populated region in south central South America, extending from southern Bolivia through Paraguay to northern Argentina. Area: 250,000 sq. mi./647,500 sq. km.

grand /grand/ *adj* **1. OUTSTANDING** outstanding and impressive in appearance, extent, or style ○ *making a grand entrance* **2. IMPRESSIVE** impressive, ambitious, and far-reaching ○ *a grand plan* **3. WORTHY OF RESPECT** worthy of great respect by virtue of exceptional ability or high rank ○ *among the grandest orchestras of our time* **4. WONDERFUL** wonderful, enjoyable, and memorable ○ *We had a grand time.* **5. PRINCIPAL** main or principal ○ *And now we move into the Grand Banqueting Hall.* ■ *n* (*informal*) **1.** (*plural same*) MONEY **1,000 DOLLARS** a thousand dollars ○ *made ten grand on the deal* **2.** MUSIC same as **grand piano** [Early 16C. Via Old French < Latin *grandis* "great, full grown"] —**grand·ly** *adv* —**grand·ness** *n*

grand- *prefix* one generation further removed ○ *grandniece* ○ *grandfather* ■ *n* one thousand (*informal*) [< GRAND]

gran·dad *n* another spelling of **granddad** (*informal*)

gran·dad·dy *n* another spelling of **granddaddy** (*informal*)

gran·dam /grán dàm, -dəm/, **gran·dame** /grán dàym, grándəm/ *n* a grandmother, or a woman who is no longer young (*archaic*) [13C. < Anglo-Norman *graund dame* "grandmother"]

~~grandaughter~~ incorrect spelling of **granddaughter**

grand·aunt /grànd ánt/ *n* same as **great-aunt**

grand·ba·by /gránd bàybee/ *n* a grandchild who is still a baby

Grand Ba·ha·ma /grànd bə haámə/ island of the western Bahamas in the Atlantic Ocean off the eastern coast of Florida. Population: 40,898 (1990). Area: 430 sq. mi./1,114 sq. km.

Grand Banks /-bángks/ shallow section of the Atlantic Ocean, off southeastern Newfoundland, Canada, that is an important fishing region. Area: 109,100 sq. mi./282,500 sq. km.

Grand Ca·nal main thoroughfare of Venice, Italy. There are almost 200 palaces on the banks of the canal. Length: 2 mi./3 km.

Barnaby's

Grand Canyon

Grand Can·yon spectacular natural gorge carved by the Colorado River in northwestern Arizona. Its width varies from 5 to 18 mi./8 to 29 km, and its depth can exceed 1 mi./1.6 km. Length: 277 mi./446 km.

Grand Can·yon Na·tion·al Park national park in northern Arizona, established in 1919. Its primary feature is the Grand Canyon of the Colorado River. Area: 1,902 sq. mi./4,927 sq. km.

Grand Can·yon State *n* a nickname for Arizona

grand·child /gránd chīld/ (*plural* **-chil·dren** /-chìldrən/) *n* a child of a son or daughter

Grand Cou·lee Dam /-kóolee-/ dam in Washington State on the Columbia River, 90 mi./145 km west of Spokane. Completed in 1942, it is the world's largest concrete structure and a major source of hydroelectric power. Height: 550 ft./168 m.

grand·dad /grán dàd/, **gran·dad** *n* (*informal*) **1.** same as

grandfather 2. a disrespectful term of address for a man of advanced years

grand·dad·dy /grán dàddee/ (*plural* **-dies**), **gran·dad·dy** *n* (*informal*) **1.** same as **grandfather 2.** something considered the oldest, first, or most important of its time

grand·daugh·ter /grán dàwtər/ *n* a daughter of a son or daughter

grand duch·ess *n* **1. GRAND DUKE'S SPOUSE** the wife or widow of a grand duke **2. NOBLEWOMAN OF HIGH RANK** a woman who holds a rank above that of duchess **3. RUSSIAN PRINCESS** in tsarist Russia, a daughter of a tsar or of a tsar's descendants

grand duch·y *n* a country, territory, or estate that has a grand duke or a grand duchess as its ruler

grand duke *n* **1.** a nobleman who holds a rank above that of a duke **2.** in tsarist Russia, a brother, son, uncle, or nephew of a tsar

grande dame /gránd dàm, graánd daám/ *n* a socially important, dignified woman, usually in later life [< French, "great lady"]

Grande Dix·ence Dam /grand diksənss-/ concrete dam on the Dixence River, southwestern Switzerland. Completed in 1962, it is one of the world's highest dams. Height: 932 ft./284 m.

gran·dee /gran deé/ *n* **1.** somebody highly influential and respected, especially a politician **2.** a high-ranking Spanish or Portuguese nobleman [Late 16C. Via Spanish and Portuguese *grande* < Latin *grandis* "great"]

gran·deur /gránjər, -joor/ *n* the quality of being great or grand and very impressive [Early 16C. < French < *grand* (see GRAND)]

grand·fa·ther /gránd faathər/ *n* **1. PARENT'S FATHER** the father of a father or mother **2. ANCESTOR** a man who is an ancestor **3. DISRESPECTFUL TERM OF ADDRESS** a disrespectful term of address for a man of advanced years (*dated informal*) ■ *vt* (**-thered, -ther·ing, -thers**) **EXEMPT** to exempt somebody from something by means of a grandfather clause —**grand·fa·ther·ly** *adj*

grand·fa·ther clause *n* **1.** a clause in some Southern US states' constitutions, subsequently declared unconstitutional, that waived electoral literacy requirements for descendants of those allowed to vote before 1867. In effect it enabled illiterate white people to vote, while excluding illiterate Black people. **2.** a clause in prohibitive legislation that makes exceptions for those already engaged in the activity that it bans or regulates

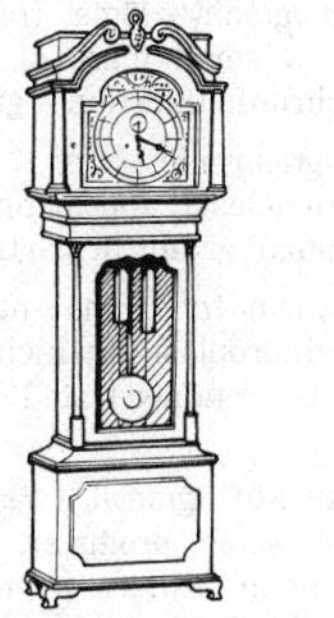

grandfather clock

grand·fa·ther clock *n* a large clock in a tall case that stands on the floor

grand fi·nal *n* the last round in a series of contests, competitions, or sports matches

grand fi·nal·e *n* the closing spectacular scene or section of a performance or other show

Grand Forks /-fáwrks/ city on the Red River, in eastern North Dakota, north of Fargo. Population: 64,920 (2002 estimate).

Grand Gui·gnol /graaN gee nyáwl/ *n* a sensational drama, often structured in short scenes with violent or horrific subject matter, that aims to horrify its audience [Early 20C. < *Le Grand Guignol*, theater in Paris] —**grand gui·gnol** *adj*

gran·dil·o·quence /gran dílləkwənss/ *n* a pompous or lofty manner of speaking or writing [Late 16C. < Latin *grandiloquus* "speaking grandly" < *grandis* "great" + *loqui* "speak"] —**gran·dil·o·quent** *adj* —**gran·dil·o·quent·ly** *adv*

gran·di·ose /grándee òss/ *adj* **1. PRETENTIOUS AND POMPOUS** pretentious, pompous, and imposing **2. MAGNIFICENT** impressive and magnificent **3. TOO COMPLEX** excessively complicated and unrealistic ○ *a grandiose plan* [Mid-19C. Via French < Italian *grandioso* "imposing" < *grande* "great" < Latin *grandis*] —**gran·di·ose·ly** *adv* —**gran·di·ose·ness** *n* —**gran·di·os·i·ty** /gràndee óssətee/ *n*

gran·di·o·so /gràndee óssō/ *adv* in a grand or imposing style (*used as a musical direction*) [Late 19C. < Italian, "grandly"] —**gran·di·o·so** *adj*

Grand Junc·tion city in Mesa County, western Colorado, where the Gunnison and Colorado rivers meet. Population: 43,170 (2002 estimate).

grand ju·ry *n* in US and Canadian law, a panel of 12 to 23 jurors called to decide whether there are grounds for a criminal prosecution in a case — **grand ju·ror** *n*

grand·kid /grán kìd/ *n* same as **grandchild** (*informal*)

grand lar·ce·ny *n* a robbery or theft of money or property with a value over the amount specified by law to constitute petit larceny

grand·ma /grán maa/ *n* (*informal*) **1.** same as **grandmother 2.** a disrespectful term of address for a woman of advanced years [Late 18C. Shortening]

grand mal /graaN maal/ *n* a serious form of epilepsy in which there is loss of consciousness and severe convulsions [< French, "great illness"]

grand·ma·ma /granmə maa, grànmə maa/ *n* same as **grandmother** (*dated*)

Grand Ma·nan Is·land /-mə nàn-/ island at the entrance to the Bay of Fundy in southwestern New Brunswick, southeastern Canada. Population: 3,000. Area: 53 sq. mi./137 sq. km.

grand mas·ter /gránd màstər/, **grand·mas·ter** *n* **1. TOP CHESS PLAYER** a champion chess player who plays at an international level **2. SOMEBODY OUTSTANDING** somebody at the top of a particular field in ability or achievement **3. GROUP HEAD** the head of a brotherhood of knights or of a fraternal organization such as the Masons

grand·moth·er /grán mùthər/ *n* **1. PARENT'S MOTHER** the mother of a father or mother **2. ANCESTOR** a woman who is an ancestor **3. DISRESPECTFUL TERM OF ADDRESS** a disrespectful term of address for a woman of advanced years (*dated informal*) —**grand·moth·er·ly** *adj*

grand·moth·er clock *n* a clock in a tall case that stands on the floor, smaller than a grandfather clock

grand·neph·ew /grán nèffyoo/ *n US* a son of a nephew or niece. Can term **great-nephew**

grand·niece /grán neéss/ *n US* a daughter of a nephew or niece. Can term **great-niece**

grand old man *n* a man, usually past middle age, who is respected for his contribution to some field of activity such as politics, music, or sports ○ *the grand old man of American jazz*

grand op·er·a *n* an opera on a serious dramatic theme in which all the words are sung and there is no spoken dialogue

grand·pa /grán paa, grám paa/ *n* (*informal*) **1.** same as **grandfather 2.** a disrespectful term of address for a man of advanced years

grand·par·ent /grán pérrənt/ *n* the mother or father of a mother or father —**grand·pa·ren·tal** /grànpə rént'l/ *adj* —**grand·par·ent·hood** *n*

grand piano

grand pi·an·o *n* a large piano in which the strings are fixed horizontally behind the keyboard in a long harp-shaped frame

Grand Prai·rie city on the Trinity River in northeastern Texas. It is an important manufacturing center. Population: 135,303 (2002 estimate).

Grand Pré /gròn práy, graaN-/ village in central Nova Scotia, Canada, on Minas Basin, the site of Grand Pré National Historic Park

Grand Prix /gròn preé, gròN-/ (*plural same* or **Grands Prix** /*pronunc. same*/) *n* **1.** any of a number of important international annual races for racecars, held to decide the world automobile-racing championship **2.** any of various competitions in a variety of sports that have the same importance and prestige as a Grand Prix in automobile racing [< French, "big prize"]

Grand Rap·ids /-ráppids/ city on the Grand River in west central Michigan. An important furniture-manufacturing center since the 19th century, it is also home to the Ford Presidential Museum. Population: 196,595 (1998).

grand·sire /gránd sìr/ *n* same as **grandfather** (*archaic*)

grand slam *n* **1.** BASEBALL **4 RUNS** in baseball, a home run made when the bases are loaded **2. WINNING OF ALL MAJOR COMPETITIONS** in sports such as tennis and golf, the winning of all of a series of major competitions by one player or team in one year **3. MAJOR COMPETITION** in sports such as tennis and golf, a major competition that is part of a series **4.** CARDS **WINNING OF ALL TRICKS** in bridge and similar card games, the winning of all 13 tricks in a game by one player or pair of players, or a contract to do so

grand·son /grán sùn/ *n* a son of a son or daughter

grand·stand /gránd stànd/ *n* **1. STRUCTURE FOR SPECTATORS' SEATS** an open structure or platform, usually with a roof, containing rows of seats for spectators at a sports stadium or racetrack **2. SEATED SPECTATORS** the spectators sitting in a grandstand ■ *adj* **UNOBSTRUCTED** clear, close, and unobstructed ○ *We had a grandstand view of the proceedings.* ■ *vi* (**-stand·ed, -stand·ing, -stands**) **SEEK ATTENTION OR ADMIRATION** to show off in order to impress people, especially spectators — **grand·stand·er** *n*

grand·stand play *n* an action or play, e.g., in sports, that is made more elaborate than necessary in order to gain attention or applause

Grand Te·ton Na·tion·al Park /-teét'n-/ national park south of Yellowstone in northwestern Wyoming, established in 1929. The highest peak is Grand Teton, 13,771 ft./4,197 m. Area: 484 sq. mi/1,255 sq. km.

grand to·tal *n* a final and complete total of all amounts to be added

grand tour *n* **1.** a trip or tour that takes in visits to several places, or a visit that allows a complete inspection of all parts of one place **2.** formerly, a tour of the main European cities and cultural centers undertaken by young upper-class Englishmen as a way of completing their education

grand·un·cle /gránd ùngk'l/ *n* same as **great-uncle**

Grand U·ni·fied The·o·ry *n* a mathematical representation linking the four fundamental forces, electromagnetic, gravitational, strong, and weak, that has been theorized but not yet achieved

grandure incorrect spelling of **grandeur**

grange /graynj/ *n* **1.** a large farm building used for storing grain or hay (*archaic*) **2.** *UK* a large farmhouse or country house with other buildings such as stables or barns attached to it (*often in house names*) ○ *Norton Grange* [13C. Via French < medieval Latin *granica villa* "grain house" < Latin *granum* "seed"]

Grange *n* **1.** the Patrons of Husbandry, an association of US farmers founded in 1867 for their mutual support **2.** a local branch of the Grange —**Grang·er** *n*

Grange /graynj/, **Red** (1903–91) US football player. Playing mostly for the Chicago Bears during a ten-year career, he was an early popularizer of the professional game, and later became a sports announcer. Born **Grange, Harold Edward**. Known as **the Galloping Ghost**

grang·er /gráynjər/ *n Northwest US* same as **farmer**

grani- *prefix* grain, seed ○ *granivorous* [< Latin *granum*]

gran·i·ta /grə neétə/ *n* a sweetened flavored water ice with a grainy texture [Mid-19C. < Italian, form of *granito* (see GRANITE)]

gran·ite /gránnit/ *n* **1. COARSE-GRAINED ROCK** a coarse-grained igneous rock made up of feldspar, mica, and at least 20 percent quartz. Use: building. **2. TOUGHNESS** determination or toughness of character **3. STONE USED IN CURLING** the rounded stone used in the sport of curling [Mid-17C. < Italian *granito* "grainy" < Latin *granum* "seed"] —**gra·nit·ic** /gra níttik, grə-/ *adj* —**gran·it·oid** *adj*

Gran·ite City /grànnit-/ city in southwestern Illinois, on the Mississippi River near St. Louis. Population: 31,622 (2002 estimate).

Gran·ite Peak mountain in the northern Rockies of southern Montana. It is the highest peak in the state. Height: 12,799 ft./3,901 m.

Gran·ite State *n* a nickname for New Hampshire

gran·ite·ware /gránnit wèr/ *n* **1.** earthenware with a speckled glaze that gives it the appearance of granite **2.** iron articles, e.g., pots and bowls, coated with a glaze that gives a finish with the appearance of granite

gra·niv·o·rous /grə nívvərəss/ *adj* used to describe birds that feed on seeds and grain

gran·ny /gránnee/ (*plural* **-nies**), **gran·nie** *n* **1.** same as **grandmother** (*informal*) **2. DISRESPECTFUL TERM OF ADDRESS** a disrespectful term of address for a woman of advanced years (*informal*) **3. FUSSY PERSON** somebody who is regarded as annoyingly fastidious or fussy (*insult*) **4.** *Southern US* **MIDWIFE** a nurse or midwife **5.** same as **granny knot** [Mid-17C. Shortening of *grannam*, common pronunciation of GRANDAM]

gran·ny dump·ing *n* the abandonment in a public place of a senior citizen who is in deteriorating mental or physical health by a family member or members (*disapproving*)

gran·ny flat *n UK* same as **in-law suite**

gran·ny gear *n* the lowest gear on a bicycle that makes it possible to pedal up steep inclines (*informal*)

gran·ny glass·es *npl* eyeglasses consisting of small lenses set in gold or steel frames (*informal*)

gran·ny knot *n* a square knot incorrectly tied and therefore likely to come apart

Gran·ny Smith *n* an eating apple with green skin and crisp white flesh [Late 19C. After the nickname of Maria Ann *Smith* (1801–70), who first grew it in Sydney, Australia]

gran·ny specs *npl* OPHTHALMOL same as **granny glasses** (*informal*)

grano- *prefix* granite ○ *granolith* [Via German < Italian *granito* (see GRANITE)]

gran·o·di·or·ite /grànnō dī ə rìt/ *n* a coarse-grained igneous rock containing plagioclase and orthoclase, whose composition is intermediate between granite and diorite —**gran·o·di·or·it·ic** /-dī ə ríttik/ *adj*

gra·no·la /grə nṓlə/ *n* a breakfast cereal consisting of rolled oats mixed with other ingredients such as dried fruit and nuts [Early 20C. Originally a trade name]

gran·o·lith /gránnə lìth/ *n* a paving material made from cement and granite chips —**gran·o·lith·ic** /grànnə líthik/ *adj*

gran·o·phyre /gránnə fìr/ *n* a medium-grained light-colored igneous rock consisting mainly of crystals of feldspar and quartz that have crystallized together [Late 19C. < German *Granophyr* < *Granit* "granite" + *Porphyr* "porphyry"] —**gran·o·phyr·ic** /grànnə feérik/ *adj*

Gran Pa·ra·di·so /graán paárə deézō/ mountain in the western Alps, northern Italy, situated within the Gran Paradiso National Park. Height: 13,323 ft./ 4,061 m.

grant /grant/ *vt* (**grant·ed, grant·ing, grants**) **1. ALLOW SOMETHING AS FAVOR** to agree to allow a request, favor, or privilege ○ *She refused to grant any interviews.* **2. ADMIT TRUTH OF SOMETHING** to acknowledge, often reluctantly the truth or efficacy of something **3.** LAW **TRANSFER PROPERTY LEGALLY** to transfer money, property or rights to somebody in a legal transaction ■ *n* **1. MONEY GIVEN FOR SPECIFIC PURPOSE** a sum of money given by the government or some other organization to fund such things as education or research **2. GIFT** something given to somebody as a favor or privilege, or the giving of it ○ *a land grant* **3.** LAW **LEGAL TRANSACTION** something transferred from one person to another in a legal transaction, or the making of such a transaction **4.** LAW **DOCUMENT TRANSFERRING SOMETHING** a legal document recording a transaction in which something is transferred from one person to another **5. AREA OF LAND** a land division in New Hampshire, Maine, or Vermont [13C. < Old French *granter*, variant of *creanter* "guarantee," via assumed Vulgar Latin *credentare* < Latin *credere* "believe"] —**grant·a·ble** *adj* —**grant·er** *n* ◇ **take somebody for granted** to fail to realize or appreciate the value of somebody ◇ **take something for granted 1.** to assume that something is true without checking **2.** to fail to appreciate or realize the value of something

SYNONYMS See *give*.

Grant /grant/, **Cary** (1904–86) British-born US movie actor. He was a sophisticated leading man in movies such as *The Philadelphia Story* (1940) and *North by Northwest* (1959). Born **Leach, Alexander Archibald**

> "In the spring a young man's fancy lightly turns to what he's been thinking about all winter."
> [Cary Grant, *The Awful Truth*; 1937]

Grant, Cuthbert (1793–1854) Canadian fur trader. He led the Metis attack on the Hudson's Bay Company's settlers at Seven Oaks (1816), the site of present-day Winnipeg.

Library of Congress

Ulysses S. Grant

Grant, Ulysses S. (1822–85) 18th president of the United States. As the Union army's greatest general, he led his troops to victory in the Civil War. His Republican administration (1869–77) is regarded as one of the most corrupt in US history. Full name **Grant, Hiram Ulysses Simpson**. See table at **president**

> "The war is over—the rebels are our countrymen again."
> [Ulysses S. Grant, ordering his Union troops not to cheer after General Robert E. Lee's surrender at Appomattox, VA; April 9, 1865]

grant-aid·ed school *n UK* a school in which independent managers control the appointment of the teachers and the religious instruction given, and are required to pay part of the upkeep costs

grant·ed /grántəd/ *adv, conj* used to acknowledge, often reluctantly, the truth of something

grant·ee /gran teé/ *n* somebody to whom something is transferred in a legal transaction

Granth /graanth, granth/, **Granth Sa·hib** /-saá hib, -saá ib/ *n* RELIG same as **Adi Granth** [Late 18C. Via Hindi < Sanskrit *granthaḥ* "book, binding"]

grant-in-aid (*plural* **grants-in-aid**) *n* a sum of money given as funding by a federal government to a state or local government, or by federal or local government to a department or institution

gran·tor /grántər, grán tàwr/ *n* somebody from whom something is transferred in a legal transaction

grants·man /grántsmən/ (*plural* **-men** /-mən/) *n* somebody who is skilled in obtaining grants —**grants·man·ship** *n*

gran·u·lar /grányələr/ *adj* **1. MADE UP OF GRAINS** consisting of small grains or particles **2. WITH TEXTURE OF GRANULES** appearing to consist of or be covered in small grains or particles **3. DIVISIBLE** made up of conveniently small and independent parts ○ *a granular interface* [Late 18C. < late Latin *granulum* (see GRANULE)] —**gran·u·lar·i·ty** /grànnyə lárrətee/ *n* —**gran·u·lar·ly** *adv*

gran·u·late /grányə làyt/ (**-lat·ed, -lat·ing, -lates**) *v* **1.** *vti* **MAKE INTO SMALL PARTICLES** to form into small grains or particles, or make something do this **2.** *vti* **BECOME OR MAKE GRAINY IN TEXTURE** to become rough and grainy in texture or appearance, or give something a rough and grainy texture or appearance **3.** *vi* MED **FORM HEALING TISSUE** to form granulation tissue over a wound [Mid-17C. < late Latin *granulum* (see GRANULE)] —**gran·u·la·tive** *adj* —**gran·u·la·tor** *n*

gran·u·lat·ed sug·ar *n* white sugar in the form of a coarse powder with large particles

gran·u·la·tion /grànnyə láysh'n/ *n* **1. MAKING OF SMALL PARTICLES** the formation of small grains or particles **2. GRAINY TEXTURE** a rough grainy texture or appearance **3. SMALL LUMP** one of the individual small lumps that, together, give something a rough grainy texture or appearance **4.** MED **FORMATION OF HEALING TISSUE** the formation of granulation tissue, or the tissue itself **5.** ASTRON **CELLULAR APPEARANCE OF SUN'S SURFACE** the cellular appearance of the Sun's disk when seen at high magnification [Early 17C. < late Latin *granulum* (see GRANULE)]

gran·u·la·tion tis·sue *n* connective tissue in the form of small grainy particles along with masses of tiny blood vessels that forms over healing wounds

gran·ule /grán yool/ *n* **1. SMALL PARTICLE** a small grain or particle **2.** GEOL **SMALL ROCK FRAGMENT** a mineral or rock particle that is the size of a small grain **3.** ASTRON **TEMPORARY BRIGHT REGION ON SUN'S SURFACE** a temporary bright region on the Sun's surface, usually with an approximate diameter of 320 mi./1,000 km [Mid-17C. < late Latin *granulum* "small seed" < Latin *granum* "seed"]

gran·u·lite /grányə lìt/ *n* a coarse-grained metamorphic rock in which the minerals are of roughly equal size —**gran·u·lit·ic** /grànnyə líttik/ *adj*

gran·u·lo·cyte /grányəlō sìt/ *n* a white blood cell that contains many granular particles in its cytoplasm —**gran·u·lo·cyt·ic** /grànnyəlō síttik/ *adj*

gran·u·lo·ma /grànnyə lṓmə/ (*plural* **-mas** or **-ma·ta** /-lṓmətə/) *n* a small mass of granulation tissue caused by chronic infection —**gran·u·lo·ma·tous** *adj*

gran·u·lose /grányə lòss/ *adj* **1.** consisting of small grains or particles **2.** appearing to consist of or be covered in small grains or particles

gra·num /gráynəm/ (*plural* **-na** /-nə/) *n* a stack of thin layers in a chloroplast in which the green pigment chlorophyll is contained [Late 19C. Via German < Latin, "seed"]

Gran·ville-Bar·ker /grànvil baárkər/, **Harley** (1877–1946) British actor, producer, and dramatist. He managed London theaters, wrote plays about social problems, and published a famous series of prefaces to William Shakespeare's plays (1927–46).

grape /grayp/ *n* **1. EDIBLE FRUIT** a green or purple berry

grape

with sweet juicy flesh that grows in bunches on a vine, eaten fresh or used to make wine or juice. Raisins, sultanas, and currants are dried grapes. **2.** PLANTS same as **grapevine** (sense 1) **3. PLANT WITH FRUIT RESEMBLING GRAPES** a plant that produces fruit resembling grapes ○ *Oregon grape* **4.** BEVERAGES same as **wine** (*humorous*) **5.** ARMS same as **grapeshot 6.** COLORS **DARK PURPLE** a dark purple color [13C. < Old French, "bunch of grapes, hook (as used to harvest grapes)" < Germanic, "hook"] —**grape** *adj*

CULTURAL NOTE ***The Grapes of Wrath***, a novel (1939) by writer John Steinbeck. A sympathetic portrayal of the plight of the rural poor during the Depression and an attack on capitalism, it tells of the tribulations suffered by the Joad family when they leave drought-stricken Oklahoma in search of work. It was made into a film by John Huston in 1940.

grape fern *n* a fern with fronds that bear spore capsules in clusters similar to those of grapes. Genus: *Botrychium*.

grape·fruit /gráyp fro͞ot/ (*plural* **-fruits** or *same*) *n* **1.** a large round yellow or pinkish citrus fruit with tart juicy flesh **2.** an evergreen tree with large white flowers that produces grapefruits. Native to: tropical and subtropical regions. Latin name: *Citrus paradisi*. [Early 19C. Probably because the fruit grows in bunches, like grapes]

grape hy·a·cinth *n* a perennial plant belonging to the lily family. Flowers: usually blue, dense, cup-shaped, in clusters. Genus: *Muscari*.

grape i·vy *n* an evergreen climbing plant commonly kept as a house plant. Native to: South America. Latin name: *Rhoicissus rhomboidea*.

grape·seed /gráyp sèed/ (*plural same* or **-seeds**) *n* a seed of a grape, from which an oil is extracted for use in cooking

grape·shot /gráyp shòt/ *n* a number of small iron balls fired simultaneously from a cannon in order to kill enemy soldiers [< the resemblance to a bunch of grapes]

grape sug·ar *n* a fruit sugar obtained from grapes

grape·vine /gráyp vìn/ *n* **1.** a climbing plant on which grapes grow. Genus: *Vitis*. **2.** the path of communication along which news, gossip, or rumor passes unofficially from person to person within a group, organization, or community (*informal*) ○ *I heard through the office grapevine that she was leaving.*

grap·ey /gráypee/ (**-i·er, -i·est**), **grap·y** *adj* looking or tasting like a grape or grapes —**grap·i·ness** *n*

graph[1] /graf/ *n* a diagram used to indicate relationships between two or more variable quantities. The quantities are usually measured along two axes set at right angles to each other. A graph may be in different forms, e.g. of a line joining points plotted between coordinates, or a series of parallel bars or boxes. ■ *vt* (**graphed, graph·ing, graphs**) to represent data by means of a graph, or add data to a graph [Late 19C. Shortening of *graphic formula*]

graph[2] /graf/ *n* a symbol, letter, or combination of letters used in writing to represent the smallest discrete unit of speech [Mid-20C. < Greek *graphē* "writing" < *graphein* "write"]

graph- *prefix* same as **grapho-** (*used before vowels*)

-graph *suffix* **1.** something written or drawn ○ *digraph* ○ *zincograph* **2.** an instrument for writing, drawing, or recording ○ *pantograph* ○ *seismograph* [Via French or Latin < Greek *graphos* "written, writing" < *graphein* "write"]

graph·eme /grá fèem/ *n* a written symbol, letter, or combination of letters that represents a single sound —**gra·phe·mic** /gra fèemik/ *adj* —**gra·phe·mi·cal·ly** *adv*

gra·phe·mics /gra fèemiks/ *n* LING same as **graphology** (sense 2)

-grapher *suffix* somebody who writes, draws, or records ○ *calligrapher* ○ *cinematographer* [< late Latin *-graphus* "writer" < Greek *-graphos* < *graphein* "write"]

graph·ic /gráffik/ *adj* **1. VIVIDLY DETAILED** including a number of vivid descriptive details, especially exciting or unpleasant ones ○ *her graphic description of the accident* **2. SHOWN IN WRITING** representing something such as a sound by means of letters or other written symbols. "Moo," "woof," and "meow" are graphic representations of the sounds made by cows, dogs, and cats respectively. **3. SHOWN IN PICTURES** representing something in the form of pictures or images **4. GRAPHS** relating to or given in the form of a graph or diagram **5. OF GRAPHIC ARTS** relating to the graphic arts **6. OF GRAPHICS** relating to graphics **7.** GEOL **CONTAINING CRYSTALS LIKE LETTERS** containing crystal structures that resemble letters ■ *n* (*often used in the plural*) **1.** COMPUT **PICTURE PRODUCED BY COMPUTER** a picture, design, or visual display of data produced by a computer program **2.** PUBL **BOOK ILLUSTRATION** an illustration or diagram in a book or magazine **3.** MOVIES, MEDIA **DISPLAYED TEXT IN MOVIE** a part of a movie that consists of illustration and text, e.g., titles, credits, or drawings [Mid-18C. Via Latin < Greek *graphikos* < *graphein* "write"] —**graph·i·cal·ly** *adv* —**graph·ic·ness** *n*

graph·i·ca·cy /gráffikəssee/ *n* the ability to use and understand such things as symbols, diagrams, plans, and maps [Mid-20C. < GRAPHIC, after *literacy*]

graph·i·cal /gráffik'l/ *adj* MATH same as **graphic** *adj* (sense 4)

graph·i·cal us·er in·ter·face *n* a user interface on a computer that relies on icons, menus, and a mouse, and not on typing in commands

graph·ic arts *npl* artistic processes based on the use of lines rather than color, e.g., drawing, calligraphy, engraving, and printmaking —**graph·ic art·ist** *n*

graph·ic de·sign *n* the art of integrating text, typography, and illustrations in the production of books and magazines —**graph·ic de·sign·er** *n*

graph·ic e·qual·iz·er *n* a device, e.g., on a radio or CD player, that allows adjustments to be made to the strength of sounds of different frequencies [Because the variable levels of the sounds are often displayed electronically in graphic format]

Graph·ic in·ter·face for·mat *n* COMPUT full form of **GIF**

graph·ic nov·el *n* a fictional story for adults published in the form of a comic book

graph·ics /gráffiks/ *n* (*takes a singular verb*) **1. DIAGRAMS AND ILLUSTRATIONS** the presentation of information in the form of diagrams and illustrations instead of as words or numbers **2.** COMPUT **DISPLAY OF COMPUTER DATA AS SYMBOLS** the art and science of storing, manipulating, and displaying computer data in the form of pictures, diagrams, graphs, or symbols **3.** ARCHIT, ENG **MATHEMATICAL DRAWING** the science of drawing something in accordance with mathematical principles, e.g., in architecture and engineering ■ *npl* ARTS same as **graphic arts**

graph·ics a·dapt·er *n* a circuit board in a computer that contains the necessary video memory to allow a bit-mapped display to be created

graph·ics card *n* a circuit board that enables a computer to display screen information

graph·ics de·vice in·ter·face *n* a set of program instructions that allows the Windows™ operating system to output graphics to a computer screen or print device

graph·ics tab·let *n* a device consisting of an electronic pen and an electronically sensitive surface, used to enter designs into a computer by drawing them

graph·ite /grá fìt/ *n* a soft dark carbon that conducts electricity, occurs naturally as a mineral, and is also produced industrially. Use: batteries, lubricants, polishes, electric motors, nuclear reactors, carbon fibers, pencil lead. [Late 18C. < German *Graphit* < Greek *graphein* "write"] —**gra·phit·ic** /gra fíttik/ *adj*

graph·i·tize /gráffi tìz/ (**-tized, -tiz·ing, -tiz·es**) *vt* **1.** to convert something into graphite **2.** to coat something with graphite, or mix graphite into it —**graph·i·tiz·a·ble** *adj* —**graph·i·ti·za·tion** /gràffiti záysh'n/ *n*

grapho- *prefix* writing ○ *graphology* [< Greek *graphein* "write"]

gra·phol·o·gy /gra fóllәjee/ *n* **1.** the study of handwriting, especially in order to assess somebody's personality from patterns or features of his or her writing **2.** the study of writing systems and their relationship to the sound systems of languages —**graph·o·log·i·cal** /gràffә lójjik'l/ *adj* —**gra·phol·o·gist** *n*

graph pa·per *n* paper on which a series of usually equally or logarithmically spaced vertical and horizontal intersecting lines has been imprinted to facilitate the drawing of graphs and diagrams

-graphy *suffix* **1.** a method of writing or making an image by means of a particular process or technique ○ *chirography* ○ *radiography* **2.** writing about or study of a particular subject ○ *biography* ○ *ethnography* [< Latin *-graphia* < Greek *graphein* "write"]

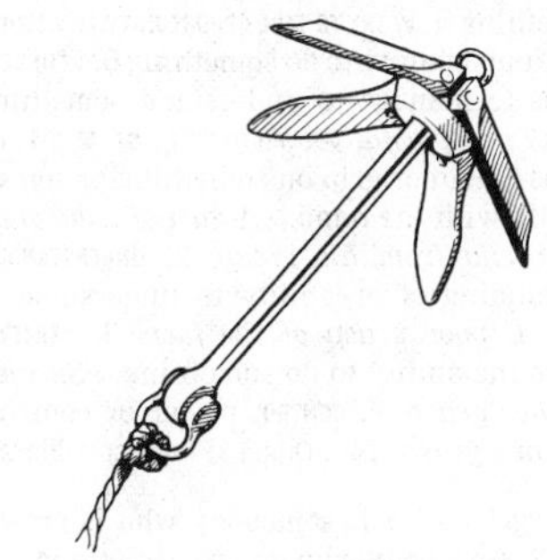

grapnel

grap·nel /grápnәl/ *n* **1.** a device consisting of an iron shaft with several hooks at one end and a rope at the other by which it can be thrown to attach itself to something **2.** an anchor with three or more arms, especially one for anchoring a small boat [14C. < Anglo-Norman < Old French *grapon* < *grape* "hook" (see GRAPE)]

grap·pa /graápә/ *n* an Italian brandy distilled from what remains of grapes after they have been pressed for winemaking [Late 19C. < Italian, "grape stalk, brandy"]

Barnaby's

Stéphane Grappelli

Grap·pel·li /grә péllee/, **Stéphane** (1908–97) French musician. He is known for his playing of the violin in the jazz style.

grap·ple /grápp'l/ *v* (**-pled, -pling, -ples**) **1.** *vi* **STRUGGLE WITH SOMEBODY** to struggle with somebody in a close hand-to-hand fight **2.** *vi* **STRUGGLE TO DEAL WITH SOMETHING** to struggle to deal with or comprehend something ○ *The government continues to grapple with the economic crisis.* **3.** *vt* **GRAB SOMEBODY** to grab hold of somebody **4.** *vt* **HOLD SOMETHING WITH HOOKED DEVICE** to hook or hold something with a grapnel or other hooked device ■ *n* **1.** same as **grapnel** (sense 1) **2. STRUGGLE** a close struggle **3. GRIP OR HOLD** in wrestling, a grip or hold on an opponent [14C. < Old French *grapil* "small hook" < *grape* "hook" (see GRAPE)]

grap·pler /grápplәr/ *n* somebody who competes in a wrestling match (*informal*)

grap·pling /grápplíng/, **grap·pling i·ron, grap·pling hook** *n* same as **grapnel** (sense 1)

grap·to·lite /gráptә lìt/ *n* a small floating sea animal that lived in colonies between about 550 million and 325 million years ago and is now found as a fossil. Graptolite fossils are often used to date rocks.

Orders: Graptoloidea or Dendroidea. [Mid-19C. < Greek *graptos*, past participle of *graphein* "write"]

grap·y *adj* FOOD another spelling of **grapey**

GRAS *abbr* generally recognized as safe (*used on food labels to show that the ingredients are not harmful to human beings*)

grasp /grasp/ *v* (**grasped, grasp·ing, grasps**) **1.** *vt* **TAKE HOLD OF SOMEBODY OR SOMETHING** to take hold of somebody or something firmly, especially with the hand **2.** *vi* **TRY TO TAKE HOLD OF SOMETHING** to attempt to take hold of somebody or something, especially with the hand ○ *He grasped at the rope.* **3.** *vt* **HOLD SOMEBODY OR SOMETHING** to hold somebody or something, especially in the hand **4.** *vt* **TAKE OPPORTUNITY** to take the opportunity to do something **5.** *vi* **TRY TO TAKE OPPORTUNITY** to attempt to take the opportunity to do something **6.** *vt* **UNDERSTAND SOMETHING** to manage to understand something ○ *I just can't grasp what you're getting at.* ■ *n* **1. HOLD ON SOMETHING** a hold or grip on something or somebody, especially with the hand ○ *A gust of wind snatched the umbrella from his grasp.* **2. UNDERSTANDING** an understanding of or ability to understand something ○ *a poor grasp of the facts* **3. ABILITY TO DO SOMETHING** the ability to do something ○ *Success was within her grasp.* **4. CONTROL** power or control ○ *in the tyrant's grasp* [14C. Origin ?] —**grasp·a·ble** *adj*

grasp·er /gráspər/ *n* **1.** somebody who is greedy for money **2.** somebody who grasps something

grasp·ing /gráspiŋ/ *adj* greedy for money —**grasp·ing·ly** *adv* —**grasp·ing·ness** *n*

grass: annual meadow grass

grass /grass/ *n* (*plural same* or **grass·es**) **1. GREEN PLANT THAT FORMS LAWNS** a low green narrow-leaved plant that grows in fields and gardens, is eaten by animals such as cows and sheep, and is used to make lawns and playing fields **2. GRASS-COVERED AREA** an area of grass such as a lawn or pasture ○ *Keep off the grass.* **3. HOLLOW-STEMMED GREEN PLANT** a plant with hollow jointed stems and long narrow, usually green leaves and tiny flowers arranged in spikes. Grasses include important food plants such as wheat, oats, barley, rice, rye, corn, millet, and sorghum as well as sugar cane and bamboo. Family: Gramineae. **4. PLANT LIKE GRASS** a green plant not related to the true grasses, e.g., cleavers or knotgrass **5.** DRUGS same as **marijuana** (*slang*) **6.** *UK* **INFORMER** somebody who informs on somebody else, especially to the police (*slang*) ■ *v* (**grassed, grass·ing, grass·es**) **1.** *vti* **COVER WITH GRASS** to become covered with grass, or cause ground to become covered with grass **2.** *vi UK* **BE INFORMER** to inform on somebody, especially to the police (*slang*) **3.** *vt* **FEED ANIMAL ON GRASS** to put an animal into a pasture to feed on grass [Old English *græs, gærs* < Indo-European] ◇ **not let the grass grow under your feet** to act without delay or wasting time ◇ **put somebody out to grass** *UK* to impose retirement on somebody, usually on grounds of age (*informal*)

CULTURAL NOTE ***Leaves of Grass***, a collection of verse (1855–92) by poet Walt Whitman. Whitman constantly revised and expanded this collection to create a work that celebrates all aspects of human life from politics to the natural world and from procreation to mortality. Both its subject matter and its self-consciously modern style, based on long, loosely rhymed lines, were highly influential.

Günter Grass

Grass /graass/, **Günter** (*b.* 1927) German writer and political activist. His novels such as *The Tin Drum* (1959) and *Dog Years* (1963) combine fantasy and symbolism with the theme of the materialism of modern life. He won the Nobel Prize in literature (1999).

> "History offers no comfort. It hands out hard lessons. It makes absurd reading, mostly. Admittedly, it moves on, but progress is not the result of history. History is never-ending. We are always inside history, never outside it."
> [Günter Grass, *Documents on the Workings of Politics*; 1971]

grass box *n UK* GARDENING same as **grass catcher**

grass carp *n* a plant-eating fish used for keeping water weeds under control. Native to: Russia, China. Latin name: *Ctenopharyngodon idella.*

grass catch·er *n* the container attached to a lawn mower that catches the grass cuttings

grass ceil·ing *n* a gender barrier preventing women golfers from participating in the sport at the highest level (*informal*) [Late 20C. Modeled on GLASS CEILING]

grass cloth *n* cloth made from loosely woven plant fibers

grass court *n* a grass-covered tennis court

grass-green *adj* having the color of green grass —**grass green** *n*

grasshopper

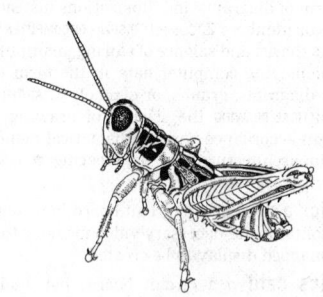

grass·hop·per /gráss hòppər/ *n* **1.** INSECTS **JUMPING INSECT** a slender plant-eating flying and jumping insect that produces a buzzing or whirring sound by rubbing its back legs against its forewings. Order: Orthoptera. **2.** BEVERAGES **CREAMY COCKTAIL** a cocktail consisting of crème de menthe, crème de cacao, and cream **3.** PLANES **RECONNAISSANCE AIRCRAFT** a light, unarmed military airplane used for reconnaissance **4.** *Southwest US* **ILLEGAL IMMIGRANT** an illegal Mexican immigrant into the US, especially a drug smuggler (*slang*) [14C. < *grasshop* < Old English *gærshoppa*]

grass·land /gráss lànd/ *n* **1.** land on which grass or low green plants are the main vegetation (*usually used in the plural*) **2.** land kept for pasture or for the production of forage crops

Grass·lands Na·tion·al Park /gràsslәndz-/ national park in southwestern Saskatchewan, Canada, on the border with the United States. It is a conservation area for grasses, animals, and birds. Area: 350 sq. mi./907 sq. km.

grass moth *n* a small straw-colored night-flying moth that spends the daytime clinging to grass stems. Family: Pyralidae.

grass·roots /gráss ro͝ots, -ro͞ots/ *npl* **1. ORDINARY PEOPLE** the ordinary people in a community or the ordinary members of an organization, as opposed to the leadership **2. BASIS OF SOMETHING** the origin, basis, fundamental aim, or basic meaning of something ○ *the grassroots of socialism* **3. RURAL AREAS** agricultural or rural areas **4. RURAL PEOPLE** the people living in rural areas

grass snake *n* **1.** a common nonpoisonous dark green snake. Native to: Europe, North Africa, Asia. Genus: *Natrix.* **2.** REPT same as **green snake**

grass tree *n* a tree with an unbranching trunk topped by a tuft of leaves resembling grass. Native to: eastern Australia. Genus: *Xanthorrhoea.*

grass wid·ow *n* a woman whose husband or partner is frequently away from home or who has divorced or completely deserted her [Originally "discarded mistress," thought of as having made love in a field]

grass wid·ow·er *n* a man whose wife or partner is frequently away from home or who has divorced or completely deserted him

grass·y /grássee/ (**-i·er, -i·est**) *adj* **1.** covered with grass **2.** looking, tasting, or feeling like grass —**grass·i·ness** *n*

grate[1] /grayt/ *n* **1. BARS IN FRONT OF FIRE** a framework of metal bars used to keep solid fuel such as coal or wood within a fireplace, stove, or furnace **2. FIREPLACE** a fireplace, stove, or furnace **3. BARS OVER OPENING** a framework of bars covering and blocking an opening **4.** MIN EXTRACT **SIEVE FOR GRADING ORE** an iron plate with holes in it for grading crushed ore [14C. Via Old French < Latin *cratis* "wickerwork"]

grate[2] /grayt/ (**grat·ed, grat·ing, grates**) *v* **1.** *vti* **MAKE INTO SMALL PIECES** to shred something by rubbing it against a rough surface or a tool with sharp-edged holes in it, or be shredded in this way ○ *He chose a cheese that grates easily.* **2.** *vi* **MAKE NOISE OF RUBBING** to make a rough, vibrating, or creaking sound by being rubbed together, or cause things to make such a sound ○ *Grasshoppers make their characteristic sound by grating their back legs against their wings.* **3.** *vi* **IRRITATE** to be a source of irritation ○ *His constant snickering really grates on me.* **4.** *vt* **SAY SOMETHING IN HARSH VOICE** to say something in a harsh rasping voice [14C. < Old French *grater* "scrape" < Germanic] —**grat·ed** *adj*

grate·ful /gráytfəl/ *adj* **1.** having or showing the desire or reason to thank somebody ○ *I'm very grateful to you for your help.* **2.** giving pleasure or comfort (*archaic or literary*) [Mid-16C. < obsolete *grate* "pleasing, thankful" < Latin *gratus*] —**grate·ful·ly** *adv* —**grate·ful·ness** *n*

grat·er /gráytər/ *n* **1.** a device with many sharp-edged holes against which something such as cheese can be rubbed to reduce it to shreds or fine particles **2.** somebody who grates something

Gra·tian /gráysh'n/ (A.D. 359–383) Western Roman emperor (A.D.367–383). He served as coemperor until A.D. 375 with his father, Valentinian I, and from then with his half-brother, Valentinian II. He spent much of his rule fighting Germanic tribes in Gaul and was a strong supporter of the Christian Church. Full name **Flavius Gratianus**

grat·i·cule /grátti kyo͞ol/ *n* OPTICS same as **reticle** [Late 19C. Via French < Latin *craticula* "small grid" < *cratis* "wickerwork"]

grat·i·fi·ca·tion /gràttəfi káysh'n/ *n* **1. SATISFACTION** a feeling of pleasure or satisfaction **2. ACT OF SATISFYING** the act of giving somebody pleasure or satisfaction **3. SOMETHING SATISFYING** something that gives pleasure or satisfaction

grat·i·fy /grátta fī/ (**-fied, -fy·ing, -fies**) *vt* **1.** to make somebody feel pleased or satisfied (*often passive*) **2.** to satisfy a desire [15C. Directly or via French *gratifier* < Latin *gratificari* < *gratus* "agreeable"] —**grat·i·fi·er** *n* —**grat·i·fy·ing** *adj* —**grat·i·fy·ing·ly** *adv*

gra·tin /grátt'n, graát'n, gra táN/ *n* **1.** a crust of browned breadcrumbs or melted grated cheese on top of food **2.** a cooked dish with a breadcrumb or melted grated cheese crust [Mid-17C. < French < Old French *grater* (see GRATE²)]

grat·i·nee /gràtt'n áy, graát'n-/ *adj* cooked or served with browned breadcrumbs or melted grated cheese on top [Early 20C. < French *gratinée*, past participle of *gratiner* "cook au gratin"]

grat·ing¹ /gráyting/ *n* **1.** a framework of metal bars covering an opening **2.** OPTICS same as **diffraction grating** ■ **grat·ings** *npl* shreds or fine particles produced by grating something

grat·ing² /gráyting/ *adj* **1.** unpleasantly rough, harsh, or vibrating **2.** irritating or annoying —**grat·ing·ly** *adv*

grat·is /gráttiss, graát-, gráyt-/ *adj, adv* received or given without payment or obligation [15C. < Latin, "out of kindness" < *gratia* (see GRACE)]

grat·i·tude /grátti tòod/ *n* a feeling of being thankful to somebody for doing something ○ *I'd like to find some way of expressing my gratitude to her for all she did.* [15C. Directly or via French < Latin *gratitudo* < *gratus* "pleasing"]

gra·tu·i·tous /grə tòo itəss/ *adj* **1.** UNNECESSARY unnecessary and unjustifiable ○ *gratuitous remarks* **2.** FREE received or given without payment or obligation **3.** LAW WITHOUT RETURN BENEFIT not requiring any benefit or compensation in return [Mid-17C. Via French < Latin *gratuitus* "freely given" < *gratus* "pleasing"] —**gra·tu·i·tous·ly** *adv* —**gra·tu·i·tous·ness** *n*

gra·tu·i·ty /grə tòo ətee/ (*plural* **-ties**) *n* a small gift, usually of money, given to somebody such as a waiter as thanks for service given [15C. Via French *gratuité* < medieval Latin *gratuitas* "gift" < Latin *gratus* "pleasing"]

Grau /grow/, **Shirley Ann** (*b.* 1929) US writer. Her fiction portrays life in the South, and includes the Pulitzer Prize-winning *The Keepers of the House* (1964).

grau·pel /grówp'l/ *n* small soft white ice particles that fall as hail or snow [Late 19C. < German, "small hulled grain" < Slavic]

Grau San Mar·tín /gròw san maar teén/, **Ramón** (1887–1969) president of Cuba (1933–34, 1944–48)

grav /grav/ *n* a unit of acceleration that corresponds to the standard acceleration of free fall. Symbol **g** [Shortening of GRAVITY]

gra·va·men /grə váymən/ (*plural* **-va·mens** or **-vam·i·na** /-vámmənə/) *n* **1.** the most serious part of an accusation or charge made against an accused person **2.** a grievance against somebody (*formal*) [Early 17C. < medieval Latin, "grievance" < Latin *gravare* "weigh upon" < *gravis* "heavy"]

grave¹ /grayv/ *n* **1.** BURIAL PLACE a burial place in the ground, or another place of interment ○ *She goes every week to put fresh flowers on her husband's grave.* ○ *as silent as the grave* **2.** LAST RESTING PLACE a final resting place ○ *the sunken ship's watery grave* **3.** DEATH the end of life ○ *health care from the cradle to the grave* **4.** END OF SOMETHING the end or destruction of something ○ *the grave of his ambition* [Old English *græf* < Indo-European, "scratch, dig"] —**grave·less** *adj* ◇ **turn over in his** *or* **her grave** used to emphasize how displeased or upset somebody who is dead would be if he or she knew what was happening ○ *If she heard this version, she'd turn over in her grave.*

grave² /grayv/ (**grav·er, grav·est**) *adj* **1.** SERIOUS IN MANNER solemn and serious in manner **2.** NEEDING SERIOUS THOUGHT important and having serious consequences, and therefore requiring careful consideration **3.** INVOLVING POSSIBLE HARM OR DANGER causing, involving, or arising from a threat of serious consequences such as danger or harm ○ *Things are looking pretty grave here as the air raid sirens wail.* [15C. Via French < Latin *gravis* "heavy"] —**grave·ly** *adv* —**grave·ness** *n*

grave³ /grayv, graav/, **grave ac·cent** *n* in some languages, a mark (`) placed above a letter to show that it is sounded in a specific way, as in ò and è. See table at [Early 17C. < French, "heavy" (see GRAVE²)]

grave⁴ /grayv/ (**graved, graved** or **grav·en** /gráyvən/, **grav·ing, graves**) *vt* **1.** to fix something firmly in the mind (*literary*) ○ *graved it in her mind* **2.** to carve or engrave something (*archaic*) [Old English *grafan* "dig, carve" < Germanic]

grave⁵ /grayv/ (**graved, grav·ing, graves**) *vt* to clean the bottom of a wooden ship and coat it with pitch [15C. Probably < French dialect *grave* "sand, shore" < Old French (see GRAVEL), because the work was done while the ship was hauled up on a beach]

gra·ve⁶ /graá vày/ *adv* to be played seriously or solemnly (*used as a musical direction*) [Late 16C. Via Italian < Latin *gravis* "heavy"] —**gra·ve** *adj*

grave ac·cent *n* LING same as **grave³**

grave·clothes /gráyv klòthz, -klòz/ *npl* the clothes or other wrappings that a dead body is buried in

grave·dig·ger /gráyv dìggər/ *n* somebody employed to dig graves

grav·el /grávv'l/ *n* **1.** SMALL STONES small stones used for paths or for making concrete **2.** GEOL ROCK FRAGMENTS a deposit or stratum of loose fragmentary sedimentary material **3.** MED SMALL PARTICLES IN KIDNEY OR BLADDER hard particles in the kidney or bladder that are much smaller than kidney stones and can pass through the urinary tract without causing a blockage, although they may cause severe pain ■ *vt* (**-eled, -el·ing, -els**) **1.** LAY GRAVEL OVER SOMETHING to cover a surface with gravel **2.** BEWILDER SOMEBODY to puzzle or confuse somebody **3.** ANNOY SOMEBODY to annoy or irritate somebody (*informal*) [13C. < Old French < *grave* "pebbles, shore" < Celtic]

grav·el-blind *adj* almost totally sightless (*archaic; usually considered offensive*) [After SAND-BLIND]

grav·el·ly /grávv'lee/ *adj* **1.** GRATING sounding rough or harsh ○ *a gravelly voice* **2.** LIKE GRAVEL like or covered with gravel **3.** WITH GRAVEL made or manufactured with gravel

grav·en past participle of **grave⁴**

grav·en im·age *n* a carving representing a god

grav·er /gráyvər/ *n* a tool used for carving or engraving

grave rob·ber *n* a thief of objects from graves or tombs, usually valuable artifacts or corpses for dissection

Graves /graav/ *n* a white or red wine from the district of Graves in southwestern France

Graves /grayvz/, **Robert** (1895–1985) British poet and novelist. A classical scholar, he was also a prolific writer of poetry and fiction. His works include *Goodbye to All That* (1929), *I, Claudius* (1934), and *The White Goddess* (1947). Full name **Graves, Robert Ranke**

> "To be a poet is a condition rather than a profession."
> [Robert Graves. Quoted in *Horizon*; September 1946]

Graves' dis·ease /gráyvz-/ *n* an inflammatory disorder of the thyroid gland commonly associated with protrusion of the eyes [Mid-19C. After Robert J. Graves (1796–1853), Irish physician]

Graves·end /gràyvz énd/ port on the Thames River in Kent, southeastern England. Population: 51,435 (1991).

grave·side /gráyv sìd/ *n* the area surrounding a grave (*often used before a noun*) ○ *a graveside service*

grave·site /gráyv sìt/ *n* the place where somebody's grave is located

grave·stone /gráyv stòn/ *n* an ornamental piece of stone put at the head of a grave, on which are written the name, birth date, and death date of the person buried there

grave·yard /gráyv yaàrd/ *n* **1.** a piece of ground, sometimes beside a church, set aside for people to be buried in **2.** a place where old, unwanted, useless objects, especially old cars, are left

grave·yard po·et·ry *n* sad reflective poems about death, often set in graveyards and usually by 18th-century British writers —**grave·yard po·et** *n*

grave·yard shift *n* a shift of work running through the early hours of the morning, especially one running from midnight till eight o'clock the following morning, or the workers on such a shift

grav·id /grávvid/ *adj* same as **pregnant** (*technical*) [Late 16C. < Latin *gravidus* < *gravis* "heavy"] —**gra·vid·i·ty** /grə víddətee/ *n* —**grav·id·ly** *adv* —**grav·id·ness** *n*

grav·i·da /grávvədə/ (*plural* **-das** or **-dae** /-deè/) *n* a pregnant woman (*technical*) [Mid-20C. < Latin, form of *gravidus* (see GRAVID)]

gra·vim·e·ter /grə vímmətər, grávvə meètər/ *n* **1.** an instrument for measuring variations in the strength of the Earth's gravitational field from one place to another **2.** an instrument used to measure the relative density of a substance [Late 18C. < French *gravimètre* < Latin *gravis* (see GRAVE²)]

grav·i·met·ric /gràvvə méttrik/ *adj* **1.** RELATING TO MEASUREMENT OF WEIGHT relating to or using the measurement of weight **2.** MEASURING GRAVITATIONAL VARIATIONS relating to the measurement of variations in the strength of the Earth's gravitational field from one place to another **3.** OF CHEMICAL ANALYSIS AND WEIGHT relating to chemical analysis involving the measurement of the weights of substances used in and produced by a chemical reaction —**grav·i·met·ri·cal** *adj* —**grav·i·met·ri·cal·ly** *adv*

gra·vim·e·try /grə vímmətree/ *n* **1.** the measurement of density or weight **2.** the measurement of variations in the strength of the Earth's gravitational field from one place to another

grav·ing dock /gráyving-/ *n* SHIPPING same as **dry dock** [< GRAVE⁵]

grav·i·tas /grávvi taàss/ *n* a serious and solemn attitude or way of behaving [Early 20C. < Latin (see GRAVITY)]

grav·i·tate /grávvi tàyt/ (**-tat·ed, -tat·ing, -tates**) *v* **1.** *vi* to move gradually and steadily toward somebody or something as if drawn by some force or attraction ○ *guests slowly gravitating to the kitchen* **2.** *vti* to move under the influence of the force of gravity, or cause something to do this [Mid-17C. < modern Latin *gravitat-*, past participle of *gravitare* < Latin *gravitas* (see GRAVITY)] —**grav·i·tat·er** *n* —**grav·i·ta·tive** *adj*

grav·i·ta·tion /gràvvi táysh'n/ *n* **1.** a gradual and steady movement toward somebody or something, as if drawn by some force or attraction **2.** the mutual force of attraction between all particles or bodies that have mass —**grav·i·ta·tion·al** *adj* —**grav·i·ta·tion·al·ly** *adv*

grav·i·ta·tion·al con·stant *n* the numerical factor relating force, mass, and distance in Newton's theory of gravitation. It has the value 6.673 ± 10^{-11} Nm^2kg^{-2}.

grav·i·ta·tion·al field *n* the region of space around an object that has mass, within which another object that has mass experiences the force of attraction

grav·i·ta·tion·al lens *n* a large astronomical object such as a galaxy whose gravitational field focuses or distorts the light from another object beyond it

grav·i·ta·tion·al red·shift *n* the displacement of the spectrum of light emitted by an astronomical object toward longer wavelengths (**redshift**) because of the difference between the gravitational potential at the observer and source

grav·i·ta·tion·al wave *n* a hypothetical wave, predicted by relativity theory, that travels at the speed of light and propagates a gravitational field

grav·i·ton /grávvi tòn/ *n* a hypothetical particle with zero charge and rest mass that is considered to be the quantum particle of the gravitational interaction [Mid-20C. < GRAVITATION]

grav·i·ty /grávvətee/ *n* **1.** GRAVITATIONAL FORCE the attraction due to gravitation that the Earth or another astronomical object exerts on an object on or near its surface **2.** PHYS same as **gravitation** (sense 2) **3.** SERIOUSNESS the seriousness of something considered in terms of its unfavorable consequences ○ *regarded it as a matter of the utmost gravity* **4.** SERIOUS BEHAVIOR solemnity and seriousness in somebody's attitude or behavior **5.** HEAVINESS the quality of being heavy **6.** WEIGHT the amount that something weighs (*formal*) [15C. Via French < Latin *gravitas* "heaviness" < *gravis* "heavy"]

CULTURAL NOTE ***Gravity's Rainbow***, a novel (1973) by writer Thomas Pynchon. Set in Europe during World War II, it describes the attempts of various interest groups to exploit the extrasensory powers of US soldier Tyrone

Slothrop, whose sexual encounters reliably predict the impact sites of German V2 rockets. It is noted for its extraordinary erudition, broad range of styles, and complex characterization.

grav·i·ty feed *n* a mechanism or process for supplying something such as fuel to a boiler or materials to a manufacturing process by their downward movement under the influence of gravity —**grav·i·ty-fed** *adj*

grav·i·ty wave *n* PHYS same as **gravitational wave**

grav·lax /graáv laàks/ *n* a Scandinavian dish consisting of thin slices of dried salmon marinated in sugar, salt, pepper, and herbs, especially dill, and usually served as an appetizer [Mid-20C. < Swedish or Norwegian *gravlaks* "buried salmon" (because originally marinated in a hole in the ground)]

gra·vure /grə vyoōr/ *n* **1.** PRINTING same as **intaglio** (sense 4) **2.** a plate used in or a print produced by intaglio printing **3.** PRINTING same as **photogravure** [Late 19C. < French < *graver* "engrave"]

gra·vy /gráyvee/ *n* the juices produced by meat while it is being roasted, fried, or broiled, or a sauce made with these juices or another liquid and poured over cooked meat and vegetables [14C. < Old French *grave*]

gra·vy boat *n* a small pitcher, usually long and narrow, in which gravy or other sauces are served

gra·vy train *n* a way of getting a large amount of money or other benefits for very little effort (*informal*) ○ *scrambling to get on the gravy train*

gray[1] /gray/ *n* the derived SI unit for the absorbed dose of ionizing radiation, equal to an absorption of 1 joule per kilogram. Symbol **Gy** [After L. H. *Gray* (1905–65), English radiobiologist]

gray[2] /gray/ *adj* **1.** OF COLOR OF ASH of the color of ash or lead **2.** DISMAL dismal or gloomy **3.** DULL dull and colorless **4.** OF SENIORS relating to, involving, or affecting senior citizens ○ *gray marketing* ■ *n* **1.** COLOR OF ASH the color of ash or lead **2.** GRAY COLORING MATTER a pigment or dye formed from a combination of black and white that is like the color of ash or lead **3.** GRAY CLOTHING fabric or clothing that is gray in color **4.** *also* **Gray** CONFEDERATE SOLDIER a soldier of the Confederacy in the Civil War **5.** CONFEDERATE ARMY the Confederate army in the Civil War, because of its gray uniforms **6.** SOMETHING GRAY a gray object ■ *vi* (**grayed, gray·ing, grays**) TURN GRAY to turn the color gray ○ *His hair is graying.* [Old English *grǣg* < Germanic] —**gray·ly** *adv* —**gray·ness** *n* —**gray·ish** *adj*

Gray /gray/, **Asa** (1810–88) US botanist. He replaced the Linnaean taxonomic system with a new method of classification and wrote the classic *Manual of Botany of the Northern United States* (1848), known as "Gray's Manual."

Gray, Elisha (1835–1901) US inventor. An inventor of telegraphic equipment, he filed his intent to patent the telephone two hours after Alexander Graham Bell (1876).

gray ar·e·a *n* **1.** a situation, subject, or category of something that is unclear or hard to define or classify **2.** a part of something that does not belong to any specific category but contains features of more than one

gray·back /gráy bàk/ *n* a soldier of the Confederacy in the Civil War

gray·bar land /gráy baàr-/ *n* the wait during a time-consuming computer operation while the graphic displaying a usually gray bar slowly moves across the screen (*informal*)

gray·beard /gráy beèrd/ *n* **1.** a man of advanced years (*dated*) **2.** an earthenware container for alcoholic drink —**gray·beard·ed** *adj*

gray em·i·nence *n* same as **éminence grise**

gray·hen /gráy hèn/ (*plural* **-hens** or *same*) *n* a female black grouse

gray·ing /gráy ing/ *n* same as **aging** *n* (sense 1) ■ *adj* same as **aging**

gray jay *n* a bird of the crow family that is gray with black markings on the head. Native to: coniferous forests, especially spruce forests, in North America. Latin name: *Perisoreus canadensis.*

gray·lag /gráy làg/, **gray·lag goose** *n* a common wild goose that is light brownish gray with a large orange or pink beak and is the ancestor of the domestic farm goose. Native to: Europe, Asia. Latin name: *Anser anser.* [Early 18C. < GRAY[2] + dialect *lag* "goose," origin ?]

gray·ling /gráyling/ (*plural* **-lings** or *same*) *n* **1.** a freshwater fish with silvery scales and a large dorsal fin, valued as a game fish. Native to: Russia, China. Genus: *Thymallus.* **2.** INSECTS a common gray butterfly. Native to: Europe. Latin name: *Eumenis semele.*

gray lit·er·a·ture *n* articles and information published, especially on the Internet, without a commercial purpose or the mediation of a commercial publisher

gray·mail /gráy màyl/ *n* a maneuver used by the defense in a spy trial whereby the government is threatened with the revelation of national secrets unless the case against the defendant is dropped [Late 20C. After BLACKMAIL]

gray mar·ket *n* **1.** trading in new shares before they have been officially issued on the stock exchange **2.** clandestine but legal trading in goods either at excessively high prices or at prices well below the manufacturer's recommended price

gray mat·ter *n* **1.** intelligence or brains (*informal*) **2.** brownish gray nerve tissue consisting mainly of nerve cell bodies within the brain and spinal cord

gray mul·let *n UK* same as **mullet** (sense 2)

gray pow·er *n* a movement of people and groups who act as advocates for issues that concern senior citizens, e.g., health care, housing, and discrimination

gray scale *n* a series of shades from white to black used in displaying or printing text and graphics

gray squir·rel *n* a large tree squirrel that has gray fur with a reddish tinge in the legs and head. Native to: North America, Great Britain, Ireland, South Africa. Latin name: *Sciurus carolinensis.*

gray vote *n* senior citizens considered as a group that can be influenced to vote in a particular way ○ *the growing political importance of the gray vote*

gray·wacke /gráy wàk, -wàkə/ *n* a conglomerate rock composed of well-rounded pebbles cemented by a sandy infill [Late 18C. < German *Grauwacke* "gray sandstone"]

gray wa·ter *n* waste water from sinks, baths, and kitchen appliances

gray·weth·er /gráy wethər/ *n* GEOL same as **sarsen**

gray whale *n* a large baleen whale that has no dorsal fin but a line of bumps along part of its back. Native to: northern Pacific coastal waters. Latin name: *Eschrichtius gibbosus.*

gray wolf *n* a large intelligent highly social wild dog, varying in color from white in the north of its range to black in the south. Native to: North America, Europe, Asia. Latin name: *Canis lupus.*

Graz /graats/ city and capital of Styria Province on the Mur River in southeastern Austria. Population: 240,513 (1999).

graze[1] /grayz/ (**grazed, graz·ing, graz·es**) *v* **1.** *vti* EAT GRASS IN FIELDS to eat grass and other green plants in a field or fields **2.** *vt* PROVIDE GRASS FOR ANIMALS to allow animals such as cows and sheep to eat grass in fields **3.** *vt* USE LAND FOR FEEDING ANIMALS to allow animals such as cows and sheep to eat the grass and green plants of a particular field or fields ○ *We usually graze those two fields over there.* **4.** *vi* EAT SNACKS to eat snacks throughout the day, instead of regular meals, especially while working (*slang*) **5.** *vi* EAT FOOD IN SUPERMARKET to eat food from the shelves of a supermarket while shopping, without subsequently paying for it at the checkout counter (*slang*) **6.** *vi* SAMPLE DIFFERENT FOODS to eat small portions of several different appetizers or entrées instead of a complete meal (*slang*) **7.** *vi* CHANGE TV CHANNELS to switch television channels frequently without watching much of any one program (*slang*) **8.** *vi* KEEP STOPPING AND STARTING to perform an activity in a desultory manner, e.g., by picking up and putting down magazines without reading much of any one (*slang*) [Old English *grasian* < *græs* (see GRASS)] —**graze·a·ble** *adj* —**graz·er** *n* ◇ **put somebody out to graze** to cause somebody to retire

graze[2] /grayz/ *vt* (**grazed, graz·ing, graz·es**) **1.** TOUCH SOMETHING LIGHTLY to touch against the surface of something lightly in passing **2.** BREAK SKIN SLIGHTLY to damage the surface of the skin of a part of the body slightly when it is rubbed against something rough and hard ■ *n* **1.** SLIGHT BREAK IN SKIN slight and shallow damage to the skin caused by rubbing against something rough and hard **2.** TOUCH OF SOMETHING the act of rubbing something or touching it lightly ○ *the graze of a bullet* [Late 16C. Origin ?]

graz·ing /gráyzing/ *n* **1.** grass and green plants for animals such as cows and sheep to eat **2.** land with grass suitable for animals such as cows and sheep to feed on

gra·zi·o·so /graàtsee óssō/ *adv* in a graceful way (*used as a musical direction*) [Early 19C. Via Italian < Latin *gratiosus* (see GRACIOUS)] —**gra·zi·o·so** *adj*

GRE *tdmk* a trademark for a standardized test taken by applicants to graduate schools in the United States. Full form **Graduate Record Examinations**

grease *n* /greess/ **1.** ANIMAL FAT thick soft animal fat, e.g., from cooked meat **2.** THICK LUBRICANT a thick oily substance, especially one used to make machinery run smoothly **3.** OIL FOR HAIR an oily substance used as a cosmetic for the hair **4.** BRIBERY bribes or bribery (*slang*) **5.** OILY WOOL untreated wool from sheep that still contains its natural oils, or the natural oils in this wool ■ *vt* /greess, greez/ (**greased, greas·ing, greas·es**) **1.** PUT GREASE ON SOMETHING to put grease on something, e.g., in order to make it move smoothly or to stop something else from sticking to it **2.** MAKE SOMETHING EASIER to make something such as progress or promotion easier or quicker (*informal*) ○ *His mother's money certainly greased his path to the boardroom.* [13C. Via Anglo-Norman *grece* < Latin *crassus* "fat, thick"] ◇ **grease somebody's palm** *or* **hand** to bribe somebody to do something (*informal*)

grease·ball /greess bàwl/ *n* **1.** somebody who is habitually dirty or unkempt (*slang insult*) **2.** *US* a highly offensive term for somebody of Mediterranean or Latin American, especially Mexican, origin (*taboo; slang*)

grease gun *n* **1.** a hand-held device for forcing grease into machinery to lubricate it **2.** a submachine gun (*dated slang*)

grease mon·key *n* an offensive term for a mechanic, especially one who works on motor vehicles or aircraft (*slang insult*)

grease·paint /greess pàynt/ *n* a thick greasy or waxy form of colored makeup used by actors

grease pen·cil *n* a pencil containing a core of a waxy colored substance that can write on glossy surfaces

grease·proof /greess proōf/ *adj* not allowing oil or grease to soak into it or pass through it

grease·proof pa·per *n UK* same as **wax paper**

greas·er /greessər, greezər/ *n* **1.** somebody whose job involves greasing machinery, especially a mechanic who works on motor vehicles (*slang*) **2.** a usually young, longhaired, leather-jacketed motorcyclist, especially a member of a motorcycle gang (*slang insult*) **3.** *US* same as **greaseball** (sense 2) (*taboo offensive*)

grease·wood /greess wòōd/ *n* **1.** a spiny desert bush that yields an oil used as fuel. Native to: western North America. Latin name: *Sarcobatus vermiculatus.* **2.** a bush that is similar to or related to the true greasewood, e.g., the creosote bush

greas·y /greessee, greezee/ (**-i·er, -i·est**) *adj* **1.** THICK WITH GREASE covered with or containing grease, often a lot or too much of it ○ *a greasy hamburger* **2.** SMARMY unpleasantly and insincerely flattering, friendly, or groveling **3.** MADE OF GREASE consisting of grease or of something with the consistency of grease **4.** HAVING EXCESSIVE NATURAL OILS producing or containing a lot of natural oils **5.** PRODUCED BY GREASE caused by grease or by something with the consistency of grease ○ *a greasy stain* **6.** SLIPPERY difficult to move, walk, or drive on because of wetness or iciness —**greas·i·ly** *adv* —**greas·i·ness** *n*

greas·y spoon *n* a small, cheap, and often dirty café, especially one that serves fried food (*informal*)

great /grayt/ *adj* **1.** IMPRESSIVELY LARGE very large and impressive **2.** LARGE IN NUMBER large in number, or with many parts ○ *a great crowd of well-wishers* **3.** BIGGER THAN OTHERS larger or more important than others of the same kind **4.** MUCH extreme or more than usual ○ *It gives me great pleasure to introduce our speaker tonight.* **5.** LASTING LONG TIME lasting a long time, or covering a long distance ○ *We endured a great delay.* ○ *one of the world's great railway journeys* **6.** IMPORTANT very significant or important ○ *a truly great novel* **7.** EXCEPTIONALLY TALENTED with exceptional talents or achievements ○ *He was a great humanitarian as well as a talented artist.* **8.** POWERFUL powerful and influential ○ *striving to make our nation great again* ○ *in this great nation* **9.** EXPERT able to do something very well, or very skillful with something (*informal*) **10.** VERY GOOD very good or pleasing ○ *We had a great time at the party.* **11.** USEFUL very useful or suitable for a particular task (*informal*) ○ *This cast-iron pan is great for making pancakes.* **12.** BEING GOOD EXAMPLE OF SOMETHING doing something often, enjoying something very much, or being a very good example of something **13.** USED FOR EMPHASIS used to emphasize how much of a quality somebody or something has (*informal*) ○ *Their new house is a great big place out in the country.* **14.** same as **pregnant** (sense 1) (*archaic*) ○ *She was great with child.* ■ *n* **1.** SOMEBODY GREAT somebody whose fame or influence has proved to be long-lasting ○ *one of the all-time greats of blues music* **2.** MUSIC PART OF PIPE ORGAN the principal division of a pipe organ ■ *adv* VERY WELL very well (*informal*) ○ *That's it; you're doing great.* ○ *Steve and I get along just great.* [Old English *grēat* "thick, coarse" < Germanic] —**great·ly** *adv*—**great·ness** *n*

CULTURAL NOTE *The Great Gatsby*, a novel (1925) by US writer F. Scott Fitzgerald. Set on Long Island, New York, it is the story of enigmatic businessman Jay Gatsby, a symbol of the American obsession with wealth and status, whose attempts to revive a relationship with an old girlfriend lead to his downfall. It was made into movies by Elliott Nugent in 1949 and by Jack Clayton in 1974. Terms such as *Gatsbyesque*, obsessed with social status and the acquisition of great riches, derive directly from the book title and the character.

great- *prefix* **1.** being a parent of somebody's grandparent ○ *great-grandmother* **2.** being a child of one of somebody's grandchildren ○ *great-grandson*

great ape *n* a large ape, e.g., a gorilla, chimpanzee, or orangutan

Great At·trac·tor *n* a large aggregation of galaxies, approximately 150 to 350 million light-years away, whose gravitational pull might account for the unexpected motions of many galaxies, including our own

great auk *n* a large flightless seabird that was hunted to extinction in the mid-19th century. Native to: formerly, North Atlantic coasts. Latin name: *Alca impennis*.

great-aunt *n* an aunt of somebody's father or mother

Great Aus·tra·lian Bight /gràyt-/ wide inlet of the Indian Ocean off the southern coast of Australia. It stretches 685 mi./1,100 km from Cape Pasley in Western Australia to Cape Carnot in South Australia.

Great Bar·ri·er Reef chain of coral reefs in the Coral Sea, located off the coast of Queensland, Australia. The largest deposit of coral in the world, the reef extends for 1,250 mi./2,010 km. Area: 134,600 sq. mi./348,600 sq. km.

Great Ba·sin /-báyss'n/ desert covering most of Nevada and parts of Utah, Oregon, Idaho, and California. Area: 210,000 sq. mi./543,900 sq. km.

Great Ba·sin Na·tion·al Park national park established in 1986 in eastern Nevada. It is noted for its limestone formations. Area: 121 sq. mi./312 sq. km.

Great Bear *n* ASTRON same as **Ursa Major**

Great Bear Lake freshwater lake in Canada's Northwest Territories, lying astride the Arctic Circle. It is the world's seventh largest lake. Area: 12,270 sq. mi./31,790 sq. km.

Great Bend city in central Kansas, on the northern bank of the Arkansas River, northeast of Dodge City. It is located on the old Santa Fe Trail. Population: 15,066 (2002 estimate).

Great Brit·ain the largest island of the British Isles in northwestern Europe. It includes England, Scotland, and Wales.

great cir·cle *n* a circle on the surface of a sphere such as the Earth that has a radius equal to the radius of the sphere, and whose center is also the sphere's center

great·coat /gráyt kòt/ *n* a long thick heavy overcoat worn especially by soldiers

Great Dane

Great Dane *n* a very large dog with long legs, a square head, a deep muzzle, and short hair, belonging to a breed originating in Germany [Because Germans were formerly called Danes]

Great De·pres·sion *n* a drastic decline in the world economy resulting in mass unemployment and widespread poverty that lasted from 1929 until 1939

Great Dis·mal Swamp /-dìzməl swómp/ low-lying marshland in southeastern Virginia and northeastern North Carolina. It is densely forested in parts and rich in wildlife. George Washington once owned most of the area. Area: 750 sq. mi./1,900 sq. km. Former name **Dismal Swamp**

great di·vide *n* a major demarcation between two contrasting things, especially life and death

Great Di·vide *n* same as **Continental Divide**

Great Di·vid·ing Range /-di vīding-/ system of mountain ranges and plateaus in Queensland, New South Wales, and Victoria, extending along the eastern border of Australia. The highest peak is Mount Kosciuszko, 7,310 ft./2,228 m.

Great·er An·til·les /gràytər an tílleez/ island group in the northern Caribbean, comprising Cuba, Jamaica, Hispaniola, and Puerto Rico

Great·er Bai·ram *n* an Islamic festival marking the end of the Islamic year. Date: 70 days after the end of Ramadan.

great·er cel·an·dine *n* PLANTS same as **celandine** (sense 1)

great·er o·men·tum *n* the fold of the peritoneum that covers the intestines

Great·er Sun·da Is·lands ➧ **Sunda Islands**

great·est com·mon di·vi·sor, **great·est com·mon fac·tor** *n* US the highest number that can be exactly divided into each member of a set of numbers. The greatest common divisor of 12, 60, and 84 is 12. Can term **highest common factor**

Great Falls city in north-central Montana, near the falls of the Missouri River. It is a major center of hydroelectric power. Population: 56,046 (2002 estimate).

greatful incorrect spelling of **grateful**

Great Glen rift valley in Scotland that extends southwestward from the Moray Firth to Loch Linnhe. It contains Loch Lochy and Loch Ness. Length: 97 mi./156 km.

great-grand·child *n* a son or daughter of somebody's grandchild

great-grand·par·ent *n* the mother or father of somebody's grandmother or grandfather

great heart·ed *adj* **1.** with a generous and forgiving nature **2.** not easily frightened or dispirited —**great heart·ed·ly** *adv*

Great In·di·an Des·ert ➧ **Thar Desert**

Great Ka·roo ➧ **Karoo**

Great Lakes

Great Lakes group of five freshwater lakes in north central North America, interconnected by natural and artificial channels. The largest group of lakes in the world, they are Lakes Superior, Michigan, Huron, Erie, and Ontario. Area: 94,250 sq. mi./244,100 sq. km.

Great Lakes State *n* a nickname for Michigan

great lau·rel *n* PLANTS same as **rosebay rhododendron**

Great Leap For·ward *n* the attempt by the People's Republic of China from 1958 to 1960 to modernize agriculture by labor-intensive methods

great-neph·ew *n* *Can, UK* a son of somebody's nephew or niece. US term **grandnephew**

great-niece *n* *Can, UK* a daughter of somebody's nephew or niece. US term **grandniece**

great north·ern div·er *n* same as **loon**[1] (sense 1)

great or·gan *n* the main keyboard of an organ, and the pipes and mechanism relating to it

Great Plains vast high plateau region in central North America that stretches from northeastern Canada to southern Texas between the Canadian Shield and Central Lowlands on the east and the Rocky Mountains on the west. Area: 1,200,000 sq. mi./3,200,000 sq. km.

Great Pow·er *n* a nation that has a far-reaching political, social, economic, and usually military influence internationally (*hyphenated when used before a noun*)

Great Rift Val·ley /-rìft-/ depression extending more than 3,000 mi./4,830 km from the valley of the Jordan River in Syria to Mozambique, forming the most extensive rift in the Earth's surface. The area is marked by a chain of seas and lakes and a series of volcanoes.

Great Rus·sian *n* (*dated*) **1.** the Russian language **2.** a member of the main Russian-speaking ethnic group in Russia —**Great Rus·sian** *adj*

Great St. Ber·nard Pass /-saynt bər naárd-/ mountain pass in western Europe, on the border between Valais, central Switzerland, and Aosta Province, Piedmont, northern Italy. Founded in the 11th century, it is named for the hospice founded at its summit by the French monk St. Bernard. Height: 8,098 ft./2,468 m.

Great Salt Lake /-sàwlt láyk/ shallow body of salt water in northwestern Utah, near Salt Lake City. It is the largest salt lake in North America. Area: 2,000 sq. mi./5,200 sq. km.

Great San·dy Des·ert /-sàndee-/ desert in northwestern Australia that contains large areas of sand dunes and salt marshes and some grassland. Area: 150,000 sq. mi./390,000 sq. km.

Great Schism *n* **1.** the period between 1378 and 1415 when there were rival popes, one reigning in Rome and the other in Avignon **2.** the separation of the Roman Catholic and Eastern Orthodox churches in 1054, as a result of theological disagreement

Great Seal *n* in the United States, the seal kept in the charge of the Secretary of State and used in sealing important state papers

Great Slave Lake /-slàyv-/ freshwater lake in the Northwest Territories, northwestern Canada. It is the deepest lake in North America. Depth: 2,015 ft./614 m. Area: 11,030 sq. mi./28,570 sq. km.

Great Smok·y Moun·tains /-smṑkee-/ mountain range in the southeastern United States, forming part of the Appalachian Mountain system, in western North Carolina and eastern Tennessee. Its highest point is Clingmans Dome (6,642 ft./2,024 km).

Great Smok·y Moun·tains Na·tion·al Park national park in the southeastern United States, in western North Carolina and eastern Tennessee. Established in 1930, it contains some of the highest peaks in eastern North America. Area: 815 sq. mi./2,111 sq. km.

Great So·ci·e·ty *n* a legislative program introduced during the presidency of Lyndon Baines Johnson (1963–69) that comprised legislation intended to improve education, health care, and housing and to reduce poverty and racism

great tit *n* a large common tit with a short beak and yellow, black, and white markings. Native to: Europe, Asia. Latin name: *Parus major.*

Great Trek *n* a mass movement between 1836 and 1844 of Boer cattlemen in South Africa from the Cape to the north that eventually resulted in the establishment of the Transvaal and the Orange Free State

great-un·cle *n* an uncle of somebody's father or mother

Great Vic·to·ri·a Des·ert desert in the states of Western Australia and South Australia, consisting of sand dunes, salt lakes, and low scrubland. Area: 150,000 sq. mi./390,000 sq. km.

Great Wall *n* **1.** a huge expanse of thousands of galaxies arranged in a supercluster that forms the largest system of astronomical objects observed in the universe **2.** HIST same as **Great Wall of China**

Barnaby's

Great Wall of China

Great Wall of Chi·na *n* a vast Chinese defensive fortification begun in the 3rd century B.C. and running along the northern border of the country for 1,500 mi./2,400 km

Great War *n* HIST same as **World War I**

great white shark *n* a large shark that is gray-brown with white underparts and preys on large fish, marine mammals, and carrion. Native to: warm and tropical waters. Latin name: *Carcharodon carcharias.*

Great White Way *n* the historic entertainment district in Manhattan stretching along Broadway north of Times Square and distinguished by its many brightly-lit signs and marquees

Great Yar·mouth /-yaármәth/ port and coastal resort in Norfolk, eastern England. Population: 90,810 (2001).

great year *n* a period of about 25,800 years, representing a complete cycle of the precession of the equinoxes

greave /greev/ *n* a piece of armor worn from the ankle to the knee (*usually used in the plural*) [14C. < Old French *greve* "calf, shin"]

grebe

grebe /greeb/ (*plural* **grebes** or *same*) *n* a mainly freshwater diving bird that has lobed toes and is a strong swimmer. Family: Podicipedidae. [Mid-18C. < French *grebe*]

Gre·cian /greésh'n/ *adj* **1.** relating to the ancient Greek style of architecture or sculpture **2.** PEOPLES same as **Greek** *n* (sense 1) (*dated*) ■ *n* (*dated*) **1.** a Hellenist **2.** LANG same as **Greek** *n* (sense 2) —**Gre·cian·ize** *vt*

Gre·cism /greé sìzzәm/ *n* **1.** an idiom of the Greek language used in another language, often for stylistic effect **2.** Greek style, spirit, or characteristics as expressed in Greek culture, arts, architecture, and philosophy

Gre·cize /grée sīz/ (**-cized, -ciz·ing, -ciz·es**) *vt* to make something Greek or Hellenic in style or form so that it becomes characteristic of the culture, civilization, or language of the ancient Greeks

Gre·co /grékō/, **El** (1541–1614) Greek-born Spanish painter. His works combine the baroque style with exaggerated mannerism, and are characterized by lambent lighting and long figures. Born **Theotokopoulos, Domenikos**

Greco-, **Graeco-** *prefix* Greece, Greek ○ *Greco-Roman* [< Latin *Graecus* (see GREEK)]

Gre·co-Ro·man /grèkō rṓmәn, greékō-/ *adj* **1.** relating to, or characteristic of, both ancient Greece and ancient Rome or the influence of their civilizations **2.** describes a style of wrestling allowing no hold below the waist and no use of the legs to obtain a fall

Greece

Greece /greess/ country in southeastern Europe, comprising the southernmost part of the Balkan Peninsula and numerous islands in the eastern Mediterranean. Language: Greek. Currency: drachma. Capital: Athens. Population: 10,665,989 (2003). Area: 50,949 sq. mi./131,957 sq. km. Official name **Hellenic Republic**

greed /greed/ *n* an overwhelming desire to have more of something such as money than is actually needed [Late 16C. Back-formation < GREEDY]

greed·y /greédee/ (**-i·er, -i·est**) *adj* **1.** having an overwhelming desire to have more of something such as money than is actually needed **2.** eating to excess, or wanting to do so [Old English *grǣdig* < Germanic, "hunger, greed"] —**greed·i·ly** *adv* —**greed·i·ness** *n*

gree·gree *n* ANTHROP another spelling of **grigri**

Greek /greek/ *n* **1.** SOMEBODY FROM GREECE somebody who comes from Greece **2.** LANGUAGE OF GREECE the official language of Greece and part of Cyprus. Native speakers: 12 million. **3.** LANG same as **Ancient Greek** **4.** FRATERNITY OR SORORITY MEMBER a member of a college or university fraternity or sorority whose name consists of Greek letters ■ *adj* **1.** OF GREECE relating to Greece or its people, language, or culture **2.** OF GREEK relating to the ancient or modern Greek language **3.** OF FRATERNITY OR SORORITY relating to a college or university fraternity or sorority or their activities **4.** OF ORTHODOX CHURCH relating to the Greek Orthodox Church ▶ See panel on next page [Old English *grecas,* via Latin *Graecus* < Greek *Graikos* "the Hellenic people"] ◇ **beware of Greeks bearing gifts** be careful of possible treachery from somebody who appears to be kind (*sometimes offensive*) ◇ **go Greek** to pledge and then join a college fraternity or sorority (*informal*) ○ *About 40% of the student body is expected to go Greek after rush.* ◇ **it's (all) Greek to me** used to say that you cannot understand something

Greek Cath·o·lic *n* **1.** a member of the Eastern Orthodox Church **2.** a member of the Uniat Greek Church

Greek Church *n* CHR same as **Greek Orthodox Church**

Greek cross *n* a cross consisting of four arms of the same length

Greek key *n* an ornate pattern for a cornice or border consisting of lines that change direction at right angles to form a continuous band

Greek Or·tho·dox Church *n* the national church of Greece, an independent branch of the Orthodox Church

Greek sal·ad *n* a salad of tomatoes, lettuce, cucumber, olives, oregano, and feta cheese

Gree·ley /greélee/ city in northern Colorado, founded as a farm cooperative and temperance colony in 1870. Population: 82,115 (2002 estimate).

Gree·ley, Horace (1811–72) US politician and journalist. He was founding editor of the *New York Tribune* (1841–72), and used the newspaper and lectures to promote his liberal political views.

> "Go West, young man, and grow up with the country."
> [Horace Greeley, *Hints Toward Reforms;* 1850]

Gree·ly /greélee/, **Adolphus Washington** (1844–1935) US explorer and army officer. He led an expedition to the Arctic (1881–84) and established a meteorological base on Ellesmere Island.

green /green/ *adj* **1.** GRASS-COLORED of a color in the spectrum between yellow and blue, like the color of grass **2.** HAVING EDIBLE GREEN LEAVES consisting of or containing green leaves of vegetables ○ *a green salad* **3.** GRASSY OR LEAFY consisting of or containing grass, plants, or foliage **4.** *also* **Green** POL ADVOCATING PROTECTION OF ENVIRONMENT supporting or promoting the protection of the environment **5.** MADE WITH LITTLE ENVIRONMENTAL HARM produced in an environmentally and ecologically friendly way, e.g., by using renewable resources **6.** NOT RIPE unripe or not mature ○ *green bananas* **7.** JEALOUS envious or jealous **8.** SICKLY-LOOKING pale and sickly-looking, especially as a result of nausea **9.** INNOCENT naive and lacking experience, especially because of being new to something **10.** NEW young, new, recent, or fresh **11.** WOODWORK UNSEASONED describes newly cut and unseasoned wood ○ *green wood* **12.** INDUST UNTANNED describes leather that is not yet tanned **13.** CERAMICS UNFIRED describes objects that are not yet fired ■ *n* **1.** COLOR OF GRASS a primary color between yellow and blue in the spectrum, like the color of grass **2.** GREEN COLORING a green pigment or dye **3.** GREEN CLOTH green fabric or clothing **4.** GREEN THING a green object **5.** GRASSY AREA an area of ground that is covered with grass, especially a public or communal area **6.** LAWN BOWLING GRASSY AREA FOR LAWN BOWLING an area of grass that is maintained for lawn bowling and similar games **7.** GOLF GRASSY AREA SURROUNDING GOLF HOLE the closely mowed area at the end of a fairway on a golf course on which the hole for the ball is located **8.** *also* **Green** POL ADVOCATE OF PROTECTION OF ENVIRONMENT a supporter or advocate of protecting the environment, especially a member of a political party concerned with environmental issues **9.** FIN MONEY

LANGUAGE HERITAGE ***Greek*** Much of English is made up of words from other languages, and a large proportion come from Greek, not usually directly, but indirectly via Latin and sometimes, again through Latin, immediately from French. The first words to migrate to English straight from Greek did not arrive until the late medieval and Renaissance periods, with the revival of classical learning, for example, in the 15th century ***aneurysm***, ***epiglottis***, and some letters of the Greek alphabet that were not already known through Latin, ***chi***, ***eta***, ***kappa***, and ***psi***; in the early 16th century ***sycamine*** (a tree mentioned in the Bible) and the letter ***omega***; in the mid-16th century ***hegemony***; in the late 16th century, when the pace of migration picks up, ***acme***, ***anaglyph*** ("decoration carved in low relief"), ***apologize***, ***epigraph***, ***euphemism***, ***nemesis***, ***pathos***, ***synchronism***, and geometric shapes including the ***hexahedron*** and ***parallelepiped*** ("polyhedron consisting of six faces that are parallelograms"). These early migrants are typical of their successors: learned, literary, linguistic, medical, mathematical, generally scientific – not for the ***hoi polloi*** (mid-17th century). The 20th century followed up with, for example, (early 20th) ***agnosia*** ("loss of the ability to recognize familiar people or objects"), ***bar*** (a unit of pressure, from *baros* "weight"), ***clone*** (from *klōn* "twig"), ***empathy***, and ***kinesis***; (mid-20th) ***deixis*** ("use of words whose full meaning depends on context") and ***topos*** ("traditional theme in literature or rhetoric," in Greek "place").

New words have continued to be formed from Greek elements combined with others, in the 20th century, for example, ***autism*** (from *autos* "self"), ***epistemic***, ***holism***, ***mastectomy*** (from *mastos* "breast"), ***podiatry*** (from *pod-* "foot"), ***Proterozoic*** (from *proteros* "former" + *zōē* "life"), and various phobias such as ***ailurophobia*** (from *ailuros* "cat") and ***triskaidekaphobia*** ("fear of the number thirteen"). The prefix ***tele-***, from Greek *tēle* "far away," has become vigorously productive, with words from ***television*** to ***teleconferencing*** and ***telemedicine***.

It may be noticed that many of these words, though directly from Greek, are spelled as if they came from Latin: the letter usually transliterated from the Greek alphabet as *k* is represented by *c*, Greek *kh* appears as *ch*, instances of *u* appear as *y*, and so on. So many Greek words passed through Latin in transit to English that the two languages readily hybridize. The process started early: ***antithetical***, for example, a late 16th century formation, is based on Greek *antithetikos* but with a suffix derived from Latin *-alis*. Early Greek migrants through Latin include ***acacia***, ***idea***, and ***tetanus*** (14th century); ***geography***, ***iris***, and ***magma*** (15th); ***asthmatic***, ***basis***, ***gymnastic***, ***proboscis***, and ***sympathy*** (16th). The earliest arrival in English from Greek via Latin is not recognizably either, however: ***bishop***, recorded in Old English and a common Germanic form with initial *b-* from a popular variant of Latin *episcopus* from Greek *episkopos*. Another Old English word with related forms in other Germanic languages is ***church***, ultimately from Greek *kuriakon dōma* "house of the lord." Ecclesiastical words often took the road from Greek, including ***ecclesiastic***, 15th century via French or ecclesiastical Latin from Greek *ekklēsiastikos*.

"Greek" alone usually refers to Ancient Greek, used from about 1500 B.C. to about A.D. 500: later periods are specified as "late Greek," "ecclesiastical Greek," etc., as appropriate. Modern Greek migrants are comparatively uncommon, but bring with them the pleasures of Greek food and drink: ***feta*** cheese, ***phyllo*** pastry (from *phullo* "leaf"), ***taramasalata*** (from *taramas* "preserved roe" + *salata* "salad"), ***ouzo***, and ***retsina*** (modern Greek from Greek *rētinē* "pine resin").

cash or paper money (*slang*) ■ **greens** *npl* **1. GREEN VEGETABLES** vegetables with green leaves and stems, e.g., cabbage and spinach **2. DECORATIVE GREEN FOLIAGE** green foliage used for decoration **3. GREEN-COLORED CLOTHING** green clothing, e.g., Army uniforms or operating room scrubs (*informal*) ■ *vti* (**greened, green·ing, greens**) **1. BECOME GREEN** to become green, or make something green **2.** ENVIRON **BECOME ENVIRONMENTAL ADVOCATE** to become aware of environmental issues, or make somebody aware of environmental issues [Old English *grene* < Germanic] —**green·ish** *adj* —**green·ly** *adv* —**green·ness** *n* ◇ **go green** to become actively interested in environmental issues and support environmental causes

green ac·count·ing *n* BUSINESS, ENVIRON same as **environmental accounting**

green al·ga *n* an alga found mostly in fresh water. Division: *Chlorophyta.*

green au·dit *n* same as **environmental audit**

green·back /green bàk/ *n* a US bank note of any denomination (*slang*)

Green·back Par·ty *n* a political party formed after the Civil War that was against reducing the amount of paper money in circulation and in favor of the use of fiat money

Green Bay /green báy/ city in Brown County, northeastern Wisconsin, on the southern shores of Lake Michigan. Population: 101,515 (2002 estimate).

green bean *n* a bean that is eaten complete with its pod, e.g., a string bean

green·belt *n* **1.** a strip of undeveloped land around a city that contains parks, farms, or vacant land **2.** an irrigated area of land on the edge of a desert, designed to prevent any further encroachment by the desert

Green·belt /green bèlt/ planned city in west central Maryland, northeast of Washington, D.C., developed in the 1930s to house government employees. Population: 22,006 (2002 estimate).

Green Be·ret *n* (*informal*) **1.** a US Special Forces soldier **2.** a British commando [< the regulation green beret worn by members]

green·bot·tle /green bòtt'l/, **green·bot·tle fly** *n* a fly that is metallic green in color and lays its eggs in rotting vegetation or flesh. Genus: *Lucilia.*

green bur·i·al *n* a burial designed to have minimal environmental impact, typically with a corpse that has not been embalmed being placed in a biodegradable coffin or bag and buried in a grave marked with a sapling

green card *n* in the United States, an identity card and work permit issued to nationals of other countries —**green-card·er** *n*

green Christ·mas *n Can* a Christmas without snow

green drag·on *n* a tuberous plant that has divided leaves. Flowers: small, green, on a stalk enclosed in a tight green sheath. Native to: North America. Latin name: *Arisaema dracontium.*

AKG London

Graham Greene

Greene /green/, **Graham** (1904–91) British writer. His major novels, including *Brighton Rock* (1938) and *The Power and the Glory* (1940), incorporate themes of spiritual and moral struggle. He wrote the screenplay for the movie *The Third Man* (1950). Full name **Greene, Henry Graham**

> "There is always one moment in childhood when the door opens and lets the future in."
> [Graham Greene, *The Power and the Glory*; 1940]

Greene, Nathanael (1742–86) US revolutionary soldier. He commanded revolutionary armies in New Jersey and South Carolina.

green earth *n* ART same as **terre verte**

green·er·y /greenəree/ *n* **1.** growing green foliage and plants **2.** *UK* same as **greens** (sense 2; *see* **green**)

green-eyed mon·ster *n* jealousy or envy personified

Green·field /green feeld/ town in northern Massachusetts, on the western bank of the Connecticut River, north of Northampton. Population: 18,005 (2002 estimate).

green·finch /green finch/ (*plural* **-finch·es** or *same*) *n* a green-gray and yellow finch. Native to: Europe. Latin name: *Carduelis chloris.*

green fin·gers *npl UK* same as **green thumb** —**green-fin·gered** *adj*

green·flag /green flàg/ (**-flagged, -flag·ging, -flags**) *vt S Asia* to give approval or permission for something to proceed [< the use of a green flag in motor racing to start a race]

green·fly /green flī/ (*plural same* or **-flies**) *n* a green winged aphid that is a pest of garden plants, houseplants, and crops

green·gage /green gàyj/ *n* **1.** a sweet green plum **2.** a tree that produces greengages. Latin name: *Prunus domestica italica.* [Early 18C. After Sir William *Gage* (1657–1727), English botanist]

green·gro·cer /green grōssər/ *n UK* a dealer in fresh fruit and vegetables

green·head /green hèd/ *n* a male mallard duck

green·heart /green haart/ (*plural* **-hearts** or *same*) *n* **1. TROPICAL WOOD** a dark greenish wood from a tropical American laurel **2. TROPICAL AMERICAN TREE** an evergreen tree of the laurel family that yields greenheart. Native to: tropical America. Latin name: *Ocotea rodiaei.* **3. TREE LIKE GREENHEART** any tree similar to the tropical American greenheart

green·horn /green hàwrn/ *n* somebody who lacks experience and may be naive or gullible

SYNONYMS See ***beginner.***

green·house /green hòwss/ (*plural* **-hous·es** /-hòwzəz/) *n* **1.** a glass or transparent plastic structure, often on a metal or wooden frame, in which plants that need heat, light, and protection from the weather are grown **2.** a transparent plastic dome or cover for part of an aircraft (*informal*)

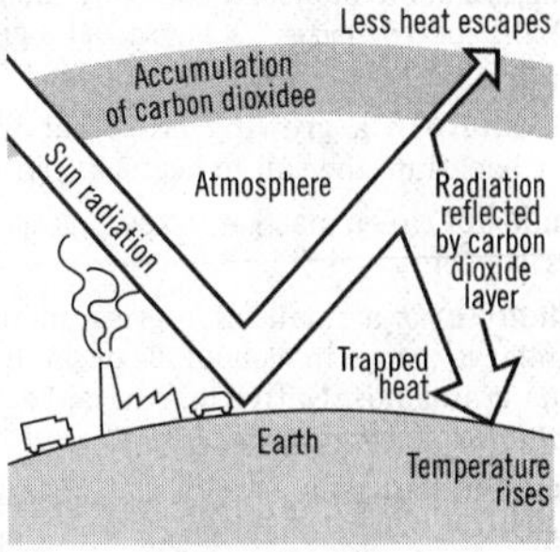

greenhouse effect

green·house ef·fect *n* warming of the Earth's surface as a result of atmospheric pollution by gases. It is now feared that the warming effects are being undesirably increased, causing climate changes and melting polar icecaps.

green·house gas *n* a gas that contributes to the warming of the Earth's atmosphere by reflecting radiation from the Earth's surface, e.g., carbon dioxide, ozone, or water vapor

green·ing /greening/ *n* **1.** the process of planting trees and other vegetation in an area **2.** the process of becoming more aware, or increasing others' awareness, of the environment and environmental issues

green keep·er *n UK* GOLF same as **greenskeeper**

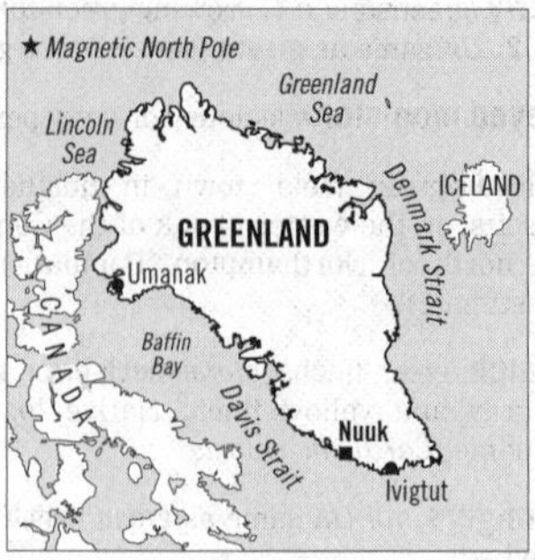

Greenland

Green·land /greénlənd/ island situated between the North Atlantic and Arctic oceans. The largest island in the world, it is a self-governing part of Denmark. Population: 56,385 (2003). Area: 840,000 sq. mi./ 2,175,600 sq. km. —**Green·land·er** *n*

Green·land·ic /greén lándik/ *n* **INUIT DIALECT** a dialect of Inuit spoken in Greenland. Native speakers: 160,000. ■ *adj* **1. OF GREENLAND DIALECT** relating to the dialect Greenlandic **2. OF GREENLAND** relating to Greenland or its language, people, or culture

Green·land right whale *n* ZOOL same as **bowhead**

Green·land Sea section of the Atlantic Ocean off the coast of northeastern Greenland that is covered by pack ice for most of the year

Green·land spar *n* MINERALS same as **cryolite**

green light *n* **1.** a light that is green in color and is used as a signal at intersections for vehicles or pedestrians to proceed **2.** permission to start work on something, especially a project or plan

green·light /greén lìt/ (**-light·ed, -light·ing, -lights**) *vt* to give approval or permission for something to proceed (*informal*) ○ *Are they going to greenlight the project?*

Green Line *n* in the state of Israel, the pre-1967 border along the West Bank and the Gaza Strip [Late 20C.]

green·ling /greénling/ (*plural* **-lings** or *same*) *n* a fish with large pectoral fins, a large head, and a skin flap over each eye. Native to: northern Pacific coastal waters. Family: Hexagrammidae.

green·mail /greén màyl/ *n* the purchase of enough of a company's stock to threaten it with takeover, thereby forcing the company to buy back the stock at a higher price to avoid the takeover ■ *vt* (**-mailed, -mail·ing, -mails**) to subject a company to greenmail [Late 20C. < GREEN "money" + BLACKMAIL] —**green·mail·er** *n*

green ma·nure *n* a growing crop that is plowed directly back into the soil to act as a fertilizer

green·mar·ket /greén maàrkət/ *n* AGRIC, COMM same as **farmers' market**

green mon·key *n* a small olive green monkey that lives in large troops in woodlands or on the edge of savanna grasslands. Native to: Africa. Latin name: *Cercophithecus aethiops sabaeus.*

green mon·key dis·ease *n* MED same as **Marburg disease**

Green Moun·tains /greén \mòwnt'nz/ mountain range in the Appalachian system, extending from Canada into western Massachusetts. The highest peak is Mount Mansfield, 4,393 ft./1,339 m.

Green Moun·tain State *n* a nickname for Vermont

green·ock·ite /greénə kìt/ *n* a yellowish crystalline mineral consisting of cadmium sulfide [Mid-18C. After Charles Murray Cathcart, Lord *Greenock* (1783–1859)]

green on·ion *n* an immature onion that is harvested before the bulb develops. Use: raw in salads.

Gree·nough /greénō/, **Horatio** (1805–52) US sculptor. He worked in Italy from 1828 to 1851, and is known for his neoclassical statue of George Washington (1832–41) at the Smithsonian Institution in Washington, D.C.

green pa·per *n* in the United Kingdom or Canada, a document that contains the government's policy proposals that are to be discussed in Parliament

Green Par·ty *n* a political party whose primary policy is the protection of the environment

Green·peace /greén peèss/ *n* an international organization that advocates the protection of the environment and takes nonviolent action to achieve its goals

green pep·per *n* an unripe sweet pepper eaten raw or cooked. Latin name: *Capsicum annuum.*

green rev·o·lu·tion *n* the introduction of modern farming techniques and higher-yielding, more pest-resistant varieties of crops in order to significantly increase crop production

green·room /greén ro͝om, -ro͞om/ *n* a room in a studio, theater, or concert hall where performers may relax before or after a performance or appearance

green sal·ad *n* a salad made of lettuce or other green leaves of vegetables, sometimes including other raw green vegetables such as cucumber or green pepper. It is usually served with a vinaigrette dressing.

green·sand /greén sànd/ *n* sandstone flecked with the dark green clay mineral glauconite

Greens·bor·o /greénz bùr ə, -bùr ō/ city in northern North Carolina. It is the site of Guilford College. Population: 228,217 (2002 estimate).

green·shank /greén shàngk/ (*plural* **-shanks** or *same*) *n* a large sandpiper with long greenish legs. Native to: Europe, Asia. Latin name: *Tringa nebularia.*

green·sick·ness /greén siknəss/ *n* MED same as **chlorosis** (sense 2) —**green·sick** *adj*

greens·keep·er /greénz keèpər/ *n* somebody employed to maintain a golf course or bowling green

green snake *n* a slender nonpoisonous snake that is yellow-green in color and feeds on insects, especially grasshoppers. Native to: North America. Genus: *Opheodryas.*

Green·span /greén spàn/, **Alan** (*b.* 1926) US economist. After serving as an economic adviser to Presidents Nixon and Ford, he was made chairman of the Federal Reserve Board by President Reagan (1987).

"Inflation is never ultimately tamed. It only becomes subdued."
[Alan Greenspan, *Financial Times (London)*; June 3, 1987]

"Monetary policy never ends. It's like the luggage carousel in the airports."
[Alan Greenspan, testimony to the US Senate Banking Committee, *Wall Street Journal*; June 23, 1995]

green·stick frac·ture /greén stik-/ *n* a bone fracture usually occurring in children, in which one side of the bone is broken and the other side is bent [< GREEN "immature" + STICK[1] because it resembles one]

green·stone /greén stòn/ *n* **1. GREEN IGNEOUS ROCK** a green igneous rock containing the minerals feldspar and hornblende **2. VARIETY OF JADE** a dark New Zealand jade. Use: Maori weapons, jewelry. **3.** GEOL **ROCK SIMILAR TO JADE** a rock that includes material similar to jade. Use: for decorative objects, e.g., ceremonial axes.

green·strip /greén strìp/ *n* a firebreak on open grassland, planted with vegetation that does not burn easily

green·sward /greén swàwrd/ *n* a grass-covered area (*archaic or literary*)

green·tail·ing /greén tàyling/ *n* environmentally responsible retailing that involves the sale of products with the least impact on the environment or that increases the ecological awareness of the consumer (*informal*) [< GREEN + *retailing*]

green tea *n* tea made from leaves that have been dried but not fermented. It is pale green in color.

green thumb *n* a natural ability to make plants grow well

green tur·tle *n* a large turtle that is sometimes killed for food. It comes to land only to bask, sleep, and lay eggs. Native to: warm oceans. Latin name: *Chelonia mydas.* [< its green shell]

Green·ville /greén vìl/ industrial city on the Reedy River in northwestern South Carolina, on the Piedmont Plateau. Population: 56,181 (2002 estimate).

green vit·ri·ol *n* CHEM same as **ferrous sulfate**

green·wash /greén wòsh, -wàwsh/ *n* public relations' initiatives by a business or organization, e.g., advertising or public consultation, that purport to show concern for the environmental impact of its activities (*disapproving*) [Late 20C. < GREEN "favorable to the environment," after WHITEWASH]

green·way /greén wày/ *n* a stretch of undeveloped land close to an urban area that is kept for recreational use

Green·wich /grénnich, -ij/ **1.** borough of London, England, on the southern bank of the Thames River. It is the site of the prime meridian, which passes through the Royal Greenwich Observatory. Population: 214,403 (2001). **2.** fashionable residential community and resort town in southwestern Connecticut, on Long Island Sound near the border with New York State. Population: 61,784 (2002 estimate).

Green·wich Mean Time *n* same as **Universal Time**

Green·wich Vil·lage /grènnich-, grìnnich-/ residential area in lower Manhattan, once popular with bohemians, artists, and writers and now a tourist attraction

green·wood /greén wo͝od/ *n* a forest or wood in the summer when the leaves are green (*archaic*)

Green·wood /greén wo͝od/ city and county seat of Greenwood County in western South Carolina, northwest of Columbia. Population: 22,181 (2002 estimate).

green wood·peck·er *n* a large woodpecker with green feathers and a red crown that often feeds on the ground. Native to: Europe. Latin name: *Picus viridis.*

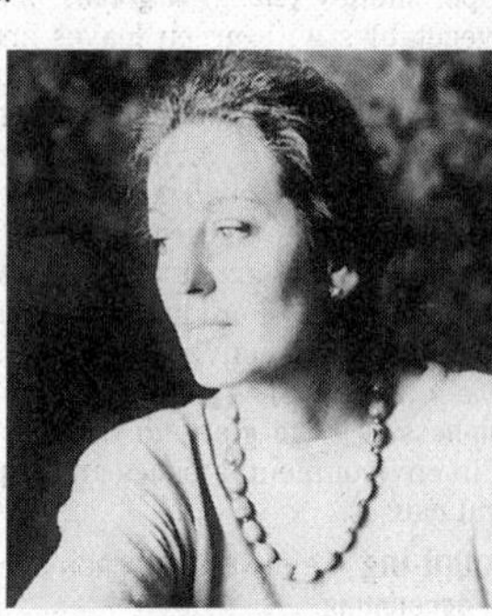
Germaine Greer

Greer /greer/, **Germaine** (*b.* 1939) Australian writer and feminist. She launched her career as a passionate advocate of women's empowerment with her first book, *The Female Eunuch* (1970).

"Human beings have an inalienable right to invent themselves; when that right is preempted, it is called brainwashing."
[Germaine Greer, *Times (London)*; February 1,1986]

greet /greet/ (**greet·ed, greet·ing, greets**) *vt* **1. WELCOME SOMEBODY** to welcome somebody in a cordial and usually conventional way **2. ADDRESS SOMEBODY COURTEOUSLY** to address somebody in a polite and usually conventional way on meeting **3. ADDRESS SOMEBODY IN LETTER** to address a person or group at the start of a letter using a set formula **4. REPLY TO SOMETHING** to receive or respond to something in a particular way ○ *The news was greeted with dismay.* **5. BECOME NOTICEABLE TO SOMEBODY** to become perceptible to somebody, especially by way of the senses such as vision, hearing, or smell ○ *The smell of a cake baking greeted them.* [Old English *gretan* < W Germanic, "resound"]

greet·er /greéter/ *n* somebody employed to greet customers in a restaurant or similar business

greet·ing /greéting/ *n* **1. FRIENDLY GESTURE** a cordial and often conventional gesture or expression used when welcoming, meeting, or addressing somebody **2. WELCOMING SOMEBODY** an act of welcoming or addressing somebody with a greeting ■ **greet·ings** *npl* **MESSAGE** a friendly message or good wishes

greet·ing card *n* a folded piece of heavy paper with an image or design and a message to somebody to mark a special occasion

greet·ings card *n UK* same as **greeting card**

greg·a·rine /gréggə rēen/ *n* a protozoan that lives as a parasite in the digestive tracts of some insects, arthropods, annelids, and other invertebrates. Order: Gregarinida. ■ *adj also* **greg·a·rin·i·an** /grèggə rínnee ən/ relating to or belonging to the order that comprises the gregarines [Mid-19C. < modern Latin *Gregarina* < Latin *gregarius* (see GREGARIOUS)]

gre·gar·i·ous /grə gérree əss/ *adj* **1. FRIENDLY** very friendly and sociable **2. LIVING COMMUNALLY** describes organisms that live in groups **3. GROWING TOGETHER** describes plants that grow in clusters [Mid-17C. < Latin *gregarius* < *grex* "flock"] —**gre·gar·i·ous·ly** *adv* —**gre·gar·i·ous·ness** *n*

ORIGIN The Latin word *grex* "flock," from which ***gregarious*** is derived, is also the source of English *aggregate, congregate,* and *egregious.*

Gre·go·ri·an cal·en·dar /gri gàwree ən-/ *n* the calendar introduced in 1582 by Pope Gregory XIII that is still in use and is a modification of the previous Roman calendar. It was not adopted by Britain and its colonies until 1752. ◊ **Hegira** (sense 2)

Gre·go·rian chant *n* a liturgical chant of the Roman Catholic Church that is sung without accompaniment [< its supposed introduction by GREGORY I]

Gre·go·ri·an tel·e·scope *n* an astronomical telescope that has a concave primary mirror with a central hole through which light is reflected from a smaller secondary concave mirror [After J. *Gregory* (1638–75), Scottish mathematician]

Greg·o·ry I /gréggəree/, **St.** (540?–604) pope (590–604). He sent St. Augustine to England to lead the country's conversion to Christianity. He is said to have introduced Gregorian chant into the Roman Catholic liturgy. Known as **Gregory the Great**

> "Not Angles but angels."
> [Gregory I. Reported in *Ecclesiastical History of the English People*, Saint Bede the Venerable; 731]

Greg·o·ry VII, St. (1020?–85) pope (1073–85). He sought to reassert papal authority within the Church and weaken secular influences. His reforms provoked the Holy Roman Emperor Henry IV to replace him with an antipope (1076).

Greg·o·ry XIII (1502–85) pope (1572–85). He built several universities and a papal palace in Rome, and devised the Gregorian calender (1582). Born **Ugo Buoncompagni**

grei·sen /grīz'n/ *n* a granite-derived rock consisting of mica and quartz [Late 19C. < German, probably < *greis* "gray with age"]

grem·lin /grémmlin/ *n* a tiny mischievous imaginary being that is blamed for faults in tools, machinery, and electronic equipment (*informal*) [Early 20C. Probably after GOBLIN]

Gre·nache /grə náash/ *n* a red grape variety. Use: to make red wine. [Mid-19C. < French]

Gre·na·da /grə náydə/ independent state in the southeastern Caribbean Sea, comprising the island of Grenada and some of the southern Grenadines. It became an independent member of the British Commonwealth in 1974. Language: English. Currency: East Caribbean dollar. Capital: St. George's. Population: 89,258 (2003). Area: 133 sq. mi./344 sq. km. —**Gre·na·di·an** *n, adj*

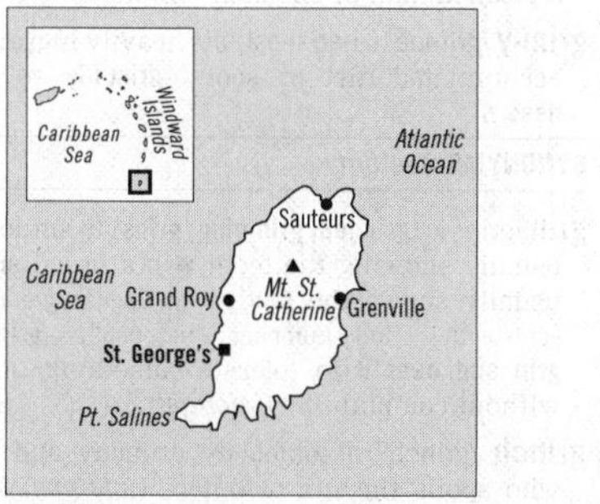

Grenada

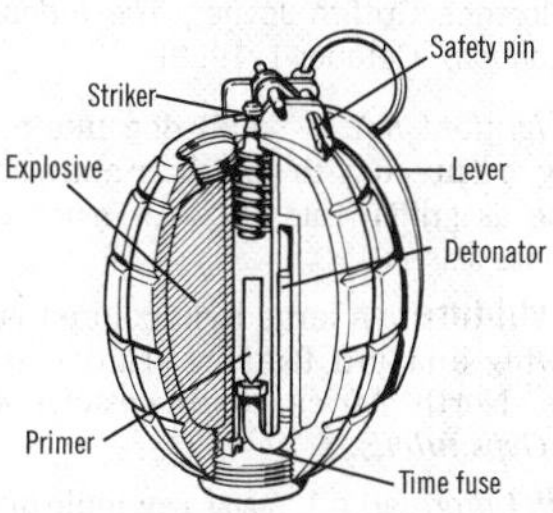

grenade

gre·nade /grə náyd/ *n* **1.** a small bomb that is thrown by hand or shot from a rifle or other weapon **2.** a sealed glass projectile that breaks on impact, releasing tear gas or chemicals to put out fires [Mid-16C. < French, alteration of *grenate* "pomegranate" (shortening of *pome grenate*) after Spanish *granada*]

gren·a·dier /grènnə dēer/ (*plural* **-diers** or *same*) *n* **1. GRENADE-CARRYING SOLDIER** formerly, a soldier armed with grenades **2. TALL STRONG SOLDIER** formerly, a soldier assigned to a special company of a regiment on the basis of exceptional height and ability **3. FISH** a bottom-dwelling sea fish with a tapering body and no tail fin. Native to: deep waters worldwide. Family: Macrouridae. **4. AFRICAN FINCH** a finch with purple patches, a red beak, and a tapering tail. Native to: eastern Africa. Latin name: *Uraeginthus ianthinogaster*. [Late 17C. < French < *grenade* (see GRENADE)]

Gren·a·dier, Gren·a·dier guard *n* a British soldier belonging to the first regiment of the Guards Division, the troops of the Royal Household

gren·a·dine[1] /grènnə dēen, grénnə dēen/ *n* **1.** a syrup made from pomegranates, used especially in cocktails **2.** a reddish orange color [Late 19C. < French (*sirop de*) *grenadine* < *grenade* (see GRENADE)] —**gren·a·dine** *adj*

gren·a·dine[2] /grènnə dēen, grénnə dēen/ *n* a gauzy silk or woolen dress fabric [Mid-19C. < French, "silk with a texture like grain" < *grain* (see GRAIN)]

Gren·a·dines /grènnə dēenz, grénnə dēenz/, **Gren·a·dine Is·lands** group of about 600 small islands, part of the Windward Islands, in the Caribbean Sea. The islands of the northern Grenadines are part of St. Vincent and the Grenadines, some of the southern Grenadines belong to Grenada.

Gre·no·ble /gri nṓb'l, -náwb'l/ industrial city and capital of Isère Department, in the Rhône-Alpes Region, southeastern France. Population: 153,317 (1999).

Gresh·am's law /gréshəmz-/, **Gresh·am's the·o·rem** *n* the theory that bad money drives good money out of circulation because a currency of lower intrinsic value will be used while one of higher intrinsic value will be hoarded [Mid-19C. After Sir Thomas *Gresham* (1519?–79), founder of the Royal Exchange in London, England]

Gret·na /grétnə/ city in the southeastern corner of Louisiana, across the Mississippi River from New Orleans. Population: 17,170 (2002 estimate).

Gret·na Green /grètnə-/ village in Dumfries and Galloway, southwestern Scotland. It was historically notable as a place where eloping couples from England could be married without parental consent. Population: 3,149 (1991).

Gretz·ky /grétskee/, **Wayne** (*b.* 1961) Canadian ice hockey player. He led the Edmonton Oilers to four Stanley Cup championships. He was named the National Hockey League's most valuable player nine times and became the league's all-time leading scorer. Known as **the Great One**

grew past tense of **grow**

grey *adj, n, vti* COLORS another spelling of **gray**[2]

Grey /gray/, **Albert Henry George, 4th Earl** (1851–1917) British colonial administrator. He was governor-general of Canada (1904–11).

Grey, Lady Jane (1537–54) queen of England. The great-granddaughter of Henry VII, she was named as the successor of Edward VI in 1553. She ruled for only nine days before being forced to abdicate, and was executed for treason.

Grey, Zane (1875–1939) US writer. His dozens of popular "dime novels" helped define the Western as a literary genre, and included *Riders of the Purple Sage* (1912). Full name **Grey, Pearl Zane**

greyhound

grey·hound /gráy hòwnd/ *n* a tall slim fast-running dog with a smooth coat, narrow head, and long legs, widely used for racing [Old English *grīghund* < Germanic]

grey·mail *n* POL Can, UK spelling of **graymail**

Grey·mouth /gráymәth/ town on the western coast of the South Island, New Zealand. A former gold-mining town, it is now the commercial center of a mining and industrial region. Population: 9,528 (2001).

grib·ble /gríbb'l/ *n* a small marine crustacean of the wood louse family that burrows into submerged wooden structures. Genus: *Limnoria*. [Late 18C. Origin ?]

grid /grid/ *n* **1. REFERENCE LINES ON MAP** a network of evenly spaced horizontal and vertical lines on a map, used as a basis for finding specific points **2. ADJACENT SQUARES** a network of squares formed by horizontal and vertical lines **3. GRATING MADE OF BARS** a set of parallel or crisscrossing bars that form a grating **4.** UTIL **NETWORK** a network of cables, lines, or pipes for distributing electricity, gas, or water ○ *the Northeast power grid* **5.** ELECTRONICS **CONTROL ELECTRODE** the part of a vacuum tube that controls the flow of current between the other electrodes, usually constructed as a metal screen or coil **6.** MOTOR SPORTS same as **starting grid** **7.** FOOTBALL same as **gridiron** (sense 2) [Mid-19C. Shortening of GRIDIRON] —**grid·ded** *adj*

grid bi·as *n* a fixed voltage applied between the control electrode and the cathode in a vacuum tube

grid·der /gríddər/ *n* a football player (*informal*)

grid·dle /grídd'l/ *n* a heavy flat metal plate heated and used for cooking food ■ *vt* (**-dled, -dling, -dles**) to cook something on a flat hot surface [Pre-12C. < Old French *gredil* "gridiron" < Latin *cratis* "crate"]

grid·dle·cake /grídd'l kàyk/ *n* a thin pancake cooked on a griddle

grid·i·ron /gríd ìrn/ *n* **1. GRATING** a structure consisting of parallel bars **2.** SPORTS **FOOTBALL FIELD** a field marked with parallel white lines, on which football is played **3.** SPORTS **FOOTBALL** the game of football (*informal*) **4.** HOUSEHOLD same as **grill**[1] *n* (sense 2) **5.** THEATER **STRUCTURE ABOVE STAGE** a structure of beams or bars above a theater stage from which lighting and scenery are suspended [13C. Alteration of GRIDDLE, by association with IRON]

grid·lock /gríd lòk/ *n* **1.** a traffic jam in which congestion at one or two intersections affects a wide area, so that traffic is unable to move in any direction **2.** a situation in which no progress can be made —**grid·locked** *adj*

grid ref·er·ence *n* a reference, usually using numbers or letters, that specifies a position on a map or chart by referring to the superimposed grid

grief /greef/ *n* **1. INTENSE SORROW** great sadness, especially as a result of a death **2. CAUSE OF INTENSE SORROW** the cause of intense, deep, and profound sorrow, especially a specific event or situation **3. TROUBLE** annoyance or trouble (*informal*) ○ *His parents gave him grief for coming home so late.* ○ *I got grief for missing the appointment.* [Pre-12C. Via Anglo-Norman *gref* < Old French *grief* "grieved" < *grever* (see GRIEVE)] ◇ **come to grief** to suffer misfortune or ruin ◇ **good grief** used to express surprise, exasperation, or dismay (*dated informal*)

grief-strick·en *adj* deeply affected by grief

Barnaby's

Edvard Grieg

Grieg /greeg/, **Edvard** (1843–1907) Norwegian composer. His work was permeated by the melodies and harmonies of Norwegian folk music. He was a noted composer of songs, and wrote the music to Henrik Ibsen's *Peer Gynt* (1875). Full name **Grieg, Edvard Hagerup**

griev·ance /gréevənss/ *n* **1. REASON FOR COMPLAINT** a cause for complaint or resentment that may or may not be well-founded **2. RESENTMENT** bitterness or anger at having received unfair treatment **3. FORMAL OBJECTION** a formal complaint made on the basis of something that somebody feels is unfair

griev·ance com·mit·tee *n* a committee in the workplace formed by management and employees to resolve workers' grievances

grieve /greev/ (**grieved, griev·ing, grieves**) *v* **1.** *vti* to experience great sadness over something such as a death **2.** *vt* to cause great sadness to somebody [Pre-12C. Via Old French *grever* "to burden" < Latin *gravare* < *gravis* "heavy, grave"] —**griev·er** *n*

griev·ous /gréevəss/ *adj* **1.** extremely serious or significant ○ *a grievous mistake* **2.** very bad or severe ○ *a grievous wound* [13C. < French < *grever* (see GRIEVE)] —**griev·ous·ly** *adv* —**griev·ous·ness** *n*

griev·ous bod·i·ly harm *n* serious physical injury intentionally done to another person

griffin

grif·fin /gríffin/, **gryph·on** *n* a monster with the head and wings of an eagle and the body and tail of a lion [13C. Via Old French *grifoun* < Latin *gryphus* < Greek *grups*]

Grif·fin /gríffin/ city and county seat of Spalding County, central Georgia, situated 42 mi./68 km southeast of Atlanta. Population: 23,226 (2002 estimate).

Grif·fith Joy·ner /grìffith jóynər/, **Florence** (1959–98) US athlete. A sprinter, she set world records in the 100- and 200-meter dashes in 1988 and won three gold medals at the 1988 Olympics (100 meters, 200 meters, 400-meter relay). Born **Griffith, Delorez Florence**. Known as **Flojo**

> "I lift and reach out when I run, more like a guy than a girl."
> [Florence Griffith Joyner, *The Independent (London)*; October 1, 1988]

grif·fon /gríffən/ *n* **1.** a small dog like a terrier belonging to a breed with wiry hair and a short muzzle **2.** same as **griffin** [Late 18C. Via French < Old French *grifoun* (see GRIFFIN)]

grif·fon vul·ture *n* a large light-colored vulture with dark wing and tail feathers. Native to: southern Europe, North Africa, southwestern Asia. Latin name: *Gyps fulvus*.

grift /grift/ (*informal*) *n* **1. FRAUD** a swindle or confidence game **2. PROCEEDS FROM FRAUD** money made from a swindle or confidence game ■ *vti* (**grift·ed, grift·ing, grifts**) **SWINDLE SOMEBODY** to carry out a swindle, or obtain something by swindling [Early 20th. Probably alteration of GRAFT[2]] —**grift·er** *n*

Gri·gnard re·a·gent /grée̅n yaar-/ *n* an organometallic compound belonging to a group whose molecules contain one magnesium and one halogen atom. Use: preparation of organic compounds. [Early 20C. After Victor *Grignard* (1871–1934), French chemist]

gri·gri /grée gree/ (*plural* **-gris** /-gree/), **gree·gree** (*plural* **-grees**), **gris-gris** (*plural* **gris-gris** /-gree/) *n* an African talisman or fetish [Late 18C. Via American Spanish < Carib *grugru* "palm"]

Grik·wa *n, adj* LANG, PEOPLES another spelling of **Griqua**

grill[1] /gril/ *v* (**grilled, grill·ing, grills**) **1.** *vti* **COOK FOOD OVER HEAT** to cook food over direct heat without fat or oil, especially outside on a barbecue, or be cooked in this way **2.** *vti UK* COOK same as **broil**[1] *v* (sense 1) **3.** *vt* **INTERROGATE SOMEBODY** to question somebody in a persistent manner (*informal*) **4.** *vti* **SUBJECT OR BE SUBJECTED TO HEAT** to subject somebody or something to great heat, or be subjected to great heat, especially from the sun **5.** *vt* **MARK SOMETHING USING GRIDIRON** to mark a gridiron pattern on something ■ *n* **1.** *UK* same as **broiler** (sense 2) **2. GRATE FOR GRILLING** a flat surface of parallel metal bars, on which food is grilled **3. GRIDIRON PATTERN** a pattern made on a surface by a grill or gridiron **4. FOOD COOKED ON GRILL** a dish or portion of food cooked on a grill **5. RESTAURANT SERVING GRILLED FOOD** an establishment that serves food cooked on a grill [Mid-17C. < French *griller* < *grille* (see GRILLE)] —**grill·er** *n*

SPELLCHECK grill or **grille**? Do not confuse the spelling of ***grill*** and ***grille***, which sound similar. ***Grill***, the more frequent of the two words, is a verb meaning "broil," "interrogate," "subject to great heat," or "mark with a gridiron pattern," or a noun denoting broiled food or a gridiron pattern. ***Grille*** is only used as a noun, denoting a lattice of bars or a metal grating, as in *a radiator grille*, and an opening in a court tennis court. Although the spelling ***grill*** is sometimes used in the place of ***grille***, the reverse should never be the case.

SYNONYMS See ***question***.

grill[2] /gril/ *n* CONSTR, RACKET GAMES another spelling of **grille**

gril·lage /grílij/ *n* a framework of beams and crossbeams built as a foundation for a building on soft ground

grille /gril/, **grill** *n* **1. CRISSCROSSED BARS** a pattern or lattice of bars, especially in front of a window **2. PART OF COOLING SYSTEM** a metal grating that allows cooling air into the radiator of a vehicle's engine **3. COURT TENNIS WALL OPENING** in court tennis, the opening in one corner of an end wall of the court [Mid-17C. < French, later form of Old French *graille* < Latin *cratis* "grating, hurdle"] —**grilled** *adj*

SPELLCHECK See ***grill***[1].

grill·ing /grílling/ *n* an act or process of interrogating a person in an intimidating and persistent manner

grill·room /gríl ro͝om, -ro͞om/ *n* COMM same as **grill**[1] *n* (sense 5)

grill·work /gríl wùrk/ *n* CONSTR same as **grille** (sense 1)

grilse /grilss/ (*plural* **grils·es** or *same*) *n* a salmon when it returns from the ocean for the first time [15C. Origin ?]

grim /grim/ (**grim·mer, grim·mest**) *adj* **1. UNPLEASANT** extremely unpleasant, distressing, or sinister ○ *a grim accident scene* **2. DEPRESSING** depressingly gloomy ○ *a grim economic forecast* **3. STERNLY SERIOUS** stern in a frightening and unnerving way ○ *a grim, set look on his face* **4. FORBIDDING** forbidding and unattractive in appearance ○ *a grim mining town* **5. IRONIC** disquietingly ironic ○ *took grim satisfaction in his opponent's misfortune* **6. UNYIELDING** refusing to give way or give up ○ *with grim determination* **7. FEROCIOUS** fierce or savage ○ *a grim gale tossing the boat at sea* [Old English, < Germanic] —**grim·ly** *adv* —**grim·ness** *n*

grim·ace /grímməss, gri máyss/ *n* a contorted twisting of the face that expresses disgust or pain [Mid-17C. Via French *grimache* < Spanish *grimazo* "caricature" < *grima* "fright"] —**grim·ace** *vi*

Grim·al·di /gri máwldee/ very large, dark-floored enclosure near the western edge of the Moon, approximately 135 mi./220 km in diameter

gri·mal·kin /gri máwlkin, -málkin/ *n* an old female cat [Late 16C. < GRAY[2] + obsolete *malkin* "cat"]

grime /grīm/ *n* dirt or soot, usually accumulated in a black layer or ingrained into a surface ■ *vt* (**grimed, grim·ing, grimes**) to coat something with dirt or soot [13C. < Middle Low German *greme*]

Grim·ké /grímkee/, **Angelina Emily** (1805–79) US abolitionist and reformer. She was a leading abolitionist and women's rights campaigner whose works include the antislavery tract *Appeal to the Christian Women of the South* (1836). Sarah Moore Grimké was her sister.

> "I know you do not make the laws but I also know that you are the wives and mothers, the sisters and daughters of those who do."
> [Angelina Emily Grimké, "Appeal to the Christian Women of the South," *The Anti-Slavery Examiner*; September 1836]

Grim·ké, Sarah Moore (1792–1873) US abolitionist and reformer. The sister of Angelina Emily Grimké, she lectured and wrote in support of women's rights and the abolition of slavery.

> "Brute force, the law of violence, rules to a great extent in the poor man's domicile; and woman is little more than his drudge."
> [Sarah Moore Grimké, *Letter from Brookline*; September 1837]

Grimm /grim/, **Jacob** (1785–1863) German philologist and folklorist. He was the founder of comparative linguistics, and formulated Grimm's Law. In collaboration with his brother, Wilhelm Karl Grimm (1786–1859), he collected old German folk tales and published them in collections now known as *Grimm's Fairy Tales* (1812–15). Full name **Grimm, Jacob Ludwig Karl**. See Cultural note at **fairy tale**

Grimm's Law /grímz-/ *n* a formula showing the systematic relationship between consonants in Germanic languages and consonants in other Indo-European languages, stating what phonetic changes took place [Mid-19C. After Jacob GRIMM]

Grim Reap·er *n* a personification of death, shown as a cloaked man or skeleton holding a scythe

grim·y /grīmee/ (**-i·er, -i·est**) *adj* heavily ingrained with accumulated dirt or soot —**grim·i·ly** *adv* —**grim·i·ness** *n*

SYNONYMS See ***dirty***.

grin /grin/ *vi* (**grinned, grin·ning, grins**) to smile broadly, usually showing the teeth ■ *n* a broad smile that usually shows the teeth [Old English *grennian* "bare your teeth" < Indo-European, "be open"] —**grin·ner** *n* ◇ **grin and bear it** to tolerate something unpleasant without complaining (*informal*)

grinch /grinch/ *n* somebody grouchy and contrary who spoils the fun of others (*informal*) [Late 20C. After a character in a children's story by Dr. Seuss]

grind /grīnd/ *v* (**ground** /grownd/, **grind·ing, grinds**) **1.** *vti* PULVERIZE to crush something into very small pieces by rubbing it between two hard surfaces, or be crushed in this way **2.** *vti* MAKE RASPING NOISE to rub two surfaces together with a grating noise, or make a grating noise by rubbing things together ○ *grinding her teeth* **3.** *vt* PUSH SOMETHING DOWN WITH TWISTING MOTION to push something down firmly or crush something on a surface with a twisting or rotating motion ○ *grinding dirt into the carpet with every step* **4.** *vt* CHOP SOMETHING INTO TINY PIECES to chop food, especially meat, into tiny pieces, using a mechanical device **5.** *vt* SMOOTH OR SHARPEN SOMETHING to make something smooth or sharp by rubbing it against an abrasive surface **6.** *vi* MOVE NOISILY to move with a grating noise **7.** *vt* TURN HANDLE OF SOMETHING to operate something such as a barrel organ by turning its handle **8.** *vi* LABOR AT to study or work hard, especially too hard (*informal*) **9.** *vi* DANCE EROTICALLY to dance erotically with a circling and thrusting of the hips (*informal*) ■ *n* **1.** GRINDING an act of grinding **2.** GRINDING NOISE a grating noise like that of something grinding **3.** TEXTURE the texture of something that is ground ○ *a fine grind of coffee* **4.** SOMETHING BORING AND REPETITIVE something that is routine, dull, and tedious (*informal*) **5.** HARD WORKER somebody who works or studies too hard (*informal*) **6.** EROTIC DANCE MOVEMENT an erotic circling and thrusting of the hips in dancing (*informal*) [Old English *grindan*, origin ?]

grind down *vt* to weaken somebody gradually by persistent oppression

grind on *vi* to continue in an unrelenting way

grind out *vt* to perform or produce something with little thought, care, or effort as a result of boredom or excessive familiarity with the process ○ *grinding out articles for the local paper*

grind·er /grīndər/ *n* **1.** SOMEBODY OR SOMETHING THAT GRINDS somebody or something that grinds something ○ *a coffee grinder* **2.** TOOTH a molar tooth **3.** *New England* LARGE SANDWICH a sandwich in a long roll with a filling of meat or seafood and chopped raw vegetables

grind·ing /grīnding/ *adj* **1.** oppressive and relentless ○ *grinding poverty* **2.** characterized by a grating sound —**grind·ing·ly** *adv*

grind·stone /grīnd stōn/ *n* **1.** an abrasive wheel that sharpens or polishes something **2.** INDUST same as **millstone** (sense 1)

grin·ga /gríng gə/ *n Hispanic* in Spain and Latin America, an offensive term for a woman who is an English-speaking foreigner (*offensive*) [Mid-20C. < Spanish, feminine of *gringo* "foreigner"] —**grin·ga** *adj*

grin·go /gríng gō/ (*plural* **-gos**) *n Hispanic* in Spain and Latin America, an offensive term for an English-speaking foreigner, especially a man (*offensive*) [Mid-19C. < Spanish, "foreigner"] —**grin·go** *adj*

grin·nie /grínnee/ *n regional* **1.** same as **chipmunk 2.** same as **ground squirrel** (sense 1) [Origin ?]

gri·ot /grée ō, gree ót/ *n* a member of a caste of professional oral historians in the Mali Empire [Early 19C. < French]

grip /grip/ *n* **1.** HOLDING ACTION an act or the action of taking or keeping a firm hold of something **2.** MANNER OF HOLDING the way that somebody holds something ○ *a firm grip* **3.** same as **handgrip** (senses 2–3) **4.** HOLDING DEVICE a device for holding something firmly **5.** ABILITY NOT TO SLIP the ability of something to adhere to a surface without slipping ○ *shoes with grip* **6.** CONTROL power over somebody or something ○ *in the grip of fear* **7.** COMPREHENSION a proper understanding of something **8.** SMALL SUITCASE a bag or carryall used for carrying clothes and other personal items when traveling **9.** MOVIES, MEDIA MEMBER OF FILM CREW a member of a film or television crew who is responsible for moving equipment **10.** THEATER STAGEHAND a worker who moves sets and props in a theater ■ *v* (**gripped, grip·ping, grips**) **1.** *vt* GRASP SOMETHING FIRMLY to take or keep a firm hold of something **2.** *vti* STICK TO SURFACE to adhere to a surface without slipping **3.** *vt* AFFECT SOMEBODY OR SOMETHING GREATLY to overwhelm or take control of somebody or something ○ *gripped by fear* **4.** *vt* CAPTURE SOMEBODY'S INTEREST to capture somebody's interest, imagination, or attention ○ *a performance that gripped the audience* [Old English *gripe* "grasp," *gripa* "handful" < Germanic] —**grip·per** *n* —**grip·py** *adj* ◇ **come to grips with something** to begin to understand and deal with something ◇ **lose your grip** to stop being as effective or as much in control as formerly

gripe /grīp/ *v* (**griped, grip·ing, gripes**) **1.** *vti* HAVE OR CAUSE STOMACH PAINS to experience severe stomach pains, or cause somebody to experience severe stomach pains **2.** *vi* GRUMBLE CONSTANTLY to complain continually and irritatingly (*informal*) **3.** *vt* ANNOY SOMEBODY to irritate somebody intensely (*slang*) ○ *It really gripes me when you do something selfish like that.* ■ *n* MINOR COMPLAINT a minor but irritating grievance (*informal*) [Old English *grīpan* "seize" < Germanic] —**grip·er** *n*

SYNONYMS See ***complain.***

grip·ing /grīping/ *adj* describes stomach pains that are sudden, sharp, and intense

grip·man /grípmən, -màn/ (*plural* **-men** /-mən, -mèn/) *n* a cable car operator who starts or stops the car by releasing or engaging a gripping device on the moving cable

grippe /grip/ *n* same as **influenza** (*dated*) [Late 18C. < French, literally "seizure"]

grip·ping /grípping/ *adj* holding the interest and attention completely —**grip·ping·ly** *adv*

Gri·qua /greékwə, gríkwə/ (*plural same* or **-quas**), **Gri·kwa** (*plural same* or **-kwas**) *n* **1.** a member of a group of people of both African and European descent in South Africa **2.** the Khoisan language of the Griqua people, of which very few, if any, speakers remain [Mid-18C. < Nama] —**Gri·qua** *adj*

Gris /greess/, **Juan** (1887–1927) Spanish-born French artist. After 1906 he lived in Paris, where he was much influenced by cubism. In addition to paintings and collages, he designed sets for Diaghilev's ballets. Born **González, José Vittoriano**

AKG London

grisaille: *David and Goliath* by Andrea Mantegna

gri·saille /gri zī, gri záyl/ *n* **1.** a method of painting that uses only shades of gray **2.** a work of art produced by the grisaille method [Mid-19C. < French < *gris* "gray"]

gris·e·o·ful·vin /grìzzee ō fóolvin/ *n* an antibiotic obtained from a fungus. Use: treatment of fungal skin conditions. [Mid-20C. < modern Latin *Griseofulvum* < medieval Latin *griseus* "gray" + Latin *fulvus* "reddish yellow"]

gri·sette /gri zét/ *n* formerly, a young working-class French woman [Early 18C. < French < *gris* "gray"]

gris-gris *n* ANTHROP another spelling of **grigri**

Grish·am /gríshəm/, **John** (*b.* 1955) US writer and lawyer. His bestselling legal thrillers include *The Firm* (1991).

> "I cannot write as well as some people; my talent is in coming up with good stories about lawyers. That is what I am good at."
> [John Grisham, *Independent on Sunday (London)*; June 5, 1994]

gris·ly /grízzlee/ (**-li·er, -li·est**) *adj* gruesomely unpleasant, or creating a sense of horror [12C. Ultimately < W Germanic, "terror"] —**gris·li·ness** *n*

SPELLCHECK Do not confuse the spelling of ***grisly*** and ***grizzly*** (a type of bear), which sound similar. ***Grisly*** is an adjective meaning "gruesomely unpleasant," as in *the grisly remains of the corpse*, whereas ***grizzly*** is a noun, short for *grizzly bear*.

gri·son /grīss'n, grízz'n/ (*plural* **-sons** or *same*) *n* a weasel that has striking gray, white, and black markings, and is sometimes used to hunt chinchillas. Native to: South America. Latin name: *Galictis vittata* or *Galictis cuja*. [Late 18C. < French < *gris* "gray"]

grist /grist/ *n* **1.** grain that is ground into flour **2.** the quantity of grain that is ground in one batch [Old English, < Germanic] ◇ **grist for the** *or* **somebody's mill** a potential source of advantage or profit to somebody

gris·tle /gríss'l/ *n* tough cartilage, especially in meat prepared for eating [Old English, origin ?] —**gris·tli·ness** *n* —**gris·tly** *adj*

grist·mill /gríst mìl/ *n* a mill where grain or corn is ground

grit /grit/ *n* **1.** SAND OR STONE GRAINS small pieces of sand or stone **2.** SANDSTONE sandstone, often used as a grindstone **3.** TEXTURE OF GRAINS the texture of stone or particles used for grinding **4.** FIRMNESS OF CHARACTER determination or strength of character ■ *vt* (**grit·ted, grit·ting, grits**) **1.** CLENCH TEETH to clench the teeth, especially when under stress **2.** PUT GRIT ON SOMETHING to cover something with grit, especially an icy road [Old English *grēot* < Germanic]

grits /grits/ *n* (*takes a singular or plural verb*) **1.** coarsely ground hulled corn that is boiled and eaten hot with butter, especially at breakfast in the southern United States **2.** grain that has had its husks removed or been coarsely ground [Late 16C. Plural of obsolete *grit* "chaff" < Old English *grytta* "coarse meal" < Germanic]

grit·stone /grít stōn/ *n* GEOL, INDUST same as **grit** *n* (sense 2)

grit·ty /grìttee/ (**-ti·er, -ti·est**) *adj* **1.** RESOLUTE courageous, resolute, or persistent **2.** REALISTIC having a stark realism ○ *a gritty detective novel* **3.** LIKE OR WITH GRIT resembling, containing, or covered with grit —**grit·ti·ly** *adv* —**grit·ti·ness** *n*

griz·zle /grízz'l/ *vti* (**-zled, -zling, -zles**) BECOME OR MAKE GRAY to make something gray, or become gray ■ *n* **1.** COLORS GRAY a gray color **2.** GRAY HAIR hair that is gray or streaked with gray [14C. < Old French *grisel* < *gris* "gray"]

griz·zled /grízz'ld/ *adj* **1.** streaked with gray, especially with gray hair ○ *his grizzled beard* **2.** with hair that is gray or streaked with gray

griz·zly bear /grízzlee-/, **griz·zly** (*plural* **-zl·ies**) *n* a brown bear that has brown fur tipped with white. Native to: northwestern North America. Latin name: *Ursus arctos horribilis*.

SPELLCHECK See ***grisly.***

groan /grōn/ *n* **1.** MOURNFUL SOUND a long low cry expressing pain or misery **2.** LOUD CREAKING SOUND a loud creaking sound of something affected by pressure **3.** GRIEVANCE an aggrieved complaint (*informal*) ■ *v* (**groaned, groan·ing, groans**) **1.** *vi* MOAN to utter a moan **2.** *vt* SAY SOMETHING WITH GROAN to express something by means of a groan **3.** *vi* MAKE LOUD CREAKING SOUND to make a loud creaking sound as a result of pressure ○ *The floorboards groaned under their weight.* **4.** *vi* COMPLAIN to complain in an aggrieved way (*informal*) [Old English *grānian* < Indo-European, "be open"] —**groan·er** *n* —**groan·ing·ly** *adv*

groats /grōts/ *n* grain, especially oats, that has been crushed or has had the husks removed (*takes a singular or plural verb*) [14C. < Old English *grotan* < Germanic]

gro·cer /grṓssər/ *n* **1.** an owner or manager of a store selling food and other household goods **2.** *also* **gro·cer's** (*plural same*) *UK* same as **grocery store** [13C. Via Old French < medieval Latin *grossarius* "wholesale dealer" < *grossus* "large"]

gro·cer·y /grṓssəree/ *n* (*plural* **-ies** /grṓssəreez/) **1.** COMM same as **grocery store 2.** the trade or profession of a grocer ■ **gro·cer·ies** *npl* goods, especially food, sold in a grocery store

gro·cer·y store *n* a store that sells food and other household goods

gro·dy /grṓdee/ (**-di·er, -di·est**) *adj* disgusting or extremely unpleasant (*slang*) [Mid-20C. Alteration of GROTESQUE]

Groen·ing /grṓning/, **Matt** (*b.* 1954) US cartoonist. He created the comic strips "Life in Hell" (1980) and television's animated cartoon show "The Simpsons" (1987).

Gro·fé /grṓ fày/, **Ferde** (1892–1972) US composer and arranger. A pianist and orchestrator for Paul Whiteman's jazz band, he wrote the atmospheric *Grand Canyon Suite* (1931). Full name **Grofé, Ferdinand Rudolph von**

grog /grog/ *n* a mixture of alcohol, especially rum, and water, now often served hot with sugar and lemon juice [Mid-18C. Shortening of *Old Grogram*, nickname of Admiral Edward Vernon (from his grogram cloak)]

grog·gy /gróggee/ (**-gi·er, -gi·est**) *adj* feeling weak or dizzy, especially because of illness or over-indulgence —**grog·gi·ly** *adv* —**grog·gi·ness** *n*

grog·ram /gróggrəm, grṓgrəm/ *n* a stiff fabric of silk and wool or mohair [Mid-16C. < French *gros grain* "coarse grain"]

groin (sense 3)

groin[1] /groyn/ *n* **1. AREA BETWEEN THIGHS AND ABDOMEN** the area between the tops of the thighs and the abdomen **2. GENITALS** the genitals, especially the testicles **3.** ARCHIT **EDGE BETWEEN VAULTS** a curved line forming the edge between two intersecting vaults [14C. Origin ?]

groin[2] /groyn/ *n* a structure resembling a wall built out into a river or the sea to protect the shore from erosion [Late 16C. < obsolete *groin* "pig's snout," via Old French < late Latin *grunium* < Latin *grunnire* "grunt"]

grok /grok/ (**grokked, grok·king, groks**) *vt* to understand something completely by intuition (*slang*) ○ *Do you grok that?* [Mid-20C. Invention by Robert HEINLEIN]

grom·met /grómmət, grúmmət/, **grum·met** /grúmm-/ *n* **1. PROTECTIVE EYELET** a protective eyelet in a material that prevents damage either to the material or to a rope passed through it **2. REINFORCEMENT AROUND EYELET** a small ring of metal or plastic that reinforces an eyelet **3.** SAILING **RING TO FASTEN SAIL** a ring used to fasten the edge of a sail to its stay [Early 17C. < obsolete French *gromette* "curb of a bridle" < *gourmer* "curb"]

grom·well /grómmwəl, gróm wèl/ *n* a hairy flowering plant of the borage family that produces hard smooth white seeds. Genus: *Lithospermum*. [13C. < Old French *gromil*]

Gro·my·ko /grə meékō/, **Andrey** (1909–89) president of the Soviet Union (1985–88). He was foreign minister (1957–85) and chairman of the Presidium of the Supreme Soviet (1985–88) of the Soviet Union during the Cold War. Full name **Gromyko, Andrey Andreyevich**

Gron·in·gen /grṓningən, grónn-/ city and capital of Groningen Province, in the northeastern Netherlands, on the Hunze River. Population: 172,701 (2000).

groom /groom, gro͝om/ *n* **1.** same as **bridegroom 2. SOMEBODY WHO CARES FOR HORSES** somebody whose job is to take care of horses by cleaning them and their stables **3. OFFICER IN ROYAL HOUSEHOLD** an officer in a royal household ■ *v* (**groomed, groom·ing, grooms**) **1.** *vt* **CARE FOR ANIMAL'S APPEARANCE** to clean and brush or comb an animal **2.** *vti* **CLEAN ANIMAL'S BODY** to clean the fur, skin, or feathers of another animal or of itself, often with the tongue **3.** *vt* **CARE FOR YOUR PERSONAL APPEARANCE** to keep somebody else's or your own personal appearance neat ○ *a well-groomed young man* **4.** *vt* **TRAIN SOMEBODY** to train and prepare somebody for a particular position ○ *being groomed for the presidency* **5.** *vt* **ESTABLISH PREDATORY RELATIONSHIP** to develop the trust of a young person or his or her family in order to engage in illegal sexual conduct **6.** *vt* SKIING **MAKE PATH IN SNOW** to clear a path or track in snow by compacting the snow [12C. Origin ?] —**groom·er** *n*

groom·ing /gro͝oming/ *n* **1.** the taking care of personal appearance, or the way in which somebody is groomed **2.** the developing of the trust of a young person or his or her family in order to engage in illegal sexual conduct ○ *Internet grooming*

grooms·man /gro͝omzmən, gro͝omz-/ (*plural* **-men** /-mən/) *n* a man who is an attendant to a bridegroom

groom wear *n S Asia* clothing for the bridegroom at a wedding

Groote Ey·landt /gro͝ot ìlənd/ island off the northeastern Northern Territory, Australia, in the Gulf of Carpentaria. Population: 14,209 (1996). Area: 882 sq. mi./2,285 sq. km.

groove /groov/ *n* **1. NARROW PASSAGE** a narrow channel or path in a surface **2. TRACK CUT IN RECORD** a spiral track cut into a vinyl record along which the needle of the record player passes **3. REGULARLY FOLLOWED PROCEDURE** a routine into which somebody has settled (*informal*) **4. SUITABLE ACTIVITY** an activity or situation suited to somebody's talents or tastes (*slang*) **5.** MUSIC **MUSICAL BEAT** a strong beat or rhythm in music (*slang*) ■ *v* (**grooved, groov·ing, grooves**) **1.** *vt* **MAKE GROOVE IN SOMETHING** to cut a groove in a surface **2.** *vi* **ENJOY YOURSELF** to enjoy yourself very much (*informal*) ○ *She's grooving on all the attention she's getting.* **3.** *vi* **PLAY MUSIC RHYTHMICALLY** to play jazz or dance music with a strong beat (*slang*) [14C. < Dutch *groeve*] —**grooved** *adj* —**groov·er** *n* ◇ **groove it** same as **groove** *v* (sense 3) (*slang*) ◇ **in the groove 1.** functioning perfectly and with great ease (*slang*) **2.** playing or performing in a highly accomplished manner (*dated slang*)

groov·y /gro͞ovee/ (**-i·er, -i·est**) *adj* used, often as an exclamation, to describe somebody or something that is fashionable, excellent, or pleasing (*dated slang*) [Mid-20C. < *in the groove*] —**groov·i·ly** *adv* —**groov·i·ness** *n*

grope /grōp/ (**groped, grop·ing, gropes**) *v* **1.** *vi* **SEARCH BY FEELING** to search for something blindly or uncertainly by feeling with the hands ○ *groping for the light switch* **2.** *vi* **BE WITHOUT GUIDANCE** to strive blindly or uncertainly for something ○ *groping for inspiration* **3.** *vt* **FEEL YOUR WAY UNCERTAINLY** to feel your way forward slowly and hesitantly, e.g., in the dark ○ *They groped their way back out of the tunnel.* **4.** *vt* **FONDLE SOMEBODY ROUGHLY** to caress or touch somebody's body for sexual pleasure, often roughly, awkwardly, or without the person's consent (*slang*) [Old English *grāpian* "grasp at" < Germanic] —**grope** *n* —**grop·er** *n*

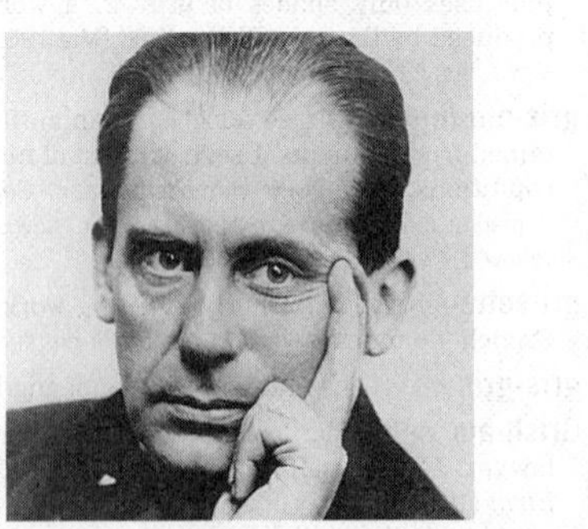

AKG London

Walter Gropius

Gro·pi·us /grṓpee əss/, **Walter** (1883–1969) German-born US architect and educator. A pioneer of the international style, he directed the Bauhaus design school in Weimar, Germany (1919–28). As head of Harvard University's architecture department (1938–52) he trained a generation of US architects in the modernist idiom. Full name **Gropius, Walter Adolph**

"Architecture begins where engineering ends."
[Walter Gropius, *Speech, Harvard Department of Architecture, Architects on Architecture*; 1978]

gros·beak /grṓss beèk/ *n* a finch with a large beak for crushing seeds. Native to: Europe, North America. Family: Fringillidae or Emberizidae. [Late 17C. < French *grosbec* "large beak"]

gro·schen /grṓsh'n/ (*plural same*) *n* **1. SUBUNIT OF FORMER AUSTRIAN CURRENCY** a subunit of the former Austrian currency **2. FORMER COIN WORTH 10 PFENNIGS** a former German coin worth 10 pfennigs (*informal*) **3. OLD GERMAN COIN** a former small German silver coin [Early 17C. Via German < medieval Latin *(denarius) grossus* "thick (penny)"]

gros·grain /grṓ gràyn/ *n* a heavy corded silk or rayon fabric. Use: trimmings, ribbons. [Mid-19C. < French, "coarse grain"]

Gros Morne Na·tion·al Park /grō máwrn-/ national park that is situated on the western coast of Newfoundland, Canada. It contains lakes and part of the Long Range Mountains. Area: 697 sq. mi./1,805 sq. km.

gros point /grṓ pòynt/ *n Can, UK* **1.** an embroidery technique using large diagonal stitches **2.** embroidery done with gros point ▶ US term **raised point** [< French *gros point (de Venise)* "large stitch (from Venice)"]

gross /grōss/ *adj, adv* **1. WITHOUT DEDUCTIONS** before any usual deductions such as tax or expenses have been made ○ *gross salary* **2. OVERALL** including all packaging and contents ○ *the gross weight of the shipment* ■ *adj* **1. OBVIOUSLY WRONG** flagrantly wrong or unmitigated ○ *gross misconduct* **2. DISGUSTING** disgusting or highly unpleasant (*slang*) ○ *The coffee in here is totally gross.* **3. VULGAR** vulgar or coarse **4. WITHOUT GOOD TASTE** not sensitive to, or not able to appreciate, the finer things in life **5. LUXURIANT** growing thickly or densely **6. EXTREMELY OVERWEIGHT** overweight to an unhealthy or repellent degree (*informal*) ■ *n* **1.** (*plural same*) **TWELVE DOZEN** a quantity of 144 or twelve dozen **2.** (*plural* **gross·es**) **SUM BEFORE DEDUCTIONS** a total, especially a total amount of money before any usual deductions are made ■ *vt* (**grossed, gross·ing, gross·es**) **EARN MONEY** to earn or make an amount of money as profit before any usual deductions are made ○ *The movie grossed $70 million.* [14C. Via French < late Latin *grossus* "bulky, coarse"] —**gross·ly** *adv* —**gross·ness** *n*

gross out *vt* to be disgusting or repellent to somebody (*slang*) ○ *language that really grossed me out*

Gross /grōss/, **Chaim** (1904–91) Austrian-born US sculptor. He is noted for his flowing expressionist figures sculpted from wood, stone, and clay.

gross a·nat·o·my *n* a branch of anatomy dealing with body parts that are visible to the naked eye

gross do·mes·tic prod·uct *n* the total value of all goods and services produced within a country in a year, minus net income from investments in other countries

Gross·glock·ner /grṓss glóknər/ mountain in southern Austria, in the Hohe Tauern range, part of the Eastern Alps. The highest peak in Austria, it rises to a height of 12,457 ft./3,797 m.

gross mar·gin *n* gross profit divided by net sales revenue, expressed as a percentage

gross mis·con·duct *n* behavior in the workplace that is illegal or is such a clear and serious violation of company rules that the employee may be dismissed immediately

gross na·tion·al prod·uct *n* the total value of all goods and services produced within a country in a year, including net income from investments in other countries

gross-out *n* something considered disgusting or repellent (*slang*)

gross prof·it *n* the difference between sales revenue and the cost of goods sold

gros·su·la·rite /gróssyələ rìt/, **gros·su·lar** /gróssyələr/ *n* a green variety of garnet. Use: gems. [Early 19C. < German *Grossularit* < modern Latin *grossularia* "gooseberry" (because the gem is green) < French *groseille*]

Grosve·nor /grṓvnər/, **Gilbert** (1875–1966) Turkish-born US editor and geographer. He edited *National Geographic Magazine* (1903–54). As president of the National Geographic Society (1920–54), he developed it into a major research organization. Full name **Grosvenor, Gilbert Hovey**

grosz /grawsh/ (*plural* **gro·szy** /gràwshee/ or **gro·sze**) *n* a subunit of Polish currency. See table at **currency** [Mid-20C. Via Polish *grosz*, Czech *groš* < medieval Latin *(denarius) grossus* "thick (penny)"]

Grosz /grōss/, **George** (1893–1959) German-born US artist. He is known for his satirical caricatures of Berlin life during the 1920s and 1930s. Born **Grosz, Georg**

> "To be a German means invariably to be crude, stupid, ugly, fat, and inflexible…to be a German means: to be a reactionary of the worst kind."
> [George Grosz, *Letter*; 1916]

gro·szy, **gro·sze** plural of **grosz**

gro·tesque /grō tésk/ *adj* **1. DISTORTED** misshapen, especially in a strange or disturbing way ○ *grotesque shadows* **2. INCONGRUOUS** seeming strange or ludicrous through being out of place or unexpected **3.** ARTS **BLENDING REALISTIC AND FANTASTIC** relating to or typical of a style of art that mixes the realistic and the fantastic ■ *n* **1. SOMETHING GROTESQUE** somebody or something considered to be grotesque **2.** ARTS **ART BLENDING REALISTIC AND FANTASTIC** a style of art, especially in 16th-century Europe, in which representations of real and fantastic figures are mixed **3.** ARTS **GROTESQUE ARTISTIC PIECE** a piece of art in the grotesque style [Mid-16C. Via French < Italian *grottesca* "like a grotto" < *grotta* (see GROTTO), from fanciful wall paintings found in excavated Roman ruins] —**gro·tesque·ly** *adv* —**gro·tesque·ness** *n*

gro·tes·que·rie /grō téskəree/, **gro·tes·que·ry** (*plural* **-ries**) *n* **1.** the grotesque quality of something **2.** something grotesque, especially a piece of art in the grotesque style

Gro·ti·us /grṓshee əss, grṓshəss/, **Hugo** (1583–1645) Dutch jurist. He is credited with writing the first works on international law, *Mare Liberum* (1609) (*The Free Sea*) and *De Jure Belli et Pacis* (1625) (*On the Law of War and Peace*).

Grot·on /gróttʼn/ town in southeastern Connecticut, situated on the Thames River opposite New London. It is the site of a US submarine base. Population: 10,078 (2002 estimate).

Gro·tow·ski /grə tófskee/, **Jerzy** (1933–99) Polish theater director. His emphasis on performance without elaborate staging, and his explorations of the relationship between performance and audience, greatly influenced late-20th-century theater.

grot·to /gróttō/ (*plural* **-toes** or **-tos**) *n* **1.** a cave, especially one with interesting natural features **2.** an imitation cave, especially as an ornamental shelter in a formal garden [Early 17C. Via Italian *grotta* < Latin *crypta* (see CRYPT)]

grot·ty /gróttee/ (**-ti·er, -ti·est**) *adj UK* (*informal*) **1.** distastefully dirty, shabby, or in poor condition **2.** generally unpleasant or despicable [Mid-20C. < GROTESQUE]

grouch /growch/ (*informal*) *n* **1. COMPLAINER** a habitually bad-tempered or complaining person **2. COMPLAINT** an instance of or cause for complaining **3. BAD MOOD** a mood characterized by complaining or sulking ○ *a day-long grouch* ■ *vi* (**grouched, grouch·ing, grouch·es**) **COMPLAIN** to complain or grumble [Late 19C. Origin ?] —**grouch·i·ly** *adv* —**grouch·i·ness** *n* —**grouch·y** *adj*

ground[1] /grownd/ *n* **1. LAND SURFACE** the surface of the land **2. EARTH** the earth or soil that covers the land **3. LAND FOR PURPOSE** an area of land used for a particular purpose (*often used in the plural*) ○ *a burial ground* **4. BATTLE AREA** the land held or fought over in battle ○ *prevent the enemy from gaining ground* **5. SUBJECT** an area of knowledge or debate ○ *The lecture covered familiar ground.* **6. FOUNDATION** a reason or basis (*often used in the plural*) ○ *grounds for believing his story* **7. BACKGROUND** a background, e.g., the background color of a flag **8.** ART **PAINTING SURFACE** an underlying surface or prepared area that paint is applied to **9.** ELEC ENG **ELECTRICAL CONNECTION TO GROUND FOR SAFETY** an electrical connection to the ground intended to carry current safely away from a circuit in the event of a fault, or a wire that makes such a connection ■ **grounds** *npl* **1. SURROUNDING LAND** the land surrounding and belonging to a building **2. DREGS** the sediment or dregs of a drink, especially coffee ■ *adj* **ON GROUND** happening, living, working, or operating on the ground ○ *ground crews* ○ *a message from ground control* ■ *v* (**ground·ed, ground·ing, grounds**) **1.** *vt* ELEC ENG **CONNECT APPLIANCE SAFELY TO GROUND** to equip an electrical circuit or appliance with a connection to the ground so that current is carried away safely in the event of a fault **2.** *vt* AVIAT **STOP PILOT OR PLANE FROM FLYING** to prevent or forbid a pilot or aircraft from flying ○ *Bad weather grounded all outgoing flights.* **3.** *vt* **MAKE SOMEBODY STAY HOME** to restrict somebody to a place, especially a child to his or her home, as a punishment (*informal*) ○ *My dad grounded me for a week.* **4.** *vti* NAUT **RUN AGROUND** to become stranded in a vessel, or cause a vessel to become stranded, by running aground ○ *The ferry grounded on a reef.* **5.** *vt* FOOTBALL **THROW FOOTBALL TO GROUND** in football, to throw the ball to the ground to avoid being tackled, in an infringement of the rules **6.** *vti* BASEBALL **HIT BALL TO GROUND** to strike a baseball so that it hits or rolls along the ground **7.** *vt* ART **PREPARE PAINTING SURFACE** to apply a preparatory coat to a surface that is to be painted **8.** *vt* **GIVE SOMEBODY BASIC INFORMATION** to teach somebody the basics about something ○ *was well grounded in machine operation* **9.** *vt* **SUPPORT SOMETHING** to base ideas, arguments, or beliefs on something ○ *a decision that was grounded in personal experience* **10.** *vi* **LAND ON GROUND** to land on the ground, or hit the ground **11.** *vt* **PUT SOMETHING ON GROUND** to put something on the ground ○ *ground your rifles* **12.** *vt* **FIX SOMETHING** to fix something on or in something else as a foundation ○ *The fence posts are grounded in concrete.* [Old English *grund* < Germanic] ◇ **break fresh** *or* **new ground** to do or discover something new ◇ **get (something) off the ground** to get something started or operating ◇ **hit the ground running** to begin to deal with a new situation with great energy and without delay, generally because of good prior preparation (*informal*) ◇ **hold** *or* **stand your ground** to stick resolutely to decisions, attitudes, or principles in the face of pressure to abandon them ◇ **run somebody** *or* **something to ground 1.** to find somebody or something finally, after a long and determined search **2.** to wear something out **3.** to manage something such as a business so badly that it fails ◇ **the moral high ground** a position of moral superiority in relation to other people

ground out *vi* in baseball, to be put out after hitting a ground ball that is fielded and thrown to first base

ground[2] /grownd/ past participle, past tense of **grind**

ground·bait /grównd bàyt/ *n UK* bait thrown into water to attract fish

ground ball *n* in baseball, a ball that bounces on the ground or rolls along it after being hit

ground bass /-bàyss/ *n* a short musical passage continually repeated by the bass as the basis for a changing melody

ground bee·tle *n* INSECTS same as **carabid**

ground·break·ing /grównd bràyking/ *adj* **1. NEW AND INNOVATIVE** new and pioneering or innovative **2. OF CEREMONY OF BREAKING GROUND** relating to a ceremony of breaking ground to begin a new building or construction project ■ *n* **CEREMONY OF BREAKING GROUND** a ceremony of breaking ground to begin a new building or construction project —**ground·break·er** *n*

ground·burst /grównd bùrst/ *n* an explosion of a bomb or warhead on the ground rather than in the air

ground cher·ry *n* **1.** a small round fruit with a papery husk **2.** a plant that produces ground cherries. Native to: North America. Genus: *Physalis.*

ground cloth *n* **1.** *US* a sheet of waterproof material placed on the ground to protect a sleeping bag or the floor of a tent from ground dampness. Can term **groundsheet 2.** a sheet of waterproof material spread over a playing surface to protect it against rain

ground con·trol *n* the staff and equipment on the ground that monitor or guide the flight of an aircraft or spacecraft (*takes a singular or plural verb*)

ground cov·er *n* plants that grow densely and close to the ground, especially growing wild in a forest or deliberately planted in a garden to prevent weeds or soil erosion

ground crew *n* people working in aviation, especially technicians or mechanics, who do not normally work in the air

ground·ed /grówndəd/ *adj* **1. IN TOUCH WITH REALITY** having a secure feeling of being in touch with reality and personal feelings **2. BASED ON EVIDENCE** based on reason, reliable evidence, or good sense **3. CONFINED AT HOME AS PUNISHMENT** not allowed out of the house as a punishment for bad behavior **4.** CONSTR **CONNECTED TO GROUND** connected with a wire to the ground so that electrical current is carried safely away from a circuit in the event of a fault

ground-ef·fect ma·chine *n US* VEHICLES same as **hovercraft**

ground el·der *n UK* PLANTS same as **goutweed**

ground·er /grówndər/ *n* BASEBALL same as **ground ball**

ground floor *n* the floor of a building that is level with or nearest to street level ◇ **in** *or* **on the ground floor** involved in something, especially a business venture, at the earliest stage

ground fog *n* fog lying at or near ground level

ground forc·es *npl* military units that operate on land

ground frost *n* a temperature below freezing as registered on a thermometer at or near the ground

ground glass *n* **1.** glass with a roughened non-transparent surface produced by abrading or etching **2.** glass that has been ground into fine particles. Use: abrasive.

ground hem·lock *n* a low-growing yew tree. Native to: northeastern North America. Latin name: *Taxus canadensis.*

ground·hog /grównd hàwg, -hòg/ *n* ZOOL same as **woodchuck**

Ground·hog Day *n* the day when groundhogs are said to emerge from hibernation, prompting the popular forecast of an early spring if the weather is cloudy or six more weeks of winter if it is sunny. Date: February 2.

ground·ing /grównding/ *n* training in or knowledge of the basics of something ○ *had a good grounding in math*

ground i·vy *n* an invasive evergreen ivy with scalloped leaves. Flowers: small, purple-blue. Native to: Europe, Asia, naturalized in North America. Latin name: *Glechoma hederacea.*

ground·keep·er *n* OCCUPATIONS same as **groundskeeper**

ground·less /grówndləss/ *adj* not based on evidence or reason and not justified or true —**ground·less·ly** *adv* —**ground·less·ness** *n*

ground lev·el *n* **1.** the level of the surface of the ground **2.** PHYS same as **ground state**

ground·ling /grówndling/ *n* **1. UNCULTURED PERSON** somebody disdained for having little or no appreciation of culture **2.** BIOL **ANIMAL OR PLANT LIVING NEAR GROUND** an animal or plant that lives on or near the ground, or at the bottom of a river, lake, or the sea **3.** THEATER **STANDING SPECTATOR** in Elizabethan England, an audience member standing in front of the stage in the cheapest part of the theater **4.** AVIATION **WORKER IN GROUND CREW** a member of the ground crew at an airport or air force base (*slang*)

ground loop *n* a sharp involuntary turn made by an aircraft that is taxiing, taking off, or landing, caused by unbalanced drag

ground·mass /grównd màss/ *n* in some kinds of rock, the fine-grained base rock in which larger crystals are embedded

ground mer·i·stem *n* tissue in the stems and roots of plants consisting of actively dividing cells that become new tissue

ground·nut /grównd nùt/ *n* **1. EDIBLE TUBER** the edible tuber of a climbing vine **2.** (*plural* **ground·nuts** or *same*) **CLIMBING PLANT** a climbing vine that produces groundnuts. Flowers: brownish, fragrant. Native to: North America. Latin name: *Apios americana.* **3. PLANT WITH EDIBLE TUBERS** a plant that produces underground pods or tubers containing edible nuts **4.** FOOD, PLANTS same as **peanut** (senses 1–2)

ground·out /grównd òwt/ *n* in baseball, a play in which a batter is put out after hitting a ground ball that is fielded and thrown to first base

ground pea *n Southern US* same as **peanut** (senses 1–2)

ground pine *n* **1.** a variety of bugle plant. Flowers: two-lipped, yellow with red spots, pine-scented if crushed. Native to: Europe, North Africa. Latin name: *Ajuga chamaepitys.* **2.** a moss with spore-producing tissues grouped in cones. Native to: North America. Genus: *Lycopodium.*

ground plan *n* **1.** a scale drawing of a floor of a building, especially the ground floor **2.** a preliminary plan or general outline of something ○ *a ground plan for corporate expansion*

ground plum *n* **1.** an edible green fruit that resembles a plum shape and a pea in flavor **2.** a flowering plant that bears ground plums. Native to: central and western United States. Genus: *Astragalus.*

ground rule *n* (*often used in the plural*) **1.** a basic rule of procedure ○ *Let's establish a few ground rules before we go any further.* **2.** a rule that applies to the conduct of a game or race on a particular court, field, or course

ground·scraper /grównd skràypər/ *n* a large low or medium-rise building, typically containing offices, that spreads horizontally and occupies a large amount of land [Late 20C. After SKYSCRAPER]

ground·sel /grówndss'l/ *n* a tall plant with deeply lobed leaves, toxic to livestock, and generally regarded as a weed. Flowers: yellow. Native to: Europe, Asia. Genus: *Senecio.* [Old English *grundeswylige*, alteration of *gundeswilgie* "pus-swallower," because of its use in poultices]

ground·sheet /grównd sheet/ *n Can, UK* CAMPING a sheet of waterproof material placed on the ground to protect a sleeping bag or the floor of a tent from ground dampness. US term **ground cloth**

ground·sill /grównd sìl/ *n* the joist in a timber structure that is nearest the ground

grounds·keep·er /grówndz keepər/, **ground·keep·er** /grównd-/ *n* somebody who maintains a playing field or the grounds of a property —**grounds·keep·ing** *n*

ground sloth *n* an extinct ground-dwelling sloth that is believed to be the ancestor of modern tree sloths. Native to: Americas. Family: Megalonychoidea.

grounds·man /grówndzmən/ (*plural* **-men**) *n UK* same as **groundskeeper**

ground speed *n* the speed of a flying aircraft measured in relation to the ground it is traveling over and used for calculating flight times

ground squir·rel *n* **1.** a ground-dwelling burrowing rodent related to the tree squirrels. Native to: North America, Europe, Africa, Asia. Family: Sciuridae. **2.** *regional* same as **chipmunk**

ground state *n* the state of lowest energy for a particle, atom, molecule, or system

ground·stroke /grównd strōk/ *n* in tennis, a shot played from any part of the court after the ball has bounced

ground sub·stance *n* the solid, semisolid, or liquid material that exists between the cells in connective tissue, cartilage, or bone

ground·swell /grównd swèl/ *n* **1.** a strong growth of feeling or opinion that is evident but not always attributable to a specific source ○ *a groundswell of public opinion* **2.** a deep wide up-and-down movement of the sea, often caused by a far-off storm or an earthquake

ground·wa·ter /-wàwtər/, **ground wa·ter** *n* water held underground in soil or permeable rock, often feeding springs and wells

ground wave *n* a radio wave transmitted directly from a transmitter to a receiver, without reflection from the ionosphere

ground·work /grównd wùrk/ *n* basic preparatory tasks that form a foundation for something else

ground ze·ro *n* **1.** POINT OF NUCLEAR EXPLOSION the point on the surface of land or water that is precisely the site of detonation of a nuclear weapon or the point immediately above or below it **2.** CENTER OF ACTIVITY the focal point or center of a particular activity or development ○ *The war-torn country has been ground zero for an international terrorist network.* **3.** BASIC LEVEL the most basic level or starting point for an activity ○ *learning programming from ground zero* **4.** DIRTY PLACE an extremely dirty messy place or room (*informal*) **5.** ASSAULT LOCATION a location targeted by police to assault, using, e.g., SWAT units or hostage rescue teams (*informal*)

Ground Ze·ro *n* the huge debris field resulting from the terrorist attacks on the World Trade Center towers in New York City on September 11, 2001

group /groop/ *n* **1.** SET OF PEOPLE OR THINGS a number of people or things considered together or regarded as belonging together **2.** PEOPLE WITH SOMETHING IN COMMON a number of people sharing something in common such as an interest, belief, or political aim ○ *an environmental group* **3.** MUSIC BAND OF MUSICIANS a small number of musicians, especially in pop music, who play together as a unit **4.** COMM COMPANIES UNDER COMMON CONTROL a number of companies all controlled by a single company or common owner **5.** MIL SET OF TWO OR MORE BATTALIONS a military formation made up of two or more battalions and a headquarters **6.** AIR FORCE AIR FORMATION BETWEEN SQUADRON AND WING an air force formation made up of two or more squadrons, but smaller than a wing **7.** CHEM COLLECTION OF ATOMS a collection of atoms that is a distinct chemical unit, e.g., the hydroxy group **8.** CHEM COLLECTION OF SIMILAR ELEMENTS a set of chemical elements classified according to the vertical column they occupy in the periodic table. There are 18 such groups, and elements in the same group have similar properties. ○ *the alkaline earth group of elements* **9.** GEOL SET OF ROCK FORMATIONS a collection of rock formations that date from the same geologic era and are considered as a stratigraphic unit **10.** MATH MATHEMATICAL SET UNDER OPERATION a set of mathematical entities that are related by a particular operation. For example, consecutive numbers are a group under addition but not under multiplication. (*often used before a noun*) ■ *vti* (**grouped, group·ing, groups**) FORM GROUP to come together as a unit, or bring people or things together to form a unit ○ *spectators grouped in ones and twos* ■ *adj* OF GROUPS relating to groups, or forming a group ○ *group tours* [Late 17C. Via French *groupe* < Italian *gruppo* "group, knot"] —**group·a·ble** *adj*

USAGE When ***group*** is used to refer to a collection of individuals regarded as a unit or a whole, a singular verb is used: *The group has decided not to go on the afternoon tour,* i.e., everybody in the group has decided unanimously to skip that tour. When the members of a group are regarded as separate individuals or factions, a plural verb is used: *The group have been arguing all morning about going or not going,* i.e., some members want to go and others do not.

group cap·tain *n UK* an officer in the Royal Air Force senior to a wing commander and junior to an air commodore

group dy·nam·ics *npl* the interpersonal processes, conscious and unconscious, that take place in the course of interactions among a group of people

grou·per /gróopər/ (*plural* **-pers** or *same*) *n* **1.** a heavy-bodied large-jawed ocean fish. Native to: tropical and temperate waters. Family: Serranidae. **2.** *regional* a rockfish. Native to: southern California. Family: Scorpaenidae. [Early 17C. < Portuguese *garupa*]

group home *n* a residential facility where physically or mentally challenged people live independently with the help of trained supervisors

group·ie /gróopee/ *n* (*informal*) **1.** an enthusiastic fan of a pop group, especially a female teenager seeking a sexual relationship with the object of her adulation **2.** an enthusiastic fan or supporter of something ○ *art groupies*

group·ing /gróoping/ *n* **1.** a set of people or things gathered into a group **2.** the act or process of forming a group or arranging people or things in groups

Group of Eight *n* INTERNAT REL full form of **G8**

Group of Se·ven *n* INTERNAT REL full form of **G7**

group prac·tice *n* a medical, dental, or veterinary practice operated by several doctors, dentists, or vets working together

group the·o·ry *n* the study of the formation and properties of mathematical groups. It has applications in the study of the symmetry of molecules and crystal shapes.

group ther·a·py *n* the treatment of psychological problems by placing patients in groups and, under the guidance of a trained therapist, encouraging them to discuss their problems with each other —**group ther·a·pist** *n*

group·think /gróop thìngk/ *n* conformity in thought and behavior among the members of a group, especially an unthinking acceptance of majority opinions

group·ware /gróop wèr/ *n* software designed to be shared collaboratively by a number of users on a computer network

grouse

grouse[1] /growss/ (*plural same*) *n* a large game bird that nests on the ground on moors and in forests and is usually reddish brown with feathered feet and legs. Family: Tetraonidae. [Early 16C. Origin ?]

grouse[2] /growss/ (**groused, grous·ing, grous·es**) *vi* to complain regularly and continually, often in a way that is not constructive (*informal*) [Early 19C. Origin ?] —**grouse** *n* —**grous·er** *n*

SYNONYMS See ***complain.***

grout /growt/ *n* **1.** MORTAR FOR FILLING GAPS thin mortar used to fill gaps, especially between tiles **2.** PLASTER fine plaster used to finish ceilings and walls ■ **grouts** *npl UK* DREGS the sediment that lies at the bottom of a liquid ■ *vt* (**grout·ed, grout·ing, grouts**) APPLY GROUT TO SOMETHING to use grout to fill gaps, especially between tiles, or to finish a ceiling or wall [Old English *grūt* < Germanic]

grove /grōv/ *n* **1.** a small group of trees **2.** an area where many trees are commercially grown, e.g., for their fruit ○ *an orange grove* [Old English *grāf*, origin ?]

Grove /grōv/, **Andy** (*b.* 1936) Hungarian-born US technology executive. After immigrating to the US in 1956, he cofounded an electronics company (1968) that became one of the world's major computer microprocessor manufacturers. Born **Grof, Andris**

> "The important things of tomorrow are probably going to be things that are overlooked today."
>
> [Andy Grove. Quoted in *In the Company of Giants*, Rama Dev Jager; 1997]

Grove, Frederick Philip (1871–1948) Russian-born Canadian writer. He is known for novels about life on the Canadian prairies such as *Our Daily Bread* (1928).

Grove, Lefty (1900–75) US baseball player. One of the best left-handed pitchers in the game, he played for the Philadelphia Athletics and the Boston Red Sox. Born **Grove, Robert Moses**

grov·el /gróvv'l, grúvv'l/ (**-eled, -el·ing, -els**) *vi* **1.** BEHAVE IN SERVILE WAY to act in a servile way, showing exaggerated and false respect in order to please somebody or out of fear ○ *I've already apologized, but now he wants me to grovel.* **2.** CRAWL to crawl or lie face down on the ground in humility or fear **3.** WALLOW to indulge in something unworthy (*literary*) [Late 19C. < obsolete *groof* "with face downward" < Old

Norse *á grúfu* < *grúfa* "proneness"] —**grov·el·er** *n* —**grov·el·ing·ly** *adv*

grow /grō/ (**grew** /groo/, **grown** /grōn/, **grow·ing**, **grows**) *v* **1.** *vi* GET BIGGER to become larger in size through natural development **2.** *vi* BECOME LARGER OR GREATER to expand or become more developed or intense ○ *The number of members will grow rapidly.* ○ *Excitement is growing.* **3.** *vi* DEVELOP NATURALLY to be capable of developing naturally and remaining in a naturally healthy state ○ *Plants won't grow in this soil.* **4.** *vi* BE PRODUCT OF SOMETHING to develop from something else ○ *Hatred grew out of mutual ignorance.* **5.** *vi* BECOME to move from one condition to another, especially gradually ○ *The night grew cold.* **6.** *vt* CAUSE SOMETHING TO GROW to make something, especially plants, grow and develop ○ *We grow tomatoes in the greenhouse.* **7.** *vt* DEVELOP SOMETHING NATURALLY to produce something or allow it to be produced as part of a natural process ○ *grow a mustache* **8.** ⚠ *vt* EXPAND SOMETHING to develop, expand, and stimulate something, especially a business, a line of business, or an economic market ○ *an attempt to grow the company's market share* [Old English *grōwan* < Indo-European] —**grow·er** *n*

USAGE Metaphorical uses of *grow* as a transitive verb are sometimes considered unacceptable: *grow the economy* and *grow a stock portfolio.* There are no grounds for objecting to literal physical senses of the transitive verb: *grow a beard; grow corn.* Nor are there grounds for objecting to metaphorical uses of the intransitive verb: *The economy grew rapidly.*

grow into *vt* to develop in size, maturity, or capability to suit something

grow on *vt* **1.** to become gradually more acceptable or pleasing to somebody ○ *a song that grows on you* **2.** to become gradually more apparent or powerful to somebody

grow out of *vt* to become too mature or too big in size for something

grow up *vi* **1.** BECOME ADULT to develop into an adult **2.** BEHAVE MORE MATURELY to behave in a more mature and sensible way **3.** COME INTO EXISTENCE to come into existence and develop ○ *A town had grown up at the junction of the two rivers.*

grow·ing /grṓ ing/ *adj* **1.** becoming greater in size or amount **2.** becoming more intense or extreme ○ *growing anxiety*

grow·ing pains *npl* **1.** pains in the limbs that sometimes affect adolescents, thought to be caused by rapid bodily growth **2.** problems associated with the early stages of something such as a developing project

grow·ing point *n* the area in a plant where the cells are actively dividing to produce new tissue in the stems and roots

grow·ing sea·son *n* the time of year during which annual plants, especially farm crops, develop to maturity

growl /growl/ *v* (**growled**, **growl·ing**, **growls**) **1.** *vti* MAKE HOSTILE SOUND to make a low nonverbal sound in the throat that expresses hostility, or communicate something by means of this sound **2.** *vti* SPEAK IN HOSTILE WAY to speak, or say something, in a deep voice that expresses impatience or hostility ○ *He was growling at the children.* **3.** *vi* MAKE RUMBLING NOISE to make a low rumbling noise ■ *n* **1.** ANIMAL'S HOSTILE NOISE the low throaty noise made by a hostile animal, especially a dog **2.** HOSTILE UTTERANCE something said in a hostile throaty voice [Mid-17C. Probably < Old French *grouler* < Germanic, an imitation of the sound] —**growl·ing** *adj* —**growl·y** *adj*

growl·er /grówlər/ *n* **1.** SMALL ICEBERG a small iceberg with very little showing above the water **2.** GROWLING PERSON OR ANIMAL a person or animal that growls **3.** BEER CONTAINER a container for beer, e.g., a pitcher, brought by a customer (*informal*)

grow light *n* a fluorescent lamp giving out light similar to sunlight and used to grow plants indoors

grown /grōn/ past participle of **grow** ■ *adj* having developed and matured

grown-up *adj* **1.** FULLY MATURE fully developed and mature **2.** FOR ADULTS relating to or for adults ■ *n* ADULT an adult person (*usually used by or to children*) ○ *Ask a grown-up to put it in the oven for you.*

growth /grōth/ *n* **1.** GROWING PROCESS the process of becoming larger and more mature through natural development ○ *nutrients needed for healthy growth* **2.** INCREASE an increase in numbers, size, power, or intensity **3.** SOMETHING THAT GROWS something that grows or has grown ○ *three days' growth of beard* **4.** MED TUMOR a mass of cells with no physiological function, e.g., a tumor that forms in or on an organ ■ *adj* EXPANDING in the process of expanding or developing, especially rapidly ○ *a growth company*

growth fac·tor *n* a substance produced by cells that stimulates them to multiply. When produced in excessive amounts, a growth factor may be associated with proliferating growth such as that seen in cancer.

growth hor·mone *n* a hormone, made and stored in the pituitary gland in the brain, that stimulates protein synthesis and the growth of the long bones of the limbs

growth in·dus·try *n* an industry that is expanding ○ *Microelectronics is one of the area's few growth industries.*

growth reg·u·la·tor *n* a natural or synthetic preparation that promotes or inhibits plant growth

growth ring *n* a concentric ring in the cross-section of a woody stem or trunk, representing the result of one year's growth

growth sub·stance *n* a chemical produced by a plant that regulates its growth and development, and is usually made in the shoot tip and transported to other regions

groyne Can, UK spelling of **groin**[2]

Groz·ny /gróznee/, **Groz·nyy** capital of the Russian republic of Chechnya, at the foot of the Caucasus Mountains. Population: 372,742 (1995).

GRP *abbr* glass-reinforced plastic

grub /grub/ *n* **1.** LARVA the larva of various insects, especially beetles **2.** FOOD food, especially a meal (*informal*) ■ *v* (**grubbed**, **grub·bing**, **grubs**) **1.** *vt* DIG SOMETHING UP to dig or pull something out of the ground, especially without proper tools ○ *grubbing potatoes in rock-hard soil* **2.** *vt* CLEAR GROUND to remove roots and stumps from an area of ground **3.** *vi* SEARCH ON GROUND to search on or in the ground for something **4.** *vi* SEARCH LABORIOUSLY to search for something laboriously, usually by moving things and looking under things ○ *grubbing around in the archives for evidence* **5.** *vi* TOIL to work hard, especially at something dull or arduous **6.** *vt* SCROUNGE SOMETHING to obtain something by scrounging or begging (*slang*) ○ *grub a couple of bucks* [14C. < assumed Old English *grybban* < Indo-European, "scratch, dig"] —**grub·ber** *n*

grub·by /grúbbee/ (**-bi·er**, **-bi·est**) *adj* **1.** DIRTY slightly dirty **2.** HAVING GRUBS infested with grubs **3.** CONTEMPTIBLE disliked or despised, especially for being sordid or dishonorable ○ *articles in his grubby little newsletter* —**grub·bi·ly** *adv* —**grub·bi·ness** *n*

SYNONYMS See *dirty.*

grub·stake /grúb stayk/ *n* **1.** MIN EXTRACT MONEY ADVANCED TO PROSPECTOR supplies or money given to a prospector in return for a share in any profits **2.** BUSINESS ADVANCE FOR STARTING UP BUSINESS money or materials given to somebody starting a business in return for a share in any profits ■ *vt* (**-staked**, **-stak·ing**, **-stakes**) ADVANCE MONEY TO to give money or supplies to somebody in business in return for a share of any profits [Mid-19C. < GRUB "food" + STAKE[2]] —**grub·stak·er** *n*

Grub Street *n* the world of literary hackwork and those who work at it [After a former street in London, England]

grudge /gruj/ *n* RESENTMENT a feeling of resentment or ill will, especially one lasting for a long time ■ *vt* (**grudged**, **grudg·ing**, **grudg·es**) **1.** GIVE SOMETHING RELUCTANTLY to allow, give, or do something reluctantly ○ *Don't grudge him this small favor.* **2.** ENVY SOMETHING to be envious or resentful of somebody for something [14C. < Old French *grouchier* "grumble"] —**grudg·er** *n*

grudge match *n* a match between players or teams who have a long-standing animosity between them or a specific past insult or injury to revenge

grudg·ing /grújjing/ *adj* done or given reluctantly, or doing or giving something reluctantly —**grudg·ing·ly** *adv*

gru·el /gro͞o əl, grool/ *n* a thin cereal made by boiling meal, especially oatmeal, in water [14C. < Old French < Germanic]

gru·el·ing /gro͞o əling, gro͞ol-/ *adj* extremely arduous or exhausting [< giving gruel as a punishment] —**gru·el·ing·ly** *adv*

grue·some /gro͞ossəm/ *adj* involving or depicting death or injury in a disturbing or sickening way ○ *gruesome photographs of the accident* [Late 16C. < obsolete *grue* "shudder" < N Germanic] —**grue·some·ly** *adv* —**grue·some·ness** *n*

gruff /gruf/ *adj* **1.** abrupt, angry, or impatient in manner or speech ○ *a gruff refusal* **2.** harsh-sounding or throaty ○ *a gruff voice* [15C. < Flemish or Dutch *grof* "rough, harsh"] —**gruff·ly** *adv* —**gruff·ness** *n*

grum·ble /grúmb'l/ *v* (**-bled**, **-bling**, **-bles**) **1.** *vi* EXPRESS DISSATISFACTION to complain or mutter in a discontented way **2.** *vt* SAY SOMETHING AS COMPLAINT to say something as a complaint ○ *Some entrants grumbled that there wasn't enough time.* **3.** *vi* MAKE RUMBLING NOISES to make rumbling or growling noises ○ *thunder grumbling in the distance* ■ *n* **1.** COMPLAINT a complaint or expression of discontent **2.** RUMBLING NOISE a rumbling or growling noise [Late 16C. Probably < Middle Dutch *grommelen* "mumble, grunt"] —**grum·bler** *n* —**grum·bly** *adj*

SYNONYMS See *complain.*

grum·bling /grúmbling/ *n* a muted complaint or protest ○ *grumblings of discontent* ■ *adj* with a tendency to complain —**grum·bling·ly** *adv*

grum·met *n* same as **grommet**

grump /grump/ (*informal*) *n* SOMEBODY IN BAD MOOD somebody regarded as bad-tempered or sullen ■ **grumps** *npl* BAD-TEMPERED MOOD a bad-tempered or sullen mood ○ *a fit of the grumps* ■ *vi* (**grumped**, **grump·ing**, **grumps**) COMPLAIN to complain or be sullen [Early 18C. An imitation of somebody expressing displeasure]

grump·y /grúmpee/ (**-i·er**, **-i·est**) *adj* bad-tempered or sullen —**grump·i·ly** *adv* —**grump·i·ness** *n*

Grun·dy·ism /grúndee ìzzəm/ *n* a prudish narrow-minded attitude toward other people (*disapproving*) [Mid-19C. < Mrs. *Grundy*, character in Thomas Moreton's play *Speed the Plough* (1798)]

grunge /grunj/ *n* **1.** FILTH filth or garbage (*informal*) **2.** KIND OF ROCK MUSIC a variety of rock music that emerged in the 1980s in the United States and owes much to punk and heavy metal (*often used before a noun*) ○ *grunge rock* **3.** UNKEMPT FASHION STYLE a style of dress, popularized by fans of grunge music, typified by second-hand clothes worn in layers, heavy footwear, unkempt hair, and an overall scruffy appearance ○ *designer grunge* **4.** UNAPPEALING PERSON somebody who looks dirty, unkempt, or otherwise unsavory (*slang insult*) [Mid-20C. Back-formation < GRUNGY]

grun·gy /grúnjee/ (**-gi·er**, **-gi·est**) *adj* **1.** dirty, shabby, inferior, or otherwise undesirable (*informal*) **2.** relating to or typical of grunge music or grunge fashions [Mid-20C. Origin ?] —**grun·gi·ness** *n*

grun·ion /grúnnyən/ *n* a small fish that spawns on beaches. Native to: coastal waters of California, Mexico. Latin name: *Leuresthes tenuis.* [Early 20C. Probably < Spanish *gruñón* "grunter" < Latin *grunnire* "to grunt"]

grunt[1] /grunt/ *v* (**grunt·ed**, **grunt·ing**, **grunts**) **1.** *vi* MAKE NOISE OF PIG to make the half-nasal, half-throaty noise that a pig makes **2.** *vti* SAY SOMETHING IN THROATY BURST to make a deep sound in the throat as an annoyed, half-hearted, or inattentive response to what somebody has said, or to indicate or say something in this way ○ *He grunted in acknowledgment of my greeting.* ■ *n* **1.** NOISE OF PIG a half-nasal, half-throaty noise that a pig makes, or a vocal sound that resembles it **2.** SOMEBODY DOING MENIAL TASKS a worker who does menial tasks (*slang*) **3.** SEA FISH a bony fish that grunts when taken out of the water. Native to:

warm and tropical oceans. Family: Pomadasyidae. [Old English *grunettan* < Indo-European] —**grunt·er** *n*

grunt[2] /grunt/ *n* an infantryman in the US Army or Marine Corps, especially one serving in Vietnam (*slang*) [Mid-20C. Alteration of *ground* < *ground man* "low-ranking railway worker"]

grun·tled /grúnt'ld/ *adj* pleased or happy (*informal humorous*) [Early 20C. Back-formation < *disgruntled*]

grunt·work /grúnt wùrk/ *n* basic work that is necessary to the completion of a task but that is uninspiring or unrewarding (*informal*)

Grus /gruss, grooss/ *n* a small constellation of the southern hemisphere situated between Tucana and Piscis Austrinus. See illustration at **constellation** [Early 18C. < Latin *grus* "crane (bird)"]

Gru·yère /groo yér/ *n* a hard Swiss cheese with occasional holes in it that has a mild nutty slightly sweet flavor. It is often used in cooking, e.g., in fondues. [Early 19C. After a town in Switzerland]

gr. wt. *abbr* COMM gross weight

gryph·on *n* another spelling of **griffin**

gs *abbr* South Georgia (*used in Internet addresses*) See table at **domain name**

GS *abbr* **1.** POL General Secretary **2.** MIL general staff **3.** AVIAT ground speed

GSA *abbr* **1.** GOV General Services Administration **2.** Girl Scouts of America

GSC *abbr* MIL general staff corps

GSL *abbr* EDUC guaranteed student loan

GSM *tdmk* a trademark for an international wireless communications network for cellular phones. Full form **Global System for Mobile Communications**

gsoh *abbr* good sense of humor (*used in personal columns*)

G-spot *n* a highly sensitive small area in the vagina that, when stimulated, gives extreme sexual pleasure (*informal*) [Late 20C. After Ernst *Gräfenberg* (1881–1957), German gynecologist]

GSR *abbr* PHYSIOL galvanic skin response

GST *abbr* FIN goods and services tax

Gstaad /gə staát/ alpine ski resort in Bern Canton, western Switzerland. Population: 2,500 (1980 estimate).

G-string *n* a piece of material covering only the pubic area, supported by a narrow cord between the buttocks and around the waist [Late 19C. Origin ?]

G-suit *n* a close-fitting garment worn by pilots and astronauts that counters the blackout effects of high acceleration by applying pressure to the legs and lower body, thereby reducing blood supply loss to the head [Mid-20C. Shortening of *gravity-suit*]

gt *abbr* Guatemala (*used in Internet addresses*) See table at **domain name**

GT *abbr* Gran Turismo (*used as part of the name of a fast car*) [Italian, "grand touring"]

gt. *abbr* **1.** gilt[1] **2.** PHARM drop (*on prescriptions*) [in sense 2 < Latin *gutta*]

Gt. *abbr* GEOG Great

G.T.C. *abbr* COMM good till canceled

gtd. *abbr* guaranteed

GTG *abbr* got to go (*used in e-mails or text messages*)

GTi *abbr* Gran Turismo injection (*used as part of the name of a fast car*) [Italian, "grand touring, injection"]

gTLD *n* the portion of an Internet address that identifies it as belonging to a specific generic domain class, e.g., com, edu, or gov. Full form **generic top-level domain**

GTP *abbr* BIOCHEM guanosine triphosphate

GTT *abbr* MED glucose tolerance test

gtt. *abbr* PHARM drops (*used in prescriptions*) [Latin *guttae*]

gu *abbr* Guam (*used in Internet addresses*) See table at **domain name**

GU *abbr* **1.** MED, PHYSIOL genitourinary **2.** GEOG Guam

g.u. *abbr* MED, PHYSIOL genitourinary

gua·ca·mo·le /gwaàkə mṓlee, -mṓ lày/ *n* avocado mashed or puréed with tomato and lightly spiced with chili, served as a dip or as an accompaniment to some Mexican-style dishes [Early 20C. Via American Spanish < Nahuatl *ahuacamolli* "avocado paste"]

gua·cha·ro /gwaáchə rō/ (*plural* **-ros**) *n* BIRDS same as **oilbird** [Early 19C. Via American Spanish *guácharo* < Quechua *wáhcha* "orphan"]

Gua·da·la·ja·ra /gwòdd'lə haárə/ city in west central Mexico, capital of Jalisco State, and the country's second largest city. Founded in 1530, it is a resort and commercial center. Population: 1,646,319 (2000).

Gua·dal·ca·nal /gwòdd'lkə nál/ mountainous island in the southwestern Pacific Ocean. It is the largest island of the Solomon Islands. In World War II, heavy fighting took place there between the United States and Japanese forces. Area: 2,500 sq. mi./6,475 sq. km.

Gua·dal·qui·vir /gwòdd'l kwívvər/ river in Andalusia, southern Spain. It rises in the Sierra de Segura and flows southwestward through Córdoba and Seville before emptying into the Gulf of Cádiz. Length: 408 mi./657 km.

Gua·da·lupe /gwaádə lóop/ **1.** river in southeastern Texas that rises north of Austin and empties into the Gulf of Mexico south of Houston. Length: 250 mi./402 km. **2.** island off the Baja California coast of Mexico in the Pacific Ocean. Area: 80 sq. mi./207 sq. km. **3.** city near Monterrey in Nuevo León State, northeastern Mexico. Population: 670,162 (2000).

Gua·da·lupe Hi·dal·go /gwaádə lóop hi daálgō/ former name for **Gustavo A. Madero**

Gua·da·lupe Moun·tains mountain range of the Rocky Mountains that runs from New Mexico to Texas. The highest peak is Guadalupe Peak, 8,749 ft./2,667 m.

Gua·da·lupe Moun·tains Na·tion·al Park national park in southwestern Texas that was established in 1972 and is Noted for its limestone formations and unusual wildlife. The highest peak is Guadalupe Peak, 8,749 ft./2,667 m. Area: 135 sq. mi./350 sq. km.

Gua·de·loupe /gwòdd'l óop/ overseas department of France consisting of a group of islands in the eastern Caribbean. Capital: Basse-Terre. Population: 431,170 (2001). Area: 687 sq. mi./1,780 sq. km.

Gua·di·a·na /gwaa dyaánə, -thyaánə/ river that rises south of Madrid, Spain, and flows westward to Portugal. It forms part of the southern border between the two countries before emptying into the Gulf of Cádiz. Length: 515 mi./829 km.

~~**guage**~~ incorrect spelling of **gauge**

gua·gua /gwaá gwaá/ *n* in Cuba and the Canary Islands, a bus [< Spanish (Cuba and Canary Islands)]

guai·ac /gwí ak, -ək/ *n* PHARM same as **guaiacum** (sense 3) [Mid-16C. Anglicization]

guai·a·col /gwí ə kàwl/ *n* a yellowish oily liquid. Source: guaiacum resin, wood creosote. Use: expectorant, antiseptic, local anesthetic. [Mid-19C. < GUAIACUM]

guai·a·cum /gwí əkəm/ *n* **1.** TROPICAL AMERICAN TREE an evergreen tree that has dark dense oily wood and yields a medicinal resin. Native to: tropical America. Latin name: *Guaiacum officinale.* **2.** GUAIACUM WOOD the hard dense oily wood of the guaiacum tree **3.** GUAIACUM RESIN the brownish green resin of the guaiacum tree. Use: in medicine, making varnishes. [Mid-16C. Via modern Latin < American Spanish *guayacán* < Taino]

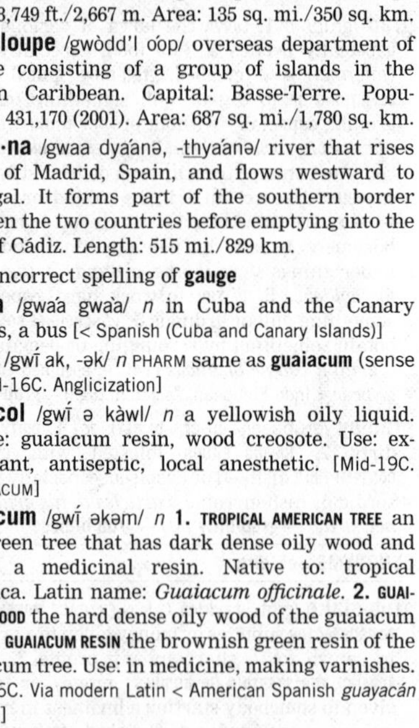

Guam

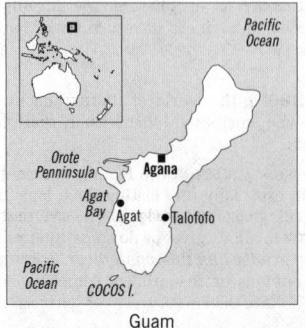

Guam /gwaam/ island and tourist resort in the northwestern Pacific Ocean. An unincorporated territory of the United States, it is the largest of the Mariana Islands. Capital: Agana. Population: 163,941 (2003). Area: 212 sq. mi./549 sq. km. —**Gua·ma·ni·an** /gwaa máynee ən/ *n, adj*

guan /gwaan/ *n* a large fruit-eating bird that lives in trees. Native to: Central and South America. Family: Cracidae. [Late 17C. Via American Spanish < Miskito *kwamu*]

gua·na·co /gwə naákō/ (*plural* **-cos**) *n* an animal similar and related to the domesticated llama and alpaca. Native to: dry regions of the Andes. Latin name: *Lama guanaco.* [Early 17C. Via Spanish < Quechua *huanacu*]

Gua·na·jua·to /gwaánə hwaátō/ **1.** state in central Mexico. Capital: Guanajuato. Population: 4,663,032 (2000). Area: 11,880 sq. mi./30,770 sq. km. **2.** capital city of Guanajuato State in central Mexico. Population: 135,611 (2000).

Guang·dong /gwaáng dóong/ province of southern China, on the South China Sea. Capital: Guangzhou. Population: 69,610,000 (1997). Area: 76,100 sq. mi./197,100 sq. km.

Guang·xi Zhuang /gwaáng shee jwaáng/ autonomous region in southeastern China, on the border with Vietnam. Capital: Nanning. Population: 42,245,765 (1990). Area: 85,100 sq. mi./220,400 sq. km.

Guang·zhou /gwaáng jṓ/ capital of Guangdong Province and chief port in southeastern China. It lies about 80 mi./129 km northwest of Hong Kong. A major international trade fair is held there twice yearly. Population: 4,490,000 (1995).

gua·ni·dine /gwaáni deen/ *n* a strongly alkaline substance found in urine as a product of protein metabolism and in plant tissues. Use: manufacture of plastics and resins. Formula: CH_5N_3. [Mid-19C. < GUANO + -IDE + -INE]

gua·nine /gwaá neen/ *n* a purine derivative that is one of the four bases in DNA and RNA. Symbol **G** [Mid-19C. < GUANO]

gua·no /gwaánō/ *n* **1.** accumulated droppings of birds, bats, or seals, occurring where large established colonies of these animals are situated **2.** fertilizer consisting of dried bird or bat droppings that is rich in nutrients, including urates, oxalates, and phosphates, or a synthetic fertilizer with properties similar to those of natural guano [Early 17C. Via American Spanish < Quechua *huanu* "dung"]

gua·no·sine /gwaánə seen, -sin/ *n* a compound containing guanine and ribose [Early 20C. < GUANINE + RIBOSE]

gua·no·sine mon·o·phos·phate *n* a constituent of the nucleic acids DNA and RNA that plays a part in various metabolic reactions and is composed of guanosine linked to a phosphate group

gua·no·sine tri·phos·phate *n* a nucleotide made of guanosine linked to three phosphate groups

Guan·ta·na·mo Bay /gwaan taánəmō-/ sheltered inlet of the Caribbean Sea, southeastern Cuba. It is the site of a major US naval base and a prison camp for suspected terrorists captured by the United States. Area: 14 sq. mi./36 sq. km.

Guan·xiu /gwaán syóo/ (832–912) Chinese artist. He is noted for his paintings of Buddhist monks with exaggerated and grotesque features.

gua·nyl·ic ac·id /gwaa nìllik-/ *n* BIOCHEM same as **guanosine monophosphate** [Late 19C. < GUANOSINE]

Gua·po·ré /gwaápə ráy, gwaápoo-/ river in central South America that rises in western Brazil and flows northwest along the Brazil-Bolivia border before joining the Mamoré River. Length: 1,087 mi./1,749 km.

guar /gwaar/ *n* **1.** a plant of dry regions widely grown as fodder and for its seeds, which are used to make gum. Native to: South Asia. Latin name: *Cyamopsis tetragonolobus.* **2.** INDUST same as **guar gum** [Late 19C. < Hindi *guār*]

gua·ra·ní /gwaárə neé/ (*plural same* or **-nís**) *n* **1.** the main unit of Paraguayan currency. See table at **currency** **2.** a coin worth one guaraní [Mid-20C. < GUARANI]

Gua·ra·ni /gwaàrə neé/ (*plural same* or **-nis**) *n* **1.** a member of a Native South American people who live in parts of Paraguay, Uruguay, Bolivia, and Brazil **2.** an official language of Paraguay, also spoken elsewhere in central South America, belonging to the Tupi-Guarani branch of Andean-Equatorial languages. Native speakers: 3 million. [Mid-18C. Via Spanish *Guaraní* < *Guarini*, a people of Paraguay] —**Gua·ra·ni** *adj*

guar·an·tee /gàrrən teé/ *n* **1.** ASSURANCE something that assures a specific outcome ○ *There's no guarantee that the plan will work.* **2.** PROMISE OF QUALITY a formal promise that a product will be repaired free of charge if it breaks or fails within a particular period or that substandard work will be redone ○ *The television came with a five-year guarantee.* **3.** LAW PROMISE TO BE RESPONSIBLE FOR ANOTHER a formal promise by one person to take responsibility for the debts or obligations of another person if that person fails to meet them **4.** LAW SOMEBODY RECEIVING FORMAL ASSURANCE a person or company given an assurance that somebody's debts or obligations will be dealt with **5.** CERTIFICATE STATING PROMISE OF QUALITY a document setting out a promise of quality made by a manufacturer or the provider of a service **6.** LAW same as **guarantor** ■ *vt* (**-teed, -tee·ing, -tees**) **1.** GIVE ASSURANCE OF SOMETHING to promise something, or make something certain ○ *We can't guarantee availability of seats on tomorrow's flight.* **2.** PROMISE QUALITY OF GOODS OR SERVICES to give a formal, usually printed promise with regard to the quality of a product, saying that it will be repaired free of charge if it fails within a particular period, or that substandard work will be redone **3.** LAW ACCEPT RESPONSIBILITY FOR SOMEBODY to promise to fulfill another person's debts or obligations if that person fails to meet them [Late 17C. Probably alteration of GUARANTY]

guar·an·teed /gàrrən teéd/ *adj* **1.** covered by a formal promise of quality and durability ○ *a fully guaranteed product* **2.** certain to happen or be done or provided ○ *a movie guaranteed to have you in tears*

guar·an·teed in·vest·ment cer·tif·i·cate *n Can* an investment that provides a guaranteed rate of interest over a specific term, usually one to five years

guar·an·tor /gàrrən táwr, gàrrəntər/ *n* somebody who gives a guarantee, especially a formal promise to be responsible for somebody else's debts or obligations [Mid-19C. < GUARANTEE]

SYNONYMS See *backer.*

guar·an·ty /gàrrəntee/ *n* (*plural* **-ties**) **1.** something used as security for a formal promise **2.** the giving of something as security for a promise **3.** LAW same as **guarantor 4.** same as **guarantee** *n* (sense 3) ■ *vt* (**-tied, -ty·ing, -ties**) LAW same as **guarantee** *v* (sense 3) [Early 16C. < Anglo-Norman *guarantie* < Old French *garantir* "to warrant" < *garant* "warrant"]

SYNONYMS See *backer*

guard /gaard/ *vt* (**guard·ed, guard·ing, guards**) **1.** PROTECT SOMEBODY OR SOMETHING to protect somebody or something against danger or loss by being vigilant and taking defensive measures **2.** PREVENT SOMEBODY FROM ESCAPING to watch over somebody held captive and prevent him or her from escaping ○ *Two MPs were guarding the prisoner.* **3.** CONTROL PASSAGE THROUGH PLACE to watch over and control passage through an entrance or across a boundary ○ *All of the mountain passes are guarded by troops.* **4.** BASKETBALL HAMPER OPPONENT in basketball, to prevent an opponent from scoring or playing effectively **5.** CONTROL SOMETHING to control or restrain something such as speech or behavior ○ *guard your tongue* **6.** PUT PROTECTIVE COVER ON SOMETHING to equip a machine or device with a protective cover ■ *n* **1.** PROTECTOR a person or group that protects, watches over, restrains, or controls somebody or something ○ *The prisoner broke away from his guards.* **2.** ACT OF GUARDING an act of guarding somebody or something, or the responsibility of guarding somebody or something **3.** DEFENSE a defensive posture or state of mind ○ *Her guard was up.* **4.** CEREMONIAL ESCORT a usually mounted or motorized group forming a ceremonial escort **5.** BODY PROTECTION a piece of tough material worn to protect a part of the body from injury **6.** PROTECTIVE DEVICE a device or part intended to protect the user against injury ○ *a guard on a lathe* **7.** MEANS OF PROTECTION any means of protection ○ *The snow fence serves as a guard against drifts.* **8.** DEFENSIVE POSITION IN BASKETBALL in basketball, either of the two players who regularly defend the backcourt and initiate offensive plays **9.** FOOTBALL LINEMAN in football, each of two offensive linemen on each side of the center **10.** *also* **Guard** SOLDIER in the British army and other armies, a soldier who belongs to any regiment originally formed to provide protection for the sovereign **11.** *UK* RAIL same as **conductor** (sense 3) **12.** *Ireland* GARDA a member of the Garda (*informal*) [15C. < French *garde* (noun), *garder* (verb) < Germanic] ◇ **stand guard** to keep a watch or defensive posture ◇ **off (your) guard** having relaxed the usual precautions against attack ◇ **on (your) guard** prepared against attack

SYNONYMS See *safeguard.*

guard against *vt* to be wary of something or take precautions against it

guar·dant /gaárd'nt/, **gar·dant** *adj* describes an animal on a coat of arms that has its face turned toward the observer ○ *a lion guardant* [Late 16C. < French *gardant*, present participle of *garder* "guard"]

guard cell *n* either of two specialized cells bordering pores in the epidermis of leaves that move to control the size of the aperture in response to changes in water levels. The guard cells and pore are called the stoma, and are situated on the underside, and sometimes the top side, of leaves and on young shoots.

guard dog *n* a dog used for guarding property or people

guard·ed /gaárdəd/ *adj* reluctant to share information with others ○ *Officials reacted with guarded optimism to the proposal.* —**guard·ed·ly** *adv* —**guard·ed·ness** *n*

SYNONYMS See *cautious.*

guard hair *n* the long coarse outer hair on some animals that forms a protective layer over softer underfur

guard·house /gaárd hòwss/ (*plural* **-hous·es** /-hòwzəz/) *n* a building used to house soldiers acting as guards and as a place for detaining military prisoners

Guar·di /gwaárdee/, **Francesco** (1712–93) Italian painter. He painted romantic landscapes of his native city, Venice, which are characterized by lively line and color and a mood of fantasy.

Guar·di·a ➧ **La Guardia, Fiorello Henry**

guard·i·an /gaárdee ən/ *n* **1.** PROTECTOR somebody who or something that guards, protects, or preserves somebody or something **2.** LEGALLY RESPONSIBLE PERSON somebody who is legally entrusted to manage somebody else's affairs, especially those of a minor **3.** SUPERIOR FRANCISCAN a superior in a Franciscan monastery [15C. < Anglo-Norman *gardein* < Old French *garder* "to guard"] —**guard·i·an·ship** *n*

guard·i·an an·gel *n* **1.** somebody seen as the special protector of somebody's interests (*informal*) **2.** an angel believed to look after a particular person

Guard·i·an An·gel *n* a member of a vigilante group that patrols the streets of a city as a volunteer crime prevention squad. New York was the birthplace of the first such group.

Guard·mem·ber /gaárd mèmbər/ *n* somebody who serves in the National Guard

guard of hon·or *n* a body of troops acting as a formal escort for somebody important during a ceremony

guard·rail /gaárd ràyl/ *n* **1.** a rail acting as a safety barrier at the side of a freeway, highway, road, or ship's deck **2.** an additional rail laid close inside the main running rail on tight curves and at a junction to help a train's wheels stay on the track

guard ring *n* a ring worn to stop another ring from slipping off the finger

guard·room /gaárd ròom, -ròom/ *n* a room used by soldiers acting as guards and as a place for detaining military prisoners

guards·man /gaárdzmən/ (*plural* **-men** /-mən/) *n* **1.** a member of the National Guard, especially a man **2.** *UK* a soldier who belongs to any of several regiments of the British army originally formed to provide protection for the sovereign

guards·per·son /gaárdz pùrss'n/ (*plural* **-peo·ple** /-peep'l/ or **-per·sons**) *n* a member of the National Guard

guards·wom·an /gaárdz wòommən/ (*plural* **-wom·en** /-wìmmin/) *n* a woman who is a member of the National Guard

guar gum *n* gum extracted from the seeds of the guar plant. Use: to thicken and stabilize processed foods, in paper manufacture.

Guar·ne·ri /gwaar nérree, -nyérree/ family of Italian violin makers, including **Andrea** (1626–98) and his grandson **Giuseppe Antonio** (1687–1745)

~~Guatamala~~ incorrect spelling of **Guatemala**

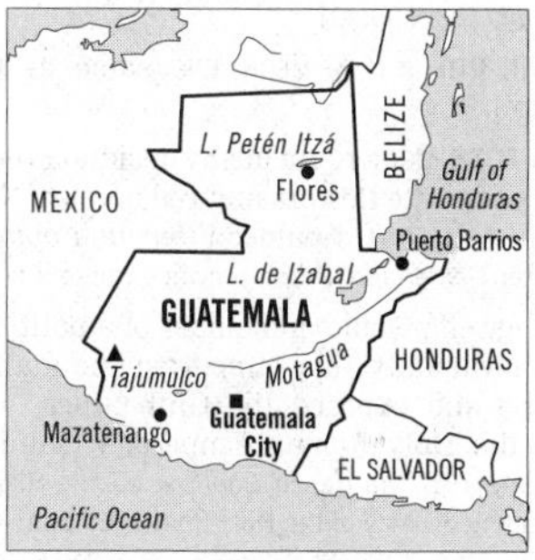

Guatemala

Gua·te·ma·la /gwaàtə maálə/ the third largest country in Central America, bordered by Belize, Mexico, the Gulf of Honduras, Honduras, and El Salvador. About two thirds of the total land area of Guatemala is mountainous. Language: Spanish. Currency: quetzal. Capital: Guatemala City. Population: 13,909,384 (2003). Area: 42,042 sq. mi./108,889 sq. km. Official name **Republic of Guatemala** —**Gua·te·ma·lan** *adj, n*

Gua·te·ma·la Cit·y capital city of Guatemala, located in the south central part of the country. It is the largest city in Central America and the nation's economic center. It was the capital of the United Provinces of Central America between 1823 and 1834. Population: 1,015,303 (2000).

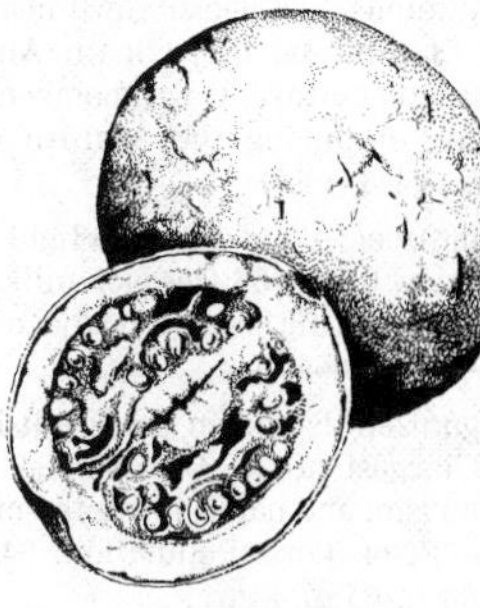

guava

gua·va /gwaávə/ *n* **1.** a pear-shaped fruit with red or yellow-green skin and cream or pink flesh. Use: eaten raw or made into jelly. **2.** a tree that produces guavas. Native to: tropical America. Genus: *Psidium.* [Mid-16C. < Spanish *guayaba*, of Caribbean Native American origin]

gua·ya·be·ra /gwaàyə bérrə/ *n Hispanic* a light short- or long-sleeved shirt, often pleated, with large pockets at the waist and usually worn outside the pants instead of a jacket [< American Spanish < *guayaba* "guava," from the large pockets supposedly used to carry guavas]

Gua·ya·quil /gwì ə keél/ largest city in Ecuador, situated in the west of the country. It is the capital of Guayas Province and Ecuador's main port. Population: 2,117,553 (2000). Full name **Santiago de Guayaquil**

gua·yu·le /gwaa yóolee/ *n Southwest US* **1.** rubber made from the sap of an American bush **2.** the bush whose sap is a source of guayule. Native to: southwestern United States, Mexico. Latin name: *Parthenium argentatum*. [Early 20C. Via American Spanish < Nahuatl *cuauhuli* "gum tree"]

gu·ber·na·to·ri·al /go͞obərnə tάwree əl/ *adj* relating to, involving, or associated with a governor [Mid-18C. < Latin *gubernator* "governor" < *gubernare* (see GOVERN)]

guck /guk/, **gook** /gook/ *n* a slimy, oily, gooey, or otherwise unpleasant substance (*informal*) [Mid-20C. Origin ?]

gudg·eon[1] /gújjən/ *n* a small freshwater fish that is often used as bait. Native to: Europe. Latin name: *Gobio gobio*. [14C. Via Old French *goujon* < Latin *gobius* (see GOBY)]

gudg·eon[2] /gújjən/ *n* a socket that a pin fits into, e.g., the pin of a hinge or the pivoting bolt of a ship's rudder [15C. < Old French *goujon* "little gouge" < late Latin *gubia* (see GOUGE)]

gudg·eon pin *n UK* MECH ENG same as **wrist pin** [< GUDGEON[2]]

guel·der rose /géldər-/ *n* a bushy deciduous bush with clusters of white flowers and red berries. Native to: Europe, Asia. Latin name: *Viburnum opulus*. [Late 16C. After *Gelderland*, Dutch province where it originated]

Guelph[1] /gwelf/, **Guelf** *n* a member of a political party in medieval Italy that supported the authority of the pope and opposed the Ghibellines, who supported the Holy Roman Emperor's claim to rule Italy [Late 16C. Via Italian *Guelfo* < Middle High German *Welf*, leading dynasty of the Holy Roman Empire] —**Guelph·ism** *n*

Guelph[2] /gwelf/ industrial city on the Speed River in southeastern Ontario, Canada, 60 mi./96 km west of Toronto. Population: 106,920 (2001).

gue·non /gə nón/ *n* a small long-tailed monkey that lives in trees. Native to: Africa. Genus: *Cercopithecus*. [Mid-19C. < French]

guer·don /gúrd'n/ *n* a reward or recompense (*literary*) [14C. Via Old French < medieval Latin *widerdonum* "repayment," partial translation of Old High German *widarlōn* "giving back"]

gue·ri·don /gérri dòn, gèrri dάwN/ *n* a small round ornate table or stand with a central pedestal [Mid-19C. After French, < a character in French farce]

gue·ril·la *n* MIL another spelling of **guerrilla**

SPELLCHECK See *gorilla*.

Guer·ni·ca /gwérnikə, ger néekə/ town near Bilbao in the Basque Country, northern Spain. An important center of Basque culture, it was bombed in 1937 by German aircraft during the Spanish Civil War. Population: 15,485 (1998).

guern·sey /gúrnzee/ (*plural* **-seys**) *n* a light-brown and white dairy cow that produces rich milk, belonging to a breed originating on the island of Guernsey [Early 19C. After GUERNSEY]

Guern·sey /gúrnzee/ island in the English Channel, the second largest of the Channel Islands. Dairy farming, tourism, and banking are the main trades. Capital: St. Peter Port. Population: 64,818 (2003). Area: 25 sq. mi./65 sq. km.

guer·ril·la /gə ríllə/, **gue·ril·la** *n* a member of an irregular paramilitary unit, usually with a political objective such as the overthrow of a government. Guerrillas usually operate in small groups to harass and carry out sabotage. ○ *guerrilla warfare* [Early 19C. < Spanish, "raiding party, skirmish" < *guerra* "war"]

SPELLCHECK See *gorilla*

guer·ril·la the·a·ter *n* THEATER same as **street theater**

guess /gess/ *v* (**guessed, guess·ing, guess·es**) **1.** *vti* PREDICT SOMETHING to form an opinion about something without enough evidence to make a definite judgment ○ *She guessed the number before he turned the card over.* ○ *Guess where I've been.* ○ *I could tell you what I think, but I'd only be guessing.* **2.** *vt* CONCLUDE SOMETHING CORRECTLY to arrive at a correct answer to or conjecture about something ○ *I guessed it would be you.* **3.** *vt* SUPPOSE SOMETHING to think or suppose something ○ *I guess I'll have the steak.* **4.** *vi* FIND CORRECT ANSWER to be correct in your thinking about what might be the case ○ *You'll never guess.* ■ *n* **1.** OPINION an opinion or answer arrived at by guessing ○ *My guess is she'll head for home.* **2.** ACT OF GUESSING an act or the process of guessing ○ *Take another guess.* [13C. < N Germanic < Germanic, "try to get"] —**guess·a·ble** *adj* —**guess·er** *n* ◇ **anybody's guess** something that cannot be reliably predicted (*informal*)

guess·ing game *n* **1.** a game in which players must identify an unknown word, person, or object by asking a series of questions to gain information **2.** a situation of which the outcome is frustratingly unpredictable

guess·ti·mate (*informal*) *n* /géstimət/ an estimate based largely on incomplete information or evidence ■ *vti* /gésti mȧyt/ (**-mat·ed, -mat·ing, -mates**) to make an estimate of something based largely on incomplete evidence or information [Mid-20C. Blend of GUESS + ESTIMATE]

guess·work /géss wùrk/ *n* the process of making guesses, or the conclusions arrived at by guessing

guest /gest/ *n* **1.** RECIPIENT OF HOSPITALITY somebody who receives hospitality from somebody else **2.** SOMEBODY ENTERTAINED AT ANOTHER'S EXPENSE a recipient of a meal or entertainment that is paid for by somebody else ○ *Club members are allowed to sign two people in as guests.* **3.** CUSTOMER somebody who pays to use the facilities of a hotel, restaurant, or other establishment **4.** SOMEBODY ASKED TO JOIN OTHERS somebody who is invited by an organization or institution to receive hospitality ○ *We have a distinguished guest at the meeting tonight.* **5.** SOMEBODY MAKING SPECIAL APPEARANCE somebody who appears by invitation on a radio or television program ○ *our special guest for tonight's show* **6.** ZOOL ANIMAL USING ANOTHER'S NEST an organism, especially an insect, that shares the shelter of another or lives alongside the other as a parasite ■ *v* (**guest·ed, guest·ing, guests**) **1.** *vi* MAKE SPECIAL APPEARANCE to appear as a guest on a radio or television program ○ *the trend for big-time movie stars to guest on sitcoms* **2.** *vt* ENTERTAIN SOMEBODY to entertain or play host to somebody ■ *adj* **1.** APPEARING AS GUEST appearing or invited as a guest ○ *a guest star* **2.** FOR GUESTS for guests to use ○ *the guest bedroom* [13C. < Old Norse *gestr*] ◇ **be my guest** used to tell people that they are welcome to do as they please (*informal*)

Guest /gest/, **Edgar A.** (1881–1959) British-born US poet. His popular verses were collected in anthologies such as *A Heap o' Livin'* (1916). Full name **Guest, Edgar Albert**

"The best of all the preachers are the men who live their creeds."
[Edgar A. Guest, "Sermons We See"; 1926]

guest book *n* a book or register that visitors or guests sign, e.g., at a bed-and-breakfast

guest·house /gést hòwss/ (*plural* **-hous·es** /-hòwzəz/) *n* **1.** a small house used to accommodate visitors to a main house **2.** *UK* a small hotel or private home that offers accommodations to paying guests

guest night *n* an evening during which nonmembers are welcome to participate in the activities of a club or society

guest of hon·or *n* somebody invited to attend a gathering or event who is seen as highly important or the most important of the invited guests

guest·room /gést ro͝om, -ro͞om/ *n* a bedroom for visitors who stay for a short time

guest star *n* a well-known performer who makes a single or occasional appearance in a television or radio program

guest-star *vti* to appear as a guest star, or feature somebody as a guest star

guest work·er *n* a foreign national allowed to come and work, but not take up permanent residence, in a European country

AKG London
Che Guevara

Gue·va·ra /gə vάarə/, **Che** (1928–67) Argentine-born South American revolutionary leader. A radical political theorist and guerrilla fighter, he played a significant part in Fidel Castro's revolution (1956–59) and early administration in Cuba. He was executed while planning an uprising in Bolivia. Born **Guevara de la Serna, Ernesto**

"In the laborious work of revolutionaries, death is a frequent accident."
[Che Guevara. Quoted in *We Say No*, Eduardo Galeano; 1992]

guff /guf/ *n* nonsense or empty talk (*informal*) [Early 19C. Probably suggesting a whiff of bad smelling air]

guf·faw /gə fάw/ *vi* (**-fawed, -faw·ing, -faws**) to laugh loudly and raucously ■ *n* a loud and raucous laugh [Early 18C. An imitation of the sound]

Gug·gen·heim /go͝oggən hīm/, **Meyer** (1828–1905) Swiss-born US financier and industrialist. With his seven sons, he established large mining and metal-processing companies.

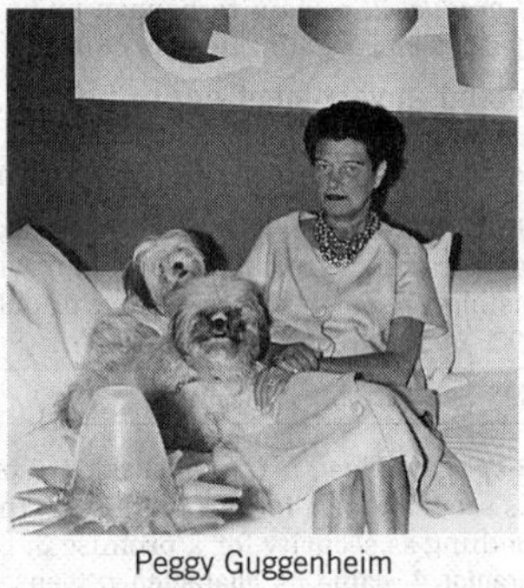
AKG London
Peggy Guggenheim

Gug·gen·heim, Peggy (1898–1979) US art collector and philanthropist. She helped to promote the careers of such avant-garde artists as Jackson Pollock and her husband Max Ernst. She was one of the earliest collectors of surrealist and abstract art. Full name **Guggenheim, Marguerite**

GUI /go͞o ee/ *abbr* COMPUT graphical user interface

Gui·an·a /gee ánnə, -άanə, gī-/ region of northeastern South America, bordering the Atlantic Ocean and including Guyana, Suriname, French Guiana, and parts of Venezuela and Brazil. Area: 690,000 sq. mi./1,787,100 sq. km.

guid·ance /gī́d'nss/ *n* **1.** LEADERSHIP leadership or direction **2.** ADVICE advice or counseling, especially counseling given to students on academic matters **3.** SYSTEMS THAT CONTROL FLIGHT the systems and devices that control the flight of an aircraft, missile, or spacecraft ○ *onboard guidance*

guid·ance coun·sel·or *n* in a high school, somebody who gives students personal, academic, and career counseling

guide /gīd/ *v* (**guid·ed, guid·ing, guides**) **1.** *vti* SHOW SOMEBODY THE WAY to lead somebody in the right direction **2.** *vt* ADVISE OR INFLUENCE SOMEBODY to advise or counsel somebody, or influence the way somebody behaves or acts ○ *Be guided by your conscience.* **3.** *vt* HELP SOMEBODY LEARN SOMETHING to teach somebody, or oversee training in something ○ *A tutor guided me through the intricacies of calculus.* **4.** *vt* RUN

ORGANIZATION to control the affairs of an organization or body **5.** *vt* STEER SOMETHING to steer a vehicle or animal ■ *n* **1.** SOMEBODY WHO SHOWS WAY somebody who leads and assists others in a place or toward a destination **2.** SOMEBODY WHO LEADS TOURISTS somebody who supervises a tour **3.** INFLUENCE ON DECISION a strong influence on the decisions and behavior of another ○ *Her grandmother's wisdom was her guide throughout life.* **4.** PUBL same as **guidebook** **5.** SOURCE OF INFORMATION a publication or a section of a magazine or newspaper giving information on a subject ○ *a movie guide* **6.** CONTROLLING DEVICE a device that controls the movement or operation of a machine **7.** SOLDIER CONTROLLING MARCH a soldier stationed at the side of a column of marching soldiers to control alignment and lead the way [14C. < Old French *guider* < Germanic] —**guid·a·ble** *adj*

SYNONYMS ***guide, conduct, direct, lead, steer, usher***

CORE MEANING: to show somebody the way to a place

guide to lead somebody in the right direction. ○ *Another rescue team, guided by a dog, located a woman alive under the rubble.* **conduct** to lead a person or group of people somewhere by going along with them ○ *He was conducted by an attendant through a maze of corridors to an enormous room.* **direct** to aim, point, or send something or somebody in a particular direction ○ *We didn't see a sign that would have directed us to the Roman site.* **lead** to show other people the way, usually by going ahead of them ○ *He led us into the house and introduced us to his two nieces.* **steer** to encourage somebody to take a particular course or route by unobtrusively guiding them ○ *She steered them all forward saying, "Let's not stand around. The car's over there."* **usher** to escort somebody to or from a place or a seat ○ *We were ushered to the front of the queue.* ○ *He ushered the young man into a comfortable chair on the far side of the room.*

guide·book /gī́d bo͝ok/ *n* a book containing information for tourists about a country, area, city, or institution

guid·ed mis·sile *n* a self-propelled missile that can be steered in flight by remote control or by an onboard homing device

guide dog *n* a dog trained to lead a sightless person

guide fos·sil *n* PALEONT same as **index fossil**

guide·line /gī́d lìn/ *n* **1.** an official recommendation indicating how something should be done or what sort of action should be taken in a particular circumstance **2.** a line that shows a correct position, route, or alignment, e.g., a fine line printed as an aid to lining up text or illustrations on a page

~~**guidence**~~ incorrect spelling of **guidance**

guide·post /gī́d pòst/ *n* something that serves as an example or is recommended as a rule to live by

guid·er /gī́dər/ *n N Ireland* a vehicle made from planks and wheels to help children learn to walk

guide·rail /gī́d ràyl/ *n* a rail designed to lead somebody in the right direction or help somebody move along, or to control the sideways movement of something

guide rope *n* a rope attached to an object or to another rope or cable and used to maneuver it into position or to steady a load

guide·way /gī́d wày/ *n* a groove or channel that controls the direction in which a moving object travels

guide word *n US* a word printed at the top of a page in a dictionary or other reference book, usually the first or last entry for that page. Can term **catchword**

guid·ing light /gī̀ding-/ *n* somebody or something that is a guide, example, or inspiration

Gui·do d'A·rez·zo /gwe̅e̅dō da rétsō/ (990?–1033?) Italian monk and music theorist. He introduced the four-line staff for musical notation and the system of using syllables to name the notes of the scale.

gui·don /gī́ dòn, gī́d'n/ *n* a regimental flag or pennant, or the soldier who carries it [Mid-16C. Via French < Italian *guidone* < *guida* "guide"]

guild /gild/, **gild** *n* **1.** ASSOCIATION OF PEOPLE WITH SIMILAR INTERESTS a club, society, or other organization of people with common interests or goals **2.** MEDIEVAL TRADE ASSOCIATION an association of merchants or craftspersons in medieval Europe, formed to give help and advice to its members and to make regulations and set standards for a particular trade **3.** GROUP OF ORGANISMS a group of organisms that use the same environmental resources in a similar way [14C. Probably < Middle Low German, Middle Dutch *gilde* < Germanic] —**guild·ship** *n* —**guilds·man** *n* —**guilds·wo·man** *n*

SPELLCHECK guild or **gild**? Do not confuse the spelling of ***guild*** and ***gild***, which sound similar. ***Guild*** is a noun denoting an association of people, as in *a guild of craftspersons.* ***Gild*** is a verb meaning "cover with gold" or "tinge with a golden color," as in *gild a picture frame, clouds gilded by the setting sun.* Note that the noun ***guild*** can also be spelled ***gild***, but the verb ***gild*** cannot be spelled ***guild***.

guil·der /gíldər/, **gul·den** /go͝oldən/ (*plural* **-dens** or *same*) *n* **1.** FORMER CURRENCY UNIT OF NETHERLANDS the main unit of the former currency of the Netherlands **2.** CURRENCY UNIT OF SURINAME the main unit of currency of Suriname. See table at **currency** **3.** OLD COIN a gold or silver coin formerly used in Germany, Austria, and the Netherlands [15C. Alteration of Dutch *gulden* "golden"]

guild·hall /gíld hàwl/ *n* the meeting place of a modern or medieval guild

guild so·cial·ism *n* a socialist movement in Great Britain in the early 20th century that advocated state ownership of industry but with each branch managed by guilds of workers —**guild so·cial·ist** *n*

guile /gīl/ *n* a cunning, deceitful, or treacherous quality [13C. Via French < Old Norse] —**guile·ful** *adj* —**guile·ful·ly** *adv* —**guile·ful·ness** *n*

guile·less /gī́l ləss/ *adj* open and honest and not expecting others to behave differently —**guile·less·ly** *adv* —**guile·less·ness** *n*

Guil·ford /gílfərd/ town in southern Connecticut, situated on Long Island Sound east of New Haven. Population: 21,868 (2002 estimate).

Gui·lin /gwày lín/ city in northeastern Guangxi Zhuangzu Province, southern China. It is located in a scenic limestone region made famous by Chinese classical painters and poets. Population: 376,362 (1991).

guil·le·mot /gíllə mòt/ *n* a black-and-white narrow-beaked diving seabird of the auk family. Native to: northern Atlantic, northern Pacific. Genera: *Uria* or *Cepphus.* [Late 17C. < French, "little William"]

guil·loche /gi lṓsh, gee yṓsh/ *n* in architecture, an ornamental border formed by two or more interlaced bands around a series of interlocking circles [19C. < French]

guil·lo·tine /gíllə te̅e̅n/ *n* **1.** MACHINE FOR BEHEADING PEOPLE a machine for executing people by beheading, consisting of a vertical wooden frame with grooves for a heavy sliding blade to be dropped from a height onto the person's neck. It became famous for its use during the French Revolution. **2.** DEATH BY GUILLOTINE execution by means of the guillotine **3.** INSTRUMENT FOR CUTTING METAL OR PAPER a cutting instrument, especially one for cutting sheet metal or paper, consisting of a platform with a sheet blade attached to one side that is pulled down like a lever **4.** *UK* TIME LIMIT ON LEGISLATIVE DEBATE a limit on the time available for debate on a piece of legislation, designed to speed up parliamentary proceedings and prevent opponents of the legislation from obstructing its progress [Late 18C. After Joseph-Ignace *Guillotin* (1738–1814), French physician] —**guil·lo·tine** *vt*

guilt /gilt/ *n* **1.** AWARENESS OF WRONGDOING an awareness of having done wrong or committed a crime, accompanied by feelings of shame and regret ○ *feelings of guilt* **2.** FACT OF WRONGDOING the fact of having committed a crime or done wrong ○ *an admission of guilt* **3.** RESPONSIBILITY FOR WRONGDOING the responsibility for committing a crime or doing wrong ○ *Some of the guilt must attach to the parents.* **4.** LEGAL CULPABILITY the responsibility, as determined by a court or other legal authority, for committing an offense that carries a legal penalty [Old English *gylt*, origin ?]

SPELLCHECK guilt or **gilt**? Do not confuse the spelling of ***guilt*** and ***gilt***, which sound similar. ***Guilt*** is a noun denoting the fact or awareness of having done wrong: *Guilt was written all over her face.* ***Gilt*** is a noun or adjective referring to a thin layer of gold (as in *lettering in gilt, gilt picture frames*).

guilt·less /gíltləss/ *adj* not responsible for a crime or wrongdoing, or not deserving blame or criticism —**guilt·less·ly** *adv* —**guilt·less·ness** *n*

guilt trip *n* an exaggerated feeling or display of shame and regret, usually lasting some time (*slang*)

guilt·y /gíltee/ (**-i·er, -i·est**) *adj* **1.** RESPONSIBLE FOR WRONGDOING responsible for a crime, wrong action, or error and deserving punishment, blame, or criticism ○ *He was guilty of a serious error of judgment.* **2.** OFFICIALLY FOUND RESPONSIBLE FOR CRIME found and declared responsible for committing an offense by a court or other legal authority **3.** ASHAMED OF WRONGDOING aware of having done wrong or committed a crime and regretful and ashamed about it ○ *I still feel guilty about having forgotten your birthday.* **4.** SHOWING GUILT indicating or suggesting that somebody feels guilt, has done wrong, or has something to hide ○ *a guilty look on his face* **5.** CAUSING GUILT causing or likely to cause emotions of shame and regret ○ *a guilty secret* —**guilt·i·ly** *adv* —**guilt·i·ness** *n*

guilt·y con·science *n* a feeling of shame at having done wrong

Gui·mard /gee maár/, **Hector** (1867–1942) French architect. One of the most important figures of the art nouveau movement, he is best known for Castel Béranger (1898) in Paris and his designs for the entrances to several Paris Métro stations (1899–1905). Full name **Guimard, Hector Germain**

guimpe[1] /gamp, gimp/ *n* **1.** a short blouse designed to be worn under a jumper **2.** a starched cloth that covers the neck and shoulders, worn by some nuns as part of their habit [Mid-19C. < French < Old French *guimple* "wimple"]

guimpe[2] *n* CLOTHING another spelling of **gimp**[1]

Guin ➧ **Le Guin, Ursula**

guin·ea /gínnee/ *n* **1.** OLD UNIT OF BRITISH CURRENCY a gold coin worth 21 shillings (£1.05p) that was a British unit of currency between 1663 and 1813 **2.** AMOUNT EQUIVALENT TO £1.05 an amount equivalent to £1.05 or 21 shillings, the value of a guinea **3.** TABOO TERM a highly offensive term for an Italian person or a person of Italian descent (*taboo*) [Mid-16C. Because first made for trade with the *Guinea* coast of W Africa, In sense 3 < earlier use of a Black person newly arrived from W Africa]

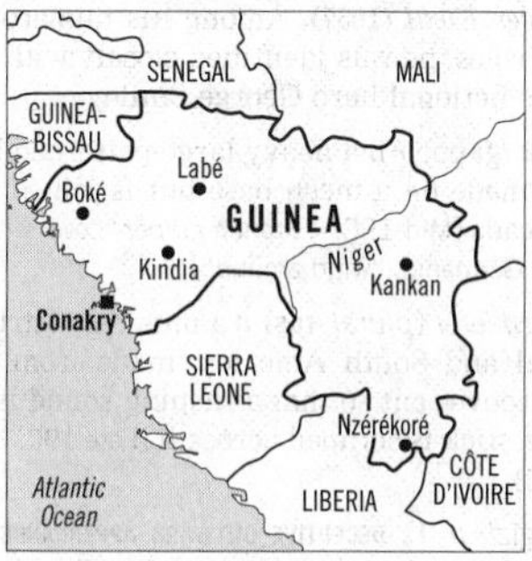

Guinea

Guin·ea /gínnee/ country in West Africa, between Guinea-Bissau and Sierra Leone. It became independent from France in 1958. Language: French. Currency: Guinean franc. Capital: Conakry. Population: 9,030,220 (2003). Area: 94,926 sq. mi./245,857 sq. km. Official name **Republic of Guinea** —**Guin·e·an** *adj, n*

Guin·ea, Gulf of arm of the Atlantic Ocean, West Africa, between Cape Palmas, at the southeastern tip of Liberia, and Cape Lopez, Gabon. The gulf forms two bays, the Bight of Benin and the Bight of Bonny (Biafra).

Guinea-Bissau

Guin·ea-Bis·sau /gìnnee bi sów/ country in West Africa, between Senegal and Guinea. It became independent from Portugal in 1974. Language: Portuguese. Currency: CFA franc. Capital: Bissau. Population: 1,360,827 (2003). Area: 13,948 sq. mi./ 36,125 sq. km. Official name **Republic of Guinea-Bissau**

guin·ea fowl /gínnee fòwl/ *n* a bird that is related to pheasants, is typically black with white speckles, and has a short tail and a bare head and neck. Raised for: food. Native to: Africa. Family: Numididae. [Late 18C. After the *Guinea* coast of W Africa]

guin·ea grass *n* a tall grass grown in Central and South America and parts of the United States. Use: animal fodder. Native to: Africa. Latin name: *Panicum maximum*. [Mid-18C. After the *Guinea* coast of W Africa]

guin·ea pig *n* **1.** a plump short-eared furry domesticated rodent that is similar to but larger than a hamster and is widely kept as a pet. Native to: South America. Latin name: *Cavia porcellus*. **2.** somebody or something used as the subject of an experiment, test, or trial [Mid-17C. After the *Guinea* coast of W Africa, probably from confusion with GUYANA]

guin·ea worm *n* a long thin worm that lives as a parasite under the skin of people and animals and can grow to several feet in length. Native to: Africa, Asia. Latin name: *Dracunculus medinensis*. [Late 17C. After the *Guinea* coast of W Africa]

guinep *n* **1.** *Carib* a small round fruit, with a hard green casing and slightly astringent edible yellowish pulp covering a large round seed **2.** a slow-growing tree that produces guineps. Native to: tropical America. Latin name: *Melicoccus bijugatus*.

Guin·e·vere /gwínni vèer/ *n* in Arthurian legend, the wife of King Arthur and the lover of the knight Sir Lancelot

Guin·ness /gínnəss/, **Sir Alec** (1914–2000) British actor. He won an Academy Award for *The Bridge on the River Kwai* (1957). Among his numerous other movie roles, he was identified closely with John Le Carré's fictional hero George Smiley.

gui·pure /gi pòor/ *n* a heavy large-patterned lace that is not made on a mesh base but is joined together by threads [Mid-19C. < French *guiper* "cover with cloth or yarn" < Germanic, "wind around"]

gui·ro /gwèerō/ (*plural* **-ros**) *n* a musical instrument of Central and South America, made from a gourd with grooves cut so that a rasping sound is created when a stick is scraped across it [Late 19C. < Spanish, "gourd"]

guise /gīz/ *n* **1.** DECEPTIVE OUTWARD APPEARANCE a false outward appearance ○ *hiding her treacherous intentions under the guise of friendship* **2.** FORM OR APPEARANCE a shape or form, especially a changed one, in which something presents itself or is presented ○ *old ideas in a new guise* **3.** COSTUME a style of dress or personal appearance [14C. < French < Germanic]

gui·tar /gi taár/ *n* a musical instrument with a long neck, a flat body shaped like a figure eight, and usually six strings that are plucked or strummed [Early 17C. Via Spanish *guitarra* < Greek *kithara* "cithara"] —**gui·tar·ist** *n*

gui·tar·fish /gi taár fish/ (*plural* **-fish·es** or *same*) *n* a ray with large curving pectoral fins that give its body a guitar shape. Native to: tropical and subtropical waters. Family: Rhinobatidae.

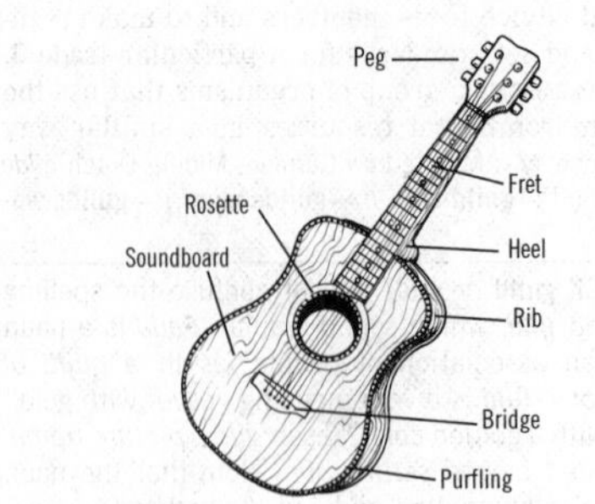

guitar

Gui·yang /gwày yáng/ industrial city in southern China and capital of Guizhou Province. Population: 1,930,000 (1995).

Gui·zhou /gwày jṓ/ province in southwestern China, dominated by a high plateau. Capital: Guiyang. Population: 35,550,000 (1997). Area: 67,182 sq. mi./ 174,000 sq. km.

Gui·zot /gee zṓ/, **François Pierre Guillaume** (1787–1874) French politician and historian. He served as minister of education (1832–37) and foreign minister (1840–47) before becoming prime minister (1847–48). The moderate liberal policies of his earlier years gave way to a more conservative philosophy toward the end of his career.

Gu·ja·rat /gòojə raát/ state in western India, bordered in the northwest by Pakistan and in the south and southwest by the Arabian Sea. Language: Gujarati. Capital: Gandhinagar. Population: 50,596,992 (2001). Area: 75,685 sq. mi./196,024 sq. km.

Gu·ja·ra·ti /gòojə raátee/ (*plural same*), **Gu·je·ra·ti** *n* **1.** an Indic language spoken in the Indian states of Gujarat and Maharashtra and in southern parts of Pakistan, belonging to the Indo-Iranian branch of Indo-European languages. Native speakers: 35 million. **2.** a member of a people living mainly in the Indian state of Gujarat [Early 19C. < Hindi] —**Gu·ja·ra·ti** *adj*

Guj·ran·wa·la /gooj raán wùllə/, **Guj·rān·wā·la** city in northeastern Pakistan, in Punjab Province. Population: 1,124,799 (1998).

gul /gool, gòol/ *n* a large octagonal motif used in the patterns on Oriental rugs and resembling a rose with straight-sided petals [Early 20C. < Persian, "rose"]

gu·lab ja·mun /gòo laáb yaámòon/ *n S Asia* in Indian cuisine, deep-fried dough served in a sugar syrup flavored with rose water [< Hindi *gulāb* "rose water" + *jāmun* "fruit"]

gu·lag /gòo laág/ *n* **1.** POLITICAL PRISON IN FORMER USSR a prison or labor camp in the former Soviet Union, to which opponents of the government were sent **2.** PRISON CAMP NETWORK IN FORMER USSR the network of political prisons and labor camps in the former Soviet Union **3.** FORMER SOVIET PRISONS DEPARTMENT the department of the former Soviet security service that was responsible for running the network of political prisons **4.** PRISON FOR DISSENTERS any place that dissenters are sent to, or the isolating or imprisoning of dissenters [Mid-20C. < Russian, acronym < *Glavnoe upravlenie ispravitelno-trudovykh lagerei* "Chief Administration for Corrective Labor Camps"]

gulch /gulch/ *n* a small rocky ravine, especially one with a fast-flowing stream running through it (*often used in place names*) [Mid-19C. Origin ?]

gules /gyoolz/ *n* the color red on a coat of arms [14C. < Old French *go(u)les* "red fur garment like a scarf" < plural of *go(u)le* (see GULLET)]

gulf /gulf/ *n* **1.** INLET OF OCEAN a large inlet of an ocean similar to a bay but often longer and more enclosed by land (*often used in place names*) ○ *the Gulf of Mexico* **2.** VAST DIFFERENCE a great difference, e.g., in points of view, regarded as dividing or separating people or groups **3.** WIDE HOLE a deep wide hole in the ground [14C. Via French *golfe* < Greek *kolfos* "bosom, bag, trough between waves, abyss"]

Gulf·port /gúlf pàwrt/ **1.** city in Pinellas County, west central Florida, a suburb of St. Petersburg. Population: 12,568 (2002 estimate). **2.** city and port in Harrison County, southeastern Mississippi, situated on the Gulf of Mexico. Population: 72,511 (2002 estimate).

Gulf States *n* **1.** the states of the southern United States that border the Gulf of Mexico, namely Florida, Alabama, Mississippi, Louisiana, and Texas **2.** the countries that border the Persian Gulf, considered as an economic or geopolitical unit, especially in their role as oil producers. The Gulf States are Iran, Iraq, Kuwait, Saudi Arabia, Bahrain, Qatar, the United Arab Emirates, and Oman.

Gulf Stream *n* a warm current that originates in the Gulf of Mexico and flows northeastward along the coast of North America toward Newfoundland then eastward across the Atlantic Ocean to the coasts of the British Isles

Gulf War *n* **1.** the war that took place in January and February 1991 in the Persian Gulf between United Nations forces and Iraq, following the invasion of Kuwait by Iraq in August 1990. It resulted in the withdrawal of Iraq from Kuwait. **2.** the war that took place in 2003 in Iraq between the attacking forces of the United States, United Kingdom, and Australia and troops loyal to Iraqi president Saddam Hussein **3.** MIL, HIST same as **Iran-Iraq War**

Gulf War syn·drome *n* a group of medical symptoms, including fatigue, skin disorders, and muscle pains, experienced by some soldiers who fought in the Gulf War of 1991. These conditions are believed by some people to have been caused by exposure to pesticides, vaccines, and chemical and biological warfare agents.

gulf·weed /gúlf wèed/ *n* a brown seaweed that forms thick floating masses. Native to: tropical Atlantic. Genus: *Sargassum*.

gull

gull[1] /gul/ *n* a common, fairly large, web-footed white-and-gray seabird usually with a yellow or red beak. Native to: North American and European coasts. Family: Laridae. [15C. < Celtic] —**gull·er·y** *n*

gull[2] /gul/ *vt* (**gulled, gull·ing, gulls**) to trick or deceive somebody (*often passive*) ■ *n* somebody regarded as easily deceived [Mid-16C. Origin ?]

Gul·lah /gúllə/ (*plural* **-lahs** or *same*) *n* **1.** a member of a people of African descent who live along the coasts of South Carolina, Georgia, and northern Florida, and on the neighboring Sea Islands **2.** the creole language of the Gullah people, a form of English that has been influenced by several West African languages. Native speakers: 300,000. [Mid-18C. Origin ?] —**Gul·lah** *adj*

gul·let /gúllət/ *n* **1.** the esophagus or throat **2.** a groove or indentation in the protoplasm of some protozoans that has a function in the intake of food [14C. < Old French *goulet* "little throat" < *go(u)le* "throat" < Latin *gula*]

gul·li·ble /gúlləb'l/ *adj* tending to trust and believe people, and therefore easily tricked or deceived [Early 19C. < GULL[2]] —**gul·li·bil·i·ty** /gùllə bíllətee/ *n* —**gul·li·bly** *adv*

gull·wing /gúl wìng/ *adj* describes a type of car door that is hinged at the top and opens upward ■ *n* an aircraft wing in which the section attached to the fuselage slants upward and the outer section is horizontal, or an aircraft with such a wing

gul·ly /gúllee/ *n* (*plural* **-lies**) **1. SMALL VALLEY** a channel or small valley, especially one carved out by persistent heavy rainfall **2. NARROW MOUNTAIN PASSAGE** a narrow passage between two rocky slopes on a mountain **3. CHANNEL MADE FOR WATER** a gutter, open drain, or other artificial channel for water, especially one at a roadside ■ *vti* (**-lied, -ly·ing, -lies**) **CUT OUT CHANNELS** to wear away channels in land or soil, or be worn into channels [Mid-17C. < French *goulet* (see GULLET)]

gul·ly·wash·er /gúllee wòshər, -wàwshər/ *n* a heavy downpour or its runoff (*informal*)

REGIONAL NOTE See ***trashmover***.

gulp /gulp/ *v* (**gulped, gulp·ing, gulps**) **1.** *vt* **SWALLOW SOMETHING FAST** to swallow something greedily, hurriedly, or frantically, taking in large amounts at a time ○ *She gulped down her coffee and grabbed her coat.* **2.** *vi* **GASP** to gasp or choke **3.** *vi* **MAKE SWALLOWING MOTION** to make a swallowing movement with the throat, especially because of being frightened or nervous ○ *He gulped and looked around nervously for the exit.* **4.** *vi* **MAKE SWALLOWING SOUND** to make a loud swallowing sound with the throat, especially because of drinking too fast ■ *n* **1. SWALLOWING MOTION OR SOUND** a swallowing movement or noise made with the throat **2. AMOUNT SWALLOWED** a quantity of something, especially drink, consumed in one large swallow [15C. Probably < Middle Dutch *gulpen* "swallow, guzzle"] —**gulp·er** *n* —**gulp·ing·ly** *adv*

gulp back *vt* to attempt to stifle tears or sobs

gum[1] /gum/ *n* **1.** same as **chewing gum** (*informal*) **2. STICKY PLANT SUBSTANCE THAT HARDENS** a sticky substance found inside some plants, especially trees, that hardens when it is exposed to air and dissolves when put in water **3. ANY STICKY PLANT SUBSTANCE** any sticky substance found inside plants, e.g., a resin **4. SOMETHING STICKY** any sticky substance or deposit **5. ADHESIVE** glue made from a sticky plant substance, or any soft synthetic glue used for sticking paper or other lightweight materials **6. TREE PRODUCING GUM** any tree that produces gum. Genera: *Eucalyptus* or *Liquidambar* or *Nyssa*. ■ *vt* (**gummed, gum·ming, gums**) **STICK SOMETHING TO SOMETHING ELSE** to stick something to something else, with or without gum or glue [14C. Via Old French *gomme* < Greek *kommi* < Egyptian *kemai*]

gum up *vt* to block or immobilize something with a sticky substance that prevents parts from moving ○ *eyes all gummed up* ◇ **gum up the works** to bring everything to a halt, usually by being obstructive or incompetent (*informal*)

gum[2] /gum/ *n* the firm flesh that surrounds the roots of the teeth (*often used in the plural*) ■ *vt* to chew food with the gums as a result of having no teeth (*informal*) [Old English *goma*, origin ?]

gum a·ca·cia *n* INDUST same as **gum arabic**

gum ac·croi·des /-ə króydeez/ *n* INDUST, MED same as **acaroid resin**

gum am·mo·ni·ac *n* INDUST same as **ammoniac**

gum a·ra·bic *n* a sticky substance taken from some acacia trees. Use: in adhesives, confectionery, medicines. [Because the trees grow in the Middle East]

gum·ball /gúm bàwl/ *n* a ball of chewing gum with a thin candy shell, bought from a machine

gum·bo /gúmbō/ (*plural* **-bos**) *n* **1. THICK STEW WITH OKRA** a stew of fish, poultry, or meat that has been thickened with okra **2.** PLANTS same as **okra** (senses 1–2) **3. STICKY SOIL** silty soil that turns very sticky and muddy when it becomes wet, found throughout the central United States **4. MIXTURE** a mixture or hodgepodge (*informal*) ○ *The band played a gumbo of Cajun, zydeco, and jazz music.* [Early 19C. < Louisiana French *gombo*, probably < Bantu]

Gum·bo *n* a French patois, incorporating aspects of African languages, that is spoken in Louisiana and the Caribbean —**Gum·bo** *adj*

gum·boil /gúm bòyl/ *n* an abscess on the gum, especially near the root of a decayed tooth

gum·bo-lim·bo *n* a deciduous tree that produces elemi resin. Native to: Florida, Central America, Caribbean. Latin name: *Bursera simaruba*. [Mid-19C. Origin ?]

gum boot *n* a waterproof boot made of rubber or plastic, especially one that comes to just below the knee (*dated*)

gum dam·mar *n* INDUST same as **dammar**

gum·drop /gúm dròp/ *n* a chewy fruit-flavored candy coated with sugar

gum·ma /gúmmə/ (*plural* **-ma·ta** /-mətə/ or **-mas**) *n* a rubbery tumor that can occur in the tertiary stage of syphilis [Early 18C. Via Modern Latin < Greek *kommi* (see GUM[1])] —**gum·ma·tous** *adj*

gum·mo·sis /gə mṓssiss/ *n* the production of too much gum by a tree, especially a fruit tree, as a result of infection, a wound, or adverse weather

gum·mous /gúmməss/ *adj* **1.** sticky like the gum from a tree **2.** containing gum

gum·my[1] /gúmmee/ (**-mi·er, -mi·est**) *adj* **1.** like gum, especially in being sticky or thick and slow-flowing **2.** covered, clogged, or stuck together with a sticky substance [14C. < GUM[1]] —**gum·mi·ness** *n*

gum·my[2] /gúmmee/ (**-mi·er, -mi·est**) *adj* with only the gums showing, but no teeth, usually because the person concerned has no teeth [Late 19C. < GUM[2]] —**gum·mi·ly** *adv*

gump /gump/ *vi* to muddle through difficult situations thanks to a series of lucky chances (*slang*) [Late 20C. < the 1994 movie *Forrest Gump*]

CULTURAL NOTE ***Forrest Gump***, a movie (1994) by Robert Zemeckis. It is the sentimental tale of a mentally challenged boy who grows up to become a sports star, war hero, and successful business executive thanks to his uncomplicated world-view, traditional moral values, and uncanny ability to be in the right place at the right time.

gum plant *n* a plant with sticky flower heads or leaves. Native to: North America. Genus: *Grindelia*.

gump·tion /gúmpshən/ *n* (*informal*) **1.** the courage to take what action is needed ○ *He wouldn't have the gumption to say so, even if he disagreed.* **2.** practical common sense and presence of mind ○ *Luckily, he had the gumption to call the police.* [Early 18C. Origin ?]

gum res·in *n* a naturally occurring mixture of gum and resin taken from some plants and trees, e.g., the yellow pigment gamboge

gum·shield /gúm shēeld/ *n UK* SPORTS same as **mouth guard**

gum·shoe /gúm shoo/ *n* a detective, especially a private investigator (*informal*) [< moving with stealth in rubber overshoes]

gum tree *n* any tree that produces gum. Genera: *Eucalyptus* or *Liquidambar* or *Nyssa*.

gum·wood /gúm wòod/ *n* wood from any gum tree, especially a eucalyptus tree

gun /gun/ *n* **1. WEAPON THAT FIRES BULLETS** any weapon, from a small handheld pistol to a large piece of artillery, that has a metal tube through which bullets or missiles are fired by an explosive charge **2. DEVICE THAT FIRES SOMETHING** any tool or instrument that forces something out under pressure ○ *a paint gun* **3. SHOT FROM GUN** a shot fired from a gun, e.g., as a military salute or a signal for a race to begin, or the sound of the shot ○ *Wait for the gun.* **4. SOMEBODY WITH GUN** somebody who is armed with a gun (*informal*) ○ *the fastest gun in the West* **5. GAS PEDAL** a vehicle's gas pedal (*informal*) ○ *Give it the gun.* **6. HUNTER** a member of a party of hunters armed with shotguns ■ *vt* (**gunned, gun·ning, guns**) **PRESS THROTTLE** to rev up an engine (*informal*) [14C. Probably < Scandinavian name *Gunnhildr* < *gunnr* "battle" + *hildr* "war," from the custom of giving women's names to weapons] ◇ **go great guns** to be working, operating, or doing something at great speed or very effectively and successfully ◇ **jump the gun 1.** to start a race before the starting gun goes off **2.** to act prematurely ◇ **stick to your guns** to refuse to change your plans or opinions even though you are under attack from other people ◇ **under the gun** under great pressure ◇ **with (both) guns blazing** in a determined aggressive way

gun down *vt* to shoot and kill or severely injure somebody (*informal*)

gun for *vt* (*informal*) **1.** to set out to attack or criticize somebody or bring about somebody's downfall **2.** to plan or intend to get something for yourself ○ *She's gunning for a position in the Paris office.*

gun·boat /gún bōt/ *n* a small fast ship with large guns mounted on it, used, e.g., by the Coast Guard

gun·boat di·plo·ma·cy *n* negotiations between nations that involve threats to use military force

gun car·riage *n* a platform with wheels on which a large military gun is mounted and transported or on which a coffin is laid during state funerals

gun con·trol *n* legal measures to license, control, or restrict the ownership of firearms by members of the public

gun·cot·ton /gún kòtt'n/ *n* CHEM, INDUST same as **nitrocellulose**

gun court *n* a court that hears only cases that deal with gun-related crimes

gun deck *n* the deck of a sailing warship, below the main deck, where the cannons were situated

gun dog *n* **1.** a dog trained to find game and to bring back any game shot by a hunter or gamekeeper **2.** a dog of a breed that is traditionally regarded as suitable for training as a hunter's or gamekeeper's dog

gun·fight /gún fìt/ *n* a fight between two or more people armed with handguns, especially in the days of the Wild West —**gun·fight·er** *n*

gun·fire /gún fìr/ *n* shots fired from a gun or guns, or the sound of shots

gun·flint /gún flint/ *n* a small piece of flint that ignites the gunpowder in an old-fashioned flintlock gun

gunge /gunj/ *n UK* an unpleasantly sticky, slimy, or messy semiliquid substance (*informal*) [Mid-20C. Origin ?] —**gun·gy** *adj*

gung ho *adj* (*informal; hyphenated when used before a noun*) **1.** extremely or excessively enthusiastic or eager **2.** eager to fight, especially in a military conflict [Mid-20C. < Chinese *hónghé* "work together" (shortening of *gongyèhézuòshè* "Chinese Industrial Cooperative Society"), motto of US marines in Asia in World War II]

gun·ite /gú nìt/ *n* a concrete building material that is sprayed from a high-pressure gun onto a mold or over reinforced concrete or steel in light construction

gunk /gungk/ *n* a greasy messy near-solid mass (*informal*) [Mid-20C. Probably invented to suggest lumpy grease] —**gunk·y** *adj*

gun lap *n* in track, the last lap of a race, signaled by the firing of a gun as the lead runner begins it

gun lob·by *n* lobbyist groups who argue for the right of ordinary members of the public to buy and own guns. The gun lobby resists legislative attempts to put conditions on the ownership and availability of firearms and ammunition.

gun·lock /gún lòk/ *n* the mechanism by which the gunpowder charge was exploded in early types of guns, e.g., flintlock, matchlock, or wheel lock

gun·man /gúnmən/ (*plural* **-men** /-mən/) *n* **1.** a man armed with a gun, especially a criminal or an assassin **2.** a man skilled in firing guns

gun·met·al /gún mètt'l/ *n* **1. GRAY BRONZE FOR CANNONS** a dark gray bronze. Use: formerly, to make cannons. **2. DARK GRAY METAL** a dark gray alloy. Use: formerly, household and industrial items, children's toys. **3.** *also* **gun·met·al gray DARK GRAY COLOR** a dark bluish gray color —**gun·met·al** *adj* —**gun·met·al-gray** *adj*

Gun·nar /gṓonaar, -ər/ *n* in Norse mythology, the husband of Brynhild, won for him by Sigurd who assumes Gunnar's form

Gunn ef·fect /gún-/ *n* in a semiconductor, the microwave oscillation produced by a steady electric field that is larger than the normal threshold value [Mid-20C. After J. B. Gunn, (1928–), Egyptian-born British physicist]

gun·nel[1] /gúnn'l/ *n* NAUT same as **gunwale**

gun·nel[2] /gúnn'l/ (*plural* **-nels** or *same*) *n* a small fish that is similar to an eel. Native to: Atlantic and Pacific coastal waters. Family: Pholidae. [Late 17C. Origin ?]

Gun·nell /gúnn'l/, **Sally** (*b.* 1966) British athlete. She dominated 400-meter hurdle running in the 1990s. Full name **Gunnell, Sally Janet**

gun·ner /gúnnər/ *n* **1. SOLDIER WHO FIRES LARGE GUN** a soldier who operates a large gun **2. NCO WITH GUN-RELATED RESPONSIBILITIES** a warrant officer in the US Marines or the British navy who is responsible for training gun operators and running the ammunition stores **3. ARTILLERY SOLDIER** a soldier in an artillery regiment, especially a private

gun·ner·a /gúnnərə/ (*plural* **-as**) *n* a tropical plant with huge leaves. Native to: South America. Genus: *Gunnera*. [Late 18C. < modern Latin, after J. E. *Gunnerus* (1718–73), Norwegian botanist]

gun·ner·y /gúnnəree/ *n* **1.** the knowledge and techniques involved in the effective use of guns or in their design and construction **2.** the use of guns, especially of large guns in battle

gun·ner·y ser·geant *n* a noncommissioned officer in the US Marine Corps of a rank above staff sergeant

gun·ny /gúnnee/ (*plural* **-nies**) *n* **1.** coarse jute or hemp cloth **2.** *UK* TEXTILES same as **gunnysack** [Early 18C. < Hindi *gonī*]

gun·ny·sack /gúnnee sàk/ *n* a sack made from coarse jute or hemp

gun·per·son /gún pùrss'n/ (*plural* **-per·sons** or **-peo·ple** /-peèp'l/) *n* somebody who is armed with a gun

gun·play /gún plày/ *n* the shooting of guns, especially by armed criminals

gun·point /gún pòynt/ *n* the muzzle of a firearm ◇ **at gunpoint** under the threat of being shot and killed if orders are not obeyed

gun·pow·der /gún pòwdər/ *n* an explosive mixture of potassium nitrate, charcoal, and sulfur. Use: in fireworks and other explosives, e.g., in quarry blasting, and, formerly, as the charge in firearms.

Gunpowder Plot *n* a conspiracy by a group of Roman Catholics, including Guy Fawkes, to blow up the English parliament in 1605

gun·pow·der tea *n* Chinese green tea with individual leaves rolled into small pellets

gun·room /gún ròom, -ròòm/ *n* **1.** a room in a house where guns are kept, especially shotguns **2.** the quarters of midshipmen and junior officers on a ship in the British navy

gun·run·ning /gún rùnning/ *n* the smuggling of illegal arms into a country, usually in order to supply terrorist or insurrectionist organizations —**gun·run·ner** *n*

gun·sel /gúnss'l/ *n* **1.** a violent criminal, especially one who carries a gun (*slang*) **2.** an offensive term for a young gay man living with and supported by an older gay man (*slang insult*) [Early 20C. Via Yiddish *gendzel* < German *Gänslein* "gosling"]

gun·ship /gún shìp/ *n* helicopter that is fitted with guns for use against ground targets

gun·shot /gún shòt/ *n* **1. GUN'S NOISE** the sound of a gun being fired **2. BULLETS FIRED** bullets or shot fired from a gun **3. GUN'S RANGE** the maximum distance that a bullet fired from a gun can travel

gun-shy *adj* **1.** extremely cautious, timid, or wary of taking risks **2.** afraid of guns or the noise they make when fired

gun·sight /gún sīt/ *n* a device on a gun, often a projection on the barrel or a small telescope attached to the gun, used to assist somebody in aiming it

gun·sling·er /gún slìngər/ *n* an armed fighter or criminal, especially in the frontier days of the Wild West (*informal*) —**gun·sling·ing** *n*

gun·smith /gún smìth/ *n* a maker, seller, or repairer of firearms

gun·stock /gún stòk/ *n* the shaped wooden or metal handle of a rifle that is pressed against the shoulder when the rifle is being fired

Gun·ther /gŏŏntər/ *n* in medieval Germanic mythology, the king of Burgundy and husband of Brunhild

Gun·tur /gŏŏn tŏŏr/ city in the Krishna River delta, in Andhra Pradesh State, southeastern India. Population: 471,051 (1991).

gun·wale /gúnn'l/, **gun·nel** *n* the top edge of a boat's sides that forms a ledge around the whole boat above the deck (*often used in the plural*) [15C. Because used in the past to support guns]

gun·wom·an /gún wŏŏmmən/ (*plural* **-wom·en** /-wìmmin/) *n* a woman armed with a gun

Guo Xi /gwō sheé/ (*fl* 1060–75) Chinese artist. He is noted for his large landscape murals and scrolls.

gup·py /gúppee/ (*plural* **-pies**) *n* a small freshwater fish that has a brightly colored tail, produces live young rather than eggs, and is popular in aquariums. Native to: Caribbean, South America. Latin name: *Poecilia reticulata*. [Early 20C. After the Reverend R. J. Lechmere *Guppy* (1836–1916), who sent the first specimen from Trinidad to the British Museum]

Gup·ta /gŏŏptə/ *n* an Indian dynasty of the 3rd to 6th centuries that established an empire in much of South Asia. Their rule, during which the arts, architecture, and literature flourished, is generally regarded as the Golden Age of India. [Late 19C. After *Chandragupta*, the dynasty's founder]

gur /gur/ *n S Asia* FOOD same as **jaggery** [< Hindi]

Gur /goor/ *n* a group of Niger-Congo languages spoken in western Central Africa. Native speakers: 10 million. —**Gur** *adj*

gur·dwa·ra /goor dwaárə/ *n* a Sikh temple or other place of worship where Sikh scriptures are kept [Early 20C. < Punjabi *gurduārā*]

gur·gle /gúrg'l/ (**-gled, -gling, -gles**) *v* **1.** *vi* to make the deep bubbling noise that liquid makes when it is poured from a bottle **2.** *vti* to make a bubbling sound in the throat, or say something with a bubbling sound in the throat [Mid-16C. < assumed Vulgar Latin *gurguliare* < Latin *gurgulio* "gullet"] —**gur·gle** *n* —**gur·gling·ly** *adv*

Gur·kha /gúrkə/ (*plural same* or **-khas**) *n* **1.** a member of a Hindu people living mainly in Nepal, with small communities in Bhutan **2.** a Gurkha serving in the British or Indian army [Early 19C. < Nepalese *Gurkha*, place name] —**Gur·kha** *adj*

gur·nard /gúrnərd/ (*plural* **-nards** or *same*) *n* **1.** a widely distributed spiny-finned ocean fish with an armored head and sets of pectoral fins modified for crawling on the ocean bottom. Family: Triglidae. **2.** FISH same as **flying gurnard** [14C. < Old French *gornart* < Latin *grunnire* "grunt"; from the sound it makes when caught]

gur·ney /gúrnee/ (*plural* **-neys**) *n* a wheeled stretcher for transporting hospital patients [Late 19C. Origin ?]

gu·ru /gŏŏ ròo/ (*plural* **-rus**) *n* **1. HINDU OR SIKH RELIGIOUS TEACHER** in Hinduism and Sikhism, a religious leader or teacher **2. LEADER OF RELIGIOUS GROUP** a spiritual leader or intellectual guide for a religious group or movement, especially one considered not to be mainstream **3. INFLUENTIAL EXPERT** somebody who has a reputation as an expert leader, teacher, or practitioner in a particular field ○ *a meeting of the world's software gurus* ○ *a style guru* **4. REVERED TEACHER AND COUNSELOR** a person's revered guide, mentor, or adviser in spiritual or intellectual matters [Early 17C. < Sanskrit, "elder, teacher"]

Gu·ru Na·nak /gŏŏ roo naánək/ ➧ **Nanak**

Gu·ru Na·nak Ja·nan·ti /-jə naántee/ *n* a Sikh festival marking the birthday of Guru Nanak. Date: November.

gu·sa·no /gŏŏ saánō, -zaá-/ *n* a Cuban, usually living in exile, opposed to the regime of Fidel Castro [< Spanish, literally "worm"]

gush /gush/ *vti* (**gushed, gush·ing, gush·es**) **1. FLOW OUT FAST** to flow out rapidly and in large quantities, or release large quantities of a liquid in a fast-flowing stream **2. SPEAK OR SAY SOMETHING EFFUSIVELY** to express yourself, or say something, in an excessively enthusiastic, affectionate, or sentimental way ○ *"Your children are simply delightful!" she gushed.* ■ *n* **1. FLOW OF LIQUID** a fast or copious flow of liquid from somewhere **2. EFFUSIVE OUTBURST** an outburst of overenthusiastic or overemotional speech or self-expression [14C. Probably an imitation of the sound of liquid gushing] —**gush·ing** *adj* —**gush·ing·ly** *adv*

gush·er /gúshər/ *n* **1.** an oil well from which oil flows freely and in large amounts, without having to be pumped **2.** somebody who speaks or behaves in an exaggeratedly emotional or enthusiastic way

gush·y /gúshee/ (**-i·er, -i·est**) *adj* characterized by overenthusiastic or overemotional speech or self-expression —**gush·i·ly** *adv* —**gush·i·ness** *n*

Gus·mão /gŏŏss maá ō, gŏŏss mów/, **Xanana** (*b.* 1946) president of Timor-Leste (East Timor). A guerrilla leader in the fight for independence in Timor-Leste he became its first president in 2002. Full name **Gusmão, José Alexandre Xanana**

gus·set /gússət/ *n* **1. INSET PIECE OF FABRIC** a piece of fabric inserted in a garment where added strength or freedom of movement is needed **2. FLAT PLATE REINFORCING JOINT** a flat, often triangular plate, usually of steel or plywood, used to connect and reinforce a joint where several members meet at different angles, e.g., in a pitched roof **3. CHAIN MAIL AT ARMOR JOINT** a section of chain mail protecting the unarmored joints of a suit of armor [14C. < French *gousset* "little pod" < *gousse* "pod, shell"]

gus·sy /gússee/ (**-sied, -sy·ing, -sies**)
gussy up *vt* to dress somebody in fancy clothes, or decorate something elaborately (*informal*; *often passive*) ○ *all gussied up in a frilly dress* ○ *The city was gussied up for the governor's visit.* [Mid-20C. Origin ?]

gust /gust/ *n* **1. BURST OF WIND** a sudden powerful rush of wind **2. BURST OF EMOTION** a sudden powerful experience or expression of an emotion ■ *vi* (**gust·ed, gust·ing, gusts**) **BLOW IN BURSTS** to blow, or be blown by the wind, in sudden powerful bursts [Late 16C. < Old Norse *gustr* < *gjósa* "to gush"]

gus·ta·tion /gu stáysh'n/ *n* the action of tasting, or the sense of taste (*formal*) [Late 16C. Directly or via French < Latin *gustation-* < *gustare* "to taste"]

gus·ta·to·ry /gústə tàwree/, **gus·ta·to·ri·al** /gùstə táwree əl/ *adj* relating to the sense of taste or to the action or experience of tasting something (*formal*) [Late 17C. < Latin *gustare* "to taste"] —**gus·ta·to·ri·ly** *adv*

Gus·tav I Vasa /gŏŏ staav vaázə/ (1496–1560) king of Sweden. The founder of the Swedish royal house of Vasa, in the course of his reign (1523–60) he proclaimed Lutheranism as the state religion (1529) and achieved independence for Sweden from the Hanseatic League (1537).

Gus·tav II Ad·olph /gŏŏ staav áddolf/ (1594–1632) king of Sweden. Regarded as the founding father of modern Sweden for the domestic reforms instituted during his reign (1611–32), he also led the Protestant forces during the early part of Thirty Years' War (1618–48). Known as **the Lion of the North**

Gus·tav V /gŏŏ staav/ (1858–1950) king of Sweden. His reign (1907–50) was characterized by progressive social reforms introduced by the ruling Social Democrat party and Sweden's neutrality in both World Wars.

Gus·tav VI Ad·olph (1882–1973) king of Sweden. Known during his reign (1950–73) for his patronage of the arts, he had a reputation as a classical archaeologist and an authority on Chinese art.

Gu·stav·o A. Ma·der·o /gŏŏ staávō aa mə dáyrō/ city in south central Mexico, near Mexico City. The Treaty of Guadalupe Hidalgo ending the Mexican War was signed there in 1848. Population: 1,309,211 (2000). Former name **Guadalupe Hidalgo** (until 1931)

Gus·ta·vus IV /gŏŏ staávəss/ (1778–1837) king of Sweden. His fierce opposition to Napoleon I and the French Republic during his reign (1792–1809) led to a loss of territory to France (1807) and Russia (1808) and to his abdication the following year.

gus·to /gústō/ *n* lively enthusiasm or enjoyment [Early 17C Via Italian < Latin *gustus* "taste"]

gust·y /gústee/ (**-i·er, -i·est**) *adj* blowing in gusts, blown on gusts of wind, or characterized by recurring gusts ○ *a gusty day* —**gust·i·ly** *adv* —**gust·i·ness** *n*

gut /gut/ *n* **1. ALIMENTARY CANAL** the whole of the alimentary canal in people and animals, from the mouth to the anus, or the lower part of it (**intestine**), from the stomach to the anus **2.** INDUST same as **catgut** **3. FISHING CORD** cord made of fibrous material taken from silkworms. Use: fishing lines. **4. PLACE WHERE INSTINCTS ARE FELT** the supposed location in the body of a person's deepest instinctively felt responses, as distinct from his or her rational or logical responses, or those instinctive responses themselves (*often used before a noun*) ○ *Let's just say, I feel in my gut something's wrong.* **5. ABDOMEN** somebody's belly, especially if it is noticeably large (*slang disapproving*) ○ *I've got to work off this gut.* ■ *npl* **1. INTESTINES** the insides of a person or animal, especially the intestines **2. INNER OR CENTRAL PARTS** the inner or central parts of something, e.g., the working parts of a machine, or the basic principles that a theory is based on **3. STRENGTH OF CHARACTER** courage or boldness (*slang*) ■ *vt* (**gut·ted, gut·ting, guts**) **1. REMOVE ANIMAL'S INSIDES** to remove the insides of a dead animal **2. DESTROY BUILDING'S INTERIOR** to destroy the internal parts of a building, leaving only the outer walls standing ○ *The factory was completely gutted in the fire.* **3. REMOVE FIXTURES FROM ROOM OR BUILDING** to remove all the internal fixtures and furnishings from a room or building **4. TAKE EXTRACTS FROM A TEXT** to select extracts from a piece of writing for use elsewhere **5. MAKE SOMETHING INEFFECTIVE** to make something powerless or ineffective, especially by removing essential parts or features from it [Old English *guttas* < Indo-European, "pour"] ◇ **bust a gut** to struggle or work exceptionally hard to get something done (*slang*)

SYNONYMS See *courage*.

GUT /gut/ *abbr* PHYS Grand Unified Theory

gut·buck·et /gút bùkət/ *n* **1.** a homemade instrument played like a double bass, made by fixing a stick to an upturned basin and stretching a string along its length **2.** a simple but highly emotional style of jazz or blues

gut course *n* a college or university course that is very easy to pass (*informal*)

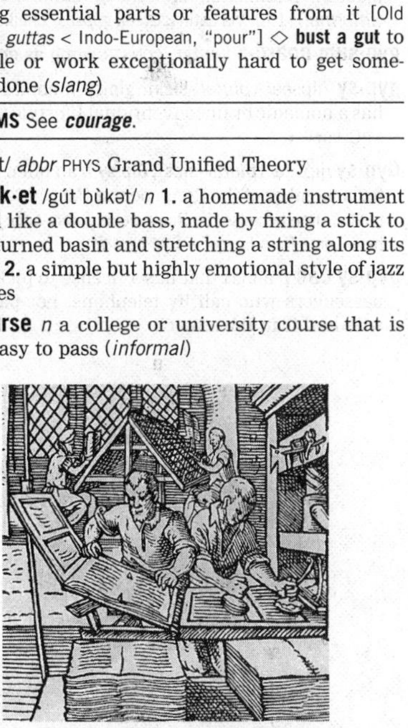
Popperfoto

Johannes Gutenberg: 15th-century engraving showing Gutenberg (left foreground) printing the Gutenberg Bible (1456?)

Gu·ten·berg /góot'n bùrg/, **Johannes** (1400?–68) German printer. He is credited with the invention of moveable type, which he used in his Mainz printing press to print the 42-line Bible, known as the Gutenberg Bible. Full name **Gutenberg, Johannes Gensfleisch**

Guth·rie /gúthree/, **Sir Tyrone** (1900–71) British stage director. He was closely identified with the Old Vic-Sadler's Wells Company, London, in the 1940s and 1950s, and founded the Tyrone Guthrie Theater in Minneapolis in 1963. Full name **Guthrie, Sir William Tyrone**

Guth·rie, Woody (1912–67) US folk singer and composer. Many of his hundreds of songs protested the social injustice of the Depression. He wrote "This Land Is Your Land" (1940). Full name **Guthrie, Woodrow Wilson**

> "You can't write a good song about a whorehouse unless you been in one."
> [Woody Guthrie, recalled on his death; October 4, 1967]

gut is·sue *n* a political issue that causes an emotional response rather than a strictly rational one

gut job *n* the restoration or repair of a building that includes the removal and rebuilding of the interior (*informal*)

gut·less /gúttləss/ *adj* seriously lacking in resolve and determination (*informal*) —**gut·less·ness** *n*

SYNONYMS See *cowardly*.

gut re·ac·tion *n* an immediate and instinctive reaction, rather than a well-thought-out response ○ *The boss's gut reaction is to be suspicious.*

gut re·ha·bil·i·ta·tion, **gut ren·o·va·tion** *n* CONSTR same as **gut job** (*informal*)

guts·y /gútsee/ (**-i·er, -i·est**) *adj* (*informal*) **1.** showing courage, boldness, and determination **2.** done or performed with a great deal of vigor, passion, or emotion —**guts·i·ly** *adv* —**guts·i·ness** *n*

gut·ta /gúttə/ (*plural* **-tae** /gú teè/) *n* **1.** one of a series of ornaments shaped like drops that are attached to the underside of a Doric entablature **2.** a drop of medicine (*dated; formerly, on prescriptions*) [14C. < Latin, "drop"]

gut·ta-per·cha /gùttə púrchə/ *n* **1.** a pliable substance made from a natural latex. Use: dental fillings, dressings, electrical insulation. **2.** a tree whose latex is a source of gutta-percha. Native to: Southeast Asia. Genera: *Palaquium* or *Payena*. [Mid-19C. Alteration (influenced by Latin *gutta* "drop") of Malay *getah perca* "gum strips of cloth"]

gut·tate /gú tàyt/, **gut·tat·ed** /-tàytəd/ *adj* having or resembling drops or spots [Early 19C. < Latin *guttatus* < *gutta* "drop"]

gut·ta·tion /gu táysh'n/ *n* the oozing out of water droplets from the uninjured surface of a plant leaf

gut·ted /gúttəd/ *adj* with the insides taken out, ready to be sold

gut·ter /gúttər/ *n* **1. RAINWATER CHANNEL ON ROOF** a metal or plastic channel attached to the eaves of a roof for carrying away rainwater **2. RAINWATER CHANNEL ON ROAD** a channel at the edge of a road that carries water into a sewer **3. POOR OR DEGRADED STATE** an impoverished and degraded existence or way of life ○ *She dragged me out of the gutter and made me respect myself.* **4.** BOWLING **CHANNEL ON BOWLING LANE** the channel on either side of a bowling lane **5.** PRINTING **INNER MARGINS OF BOOK** the blank space formed by the inner margins of two facing pages of a book **6.** STAMPS **SPACE BETWEEN STAMPS ON SHEET** the space between the printed design of one stamp and the next one on the sheet, where the perforations lie ■ *v* (**-tered, -ter·ing, -ters**) **1.** *vi* **MELT QUICKLY** to burn down more quickly than usual because melting wax has formed a channel on one side (*refers to candles*) **2.** *vi* **FLICKER** to flicker when on the point of being extinguished **3.** *vt* **FORM CHANNELS IN SOMETHING** to wear away channels in the surface of something **4.** *vi* **TRICKLE** to run in a narrow stream or trickle ■ *adj* **OF WORST KIND** of the most vulgar, corrupt, or morally degraded kind (*disapproving*) [13C. < Anglo-Norman *gotere* < Latin *gutta* "drop"]
gutter out *vi* **1.** to go out after flickering for a while **2.** to come to an end finally, after gradually declining

~~gutteral~~ incorrect spelling of **guttural**

gut·ter ball *n* in bowling, a ball that, when bowled, rolls into the gutter and does not knock over any pins

gut·ter press *n UK* low-quality newspapers and magazines that deal mostly with scandal and gossip rather than serious news

gut·ter·snipe /gúttər snìp/ *n* **1.** somebody regarded as having a rough or vulgar manner, especially somebody with a lower-class background (*insult*) **2.** a child who wears dirty ragged clothes, has rough manners, and lives in the streets (*dated insult*) [Mid-19C. Via "street cleaner" < "common snipe" (a bird that likes wet muddy conditions)] —**gut·ter·snip·ish** *adj*

gut·tur·al /gúttərəl/ *adj* **1.** characterized by harsh and grating speech sounds made in the throat or toward the back of the mouth **2.** PHON same as **velar** *adj* (sense 1) ■ *n* a speech sound produced in the throat or at the back of the mouth [Late 16C. Directly or via French < medieval Latin *gutturalis* < Latin *guttur* "throat"] —**gut·tur·al·ism** *n* —**gut·tur·al·i·ty** /gùttə rállətee/ *n* —**gut·tur·al·ly** *adv* —**gut·tur·al·ness** *n*

gut·tur·al·ize /gúttərə lìz/ (**-ized, -iz·ing, -iz·es**) *v* **1.** *vt* to pronounce a speech sound in the throat or toward the back of the mouth **2.** *vti* to speak or say something in a harsh rasping way —**gut·tur·al·i·za·tion** /gùttərəli záysh'n/ *n*

gut-wrench·ing *adj* having a very powerful effect on the feelings, especially in stirring up pity or sympathy (*informal*)

guv /guv/ *n UK* (*informal*) **1.** used as a familiar term of address by one man to another, especially to one in a superior position **2.** used by men and women as a term of address for their boss [Mid-19C. Shortening of GUVNOR]

guv·nor /gúvnər/ *n UK* **1.** same as **guv** (*informal*) **2.** used by upper-class young men to refer to or address their father (*dated informal*) ○ *The guvnor won't increase my allowance.* [Mid-19C. Representing a pronunciation of GOVERNOR]

guy[1] /gī/ (*informal*) *n* same as **man** *n* (sense 1) ■ **guys** *npl* used to address a group of people of either sex ○ *Hey, guys, where are you off to?* [Early 19C. < Guy Fawkes (see GUY FAWKES NIGHT)]

USAGE ***Guy*** has two contrary meanings. It is used to mean "man," often in contexts relating to the two sexes: *Guys like her because she's smart.* And in the plural it can mean people of either sex: *You guys are my best friends*, though this use may not receive universal approval.

CULTURAL NOTE ***Guys and Dolls***, a musical (1950) by Frank Loesser. It transforms a story by Damon Runyon into a classic American musical comedy. Nathan Detroit, a gambler in New York City, bets that gangster Sky Masterson can't persuade the next woman he sees to go to Havana with him. The woman in question turns out to be a prim reformer who runs a mission to save sinners. In the meantime, Detroit's own long-suffering fiancée is demanding a wedding. These two-bit gangsters roister their way to an improbably happy ending. Frank Sinatra and Marlon Brando starred in a 1955 movie version.

guy[2] /gī/ *n* same as **guywire** ■ *vt* (**guyed, guy·ing, guys**) to support or anchor something using ropes, cables, or chains [14C. Probably < Low German]

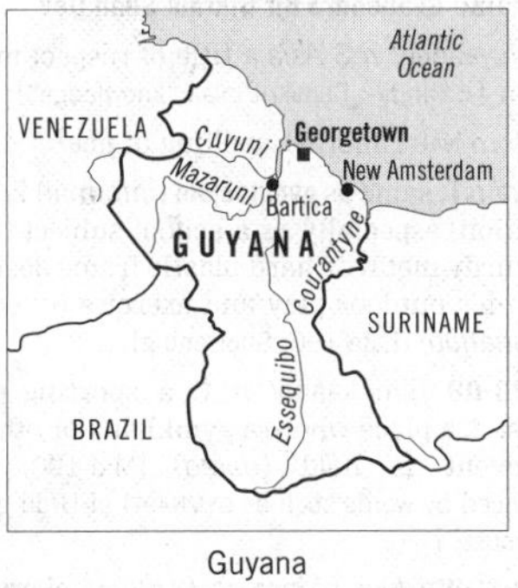

Guyana

Guy·a·na /gee ánnə, -aánə/ country on the North Atlantic coast of South America bordered by Venezuela, Brazil, and Suriname. It became an independent member of the British Commonwealth in 1966. Venezuela claims Guyana's territory west of the Essequibo river. Language: English. Currency: Guyana dollar. Capital: Georgetown. Population: 702,100 (2003). Area: 83,000 sq. mi./214,969 sq. km. Official name **Cooperative Republic of Guyana** —**Guy·a·nese** /gì ə neéz/ *adj, n*

Guy Fawkes Night /gī fáwks-/ *n* CALENDAR same as **Bonfire Night** [After *Guy Fawkes* (1570–1606), conspirator in the Gunpowder Plot]

guy·line *n* same as **guywire**

guy·ot /gee ṓ/ *n* a flat-topped underwater mountain of a type commonly found in the Pacific Ocean and considered to be an extinct volcano [Mid-20C. After Arnold Henri *Guyot*, (1807–84), Swiss-born US geologist and geographer]

guy·rope /gí rṑp/ *n UK* TELECOM same as **guywire**

guy·wire /gí wìr/ *n* a wire or chain tightened to hold something in position, e.g., any of the wires that hold up a telephone pole

Guz·mán Blan·co /gooss maàn blaángkō/, **Antonio** (1829–99) president of Venezuela (1870–77, 1879–84,

1886–88). During his presidency, he promoted public education and foreign investment.

guz·zle /gúzz'l/ (**-zled, -zling, -zles**) *vti* to drink something rapidly and in large quantities (*informal*) [Late 16C. Origin ?] —**guz·zler** *n*

gw *abbr* ONLINE Guinea-Bissau (*used in Internet addresses*) See table at **domain name**

GW *symbol* MEASURE gigawatt

GW 2 *abbr* MIL Gulf War II, fought in the spring of 2003 against Iraq [Early 21C.]

Gwa·dar /gwə daár/ port in southwestern Pakistan. Population: 17,000 (1981).

Gwa·li·or /gwaálee àwr/ city near Agra in Madhya Pradesh State, central India. Population: 690,765 (1991).

gwe·duc *n* ZOOL same as **geoduck**

gwei·lo /gwì lṓ/ *n Hong Kong* a foreigner from the West (*informal*) [< Japanese]

Gwe·lo /gwéelō/ former name for **Gweru** (until 1982)

Gwe·ru /gwáy roo/ city on the Gweru River in central Zimbabwe. It is a commercial, manufacturing, and transportation center. Population: 128,027 (1992). Former name **Gwelo** (until 1982)

Gwin·nett /gwə nét/, **Button** (1735?–77) British-born American patriot. A member of the Continental Congress, he was one of the signers of the Declaration of Independence.

Gwy·nedd /gwínnə<u>th</u>/ mountainous county in northwestern Wales, dominated by Snowdonia National Park. Population: 116,843 (2001).. Area: 1,494 sq. mi./3,867 sq. km.

gy *abbr* ONLINE Guyana (*used in Internet addresses*) See table at **domain name**

Gy *symbol* PHYS gray[1]

Gya·nen·dra /gya néndrə/ (*b.* 1947) king of Nepal (2001–). He was crowned king after his older brother, King Birendra, and several other members of the royal family were killed in a palace massacre. Full name **Gyanendra Bir Bikram Shah Dev**

Gya·ni /gyaánee/ *n S Asia* a title of respect for a Sikh scholar [< Hindi < Sanskrit *gyan* "knowledge"]

gybe *vti, n* NAUT another spelling of **jibe**[1]

gym /jim/ *n* **1.** same as **gymnasium** (*informal*) **2.** physical education, especially as a school subject (*informal*) **3.** a sturdy metal or hard plastic frame designed for children's outdoor play and exercise (*often used in combination*) [Late 19C. Shortening]

gym·kha·na /jim kaánə/ *n* **1.** a sporting event or contest **2.** a place where a gymkhana or other sporting event is held (*dated*) [Mid-19C. Alteration (influenced by words such as GYMNAST) of Urdu *gendk<u>h</u>anah* "ball house"]

gym·na·si·um /jim náyzee əm/ (*plural* **-si·ums** or **-si·a** /-zee ə/) *n* **1.** a large room equipped for physical exercise or training of various kinds, e.g., in a school or a private club **2.** in Europe, principally Germany and other German-speaking countries, a secondary school where the emphasis is on academic subjects rather than on technical training [Late 16C. Via Latin, "school" < Greek *gumnasion* < *gumnazein* "exercise naked, train" < *gumnos* "naked"]

gym·nast /jímnəst, jím nàst/ *n* an athlete who performs gymnastics, especially as a competitive sport [Late 16C. Directly or via French < Greek *gumnastēs* "trainer of athletes" < *gumnazein* (see GYMNASIUM)]

gym·nas·tic /jim nástik/ *adj* **1.** relating to or involving gymnastics ○ *gymnastic equipment* **2.** involving or demonstrating athleticism and agility ○ *a gymnastic dancing style* [Late 16C. Via Latin < Greek *gumnastikos* < *gumnazein* (see GYMNASIUM)] —**gym·nas·ti·cal·ly** *adv*

gym·nas·tics /jim nástiks/ *n* (*takes a singular verb*) **1.** EXERCISE USING GYMNASTIC EQUIPMENT exercise using equipment such as bars, rings, and vaulting horses, designed to develop agility and muscular strength **2.** COMPETITIVE SPORT USING GYMNASTIC EQUIPMENT the competitive sport in which athletes perform a series of exercises on pieces of gymnastic equipment ■ *npl* (*takes a plural verb*) **1.** PHYSICAL EXERCISES movements, exercises, or activities that involve feats of physical strength and agility **2.** ACTIONS DEMONSTRATING AGILITY AND SKILL the performance of a series of complex mental or physical operations of a particular kind, usually rapidly and with great agility and skill ○ *verbal gymnastics*

gym·no·sperm /jímnə spùrm/ *n* a woody vascular plant in which the ovules are carried naked on the scales of a cone, e.g., a conifer, cycad, or ginkgo [Mid-19C. Via modern Latin < Greek *gumnospermos* "naked seed"] —**gym·no·sper·mous** /jìmnə spúrməss/ *adj* —**gym·no·sper·my** *n*

Gym·pie /gímpee/ town in southeastern Queensland, Australia, noted as an agricultural center. Population: 10,784 (1991).

gym rat *n* somebody who spends a lot of time exercising or playing a sport at a gymnasium (*informal*)

gyn. *abbr* MED **1.** gynecological **2.** gynecologist **3.** gynecology

gyn- *prefix* same as **gyno-** (*used before vowels*)

gynaec-, etc *prefix* UK spelling of **gynec-, etc**

gy·nan·dro·morph /gī nándrə màwrf, ji-/ *n* an organism, especially an insect, that has both male and female characteristics in a way that is atypical for its species [Late 19C. < GYNANDROUS] —**gy·nan·dro·mor·phic** /gī nàndrə máwrfik, ji-/ *adj* —**gy·nan·dro·mor·phism** /-máwr fizzəm/ *n* —**gy·nan·dro·mor·phous** /-máwrfəss/ *adj* —**gy·nan·dro·mor·phy** *n*

gy·nan·drous /gī nándrəss, ji-/ *adj* describes flowers such as orchids that have pistils and stamens united in a column [Early 19C. < Greek *gunandros* "of doubtful sex" < *gunē* "woman" + *andr-* "man"]

gyn·ar·chy /jín aàrkee, jī́n-/ (*plural* **-chies**) *n* POL same as **gynecocracy** —**gyn·ar·chic** /gī naárkik, ji-/ *adj*

-gyne *suffix* **1.** female ○ *androgyne* **2.** female reproductive organ ○ *trichogyne* [< Greek *gunē* "woman"] —**-gynous** *suffix* —**-gyny** *suffix*

gynec- *prefix* same as **gyneco-** (*used before vowels*) [< Greek *gunaik-*, stem of *gunē* "woman"]

gyneco- *prefix* woman ○ *gynecology*

gyn·e·coc·ra·cy /gìnə kókrəssee/ (*plural* **-cies**) *n* political dominance by women, or a political system that gives supreme power to women

gy·ne·coid /gī́nə kòyd/ *adj* physically resembling a woman, or physiologically typical of a woman ○ *a gynecoid pelvis*

gynecol. *abbr* MED **1.** gynecological **2.** gynecologist **3.** gynecology

gy·ne·col·o·gy /gìnə kóllǝjee/ *n* the branch of medicine that deals with women's health, especially with the health of women's reproductive organs —**gy·ne·co·log·i·cal** /gìnəkə lójjik'l/ *adj* —**gy·ne·col·o·gist** *n*

gy·ne·co·mas·ti·a /gìnə kō mástee ə/ *n* enlarged breasts on a man caused by hormonal imbalance or hormone therapy [Mid-19C. < GYNECO- + Greek *mastos* "breast"]

gyn·e·cop·a·thy /gìnə kóppəthee/ (*plural* **-thies**) *n* a disease that affects only women

gy·ne·pho·bi·a /gìnə fṓbee ə/ *n* an irrational and pathological fear of women

gyno- *prefix* **1.** female reproductive organ ○ *gynophore* **2.** woman ○ *gynocracy* [< Greek *gunē* "woman"]

gy·noc·ra·cy /gī nókrəssee, ji-/ (*plural* **-cies**) *n* POL same as **gynecocracy**

gyn·o·di·oe·cious /gìnō dī éeshəss/ *adj* describes a plant species that has bisexual flowers on some plants and single-sex flowers on others —**gy·no·di·oe·cism** /-ée sìzzəm/ *n*

gy·noe·ci·um /gī néeshee əm, -shəm/ (*plural* **-ci·a** /-shə/) *n* the carpels of a plant considered together [Mid-19C. Alteration (influenced by Greek *oikos* "house") of modern Latin *gynaeceum* "women's apartments" < Greek *gunaikeios* "of women" < *gunē* "woman"]

gyn·o·gen·e·sis /gìnə jénnəssiss/ *n* the development of an embryo without fusion of the egg and sperm nuclei, so that the embryo has only maternal chromosomes

gyn·o·phore /gínə fàwr/ *n* a pistil stalk that has its gynoecium raised above the rest of the flower —**gyn·o·phor·ic** /gìnə fáwrik/ *adj*

Gyor /dyur, dyör/ port in northwestern Hungary, situated on the Danube River between Budapest and Vienna. Population: 127,275 (1999).

gyo·za /gyṓzə/ *n* a Japanese dish consisting of cases of dough stuffed with ground meat, fish, or vegetables, and fried [< Japanese]

gyp /jip/, **gip** (*sometimes considered offensive*) *vt* (**gypped, gyp·ping, gyps; gipped, gip·ping, gips**) CHEAT SOMEBODY to cheat somebody, especially by overcharging (*informal*) ■ *n* **1.** SCAM a scheme to trick or swindle people (*informal*) **2.** CHEATER a cheater or swindler (*insult*) [Late 19C. Origin ? Sometimes taken to be a shortening of GYPSY and so offensive] —**gyp·per** *n*

gyp·sif·er·ous /jip síffərəss/ *adj* containing gypsum

gyp·soph·i·la /jip sóffilə/ *n* a plant of the carnation family popular in bouquets. Flowers: tiny, white or pink, on long branching stalks. Native to: Mediterranean. Genus: *Gypsophila*. [Late 18C. < modern Latin, "chalk-loving" < Greek *gupsos* "chalk," because it grows in chalky soil]

gyp·sum /jípsəm/ *n* **1.** a white or colorless mineral consisting of hydrated calcium sulfate. Use: cement, plaster, fertilizers. **2.** CONSTR same as **drywall** (*informal*) [14C. Via Latin < Greek *gupsos* "chalk, gypsum"]

gyp·sum board *n* INDUST, CONSTR same as **drywall**

gyp·sy /jípsee/ (*plural* **-sies**), **gip·sy** *n* somebody who has a nomadic or unconventional lifestyle (*informal*) [< GYPSY]

Gyp·sy /jípsee/ (*plural* **-sies**), **Gip·sy** *n* an offensive term for a member of the Roma people [Mid-16C. Shortening of EGYPTIAN; because the Roma people were once thought to have come from Egypt] —**Gyp·sy** *adj*

gyp·sy cab *n* a taxi that has a license to pick up only passengers who call by telephone, not passengers who hail it in the street

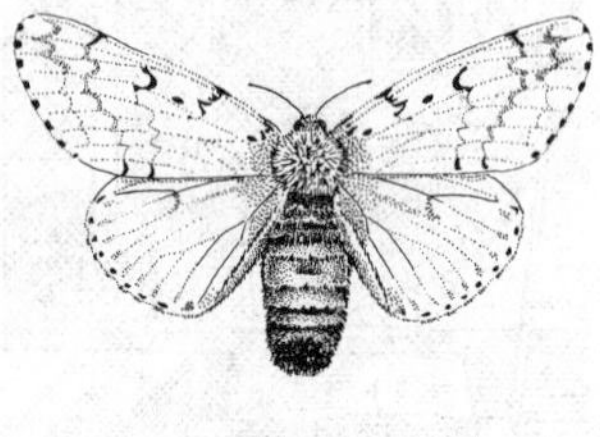

gypsy moth

gyp·sy moth *n* a tussock moth with a spotted hairy caterpillar that is a serious pest of trees. Native to: Europe, but common in North America since the 19th century. Latin name: *Lymantria dispar*.

gy·ral /jī́rəl/ *adj* moving in a path that is spiral or circular —**gy·ral·ly** *adv*

gy·rate /jī ràyt/ *vi* (**-rat·ed, -rat·ing, -rates**) to move with a circular or spiral motion, especially around a fixed central point ■ *adj* BIOL growing in a winding spiral or coil [Early 19C. < late Latin *gyrat-*, past participle of *gyrare* "revolve" < Latin *gyrus* (see GYRUS)] —**gy·ra·tor** *n* —**gy·ra·to·ry** /jī́rə tàwree/ *adj*

gy·ra·tion /jī ráysh'n/ *n* **1.** movement in a circle around a fixed center ○ *the gyration of the rotor* **2.** a spiral or coil-shaped thing or part

gyre /jīr/ *n* a circle or spiral (*literary*) [Mid-16C. < Latin *gyrus* (see GYRUS)]

gy·rene /jī reen, jī réen/ *n* a soldier in the US Marine Corps (*slang*) [Mid-20C. Origin ?]

gyr·fal·con /júr fàlkən/ *n* a large falcon varying in color from white to dark brown. Native to: cold northern regions. Latin name: *Falco rusticolus*. [14C. Alteration (by association with Latin *gyrare* "revolve") of Old French *gerfaucon*]

gy·ro /jī́rō, jée-/ (*plural* **-ros**) *n* minced lamb that has been cooked on a spit in a molded block, then sliced thin and served in pita bread with onion and tomato [Late 20C. < modern Greek *guros* "turning"]

gyro- *prefix* **1.** spinning or rotating in a circle ○ *gyrostatics* **2.** gyroscope, gyroscopic ○ *gyrostabilizer* [< Greek *guros* "ring, circle"]

gy·ro·com·pass /jīrō kùmpəss, -kòmpəss/ *n* a navigational compass fitted with a gyroscope instead of a magnet

gy·ro·mag·net·ic /jìrō mag néttik/ *adj* relating to or caused by the magnetism produced by the spinning motion of a charged particle ○ *gyromagnetic effect*

gy·ro·mag·net·ic ra·tio *n* the ratio of the magnetic moment to the angular momentum of a system

gy·ron /jīrən, -ròn/, **gi·ron** *n* in heraldry, a triangular form made by two blinds drawn from the edge of an escutcheon to meet at the fesse-point and occupying half of the quarter [Late 16C. < French, "gusset" < Germanic]

gy·ro·plane /jīrə plàyn/ *n* an aircraft fitted with an unpowered rotor for producing lift

gy·ro·scope /jīrə skōp/ *n* a device consisting of a rotating heavy metal wheel pivoted inside a circular frame whose movement does not affect the wheel's orientation in space. Use: in compasses and other navigational aids, in stabilizing mechanisms on ships and aircraft. —**gy·ro·scop·ic** /jīrə skóppik/ *adj* —**gy·ro·scop·i·cal·ly** *adv*

gy·ro·sta·bi·liz·er /jìrō stáyb'l īzər/ *n* a stabilizing system that uses gyroscopes to compensate and reduce the rolling or pitching motion of a ship or aircraft

gy·ro·stat /jīrō stàt/ *n* a gyroscope or gyrostabilizer in which the rotating wheel is pivoted within a rigid case [Late 19C. < GYRO- + Greek *statos* "standing"]

gy·ro·stat·ics /jìrō státtiks/ *n* the branch of science that deals with rotating bodies (*takes a singular verb*) —**gy·ro·stat·ic** *adj* —**gy·ro·stat·i·cal·ly** *adv*

gy·rus /jīrəss/ (*plural* **-ri** /-rī/) *n* a rounded ridge on the outer layer of the brain [Mid-19C. Via Latin, "circle" < Greek *guros* "ring, circle"]

Gyum·ri /gyŏommree/ city in northwestern Armenia, the country's second most populated urban area. Population: 206,600 (1990). Former name **Leninakhan** (1924–90)

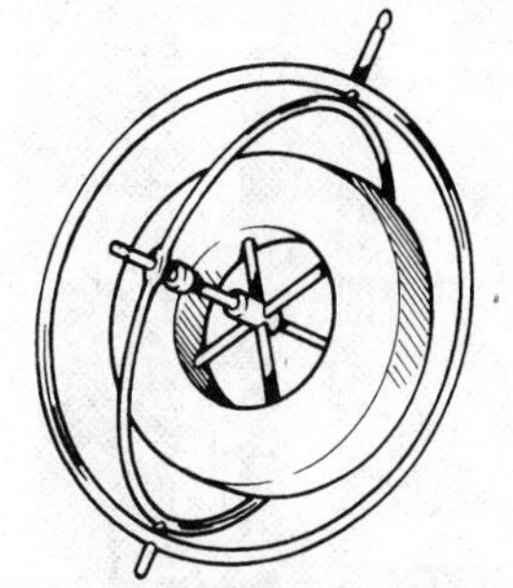

gyroscope

gyve /jīv/ (*archaic*) *n* a shackle or fetter, usually for the leg (*usually used in the plural*) ■ *vt* (**gyved, gyv·ing, gyves**) to shackle or fetter somebody, especially by the leg [13C. Origin ?]

Hh

h[1] /aych/ (*plural* **h's**), **H** (*plural* **H's** or **Hs**) *n* **1.** the eighth letter of the English alphabet, representing a consonant sound **2.** a written representation of the letter "h"

h[2] *symbol* **1.** hecto- **2.** PHYS Planck's constant **3.** used to refer to the eighth vertical row of squares from the left on a chessboard

H[1] *symbol* **1.** PHYS enthalpy **2.** MATH, PHYS Hamiltonian function **3.** ELECTRONICS henry **4.** CHEM ELEM hydrogen

H[2] /aych/ (*plural* **H's** or **Hs**) *n* something shaped like a letter "H"

h. *abbr* **1.** harbor **2.** hard **3.** hardness **4.** height **5.** high **6.** BASEBALL hit **7.** horizontal **8.** MUSIC horn **9.** hospital **10.** MATH hundred **11.** husband

H. *abbr* **1.** harbor **2.** hard **3.** hardness **4.** height **5.** high **6.** hospital

H2 *abbr* ONLINE how to (*used in e-mails or text messages*)

H_2O *n* CHEM same as **water** (sense 1) (*informal*)

ha[1] /haa/, **hah** *interj* **1.** used to express surprise, triumph, scorn, or happiness, depending on the way the speaker says it **2.** a word used in writing to represent the sound of laughter [13C. Natural exclamation]

ha[2] *symbol* MEASURE hectare

ha[3] *abbr* **1.** ARMS high angle **2.** hoc anno **3.** ASTRON hour angle

Ha. *abbr* **1.** Haiti **2.** Haitian **3.** *also* **HA** Hawaii **4.** Hawaiian

Haa·kon VII /háw kaan, háwkən/ (1872–1957) **king of Norway** He was elected king in 1905, when the union between Norway and Sweden was dissolved. His reign (1905–57) included a period in exile, leading Norwegian resistance during World War II.

Haar·lem /haárləm/, **Har·lem** city in North Holland Province, western Netherlands. Population: 148,772 (2000).

Hab. *abbr* Habakkuk

Ha·bak·kuk /hábbə kòok, hə bákək/ *n* **1.** in the Bible, a Hebrew priest who lived in the 7th century B.C. **2.** a book of the Bible that contains the prophecies traditionally attributed to Habakkuk. See table at **Bible**

ha·ba·ne·ra /haàbə nérrə/ *n* **1.** SLOW DANCE a slow dance of Cuban origin in 2/4 time **2.** MUSIC the music for a habanera. There is a famous example in the opera "Carmen," sung by Carmen herself. **3.** HOT CHILI PEPPER a hot chili pepper, originally from Cuba [Late 19C. < Spanish, "of Havana"]

hab·da·lah /haàvdə laá, haav dáwlə/, **hav·da·lah** *n* a Jewish ceremony that marks the end of the Sabbath or another holy day, or a prayer said during the ceremony [Mid-18C. < Hebrew *habdālāh* "separation, division"]

ha·be·as cor·pus /hàybee əss káwrpəss/ *n* a writ issued in order to bring somebody who has been detained into court, usually for a decision on whether the detention is lawful [15C. < Latin, "you may have the body"]

Ha·ber-Bosch proc·ess /hàybər báwsh-, -bósh-/ *n* CHEM same as **Haber process** [After Fritz *Haber* (1868–1934) and Karl *Bosch* (1874–1940), German chemists]

hab·er·dash·er /hábbər dàshər/ *n* **1.** a dealer in men's clothing and accessories **2.** *UK* a dealer in small articles used in sewing, e.g., thread, ribbons, and buttons [14C. Probably < Anglo-Norman *hapertas* "small items of merchandise"]

hab·er·dash·er·y /hábbər dàsharee/ (*plural* **-ies**) *n* **1.** goods sold by a haberdasher **2.** a store that sells haberdashery

hab·er·geon /hábbərjən, hə búrjən/ *n* a sleeveless chain mail jacket worn under armor [14C. < French *haubergeon* < Old French *hauberc* (see HAUBERK)]

Ha·ber proc·ess /háybər-/ *n* a commercial process for catalytically producing ammonia from atmospheric nitrogen and hydrogen at high temperature and pressure [See HABER-BOSCH PROCESS]

~~habeus corpus~~ incorrect spelling of **habeas corpus**

hab·ile /hább'l/ *adj* able to do something with ease (*formal*) [Late 15C. Via French < Latin *habilis* "able, easy to hold" < *habere* "have, hold"]

ha·bil·i·ment /hə bíllәmənt/ *n* GARMENT OR GARMENTS clothing, or an item of clothing (*archaic; usually used in the plural*) ■ **ha·bil·i·ments** *npl* (*formal*) **1.** SPECIALIZED EQUIPMENT the equipment and gear needed for a task or activity **2.** SPECIAL CLOTHES items of clothing associated with somebody's work or position or an occasion [Early 17C. < Old French *habillement* < *habiller* "fit out" < *habile*"able, easy to hold" < *habere*"have, hold"]

ha·bil·i·tate /hə bíllə tàyt/ (**-tat·ed, -tat·ing, -tates**) *v* **1.** *vi* PREPARE FOR POSITION to qualify for employment or an office (*formal*) **2.** *vt* CLOTHE SOMEBODY to clothe somebody in a particular way (*literary*) **3.** *vt* EQUIP MINING OPERATION to provide a mine with the equipment and money needed for operation [Early 17C. < medieval Latin *habilitat-*, past participle of *habilitare* < Latin *habilitas* (see ABILITY)] —**ha·bil·i·ta·tion** /hə bìllə táysh'n/ *n* —**ha·bil·i·ta·tor** *n*

hab·it /hábbit/ *n* **1.** REGULARLY REPEATED BEHAVIOR PATTERN an action or pattern of behavior that is repeated so often that it becomes typical of somebody, although he or she may be unaware of it ○ *I really need to get into the habit of writing down what I spend.* ○ *the annoying habit of finishing someone else's sentences* **2.** ATTITUDE somebody's attitude or general disposition **3.** ADDICTION an addiction to a drug (*slang*) **4.** CLOTHING OF RELIGIOUS ORDER a long loose gown, usually black, brown, gray, or white, traditionally worn by nuns, friars, and monks **5.** BOT, ZOOL GROWTH PATTERN the characteristic appearance, behavior, or growth pattern of a plant or animal **6.** SHAPE OF CRYSTAL the characteristic growth pattern or shape of a crystal ■ *vt* (**-it·ed, -it·ing, -its**) CLOTHE SOMEBODY SPECIALLY to dress somebody in clothing distinctive to a particular position or office (*literary*) [12C Via French < Latin *habitus* < *habere* "have, wear"] ◇ **kick the habit** to become free of an addiction, or stop doing something that has been a long-standing practice (*informal*)

ORIGIN The Latin word *habere* from which ***habit*** is derived was used reflexively to mean "to be," and so its past participle *habitus* came to be used as a noun for "how you are," that is, your "state" or "condition." Subsequently this noun developed in two directions, coming to mean both "outward condition or appearance," hence, eventually, "clothing," and "inner condition, quality, nature, character," and later "usual way of behaving." (The notion of adapting a verb meaning "to have" to express "how you are, how you act in particular situations" is duplicated in the English word "behave").

SYNONYMS ***habit, custom, tradition, practice, routine, wont***

CORE MEANING: established pattern of behavior

habit an action or pattern of behavior that is repeated so often that it becomes typical of somebody, although he or she may be unaware of it ○ *She had an irritating habit of phoning just as we were about to eat.* **custom** the way somebody usually or traditionally behaves in a situation ○ *It was his custom to walk three miles a day for health reasons.* ○ *The custom is for someone to give a short speech of thanks after the meal.* ○ *He wrote a book on local customs after he retired.* **tradition** a long-established action or pattern of behavior in a community or group of people, often one that has been handed down from generation to generation ○ *They maintain the old local tradition of decorating the wells in spring.* **practice** an established way of doing something, especially one that has developed through experience and knowledge; **routine** the usual sequence for a set of activities, sometimes with the suggestion that this is monotonous and tedious ○ *The visit was clearly going to disrupt our daily routine.* ○ *Life settled into a routine of writing in the mornings and long walks in the afternoons.* **wont** (*formal*) something that somebody does regularly or habitually ○ *I went to the library on Thursday, as is my wont.*

hab·it·a·ble /hábbitəb'l/ *adj* considered fit to be lived in ○ *A lot of structural work will be needed before the house is habitable.* [14C. Via French < Latin *habitabilis* < *habitare* (see HABITAT)] —**hab·it·a·bil·i·ty** /hàbbitə bíllətee/ *n* —**hab·it·a·ble·ness** *n* —**hab·it·a·bly** *adv*

hab·i·tant /hábbitənt/ *n* **1.** a farmer of French descent living in Canada or the United States **2.** somebody living in a place (*literary*) [15C. < French < Old French *habiter* "dwell" < Latin *habitare* (see HABITAT)]

hab·i·tat /hábbi tàt/ *n* **1.** ECOL HOME ENVIRONMENT the natural conditions and environment in which a plant or animal lives, e.g., forest, desert, or wetlands **2.** TYPICAL LOCATION the place in which a person or group is usually found **3.** ARTIFICIALLY CREATED ENVIRONMENT a sealed controlled environment in which people can live in unusual conditions such as under the sea or in space [Late 18C. < 3rd person present singular of Latin *habitare* "possess, inhabit" < *habere* "have"]

hab·i·ta·tion /hàbbi táysh'n/ *n* **1.** OCCUPANCY the state of being lived in by people or animals, or the act of living in a place ○ *unfit for human habitation* **2.** DWELLING PLACE a place in which to live ○ *The squirrels found a new habitation in a hollow tree.* **3.** DWELLINGS a group of dwellings and their inhabitants ○ *There is little evidence remaining of the ancient habitation.* [14C. Via French < Latin *habitation-* < *habitare* (see HABITAT)] —**hab·i·ta·tion·al** *adj*

hab·it-form·ing *adj* capable of causing a physiological or psychological need in somebody ○ *habit-forming drugs*

ha·bit·u·al /hə bíchoo əl/ *adj* **1.** DONE AS HABIT done so frequently and predictably as to constitute a habit **2.** PERSISTING IN BEHAVIOR continuing in a particular practice as a result of an ingrained tendency ○ *a habitual criminal* **3.** CHARACTERISTIC characteristic of somebody's character or behavior ○ *She tackled the problem with her habitual single-mindedness.* —**ha·bit·u·al·ly** *adv* —**ha·bit·u·al·ness** *n*

SYNONYMS See ***usual.***

ha·bit·u·ate /hə bíchoo àyt/ (**-at·ed, -at·ing, -ates**) *v* **1.** *vt* MAKE SOMEBODY USED TO SOMETHING to accustom a person or animal to something through prolonged and regular exposure (*formal*) ○ *People living in cities become habituated to crowds.* **2.** *vti* PSYCHOL LEARN TO

IGNORE STIMULUS to learn not to respond to a stimulus that is frequently repeated, or teach a person or animal to do this **3.** *vi* BECOME ACCUSTOMED TO DRUG to become dependent on or less affected by a medical or illegal drug through frequent use [16C. < late Latin *habituat-*, past participle of *habituare* "bring into a state" < Latin *habitus* (see HABIT)] —**ha·bit·u·a·tion** /hə bìchoo áysh'n/ *n*

hab·i·tude /hábbi to͞od/ *n* a tendency to act in a particular way (*formal*) —**hab·i·tu·di·nal** /hàbbi to͞od'nəl/ *adj*

ha·bit·u·é /hə bíchoo ày, hə bìchoo áy/ *n* a regular visitor of a place [Early 19C. < French < past participle of *habituer* < late Latin *habituare* (see HABITUATE)]

hab·i·tus /hábbitəss/ (*plural same*) *n* the general appearance, posture, or physical state of a patient, especially with regard to susceptibility to disease [Late 19C. < Latin (see HABIT)]

ha·boob /hə bo͞ob/ *n* a violent sandstorm or dust storm that sweeps across the deserts of northern Africa and Arabia and the plains of South Asia [Late 19C. < Arabic *habub* "violent storm"]

Habs·burg *n* HIST another spelling of **Hapsburg**

ha·bu /haá bo͞o/ (*plural* **-bus**) *n* a large light brown poisonous snake with black markings. Native to: Okinawa and neighboring Pacific islands. Latin name: *Trimeresurus flavoviridis.* [Late 19C. < Japanese]

há·ček /há chèk/ *n* in some Slavic and other languages, a mark (ˇ) placed over a letter to indicate a change in pronunciation. For example, in Czech it changes the sound of the letter "c" to "ch." See table at **diacritic** [Mid-20C. < Czech, "small hook" < *hak* "hook"]

ha·cen·da·do /haà sen daádō/ (*plural* **-dos**), **ha·ci·en·da·do** /haàssee en-/ *n Hispanic* an owner or manager of a hacienda [Mid-19C. < Spanish < *hacienda* (see HACIENDA)]

ha·chure /ha sho͝or, háshər/ *n* a short shading line, usually one of a group of such lines drawn in parallel, used on a map to indicate the direction and steepness of a slope [Mid-19C. < French < *hacher* "mark with hatches, chop" (see HATCH[3])]

ha·ci·en·da /haàssee éndə/ *n Hispanic* **1.** in Spain or Spanish-speaking parts of America, a large estate, farm, or ranch **2.** in Spain or Spanish-speaking parts of America, the main residence on a hacienda [Mid-18C. Via Spanish, "domestic work, large estate" < Latin *facienda* "things needing to be done" < *facere* "do"]

ha·ci·en·da·do *n* AGRIC another spelling of **hacendado**

Ha·ci·en·da Heights /haàssee endə hīts/ city in SW California. Population: 52,354 (2002 estimate).

hack[1] /hak/ *v* (**hacked, hack·ing, hacks**) **1.** *vti* CUT SOMETHING USING REPEATED BLOWS to cut or chop something by striking it with short repeated blows using a sharp tool such as a knife or an ax **2.** *vt* CUT WAY THROUGH OBSTRUCTION to cut a path or way through an obstruction, e.g., undergrowth ○ *I had to hack my way through the bureaucracy to get the job done.* **3.** *vt* CHOP SOMETHING OFF OR INTO PARTS to cut, shape, or divide something roughly or carelessly (*informal*) ○ *He's hacked a whole chunk off that article I wrote for the magazine.* **4.** *vi* COMPUT GAIN UNAUTHORIZED ACCESS TO COMPUTER DATA to use a computer or other technological device or system in order to gain unauthorized access to data held by another person or organization **5.** *vt* COPE WITH SOMETHING to succeed at or endure something (*informal*) ○ *I wonder if he can hack getting up at five every day.* **6.** *vi* COUGH WITH RASPING NOISE to cough persistently in short dry bursts with a rasping noise **7.** *vt* SOCCER, RUGBY KICK SOCCER PLAYER'S SHINS in soccer, to commit a foul by kicking the shins of an opposing player **8.** *vt* BASKETBALL HIT BASKETBALL PLAYER'S ARM in basketball, to commit a foul by striking another player on the arm ■ *n* **1.** QUICK CHOP a short violent blow with a sharp tool **2.** CUT MADE BY HACKING SOMETHING a rough cut made by a quick blow with a sharp tool, e.g., a notch in a tree made with an ax **3.** TOOL FOR HACKING a tool used for chopping something or breaking up hard ground, e.g., a pickax **4.** COUGHING NOISE a short dry cough **5.** WOUND FROM KICK a wound from being kicked **6.** SOCCER, RUGBY DISABLING KICK IN SOCCER a kick on the shins in soccer, meant to disable a player temporarily **7.** COMPUT SUCCESSFUL EFFORT an extremely good, often very time-consuming, work effort that produces exactly what is needed (*informal*) [Old English *haccian* "cut in pieces" < W Germanic] ◇ **not be able to hack it** not be able to manage or cope (*informal*)

hack around *vi* to spend time doing silly or unimportant things or doing nothing at all (*informal*)

hack[2] /hak/ *n* **1.** POL UNCRITICAL POLITICAL PARTY WORKER a political party member who serves the party uncritically and in a routine capacity **2.** same as **taxi** (*informal*) **3.** TRANSP same as **hackie** (*informal*) **4.** DRUDGE a mediocre and unimaginative person, especially somebody engaged in dull or uninspired work **5.** UNORIGINAL WRITER a writer who produces routine unoriginal writing, especially for newspapers, magazines, television, or movies **6.** CAR OR CARRIAGE FOR HIRE an automobile or a carriage for hire **7.** OLD HORSE a horse that is in bad condition through age or overwork **8.** HORSE FOR HIRE a horse that is hired out **9.** HORSE FOR RIDING a horse for riding or driving ■ *adj* TRITE lacking quality and originality ○ *The movie had a really hack plot.* ■ *v* (**hacked, hack·ing, hacks**) **1.** *vi* DRIVE TAXICAB to work as a taxi driver (*informal*) **2.** *vi* RIDING GO HORSEBACK RIDING to ride a horse for exercise at a normal pace **3.** *vt* MAKE SOMETHING HACKNEYED to make an expression or phrase trite through overuse [Early 18C. Shortening of HACKNEY]

hack·a·more /hákə màwr/ *n* a bridle without a bit but with an adjustable band by which a rider can exert pressure on a horse's nose, used especially to break young horses [Mid-19C. Alteration (by association with HACK[2]) of Spanish *jaquima* < Arabic *shaqīmah* "restraint, bit"]

REGIONAL NOTE The term ***hackamore*** was originally used in the Western states before the Civil War. Not limited to the Mexican-American settlements, this ranching term spread from Texas and New Mexico to Oregon, but is virtually unknown east of Texas.

---

hack and slash·er *n* a computer game that features a great deal of violence (*slang*)

hack·ber·ry /hák bèrree/ (*plural* **-ries**) *n* a tree of the elm family with soft yellowish wood and fruit resembling cherries. Native to: North America. Latin name: *Celtis occidentalis.* [Mid-18C. < variant of *hag* < N Germanic]

hacked off *adj UK* annoyed or dissatisfied (*informal*)

Hack·en·sack /hákən sàk/ city in northeastern New Jersey, originally settled by the Dutch and now a suburb of New York City. Population: 43,525 (2002 estimate).

hack·er /hákər/ *n* **1.** SOMEBODY ACCESSING ANOTHER'S COMPUTER WITHOUT AUTHORIZATION a computer user who gains unauthorized access to a computer system or data belonging to somebody else **2.** COMPUTER ENTHUSIAST somebody who is interested or skilled in computer technology and programming **3.** AMATEUR PLAYER somebody who enjoys a sport but lacks skill in it **4.** SOMEBODY WHO CHOPS somebody who cuts or chops something

hack·er eth·ic *n* the belief that all technical information should be freely shared and that gaining unauthorized access to computer systems is acceptable if there is no injury or expense to others

hack·ie /hákee/ *n* a taxicab driver (*informal*)

hack·ing coat /háking-/ *n UK* CLOTHING same as **hacking jacket**

hack·ing cough /hàking-/ *n* a repeated cough that is short, dry, and rasping

hack·ing jack·et /háking-/ *n* a tweed or woolen jacket with side or back vents and a full skirt, worn especially for horseback riding

hack·le[1] /hák'l/ *n* **1.** BIRDS BIRD'S NECK FEATHER a long slender feather on the neck or lower back of a male bird, especially a domestic fowl **2.** FISHING FEATHERS USED FOR FISHING FLY a tuft of feathers from the neck of a bird used in making an artificial fly for fishing **3.** FISHING FISHING FLY MADE FROM FEATHERS an artificial fly for fishing made from the neck feathers of a bird **4.** TEXTILES FLAX COMB a steel comb with long teeth used to comb out flax, hemp, or jute fibers ■ **hack·les** *npl* HAIRS ON ANIMAL'S NECK the line of hairs on the back of the neck and along the spine of an animal, especially a dog or cat, that stand up when it is threatened or angry ■ *vt* (**-led, -ling, -les**) **1.** FISHING PUT FEATHERS ON FISHING FLY to trim an artificial fly with the neck feathers of a bird **2.** TEXTILES COMB FLAX BEFORE SPINNING to comb out flax, hemp, or jute fibers using a hackle [15C. Probably < assumed Old English *hacule* "little hook" < Germanic] —**hack·ler** *n* ◇ **make somebody's hackles rise, raise somebody's hackles, get somebody's hackles up** to make somebody angry or hostile

hack·le[2] /hák'l/ (**-led, -ling, -les**) *vti* to mangle something by cutting it roughly [Late 16C. < HACK[1]]

hack·ly /háklee/ (**-li·er, -li·est**) *adj* having a rough jagged surface

hack·man /hákmən/ (*plural* **-men** /-mən/) *n* the driver of a taxi

Hack·man /hákmən/, **Gene** (*b.* 1930) US movie actor. He won Academy Awards for *The French Connection* (1971) and *Unforgiven* (1992). Full name **Hackman, Eugene Alden**

hack·ma·tack /hákmə tàk/ *n* **1.** TREES, INDUST same as **tamarack 2.** TREES same as **balsam poplar** [Late 18C. < Algonquian *akemantek* "snowshoe wood"]

hack·ney /háknee/ (*plural* **-neys**) *n* **1.** an automobile or carriage for hire **2.** a horse for riding or driving [13C. Probably after *Hackney*, NE London]

hack·neyed /hákneed/ *adj* made commonplace and stale by overuse ○ *the same old hackneyed sales talk*

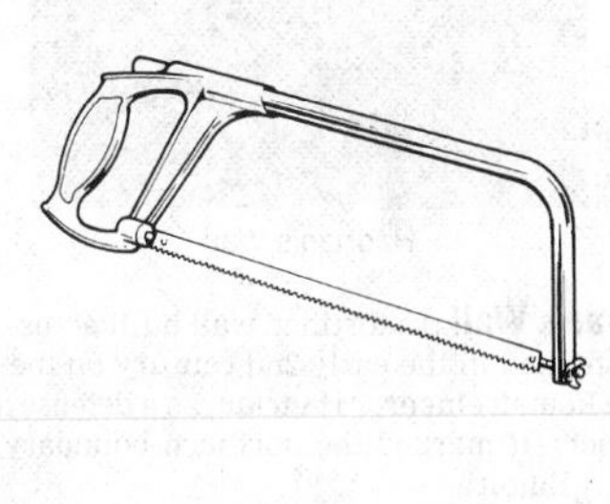

hacksaw

hack·saw /hák sàw/ *n* a handsaw with a small-toothed steel blade stretched taut across a frame, used for cutting metal ■ *vt* (**-sawed, -sawn** /-sawn/ or **-sawed, -saw·ing, -saws**) to cut something using a hacksaw

hack·tiv·ism /háktəv ìzzəm/ *n* the activity of breaking into and sabotaging a computer system via the Internet as a political protest ○ *"The apparent increase in hacktivism may be due in part to the growing importance of the Internet as a means of communication."* (*Wired Web site*; April 1999) [Late 20C. Blend of HACKER + ACTIVISM] —**hack·tiv·ist** *n, adj*

hack·work /hák wùrk/ *n* ordinary literary, artistic, or professional work that somebody is hired to do (*disapproving*)

had past participle, past tense of **have**

had·dock /háddək/ (*plural same* or **-docks**) *n* **1.** a fish that is related to but smaller than the cod. Native to: northern Atlantic. Latin name: *Melanogrammus aeglefinus.* **2.** the flesh of a haddock used as food [14C. Via Anglo-Norman *hadoc* < Old French *(h)adot*]

hade /hayd/ *n* GEOL the angle between the vertical plane and a plane containing a vein, fault, or lode ■ *vi* (**had·ed, had·ing, hades**) to be at an angle with the vertical [Late 17C. Origin ?]

Had·e·an /hàydee ən/ *adj* **1.** relating to Hades **2.** relating to the Hadean eon

Had·e·an e·on *n* the period of geologic time not confirmed by rock formation records, beginning approximately 4.6 billion years ago with the formation of the Earth

Ha·des /háy deez/ *n* **1.** *also* **ha·des** same as **hell** (*informal*) **2.** in Greek mythology, the underworld kingdom inhabited by the souls of the dead. Roman equivalent **Dis 3.** in Greek mythology, the god of the underworld and husband of Persephone. Roman equivalent **Pluto** (sense 2) [Late 16C. < Greek *Haidēs*, god of the dead]

Ha·dhra·maut /haàdrə máwt/, **Ha·dra·maut** coastal region in the southern Arabian peninsula, shared between Yemen and Oman. The ancient civilization that flourished there is called "Hazarmaveth" in the Bible. Area: 60,000 sq. mi./155,400 sq. km.

Ha·dith /hə déeth/, **ha·dith** *n* the collected traditions, teachings, and stories of the prophet Muhammad, accepted as a source of Islamic doctrine and law second only to the Koran [Early 18C. < Arabic *ḥadīṯ* "tradition"]

hadj, etc. ISLAM another spelling of **hajj, etc.**

had·n't /hádd'nt/ *contr* had not

Had·ra·maut another spelling of **Hadhramaut**

Ha·dri·an /háydree ən/ (76–138) Roman emperor. As emperor (117–138) he consolidated the Roman Empire by establishing a series of defense fortifications, including Hadrian's Wall, that marked the end of Roman territorial expansion.

> "Little soul, wandering, gentle guest and companion of the body, into what places will you now go?"
> [Hadrian, *Dying words*; 138]

Barnaby's
Hadrian's Wall

Ha·dri·an's Wall *n* a fortified wall built across northern England in the early 2nd century on the orders of the Roman emperor Hadrian, as a defense against the Picts. It marked the northern boundary of the Roman Empire.

had·ron /háddrən, hád ròn/ *n* an elementary particle that is made up of gluons or quarks or both and participates in the strong interaction [Mid-20C. < Greek *hadros* "bulky"] —**had·ron·ic** /ha drónnik, hə-/ *adj*

had·ro·saur /háddrə sàwr/ *n* an amphibious plant-eating dinosaur with a snout resembling a duck's bill and strong hind legs for walking in swamps. Hadrosaur fossils have been found in sediments from the Upper Cretaceous period. Genus: *Anatosaurus*. [Late 19C. < modern Latin *hadrosaurus* < Greek *hadros* "bulky" + *sauros* "lizard"]

hadst /hadst/ *v* 2nd person singular past of **have** (*archaic*)

haec·ce·i·ty /hek sée ətee/ *n* the essential property that makes an individual uniquely that individual [Mid-17C. < medieval Latin *heicceitas* < Latin *haec* "this"]

Haeck·el /hék'l/, **Ernst** (1834–1919) German zoologist and evolutionist. He was an early advocate of Charles Darwin's theories, and is chiefly remembered for producing genealogical trees of species development. Full name **Haeckel, Ernst Heinrich Philipp August**

Haeck·el's law *n* the theory proposing as a law that an embryo in each stage of development resembles an organism that its species descended from [After Ernst HAECKEL]

haem /heem/ *n* BIOCHEM UK spelling of **heme**

haema-, etc. another spelling of **hema-, etc.**

-haemia *suffix* another spelling of **-emia**

ha·fiz /haáfiz/ *n* the title used to address somebody who has committed the Koran to memory [Mid-17C. Via Persian < Arabic *ḥāfiẓ* "guardian"]

haf·ni·um /háfnee əm/ *n* a bright silvery metallic element. Source: zirconium ores. Use: absorption of neutrons in nuclear reactor rods, manufacture of tungsten filaments. Symbol **Hf**. See table at **element** [Early 20C. < modern Latin < *Hafnia*, Latin name for Copenhagen, Denmark]

haft /haft/ *n* the handle of a knife, ax, or other weapon or tool (*literary*) [Old English *hæft(e)* < Germanic] —**haft** *vt* —**haft·er** *n*

haf·ta·rah /hàftə raá/ (*plural* **-rahs** or **-roth** /-rṓth/ or **-rot** /-rṓt/), **haf·to·rah** (*plural* **-rahs** or **-roth** or **-rot**), **haph·ta·rah** *n* a reading from the Prophets following each lesson from the Torah in synagogue services on the Sabbath [Early 18C. < Hebrew *haphṭārāh* "conclusion"]

hag /hag/ *n* **1.** an offensive term that deliberately insults a woman's appearance, temperament, and age (*slang*) **2.** a witch, especially an elderly one **3.** FISH same as **hagfish** [14C. Origin ?] —**hag·gish** *adj*

Hag. *abbr* BIBLE Haggai

Ha·gar /háy gaàr, háygər/ *n* in the Bible, an Egyptian servant of Sarah who bore Sarah's husband, Abraham, a son named Ishmael (Genesis 16, 21:1–21) [< Hebrew *Haghar*]

Ha·gen /háygən/, **Walter** (1892–1969) US golfer. He won the US Open (1914 and 1919) and the British Open (1922, 1924, and 1928–29). Full name **Hagen, Walter Charles**

Hag·ers·town /háygərz tòwn/ industrial city in northwestern Maryland, near the Potomac River, founded in 1762. Population: 36,659 (2002 estimate).

hag·fish /hág fish/ (*plural same* or **-fish·es**) *n* a primitive jawless fish with a long body and a sucking mouth that it uses for feeding off other fishes. Native to: oceans worldwide. Family: Myxinidae.

Hag·ga·dah /hə gaádə/ (*plural* **-dahs** or **-doth** /hə gaádōth/), **Hag·ga·da** (*plural* **-das** or **-doth**), **Ag·ga·dah** /aà gaa daá, ə gaádə/ (*plural* **Ag·ga·doth** /aà gaa dáwt, ə gaá dòt/) *n* **1.** PASSOVER SERVICE, OR BOOK CONTAINING IT the service for the ritual meal (**Seder**) celebrated by Jews at Passover, or the book containing this service. It includes the story of the Exodus from Egypt. **2.** RABBINICAL LITERATURE ON BIBLICAL STORIES those sections of the Talmud and other rabbinical literature that deal with biblical narrative and stories and legends on biblical themes, rather than with religious law and regulations **3.** STORY OF ISRAELITES' EXODUS FROM EGYPT the account of the Exodus of the Israelites from Egypt that is central to the Jewish Passover ritual [Mid-19C. < Hebrew *haggāḏāh* "tale" < *higgîḏ* "tell"] —**hag·gad·ic** /hə gáddik/ *adj*

Hag·ga·i /há gì, hággee ì/ *n* **1.** in the Bible, a Hebrew prophet who urged the Israelites to rebuild their temple in Jerusalem in prophecies believed to have been made in 520 B.C. **2.** a book of the Bible that describes the rebuilding of the Israelites' temple after their return to Jerusalem from exile in Babylon and records the prophecies traditionally attributed to Haggai. See table at **Bible**

hag·gard /hággərd/ *adj* **1.** TIRED-LOOKING showing signs of tiredness, anxiety, or hunger on the face, e.g., dark rings around the eyes **2.** UNRULY wild and unruly in appearance **3.** BIRDS UNMANAGEABLE in falconry, used to describe a hawk that has reached maturity before being captured and is therefore wild and unmanageable ■ *n* HAWK in falconry, a captured wild adult hawk [Late 16C. < French *hagard* "untamed" (used of hawks)] —**hag·gard·ly** *adv* —**hag·gard·ness** *n*

hag·gis /hággiss/ (*plural* **-gis·es**) *n* a Scottish dish made from chopped lamb's heart, lungs, and liver mixed with suet, oats, onions, and seasonings, which is packed into a round sausage skin and usually boiled. Haggis is traditionally cooked in a cleaned sheep's stomach, but artificial casings are now frequently used. [15C. Origin ?]

ORIGIN One possible source of ***haggis*** is Middle English *haggen*, meaning "to chop," a northern variant of *hack*. From this view, its name would refer to its chopped-up contents. An alternative possibility is Old French *agace*, meaning "magpie." This is supported by a parallel semantic development of English *pie*, which originally meant "magpie" but was apparently applied to a "pastry case with a filling" from the notion that the collection of edible odds and ends in a pie resembles the collection of trinkets assembled by the acquisitive magpie. The miscellaneous assortment of sheep's entrails and other ingredients in a haggis would therefore represent the magpie's hoard.

hag·gle /hágg'l/ (**-gled, -gling, -gles**) *vi* to argue over something such as a price or contract in order to reach an agreement [Late 16C. < variant of HACK[1]] —**hag·gle** *n* —**hag·gler** *n*

hagio- *prefix* saints, holy ○ *hagiolatry* ○ *hagioscope* [< Greek *hagios* "holy"]

hag·i·oc·ra·cy /hàggee ókrəssee, hàyjee-/ (*plural* **-cies**) *n* **1.** government by saints, prophets, or other holy people **2.** a state or community governed by holy people

Hag·i·og·ra·pha /hàggee óggrəfə, hàyjee-/ *n* the last of the three main parts into which the Hebrew Bible is divided [Late 16C. Via late Latin < Greek < *hagios* "holy" + *grapha* "writings"]

hag·i·og·raph·er /hàggee óggrəfər, hàyjee-/, **hag·i·og·raph·ist** /-fist/ *n* **1.** BIOGRAPHER OF SAINTS a writer of biographies of the saints **2.** REVERENTIAL BIOGRAPHER a writer of biographies that treat their subjects with undue reverence **3.** WRITER OF HEBREW BIBLE a writer of the Hagiographa

hag·i·og·ra·phy /hàggee óggrəfee, hàyjee-/ (*plural* **-phies**) *n* **1.** biography of a saint or the saints **2.** biography that treats its subject with undue reverence —**hag·i·o·graph·ic** /-ə gráffik/ *adj*

hag·i·ol·a·try /hàggee óllətree, hàyjee-/ *n* the worship or idolizing of saints

hag·i·ol·o·gy /hàggee óllәjee, hàyjee-/ (*plural* **-gies**) *n* **1.** WRITINGS ABOUT SAINTS literature about the lives of the saints **2.** BIOGRAPHY OF SAINT a biography of a saint, or a collection of such biographies **3.** LIST OF SAINTS an authoritative list of saints **4.** SACRED WRITINGS a collection or history of sacred writings —**hag·i·o·log·ic** /-ə lójjik/ *adj* —**hag·i·ol·o·gist** *n*

hag·i·o·scope /hággee ə skòp, háyjee-/ *n* a narrow opening in an interior wall of a church that allows members of the congregation seated at the sides to see the altar —**hag·i·o·scop·ic** /-skóppik, hàyjee-/ *adj*

hag·rid·den *adj* plagued by fear or mental anguish

Hague, The /háyg/ city in the western Netherlands, seat of the Dutch government and capital of South Holland Province. Population: 440,900 (2000). Dutch name **Den Haag**

hah *interj* another spelling of **ha**[1]

ha-ha[1] /haá haá/, **haw-haw** /háw hàw/ *interj* **1.** in writing used to indicate the sound of somebody laughing **2.** used to tease or ridicule somebody (*informal*) ○ *"Where is it?" "Ha-ha, wouldn't you like to know?"* [Old English. Natural exclamation]

ha-ha[2] /haá haá/, **haw-haw** /hàw háw/ *n* a deep ditch or steep change in level, sometimes supported by a wall, that marks the boundary of a large garden but is not visible from within it [Early 18C. < French; probably < a cry of surprise when finding one]

hah·ni·um /haánee əm/ *n* dubnium or hassium [Late 20C. After Otto *Hahn* (1879–1968), German chemist]

haick *n* CLOTHING another spelling of **haik**

Hai·da /hídə/ (*plural same* or **-das**) *n* **1.** a member of a Native North American people living along and off the coast of British Columbia and the adjoining Alaskan coast. The Haida are particularly noted for their intricately carved dugout canoes and miniature totems. **2.** the language of the Haida, now spoken by very few people [Early 20C. < Haida, "people"] —**Hai·da** *adj* —**Hai·dan** *adj*

Hai·da Gwai'i /-gwí/ *n* the traditional territory of the Haida

Hai·dar A·li /hídər aa lée/ (1722–82) Indian soldier and ruler. The sultan of Mysore (1759–82), he waged war against the British in India and was defeated by Sir Eyre Coote (1781–82).

Hai·fa /hífə/ city and chief seaport of Israel, situated in the northern part of the country. Population: 265,700 (1999).

Haig /hayg/, **Alexander** (*b.* 1924) US general and secretary of state (1981–82). He commanded an infantry division in Vietnam and later served as White House chief of staff (1973–74) and NATO commander (1974–79) before becoming Ronald Reagan's secretary of state in 1981.

Haig, Douglas, 1st Earl Haig (1861–1928) British field marshal. During World War I, he was made commander of the British Expeditionary Forces in France.

> "Every position must be held to the last man: there must be no retirement. With our backs to the wall, and believing in the justice of our cause, each one of us must fight on to the end."
> [Douglas Haig, *Order to the British troops*; April 2, 1918]

haik /hīk, hayk/, **haick** *n* a loose-fitting North African garment made from a rectangle of cloth, usually white, that is wrapped around the head and body. It is worn by men and women. [Early 18C. < Arabic *hā'ik*]

Hai·kou /hī kṓ/ capital of Hainan Province in China, on the northern side of the island of Hainan. Population: 280,153 (1991).

hai·ku /hī ko͝o/ (*plural same*) *n* a form of Japanese poetry with 17 syllables in three unrhymed lines of five, seven, and five syllables, often describing nature or a season [Late 19C. < Japanese < *hai* "amusement" (< Middle Chinese *b@ij*) + *ku* "sentence" (< Middle Chinese *ku@h*)]

hail[1] /hayl/ *n* **1.** small balls of ice and hardened snow that fall like rain **2.** a barrage of something such as missiles or insults ○ *a hail of exploding flying glass* [Old English *hagol, hægl* < Indo-European] —**hail** *vi*

hail[2] /hayl/ *vt* (**hailed, hail·ing, hails**) **1.** ACCLAIM SOMEBODY OR SOMETHING to praise or approve a person, action, or accomplishment with enthusiasm ○ *The press hailed her as a child prodigy.* **2.** GET SOMEBODY'S ATTENTION BY SHOUTING to attract the attention of somebody or something such as a taxicab or ship by calling or signaling ○ *hail a taxi* **3.** GREET SOMEBODY to welcome or greet somebody upon meeting ○ *We hailed each other like long-lost buddies.* ■ *interj* EXCLAMATION OF GREETING used to greet, welcome, or acclaim somebody (*archaic or literary*) [12C. Variant of HALE[1]] —**hail** *n* —**hail·er** *n* ◇ **within hail** near enough to hear a shout or see a signal (*dated*)

hail from *vt* to live in or come from a particular place, especially as a birthplace or place of origin ○ *Her husband hails from Seattle.*

Hai·le Se·las·sie I /hīlee sə lássee/, **emperor of Ethiopia** (1892–1975) He acceded to the Ethiopian throne in 1916 and was a modernizing emperor (1930–36, 1942–74). Born **Makonnen, Ras Tafari**

hail-fel·low-well-met, hail-fel·low *adj* very friendly, especially in a way that presumes an intimacy that does not exist ■ *n* an exuberantly friendly person (*archaic*) [< the greeting *Hail, fellow! Well met!*]

Hail Mar·y (*plural* **Hail Mar·ys**) *n* **1.** PRAYER INVOKING VIRGIN MARY'S INTERCESSION a Roman Catholic prayer to the Virgin Mary based on Gabriel's and Elizabeth's greetings to her as recorded in the Gospel of Luke in the Bible. Churchgoers are often required to repeat the prayer as a penance, given in the sacrament of reconciliation. **2.** FOOTBALL LAST-MINUTE PASS in football, a long high pass into the end zone, in an effort to score a touchdown before time runs out in the half or game (*slang*) **3.** LAST-DITCH EFFORT OR PLAN a proposition, plan, request, or effort that is made as a last resort or final recourse (*slang*) [Translation of medieval Latin *Ave, Maria*, opening words of the prayer]

Hail·sham /háylshəm/, **Quintin Hogg, 2nd Viscount, Baron Hailsham of St. Marylebone** (1907–2001) British politician. First elected to Parliament in 1938, he held many government posts, and was Lord Chancellor (1970–74, 1979–87). Full name **Hogg, Quintin McGarel**

hail·stone /háyl stṓn/ *n* a pellet of ice and hardened snow that falls like rain

hail·storm /háyl stàwrm/ *n* a storm that includes a downpour of hail

haim·ish /háymish/, **heim·ish** *adj* possessing the warmth, comfort, and informality associated with somebody's own home (*informal*) ○ *The inn was very haimish and comfortable.* [Mid-20C. Via Yiddish *heymish* "like home" < Middle High German *heimisch* "of the home"]

Hai·nan /hī naán/ province in southeastern China comprising the island of Hainan in the South China Sea. Capital: Haikou. Population: 7,340,000 (1997). Area: 13,200 sq. mi./34,300 sq. km.

haint /haynt/ *n Southern US* a ghost or other phenomenon believed to be supernatural [Variant of HAUNT *n* (sense 2)]

Hai·phong /hī fóng/ city and seaport in northern Vietnam, on the Red River delta. Population: 783,133 (1992).

hair /hər/ *n* **1.** STRANDS GROWING ON HEAD OR BODY the mass of fine flexible protein strands that grow from follicles on the skin of a person or animal, especially those on somebody's head **2.** SINGLE STRAND a fine strand that grows out of the skin of a person or animal ○ *The rug was covered with dog hairs.* **3.** FINE GROWTH ON PLANT a thin flexible growth on a plant resembling a human or animal hair **4.** FABRIC fabric made from animal hair **5.** TINY AMOUNT a tiny amount or degree ○ *won by a hair* [Old English *hær* < Germanic] —**haired** /haird/ *adj* —**hair·less** *adj* —**hair·less·ness** *n* ◇ **be tearing your hair out** to be very irritated or frustrated ◇ **have somebody by the short hairs** *UK* to have somebody in your control or power (*informal*) ◇ **let your hair down** to behave in a more relaxed way than usual (*informal*) ◇ **not turn a hair** to remain completely calm ◇ **split hairs** to argue about or give undue significance to fine distinctions and details ◇ **the hair of the dog (that bit you)** an alcoholic drink taken as a supposed cure for a hangover (*informal*)

SPELLCHECK hair or **hare**? Do not confuse the spelling of ***hair*** and ***hare***, which sound similar. The word ***hair*** means "a strand or mass of fine strands growing out of the skin" (*a girl with black hair, dog hairs all over my pants*), or "a tiny amount" (*to win by a hair*). The word ***hare*** denotes an animal resembling a large rabbit.

hair·ball /hér bàwl/ *n* a ball of hair that accumulates in the stomach of some animals such as cats and cows when they clean themselves. It often causes indigestion and retching.

hair·band /hér bànd/ *n* a strip of fabric worn on the head to keep the hair in place or out of the eyes

~~hair-brained~~ incorrect spelling of **harebrained**

hair·breadth /hér brèdth/ *n* same as **hairsbreadth** ■ *adj* exceedingly narrow

hair·brush /hér brùsh/ *n* a brush for smoothing and styling hair

hair cell *n* a sensory cell with fine projections resembling hairs, especially one in the inner ear that transmits information on sound or movement to the brain

hair·cloth /hér klàwth, -klòth/ *n* a thick coarse fabric made from horse's or camel's hair. Use: upholstery.

hair·cut /hér kùt/ *n* **1.** a session in which somebody's hair is cut **2.** the shape or style in which somebody's hair is cut ○ *How do you like my new haircut?* —**hair·cut·ter** *n* —**hair·cut·ting** *n, adj*

hair·do /hér do͞o/ (*plural* **-dos**) *n* the way in which somebody's hair has been cut or styled (*informal*)

hair·dress·er /hér drèssər/ *n* **1.** somebody whose job is to cut and style people's hair **2.** a shop or salon where a hairdresser works

hair·dress·ing /hér drèssing/ *n* **1.** CARE OF HAIR the cutting or styling of hair **2.** HAIRDRESSER'S PROFESSION the occupation of a hairdresser **3.** HAIR CARE PRODUCT a preparation used to style or care for the hair, especially an oil, cream, or gel

hair dry·er *n* a device that uses heated air for drying hair, either handheld or in the shape of a dome that fits over the head

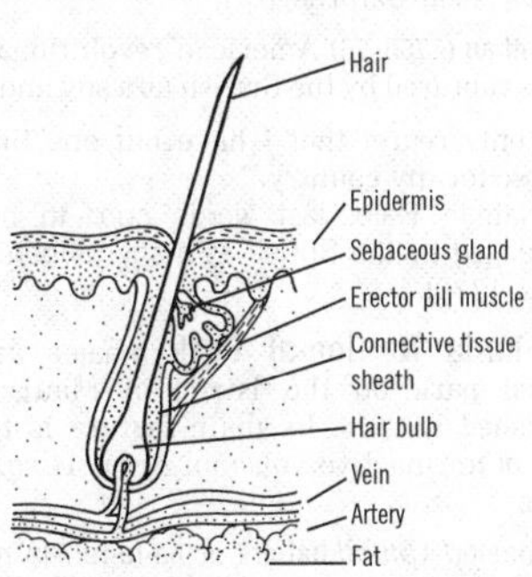

cross section of hair follicle

hair fol·li·cle *n* a small tubular pit in the outer layer of skin (**epidermis**) enclosing the base of a growing hair

hair·line /hér līn/ *n* **1.** WHERE HAIR BEGINS ON HEAD the line across the top of the forehead behind which the hair grows **2.** THIN LINE a very narrow line that is barely visible **3.** THIN STROKE a very thin line on a typeface, or a typeface containing thin lines **4.** FABRIC WITH FINE STRIPES a textile pattern of very thin stripes, or a fabric with such stripes

hair·net /hér nèt/ *n* a circular piece of fine netting with an elastic edge, worn to hold the hair in place, especially in bed

hair·piece /hér pēess/ *n* a wig, toupee, or other piece of false hair, worn to conceal hair loss or to add bulk or length to somebody's natural hair

hair·pin /hér pìn/ *n* **1.** BENT WIRE FOR HOLDING HAIR a U-shaped piece of metal wire used to hold the hair in place **2.** U SHAPE something with a U shape, especially a sharp bend in a road **3.** SYMBOL FOR CRESCENDO OR DECRESCENDO a long V-shaped mark used in written music to indicate an increase or decrease in loudness (*informal*)

hair·pin curve, hair·pin turn *n* a very sharp curve in a road or on a racing circuit that almost doubles back on itself

hair-rais·ing /hér ràyzing/ *adj* causing intense fear or excitement —**hair-rais·er** *n* —**hair-rais·ing·ly** *adv*

hairs·breadth /hérz brèdth/, **hair's-breadth** *n* a very small margin or distance

hair shirt *n* **1.** a shirt made from a harsh scratchy haircloth that was once worn next to the skin by religious people as a form of self-imposed punishment **2.** a self-imposed punishment in the form of private suffering

hair space *n* the thinnest space used to separate words and letters in typesetting

hair·split·ting /hér splìtting/ *n* overattention to unimportant details and fine distinctions, especially in an argument —**hair·split·ter** *n* —**hair·split·ting** *adj*

hair spray /hér sprày/, **hair·spray** (*plural* **hair sprays** or **hair·sprays**) *n* a substance sprayed onto the hair to hold it in place

hair·spring /hér sprìng/ *n* a very fine coiled spring that controls the movement of the balance wheel in a watch or clock

hair·streak /hér strēek/ *n* a brown or grayish butterfly with delicate streaks on the underside of its wings and fine tails resembling hairs on its hind wings. Subfamily: Theclinae. Native to: tropical America.

hair stroke *n* a very fine line in writing or printing

hair·style /hér stīl/ *n* the way in which somebody's hair is cut and arranged ○ *How do you like my new hairstyle?* —**hair·styl·ing** *n* —**hair·styl·ist** *n*

hair trig·ger *n* **1.** a gun trigger that needs very little pressure to activate it **2.** a response or mechanism that reacts to the slightest provocation or impulse (*hyphenated before a noun*) [< the thin spring that it activates]

hair·weav·ing /hér wēeving/ *n* the interweaving of a hairpiece with somebody's own hair, often done to disguise hair loss —**hair·weave** *n, vt* —**hair·weav·er** *n*

hair·worm /hér wùrm/ *n* **1.** a nematode worm that lives as a parasite in the digestive tracts of domestic animals. Genus: *Trichostrongylus*. **2.** a long slender worm found in water or damp soil whose larvae live as parasites on arthropods. Phylum: Nematomorpha.

hair·y /hérree/ (**-i·er, -i·est**) *adj* **1.** COVERED WITH HAIR covered with hair or filaments resembling hair **2.** MADE OF HAIR made of hair, or similar in texture to something made of hair **3.** FRIGHTENING filled with dangers or difficulties (*informal*) —**hair·i·ness** *n*

hair·y wood·peck·er *n* a common large woodpecker with black-and-white markings and a long beak. Native to: North America. Latin name: *Picoides villosus*.

Hai·ti /háytee/ country occupying the western third of the island of Hispaniola in the northern Caribbean. Language: French, Haitian Creole. Currency: gourde. Capital: Port-au-Prince. Population: 7,527,817 (2003). Area: 10,714 sq. mi./27,750 sq. km. Official name **Republic of Haiti**. See map on next page —**Hai·tian** /háysh'n/ *n, adj*

Hai·tian Cre·ole *n* the French-based creole spoken in Haiti. Native speakers: 4 million. —**Hai·tian Cre·ole** *adj*

Hai·tink /hítingk/, **Bernard** (*b.* 1929) Dutch conductor. One of the leading conductors of the later 20th century, he led the Concertgebouw Orchestra in Amsterdam, the Netherlands (1961–88) and the London Philharmonic Orchestra (1967–79).

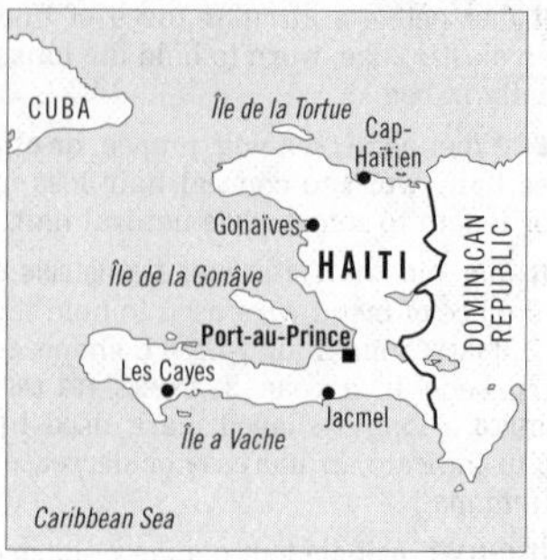

Haiti

halberd

haj, etc. ISLAM another spelling of **hajj, etc.**

hajj /haj/, **hadj, haj** *n* the pilgrimage to Mecca, Saudi Arabia, that is a principal religious obligation of adult Muslims [Late 17C. < Arabic, "pilgrimage"]

haj·ja /hájjə/, **had·ja, haj·a** *n* a Muslim woman who has made the pilgrimage to Mecca (*also used as a title*) [< form of Turkish, Persian *ḥājī* (see HAJJI)]

Haj·jaj /ha jaáj, kha jaáj/ *n* the governor of the eastern provinces of India during the Arab Umayyad dynasty

haj·ji /hájjee/ (*plural* **-jis**), **had·ji, haj·i** (*plural* **-is**) *n* a Muslim who has made the pilgrimage to Mecca (*also used as a title*) [Early 17C. Directly or via Turkish < Persian *ḥājī* "pilgrim" < Arabic *hajj* "pilgrimage"]

hake /hayk/ (*plural same or* **hakes**) *n* **1.** a valuable food fish similar to cod that has two dorsal fins and an elongated body. Native to: oceans worldwide. Genus: *Merluccius*. **2.** the flesh of a hake used as food [15C. Origin ?]

ha·kim[1] /haá keém/, **ha·keem** *n* a Muslim doctor who uses traditional remedies [Mid-17C. < Arabic *ḥakīm* "wise man"]

ha·kim[2] /haákim/ *n* a Muslim judge, ruler, or administrator [Early 17C. < Arabic *ḥākim* "ruler"]

Hak·luyt /hák lo͝ot/, **Richard** (1552?–1616) English geographer. His works on English naval exploration include *Divers Voyages Touching the Discovery of America and the Islands Adjacent* (1582).

Ha·ko·da·te /haákō daát ay/ seaport on Tsugaru Strait in southern Hokkaido, Japan, famous for its breweries. Population: 284,690 (2002).

ha·ku /haá ko͞o/ *n Hawaii* a crown made of fresh flowers

hal- *prefix* same as **halo-** (*used before vowels*)

Ha·lab /há làb/ ♦ **Aleppo**

Ha·la·cha /haá laa khaá, haa laákhə/, **Ha·la·kha, Ha·la·khah** *n* the body of Jewish law beginning with the Pentateuch, developed by the rabbis [Mid-19C. < Hebrew *hă lāḵāh* "law"]

ha·lal /hə laál/ *adj* **1.** RITUALLY SLAUGHTERED describes meat from animals that have been slaughtered in the ritual way prescribed by Islamic law **2.** OF HALAL MEAT relating to halal meat ■ *n* MEAT FROM RITUALLY SLAUGHTERED ANIMALS meat from animals that have been slaughtered in the ritual way prescribed by Islamic law ■ *vt* **(-lalled, -lal·ling, -lals)** SLAUGHTER ANIMALS RITUALLY to slaughter animals for meat in the ritual way prescribed by Islamic law [Mid-19C. < Arabic *ḥalāl* "lawful"]

ha·la·la /hə laálə/ (*plural same or* **-las**) *n* a subunit of Saudi Arabian currency. See table at **currency** [Mid-20C. < Arabic]

ha·la·tion /hə láysh'n/ *n* **1.** a blurred bright patch around a light source on a photographic image. It is caused by light being reflected off the film base and back onto the light-sensitive layer. **2.** a patch or ring of glowing light around a bright object on a television screen [Mid-19C. < HALO]

hal·berd /hálbərd, háwl-/, **hal·bert** /-bərt/ *n* an ax blade and pick with a spearhead on top, mounted on a long handle and used as a weapon in the 15th and 16th centuries [15C. Via French < Middle High German *helmbarde* < *helm* "handle" + *barde* "hatchet"] —**hal·ber·dier** /hàlbər deér, hàwl-/ *n*

hal·cy·on /hálssee ən/ *adj* tranquil and free from disturbance or care (*literary*) ■ *n* **1.** in Greek mythology, a bird resembling the kingfisher, believed to have had the power to calm the waves at the time of the winter solstice when it nested at sea **2.** same as **kingfisher** [14C. Via Latin < Greek *(h)alkuōn*, mythical bird]

hal·cy·on days *npl* **1.** a time of happiness and tranquillity (*literary*) **2.** two weeks of calm weather during the winter solstice

hal·di /húldee/ *n S Asia* turmeric used as a spice in Indian cuisine [Mid-19C. Via Hindi < Sanskrit *haridrā*]

hale[1] /hayl/ **(hal·er, hal·est)** *adj* in robust good health [Old English *hāl* (see WHOLE)] —**hale·ness** *n*

hale[2] /hayl/ **(haled, hal·ing, hales)** *vt* **1.** to compel somebody to go somewhere, especially to court (*formal*) **2.** to pull or drag somebody or something with great effort (*archaic*) [13C. Via French < Old Norse *hala*] —**hal·er** *n*

Hale /hayl/, **Edward Everett** (1822–1909) US cleric and writer. A noted abolitionist, he was a prolific and influential writer. His works include "The Man Without a Country" (1863).

> "'Do you pray for the senators, Dr. Hale?' / 'No, I look at the senators and I pray for the country.'"
> [Edward Everett Hale. Quoted in *New England Indian Summer*, Van Wyck Brooks; 1940]

Hale, George Ellery (1868–1938) US astronomer. He established the Yerkes Observatory, Wisconsin (1895) and Mount Wilson Observatory, California (1904) and helped design the world's first giant reflecting telescope, later installed on Mount Palomar, near San Diego.

Hale, Nathan (1755–76) American revolutionary hero. He was captured by the British as a spy and hanged.

> "I only regret that I have but one life to lose for my country."
> [Nathan Hale, last words prior to being hanged by the British as a spy; September 22, 1776]

Ha·le·a·ka·la Na·tion·al Park /haálee aakə laá-/ national park on the island of Maui, Hawaii, established in 1916. Its main feature is the large crater of an inactive volcano. Area: 44 sq. mi./115 sq. km.

ha·ler /haálər/ (*plural* **hal·ers** or **ha·le·ru** /-lə ro͞o/), **hel·ler** /héllər/ (*plural* **-lers** or **-le·ru**) *n* a minor unit of currency in the Czech Republic. See table at **currency** [Mid-20C. Via Czech < Middle High German *haller* "silver coin," after *Hall*, town in SW Germany]

Ha·ley /háylee/, **Alex** (1921–92) US writer. He is best known for his autobiographical novel *Roots* (1976), which won a Pulitzer citation and was made into an acclaimed TV miniseries. Full name **Haley, Alexander Murray Palmer**

> "History is written by the winners."
> [Alex Haley, *Interview, The David Frost Television Show*; April 20, 1972]

Ha·ley, Bill (1925–81) US musician. He drew on his background in country and western and rhythm and blues in recording some of the first rock-and-roll hits, including "Rock Around the Clock" (1955), with the Comets, the band he formed in 1952. Full name **Haley, William John Clifton**

> "*We* never sold no sex or sideburns. If we wanted to sell sex or sideburns, we'd have dressed differently."
> [Bill Haley. Quoted in *All You Need is Love*, Tony Palmer; 1977]

half /haf/ *n* (*plural* **halves** /havz/), *adj, pron* ONE OF TWO EQUAL PARTS either of two equal or nearly equal parts into which a whole can be divided ○ (n) *Arrange the apricot halves in a gratin dish.* ○ (n) *The recession began in the second half of 1990.* ○ (adj) *You don't have to pay for the first half hour.* ○ (adj) *I'll pay half the bill.* ○ (pron) *I invited 20, but only half showed up.* ■ *n* **1.** *US* SPORTS TIME BETWEEN PERIODS the break between two playing periods in a game ○ *The score was tied at the half.* Can term **halftime 2.** SPORTS PLAYING PERIOD either of two periods of play into which some games are divided ○ *We started off well but failed to score in the second half.* **3.** MONEY same as **half-dollar 4.** SPORTS HALFBACK a halfback in any sport **5.** *UK* LOWER FARE a fare costing more or less half the ordinary amount on public transportation, usually for a child or senior citizen ○ *Two and two halves please.* **6.** *UK* MEASURE OF BEER a half pint of beer, lager, or cider ■ *adj, adv* **1.** PARTIAL to some extent but not complete or completely ○ (adj) *She gave me a half-smile* ○ (adv) *She was half laughing, half crying* **2.** EQUALLY in equal parts ○ (adj) *We each have half ownership in the building.* ○ (adv) *He's half French, half Spanish.* [Old English *healf* < Germanic] ◇ **by half** to a too great extent ○ *I don't trust him – he's too friendly by half.* ◇ **go halves (with somebody)** to share something equally with somebody ○ *If we go halves on the gas the trip shouldn't be too expensive.* ◇ **not do things by halves** to do things thoroughly and often on a large scale ◇ **not half 1.** not at all ○ *Mmm! This cake's not half bad!* **2.** much less than half ○ *She's not half as busy as you are.* ○ *This isn't half the fun I thought it would be.* **3.** *UK* used as an understatement to indicate enthusiasm (*informal*) ○ *Just look at them – his new girlfriend can't half dance!*

USAGE Singular or plural? The pronoun ***half*** is singular, but the word is treated as plural when followed by a plural noun (with or without *of*) or when it refers to a plural: *Half the people are late. The other half of them aren't coming at all. At least half are behaving inexcusably.* With many singular nouns, ***half*** can be used in the forms *half a share, half of a share*, and *a half share*.

half-a-crown *n UK* same as **half-crown**

half-and-half *n* **1.** DAIRY PRODUCT FOR COFFEE a mixture of cream and milk in equal parts, used in coffee and tea **2.** TWO THINGS MIXED EQUALLY a mixture of two things in equal parts ■ *adj* WITH HALF OF EACH containing half each of two things ■ *adv* IN HALF in two equal portions

half-assed *adj* (*slang*) **1.** an offensive term meaning badly organized or carried out **2.** an offensive term meaning lacking forcefulness or effectiveness

half·back /háf bàk/ *n* **1.** FOOTBALL PLAYER BEHIND FRONT LINE in football, the player who is positioned next to the fullback and behind the front line at the start of play **2.** SOCCER same as **midfielder 3.** SPORTS PLAYER NEAR DEFENSIVE LINE in a team sport, any player who is positioned just in front of the last defensive line **4.** SPORTS POSITION OF HALFBACK the position of somebody playing as a halfback

half-baked *adj* **1.** POORLY PLANNED not well thought out and likely to fail (*informal*) **2.** UNINTELLIGENT lacking the ability to act with reason and common sense (*informal*) ○ *That's about what you'd expect from a department run by a bunch of half-baked idealists.* **3.** UNDERCOOKED not baked enough

half·beak /háf beek/ *n* a small fish with a short upper jaw and long lower jaw. Native to: warm seas, lakes, and rivers. Family: Hemiramphidae.

half bind·ing *n* bookbinding in which the back and sometimes the corners of a book are bound in one material and the sides in another

half blood *n* **1.** HALF BROTHER OR HALF SISTER somebody who is related to somebody else by having one parent in common **2.** *also* **half-blood** RELATIONSHIP SHARING ONE PARENT the relationship between two people who have one parent in common **3.** OFFENSIVE TERM an offensive term for somebody of racially mixed parentage, especially Native American and white

half-blood·ed *adj* **1.** having only one parent in common **2.** an offensive term meaning with racially different parents **3.** ZOOL same as **half-bred**

half board *n UK* the price of a room in a hotel for a night with breakfast and one main meal included (*hyphenated before a noun*)

half boot *n* a boot that reaches anywhere from the top of the ankle to mid-calf

half-bound *adj* describes a book that is bound on the back and sometimes the corners in one material and on the sides in another

half-bred *adj* used to describe a domestic animal that has only one parent of a known pedigree

half-breed *n* **1.** OFFSPRING OF ONLY ONE PUREBRED PARENT a domestic animal with only one parent of known pedigree **2.** HYBRID ANIMAL OR PLANT an animal or plant that is a hybrid product of two distinct types **3.** OFFENSIVE TERM an offensive term for a person of mixed racial parentage, especially Native American and white (*insult*)

half broth·er *n* a son of one of your parents by a different partner

half-caste *n* an offensive term for somebody of mixed racial parentage —**half-caste** *adj*

half cock *n* a position on a single-action firearm in which the hammer is half-raised and locked so that the trigger cannot be pulled

half-cocked *adj* **1.** describes a single-action firearm with the hammer half-raised and locked so that the trigger cannot be pulled **2.** lacking adequate planning, thought, or preparation ◇ **go off half-cocked** to start doing something too soon, especially without adequate planning (*informal*)

half-crown *n* a former British coin worth two shillings and sixpence

half-day *n* either the morning or the afternoon of a regular workday, especially when taken as vacation time

half-dead *adj* tired and worn-out (*informal*)

half dime *n* a former US coin worth five cents

half-dol·lar *n* a US coin worth 50 cents

half-dug·out *n regional* a house, shelter, or dwelling built several feet underground with logs

REGIONAL NOTE Once common as far north as Montana, the term ***half-dugout*** is today characteristic of Oklahoma speech.

half ea·gle *n* a former US coin worth five dollars

half gain·er *n* a dive in which the diver jumps from the board facing forward and then does a half backward somersault to enter the water headfirst, facing the board

half-hard·y *adj* describes a plant that can survive outdoors in mild frosts

half-heart·ed *adj* with little enthusiasm and no real interest in the result —**half-heart·ed·ly** *adv* —**half-heart·ed·ness** *n*

half hitch *n* a knot made by looping a piece of rope around an object then passing the end of the rope around itself and through the loop

half-hol·i·day *n UK* either the morning or afternoon of a regular workday or school day taken as a holiday

half-hour *n* **1.** a period of 30 minutes ○ *I'll be gone for about a half-hour.* **2.** the point in time 30 minutes after the start of an hour ○ *Isn't that clock supposed to chime on the half-hour?* —**half-hour·ly** *adv, adj*

half-inch *n* a measurement of length equal to half an inch or roughly 13 mm

half-length *adj* **1.** SHOWN ABOVE WAIST describes a portrait depicting the subject from the waist up but including the hands **2.** REACHING TO KNEE coming down to the knee rather than the ankles ■ *n* PORTRAIT FROM WAIST UP a portrait depicting the subject from the waist up but including the hands

half-life *n* **1.** the time a radioactive substance takes to lose half its radioactivity through decay. Symbol $T_{\frac{1}{2}}$ **2.** the time it takes for half a given amount of a substance such as a drug to be removed from living tissue through natural biological activity

half-light *n* the soft dim light seen at dawn and dusk

half-line *n* MATH same as **ray**[1] (sense 4)

half-mar·a·thon *n* a race on foot covering 13 mi. 352 yd./21.243 km

half-mast *n* the position, roughly halfway down a flagpole, to which a flag is lowered as a sign of respect when an important person dies —**half-mast** *vt*

half meas·ure *n* an inadequate or ineffectual action

half-moon *n* **1.** MOON VISIBLE AS SEMICIRCLE the moon when only half its face is illuminated during the first or last quarter **2.** SOMETHING SEMICIRCULAR anything with the shape of a semicircle or crescent **3.** AREA OF FINGERNAIL a pale semicircle at the base of the fingernail

half nel·son *n* a hold in which a wrestler passes an arm under the opponent's arm from behind to the back of the neck and then levers the opponent's arm backward [Because only one arm is held, whereas both are held in a full nelson]

half note *n* a musical note that has the time value of one half of a whole note. It is written as an open note-head with a stem.

half·pen·ny /háypnee, háypənee/ (*plural same* or **-nies**) *n* a former British coin worth half an old or new penny, withdrawn in 1985

half·pen·ny·worth /háypnee wùrth, háypənee-/ *n UK* **1.** an amount of something that could be bought for half a penny (*dated*) **2.** a very small amount (*dated informal*)

half-pint *n* **1.** half of a pint **2.** an offensive term for a short person (*insult*)

half·pipe /háf pĭp/ *n* a structure in the shape of the bottom half of a pipe, built for freestyle snowboarding, in-line skating, and skateboarding

half-price *n* half the regular price ■ *adj, adv* at half the usual price

half re·lief *n* sculptural relief that projects roughly halfway from the background

half rest *n* a musical rest that has the time value of a half note

half rhyme *n* an imperfect rhyme where there is a similarity in the sounds but not the identity of stressed vowels that is found in full rhymes

half-run·ner, **half-run·ner bean** *n Southern US* a rambling white bean

REGIONAL NOTE The term ***half-runner*** is used in the South Midland and Southern regions, being most common in West Virginia, Kentucky, and Tennessee. It is sometimes also called *white half-runner*. The legume takes its name from its growing closer to the ground than higher-rising running beans.

half shell *n* one half of the shell of a bivalve mollusk, often served containing the soft edible part of the animal, eaten raw as an appetizer ○ *Do you like oysters on the half shell?*

half sis·ter *n* a daughter of one of your parents by a different partner

half-size *n* **1.** a size that is halfway between two whole-numbered sizes ○ *Do you have half-sizes in this style?* **2.** any clothing size that is designed for a short-waisted full-figured woman

half-slip *n* a woman's undergarment that hangs from the waist and is worn as a lining for a skirt or dress

half sole *n* an additional layer on a piece of footwear that covers the wide part of the base

half-sole *vt* to put a new half sole on a shoe or boot

half-staff *n* MIL same as **half-mast**

half step *n* **1.** *US* MUSIC same as **semitone** **2.** a marching step that is 15 in./38 cm long in quick time and 18 in./46 cm long in double time

half term *n UK* a short vacation for schools halfway through a semester (*hyphenated when used before a noun*)

half tide *n* the time during which the tide is halfway between its high and low levels

half-timbered

half-tim·bered, **half-tim·ber** *adj* built with a visible frame of wooden beams as well as plaster, stone, or brick. Many Tudor buildings in England were half-timbered. —**half-tim·ber·ing** *n*

half·time /háf tĭm/ *n* a short break between the halves of a game, during which players rest

half ti·tle *n* the title of a book printed on the right-hand page before the main title page

half tone *n US* MUSIC same as **semitone**

half·tone /háf tōn/ *n* **1.** a shade or tone halfway between light and dark **2.** a photoengraving process by which shading is produced by photographing an image through a screen, then etching a plate so that the shading is reproduced as dots

half-track *n* a military vehicle with wheels on the front axles and continuous chain treads on the axles that supply motive power

half-truth *n* a statement that includes only some of the relevant facts or information and so is intended or likely to be misleading

half vol·ley *n* a stroke or shot that makes contact with the ball immediately after it has bounced

half-vol·ley *vti* to strike a ball immediately after it has bounced

half·way /hàf wáy, háf wày/ *adv, adj* **1.** at or to the middle point between two things in space or time ○ *reach the halfway point* **2.** to only some extent, degree, or distance

half·way house *n* **1.** STOPPING PLACE a resting place for travelers halfway through a long journey **2.** REHABILITATION CENTER a residence or center designed to ease people back into society after their release from an institution such as prison or a psychiatric hospital **3.** HALFWAY TO END OF SOMETHING the halfway point in progress toward a goal

half-white run·ner *n Southern US* PLANTS same as **half-runner**

half·wit /háf wit/ *n* an offensive term for somebody who is regarded as behaving in a thoughtless or unintelligent way (*insult*) —**half-wit·ted** *adj* —**half-wit·ted·ly** *adv* —**half-wit·ted·ness** *n*

half-year·ly *adv, adj UK* done or happening every six months or in the middle of the calendar or financial year

Hal·i·bur·ton /hálli bùrt'n/, **Thomas Chandler** (1796–1865) Canadian judge and writer. He created the Yankee peddler and philosopher Sam Slick (1835–55).

> "A college education shows a man how little other people know."
> [Thomas Chandler Haliburton. In *Dictionary of Quotations*, H. L. Mencken (ed.); 1942]

hal·i·but /hálləbət/ (*plural* **-buts** or *same*) *n* **1.** a large flatfish. Native to: northern Atlantic, Pacific oceans. Genus: *Hippoglossus.* **2.** the flesh of a halibut used as food [15C. < form of HOLY + dialect *butt* "flatfish" (< Middle Low German or Middle Dutch)]

Hal·i·car·nas·sus /hàlli kaar nássəss/ ancient city near Bodrum in the southwestern part of present-day Turkey. It was the site of the Mausoleum, the tomb of King Mausolus, which was one of the Seven Wonders of the World.

hal·ide /há lìd, háy-/ *n* a chemical compound of a halogen with another element or group of atoms [Late 19C. < HALOGEN]

ha·lier /hállyər/ *n* a subunit of Slovakian currency. See table at **currency** [Mid-20C. Via Czech < Middle High German *haller* (see HALER)]

Hal·i·fax /hálli fàks/ **1.** manufacturing city in West Yorkshire, northern England, that grew up as a center of textile making. Population: 91,069 (1991). **2.** Atlantic seaport and capital of Nova Scotia Province, Canada. Population: 276,221 (2001).

hal·i·plank·ton /hàlli plángktən/ *n* plankton found in the ocean [< Greek *hals*"salt"]

hal·ite /há lìt, háy-/ *n* a colorless or white crystalline mineral consisting of sodium chloride. Source: dried up lake beds. Use: table salt, source of chlorine. [Mid-19C. < Greek *hals* "salt"]

hal·i·to·sis /hàlli tṓsiss/ *n* MED same as **bad breath** [Late 19C. < Latin *halitus* "health"]

hall /hawl/ *n* **1.** CORRIDOR a connecting passage or corridor with doors leading to other rooms **2.** ENTRANCE ROOM an entrance room in a house, apartment, or building, with doors leading to other rooms **3.** BUILDING WITH LARGE PUBLIC ROOM a building with a large room used for public events or activities such as meetings, entertainment, and exhibitions **4.** LARGE ROOM a large room in a building such as a school, university, or castle, used for such purposes as dining or receptions **5.** CAMPUS BUILDING a building at a university, college, or school used as a dormitory or for classrooms **6.** LARGE HOUSE the main house on a large estate **7.** DINING ROOM a large dining room in a university, college, or school **8.** *UK* EDUC same as **dormitory** (sense 2) [Old English < Germanic, "cover, conceal"]

Hall /hawl/, **Lyman** (1724–90) American patriot, politician, and physician. He signed the Declaration of Independence (1776) and served as governor of Georgia (1783).

hal·lah *n* JUDAISM another spelling of **challah**

Hal·lan·dale /hállən dàyl/ city in southeastern Florida on the Atlantic Ocean, north of Miami. Population: 35,295 (2002 estimate).

Hal·le /hállə, haálə/ city in central Germany, situated on the Saale River. Population: 290,051 (1997).

Hal·lé /hál ay/, **Sir Charles** (1819–95) German-born British conductor and pianist. He founded the Hallé Orchestra in Manchester, England, in 1858. Born **Halle, Karl**

Hal·leck /hállik/, **Henry Wager** (1815–72) US army officer. He served as general in chief (1862–64) and chief of staff (1864–65) of the Union army during the Civil War.

Hal·lel /haa láyl, haá làyl/, **hal·lel** *n* Psalms 113 through 118, recited during the Jewish morning service at festivals as an expression of joy [Early 18C. < Hebrew, "praise"]

hal·le·lu·jah /hàllə lóoyə/, **hal·le·lu·iah, al·le·lu·ia** /àllə-/ *interj* **1.** USED TO EXPRESS PRAISE TO GOD used to express praise or thanks to God **2.** USED TO EXPRESS RELIEF used to express relief, welcome, or gratitude ○ *Hallelujah! The old car finally started.* ■ *n* **1.** CRY OF "HALLELUJAH!" a thankful cry of "hallelujah!" **2.** HYMN OF PRAISE a song or piece of religious music expressing praise to God [Pre-12C. Via Latin and Greek < Hebrew *hallĕlūyāh* "praise ye the Lord"]

Hal·ler /hállər/, **Albrecht von** (1707–77) Swiss biologist. He wrote the great neurological and physiological treatise *Elements of the Physiology of the Human Body* (1757–66).

hal·liard *n* NAUT another spelling of **halyard**

hall·mark /háwl maark/ *n* **1.** MARK OF QUALITY a mark showing that something is of high quality **2.** DISTINGUISHING MARK a feature of something that distinguishes it from others ○ *Discreet service is the hallmark of a fine restaurant.* **3.** OFFICIAL MARK ON PRECIOUS METAL in Great Britain, a mark stamped on articles made of gold, silver, or platinum to show that the metal used meets the proper standards of purity ■ *vt* (**-marked, -mark·ing, -marks**) STAMP SOMETHING WITH MARK INDICATING QUALITY to stamp an object made of gold, silver, or platinum to show that the metal used meets the proper standards of purity [Early 18C. After *Goldsmiths' Hall* in London]

hallmark (sense 3)

hal·lo *interj, n, vti* another spelling of **halloo**

hall of fame *n* **1.** a museum where portraits, memorabilia, or belongings of people who have excelled in a particular sphere of activity are displayed **2.** the group of people whose achievements in a particular field are at the highest level

hall of res·i·dence *n UK* EDUC same as **dormitory** (sense 2)

hal·loo /hə lóo/, **hal·loa** /hə lṓ/, **hal·lo** *interj* **1.** CALL TO ATTRACT ATTENTION used to try to attract somebody's attention **2.** CALL TO URGE ON HUNTING DOGS used to spur on dogs in a hunt ■ *v* (**-looed, -loo·ing, -loos; -loaed, -loa·ing, -loas; -loed, -lo·ing, -los**) **1.** *vi* CALL OUT "HALLOO!" to utter a call of "halloo!" **2.** *vt* SPUR DOGS ON to spur hunting dogs on by shouting halloos **3.** *vt* SHOUT SOMETHING to shout out something to somebody ○ *hallooed a warning from the shore* [Late 17C. Alteration of *holla* < French *holà*] —**hal·loo** *n*

hal·lou·mi *n* FOOD another spelling of **haloumi**

hal·low /hállō/ (**-lowed, -low·ing, -lows**) *vt* **1.** to make somebody or something holy **2.** to have great respect or reverence for somebody or something [Old English *hālgian* < Indo-European] —**hal·low·er** *n*

hal·lowed /hállōd/ *adj* **1.** holy or kept for religious use ○ *buried in hallowed ground* **2.** regarded with great respect or reverence ○ *the hallowed pages of our country's history* —**hal·lowed·ness** *n*

Hal·low·een /hàllə wéen/, **Hal·low·e'en** *n* the eve of All Saints' Day, originally celebrated by Celtic peoples but now popular with children in the United States, Canada, and the United Kingdom. The children dress up, often as witches or ghosts, and go from door to door asking for candy and saying "trick or treat." Date: the night of October 31. [Late 18C. Shortening of *All Hallow Even*, the eve of All Saints' Day (see ALLHALLOWS, EVEN[2])]

halls of i·vy *npl* institutions or an institution of higher learning, especially those regarded as particularly prestigious ○ *After four years in the halls of ivy, she had to adjust to a 9 to 5 job.* [< the traditional ivy-covered buildings]

hall stand *n UK* FURNITURE same as **hall tree**

Hall·statt /háwl stàt, haál shtaàt/, **Hall·stat·ti·an** /hàwl státtee ən, haàl-/ *adj* relating to or characteristic of a European culture of the late Bronze Age and early Iron Age [Mid-19C. After a town in Austria where a burial ground of this culture was found]

hall tree *n* a piece of furniture, usually kept in the hall of a house, on which people can hang their coats, hats, and umbrellas

hal·lu·ces ANAT plural of **hallux**

hal·lu·ci·nate /hə lóoss'n àyt/ (**-nat·ed, -nat·ing, -nates**) *vti* to imagine seeing, hearing, or otherwise sensing people, things, or events that are not present or actually occurring at the time [Early 19C. < Latin *hallucinat-*, past participle of *hallucinari* "dream, be distracted"] —**hal·lu·ci·na·tive** *adj* —**hal·lu·ci·na·tor** *n*

hal·lu·ci·na·tion /hə lòoss'n áysh'n/ *n* **1.** the perception of somebody or something that is not really there, which is often a symptom of a psychiatric disorder or a response to some drugs **2.** something that somebody imagines seeing, hearing, or otherwise sensing when it is not present or actually occurring at the time (*often used in the plural*) —**hal·lu·ci·na·tion·al** *adj*

hal·lu·ci·na·to·ry /hə lóoss'nə tàwree/ *adj* **1.** relating to or involving the belief that something is being seen, heard, or otherwise sensed when it is not present or actually occurring at the time **2.** causing somebody to believe that he or she is seeing, hearing, or otherwise sensing things that are not present or actually occurring at the time

hal·lu·cin·o·gen /hə lóoss'nəjən/ *n* a substance, especially a drug such as LSD, that causes hallucinations —**hal·lu·cin·o·gen·ic** /hə lòoss'nə jénnik/ *adj*

hal·lu·ci·no·sis /hə lòoss'n ṓsiss/ *n* a psychiatric disorder that involves hallucinations

hal·lux /hálləks/ (*plural* **-lu·ces** /hállyə seèz, hállə-/) *n* the big toe on a human foot, or the first digit on the hind foot of some mammals, birds, reptiles, and amphibians (*technical*) [Mid-19C. Via modern Latin < Latin *hallus*]

hal·lux val·gus /hàlləks válgəss/ *n* a medical condition affecting the big toe in which its tip points toward the little toe and its base sticks out on the inner edge of the foot [*Valgus* < Latin, "bowlegged"]

hall·way /háwl wày/ *n* BUILDINGS same as **hall** (sense 2)

hal·ma /hálmə/ *n* a board game similar to Chinese checkers [Late 19C. < Greek, "leap"]

Hal·ma·he·ra /hàlmə heérə/ largest island of the Moluccas, Indonesia, situated on the equator. Area: 6,873 sq. mi./17,800 sq. km.

ha·lo /háylō/ *n* (*plural* **-loes** or **-los**) **1.** CIRCLE OF LIGHT AROUND SAINT'S HEAD a ring or circle of light around the head of a saint in a religious painting **2.** IMAGINED AURA OF GLORY an aura of glory imagined to surround somebody or something famous or revered **3.** SOMETHING RESEMBLING RING OF LIGHT something that resembles or suggests a ring of light **4.** LIGHT CIRCLE AROUND MOON OR SUN a circle of light around the Moon or Sun, caused by light refracting from ice crystals in the atmosphere **5.** BODY OF STARS a thinly populated spherical region of stars and other luminous objects surrounding a galaxy ■ *vt* (**-loed, -lo·ing, -los**) SURROUND SOMEBODY OR SOMETHING WITH HALO to surround somebody or something with a halo [Mid-16C. Via medieval Latin < Greek *halos* "disk around the Sun or Moon"]

halo- *prefix* **1.** salt ○ *halobiont* **2.** halogen ○ *halocarbon* [Via French < Greek *hals* < Indo-European]

hal·o·bi·ont /hàllō bī ònt/ *n* an organism that flourishes in a salty environment —**hal·o·bi·on·tic** /hàllō bī óntik/ *adj*

hal·o·car·bon /hállə kaárbən/ *n* a compound such as a fluorocarbon that contains carbon and a halogen

hal·o·cline /hállə klīn/ *n* a vertical gradient in the saltiness of the ocean

ha·lo ef·fect *n* the tendency to judge somebody as being totally good because one aspect of his or her character is good [< the haloes of angels]

hal·o·gen /hálləjən/ *n* any of the five electronegative elements, namely fluorine, chlorine, iodine, bromine, or astatine ■ *adj* describes lamps or heat sources that have a filament surrounded by halogen vapor ○ *a halogen bulb* [Mid-19C. < HALO-; because they readily form salts when combined with metals]

hal·o·ge·nate /hálləjə nàyt, hə lójjə-/ (**-nat·ed, -nat·ing, -nates**) *vt* to treat or combine something with a halogen —**hal·o·ge·na·tion** /hàlləjə náysh'n, hə lòjjə-/ *n*

ha·lon /háy lòn/ *n* a stable halocarbon used to put out fires [Mid-20C. < HALOGEN]

hal·o·per·i·dol /hàllō pérri dàwl/ *n* a tranquilizing drug. Use: treatment of schizophrenia, mania, and psychoses. [Mid-20C. < HALO- + PIPERIDINE]

hal·o·phile /hállə fīl/ *n* an organism that lives in salty conditions —**hal·o·phil·ic** /hàllə fíllik/ *adj*

hal·o·phyte /hállə fīt/ *n* a plant capable of growing in salty soil —**hal·o·phyt·ic** /hàllə fíttik/ *adj* —**ha·lo·phyt·ism** *n*

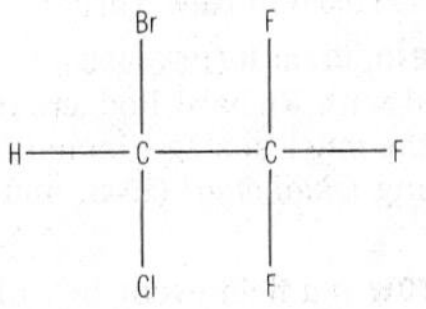

halothane

hal·o·thane /hállə thàyn/ *n* a colorless liquid. Use: anesthetic. Formula: $C_2HBrClF_3$. [Mid-20C. < HALO- + ETHANE]

ha·lou·mi /hə lóomi/ *n* a salty white Greek cheese with a rubbery texture that is usually grilled and eaten hot [< modern Greek]

Hals /haalss/, **Frans** (1580?–1666) Flemish-born Dutch painter. He was known principally as a painter of lighthearted portraits. His work includes *The Laughing Cavalier* (1624).

Hal·sey /háwlzee/, **William F.** (1882–1959) US admiral. In 1944 he commanded the US Third Fleet in the battle for the Philippines. Full name **Halsey, William Frederick**. Known as **Bull Halsey**

> "Our ships have been salvaged and are retiring at high speed toward the Japanese fleet."
> [William F. Halsey, *Report*; October 14, 1944]

halt[1] /hawlt/ *n* TEMPORARY STOP an end or temporary stop ○ *The sudden rain brought the game to an abrupt halt.* ■ *interj* COMMAND USED TO MAKE SOMEBODY STOP used to command somebody to stop ○ *Halt! Identify yourself!* ■ *vti* (**halt·ed, halt·ing, halts**) STOP to stop, or make somebody or something stop [Late 16C. < German *halten* "to stop, hold"] ◇ **grind to a halt** to come gradually to a complete stop

halt[2] /hawlt/ *vi* (**halt·ed, halt·ing, halts**) **1.** ACT HESITANTLY to act or behave without certainty or confidence **2.** BE DEFECTIVE to have flaws or inconsistencies in logical development or in poetic rhythm **3.** OFFENSIVE TERM an offensive term meaning to have difficulty in walking (*archaic*) ■ *adj* OFFENSIVE TERM an offensive term meaning walking with difficulty (*archaic*) [Old English *healtian* "walk with a limp" < Germanic]

hal·ter[1] /háwltər/ *n* **1.** BACKLESS GARMENT a woman's garment, worn between the shoulders and waist, that fastens or passes behind the neck and leaves the arms, shoulders, and back bare ○ *wore shorts and a halter on hot summer days* **2.** DEVICE FOR LEADING ANIMAL an arrangement of ropes or leather straps put over the head of an animal, especially a horse, and used to lead it **3.** ROPE FOR HANGING SOMEBODY a rope with a noose, used to hang somebody **4.** HANGING death by hanging ○ *destined for the halter* [< Old English *hælftre* < Germanic, "hold on to"] —**hal·ter** *vt*

hal·ter[2] *n* INSECTS another spelling of **haltere**

hal·tere /háwl tèer, hál tèer/ (*plural* **-ter·es** /hawl tèer eez, hal \tèer eez/) *n* either of a pair of projecting parts in insects of the fly family that are rudimentary hind wings and are used to maintain balance in flight [Mid-16C. < Greek *haltēres* (plural) "weights like dumbbells used in jumping" < *hallestai* "to jump"]

hal·ter-top *n* CLOTHING same as **halter**[1] (sense 1)

halt·ing /háwlting/ *adj* hesitant or done with frequent irregular pauses ○ *halting speech* —**halt·ing·ly** *adv* —**halt·ing·ness** *n*

ha·lutz *n* JUDAISM another spelling of **chalutz**

hal·vah /haal vaá, haál vaà/, **hal·va** *n* a confection made from crushed sesame seeds and honey with various flavorings, originally from Southwest Asia [Mid-17C. Via Turkish < Arabic *ḥalwā*]

halve /hav/ (**halved, halv·ing, halves**) *v* **1.** *vt* DIVIDE SOMETHING IN TWO to divide something into two equal parts **2.** *vt* DISTRIBUTE SOMETHING EQUALLY to divide something equally between two people **3.** *vti* REDUCE SOMETHING BY HALF to reduce something by half, or be reduced by half **4.** *vt* GOLF DRAW HOLE OR MATCH in golf, to draw at a hole or match by playing the same number of strokes as an opponent [14C. < HALF]

halves plural of **half**

hal·wa /hál waà/ *n* in Indian cuisine, a dish made of almonds, carrots, or semolina boiled with milk, sweetened with sugar and spiced with cardamom [< Arabic *ḥalwā* "halvah"]

hal·yard /hállyərd/, **hal·liard** *n* a rope used to raise or lower something such as a sail or flag [14C. Alteration of *halier* < HALE[2]]

ham[1] /ham/ *n* **1.** MEAT FROM HOG'S THIGH meat cut from the thigh of the hind leg of a hog after curing by salting or smoking ○ *a slice of ham* ○ *a ham sandwich* **2.** HOG'S THIGH the thigh of the hind leg of a hog **3.** HOLLOW AREA BEHIND KNEE the hollow area behind somebody's knee ■ **hams** *npl* BUTTOCKS the back of somebody's thighs including the buttocks [Old English *hamm* "back of the knee" < Germanic, "be crooked"]

ham[2] /ham/ *n* somebody, especially an actor, who performs in an exaggerated showy style ■ *vti* (**hammed, ham·ming, hams**) to behave, overact, or perform a role in an exaggerated showy style ○ *always hamming it up* [Late 19C. Origin ?] —**ham** *adj* —**ham·my** *adj*

ham[3] /ham/ *n* a licensed amateur radio operator [Early 20C. Origin ?]

Ham /ham/ *n* in the Bible, the second son of Noah, formerly considered to be the ancestor of the Hamite people (Genesis 10:1)

Ha·ma /haá maa/, **Ha·māh** ancient city in west central Syria, 75 mi./121 km southwest of Aleppo. Population: 264,348 (1994).

ham·a·dry·ad /hàmmə drī́ əd/ *n* **1.** in Greek and Roman mythology, a minor deity who lives in a tree and dies when the tree dies **2.** ZOOL same as **king cobra** [14C. Via Latin *Hamadryad-*, *Hamadryas* < Greek *Hamadruad-* < *hama* "together" + *Druad-* (see DRYAD)]

ham·a·dry·as ba·boon /hàmmə drī́ əss-/ *n* a baboon, the adult male of which has a long silvery mane, that was sacred to the ancient Egyptians. Native to: northeastern Africa, Arabia. Latin name: *Papio hamadryas*. [Late 19C. Via modern Latin < Latin *Hamadryas* (see HAMADRYAD)]

Ha·māh another spelling of **Hama**

ha·mal /hə maál/, **ham·mal** *n* in an Islamic country, a porter or servant [Mid-18C. < Arabic *ḥammāl* < *ḥamala* "carry"]

Ha·ma·ma·tsu /hàmmə mátsoo/ coastal manufacturing city in southern Honshu, Japan. Population: 573,504 (2002).

ha·man·tasch /haámən taàsh/ (*plural* **-tasch·en** /-taàshən/) *n* a triangular pastry filled with spiced dried fruit or poppy seeds and eaten during the Jewish feast of Purim [< Yiddish < *Haman*, persecutor of the Jews in the Book of Esther + *tasch* < German *Tasche* "bag, pocket"]

ha·mar·ti·a /haà maar tée ə/ *n* a flaw in the character of the protagonist of a literary tragedy that brings about his or her downfall [Late 18C. < Greek, "error, sin" < *hamartanein* "miss the mark, make a mistake"]

Ha·mas /ha máss/ *n* a fundamentalist Islamic Palestinian organization supporting and engaging in resistance to Israel in the Israeli-occupied territories [Late 20C. < Arabic *hamas* "enthusiasm, zeal," identified with acronym < *harakat al-Muqawama al-Islamiyya* "Islamic Resistance Movement"]

ha·mate /háy màyt/ *adj* shaped like a hook ■ *n* a small hook-shaped bone in the wrist, at the base of the third and little fingers [Early 18C. < Latin *hamatus* < *hamus* "hook"]

ham·burg /hám bùrg/ *n regional* FOOD same as **hamburger** [Late 19C. Shortening]

REGIONAL NOTE The term ***hamburg*** is used in New England and the North Central States, as far west as Michigan. The Northern usage contrasts with the general-currency terms *hamburger* and *hamburger steak* used elsewhere in the United States. And in the North, especially among the young, the ***hamburg*** forms are less frequent than the primary American terms.

Ham·burg /hám bùrg, haám bòorg/ city and major seaport in north central Germany, situated on the Elbe and Alster rivers. Population: 1,705,872 (1997).

ham·burg·er /hám bùrgər/ *n* **1.** PATTY OF GROUND MEAT a flat patty of ground meat, usually beef, that is broiled, grilled, or fried and usually served in a bun **2.** GROUND-BEEF SANDWICH a sandwich containing a flat patty of broiled, grilled, or fried ground beef or other meat in a bun, usually with other ingredients such as lettuce and condiments **3.** BEEF ground beef [Late 19C. < *Hamburg steak*, after HAMBURG, Germany]

ham·burg·er steak, ham·burg steak *n* FOOD same as **hamburger** (senses 1, 3)

Ham·den /hámdən/ town in southern Connecticut near New Haven, first settled in 1664. Population: 57,927 (2002 estimate).

hame /haym/ *n* either of a pair of metal or wooden bars curved to fit over the neck of a draft animal and to which the traces are attached [14C. < Middle Dutch]

Ham·er·sley Range /hámmərzlee-/ range of mountains in northwestern Western Australia, containing large iron ore deposits

ha·metz *n* JUDAISM another spelling of **chametz**

ham-fist·ed *adj UK* same as **ham-handed** (*informal*) —**ham-fist·ed·ly** *adv* —**ham-fist·ed·ness** *n*

ham-hand·ed *adj* **1.** clumsy with the hands (*informal*) **2.** having hands that are very large —**ham-hand·ed·ly** *adv* —**ham-hand·ed·ness** *n*

Ham·hung /haám hòong/, **Ham·hŭng** industrial city in South Hamgyŏng Province, North Korea. Population: 709,730 (1993).

Ham·ill /hámməl/, **Dorothy** (*b.* 1956) US figure skater. After winning the Olympic gold medal and World Championship (1976), she became a professional ice skater, starring in popular touring shows and television specials. Full name **Hamill, Dorothy Stuart**

Ham·il·ton /hámm'ltən/ **1.** industrial town in central Scotland, near Glasgow. Population: 49,991 (1991). **2.** seaport and capital of Bermuda, situated on Bermuda Island. Population: 1,000 (1990 estimate). **3.** city in southeastern Ontario, Canada, at the western end of Lake Ontario. Population: 618,820 (2001). **4.** city in the west of the North Island, New Zealand, situated on the Waikato River. Population: 138,792 (2001).

Ham·il·ton, Alexander (1757–1804) US lawyer and politician. He was the principal author of *The Federalist* (1787–88) and the first secretary of the US Treasury (1789–95).

> "Justice is the end of government. It is the end of civil society. It ever has been and ever will be pursued until it be obtained, or until liberty be lost in the pursuit."
> [Alexander Hamilton, *The Federalist*; 1787–88]

Ham·il·ton, Emma, Lady (1765–1815) British courtier. She is remembered as the mistress of Horatio Nelson, with whom she had a child, Horatia Nelson (1801–81). Born **Lyon, Emma**

Ham·il·ton, Scott (*b.* 1958) US figure skater. He was world champion four times (1981–84) and Olympic gold medalist (1984).

Ham·il·ton, Sir William (1805–65) Irish mathematician. He introduced the method of quaternions into algebra and helped to discover the wave theory of light. Full name **Hamilton, Sir William Rowan**

Ham·il·to·ni·an func·tion /hàmm'l tṓnee ən-/ *n* a mathematical function used to describe the dynamics of a system such as particles in motion that uses momentum and spatial coordinates. Symbol *H* [Mid-19C. After Sir William Rowan HAMILTON] —**Ham·il·to·ni·an·ism** *n*

Ham·il·ton Is·land island and tourist destination off the east of Queensland, Australia, situated 719 mi./1,160 km north of Brisbane. Population: 1,500 (1996).

Ham·ite /há mīt/ *n* a member of a group of peoples who live in North Africa [Mid-19C. After HAM]

Ha·mit·ic /ha míttik/ *n* GROUP OF AFRICAN LANGUAGES a group of languages spoken in parts of northeastern Africa. Native speakers: 6 million. ■ *adj* **1.** OF HAMITES relating to the Hamites **2.** OF HAMITIC relating to Hamitic

Ham·i·to-Se·mit·ic /hàmmitō-/ *n, adj* LANG same as **Afro-Asiatic** (*not in technical use*)

ham·let /hámmlət/ *n* a small village or group of houses [14C. < Old French *hamelet* "small village" < *ham* "village" < W Germanic]

Ham·lin /hámmlin/, **Hannibal** (1809–91) vice president of the United States. A Democrat from Maine, his long congressional career (1843–81) was interrupted by a term as Abraham Lincoln's vice president (1861–65).

ham·mal *n* another spelling of **hamal**

Ham·mar·skjöld /hámmər shòld/, **Dag** (1905–61) Swedish diplomat. As secretary-general of the United Nations (1953–61), he was known as a skillful mediator, and won a Nobel Peace Prize posthumously (1961). Full name **Hammarskjöld, Hjalmar Agne Carl**

"Never measure the height of a mountain, until you have reached the top. Then you will see how low it was."
[Dag Hammarskjöld, *Markings*; 1964]

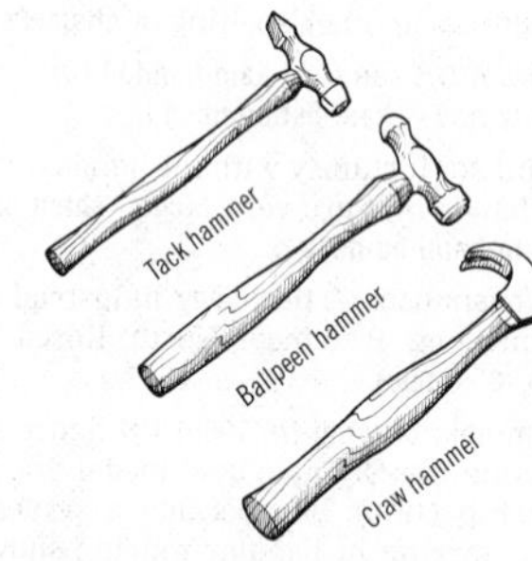

hammer

ham·mer /hámmər/ *n* **1.** POUNDING TOOL a hand tool consisting of a shaft with a metal head at right angles to it, used mainly for driving in nails and beating metal **2.** MECHANICAL STRIKING TOOL a powered mechanical striking tool used mainly in forging metal ○ *a steam hammer* **3.** STRIKING PART a part that strikes another in various devices, e.g., in a piano or striking clock **4.** ARMS PART OF GUN the part of the firing mechanism of a gun that delivers the impact that detonates the cartridge **5.** TRACK AND FIELD OBJECT FOR THROWING a heavy metal ball attached to a handle of flexible wire, thrown in an athletics field event **6.** TRACK AND FIELD same as **hammer throw 7.** AUCTIONEER'S GAVEL a gavel used by an auctioneer **8.** ANAT same as **malleus** ■ *v* **(-mered, -mer·ing, -mers) 1.** *vti* POUND SOMETHING IN to force something such as a nail into something else by pounding it with a hammer **2.** *vt* BEAT SOMETHING INTO SHAPE to beat something with a hammer, especially to shape it ○ *hammering tin into bowls* **3.** *vti* HIT SOMETHING HARD AND REPEATEDLY to hit or strike something hard and repeatedly ○ *hammering at the door* **4.** *vt* CAUSE SOMETHING TO BE REMEMBERED to cause something to be remembered, realized, or understood by repeating it forcefully and frequently ○ *hammered the multiplication table into our heads* **5.** *vi* MOVE WITH POWERFUL RHYTHM to produce fast powerful rhythmic movements or beats ○ *Their hearts were hammering.* **6.** *vt* DAMAGE SOMETHING SEVERELY to inflict serious damage on something **7.** *vt* BEAT SOMEBODY UP to beat somebody severely (*informal*) **8.** *vt* DEFEAT SOMEBODY BY LARGE MARGIN to inflict a convincing defeat on somebody, especially an opponent in a competitive sport (*slang*) ○ *Our team got hammered in last week's game.* **9.** *vt* CRITICIZE SOMEBODY OR SOMETHING HEAVILY to subject somebody or something to severe criticism (*slang*) ○ *The critics really hammered his last play.* [Old English *hamor* < Germanic, "stone, stone tool"] —**ham·mer·er** *n* ◇ **go at it hammer and tongs 1.** to do something with maximum energy and force **2.** to fight or argue violently ◇ **go** *or* **come under the hammer** to be up for auction or sale

hammer away at *vt* to work hard, determinedly, and steadily at something ○ *hammering away at the new novel*

hammer out *vt* **1.** SHAPE METAL WITH HAMMER to shape or reshape metal with a hammer **2.** AGREE ON OR ESTABLISH SOMETHING to agree on or establish something after prolonged discussion or argument ○ *hammer out a new contract* **3.** PLAY MUSIC ENERGETICALLY to play a piece of music on a piano energetically and forcefully ○ *She can really hammer out a tune.*

Ham·mer /hámmər/, **Armand** (1898–1990) US industrialist, art collector, and philanthropist. He established trade links with the Soviet Union in the 1920s and increased his personal fortune in a long career in the oil industry. He made major gifts to art and educational institutions.

"When I work 14 hours a day, seven days a week, I get lucky."
[Armand Hammer, *Guardian (London)*; December 30, 1990]

hammer and sickle

ham·mer and sick·le *n* a symbol of Soviet Communism representing industrial and agricultural workers, used on the flag of the former Soviet Union

ham·mer blow *n* something that has a damaging or destructive effect ○ *This year's drought has been a hammer blow to farmers.*

ham·mer dul·ci·mer *n* a large dulcimer played with light hammers and supported by a stand

Ham·mer·fest /hámmər fèst/ fishing port in northern Norway, the northernmost town in Europe. Population: 9,216 (1998).

ham·mer·head /hámmər hèd/ (*plural* **-heads** or *same*) *n* **1.** FISH same as **hammerhead shark 2.** a large brown wading bird with a prominent crest on the back of its head. Native to: tropical African wetlands, ponds, and lakes. Latin name: *Scopus umbretta*. **3.** a fruit bat, the male of which has an enlarged square head and a muzzle shaped like the head of a hammer. Native to: Africa. Latin name: *Hypsignathus monstrosus*.

ham·mer·head·ed /hàmmər héddəd/ *adj* having a head that is wide and extends to each side of the body

hammerhead shark

ham·mer·head shark *n* a shark with a head that has a lateral extension on each side with an eye at the end. Genus: *Sphyrna*.

ham·mer·kop /hámmər kòp/ (*plural* **-kops** or *same*) *n* BIRDS same as **hammerhead** (sense 2) [Mid-19C. < Afrikaans *hamerkop* "hammerhead"]

ham·mer·lock /hámmər lòk/ *n* a wrestling hold in which an opponent's arm is twisted upward behind the back [Origin ?]

Ham·mer·stein /hámmər stìn/, **Oscar** (1846?–1919) German-born US impresario. He founded the Harlem Opera House (1888) and the Manhattan Opera House (1906) in New York.

Ham·mer·stein, Oscar II (1895–1960) US librettist. He collaborated with Richard Rodgers on some of the classics of the musical stage, including the Pulitzer Prize-winning *Oklahoma!* (1943) and *South Pacific* (1949).

ham·mer throw *n* a field event in which competing athletes try to throw a heavy metal ball attached to a handle of flexible wire as far as they can

ham·mer·toe /hámmər tṑ/ *n* **1.** a medical condition in which the joint between the two small bones of a toe is permanently bent downward in a claw shape **2.** a toe affected by hammertoe

Ham·mett /hámmit/, **Dashiell** (1894–1961) US writer. He helped to establish and define the detective genre with *The Maltese Falcon* (1930) and *The Thin Man* (1932). Full name **Hammett, Samuel Dashiell**

"Talking's something you can't do judiciously unless you keep in practice."
[Dashiell Hammett, *The Maltese Falcon*; 1930]

ham·mock[1] /hámmək/ *n* a hanging bed made of canvas or netting and suspended between two supports [Mid-16C. Via Spanish *hamaca* < Taino]

ham·mock[2] /hámmək/ *n US regional, Can* in the southern United States, an area of forested land that rises above a marsh [Mid-16C. Origin ?]

Ham·mond /hámmənd/ **1.** industrial city in northwestern Indiana on Lake Michigan, near Chicago. Population: 81,413 (2002 estimate). **2.** city in southeastern Louisiana, east of Baton Rouge. Population: 17,624 (2002 estimate).

Ham·mu·ra·bic code /hàmmə ra̎abik-/ *n* the first known code of law, written down by Hammurabi, king of Babylonia (1792–50 B.C.)

ham·per[1] /hámpər/ *vt* **(-pered, -per·ing, -pers)** to restrict the free movement or progress of somebody or something ■ *n* equipment on board a ship that is essential but likely to get in the way [14C. Origin ?]

SYNONYMS See ***hinder***[1].

ham·per[2] /hámpər/ *n* **1.** a large basket with a cover that is used for holding soiled laundry **2.** a large basket with a cover that is used for carrying food, especially for picnics [14C. < Anglo-Norman *hanaper* "basket for holding goblets" < Old French *hanap* "goblet" < Germanic]

Hamp·shire[1] /hámp shee̊r, -shər/ (*plural* **-shires** or *same*) *n* **1.** a black-and-white pig belonging to a breed developed in the United States from stock imported from Hampshire, England **2.** a large sheep with a black face and no horns, belonging to an English breed [Mid-17C. After HAMPSHIRE[2]]

Hamp·shire[2] /hámp shee̊r, -shər/ county in southern England, bordering the English Channel. Area: 1,455 sq. mi./3,769 sq. km.

Hamp·shire Down *n* BREED same as **Hampshire**[1] (sense 2)

Hamp·ton /hámptən/ city and port in southeastern Virginia, situated on Hampton Roads opposite Norfolk. It is the home of Langley Air Force Base and Hampton University. Population: 145,921 (2002 estimate).

Hamp·ton, Wade (1818–1902) US Confederate army general and politician. He led the Confederate cavalry (1864–65) during the Civil War and later served as US senator for South Carolina (1879–91).

Hamp·ton Court /hàmptən-/ *n* a royal palace by the Thames River in southwestern London, mainly dating from the Tudor period

Hamp·ton Roads /-rōdz/ deep-water channel and commercial waterway in southeastern Virginia at the point where the James, Nansemond, and Elizabeth rivers empty into Chesapeake Bay. The Port of Hampton Roads comprises the cities of Newport News, Hampton, Portsmouth, and Norfolk and is one the country's busiest ports and shipbuilding centers. In 1862 Hampton Roads was the site of a Civil War naval confrontation between the ironclads *Monitor* and *Merrimack*.

hamster

ham·ster /hámstər/ *n* **1.** a small rodent with a short tail and large cheek pouches for storing food, often kept as a pet. Native to: Europe, Asia. Family: Muridae. **2.** a cordless computer mouse that operates through an infrared connection [Early 17C. Via German < Old High German *hamustro*]

ham·string /hám strìng/ *n* **1.** ANAT **LEG TENDON** either of the two prominent common tendons of the muscles (**hamstring muscle**)behind the knee **2.** ANAT same as **hamstring muscle 3.** ZOOL **TENDON IN ANIMAL'S LEG** a large tendon at the back of the hock of an animal's hind leg ■ *vt* (**-strung** /-strùng/, **-string·ing, -strings**) **1. CUT HAMSTRING OF PERSON OR ANIMAL** to cut the hamstring of a person or animal causing inability to use the leg normally (*often considered offensive*) **2. THWART SOMEBODY OR SOMETHING** to make somebody or something powerless or ineffective ○ *hamstrung by a lack of funds*

ham·string mus·cle *n* a muscle belonging to a group of three at the back of the thigh that control leg movements such as flexing the knee

ham·strung past participle, past tense of **hamstring**

Ham·sun /hámss'n, -sŏŏn/, **Knut** (1859–1952) Norwegian author. His best-known work is *Growth of the Soil* (1917). He won a Nobel Prize in literature (1920). Pseudonym of **Pedersen, Knut**

ham·u·lus /hámmyələss/ (*plural* **-li** /-lī/) *n* a hook-shaped part at the end of a bone [Early 18C. < Latin, "small hook" < *hamus* "hook"]

ham·za /hámzə, haám zaá/, **ham·zah** *n* a sign (ʼ) used in Arabic script to represent a glottal stop [Early 19C. < Arabic]

Han[1] /haan/ (*plural same* or **Hans**) *n* **1.** a member of a Chinese dynasty that ruled from 206 B.C. to A.D. 220 and was responsible for systematizing Chinese bureaucracy, promoting Confucianism, and consolidating Chinese government and territory **2.** PEOPLES same as **Han Chinese** [Mid-18C. < Chinese *Hàn*] —**Han** *adj*

Han[2] /haan/ ➧ **Han Jiang**

Ha·na·bu·sa It·cho /hànnə bŏŏssə íchō/ (1652–1724) Japanese painter. He was noted for his caricatures and his depictions of city life. Born **Tage, Shinko**

Han Chi·nese *n* a member of the largest ethnic group in China, making up approximately 93% of the Chinese population —**Han Chi·nese** *adj*

Han·cock /hán kòk/, **John** (1737–93) US patriot and politician. As president of the Continental Congress (1775–77) he was the first to sign the Declaration of Independence (1776). He was the first governor of Massachusetts (1780–85, 1789–93).

Han·cock, Winfield Scott (1824–86) US army officer. A Union commander during the Civil War, he was noted for rallying his troops at the Battle of Gettysburg (1863).

hand /hand/ *n* **1. END OF HUMAN ARM** the part of the human arm below the wrist, consisting of a thumb, four fingers, and a palm and capable of holding and manipulating things **2. ANIMAL PART CORRESPONDING TO HUMAN HAND** the part of an animal's limb that corresponds to a human hand in shape or function **3. POINTER ON CLOCK** a pointer on a clock, watch, dial, or gauge **4. PLAYER'S CARDS** the cards dealt to a player in a card game ○ *a losing hand* **5. ROUND IN CARD GAME** a round in a card game ○ *played one last hand of bridge* **6. CARD PLAYER** somebody who plays a card game **7. PART IN DOING SOMETHING** a share in the performance of an action ○ *Who else had a hand in this?* **8. HELP** help to do something ○ *Give me a hand.* **9. OFFER OF AGREEMENT** a sign of agreement or acceptance, especially of an offer of marriage ○ *Here's my hand on it.* **10. SIDE** side or direction ○ *surrounded by enemies at every hand* **11. CLAP** a round of applause ○ *a big hand for our next contestant* **12. POSSESSION OR POWER** the possession, power, responsibility, or care of somebody (*usually used in the plural*) ○ *Your future is in your own hands.* **13. DEGREE OF CLOSENESS TO SOURCE** a degree of closeness to actual involvement in something being talked about ○ *I heard about it third hand.* **14. MEMBER OF SHIP'S CREW** a member of the crew of a vessel ○ *Attention, all hands!* **15. SOMEBODY DOING OR MAKING SOMETHING** a maker or doer of something, especially to a particular level of competence or experience ○ *I'm an old hand at this.* **16. WORKER** a worker, especially one doing manual or farm work ○ *a ranch hand* **17. HANDWRITING** somebody's handwriting ○ *an admirably clear hand* **18. SKILL** ability or skill ○ *She has a good hand for gardening.* **19. APPROACH OR METHOD** a distinctive way of doing something ○ *This drawing is executed with the hand of a master.* **20.** US TEXTILES **FABRIC TEXTURE** the feel of a textile, used to determine its quality. Can term **handle 21.** SHOW JUMPING **MEASURE OF HORSE'S HEIGHT** a measure of the height of a horse, equal to 4 in./10.2 cm ■ *v* (**hand·ed, hand·ing, hands**) **1.** *vt* **PASS SOMETHING BY HAND** to pass something to somebody by hand ○ *She handed me a glass.* **2.** *vt* **LEAD SOMEBODY BY HAND** to help or lead somebody by the hand ○ *She handed her aunt into the taxi.* **3.** *vti* SAILING **FURL** to furl a sail [Old English < Germanic] ◇ **all hands on deck 1.** used as a call or signal for all members of a ship's crew to assemble on deck, e.g., in an emergency **2.** used to indicate that help is required from everybody available ○ *When the truck arrives, we'll need all hands on deck.* ◇ **at hand 1.** nearby **2.** about to happen ◇ **by hand** not using a machine ◇ **change hands** to pass to a different owner ◇ **force somebody's hand** to pressure somebody to do something against his or her will or earlier than planned ◇ **(from) hand to mouth** with barely enough to live on for your daily needs ◇ **hand in glove** in cooperation with somebody, usually for some secret or illegal purpose ◇ **hand in hand 1.** in close cooperation **2.** inseparably closely **3.** holding hands ◇ **hand over fist** in large quantities or amounts ○ *losing money hand over fist* ◇ **hold somebody's hand** to provide reassurance, guidance, and support to somebody ◇ **in hand 1.** under control **2.** remaining or unused ◇ **not turn a hand** to make no attempt to help somebody ◇ **off somebody's hands** no longer somebody's responsibility or problem ◇ **on hand** near and available ◇ **on the one hand…on the other hand…** used to present two conflicting aspects of a situation ○ *On the one hand we have plenty of time, but on the other hand our resources are limited.* ◇ **out of hand 1.** out of control ○ *The situation's getting out of hand.* **2.** immediately and without consideration or explanation ○ *My suggestions were dismissed out of hand.* ◇ **out of somebody's hands** unable to be influenced by somebody ◇ **overplay your hand** to make overconfident use of an advantage and fail as a result ◇ **put your hand up to 1.** to volunteer to do something ○ *If you want to get into this type of work, put your hand up to do unpaid work experience.* **2.** to acknowledge or accept something ○ *You have an ethical and professional obligation to put your hand up to this problem.* ◇ **show** *or* **tip your hand** to reveal your plans or intentions ◇ **take somebody** *or* **something in hand** to begin to bring somebody *or* something under control ◇ **throw in your hand 1.** to admit defeat in a card game by laying your cards down **2.** to admit or accept defeat ◇ **to hand** close by ◇ **try your hand at something** to make an attempt at something, usually for the first time ◇ **turn your hand to something** to do something for the first time and be competent at it ◇ **wait on somebody hand and foot** to attend to somebody's every need, often with bad grace ◇ **wash your hands of somebody** *or* **something** to refuse to continue being responsible for somebody or something

REGIONAL NOTE Referring to a farm worker, the term ***hand*** is most commonly found in the South Midland territory, from Kentucky to Texas, and the Lower South. The terms *cowhand, farm hand,* and *field hand* respectively characterize Western, Northern, and Southern dialects. The general-currency words are *hired hand* and *hired man,* which recur throughout the country but are most common in the North.

hand down *vt* **1. BEQUEATH SOMETHING** to pass something on to a later generation or time **2. PASS CLOTHES ON** to pass clothes on from an older to a younger child **3. PRONOUNCE VERDICT OR SENTENCE** to decide on a verdict or sentence and announce it in court

hand in *vt* **1.** to give or submit something to somebody ○ *handed in her resignation* **2.** to return or surrender something, especially something lost or illegal

hand off /-ôf/ *vt* **1.** in football, to hand the ball to a teammate during play ○ *The quarterback handed off the ball to the running back.* **2.** to pass control of something to another party ○ *handed off the blueprints to the builder*

hand on *vt* to pass something to the next person or generation

hand out *vt* **1.** to distribute or give something by hand **2.** to administer or award something

hand over *v* **1.** *vt* to surrender somebody, or give something away to somebody else ○ *handed over the suspects* **2.** *vti* to transfer control of a commentary during a broadcast to somebody else ○ *Now we'll hand you over to our reporter at the scene.*

hand up *vt* to deliver an indictment, especially from a grand jury to a court for further action [Because the judge's bench is higher than the jury box]

Hand /hand/, **Learned** (1872–1961) US jurist. His more then 2,000 opinions, issued during the course of a 52-year career in district and appeals courts, were important contributions to US jurisprudence. Full name **Hand, Billings Learned**

"Liberty is so much latitude as the powerful choose to accord to the weak."
[Learned Hand, *Address to University of Pennsylvania Law School*; May 21, 1944]

HAND *abbr* ONLINE have a nice day (*used in e-mails or text messages*)

hand ax *n* **1.** an ax with a short handle, for use with one hand **2.** a chipped stone tool rounded at one end and pointed at the other, used for a variety of purposes during the Lower and Middle Paleolithic periods

hand·bag /hánd bàg/ *n* **1.** *UK* same as **purse** *n* (sense 1) **2.** a small light traveling bag that is easily carried by hand

hand·ball /hánd bàwl/ *n* **1. BALL GAME PLAYED AGAINST WALL** a game for two or four people in which players hit a small hard ball against a wall with their hands **2. BALL USED IN HANDBALL** the small hard rubber or synthetic ball used in the game of handball **3. GOAL-SCORING BALL GAME** a team game similar to basketball in which players dribble the ball and pass it, and goals are scored by hitting the ball into the goal with the hand

hand·bar·row /hánd bàrrō/ *n* a flat rectangular board for transporting loads that has a pair of handles at each end and is carried by two people

hand·bas·ket /hánd bàskət/ *n* a small basket carried by hand ◇ **go to hell in a handbasket** to deteriorate quickly and utterly (*informal*)

hand·bell /hánd bèl/ *n* a small bell held in the hand to be rung, often one of a tuned set used to play a musical piece or to practice change ringing

hand·bill /hánd bìl/ *n* a small sheet of paper with a notice or advertisement printed on it, distributed by hand

hand·blown /hánd blōn/ *adj* describes glassware blown using a handheld tube ○ *a handblown vase*

hand·book /hánd bŏŏk/ *n* **1. REFERENCE BOOK** a reference book, especially one small enough to be carried in the hand, giving concise information on a particular subject ○ *a handbook of English–French expressions* **2. SHORT TRAVEL GUIDE** a concise guide designed to help travelers and tourists find their way around a region, city, or other geographic location **3.** BOOKMAKER'S RECORD a notebook in which a bookmaker records bets, or a place where bets are taken

hand·brake /hánd bràyk/ *n* **1.** *UK* AUTOMOT same as **emergency brake** (sense 1) **2.** either of two manual brakes on the handlebars of a bicycle or motorcycle, used to slow or stop the vehicle

hand·breadth /hánd brèdth/, **hand's-breadth** *n* the width of a hand, used as an approximate measure of length

hand·car /hánd kaar/ *n* a small, open, four-wheeled railroad vehicle propelled by a manual pumping mechanism or a small motor

hand·cart /hánd kaart/ *n* a small cart with two or four wheels, pulled or pushed by hand

hand·clap /hánd klàp/ *n* a clapping of the hands, done to gain attention, applaud, or keep a rhythm

hand·clasp /hánd klàsp/ *n* same as **handshake** (sense 1)

hand·craft /hánd kràft/ *n* ARTS same as **handicraft** (sense 3) ■ *vt* (**-craft·ed, -craft·ing, -crafts**) to make something using manual skill —**hand·craft·er** *n* —**hand·crafts·man·ship** *n*

hand·cuff /hánd kùf/ *n* WRIST RESTRAINTS either of a pair of joined metal rings locked around somebody's wrists as a restraint (*usually used in the plural*) ■ *vt* (**-cuffed, -cuff·ing, -cuffs**) **1.** PUT SOMEBODY IN HANDCUFFS to restrain somebody by using handcuffs **2.** GREATLY HAMPER SOMEBODY OR SOMETHING to make somebody or something ineffective ○ *handcuffed by bureaucratic regulations*

-handed *suffix* **1.** using or involving a particular hand ○ *right-handed* **2.** involving a particular number of people ○ *four-handed chess*

hand·ed·ness /hándədnəss/ *n* **1.** the tendency to prefer the use of one hand over the other **2.** the property of some objects whereby they cannot be superimposed on their mirror images

George Frederick Handel

Han·del /hánd'l/, **George Frederick** (1685–1759) German-born British composer. He is best known for his oratorio *Messiah* (1742) and the orchestral suites *Music for the Royal Fireworks* (1749) and *Water Music* (1717). Born **Händel Georg Friedrich**

hand-eye co·or·di·na·tion *n* the ability to perform tasks that involve coordinating the movement of the hands and eyes, e.g., catching or hitting a ball

hand-feed *vt* **1.** to feed a person or animal by hand **2.** to feed material into a machine by hand rather than by means of an automatic or machine feed

hand·ful /hánd fòol/ *n* **1.** AMOUNT CONTAINED BY HAND an amount that can be held in the hand **2.** SMALL AMOUNT OR NUMBER a small amount or number of people or things ○ *Only a handful of students turned up for the lecture.* **3.** SOMEBODY OR SOMETHING DIFFICULT somebody or something that is difficult to cope with or control (*informal*) ○ *Together those two are a real handful!*

CULTURAL NOTE ***A Handful of Dust***, a novel (1934) by British writer Evelyn Waugh. One of Waugh's early satires, it tells the story of Tony Last, a haughty country gentleman whose wife leaves him for a young socialite. His response is to set off on an ill-advised expedition to South America, where he ends up the captive of an eccentric local with a penchant for Dickens.

hand glass *n* **1.** a magnifying glass with a handle for holding in the hand **2.** a small mirror for holding in the hand (*dated*)

hand gre·nade *n* a small bomb designed to be thrown by hand and detonated by a time fuse

hand·grip /hánd grìp/ *n* **1.** same as **grip** *n* (sense 2) **2.** HANDLE a handle, or the part of something that can be held with the hand **3.** COVERING FOR HANDLE a piece of material that covers a handle and makes it easier to keep hold of ■ **hand·grips** *npl* HAND-TO-HAND FIGHTING fighting carried out hand-to-hand

hand·gun /hánd gùn/ *n* a gun that can be held and fired in one hand

hand·held /hánd hèld/, **hand-held** *adj* **1.** HELD IN HAND made to be operated while held in the hand **2.** MOVIES, MEDIA SHOT WITH PORTABLE CAMERA filmed with a camera that is carried by the operator rather than mounted on a support ○ *black-and-white handheld footage* ■ *n* COMPUT SMALL COMPUTER a pocket-sized computer or personal digital assistant that accepts handwritten or keyboard input

hand·hold /hánd hòld/ *n* **1.** something that somebody climbing can grasp for support, e.g., a projecting piece of rock or a fissure in a cliff face **2.** a firm grip with the hand or hands

hand·hold·ing /hánd hòlding/ *n* the giving of reassurance and guidance to somebody

hand-hot *adj* describes hot water that is not too hot for putting the bare hands into

hand·i·cap /hándee kàp/ *n* **1.** HINDRANCE something that hinders or is a disadvantage to somebody or something **2.** GOLF GOLFER'S COMPENSATION IN STROKES a compensation in strokes given to a golfer on the basis of skill in past performances **3.** HORSERACING, SPORTS BALANCED CONTEST a contest, especially a horserace, in which individual competitors are given an advantage or disadvantage in an attempt to give every contestant an equal chance ○ *a handicap race* **4.** ADDED ADVANTAGE OR DISADVANTAGE an advantage or disadvantage given to a competitor in a handicap **5.** MED MEDICAL CONDITION a specific way in which somebody is physically or mentally challenged (*often considered offensive*) ■ *vt* (**-capped, -cap·ping, -caps**) **1.** HINDER SOMEBODY OR SOMETHING to hinder or be a disadvantage to somebody or something **2.** HORSERACING, SPORTS GIVE HANDICAP TO COMPETITOR to give an advantage or disadvantage to a competitor in a contest, especially a horserace **3.** SPORTS ASSESS COMPETITORS' CHANCES to assess the chances of competitors in a contest [Mid-17C. < *hand in cap* "betting game in which contestants place their hands in a hat with their wagers"]

ORIGIN In the original game of ***handicap***, one contestant put up an item of personal property against something belonging to the other contestant, offering to exchange the one for the other. An umpire adjudicated on the difference in value between the two articles. The contestants then placed their hands in a hat, along with some forfeit money, and the way in which they withdrew their hands – full or empty – signified whether they accepted the adjudication. If they both either accepted or rejected it, the umpire got the forfeit money; if they disagreed, the one who accepted it got the money. The application to horseracing arose in the 18th century from the notion of an umpire adjudicating on the weight disadvantage to be given to a specific horse.

hand·i·capped /hándee kàpt/ *adj* **1.** PHYSICALLY OR MENTALLY CHALLENGED physically or mentally challenged (*often considered offensive*) **2.** FOR PEOPLE WITH DISABILITIES for use by people with disabilities ○ *the handicapped entrance near the parking lot* ■ *npl* OFFENSIVE TERM an offensive term for people who are physically or mentally challenged

USAGE Although ***handicapped*** has a long history of use by those so affected, *physically challenged* and *people with disabilities* are preferred over the adjective and noun uses of ***handicapped*** when referring to people.

hand·i·cap·per /hándee kàppər/ *n* **1.** somebody who assigns handicaps to competitors in a contest, especially to racehorses **2.** somebody who forecasts horserace results, especially somebody who provides published advice to bettors

hand·i·craft /hándee kràft/ *n* **1.** CRAFT a craft or occupation in which manual skill is needed, e.g., weaving **2.** OBJECT MADE BY HAND something made using manual skill **3.** MANUAL SKILL skill in making things with the hands [13C. Alteration of HANDCRAFT, after HANDIWORK] —**hand·i·craft·er** *n*

hand·i·ly /hándilee/ *adv* **1.** EASILY in an easy way ○ *She took the second set handily.* **2.** CONVENIENTLY in a convenient way ○ *handily located close to the train station* **3.** SKILLFULLY in a skillful way

hand·i·work /hándee wùrk/ *n* **1.** the result of a particular person's action ○ *The street names are the handiwork of city planners.* **2.** work done or produced by hand [Old English *handgeweorc* < *hand* "hand" + *geweorc* "body of work" < *weorc* "work"]

hand-jam *n* an act of wedging the hand into a rock crack to aid in climbing

hand job *n* an offensive term for the act of masturbation (*slang*)

hand·ker·chief /hángkərchif, -cheef/ (*plural* **-chiefs** or **-chieves** /-chivz, -cheevz/) *n* **1.** a square of cloth or absorbent paper used mainly to wipe areas of the face, especially the nose **2.** CLOTHING same as **kerchief**

han·dle /hánd'l/ *v* (**-dled, -dling, -dles**) **1.** *vt* TOUCH SOMETHING to touch, pick up, or move something with the hands ○ *Don't handle the merchandise.* **2.** *vt* OPERATE SOMETHING to operate or make use of something with the hands **3.** *vt* TAKE CHARGE OF SOMETHING to take care of or be responsible for something ○ *Who handles the import side of the business?* **4.** *vt* DEAL WITH SOMEBODY OR SOMETHING to deal with or cope with somebody or something ○ *She's good at handling difficult customers.* **5.** *vt* BE MANAGER OF SOMEBODY to manage or supervise somebody ○ *He handles a string of professional boxers.* **6.** *vt* BE ABOUT SOMETHING to discuss or deal with a subject ○ *an article handling the subject of global warming* **7.** *vt* TRADE IN SOMETHING to deal in particular goods, sometimes illegally **8.** *vi* RESPOND TO CONTROL to respond to control or use, often in a particular way ○ *The little yacht handled like a dream.* ■ *n* **1.** PART FOR HOLDING OR OPERATING SOMETHING a part of a thing by which it is held, moved, or operated **2.** MEANS an opportunity, pretext, or means of doing something **3.** GAMBLING TOTAL AMOUNT BET the total sum of money bet on a race, series of races, or other event **4.** NAME somebody's name (*slang*) **5.** *Can, UK* TEXTILES the feel of a fabric, used to determine its quality. US term **hand** [Old English *handlian* (verb), *handle* (noun) < HAND] —**han·dle·a·ble** *adj* —**han·dle·less** *adj* ◇ **fly off the handle** to lose your temper, especially without justification (*informal*) ◇ **get a handle on something** to understand or be able to control a situation fully ○ *It's a difficult problem to get a handle on.*

han·dle·bar /hánd'l baar/ *n* a bar with handles at each end, used to steer a vehicle such as a bicycle or motorcycle

handlebar mustache: William II, Emperor of Germany and King of Prussia (photographed in 1898)

han·dle·bar mus·tache *n* a thick broad mustache that curls up at the ends

hand lens *n* OPTICS same as **hand glass** (sense 1)

han·dler /hándlər/ *n* **1.** ANIMAL TRAINER somebody who trains or manages a working animal, e.g., a police dog or a show dog **2.** DEALER OR OPERATOR somebody who works or deals with a particular thing ○ *a baggage handler* **3.** BOXER'S TRAINER a boxer's trainer or second **4.** MANAGER somebody who manages the career of somebody or the running of something **5.** COMPUT **PART OF COMPUTER PROGRAM** a part of a computer program that handles a particular operation or problem

han·dling /hándling/ *n* **1. WAY SOMEBODY HANDLES SOMETHING** the way in which somebody handles or deals with something ○ *The report criticized his handling of the affair.* **2. TREATMENT** the way in which a subject is treated or dealt with in a written work or other work of art **3. SOMETHING'S RESPONSE** the way in which something responds to control or use ○ *the car's excellent handling* **4. USE OF HANDS TO DO SOMETHING** the act of touching, moving, or operating something with the hands ○ *baggage handling* **5. COPING WITH SOMEBODY OR SOMETHING** the act of dealing with something, or of managing or supervising somebody **6.** COMM **TRANSPORTATION AND PACKAGING** the transportation and packaging of goods ○ *The cost includes a charge for handling.*

han·dling charge *n* a charge levied by a retailer or other organization for obtaining, packaging, and sending a particular item

hand·made /hànd máyd, hánd màyd/ *adj* made by hand, not by machine ○ *handmade furniture*

hand·maid /hánd màyd/, **hand·maid·en** /-màyd'n/ *n* **1.** something that provides help or support in a subsidiary role (*literary*) ○ *Hard work and focus are the handmaids of genius.* **2.** a woman or girl servant (*archaic*)

hand-me-down *n* **1.** an item of clothing, usually outgrown, passed down from a family member or friend to another **2.** something taken up or used by a person or group that has been used before and discarded

hand·off /hánd àwf/ *n* **1.** FOOTBALL **GIVING OF FOOTBALL TO ANOTHER PLAYER** in football, a handing of the ball to a teammate during play **2.** FOOTBALL **BALL IN HANDOFFHANDOFF** the ball played in a handoff **3. RELINQUISHMENT OF CONTROL** the passage of control over something from one party to another ○ *the handoff of flight 796*

hand or·gan *n* a mechanical musical instrument with a bellows, played by turning a crank

hand·out /hánd òwt/ *n* **1.** something given as charity to somebody in need, e.g., money or food **2.** a document that is distributed to a group, e.g., a press release, an advertisement, or material accompanying a meeting or lecture

hand·o·ver /hánd ōvər/ *n* **1.** a surrendering of somebody or a giving away of something to somebody else ○ *the handover of power to the civilian authorities* **2.** a transfer of the control of the commentary during a broadcast to somebody else

hand·paint·ed /hànd páyntəd/ *adj* painted individually by hand

hand·phone /hánd fōn/ *n Malaysia, Singapore* TELECOM same as **cell phone**

hand·pick /hànd pík/ (**-picked, -pick·ing, -picks**) *vt* **1.** to choose somebody or something with care and personal attention, especially for a particular purpose ○ *handpicked the starting lineup* **2.** to pick or harvest something by hand, not by machine —**hand·picked** *adj*

hand plant *n* in skateboarding, a move in which the board is held to the feet with one hand while the skateboarder performs a handstand on a ramp or obstacle with the other

hand press, hand·press /hánd prèss/ *n* a printing press operated by hand

hand·print /hánd prìnt/ *n* a mark or impression made by the palm of the hand and fingers

hand pup·pet *n US* a puppet that fits over the hand like a glove and is operated by the user's thumb and fingers. Can term **glove puppet**

hand·rail /hánd ràyl/ *n* a rail to hold with the hand for support, e.g., at the side of stairs or a ramp

hand·saw /hánd sàw/ *n* a saw for use with one hand

hand's-breadth *n* MEASURE same as **handbreadth**

hands down *adv* **1.** without encountering any problems, obstacles, or opposition ○ *whizzed through the exam hands down* **2.** in a way that is not open to question ○ *They won hands down.* [< a jockey not needing to ride hard to win] —**hands-down** *adj*

hand·set /hánd sèt/ *n* the part of a telephone that is held in the hand and contains the parts used for speaking into and listening to

hands-free *adj* used to describe devices that allow somebody to use portable communications equipment such as cell phones or two-way radios without having to hold them —**hands-free** *adv*

hand·shake /hánd shàyk/ *n* **1.** a gesture of gripping and shaking another person's hand, used as a greeting or farewell and to seal an agreement **2.** an exchange of signals between a computer and another computer or external device indicating that a link is established and communication is possible —**hand·shak·ing** *n*

hands-off *adj* not wanting or needing to interfere in or control something ○ *a hands-off policy with respect to the running of the business*

hand·some /hánssəm/ *adj* **1. GOOD-LOOKING** with good-looking facial features or a pleasing general appearance **2. SUBSTANTIAL** pleasingly large in extent or size ○ *a handsome victory* ○ *earning a handsome salary* **3. IMPRESSIVE** well-made or skillfully executed ○ *a handsome piece of jewelry* [15C. Originally "easy to handle," then "handy, suitable"] —**hand·some·ness** *n*

SYNONYMS See ***good-looking***.

hand·some·ly /hándssəmlee/ *adv* **1. GENEROUSLY** in an amount that is more than expected **2. IMPRESSIVELY** in a way that requires great skill or agility **3. WITH GREAT SIZE OR EXTENT** in a way that is very large in extent or size

hands-on *adj* **1. USING SOMETHING** involving the actual use or doing of something ○ *a hands-on carpentry course* **2. INVOLVING PHYSICAL TOUCHING** involving physical touching of something ○ *a museum with hands-on exhibits for children* **3. PERSONALLY INVOLVED** giving personal attention to or taking personal control of somebody or something ○ *a hands-on manager*

hand·spike /hánd spìk/ *n* a metal bar used as a lever [Early 16C. Alteration of Dutch *handspaak* < *hand* "hand" + *spaak* "spoke"]

hand·spring /hánd sprìng/ *n* a gymnastic movement in which somebody flips the body forward or backward and lands briefly on the hands before continuing the flip so as to land on the feet again

hand·stand /hánd stànd/ *n* an act of balancing the body on the hands with the legs straight up in the air

hand-to-hand *adj* taking place at close quarters and involving bodily contact ○ *hand-to-hand fighting* —**hand to hand** *adv*

hand-to-mouth *adj* having barely enough money or food for daily needs —**hand to mouth** *adv*

hand truck *n* an upright rectangular frame with handles at the top and, at the bottom, two wheels and a shallow platform for sliding under a heavy load to be moved by hand

hand·work /hánd wùrk/ *n* work done by hand, not by a machine —**hand·work·er** *n*

hand·wo·ven /hánd wōvən/ *adj* **1.** woven on a hand-operated loom, not a mechanical one **2.** woven using the hands

hand·wring·ing /hánd rìnging/ *n* **1.** the demonstration or expression of concern about something, often without any constructive action being taken **2.** the repeated clasping and squeezing of the hands together as a result of anxiety or grief

hand·write /hánd rìt/ (**-wrote** /-ròt/, **-writ·ten** /-rìtt'n/, **-writ·ing, -writes**) *vt* to write something by hand using a pen or pencil

hand·writ·ing /hánd rìting/ *n* **1.** writing done by hand using a pen or pencil **2.** somebody's individual way of writing by hand ○ *I recognized my father's handwriting on the envelope.* ◇ **see the handwriting on the wall** foresee a future disaster or decline in somebody's fortunes

hand·writ·ten /hànd rítt'n, hánd rìtt'n/ past participle of **handwrite** ■ *adj* written by hand rather than typed or printed ○ *a handwritten letter*

hand·wrote past tense of **handwrite**

hand·wrought /hànd ráwt, hánd ràwt/ *adj* shaped by hand, especially by hammering

hand·y /hándee/ (**-i·er, -i·est**) *adj* **1. USEFUL** useful or easy to use **2. CONVENIENT** located in a convenient place, especially nearby and easy to reach **3. SKILLFUL** skillful at doing a number of different things —**hand·i·ness** *n*

Han·dy /hándee/, **W. C.** (1873–1958) US composer. He was known for blues compositions including "St. Louis Blues" (1914), and brought blues to a wide audience. Full name **Handy, William Christopher**

> "Hits are like babies. To some they come every year or so and to others they never come."
> [W. C. Handy, *Father of the Blues*; 1941]

hand·y·man /hándee màn/ (*plural* **-men** /-mèn/) *n* somebody who is skilled at doing, or paid to do, small jobs such as household repairs

han·dy·per·son /hándee pùrss'n/ (*plural* **-per·sons** or **-peo·ple** /-peèp'l/) *n* **1.** somebody who earns pay by doing varied small maintenance and repair jobs **2.** somebody who has the experience and skill to perform a variety of small maintenance and repair jobs

han·dy·wom·an /hándee wòommən/ (*plural* **-wom·en** /-wìmmin/) *n* **1.** a woman who has the experience and skill to perform a variety of small maintenance and repair jobs **2.** a woman who earns pay by doing varied small maintenance and repair jobs

Han·ford /hánfərd/ city in central California, 30 mi./49 km south of Fresno. Population: 44,350 (2002 estimate).

hang /hang/ *v* (**hung** /hung/, **hang·ing, hangs**) **1.** *vti* **SUSPEND** to suspend or fasten something so that it is held up from above and not supported from below, or be suspended or fastened in this way **2.** *vt* **PUT SOMETHING ON HINGES** to put something such as a door on hinges so that it can move freely **3.** *vti* **DISPLAY PAINTING** to put pictures or paintings on display, or be put on display **4.** *vt* **PUT DECORATIONS ON SOMETHING** to decorate or furnish a place or object with something ○ *trees hung with lights* **5.** *vt* **PUT UP WALLPAPER** to attach wallpaper to walls, usually using a paste solution **6.** (*past and past participle* **hanged**) *vti* **KILL SOMEBODY WITH ROPE** to kill somebody or yourself by fastening a rope around the neck and removing any other support for the body, or die in this way, especially as a form of legal execution **7.** *vt* **LET SOMETHING DROOP** to let something, especially the head, droop ○ *hung their heads in shame* **8.** *vi* **BE UNRESOLVED** to be unresolved or in doubt ○ *His academic future hangs in the balance.* **9.** *vi* **DRAPE** to drape from a point of suspension in a particular way ○ *The jacket hung badly on her.* **10.** *vi* **ELAPSE SLOWLY** to pass by or elapse slowly ○ *Time hung heavily when she was away.* **11.** *vt* LAW **PREVENT JURY FROM DECIDING** to prevent a jury from reaching a verdict (*usually used in the passive*) **12.** *vti* BASEBALL **PITCH BASEBALL THAT FAILS TO BREAK** in baseball, to pitch the ball in such a way that it fails to break, or be pitched in this way **13.** *vi* COMPUT **ALLOW NO INPUT OR OUTPUT** to refuse additional input and be unable to generate output until rebooted (*refers to computers*) **14.** *vt* COOK **SUSPEND GUTTED ANIMAL** to suspend meat or a recently killed game animal until the flesh begins to decompose slightly and becomes more tender and highly flavored **15.** *vt* **MAKE TURN** to make a particular turn, especially when driving a car (*informal*) ○ *hang a left* **16.** (*past and past participle* **hanged**) *vt* **EXCLAMATION INDICATING ANNOYANCE** used to express annoyance at something (*dated informal*) ○ *Hang it all!* **17.** *vi* same as **hang out** (*slang*) ■ *n* **1. WAY OF HANGING** the way that something hangs **2. SLOPE** a downward slope [Old English *hangian* (intransitive) < W Germanic] ◇ **get the hang of something** to learn a skill or activity ◇ **hang somebody out to dry** to leave somebody to struggle through a bad situation without support (*slang*) ◇ **hang your hat** to live in a particular place (*informal*) ○ *So this is where you hang your hat!*

hang around *vi* **1.** to loiter or waste time ○ *kids hanging around in the mall* **2.** to spend time regularly with somebody ○ *He hangs around with the drama crowd.*

hang back *vi* to show reluctance to do something

hang in *vi* to endure or persevere in doing something (*informal*) ○ *She hung in as long as she could.*

hang on *v* **1.** *vi* HOLD ON TIGHTLY to hold on tightly to something **2.** *vi* KEEP GOING to persist in an endeavor in spite of obstacles or difficulties **3.** *vt* CLING TO SOMEBODY to cling to somebody in a possessive or dependent way **4.** *vi* WAIT to wait or show patience for a short time ○ *Hang on a minute while I find out.* **5.** *vt* LISTEN CLOSELY TO SOMEBODY to listen attentively to what somebody says ○ *hanging on his every word*

hang on in *vi* same as **hang in** (*informal*)

hang out *v* **1.** *vti* SUSPEND OUTSIDE to suspend something in the open air so that it will dry or so that it can be seen, or be suspended in this way ○ *hang the washing out* **2.** *vi* SPEND TIME SOMEWHERE to spend time somewhere in a casual or relaxed way (*informal*) ○ *Do you want to hang out at my house?* **3.** *vi* ASSOCIATE to spend time regularly with somebody (*slang*) **4.** *vi* BE AROUND SOMEWHERE to be regularly present somewhere (*slang*) ○ *usually hangs out in the cafeteria*

hang over *vt* to be imminent or threatening for somebody or something, or be unwelcomely associated with somebody or something

hang together *vi* to be consistent or cohesive ○ *Everything in his story hangs together.*

hang tough *vi* to remain resistant or unyielding (*slang*) ○ *He hung tough all through the negotiations.*

hang up *v* **1.** *vt* SUSPEND SOMETHING to put something on a peg, hook, or hanger **2.** *vi* REPLACE PHONE IN ITS CRADLE to end a telephone call by returning the receiver to its original position **3.** *vti* CAUSE DELAY to delay somebody or something, or be delayed

han·gar /hángər/ *n* a large building in which aircraft are kept or repaired [Late 17C. < French, "shed"]

SPELLCHECK hangar or **hanger**? Do not confuse the spelling of ***hangar*** and ***hanger***, which sound similar. The noun ***hangar*** refers only to a large building for aircraft. The noun ***hanger*** has a wider range of meaning, denoting a support or frame for hanging something (as in *a clothes hanger*) or a short sword worn on a belt.

hang·dog /háng dàwg, -dòg/ *adj* having an expression that indicates guilt or sadness [Late 17C. Originally referring to somebody who deserved to be hanged like a dog]

hang·er /hángər/ *n* **1.** FRAME FOR HANGING GARMENT a triangular frame of metal, wood, or plastic over which clothes can be draped for storage or display **2.** NAIL OR HOOK FOR HANGING SOMETHING a support from which something can be hung, e.g., a nail or hook **3.** SOMEBODY WHO HANGS SOMETHING somebody who hangs or suspends something **4.** SHORT SWORD a short sword worn on a belt

SPELLCHECK See *hangar.*

hang·er-on (*plural* **hang·ers-on**) *n* somebody who latches on to a richer or more prominent person or group in the hope of gain

Barnaby's

hang glider

hang glid·er *n* an aircraft without an engine that consists of a rigid frame in the shape of a wing, with the pilot usually suspended in a harness below the wing —**hang-glide** *vi* —**hang glid·ing** *n*

hang·ing /hánging/ *n* **1.** METHOD OF KILLING the act of killing somebody by putting the neck in a noose and removing any other support for the body, especially as a form of legal execution **2.** FABRIC HUNG ON WALL a drapery, tapestry, or decorative fabric hung on a wall (*often used in the plural*) ■ *adj* **1.** PUNISHABLE BY DEATH punishable by death, or seen as deserving the death penalty ○ *a hanging offense* **2.** SEVERE OR UNMERCIFUL tending to impose severe punishments, especially the death penalty ○ *a hanging judge* **3.** AT TOP OF SLOPE positioned at the top of a steep slope or height

hang·ing bas·ket *n* a container for plants, usually trailing plants, that is hung up outside

hang·ing in·den·ta·tion *n* an indenting of all the lines of a paragraph of text except the first

hang·ing par·ti·ci·ple *n* GRAM same as **dangling participle**

hang·ing wall *n* the rocks that hang over a seam of coal or other mineral vein

hang·man /hángmən, háng màn/ (*plural* **-men** /-mən, -mèn/) *n* **1.** an official who carries out the death penalty of hanging **2.** a game in which one player has to guess the letters of a word before the other player has drawn a person being hanged, with one line being added to the figure for every wrong guess

hang·nail /háng nàyl/ *n* a small piece of skin partly detached from the side or base of a fingernail [Late 17C. By folk etymology < *agnail* "corn on the foot" < Old English *angnægl* < *ang-* (< Germanic, "tight") + NAIL]

hang·out /háng òwt/ *n* a place frequented by a particular person or group of people, especially for relaxation (*slang*) ○ *The café is a favorite teen hangout.*

hang·o·ver /háng ŏvər/ *n* **1.** a set symptoms including headache, nausea, thirst, and sickness that result from drinking too much alcohol **2.** something that remains from an earlier time

Hang Seng in·dex /hàng séng-/ *n* an index based on the relative prices of selected stocks on the Hong Kong Stock Exchange [After the *Hang Seng Bank*, Hong Kong]

hang·tag /háng tàg/ *n* a small slip attached to an item being sold and giving information about it

hang time *n* **1.** SPORTS TIME BALL IS IN AIR the amount of time a ball remains in the air after being kicked, or an athlete remains in the air after leaping **2.** SPORTS TIME ATHLETE IS IN AIR the amount of time an athlete remains in the air after leaping **3.** TIME COMPUTER IS DOWN the time that elapses between the time a computer freezes, preventing the user from accomplishing any useful work, and restarts, allowing work to resume **4.** TIME SPENT AT WEBSITE the amount of time spent viewing a website. Longer viewing times are considered commercially more valuable, on the assumption that the message is holding the viewer's interest.

Hang·town fry /háng tòwn-/ (*plural* **Hang·town fries**) *n* an omelet made with a filling of fried bacon and oysters [Mid-20C. After the nickname of Placerville, California]

Han·gul /haáng gŏŏl, háng-/, **han·gul** *n* the alphabet used for Korean writing [Mid-20C. < Korean *han kul* "Korea alphabet"]

hang-up *n* **1.** a psychological or emotional problem or fixation about something (*informal*) **2.** a persistent impediment or source of delay ○ *Bureaucratic inefficiency was the main hang-up.*

Hang·zhou /haáng jṓ/ seaport and capital city of Zhejiang Province in southeastern China. Population: 4,210,000 (1995).

Han Jiang /haán jyaáng/, **Han** river of central China, a tributary of the Yangtze River and major trade artery. Length: 952 mi./1,532 km.

hank /hangk/ *n* **1.** LOOSE COIL OF FIBER a length of fiber such as rope or wool that has been wrapped around itself to form a loose coil **2.** SAILING ATTACHMENT FOR SAIL a ring-shaped fitting that can be opened to secure the leading edge of a sail **3.** MEASURE LENGTH OF YARN a length of yarn when reeled. A hank of cotton is 840 yd./767 m. [14C. < Old Norse *hönk* < Germanic]

han·ker /hángkər/ (**-kered, -ker·ing, -kers**) *vi* to want something very badly and persistently ○ *hankers after something she can't have* [Early 17C. Origin ?]

~~**hankerchief**~~ incorrect spelling of **handkerchief**

han·kie /hángkee/, **han·ky** (*plural* **-kies**) *n* same as **handkerchief** (*informal*) [Late 19C. Shortening]

Hanks /hangks/, **Tom** (*b.* 1956) US actor. He won Academy Awards for *Philadelphia* (1993) and *Forrest Gump* (1994). Full name **Hanks, Thomas J.**

han·ky *n* another spelling of **hankie** (*informal*)

han·ky-pan·ky /hàngkee pángkee/ *n* **1.** illicit or suspicious behavior ○ *suspected financial hanky-panky* **2.** frivolous and slightly indecent sexual activity [Mid-19C. Alteration of HOCUS-POCUS]

Han·na /hánnə/, **Mark** (1837–1904) US entrepreneur and politician. He took US presidential campaigns to new levels of sophistication and expense in masterminding the election of William McKinley (1896). Full name **Hanna, Marcus Alonzo**

Han·ni·bal /hánnəb'l/ city and port in eastern Missouri, on the Mississippi River. It was the boyhood home of Mark Twain. Population: 17,517 (2002 estimate).

Han·ni·bal (247–183 B.C.) Carthaginian general. At the beginning of the Second Punic War (218–202 B.C.), he marched across the Alps to northern Italy with elephants and a 40,000-strong army. It is one of the most famous military exploits in history. He was less successful in a subsequent African campaign against Scipio, and died in exile.

Ha·noi /ha nóy/ capital city of Vietnam, located in the northern part of the country. Population: 3,734,000 (2000).

Han·o·ver[1] /hán ŏvər/ city in northwestern Germany, situated on the Leine River. Population: 525,763 (1997). ■ former state and province in northern Germany

Han·o·ver[2] /hán ŏvər/ *n* the royal house of Great Britain from 1714, when the elector of Hanover ascended the British throne as George I, until 1901, when Queen Victoria died

Han·o·ve·ri·an /hànnə veéree ən/ *adj* **1.** OF HOUSE OF HANOVER relating to the British rulers from 1714 to 1901, belonging to the house of Hanover **2.** OF HANOVER relating to Hanover, Germany ■ *n* HANOVERIAN MONARCH a supporter or monarch of the British Hanoverian line

Han·o·ver Park village in northeastern Illinois, a western suburb of Chicago. Population: 38,037 (2002 estimate).

Han·sard /hánssərd/ *n* the official published reports of proceedings in the British or Canadian parliaments or of similar legislative bodies in the British Commonwealth [Late 19C. After Luke *Hansard* (1752–1828), British printer]

Han·se /haánzə, hanss/ *n* **1.** HIST same as **Hanseatic League 2.** the fee paid by a new member of the Hanseatic League [12C. < Old High German *hansa* "troop, company"]

Han·se·at·ic /hànssee áttik/ *adj* relating to the Hanseatic League or one of the towns in it [Early 17C. < medieval Latin *Hanseaticus* < *Hansa* "the Hanseatic League"]

Han·se·at·ic League *n* an organized network of towns in northern Europe between the 15th and 17th centuries that protected each other and promoted trade with each other

Han·sen's dis·ease /hànss'nz-/ *n* MED same as **leprosy** [Early 20C. After Gerhard *Hansen* (1841–1921), Norwegian physician]

han·som /hánssəm/, **han·som cab** *n* a covered two-

hansom

wheeled vehicle drawn by one horse and carrying two passengers inside while the driver sits outside on a raised seat at the rear [Mid-19C. After Joseph Aloysius *Hansom* (1803–82), British architect]

han·ta·vi·rus /hántə vìrəss/ *n* a virus belonging to a group that affects small rodents and can be passed to humans, causing fever, headache, nausea, and vomiting [Late 20C. < *Hantaan*, river in Korea]

Ha·nuk·kah /haánəkə, kha̲a̲n-/, **Ha·nu·kah**, **Cha·nu·kah** *n* a Jewish festival marking the rededication to Judaism of the Temple in Jerusalem in 165 B.C. and celebrated by the kindling of eight lights. Date: from 25th day of Kislev, in December, for eight days. [Late 19C. < Hebrew *hanukkah* "consecration"]

han·u·man /húnnoo maán, haánoo-/ *n* a slender long-tailed langur monkey, considered sacred in South Asia. Native to: South Asia. Latin name: *Presbytis entellus*. [Mid-19C. < HANUMAN]

Han·u·man /húnnoo maán, haánoo-/ *n* in Hinduism, a leader of monkeys who assists Rama [Early 19C. < Sanskrit, "large-jawed"]

hao /how/ (*plural same*) *n* a minor currency unit of Vietnam. See table at **currency** [Mid-20C. < Vietnamese]

hao·le /hówlee/ *n Hawaii* somebody, especially a white person, who lives in Hawaii but is not of Polynesian descent [Mid-19C. < Hawaiian] —**hao·le** *adj*

Hao·ra /hówrə/, **How·rah** industrial port in Bangla state, eastern India, on the Hugli River, opposite Kolkata. Population: 1,008,704 (2001).

hap[1] /hap/ (*archaic*) *n* a happening or occurrence ■ *vi* (**happed, hap·ping, haps**) to happen or occur [13C. < Old Norse *happ*]

hap[2] /hap/ *n Scotland* something used to cover a person or bed, e.g., a cloak or comforter ■ *vt* (**happed, hap·ping, haps**) *US regional, Scotland* to wrap somebody up in warm clothes [13C. Origin ?]

ha·pa hao·le /hàppə-/ *adj* of descent that is both Hawaiian and European [Early 19C. < Hawaiian *hapa* + HAOLE]

ha·pax le·go·me·non /hà paks lə gómmə nòn, -gómmənən/ (*plural* **ha·pax le·go·me·na** /-gómmənə/) *n* a word of which there is only one recorded use [Mid-17C. < Greek, "said only once"]

~~**hapen**~~ incorrect spelling of **happen**

ha'pen·ny /háypnee, háypənee/ (*plural* **-nies**) *n UK* COINS same as **halfpenny** [Mid-16C. Contraction]

hap·haz·ard /hap házzərd/ *adj* happening or done in a way that has not been planned [Late 16C. < HAP[1] + HAZARD, literally "hazard of chance"] —**hap·haz·ard·ly** *adv* —**hap·haz·ard·ness** *n*

haph·ta·rah *n* JUDAISM another spelling of **haftarah**

hapl- *prefix* same as **haplo-** (*used before vowels*)

hap·less /hápplәss/ *adj* unlucky or unfortunate —**hap·less·ly** *adv* —**hap·less·ness** *n*

hap·lite /háp lìt/ *n* GEOL same as **aplite** [Variant] —**hap·lit·ic** /ha plíttik/ *adj*

haplo- *prefix* **1.** single ○ *haplology* **2.** haploid ○ *haplont* [< Greek *haplous* "single" < Indo-European]

hap·log·raph·y /hap lóggrəfee/ *n* the accidental omission of a letter or written syllable that should be repeated, e.g., in writing "mispell" for "misspell"

hap·loid /háp lòyd/ *adj* having a single set of unpaired chromosomes —**hap·loid** *n*

hap·lol·o·gy /hap lólləjee/ *n* the accidental omission of one or more repeated syllables or sounds when speaking —**hap·lo·log·ic** /hàpplə lójjik/ *adj*

hap·lont /háp lònt/ *n* an organism, especially an algal plant, that is haploid at one stage of its life cycle [Early 20C. < HAPLO- + -ONT] —**hap·lon·tic** /hap lóntik/ *adj*

hap·lo·sis /hap lóssiss/ *n* the production of haploids during cell division (**meiosis**)

hap·lo·type /háppl ə tìp/ *n* a segment of DNA that contains closely linked gene variations that are inherited as a unit [Mid-20C. < HAPLO- + TYPE]

hap·ly /hápplee/ *adv* used to express the possibility or hope that something is or will be the case (*archaic*) ○ *"I will kiss thy lips; haply some poison yet doth hang on them"* (William Shakespeare, *Romeo and Juliet*; 1594)

ha'p'·orth /háypərth/ (*plural same*) *n UK* same as **halfpennyworth** (*dated*) [Late 17C. Contraction]

hap·pen /hápp'n/ (**-pened, -pen·ing, -pens**) *v* **1.** *vi* OCCUR to take place ○ *How did it happen?* ○ *a go-getter who can really make things happen* **2.** *vt* DO SOMETHING BY CHANCE to do something by chance and without a previous plan ○ *If you happen to see him, give him these keys.* **3.** *vi* AFFECT SOMEBODY OR SOMETHING to affect somebody or something, especially in an unpleasant way ○ *If anything happens to him, you'll regret it.* **4.** *vti* OCCUR BY CHANCE to occur or exist by chance ○ *It happened to be the last one in the store.* [14C. < HAP[1]]

happen along, happen by *vi* to appear or pass by chance or unexpectedly (*informal*)

happen on, happen upon *vt* to discover or encounter somebody or something by chance

hap·pen·chance /hápp'n chànss/ *n* same as **happenstance** [Mid-20C. Alteration]

hap·pen·ing /háppəning/ *n* **1.** OCCURRENCE something that occurs **2.** ARTISTIC PERFORMANCE an improvised or informal performance or demonstration, often dramatic in form and using audience participation (*informal*) ■ *adj* FASHIONABLE at the forefront of what is fashionable and exciting (*informal*)

hap·pen·stance /háppən stànss/ *n* a chance occurrence or event [Late 19C. Blend of HAPPENING + CIRCUMSTANCE]

hap·pi coat /háppee-/ *n* an open Japanese jacket that has wide loose sleeves and is usually tied with a sash, or a fashion garment resembling this [Late 19C. < Japanese *happi*]

hap·pi·ly /háppilee/ *adv* **1.** FORTUNATELY used to indicate that something that could have been difficult or disastrous is luckily not so ○ *Happily, no one was hurt.* **2.** WILLINGLY with willingness ○ *I'd happily contribute.* **3.** IN HAPPY WAY in a pleased, contented, or joyful way

hap·py /háppee/ (**-pi·er, -pi·est**) *adj* **1.** FEELING PLEASURE feeling or showing pleasure, contentment, or joy ○ *happy smiling faces* **2.** CAUSING PLEASURE causing or characterized by pleasure, contentment, or joy ○ *a happy childhood* **3.** SATISFIED feeling satisfied that something is right or has been done right ○ *Are you happy with your performance?* **4.** WILLING willing to do something ○ *I'd be only too happy to help.* **5.** FORTUNATE resulting in something pleasant or welcome ○ *a happy coincidence* **6.** TIPSY slightly drunk (*informal*) **7.** USED IN GREETINGS used in formulae to express a hope that somebody will enjoy a special day or holiday ○ *Happy birthday!* **8.** TOO READY TO USE SOMETHING inclined to use a particular thing too readily or be too enthusiastic about a particular thing (*used in combination*) ○ *trigger-happy* [14C. < HAP[1]] —**hap·pi·ness** *n*

hap·py e·vent *n UK* the birth of a baby (*informal*)

hap·py-go-luck·y *adj* tending not to worry about the future

hap·py hard core *n* uplifting hard core music, often achieving its emotional effect by the use of piano riffs over straightforward rhythms

hap·py hour *n* a period of time, usually in the late afternoon or early evening, during which a bar serves alcoholic drinks at reduced prices

hap·py hunt·ing ground *n* **1.** among some Native American peoples, a place of peace and abundance to which people are believed to go after death **2.** a place that provides plenty of something desired ○ *The arcade was a happy hunting ground for somebody looking for gifts.*

hap·py me·di·um *n* a satisfying compromise

~~**happyness**~~ incorrect spelling of **happiness**

hap·py talk *n* informal or entertaining conversation among broadcasters during a television news show (*slang*)

Haps·burg /háps bùrg, haáps boorg/, **Habs·burg** *n* a member of a German royal family, prominent between the 13th and 20th centuries in Europe, that included rulers of the Holy Roman Empire, Spain, and Austria-Hungary

hap·ten /háp tèn/, **hap·tene** /-teen/ *n* an antigen that can only stimulate antibody production when combined with a specific protein [Early 20C. < Greek *haptein* "fasten"]

hap·tic /háptik/ *adj* relating to the sense of touch [Late 19C. < Greek *haptikos* < *haptesthai* "grasp, touch" < *haptein* "fasten"]

hap·to·glo·bin /hàptə glóbin/ *n* a plasma protein that combines with free hemoglobin in the bloodstream [Mid-20C. < Greek *haptein* "fasten"]

hap·to·trop·ism /hàp tóttrə pìzzəm/ *n* BOT same as **thigmotropism** [Late 19C. < Greek *haptein* "fasten"]

ha·ra-ki·ri /hàrrə keeree/ *n* in Japan, a traditional form of suicide, sometimes ritually performed as a point of honor, involving disembowelment with a sword [Mid-19C. < Japanese, "belly-cutting"]

ha·ram /hérrəm, hárrəm/, **ha·raam** *adj* describes food forbidden by Islamic law [Early 17C. < Arabic *harām* "forbidden"]

ha·rangue /hə ráng/ (**-rangued, -rangu·ing, -rangues**) *vti* to criticize or question somebody, or try to persuade somebody to do something in a forceful angry way [15C. Via French < medieval Latin *harenga*] —**ha·rangue** *n* —**ha·rangu·er** *n*

Ha·rar ➧ **Harer**

Ha·ra·re /hə raáree/ capital city of Zimbabwe, located in the northeastern part of the country. Population: 1,752,000 (2000).

ha·rass /hə ráss, hárrəss/ (**-rassed, -rass·ing, -rass·es**) *vt* **1.** to persistently annoy, attack, or bother somebody **2.** to exhaust an enemy by attacking repeatedly [Early 17C. < French *harasser* < *harer* "set a dog on (by crying 'hare')"] —**ha·rass·er** *n*

USAGE In US English the traditional pronunciation of *harass* (and its derivatives *harassed* and *harassment*) has the stress on the second syllable, but the variant pronunciation, with the stress on the first syllable, is now equally common.

USAGE See *embarrass*.

ha·rass·ment /hérrəsmənt, hə rásmənt/ *n* behavior that threatens or torments somebody, especially persistently

ha·rass·ment re·strain·ing or·der *n* LAW same as **restraining order** (sense 1)

Har·bin /haar bín/ capital city of Heilongjiang Province in northeastern China. Population: 4,470,000 (1995).

har·bin·ger /haárbinjər/ *n* somebody or something that foreshadows or anticipates a future event [12C. < Old French *herberger* < *herbergier* "provide shelter for an army" < Germanic] —**har·bin·ger** *vt*

har·bor /haárbər/ *n* **1.** PORT a part of a body of water near a coast in which ships can anchor safely (*often used in place names*) **2.** PLACE OF REFUGE a place that is safe and sheltered ■ *v* (**-bored, -bor·ing, -bors**) **1.** *vt* SHELTER SOMEBODY to provide somebody with shelter or sanctuary ○ *accused of harboring a fugitive* **2.** *vt* KEEP SOMETHING IN MIND to privately have and continue to keep in mind an emotion or thought ○ *had harbored a secret fear of the dark since childhood* **3.** *vt* BE HABITAT FOR SOMEBODY OR SOMETHING to be a place where somebody or something can live or be found ○ *Many patients now harbor bacteria resistant to these antibiotics.* **4.** *vti* NAUT KEEP SHIP IN HARBOR to take shelter in a harbor, or shelter a ship in a harbor [Old English *herebeorg* "lodging" < Germanic, "army shelter"] —**har·bor·er** *n* —**har·bor·less** *adj*

har·bor·age /haárbərij/ *n* NAUT same as **harbor** *n* (sense 1)

har·bor mas·ter *n* an official who supervises and administers the general activities of a harbor or port

har·bor seal *n* a small seal that is grayish black with paler spots. Native to: northern coasts of North America, Europe, and Asia. Latin name: *Phoca vitulina*.

har·bour *n, vi, vi* NAUT Can, UK spelling of **harbor**

hard /haard/ *adj* **1.** NOT EASILY BENT firm, stiff, or rigid, and not easily cut, pierced, or bent ○ *a hard mattress* ○ *Do not move the object until the glue is hard.* **2.**

DIFFICULT OR AWKWARD difficult or awkward to do or achieve ○ *a hard decision* **3. INVOLVING EFFORT** involving a great deal of mental or physical effort or exertion ○ *a hard climb* **4. PERFORMING ENERGETICALLY** doing something with energy or industriousness ○ *a hard worker* **5. MIGHTY** using a lot of force or violence ○ *a hard tug on the rope* **6. DEMANDING AND STRICT** making inflexible and heavy demands ○ *a hard taskmaster* **7. PROBLEMATIC** difficult to endure and full of problems ○ *a hard life* **8. UNSYMPATHETIC** showing little or no sympathy, compassion, or gentleness ○ *She's as hard as nails.* **9. RESENTFUL** marked by resentment or bitterness ○ *no hard feelings* **10. REAL OR TRUE** demonstrably real, true, or certain ○ *cold hard facts* **11. DIFFICULT TO UNDERSTAND** difficult to understand or explain **12.** POL **RADICAL** politically radical or extreme ○ *the hard left* **13. SEVERE** marked by weather conditions such as extreme cold or severe storms ○ *a hard winter* **14. TOUGHENED** rough or leathery, and unyielding ○ *hard skin* **15.** CHEM **CONTAINING MINERAL SALTS** containing mineral salts and preventing soap from lathering well ○ *hard water* **16. PENETRATING** seeming to penetrate and discover intentions or thoughts ○ *a hard stare* **17. FIRM OR CRISP IN TEXTURE** having a crisp, firm, or stale crust or texture **18. ERECT** stiff and erect (*informal*) **19.** PHYS **EASILY ABLE TO PENETRATE SUBSTANCES** describes radiation, especially high frequency X-rays, that has a high energy and is thus easily able to penetrate substances including metals, or relating to this type of radiation ○ *hard vacuum* **20.** BEVERAGES **HIGH IN ALCOHOL** describes beverages that have a high alcoholic content, especially alcohol produced by distillation ○ *hard liquor* **21.** DRUGS **ADDICTIVE AND DANGEROUS TO HEALTH** describes drugs that are highly addictive and particularly dangerous to the health ○ *hard drugs* **22.** PHON **PRONOUNCED LIKE "K" OR "G"** describes the consonants "c" and "g" when they are pronounced with a "k" sound, as in "come," and a "g" sound, as in "go" ■ *adv* **1. FORCEFULLY** with a lot of force ○ *hit the ball hard* **2. ALL THE WAY** to the greatest degree or extent ○ *pulled the truck over hard* **3. ENERGETICALLY** with vigor and energy or industriousness ○ *worked hard* **4. WITH CONCENTRATION** with great mental concentration ○ *studied hard* **5. WITH DIFFICULTY** with effort and great difficulty ○ *Her victory was hard won.* **6. COMPACTLY** into a solid or compact state ○ *set hard* **7. SEVERELY** in a way that causes anguish or hardship ○ *hit hard by the recession* **8. SLOWLY** slowly and with difficulty ○ *hatred that dies hard* [Old English *heard* < Indo-European, "strength"] ◇ **be hard on somebody 1.** to treat somebody severely **2.** to be unfortunate for somebody ◇ **be hard put to do something** to find it difficult to do something ◇ **go hard with somebody** to cause difficulty or distress to somebody (*dated*) ◇ **hard by** close by

USAGE See ***hardly***.

CULTURAL NOTE ***Hard Times***, a novel (1854) by British writer Charles Dickens. This story of the loveless upbringing of Tom and Louisa Gradgrind contrasts the soullessness of utilitarianism, as personified by their father Thomas Gradgrind, with the natural warmth and generosity of the human spirit, symbolized by their adopted sister Sissy Jupe, a member of a traveling circus.

SYNONYMS ***hard, difficult, strenuous, tough, arduous, laborious***

CORE MEANING: requiring effort or exertion

hard requiring mental or physical effort or exertion ○ *The work was always hard and sometimes dangerous.* ○ *It is hard to imagine Pauline being afraid of anything.* **difficult** requiring a lot of planning or effort to do, understand, or deal with ○ *Some of the questions on this paper are too difficult for the children.* ○ *Improvements in this area may turn out to be the most difficult to achieve.* **strenuous** requiring physical effort, energy, stamina, or strength ○ *strenuous physical activity* ○ *The fittest men are involved in the more strenuous tasks, while the less fit do other work.* **tough** physically or mentally challenging ○ *Tough decisions await the government, not least over public spending.* ○ *It will be tough for him, but I think he'll cope.* **arduous** requiring hard work or continuous physical effort ○ *a long and arduous task* ○ *He left the comforts of the capital to make the arduous journey north.* **laborious** requiring much unwelcome, often tedious effort. ○ *slow laborious manual methods* ○ *Producing charts and graphs on conventional printers is a very laborious process.*

hard-and-fast *adj* unable to be changed or adapted

Har·dan·ger Fjord /haárd angər-/ large fjord on the southwestern coast of Norway. Length: 114 mi./183 km.

hard-ass *n* an offensive term for somebody who is perceived as inflexible and uncompromising (*slang insult*) —**hard-assed** *adj*

hard·back /haárd bàk/ *n* a book with a rigid cover

hard·ball /haárd bàwl/ *n* **1.** SPORTS same as **baseball** (sense 1) **2.** tough or ruthless behavior, especially in politics or business (*informal*) ○ *These guys play hardball.*

hard-bit·ten *adj* tough and experienced

hard·board /haárd bàwrd/ *n* thin stiff sheets of compressed sawdust and wood chips, often used in constructing walls

hard-boil (**hard-boiled, hard-boil·ing, hard-boils**) *vt* to boil an egg until both the white and the yolk are firm

hard-boiled *adj* **1.** describes an egg boiled until the yolk and white are firm **2.** tough, realistic, and unsentimental (*informal*)

hard·boot /haárd bòot/ (**-boot·ed, -boot·ing, -boots**) *vt UK* COMPUT same as **coldboot**

hard·bound /haárd bòwnd/ *adj* bound as a book in a stiff cover

hard can·dy *n* a crunchy candy made from boiled corn syrup and sugar and flavored with fruit, herbs, or spices

hard case *n* somebody who is rough, tough, and ruthless (*informal*)

hard cash *n* money in the form of coins or bills

hard ci·der *n* an alcoholic drink made by pressing and fermenting apples

hard coal *n* INDUST same as **anthracite**

hard cop·y *n* data from a computer printed out on paper

hard core *n* **1. COMMITTED NUCLEUS OF GROUP** the most committed, faithful, and active members of a group or organization **2.** MUSIC **FAST ROCK MUSIC** rock music with repetitive rhythmic synthesized sounds and a fast tempo **3.** *UK* ROADS **FOUNDATION FOR ROADS OR PAVING** stones and other rubble used to form a foundation under roads or paving

hard-core, hard·core /haárd kàwr/ *adj* **1. UNCOMPROMISING** uncompromising and committed **2. SHOWING EXPLICIT SEX** depicting sexual acts in an explicit way **3.** MUSIC **RELATING TO FAST ROCK MUSIC** describes rock music with repetitive rhythmic synthesized sounds and a fast tempo

hard·cov·er /haárd kùvvər/ *n* PUBL same as **hardback**

hard disk, hard drive *n* a rigid disk inside a computer that holds a large quantity of data and programs

hard·ears /haárd eèrz/ *adj Carib* stubborn and unwilling to take orders or advice

hard-edge *adj* describes a US style of abstract painting that developed in the 1960s, marked by sharply outlined colored forms

hard-edged *adj* realistic, direct, and uncompromising

hard·en /haárd'n/ (**-ened, -en·ing, -ens**) *v* **1.** *vti* **BECOME OR MAKE HARD** to become hard, firm, or solid, or make something do this ○ *The glue hardened overnight.* **2.** *vti* **MAKE OR BECOME LESS SYMPATHETIC** to become more tough, callous, or unfeeling, or make somebody do this **3.** *vti* **MAKE OR BECOME MORE DETERMINED** to become more determined and resolute, or make somebody do this **4.** *vti* **MAKE OR BECOME STRONGER** to become stronger or more resistant, or make somebody or something do this **5.** *vi* COMM **STABILIZE** to become stable after fluctuation ○ *Prices are hardening.*

harden off *vti* to accustom a plant grown indoors to outdoor conditions by gradually exposing it to cold, wind, or sunlight before planting it outdoors, or become accustomed to outdoor conditions in this way

hard·ened /haárd'nd/ *adj* made harder or stronger ○ *hardened steel*

hard·en·er /haárd'nər/ *n* an ingredient or element that makes something hard, e.g., a substance added to paint to make it more durable

hard·en·ing of the ar·ter·ies *n* MED same as **atherosclerosis** (*not in technical use*)

hard-fist·ed *adj* not generous with money

hard goods *npl* COMM same as **durables**

hard·hack /haárd hàk/ (*plural* **-hacks** or *same*) *n* a bush of the rose family with downy leaves. Flowers: pink or white, in clusters. Native to: North America. Latin name: *Spiraea tomentosa*. [Mid-19C. Origin ?]

hard·hand·ed /haárd hàndəd/ *adj* showing little or no sympathy or pity —**hard·hand·ed·ness** *n*

hard·hat /haárd hàt/ *n* **1. PROTECTIVE HELMET** a helmet made of metal or plastic worn for protection by workers in a factory or on a construction site **2. CONSTRUCTION WORKER** a worker in the construction industry (*informal*) **3. CONSERVATIVE** a politically very conservative patriot (*informal*) —**hard-hat** *adj*

hard·head /haárd hèd/ *n* a logical and unsentimental person

hard·head·ed /haárd héddəd/ *adj* **1.** behaving in a logical and unsentimental way **2.** determined not to give in —**hard·head·ed·ly** *adv* —**hard·head·ed·ness** *n*

hard·heart·ed /haárd haártəd/ *adj* showing no sympathy for other people's feelings —**hard·heart·ed·ly** *adv* —**hard·heart·ed·ness** *n*

hard-hit·ting *adj* direct and uncompromising ○ *a hard-hitting documentary*

har·di·hood /haárdee hòod/ *n* **1.** the quality of being tough and able to withstand difficulty or hard work **2.** bold audacity

Har·ding /haárding/, **Florence** (1860–1924) US first lady (1921–23). Full name **Harding, Florence Mabel King**

Library of Congress

Warren G. Harding

Har·ding, Warren G. (1865–1923) 29th president of the United States. A conservative Republican from Ohio elected on the promise of a "return to normalcy" after World War I, he presided (1921–23) over a federal administration distinguished primarily by its flagrant corruption. Full name **Harding, Warren Gamaliel**. See table at **president**

> "I wish for an America no less alert in guarding against dangers from within than it is watchful against enemies from without."
> [Warren G. Harding, *New York Times*; March 5, 1921]

hard la·bor *n* a sentence of compulsory work imposed in addition to a term of imprisonment

hard land·ing *n* **1.** an uncontrolled landing by an aircraft or spacecraft that results in its being damaged or destroyed **2.** a downward trend in economic activity after a period of expansion

hard·line /haárd lìn/ *adj* inflexible and uncompromising —**hard·lin·er** *n*

hard-luck *adj* involving or suffering a lot of personal misfortune ○ *She had a soft spot for other people's hard-luck stories.*

hard·ly /haárdlee/ CORE MEANING: an adverb with negative meaning, used to indicate that something is true or exists to a very minimal extent ○ *She lived*

so privately, hardly anyone even spoke to her. ○ *Though we hardly knew him, we could sense his good humour.* ○ *I looked out of the window; it was hardly raining.*
adv **1. NOT** indicates that something is almost entirely untrue or impossible ○ *We are hardly going to give up with success in view.* ○ *It's hardly likely that I would tell you.* **2. ONLY WITH DIFFICULTY** only with great awkwardness, difficulty, or embarrassment ○ *I was so shocked I could hardly speak.* **3. SELDOM** indicates that something seldom occurs (*used with a negative such as "without"*) ○ *Hardly a day passes without acclaim for this exciting new invention.* **4. AS SOON AS** indicates that one event follows quickly after another ○ *Hardly had I rung the bell when the bolt was shot back.* **5. USED TO DISAGREE** used to indicate surprise, disagreement, or annoyance ○ *"I thought you were going at about sixty miles an hour." "Well, hardly. Maybe forty."*

USAGE ***Hardly***, like *barely* and *scarcely*, has a negative force, rendering unnecessary the use of another negative in the clause or sentence: *I can* [not: *can't*] *hardly see you.* Note that *when* and not *than* is used in any continuation of the sentence: *Hardly* [or *barely* or *scarcely*] *had I begun to speak when* [not *than*] *she interrupted me.* (After *no sooner*, however, *than* is correct. *No sooner had I begun to speak than* [not *when*] *she interrupted me.*) ***Hardly*** is limited to these special uses; the usual adverb from the adjective *hard* is also *hard*: *They are all working hard to get ready for their exams.*

hard man *n* a man who is perceived as vicious and ruthless, often with criminal tendencies

hard ma·ple *n* TREES same as **sugar maple**

hard mouth *n* a horse's mouth that is insensitive to pressure from the bit, or a horse's ability to resist this pressure

hard·mouthed /haárd mòwthd, -mòwtht/ *adj* describes a horse that fails to respond when the rider pulls on the bit in its mouth

hard·ness /haárdnəss/ *n* **1. FIRMNESS, SOLIDITY, AND COMPACTNESS** the state or quality of being firm, solid, and compact **2. UNYIELDING TOUGHNESS** the state or quality of being tough and unyielding **3.** CHEM **WATER QUALITY** the degree to which water contains mineral salts **4.** METALL, MEASURE **DEGREE TO WHICH A METAL IS HARD** the degree to which a metal may be scratched, abraded, indented, or machined, measured according to any of several scales

hard news *n* news that concerns specific events and is strictly factual —**hard-news** *adj*

hard-nosed *adj* tough, realistic, and unsentimental (*informal*)

hard-of-hear·ing *adj* MED same as **hearing-impaired** (*sometimes considered offensive*)

hard-on *n* a highly offensive term for an erect penis (*slang taboo*)

hard pal·ate *n* the bony front portion of the roof of the mouth

hard·pan /haárd pàn/ *n* a layer of hard matter, especially clay, that lies under soft soil and that plant roots cannot penetrate

hard-pressed *adj* **1.** subject to a lot of pressure and lacking sufficient resources **2.** finding something very difficult

hard rock *n* a form of rock music that has simple lyrics and a strong insistent beat

hard·rock /haárd ròk/ *adj Can* relating to the extraction of minerals from igneous and metamorphic rocks by blasting or drilling

hard rub·ber *n* rubber treated with sulfur to make it hard and stiff

hard sauce *n* butter creamed with sugar and often flavored with brandy or whiskey, usually served with plum pudding

hard sci·ence *n* a science such as physics, chemistry, geology, or astronomy in which data can be precisely quantified and theories tested

hard·scrab·ble /haárd skràbb'l/ *adj* yielding or earning very little in return for hard effort (*informal*)

hard sell *n* a direct, aggressive, and insistent way of selling or advertising

hard-set *adj* firmly or rigidly fixed

hard-shell, **hard-shelled** *adj* rigid and uncompromising in attitude

hard-shell clam *n* ZOOL same as **quahog**

hard-shell crab *n* a crab that has not recently shed its shell and as a result has a shell that is particularly tough

hard-shelled *adj* same as **hard-shell**

hard·ship /haárd shìp/ *n* **1.** difficulty or suffering caused by a lack of something, especially money **2.** something that causes difficulty or suffering

hard shoul·der *n UK* ROADS same as **shoulder** (sense 6)

hard·stand /haárd stànd/ *n* a hard surface on which aircraft or heavy motor vehicles may be parked

hard stand·ing *n UK* TRANSP same as **hardstand**

hard stuff *n* something that is intoxicating, addictive, and potentially very dangerous to the health, especially strong alcohol (*informal*)

hard·tack /haárd tàk/ *n* a hard thin unsalted bread or biscuit formerly eaten aboard ships or as military rations

hard-times to·ken *n* a US copper token, issued between 1834 and 1841, that carried an advertising or political message and served as currency during coin shortages

hard up *adj* short of money (*informal*)

hard·ware /haárd wèr/ *n* **1.** COMPUT **COMPUTER EQUIPMENT AND PERIPHERALS** the equipment and devices that make up a computer system as opposed to the programs used on it **2. TOOLS AND IMPLEMENTS** tools and implements, usually made of metal, e.g., hinges, screws, and hammers **3.** ARMS **MILITARY WEAPONS** heavy military weapons and equipment **4.** ARMS **GUN** a gun or guns (*informal*)

hard-wear·ing *adj* not easily damaged or worn out despite frequent use

hard wheat *n* a wheat with hard kernels and a high gluten content. Use: flour for bread.

hard·wire /haárd wīr/ (**-wired, -wir·ing, -wires**) *vt* to build a function into a computer with hardware rather than programming

hard·wired /haárd wīrd/ *adj* directly wired into a computer or physically connected to a computer system or network ○ *a hardwired circuit*

hard-won *adj* achieved after much effort

hard·wood /haárd wòod/ *n* **1.** wood from a broad-leaved tree as opposed to from a conifer **2.** a tree that produces hardwood

hard-work·ing *adj* tending to work industriously

har·dy /haárdee/ (**-di·er, -di·est**) *adj* **1. ROBUST** sufficiently robust to withstand fatigue, hardship, or adverse physical conditions **2.** BOT **NOT SENSITIVE TO COLD** describes plants that are able to live outdoors during the winter ○ *a hardy shrub* **3. COURAGEOUS** courageous and daring [13C. < French *hardi* < *hardir* "become bold" < Germanic] —**har·di·ly** *adv* —**har·di·ness** *n*

Har·dy /haárdee/, **Oliver** (1892–1957) US comedian. He appeared with Stan Laurel in a series of classic comedy movies in the 1920s and 1930s.

> "Here's another fine mess you've gotten me into."
> [Oliver Hardy. Quoted in *Filmgoer's Book of Quotes*, Leslie Halliwell; 1973]

Har·dy, Thomas (1840–1928) British novelist and poet. He wrote brooding novels of the British West Country including *The Mayor of Casterbridge* (1886), and from the 1890s devoted himself to poetry. See Cultural note at **madding, mayor**

> "It is hard for a woman to define her feelings in language which is chiefly made by men to express theirs."
> [Thomas Hardy, *Far from the Madding Crowd*; 1874]

> "A novel is an impression, not an argument."
> [Thomas Hardy. Preface, *Tess of the D'Urbervilles*, 5th ed.; 1892]

Har·dy-Wein·berg law /-wīn burg-/, **Har·dy-Wein·berg dis·tri·bu·tion** *n* a principle of genetics stating that gene frequencies remain constant from one generation to the next if mating is random and there are no outside influences such as mutation and immigration [Mid-20C. After G. H. *Hardy* (1877–1947), British mathematician, and Wilhelm *Weinberg* (1862–1937), German physician]

hare

hare /her/ (*plural same* or **hares**) *n* a fast-running animal that resembles a rabbit but is larger, has longer ears and large hind legs, and does not burrow. Genus: *Lepus*. [Old English *hara* < Germanic]

SPELLCHECK See *hair*.

hare and hounds, **hare and hounds race** *n* an outdoor game in which one group of players, the hounds, follows a trail of scraps of paper left by another group, the hares, and tries to catch them before they reach a designated point

harebell

hare·bell /hér bèl/ *n* a low-growing delicate wild plant with slender stems. Flowers: blue, bell-shaped. Native to: northern temperate regions. Latin name: *Campanula rotundiflora*.

hare·brained /hér bràynd/ *adj* regarded as impractical and likely to fail

Ha·re Krish·na /haaree-/ *n* **1.** a religious group that bases its practice on worship of the god Krishna **2.** a member of Hare Krishna [Late 20C. < Sanskrit, "O Lord Krishna," chant used by devotees]

hare·lip /hér lip/ *n* same as **cleft lip** (*offensive*) —**hare·lipped** *adj*

har·em /hérrəm, hárrəm/ *n* **1. WOMEN'S PART OF HOUSE** in a traditional Muslim home, the separate private quarters reserved for wives and concubines **2. GROUP OF WOMEN** the wives and concubines who live in a harem **3. WOMEN FOLLOWERS** a group of women admirers or followers (*humorous; sometimes considered offensive*) **4.** ZOOL **GROUP OF ANIMALS** a group of female animals of the same species associated for breeding purposes with one male [Mid-17C. Via Turkish < Arabic *ḥaram* "prohibited (place), women's quarters"]

har·em pants *npl* women's pants made of soft thin cloth, with wide legs that are gathered at the ankle

Ha·rer /haárər/, **Hä·rer**, **Ha·rar** city in eastern Ethiopia, the center of a coffee-growing area. Population: 131,139 (1994).

hare's-foot (*plural same* or **hare's-foots**), **hare's-foot clo·ver** *n* a clover that grows on sandy soil. Flowers: white or pink, almost hidden by their calyx. Latin name: *Trifolium arvense.* [< the appearance of the soft hair around the flowers]

hares·tail /hérz tàyl/ *n* a variety of cotton grass that grows on moors and has a single flower head [< its similarity to a hare's tail]

hare·wood /hér wŏŏd/ *n* the greenish colored wood of the sycamore maple. Use: furniture. [Late 17C. < German dialect *Ehre* < Latin *acer* "maple, sycamore"]

har·i·cot /hárri kō, -kòt/ *n* **1.** a small white oval dried bean, cooked and eaten as a vegetable **2.** a bean plant whose seeds are dried and stored as haricots. Latin name: *Phaseolus vulgaris.* [Mid-17C. < French]

Har·i·jan /hárri jàn/ *n S Asia* same as **Dalit** [Mid-20C. < Sanskrit, "God's people"]

Har·ing /hérring/, **Keith** (1958–90) US painter. He is best known for his graffiti art works inspired by the urban culture of New York.

ha·ris·sa /hə ríssə/ *n* a spicy oily paste made from chili and tomatoes, used as an ingredient in North African cooking or as an accompaniment for dishes such as couscous

hark /haark/ (**harked, hark·ing, harks**) *vi* to listen to somebody or something (*archaic*) [12C. Probably < assumed Old English *heorcnian* < Germanic]

hark back *vi* **1.** to think or speak again about something from the past **2.** to be similar in some respects to something in the past

har·ken *vi* another spelling of **hearken**

Hark·ness /ha̋arknəss/, **Edward Stephen** (1874–1940) US philanthropist, who gave funds to US and European educational and medical institutions

harl /haarl/ *Scotland vt* (**harled, harl·ing, harls**) to cover the exterior walls of a building with lime and gravel or sand ■ *n* a mixture of lime and gravel or sand used for covering a building's exterior walls [13C. Origin ?]

Har·lan /ha̋arlən/, **John Marshall** (1833–1911) associate justice of the US Supreme Court (1877–1911). He was a Union army colonel and attorney general of Kentucky before his appointment to the US Supreme Court.

> "The law regards man as man and takes no account of his surroundings or of his color when his civil rights as guaranteed by the supreme law of the land are involved."
> [John Marshall Harlan, *Plessy v. Ferguson*; 1896]

Har·lan, John Marshall (1899–1971) associate justice of the US Supreme Court (1955–71). The grandson of John Marshall Harlan, he held government positions before his tenure on the US Supreme Court.

Har·lem /ha̋arləm/ *n* **1.** district of New York City, on Manhattan Island, originally named Nieuw Haarlem by Dutch settlers in 1658 **2.** another spelling of **Haarlem**

Har·lem Globe·trot·ters *npl* a US basketball team that tours widely to play exhibition matches during which the team displays skilled comic maneuvers

har·le·quin /ha̋arləkwən, -kən/ *n* a clown or buffoon ■ *adj* varied in color and having a pattern of irregular shapes [Late 18C. < HARLEQUIN]

Har·le·quin /ha̋arləkwən, -kən/ *n* a comic dramatic character featured in the Italian commedia dell'arte and the English harlequinade, usually shown wearing multicolored diamond-patterned tights and a black mask [Late 16C. < obsolete French, variant of *Hellequin*, legendary leader of night-raiding demon horsemen]

har·le·quin·ade /ha̋arləkwə náyd, -kə-/ *n* **1.** a pantomime, play, or other performance featuring a harlequin as a character **2.** clowning or silly behavior

har·le·quin bug *n* a stinkbug that has black and red markings and feeds on cabbages and other plants of the same family. Native to: North and Central America. Latin name: *Murgantia histrionica.*

har·le·quin duck *n* a small diving duck that has blue and red feathers with black and white markings. Native to: North America, Iceland, eastern Siberia. Latin name: *Histrionicus histrionicus.*

har·ling /ha̋arling/ *n Scotland* CONSTR same as **harl**

har·lot /ha̋arlət/ *n* same as **prostitute** (*archaic or literary*) [13C. < Old French, "vagabond, rogue, beggar"]

Har·low /ha̋arlō/ city in Essex, southeastern England. Population: 78,768 (2001).

Har·low, Jean (1911–37) US actor. Her platinum-blond hair and frankly sexual screen presence characterized her movies, including *Dinner at Eight* (1933). Born **Carpenter, Harlean**

harm /haarm/ *n* physical, mental, or moral impairment or deterioration ■ *vt* (**harmed, harm·ing, harms**) to cause physical, mental, or moral impairment or deterioration [Old English *hearm* < Germanic]

SYNONYMS ***harm, damage, hurt, injure, wound***

CORE MEANING: to weaken or impair somebody or something

harm to cause physical, mental, moral or social impairment or deterioration. ○ *Smoking while pregnant harms your baby.* ○ *decisions that will harm the economy* **damage** to cause physical injury that makes something less useful, valuable, or able to function, or to have a harmful effect on something ○ *The storm caused severe damage to the roof.* ○ *The bombings have damaged the prospects for a negotiated settlement.* **hurt** to cause somebody, yourself, or an animal physical injury or pain, or cause emotional distress ○ *Laura tripped and fell, but didn't hurt herself.* ○ *His words hurt.* **injure** to cause physical damage to a person, animal, or body part, or cause emotional distress ○ *Two other people were seriously injured in the accident.* ○ *The reviews were cruel and badly injured their pride.* **wound** to cause physical damage to a person, animal, or body part, or to upset or offend somebody ○ *wounded in battle* ○ *He feels wounded by the accusations.*

har·mat·tan /ha̋armə ta̋an, haar mátt'n/ *n* an extremely dry dusty wind that blows from the Sahara toward the western coast of Africa, especially between November and March [Late 17C. < Twi *haramata*]

harm·ful /ha̋armfəl/ *adj* causing damage or injury ○ *The plant is harmful to humans.* —**harm·ful·ly** *adv* —**harm·ful·ness** *n*

harm·less /ha̋armləss/ *adj* **1.** not likely to cause damage or injury **2.** not likely to cause offense or upset ○ *Don't worry; he's harmless enough.* —**harm·less·ly** *adv* —**harm·less·ness** *n*

har·mon·ic /haar mónnik/ *adj* **1.** PRODUCED BY HARMONY relating to, produced, or marked by harmony **2.** PHYS RELATING TO INTEGRAL MULTIPLE OF FREQUENCY describes a frequency that is an integral multiple of a fundamental frequency ■ *n* **1.** PHYS MULTIPLE OF FUNDAMENTAL FREQUENCY a single oscillation having a frequency that is an integral multiple of a fundamental frequency, e.g., 220 Hz and 330 Hz are both harmonics of 110 Hz **2.** OVERTONE ON STRINGED INSTRUMENT an overtone produced on an instrument, e.g., by lightly touching a vibrating string at a point where the string to either side will continue to vibrate [Late 16C. Via Latin *harmonicus* < Greek *harmonikos* < *harmonia* (see HARMONY)] —**har·mon·i·cal·ly** *adv*

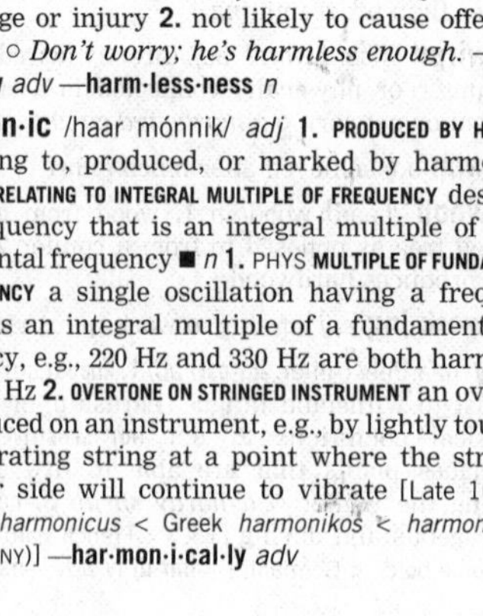

harmonica

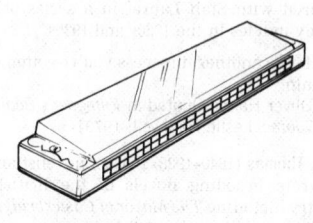

har·mon·i·ca /haar mónnikə/ *n* a small musical instrument whose narrow metal case houses a set of metal reeds that are made to sound by exhaling or inhaling air past them [Mid-18C. Via Italian *armonica* < Latin *harmonicus* (see HARMONIC)]

har·mon·ic a·nal·y·sis *n* the representation of a periodic function by a series of sines and cosines, especially by a Fourier series

har·mon·ic dis·tor·tion *n* the unwanted presence of distorted frequencies at the output of an electronic device such as an audio amplifier

har·mon·ic mean *n* the reciprocal of the arithmetic mean of the reciprocals of a finite set of numbers

har·mon·ic mo·tion *n* a periodic vibration, e.g., of a violin string or pendulum, that has a single frequency or an even multiple of one or is symmetrical about a point of equilibrium

har·mon·ic pro·gres·sion *n* a sequence of numbers whose reciprocals form an arithmetic progression, e.g., 1/2, 1/5, 1/8, 1/11

har·mon·ics /haar mónniks/ *n* the branch of science that deals with the physical properties of musical sound (*takes a singular verb*)

har·mon·ic se·ries *n* an infinite series of numbers constructed by adding the numbers in a harmonic progression to one another, e.g., 1/2+1/5+1/8+1/11

har·mo·ni·ous /haar mṓnee əss/ *adj* **1.** SHOWING ACCORD characterized by friendly agreement or accord **2.** RELATING TO HARMONY relating to or sounding in musical harmony **3.** BLENDING PLEASANTLY having a pleasing combination of parts or colors —**har·mo·ni·ous·ly** *adv* —**har·mo·ni·ous·ness** *n*

har·mo·nist /ha̋armənist/ *n* **1.** somebody who is skilled in creating musical harmony **2.** somebody who researches and tries to find similarities in parallel texts, especially the four Gospels —**har·mo·nis·tic** /ha̋armə nístik/ *adj* —**har·mo·nis·ti·cal·ly** *adv*

har·mo·ni·um /haar mṓnee əm/ *n* an organ in which a pair of bellows operated by the player's feet blow air into the reeds to produce musical sound [Mid-19C. < French < Latin *harmonia* (see HARMONY) or Greek *harmonios* "harmonious"]

har·mo·nize /ha̋armə nīz/ (**-nized, -niz·ing, -niz·es**) *v* **1.** *vti* BLEND PLEASINGLY to combine pleasingly, or make things combine pleasingly **2.** *vt* MAKE SYSTEMS AGREE to make rules, regulations, or systems similar or in accord with each other **3.** *vt* ADD HARMONY TO MELODY to provide a harmony for a melody **4.** *vi* PLAY IN HARMONY to sing or play musical instruments in harmony —**har·mo·niz·a·ble** /ha̋armə nīzəb'l/ *adj* —**har·mo·ni·za·tion** /ha̋armənī záysh'n/ *n* —**har·mo·niz·er** *n*

har·mo·nized sales tax *n* in the provinces of Nova Scotia, New Brunswick, and Newfoundland, a tax combining the goods and services tax and the provincial sales tax

har·mo·ny /ha̋armənee/ (*plural* **-nies**) *n* **1.** FRIENDLY AGREEMENT a situation in which there is friendly agreement or accord **2.** PLEASING COMBINATION OF SOUNDS a pleasing combination of musical sounds **3.** NOTES SUNG OR PLAYED TOGETHER a combination of notes that are sung or played at the same time. Changing harmony is one of the most characteristic features of Western music, providing momentum and richness to the melody. **4.** STUDY OF CHORDS IN MUSIC the study of the way in which musical chords are constructed and function in relation to one another **5.** PLEASANTNESS IN ARRANGEMENT a pleasing effect produced by an arrangement of things, parts, or colors **6.** STUDY OF TEXTS a study or collation of the similarities in parallel texts, especially the four Gospels **7.** PARALLEL TEXT a book or manuscript in which several versions of the same text, often a biblical text, are laid out in parallel columns ○ *a Gospel harmony* [14C. Via French and Latin < Greek *harmonia* "agreement, concord" < *harmozein* "fit together"]

Har·nack /ha̋ar nàk/, **Adolf von** (1851–1930) German theologian. One of the leading Protestant scholars of his day, he advocated a return to biblical Christianity. His major work was *History of Dogma* (1886–90).

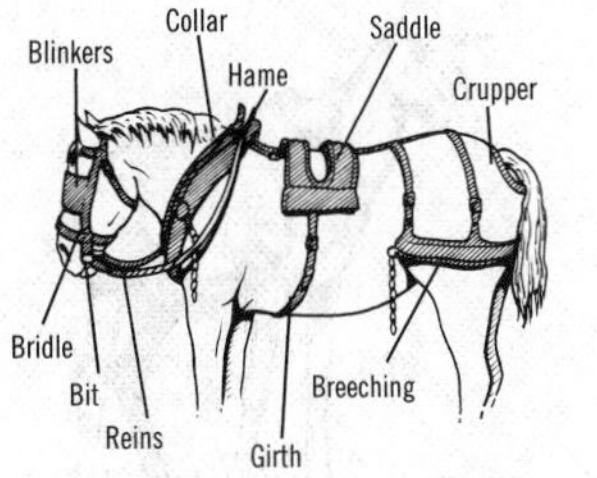

harness

har·ness /haárnəss/ *n* **1. STRAPS FOR ANIMAL** a set of leather straps fitted to an animal such as a horse so that it can be attached to a cart or carriage for pulling **2. STRAPS FITTED TO PERSON** a set of straps fitted to somebody to fasten him or her to something or to keep the him or her in position ■ *vt* (**-nessed, -ness·ing, -ness·es**) **1. GET CONTROL OF AND USE SOMETHING** to gain control of something and use it for some purpose ○ *seek to harness the skills and resources of a number of agencies* **2. FIT ANIMAL WITH HARNESS** to put a harness on an animal [13C. Via Old French *harneis* < assumed Old Norse *hernest* "provisions for an army" < *herr* "army"] —**har·ness·er** *n* ◇ **in harness 1.** doing your usual work **2.** working cooperatively with a person or group

har·ness hitch *n* a knot with one loop and no free ends, used in tying harnesses

har·ness race *n* a horse race in which trotters or pacers pull small carriages around a course wearing special harnesses to ensure that they move as required by the race rules —**har·ness rac·ing** *n*

Har·ney Peak /haárnee-/ mountain in the Black Hills, southwestern South Dakota, and the highest peak in the state. Height: 7,242 ft./2,207 m.

Har·old I /hárrəld/ (*d.* 1040) Danish-born king of the English. He was the illegitimate son of Canute II and ruled England (1037–40) in constant strife with his half-brother, Hardecanute. Known as **Harold Harefoot**

Har·old II (1020?–66) king of the English. The last Saxon king of England (1066), he was killed fighting William the Conqueror at the Battle of Hastings.

> "He will give him seven feet of English ground, or as much more as he may be taller than other men."
> [Harold II, *King Harald's Saga*, Snorri Sturluson; 1260]

ha·ro·seth /hə rṓ seth/, **ha·ro·set** /-rṓ set/, **cha·ro·seth** /k͟hə-/, **cha·ro·set** /k͟hə-/ *n* a mixture of apples, nuts, spices, and wine, eaten as part of the Passover Seder meal. The mixture symbolizes the clay used by the Israelites to make bricks during their enslavement in Egypt. [Late 19C. < Hebrew *ḥarōset* < *ḥeres* "earthenware"]

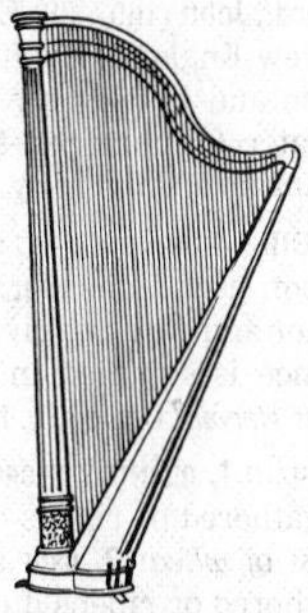
harp

harp /haarp/ *n* **1. TRIANGULAR STRINGED INSTRUMENT** a triangular-shaped instrument that has a curved neck and strings stretched between the neck and the body, at an angle to the sound box. The modern orchestral harp is large and played by a seated player. **2. HARMONICA** a reed harmonica (*informal*) ■ *vi* (**harped, harp·ing, harps**) **PLAY HARP** to play the harp [Old English *hearpe* < Germanic] —**harp·er** *n* —**harp·ist** *n*
harp on *vti* to repeat or stress something in a way that becomes tiresome

Har·pers Fer·ry /haárpərz-/ historic town and tourist resort in eastern West Virginia, situated at the confluence of the Potomac and Shenandoah rivers. Population: 304 (2002 estimate).

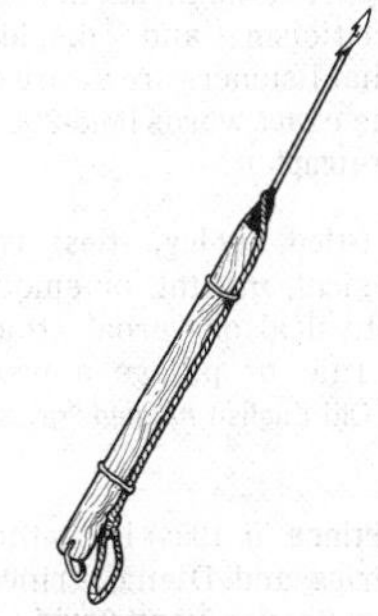
harpoon

har·poon /haar poón/ *n* a long pointed piece of metal attached to a cord and thrown or fired from a gun in order to capture whales or other large sea animals ■ *vt* (**-pooned, -poon·ing, -poons**) to catch a whale or other large sea animal using a harpoon [Early 17C. < Old French *harpon* "clamp" < *harpe* "dog's claw, clamp" < Greek *harpē* "sickle"] —**har·poon·eer** /haàr poo neér/ *n* —**har·poon·er** *n*

harp seal *n* a brownish gray earless seal that is whitish when very young, formerly hunted for its fur. Native to: coastal regions and ice floes of the North Atlantic Ocean. Latin name: *Pagophilus groenlandicus.* [< the shape of its markings]

harp·si·chord /haárpsi kàwrd/ *n* a keyboard instrument resembling a piano that has horizontal strings plucked by leather or quill points connected to the keys. It was superseded by the piano in the 19th century. [Early 17C. < French *harpechorde* < Latin *harpa* "harp" + *chorda* "string"] —**harp·si·chord·ist** *n*

Har·pur /haárpər/, **Charles** (1813–68) Australian poet and playwright. Considered by many to be Australia's first major poet, he wrote *The Creek of the Four Graves* (1853).

har·py /haárpee/ (*plural* **-pies**) *n* **1.** an offensive term for a woman regarded as bad-tempered or nagging (*insult*) **2.** somebody who preys on others [< HARPY]

Har·py /haárpee/ (*plural* **-pies**) *n* in Greek mythology, a monster that was half woman and half bird of prey. The Harpies were thought to live on the Strophades Islands and carry out acts of vengeance on behalf of the gods. [14C. Directly or via French < Latin *harpyia* < Greek *harpuiai* (plural) "snatchers" < *harpazein* "seize"]

har·py ea·gle *n* a huge eagle with a blackish back, white underparts, and a gray head with a double crest. Native to: lowland forests of southern Mexico to northern Argentina. Latin name: *Harpia harpyja.*

har·que·bus /haárkəbəss, haárkwə-/, **ar·que·bus** /aár-/ *n* an early portable gun with a long barrel, supported on a tripod by a hook or on a forked post [Mid-16C. Via French *(h)arquebuse* < Middle Dutch *hakebus* < *hake(n)* "hook" + *bus(se)* "gun"; from the hook supporting it] —**har·que·bus·ier** /haàrkəbə seér, haàrkwə-/ *n*

~~**harrass**~~ incorrect spelling of **harass**

har·ri·dan /hárrid'n/ *n* an offensive term for a woman that deliberately insults her age as advanced and her temperament as assertive (*insult*) [Late 17C. Origin ?]

har·ried *adj* looking or feeling tired and annoyed

har·ri·er[1] /hárree ər/ (*plural* **-ers** or *same*) *n* a slender graceful hawk with long wings and a long tail that hunts by flying low over marshland and grassland to catch mice, snakes, frogs, and fish. Native to: all continents except Antarctica. Genus: *Circus.* [Mid-16C. < *harrow* "rob," variant of HARRY; later influenced by HARRIER[3]]

har·ri·er[2] /hárree ər/ *n* **1.** a small hound resembling a foxhound used for hunting hares or rabbits **2.** a

harrier

cross-country runner (*often used in the name of athletics clubs*) [15C. Origin ?]

har·ri·er[3] /hárree ər/ *n* **1.** somebody who repeatedly attacks another person or group physically or verbally **2.** somebody who raids or pillages a place [Early 16C. < HARRY]

Har·ri·man /hárrimən/, **Averell** (1891–1986) US diplomat and politician. He was appointed ambassador to the U.S.S.R. (1943) and secretary of commerce (1946) and was later elected governor of New York (1954). He served as chief US negotiator at the Paris peace talks attempting to end the Vietnam War. Full name **Harriman, William Averell**

Har·ri·man, Edward H. (1848–1909) US financier and railroad executive. He reorganized the Union Pacific Railroad (1898). He was renowned for his ruthlessness in pursuing his extensive business interests. Full name **Harriman, Edward Henry**

Har·ris /hárriss/, **Frank** (1856–1931) Irish-born US journalist and writer. He gained notoriety for his scandalous semifictional autobiography, *My Life and Loves*, published in three volumes (1922, 1925, 1927). Born **Harris, James Thomas**

> "A history of humanity to the present time in which Shakespeare is not mentioned and Jesus is dismissed in a page carelessly, as if not worth contempt, shocks me."
> [Frank Harris, *My Life and Loves*; 1925]

Har·ris, Joel Chandler (1848–1908) US writer. He published several collections of whimsical tales from the southern US states, narrated by the fictional Uncle Remus.

> "Tar-baby ain't sayn' nuthin', en Brer Fox, he lay low."
> [Joel Chandler Harris, "The Wonderful Tar-Baby Story," *Uncle Remus and His Legends of the Old Plantation*; 1881]

Har·ris, Lawren (1885–1970) Canadian artist. A founder member of the Group of Seven, he is noted for his Arctic landscapes such as *Icebergs* (1930). Full name **Harris, Lawren Stewart**

Har·ris, Townsend (1804–78) US diplomat. As US consul to Japan (1856–61), he negotiated a treaty that greatly increased Japan's international trade.

Har·ris·burg /hárriss bùrg/ city and capital of Pennsylvania, located in the southern part of the state. Population: 48,540 (2002 estimate).

Har·ri·son /hárriss'n/ **1.** town in northeastern New Jersey, on the Passaic River opposite Newark. Population: 14,378 (2002 estimate). **2.** village in southeastern New York. It is a northeastern suburb of New York City. Population: 24,951 (2002 estimate).

Har·ri·son, Benjamin (1726?–91) American patriot. A longtime member of the Virginia House of Burgesses (1749–75), he presided over the Continental Congress (1774–77) and signed the Declaration of Independence (1776). He was governor of Virginia (1781–84).

Library of Congress

Benjamin Harrison

Har·ri·son, Benjamin (1833–1901) 23rd president of the United States. The grandson of William Henry Harrison, he was a Republican senator (1881–87) before his election as president. His administration (1889–93) enacted protectionist tariffs and other pro-business legislation. See table at **president**

> "Lincoln had faith in time, and time has justified his faith."
> [Benjamin Harrison, *Lincoln Day Address*; 1898]

Har·ri·son, George (1943–2001) British musician. The lead guitarist with the Beatles, he later turned to solo music projects and movie production.

> "All things must pass, all things must pass away."
> [George Harrison, *All Things Must Pass*; 1971]

Har·ri·son, Sir Rex (1908–90) British actor. He starred in comedies including *Blithe Spirit* (1945) and *My Fair Lady* (1964), for which he won an Academy Award. Full name **Harrison, Sir Reginald Carey**

US Military History Institute

William Henry Harrison

Har·ri·son, William Henry (1773–1841) 9th president of the United States. He was elected president in 1840 on the strength of his military successes against the Native North Americans and in the War of 1812, but died after one month in office. See table at **president**

> "We admit of no government by divine right...the only legitimate right to govern is an express grant of power from the governed."
> [William Henry Harrison, *Inaugural presidential address*; March 4, 1841]

Har·ris tweed *n* a thick woven woolen cloth traditionally made in Harris, the southern part of the island of Lewis, in the Outer Hebrides, Scotland

har·row[1] /hárrō/ *n* a piece of farm equipment with sharp teeth or disks that is used to break up soil and clods of dirt and to even up a plowed field ■ *vti* (**-rowed, -row·ing, -rows**) to break up land by pulling a harrow over it, or be broken up with a harrow [12C. < Old Norse *herfi*] —**har·row·er** *n*

har·row[2] /hárrō/ (**-rowed, -row·ing, -rows**) *vt* same as **harry** (*archaic*) [14C. Variant]

har·row·ing /hárrō ing/ *adj* causing feelings of fear, horror, or distress ○ *harrowing scenes of hurricane devastation* [Early 19C. < HARROW[2] in archaic sense "wound, distress"] —**har·row·ing·ly** *adv*

Har·row School /hàrrō-/ *n* a private school for boys in northwestern London, England. It was founded in 1571. —**Har·ro·vi·an** /hə rṓvee ən/ *n*

har·rumph /hə rúmf/ (**-rumphed, -rumph·ing, -rumphs**) *vti* **1.** to clear the throat, or make a noise that resembles the sound of clearing the throat **2.** to say something expressing criticism and displeasure, often muttering so that listeners are aware of the tone but cannot hear the exact words [Mid-20C. An imitation of the sound] —**har·rumph** *n*

har·ry /hárree/ (**-ried, -ry·ing, -ries**) *vt* **1.** to cause somebody physical, mental, or emotional distress by repeated physical or verbal attacks ○ *harried parents* **2.** to raid or pillage a place, especially during a war [Old English *hergian* "ravage" < Germanic, "army"]

Har·ry /hárree/, **Prince** (*b.* 1984) He is the younger son of Prince Charles and Diana, Princess of Wales. Full name **Henry Charles Albert David**

harsh /haarsh/ *adj* **1.** DIFFICULT TO ENDURE bleak or inhospitable and therefore difficult to endure ○ *a harsh winter* ○ *harsh prison conditions* **2.** SEVERELY CRITICAL severely scrutinizing, critical, and rigid in manner ○ *harsh criticism* **3.** PUNITIVE exacting to the point of being punitive ○ *Harsh penalties will be imposed.* **4.** JARRING jarring or unpleasant to the senses ○ *a harsh voice* ○ *a harsh light* [14C. Ultimately < Germanic] —**harsh·ly** *adv* —**harsh·ness** *n*

Har·sha /haárshə/ *n* a descendant of the Guptas in India, who created a large empire in northern India between A.D. 616 and 654

harsh·en /haársh'n/ (**-ened, -en·ing, -ens**) *vti* to make something harsh or harsher, or become harsh or harsher

hars·let *n* COOK another spelling of **haslet**

hart /haart/ (*plural* **harts** or *same*) *n* a male deer, especially a male red deer over five years of age [Old English *heor(o)t* < Indo-European, "horn, head"]

Hart /haart/, **John** (1711?–79) American patriot. He signed the Declaration of Independence (1776) as a New Jersey delegate to the Continental Congress.

Hart, Lorenz (1895–1943) US lyricist. He collaborated with Richard Rodgers for 20 years, producing a string of classic musicals including *On Your Toes* (1936) and *Pal Joey* (1940). Full name **Hart, Lorenz Milton**

> "Bewitched, bothered, and bewildered am I."
> [Lorenz Hart, "Bewitched," *Pal Joey*; 1941]

Hart, Moss (1904–61) US playwright and director. In the 1930s he collaborated with George S. Kaufman on witty social comedies, including the Pulitzer Prize-winning *You Can't Take It With You* (1936).

> "The only credential the city asked was the boldness to dream. For those who did, it unlocked its gates and its treasures, not caring who they were or where they came from."
> [Moss Hart, *Act One*; 1959]

har·tal /haar taál/ *n S Asia* a general closing of stores and suspending of work, especially as an indication or means of political protest [Early 20C. < Hindi *hartāl* "shop locking"]

Harte /haart/, **Bret** (1836–1902) US poet and writer. He is best known for his colorful stories set in California's mining towns. Born **Harte, Francis Brett**

> "Behind the curtain's mystic fold / The glowing future lies unrolled."
> [Bret Harte, *Speech, San Francisco*; January 19, 1870]

hartebeest

har·te·beest /haártə beèst, haárt beèst/ (*plural* **-beests** or *same*) *n* a large antelope with humped shoulders, a long narrow face, and lyre-shaped horns. Native to: eastern and southern Africa. Genus: *Alcelaphus*. [Late 18C. < obsolete Afrikaans]

Hart·ford /haártfərd/ city and capital of Connecticut, situated on the Connecticut River 36 mi./58 km northeast of New Haven. It is home to Trinity College. Population: 124,558 (2002 estimate).

Hart·ford Wits *npl* a group of writers, most of whom attended Yale College (later Yale University), who collaborated on works of political satire at the end of the 18th and beginning of the 19th centuries

Har·tle·pool /haártlee pool/ industrial city and seaport in northeastern England. Population: 87,310 (1991).

Hart·ley /haártlee/, **Marsden** (1877–1943) US painter. Strongly influenced by contemporary European artists, he developed a bold personal style exemplified in works such as *Evening Storm, Schoodic, Maine* (1942). Full name **Hartley, Edmund Marsden**

Har·tog /haár tàwg/, **Dirk** (*fl* 16th-17th centuries) Dutch navigator. His Dutch East India Company expedition to Java in 1616 instead reached Australia, where he made the earliest recorded European exploration of the west coast.

hart's-tongue (*plural* **hart's-tongues** or *same*) *n* an evergreen fern that has narrow undivided fronds bearing rows of spore-producing organs. Native to: Europe, Asia. Latin name: *Phyllitis scolopendrium*. [< the shape of its fronds]

har·um-scar·um /hèrrəm skérrəm/ *adj* careless or irresponsible ○ *harum-scarum methods* [Late 17C. Probably rhyming alteration of HARE (verb) + SCARE] —**har·um-scar·um** *adv*

Ha·run ar-Ra·shid /haa roón aar raa sheéd/ (766–809) Abbasid caliph of Baghdad. His splendid court, a center of Islamic culture, is described in the *Arabian Nights*.

ha·rus·pex /hə rú spèks, hárrə-/ (*plural* **-pi·ces** /-pi seèz/), **a·rus·pex** /ə rú-, árrə-/ *n* in ancient Rome, a priest who attempted to foretell the future, especially by examining the entrails of animals [15C. < Latin]

Har·vard /haárvərd/, **John** (1607–38) English cleric who emigrated to New England. Upon his death he left half his fortune and his library to the college at New Towne (later Cambridge), Massachusetts. It later became Harvard University (1780).

Har·vard sys·tem /haárvərd-/ *n* a bibliographic reference system, used in academic publishing, in which the author and date are given in the text and the full reference is supplied in a general list of references [After *Harvard* University, Massachusetts]

har·vest /haárvəst/ *n* **1.** QUANTITY OF CROP the quantity of a crop that is gathered or ripens during a season ○ *a record harvest of wheat* **2.** CROP THAT IS GATHERED the crop that is gathered or ripens during a season ○ *A few days of rain can destroy an entire harvest of strawberries.* **3.** SEASON IN WHICH CROPS ARE GATHERED the season during which crops ripen and are gathered **4.** CONSEQUENCES the consequences of previous actions or behavior **5.** BIOL REMOVAL OF BIOLOGICAL MATERIAL the removal of an organ, fluid, cells, or tissue for transplantation, testing, or research ■ *v* (**-vest·ed, -vest·ing, -vests**) **1.** *vti* GATHER CROP to gather a crop for use or sale ○ *Farmers expect to harvest a bumper crop this year.* **2.** *vt* KILL ANIMALS to kill animals for food, sport, or to control their population ○ *The deer are being harvested to control the spread of the disease.* **3.** *vt* REAP RESULTS OF SOMETHING to experience the consequences of previous actions or behavior **4.** *vt* BIOL REMOVE BIOLOGICAL MATERIAL to remove an organ, fluid, cells, or tissue for transplantation, testing, or research [Old English *hærfest* "autumn" < Indo-European, "gather"] —**har·vest·a·bil·i·ty** /haárvəstə bíllətee/ *n* —**har·vest·a·ble** *adj*

har·vest·er /haárvəstər/ *n* **1.** a machine that gathers crops from the fields, especially a combine harvester **2.** somebody who gathers in crops, especially by hand

har·vest fly *n* a cicada that sings loudly near the end of the summer. Native to: United States. Genus: *Tibicen*.

har·vest home *n* the gathering of the harvest, especially its safe completion

har·vest·man /haárvəstmən/ (*plural* **-men** /-mən/) *n* **1.** INSECTS same as **daddy longlegs** (sense 1) **2.** an agricultural worker, especially, before agriculture became mechanized, one who left home to find work at harvest time

har·vest mite *n UK* same as **chigger** (sense 1) [Because common at harvest time]

har·vest moon *n* the full moon nearest to the autumnal equinox. It rises for several nights at nearly the same time at points successively further north on the eastern horizon.

Har·vey /haárvee/ **1.** city in northeastern Illinois, an industrial center near Chicago. Population: 29,714 (2002 estimate). **2.** city in Jefferson County, Louisiana. Population: 21,222 (2002 estimate).

Har·vey, William (1578–1657) English physician. He discovered the circulation of blood and the role of the heart. He formally published his work on the circulatory system in 1628.

> "Everything from an egg."
> [William Harvey, *On the Generation of Animals*; 1651]

Har·wich /hárrij, -ich/ town and summer resort in southeastern Massachusetts, on south central Cape Cod. Population: 12,801 (2002 estimate).

Ha·ry·a·na /hùrree aánə/ state in Northwestern India. The union territory of Delhi forms an enclave on its eastern boundary. Capital: Chandigarh. Population: 21,082,989 (2000). Area: 17,070 sq. mi./44,212 sq. km.

Harz Moun·tains /haárts-/ mountain range in central Germany, between the Elbe and Weser rivers south of Brunswick. The highest peak is the Brocken. Height: 3,743 ft./1,141 m.

has 3rd person singular present of **have**

Ha·san /haa saán/ (625?–669?A.D.) Arabian religious figure. The son of Fatima, grandson of Muhammad, and elder brother of Husain, he is revered as a martyr by Shiite Muslims.

has-been *n* somebody who formerly was successful, important, or popular, but is no longer (*informal*) ○ *It's hard to be a hero one day and a has-been the next.*

Has·brouck Heights /hàzbròok-/ borough in Northeastern New Jersey, southeast of Paterson. Population: 11,647 (2002 estimate).

Ha·se·ga·wa To·ha·ku /haássə gaáwə to haá koo/ (1539–1610) Japanese artist. He was noted for his ink screen paintings, which often featured monkeys, and founded his own school of painting.

Ha·šek /hásh ek/, **Jaroslav** (1883–1923) Czech writer. He is best known for his four-volume unfinished satirical novel *The Good Soldier Schweik* (1921–23).

ha·sen·pfef·fer /haáz'n fèffər, haáss'n-/ *n* marinated rabbit, highly seasoned and served as a hot stew [Late 19C. < German < *Hase* "hare" + *Pfeffer* "pepper"]

hash[1] /hash/ *n* **1.** FRIED DISH OF POTATOES AND MEAT a dish made of cooked potatoes or other vegetables, usually combined with chopped-up pieces of cooked meat, and reheated, usually by frying until golden brown ○ *corned-beef hash* **2.** *Can, UK* the symbol #, especially on a telephone keypad or a computer keyboard. US term **pound sign** ■ *vt* (**hashed, hash·ing, hash·es**) **1.** COMPUT APPLY ALGORITHM TO CHARACTER STRING to apply an algorithm to a character string, especially in order to find an address of a record **2.** CUT FOOD INTO TINY PIECES to chop meat or vegetables into tiny pieces [Late 16C. < French *hacher* "hack, cut into small pieces" < *hache* (see HATCHET)] ◇ **make a hash of something** to do something very badly (*informal*) ○ *I made a real hash of the exam.* ◇ **settle somebody's hash** to assert yourself over somebody, especially somebody hostile or troublesome (*informal*)

hash out, hash over *vt US* to have a long, drawn-out, and usually involved discussion of a matter or a problem ○ *They hashed out their differences with an arbitrator.* Can term **thrash out**

hash[2] /hash/ *n* same as **hashish** (*slang*) [Mid-20C. Shortening]

hash browns *npl* cooked potatoes chopped up, sometimes with onions, and fried until golden brown. Occasionally hash browns are formed into small cakes or patties.

hash·eesh *n* DRUGS another spelling of **hashish**

Ha·Shem /haa shém/ *n* in Judaism, a substitute word used when referring to God in contexts other than prayers or scriptural readings, because the name for God is considered too holy for such use [< Hebrew, "the name"]

Hash·e·mite /háshə mìt/ *n* **1.** a member of an ancient Arabian dynasty that included the prophet Muhammad and claimed to be directly descended from his great-grandfather, Hashim. The Hashemites were traditionally the custodians of the Kaaba, the sacred Muslim shrine at Mecca. **2.** a member of a modern Arabian dynasty that traces its lineage, via the prophet Muhammad's daughter Fatima, directly to the prophet Muhammad. The dynasty has ruled Jordan since 1926. [Late 17C. After *Hashim*, Muhammad's great-grandfather] —**Hash·e·mite** *adj*

hash house *n* a restaurant that serves cheap food (*informal*)

hash·ish /há sheèsh, há shìsh, haa sheésh/, **hash·eesh** /há sheèsh, haa sheésh/ *n* a purified resin, prepared from the flowering tops of the female cannabis plant, that is smoked or chewed for its narcotic and intoxicating properties and is widely illegal [Late 16C. < Arabic *ḥašīš* "dry herb, powdered hemp"]

hash mark *n* **1.** a stripe sewn on US Army uniforms, one for every two years of active duty **2.** *Can, UK* COMPUT same as **hash**[1] *n* (sense 2) **3.** in football, a line indicating how close to a sideline a football may be at the start of a play

hash sling·er *n* somebody employed as a cook in a cheap restaurant (*slang*)

Ha·sid /khaássid, haá-/, **Has·sid, Cha·sid, Chas·sid** *n* a member of a Jewish movement of popular mysticism founded in Eastern Europe in the 18th century. It emphasized a person's emotional relationship with God, and is now represented by a number of different religious groups. [Early 19C. < Hebrew *ḥāsīd* "pious"] —**Ha·si·dic** /khaa síddik, haa-/ *adj* —**Ha·si·dism** *n*

Ha·ska·lah /hàskə laá/, **Ha·ska·la** *n* the Jewish enlightenment movement, which originated in 18th-century Germany and aimed to integrate Jews into western European society, e.g., by the use of German instead of Yiddish. It also emphasized secular intellectualism rather than religious learning. [< Hebrew *haśkālāh* "enlightenment"]

has·let /hásslət, házz-/, **hars·let** /haárss-/ *n* internal organs such as the heart and liver, usually of a hog, used as food [14C. < Old French *hastelet* "small piece of meat roasted on a spit" < *haste* "spit"]

has·n't /házz'nt/ *contr* has not

hasp /hasp/ *n* a hinged metal fastening that fits over a staple and is secured by a pin, bolt, or padlock [Old English *hæpse* "fastening" < Germanic] —**hasp** *vt*

Has·sam /hássəm/, **Childe** (1859–1935) US artist. His impressionist paintings are distinctive for the brilliant coloring of their street scenes and landscapes. Full name **Hassam, Frederick Childe**

Has·san II /haa saán, hə saán/ (1929–99) king of Morocco. Educated in France, he ruled Morocco from 1961 to 1999. Born **Moulay Hassan ben Mohammed Alaoui**

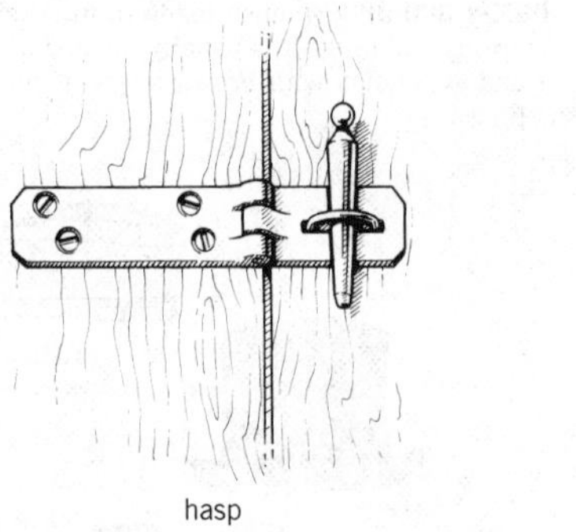

hasp

Has·san /haa saán/, **Abdiqasim Salad** (*b.* 1942) president of Somalia (2000–). A former deputy premier and interior minister, he was elected president by the transitional national government of clan elders established in 2000.

~~hassel~~ incorrect spelling of **hassle**

Has·sid *n* JUDAISM another spelling of **Hasid**

has·sium /hássee əm/ *n* an extremely rare unstable element. Source: high-energy atomic collisions. Symbol **Hs**. See table at **element** [Late 20C. < modern Latin < Latin *Hassias* "Hesse," Germany]

has·sle /háss'l/ (*informal*) *n* a source or the experience of aggravation or annoying difficulty ○ *It's just not worth the hassle.* ■ *vt* (**-sled, -sling, -sles**) to bother or annoy somebody, especially by continually asking that person to do something ○ *Stop hassling me about washing the car.* [Late 19C. Origin ?]

has·sock /hássək/ *n* **1.** FURNITURE PADDED STOOL a piece of furniture that is round or square, and padded, with an upholstered cover, used as a seat or footrest **2.** CUSHION ON WHICH TO KNEEL a thick firm cushion used for kneeling on, especially in a Christian church **3.** GRASS CLUMP a thick clump of grass [Old English *hassuc* "clump of grass," origin ?]

hast /hast/ 2nd person singular present of **have** (*archaic*)

has·tate /háss tàyt/ *adj* describes a leaf that is shaped like an arrowhead, with a tip pointing forward and two sideways-pointing lobes at the base [Late 18C. < Latin *hastatus* "armed with a spear" < *hasta* "spear"]

haste /hayst/ *n* great speed, especially in situations where time is limited (*formal*) ○ *Act in haste, repent at leisure.* ■ *vti* (**hast·ed, hast·ing, hastes**) same as **hasten** (senses 2–3) (*literary or archaic*) [13C. < Old French < Germanic] ◇ **more haste less speed** *UK* a way of saying that it is not worth rushing something because too many mistakes will be made

has·ten /háyss'n/ (**-tened, -ten·ing, -tens**) *v* **1.** *vi* DO SOMETHING IMMEDIATELY to do or say something without delay, often in order to correct what might otherwise be a misleading impression ○ *"But she's perfectly right," he hastened to add.* **2.** *vt* SPEED SOMETHING UP to make something happen more quickly ○ *A vacation would hasten his recovery.* **3.** *vi* GO SOMEWHERE QUICKLY to go somewhere quickly or without delay (*literary*) ○ *hastened to her side*

Has·tings /háystingz/ **1.** historic seaside city in East Sussex, southern England. The Battle of Hastings was fought nearby in 1066. Population: 85,029 (2001). **2.** city in the eastern part of the North Island, New Zealand. It is a major agricultural center. Population: 59,139 (2001).

Has·tings, Warren (1732–1818) British colonial administrator. As the first governor-general of India (1773–85), he secured British rule and enacted legal and administrative reforms. He was impeached in Parliament for high crimes and misdemeanors (1788–95) and, although he was eventually acquitted, his career and fortune were destroyed.

hast·y /háystee/ (**-i·er, -i·est**) *adj* done, taking place, or acting in a hurry because of impetuosity or lack of time ○ *a hasty marriage* —**hast·i·ly** *adv* —**hast·i·ness** *n*

hast·y pud·ding *n* mush made from crushed cereal grains and milk. It is usually made with cornmeal and sweetened with brown sugar or maple syrup. [Origin ?]

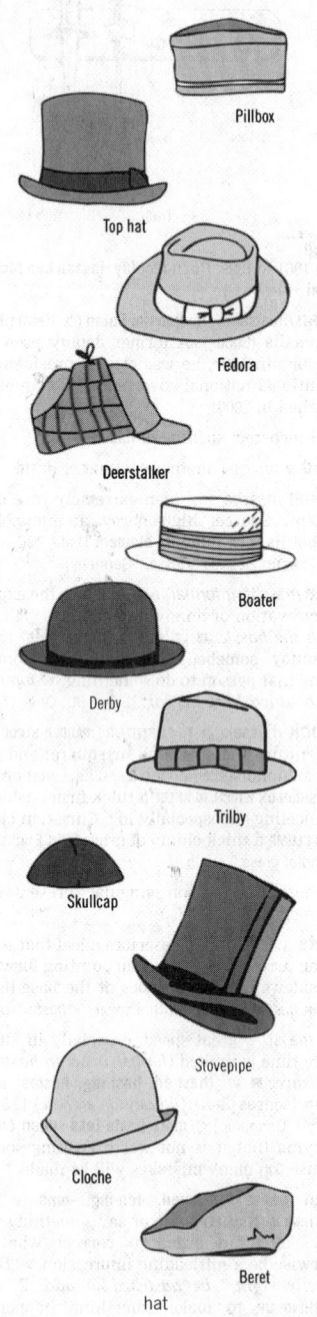

hat

hat /hat/ *n* **1.** a covering for the head, worn for protection from the weather or as a fashion accessory **2.** an area of interest or responsibility of somebody who has more than one interest or responsibility in a particular situation ○ *Which hat will you be wearing at the meeting – parent or teacher?* [Old English *hæt(t)*, via Germanic, "hood, cowl" < Indo-European, "to cover"] —**hat·ted** *adj* ◇ **hang up your hat 1.** to retire from work ○ *When this project's finished he's going to hang up his hat and retire to the country.* **2.** to settle down to a calmer, more stable lifestyle after an extended period of stress or activity ○ *Children of military personnel move so frequently that they'd like to find just one place in which to hang up their hats.* ◇ **hat in hand** asking or begging for something such as assistance or money ○ *He had to go hat in hand to the courthouse, asking for legal relief in the matter.* ◇ **hats off to somebody** a way of saying that somebody has gained your respect or admiration ◇ **keep something under your hat** to keep something secret ◇ **pass the hat** to collect contributions for somebody or something ◇ **pull something out of a** *or* **your hat** to do something that seemed very difficult or impossible to achieve, as if by a magic trick (*informal*) ◇ **take your hat off to somebody** to acknowledge admiration or respect for somebody ◇ **talk through your hat** to talk nonsense (*informal*) ◇ **throw your hat into the ring** to volunteer to take part in a particular contest

hat·band /hát bànd/ *n* a thin strip of leather, cloth, ribbon, or other material that is attached to and wound around a hat just above the brim

hat·box /hát bòks/ *n* a large hard box with a removable or liftable lid, used for storing, carrying, or protecting a hat or hats

hatch[1] /hach/ *n* **1.** a door cut into the floor or ceiling of something, especially on a boat or an aircraft. It is lifted to provide access to the area below or above it. A hatch may also provide access to an attic or cellar in a building. **2.** a small connecting hole in a wall between two rooms, or the small doors that cover this hole ○ *an escape hatch* **3.** CARS same as **hatchback** [Old English *hæcc* "lower half of a door, wicket" < Germanic]

hatch[2] /hach/ (**hatched, hatch·ing, hatch·es**) *v* **1.** *vi* **COME OUT OF EGG** to emerge from an egg **2.** *vi* **BREAK OPEN FOR RELEASE OF YOUNG** to break open so that the young inside may be released (*refers to eggs*) **3.** *vt* **CAUSE YOUNG TO EMERGE FROM EGG** to cause a young organism such as a chick, fish, or insect, to emerge from its egg ○ *Birds hatch their chicks by sitting on the nests.* **4.** *vt* **SECRETLY DEVISE PLOT** to secretly devise a plot, plan, or scheme, usually an illicit or illegal one, or one that is ill-advised in some way [15C. Origin ?]
hatch out *vi* to emerge from an egg

hatch[3] /hach/ (**hatched, hatch·ing, hatch·es**) *vti* in graphic art, to mark or cover something with parallel crossed lines to show shading, or be marked in this way [15C. < French *hacher* "to chop" < *hache* (see HATCHET)] —**hatch·ing** *n*

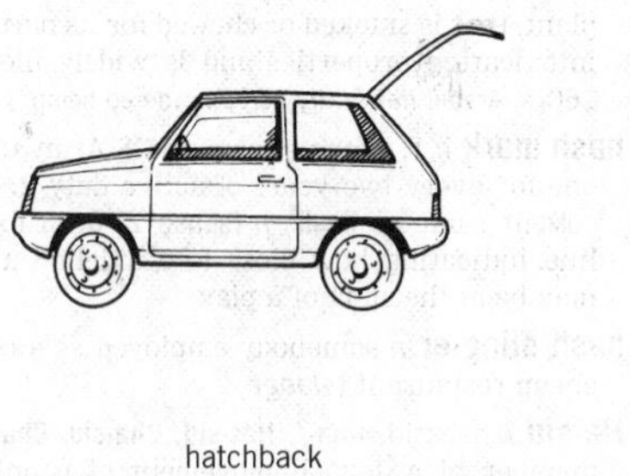
hatchback

hatch·back /hách bàk/ *n* a car with a rear door that is hinged from the roof to allow easy access to storage space behind the rear seats. The storage space usually has a removable shelf between the top of the seats and the rear window. ○ *a five-door hatchback*

hat·check /hát chèk/ *n* a room where hats, coats, and other outerwear are checked with an attendant for safekeeping, e.g., in a bar or restaurant (*dated*)

hatch·er·y /hácharee/ (*plural* **-ies**) *n* a place where fish or poultry eggs are hatched commercially under artificial conditions

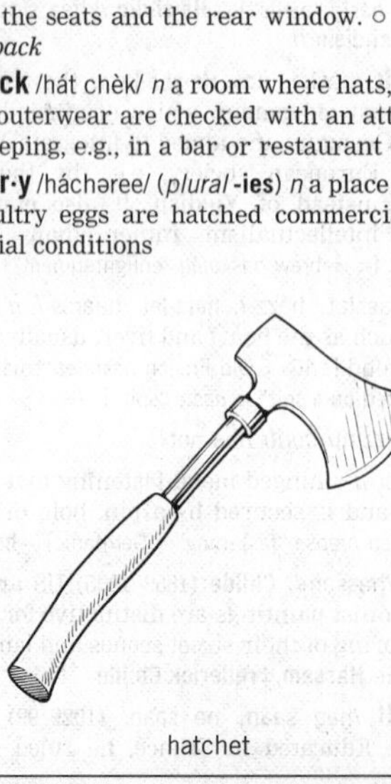
hatchet

hatch·et /háchət/ *n* a small ax that can be used with one hand ○ *wield a hatchet* [14C. < French *hachette* "small ax" < *hache* "ax" < medieval Latin *hapia* < Germanic] ◇ **bury the hatchet** to make peace with somebody after a disagreement ◇ **do a hatchet job on somebody** *or* **something** to criticize somebody or something severely, especially in print (*informal*)

hatch·et face *n* an unpleasantly long thin face with sharp or gaunt features —**hatch·et-faced** *adj*

hatch·et man *n* (*informal*) **1.** somebody who is hired to do something unpopular, especially to make cuts in staff or funding **2.** a hired killer

hatch·ling /háchling/ *n* a bird, fish, insect, or other organism that has just hatched from an egg

hatch·ment /háchmənt/ *n* a diamond-shaped panel bearing the coat of arms of somebody who has died [Early 16C. Probably < obsolete French *hachement*, alteration of Old French *acesmement* "adornment" < *acesmer* "adorn"]

hatch·way /hách wày/ *n* BUILDINGS same as **hatch**[1] (sense 2)

hate /hayt/ *v* (**hat·ed, hat·ing, hates**) **1.** *vt* **DISLIKE SOMEBODY OR SOMETHING INTENSELY** to dislike somebody or something intensely, often in a way that evokes feelings of anger, hostility, or animosity **2.** *vti* **HAVE STRONG DISTASTE FOR SOMETHING** to have strong distaste or aversion for something, somebody, or something that has to be done ○ *I hate this show; it's so boring.* ○ *I hate to say it, but I know we're going to lose.* ○ *Some people seem to have been born to hate.* ■ *n* **1. FEELING OF INTENSE HOSTILITY** a feeling of intense hostility toward somebody or something ○ *You could see the hate in his eyes.* **2. SOMETHING HATED** something that is hated [Old English *hete* (noun), *hatian* (verb) < Indo-European] —**hate·a·ble** *adj* —**hat·ed** *adj* —**hat·er** *n*

SYNONYMS See ***dislike***.

hate crime *n* a crime that is motivated by hate, prejudice, or intolerance of somebody's religion, ethnicity, or sexual orientation ○ *hate crimes such as car bombings of civil rights activists*

hate·ful /háytfəl/ *adj* **1.** characterized by malevolence or spite **2.** eliciting feelings or reactions of hatred, detestation, or abhorrence —**hate·ful·ly** *adv* —**hate·ful·ness** *n*

hate mail *n* mail that expresses the sender's anger about something, usually toward the recipient, in a threatening or offensive way

hat·ful /hát fòol/ *n* a large quantity or number of something ○ *received a hatful of compliments on the performance*

hath /hath/ 3rd person singular present of **have** (*archaic*)

Hath·a·way /háthə wày/, **Anne** (1556–1623) English wife of William Shakespeare. She was born into a farming family, and married William Shakespeare, eight years her junior, in 1582.

ha·tha yo·ga /háthə-, hùttə-/ *n* a low-impact yoga that helps to regulate breathing by exercises consisting of postures and stretches intended to sustain healthy bodily functioning and induce emotional calmness [< Sanskrit, "force yoga"]

hat·pin /hát pìn/ *n* a long thin pin, often with a decoration at the end, that is pushed through a hat and into the hair to keep the hat securely on the head

ha·tred /háytrəd/ *n* a feeling of intense hostility towards somebody or something [12C. < HATE + suffix < Old English *ræden* "state, condition"]

SYNONYMS See ***dislike***.

Hat·shep·sut /hàt shép sòot/, **queen of Egypt of the 18th Dynasty** (*fl* 15th century B.C.) She ruled from 1479–57 and crowned herself pharaoh in 1473 after years of ruling jointly with her husband, Thutmose II, and his son, Thutmose III

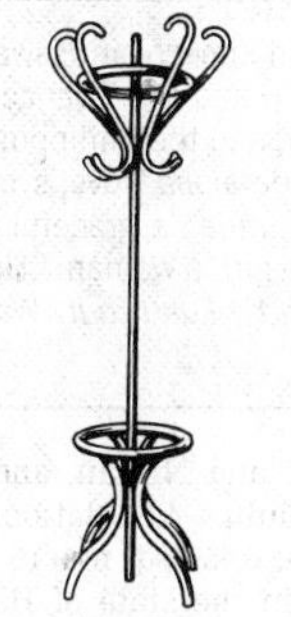
hat stand

hat stand *n* a tall freestanding piece of furniture consisting of a base with a pole embedded in it with hooks around the top on which hats, coats, and umbrellas can be hung

hat·ter /háttər/ *n* a maker or seller of hats

Hat·ter·as, Cape /háttərəss/ headland projecting into the Atlantic Ocean in eastern North Carolina. It is renowned for treacherous weather conditions.

hat tree *n* FURNITURE same as **hat stand**

hat trick *n* in ice hockey or soccer, a series of three wins or successes, especially three goals scored by the same player [Probably < the former practice in cricket of awarding a hat to a bowler who took three wickets with three consecutive balls]

hau·berk /háwbərk/ *n* a long, often sleeveless, tunic made of chain mail. It was originally intended as protection just for the neck and shoulders but it developed into a longer tunic in the 12th and 13th centuries. [13C. < Old French *hau(s)berc* < Germanic, "neck-protector"]

haugh /haw, hawkh/ *n Scotland* a low-lying stretch of land in a river valley, often unproductive because of frequent flooding [14C. Probably < Old English *healh* "corner, nook, small hollow in a slope"]

Haugh·ey /háw hee, háwkhee/, **Charles** (*b.* 1925) Irish politician. He was leader of the Fianna Fáil Party (1979–92) and prime minister of Ireland (1979–81, 1982, and 1987–92).

> "If you were to elect the head of the Orange Order as President of this Republic, the Unionists would still find we are doing something dishonest, deceitful, and totally unacceptable to them."
> [Charles Haughey, *Irish Times (Dublin)*; June 30, 1986]

haugh·ty /háwtee/ (**-ti·er, -ti·est**) *adj* behaving in a superior, condescending, or arrogant way ○ *haughty self-assurance* [Mid-16C. < archaic *haught* < French *haut(e)* "high"] —**haugh·ti·ly** *adv* —**haugh·ti·ness** *n*

haul /hawl/ *v* (**hauled, haul·ing, hauls**) **1.** *vt* PULL OR DRAG SOMETHING to pull or drag something with continuous and laborious movements **2.** *vt* MOVE SOMETHING WITH EFFORT to transport something that is heavy and bulky from one place to another **3.** *vt* SAILING CHANGE BOAT'S COURSE to change a vessel's course so as to sail closer to the wind **4.** *vi* NAUT BLOW CLOSER TO BOW to blow from a direction that is closer to a vessel's bow (*refers to winds*) **5.** *vt* NAUT HOIST VESSEL INTO DRY DOCK to hoist a vessel from the water into a dry dock, e.g., to make repairs ■ *n* **1.** STOLEN ITEMS goods that have been stolen, or the value of these stolen goods **2.** DISTANCE SOMETHING IS TRANSPORTED a distance over which something is transported or pulled, or which somebody travels with difficulty ○ *a long haul* **3.** FISHING SINGLE CATCH OF FISH the amount of fish caught in a single catch **4.** CONFISCATED CONTRABAND illegal goods that are confiscated by the authorities [13C. Variant of HALE[2]]

SYNONYMS See *pull*.

haul off *vi* **1.** to pull back the arm in preparation for striking somebody or something (*informal*) ○ *She hauled off and swung the swatter at the hornet.* **2.** to maneuver a vessel in order to avoid something

haul up *vt* to force somebody to appear before a court or another disciplinary body for judgment ○ *witnesses who were hauled up before a grand jury*

haul·age /háwlij/ *n* **1.** the business or process of transporting goods, usually by road or rail **2.** the cost of transporting goods, or the rate charged for transporting goods

haul·er /háwlər/ *n* a person or company whose business is transporting goods, especially by road

haul·ier /háwlyər, -lee ər/ *n UK* TRANSP same as **hauler**

haunch /hawnch/ *n* **1.** HIP, BUTTOCK, AND UPPER THIGH the part of the body comprising the hip, buttock, and upper thigh ○ *She sat back on her haunches.* **2.** ANIMAL LEG one of the back legs of a four-legged animal, either when it is alive, or as a cut of meat **3.** ARCHIT UPPER PART OF ARCH the upper curving part of either side of an arch [12C. < French *hanche* < Germanic]

haunt /hawnt/ *vt* (**haunt·ed, haunt·ing, haunts**) **1.** DISCOMFIT SOMEBODY BY UNPLEASANT REMINDERS to cause somebody unease, worry, or regret by continual presence or recurrence in his or her life ○ *haunted by doubt* **2.** VISIT SOMEWHERE CONTINUALLY to go often to a place **3.** PARANORMAL APPEAR TO SOMEBODY AS GHOST to frequent a place or appear to somebody in the form of a ghost or other supposed supernatural being ■ *n* **1.** PLACE SOMEBODY OFTEN VISITS a place that somebody likes and often visits **2.** PARANORMAL GHOST a supposed supernatural being or a manifestation of one, especially one associated with a particular place [12C. < French *hanter* "frequent a place" < Germanic, "home"] —**haunt·er** *n*

haunt·ed /háwntəd/ *adj* **1.** inhabited by or visited regularly by a ghost or other supposed supernatural being **2.** looking strangely frightened or worried

haunt·ing /háwnting/ *adj* evoking strong emotion, especially a sense of sadness, that persists for a long time ○ *a tender, haunting melody* —**haunt·ing·ly** *adv*

Hau·ra·ki Gulf /how ráakee-/ bay on the northeastern coast of the North Island, New Zealand. The city of Auckland is located on its southwestern shore. Area: 884 sq. mi./2,290 sq. km.

Hau·sa /hówssə, -zə/ (*plural same* or **-sas**) *n* **1.** PEOPLES MEMBER OF W AFRICAN PEOPLE a member of a people living mainly in northern Nigeria and southern Niger **2.** LANG LANGUAGE OF W AFRICA a language spoken in Nigeria, Niger, and other parts of eastern West Africa, belonging to the Chadic branch of Afro-Asiatic. Native speakers: 25 million. Other speakers: 40 million. **3.** RELIG SPIRITUAL TRADITION OF NIGERIA the tradition combining aspects of Islam and of local religious beliefs associated with the Hausa, after the collapse of the Songhay Empire [Early 19C. < Hausa] —**Hau·sa** *adj*

haus·frau /hówss fròw/ (*plural* **-fraus**) *n* a traditional housewife, conventionally believed to be interested mostly in her home and family (*sometimes offensive*) ○ *She wanted a career, not a life as a hausfrau.* [Late 18C. < German < *Haus* "house" + *Frau* "wife, woman"]

Haus·mann /hówssmən/, **Raoul** (1886–1971) Austrian poet and artist. He was a founding member of the Dada movement in Berlin. His work includes photomontages and "phonetic poems," several of which he recorded.

haus·tel·lum /haw stélləm/ (*plural* **-la** /-lə/) *n* the tip of the proboscis, or elongated mouthpart, that is adapted for sucking food in many insects such as flies [Early 19C. < modern Latin, "small scoop" < Latin *haustrum* "scoop" < *haurire* "draw up"]

haus·to·ri·um /haw stáwree əm/ (*plural* **-ri·a** /-ree ə/) *n* a structure of a parasitic plant or fungus that penetrates host tissues to obtain food and water [Late 19C. < Latin *haustor* "water-drawer, drinker" < *haurire* "draw up"]

haut·boy /ṓ bòy, hṓ-/ (*plural* **-boys**), **haut·bois** (*plural same*) *n* MUSIC same as **oboe** (*archaic*) [Mid-16C. < French *hautbois* "oboe" < *haut* "high" (from its high pitch) + *bois* "wood" < Germanic]

haute cou·ture /ōt koo tóor/ *n* exclusive and expensive clothing made for an individual customer by a fashion designer, or the industry that produces such clothing [Early 20C. < French, "high dressmaking"]

haute cui·sine /ōt kwi zéen/ *n* classic high-quality French cooking (*hyphenated when used before a noun*) [Early 20C. < French, "high cooking"]

haute é·cole /ōt ay káwl/ *n* the skill and art of expert horsemanship [Mid-19C. < French, "high school"]

hau·teur /hō túr, haw-/ *n* a haughty manner, feeling, or quality [Early 17C. < French < *haute* "high" < Latin *altus*]

haut monde /ō máwNd/ *n* the highest stratum of society, international or domestic, and those in it [Mid-19C. < French, "high world"]

ha·va·la /hə vaálə/, **ha·wa·la** *n S Asia* FIN a means of exchanging foreign currency unofficially and sometimes illegally without records [< Hindi]

Ha·van·a[1] /hə vánnə, -vaánə/ capital, port, and largest city of Cuba, on the northwestern coast of the country. Population: 2,189,716 (2000). —**Ha·van·an** *adj*, *n*

Ha·van·a[2] /hə vánnə/, **Ha·van·a ci·gar** *n* a high-quality cigar made in Cuba [Early 19C. < HAVANA[1]]

Ha·var·ti /hə vaártee/ *n* a pale, moist, semihard Danish cheese with tiny holes, a slightly rubbery texture, and a mild buttery flavor [Mid-20C. After the farm of a 19C Danish cheese maker]

Ha·va·su·pai /haavə sòo pì/ (*plural same*) *n* **1.** a member of a Native North American people living in Arizona, southeast of the Grand Canyon **2.** the Yuman language of the Havasupai people [Late 19C. < Yuman, "blue or green water people"] —**Ha·va·su·pai** *adj*

hav·da·lah *n* JUDAISM another spelling of **habdalah**

have *stressed* /hav/; *unstressed* /həv, əv/ (**had** *stressed* /had/; *unstressed* /həd, əd/, **hav·ing, has** *stressed* /haz/; *unstressed* /həz, əz/) CORE MEANING: a verb indicating that somebody possesses something, either materially or as a characteristic or attribute ○ *She has a small cottage in the country.* ○ *He has beautiful eyes.*

1. *vt* OWN SOMETHING to be the owner or possessor of something ○ *I don't have a lot of money.* **2.** *vt* POSSESS CHARACTERISTIC to be the possessor of a quality or characteristic ○ *She had long blond hair.* **3.** *aux v* FORMS PERFECT TENSES used to form the following tenses or aspects: the present perfect, the past perfect, the future perfect, and the continuous forms of these (*used before the past participle of a verb or at the beginning of a question, or with "got" to indicate possession*) ○ *I have finished my dinner, thank you.* ○ *Have you finished yet?* ○ *I have got a new car.* **4.** *modal v* EXPRESSES COMPULSION expresses compulsion, obligation, or necessity ○ *We have to go now.* ○ *said he'd do it if he had to* **5.** *modal v* EXPRESSES CERTAINTY expresses conviction or certainty ○ *There just has to be a solution to the problem.* **6.** *vt* RECEIVE SOMETHING to receive or obtain something ○ *I had a Christmas card from him.* **7.** *vt* EAT SOMETHING to eat or drink something ○ *We have breakfast at eight.* **8.** *vt* THINK OF SOMETHING to think of something, or hold something in the mind ○ *Listen! I have a good idea.* **9.** *vt* EXPERIENCE SOMETHING to experience or undergo something ○ *He went to the carnival to have a good time.* ○ *I had a shock.* **10.** *vt* BE AFFECTED BY SOMETHING to be affected by something, especially something of a medical nature ○ *I've had the flu for the last week.* **11.** *vt* ENGAGE IN SOMETHING to engage or participate in something ○ *They had a long talk about cars.* **12.** *vt* ARRANGE SOMETHING to organize or arrange something ○ *We had a party last week.* **13.** *vt* ARRANGE FOR SOMETHING TO BE DONE to arrange for somebody to do something for you or on your behalf ○ *I've just had my hair cut.* **14.** *vt* TOLERATE SOMETHING to tolerate or put up with something (*usually used in negative statements*) ○ *I won't have such behavior any longer!* **15.** *vt* RECEIVE SOMEBODY to receive somebody as a guest ○ *We had Mother to stay over Christmas.* **16.** *vt* BRING CHILD INTO EXISTENCE to be the parent of a child, or conceive, carry, or give birth to a child ○ *She's had three children and now she's having another one.* **17.** *vt* PUT SOMEBODY OR SOMETHING SOMEWHERE to put or place somebody or something in a particular place ○ *I'll have you two in the front row, please.* ○ *I'll have the desk over there.* **18.** *vt* UNDERGO SOMETHING to be the victim of an unpleasant action or experience ○ *I had my car stolen.* **19.** *vt* MAKE SOMETHING HAPPEN to direct or cause somebody to do something, or cause something to happen ○ *If you see him tomorrow, have him call me.* **20.** *vt* CHEAT SOMEBODY to cheat or outwit somebody (*slang; usually passive*) ○ *I think* *you've been had in this deal.* [Old English *habban* < Indo-European, "grasp"] ◇ **have done with something** to finish with something ○ *Let's put everything else in this box and have done with it.* ◇ **have had it 1.** to have no prospect of success ○ *We've had it now.* **2.** to be too worn out, damaged, or exhausted to function properly (*informal*) ○ *I'm afraid this printer has just about had it.* ○ *I've had it – you go on, I'm turning back.* ◇ **have had it with somebody** *or* **something** to have lost patience with somebody or something ○ *I've had it with delays.* ◇ **have it** to declare or assert something ○ *Rumor has it that they are planning to get engaged.* ◇ **have it in for somebody** to dislike somebody and want to do that person harm ◇ **have it out (with somebody)** to engage in a spirited, aggressive argument over an issue with somebody ○ *OK, let's have it out now and get this settled once and for all.* ◇ **have something on somebody** to have unfavorable information about somebody's activities ◇ **have to do with 1.** to be relevant to ○ *Does your question have anything to do with the topic under discussion?* **2.** to have a friendship or relationship with ○ *She will have nothing to do with him anymore.* ◇ **have what it takes** to have the necessary skills, personality, or attitude to be successful at something ○ *He doesn't really have what it takes to be a professional actor.* ◇ **not having any (of something)** refusing to take part or become involved in something ○ *They tried to involve him in the conspiracy, but it soon became clear that he wasn't having any.*

USAGE See *do*[1].

have at *vt* attack somebody ◇ **have at it** to set to work with vigor ○ *Let's have at it – this project has to be done in June.*

have on *vt* to have an item of clothing on your body

Hav·el /hávv'l/, **Václav** (*b.* 1936) Czech dramatist and statesman. He was a dissident playwright who became a leader of the Charter 77 Czech democracy movement under Communist rule. After the democratic revolution in 1989 he became president of Czechoslovakia (1989) and then of the Czech Republic (1993–2003).

> "Truth is not merely what we are thinking, but also why, to whom, and under what circumstances we say it."
> [Václav Havel, *Temptation*; 1985]

ha·ve·li /hùvvə leé/ (*plural* **-lis**) *n S Asia* a large stately house [Via Hindi < Arabic *havelī*]

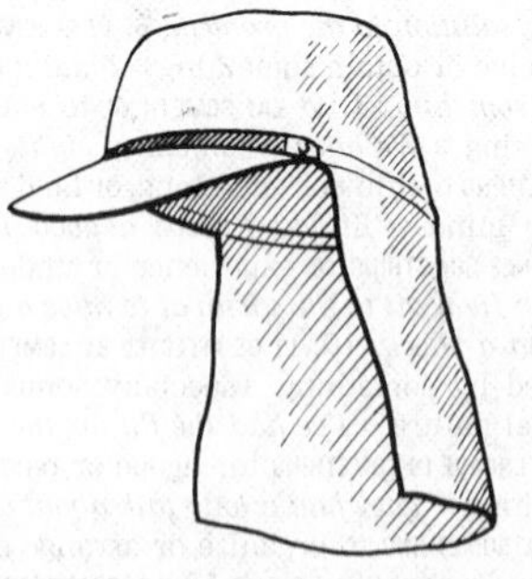

havelock

have·lock /háv lòk, hávvlək/ *n* a light-colored cover for a soldier's cap, with a flap extending over the back of the neck to protect the head and neck from the sun [Mid-19C. After Sir Henry *Havelock* (1795–1857), British major general]

ha·ven /háyvən/ *n* **1.** a place sought for rest, shelter, or protection ○ *a haven for wildlife* **2.** a harbor or port facility where ships and boats come in and tie up (*literary*) [Pre-12C. < Old Norse *hǫfn* "place that holds (ships)"]

have-nots *npl* people who are not rich or privileged, especially compared with those who are ○ *a country with the highest income inequality between the haves and have-nots*

have·n't /hávvənt/ *contr* have not

Hav·er·ford·west /hàvvərfərd wést/ market town in Pembrokeshire, southwestern Wales. It is the administrative center of the county. Population: 13,454 (1991).

WORLD ENGLISH ***Hawaiian English*** is the variety of English used, mainly in speech, in Hawaii, a state of the United States. It ranges from Hawaii Pidgin English to standard US English, and is influenced by Hawaiian, a Polynesian language, and by the languages of immigrants from China, Japan, and the Philippines among others, as well as by usage from the US mainland. Expressions from Hawaiian include *aloha* "love, sympathy, welcome, farewell," *haole* "foreigner, especially a white person," *heiau* "a temple," *hula* "a graceful swaying dance," *kahuna* "a traditional priest or shaman," *lei* "a garland of flowers," *wahine* "a girl, a woman." Hybrid expressions are commonplace, usually with the Hawaiian element first, as in *aloha party, kukui nut, Waikiki Beach,* and *Waimea Arboretum.*

Hav·er·hill /háyvəril/ city in northeastern Massachusetts on the Merrimack River. Population: 59,634 (2002 estimate).

hav·er·sack /hávvər sàk/ *n* a strong bag carried on the back or the shoulder, used especially by travelers or hikers [Mid-18C. Via French *havresac* < obsolete German *Habersack* < *Haber* "oats" + *Sack* "bag"]

Ha·ver·sian ca·nal /hə vúrzh'n-/ *n* a tiny longitudinal channel in bone tissue. The canals form a network that contains blood vessels and nerve fibers. [Mid-19C. After Clopton *Havers* (1650?–1702), English physician and anatomist]

Ha·ver·sian sys·tem *n* a Haversian canal along with the concentric layers of compact bone surrounding it [See HAVERSIAN CANAL]

hav·er·sine /hávvər sīn/ *n* in mathematics, half the value of the versed sine [Late 19C. Contraction of *half versed sine*]

haves /havz/ *npl* people who are rich and privileged, especially compared with those who are not [Mid-18C. < HAVE]

hav·il·dar /hávv'l daar/ *n S Asia* an army or police officer of a rank equivalent to sergeant [Late 17C. Via Urdu *hawildār* < Persian *hawāl(a)dār* "charge holder"]

Ha·vil·land ➧ **De Havilland, Sir Geoffrey**

Ha·vil·land ➧ **de Havilland, Olivia**

hav·oc /hávvək/ *n* **1. DEVASTATION** widespread damage, destruction, or devastation ○ *the havoc wreaked by the storm* **2. CHAOS** a condition or situation of disruptive chaos ■ *adj Malaysia, Singapore* **DIFFICULT TO CONTROL** difficult to control, manage, discipline, or govern (*informal*) ○ *Her kids look really havoc!* [15C. < Anglo-Norman *(crier) havok* "(to cry) havoc," signal to an army to seize plunder, alteration of Old French *havo(t)* "pillage"]

Ha·vre de Grace /hàvvər dee gráyss/ town in northeastern Maryland, on the Chesapeake Bay at the mouth of the Susquehanna River. Population: 11,318 (2002 estimate).

haw[1] /haw/ *n* **1.** PLANTS same as **hawthorn 2.** the round or oval fruit of the hawthorn, usually red or yellow and containing seeds [Old English *haga*, origin ?]

haw[2] /haw/ *n* a sound that people make when they are hesitating to speak ■ *vi* (**hawed, haw·ing, haws**) to make a sound indicative of hesitation while speaking [Mid-17C. An imitation of the sound]

haw[3] /haw/ *interj* used to command an animal or a team of animals to turn left [Late 17C. Origin ?]

haw[4] /haw/ *n* VET same as **nictitating membrane** [Early 16C. Origin ?]

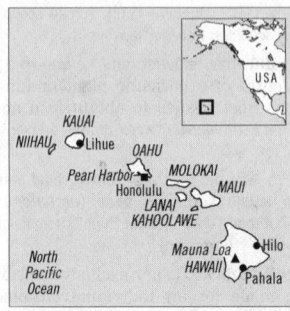

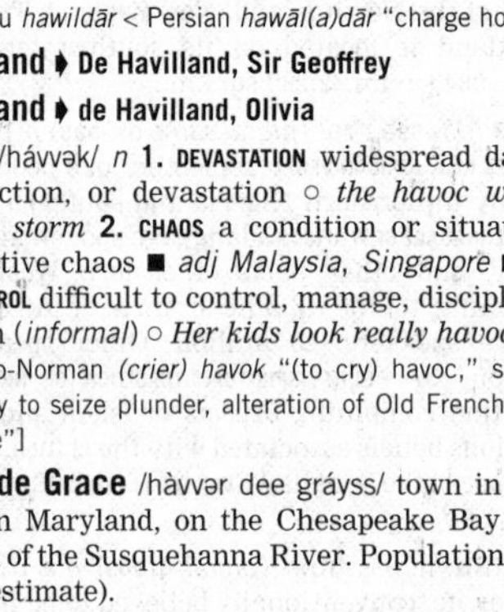

Hawaii

Ha·wai·i /hə waá ee/ **1.** state of the United States in the northern Pacific Ocean, consisting of eight main islands, Oahu, Hawaii, Kahoolawe, Kauai, Lanai, Maui, Molokai, and Niihau, and over 100 others. Capital: Honolulu. Population: 1,244,898 (2002 estimate). Area: 6,459 sq. mi./16,729 sq. km. **2.** the largest island in the state of Hawaii. Population: 154,794 (2002 estimate). Area: 4,028 sq. mi./10,432 sq. km.

Ha·wai·i-A·leu·tian Stan·dard Time *n* the standard time in the time zone centered on 150° west longitude, which includes Hawaii and the western Aleutian Islands. It is ten hours behind Universal Time.

Ha·wai·ian /hə waá yən/ *n* **1.** somebody who comes from Hawaii **2.** a language spoken in Hawaii and other neighboring islands, belonging to the Polynesian branch of Austronesian. Native speakers: 70,000. —**Ha·wai·ian** *adj*

Ha·wai·ian ap·pli·qué *n* appliqué in which a large central motif, from a design cut from folded paper, is applied to a foundation fabric and made into a quilt. Traditional Hawaiian appliqué is made in two solid colors, typically red, green, orange, or blue on white.

Ha·wai·ian Eng·lish *n* a variety of English spoken in Hawaii

Ha·wai·ian goose *n* BIRDS same as **nene**

Ha·wai·ian gui·tar *n* a small steel-strung guitar with a sliding glass or metal bar that fits across the strings in order to change the pitch of the whole instrument. It is usually played horizontally on a stand, and the strings are plucked with a thimble.

Ha·wai·ian Is·lands island group in the central North Pacific Ocean, consisting of eight main islands: Hawaii, Maui, Oahu, Kauai, Molokai, Lanai, Niihau, and Kahoolawe, and many islets, making up most of the US state of Hawaii

Ha·wai·i Stan·dard Time, Ha·wai·i Time *n* TIME same as **Hawaii-Aleutian Standard Time**

Ha·wai·i Vol·ca·noes Na·tion·al Park /-vol kàynōz-/ national park on the island of Hawaii, in Hawaii State, established in 1916. Its features include the active volcanoes of Mauna Loa and Kilauea. Area: 328 sq. mi./849 sq. km.

hawfinch

haw·finch /háw finch/ (*plural* **-finch·es** or *same*) *n* a songbird with a thick conical silvery beak, brown feathers, and black-and-white wings, and a white-tipped tail. Native to: Europe, Asia. Latin name: *Coccothraustes coccothraustes.* [< HAW[1]]

haw-haw[1] *interj* same as **ha-ha**[1]

haw-haw[2] *n* GARDENING same as **ha-ha**[2]

Haw·ick /háw ik/ historic town in the Scottish Borders district on the Teviot River. Population: 15,812 (1991).

hawk[1] /hawk/ *n* **1. BIRD OF PREY** a bird of prey that is active in the daytime, typically having broad wings, a short hooked beak, strong talons, and a long tail.

Family: Accipitridae. **2.** BIRDS **SMALL BIRD OF PREY** a small bird of prey, e.g., a falcon. Order: Falconiformes. **3. SOMEBODY FAVORING FORCE** somebody who favors the use of military force in implementing foreign policy **4. AGGRESSIVE COMPETITOR** a fiercely competitive, aggressive, predatory, or combative person ○ *a marketing hawk who wanted to put the competition out of business* **5. RUTHLESS SWINDLER** a ruthless con man or other swindler who preys on unsuspecting victims ■ *v* **(hawked, hawk·ing, hawks) 1.** *vi* HUNTING **HUNT WITH HAWKS** to hunt for prey on the wing, or hunt for prey using hawks and similar birds of prey **2.** *vti* BIRDS **ATTACK ON WING** to pursue or attack something while flying in a way similar to that of a hawk ○ *tiny birds hawking insects in the morning sky* [Old English *h(e)afoc* < Indo-European, "grasp"] —**hawk·er** *n* —**hawk·ing** *n*

hawk[2] /hawk/ **(hawked, hawk·ing, hawks)** *vti* to engage in selling merchandise on the street or from door to door [14C. Probably back-formation < *hawker*, probably < Middle Low German *höker* < *höken* "peddle"] —**hawk·er** *n*

hawk[3] /hawk/ *vti* **(hawked, hawk·ing, hawks)** to clear the throat noisily of phlegm ■ *n* a noisy attempt to clear the throat of phlegm [Late 16C Probably an imitation of the sound]

hawk[4] /hawk/ *n* a metal square with a wooden handle underneath, used by a plasterer to hold wet plaster or mortar before applying it to a surface [15C. Origin ?]

hawk·bill *n* ZOOL same as **hawksbill**

hawk·bit /háwk bìt/ (*plural* **-bits** or *same*) *n* a perennial plant with lobed leaves. Flowers: yellow. Native to: grasslands. Genus: *Leontodon.* [Early 18C. Blend of HAWKWEED + *devil's bit*, wild plant with a short rootstock, popularly said to have been bitten off by the devil]

Hawke /hawk/, **Bob** (*b.* 1929) Australian politician. He was leader of the Australian Labor Party and prime minister of Australia (1983–91). Full name **Hawke, Robert James Lee**. See table at **prime minister**

Hawke Bay /hàwk báy/ bay on the eastern coast of the North Island, New Zealand. It extends from Mahia Peninsula in the north to Cape Kidnappers in the south.

Hawke's Bay /hàwks báy/ administrative region of New Zealand, located in the east of the North Island and bordering Hawke Bay. Population: 142,947 (2001). Area: 8,177 sq. mi./21,178 sq. km.

Hawkes·bur·y /háwksbəree/ river in eastern New South Wales, Australia, which rises in the Great Dividing Range. Length: 298 mi./480 km.

Hawk·eye /háwk ì/ *n* somebody who comes from the state of Iowa (*informal*) [Early 19C. < Iowa's popular name "the Hawkeye State"]

hawk-eyed *adj* quick to see things that are not obvious, often as a result of having very keen eyesight ○ *The hawk-eyed appraiser spotted a tiny chip in the antique teapot.*

Hawk·eye State *n* a nickname for Iowa

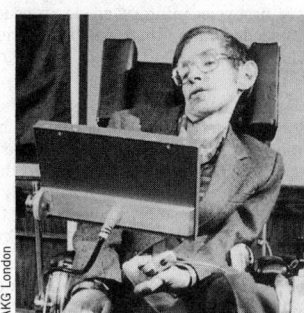

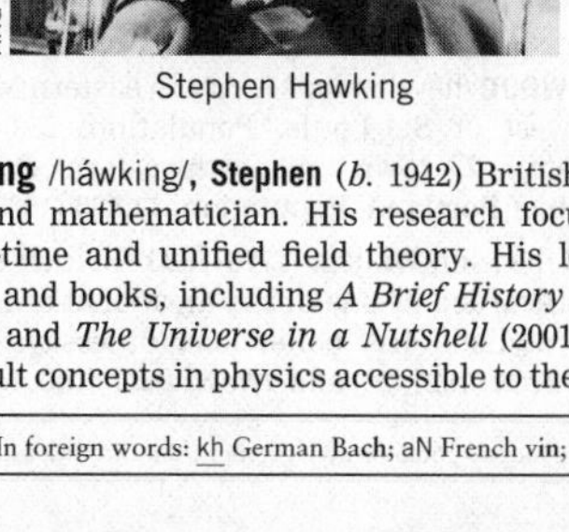
AKG London

Stephen Hawking

Hawk·ing /háwking/, **Stephen** (*b.* 1942) British physicist and mathematician. His research focused on space-time and unified field theory. His lectures, films, and books, including *A Brief History of Time* (1988) and *The Universe in a Nutshell* (2001), made difficult concepts in physics accessible to the public. Full name **Hawking, Stephen William**. See Cultural note at **time**

> "Even if there is only one possible unified theory, it is just a set of rules and equations. What is it that breathes fire into the equations and makes a universe for them to describe?... Why does the universe go to all the bother of existing?"
> [Stephen Hawking, *A Brief History of Time*; 1988]

Haw·kins /háwkinz/, **Coleman** (1904–69) US musician. His technique and improvisational skills laid the foundations for the tenor saxophone in bebop jazz. His best known album is *Body and Soul* (1939).

> "I like most music unless it's wrong."
> [Coleman Hawkins. Quoted in *The World of Swing*, Stanley Dance; 1974]

hawk·ish /háwkish/ *adj* favoring the use of military force in implementing foreign policy rather than diplomatic solutions ○ *The senator was hawkish on the use of preemptive air strikes.* —**hawk·ish·ly** *adv* —**hawk·ish·ness** *n*

hawk moth

hawk moth (*plural* **hawk moths** or *same*), **hawk·moth** /háwk màwth/ (*plural* **-moths** or *same*) *n* a moth with a thick body and long narrow wings that enable it to hover over flowers and feed on their nectar. Family: Sphingidae.

hawk owl

hawk owl *n* an owl with a long slender tail and brownish speckled feathers that resembles a hawk when in flight. Native to: North America, Europe, Asia. Latin name: *Surnia ulula.*

Hawks /hawks/, **Howard** (1896–1977) US movie director. During his 45-year career, he directed many Hollywood classics, including *Bringing Up Baby* (1938) and *The Big Sleep* (1946). Full name **Hawks, Howard Winchester**

hawk's beard (*plural* **hawk's beards** or *same*) *n* a composite plant with milky juice. Flowers: small, yellow, resembling the dandelion. Genus: *Crepis.*

hawks·bill /háwks bìl/ (*plural* **-bills** or *same*), **hawks·bill tur·tle, hawk·bill** /háwk bìl/ (*plural* **-bills** or *same*) *n* a sea turtle, reaching 2 ft./61 cm in length, that has a yellowish brown shell of overlapping plates. Native to: tropics. Latin name: *Eretmochelys imbricata.* [< the shape of its mouth]

hawk's-eye *n* a dark blue semiprecious stone that is a variety of crocidolite. Use: gems.

Hawks·moor /háwks moŏr/, **Nicholas** (1661–1736) British architect. He was a pupil of Sir Christopher Wren and assistant to Sir John Vanbrugh. His work includes several London churches, parts of Westminster Abbey, London, and All Souls, Oxford, England.

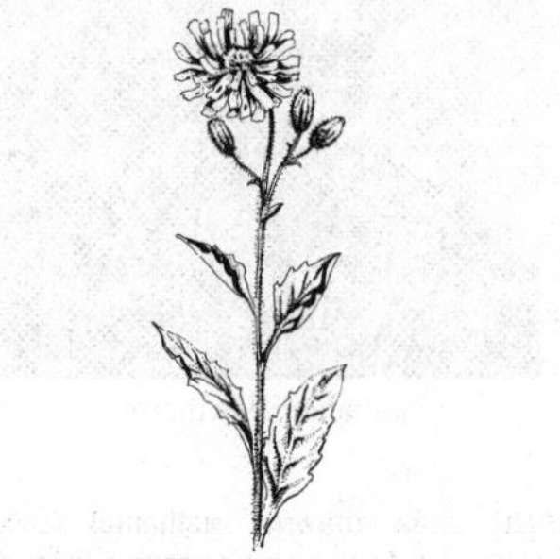

hawkweed

hawk·weed /háwk wèed/ (*plural same* or **-weeds**) *n* a plant typically with hairy leaves, sometimes found as a weed. Flowers: yellow or orange, resembling dandelions. Genus: *Hieracium.*

Ha·worth /hów ərth/ historic village in West Yorkshire, northern England. It was once home to the Brontë family. Population: 4,956 (1991).

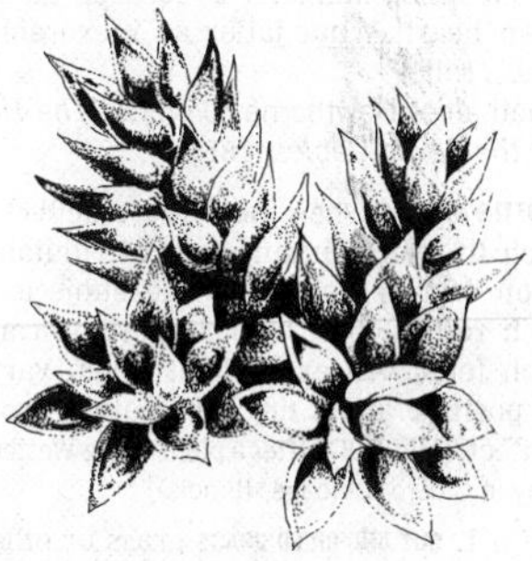

haworthia

ha·wor·thi·a /haw wúrthee ə, -thee ə/ (*plural* **-as** or *same*) *n* a succulent plant with densely overlapping, often warty leaves, clustered in rosettes. Native to: southern Africa. Genus: *Haworthia.* [After Adrian Hardy *Haworth* (1768–1833), British writer on succulent plants]

hawse /hawz/ *n* **1. LOCATION OF SHIP'S HAWSEHOLES** the area of a ship in which the hawseholes are to be found **2.** same as **hawsehole 3. SPACE BETWEEN BOW AND ANCHOR** the space between the bow and the anchors of a ship lying at anchor **4. ANCHOR DEPLOYMENT** the way in which a ship's anchor lines are deployed, starboard and port, when both are deployed together at the same time ■ *vi* **(hawsed, haws·ing, haws·es) PITCH VIOLENTLY WHEN AT ANCHOR** to pitch violently when lying at anchor [13C < Old Norse *hals*, Old English *h(e)als* "neck, ship's prow" < Indo-European, "revolve"]

hawse·hole /háwz hòl/ *n* an opening in the bow of a ship through which a large heavy line is passed for towing or mooring the ship

hawse·pipe /háwz pìp/ *n* a pipe on each side of a ship's bow for use in deploying and weighing anchor, with the anchor lines running through each pipe

haw·ser /háwzər/ *n* a large heavy cable that is used when mooring or towing a ship [13C. < Anglo-Norman *haucer* < Old French *haucier* "to hoist" < Latin *altus* "high"]

haw·ser-laid *adj* describes rope composed of three strands that are made by being twisted in a left-handed direction, then twisted together in a right-handed direction

haw·thorn /háw thàwrn/ *n* a thorny bush or tree of the rose family with white or pink flowers and reddish berries. Genus: *Crataegus.*

Haw·thorne /háw thàwrn/ industrial and residential city in southwestern California, situated 5 mi./8 km south of the city of Los Angeles. Population: 85,934 (2002 estimate).

Nathaniel Hawthorne

Haw·thorne /háw thàwrn/, **Nathaniel** (1804–64) US writer. His novels and short stories frequently deal with Puritan sin and atonement, and include *The Scarlet Letter* (1850). Born **Hathorne, Nathaniel.** See Cultural note at **scarlet letter**

> "No man, for any considerable period, can wear one face to himself, and another to the multitude, without finally getting bewildered as to which may be the true."
> [Nathaniel Hawthorne, *The Scarlet Letter*; 1850]

> "What other dungeon is so dark as one's own heart! What jailer so inexorable as one's self!"
> [Nathaniel Hawthorne, preface, *The House of the Seven Gables*; 1851]

Haw·thorne ef·fect /háw thàwrn-/ *n* an effect in social research in which findings are attributable to the attention of researchers to the subjects of their research rather than to factors significant to the research topic. An example is when variables of both a positive and a negative nature produce the same effect. [Mid-20C. After a plant of the Western Electric Company in Cicero (Chicago, Illinois)]

hay /hay/ *n* **1.** CUT AND DRIED GRASS grass or other plants that are cut, dried, and then often used as fodder **2.** MINUSCULE AMOUNT OF MONEY a very small amount of money (*slang; usually in negative statements*) ○ *He made five thousand bucks out of the deal, and that isn't hay.* ■ *v* **(hayed, hay·ing, hays) 1.** *vi* CUT, BALE, AND STORE HAY to mow hay and bale or roll it, and then store it ○ *He's been haying all day.* **2.** *vt* GIVE HAY TO ANIMAL to feed an animal or animals with hay [Old English *hēg* "something that can be cut down" < Indo-European, "hew, strike"] ◇ **hit the hay** to go to bed (*slang*) ◇ **make hay while the sun shines** to take advantage of opportunities when they present themselves (*slang*)

Hay /hay/, **John** (1838–1905) US diplomat and writer. He was Abraham Lincoln's private secretary (1861–65), and wrote a monumental ten-volume biography of him (1890). Full name **Hay, John Milton**

> "There is a sanction like that of religion which binds us in partnership in the serious work of the world...We are joint ministers in the same sacred mission of freedom and progress."
> [John Hay, *Speech, London*; April 21, 1898]

hay·cock /háy kòk/ *n UK* a cone-shaped pile of hay that is left in a field until it is dry enough to be stored

Hay·den /háyd'n/, **Melissa** (*b.* 1923) Canadian ballet dancer. She danced with the New York City Ballet from 1950 and appeared in the movie *Limelight* (1952). Born **Herman, Mildred**

Hay di·et /háy-/ *n* a diet in which protein and carbohydrate foods are not eaten at the same time, claimed to be helpful for digestive complaints and weight loss [Mid-20C. After William Howard *Hay* (1866–1940), US physician]

Hay·dn /hī́d'n/, **Joseph** (1732–1809) Austrian composer. His hundreds of symphonies, concertos, string quartets, and operas helped define the classical style, and include the popular oratorio *The Creation* (1798). Full name **Haydn, Franz Joseph**

Hayes /hayz/, **Helen** (1900–93) US actor. One of the most distinguished stage performers of the century, she was closely identified with the title role in *Victoria Regina* (1935). She won Academy Awards for *The Sin of Madelon Claudet* (1931) and *Airport* (1970). Born **Brown, Helen Hayes**

> "I decided long ago never to look at the right-hand side of the menu or the price tag of clothes—otherwise I would starve, naked."
> [Helen Hayes, *Washington Post*; May 7, 1990]

Rutherford B. Hayes

Hayes, Rutherford B. (1822–93) 19th president of the United States. A Republican, he reformed the civil service and withdrew the last federal troops from the Reconstruction South during his presidential term (1877–81). Full name **Hayes, Rutherford Birchard.** See table at **president**

> "He serves his party best who serves his country best."
> [Rutherford B. Hayes, *Inaugural address, Washington, D.C.*; March 5, 1877]

hay fe·ver *n* an allergic reaction to pollen that irritates the upper respiratory tract and the eyes, resulting in symptoms including a runny and itchy nose, itchy and watering eyes, and sneezing. Technical name **pollinosis**

hay·fork /háy fàwrk/ *n* **1.** AGRIC same as **pitchfork 2.** a machine-operated fork for moving hay

hay·lage /háylij/ *n* silage made from partially dried grass [Mid-20C. Blend of HAY + SILAGE]

hay·loft /háy lòft/ *n* a loft for storing hay over a stable or a barn

hay·mak·er /háy màykər/ *n* **1.** BOXING POWERFUL SWINGING PUNCH a powerful swinging punch, especially in a boxing match (*slang*) **2.** AGRIC MACHINE PROCESSING HAY a machine for breaking down stems of hay to improve the drying process **3.** AGRIC WORKER PROCESSING HAY an agricultural worker whose job it is to cut, turn, toss, spread, or carry hay after it has been mown

hay·rack /háy ràk/ *n* **1.** RACK HOLDING FEED a rack that holds hay and from which livestock feed **2.** RACK ON WAGON a rack attached to a wagon to increase its capacity for carrying hay **3.** WAGON WITH HAYRACK a wagon equipped with a hayrack

hay·ride /háy rīd/ *n* a ride taken for pleasure by a group of people in a wagon or other vehicle that is full of hay or straw

Hays /hayz/ town in central Kansas, west of Salina and northwest of Great Bend. Population: 19,908 (2002 estimate).

hay·seed /háy sèed/ *n* **1.** OFFENSIVE TERM an offensive term that deliberately insults somebody's rural residence or background and his or her intelligence and level of sophistication (*slang insult*) **2.** GRASS SEED FROM HAY grass seed that is shaken out of hay **3.** PIECES OF GRASS pieces of grass or straw that fall from hay

hay·stack /háy stàk/ *n* a large pile of hay, especially one that is built in the open

Hay·ward /háywərd/ city in northwestern California, on San Francisco Bay. Population: 142,718 (2002 estimate).

Hay·ward, Susan (1917?–75) US actor. She won an Academy Award for *I Want to Live!* (1958). Born **Marrener, Edythe**

hay·wire /háy wìr/ *adj* (*informal*) **1.** functioning erratically, or not functioning at all ○ *A powerful magnet can make the television set go haywire.* **2.** behaving unpredictably or extravagantly [< the springy nature of wire used to tie up bundles of hay, and sometimes for makeshift repairs]

Hay·wood /háywòod/, **William Dudley** (1869–1928) US labor leader. He cofounded the radical Industrial Workers of the World (1905) and advocated the violent overthrow of capitalism. Known as **Big Bill**

Hay·worth /háywərth/, **Rita** (1918–87) US actor. A dancer from her childhood, she appeared in movies including *Gilda* (1946). Born **Cansino, Margarita Carmen**

ha·zan *n* JUDAISM another spelling of **chazan**

haz·ard /házzərd/ *n* **1.** POTENTIAL DANGER something that is potentially very dangerous **2.** ENG DANGEROUS OUTCOME a dangerous or otherwise unwanted outcome, especially one resulting from the failure of an engineered system **3.** GOLF OBSTACLE ON GOLF COURSE a natural or constructed obstacle on a golf course, e.g., a sand trap or a lake **4.** GAMBLING DICE GAME a dice game resembling craps **5.** CUE GAMES SCORING STROKE IN BILLIARDS in billiards, a scoring stroke made when a ball is pocketed, either a ball other than the striker's (**winning hazard**) or the striker's cue ball itself (**losing hazard**) **6.** RACKET GAMES RECEIVER'S SIDE IN COURT TENNIS in court tennis, the receiver's side of the court ■ *vt* **(-ard·ed, -ard·ing, -ards) 1.** SUGGEST SOMETHING TENTATIVELY to offer a tentative explanation of something ○ *Would anyone like to hazard a guess as to what this could possibly mean?* **2.** RISK LOSS OF SOMETHING to chance or risk something, especially in order to gain something else [13C. Via Old French *hasard* "game of chance played with dice" < Arabic *az-zahr* "the die, the chance"]

haz·ard light *n* either of a pair of car lights, usually the blinkers, that flash on and off to warn other drivers of potential danger

haz·ard·ous /házzərdəss/ *adj* potentially very dangerous to living beings or the environment —**haz·ard·ous·ly** *adv* —**haz·ard·ous·ness** *n*

haz·ard·ous waste *n* a byproduct of manufacturing processes or nuclear processing that is toxic and presents a potential threat to people and the environment

haz·ard pay *n* extra money given to employees because of the dangerous nature of their work

haz·ard warn·ing light *n* AUTOMOT same as **hazard light**

haze[1] /hayz/ *n* **1.** PARTICLES IN ATMOSPHERE mist, cloud, or smoke suspended in the atmosphere and obscuring or obstructing the view **2.** VAGUE OBSCURING FACTOR something that is vague and serves to obscure something **3.** DISORIENTED MENTAL OR PHYSICAL STATE a mental or physical state or condition when feelings and perceptions are vague, disorienting, or obscured ■ *vi* **(hazed, haz·ing, haz·es)** BECOME FILLED WITH PARTICLES to become saturated with suspended particles ○ *As the temperatures rose, the sky began to haze over.* [Early 18C. Probably back-formation < HAZY]

haze[2] /hayz/ **(hazed, haz·ing, haz·es)** *vti* to persecute or torture somebody in a subordinate position, especially a first-year military academy cadet or a fraternity pledge. Many institutions have now prohibited hazing. [Late 17C. Origin ?] —**haz·er** *n* —**haz·ing** *n*

ha·zel /háyz'l/ (*plural* **-zels** or *same*) *n* **1.** FOOD same as **hazelnut 2.** TREES SMALL TREE WITH EDIBLE NUTS a bush or small tree of the birch family with edible brown nuts. Genus: *Corylus.* **3.** INDUST WOOD OF HAZEL the wood of the hazel tree. Use: baskets, hurdles. **4.** COLORS LIGHT BROWN COLOR a light brown color with a tinge of green or gold, like a ripe hazelnut ○ *hazel eyes* [Old English *hæsel* < Indo-European] —**ha·zel** *adj*

ha·zel·nut /háyz'l nùt/ *n* an edible nut from a hazel tree

Ha·zel·wood /háyz'l wòod/ **1.** city in eastern Missouri, northwest of St. Louis. Population: 26,042 (2002 estimate). **2.** town in northwestern Oregon, a suburb of Portland. Population: 11,480 (1998).

Haz·litt /házzlit/, **William** (1778–1830) British essayist. He is regarded as one of the most brilliant English prose stylists. His collections of essays include *Table Talk* (1821–22) and *The Spirit of the Age* (1825).

"The least pain in our little finger gives us more concern and uneasiness than the destruction of millions of our fellow beings."
[William Hazlitt, "American Literature—Dr. Channing," *Edinburgh Review*; October 1829]

"There is not a more mean, stupid, dastardly, pitiful, selfish, spiteful, envious, ungrateful animal than the public. It is the greatest of cowards, for it is afraid of itself."
[William Hazlitt, "On Living to One's Self," *Table Talk*; 1821–22]

HAZMAT /ház màt/, **haz/mat** *abbr* INDUST hazardous material

haz·y /háyzee/ (**-i·er, -i·est**) *adj* **1.** VISUALLY OBSCURED unclear, especially because partially obscured or obstructed by mist, cloud, or smoke **2.** IMPRECISE not specific or clearly remembered ○ *I have a hazy recollection of having met her.* **3.** NOT KNOWLEDGEABLE showing a lack of understanding or knowledge [Early 17C. Origin ?] —**haz·i·ly** *adv* —**haz·i·ness** *n*

haz·zan *n* JUDAISM another spelling of **chazan**

H-beam *n* a structural steel member shaped like an H in section. It is similar to an I-beam.

H-bomb *n* ARMS same as **hydrogen bomb**

H.C. *abbr* House of Commons

HCF, **hcf** *abbr* MATH highest common factor

HCFC *n* a gas containing carbon, chlorine, fluorine, and hydrogen that has been identified as being less damaging to the ozone layer than CFCs. Full form **hydrochlorofluorocarbon**

HCI *abbr* human-computer interaction

HD *abbr* **1.** COMPUT hard disk **2.** COMPUT hard drive **3.** heavy-duty **4.** BIOCHEM, ELECTRONICS high-density

hd. *abbr* **1.** hand **2.** head

HDL *abbr* high-density lipoprotein

hdqrs. *abbr* headquarters

HDR *abbr* MIL humanitarian daily ration

HDSL *abbr* TELECOM, ONLINE **1.** High-Bit-Rate Digital Subscriber Line **2.** High-Data Rate Digital Subscriber Line

HDTV *abbr* high-definition television

he[1] *stressed* /hee/; *unstressed* /ee/ *pron* used to refer to a male person or animal that has been previously mentioned or whose identity is known (*used as the subject of a verb*) ■ *n* a male animal or boy, especially used of a new baby ○ *Is your pup a he or a she?* [Old English < Indo-European, "this (here)"]

USAGE Formerly, ***he*** was often used to refer to somebody whose gender was not specified: *A child needs time to learn and can then move at his own pace.* More recently this usage has been avoided. Because English does not have a gender-neutral pronoun in the third person singular that can be used to refer to people, "he or she" may need to be used, especially in formal contexts. In informal contexts *they* is often used instead. Another alternative is to use the plural: *Children need time to learn and can then move at their own pace.* See also ***they***.

he[2] /hay/ *n* the fifth letter of the Hebrew alphabet, represented in the English alphabet as "h." See table at **alphabet** [Mid-17C. < Hebrew *hē'*]

He *symbol* CHEM ELEM helium

H.E. *abbr* **1.** His Eminence **2.** His Excellency

head /hed/ *n* **1.** TOP PART OF BODY the topmost part of a vertebrate body, where the brain, eyes, nose, ears, mouth, and jaws are situated **2.** MOST FORWARD SECTION OF BODY the section of the body of an invertebrate that is forward of all other segments **3.** CENTER OF INTELLECT the center of a human being's faculties of intellect, emotion, and reasoning ○ *a good head for figures* **4.** LEADER OF OTHERS the chief leader, supervisor, or manager ○ *All department heads attended the meeting.* **5.** TOP OF LONG THIN OBJECT the wider top of a long thin object ○ *the head of a nail* ○ *a hammer head* **6.** HIGHEST PART the highest, uppermost, or foremost part of something ○ *was invited to sit at the head of the table* ○ *standing by the head of the bed* **7.** SECTION IN SPEECH OR TEXT one of the main sections or topics of a written or spoken discourse ○ *listed under three main heads* **8.** CRISIS POINT a critical juncture in a situation or series of events, at which time some action must be taken, however painful ○ *The looming deadline brought matters to a head.* **9.** *Carib* STATE OF MIND somebody's state of mind at a specific time, especially as perceived by others ○ *Wha' head you pushing?* **10.** (*plural same*) COUNTABLE UNIT a single unit in a number of people or animals, especially when they are being counted ○ *500 head of cattle* **11.** MEASURE OF DISTANCE the height or length of a head, used as a measure of distance between two individuals, especially racehorses at the winning post ○ *The favorite won by a head.* **12.** TABOO TERM a highly offensive term for an act of performing oral sex on somebody (*taboo*) **13.** ARTS REPRESENTATION OF HUMAN HEAD an artistic, photographic, or televised representation or image of a human being's face, hair, eyes, mouth, nose, and ears **14.** BOT TOP OF PLANT the top part of a plant where a flower or a cluster of leaves grows **15.** FROTH ON BEER the froth that forms on the top of beer when it is poured into a glass **16.** TOP OF PIMPLE the visible pus-filled center of a pimple or boil **17.** COINS OBVERSE OF COIN the side of a coin that shows a leader's head or other main design **18.** ELECTRONICS ELECTROMAGNETIC RECORDING DEVICE the part of a machine that records, reads, or erases sounds, images, or data, e.g., on a tape recorder or video cassette recorder (*often used in the plural*) **19.** TITLE a heading, e.g., a newspaper headline or a title before a section in a text **20.** MED same as **headache** (sense 1) (*informal*) ○ *I've got a terrible head.* **21.** USER OF ILLICIT DRUGS a habitual user of a drug (*slang; only in combination*) ○ *a cokehead* **22.** GEOG SOURCE OF RIVER the source of a river or stream, or the point at which a river or stream enters a lake **23.** GEOG PROMONTORY a headland that juts out into the sea or other stretch of water (*often used in place names*) **24.** GEOG TOP OF VALLEY the high end of a valley **25.** MUSIC PART OF DRUM the stretched membrane of a drum or tambourine **26.** PHYS REQUIRED HEIGHT OF LIQUID SURFACE the height that the surface of a liquid has to be above a specific level to produce a stated pressure at that level **27.** PHYS PRESSURE OF LIQUID the pressure at the lower of two points in a column of liquid resulting from the difference in height **28.** PHYS PRESSURE the pressure exerted by a liquid or gas ○ *a head of steam* **29.** NAUT SHIP'S TOILET a lavatory on a ship **30.** MIN EXTRACT PART OF COAL MINE a passage where coal is mined underground **31.** TRANSP TERMINAL the destination point of a transport route **32.** MECH ENG DEVICE FOR HOLDING CUTTING TOOLS a part of a boring or turning machine such as a lathe that holds cutting tools to the work in progress **33.** MECH ENG same as **cylinder head** **34.** REGATTA a regatta held on a river involving a series of races for rowing crews ○ *the head of the Charles* **35.** VICTOR IN REGATTA the winner of a regatta held on a river **36. heads** COINS POSITION OF COIN WITH HEAD UPWARD the head of a coin turned up after a toss ■ *adj* CHIEF IN RANK most important in rank ○ *the head gardener* ○ *I had a call from head office.* ■ *v* (**head·ed, head·ing, heads**) **1.** *vt* CONTROL OTHERS OR ORGANIZATION to be in the first position of authority and exercise control over people or an organization **2.** *vt* BE AT FRONT OF GROUP to be at the front or the top of something ○ *The mayor headed the parade as it entered the town.* **3.** *vi* GO IN PARTICULAR DIRECTION to move or go in a particular direction or to a particular position ○ *He headed toward the station.* **4.** *vt* CAUSE SOMETHING TO GO SOMEWHERE to make something move in a particular direction or to a particular place ○ *The pilot headed the plane on a northeasterly course.* **5.** *vt* BE OR GIVE HEADING FOR TEXT to act as or supply a heading on a written page ○ *Let's head the letter with our logo.* **6.** *vt* SOCCER HIT BALL WITH HEAD to use the head to hit a soccer ball ○ *He headed the ball into the goal.* [Old English *hēafod* < Indo-European] —**head·ed** *adj* ◇ **be above** *or* **over somebody's head** to be too difficult for somebody to understand ◇ **be head and shoulders above somebody** to be notably superior to somebody ◇ **be off your head** to be mentally or emotionally challenged or highly upset ◇ **give somebody his** *or* **her head** to relax control or supervision of somebody ◇ **go off your head** to become completely irrational (*informal*) ◇ **go over somebody's head** to bypass the usual person and address a request or complaint to a more important person in order to get what you want ○ *If he refuses to cooperate, I'll go over his head and speak to his superiors.* ◇ **go to somebody's head 1.** to make somebody conceited or overconfident **2.** to make somebody dizzy or lightheaded ○ *The high altitudes of the Rocky Mountains went right to my head.* ◇ **have your head in the clouds** to be completely unrealistic, overoptimistic, or engaged in daydreaming ◇ **head over heels 1.** completely ○ *They fell head over heels in love.* **2.** rolling or turning so that the feet are in the air and the head below them so as to land on the back or the feet ◇ **keep your head** to remain calm or unexcited ◇ **keep your head down** to avoid drawing attention to yourself at a time of danger or difficulty ◇ **knock something on the head** to put an end to something, or prevent it from developing any further (*informal*) ◇ **let somebody have his** *or* **her head** same as **give somebody his** *or* **her head** ◇ **lose your head** to panic or lose self-control ◇ **rear its ugly head** used to say that something unpleasant appears or happens

head off *v* **1.** *vt* INTERCEPT PERSON OR ANIMAL to stop a person or animal from proceeding in a particular direction by placing yourself between the person or animal and the goal sought ○ *Let's try to head the rustlers off at the pass.* ○ *We took a shortcut to head her off before she reached the station.* **2.** *vt* FORESTALL SOMETHING to try in advance to prevent something from taking place, or to prevent somebody from doing something, that might prove difficult or unpleasant ○ *We need to head off any attempt to have the matter raised again in committee.* **3.** *vi* GO to go off, or leave a place and go in a particular direction ○ *The others headed off down the hill while we stayed to enjoy the view a little longer.*

Head /hed/, **Edmund Walker, 8th Baronet** (1805–68) British-born Canadian administrator, who served as lieutenant governor of New Brunswick (1848–54), governor-general of British North America (1854–61), and governor of the Hudson's Bay Company (1863–68)

head·ache /héd àyk/ *n* **1.** a pain in the head lasting for some time caused by changes in pressure in the blood vessels leading to and from the brain **2.** something that causes worry or difficulty (*informal*) —**head·ach·y** *adj*

head bag, **head·bag** /héd bàg/ *n* **1.** a bag that is placed over the head in order to prevent somebody from being identified **2.** an air bag in an automobile designed to protect the head in the event of a collision

head·band /héd bànd/ *n* **1.** a band worn on or around the head to keep the hair in place or as decoration **2.** a band of usually absorbent material worn around the head across the forehead to absorb sweat and keep hair off the face

head·bang /héd bàng/ (**-banged, -bang·ing, -bangs**) *vi* to dance to heavy metal music by moving the head violently backward and forward to the beat of the music (*slang*)

head·bang·er /héd bàngər/ *n* somebody whose favorite music is heavy metal (*slang*)

head-bath *n S Asia* a bath that includes washing the hair

head·board /héd bàwrd/ *n* an upright board, often padded or covered in fabric, used to form the head of a bed

head boy *n UK* a boy in the senior years at a British school who has been elected to represent the school and to act as a role model for younger students

head-butt *vt* to hit somebody a deliberate hard blow with the forehead or the top of the head ■ *n* a deliberate blow with the forehead or the top of the head

head·cam /héd kàm/ *n* a video camera mounted on a person's head or on headgear

head·case /héd kàyss/ *n* an offensive term that deliberately shows contempt for or ridicules somebody's mental condition (*slang insult*)

head·cheese /héd cheez/ (*plural* **-chees·es** or *same*) *n* a mixture of chopped cooked meat, mainly from the head and feet of a hog, that is pressed into the form of a loaf or sausage and eaten cold [Because the ingredients are pressed together as in cheese-making]

REGIONAL NOTE The word ***headcheese*** prevails in all parts of the country except in the South Midland and Southern regions. In the South Midland, usual terms include *press meat, pressed meat, souse, souse meat, hog souse*, and *pressed souse meat.* The *souse* forms prevail across all of the South as well, except in the coastal regions. There, the terms *hoghead cheese* and *hog's head cheese* are mainly used.

head cold *n* a viral infection of the nose, throat, and bronchial tubes, characterized by sneezing, headaches, nasal congestion, and coughing

head count *n* the process of counting the people in a group one by one, or the number arrived at by this process ○ *After a head count, we found there were 265 people in the hall.*

head·dress /héd drèss/ *n* a decorative covering worn on the head, usually as a sign of rank, for ceremonial purposes, or as personal display

head·er /héddər/ *n* **1.** SOCCER **SHOT WITH HEAD** a deliberate use of the head to play, pass, or shoot the ball in soccer ○ *He scored with a flying header.* **2. HEADLONG FALL** a headlong plunge or fall **3.** COMPUT **HEADING FOR PAGE** a heading for each page of a word-processed or faxed document, usually automatically inserted and consisting of text or a page number **4.** COMPUT **PLACE FOR INFORMATION ABOUT MESSAGE** a place at the top of an e-mail for information about the message, including subject, sender, and receiver **5.** CONSTR **CROSSWISE BRICK** a brick or stone positioned crosswise in a wall and level with its outer surface **6.** MECH ENG, AUTOMOT **PIPE CONNECTING OTHER PIPES** a pipe that links other pipes to direct the flow of fluid to a system, especially an exhaust system **7.** ENG same as **header tank** **8.** INDUST **MAKER, FITTER, OR REMOVER OF TOPS** a person or machine that makes, fits, or removes the tops of something

head·er tank *n* a raised tank that ensures a constant pressure or supply of fluid to a system, especially water to a central heating system

head·fast /héd fàst/ *n* a mooring rope at the bow of a ship

head·first /hèd fúrst/, **head·fore·most** /hèd fáwr mōst/ *adv, adj* in a movement or position where the head is in front of the rest of the body and is the first thing that reaches, enters, or strikes something ○ *He insisted on going down the slide headfirst.* ○ *taking a headfirst dive into the pool* ■ *adv* abruptly and without taking time to think about or prepare for something ○ *They rush into things headfirst and think about the consequences afterward.*

head·fore·most *adv, adj* same as **headfirst**

head·frame /héd fràym/ *n* the framework at the top of a mineshaft that supports the pulleys for the winding mechanism

head·ful /héd fŏŏl/ *n* **1.** a large amount of something that has been learned, thought, or imagined (*informal*) ○ *a headful of facts* **2.** a thick mass of hair ○ *a headful of curls*

head game *n* the psychological aspect of a competitive endeavor, especially a sport

head gate *n* **1.** the gate that controls the flow of water into the upstream end of a canal lock **2.** CIV ENG same as **floodgate**

head·gear /héd gèer/ *n* **1.** CLOTHING **SOMETHING COVERING HEAD** something worn on the head, especially a hat ○ *wearing some pretty impressive headgear* **2.** MIN EXTRACT **HOISTING MECHANISM AT MINESHAFT** an apparatus at the top of a mineshaft for lifting things out of and lowering them into a mine **3.** RIDING **PART OF HARNESS** the part of a harness that fits over a horse's head

head girl *n UK* a girl in the senior years at a British school who has been elected to represent the school and to act as a role model for younger students

head·hunt /héd hùnt/ (**-hunt·ed, -hunt·ing, -hunts**) *v* **1.** *vt* BUSINESS **RECRUIT SOMEBODY FROM ANOTHER COMPANY** to recruit, or attempt to recruit, an executive or highly valued employee from one company to fill a similar position in another enterprise ○ *The agency headhunted her to work for an investment bank.* **2.** *vi* HR **ENGAGE IN EMPLOYEE RECRUITING** to engage in the profession of employee recruitment ○ *an agency that headhunts for engineers only* **3.** *vi* CULTL ANTHROP **COLLECT HEADS** to seek, collect, and preserve the heads of enemies as trophies or ceremonial objects —**head·hunt·er** *n* —**head·hunt·ing** *n*

head·ing /hédding/ *n* **1.** PRINTING **TITLE** something that forms the head, top, edge, or front of something, especially as a title for a paragraph, section, chapter, or page ○ *The chapter headings are to be set in 24-point bold.* **2. CATEGORY OF SUBJECT MATTER** a division into which the subject matter of a document, discourse, or discussion is divided ○ *That information definitely comes under the heading of matters not to be aired in public.* **3.** NAVIG **COURSE** the direction in which a ship or aircraft is traveling, often given as a compass bearing ○ *If we continue on our present heading we should sight land in one hour.* **4.** MIN EXTRACT **MINE TUNNEL** a horizontal tunnel in a mine, or the end of such a tunnel

head·lamp /héd làmp/ *n* AUTOMOT same as **headlight**

head·land /hédlənd, héd lànd/ *n* **1.** a narrow piece of land jutting out into water, usually with steep high cliffs **2.** a strip of land left unplowed at the edge of a field

head·less /hédləss/ *adj* **1.** having no head on the body **2.** having no leader, guide, or director —**head·less·ness** *n*

head·light /héd lìt/ *n* a powerful light attached to the front of a motor vehicle or a locomotive, or the beam of light cast by it ○ *He was driving without headlights.*

head·line /héd lìn/ *n* **1.** MEDIA **TITLE OF NEWSPAPER ARTICLE** a caption printed at the top of a page or article in a newspaper, usually in large heavy letters and often summarizing the content that follows it ○ *an article with the headline "Sharp Fall in Stock Prices"* **2.** PRINTING **LINE AT TOP OF PAGE** a line printed at the top of a page of a book or document giving the page number and sometimes other information such as the title or the author's name ■ **head·lines** *npl* MEDIA, BROADCAST **MAIN NEWS ITEMS** the most important items of news covered by a newspaper or a news broadcast ○ *Her name has seldom been out of the headlines since she announced her intention to sue.* ○ *We bring you the headlines every hour on the hour.* ■ *v* (**-lined, -lin·ing, -lines**) **1.** *vt* MEDIA **PROVIDE HEADING FOR TEXT** to give a prominent title or caption to something ○ *a story headlined "POP STAR ENTERS HOSPITAL"* **2.** *vt* **PUBLICIZE SOMEBODY AS STAR** to present somebody as the leading attraction of a show **3.** *vti* **APPEAR AS STAR** to appear as the leading attraction of a show

head·lin·er /héd lìnər/ *n* a performer who is advertised as a leading attraction in a show

head·lock /héd lòk/ *n* a hold in which a wrestler tightly grips an arm around an opponent's head

head·long /hèd láwng/ *adv, adj* **1. WITH HEAD FOREMOST** with the head in front of the rest of the body, especially in a rapid uncontrolled movement **2. MOVING FAST AND OUT OF CONTROL** moving or traveling in a fast uncontrolled way **3. WITH TOO MUCH HASTE** acting, happening, or done in an impetuous way with little or no thought for the consequences ○ *She had thrown herself headlong into an even worse situation.* [14C. < HEAD + -LING[2], altered by association with *-long* "foremost"]

head louse *n* a louse that lives on a human head among the hair, feeding by sucking blood and gluing its eggs to the hair shafts near the skin surface. Latin name: *Pediculus humanus capitis.*

head·man /héd màn/ (*plural* **-men** /-mèn/) *n* **1.** in some small-scale societies, a man who is the leader of a community or village **2.** a leader or overseer, e.g., of a group of workers

head·mas·ter /héd màstər/ *n* a man who is in charge of a private school

head·mis·tress /héd mìstrəss/ *n* a woman who is in charge of a private school

head mon·ey *n* a reward paid for the capture or killing of a fugitive or outlaw

head·most /héd mōst/ *adj* forward to the greatest extent (*archaic*)

head·note /héd nōt/ *n* a brief note at the top of a chapter or a page that summarizes what follows, especially points of law or a legal decision

head of·fice *n* **1.** the administrative center from which the affairs of an organization are directed ○ *Have you discussed it with head office?* **2.** the senior employees who direct the affairs of an organization ○ *Have you discussed it with head office?*

head of gov·ern·ment *n* the person in charge of a country's or state's government

head of pro·gram·ming *n UK* BROADCAST same as **program director**

head of state *n* the chief representative of a country or state, who may or may not also be the head of government

head-on *adv, adj* **WITH FRONT FACING FORWARD** with the front facing toward something ○ *We were sailing head-on into the teeth of the gale.* ○ *a head-on collision* ■ *adv* **WITHOUT EVASION OR COMPROMISE** making no attempt to avoid the dangers or difficulties involved in something ○ *addressed the controversy head-on* ■ *adj* **UNCOMPROMISING** involving direct, fundamental, and uncompromising opposition ○ *He tried to avoid a head-on clash with his business partner.*

head·per·son /héd pùrss'n/ *n* in some small-scale societies, the leader of a community or village

head·phones /héd fōnz/ *npl* a pair of listening devices joined by a band across the top of the head and worn in or over the ears

head·piece /héd pèess/ *n* **1.** CLOTHING **HEAD DECORATION** an ornamental accessory for the head ○ *The bride wore a headpiece adorned with crystals.* **2.** PRINTING **DESIGN AT TOP OF PAGE** an ornamental design printed at the beginning of a text **3.** RIDING **BRIDLE PART** the part of a horse's bridle that fits around the head

head pin *n* BOWLING, LEISURE same as **kingpin** (sense 3)

head·quar·ter /héd kwàwrtər/ (**-tered, -ter·ing, -ters**) *v* **1.** *vt* to provide somebody with a center of operations ○ *They headquartered their office in a former barracks.* **2.** *vi* to set up a headquarters ○ *She headquartered in Paris.*

head·quar·ters /héd kwàwrtərz/ *n* (*takes a singular or plural verb*) **1.** a military commander's central office, from which operations are controlled and orders issued ○ *Napoleon's headquarters were in a disused windmill.* ○ *Headquarters is on the radio, wanting to know our precise position.* **2.** the administrative center from which the affairs of an organization are directed

head·race /héd ràyss/ *n* a channel conveying water to a water wheel or turbine

head·rail /héd ràyl/ *n* **1.** the end of the table from which a game of billiards is started, nearest the balk line **2.** a railing on a sailing vessel extending from the rear of the bow to the back of the figurehead

head·reach /héd rèech/ *n* the distance that a sailboat makes to windward when tacking ■ *vt* (**-reached, -reach·ing, -reach·es**) to make a better distance than another boat when tacking

head reg·is·ter *n* the higher register or falsetto of men's and boys' singing voices in which tone production is concentrated in the head and assisted by sympathetic vibration of the nasal and skull cavities

head·rest /héd rèst/ *n* an often padded support for the head, usually on the back of a seat, especially in a motor vehicle

head re·straint *n* an adjustable headrest fitted to the back of a seat of a motor vehicle, designed to prevent neck injuries in an accident

head rhyme *n* LITERAT same as **alliteration**

head·room /héd rŏŏm, -rōōm/ *n* the space or clearance overhead, e.g., in a room, doorway, the interior of a motor vehicle, or the underside of a bridge ○ *There's plenty of headroom in this car, even in the back seat.*

head·sail /héd sàyl/ *n* a sail attached to or set forward of the foremost of a vessel

head·scarf /héd skaàrf/ (*plural* **-scarves** /-skaàrvz/) *n* a woman's scarf in the form of a square of fabric, for wearing on the head or around the neck

head sea *n* waves or a current running in a direction opposite to the course of a ship

head·set /héd sèt/ *n* a pair of earphones, often with a small mouthpiece attached to enable two-way communication

head·shak·ing /héd shàyking/ *n* a series of side-to-side movements of the head, communicating or suggesting something such as disagreement, doubt, or refusal ○ *I noticed a lot of headshaking in the audience as you made that claim.*

head·ship /héd shìp/ *n* **1.** somebody's position or authority as a leader **2.** *UK* a position as the principal of a school

head shop *n* a shop that specializes in selling articles associated with the use of drugs such as hashish and marijuana (*slang*)

head·shot /héd shòt/ *n* **1.** a photograph or cinematic shot of a head, especially a person's head **2.** a gunshot aimed to hit the head of a person or animal

head·shrink·er /héd shrìngkər/ *n* same as **psychiatrist** (*dated informal insult*)

heads·man /hédzmən/ (*plural* **-men** /-mən/) *n* a public executioner who beheaded prisoners condemned to death

head·square /héd skwèr/ *n UK* CLOTHING same as **headscarf**

head·stall /héd stàwl/ *n* RIDING same as **headpiece** (sense 3) [< STALL[1] "position, place"]

head·stand /héd stànd/ *n* a position in gymnastics or yoga in which the body is balanced upside down on the head, usually using the hands for support

head start *n* an advantage in a competition or endeavor ○ *A good education gives you a head start when it comes to getting a job.*

head·stock /héd stòk/ *n* an assembly or part of a machine, especially in a lathe, that holds and supports a revolving part

head·stone /héd stōn/ *n* **1.** a slab of stone placed at the head of a grave as a memorial to the person or people buried there **2.** *also* **head stone** ARCHIT same as **keystone** (sense 1)

head·stream /héd streem/ *n* a stream that is the source, or one of the sources, of a river

head·strong /héd stròng/ *adj* self-willed and determined not to follow orders or advice —**head·strong·ly** *adv* —**head·strong·ness** *n*

heads up *interj* a command to watch out, especially for danger from overhead such as a falling object or a ball coming through the air

heads-up *n* **1.** WARNING an early warning to somebody that something, typically something undesirable, is soon to happen ○ *gave the law firm a heads-up on the impending subpoena* **2.** SOMETHING REQUIRING ATTENTION something that requires alert attention ■ *adj* ALERT AND RESOURCEFUL showing quick resourcefulness and alertness in doing or observing something

heads-up dis·play *n* **1.** a display of instrument data projected onto a screen at eye level so that a pilot or driver does not have to look down to see it **2.** in computer games, a display of meters, dials, and other indicators around the margins of the screen

head teach·er *n UK* a teacher who is in charge of a school, supervising teaching staff and overseeing day-to-day operations

head-tie *n Carib* a piece of cloth, usually square, that is wrapped and tied around the top of a woman's head, covering the hair

head-to-head *adv, adj* WITH DIRECT ENCOUNTER in or involving direct contact or confrontation ■ *adv* WITH HEADS ADJACENT placed or arranged with heads adjacent ○ *We put the beds head-to-head.* ■ *n* DIRECT ENCOUNTER a direct and immediate encounter

head trip *n* (*dated slang*) **1.** an experience that stimulates or excites somebody mentally **2.** something done or a way of behaving that is intended mainly for personal gratification

head-up dis·play *n UK* COMPUT GAMES same as **heads-up display**

head voice *n* MUSIC same as **head register**

head·wait·er /héd wàytər/ *n* the person in charge of a group of servers at a restaurant, often also responsible for taking reservations and seating customers ○ *She has been headwaiter at the club for five years.*

head wall *n* a cliff forming one end of a valley

head·wa·ters /héd wàwtərz/ *npl* the streams that make up the beginnings of a river

head·way /héd wày/ *n* **1.** PROGRESS progress toward achieving something ○ *We're unable to make much headway with the project.* **2.** FORWARD MOVEMENT movement or rate of progress forward **3.** CONSTR same as **headroom** **4.** TRANSP DIFFERENCE IN TIME OR DISTANCE the interval or distance between two vehicles, trains, or ships traveling in the same direction along the same route ◇ **make headway** to make progress in doing something or going somewhere

head·wind /héd wìnd/ *n* a wind blowing against the direction of travel

head·wo·man /héd wòommən/ (*plural* **-wo·men** /-wìmmin/) *n* in some small-scale societies, a woman who is the leader of a community or village

head·word /héd wùrd/ *n* a word or phrase that forms a heading at the start of a text and is usually printed in distinctive type, especially a main entry word in a dictionary

head·work /héd wùrk/ *n* **1.** mental activity or effort **2.** decoration on the keystone of an arch

head·y /héddee/ (**-i·er, -i·est**) *adj* **1.** EXHILARATING causing or involving a feeling of energy, confidence, and elation **2.** INTOXICATING causing a feeling of light-headedness or intoxication **3.** IMPETUOUS impulsive and rash in behavior —**head·i·ly** *adv* —**head·i·ness** *n*

heal /heel/ (**healed, heal·ing, heals**) *v* **1.** *vt* CURE SOMEBODY OR SOMETHING FROM AILMENT to restore a person, body part, or injury to health **2.** *vi* BE REPAIRED NATURALLY to be repaired and restored naturally, e.g., by the formation of scar tissue ○ *The broken bone seems to be healing quite nicely.* **3.** *vt* PUT SOMETHING RIGHT to repair or rectify something that causes discord and animosity ○ *Unless she can heal the rift within her party, she stands little chance in the election.* **4.** *vti* RECOVER SPIRITUALLY OR EMOTIONALLY to get rid of a wrong, evil, or painful affliction ○ *After losing his business, he's taken a while to heal.* [Old English *hǣlan* < Germanic] —**heal·a·ble** *adj*

SPELLCHECK heal or **heel**? Do not confuse the spelling of ***heal*** and ***heel***, which sound similar. ***Heal*** is only used as a verb, meaning "restore or be restored to health" or "put right": *His wounds have healed. Nothing could heal the rift between them.* ***Heel*** is chiefly used as a noun, denoting the back part of a foot, shoe, or sock (as in *her Achilles heel, head over heels in love, boots with high heels*) or the end part of something such as a loaf of bread or a violin bow. ***Heel*** is also used as a derogatory term, as a verb meaning "repair or replace the heel of" or "strike with the heel," and in the adjective compound *well-heeled.*

heal-all *n* PLANTS same as **selfheal**

heal·er /heélər/ *n* somebody who cures or treats illnesses or injuries

Hea·ley /heélee/, **Denis, Baron Healey of Riddlesden** (*b.* 1917) British politician. A Labour member of parliament from 1952, he was Chancellor of the Exchequer (1974–79) and deputy leader of the Labour Party (1980–83). Full name **Healey, Denis Winston**

heal·ing /heéling/ *n* the process of curing somebody or something or of becoming well ○ *spiritual healing* ■ *adj* having the effect of curing or improving something ○ *healing lotions*

health /helth/ *n* **1.** GENERAL PHYSICAL CONDITION the general condition of the body or mind, especially in terms of the presence or absence of illnesses, injuries, or impairments **2.** OVERALL CONDITION OF SOMETHING the general condition of something in terms of soundness, vitality, and proper functioning ○ *There is concern about the financial health of the company.* **3.** DRINKING TOAST a toast drunk to wish for somebody's well-being and prosperity ○ *He drank a health to all his guests.* ■ *adj* **1.** DEVOTED TO GENERAL WELL-BEING having the function of maintaining physical and mental well-being among the general public and the administration of medical and related services **2.** GOOD FOR PEOPLE promoting physical and mental well-being [Old English *hǣlþ* < Germanic] ◇ **drink somebody's health** to drink a toast to somebody

Health Can·a·da *n* the Canadian government department that is responsible for protecting the health and safety of the people of Canada

health·care /hélth kèr/ *n* the provision of medical and related services aimed at maintaining good health, especially through the prevention and treatment of disease —**health·care** *adj*

health·care as·sis·tant *n UK* same as **nurse's aide**

health cen·ter *n* a place that houses a medical practice and offers healthcare services

health club *n* a private club that offers fitness and leisure facilities such as a gym and a swimming pool

health farm *n* same as **health spa**

health food *n* food that is considered to be more beneficial to health than ordinary food, especially products that are organically grown or without chemical additives

health·ful /hélthfəl/ *adj* beneficial to physical or mental health —**health·ful·ly** *adv* —**health·ful·ness** *n*

USAGE See *healthy.*

health in·sur·ance *n* insurance to cover the costs or losses incurred if an insured person falls ill

health main·te·nance or·gan·i·za·tion *n* HEALTH SERVICES full form of **HMO**

health pack *n* **1.** a dietary supplement consisting of a combination of ingredients, with supposed benefits for a specific aspect of health **2.** in computer games, an object that restores a number of points lost, thus postponing the death of a character in the game

health spa *n* **1.** a commercial establishment similar to a hotel, usually rural, that offers ways of improving health and fitness such as a controlled diet, exercise, and massage **2.** a commercial establishment without accommodation that offers facilities for health and fitness

health tour·ism *n* the practice of visiting other countries specifically to benefit from the medical services available there, often because they are cheaper than at home —**health tour·ist** *n*

health vis·i·tor *n UK* a trained nurse who gives medical care and advice to people in their homes, especially to mothers of babies and young children, senior citizens, and physically challenged people

health·y /hélthee/ (**-i·er, -i·est**) *adj* **1.** IN GOOD CONDITION in good physical or mental condition **2.** BENEFICIAL TO HEALTH helping to maintain or bring about good health ○ *a healthy diet* **3.** SUGGESTIVE OF GOOD HEALTH showing that somebody is in good health **4.** PSYCHOLOGICALLY SOUND showing or encouraging moral or psychological soundness **5.** FUNCTIONING WELL in a prosperous and efficient condition ○ *a healthy economy* **6.** BIG large, usually satisfyingly large, in size or quantity (*informal*) ○ *a healthy dose of skepticism* —**health·i·ly** *adv* —**health·i·ness** *n*

USAGE healthy or **healthful**? It is sometimes argued that ***healthy*** should be used only to describe a living being in good health, and that ***healthful*** is the word for such things as habits or foods promoting good health. There is nothing wrong with observing this distinction, but there is also nothing wrong with using ***healthy*** as a synonym for ***healthful***, as reputable writers have been doing for centuries. Indeed, this usage received federal sanction in 1995, when the US Department of Agriculture and the Food and Drug Administration issued regulations governing the ways ***healthy*** may be used on labels to describe food products.

Hea·ney /heénee/, **Seamus** (*b.* 1939) Irish poet. His poems explore his native Northern Irish culture and language, although he has lived primarily in the Republic of Ireland since 1972. One of the leading English-language poets of his generation, he won a Nobel Prize in literature (1995). Full name **Heaney, Seamus Justin**

"Rained-on, flower-laden / Coffin after coffin / Seemed to float from the door / Of the packed cathedral/Like blossoms on slow water."
[Seamus Heaney, "Casualty," *Field Work*; 1979]

heap /heep/ *n* **1.** ROUNDED PILE a large number of things lying on top of one another, or a large quantity of material, forming a roughly rounded shape ○ *They'd left all their dirty clothes in a heap on the floor.* **2.** LARGE AMOUNT a large quantity or amount (*informal*) ○ *I've got a heap of things to see to before I can go home.* **3.** SOMETHING OLD OR RUNDOWN something that is old, rundown, or messy, especially an old building or car (*slang*) ■ *vt* **(heaped, heap·ing, heaps) 1.** PUT THINGS IN PILE to collect or arrange something into a loose pile ○ *heaping the stuff all together in the middle of the yard* **2.** FILL SOMETHING UP to load or fill a shallow container, forming a roughly rounded mound **3.** GIVE SOMETHING IN ABUNDANCE to supply something in large quantities or amounts ○ *They heaped scorn on my suggestion.* [Old English *hēap* < Germanic]
heap up *v* **1.** *vti* to accumulate something, or be gathered, into a roughly rounded mound **2.** *vt* to collect or acquire something in large amounts

heap·ing /heéping/ *adj* in sufficient quantity to rise above the rim of a shallow container, especially a spoon or plate, in a small heap

heaps /heeps/ *adv UK* very much or greatly (*informal*) ○ *I feel heaps better since I went to the doctor.*

hear /heer/ **(heard, heard** /hurd/, **hear·ing, hears)** *v* **1.** *vti* PERCEIVE SOUNDS to perceive or be able to perceive sound **2.** *vti* GET TO KNOW SOMETHING to be informed of something, especially by being told about it **3.** *vt* LISTEN TO SOMETHING to listen to somebody or something ○ *I've heard him on the radio.* **4.** *vti* UNDERSTAND to understand fully by listening attentively ○ *Did you hear what I just said?* ○ *I won't stand for it, do you hear?* **5.** *vt* LAW PRESIDE OVER SOMETHING to consider something officially as a judge, commissioner, or member of a jury **6.** *vt* CHR ATTEND MASS to attend Mass in a Roman Catholic church [Old English *hīeran* < Germanic] —**hear·a·ble** *adj* —**hear·er** *n* ◇ **hear, hear** used as an exclamation to show great approval

SPELLCHECK hear or **here**? Do not confuse the spelling of ***hear*** and ***here***, which sound similar. ***Hear*** is a verb meaning "perceive a sound," "listen," or "be informed": *Did you hear that noise? She nodded in agreement and said, "Hear, hear!" I hear they're getting married.* ***Here*** is an adverb meaning "in this place": *Come here! Here you are!*

hear from *vt* to receive a communication such as a letter or telephone call from a person, place, or organization
hear of *vt* to consider something as a possibility ○ *She wouldn't hear of their paying their own way.*
hear out *vt* to continue listening until somebody or something has finished

heard past participle, past tense of **hear**

SPELLCHECK heard or **herd**? Do not confuse the spelling of ***heard*** and ***herd***, which sound similar. ***Heard*** is the past tense of the verb *hear*: *A scream was heard. I've never heard of him.* ***Herd*** is a noun or verb referring to a large group of animals or people: *The road was blocked by a herd of cattle. We were herded into the room.*

Heard and Mc·Do·nald Is·lands /hùrd ənd mək dónn'ld-/ dependency of Australia consisting of four small uninhabited islands in the southern Indian Ocean. Area: 159 sq. mi./412 sq. km. Official name **Territory of Heard Island and McDonald Islands**

hear·ing /heéring/ *n* **1.** AWARENESS OF SOUND the perception of sound, made possible by vibratory changes in air pressure on the ear drums ○ *My hearing's going, so you'll have to speak louder.* **2.** EARSHOT the range within which something can be heard ○ *She moved out of hearing and I lost the end of the sentence.* **3.** CHANCE TO BE HEARD an opportunity to be heard, especially a chance to state an opinion or fact ○ *All I want is for my views to get a fair hearing.* **4.** LAW TRIAL the trial of a case in a court of law **5.** LAW PRELIMINARY EXAMINATION OF ACCUSED a preliminary judicial examination of an accused person to decide whether the case should proceed to trial **6.** LAW SESSION TO HEAR EVIDENCE a session of an investigative or legislative body at which witnesses are heard ◇ **hard of hearing** unable to hear well

hear·ing aid *n* a small amplifying device to enable somebody to hear better, usually worn in or behind the ear

hear·ing-and-speech-im·paired *adj* unable to speak or hear

hear·ing dog *n* a dog trained to help a hearing-impaired person by indicating that it has heard a sound such as the ringing of a telephone or doorbell

hear·ing-im·paired *adj* having a reduced or deficient ability to hear

USAGE See *deaf*.

hear·ing loss *n* a measurable reduction of the ability to hear or distinguish sounds, especially of a specific frequency

hear·ken /haárkən/ **(-kened, -ken·ing, -kens), har·ken** *vi* to listen and pay attention (*archaic*) [Old English *he(o)rcnian* < HARK] —**hear·ken·er** *n*

Hearn /hurn/, **Lafcadio** (1850–1904) Japanese writer and teacher of Irish-Greek descent. A translator and journalist, he moved to Japan in 1890, became a Japanese citizen, and wrote a stream of books that introduced Japanese culture and literature to the West. Full name **Hearn, Patricio Lafcadio Tessima Carlos**. Japanese name **Koizumi, Yakumo**

Hearne /hurn/, **Samuel** (1745–92) British explorer. Working for the Hudson's Bay Company, he was the first European to travel overland to the North American coast on the Arctic Ocean (1770–72).

hear·say /heér sày/ *n* information that is heard from other people —**hear·say** *adj*

hear·say ev·i·dence *n* evidence consisting of testimony about other people that is not based on direct or personal knowledge. Hearsay evidence is not usually admissible in a court of law.

hearse /hurss/ *n* a vehicle in which a coffin is carried to a funeral or a dead person is transported to a funeral home immediately after death [13C. Via French *herse* < Latin *hirpex* "rake, harrow"]

ORIGIN Agricultural harrows in the Middle Ages were typically toothed triangular frames, so the word for a harrow came to be applied in French to a similar frame for holding candles, particularly those placed over a coffin at funeral services. This was the meaning of ***hearse*** when English acquired it, and its meaning gradually developed from "canopy placed over a coffin" and "coffin, bier" to the modern sense of "funeral vehicle."

Hearst /hurst/, **William Randolph** (1863–1951) US publisher and politician. He built up a vast national newspaper and media empire, and after 1927 lived in seclusion at his Californian castle, San Simeon. Orson Welles's movie *Citizen Kane* (1941) is based on his career.

"A politician will do anything to keep his job—even become a patriot."
[William Randolph Hearst, *Syndicated editorial*; August 28, 1933]

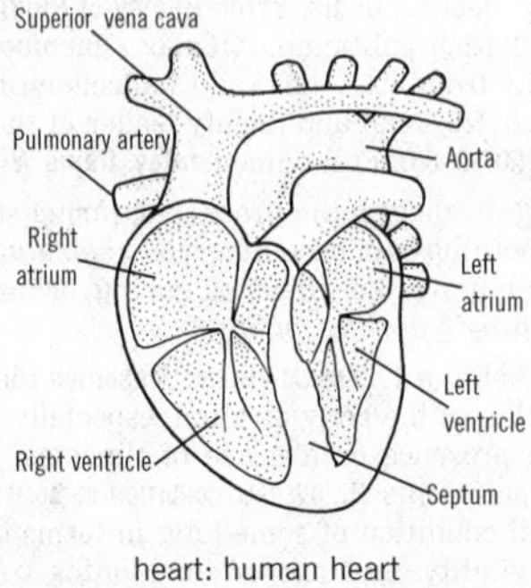

heart: human heart

heart /haart/ *n* **1.** BLOOD-PUMPING ORGAN a hollow muscular organ that pumps blood around the body, in humans situated in the center of the chest with its apex directed to the left **2.** LEFT SIDE OF CHEST the area on the front of the human body that corresponds roughly to the position of the heart **3.** BASIS OF EMOTIONAL LIFE the source and center of emotional life, where the deepest and sincerest feelings are located and a person is most vulnerable to pain **4.** CHARACTER somebody's essential character ○ *He's an abrupt-sounding cuss, but he's got a very good heart.* **5.** COMPASSION the ability to feel humane and altruistic feelings ○ *If she had any heart she would forgive him.* **6.** AFFECTION affection, love, or warm admiration ○ *The chorus's singing won the hearts of the audience.* **7.** SPIRIT the capacity for courage and determination ○ *She put her whole heart into making a go of the business.* **8.** DISPOSITION a mood, mental state, or frame of mind ○ *took the remark in good heart* **9.** DEPICTION OF HEART a simplified and conventionalized picture of a heart as a rounded, roughly triangular shape, often used to signify love **10.** CENTRAL PART the distinctive, significant, and characteristic center of something ○ *the heart of rural America* **11.** CENTRAL PART OF LEAFY VEGETABLE the compact central part of a vegetable such as lettuce, cabbage, or celery, where the leaves or stalks curl in tightly **12.** ANIMAL HEART USED AS FOOD the heart of an animal that is cleaned and trimmed, then cooked as food **13.** BELOVED PERSON somebody who is intensely loved ○ *Come to me, dear heart.* **14.** CARDS CARD WITH HEART-SHAPED SYMBOL a playing card of the suit of hearts [Old English *heorte* < Indo-European] —**heart·ed** *adj* ◇ **a man** *or* **woman after your own heart** somebody with tastes, interests, or opinions that are similar to your own ◇ **at heart** in essence or reality, and despite contrary appearances ◇ **break somebody's heart** to cause somebody intense unhappiness and suffering ◇ **do somebody's heart good** to make somebody feel happy or satisfied ◇ **eat your heart out** (*informal*) **1.** to brood about something that makes you feel unhappy **2.** to be consumed with envy ◇ **have somebody's welfare** *or* **interests at heart** to have somebody's well-being or interests in mind ◇ **heart and soul** completely, or with the greatest devotion ◇ **in your heart of hearts** in your deepest inner feelings ◇ **learn** *or* **know something by heart** to memorize *or* have memorized something ◇ **lose heart** to become discouraged ◇ **not have the heart to do something** to be unable to bring yourself to do something that is liable to hurt somebody else ◇ **set your heart on something, have your heart set on something** to have something as your ambition or greatest wish ◇ **somebody's heart is in his** *or* **her mouth** somebody is very afraid or apprehensive, usually at a moment of great danger or uncertainty ○ *My heart was in my mouth as I opened the envelope.* ◇ **somebody's heart is in the right place** somebody is kind or well-intentioned, often contrary to appearances ○ *Her brusque manner can be somewhat disturbing, but her heart is in the right place.* ◇ **take heart** to become encouraged and more confident ◇ **take something to heart 1.** to take something seriously **2.** to be upset by something ◇ **wear your heart on your sleeve** to reveal your feelings openly ◇ **with all your heart 1.** completely **2.** sincerely

CULTURAL NOTE ***Heart of Darkness***, a novel (1902) by British writer Joseph Conrad. Based on Conrad's own experience in the Congo, it tells the story of Marlow, a young English steamboat captain who travels upriver deeper and deeper into the African jungle. He despises the European traders for their exploitation of Black Africans, who are themselves brutal, but when Marlow comes upon the mysterious Kurtz, an evil, charismatic white man ruling over an inland territory like a god, the young man is fascinated as well as repelled. *Heart of Darkness* was the inspiration for Francis Ford Coppola's 1979 movie *Apocalypse Now*.

ORIGIN The Indo-European word from which ***heart*** is derived is also the source of English *accord, cardiac, concord, cordial, courage, discord, quarry*[2], and *record*.

heart·ache /haárt àyk/ *n* a powerful feeling of sorrow, anguish, or regret

heart at·tack *n* **1.** a sudden, serious, painful, and sometimes fatal interruption of the heart's normal functioning, especially due to a blockage in the coronary artery **2.** a sudden severe shock (*informal*) ○ *I had a heart attack when I looked in the drawer and saw that the money was gone.*

heart·beat /haárt beet/ *n* **1. CONTRACTION OF HEART MUSCLE** a single contraction of the lower chambers of the heart that drives blood through the body **2. CONTINUOUS PULSATION OF HEART** the continuous pulsating movement and sound made by a beating heart **3. DRIVING FORCE** the driving force behind something ○ *Caucus discussion is the party's heartbeat.*

heart block *n* a condition in which the nerve impulses that control the heartbeat are irregular so that the ventricles and the atria no longer beat in time with one another

heart·break /haárt bràyk/ *n* intense unhappiness or grief

heart·break·er /haárt bràykər/ *n* somebody or something that creates intense unhappiness, especially somebody with whom people fall in love and by whom they are later hurt

heart·break·ing /haárt bràyking/ *adj* causing intense sadness or distress —**heart·break·ing·ly** *adv*

heart·bro·ken /haárt brṓkən/ *adj* intensely unhappy or disappointed because of something that has happened ○ *The children were heartbroken when we had to cancel the trip.* —**heart·bro·ken·ly** *adv* —**heart·bro·ken·ness** *n*

heart·burn /haárt bùrn/ *n* an uncomfortable burning sensation in the lower chest, usually caused by stomach acid flowing back into the lower end of the esophagus [< HEART in the obsolete sense "stomach"]

heart dis·ease *n* any medical condition of the heart or the blood vessels supplying it that impairs cardiac functioning

heart·en /haárt'n/ (**-ened, -en·ing, -ens**) *vt* to make somebody feel more cheerful and hopeful [< HEART in the obsolete sense "encourage"] —**heart·en·ing** *adj*

heart fail·ure *n* **1.** cessation of the normal functioning of the heart, leading to death **2.** a condition in which the heart cannot pump blood in sufficient volume to meet the needs of the body, causing breathlessness, enlargement of the liver, swollen ankles, and other symptoms

heart·felt /haárt fèlt/ *adj* arising from strong and sincere emotion

Heart·field /haárt feeld/, **John** (1891–1968) German painter and graphic artist. A leading member of the Dada movement after World War I, he pioneered the technique of photomontage. Many of his works such as *German Acorns* (1933) satirize Hitler, Nazism, or the Weimar Republic. Born **Herzfeld, Helmut**

hearth /haarth/ *n* **1. FLOOR OF FIREPLACE** the floor of a fireplace, especially when it extends into the room **2. HOME LIFE** the fireplace of a home, thought of as a symbol of the home and the life of the family who live in it **3.** METALL **PART OF FOUNDRY FURNACE** the lowest part of a foundry furnace where molten metal collects or ore is smelted [Old English *heorþ* < Germanic]

hearth·rug /haárth rùg/ *n* a rug for the floor in front of a fireplace

hearth·side /haárth sīd/ *n* same as **fireside**

hearth·stone /haárth stṓn/ *n* **1.** a large stone used to form the hearth in a fireplace **2.** a soft variety of stone or a compound of pipe clay and stone used to clean and whiten fireplaces and doorsteps

heart·i·ly /haártilee/ *adv* **1. ENTHUSIASTICALLY** in a sincere and enthusiastic way **2. GOOD-NATUREDLY** in a loud, vigorous, good-natured way **3. COMPLETELY** in a full and complete way **4. HUNGRILY** with a good appetite

heart·land /haárt lànd/ *n* a central area of a country or region that has special economic, political, military, or sentimental significance

heart·leaf /haárt leef/ *n* PLANTS same as **wild ginger** [< the heart-shaped leaves]

heart·less /haártləss/ *adj* having or showing no pity or kindness —**heart·less·ly** *adv* —**heart·less·ness** *n*

heart-lung ma·chine *n* a machine that is used to take over the functions of the heart and lungs in pumping and oxygenating the blood, chiefly during heart surgery

heart mas·sage *n* MED same as **cardiac compression**

heart mur·mur *n* an unusual sound coming from the heart that can be detected by a stethoscope and may indicate the presence of a heart disorder

Heart of Dix·ie *n* a nickname for Alabama

heart of palm *n* the terminal bud of the cabbage palm, cooked and served as a vegetable or in salads

heart rate *n* the number of heartbeats occurring within a specific length of time

heart·rend·ing /haárt rènding/ *adj* causing intense sadness or distress, especially in sympathy with somebody else's unhappiness or hardship —**heart·rend·ing·ly** *adv*

SYNONYMS See *moving.*

hearts /haarts/ *n* **1.** one of the four suits used in cards, with a red heart shape as its symbol (*takes a singular or plural verb*) **2.** a card game in which players try either to avoid winning cards of the suit hearts and the queen of spades or to win all of these (*takes a singular verb*)

heart-search·ing /haárt sùrching/ *n* a thorough and often distressing self-examination of feelings and motives

hearts·ease /haárts eez/ (*plural* **-eas·es** or *same*) *n* a pansy, especially a wild pansy. Latin name: *Viola tricolor.*

heart·sick /haárt sìk/ *adj* deeply disappointed or sad (*literary*) —**heart·sick·ness** *n*

heart smart *adj* describes food that is low in fat and cholesterol and therefore reduces the risk of heart disease (*informal*)

heart·sore /haárt sàwr/ *adj* extremely sad or regretful (*archaic or literary*)

heart-stop·ping *adj* extremely frightening, unnerving, or exhilarating

heart·strings /haárt strìngz/ *npl* somebody's feelings, especially tender emotions ○ *a doleful expression that tugged at my heartstrings* [< STRING "tendon," from the earlier belief that tendons brace the heart]

heart·throb /haárt thròb/ *n* an extraordinarily attractive person, especially a young movie star or singer (*informal*)

heart-to-heart *n* a frank, intimate conversation ○ *had a heart-to-heart about their feelings for each other* —**heart-to-heart** *adj*

heart·warm·ing /haárt wàwrming/ *adj* inspiring warm or kindly feelings, usually by showing life and human nature in a positive and reassuring light —**heart·warm·ing·ly** *adv*

SYNONYMS See *moving.*

heart·wood /haárt wòod/ *n* the wood at the center of a tree trunk or branch that is older, darker, and harder than the wood surrounding it

heart·worm /haárt wùrm/ (*plural* **-worms** or *same*) *n* **1.** a parasitic filarial worm that lives in the heart and associated blood vessels of members of the dog family, and occasionally in cats and seals **2.** an infection of the heart in members of the dog family, and occasionally in cats and seals, that is caused by parasitic worms

heart·y /haártee/ (**-i·er, -i·est**) *adj* **1. SINCERE AND ENTHUSIASTIC** sincere and expressed in a cheerful, enthusiastic way **2. LOUD AND ENTHUSIASTIC** done in an unrestrainedly loud, vigorous, but usually good-humored way **3. HEALTHY** showing physical health, strength, and vigor **4. STRONGLY FELT** sincerely and strongly felt **5. SUBSTANTIAL AND NOURISHING** substantial and giving considerable satisfaction and nourishment ○ *a hearty breakfast* **6.** *UK* **EXCESSIVELY LOUD AND ENTHUSIASTIC** annoyingly loud or boisterous, especially about sports or outdoor activities (*informal*) —**heart·i·ness** *n*

heat /heet/ *n* **1. ENERGY PERCEIVED AS TEMPERATURE** a form of transferred energy that arises from the random motion of molecules and is felt as temperature, especially as warmth or hotness. Heat is transmitted by conduction, convection, or radiation. Symbol **Q 2. DEGREE OF HOTNESS** the perceptible or measurable degree of hotness ○ *The heat in that kitchen is absolutely unbearable.* ○ *At what heat do I cook this?* **3. SOURCE OF HIGHER TEMPERATURE** a source of warmth, e.g., for cooking something or keeping a building warm ○ *The heat turns off automatically when the room reaches a certain temperature.* **4. INTENSE EMOTION** emotional intensity, especially in the form of anger or excitement ○ *I replied with some heat that my conscience was perfectly clear.* **5. TIME OF MOST ACTIVITY** the period or phase of something at which activity and excitement is at its most intense ○ *During the heat of the campaign, many rash promises were made.* **6. MENTAL PRESSURE** psychological pressure on a person or group, especially to produce or achieve something (*informal*) ○ *We're beginning to feel the heat as the deadline gets closer and closer.* **7. CRITICISM** harsh criticism or reproach (*slang*) ○ *What's your problem? Can't you take the heat?* **8.** FOOD **SPICY HOTNESS** the hot or burning sensation produced in the mouth by spicy foods **9.** ZOOL **SEXUALLY RECEPTIVE STAGE** a time during a female mammal's reproductive cycle when she is fertile and ready to mate **10.** SPORTS **PRELIMINARY ROUND** one of several preliminary rounds before a race or contest, especially one in which competitors are eliminated, or one that determines players' starting order for the main event **11.** POLICE **INTENSE POLICE ACTIVITY** intensive police activity carried out in order to catch criminal suspects (*slang*) **12.** POLICE **POLICE** the police (*slang*) ■ *vti* (**heat·ed, heat·ing, heats**) **RAISE TEMPERATURE** to become or make something warm or hot [Old English *hǣtu* < Germanic, "hot"] —**heat·less** *adj* ◇ **in the heat of the moment** during a brief period of anger, enthusiasm, or other strong emotion, and usually without thinking ○ *remarks made in the heat of the moment and later regretted* ◇ **turn on** *or* **up the heat (on somebody)** to apply increased pressure on somebody (*slang*)

heat up *vti* **1.** to make something hotter, or become hotter **2.** to become or make something more intense, exciting, or excited

heat bal·ance *n* INDUST same as **energy balance**

heat bar·ri·er *n* SCI same as **thermal barrier**

heat ca·pac·i·ty *n* the quantity of heat required to raise the temperature of one mole or gram of a substance by one degree Celsius. Symbol *C*

heat death *n* a condition of a closed system in which energy is uniformly distributed throughout it, with none available for use. The universe might ultimately suffer heat death if it is a closed system.

heat·ed /heetəd/ *adj* **1.** made warm by artificially generated heat **2.** showing emotional intensity or anger ○ *a heated argument* —**heat·ed·ly** *adv* —**heat·ed·ness** *n*

heat en·gine *n* a machine that transforms heat into mechanical power, e.g., a steam or gasoline engine

heat·er /heetər/ *n* **1. HEATING DEVICE** a device that uses fuel to produce heat in order to make something else warm or hot, especially a device to heat the air in a room or vehicle **2. HEATING ELEMENT IN VACUUM TUBE** an element in a vacuum tube that carries the current for heating a cathode **3. HANDGUN** a revolver or other handgun (*slang dated*)

heat ex·chang·er *n* a device that transfers heat from one medium to another, usually by conduction through a solid barrier, e.g., a car radiator transferring heat from water to air

heat ex·haus·tion *n* a condition of physical weakness or collapse often accompanied by nausea, muscle cramps, and dizziness, that is caused by exposure to intense heat

heath /heeth/ (*plural* **heaths** or *same*) *n* **1.** GEOG **SHRUBBY UNCULTIVATED LAND** a tract of uncultivated, open land with infertile, often sandy soil covered with rough grasses and small bushes or heather **2.** PLANTS **LOW BUSH** a plant of a family that includes heather and some other low-growing evergreen bushes, commonly found on heaths. Genera: *Erica* or *Calluna.* **3.** INSECTS **BROWN BUTTERFLY** a butterfly with coppery-brown wings. Genus: *Coenonympha.* [Old English *hǣþ* < Germanic, "unplowed land"]

Heath /heeth/, **Ted** (*b.* 1916) prime minister of Great Britain (1970–74). A Conservative member of parliament from 1950, he was prime minister during a period of industrial unrest and Britain's accession to the European Economic Community. Full name **Heath, Sir Edward Richard George**. See table at **prime minister**

"We may be a small island, but we are not a small people."
[Ted Heath, *Observer (London)*; June 21, 1970]

hea·then /heéthən/ (*plural* **-thens** or *same*) *n* **1.** an offensive term that deliberately insults somebody who does not acknowledge the God of the Bible, Torah, or Koran **2.** an offensive term that deliberately insults somebody's way of life, degree of knowledge, or nonbelief in religion [Old English *hǣþen* < Germanic, "heath"] —**hea·then** *adj*—**hea·then·ish** *adj*—**hea·then·ish·ly** *adv* —**hea·then·ize** *vti*

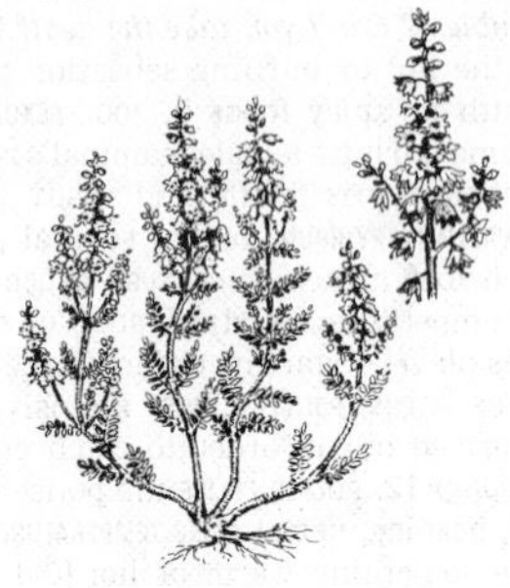

heather

heath·er /héthər/ *n* **1.** a low-growing evergreen plant with spiky leaves that grows in clusters. Flowers: small purple, pink, or white, bell-shaped. Native to: heaths and mountainsides in Europe and Asia. Latin name: *Calluna vulgaris*. **2.** a purple color tinged with pink and blue [14C. Origin ?] —**heath·er** *adj* —**heath·er·y** *adj*

heath·er grass *n* a perennial grass with flat hairless leaves. Native to: Europe. Latin name: *Sieglingia decumbens*. [Because it grows in the same places as heather]

Heath Rob·in·son /heeth rάwbənsʼn/ *adj UK* CONSTR same as **Rube Goldberg** (*humorous*) [Early 20C. After W. *Heath Robinson* (1872–1944), British humorous artist]

Heath·row /heéth rō/ largest and busiest airport serving London, England, situated on the western outskirts of the capital

heat·ing /heéting/ *n* **1.** the operation of warming something such as food, a room, or the interior of a building **2.** *UK* the equipment that produces heat to warm something, e.g., a central heating system ○ *The heating doesn't come on again until six o'clock in the evening.*

heat·ing el·e·ment *n* an insulated or covered wire whose high resistance to an electrical current causes its temperature to rise, providing heat to surrounding materials such as an electric blanket

heat·ing pad *n* a fabric-covered pad that contains an electric heating element and is used to apply heat to various parts of the body

heat is·land *n* an urban area where the air temperature is consistently higher than in the surrounding region because of the generation and retention of heat created by human activity and human-made structures

heat light·ning *n* lightning seen near the horizon, especially on hot evenings, without the sound of thunder, thought to be a reflection on clouds. The thunder accompanying the lightning is too distant to be heard.

heat of com·bus·tion *n* the amount of heat produced when one mole of a substance is burned in oxygen

heat·proof /heét proof/ *adj* not damaged or affected when exposed to heat, e.g., in an oven or over a flame

heat pros·tra·tion *n* MED same as **heat exhaustion**

heat pump *n* a mechanical or chemical device used to heat and air-condition buildings

heat rash *n* MED same as **prickly heat**

heat-re·sis·tant *adj* able to withstand the kind of damage normally caused by heat, but not completely flameproof or nonflammable

heat-seal *vt* to make packaging material, usually a thin clear plastic film, airtight around something by applying heat and pressure

heat·seek·er /heét seèkər/ *n* a customer who always purchases the latest version or most recent update of an existing product (*slang*)

heat-seek·ing *adj* able to detect and follow infrared radiation from heat ○ *The aircraft was brought down by a heat-seeking missile.*

heat shield *n* a coating or structure designed to protect against the effects of very high temperatures, especially the coating that protects spacecraft during re-entry into the Earth's atmosphere

heat-shock pro·tein *n* a peptide that is released in response to adverse conditions, e.g., heart attacks, strokes, and breast cancer in humans or environmental stress in plants

heat sink *n* a device, often a metal plate, that conducts and dissipates unwanted heat generated by an electronic component or power supply

heat·stroke /heét strōk/ *n* a condition caused by prolonged exposure to high temperatures, in which people experience high fever, headaches, hot dry skin, physical exhaustion, and sometimes physical collapse and coma

heat-treat *vt* **1.** to bring metal to the desired hardness by alternately heating and cooling it **2.** to use heat such as that generated by massage as a means of treating rheumatism or muscular injuries —**heat treat·ment** *n*

heat wave *n* a period of unusually hot weather

heave /heev/ *v* (**heaved, heav·ing, heaves**) **1.** *vt* MOVE SOMETHING USING MUCH EFFORT to pull, push, lift, or throw something heavy by exerting great physical effort, especially in a concentrated or concerted burst ○ *We picked up the sack and heaved it into the truck.* **2.** *vi* EXERT PHYSICAL EFFORT IN RHYTHMIC BURST to exert great physical effort, especially in concentrated or concerted rhythmic bursts, when pulling on a rope or attempting to move something heavy ○ *All together now, heave!* ○ *heave on a rope* **3.** *vi* RISE AND FALL RHYTHMICALLY to rise and fall in a rhythmic or spasmodic way ○ *After the footraces his chest was heaving.* **4.** *vt* LABORIOUSLY UTTER SOMETHING to utter a sound, especially a sigh, with a long outflow of breath or with effort and pain ○ *We can heave a sigh of relief now that the waiting is over.* **5.** *vi* MAKE A SUDDEN INVOLUNTARY MOVEMENT to move suddenly in a violent involuntary motion, often associated with feelings of nausea ○ *The sight made my stomach heave.* **6.** *vti* VOMIT to vomit something up or try to vomit (*informal*) **7.** (*past* **hove** /hōv/) *vti* NAUT MOVE A SHIP to move or make a ship move in a particular direction **8.** (*past* **hove**) *vi* APPEAR to become visible, like a ship appearing over the horizon ○ *Gradually, the end of summer hove into sight.* **9.** *vt* GEOL DISPLACE SOMETHING HORIZONTALLY to displace rock strata or a mineral lode in a horizontal direction, usually by the intersection of other strata or another lode ■ *n* **1.** EFFORTFUL BURST a burst of physical effort to pull on something or move something heavy ○ *We gave one final heave and the tree began to topple over.* **2.** THROW an act of throwing something fairly heavy, or the distance something is thrown **3.** UP-AND-DOWN MOVEMENT a rhythmic or spasmodic movement that rises and falls ○ *the heave of a heavy ocean swell* **4.** ACT OF VOMITING an act of or attempt at vomiting (*informal*) **5.** GEOL HORIZONTAL DISPLACEMENT rock strata or a lode that is displaced horizontally ■ *interj Carib* USED TO REPORT FIGHT in Trinidad, used to report that a fight has started (*informal*) [Old English *hebban* "lift" < Germanic] —**heav·er** *n*

heave down *vt* to turn a boat over for cleaning

heave to *vti* to bring a ship, especially a sailing vessel, to a stop

heave-ho *interj* used to command or encourage sailors to pull together on a rope ■ *n* dismissal from something or rejection by somebody (*informal*) ○ *He's just been given the heave-ho from his job.*

heav·en /hévvən/ *n* **1.** *also* **Heav·en** RELIG PERFECT DWELLING PLACE AFTER DEATH a place or condition of supreme happiness and peace where good people are believed to go after death, and, especially in Christianity, where God and the angels are believed to dwell **2.** BLISSFUL EXPERIENCE an experience of blissful happiness ○ *It's heaven not to have get up early in the morning.* **3.** SKY the sky as seen from Earth (*literary*; *often plural*) **4.** *also* **Heav·en** RELIG GOD God, gods, or other divine agency ○ *Heaven protect us!* ○ *a gift from Heaven* ■ *interj also* **heav·ens** EXPRESSING ASTONISHMENT used to express great surprise, annoyance, or gratitude (*informal*) ○ *Heavens, is that the time?* [Old English *heofon*, origin ?] ◇ **for heaven's sake** used to express annoyance or exasperation ◇ **heaven knows** used to emphasize the truth of what somebody is saying ○ *Heaven knows, I've warned you about that already.* ◇ **heaven (only) knows** used to emphasize the fact that somebody is unable even to make a reasonable guess at something unknown or mysterious ○ *Heaven only knows what he's done with my keys.* ◇ **move heaven and earth** to do everything possible to make something happen

heav·en·ly /hévvənlee/ (**-li·er, -li·est**) *adj* **1.** *also* **Heav·en·ly** OF GOD AND HEAVEN belonging to the heaven and God of Christian belief ○ *A heavenly voice spoke to him out of the clouds.* **2.** IN THE SKY in the sky or space as seen from Earth **3.** LOVELY supremely delightful, delicious, or beautiful (*informal*) ○ *The chocolate mousse was heavenly.* —**heav·en·li·ness** *n*

heav·en·ly bod·y *n* ASTRON same as **celestial body**

heav·en-sent *adj* happening or arriving at just the right time to help or benefit somebody greatly

heav·en·ward /hévvənwərd/ *adj* moving or directed upward toward the sky or heaven ■ *adv also* **heav·en·wards** /-wərdz/ upward toward the sky or heaven ○ *He rolled his eyes heavenward.*

heaves /heevz/ *n* a chronic lung disorder in horses marked by difficulty in breathing and believed to be caused by dust, molds, or other air pollutants. The heaves resembles asthma in human beings. (*informal*; *takes a singular or plural verb*) ■ *npl* an attack of vomiting or retching (*slang*; *takes a plural verb*) ○ *The smell gave me the heaves.*

heav·i·er-than-air *adj* unable to float in air because it weighs more than the air it displaces, and thus only able to fly under power using aerodynamic lift

heav·i·ly /hévvilee/ *adv* **1.** WITH GREAT WEIGHT with a great weight **2.** LABORIOUSLY in a slow, clumsy, or laborious way **3.** SEVERELY in a severe, onerous, or comprehensive way ○ *heavily dependent on their parents* **4.** IN LARGE NUMBERS in large numbers or quantities **5.** SADLY in a sad and resigned way ○ *"It was my fault," he replied heavily.* ◇ **be heavily into** to be seriously or enthusiastically interested in something (*informal*) ○ *I didn't know you were heavily into astrology.*

heav·ing /heéving/ *adj* **1.** gently rising and falling in regular alternation **2.** *UK* uncomfortably full of people (*informal*)

Heav·i·side /hévvee sīd/, **Oliver** (1850–1925) British physicist. He predicted the existence of the ionosphere and contributed to the development of radio communications.

Heav·i·side lay·er *n* PHYS same as **E region**

heav·y /hévvee/ *adj* (**-i·er, -i·est**) **1.** WEIGHING A LOT weighing a relatively large amount and thus difficult to lift, carry, or move ○ *We put heavy stones on the corners of the blanket to stop it from blowing away.* **2.** PRESENT IN LARGE AMOUNTS occurring or produced in large amounts or in greater amounts than normal ○ *heavy rain* **3.** FULL OR DENSE involving or using a larger amount of material, or having a thicker, denser texture than usual **4.** USING SOMETHING ABUNDANTLY using or consuming something a great deal ○ *heavy on gas* **5.** NEEDING STRENGTH needing much strength and effort ○ *heavy road work* **6.** DEMANDING difficult to fulfill or cope with, and often burdensome or oppressive **7.** BUSY filled with a large or larger than normal amount of activity, business, or commitments ○ *a heavy day at work* **8.** POWERFUL struck or striking with a great deal of weight or force ○ *a heavy blow* **9.** BROAD AND DARK thick and dark-colored or made with thick dark lines ○ *heavy underlining* **10.** EXPLICIT intended to give emphasis to something and to make the meaning or intention obvious **11.** UNSUBTLE lacking subtlety or delicacy ○ *heavy sarcasm* **12.** FLESHY large and solidly fleshy ○

a man of heavy build **13.** CLUMSY characteristic of somebody who is large and who moves slowly and deliberately or clumsily **14.** AFFECTED BY TIREDNESS tending to close or droop or feel weighed down by tiredness ○ *eyes heavy with sleep* **15.** SOUNDING LOUD AND DULL loud and dull in sound, as if produced by something large hitting or falling onto something ○ *a heavy thud* **16.** INDUSTRIAL-SCALE involved in large-scale industrial processes requiring large premises and a lot of equipment ○ *heavy industry* **17.** RUGGED AND STRONG specially adapted for rough work or for carrying large loads ○ *heavy excavating equipment* **18.** SAD sad or likely to make somebody feel sad ○ *a heavy heart* **19.** REQUIRING CONCENTRATION requiring concentrated attention to be understood or appreciated ○ *a heavy novel* **20.** STRICT strict or severe in behavior **21.** POWERFUL AND LINGERING strong and lingering in smell ○ *a heavy odor of leeks* **22.** VIOLENT using or prepared to use violence (*informal*) ○ *the heavy mob* **23.** SERIOUS AND OPPRESSIVE significant, oppressively serious, or emotionally demanding (*slang*) ○ *I had a heavy scene with my friend tonight.* **24.** MIL LARGE-CALIBER firing large-caliber ammunition **25.** MIL WITH LARGE WEAPONS carrying more or larger guns and armaments than is standard ○ *building a new heavy cruiser* **26.** NAUT, OCEANOG ROUGH with large waves causing difficulties for boats ○ *heavy winds and seas* **27.** METEOROL DARK AND OVERCAST dark in color and threatening rain or snow ○ *heavy skies* **28.** FOOD HARD TO DIGEST large in quantity and difficult to digest ○ *a heavy meal* **29.** MUSIC WITH POWERFUL BEAT describes rock music with a powerful, insistent beat **30.** CHEM WITH HIGH ATOMIC WEIGHT with a higher than normal atomic weight **31.** PHYS WITH HIGH SPECIFIC GRAVITY with a specific gravity that is higher than usual ■ *n* (*plural* **-ies**) **1.** VILLAIN a villain in a play, movie, or other dramatic performance (*informal*) ○ *He played the heavy in a couple of westerns.* **2.** SOMEBODY WHO IS VIOLENT somebody hired to persuade people, by threats or violence, to do something (*slang; often used in the plural*) ○ *He sent in a bunch of heavies to do his dirty work.* **3.** IMPORTANT PERSON an important or influential person (*slang*) **4.** HEAVYWEIGHT a heavyweight, e.g., a heavyweight boxer (*informal*) [Old English *hefig* < Germanic, "lift"] —**heav·i·ness** *n*

heav·y breath·er *n* **1.** an anonymous telephone caller who breathes loudly into the mouthpiece as a means of suggesting sexual excitement or a physical threat **2.** somebody who breathes noisily or with difficulty, usually because of a medical condition —**heav·y breath·ing** *n*

heav·y chain *n* either of the larger polypeptide chains in an antibody

heav·y cream *n* cream with a high fat content that can be whipped to make it thicker

heav·y-dut·y *adj* **1.** designed for hard wear or use in rough conditions **2.** more serious, substantial, or intensive than usual (*informal*) ○ *a heavy-duty meeting*

heav·y-foot·ed *adj* slow, lumbering, or clumsy in walking

heav·y-hand·ed *adj* **1.** lacking skill or delicacy in handling objects or dealing with people **2.** relying on force or intimidation to exercise authority —**heav·y-hand·ed·ly** *adv* —**heav·y-hand·ed·ness** *n*

heav·y-heart·ed *adj* feeling or showing sadness —**heav·y-heart·ed·ly** *adv* —**heav·y-heart·ed·ness** *n*

heav·y hit·ter *n* **1.** somebody with power or influence (*slang*) **2.** in baseball, a batter of great strength, capable of hitting long balls and home runs

heav·y hy·dro·gen *n* an isotope of hydrogen with a mass number greater than one, especially deuterium

heav·y-lad·en *adj* carrying a heavy burden, e.g., of sorrow or guilt

heav·y lift·ing *n* **1.** STRENUOUS LIFTING the lifting of heavy objects **2.** SUSTAINED EFFORT serious or sustained effort in a demanding task ○ *Who's going to do the heavy lifting on this project?* **3.** MENTAL OR PHYSICAL EFFORT labor- or brain-intensive activity (*slang*) ○ *wanted a position involving no heavy lifting*

heav·y met·al *n* **1.** a style of loud rock music with a very strong beat (*hyphenated when used before a noun*) **2.** a metal, often toxic to organisms, that has a relative density of 5.0 or higher, e.g., lead, mercury, copper, and cadmium

heav·y oil *n* a mixture of hydrocarbons distilled from coal tar that is heavier than water

heav·y par·ti·cle *n* CHEM same as **baryon**

heav·y·set /hévvee sét/ *adj* with a compact and powerful-looking build

heav·y spar *n* the mineral form of barium sulfate

heav·y wa·ter *n* water that has had its hydrogen atoms replaced with the hydrogen isotope deuterium. Use: nuclear reactors. Formula: D_2O.

heav·y-wa·ter re·ac·tor *n* a nuclear reactor in which heavy water is used as a moderator

heav·y·weight /hévvee wàyt/ *n* **1.** WEIGHT CATEGORY IN PROFESSIONAL BOXING in professional boxing, the heaviest weight category, for competitors whose weight does not exceed 175 lb./79.5 kg **2.** WEIGHT CATEGORY IN AMATEUR BOXING in amateur boxing, the heaviest weight category, for competitors whose weight does not exceed 201 lb./91 kg **3.** BOXER AT HEAVYWEIGHT LEVEL a professional or amateur boxer who competes at heavyweight level **4.** CONTESTANT IN HEAVIEST WEIGHT CLASS a contestant in the heaviest weight class of a sport **5.** HEAVY PERSON OR THING somebody or something whose weight is considerably above the average **6.** SOMEBODY OR SOMETHING POWERFUL OR INFLUENTIAL a person or organization with considerable power or influence, usually in a particular area (*informal*)

Heb. *abbr* **1.** Hebrew **2.** BIBLE Hebrews

heb·do·mad /hébdə màd/ *n* (*formal*) **1.** a group of seven people or things **2.** a period of seven days [Mid-16C. Via late Latin < Greek *hebdomad-* "the number seven, period of seven days" < *hepta* "seven"]

heb·dom·a·dal /heb dómməd'l/ *adj* occurring on a weekly basis (*formal*)

he·be /heébee/ *n* an evergreen bush widely cultivated for its blue, mauve, or white flowers. Native to: southern temperate regions. Genus: *Hebe*. [Mid-20C. After HEBE]

He·be /heébee/ *n* in Greek mythology, the goddess of youth and the daughter of Zeus and Hera [Early 17C. < Greek *Hēbē*, literally "youthful prime"]

He·bei /hŏ báy/, **Ho·peh** /hŏ páy/ province in northern China. Its territories include the economic heartland of ancient Chinese civilization. Capital: Shijiazhuang. Population: 64,840,000 (1997). Area: 72,600 sq. mi./188,000 sq. km.

heb·e·tude /hébbə tood/ *n* mental lethargy (*literary*) [Early 17C. < late Latin *hebetudo* < Latin *hebet-* "dull"]

Hebr. *abbr* **1.** Hebrew **2.** BIBLE Hebrews

He·bra·ic /hi bráy ik/, **He·bra·i·cal** /-ik'l/ *adj* relating to the Israelites, or their language or culture [14C. Via late Latin < Greek *Hebraikos* < *Hebraios* (see HEBREW)] —**He·bra·i·cal·ly** *adv*

He·bra·ism /heé bray ìzzəm/, **He·bra·i·cism** /hee bráy i sìzzəm/ *n* a feature of the Hebrew language, especially one borrowed by another language, or something frequently found among Hebrews or their culture [Late 16C. Via French or modern Latin < late Greek *Hebraismos* < *Hebraios* (see HEBREW)]

He·bra·ist /heé bràу ist/ *n* a specialist in the study of Hebrew

He·bra·ize /heé bray ìz/ (**-ized, -iz·ing, -iz·es**) *v* **1.** *vt* to give a language or culture Hebrew characteristics **2.** *vi* to adopt Hebrew idioms or customs [Mid-17C. < late Greek *Hebraizein* < *Hebraios* (see HEBREW)] —**He·bra·i·za·tion** /heé bray i záysh'n/ *n* —**He·bra·iz·er** *n*

He·brew /heébroo/ *n* **1.** LANG a Semitic official language of Israel, also spoken elsewhere in the world. Native speakers: 5 million. See panel on next page **2.** PEOPLES, HIST same as **Israelite** (sense 1) ■ *adj* **1.** relating to Hebrew **2.** LANG, HIST same as **Hebraic** [13C. Via Old French *ebreu* < late Greek *Hebraios* < Aramaic *ibrāy*]

He·brew cal·en·dar *n* CALENDAR same as **Jewish calendar**

He·brews /heébrooz/ *n* a book of the Bible, originally a letter and thought to have been written toward the end of the 1st century A.D. (*takes a singular verb*) See table at **Bible**

He·brew Scrip·tures *npl* the Bible of Judaism, consisting of the Pentateuch, the Prophets, and the Hagiographa

Heb·ri·des /hébbrə deez/ collective name for the islands off the western coast of Scotland, comprising an outer chain of islands, the Outer Hebrides, separated by a sea channel from the Inner Hebrides nearer the mainland —**He·bri·de·an** /hèbbrə deé ən/ *adj, n*

He·bron /heé bron, hébbron/ city in the West Bank territory, situated 20 mi./32 km southwest of Jerusalem. Population: 119,401 (1997).

Hec·a·te /hékətee/, **Hek·a·te** *n* in Greek mythology, the goddess of darkness, witchcraft, and crossroads. She was the daughter of the Titans Perses and Asteria. [Late 16C. < Greek *Hekatē*, form of *hekatos* "far-darting"]

hec·a·tomb /hékə tŏm/ *n* **1.** in ancient Greece or Rome, a public sacrifice and feast, originally involving the slaughter of 100 oxen **2.** any large-scale sacrifice (*literary*) [Late 16C. Via Latin < Greek *hekatombē* < *hekaton* "hundred" + *bous* "ox"]

Hecht /hekt/, **Ben** (1894–1964) US writer. The author of fiction, plays, and screenplays, he is best remembered for his collaborations with Charles MacArthur on the plays *The Front Page* (1928) and *Twentieth Century* (1933).

> "There is hardly one in three of us who live in the cities who is not sick with unused self."
>
> [Ben Hecht, *Child of the Century*; 1954]

heck /hek/ (*informal*) *interj* used as a mild way of expressing annoyance, frustration, or of emphasizing a statement ○ *Oh heck, I suppose that means we can't go.* ■ *n* sometimes used as a less offensive alternative for the word "hell" ○ *What the heck is going on?* [Late 19C. Euphemistic alteration of HELL] ◇ **a** *or* **one heck of a** used to indicate that something is particularly large, intense, or impressive (*informal*) ○ *There's still a heck of a lot to do before closing time.*

heck·el·phone /hék'l fōn/ *n* a bass musical instrument of the oboe family, in pitch between the English horn and the bassoon [Early 20C. < German *Heckelphon*, after Wilhelm *Heckel* (1856–1909), German instrument maker]

heck·le /hék'l/ *v* (**-led, -ling, -les**) **1.** *vti* INTERRUPT SOMEBODY WITH SHOUTING to shout remarks, insults, or questions in order to disconcert somebody who is making a speech or giving a performance ○ *A very angry crowd of voters heckled the candidate for mayor.* **2.** *vt* DRESS FLAX OR HEMP to comb flax or hemp ■ *n* COMB FOR FLAX OR HEMP a comb used for dressing flax or hemp [14C. Variant of HACKLE[1]] —**heck·ler** *n*

hect- *prefix* same as **hecto-** (*used before vowels*)

hec·tare /hék tair/ *n* a metric unit of area equal to 100 ares or 10,000 sq. m (2.471 acres) [Early 19C. < French < Greek *hekaton* "hundred" + French *are*, unit of area < Latin *area* "open space"]

hec·tic /héktik/ *adj* **1.** characterized by continual activity and haste, the lack of any time to rest or relax, and a sense of things barely under control ○ *Things have been pretty hectic at work this week.* **2.** MED symptomatic of or involving a recurrent afternoon fever, especially one accompanying tuberculosis ○ *a hectic flush* [14C. Via French < Greek *hektikos* "habitual, consumptive" < *ekhein* "have"] —**hec·tic·al·ly** *adv*

hecto- *prefix* one hundred ○ *hectogram* Symbol **h** [Via French < Greek *hekaton* < Indo-European]

hec·to·cot·y·lus /hèktō kótt'ləss/ (*plural* **-li** /-lī/) *n* a tentacle with which male octopuses and related mollusks transfer sperm to the female during mating [Mid-19C. < modern Latin < French *hecto-* (see HECTO-) + Greek *kotulē* "cup, something hollow"]

LANGUAGE HERITAGE ***Hebrew*** Much of English is made up of words from other languages, and Hebrew is an important contributor in this respect. To begin with, quite a few English first names, for example, *Elizabeth, Emanuel, Gabriel, Jonathan, Joan,* and *Josephine,* have internal elements derived from Hebrew. ***Jehovah*** and some other Judeo-Christian terms for "God" go back to Hebrew. ***Passover,*** first recorded in the 16th century, is a translation of Hebrew *pesaḥ* "to pass without affecting," an allusion to Exodus 12:11–27, in which it is said that God passes over the Israelites, while the first-born of other families are killed.

A good many Hebrew émigrés into English are, of course, integral to Judaism and Jewish life and culture, in the manner of ***Passover. Bar mitzvah, bat mitzvah, huppah, menorah, Seder, Torah, tref, yeshiva,*** and ***Yom Kippur*** are but a few. Some of these have become generalized into the secular cultures of the English-speaking world: ***kosher, megillah,*** and ***shekel*** are representative. Still others, for example, ***amen, hallelujah, manna,*** and ***Sabbath,*** which are associated with both Judaism and Christianity, came into English via Latin and Greek but are ultimately of Hebrew origin.

Two English words of Hebrew origin that migrated into English in the 13th and 14th centuries, respectively are ***cider*** and ***jubilee. Cider*** came into English via French, Latin, and Greek, but goes back to Hebrew *šēkār* "alcoholic drink." ***Jubilee*** also entered English via French from Latin and Greek, and goes back to Hebrew *yōbēl* "ram," from the ram's horn with which the year of restoration and restitution was proclaimed every 50 years. And some Hebrew émigrés into English entered Hebrew from other languages: ***cherub*** is probably of Akkadian origin, and ***hora*** is of Romanian origin. See also ***Yiddish.***

hec·to·gram /héktə gràm/ *n* a metric unit of mass equal to 100 grams [Late 18C. < French *hectogramme* < *hecto-* (see HECTO-) + *gramme* (see GRAM[1])]

hec·to·li·ter /héktə leetər/ *n* a metric unit of capacity equal to 100 liters [Early 19C. < French *hectolitre* < *hecto-* (see HECTO-) + *litre* (see LITER)]

hec·to·me·ter /héktə meetər, hek tómmətər/ *n* a metric unit of length equal to 100 meters [Early 19C. < French *hectomètre* < *hecto-* (see HECTO-) + *mètre* (see METER[3])]

hec·tor /héktər/ (**-tored, -tor·ing, -tors**) *vti* to speak to somebody in a loud, threatening, or domineering tone intended to intimidate [Mid-17C. After HECTOR]

Hec·tor /héktər/ *n* in Greek mythology, the main Trojan hero in the Trojan War and a son of King Priam and Queen Hecuba [14C. Via Latin < Greek *Hektōr* "holding fast" < *ekhein* "hold"]

Hec·u·ba /hékyəbə/ *n* in Greek mythology, the wife of King Priam of Troy and mother of 16 children, including Cassandra, Hector, and Paris [Via Latin < Greek *Hekabē*]

he'd /heed/ *contr* **1.** he had **2.** he would

hed·dle /hédd'l/ *n* one of the sets of vertical cords or wires in the frame on a loom that guides the warp threads [Early 16C. Origin ?]

hedge /hej/ *n* **1.** ROW OF BUSHES a close-set row of bushes, usually with their branches intermingled, forming a barrier or boundary in a garden, lawn, or field **2.** PROTECTIVE METHOD a means of protection against something, especially a means of guarding against financial loss ○ *a hedge against inflation* **3.** EVASIVE STATEMENT an evasive or noncommittal statement ■ *v* (**hedged, hedg·ing, hedg·es**) **1.** *vt* PUT BUSHES AROUND SOMETHING to put a row of intermingled bushes around an area of ground **2.** *vi* WORK ON HEDGES to work at repairing, trimming, or planting a hedge **3.** *vt* RESTRICT SOMETHING to restrict the scope or applicability of something by setting conditions ○ *It was a promise, but hedged in with so many ifs and buts that I wouldn't rely on it.* **4.** *vi* BE EVASIVE to avoid answering a question directly or definitely ○ *She could have given a straight answer, but instead she hedged.* **5.** *vi* FIN TRY TO OFFSET POSSIBLE LOSSES to take measures to offset any possible loss on a financial transaction, especially by investing in counterbalancing securities as a guard against price fluctuations [Old English *hegg* < Germanic, "grasp"] —**hedg·er** *n* —**hedg·y** *adj*

hedge·ap·ple /héj àpp'l/, **hedge·ball** /héj bàwl/ *n regional* the inedible fruit of the Osage orange tree

REGIONAL NOTE **Hedgeapple** is a West Midland designation for the fruit of the Osage orange, most common in Ohio, Indiana, Illinois, Kentucky, and Tennessee. ***Hedgeball*** is used in Illinois, Kentucky, and Kansas.

hedge fund *n* an investment company that is organized as a limited partnership and uses high-risk techniques in the hope of making large profits

hedge·hog /héj hàwg, -hòg/, **hedge·hock** /héj hòk/ *n* **1.** a small animal that has a round body with stiff spines on the back and a small pointed snout. It can roll itself into a ball when attacked. Native to: Europe, Africa, Asia. Family: Erinaceidae. **2.** an underwater obstacle designed to keep landing craft

hedgehog

from reaching a beach by ripping holes in the hulls [15C. Because the animal makes noises reminiscent of the squeals and grunts of pigs]

hedge·hog cac·tus *n* a low-growing round or cylindrical cactus. Flowers: white, yellow, red, or purple, bell-shaped. Native to: Mexico, southwestern United States. Genus: *Echinocereus.*

hedge·hop /héj hòp/ (**-hopped, -hop·ping, -hops**) *vi* to fly very low above the ground, often so low that the aircraft must ascend to avoid obstacles on the ground (*refers to aircraft*) —**hedge·hop·per** *n*

hedge·row /héj rō/ *n* a row of bushes or small trees forming a hedge, especially around a field or along a rural road or path

he·don·ic /hi dónnik/ *adj* **1.** concerned with pleasure **2.** characteristic of or relating to hedonism or hedonists [Mid-17C < Greek *hēdonikos* < *hēdonē* "pleasure"]

he·don·ism /heéd'n ìzzəm/ *n* **1.** a devotion, especially a self-indulgent one, to pleasure and happiness as a way of life **2.** a philosophical doctrine that holds that pleasure is the highest good or the source of moral values [Mid-19C. < Greek *hēdonē* "pleasure"] —**he·don·ist** *n* —**he·don·is·tic** /heéd'n ístik/ *adj* —**he·don·is·ti·cal·ly** *adv*

-hedron *suffix* a figure or crystal having a particular number or kind of surfaces ○ *pentahedron* [< modern Latin < Greek *hedra* "seat, base"] —**-hedral** *suffix*

hee·bie-jee·bies /heébee jeébeez/ *npl* uncomfortable nervous or anxious feelings (*slang*) ○ *There's something about thick fog that gives me the heebie-jeebies.* [Early 20C. Coined by Billy DeBeck (1890–1942), US cartoonist]

heed /heed/ *vti* (**heed·ed, heed·ing, heeds**) to give serious attention to a warning or advice and take it into account when acting ■ *n* serious attention paid to somebody or to something such as a warning, piece of advice, or request [Old English *hēdan* < Germanic] —**heed·er** *n*

heed·ful /heédfəl/ *adj* paying attention to somebody or to something such as a warning, piece of advice, or danger —**heed·ful·ly** *adv* —**heed·ful·ness** *n*

heed·less /heédləss/ *adj* not paying attention to somebody or to something such as a warning, piece of advice, or danger —**heed·less·ly** *adv* —**heed·less·ness** *n*

hee·haw /heé hàw/ *n* **1.** the natural sound made by a donkey **2.** an unrefined noisy laugh (*informal*) [Early 19C. An imitation of the sound] —**hee·haw** *vi*

he'e ho·lu·a /heé hə lóoə/ *n Hawaii* SPORTS same as **lava sledding** (*regional*)

heel[1] /heel/ *n* **1.** BACK OF FOOT the back part of a person's foot immediately below the ankle, or the same part of an animal's foot or paw **2.** BACK OF SHOE OR SOCK the part of a sock, stocking, shoe, or boot that covers the back part of somebody's foot **3.** BACK OF SHOE SOLE the back, usually thicker, portion of the sole of a shoe or other footwear that raises the foot off the ground ○ *I'll need to get new heels on these boots.* **4.** PHYSIOL THICKER PART OF PALM the thicker part of the palm of the hand, located next to the wrist **5.** CLOTHING PART OF GLOVE the part of a glove that covers the part of the palm located next to the wrist **6.** FOOD BREAD CRUST a crusty end of a loaf of bread **7.** FOOD CHEESE RIND the hard rind from a wedge of cheese **8.** GOLF PART OF GOLF CLUB the part of the head of a golf club where the shaft is attached **9.** MUSIC NECK SUPPORT a part that supports the neck of a stringed instrument at the point where it is attached to the body **10.** MUSIC END OF VIOLIN BOW the end of a violin bow that is held while playing the violin **11.** GARDENING PIECE ATTACHED TO CUTTING a small piece of a plant stem or tuber left attached to a cutting to promote the growth of new roots **12.** NAUT BOTTOM OF MAST the bottom end of a boat's mast **13.** NAUT STERN the stern end of a ship's keel **14.** OFFENSIVE TERM an offensive term that deliberately insults somebody's, especially a man's, behavior (*insult*) ■ **heels** *npl* CLOTHING HIGH-HEELED SHOES shoes with high heels ■ *v* (**heeled, heel·ing, heels**) **1.** *vt* RENEW HEEL OF SHOE to fit, replace, or repair the heel of a shoe or boot **2.** *vi* FOLLOW BY SOMEBODY'S HEELS to follow closely at somebody's heels when commanded (*refers to dogs*) **3.** *vt* RIDING DIG HEELS INTO HORSE to hit or prod an animal being ridden with the heel **4.** *vi* DANCE MOVE HEELS to move the heels to music or touch a surface with the heels when dancing **5.** *vt* GOLF MISHIT GOLF BALL to mishit a golf ball with the heel of a club [Old English *hēla* < Germanic] —**heeled** *adj* —**heel·less** *adj* ◇ **cool your heels** to wait or be kept waiting for a long time (*informal*) ◇ **dig in your heels** to hold stubbornly to a position or attitude ◇ **(hard) on the heels of somebody** *or* **something 1.** close behind somebody or something **2.** soon after somebody or something ◇ **show (somebody) a clean pair of heels** to run away from somebody ◇ **take to your heels** to run off ◇ **to heel 1.** directly behind the person with whom a dog is walking **2.** under control or discipline ◇ **turn on your heel** to turn around suddenly

SPELLCHECK See ***heal.***

heel[2] /heel/ *vti* (**heeled, heel·ing, heels**) to lean over to one side so far as to be in danger of falling, or cause a boat to lean in this way ○ *The ship heeled in the wind.* ■ *n* a leaning to one side, or the degree to which a boat is leaning [Late 16C. Alteration of *hield* (taken as past participle) < Old English *hieldan* "lean, bend" < W Germanic]

heel[3]

heel in *vt* to place a plant in a hole and cover the roots with soil until it can be planted in its permanent place

heel-and-toe *adj* describes walking or racing that requires the heel of one foot to touch the ground before the toe of the other is lifted from the ground ■ *vi* (**heel-and-toed, heel-and-toe·ing, heel-and-toes**) to operate the brake and accelerator pedals at the same time with one foot, usually to keep the engine revolutions high when shifting to a lower gear while racing

heel·ball /heél bàwl/ *n* a black waxy substance used by shoemakers to blacken the edges of the heels and soles of shoes and boots or a similar substance used for making brass rubbings

heel·bar /heél baàr/ *n UK* a small shop or a counter in a large store where repairs are made to shoe soles and heels, often while the customer waits

heel bone *n* the quadrangular bone that forms the heel of the foot. Technical name **calcaneus**

heel·er /heélər/ *n* **1.** a person or machine that fits, replaces, or repairs the heels of shoes or boots **2.** POL same as **ward heeler** (*informal*)

heel·piece /heel peess/ *n* the part of a sock, stocking, shoe, or boot that fits around the heel of the foot

heel·post /heel pōst/ *n* a post to which the hinges of a gate or door are attached

heel·tap /heel tàp/ *n* **1.** a small quantity of an alcoholic drink remaining at the bottom of a glass after the rest has been swallowed **2.** a layer of leather or other material in the heel of a shoe or boot

He·fei /hō fáy/, **Ho·fei** /hō fáy/ capital city of Anhui Province, west of Nanjing, eastern China. Population: 1,320,000 (1995).

Hef·ner /héfnər/, **Hugh** (*b.* 1926) US publisher. He founded *Playboy* in 1953, and a string of related nightclubs. His own much publicized hedonistic lifestyle epitomized the sexual revolution of the 1960s and 1970s. Full name **Hefner, Hugh Marston**

heft /heft/ *vt* (**heft·ed, heft·ing, hefts**) **1.** LIFT SOMETHING to lift up something heavy, especially with a burst of effort **2.** ESTIMATE WEIGHT OF SOMETHING to lift something in order to estimate its weight ■ *n* GREAT WEIGHT substantial heaviness or bulk [15C. Probably < HEAVE, after pairs such as *cleave, cleft*] —**heft·er** *n*

heft·y /héftee/ (**-i·er, -i·est**) *adj* **1.** POWERFULLY BUILT big and strong in physique **2.** HEAVY large and heavy to lift **3.** EXPENSIVE involving a large sum of money **4.** FORCEFUL delivered with or characterized by great force and power **5.** STRENUOUS requiring a lot of effort to do **6.** LARGER THAN USUAL much larger than is usual or required ○ *a hefty sum* —**heft·i·ly** *adv* —**heft·i·ness** *n*

he·ga·ri /hə gérree, héggəree/ *n* any originally Sudanese variety of sorghum grown for grain [Early 20C. < Arabic (Sudanese) dialect *hegiri*]

He·gel /háyg'l/, **G. W. F.** (1770–1831) German philosopher. His idealist metaphysics exerted an enormous influence on 19th-century European thought. His works include *The Phenomenology of Mind* (1807) and the *Encyclopedia of the Philosophical Sciences in Outline* (1817). Full name **Hegel, Georg Wilhelm Friedrich** —**He·ge·li·an** /hə gáylee ən/ *adj, n*

> "The nature of Spirit may be understood by a glance at its direct opposite—Matter. As the essence of Matter is Gravity, so...we may affirm that the substance, the essence of Spirit is Freedom."
> [G. W. F. Hegel, *Reason in History*; 1953]

> "What experience and history teach is this-that nations and governments have never learned anything from history, or acted upon any lessons they might have drawn from it."
> [G.W.F. Hegel, *Lectures in the Philosophy of World History: Introduction*; 1830]

He·ge·li·an·ism /hə gáylee ə nìzzəm/ *n* the philosophy of G. W. F. Hegel, which proposes a unified solution to all philosophical problems through development of a reasoning process that ultimately interprets reality by way of the dialectic method.

he·gem·o·ny /hə jémmənee, héjjə mōnee/ *n* control or dominating influence by one person or group, especially by one political group over society or one nation over others [Mid-16C. < Greek *hēgemonia* "leadership" < *hēgisthai* "lead"] —**heg·e·mon·ic** /hèjjə mónnik/ *adj* —**he·gem·o·nism** *n* —**he·gem·o·nist** *n*

he·gi·ra /hə jīrə, héjjərə/, **he·ji·ra** *n* a flight or withdrawal from somewhere, especially to escape from danger [Mid-18C. < HEGIRA]

He·gi·ra /hə jīrə, héjjərə/, **He·ji·ra** *n* **1.** the withdrawal of the Prophet Muhammad from Mecca to Medina to escape persecution **2.** the Muslim era, dated from the first day of the lunar year in which Muhammad's withdrawal to Medina took place. This was July 16, A.D. 622 in the Gregorian calendar. [Late 16C. Via medieval Latin < Arabic *hijra* "the leaving of home and friends"]

Hei·an /háy ən/ *adj* characteristic of or relating to Japan from 794–1185, when Confucianism and other Chinese influences were at their height [Late 19C < Japanese *Heian-kyo*, now Kyoto, former capital of Japan]

hei·au /háy òw/ *n Hawaii* an ancient temple or sacred place [Early 19C. < Hawaiian]

Hei·deg·ger /hīd èggər/, **Martin** (1889–1976) German philosopher. He greatly influenced the development of phenomenology and existentialism in the 20th century. His most important work is *Being and Time* (1927).

> "We are too late for the gods / and too early for Being. Being's poem, / just begun, is man."
> [Martin Heidegger, *Poetry, Language, Thought*; 1971]

> "Thinking only begins at the point where we have come to know that Reason, glorified for centuries, is the most obstinate adversary of thinking."
> [Martin Heidegger, *Being and Time*; 1927]

Hei·del·berg /hīd'l bùrg/ university city in Baden-Württemberg, southwestern Germany, situated on the Neckar River. Population: 138,964 (1997).

Hei·del·berg man /hīd'l bùrg-/ *n* an extinct early human of the Pleistocene epoch that is known mainly from a fossilized jawbone

Hei·del·berg School /hīd'l burg-/ *n* a late 19th-century school of Australian artists who painted outdoors [After a suburb of Melbourne, Australia, near painting sites]

Hei·den /hīd'n/, **Eric** (*b.* 1958) US ice skater. He was world speed-skating champion (1977–79) and won five gold medals in the 1980 Olympics. Full name **Heiden, Eric Arthur**

heif·er /héffər/ *n* a young cow, especially one that has never had a calf [Old English *heahfore*, origin ?]

Hei·fetz /hīfits/, **Jascha** (1901–87) Lithuanian-born US violinist. Noted for his technical mastery, he was considered one of the greatest classical violinists of his time.

heigh-ho /hī-, hay-/ *interj* **1.** used to express boredom, disappointment, or weary resignation ○ *Heigh-ho. Here we go again.* **2.** used to express happiness or encouragement [15C. < *heigh*, natural exclamation]

height /hīt/ *n* **1.** LENGTH UPWARD the distance between the lowest and highest point of somebody or something ○ *a steep cliff about 200 feet in height* **2.** DISTANCE ABOVE POINT the distance that somebody or something is above the ground, sea, or another reference point **3.** NOTICEABLE TALLNESS the condition of being noticeably high or tall compared to others ○ *His height makes him stand out in a crowd.* **4.** HIGHEST POINT the top or highest point of something ○ *When you reach the height, you'll get a wonderful view.* **5.** HIGH POSITION a high place or position, especially one where somebody can see a view or how high up he or she is (*often used in the plural*) ○ *afraid of heights* **6.** MOST IMPORTANT OR ACTIVE LEVEL the level of greatest intensity, activity, importance, or success ○ *She was at the height of her powers.* **7.** MOST INTENSE LEVEL a high level of intensity or severity (*often used in the plural*) ○ *Their arrogance is reaching new heights.* **8.** EXTREME EXAMPLE the most extreme example of something ○ *It was the height of folly to have gone there on your own.* ■ **heights** *npl* HILLS OR MOUNTAINS an area of hilly or mountainous terrain, especially one that is noticeably elevated above the surrounding region (*often used in place names*) [Old English *hēhþu* "highest part" < Germanic]

CULTURAL NOTE ***Wuthering Heights***, a novel (1847) by British writer Emily Brontë. Brontë's only novel, it is the story of a foundling, Heathcliff, whose mistreatment at the hands of his adoptive family leads him to seek revenge later in life. The novel is noted for its evocative descriptions of the Yorkshire moors, its complex morality, and its intensity of feeling.

height·en /hīt'n/ (**-ened, -en·ing, -ens**) *vti* **1.** INCREASE to make something such as a feeling or emotion greater or more intense, or become greater or more intense ○ *His attempts to reassure them served only to heighten their fears.* **2.** INTENSIFY IN BRIGHTNESS to make something such as a color appear brighter or stronger, or appear to become brighter or stronger ○ *The sunlight heightened the flush on her cheeks.* **3.** EXTEND UPWARD to make something higher, or become higher ○ *As protection, they heightened the city walls by another three feet.* —**height·ened** *adj* —**height·en·er** *n*

~~**heighth**~~ incorrect spelling of **height**

height of land *n Can* a ridge of high land that is a watershed

Hei·long·jiang /hày lòong jyaáng/ province in northeastern China, bordering Russia. Capital: Harbin. Population: 37,280,000 (1997). Area: 179,000 sq. mi./463,600 sq. km.

Hei·long Jiang /hày lòong jyaáng/, **Hei·lung Chiang** Chinese name for **Amur**

Heim·dall /háym daál/, **Heim·dal, Heim·dallr** /háym daálər/ *n* in Norse mythology, a giant warrior who was the god of light and dawn [< Old Norse *Heimdallr* < *heimr* "home, world"]

heim·ish *adj* another spelling of **haimish**

Heim·lich ma·neu·ver /hīmlik-/ *n* an emergency method for treating choking that uses an upward thrust immediately below the breastbone to expel food or another blockage from the windpipe [Late 20C. After Henry J. *Heimlich* (b. 1920), US surgeon]

Hei·ne /hīnə/, **Heinrich** (1797–1856) German poet. One of Germany's greatest lyric poets, he spent his last 25 years in France. The poems in his *Book of Songs* (1827) inspired numerous musical settings by leading European composers.

> "The arrow belongs not to the archer when it has once left the bow; the word no longer belongs to the speaker when it has once passed his lips."
> [Heinrich Heine, *Religion and Philosophy*; 1840]

> "Wherever books will be burned, men also, in the end, are burned."
> [Heinrich Heine, *Almansor*; 1823]

hei·nie /hīnee/ *n* the human buttocks (*slang*) [Mid-20C. Alteration of HINDER[2]]

Hein·kel /hīngk'l/, **Ernst** (1888–1958) German engineer. He designed aircraft used by the German air force in both world wars, and built the first jet-propelled plane (1939). Full name **Heinkel, Ernst Heinrich**

Hein·lein /hīn līn/, **Robert** (1907–88) US writer. His many works of science fiction, known for their technological sophistication, include *Stranger in a Strange Land* (1961). Full name **Heinlein, Robert Anson**

> "The Earth is just too small and fragile a basket for the human race to keep all its eggs in."
> [Robert Heinlein, *Speech*; Undated]

hei·nous /háynəss/ *adj* shockingly evil or wicked [14C. < Old French *haineus* < *hair* "to hate" < Germanic] —**hei·nous·ly** *adv* —**hei·nous·ness** *n*

heir /er/ *n* **1.** somebody who holds the right to receive a property, position, or title of somebody else when that person dies **2.** an inheritor of something such as a tradition, problem, or characteristic ○ *Our generation is the unfortunate heir to decades of pollution.* [14C. Via Old French *(h)eir* < Latin *heres*] —**heir·less** *adj* —**heir·ship** *n*

SPELLCHECK See *air*.

heir ap·par·ent (*plural* **heirs ap·par·ent**) *n* **1.** an heir whose entitlement to receive an inheritance cannot be altered by the birth of another heir **2.** the expected inheritor of somebody else's position, status, or influence

~~**heirarchy**~~ incorrect spelling of **hierarchy**

heir at law (*plural* **heirs at law**) *n* the heir of somebody's property under the law if that person dies without a valid will

heir·ess /érəss/ *n* a woman or girl who receives or has by law the right to receive the property, position, or title of another when that person dies

heir·loom /ér lòom/ *n* **1.** something valuable that has been in the possession of a family for a long time and has been passed on from one generation to the next **2.** an item of personal property that is attached to the estate that a legal heir will inherit [< LOOM[2] in obsolete sense "tool, utensil"]

heir pre·sump·tive (*plural* **heirs pre·sump·tive**) *n* an heir whose entitlement to an inheritance will cease if another heir is born whose entitlement is greater

Hei·sen·berg un·cer·tain·ty prin·ci·ple /hīz'n burg-/ *n* PHYS same as **uncertainty principle**

heist /hīst/ (*slang*) *n* a theft or robbery, especially of money or valuables, usually involving the use of weapons ■ *vt* (**heist·ed, heist·ing, heists**) to steal or rob something, especially money or valuables, usually while carrying weapons [Mid-19C. Representing a local N American pronunciation of HOIST] —**heist·er** *n*

He·jaz /hee jáz/ province of western Saudi Arabia, bordering the Red Sea. Capital: Mecca. Area: 134,600 sq. mi./348,600 sq. km.

he·ji·ra, He·ji·ra *n* another spelling of **hegira, Hegira**

Hek·a·te *n* MYTHOL another spelling of **Hecate**

He·ke Po·kai /hè kay pṓ kī/, **Hone** (1810?–50) Maori leader. He was head of the Ngapuhi people and a strong opponent of British colonial government in New Zealand.

Hek·la /héklə/ active volcano in southwestern Iceland. Height: 4,892 ft./1,491 m.

Hel /hel/, **Hel·a** /hé laa/ *n* **1.** in Norse mythology, the goddess of the dead and the underworld **2.** in Norse mythology, the underworld of the dead [< Old Norse]

He·La cell /héllə-/, **He·la cell** *n* a cell from a strain of human cervical cancer cells that is used in medical and biological research [Mid-20C. Acronym < *Henrietta Lacks*, from whom the original cells were taken]

held past participle, past tense of **hold**[1]

hel·den·te·nor /héld'ntə nàwr/, **Hel·den·te·nor** *n* a tenor or tenor voice with a robust dramatic quality that is suited especially for heroic roles in the operas of Richard Wagner [Early 20C. < German, "hero tenor"]

Hel·en /héllən/, **Hel·en of Troy** *n* in Greek mythology, the daughter of Zeus and Leda and the most beautiful woman in Greece. Her husband was Menelaus, the king of Sparta. Her abduction by Paris sparked the Trojan War.

Hel·e·na /héllənə/ city and capital of Montana, located in the western part of the state. Population: 26,353 (2002 estimate).

Hel·e·na, St. (248?–328?) Roman empress. She was the mother of Constantine I. Among her religious pilgrimages, she visited Jerusalem in about 325, where she founded the Church of the Holy Sepulchre and is said to have discovered the True Cross, an important Christian relic.

He·le·ne /hə léenee/ *n* a very small natural satellite of Saturn, discovered in 1980. It is irregular in shape, with a maximum dimension of 22 mi./36 km, and occupies an intermediate orbit.

he·le·ni·um /hə léenee əm/ (*plural* **-ums** or *same*) *n* a plant of the daisy family. Flowers: yellow, dark reddish, or in some cultivated varieties bicolored. Native to: North and South America. Genus: *Helenium*. [Early 17C. Via modern Latin < Greek *helenion*]

Hel·en of Troy *n* MYTHOL same as **Helen**

He·lens·vale /héllənz vàyl/ town in southeastern Queensland, Australia, a residential, tourist, and cattle-grazing center. Population: 13,823 (1996).

hel·i /héllee/ (*plural* **-is**) *n* a rotary-wing aircraft (*informal*) [Shortening of HELICOPTER]

heli- *prefix* helicopter ○ *helipad* [< HELICOPTER]

he·li·a·cal /hə lī ək'l/ *adj* describes the rising or setting of a star that occurs at the same time as the rising or setting of the Sun, because of their near conjunction [Mid-16C. < late Latin *heliacus* < Greek *hēlios* "sun"] —**he·li·a·cal·ly** *adv*

he·li·an·the·mum /héelee ánthəməm/ *n* an evergreen perennial that forms a low mound. Flowers: white, yellow, pink, orange. Native to: United States, Europe, Asia Minor. Genus: *Helianthemum*. [Early 19C. < modern Latin < Greek *hēlios* "sun" + *anthemon* "flower"; because the flower turns with the sun]

he·li·an·thus /héelee ánthəss/ (*plural* **-thus·es** or *same*) *n* a tall perennial plant of the sunflower family. Flowers: yellow, like daisies. Genus: *Helianthus*. [Late 18C. < modern Latin < Greek *hēlios* "sun" + *anthos* "flower"; because the flower turns with the sun]

hel·i·bik·ing /héllə bīking/ *n* a sport in which mountain-bike riders are taken by helicopter to the top of a mountain and then ride down

hel·i·borne /héllə bàwrn/ *adj* transported by helicopter

helic- *prefix* same as **helico-** (*used before vowels*)

hel·i·cal /héllik'l, hée-/ *adj* in the shape of a helix or spiral [Late 16C. < Latin *helix* (see HELIX)] —**hel·i·cal·ly** *adv*

hel·i·cal gear *n* a gear whose teeth are formed to curve along a spiral path on the surface of the gear on an axis oblique to the axis of the gear itself

hel·i·ces MATH, ANAT plural of **helix**

hel·i·chry·sum /hèllə krī́ssəm/ (*plural* **-sums** or *same*) *n* an annual or perennial plant of the daisy family with flowers that retain their color when dried. Genus: *Helichrysum*. [Mid-16C. < Latin < Greek *helix* "spiral" + *khrusos* "gold"]

helico- *prefix* helix, spiral ○ *helicograph* [< Greek *helik-*, stem of *helix*]

he·li·co·graph /héllikə gràf, héeli-/ *n* an instrument for drawing spiral curves on a flat surface

hel·i·coid /hélli kòyd, héeli-/ *adj* shaped or coiled like a spiral (*technical*) ○ *a helicoid shell* ■ *n* a spiral geometric surface that resembles a thread on a screw [Late 17C. < Greek *helicoidēs* < *helix* "spiral"] —**he·li·coid·al** /hèlli kóyd'l, héeli-/ *adj* —**he·li·coid·al·ly** *adv*

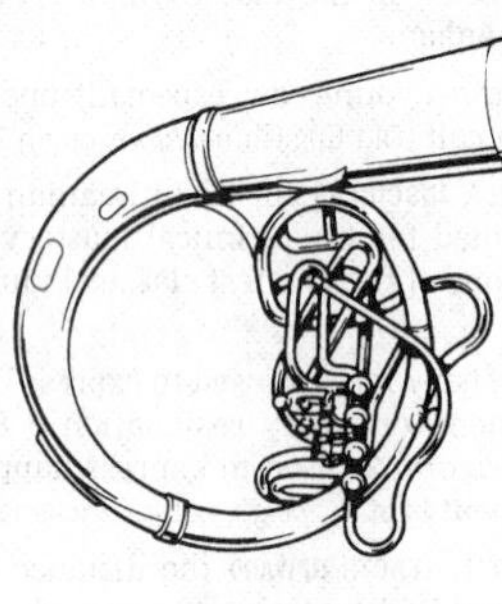

helicon

hel·i·con /hélli kòn, -kən/ *n* a large bass tuba that encircles the player's body, used in marching bands [Late 19C. < Mount *Helicon* in Greece, reputed home of the Muses; influenced by HELIX]

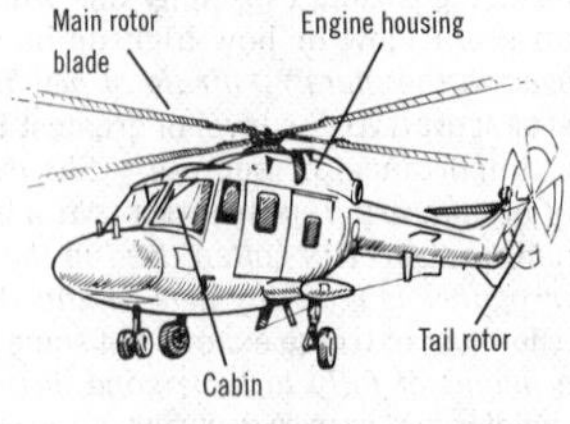

helicopter

hel·i·cop·ter /hélli kòptər/ *n* an aircraft without wings that moves by means of large blades (**rotors**) that spin around above it. It can fly vertically and horizontally and can hover. ■ *vti* (**-tered, -ter·ing, -ters**) to travel or transport somebody or something in a helicopter ○ *The survivors were helicoptered to a hospital.* [Late 19C. < French *hélicoptère* < Greek *helix* "spiral" + *pteron* "wing"]

hel·i·cop·ter gun·ship *n* a large heavily armed helicopter used to protect troops on the ground

hel·i·cop·ter view *n* a general outline or brief summary of a situation or subject ○ *a helicopter view of the state of the industry*

hel·i·cul·ture /hélli kùlchər, héeli-/ *n* the science or profession of raising snails for food [< modern Latin *Helix*, genus of spiral-shelled mollusks < Greek *helix* "spiral"] —**hel·i·cul·tur·al** /hèlli kúlchərəl, hèeli-/ *adj* —**he·li·cul·tur·al·ist** *n*

hel·i·deck /héllə dèk/ *n* a deck on something such as a ship or offshore oil platform that is used as a landing site for helicopters

helio- *prefix* sun ○ *heliostat* [< Greek *hēlios* < Indo-European]

he·li·o·cen·tric /héelee séntrik/, **he·li·o·cen·tri·cal** /-séntrik'l/ *adj* **1.** with the Sun at the center ○ *a heliocentric orbit* **2.** measured from or considered as if viewed from the center of the Sun —**he·li·o·cen·tri·cal·ly** *adv* —**he·li·o·cen·tric·i·ty** /-sen tríssətee/ *n*

he·li·o·dor /héelee ə dàwr/ *n* a clear yellow variety of beryl from southwestern Africa. Use: gems. [Early 20C. < HELIO- + Greek *dōron* "gift"]

he·li·o·graph /héelee ə gràf/ *n* **1.** an apparatus that is used to send messages in Morse code by flashes of reflected sunlight **2.** an apparatus used to photograph the Sun —**he·li·og·raph·er** /hèelee óggrəfər/ *n* —**he·li·o·graph·ic** /hèelee ə gráffik/ *adj*

he·li·o·la·try /hèelee óllətree/ *n* worship of the Sun —**he·li·o·lat·er** *n* —**he·li·o·la·trous** *adj*

he·li·o·li·thic /hèelee ə líthik/ *adj* describes a culture or society characterized by worship of the Sun and the construction of monuments or temples using huge stones (**megaliths**)

he·li·om·e·ter /hèelee ómmətər/ *n* a refracting telescope with a divided objective that is used to measure small angular distances between astronomical objects or points on the Moon —**he·li·o·met·ric** /hèelee ə méttrik/ *adj* —**he·li·o·met·ri·cal** *adj* —**he·li·o·met·ri·cal·ly** *adv* —**he·li·om·e·try** *n*

he·li·o·pause /héelee ə pàwz/ *n* the point marking the beginning of interstellar space and the endpoint boundary of our solar system, 10–15 billion miles from the Sun, where the pressure from solar winds is in balance with that of interstellar winds

he·li·o·phyte /héelee ə fīt/ *n* a plant that can survive and grow in direct sunlight or that grows best in direct sunlight

He·li·op·o·lis /hèelee óppəliss/ city of ancient Egypt, northeast of present-day Cairo in the Nile delta. The great temple there was the center of Sun worship, and reached the height of its influence in the 13th century B.C.

He·li·os /héelee òss/ *n* in Greek mythology, the god of the sun. The son of Hyperion and Thea, he drove his golden chariot across the sky from east to west each day. Roman equivalent **Sol** (sense 2)

he·li·o·seis·mol·o·gy /hèelee ō sīz móllәjee/ *n* the scientific study of the sound waves in the Sun's atmosphere

he·li·o·sphere /héelee ə sfeer/ *n* a spherical region around the Sun, approximately 100 astronomical units in radius, outside which interstellar space begins —**he·li·o·spher·ic** /hèelee ō sférrik/ *adj*

he·li·o·stat /héelee ə stàt/ *n* an instrument with an automatically rotated mirror that reflects the Sun's light in a constant direction, used to measure the Sun's radiation [Mid-18C. < modern Latin *heliostata* or French *héliostat*, both < Greek *hēlios* "sun" + *statos* "standing"] —**he·li·o·stat·ic** /hèelee ə státtik/ *adj*

he·li·o·tax·is /hèelee ə táksiss/ *n* movement toward or away from sunlight in an organism that is able to move about freely —**he·lio·tac·tic** *adj*

he·li·o·ther·a·py /hèelee ə thérrəpee/ *n* treatment of illness by exposure to direct sunlight

he·lio·trope /héelee ə trōp/ (*plural* **-tropes** or *same*) *n* **1. PLANT WITH FRAGRANT FLOWERS** a hairy plant of the borage family. Flowers: small, fragrant, white or purple, in clusters. Genus: *Heliotropium*. **2. CULTIVATED PURPLE FLOWER** a cultivated species of heliotrope. Flowers: small purple, very fragrant. Native to: South America. Latin name: *Heliotropium arborescens*. **3.** PLANTS same as **garden heliotrope** **4. FLOWER THAT TURNS TOWARD SUN** a plant with flowers that turn toward the sun **5.** COLORS **BLUISH COLOR** a bluish purple color **6.** (*plural* **he·li·o·tropes**) MINERALS same as **bloodstone** **7.** (*plural* **he·li·o·tropes**) CIV ENG **SURVEY INSTRUMENT** an instrument used in geodesic surveying to reflect the Sun's rays over long distances [Pre-

12C. Via Latin < Greek *heliotropion* < *helios* "sun" + *tropos* "turning"] —**he·lio·trope** *adj*

he·li·ot·ro·pism /hèelee óttrə pìzzəm/ *n* growth toward sunlight by a plant —**he·li·o·trop·ic** /hèelee ə tróppik/ *adj* —**he·li·o·trop·i·cal** *adj* —**he·li·o·trop·i·cal·ly** *adv*

he·li·o·zo·an /hèelee ə zṓ ən/ *n* a free-living, usually freshwater, protozoan that has a spherical shell and radiating projections **(pseudopodia)**. Class: Heliozoa. [Late 19C. < modern Latin *Heliozoa* < Greek *hēlios* "sun" + *zōion* "animal"] —**he·li·o·zo·ic** *adj*

hel·i·pad /héllə pàd/ *n* an area where helicopters take off and land

hel·i·port /héllə pàwrt/ *n* an airport designed for helicopters

hel·i·ski·ing /hélli skèe ing/ *n* skiing in which skiers are taken to a usually remote ski slope by helicopter

hel·i·stop /héllə stòp/ *n* a place where helicopters can take off and land, usually without the support facilities found at a heliport

he·li·um /héelee əm/ *n* a nonflammable inert gaseous element that is colorless and odorless. Source: natural gas. Use: inert atmospheres, cryogenic research, lasers, inflating balloons. Symbol **He**. See table at **element** [Late 19C. < Greek *hēlios* "sun"; because its existence was deduced from its emission line in the solar spectrum]

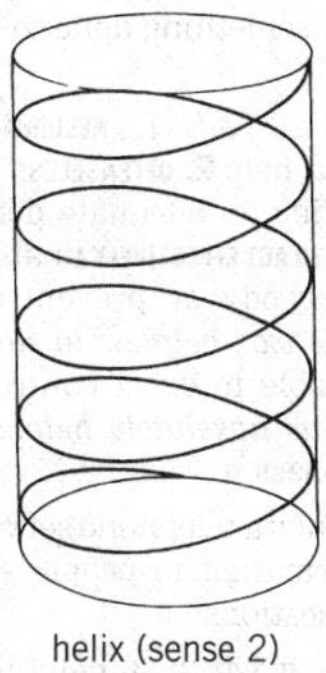

helix (sense 2)

he·lix /héeliks/ (*plural* **he·lix·es** or **hel·i·ces** /hélli sèez, héeli-/) *n* **1. SPIRAL OR COIL** something in the form of a spiral or coil, e.g., a corkscrew or a coiled spring **2.** MATH **SPIRAL CURVE** a mathematical curve that lies on a cylinder or cone and makes a constant angle with the straight lines lying in the cylinder or cone **3.** ANAT **RIM OF EAR** the rim of the external ear [Mid-16C. Via Latin < Greek]

CULTURAL NOTE ***The Double Helix***, a memoir (1968) by James D. Watson. In this personal account of the landmark discovery of the structure of the DNA molecule in 1953, for which Watson later shared a Nobel Prize with Francis Crick and Maurice Wilkins, scientific research is shown to be a competitive race in which ego, politics, and luck play prominent roles. Watson's less than generous treatment of Maurice Wilkins' and Rosalind Franklin's contribution to his work caused much controversy when the book was published.

hell /hel/ *n* **1.** *also* **Hell PLACE OF PUNISHMENT AFTER DEATH** according to many religions, the place where the souls of people who are damned suffer eternal punishment after death **2.** *also* **Hell DEVILISH POWER** according to some religions, Satan or the powers of evil that live in hell **3. UNDERWORLD** according to some religions, the place where the spirits of all people go after death **4. SUFFERING** a state or place of extreme pain or misery, or something or somebody that causes extreme pain or misery ○ *I tell you, migraine is just hell.* ○ *Finals are absolute hell.* ○ *She went through hell until she heard they were safe.* ■ *interj* **EXPRESSING ANNOYANCE** used to express annoyance or surprise or for emphasis (*sometimes considered offensive*) ○ *Hell! I've lost the key.* ○ *Oh, hell. The store is closed.* ○ *Hell, no. I don't want that.* ■ *vi* **(helled, hell·ing, hells) BEHAVE WILDLY** to live or behave recklessly or riotously (*slang*) ○ *sailors helling around port while on leave* [Old English *hel(l)* < Indo-European, "conceal"] ◇ **a** *or* **one hell of a** used as an intensifier (*informal*) ◇ **come hell or high water** whatever difficulties there may be ◇ **from hell** of the worst sort imaginable (*informal*) ○ *The bus ride in the blizzard was a trip from hell.* ◇ **give somebody hell** (*informal*) **1.** to scold somebody severely **2.** to cause somebody trouble or pain ◇ **go to hell in a handbasket** to deteriorate quickly and utterly (*informal*) ◇ **hell to pay** serious trouble or punishment that is sure to result from something (*informal*) ◇ **(just) for the hell of it** just for the sake of doing it and without any specific reason (*informal*) ◇ **like hell** (*informal*) **1.** very fast or very intensely **2.** used to emphasize disagreement or denial ◇ **play** *or* **raise hell with something** to cause harm, disruption, or damage to something (*informal*) ◇ **raise hell** (*informal*) **1.** to object to something strongly and loudly **2.** to celebrate or party wildly ◇ **the hell** (*informal*) **1.** used to emphasize annoyance ○ *Get the hell out of here. I'm trying to work.* **2.** used to emphasize disagreement or denial ○ *Did he offer to help? The hell he did.*

he'll /heel/ *contr* **1.** he shall **2.** he will

hel·la·cious /he láyshəss/ *adj* **1.** extremely bad, unpleasant, or unbearable (*informal*) **2.** extremely large (*slang*)

Hel·lad·ic /he láddik/ *adj* associated with or characteristic of the Bronze Age civilization that flourished in Greece from 3000 to 1100 B.C. [Early 19C. < Greek *Helladikos* < *Hellas* "Greece"]

Hel·las /hélləss/ *n* **1.** the Greek name for Greece **2.** an extensive plain on the surface of Mars in the southern hemisphere, approximately 1100 mi./1800 km across

hell·bend·er /hél bèndər/ *n* a large, dark gray salamander. Native to: rivers in eastern and central United States. Latin name: *Cryptobranchus alleganiensis*.

hell-bent *adj* absolutely determined to do something, regardless of the consequences (*informal*)

hell-bent-for-leath·er *adv, adj* same as **hell-for-leather** (*informal*)

hell·cat /hél kàt/ *n* an offensive term for a woman regarded as being quick to lose her temper and likely to be violent (*informal*)

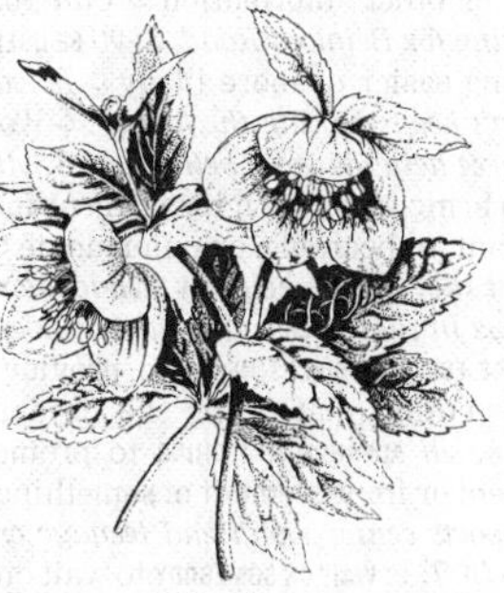

hellebore

hel·le·bore /héllə bàwr/ (*plural* **-bores** or *same*) *n* **1.** an early-flowering, often poisonous perennial plant that has large divided leaves. Flowers: drooping white, pink, dark purple, sometimes green. Native to: Europe, Asia. Genus: *Helleborus*. **2.** a poisonous plant of the buttercup family with large leaves. Flowers: greenish. Native to: North America. Genus: *Veratrum*. [Pre-12C. Via French < Greek *helleboros*]

Hel·len /héllən/ *n* in Greek mythology, a king of Thessaly and ancestor of the ancient Hellenic peoples

Hel·lene /hé lèen/, **Hel·le·ni·an** /he léenee ən/ *n* (*formal*) **1.** an ancient Greek **2.** somebody who comes from Greece [Mid-17C. < Greek *Hellēn* "a Greek"]

Hel·len·ic /he lénnik/ *adj* **1.** ANCIENT HIST **OF ANCIENT GREECE** relating to ancient Greece **2.** LANG **OF GREEK** belonging or relating to the branch of Indo-European consisting of the ancient and modern forms of Greek ■ *n* LANG **GREEK LANGUAGE** the Hellenic branch of Indo-European [Mid-17C. < Greek *Hellēnikos* < *Hellēn* "a Greek"] —**Hel·len·i·cal·ly** *adv*

Hel·le·nism /héllə nìzzəm/ *n* **1. ANCIENT GREEK CULTURE** the culture and civilization of ancient Greece, especially in the period after Alexander the Great when it spread to other parts of the Mediterranean, Southwest Asia, and North Africa **2. ADMIRATION FOR ANCIENT GREEK CULTURE** the enthusiasm for or adoption of ancient Greek culture or customs **3. GREEK CHARACTERISTIC** a Greek custom or idiom **4. GREEK NATIONAL CHARACTER** the supposed national character of the Greeks [Early 17C. < Greek *Hellēnismos* < *Hellēnizein* (see HELLENIZE)]

Hel·le·nist /héllənist/ *n* **1.** a specialist in the study of Greek language, literature, culture, or history, or an admirer of the Greeks and their culture **2.** somebody, especially somebody Jewish, who adopted Greek customs, language, and culture during the 4th to 1st centuries B.C. [Early 17C. < Greek *Hellēnistēs* < *Hellēnizein* (see HELLENIZE)]

Hel·le·nis·tic /hèllə nístik/ *adj* **1. OF ANCIENT GREEK CIVILIZATION** characteristic of or relating to ancient Greek civilization during the late 4th to 1st centuries B.C. **2. OF GREEKS** characteristic of or associated with the Greeks **3. PREFERRING GREEK CULTURE** enthusiastic for or adopting ancient Greek culture or customs ○ *the Hellenistic Jews of Alexandria* —**Hel·len·is·ti·cal·ly** *adv*

Hel·le·nize /héllə nīz/ (**-nized, -niz·ing, -niz·es**) *vti* to adopt the language and culture of the ancient Greeks, or make something closer in character to the language and culture of the ancient Greeks [Early 17C. < Greek *Hellēnizein* "speak Greek, make Greek" < *Hellēn* "a Greek"] —**Hel·le·ni·za·tion** /hèlləni záysh'n/ *n* —**Hel·le·niz·er** *n*

hel·ler[1] /héllər/ (*plural same*) *n* **1.** a former German or Austrian coin **2.** MONEY, COINS another spelling of **haler** [Late 16C. < German, later form of *haller* (see HALER)]

hell·er[2] /héllər/ *n regional* same as **hellion** (*informal*) [< HELL]

Hel·ler /héllər/, **Joseph** (1923–99) US writer. He is best known for his antiwar novel *Catch-22* (1961). See Cultural note at **Catch-22**

> "He was a self-made man who owed his lack of success to nobody."
> [Joseph Heller, *Catch-22*; 1961]

hel·ler·i /héllə rī/ (*plural* **-is**) *n* a brightly colored freshwater aquarium fish that is a hybrid of a swordtail and platy [Mid-20C. After C. *Heller*, tropical fish collector]

Hel·les·pont /hélliss pònt/ ➧ **Dardanelles**

hell·fire /hél fīr/ *n* punishment in hell according to some religions, often described as eternal torment in the flames of hell's fires ■ *adj* detailing in a vigorous and emotional way the punishment sinners can expect in hell, according to some religions

hell-for-leath·er *adv* extremely quickly and often recklessly (*informal*) —**hell-for-leath·er** *adj*

hell·gram·mite /hélgrə mīt/ *n* the large carnivorous larva of a dobsonfly, occurring in water and often used as fish bait [Mid-19C. Origin ?]

hell·hole /hél hōl/ *n* a terrifying, unbearable, or evil place

hell·hound /hél hòwnd/ *n* **1.** a supposed fiend, or a fiendish person **2.** especially in Greek mythology, a hound said to guard the gates of hell

hel·lion /héllyən/ *n* a troublesome or rowdy person, especially a child (*informal*) [Mid-19C. Probably alteration, influenced by HELL, of Scots and N English dialect *hallion* "idler," origin ?]

hell·ish /héllish/ *adj* **1.** like, from, or typical of hell ○ *a hellish scene of blazing homes and streets jammed with debris* **2.** extremely unpleasant or difficult (*informal*) ○ *The exam was absolutely hellish.* —**hell·ish·ly** *adv* —**hell·ish·ness** *n*

Lillian Hellman

Hell·man /hélmən/, **Lillian** (1905–84) US playwright. She was known for her powerful moral dramas such as *The Watch on the Rhine* (1941) and *Toys in the Attic* (1960). Full name **Hellman, Lillian Florence**

"Fashions in sin change."
[Lillian Hellman, *The Watch on the Rhine*; 1941]

hel·lo /hə lṓ, he-/ *interj, n* (*plural* **-los**) **1.** WORD USED AS GREETING a word used to greet somebody you meet, to answer a telephone call, or to begin a radio or television program ○ *Hello. Pleased to meet you.* ○ *Hello, and welcome to the show.* ○ *After we had all said our hellos, we settled down to eat.* **2.** WORD TO ATTRACT ATTENTION a word used to attract attention ○ *Hello! Is anyone there?* **3.** WORD EXPRESSING SURPRISE a word used to express surprise ○ *Hello! What's that doing here?* ■ *interj* ADDS IRONIC EMPHASIS adds ironic, sarcastic, or sometimes angry emphasis (*slang*) ○ *He's like, hello? who do you think you are?* ○ *I'm living my own life now, hello? Please mind your own business.* [Late 19C. Probably < French *holá* "stop there!", used to attract attention]

hell-rais·er *n* somebody who behaves in a drunken, rowdy, or disruptive way

Hells Can·yon /hèlz-/ gorge of the Snake River on the Idaho-Oregon border. It is the deepest canyon in the United States. Depth: 7,900 ft./2,400 m. Length: 40 mi./64 km.

hell·uv·a /héllәvә/ *adj* used as an intensifier (*informal*) ○ *a helluva party* [Early 20C. Representing *hell of a*]

hell week *n* the week when college fraternity or sorority pledges are subjected to hazing before their initiation

helm[1] /helm/ *n* **1.** NAUT SHIP'S STEERING APPARATUS the apparatus used to steer a ship, especially the wheel or handle (**tiller**) by which the rudder is turned **2.** POSITION OF CONTROL a position of leadership or control within an organization, country, or endeavor ○ *The failing company needed a new chief at its helm.* ■ *vt* (**helmed, helm·ing, helms**) **1.** NAUT STEER SHIP to be at the helm of a ship steering it **2.** DIRECT SOMETHING to be at the head of an organization, country, or endeavor directing it [Old English *helma* < Germanic, "handle"] —**helm·less** *adj*

helm[2] /helm/ *n* a military helmet, especially of an ancient or medieval type (*archaic or literary*) [Old English < Germanic, "conceal, cover"]

hel·met /hélmət/ *n* **1.** HARD PROTECTIVE HEAD COVERING a hat or other head covering made of a hard material and worn to protect the head from injury, often part of a uniform, suit of armor, or protective clothing **2.** PROTECTIVE HAT any protective hat, e.g., against cold weather or the heat of the sun **3.** BIOL PART SHAPED LIKE HELMET a part of an organism resembling a helmet, e.g., a flower's sepal or corolla [15C. < Old French, diminutive of *helme* "helmet" < Germanic] —**hel·met·ed** *adj*

hel·minth /hélminth/ *n* a parasitic worm, e.g., a fluke, nematode, or tapeworm [Mid-19C. < Greek *helminth-* "intestinal worm"] —**hel·min·thoid** /hel mín thòyd, hélmin-/ *adj*

hel·min·thi·a·sis /hèlmin thī́ əssiss/ *n* infestation by parasitic worms, often causing disease

hel·min·thic /hel mínthik/ *adj* **1.** caused by or relating to flukes, nematodes, or other parasitic worms (**helminths**) **2.** eradicating or expelling parasitic worms ■ *n* MED, VET same as **vermifuge**

hel·min·thol·o·gy /hèlmin thólləjee/ *n* the scientific study of parasitic worms —**hel·min·thol·o·gist** *n*

Hel·mont /hél mònt/, **Jan Baptista van** (1580–1644) Flemish chemist and physiologist. An early experimental chemist, he coined the term "gas."

helms·man /hélmzmən/ (*plural* **-men** /-mən/) *n* **1.** the steerer of a ship, especially a man **2.** somebody, especially a man, who is the director of an organization, country, or endeavor ○ *the country's helmsman in the crisis* —**helms·man·ship** *n*

helms·per·son /hélmz pùrss'n/ (*plural* **-per·sons** or **-peo·ple** /-peep'l/) *n* **1.** the steerer of a ship **2.** the director of an organization, country, or endeavor

helms·wo·man /hélmz wŏŏmmən/ (*plural* **-wo·men** /-wimmin/) *n* **1.** a woman who is the steerer of a ship **2.** a woman who is the director of an organization, country, or endeavor

hel·o /héllō/ (*plural* **-os**) *n* (*informal*) **1.** a rotary-winged aircraft **2.** AVIAT same as **heliport** [Mid-20C. Shortening and alteration of HELICOPTER]

Hé·lo·ïse /èllō éez/ (1098?–1164) French abbess. Her love affair with Peter Abelard, and their subsequent separation and correspondence, provided one of the world's great love stories.

hel·ot /héllət/ *n* an enslaved person or serf [Early 19C. < HELOT] —**hel·ot·age** *n*

Hel·ot /héllət/ *n* in ancient Sparta, a member of a class of serfs claimed as property by the state but assigned to individual Spartans to work on their land [Late 16C. Via Latin *Helotes* < Greek *Heilōtes*, probably after *Helos*, town in Laconia whose inhabitants were enslaved]

hel·ot·ism /héllə tìzzəm/ *n* **1.** a political or social system in which one group, class, or nation is systematically oppressed by another **2.** symbiosis found especially among ants, in which one species acts as workers for another, dominant species

help /help/ *v* (**helped, help·ing, helps**) **1.** *vti* ASSIST SOMEBODY to make it easier or possible for somebody to do something that one person cannot do alone by providing assistance ○ *Can you help me solve this problem?* ○ *Can I help with those bags?* **2.** *vti* ADVISE SOMEBODY to provide somebody with advice, directions, or other information ○ *Can you help me? I'm looking for Belmont Road.* **3.** *vti* BE USEFUL to make something easier or more likely ○ *It would help if you didn't keep shaking the ladder.* ○ *Would a business degree help me get a better job?* **4.** *vti* MAKE THINGS BETTER to bring about an improvement in something unpleasant, unbearable, or unfortunate ○ *I took two pills, but they didn't help my headache.* ○ *You look ridiculous in that dress, and the hat doesn't help.* **5.** *vti* PROVIDE FOR SOMEBODY'S NEEDS to provide somebody with something that he or she needs, especially money **6.** *vti* ADVANCE SOMETHING to promote the advancement or improvement of something ○ *Opening a new sports center won't end teenage crime, but it might help.* **7.** *vt* WAIT ON SOMEBODY to wait on somebody in a store, restaurant, or other establishment ○ *Can I help you, sir?* **8.** *vt* BRING SOMEBODY FOOD to give somebody or yourself a serving of food ○ *He helped us all to some cake.* **9.** ⚠ *vt* KEEP SOMEBODY FROM DOING SOMETHING to keep somebody or yourself from doing something (*usually used in negative statements*) ○ *We couldn't help overhearing your conversation.* ○ *I didn't want to laugh, but I couldn't help myself.* **10.** *vt* PREVENT SOMETHING to prevent something from happening (*usually used in negative statements*) ○ *The child couldn't have helped the accident.* ■ *n* **1.** ASSISTANCE something that is done for or given to somebody in order to make something easier, possible, or better ○ *I could do with some help in the kitchen.* **2.** SOMEBODY OR SOMETHING THAT ASSISTS somebody who provides aid or assistance to somebody ○ *The headaches are pretty bad, but the new medicine is a help.* **3.** WAY OUT OF SOMETHING a way of avoiding doing something or of undoing something (*often used in negative statements*) ○ *a situation for which there was no help* **4.** SERVANT OR LABORER a person or persons who are paid to help, especially servants or farm hands (*often considered offensive*) ○ *He treated all the employees like help, and they resented it.* ■ *interj* CALLS FOR ASSISTANCE used to call for assistance when somebody is in danger or difficulty [Old English *helpan* < Germanic] ◇ **help yourself** to take something for your own use, usually without permission

USAGE Can't help but Traditionally, speakers and writers had a choice between, for example, *can't help doing* and *can't* [or *cannot*] *but do*. The latter (i.e., *cannot but do*) is now uncommon. *Can't help but do* is sometimes seen, but it is a redundant mixture of the two forms, and should be avoided in favor of *can't help doing*.

SYNONYMS See ***assistant***.

help out *vti* to give somebody some help, e.g., by doing some work or giving money

help desk *n* a service providing technical help and support for people using a computer package or network

help·er /hélpər/ *n* somebody who helps with something, often in an informal or voluntary capacity

help·er T cell, **help·er cell** *n* a white blood cell that is part of the body's immune response, recognizing foreign antigens and stimulating the production of cells to control them

help·ful /hélpfəl/ *adj* providing or willing to provide assistance, information, or other aid ○ *You might find this book helpful.* —**help·ful·ly** *adv* —**help·ful·ness** *n*

help·ing /hélping/ *n* an amount of food served to somebody at one time

help·ing hand *n* something done to assist somebody else

help·less /hélpləss/ *adj* **1.** NEEDING HELP unable to manage without help **2.** DEFENSELESS unprotected and unable to provide an adequate defense against an attack **3.** UNABLE TO ACT EFFECTIVELY unable to do anything to protect somebody or prevent something from happening ○ *He was helpless to stop the assault.* **4.** UNRESTRAINED unable to exert control or restraint ○ *His jokes had us absolutely helpless.* —**help·less·ly** *adv* —**help·less·ness** *n*

help·line /hélp lìn/ *n* a telephone service that provides advice or information to people who call in with problems or questions

help·mate /hélp màyt/ *n* a helpful companion or partner, especially a spouse

help·meet /hélp meet/ *n* a helpmate, especially a wife (*archaic; sometimes considered offensive*) [Late 17C. < "an help meet for him" (Genesis 2:18, 20), with misinterpretation of MEET[2] "suitable"]

help screen *n* a pop-up screen in a computer program or website that contains advice on how to navigate the program or site

Hel·sing·borg /hélssing bàwrg/ city and seaport in Skåne province, southern Sweden, on the Øresund, opposite Denmark. Population: 116,337 (1998).

Hel·sing·ør /hèl seng úr, -ṓr/ town and seaport in eastern Denmark on the island of Zealand, the setting of Shakespeare's play *Hamlet*, in which it is called Elsinore. Population: 44,860 (1998).

Hel·sin·ki /hel síngkee/ capital city and chief seaport of Finland, situated on the Gulf of Finland in the south of the country. Population: 551,123 (2000).

hel·ter-skel·ter /hèltər skéltər/ *adv, adj* **1.** WITH HASTE with hurry and confusion ○ *The prairie dogs rushed helter-skelter down their burrows.* **2.** IN DISORDER without order or organization ○ *The winds had knocked the huge trees helter-skelter all over the park.* ■ *n* CONFUSED STATE a hurried or disorganized situation or state ○ *the helter-skelter in the junk shop* [Late 16C. Probably formed to suggest hurried action]

~~**helth**~~ incorrect spelling of **health**

helve /helv/ *n* the handle of a tool such as an ax, pick, or hammer [Old English *helfe* < Germanic]

Hel·ve·tia /hel véeshə/ *n* the Latin name for Switzerland

Hel·ve·tian /hel véesh'n/ *n* **1.** somebody who comes from Switzerland **2.** a member of the Helvetii [Mid-16C. < Latin *Helvetia* "Switzerland" < *Helvetius* "of or with the Helvetii"] —**Hel·ve·tian** *adj*

Hel·ve·tic /hel véttik/ *adj* **1.** relating to Switzerland **2.** relating to the religious teachings of Ulrich Zwingli and other Swiss Protestant reformers [Early 18C. < Latin *Helvetia* (see HELVETIAN)] —**Hel·ve·tic** *n*

Hel·ve·ti·i /hel véeshee ī/ *npl* a Celtic people who came from southern Germany and migrated to the area that is now Switzerland, where they settled during the 2nd century B.C. [Late 19C. < Latin]

hem[1] /hem/ *n* **1.** FOLDED FABRIC EDGE a neat nonfraying edge made by folding fabric over and stitching it down **2.** HANDICRAFT same as **hemline** (sense 1) ■ *v* (**hemmed, hem·ming, hems**) **1.** *vti* MAKE HEM ON SOMETHING to fold over and stitch down fabric to make a hem on something ○ *hem curtains* **2.** *vt* ENCLOSE SOMEBODY OR SOMETHING to surround and enclose somebody or something ○ *The small yard was hemmed about by a tall hedge.* [Old English, related to Old Frisian *hemme* "enclosed land"]

hem in *vt* to confine and restrict somebody or something

hem[2] /hem/ *interj, n* a word used to represent the sound made by somebody clearing his or her throat or coughing quietly in order to attract attention, warn somebody else, or hide embarrassment or uncertainty ■ *vi* (**hemmed, hem·ming, hems**) to make the sound "hem," or otherwise hesitate in speech [15C. An imitation of the sound] ◇ **hem and haw** to hesitate while speaking or deciding something

hem- *prefix* same as **hemo-** (*used before vowels*)

hema- *prefix* blood ○ *hemangioma* [< Greek *haima*]

he·mag·glu·ti·nate /hèema glóot'n àyt/ (**-nat·ed, -nat·ing, -nates**) *vti* to cause red blood cells to clump together, or become clumped together —**he·mag·glu·tin·a·tion** /hèema gloot'n áysh'n/ *n*

he·mag·glu·ti·nin /hèema glóot'nin/ *n* an agent that causes red blood cells to clump together, e.g., a virus or an antibody

he·mal /héem'l/ *adj* **1.** found in or associated with the blood or blood vessels **2.** located on or associated with the side of the body where the heart and major arteries and veins are found [Mid-19C. < Greek *haima* "blood"]

he-man *n* a strong, muscular man (*informal*)

he·man·gi·o·ma /hi mànjee ṓmə/ (*plural* **-ma·ta** /-mətə/ or **-ma·s**) *n* a benign tumor or birthmark consisting of a dense, often raised cluster of blood vessels in the skin

he·ma·pher·e·sis /hèema férrəssiss/ *n* MED same as **apheresis** (sense 1)

hemat- *prefix* same as **hemato-** (*used before vowels*)

he·ma·te·in /hèemmə tée in, hèemə téen/ *n* a red-brown compound used to stain samples for microscope study

he·mat·ic /hi máttik/ *adj* relating to or acting on blood

he·ma·tin /héemətin/ *n* a breakdown product of hemoglobin

he·ma·tin·ic /hèemə tínnik/ *adj* describes a drug or other agent that increases blood hemoglobin

he·ma·tite /héemə tīt/ *n* a black, brown, or red mineral consisting of iron oxide, often in very large deposits. Use: source of iron. [15C. Via Latin < Greek *haimatitēs* "blood-like (stone)"] —**he·ma·tit·ic** /hèemə títtik/ *adj*

hemato- *prefix* blood ○ *hematoblast* [< Greek *haimat-*, stem of *haima*]

he·ma·to·blast /héemətə blàst, hi máttə-/ *n* an immature blood cell, especially a red blood cell

he·mat·o·crit /hi máttə krìt/ *n* **1.** the percentage of a blood sample that consists of red blood cells, measured after the blood has been centrifuged and the cells compacted **2.** a centrifuge used to compact the red blood cells in a blood sample in order to determine the percentage of the blood that consists of cells [Late 19C. < HEMATO- + Greek *kritēs* "judge" (see CRITIC)]

he·ma·to·gen·e·sis /hèemətə jénnəssiss, hi màttə-/ *n* PHYSIOL same as **hematopoiesis** —**he·ma·to·gen·ic** *adj*

he·ma·tog·e·nous /hèemə tójjənəss/ *adj* **1.** MAKING BLOOD producing blood **2.** OF BLOOD originating in or derived from blood **3.** SPREAD BY BLOOD spread by means of blood

he·ma·tol·o·gy /hèemə tóllәjee/ *n* the branch of medicine devoted to the study of blood, blood-producing tissues, and diseases of the blood —**he·ma·to·log·ic** /hèemәtə lójjik/ *adj* —**he·ma·to·log·i·cal·ly** *adv* —**he·ma·tol·o·gist** *n*

he·ma·to·ma /hèemə tṓmə/ (*plural* **-mas** or **-ma·ta** /-mətə/) *n* a semisolid mass of blood in the tissues, caused by injury, disease, or a clotting disorder

he·ma·to·pha·gous /hèemə tóffəgəss/ *adj* feeding on blood [Mid-19C. < HEMATO- + Greek *phagein* "eat"]

he·ma·to·poi·e·sis /hèemətō poy éessiss, hi màttə-/, **he·mo·poi·e·sis** /hèemə poy-/ *n* the formation of red blood cells in the blood-forming tissues of the body —**he·ma·to·poi·et·ic** /hèemətō poy éttik/ *adj*

he·ma·tox·y·lin /hèemə tóksəlin/ *n* a dye used to stain microscope slides for study [Mid-19C. < modern Latin *Haematoxylum* < Greek *haimat-* "blood" + *xulon* "wood"]

he·ma·to·zo·on /hèemətō zṓ òn, hi màttə-/ (*plural* **-zo·a** /-zṓ ə/) *n* a parasitic protozoan or other microorganism that lives in blood —**he·ma·to·zo·al** *adj*

he·ma·tu·ri·a /hèemə tóoree ə/ *n* the presence of blood in the urine, as a result of injury to or disease of the kidneys, ureters, bladder, or urethra —**he·ma·tu·ric** *adj*

heme /heem/ *n* the deep red, nonprotein portion of hemoglobin that contains iron [Early 20C. Back-formation < HEMOGLOBIN]

Hem·el Hemp·stead /hèmm'l hémpstid/ city in Hertfordshire, south central England. Population: 79,235 (1991).

hem·er·a·lo·pi·a /hèmmərə lṓpee ə/ *n* impaired vision in daylight (*technical*) [Early 18C. < modern Latin < Greek *hēmeralōps* "day-blind eye"] —**hem·er·a·lop·ic** /-lóppik/ *adj*

hem·er·o·cal·lis /hèmmərō kálləss/ *n* PLANTS same as **day lily** [Mid-17C. < Greek *hēmerokallis* "lily that flowers for a day" < *hēmera* "day" + *kallos* "beauty"]

Hem·et /hémmət/ city in southeastern California, situated southeast of San Bernardino. Population: 63,367 (2002 estimate).

hemi- *prefix* half, partial ○ *hemihydrate* ○ *hemimetabolous* [< Greek *hēmi-* < Indo-European]

-hemia *suffix* same as **-emia**

he·mic /héemik/ *adj* relating to blood [Mid-19C. < Greek *haima* "blood"]

hem·i·cel·lu·lose /hèmmi séllyə lṑss, -lṑz/ *n* any polysaccharide found in plant cell walls [Because less complex than cellulose]

hem·i·chor·date /hèmmi káwr dàyt, -káwrdət/ *n* a marine animal resembling a worm that has a rudimentary cartilaginous skeleton (**notochord**) and numerous gill slits. Phylum: Hemichordata. [Late 19C. < modern Latin *Hemichordata* < Greek *hēmi-* "half" + Latin *chorda* (see CORD)] —**hem·i·chor·date** *adj*

hem·i·cy·cle /hémmi sīk'l/ *n* a structure or arrangement that has a semicircular shape [15C. Via French and Latin < Greek *hēmikuklion* "semicircle"] —**hem·i·cy·clic** /hèmmi sīklik, -síklik/ *adj*

hem·i·dem·i·sem·i·qua·ver /hèmmee dèmmee sémmee kwàyvər/ *n UK* MUSIC same as **sixty-fourth note**

hem·i·he·dral /hèmmi héedrəl/ *adj* describes crystals that have only half the number of faces needed for complete symmetry

hem·i·hy·drate /hèmmi hī dràyt/ *n* a hydrate that consists of two parts anhydrous compound to one part water, e.g., plaster of Paris

hem·i·me·tab·o·lous /hèmmee mə tábbələss/, **hem·i·met·a·bol·ic** /-mettə bóllik/ *adj* describes winged insects that lack complete metamorphosis, e.g., grasshoppers, whose increasingly larger nymphs approach adult form without going through a pupal stage

hem·i·mor·phic /hèmmi máwrfik/ *adj* describes crystals that do not have a horizontal axis of symmetry, so that the top and bottom of the crystal display different forms [Mid-19C. < HEMI- + Greek *morphē* "form"]

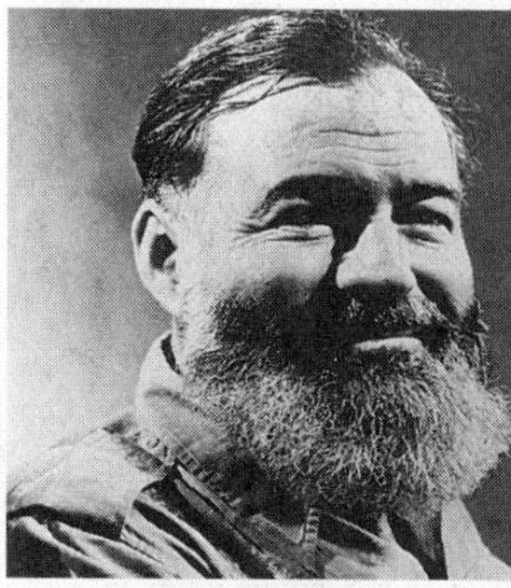
US Office of War Information

Ernest Hemingway

Hem·ing·way /hémming wày/, **Ernest** (1899–1961) US writer. He wrote fiction including *A Farewell to Arms* (1929) and *For Whom the Bell Tolls* (1940) in a distinctive terse style that complemented his own macho image and made him one of the century's leading novelists. He won the Nobel Prize in literature (1954). Full name **Hemingway, Ernest Miller**. See Cultural note at **bell**[1]

> "The world breaks everyone and afterward many are strong at the broken places. But those that do not break it kills. It kills the very good and the very gentle and the very brave impartially. If you are none of these you can be sure it will kill you too but there will be no special hurry."
> [Ernest Hemingway, *A Farewell to Arms*; 1929]

hem·i·o·la /hèmmee ṓlə/ *n* a rhythmic alternation of two musical notes in the place of three, or of three notes in place of two [14C. Via medieval Latin < Greek *hēmiolia* "in the ratio of one and a half to one" < *holos* "whole"]

hem·i·ple·gia /hèmmi pleejə/ *n* total or partial inability to move experienced on one side of the body, caused by brain disease or injury [Early 17C. Via modern Latin < Greek *hēmiplēgia* < *plēgē* (see -PLEGIA)] —**hem·i·ple·gic** *adj, n*

he·mip·ter·an /hə míptərən/ *n* any insect that has mouthparts adapted for piercing and sucking and two pairs of wings, belonging to an order that includes stinkbugs, bedbugs, and other true bugs. Order: Hemiptera. [Late 19C. < modern Latin *Hemiptera*, literally "with half a wing" < Greek *pteron* "wing"; from the partly hardened forewings of bugs] —**he·mip·ter·an** *adj* —**he·mip·ter·ous** *adj*

hem·i·sphere /hémmi sfeer/ *n* **1.** HALF OF EARTH one half of the Earth, especially a half north or south of the equator or west or east of the prime meridian **2.** HALF OF SPHERE one half of a sphere or of anything spherical in shape **3.** ANAT same as **cerebral hemisphere 4.** ASTRON HALF OF CELESTIAL SPHERE one half of the celestial sphere, north or south of the celestial equator [14C. Via French or Latin < Greek *hēmisphairion* < *sphaira* "ball"] —**hem·i·spher·ic** /hèmmi sféerik, -sférrik/ *adj* —**hem·i·spher·i·cal** *adj* —**hem·i·spher·i·cal·ly** *adv*

Hem·i·sphere *n* North, South, and Central America —**Hem·i·spher·ic** *adj*

Hem·i·spher·ic Eng·lish *n* the English spoken in the southwestern United States

hem·i·stich /hémmi stìk/ *n* one half of a line of poetry, usually separated from the rest by a caesura [Late 16C. Via late Latin < Greek *hēmistikhion* < *stikhos* "line of verse"]

hem·i·zy·gous /hèmmi zígəss/ *adj* having only one of a pair of genes, e.g., an unpaired X chromosome in males

hem·line /hém līn/ *n* **1.** the bottom edge of a skirt, dress, or coat **2.** the height of the bottom edge of a woman's skirt, dress, or coat, especially the typical height on fashionable women's clothing during a specific period ○ *Hemlines are up again.*

hemlock

hem·lock /hém lòk/ (*plural* **-locks** or *same*) *n* **1.** POISONOUS PLANT a very poisonous herb of the carrot family that has finely cut leaves, especially poison hemlock. Genus: *Conium*. **2.** POISON a poison obtained from the fruit of the poison hemlock plant. Hemlock was used in ancient Greece to execute people, and Socrates was forced to drink it when he was condemned to death. **3.** *also* **hem·lock fir** *or* **hem·lock spruce** TREES EVERGREEN TREE an evergreen tree of the pine family with short blunt needles and small cones. Genus: *Tsuga*. **4.** INDUST HEMLOCK WOOD the wood of the hemlock tree. Use: construction, paper pulp. [Old English *hymlic(e), hemlic*, origin ?]

hem·mer /hémmər/ *n* **1.** somebody who sews hems in clothes or other items **2.** a sewing machine attachment for sewing hems

hemo- *prefix* blood ○ *hemolysis* [< Greek *haima*]

he·mo·chro·ma·to·sis /heemə krōmə tṓsiss/ *n* a genetic disorder in which there is excess accumulation of iron in the body leading to damage of many organs, especially the liver and pancreas [Late 19C. < HEMO- + Greek *khromat-* "color"]

he·mo·coel /heemə seel/ *n* a body cavity in spiders, crustaceans, and other arthropods through which the blood or hemolymph circulates [Mid-19C. < HEMO- + Greek *koilos* "hollow"]

he·mo·cy·a·nin /heemō sī́ ənin/ *n* a bluish pigment found in the blood or hemolymph of some arthropods and mollusks that functions like hemoglobin, transporting oxygen to tissues [Late 19C. < HEMO- + Greek *kuan(e)os* "dark blue"]

he·mo·cyte /heemə sīt/ *n* a blood cell (*technical*)

he·mo·di·al·y·sis /heemō dī álləssiss/ *n* dialysis of the blood (*technical*)

he·mo·flag·el·late /heemō flájjə làyt, -lət, -flə jéllət/ *n* a flagellate protozoan that lives as a parasite in blood

he·mo·glo·bin /heemō glōbin/ *n* an iron-containing protein in red blood cells that transports oxygen around the body

he·mo·glo·bi·nu·ri·a /heemō glōbə nóoree ə/ *n* the presence in the urine of hemoglobin that has been freed from red blood cells —**he·mo·glo·bi·nu·ric** *adj*

he·mo·lymph /heemə lìmf/ *n* a fluid in some invertebrates that functions like the blood in vertebrates [Late 19C. < HEMO- + Latin *lympha* "clear liquid"] —**he·mo·lym·phat·ic** /heemə lim fáttik/ *adj*

he·mo·ly·sin /heemə lī́ssin, hi mólləssin/ *n* a bacterial toxin, antibody, or other agent that destroys red blood cells, releasing free hemoglobin

he·mol·y·sis /hi mólləssiss, heemə lī́ssiss/ *n* the destruction of red blood cells and the release of the hemoglobin they contain —**he·mo·lyt·ic** /heemə líttik/ *adj*

he·mo·lyt·ic a·ne·mi·a *n* anemia that results from the destruction of red blood cells and may be caused by bacteria, genetic disorders, or toxic chemicals

he·mo·lyze /heemə līz/ (**-lyzed, -lyz·ing, -lyz·es**) *vti* to destroy red blood cells and release hemoglobin, or undergo destruction and release hemoglobin

Hé·mon /ay maán/, **Louis** (1880–1913) French writer. He went to Canada in 1911, and is best known for his novel of French-Canadian pioneer life, *Maria Chapdelaine* (1914).

he·mo·phil·i·a /heemə fíllee ə, -féelyə/ *n* a disorder linked to a recessive gene on the X-chromosome and occurring almost exclusively in men and boys, in which the blood clots much more slowly than normally, resulting in extensive bleeding from even minor injuries

he·mo·phil·i·ac /heemə fíllee àk, -féelee àk/ *n* somebody who has hemophilia

he·mo·phil·ic /heemə fíllik/ *adj* **1.** relating to, resembling, or affected with hemophilia **2.** describes bacteria that are adapted to thrive in blood or a medium rich in blood

he·mo·poi·e·sis *n* PHYSIOL same as **hematopoiesis**

he·mop·ty·sis /hi móptəssiss/ *n* the coughing up of blood or mucus containing blood (*technical*) [Mid-17C. < HEMO- + Greek *ptusis* "act of spitting"]

~~**hemorrage**~~ incorrect spelling of **hemorrhage**

hem·or·rhage /hémmərij/ *n* **1.** EXCESSIVE BLEEDING the loss of blood from a ruptured blood vessel, either internally or externally ○ *a cerebral hemorrhage* **2.** UNCONTROLLED LOSS a large uncontrolled loss of something valuable ○ *a hemorrhage of cash that threatened the firm* ■ *v* (**hem·or·rhaged, hem·or·rhag·ing, hem·or·rhag·es**) **1.** *vi* BLEED HEAVILY to bleed profusely and uncontrollably ○ *The wound was hemorrhaging badly.* **2.** *vti* LOSE SOMETHING VALUABLE to experience a sudden, uncontrolled, and massive loss of something valuable ○ *The failed business had been hemorrhaging money for months.* [15C. Via French or medieval Latin < Greek *haimorrhagia* < *haima* "blood" + *rhēgnunai* "break, burst"] —**hem·or·rhag·ic** /hèmmə rájjik/ *adj*

hem·or·rhag·ic fe·ver *n* a viral infection that results in fever, chills, and profuse internal bleeding from the capillaries, e.g., dengue or Ebola

hem·or·rhoid·ec·to·my /hèmmə roy déktəmee/ (*plural* **-ec·to·mies**) *n* a surgical procedure to remove hemorrhoids

hem·or·rhoids /hémmə ròydz/ *npl* painful varicose veins in the canal of the anus —**hem·or·rhoid·al** /hèmmə róyd'l/ *adj*

hem·o·sid·er·in /hèmmō síddərin/ *n* a protein that stores iron

he·mo·sta·sis /heemə stáyssiss, hi móstəssiss/, **he·mo·sta·sia** /heemə stáyzhə/ *n* **1.** the stopping of bleeding or hemorrhaging in an organ or body part **2.** the stopping of the blood flow through an organ or body part

he·mo·stat /heemə stàt/ *n* **1.** a surgical instrument that stops bleeding by clamping a blood vessel **2.** a chemical agent that stops bleeding

he·mo·stat·ic /heemə státtik/ *adj* stopping or slowing down the flow of blood ■ *n* an agent that stops or slows down the flow of blood

hemp /hemp/ *n* **1.** TEXTILES TOUGH FIBER FROM ASIAN PLANT a tough fiber made from the stems of an Asian plant. Use: canvas, rope, paper, cloth. **2.** DRUGS NARCOTIC DRUG a narcotic drug made from an Asian plant that is smoked, chewed, eaten, or drunk to produce a mildly euphoric reaction **3.** (*plural same* or **hemps**) PLANTS PLANT a plant that produces hemp. Native to: Asia. Latin name: *Cannabis sativa*. **4.** TEXTILES TOUGH FIBER LIKE HEMP any strong fiber obtained from plant stems and used like hemp [Old English *henep* < Indo-European] —**hemp·en** *adj*

hemp ag·ri·mo·ny *n* a tall composite plant with leaves like those of the hemp plant. Flowers: red, pink, or purple, in clusters. Native to: Europe, Asia, North Africa. Latin name: *Eupatorium cannabinum*.

hemp net·tle *n* a bristly plant resembling a nettle with serrated leaves. Flowers: red, pink, purple, or white, two-lipped. Native to: Europe, Asia, naturalized in the United States. Latin name: *Galeopsis tetrahit*.

Hemp·stead /hémpstid, -sted/ village on western Long Island, southeastern New York State. It is a residential suburb of New York City. Population: 53,474 (2002 estimate).

hem·stitch /hém stìch/ *n* **1.** STITCH USED FOR HEMMING a small overcast stitch used to secure a hem **2.** DECORATIVE STITCH a decorative stitch used to ornament the edge of a piece of material, in which, after horizontal threads are removed, vertical threads are gathered in small regular bunches ■ *vti* (**-stitched, -stitch·ing, -stitch·es**) EDGE SOMETHING WITH HEMSTITCH to hem or decorate an edge of material using hemstitch —**hem·stitch·er** *n*

hen /hen/ *n* **1.** CHICKEN an adult female chicken **2.** BIRDS FEMALE BIRD any adult female bird **3.** MARINE BIOL FEMALE SEA ANIMAL a female octopus, crab, or lobster **4.** OFFENSIVE TERM an offensive term that deliberately insults a woman's personality, activity, and age (*dated*) [Old English *henn* < Indo-European, "sing"] —**hen·nish** *adj* —**hen·nish·ly** *adv* —**hen·nish·ness** *n* ◇ **scarce as hen's teeth** *UK* extremely valuable and hard to find

He·nan /hṑ naán/ densely populated province in eastern China, including important sites of early Chinese civilization. Capital: Zhengzhou. Population: 91,720,000 (1997). Area: 64,479 sq. mi./167,000 sq. km.

hen-and-chick·ens (*plural same* or **hens-and-chick·ens**) *n* a plant, especially the houseleek, that produces new plants as offsets that grow at the end of horizontal shoots or runners from the main plant [< the resemblance to chicks surrounding the mother hen]

hen·bane /hén bàyn/ *n* a poisonous plant of the nightshade family with hairy sticky leaves and a strong unpleasant smell. Use: source of the drugs hyoscyamine and scopolamine. Native to: Europe, Asia. Latin name: *Hyoscyamus niger*.

hen·bit /hén bìt/ *n* a plant of the mint family. Flowers: small, white or reddish purple, lipped. Native to: Europe, Asia, naturalized in the United States. Latin name: *Lamium amplexicaule*. [< BIT[1] in the obsolete sense "morsel of food"]

hence /henss/ *adv* **1.** BECAUSE OF THIS from this cause or for this reason (*formal*) ○ *I lent him money before, and he never paid it back; hence my reluctance to lend him more.* ○ *Her grandfather was Polish, hence her interest in Polish culture.* **2.** LATER THAN NOW later than the present time (*formal*) ○ *I'm sure the company will be in a much better financial position a year hence.* **3.** AWAY FROM HERE away from this place (*archaic*) ○ *Get you hence.* [13C. < Old English *heonan* "hence" + adverb suffix *-s* (as in *backwards, besides*)]

hence·forth /hénss fàwrth/, **hence·for·ward** /henss fáwrwərd/ *adv* from this time forward

Hench /hench/, **Philip Showalter** (1896–1965) US pathologist. He shared the Nobel Prize in physiology or medicine (1950) with biochemists Edward C. Kendall and Tadeus Reichstein for their research on hormones such as cortisone.

hench·man /hénchmən/ (*plural* **-men** /-mən/) *n* **1.** SUPPORTER OF SOMEBODY DUBIOUS somebody, especially a man, who is a supporter or associate of somebody in a dubious cause, e.g., a member of a criminal's entourage, or somebody whose status comes from supporting a politician (*disapproving*) **2.** LOYAL FOLLOWER somebody, especially a man, who is a loyal supporter or follower, especially of somebody who holds a high office or position **3.** PAGE OR SQUIRE a page or squire to somebody of high rank (*archaic*) [14C. < Old English *hengest* "stallion"]

hench·wo·man /hénch wŏŏmmən/ (*plural* **-men** /-wìmmin/) *n* **1.** a woman who is a supporter or associate of somebody in a dubious cause, e.g., a member of a criminal's entourage, or somebody whose status comes from supporting a politician (*disapproving*) **2.** a woman who is a loyal supporter or follower, especially of somebody who holds a high office or position [Late 19C. After HENCHMAN]

hen·coop /hén kòop/ *n* a cage, hutch, or small building where hens or other domestic birds are kept

hendeca- *prefix* eleven of something such as sides, facets, or units ○ *hendecasyllable* [< Greek *hendeka* "eleven"]

hen·dec·a·syl·la·ble /hen dèkə síllәb'l/ *n* a line of verse that consists of 11 syllables —**hen·dec·a·syl·lab·ic** /hen dèkə si lábbik/ *adj*

Hen·der·son /héndərss'n/ city in northwestern Kentucky on the Ohio River, on the border with Indiana. Population: 27,426 (1998).

hen·di·a·dys /hen dī́ ədiss/ *n* a literary device expressing an idea by means of two words linked by "and," instead of a grammatically more complex form such as an adverb qualifying an adjective. Everyday examples of hendiadys are the expressions "nice and soft," rather than "nicely soft," and "good and tight." [Late 16C. < medieval Latin < Greek *hen dia duoin* "one through two"]

Hen·dricks /héndriks/, **Thomas A.** (1819–85) vice president of the United States (1885). A Democrat from Ohio, he served in the House of Representatives (1851–55) and Senate (1862–69) before becoming Grover Cleveland's vice president. He died within a year of taking office.

Popperfoto

Jimi Hendrix

Hen·drix /héndriks/, **Jimi** (1942–70) US musician. A virtuoso blues-rock guitarist, he was known for songs like "Wild Thing" and albums including *Are You Experienced?* (1967). His charismatic stage performance was captured in the movie *Woodstock* (1970). Full name **Hendrix, James Marshall**

> "A musician, if he's a messenger, is like a child who hasn't been handled too many times by man, hasn't had too many fingerprints across his brain."
> [Jimi Hendrix, *Life*; 1969]

hen·e·quen /hénnikwən/, **hen·e·quin** *n* **1.** a reddish fiber obtained from the leaves of a tropical American plant. Use: rope, twine, coarse fabric. **2.** a plant that has large thick fibrous leaves shaped like swords that yield henequen. Native to: tropical America, chiefly the Yucatán peninsula of Mexico. Latin name: *Agave fourcroydes.* [Early 17C. < Spanish]

hen·house /hén hòwss/ (*plural* **-hous·es** /-hòwzəz/) *n* a shelter or small shed where hens or other domestic birds are housed

Hen·le's loop /hènleez-/ *n* ANAT same as **loop of Henle**

Hen·man /hénmən/, **Tim** (*b.* 1974) British tennis player. He has won nine singles titles and been a semifinalist at Wimbledon three times (1998, 1999, 2001). Full name **Henman, Timothy Henry**

hen·na /hénnə/ *n* **1.** COSMETICS, INDUST **RED DYE** a deep red dye made from plant leaves. Use: hair dye, cosmetics, fabric colorant. **2.** PLANTS **SHRUB** a bush with leaves that yield the red dye henna. Native to: Asia, North Africa. Latin name: *Lawsonia inermis.* **3.** COLORS **REDDISH BROWN COLOR** a rich reddish brown color ■ *adj* COLORS **OF REDDISH BROWN COLOR** of a rich reddish brown color ■ *vt* (**-naed, -na·ing, -nas**) COSMETICS, INDUST **USE HENNA TO COLOR SOMETHING** to dye or color something with henna [Early 17C. < Arabic *ḥinnā'*]

Hen·ne·pin /hénnəpən/, **Louis** (1626–1705?) Flemish-born American missionary and explorer. A missionary among the Iroquois people, he explored the upper Mississippi River. Born **Hennepin, Johannes**

Hen·ning /hénning/, **Doug** (1947–2000) Canadian magician and performer on television, in movies, and in the Broadway musicals *The Magic Show* (1974) and *Merlin* (1983)

hen·o·the·ism /hénnə thee ìzzəm/ *n* the worship of one god while acknowledging the existence of other gods [Mid-19C. < Greek *heno-* "one" + *theos* "god"] —**hen·o·the·ist** *n* —**hen·o·the·is·tic** /hènnə thee ístik/ *adj*

hen·peck /hén pèk/ (**-pecked, -peck·ing, -pecks**) *vt* an offensive term meaning to annoy or torment a husband or partner through continual nagging and faultfinding [< hens' practice of plucking the rooster]

Hen·ri /hénnree/, **Robert** (1865–1929) US artist. He was the guiding force behind The Eight, the so-called Ashcan School of realistic painting formed in 1908.

> "The object of painting is not to make a picture...The object, which is at the back of every true work of art is *the attainment of a state of being*, a state of high functioning, a more than ordinary moment of existence."
> [Robert Henri, *The Art Spirit*; 1923]

Hen·ri·et·ta Ma·ri·a /henree èttə mə rée ə/ (1609–69) French-born queen consort of England. After her marriage to Charles I (1625), her involvement in English politics made her highly unpopular.

hen·ry /hénnree/ (*plural* **-ries**) *n* the SI unit of electrical inductance, equal to an electrical potential of one volt induced in a closed circuit by a current varying uniformly by one ampere per second. Symbol **H** [Late 19C. After Joseph HENRY]

Hen·ry I /hénree/ (1068–1135) king of the English. He was the youngest son of William the Conqueror. His reign (1100–35) is notable for his conquest of Normandy (1106) and consolidation of his English and French realms.

> "An illiterate king is a crowned ass."
> [Attributed to Henry I. Described as a proverbial expression of Henry's in *De Gestis Regum Anglorum*, William of Malmesbury]

Hen·ry II (1133–89) king of the English. French-born English monarch. The first Plantagenet English king (1154–89), he imposed a strong central administration and judicial reform and annexed Ireland (1171–72). His knights murdered Thomas à Becket (1170) after a long dispute over the power of the Church.

> "Will no one rid me of this turbulent priest?"
> [Oral tradition, attributed to Henry II; 1170]

Hen·ry III (1207–72) king of England. The son of King John, he began his long reign (1216–72) at the age of nine. His rule was marked by tensions with the nobility, which came to a head in 1264 with the short-lived rebellion of the English soldier and aristocrat Simon de Montfort.

Hen·ry IV (1367–1413) king of England. The son of John of Gaunt, he was the first Lancastrian English king. His reign (1399–1413) was marked by baronial revolts, Owen Glendower's Welsh rebellion (1400–09), and conflicts with Parliament over royal finance. Born **Bolingbroke, Henry**

Hen·ry IV (1553–1610) king of France (1589–1610). The first Bourbon king of France, Henry was an effective military leader and brought stability to the country after years of religious warfare. He was assassinated by a Catholic extremist in 1610.

> "I want there to be no peasant in my kingdom so poor that he is unable to have a chicken in his pot every Sunday."
> [Henry IV. Quoted in *Histoire de Henri le Grand*, Hardouin de Péréfixe; 1681]

Hen·ry V (1387–1422) king of England. He was the son of Henry IV. During his reign (1413–22) he invaded France, winning the Battle of Agincourt (1415) against superior forces, conquering Normandy (1417–20), and being declared heir to the French throne (1420).

Hen·ry VI (1165–97) king of Germany and Holy Roman emperor. As German king (1190–97), he conquered and annexed Sicily (1194). He became Holy Roman emperor in 1191.

Hen·ry VI (1421–71) king of England. The son of Henry V, he lost all of England's French possessions except Calais during his reign (1422–61, 1470–71). His ineffectual leadership at home sparked the Wars of the Roses (1455–85).

Hen·ry VII (1457–1509) king of England. He ended the Wars of the Roses by defeating Richard III at Bosworth (1485), and founded the Tudor dynasty. His reign (1485–1509) was noted for national unity and efficient government administration. Born **Tudor, Henry**

Hen·ry VIII (1491–1547) king of England and Ireland. He succeeded his father, Henry VII. During his reign (1509–47), he broke with the Roman Catholic Church (1534) and assumed control over the Church of England. He is notorious for his six marriages and execution of two of his wives.

> "The kings of England in times past never had any superior but God. Wherefore know you that we will maintain the rights of the Crown...as any of our progenitors."
> [Henry VIII, *Remark*; 1515]

Hen·ry (the Lion) (1129?–95) duke of Saxony and of Bavaria. He expanded his territories to the east of Saxony and challenged the power of the Holy Roman Empire, but lost his duchies in 1180 to Frederick I.

Hen·ry, Alexander (1739–1824) Canadian fur trader. He wrote of his experiences in *Travels and Adventures in Canada and the Indian Territories* (1809).

Hen·ry, Joseph (1797–1878) US physicist. He discovered electromagnetism independent of Michael Faraday, and developed the first electric motor (1829), telegraph (1831), and electric relay (1835). He was the Smithsonian Institution's first secretary and director (1846–78).

Hen·ry, Lenny (*b.* 1958) British comedian. A popular television performer, his appearances included the British series *Tiswas* (1979–82) and *The Lenny Henry Show* (1984–95). Full name **Henry, Lehworth George**

Hen·ry, O. (1862–1910) US writer. His short stories relied heavily on coincidence, dramatic irony, and surprise endings. Among the most famous is *The Gift of the Magi* (1906). Born **Porter, William Sydney**

> "Life is made up of sobs, sniffles and smiles, with sniffles predominating."
> [O. Henry, *The Gift of the Magi*; 1906]

Hen·ry, Patrick (1736–99) American orator and revolutionary. He was Virginia's first nonroyal governor (1776–79, 1784–86).

> "I know not what course others may take; but as for me, give me liberty or give me death!"
> [Patrick Henry, *Speech to the Virginia Assembly*; May 1765]

> "Caesar had his Brutus—Charles the First, his Cromwell—and George the Third ('Treason!' cried the Speaker)...may profit by their example. If *this* be treason, make the most of it."
> [Patrick Henry, *Speech to the Virginia Convention*; March 23, 1775]

Hen·ry's law /hénreez-/ *n* the principle that the amount of gas dissolved under equilibrium in a volume of liquid is in direct proportion to the pressure of the gas that contacts the liquid surface [Late 19C. After William *Henry* (1774–1836), British chemist]

Hen·son /hénss'n/, **Jim** (1936–90) US puppeteer. He invented the Muppets, which appeared on the television programs *Sesame Street* and *The Muppet Show* (1976–81). Full name **Henson, James Maury**

Hen·son, Matthew (1866–1955) US explorer. As Robert Peary's assistant, he participated in seven polar expeditions, including the one credited with the discovery of the North Pole (1909). Full name **Henson, Matthew Alexander**

hep[1] /hep/ (**hep·per, hep·pest**) *adj* same as **hip**[2] (*dated slang*) [Early 20C. Origin ?]

hep[2] /hep/ *n* MED same as **hepatitis** (*informal*) [Shortening]

hep·a·rin /héppərin/ *n* an anticlotting agent present in the body. Use: produced synthetically to treat thrombosis. [Early 20C. < obsolete *hepar* "sulfur compound," via late Latin < Greek *hēpar* "liver (the organ)"] —**hep·a·rin·oid** *adj*

hepat- *prefix* same as **hepato-** (*used before vowels*)

hep·a·tec·to·my /hèppə téktəmee/ (*plural* **-mies**) *n* surgical removal of all or part of the liver

he·pat·ic /hi páttik/ *adj* **1.** ANAT **OF LIVER** relating to or affecting the liver **2.** COLORS **LIVER-COLORED** of a brownish red color like that of liver **3.** BOT **OF LIVERWORT FAMILY** relating to, belonging to, or resembling the members of the liverwort family of flowerless green plants ■ *n* **1. DRUG FOR LIVER DISEASE** a drug that treats liver disease **2.** PLANTS same as **liverwort** [14C. Via Latin < Greek *hēpatikos* < *hēpat-* "liver (the organ)"]

he·pat·i·ca /hi páttikə/ *n* a woodland plant, related to the buttercup, that has three-lobed leaves. Flowers: white, lilac, purple. Native to: northern temperate regions. Genus: *Hepatica*. [15C. Via medieval Latin < Greek *hēpatikos* (see HEPATIC); from the shape of the leaves]

hep·a·ti·tis /hèppə tītiss/ *n* inflammation of the liver, causing fever, jaundice, abdominal pain, and weakness

hep·a·ti·tis A *n* a relatively mild form of hepatitis that is caused by a virus and transmitted through contaminated food and water

hep·a·ti·tis B *n* a sometimes recurring or fatal form of hepatitis that is caused by a virus and transmitted through contact with infected blood, blood products, and bodily fluids

hepato- *prefix* person's or animal's liver ○ *hepatotoxic* [< Greek *hēpat-*, stem of *hēpar* < Indo-European]

hep·a·to·cel·lu·lar /hèppətō séllyələr, hi pàttə-/ *adj* relating to liver cells

hep·a·to·cyte /héppətə sīt, hi páttə-/ *n* a cell of the liver

hep·a·tog·e·nous /hèppə tójjənəss/ *adj* originating in the liver

hep·a·to·ma /hèppə tṓmə/ (*plural* **-mas** or **-ma·ta** /-mətə/) *n* a tumor of the liver

hep·a·to·meg·a·ly /hèppətə méggəlee, hi pàttə-/ *n* enlargement of the liver

hep·a·to·pan·cre·as /hèppətə pángkree əss, -pánkree-, hi pàttə-/ *n* a glandular digestive organ of some invertebrates and fish that combines the digestive functions of the mammalian liver and pancreas

hep·a·to·tox·ic /hèppətō tóksik, hi pàttə-/ *adj* describes a condition in which the liver is damaged

hep·a·to·tox·ic·i·ty /hèppətō tok síssətee, hi pàttə-/ *n* **1.** a condition in which the liver is damaged **2.** the capacity or tendency of something to damage the liver

hep·a·to·tox·in /hèppətō tóksin, hi pàttə-/ *n* a substance that causes damage to the liver

Audrey Hepburn

Hep·burn /hép bùrn/, **Audrey** (1929–93) Belgian-born US actor. She starred in numerous movies, including *Funny Face* (1957) and *Breakfast at Tiffany's* (1961). During her last years she was a roving ambassador for UNICEF. Born **Heemstra Hepburn-Ruston, Edda van**

Katharine Hepburn

Hep·burn, Katharine (1907?–2003) US actor. She is known for her roles as strong-willed heroines, and won Academy Awards for *Morning Glory* (1933), *Guess Who's Coming to Dinner* (1967), *The Lion in Winter* (1968), and *On Golden Pond* (1981). Full name **Hepburn, Katharine Houghton**

"First God made England, Ireland, and Scotland. That's when he corrected his mistakes and made Wales."
[Katharine Hepburn, *Time*; August 7, 1978]

"When a man says he likes a woman in a skirt, I tell him to try one."
[Katharine Hepburn, *WETA-TV, Washington, D.C.*; June 27, 1994]

hep·cat /hép kàt/ *n* a knowing and aware person, especially a jazz fan in the 1940s (*dated slang*) [Mid-20C. < HEP[1]]

He·phaes·tus /hi féstəss/, **He·phais·tos** /hi fístəss/ *n* in Greek mythology, the god of fire and fire-based arts such as metalwork. He was the son of Hera and Zeus. Roman equivalent **Vulcan**

Hepplewhite: 18th-century chair

Hep·ple·white /hépp'l wīt, -hwīt/ *adj* in or relating to the style of furniture designed by George Hepplewhite, characterized by graceful curving lines, delicate inlays, and often floral or ribbon designs. Open chair backs in the shape of a heart or shield are a feature of the style. ■ *n* furniture or a piece of furniture made by or in the style of Hepplewhite

Hep·ple·white /hépp'l wīt, -hwīt/, **George** (*d.* 1786) British furniture designer. He produced over 300 designs in *The Cabinet-Maker and Upholsterer's Guide* (1788) that are characterized by a combination of simplicity and delicacy.

hept- *prefix* same as **hepta-** (*used before vowels*)

hepta- *prefix* seven ○ *heptahedron* [< Greek *hepta* < Indo-European]

hep·ta·chlor /héptə klàwr/ *n* a chlorinated hydrocarbon. Use: pesticide. Formula: $C_{10}H_5Cl_7$.

hep·tad /hép tàd/ *n* a set or series of seven [Mid-17C. < Greek *heptad-* "the number seven" < *hepta* "seven"]

hep·ta·gon /héptə gòn/ *n* a two-dimensional geometric figure formed of seven angles and seven sides [Late 16C. Directly or via French < medieval Latin *heptagonum* < Greek *heptagōnos* "having seven angles"] —**hep·tag·o·nal** /hep tággən'l/ *adj*

hep·ta·he·dron /hèptə heedrən/ (*plural* **-drons** or **-dra** /-drə/) *n* a three-dimensional geometric figure formed of seven plane faces —**hep·ta·he·dral** *adj*

hep·tam·er·ous /hep támmərəss/ *adj* describes plant parts such as petals or sepals that grow or are arranged in groups of seven

hep·tam·e·ter /hep támmətər/ *n* a line of poetry or verse composed of seven metric feet [Late 19C. Via late Latin < Greek *heptametron* < *hepta* "seven" + *metron* "meter"] —**hep·ta·met·ri·cal** /hèptə méttrik'l/ *adj*

hep·tane /hép tàyn/ *n* an isomeric form of an organic chemical, especially a colorless flammable liquid alkane hydrocarbon. Source: petroleum. Use: solvent, anesthetic, determination of octane ratings. Formula: C_7H_{16}.

hep·tarch /hép taark/ *n* one of the seven rulers in a heptarchy

hep·tar·chy /hép taarkee/ (*plural* **-chies**) *n* **1.** government by seven rulers or leaders **2.** a state governed by seven rulers, or one divided into seven parts, each ruled by a different head —**hep·tar·chic** /hep taarkik/ *adj* —**hep·tar·chic·al** *adj*

Hep·tar·chy *n* the association consisting of the seven English kingdoms of Kent, Sussex, Wessex, Essex, Northumbria, East Anglia, and Mercia during the period from the 5th to the 9th centuries A.D.

hep·ta·stich /héptə stìk/ *n* a seven-line stanza or poem

Hep·ta·teuch /héptə tōōk, -tyōōk/ *n* the first seven books of the Bible, comprising Genesis, Exodus, Leviticus, Numbers, Deuteronomy, Joshua, and Judges [Late 17C. Via late Latin < Greek *heptateukhos* < *hepta* "seven" + *teukhos* "book"]

hep·tath·lon /hep táth lòn, -lən/ *n* an athletic competition, usually for women, in which the contestants compete in seven different track-and-field events and are awarded points for each to find the best all-around athlete. The events are the javelin, hurdles, high jump, long jump, shot put, sprint, and 800-meter race. [Late 20C. < HEPTA- + Greek *athlon* "contest"] —**hep·tath·lete** *n*

hep·tose /hép tōss, -tōz/ *n* a sugar with seven carbon atoms in the molecule

Dame Barbara Hepworth: Working on the plaster model for the bronze sculpture *Rock (Porthcurno)*

Hep·worth /hépwərth/, **Dame Barbara** (1903–75) British sculptor. Many of her works, e.g., the Dag Hammarskjöld Memorial (1964) at the U.N. headquarters in New York, are massive abstract shapes in stone or wood, pierced by holes. Full name **Hepworth, Dame Jocelyn Barbara**

her /hur/; *unstressed form* /hər, ər/ *pron* (*as the object or complement of a verb or preposition*) **1. WOMAN OR GIRL NOT REFERRED TO BY NAME** used to refer to a woman, girl, or female animal who has been previously mentioned or whose identity is known ○ *Ask her to wait.* ○ *We left the report with her.* ○ *I know it's her.* **2. MACHINE** used to refer to a car, machine, or ship that has been previously mentioned or whose identity is known ○ *Fill her up, please.* **3. COUNTRY** used to refer to a country or nation when it has been mentioned or its identity is known (*formal*) ○ *the United States and those who trade with her* ■ *adj* **RELATING TO HER** belonging to or associated with a woman, girl, female animal, car, machine, ship, country, or nation that has been mentioned earlier or whose identity is known ○ *That's her coat.* ○ *the Bismarck and her crew* [Old English *hire* < Indo-European, "this"]

her. *abbr* **1.** heraldic **2.** heraldry

He·ra /hééra, hérrə/, **He·re** /héeree, hérree/ *n* in Greek mythology, the goddess of marriage and the wife of Zeus. She was often portrayed as jealous and resentful of infidelity. Roman equivalent **Juno** (sense 1)

Her·a·cles /hérrə kleez/, **Her·a·kles** *n* in Greek mythology, the son of Zeus and Alcmene, noted for his courage and great strength and the performing of 12 near-impossible labors. Roman equivalent **Hercules** (sense 1) —**Her·a·cle·an** /hèrrə klée ən/ *adj*

Her·a·cli·tus /hèrrə klítəss/ (*fl* 500? B.C.) Greek philosopher. He was an early metaphysician. Only fragments remain of his major work, *On Nature*. —**He·ra·cli·te·an** /hèrrə klítee ən/*adj*

> "The way up and the way down are one and the same."
> [Heraclitus. Quoted in *The Presocratic Philosophers*, G. S. Kirk, J. E. Raven, and M. Schofield; 1983]

Her·a·cli·us /he ráklee əss/ (575?–641) Byzantine emperor. He came to power in a coup (610) after deposing Phocas. He successfully repelled a Persian invasion (622–28), and reclaimed the True Cross, an important Christian relic (630).

Her·a·kles *n* MYTHOL another spelling of **Heracles**

Her·ak·li·on /he ráklee òn/ seaport and the largest city on the Greek island of Crete. Population: 116,178 (1991). Greek name **Iráklion**

her·ald /hérrəld/ *n* **1.** BRINGER OF NEWS somebody who brings or announces important news **2.** SIGN OF WHAT WILL HAPPEN somebody or something that is a forerunner of something or gives an indication of something that is going to happen (*literary*) ○ *The robin is the herald of spring.* **3.** HIST OFFICIAL MESSENGER an official messenger and representative of a king or leader in former times **4.** HIST OFFICIAL AT MEDIEVAL TOURNAMENTS at medieval tournaments and jousting contests, somebody who performed official duties **5.** HERALDRY HERALDIC OFFICIAL in England, an official who is concerned with heraldry ■ *vt* (**-ald·ed, -ald·ing, -alds**) **1.** SIGNAL SOMETHING to give or be a sign that something is going to happen **2.** WELCOME SOMEBODY OR SOMETHING to welcome or announce somebody or something with enthusiasm [14C. < Old French *herault* < Germanic, "commander of the army"]

he·ral·dic /hə ráldik/ *adj* belonging or relating to heraldry or heralds —**he·ral·di·cal·ly** *adv*

her·ald moth *n* a nocturnal hibernating moth marked by mottled brown forewings and dull gray hind wings. Native to: northern Europe. Latin name: *Scoliopteryx libatrix*.

her·ald·ry /hérrəldree/ *n* **1.** STUDY OF COATS OF ARMS the profession or study of the devising and granting of coats of arms and of determining who is entitled to bear them **2.** COATS OF ARMS coats of arms and the symbols and conventions connected with them **3.** POMP pomp and ceremony

her·alds' col·lege *n* HERALDRY same as **College of Arms**

He·rat /he rát/ city in northwestern Afghanistan, situated on the Hari River. Population: 177,300 (1988 estimate).

herb /urb, hurb/ *n* **1.** a low-growing aromatic plant used fresh or dried for seasoning, for its medicinal properties, or in perfumes. Sage and rosemary are herbs. **2.** BOT a seed-producing flowering plant that does not produce woody stems and that forms new stems and leaves each season **3.** DRUGS same as **marijuana** (*slang*) [13C. Via French < Latin *herba* "grass, herb"]

her·ba·ceous /hur báyshəss, ur-/ *adj* **1.** WITHOUT WOODY STEMS describes plants or plant parts that are fleshy and wither after each growing season, as opposed to plants such as trees that grow woody stems and are persistent **2.** RESEMBLING LEAVES similar to leaves in color and general appearance **3.** OF AROMATIC PLANTS relating to aromatic herbs such as sage, dill, or thyme [Mid-17C. < Latin *herbaceus* < *herba* "grass, herb"] —**her·ba·ceous·ly** *adv*

her·ba·ceous bor·der *n* a flower bed that is mainly planted with perennial plants rather than with annuals

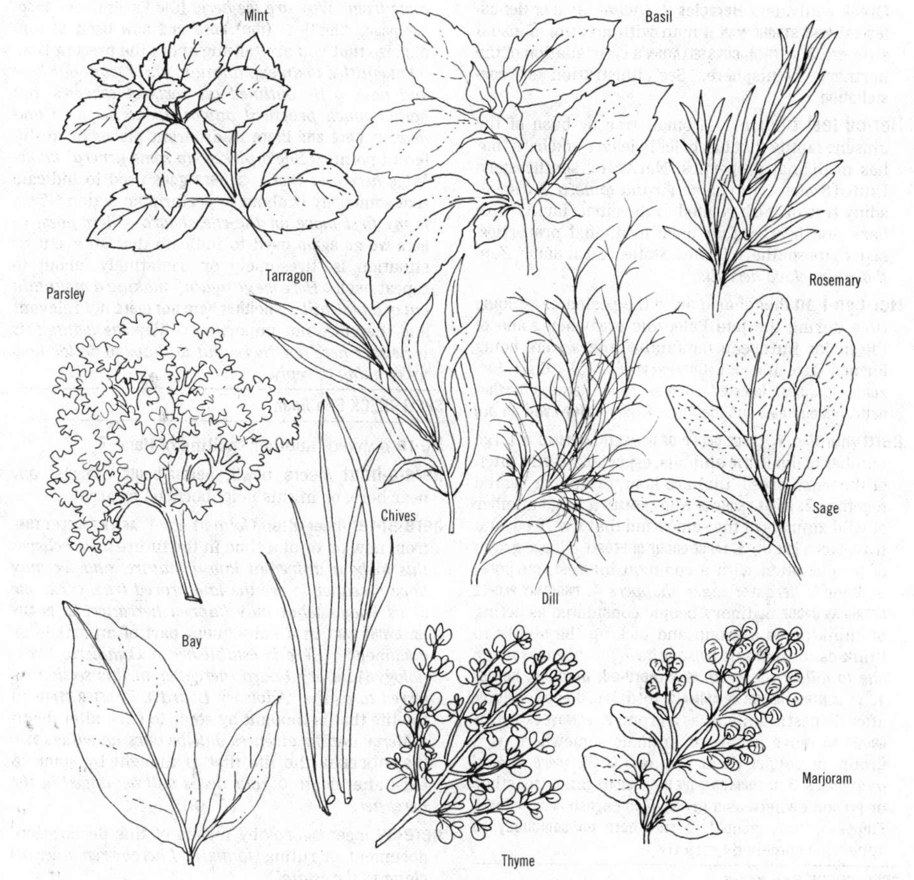

herb

herb·age /úrbij, húrbij/ *n* **1.** herbaceous plants, especially their leafy or succulent and edible parts **2.** grass and other vegetation growing in fields, pasture land, and meadows [14C. Via French < medieval Latin *herbagium* < Latin *herba* "grass, herb"]

herb·al /úrb'l, húr-/ *adj* characteristic of, consisting of, or made with aromatic herbs ○ *an herbal remedy* ■ *n* a book that lists individual herbs and describes their properties and possible uses [Early 16C. < medieval Latin *herbalis* < Latin *herba* "grass, herb"]

herb·al·ism /úrbə lìzzəm, húr-/ *n* **1.** same as **herbal medicine** (sense 1) **2.** the study of herbs and their medicinal uses **3.** the growth, collection, and sale or dispensing of aromatic herbs, especially those considered to have medicinal properties

herb·al·ist /úrbəlist, húr-/ *n* **1.** a grower, collector, or seller of aromatic herbs, especially those considered to have medicinal properties **2.** *Can, UK* ALTERN MED same as **herb doctor** **3.** a botanist, especially one concerned with the classification of plants (*archaic*)

herb·al med·i·cine *n* **1.** a system of medical treatment based on the properties of medicinal herbs **2.** a medication made from herbs

her·bar·i·um /hur bérree əm, ur-/ (*plural* **-i·ums** or **-i·a** /-ee ə/) *n* **1.** a collection of dried plants, especially one in which the plants have been mounted, systematically classified, and labeled for use in scientific studies **2.** a building, room, or other place where an herbarium is kept [Late 18C. < late Latin < Latin *herbarius* "herbalist" < *herba* "grass, herb"] —**her·ba·ri·al** *adj*

herb ben·net /-bénnət/ *n* a common wild plant that has long hairy stems and hooked seeds. Flowers: small, yellow. Native to: Europe, Asia, North Africa. Latin name: *Geum urbanum*.

herb doc·tor *n US* a traditional doctor who uses herbs and other medicines to remedy illness and discomfort. Can term **herbalist**

herbed /urbd, hurbd/ *adj* flavored with herbs

Her·bert /húrbərt/, **Victor** (1859–1924) Irish-born US composer. He wrote more than 40 operettas including *Babes in Toyland* (1903) and *Naughty Marietta* (1910).

her·bi·cide /húrbə sìd, úr-/ *n* a chemical preparation designed to kill plants, especially weeds, or to inhibit their growth —**her·bi·cid·al** /hùrbi síd'l, ùrbi-/ *adj* —**her·bi·ci·dal·ly** *adv*

her·bi·vore /húrbi vàwr, úr-/ *n* an animal that feeds only or mainly on grass and other plants [Mid-19C. < French, or back-formation < HERBIVOROUS]

her·biv·o·rous /hur bívvərəss, ur-/ *adj* eating only or mainly grass or other plants, or relating to the eating of such plants [Mid-17C. < modern Latin *herbivorus* "eating grass" < Latin *herba* "grass, herb"]

herb Par·is (*plural* **herbs Par·is**) *n* a woodland plant having a whorl of four leaves at right angles to the stem and bearing a single black berry. Flowers: single, greenish yellow. Native to: Europe. Latin name: *Paris quadrifolia*. [Partial translation of medieval Latin *herba paris* "herb of a pair," assimilated to PARIS[2]]

herb Rob·ert (*plural* **herbs Rob·ert**) *n* a common wild plant of the cranesbill family that has red-tinged leaves and stems with a strong unpleasant odor. Flowers: small, pink. Native to: temperate northern Europe, Asia. Latin name: *Geranium robertianum*. [Origin ?]

herb·y /úrbee, húrbee/ (**-i·er, -i·est**) *adj* **1.** WITH HERBAL TASTE OR SMELL tasting or smelling of herbs **2.** OF AROMATIC HERBS relating to aromatic or medicinal herbs **3.** FULL OF GROWING HERBS having a lot of growing herbs or grass

Her·cu·la·ne·um /hùrkyə láynee əm/ ancient Roman town near modern Naples, destroyed with its neighbor Pompeii in the eruption of Vesuvius in A.D. 79

Her·cu·le·an /hùrkyə lée ən, hur kyóolee ən/ *adj* **1.** relating to or associated with Hercules **2.** *also* **her·cu·le·an** requiring a great deal of strength, effort, stamina, or resources

Her·cu·les /húrkyə leez/ *n* **1.** MYTHOL ROMAN MYTHOLOGICAL HERO in Roman mythology, the son of Jupiter and Alcmene, noted for his courage and great strength and the performing of 12 near-impossible labors.

Greek equivalent **Heracles** **2.** (*plural same* or **Her·cu·les·es**) VERY STRONG MAN a man with great or unusual strength **3.** ASTRON CONSTELLATION a constellation of the northern hemisphere. See illustration at **constellation**

Her·cu·les' club *n* **1.** a small tree or bush of the ginseng family that has prickly leaves and bark that has medicinal properties. Native to: southeastern United States. Latin name: *Aralia spinosa*. **2.** a small spiny tree or bush related to the citrus family with bark and berries that have medicinal properties. Native to: southern United States. Latin name: *Zanthoxylum clava-herculis.*

Her·cyn·i·an /hur sínnee ən/ *n* the period of geologic time during the late Paleozoic era when some of the major European mountain ranges were being formed [Late 16C. < Latin *Hercynia (silva)* < Greek *Herkunios (drumos)*, forested mountain region between the Carpathian Mountains and the Rhine River] —**Her·cyn·i·an** *adj*

herd /hurd/ *n* **1.** LARGE GROUP OF DOMESTIC ANIMALS a large number of domestic animals, especially cattle, often of the same breed, that are kept, driven, or reared together **2.** LARGE GROUP OF WILD ANIMALS a large number of wild animals of the same kind that live, feed, and travel as a group **3.** LARGE GROUP OF PEOPLE a large group of people, often with a common interest, purpose, or bond ○ *herds of eager shoppers* **4.** ORDINARY PEOPLE ACTING AS GROUP ordinary people considered as acting or thinking as a group and lacking the ability to think as individuals (*disapproving*) ○ *She was never one to follow the herd.* ■ *v* (**herd·ed, herd·ing, herds**) **1.** *vt* CONTROL GROUP OF ANIMALS to drive, keep, or look after domestic animals as a group **2.** *vt* MOVE OR COLLECT GROUP to move people or animals somewhere as a group, or collect them into one ○ *We were herded onto buses.* **3.** *vi* FORM OR MOVE IN GROUP to gather together or go somewhere as a group [Old English *heord* < Indo-European, "row, group"] ◇ **ride herd on somebody** to supervise somebody strictly

SPELLCHECK See *heard.*

herd·book /húrd bo͝ok/ *n* a book that gives details of the pedigrees of domestic animals, especially cattle or hogs

herd·er /húrdər/ *n* **1.** somebody who tends or drives domestic animals in groups, especially on open pasture or land **2.** AGRIC same as **herdsman** (sense 1)

Her·der /hérdər/, **Johann Gottfried von** (1744–1803) German philosopher and critic. He is an important figure in the development of German romanticism, whose most important work is *Outline of a Philosophy of the History of Man* (1784–91).

herd in·stinct *n* the innate desire to belong to, be associated with, or imitate the behavior of a group

herds·man /húrdzmən/ (*plural* **-men** /-mən/) *n* **1.** somebody, especially a man, who owns or breeds cattle or other livestock **2.** *UK* same as **herder** (sense 1) [Alteration of Old English *heordman* "herdsman," after such words as *craftsman*]

herds·per·son /húrdz pùrss'n/ (*plural* **-peo·ple** /-peep'l/ or **-per·sons**) *n* same as **herder**

herds·wom·an /húrdz wo͝ommən/ (*plural* **-wom·en** /-wìmmin/) *n* **1.** a woman who owns or breeds cattle or other livestock **2.** a woman who tends or drives domestic animals in groups, especially on open pasture or land

here /heer/ CORE MEANING: an adverb used to refer to this place or this time ○ *How long have you been waiting here?* ○ *Winter is here.*

adv **1.** IN THIS PLACE in, at, or to the place where you are, or at a place near you ○ *Have you been here before?* ○ *Come and sit here, beside me.* **2.** AT THIS POINT OR STAGE used to draw attention to a particular point or stage in a situation ○ *I want to say here, before I go further, that only part of the credit should be mine.* **3.** NOW indicates a situation or event that is happening at the present time ○ *The time for celebrations is here.* **4.** INDICATES OFFER indicates that somebody is offering something to somebody ○ *Here are some general guidelines.* ○ *Here's my card.* **5.** INTRODUCES SOMETHING used to introduce or draw attention to a topic ○ *Now, here is a question for everybody.* **6.** LIFE ON EARTH used to refer to people in general and their life on Earth ○ *Where did we come from? Why are we here?* [Old English *hēr* < Indo-European, "this"] ◇ **(the) here and now** used to emphasize that you are talking about the present time ○ *I'm entitled to an explanation, and I want one here and now.* ○ *He outlined all sorts of schemes, but hadn't much practical advice about the here and now.* ◇ **here and there** in different places or at different points ○ *She'd picked up some general knowledge here and there.* ◇ **here goes** used to indicate that somebody is about to perform an action ○ *This is my first move on the chessboard – here goes!* ◇ **here we go again** used to indicate that an event or situation is, tiresomely or irritatingly, about to repeat itself ○ *Here we go again – making a mountain out of a molehill.* ◇ **neither here nor there** not relevant and therefore not important ○ *Why she wants this is neither here nor there, but we have to decide how we're going to reply.*

SPELLCHECK See *hear.*

He·re *n* MYTHOL another spelling of **Hera**

here·a·bout /hééra bòwt/, **here·a·bouts** /-bòwts/ *adv* near here, or in this neighborhood or area

here·af·ter /heer áftər/ (*formal*) *adv* **1.** AFTER PRESENT TIME from now on or at a time in the future ○ *He believes this to be a universal law of nature; and we may hope hereafter to see the law proved true.* ○ *No one of us knows what may happen hereafter.* **2.** IN ANY FOLLOWING PART in a subsequent part of an article or document ○ *Here is established a Commerce Technology Advisory Board (hereafter in this section referred to as the "Advisory Board").* **3.** AFTER DEATH in the life that is thought by some to exist after death ○ *Mercy and forgiveness will be ours hereafter.* ■ *n* LIFE AFTER DEATH the life that is thought by some to exist after death ○ *Your deeds will be judged in the hereafter.*

here·by /heer bī́/ *adv* by means of this declaration, document, or ruling (*formal*) ○ *I hereby renounce all claim to the estate.*

he·red·it·a·ble /hə rédditəb'l/ *adj* capable of being inherited [15C. < obsolete French *héréditable* or medieval Latin *hereditabilis*, both < ecclesiastical Latin *hereditare* "inherit" (see HEREDITAMENT)] —**he·red·it·a·bil·i·ty** /hə rèdditə bíllətee/ *n*

her·e·dit·a·ment /hèrrə díttəmənt/ *n* a piece of property that can be inherited [15C. < medieval Latin *hereditamentum* < ecclesiastical Latin *hereditare* "inherit" < Latin *hered-* "heir"]

he·red·i·tar·i·an /hə rèddi térree ən/ *n* somebody who believes that inherited characteristics are more important in determining a person's character and behavior than environmental and social factors —**he·red·i·tar·i·an** *adj* —**he·red·i·tar·i·an·ism** *n*

he·red·i·tar·y /hə réddi tèrree/ *adj* **1.** TRANSMITTED GENETICALLY passed genetically, or capable of being passed genetically, from one generation to the next **2.** HANDED DOWN THROUGH GENERATIONS handed down, or legally capable of being handed down, through generations by inheritance **3.** HAVING INHERITED STATUS holding a right, function, or property by right of inheritance **4.** TRADITIONALLY HELD possessed by or characteristic of both ancestors and descendants although not physically transmitted ○ *the family's hereditary fondness for city life* **5.** RELATING TO INHERITANCE relating to inheritance or heredity **6.** MATH, LOGIC SHARING A RELATIONSHIP OR PROPERTY sharing or transmitting a relationship or property [15C. < Latin *hereditarius* < *hereditas* "inheritance" (see HEREDITY)] —**he·red·i·tar·i·ly** /hə rèddi térrəlee/ *adv* —**he·red·i·tar·i·ness** *n*

he·red·i·ty /hə réddətee/ *n* **1.** ANCESTRY ancestral background **2.** INHERITANCE the inherited right to something ○ *based on heredity* **3.** PASSING ON OF GENETIC FACTORS the transfer of genetically controlled characteristics such as hair color or flower color from one generation to the next in living organisms **4.** SET OF INHERITED CHARACTERISTICS in genetics, the complete set of inherited characteristics of an organism [Mid-16C. Directly or via French < Latin *hereditas* "inheritance" < *hered-* "heir"]

Here·ford /hérrifərd, húrfərd/ *n* a hardy cow that has a distinctive red coat with white markings, belonging to a breed originating in England and bred for beef [Early 19C. After HEREFORDSHIRE]

He·re·ford·shire /hérrifərd sheer, -shər/ county in western England. It was disbanded in 1974 and reinstated as a unitary authority in 1998. Area: 842 sq. mi./2,181 sq. km.

here·in /heer ín/ *adv* (*formal*) **1.** in this document, article, or proceeding ○ *Disclaimer: The views represented herein do not necessarily represent the views of the moderators.* **2.** introduces a clause in which somebody states an opinion about the nature or cause of something or goes on to give further detail ○ *People are not always conscious of the effect their behavior is having on others, and herein lies the main problem.*

here·in·af·ter /hèerin áftər/ *adv* later in this document, article, or proceeding (*formal*) ○ *the Federal Reserve Board (hereinafter referred to as FRB)*

here·in·be·fore /hèerinbi fáwr/ *adv* earlier in this document, article, or proceeding (*formal*)

he·rem *n* JUDAISM another spelling of **cherem**

here·of /heer úv, -óv/ *adv* of or concerning this (*formal*)

He·re·ro /hə rérrō, hérrə rō/ (*plural same* or **-ros**) *n* **1.** a member of a people living mainly in Namibia and Botswana **2.** a Bantu language spoken by the Herero. Native speakers: 25,000. [Mid-19C. < Bantu] —**He·re·ro** *adj*

he·re·si·arch /hə reezee àark, hérrəssee-/ *n* a leader or founder of a heretical religious group or movement [Mid-16C. Via ecclesiastical Latin < ecclesiastical Greek *hairesiarkhēs* < Greek *hairesis* "choice, group" (see HERESY) + *-arkhēs* "ruler"]

her·e·sy /hérrəssee/ (*plural* **-sies**) *n* **1.** UNORTHODOX RELIGIOUS OPINION an opinion or belief that contradicts established religious teaching, especially one that is officially condemned by a religious authority **2.** HOLDING OF UNORTHODOX RELIGIOUS BELIEF the holding of, or adherence to, an opinion or belief that contradicts established religious teaching, especially one that is officially condemned by religious authorities ○ *guilty of heresy* **3.** UNORTHODOX OPINION an opinion or belief that does not coincide with established or traditional theory, especially in philosophy, science, or politics ○ *His views on child development were regarded as heresy.* **4.** HOLDING OF UNORTHODOX OPINION the holding of an unorthodox opinion that is in conflict with established or traditional theory, especially in philosophy, science, or politics [12C. Via French < Greek *hairesis* "choice, group" < *haireisthai* "choose"]

her·e·tic /hérrətik/ *n* **1.** a holder or adherent of an opinion or belief that contradicts established religious teaching **2.** somebody whose opinions, beliefs, or theories in any field are considered by others in that field to be extremely unconventional or unorthodox [14C. Via French < Greek *hairetikos* "able to choose" < *haireisthai* "choose"] —**he·ret·i·cal** /hə réttik'l/ *adj*

here·to /heer to͞o/ *adv* to this document, proceeding, or matter (*formal*)

here·to·fore /hèertə fáwr/ *adv* up until this time (*formal*) ○ *He had more liberty now than he had known heretofore.*

here·un·der /heer úndər/ *adv* (*formal*) **1.** after this introduction, heading, or sentence **2.** by the terms of this instruction, agreement, or ruling

here·un·to /heer ún to͞o/ *adv* to this document, proceeding, or matter (*formal*)

here·up·on /hèerə pón/ *adv* (*formal*) **1.** immediately after or in response to this ○ *Hereupon the entire delegation left.* **2.** on this point, subject, or matter ○ *retired to deliberate before pronouncing hereupon*

here·with /heer wi*th*, -wíth/ *adv* **1.** with this letter or other written, typed, or printed message ○ *Herewith the documents you requested.* **2.** by this statement, ruling, or document (*formal*) ○ *I herewith pronounce sentence of banishment.*

He·rez /hə réz/, **He·riz** /-ríz/ *n* a high quality Persian rug woven with a pattern of flowers or trees [After *Heris*, Iranian town]

her·i·ot /hérree ət/ *n* in feudal England, a tribute or gift, often a prized animal or a treasured possession, given by a tenant's or villein's family to his lord at the tenant's death [Old English *heregeatwa* "army trappings"; originally referring to the return of weapons]

her·i·ta·ble /hérritəb'l/ *adj* **1.** able to be passed on to an heir by the laws of inheritance **2.** having the legal right or qualification to inherit something [14C. < French < *hériter* "inherit" < ecclesiastical Latin *hereditare* (see HEREDITAMENT)] —**her·i·ta·bil·i·ty** /hèrritə bíllətee/ *n* —**her·i·ta·bly** *adv*

her·i·tage /hérritij/ *n* **1. SOMETHING SOMEBODY IS BORN TO** the status, conditions, or character acquired by being born into a particular family or social class ○ *Respect for education was part of their Scottish heritage.* **2. RICHES OF PAST** a country's or area's history and historical buildings and sites that are considered to be of interest and value to present generations (*often used before a noun*) ○ *the town's heritage trail* **3. SOMETHING PASSING FROM GENERATION TO GENERATION** something that passes from one generation to the next in a social group, e.g., a way of life or traditional culture ○ *The celebration of Passover is part of the Jewish heritage.* **4. LEGAL INHERITANCE** property or land that is or can be passed on to an heir [13C. < Old French < *hériter* (see HERITABLE)]

her·i·tage in·dus·try *n* a branch of the tourism industry responsible for preserving the art and artifacts of a place

her·i·tage lan·guage *n* in English-speaking countries, a language other than English that is spoken at home or was spoken by somebody's ancestors

her·i·tor /hérritər/ *n* an inheritor of property by law (*archaic or technical*) [15C. < Anglo-Norman < French *hériter* (see HERITABLE)]

her·i·tress /hérritrəss/ *n* a woman or girl who is inheritor of property by law (*archaic or technical*)

He·riz *n* TEXTILES same as **Herez**

Her·ki·mer /húrkimər/, **Nicholas** (1728–77) American soldier. Defending the Mohawk Valley in New York during the American Revolution, his troops weakened British forces at the Battle of Oriskany (1777).

herk·y-jerk·y /hùrkee júrkee/ *adj* moving in an irregular or spasmodic way (*informal*) [Late 20C. Rhyming expansion of JERKY[1]]

herl /hurl/ *n* **1.** the barb or barbs of a feather used for trimming an artificial fishing fly **2.** a fishing fly trimmed with a barb or barbs of a feather [14C. Probably < Middle Low German *herle* "fiber of hemp or flax"]

herm /hurm/, **her·ma** /húrmə/ (*plural* **-mae** /-mee/ or **-mai** /-mī/) *n* a square pillar topped with a bust, usually of the god Hermes, used as a marker in ancient Greece and Rome, and as an ornament in classical architecture [Late 16C. Via Latin < Greek *Hermēs* "Hermes"]

her·maph·ro·dite /hər máffrə dīt/ *n* **1. ORGANISM THAT HAS BOTH SEXES** a plant or animal that has both male and female reproductive organs and secondary sexual characteristics **2. PERSON WHO HAS BOTH SEXES** somebody who has both male and female sexual characteristics **3. SOMEBODY OR SOMETHING COMBINING CONTRADICTORY ELEMENTS** somebody or something that combines two very different features or qualities or seems to belong to two different classifications at once [15C. Via Latin < Greek *Hermaphroditos* "Hermaphroditus"] —**her·maph·ro·dism** *n* —**her·maph·ro·dite** *adj* —**her·maph·ro·dit·ic** /hər màffrə díttik/ *adj* —**her·maph·ro·dit·i·cal** *adj*—**her·maph·ro·dit·i·cal·ly** *adv*—**her·maph·ro·dit·ism** *n*

her·maph·ro·dite brig *n* a two-masted sailing vessel with a square-rigged foremast and a square-rigged topsail above a schooner rig on the mainmast

Her·maph·ro·di·tus /hər màffrə dítəss/ *n* in Greek mythology, the son of Hermes and Aphrodite, whose body was merged with the body of the nymph Salmacis to become half male and half female

her·me·neu·tic /hùrmə nóotik/, **her·me·neu·ti·cal** /-nóotik'l/ *adj* **1.** relating to or consisting in the interpretation of texts, especially the books of the Bible **2.** serving to interpret or explain something (*formal*) [Late 17C. < Greek *hermēneutikos* "of interpreting" < *hermēneuein* "interpret" < *hermēneus* "interpreter"] —**her·me·neu·ti·cal·ly** *adv*—**her·me·neu·tist** *n*

her·me·neu·tics /hùrmə nóotiks/ *n* (*takes a singular verb*) **1.** the science and methodology of interpreting texts, especially the books of the Bible **2.** the branch of theology that is concerned with explaining or interpreting religious concepts, theories, and principles

Her·mes /húr meez/ *n* in Greek mythology, the messenger of the gods and a son of Zeus. He was the patron of athletes, thieves, and trade, and was usually depicted with wings on his cap and sandals. Roman equivalent **Mercury** (sense 1)

Her·mes Tris·me·gis·tus /-trismə jístəss, -trizmə-/ *n* a name given to the Egyptian god Thoth by Greek neo-Platonists, who regarded him as a teacher of religion, magic, and alchemy

her·met·ic /hər méttik/, **her·met·i·cal** /-ik'l/ *adj* **1. AIRTIGHT** so tightly or perfectly fitting as to exclude the passage of air **2. PROTECTED FROM OUTSIDE INFLUENCE** protected from or preventing any outside interference or influence ○ *lead a solitary, hermetic existence* **3. HARD TO UNDERSTAND** obscure and difficult for outsiders to understand **4.** *also* **Her·met·ic INVOLVING ALCHEMY OR MAGIC** associated with alchemy or magic [Mid-17C. < modern Latin *hermeticus* < HERMES TRISMEGISTUS] —**her·met·i·cal·ly** *adv*

her·mit /húrmit/ *n* **1. SOMEBODY WHO CHOOSES TO LIVE ALONE** somebody who chooses to live alone and to have little or no social contact **2. EARLY CHRISTIAN LIVING APART** somebody who, in early Christian times, chose to reject material things and to live apart from the rest of society, especially in order to be completely devoted to God **3.** FOOD **SOFT SPICY COOKIE** a soft cookie containing molasses, raisins, nuts, and spices [12C. Via Old French *hermite* or medieval Latin *heremita* < Greek *erēmitēs* < *erēmia* "desert" < *erēmos* "solitary"] —**her·mit·ic** /hur míttik/ *adj* —**her·mit·i·cal** *adj* —**her·mit·i·cal·ly** *adv*

her·mit·age /húrmitij/ *n* **1.** a building or shelter where a hermit lives or where a group of people live an isolated religious life **2.** a place of isolation or solitude where somebody can live apart from society [13C. < Old French < *hermite* (see HERMIT)]

Her·mit·age /húrmitij/ *n* a museum in St. Petersburg, Russia, that contains one of the world's major collections of paintings. The nucleus of its collection was the art collection of Catherine the Great.

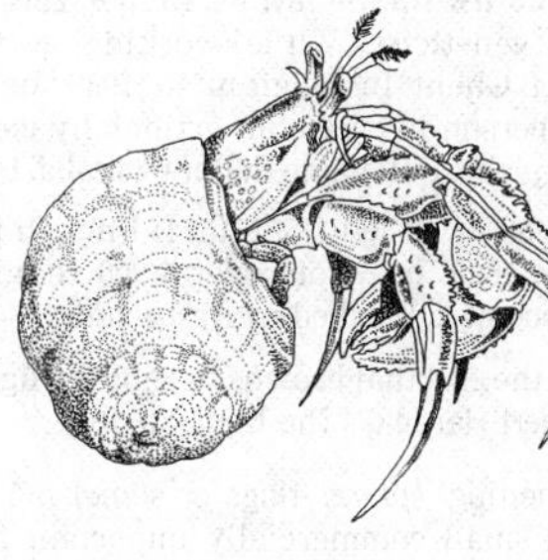

hermit crab

her·mit crab *n* a soft-bodied crab that takes over an empty mollusk shell, usually a whelk shell, and carries it around on its back for protection and to hide in. It starts off with a small shell that, as it grows, is discarded for increasingly larger ones, so that it may change shells several times during its life span. Order: Decapoda.

her·mit thrush *n* a brownish songbird with a speckled breast, reddish tail, and a distinctive spiraling song reminiscent of the sound of a flute. Native to: North America. Latin name: *Catharus guttatus*.

Her·mon, Mount /húrmən/ highest peak in the Anti-Lebanon Mountains, on the Syria-Lebanon border. It has many associations with ancient Palestine. Height: 9,232 ft./2,814 m.

Her·mo·sa Beach /hər mṓssə-/ city and coastal resort in southwestern California, southwest of the city of Los Angeles. Population: 19,281 (2002 estimate).

her·ni·a /húrnee ə/ (*plural* **-as** or **-ae** /-ee/) *n* a condition in which part of an internal organ projects through the wall of the cavity that contains it, especially the projection of the intestine from the abdominal cavity. It may be present at birth, especially in the region of the navel, be caused by muscular strain or injury, or result from a congenital weakness in the cavity wall. [14C. < Latin] —**her·ni·al** *adj*

her·ni·ate /húrnee àyt/ (**-at·ed, -at·ing, -ates**) *vi* to project through a rupture in the wall of a body cavity, or through a normal or potential opening that has become enlarged (*refers to organs or body parts*) —**her·ni·at·ed** *adj* —**her·ni·a·tion** /hùrnee áysh'n/ *n*

her·ni·or·rha·phy /hùrnee áwrəfee/ (*plural* **-phies**) *n* the surgical repair of a rupture in the wall of a body cavity

he·ro /héerō/ (*plural* **-roes**) *n* **1. REMARKABLY BRAVE PERSON** somebody who commits an act of remarkable bravery or who has shown an admirable quality such as great courage or strength of character ○ *a war hero* **2. SOMEBODY ADMIRED** somebody who is admired for outstanding qualities or achievements ○ *heroes of the war against poverty* **3.** ARTS **MAIN CHARACTER IN FICTIONAL PLOT** the principal male character in a movie, novel, or play, especially one who plays a vital role in plot development or around whom the plot is structured ○ *"Whether I shall turn out to be the hero of my own life, or whether that station will be held by anybody else, these pages must show."* (Charles Dickens, *David Copperfield*; 1849–50) **4.** MYTHOL **MAN WITH SUPERHUMAN POWERS** in classical mythology, a man, especially the son of a god and a mortal, who is famous for possessing some extraordinary gift such as superhuman strength ○ *the Greek heroes* **5.** FOOD **LONG SANDWICH** a sandwich made from a long roll or loaf of bread with a filling of meat and cheese with lettuce and tomato [Mid-16C. Via Latin < Greek *hērōs* "hero, warrior"]

He·ro /héerō/ *n* in Greek mythology, a priestess of Aphrodite whose lover Leander swam the Hellespont to visit her every night, and who drowned herself after he drowned in the strait

He·ro (of Al·ex·an·dri·a) /héerō/ (*b.* A.D. 20?) Greek mathematician and inventor. He designed numerous mechanical devices and devised a formula for calculating the area of a triangle.

Her·od (the Great) /hèrrəd-/ (73–4 B.C.) king of Judea. Born in Palestine and supported by the Romans, he ruled Judea from 37 B.C. to 4 B.C. in a period of relative prosperity. He is remembered in Jewish and Christian tradition as a tyrant and, according to the Bible, ordered the massacre of every male baby in Jerusalem (Matthew 2:16).

Her·od A·grip·pa I /-ə gríppə/ (10? B.C.–A.D. 44) king of Judea. He was the grandson of Herod the Great. As the Roman-appointed king of Judea (41–44), he adopted policies favorable to the Jews. In the New Testament, he is said to have imprisoned St. Peter and executed St. James.

Her·od A·grip·pa II (27–93?) Roman ruler in Palestine. The son of Herod Agrippa I, he was the Roman-appointed ruler in northern Palestine, where he supported Rome during the Jewish revolt (66–73).

Her·od An·ti·pas /-ánti pàss/ (21 B.C.–A.D. 39) Galilean leader. The son of Herod the Great, he was tetrarch of Galilee and Perea (4 B.C.–A.D. 39) and ordered the execution of John the Baptist.

He·rod·o·tus /hə róddətəss/ (484?–425? B.C.) Greek historian. His anecdotal *History* includes a description of the war between the Greeks and Persians in the 5th century B.C. He has been called "the father of history."

> "Death is a delightful hiding place for weary men."
> [Herodotus, *The Histories*; 450? B.C.]

he·ro·ic /hi rṓ ik/, **he·ro·i·cal** /-ik'l/ *adj* **1. COURAGEOUS** showing great bravery, courage, or determination ○ *a heroic fight against a disease* **2. SUITABLE FOR HERO** characteristic of or suitable for a hero **3. LARGE OR EXTREME** large, extensive, or extreme, often daunting in aspect or done in response to a desperate situation ○ *heroic measures to save a person's life* **4.** MYTHOL **RELATING TO MYTHICAL HERO** characteristic of or involving the heroes of legend or mythology **5.** LITERAT **OF HEROIC VERSE** written in or characteristic of heroic verse **6.** SCULPTURE **LARGER THAN LIFE-SIZE**

describes a piece of sculpture that is larger than life-size —**he·ro·i·cal·ly** *adv* —**he·ro·i·cal·ness** *n*

he·ro·ic age *n* a time in a culture's mythology when heroes were believed to exist, especially the time in ancient Greek mythology up to and including the return from Troy

he·ro·i·cal *adj* same as **heroic**

he·ro·ic cou·plet *n* a two-line unit of verse consisting of rhyming iambic pentameters, usually part of a series of rhyming pairs

he·ro·ic dra·ma *n* a play popular during the Restoration period, generally involving a warrior hero who must find a way to resolve a dilemma. This often involves finding a way of preserving both his honor and his love for a woman.

he·ro·ic me·ter *n* LITERAT same as **heroic verse**

he·ro·ic quat·rain *n* a four-line unit of verse in which each line consists of five iambic feet and either alternate or adjacent lines rhyme

he·ro·ics /hi rṓ iks/ *npl* **1.** rash, inappropriate, or extravagantly courageous behavior or talk ○ *There is no room for heroics on this expedition.* **2.** LITERAT same as **heroic verse**

he·ro·ic stan·za *n* four lines of verse in which the first and third lines and the second and fourth lines rhyme

he·ro·ic ten·or *n* MUSIC same as **heldentenor**

he·ro·ic verse *n* a verse form used in epic poetry or other narrative poetry on heroic subjects, especially the ancient Greek and Latin hexameter, the iambic pentameter, or the alexandrine

her·o·in /hérrō in/ *n* a white powder derived from morphine that is a highly addictive narcotic drug. It is prohibited for medical use in most countries. (*often used before a noun*) ○ *a heroin addict* [Late 19C. < German]

SPELLCHECK heroin or **heroine**? Do not confuse the spelling of ***heroin*** and ***heroine***, which sound similar. ***Heroin*** is an addictive drug, as in *heroin users, an overdose of heroin*. A ***heroine*** is a brave woman or girl or the main woman or girl character of a novel, play, or movie.

her·o·ine /hérrō in/ *n* **1.** REMARKABLY BRAVE WOMAN a woman who commits an act of remarkable bravery or who has shown great courage, strength of character, or another admirable quality **2.** ADMIRED WOMAN a woman who is admired or looked up to for her qualities or achievements ○ *heroines of the women's suffrage movement* **3.** ARTS MAIN FEMALE CHARACTER IN FICTIONAL PLOT the principal female character in a movie, novel, or play, especially one who plays a vital role in plot development or around whom the plot is structured

SPELLCHECK See ***heroin***.

her·o·ism /hérrō izzəm/ *n* remarkable physical or moral courage

heron

her·on /hérrən/ *n* a freshwater wading bird with a long neck, tapered beak, and often a crested head, that feeds mainly on fish, frogs, and small mammals. Family: Ardeidae. [14C. < Old French < Germanic]

her·on·ry /hérrənree/ (*plural* **-ries**) *n* a small area within which herons nest and raise their young

He·roph·i·lus /heer óffiləss/ (335?–280? B.C.) Greek anatomist. Considered the founder of scientific anatomy, he is known for his detailed description of the brain and nervous system.

"Medicines are nothing in themselves, if not properly used, but the very hands of the gods, if employed with reason and prudence."
[Attributed to Herophilus]

~~**heros**~~ incorrect spelling of **heroes**

he·ro wor·ship *n* **1.** great admiration for somebody, especially if it borders on the excessive **2.** the ancient Greek or Roman practice of worshiping a mythological hero or heroes —**he·ro-wor·ship** *vt* —**he·ro-wor·ship·er** *n*

her·pes /húrpeez/ *n* a viral infection causing small painful blisters and inflammation, most commonly at the junction of skin and mucous membrane in the mouth or nose or in the genitals [14C. Via Latin < Greek < *herpein* "creep"]

her·pes sim·plex /-sím plèks/ *n* either of two viral diseases marked by clusters of small watery blisters, one affecting the area of the mouth and lips and the other the genitals [< modern Latin, "simple herpes"]

her·pes·vi·rus /húrpeez vīrəss/ *n* a DNA-containing virus that replicates in cell nuclei and causes diseases such as chickenpox, herpes, and shingles

her·pes zos·ter /-zóstər/ *n* MED same as **shingles** (*technical*) [< modern Latin; *zoster* via Latin < Greek, "girdle"]

her·pet·ic /hər péttik/ *adj* relating to, affected by, or indicative of herpes

her·pe·tol·o·gy /hùrpə tólləjee/ *n* the scientific study of reptiles and amphibians [Early 19C. < Greek *herpeton* "creeping thing, reptile" < *herpein* "creep"] —**her·pe·to·log·ic** /hùrpətə lójjik/ *adj* —**her·pe·to·log·i·cal** *adj* —**her·pe·to·log·i·cal·ly** *adv* —**her·pe·tol·o·gist** *n*

Herr /her, hur/ (*plural* **Her·ren** /hérrən/) *n* the German equivalent of "Mister," used as a title before a surname or profession [Mid-17C. < German]

Her·ren·volk /hérrən fōk, -fàwlk/ *n* in Nazi ideology, the German nation as a master race (*often offensive*) [Mid-20C. < German, "master people"]

Her·re·ra-Es·tre·lla /hə ràyrə e stréllə/, **Luis** (*b.* 1956) Mexican geneticist. While working at the University of Ghent in Belgium in 1983, he became the first person to create an artificially genetically modified plant. Full name **Herrera-Estrella, Luis Rafael**

Her·rick /hérrik/, **Robert** (1591–1674) English poet. Ordained in 1623, he wrote over 1,200 religious and secular poems published in *Hesperides* (1648).

"It is the end that crowns us, not the fight."
[Robert Herrick, "The End"; 1648]

her·ring /hérring/ (*plural* **-rings** or *same*) *n* **1.** FISH OF N ATLANTIC a small commercially important fish with silvery scales. Native to: northern Atlantic. Latin name: *Clupea harengus.* **2.** FISH LIKE HERRING any fish related to and resembling the herring. Family: Clupeidae. **3.** HERRING AS FOOD the flesh of a herring used as food [Old English *hǣring* < W Germanic]

her·ring·bone /hérring bōn/ *n* **1.** PATTERN OF INTERLOCKING "V" SHAPES a regular geometric pattern made by placing two contrasting rows of slanting lines or blocks together so that they form rows of "V"s, zigzags, or chevrons. Use: bricklaying, textiles, parquet flooring, weaving, embroidery. **2.** TEXTILES CLOTH WITH HERRINGBONE fabric woven in a herringbone pattern (*often used before a noun*) ○ *a herringbone jacket* **3.** SKIING METHOD FOR ASCENDING ON SKIS a method for climbing a slope on skis by facing the peak, with skis pointing out at an angle, and moving them upward one step after the other ■ *v* (**-boned, -bon·ing, -bones**) **1.** *vti* DECORATE SOMETHING WITH HERRINGBONE to decorate or make something such as cloth with a herringbone pattern **2.** *vi* SKIING GO UP SLOPE ON SKIS to ascend a slope on skis using the herringbone method ■ *n* HANDICRAFT same as **herringbone stitch**

her·ring·bone bond *n* decorative bricklaying in which the bricks are placed at an angle to one another to form a herringbone pattern

her·ring·bone gear *n* a gearwheel in which two sets of teeth interlock in a series of "V" shapes

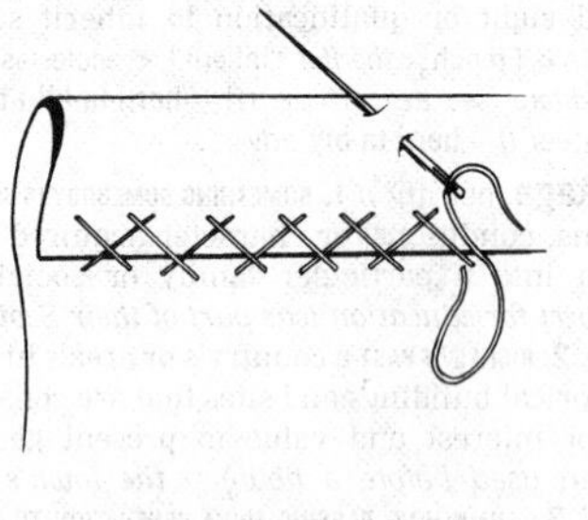

herringbone stitch

her·ring·bone stitch *n* an embroidery or hemming stitch made with overlapping cross stitches that form a zigzag line

her·ring gull *n* a common gull with a body that is mainly white, a gray back, and gray wings with black tips. Native to: northern hemisphere. Latin name: *Larus argentatus.*

Her·ri·ot /hérree ət/, **Édouard** (1872–1957) French prime minister (1924–25, 1926, 1932). He was imprisoned (1942–45) for resisting the Vichy government during World War II.

hers /hurz/ *pron* **1.** SOMETHING BELONGING TO HER indicates that something belongs or relates to a woman, girl, or female animal who has been previously mentioned or whose identity is known ○ *She drew my face to hers and kissed me.* ○ *I knew an uncle of hers.* **2.** BELONGING TO COUNTRY indicates that something belongs to or is associated with a country or nation when its identity is known (*formal*) **3.** BELONGING TO MACHINE indicates that something belongs to or is associated with a car, machine, or ship [14C. < HER + -'s]

Her·schel /húrsh'l/, **Caroline** (1750–1848) German-born British astronomer. She worked with her brother William Herschel on numerous astronomical investigations. She discovered eight comets and three nebulae. Full name **Herschel, Caroline Lucretia**

Her·schel, Sir John Frederick William (1792–1871) British astronomer. The son of William Herschel, he furthered his father's systematic studies of the skies, studied the stars of the southern hemisphere, and invented a photographic fixing agent.

Her·schel, Sir William (1738–1822) German-born British astronomer. Assisted in his researches by his sister Caroline Herschel, he pioneered the study of stars. He cataloged double stars and nebulae and discovered the planet Uranus (1781). Born **Herschel, Friedrich Wilhelm**

her·self /hər sélf/; *unstressed also* /ər sélf/ CORE MEANING: the form of "her" used in reflexive and emphatic contexts ○ *She did it herself.*

pron **1.** REFERRING TO FEMALE SUBJECT OF VERB used to refer to the same woman, girl, or female animal as the subject of the verb ○ *She put her hand on the rail to support herself.* ○ *She decided to treat herself.* **2.** USED FOR EMPHASIS used to emphasize or clarify which woman, girl, or female animal is being referred to, often introducing a note of surprise or awe ○ *I received a letter from the author herself.* **3.** ALONE OR WITHOUT HELP used to show that a woman, girl, or female animal is alone or unaided ○ *sitting by herself in the garden* ○ *wrote the song herself* **4.** COUNTRY used to refer to a nation or country whose identity is known (*formal*) ○ *The United States is causing problems for herself with this policy.* **5.** MACHINE used to refer to a car, machine, or ship **6.** NORMAL SELF her normal self in terms of personality, health, or behavior ○ *She's not herself today – I don't know what's the matter with her.*

Her·sey /húrssee, húrzee/, **John** (1914–93) US writer and journalist. His most famous work is his graphic account of nuclear war, *Hiroshima* (1946). Full name **Hersey, John Richard**

Her·shey /húrshee/ town in central Pennsylvania. It is

a confectionery manufacturing center. Population: 11,860 (2002 estimate).

Her·shey, Alfred Day (1908–97) US geneticist. He shared the Nobel Prize in physiology or medicine (1969) for his work on the replication of viruses and their genetic structure.

her·sto·ry /húrstəree/ (*plural* **-ries**) *n* **1.** history as it affects women or looked at from the point of view of women, especially in contrast to conventional treatment of history, seen in feminist terms as having favored men **2.** the study or recording of the life experiences, achievements, or expectations of a particular woman or group of women [Late 20C. < HISTORY, as if *his-* were "of him"]

Hert·ford·shire /haártfərd sheèr, -shər/ county in southeastern England. Its administrative center is Hertford. Area: 632 sq. mi./1,634 sq. km.

hertz /hurts/ (*plural same*) *n* the SI unit of frequency equal to one cycle per second. Symbol **Hz** [Late 19C. After Heinrich HERTZ]

Hertz /hurts, herts/, **Heinrich** (1857–94) German physicist. He was the first to produce electromagnetic waves under laboratory conditions, leading to the development of the telegraph and radio. The unit of frequency hertz is named for him. Full name **Hertz, Heinrich Rudolf** —**Hertz·i·an** *adj*

Hertz·i·an wave /hùrtsee ən-, hèrrtsee ən-/ *n* a radio wave

Hert·zog /húrts òg/, **J. B. M.** (1866–1942) South African prime minister (1924–39). He founded the Nationalist Party (1914) and, as prime minister, secured the rights of Dutch-descended Afrikaners in South Africa while pursuing a policy of racial segregation. Full name **Hertzog, James Barry Munnik**

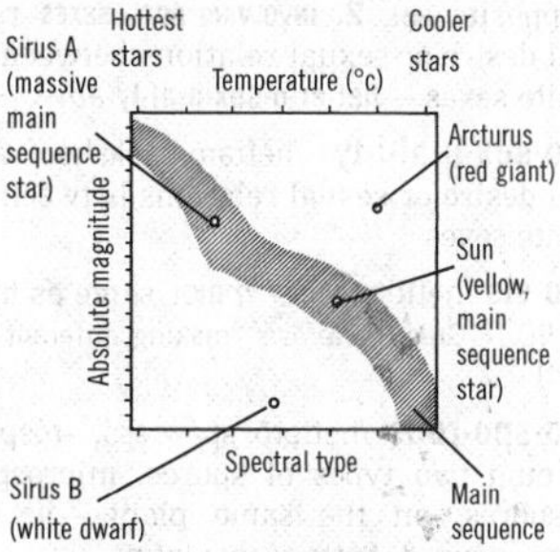

Hertzsprung-Russell diagram

Hertz·sprung-Rus·sell di·a·gram /hùrts sprung-/ *n* a graph that plots the brightness of stars against their spectral type or color [After Ejnar *Hertzsprung* (1873–1967), Danish astronomer, and Henry Norris *Russell* (1877–1957), US astronomer, who independently devised it]

Her·vey Bay /hùrvee-/ town located on a bay of the same name in southern Queensland, Australia. Population: 44,402 (2002 estimate).

Herz·berg /húrts bùrg/, **Gerhard** (1904–99) German-born Canadian physicist. He won the Nobel Prize in chemistry (1971) for his work in molecular spectroscopy.

Her·ze·go·vi·na /hèrtsə gō veénə/ ♦ **Bosnia and Herzegovina**

Her·zog /húrts òg/, **Chaim** (1918–97) British-born Israeli president (1983–93). Before becoming president, he held several military and diplomatic posts, including Israeli ambassador to the United Nations (1975–78).

he's /heez/ *contr* **1.** he has ○ *He's finished his lunch.* **2.** he is ○ *He's not the man I saw.*

Hesh·van /héshvən, khésh vaan/, **Chesh·van** *n* in the Jewish calendar, the eighth month of the religious year, lasting 29 or 30 days and falling about the same time as October to November. See table at **calendar** [Mid-19C. < Hebrew *ḥešwān*, shortening of *marḥešwān* < Akkadian *araḫ samna* "eighth month"]

He·si·on·e /hi sī́ ənee/ *n* in Greek mythology, a princess whom Heracles rescued from a sea monster

hes·i·tant /hézzit'nt/ *adj* slow to do or say something because of indecision or lack of confidence —**hes·i·tance** *n* —**hes·i·tan·cy** *n* —**hes·i·tant·ly** *adv*

SYNONYMS See *unwilling*.

hes·i·tate /hézzi tàyt/ (**-tat·ed, -tat·ing, -tates**) *vi* **1.** to be slow in doing something, or pause while doing or saying something, often because of uncertainty or reluctance **2.** to be reluctant to do or say something ○ *If you're puzzled by anything, don't hesitate to ask.* [Early 17C. < Latin *haesitat-*, past participle of *haesitare* "stick fast" < *haerere* "stick"] —**hes·i·tat·er** *n* —**hes·i·tat·ing·ly** *adv* —**hes·i·ta·tive** *adj*

SYNONYMS ***hesitate, pause, falter, stumble, waver, vacillate***

CORE MEANING: to show uncertainty or indecision

hesitate to be slow in doing something, or pause while doing or saying something, as a result of uncertainty or reluctance ○ *He hesitated for a moment, then walked swiftly to the door.* ○ *Please do not hesitate to call me if you have any questions.* **pause** to stop doing something briefly before continuing, or to wait intentionally for a short period before doing something ○ *She paused for a moment to recover her self-possession.* ○ *Scarcely pausing for thought, she sat herself down at the keyboard and started to play.* **falter** to show a loss of confidence, especially to speak or act with hesitation ○ *new anchors who falter when they read the news* ○ *In such circumstances, our allies might falter in their commitment to the defense treaty.* **stumble** to speak or act in a halting, confused, or blundering way ○ *stumbling through polite replies as to her health* ○ *He stumbled over the words, not knowing how to express his sympathy.* **waver** to become unsure or begin to change from a previous opinion ○ *The defendant never wavered from his claim.* ○ *He saw the agony in her eyes and his resolve wavered.* **vacillate** to be indecisive or irresolute, changing between one opinion and another ○ *Her mind vacillated between laughing at her fears and suspecting something terrible.* ○ *The advantages the country once had have been squandered by vacillating political leadership.*

hes·i·ta·tion /hèzzi táysh'n/ *n* **1.** the act of hesitating or pausing **2.** the state of being reluctant or undecided

~~**hesitent**~~ incorrect spelling of **hesitant**

Hes·pe·ri·a /he speéree ə/ city in southeastern California, north of San Bernardino. Population: 67,021 (2002 estimate).

Hes·pe·ri·an /he speéree ən/ *adj* **1.** belonging to or connected with the west (*literary*) **2.** relating to the Hesperides [Late 15C. < Latin *hesperius* "western" < Greek *hesperios* < *hesperos* "western, evening"]

Hes·per·i·des /he spérri deez/ *npl* **1.** in Greek mythology, the daughters of Atlas and Hesperus and the guards of a tree bearing golden apples from which Heracles was required to gather fruit as one of his 12 labors **2.** in Greek mythology, islands far to the west in which a tree with golden apples grew [Late 16C. < Greek, plural of *hesperis* "western" < *hesperos* "western, evening"] —**Hes·per·id·e·an** /hèspə ríddee ən/ *adj*

hes·per·i·din /he spérridin, -d'n/ *n* a white or colorless crystalline glycoside. Source: citrus fruits. Use: treatment of capillary disease. [Mid-19C. < Greek *hesperid-*, stem of *hesperis* "western" (see HESPERIDES)]

hes·per·id·i·um /hèspə ríddee əm/ *n* a fruit, e.g., a citrus fruit, consisting of a thick leathery rind and soft segmented pulp [Mid-19C. < HESPERIDES, with reference to the golden apples]

Hes·per·us /héspərəss/ *n* the planet Venus, especially just after sunset when it shines brightly (*literary*) [< Latin < Greek *hesperos* "western, evening"]

Hess /hess/, **Rudolf** (1894–1987) German Nazi deputy leader. Adolf Hitler's private secretary and deputy in the 1920s and 1930s, he was captured as a prisoner of war in Scotland (1941), convicted of war crimes at Nuremberg (1945–46), and imprisoned for life in Spandau Prison, West Berlin. Full name **Hess, Walter Richard Rudolf**

Hes·se /hess, héssə/ state and historic duchy in west central Germany. Largely an agricultural region, it is drained by the Rhine and Main rivers in the west and, in the northeast, by the Weser River. Capital: Wiesbaden. Population: 5,837,000 (1992). Area: 8,152 sq. mi./21,114 sq. km.

Hes·se /héssə/, **Hermann** (1877–1962) German novelist and poet. His spiritually probing novels include *Siddhartha* (1922) and *Steppenwolf* (1927).He was awarded the Nobel Prize in literature (1946).

> "If you hate a person, you hate something in him that is part of yourself. What isn't part of ourselves doesn't disturb us."
> [Hermann Hesse, *Demian*; 1919]

hes·sian /hésh'n/ *n UK* a coarse strong jute or hemp fabric. Use: bags, upholstery. [Late 19C. < HESSIAN]

Hes·sian *n* somebody who comes from Hesse in Germany ■ *adj* relating to Hesse in Germany [Late 17C. < HESSE]

Hes·sian boot *n* a men's knee-high boot with a tasseled top, first worn by Hessian soldiers and fashionable at the beginning of the 19th century

Hes·sian fly *n* a small fly of the gallfly family that lays its eggs on grain plants, where the larvae bore into the stems and weaken them. It causes severe damage to crops, especially wheat, barley, and rye. Latin name: *Mayetiola destructor*. [Because inadvertently brought to N America by Hessian troops]

hes·site /hé sīt/ *n* a gray metallic mineral composed of silver telluride. Use: source of silver. [Mid-19C. After G. H. *Hess* (see HESS'S LAW)]

hes·so·nite /héssə nīt/ *n* MINERALS same as **essonite**

Hess's law /héssiz-/ *n* a law in chemistry stating that the heat absorbed or released during a reaction is the same whether the reaction occurs in one or several steps [After Germain Henri *Hess* (1802–50), Swiss-born Russian chemist]

Hes·ti·a /héstee ə/ *n* in Greek mythology, the goddess of the hearth. Roman equivalent **Vesta** (sense 1)

Hes·ton /hést'n/, **Charlton** (*b.* 1924) US actor. He specialized in heroic roles that capitalized on his rugged good looks and powerful physique, and won an Academy Award for *Ben-Hur* (1959). In his later years he has frequently appeared on behalf of conservative political causes, notably as president of the National Rifle Association. Born **Carter, John Charlton**

Hes·y·chast /héssi kàst/ *n* a member of a school of meditative devotion developed by monks of the Greek Orthodox Church on Mount Athos in the 14th century and popular in 19th-century Russia [Mid-19C. < late Greek *hēsukhastēs* "hermit" < *hēsukhazein* "be still" < *hēsukhos* "still, quiet"] —**Hes·y·chas·tic** /hèssi kástik/ *adj*

he·tae·ra /hi teérə/ (*plural* **-rae** /-reè/ or **-ras**), **he·tai·ra** /-tī́rə/ (*plural* **-rai** /-rī/ or **-ras**) *n* in ancient Greece, one of a special class of women who were used as prostitutes and who were valued as highly cultured companions [Early 19C. < Greek, form of *hetairos* "companion"] —**he·tae·ric** *adj*

he·tae·rism /hi teér ìzzəm/, **he·tai·rism** /-tī́r-/ *n* **1.** the social condition or institution of concubinage **2.** the practice in some societies of sharing spouses or sexual partners —**he·tae·rist** *n* —**he·tae·ris·tic** /hèttə rístik/ *adj*

he·tai·ra, etc. ANCIENT HIST another spelling of **hetaera, etc.**

heter- *prefix* same as **hetero-** (*used before vowels*)

het·er·o /héttərō/ (*plural* **-os**) *n* a heterosexual person (*informal*) [Mid-20C. Shortening] —**het·er·o** *adj*

hetero- *prefix* **1.** different, other ○ *heterochromatic* **2.** containing atoms of different kinds ○ *heterocyclic* [< Greek *heteros* "other" < Indo-European, "one of two"]

het·er·o·at·om /héttərō àttəm/ *n* a noncarbon atom in a heterocyclic compound

het·er·o·cer·cal /hèttərō súrk'l/ *adj* describes a fish's tail in which the vertebral column bends upward and extends into the upper and larger lobe of the tail fin, as in some sharks [Mid-19C. < HETERO- + Greek *kerkos* "tail"]

het·er·o·chro·mat·ic /hèttərō krō máttik/ *adj* containing many different colors —**het·er·o·chro·ma·tism** /-krṓmə tizzəm/ *n*

het·er·o·chro·ma·tin /hèttərō krṓmətin/ *n* chromatic

material that contains few genes but stains readily with basic dyes and appears as nodules between chromosomes

het·er·o·chro·mo·some /hèttərō krṓmə sòm/ *n* a chromosome consisting mainly of heterochromatin, especially a sex chromosome

het·er·o·chro·mous /hèttərə krṓməss/ *adj* describes plant parts that exhibit different colors

het·er·o·clite /héttərō klìt/, **het·er·o·clit·ic** /hèttərō klíttik/ *adj* describes a word that is formed in an unusual or irregular way [Late 15C. Via late Latin < Greek *heteroklitos* < *heteros* "the other" + *klīnein* "to lean"] —**het·er·o·clite** *n*

het·er·o·cy·clic /hèttərō sī́klik, -síklik/ *adj* describes or relating to a ring system composed of atoms in which at least one is not a carbon atom

het·er·o·dact·y·lous /hèttərō dákt'ləss/, **het·er·o·dact·yl** /-dákt'l/ *adj* describes the feet of birds in which the first and second toes face backward and the third and fourth toes face forward. ◊ **zygodactyl**

het·er·o·dont /héttərə dònt/ *adj* used to describe a mammal that has teeth of different types such as incisors, canines, premolars, and molars

het·er·o·dox /héttərə dòks/ *adj* at variance with established or accepted beliefs or theories, especially in the field of religion [Early 17C. Via late Latin < Greek *heterodoxos* < *heteros* "the other" + *doxa* "opinion"]

het·er·o·dox·y /héttərə dòksee/ (*plural* **-ies**) *n* (*formal*) **1.** the condition of being at variance with established or accepted beliefs or theories, especially in the field of religion **2.** an opinion, belief, or theory that is at variance with those that are established or accepted

het·er·o·dyne /héttərə dīn/ *vt* (**-dyned, -dyn·ing, -dynes**) to combine a received radio-frequency wave with a wave of a different frequency to produce frequencies equal to the sum of and the difference between the original two signals ■ *adj* consisting of, produced by, or operated by heterodyning signals

het·er·oe·cious /hèttə réeshəss/ *adj* describes a parasite such as a tapeworm that lives in two or more hosts in the course of its life cycle [Late 19C. < HETERO- + Greek *oikia* "house"] —**het·er·oe·cism** /-rée sìzzəm/ *n*

het·er·o·gam·ete /hèttərō gá meet, hèttərōgə méet/ *n* **1.** either of two reproductive cells (**gametes**) that differ in size, structure, and function, and that unite in the process of reproduction, e.g., the small sperm and large ova in humans **2.** a reproductive cell produced by the sex that carries the chromosomes that determine the sex of the offspring

het·er·o·ga·met·ic /hèttərōgə méttik/ *adj* **1.** describes the sex that produces reproductive cells (**gametes**) of two different types, one type producing males and the other females **2.** relating to heterogametes

het·er·og·a·my /hèttə róggəmee/ *n* **1.** BIOL **UNION OF DISSIMILAR REPRODUCTIVE CELLS** in sexual reproduction, the union of two types of sex cells (**heterogametes**) that are dissimilar in size, structure, and function **2.** BIOL **ALTERNATING OF FORMS OF REPRODUCTION** the alternation of sexual and asexual reproduction in some species such as aphids in which every other generation is produced from the female with no need for a male **3.** BOT **PRESENCE OF DIFFERENT FLOWERS ON PLANT** the production on the same plant of two kinds of flower, one bearing both male and female organs and the other bearing only female organs or being asexual —**het·er·o·gam·ic** /hèttərō gámmik/ *adj* —**het·er·og·a·mous** *adj*

het·er·o·ge·ne·i·ty /hèttərō jə née ətee/ *n* **1.** the diverse nature of something **2.** the state of being chemically heterogeneous

het·er·o·ge·ne·ous /hèttərō jéenee əss/, **het·er·og·e·nous** /hèttə rójjənəss/ *adj* **1. CONSISTING OF DISSIMILAR PARTS** consisting of parts or aspects that are unrelated or unlike each other **2. UNRELATED** not related or similar **3.** CHEM **WITH TWO OR MORE PHASES** describes a chemical substance that has two or more phases **4.** MED **NOT FROM SAME BODY** originating outside the body, from another individual or species [Early 17C. < medieval Latin *heterogeneus* < Greek *heterogenēs* "other kind" < *heteros* "other" + *genos* "kind"] —**het·er·o·ge·ne·ous·ly** *adv* —**het·er·o·ge·ne·ous·ness** *n*

het·er·o·gen·e·sis /hèttərō jénnəssiss/ *n* the appearance of a mutation in a population

het·er·o·ge·net·ic /hèttərō jə néttik/ *adj* **1. OF HETEROGENESIS** relating to heterogenesis **2.** BIOL **FROM DISPARATE ANCESTORS** derived from ancestors not closely related **3. MUTATING** reproducing by heterogenesis —**het·er·o·ge·net·i·cal·ly** *adv*

het·er·o·gen·ic /hèttərō jénnik/ *adj* describes a reproductive cell (**gamete**), individual, or population that has more than one variant (**allele**) of a specific gene

het·er·og·e·nous *adj* same as **heterogeneous**

het·er·og·o·ny /hèttə róggənee/ *n* a life cycle involving alternating parasitic and free-living generations —**het·er·og·o·nous** *adj* —**het·er·og·o·nous·ly** *adv*

het·er·o·graft /héttərō gràft/ *n* a graft of living tissue from one animal to another of a different species

het·er·og·ra·phy /hèttə róggrəfee/ (*plural* **-phies**) *n* **1.** the use of different letters or groups of letters to represent the same sound or sounds **2.** a writing system that uses different combinations of letters to represent the same sound or sounds [Late 18C. < HETERO-, after ORTHOGRAPHY] —**het·er·o·graph·ic** /hèttərō gráffik/ *adj*

het·er·o·kar·y·on /hèttərō kárree òn/ (*plural* **-y·a** /-ee ə/) *n* a cell that has two or more genetically different nuclei

het·er·o·kar·y·o·sis /hèttərō kàrri óssiss/ *n* the presence in a cell of two or more nuclei of different genetic origin. Heterokaryosis occurs naturally in some fungi when cells fuse but their nuclei do not, and can be induced artificially to study the interaction of cellular components of different species. —**het·er·o·kar·y·ot·ic** /-óttik/ *adj*

het·er·ol·o·gous /hèttə róllǝgəss/ *adj* **1.** MED **FROM DIFFERENT SPECIES** derived or taken from a different species **2.** IMMUNOL **NOT CORRESPONDING** describes an antigen and an antibody that do not correspond to each other **3.** BIOL **IN UNUSUAL LOCATION** not normally found in the part of the body in which it has been found **4.** BIOL **DIFFERING IN STRUCTURE AND ORIGIN** describes organisms or parts that differ from each other in structure or origin [Mid-19C. < HETERO- + Greek *logos* "relation, ratio"] —**het·er·ol·o·gous·ly** *adv*

het·er·ol·y·sis /hèttə rólləssiss/ *n* **1.** the breaking of a chemical bond in a compound, producing particles or ions of opposite charge, e.g., the formation of sodium and chloride ions in a salt solution **2.** the destruction of cells or proteins of one species by the action of enzymes or lysins from another, e.g., when the blood of one species causes the red blood cells of another species to rupture —**het·er·o·lyt·ic** /hèttərō líttik/ *adj*

het·er·om·er·ous /hèttə rómmərəss/ *adj* **1.** with parts of different types **2.** describes plants whose flowers do not have the same number of petals in each case or whose other parts are made up of different numbers of elements

het·er·o·mor·phic /hèttərō máwrfik/, **het·er·o·mor·phous** /-fəss/ *adj* **1.** BIOL **HAVING DIFFERENT APPEARANCE** differing in shape, size, or structure ○ *heteromorphic sex chromosomes* **2.** BIOL **TAKING DIFFERENT FORMS DURING LIFE CYCLE** taking different forms at different stages of its life cycle **3.** MED **INVOLVING ATYPICAL FORM** characterized by an atypical form or forms —**het·er·o·mor·phism** *n* —**het·er·o·mor·phy** /héttərō màwrfee/ *n*

het·er·on·o·mous /hèttə rónnəməss/ *adj* **1.** subject to other laws or rules or to laws and rules imposed by other people or institutions **2.** describes parts of an organism that have different modes of development and growth, and different functions [Early 19C. < HETERO- + Greek *nomos* "law"] —**het·er·on·o·mous·ly** *adv* —**het·er·on·o·my** *n*

het·er·o·nym /héttərənim/ *n* each of two or more words that are spelled the same, but differ in meaning and often in pronunciation, e.g., "bow" (a ribbon) and "bow" (of a ship) [Late 19C. < HETERO- + *-nym* as in SYNONYM] —**het·er·on·y·mous** /hèttə rónniməss/ *adj* —**het·er·on·y·my** *n*

het·er·o·ou·si·an /hèttərō óossee ən, -ówssee ən/, **het·er·ou·si·an** /hèttə róossee ən, -rówssee ən/ *n* in Christian theology, somebody who believes that God the Father and God the Son are not formed of the same substance [Late 17C. < Greek *heter(o)ousios* "other substance" < *heteros* "other" + *ousia* "substance"] —**het·er·o·ou·si·an** *adj*

het·er·o·phyl·lous /hèttərō fílləss/ *adj* describes plants that have leaves of different shapes on the same plant. The sassafras tree is heterophyllous. —**het·er·o·phyl·ly** /héttərō fillee/ *n*

het·er·o·plas·ty /héttərō plàstee/ (*plural* **-ties**) *n* **1.** a surgical procedure to graft or transplant tissues or organs from one person or animal to another **2.** SURG same as **heterograft** —**het·er·o·plas·tic** /hèttərō plástik/ *adj*

het·er·o·ploid /héttərō plòyd/ *adj* with a number of chromosomes that is, unusually, not an exact multiple of the basic chromosome number for that species ■ *n* a heteroploid cell or organism

het·er·o·po·lar /hèttərō pṓlər/ *adj* CHEM same as **polar** (sense 7) —**het·er·o·po·lar·i·ty** /-pō lárrətee, -pə-/ *n*

het·er·o·pol·y·mer /hèttərō póllimər/ *n* CHEM same as **copolymer** —**het·er·o·pol·y·mer·ic** /-polə mérrik/ *adj*

het·er·op·ter·an /hèttə róptərən/ *n* an insect with mouthparts adapted for piercing and sucking, and partially hardened forewings with membranous tips. Bedbugs and other true bugs are heteropterans. Order: Heteroptera. [Mid-19C. < HETERO- + Greek *pteron* "wing"] —**het·er·op·ter·an** *adj*

het·er·o·sex·ism /hèttərō sék sìzzəm/ *n* discrimination against gays and lesbians by heterosexuals —**het·er·o·sex·ist** *n, adj*

het·er·o·sex·u·al /hèttərō sékshoo əl/ *n* **SOMEBODY SEXUALLY DESIRING OPPOSITE SEX** somebody who is sexually attracted to members of the opposite sex ■ *adj* **1. DESIRING OPPOSITE SEX** sexually attracted to members of the opposite sex **2. INVOLVING BOTH SEXES** relating to sexual desire or sexual relations between people of opposite sexes —**het·er·o·sex·u·al·ly** *adv*

het·er·o·sex·u·al·i·ty /hèttərō sekshoo állətee/ *n* sexual desire or sexual relations between people of opposite sexes

het·er·o·sis /hèttə róssiss/ *n* BIOL same as **hybrid vigor** [Mid-19C. < Greek *heterōsis* "making different" < *heteros* "other"]

het·er·o·spo·rous /hèttərō spáwrəss, -róspərəss/ *adj* producing two types of spores, microspores and megaspores, on the same plant —**het·er·o·spo·ry** /héttərō spàwree, hèttə róspəree/ *n*

het·er·o·sty·ly /héttərō stìlee/ *n* the possession of styles of different lengths on different plants of the same species, which is an aid to cross-pollination by insects —**het·er·o·styled** *adj* —**het·er·o·sty·lous** /hèttərō stī́ləss/ *adj*

het·er·o·tro·phic /hèttərō trṓfik, -tróffik/ *adj* obtaining nourishment by digesting plant or animal matter, as animals do, as opposed to photosynthesizing food, as plants do —**het·er·o·troph** /héttərə tròf/ *n* —**het·er·ot·ro·phy** /hèttə róttrəfee/ *n*

het·er·o·tro·pi·a /hèttərō trṓpee ə/ *n* an alignment of the eyes that differs from the usual

het·er·o·typ·ic /hèttərō típpik/, **het·er·o·typ·i·cal** /-típpik'l/ *adj* **1.** differing from the standard or usual type in an organism **2.** relating to a form of division of the nucleus of a cell in which the nuclei produced contain half the chromosomes of the parent cell

het·er·ou·si·an *n, adj* CHR same as **heteroousian**

het·er·o·zy·gote /hèttərō zī́ gòt/ *n* an organism possessing two dissimilar forms of a gene for a heritable characteristic, which may therefore produce offspring differing from the parents and each other in that characteristic

het·er·o·zy·gous /hèttərō zī́gəss/ *adj* describes a cell or organism that has two or more different versions (**alleles**) of at least one of its genes. The offspring of such an organism may thus differ with regard to the characteristics determined by the gene or genes involved, depending on which version of the gene they inherit.

heth /het, heth, khet, kheth/ *n* the eighth letter of the Hebrew alphabet, represented in the English alphabet as "h." See table at **alphabet** [Early 19C. < Hebrew *ḥēth*]

het·man /hétmən/ (*plural* **-mans**) *n* MIL same as **ataman** [Mid-18C. < Polish]

het up /het-/ *adj* extremely excited as a result of anticipation, anger, or anxiety (*regional*) [A past participle of HEAT]

heu·che·ra /hyookərə/ *n* a cultivated plant with low-growing heart-shaped leaves. Flowers: small, usually red, in sprays. Native to: North America. Genus: *Heuchera*. [Late 19C. < modern Latin, after J. H. *Heucher* (1677–1747), German botanist]

heu·land·ite /hyoolən dīt/ *n* a variously colored crystalline mineral of the zeolite family, containing calcium and sodium [Early 19C. After H. *Heuland* (1777–1856), British mineralogist]

heu·ris·tic /hyoo rístik/ *adj* **1.** EDUC **ENCOURAGING DISCOVERY OF SOLUTIONS** relating to or using a method of teaching that encourages learners to discover solutions for themselves **2.** PHILOSOPHY, SCI **INVOLVING TRIAL AND ERROR** using or arrived at by a process of trial and error rather than set rules **3.** COMPUT **ABLE TO CHANGE** describes a computer program that modifies itself in response to the user, e.g., a spellchecker ■ *n* LOGIC **PROCEDURE FOR GETTING SOLUTION** a helpful procedure for arriving at a solution but not necessarily a proof [Early 19C. < alteration of Greek *heuriskein* "find"] —**heu·ris·ti·cal·ly** *adv*

heu·ris·tics /hyoo rístiks/ *n* a method of solving a problem for which no formula exists, based on informal methods or experience, and employing a form of trial and error (**iteration**) (*takes a singular verb*)

he·ve·a /heevee ə/ *n* a tree whose bark contains a milky sap that provides rubber. Native to: Amazon jungle. Genus: *Hevea*. [Late 19C. Via modern Latin < Quechua *hyeve*]

~~**heven**~~ incorrect spelling of **heaven**

hew /hyoo/ (**hewed, hewn** /hyoon/ or **hewed, hew·ing, hews**) *v* **1.** *vti* **CUT DOWN OR UP** to cut, break, or destroy something, especially wood or stone, with a cutting implement, especially an ax **2.** *vt* **MAKE SOMETHING BY CUTTING OR CARVING** to form or create something by cutting wood or stone ○ *hewed a path through the forest* **3.** *vt* **SEVER SOMETHING FROM SOMETHING ELSE** to cut something off from a larger block or mass [Old English *hēawen* < Germanic] —**hew·er** *n*

SPELLCHECK hew or **hue**? Do not confuse the spelling of ***hew*** and ***hue***, which sound similar. ***Hew*** is a verb meaning "cut," as in *hew down a tree, roughly hewn wood, hew a path through the forest.* ***Hue*** is a noun denoting a shade of color, a type, or the way something looks, as in *flowers of every hue, to put a different hue on the matter.* ***Hue*** is also the spelling used in the phrase *hue and cry.*

hew to *vt* to conform closely to something such as a code or procedure

Hewes /hyooz/, **Joseph** (1730–79) American patriot. He signed the Declaration of Independence (1776) as a North Carolina delegate to the Continental Congress.

hex /heks/ *n* **1.** **CURSE** a curse or evil spell **2.** **BRINGER OF BAD LUCK** somebody believed to bring bad luck or misfortune ■ *vt* (**hexed, hex·ing, hex·es**) **1.** **CURSE OR BEWITCH SOMEBODY OR SOMETHING** to put a curse or spell on somebody or something **2.** **HAVE BAD EFFECT ON SOMETHING** to appear to have a bad effect on something, as if it were cursed or bewitched ○ *A string of accidents hexed their first attempt to climb the mountain.* [Mid-19C. Via Pennsylvanian Dutch < German *Hexe* "witch"] —**hex·er** *n*

hex. *abbr* **1.** hexagon **2.** hexagonal

hex- *prefix* same as **hexa-** (*used before vowels*)

hexa- *prefix* six ○ *hexagon* [< Greek *hex* < Indo-European]

hex·a·chlo·ro·phene /hèksə kláwrə feen/ *n* a white odorless organic compound that has antibacterial and antiseptic properties. Use: soaps, toothpaste, deodorants. Formula: $(C_6HCl_3OH)_2CH_2$. [Late 20C. < HEXA- + CHLORO- + Greek *phaino-* "shining"]

hex·a·chord /héksə kawrd/ *n* a series of six adjacent diatonic notes forming the basis of classical Greek and medieval music theory. There were three variants, the so-called natural, hard, and soft hexachords, which approximate to the modern C major, G major, and F major scales respectively.

hex·a·dec·a·nol /hèksə dékə nàwl/ *n* CHEM, PHARM same as **cetyl alcohol**

hex·a·dec·i·mal /hèksə déssim'l/ *adj* **BASED ON NUMBER 16** using units of 16, in which the letters A to F are used as digits as well as the digits 0 to 9, as a basis for counting and ordering. Hexadecimal notation is used especially to represent binary code in computers. ■ *n* **1.** **NUMBER WITH BASE 16** a number used to count or order in units of 16 **2.** **NOTATION FOR NUMBERS WITH BASE 16** the notation used to represent numbers with a base 16

hex·a·gon /héksə gòn/ *n* a two-dimensional geometric figure formed of six sides [Late 16C. Via late Latin < Greek *hexagōnon* "six-angled" < *hexa-* "six" + *gōnia* "angle"] —**hex·ag·o·nal** /hek sággən'l/ *adj*

hex·a·gram /héksə gràm/ *n* **1.** a six-pointed star-shaped figure formed by extending the sides of a regular hexagon until they meet at six points **2.** any of the 64 possible combinations of six broken or unbroken lines, used in divination, especially in the *I Ching*

hex·a·he·dron /hèksə heedrən/ *n* a three-dimensional geometric figure formed of six plane faces, e.g., a cube [Late 16C. < Greek *hexaedron*, form of *hexaedros* "six-sided" < *hexa-* "six"] —**hex·a·he·dral** *adj*

hex·a·hy·drate /hèksə hī dràyt/ *n* a crystalline compound, each molecule of which contains six loosely bound water molecules (**water of crystallization**) from which the water escapes when the compound is heated, leaving the compound unchanged

hex·am·er·ous /hek sámmərəss/, **hex·am·er·al** /-rəl/ *adj* with parts, especially petals or stamens, arranged in sets of six —**hex·am·er·ism** *n*

hex·am·e·ter /hek sámmətər/ *n* a line of verse that has six metrical feet, usually all in the same or a related meter. The Greek and Latin poems the *Iliad*, *Odyssey*, and *Aeneid* are composed in hexameters. [14C. < Latin < Greek *hexametros* "of six measures" < *hexa-* "six" + *metron* "measure"] —**hex·a·met·ric** /hèksə méttrik/ *adj*

hex·am·ine /hek sá meen, héksə meen/ *n* *UK* a solid camping fuel sold in blocks [Mid-20C. Contraction of *hexamethylenetetramine*, an antibacterial agent]

hex·ane /hék sàyn/ *n* a volatile hydrocarbon. Source: petroleum. Use: ingredient of gasoline, solvent. Formula: C_6H_{14}.

Hex·a·pla /héksəplə/ *n* an ancient version of the Hebrew Scriptures, compiled by the early Christian theologian Origen, that contains six parallel versions of the text [Early 17C. < Greek *(ta) hexapla*, its title, form of *hexaplous* "sixfold" < *hexa-* "six"]

hex·a·po·dy /hek sáppədee/ (*plural* **-dies**) *n* a line of poetry consisting of six feet —**hex·a·po·dic** /hèksə póddik/ *adj*

hex·a·stich /héksə stìk/, **hex·a·sti·chon** /hek sásti kòn/ (*plural* **-cha** /-kə/) *n* a unit of verse, e.g., a stanza or a short poem, that contains six lines [Late 16C. Via modern Latin < Greek *hexastikhon*, "of six rows" < *hexa-* "six" + *stikhos* "row"]

hex·a·style /héksə stīl/ *adj* having six architectural columns or in the form of six columns ■ *n* a building, or a portico or other part, that has six columns

Hex·a·teuch /héksə took/ *n* the first six books of the Bible, comprising Genesis, Exodus, Leviticus, Numbers, Deuteronomy, and Joshua [Late 19C. < HEXA- + Greek *teukhos* "book," after PENTATEUCH]

hex·a·va·lent /hèksə váylənt/ *adj* having a chemical valence of six

hex·cen·tric /hèks séntrik/ *n* a six-sided metal chock used in rock climbing

hex·o·san /héksō sàn/ *n* a polysaccharide made of linked hexose units

hex·ose /hék sōss/ *n* a simple sugar containing six carbon atoms

hex sign *n* a stylized sign incorporating a circle and other elements that was formerly painted on barns to ward off evil or bad luck

hex·yl /héks'l/ *adj* relating to the group of atoms derived from hexane after the the loss of a hydrogen atom. Formula: C_6H_{13}.

hey /hay/ *interj* **1.** **DEMANDING ATTENTION** used to get somebody's attention **2.** **EXPRESSING EMOTION** used to express amazement, delight, disappointment, or irritation **3.** **GREETING** used as a greeting (*informal*) [12C. Natural exclamation]

hey·day /háy dày/ *n* the time of somebody's or something's greatest success, popularity, or power [Late 16C. < obsolete *heyda* "hurrah," origin ?, by association with DAY]

Hey·er·dahl /háy ər daal, hī-/, **Thor** (1914–2002) Norwegian anthropologist. He successfully crossed the Pacific in the balsa raft *Kon-Tiki* (1947) in an attempt to prove that Native South Americans could have migrated to Polynesia.

Hey·ward /háywərd/, **Thomas Jr.** (1746–1809) American patriot. He signed the Declaration of Independence (1776) as a South Carolina delegate to the Continental Congress.

Hez·e·ki·ah /hèzzi kī ə/ (*fl* 715 B.C.) Judean king. An important religious reformer, he ruled Judah from 715 B.C. to 687 B.C.

Hf *symbol* CHEM ELEM hafnium

hf. *abbr* MEASURE half

hg[1] *symbol* MEASURE hectogram

hg[2] *abbr* BIOCHEM hemoglobin

Hg *symbol* CHEM ELEM mercury

HGH *abbr* BIOCHEM human growth hormone

hgt. *abbr* MEASURE height

hgwy. *abbr* highway

H.H. *abbr* **1.** Her Highness **2.** LAW Her Honor **3.** His Highness **4.** RELIG His Holiness **5.** LAW His Honor

hhd *abbr* MEASURE hogshead

H-Hour *n* the appointed time for a military event such as a planned attack to take place [*H* abbreviation of "hour"]

HHS *abbr* (Department of) Health and Human Services

hi /hī/ *interj* used as a greeting (*informal*) [12C. Natural exclamation]

HI *abbr* **1.** MAIL Hawaii **2.** MED hearing-impaired **3.** METEOROL humidity index

H.I. *abbr* GEOG Hawaiian Islands

Hi·a·le·ah /hī ə lee ə/ city in southeastern Florida, 5 mi./8 km north and west of Miami. Population: 228,149 (2002 estimate).

hi·a·tal /hī áyt'l/ *adj* relating to an opening, gap, or aperture in an organ of the body

hi·a·tal her·ni·a *n* a hernia in which the part of the stomach around the esophagus entrance is forced up into the chest cavity through the normal opening in the diaphragm for the esophagus. Hiatal hernia is associated with heartburn and can usually be corrected by surgery.

hi·a·tus /hī áytəss/ (*plural* **-tus·es** or *same*) *n* **1.** **UNEXPECTED GAP** a break in something where there should be continuity **2.** ANAT **OPENING** an opening or aperture in an organ, e.g., the opening in the diaphragm for the esophagus **3.** PHON **SEPARATION BETWEEN VOWELS** a break in pronunciation between two vowels that are next to each other in consecutive syllables without an intervening consonant, as in "reexamine" **4.** PRINTING **OMISSION** a gap where something is missing, especially in manuscripts [Mid-16C. < Latin, "gaping, opening" < *hiare* "gape" < Indo-European]

hi·a·tus her·ni·a *n* *UK* MED same as **hiatal hernia**

Hi·a·wa·tha /hī ə wáwthə/ (*fl* 1550) Onondaga leader. He was instrumental in uniting the Iroquois League of Five Nations in about 1550. Known only through Iroquois legend, and as the hero of a narrative poem by Henry Wadsworth Longfellow, he is nevertheless believed by historians to have been a real person. Born **Heowenta**

hi·ba·chi /hi baatchee/ (*plural* **-chis**) *n* a portable barbecue of Japanese design, with a base for the fire with vents under it and one or more adjustable cooking racks [Mid-19C. < Japanese, "fire bowl"]

hi·ba·ku·sha /híbbə kóoshə/ (*plural same* or **-shas**) *n* a survivor of the atomic bombing of Hiroshima or Nagasaki in 1945 [Mid-20C. < Japanese, "somebody who suffers an explosion"]

hi·ber·nac·u·lum /hībər nákyələm/ (*plural* **-la** /-lə/) *n* **1.** the winter den of a hibernating animal or insect **2.** the covering of a plant bud that protects it during its dormant phase [Late 17C. < Latin < *hibernare* (see HIBERNATE)]

hi·ber·nal /hī búrn'l/ *adj* relating to winter as one of the six divisions of the year used to describe ecological communities [Early 17C. < late Latin *hibernalis* < *hibernus* "wintry"]

hi·ber·nate /hībər nàyt/ (**-nat·ed, -nat·ing, -nates**) *vi* **1.** to be in a dormant state resembling sleep over the winter while living off reserves of body fat, with a decrease in body temperature and pulse rate and slower metabolism. Animals that hibernate include bears, bats, and many amphibians. **2.** to become less active, especially by staying at home rather than going out to socialize (*informal humorous*) [Early 19C. < Latin *hibernat-*, past participle of *hibernare* < *hiberna* "winter quarters" < *hibernus* "wintry"] —**hi·ber·na·tion** /hībər náysh'n/ *n* —**hi·ber·na·tor** *n*

Hi·ber·ni·a /hī búrnee ə/ *n* Ireland (*archaic or literary*) [< Latin, alteration of *Iverna*, via Greek *I(w)ernē* < Celtic] —**Hi·ber·ni·an** *adj, n*

Hi·ber·ni·cism /hī búrni sìzzəm/, **Hi·ber·ni·an·ism** /-ə nìzzəm/ *n UK* LANG same as **Irishism**

Hiberno- *prefix* Irish [< medieval Latin *Hibernus* < Latin *Hibernia* (see HIBERNIA)]

Hi·ber·no-Eng·lish /hī bùrnō-/ *n* the variety of English spoken in Ireland that has features from Irish Gaelic, including intonation and some Gaelic words and phrases —**Hi·ber·no-Eng·lish** *adj*

hibiscus

hi·bis·cus /hī bískəss, hi-/ *n* a bush or small tree of the mallow family. Flowers: large, brightly colored, with prominent stamen tubes. Genus: *Hibiscus*. [Early 18C. Via Latin < Greek *hibiskos* "marshmallow"]

hic /hik/ *interj* used to represent the sound of a hiccup [Late 19C. An imitation of the sound]

hic·cup /hí kùp, híkəp/, **hic·cough** *n* **1.** SUDDEN CONTRACTION OF DIAPHRAGM an abrupt involuntary contraction of the diaphragm that causes an intake of breath and closes the vocal cords, resulting in a convulsive gasp **2.** GULPING SOUND the gulping sound that accompanies a hiccup or a sound like this **3.** HITCH IN ARRANGEMENTS a temporary setback to somebody's plans or arrangements (*informal*) ■ **hic·cups** *npl* GULPING INTAKES OF BREATH an attack of repeated involuntary spasms of the diaphragm, resulting in periodic noisy gulps of breath ■ *v* (**-cuped** or **-cupped, -cup·ing** or **-cup·ping, -cups; -coughed, -cough·ing, -coughs**) **1.** *vi* PRODUCE HICCUP to have a spasm of the diaphragm resulting in a hiccup **2.** *vi* MAKE HICCUP NOISES to make the sound of, or a sound like, a hiccup **3.** *vt* UTTER SOMETHING WHILE HICCUPING to say something with a hiccup or hiccups [Late 16C. An imitation of the sound]

hic ja·cet /hìk jáyssət/ an inscription often found on gravestones, meaning "here lies" [< Latin]

hick /hik/ *n* an offensive term that deliberately insults somebody's rural residence or background and his or her intelligence and level of sophistication (*slang insult*) ■ *adj* remote from big cities and regarded as lacking in sophistication (*informal*) [Mid-16C. < *Hick*, old nickname for *Richard*]

hick·ey /híkee/ (*plural* **-eys** or **-ies**) *n* **1.** same as **doohickey** (*informal*) **2.** BRUISING ON SKIN a mark on the skin caused especially by kissing, biting, or sucking and associated with physical intimacy (*informal*) **3.** PIMPLE a pimple on the skin (*informal*) **4.** PRINTING PRINTING ERROR a printing error or imperfection **5.** MECH ENG PIPE-BENDING TOOL a device for bending pipes **6.** MECH ENG THREADED FITTING a threaded fitting for joining two parts [Early 20C. Origin ?]

US Signal Corps

Wild Bill Hickok

Hick·ok /hík ok/, **Wild Bill** (1837–76) US lawman, gunfighter, and scout. He was a Union spy and scout during the Civil War and later a Kansas marshal known for his marksmanship. He also toured with Buffalo Bill's Wild West Show (1872–73). Born **Hickok, James Butler**

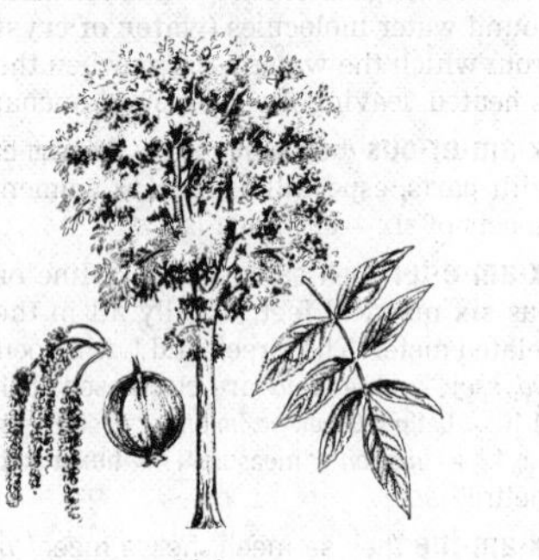

hickory

hick·o·ry /híkəree/ (*plural* **-ries**) *n* **1.** WOOD the hard light-colored wood of a North American walnut tree. Use: tool handles, sports equipment, furniture. **2.** N AMERICAN NUT TREE a deciduous tree of the walnut family that has compound leaves and nuts that are edible in some species and whose wood is hickory. Native to: North America. Genus: *Carya*. ○ *a hickory nut* **3.** HICKORY STICK a walking stick or switch made of hickory wood [Late 17C. < Virginia Algonquian *pocohiquara*, "food or drink made from pounded nuts"]

Hick·o·ry /híkəree/ city in central North Carolina, west of Statesville. Population: 39,310 (2002 estimate).

Hicks·ville[1] /híksvil/ unincorporated village in southeastern New York State, on Long Island. It is a residential and industrial center. Population: 40,174 (1996).

Hicks·ville[2], **hicks·ville** *n* a place regarded as rural and backward (*slang*)

hid past participle, past tense of **hide**[1]

hi·dal·go /hi dálgō/ (*plural* **-gos**) *n* a Spanish nobleman of the lowest rank [Late 16C. < Spanish, contraction of *hijo de algo* "son of something"]

Hi·dal·go /ee dálgō/ state in east central Mexico. Capital: Pachuca. Population: 2,235,591 (2000). Area: 8,103 sq. mi./20,987 sq. km.

Hi·dat·sa /hee dáatsə/ (*plural same* or **-sas**) *n* **1.** a member of a Native North American people living along the Missouri valley in North Dakota **2.** the Siouan language of the Hidatsa people [Late 19C. < Hidatsa *hiratsa* "willow wood lodge"] —**Hi·dat·sa** *adj*

hid·den past participle of **hide**[1] ■ *adj* **1.** made difficult to find or see ○ *a hidden doorway* **2.** not immediately obvious ○ *The package included a number of hidden costs.* —**hid·den·ness** *n*

hid·den a·gen·da *n* a plan, motive, or objective underlying somebody's actions that is kept secret from others

hid·den·ite /hídd'n īt/ *n* a semiprecious stone that is a rare green variety of spodumene. Use: gems. [Late 19C. After William E. *Hidden* (1853–1918), US mineralogist]

hid·den tax *n* FIN same as **indirect tax**

hide[1] /hīd/ *v* (**hid, hid·den** /hídd'n/ or **hid** /hid/, **hid·ing, hides**) **1.** *vti* MOVE OUT OF SIGHT to conceal yourself, or something or somebody else, from view **2.** *vt* KEEP SOMETHING SECRET to prevent something from becoming known **3.** *vt* BLOCK VIEW OF SOMETHING to obscure something by passing, or passing something, in front of it, or by being temporarily or permanently in front of it ○ *The clouds hid the sun for a while.* **4.** *vt* TURN FACE AWAY to turn away or cover the face or eyes with the hands, e.g., so that the expression cannot be seen or in order to avoid seeing something ■ *n UK* same as **blind** *n* (sense 5) [Old English *hȳdan* < W Germanic]

hide out *vi* to be in hiding, or go into hiding

hide[2] /hīd/ *n* **1.** the skin of some larger animals, e.g., deer, cattle, or buffalo (*often used in combination*) **2.** a person's skin (*informal*) ○ *"A vengeance on your crafty wither'd hide!"* (William Shakespeare, *The Taming of the Shrew*; 1593) [Old English *hȳd* < Indo-European] ◇ **neither hide nor hair of somebody** *or* **something** no trace of somebody or something (*informal*) ○ *We could see neither hide nor hair of the lost keys.* ◇ **tan somebody's hide** to beat or whip somebody (*informal*)

hide[3] /hīd/ *n* in Old English law, a measure of land equal to 120 acres [Old English *hīd* "measure of land for supporting a family" < Germanic]

hide-and-seek, **hide-and-go-seek** *n* a children's game in which one player lets the others hide, and then tries to find them

hide·a·way /hīdə wày/ *n* a secluded place of retreat or concealment [Late 19C. < HIDE[1]]

hide·bound /hīd bòwnd/ *adj* **1.** unwilling to consider new ideas or new ways of doing things **2.** having skin that is dry, stiff, and closely attached to the flesh, as a result of poor feeding ○ *hidebound cattle* [Mid-19C. < HIDE[2]]

hide-hole *n* a place in which to secrete valuable things, e.g., weaponry, or in which to escape notice by pursuers (*slang*)

hid·e·ous /híddee əss/ *adj* **1.** HORRIBLE TO SEE extremely unpleasant or horrible to see **2.** HORRIBLE TO HEAR frighteningly horrible to hear ○ *a hideous shriek* **3.** MORALLY REPULSIVE morally repulsive or disgusting **4.** CAUSING SUFFERING causing a great deal of suffering [14C. < Anglo-Norman *hidous*, Old French *hidos* < *hi(s)de* "fear"] —**hid·e·ous·ly** *adv* —**hid·e·ous·ness** *n*

SYNONYMS See ***unattractive***.

hide·out /hīd òwt/ *n* a place where somebody is hiding, especially somebody wanted by the police [Late 19C. < HIDE[1]]

hid·ey-hole /hīdee-/, **hid·y-hole** *n* a place of concealment for somebody or something (*informal*) [< variant of HIDING[1]]

hid·ing[1] /hīding/ *n* a place where somebody is hiding or can hide, or the state of being hidden [13C. < HIDE[1]]

hid·ing[2] /hīding/ *n* the punishment of being beaten (*informal*) [Early 19C. < HIDE[2]]

hi·dro·sis /hī dróssiss/ *n* **1.** the production or excretion of sweat (*technical*) **2.** a skin disease that affects the sweat glands [Mid-19C. < Greek *hidrōsis* < *hidrōs* "sweat"] —**hi·drot·ic** /-dróttik/ *adj*

hid·y-hole *n* another spelling of **hidey-hole** (*informal*)

hie /hī/ (**hied, hie·ing** or **hy·ing, hies**) *vi* to go somewhere in a hurry (*archaic*) [Old English, origin ?]

~~**hiefer**~~ incorrect spelling of **heifer**

~~**hieght**~~ incorrect spelling of **height**

hier- *prefix* same as **hiero-** (*used before vowels*)

hi·er·arch /hī ràark, hī ə-/ *n* somebody of high rank in a hierarchy, especially a priestly hierarchy [15C. Via medieval Latin < Greek *hierarkhēs* "ruling sacred person" < *hieros* "sacred" + *arkhēs* "ruling"]

hi·er·ar·chi·cal /hī ra̋arkik'l, hī ə-/, **hi·er·ar·chic** /-ra̋arkik/ *adj* **1.** relating to or arranged in a formally ranked order **2.** administered by a hierarchy composed of members of the clergy —**hi·er·ar·chi·cal·ly** *adv*

hi·er·ar·chize /hī raar kīz, hī ə-/ (**-chized, -chiz·ing, -chiz·es**) *vt* to arrange something such as an organization in graduated ranks —**hi·er·ar·chi·za·tion** /hī raarki záysh'n, hī ə-/ *n*

hi·er·ar·chy /hī ra̋arkee, hī ə-/ (*plural* **-chies**) *n* **1.** FORMALLY RANKED GROUP an organization or group whose members are arranged in ranks, e.g., in ranks of power and seniority **2.** FORMAL GRADING OF GROUP the categorization of members of a group according to importance **3.** ANIMAL GROUP ORGANIZATION a form of social organization in animals in which different members of a group possess different levels of status, affecting their feeding and mating behavior **4.** RELIG RANKED GROUP OF CLERGY a body of clergy organized into ranks **5.** CONTROLLING GROUP IN FORMAL ORGANIZATION those who are in charge of a formally organized group, especially the priests in control of the Roman Catholic Church or a local part of it **6.** BIOL SUBSET WITHIN RANKED SYSTEM a subset within a classification system, e.g., that for plants or animals

hi·er·at·ic /hī ráttik, hī ə ráttik/, **hi·er·at·i·cal** /-ráttik'l/ *adj* **1.** RELIG OF PRIESTS relating to priests **2.** LING OF ANCIENT WRITING SYSTEM relating to a cursive version of ancient Egyptian hieroglyphics **3.** ARTS IN STYLIZED FORM fixed, formal, and stylized in a traditional way, e.g., as ancient Egyptian art is ■ *n* LING ANCIENT WRITING SYSTEM a cursive version of ancient Egyptian hieroglyphics [Mid-17C. Via Latin < Greek *hieratikos* "priestly" < *hiereus* "sacred person" < *hieros* "sacred"] —**hi·er·at·i·cal·ly** *adv*

hiero- *prefix* holy, sacred ○ *hierocracy* [< Greek *hieros* < Indo-European]

hi·er·oc·ra·cy /hī rókrəssee, hī ə-/ (*plural* **-cies**) *n* **1.** government by clergy **2.** a body of clergy that rules a place or country —**hi·er·o·crat·ic** /hīrə kráttik, hī ərə-/ *adj*

hi·er·o·dule /hīrə do͞ol, hī ərə-/ *n* in ancient Greece, an enslaved person kept in or associated with a temple, especially as a prostitute [Mid-19C. Via late Latin < Greek *hierodoulos* "temple slave" < *hieron* "sacred place" < *hieros* "sacred" + *doulos* "slave"] —**hi·er·o·du·lic** /hīrə do͞olik, hī ərə-/ *adj*

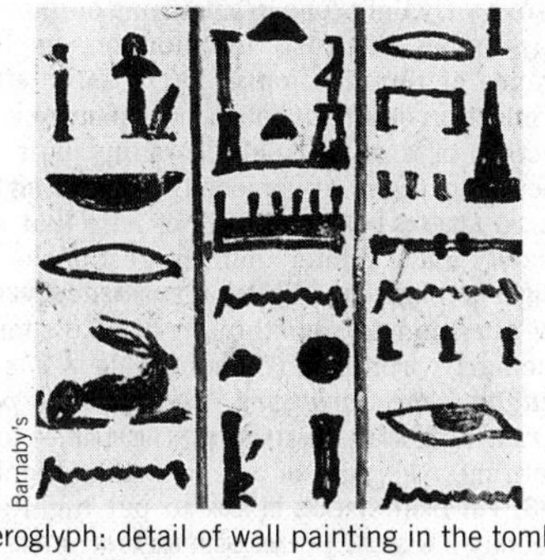

hieroglyph: detail of wall painting in the tomb of Inherkha, Thebes, Egypt (1279 B.C.–1212 B.C.)

hi·er·o·glyph /hīrə glif, hī ərə-/ *n* a symbol or picture used in a writing system to denote an object, concept, sound, or sequence of sounds, originally and especially in the writing system of the ancient Egyptians [Late 16C. Back-formation < HIEROGLYPHIC]

hi·er·o·glyph·ic /hīrə glíffik, hī ərə-/ *adj* **1.** *also* **hi·er·o·glyph·i·cal** /hīrə glíffik'l, hī ərə-/ relating to or written in hieroglyphs **2.** difficult to read (*informal*) ■ *n* same as **hieroglyph** [Late 16C. Directly or via French < late Latin *hieroglyphicus* < Greek *hierogluphikos* "sacred carving" < *hieros* "sacred" + *gluphē* "carving"] —**hi·er·o·glyph·i·cal·ly** *adv*

hi·er·o·glyph·ics /hīrə glíffiks, hī ərə-/ *n* a writing system that uses symbols or pictures to denote objects, concepts, or sounds, originally and especially in the writing system of ancient Egypt (*takes a singular verb*) ■ *npl* writing that is difficult to decipher, or other indecipherable symbols (*informal; takes a plural verb*)

hi·er·o·gram /hīrə gràm, hī ərə-/ *n* a symbol with religious significance

Hi·er·o·nym·i·an /hīrə nímmee ən, hī ərə-/, **Hi·er·o·nym·ic** /-nímmik/ *adj* relating to St. Jerome. [Mid-17C. < Latin *Hieronymus* "Jerome"]

hi·er·o·phant /hīrə fànt, hī ərə-, hī érrə-/ *n* **1.** EXPLAINER OF MYSTERIES somebody who interprets and explains obscure and mysterious matters, especially sacred doctrines or mysteries **2.** INTERPRETER OF EVENTS somebody who explains or comments on everyday matters (*formal*) **3.** ANCIENT GREEK PRIEST in ancient Greece, a priest who revealed the mysteries at the annual festival of Eleusis [Late 17C. Via late Latin < Greek *hierophantēs* "sacred person who reveals something" < *hieros* "sacred" + *phen-*, stem of *phainein* "reveal"] —**hi·er·o·phan·tic** /hīrə fántik, hī ərə-, hī èrrə-/ *adj* —**hi·er·o·phan·ti·cal·ly** *adv*

hi·fa·lu·tin *adj* another spelling of **highfalutin** (*informal*)

hi-fi /hī fī/ (*plural* **hi-fis**) *n* **1.** a set of high-quality equipment for reproducing and usually recording sound, which may include a CD player, tape deck, turntable, tuner, amplifier, and speakers (*dated*) **2.** RECORDING same as **high fidelity** [Mid-20C. Shortening of HIGH FIDELITY]

Hig·gin·son /hígginss'n/, **Thomas Wentworth** (1823–1911) US writer and reformer. He led the first African American regiment in the US Army and wrote about his experience in *Army Life in a Black Regiment* (1870). He also championed women's rights and edited Emily Dickinson's poetry. Full name **Higginson, Thomas Wentworth Storrow**

> "Great men are rarely isolated mountain peaks; they are the summits of ranges."
> [Thomas Wentworth Higginson, "A Plea For Culture," *Atlantic Essays*; 1871]

hig·gle·dy-pig·gle·dy /hìgg'ldee pígg'ldee/ *adj* disorganized and messy ■ *adv* in a disorganized, messy state [Late 16C. Probably < the idea of pigs being messy, or being huddled together when herded]

Higgs bo·son /hìgz-/ *n* a hypothetical subatomic particle with zero spin predicted in some gauge theories and thought to be the source of the mass of all other particles [Late 20C. After Peter Ware *Higgs* (b. 1929), British physicist]

high /hī/ *adj* (**high·er, high·est**) **1.** OF GREAT HEIGHT extending a long way from bottom to top, especially when viewed from the bottom ○ *a high wall* **2.** ABOVE SOMEBODY OR SOMETHING situated in a position above the onlooker, or above somebody or something else referred to ○ *The window was too high for him to see in.* **3.** IN HEIGHT ABOVE SOMETHING above or stretching upward from a known base level such as sea or ground level ○ *ten feet high* **4.** ABOVE AVERAGE greater than the normal or average, e.g., in quantity, number, quality, intensity, or cost, or well above a smaller or lower level or amount ○ *a high cost of living* **5.** MUSIC RAISED IN PITCH raised in pitch toward the upper end of a range of sound ○ *can hit the high notes* **6.** METEOROL BLOWING STRONGLY blowing with a great deal of force ○ *a high wind* **7.** DEVELOPMENTALLY ADVANCED advanced in development or complexity ○ *high finance* **8.** BETTER THAN OTHERS superior in quality, character, or morals ○ *sets a high example* ○ *high standards* **9.** OF ELEVATED RANK important in status or rank ○ *a high official* **10.** VERY FAVORABLE considering somebody or something to be particularly good ○ *held in high esteem* **11.** AT PEAK at the busiest or most important stage ○ *high summer* **12.** HAPPY animated and cheerful ○ *in high spirits* **13.** OVEREXCITED overexcited or overly stimulated **14.** DRUGS INTOXICATED under the influence of alcohol or drugs (*slang*) **15.** GEOG FAR FROM EQUATOR at a considerable distance either north or south of the equator ○ *high latitude* **16.** PHON WITH TONGUE RAISED IN MOUTH formed with the back of the tongue close, or relatively close, to the roof of the mouth ○ *high vowel sounds* **17.** AUTOMOT PRODUCING TOP SPEEDS resulting in a relatively large number of revolutions of the driven part as compared with the driving part in a transmission gear, and giving the top speed of travel or rotation ■ *adv* UPWARD at, in, or into an elevated position ○ *The balloon rose high in the sky.* ■ *n* **1.** TOP PLACE a greater than usual level or position ○ *an all-time high* **2.** METEOROL same as **anticyclone** **3.** METEOROL TOP TEMPERATURE the maximum temperature reached or expected to be reached in a particular period ○ *Today's high will be in the nineties.* **4.** ELATED STATE a state of euphoria (*informal*) **5.** INTOXICATED STATE a state of intoxication by drugs or alcohol **6.** AUTOMOT same as **high gear** (sense 1) (*informal*) [Old English *hēah* < Germanic] ◇ **high and dry 1.** stranded and abandoned, and perhaps helpless **2.** beyond the reach of water ◇ **high and low** in every conceivable place ◇ **high and mighty** arrogant and self-important ◇ **run high** to be at a level of great intensity ○ *Emotions ran high during the moving commemoration.*

SPELLCHECK higher or **hire**? Do not confuse the spelling of ***higher*** and ***hire***, which sound similar. ***Higher*** is an adjective or adverb, the comparative of *high*, as in *a higher shelf, flying higher.* ***Hire*** is a verb or noun that refers to employing somebody or renting something, as in *hire extra staff, boats for hire.*

High *n* a particular high school (*informal*) ○ *She goes to Valley High.*

high·ball /hī bàwl/ *n* **1.** LIQUOR WITH WATER OR CARBONATED DRINK a drink consisting of liquor mixed with ice and water or a carbonated drink, usually served in a tall glass **2.** RAIL RAILROAD SIGNAL a railroad signal indicating that the way ahead is clear and that a train may go ahead at full speed ■ *vti* (**-balled, -ball·ing, -balls**) GO AT HIGH SPEED to travel at high speed, or drive a vehicle at high speed (*slang*) [Earlier "type of poker played with balls and a tall glass receptacle"]

high beam *n* the setting of a vehicle's headlights that sheds light far in front of the vehicle

high·bind·er /hī bīndər/ *n* **1.** POL CORRUPT POLITICIAN a corrupt or unscrupulous politician (*dated informal*) **2.** CRIME GANGSTER a thug or gangster (*dated informal*) **3.** CRIME CHINESE GANGSTER IN US a member of a Chinese secret society of blackmailers and assassins formerly operating in US cities (*dated*) [Early 19C. After the *Highbinders*, former New York gang, probably alteration of *hellbender*]

high blood pres·sure *n* unusually high blood pressure in the arteries. It encompasses atypical elevation of either the peak blood pressure at each heartbeat (**systolic pressure**), or the running pressure between heart beats (**diastolic pressure**), or both.

high·born /hī bàwrn/ *adj* born into an aristocratic or wealthy family (*literary*)

high·boy /hī bòy/ *n* a tall chest of drawers, sometimes in two sections

high·bred /hī brèd/ *adj* born of or descended from superior breeding stock

high·brow /hī bròw/ *adj* dealing with serious subjects, especially cultural subjects, in an intellectual way ○ *"Conceits which would be only highbrow wisecracks in inferior writing have fused into a form that can only be called inevitable, the way it should be"* (Northrop Frye, *The Bush Garden*; 1972) ■ *n* somebody with highbrow interests or tastes [< the idea that a high forehead signifies greater brain power] —**high·brow·ism** *n*

high·bush blue·ber·ry /hī bo͝osh-/ *n* a bush cultivated for the commercial production of blueberries. Native to: eastern North America. Latin name: *Vaccinium corymbosum.*

high·bush cran·ber·ry *n* PLANTS same as **cranberry bush**

high cal, high cal·o·rie *adj* with many calories or more calories than usual

high·chair /hī chèr/ *n* a small chair with long legs and often a detachable tray, for older babies and toddlers to use at mealtimes

High Church *n* a section of the Episcopal Church that stresses the essential unity of Episcopal Christianity with Roman Catholicism and Orthodoxy, holds traditional views about the sacraments, and favors ritual and ceremony

high-class *adj* **1.** appealing to the rich or sophisticated, and therefore usually expensive **2.** showing or having the kind of sophistication associated with wealth

high com·e·dy *n* comedy with humor depending on witty dialogue and a clever plot rather than slapstick

high com·mand *n* **1.** the senior officers in a country's armed forces, who jointly make decisions on strategy and tactics **2.** the main headquarters of a military force

High Com·mis·sion *n* the embassy of one country of the British Commonwealth of Nations in another Commonwealth country

high com·mis·sion·er *n* **1.** the person leading an international commission **2.** the chief representative of a country of the British Commonwealth of Nations in another Commonwealth country

high-con·cept *adj* describes a movie that contains features likely to attract a large audience, e.g., big stars, fast action, and glamour

high-count *adj* with a large number of threads per square inch

high coun·try *n* lands that are in a mountainous region, but not so high as to have no pastoral or agricultural use (*hyphenated before a noun*)

high court *n* a superior court, or a state's supreme court

High Court *n* **1.** the Supreme Court of the United States **2.** in India, the highest court of a state

high-def·i·ni·tion tel·e·vi·sion *n* a television system with twice the scanning capacity of normal television systems, allowing for far greater definition and less flickering

high-den·si·ty lip·o·pro·tein *n* an aggregate of fat and protein that transports cholesterol away from the arteries. High levels of high-density lipoproteins are associated with a decreased risk of heart disease.

high-end *adj* expensive and likely to appeal to sophisticated and discerning people ○ *high-end products*

high-en·er·gy *adj* **1.** describes chemical reactions that take place with the release of substantial amounts of energy **2.** used in marketing to describe foods such as glucose drinks or high-sugar items such as honey that can be broken down easily by the body to provide a rapid supply of energy

high-en·er·gy phys·ics *n* PHYS same as **particle physics**

high·er crit·i·cism *n* the establishment of the sources of biblical texts, using the techniques of textual criticism —**high·er crit·ic** *n*

high·er ed·u·ca·tion *n* education generally begun after high school, usually carried out at a university or college, and usually involving study for a degree or diploma

high·er law *n* a moral law or ethical principle that is believed to be of greater validity than civil law

high·er learn·ing *n* education or study at college or university level

high·er math·e·mat·ics *n* mathematics at an abstract and sophisticated level, including number theory and topology (*takes a singular verb*)

high·er-up *n* somebody in a position of authority or at a higher level in a hierarchy (*informal*)

high·est com·mon fac·tor *n Can, UK* MATH the highest number that can be exactly divided into each member of a set of numbers. For example, the highest common factor of 12, 60, and 84 is 12. US term **greatest common divisor**

high ex·plo·sive *n* a liquid or solid substance that detonates without burning to produce a large release of energy. Use: rock blasting, military applications.

high·fa·lu·tin /hì fə lo͞ot'n/, **hi·fa·lu·tin**, **high·fa·lu·ting** /-lo͞oting/ *adj* affecting a grand style in an unconvincing way (*informal*) [Mid-19C. Origin ?]

high fash·ion *n* FASHION same as **haute couture**

high fi·del·i·ty *n* extremely high-quality sound reproduction with minimal distortion, achieved with electronic equipment (*hyphenated when used before a noun*)

high-five *n* an informal greeting or gesture of elation or victory in which somebody slaps a raised palm against the raised palm of somebody else (*slang*) — **high-five** *vti*

high-fli·er, **high-fly·er** *n* a highly successful person, or somebody who seems destined for great achievement

high-flown *adj* giving an unconvincing appearance of being elegant, refined, or exalted ○ *a high-flown prose style* ○*"a warning against high-flown pretensions"* (Henry James, *Roderick Hudson*; 1876)

high-fly·er *n* another spelling of **high-flier**

high-fly·ing *adj* **1.** highly successful, or having the potential for great achievement **2.** flying or located at a great height

high fre·quen·cy *n* a radio frequency in the range 3–30 MHz or of wavelength 10–100 meters (*hyphenated when used before a noun*)

high gear *n* **1.** the highest gear of a transmission system, giving the greatest speed of travel **2.** a very quick pace or rate of development

High Ger·man *n* the form of German spoken originally in the southern part of the country that has become standard German —**High-Ger·man** *adj*

high-grade *adj* of a high quality, especially because of purity or concentration of contents

high ground *n* **1.** an area of land higher than its surroundings **2.** a position of superiority or advantage over others

high-hand·ed *adj* overbearing and inconsiderate of other people's views or feelings —**high-hand·ed·ly** *adv* —**high-hand·ed·ness** *n*

high-hat (*dated*) *adj* snobbish and arrogant ■ *vti* (**high-hat·ted, high-hat·ting, high-hats**) to treat somebody in a haughty, disdainful way

high-hat cym·bals *npl* a pair of cymbals held horizontally on a stand, with the upper one made to rise and fall against the lower one by the drummer's foot

high heels *npl* women's shoes with tall, often slender, heels that raise the back of the foot off the ground

High Hol·i·days, **High Ho·ly Days** *npl* the period of Jewish festivals from Rosh Hashanah to Yom Kippur

high horse *n* an attitude of arrogance and haughty disregard for others (*informal*) ○ *told him to get off his high horse*

high hur·dles *n* a track-and-field event for men, in which the athletes cover a distance of 110 m outdoors, jumping over hurdles 42 in./107 cm high (*takes a singular or plural verb*) —**high hur·dler** *n*

high·jack, etc. CRIME another spelling of **hijack, etc.**

high jinks, **hi-jinks** /hī́ jìngks/ *n* good-humored boisterousness, frequently including mischievousness and pranks (*informal*; *takes a singular or plural verb*)

high jump *n* a track-and-field event in which the contestants run forward to gain momentum and then jump over a horizontal pole. The pole is raised higher in each successive round until all competitors have failed to get over it. —**high jump·er** *n* — **high jump·ing** *n*

high·land /hī́lənd/ *n* HILLY LAND hilly ground, higher than its surroundings ■ **high·lands** *npl* HILLY AREA an area or region that is largely hilly or mountainous ■ *adj* RELATING TO HIGHLANDS relating to or coming from highlands, especially those in Scotland —**high·land·er** *n*

High·land[1] /hī́lənd/ *adj* relating to, found in, or originating from the Scottish Highlands —**High·land·er** *n*

High·land[2] /hī́lənd/ town in northwestern Indiana, south of Lake Michigan, part of the suburban area of Chicago. Population: 23,589 (2002 estimate).

High·land cow *n* a cow belonging to a hardy breed with long shaggy reddish brown hair and long curved horns, originally developed in the Scottish Highlands

High·land dress *n* a modern version of the traditional clothing of men from the Scottish Highlands, comprising a tartan kilt, a sporran, knee-length socks, a tweed or plain wool jacket, and brogues. Highland dress is worn, e.g., by some Scottish regiments, by pipe bands, and by some Scotsmen or men of Scottish descent on special occasions.

High·land fling *n* an energetic Scottish solo dance originally danced by men in Highland dress, but now also by women and children

High·land Games *n* an outdoor meeting at which there are competitions in various traditional Scottish sports such as tossing the caber, in Scottish dancing, and in piping (*takes a singular or plural verb*)

High·land Park **1.** city in northeastern Illinois, on Lake Michigan. It is a northern suburb of Chicago. Population: 26,376 (2002 estimate). **2.** town in southeastern Michigan. Surrounded by Detroit, it evolved as a community after Henry Ford located his mass-production Model T factory there in 1909. Population: 16,281 (2002 estimate).

High·lands /hī́ləndz/ mountainous area of mainland Scotland, north and west of a line from Dumbarton in the west to Stonehaven in the east

high-lev·el *adj* involving participation by people at a high level in their organization or country, e.g., politicians, civil servants, or corporate directors

high-lev·el lan·guage *n* a computer programming language with syntax and grammar crudely approximating a natural language. The pioneering high-level languages, FORTRAN, COBOL, and ALGOL, have largely been supplanted by BASIC, FORTH, Pascal, and C, especially for educational and personal-computer applications.

high-lev·el waste *n* radioactive waste material retaining sufficient activity to need to be continuously cooled

high life *n* the luxurious lifestyle of fashionable society (*informal*; *often ironic*) —**high lif·er** *n*

high·life /hī́ lìf/ *n* a style of music that blends West African features with American jazz forms and is popular in West Africa

high·light /hī́ lìt/ *n* **1.** BEST PART the most memorable, important, or exciting part of an experience or event **2.** REPRESENTATIVE PART an exemplary extract from a larger work that, along with others, is meant to represent it ○ *gave us highlights of the president's speech* **3.** ART, PHOTOGRAPHY CONTRASTING PALE AREA an area in a very light tone in a painting or photograph that provides contrast, illumination, or the appearance of illumination **4.** PHOTOGRAPHY REFLECTION the reflection of a light source in a picture, e.g., the reflection of a studio light in shiny hair or the reflection of light in somebody's eye ■ **high·lights** *npl* LIGHT STREAKS IN HAIR strands of hair that are deliberately made lighter than the rest of the hair ■ *vt* (**-light·ed, -light·ing, -lights**) **1.** EMPHASIZE SOMETHING to draw attention to something, or make something particularly prominent or noticeable ○ *The report highlights the problems caused by polluted waterways.* **2.** MARK SOMETHING WITH HIGHLIGHTER to mark something, e.g., part of a text, with a highlighter pen **3.** PUT LIGHT STREAKS IN HAIR to put highlights in somebody's hair **4.** ART ADD LIGHT AREAS IN PICTURE to add highlights to parts of a picture to provide contrast, illumination, or the appearance of illumination

high·light·er /hī́ lìtər/ *n* **1.** a broad-tipped felt pen, often with transparent, brightly colored ink, for marking important passages of text **2.** a cosmetic for the face that is used to emphasize features such as the eyes or cheekbones

high-low *n* **1.** a variety of poker in which both high and low hands win **2.** in bridge, a signal to a partner to lead a particular suit

high·ly /hī́lee/ *adv* **1.** EXTREMELY to a great extent, or in many ways ○ *highly likely to succeed* ○ *highly recommended* ○ *highly improbable* **2.** FAVORABLY very favorably ○ *highly regarded* **3.** IN HIGH PLACE in a high position or rank ○ *highly placed officials who denied the story*

high·ly-strung *adj UK* same as **high-strung**

high-main·te·nance *adj* requiring an excessive amount of attention or effort to maintain ○ *a high-maintenance car* ○ *a high-maintenance relationship*

High Mass *n* an elaborate Roman Catholic Mass in which a choir sings much of the service. It is usually celebrated by more than one priest.

high-mind·ed *adj* having or showing high moral principles —**high-mind·ed·ly** *adv* —**high-mind·ed·ness** *n*

high-muck-a-muck /hī mùkə múk/, **high-muck·et·y-muck** /-mùkətee-/ *n* somebody in a position of importance and authority who behaves in an overbearing way (*informal*) [Mid-19C. Probably < Chinook Jargon *hiyu muckamuck*, literally "plenty to eat" < Nootka, by association with HIGH]

high·ness /hīnəss/ *n* the condition, state, or extent of being high

High·ness *n* a title and style of address for members of a royal family other than a sovereign

high noon *n* **1.** NOON EXACTLY the exact moment of noon **2.** PEAK OF ACHIEVEMENT the high point or most creative part of somebody's career or achievements **3.** *also* **High Noon** CRUCIAL TIME a time of confronting a serious problem or making a hard decision

CULTURAL NOTE *High Noon*, a movie (1952) by director Fred Zinnemann. In this classic western, lawman Will Kane (Gary Cooper) valiantly awaits and then confronts a killer seeking revenge for his recent incarceration. Shot in real time, the film's suspense is heightened by close-ups of Kane's anxious expressions and of clocks ticking steadily toward the moment of truth.

high-oc·tane *adj* **1.** describes fuel that has a high octane content **2.** showing or demanding a high degree of commitment and effort in a drive for success (*informal*) ○ *high-octane lawyers*

high-per·form·ance *adj* designed to operate at greater speed or with greater power than other things of the same kind ○ *a high-performance sports car*

high-pitched *adj* **1.** AT TOP OF SOUND RANGE toward the upper end of the range of audible sound **2.** EMOTIONAL extremely emotional and intense **3.** CONSTR WITH STEEP SLOPE having a very steep slope

high plac·es *npl* positions of power, authority, or influence

high point *n* the most successful, enjoyable, or important part of a period of time, activity, or experience ○ *This new promotion marked the high point of his career.*

High Point /hī póynt/ city in central North Carolina, a major furniture-manufacturing center. Population: 90,639 (2002 estimate).

high-pow·ered, high-pow·er *adj* **1.** DYNAMIC possessing great energy and impressive ability, especially as displayed in a professional environment ○ *a high-powered sales pitch* **2.** INFLUENTIAL having much power or influence **3.** OPTICS GREATLY ENLARGING giving a high magnification **4.** TECH VERY POWERFUL operating much more powerfully, or able to handle material of greater complexity and more quickly, than other equipment of the same type **5.** ENG NEEDING OR MAKING LOTS OF POWER requiring or producing a great deal of power

high-pres·sure *adj* **1.** STRESSFUL causing stress, e.g., from deadlines or excessive demands ○ *She's at her best in high-pressure situations.* **2.** PERSISTENT aggressively persistent in seeking to bring about a result ○ *a high-pressure sales pitch* **3.** OPERATING AT GREATER THAN NORMAL PRESSURE using, or designed to withstand, forces exerted by liquid or gas at pressures higher than normal atmospheric pressure

high priest *n* **1.** MAIN PROPONENT the leading figure propounding a doctrine or ideology **2.** JUDAISM JEWISH CHIEF PRIEST a Jewish chief priest, especially the head of the priestly caste at the time of the Temple in Jerusalem **3.** CHR MORMON PRIEST a man who is a priest in the Church of Jesus Christ of Latter-Day Saints, belonging to the order of Melchizedek

high priest·ess *n* **1.** a woman who leads a religion or a religious group **2.** the leading woman propounding a doctrine or ideology

high pro·file *n* a prominent position or presence in the public eye

high-pro·file *adj* in or intended to be in the public eye, e.g., to attract attention, support, or business

high-rank·ing *adj* of high status or holding great responsibility in a hierarchical organization

high re·lief *n* a version of relief sculpture in which the carving projects from the background to more than half its natural depth

High Re·nais·sance *n* the period in European art between about 1490 and 1520, when the work of Leonardo da Vinci, Michelangelo, Raphael, and other great artists reached the highest point of Renaissance perfection

high-rent *adj* costing or charging a large amount of money (*informal*)

high-res *adj* COMPUT another spelling of **hi-res** (*informal*)

high-res·o·lu·tion *adj* using a large number of dots or lines to portray an image in great detail in a video display or printed image

high-rise *adj* **1.** ARCHIT MULTISTORY consisting of several stories, but usually fewer than for a skyscraper **2.** CYCLING WITH HIGH HANDLEBARS describes a child's bicycle that has small wheels, very high handlebars, and a long narrow seat ■ *n* **1.** ARCHIT TALL BUILDING a multistory building **2.** CYCLING HIGH-RISE BICYCLE a child's high-rise bicycle

high road *n* **1.** DIRECT ROUTE the easiest or most direct way to a place **2.** *UK* MAIN ROAD a main road, usually in a town or village **3.** RIGHT MORAL COURSE the most ethical course of action ○ *was commended for taking the high road and resigning*

high roll·er *n* (*slang*) **1.** a person or organization that spends money freely and extravagantly **2.** a gambler who plays for high stakes —**high-roll·ing** *adj*

high school *n* a school that includes grades 9 or 10 through 12 —**high school·er** *n*

high seas *npl* the open ocean, not under any nation's jurisdiction

high sea·son *n UK* TRAVEL same as **peak season**

high sign *n* a secret signal, often prearranged, given as a warning or to convey information

High·smith /hī smìth/, **Patricia** (1921–95) US writer. She wrote literary crime novels such as *Strangers on a Train* (1950) and *The Talented Mr. Ripley* (1955). Born **Plangman, Mary Patricia**

high so·ci·e·ty *n* the fashionable wealthy people in society as a group

high-sound·ing *adj* grandiose and pretentious but unlikely to come to anything

high-speed *adj* **1.** TRANSP CAPABLE OF GREAT SPEED moving or functioning at high speed, or capable of moving or functioning at high speed **2.** PHOTOGRAPHY NEEDING LITTLE EXPOSURE needing a very short exposure time ○ *high-speed film* **3.** PHOTOGRAPHY OPERATING AT FAST SPEEDS operating, done, or capable of making exposures at a very fast rate, at between 50 and several million frames per second ○ *a high-speed shutter*

high-spir·it·ed *adj* lively and full of fun or mischief —**high-spir·it·ed·ly** *adv* —**high-spir·it·ed·ness** *n*

high-stakes *adj* describes a risky situation in which somebody is likely to win or lose a great deal ○ *"Everyone is getting in the starting blocks for a high-stakes fight."* (*Washington Post*; November 1998)

high-stick *vt* in ice hockey, to strike an opponent with the blade of the stick above the legally specified height —**high-stick·ing** *n*

high street *n UK* in the United Kingdom, a principal street where the main stores of a town are located

high-strung *adj* tense, nervous, or easily upset by nature

high style *n* the most up-to-date and stylish fashion, especially in clothing (*hyphenated before a noun*)

~~**hight**~~ incorrect spelling of **height**

high ta·ble *n UK* in the United Kingdom, a table in a large dining hall in some schools and university colleges at which the staff, principal teachers, or fellows sit

high·tail /hī tàyl/ (**-tailed, -tail·ing, -tails**) *vi* to rush away from a place (*slang*) [< the erect tail of a fleeing animal]

high tea *n UK* in the United Kingdom, a meal served in the late afternoon or early evening, consisting of a cooked dish, usually hot, with bread and butter, cakes, and tea

high tech, hi-tech *n* **1.** advanced technology and state-of-the-art devices and methods, especially in electronic engineering **2.** a style of architecture and interior design that makes use of metal, glass, and plastic in a simple utilitarian way

high-tech /hī ték/, **hi-tech** *adj* **1.** using or relating to advanced technological devices and methods **2.** using metal, glass, and plastic in a simple utilitarian way in architecture and interior design

high tech·nol·o·gy *n* **1.** TECH same as **high tech** (sense 1) **2.** the computing and telecommunications industries, collectively

high-ten·sion *adj* designed for or operating at high voltage

high-test *adj* same as **high-octane** (sense 1)

high tide *n* **1.** HIGHEST POINT OF TIDE the tide at its highest level **2.** MOMENT OF HIGHEST TIDE the time when the tide reaches its highest level **3.** PEAK OF SOMETHING the culmination or high point of something

high-toned *adj* culturally, morally, or socially superior (*dated slang*)

high-top *n* a sneaker or other athletic shoe that covers the foot up to the ankle, e.g., those worn by basketball players

high trea·son *n* treason perpetrated by somebody against his or her own country

high-val·ue tar·get *n* an enemy person or site regarded by military personnel as of the highest priority and therefore essential to the successful completion of a mission [Late 20C.]

high·veld /hī vélt/ *n* in South Africa, the high-altitude grassy plateau of Gauteng and neighboring Northern provinces

high-volt·age *adj* **1.** involving a voltage higher than 650 volts **2.** virtuosic in skill, delivery, style, and performance ○ *a high-voltage rendition of the piano concerto*

high wa·ter *n* **1.** same as **high tide** (senses 1–2) **2.** the highest level reached by any stretch of water, e.g., during a flood (*hyphenated before a noun*) **3.** the time when the water level of a river or other stretch of water is at its highest

high-wa·ter mark *n* **1.** HIGHEST WATER LEVEL the highest level reached by any natural stretch of water, especially by the sea at high tide, but also by inland water such as a river during a flood **2.** MARK SHOWING HIGHEST LEVEL a mark drawn to indicate the highest level reached by any natural stretch of water **3.** PEAK OF SOMETHING a high point in an enterprise ○ *Winning the book award was the high-water mark in her career.*

high-wa·ter pants *npl* pants that are too short, especially because the person wearing them has grown out of them (*slang*)

high·way /hī wày/ *n* **1.** a principal road, especially one that connects towns or cities and is part of a numbered system (*often used before a noun*) **2.** a direct route or course ○ *the highway to fame*

high·way·man /hī wàymən/ (*plural* **-men** /-mən/) *n* formerly, somebody who forced people traveling by road to stop, usually at gunpoint, and robbed them

high·way pa·trol *n* the law enforcement agency that patrols the public highways in some states of the United States

high·way rob·ber·y *n* **1.** the charging of inflated prices for goods or services (*informal*) **2.** a robbery, usually of a traveler, committed on or near a public road

high wire *n* a tightrope stretched high above the ground on which circus performers balance and perform acrobatics

high-wire *adj* holding the possibility of great risk, e.g., to life or reputation

hi·jab /hee jáab/ *n* **1.** a head covering worn by some

Muslim women to conceal their hair and neck **2.** the Islamic practice of dressing modestly in clothing that covers most of the body [Via Persian < Arabic *ḥajaba* "to veil"]

hi·jack /hī́ jàk/, **high·jack** *vt* (**-jacked, -jack·ing, -jacks**) **1. SEIZE TRANSPORT VEHICLE** to take forcible control of a public transport vehicle, e.g., a passenger aircraft while in transit, taking the people on board hostage, and often diverting it to another destination **2. STOP VEHICLE TO ROB IT** to seize a motor vehicle, e.g., an armored car carrying money, in order to rob it of its contents **3. STEAL SOMETHING FROM SEIZED VEHICLE** to steal merchandise, money, or any other items from a hijacked motor vehicle **4. STEAL IDEA** to take somebody else's idea and use it, especially to the exclusion or detriment of the person from whom it was taken (*informal*) ■ *n* TRANSP same as **hijacking** [Early 20C. Origin ?] —**hi·jack·er** *n*

hi·jack·ing /hī́ jàking/, **high·jack·ing** *n* the forcible seizure of a public transport vehicle, e.g., a passenger aircraft while in transit, taking those on board hostage, and often diverting it to another destination

hi·ji·ki /hee jéekee/, **hi·zi·ki** /-zée-/ *n* a Japanese seaweed that turns black when dried and is sold shredded to be used in cooking [Late 20C. < Japanese]

hi·jinks *n* another spelling of **high jinks** (*informal*)

hij·ra /híjjrə/ *n* in South Asia, a member of a community of male transvestites or eunuchs, traditionally performing as singers or dancers at religious festivals or on social occasions such as baptisms or weddings [< Hindi]

hike /hīk/ *v* (**hiked, hik·ing, hikes**) **1.** *vti* **TAKE LONG WALK** to go for a long walk in the countryside, usually for pleasure **2.** *vi* MIL **GO ON TRAINING MARCH** to march in a training exercise **3.** *vt* **RAISE AMOUNT OF SOMETHING** to increase taxes, prices, or the level or quantity of something suddenly and by a large amount ○ *rumors that they plan to hike oil prices* **4.** *vt* **PULL SOMETHING UPWARD** to pull or raise something with a sudden strong movement **5.** *vt* FOOTBALL same as **snap** *v* (sense 12) ■ *n* **1. PLEASURABLE LONG WALK** a long walk, usually in the country for pleasure **2.** MIL **MILITARY MARCH** a long military march, usually as a training exercise **3. SUDDEN LARGE INCREASE** a sudden large increase in prices, taxes, or the level or quantity of something ○ *an unexpected hike in gas prices* **4.** FOOTBALL same as **snap** *n* (sense 9) [Early 19C. Origin ?] —**hik·er** *n* ◇ **take a hike** to leave abruptly, or, more often, used to tell somebody who is unwelcome to leave (*slang*)

hike out *vi* to lean backward over the side of a sailboat to counterbalance the wind in the sails and keep the boat flat in the water

hike up *vti* to move something up from the proper position, or become moved up from the proper position ○ *Her coat had hiked up at the back.*

hi·la·hi·la /héelə hèelə/ *adj Hawaii* bashful, shy, or ashamed [< Hawaiian]

Hi·lar·i·on /hi láree ən/, **St.** (290?–371) Palestinian monk. He was educated in Alexandria, Egypt, where he converted to Christianity. On his return to Palestine, he lived as a hermit in marshes near Gaza.

hi·lar·i·ous /hi lérree əss/ *adj* extremely funny [Early 19C. < Latin *hilaris* "cheerful" < Greek *hilaros*] —**hi·lar·i·ous·ly** *adv* —**hi·lar·i·ous·ness** *n*

SYNONYMS See *funny.*

hi·lar·i·ty /hi lárrətee/ *n* amusement or merry laughter [15C. Via French < Latin *hilaritas* < *hilaris* (see HILARIOUS)]

Hil·bert /hílbərt/, **David** (1862–1943) German mathematician. He is best known for reducing geometry to a series of abstract equations, thereby giving it a more mathematical foundation.

> "The importance of a scientific work can be measured by the number of previous publications it makes superfluous to read."
> [David Hilbert. Quoted in *The Unnatural Nature of Science*, Lewis Wolpert; 1993]

Hil·de·gard (of Bin·gen) /híldə gaàrd əv bíngən/, **St.** (1098–1179) German writer and composer. A nun, she is remembered for her book of visions, *Scivias* (1141–52), and for her devotional music and poetry. She also developed the idea of universal gravitation.

hill /hil/ *n* **1. HIGH LAND** an area of land, usually rounded in shape, that is higher than the surrounding land but not as high as a mountain ○ *the hills surrounding Colorado Springs* **2. GRADIENT IN ROAD** a slope or gradient in a road ○ *You'll need to shift down into second gear for this hill.* **3. PILE OF EARTH** a pile of something such as earth **4. GROUP OF PLANTS OR SEEDS** plants or seeds arranged in a cluster rather than planted in rows ○ *a hill of squash* **5.** *regional* **PILE OF STORED VEGETABLES** a heap of vegetables, usually potatoes, covered with earth and mulch and sometimes stored in a shed ■ *vt* (**hilled, hill·ing, hills**) **MAKE EARTH INTO PILE** to pile up earth, especially around the base of plants [Old English *hyll* < Indo-European, "be prominent"] —**hill·er** *n* ◇ **over the hill** at an age considered too advanced in years for something, or supposedly past the prime of life (*informal*)

REGIONAL NOTE See *bank*[2].

Hill *n* same as **Capitol Hill** (*informal*) ○ *has worked on the Hill for two years*

Hill /hil/, **Ambrose** (1825–65) US army officer. A Confederate corps commander, he initiated the battle of Gettysburg (1863) and died when his troops were defeated at the Siege of Petersburg (1865). Full name **Hill, Ambrose Powell**

Hill, Graham (1929–75) British racing driver. He was winner of the Grand Prix world championship (1962, 1968) and the Indianapolis 500 (1966). Full name **Hill, Norman Graham**

Hill, James Jerome (1838–1916) Canadian-born US entrepreneur and financier. He managed and controlled the Great Northern Railway Company (1890–1912).

Hil·la·ry /híllaree/, **Sir Edmund** (*b.* 1919) New Zealand mountaineer and explorer. On May 29, 1953, he and Tenzing Norkay became the first climbers to reach the summit of Mount Everest. Full name **Hillary, Sir Edmund Percival**

> "Well, we knocked the bastard off!"
> [Edmund Hillary. On summiting Mount Everest (1953), *Nothing Venture, Nothing Win*; 1975]

hill·bil·ly /híl billee/ (*plural* **-lies**) *n* a term used by people from the country to describe themselves with pride, but used by others as an insult for people whom they regard as ignorant and unsophisticated (*informal; offensive in some contexts*) [Early 20C. < pet form of the name *William*]

hill·bil·ly mu·sic *n* a variety of country music, especially the music of the Appalachian Mountains, that features fiddles, banjos, guitars, and hammer dulcimers

hill climb *n* a competition in which automobile or motorcycle drivers compete to set the fastest time in reaching the top of a steep slope

hill coun·try *n US* hilly rural land, especially when used as pasture for sheep or cattle

hill·crest /híl krèst/ *n* the summit or the highest ridge of a hill

Hil·lel (the El·der) /hìl el-/ (70? B.C. - A.D. 10?) Jewish rabbi and teacher. He founded a liberal school of scriptural interpretation that influenced later Jewish religious leaders.

Hil·liard /híllyərd, híllee ərd/, **Nicholas** (1547–1619) English painter and goldsmith. He is regarded as the founder of the English school of painting miniatures, and his portraits include Mary, Queen of Scots, and Elizabeth I.

Hill·man /hílmən/, **Sidney** (1887–1946) Lithuanian-born US labor leader. A skilled negotiator, he was president of the Amalgamated Clothing Workers of America (1914–46).

hill my·na *n* a black bird of the starling family often kept as a cagebird because of its ability to mimic human words. Native to: South Asia. Latin name: *Gracula religiosa.*

hill·ock /híllək/ *n* a small hill or mound —**hill·ocked** *adj* —**hill·ock·y** *adj*

Hills·bor·ough /hílz bùrō/ town in northern North Carolina. It was a site of patriot resistance before and during the American Revolution. Population: 5,406 (2002 estimate).

hill·side /híl sīd/ *n* the slope or side of a hill

Hill·side /híl sīd/ town in northeastern New Jersey, north of Elizabeth. Population: 21,993 (2002 estimate).

hill·top /híl tòp/ *n* the summit of a hill

hill·y /híllee/ (**-i·er, -i·est**) *adj* **1.** having many hills ○ *hilly countryside* **2.** having a steep incline —**hill·i·ness** *n*

Hi·lo /héelō/ town and county seat of the island of Hawaii, situated on the eastern coast of the island. Population: 37,728 (1996).

hilt /hilt/ *n* the handle of a sword, knife, or dagger [Old English *hilt(e)* < Germanic] ◇ **(up) to the hilt** to the maximum

Hil·ton /híltən/, **Conrad** (1887–1979) US hotel-chain owner and executive. He bought many hotels and founded the Hilton Hotel Corporation in 1946.

Hil·ton, James (1900–54) British novelist. He wrote *Lost Horizon* (1933) and *Good-bye, Mr. Chips* (1934).

Hil·ton Head /hìltən-/ island in the Sea Islands, off the southern coast of South Carolina. It is a popular resort.

hi·lum /hī́ləm/ (*plural* **-la** /-lə/) *n* **1.** a scar on the seed of a plant indicating where it was attached to the ovule **2.** an opening through which blood vessels and nerves enter and leave an organ [Mid-17C. < Latin, "trifle"]

hi·lus /hī́ləss/ (*plural* **-li** /hī́ lī/) *n UK* same as **hilum** (sense 2) [Mid-19C. < modern Latin, alteration of HILUM]

him *stressed* /him/; *unstressed* /im/ *pron* used to refer to a man, boy, or male animal who has been previously mentioned or whose identity is known (*used as the object or complement of a verb or preposition*) ○ *She handed him the phone without a word.* ○ *John closed the door behind him.* [Old English < Germanic]

Hi·ma·chal Pra·desh /hi maáchəl prə désh/ mountainous state in northern India. Capital: Simla. Population: 6,077,248 (2001). Area: 21,495 sq. mi./55,673 sq. km.

Himalaya

Him·a·la·ya /hìmmə láy ə/, **Him·a·la·yas** /-láy əz/ mountain system in southern Asia. Its highest peak, and the highest mountain in the world, is Mount Everest, 29,028 ft./8,848 m. Length: 1,500 mi./2,400 km. —**Him·a·la·yan** *adj*

Him·a·la·yan cat *n* a longhaired cat with the markings of a Siamese cat, bred by crossing a Persian cat with a Siamese cat

Hi·ma·lia /hi maályə/ *n* a small natural satellite of Jupiter, discovered in 1904. It is approximately 112 mi./180 km in diameter. [Late 20C. Probably < Greek *himalis*, name for DEMETER < *himalios* "abundant"]

hi·mat·i·on /hi máttee òn/ *n* in ancient Greece, a loose outer garment worn by men and women, consisting of a large rectangular piece of cloth draped over one shoulder and under the opposite arm [Mid-19C. < Greek, "small garment" < *hima* "garment" < *hennunai* "clothe"]

him/her /hìm ər húr/ *pron* him or her, used to avoid the sexist use of "him" in reference to somebody whose sex is unknown

Himm·ler /hímmlər/, **Heinrich** (1900–45) German Nazi official. The head of the Nazi police forces (1936–45), he committed suicide rather than face trial for his part in the Holocaust.

> "Most of you know what it means when a hundred corpses are lying together, when five hundred are lying there, or when a thousand are lying there...This is an unwritten and never-to-be-written page of glory in our history."
> [Heinrich Himmler, *Speech to the S.S. (Nazi security forces), Poznan, Poland*; October 1943]

him·self *stressed* /him sélf/; *unstressed* /im sélf/ CORE MEANING: the form of "him" used in reflexive and emphatic contexts ○ *After a final struggle with himself, he handed the papers over.* ○ *If he himself doesn't know what he's doing, I don't see how I can help him.* ○ *He did it himself.*

■ *pron* **1.** REFERRING TO MALE SUBJECT OF VERB used to refer to the same man, boy, or male animal as the subject of the verb ○ *He decided to treat himself.* ○ *his sense of pride in himself* **2.** USED FOR EMPHASIS used to emphasize or clarify which man, boy, or male animal is being referred to, often introducing a note of surprise or awe ○ *a visit from the Prince himself* **3.** ALONE OR WITHOUT HELP used to show that a man, boy, or male animal is alone or unaided ○ *sitting by himself in a corner* ○ *tied his shoelaces himself* **4.** NORMAL SELF his normal self in terms of personality, health, or behavior ○ *not feeling himself* **5.** *also* **Him·self** *Ireland, Scotland* IMPORTANT MALE PERSON an important, or often self-important, man or boy (*informal; often used ironically*) ○ *Himself is wanting a word.*

Him·yar·ite /hímmyə rīt/ *n* (*plural* **-ites** or *same*) a member of an ancient people who lived in the southern Arabian Peninsula ■ *adj* relating to the Himyarites [Mid-19C. After *Himyar*, legendary king of Yemen]

Him·yar·it·ic /hìmmyə ríttik/ *n* an extinct language spoken by the ancient Himyarites in southwestern Arabia. It belongs to the Semitic branch of the Afro-Asiatic family of African languages. —**Him·yar·it·ic** *adj*

Hi·na·ya·na /hèenə yaánə/ *n* a form of Buddhism characterized by adherence to the early Pali scriptures and the nontheistic pursuit of purification through Nirvana. It is found mainly in Sri Lanka and Southeast Asia. [Mid-19C. < Sanskrit, "lesser vehicle"] —**Hi·na·ya·nist** *n* —**Hi·na·ya·nis·tic** /hèenə yaa nístik/ *adj*

Hincks /hingks/, **Sir Francis** (1807–85) Irish-born Canadian colonial administrator. He advocated a bicultural nation, and cofounded the Reform Party in 1841.

hind¹ /hīnd/ *adj* at or forming the back part of something, especially a bodily organ or an animal ○ *the hind legs of a donkey* [13C. Probably shortening of BEHIND]

hind² /hīnd/ *n* **1.** a female red deer **2.** a spotted ocean fish that is a type of grouper. Native to: Atlantic Ocean. Genus: *Epinephelus.* [Old English < Indo-European, "hornless"]

Hind. *abbr* **1.** Hindi **2.** Hindu **3.** Hindustan **4.** Hindustani

hind·brain /hīnd bràyn/ *n* the rearmost part of the brain in a vertebrate embryo, which develops into the cerebellum, pons, and medulla oblongata

Hin·de·mith /híndə mìt/, **Paul** (1895–1963) German composer and violinist. A pioneer of *Gebrauchsmusik*, a utilitarian approach to composition, he also wrote ballets, concertos, and operas, including *Mathis der Maler* (1935).

Hin·den·burg /híndən bùrg/, **Paul von** (1847–1934) Prussian-born president of the German Republic (1925–34). A general in World War I, he became second president of the German Republic in 1925, and appointed Adolf Hitler chancellor in 1933.

> "That man for a Chancellor? I'll make him a postmaster and he can lick the stamps with my head on them."
> [Paul von Hindenburg, referring to Hitler, August 13, 1932, *Hindenburg: The Wooden Titan*, J.W. Wheeler-Bennett; 1936]

LANGUAGE HERITAGE ***Hindi*** Much of English is made up of words from other languages, and Hindi is a contributor in this respect. Many Hindi terms are used in South Asian English; others that were once the preserve of traders and colonial settlers are familiar outside the subcontinent through emigrant communities; others are completely naturalized in English, often to the extent that any sense of their origins is lost.

In this last category are, for example, ***bandanna***, ***bangle***, ***bungalow***, ***cushy***, ***dinghy***, ***loot***, and ***shampoo***, and from Hindi in transit from Sanskrit, ***cheetah***, ***chit***, ***jungle***, ***pundit***, and ***thug***. ***Bandanna***, for example, arrived in the mid-18th century, probably via Portuguese, from Hindi *bāndhnū*, a method of tie-dyeing; ***bungalow*** (late 17th) is from Hindi *banglā* "of Bengal" (a former province of northeastern India); ***cushy*** (early 20th), from Hindi *khūsh* "pleasant," is so much part of the English language that it has developed derivatives *cushily* and *cushiness*; ***shampoo*** (mid-18th) was adopted from Hindi *cāpō*, from *cāpnā* "knead, massage." Europeans trading and empire-building in South Asia not only received words from, but also gave words to, the contact languages, and in the case of ***veranda*** were given one back: Hindi-speakers took Portuguese *varanda* "railing, balcony" as *varaṇḍā* and in the early 18th century passed it on to English.

Names of flora and fauna inevitably were adopted into English, for example, ***chukar*** (a partridge that has been introduced into the western United States as a game bird), ***guar*** (a plant with seeds used for gum), ***krait*** (a poisonous snake), and ***mugger*** (a crocodile).

South Asian cuisine has had considerable impact on English: migrants include ***basmati*** rice (from Hindi *bāsamatī* "fragrant"), ***bhaji*** (Hindi *bhājī* "fried vegetables"), ***chapati*** (from Hindi *capātī*, from *capānā* "flatten"), ***chutney***, ***dahl***, ***garam masala*** (literally "hot spices"), ***jalebi***, ***lassi***, ***mung bean***, and ***paratha***. Dishes have been adapted and created for Western tastes: ***kedgeree*** (from Hindi *khicṛī*), a dish consisting of rice with flaked smoked fish and hard-boiled eggs, is of British origin.

Numerous Hindi terms for cloth and clothing have also moved into English: *dungarees* are made of ***dungaree*** (from Hindi *dungrī* "kind of coarse cloth," named after a village near Mumbai [Bombay]). Other migrants in this category include ***chappal***, ***churidars***, ***dhoti***, and ***nainsook***.

Within South Asian English, Hindi and English freely interact. English suffixes combine with Hindi forms (***goondaism*** from ***goonda*** "ruffian, hooligan"), and Hindi suffixes combine with English (***filmi***, with the Hindi adjective suffix *-i*); Hindi and English nouns make hybrid compounds (***cyber dhaba*** "roadside stall where people can use computers or the Internet," with *dhaba* a Hindi word for a roadside food stall); and Hindi terms are translated into English (***good name*** "somebody's last name or family name," a loan translation from Hindi *shubh naam*).

South Asian immigrants to the Caribbean also brought some Hindi words, for example, ***aja*** "the father of somebody's father" (from Hindi *daadaa*), ***aji*** "the mother of somebody's father" (from Hindi *daadii*), and ***bhaigan*** "eggplant"; shared South Asian and Caribbean cuisine is reflected in words such as ***anchar*** and ***roti***. And elsewhere in the world South Asian traders have left their mark on the names of currencies: in Oman the ***baiza*** (via Arabic from Hindi *paisā*) and in the Maldives the ***rufiyaa*** (via Divehi, a form of Sinhalese, from Hindi *rūpiyā* "rupee"). See also ***Sanskrit***

Hin·den·burg line /híndən bùrg-/ *n* a strong defensive line of fortifications built by the German army near the border with France and Belgium in 1916–17 and breached by an Allied offensive in 1918 [Because Paul von Hindenburg directed retreat to it]

hin·der¹ /híndər/ *vt* (**-dered, -der·ing, -ders**) to delay or prevent the development or progress of somebody or something ○ *A heavy snowfall has hindered rescuers' attempts to reach the stranded climbers.* ■ *n* in squash and handball, an opponent's accidental interference, preventing fair and unobstructed return of the ball [Old English *hindrian* < Germanic] —**hin·der·er** *n*

SYNONYMS ***hinder, block, hamper, hold back, restrain, impede, obstruct***

CORE MEANING: to put difficulties in the way of progress

hinder to delay or prevent the development or progress of somebody or something ○ *Does migration help or hinder a country's development?* ○ *Nothing in the bylaws can hinder the party from pushing its proposed measures through.* **block** to prevent or restrict movement through, into, or out of something, or prevent something from taking place ○ *Guards stepped forward to block the vehicle trying to enter the air base.* ○ *The company's operations were totally blocked by the injunction.* **hamper** to restrict the free movement or progress of somebody or something ○ *The rescue effort, hampered by foul weather over the weekend, was again halted on Monday.* ○ *She claimed her injury did not hamper her in today's race.* **hold back** to keep something from happening, or keep somebody from doing something ○ *The expense of data is holding back development in this area.* ○ *He stopped suddenly and held the child back.* **restrain** to keep somebody or something under control or within limits ○ *There were crash barriers along the route to restrain the crowds.* **impede** to interfere with the movement, progress, or development of somebody or something ○ *We had no flashlights, but darkness did not impede our progress.* ○ *The two leaders agreed not to let their rival claims to offshore oil fields impede the development of trade.* **obstruct** to cause a serious delay in action or progress, or to cause a blockage in a road, course, or passage ○ *pleaded guilty to charges of conspiring to obstruct justice* ○ *Obstructing the doors causes delay and can be dangerous.*

hind·er² /hīndər/ *adj UK* at or toward the rear of something ○ *at the hinder end of the conference* [Old English, origin ?]

~~**hinderance**~~ incorrect spelling of **hindrance**

Hin·di /híndee/ *n* an Indic official language of India that developed from a literary form of Hindustani and is widely used as a lingua franca in many parts of the country. Native speakers: 200 million. Other speakers: 700 million. [Early 19C. < Urdu *hindī* < *Hind* "India"] —**Hin·di** *adj*

hind·milk /hīnd mìlk/ *n* the milk produced after foremilk during breast-feeding, which is rich in fat content and high in calories

hind·most /hīnd mōst/ *adj* farthest back, or last (*literary*)

hind·quar·ter /hīnd kwàwrtər/ *n* either of the two back quarters of a carcass of beef, lamb, veal, or mutton consisting of one leg and one or two ribs ■ **hind·quar·ters** *npl* the hind legs and adjoining parts of a four-legged animal

hin·drance /híndrənss/ *n* **1.** somebody or something that prevents or makes it difficult for somebody to do something **2.** the act of obstructing progress

hind·sight /hīnd sīt/ *n* the ability or opportunity to understand and judge an event or experience after it has occurred ○ *That's easy to say with the benefit of hindsight.*

Hin·du /híndoo/ *n* **1.** FOLLOWER OF HINDUISM somebody whose religion is Hinduism **2.** SOMEBODY FROM HINDUSTAN somebody who comes from Hindustan ■ *adj* **1.** OF HINDUISM relating to Hinduism **2.** OF HINDUS relating to Hindus or their culture [Mid-17C. Via Urdu < Persian *Hindū* < *Hind* "India"]

Hin·du·ism /híndoo ìzzəm/ *n* a major religion and religious tradition of South Asia, the oldest worldwide religion, characterized by a belief in reincarnation and a large pantheon of gods and goddesses

Hin·du Kush /hìndoo ko͝osh/ mountain system in Central Asia mainly in Afghanistan but extending into Jammu and Kashmir. The highest peak is Tirich Mir, 25,230 ft./7,690 m. Length: 600 mi./1,000 km.

Hin·du·stan /hìndoo staán/ *n* the Hindi-speaking region of Northern India, stretching from the Himalayan range to the Deccan and from Assam to Punjab, or the wider Hindi-speaking area of South Asia. The term is sometimes used to indicate the Ganges Plain, or sometimes the whole of India or parts of South Asia.

Hin·du·sta·ni /hindoo staanee/ *n* **GROUP OF S ASIAN LANGUAGES** a group of South Asian languages and dialects that includes all forms of Urdu and Hindi ■ *adj* **1.** **OF HINDUSTAN** relating to Hindustan **2.** **OF HINDUSTANI** relating to Hindustani [Early 17C. Via Urdu < Persian *Hindūstānī* "of the Indian country"]

Hin·dut·va /hin dóotvə/ *n S Asia* great enthusiasm for the Hindu way of life, especially when including the desire for a Hindu state [< Hindi]

Hine /hīn/, **Lewis** (1874–1940) US photographer. His works show a concern for social justice, frequently depicting subjects such as child laborers in sweatshops and mines. Full name **Hine, Lewis Wickes**

Hines /hīnz/, **Earl** (1905–83) US musician. A jazz pianist, he formed his own band (1928) and collaborated with Charlie Parker, Dizzy Gillespie, and Louis Armstrong. Full name **Hines, Earl Kenneth.** Known as **Fatha Hines**

Hines, Gregory (1946–2003) US dancer and actor. A skilled tap dancer, he is known for his appearances in the musicals *Sophisticated Ladies* (1981) and *Jelly's Last Jam* (1992).

Hines·ville /hínz vìl/ town in southeastern Georgia. Population: 30,541 (2002 estimate).

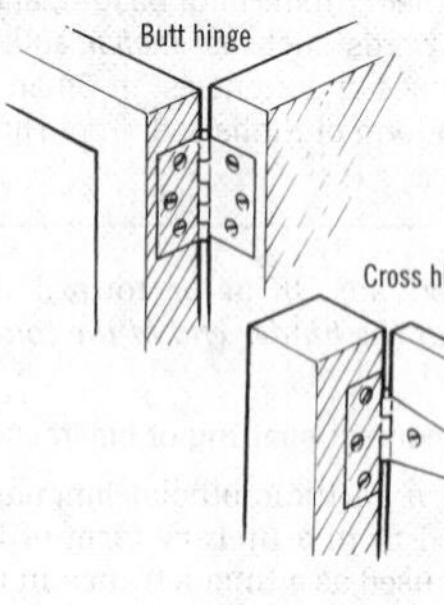

hinge

hinge /hinj/ *n* **1.** **JOINT** a movable joint of metal or plastic used to fasten two things, e.g., a box and its lid, together and allow one of them to pivot ○ *The hinges on the door need oiling.* **2.** ZOOL **LIGAMENT** a part in animals that operates like a hinge, e.g., the ligament that opens and closes the two halves of a clam or other bivalve mollusk **3.** ANAT same as **hinge joint** **4.** **SOMETHING VITAL** something on which a subsequent action or an outcome depends **5.** **STICKY PAPER STRIP** a thin gummed paper strip that is folded in half to affix postage stamps to the pages of an album [13C. Probably ultimately < Germanic] —**hinged** *adj* —**hinge·less** *adj*

hinge on (**hinged on, hinging on, hinges on**) *vt* to depend completely on something ○ *The success of the plan hinges on your full cooperation.*

hinge joint *n* a joint that allows movement in only one plane, e.g., a knee or elbow joint. Technical name **ginglymus**

Hing·ham /híngəm/ coastal town in eastern Massachusetts southeast of Boston, first settled about 1633. Population: 20,221 (2002 estimate).

hink·y /híngkee/ (**-i·er, -i·est**) *adj US* (*slang*) **1.** unstable or subject to sudden change ○ *hinky weather* ○ *My computer's been acting hinky.* **2.** unusual in a way that is hard to describe ○ *something a little hinky in his behavior*

hin·ny /hínnee/ (*plural* **-nies**) *n* the offspring of a stallion and a female donkey [Early 17C. Via Latin *hinnus* < Greek *(g)innos*]

Hins·dale /hínz dàyl/ village in northeastern Illinois, northeast of Downers Grove. It is a western suburb of Chicago. Population: 17,855 (2002 estimate).

Hin·shel·wood /hínsh'l wòod/, **Sir Cyril Norman** (1897–1967) British chemist. He was joint winner of the Nobel Prize in chemistry (1956) for his research into the kinetics of chemical chain reactions.

hint /hint/ *vti* (**hint·ed, hint·ing, hints**) **SUGGEST SOMETHING INDIRECTLY** to convey an idea or information in a roundabout way ○ *The President hinted that he might not seek a second term.* ■ *n* **1.** **INDIRECT SUGGESTION** an idea or information conveyed in a roundabout way ○ *Our daughter has been dropping hints that she'd like a guitar for her birthday.* **2.** **PIECE OF ADVICE** a useful piece of advice, or a practical suggestion ○ *The book had lots of useful hints on how to grow vegetables.* **3.** **VERY SMALL AMOUNT** an amount or trace of something that is so small that it can only just be noticed ○ *The walls need a hint of yellow.* [Early 17C. Probably alteration of obsolete *hent* "grasp" < Germanic] —**hint·ing·ly** *adv* ◇ **take the hint** to understand what is being implied or suggested and to act accordingly

hin·ter·land /híntər lànd/ *n* **1.** a region that is remote from cities or their cultural influence **2.** the land that lies next to coastline or a river [Late 19C. < German < *hinter* "behind" + *Land* "land"]

hip[1] /hip/ *n* **1.** **SIDE OF BODY BELOW WAIST** the area on each side of the body between the waist and the thigh **2.** ANAT same as **hip joint** **3.** **ROOF ANGLE** the angle formed where two adjacent sides of a sloping roof meet **4.** **POINTED END OF OBSTACLE** in skateboarding, the place where a ramp or obstacle comes to a point [Old English *hype* < Germanic] —**hipped** *adj*

hip[2] /hip/ (**hip·per, hip·pest**) *adj* aware of and influenced by the latest fashions in clothes, music, or ideas (*slang*) [Early 20C. Alteration of HEP[1]] —**hip·ly** *adv* —**hip·ness** *n* ◇ **be hip to something** to be aware of something that is going on (*informal*)

hip[3] /hip/ *n* BOT same as **rosehip** [Old English *hēope* < Indo-European, "thorn"]

HIP *abbr* health insurance plan

hip·bone /híp bòn/ *n* either of the two large bones forming the sides of the pelvis and made up of the ilium, ischium, and pubis, fused together in adults. Technical name **innominate bone**

hip boot *n* a boot reaching to the hip, usually worn by people who fish

hip flask *n* same as **flask** (sense 2)

hip hip hoo·ray *interj* used as a cheer to express joy or approval of somebody or something [*Hip*, origin ?]

hip-hop *n* a form of popular culture that started in African American inner-city areas, characterized by rap music, graffiti art, and breakdancing [< HIP[2]]

hip-hug·gers *npl* pants that end at the hips instead of the waist

hip joint *n* the joint formed between the head of the thigh bone and the hipbone

~~**hipocrisy**~~ incorrect spelling of **hypocrisy**

Hip·par·chus /hi paarkəss/ (190?–120? B.C.) Greek astronomer and mathematician. The inventor of trigonometry, he also produced the earliest known star catalog and discovered the precession of the equinoxes.

hip·pe·as·trum /hìppee ástrəm/ *n* a cultivated plant belonging to the daffodil family. Flowers: huge, red or pink, funnel-shaped. Native to: Central and South America. Genus: *Hippeastrum.* [Early 19C. < modern Latin < Greek *hippeus* "horseman" + *astron* "star"]

hipped /hipt/ *adj* preoccupied or obsessed with something (*informal*) ○ *She's just hipped on clothes.* [Early 20C. < HIP[2]]

hipped roof *n* ARCHIT same as **hip roof**

hip·pie /híppee/, **hip·py** (*plural* **-pies**) *n* a young person, especially in the 1960s, who rejected accepted social and political values and proclaimed a belief in universal peace and love. Hippies often dressed unconventionally, lived communally, and used psychedelic drugs. (*informal*) [Mid-20C. < HIP[2]] —**hip·pie·dom** *n* —**hip·pie·hood** *n* —**hip·pie·ness** *n*

hip·po /híppō/ (*plural* **-pos**) *n* same as **hippopotamus** (*informal*) [Late 19C. Shortening]

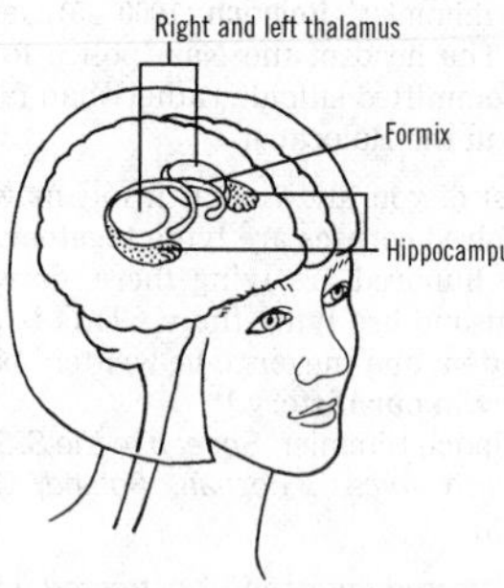

hippocampus (sense 2)

hip·po·cam·pus /hìppə kámpəss/ (*plural* **-pi** /-pī/) *n* a mythological sea creature with the head and forelegs of a horse and the tail of a fish **2.** a curved ridge of tissue in each cerebral hemisphere of the brain, concerned with basic drives, emotions, and short-term memory and forming part of the limbic system [Late 16C. Via Latin < Greek *hippokampos* < *hippos* "horse" + *kampos* "sea monster"] —**hip·po·cam·pal** *adj*

hip·pock·et *n* a pocket at the back of a pair of pants or a skirt

hip·po·cras /híppə kràss/ *n* a medieval drink of spiced wine sweetened with honey [14C. Via Old French *hypocras* < medieval Latin *(vinum) Hippocraticum* "(wine of) Hippocrates"]

Hip·poc·ra·tes /hi pókrə teez/ (460?–377? B.C.) Greek physician. Known as "the father of medicine," he gave his name to the hippocratic oath. —**Hip·po·crat·ic** /hìppə kráttik/ *adj*

> "Extreme remedies are most appropriate for extreme diseases."
> [Hippocrates, *Aphorisms*; 415? B.C.]

Hip·po·crat·ic oath *n* an oath traditionally taken by newly graduated physicians to observe the ethical standards of their profession, specifically to seek to preserve life [Because Hippocrates was the supposed author of such an oath]

hip·po·drome /híppə dròm/ *n* **1.** an open-air stadium in ancient Greece or Rome with an oval track that was used for horse or chariot racing **2.** an arena for equestrian events [Late 16C. Via French and Latin < Greek *hippodromos* < *hippos* "horse" + *dromos* "racecourse"]

hip·po·griff /híppə grìf/ *n* in Greek mythology, a monster with the body of a horse and the head, wings, and claws of a griffin [Mid-17C. Via French *hippogriffe* < Italian *ippogrifo* < Greek *hippos* "horse" + Italian *grifo* "griffin"]

Hip·pol·y·ta /hi póllətə/ *n* in Greek mythology, a queen of the Amazons. She was killed by Heracles because she refused to give up her girdle, which he had been sent to get as one of his labors.

Hip·pol·y·tus /hi póllətəss/ *n* in Greek mythology, the son of Theseus. He was killed by Poseidon after rejecting the advances of his stepmother, Phaedra.

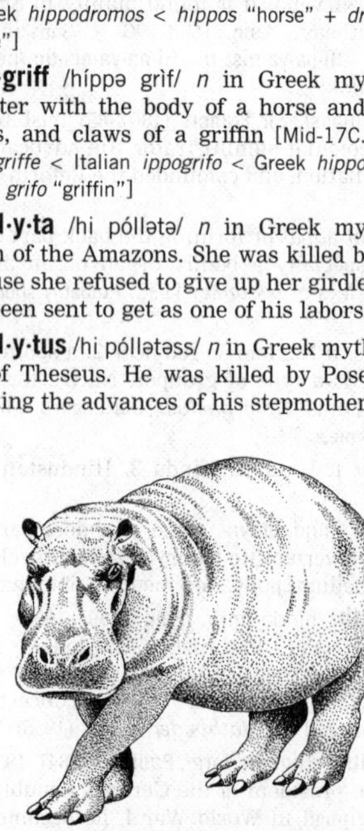

hippopotamus

hip·po·pot·a·mus /hìppə póttəməss/ (*plural* **-mus·es** or **-mi** /-mī/) *n* a large amphibious animal that has a large head with a wide mouth, short legs, and a thick gray skin. Native to: rivers of eastern equatorial Africa. Latin name: *Hippopotamus* *amphibius.* [Mid-16C. Via Latin < Greek *hippopotamos* < *hippos* "horse" + *potamos* "river"]

hip·py[1] /híppee/ (**-pi·er, -pi·est**) *adj* having wide hips

hip·py[2] /híppee/ *n* another spelling of **hippie**

hip roof *n* a roof with sloping ends as well as sides

hip-shoot·ing *adj* too quick to take action or make decisions (*slang*) [< shooting from a holster without taking formal aim] —**hip-shoot·ing** *n*

hip·ster /hípstər/ *n* somebody conversant with fashions in music, clothes, and social attitudes, especially an enthusiast of modern jazz (*dated slang*) [< HIP[2]]

hip·ster·ism /hípstər ìzzəm/ *n* the quality of being hip (*dated slang*)

hip·sters /hípstərz/ *npl UK* CLOTHING same as **hip-huggers** [< HIP[1]]

hi·ra·ga·na /heèrə gaánə/ *n* a set of curly symbols, representing syllables and often conveying grammatical information when combined with pictorial symbols (**kanji**), used in writing Japanese. ◊ **kana** (sense 1), **katakana** [Early 19C. < Japanese, "plain syllabary"]

hire /hīr/ *v* (**hired, hir·ing, hires**) **1.** *vti* GIVE SOMEBODY WORK to employ somebody to work for you, or pay somebody to do a job for you **2.** *vt* PAY FOR USE OF SOMETHING to rent something from somebody for a period of time ○ *hired the Women's Club for the wedding reception* ■ *n* **1.** ACT OF HIRING SOMETHING OR SOMEBODY the activity of renting something to somebody or of making the services of somebody available to another person for pay **2.** EMPLOYEE an employed person [Old English *hȳr* < Germanic] —**hir·a·ble** *adj* —**hir·er** *n*

hire on *vti* to obtain work, or provide work for somebody ○ *He hired on as an oil rig wildcatter.*

hire out *vt* to rent something to somebody or make the services of somebody available to another person for pay

hired gun /hīrd-/ *n* (*slang*) **1.** a professional killer **2.** an expert brought in to solve a particularly complex or intractable problem ○ *The law firm brought in a hired gun from New York to handle the cross-examination of the prosecution's genetics expert.*

hired hand *n* a paid manual worker employed on a short-term basis, usually on a farm or ranch

hire·ling /hīrling/ *n* somebody who works only for money, especially at menial or unpleasant tasks (*disapproving*)

hire pur·chase *n UK* a financing arrangement that enables somebody to take possession of an expensive item while making regular payments on it, with legal ownership transferred only after it is paid for. ◊ **installment plan**

hi-res /hī réz/, **high-res** *adj* COMPUT same as **high-resolution** (*informal*) [Shortening]

Hi·ri Mo·tu /heèree mṓ tòo/ *n* a pidginized form of Motu that is an official language of Papua New Guinea. Native speakers: 150,000. —**Hi·ri Mo·tu** *adj*

hir·ing hall *n* a union-operated employment agency where registered applicants are given jobs on a seniority basis or by rotation

AKG London

Hirohito, emperor of Japan

Hi·ro·hi·to /heèrō heétō/ (1901–89) emperor of Japan. His reign (1926–89) was the longest in Japanese history. He renounced the belief that Japanese rulers are divine at the end of World War II (1945) and oversaw the transition to a constitutional monarchy.

> "The war situation has developed not necessarily to Japan's advantage."
> [Hirohito, announcing Japan's surrender, *Radio broadcast*; August 15, 1945]

Hi·ro·shi·ma /hìrrə sheémə, hi róshimə/ city in southwestern Honshu, Japan. It was devastated by the first atomic bomb to be used in war, in August 1945. Population: 1,113,786 (2002).

Hirst /hurst/, **Damien** (*b.* 1965) British artist. He is known for his controversial experimental works, especially his series of animal carcasses preserved in formaldehyde.

hir·sute /húr sòot, heér-, hər sóot/ *adj* **1.** having a large amount of hair ○ *a hirsute young man* **2.** describes a plant or plant part covered with long stiff hairs ○ *a hirsute leaf* [Early 17C. < Latin *hirsutus* "shaggy"] —**hir·sute·ness** *n*

hir·sut·ism /húr soo tìzzəm, heér-, hər sóo tìzzəm/ *n* excessive growth of hair, e.g., on a woman's face or body

hir·u·din /heérəd'n, heer óod'n/ *n* a substance produced by the salivary glands of leeches that prevents blood from clotting [Early 20C. < Latin *hirudo* "leech"]

his *stressed* /hiz/; *unstressed* /iz/ *adj, pron* indicates something belonging or relating to a man, boy, or male animal who has been previously mentioned or whose identity is known ○ *He stood at the sink washing his hands.* ○ *The fault was all his.* ○ *I went to school with a cousin of his.*

his/her /hìz ər húr/ *pron* his or her, used to avoid the sexist use of "his" in reference to somebody whose sex is unknown

His·pan·ic /hi spánnik/ *adj* **1.** OF PEOPLE OF SPANISH DESCENT relating to people descended from Spanish or Latin American people or their culture **2.** OF SPANISH-SPEAKING PEOPLE relating to Spanish-speaking people or their culture **3.** OF SPAIN relating to Spain, or its language, people, or culture ■ *n* PEOPLES same as **Hispanic American** [Late 16C. < Latin *Hispanicus* < *Hispania* "Spain"]

USAGE See ***Anglo*** and ***Amexican***.

USAGE Hispanic and **Latino/Latina**: ***Hispanic*** and ***Latino/Latina*** are not identical in meaning and use, though many people use them interchangeably. ***Hispanic***, the broader term, comes from a Spanish word for "Spain." As such, it can refer to not only the Spanish-speaking people of North, Central, and South America (*the Hispanic communities of South Florida*; *a university population composed chiefly of Hispanics from Argentina and Colombia*), but to all such speakers worldwide whose first language is Spanish and whose descent is from Spain (*Hispanic students from Madrid are studying at our college*). By contrast, ***Latino*** and the feminine form ***Latina*** are shortened from Spanish *latinamericano*, "Latin American," thus narrowing the scope of meaning to North, Central, and South America, as in the *Latino cultural centers of San Diego* and *Many of our exchange students in the women's studies program are Latinas.* Within the many Spanish-speaking communities of the United States, local or regional preferences are also in play, with ***Latino/Latina*** used more often on the West Coast and especially California, and ***Hispanic*** used more often in states such as Florida and Texas.

His·pan·ic A·mer·i·can *n* somebody who comes from the United States and is of Spanish or Latin American descent —**His·pan·ic A·mer·i·can** *adj*

His·pan·i·cism /hi spánni sìzzəm/ *n* a Spanish word, expression, or other linguistic feature that has been adopted into another language [Mid-20C. < Latin *Hispania* "Spain"]

His·pan·i·cist /hi spánnissist/ *n* a scholar of the languages and cultures of Spain and Spanish-speaking countries

His·pan·i·cize /hi spánni sīz/ (**-cized, -ciz·ing, -ciz·es**) *vt* to make somebody or something Spanish in character, style, or culture —**His·pan·i·ci·za·tion** /hi spànnəssi záysh'n/ *n*

His·pan·io·la /hìspən yṓlə/ island in the Caribbean Sea, lying southeast of Cuba and west of Puerto Rico, and divided between Haiti and the Dominican Republic. Originally the home of an Arawak people, it was colonized by Spain after Christopher Columbus landed there in 1492 and named it Española. The western part, now Haiti, was ceded to France in 1697. Area: 30,290 sq. mi./78,460 sq. km.

His·pan·ism /híspə nìzzəm/ *n* LING same as **Hispanicism**

His·pa·nist /híspənist/ *n* LING same as **Hispanicist**

His·pa·no /hi spánnō, hi spaánō/ (*plural* **-nos**) *n* *Hispanic* **1.** somebody of Spanish descent who lives in the southwestern United States. Many Hispanos are descended from people who lived in the region before its annexation by the United States. **2.** PEOPLES same as **Hispanic American** [Mid-20C. < Latin *Hispanus* "Spanish"]

His·pa·no-A·mer·i·can /hi spànnō ə mérrikən, hi spaànō-/ *n* PEOPLES same as **Hispanic American** —**His·pa·no-A·mer·i·can** *adj*

his·pid /híspid/ *adj* rough, especially covered with stiff hairs or bristles ○ *a hispid leaf* [Mid-17C. < Latin *hispidus*] —**his·pid·i·ty** /hi spíddətee/ *n*

hiss /hiss/ *v* (**hissed, hiss·ing, hiss·es**) **1.** *vi* MAKE "S" SOUND to make a sound like a loud continuous "s" ○ *the sound of car tires hissing over a wet road* **2.** *vti* SHOW NEGATIVE OPINION OF SOMETHING to show disapproval or dislike of somebody or something, e.g., a performance, by making a hissing sound **3.** *vti* WHISPER LOUDLY to whisper loudly and angrily ○ *"Stop biting your nails," she hissed.* ■ *n* **1.** SOUND LIKE "S" a sound like a loud continuous "s" ○ *the hiss of escaping air* **2.** SOUND EXPRESSING DISAPPROVAL a hissing sound used to express disapproval or dislike [14C An imitation of the sound] —**hiss·er** *n*

Hiss /hiss/, **Alger** (1904–96) US lawyer and government official. A former senior State Department official, he was accused by the journalist Whittaker Chambers (1948) of spying for the Soviet Union, and imprisoned for perjury despite his protestations of innocence.

his·self *stressed* /hiss sélf/; *unstressed* /iss sélf/ *pron* same as **himself** (*nonstandard*)

his·sy fit /híssee-/ *n Can, Southern US* a temper tantrum [Origin ?]

hist. *abbr* **1.** MED histology **2.** historic **3.** historical **4.** history

hist- *prefix* same as **histo-** (*used before vowels*)

his·tam·i·nase /hi stámmi nàyss, hístəmi-, -nàyz/ *n* an enzyme in the digestive system that inactivates histamine

his·ta·mine /hístə meèn/ *n* an amine released by immune cells that produces allergic reactions [Early 20C. Blend of HISTIDINE + AMINE] —**his·ta·min·ic** /hìstə mínnik/ *adj*

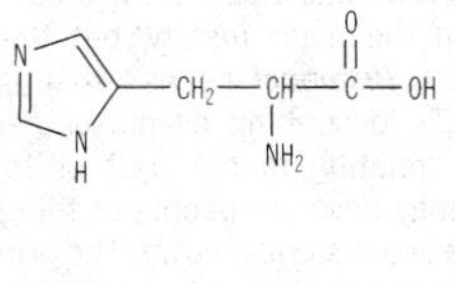

histidine

his·ti·dine /hísti deèn/ *n* an amino acid involved in the repair of tissues that is also the precursor of histamine. Formula: $C_6H_9N_3O_2$.

his·ti·o·cyte /hístee ə sīt/ *n* a large immobile scavenging cell (**macrophage**) found in connective tissue —**his·ti·o·cyt·ic** /hìstee ə síttik/ *adj*

histo- *prefix* living tissue ○ *histochemistry* [< Greek *histos* "web"]

his·to·chem·is·try /hìstō kémmistree/ *n* the biochemistry of cells and tissues —**his·to·chem·i·cal** *adj* —**his·to·chem·i·cal·ly** *adv*

his·to·com·pat·i·bil·i·ty /hìstō kəm pàttə bíllətee/ *n* the degree of similarity between some antigens that determines the degree of success of a tissue graft or blood transfusion —**his·to·com·pat·i·ble** /hìstō kəm páttəb'l/ *adj*

his·to·com·pat·i·bil·i·ty an·ti·gen *n* an antigen occurring on the surface of tissue cells that is used in self-identification and determines the acceptance of a tissue graft or blood transfusion

his·to·di·al·y·sis /hìstō dī álləssəss/ *n* MED same as **histolysis**

his·to·gen·e·sis /hìstō jénnəssiss/ *n* the development of tissues —**his·to·ge·net·ic** /hìstōjə néttik/ *adj* —**his·to·ge·net·i·cal·ly** *adv* —**his·to·gen·ic** /hìstə jénnik/ *adj* —**his·to·gen·i·cal·ly** *adv*

his·to·gram /hístə gràm/ *n* a statistical graph of a frequency distribution in which vertical rectangles of different heights are proportionate to corresponding frequencies

his·tol·o·gy /hi stólləjee/ *n* a branch of anatomy concerned with the study of the microscopic structures of animal and plant tissue —**his·to·log·ic** /hìstə lójjik/ *adj* —**his·to·log·i·cal** *adj* —**his·to·log·i·cal·ly** *adv* —**his·tol·o·gist** *n*

his·tol·y·sis /hi stólləssiss/ *n* the breakdown and disintegration of bodily tissue —**his·to·lyt·ic** /hìstə líttik/ *adj* —**his·to·lyt·i·cal·ly** *adv*

his·tone /hí stōn/ *n* a simple protein bound to DNA, involved in the coiling of chromosomes. There are five types, together constituting about half the mass of chromosomes. [Late 19C. < German *Histon*]

his·to·pa·thol·o·gy /hìstōpə thólləjee/ *n* a branch of pathology concerned with the study of the microscopic changes in diseased tissues —**his·to·path·o·log·ic** /hìstō pathə lójjik/ *adj* —**his·to·path·o·log·i·cal** *adj* —**his·to·path·o·log·i·cal·ly** *adv* —**his·to·pa·thol·o·gist** *n*

his·to·phys·i·ol·o·gy /hìstō fizee ólləjee/ *n* a branch of physiology concerned with the structure and function of tissues —**his·to·phys·i·o·log·ic** /-fizee ə lójjik/ *adj* —**his·to·phys·i·o·log·i·cal** *adj*

his·to·plas·mo·sis /hìstō plaz mṓssiss/ *n* a severe disease of the lungs with symptoms resembling flu, caused by the fungus *Histoplasma capsulatum* [Early 20C. < modern Latin *Histoplasma*, genus name]

his·to·ri·an /hi stáwree ən/ *n* **1.** a student of or expert in history **2.** a writer of an account of historical events [15C. < French *historien* < Latin *historia* (see HISTORY)]

his·to·ri·at·ed /hi stáwree àytəd/ *adj* describes decorative initials in books or maps and plans that are illustrated with symbolic flowers and animals or symbols in the form of flowers or animals [Late 19C. < French *historié* or directly < medieval Latin *historiare* "adorn (with historical scenes), relate" < Latin *historia* (see HISTORY)]

his·tor·ic /hi stáwrik/ *adj* **1.** important in or affecting the course of history ○ *a historic election victory* **2.** same as **historical** (sense 1)

USAGE historic or **historical**? Both these adjectives are derived from the noun *history*, but they are used in different ways. ***Historical*** means "existing or happening in the past," "describing events or people from the past," and "relating to the past or to the study of history"; it may describe people or things, as in *a historical figure* or *a historical novel*. The principal meaning of ***historic***, on the other hand, is "important in history": *the historic moment when the Berlin Wall came down; the preservation of our city's historic district.* ***Historic*** can sometimes be used in place of ***historical*** in the sense "existing in, happening in, or relating to the past," but ***historical*** should never be used in place of ***historic***.

his·tor·i·cal /hi stáwrik'l/ *adj* **1.** FORMERLY EXISTING OR HAPPENING existing, happening, or relating to the past ○ *an important historical personage* **2.** FORMERLY USED worn or used by people in the past ○ *historical uniforms of the 18th century* **3.** SUPPORTED BY FACTS FROM HISTORY based on the past, or describing people who lived in the past or events that happened in the past ○ *historical fiction* ○ *a historical movie* **4.** RELATING TO STUDY OF HISTORY relating to or involving the study of history ○ *a series of historical monographs* **5.** RELATING TO EVOLUTION OF SOMETHING relating to the gradual change and development of phenomena such as languages or societies ○ *historical sociology* —**his·tor·i·cal·ness** *n*

USAGE See ***historic***.

his·tor·i·cal ge·ol·o·gy *n* a branch of geology that deals with the geologic history of Earth

his·tor·i·cal lin·guis·tics *n* the study of language as it changes and develops through time (*takes a singular verb*)

his·tor·i·cal·ly /hi stáwrikəlee/ *adv* **1.** according to or with reference to history or its course ○ *The law will prove to be historically significant.* **2.** used to indicate that something has happened often in the past ○ *Historically, a rise in interest rates slows the rate of inflation.*

his·tor·i·cal ma·te·ri·al·ism *n* the part of Marx's theory of dialectical materialism that maintains that the development of social thought and institutions is based on material economic forces

his·tor·i·cal nov·el *n* a novel set in the past that includes real events and people from that period

his·tor·i·cism /hi stáwrə sìzzəm/ *n* **1.** the belief that natural laws beyond human control determine historical events **2.** the theory that each period of history has its own unique beliefs and values and can only be understood in its historical context —**his·tor·i·cist** *n*

his·to·ric·i·ty /hìstə ríssətee/ *n* the state or fact of being historically authentic

his·tor·i·cize /hi stáwrə sīz/ (**-cized, -ciz·ing, -ciz·es**) *vt* to give something the appearance of historical truth —**his·tor·i·ci·za·tion** /hi stàwrəssi záysh'n/ *n*

his·tor·ic pres·ent *n* the present tense used to narrate actions that happened in the past to make them seem more vivid

his·to·ri·og·ra·phy /hi stàwree óggrəfee/ *n* **1.** METHODS OF HISTORICAL RESEARCH the principles, theories, or methods of historical research or writing **2.** WRITING OF HISTORY the writing of history based on scholarly disciplines such as the analysis and evaluation of source materials **3.** AVAILABLE DATA ON HISTORICAL TOPIC the existing findings and interpretations relating to a particular historical topic **4.** HISTORICAL LITERATURE a body of historical literature [Mid-16C. Via medieval Latin < Greek *historiographia* < *historia* (see HISTORY) + *graphia* "writing"] —**his·to·ri·o·graph·ic** /hi stàwree ə gráffik/ *n* —**his·to·ri·o·graph·i·cal** *adj* —**his·to·ri·o·graph·i·cal·ly** *adv*

his·to·ry /hístəree/ (*plural* **-ries**) *n* **1.** WHAT HAS HAPPENED the past events of a period in time or in the life or development of a people, an institution, or a place **2.** STUDY OF PAST EVENTS the branch of knowledge that records and analyzes past events **3.** RECORD OF EVENTS a chronological account of past events of a period or in the life or development of a people, an institution, or a place ○ *a history of Byzantium* **4.** PERSONAL BACKGROUND the events and experiences of an individual's past ○ *We don't know very much about her personal history.* **5.** INTERESTING PAST an interesting or colorful past ○ *The car has something of a history attached to it.* **6.** HISTORICAL PLAY a play that deals with historical events [15C. Via Latin < Greek *historia* "history, knowledge, narrative" < *histōr* "learned man"] ◇ **be (ancient) history** to be something that happened a long time ago, or perhaps only recently in the past, and is no longer important or relevant ○ *The scandal is history, as far as I'm concerned.* ◇ **be history** used to indicate that somebody's life or influence, or something's importance, will be abruptly brought to an end ○ *If he's found guilty of bribery, he's history as far as the Senate is concerned.*

his·to·ry list *n* a record of the input of previous users of a computer

his·tri·on·ic /hìstree ónnik/, **his·tri·on·i·cal** /-ik'l/ *adj* **1.** overdramatic in reaction or behavior ○ *Paul gave a histrionic sigh and slumped in his chair.* **2.** relating to acting or actors (*formal*) [Mid-17C. < late Latin *histrionicus* < Latin *histrion-* "actor"] —**his·tri·on·i·cal·ly** *adv*

his·tri·on·ics /hìstree ónniks/ *n* exaggerated emotional behavior done for show or to get a reaction from somebody (*takes a singular or plural verb*) ○ *Let's hope there won't be any histrionics when you tell them.* ■ *npl* performances of dramatic works (*formal; takes a plural verb*)

hit /hit/ *v* (**hit, hit·ting, hits**) **1.** *vti* STRIKE DELIBERATELY to strike somebody or something deliberately with the hand or something held in it ○ *He hit me on the jaw.* **2.** *vti* COME INTO CONTACT to come into violent contact with something ○ *His van skidded and hit a parked car.* **3.** *vt* MAKE BALL MOVE to make something such as a ball move by striking it with a bat or racket ○ *She kept hitting the ball over the fence into the next yard.* **4.** *vt* SCORE WITH BALL to score points in a sport by striking a ball well or delivering it successfully to a target **5.** *vt* STRIKE TARGET to reach an intended target with a ball or missile **6.** *vti* OCCUR TO SOMEBODY to be suddenly realized by somebody ○ *It suddenly hit him that he was unlikely to see her again.* **7.** *vt* AFFECT SOMEBODY OR SOMETHING BADLY to have an adverse effect on somebody or something ○ *The rise in interest rates is going to hit exporters hard.* **8.** *vt* ARRIVE AT PARTICULAR LEVEL to reach a particular level on a scale ○ *Unemployment has hit the 2 million mark.* **9.** *vt* PRODUCE SOMETHING ACCURATELY to render or represent something accurately ○ *hit a high C* **10.** *vt* CONFORM TO SOMETHING to conform to or agree with something ○ *Your comments hit a sympathetic note.* **11.** *vt* STRIKE BUTTON OR KEY to press or push a button or part of a machine (*informal*) ○ *Hit the accelerator.* **12.** *vi* HAPPEN to take place, usually with undesirable or adverse effects (*informal*) ○ *The storm hit before we could get home.* **13.** *vt* VIEW WEBPAGE to visit or view a particular webpage (*informal*) **14.** *vt* REACH PLACE to reach a particular place (*slang*) ○ *You'll hit a toll-free road about five miles farther on.* **15.** *vt* GIVE SOMEBODY INFORMATION to tell somebody something that may be of interest (*slang*) ○ *"I've got a great idea. Want to hear it?" "OK, hit me. I'm listening."* **16.** *vt* KILL SOMEBODY USING PROFESSIONAL KILLER to murder somebody, especially by employing a professional killer (*slang*) **17.** *vt* GIVE SOMEBODY SOMETHING to give somebody something such as a drink or a card in the game of twenty-one (*slang*) **18.** *vt* BASEBALL MAKE BASE HIT in baseball, to make a base hit ○ *hit a double* **19.** *vi* BASEBALL BAT in baseball, to be at bat **20.** *vi* MIL ATTACK to launch an attack on something or somebody ○ *The troops hit before daylight.* **21.** *vi* AUTOMOT IGNITE AND START to ignite the fuel and air mixture in the cylinders (*refers to internal combustion engines*) ○ *The engine finally hit and we could leave.* ■ *n* **1.** HARD BLOW a hard blow delivered with the hand or something held in it **2.** COLLISION a violent impact between things **3.** SOMETHING THAT HITS TARGET a ball or missile that successfully strikes the target ○ *We've taken a couple of hits, but nothing serious.* **4.** SUCCESS a person who or thing that is popular or successful ○ *That rock band had a big hit with its last CD.* ○ *The clown was a hit with the kids.* **5.** ACCESSING OF DATABASE OR INTERNET FILE an instance of a user retrieving an item from a database or contacting a file such as a home page through the Internet ○ *Her home page has received 3,000 hits since she opened it last month.* **6.** SOMETHING GIVEN a single item given or taken, e.g., a drink, or a card in the game of blackjack (*slang*) **7.** EFFECT OF DRUG a sense of a drug's effect (*slang*) **8.** PROFESSIONAL KILLING a murder, especially one committed by a professional killer (*slang*) **9.** BASEBALL same as **base hit** [Pre-12C. < Old Norse *hitta* "find"] —**hit·ta·ble** *adj* —**hit·ter** *n* ◇ **hit it off** to get along very well with somebody (*informal*)

hit back *vi* to retaliate against somebody or something for an attack

hit on *vt* **1.** *also* **hit upon** FIND ANSWER to think of a solution to a problem, especially by chance ○ *She then hit on the idea of painting the inside of the box black.* **2.** APPROACH SOMEBODY SEXUALLY to make sexual advances to somebody (*slang*) **3.** ASK FAVOR FROM SOMEBODY to ask somebody to do you a favor (*slang*)

hit out at *vi* **1.** to criticize somebody or something severely ○ *The bishop hit out at their human rights record.* **2.** to try to strike somebody repeatedly ○ *When the baby is in a tantrum, she hits out at people trying to comfort her.*

hit up *vt* US to ask somebody for something, especially money (*slang*) ○ *How come you're suddenly hitting me up for the cab fare?*

hit upon *vt* same as **hit on** (sense 1)

Hi·ta·chi /hi táchee/ coastal industrial city in eastern Honshu, Japan. Population: 193,080 (2002).

hit-and-miss *adj* **1.** sometimes successful and sometimes not ○ *He ran a hit-and-miss travel agency, never making much money.* **2.** *UK* same as **hit-or-miss** (sense 1)

hit-and-run *adj* **1. NOT STOPPING AFTER CAUSING ACCIDENT** describes a road accident in which the driver who has hit another person or motor vehicle leaves the scene without stopping ○ *a hit-and-run driver* **2. FAST AND WITHOUT WARNING** relying on surprise and speed to overcome an enemy ○ *Three fighter planes launched a hit-and-run attack at dawn.* **3.** BASEBALL **SWINGING AT BASEBALL TO PROTECT RUNNER** describes a baseball play in which a base runner starts for the next base as the pitcher throws the ball, which the batter must swing at to protect the runner from being thrown out ■ *n* **HIT-AND-RUN ACCIDENT** a hit-and-run road accident

hitch /hich/ *v* (**hitched, hitch·ing, hitch·es**) **1.** *vt* **JOIN SOMETHING TO SOMETHING ELSE** to connect two things so that one can move the other, e.g., a horse to a wagon or a trailer to a car **2.** *vt* **FASTEN SOMETHING TO STOP IT** to fasten or tie something temporarily to keep it from moving away ○ *Hitch the boat to the dock before the current catches it.* **3.** *vi* **MOVE IN JERKY WAY** to move in an awkward jerky way **4.** *vti* **HITCHHIKE** to hitchhike a ride (*informal*) ■ *n* **1. OBSTACLE** an obstacle in the way of progress ○ *There's been a slight technical hitch.* **2. MEANS OF CONNECTING TWO THINGS** a device used to connect two things, e.g., a ball on a vehicle for connecting a trailer **3. KNOT THAT UNTIES EASILY** a knot that can be easily untied, used for temporarily securing a line to something **4.** TRANSP **FREE RIDE** a ride solicited by means of hitchhiking (*informal*) **5. TUG** a sudden pull on something **6. WAY OF WALKING** an awkward jerky manner of walking **7.** MIL **TIME IN THE MILITARY** a period of time spent in military service [14C. Origin ?] —**hitch·er** *n*

hitch up *v* **1.** *vt* to pull up an item of clothing **2.** *vi* get together with somebody else, especially in partnership or marriage (*informal*)

Sir Alfred Hitchcock

Hitch·cock /hích kòk/, **Sir Alfred** (1899–1980) British movie director. A prolific director and master of suspense, his movies include *The 39 Steps* (1935), *Rebecca* (1940), and *Psycho* (1960). Full name **Hitchcock, Sir Alfred Joseph**

> "A good film is when the price of the admission, the dinner, and the babysitter was well worth it."
> [Sir Alfred Hitchcock. Quoted in *Halliwell's Filmgoer's Companion*, Leslie Halliwell; 1993]

hitched /hicht/ *adj* married (*informal*) ○ *They're getting hitched in a couple of weeks.*

hitch·hike /hích hìk/ (**-hiked, -hik·ing, -hikes**) *vti* to get a ride from a passing vehicle, usually by standing at the side of the road and holding out the hand with the thumb raised —**hitch·hik·er** *n*

hitch·ing post /híching-/ *n* a post or rail used to tie the reins of a horse to

Hitch·ings /hichingz/, **George Herbert** (1905–98) US biochemist. He and fellow researcher Gertrude Elion pioneered research into drugs that kill harmful invading cells without damaging healthy body cells, which led to the development of AZT. They shared the 1988 Nobel Prize in physiology or medicine with James Black.

hi-tech *n, adj* TECH another spelling of **high tech, high-tech**

hith·er /hí*th*ər/ *adv* to this place (*archaic or humorous*) ○ *Come hither, child.* ■ *adj* on the near side of something (*archaic*) [Old English *hider* < Indo-European, "here, this"] ◇ **hither and thither** in many directions in a disorderly way

hith·er·to /hì*th*ər tóo, hí*th*ər tòo/ *adv* up to the present time or the time in question

hit in (*plural* **hit ins** or **hits in**) *n* in field hockey, a hit from the sideline awarded to the opposition when the team in possession of the ball fails to keep it in bounds

Hit·ler /híttlər/, **Adolf** (1889–1945) Austrian-born German Nazi leader. He cofounded the Nazi Party in Germany (1919) and became chancellor in 1933. His invasion of Poland in 1939 led to the outbreak of World War II. He implemented anti-Semitic policies that led to the Holocaust.

> "All those who are not racially pure are mere chaff."
> [Adolf Hitler, *Mein Kampf*; 1933]

Hit·ler·ism /híttlə rìzzəm/ *n* the extreme nationalistic ideology and fascistic policies developed by the Nazi Party under Adolf Hitler —**Hit·ler·ist** *n* —**Hit·ler·ite** *adj*

hit list *n* (*slang*) **1.** a list of things or people considered problems to be dealt with in the near future **2.** a list of potential murder victims

hit man *n* a hired killer, especially a man (*slang*)

hit-or-miss *adj* **1.** done in a careless haphazard way ○ *The survey was hit-or-miss, so we cannot trust the results.* **2.** *UK* same as **hit-and-miss** (sense 1)

hit out (*plural* **hit outs** or **hits out**) *n* in field hockey, a hit taken from the 16-yard line that is awarded to the defense when the attacking team hit the ball over the goal line without scoring a goal

hit pa·rade *n* a list of the best-selling pop records in the previous week (*dated*)

hit·per·son /hít pùrss'n/ (*plural* **-per·sons** or **-peo·ple** /-pèep'l/) *n* same as **hired gun** (sense 1) (*slang*)

hit squad *n* (*slang*) **1.** a team of hired assassins or other killers **2.** a team of experts sent in to solve serious problems

Hit·tite /hí tìt/ *n* **1.** a member of an ancient Anatolian people whose empire was based in Asia Minor during the second millennium B.C. **2.** an extinct Indo-European language spoken in Anatolia, parts of Syria, and surrounding areas during the second millennium B.C. Despite evidence from ample cuneiform inscriptions, there is no consensus over which branch of Indo-European it belongs to. [Mid-16C. < Hebrew *Ḥittīm* < Hittite *Hatti*] —**Hit·tite** *adj*

HIV *n* either of two strains of a retrovirus, HIV-1 or HIV-2, that destroys the immune system's helper T cells, the loss of which causes AIDS. Full form **human immunodeficiency virus**

hive[1] /hīv/ *n* **1. HOME FOR BEES** a shelter in which a colony of social bees, especially honeybees, builds its nest **2. COLONY OF BEES** a colony of honeybees ■ *v* (**hived, hiv·ing, hives**) **1.** *vti* **GATHER IN HIVE** to gather in a hive, or cause bees to gather in a hive ○ *hive a swarm* **2.** *vt* **KEEP HONEY IN HIVE** to store honey in a hive **3.** *vt* **KEEP SOMETHING TO USE LATER** to store something for later use **4.** *vi* **LIVE CLOSELY TOGETHER** to live closely in a group [Old English *hȳf* < Indo-European, "round container"] —**hive·less** *adj* ◇ **a hive of industry** *or* **activity** a very busy, active place

hive off *vt* to separate something from the whole or from a larger group, e.g., to divert work to a subsidiary company or to split a branch of knowledge into specialties

hive[2] /hīv/ *n* a lesion due to urticaria [Back-formation < HIVES]

hives /hīvz/ *n* MED same as **urticaria** (*takes a singular or plural verb*) [Early 16C. Origin ?]

HIV-neg·a·tive *adj* having taken a test that revealed no antibodies to HIV in the bloodstream

HIV-pos·i·tive *adj* shown by a test for antibodies to HIV in the bloodstream to be infected with HIV

hi·ya /hí yaa/ *interj* a word used to say hello to somebody [Mid-20C. Apparently contraction of *how are you*, influenced by *hi* (interjection)]

hi·zi·ki *n* FOOD another spelling of **hijiki**

hiz·zon·er /hi zónnər/ *n* used jokingly to refer to a man who is a mayor (*slang*) [Early 20C. Alteration of *his honor*]

HJ *abbr* here lies (*on gravestones*) [Latin *hic jacet*]

hk *abbr* Hong Kong (*used in Internet addresses*) See table at **domain name**

hl *symbol* MEASURE hectoliter

H.L. *abbr* House of Lords

HLA *n* the major antigen compatibility complex in humans that is genetically determined and is involved in cell self-identification and histocompatibility. Full form **human lymphocyte antigen**

HLL *abbr* COMPUT high-level language

HLZ *abbr* MIL helicopter landing zone

hm *abbr* **1.** MEASURE hectometer **2.** Heard and McDonald Islands (*used in Internet addresses*) See table at **domain name**

h'm /m, hm/ *interj* used to represent a sound made while pausing during a conversation to consider something ○ *H'm, it'll take about two weeks.* [Mid-19C. Natural utterance]

H.M. *abbr* **1.** EDUC headmaster **2.** EDUC headmistress **3.** MUSIC heavy metal

HMAS, H.M.A.S. *abbr UK* **1.** Her Majesty's Australian ship **2.** His Majesty's Australian ship

HMCS, H.M.C.S. *abbr UK* **1.** Her Majesty's Canadian Ship **2.** His Majesty's Canadian Ship

HMF, H.M.F. *abbr* **1.** Her Majesty's Forces **2.** His Majesty's Forces

HMI *abbr* **1.** His Majesty's Inspector (of Schools) **2.** COMPUT human-machine interface

HMO *n* a healthcare organization whose members pay fees and receive medical care from participating physicians, hospitals, and other providers. Full form **health maintenance organization**

Hmong /mawng, hə máwng/ (*plural* **Hmongs** or *same*) *n* **1.** a member of a people living in southern China and mainly remote areas of northern Laos, Thailand, and Vietnam **2.** a language spoken in parts of southern China and in Laos, Thailand, Vietnam, and the United States, forming a main branch of the Miao-Yao language family. Native speakers: 5 million. —**Hmong** *adj*

hMPV *abbr* MICROBIOL human metapneumovirus

HMS *abbr* **1.** Her Majesty's Ship **2.** His Majesty's Ship

hn *abbr* Honduras (*used in Internet addresses*) See table at **domain name**

Hn *symbol* CHEM ELEM hahnium

ho[1] /hō/ (*plural* **hos** or **hoes**) *n* **1.** an offensive term for a prostitute (*slang*) **2.** an offensive term for a woman (*slang offensive insult*) [Late 20C. Pronunciation of WHORE]

ho[2] /hō/ *interj* **1. EXPRESSING VARIOUS EMOTIONS** used to express surprise, triumph, admiration, or derision, depending on the way the speaker says it **2. CALL FOR ATTENTION** used to attract somebody's attention **3. USED TO POINT OUT SOMETHING** used to draw somebody's attention to something (*used in combinations*) ○ *Land ho!* [13C. Natural exclamation]

Ho *symbol* CHEM ELEM holmium

HO, H.O. *abbr* **1.** LAW habitual offender **2.** BUSINESS head office

hoac·tzin *n* BIRDS same as **hoatzin**

hoa·gie /hógee/ *n US regional, Can* a large sandwich made from a long roll split lengthwise and filled with layers of meat, cheese, and vegetables [Mid-20C. Alteration of *hoggy*]

hoar /hawr/ *adj* white or grayish white in color, usually as a result of age or frost (*literary*) [Old English *hār* < Indo-European, "shine"]

hoard /hawrd/ (**hoard·ed, hoard·ing, hoards**) *vti* to collect and store, often secretly, large amounts of things such as food or money for future use [Old English *hord* < Indo-European] —**hoard** *n* —**hoard·er** *n*

SPELLCHECK hoard or **horde**? Do not confuse the spelling of ***hoard*** and ***horde***. ***Hoard*** is used as a verb meaning "collect and store for future use" (as in *to hoard money*) or as a noun denoting such a collection (as in *a hoard of valuables*). ***Horde*** is chiefly used as a noun, denoting a large group of people or animals (as in *hordes of visitors*); it is only occasionally used as a verb, meaning "gather, move, or live in a large group."

SYNONYMS See ***collect***[1].

hoar frost *n* the white frost that forms on grass or leaves in the morning when the dew freezes

hoarse /hawrss/ (**hoars·er, hoars·est**) *adj* **1.** sounding rough and grating **2.** having a rough, harsh, grating voice [Old English *hās* < Germanic] —**hoarse·ly** *adv* —**hoarse·ness** *n*

SPELLCHECK hoarse or **horse**? Do not confuse the spelling of ***hoarse*** and ***horse***, which sound similar. The word ***hoarse*** is only used as an adjective, meaning "rough or grating," as in *a hoarse voice*. The correct spelling of the noun, denoting an animal used for riding, is ***horse***.

hoars·en /háwrss'n/ (**-ened, -en·ing, -ens**) *vti* to become hoarse, or make the voice hoarse

hoar·y /háwree/ (**-i·er, -i·est**) *adj* **1.** OVERUSED old and stale from overuse ○ *Do we have to hear those hoary knock-knock jokes again?* **2.** WHITE WITH AGE describes hair that has become white or gray with age **3.** COVERED WITH PALE HAIRS covered with gray or white hairs ○ *a plant with hoary leaves* —**hoar·i·ly** *adv* —**hoar·i·ness** *n*

hoat·zin /waat seen/, **hoac·tzin** /waak seen, waakt seen/ *n* a bird with brownish feathers, a very small crested head, and a specialized digestive system for leaves. Young birds have a digit resembling a claw on each wing, used for climbing and swimming. Native to: South America. Latin name: *Opisthocomus hoazin.* [Mid-17C. Via American Spanish < Nahuatl *uatzin*]

hoax /hōks/ *n* an act intended to trick people into believing something is real when it is not ■ *vt* (**hoaxed, hoax·ing, hoax·es**) to trick people into believing something is real when it is not [Late 18C. Probably alteration of HOCUS] —**hoax·er** *n*

hob[1] /hob/ *n* a small shelf or rack level with the top of the grate of a fireplace on which to set pans to keep them warm [Late 17C. Alteration of *hub*, origin ?]

hob[2] /hob/ *n* a hobgoblin or elf (*archaic*) [15C. < the name *Robert* or *Robin*]

Ho·ban /hóban/, **James** (1762?–1831) Irish-born US architect. He designed and supervised the construction of the White House (1792–99 and 1815–29) and the US Capitol in Washington, D.C.

Ho·bart /hō baart/ **1.** capital city of the island state of Tasmania in Australia, located on the Derwent River. Population: 195,000 (2002 estimate). **2.** city in northwestern Indiana, southeast of Gary. Population: 26,464 (2002 estimate).

Ho·bart, Garret A. (1844–99) vice president of the United States (1897–99). A Republican from New Jersey, he served in the state senate (1876–82) before becoming William McKinley's vice president.

Hobbes /hobz/, **Thomas** (1588–1679) English philosopher and political theorist. In *Leviathan* (1651) he advocated absolute monarchy as the only means of controlling clashing human interests and desires and guaranteeing people's rights of self-preservation and happiness. —**Hobbes·i·an** *adj, n* —**Hobb·ism** *n* —**Hobb·ist** *adj, n*

> "Liberties...depend on the silence of the law."
> [Thomas Hobbes, *Leviathan*; 1651]

hob·bit /hóbbit/ *n* in the novels of J. R. R. Tolkien, a member of an imaginary good-natured little people who have brown furry legs and live underground. Tolkien's most famous hobbits are Bilbo Baggins, the hero of *The Hobbit*, and Frodo Baggins, the hero of *Lord of the Rings*. [Mid-20C. Coined by J. R. R. TOLKIEN]

hob·ble /hóbb'l/ *v* (**-bled, -bling, -bles**) **1.** *vt* RESTRICT SOMEBODY'S ACTIONS to put restrictions on somebody or something to slow or prevent progress **2.** *vt* LIMIT HORSE'S MOVEMENT to tie the legs of a horse loosely together with a rope or strap to prevent it from moving away **3.** *vi* LIMP ALONG to walk haltingly and unsteadily, taking short steps ■ *n* **1.** ROPE OR STRAP something, e.g., a loop of rope or a strap, used to tie the legs of a horse **2.** UNSTEADY WALK a halting unsteady walk [13C. Probably < Low German]

hob·ble·bush /hóbb'l bŏŏsh/ *n* a deciduous bush with rounded leaves and red berries. Flowers: white, in clusters. Native to: eastern North America. Latin name: *Viburnum alnifolium.* [Mid-19C. Because it obstructs the way with its branches]

hob·ble·de·hoy /hóbb'ldee hòy/ *n* a clumsy or rude young man (*archaic*) [Mid-16C. Origin ?]

hob·ble skirt *n* a long skirt designed to be full at the hips but narrow at the ankles, first popular between 1910 and 1914

Hobbs /hobz/ city in southeastern New Mexico, on the Texas border, northeast of Carlsbad. Population: 28,479 (2002 estimate).

hob·by[1] /hóbbee/ (*plural* **-bies**) *n* an activity engaged in for pleasure and relaxation during spare time [14C. Probably < *Hobin*, variant of the name *Robin*]

hob·by[2] /hóbbee/ (*plural* **-bies**) *n* a small blackish falcon with a whitish chest and chestnut legs. Native to: Europe, Asia, migrating to Africa. Latin name: *Falco subbuteo.* [15C. < Old French *hobé, hobet*, diminutive of *hobe* "falcon"]

hob·by·horse /hóbbee hàwrss/ *n* **1.** LEISURE same as **rocking horse 2.** TOY HORSE a toy consisting of a long stick with the shape of a horse's head at one end **3.** HORSE FIGURE IN FOLK DANCES a representation of a horse that a Morris dancer or mummer wears around the waist so that it appears that the horse is being ridden **4.** FAVORITE TOPIC a favorite subject about which somebody will talk given the slightest opportunity

hob·by·ist /hóbbee ist/ *n* somebody who pursues a hobby or leisure activity [Late 19C. < HOBBY[1]]

hob·gob·lin /hób gòbblin/ *n* **1.** same as **goblin 2.** a source of fear or worry [< HOB[2]]

hob·nail /hób nàyl/ *n* a short nail with a broad head that is used to protect the soles of boots —**hob·nailed** *adj*

hob·nob /hób nòb/ (**-nobbed, -nob·bing, -nobs**) *vi* to socialize in a familiar manner with somebody, especially somebody considered to be of a higher social class (*disapproving*) [Mid-18C. Probably < obsolete *hob or nob* "have or not have"]

ho·bo /hō bō/ (*plural* **-boes**) *n* a poor and homeless person, especially somebody who traveled around the United States looking for work in the 1920s and 1930s [Late 19C. Origin ?]

Ho·bo·ken /hō bōkən, hō bōkən/ city in northeastern New Jersey, on the Hudson River opposite New York City. It is Frank Sinatra's birthplace. Population: 39,507 (2002 estimate).

Hob·son's choice /hóbss'nz-/ *n* a choice between what is offered and nothing at all [Mid-17C. After Thomas *Hobson* (1554–1631), English liveryman who would let his customers take only the horse nearest the door]

Ho Chi Minh /hō chee mín/ (1890–1969) Vietnamese politician. A founding member of the Communist Party (1918), he led Vietnamese resistance to French colonial rule (1946–54), and was prime minister (1954–55) and president of North Vietnam (1955–69). Born **Nguyen Tat Thanh**

> "You will kill 10 of our men and we will kill 1 of yours and in the end it will be you who tire of it."
> [Ho Chi Minh. Recalled on his death; September 3, 1969]

Ho Chi Minh Cit·y the largest city of Vietnam, in the southern part of the country. Population: 4,615,000 (2000). Former name **Saigon** (until 1975)

hock[1] /hok/ *n* **1.** the joint in the hind leg of a four-legged animal such as a horse or cow, corresponding to the human ankle **2.** a cut of cured meat, especially ham, taken from the lower joint of the leg immediately above the foot. It contains a comparatively small amount of meat but has a good flavor and jelly properties and is often used in stocks and soups. [Mid-16C. Shortening of obsolete *hockshin* < Old English *hōhsinu* "heel-sinew" < *hōh* "heel"]

hock[2] /hok/ *n* a German white wine, especially from the Rhineland [Early 17C. Shortening of obsolete *hockamore*, Anglicization of German *Hochheimer* < *Hochheim*, German town]

hock[3] /hok/ (**hocked, hock·ing, hocks**) *vt* to deposit something as security against money borrowed, with the risk of losing it if the money is not paid back within a specific period (*slang*) [Mid-19C. < Dutch *hok* "prison, debt"] ◇ **in hock 1.** left as security against money borrowed (*informal*) **2.** in debt (*slang*)

hock·ey /hókee/ *n* **1.** a game played on ice between two teams of six, using long sticks with curved ends. The objective is to hit a small hard rubber disk into the opposing goal. **2.** *UK* same as **field hockey** [Early 16C. Origin ?]

David Hockney

Hock·ney /hóknee/, **David** (*b.* 1937) British painter. He was closely associated with the Pop Art movement. His fascination with water inspired "swimming pool" paintings such as *A Bigger Splash* (1967).

> "Art has to move you and design does not, unless it's a good design for a bus."
> [David Hockney, *Guardian (London)*; October 26, 1988]

hock·shop /hók shòp/, **hock shop** *n* a pawnshop (*slang*)

ho·cus /hōkəss/ (**-cused, -cus·ing, -cus·es** or **-cus·ses**) *vt* (*archaic*) **1.** DECEIVE SOMEBODY to deceive or trick somebody **2.** DOPE SOMEBODY to drug somebody or an animal by deception **3.** DRUG ALCOHOLIC DRINK to secretly add a drug to an alcoholic drink [Late 17C. Shortening of HOCUS-POCUS]

ho·cus-po·cus /hōkəss pōkəss/ *n* **1.** CONJURER'S INCANTATION a phrase or chant used by a magician or conjurer during a performance **2.** MAGIC TRICK a trick performed by a magician or conjurer **3.** TRICKERY a hoax or trickery ○ *The negotiations were ruined by the parties' hocus-pocus.* **4.** CONJURER a juggler or magician (*dated*) ■ *vti* (**ho·cus-po·cused, ho·cus-po·cus·ing, ho·cus-po·cus·es**) DECEIVE to deceive or trick somebody [< pseudo-Latin *hax pax max Deus adimax*, used by conjurers]

hod /hod/ *n* **1.** a V-shaped tray on the end of a long pole, usually carried on the shoulder. Use: carrying bricks, mortar, and other building materials. **2.** HOUSEHOLD same as **coal scuttle** [Late 16C. < Old French *hotte* "pannier, basket" < Germanic]

hod car·ri·er *n* somebody hired to carry bricks and mortar in a hod

Ho·dei·da /hō dáydə/ seaport in western Yemen, situated on the Red Sea. Population: 155,110 (1995).

hodge·podge /hój pòj/ *n* a mixture of several unrelated things. Can term **hotchpotch** [14C. Variant of HOTCHPOTCH]

Hodg·kin /hójkin/, **Alan** (1914–98) British physiologist. He shared the Nobel Prize in physiology or medicine (1963) for his research into the chemical processes of nerve impulses. Full name **Hodgkin, Alan Lloyd**

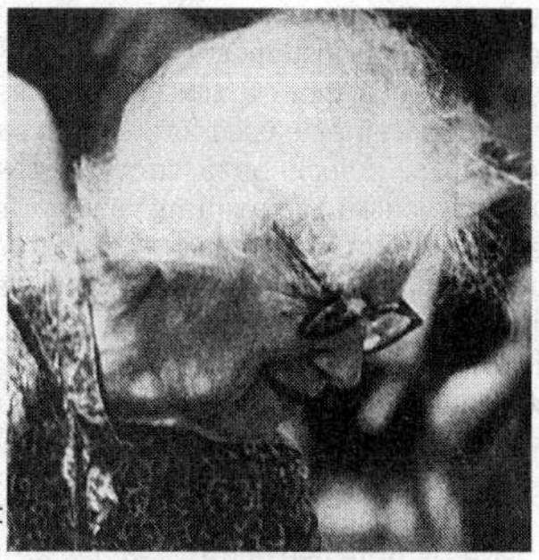

Dorothy Mary Hodgkin

Hodg·kin, Dorothy Mary (1910–94) Egyptian-born British chemist. She was awarded the Nobel Prize in chemistry (1964) for work on X rays, molecular science, and penicillin.

> "I'm really an experimentalist. I used to say 'I think with my hands.' I just like manipulation."
> [Dorothy Mary Hodgkin. Quoted in *A Passion for Science*, Lewis Wolpert and Alison Richards; 1988]

Hodg·kin, Thomas (1798–1866) British pathologist. He was the first person to detect the glandular disease of the lymph tissue later named "Hodgkin's disease."

Hodg·kins /hójkinz/, **Frances Mary** (1869–1947) New Zealand painter. Noted for her watercolor still lifes and landscapes, she spent most of her working life in Europe.

Hodg·kin's dis·ease *n* a malignant form of lymphoma marked by progressive enlargement of the lymph nodes and spleen and sometimes of the liver [Mid-19C. After Thomas HODGKIN]

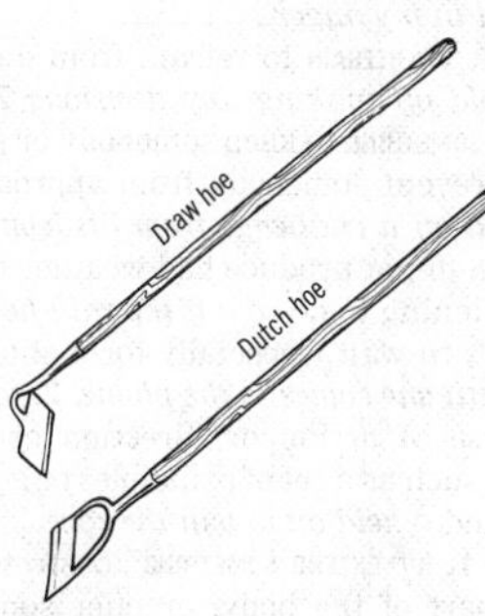

hoe

hoe /hō/ *n* a garden implement consisting of a long pole with a small flat metal blade set into one end at a right angle to the pole. Use: weeding, turning over soil. [14C. < Old French *houe* < Germanic, "cut down"] —**hoe** *vti* —**ho·er** *n*

Hoe /hō/, **Richard M.** (1812–86) US inventor. He revolutionized the daily newspaper industry from 1847 with his new printing presses. Full name **Hoe, Richard March**

hoe·cake /hṓ kàyk/ *n Southern US* a bread made with cornmeal, originally baked in a fireplace on the blade of a hoe [Because originally baked on the blade of a hoe]

hoe·down /hṓ dòwn/ *n Can, Southern US* **1.** a noisy lively dance, especially a square dance, or a party for square dancing **2.** the music for a hoedown [< the idea of stopping work]

HOF *abbr* ONLINE hall of fame

Ho·fei /hō fáy/ ➧ **Hefei**

Hof·fa /hóffə/, **Jimmy** (1913–75?) US labor leader. He was president of the International Brotherhood of Teamsters (1957–71) and disappeared in 1975, presumed murdered. Full name **Hoffa, James Riddle**

> "You will only get what you are big enough to take."
> [Attributed to Jimmy Hoffa, on labor unions and business management]

Hoff·man /hófmən/, **Dustin** (*b.* 1937) US actor. He starred in *The Graduate* (1967), and won Academy Awards for *Kramer vs. Kramer* (1979) and *Rain Man* (1988). Full name **Hoffman, Dustin Lee**

Hoff·man Es·tates /hòfmən-/ village in northeastern Illinois, a residential suburb of Chicago. Population: 49,795 (2002 estimate).

Hof·mann /hófmən/, **Hans** (1880–1966) German-born US painter. He opened the Hans Hofmann School of Fine Art in New York. He was a pioneer of improvisatory abstract painting.

> "The ability to simplify means to eliminate the unnecessary so that the necessary may speak."
> [Hans Hofmann, *Search for the Real*; 1967]

Hof·stadt·er /hóf stàttər/, **Robert** (1915–90) US physicist. He was joint winner of the Nobel Prize in physics (1961) for his research into the structure of atom nuclei.

hog /hawg, hog/ *n* **1.** PIG a full-grown domestic pig, especially a castrated male pig **2.** MEMBER OF PIG FAMILY any animal of the pig family, including both domesticated and wild species, e.g., the wild boar. Family: Suidae. **3.** SHIP'S BROOM a broom used to clean the bottom of a ship while it is in the water **4.** OFFENSIVE TERM an offensive term that deliberately insults somebody's appetite, consideration for others, tidiness, or cleanliness (*informal insult*) **5.** LARGE MOTORCYCLE a large powerful motorcycle or any large car or truck that consumes a large amount of gas (*slang*) ■ *v* (**hogged, hog·ging, hogs**) **1.** *vt* TAKE EXCESS OF SOMETHING to take more of something or keep something for longer than is fair or polite (*informal*) ○ *He's been hogging the fast lane for the past two miles.* **2.** *vt* ARCH BACK to arch the back upward **3.** *vt* TRIM HORSE'S MANE to trim the mane of a horse very short, causing it to stand up like the bristles of a hog's back **4.** *vti* WARP to cause the keel or plank of a ship to curve upward in the middle, or curve in this way **5.** *vt* SCRUB SHIP'S BOTTOM to clean a ship's bottom with a broom while the ship is in the water [Pre-12C. Origin ?] —**hog·like** *adj* ◇ **go the whole hog, go whole hog** to do something wholeheartedly or completely and without restraint (*slang*) ◇ **live high off** *or* **on the hog** to have a luxurious standard of living (*slang*)

ho·gan /hṓgən/ *n* a traditional Navajo dwelling made of logs and mud, with a roof of earth [Late 19C. < Navajo]

Ho·gan /hṓgən/, **Ben** (1912–97) US golfer. He won over 60 major golfing tournaments including four US Open championships (1948, 1950, 1951, 1953). Full name **Hogan, William Benjamin**

Ho·gan, Paul (*b.* 1939) Australian actor. Originally a television performer, he starred in the movie *Crocodile Dundee* (1986) and cowrote and produced *Crocodile Dundee II* (1988).

Ho·garth /hṓ gaàrth/, **William** (1697–1764) British painter and engraver. He is best known for his series of satirical engravings, including *A Rake's Progress* (1733–35). —**Ho·garth·i·an** /hō gaàrthee ən/ *adj*

> "Comedy in painting, as well as in writing, ought to be allotted the first place."
> [William Hogarth. Quoted in *Hogarth Illustrated*, John Ireland; 1812]

hog·back /háwg bàk, hóg-/ *n* **1.** a steep and narrow low ridge produced by the erosion of the softer surrounding rock strata **2.** an arched back, similar to a hog's back (*slang*)

hog badg·er *n* a nocturnal badger with a long snout with which it roots for insects and grubs. Native to: Southeast Asia. Latin name: *Arctonyx collaris.* [< its cloven hooves]

hog chol·er·a *n* VET same as **swine fever**

hog·fish /háwg fish, hóg-/ (*plural same* or **-fish·es**) *n* **1.** a brightly colored fish of the wrasse family, especially one in which the first three spines of its dorsal fin are thicker and longer than the rest. Native to: tropical coral reefs. Latin name: *Lachnolaimus maximus.* **2.** FISH same as **pigfish** [< its grunting sound]

hog·gish /háwggish, hóggish/ *adj* **1.** greedy, selfish, or slovenly **2.** filthy dirty —**hog·gish·ly** *adv* —**hog·gish·ness** *n*

hog·head cheese /háwg hèd-, hóg \hèd cheéz/, **hog's head cheese** /hógz hèd-, hógz \hed cheéz/ *n regional* FOOD same as **headcheese** [Because its ingredients are pressed together as in cheese-making]

REGIONAL NOTE See *headcheese*.

hog heav·en *n* a state of complete contentment or satiation (*slang*) ○ *He'll be in hog heaven when he finds out.*

Hog·ma·nay /hógmə này, hògmə náy/, **hog·ma·nay** *n Scotland* New Year's Eve as celebrated in Scotland and in parts of northern England [Early 17C. Probably < Norman dialect *hoguinané*, said when exchanging New Year's gifts < Old French *aguillanneuf*, contraction of *accueillis l'an neuf* "welcome the new year"]

hog·nose snake /háwg nōz-, hòg-/, **hog·nosed snake** /-nōzd-/ *n* a nonvenomous snake with a thick body and an upturned snout resembling a hog's that is used for burrowing. Native to: North America. Genus: *Heterodon.* [< its upturned snout]

hog·nut /hóg nut/ *n* FOOD, TREES same as **pignut**

hog pea·nut *n* a vine of the legume family that has edible, fleshy, single-seeded pods that ripen on or beneath the ground. Flowers: white or pinkish, in clusters. Native to: North America. Latin name: *Amphicarpaea bracteata.*

hog's back /háwgz bák, hògz-/ *n* GEOG same as **hogback** (sense 1)

hogs·head /háwgz hèd, hógz-/ *n* **1.** a large cask or barrel, especially one having a capacity of one hogshead **2.** a unit of capacity for liquids or dry goods, used especially for alcohol, having various values but typically 63 US gallons or 54 British imperial gallons [14C. Origin ?]

hog souse *n regional* FOOD same as **headcheese**

REGIONAL NOTE See *headcheese*.

hog-tie *vt* **1.** to tie the legs of an animal or the feet and hands of a person together **2.** to hamper or impede somebody or something (*informal*) ○ *Without that evidence, I'm hog-tied.*

hog·wash /háwg wàwsh, hóg wòsh/ *n* **1.** worthless stuff or nonsense (*informal*) ○ *What a pile of hogwash!* **2.** leftovers of food that are given to hogs to eat

hogweed

hog·weed /háwg weèd, hóg-/ *n* any coarse weed, e.g., sow thistle or knotweed

hog-wild *adj* excited or enthusiastic to the point of losing any inhibitions (*slang*) ○ *He's gone hog-wild ever since he inherited the money.*

hog wire *n regional* wire fencing, usually of square mesh narrower toward the bottom

Hoh·hot /hō hṓt/ capital city of Nei Monggol Autonomous Region in northeastern China. Population: 1,090,000 (1995).

ho hum *interj* used to express boredom, disappointment, or resignation (*informal*) [Probably formed to suggest a yawn]

ho-hum *adj* **1.** boring or lacking in originality (*informal*) ○ *All in all it was a pretty ho-hum affair.* **2.** indifferent or lacking enthusiasm (*slang*) ○ *He had a very ho-hum attitude toward my project.*

hoick /hoyk/ (**hoicked, hoick·ing, hoicks**) *vti* to pull or lift something or somebody violently or suddenly (*informal*) [Late 19C. Origin ?]

hoicks /hoyks/ *n* a shout in hunting, used to urge hounds to move along faster [Early 17C. Origin ?]

hoi pol·loi /hòy pə lóy/ *n* ordinary people, as opposed to the wealthy, well-educated, and cultivated elite (*disapproving*) [Mid-17C. < Greek, "the many"]

hoi·sin sauce /hoy sín-, hóyssin-/ *n* a dark sweet and spicy sauce of thick consistency made from fermented soybeans. Use: to flavor Chinese dishes, as a condiment. [< Chinese (Cantonese), "delicacy of the sea"]

hoist /hoyst/ *vt* (**hoist·ed, hoist·ing, hoists**) LIFT SOMEBODY OR SOMETHING UP to raise or lift somebody or something up, especially using a mechanical device such as a winch ■ *n* **1.** DEVICE FOR LIFTING a mechanical device or apparatus, e.g., a winch or elevator, designed for lifting people or heavy objects **2.** LIFTING UP an act of hoisting somebody or something **3.** SIGNAL MADE WITH FLAGS a message or signal conveyed from ship to ship by flags hoisted up the mast **4.** SIZE OF SAIL the height of a sail or flag [15C. Alteration of *hoise*, origin ?] —**hoist·er** *n*

SYNONYMS See *raise*.

hoi·ty-toi·ty /hòytee tóytee/ *adj* **1.** arrogant and self-important (*informal*) **2.** silly, giddy, or frivolous ○ *We were confronted by giggling, hoity-toity nonsense.* [Alteration and repetition of obsolete *hoit* "romp," origin ?]

Ho·kan /hṓkən/ *n* a group of Native American languages of the southwestern United States, including Chumash, Yuman, and other languages and linguistic groups [Early 20C. < Hokan *hok* "two"] —**Ho·kan** *adj*

hoke /hōk/ (**hoked, hok·ing, hokes**) *vt* to introduce highly melodramatic or broadly comic features into a story, play, or speech, in order to captivate an audience [Early 20C. Back-formation < HOKUM]

hok·ey /hṓkee/ (**-i·er, -i·est**) *adj* (*informal*) **1.** obviously contrived or clearly not genuine **2.** corny, sentimental, or melodramatic [Mid-20C. < HOKE or HOKUM] —**hok·ey·ness** *n* —**hok·i·ly** *adv*

hok·ey cok·ey /hṓkee kṓkee/ *n UK* DANCE same as **hokey-pokey** (sense 1) [Mid-20C. Origin ?]

hok·ey-poke·y /hòkee pṓkee/ (*plural* **hok·ey-po·keys**) *n* **1.** a dance in which a circle of people, especially children, sing out instructions for movements that they perform at the same time **2.** same as **hocus-pocus** *n* (sense 3) [Mid-19C. In sense 2 alteration; in sense 1, origin ?]

Hok·kai·do /ho kī́dō/ the second largest island of Japan, situated north of the main island of Honshu. Population: 5,643,647 (1990). Area: 30,290 sq. mi./78,460 sq. km.

Hok·ki·en /hókee èn/ *n* the form of the Chinese language that is most widely used in Singapore. Native speakers: 700,000. —**Hok·ki·en** *adj*

hok·ku /hṓkoo/ (*plural same*) *n* LITERAT another spelling of **haiku** [Late 19C. < Japanese, "opening verse (of a sequence of comic verses)"]

ho·kum /hṓkəm/ *n* **1.** something that on the surface appears to be true or credible but is in fact meaningless or untrue (*informal*) ○ *a load of hokum* **2.** highly melodramatic or broadly comic features introduced into a story, play, or speech, in order to captivate an audience [Early 20C. Origin ?]

Ho·ku·sai /hṓkŏŏ sī́/ (1760–1849) Japanese painter and book illustrator. The finest Japanese printmaker of his time, he was the leading member of the Ukiyo-e school. His best known work is *Thirty-Six Views of Mount Fuji* (1826–33). Full name **Hokusai, Katsushika**

hol- *prefix* same as **holo-** (*used before vowels*)

ho·lan·dric /hō lándrik, ho-/ *adj* describes genetic traits carried on the Y chromosome and therefore carried and inherited only by males [Mid-20C. < HOLO- + ANDRO-]

Hol·arc·tic /hō laárktik, -laártik, ho-/ *adj* found in or characteristic of the regions of North America, Europe, and Asia combined, which share many faunal characteristics

Hol·bein (the El·der) /hṓl bīn-/, **Hans** (1460?–1524) German painter. The father and teacher of Hans Holbein the Younger, his most famous work is the St. Sebastian Altar, Munich, Germany (1493).

Hol·bein (the Young·er), Hans (1497–1543) German painter. The son of Hans Holbein the Elder, he is best remembered for his portraits of the court of Henry VIII of England.

hold[1] /hōld/ *v* (**held** /held/, **hold·ing, holds**) **1.** *vt* GRASP SOMETHING to take something firmly and retain it in the hand or arms **2.** *vt* LIFT AND SUPPORT SOMETHING to carry, lift, or support temporarily an object or part of the body in a particular position ○ *Hold the rope a little higher.* **3.** *vt* FIX SOMETHING IN POSITION to keep something fixed in a particular position ○ *The picture is held in place by two large hooks.* **4.** *vt* EMBRACE SOMEBODY to bring or have somebody within an embrace or supported by the arms **5.** *vt* CONTAIN SOMETHING to be the place where something is or can be kept ○ *a basket to hold all your sewing equipment* **6.** *vt* KEEP SOMEBODY IN CUSTODY to keep somebody in a particular place or condition, especially in custody **7.** *vt* RETAIN OR RESERVE SOMETHING to retain or reserve something for later use or collection by somebody else ○ *Ask if they can hold the tickets for us at the box office.* **8.** *vt* REFRAIN FROM SOMETHING to refrain from doing or saying something ○ *Please hold your applause until the end.* **9.** *vt* STOP SOMETHING FROM LEAVING OR OCCURRING to stop something leaving or happening at the appointed time, usually for a particular purpose ○ *The conductor held the train so we could board.* **10.** *vt* MIL KEEP SOMETHING BY FORCE to keep possession of something by force, especially while under attack ○ *The insurgents held the town for some time before retreating.* **11.** *vt* HAVE PARTICULAR CAPACITY to contain or be able to contain a particular number or amount ○ *holds 20 passengers* **12.** *vt* BE ABLE TO CONSUME SOMETHING to consume something, especially alcohol, without ill effect **13.** *vt* ARRANGE SOMETHING to arrange, take part in, or observe an activity or event ○ *They hold a party every Friday night.* **14.** *vt* POSSESS SOMETHING to have the right to something as a possession or achievement ○ *The author holds the copyright to this book.* ○ *holds the property on a long lease* **15.** *vt* HAVE PARTICULAR POSITION to fulfill the duties of a particular title, office, or position ○ *held the office of treasurer* **16.** *vti* KEEP PROMISE to keep a promise or carry out an intention, or make sure that somebody does this ○ *held her to her agreement* **17.** *vt* BELIEVE OR FEEL SOMETHING to have a particular belief, opinion, or feeling ○ *We hold these truths to be self-evident.* **18.** *vt* REGARD SOMEBODY IN PARTICULAR WAY to regard somebody or something in a particular way ○ *She holds her professor in very high esteem.* **19.** *vt* HAVE PARTICULAR BEARING to keep or carry the body or a part of it in a particular attitude or position ○ *She holds herself well.* **20.** *vt* ENGROSS SOMEBODY to engage or captivate somebody or somebody's attention ○ *She held their attention with the dramatic tale of her solo crossing.* **21.** *vt* SUSTAIN SOMEBODY to be enough to satisfy or sustain somebody ○ *a breakfast that will hold us all day* **22.** *vt* LAW DECIDE SOMETHING LEGALLY to decide or lay down something legally or authoritatively ○ *The appeals court held that the lower court acted properly.* **23.** *vt* MUSIC SUSTAIN MUSICAL NOTE to continue singing or playing a note or a chord for a length of time ○ *The trumpeter held the note for at least a full minute.* **24.** *vi* PERSIST to continue in a particular state or course **25.** *vi* REMAIN FIRM to remain fast or firm and not break or give way ○ *The levee held against the floods.* **26.** *vi* STAND FIRM to maintain a position against attack or opposition ○ *Their defensive line held.* **27.** *vi* REMAIN VALID to remain in force or continue to be valid ○ *Many old sayings still hold true.* **28.** *vi* STAY FINE to continue to be fine and not become wet or cold (*refers to the weather*) ○ *I hope the weather holds through the weekend.* **29.** *vti* COMMUNICATION WAIT ON TELEPHONE to maintain the connection on a telephone line while not talking, usually so that the person being called can speak to somebody else or transfer the call ○ *Hold, please, while I try to connect you.* ■ *n* **1.** GRASPING the act or position of grasping or keeping possession of something ○ *She grabbed hold of the rope and pulled herself aboard.* ○ *has no hold on reality* **2.** WRESTLING TECHNIQUE in wrestling, a position or manner of grasping an opponent **3.** SOMETHING GIVING SUPPORT something that may be grasped or used as a support ○ *There were few holds on the sheer rock face.* **4.** SOMETHING THAT RESTRAINS a structure or receptacle used for keeping something in check, e.g., a lock on a canal **5.** CONTROL OVER SOMEBODY OR SOMETHING a controlling power or influence over somebody or something ○ *a firm hold on the public imagination* **6.** DELAYING OF SOMETHING an act of delaying or restraining something, or an order to do this ○ *Put a hold on their dinner order.* **7.** MUSIC MUSICAL NOTATION a symbol appearing above or below a note or rest signaling that it can be prolonged beyond its prescribed time **8.** PRISON a prison cell or place of confinement **9.** STRONGHOLD a fortified place in a castle or other structure (*archaic*) [Old English *haldan, healdan* < Germanic, "guard, watch"] ◇ **hold good** to apply to something, or be true or valid ◇ **hold it** used to tell somebody to stop or wait ◇ **hold something against somebody** to resent something that somebody has done and to bear a grudge because of it ◇ **no holds barred** with no restrictions on what is allowed or included ◇ **on hold 1.** waiting to be connected or reconnected to somebody during a telephone call **2.** into or in a state of suspension or postponement ○ *put our vacation plans on hold*

hold back *v* **1.** *vti* to keep something from happening, or keep somebody from doing something ○ *His shyness holds him back from making friends.* **2.** *vt* to withhold something or retain something within your own control ○ *accused of holding back vital information* ○ *holding back tears*

SYNONYMS See *hinder*[1].

hold down *vt* to do enough in a job or position in order to keep it (*informal*) ○ *She holds down two jobs.*

hold forth *vi* to speak at length and sometimes tediously on a subject ○ *holding forth on the ins and outs of parliamentary procedure*

hold in *vt* **1.** to keep back or in check **2.** to suppress something such as an emotion or feeling ○ *could barely hold in my anger*

hold off *v* **1.** *vti* REFRAIN to refrain from doing something ○ *hold off making any decisions* **2.** *vt* RESIST SOMEBODY OR SOMETHING to keep somebody or something away or prevent somebody from approaching too close ○ *held off a challenge from his competitors* **3.** *vi* NOT HAPPEN to not produce bad weather conditions after threatening to do so ○ *if the rain holds off*

hold on *vi* **1.** to wait, especially for a short while ○ *Hold on until she comes to the phone.* **2.** to continue on a course of action or direction or maintain something such as a set of principles or a particular state of mind ○ *held on to win the race*

hold out *v* **1.** *vt* EXTEND SOMETHING to stretch out or extend a part of the body, or offer something to somebody by doing this ○ *She held out her hand.* **2.** *vi* LAST to keep up or continue to be in supply ○ *Is the food holding out?* **3.** *vi* ENDURE to continue to resist and not give in to something ○ *held out for two days without food or water* **4.** *vi* RESIST to refuse to settle something or accept something until all demands or conditions are met ○ *holding out for a 6% raise*

hold over *v* **1.** *vt* DEFER SOMETHING to postpone action on or consideration of something until a later date **2.** *vi* MUSIC HOLD MUSICAL NOTE to hold a note from one bar of music to the next **3.** *vt* THREATEN SOMEBODY WITH UNWELCOME FACTS to use something, often information or photographs, to threaten or influence somebody (*informal*) ○ *You're not going to keep holding that over me, are you?*

hold together *vti* to remain united, or cause a group of people to remain united, often despite problems or disagreements ○ *He held the family together single-handed.*

hold up *v* **1.** *vt* CAUSE DELAY TO SOMEBODY OR SOMETHING to cause somebody or something to be late or take longer than intended ○ *I was held up in traffic.* **2.** *vt* CRIME ROB SOMEBODY OR SOMETHING to rob a person or place using violence or threats, usually at gunpoint **3.** *vt* PRESENT SOMEBODY OR SOMETHING to show or display somebody or something for a particular reason ○ *The firefighter was held up as a hero.* **4.** *vi* ENDURE to continue to function or survive ○ *How's the bike holding up?* ○ *You've been holding up well under the strain.* **5.** *vi* REMAIN SAME to remain or be maintained at a particular level or in a particular state ○ *The* *stock market held up reasonably well this month.* **6.** *vi* **STAND UP TO SCRUTINY** to remain persuasive or convincing even after closer examination ○ *I don't think these ideas will hold up.*

hold with *vt* to approve or agree with something ○ *She doesn't hold with that kind of thinking.*

hold[2] /hōld/ *n* the area below the deck of a ship or inside an aircraft in which cargo is carried [Late 16C. Alteration of HOLE, influenced by HOLD[1]]

hold·all /hṓld àwl/ *n UK* same as **carryall** (sense 1)

hold·back /hṓld bàk/ *n* **1. SOMETHING HELD BACK** something withheld, usually wages or money **2. BONUS FOR CAR DEALER** an amount of money that an automobile manufacturer gives a dealer for each car sold, increasing the dealer's profit **3. SOMETHING THAT HINDERS** something that prevents somebody from doing or achieving something, or prevents an event or plan from going ahead **4. DEVICE ON HORSE-DRAWN WAGON** a device on the shaft of a horse-drawn wagon or carriage that attaches to the harness, allowing the horse to hold back or back up the vehicle

hold but·ton *n* a button on a telephone that allows somebody to put a caller on hold

hold-down *n* **1.** a restraint or limitation of price increases or pay raises **2.** something that holds another thing in place

Hol·den /hṓldən/, **William** (1918–81) US actor. He was a popular clean-cut hero in many 1940s and 1950s Hollywood movies such as *Sunset Boulevard* (1950) and *Bridge on the River Kwai* (1957).

hold·er /hṓldər/ *n* **1. OWNER** somebody who owns, occupies, or is in possession of something such as property or a title ○ *the current holder of the world title* **2. CONTAINER** something designed to hold another thing (*often used in combination*) ○ *a coin holder* **3.** FIN **SOMEBODY WITH PROMISE OF PAYMENT** somebody in possession of and legally entitled to receive payment on or to negotiate a note, bill, or check

hold·fast /hṓld fàst/ *n* **1. CLAMP** a device designed to hold something securely, e.g., a clamp or grip **2.** BOT **PLANT'S MEANS OF ATTACHING ITSELF** an organ at the base of a seaweed, water plant, or fungus that attaches the organism to a surface **3. FIRM GRASP** the action or fact of holding something fast or firmly

hold·ing /hṓlding/ *n* **1. LEASED LAND** a piece of land that is leased from somebody else, especially when used for agricultural purposes **2. PROPERTY** legally owned property, especially stocks or bonds (*often used in the plural*) **3.** LAW **LEGAL RULING** a ruling of a court of law, especially one that decides a legal issue raised in a particular case **4.** SPORTS **HOLDING OR OBSTRUCTING OF OPPONENT** in some sports such basketball or football, the illegal use of the arms to hold or obstruct an opponent **5.** PSYCHOL **SENSE OF SECURITY** the ability of a therapist or parent to make a client or child feel contained and secure during times of growth or change

hold·ing com·pa·ny *n* a company that has a controlling interest in one or more other companies through ownership of their stocks or bonds

hold·ing op·er·a·tion *n* a procedure or operation designed to maintain the present situation as it is

hold·ing pat·tern *n* **1.** a usually circular course taken by an aircraft while awaiting permission to land **2.** a state of suspended action or progress ○ *The team is in a holding pattern until organizers decide whether the races can go ahead.*

hold·out /hṓld òwt/ *n* **1.** a person or group that refuses to submit to or comply with a situation, trend, or order ○ *persuaded the last holdouts to evacuate* **2.** a refusal to agree or compromise in order to obtain better terms in a settlement ○ *The holdout lasted three weeks.*

hold·o·ver /hṓld ȍvər/ *n* **1. RETAINED EMPLOYEE** somebody who remains in a job or other position that has come under the control of a different organization ○ *keeping the personnel files of holdover employees* **2. REMAINDER** somebody or something held over from a previous period or time **3.** EDUC **REPEATING STUDENT** a student who repeats a course or grade **4.** ARTS **SOMEBODY OR SOMETHING GIVEN EXTENDED RUN** a performer's engagement or a set of performances of a production that is allowed to continue beyond the term originally agreed

hold·up /hṓld ùp/ *n* **1.** an act of robbing a person or place using violence or threats, usually at gunpoint **2.** a situation in which somebody or something is delayed or takes longer than planned ○ *delayed by holdups on the interstate*

hole /hōl/ *n* **1. CAVITY** a hollow space in a solid object or area ○ *The hole had filled with water.* **2. APERTURE** a gap or opening in or through something ○ *a hole in my socks* ○ *a hole in the defensive line* **3. BURROW** a hollowed-out area in the ground where an animal such as a rabbit or mouse lives **4. FLAW** a fault or flaw in something such as logic, an argument, or a position ○ *But there are so many holes in her theory.* **5. UNPLEASANT PLACE** a dark or dirty place, especially a place where somebody lives (*informal*) **6. AWKWARD SITUATION** an awkward or embarrassing situation (*informal*) **7. PRISONER'S CELL** a prison cell or dungeon, or solitary confinement (*informal*) **8.** GOLF **TARGET IN GOLF** in golf, a small round cavity or cup on a green into which the ball is hit **9.** GOLF **AREA OF GOLF COURSE** a part of a golf course that consists of a tee, a fairway, and a green with a hole and is a basic element in scoring. A golf course usually has 18 holes. **10.** ELECTRONICS **MOBILE SPACE IN SEMICONDUCTOR** a space normally occupied by an electron in the lattice structure of a semiconductor material that is mobile and can act as a carrier of a positive charge **11.** GEOG **COVE** a small bay or harbor on the coast **12.** *regional* AGRIC **PILE OF VEGETABLES** a heap of vegetables, usually potatoes, covered with earth and mulch and sometimes stored in a shed ■ *v* (**holed, hol·ing, holes**) **1.** *vt* **PERFORATE SOMETHING** to make a hole or holes in something ○ *This new device holes a ream of paper perfectly.* **2.** *vt* **PUT BALL IN HOLE** to hit or drive a ball into one of the holes of a golf course **3.** *vi* **GO INTO HOLE** to go or climb into a hole [Old English *hol* "hollow," probably < Indo-European, "hide, conceal"] —**hol·ey** *adj*
◇ **in the hole** (*informal*) **1.** owing money **2.** having a score of less than zero **3.** in a position of disadvantage ◇ **make a hole in something** to use up a large part of something (*slang*) ○ *The monthly rent makes a considerable hole in my salary.* ◇ **pick holes in something** to look for and find minor mistakes in something, particularly in an argument

SPELLCHECK hole or **whole**? Do not confuse the spelling of ***hole*** and ***whole***, which sound similar. ***Hole*** is chiefly used as a noun, denoting a hollow space, a gap, an unpleasant place, or an awkward situation, as in *a hole in the ground*; it is also used as a verb, meaning "make a hole in" or "put in a hole." ***Whole*** is an adjective, noun, or adverb referring to something in its entirety, as in *the whole world, the whole of the summer, a whole new ball game.*

REGIONAL NOTE See ***bank***[2].

SYNONYMS See ***criticize***.

hole out *vi* to hit a golf ball into a hole

hole up *vi* **1.** to hide away somewhere (*slang*) **2.** to go into a hole, cave, or other similar place to shelter or hibernate

hole card *n* **1.** in stud poker, a card dealt face down that only the holder can see **2.** an advantage hidden or held in reserve (*informal*)

hole in one (*plural* **holes in one**) *n* a golf shot that enters the hole directly from the tee

hole-in-the-wall (*plural* **holes-in-the-wall**) *n* a small unpretentious out-of-the-way place such as a restaurant or other business (*informal*) ○ *It's only a little hole-in-the-wall, but they serve great food.*

Ho·li /hṓlee/ *n* a Hindu festival during which people celebrate the time when Krishna paid amorous attention to young women tending cows by spraying colored water over each other. Date: early Phalguna. [Late 17C. < Hindi *holī*]

hol·i·day /hóllə dày/ *n* **1.** a day set aside by law or statute as exempt from regular labor or business activities, usually to celebrate or commemorate something that happened on or near that date ○ *a public holiday* **2.** the day or days of a religious festival **3.** *UK* same as **vacation** *n* (sense 3) ■ *vi* (**-dayed, -day·ing, -days**) *UK* same as **vacation** [Old English *hāligdæg* "holy day"]

Hol·i·day /hóllə dày/, **Billie** (1915–59) US jazz singer. Known for her emotionally charged renditions of popular songs, she collaborated with Count Basie and Artie Shaw. Her autobiography *Lady Sings the Blues* (1956) was later made into a movie. Born **Holiday, Eleanora**. Known as **Lady Day**

> "I can't stand to sing the same song the same way two nights in succession, let alone two years or ten years. If you can, then it ain't music, it's close-order drill, or exercise or yodeling or something, not music."
> [Billie Holiday, *Lady Sings the Blues*; 1956]

hol·i·day·mak·er /hólli day màykər/ *n UK* same as **vacationer**

ho·li·er-than-thou *adj* aggressively or offensively pompous or self-righteous (*disapproving*) ○ *Her holier-than-thou attitude alienates people.*

ho·li·ness /hṓleenəss/ *n* the state or quality of being holy

Ho·li·ness *n* a title used in addressing or referring to the pope

ho·lism /hṓ lìzzəm/ *n* **1.** the view that a whole system of beliefs must be analyzed rather than simply its individual components **2.** the theory of the importance of taking all of somebody's physical, mental, and social conditions into account in the treatment of illness [Early 20C. < Greek *holos* "whole"] —**ho·list** *n*

ho·lis·tic /hō lístik/ *adj* **1.** characterized by the view that a whole system of beliefs must be analyzed rather than simply its individual components **2.** taking into account all of somebody's physical, mental, and social conditions in the treatment of illness —**ho·lis·ti·cal·ly** *adv*

hol·land /hóllənd/ *n* a strong smooth linen fabric. Use: upholstery. [14C. After HOLLAND]

Hol·land /hóllənd/ ▸ **Netherlands** (*informal*)

hol·lan·daise sauce /hóllən dàyz-/, **hol·lan·daise** *n* a rich creamy piquant sauce made from butter, egg yolks, and vinegar or lemon juice [< French, form of *Hollandais* "Dutch"]

hol·ler[1] /hóllər/ (*informal*) *vti* (**-lered, -ler·ing, -lers**) **YELL** to call out or shout something ○ *If you need me, just holler!* ■ *n* **1. LOUD CRY** a loud cry or shout **2. WORK SONG** a work song originally sung by enslaved African American people [Late 17C. Probably partly < Old French *halloer* "pursue with shouting," an imitation of the sound, partly < French *holà* "stop!" < *ho* "ho" + *là* "there"]

hol·ler[2] /hóllər/ *n regional* a small valley or hollow [Variant of HOLLOW]

Hol·li·day /hóllə dày/, **Judy** (1921–65) US actor. She is known for her roles in the stage and screen versions of *Born Yesterday* (1946, 1950) and *Bells are Ringing* (1956, 1960).

hol·low /hóllō/ *adj* **1. NOT SOLID** having empty space inside ○ *a hollow tree trunk* **2. CONCAVE** sunk deep into the surface of something **3. NOT FULL-TONED** resonating or echoing as if in an empty space ○ *a hollow, booming sound* **4. INSINCERE** not sincere or genuine ○ *a hollow laugh* **5. MEANINGLESS** lacking meaning or substance ○ *a hollow victory* **6. HUNGRY** having the feeling of an empty stomach ■ *n* **1. CAVITY** a hollow or concave place or area ○ *held the chick in the hollow of his hand* **2. SMALL SHALLOW VALLEY** a sunken or low-lying area of ground ■ *v* (**-lowed, -low·ing, -lows**) **1.** *vt* **MAKE CAVITY IN SOMETHING** to form a concave area or cavity in something by removing contents **2.** *vti* **MAKE OR BECOME HOLLOWED** to make something hollow, or become hollow ○ *hollow out a pumpkin* ■ *adv* **HOLLOWLY** in a hollow way ○ *Their voices rang hollow in the emptied streets.* [Old English *holh* "hollow place, hole, cave," related to HOLE] —**hol·low·ly** *adv* —**hol·low·ness** *n*

CULTURAL NOTE ***The Hollow Men***, a poem (1925) by US-born British writer T. S. Eliot. One of Eliot's most pessimistic works, it depicts a barren, ghostly land peopled by soulless beings. Its imagery and concern with the sterility of modern civilization link it to "The Waste Land," but in "The Hollow Men" the message, conveyed in short lines and repetitive phrases, is more direct and bereft of any hope of redemption. The oft-quoted words "This is the way the world ends/ Not with a bang but a whimper" come from this poem.

hol·low·ware /hóllō wèr/ *n* articles of tableware and

kitchenware, e.g., bowls, cups, and pitchers that are hollow, as opposed to items such as plates and saucers

holly

hol·ly /hóllee/ (*plural* **-lies**) *n* **1.** an evergreen tree or bush with glossy, prickly leaves and bright red berries. Genus: *Ilex*. **2.** the leaves and berries of holly, used especially as a Christmas decoration [12C. Shortening of Old English *hole(g)n* < Germanic]

Hol·ly /hóllee/, **Buddy** (1938–59) US musician. His band, the Crickets, was one of the earliest rock-and-roll groups, and helped establish the standard lineup of two guitars, bass, and drums. His hit songs included "That'll Be the Day" and "Peggy Sue" (both 1957). He became a popular icon after his early death in a plane crash. Born **Holley, Charles Hardin**

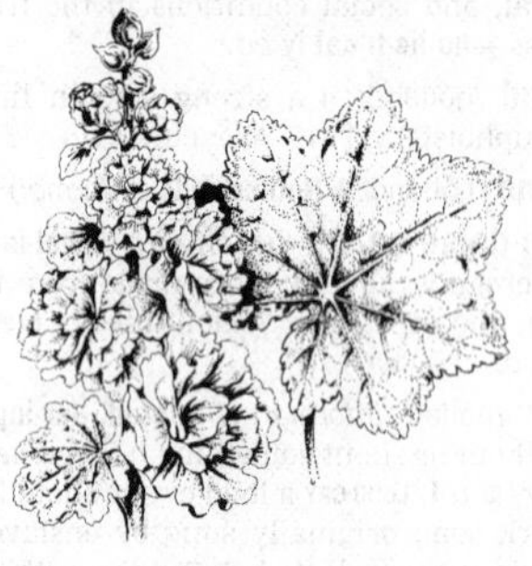

hollyhock

hol·ly·hock /hóllee hòk/ *n* a very tall flowering plant of the mallow family with hairy stems. Latin name: *Alcea rosea*. [13C. < alteration of HOLY + obsolete *hock* "mallow," origin ?]

hol·ly oak *n* TREES same as **holm oak** [Because its foliage resembles holly]

Hol·ly·wood[1] /hóllee wòòd/ *n* the US movie industry as a whole

Hol·ly·wood[2] /hóllee wòòd/ **1.** district of Los Angeles, California, a center of the US movie and television industry **2.** city in southeastern Florida, on the Atlantic Ocean, north of Miami. Population: 143,213 (2002 estimate).

holm[1] /hōm, hōlm/, **holme** *n* **1.** a piece of low-lying flat land next to a river or stream **2.** a small island in a river, lake, or estuary, or near the coastal mainland [Pre-12C. < Old Norse *holmr* "islet in a bay, meadow" < Indo-European, "be prominent"]

holm[2] /hōm/ *n* TREES same as **holm oak** [14C. Alteration of obsolete *hollin* < Old English *hole(g)n* (see HOLLY)]

holme *n* GEOG another spelling of **holm**[1]

Holmes /hōmz, hōlmz/, **Oliver Wendell** (1809–94) US physician and writer. He is best known for his essays collected in volumes including *The Autocrat of the Breakfast-Table* (1858). His poems "Old Ironsides" and "Chambered Nautilus" are considered classics of American literature.

> "Put not your trust in money, but put your money in trust."
> [Oliver Wendell Holmes, *The Autocrat of the Breakfast-Table*; 1858]

> "It is the province of knowledge to speak and it is the privilege of wisdom to listen."
> [Oliver Wendell Holmes, *The Poet at the Breakfast-Table*; 1872]

Holmes /hōmz/, **Oliver Wendell, Jr.** (1841–1935) associate justice of the US Supreme Court (1902–32). He was known for his liberal interpretations of the US Constitution. Known as **the Great Dissenter**

> "The life of the law has not been logic: it has been experience."
> [Oliver Wendell Holmes, Jr., *Common Law*; 1881]

> "The most stringent protection of free speech would not protect a man falsely shouting fire in a theater and causing a panic."
> [Oliver Wendell Holmes, Jr., *Schenck v. United States, 249 US 47*; 1919]

hol·mic /hṓlmik/ *adj* resembling or containing holmium

hol·mi·um /hṓlmee əm/ *n* a silvery white malleable metallic element of the rare-earth group. Source: gadolinite, monazite. Symbol **Ho**. See table at **element** [Late 19C. < *Holmia*, Latinized form of STOCKHOLM]

holm oak *n* a broad-leaved evergreen tree grown widely for ornament. Native to: southern Europe. Latin name: *Quercus ilex*. [< HOLM[2]]

holo- *prefix* whole, complete ○ *hologynic* [< Greek *holos* "whole, entire" < Indo-European]

hol·o·caust /hóllə kàwst, hṓlə-/ *n* **1.** DESTRUCTION OF HUMAN LIFE wholesale or mass destruction, especially of human life ○ *a nuclear holocaust* **2.** COMPLETE DESTRUCTION BY FIRE complete consumption by fire, especially of a large number of human beings or animals **3.** BURNT OFFERING a religious sacrifice that is totally consumed by fire [13C. < Old French *holocauste* < Greek *holokaustos* "burned whole" < *kaiein* "burn"]

ORIGIN ***Holocaust*** was originally used in English for a "burnt offering," a "sacrifice completely consumed by fire" (Mark 12:33, "more than all whole burnt offerings and sacrifices" in the King James Version of the Bible, was translated by William Tyndale in 1526 as "a greater thing than all holocausts and sacrifices"). John Milton is the first English writer recorded as using it in the wider sense "complete destruction by fire," in the late 17th century, and succeeding centuries its modern application to "nuclear destruction" and "mass murder" – Bishop Ken, for instance, wrote in 1711 "Should general Flame this World consume ... An Holocaust for Fontal Sin," and Leitch Ritchie in 1833 refers to Louis VII making "a holocaust of thirteen hundred persons in a church." The specific application to the mass murder of the Jews by the Nazis during World War II was introduced by historians during the 1950s, probably as an equivalent to Hebrew *ḥurban* and *shoah* "catastrophe" (used in the same sense).

Hol·o·caust *n* the systematic extermination of millions of European Jews, as well as Roma, Slavs, intellectuals, gay people, and political dissidents, by the Nazis and their allies during World War II. In popular usage, Holocaust refers particularly to the extermination of European Jews.

Hol·o·caust Day, **Hol·o·caust Me·mo·ri·al Day** *n* an annual commemoration of the Holocaust. Date: 27th of Nisan in many countries.

Hol·o·cene /hóllə sèen, hṓlə-/ *n* the present epoch of geologic time, which began 10,000 years ago. See table at **geologic time** [Late 19C. < French < Greek *holos* "whole" + *kainos* "new, recent"] —**Hol·o·cene** *adj*

hol·o·crine /hóllәkrin, -krīn, hṓlə-/ *adj* relating to a gland whose secretions are derived from the substance of the gland itself, e.g., a sebaceous gland

hol·o·en·zyme /hòllō én zīm, hòlō-/ *n* an active enzyme composed of a protein and coenzyme

hol·o·gram /hóllə gràm, hṓlə-/ *n* **1.** a three-dimensional image of an object that is a photographic record of light interference patterns produced using a photographic plate and light from a laser **2.** the image produced by a hologram

hol·o·graph[1] /hóllə gràf, hṓlə-/ *n* a document entirely handwritten by its author, especially a manuscript, letter, or unwitnessed will [Early 17C. Via late Latin < Greek *holographos* "written whole"] —**hol·o·graph** *adj*

ho·lo·graph[2] /hóllə gràf, hṓlə-/ *n* OPTICS same as **hologram**

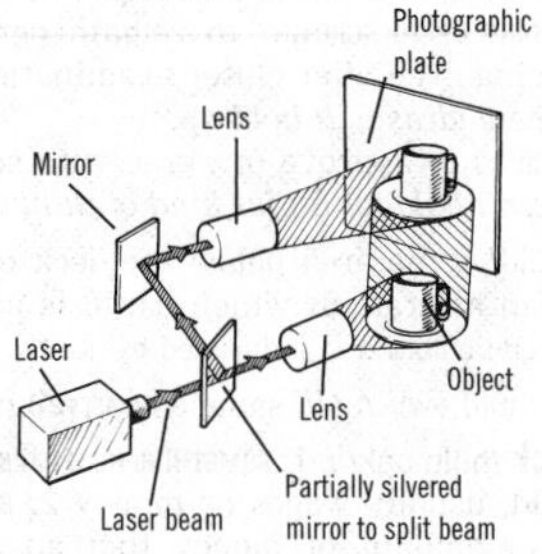

holography

ho·log·raph·y /hō lóggrəfee/ *n* a method of recording and showing a three-dimensional image of an object using a photographic plate and light from a laser —**hol·o·graph·ic** /hòllə gráffik, hòlə-/ *adj* —**ho·lo·graph·i·cal·ly** *adv*

hol·o·gyn·ic /hòllə jínnik, -gínik, hòlə-/ *adj* describes genetic traits that are inherited and passed on only by females [< HOLO- + Greek *gunē* "woman"]

hol·o·he·dral /hòllə hèedrəl, hòlə-/ *adj* describes crystals that have all the faces required for complete symmetry

ho·lo·ku /hṓlō kòò/ (*plural same*) *n* a floor-length Hawaiian dress with a train, closely fitted and without a waistline, worn on formal occasions and traditionally by brides [Late 19C. < Hawaiian]

hol·o·mor·phic /hòllə máwrfik, hòlə-/ *adj* CRYSTALS same as **holohedral** —**hol·o·mor·phism** *n*

ho·lo·mu'·u /hòlō mòò oo/ (*plural same*) *n* an ankle-length Hawaiian dress, closely fitted and without a waistline, often worn on formal occasions [< Hawaiian]

hol·o·phras·tic /hòllə frástik, hòlə-/ *adj* containing the idea of a sentence or phrase in one word, e.g., "goodbye" [Mid-19C. < HOLO- + Greek *phrastikos* < *phrazein* "tell"]

hol·o·phyte /hóllə fīt, hṓlə-/ *n* an organism that synthesizes complex organic molecules by photosynthesis

hol·o·phyt·ic /hòllə fíttik, hòlə-/ *adj* able to synthesize complex organic molecules by photosynthesis

hol·o·plank·ton /hòllə plángktən, hòlə-/ *n* organisms that remain free-swimming plankton throughout their life cycle

hol·o·thu·ri·an /hòllə thòòree ən, hòlə-/ *n* an invertebrate sea animal (**echinoderm**) of the class that includes the sea cucumber. Holothurians have a mouth surrounded by tentacles at one end, an anus at the other, and a body that contains calcitic material but is not rigid. Class: Holothuroidea. [Mid-19C. < modern Latin *Holothuria* < Latin *holothurion*, a sea creature] —**hol·o·thu·ri·an** *adj*

hol·o·type /hóllə tīp, hṓlə-/ *n* the individual organism used in naming and describing a new species and usually preserved afterward —**hol·o·typ·ic** /hòllə típpik, hòlə-/ *adj*

hol·o·zo·ic /hòllə zṓ ik, hòlə-/ *adj* obtaining nutrition from other organisms or organic matter, as most animals do

hols /holz/ *n UK* holidays, especially school vacations or somebody's main annual vacation (*informal*) ○ *during the hols* [Early 20C. Contraction of *holidays*]

Holst /hōlst/, **Gustav** (1874–1934) British composer. He is best remembered for his popular orchestral suite *The Planets* (1914–16). Full name **Holst, Gustav Theodore**

> "Never compose anything unless the not composing of it becomes a positive nuisance to you."
> [Gustav Holst, *Letter to W. G. Whittaker*; 1921]

Hol·stein /hṓl stīn, -stèen/, **Hol·stein-Frie·sian** *n* a large black-and-white dairy cow belonging to a breed known for its abundant milk production [Mid-19C. After a region, formerly of the Netherlands, now of N Germany]

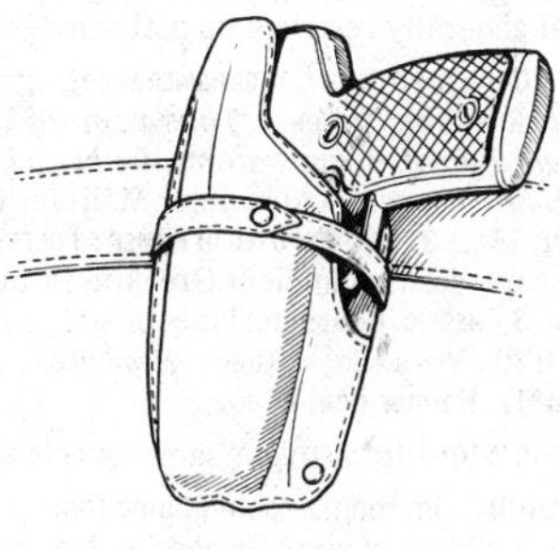

holster

hol·ster /hṓlstər/ *n* a holder for a pistol, usually worn on the hip or shoulder [Mid-17C. Probably < Dutch < Indo-European, "to cover"] —**hol·ster** *vt* —**hol·stered** *adj*

ho·lus-bo·lus /hṓləss bṓləss/ *adv Can* all at once or all together [Mid-19C. Origin ?]

ho·ly /hṓlee/ *adj* (**-li·er, -li·est**) **1. CONSECRATED** dedicated or set apart for religious purposes ○ *holy water* ○ *Native American holy ground* **2. SAINTLY** devoted to the service of God, a god, or a goddess ○ *a holy man* **3. SACRED** relating to, belonging to, or coming from a divine being or power ○ *holy relics* **4. AWE-INSPIRING** having a character that evokes reverence ○ *Arlington National Cemetery is a holy place for many people of the United States.* **5. USED IN EXPRESSIONS OF SURPRISE** used in various expressions to show surprise (*informal*) ○ *Holy mackerel!* ■ *n* (*plural* **-lies**) **1. HOLY THING** something sanctified or venerated **2. HOLY PERSON** a devoutly religious or saintly person [Old English *hālig* < Germanic] —**ho·li·ly** *adv*

Ho·ly Al·li·ance *n* an alliance between Russia, Prussia, and Austria in 1815 advocating government according to Christian principles

Ho·ly Ark *n* JUDAISM same as **ark** (sense 2)

Ho·ly Bi·ble *n* CHR same as **Bible** (sense 1)

Ho·ly Cit·y *n* **1.** Jerusalem as a city of great religious significance **2.** heaven in Christian tradition

Ho·ly Com·mu·nion *n* CHR same as **Communion** (senses 1, 3)

ho·ly cow *interj* used to express surprise or annoyance

Ho·ly Cross *n* in Christianity, the cross that Jesus Christ died on

ho·ly day *n* a day set aside for the celebration of a religious festival

ho·ly day of ob·li·ga·tion *n* a Roman Catholic festival during which Catholics are required to attend Mass and abstain from some types of work

Ho·ly Fam·i·ly *n* in Christianity, the young Jesus Christ, his mother Mary, and Mary's husband Joseph, especially as represented in art

Ho·ly Fa·ther *n* in the Roman Catholic Church, the pope

Ho·ly Ghost *n* CHR same as **Holy Spirit**

ho·ly grail *n* same as **grail**

Ho·ly Grail *n* CHR same as **Grail**

Hol·y·head /hóllee hèd/ seaport and resort on the northern coast of Holy Island, northwestern Wales. Population: 11,796 (1991).

Ho·ly In·no·cents' Day *n* in the Christian church, the day that commemorates the order given by Herod to massacre all baby boys in Bethlehem. December 28.

Ho·ly Is·land /hṓlee-/ ➧ **Lindisfarne**

Ho·ly Joe *n* (*dated slang*) **1. ARMED FORCES CHAPLAIN** a chaplain in the armed forces **2. CLERIC** a priest or other cleric **3. SOMEBODY SANCTIMONIOUS** a sanctimonious or self-righteous person

Ho·ly Land region on the eastern shore of the Mediterranean Sea, comprising the historic region of Palestine. It is regarded as holy by Christians, Jews, and Muslims.

Ho·ly Of·fice *n* **1.** a permanent committee of the Roman Catholic College of Cardinals that deals with doctrine and morals **2.** HIST same as **Inquisition**

ho·ly of ho·lies *n* **1.** the innermost chamber in the Jewish Temple in Jerusalem, where the Ark of the Covenant was kept **2.** a place considered to be especially sacred

Hol·yoke /hṓl yṑk, hṓlee ṑk, hóy ṑk/ manufacturing city in southwestern Massachusetts, on the Connecticut River. Population: 39,869 (2002 estimate).

ho·ly or·ders *npl* **1. RITE OF CHRISTIAN ORDINATION** in the Christian church, the rite or sacrament of ordination as a minister or priest **2. CHRISTIAN CLERICAL RANK** the rank or position of a Christian minister or priest **3. ROMAN CATHOLIC OR ANGLICAN RANKS** in the Roman Catholic Church, the ranks of priest, deacon, and subdeacon, or in the Anglican Church, the ranks of bishop, priest, and deacon

Ho·ly Roll·er *n* an offensive term for a member of a Christian group that worships in what is perceived to be an ecstatic or frenzied way, with shouting, bodily movements, and trances (*slang*) [< the movement of the body during worship]

Ho·ly Ro·man Em·pire *n* an empire in Germany and northern Italy from 800 to 1806, initially a revival of the Western Roman Empire. It became confined to Germany, and the emperor's authority was negligible after 1254. From 1438 the imperial crown was held almost continuously by the Hapsburg family. —**Ho·ly Ro·man Em·per·or** *n*

Ho·ly Sat·ur·day *n* in Christianity, the Saturday preceding Easter Sunday

Ho·ly Scrip·ture *n* all or part of the Christian Bible

Ho·ly See *n* **1.** in the Roman Catholic Church, the see of the pope as Bishop of Rome **2.** in the Roman Catholic Church, the government departments, jurisdiction, and authority of the Vatican

Ho·ly Sep·ul·chre *n* in Christianity, the tomb in which the body of Jesus Christ was laid after the Crucifixion

ho·ly smoke *interj* used to express surprise or annoyance

Ho·ly Spir·it *n* in Christianity, the third person of the Trinity, understood as the spiritual force of God

ho·ly·stone /hṓlee stṑn/ *n* a piece of soft sandstone used for scouring the decks of ships [Origin ?] —**ho·ly·stone** *vt*

Ho·ly Syn·od *n* the governing body of any of the Eastern Orthodox Christian churches

Ho·ly Thurs·day *n* **1.** in the Roman Catholic Church, Maundy Thursday, the Thursday before Easter, commemorating the Last Supper and the day before Jesus Christ was crucified **2.** in the Anglican Church, Ascension Day, the 40th day after Easter

Ho·ly Trin·i·ty *n* CHR same as **Trinity** (sense 1)

ho·ly war *n* a war undertaken in the name of a religion

ho·ly wa·ter *n* in Christianity, water that has been blessed by a priest and is used in a church for blessings, baptisms, and other holy rituals

Ho·ly Week *n* in the Christian calendar, the final week of Lent, beginning on Palm Sunday and including Maundy Thursday, Good Friday, and Holy Saturday

Ho·ly Writ *n* sacred Christian writings, especially the Bible

Ho·ly Year *n* in the Roman Catholic Church, a period of remission from sin declared by the pope with some conditions attached, usually at 25-year intervals

hom- *prefix* same as **homo-** (*used before vowels*)

hom·age /hómmij, ómmij/ *n* **1.** a show of reverence and respect toward somebody **2.** allegiance or a formal public acknowledgment of allegiance on the part of a vassal toward a feudal lord [13C. < Old French]

hom·bre /óm bràу, ómbree/ *n* (*informal*) **1.** same as **man** *n* (sense 1) **2.** a macho or very strong, tough, and masculine man [Mid-19C. Via Spanish < Latin *homo* "human being"]

hom·burg /hóm bùrg/ *n* a man's felt hat with an upturned brim and a lengthwise crease in the crown [Late 19C. After *Homburg*, town in W Germany]

home /hōm/ *n* **1.** ⚠ **RESIDENCE** the place where a person, family, or household lives ○ *invited them home* **2. FAMILY GROUP** a family or any other group that lives together ○ *Theirs was a happy home, full of love.* **3. BIRTHPLACE** the place where somebody was born or raised or feels that he or she belongs ○ *Home is New York.* **4. NATIVE HABITAT** the place where an animal is most common or indigenous ○ *home to the grizzly bear* **5. PLACE OF ORIGIN OF SOMETHING** the place where something originated or is based ○ *the home of basketball* ○ *home to the state university* **6. HEADQUARTERS** the headquarters or main place of operations of an organization, especially a sports team ○ *The team plays at home this weekend.* **7. SAFE PLACE** a place where a person or animal can find refuge and safety or live in security **8. PLACE OF ASSISTANCE** an establishment where somebody who is in need of care, rest, or medical attention can stay or find help ○ *My grandmother moved into a home.* **9.** COMPUT same as **homepage** **10.** COMPUT **STARTING POINT OF CURSOR** the starting position of a cursor in an application or text **11.** SPORTS **GOAL** in many games, the place or point that must be hit in order to score or reached in order to be safe from attack **12.** BASEBALL same as **home plate** ■ *adj* **1. DOMESTIC** relating to somebody's own home or country ○ *home cooking* **2. OF HOUSEHOLD** for, belonging to, or produced in a dwelling or household ○ *home life* **3. NATIVE** happening in or coming from somebody's native territory or permanent base, especially a sports team's own ground ○ *home news* ○ *a home game* **4. EFFECTIVE** to the point or central to achieving a goal **5. PRINCIPAL** relating to or belonging to the headquarters of a business or enterprise ○ *received a directive from home office* **6.** BASEBALL **INVOLVING HOME PLATE** in baseball, occurring at or near home plate ■ *adv* **1. AT OR TO SOMEBODY'S HOME** at or to the house, household, or country where somebody lives ○ *He desperately wanted to get home.* **2. EFFECTIVELY** to the point or to a desired goal ○ *criticism that hit home* **3. TO CENTER** to the center or heart of something or as far as possible into a desired position ○ *drove the nail home* ■ *v* (**homed, hom·ing, homes**) **1.** *vi* **GO HOME** to go back to the house, household, or country where you live **2.** *vi* **RETURN TO BASE** to return home, especially to fly home accurately (*refers to animals and birds*) **3.** *vi* **DWELL** to have a home and live in it (*dated*) **4.** *vt* **DIRECT SOMEBODY OR SOMETHING HOME** to take or send somebody or something home (*dated*) **5.** *vt* **PROVIDE SOMEBODY OR SOMETHING WITH HOME** to give a home to somebody or something [Old English *hām* < Germanic] —**home·like** *adj* ◇ **at home** **1.** at ease or in a familiar and friendly place **2.** having knowledge of or familiarity with a subject or activity ◇ **come** *or* **be brought home to somebody** to be fully understood and appreciated by somebody ◇ **home alone** left alone in a house or apartment when supervision or companionship is required or desired (*informal*) ◇ **home free** with something successfully completed ◇ **take home something** to earn a particular amount of money after all deductions, e.g., for tax, have been made

USAGE home or **house**? Many consider ***home*** an affectation when used anywhere that ***house*** would be appropriate, as in *Home for Sale.* **Home** is nonetheless useful to express the idea of dwelling places of various sorts, including apartments and condominiums, hogans and huts, and other dwellings that are not accurately described as houses; it can also add a connotation of warmth and security when appropriate. ***House***, in many contexts, suggests a single-family dwelling. For example, if *The tornado destroyed 17 homes* is meant to convey that 17 residential structures were demolished, the word should have been ***houses***. *Most homes in town lost electricity*, however, no doubt refers to households of all descriptions, so here ***homes*** is the better choice.

home in on *vt* **1.** to locate and proceed straight toward a particular target **2.** to direct all attention or energy toward something ○ *homing in on the classified ads*

USAGE See ***hone***[1].

Home (of the Hir·sel) /hyoom əv thə húrss'l/, **Sir Alec Douglas-Home, Baron** ➧ **Douglas-Home, Sir Alec**

home bank·ing *n* an electronic banking system that allows a customer to conduct transactions at home

home base *n* **1.** BASEBALL same as **home plate** **2.** the administrative center from which operations or activities are directed

home·bod·y /hṓm bòddee/ (*plural* **-ies**) *n* somebody who prefers home to other places (*informal*)

home·bound /hṓm bównd/ *adj* **1.** confined to the home, usually because of illness, age, or inability to travel **2.** moving or traveling toward home

home·boy /hṓm bòy/ *n* a man or boy from somebody's home town, state, or neighborhood, especially somebody who shares that person's own culture and customs (*slang*)

home·bred /hṑm bréd/ *adj* **1.** bred or raised at home **2.** lacking worldly experience

home·brew /hṓm bro͞o/ *n* an alcoholic beverage, especially beer, that has been brewed at home for personal consumption —**home·brewed** *adj*

home·build·er /hṓm bìldər/ *n* a builder or designer of houses —**home·build·ing** *n*

home·buy·er /hṓm bī ər/ *n* somebody who is buying or is interested in buying a house or apartment

home care *n* HEALTH SERVICES same as **home healthcare**

home·com·ing /hṓm kùmming/ *n* **1.** the annual return to somebody's old school or college, usually at a prescribed time of year, for celebrations with other alumni **2.** the arrival home of somebody who has been away ○ *an emotional homecoming*

home ec·o·nom·ics *n* the science or study of diet, cookery, sewing, childcare, and other subjects related to the running of a home, as taught in schools (*takes a singular or plural verb*)

home eq·ui·ty loan *n* a loan by which the borrower's home is used as collateral, usually secondary to a first mortgage

home fries *npl* boiled sliced potatoes fried in butter or oil, sometimes with onions and seasonings

home front *n* **1.** the civilian effort and activity at home in support of a war waged overseas ○ *On the home front, factories went into 24-hour production.* **2.** somebody's life at home

home fur·nish·ings *npl* articles that decorate a house and make it more comfortable, e.g., furniture, lighting, and carpets

home·girl /hṓm gùrl/ *n* a girl or woman from somebody's home town, state, or neighborhood, especially one who shares that person's own culture and customs (*slang*)

home ground *n* **1.** surroundings that are familiar to somebody ○ *They're performing here on home ground before starting their tour.* **2.** an area of knowledge or a situation that somebody is familiar with and feels confident about ○ *was back on home ground when the discussion returned to politics*

home·grown /hṓm grṓn/ *adj* **1.** grown in somebody's own garden or on somebody's own land **2.** produced by or coming from a specific area or region ○ *homegrown talent*

home health aide *n* a healthcare worker who gives assistance to a sick or physically challenged person in the person's home

home health·care *n* US care provided at home by family members or professional caregivers for people who otherwise might require institutional care

home im·prove·ment *n* **1.** a change or addition made to a house or apartment that improves living conditions and increases its market value, or the making of such changes or additions **2.** the act of making home improvements

home·land /hṓm lànd/ *n* **1.** the country where somebody was born or where somebody lives and feels that he or she belongs **2.** in South Africa during the apartheid era, a partially self-governing region created and set aside for the Black population

home lan·guage *n* **1.** LANG same as **native tongue 2.** the language spoken regularly or most often in the home by the people living there

home·less /hṓmləss/ *adj* having no home of any kind ■ *npl* people without a home of any kind —**home·less·ness** *n*

home·ly /hṓmlee/ (**-li·er, -li·est**) *adj* **1.** NOT GOOD-LOOKING plain or less than pleasing in appearance ○ *a homely face* **2.** COZY simple, comfortable, and unpretentious **3.** UNPRETENTIOUS IN MANNER having a simple, unpretentious, and warm-hearted manner —**home·li·ness** *n*

SYNONYMS See ***unattractive***.

home·made /hṓm màyd/ *adj* **1.** made at home using traditional methods, instead of by a manufacturer ○ *homemade jam* **2.** roughly or crudely constructed to perform a specific function or purpose

home·mak·er /hṓm màykər/ *n* somebody who manages a household, especially his or her own home, as a primary job

home mov·ie *n* an amateur movie recording everyday events or a special occasion in somebody's life, e.g., a family vacation

homeo- *prefix* similar, alike ○ *homeotherm* [< Greek *homoios* "similar" < *homos* (see HOMO-)]

ho·me·o·box /hṓmee ō bòks/ *n* a short section of nucleotides with a base sequence that is almost identical in all genes that contain it

ho·me·op·a·thy /hṑmee óppəthee/ *n* a complementary disease-treatment system in which a patient is given minute doses of natural substances that in larger doses would produce symptoms of the disease itself —**ho·me·o·path** /hṓmee ə pàth/ *n* —**ho·me·o·path·ic** /hṑmee ə páthik/ *adj* —**ho·me·o·path·i·cal·ly** *adv* —**ho·me·op·a·thist** *n*

USAGE ***Homeopathic*** is sometimes used in a general way to refer to treatments for health when *herbal* or *natural* would be more appropriate.

ho·me·o·sta·sis /hṑmee ō stáyssiss/ *n* a state of equilibrium or a tendency to reach equilibrium, either metabolically within a cell or organism or socially and psychologically within an individual or group —**ho·me·o·stat·ic** /-státtik/ *adj*

ho·me·o·therm /hṓmee ə thùrm/, **ho·moi·o·therm** /hō móyə thùrm/ *n* an organism whose stable body temperature is generally independent of the temperature of its surrounding environment [Late 19C. < HOMEO- + Greek *thermē* "heat"] —**ho·me·o·therm·ic** /hṑmee ō thúrmik/ *adj* —**ho·me·o·therm·y** *n*

ho·me·o·tic /hṑmee óttik/ *adj* describes mutation in which one part or organ is transformed into another part associated with a different segment of the organism [Late 19C. < Greek *homoiōtikos* "becoming like" < *homoios* (see HOMEO-)]

home·own·er /hṓm ōnər/ *n* somebody who owns a home

home·page /hṓm pàyj/ *n* **1.** the opening page of an Internet website **2.** somebody's personal website on the Internet, often containing personal data, photographs, or contact information

home plate *n* in baseball, a flat slab marking the area over which a pitcher must throw the ball for a strike and on which a base runner must land in order to score

home port *n* the place of registry or regular base of a ship

home·port (**home·port·ed, home·port·ing, home·ports**) *vt* to base a vessel at a particular port

hom·er /hṓmər/ *n* **1.** BASEBALL same as **home run** (*informal*) **2.** ELECTRONICS a device that provides signals for guiding missiles, ships, or aircraft to their destinations **3.** BIRDS same as **homing pigeon** (*informal*) ■ *vi* (**-ered, -er·ing, -ers**) BASEBALL in baseball, to score a home run (*slang*) ○ *He homered in the last seconds of the third inning.*

Ho·mer /hṓmər/ city in southern Alaska, on the southeastern shore of Cook Inlet. Population: 4,181 (2002 estimate).

Ho·mer (*fl* 8th century B.C.) Greek poet. He is credited as the author of the *Iliad* and the *Odyssey*. See Cultural note at **odyssey**

"Hunger is insolent, and will be fed."
[Homer, *Odyssey*; Late 8th century B.C.]

Ho·mer, Winslow (1836–1910) US artist. He is best known for his use of light and color in his watercolor seascapes and landscapes such as *Gulf Stream* (1899).

home range *n* the geographic area to which an animal generally restricts its activities

Ho·mer·ic /hō mérrik/ *adj* **1.** OF HOMER relating to Homer, his work, or his times ○ *"Thus vain and false are the mere human surmises and doubts which clash with Homeric writ!"* (Alexander William Kinglake, *Eothen*; 1844) **2.** OF GREEK USED IN HOMER'S POETRY relating to the early form of ancient Greek used in Homer's poetry **3.** HEROIC characteristic of a hero (*literary*) [Early 17C. Via Latin < Greek *Homērikos* < *Homēros* "Homer"] —**Ho·mer·i·cal·ly** *adv*

Ho·mer·ic sim·i·le *n* LITERAT same as **epic simile**

home·room /hṓm ro͝om, -ro͞om/, **home room** *n* the room to which a class of secondary-school students must report at specific times each day

home rule *n* the principle or practice of self-government by a part of a larger country or commonwealth such as a municipality, colony, territory, or principality

home run *n* in baseball, a hit that allows a player to make a circuit of all four bases and score a run, usually by hitting the ball out of the playing area

home·school /hṓm sko͞ol/ *vti* (**-schooled, -school·ing, -schools**) to teach somebody at home, or be taught at home rather than in the public school system ○ *She's homeschooling her boys from K through 12.* ■ *n* a school run usually by parents in the home for their children, using an approved curriculum

home·school·er /hṓm sko͞olər/ *n* **1.** a child who is undergoing or has undergone private education, typically by the parents at home rather than in the public schools **2.** a parent who educates his or her child or children at home rather than in the public school system

home shop·ping *n* shopping done electronically from home either through an online retail service or a television shopping channel

home·sick /hṓm sìk/ *adj* feeling sadness and longing to be at home with family and friends when away from them —**home·sick·ness** *n*

home·site /hṓm sīt/ *n* a plot of land on which a new home can be or is constructed

home·spun /hṓm spùn/ *adj* **1.** PLAIN AND SIMPLE plain, simple, and unpretentious ○ *inspired us with his homespun wisdom* **2.** HANDICRAFT MADE BY HAND AT HOME spun or woven by hand at home ○ *homespun cotton* **3.** CLOTHING, HOUSEHOLD MADE OF HOMESPUN FABRIC made of fabric spun or woven by hand at home ○ *a homespun shirt* ■ *n* TEXTILES **1.** CLOTH FROM HOMESPUN THREAD a coarse plain, usually woolen or linen, cloth woven from homespun thread **2.** ROUGH CLOTH WOVEN ON POWER LOOM a cloth similar to homespun, but woven on an automatic or electric loom

home stand *n* a series of games played on a sports team's home field, especially in baseball

home·stay /hṓm stày/ *n* a visit to somebody's home in a foreign country, often a stay by an exchange student in a family's home (*informal*)

home·stead /hṓm stèd/ *n* **1.** HOUSE, OUTBUILDINGS, AND LAND a house, especially a farmhouse, with its dependent buildings and land, considered as a whole **2.** HIST LAND CLAIMED BY SETTLER formerly, a piece of land occupied by a settler or squatter under the terms of the US Homestead Act or the Canadian Dominion Lands Act **3.** LAW RESIDENCE EXEMPT FROM FORCED SALE a house, adjoining land, and buildings declared as the owner's fixed residence and therefore exempt from seizure and forced sale for the recovery of debts ■ *vi* (**-stead·ed, -stead·ing, -steads**) CLAIM AND WORK FARMLAND to settle and farm land, especially under the terms of the Homestead Act —**home·stead·er** *n*

Home·stead /hṓm stèd/ city in southeastern Florida, southwest of Miami. Population: 33,727 (2002 estimate).

Home·stead Act *n* **1.** an act passed by the US Congress in 1862, promising ownership of 160 acres of public land to a citizen who lived on and cultivated it for five years **2.** the Dominion Lands Act, passed by the Canadian Parliament in 1872, and modeled after the US Homestead Act of 1862

home·stead law *n* a law granting homesteaders privileges such as exemption from having their property sold to recover debts

home straight *n UK* HORSERACING same as **home stretch**

home stretch *n* **1.** the part of a racecourse between the last turn and the finish line **2.** the last part of a trip, task, or operation

home·style /hṓm stīl/, **home-style** *adj* made or presented as in somebody's home ○ *were served a home-style meal in the inn* —**home·style** *adv*

home teach·er *n UK* EDUC same as **visiting teacher**

home·town /hṓm tòwn/ *n* the town or city where somebody was born or raised

home truth *n* an unpleasant but true basic fact about somebody's character or behavior

home truths *npl* true statements that are unpleasant or upsetting to the person they concern

ho·metz *n* JUDAISM same as **chametz**

home vid·e·o *n* a video recording produced at home, often a recording of family celebrations or events

home·ward /hṓmwərd/ *adj* going home or in the direction of home ■ *adv also* **home·wards** /-wərdz/ toward or in the direction of home ○ *homeward bound*

Home·wood /hṓm wŏŏd/ **1.** city in northern Alabama, a southeastern suburb of Birmingham. Population: 24,872 (2002 estimate). **2.** town in northeastern Illinois, a southern suburb of Chicago. Population: 19,540 (2002 estimate).

home·work /hṓm wùrk/ *n* **1.** SCHOOLWORK DONE AT HOME schoolwork that students do outside of class or after school at home **2.** PREPARATORY WORK preliminary research and study about a particular subject, especially in preparation for writing or talking about it (*informal*) **3.** PAID WORK DONE AT HOME work done at home for money, especially piecework —**home·work·er** *n* —**home·work·ing** *n* ◇ **do your homework** to do all the necessary research and preparation for something in a thorough manner

hom·ey[1] /hṓmee/ (**-i·er, -i·est**), **hom·y** *adj* feeling as comfortable and familiar as somebody's own home ○ *a homey little hotel* [Mid-19C. < HOME] —**hom·ey·ness** *n*

hom·ey[2] /hṓmee/, **hom·ie** *n* same as **homeboy, homegirl** (*slang*) [Late 20C. Shortening and alteration]

hom·i·cid·al /hòmmi sī́d'l/ *adj* capable of or intending to kill another human being unlawfully —**hom·i·cid·al·ly** *adv*

hom·i·cide /hómmi sīd/ *n* **1.** the act or an instance of unlawfully killing another human being **2.** somebody who kills another human being unlawfully [13C. Via French < Latin *homicidium, homicida* < *homo* "human being" + *caedere* "kill"]

hom·i·cide bomb·er *n* somebody, often a suicide bomber, who uses a bomb to attack others with the intention of killing them —**hom·i·cide bomb·ing** *n*

hom·i·let·ic /hòmmə léttik/, **hom·i·let·i·cal** /-léttik'l/ *adj* **1.** relating to, or in the style of, a sermon or homily **2.** relating to the art of writing and preaching sermons [Mid-17C. Via late Latin < Greek *homilētikos* < *homilein* "associate with, converse" < *homilos* "crowd"]

hom·i·let·ics /hòmmə léttiks/ *n* the art of writing and preaching sermons (*takes a singular verb*)

hom·i·ly /hómməlee/ (*plural* **-lies**) *n* **1.** RELIGIOUS LECTURE a sermon or other piece of writing on a moral or religious topic **2.** MORALIZING SPEECH a speech or other piece of writing with a moralizing theme (*disapproving*) **3.** CHR TALK BASED ON BIBLICAL PASSAGE in the Roman Catholic Church, an address based on the scriptures of the day **4.** SHORT SAYING a short inspirational saying ○ *a calendar that gives a little homily for each day* [14C. Via French < Greek *homilia* "sermon" < *homilos* "crowd"] —**hom·i·list** *n*

hom·ing /hṓming/ *adj* **1.** relating to or possessing the ability to find the way home after traveling a long distance **2.** describes a missile or aircraft that has equipment that enables it to guide itself to its target

hom·ing guid·ance *n* a system that enables a missile or aircraft to guide itself to its target

hom·ing pi·geon *n* a domestic pigeon that is trained to return to its roost, used for racing

hom·i·nid /hómmənid/ *n* a primate belonging to a family of which the modern human being is the only species still in existence. Family: Hominidae. [Late 19C. < modern Latin *Hominidae* < Latin *homin-*, stem of Latin *homo* "human being"] —**hom·i·nid** *adj*

hom·i·ni·za·tion /hòmməni záysh'n/ *n* the theorized evolutionary development of human characteristics that set hominids apart from other primates [Mid-20C. < French *hominisation* < Latin *homin-* (see HOMINID)]

hom·i·noid /hómmə nòyd/ *adj* **1.** resembling a human being **2.** relating to or belonging to the superfamily that includes human beings and apes. Superfamily: Hominoidea. [Early 20C. < Latin *homin-* (see HOMINID)]

hom·i·ny /hómmənee/ *n* dried and puffed whole kernels of corn that are eaten boiled, especially in the Southwestern dish known as "posole" [Early 17C. Contraction of Virginia Algonquian *uskatahomen*, "that which is ground"]

hom·i·ny grits *n* FOOD same as **grits**

hom·mos *n* FOOD another spelling of **hummus**

ho·mo /hṓmō/ (*plural* **-mos**) *n* an offensive term for a gay man (*dated slang insult*) [Early 20C. Shortening]

homo- *prefix* alike, same ○ *homograph* [< Greek *homos* < Indo-European, "one"]

ho·mo·cen·tric /hōmə séntrik/ *adj* describes circles and spheres that have the same center

ho·mo·cer·cal /hōmə súrk'l, hòmmə-/ *adj* describes a fish that has a tail with two symmetrical lobes that extend beyond the end of the vertebral column, or a tail of this kind

ho·mo·chro·mat·ic /hōmə krō máttik, hòmmə-/ *adj* COLORS same as **monochromatic** (sense 1)

ho·mo·chro·mous /hōmə krṓməss, hòmmə-/ *adj* being of just one color [Mid-19C. < HOMO- + Greek *khrōma* "color"]

ho·mo·cy·clic /hōmə sī́klik, -síklik, hòmə-/ *adj* describes a chemical compound in which molecules take the form of a ring in which all the atoms are the same

ho·mo·cys·teine /hōmə síss teen/ *n* an amino acid found in animals and humans that is involved in cell metabolism and the manufacture of proteins. High concentrations are implicated in heart disease.

ho·mo·dont /hṓmə dònt/ *adj* used to describe vertebrates that have teeth that are all similar in shape, as in most nonmammalian vertebrates [Late 19C. < HOMO- + Greek *odont-* "tooth"]

homoeo- *prefix UK* another spelling of **homeo-**

Ho·mo e·rec·tus /hōmō i réktəss/ *n* an extinct ancestor of the modern human being (**Homo sapiens**) living approximately 1.5 million years ago and known by fossils to have had an upright stature, a smallish brain, and a low forehead [< modern Latin, "upright man"]

ho·mo·e·rot·ic /hōmō i róttik/ *adj* relating to or characterized by eroticism that is focused on or inspired by people of the same sex

ho·mo·e·rot·i·cism /hōmō i rótti sìzzəm/, **ho·mo·er·o·tism** /hōmō érrə tìzzəm/ *n* eroticism that is focused on or inspired by people of the same sex

ho·mo·ga·met·ic /hōmō gə méttik/ *adj* producing gametes that have the same type of sex chromosome

ho·mog·a·my /hō móggəmee, ho-/ *n* the condition of a flower in which male and female organs mature at the same time

ho·mog·e·nate /hō mójjə nàyt, hə-/ *n* a substance produced by homogenizing

ho·mo·ge·ne·i·ty /hōmə jə née ətee, -náy-, hòmmə-/ *n* **1.** the quality of being of the same or a similar nature **2.** the quality of having a uniform appearance or composition [Early 17C. < medieval Latin *homogeneitas* < *homogeneus* (see HOMOGENEOUS)]

ho·mo·ge·ne·ous /hōmə jeenee əss, hòmmə-/, **ho·mog·e·nous** /hə mójjənəss, hō-/ *adj* **1.** having the same kind of constituent elements, or being similar in nature ○ *a relatively small, culturally homogeneous community* **2.** having a uniform composition or structure [Mid-17C. < medieval Latin *homogeneus* < Greek *homogenēs* "of the same kind"] —**ho·mo·ge·ne·ous·ly** *adv* —**ho·mo·ge·ne·ous·ness** *n*

ho·mog·e·nize /hə mójjə nīz, hō-/ (**-nized, -niz·ing, -niz·es**) *v* **1.** *vt* to emulsify the fat particles in milk or cream in order to give it an even consistency and prevent cream from separating from the rest of the milk **2.** *vti* to become homogeneous, or cause something to become homogeneous [Late 19C. < HOMOGENEOUS] —**ho·mog·e·ni·za·tion** /hə mòjjəni záysh'n, hō-/ *n* —**ho·mog·e·niz·er** *n*

ho·mog·e·nous *adj* another spelling of **homogeneous**

ho·mog·e·ny /hə mójjənee, hō-/ *n* a similarity in individuals, organs, or parts caused by a common ancestry

ho·mo·graft /hómmə gràft, hṓmə-/ *n* same as **allograft**

hom·o·graph /hómmə gràf, hṓmə-/ *n* a word that is spelled in the same way as one or more other words but is different in meaning, e.g., the verb "project" and the noun "project" —**hom·o·graph·ic** /hòmmə gráffik, hōmə-/ *adj*

Ho·mo hab·i·lis /hōmō hábbiliss/ *n* an extinct ancestor of the modern human being (**Homo sapiens**) living approximately 1.5 million years ago and characterized by its ability to make and use tools [< modern Latin, "skillful man"]

homoio- *prefix* another spelling of **homeo-**

ho·moi·o·therm *n* ZOOL another spelling of **homeotherm**

Ho·moi·ou·si·an /hō moy óossee ən, -óozee-/ *n* a Christian who believes that Jesus Christ is of a similar, but not identical, substance to God ■ *adj* relating to the doctrine of the Homoiousians [Late 17C. < Greek *homoiousios* "of similar substance" < *homoios* "similar" + *ousia* "substance"] —**Ho·moi·ou·si·an·ism** *n*

hom·o·log *n* BIOL, CHEM another spelling of **homologue**

ho·mol·o·gate /hə móllə gàyt, hō-/ (**-gat·ed, -gat·ing, -gates**) *v* **1.** *vti* LAW to confirm or sanction the validity of something **2.** *vt* to give official recognition to a prototype car or car component, thus allowing it to be used in a race [Early 16C. < medieval Latin *homologat-*, past participle of *homologare* "agree" < Greek *homologos* "agreeing" (see HOMOLOGOUS)]

ho·mo·log·i·cal /hōmə lójjik'l, hòmmə-/ *adj* SCI same as **homologous** —**ho·mo·log·i·cal·ly** *adv*

ho·mol·o·gize /hə móllə jīz, hō-/ (**-gized, -giz·ing, -giz·es**) *vt* to make something have a similar or related structure, position, function, or value to something else —**ho·mol·o·giz·er** *n*

ho·mol·o·gous /hə mólləgəss, hō-/ *adj* **1.** SIMILAR sharing a similar or related structure, position, function, or value **2.** BIOL HAVING SAME ORIGIN BUT DIFFERENT FUNCTION describes biological structures such as the wing of a bird and the fin of a fish that share the same origin but have a different function **3.** CHEM OF RELATED CHEMICAL COMPOUNDS relating to a series of organic chemical compounds such as a methylene group, each of which differs from the preceding by the addition of a constant component **4.** MED HAVING IDENTICAL TISSUE produced from identical tissue [Mid-17C. < medieval Latin *homologus* < Greek *homologos* "agreeing" < *homos* "same" + *legein* "speak"]

hom·o·lo·graph·ic /hòmmələ gráffik/ *adj* MAPS same as **equal-area** [Mid-19C. Alteration (after HOMO-) of *homalographic* < Greek *homalos* "even, level"]

hom·o·logue /hómmə lòg, hṓmə-/, **hom·o·log** *n* **1.** a part or organ that has the same evolutionary origin as another but differs in function, e.g., a bird's wing in relation to the fin of a fish **2.** a homologous chemical compound [Mid-19C. < French < Greek *homologos* "agreeing" (see HOMOLOGOUS)]

ho·mol·o·gy /hə mólləjee, hō-/ *n* **1.** similar characteristics in two animals that are a product of descent from a common ancestor rather than a product of a similar environment **2.** the correspondence between chemical compounds in a homologous series [Early 17C. Via late Latin < Greek *homologia* "agreement" < *homologos* (see HOMOLOGOUS)]

ho·mol·o·sine pro·jec·tion /hō mòllə sīn-/ *n* a map of the Earth's surface that distorts the oceans in order to represent the continents with a minimum of distortion [< HOMOLOGRAPHIC + SINE, because it is a homolographic projection based on sinusoidal curves]

ho·mol·y·sis /hō mólləssiss/ *n* the breakdown of a molecule into neutral atoms or radicals —**ho·mo·lyt·ic** /hōmə líttik, hòmmə-/ *adj*

hom·o·nym /hómmənim/ *n* **1. WORD WITH SAME SPELLING OR SOUND** a word that is spelled or pronounced in the same way as one or more other words but has a different meaning. Examples include the noun and adjective "fleet," "plane" and "plain," pronounced the same but spelled differently, and the verb and noun "sow," spelled the same but pronounced differently. **2. SOMEBODY WITH SAME NAME** somebody with the same name as somebody else **3.** BIOL **DUPLICATE TAXONOMIC NAME** a taxonomic name that is the same as one already designating a different species or genus and cannot therefore be used [Late 17C. < Latin *homonymum* < Greek *homōnumos* (see HOMONYMOUS)] —**hom·o·nym·ic** /hòmmə nímmik/ *adj* —**hom·o·nym·i·ty** /-nímmətee/ *n* —**ho·mon·y·my** /hə mónnəmee/ *n*

ho·mon·y·mous /hə mónniməss/ *adj* **1.** having the same spelling or pronunciation but a different meaning, as do the words "peace" and "piece" **2.** having the same name as somebody or something else [Early 17C. Via Latin < Greek *homōnumos* "having the same name" < *onuma* "name"] —**ho·mon·y·mous·ly** *adv*

Ho·mo·ou·si·an /hōmō óossee ən, -óozee-/ *n* a Christian who believes that Jesus Christ is of the same substance as God, in accordance with the Council of Nicaea's definition of the Trinity ■ *adj* relating to the doctrine of the Homoousians [Mid-16C. < Greek *homoousios* "of the same substance" < *homos* "same" + *ousia* "substance"] —**Ho·mo·ou·si·an·ism** *n*

ho·mo·phile /hṓmə fīl/ *adj* **1. ADVOCATING GAY RIGHTS** supporting the rights of gay and lesbian people and appreciating their culture **2. GAY OR LESBIAN** relating to or being gay or lesbian ■ *n* **1. GAY OR LESBIAN** a gay man or lesbian **2. SUPPORTER OF GAY RIGHTS** somebody who is sympathetic to gay and lesbian people and supports their rights

ho·mo·pho·bi·a /hòmə fóbee ə/ *n* an irrational hatred, disapproval, or fear of homosexuality, gay and lesbian people, or their culture [Mid-20C. < HOMOSEXUAL]

ho·mo·pho·bic /hòmə fóbik/ *adj* showing an irrational hatred, disapproval, or fear of homosexuality, gay and lesbian people, or their culture —**ho·mo·phobe** /hṓmə fōb/ *n*

hom·o·phone /hómmə fōn, hṓmə-/ *n* **1.** a word that is pronounced in the same way as one or more other words but is different in meaning and sometimes spelling, as are "hair" and "hare" **2.** a letter or diphthong that has the same sound as one or more other letters or diphthongs [Early 17C. < Greek *homophōnos* "having the same sound"]

hom·o·phon·ic /hòmmə fónnik, hṑmə-/ *adj* **1.** relating to part music in which the parts move together in simple harmonization **2.** LING same as **homophonous** (sense 1) —**ho·mo·phon·i·cal·ly** *adv*

ho·moph·o·nous /hō móffənəss, hə-/ *adj* **1.** having the same sound or pronunciation but a different meaning or spelling, as do the words "pale" and "pail" **2.** MUSIC same as **homophonic** (sense 1)

ho·moph·o·ny /hō móffənee, hə-/ *n* **1.** LING the quality of having the same pronunciation as one or more other words with a different origin and meaning **2.** MUSIC music of a largely chordal style in which there is no independence of voice parts, but rather a simple harmonization of a melody [Mid-18C. < Greek *homophōnia* "unison" < *homophōnos* "having the same sound"]

ho·mo·plas·tic /hòmə plástik, hòmmə-/ *adj* describes a tissue graft that is obtained from a member of the same species as the recipient —**ho·mo·plas·ti·cal·ly** *adv*

ho·mo·po·lar /hòmə pṓlər, hòmmə-/ *adj* having uniform polarity —**ho·mo·po·lar·i·ty** /-pō lárrətee/ *n*

ho·mop·ter·an /hō móptərən/ *n* an insect that has the ability to suck plant juices through its mouthparts, e.g., a cicada, scale insect, or aphid. Order: Homoptera. [Mid-19C. < modern Latin *Homoptera* < Greek *homos* "same" + *pteron* "wing"] —**ho·mop·ter·an** *adj*

Ho·mo sa·pi·ens /hōmō sáypee ənz, -ènz/ *n* the species of modern human beings, the only extant species of the family that also included other species named Homo. Family: Hominidae. [< modern Latin, "wise man"]

ho·mo·sce·das·tic /hòmō sə dástik, hòmō skə-/ *adj* characterized by equal statistical variances [Early 20C. < HOMO- + Greek *skedastos* "able to be scattered" < *skedannunai* "scatter"] —**ho·mo·sce·das·tic·i·ty** /-sə dass tíssətee/ *n*

ho·mo·sex·u·al /hòmə sékshoo əl, hòmō-/ *n* **SOMEBODY ATTRACTED TO SAME SEX** somebody who is sexually attracted to members of his or her own sex ■ *adj* **1. ATTRACTED TO SAME SEX** sexually attracted to members of the same sex **2. OF HOMOSEXUALITY** relating to sexual attraction or activity among members of the same sex

USAGE See *gay*.

ho·mo·sex·u·al·i·ty /hòmə sekshoo állətee, hòmō-/ *n* sexual attraction to or sexual relations with somebody of the same sex

ho·mo·spo·rous /hòmō spáwrəss, hòmmō-, ho móspərəss/ *adj* producing asexual spores of only one type

ho·mo·tax·is /hòmō táksiss, hòmmō-/ *n* a similarity of composition, arrangement, or fossil content among rock strata of different ages or locations —**ho·mo·tax·i·al** *adj* —**ho·mo·tax·i·al·ly** *adv* —**ho·mo·tax·ic** *adj*

ho·mo·thal·lic /hòmō thállik, hòmmō-/ *adj* describes a plant that has both male and female reproductive organs on one thallus and is therefore able to fertilize itself —**ho·mo·thal·lism** *n*

ho·mo·zy·gote /hòmō zī gōt, hòmmō-/ *n* an organism that has two identical genes at the same place on two corresponding chromosomes —**ho·mo·zy·got·ic** /-zī góttik/ *adj*

ho·mo·zy·gous /hòmō zígəss, hòmmō-/ *adj* having two identical genes at the corresponding loci of homologous chromosomes —**ho·mo·zy·gous·ly** *adv*

Homs /homz, homs/ historic city in western Syria, situated on the Orontes River. Population: 540,133 (1994).

ho·mun·cu·lus /hō múngkyələss/ (*plural* **-li** /-lī/), **ho·mun·cule** /-kyool/ *n* **1.** a diminutive human being **2.** in early biological theory, the fully formed human being that was thought to exist inside an egg or spermatozoon [Mid-17C. < Latin, "little person" < *homo* "human being"] —**ho·mun·cu·lar** *adj*

hom·y *adj* another spelling of **homey**[1]

hon /hun/ *n* used as an affectionate term of address (*informal*) [Early 20C. Shortening of HONEY]

hon. *abbr* **1.** honorable **2.** honorary

Hon. *abbr* Honorable

ho·nan /hō naan/ *n* a rough-woven raw silk fabric, originally from China [Early 20C. After *Honan*, province of N China]

hon·cho /hónchō/ (*slang*) *n* somebody who dominates a project, situation, or other people, or who behaves in a self-important way ■ *vt* (**-choed, -cho·ing, -chos**) to manage or organize people or events ○ *He's the one who honchoed their election campaign.* [Mid-20C. < Japanese *hanchō* "group leader"]

Hon·da /hóndə/, **Soichiro** (1906–92) Japanese engineer and business executive. He founded the Honda Motor Company to manufacture motorcycles (1948) and cars (1963).

> "To me success can only be achieved through repeated failure and introspection. In fact, success represents 1 percent of your work which results from the 99 percent that is called failure."
> [Soichiro Honda. Quoted in *Thriving on Chaos*, Tom Peters; 1988]

hon·dle /hónd'l/ (**-dled, -dling, -dles**) *vti* to haggle, bargain, or maneuver in order to get something desired (*informal*) [< Yiddish]

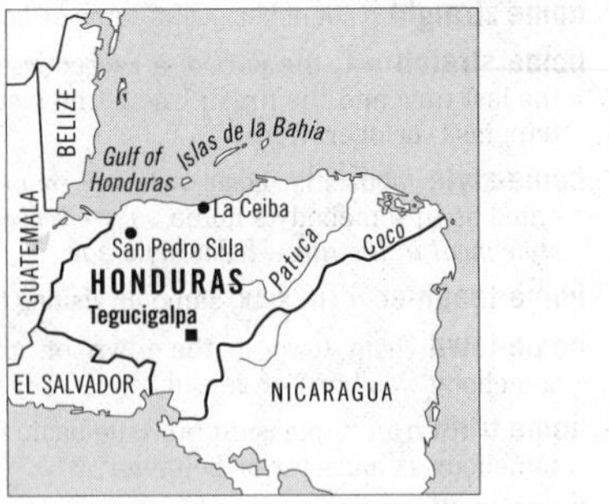

Honduras

Hon·du·ras /hon dóorəss/ country in Central America, with coastlines on the Caribbean Sea and the Pacific Ocean. Language: Spanish. Currency: lempira. Capital: Tegucigalpa. Population: 6,669,789 (2003). Area: 43,433 sq. mi./112,492 sq. km. Official name **Republic of Honduras** —**Hon·du·ran** *adj, n*

Hon·du·ras, Gulf of inlet of the Caribbean Sea, situated between southern Belize, eastern Guatemala, and northern Honduras

hone[1] /hōn/ *vt* (**honed, hon·ing, hones**) **1. IMPROVE SOMETHING WITH REFINEMENTS** to bring something to a state of increased intensity, excellence, or completion, especially over a period of time ○ *honed the speech through rewrites* **2. SHARPEN BLADE ON WHETSTONE** to sharpen a blade on a fine whetstone ■ *n* **1. WHETSTONE** a fine-grained sedimentary rock used as a whetstone for sharpening razors and other cutting tools. Emery and silicon carbide products are now largely used instead. **2. MACHINE TOOL** a tool with a rotating abrasive head, used to bore holes [Old English *hān* "whetstone" < Indo-European, "sharpen"] —**hon·er** *n*

USAGE hone in or **home in**? Avoid using the incorrect ***hone in***. ***Hone*** is a transitive verb meaning "sharpen" (*hone a blade*) or, in a figurative sense, "perfect or refine" (*I honed my ideas before publishing them*). It is the verb ***home***, generally intransitive, whose meanings include "return home accurately," that makes sense with the particle *in*: *He homed in on his opponent's weaknesses.*

hone[2] /hōn/ (**honed, hon·ing, hones**) *vi regional* **1.** to long for somebody or something **2.** to complain about somebody or something, especially in a whining manner [Early 17C. < Old French *hognier* "grumble"]

Ho·neck·er /hṓnəkər/, **Erich** (1912–94) secretary general of East Germany (1971–89). He served as East German head of state from 1971 until he was ousted in 1989, a year before the reunification of East and West Germany.

Ho·neg·ger /hónnigər/, **Arthur** (1892–1955) French composer. He was a member of the Paris-based group of composers known as "Les Six." His works include *Pacific 231* (1923) and *King David* (1921).

> "The first requirement for a composer is to be dead."
> [Arthur Honegger, *Je suis compositeur (I am a Composer)*; 1951]

hon·est /ónnəst/ *adj* **1. MORALLY UPRIGHT** never cheating, lying, or breaking the law **2. TRUTHFUL OR TRUE** expressing or embodying the truth **3. IMPARTIAL** presenting information in an impartial way **4. REASONABLE IN PARTICULAR SITUATION** reasonable and acceptable, given the circumstances ○ *an honest mistake* **5. UNPRETENTIOUS** having simple manners and no pretensions ○ *honest country folk* **6. RESPECTABLE** respectable and virtuous (*dated*) [13C. Via French < Latin *honestus* "honorable" < *honos* "honor"] —**hon·est·ness** *n* ◇ **honest to God** *or* **goodness 1.** used to express surprise or shock **2.** used to emphasize the truth of a statement

hon·est bro·ker *n* a person, country, or organization that mediates in disputes [Translation of German *ehrlicher Makler*, describing Otto von BISMARCK]

hon·est·ly /ónnəstlee/ *adv* **1. IN FAIR WAY** in a way that is fair, truthful, and morally upright **2. GENUINELY** really and truly ○ *Can you honestly say that you* *care?* ■ *interj* USED TO EXPRESS SURPRISE used to express surprise, annoyance, or disapproval

hon·est-to-God, **hon·est-to-good·ness** *adj* completely real or authentic (*informal*) ○ *You made a real, honest-to-God mess of that.*

hon·es·ty /ónnəstee/ (*plural* **-ties**) *n* **1.** MORAL UPRIGHTNESS the quality, condition, or characteristic of being fair, truthful, and morally upright **2.** TRUTHFULNESS truthfulness, candor, or sincerity ○ *In all honesty, I really didn't know.* **3.** PLANT a hardy plant with flat silvery seed pods that are often used for indoor decoration. Flowers: purplish or white. Native to: Europe. Latin name: *Lunaria annua.*

hone·wort /hṓn wùrt, -wàwrt/ *n* **1.** a perennial plant that has compound leaves. Flowers: small, white, in clusters. Native to: eastern North America. Latin name: *Cryptoaenia canadensis.* **2.** a perennial plant. Flowers: small, white, in clusters. Native to: Europe. Latin name: *Trinia glauca.* [Mid-17C. *Hone*, origin ?]

hon·ey /húnnee/ *n* **1.** SWEET SUBSTANCE MADE BY BEES a sweet sticky golden-brown fluid produced by bees from the nectar of flowers. Use: in cooking, spread on bread, or added to tea. **2.** SWEET SUBSTANCE MADE BY OTHER INSECTS a sweet sticky substance produced from nectar by insects other than bees **3.** AFFECTIONATE TERM OF ADDRESS used as an affectionate term of address (*informal*) **4.** SOMEBODY VERY NICE an attractive, endearing, or lovable person (*informal*) **5.** SOMETHING EXTREMELY GOOD an object, situation, or idea that is exceptionally good (*informal*) ○ *That's a honey of a motorboat!* **6.** YELLOWISH COLOR a yellowish brown color ■ *vt* (**-eyed** or **-ied, -ey·ing, -eys**) TALK FLATTERINGLY TO SOMEBODY to talk to somebody in an affectionate and flattering way, especially insincerely and for selfish reasons (*informal*) [Old English *hunig* < Germanic] —**hon·ey** *adj*

hon·ey badg·er *n* ZOOL same as **ratel** [< its fondness for honey]

hon·ey bear *n* ZOOL same as **kinkajou** [< its practice of sucking honey from the nests of bees]

hon·ey·bee /húnnee bee/ *n* a honey-producing bee that lives in organized groups and has been domesticated for its honey and beeswax since ancient times. Latin name: *Apis mellifera.*

hon·ey·bun /húnnee bùn/, **hon·ey·bunch** /-bùnch/ *n* used as an affectionate term of address (*informal*)

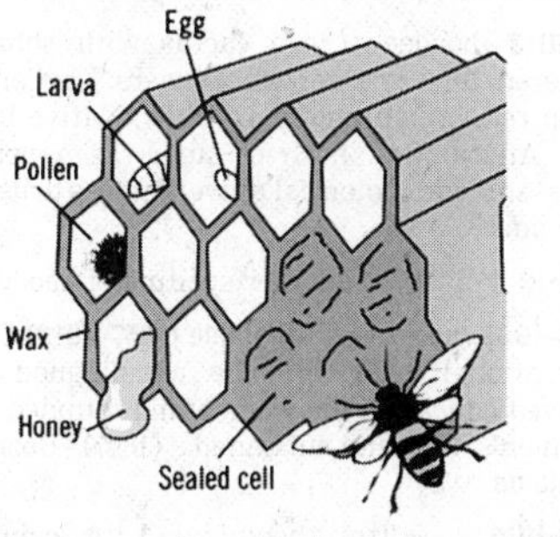

honeycomb

hon·ey·comb /húnnee kṑm/ *n* **1.** STRUCTURE OF SIX-SIDED CELLS a collection of hexagonal cells constructed of wax by bees inside a hive or nest in which honey is stored, eggs are laid, and larvae develop **2.** CELLS CONTAINING HONEY EATEN AS FOOD a structure made up of waxy hexagonal cells containing honey that is extracted from a bees' hive or nest and eaten by animals and humans **3.** SOMETHING LIKE HONEYCOMB an object resembling a honeycomb in pattern or structure, especially by consisting of a network of hexagons **4.** HONEYCOMB-PATTERNED FABRIC a soft fabric woven in a pattern of ridges and hollows like those in a honeycomb. Use: towels, bedspreads. ■ *vt* (**-combed, -comb·ing, -combs**) **1.** PROVIDE SOMETHING WITH HOLES to fill a wall, cliff, or structure with many cavities **2.** INFILTRATE SOMETHING THOROUGHLY to infiltrate a place or organization thoroughly ○ *an intelligence agency honeycombed by double agents* —**hon·ey·combed** *adj*

hon·ey·comb moth *n* INSECTS same as **wax moth**

hon·ey·creep·er /húnnee kreepər/ *n* **1.** a small bird with brightly colored feathers and a long slender beak for sucking nectar from flowers. Native to: tropical America. Family: Coerebidae. **2.** a bird that resembles the honeycreeper of tropical America. Native to: Hawaii. Family: Drepanididae.

WORLD ENGLISH ***Hong Kong English*** is the variety of English used in Hong Kong, ranging from forms close to British, US, and Australian usage to those influenced by and mixed with Cantonese, the language of some 98% of the population. In Hong Kong English pronunciation "r" is not pronounced in such words as *art, door,* and *worker.* It generally shares features with English as used in mainland China, Taiwan, and Singapore: e.g. glottal stops replacing the /p, t, k/ consonants at the ends of such words as *map, pat,* and *tack.* In grammar, there is a tendency to use the present tense when describing events in the past and future ("When I see him in school yesterday" and "Tomorrow I ask him about it").

Hong Kong English has three sources of distinctive vocabulary. The first is represented by items taken directly from Chinese (especially Cantonese), e.g. *gweilo* (ghost man/person) for "a European" and *feng shui* (wind-water) denoting a system of laws that govern spatial relationships with respect to the flow of energy, used in situating buildings advantageously. The second vocabulary source is represented by items that translate Chinese words and phrases, such as *dragon boat*, a long decorated boat configured as a dragon, used in racing at festivals, and *snakehead*, a smuggler of illegal immigrants from mainland China. A third vocabulary source is represented by items common to former British colonies, especially in Asia, e.g. *expat* (English), short for "expatriate," *godown* (probably from Tamil), "warehouse," and *shroff* (from Arabic through Indian languages), "cashier."

hon·ey·dew /húnnee dōō/ *n* **1.** a sweet sticky substance deposited on leaves by aphids and some other insects as a byproduct of the juices they suck from plants **2.** a sweet sticky substance produced by the leaves of some plants **3.** FOOD same as **honeydew melon** [< the belief that the substance was distilled from the air like dew] —**hon·ey·dewed** *adj*

hon·ey·dew mel·on *n* a melon with sweet pale green flesh and a smooth greenish white rind. Latin name: *Cucumis melo.*

hon·ey·eat·er /húnnee eetər/ *n* a slender bird with a long beak and a long brush-tipped tongue for extracting nectar from flowers. Native to: Australia to Hawaii. Family: Meliphagidae.

hon·eyed /húnneed/, **hon·ied** *adj* **1.** INGRATIATING intended to flatter or soothe **2.** PLEASANT-SOUNDING sweet and pleasant to hear **3.** SWEETENED WITH HONEY containing or sweetened with honey —**hon·eyed·ly** *adv*

hon·ey fun·gus *n* a destructive fungus that grows in small tight clusters at the base of trees, with a golden or brown cap and black spreading filaments (**hyphae**). It is possibly the most serious fungal parasite affecting coniferous trees. Latin name: *Armillaria mellea.* [< its color]

hon·ey guide *n* **1.** a small bird that feeds on the wax and larvae remaining after people or animals have removed the honey from bees' nests. Native to: tropical forests of Africa and Asia. Family: Indicatoridae. **2.** a series of dots or lines on the perianth of a flower that guide insects toward the nectar. They are sometimes only visible to the human eye in ultraviolet photographs.

hon·ey lo·cust *n* a thorny tree with compound leaves and pods containing a sweet pulp. Native to: eastern North America. Genus: *Gleditsia.*

hon·ey mes·quite *n* a tree that has nutritious pods. Native to: southwestern United States. Latin name: *Prosopis juliflora.* [< the sweet taste of its pods]

hon·ey·moon /húnnee mōōn/ *n* **1.** a period of time spent alone together, especially away, by a newly-married couple, usually immediately following the wedding or reception **2.** a short period of harmony or goodwill at the beginning of a relationship, especially in politics or business [Mid-16C. Originally "waning affection," from the idea that although married love is at first as sweet as honey, it soon wanes like the moon] —**hon·ey·moon** *vi* —**hon·ey·moon·er** *n*

hon·ey·pot /húnnee pòt/ *n* **1.** anything that attracts or appeals to large numbers of people (*informal*) **2.** a server connected to the Internet that is used as a decoy to attract potential hackers in order to study their activities and techniques

hon·ey·suck·le /húnnee sùk'l/ *n* **1.** a climbing bush with twining stems. Flowers: fragrant, tubular, with spreading twin-petal lobes. Genus: *Lonicera.* **2.** a plant with large woody seed cones. Flowers: yellow, orange, red, gray, and green, in spike-shaped clusters. Native to: Australia. Genus: *Banksia.* [< the belief that bees suck honey from it]

hon·ey·suck·le or·na·ment *n* ARTS, ARCHIT same as **anthemion**

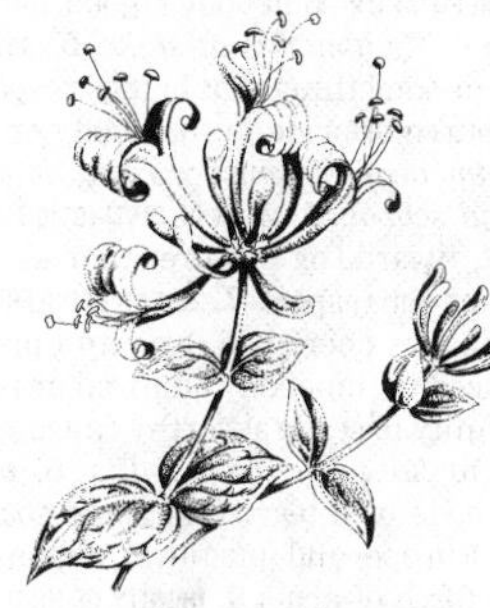

honeysuckle

hon·ey-sweet *adj* sounding or appearing sweet and attractive

hong·i /hóngee/ *n* a Maori greeting in which two people press or touch the side of each other's noses together, usually three times [Mid-19C. < Maori]

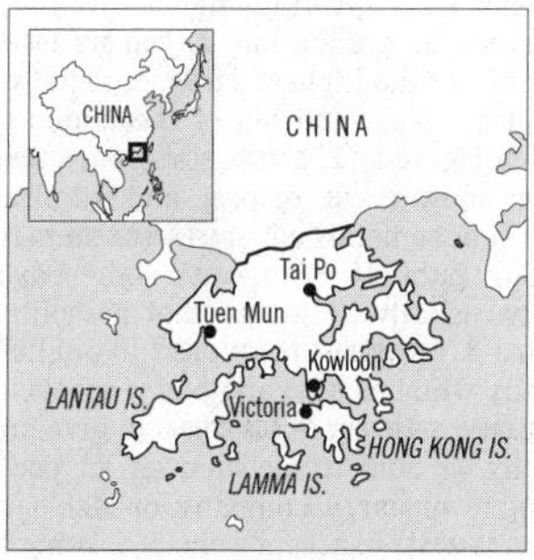

Hong Kong

Hong Kong /hóng kòng/ seaport and major commercial center on the southeastern coast of China. A former British colony, it is now a Chinese Special Administrative Region. Population: 7,210,505 (2001). Area: 422 sq. mi./1,092 sq. km.

Hong Kong Eng·lish *n* a variety of English spoken in Hong Kong

Ho·ni·a·ra /hō nee áarə/ port and capital of the Solomon Islands, situated on the northern coast of Guadalcanal. Population: 35,288 (1990).

hon·ied *adj* another spelling of **honeyed**

honk /hongk/ *n* **1.** SOUND OF CAR HORN the sound made by a car horn **2.** CRY OF GOOSE the raucous sound made by a goose **3.** SOUND RESEMBLING GOOSE OR CAR HORN any sound, e.g., a laugh or a blowing of the nose, that resembles the sound made by a goose or a car horn ■ *v* (**honked, honk·ing, honks**) **1.** *vti* SOUND CAR HORN to cause a car horn to make a honk **2.** *vi* PRODUCE HONK to let out or give out a honk [Mid-19C. An imitation of the sound]

honk·er /hóngkər/ *n* **1.** a person, animal, or object that makes a honking sound, e.g., a goose or a car horn **2.** a nose, especially a large one (*informal*) **3.** *Can* same as **Canada goose** (*informal*)

hon·ky /hóngkee/ (*plural* **-kies**), **hon·kie, hon·key** (*plural* **-keys**) *n* a highly offensive term for a white person (*slang*) [Mid-20C. Origin ?]

hon·ky-tonk /hóngki tòngk/ *n* **1.** COUNTRY MUSIC a style of country music associated with cheap, noisy, and often disreputable bars or nightclubs ○ *honky-tonk blues* **2.** RAGTIME PIANO-PLAYING a style of ragtime with a heavy beat, usually played on an upright piano with a tinny sound **3.** CHEAP NIGHTCLUB a cheap, noisy, and often disreputable bar or nightclub (*slang*) ■ *vi* (**hon·ky-tonked, hon·ky-tonk·ing, hon·ky-tonks**) VISIT HONKY-TONKS to frequent cheap noisy bars and nightclubs [Late 19C. Origin ?]

Hon·o·lu·lu /hònnə lóoloo/ urban area and capital of Hawaii, located on Oahu Island. Population: 378,155 (2002 estimate).

hon·or /ónnər/ *n* **1.** PERSONAL INTEGRITY strong moral character or strength, and adherence to ethical principles ○ *It's a matter of honor.* **2.** RESPECT great respect and admiration ○ *a mark of honor* **3.** DIGNITY personal dignity that sometimes leads to recognition and glory ○ *Although defeated, he accepted the loss with honor.* **4.** REPUTATION somebody's good name or good reputation ○ *My honor is at stake.* **5.** SOURCE OF PRIDE somebody or something that brings respect or glory and is a source of pride to somebody or something else ○ *Your achievements are an honor to your parents and school.* **6.** MARK OF DISTINCTION something, e.g., a gift, award, or gesture, that signifies high achievement or respect **7.** GREAT PRIVILEGE a special privilege that is cherished, e.g., an opportunity to be introduced to somebody admired or respected or an opportunity to serve a worthy cause ○ *It is indeed an honor to have you here today.* **8.** MEN'S CODE OF INTEGRITY a code of integrity in some societies, e.g., in feudal Europe and medieval Japan, that men upheld by force of arms **9.** DIGNITY OF HIGH POSITION the degree of dignity with which high positions such as the presidency are regarded by those elected to them and by the people they serve ○ *actions detrimental to the honor of his office* **10.** RIGHT TO TEE OFF FIRST in golf, the right to drive off first from the tee **11.** WOMAN'S REPUTATION a woman's virginity or reputation for chastity (*dated*) ■ *npl* **1. hon·ors, Hon·ors** ACADEMIC DISTINCTION official recognition of academic excellence given to students by colleges and universities at graduation **2. hon·ors** HIGHEST CARDS four or five of the highest cards, especially the ace, king, queen, jack, and ten of the trump suit ■ *vt* (**-ored, -or·ing, -ors**) **1.** ESTEEM SOMEBODY OR SOMETHING to have or show great respect and admiration for somebody or something **2.** EXALT SOMEBODY to recognize somebody publicly or elevate somebody's status officially, usually by giving that person a title or an award **3.** PAY TRIBUTE TO SOMEBODY to publicly praise somebody who has died and pay respects to him or her **4.** DIGNIFY SOMEBODY OR SOMETHING to give prestige to somebody or something such as an occasion by choosing to appear, accompany, or take part **5.** TREAT SOMETHING AS MONEY to accept a check or other financial instrument as money or as a substitute for money and pay it when it is due ○ *The bank won't honor a check without a signature.* **6.** KEEP PROMISE to keep a promise, or fulfill the terms of an agreement or contract **7.** BOW TO PARTNER to bow to another dancer in square dancing [12C. Via French < Latin *honor-*, stem of *honos*] —**hon·or·er** *n* —**hon·or·less** *adj* ◇ **do somebody the honor of doing something** to make somebody feel proud and pleased by agreeing to do something for that person (*formal*) ○ *Will you do me the honor of dancing the last waltz with me?* ◇ **do the honors** to act as host or hostess by doing something for a group of guests, e.g., pouring wine, carving meat, or cutting a cake (*informal*) ◇ **honor bound** obligated by a promise or ethical principles to do something ◇ **in honor of somebody** *or* **something** in recognition of or for the glorification of somebody or something ○ *I'd like to propose a toast in honor of the bride and groom.* ◇ **on your honor 1.** staking your reputation on something ○ *On my honor, I will tell the truth.* **2.** being trusted to act in a particular way ○ *You are on your honor to behave well.*

Hon·or *n* used as a form of address to dignitaries such as judges and mayors ○ *Your Honor, may we approach the bench?*

hon·or·a·ble /ónnərəb'l/ *adj* **1.** HAVING PERSONAL INTEGRITY guided by, or with a reputation for having, strong moral and ethical principles **2.** DESERVING OR GAINING HONOR worthy of or winning honor, respect, recognition, or glory **3.** MORALLY UPRIGHT upright and moral in intent (*formal*) ○ *I hope his intentions are honorable.* —**hon·or·a·bil·i·ty** /ònnərə bíllətee/ *n* —**hon·or·a·ble·ness** *n* —**hon·or·a·bly** *adv*

Hon·or·a·ble *adj* **1.** used as a title of respect before somebody's name to indicate entitlement to respect because of an official position held, or used to address a parliamentary colleague ○ *The Honorable Mr. Smith, the presiding judge, is on the bench.* **2.** *UK* used as a courtesy title in the United Kingdom for the children of some members of the aristocracy

hon·or·a·ble dis·charge *n* an official separation from the armed forces, signifying that all duties have been honorably fulfilled

hon·or·a·ble men·tion *n* an official or public commendation, usually granted to somebody who has done well in a competition but has not actually won an award

hon·o·rar·i·um /ònnə réree əm/ (*plural* **-i·ums** *or* **-i·a** /-ee ə/) *n* an amount of money paid to somebody, especially a professional or famous person, for providing a service such as addressing a conference [Mid-17C. < Latin, "gift made on being admitted to a post of honor" < *honor-* (see HONOR)]

SYNONYMS See *wage.*

---

hon·or·ar·y /ónnə rèrree/ *adj* **1.** AWARDED AS HONOR given, elected, or awarded for outstanding service or distinguished achievements, rather than for the completion of formal educational or legal requirements **2.** SYMBOLIZING HONOR CONFERRED representing the bestowal of an honor or distinction on somebody **3.** UNPAID holding an office awarded as an honor and receiving no payment for services provided in that office **4.** NOT LEGALLY ENFORCEABLE dependent on somebody's sense of honor and honesty for fulfillment, rather than on a legal agreement

hon·or·ee /ònnə rée/ *n* somebody who receives an honor

hon·or guard *n* a group of US Army, Navy, or Air Force personnel or Marines who perform a ceremonial duty such as attending a casket at a military funeral or raising and lowering a flag

hon·or·if·ic /ònnə ríffik/ *adj* CONFERRING HONOR given as a mark of distinction, esteem, or respect ■ *n* **1.** TITLE OF RESPECT a title of respect, e.g., "The Honorable," used in speech or writing before the full name or the surname of a social or governmental superior **2.** GRAMMATICAL FORM ACKNOWLEDGING INFERIORITY a phrase or word, e.g., a pronoun or a verb inflection, that is used to show respect to somebody of a higher status

hon·or·is cau·sa /o nàwriss kówssə, -ków zaa/ *adv* as a mark of honor ○ *a doctorate in humane letters conferred honoris causa* [< Latin, "for the sake of honor"]

hon·or roll *n* a list of school students who have excellent grades or a high grade point average ○ *Seven seniors made the honor roll first semester.*

Hon·ors List *n* a list of the people who have been or are to be awarded honors such as a peerage or membership in a chivalric order by the British monarch

hon·or so·ci·e·ty *n* a club, usually in high school, for students who have excellent grades or a high grade point average

hon·ors of war *npl* **1.** the privileges that are accorded members of a defeated army **2.** marks of respect paid by troops at the burial of another soldier

hon·or sys·tem *n* a system under which people are relied on to be honest without direct supervision

hon·our *n, vt* Can, UK spelling of **honor**

Hon·shu /hónshoo/ largest and most populous island of Japan. Area: 88,979 sq. mi./230,455 sq. km. Population: 99,254,194 (1990).

hoo /hoo/ (*plural* **hoos**) *n* the hooting sound made by an owl [15C. An imitation of the sound]

hooch[1] /hooch/, **hootch** *n* (*slang*) **1.** hard liquor, especially when very cheap or illegally obtained or distilled **2.** same as **marijuana** [Late 19C. Shortening of *hoochinoo*, after *Hoochinoo*, Tlingit village in Alaska where illegal liquor was thought to be distilled]

hooch[2] /hooch/, **hootch** *n* a semipermanent structure, e.g., a hut, used as a quarters for troops in Southeast Asia (*dated slang*) [Mid-20C. Origin ?]

hood[1] /hŏŏd/ *n* **1.** COVERING FOR HEAD a loose covering for the head that is usually attached to the neck of a coat **2.** COVER FOR DEVICE a cover for an appliance or machine, or for a part such as a camera lens **3.** ENGINE COVER the hinged cover over the engine of a car or other vehicle ○ *Let's check under the hood to see what's wrong.* **4.** FOLDING ROOF the folding roof of a vehicle such as a carriage or convertible car **5.** PART OF ACADEMIC ROBE an ornamental piece of cloth, often trimmed with fur or luxurious fabric, that hangs from the shoulders of an academic or ecclesiastical robe to indicate the status of the wearer **6.** COVER FOR CHIMNEY a fixed or revolving cover attached to the top of a chimney to prevent downdrafts **7.** HEAD COVERING FOR FALCON a bag placed over the head of a falcon to keep it calm when it is not hunting **8.** MARKING ON ANIMAL'S HEAD a crest, marking, or other conspicuous part on the head of an animal ■ *vt* (**hood·ed, hood·ing, hoods**) PUT HOOD ON HEAD to cover the head of a person, animal, or bird with a hood [Old English *hōd* < Indo-European, "to cover"] —**hood·less** *adj* —**hood·like** *adj*

hood[2] /hŏŏd/ *n* same as **hoodlum** (*slang*) [Late 19C. Shortening]

hood[3] /hŏŏd/ *n* same as **neighborhood** (sense 1) (*slang*) [Late 20C. Shortening]

Hood /hŏŏd/, **John Bell** (1831–79) US Confederate general. A graduate of West Point who showed great promise and bravery in his early career, he fought a series of disastrous encounters as acting general of the Army of Tennessee against General Sherman's Union army in Atlanta.

-hood *suffix* **1.** quality, state, condition ○ *knighthood* **2.** a group of people ○ *brotherhood* **3.** time, stage of life ○ *adulthood* [Old English *-hād* < Germanic]

hood·ed /hŏŏddəd/ *adj* **1.** COVERED BY HOOD covered by or having a hood **2.** PARTLY HIDDEN partly concealed or covered ○ *dark, hooded eyes* **3.** HAVING CREST having a crest, markings, or a specialized structure on the head —**hood·ed·ness** *n*

hood·ed crow *n* a crow that is a subspecies of the carrion crow with a black head, tail, and wings, and a gray body. Native to: Europe, Asia. Latin name: *Corvus corone cornix*.

hood·ed seal *n* a large gray-spotted seal, the mature male of which has an inflatable sac near its nose. Native to: the North Atlantic and Arctic oceans. Latin name: *Cystophora cristata*.

hoo·di·a /hŏŏdee ə/ *n* a cactus with short stems covered in white spikes. Flowers: saucer-shaped, deep red, brown, mottled yellow. Native to: southern Africa. Use: flesh of stems as appetite suppressant, with potential as weight-loss drug. Genus: *hoodia*.

hood·ie *n* CLOTHING another spelling of **hoody**

Hood·less /hŏŏddləss/, **Adelaide** (1857–1910) Canadian educational reformer. She campaigned for improved education for women and founded the first Women's Institute in Canada (1897). Born **Hunter, Adelaide**

hood·lum /hŏŏdləm, hŏŏd-/ *n* **1.** a criminal or gangster, especially one prone to violence **2.** a young person who is violent or prone to committing crimes [Late 19C. Origin ?] —**hood·lum·ish** *adj* —**hood·lum·ism** *n*

hood·mold /hŏŏd mōld/ *n* CONSTR same as **dripstone** (sense 1)

hoo·doo /hŏŏdoo/ *n* (*plural* **-doos**) **1.** RELIG same as **voodoo** *n* (sense 2) **2.** BAD LUCK bad luck or misfortune **3.** BRINGER OF BAD LUCK somebody or something believed to bring bad luck **4.** ODDLY-SHAPED ROCK COLUMN in the western United States and Canada, a column of rock that has been weathered into a strange shape ■ *vt* (**-dooed, -doo·ing, -doos**) JINX SOMEBODY OR SOMETHING to appear to bring bad luck or misfortune to somebody or something [Late 19C. Origin ?] —**hoo·doo·ism** *n*

hood·wink /hŏŏd wìngk/ (**-winked, -wink·ing, -winks**) *vt* to deceive or dupe somebody, especially by trickery —**hood·wink·er** *n*

hood·y /hŏŏdee/ (*plural* **-ies**), **hood·ie** *n* a sweatshirt or fleece with a hood

hoo·ey /hoó ee/ *n* empty or nonsensical talk or ideas (*informal*) [Early 20C. Origin ?]

hoof /hòòf, hoof/ *n* (*plural* **hooves** /hòòvz, hoovz/ or **hoofs**) **1.** ANIMAL'S FOOT the foot of a horse, deer, cow, or similar animal, covered with horny material **2.** HORNY COVERING OF FOOT the horny material covering the feet of animals such as horses, deer, and cattle **3.** ANIMAL WITH HOOVES an animal that has hooves, e.g., a horse, deer, or cow **4.** HUMAN FOOT the foot of a human being (*slang humorous*) ■ *v* (**hoofed, hoof·ing, hoofs**) **1.** *vt* TRAVEL DISTANCE ON FOOT to walk a particular distance (*slang*) **2.** *vt* KICK SOMEBODY OR SOMETHING to kick or trample a person or animal **3.** *vi* same as **dance** (*slang*) [Old English *hōf* < Indo-European] —**hoof·less** *adj* ◇ **hoof it** (*slang*) **1.** same as **walk** *v* (sense 1) **2.** same as **dance** *v* (sense 1) ◇ **hoof it up** same as **dance** *v* (sense 1) (*slang*) ◇ **on the hoof 1.** used to describe an animal that is alive and has not yet been butchered **2.** without sufficient thought or attention (*informal*)

hoof-and-mouth dis·ease *n* VET same as **foot-and-mouth disease**

hoofed /hòòft, hooft/, **hooved** /hòòvd, hoovd/ *adj* having hooves, or with hooves of a particular size and type

hoof·er /hóofər, hòòffər/ *n* a professional dancer, especially a tap dancer (*slang*)

hoof·print /hòòf prìnt, hóof-/ *n* an imprint of an animal's hoof

Hoogh·ly another spelling of **Hugli**

hoo-hah /hoó haa/, **hoo-ha** *n* a loud noisy aggressive public controversy or disturbance (*slang*) [Mid-20C. Probably < Yiddish *hu-ha*, an imitation of the sound of a disturbance]

hook /hòòk/ *n* **1.** BENT PIECE OF METAL a bent or curved piece of metal or other material, used to attach, suspend, fasten, or lift another object **2.** SOMETHING LIKE HOOK something resembling a curved piece of metal, especially a plant or animal part **3.** FISHING same as **fishhook 4.** SNARE a stratagem for trapping or snaring somebody **5.** SOMETHING THAT ATTRACTS a means of attracting or interesting somebody, especially a potential customer (*informal*) **6.** BOXING SHORT SWINGING BLOW in boxing, a short blow to an opponent delivered with a swing and a bent arm **7.** GOLF SWERVING SHOT a golf shot that swerves sharply from right to left in the case of a right-handed player **8.** BASEBALL same as **curveball 9.** HOCKEY ACT OF RESTRAINING PLAYER the act of using an ice hockey stick to prevent another player from moving freely **10.** MUSIC CATCHY REFRAIN a pleasing and easily remembered refrain in a pop song **11.** BASKETBALL same as **hook shot 12.** PRINTING PART OF LETTER in writing or printing, a short curve of a letter that extends above or below the line ○ *the hook of the "g"* **13.** CREST OF WAVE the crest of a wave that is about to break **14.** AGRIC same as **sickle** *n* (sense 1) ■ *v* (**hooked, hook·ing, hooks**) **1.** *vti* FASTEN WITH HOOK to fasten something by means of hooks, or hooks and eyes, or be fastened in this way **2.** *vt* ATTACH ONE THING TO ANOTHER to attach one thing to another by means of a specially designed mechanical device ○ *hook the trailer to the car* **3.** *vti* BEND LIKE HOOK to curve in the shape of a hook, or cause something to curve in the shape of a hook ○ *The road hooks sharply to the left.* **4.** *vt* ENSNARE SOMETHING to catch or ensnare something using a hook **5.** *vt* CATCH SOMEBODY'S ATTENTION to attract and hold somebody's interest or attention **6.** *vt* BOXING HIT SOMEBODY WITH CURVING BLOW in boxing, to deliver a sharp curving blow to an opponent, using a curved or bent arm **7.** *vt* GOLF STRIKE SWERVING BALL in golf, to strike the ball so that it swerves sharply from right to left in the case of a right-handed player **8.** *vt* BASEBALL THROW CURVED BALL in baseball, to pitch the ball with a curve **9.** *vt* BASKETBALL SHOOT BALL INTO BASKET in basketball, to shoot the ball by sweeping the hand upward and farther away from the basket while moving sideways toward the basket **10.** *vt* HOCKEY RESTRAIN PLAYER WITH STICK to use an ice hockey stick to prevent another player from moving freely **11.** *vt* DRUGS MAKE SOMEBODY ADDICTED to cause somebody to become addicted or dependent on something, especially a drug (*slang*) **12.** *vt* GORE SOMEBODY OR SOMETHING to gore a person or animal with the horns or tusks **13.** *vt* AGRIC CUT SOMETHING WITH SICKLE to cut grass or similar plants with a sickle **14.** *vt* HANDICRAFT MAKE RUG to make a rug by pulling pieces of wool through holes in stiff canvas using a special hook **15.** *vt* STEAL SOMETHING to seize and steal something (*slang*) **16.** *vi* BE PROSTITUTE to work as a prostitute (*slang*) [Old English *hōc* < Indo-European, "hook, tooth"] —**hook·less** *adj* ◇ **by hook or by crook** by some means or other ◇ **get the hook** to be removed unceremoniously from a place or position (*slang*) ◇ **give somebody the hook** to remove somebody abruptly from a place or position (*informal*) ◇ **hook, line, and sinker** to the fullest possible extent (*informal*) ◇ **off the hook 1.** free of a difficult situation (*informal*) **2.** with the receiver off its cradle so that no telephone calls can be received ◇ **on the hook** caught in a difficult situation (*informal*) ◇ **on your own hook** by your own efforts (*informal*)

hook up *v* **1.** *vt* to set up or connect electronic or electric devices ○ *Is the microphone hooked up?* **2.** *vti* to meet and become associated, or cause somebody to meet and become associated, with somebody else (*informal*)

hook·ah /hòòkə, hóokə/ *n* in Southwest and South Asia, a pipe for smoking tobacco or marijuana, consisting of a flexible tube with a mouthpiece attached to a container of water through which smoke is drawn and cooled [Mid-18C. Via Urdu < Arabic *ḥukka* "jar"]

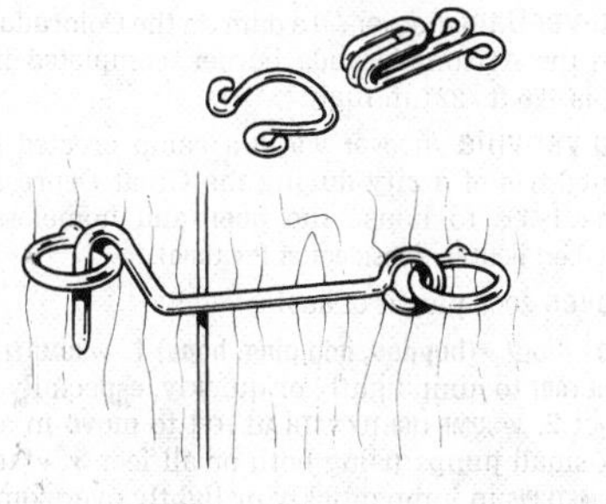

hook and eye: clothes fastener (top) and latch (bottom)

hook and eye (*plural* **hooks and eyes**) *n* **1.** a fastening for clothes consisting of a small hook inserted into a metal or thread loop **2.** a latch for a gate or door consisting of a metal hook inserted into a metal loop

hook-and-lad·der truck *n* a fire engine equipped with extension ladders and hooked poles

hook·check /hòòk chèk/ *n* HOCKEY same as **hook** *n* (sense 9)

hooked /hòòkt/ *adj* **1.** SHAPED LIKE HOOK bent or shaped like a hook **2.** WITH HOOK AT END ending in a hook **3.** ADDICTED addicted to a drug (*slang*) **4.** OBSESSED WITH SOMEBODY OR SOMETHING in love with, compulsively attracted to, or obsessed with somebody or something (*slang*) **5.** MADE USING YARN HOOK made by hooking yarn through canvas

hook·er[1] /hòòkər/ *n* an offensive term for a prostitute (*slang*) [Mid-19C. Origin ?]

hook·er[2] /hòòkər/ *n* a drink of hard liquor, typically a big one (*slang*) [Mid-19C. Origin ?]

hook·er[3] /hòòkər/ *n* a person, animal, or object that catches something by hooking it [Mid-16C. < HOOK]

hook·er[4] /hòòkər/ *n* **1.** FISHING BOAT a commercial fishing vessel that uses hooks and lines instead of nets **2.** CARGO BOAT a large cargo boat with several sails, formerly used off the western coast of Ireland and now used as a pleasure craft **3.** SHABBY BOAT an old, shabby, or ungraceful boat [Mid-17C. < Dutch *hoeker*, shortening of Middle Dutch *hoeckboot* "fishing boat" < *hoec* "fishhook"]

Hook·er /hòòkər/, **Joseph** (1814–79) US Union general. Known as an aggressive leader, he commanded the Army of the Potomac (1863). Known as **Fighting Joe**

hook·ey *n* another spelling of **hooky** (*informal*)

hook·nose /hòòk nōz/ *n* a nose with a noticeable curve at the end, like an eagle's beak —**hook·nosed** *adj*

Hook of Hol·land /hòòk-/ **1.** cape on the North Sea coast in the southwestern Netherlands. Dutch name **Hoek van Holland 2.** seaport on the Hook of Holland, situated approximately 6 mi./10 km northwest of Rotterdam

hook shot *n* in basketball, a shot that is made by sweeping the hand upward and farther away from the basket while moving sideways toward the basket

hook·tip /hòòk tìp/ *n* a moth that has forewings ending in a hooked point. Genus: *Daepana.*

hook·up /hòòk ùp/ *n* **1.** LINK BETWEEN SOURCE AND USER a connection allowing a user access to a utility such as electricity, gas, or water ○ *a gas hookup* **2.** ELECTRONIC SYSTEM a number of items of electronic equipment designed to operate together (*informal*) **3.** RELATIONSHIP an alliance between people, groups, or things, especially an unlikely one (*informal*) ○ *a bizarre hookup between political enemies over an issue* **4.** FISHING CATCH IN OFFSHORE FISHING in offshore big game fishing, an act of catching a fish on the end of the line

hook·worm /hòòk wùrm/ *n* **1.** a blood-sucking, disease-causing nematode worm that bores through the skin, attaching itself to the intestinal walls with its hooked mouthparts. Family: Ancylostomatidae. **2.** MED same as **ancylostomiasis**

hook·y /hòòkee/, **hook·ey** *n* absence, especially from school, without permission (*informal*) [Mid-19C. Origin ?] ◇ **play hooky** to be absent without permission, especially from school

hoo·ley /hóolee/ (*plural* **-leys**) *n Ireland* a noisy merry party (*informal*) [Late 19C. Origin ?]

hoo·li·gan /hóoligən/ *n* a young person who is violent or prone to committing crimes (*informal*) [Late 19C. Origin ?]

hoo·li·gan·ism /hóoligə nìzzəm/ *n* acts of vandalism and violence in public places, committed especially by youths

hoop /hoop, hòòp/ *n* **1.** RING HOLDING BARREL TOGETHER the metal or wooden ring used to hold the staves of a barrel in place **2.** RING a large light ring, often with paper stretched over it, through which trained animals or performers jump **3.** EARRING an earring formed from a continuous ring of metal **4.** PART OF FINGER RING the part of a ring that the finger fits through **5.** RING HOLDING NET IN BASKETBALL in basketball, the metal ring from which an open-bottomed net is suspended, through which the ball is thrown in order to score points **6.** HANDICRAFT BAND FOR EMBROIDERY FABRIC either of a pair of wooden or metal bands used to keep fabric taut when it is being embroidered **7.** CROQUET HOOP in croquet, a metal arch through which the ball is driven **8.** CLOTHING SUPPORT FOR SKIRT a lightweight cane, wire, or whalebone ring, or a structure made of several such rings, used, especially formerly, to stiffen a woman's skirt or petticoat **9.** CLOTHING WIDE STIFF SKIRT a petticoat or skirt stiffened by rings **10.** BASKETBALL GAME the game of basketball (*slang*) ■ *vt* (**hooped, hoop·ing, hoops**) PUT HOOP AROUND SOMETHING to surround something with a hoop or band [Old English *hōp* < W Germanic] ◇ **jump** *or* **go through hoops (for somebody)** to go to extreme lengths to gain favor with somebody or to carry out somebody's wishes (*informal*)

hoop·er /hóopər, hòòppər/ *n* somebody who makes or repairs barrels

hoop·la /hoop laa, hòòp laa/ *n* **1.** MISLEADING TALK intentionally misleading talk or propaganda (*informal*) **2.** LOUD CELEBRATION a noisy excited commotion or joyous celebrating (*slang*) **3.** GREAT PUBLIC UPROAR a great amount of public fuss, commotion, or uproar with attendant publicity or media interest (*slang*) [Late 19C. Origin ?]

hoo·poe /hoó pō, -poo/ (*plural* **-poes** or *same*) *n* a bird with a pinkish brown head and back, a very prominent crest, a downward curving beak, and a loud cry. Native to: Europe, Asia, Africa. Latin name: *Upupa epops.* See illustration on next page [Mid-17C. Alteration of *hoop*, via Old French *huppe* < Latin *upupa*, an imitation of the bird's cry]

hoop skirt *n* a long full skirt held out in the shape of a bell by a series of connected hoops, fashionable in the 18th and early 19th centuries

hoop snake *n* any harmless North American snake that was once believed to be able to take its tail in its mouth and roll along like a hoop, e.g., the mud snake

hoopoe

hoop·ster /hŏŏpstər/ *n* a basketball player (*informal*)

hoo·ray /hŏŏ ráy/, **hur·ray** /hŏŏ ráy, hə-/ *n* a shout of happy excitement, victory, or jubilation ■ *interj* used as a shout of happy excitement, victory, or jubilation [Late 17C. Alteration of HURRAH]

hoose·gow /hŏŏss gòw/ *n* same as **jail** (*slang*) [Early 20C. Via Mexican Spanish *jusgado* < Spanish *juzgado* "courtroom" < past participle of *juzgar* "judge" < Latin *judicare* (see JUDICATURE)]

Hoo·sier /hŏŏzhər/ *n* somebody who comes from the state of Indiana (*informal*) [Early 19C. Origin ?]

Hoo·sier State *n* a nickname for Indiana

hoot /hoot/ *n* **1.** OWL'S CRY the long cry, including a sound like "hoo," of some owls **2.** SOUND LIKE OWL'S CRY a sound similar to an owl's cry, e.g., the sound made by a train whistle or car horn **3.** LAUGHING SOUND a shout, especially of laughter, derision, or scorn **4.** SOMEBODY OR SOMETHING HILARIOUS a highly amusing person, object, or situation (*slang*) ■ *v* (**hoot·ed, hoot·ing, hoots**) **1.** *vi* EMIT HOOT to produce a hoot **2.** *vi* MAKE LAUGHING SOUND to utter a sound of laughter, derision, or scorn **3.** *vt* DRIVE PERFORMER OFF STAGE to drive a public performer or speaker off a stage by jeering **4.** *vt* EXPRESS FEELING WITH JEERS to express a feeling such as contempt, derision, or scorn by jeering [12C. Probably an imitation of the sound] ◇ **not care** *or* **give a hoot** to show no interest or concern for something (*informal*)

hootch[1] *n* BEVERAGES, DRUGS another spelling of **hooch**[1]

hootch[2] *n* BUILDINGS another spelling of **hooch**[2]

hootch·y-kootch·y /hŏŏchee kŏŏchee/ (*plural* **hootch·y-kootch·ies**) *n* a sensual belly dance (*dated slang*) [Late 19C. Origin ?]

hoot·en·an·ny /hŏŏt'n ànnee/ (*plural* **-nies**) *n* (*informal*) **1.** an informal or impromptu performance by folk singers, in which the audience often participates **2.** an object or gadget for which the name is not known [Early 20C. Origin ?]

hoot·er /hŏŏtər/ *n* a person, animal, or object that hoots, especially a horn ■ **hoot·ers** *npl* an offensive term for a woman's breasts, especially when large (*slang*)

hoots /hoots/ *interj Scotland* used to express impatience, disbelief, or annoyance (*informal*)

hooved *adj* ZOOL another spelling of **hoofed**

Hoo·ver /hŏŏvər/ city in northern Alabama, a suburb of Birmingham. Population: 65,265 (2002 estimate).

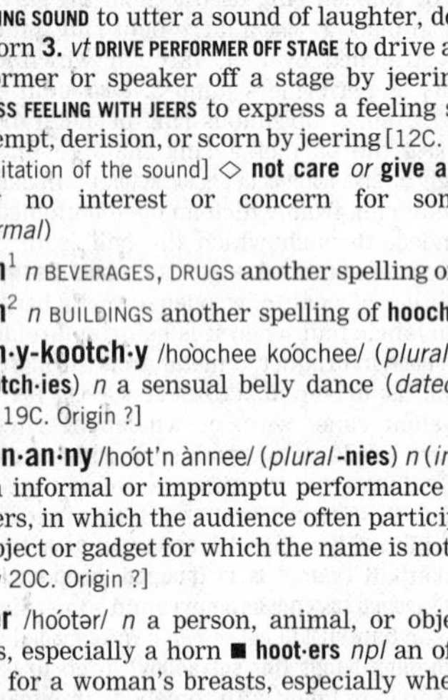

Herbert Hoover

Hoo·ver, Herbert (1874–1964) 31st president of the United States. A Republican president (1929–33), he opposed government assistance during the Great Depression. This made him unpopular, and he was defeated after one term by Franklin D. Roosevelt. Full name **Hoover, Herbert Clarke**. See table at **president**

> "We are nearer today to the ideal of the abolition of poverty and fear from the lives of men and women than ever before in any land."
> [Herbert Hoover, *Speech, New York City*; October 22, 1928]

Hoo·ver, J. Edgar (1895–1972) US director of the FBI (1924–72). Under his long and controversial leadership, the FBI targeted gangsters in the 1930s, Communists in the 1940s and 1950s, and liberals and opponents of the Vietnam War in the 1960s. Full name **Hoover, John Edgar**

> "You are honored by your friends... distinguished by your enemies. I have been very distinguished."
> [J. Edgar Hoover. Quoted in *J. Edgar Hoover*, Curt Gentry; 1991]

Hoo·ver, Lou Henry (1874–1944) US first lady (1929–33). She took a strong interest in education and the Girl Scout movement.

Hoo·ver Dam /hŏŏvər-/ *n* a dam on the Colorado River, on the Arizona-Nevada border, completed in 1936. It is 726 ft./221 m high.

Hoo·ver·ville /hŏŏvər vìl/ *n* a camp erected on the outskirts of a city during the Great Depression of the 1930s to house the poor and homeless [After Herbert HOOVER, president at the time]

hooves ZOOL plural of **hoof**

hop[1] /hop/ *v* (**hopped, hop·ping, hops**) **1.** *vi* JUMP LIGHTLY ON ONE FOOT to jump lightly or quickly, especially on one foot **2.** *vi* JUMP LIGHTLY WITH ALL FEET to move in a series of small jumps using both or all feet **3.** *vt* LEAP OVER SOMETHING to jump quickly or lightly over something **4.** *vi* GET ON OR OFF to move quickly or lightly into, onto, out of, or off something, especially a vehicle (*informal*) **5.** *vt* JUMP ABOARD VEHICLE to get on a plane, train, bus, or other vehicle, usually quickly or after a sudden decision to do so (*informal*) ○ *hop a plane to California* **6.** *vt* RIDE TRAIN WITHOUT TICKET to ride on a train secretly without paying (*informal*) **7.** *vi* TRAVEL BY AIRPLANE to make a short trip by airplane (*informal*) ○ *hop to Chicago for the convention* ■ *n* **1.** SMALL QUICK JUMP a small jump on one, both, or all feet **2.** BOUNCE a bounce or rebound of a ball ○ *caught the grounder on its second hop* **3.** FREE RIDE a free ride in a vehicle **4.** FLIGHT a flight or leg of a flight in an airplane (*informal*) ○ *a short hop from New York to Washington* **5.** JOURNEY a usually short journey (*informal*) ○ *a weekend hop to the mountains* **6.** DANCE a social occasion at which people dance together, usually to popular music (*informal*) [Old English *hoppian* "leap, limp" < Germanic]

hop[2] /hop/ *n* **1.** CLIMBING VINE a climbing vine of the mulberry family with lobed leaves. Flowers: green, arranged in spikes that look like pine cones. Latin name: *Humulus lupulus.* **2.** DRUG a narcotic drug, e.g., opium (*dated slang*) ■ **hops** *npl* DRIED HOP FLOWERS the dried flowers of the hop plant. Use: in brewing, to add flavor to beer. [15C. < Middle Low German, Middle Dutch *hoppe*] —**hop·py** *adj*

hop up *vt* (*slang*) **1.** to make somebody excited, or intoxicated, especially with drugs (*often passive*) **2.** AUTOMOT same as **soup up**

hop, skip, and jump *n* a short distance (*informal*) ○ *It's just a hop, skip, and jump to the station.*

hop, step, and jump *n* TRACK AND FIELD same as **triple jump**

hop clo·ver *n* a plant that is related to peas, beans, and clover and has yellow flowers that resemble hop flowers. Native to: northern temperate grasslands. Latin name: *Trifolium campestre.*

hope /hōp/ *vti* (**hoped, hop·ing, hopes**) WANT OR EXPECT SOMETHING to have a wish to get or do something or for something to happen or be true, especially something that seems possible or likely ■ *n* **1.** CONFIDENT DESIRE a feeling that something desirable is likely to happen ○ *The research offers hope to sufferers.* **2.** LIKELIHOOD OF SUCCESS a chance that something desirable will happen or be possible ○ *There's not much hope that things will improve.* **3.** WISH OR DESIRE something that somebody wants to have or do or wants to happen or be true ○ *My hope is that she will change her mind.* **4.** SOURCE OF SUCCESS somebody or something that seems likely to bring success or relief ○ *We have to do this, it's our only hope.* **5.** TRUST a feeling of trust (*archaic*) [Old English *hopian* (verb), *hopa* (noun), origin ?] —**hop·er** *n*

Hope /hōp/, **Bob** (1903–2003) British-born US comedian. Highlights of his long career in show business include his traveling revues entertaining US service personnel stationed abroad during World War II and his "Road" movies with Bing Crosby and Dorothy Lamour (1940–52), including *The Road to Singapore* (1940). Born **Hope, Leslie Townes**

> "A bank is a place that will lend you money if you can prove that you don't need it."
> [Bob Hope, *Life in the Crystal Palace*, Alan Harrington; 1959]

HOPE /hōp/ *abbr* Health Opportunity for People Everywhere

hope chest *n* **1.** a collection of household items such as linens, silver, and clothing that a young woman traditionally accumulates in anticipation of marriage **2.** a chest used to store household items traditionally accumulated by a young woman before marriage

hoped-for *adj* awaited with longing

hope·ful /hṓpfəl/ *adj* **1.** HAVING HOPE feeling fairly sure that something that is wanted will happen **2.** GIVING HOPE making somebody feel confident that something desirable will happen ○ *It looks hopeful that she'll be able to dance again.* **3.** SHOWING HOPE showing a desire for something ■ *n* SOMEBODY DESIRING SUCCESS somebody who desires achievement, especially somebody who hopes to be successful in sports, the arts, or politics —**hope·ful·ness** *n*

hope·ful·ly /hṓpfəlee/ *adv* **1.** in a way that shows somebody's hope of having or receiving something ○ *a hopefully worded apology* **2.** ⚠ used to indicate that somebody hopes something will happen or will be the case

USAGE Many people object when ***hopefully*** is used as a so-called sentence adverb (i.e., a sentence introducer that qualifies the entire sentence), as in *Hopefully, someone can resolve this.* The criticism arises from the fact that in this sentence no one is present who is meant to be doing the hoping. You can avoid the whole problem by saying *Let's hope, Let us hope*, or *It is to be hoped.*

Ho·peh /hō páy/ ➧ **Hebei**

~~**hopeing**~~ incorrect spelling of **hoping**

hope·less /hṓpləss/ *adj* **1.** WITH NO HOPE OF SUCCESS unable to succeed or improve, or unable to be resolved, helped, or cured **2.** DESPAIRING feeling or showing no hope **3.** VERY BAD showing a complete lack of ability, competence, or efficiency —**hope·less·ness** *n*

hope·less·ly /hṓpləsslee/ *adv* **1.** in a way that shows somebody has no hope of success, relief, or of getting what he or she wants **2.** actually or supposedly to too great a degree to be improved or to be of use

Hope·well[1] /hṓp wèl/ *adj* relating to an early Native North American culture of the Ohio and Illinois river valleys from A.D. 300 to A.D. 500, known especially for large-scale earthworks such as burial mounds [Late 19C. After Cloud *Hopewell*, owner of a farm in Ohio where remains were first identified]

Hope·well[2] /hṓp wèl/ city in eastern Virginia, used as a base by Ulysses S. Grant during the Civil War. Population: 22,525 (2002 estimate). Area: 7 sq. mi./18 sq. km.

hop·head /hóp hèd/ *n* somebody addicted to a narcotic drug such as heroin (*slang*)

hop horn·beam *n* a tree of the birch family whose fruit clusters resemble hops. Native to: eastern United States. Latin name: *Ostrya virginiana.*

Ho·pi /hṓpee/ (*plural same* or **-pis**) *n* **1.** a member of a Native North American people of northeastern Arizona **2.** a Shoshonean language spoken in northeastern Arizona. Native speakers: 5,000. [Late 19C. < Hopi, "peaceable"] —**Ho·pi** *adj*

Hop·kins /hópkinz/, **Sir Anthony** (*b.* 1937) Welsh actor. His movies include *Silence of the Lambs* (1991), *Remains of the Day* (1993), and *Shadowlands* (1993).

Hop·kins, Sir Frederick (1861–1947) British biochemist. He was the joint winner of the Nobel Prize in physiology or medicine (1929) for research into the role of vitamins in diet. Full name **Hopkins, Sir Frederick Gowland**

Hop·kins, Gerard Manley (1844–89) British poet. He was a technical innovator and is best remembered for his poem *The Wreck of the Deutschland* (1875).

> "I have desired to go / Where springs not fail, / To fields where flies no sharp and sided hail / And a few lilies blow."
> [Gerard Manley Hopkins, "Heaven-Have"; 1864]

Hop·kins, Harry Lloyd (1890–1946) US administrator and presidential aide. He headed the Works Progress Administration (1935–38), working closely with Franklin D. Roosevelt.

Hop·kins, Stephen (1707–85) American patriot. He served as governor of Rhode Island four times between 1755 and 1768.

Hop·kin·son /hópkinss'n/, **Francis** (1737–91) American writer and composer. He wrote satires such as *The Battle of the Kegs* (1778) attacking British rule, composed the first American opera, and signed the Declaration of Independence.

Hop·kins·ville /hópkinz vìl/ city in southwestern Kentucky, a manufacturing and tobacco marketing center. Population: 29,279 (2002 estimate).

hop·lite /hóp lìt/ *n* in ancient Greece, a heavily armed foot soldier [Early 18C. < Greek *hoplitēs* < *hoplon* "weapon" < *hepein* "care for, work at"] —**hop·lit·ic** /hop líttik/ *adj*

hop·lol·o·gy /hop lóllәjee/ *n* the study of weapons and armor [Late 19C. < Greek *hoplon* (see HOPLITE)] —**hop·lol·o·gist** *n*

hopped-up *adj* (*slang*) **1.** excited, exhilarated, or intoxicated, especially by drugs **2.** made more powerful by mechanical modification

hop·per[1] /hóppәr/ *n* **1.** FUNNEL-SHAPED DISPENSER a large funnel-shaped container for storing and dispensing grain, fuel, or other materials **2.** VEHICLE THAT DISCHARGES LOAD THROUGH FLOOR a truck or railroad car with sloping floors designed to carry dry bulk goods such as grain or cement that are discharged through an opening in the bottom **3.** SOMEBODY OR SOMETHING THAT HOPS somebody who or something that hops **4.** JUMPING INSECT a jumping insect, e.g., a leafhopper or treehopper. Order: Homoptera. [13C. < HOP[1]]

hop·per[2] /hóppәr/ *n* a machine used to harvest hops [Early 18C. < HOP[2]]

UPI/Corbis-Bettmann

Edward Hopper

Hop·per /hóppәr/, **Edward** (1882–1967) US artist. His work, e.g., *Nighthawks* (1942), is known for its stark realism.

> "A nation's art is greatest when it most reflects the character of its people."
> [Edward Hopper. Quoted in *Aroused by Books*, Anatole Broyard; 1974]

hop-pick·er *n* a person or machine that harvests hops

hop·ping /hópping/ *adj* very active or busy (*informal*) ■ *n* going from one place of a particular kind to another of the same kind (*usually used in combination*) ○ *job-hopping*

hop·ping John /hòppin-/, **hop·pin' John** *n* a dish of black-eyed peas, spices, and bacon or salt pork

hop·ping mad *adj* extremely angry (*informal*)

hop·pin' John *n* FOOD same as **hopping John**

hop·ple /hópp'l/ HORSERACING *vt* same as **hobble** *v* (sense 2) ■ *n* same as **hobble** *n* (sense 1) [Late 16C. Probably < Low German] —**hop·pler** *n*

hop·sack /hóp sàk/ *n* **1.** a coarsely woven cotton or woolen fabric. Use: clothes. **2.** a coarse hemp or jute fabric. Use: sacks, bags.

Barnaby's

hopscotch

hop·scotch /hóp skòch/ *n* a children's game in which players hop along squares marked in a pattern on the ground to pick up a small object thrown into one of the squares [Early 19C < SCOTCH[1], "scratched line"]

hop tre·foil *n UK* PLANTS same as **hop clover**

hor. *abbr* **1.** horizon **2.** horizontal **3.** horology

ho·ra /háwrә/, **ho·rah** *n* **1.** a traditional circle dance of Israel and Romania **2.** the music for a hora [Late 19C. Directly or via modern Hebrew < Romanian *horă*]

Hor·ace /háwrәss/ (65–8 B.C.) Roman poet. The son of a freedman, he was educated in Rome and Athens, and became the preeminent lyric poet of his time. His most famous works are *Odes* (23 B.C.) and *Epistles* (20? B.C.). Full name **Flaccus, Quintus Horatius**

> "Seize the day, and put as little trust as you can in the morrow."
> [Horace, *Odes*; 23 B.C.]

Ho·rae /háw rèe/ *npl* in Greek mythology, the goddesses of the seasons and the order of nature

ho·rah *n* DANCE, MUSIC another spelling of **hora**

ho·ra·ry /háwrәree/ *adj* (*formal*) **1.** relating to an hour or hours **2.** same as **hourly** *adj* (sense 1) [Early 17C. < medieval Latin *horarius* < Latin *hora* (see HOUR)]

Ho·ra·tian /hә ráysh'n/ *adj* written by or in the style of the ancient Roman poet Horace [Early 17C. < Latin *Horatianus* < Quintus *Horatius* Flaccus, Latin name of HORACE]

Ho·ra·tian ode *n* an ode that has several stanzas, each of which has the same rhythmic pattern

hor·cha·ta /awr chaátә/ *n Hispanic* a sweet drink, usually made in Mexico from ground rice or cantaloupe melon seeds and in Spain from chufas or hazelnuts [Mid-19C. < Spanish]

horde /hawrd/ *n* **1.** LARGE CROWD a large group of people (*often used in the plural*) **2.** NOMADIC GROUP a group of nomads, especially of a people who live by hunting and foraging for food (**hunter-gatherers**) **3.** SWARM OR PACK a large group of insects or other animals moving in a mass ■ *vi* (**hord·ed, hord·ing, hordes**) **1.** FORM OR LIVE IN CROWD to gather together, move, or live in a large crowd or mass **2.** LIVE IN GROUP to live together in a nomadic group [Mid-16C. Directly or via French and German < Polish *horda* < Turkish *ordu* "camp, army"]

SPELLCHECK See ***hoard***.

hore·hound /háwr hòwnd/ *n* **1.** a bitter perennial mint with downy leaves and square stems. Flowers: small white, yielding juice used as a flavoring and in cough remedies. Native to: Europe, Asia. Latin name: *Marrubium vulgare*. **2.** an extract of the horehound plant, or something flavored with it, e.g., cough drops [Old English *hāre hūne* < *hār* "hoar" + *hūne* "horehound," origin ?]

~~**horizen**~~ incorrect spelling of **horizon**

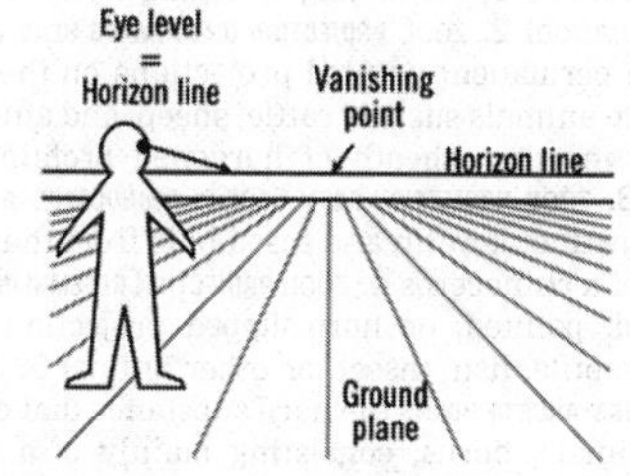

horizon

ho·ri·zon /hә rīz'n/ *n* **1.** PLACE WHERE EARTH MEETS SKY the line in the farthest distance where the land or sea seems to meet the sky **2.** ASTRON CIRCLE ON APPARENT SPHERE OF SKY a circle formed on the celestial sphere by a plane tangent to a point on the Earth's surface **3.** ASTRON CIRCLE ON CELESTIAL SPHERE a circle formed on the celestial sphere by a plane through the center of the Earth and parallel to the tangent of a point on Earth's surface **4.** GEOG DISTINCT LAYER OF SOIL a layer of soil having characteristics that distinguish it from other layers **5.** PALEONT, GEOL GEOLOGIC LAYER a distinct layer of rock or geologic deposit within a stratum that can be dated, e.g., by its fossil content ■ **ho·ri·zons** *npl* RANGE OF EXPERIENCE the range or limits of somebody's interests, knowledge, or experience [14C. Via French < late Latin < Greek *horizōn (kuklos)* "limiting (circle)," present participle of *horizein* "to limit" < *horos* "limit"] —**ho·ri·zon·al** *adj*

hor·i·zon·tal /hàwri zónt'l/ *adj* **1.** LEVEL parallel to the horizon **2.** MEASURED PARALLEL TO HORIZON measured or operating in a plane parallel to the horizon **3.** HAVING SAME STATUS at the same level within an organization ○ *a horizontal promotion* **4.** APPLIED TO ALL applied equally to all members, parts, or aspects of something ○ *a horizontal bonus* **5.** OF HORIZON relating to the horizon **6.** LYING DOWN lying down or in a reclining position (*informal*) **7.** GENETICS OF TRANSFER OF GENETIC MATERIAL relating to the transfer of genetic material from one individual to another of a different species ■ *n* SOMETHING HORIZONTAL a horizontal line, surface, or position [Mid-16C. < French, or modern Latin *horizontalis* < late Latin *horizont-*, stem of *horizon* (see HORIZON)] —**hor·i·zon·tal·i·ty** /-zon tállәtee/ *n* —**hor·i·zon·tal·ly** *adv* —**hor·i·zon·tal·ness** *n*

hor·i·zon·tal bar *n* **1.** a metal bar fixed in a horizontal position and used for gymnastic exercises **2.** a competitive gymnastics event involving feats of skill and strength on the horizontal bar

hor·i·zon·tal mo·bil·i·ty *n* a change in social situation that does not involve a change in social status

hor·i·zon·tal un·ion *n* HR same as **craft union**

Hor·liv·ka /háwr lәvkә, -lèewkә/ industrial city in eastern Ukraine. Population: 303,593 (1999).

hor·mo·go·ni·um /hàwrmә gónee әm/ (*plural* **-ni·a** /-nee ә/) *n* a section of a filament in some cyanobacteria that detaches and reproduces by cell division [Late 19C. < modern Latin < Greek *hormos* "chain" + *gonos* "generation, seed"]

hor·mone /háwr mōn/ *n* **1.** CHEMICAL IN BODY a chemical secreted by an endocrine gland or some nerve cells that regulates the function of a specific tissue or organ **2.** CHEMICAL IN PLANTS a substance synthesized by plants that regulates their growth and development **3.** REGULATING CHEMICAL IN INSECTS a substance produced in the body of an insect that regulates various aspects of growth and development such as the change from larva to adult **4.** REGULATING CHEMICAL a synthetic chemical that acts like a hormone [Early 20C. < Greek *hormōn*, present participle of *horman* "set in motion" < *hormē* "assault"] —**hor·mon·al** /hawr mōn'l/ *adj* —**hor·mon·al·ly** *adv*

hor·mone re·place·ment ther·a·py *n* treatment to maintain previous levels of estrogen and other hormones in women during and after the menopause, to avoid bone fragility (**osteoporosis**) and protect against heart disease. ◊ **estrogen-replacement therapy**

Hor·muz, Strait of /hawr mo͞oz, háwr mooz/ narrow waterway between Iran and the Arabian Peninsula, linking the Persian Gulf with the Arabian Sea

horn /hawrn/ *n* **1.** AUTOMOT, EMERGENCIES **NOISE-MAKING WARNING DEVICE** a device, e.g., in a car, that produces a loud noise as a warning or signal (*often used in combination*) **2.** ZOOL **PROJECTION ON ANIMAL'S HEAD** either of two permanent pointed projections on the head of some animals such as cattle, sheep, and antelope, consisting of a sheath of hardened protein over bone **3.** ZOOL **PROJECTION FROM NOSE OF RHINOCEROS** a solid outgrowth of keratin and fused hair from the nasal bone of a rhinoceros **4.** ZOOL **PROJECTION RESEMBLING HORN** a hard, pointed, or horn-shaped projection on a bird, reptile, fish, insect, or other animal **5.** INDUST **HARD SUBSTANCE OF HORNS** the hard substance that covers an animal's horns, consisting mainly of a tough protein (**keratin**) **6.** **SOMETHING MADE OF HORN** something made with a piece of horn or from a synthetic substance resembling it **7.** **PROJECTION ON DEVIL'S HEAD** either of a pair of parts resembling an animal's horns supposed to grow on the head of the devil or a cuckold **8.** **HORN-SHAPED THING** something shaped like a horn, e.g., either of the tips of a crescent moon, the pommel of a saddle, or the pointed end of an anvil **9.** GEOG **SHARP PEAK** a sharp pyramid-shaped mountain peak **10.** GEOG **HORN-SHAPED AREA** a horn-shaped body of water or land **11.** MUSIC **BRASS INSTRUMENT** a wind instrument, usually made of brass, with a long tube whose flared end produces a sound when the player's lips vibrate together into the mouthpiece **12.** MUSIC **WIND INSTRUMENT** any wind instrument used in a jazz band, especially a trumpet (*informal*) **13.** MUSIC **SIMPLE WIND INSTRUMENT** a simple or early musical instrument made from an animal's horn **14.** TELECOM same as **telephone** (*slang*) ■ *v* (**horned, horn·ing, horns**) **1.** *vt* **PROVIDE SOMETHING WITH HORNS** to give something a horn or horns **2.** *vt* **ATTACK SOMEBODY WITH HORNS** to butt or gore somebody with the horns **3.** *vt US, Carib* **CUCKOLD SOMEBODY** to make a cuckold of somebody by having a sexual relationship with that person's spouse or partner (*informal*) **4.** *vi Malaysia, Singapore* **BLOW CAR HORN** to cause a car horn to make a warning sound ○ *Don't horn at other drivers except in an emergency.* [Old English, < Indo-European, "horn, head"] —**horn·less** *adj* ◇ **pull in your horns 1.** to spend or invest less money than usual or before **2.** to adopt a less active or less assertive position ◇ **lock horns (with somebody)** to engage in an argument or quarrel with somebody ◇ **on the horns of a dilemma** faced with making a decision between two things or two courses of action, each of which is problematic or unattractive

ORIGIN The Indo-European word from which ***horn*** is ultimately derived, is also the ancestor of English *carrot, corn²*, *cornea, corner, cornet, cranium, ginger, hart, hornet, keratin, rhinoceros*, and *triceratops*.

horn in *vi* to intrude, interfere, or get involved in something without invitation (*informal*)

Horn, Cape /hawrn/ cape at the southern extremity of South America. Height: 1,391 ft./424 m. Spanish name **Cabo de Hornos**

horn·beam /háwrn bēem/ *n* **1.** a tree with smooth grayish bark and hard white wood. Genus: *Carpinus.* **2.** the hard white wood of the hornbeam tree

hornbill

horn·bill /háwrn bìl/ *n* a noisy tropical bird that has a large curved beak with a horny protuberance and is often found in large groups. Family: Bucerotidae.

horn·blende /háwrn blènd/ *n* a dark green to black mineral of the amphibole group, containing calcium, iron, magnesium, and sodium [Late 18C. < German] —**horn·blend·ic** /hawrn bléndik/ *adj*

horn·book /háwrn bo͝ok/ *n* **1.** formerly, a page of text used as an aid in teaching reading, usually printed with the alphabet, letter combinations, and a religious passage, covered with a thin layer of horn **2.** a book containing elementary teaching material for those learning a subject or skill

Horne /hawrn/, **Marilyn** (*b.* 1934) US mezzo-soprano. She is known for her roles in operas by Rossini, Berg, and Stravinsky.

> "The thing to do for insomnia is to get an opera score and read *that.* That will bore you to death."
> [Marilyn Horne. Quoted in "Marilyn Horne," *Divas: Impressions of Six Opera Superstars*, Winthrop Sargeant; 1959]

horned /hawrnd/ *adj* having a horn or horns, or one or more projections that resemble horns

horned liz·ard *n* a small insect-eating lizard that has a flattened body, a short tail, and spikes like horns on its head. Native to: desert regions of the southwestern United States and Mexico. Genus: *Phrynosoma.*

horned owl *n* a large owl with prominent ear tufts resembling horns. Latin name: *Bubo virginianus.*

horned pout *n* FISH same as **hornpout**

horned toad *n* REPT same as **horned lizard**

horned vi·per *n* a poisonous snake that has spines on its head that look like horns. Native to: dry regions of the Near East and Africa. Latin name: *Cerastes cornutus.*

hor·net /háwrnət/ *n* a large stinging wasp that builds large group nests underground or hanging from a tree. Family: Vespidae. [Old English *hyrnet(u)* < Indo-European]

hor·net's nest *n* a highly controversial issue or situation that is likely to lead to confrontation, opposition, or argument

Hor·ney /háwrnee/, **Karen** (1885–1952) German-born US psychoanalyst. She advanced and developed Freudian theory in books such as *New Ways in Psychoanalysis* (1939).

> "The most comprehensive formulation of therapeutic goals is the striving for *wholeheartedness*: to be without pretense, to be emotionally sincere, to be able to put the whole of oneself into one's feelings, one's work, one's beliefs."
> [Karen Horney, *Our Inner Conflicts*; 1945]

horn·fels /háwrn fèlz/ *n* a fine-grained metamorphic rock composed of silicate minerals and formed through the action of heat and pressure on shale [Mid-19C. < German, "horn rock"]

horn fly *n* a small bloodsucking black fly that is a pest of cattle. Latin name: *Haematobia irritans.* [< its sucking blood from the base of the horns]

horn·ing /háwrning/ *n Northeast US* same as **shivaree**

hor·nist /háwrnist/ *n* a musician who plays a horn

horn of plen·ty *n* **1.** ARTS same as **cornucopia** (sense 2) **2.** a funnel-shaped black and brown edible fungus found in deciduous woodland in fall. Latin name: *Craterellus cornucopioides.*

horn·pipe /háwrn pīp/ *n* **1.** DANCE **SAILORS' DANCE** a lively British dance traditionally performed by sailors **2.** MUSIC **MUSIC ACCOMPANYING HORNPIPE** the music for a hornpipe, or an orchestral piece based on this **3.** MUSIC **REED INSTRUMENT** a musical instrument with a single reed and a mouthpiece made of horn, traditionally used to play the music for a hornpipe

horn·pout /háwrn pòwt/ *n* a small freshwater catfish with a large head and eight barbels. Native to: North America. Latin name: *Ictalurus nebulosus.*

horn-rims, horn-rimmed glasses *npl* glasses with frames made from dark-colored horn or a synthetic substance resembling this —**horn-rimmed** *adj*

Horns·by /háwrnzbee/, **Rogers** (1896–1963) US baseball player and manager. Considered one of the best batters of all time, he was inducted into the Baseball Hall of Fame (1942). Also known as **The Rajah**

horn·stone /háwrn stōn/ *n* GEOL same as **hornfels** [Early 18C. Translation of German *Hornstein*]

horn·swog·gle /háwrn swògg'l/ (**-gled, -gling, -gles**) *vt* to cheat, trick, or deceive somebody (*informal*) [Early 19C. Origin ?]

horn·tail /háwrn tàyl/ *n* an insect that resembles a wasp and whose larvae burrow in wood. The female has a specialized egg-laying organ (**ovipositor**) used to lay eggs in wood. Family: Siricidae.

horn·worm /háwrn wùrm/ *n* the caterpillar of some hawk moths, with a projection on its tail that resembles a horn. Hornworms are often destructive agricultural pests.

horn·wort /háwrn wùrt, -wàwrt/ *n* a rootless water plant that grows in branching submerged masses and has finely dissected leaves and tiny flowers. Genus: *Ceratophylum.* [< its branching stem]

horn·y /háwrnee/ (**-i·er, -i·est**) *adj* **1.** **OF OR LIKE HORN** made of or resembling horn **2.** **AS TOUGH AS HORN** hard or rough like horn **3.** **FEELING SEXY** sexually excited, or easily aroused sexually (*slang*) **4.** **WITH HORNS** having a horn or horns —**horn·i·ly** *adv* —**horn·i·ness** *n*

horol. *abbr* **1.** horological **2.** horology

Hor·o·lo·gi·um /hàwrə lṓjee əm, -lṓjəm/ *n* a faint constellation of the southern hemisphere situated between Hydrus and Eridanus

ho·rol·o·gy /haw róllәjee/ *n* **1.** the study or science of measuring time **2.** the art or skill of making clocks, watches, or other devices for telling the time [Early 19C. < Greek *hōra* "time, hour"] —**hor·o·log·ic** /hàwrə lójjik/ *adj* —**hor·o·log·i·cal** *adj* —**hor·o·log·i·cal·ly** *adv* —**ho·rol·o·gist** *n*

hor·o·scope /háwrə skōp/ *n* **1.** an astrologer's description of the personality and future of a person based on the position of the planets in relation to the sign of the zodiac under which the person was born **2.** the positions of the stars or planets relative to each another at a specific moment, especially the time of somebody's birth, or a diagram of these positions [Pre-12C. Via Latin < Greek *hōroskopos* "time observer" < *hōra* "time, hour" (of birth)] —**hor·o·scop·ic** /hàwrə skóppik/ *adj*

ho·ros·co·py /hə róskəpee/ *n* the making and interpretation of horoscopes

Ho·ro·witz /háwrə wìts/, **Vladimir** (1904–89) Russian-born US pianist. He was known for his brilliant virtuosity. His interpretations of works by Liszt and Rachmaninoff achieved popular and critical acclaim.

hor·ren·dous /hə réndəss, haw-/ *adj* **1.** sufficiently unpleasant, frightening, or shocking as to provoke horror **2.** very large, great, or high, often unreasonably or excessively so (*informal*) ○ *horrendous prices* [Mid-17C. < Latin *horrendus* "to be shuddered at," form of *horrere* "bristle, shudder with fear at"] —**hor·ren·dous·ness** *n*

hor·ren·dous·ly /hə réndəsslee, haw-/ *adv* to a very great and often unreasonable or excessive degree

hor·ri·ble /háwrəb'l/ *adj* **1.** **VERY UNPLEASANT** very bad, unpleasant, or unsightly ○ *a horrible smell* **2.** **CAUSING HORROR** sufficiently frightening, distressing, or shocking as to provoke horror ○ *a horrible crime* **3.** **NASTY** unkind, rude, or ill-behaved (*informal*) [13C. Via French < Latin *horribilis* < *horrere* "bristle, shudder with fear at"] —**hor·ri·ble·ness** *n*

hor·ri·bly /háwrəblee/ *adv* **1.** in an unpleasant, frightening, distressing, or shocking way **2.** to a great or excessive extent ○ *horribly late*

hor·rid /háwrid/ *adj* **1.** **NASTY** callously unkind or nasty (*informal*) ○ *a horrid thing to say* **2.** **CAUSING DISGUST** provoking disgust or extreme displeasure ○ *a horrid taste* **3.** **CAUSING HORROR** dreadful, shocking, or frightening enough to cause horror ○ *a horrid accident* **4.** **BRISTLY** rough, shaggy, or bristly (*archaic*) [Late 16C. < Latin *horridus* "bristly, rough, horrid" < *horrere* "bristle, shudder with fear at"] —**hor·rid·ly** *adv* —**hor·rid·ness** *n*

hor·rif·ic /haw ríffik/ *adj* frightening or disturbing enough to cause horror [Mid-17C. Directly or via French < Latin *horrificus* < *horrere* "bristle, shudder with fear at"] —**hor·rif·i·cal·ly** *adv*

hor·ri·fy /háwrə fī/ (**-fied, -fy·ing, -fies**) *vt* **1.** to make somebody feel horror, disgust, or fright **2.** to make somebody shocked or dismayed [Late 18C. < Latin *horrificare* "cause horror" < *horrere* "bristle, shudder with fear at"] —**hor·ri·fi·ca·tion** /hàwrəfi káysh'n/ *n* —**hor·ri·fied** *adj* —**hor·ri·fy·ing** *adj* —**hor·ri·fy·ing·ly** *adv*

hor·rip·i·la·tion /haw rìppi láysh'n/ *n* the standing on end of somebody's hair, e.g., because of fear or cold [Mid-17C. < late Latin *horripilation-* < Latin *horripilare* "become hairy" < *horrere* "to bristle" + *pilus* "hair"]

hor·ror /háwrər/ *n* **1.** INTENSE FEAR a very strong feeling of fear, shock, or disgust **2.** INTENSE DISLIKE a feeling of distress or distaste ○ *He has a horror of spiders.* **3.** SOMETHING CAUSING HORROR something that causes a very strong feeling of fear, shock, or disgust ○ *the horrors of war* **4.** SOMETHING UNPLEASANT a very unpleasant or unsightly thing (*informal*) ○ *The new building is an absolute horror.* ■ **hor·rors** *npl* (*informal*) **1.** FEELING OF TERROR a feeling of intense fear, anxiety, or hopelessness **2.** MED same as **delirium tremens** ■ *adj* MOVIES, LITERAT GROTESQUE AND TERRIFYING describes a genre of motion picture or literature intended to thrill viewers or readers by provoking fear or revulsion through the portrayal of grotesque, violent, or supernatural events [14C. Directly or via French < Latin < *horrere* "bristle, shudder with fear at"]

hor·ror sto·ry *n* **1.** a story that is intended to frighten people, usually by describing gruesome or supernatural events **2.** a true account of something very unpleasant or shocking

hor·ror-struck, hor·ror-strick·en *adj* suddenly shocked, frightened, or dismayed

hors con·cours /àwr kawN ko͞or/ *adj* not participating in a competition or contest [< French, "out of the competition"]

hors de com·bat /àwr də kawN baá/ *adj* out of action and often in a seriously wounded condition [< French, "out of the fight"]

hors d'oeuvre /awr dúrv/ (*plural same* or **hors d'oeuvres** /-dúrvz/) *n* a small portion of food served cold or hot before a meal to stimulate the appetite [< French, "outside the work"]

horse /hawrss/ *n* **1.** FOUR-LEGGED ANIMAL a large four-legged animal with a mane, tail, hooves, and a long head. Raised for: riding, pulling vehicles, carrying loads. Latin name: *Equus caballus*. **2.** STALLION OR GELDING an adult male horse **3.** ANIMAL OF HORSE FAMILY an animal that belongs to the horse family, e.g., a donkey or zebra. Family: Equidae. **4.** GYMNASTICS same as **vaulting horse** **5.** FRAME OR SUPPORT a frame or support, especially one mounted on four legs **6.** MIL MOUNTED SOLDIERS a unit of soldiers riding horses (*takes a singular verb*) **7.** GEOL MASS OF ROCK IN ORE a mass of rock located in an ore vein **8.** DRUGS same as **heroin** (*dated slang*) **9.** AUTOMOT same as **horsepower** (*informal; usually used in the plural*) ■ **hors·es** *npl* HORSERACING horseracing, especially as a gambling activity (*informal*) ■ *v* (**horsed, hors·ing, hors·es**) **1.** *vt* GIVE SOMEBODY HORSE to provide somebody with a horse **2.** *vti* RIDING PUT OR GET ON HORSE to put a rider on a horse's back, or mount a horse **3.** *vi* ZOOL BE IN HEAT to be ready to mate with a male horse (*refers to mares*) [Old English *hors* < Germanic] ◇ **back** *or* **pick the wrong horse** to make a bad choice ◇ **beat a dead horse** to pursue a topic or course of action that is likely to be totally unproductive ◇ **from the horse's mouth** from a well-informed and reliable source ◇ **look a gift horse in the mouth** to criticize something that has been given to you ◇ **wild horses would** *or* **could not...** no amount of force or persuasion could make somebody do a particular thing (*informal*) ○ *Wild horses wouldn't drag the secret out of me.*

SPELLCHECK See *hoarse*.

horse around *vi* to play or fool around in a boisterous manner

horse-and-bug·gy *adj* **1.** belonging or relating to the era before the invention of the automobile **2.** adhering to things, fashions, or ideas that are old-fashioned and out of date (*informal*)

horse·back /háwrss bàk/ *adj, adv* sitting on or riding a horse ◇ **on horseback** sitting on or riding a horse

horse·back rid·ing *n* the practice of riding on horseback, especially as a recreation

horse bean *n* same as **broad bean** (sense 1) [< its use as fodder for horses]

horse·box /háwrss bòks/ *n UK* same as **horsecar**

horse·car /háwrss kaàr/ *n* a vehicle used to transport horses, e.g., a truck or railroad car

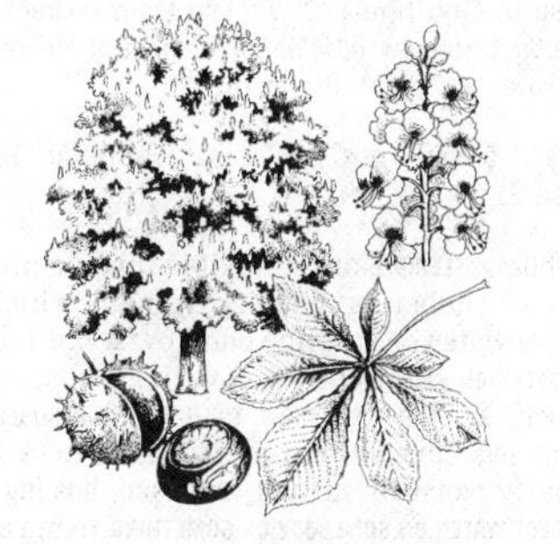

horse chestnut

horse chest·nut *n* **1.** SEED a large shiny brown inedible seed with a fleshy, sometimes spiny husk **2.** TREE a large tree that has compound leaves, conical flower clusters, and sticky winter buds, and produces horse chestnuts. Native to: northern hemisphere. Genus: *Aesculus*. **3.** WOOD the soft wood of the horse chestnut tree

horse·feath·ers /háwrss fèthərz/ *n, interj* nonsense (*slang humorous; takes a singular verb*) [Early 20C. Alteration of HORSESHIT]

horse·flesh /háwrss flèsh/ *n* **1.** horses collectively **2.** the flesh of a horse, especially when sold or eaten as meat

horse·fly /háwrss flī/ (*plural* **-flies**) *n* a large two-winged fly, the female of which sucks the blood of horses and other animals. Genus: *Tabanus*.

horse gen·tian *n* a plant of the honeysuckle family with orange fruit. Flowers: purplish brown. Native to: North America. Genus: *Triosteum*. [*Horse* because large or coarse]

horse·hair /háwrss hèr/ *n* **1.** hair from a horse's mane and tail. Use: upholstery, mattress filling, cloth. **2.** fabric woven from the hair of a horse's mane and tail

horse·hair worm *n* ZOOL same as **hairworm**

Horse·head neb·u·la /háwrss hed-/ *n* a dark nebula in the constellation Orion, shaped like a horse's head

horse·hide /háwrss hīd/ *n* **1.** the tough thick skin of a horse, or leather made from a horse's skin **2.** the ball used in the game of baseball (*informal*)

horse lat·i·tudes *npl* either of two regions at sea near the latitudes 30° S and 30° N marked by high atmospheric pressure and light variable winds or calms [Origin ?]

horse·laugh /háwrss làf/ *n* a loud, coarse, and often scornful laugh

horse·leech /háwrss leèch/ *n* a large freshwater leech. Genus: *Haemopis*. [*Horse* because large or coarse]

horse·less car·riage /hàwrssləss \kàrrij/ *n* an automobile, at a time when horse-drawn vehicles were still the usual form of transport (*archaic*)

horse mack·er·el *n* a swift torpedo-shaped fish. Native to: Atlantic Ocean, Mediterranean Sea, Black Sea. Latin name: *Trachurus trachurus*. [*Horse* because large or coarse]

horse·man /háwrssmən/ (*plural* **-men** /-mən/) *n* **1.** a man who rides or is riding a horse, especially one who does so with skill **2.** a man who owns or breeds horses —**horse·man·ship** *n*

horse·mint /háwrss mìnt/ *n* **1.** a coarse mint. Flowers: showy, yellow with purple spots. Native to: North America. Latin name: *Monarda punctata*. **2.** a hairy wild mint. Flowers: small, pinkish purple, in elongated clusters. Native to: Europe, Asia. Latin name: *Mentha longifolia*. [*Horse* because large or coarse]

horse net·tle *n* a coarse prickly weed of the nightshade family with yellow berries. Flowers: white, blue. Native to: North America. Latin name: *Solanum carolinese*. [*Horse* because large or coarse]

horse o·pe·ra *n* MOVIES same as **western** (*informal*)

horse pis·tol *n* a large pistol formerly used by horsemen and carried in a holster

horse·play /háwrss plày/ *n* rough boisterous playful behavior

horse·play·er /háwrss plày ər/ *n* a frequent better on horse races

horse·pow·er /háwrss pòwr/ *n* a unit of power equal in the United States to 745.7 watts and in the United Kingdom to 550 foot-pounds per second [Supposedly equivalent to the work rate of a horse]

horse puck·ey /háwrss pùkee/, **horse puck·y** *interj* used to express disbelief or scorn (*slang; regional*) [Late 20C. Modeled on *horse hockey*, a euphemism for *horse crap*]

horse·race *n* a race between horses ridden by jockeys on a flat circuit or over obstacles

horse·rac·ing /háwss ràyssing/ *n* a sport in which horses ridden by jockeys race against each other, usually with spectators and others betting on the result

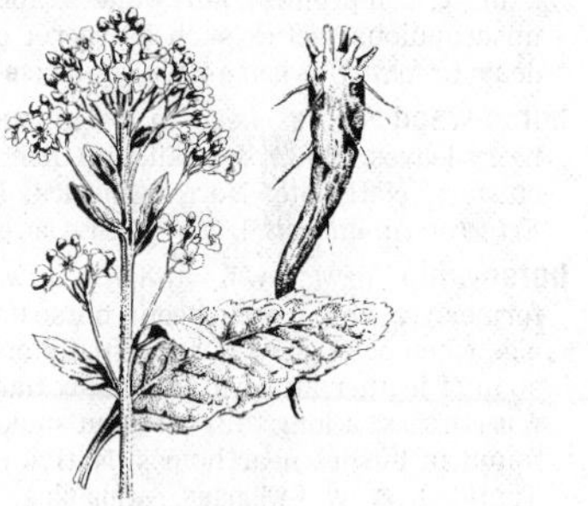

horseradish

horse·rad·ish /háwrss ràddish/ *n* **1.** a long slim pungent root. Use: in cooking, especially peeled and grated to make a hot sharp-tasting sauce often served with beef. **2.** a tall coarse plant that yields horseradish. Flowers: white. Native to: North America. Latin name: *Amoracia lapathifolia*. [*Horse* because large or coarse]

horse rid·ing *n* SHOW JUMPING same as **horseback riding**

hors·e's ass *n* an offensive term for somebody who is disliked or considered objectionable (*insult*)

horse sense *n* same as **common sense** (*informal*)

horse·shit /háwrss shìt/ *n* (*slang*) **1.** an offensive term for nonsense **2.** an offensive term for the excrement of a horse

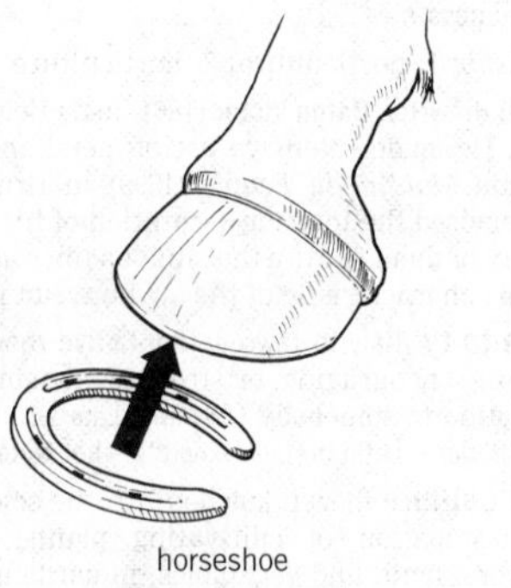

horseshoe

horse·shoe /háwrss sho͞o/ *n* **1.** PROTECTION FOR HORSE'S HOOF a flat U-shaped piece of iron nailed to the bottom of a horse's hoof to protect it against hard surfaces. Horseshoes are regarded as symbols of good luck. **2.** GOOD-LUCK TOKEN a representation of a horseshoe regarded as a symbol of good luck **3.** SOMETHING HORSESHOE-SHAPED something that has the curved shape of a horseshoe ○"*... every known superstition in the world is gathered into the horseshoe of the Carpathians ...*" (Bram Stoker, *Dracula*; 1897) ■ *vt* (**-shoed, -shoe·ing, -shoes**) RIDING same as **shoe** *v* (sense 1) —**horse·sho·er** *n*

horse·shoe arch *n* an arch that narrows slightly below the upper rounded part. Horseshoe arches are characteristic of the Islamic architecture of southern Spain and North Africa.

horse·shoe crab *n* an invertebrate sea animal that has a stiff pointed tail and rounded brown body resembling a horseshoe. Native to: eastern North America, Asia. Class: Merostomata.

Horse·shoe Falls /háwrss shoo-/ crescent-shaped Canadian section of Niagara Falls on the US-Canadian border. Height: 161 ft./49 m.

horse·shoes /háwrss shōōz/ *n* a game in which players throw horseshoes at a post and score points according to how close the horseshoes land to the post (*takes a singular verb*)

horse show *n* a sporting event in which horses and usually riders are judged on their skills in a variety of competitions such as riding or jumping

horse·tail /háwrss tàyl/ *n* **1.** a nonflowering plant that has a hollow jointed stem, tiny thin leaves, and spore-producing cones at the top of the stems. Genus: *Equisetum*. **2.** an object resembling a horse's tail, formerly used as a emblem of rank by Turkish pashas in the Ottoman Empire

horse-trad·ing *n* negotiation that involves hard bargaining, compromise, shrewdness, and sometimes unscrupulous tactics such as secret or unofficial deals (*informal*) —**horse-trade** *vi* —**horse-trad·er** *n*

horse·weed /háwrss wēed/ *n* a fleabane with thin hairy leaves. Flowers: small, greenish or white, in clusters. Native to: North America. Latin name: *Erigeron canadensis*. [*Horse* because large or coarse]

horse·whip /háwrss wìp, -hwìp/ *n* **1.** WHIP FOR HORSE formerly, a whip used to keep a horse under control, e.g., when being driven, and usually made of a long strip of leather attached to a short handle **2.** *Carib* W INDIAN SNAKE a long thin common snake frequently found in bushes near homes. Native to: forests of Trinidad. ■ *vt* (**-whipped, -whip·ping, -whips**) BEAT PERSON OR ANIMAL SEVERELY to flog a person or animal with a horsewhip or with something similar, usually as a punishment

horse·wom·an /háwrss wŏŏmmən/ (*plural* **-wom·en** /-wìmmin/) *n* **1.** a woman who rides or is riding a horse, especially one who does so with skill **2.** a woman who owns or breeds horses

hors·ey *adj* another spelling of **horsy**

horst /hawrst/ *n* an elevated block of the Earth's crust forced upward between faults [Late 19C. < German, "heap, mass"]

hors·y /háwrssee/ (**-i·er, -i·est**), **hors·ey** *adj* **1.** RELATING TO HORSES relating to or characteristic of a horse **2.** LOOKING LIKE HORSE heavy, awkward, and unattractive in appearance **3.** INTERESTED IN HORSES very fond of horses and interested in activities involving horses such as riding, racing, show jumping, or hunting —**hors·i·ness** *n*

hort. *abbr* **1.** horticultural **2.** horticulture

Hor·ta /háwrtə/, **Baron Victor** (1861–1947) Belgian architect. He made extensive use of metal and glass, as in the *Maison du Peuple* (1899) in Brussels, and supervised the interior decoration of his buildings. Many of them feature the sinuous lines and organic forms characteristic of the art nouveau movement.

hor·ta·to·ry /háwrtə tàwree/, **hor·ta·tive** /háwrtətiv/ *adj* urging, encouraging, or strongly advising a course of action to somebody (*formal*) [Late 16C. < late Latin *hortatorius* < Latin *hortari* "exhort"] —**hor·ta·to·ri·ly** *adv*

hor·ti·cul·ture /háwrti kùlchər/ *n* **1.** the science, skill, or occupation of cultivating plants, especially flowers, fruit, and vegetables, in gardens or greenhouses **2.** a simple form of agriculture based on working small plots of land without using draft animals, plows, or irrigation [Late 17C. < Latin *hortus* "garden"] —**hor·ti·cul·tur·al** /hàwrti kúlchərəl/ *adj* —**hor·ti·cul·tur·al·ly** *adv* —**hor·ti·cul·tur·ist** /hàwrti kúlchərist/ *n*

Ho·rus /háwrəss/ *n* in Egyptian mythology, the god of the Sun, the sky, and goodness, usually depicted as having a falcon's head. Horus was the son of Isis and Osiris.

Hor·vitz /háwr vìtz/, **H. Robert** (*b.* 1947) US molecular biologist. He worked on molecular genetics and the degeneration of cells, and shared the 2002 Nobel Prize in physiology or medicine with John Sulston and Sydney Brenner.

Hos. *abbr* BIBLE Hosea

ho·san·na /hō zánnə/, **ho·san·nah** *n, interj* a cry of praise to God [Pre-12C. Via late Latin < Greek *hōsanna* < Rabbinic Hebrew *hōša'nā*, shortening of Hebrew *hōšī'ā-nnā* "save, (we) pray" (Psalm 118:25)]

Ho·say /hō sáy/ *n Carib* ISLAM same as **Muharram** (sense 2)

hose /hōz/ *n* FLEXIBLE TUBE a flexible tube or pipe, often made of rubber or plastic, through which fluids such as water or gasoline can flow ■ *npl* **1.** CLOTHING LEG COVERINGS skintight leg coverings, e.g., stockings or socks **2.** CLOTHING, HIST TIGHT-FITTING TROUSERS close-fitting leg coverings that attached to a doublet, formerly worn by men ■ *vt* (**hosed, hos·ing, hos·es**) **1.** DIRECT WATER ON SOMEBODY OR SOMETHING to spray, soak, wash, or rinse somebody or something with water from a hose **2.** TRICK SOMEBODY to deceive or trick somebody (*slang*) **3.** DEGRADE COMPUTER'S PERFORMANCE to make a computer system nonfunctional, or greatly degrade the performance of a computer system (*slang*) [Old English *hosa* "leg covering, husk" < Indo-European, "to cover"]

Ho·se·a /hō záy ə/ *n* a book of the Bible that contains the prophecies traditionally attributed to the Hebrew prophet Hosea. See table at **Bible**

Ho·sein /hō sáyn/ *n Carib* ISLAM same as **Ashora** [Late 20C. Variant of HUSAIN]

ho·sel /hṓz'l/ *n* the socket in the head of a golf club where the shaft is attached [Late 19C. < HOSE + *-el* "small" < Latin *-ellus*]

hos·er /hṓzər/ *n Can* an offensive term for somebody regarded as unintelligent and vulgar, especially a man whose main interests are hockey and drinking beer (*slang*)

ho·sier /hṓzhər/ *n* somebody who makes or sells hosiery (*archaic*)

ho·sier·y /hṓzhəree/ *n* socks, stockings, pantyhose, and tights, considered collectively

hos·pice /hóspiss/ *n* **1.** MED, SOC WELFARE NURSING HOME FOR DYING a usually small residential institution for terminally ill patients where treatment focuses on the patient's well-being rather than a cure and includes drugs for pain management and often spiritual counseling **2.** MED HOME CARE FOR DYING a program of hospice care for the terminally ill that includes home visits by professionals such as nurses and clergy to provide for the person's physical and emotional needs **3.** REFUGE FOR TRAVELERS formerly, a place where pilgrims, travelers, and the homeless or destitute were offered lodging, usually by a religious order [Early 19C. Via French < Latin *hospitium* "guesthouse, hospitality" < *hospit-* "host, guest"]

hos·pi·ta·ble /ho spíttəb'l, hóspitəb'l/ *adj* **1.** friendly, welcoming, and generous to guests or strangers ○ *That's very hospitable of you.* **2.** pleasant, agreeable, and providing what somebody needs to live comfortably ○ *a hospitable climate* [Late 16C. < French < obsolete *hospiter* "receive a guest" < Latin *hospit-* "host, guest"] —**hos·pi·ta·bil·i·ty** /hòspitə bíllətee/ *n* —**hos·pi·ta·bly** *adv*

hos·pi·tal /hóspit'l/ *n* **1.** BUILDING FOR MEDICAL CARE an institution where people receive medical, surgical, or psychiatric treatment and nursing care **2.** PLACE FOR REPAIRING THINGS a place where something is repaired **3.** SOC WELFARE CHARITABLE HOME a charitable institution providing shelter, care, or education for orphaned children, senior citizens, or the homeless or destitute (*archaic*) [13C. Via Old French, "hostel" < medieval Latin *hospitale* "guesthouse, inn" < Latin *hospit-* "host, guest"]

hos·pi·tal-ac·quired in·fec·tion *n* a disease caught by somebody while being treated in the hospital for something else

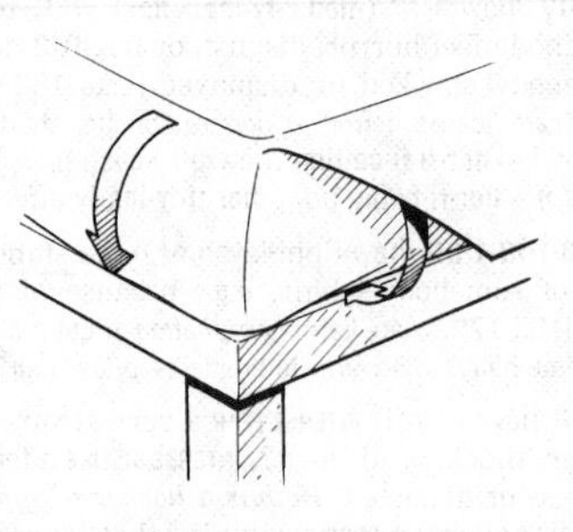

hospital corner

hos·pi·tal cor·ner *n* a neat overlapping fold of the bedding at each corner of a bed

Hos·pi·tal·er /hóspitlər/, **Hos·pi·tal·ler** *n* **1.** a member of a military religious order, the Knights of the Hospital of St John, founded in the late 11th century by European crusaders to care for sick pilgrims in Jerusalem **2.** a member of a religious order or charitable institution involved in the care of the sick, especially in the hospital [14C. Via Old French *hospitalier* < medieval Latin *hospitalarius* < *hospitale* (see HOSPITAL)]

hos·pi·tal·i·ty /hòspi tállətee/ *n* KINDNESS TO VISITORS friendly, welcoming, and generous treatment offered to guests or strangers ■ *adj* **1.** FOR GUESTS for the use of clients, guests, or visitors who are being entertained, especially by a company at a convention ○ *a hospitality suite* **2.** BUSINESS OF CATERING AND ENTERTAINMENT describes the business of providing services such as catering and entertainment ○ *the hospitality industry*

hos·pi·tal·i·ty box *n* a private room or enclosure in a sports stadium or arena with a view of the playing area that is rented by a person or organization for the use of guests

hos·pi·tal·i·ty suite *n* a room or suite of rooms where invited guests or clients of a company, delegates to a conference, or other official visitors are welcomed and usually provided with free refreshments

hos·pi·tal·ize /hóspit'l ìz/ (**-ized, -iz·ing, -iz·es**) *vt* to admit somebody to the hospital for treatment, diagnosis, or observation, usually as an inpatient —**hos·pi·tal·i·za·tion** /hòspit'li záysh'n/ *n*

Hos·pi·tal·ler /hóspit'lər/ *n* RELIG, HIST another spelling of **Hospitaler**

hos·po·dar /hóspə daar/ *n* a prince or governor of Moldavia or Walachia during the time of Ottoman rule [Late 16C. Via Romanian < Ukrainian]

host[1] /hōst/ *n* **1.** SOMEBODY ENTERTAINING GUESTS somebody who invites and entertains guests **2.** BROADCAST SOMEBODY INTRODUCING GUESTS ON SHOW somebody who presents and interviews guests on a radio or television program **3.** PLACE WHERE EVENT IS HELD a place or organization that provides the space and facilities for an event such as an international sporting competition **4.** BIOL ORGANISM INFECTED BY PARASITE a human, animal, plant, or other organism in or on which another organism, especially a parasite, lives **5.** MED GRAFT OR TRANSPLANT RECIPIENT the recipient of a transplanted or grafted embryo, tissue, or organ **6.** LEISURE LANDLORD OF INN the owner or manager of a bed and breakfast, guest house, or hotel **7.** *also* **host com·pu·ter** COMPUT MAIN COMPUTER IN NETWORK the main computer that controls specific functions or files in a network **8.** RESTAURANT GREETER somebody employed in a restaurant to greet and seat customers ■ *vt* (**host·ed, host·ing, hosts**) **1.** ACCOMMODATE EVENT to provide the space and facilities for an event such as an international sporting competition **2.** BROADCAST INTRODUCE GUESTS ON SHOW to act as the host of a television or radio program **3.** ENTERTAIN GUESTS to be the host of a social or official gathering **4.** ONLINE CREATE WEBSITE FOR SOMEBODY to create and maintain a website for somebody as a service [13C. Via Old French *(h)oste* "host, guest" < Latin *hospit-*]

host[2] /hōst/ *n* **1.** a very large number of people or things **2.** MIL same as **army** (*archaic*) [14C. Via French < Latin *hostis* "stranger, enemy" (in medieval Latin, "army")]

Host /hōst/, **host** *n* the bread or wafer consecrated and eaten during the Christian ceremony of Communion [14C. Via French < Latin *hostia* "sacrificial animal, victim"]

hos·ta /hóstə, hóstə/ *n Can, UK* PLANTS a perennial shade-loving plant with broad ribbed leaves. Flowers: white, blue, or lilac, tubular, in clusters. Genus: *Hosta.* US term **plantain lily** [Early 19C. < modern Latin, after Nicolaus T. *Host* (1761–1834), Austrian botanist]

hos·tage /hóstij/ *n* **1.** somebody held prisoner by a person or group such as a criminal or a terrorist organization until specific demands are met or money is handed over **2.** a person or group of people whose freedom of action is restricted or controlled by a more powerful organization by implied threats or other means [13C. < Old French *(h)ostage* < late Latin *obsidiatus* "state of being a hostage" < *sedere* "sit"] ◇ **a hostage to fortune** a remark or action that could potentially lead to trouble or difficulty and so is better avoided

host com·puter *n* COMPUT same as **host**[1] *n* (sense 7)

hos·tel /hóst'l/ *n* **1.** TRAVEL same as **youth hostel 2.** an inexpensive inn or place of lodging [13C. < Old French *(h)ostel* < medieval Latin *hospitale* (see HOSPITAL)]

hos·tel·er /hóstələr/ *n* somebody who stays at hostels while traveling for pleasure, especially a young person who stays at youth hostels

hos·tel·ing /hóstəling/ *n* the practice of staying at hostels, especially youth hostels, while traveling for pleasure

hos·tel·ler *n* TRAVEL Can, UK spelling of **hosteler**

hos·tel·ling *n* TRAVEL Can, UK spelling of **hosteling**

hos·tel·ry /hóstəlree/ (*plural* **-ries**) *n* a hotel, pub, or inn (*archaic*)

host·ess /hōstəss/ *n* **1.** WOMAN ENTERTAINING GUESTS a woman who invites, welcomes, and entertains guests, often providing them with food and drink **2.** BROADCAST **WOMAN INTRODUCING GUESTS ON SHOW** a woman who presents a television or radio program such as a talk show or game show in which invited guests take part **3. PAID DANCE PARTNER** a woman who is paid to be a dancing partner at a nightclub or dance hall **4. WOMAN GREETER IN RESTAURANT** a woman who is employed in a restaurant to greet and seat customers **5.** TRAVEL **WOMAN ATTENDANT FOR PASSENGERS** a woman who is employed to provide for the safety and comfort of passengers on an aircraft, ship, train, or bus (*dated*) [12C. < Old French *(h)ostesse* < *(h)oste* (see HOST[1])] —**host·ess** *vti*

hos·tile /hóst'l/ *adj* **1. VERY UNFRIENDLY** showing or feeling hatred, enmity, antagonism, or anger toward somebody **2. AGAINST** strongly opposed to somebody or something ○ *hostile to the idea* **3.** MIL **RELATING TO ENEMY** relating to, characteristic of, or belonging to an enemy, especially in warfare ○ *hostile fire* **4. ADVERSE** not favorable to life, health, development, or success ○ *a hostile environment* **5.** BUSINESS **AGAINST MANAGEMENT'S WILL** opposed by the owner or management of a corporation ○ *a hostile takeover* ■ *n* **HOSTILE PERSON** an enemy, especially in warfare [Late 16C. Directly or via French < Latin *hostilis* < *hostis* "enemy, stranger"] —**hos·tile·ly** *adv*

hos·tile wit·ness *n* a witness called by a party who gives evidence against that party

hos·til·i·ty /ho stíllətee/ *n* (*plural* **-ties**) **1. INTENSE AGGRESSION OR ANGER** a feeling or attitude of hatred, enmity, antagonism, or anger toward somebody **2. STRONG OPPOSITION** strong opposition to somebody or something **3. HOSTILE ACT** an act of hatred, enmity, antagonism, or anger against somebody ■ **hos·til·i·ties** *npl* MIL **ATTACKS** open acts of warfare

host·ing cen·ter *n* a business that provides Internet access and guarantees maintenance of Internet links to clients housing their own processors and software with it

hos·tler /hósslər, ósslər/, **os·tler** /ósslər/ *n* **1.** somebody employed to service a large vehicle or machine such as a locomotive or crane **2.** formerly, somebody employed to take care of horses at an inn [14C. Variant of HOSTELER]

hot /hot/ *adj* (**hot·ter, hot·test**) **1. VERY WARM** at a high, relatively high, or very high temperature ○ *the hottest day of the year* **2. TOO WARM FOR COMFORT** feeling warmer than usual or desirable ○ *If you're hot, take your sweater off.* **3.** FOOD **VERY SPICY** spicy or peppery enough to cause a burning sensation in the mouth or throat **4. CAUSING CONTROVERSY** causing much discussion, disagreement, or controversy ○ *a hot topic* **5. DANGEROUS** unpleasant or uncomfortable because of antagonism, trouble, or danger (*informal*) ○ *It got too hot for him to handle.* **6. QUICKLY ANGERED** easily provoked or aroused ○ *a hot temper* **7. INTENSE** felt, done, or expressed with forceful intense energy ○ *hot competition* **8.** COLORS **BRIGHT** bright and vivid ○ *hot pink* **9. CLOSE** following somebody or something very closely ○ *hot on the trail* **10. PROMISING** offering potential success or good fortune ○ *a hot tip* **11. TOPICAL** very recent or new and therefore of interest or importance ○ *hot off the press* **12. EXCITING** fresh and exciting (*informal*) ○ *a hot new talent* **13. SUCCESSFUL** very popular or successful (*informal*) ○ *one of the hottest items in the range* **14. KNOWLEDGEABLE** having, showing, or characterized by particular skill or knowledge (*informal*) ○ *not very hot at math* **15. LUCKY** very lucky, e.g., in gambling (*informal*) **16. WISE** very good, wise, or sensible (*informal*) ○ *That idea's not so hot.* **17. WELL** well or good (*informal*) ○ *I don't feel too hot.* **18. ANGRY** angry or agitated about something (*informal*) ○ *Watch out, the captain is hot!* **19. KEEN** enthusiastically eager (*informal*) ○ *She's really hot on jazz.* **20.** *UK* **STRICT** very strict about something (*informal*) ○ *He's hot on getting the paperwork right.* **21. PHYSICALLY ATTRACTED** physically attracted or aroused (*slang*) **22. PHYSICALLY ATTRACTIVE** physically attractive or exciting (*slang*) **23. STOLEN** obtained illegally, especially by stealing (*slang*) ○ *hot jewels* **24. ON RUN** wanted by the police (*slang*) ○ *a hot suspect* **25. EAGER** full of activity, energy, enthusiasm, or excitement ○ *I'm really hot to get started.* **26.** MUSIC **INVENTIVE AND EXCITING** with strong rhythms or exciting improvisation (*informal*) **27.** AUTOMOT **POWERFUL** very fast and powerful (*slang*) ○ *a hot car* **28.** ELEC **LIVE** electrically charged ○ *a hot wire* **29.** PHYS **RADIOACTIVE** dangerously radioactive **30.** BIOL **INFECTIOUS** extremely infectious or lethal, or containing infectious viruses ○ *a hot zone* **31.** PHYS **IN ELEVATED ENERGY STATE** in an elevated energy state, usually caused by nuclear processes ○ *a hot atom* **32. NEAR ANSWER** very close to something to be found or discovered in a hunting or guessing game (*informal*) ○ *You're getting hotter.* **33. ABSURD** funny, absurd, or unbelievable (*slang*) ○ *told a hot one about his hunting experiences* ■ **hots** *npl* **DESIRE** strong physical desire (*informal*) ■ *adv* **INTENSELY** in an eager, intense, or angry way ○ *They argued hot and long.* [Old English *hāt* < Germanic] —**hot·ness** *n* ◇ **blow** *or* **run hot and cold** to vacillate between emotions, opinions, or ideas, e.g., by being enthusiastic about somebody or something and then unenthusiastic ◇ **hot to trot** eager and willing (*slang*)

hot air *n* impressive or boastful talk about achievements or intentions that has no substance (*informal*)

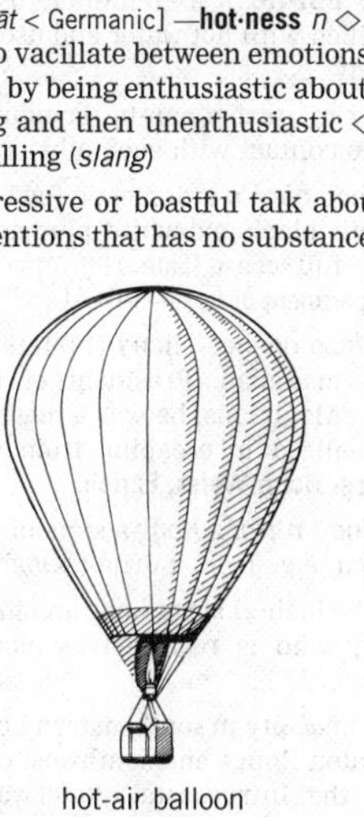

hot-air balloon

hot-air bal·loon *n* a lighter-than-air craft in which a compartment for pilot and passengers is suspended from a large nylon balloon that holds heated air or helium

hot·bed /hót bèd/ *n* **1.** an environment in which something flourishes or happens frequently, especially something undesirable ○ *a hotbed of corruption.* **2.** a planting bed covered with glass and heated with electricity or by the action of fermenting manure to aid in quick germination of seeds and growth of plants

hot-blood·ed *adj* easily angered, excited, or physically aroused —**hot-blood·ed·ness** *n*

hot but·ton *n* something that is known or likely to provoke a strong response, especially among voters or consumers ◇ **press somebody's hot button** to provoke a strong immediate reaction, usually a predictable one

hot-but·ton *adj* arousing strong feelings (*slang*)

hot·cake /hót kàyk/ *n* FOOD same as **pancake** *n* (sense 1) ◇ **sell like hotcakes** to sell very quickly (*informal*)

hotch /hoch/ (**hotched, hotch·ing, hotch·es**), **hoatch** (**hoatched, hoatch·ing, hoatch·es**) *vi Scotland* to be surrounded by or full of a large number of people or things, especially when these are unpleasant or undesirable ○ *hotching with maggots* [14C. Origin ?]

hotch·pot /hóch pòt/ *n* in law, the gathering together of property belonging to different people in order to divide it equally [14C. < Old French *hochepot* < *hocher* "shake" + *pot* "pot"]

hotch·potch /hóch pòch/ *n UK* same as **hodgepodge** [Late 16C. Rhyming alteration of HOTCHPOT]

hot comb *n* a comb that can be heated, usually electrically, and used to style or straighten the hair

hot cor·ner *n* in baseball, the fielding position covering third base

hot cross bun *n* a sweet bun containing yeast, spices, and dried fruit, and marked with a cross on the top, traditionally eaten hot on Good Friday

hot-desk·ing *n* the practice of using any available desk at work, instead of having a desk assigned to you —**hot-desk** *vi*

hot dish *n* a dish of hot food cooked and served in a casserole, usually consisting of meat and vegetables, often with pasta

hot dog *n* **1. FRANKFURTER IN A BUN** a long frankfurter usually served hot on a bread roll with toppings such as mustard, ketchup, or relish **2.** FOOD same as **frankfurter 3. PERFORMER OF STUNTS** a performer of difficult, dangerous, or acrobatic stunts in skiing, surfing, and other sports (*slang*) ■ *interj* **EXPRESSING ENTHUSIASTIC PLEASURE** used to express strong approval, delight, or surprise (*informal*)

hot-dog (**hot-dog·ged, hot-dog·ging, hot-dogs**) *vi* to perform difficult, dangerous, or acrobatic stunts in a showy or impressive manner in skiing, surfing, or similar sports (*slang*) —**hot-dog·ger** *n* —**hot-dog·ging** *n*

ho·tel /hō tél/ *n* **1.** a building or commercial establishment where people pay for lodging, and where meals and other facilities such as conference rooms are often available **2.** *S Asia* FOOD same as **restaurant 3.** a code word for the letter "H," used in international radio communications [Mid-17C. < French *hôtel*, modern form of Old French *(h)ostel* (see HOSTEL)]

ho·te·lier /ō tel yáy, hō téllyər/ *n* somebody who owns or runs a hotel [Early 20C. < French *hôtelier*, modern form of Old French *hostelier* "hosteler" < *(h)ostel* (see HOSTEL)]

ho·tel·ing /hō télling/ *n* the practice of providing temporary desk space for an employee [Because a hotel is a temporary place to stay]

ho·tel·keep·er /hō tél keèpər/ *n* TRAVEL same as **hotelier**

hot flash *n* a sudden hot feeling, sometimes accompanied by sweating and redness of the face, experienced by some women during menopause and caused by an endocrine imbalance

hot flush *n UK* MED same as **hot flash**

hot·foot /hót fòot/ *adv* as quickly as possible ■ *n* a practical joke in which a match is put between the sole and upper of somebody's shoe, without the person's knowledge, and then lit ◇ **hotfoot it** to go with great haste and eagerness, usually on foot (*slang*)

hot-gos·pel·er *n* somebody who preaches religion or spreads propaganda in a very forceful or enthusiastic way (*informal; sometimes considered offensive*)

hot·head /hót hèd/ *n* somebody who is too easily angered or excited and who usually acts impetuously

hot·head·ed /hòt héddəd/ *adj* too easily angered or

excited and usually acting impetuously —**hot·head·ed·ly** *adv* —**hot·head·ed·ness** *n*

hot·house /hót hòwss/ *n* (*plural* **-hous·es** /-hòwzəz/) **1.** HEATED GREENHOUSE a heated building, usually with glass walls and a glass roof, in which tropical or delicate plants can grow at a stable warm temperature **2.** CENTER OF ACTIVITY a place where a particular thing flourishes and develops, usually in an intensive way ○ *a hothouse of technological innovation* ■ *adj* SENSITIVE sensitive and delicate (*informal disapproving*) ○ *hothouse views on political strategy*

hot·hous·ing /hót hòwzing/ *n* a program of providing children with intensive education

hot key *n* a computer key or combination of keys that provides a shortcut for a specific function

hot·line /hót lìn/ *n* **1.** a telephone connection or similar link that allows direct communication between heads of government or other important people, especially in an emergency ○ *The Chief of Staff has a hotline to the President.* **2.** a telephone number that enables members of the public to make direct contact with a special service offering information, advice, or help, usually on a serious or urgent matter

hot·link /hót lingk/ *n* COMPUT same as **hyperlink**

hot·list /hót list/ *n* a browser configuration file of a computer user's most recent hypertext link selections

hot·ly /hóttlee/ *adv* **1.** in an angry way **2.** in an intense and committed way ○ *hotly contested*

hot-melt *n* a fast-drying adhesive applied in a molten state

hot met·al *n* **1.** printing type cast from molten metal in a crucible beside the printing machine **2.** a method of printing using hot metal type

hot mon·ey *n* funds transferred from one form of currency to another in order to take advantage of better exchange rates

hot pants *npl* **1.** very brief close-fitting shorts for women, first fashionable in the early 1970s **2.** very strong physical desire (*slang*)

hot pep·per *n* **1.** a hot-tasting, often elongated, green or red fruit. Use: in cooking. **2.** a variety of pepper that produces hot-tasting fruits. Latin name: *Capsicum frutescens.*

hot plate *n* **1.** a one- or two-burner electrically heated device on which food can be cooked **2.** a portable device with a flat heated surface on which cooked food can be heated or kept warm

hot plug *vt* COMPUT same as **hot-swap**

hot pot *n* a small heated pot of boiling water or broth used to cook pieces of food at the table, especially in Southeast Asian cooking

hot po·ta·to *n* a sensitive or controversial issue that is awkward or difficult to deal with (*informal*)

hot press *n* a machine used to apply heat and pressure to a material such as paper or cloth —**hot-press** *vt*

hot rod *n* a car that has been modified to make it go very fast (*slang*)

hot-rod (**hot-rod·ded, hot-rod·ding, hot-rods**) *v* (*slang*) **1.** *vt* to modify a car or its engine to make it very fast or powerful **2.** *vi* to drive a hot rod —**hot-rodd·er** *n*

hot seat *n* the electric chair (*slang*) ◇ **in the hot seat** facing or liable to face criticism or intense questioning (*informal*) ○ *in the hot seat after the latest round of allegations*

hot shoe *n* a camera accessory used to connect the camera and an electric flash

hot·shot /hót shòt/ *n* **1.** a successful, important, or highly skilled person, especially one who is showily confident (*informal disapproving*) **2.** a very fast freight train

hot spot *n* **1.** MIL PLACE OF POTENTIAL UNREST an area where fighting or trouble is likely to break out **2.** LEISURE CENTER OF ENTERTAINMENT a place that is a center of entertainment and social activity, e.g., a popular nightclub (*informal*) **3.** CENTER FOR ACTIVITY a place where a lot of activity of a particular type takes place ○ *a biodiversity hot spot* **4.** ENG SMALL AREA OF INTENSE HEAT a small area of something such as an engine that is at a much higher temperature than the rest **5.** COMPUT WIRELESS INTERNET CONNECTION a building or locale in which wireless Internet users can access a high-speed Internet connection **6.** GEOG AREA OF GEOTHERMAL ACTIVITY a part of the Earth's surface subject to greater than usual geothermal activity **7.** COMPUT SELECTABLE HYPERLINK a clickable image on a computer screen that acts as a hyperlink to another location

hot spring *n* a spring of water heated by geothermal energy

Hot Springs /hòt-/ city in central Arkansas in the eastern Ouachita Mountains, on the Ouachita River. Population: 36,356 (2002 estimate).

Hot Springs Na·tion·al Park national park in west central Arkansas, established in 1921, with 47 thermal springs that have an average temperature of 60°C/140°F. Area: 9 sq. mi./22 sq. km.

hot·spur /hót spùr/ *n* a rash or impetuous person (*archaic*) [< *Hotspur,* nickname of Henry Percy (1364–1403), English military leader]

hot stuff *n* (*slang*) **1.** an impressive, attractive, exciting, or important person or thing **2.** a physically attractive person

hot-swap *vt* to add or remove hardware devices to or from a computer while it is running and have the operating system automatically recognize the change

hot-tem·pered *adj* having or showing a short temper

Hot·ten·tot /hótt'n tòt/ (*plural same* or **-tots**) *n* (*dated*) **1.** an offensive term for a member of the Khoikhoi people **2.** an offensive term for the languages of the Khoikhoi people [Late 17C. < Dutch, probably < a formula in a Nama song]

hot tick·et *n* a popular or fashionable person or thing (*informal*)

hot·tie /hóttee/ *n also* **hot·ty** (*plural* **-ties**) somebody who is sexually attractive (*slang*)

hot·tish /hóttish/ *adj* fairly, but not excessively hot

hot tod·dy *n* BEVERAGES same as **toddy** (sense 1)

hot tub *n* a large round bathtub filled with hot water for one or more people to relax, bathe, or socialize in —**hot-tub·bing** *n*

hot·ty *n* another spelling of **hottie** (*slang*)

hot war *n* armed conflict between groups or nations, as opposed to political hostility

hot-wa·ter bot·tle *n* a container, usually made of rubber, filled with hot water and used to warm part of the body

hot-wire *vt* to start a car by bringing the ignition wires into contact with each other (*informal*)

Hou·dan /hoó dàn/ *n* a domestic fowl belonging to a breed with black-and-white plumage and a characteristic full crest [Late 19C. After a village in the French department of Seine-et-Oise]

Hou·di·ni /hoo deénee/, **Harry** (1874–1926) Hungarian-born US magician. President of the Society of American Magicians, he was a master escapologist and specialized in escaping from various locked containers. Born **Weiss, Ehrich**

hou high /hō-/ *n Hong Kong* a state of intoxication or excitement, e.g., from a drug (*slang*)

hou inch /hṓ inch/ *n Hong Kong* an offensive term for somebody who is regarded as aloof or arrogant (*insult*)

Hou·ma /hṓmə/ city in southeastern Louisiana, southeast of Baton Rouge and southwest of New Orleans. It is on the Intracoastal Waterway. Population: 32,130 (2002 estimate).

hound /hownd/ *n* **1.** DOG BRED FOR HUNTING a dog with floppy ears, short hair, and a deep bark, belonging to a breed originally developed for hunting (*often used in combination*) **2.** DOG a domestic dog, especially one viewed with disapproval (*informal*) **3.** UNPLEASANT PERSON somebody regarded as contemptible or despicable (*dated*) **4.** ENTHUSIAST somebody who pursues a particular activity with great enthusiasm or determination (*informal*) ○ *a media hound* ■ *vt* (**hound·ed, hound·ing, hounds**) **1.** PURSUE DOGGEDLY to follow, chase, or pester somebody in a persistent or relentless manner **2.** URGE OR NAG SOMEBODY to urge or force somebody to do something by nagging or harassment ○ *hounded out of office by a hostile press* [Old English *hund* "dog" < Indo-European] —**hound·er** *n*

ORIGIN The Indo-European word from which ***hound*** is ultimately derived, is also the ancestor of English *canary, canine, chenille, corgi, cynic, dachshund,* and *kennel.*

hounds /howndz/ *npl* the part of a sailing ship's masthead that supports the topmast and the rigging [15C. Alteration of *hune* "wooden projection below a masthead," origin ?]

hound's-tongue *n* a coarse plant of the borage family with spiny clinging fruit. Flowers: small, reddish purple. Native to: Europe, Asia. Genus: *Cynoglossum.* [< the shape and texture of its leaves]

hounds·tooth check /hówndz toòth-/, **hound's-tooth check** *n* a fabric design of small jagged checks

hour /owr/ *n* **1.** 60 MINUTES one of the 24 equal parts of a day, equivalent to 60 minutes or 3,600 seconds **2.** 60-MINUTE INTERVAL SHOWN ON TIMEPIECE one of the intervals of 60 minutes shown on a clock or watch ○ *There's a bus at 20 past the hour.* **3.** TIME OF DAY a time of day, with emphasis on the general portion of day or night being referred to ○ *at this unearthly hour* **4.** REGULAR TIME FOR SOMETHING the time at which something usually takes place or is done ○ *my lunch hour* **5.** SIGNIFICANT PERIOD a period during which something particularly significant happens **6.** TIME OF SUCCESS a time when somebody is powerful, successful, or famous ○ *their finest hour* **7.** TIME OF DEATH the time when somebody is going to die ○ *As he started falling, he thought his hour had surely come.* **8.** WORK DONE IN 60 MINUTES the amount of work done in a period of sixty minutes ○ *I have a couple of hours left to do in the yard.* **9.** DISTANCE TRAVELED IN 60 MINUTES the distance that can be traveled in sixty minutes ○ *My office is only an hour away.* **10.** MEASURE, NAVIG MEASURE OF LONGITUDE a measure of longitude equal to 15 degrees or one twenty-fourth of a great circle **11.** SINGLE SESSION a meeting of a class or course of therapeutic treatment, usually 50 or 55 minutes ○ *I missed my hour with the therapist last week.* **12.** EDUC same as **credit hour** ■ **hours** *npl* **1.** LONG TIME a long but unspecified amount of time (*informal*) **2.** TIMES FOR DOING PARTICULAR THINGS the times of day during which particular things are done ○ *during school hours* **3.** TIME IN 24-HOUR CLOCK the time of day, when using a 24-hour clock ○ *The flight leaves at 1300 hours.* **4.** CHR **CANONICAL HOURS** the canonical hours taken as a whole [12C. Via Old French *houre* < Latin *hora* < Greek *hōra* "time, hour"] ◇ **at any hour** at any time, day or night ◇ **of the hour** enjoying the highest degree of relevance, importance, or popularity at the current moment or a particular time ○ *The question of the hour is whether war is justified.*

SPELLCHECK hour or **our**? Do not confuse the spelling of ***hour*** and ***our***, which sound similar. The word ***hour*** denotes a unit, period, or moment of time, as in *half an hour earlier, at this late hour.* The word ***our*** means "belonging to us," as in *our parents.*

hour an·gle *n* the angle, measured positively westward, between the plane containing the observer and the Earth's poles and the plane containing a specific astronomical object and the Earth's poles

hour cir·cle *n* a great circle passing through the poles of the celestial sphere and intersecting the celestial equator at right angles, containing a point on the celestial sphere such as a star

hourglass

hour·glass /ówr glàss/ *n* **1.** a time-measurement device consisting of two transparent bulbs connected by a narrow tube and containing an amount of sand that takes a specific time to flow between the bulbs after inversion. See illustration on previous page **2.** an hourglass-shaped computer icon that shows that a task is being performed but is not yet completed

hour·glass fig·ure *n* a woman's body shape, curving out above and below a narrow waist like the shape of an hourglass

hour hand *n* the shorter wider hand on a nondigital clock or watch that indicates the hour

hou·ri /hŏoree/ *n* **1.** in Islamic belief, one of the beautiful young women who attend Muslim men in paradise **2.** an attractive woman (*dated; sometimes considered offensive*) [Mid-18C. Via French < Arabic *ḥawrā'* "woman with dark eyes"]

hour·ly /ówrlee/ *adj* **1. HAPPENING EACH HOUR** happening at 60 minute intervals ○ *hourly news* **2. OCCURRING OFTEN** happening frequently or continually ○ *hourly changes* **3. CALCULATED BY HOUR** calculated as a particular amount for each hour worked ○ *hourly wages* **4. PAID BY HOUR** working for pay that is calculated as a particular amount for each hour worked ○ *an hourly employee* ■ *adv* **1. ONCE AN HOUR** happening once during an hour ○ *The news is broadcast hourly.* **2. SOON** at any time not long from now ○ *Her arrival is expected hourly.* **3. OFTEN** frequently or continually ○ *The situation is changing hourly.* **4. BY THE HOUR** with a specific amount being paid for each hour worked ○ *paid hourly* ■ *n* (*plural* **-lies**) **WORKER PAID BY HOURS WORKED** an employee paid by the number of hours worked ○ *The factory is hiring more hourlies.*

Hou·sa·ton·ic /hòssə tónnik/ river in northwestern Massachusetts and Connecticut, rising in the Berkshire Hills. Length: 148 mi./238 km.

house *n* /howss/ (*plural* **hous·es** /hówzəz, hówssəz/) **1. DWELLING** a building made for people to live in, especially one built for a single family of occupants **2. OCCUPANTS OF HOUSE** all of the people who are in a house at one time, particularly the people who usually live there **3. BUILDING FOR ANIMALS** a building where animals are kept, especially in a zoo ○ *the monkey house* **4. PLACE OF ENTERTAINMENT** a place where members of the public pay for food, drink, or other entertainment, e.g., a restaurant or club ○ *the specialty of the house* **5. THEATER** a theater, especially the auditorium ○ *played to a full house* **6. THEATER AUDIENCE** the audience at a theater ○ *The dancers performed to an appreciative house.* **7. GAMBLING CASINO** a gambling casino, or the people who manage it ○ *The odds always favor the house.* **8. BUSINESS OPERATION** a company or a corporation creating or selling a particular product ○ *a publishing house* **9. COLLEGE OR UNIVERSITY RESIDENCE HALL** a residential college, or a residence hall within a university **10.** *also* **House LEGISLATIVE GROUP** a legislative group in a government, or the place where it meets **11.** *also* **House FAMILY LINE** a family line, including ancestors and descendants, especially a royal family **12.** same as **brothel** (*dated*) **13. DIVISION OF ZODIAC** in astrology, one of the 12 divisions of the zodiac **14. ZODIAC SIGN WHERE PLANET LIES** in astrology, the sign of the zodiac in which a planet is found at a specific time **15. CURLING TARGET** in curling, an area of concentric circles marked at each end of an ice rink, with the target in its center **16.** *regional* AGRIC **PILE OF VEGETABLES** a heap of vegetables, usually potatoes, covered with earth and mulch and sometimes stored in a shed **17. FAST DANCE MUSIC** a style of dance music first developed by adding electronic beats to disco records, and later characterized by the addition of repetitive vocals, extracts from other recordings, or synthesized sounds ■ *vt* /howz/ (**housed, hous·ing, hous·es**) **1. GIVE SOMEBODY SOMEWHERE TO LIVE** to provide somebody with a place to live **2. CONTAIN SOMETHING** to contain, keep, or store something ○ *a shed that houses our lawn mowers* **3. PUT SOMETHING AWAY SAFELY ON BOAT** in sailing, to safely stow something such as oars or an anchor [Old English *hūs* < Germanic] ◇ **bring the house down** to provoke a great deal of laughter or applause ◇ **like a house on fire** very quickly, successfully, or strongly ○ *They got along like a house on fire.* ◇ **on the house** given free by somebody who would normally charge ◇ **play house** to take part in a children's game of pretending to be a family, with children playing the roles of both adults and children (*informal*) ◇ **put your house in order** to organize your life, work, or other enterprise properly

USAGE See *home*.

REGIONAL NOTE See *bank*².

house ar·rest *n* a form of legal confinement in which people who have been arrested are not allowed to leave their own homes

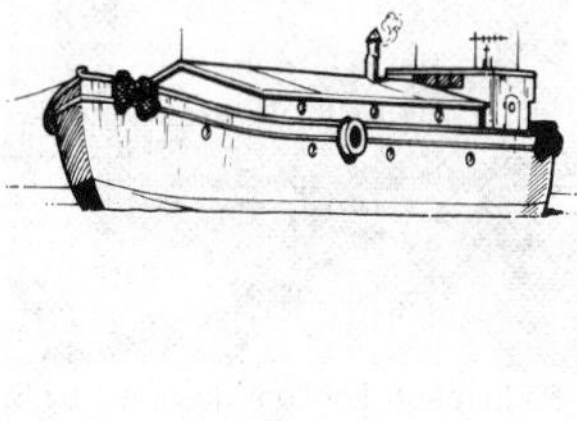

houseboat

house·boat /hówss bŏt/ *n* a boat, especially a flat-bottomed riverboat or barge, that is permanently moored and used as a house

house·bound /hówss bòwnd/ *adj UK* same as **homebound**

house·boy /hówss bòy/ *n* a man employed to perform various household tasks (*often offensive*)

house brand *n* a product made by or for a specific retailer and often sold under that retailer's name

house·break /hòwss bràyk/ *vt* (**-broke** /-brōk/, **-bro·ken** /-brōkən/, **-break·ing, -breaks**) **1.** to teach an animal to excrete outdoors or in a specific place **2.** to teach acceptable behavior to somebody (*informal humorous*) ○ *Do you think we can ever housebreak those kids?* ■ *n* CRIME same as **break-in** (sense 1)

house·break·ing /hówss bràyking/ *n* the action of illegally forcing entry into a house or other building in order to commit a crime —**house·break·er** *n*

house·bro·ken /hówss brŏkən/ *adj* **1.** having learned to excrete outdoors or in a specific place **2.** behaving in a socially acceptable way (*humorous*)

house call *n* a visit made by a doctor or other professional to a patient or client at home

house cat *n* a cat that lives with people as a pet

house·clean·ing /hówss klèening/ *n* **1.** the performance of a range of tasks to make a house clean such as dusting,vacuuming, and washing windows **2.** the process of getting rid of unwanted employees, policies, or other practices in order to make a business more efficient (*informal*)

house·coat /hówss kŏt/ *n* a woman's outer garment, often loose and comfortable, worn at home

house crick·et *n* a dark brown cricket that can become a nuisance indoors. Native to: North America, Europe. Latin name: *Acheta domesticus.*

house de·tec·tive *n* somebody employed by a business such as a hotel to patrol the premises and guard against theft or other unlawful behavior

house doc·tor *n* a physician on duty in a hotel or other business organization

house·dress /hówss drèss/ *n* a loose comfortable dress worn around the house

house·fa·ther /hówss faàthər/ *n* a man who is responsible for a group of young people living in a dormitory or an institution such as a hostel

house finch *n* a small common finch, the male of which has a red forehead, throat, breast, and rump. Native to: United States, Mexico. Latin name: *Carpodacus mexicanus.*

house fluf·fing *n* the practice of changing the appearance of a house or room by rearranging existing items

house·fly /hówss flī/ (*plural* **-flies**) *n* a common fly that lives in and around human dwellings in most parts of the world and is responsible for spreading numerous diseases. Latin name: *Musca domestica.*

house·ful /hówss fŏŏl/ *n* the quantity of people or objects that a house can hold ○ *a houseful of antique furniture* ○ *We had a houseful last week when all our grandchildren were here.*

house guest *n* a guest in somebody's home

house·hold /hówss hōld/ *n* **PEOPLE WHO LIVE TOGETHER** the people who live together in a single home ■ *adj* **1. OF HOUSEHOLD** relating to, belonging to, or used in a household **2. FAMILIAR TO ALL** very widely known ○ *a household word*

house·hold arts *npl* all the skills useful or essential in running a house, e.g., cooking, cleaning, and childcare

house·hold·er /hówss hōldər/ *n* **1.** an owner or renter of a house **2.** the head of a household

house·hold gods *npl* the deities believed to protect the home and its inhabitants, especially in the religion of ancient Rome

house·hold goods *npl UK* same as **housewares**

house·hold name *n* somebody or something that most people have heard of

house·hold word *n* a popular saying, the name of a famous person, or an event that is very well known

house-hunt *v* to look for a residential property to buy or rent —**house-hunt·er** *n* —**house-hunt·ing** *n*

house·hus·band /hówss hùzbənd/ *n* a man who does not go out to work but stays at home to manage a household [Mid-20C. After HOUSEWIFE]

house·keep·er /hówss keèpər/ *n* **1. SOMEBODY RUNNING SOMEBODY ELSE'S HOUSE** somebody employed to perform or manage the work of taking care of somebody else's house and the people who live there **2. EMPLOYEE WHO CLEANS** somebody employed by a hotel, hospital, or other establishment to clean and do other housekeeping tasks or manage the people who do this **3. SOMEBODY RUNNING HOUSEHOLD** somebody who takes care of his or her own house and its residents

house·keep·ing /hówss keèping/ *n* **1. HOUSEHOLD MAINTENANCE** the maintenance of a household, or the range of tasks involved in this **2. COMMERCIAL CLEANING DEPARTMENT** a work unit in a hotel or other such establishment tasked with cleaning rooms, changing linens, and related jobs **3. MANAGEMENT OF PROPERTY AND EQUIPMENT** the management and upkeep of equipment and property for a business or other organization **4. MAINTENANCE OF COMPUTER SYSTEM** the performance of routine tasks needed to keep a computer system working efficiently, e.g., deletion of unwanted files

House Lead·er *n Can* a member of the Canadian government who initiates and supervises business in the legislature

house·leek /hówss leèk/ *n* a flowering succulent plant with rosettes of leaves at the base of the stems. Native to: Europe. Genus: *Sempervivum.* [Because formerly planted on walls and roofs to protect the house from lightning]

house·lights /hówss līts/ *npl* the lights inside a theater or auditorium that illuminate the area where the audience sits

house·maid /hówss màyd/ *n* a woman employed to do housework (*dated*)

house·maid's knee *n* a swelling of the fluid-filled sac in front of the kneecap, caused by kneeling too much

house·man /hówssmən/ (*plural* **-men** /-mən/) *n* **1.** a man whose job is to perform routine tasks of cleaning and maintenance in a house or hotel **2.** same as **househusband**

house man·ag·er *n* somebody in charge of managing the ushers and the area in a theater where the audience sits

house mar·tin *n* a small swallow with blue-black feathers, a white rump, and a forked tail. Native to: Europe, China, Africa. Latin name: *Delichon urbica.* [< its habit of nesting under the eaves of houses]

house·mas·ter /hówss màstər/ *n* a man who is in charge of the students living together in a dormitory or residence hall at some preparatory schools and colleges or universities

house·mate /hówss màyt/ *n* somebody who shares a house with one or more other people who are not relatives

house·moth·er /hówss mùthər/ *n* a woman who is responsible for a group of young people living in an institution such as a college residence hall or a sorority house

house mouse *n* a gray or brownish gray mouse that is common worldwide and is a household pest. Latin name: *Mus musculus*.

house mu·sic *n* MUSIC same as **house** *n* (sense 17) [Probably after the *Warehouse*, nightclub in Chicago]

house of as·sem·bly *n* the lawmaking body or lower house of the legislature in some countries of the Commonwealth of Nations

House of As·sem·bly *n* the provincial legislative body in Nova Scotia and Newfoundland

House of Bur·gess·es *n* the lower house of the colonial legislature in Virginia

house of cards *n* something that is unstable and likely to fall down, like a structure built of playing cards

House of Com·mons *n* the lower house of Parliament in the United Kingdom and Canada

house of cor·rec·tion *n* an institution where people convicted of minor offenses are imprisoned

House of Del·e·gates *n* the lower house in the legislatures of Maryland, Virginia, and West Virginia

house officer *n UK* a hospital doctor who is training to become a registrar, and eventually a GP or consultant

house of God *n* RELIG same as **house of worship**

house of ill fame *n* same as **brothel**

House of Lords *n* the nonelected upper house of Parliament in the United Kingdom, made up of life peers, some hereditary peers, and some bishops

House of Rep·re·sen·ta·tives *n* the lower house of Congress and of most state legislatures in the United States

House of the Peo·ple *n* POL same as **Lok Sabha**

house of wor·ship, house of God *n* a church, temple, synagogue, or other building used for religious services

house or·gan *n* a magazine published by a business or other organization for its employees or customers, containing information about the company, its products, and its employees

house·paint·er /hówss pàyntər/ *n* a professional painter of houses

house·par·ent /hówss pérrənt/ *n* an adult who is responsible for a group of young people living in an institution such as a dormitory or hostel

house par·ty *n* **1.** a party at somebody's home or at a residence such as a fraternity or sorority house at which the guests stay overnight or for several days **2.** the group of guests attending a house party

house·per·son /hówss pùrss'n/ (*plural* **-per·sons** or **-peo·ple** /-pèep'l/) *n* somebody whose job is to perform routine tasks of cleaning and maintenance in a house or hotel

house phy·si·cian *n* **1.** a doctor employed in a hospital, especially a resident or an intern who cares for patients under the supervision of the regular medical staff **2.** MED same as **house doctor**

house·plant /hówss plànt/ *n* a decorative plant grown indoors, especially one that would die if planted outdoors in a cold climate

house-poor *adj* financially encumbered because of having purchased property, especially a house for which mortgage payments, repairs, and maintenance are very expensive

house-proud *adj* taking pride in the appearance of the home and its state of cleanliness or repair, sometimes in an excessive or fussy way

house-rais·ing *n* a gathering of friends and neighbors, especially in a rural community, to help somebody build a house

house rule *n* a rule, usually not one of the regular rules in a game, that is observed in a casino or among a group of friends

house seat *n* a seat in a theater reserved for friends of members of the cast or the producers or other special guests

house-sit *vi* to live in temporarily and take care of somebody else's house and property while that person is away —**house-sit·ter** *n* —**house-sit·ting** *n*

Houses of Parliament, London, designed by Sir Charles Barry (1840–60)

Houses of Par·lia·ment *npl* the building in London, England, in which the House of Commons and the House of Lords of the United Kingdom meet and work

house spar·row *n* a small hardy brown-and-gray bird with a black throat. Native to: Europe, Asia. Latin name: *Passer domesticus*. [< its living in or near human settlements]

house-to-house *adj* going or done from one house to the next ○ *a house-to-house search*

house·top /hówss tòp/ *n* the very top or roof of a house

house trail·er *n* a trailer used as a dwelling or an office and containing facilities such as a bathroom, bedroom, and kitchen (*dated*)

house·train /hówss tràyn/ (**-trained, -train·ing, -trains**) *vt UK* same as **housebreak** *v* (sense 1) —**house-trained** *adj*

House Un-A·mer·i·can Ac·tiv·i·ties Com·mit·tee *n* a former Congressional committee created in 1938 to investigate possibly subversive activities and responsible in the 1950s for publicly accusing a number of writers and artists of being Communists

house·wares /hówss wérz/ *npl* things that people use in a house, especially kitchen utensils and small electrical appliances

house·warm·ing /hówss wàwrming/, **house-warm·ing par·ty** *n* a party that somebody gives to celebrate moving into a new house

house·wife /hówss wīf/ (*plural* **-wives** /-wīvz/) *n* a woman who does not go out to work but stays at home to manage a household

house·wife·ly /hówss wīflee/ *adj* relating to, done by, or thought appropriate for a housewife

house·wom·an /hówss wŏŏmmən/ (*plural* **-wom·en** /-wìmmin/) *n* same as **housewife**

house·work /hówss wùrk/ *n* tasks that are regularly done in a house, e.g., dusting, vacuuming, washing clothes, and cooking

hous·ing[1] /hówzing/ *n* **1.** ACCOMMODATION houses and other buildings where people live, considered collectively ○ *Decent housing is often hard to find.* **2.** PROVISION OF ACCOMMODATION the provision of places to live ○ *Housing of homeless families is our first priority.* **3.** MACHINE'S PROTECTIVE STRUCTURE a frame or structure that protects part of a machine ○ *a wheel housing* **4.** PLACE THAT PIECE FITS INTO a slot, groove, or hole in one piece of wood into which another piece is inserted **5.** NICHE FOR STATUE a small recess or hollow in which a statue can be placed **6.** NAUT BELOW-DECK PART OF MAST the portion of a mast that is below the deck [13C. < HOUSE]

hous·ing[2] /hówzing/ *n* **1.** a piece of cloth that covers the back of a horse, used for protection or decoration **2.** the ornamental trappings for a horse (*often used in the plural*) [Mid-17C. < Old French *houce* < medieval Latin *hultia* "protective covering" < Germanic]

hous·ing de·vel·op·ment *n* a planned area of houses or apartment buildings, usually built at the same time to a similar design

hous·ing es·tate *n UK* same as **housing development**

hous·ing pro·ject *n* a group of houses or apartment buildings built with public money for low-income families

Hous·man /hówssmən/, **A. E.** (1859–1936) British poet and scholar. His verse collections include *A Shropshire Lad* (1896) and *Last Poems* (1922). Full name **Housman, Alfred Edward**

> "Clay lies still, but blood's a rover; / Breath's a ware that will not keep/Up, lad: when the journey's over / There'll be time enough to sleep."
> [A. E. Housman, "Reveillé," *A Shropshire Lad*; 1896]

Hou·ston /hyŏŏst'n/ city in Texas, the fourth largest city in the United States. It is a major port and one of the world's chief oil centers. Population: 2,009,834 (2002 estimate).

Hous·ton /hyŏŏstən/, **Sam** (1793–1863) US frontiersman and politician. He served as president of the Republic of Texas (1836–38 and 1841–44) and then as the new state's US senator (1845–59) and governor (1859–61). Full name **Houston, Samuel**

hous·to·ni·a /hyoo stṓnee ə, yoo-/ *n* a small flowering plant of the mallow family, e.g., the bluet. Native to: North America. Genus: *Houstonia*. [Early 19C. < modern Latin, after William *Houston* (d. 1733), Scottish botanist]

HOV *abbr* high-occupancy vehicle

hove /hōv/ NAUT past tense of **heave** *v* (senses 7–8) (*formal*)

hov·el /húvv'l/ *n* a small, dirty, or poorly built house [14C. Origin ?]

hov·er /húvvər/ (**-ered, -er·ing, -ers**) *v* **1.** *vi* FLOAT IN AIR to float or flutter in the air without moving very far from the same spot **2.** *vi* WAIT NEAR BY to wait near a person or place, usually in a nervous, inquisitive, or expectant way **3.** *vi* BE UNDECIDED to be unable to decide between alternatives **4.** *vi* BE UNSTABLE to be in a condition that is neither one of two alternatives nor the other ○ *hovering between life and death* **5.** *vi* STAY AROUND SAME LEVEL to stay near a particular point, changing only slightly ○ *temperatures hovering in the low teens* **6.** *vti* COMPUT PUT CURSOR OVER ICON to position the cursor over an icon on a computer screen to get pop-up information without clicking, or be positioned in this way [14C. < obsolete *hove* "linger," origin ?] —**hov·er** *n* —**hov·er·er** *n* —**hov·er·ing·ly** *adv*

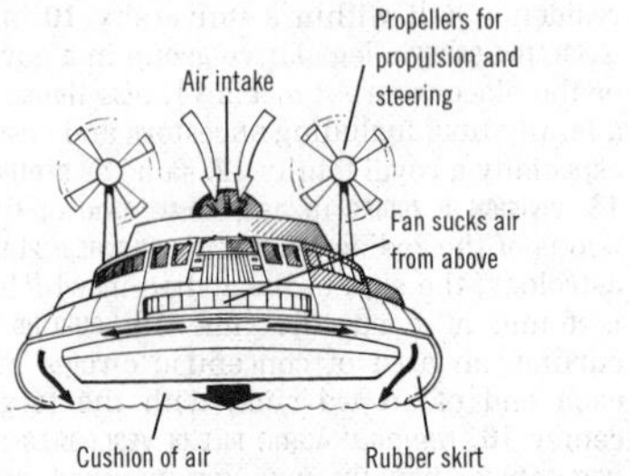

hovercraft

hov·er·craft /húvvər kràft/ (*plural* **-crafts** or *same*) *n* a vehicle that can travel over land and water supported by a cushion of air that it creates by blowing air downward

hov·er·port /húvvər pàwrt/ *n* a place where hovercrafts load and unload [Mid-20C. Blend of HOVERCRAFT + AIRPORT]

how /how/ *adv* **1.** IN WHAT WAY used to ask or report questions or to introduce statements about the manner in which something happens or is done ○ *How do I open the window?* ○ *I don't know how you manage to sew so neatly.* **2.** TO WHAT EXTENT used to ask or report questions or to introduce statements about the quantity or degree of something ○ *How high is* *the roof?* **3.** LIKE WHAT used to ask or report questions or to introduce statements about the quality or success of something ○ *How was the movie?* ○ *We didn't realize how interesting the lecture would be.* **4.** USED IN EXCLAMATIONS used in exclamations to emphasize a word or statement ○ *How nice to see you!* **5.** IN WHATEVER WAY used to indicate that it does not matter in what way somebody does something ○ *Do it how you want.* ■ *conj* THAT used to mention a fact or event ○ *Do you remember how we were ridiculed?* [Old English *hū* < Indo-European] ◇ **how about** (*informal*) **1.** used to make a suggestion ○ *How about some lunch?* **2.** used to change the subject of a conversation ○ *That's enough of my ideas. How about your own policies?* ◇ **how are you (doing)?** used to ask about somebody's health, or simply as a greeting when you meet somebody, especially somebody already known ◇ **how do you do?** used when meeting somebody for the first time

How·ard /hów ərd/, **Catherine** (1520?–42) queen of England. She became the fifth wife of Henry VIII in 1540 and was beheaded when her premarital affairs were revealed.

How·ard, Leslie (1893–1943) British actor. He is best known for his roles as Henry Higgins in *Pygmalion* (1938) and Ashley Wilkes in *Gone With the Wind* (1939). Born **Steiner, Leslie Howard**

How·ard, Trevor (1916–88) British actor. An accomplished stage and screen performer, his movies include *Brief Encounter* (1945) and *Mutiny on the Bounty* (1962). Full name **Howard, Trevor Wallace**

how·be·it /how bée it/ *adv* however or nevertheless (*formal*)

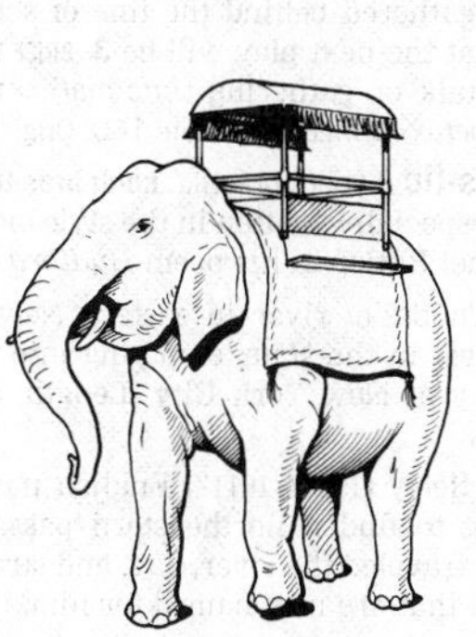

howdah

how·dah /hówdə/ *n* a large seat for several people, often with a canopy, that rests on the back of an elephant [Late 18C. Via Urdu *haudah* < Arabic *hawdaj* "litter carried by a camel"]

how-do-you-do (*plural* **how-do-you-dos**) *n* **1.** a greeting or welcome ○ *got to business as soon as the how-do-you-dos were finished* **2.** a difficult or unsatisfactory situation (*informal*) ○ *a fine how-do-you-do* [< the greeting *How do you do?*]

how·dy /hówdee/ (*informal*) *interj* used as a greeting ■ *n* (*plural* **-dies**) a greeting or welcome ○ *"Give your granddad a big howdy!"* [Early 19C. < *How d'ye*, variant of *How do you do?*]

Howe /how/, **Elias** (1819–67) US inventor. He developed and patented the first sewing machine (1846).

Howe, Gordie (*b.* 1928) Canadian ice-hockey player. He played for the Detroit Red Wings (1946–71), the Houston Aeros (1973–77), and the New England Whalers (1977–80). Full name **Howe, Gordon**

Howe, Joseph (1804–73) Canadian journalist and politician. He served as prime minister of Nova Scotia (1860–63) and president of the council in the first Canadian government (1869–73).

> "We seek for nothing more than British subjects are entitled to; but we will be contented with nothing less."
> [Joseph Howe, *Letter to Lord John Russell*; 1839]

Howe, Julia Ward (1819–1910) US writer and reformer. She wrote the poem "Battle Hymn of the Republic" (1862) and was the first woman to be elected to the American Academy of Arts and Letters (1908).

> "Mine eyes have seen the glory of the coming of the Lord: / He is trampling out the vintage where the grapes of wrath are stored."
> [Julia Ward Howe, "Battle Hymn of the Republic"; 1862]

Howe, William, 5th Viscount (1729–1814) British military commander. Second in command at the Battle of Bunker Hill (1775), he became commander in chief of the British Army in North America (1776–78).

how·e'er /how ér/ *contr* same as **however** (*literary*)

How·ells /hów əlz/, **William Dean** (1837–1920) US writer and critic. He is best known for his novel *The Rise of Silas Lapham* (1885).

> "The wrecks of slavery are fast growing a fungus crop of sentiment."
> [William Dean Howells, *Their Wedding Journey*; 1872]

how·ev·er /how évvər/ CORE MEANING: an adverb introducing some form of contrast ○ *The letters are stained and faded. I do, however, believe they're legible.*

adv **1.** TO WHATEVER DEGREE used to indicate that no matter what happens, a situation remains the same ○ *However much we disagree about the details, the basic facts remain the same.* **2.** IN WHATEVER WAY used to indicate that it does not matter in what way somebody does something ○ *Prepare the potatoes however you like.* **3.** HOW used as an emphatic form of "how" ○ *What a surprise to see you! However did you find us?* **4.** NEVERTHELESS used to introduce a restricting or counterbalancing consideration

USAGE See *although*.

USAGE People disagree as to whether we should put ***however***, meaning "nevertheless," "nonetheless," "but," at the beginning of new sentences. Therefore, it is wise to avoid it by combining two main, contrasting, clauses and linking them with ***however***: *He was indicted for the crime; however, he was acquitted by the jury at trial.* Notice that a semicolon must precede ***however*** and a comma must follow it when two main clauses are linked like this. A common error is to set ***however*** off with commas, as in this incorrectly punctuated sentence: *He was indicted for the crime, however, he was acquitted by the jury at trial.*

When ***however*** in the senses mentioned here appears in the midst of a sentence expressing ideas contrasting with what has been said in a previous sentence, put one comma before ***however*** and another after it: *The resort has closed for the season. Its staff members, however, are remaining on the property to service and repair the ski lifts.* ***However*** can also appear at the end of such a sentence, punctuated by a single comma just before it: *Its staff members are remaining on the property to service and repair the ski lifts, however.*

However has other meanings, and those meanings dictate whether or not you punctuate the word and how. If you use ***however*** to mean "to whatever degree," "in whatever way," or "how" at the outset of an introductory main clause, put a comma after the clause, as in *However hard it snowed during the night, the road crews were able to clear the main arteries before the rush hour.* If ***however***, meaning "in whatever way," modifies another adverb and the two appear as a pair in mid-sentence, put a comma before and after the two words: *The coaching staff has begun, however reluctantly, to admit major flaws in the offensive team's tactics.*

It is redundant to pair *but* with ***however***. Use one word or the other, not both. Thus, this sentence is poor: *The flight was initially canceled but it did manage to take off five hours late, however.* Keep *but* and drop ***however***.

howff /howf/, **howf** *n Scotland* a place where people often go to meet, especially a bar [Early 18C. Origin ?]

how·it·zer /hówitsər/ *n* a cannon with a bore diameter greater than 30 mm and a maximum elevation of 60 degrees that fires projectiles in a curved trajectory [Late 17C. Via Dutch *houwitser* < Czech *haufnice* "catapult" < *hauf* "heap" (of stones) < Germanic]

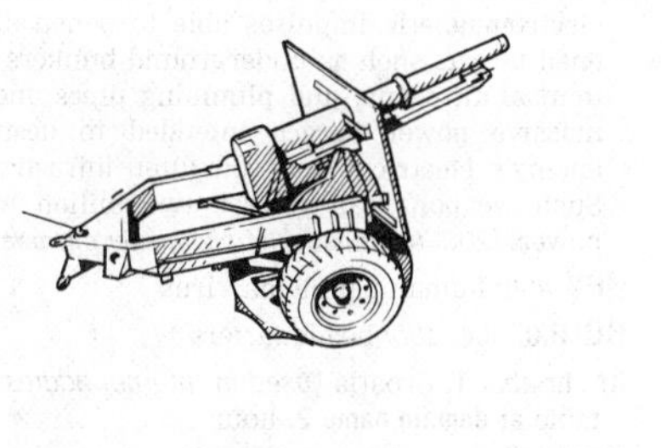

howitzer

howl /howl/ *v* (**howled, howl·ing, howls**) **1.** *vi* MAKE WHINING SOUND to make a long wavering or whining sound ○ *a coyote howling* **2.** *vi* CRY OUT to cry out in pain, anger, or distress **3.** *vt* EXPRESS LOUDLY to express an emotion or opinion loudly and forcefully ○ *The crowd howled its disapproval.* **4.** *vi* ROAR WITH LAUGHTER to laugh loudly and unrestrainedly (*slang*) **5.** *vi* CAROUSE to go on a spree (*slang*) ○ *out howling all night* ■ *n* **1.** MOANING CRY a long sad wavering cry **2.** LOUD CRY a cry of pain, anger, or distress **3.** DRAWN-OUT WAVERING SOUND a long loud high wavering noise ○ *the howl of the wind* **4.** SOMETHING OR SOMEBODY HILARIOUS an extremely funny person or thing (*slang*) [13C. Probably an imitation of the sound]

howl down *vt* to prevent somebody or something from being heard by making loud cries of protest or mockery

howl·er /hówlər/ *n* **1.** a mistake that is so bad that it is funny (*slang*) **2.** somebody or something that makes a howling noise **3.** VERTEB same as **howler monkey**

howl·er mon·key *n* any one of various mainly leaf-eating monkeys that live in trees and have a very loud booming call. Native to: tropical America. Genus: *Alouatta.*

howl·ing /hówling/ *adj* **1.** LOUD AND WAVERING making a long loud high wavering noise ○ *a howling wind* **2.** VERY GREAT extreme or great in degree (*informal*) ○ *a howling success* **3.** DISMALLY DESOLATE desolate or drearily empty of human beings (*literary*) ■ *n* NOISE a succession of long high wavering noises such as animal cries or the sound of a strong wind —**howl·ing·ly** *adv*

howl·ing der·vish *n* a member of an ascetic Muslim religious group known for very energetic chanting and singing

Howl·in' Wolf /hówlən wŏolf/ (1910–76) US musician. He was an electric blues singer who profoundly influenced rock and roll during its early years. His most famous song was "Smokestack Lightnin'" (1956). Born **Burnett, Chester Arthur**

How·rah another spelling of **Haora**

how·so·ev·er /hòwssō évvər/ *adv* same as **however** (*formal or archaic*)

how-to (*informal*) *adj* giving practical information and instructions on the way to do something ○ *another how-to guide on home decorating* ■ *n* (*plural* **how-tos**) a book, manual, or experience that gives practical information and detailed instructions ○ *Before you tinker with your car, read a how-to.*

how·zit /hówzit/ *interj S Africa* used as a greeting or to ask about another person's health or progress (*informal*) [Late 20C. Contraction of *How is it?*]

hoy·a /hóy ə/ *n* TREES same as **wax plant** [Mid-19C. < modern Latin, after Thomas *Hoy* (d. 1821), British gardener]

hoy·den /hóyd'n/ *n* an offensive term that deliberately insults a young woman's self-control and thoughtfulness (*dated*) [Late 17C. Probably < Dutch *heiden* "lout, heathen"]

Hoyle /hoyl/, **Sir Fred** (1915–2001) British astronomer and writer. An expert in astrophysics, he wrote books on astronomy and works of science fiction. Although an advocate of the steady-state theory, he coined the term big bang to describe the theory that the universe originated from an explosion. Full name **Hoyle, Sir Frederick**

> "Space isn't remote at all. It's only an hour's drive away if your car could go straight upward."
> [Sir Fred Hoyle, *Observer (London)*; September 9, 1979]

hp *abbr* MEASURE horsepower

h.p. *abbr* high pressure

HPM *n* an e-bomb with capacitors that emit powerful electromagnetic impulses able to penetrate hardened targets such as underground bunkers via antennas, air vents, and plumbing pipes and cause massive power surges intended to destroy an enemy's electrical and computer infrastructures. Such weapons can release two billion watts of power. [20C. Abbreviation of *high-power microwave*]

HPV *abbr* human papilloma virus

HQ, **H.Q.**, **h.q.** *abbr* headquarters

hr., **hr** *abbr* **1.** Croatia (*used in Internet addresses*) See table at **domain name** **2.** hour

H.R. *abbr* **1.** homeroom **2.** BASEBALL home run **3.** human resources **4.** GOV House of Representatives

H.R.E. *abbr* **1.** Holy Roman Emperor **2.** Holy Roman Empire

H.R.H. *abbr* **1.** Her Royal Highness **2.** His Royal Highness

HRSD *abbr* GOV Department of Human Resources and Skills Development

HRT *abbr* **1.** hormone replacement therapy **2.** hostage rescue team

hryv·ni·a /hrívnee ə/ (*plural same* or **-as**) *n* the main unit of Ukrainian currency. See table at **currency** [< Ukrainian]

Hs *symbol* CHEM ELEM hassium

HS, **H.S.** *abbr* EDUC high school

HSGT *abbr* high-speed ground transportation

H.S.H. *abbr* **1.** Her Serene Highness **2.** His Serene Highness

Hsi·en Nien /syèn nyén/ *n* CALENDAR same as **Chinese New Year**

HST *abbr* **1.** harmonized sales tax **2.** hypersonic transport

ht *abbr* **1.** Haiti (*used in Internet addresses*) See table at **domain name** **2.** heat **3.** height

HT *abbr* **1.** SPORTS halftime **2.** ELEC ENG high tension **3.** high tide

HTH *abbr* ONLINE (*used in e-mails or text messages*) **1.** happy to help **2.** hope this helps

HTLV *abbr* human T-cell lymphotropic virus

HTLV-I *n* a virus associated with cancers of the lymphatic system. Full form **human T-cell lymphotropic virus I**

HTLV-II *n* a virus associated with leukemia. Full form **human T-cell lymphotropic virus II**

html, **htm** *abbr* a file extension for an HTML file. Full form **HyperText Markup Language**

HTML *n* the markup language used for creating documents on the World Wide Web. Full form **HyperText Markup Language**

Hts. *abbr* GEOG Heights

HTTP, **http** *n* the client/server protocol that defines how messages are formatted and transmitted on the World Wide Web. Full form **HyperText Transfer Protocol**

hu *abbr* Hungary (*used in Internet addresses*) See table at **domain name**

HUAC /hyŏŏ ak/ *abbr* House Un-American Activities Committee

hua·ca /waakə/ *n* one of the sacred spirits and powers whom Native South American peoples of the Andes believe to live in caves, rocks, and other natural formations [Early 17C. Via Spanish < Quechua *waca* "god of the house"]

hu·ah /hŏŏ ə/ *interj* used as a loud expression of great enthusiasm or aggression by members of the US Army (*informal*)

Huai·nan /hwī naan/ industrial city in Anhui Province, eastern China. It is the center of a large coalmining area. Population: 1,310,514 (1991).

Huang Hai /waang hī/ ♦ **Yellow Sea**

Huang He /hwaang hő/ second longest river in China, flowing through the north central part of the country. Length: 3,395 mi./5,464 km.

hua·ra·che /wə raachee/ *n Hispanic* a sandal of a type originally worn in Mexico, with the upper part made of woven leather straps and a rubber sole [Late 19C. < Mexican Spanish]

Huas·ca·rán /wàskə rán/ mountain in the Andes in west central Peru. Snowcapped all year round, it is the highest peak in the country. Height: 22,205 ft./6,768 m.

hub /hub/ *n* **1.** CENTRAL PART the central part of a wheel or a similar rotating device such as a propeller **2.** CENTER OF ACTIVITY a place that is a center of activity or interest ○ *the region's financial hub* **3.** *also* **hub air·port** CENTRAL AIRPORT a central airport that passengers can fly to from smaller local airports in order to catch an international or long-distance flight [Early 16C. Probably alteration of HOB[1]]

Hub /hub/ *n* the city of Boston, Massachusetts (*informal*) [Because most of its main roads lead into the central city like the spokes of a wheel]

hub air·port *n* AVIAT same as **hub** (sense 3)

hub·ba-hub·ba /hùbbə húbbə/ *interj* used to express approval, enthusiasm, or pleasure (*dated slang*) [Mid-20C. Origin ?]

Hub·bard squash /húbbərd-/, **hub·bard squash** *n US regional, Can* PLANTS same as **winter squash** [Mid-19C. After a surname]

Hub·ble /húbb'l/, **Edwin** (1889–1953) US astronomer. Through his study of galaxies, he proved that the universe is larger than had previously been thought and is still expanding. Full name **Hubble, Edwin Powell**

hub·ble-bub·ble /hùbb'l-/ *n* **1.** same as **hookah** **2.** same as **hubbub** [Early 17C. Alteration of BUBBLE]

Hub·ble con·stant, **Hub·ble's con·stant** *n* the ratio that expresses the rate of the universe's expansion, equal to the speed at which galaxies appear to be moving away from Earth divided by their distance [Mid-20C. After Edwin HUBBLE]

Hub·ble's law *n* the law holding that the speed at which distant galaxies are moving away from Earth is proportional to their distance from the observer [Mid-20C. After Edwin HUBBLE]

Popperfoto

Hubble Telescope: a space shuttle astronaut repairs the Hubble Telescope

Hub·ble Tel·e·scope, **Hub·ble Space Tel·e·scope** *n* a telescope mounted on a satellite that orbits the Earth, used to observe distant parts of the universe and photograph them. It was launched in 1990. [Late 20C. After Edwin HUBBLE]

hub·bub /hú bùb/ *n* **1.** a confused din, especially a number of voices speaking at once **2.** a fuss or period of excitement [Mid-16C. Probably < Celtic]

hub·by /húbbee/ (*plural* **-bies**) *n* same as **husband** (*informal*) [Late 17C. Alteration of HUSBAND]

hub·cap /húb kàp/ *n* a round cover that protects the outside of the central part of a vehicle's wheel

Hu·bei /hŏŏ báy/ province in central China comprising both mountainous territory and the lake-studded plain of the Yangtze River. Capital: Wuhan. Population: 58,250,000 (1997). Area: 72,390 sq. mi./187,500 sq. km.

hu·bris /hyŏŏbriss/ *n* **1.** excessive pride or arrogance **2.** the excessive pride and ambition that usually leads to the downfall of a hero in classical tragedy [Late 19C. < Greek] —**hu·bris·tic** /hyoo brístik/ *adj*

huck·a·back /húkə bàk/, **huck** /huk/ *n* a coarse absorbent cotton or linen fabric. Use: towels. [Late 17C. Origin ?]

huck·le·ber·ry /húk'l bèrree/ (*plural* **-ries**) *n* **1.** the edible dark-blue fruit of a bush related to the blueberry **2.** a bush that bears huckleberries. Native to: North America. Genus: *Gaylussacia*. [Late 16C. Probably alteration of *hurtleberry* "whortleberry"]

huck·ster /húkstər/ *n* **1.** AGGRESSIVE SALESPERSON an aggressive salesperson or promoter **2.** RETAILER somebody who sells small articles, especially a street peddler **3.** COPYWRITER a writer of advertising copy, especially for broadcast (*informal*) ■ *v* (**-stered, -ster·ing, -sters**) **1.** *vt* PEDDLE MERCHANDISE to sell or peddle something **2.** *vti* SELL SOMETHING AGGRESSIVELY to use aggressive methods to sell or promote something [12C. Origin ?]

HUD /hud/ *abbr* **1.** COMPUT heads-up display **2.** (Department of) Housing and Urban Development

Hud·ders·field /húddərz fèeld/ industrial city in West Yorkshire, northern England. Population: 143,726 (1991).

hud·dle /húdd'l/ *v* (**-dled, -dling, -dles**) **1.** *vti* GATHER TIGHTLY TOGETHER to gather together in a tightly packed group, or make people or things do this ○ *huddled together for warmth* **2.** *vi* CROUCH to draw your arms and legs tightly into your body, or move in close to something, often for shelter or comfort ○ *He huddled in a doorway.* **3.** *vi* FOOTBALL GATHER TO PLAN PLAY in football, to gather together behind the line of scrimmage in order to plan the next play **4.** *vi* TALK PRIVATELY to gather privately to confer, make plans, or gossip (*informal*) ■ *n* **1.** TIGHT GROUP a group of people or things gathered closely together **2.** FOOTBALL GATHERING OF FOOTBALL PLAYERS a group of football players gathered behind the line of scrimmage to hear what the next play will be **3.** BRIEF TALK a quick private talk or gathering (*informal*) ○ *went into a huddle between meetings* [Late 16C. Origin ?]

Hu·di·bras·tic /hyŏŏdi brástik/, **hu·di·bras·tic** *adj* mock-heroic, especially written in the style or meter used by Samuel Butler in his poem *Hudibras*

Hud·son /húdss'n/ river in eastern New York, and the longest in the state, emptying into Upper New York Bay at New York City. Length: 306 mi./492 km.

Hud·son, Henry (1565?–1611?) English navigator. Attempting to find a northeastern passage to East Asia, he traveled the river, bay, and strait in North America that are now named for him.

Hud·son, Rock (1925–85) US actor. He was a handsome romantic lead in movies such as *Pillow Talk* (1959). Born **Scherer, Jr., Roy Harold**

Hud·son Bay almost landlocked inland sea of east central Canada, rich in wildlife. Native Americans and Inuit are the chief inhabitants of the region. Area: 475,000 sq. mi./1,230,000 sq. km. Depth: 846 ft./258 m.

Hud·son's Bay blan·ket *n Can* a wool blanket, usually cream-colored with distinctive red, black, yellow, and indigo stripes [Because originally traded by the HUDSON'S BAY COMPANY]

Hud·son's Bay Com·pa·ny *n* a fur-trading company chartered in England in 1670 to trade in North America and later much involved in fur trading, exploring, and claiming territory for the British crown [Because its original charter was to trade around Hudson Bay]

Hud·son Strait body of water in northeastern Canada connecting Hudson Bay with the Atlantic Ocean and separating Baffin Island from northern Quebec. Depth: 2,890 ft./880 m. Length: 450 mi./720 km.

hue /hyoo/ *n* **1.** COLOR a color or shade of a color ○ *flowers of every hue* **2.** SHADE OF COLOR a particular shade of a color ○ *a pleasing hue of green* **3.** PHYS PROPERTY OF COLOR a property of a color that enables it to be perceived, determined by its dominant wavelength **4.** TYPE a type or kind in a particular range ○ *all hues of political opinion* **5.** ASPECT the way that something looks ○ *This puts a completely different hue on the matter.* [Old English *hē(o)w* < Germanic]

SPELLCHECK See *hew*.

Hue /hway/ historic city in central Vietnam on the Huong River, near the South China Sea. It was the Nguyen royal capital from 1802 to 1945. Population: 219,149 (1992).

hue and cry *n* **1.** a great uproar or commotion about something **2.** formerly, a pursuit of somebody accused of a crime, with the pursuers calling on bystanders to join in the chase [< Anglo-Norman *hu e cri* "outcry and cry"]

-hued *suffix* of a particular color or number of colors ○ *the many-hued rainbow* ○ *a rose-hued sunset*

Huer·ta /wértə/, **Victoriano** (1854–1916) general and president of Mexico (1913–14). He became provisional president of Mexico (1913), but resigned and fled amid rebellions (1914).

hue·vos ran·che·ros /wàyvōss ran chérrōss/ *npl Hispanic* a Mexican dish of fried or poached eggs covered with chili, salsa, or tomato sauce and cheese, often served on a corn tortilla and accompanied by refried beans and sour cream [< American Spanish, "ranch-style eggs"]

huff /huf/ *n* **FIT OF ANGER** a brief mood of anger or resentment at something somebody has done ○ *walked out in a huff* ■ *v* (**huffed, huff·ing, huffs**) **1.** *vti* **ANGER SOMEBODY, OR GET ANGRY** to anger or offend somebody, or become angry or offended **2.** *vi* **BLOW OR PANT** to blow, pant, or breathe laboriously [Late 16C. An imitation of the sound of blowing] ◇ **huff and puff 1.** to blow or pant, or do this while moving with great difficulty **2.** to make noisy but empty threats or objections

huff·y /húffee/ (**-i·er, -i·est**) *adj* **1. TOUCHY** easily offended or put into a huff **2. IRRITATED** annoyed or irritated about something ○ *a huffy silence* **3. ARROGANT** haughtily arrogant and condescending —**huff·i·ly** *adv* —**huff·i·ness** *n*

hug /hug/ *v* (**hugged, hug·ging, hugs**) **1.** *vti* **EMBRACE AFFECTIONATELY** to put your arms around somebody's body and hold the person tight to show affection or pleasure **2.** *vt* **PUT YOUR ARMS AROUND SOMETHING** to clasp your arms around a part of your own body ○ *hugging her knees to her chest* **3.** *vt* **KEEP CLOSE TO SOMETHING** to remain in close linear proximity to something while moving in a forward direction ○ *This car really hugs the road.* ■ *n* **AN EMBRACE** an affectionate embrace [Mid-16C. Probably < N Germanic] —**hug·ga·ble** *adj* —**hug·ger** *n*

huge /hyooj/ (**hug·er, hug·est**) *adj* **1. ENORMOUS** very big in size or amount **2. LARGE IN SCOPE** very large in scope or scale ○ *huge talent* **3. SIGNIFICANTLY SUCCESSFUL** very important or successful (*informal*) ○ *This band is going to be huge.* [12C. Shortening of Old French *ahuge*] —**huge·ness** *n*

huge·ly /hyóojlee/ *adv* to a great degree ○ *hugely successful*

hug·ger·mug·ger /húggər mùggər/ *n* **1. MUDDLED MESS** a disorderly mess or muddle **2. SECRECY** secretive behavior or concealment ■ *adj* **1. DISORDERED** confused or jumbled **2. SECRETIVE** clandestine or secret ■ *v* (**-gered, -ger·ing, -gers**) **1.** *vt* **CONCEAL SOMETHING** to keep something secret **2.** *vi* **ACT SECRETIVELY** to behave in a secretive manner [Early 16C. Origin ?] —**hug·ger·mug·ger** *adv*

Hughes /hyooz/, **Charles** (1862–1948) chief justice of the US Supreme Court (1930–41). He also served as governor of New York (1907–10) and US secretary of state (1921–25). Full name **Hughes, Charles Evans**

> "We are under a constitution, but the constitution is what the judges say it is, and the judiciary is the safeguard of our liberty and of our property under the constitution."
> [Charles Hughes, *Speech as Governor of New York State, Addresses 1906–16*; 1916]

Hughes, Howard (1905–76) US industrialist. He became one of the richest people in the United States by expanding his family manufacturing business into a huge corporate conglomerate. A record-setting pilot during the 1930s, he became notorious for his reclusiveness and eccentricity in his later years. Full name **Hughes, Howard Robard**

> "Never make a decision. Let someone else make it and then if it turns out to be the wrong one, you can disclaim it, and if it is the right one you can abide by it."
> [Howard Hughes. Quoted in *The Hughes Legacy: Scramble for the Billion*; 1976]

Library of Congress

Langston Hughes

Hughes, Langston (1902–67) US writer. A leader of the Harlem Renaissance, he incorporated the rhythms of jazz into his poems and stories about African American urban life. Full name **Hughes, James Mercer Langston**

> "What happens to a dream deferred? / Does it dry up / like a raisin in the sun? / Or fester like a sore— / and then run?"
> [Langston Hughes, "Harlem," *Montage of a Dream Deferred*; 1951]

Hughes, Ted (1930–98) British poet. He was poet laureate (1984–98) and married the poet Sylvia Plath in 1956. His works include *Lupercal* (1960) and *Wodwo* (1967). Full name **Hughes, Edward James**

> "He spins from the bars, but there's no cage to him / More than to the visionary his cell: / His stride is wildernesses of freedom: / The world rolls under the long thrust of his heel. / Over the cage floor the horizons come."
> [Ted Hughes, "The Jaguar," *The Hawk in the Rain*; 1957]

Hughes·i·an /hyóozee ən/ *adj* relating to or representative of the works of the British poet Ted Hughes ■ *n* a supporter of the British poet Ted Hughes

Hug·li /hóoglee/, **Hoogh·ly** river in northeastern India. It is the most westerly of the channels by which the Ganges River reaches the Bay of Bengal. Length: 160 mi./257 km.

Hu·go /hyóogō/, **Victor** (1802–85) French poet, novelist, and dramatist. A leading writer of the 19th century, he wrote *The Hunchback of Notre Dame* (1831) and *Les Misérables* (1862). Full name **Hugo, Victor Marie**

> "The misery of a child is interesting to a mother, the misery of a young man is interesting to a young woman, the misery of an old man is interesting to nobody."
> [Victor Hugo, "Saint Denis," *Les Misérables*; 1862]

Hu·gue·not /hyóogə nòt/ *n* a French Protestant, especially in the 16th and 17th centuries [Mid-16C. < French, alteration (based on the name of Besançon *Hugues*, leader of a Swiss political movement) of obsolete *eiguenot* < Swiss German *Eidgenosse* "confederate," literally "oath-companion"]

huh /hu/ *interj* **1.** used to show surprise, inquiry, disdain, or lack of interest **2.** used to invite comment, especially agreement, after an expressed opinion ○ *Great shot, huh?* [Early 17C. Natural exclamation]

hui·a /hóo yə/ (*plural same*) *n* an extinct bird that had feathers that were much prized by the Maori. Native to: formerly, New Zealand. Latin name: *Heteralocha acutirostris.* [Mid-19C. < Hawaiian; an imitation of its whistling cry]

hui·sa·che /wee sáachee/ *n* a thorny bush with fragrant clusters of deep yellow flowers. Native to: southern United States, Mexico. Latin name: *Acacia farnesiana.* [Mid-19C. Via Mexican Spanish < Nahuatl *huixachi* "many-thorn(ed) shrub"]

Hu Jin·tao /hoo jin tów/ (*b.* 1942) Chinese president of the People's Republic of China (2003–). He was vice president of Jiang Zemin and was named in 2002 as the new leader of the Communist Party from March 2003.

hu·la /hóolə/ *n* a Polynesian or Hawaiian dance involving swaying the hips and miming gestures with the hands ■ *vi* (**-laed, -la·ing, -las**) to dance a hula [Early 19C. < Hawaiian]

Hu·la-Hoop *tdmk* a trademark for a plastic ring that people place around the waist and keep twirling by rhythmically moving the hips

hulk /hulk/ *n* **1. SOMEBODY BIG** a big, powerful, and often clumsy person **2. EMPTY HULL** the empty hull of a ship that has been wrecked or is too old to be sailed **3. UNWIELDY SHIP** a heavy ship that is difficult to steer **4. SHELL OF STRUCTURE** the shell of any old, abandoned, or burned-out structure or vehicle ■ *vi* (**hulked, hulk·ing, hulks**) **1. APPEAR AS LARGE OBJECT** to appear as a large looming object **2. MOVE CLUMSILY** to move in a clumsy or awkward way [Pre-12C. Probably via Anglo-Latin *hulcus* < Greek *holkas* "merchant barge, ship that is towed" < *helkein* "pull"]

hulk·ing /húlking/, **hulk·y** /húlkee/ (**-i·er, -i·est**) *adj* large, bulky, and often clumsy (*informal*)

hull /hul/ *n* **1. BODY OF SHIP** the body of a ship, excluding other parts such as the masts and engines **2. BODY OF VEHICLE** the main body of a large vehicle such as a tank or airplane **3. ROCKET CASING** the external casing of a rocket, missile, or spaceship **4. OUTER COVERING** the outer covering of a seed or fruit **5. CALYX ON STRAWBERRY** the calyx on a strawberry that stays attached to the fruit when it is picked but is not eaten ■ *vt* (**hulled, hull·ing, hulls**) **1. REMOVE OUTER RIND** to remove the outer rind or shell from a fruit or vegetable **2. TAKE STRAWBERRY CALYX OFF** to remove the calyx from a strawberry [Old English *hulu* < Indo-European, "cover, conceal"]

Hull /hul/ **1.** industrial and port city in northeastern England, situated on the Humber Estuary. Population: 243,595 (2001). Official name **Kingston-upon-Hull 2.** city in southwestern Quebec, Canada, situated on the Ottawa River opposite Ottawa. Population: 62,339 (1996).

Hull, Bobby (*b.* 1939) Canadian ice-hockey player. He played left wing for the Chicago Blackhawks (1957–72) and was the first to score over 50 goals in a season. Full name **Hull, Robert Marvin**

Hull, Cordell (1871–1955) US secretary of state (1933–44). During World War II, he planned the postwar United Nations and was awarded the Nobel Peace Prize (1945).

hul·la·ba·loo /hùlləbə lóo/, **hul·la·bal·loo** *n* noisy excitement or fuss (*informal*) [Mid-18C. Alteration of *hollo-ballo* < *holla*, early variant of HELLO]

hul·lo /hu lṓ, hə-/ *interj, n UK* another spelling of **hello**

Hulme /hyoom/, **T. E.** (1883–1917) British poet, critic, and philosopher. A founding member of the imagist movement, he championed modern abstract art and attacked liberalism as a spent political force. His extensive collection of notes were published posthumously as *Speculations* (1924) and *Further Speculations* (1955). Full name **Hulme, Thomas Ernest**

Hulse /hulss/, **Russell A.** (*b.* 1951) US physicist. He shared the Nobel Prize in physics with Joseph Taylor (1993) for discovering and studying the first binary pulsar.

hum /hum/ *v* (**hummed, hum·ming, hums**) **1.** *vti* **SING WITH LIPS CLOSED** to sing with lips closed and without words, or sing something in this way **2.** *vi* **MAKE DRONING SOUND** to make a steady prolonged droning sound ○ *bees humming* **3.** *vi* **GIVE OFF LOW INDISTINCT NOISE** to be filled with a low, continuous, indistinct noise ○ *a room that hummed with strange electronic equipment* **4.** *vi* **BE EXTREMELY BUSY** to be very busy or active (*informal*) ○ *This place is really humming.* ■ *n* **DRONING NOISE** a steady droning sound ■ *interj* **EXPRESSION OF DISPLEASURE OR INDECISION** a low sound made to express displeasure, doubt, surprise, or indecision [14C. An imitation of the sound] —**hum·ma·ble** *adj*

hu·man /hyóomən/ *adj* **1. OF PEOPLE** relating to, involving, or characteristic of human beings ○ *human nature* ○ *human frailty* **2. MADE UP OF PEOPLE** composed of people ○ *the human race* ○ *a human chain* **3. COMPASSIONATELY KIND** showing kindness, compassion, or approachability **4. IMPERFECT** having the imperfections and weaknesses of a human being ○ *She's only human, so give her a break!* ■ *n* same as

human being [14C. Via French < Latin *humanus*] —**hu·man·ness** *n*

USAGE human or **humane**? Do not confuse the spelling of ***human*** and ***humane***. Although the two words sound different, they share the meaning of "compassionate," which is why they are sometimes confused. ***Human*** is chiefly used as an adjective or noun referring to a person or people (as in *a human being, human weaknesses, humans and other animals*), and it cannot be replaced by ***humane*** in such contexts. ***Humane*** also means "involving minimal pain," as in *the humane killing of sick animals*, and it cannot be replaced by ***human*** in this sense.

CULTURAL NOTE ***The Human Comedy***, a collection of novels and stories (1833–50) by French writer Honoré de Balzac. By linking his novels and stories through the use of common themes and characters, Balzac planned a work that would portray the human species in all stages of its development and all aspects of its behavior. At the time of his death, the collection included a hundred novels and stories and about fifty incomplete works.

hu·man be·ing *n* **1.** a member of the species to which men and women belong. Latin name: *Homo sapiens.* **2.** a person, viewed especially as having imperfections and weaknesses ○ *I'm a human being, not a machine.*

hu·mane /hyoo máyn/ *adj* **1. COMPASSIONATE** showing the better aspects of the human character, especially kindness and compassion **2. INVOLVING MINIMAL PAIN** done without inflicting any more pain than is necessary **3. WITH EMPHASIS ON LIBERAL VALUES** with an emphasis on respect for other people's views [15C. Variant of HUMAN] —**hu·mane·ly** *adv* —**hu·mane·ness** *n*

USAGE See *human.*

hu·man e·col·o·gy *n* a branch of sociology that studies the relationships between human beings and their natural and social environments

hu·man en·gi·neer·ing *n* COMM same as **ergonomics**

hu·man er·ror *n* a mistake made by a person rather than being caused by a poorly designed process or the malfunctioning of a machine such as a computer ○ *Most of the accidents are attributable to human error.*

hu·mane so·ci·e·ty *n* an organization that promotes the compassionate treatment of animals

hu·man e·thol·o·gy *n* the study of human behavior, especially aggressive and submissive behavior in social contexts

hu·man fac·tors en·gi·neer·ing *n* COMM same as **ergonomics**

Hu·man Ge·nome Proj·ect *n* a publicly funded international research initiative to sequence and identify human genes and record their positions on chromosomes

hu·man im·mun·o·de·fi·cien·cy vi·rus *n* MED full form of **HIV**

hu·man in·ter·est *n* an element in something, especially a news report, that is about somebody's personal life or feelings and is expected to appeal to the public's sympathy or curiosity —**hu·man-in·ter·est** *adj*

hu·man·ism /hyoómə nìzzəm/ *n* **1. BELIEF IN HUMAN-BASED MORALITY** a system of thought that is based on the values, characteristics, and behavior that are believed to be best in human beings, rather than on any supernatural authority **2. CONCERN FOR PEOPLE** a concern with the needs, well-being, and interests of people **3.** *also* **Hu·man·ism RENAISSANCE CULTURAL MOVEMENT** the secular cultural and intellectual movement of the Renaissance that spread throughout Europe as a result of the rediscovery of the arts and philosophy of the ancient Greeks and Romans —**hu·man·ist** *n, adj* —**hu·man·ist·ic** /hyoómə nístik/ *adj* —**hu·man·is·ti·cal·ly** *adv*

hu·man·i·tar·i·an /hyoo mànni térree ən/ *adj* **1. CARING** committed to improving the lives of other people ○ *a humanitarian organization* **2. HUMAN** involving and affecting human beings, especially in a harmful way (*informal*) ○ *a humanitarian disaster* ■ *n* **1. CARING PERSON** somebody who seeks to improve the lives of other people **2. SOMEBODY BELIEVING IN HUMANITARIANISM** somebody who believes in the philosophical theory of humanitarianism [Mid-19C. < HUMAN, after UNITARIAN and EGALITARIAN]

hu·man·i·tar·i·an·ism /hyoo mànni térree ə nìzzəm/ *n* **1.** a commitment to improving the lives of other people **2.** the philosophical doctrine holding that it is a human being's duty to improve the lives of other people

hu·ma·ni·ta·ri·an space *n* a neutral and impartially administered zone occupied by international aid agencies in a region in which armed conflict is occurring

hu·man·i·ty /hyoo mánnətee/ *n* **1. HUMAN RACE** the human race considered as a whole **2. QUALITIES OF HUMAN BEING** the qualities or characteristics considered as a whole to be characteristic of human beings **3. KINDNESS** kindness or compassion for others ■ **hu·man·i·ties, Hu·man·i·ties** *npl* **1. LIBERAL ARTS** subjects such as history, languages, and philosophy that involve the study of culture and ideas, as distinct from the sciences **2. CLASSICAL STUDIES** the study of the language and literature of the ancient Greeks and Romans

hu·man·ize /hyoómə nìz/ (**-ized, -iz·ing, -iz·es**) *vti* **1.** to make somebody or something humane in character, characteristics, or nature, or become humane **2.** to make something human or like humans, or become human or like humans —**hu·man·i·za·tion** /hyoòməni záysh'n/ *n*

hu·man·kind /hyoómən kìnd/, **hu·man kind** *n* all human beings considered as a whole ○ *"Human kind cannot bear very much reality."* (T. S. Eliot, *Four Quartets, Burnt Norton*; 1935)

hu·man·ly /hyoómənlee/ *adv* **1. WITHIN LIMITS OF HUMAN ABILITY** within the limits of human ability and knowledge ○ *if humanly possible* **2. IN WAY CHARACTERISTIC OF HUMANS** in a way generally considered to be characteristic of humans **3. ACCORDING TO HUMAN EXPERIENCE** as far as human knowledge or experience can judge

hu·man·made /hyoómən màyd/ *adj* made by human beings and not occurring naturally ○ *"Humanmade materials gradually deteriorate even when exposed to unpolluted rain, but acid rain accelerates this process."* (*United States Environmental Protection Agency website*; April 1999)

hu·man met·a·pneu·mo·vi·rus *n* a single-stranded RNA virus discovered in 2001 that is a major cause of respiratory infections with symptoms similar to the common cold

hu·man na·ture *n* the typical character that all human beings share, often seen as being imperfect

hu·man·oid /hyoómə nòyd/ *adj* describes a being from another planet that has the appearance or characteristics of a human —**hu·man·oid** *n*

hu·man pap·il·lo·ma vi·rus *n* a virus that causes warts in the genital area of humans

hu·man race *n* all people considered as a group

hu·man re·la·tions *n* **1.** the study of the ways in which people relate to each other in group situations, especially work, and how communication skills and sensitivity to other people's feelings can be improved (*takes a singular verb*) **2.** the department of an organization or business that deals with employees' hiring, records, and problems

hu·man re·sourc·es *n* the field of business concerned with recruiting and managing employees (*takes a singular verb*) ○ *a career in human resources* ■ *npl* all the people who work in a business or organization, considered as a whole (*takes a plural verb*)

hu·man rights *npl* the rights that are considered by most societies to belong automatically to everyone, e.g., the rights to freedom, justice, and equality

Hum·ber Es·tu·ary /hùmbər-/ navigable estuary in northeastern England. The Trent, Yorkshire, Ouse, and Hull rivers flow into it. Length: 40 mi./60 km.

hum·ble /húmb'l/ *adj* (**-bler, -blest**) **1. MODEST** modest and unassuming in attitude and behavior **2. RESPECTFUL** feeling or showing respect and deference toward other people **3. LOWLY** relatively low in rank and without pretensions ○ *of humble origins* ■ *vt* (**-bled, -bling, -bles**) **1. MAKE SOMEBODY FEEL LESS IMPORTANT** to make somebody feel less proud or convinced of his or her own importance **2. DEGRADE SOMEBODY** to lower somebody in rank or importance [13C. Via Old French *(h)umble* < Latin *humilis* "lowly" < *humus* "earth"] —**hum·ble·ness** *n* —**hum·bly** *adv*

hum·ble·bee /húmb'l bèe/ *n* INSECTS same as **bumblebee** [15C. Probably alteration of Middle Low German *hummelbē* "humming bee" < *hummel* "hum, buzz" + *bē* "bee"]

hum·ble pie *n* formerly, a pie made using the entrails of a newly killed animal, especially a deer (*archaic*) [Mid-17C. Alteration of *umble pie* < *umbles* "edible animal entrails," via French dialect *nombles* < Latin *lumbulus* "small loin"] ◇ **eat humble pie** to apologize or admit you have been wrong, especially in a way that makes you feel humiliated

hum·bling /húmbling/ *adj* making somebody lose confidence, self-importance, or pride

Hum·boldt Cur·rent /húmbōlt-/ *n* a cold current of the South Pacific Ocean that flows north along the western coastline of South America, carrying nutrients that support rich fishing grounds

hum·bug /húm bùg/ *n* **1. NONSENSE** something that is silly or makes no sense **2. DECEPTION** something that is meant to deceive or cheat people **3. FRAUD** somebody who deceives others by making false claims ■ *v* (**-bugged, -bug·ging, -bugs**) **1.** *vti* **DECEIVE** to take part in a deception or deceive somebody **2.** *vt Carib* **HINDER** to hamper or prevent somebody from working ■ *interj* **EXPRESSES DISAGREEMENT** used to express the opinion that something is nonsense or deception (*archaic*) [Mid-18C. Origin ?]

hum·ding·er /hùm díngər/ *n* an exceptional or outstanding person or thing (*slang*) [Early 20C. Probably < HUM "approving murmur" + *dinger* "superlative thing"]

hum·drum /húm drùm/ *adj* dull because of being too familiar and lacking variety [Mid-16C. Probably expressive alteration of HUM]

Hume /hyoom/, **David** (1711–76) Scottish philosopher and historian. His major works are *A Treatise of Human Nature* (1739–40) and *An Enquiry Concerning Human Understanding* (1748).

> "Good and ill, both natural and moral, are entirely relative to human sentiment and affection."
> [David Hume, "The Skeptic," *Essays, Moral and Political*; 1741]

> "Our reason must be consider'd as a kind of cause, of which truth is the natural effect."
> [David Hume, *A Treatise of Human Nature*; 1739–40]

hu·mec·tant /hyoo méktənt/ *n* a substance that absorbs or helps retain moisture, e.g., a skin lotion [Early 19C. < Latin *(h)umectant-*, present participle of *(h)umectare* "moisten" < *(h)umectus* "moist" < *(h)umere* "be moist"] —**hu·mec·tant** *adj*

hu·mer·al /hyoómərəl/ *adj* relating to, involving, or located in the humerus of the upper arm or forelimb ○ *a humeral injury*

hu·mer·al veil *n* a silk shawl covering the shoulders and hands, worn by a Roman Catholic priest while holding sacred vessels

hu·mer·us /hyoómərəss/ (*plural* **-mer·i** /-mə rì/) *n* the long bone of the human upper arm or of a forelimb in other animals [14C. < Latin, "upper arm"]

hu·mic /hyoómik/ *adj* relating to, involving, containing, or typical of humus [Mid-19C. < HUMUS[1]]

hu·mid /hyoómid/ *adj* with a relatively high level of moisture in the air [14C. < Latin *(h)umidus* < *(h)umere* "be moist"] —**hu·mid·ly** *adv*

SYNONYMS See *wet.*

hu·mi·dex /hyoómi dèks/ *n Can* an index of the level of discomfort likely to be experienced as a result of the combined effects of humidity and heat [Late 20C. Contraction of *humidity index*]

hu·mid·i·fi·er /hyoo míddi fì ər/ *n* a device or machine that keeps the air moist inside an enclosed space

hu·mid·i·fy /hyoo míddə fì/ (**-fied, -fy·ing, -fies**) *vt* to make something, especially the air, more moist or damp —**hu·mid·i·fi·ca·tion** /hyoo mìddəfi káysh'n/ *n*

hu·mid·i·stat /hyoo míddi stàt/ *n* an instrument that measures or controls the relative humidity of the air [Early 20C. < HUMIDITY, after THERMOSTAT]

hu·mid·i·ty /hyoo míddətee/ *n* **1.** the amount of moisture in the air **2.** the condition of having a high amount of moisture in the air **3.** METEOROL same as **relative humidity**

hu·mi·dor /hyóomi dàwr/ *n* a container, often a box or jar, in which tobacco products, especially cigars, can be stored to prevent them from drying out [Early 20C. < HUMID, after CUSPIDOR]

hu·mi·fy /hyóomi fī/ (**-fied, -fy·ing, -fies**) *vti* to turn a substance into humus, or turn into humus

hu·mil·i·ate /hyoo míllee àyt/ (**-at·ed, -at·ing, -ates**) *vt* to damage somebody's dignity or pride, especially publicly [Mid-16C. < late Latin *humiliat-*, past participle of *humiliare* < Latin *humilis* (see HUMBLE)] —**hu·mil·i·at·ing** *adj* —**hu·mil·i·at·ing·ly** *adv* —**hu·mil·i·a·tor** *n*

hu·mil·i·a·tion /hyoo mìllee áysh'n/ *n* **1. LOSS OF DIGNITY** the feeling or condition of being lessened in dignity or pride **2. LESSENING OF SOMEBODY'S DIGNITY** the act of damaging somebody's dignity or pride **3. SOMETHING THAT HUMILIATES** something that damages somebody's pride or dignity

hu·mil·i·ty /hyoo míllətee/ *n* the quality of being modest or respectful [13C. Via French < Latin *humilitas* < *humilis* (see HUMBLE)]

~~**huminist**~~ incorrect spelling of **humanist**

hum·int /hyóomint/, **HUMINT** *n* intelligence information acquired from people in enemy territory. Full form **human intelligence**

hummingbird

hum·ming·bird /húmming bùrd/ *n* a small brightly colored nectar-eating bird that hovers, especially while feeding, by beating its wings rapidly, producing a humming sound. Native to: tropical America. Family: Trochilidae.

hum·ming·bird moth *n* INSECTS same as **hawk moth** [< its flight, likened to that of a hummingbird]

hum·mock /húmmək/ *n* **1.** a small hill or mound **2.** GEOG another spelling of **hammock**[2] **3.** a ridge of ice in an ice field [Mid-16C. Origin ?] —**hum·mock·y** *adj*

hum·mus /hóommәss, húmmәss/, **hu·mus, hom·mos** *n* a dish made with mashed chickpeas, tahini, oil, lemon juice, and garlic combined into a thick paste, originating in southwestern Asia [Mid-20C. < Arabic *ḥummuṣ* "chickpea"]

hu·mon·gous /hyoo múng gəss/, **hu·mun·gous** *adj* extremely large in size or amount (*informal*) [Mid-20C. Origin ?] —**hu·mon·gous·ly** *adv*

hu·mor /hyóomər/ *n* **1. FUNNY QUALITY** the quality or content of something such as a story, performance, or joke that elicits amusement and laughter ○ *couldn't see the humor in it* **2. ABILITY TO SEE SOMETHING AS FUNNY** the ability to see that something is funny, or the enjoyment of things that are funny ○ *He has no sense of humor.* **3. FUNNY THINGS AS GENRE** writings and other material created to make people laugh **4. SOMEBODY'S USUAL TEMPERAMENT** somebody's character or usual attitude ○ *a writer of melancholy humor* **5. MOOD** a temporary mood or state of mind **6.** HIST **BODY FLUID** according to medieval science and medicine, any of the four main fluids of the human body, blood, yellow bile, black bile, or lymph, that determined somebody's mood and temperament ■ *vt* (**-mored, -mor·ing, -mors**) **1. DO WHAT SOMEBODY WANTS** to do what somebody wants in order to keep him or her happy **2. COMPLY WITH SOMETHING** to act in accordance with something [14C. Via Anglo-Norman < Latin, "body fluid" < *humere* "be moist"]

hu·mor·al /hyóomərəl/ *adj* relating to, involving, or typical of body fluids, especially blood serum

hu·mored /hyóomərd/ *adj* having a particular character or frame of mind (*usually used in combination*) ○ *good-humored*

hu·mor·esque /hyòomə résk/ *n* a light or whimsical piece of music, especially 19th-century music [Late 19C. Alteration of German *Humoreske* < *Humor* "humor" < English]

hu·mor·ist /hyóomərist/ *n* **1.** somebody known to be amusing and to have a quick wit **2.** somebody who writes or performs comic material

hu·mor·less /hyóomərləss/ *adj* **1.** lacking a sense of humor **2.** having no amusing aspect —**hu·mor·less·ly** *adv* —**hu·mor·less·ness** *n*

hu·mor·ous /hyóomərəss/ *adj* **1.** intended to be amusing and make people laugh **2.** witty or able to make people laugh —**hu·mor·ous·ly** *adv* —**hu·mor·ous·ness** *n*

SYNONYMS See ***funny***.

hu·mour *n, vt* Can, UK spelling of **humor**

~~**humourous**~~ incorrect spelling of **humorous**

hump /hump/ *n* **1. BUMP ON ANIMAL'S BACK** a rounded protuberance on the back of some animals such as camels and some cattle **2. CURVE OF BACK** a pronounced convex curvature of somebody's upper spine resulting from injury or disease, a congenital condition, or an accumulation of fat **3. BUMP IN SURFACE OF SOMETHING** a rounded protruding mass, e.g., a mound of earth ■ *v* (**humped, hump·ing, humps**) **1.** *vt* **MOVE SOMETHING WITH EFFORT** to carry something heavy with difficulty (*informal*) **2.** *vti* **OFFENSIVE TERM** an offensive term meaning to have sexual intercourse with somebody (*slang*) **3.** *vt* **MAKE SOMETHING INTO HUMP** to form something into a hump [Mid-17C. Probably < Dutch *homp*, Low German *humpe*] ◇ **over the hump** past the worst or most difficult part of something

hump·back /húmp bàk/ *n* **1.** MED same as **hunchback** **2.** MARINE BIOL same as **humpback whale** **3.** FISH same as **pink salmon** (sense 1) —**hump·backed** *adj*

hump·back salm·on *n* FISH same as **pink salmon** (sense 1) [Because the male develops a humped back during the breeding season]

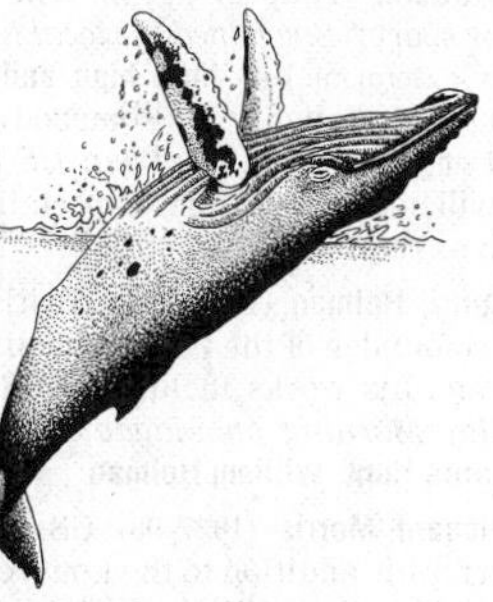

humpback whale

hump·back whale *n* a large dark-gray or black whale, up to 50 ft./15.2 m long, with a humped back and long white flippers, that feeds by sieving plankton and fish through baleen plates. Humpback whales communicate with each other using distinctive complex sounds that can travel over considerable distances. Latin name: *Megaptera novaengliae*.

Hum·per·dinck /hóompər dingk/, **Engelbert** (1854–1921) German composer. He wrote numerous operas, the most famous of which is *Hansel and Gretel* (1893).

humph /humf/ *interj* used to express annoyance, doubt, or dissatisfaction [Mid-16C. Natural exclamation]

Hum·phrey /húmfree/, **Hubert H.** (1911–78) vice president of the United States (1965–69). He served as Democratic vice president under Lyndon Johnson, and ran unsuccessfully for the presidency in 1968. Full name **Humphrey, Hubert Horatio, Jr.**

> "There are those who say to you—we are rushing this issue of civil rights. I say we are 172 years late."
>
> [Hubert H. Humphrey, *Speech, Democratic National Convention*; July 14, 1948]

Hum·phreys Peak /hùmfreez-/ mountain in northern Arizona in the San Francisco Mountains, and the highest peak in the state. Height: 12,633 ft./3,851 m.

hump·ty-dump·ty /hùmptee dúmptee/ (*plural* **hump·ty-dump·ties**) *n* an offensive term for somebody perceived as being short and overweight (*informal*) [Late 18C. After *Humpty-Dumpty*, nursery-rhyme character]

hump·y /húmpee/ (**-i·er, -i·est**) *adj* having or full of humps [Early 18C. < HUMP] —**hump·i·ness** *n*

hu·mun·gous *adj* another spelling of **humongous**

hu·mus[1] /hóommәss, húmmәss/ *n* a dark-brown organic component of soil that is derived from decomposed plant and animal remains and animal excrement. Humus improves the water-retaining properties of soil, adds nutrients, and makes it more workable. [Late 18C. < Latin, "soil"]

hu·mus[2] *n* FOOD another spelling of **hummus**

Hum·vee /húm vèe/ *tdmk* a trademark for a type of military vehicle that combines the features of a light truck and a four-wheel-drive vehicle, used for transporting troops and supplies

Hun /hun/ *n* **1. MEMBER OF EARLY ASIAN NOMADIC PEOPLE** a member of a nomadic people, probably originating in north central Asia, who invaded China in the 3rd century B.C. and then spread westward across Asia and into Europe. During the 4th century A.D., under their leader Attila, they overran much of the Roman Empire. **2. DESTRUCTIVE PERSON** a barbaric and destructive person **3. OFFENSIVE TERM** an offensive term for a German person or the German people, used especially by their opponents during World Wars I and II (*dated slang*) [Old English *Hūne*, via Germanic < late Latin *Hunni* < Sogdian *xwn*]

Hu·nan /hóo naán/ province in central China, and an important agricultural and mineral producing region. Capital: Changsha. Population: 64,280,000 (1997). Area: 81,270 sq. mi./210,500 sq. km.

hunch /hunch/ *n* **1. FEELING** an intuitive feeling about something **2. STOOP** a curved posture of the body with the head down and shoulders forward **3.** MED same as **hump** *n* (sense 2) **4. PIECE** a large lump or slice of something (*dated*) ■ *v* (**hunched, hunch·ing, hunch·es**) **1.** *vti* **BEND UPPER BODY FORWARD** to bend the head down and the shoulders forward, e.g., because of bad posture, illness, or the cold ○ *a typist hunching over the keyboard* ○ *hunched her shoulders against the wind* **2.** *vt* **PUSH OR SHOVE SOMEBODY** to push or jostle somebody **3.** *vi* **MOVE FORWARD CLUMSILY** to lunge forward in a clumsy manner [15C. Origin ?]

hunch·back /húnch bàk/ *n* **1.** a back that shows a pronounced curvature of the spine **2.** somebody with a hump on his or her back —**hunch·backed** *adj*

CULTURAL NOTE ***The Hunchback of Notre Dame***, a novel (1831) by French writer Victor Hugo. In this richly evocative medieval tragedy, Quasimodo, the hunchbacked bell-ringer at the Cathedral of Notre Dame in Paris, falls in love with a beautiful girl, Esmerelda. When corrupt priest Claude Frollo's harassment of Esmerelda results in her being executed for sorcery, Quasimodo murders Frollo by pushing him off the bell tower.

hun·di /hóondee/ *n S Asia* an informal banker's draft, especially used in transmitting currency from one country to another

hun·dred /húndrəd/ *n* **1. 100** the number 100 **2. GROUP OF 100** a group of a hundred people or objects **3. LARGE NUMBER** an unspecified large number ○ *attended by hundreds* **4. THIRD DIGIT TO LEFT OF DECIMAL** the number that is three places to the left of the decimal point in an Arabic numeral **5.** MONEY **$100 BILL** a bill worth a hundred dollars **6.** HIST **COUNTY SUBDIVISION** a historical subdivision of English, Irish, and some North American counties ■ **hun·dreds** *npl* **1. 100 TO 999** the numbers 100 to 999 **2. YEARS OF CENTURY** the years of a particular century ○ *the seventeen-hundreds* **3. TEMPERATURES OVER 100** numbers over 100, particularly as a range of Fahrenheit temperatures ○ *For three days the temperature was in the hundreds.* **4. LARGE NUMBERS** unspecified large numbers [Old English < Indo-European] —**hun·dred·fold** *adj, adv*

hun·dredth /húndrədth/ *n* one of 100 equal parts of something

hun·dred·weight /húndrəd wàyt/ *n* **1.** a unit of mass in the US customary system equal to 100 lb. (45.36 kg) **2.** *UK* a unit of mass in the British imperial system equal to 112 lb. (50.80 kg) [Probably originally 100 pounds]

Hun·dred Years' War *n* a series of wars fought between England and France from 1337 to 1453 that resulted in the final expulsion of the English from all French territories except Calais

hung /hung/ past participle, past tense of **hang** ■ *adj* **1.** unable to form a required consensus to make decisions or reach a verdict ○ *a hung jury* ○ *a hung parliament* **2.** an offensive term meaning having male sexual organs of a particular size (*slang*)

Hung. *abbr* **1.** Hungarian **2.** Hungary

Hun·gar·i·an /hung gérree ən/ *n* **1.** somebody who comes from Hungary **2.** the official language of Hungary, also spoken in parts of neighboring countries, belonging to one of the Ugric subgroups of Finno-Ugric. Native speakers: 14 million. —**Hun·gar·i·an** *adj*

Hun·gar·i·an gou·lash *n* FOOD same as **goulash** (sense 1)

Hungary

Hun·ga·ry /húng gəree/ country in central Europe, first united as a country around A.D. 1000. It became a member of the European Union in 2004. Language: Hungarian. Currency: forint. Capital: Budapest. Population: 10,045,407 (2003). Area: 35,919 sq. mi./93,030 sq. km. Official name **Republic of Hungary**

hun·ger /húng gər/ *n* **1.** NEED TO EAT the need or desire for food **2.** STARVATION a lack of food leading to sickness or death ○ *children dying of hunger* **3.** CRAVING a great need or desire for something ○ *a hunger for knowledge* ■ *vi* (**-gered, -ger·ing, -gers**) CRAVE to feel a great need or desire for something [Old English *hungur* < Germanic]

hun·ger march *n* a march organized to focus attention on world hunger and to raise funds to eradicate it

hun·ger strike *n* a refusal to eat over a period of time as a form of protest, especially by a prisoner —**hun·ger strik·er** *n*

hung·o·ver, **hung o·ver**, **hung·o·ver** /hung óvər/ *adj* suffering from the aftereffects of drinking too much alcohol or using drugs

hun·gry /húng gree/ (**-gri·er, -gri·est**) *adj* **1.** WANTING TO EAT wanting or needing food **2.** CAUSING HUNGER using up a lot of energy and making somebody want or need food ○ *hungry work* **3.** AVID wanting or desiring something very much ○ *hungry for new experiences* **4.** AMBITIOUS having great ambition or a powerful desire to win (*informal*) ○ *They won because they were hungrier than we were.* [Old English *hungrig*, related to HUNGER] —**hun·gri·ly** *adv* —**hun·gri·ness** *n* ◇ **go hungry** to go without food

hung up *adj* (*informal*) **1.** OBSESSED obsessed with somebody or something ○ *He's completely hung up on her.* **2.** WORRIED in a state of worry or anxiety over something ○ *hung up over minor details* **3.** DELAYED held up or otherwise delayed ○ *hung up in rush hour traffic*

hunk /hungk/ *n* **1.** a large piece of something such as bread or cheese that is cut or torn off a larger portion **2.** a man who is well-built and very attractive physically (*informal*) [Early 19C. Origin ?]

hun·ker /húngkər/ (**-kered, -ker·ing, -kers**) *vi* to squat down close to the ground [Early 18C. Origin ?]

hunker down *vi* **1.** to settle down seriously to try to achieve something ○ *time to hunker down and start studying* **2.** to hold stubbornly to an opinion (*informal*)

hun·kers /húngkərz/ *npl* the hips, buttocks, and upper thighs of a person or animal (*dated informal*) [Mid-18C. Probably < HUNKER]

Hunk·pa·pa /húngk paapə/ (*plural same or* **-pas**) *n* a member of a Native North American people, a branch of the Teton, who now live on both sides of the border between North and South Dakota. The Hunkpapa formerly lived in the border regions between Montana and North and South Dakota. [< Siouan, "at the end of the circle" (of the Teton camp)] —**Hunk·pa·pa** *adj*

hunk·y /húngkee/ (**-i·er, -i·est**) *adj* masculine, well-built, and very attractive physically (*informal*) [Early 20C. < HUNK]

Hun·ky *n* an offensive term for a laborer or other worker of eastern European origins (*dated slang*) [Early 20C. Probably < HUNGARIAN]

hun·ky-do·ry /hùngkee dáwree/ *adj* absolutely fine or satisfactory (*informal*) [Probably alteration of *hunky* "all right" < obsolete *hunk* "place where a game player is safe from capture" < Dutch *honk* "home"]

Hun·nish /húnnish/ *adj* **1.** relating to the Huns **2.** *also* **hun·nish** destructive and barbarous

hunt /hunt/ *v* (**hunt·ed, hunt·ing, hunts**) **1.** *vti* SEEK PREY to pursue an animal with the intention of capturing or killing it for sport or food ○ *Cats hunt mice and small birds.* ○ *They've been hunting together for years.* **2.** *vt* SEEK OUT SOMEBODY to search for and try to capture somebody **3.** *vi* SEARCH to search persistently for something difficult to find ○ *hunting for his missing keys* **4.** *vt* HOUND SOMEBODY to seek out and harass or persecute somebody **5.** *vi* CHASE ANIMALS WITH HOUNDS to engage in a sport involving the pursuit of an animal, usually a fox, on horseback and with the aid of hounds **6.** *vt* USE PARTICULAR PLACE FOR BLOOD SPORT to search a particular area for animals to capture or kill for sport or food **7.** *vi* ENG OSCILLATE AROUND POSITION to oscillate around a fixed point ■ *n* **1.** ACT OF SEARCHING the act of looking for somebody or something carefully, thoroughly, and persistently **2.** SEEKING OF PREY an attempt to capture or kill animals for sport or food **3.** *also* **Hunt** ORGANIZED GROUP OF HUNTERS an organized group of people who hunt foxes or deer for sport ○ *She joined the local hunt.* [Old English *huntian* < Germanic] ◇ **hunt high and low** to search extremely thoroughly for somebody or something ◇ **that dog won't hunt** *Southern US* that person or thing will not perform up to expectations or perform the job as required (*informal*)

Hunt /hunt/, **Holman** (1827–1910) British painter. He was a cofounder of the Pre-Raphaelite Brotherhood (1848) and his works include *The Scapegoat* (1854) and *May Morning on Magdalen Tower* (1888–91). Full name **Hunt, William Holman**

Hunt, Richard Morris (1827–95) US architect. He is known for his addition to the Louvre in Paris (1854–55) and the Great Hall (1895–1902) of the Metropolitan Museum of Art in New York.

hunt-and-peck *n* a slow and inefficient typing technique used by untrained typists in which each key is laboriously searched for before being struck (*informal*)

hunt·ed /húntəd/ *adj* startled and panic-stricken, as if being pursued ○ *a hunted look*

hunt·er /húntər/ *n* **1.** PREDATOR a person or animal that hunts birds or animals for food or sport **2.** HORSE a powerful fast horse that is bred for and used in hunting **3.** DOG a dog that is bred for and used in hunting **4.** SEEKER somebody who seeks out a particular type of person or thing, especially as an occupation or hobby ○ *fossil hunters* **5.** WATCH a watch with a hinged metal cover to protect the watch face

CULTURAL NOTE ***The Heart is a Lonely Hunter***, a novel (1940) by writer Carson McCullers. A work about isolation, alienation, and the search for love, it is the story of four lonely individuals, all of whom find themselves drawn to a local boy who is unable to hear or speak. The novel's central irony is that the boy is even more isolated than they are, his loneliness eventually leading him to suicide.

hunt·er-gath·er·er *n* a member of a society in which people live by hunting game and gathering edible plants only, and grow no crops and raise no livestock

hunt·er green *adj* of a dark green color

hunt·er-kill·er *adj* describes a naval vessel or force equipped with antisubmarine devices and designed to search for and destroy submarines

hunt·er's moon *n* the first full moon after the harvest moon

Hun·ter Val·ley /húntər-/ agricultural and industrial region in eastern New South Wales, Australia. Area: 8,495 sq. mi./22,000 sq. km.

hunt·ing /húnting/ *n* **1.** the sport or practice of pursuing and killing or capturing wild animals **2.** the process of searching carefully for something, usually over a period of time ○ *job hunting*

hunt·ing and gath·er·ing *n* the seeking of game and edible plants for subsistence, as practiced by preagricultural and nomadic people, instead of raising livestock and growing crops for food

hunt·ing ground *n* **1.** a place where hunting is pursued or that is suitable for hunting **2.** a source of useful or desired objects or information ○ *The town is a great hunting ground for antiques.*

hunt·ing knife *n* a broad knife used for killing or gutting game

hunt·ing spi·der *n* ZOOL same as **wolf spider**

hun·ting·tin /húntingtin/ *n* a protein that occurs naturally in nerve cells, but when mutated can cause Huntington's chorea [< HUNTINGTON'S CHOREA]

Hunt·ing·ton /húntingtən/ **1.** town on the northern shore of Long Island, in southeastern New York. Population: 198,430 (2002 estimate). **2.** city and river port in West Virginia on the Ohio River, near the Kentucky border. Population: 49,910 (2002 estimate).

Hunt·ing·ton Beach coastal city in southern California, 14 mi./23 km southeast of Long Beach. It was formerly an oil-producing center. Population: 193,799 (2002 estimate).

Hunt·ing·ton Park city in southwestern California, near Los Angeles. Population: 62,976 (2002 estimate).

Hunt·ing·ton's cho·re·a *n* a hereditary disorder of the nervous system that manifests as jerky involuntary movements in early middle age, with behavioral changes and progressive dementia [Late 19C. After George *Huntington* (1851–1916), US neurologist]

Hunt·ing·ton Sta·tion town in southeastern New York, on the northern shore of Long Island. Population: 28,247 (2002 estimate).

hunt·ing watch *n* JEWELRY same as **hunter** (sense 5)

hunt·ress /húntrəss/ *n* a woman or goddess who hunts (*literary*)

hunts·man /húntsmən/ (*plural* **-men** /-mən/) *n* **1.** a man who hunts, either for a living or for sport **2.** an official who is in charge of the hounds belonging to a hunt

hunts·man's-cup *n* PLANTS same as **pitcher plant**

Hunts·ville /húnts vìl/ city in northern Alabama, a major center of aerospace research and manufacture, home to Redstone Arsenal. Population: 162,536 (2002 estimate).

hunts·wom·an /húnts wŏŏmmən/ (*plural* **-wom·en** /-wìmmin/) *n* a woman who hunts, either for a living or for sport

hup /hup/ *interj* used when marching to mark time or when lifting or raising something (*informal*) [Mid-20C. Origin ?]

hup·pah /khŏŏpə, khŏŏ paá/ (*plural* **hup·pahs** *or* **hup·pot** /khŏŏ-/ *or* **hu·pot**), **chup·pah** (*plural* **chup·pahs** *or* **chup·pot** *or* **chu·pot**) *n* **1.** a canopy under which a Jewish wedding ceremony is performed **2.** a Jewish wedding ceremony [Late 19C. < Hebrew *ḥuppāh* "cover, canopy"]

hur·dle /húrd'l/ *n* **1.** DIFFICULTY OR OBSTACLE a difficulty or obstacle that has to be overcome **2.** BARRIER FOR RUNNER TO JUMP OVER one of a number of light barriers over which runners have to jump in some track-and-field events **3.** HORSERACING FENCE USED IN HORSE RACE a fence of intertwined branches or wattle that horses jump over in a race, or a race over fences of this type ■ *v* (**-dled, -dling, -dles**) **1.** *vi* **RACE OVER HURDLES** to run in a track-and-field event in which hurdles must be jumped **2.** *vt* **CLEAR RACING BARRIER** to clear a barrier in a race **3.** *vt* **OVERCOME DIFFICULTY** to overcome a difficulty or obstacle [Old English *hyrdel* < Indo-European, "to turn"] —**hur·dler** *n*

hur·dles /húrd'lz/ *n* a track-and-field event in which runners have to race to clear a series of light barriers (*takes a singular or plural verb*)

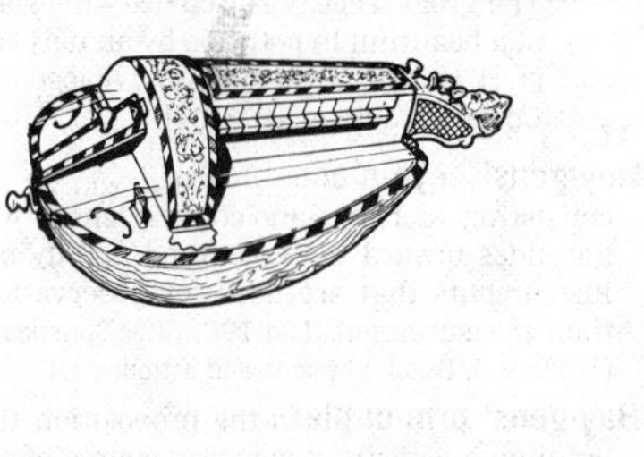

hurdy-gurdy (sense 2)

hur·dy-gur·dy /hùrdee gúrdee, húrdee gùrdee/ (*plural* **hur·dy-gur·dies**) *n* **1.** a mechanical musical instrument that is played by turning a handle, e.g., a barrel organ **2.** a medieval string instrument played by turning a crank attached to a rosined wheel that causes strings to vibrate while being controlled by a keyboard [Mid-18C. An imitation of the sound]

hurl /hurl/ *v* (**hurled, hurl·ing, hurls**) **1.** *vt* **FLING SOMETHING** to throw something with great force **2.** *vt* **YELL SOMETHING** to utter something with great vehemence ○ *hurling abuse* **3.** *vti* BASEBALL **PITCH** to pitch a baseball **4.** *vi* **VOMIT** to vomit, especially with considerable force (*slang*) ■ *n* **STRONG THROW** a forceful throw, or the act of throwing something with great force [12C. Probably suggesting the action] —**hurl·er** *n*

SYNONYMS See *throw.*

hur·ley /húrlee/ *n* a long wooden stick with a curved end used in the game of hurling [Early 19C. < HURL]

hurl·ing /húrling/ *n* an Irish field sport resembling hockey and lacrosse that is played with broad sticks and a leather ball that is passed from player to player through the air

hur·ly-bur·ly /hùrlee búrlee, húrlee bùrlee/ *n* noisy and bustling activity [Alteration of *hurling and burling*, playful formation based on HURL]

Hu·ron[1] /hyoǒ ron/ (*plural same* or **-rons**) *n* a member of a confederacy of Iroquoian peoples who lived around the Great Lakes and now live in Quebec, Ontario, and Oklahoma. During the 17th century, the population was greatly reduced by continual warring with the Iroquois and the arrival of smallpox and other European diseases. [Mid-17C. < French, "boar" < Old French *hure* "bristling hair"] —**Hu·ron** *adj*

Hu·ron[2] /hyoǒ ron/ city in eastern South Dakota, east of Pierre and northwest of Sioux Falls. Population: 11,569 (2002 estimate).

Hu·ron, Lake second largest of the Great Lakes, lying between the state of Michigan, United States, and the province of Ontario, Canada. Area: 23,000 sq. mi./59,600 sq. km. Depth: 751 ft./229 m.

hur·rah /hoǒ raá, hə-/ *interj, n* same as **hooray** [Late 17C. Alteration of HUZZAH] ◇ **(the) last hurrah** a final experience in the limelight, brush with fame, or spree (*informal*)

hur·ray *interj, n* another spelling of **hooray**

Hur·ri·an /hoóree ən/ *n* **1.** a member of an ancient people who lived in Syria and Mesopotamia around 1500 B.C. **2.** the unaffiliated language of the Hurrian people [Early 20C. < Hittite, Assyrian *Harri, Hurri*] —**Hur·ri·an** *adj*

hur·ri·cane /húrri kàyn/ *n* **1.** **SEVERE STORM** a severe tropical storm with torrential rain and extremely strong winds. Hurricanes originate in areas of low pressure in equatorial regions of the Atlantic or Caribbean, and then strengthen, traveling northwest, north, or northeast. **2.** **HIGH WIND** a wind of above 74 mi./119 km per hour, classified as force 12 or above on the Beaufort scale **3.** **FAST AND FORCEFUL PERSON OR THING** somebody or something resembling a violent storm in force, speed, or effect [Mid-16C. Via Spanish < Taino *hurakán* "god of the storm"]

hur·ri·cane deck *n* a deck on a ship with a cover from the sun

hur·ri·cane lamp *n* an oil or kerosene lamp with a glass cover to prevent the wick from being extinguished in wind or rain

hur·ried /húrreed/ *adj* done, made, or performed too quickly because of a real or perceived lack of time —**hur·ried·ly** *adv* —**hur·ried·ness** *n*

hur·ry /húrree/ *v* (**-ried, -ry·ing, -ries**) **1.** *vi* **RUSH** to move or do something with great or excessive speed because of a real or perceived lack of time **2.** *vt* **SPEED SOMEBODY OR SOMETHING UP** to make or encourage somebody or something to act with greater speed ○ *Hurry up and put your coat on!* ■ *n* **1.** **HASTE** a state in which somebody is moving or doing something with great or excessive speed because of a real or perceived lack of time ○ *We were in such a hurry we left the tickets behind.* **2.** **URGENCY** the need to do something quickly ○ *What's the hurry?* [Early 17C. Origin ?] —**hur·ri·er** *n*

hur·ry-scur·ry *n* an undue rush to do something [Mid-18C. Repetition of HURRY]

hur·ry sick·ness *n* a compulsion to do everything quickly, or a chronic feeling of being short of time, attributed to the fast pace of modern life and causing symptoms such as anxiety and insomnia

Hurst /hurst/, **Fannie** (1889–1968) US writer. A prolific and popular writer, she is best known for her novels *Back Street* (1931) and *Imitation of Life* (1933). Born **Danielson, Fannie**

> "It's hard for a young girl to have patience for old age sitting and chewing all day over the past."
> [Attributed to Fannie Hurst]

Hur·ston /húrst'n/, **Zora Neale** (1891–60) US writer and folklorist. She collected and published folklore of the South and the Caribbean, and her studies of African American culture influenced the Harlem Renaissance writers of the 1920s and 1930s. Her works include the novel *Their Eyes Were Watching God* (1937).

> "People are prone to build a statue of the kind of person that it pleases them to be. And few people want to be forced to ask themselves, 'What if there is no me like my statue?'"
> [Zora Neale Hurston, *Dust Tracks on a Road*; 1942]

> "Sometimes, I feel discriminated against, but it does not make me angry. It merely astonishes me. How *can* any deny themselves the pleasure of my company? It's beyond me."
> [Zora Neale Hurston, "How It Feels To Be Colored Me," *I Love Myself, a Zora Neale Hurston Reader*, Alice Walker (ed.); 1979]

hurt /hurt/ *v* (**hurt, hurt·ing, hurts**) **1.** *vti* **INJURE SOMEBODY OR SOMETHING** to cause somebody, yourself, or an animal physical injury or pain ○ *hurt his back when he fell down* ○ *Ouch! That hurts!* **2.** *vti* **EXPERIENCE PAIN** to experience physical pain, or be a source of physical pain for a person or animal ○ *I hurt all over.* ○ *My arm's hurting me.* **3.** *vti* **UPSET** to feel emotional pain, or make somebody feel emotional pain ○ *was hurt by his unkind remarks* **4.** *vti* **IMPAIR** to have a negative effect on something ○ *This could hurt her chances of reelection.* **5.** *vi* **EXPERIENCE DIFFICULTIES** to undergo or experience difficulties or setbacks, e.g., in business or financial affairs (*informal*) ○ *The business is really hurting.* ■ *n* **1.** **PAIN** emotional or mental pain or suffering ○ *after all the hurt he's caused* **2.** **INJURY** an injury or wound, whether emotional, mental, or physical ○ *old hurts* [12C. < Old French *hurter* "ram, collide," probably < Germanic] —**hurt** *adj* —**hurt·er** *n*

SYNONYMS See *harm.*

hurt·ful /húrtfəl/ *adj* causing emotional pain or suffering —**hurt·ful·ly** *adv* —**hurt·ful·ness** *n*

hur·tle /húrt'l/ (**-tled, -tling, -tles**) *vi* to move or travel at very high speed [13C. < HURT]

Hu·sain /hoǒ sáyn/ (626?–680A.D.) Arabian Muslim saint. The son of Fatima, grandson of Muhammad, and younger brother of Hasan, he was killed defending Islam and his death is commemorated in the festival of Ashora.

hus·band /húzbənd/ *n* the man to whom a woman is married ■ *vt* (**-band·ed, -band·ing, -bands**) to use and manage something economically and sensibly, e.g., resources or money [Pre-12C. < Old Norse *húsbóndi* "man in charge of the house, farmer" < *hús* "house" + *bóndi* "dweller," present participle of *búa* "dwell"] —**hus·band·age** *n* —**hus·band·er** *n*

hus·band·man /húzbəndmən/ (*plural* **-men** /-mən/) *n* AGRIC, OCCUPATIONS same as **farmer** (*archaic*)

hus·band·ry /húzbəndree/ *n* **1.** the science, skill, or art of farming **2.** the economical and sensible management of resources

Hu·sein ♦ **Abdullah ibn Husein**

hush /hush/ *vti* (**hushed, hush·ing, hush·es**) **MAKE SOMEBODY BE QUIET** to become silent, or make somebody do this ■ *interj* **BE QUIET** used to request or demand silence ■ *n* **SILENCE** a silence, especially after a period of noise or in expectation of something [Mid-16C. Probably back-formation < obsolete *husht* "hush!", natural exclamation]

hush up *v* **1.** *vt* to prevent something, especially something dishonorable or discreditable, from becoming publicly known (*informal*) **2.** *vi* to ask or tell somebody to become silent or quieter

hushed *adj* made quiet, or quieter than usual ○ *speaking in hushed tones*

hush-hush *adj* secret or confidential (*informal*)

hush mon·ey *n* money paid as a bribe not to disclose information (*informal*)

hush pup·py *n* a small deep-fried ball of cornmeal dough, originally a strictly Southern form of bread

husk /husk/ *n* **1.** BOT **OUTER PLANT COVERING** the outer membranous covering of some fruits, nuts, and grains **2.** **USELESS OUTER SHELL** an empty outer shell or covering that no longer serves any useful purpose ■ *vt* (**husked, husk·ing, husks**) **REMOVE HUSK FROM SOMETHING** to remove the husks from fruits, nuts, or grains [14C. Origin ?] —**husk·er** *n*

hus·kie *n* ZOOL another spelling of **husky**[2]

husk·ing bee *n* a gathering of people, usually farm families, for the purpose of husking corn

husk to·ma·to *n* PLANTS same as **ground cherry** (sense 2)

husk·y[1] /húskee/ (**-i·er, -i·est**) *adj* **1.** **BURLY AND COMPACT IN PHYSIQUE** having a solid, burly, compact physique ○ *a husky boy* **2.** **THROATY** hoarse and dry, either naturally or as a result of illness or emotion ○ *a husky voice* **3.** **RELATING TO HUSKS** relating to, containing, or resembling husks [Mid-16C. < HUSK] —**husk·i·ly** *adv* —**husk·i·ness** *n*

hus·ky[2] /húskee/ (*plural* **-kies**), **hus·kie** *n* a large long-haired dog with a curled tail and pricked ears, belonging to a breed originally developed in Arctic regions and trained to pull sleds [Mid-19C. Probably alteration of ESKIMO in *Eskimo dog*]

Huss /huss/, **John** (1372?–1415) Bohemian religious reformer. He was burned at the stake for supporting the teachings of the English reformer John Wycliffe. His execution led to the outbreak of the Hussite Wars (1419–36).

> "O holy simplicity!"
> [John Huss. While at the stake, *Apophthegmata*, Zincgreff-Weidner; 1653]

hus·sar /hə zaár, hoǒ-/ *n* **1.** a member of the Hungarian cavalry in the 15th century **2.** a soldier in any European light cavalry unit in the 18th and 19th centuries that adopted an ornate uniform similar to that of the Hungarian cavalry in the 15th century [Mid-16C. Via Hungarian *huszár* "light horseman" < Italian *corsaro* "corsair"]

Hus·sein I /hoǒ sáyn/ (1935–99) king of Jordan. Throughout his reign (1952–99), he was regarded by many as a moderating influence in the politics of Southwest Asia.

> "We should face reality and our past mistakes in an honest, adult way. Boasting of glory does not make glory, and singing in the dark does not dispel fear."
> [Hussein I, *Conference for Arab heads of state, Sudan*; August 30, 1967]

Hus·sein, Saddam (*b.* 1937) Iraqi national leader. As leader of the Baath Party, he became president of Iraq in 1979. Two years after the end of the Iran-Iraq War (1980–88), his invasion of Kuwait in August 1990 led to the Gulf War (1991). He was deposed and captured during the Iraq War of 2003.

> "The mother of battles will be our battle of victory and martyrdom."
> [Saddam Hussein, *Speech, Baghdad, Times (London)*; January 7, 1991]

Huss·ite /hú sìt, hŏŏ-/ *n* a follower of the teachings of John Huss —**Huss·it·ism** /hússi tìzzəm, hŏŏssi-/ *n*

hus·sy /hússee/ (*plural* **-sies**) *n* **1.** an offensive term that deliberately insults a woman's manner or behavior (*dated*) **2.** an offensive term for a young woman that deliberately insults her tact and self-restraint (*dated or humorous*) [Mid-16C. Contraction of HOUSEWIFE (the original sense)]

hust·ings /hústingz/ *npl* **1.** the rounds of political activities, e.g., speech-making and the organization of public rallies, that take place before an election **2.** in Great Britain before 1872, a platform from which parliamentary candidates were nominated and addressed electors [Pre-12C. < Old Norse *húsþing* "king's council" < *hús* "house" + *þing* "meeting"]

hus·tle /húss'l/ *v* (**-tled, -tling, -tles**) **1.** *vti* **HURRY** to go somewhere or deal with something fast or hurriedly ○ *We'd better hustle, or we'll be late.* ○ *They hustled the legislation through before the recess.* **2.** *vi* CRIME **ENGAGE IN SMALL-TIME ILLEGAL DEALS** to engage in small-time illegal activity such as petty theft or prostitution (*slang*) **3.** *vt* **SELL SOMETHING AGGRESSIVELY** to sell goods or services using aggressive sales techniques **4.** *vti* CRIME **SOLICIT CUSTOMERS IN SHADY DEALS** to solicit customers in shady or illegal deals, e.g., as a prostitute (*slang*) **5.** *vt* **HURRY SOMEBODY SOMEWHERE** to convey somebody roughly or hurriedly to or from a place ○ *hustled her into a waiting car* **6.** *vi* **PLAY SPORT AGGRESSIVELY** to play a sport with great aggressiveness, intensity, and concentration **7.** *vt* **PUSH SOMEBODY** to jostle or push somebody roughly ○ *One hustled me while the other stole my purse.* **8.** *vt* **COERCE SOMEBODY** to put pressure on somebody to do something without due thought ○ *hustled them into the purchase* ■ *n* **1. NOISY ACTIVITY** lively noisy continual activity ○ *enjoyed the hustle and bustle of the big city* **2. ENERGY AND AGGRESSION** energetic and aggressive initiative in pursuing personal goals (*slang*) **3.** CRIME **RACKET OR SWINDLE** an act or scheme involving deceit, swindling, fraud, or petty theft (*slang*) [Late 17C. < Dutch *hutselen* "shake (repeatedly), toss," < *hotsen* "shake"]

hus·tler /hússlər/ *n* **1. PETTY CRIMINAL** a small-time operator who engages in illegal activities such as petty theft or illegal gambling (*informal*) **2. PROSTITUTE** a prostitute, especially a streetwalker or one who solicits in bars (*slang*) **3. AGGRESSIVELY DETERMINED PERSON** somebody who works aggressively and determinedly, especially to advance his or her career (*informal*)

Hus·ton /hyŏŏstən/, **John** (1906–87) US movie director and actor. The son of Walter Huston, he directed *The Maltese Falcon* (1941), *The African Queen* (1951), and won two Academy Awards for *The Treasure of the Sierra Madre* (1948).

> "The directing of a picture involves coming out of your individual loneliness and taking a controlling part in putting together a small world."
> [John Huston, *New York Journal*; March 31, 1960]

Hus·ton /hyŏŏst'n/, **Walter** (1884–1950) Canadian-born US actor. He won an Academy Award for *The Treasure of the Sierra Madre* (1948).

hut[1] /hut/ *n* a small single-story building, often made of wood, that is used as a simple house or shelter, or for storage, temporary accommodation, or leisure activities ○ *a fishing hut* ■ *vt* (**hut·ted, hut·ting, huts**) to provide huts for a place, especially for accommodation [Mid-16C. Origin ?]

hut[2] /hut/ *interj* used to mark time while marching (*informal*) [Mid-20C. Origin ?]

hutch /huch/ *n* **1.** a cupboard with drawers and usually open shelves on top, often used for storing and displaying dishes and kitchen utensils **2.** a small shelter, usually constructed from wire and wood, for keeping small animals such as rabbits [12C. Via French *huche* < medieval Latin *hutica*]

Hutch·ins /húchinz/, **Robert Maynard** (1899–1977) US educator. He was a reforming president and chancellor of the University of Chicago (1929–51), where he introduced, most notably, the Great Books program.

> "We do not know what education can do for us, because we have never tried it."
> [Robert Maynard Hutchins, *The Atomic Bomb Versus Civilization*; 1945]

Hutch·in·son /húchinss'n/ city in central Kansas on the Arkansas River. Population: 40,741 (2002 estimate).

Hutch·in·son, Anne (1591–1643) English-born American colonial religious reformer. She was banished from Massachusetts for preaching her liberal religious doctrine that was opposed to the Puritans. Born **Marbury, Anne**

> "What from the Church at Boston? I know no such church, neither will I own it. Call it the whore and strumpet of Boston, no Church of Christ."
> [Anne Hutchinson, *Remark*; 1638?]

Hutch·in·son-Gil·ford syn·drome /-gílfərd-/ *n* MED same as **progeria** [After Sir Jonathan *Hutchinson* (1828–1913) and Hastings *Gilford* (1861–1941), British physicians]

hut·ment /hútmənt/ *n* a group of huts forming a military encampment

Hut·ter·ite /húttə rìt/ *n* a member of an Anabaptist religious group who immigrated from Moravia mainly to Alberta and Manitoba in Canada, but also to areas of the northwestern United States where they formed farming communities [Late 19C. After Jacob *Hutter* (d. 1536), Moravian Anabaptist]

Hut·ton /hútt'n/, **James** (1726–97) Scottish geologist. He outlined the principles of uniformitarianism in *Theory of the Earth* (1795).

Hutt Val·ley /hùt-/ urban area in the south of the North Island, New Zealand, near the city of Wellington. Population: 131,000 (2001).

Hu·tu /hoo too/ (*plural same* or **-tus**) *n* **1.** a member of a people who are the most populous in Rwanda and Burundi **2.** a Bantu language spoken in Rwanda and Burundi. Native speakers: 14 million. [Mid-20C. < Bantu] —**Hu·tu** *adj*

hutz·pah *n* another spelling of **chutzpah**

Hux·ley /húkslee/, **Aldous** (1894–1963) British novelist and essayist. His novels include *Point Counter Point* (1928), *Brave New World* (1932), and *Eyeless in Gaza* (1936). Full name **Huxley, Aldous Leonard**. See Cultural note at **brave new world**

> "It takes two to make a murder. There are born victims, born to have their throats cut."
> [Aldous Huxley, *Point Counter Point*; 1928]

> "There can be no doubt that if tranquilizers could be bought as easily and cheaply as aspirin they would be consumed, not by the billions, as they are at present, but by the scores and hundreds of billions."
> [Aldous Huxley, *Brave New World Revisited*; 1958]

Hux·ley, Andrew (*b.* 1917) British physiologist. He was joint winner of the Nobel Prize in physiology or medicine (1963) for his work on nerve impulses. Full name **Huxley, Andrew Fielding**

Hux·ley, Sir Julian (1887–1975) British biologist. He was the first director-general of UNESCO (1947–48) and the author of *Essays of a Biologist* (1923). Full name **Huxley, Sir Julian Sorell**

> "The human race will be the cancer of the planet. Operationally, God is beginning to resemble not a ruler but the last fading smile of a cosmic Cheshire cat."
> [Sir Julian Huxley, *Religion without Revelation*; 1957 ed.]

Hux·ley, T. H. (1825–95) British biologist. A supporter of Darwin, he wrote *Zoological Evidences as to Man's Place in Nature* (1863) and *Collected Essays* (1893–94). Full name **Huxley, Thomas Henry**

> "The great tragedy of Science—the slaying of a beautiful hypothesis by an ugly fact."
> [T. H. Huxley, "Biogenesis and Abiogenesis," *Collected Essays*; 1893–94]

Huy·gens' eye·piece /hígənz-/ *n* an eyepiece consisting of two plano-convex lenses with their flat sides toward the eye, fitted mainly on optical instruments that are used for observation rather than measurement [Mid-19C. After Christiaan *Huygens* (1629–95), Dutch physicist and astronomer]

Huy·gens' prin·ci·ple *n* the proposition that every point on a wavefront acts as a source of secondary waves of light and that the wavefront at a later time is the envelope of these secondary waves [See HUYGENS' EYEPIECE]

huz·zah /hə zaá/ *interj, n* same as **hooray** (*archaic*) [Late 16C. Origin ?]

H.V. *abbr* **1.** PHYS high velocity **2.** ELEC high voltage

HVAC *abbr* CIV ENG heating, ventilating, and air conditioning

HVT *abbr* MIL high-value target [Late 20C.]

HW *abbr* **1.** ONLINE hardware **2.** hazardous waste **3.** high water **4.** hot water

Hwan·ge Na·tion·al Park /hwàng gay-/ the largest national park in Zimbabwe, established in 1929. Area: 5,657 sq. mi./14,651 sq. km.

hwy *abbr* TRANSP highway

hwyl /hoó il/ *Wales* (*informal*) *n* good spirit or enthusiasm ■ *interj* used as a toast or to say goodbye [< Welsh]

hyacinth

hy·a·cinth /hí ə sìnth/ *n* a cultivated plant of the lily family. Flowers: fragrant pink, white, or blue, in spikes. Native to: northeastern Mediterranean. Latin name: *Hyacinthus orientalis*. [Mid-16C. Via French and Latin < Greek *huakinthos* "plant sprung from the blood of Hyacinthus"] —**hy·a·cin·thine** /hì ə sínthin, -sín thìn/ *adj*

hy·a·cinth bean *n* a deciduous woody-stemmed leguminous climbing plant. Flowers: pink, white. Latin name: *Dolichos lablab*.

hy·a·cinth or·chid *n* a leafless orchid that usually grows near eucalyptus trees. Flowers: dark pink with white spots. Native to: Australia. Latin name: *Dipodium punctatum*.

Hy·a·cin·thus /hì ə sínthəss/ *n* in Greek mythology, a young boy who was loved and accidentally killed by the god Apollo, who made a flower grow on the spot where the boy died

Hy·a·des /hí ə deez/ *n* a cluster of over 200 stars in the constellation Taurus, whose five brightest members form a V-shaped group

hy·ae·na *n* ZOOL another spelling of **hyena**

hyal- *prefix* same as **hyalo-** (*used before vowels*)

hy·a·lin /hī́ əlin/ *n* a clear glassy material found in hyaline cartilage or formed as a product of some skin diseases

hy·a·line /hī́ əlin, -līn/ *adj* clear, translucent, and containing no fibers or granular material

hy·a·line car·ti·lage *n* the most common type of cartilage, consisting of a bluish white elastic material containing fine collagen fibers and providing flexibility and support at the joints. Hyaline cartilage is found at the ends of the long bones and in the nose and the larynx, and forms most of the fetal skeleton.

hy·a·line mem·brane dis·ease *n* MED same as **respiratory distress syndrome**

hy·a·lite /hī́ ə līt/ *n* a clear colorless variety of opal. Use: gems.

hy·a·li·tis /hī́ ə lītiss/ *n* inflammation of the transparent jelly **(vitreous humor)** that fills the chamber of the eye behind the lens

hyalo- *prefix* glass, glassy [< Greek *hualos* "glass"]

hy·a·loid /hī́ ə lòyd/ *adj* clear and glassy in appearance

hy·a·loid mem·brane *n* a transparent insubstantial membrane surrounding the transparent jelly **(vitreous humor)** of the eye and separating it from the retina

hy·al·u·ron·ic ac·id /hīə lōō rònnik-/ *n* a complex viscous substance that lubricates joints and is present in connective tissue. It also plays a role in the healing of wounds. [< HYALOID (because first isolated in the vitreous humor) + *uronic* "connected with urine"]

hy·a·lu·ron·i·dase /hī́ əlōō rónni dàyss, -dàyz/ *n* an enzyme that breaks down hyaluronic acid, increasing the permeability of connective tissues

Hy·an·nis /hī ánniss/ resort village and commercial center in southeastern Massachusetts, on the southern coast of Cape Cod. Population: 14,120 (2002 estimate).

Hy·atts·ville /hī́ əts vìl/ city in west central Maryland, a northeastern suburb of Washington, D.C. Population: 15,121 (2002 estimate).

hy·brid /hī́brid/ *n* **1.** BOT **PLANT RESULTING FROM CROSSING** a plant produced from a cross between two plants with different genetic constituents. Hybrids from crosses between crop varieties are often stronger and produce better yields than the original stock. **2.** ZOOL **ANIMAL RESULTING FROM CROSS-SPECIES MATING** an animal that results from the mating of parents from two distinct species or subspecies **3. RESULT OF MIXING ELEMENTS** something made up of a mixture of different aspects or components **4.** LING **WORD DERIVED FROM TWO LANGUAGES** a word that has derived from two different languages, e.g., "appendicitis," in which "appendic" is from Latin and "itis" is from Greek **5.** AUTOMOT **USING TWO FUELS** a vehicle with an engine that runs on electricity and gasoline, which it can alternate between ■ *adj* **1.** BIOL **CROSSBRED** bred from two distinct species or subspecies **2. CONTAINING MIXED ELEMENTS** made up of different aspects or components ○ *a hybrid literary form* **3.** ELECTRONICS **UNUSUAL AS ELECTRONIC CIRCUIT** describes an electronic circuit that consists of two or more components not ordinarily combined with one another, e.g., a circuit that has integrated circuitry, transistors, and vacuum tubes **4.** ELECTRONICS **WITH MULTIPLE INTEGRATED CIRCUITRY** describes an electronic circuit containing more than one integrated circuit, all of which are attached to the same ceramic substrate [Early 17C. < Latin *hybrida*] —**hy·brid·ism** *n* —**hy·brid·ist** *n* —**hy·brid·i·ty** /hī bríddətee/ *n*

hy·brid an·ti·bod·y *n* an artificial antibody synthesized to attach to two different antigens

hy·brid bill *n* a legislative bill that includes a number of largely unrelated subject areas

hy·brid com·put·er *n* a computer employing both analog and digital techniques

hy·brid·ize /hī́bri dīz/ (**-ized, -iz·ing, -iz·es**) *vti* to generate a new form of plant or animal, either by human intervention or naturally, by combining the genes of two different species or subspecies —**hy·brid·iz·a·ble** *adj* —**hy·brid·i·za·tion** /hìbridi záysh'n/ *n* —**hy·brid·iz·er** *n*

hy·brid·o·ma /hìbri dṓmə/ *n* a hybrid cell produced by the fusion of a tumor cell with an ordinary antibody-producing cell, which then proliferates and yields large amounts of a monoclonal antibody

hy·brid rock *n* rock formed when molten magma incorporates solid material from the rock through which it flows, yielding a mixture of rock types

hy·brid vig·or *n* the increased growth, disease resistance, or fertility seen in hybrid species. For example, mules, the offspring of mares and donkeys, are stronger and longer-lived than the parent animals.

hy·da·thode /hī́də thṑd/ *n* a pore in the outer layer of a leaf that secretes water when the rate of transpiration is low, e.g., in humid conditions [Late 19C. < Greek *hudat-* "water" + *hodos* "way"]

hy·da·tid /hī́dətid/, **hy·da·tid cyst** *n* a cyst formed in human tissue that contains the larvae of a tapeworm [Late 17C. < modern Latin < Greek *hudatis* "drop of water, watery vesicle" < *hudat-* "water"]

hy·da·tid dis·ease *n* a condition resulting from the presence of hydatid cysts in the liver, lungs, or brain, which can cause malignancies, blindness, epilepsy, or fever

Hyde Park /hīd-/ town in eastern New York, on the Hudson River. It was the home of President Franklin D. Roosevelt, whose presidential library is located there. Population: 21,020 (2002 estimate).

Hy·der·a·bad /hī́dərə bàd/, **Hy·der·ā·bād** **1.** city and capital of Andhra Pradesh State, India, founded in 1589, situated on the Musi River. Population: 5,533,640 (2001). **2.** city in Sind Province, southeastern Pakistan, situated on the Indus River. Population: 1,151,274 (1998). **3.** former state in central India, now divided between the states of Andhra Pradesh, Karnataka, and Maharashtra

hyd·no·car·pate /hìdnə kaárr pàyt/ *n* a salt of hydnocarpic acid

hyd·no·carp·ic ac·id /hìdnə kaárpik-/ *n* a fatty acid containing a carbon ring in its structure. Source: glycerides in chaulmoogra oil. Formula: $C_{16}H_{28}O_2$. [< *hydnocarpus*, plant yielding an oil containing this acid < Greek *hudnon* "truffle" + *karpos* "fruit," from the fruit's appearance]

hydr- *prefix* same as **hydro-** (*used before vowels*)

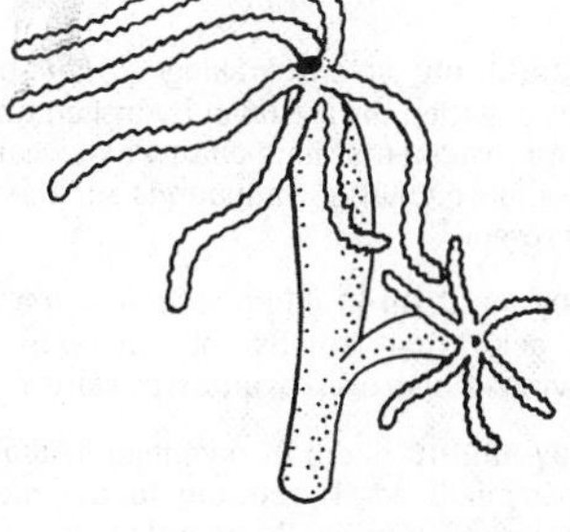

hydra

hy·dra /hī́drə/ (*plural* **-dras** or **-drae** /-dree/) *n* a freshwater polyp with a cylindrical body at one end and a mouth surrounded by tentacles at the other. Genus: *Hydra*. [Late 18C. Via modern Latin < Greek *hudra* "water snake"]

Hy·dra /hī́drə/ *n* **1.** a constellation near the celestial equator. See illustration at **constellation 2.** in Greek mythology, a monster that had nine heads and was killed by Heracles. When one head was cut off, another grew instantly in its place.

hy·drac·id /hī drássid/ *n* an acid such as hydrochloric acid in which the hydrogen atoms are bound to an atom other than oxygen

hy·dra·gogue /hī́drə gòg/ *n* a laxative that acts by osmosis by drawing water into the intestinal canal from the blood, thereby softening the contents. Epsom salts, once the principal hydragogue, has now been superseded by complex sugars such as lactulose that work in the same way. [Mid-17C. Via late Latin < Greek *hudragōgos* "conveying water" < *hudr-* "water"]

hy·dra-head·ed *adj* having many heads or parts like heads

hy·dral·a·zine /hī dràllə zeén/ *n* a drug that lowers blood pressure, usually given with drugs that cause increased urine output [Mid-20C. < HYDRO- + PHTHALIC ACID + AZINE]

hy·dran·gea /hī dráynjə/ *n* an erect or climbing evergreen or deciduous bush. Flowers: white, pink, or blue, in large clusters in a variety of shapes. Native to: Asia. Genus: *Hydrangea*. [Mid-18C. < modern Latin, literally "water pot"; from its cup-shaped seed pod]

hy·drant /hī́drənt/ *n* an upright pipe, usually in a street, connected to a water main with a valve to which a hose can be attached, e.g., by the fire department [Early 19C. < HYDRO-]

hy·dranth /hī́ drànth/ *n* the sedentary form in the life cycle of a cnidarian such as a sea anemone or a hydra [Late 19C. < HYDRA + Greek *anthos* "flower"]

hy·drarch /hī́ draárk/ *adj* describes the development of a sequence of ecological stages that begins in a freshwater habitat such as a pond [Early 20C. < HYDRO- + Greek *arkhē* "beginning"]

hy·drase /hī́ dràyss, -dràyz/ *n* an enzyme that catalyzes the addition or removal of water

hy·dras·tine /hī drá steén, -drástin/ *n* a poisonous white substance. Source: roots of the goldenseal plant. Use: formerly, to stop hemorrhaging, shrink the uterus, reduce inflammation of mucous membranes. Formula: $C_{21}H_{21}NO_6$. [Mid-19C. < modern Latin *Hydrastis*, plant genus name < HYDRO-]

hy·dras·ti·nine /hī drásti neén, -drástinin/ *n* an organic compound forming colorless crystals, soluble in water and resembling hydrastine in its medicinal properties. Formula: $C_{11}H_{13}NO_3$.

hy·drate /hī́ dràyt/ *vt* (**-drat·ed, -drat·ing, -drates**) **1. GIVE WATER TO SOMEBODY OR SOMETHING** to provide water for somebody or something in order to reestablish or maintain a correct fluid balance **2.** CHEM **ADD WATER TO SOMETHING** to add water to a chemical compound so that different crystals are formed ■ *n* CHEM **COMPOUND CONTAINING WATER** a chemical compound containing water molecules that can usually be expelled by heating, without decomposition of the compound [Early 19C. < French (noun) < Greek *hudr-* "water"] —**hy·dra·tion** /hī dráysh'n/ *n* —**hy·dra·tor** *n*

hy·drat·ed /hī́ dràytəd/ *adj* describes a chemical compound that contains water

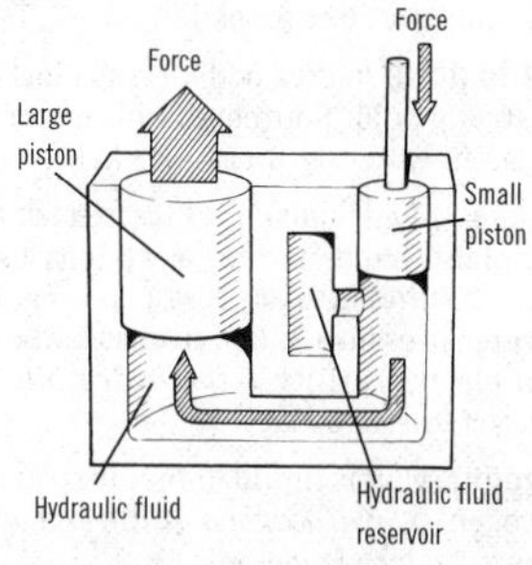

hydraulic: cross section of hydraulic mechanism

hy·drau·lic /hī dráwlik/ *adj* relating to or operated by a device in which pressure applied to a piston is transmitted by a fluid to a larger piston, so as to give rise to a larger force [Early 17C. Via Latin < Greek *hudraulikos* < *hudōr* "water" + *aulos* "pipe"] —**hy·drau·li·cal·ly** *adv*

hy·drau·lic brake *n* a brake in which force applied to a pedal is transmitted to the brake pads by an enclosed liquid, usually a glycol mixture

hy·drau·lic cou·pling *n* an arrangement in which two pistons of different sizes are connected by an enclosed fluid that can transmit pressure from one piston to the other

hy·drau·lic press *n* a device in which a relatively small force applied to a piston results in movement of a larger piston to which it is hydraulically coupled by an enclosed liquid. A hydraulic press is often the key part of machinery that forces materials to flow into a preformed shape.

hy·drau·lic ram *n* **1.** the larger working piston of a hydraulic press **2.** a device that uses the kinetic energy of a flow of water to raise water to a reservoir that is higher than the water source itself

hy·drau·lics /hī dráwliks/ *n* the study of water or other fluids at rest or in motion, especially with respect to engineering applications (*takes a singular verb*)

hy·dra·zide /hīdrə zīd/ *n* a compound formed by the reaction of hydrazine with a carboxylic acid [Late 19C. < HYDR- + AZO-]

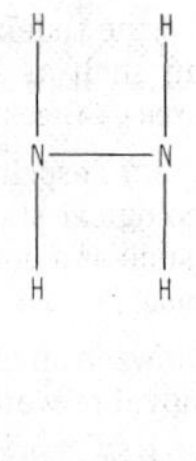

hydrazine

hy·dra·zine /hīdrə zeen/ *n* a highly reactive colorless liquid or white crystalline solid made from sodium hypochlorite and ammonia. Use: in rocket fuel. Formula: $H_2N.NH_2$. [Late 19C. < HYDR- + AZO-]

hy·dra·zo·ic ac·id /hīdrə zō ik-/ *n* a colorless liquid that is highly toxic and explosive in the presence of oxygen. Formula: HN_3. [< HYDR- + AZO-]

hy·dric /hīdrik/ *adj* **1.** containing or using considerable amounts of water **2.** relating to an environment that is extremely wet

hy·dride /hī drīd/ *n* a chemical compound formed between hydrogen and a more electropositive atom, e.g., sodium hydride, or via a covalent bond, e.g., boron hydride. Hydrides can also be formed with transition metals such as platinum and palladium.

hy·dril·la /hī drillə/ (*plural* **-las** *or same*) *n* a plant that grows underwater in large masses and oxygenates the water. Introduced into the southern United States, it has proliferated to such an extent that in some places it chokes fish and blocks water traffic. Genus: *Hydrilla*. [Early 19C. < modern Latin, "little hydra" < Latin *hydra* (see HYDRA)]

hy·dri·od·ic ac·id /hīdree òddik-/ *n* a colorless or pale yellow strong acid. Source: dissolving of hydrogen iodide gas in water. [< HYDR- + IODINE]

hy·dro /hīdrō/ (*plural* **-dros**) *n* **1.** HYDROELECTRIC POWER PLANT a power plant that generates electricity using water pressure **2.** HYDROELECTRIC POWER power generated using water pressure **3.** *Can* ELECTRIC POWER electricity from an electric utility ○ *the hydro bill* [Early 20C. Shortening of HYDROELECTRIC]

hydro- *prefix* **1.** water, liquid, moisture ○ *hydrobiology* **2.** hydrogen ○ *hydrocarbon* [< Greek *hudr-*, stem of *hudōr* "water" < Indo-European]

hy·dro·a·cous·tics /hīdrō ə kōōstiks/ *n* the branch of acoustics that studies how sound travels in water (*takes a singular verb*)

hy·dro·bi·ol·o·gy /hīdrō bī óllәjee/ *n* the branch of biology that studies water animals and plants —**hy·dro·bi·o·log·i·cal** /-bī ə lójjik'l/ *adj* —**hy·dro·bi·ol·o·gist** *n*

hy·dro·bro·mic ac·id /hīdrə brōmik-/ *n* a colorless or pale yellow strong acid. Source: dissolving hydrogen bromide gas in water. Formula: HBr.

hy·dro·car·bon /hīdrə kaarbən/ *n* an organic chemical compound containing only hydrogen and carbon atoms arranged in rows, rings, or both, and connected by single, double, or triple bonds. Hydrocarbons constitute a very large group including alkanes, alkenes, and alkynes. —**hy·dro·car·bo·na·ceous** /-kaarbə náyshəss/ *adj* —**hy·dro·car·bon·ic** /-kaar bónnik/ *adj* —**hy·dro·car·bon·ous** /-kaarbənəss/ *adj*

hy·dro·cele /hīdrə seel/ *n* an accumulation of watery liquid in a body cavity, especially in the sac around the testes. It is a painless condition that can be treated surgically by draining the fluid.

hy·dro·cel·lu·lose /hīdrə séllyə lōss/ *n* a gelatinous substance formed when cellulose is mixed with water, acids, or alkalis, e.g., in the manufacture of paper or rayon

hy·dro·ceph·a·lus /hīdrō séffələss/, **hy·dro·ceph·a·ly** /-séffəlee/ *n* an increase of cerebrospinal fluid around the brain, resulting in an enlargement of the head in infants, because the bones of the skull are still unfused. The fluid is blocked by a congenital condition or a disease, and can be drained into the abdominal cavity. [Late 17C. < modern Latin < Greek *hudōr* "water" + *kephalē* "head"] —**hy·dro·ce·phal·ic** /-sə fállik/ *adj* —**hy·dro·ceph·a·loid** /-séffə lòyd/ *adj* —**hy·dro·ceph·a·lous** *adj*

hy·dro·chlo·ric ac·id /hīdrə klàwrik-/ *n* a strong colorless acid. Source: dissolving hydrogen chloride gas in water. Use: industrial and laboratory processes. Formula: HCl.

hy·dro·chlo·ride /hīdrə kláw rīd/ *n* a salt formed when hydrochloric acid reacts with an organic base, e.g., aniline

hy·dro·chlo·ro·fluor·o·car·bon /hīdrō klawrō floorō kaarbən, -flawrō-/ *n* CHEM full form of **HCFC** [Late 20C. < HYDROCHLORIDE]

hy·dro·chlo·ro·thi·a·zide /hīdrə klàwrə thī ə zīd/ *n* a drug used in the treatment of fluid retention and high blood pressure

hy·dro·col·loid /hīdrə kó lòyd/ *n* a substance that forms a gel when mixed with water —**hy·dro·col·loid·al** /hīdrəkə lóyd'l/ *adj*

hy·dro·col·loid strip *n* a gelatinous waterproof bandage that seals a wound, retaining moisture and protecting from germs and dirt

hy·dro·cor·al /hīdrə káwrəl/ *n* a multicellular organism that lives in the ocean in colonies and builds calcareous skeletons within which the animals live. Order: Milleporina or Stylasterina.

hy·dro·cor·ti·sone /hīdrə káwrti sōn, -zōn/ *n* **1.** a steroid hormone secreted by the adrenal cortex, involved in carbohydrate metabolism and the stress reaction **2.** a synthetic form of hydrocortisone. Use: treatment of allergies, inflammation, and adrenal failure.

hy·dro·crack·ing /hīdrō kràking/ *n* an industrial process in which the action of hydrogen under high pressure fragments long-chain hydrocarbons to produce more volatile compounds such as gasoline and kerosene

hy·dro·cy·an·ic ac·id /hīdrō sī ánnik-/ *n* a colorless weak acid that smells of almonds. Source: dissolving of hydrogen cyanide in water.

hy·dro·dy·nam·ic /hīdrō dī námmik/, **hy·dro·dy·nam·i·cal** /-námmik'l/ *adj* **1.** relating to the mechanical properties of liquids **2.** operated by a moving liquid —**hy·dro·dy·nam·i·cal·ly** *adv*

hy·dro·dy·nam·ics /hīdrō dī námmiks/ *n* the area of fluid dynamics that is concerned with the study of liquids (*takes a singular verb*) —**hy·dro·dy·nam·i·cist** /-námmissist/ *n*

hy·dro·e·lec·tric /hīdrō i léktrik/ *adj* **1.** generated by converting the pressure of falling or running water to electricity by means of a turbine coupled to a generator **2.** relating to the generation of electricity by means of water pressure —**hy·dro·e·lec·tri·cal·ly** *adv* —**hy·dro·e·lec·tric·i·ty** /hīdrō i lek tríssətee, -ee lek-/ *n*

hy·dro·fluor·ic ac·id /hīdrō floorrik-, -flàwrik-/ *n* an extremely poisonous corrosive colorless liquid. Source: dissolving of hydrogen fluoride in water. Use: etching glass, treatment of metal surfaces, cleaning masonry. Formula: HF.

hy·dro·fluor·o·car·bon /hīdrō floorō kaarbən/ *n* a chemical compound composed of hydrogen, fluorine, and carbon. Use: preparation of plastics and pharmaceuticals.

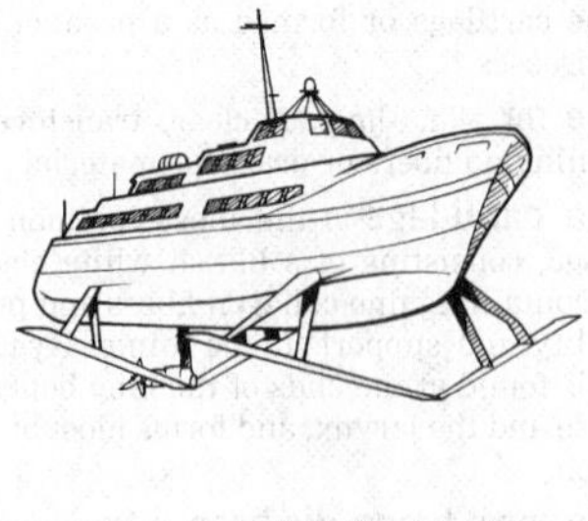

hydrofoil

hy·dro·foil /hīdrə fòyl/ *n* **1.** a boat with wing-shaped blades attached to struts under the hull that lift the boat out of the water as the speed increases **2.** a wing-shaped blade that lifts a hydrofoil out of the water

hy·dro·form·ing /hīdrə fàwrming/ *n* **1.** a high-temperature process in which hydrogen, with other catalysts, causes some hydrocarbons to break down, lose hydrogen, and rearrange themselves into aromatic or cyclic forms. It is used in the petroleum industry to impart better antiknock properties to gasoline. **2.** a process in which sheet metal is shaped by a punch forced against a flexible shaped block resting on a fluid-filled bag

hy·dro·gel /hīdrə jèl/ *n* a thick fluid like a jelly, formed by the addition of a substance to water

hy·dro·gen /hīdrəjən/ *n* a highly reactive colorless gas, the lightest element and the most abundant in the universe. Source: water, most organic compounds. Use: industrial processes, production of ammonia, reduction of metal ores to metals. Symbol **H**. See table at **element** [Late 18C. < French *hydrogène* < Greek *hudōr* "water" + French *-gène* (see -GEN)]

hy·drog·e·nase /hī drójjə nàyss, -nàyz/ *n* an enzyme that catalyzes reduction reactions by hydrogen

hy·dro·gen·ate /hī drójjə nàyt/ (**-at·ed, -at·ing, -ates**) *vt* to add hydrogen to a compound in a chemical reaction —**hy·dro·gen·a·tion** /hī drójjə náysh'n/ *n* —**hy·dro·gen·a·tor** *n*

hy·dro·gen bomb *n* an explosive weapon of mass destruction in which huge amounts of energy are released by the fusion of hydrogen nuclei

hy·dro·gen bond *n* an electrostatic interaction between molecules of compounds in which hydrogen atoms are bound to electronegative atoms such as oxygen or nitrogen. The attraction between water molecules due to hydrogen bonds accounts for the relatively high boiling point of water.

hy·dro·gen bro·mide *n* a colorless gas usually made by the combination of hydrogen and bromine in the presence of a catalyst such as platinum. It forms hydrobromic acid in water solution. Formula: HBr.

hy·dro·gen car·bon·ate *n* a salt of carbonic acid in which one hydrogen atom has been replaced, usually by a metal

hy·dro·gen chlo·ride *n* a colorless fuming corrosive gas. Source: byproduct of organic chlorination reactions. Use: manufacture of PVC. Formula: HCl.

hy·dro·gen cy·a·nide *n* an extremely poisonous colorless liquid or gas with a characteristic smell of almonds. Source: reaction between an acid and a metal cyanide. Formula: HCN.

hy·dro·gen em·brit·tle·ment /-em britt'lmənt/ *n* a process in which a metal is weakened by the incorporation of hydrogen in or below its surface, e.g., during plating or etching

hy·dro·gen fluor·ide *n* a colorless corrosive liquid. Source: action of sulfuric acid on a metal fluoride. Formula: HF.

hy·dro·gen i·o·dide *n* a colorless poisonous gas. Source: reaction of hydrogen and iodine in the presence of a catalyst, usually platinum. Formula: HI.

hy·dro·gen i·on *n* a positively charged ion of hydrogen that is formed by the removal of an electron from a hydrogen atom and is present in solutions of acids in water. The degree to which a compound produces hydrogen ions in solution is measured on the pH scale, 1 being highly acidic, 7 being neutral, and 14 being highly alkaline.

hy·dro·ge·nize /hī drójjə nīz, hídrəjə nīz/ (**-nized, -niz·ing, -niz·es**) *vt* CHEM same as **hydrogenate** —**hy·dro·ge·ni·za·tion** /hī dròjjəni záysh'n, hìdrəjəni-/ *n*

hy·dro·gen·ol·y·sis /hìdrəjə nólləssiss/ *n* the breaking of a bond in a molecule of an organic compound by the action of hydrogen, accompanied by the addition of a hydrogen atom to each of the fragments

hy·drog·e·nous /hī drójjənəss/ *adj* containing hydrogen

hy·dro·gen per·ox·ide *n* a colorless viscous unstable liquid that readily decomposes in water and oxygen. Use: bleach, mild antiseptic, component in rocket fuel. Formula: H_2O_2.

hy·dro·gen sul·fate *n* a salt containing the ion HSO_4O^-, formed when one hydrogen atom is removed from sulfuric acid by reaction with a metal, metal salt, or organic group

hy·dro·gen sul·fide *n* a colorless flammable poisonous gas with a characteristic smell of rotten eggs. Source: action of a mineral acid such as hydrochloric acid on a metal sulfide. Formula: H_2S.

hy·dro·gen sul·fite *n* a salt containing the ion HSO_3^-

hy·dro·gen tar·trate *n* a salt or ester of tartaric acid, e.g., potassium hydrogen tartrate, that forms deposits in wine vats

hy·dro·ge·o·lo·gy /hìdrō jee óllajee/ *n* the branch of geology that studies the movement of subsurface water through rocks and the effect of moving water on rocks, including their erosion —**hy·dro·ge·o·log·ic** /hìdrō jee ə lójjik/ *adj* —**hy·dro·ge·o·log·i·cal** *adj* —**hy·dro·ge·ol·o·gist** *n*

hy·drog·ra·phy /hī dróggrəfee/ *n* the scientific study of seas, lakes, and rivers, especially the charting of tides and changes in coastal bathymetry or the measurement and recording of river flow —**hy·dro·graph** /hídrə gràf/ *n* —**hy·drog·ra·pher** *n* —**hy·dro·graph·ic** /hìdrə gráffik/ *adj* —**hy·dro·graph·i·cal·ly** *adv*

hy·droid /hí dròyd/ *n* **1.** an invertebrate sea animal with an internal body cavity that lives in colonies, forming growths like tufts. Order: Hydroida. **2.** an asexual polyp that is part of the life cycle of hydrozoans [Mid-19C. < HYDRA]

hy·dro·ki·net·ics /hìdrōki néttiks, -kī-/ *n* the branch of physics concerned with the scientific study of the properties and behavior of fluids in motion (*takes a singular verb*)

hy·dro·lase /hídrə làyss, -làyz/ *n* an enzyme that controls hydrolysis, e.g., an esterase [Early 20C. < HYDROLYSIS]

~~hydrolic~~ incorrect spelling of **hydraulic**

hy·dro·log·ic cy·cle /hìdrə lójjik-/, **hy·dro·log·i·cal cy·cle** /hìdrə lójjik'l-/ *n* METEOROL same as **water cycle** (*technical*)

hy·drol·o·gy /hī dróllәjee/ *n* the scientific study of the properties, distribution, use, and circulation of the water on Earth and in the atmosphere in all of its forms —**hy·drol·o·gist** *n*

hy·drol·y·sate /hī dróllə sàyt/ *n* a substance produced by hydrolysis

hy·drol·yse *vti* CHEM UK spelling of **hydrolyze**

hy·drol·y·sis /hī drólləssis/ *n* a chemical reaction in which a compound reacts with water, causing decomposition and the production of two or more other compounds, e.g., in the conversion of starch to glucose —**hy·dro·lyt·ic** /hìdrə líttik/ *adj* —**hy·dro·lyt·i·cal·ly** *adv*

hy·dro·lyze /hídrə līz/ (**-lyzed, -lyz·ing, -lyz·es**) *vti* to undergo hydrolysis, or make a substance undergo hydrolysis [Late 19C. < HYDROLYSIS, after ANALYSIS, ANALYZE] —**hy·dro·lyz·a·ble** *adj* —**hy·dro·ly·za·tion** /hìdrəli záysh'n/ *n*

hy·dro·mag·net·ics /hìdrō mag néttiks/ *n* MECH ENG same as **magnetohydrodynamics** (*takes a singular verb*) —**hy·dro·mag·net·ic** *adj*

hy·dro·man·cy /hídrə mànssee/ *n* the practice of attempting to foretell events or discover unknown knowledge by studying the appearance or movement of water —**hy·dro·manc·er** *n* —**hy·dro·man·tic** /hìdrə mántik/ *adj*

hy·dro·me·chan·ics /hìdrō mə kánniks/ *n* MECH ENG same as **hydrodynamics** (*takes a singular verb*) —**hy·dro·me·chan·i·cal** *adj*

hy·dro·me·du·sa /hìdrōm doóssə, -dyoó-/ (*plural* **-sae** /-ssee/) *n* a free-swimming invertebrate ocean animal, resembling a tiny jellyfish, that is the reproductive stage of a hydroid

hy·dro·mel /hídrə mèl/ *n* a drink made of honey mixed in water. If allowed to ferment, it turns into mead. [15C. Via Latin < Greek *hudromeli* "water honey" < *meli* "honey"]

hy·dro·met·al·lur·gy /hìdrō mét't'l ùrjee/ *n* the extraction of metals from ores by treating them with aqueous chemical solutions, including extraction by electrolysis and ion exchange —**hy·dro·met·al·lur·gi·cal** /hìdrō mètt'l úrjik'l/ *adj*

hy·dro·me·te·or /hìdrō meétee ər/ *n* a weather condition caused by condensation of water in the atmosphere, e.g., rain, snow, or fog —**hy·dro·me·te·or·o·log·i·cal** /-meetee ərə lójjik'l/ *adj* —**hy·dro·me·te·or·ol·o·gist** /-róllәjist/ *n* —**hy·dro·me·te·or·ol·o·gy** /-róllәjee/ *n*

hy·drom·e·ter /hī drómmətər/ *n* a device, usually a sealed graduated tube containing a weighted bulb, used to determine the specific gravity or density of a liquid —**hy·dro·met·ric** /hìdrə méttrik/ *adj* —**hy·dro·met·ri·cal·ly** *adv* —**hy·drom·e·try** *n*

hy·dro·mor·phic /hìdrə máwrfik/ *adj* relating to or typical of a soil that has built up in the presence of excess water

hy·drop·a·thy /hī dróppəthee/ *n* the treatment of injuries or disease by applying water both internally and externally —**hy·dro·path** /hídrə pàth/ *n* —**hy·dro·path·ic** /hìdrə páthik/ *adj* —**hy·dro·path·i·cal** *adj* —**hy·dro·path·i·cal·ly** *adv*

hy·dro·per·ox·ide /hìdrōpə rók sīd/ *n* an intermediate compound formed during the oxidation of unsaturated organic substances and containing the group -OOH

hy·dro·phane /hídrə fàyn/ *n* a translucent lustrous form of opal —**hy·droph·a·nous** /hī dróffənəss/ *adj*

hy·dro·phil·ic /hìdrə fíllik/ *adj* dissolving in, absorbing, or mixing easily with water —**hy·dro·phile** /hídrə fīl/ *n* —**hy·dro·phi·lic·i·ty** /hìdrə fi líssətee/ *n*

hy·dro·pho·bi·a /hìdrə fóbee ə/ *n* **1.** MED same as **rabies 2.** an extremely intense aversion to water, especially the fear of drinking water or other liquids

hy·dro·pho·bic /hìdrə fóbik/ *adj* **1.** relating to or affected by an extreme fear of water **2.** CHEM not dissolving in, absorbing, or mixing easily with water —**hy·dro·phobe** /hídrə fòb/ *n* —**hy·dro·pho·bic·i·ty** /hìdrəfō bíssətee/ *n*

hy·dro·phone /hídrə fōn/ *n* an electronic receiver that can pick up sound traveling through water by converting acoustic energy into electromagnetic waves. One use is tracking submarines.

hy·dro·phyte /hídrə fīt/ *n* a plant that will only grow in water or in a very damp environment —**hy·dro·phyt·ic** /hìdrə fíttik/ *adj*

hy·dro·plane /hídrə plàyn/ *n* **1.** FAST BOAT a motorboat designed so that it rises up out of the water at high speed and skims along the surface **2.** same as **hydrofoil** (sense 1) **3.** DIVING PLANE ON SUBMARINE a horizontal diving plane on a submarine, used to control its vertical movement **4.** AEROSP same as **seaplane** ■ *vi* (**-planed, -plan·ing, -planes**) **1.** SKIM SURFACE to skim along on the surface of the water **2.** SKID ON WET ROAD to skid on a wet road because a film of surface water prevents a vehicle's tires from making firm contact with the road surface

hy·dro·pon·ics /hìdrə pónniks/ *n* the cultivation of plants in a nutrient liquid with or without gravel or another supporting medium (*takes a singular verb*) [Mid-20C. < HYDRO- + Greek *ponos* "work"] —**hy·dro·pon·ic** *adj* —**hy·dro·pon·i·cal·ly** *adv* —**hy·dro·pon·i·cist** *n* —**hy·drop·on·ist** /hī dróppənist, hìdrə pónnist/ *n*

hy·dro·pow·er /hídrə pòwr/ *n* electric power generated using water power

hy·dro·qui·none /hìdrəkwi nōn, -kwí nōn/, **hy·dro·quin·ol** /-kwí nàwl/ *n* a white crystalline compound. Use: photographic developer, in paints, in motor oils, in medicines. Formula: $C_6H_4(OH)_2$.

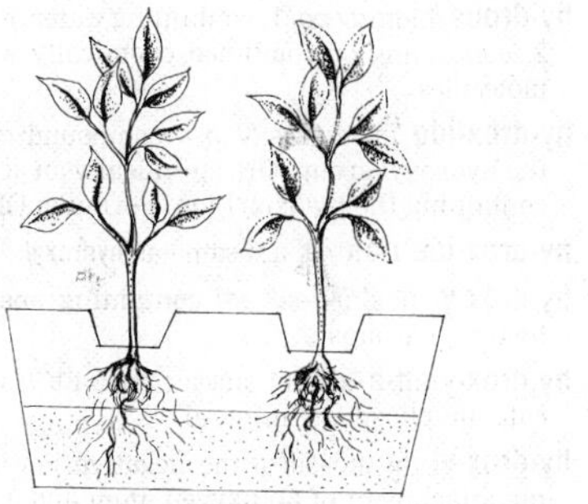
hydroponics

hy·dro·scope /hídrə skōp/ *n* an optical instrument constructed from a series of mirrors encased in a tube, used for observing objects deep beneath the surface of a body of water —**hy·dro·scop·ic** /hìdrə skóppik/ *adj* —**hy·dro·scop·i·cal** *adj* —**hy·dro·scop·i·cal·ly** *adv*

hy·dro·ski /hídrō skeè/ *n* a hydrofoil on a seaplane, usually ski-shaped and retractable, used to give extra lift on takeoff

hy·dro·sol /hídrə sàwl/ *n* a colloidal solution in which the particles are suspended in water [Mid-19C. < HYDRO- + SOLUTION] —**hy·dro·sol·ic** /hìdrə sóllik/ *adj*

hy·dro·space /hídrə spàyss/ *n* the area beneath the surface of the seas

hy·dro·sphere /hídrə sfeèr/ *n* the portion of Earth's surface that is water, including the seas and water in the atmosphere —**hy·dro·spher·ic** /hìdrə sféerik, -sférrik/ *adj*

hy·dro·stat /hídrə stàt/ *n* a device designed to regulate the height of fluid in a column or container. Use: measurement and control of relative humidity or, in steam boilers, to detect a low water level.

hy·dro·stat·ic /hìdrə státtik/, **hy·dro·stat·i·cal** /-k'l/ *adj* **1.** relating to, involving, or typical of fluids that are at rest and the forces and pressures they exert **2.** relating to, involving, or typical of hydrostatics [Mid-17C. Probably < modern Latin *hydrostaticus* or < its source Greek *hudrostatēs* "hydrostatic balance" < *statikos* "causing to stand"] —**hy·dro·stat·i·cal·ly** *adv*

hy·dro·stat·ics /hìdrə státtiks/ *n* the scientific study of the equilibrium of liquids at rest and the forces and pressures exerted by them (*takes a singular verb*) —**hy·dro·stat·i·cal·ly** *adv*

hy·dro·stat·ic skel·e·ton *n* the most primitive form of skeletal structure, found in animals such as jellyfish and worms, that consists of layers of muscle around a fluid-filled body cavity

hy·dro·tax·is /hìdrə táksiss/ *n* the response of an organism or cell to the presence of water or moisture, usually detected as movement —**hy·dro·tac·tic** /-táktik/ *adj*

hy·dro·ther·a·peu·tics /hìdrə therə pyoótiks/ *n* the scientific study and theory of the external use of water for healing (*takes a singular verb*) —**hy·dro·ther·a·peu·tic** *adj*

hy·dro·ther·a·py /hìdrə thérrəpee/ *n* the treatment of disease by the external use of water, e.g., by exercising weakened limbs in a pool —**hy·dro·ther·a·pist** *n*

hy·dro·ther·mal /hìdrə thúrm'l/ *adj* relating to, or produced by, the action of extremely hot water on the Earth's crust ○ *hydrothermal deposits* —**hy·dro·ther·mal·ly** *adv*

hy·dro·tho·rax /hìdrə tháw ràks/ *n* a buildup of fluid in a pleural cavity, e.g., as a result of failing circulation caused by heart disease [Late 18C. < modern Latin < Greek *hudōr* "water" + *thōrax* "chest"] —**hy·dro·tho·rac·ic** /-thaw rássik/ *adj*

hy·drot·ro·pism /hī dróttrə pìzzəm/ *n* movement by a plant part such as a root toward or away from a source of water —**hy·dro·tro·pic** /hìdrə trópik, -tróppik/ *adj* —**hy·dro·tro·pi·cal·ly** *adv*

hy·drous /hī́drəss/ *adj* **1.** containing water or moisture **2.** containing or combined chemically with water molecules

hy·drox·ide /hī drók sīd/ *n* a compound containing the hydroxyl group -OH, specifically an acid or base containing the hydroxyl ion. Formula: OH^-.

hy·drox·ide i·on *n* CHEM same as **hydroxyl**

hy·drox·y /hī dróksee/ *adj* containing one or more hydroxyl groups

hy·drox·y·ap·a·tite /hī dròksee áppə tīt/ *n* a hydrated calcium phosphate mineral

hy·drox·yl /hī dróksil/ *n* the negative ion formed by the attachment of an oxygen atom and a hydrogen atom. Formula: OH^-. [Mid-19C. < HYDRO- + OXY- + -YL] —**hy·drox·yl·ic** /hī drok síllik/ *adj*

hy·drox·yl·a·mine /hī dròksələ meén, hī drok sílla meén, -sə lá meén/ *n* a colorless crystalline compound that decomposes at room temperature and explodes on heating. Use: reducing agent, in the synthesis of organic molecules. Formula: NH_2OH.

hy·drox·yl·ate /hī dróksə làyt/ (**-at·ed, -at·ing, -ates**) *vt* to introduce hydroxyl into a compound —**hy·drox·y·la·tion** /hī dròksə láysh'n/ *n*

hy·drox·yl i·on *n* CHEM same as **hydroxyl**

hy·drox·y·pro·line /hī dròksi prṓ leén/ *n* an amino acid derived from proline that is a component of collagen

hy·dro·zo·an /hīdrə zṓ ən/ *n* a ocean or freshwater invertebrate animal, e.g., a polyp or jellyfish. Class: Hydrozoa. [Late 19C. < modern Latin *Hydrozoa* "water animals" < Greek *hudōr* "water" + *zōia*, plural of *zōion* "animal"]

Hy·drus /hī́drəss/ *n* a constellation of the southern hemisphere. See illustration at **constellation**

hyena

hy·e·na /hī éenə/, **hy·ae·na** *n* a carnivorous scavenging animal resembling a dog, with a sloping back and loping gait. Native to: Africa, South Asia. Family: Hyaenidae. [14C. Directly or via French < Latin *hyaena* < Greek *huaina*, form of *hus* "pig"] —**hy·en·ic** *adj*

hy·e·tal /hī́ ət'l/ *adj* relating to rain or rainfall [Mid-19C. < Greek *huetos* "rain" (see HYETO-)]

hyeto- *prefix* rain ○ *hyetograph* [< Greek *huetos* < *huein* "to rain"]

hy·e·to·graph /hī étto gràf/ *n* **1.** a chart or graph showing the pattern of rainfall in an area **2.** an instrument that automatically collects rain and measures its amount —**hy·e·to·graph·i·cal·ly** /hī èttə gráffikəlee/ *adv* —**hy·e·tog·ra·phy** /hī ə tóggrəfee/ *n*

Hy·ge·ia /hī jée ə/ *n* in Greek mythology, the goddess of health. The daughter of Asclepius, she is often represented as a maiden feeding a snake.

~~**hygeine**~~ incorrect spelling of **hygiene**

Hy·gi·ea /hī jée ə/ *n* the fourth-largest asteroid, discovered in 1849. It has a diameter of approximately 420 km (260 mi.).

hy·giene /hī́ jeen/ *n* **1.** the science dealing with the preservation of health **2.** the practice or principles of cleanliness [Late 17C. Directly or via French *hygiène* < modern Latin *(ars) hygieina* "healthful art" < Greek *hugiēs* "healthy"]

hy·gien·ic /hī jénnik, -jéenik, hī jee énnik/ *adj* **1.** OF CLEANLINESS relating to the scientific study or principles of cleanliness **2.** PROMOTING HEALTH promoting health or cleanliness **3.** GERM-FREE clean or free from disease-causing microorganisms —**hy·gien·i·cal·ly** *adv*

hy·gi·en·ics /hījee énniks, hī jénniks, -jéeniks/ *n* HEALTH same as **hygiene** (sense 1) (*takes a singular verb*)

hy·gien·ist /hī jéenist, -jénnist/ *n* a student of or expert in the maintenance of hygiene

hygro- *prefix* moisture, humidity ○ *hygrometer* [< Greek *hugros* "moist" < Indo-European]

hy·gro·graph /hī́grə gràf/ *n* an automatic hygrometer that records the humidity of the air

hy·grom·e·ter /hī grómmətər/ *n* an instrument used to measure humidity —**hy·gro·met·ric** /hīgrə méttrik/ *adj* —**hy·gro·met·ri·cal·ly** *adv*

hy·groph·il·ous /hī gróffələss/ *adj* describes plants that are adapted to growing in damp places

hy·gro·phyte /hī́grə fīt/ *n* BOT same as **hydrophyte** —**hy·gro·phyt·ic** /hīgrə fíttik/ *adj*

hy·gro·scope /hī́grə skōp/ *n* an instrument that shows changes in the humidity of the air but does not measure the changes

hy·gro·scop·ic /hīgrə skóppik/, **hy·gro·scop·i·cal** /-ik'l/ *adj* capable of easily absorbing moisture, e.g., from the air —**hy·gro·scop·i·cal·ly** *adv* —**hy·gro·sco·pic·i·ty** /hīgrə skō píssətee/ *n*

hy·gro·stat /hī́grə stàt/ *n* METEOROL same as **humidistat**

hy·ing present participle of **hie**

Hyk·sos /híksōss/ (*plural same*) *n* a member of an ancient nomadic people from western Asia, probably of Semitic ancestry, who conquered and ruled Egypt between 1720 B.C. and 1560 B.C. [Early 17C. Via Greek *Huksōs* < Egyptian *heqa khoswe* "foreign rulers"] —**Hyk·sos** *adj*

hy·la /hī́lə/ *n* a tree frog of a genus found all over the world. Genus: *Hyla*. [Mid-19C. Via modern Latin < Greek *hulē* "wood"]

hylo- *prefix* matter ○ *hylotheism* [< Greek *hulē* "wood, matter"]

hy·lo·bate /hī lóbbət/ *n* same as **gibbon** (*technical*) [Late 20C. < modern Latin *Hylobates*]

hy·lo·mor·phism /hīlə máwr fìzzəm/ *n* the belief that all material objects are made up of matter, which is only potential, and form, which makes the object an actuality

hy·lo·the·ism /hīlə theé ìzzəm/ *n* the belief that God and the material world are the same

hy·lo·zo·ism /hīlə zṓ ìzzəm/ *n* the belief that all matter is living [Late 17C. < HYLO- + Greek *zōē* "life"] —**hy·lo·zo·ic** *adj*

hy·men /hī́mən/ *n* a thin mucous membrane that completely or partially covers the opening of the vagina [Mid-16C. Directly or via French < late Latin < Greek *humēn* "membrane"]

Hy·men /hī́mən/ *n* in Greek mythology, the god of marriage, often represented as a youth holding a torch

hy·me·ne·al /hīmə neé əl/ (*literary*) *adj* relating to, involving, or characteristic of marriage ■ *n* a song or poem celebrating a wedding [Early 17C. < Latin *hymenaeus* "wedding song, wedding" < Greek *humenaios* < *Humēn* "Hymen"] —**hy·me·ne·al·ly** *adv*

hy·me·ni·um /hī meénee əm/ (*plural* **-ni·a** /-nee ə/ or **-ni·ums**) *n* a layer of spore-bearing structures within or on the surface of the fruiting body of a fungus [Early 19C. Via modern Latin < Greek *humenion* "small membrane" < *humēn* "membrane"] —**hy·me·ni·al** *adj*

hy·me·nop·ter·an /hīmə nóptərən/, **hy·me·nop·ter·on** /-nóptə ròn, -nóptərən/ *n* an insect that has two pairs of membranous wings and a very thin waist and that lives in socially complex colonies, e.g., the wasp, ant, and sawfly. Order: Hymenoptera. [Mid-19C. < modern Latin *Hymenoptera* < form of Greek *humenopteros* "membrane-winged" < *humēn* "membrane" + *pteron* "wing"] —**hy·me·nop·ter·an** *adj* —**hy·me·nop·ter·ous** *adj*

Hy·mie /hī́mee/ *n* a highly offensive term for a Jew (*taboo*) [Late 20C. Alteration of *Hyman*, Jewish man's name]

hymn /him/ *n* **1.** RELIGIOUS SONG a song of praise to God, a god, or a saint **2.** SONG OF PRAISE a song of praise to somebody or something other than a deity ■ *v* (**hymned, hymn·ing, hymns**) **1.** *vt* PRAISE SOMEBODY OR SOMETHING IN SONG to sing in praise of somebody or something **2.** *vi* SING HYMNS to sing songs of praise [Pre-12C. Via Latin < Greek *humnos* "song in praise of gods or heroes"]

hym·nal /hímnəl/ *n* same as **hymnbook** (*dated*)

hymn·book /hím bo͝ok/ *n* a book that contains the words and sometimes the music of hymns sung in church

hym·nist /hímnist/ *n* a composer of hymns

hym·no·dy /hímnədee/ (*plural* **-dies**) *n* **1.** the composition or singing of hymns **2.** hymns collectively, especially a group of hymns that share a characteristic such as time of composition or use in a particular church [Early 18C. Via medieval Latin < Greek *humnōidia* "singing of hymns" < *humnos* "song in praise of gods or heroes"]

hym·nol·o·gy /him nóllәjee/ (*plural* **-gies**) *n* **1.** the study of religious hymns **2.** CHR same as **hymnody** —**hym·no·log·ic** /hìmnə lójjik/ *adj* —**hym·no·log·i·cal** *adj* —**hym·nol·o·gist** *n*

hy·oid /hī óyd/ *n* ANAT same as **hyoid bone** ■ *adj* relating to or involving the hyoid bone [Early 19C. Via French *hyoïde* < Greek *huoeidēs* "shaped like the Greek letter upsilon" < *hu* "upsilon"]

hy·oid bone *n* a U-shaped bone positioned at the base of the tongue and above the thyroid cartilage that supports the tongue and its muscles

hy·o·scine /hī́ ə seén/ *n* CHEM same as **scopolamine** [Late 19C. < modern Latin *Hyoscyamus* (see HYOSCYAMINE)]

hy·o·scy·a·mine /hī ə sī́ ə meén/ *n* a poisonous alkaloid that resembles atropine. Source: henbane, belladonna. Use: dilates blood vessels, prevents or controls spasms. [Mid-19C. < modern Latin *Hyoscyamus*, genus name of the henbane < Greek *huoskuamos* "pig's bean" < genitive of *hus* "pig" + *kuamos* "bean"]

hyp. *abbr* **1.** MATH hypotenuse **2.** hypothesis **3.** hypothetical

hyp- *prefix* same as **hypo-** (*used before vowels*)

hyp·a·bys·sal /hìppə bíss'l, hīpə-/ *adj* describes igneous rocks, especially in the form of dikes or sills, created when molten magma rose to the surface of the Earth's crust but solidified before reaching it —**hyp·a·bys·sal·ly** *adv*

hy·paes·the·sia *n* MED Can, UK spelling of **hypoesthesia**

hy·pae·thral /hī peéthrəl, hi-/, **hy·pe·thral** *adj* lacking a roof, or having a roof that is partly open to the sky, in the style of a classical temple [Late 18C. < Latin *hypaethrus* "in the open air" < Greek *hupo-* (see HYPO-) + *hupaithros* < *aithēr* "air"]

hy·pal·la·ge /hi pállәjee, hī-/ *n* a figure of speech in which the usual relations of words or phrases are interchanged, e.g., "He nodded his agreeing head" [Late 16C. Via late Latin < Greek *hupallagē* "interchange" < *hupo-* (see HYPO-) + *allag-*, stem of *allassein* "to exchange" < *allos* "other"]

hy·pan·thi·um /hī pánthee əm/ (*plural* **-thi·a** /-thee ə/) *n* the flat or cup-shaped area that bears the stamens, petals, and sepals of plants such as roses and cherries [Mid-19C. < modern Latin, "structure under the flower" < Greek *hupo-* (see HYPO-) + *anthos* "flower"] —**hy·pan·thi·al** *adj*

hype[1] /hīp/ (*informal*) *n* **1.** PUBLICITY greatly exaggerated publicity intended to excite public interest in something such as a movie or theatrical production **2.** SOMEBODY OR SOMETHING OVERPUBLICIZED a widely publicized person or thing **3.** DECEPTION a deception or dishonest scheme ■ *vt* (**hyped, hyp·ing, hypes**) **1.** PUBLICIZE SOMEBODY OR SOMETHING to promote somebody or something with intense publicity **2.** ARTIFICIALLY BOOST SALES OF RECORDING to boost sales of a pop recording artificially by employing people to buy quantities of it at numerous outlets [Early 20C. Partly back-formation < HYPERBOLE, partly < slang *hyper* "somebody giving short change" (< HYPER-)]

hype[2] /hīp/ *n* (*slang*) **1.** a hypodermic needle or injection **2.** a drug addict [Early 20C shortening of HYPODERMIC]

hyped-up /hīpt-/ *adj* highly stimulated or excited, especially by drugs (*slang*) [Early 20C. < shortening of HYPODERMIC]

hy·per /hīpər/ *adj* (*informal*) **1.** behaving in an overexcited or hyperactive way **2.** easily excited, or having a high-strung temperament [Mid-20C. Shortening of HYPERACTIVE]

hyper- *prefix* **1.** over, above, beyond ○ *hyperextension* **2.** excessive, unusually high ○ *hypertension* [< Greek *huper* "above, beyond" < Indo-European]

hy·per·a·cute *adj*
hy·per·ag·gres·sive *adj*
hy·per·alert *adj*
hy·per·a·rous·al *n*
hy·per·a·ware *adj*
hy·per·a·ware·ness *n*
hy·per·cau·tious *adj*
hy·per·civ·i·lized *adj*
hy·per·com·pet·i·tive *adj*
hy·per·con·cen·tra·tion *n*
hy·per·con·scious *adj*
hy·per·con·scious·ness *n*
hy·per·ef·fi·cient *adj*
hy·per·e·mo·tion·al *adj*
hy·per·en·er·get·ic *adj*
hy·per·ex·cit·a·ble *adj*
hy·per·fas·tid·i·ous *adj*
hy·per·fem·i·nine *adj*
hy·per·in·tel·lec·tual *adj*
hy·per·in·tel·li·gent *adj*
hy·per·in·tense *adj*
hy·per·ir·ri·ta·bil·i·ty *n*
hy·per·ir·ri·ta·ble *adj*
hy·per·mas·cu·line *adj*
hy·per·mod·ern *adj*
hy·per·na·tion·al·is·tic *adj*
hy·per·pro·duc·tion *n*
hy·per·ra·tion·al *adj*
hy·per·re·ac·tive *adj*
hy·per·re·ac·tor *n*
hy·per·re·spon·sive *adj*
hy·per·sal·i·va·tion *n*
hy·per·secre·tion *n*
hy·per·sen·si·ti·za·tion *n*
hy·per·sen·si·tize *vt*
hy·per·som·no·lence *n*
hy·per·stim·u·late *vt*
hy·per·stim·u·la·tion *n*
hy·per·sus·cep·ti·bil·i·ty *n*
hy·per·sus·cep·ti·ble *adj*
hy·per·tense *adj*
hy·per·vig·i·lant *adj*
hy·per·vir·u·lent *adj*
hy·per·vis·cos·i·ty *n*

hy·per·ac·cum·u·late /hīpərə kyōōmyə làyt/ (**-lated, -lat·ing, -lates**) *vti* to take up and accumulate an unusually high concentration of metal from the environment (*refers to plant tissue*) —**hy·per·ac·cum·u·la·tion** /hīpərə kyoomyə láysh'n/ *n* —**hy·per·ac·cum·u·la·tor** *n*

hy·per·a·cid·i·ty /hīpər ə síddətee/ *n* a condition in which excess stomach acid is produced, usually associated with the formation of a peptic or duodenal ulcer

hy·per·ac·tive /hīpər áktiv/ *adj* unusually active, restless, and lacking the ability to concentrate for any length of time, especially as a result of attention deficit disorder —**hy·per·ac·tion** *n* —**hy·per·ac·tive·ly** *adv* —**hy·per·ac·tiv·i·ty** /hīpər ak tívvətee/ *n*

hy·per·ae·mi·a *n* MED UK spelling of **hyperemia**

hy·per·aes·the·sia *n* another spelling of **hyperesthesia**

hy·per·bar·ic /hīpər bárrik/ *adj* relating to, involving, or occurring at pressures higher than normal [Mid-20C. < HYPER- + Greek *baros* "weight"] —**hy·per·bar·i·cal·ly** *adv*

hy·per·ba·ton /hī púrbə tòn/ *n* a figure of speech in which the expected word order is inverted for emphasis, e.g., in "you I hate" [Mid-16C. Via Latin < Greek *huperbaton* "overstepping" < *huperbainein* "step over" < *bainein* "step, walk"]

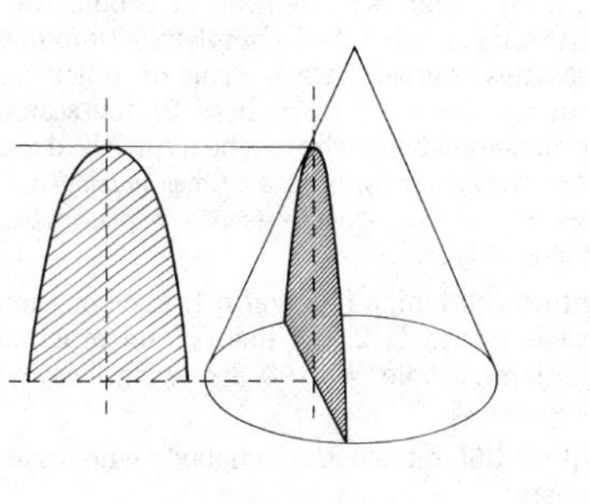

hyperbola

hy·per·bo·la /hī púrbələ/ (*plural* **-las** or **-lae** /-lee/) *n* a conic section formed by a point that moves in a plane so that the difference in its distance from two fixed points in the plane remains constant [Mid-17C. Via modern Latin < Greek *huperbolē* "excess" (see HYPERBOLE)]

hy·per·bo·le /hī púrbəlee/ *n* deliberate and obvious exaggeration used for effect, e.g., "I could eat a million of these" [15C. Via Latin < Greek *huperbolē* "excess," literally "overthrow" < *ballein* "to throw"]

hy·per·bol·ic /hīpər bóllik/, **hy·per·bol·i·cal** /-ik'l/ *adj* **1.** OF HYPERBOLA relating to, involving, or typical of a hyperbola **2.** OF GEOMETRIC SYSTEM produced by or relating to a geometric system in which two lines can pass through any point in a plane without intersecting a specific line in the same plane **3.** OF HYPERBOLIC FUNCTION connected with or relating to a hyperbolic function **4.** OF HYPERBOLE relating to or constituting hyperbole —**hy·per·bol·i·cal·ly** *adv*

hy·per·bol·ic func·tion *n* any of six functions analogous to trigonometric functions but related to a hyperbola rather than a circle. Hyperbolic functions include the hyperbolic sine, hyperbolic cosine, hyperbolic tangent, hyperbolic cotangent, hyperbolic secant, and hyperbolic cosecant.

hy·per·bo·lize /hī púrbə līz/ (**-lized, -liz·ing, -liz·es**) *vti* to use deliberate and obvious exaggeration for effect, or describe something in obviously exaggerated terms

hy·per·bo·loid /hī púrbə lòyd/ *n* a mathematical surface whose sections parallel to one coordinate plane form ellipses and those parallel to the other two coordinate planes form hyperbolas —**hy·per·bo·loid·al** /hī pùrbə lóyd'l/ *adj*

hy·per·bo·re·an /hīpər báwree ən/ *adj* **1.** relating to the far northern regions of the world **2.** relating to peoples who live in the Arctic [Late 16C. < late Latin *hyperboreanus* < Latin *hyperboreus* < Greek *huperbore(i)os* < *boreios* "northern" or *Boreas* "north wind"]

Hy·per·bo·re·an /hīpər báwree ən/ *n* in Greek mythology, a member of a people who lived beyond the north wind in a land that was always sunny and warm [15C. < late Latin *hyperboreanus* (see HYPERBOREAN)]

hy·per·cal·ce·mi·a /hīpər kal seémee ə/ *n* an unusually high amount of calcium in the blood

hy·per·cap·ni·a /hīpər kápnee ə/ *n* an unusually high level of carbon dioxide in the blood [Early 20C. < modern Latin, "condition of excessive smoke" < Greek *kapnos* "smoke"] —**hy·per·cap·nic** *adj*

hy·per·charge /hīpər chaarj/ *n* a property of elementary particles that is calculated by adding together a particle's baryon number and its quantum property of strangeness [Mid-20C. Contraction of *hyperonic charge* (< HYPERON)]

hy·per·charged *adj* **1.** imbued with an atmosphere of exceptionally intense interest, excitement, or other strong emotion **2.** describes elementary particles with the property of hypercharge

hy·per·cho·les·ter·ol·e·mi·a /hīpərkə lestərə leémee ə/ *n* an unusually high level of cholesterol in the blood —**hy·per·cho·les·ter·ol·em·ic** *adj*

hy·per·cor·rect /hīpərkə rékt/ *adj* **1.** too greatly concerned about correctness **2.** showing or being the result of hypercorrection —**hy·per·cor·rect·ly** *adv* —**hy·per·cor·rect·ness** *n*

hy·per·cor·rec·tion /hīpərkə rékshən/ *n* a grammatical mistake or mispronunciation made by correcting something that is not actually wrong, e.g., saying "between you and I" instead of "between you and me"

hy·per·crit·i·cal /hīpər kríttik'l/ *adj* criticizing somebody or something too severely or too much —**hy·per·crit·i·cal·ly** *adv* —**hy·per·crit·i·cism** /-krítti sìzzəm/ *n*

hy·per·cube /hīpər kyoob/ *n* a figure in four or more dimensions with sides that are all of the same length and angles that are all right angles

hy·per·e·mi·a /hīpə reémee ə/ *n* an unusually high level of blood in some part of the body —**hy·per·e·mic** *adj*

hy·per·es·the·sia /hīpərəss theézhə/, **hy·per·aes·the·sia** *n* a heightened sensitivity of a part of the body such as the skin, or of any of the senses [Mid-19C. < modern Latin, "condition of extreme sensation" < Greek *aisthēsis* "sensation"] —**hy·per·es·thet·ic** /-əss théttik/ *adj*

hy·per·eu·tec·tic /hīpəryoo téktik/, **hy·per·eu·tec·toid** /-tòyd/ *adj* describes a compound or alloy that contains a minor component in a higher proportion than in the mixture of the same elements that has the lowest melting point

hy·per·ex·ten·sion /hīpərik sténshən/ *n* the movement of a limb beyond its normal range —**hy·per·ex·tend** *vt* —**hy·per·ex·tend·ed** *adj*

hy·per·fine struc·ture /hīpər fīn-/ *n* the splitting of lines in a spectrum into two or more closely spaced fine lines, caused by magnetic interactions within atoms

hy·per·fo·cal dis·tance /hīpər fōk'l-/ *n* the distance between a camera lens and the closest object that is in focus when the lens is focused at infinity

hy·per·func·tion /hīpər fúngksh'n/ *n* overactivity of a gland or other bodily organ

hy·per·ga·my /hī púrgəmee/ *n* a custom in some societies that requires a woman to marry a man of a higher social class than the one to which she belongs

hy·per·gly·ce·mi·a /hīpər glī seémee ə/ *n* an unusually high level of sugar in the blood —**hy·per·gly·ce·mic** *adj*

hy·per·gol·ic /hīpər góllik/ *adj* describes a rocket propellant that ignites on contact with an oxidizer [Mid-20C. < German *Hypergol* "hypergolic fuel" < *hyper-* "hyper-" + *erg-* "work" < Greek *ergon*] —**hy·per·gol** /hīpər gàwl/ *n* —**hy·per·gol·i·cal·ly** *adv*

hy·per·hi·dro·sis /hīpər hī drṓssiss/ *n* excessive sweating, either generalized or localized to a particular part of the body

hy·per·i·cum /hī pérrikəm/ (*plural same* or **-cums**) *n* a herbaceous plant such as St. John's wort that grows in temperate regions in many cultivated forms. Genus: *Hypericum*. [15C. Via Latin < Greek *hupereikon* < *huper-* (see HYPER-) + *ereikē* "heath, heather"]

hy·per·in·fla·tion /hīpərin fláysh'n/ *n* very high, rapid monetary inflation that is great enough to threaten a nation's economic stability —**hy·per·in·flat·ed** *adj* —**hy·per·in·fla·tion·ar·y** *adj*

hy·per·in·su·lin·ism /hīpər ínssələ nìzzəm/ *n* an unusually high level of insulin in the blood, causing hypoglycemia

Hy·pe·ri·on /hī peéree ən/ *n* **1.** a large satellite of Saturn **2.** in Greek mythology, one of the Titans, son of Gaia and Uranus

hy·per·ker·a·to·sis /hīpər kerə tṓssiss/ *n* an excessive thickening of the outer layer of the skin —**hy·per·ker·a·tot·ic** /hīpər kerə tóttik/ *adj*

hy·per·ki·ne·sia /hīpər ki neézhə, -kī-/, **hy·per·ki·ne·sis** /-neéssiss/ *n* **1.** unusually increased movement in a muscle, e.g., in a spasm **2.** excessive activity in children, e.g., in those affected by attention deficit disorder [Mid-19C. < HYPER- + Greek *kinēsis* (see KINESIS) + -IA] —**hy·per·ki·net·ic** /hīpərki néttik, -kī-/ *adj*

hy·per·link /hīpər lingk/ *n* a word, symbol, image, or other element in a hypertext document that links to another element in the same document or in another hypertext document

hy·per·li·pe·mi·a /hīpərli peémee ə/, **hy·per·li·pi·de·mi·a** /hīpər lipi deémee ə/ *n* an excessive level of fats or lipids in the blood —**hy·per·li·pe·mic** *adj* —**hy·per·li·pi·de·mic** *adj*

hy·per·mar·ket /hīpər maarkət/ *n* a very large self-service store that sells products usually sold in department stores as well as those sold in supermarkets, e.g., clothes, hardware, electrical goods, and food [Late 20C. Translation of French *hypermarché*]

hy·per·me·di·a /hīpər meédee ə/ *n* a hypertext system that supports the linking of graphics, audio and video elements, and text. The World Wide Web has many aspects of a complete hypermedia system.

hy·per·me·ter /hī púrmətər/ *n* a line of poetry or a metrical foot that has one or more syllables in addition to those usually occurring in a metrical foot or completed line of verse [Mid-17C. Via late Latin < Greek *hupermetros* (see HYPERMETROPIA)] —**hy·per·met·ric** /hīpər méttrik/ *adj* —**hy·per·met·ri·cal** *adj*

hy·per·me·tro·pi·a /hīpərmə trṓpee ə/, **hy·per·met·ro·py** /-méttrəpee/ *n* MED same as **hyperopia** (*technical*) [Mid-19C. < modern Latin < Greek *hupermetros* "beyond measure" < *metron* "measure"] —**hy·per·me·tro·pic** /hīpərmə tróppik/ *adj* —**hy·per·me·tro·pi·cal** *adj*

hy·perm·ne·sia /hīpərm neézhə/ *n* an unusually powerful ability to remember exactly, sometimes a symptom of a psychiatric disorder [Mid-19C. < modern Latin, "condition of extreme memory" < Greek *mnēsis* "memory"] —**hy·perm·ne·sic** *adj*

hy·per·mo·bile /hìpər mṓ b'l, -mṓ bèel, -mṓ bìl/ *adj* BIOL same as **double-jointed** —**hy·per·mo·bil·i·ty** /-mō bíllətee/ *n*

hy·per·no·va /hípər nṑvə/ (*plural* **-vae** /-nṑvee/ or **-vas**) *n* a large, very energetic supernova that is believed to be a source of intense gamma-ray emissions

hy·per·nym /hípərnim/ *n* LING same as **superordinate** (sense 1)

hy·per·on /hípə ròn/ *n* a comparatively massive baryon that may be unstable or partially stable and is short-lived [Mid-20C. < HYPER- + -ON[1]]

hy·per·o·pi·a /hìpər ṓpee ə/ *n* far-sightedness —**hy·per·ope** /hípə rōp/ *n* —**hy·per·o·pic** /hìpər óppik/ *adj*

hy·per·os·to·sis /hìpər o stṓssiss/ *n* an unusual growth or thickening of bone [Mid-19C. < modern Latin, "condition of excessive bone" < Greek *osteon* "bone"] —**hy·per·os·tot·ic** /-o stóttik/ *adj*

hy·per·par·a·site /hìpər párrə sìt/ *n* a parasite living on another parasite —**hy·per·par·a·sit·ic** /-parə síttik/ *adj* —**hy·per·par·a·sit·ism** /hìpər párrəssi tìzzəm, -párrə sì-/ *n*

hy·per·par·a·thy·roid·ism /hìpər parə thí roy dìzzəm/ *n* an unusually high level of parathyroid hormone in the body, causing various disorders including kidney damage

hy·per·pha·gia /hìpər fáyjə/ *n* a condition in which somebody compulsively overeats over a long period —**hy·per·phag·ic** /-fájjik/ *adj*

hy·per·phys·i·cal /hìpər fízzik'l/ *adj* not governed by the natural laws of physics —**hy·per·phys·i·cal·ly** *adv*

hy·per·pi·tu·i·ta·rism /hìpərpi tóo itə rìzzəm/ *n* excessively high activity of the pituitary gland, sometimes causing unusual bodily growth —**hy·per·pi·tu·i·tar·y** *adj*

hy·per·plane /hípər plàyn/ *n* a figure in hyperspace that is the three-dimensional equivalent of a plane in ordinary space

hy·per·pla·sia /hìpər pláyzhə/ *n* unusual growth in a part of the body, caused by an excessive multiplication of cells —**hy·per·plas·tic** /-plástik/ *adj*

hy·per·ploid /hípər plòyd/ *adj* having an extra chromosome or section of a chromosome. In Down syndrome, there is an extra copy or segment of chromosome 21. —**hy·per·ploi·dy** *n*

hy·perp·ne·a /hìpər née ə, -pərp-/ *n* unusually deep or fast breathing, e.g., after physical exertion. UK spelling **hyperpnoea** [Mid-19C. < modern Latin, "extreme breathing" < Greek *pnoē* "breathing"] —**hy·perp·ne·ic** *adj*

hy·per·py·rex·i·a /hìpər pī réksee ə/ *n* a very high fever (*technical*) [Late 19C. < modern Latin, "extreme fever" < *pyrexia* (see PYREXIA)] —**hy·per·py·ret·ic** /hìpər pī réttik/ *adj* —**hy·per·py·rex·i·al** *adj*

hy·per·re·ac·tiv·i·ty /hìpər ree ak tívvətee/ *n* a condition of hypersensitivity resulting in an often severe reaction to a minimal stimulus, as happens, e.g., in asthma

hy·per·re·al·ism /hìpər rée ə lìzzəm/ *n* a style in the visual arts that uses realism to achieve a striking effect rather than photographic representation of real life —**hy·per·re·al·ist** *adj, n* —**hy·per·re·al·is·tic** /hìpər rée ə lístik/ *adj*

hy·per·sen·si·tive /hìpər sénssətiv/ *adj* **1.** very easily upset or offended **2.** showing a strong reaction to a drug, allergen, or other agent —**hy·per·sen·si·tive·ness** *n* —**hy·per·sen·si·tiv·i·ty** /-senssə tívvətee/ *n*

hy·per·sex·u·al /hìpər sékshoo əl/ *adj* interested in or engaging in sexual activity to an unusual extent —**hy·per·sex·u·al·i·ty** /hìpər sekshoo állətee/ *n*

hy·per·son·ic /hìpər sónnik/ *adj* relating to or moving at a speed of at least five times the speed of sound —**hy·per·son·i·cal·ly** *adv*

hy·per·space /hípər spàyss/ *n* **1.** space with more than three dimensions **2.** in science fiction, a theoretical dimension in which things not physically possible in ordinary space such as intergalactic travel can happen —**hy·per·spa·tial** /hìpər spáysh'l/ *adj*

hy·per·sthene /hípər sthèen/ *n* a green, brown, or black pyroxene mineral containing iron and magnesium [Early 19C. < French *hypersthène* "extremely strong (mineral)" < Greek *sthenos* "strength"] —**hy·per·sthen·ic** /hìpər sthénnik/ *adj*

hy·per·sur·face /hípər sùrfəss/ *n* a mathematical surface in hyperspace, analogous to a surface in three-dimensional space

hy·per·ten·sion /hìpər ténshən/ *n* **1.** unusually high blood pressure **2.** arterial disease accompanied by high blood pressure —**hy·per·ten·sive** /-ténssiv/ *adj*

hy·per·ten·sive ret·i·nop·a·thy *n* retinal changes resulting from local bleeding and impaired blood supply that threaten eyesight and even life. Hypertensive retinopathy indicates that blood pressure is excessively high.

hy·per·text /hípər tèkst/ *n* a system of storing images, text, and other computer files that allows direct links to related text, images, sound, and other data

Hy·per·Text Mark·up Lan·guage *n* full form of **HTML**

Hy·per·Text Trans·fer Pro·to·col *n* full form of **HTTP**

hy·per·ther·mi·a /hìpər thúrmee ə/ *n* unusually high body temperature, especially when induced for therapeutic reasons [Late 19C. < modern Latin, "condition of extreme heat" < Greek *thermē* "heat"] —**hy·per·ther·mal** *adj* —**hy·per·ther·mic** *adj*

hy·per·thy·roid·ism /hìpər thí roy dìzzəm/ *n* **1.** the overproduction of thyroid hormones at dangerously high levels **2.** the condition in which basal metabolism increases as a result of overactivity of the thyroid gland —**hy·per·thy·roid** *adj*

hy·per·ton·ic /hìpər tónnik/ *adj* **1.** describes a body part such as a muscle or artery that is under unusually high tension **2.** describes a fluid that has a higher osmotic pressure than another fluid —**hy·per·to·ni·a** /-tṓnee ə/ *n* —**hy·per·to·nic·i·ty** /hìpər tō níssətee/ *n*

hy·per·tro·phy /hī púrtrəfee/ *n* (*plural* **-phies**) **1.** ENLARGEMENT BY CELL GROWTH a growth in size of an organ through an increase in the size, rather than the number, of its cells **2.** UNNECESSARY COMPLEXITY exaggerated or unnecessary growth or complexity ■ *vti* (**-phied, -phy·ing, -phies**) GET BIGGER BY CELL GROWTH to grow larger through an increase in the size, rather than the number, of cells, or cause something to grow larger in this way —**hy·per·tro·phic** /hìpər trṓfik, -tróffik/ *adj*

hy·per·ven·ti·late /hìpər véntə làyt/ (**-lated, -lat·ing, -lates**) *vi* to breathe unusually deeply or rapidly because of anxiety or organic disease and in excess of the body's requirements, causing too much loss of carbon dioxide —**hy·per·ven·ti·la·tion** /hìpər venti láysh'n/ *n*

hy·per·vi·ta·min·o·sis /hìpər vìtəmə nṓssiss/ *n* a condition in which adverse effects are caused by taking in too much of one or more vitamins

hy·pes·the·sia *n* MED same as **hypoesthesia**

hy·pe·thral *adj* ARCHIT another spelling of **hypaethral** (*technical*)

hy·pha /hífə/ (*plural* **-phae** /-ee/) *n* a part of the vegetative portion of a fungus that resembles threads [Mid-19C. Via modern Latin < Greek *huphē* "web"] —**hy·phal** *adj*

hy·phen /hífən/ *n* a punctuation mark (-) used at the end of a line when a word must be divided or to link the parts of a compound word or phrase ■ *vt* (**-phened, -phen·ing, -phens**) GRAM same as **hyphenate** [Early 17C. Via late Latin < late Greek *huphen* "sign joining two syllables or words" < *hupo* "under" + *hen*, neuter of *heis* "one"]

USAGE Use of **hyphen**. A number of compound words and phrases are joined by hyphens: *thirty-seven; well-wisher; old-fashioned; mother-in-law*. For some the hyphens are optional, or inserted only when the word or phrase is used before a noun: *a coffee-table book; a well-timed attack* (but *the book on the coffee table; if the attack is well timed*). Most words with prefixes do not have a hyphen, exceptions being those where a capital letter follows the prefix (e.g., *pre-Christian*) and those where the word could be confused with another (e.g., *re-form* meaning "form again" as distinct from *reform*). A hyphen is sometimes inserted when a prefix ending in a vowel is added to a word beginning with a vowel (e.g., *co-opt, de-ice*). In writing and printing, a hyphen may also be used to show that a word has been broken at the end of a line. Note that the word must be divided between syllables (e.g., *stream-ing,* not *stre-aming*) and the hyphen is attached to the end of the first part, not the beginning of the second part. Ideally there should be at least two letters in each part of the divided word. See ***dash***.

hy·phen·ate /hífə nàyt/ (**-at·ed, -at·ing, -ates**) *vt* to separate or join words or parts of words using a hyphen —**hy·phen·a·tion** /hìfə náysh'n/ *n*

hy·phen·at·ed /hífə nàytəd/ *adj* **1.** split or joined by a hyphen **2.** belonging to a group of people identified in two ways that may be joined as one term e.g., "Irish Americans" (*offensive in some contexts*)

hypn- *prefix* same as **hypno-** (*used before vowels*)

hyp·na·gog·ic /hìpnə gójjik/, **hyp·no·gog·ic** *adj* in or relating to the state of drowsiness immediately before sleep [Late 19C. < French *hypnagogique* < Greek *hupno-* "sleep" + *agōgos* "leading" (see -AGOGUE)]

hyp·na·gog·ic im·age *n* something of the nature of a hallucination seen or imagined by somebody just before falling asleep

hypno- *prefix* **1.** sleep ○ *hypnopompic* **2.** hypnosis ○ *hypnoanalysis* [< Greek *hupnos* "sleep" < Indo-European]

hyp·no·a·nal·y·sis /hìpnō ə nálləssiss/ (*plural same* or **-y·ses** /-ə sèez/) *n* psychoanalysis carried out on people who are in a state of hypnosis —**hyp·no·an·a·ly·tic** /hìpnō anə líttik/ *adj*

hyp·no·gen·e·sis /hìpnō jénnəssiss/ *n* the process of inducing sleep or a state of hypnosis —**hyp·no·ge·net·ic** /hìpnōjə néttik/ *adj* —**hyp·no·ge·net·i·cal·ly** *adv*

hyp·no·gog·ic *adj* same as **hypnagogic**

hyp·noid /híp nòyd/, **hyp·noi·dal** /hip nóyd'l/ *adj* relating to, involving, or resembling sleep or hypnosis

hyp·nol·o·gy /hip nólləjee/ *n* the scientific study of sleep or hypnosis —**hyp·no·log·ic** /hìpnə lójjik/ *adj* —**hyp·nol·o·gist** *n*

hyp·no·pe·di·a /hìpnə péedee ə/ *n* same as **sleep-learning** (*technical*) [Mid-20C. < HYPNO- + Greek *paideia* "education"]

hyp·no·pom·pic /hìpnə pómpik/ *adj* involving, typical of, or in the state between sleeping and waking [Early 20C. < HYPNO- + Greek *pompē* "a sending away"]

Hyp·nos /híp nòss/ *n* in Greek mythology, the god of sleep [< Greek *Hupnos*, literally "sleep"]

hyp·no·sis /hip nṓssiss/ (*plural* **-no·ses** /-nō sèez/) *n* **1.** a condition that can be artificially induced in people, in which they can respond to questions and are very susceptible to suggestions from the hypnotist **2.** the technique or practice of inducing a state of hypnosis in people

hyp·no·ther·a·py /hìpnō thérrəpee/ *n* the use of hypnosis in treating illness, e.g., in dealing with physical pain or psychological problems —**hyp·no·ther·a·pist** *n*

hyp·not·ic /hip nóttik/ *adj* **1.** OF SLEEP OR HYPNOSIS producing sleep or hypnosis **2.** SUSCEPTIBLE TO HYPNOSIS susceptible to being hypnotized **3.** FASCINATING so fascinating that the attention of people watching or listening is absorbed completely (*informal*) ■ *n* **1.** SOMETHING CAUSING SLEEP a drug or other agent that causes sleep or drowsiness **2.** SOMEBODY EASILY HYPNOTIZED somebody who can be hypnotized easily [Early 17C. Via French *hypnotique* < Greek *hupnōtikos* "putting to sleep" < *hupnoun* "put to sleep" < *hupnos* "sleep"] —**hyp·not·i·cal·ly** *adv*

hyp·no·tism /hípnə tìzzəm/ *n* **1.** PSYCHOL same as **hypnosis** (sense 1) **2.** the theory and practice of hypnotizing people [Mid-19C. Shortening of *neuro-hypnotism* < HYPNOTIC]

hyp·no·tist /hípnətist/ *n* somebody who performs hypnosis

hyp·no·tize /hípnə tìz/ (**-tized, -tiz·ing, -tiz·es**) *vt* **1.** to put somebody into a state of hypnosis **2.** to fascinate or charm somebody utterly —**hyp·no·tiz·a·bil·i·ty** /hìpnə tìzə bíllətee/ *n* —**hyp·no·tiz·a·ble** *adj* —**hyp·no·ti·za·tion** /hìpnəti záysh'n/ *n* —**hyp·no·tiz·er** *n*

hy·po[1] /hípō/ *n* (*plural* **-pos**) a hypodermic injection, needle, or syringe (*informal*) ■ *vt* (**-poed, -po·ing, -pos**) to stimulate somebody or something to action in order to achieve some purpose or goal (*dated informal*) [Early 20C. Shortening of HYPODERMIC]

hy·po[2] /hípō/ *n* sodium thiosulfate, used in photographic processing as a fixing agent (*informal*) [Mid-20C. Shortening of *hyposulfite*, another name for thiosulfate]

hy·po[3] /hī́pō/ (*informal*) *n* a hypoglycemic episode, as sometimes experienced by people being treated with insulin ■ *adj* experiencing hypoglycemia [Shortening of *hypoglycemic*]

hypo- *prefix* **1.** under, below ○ *hypodermis* **2.** unusually low ○ *hypotonia* **3.** in a lower state of oxidation [< Greek *hupo* < Indo-European, "under"]

hy·po·a·cid·i·ty /hīpō ə síddətee/ *n* an unusually low level of acidity, especially in the stomach

hy·po·al·ler·gen·ic /hīpō àllər jénnik/ *adj* not likely to cause an allergic reaction

hy·po·blast /hī́pə blàst/ *n* **1.** the inner germ layer of an embryo, which develops into the endoderm **2.** BIOL same as **endoderm** (*dated*) —**hy·po·blas·tic** /hīpə blástik/ *adj*

hy·po·cal·ce·mi·a /hīpō kal séemee ə/ *n* an unusually low level of calcium in the blood —**hy·po·cal·ce·mic** *adj*

hy·po·cen·ter /hī́pə sèntər/ *n* ARMS same as **ground zero** (sense 1) —**hy·po·cen·tral** /hīpə séntrəl/ *adj*

hy·po·chlo·rite /hīpə kláw rìt/ *n* a salt or ester of hypochlorous acid

hy·po·chlo·rous ac·id /hīpə kláwrəss-/ *n* a weak unstable greenish yellow acid that occurs only in solution or in its salts. Source: dissolving of chlorine in water. Use: in bleach, disinfectants. Formula: HOCl.

hyp·o·chon·dri·a /hīpə kóndree ə/ *n* **1.** an excessive, usually long-term preoccupation with health and bodily sensations, accompanied by a deluded conviction of having a serious disease without objective evidence **2.** ANAT plural of **hypochondrium** [Mid-16C. < late Latin (plural) "upper abdomen" (formerly believed to be the seat of melancholy) < Greek *hupokhondrios* "under the cartilage of the breastbone" < *khondros* "cartilage"]

hy·po·chon·dri·ac /hīpə kóndree àk/ *n* SOMEBODY WITH IMAGINARY ILLNESS somebody who is unduly preoccupied with personal health and believes that illness is nearly always present or imminent ■ *adj* **1.** BELIEVING IN NONEXISTENT ILLNESS excessively preoccupied with health and persistently believing in a nonexistent illness, or relating to the attitudes or state of mind of somebody with this condition **2.** ANAT OF HYPOCHONDRIUM relating to, involving, or typical of the hypochondrium —**hy·po·chon·dri·a·cal** /hīpəkən drī́ ək'l/ *adj* —**hy·po·chon·dri·a·cal·ly** *adv*

hy·po·chon·dri·a·sis /hīpəkən drī́ əssiss/ (*plural* **-a·ses** /-ə seez/) *n* PSYCHOL same as **hypochondria** (sense 1)

hy·po·chon·dri·um /hīpə kóndree əm/ (*plural* **-dri·a** /-dree ə/) *n* the area of the upper abdomen on each side of the epigastrium below the lower ribs [Mid-17C. Back-formation < HYPOCHONDRIA (originally a plural form)]

hy·poc·o·rism /hī pókə rìzzəm, hīpə káw-/ *n* **1.** a pet name, especially a diminutive or abbreviated form of somebody's full name (*formal*) **2.** the use of a pet name to address somebody, instead of his or her full name [Early 16C. Via late Latin < Greek *hupokorisma* < *hupokorizesthai* "play the child" < *korē* "child"] —**hy·po·co·ris·tic** /hīpəkə rístik/ *adj* —**hy·po·co·ris·ti·cal** *adj* —**hy·po·co·ris·ti·cal·ly** *adv*

hy·po·cot·yl /hīpə kòtt'l/ *n* the part of an embryo plant lying between its cotyledons and its radicle [Late 19C. < HYPO- + COTYLEDON] —**hy·po·cot·y·lous** *adj*

~~**hypocrasy, hypocricy**~~ incorrect spelling of **hypocrisy**

hy·poc·ri·sy /hi pókrəssee/ (*plural* **-sies**) *n* **1.** the false claim to or pretense of having admirable principles, beliefs, or feelings ○ *It would be sheer hypocrisy for them to turn around and do what they criticize in others.* **2.** an act or instance of hypocrisy ○ *After his hypocrisies became widely known, he decided not to run for re-election.* [12C. Via Old French *ypocrisie* < Greek *hupokrisis* "acting a part" < *hupokrinesthai* "act a part" < *krinein* "to separate"]

hyp·o·crite /híppə krìt/ *n* somebody who pretends to have admirable principles, beliefs, or feelings but behaves otherwise [12C. Via Old French *ypocrite* < Greek *hupokritēs* "actor, pretender" < *hupokrinesthai* (see HYPOCRISY)]

hy·po·crit·i·cal /hìppə kríttik'l/ *adj* showing, originating from, or of the nature of hypocrisy ○ *It would be hypocritical of me to congratulate you on defeating me.* —**hyp·o·crit·i·cal·ly** *adv*

hy·po·cy·cloid /hīpə sī́ klòyd/ *n* in geometry, a curve traced by a point on the circumference of a circle as it rolls along the inside circumference of another circle —**hy·po·cy·cloid·al** /hīpə sī klóyd'l/ *adj*

hy·po·derm *n* BOT, ANAT same as **hypodermis**

hy·po·der·mic /hīpə dúrmik/ *adj* relating to or involving the area of tissue lying beneath the skin ■ *n* a hypodermic injection, needle, or syringe [Mid-19C. < HYPO- + Greek *derma* "skin"] —**hy·po·der·mi·cal·ly** *adv*

hy·po·der·mic in·jec·tion *n* an injection into tissue under the skin

hy·po·der·mic nee·dle *n* **1.** a thin hollow needle used with a syringe, suitable for administering hypodermic injections **2.** a hypodermic syringe to which a needle has been fitted (*informal*)

hy·po·der·mic sy·ringe *n* a plastic or glass syringe to which a thin hollow needle is attached, used to inject medicine under the skin or to withdraw fluids, especially blood, from under the skin

hy·po·der·mis /hīpə dúrmiss/, **hy·po·derm** /hīpə dùrm/ *n* **1.** TISSUE UNDER SKIN the layer of fatty tissue beneath the skin **2.** SKIN BENEATH ANIMAL'S SHELL the epidermis of some animals such as arthropods that secretes a shell or other outer covering **3.** CELLS UNDER PLANT SURFACE the usually supportive and protective layer of cells immediately under the outer covering of a plant [Mid-19C. < HYPO-, after EPIDERMIS] —**hy·po·der·mal** *adj*

hy·po·es·the·sia /hīpō iss théezhə/, **hy·pes·the·sia** /hīppə sthéezhee ə/ *n* an unusually reduced sensitivity to touch [Late 19C. < modern Latin, "condition of sensation being below normal" < Greek *hupo-* (see HYPO-) + *aisthēsis* "sensation"] —**hy·poes·thet·ic** /-théttik/ *adj*

hy·po·gas·tri·um /hīpə gástree əm/ (*plural* **-tri·a** /-tree ə/) *n* the part of the front of the human abdomen that lies below the navel [Late 17C. Via modern Latin < Greek *hupogastrion* "lower part of the belly" < *gastr-* "belly"] —**hy·po·gas·tric** *adj*

hy·po·ge·a ANCIENT HIST plural of **hypogeum**

hy·po·ge·al /hīpə jée əl/, **hy·po·ge·an** /-ən/, **hy·po·ge·ous** /-əss/ *adj* **1.** happening or living below ground **2.** describes a plant part that remains below ground while the stem of the plant grows [Late 17C. < late Latin *hypogeus* < Greek *hupogeios* "underground" < *gē* "ground, earth"] —**hy·po·ge·al·ly** *adv*

hy·po·gene /hīpə jeen/ *adj* describes rocks that are formed or lying beneath the Earth's surface —**hy·po·gen·ic** /hīpə jénnik/ *adj*

hy·pog·e·nous /hī pójjənəss/ *adj* on or growing on the underside of something such as a leaf. ◊ **epigenous**

hy·po·ge·ous *adj* same as **hypogeal**

hy·po·ge·um /hīpə jée əm/ (*plural* **-ge·a** /-jée ə/) *n* an underground room or space in an ancient building, or an ancient underground burial chamber [Mid-17C. Via Latin < Greek *hupogeion*, form of *hupogeios* "underground" (see HYPOGEAL)]

hy·po·glos·sal /hīpə glóss'l/ *adj* **1.** beneath or on the underside of the tongue **2.** relating to or involving the hypoglossal nerve [Mid-19C. < *hypoglossus* "hypoglossal nerve" < HYPO- + Greek *glōssa* "tongue"]

hy·po·glos·sal nerve *n* either of the 12th pair of cranial nerves that serve the muscles of the tongue

hy·po·gly·ce·mi·a /hīpō glī séemee ə/ *n* the medical condition of having an unusually low level of sugar in the blood —**hy·po·gly·ce·mic** *adj*

hy·pog·y·nous /hī pójjənəss/ *adj* describes a flower such as a buttercup that has its petals, sepals, or other parts situated below and apart from its ovary [Early 19C. < modern Latin *hypogynus* < *hypo-* "below" + Greek *gunē* "woman," used to mean "pistil"] —**hy·pog·y·ny** *n*

hy·poid gear /hī́ pòyd-/ *n* a gear often used in the transmission of motor vehicles, in which a hypocycloidal curve is used in arranging the meshing of the teeth [Early 20C. Origin ?]

hy·po·lim·ni·on /hīpə límnee òn, hīpə límnee ən/ (*plural* **-a** /-nee ə/) *n* the lower and colder layer of water in a lake, largely stagnant and remaining at a constant temperature (*technical*) [Early 20C. < HYPO- + Greek *limnion* "small lake" < *limnē* "lake"]

hy·po·ma·ni·a /hīpō máynee ə/ *n* a condition of mild mania or overexcitement, especially when part of a bipolar manic-depressive cycle —**hy·po·man·ic** /-mánnik/ *adj*

hy·po·nas·ty /hīpə nàstee/ *n* greater than normal growth on the underside of a plant part, causing the part to bend upward [Late 19C. < HYPO- + Greek *nastos* "pressed close, compact"] —**hy·po·nas·tic** /hīpə nástik/ *adj* —**hy·po·nas·ti·cal·ly** *adv*

hy·po·nym /hī́pənim/ *n* a word whose meaning is both narrower than and included in the meaning of a more general term. The words "tulip" and "rose" are hyponyms of "flower." —**hy·po·ny·my** /hī pónnəmee/ *n*

hy·po·phy·sec·to·my /hī pòffi séktəmee/ (*plural* **-mies**) *n* surgical removal of the pituitary gland

hy·poph·y·sis /hī póffəssiss/ (*plural* **-y·ses** /-ə seez/) *n* same as **pituitary gland** (*technical*) [Late 17C. Via modern Latin < Greek *hupophusis* "offshoot" < *phusis* "growth"] —**hy·po·phys·e·al** /hī pòffə sée əl, hīpə fízzee əl/ *adj*

hy·po·pi·tu·i·ta·rism /hīpōpi tóo itə rìzzəm/ *n* failure of the pituitary gland to produce hormones, especially a deficiency in growth hormone, which can result in dwarfism —**hy·po·pi·tu·i·tar·y** *adj*

hy·po·pla·sia /hīpə pláyzhə/, **hy·po·plas·ty** /hīpə plàstee/ *n* the failure of an organ or body part to grow or develop fully —**hy·po·plas·tic** /-plástik/ *adj*

hy·po·ploid /hīpə plòyd/ *adj* having a chromosome number slightly less than the diploid number —**hy·po·ploi·dy** *n*

hy·pop·ne·a /hī pópnee ə, hīpō née ə/ *n* breathing that is unusually shallow and slow [Via modern Latin < Greek *hupopnoia* < *pnoia* "breathing"] —**hy·pop·ne·ic** /hīpō née ik/ *adj*

hy·pop·noe·a *n* MED UK spelling of **hypopnea**

hy·po·sen·si·tiv·i·ty /hīpō senssə tívvətee/ *n* an unusually low sensitivity to stimuli such as allergens —**hy·po·sen·si·tive** /hīpō sénssətiv/ *adj*

hy·po·sen·si·tize /hīpō sénssə tīz/ (**-tized, -tiz·ing, -tiz·es**) *vt* to lower somebody's sensitivity to something, e.g., in the treatment of allergies —**hy·po·sen·si·ti·za·tion** /hīpō sènssəti záysh'n/ *n*

hy·pos·ta·sis /hī póstəssiss/ (*plural* **-ta·ses** /-tə seez/) *n* **1.** ESSENCE in philosophy, the essence or reality of something **2.** ONE ELEMENT OF TRINITY in Christian doctrine, one of the three parts of the Trinity **3.** ESSENTIAL NATURE OF JESUS CHRIST in Christian doctrine, the essential nature of Jesus Christ, in which the divine and the human are believed to be combined **4.** SETTLING OF BODY FLUID the settling of fluid in an organ or other part of the body, as a result of poor circulation, in patients kept in bed, and after death [Early 16C. Via late Latin < Greek *hupostasis* "sediment, foundation, essence" < *huphistasthai* "stand under, support" < *histasthai* "stand"] —**hy·po·stat·ic** /hīpə státtik/ *adj* —**hy·po·stat·i·cal** *adj* —**hy·po·stat·i·cal·ly** *adv*

hy·pos·ta·tize /hī póstə tīz/ (**-tized, -tiz·ing, -tiz·es**) *vt* to treat something conceptual as if it were real —**hy·pos·ta·ti·za·tion** /hī pòstəti záysh'n/ *n*

hy·po·style /hīpə stīl/ *adj* describes a classical building with a roof or ceiling that rests on many columns [Mid-19C. < Greek *hupostulos* "resting upon pillars" < *stulos* "pillar"] —**hy·po·style** *n*

hy·po·tax·is /hīpə táksiss/ *n* the subordinate status of one clause in relation to another separated from it by a subordinating conjunction. For example, in "I will go when I am ready," the relationship between "I am ready" and "I will go" is one of hypotaxis. [Late 19C. < Greek *hupotaxis* "subjection" < *hupotassein* "arrange under" < *tassein* "arrange"] —**hy·po·tac·tic** *adj*

hy·po·ten·sion /hīpō ténsh'n/ *n* unusually low blood pressure —**hy·po·ten·sive** *adj, n*

hy·pot·e·nuse /hī pótt'n òoss/ *n* the longest side of a right triangle, opposite the right angle. See illustration on next page [Late 16C. Via Latin *hypotenusa* < Greek *hupoteinousa* "(line) stretching under (the right angle)" < present participle of *hupoteinein* "stretch under" < *teinein* "stretch"]

hypoth. *abbr* **1.** hypothesis **2.** hypothetical

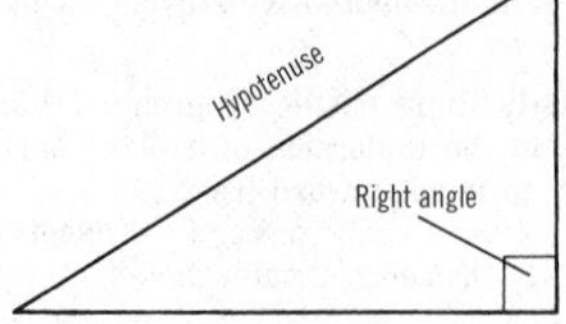

hypotenuse

hy·po·thal·a·mus /hīpə thálləməss/ (*plural* **-mi** /-mī/) *n* a central area on the underside of the brain, controlling involuntary functions such as body temperature and the release of hormones —**hy·po·tha·lam·ic** /hīpōthə lámmik/ *adj*

hy·poth·e·cate /hī póthə kàyt/ (**-cat·ed, -cat·ing, -cates**) *vt* **1.** to designate money, especially public revenue, to be used for a specific purpose **2.** to pledge property or goods as security for a debt without surrendering ownership [Early 17C. < medieval Latin *hypothecat-*, past participle of *hypothecare* < late Latin *hypotheca* "deposit" < Greek *hupothēkē* < *hupotithenai* "deposit as a pledge"] —**hy·poth·e·ca·tion** /hī pòthə káysh'n/ *n* —**hy·poth·e·ca·tor** *n*

hy·po·ther·mal /hīpō thúrm'l/ *adj* describes rocks and minerals formed deep underground at high temperatures

hy·po·ther·mi·a /hīpō thúrmee ə/ *n* **1.** dangerously low body temperature caused by prolonged exposure to cold **2.** lower-than-normal body temperature induced medically, e.g., to slow a patient's metabolism during heart surgery [Late 19C. < HYPO- + Greek *thermē* "heat"] —**hy·po·ther·mic** *adj*

hy·poth·e·sis /hī póthəssiss/ (*plural* **-e·ses** /-ə seez/) *n* **1.** THEORY NEEDING INVESTIGATION a tentative explanation for a phenomenon, used as a basis for further investigation ○ *The hypothesis of the big bang is one way to explain the beginning of the universe.* **2.** ASSUMPTION a statement that is assumed to be true for the sake of argument ○ *That is what would logically follow if you accepted the hypothesis.* **3.** ANTECEDENT CLAUSE in logic, the antecedent of a conditional statement [Late 16C. Via late Latin < Greek *hupothesis* "foundation, base" < *thesis* "placing"] —**hy·poth·e·sist** *n*

hy·poth·e·size /hī póthə sīz/ (**-sized, -siz·ing, -siz·es**) *vti* to offer something as a hypothesis, or form a hypothesis ○ *Let us, for the moment, hypothesize that the Earth is flat.* —**hy·poth·e·siz·er** *n*

hy·po·thet·i·cal /hīpə théttik'l/, **hy·po·thet·ic** /-théttik/ *adj* **1.** existing as or involving something that exists as an unproven idea, theory, or possibility ○ *the hypothetical existence of a Loch Ness monster* **2.** assumed or proposed for further investigation ○ *The question is purely hypothetical.* —**hy·po·thet·i·cal·ly** *adv*

hy·po·thet·i·cal im·per·a·tive *n* in philosophy, an imperative that depends on a condition, e.g., "be kind to people if they are kind to you"

hy·po·thy·roid·ism /hīpō thī royd ìzzəm/ *n* a deficiency in the production of thyroid hormones, or the slowing of the metabolic rate that results. A severe deficiency can result in sluggishness and weight gain (**myxedema**). —**hy·po·thy·roid** *adj*

hy·po·ton·ic /hīpō tónnik/ *adj* **1.** with low or diminished muscle tone or tension **2.** with a lower osmotic pressure than another fluid —**hy·po·to·nic·i·ty** /hīpōtō nissətee/ *n*

hy·po·ven·ti·late /hīpō véntə làyt/ (**-lat·ed, -lat·ing, -lates**) *vi* to breathe in an unusually slow and shallow way leading to a dangerous buildup of carbon dioxide in the blood —**hy·po·ven·ti·la·tion** /-ventə láysh'n/ *n*

hy·pox·ae·mi·a *n* MED UK spelling of **hypoxemia**

hy·pox·e·mi·a /hī pok seemee ə/ *n* inadequate oxygen in the blood [Late 19C. < HYP- + OXYGEN] —**hy·pox·e·mic** *adj*

hy·pox·i·a /hī póksee ə/ *n* an inadequacy in the oxygen reaching the body's tissues [Mid-20C. < HYP- + OXYGEN] —**hy·pox·ic** *adj*

hypso- *prefix* height ○ *hypsometer* [< Greek *hupsos*]

hyp·sog·ra·phy /hip sóggrəfee/ (*plural* **-phies**) *n* **1.** the measurement and mapping of the contours and elevations of natural features of Earth above sea level **2.** the depiction of the contours and elevations of the natural features on the surface of the land **3.** GEOG same as **hypsometry** —**hyp·so·graph·ic** /hìpsə gráffik/ *adj* —**hyp·so·graph·i·cal** *adj*

hyp·som·e·ter /hip sómmətər/ *n* **1.** an instrument that uses the boiling point of water at different altitudes to measure the elevation of a specific point on the Earth's surface **2.** an instrument for calculating the heights of trees by using the principles of geometric triangulation

hyp·som·e·try /hip sómmətree/ *n* the measurement of the elevation of land above sea level —**hyp·so·met·ric** /hìpsə méttrik/ *adj* —**hyp·so·met·ri·cal** *adj* —**hyp·so·met·ri·cal·ly** *adv* —**hyp·som·e·trist** *n*

hy·rax /hī ràks/ (*plural* **-rax·es** or **-ra·ces** /-rə seez/) *n* a small gregarious plant-eating mammal that resembles a rabbit with short ears and has toenails resembling hooves. Native to: Mediterranean, Southwest Asia. Family: Procaviidae. [Mid-19C. Via modern Latin < Greek *hurax* "shrew mouse"]

hy·son /hīss'n/ *n* a Chinese green tea [Mid-18C. < Chinese *xīchūn* "bright spring"]

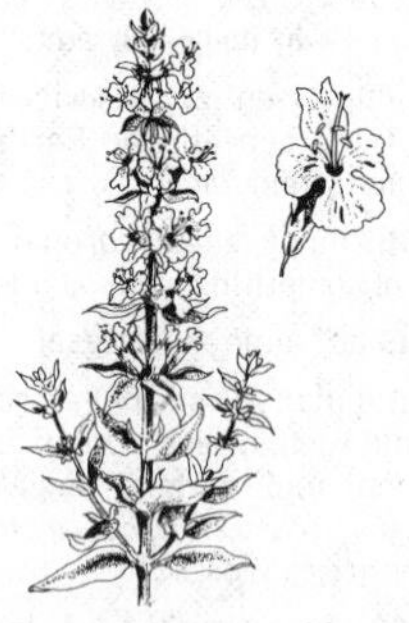

hyssop

hys·sop /híssəp/ *n* **1.** AROMATIC HERB a fragrant plant similar to mint. Flowers: fragrant, pink, white, or blue, in spikes. Use: in aromatherapy and alternative medicine. Native to: Europe, Asia. Latin name: *Hyssopus officinalis.* **2.** PLANT LIKE HYSSOP a plant related to or similar to true hyssop **3.** BIBLICAL PLANT an unidentified plant whose twigs are described in the Bible as being used to sprinkle water during Hebrew religious ceremonies [Pre-12C. Via Latin < Greek *hussōpos*]

hyster- *prefix* same as **hystero-** (*used before vowels*)

hys·ter·ec·to·my /hìstə réktəmee/ (*plural* **-mies**) *n* a surgical operation to remove a womb —**hys·ter·ec·to·mize** *vt*

hys·ter·e·sis /hìstə reessiss/ *n* a delayed response by an object to changes in the forces acting on it, especially magnetic forces [Late 19C. < Greek *husterēsis* "deficiency" < *husterein* "be behind, come late" < *husteros* "late"] —**hys·ter·et·ic** /hìstə réttik/ *adj*

hys·ter·i·a /hi steeree ə/ *n* **1.** EMOTIONAL INSTABILITY CAUSED BY TRAUMA an emotionally unstable state brought about by a traumatic experience **2.** STATE OF EXTREME EMOTION a state of extreme or exaggerated emotion such as excitement or panic, especially among large numbers of people ○ *media hysteria about the latest scandals* **3.** LAUGHING OR CRYING uncontrollable laughter or crying **4.** PSYCHIAT same as **conversion disorder** (*dated*) [Early 19C. < Latin *hystericus* (see HYSTERIC)]

CULTURAL NOTE ***Studies in Hysteria***, a book (1895) by Austrian psychologists Joseph Bauer and Sigmund Freud. A pioneering work in the field of psychoanalysis, it suggests that hysterical symptoms are the result of the memory's suppression of earlier traumatic events. The authors recommend that patients recall and confront these experiences in the hope of achieving catharsis.

hys·ter·ic /hi stérrik/ *n* somebody affected by hysteria (*dated; sometimes considered offensive*) ■ *adj* same as **hysterical** (senses 1–3) [Mid-17C. Via Latin *hystericus* < Greek *husterikos* "affected in the womb" < *hustera* "womb"]

hys·ter·i·cal /hi stérrik'l/ *adj* **1.** AFFECTED BY HYSTERIA in a state of hysteria ○ *hysterical with grief* **2.** RELATING TO HYSTERIA relating to, caused by, or subject to hysteria **3.** UNCONTROLLABLE impossible to hold back or control ○ *hysterical sobbing coming from the next room* **4.** EXTREMELY FUNNY causing uncontrollable laughter (*informal*) ○ *one hysterical sketch after another*

hys·ter·ics /hi stérriks/ *n* (*takes a singular or plural verb*) **1.** a state of uncontrollable laughter (*informal*) ○ *had them in hysterics with her stories* **2.** a state of hysteria, or an episode of hysterical behavior

hystero- *prefix* **1.** womb ○ *hysterotomy* **2.** hysteria ○ *hysterogenic* [< Greek *hustera* "womb" < Indo-European]

hys·ter·o·gen·ic /hìstərō jénnik/ *adj* bringing about a state of emotional instability or hysteria

hys·ter·on prot·er·on /hìstə ron próttə ròn/ *n* a figure of speech in which the order of words or phrases is the reverse of what is usual, e.g., "photographed in white and black" [Mid-16C. Via late Latin < Greek *husteron proteron* "latter first"]

hys·ter·ot·o·my /hìstə róttəmee/ (*plural* **-mies**) *n* a surgical incision into a womb, carried out especially in order to perform a cesarean section

Hz *symbol* MEASURE, PHYS hertz

I i

i[1] /ī/ (*plural* **i's**), **I** (*plural* **I's** or **Is**) *n* **1.** **9TH LETTER OF ENGLISH ALPHABET** the ninth letter of the English alphabet, representing a vowel sound **2.** **LETTER "I" WRITTEN** a written representation of the letter "i" **3.** **ROMAN NUMERAL** the Roman numeral for 1 ◇ **dot the i's and cross the t's** to be careful with the details of something ○ *We're in general agreement on the contract, but we still have to dot the i's and cross the t's.*

i[2] *symbol* **1.** one **2.** MATH imaginary unit

I[1] /ī/ *n* a syllable of special significance in Rastafarian theology. It combines the notions of self (I) and vision (**eye**). (*used in Black English*)

I[2] /ī/ *pron* a pronoun used by a speaker or writer to refer to himself or herself (*as the subject of a verb*) [Old English *ic* < Indo-European]

I[3] /ī/ (*plural* **I's** or **Is**) *n* something shaped like a letter "I"

I[4] *symbol* **1.** ELEC electric current **2.** CHEM ELEM iodine **3.** CHEM ionization potential **4.** QUANTUM PHYS isospin **5.** PHYS moment of inertia **6.** one **7.** LOGIC a particular affirmative categorical statement **8.** MATH unit matrix

I[5] *abbr* interstate

i. *abbr* **1.** DENT incisor **2.** indicate **3.** BANKING interest **4.** GRAM intransitive **5.** island **6.** isle

I. *abbr* **1.** Imperial **2.** (single column) inch (*in advertisements*) **3.** incumbent **4.** independence **5.** Independent **6.** Inspector **7.** Institute **8.** Instructor **9.** intelligence **10.** International **11.** interpreter **12.** Island **13.** Isle **14.** issue

-i- *infix* used as a connector to join word parts ○ *fossiliferous* [Via French < Latin]

IA *abbr* **1.** infected area **2.** Institute of Actuaries **3.** MAIL Iowa

Ia. *abbr* Iowa

-ia *suffix* **1.** place names ○ *Australia* ○ *India* **2.** plurals ○ *genitalia* **3.** diseases or medical conditions ○ *dyslexia* **4.** classes or genera, or a specific example of a genus ○ *Mammalia* ○ *gardenia* **5.** things belonging to or associated with something ○ *regalia* [Directly or via modern Latin < Latin and Greek]

IAA *abbr* **1.** indoleacetic acid **2.** International Advertising Association

IAAF *abbr* **1.** International Amateur Athletic Federation **2.** International Association of Athletics Federations

IAB *abbr* **1.** Industrial Advisory Board **2.** Industrial Arbitration Board **3.** Inter-American Bank

I·a·coc·ca /ī ə kṓkə/, **Lee** (*b.* 1924) US automobile executive. After a 32-year career at Ford, he became the president and chief executive officer of Chrysler Corporation (1978–92), which he helped rescue from failure. Full name **Iacocca, Lido Anthony**

> "The cement in our whole democracy today is the worker who makes $15 an hour. He's the guy who will buy a house and a car and a refrigerator. He's the oil in the engine."
> [Lee Iacocca, *Iacocca: An Autobiography*; 1985]

IACP *abbr* **1.** International Association of Chiefs of Police **2.** International Association of Computer Programmers

IADB *abbr* **1.** Inter-American Defense Board **2.** Inter-American Development Bank

IAEA *abbr* International Atomic Energy Agency

-ial *suffix* connected with or belonging to something ○ *secretarial* ○ *imperial* [Directly or via French < Latin *-ialis, -iale*]

IAM *abbr* **1.** Institute of Administrative Management **2.** internal auditory meatus

i·amb /ī̀ àm/ *n* a metrical foot of one short or unstressed syllable followed by one long or stressed syllable. "The plowman homeward plods his weary way" consists of five iambs. [Mid-19C. Anglicization of IAMBUS]

i·am·bi LITERAT plural of **iambus**

i·am·bic /ī ámbik/ *adj* relating to or consisting of iambs ■ *n* **1.** LITERAT same as **iamb** **2.** a poem or a line of poetry written in iambs (*often used in the plural*)

i·am·bic pen·tam·e·ter *n* the most common rhythm in English poetry, consisting of five iambs in each line. "The quality of mercy is not strained" is an iambic pentameter.

i·am·bus /ī ámbəss/ (*plural* **-bus·es** or **-bi** /-bī/) *n* LITERAT same as **iamb** [Late 16C. Via Latin < Greek *iambos* "iamb, lampoon" < *iaptein* "attack in words"]

-ian *suffix* belonging to, coming from, being involved in, or being like something ○ *Italian* ○ *Smithsonian* ○ *mathematician* [Directly or via French < Latin *-ianus*]

IAP *abbr* ONLINE Internet access provider

I·ap·e·tus /ī áppətəss/ *n* a natural satellite of Saturn, discovered in 1671. It is 892 mi./1,436 km in diameter and occupies an outer orbit.

IAS *abbr* **1.** COMPUT image analysis system **2.** COMPUT immediate access store **3.** AVIAT indicated air speed

Ia·şi /yaash, yáashee/ city and capital of the county of the same name in eastern Romania, situated on a tributary of the Prut River. Population: 346,613 (1997).

-iasis *suffix* a disease characterized by or caused by a particular thing ○ *filariasis* [< -I- + Latin or Greek *-asis*, suffix of state or process]

IATA /ī aátə/ *abbr* International Air Transport Association

-iatric *suffix* of a particular field of medicine ○ *psychiatric* [< Greek *iatrikos* < *iatros* "physician" < *iasthai* "heal"]

-iatrics *suffix* a particular field of medicine ○ *pediatrics*

i·at·ro·gen·ic /ī àttrə jénnik/ *adj* describes a symptom or illness brought on unintentionally by something that a doctor does or says ○ *iatrogenic disorders* [Early 20C. < Greek *iatros* "physician"] —**i·at·ro·gen·i·cal·ly** *adv*

-iatry *suffix* a particular field of medicine or medical treatment ○ *podiatry* ○ *psychiatry* [< Greek *-iatreia* "art of healing" < *iatros* "physician"]

IAU *abbr* **1.** International Association of Universities **2.** International Astronomical Union

IB *abbr* **1.** COMM in bond **2.** ARMS incendiary bomb **3.** COMM industrial business **4.** EDUC International Baccalaureate **5.** COMM invoice book

ib. *abbr* ibidem

IBA *abbr* **1.** CHEM indolebutyric acid **2.** LAW International Bar Association **3.** BANKING Investment Bankers' Association

I·ba·dan /ee baád'n, -daán/ city and capital of Oyo State, southwestern Nigeria, situated 89 mi./143 km northeast of Lagos. Population: 1,365,000 (1995).

I·ba·gué /éeba gáy/ city and capital of Tolima department, central Columbia, situated on a high plain at an altitude of 4,300 ft./1,311 m. Population: 334,100 (1992).

IBD *abbr* **1.** inflammatory bowel disease **2.** ENG ion-beam deposition

I-beam *n* **1.** a metal beam or girder that is shaped like a capital "I" in cross section **2.** *also* **I-beam cursor** a cursor shaped like a capital I that appears over text in Microsoft Windows applications

I·be·ri·a /ī béeree ə/ *n* **1.** the Iberian Peninsula **2.** ancient region in the Caucasus, roughly equivalent to present-day eastern Georgia

I·be·ri·an /ī béeree ən/ *n* **1.** a member of an ancient people who lived on the iberian peninsula or in the Caucasian state of Iberia **2.** somebody who comes from Spain or Portugal —**I·be·ri·an** *adj*

I·be·ri·an Pen·in·su·la /ī béeree ən-/ peninsula in southwestern Europe, divided into Spain and Portugal, together with Gibraltar

ibex

i·bex /ī bèks/ (*plural same* or **i·bex·es**) *n* a wild mountain goat with long knobby backward-curving horns. Native to: Europe, Asia, North Africa. Genus: *Capra*. [Early 17C. < Latin]

I·bib·i·o /i bíbbee ṑ/ (*plural same* or **-os**) *n* **1.** a member of a people living in southwestern Nigeria **2.** the Benue-Congo language of the Ibibio people. Native speakers: 2 million. [Early 19C. < Ibibio] —**I·bib·i·o** *adj*

ibid. /íbbid/ *abbr* ibidem

i·bi·dem /íbbi dèm/ *adv* used to cite the same book, publication, chapter, or page previously cited [Mid-18C. < Latin, "in the same place" < *ibi* "there" + *-dem* "that"]

ibis

i·bis /ībiss/ (*plural* **i·bis·es** or *same*) *n* a gregarious wading bird with a downward-curving beak. Native to: warm climates. Family: Threskiornithidae. [14C. Via Latin < Egyptian *hbj*]

I·bi·za /ee beéssə/ **1.** third-largest island in the Balearic Islands, Spain, situated in the western Mediterranean Sea approximately 60 mi./96 km from the eastern coast of the mainland. Area: 220 sq. mi./570 sq. km. **2.** seaport and capital of the island of Ibiza, situated 80 mi./129 km southwest of Palma. Population: 34,826 (2001). —**I·bi·zan** *adj, n*

I·bi·zan hound /i beéz'n-/ *n* a smooth-haired dog like a small German shepherd, with a light brown or reddish coat that is sometimes spotted. It belongs to a breed originally developed in the Balearic Islands for hunting.

-ible *suffix* same as **-able** ○ *audible* [< Latin *-ibilis*] —**-ibility** *suffix*

Ibn Sa·ud /ibbən saa o͝od, -sówd/, **Abdul Aziz,** (1880?–1953) king of Saudi Arabia. As the first king of Saudi Arabia (1932–53), he helped to found the Arab League (1945) and opened up his country's oil reserves.

I·bo /eé bō/ (*plural same* or **I·bos**), **Ig·bo** /íg bō/ (*plural same* or **-bos**) *n* **1.** a member of a people living in western Africa, especially in southeastern Nigeria. During the 1960s, the Ibo formed the breakaway state of Biafra. Fighting with Nigerian troops and severe famine led to enormous loss of life, and the Ibo capitulated in 1970. **2.** a language spoken in southern parts of Nigeria and in some areas of Niger, belonging to the Kwa group of Niger-Congo languages. Native speakers: 17 million. [Mid-18C. < Ibo] —**I·bo** *adj*

I·bra·him /eé braa heém/ *n* BIBLE Arabic name for **Abraham**

IBRD *abbr* International Bank for Reconstruction and Development

IBS *abbr* irritable bowel syndrome

AKG London

Henrik Ibsen

Ib·sen /íbss'n/, **Henrik** (1828–1906) Norwegian playwright. The pioneering psychological realism of such works as *A Doll's House* (1879) and *Hedda Gabler* (1890) had a profound impact on 20th-century drama. Full name **Ibsen, Henrik Johan**. See Cultural note at **master builder**

> "It's not just what we inherit from our mothers and fathers that haunts us. It's all kinds of old defunct theories, all sorts of old defunct beliefs, and things like that. It's not that they actually live on in us; they are simply lodged there, and we cannot get rid of them. I've only to pick up a newspaper and I seem to see ghosts gliding between the lines."
> [Henrik Ibsen, *Ghosts*; 1881]

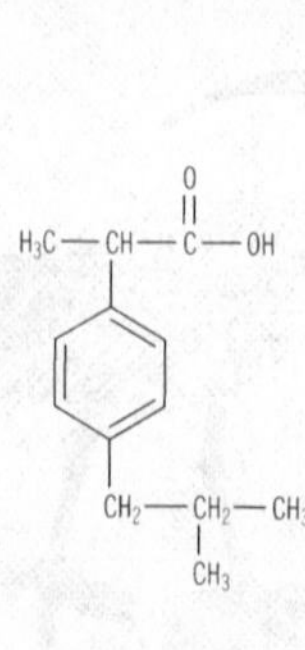

ibuprofen

i·bu·pro·fen /ībyoo prṓfən/ *n* a nonsteroid anti-inflammatory drug. Use: relief of pain and swelling, especially in arthritis and rheumatism. [Mid-20C. < ISO- + BUTYL + PROPIONIC + alteration of PHENYL]

-ic *suffix* **1.** of or relating to, having the nature of ○ *anarchic* ○ *Indic* **2.** with a valence that is higher than that of a related compound or ion ending in *-ous* ○ *cobaltic* [Directly or via French *-ique* < Latin *-icus* < Greek *-ikos*]

i/c *abbr* **1.** in charge (of) **2.** in command

ICA *abbr* **1.** International Coffee Agreement **2.** International Commodity Agreement **3.** International Cooperation Administration

ICAEW *abbr* Institute of Chartered Accountants in England and Wales

ICAO *abbr* **1.** International Civil Aeronautics Organization **2.** International Civil Aviation Organization

Ic·a·rus /íkərəss/ *n* **1.** in Greek mythology, the son of Daedalus, who drowned in the sea while attempting to escape from Crete after the sun melted his wings of wax and feathers **2.** an asteroid whose orbit is within 19 million mi./30 million km of the Sun, closer than any other orbiting object —**I·car·i·an** /i kéree ən/ *adj*

ICBM *abbr* intercontinental ballistic missile

ICC *abbr* **1.** Indian Claims Commission **2.** International Chamber of Commerce **3.** International Criminal Court **4.** Interstate Commerce Commission

ice /īss/ *n* **1.** FROZEN WATER water that has frozen into solid form ○ *puddles turning to ice* **2.** EXPANSE OF FROZEN WATER an area, layer, or body of frozen water ○ *a polar bear far out on the ice* **3.** SUBSTANCE LIKE ICE any substance resembling ice, e.g., the frozen form of carbon dioxide, known as dry ice **4.** PIECES OF FROZEN WATER ice, either crushed or in cubes, used to cool drinks or food **5.** UNFRIENDLINESS animosity or excessive formality between people ○ *The atmosphere turned to ice when her ex-husband walked in.* **6.** FROZEN DESSERT a dessert or snack of crushed ice flavored with sweetened juice **7.** HOCKEY, ICE SKATING SKATING SURFACE a prepared frozen surface for ice skaters or hockey players **8.** DIAMONDS diamonds, or jewelry, especially stolen merchandise or flashy diamond jewelry (*slang*) **9.** ILLEGAL DRUG a smokable form of methamphetamine used as an illegal drug (*slang*) ■ *v* (**iced, ic·ing, ic·es**) **1.** *vi* FREEZE UP to freeze and develop a thin coating of ice on the surface ○ *The bridge iced, making it dangerous.* **2.** *vt* PUT ICING ON FOOD to cover something such as a cake with icing **3.** *vt* COOL DRINK to chill a drink with ice, or stir ice cubes into a drink **4.** *vt* KILL SOMEBODY to kill another person (*slang*) **5.** *vt* HOCKEY SEND PUCK OUT OF DEFENSIVE TERRITORY to shoot a hockey puck out of defensive territory and far into the opposing team's territory **6.** *vt* MAKE CERTAIN OF SOMETHING to make certain of something, especially of winning a game (*slang*) ○ *They iced the game with a late field goal.* [Old English *īs* < Germanic] —**iced** *adj* —**ice·less** *adj* ◇ **break the ice** to ease the initial restraint or awkwardness of a meeting or social gathering ◇ **cut no ice** to fail to impress or make a difference ◇ **on ice 1.** in abeyance or in a state of being postponed ○ *We had so much work that we had to put the idea of a vacation on ice.* **2.** in a place of safekeeping (*slang*) **3.** being chilled in a freezer, refrigerator, or among ice cubes ◇ **on thin ice** in an unsafe, difficult, or vulnerable situation (*informal*)

USAGE ice or **iced**? For most cold beverages, ***iced*** is by far the more common form for the adjective: *iced tea, iced coffee. Ice beer* and *ice water* are exceptions; in the first the meaning is not that the drink is being served with ice but that ice figured in the production of it, and in the second the water may be turning into ice rather than poured over ice cubes.

ice over *vi* to become covered with a layer of ice ○ *As soon as the lake iced over, people were out there with their skates.*

ice up *vi* to become coated with a layer of ice ○ *The windshield will ice up if you don't put the car in the garage.*

ICE *abbr* **1.** ice, compress, elevation (*refers to first-aid treatment of injuries and bruises*) **2.** Institution of Civil Engineers **3.** internal-combustion engine **4.** International Cultural Exchange

ice age *n* a period in the Earth's history when temperatures fell worldwide and large areas of the Earth's surface were covered with glaciers

Ice Age *n* the most recent ice age during which most of the northern hemisphere was covered with glaciers, occurring during the Pleistocene epoch

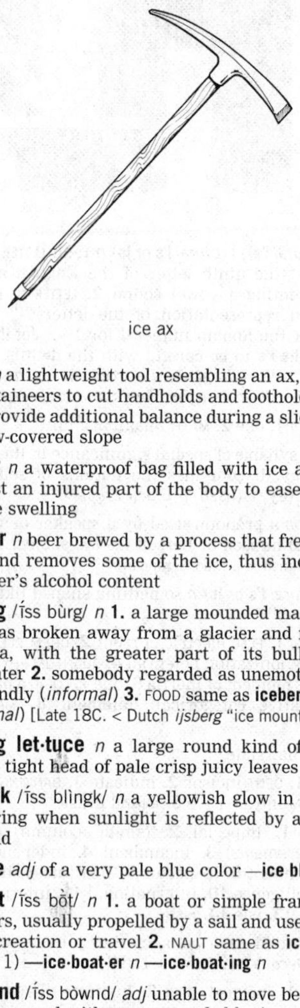

ice ax

ice ax *n* a lightweight tool resembling an ax, used by mountaineers to cut handholds and footholds in ice and provide additional balance during a slide down a snow-covered slope

ice bag *n* a waterproof bag filled with ice and held against an injured part of the body to ease pain or reduce swelling

ice beer *n* beer brewed by a process that freezes the beer and removes some of the ice, thus increasing the beer's alcohol content

ice·berg /īss bùrg/ *n* **1.** a large mounded mass of ice that has broken away from a glacier and floats in the sea, with the greater part of its bulk under the water **2.** somebody regarded as unemotional or unfriendly (*informal*) **3.** FOOD same as **iceberg lettuce** (*informal*) [Late 18C. < Dutch *ijsberg* "ice mountain"]

ice·berg let·tuce *n* a large round kind of lettuce with a tight head of pale crisp juicy leaves

ice·blink /īss blìngk/ *n* a yellowish glow in the sky, occurring when sunlight is reflected by a distant ice field

ice blue *adj* of a very pale blue color —**ice blue** *n*

ice·boat /īss bṑt/ *n* **1.** a boat or simple frame with runners, usually propelled by a sail and used on ice for recreation or travel **2.** NAUT same as **icebreaker** (sense 1) —**ice·boat·er** *n* —**ice·boat·ing** *n*

ice·bound /īss bòwnd/ *adj* unable to move because of being covered with or surrounded by ice

ice·box /īss bòks/ *n* **1.** same as **refrigerator 2.** an insulated container filled with ice and used to keep food and drinks cool and fresh

ice·break·er /īss bràykər/ *n* **1.** a ship with a reinforced bow used to break up ice and cut a passage through frozen navigable waters **2.** something used to ease the initial tension, restraint, or awkwardness of a meeting or social gathering, e.g., a joke or game

ice buck·et *n* a container in which ice cubes are kept cold, ready to be served in drinks

ice·cap /īss kàp/, **ice cap** *n* a thick permanent covering of ice and snow such as at the North and South Poles or on a mountain top

ice-cold *adj* extremely cold

ice cream *n* a sweet frozen dessert or snack traditionally made with cream and egg yolks and flavored with a variety of fruits or other extracts [Alteration of *iced cream*]

ice-cream chair *n* a wire chair with a round seat and without arms, formerly popular in ice-cream parlors and used in a variety of cafés

ice-cream cone *n* **1.** a hollow cone-shaped wafer designed to hold a serving of ice cream **2.** an ice-cream cone containing a serving of ice cream

ice-cream par·lor *n* a small store that sells ice cream to be eaten on or off the premises, typically having small tables and chairs for customers

ice-cream so·da *n* a refreshment consisting of ice cream in any kind of soda, sometimes with the addition of a flavored syrup, served in a tall glass

ice dancing: Jayne Torvill and Christopher Dean

ice danc·ing *n* figure skating in which a pair of skaters perform routines based on ballroom dancing, and in which lifts and separation are restricted in competition. Competitive ice dancing also requires that the two skaters remain in close physical contact throughout their routine.

ice·fall /íss fàwl/ *n* **1.** a waterfall that has frozen solid **2.** a face of a glacier on which the gradient is so steep that the ice breaks up into a jumble of blocks [After WATERFALL]

ice field *n* a large flat expanse of ice formed where the land surface is level, therefore making it easy for ice to accumulate

ice floe *n* a sheet of floating ice smaller than an ice field

ice fog *n* a fog that is made up of ice particles rather than water droplets

ice foot *n* a permanent band of ice along the coast of a polar region

ice hock·ey *n UK* SPORTS same as **hockey** (sense 1)

ice·house /íss hòwss/ (*plural* **-hous·es** /-hòwzəz/) *n* a building where ice is made, stored, and sometimes sold

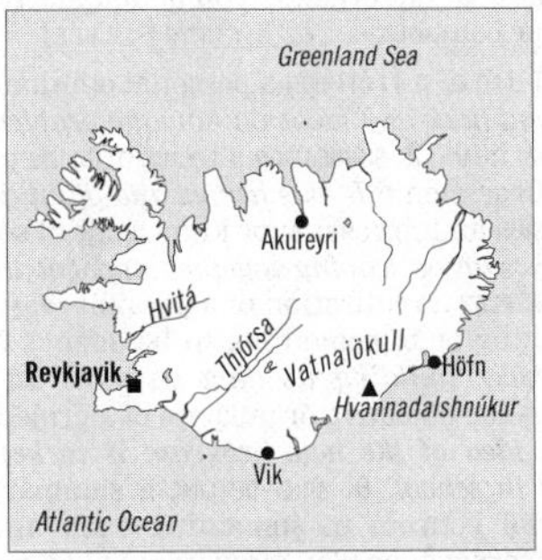

Iceland

Ice·land /íssland/ island country in the North Atlantic Ocean, 185 mi./300 km east of Greenland and 620 mi./1,000 km west of Norway. Language: Icelandic. Currency: króna. Capital: Reykjavik. Population: 280,798 (2003). Area: 39,800 sq. mi./103,000 sq. km. Official name **Republic of Iceland** —**Ice·land·er** *n*

Ice·land·ic /īss lándik/ *adj* **1.** OF ICELAND relating to Iceland, or its people **2.** OF ICELANDIC LANGUAGE relating to the North Germanic language of modern Iceland ■ *n* LANGUAGE OF ICELAND the North Germanic language of modern Iceland. Native speakers: 250,000.

LANGUAGE HERITAGE See ***Scandinavian.***

Ice·land moss *n* a grayish brown lichen grown as a food and also used medicinally. Native to: Arctic, northern Europe. Latin name: *Cetraria islandica.*

Ice·land pop·py *n* a poppy with leafless stems. Flowers: white, yellow. Native to: Arctic. Latin name: *Papaver nudicaule.*

Ice·land spar *n* a transparent form of calcite. Use: optical instruments.

ice ma·chine *n UK* same as **icemaker**

ice·mak·er /íss màykər/ *n* a machine that produces ice cubes, often built into a refrigerator

ice·man /íss màn/ (*plural* **-men** /-mèn/) *n* a dealer or deliverer of ice for public or commercial use

ice milk *n* a sweet frozen food like ice cream but made with skim milk

ice nee·dle *n* a tiny needle-shaped ice crystal that forms in cold moist air and gathers with others into masses resembling clouds, often at high altitudes and in otherwise clear weather

I·ce·ni /ī seé nī/ *npl* an ancient people of Britain who, under Queen Boudicca, attempted to overthrow the Romans in A.D. 61. The Romans fought off the Iceni and Boudicca committed suicide. [< Latin]

ice-out *n* a thawing of the ice covering a lake or other body of water

ice pack *n* **1.** an ice-filled cloth or bag held against an injured part of the body to ease pain or reduce swelling **2.** an area of pack ice

ice pick *n* a lightweight hand-held pick for chipping away or breaking up ice

ice plant *n* **1.** a clump-forming plant with thick pale-green leaves. Flowers: dark pink, flat-topped. Native to: Mediterranean. Latin name: *Sedum spectabile.* **2.** a low-growing plant with leaves that are covered with fine protruding sacs that glisten like ice crystals. Flowers: pink, white, resembling daisies. Native to: southern Africa. Latin name: *Mesembryanthemum crystallinum.*

ice point *n* the temperature, 0°C or 32°F, at which water freezes under a pressure of one atmosphere

ice road *n Can* a stretch of road that runs on a frozen body of water

ice sheet *n* a thick covering of ice over a large area that remains for a long period of time

ice shelf *n* a thick mass of ice covering coastal land and extending out over the sea so that the extended portion floats

ice show *n* an entertainment performed by skaters on ice

ice skate *n* a boot with a metal blade fixed along the length of its sole, allowing the wearer to glide over an ice-covered surface

ice skat·ing *n* the sport or pastime of using ice skates to glide over an ice-covered surface —**ice-skate** *vi* —**ice skat·er** *n*

ice storm *n* a rainstorm in conditions so cold that the rain freezes as it hits the ground, forming sheets of ice

ice wa·ter *n* **1.** very cold water or water chilled in a refrigerator or with ice cubes, served as a drink **2.** water produced when ice melts

ICFTU *abbr* International Confederation of Free Trade Unions

I Ching /eè jíng/ *n* **1.** an ancient Chinese system of divination, based on a book of Taoist philosophy and expressed in hexagrams chosen at random and interpreted to answer questions and give advice **2.** the book containing the symbols used in I Ching divination and an accompanying text that the reader may consult for help in interpreting the symbols [Late 19C. < Chinese, literally "Book of Changes"]

ich·neu·mon fly /ik nóomən-/, **ich·neu·mon wasp, ich·neu·mon** *n* a slender insect related to and resembling a wasp that is a parasite of many insect pests, laying its eggs in insect larvae. Family: Ichneumonidae. [Via Latin < Greek *ikhneumōn* "mongoose," literally "tracker" < *ikhneuein* "to track" < *ikhnos* "track, footprint"]

ich·nog·ra·phy /ik nóggrəfee/ (*plural* **-phies**) *n* **1.** the art or practice of drawing ground plans of the layout of buildings **2.** a ground plan of the layout of a building [Late 16C. Directly or via French < Latin *ichnographia* < Greek *ikhnographia* "track-drawing" < *ikhnos* "track, footprint"] —**ich·no·graph·ic** /iknə gráffik/ *adj* —**ich·no·graph·i·cal** *adj* —**ich·no·graph·i·cal·ly** *adv*

ich·nol·o·gy /ik nóllәjee/ *n* the scientific study of fossilized footprints [Mid-19C. < Greek *ikhnos* "track, footprint"] —**ich·no·log·i·cal** /iknə lójjik'l/ *adj*

i·chor /ī kàwr, íkər/ *n* **1.** a watery or slightly bloody discharge from a wound or an ulcer **2.** in Greek mythology, the fluid said to run instead of body fluid through the veins of the gods [Mid-17C. < Greek *ikhōr*] —**i·chor·ous** /íkərəss/ *adj*

ich·thus /íkthəss/, **ich·thys** /íkthiss/ *n* a simple symbol that resembles a fish, consisting of two curves that bisect each other. It is a symbol of Christianity. [< Greek *ikhthus* "fish"]

ichthy- *prefix* same as **ichthyo-** (*used before vowels*)

ichthyo- *prefix* fish ○ *ichthyology* [Via Latin < Greek *ikhthus* "fish"]

ich·thy·oid /íkthee òyd/ *n* a fish, or a vertebrate that is similar to a fish, e.g., a lamprey or hagfish —**ich·thy·oid** *adj* —**ich·thy·oi·dal** /íkthee óyd'l/ *adj*

ich·thy·ol·o·gy /íkthee óllәjee/ *n* the branch of zoology that deals with the scientific study of fish —**ich·thy·o·log·ic** /íkthee ə lójjik/ *adj* —**ich·thy·o·log·i·cal** *adj* —**ich·thy·o·log·i·cal·ly** *adv* —**ich·thy·ol·o·gist** *n*

ich·thy·oph·a·gous /íkthee óffəgəss/ *adj* eating or feeding on fish

ich·thy·or·nis /íkthee áwrniss/ *n* an extinct toothed bird, similar to a gull, that lived during the Cretaceous period. Genus: *Ichthyornis.* [Late 19C. < modern Latin < Greek *ikhthus* "fish" + *ornis* "bird"]

ich·thy·o·saur /íkthee ə sàwr/, **ich·thy·o·sau·rus** /íkthee ə sáwrəss/ (*plural* **-rus·es** or **-ri** /-rī/) *n* a prehistoric reptile with a long snout and paddle-shaped limbs that lived in the sea during the Mesozoic era. Order: Ichthyosauria. [Mid-19C. < modern Latin *Ichthyosauria* < Greek *ikhthus* "fish" + *sauros* "lizard"] —**ich·thy·o·sau·ri·an** /íkthee ə sáwree ən/ *adj*

ich·thy·o·sis /íkthee óssiss/ *n* a disease that causes the skin to become dry, thick, and scaly

ich·thys *n* CHR same as **ichthus**

-ician *suffix* somebody who practices or specializes in a particular thing ○ *musician* ○ *statistician* [< Old French *-icien* < *-ique* (see -IC)]

i·ci·cle /íssik'l/ *n* **1.** HANGING ICE a hanging tapered rod of ice, formed when dripping water freezes **2.** SOMEBODY VERY RESERVED somebody regarded as aloof or unemotional (*informal*) **3.** DECORATION ON CHRISTMAS TREE a decoration for Christmas trees resembling an icicle, made of a thin strip of foil or formed from plastic or glass [14C. < ICE + obsolete *ickle* "icicle" < Old English *gicel* < Germanic]

i·ci·ly /íssəlee/ *adv* in a very aloof or unfriendly manner

ic·ing /íssing/ *n* **1.** GLAZING OR FROSTING FOR CAKES a sugar-based decorative coating for cakes, either soft or hardened, made by mixing powdered sugar with water or another binding substance and often other ingredients or flavorings **2.** FORMATION OF ICE the formation of ice on exposed surfaces ○ *Some bridges and overpasses are more predisposed to icing than paved roads.* **3.** SHOOTING PUCK INTO OPPOSING TERRITORY in hockey, the action of shooting the puck out of defensive territory and far into the opposing team's territory ◇ **the icing on the cake** something additional that makes something that was already good even better

ic·ing sug·ar *n Can, UK* powdered white sugar used to make icing, for sweetening, or for sprinkling. US term **confectioners' sugar**

ICJ *abbr* International Court of Justice

Ick·es /íkəss/, **Harold L.** (1874–1952) US lawyer and public official. He was secretary of the interior under Franklin D. Roosevelt (1933–46). Full name **Ickes, Harold Leclair**

> "I am against government by crony."
> [Harold L. Ickes, *Remark*; February 1946]

ick·y /íkee/ (**-i·er, -i·est**) *adj* (*informal*) **1.** STICKY disgustingly and messily sticky **2.** NASTY generally nasty or unpleasant ○ *I had an icky feeling in their presence.* **3.** SENTIMENTAL sentimental in a silly or childish way ○ *a script with some pretty icky lines* [Early 20C. Origin ?] —**ick·i·ness** *n*

ICM *abbr* **1.** Institute of Credit Management **2.** Intergovernmental Committee for Migrations (*part of the UN*)

i·con /ī kòn/ *n* **1.** *also* **i·kon** IMAGE OF HOLY PERSON a holy picture, carving, or statue of Jesus Christ, the Virgin Mary, or a saint, especially an oil painting on a wooden panel, of a type revered in the Eastern Orthodox churches **2.** SOMEBODY FAMOUS FOR SOMETHING somebody or something widely and uncritically admired, especially somebody or something symbolizing a movement or field of activity ○ *the all-time rock'n'roll icon* **3.** PICTURE ON COMPUTER SCREEN a small image on a computer screen that represents something such as a program or device, that is activated by a mouse click ○ *Open the program by clicking on its icon.* **4.** RECOGNIZABLE SYMBOL a picture or symbol that is universally recognized to be rep-

icon: Eastern Orthodox icon of *Christus Acheiropoietus* in the Cathedral of the Assumption, Moscow

resentative of something **5.** SIGN a word or sign that stands for something else, e.g., the Roman numeral "II" representing the number two [Mid-16C. Via Latin < Greek *eikōn* "image"]

icon- *prefix* same as **icono-** (*used before vowels*)

i·con·ic /ī kónnik/ *adj* **1.** CHARACTERIZED BY FAME relating to or characteristic of somebody or something admired as an icon ○ *Their fame has grown to iconic proportions.* **2.** TYPICAL OF RELIGIOUS ICON relating to or characteristic of a religious icon ○ *iconic images* **3.** CONVENTIONAL made in a conventional style or pose, especially that of ancient Greek statues of athletes —**i·con·i·cal·ly** *adv*

i·con·ic mem·o·ry *n* a form of memory in which objects are retained briefly but clearly as a visual image after the stimulus has been removed. It develops between the ages of two and six, when a child begins to use images to stand for objects.

icono- *prefix* icon, image ○ *iconolatry* ○ *iconoscope* [< Greek *eikōn*]

i·con·o·clasm /ī kónnə klàzzəm/ *n* **1.** a challenge to or overturning of traditional beliefs, customs, and values **2.** the destruction of religious images used in worship, or opposition to their use in worship

i·con·o·clast /ī kónnə klàst/ *n* **1.** SOMEBODY CHALLENGING TRADITION somebody who challenges or overturns traditional beliefs, customs, and values **2.** DESTROYER OF RELIGIOUS IMAGES somebody who destroys religious images or opposes their use in worship **3.** HERETIC IN GREEK ORTHODOX CHURCH a member of an 8th-century movement in the Greek Orthodox Church that tried to end the use of icons [Mid-17C. Via medieval Latin < medieval Greek *eikonoklastēs* "image-breaker" < Greek *eikōn* "image"] —**i·con·o·clas·tic** /ī kònnə klástik/ *adj* —**i·con·o·clas·ti·cal·ly** *adv*

i·co·nog·ra·phy /ìkə nóggrəfee/ *n* **1.** SET OF RECOGNIZED IMAGES the set of symbols or images used in a particular field of activity such as music or the movies and recognized by people as having a particular meaning ○ *In the 1960s, peace signs, long hair, work shirts, and blue jeans were part of the iconography of rebellion.* **2.** SYMBOLS IN PAINTING the symbols and images used conventionally in a genre of painting, or the study and interpretation of these symbols and images ○ *the iconography used in Renaissance paintings of the Virgin and Child* **3.** IMAGES OF SOMEBODY OR SOMETHING SPECIFIC the collection, description, or study of images of somebody or something specific —**i·co·nog·ra·pher** *n* —**i·con·o·graph·ic** /ī kònnə gráffik/ *adj* —**i·con·o·graph·i·cal** *adj*

i·co·nol·a·try /ìkə nóllətree/ *n* the worshiping of religious images rather than of what they represent (*disapproving*) —**i·co·nol·a·ter** *n*

i·co·nol·o·gy /ìkə nólləjee/ *n* the study of artistic images and their symbolism and interpretation —**i·con·o·log·i·cal** /ī kònnə lójjik'l/ *adj* —**i·co·nol·o·gist** *n*

i·con·o·mat·ic /ī kònnə máttik/ *adj* using images to represent the sounds of the names of things rather than the things themselves, e.g., in the transition from pictorial to phonetic representation, seen in the history of some languages [Late 19C. Contraction of *icononomatic* < Greek *eikōn* "image" + *onomat-* "name"] —**i·con·o·mat·i·cism** /ī kònnə mátti sìzzəm/ *n*

i·con·o·scope /ī kónnə skōp/ *n* an early form of television camera tube in which an image is converted into electrical impulses

i·co·nos·ta·sis /ìkə nóstəssiss/ (*plural* **-ta·ses** /-tə seèz/), **i·co·nos·tas** /ī kónnə stàss/ (*plural* **-ta·ses** /-stàsseez/) *n* a screen on which icons are mounted, used in Eastern Orthodox churches to separate the area around the altar from the main part of the church [Mid-19C. < modern Greek *eikonostasis* "place where images stand"]

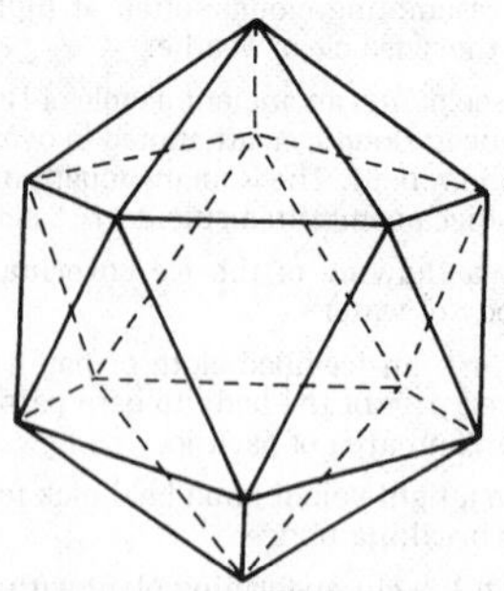

icosahedron

i·co·sa·he·dron /ī kòssə heédrən/ (*plural* **-drons** or **-dra** /-drə/) *n* a three-dimensional geometric figure formed of 20 sides or faces [Late 16C. Via late Latin < Greek *eikosaedron* < *eikosi* "twenty" + *hedra* "base"] —**i·co·sa·he·dral** *adj*

i·co·si·tet·ra·he·dron /ī kòssə tèttrə heédrən/ (*plural* **-drons** or **-dra** /-drə/) *n* a three-dimensional geometric figure formed of 24 sides or faces [Mid-19C. < Greek *eikosi* "twenty" + *tetra-* "four"]

ICQ *n* a computer program that makes contact with a user who is chatting online [Late 20C. After *ICQ* Inc., name representing "I seek you"]

ICR *abbr* **1.** Institute for Cancer Research **2.** COMPUT intelligent character recognition

ICRC *abbr* International Committee of the Red Cross

ICS *abbr* **1.** installment credit selling **2.** Institute of Chartered Shipbrokers **3.** International Chamber of Shipping **4.** international consultancy service

-ics *suffix* **1.** a science, art, or knowledge ○ *physics* ○ *mathematics* **2.** an activity or action ○ *calisthenics* [< -IC + -S; translation of Greek *-ika* (plural)]

ic·ter·us /íktərəss/ *n* MED same as **jaundice** (*technical*) [Early 18C. Via Latin < Greek *ikteros*] —**ic·ter·ic** /ik térrik/ *adj*

ic·tus /íktəss/ (*plural same or* **-tus·es**) *n* **1.** MED same as **seizure** (sense 2) (*technical*) **2.** the stress that falls on syllables in poetic rhythm [Early 18C. < Latin, "stroke" < past participle of *icere* "strike"] —**ic·tal** *adj*

ICU *abbr* HEALTH SERVICES intensive care unit

ic·y /íssee/ (**-i·er, -i·est**) *adj* **1.** ICE-COVERED covered in or involving ice **2.** VERY COLD extremely cold, like ice ○ *Your hands are icy.* **3.** UNFRIENDLY very aloof or unfriendly ○ *his reserved manner and icy voice* —**i·ci·ness** *n*

id[1] /id/ *n* in Freudian psychoanalytic theory, the part of the psyche that is unconscious and the source of primitive instinctive impulses and drives. The other parts of the psyche are the ego and the superego. [Early 20C. < Latin, "it"]

id[2] *abbr* ONLINE Indonesia (*used in Internet addresses*) See table at **domain name**

I'd /īd/ *contr* **1.** I had ○ *I'd forgotten you were coming.* **2.** I would or I should ○ *I'd leave now, if I were you.*

Id *n* ISLAM another spelling of **Eid**

ID[1] *abbr* **1.** MAIL Idaho **2.** MED infectious disease(s) **3.** *also* **i.d.** MED intradermal

ID[2] *n* material or an official document that identifies somebody ■ *vt* (**IDed, ID·ing, IDs**) to identify somebody or check somebody's identity (*informal*) ○ *police to ID the suspect* [Abbreviation IDENTIFICATION]

id. *abbr* idem

Id. *abbr* Idaho

-id *suffix* **1.** objects, especially meteors, that appear to come from a particular constellation ○ *Perseids* **2.** particular kinds of particle or body ○ *plastid* **3.** a member of a zoological family ○ *camelid* **4.** a member of a dynasty ○ *Abbasid* [Directly or via French *-ide* < Latin *-ides* < Greek *-idēs* "offspring of"]

IDA *abbr* International Development Association

Ida. *abbr* Idaho

I·da·ho /īdə hō/ state in the western United States bordered by Montana, Nevada, Oregon, Utah, Washington, and Wyoming, and British Columbia, Canada. Capital: Boise. Population: 1,341,131 (2002 estimate). Area: 83,574 sq. mi./216,456 sq. km. —**I·da·ho·an** *adj, n*

Idaho

I·da·ho Falls city in southeastern Idaho, on the Snake River, northeast of Pocatello. Population: 51,096 (2002 estimate).

I·da·ho rain·storm *n regional* a dust storm (*humorous*)

Id al-Ad·ha, etc. *n* ISLAM another spelling of **Eid al-Adha, etc.**

I·da Mountains /īdə-/ mountain range in northwestern Turkey, southeast of the ancient site of Troy. The highest peak is Mount Gargarus, 5,797 ft./1,767 m.

IDB *abbr* **1.** Industrial Development Bank **2.** Inter-American Development Bank

ID card *n* a card identifying its carrier, having on it information such as name, age, and often an address and a physical description or photograph (*informal*)

IDD *abbr* **1.** MED insulin-dependent diabetes **2.** TELECOM international direct dialing

IDDD *abbr* international direct distance dialing

-ide *suffix* **1.** a class of elements or compounds ○ *actinides* **2.** an organic compound derived from another compound ○ *anhydride* [< OXIDE]

i·de·a /ī deé ə/ *n* **1.** OPINION a personal opinion or belief ○ *Do you have any ideas on how the problem should be dealt with?* **2.** SUGGESTION a thought to be presented as a suggestion ○ *It was her idea to plant daisies.* **3.** IMPRESSION an impression or knowledge of something ○ *They saw us leaving together and got the wrong idea.* **4.** PLAN a realization of a possible way of doing something or of something to be done ○ *Watching the beaver building its dam gave me an idea.* **5.** OBJECTIVE the objective or purpose of a project or plan ○ *The idea of the new program is to keep young people in school.* **6.** BRIEF OUTLINE a summary or the essential concept of something such as a book, report, project, or plan ○ *give you only a broad idea now, with a detailed outline to follow* **7.** THOUGHT a thought about or mental picture of something such as a future or possible event ○ *Sometimes the idea of having to speak in public is worse than actually doing it.* **8.** CONCEPT a concept that exists in the mind only ○ *discussing the idea of morality* **9.** MENTAL IMAGE a mental image that reflects reality [14C. Via Latin < Greek, "look" < *idein* "to see"] —**ide·a·less** *adj* ◇ **get ideas** to become ambitious or begin thinking undesirable thoughts (*informal*) ◇ **have no idea** to know nothing at all, especially about a particular subject ◇ **what's the big idea?** used, often angrily, to ask about somebody's intention or about what is happening

i·de·al /ī deé əl/ *n* **1.** PERFECT EXAMPLE an excellent or perfect example of something or somebody, or something that is considered a perfect example ○ *By her third movie, she had become the world's ideal of beauty and grace.* **2.** PRINCIPLE a standard or principle to which people aspire ○ *political ideals* **3.** IMAGINARY OBJECT OR CONCEPT a concept that exists in the imagination only ■ *adj* **1.** BEST serving as the best or most perfect example **2.** PERFECT perfect but existing only in the imagination ○ *In an ideal world, such horrors wouldn't happen.* **3.** EXCELLENT excellent or perfectly suitable ○ *A later meeting would be ideal for me.* [15C. Directly or via French < late Latin *idealis* < Latin *idea* (see IDEA)] —**ide·al·less** *adj* —**ide·al·ness** *n*

USAGE See *idyll.*

i·de·al gas *n* a hypothetical gas that obeys the gas laws perfectly at all temperatures and pressures

i·de·al·ism /ī dée ə lìzzəm/ *n* 1. BELIEF IN PERFECTION belief in and pursuit of perfection as an attainable goal ○ *youthful idealism* 2. LIVING BY HIGH IDEALS aspiring to or living in accordance with high standards or principles 3. BELIEF THAT MATERIAL THINGS ARE IMAGINARY the philosophical belief that material things do not exist independently but only as constructions in the mind

i·de·al·ist /ī dée əlist/ *n* 1. IMPRACTICAL PERSON a perfectionist who rejects practical considerations ○ *too much of an idealist to compromise with her opponents* 2. SOMEBODY WITH HIGH IDEALS somebody who aspires to or abides by high standards or principles 3. PHILOSOPHY BELIEVER IN IDEALISM a believer in a philosophy holding that material objects do not exist independently of the mind —**i·de·al·is·tic** /ī dée ə lístik/ *adj* —**i·de·al·is·ti·cal·ly** *adv*

i·de·al·i·ty /ìdee állətee/ *n* 1. the condition or quality of being ideal 2. existence as an idea only, rather than as a concrete object

i·de·al·ize /ī dée ə lìz/ (**-ized, -iz·ing, -iz·es**) *v* 1. *vt* to think of or represent somebody or something as being perfect, ignoring any imperfections that exist or may exist in reality ○ *paintings that idealize feminine beauty* 2. *vi* to form ideals in the mind ○ *He has a tendency to idealize.* —**i·de·al·i·za·tion** /ī dèe əli záysh'n/ *n* —**i·de·al·ized** *adj* —**i·de·al·iz·er** *n*

i·de·al·ly /ī dée əlee/ *adv* 1. IN IDEAL SITUATION if everything were perfect or as desired ○ *Ideally, I'd like to finish the job by next week.* 2. PERFECTLY in a perfect manner ○ *She is ideally suited to the post.* 3. THEORETICALLY in theory or in the imagination ○ *Ideally, there would be no prejudice or persecution in the world.*

~~**idealy**~~ incorrect spelling of **ideally**

i·de·ate /ìdee àyt/ (**-at·ed, -at·ing, -ates**) *vti* to form an idea of something, or form ideas [Early 17C. < medieval Latin *ideat-*, past participle of *ideare* "form an idea" < Latin *idea* (see IDEA)] —**i·de·a·tion** /ìdee áysh'n/ *n* —**i·de·a·tion·al** *adj* —**i·de·a·tion·al·ly** *adv* —**i·de·a·tive** /ìdee ətiv, -àytiv/ *adj*

i·dée fixe /ee dày féeks/ (*plural* **i·dées fixes** /*pronunc. same*/) *n* an idea that remains fixed and unchanging in the mind and often becomes an obsession [< French, "fixed idea"]

i·dée re·çue /ee dày rə sóo, -sǘ/ (*plural* **i·dées re·çues** /*pronunc. same*/) *n* a conventional or commonplace idea [< French, "received idea"]

i·dem /í dèm, í dèm/ *pron* the same, especially a book, article, or chapter previously referred to [14C. < Latin (see IDENTITY)]

i·dem·po·tent /ī dem pōt'nt, ì dem-/ *adj* describes a mathematical quantity that remains unchanged when multiplied by itself [Late 19C. < Latin *idem* (see IDENTITY) + *potent-* "powerful"]

i·den·tic /ī déntik/ *adj* describes diplomatic notes sent, or diplomatic action taken, by two or more governments in exactly the same form [Mid-17C. < medieval Latin *identicus* "identical" < *ident-* (see IDENTITY)]

i·den·ti·cal /ī déntik'l/ *adj* 1. exactly the same as or equal to something else, or alike in every respect ○ *wearing identical dresses* ○ *His name was identical to mine.* 2. describes twins of the same sex and with the same genetic makeup that have developed from a single fertilized egg —**i·den·ti·cal·ly** *adv* —**i·den·ti·cal·ness** *n*

i·den·ti·cal rhyme *n* 1. perfect rhyme of a whole syllable, including consonants and vowels, e.g., "describe" and "inscribe" 2. LITERAT same as **rime riche**

~~**identicle**~~ incorrect spelling of **identical**

i·den·ti·fi·ca·tion /ī dèntəfi káysh'n/ *n* 1. NAMING SOMEBODY the action of identifying somebody or something, or an act of recognizing and naming somebody or something 2. PROOF OF IDENTITY something, especially a card or document, to prove that somebody is who he or she claims to be 3. STRONG FEELING OF AFFINITY a powerful feeling of affinity with another person or group, which sometimes involves regarding somebody as a model and adopting his or her beliefs, values, or other characteristics

i·den·ti·fi·ca·tion card *n* a small card holding information sufficient to prove that a claim or description of somebody bearing it is accurate

i·den·ti·fi·ca·tion pa·rade *n UK* CRIME same as **lineup** (sense 3)

i·den·ti·fi·er /ī déntə fì ər/ *n* a symbol that identifies, indicates, or names a body of data

i·den·ti·fy /ī dénti fì/ (**-fied, -fy·ing, -fies**) *vt* 1. to recognize somebody or something and to be able to say who or what he, she, or it is 2. to consider two or more things as being entirely or essentially the same [Mid-17C. Directly or via French *identifier* < medieval Latin *identificare* "make the same" < *ident-* (see IDENTITY)] —**i·den·ti·fi·a·bil·i·ty** /ī dènti fì ə bíllətee/ *n* —**i·den·ti·fi·a·ble** *adj* —**i·den·ti·fi·a·bly** *adv*

identify with *vi* 1. to feel a strong sympathetic or imaginative bond with somebody or something and a sense of understanding and sharing his, her, or its nature or concerns 2. to consider somebody or something as closely linked with somebody or something such as a school of thought or political movement (*often passive*)

i·den·ti·ty /ī déntətee/ (*plural* **-ties**) *n* 1. WHAT IDENTIFIES SOMEBODY OR SOMETHING the name or essential character that identifies somebody or something 2. ESSENTIAL SELF the set of characteristics that somebody recognizes as belonging uniquely to himself or herself and constituting his or her individual personality for life 3. SAMENESS the fact or condition of being the same or exactly alike 4. MATH EQUATION TRUE FOR ALL ITS VARIABLES a mathematical equation that remains valid whatever values are taken by its variables 5. MATH same as **identity element** [Late 16C. < late Latin *identitas* < *ident-*, combining form of Latin *idem* "same" < *id* "that"]

i·den·ti·ty card *n UK* same as **identification card**

i·den·ti·ty cri·sis *n* 1. a period during which somebody feels great anxiety and uncertainty about his or her identity and role in life and society, typically experienced in adolescence or middle age 2. a period of anxiety or confusion about the nature, aims, and role of a group, organization, or business

i·den·ti·ty el·e·ment *n* an element of a mathematical set that leaves other elements unchanged when combined with them

i·den·ti·ty ma·trix *n* a square matrix that has the numeral 1 in each position on the principal diagonal and 0 in all other positions

i·den·ti·ty theft *n* theft of personal information such as somebody's credit card details

ideo- *prefix* ideas ○ *ideomotor* [Via French < Greek *idea* (see IDEA)]

id·e·o·gram /ìdee ə gràm, íddee-/, **id·e·o·graph** /-gràf/ *n* 1. a symbol used in some writing systems, e.g., those of Japan and China, that directly but abstractly represents a thing or concept itself rather than the word for it 2. a symbol or graphic character used to represent a word, e.g., "@" or "&" —**id·e·o·gram·mat·ic** /ìdee əgrə máttik, iddee-/ *adj* —**id·e·o·gram·mat·i·cal·ly** *adv* —**id·e·o·graph·ic** /ìdee ə gráffik, iddee-/ *adj* —**id·e·o·graph·i·cal·ly** *adv* —**id·e·og·ra·phy** /ìdee óggrəfee, iddee-/ *n*

i·de·o·logue /ìdee ə lòg, íddee-/ *n* a particularly zealous or doctrinaire supporter of an ideology

i·de·ol·o·gy /ìdee óllәjee, iddee-/ (*plural* **-gies**) *n* 1. a closely organized system of beliefs, values, and ideas forming the basis of a social, economic, or political philosophy or program 2. a set of beliefs, values, and opinions that shapes the way a person or a group such as a social class thinks, acts, and understands the world —**i·de·o·log·i·cal** /ìdee ə lójjik'l, iddee-/ *adj* —**i·de·ol·o·gist** *n*

i·de·o·mo·tor /ìdee ə mōtər, iddee-/ *adj* describes body movements triggered by thoughts rather than by external stimuli

ides /īdz/, **Ides** *n* in the ancient Roman calendar, the 15th day of March, May, July, and October, or the 13th day of any other month (*takes a singular or plural verb*) [12C. Directly or via French < Latin *idus* (plural)]

id·gah /íd gaà/ *n S Asia* a mosque or other place of prayer for Muslims [< Arabic *id* "place" + Persian *gah* "prayer"]

-idine *suffix* a chemical compound related to another compound ○ *histidine* [< -IDE + -INE]

idio- *prefix* private, individual, proper, or distinctive ○ *idiolect* ○ *idiomorphic* [< Greek *idios* "your own, private" < Indo-European, "self"]

id·i·o·blast /íddee ə blàst/ *n* a specialized plant cell that differs from others in the same area of tissue. An idioblast is usually thick-walled and lacks chlorophyll. —**id·i·o·blas·tic** /iddee ə blástik/ *adj*

id·i·o·cy /íddee əssee/ *n* 1. an offensive term meaning extreme lack of intelligence or foresight 2. an offensive term for an extremely unintelligent or thoughtless act 3. an offensive term in a now disused classification system for mental disability (*dated*) [Early 16C. < IDIOT]

id·i·o·glos·si·a /iddee ə glóssee ə/ *n* 1. a developmental speech difficulty in which a child substitutes different sounds for the correct ones, so that speech is intelligible only to parents or others familiar with it 2. the invention and use by a child or closely involved siblings of language that is unintelligible to anyone else [Late 19C. < Greek *idioglōssos* < *idios* "distinct" + *glōssa* "tongue"]

id·i·o·gram /íddee ə gràm/ *n* a photograph or diagram showing the chromosomes of a cell or organism arranged in their homologous pairs according to the standard numbering system for that organism

id·i·o·graph·ic /iddee ə gráffik/ *adj* concentrating on specific cases and the unique traits or functioning of individuals, rather than on broad generalizations about human behavior. Idiographic research methods in psychology include the case study, which is characterized by the distinctiveness of each case.

id·i·o·lect /íddee ə lèkt/ *n* an individual person's vocabulary and unique way of using language [Mid-20C. < IDIO- + DIALECT] —**id·i·o·lec·tal** /iddee ə lékt'l/ *adj*

SYNONYMS See ***language***.

id·i·om /íddee əm/ *n* 1. FIXED EXPRESSION WITH NONLITERAL MEANING a fixed distinctive expression whose meaning cannot be deduced from the combined meanings of its actual words 2. NATURAL WAY OF USING LANGUAGE the way of using a language that comes naturally to its native speakers 3. STYLISTIC EXPRESSION the style of expression of a specific person or group 4. DISTINGUISHING ARTISTIC STYLE the characteristic style of an artist or artistic group [Late 16C. Directly or via French < late Latin *idioma* < Greek, "property, peculiarity" < *idios* (see IDIO-)]

SYNONYMS See ***jargon***[1].

id·i·o·mat·ic /iddee ə máttik/, **id·i·o·mat·i·cal** /-máttik'l/ *adj* 1. CHARACTERISTIC OF NATIVE-SPEAKER USE characteristic of, or in keeping with, the way a language is ordinarily and naturally used by its native speakers 2. OF NATURE OF IDIOM having a meaning not deducible from the combined meanings of the constituent words ○ *an idiomatic phrase* 3. CHARACTERISTIC OF STYLE characteristic of a specific style, or using a distinctive style, especially in the arts —**id·i·o·mat·i·cal·ly** *adv*

id·i·o·mor·phic /iddee ə máwrfik/ *adj* describes minerals that occur naturally in the form of fully developed crystals —**id·i·o·mor·phi·cal·ly** *adv* —**id·i·o·mor·phism** *n*

id·i·o·path·ic /iddee ə páthik/ *adj* describes a disease or disorder that has no known cause —**id·i·o·path·i·cal·ly** *adv* —**id·i·op·a·thy** /iddee óppəthee/ *n*

id·i·o·phone /íddee ə fōn/ *n* a percussion instrument that is made from resonating material that does not have to be tuned e.g., a gong or xylophone —**id·i·o·phon·ic** /iddee ə fónnik/ *adj*

~~**idiosyncracy**~~ incorrect spelling of **idiosyncrasy**

id·i·o·syn·cra·sy /iddee ə síngkrəssee/ (*plural* **-sies**) *n* 1. a way of behaving, thinking, or feeling that is peculiar to an individual or group, especially an odd or unusual one 2. an unusual or exaggerated reaction to a drug or food that is not caused by an allergy [Early 17C. Directly or via French *idiosyncrasie* < Greek *idiosugkrasia*, literally "personal mixing together" < *krasis* "mixing"] —**id·i·o·syn·crat·ic** /-ə sing kráttik/ *adj* —**id·i·o·syn·crat·i·cal·ly** *adv*

id·i·ot /íddee ət/ *n* 1. an offensive term that deliberately insults somebody's intelligence (*insult*) 2. an offensive term in a now disused classification system for somebody with an IQ of about 25 or under and a mental age of less than 3 years (*dated*) [14C. Via French and Latin < Greek *idiōtēs* "private person, layperson" < *idios* (see IDIO-)]

id·i·ot board *n* a placard, projector, or continuous

roll of paper that prompts a television performer with lines to be spoken (*slang*)

id·i·ot box *n* television, or a television set (*slang*) [< the belief that watching too much television causes stupidity]

id·i·ot card *n* MEDIA same as **idiot board** (*slang*)

id·i·ot·ic /iddee óttik/ *adj* an offensive term meaning showing a lack of good sense or intelligence —**id·i·ot·i·cal·ly** *adv*

id·i·ot light *n* a warning light on a device or instrument panel, especially in a car (*slang*) [< the idea that it is for people unable to read the gauges on an instrument panel]

id·i·ot-proof *adj* constructed or designed so as not to fail or go wrong even if misused (*informal*)

id·i·ot sa·vant /iddee ət sa vaánt, -sə vaánt/ (*plural* **id·i·ot sa·vants** /*pronunc. same*/ or **id·i·ots sa·vants** /iddee əts sa vaánt, -sə vaánt/) *n* same as **autistic savant** (*dated offensive*) [< French, "learned idiot"]

id·i·ot tape *n* a tape for a typesetting machine that contains text but no formatting except markers for new paragraphs

IDK *abbr* I don't know (*used in e-mails or text messages*)

i·dle /íd'l/ *adj* (**i·dler, i·dlest**) **1.** NOT WORKING OR IN USE not working, operating, producing, or in use **2.** LAZY lazy and unwilling to work **3.** FRIVOLOUS frivolous and a waste of time ○ *idle pleasures* **4.** UNFOUNDED having no basis in fact ○ *idle gossip* **5.** INEFFECTIVE unlikely to be carried out or impossible to put into effect ○ *idle threats* **6.** NOT EARNING MONEY not being used to yield a financial return ○ *idle funds* **7.** NOT PLAYING not playing or competing ○ *Green Bay and Minnesota are idle this weekend.* ■ *n* SPEED OF ENGINE WITH GEAR DISENGAGED the state in which a motor vehicle engine is running but is not in gear ■ *v* (**i·dled, i·dling, i·dles**) **1.** *vti* RUN WITHOUT APPLYING POWER to run gently with the gear disengaged, or allow a motor vehicle engine to do this **2.** *vt* MAKE SOMEBODY UNEMPLOYED to make somebody unemployed or inactive **3.** *vti* PASS TIME AIMLESSLY to be lazy and avoid work, or pass the time in this way ○ *He idled away the morning.* **4.** *vi* MOVE SLOWLY AND AIMLESSLY to move in a slow and lazy or aimless way [Old English *īdel* "worthless, empty" < Germanic] —**i·dle·ness** *n* —**i·dly** *adv*

SPELLCHECK idle or **idol**? Do not confuse the spelling of ***idle*** and ***idol***, which sound similar. ***Idle*** is an adjective meaning "lazy" or "not in use," as in *machines lying idle*, or a verb meaning "move slowly" or "pass time lazily," as in *idle away the afternoon.* ***Idol*** is a noun denoting an object of adoration, as in *a pop idol, worshiping idols.*

i·dle gear *n* a gear placed between two others to transmit motion, but not direction or speed

i·dle pul·ley *n* a freely rotating pulley wheel that guides or takes up slack from a drive belt by pressing against it

i·dler /ídlər/ *n* **1.** somebody who spends time in a lazy or relaxed way and habitually avoids work **2.** MECH ENG same as **idle wheel** (sense 1)

i·dler gear *n* MECH ENG same as **idle gear**

i·dler pul·ley *n* MECH ENG same as **idle pulley**

i·dler wheel *n* MECH ENG same as **idle wheel**

i·dle time *n* a period during which a device, machine, or employee is temporarily inactive

i·dle wheel *n* **1.** a gear wheel or roller placed between two others to transmit motion between them without changing their speed or direction or to provide support **2.** MECH ENG same as **idle pulley**

i·do·crase /ídə kràyss, -kràyz, íddə-/ *n* MINERALS same as **vesuvianite** [Early 19C. < Greek *eidos* "form" + *krasis* "mixture"]

i·dol /íd'l/ *n* **1.** OBJECT OF ADORATION somebody or something greatly admired or loved, often to excess **2.** OBJECT WORSHIPED AS GOD something that is worshiped as a god, e.g., a statue or carved image **3.** FORBIDDEN OBJECT OF WORSHIP in monotheistic religions, an object of worship other than the one God [13C. Via French *idole* < Greek *eidōlon* "image" < *eidos* "form, shape"]

SPELLCHECK See *idle.*

i·dol·a·ter /ī dóllətər/ *n* (*disapproving*) **1.** a worshiper of idols **2.** somebody who shows excessive admiration or love for somebody or something [14C. < French *idolâtre* < Greek *eidōlolatrēs* "image worshiper" < *eidōlon* (see IDOL)]

i·dol·a·try /ī dóllətree/ *n* (*disapproving*) **1.** the worship of idols or false gods **2.** excessive admiration or love shown for somebody or something [13C. Via French *idolâtrie* < Greek *eidōlolatreia* "image-worship" < *eidōlon* (see IDOL)] —**i·dol·a·trous** *adj*

i·dol·ize /íd'l ìz/ (**-ized, -iz·ing, -iz·es**) *vt* **1.** to feel great admiration or love for somebody or something, often to excess **2.** to worship something as an idol (*disapproving*) —**i·dol·i·za·tion** /íd'li záysh'n/ *n*

IDP *abbr* integrated data processing

IDTS *abbr* ONLINE I don't think so (*used in e-mails or text messages*)

Id ul-Ad·ha, etc. *n* ISLAM another spelling of **Eid al-Adha, etc.**

i·dyl·ist *n* ARTS another spelling of **idyllist**

i·dyll /íd'l/, **i·dyl** *n* **1.** EXPERIENCE OF SERENE HAPPINESS an experience or period of serene and carefree happiness, usually in beautiful surroundings and often idealized **2.** TRANQUIL CHARMING SCENE a scene or event characterized by tranquillity, simple beauty, and innocent charm, usually in a rural setting **3.** ARTS LITERARY PIECE ABOUT CHARMING RURAL LIFE a short work in verse or prose, a painting, or a piece of music depicting simple pastoral or rural scenes and the life of country folk, often in an idealized way [Late 16C. Via Latin *idyllium* "pastoral poem" < Greek *eidullion* "small picture" < *eidos* "form"]

USAGE idyll, idyllic, or **ideal**? Do not confuse ***idyll*** and ***idyllic*** with the noun and adjective ***ideal***. ***Idyll*** and ***idyllic*** are narrower in meaning, referring to carefree happiness, unspoiled beauty, and serenity, as in *a pastoral idyll* or *an idyllic way to spend a summer afternoon.* ***Ideal*** refers to perfection, or to being the best in every respect, as in *the ideal of beauty* or *the ideal way to tackle the problem.* An ***idyllic*** setting for a hotel, perhaps in the middle of the countryside, is not necessarily ***ideal***; an ***ideal*** setting for a hotel, perhaps near a major airport, may be far from ***idyllic***. Note that the title of Tennyson's *Idylls of the King*, a set of poems about Arthur, Guinevere, and Lancelot, does not refer to the ***ideals*** of the Knights of the Round Table.

i·dyl·lic /ī díllik/ *adj* **1.** serenely beautiful, untroubled, and happy **2.** like an idyll, especially in having a simple, unspoiled, and especially rural charm (*See usage note at idyll*) —**i·dyl·li·cal·ly** *adv*

i·dyl·list /íd'list/, **i·dyl·ist** *n* a writer, composer, or painter of idylls

ie *abbr* Ireland (*used in Internet addresses*) See table at **domain name**

IE *abbr* **1.** LING Indo-European **2.** ENG industrial engineer **3.** ENG industrial engineering **4.** CHEM ion exchange **5.** CHEM ionization energy

i.e. *abbr* that is to say [Latin *id est* "that is"]

USAGE See ***e.g.***

-ie *suffix* **1.** somebody or something that is small or dear ○ *doggie* ○ *auntie* **2.** somebody or something that has a particular character ○ *sweetie* **3.** somebody or something that has to do with ○ *townie* [Origin ?]

IEEE /ī tripp'l ée/ *abbr* Institute of Electrical and Electronic Engineers

-ier *suffix* same as **er**[1]

~~**iether**~~ incorrect spelling of **either**

if /if/ CORE MEANING: a conjunction used to indicate the circumstances that would have to exist in order for an event to happen ○ *You can come with us if you want to.* ○ *Are you thinking of buying a new car? If so, talk to us first.*

1. *conj* USED IN INDIRECT QUESTIONS used in indirect speech to introduce a question that in direct speech requires the answer "yes" or "no" ○ *asked if I would stay* **2.** *conj* MODIFYING STATEMENT used to indicate a modification to a statement, usually to add something negative or to indicate that there is less of something than originally expected ○ *a gallant, if misguided, attempt* ○ *by Thursday, if not earlier* **3.** *conj* INTRODUCING EXCLAMATION used to introduce an exclamation expressing surprise or dismay ○ *If that isn't the last straw!* **4.** *n* DOUBT a doubt or uncertainty ○ *The proposal contains too many ifs for us to be enthusiastic about it.* **5.** *n* CONDITION a condition or qualification ○ *I'm not very happy about the ifs written into the contract.* [Old English *gif* < Germanic] ◇ **if only** used to introduce an expression of a hopeless wish or regret ○ *If only you had told me sooner!* ◇ **ifs, ands, or buts** excuses or protests

USAGE Ambiguity of **if**: In *We have hundreds, if not thousands, of items in stock*, the *if not* fairly plainly means "or even." In *It's a clever idea, if not a practical one*, it fairly plainly means "although not a practical one." But in *He's good-looking, if not really handsome*, it is unclear which of those meanings is intended — at least out of context. Often it is clear what *if not* means only because the context shows what the phrase must mean. When you think it may be unclear, choose another wording.

In an ***if***-clause expressing a condition contrary to fact, you must use the subjunctive mood of the verb in that clause (*If I were* [not "was"] *you*), and you must use the modal auxiliary verb *would* (or, less commonly, *should*) in the main clause: *If I were you, I would not try that at home.* When the ***if***-clause expresses a condition not contrary to fact, you must use the indicative mood of the verb in that clause: *If Jon was still on the road during the blizzard, he probably tried to stop at a motel for the night.* Notice that the mood and tenses of the main-clause verbs are dependent on the verbs in the ***if***-clauses. The sense is that we know that Jon has been on the road. We are not sure, however, whether he is still there. Hence, we can use the indicative, not the subjunctive.

USAGE Substituting ***would have*** for *had* in an *if* clause (one stating a condition contrary to fact) is a grammatical error. Do not write: *If they would have done it properly to begin with, these problems would not exist.* Write instead: *If they had done it properly...* or, more formally, *Had they done it properly to begin with, these problems would not exist.* Avoid the incorrect form *they'd + have*, as in *If they'd have done it properly...* Here *they'd* is a contraction for *they had.* Write instead *If they'd done it properly...* or *If they had done it properly...*

IF *abbr* ELECTRONICS intermediate frequency

IFC *abbr* International Finance Corporation (*of the United Nations*)

I·fe /ée fày/ city in southwestern Nigeria, situated 54 mi./87 km east of Ibadan. Population: 289,500 (1995).

if·fy /iffee/ (**-fi·er, -fi·est**) *adj* (*informal*) **1.** UNCERTAIN uncertain or unlikely to happen **2.** UNDECIDED undecided or unsure about something ○ *feeling iffy about applying to law school* **3.** DUBIOUS dubious, suspicious, or unreliable ○ *My car is iffy at the moment: will you drive?* —**if·fi·ness** *n*

If·ni /éefnee/ region of Morocco, situated on the southwestern coast of the country. Formerly an overseas province of Spain, it was ceded to Morocco in 1969. Sidi Ifni is the only city. Area: 580 sq. mi./1,502 sq. km.

I for·ma·tion *n* in football, an alignment of the offensive team in which all the backs line up in single file behind the center

IFR *abbr* AVIAT instrument flight rules

Ig *abbr* BIOCHEM immunoglobulin

IG, I.G. *abbr* **1.** MEASURE imperial gallon **2.** GOV Inspector General

IgA *n* a class of antibodies, found in respiratory and alimentary secretions as well as in saliva and tears, that help the body to neutralize harmful bacteria and viral antigens [Shortening of *immunoglobulin A*]

Ig·bo *n, adj* PEOPLES, LANG same as **Ibo**

IgD *n* a class of antibodies, present on most cell surfaces and predominant in B cells, that help the body to resist antigens [Abbreviation of *immunoglobulin D*]

IgE *n* a class of antibodies, abundant in tissues, that help the body to expel intestinal parasites and cause allergic reactions in response to antigens [Abbreviation of *immunoglobulin E*]

igg /ig/ (**igged, ig·ging, iggs**) *vt* to ignore somebody or something (*slang*) [Shortening]

IgG *n* a class of antibodies, predominant in serum, that pass through the placental wall into fetal circulation and help to prepare the immune system for the period of infancy [Abbreviation of *immunoglobulin G*]

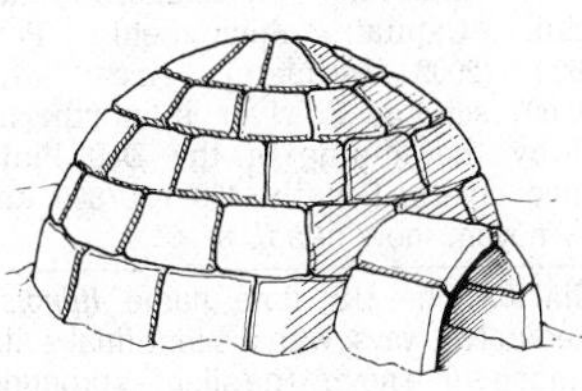

igloo

ig·loo /íggloo/ *n* **1.** an Inuit dwelling, usually dome-shaped and built from blocks of packed snow **2.** a small dome-shaped shelter or structure [Mid-19C. < Inuit *iglu* "house"]

IgM *n* a class of antibodies, circulating in the blood and secretions, that help the body to resist viruses [Abbreviation of *immunoglobulin M*]

ign.[1] *abbr* **1.** ignites **2.** ignition

ign.[2] *abbr* unknown [Latin *ignotus*]

Ig·na·tius (of An·ti·och) /ig nàyshəss-/, **St.** (35?–107) bishop and martyr. He was one of the Apostolic Fathers of the Christian Church, and his seven epistles give important historical information about the early Church.

Ig·na·tius Loy·o·la /-loy ṓlə/, **St.** (1491–1556) Spanish priest who was cofounder of the Society of Jesus in 1534. He also produced a Jesuit training manual, *Spiritual Exercises* (1548).

ig·ne·ous /ígnee əss/ *adj* **1.** describes rock formed under conditions of intense heat or produced by the solidification of volcanic magma on or below the Earth's surface **2.** relating to or characteristic of fire (*formal*) [Mid-17C. < Latin *igneus* < *ignis* "fire"]

ig·nes·cent /ig néss'nt/ *adj* giving off sparks when struck, as a flint does [Early 19C. < Latin *ignescent-*, present participle of *ignescere* "catch fire" < *ignis* "fire"]

ig·nim·brite /ígnim brīt/ *n* a volcanic rock consisting of droplets of lava and glass that were welded together by intense heat [Mid-20C. < Latin *ignis* "fire" + *imbr-* "rain"]

ig·nis fat·u·us /ígniss fáchoo əss/ (*plural* **ig·nes fa·tu·i** /ígneez fáchoo ī/) *n* **1.** SCI same as **will-o'-the-wisp** (sense 1) **2.** something such as a hope or an aim that proves illusory or leads somebody astray (*literary*) [< Latin, "foolish fire"; from its erratic movements]

ig·nite /ig nīt/ (**-nit·ed, -nit·ing, -nites**) *v* **1.** *vti* **LIGHT OR CATCH FIRE** to set fire to something, or catch fire **2.** *vti* **HEAT GAS UNTIL IT BURNS** to heat a gas to the temperature at which it begins to burn, or be heated in this way **3.** *vt* **AROUSE EMOTION** to cause a strong emotion to arise or show itself in somebody [Mid-17C. < Latin *ignit-*, past participle of *ignire* "set on fire" < *ignis* "fire"] —**ig·nit·a·bil·i·ty** /ig nītə bíllətee/ *n* —**ig·nit·a·ble** *adj* —**ig·nit·er** *n*

ig·ni·tion /ig nísh'n/ *n* **1. MEANS OF STARTING ENGINE** a mechanism that determines when, where, and how a spark is delivered to an engine cylinder to ignite the fuel and start or run the engine **2. SPARK THAT IGNITES FUEL-AIR MIXTURE** a spark in an internal-combustion engine that ignites and explodes a mixture of fuel and air **3. PROCESS OF IGNITING** the process of setting something on fire

ig·ni·tion point *n* the temperature at which a substance begins to burn and will remain alight

ig·no·ble /ig nṓb'l/ *adj* **1.** dishonorable and contrary to the high standards of conduct expected of somebody **2.** not belonging to the nobility (*formal*) [15C. Directly or via French < Latin *ignobilis* "not noble" < *(g)nobilis* (see NOBLE)] —**ig·no·bly** *adv*

SYNONYMS See *mean*[2].

ig·no·min·i·ous /ìgnə mínnee əss/ *adj* **1.** involving a total loss of dignity and self-respect, and making somebody or something appear shamefully weak and ineffective **2.** deserving condemnation and contempt (*formal*) —**ig·no·min·i·ous·ly** *adv* —**ig·no·min·i·ous·ness** *n*

ig·no·min·y /ígnə mìnnee/ (*plural* **-ies**) *n* **1.** a total loss of dignity and self-respect, or an incurring of public disgrace **2.** a disgraceful act (*formal*) [Mid-16C. Directly or via French < Latin *ignominia* "lacking name" < *nomin-* "name, reputation"]

ig·no·ra·mus /ìgnə ráyməss/ *n* an offensive term that deliberately insults somebody's level of intelligence or education (*insult*) [Late 16C. < modern Latin < Latin "we do not know," form of *ignorare* (see IGNORE)]

ig·no·rance /ígnərənss/ *n* **1.** lack of knowledge or education **2.** unawareness of something, often of something important ◇ **ignorance is bliss** it is often better not to know about something unpleasant

ig·no·rant /ígnərənt/ *adj* **1. LACKING KNOWLEDGE** lacking knowledge or education in general or in a specific subject **2. UNAWARE** unaware of something ○ *ignorant of the danger* **3. RESULTING FROM LACK OF KNOWLEDGE** caused by a lack of knowledge, understanding, or experience ○ *an ignorant mistake* **4.** *Carib* **QUARRELSOME** quarrelsome and aggressive —**ig·no·rant·ly** *adv*

ig·nore /ig náwr/ (**-nored, -nor·ing, -nores**) *vt* to refuse to notice or pay attention to somebody or something [15C. Directly or via French < Latin *ignorare* "not know, ignore" < *(g)noscere* "know"]

~~**ignorent**~~ incorrect spelling of **ignorant**

I·go·rot /íggə rṓt, èegə-/ (*plural same* or **-rots**) *n* a member of a people living in the mountainous northern part of Luzon in the Philippines [Early 19C. Via Spanish *Ygolote* < the local Philippine name] —**I·go·rot** *adj*

I·gua·çu /èe gwaa sṓo/ river in southern Brazil and northeastern Argentina. Length: 745 mi./1,200 km.

Barnaby's

Iguaçu Falls

I·gua·çu Falls waterfalls on the Iguaçu River, in southern Brazil. In the wet season they form a single waterfall over 2.5 mi./4 km wide and up to 260 ft./80 m high.

iguana

i·gua·na /i gwáanə/ (*plural* **-nas** or *same*) *n* a large plant-eating lizard with a serrated fringe or crest running along its back from head to tail. Native to: tropical South and Central America. Family: Iguanidae. [Mid-16C. Via Spanish < Arawak *iwana*]

i·guan·o·don /i gwáanə dòn/ *n* a large long-tailed plant-eating dinosaur of the Jurassic and early Cretaceous periods. Genus: *Iguanodon*. [Early 19C. < IGUANA + Greek *odōn*, variant of *odous*, *odont-* "tooth"; from the similarity of its teeth to those of an iguana]

IGY *abbr* International Geophysical Year

i.h.p., ihp *abbr* AUTOMOT indicated horsepower

ih·ram /ee ráam/ *n* **1.** a white cotton robe worn by Muslim men when they are pilgrims to Mecca, formed from pieces of cloth wound around the waist and over the shoulder **2.** the state of holiness conferred on Muslims or symbolized by the wearing of the ihram [Early 18C. < Arabic *'iḥrām*]

IHS *abbr* CHR Jesus [< three letters of the capitalized form of the name of Jesus in Greek; later also taken as abbreviation of Latin *Iesus hominum salvator* "Jesus savior of humankind," *in hoc signo* "in this sign (you shall conquer)," *in hac salus* "in this (cross) is salvation," and other religious phrases]

IINM *abbr* ONLINE if I'm not mistaken (*used in e-mails*)

IIRC *abbr* ONLINE if I recall/remember correctly (*used in e-mails*)

IJs·sel·meer /ʼíss'l mèer/, **Ijs·sel·meer** shallow freshwater lake in the northern Netherlands that occupies part of what was formerly the Zuider Zee. The IJssel River flows into it.

i·kat /èe kàat/ *n* a technique for making patterned fabric by using tie-dyed yarn [Mid-20C. < Malay, "tie, fasten"]

i·ke·ba·na /ìkə báanə, èeke-/ *n* the Japanese art of arranging flowers in a formal balanced composition [Early 20C. < Japanese, "living flowers"]

I·ke Tai·ga /èe kay tī́gə/ (1723?–76) Japanese painter. His works, using ancient forms of calligraphy, are in the Bunjinga style. Also known as **Ikeno Taiga**

Ikh·na·ton another spelling of **Akhenaton**

Ikh·wan /ík wàan/ *npl* in 20th-century Islam, a religious and military movement whose members practice Wahhabism. The Ikhwan played an important role in the unification of Saudi Arabia.

i·kon *n* RELIG another spelling of **icon** (sense 1)

IKWUM *abbr* ONLINE I know what you mean (*used in e-mails*)

il *abbr* Israel (*used in Internet addresses*) See table at **domain name**

IL *abbr* MAIL Illinois

il- *prefix* same as **in-**[1], **in-**[2] (*used before l*)

-il *suffix* forming nouns and adjectives ○ *utensil* ○ *civil* [< Latin *-ilis*]

ILA *abbr* International Longshoremen's Association

i·lang-i·lang *n* TREES another spelling of **ylang-ylang**

il Bron·zi·no /il brōn zéenō/ (1503–72) Italian painter. Known as a portraitist of the Medici family, Dante, and Boccaccio, he also painted religious pictures. Born **di Mariano, Agnolo di Cosimo**

-ile[1] *suffix* of, relating to, capable of ○ *volatile* [Via French < Latin *-ilis*]

-ile[2] *suffix* a portion of a particular size in a frequency distribution ○ *quartile* ○ *percentile* [Origin ?]

il·e·a ANAT plural of **ileum**

il·e·ac /íllee àk/, **il·e·al** /-əl/ *adj* relating to the ileum [Early 19C. Alteration of ILIAC, after ILEUM, ILEUS]

~~**ilegal**~~ incorrect spelling of **illegal**

il·e·i·tis /ìllee ī́tiss/ *n* inflammation of the ileum

il·e·os·to·my /ìllee óstəmee/ (*plural* **-mies**) *n* **1.** a surgical operation in which an opening is made through the abdominal wall into the ileum, so that waste can be discharged out of the body without passing through the colon **2.** a surgical opening through the abdominal wall into the ileum

I·le·sa /i léshə/, **I·le·sha** city in Kwara State, southwestern Nigeria, situated approximately 15 mi./24 km southeast of Oshogbo. Population: 369,000 (1995).

il·e·um /íllee əm/ (*plural* **-e·a** /-ee ə/) *n* the third and lowest portion of the small intestine, extending from the jejunum to the pouch-shaped cecum at the beginning of the large intestine [Late 17C. < medieval Latin, variant of Latin *ilium* "entrails"]

il·e·us /íllee əss/ *n* a medical condition in which the contents of the intestines are unable to pass through owing to a physical obstruction or muscular inadequacy, often accompanied by extreme pain and vomiting [Late 17C. Via Latin < Greek *ileos* "colic"]

i·lex /ī lèks/ *n* **1.** a tree or bush belonging to a genus whose best-known member is the holly tree. Genus: *Ilex*. **2.** TREES same as **holm oak** [< Latin, "holm oak"]

ILGWU, I.L.G.W.U. *abbr* International Ladies' Garment Workers' Union

il·i·a ANAT plural of **ilium**

il·i·ac /íllee àk/ *adj* relating to the ilium and its surroundings [Early 16C. < late Latin *iliacus* "relating to colic" < Latin *ilia* (plural) "flanks"]

Il·i·ad /íllee əd, -àd/ *n* an ancient Greek epic poem, describing the siege and capture of Troy, ascribed to Homer and probably composed by oral tradition over several centuries before 700 B.C. [Early 17C. < Latin *Iliad-* < Greek *Ilias* "of Troy" < *Ilion* "Troy"]

Il·i·am·na /íllee ámnə/ volcanic peak in southwestern Alaska, situated on the western side of Cook Inlet. Height: 10,020 ft./3,053 m.

Il·i·am·na, Lake largest lake in Alaska, in the southwest of the state, west of Cook Inlet. Area: 1,022 sq. mi./2,647 sq. km.

il·i·um /íllee əm/ (*plural* **-i·a** /-ee ə/) *n* the wide flat upper portion of the pelvis that is connected to the base of the vertebral column. The ilium is a separate bone at birth but later becomes fused with two other bones to form the hip bone (**innominate bone**). [14C. < late Latin, "flank, groin" < Latin *ilia* (plural) "flanks"]

ilk /ilk/ *n* a kind or sort of person or thing ○ *journalists and others of that ilk* ○ *"save forlorn hopes and their ilk"* (Stephen Crane, *The Red Badge of Courage*; 1895) [Old English *ilca* "same," compound < Indo-European, "same" + Germanic, "form"] ◇ **of that ilk** *Scotland* coming from or owning the place of the same name as your own

ill /il/ *adj* (**worse** /wurss/, **worst** /wurst/) **1. UNWELL** not in good health, having a disease, or feeling unwell or nauseated **2. HARMFUL** resulting in harm, pain, or trouble for somebody or something ○ *ill effects from the accident* **3. UNKIND** unkind and unfriendly ○ *ill feeling* **4. UNFAVORABLE** predicting a bad future or outcome ○ *an ill wind* **5. MORALLY BAD** resulting from the actual or supposed moral badness of somebody or something ○ *of ill repute* **6. BAD** not up to the expected or required standard, e.g., of behavior or competence ■ *adv* (**worse, worst**) **1. BADLY** badly, inadequately, or inappropriately ○ *treated them ill* **2. UNFAVORABLY** in an adverse or unfavorable way, or so as to reflect badly on somebody or something ○ *bodes ill* **3. WITH DIFFICULTY** only with great difficulty and trouble ○ *can ill afford it* ■ *n* **1. PROBLEM** a serious problem or difficulty ○ *social ills* **2. HARM** evil or harm, especially as a fate wished on somebody ○ *wished them ill* [12C. < Old Norse *illr* "evil, difficult," *illa* "badly," *ilt* "evil"]

ill-ad·just·ed *adj*	**ill-e·quipped** *adj*
ill-be·haved *adj*	**ill-fit·ting** *adj*
ill-con·ceived *adj*	**ill-found·ed** *adj*
ill-con·sid·ered *adj*	**ill-nour·ished** *adj*
ill-de·fined *adj*	**ill-pre·pared** *adj*
ill-dis·guised *adj*	**ill-suit·ed** *adj*
ill-dis·posed *adj*	**ill-tem·pered** *adj*
ill-dressed *adj*	**ill-timed** *adj*

I'll /īl/ *contr* I will or I shall

ill. *abbr* **1.** illustrated **2.** illustration **3.** illustrator

Ill. *abbr* Illinois

ill-ad·vised *adj* not wise, prudent, or sensible —**ill-ad·vis·ed·ly** *adv*

ill-as·sort·ed *adj* mismatched or incompatible

ill at ease *adj* uncomfortable and nervous

il·la·tion /i láysh'n/ *n* (*formal*) **1.** an inference drawn from something **2.** the act or process of drawing an inference from something [Mid-16C. < Latin *illation-* < *illat-* (see ILLATIVE)]

il·la·tive /illətiv, i láy-/ *adj* **1. INFERENTIAL** relating to or involving the drawing of inferences (*formal*) **2. LING STATING INFERENCE** describes a word or phrase such as "thus," "therefore," or "as a result" that marks or introduces an inference **3. LING OF CASE OF FINNISH NOUN** describes a case of nouns in Finnish and some other languages that indicates motion toward something. It is usually translated into English using the prepositions "into" or "toward." ■ *n* LING **1. SOMETHING THAT STATES INFERENCE** a word, phrase, or morpheme that marks or introduces an inference **2. CASE OF FINNISH NOUN** the illative grammatical case in Finnish and some other languages [Late 16C. < Latin *illativus* < *illat-*, past participle of *inferre* (see INFER)]

Il·la·war·ra /illə wórrə/ district in southeastern New South Wales, Australia, situated approximately 30 mi./48 km south of Sydney. Population: 380,660 (1998).

ill-be·ing *n* a feeling or condition of illness, unhappiness, or lack of prosperity [After WELL-BEING]

ill-bred *adj* rude, impolite, or otherwise showing a lack of good manners or the results of a bad upbringing —**ill-breed·ing** *n*

il·le·gal /i lēeg'l/ *adj* **1. AGAINST LAW** contravening a specific law, especially a criminal law **2. AGAINST RULES** not allowed by the rules of something such as a game **3. NOT PERMITTED BY COMPUTER** not permitted in a computer program ■ *n* **ILLEGAL IMMIGRANT** somebody who has entered a country illegally —**il·le·gal·ly** *adv*

SYNONYMS See *unlawful*.

il·le·gal·i·ty /illee gállətee/ (*plural* **-ties**) *n* **1.** the fact of being forbidden by law or by the rules of something **2.** an act that is against the law

il·le·gal·ize /i lēegə līz/ (**-ized, -iz·ing, -iz·es**) *vt* to declare officially and by law that something is illegal —**il·le·gal·i·za·tion** /i lēegəli záysh'n/ *n*

il·leg·i·ble /i léjjəb'l/ *adj* impossible or very difficult to read —**il·leg·i·bil·i·ty** /i lèjjə bíllətee/ *n* —**il·leg·i·bly** *adv*

il·le·git·i·mate /illi jíttəmət/ *adj* **1.** born to parents who are not married to each other **2.** not carried out, made, or constituted in accordance with the law, the rules governing a specific activity, or social norms and customs —**il·le·git·i·ma·cy** *n* —**il·le·git·i·mate·ly** *adv*

ill-fat·ed *adj* ending in or doomed to disaster

ill-fa·vored *adj* **1.** unattractive in appearance, especially having an unattractive face **2.** offensively objectionable (*literary*)

ill feel·ing *n* animosity or resentment toward somebody or something

ill-got·ten *adj* acquired dishonestly or illegally ○ *ill-gotten gains*

ill health *n* the state of being in poor physical or mental condition

ill hu·mor *n* a bad mood or bad temper —**ill-hu·mored** *adj*

il·lib·er·al /i líbbərəl, -brəl/ *adj* **1.** narrow-minded and intolerant of ideas and behavior that vary from a conservative standard **2.** not generous with something such as money or time (*formal*) —**il·lib·er·al·ism** *n* —**il·lib·er·al·i·ty** /i lìbbə rállətee/ *n* —**il·lib·er·al·ly** *adv*

il·lic·it /i líssit/ *adj* **1.** not allowed by the law **2.** considered wrong or unacceptable by prevailing social customs or standards —**il·lic·it·ly** *adv* —**il·lic·it·ness** *n*

SPELLCHECK See *elicit*.

SYNONYMS See *unlawful*.

Il·li·lou·ette Falls /illə loo ét-/ waterfall in Yosemite National Park, central California. Height: 370 ft./113 m.

Il·li·ma·ni /éelyee maánee/ mountain in western Bolivia, situated south of La Paz. Highest peak: Nevada Illimani 21,201 ft./6,462 m.

il·lim·it·a·ble /i límmitəb'l/ *adj* having no limits or bounds (*formal*) —**il·lim·it·a·bly** *adv*

ill-in·formed *adj* having or showing a lack of knowledge about something

Il·li·nois[1] /illə nóy/ (*plural* same) *n* a member of a confederacy of Algonquian peoples who lived in an area covering northern Illinois, eastern Iowa, and southern Wisconsin, and now live in northeastern Oklahoma [Early 18C. Via French < Algonquian] —**Il·li·nois** *adj*

Illinois

Il·li·nois[2] /illə nóy, -nóyz/ **1.** state in the north central United States, bordered by Indiana, Iowa, Kentucky, Missouri, Wisconsin, and Lake Michigan. Capital: Springfield. Population: 12,600,620 (2002 estimate). Area: 57,918 sq. mi./150,007 sq. km. **2.** river in northern Illinois formed by the joining of the Des Plaines and Kankakee rivers. Length: 420 mi./680 km. —**Il·li·nois·an** /-nóyən, -nóyz'n/ *adj, n*

PRONUNCIATION The US state name ***Illinois*** can be pronounced in two ways: with a silent final *s* /illə nóy/ or with a sounded *s* /illə nóyz/. The silent *-s* pronunciation is generally the more common. The name derives from a name that late-17th-century French explorers had used for a Native American people then living in the region of the Illinois River. The name the French picked up is of the Algonquian family of languages, and it was pronounced /ill ə nō ay/. The French then added a final *s* to create a plural for the people regarded as a group of individuals.

Il·li·nois Wa·ter·way system of rivers and canals in Illinois that connects Lake Michigan at Chicago with the Mississippi River at Grafton. Length: 325 mi./523 km.

il·liq·uid /i líkwid/ *adj* **1.** not easily convertible into cash ○ *illiquid shares* **2.** lacking sufficient ready cash —**il·li·quid·i·ty** /illi kwíddətee/ *n*

il·lite /i līt/ *n* a clay mineral of the mica group containing potassium and aluminum. Source: shale, mudstone. [Mid-20C. After ILLINOIS[2]] —**il·lit·ic** /i líttik/ *adj*

il·lit·er·ate /i líttərət/ *adj* **1. OFFENSIVE TERM** an offensive term meaning not able to read or write **2. UNEDUCATED** having or showing little or no knowledge of a particular subject ○ *artistically illiterate* **3. MAKING MANY LANGUAGE MISTAKES** full of or making many basic errors in the use of language ○ *illiterate prose* ■ *n* **OFFENSIVE TERM** an offensive term for somebody who lacks education and knowledge, especially somebody who cannot read or write —**il·lit·er·a·cy** *n* —**il·lit·er·ate·ly** *adv* —**il·lit·er·ate·ness** *n*

ill-judged *adj* showing a lack of good judgment or an incorrect assessment of a situation

ill-man·nered *adj* rude or impolite in behavior

ill na·ture *n* a bad-tempered, unpleasant, or unkind disposition (*dated*)

ill-na·tured *adj* having a bad-tempered, unpleasant, or unkind disposition —**ill-na·tured·ly** *adv*

ill·ness /ilnəss/ *n* **1.** a disease, sickness, or indisposition **2.** a state of bad health

il·lo·cu·tion /illə kyóosh'n/ *n* PHILOSOPHY, LING the intention of a speaker in saying a particular thing, e.g., naming, threatening, warning, or promising, as opposed to the literal meaning of the words spoken [Mid-20C. < IL- + LOCUTION] —**il·lo·cu·tion·ar·y** *adj*

il·log·ic /i lójjik/ *n* the quality or condition of having no basis in logic

il·log·i·cal /i lójjik'l/ *adj* **1.** apparently unreasonable or perverse, especially in not being or not giving the expected response **2.** not following the rules of logic, or not following logically from a previous premise, statement, or action —**il·log·i·cal·i·ty** /i lòjji kállətee/ *n* —**il·log·i·cal·ly** *adv*

ill-o·mened *adj* accompanied by signs suggesting disaster or failure

ill-sort·ed *adj* same as **ill-assorted**

ill-starred *adj* doomed to end in failure or disaster [< the belief that an unpropitious arrangement of the astronomical objects at the start of an undertaking predetermined an unhappy outcome]

ill-treat *vt* **1.** to behave cruelly or unkindly toward a person or animal **2.** to give something rough or careless treatment —**ill-treat·ed** *adj* —**ill-treat·ment** *n*

SYNONYMS See *mistreat*.

il·lume /i lóom/ (**-lumed, -lum·ing, -lumes**) *vt* to cast illumination onto somebody or something (*literary or archaic*) [Early 17C. Contraction of ILLUMINE]

il·lu·mi·nance /i lóominənss/ *n* the amount of light, evaluated according to its capacity to produce visual stimulation, that reaches a unit of surface area during a unit of time. It is measured in lux. Symbol E_v

il·lu·mi·nant /ló͞ominənt/ *n* something that gives off or provides light ■ *adj* giving off light (*technical*) [Mid-17C. < Latin *illuminant-*, present participle of *illuminare* (see ILLUMINATE)]

il·lu·mi·nate /i ló͞omi nàyt/ (**-nat·ed, -nat·ing, -nates**) *v* **1.** *vti* SHINE LIGHT ON SOMEBODY OR SOMETHING to make somebody or something visible or bright with light, or be lit up **2.** *vt* DECORATE SOMETHING WITH LIGHTS to decorate something with lights for a celebration **3.** *vt* CLARIFY SOMETHING to make something easier to understand **4.** *vt* CAUSE SOMEBODY TO LOOK HAPPY to make something, especially somebody's face, look happy and animated **5.** *vti* ENLIGHTEN SOMEBODY to provide somebody with knowledge or with intellectual or spiritual enlightenment (*literary; often passive*) **6.** *vt* PRINTING ADD COLORED ELEMENTS TO PAGE to add colored letters, illustrations, or designs to a manuscript or the borders of a page [15C. < Latin *illuminat-*, past participle of *illuminare* "light up" < *lumin-* "light"] —**il·lu·mi·na·tive** *adj* —**il·lu·mi·na·tor** *n*

il·lu·mi·na·ti /i ló͞omi naátee/, **Il·lu·mi·na·ti** *npl* a group claiming to have received special religious or spiritual enlightenment, especially an 18th-century German secret society with deist and republican ideas [Late 16C. Via Italian < Latin, plural of *illuminatus* < past participle of *illuminare* (see ILLUMINATE)]

il·lu·mi·nat·ing /i ló͞omi nàyting/ *adj* informative and enlightening, often by revealing or emphasizing facts that were previously obscure —**il·lu·mi·nat·ing·ly** *adv*

illumination: title page of the manuscript *Augustinus Questiones in Heptateuchon* (8th century)

il·lu·mi·na·tion /i ló͞omi náysh'n/ *n* **1.** ACT OF ILLUMINATING the provision of light to make something visible or bright, or the fact of being lit up **2.** USABLE LIGHT the amount or strength of light available in a place or for a purpose **3.** CLARIFICATION OF SOMETHING the process of making something easier to understand **4.** ENLIGHTENMENT intellectual or spiritual enlightenment **5.** PRINTING DECORATION ON PAGE a colored letter, design, or illustration decorating a manuscript or page, or the art or act of decorating written texts **6.** PHYS same as **illuminance**

il·lu·mine /i ló͞omin/ (**-mined, -min·ing, -mines**) *vti* to illuminate somebody or something, or become illuminated (*formal*) [14C. Via French < Latin *illuminare* (see ILLUMINATE)]

il·lu·mi·nism /i ló͞omi nìzzəm/ *n* the beliefs held by illuminati, especially their belief in or claim to special enlightenment

illus. *abbr* **1.** illustrated **2.** illustration **3.** illustrator

ill-use /-yó͞oz/ *vt* to treat somebody or something harshly or inappropriately —**ill-us·age** *n* —**ill-use** /-yó͞oss/ *n* —**ill-used** *adj*

il·lu·sion /i ló͞ozh'n/ *n* **1.** SOMETHING WITH DECEPTIVE APPEARANCE something that deceives the senses or mind, e.g., by appearing to exist when it does not or appearing to be one thing when it is in fact another **2.** FALSE IDEA a false idea, conception, or belief about somebody or something **3.** DECEPTIVE POWER OF APPEARANCES the ability of appearances to deceive the mind and senses, or the capacity of the mind and senses to be deceived by appearances **4.** PSYCHOL MISTAKEN SENSORY PERCEPTION a misinterpretation of an experience of sensory perception, especially a visual one, where the stimuli are objectively present and the mistaken perception is due to physical rather than psychological causes [14C. Via French < Latin *illusion-* < *illus-*, past participle of *illudere* "play at" < *ludus* "play, sport"] —**il·lu·sion·ar·y** *adj*

USAGE See *allusion.*

il·lu·sion·ism /i ló͞ozh'n ìzzəm/ *n* the use of pictorial techniques to create illusions

il·lu·sion·ist /i ló͞ozh'nist/ *n* **1.** somebody who performs magical tricks **2.** an artist who creates pictorial illusions —**il·lu·sion·is·tic** /i ló͞ozh'n ístik/ *adj*

il·lu·sive /i ló͞ossiv/ *adj* same as **illusory** [Early 17C. < medieval Latin *illusivus* "deceptive" < Latin *illus-* (see ILLUSION)] —**il·lu·sive·ly** *adv* —**il·lu·sive·ness** *n*

SPELLCHECK See *elusive.*

il·lu·so·ry /i ló͞ossəree, i ló͞ozəree/ *adj* produced by, based on, or consisting of an illusion [Late 16C. Directly or via French < ecclesiastical Latin *illusorius* "ironic" < Latin *illus-* (see ILLUSION)] —**il·lu·so·ri·ly** *adv* —**il·lu·so·ri·ness** *n*

il·lus·trate /íllə stràyt/ (**-trat·ed, -trat·ing, -trates**) *v* **1.** *vt* ACCOMPANY SOMETHING WITH PICTURES to provide explanatory or decorative pictures to accompany a printed, spoken, or electronic text ○ *The book was illustrated with diagrams.* **2.** *vti* FULLY EXPLAIN SOMETHING to clarify or explain something by giving examples or making comparisons **3.** *vt* BE CHARACTERISTIC OF SOMETHING to be a good example of something, or serve to demonstrate something and make it clear ○ *a case that illustrates the need for legislation* [Early 16C. < Latin *illustrat-*, past participle of *illustrare* "light up" < *lustrare* (see LUSTER)] —**il·lus·tra·tor** *n*

il·lus·tra·tion /íllə stráysh'n/ *n* **1.** PICTURE THAT COMPLEMENTS TEXT a drawing, picture, photograph, or diagram that accompanies and complements a printed, spoken, or electronic text **2.** PROVISION OF PICTURES ACCOMPANYING TEXT the art or process of producing or providing drawings, pictures, photographs, or diagrams to accompany a text **3.** SOMETHING THAT HELPS TO EXPLAIN SOMETHING an example or comparison that helps to clarify or explain something —**il·lus·tra·tion·al** *adj*

il·lus·tra·tive /i lústrətiv/ *adj* serving to illustrate or explain something —**il·lus·tra·tive·ly** *adv*

il·lus·tri·ous /i lústree əss/ *adj* extremely distinguished and deservedly famous [Mid-16C. < Latin *illustris* "bright, famous" < *illustrare* (see ILLUSTRATE)] —**il·lus·tri·ous·ly** *adv* —**il·lus·tri·ous·ness** *n*

il·lu·vi·a GEOL plural of **illuvium**

il·lu·vi·a·tion /i ló͞ovee áysh'n/ *n* the process by which materials such as colloids and salts are washed from an upper layer of soil to a lower one [Early 20C. < IL- + ELUVIATION] —**il·lu·vi·at·ed** *adj*

il·lu·vi·um /i ló͞ovee əm/ (*plural* **-vi·ums** or **-vi·a** /-vee ə/) *n* colloids, salts, or other material washed out from an upper to a lower layer of soil [Early 20C. < modern Latin < *-luvium* (as in ALLUVIUM)]

ill will *n* a feeling or attitude of hostility, unfriendliness, or dislike toward somebody ○ *They bore us no ill will.*

ill-wish·er *n* somebody who wishes misfortune or evil to come to another person

Il·lyr·i·a /i léeree ə/ ancient region along the coast of the Adriatic Sea from Albania northward

Il·lyr·i·an /i léeree ən/ *n* **1.** a member of a people who occupied Illyria from the late 3rd century B.C. until they were conquered by the Romans around 33 B.C. **2.** an extinct Indo-European language that was spoken in Illyria in ancient times, considered to be related to Albanian

il·men·ite /ílmə nìt/ *n* a mixed oxide mineral containing iron and titanium. Source: igneous and metamorphic rocks. [Early 19C. After the *Ilmen* Mountains in the S Urals, Russia]

~~**illness**~~ incorrect spelling of **illness**

I·lo·i·lo /éelō éelō/ city and capital of Iloilo Province, on the southeastern coast of Panay, Philippines, on the Iloilo Strait. Population: 363,778 (1999).

I·lo·rin /éelə rèen, i láwrən/ city and capital of Kwara State, southwestern Nigeria, situated approximately 170 mi./274 km northeast of Lagos. Population: 464,000 (1995).

ILS *abbr* AEROSP instrument landing system

im *abbr* Isle of Man (*used in Internet addresses*) See table at **domain name**

I'm /īm/ *contr* I am

IM *abbr* **1.** ONLINE instant messaging **2.** CHESS International Master **3.** MED intramuscular

im-[1] *prefix* same as **in-**[1] (*used before b, m, and p*)

im-[2] *prefix* same as **in-**[2] (*used before b, m, and p*)

im·age /ímmij/ *n* **1.** ACTUAL OR MENTAL PICTURE a picture or likeness of somebody or something, produced either physically by a sculptor, painter, or photographer, or formed in the mind ○ *concerned about his public image* **2.** LIKENESS SEEN OR PRODUCED the likeness of somebody or something that appears in a mirror, through a lens, or on the retina of the eye, or is produced electronically on a screen **3.** SOMEBODY CLOSELY RESEMBLING SOMEBODY ELSE a person or thing bearing a close likeness to somebody or something else ○ *She's the image of her father.* **4.** CONSPICUOUS EXAMPLE a very typical or extreme example of something ○ *the very image of greed* **5.** EXAMPLE OF FIGURATIVE LANGUAGE a figure of speech, especially a metaphor or simile **6.** MATH SET OF FUNCTION'S VALUES the value of a mathematical function corresponding to a specific value of the function's variable ■ *vt* (**-aged, -ag·ing, -ag·es**) **1.** CREATE IMAGE OF SOMEBODY OR SOMETHING to produce a physical or mental image of somebody or something **2.** MAKE VISUAL IMAGE OF BODY STRUCTURES to produce a visual representation of bodily structures, using X-rays, ultrasound, radioactivity, heat, or magnetism and, usually, computerized scanning devices, as an aid to diagnosis and treatment **3.** DESCRIBE SOMETHING IN VISUAL TERMS to describe something vividly or in visual terms **4.** TYPIFY SOMETHING to embody or typify something [12C. Via French < Latin *imago* "likeness"] —**im·age·a·ble** *adj* —**im·ag·er** *n*

im·age com·pres·sion *n* a technique for reducing the amount of digitized information needed to store a visual image electronically

im·age con·vert·er *n* an optical-electronic device that reproduces an image formed by invisible radiation such as ultraviolet or infrared on a photoemissive surface as a visible-light image on a luminescent surface

im·age in·ten·si·fi·er *n* an optical-electronic device that amplifies an image formed by visible radiation on a photoemissive surface to present an enhanced image on a luminescent surface

im·age-mak·er *n* somebody employed to create a favorable public image of a business, organization, product, or public figure

im·age map *n* an electronic graphic image with variable areas that computer users can click on to activate hypertext links

im·age·ry /ímmijree/ *n* **1.** METAPHORS AND SIMILES the figurative language, especially metaphors and similes, used in poetry, plays, and other literary works **2.** MENTAL IMAGES a set of mental pictures produced by the memory or imagination or conjured up by a stimulus ○ *dreams filled with surreal imagery* **3.** IMAGES IN ARTISTIC WORK the pictorial images found in works of art such as paintings and sculptures, or the art or process of making such images **4.** IMAGES COLLECTIVELY a group or set of images considered together ○ *studying the satellite imagery*

im·age tube *n* an optical-electronic device that converts invisible radiation into a visible image, as in an image converter, or amplifies visible radiation into an enhanced image, as in an image intensifier

i·mag·i·na·ble /i májjənəb'l/ *adj* capable of being imagined ○ *the worst meal imaginable* —**i·mag·i·na·bly** *adv*

i·mag·i·nar·y /i májjə nèrree/ *adj* **1.** existing only in the mind, not in reality **2.** relating to or containing imaginary numbers, or being the coefficient of the imaginary part in a complex number ■ *n* (*plural* **-ies**) MATH same as **imaginary number** [14C. < Latin *imaginarius* < *imagin-* "likeness"] —**i·mag·i·nar·i·ly** /i màjjə nérrəlee/ *adv*

i·mag·i·nar·y num·ber *n* a complex number in the form $a + ib$ where i is the square root of minus one, and b is not equal to zero

i·mag·i·nar·y part *n* the real number, b, in the complex number $a + ib$, where i is the square root of minus one

i·mag·i·nar·y u·nit *n* the positive square root of minus one

i·mag·i·na·tion /i màjjə náysh'n/ *n* **1.** ABILITY TO VISUALIZE the ability to form images and ideas in the mind, especially of things never seen or experienced directly **2. CREATIVE PART OF MIND** the part of the mind where ideas, thoughts, and images are formed **3. RESOURCEFULNESS** the ability to think of ways of dealing with difficulties or problems ○ *used real imagination in designing the experiment* **4. CREATIVE ACT** an act of creating a semblance of reality, especially in literature —**i·mag·i·na·tion·al** *adj*

i·mag·i·na·tive /i májjənətiv, -nàytiv/ *adj* **1. SKILLED AT VISUALIZING OR THINKING ORIGINALLY** good at thinking of new ideas or at visualizing things that have never been seen or experienced directly **2. ORIGINAL** new and original, or not likely to have been easily thought up by somebody else ○ *an imaginative solution to a long-standing problem* **3. TENDING TO FANTASIZE** with a tendency to pretend or fantasize **4. UNLIKELY** seeming untrue, implausible, or unlikely (*often used ironically*) **5. OF IMAGINATION** relating to the ability to form images and ideas in the mind, or to think of new things —**i·mag·i·na·tive·ness** *n*

i·mag·i·na·tive·ly /i májjənətivlee, i májjə nàytivlee/ *adv* in a new and original way that would not have occurred readily to most people

i·mag·ine /i májjin/ *v* (**-ined, -in·ing, -ines**) **1.** *vti* **FORM IMAGE OF SOMETHING IN MIND** to form an image or idea of somebody or something in the mind ○ *I can just imagine his reaction!* **2.** *vt* **SEE OR HEAR SOMETHING UNREAL** to see or hear something that is not there, or think something that is not true ○ *There's nothing there—you're imagining things!* **3.** *vt* **ASSUME SOMETHING** to suppose or assume something ■ *interj* **EXPRESSION OF SURPRISE** used to express surprise or indignation [14C. Via French < Latin *imaginare* "make an image of," *imaginari* "picture to yourself" < *imagin-* "likeness"] —**i·mag·ined** *adj* —**i·mag·in·er** *n* —**i·mag·in·ing** *n* ◇ **imagine that!** used to express surprise or indignation

i·mag·i·neer /i màjjə néer/ *n* somebody who has a creative imagination and is able to put it to practical use, e.g., in design or engineering projects ■ *vt* (**-neered, -neer·ing, -neers**) to design or produce something by putting the imagination to practical use [Mid-20C. Blend of IMAGINE + ENGINEER] —**i·mag·i·neer·ing** *n*

~~**imaginery**~~ incorrect spelling of **imaginary**

i·ma·gi·nes INSECTS, PSYCHOANAL plural of **imago**

im·ag·ing /ímmәjing/ *n* **1.** a technique, often computerized, for obtaining images of bodies or body parts for diagnosis, emergency rescue, or surveillance **2.** the use of mental images to try to ease pain, alter the course of a disease, or help in achieving a goal

im·a·gism /ímmə jìzzəm/ *n* a literary movement of early 20th-century US and UK poets that sought to modernize poetic language by the use of ordinary language, free verse, and precise everyday imagery —**im·a·gist** *n* —**im·a·gis·tic** /ìmmə jístik/ *adj* —**im·a·gis·ti·cal·ly** *adv*

i·ma·go /i máygō, i maá-/ (*plural* **-goes** or **-gi·nes** /-máygə neez, -maágə-/) *n* **1.** an insect in its sexually mature adult state **2.** in psychoanalysis, an unconscious idealized mental picture, especially of a parent, that is formed early in life and retained in adulthood [Late 18C. < Latin, "likeness"]

i·mam /i maám/ *n* **1. LEADER OF MOSQUE PRAYERS** in Islam, a man who leads the prayers in a mosque **2.** *also* **I·mam RELIGIOUS LEADER DESCENDED FROM MUHAMMAD** in the Shia branch of Islam, an Islamic religious leader regarded as a direct descendant of Muhammad or Ali and appointed by Allah **3. ISLAMIC COMMUNITY LEADER** in the Sunni branch of Islam, a leader of an Islamic community **4. ISLAMIC SCHOLAR** a respected Islamic scholar, especially a founder of a school of theology or law [Early 17C. < Arabic *'imām* "leader"]

i·mam·ate /i maá màyt/ *n* **1.** the title or position of an imam, or the period somebody spends as an imam **2.** the area of which an imam is in charge

i·ma·ret /i maárət/ *n* in Turkey, a place providing food and shelter for travelers and pilgrims [Early 17C. Via Turkish < Arabic *'imāra* "building"]

I·mar·i /i maáree/ *n* a Japanese porcelain that is brightly decorated, especially with a floral design [Late 19C. After a port in Kyushu, Japan]

I·MAX /ī màks/ *tdmk* a trademark for a giant-screen, large-format movie and motion-simulation entertainment complex, with a motion-picture screen that is ten times larger than a conventional screen and compatible with 3-D technology

im·bal·ance /im bállənss/ *n* **1.** an unevenness, inequality, or bias existing between two or more people or things, especially in their degree of emphasis, proportions, or function **2.** a lack of harmony or an inability to function well or harmoniously, or something causing this state ○ *a hormonal imbalance* —**im·bal·anced** *adj*

im·be·cile /ímbəss'l, ímbə sīl/ *n* **1.** an offensive term that deliberately insults somebody's intellect (*insult*) **2.** in a former classification system, somebody with an IQ between 25 and 50 and a mental age of between three and seven years (*dated; now considered offensive*) [15C. Via French < Latin *imbecillus* "without support" < *baculum* "stick, staff"] —**im·be·cil·ic** /ìmbə síllik/ *adj* —**im·be·cil·i·ty** /ìmbə sílləteе/ *n*

im·bed *vt* same as **embed**

im·bibe /im bíb/ (**-bibed, -bib·ing, -bibes**) *v* **1.** *vti* **DRINK SOMETHING** to drink something, especially alcohol (*formal or humorous*) **2.** *vt* **TAKE IN SOMETHING MENTALLY** to take in and assimilate something such as an idea or experience (*literary*) **3.** *vti* **ABSORB SOMETHING** to absorb moisture, gas, light, or heat (*formal*) [14C. < Latin *imbibere* "drink in" < *bibere* "to drink"] —**im·bib·er** *n*

im·bi·bi·tion /ìmbə bísh'n, im bī-/ *n* the absorption or adsorption of something such as liquid or heat by a mixture (**colloid**) such as a gel [15C. < medieval Latin *imbibition-* "absorption" < Latin *imbibere* (see IMBIBE)]

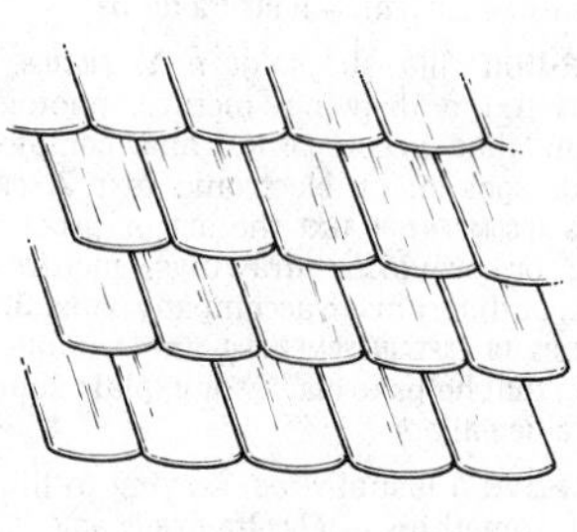

imbricate

im·bri·cate /ímbrə kàyt/ *adj* **1.** ARCHIT **MADE OF OVERLAPPING TILES** consisting of overlapping tiles or slates **2.** BOT, ZOOL **OVERLAPPING LIKE ROOF TILES** describes plant or animal parts that overlap in a regular pattern ■ *vti* (**-cat·ed, -cat·ing, -cates**) **OVERLAP OR BE OVERLAPPING** to lay things so that they overlap in layers in a similar way to roof tiles, or be laid in this way [Mid-17C. < Latin *imbricat-*, past participle of *imbricare* "cover with pantiles" < *imbric-* "roof tile" < *imber* "rain"] —**im·bri·cat·ed** *adj* —**im·bri·ca·tion** /ìmbrə káysh'n/ *n*

im·bro·glio /im brṓlyō/ (*plural* **-glios**) *n* a confusing, messy, or complicated situation, especially one that involves disagreement or intrigue [Mid-18C. < Italian < *brogliare* "mix up," probably < Old French *brōoillier*]

im·brue /im bróo/ (**-brued, -bru·ing, -brues**) *vt* to stain something, especially with blood (*archaic or literary*) [Early 16C. < Old French *embruer* "to soil, spatter"]

im·bue /im byóo/ (**-bued, -bu·ing, -bues**) *vt* **1.** to make somebody or something rich with a particular quality (*usually passive*) ○ *poetry imbued with melancholy* **2.** to saturate something with a substance, especially dye (*formal*) [Late 16C. < Latin *imbuere* "moisten, stain"]

~~**imediately**~~ incorrect spelling of **immediately**

IMF *abbr* International Monetary Fund

~~**imformation**~~ incorrect spelling of **information**

IMHO *abbr* in my humble opinion (*used in e-mails or text messages*)

im·id·az·ole /ìmmə dá zṓl/ *n* an organic white crystalline base that inhibits the action of histamine. Formula: $C_3H_4N_2$. [Late 19C. < IMIDE + AZO- + -OLE]

im·ide /ím īd/ *n* an organic compound containing an NH group combined with an acid group and derived from ammonia [Mid-19C. < French, alteration of *amide* (see AMIDE)] —**i·mid·ic** /i míddik/ *adj*

i·mine /ìm een, ímmin, i méen/ *n* an organic compound containing an NH group combined with a nonacid group and derived from ammonia [Late 19C. Alteration of AMINE]

~~**iminent**~~ incorrect spelling of **imminent**

i·mip·ra·mine /i míppra meen/ *n* a tricyclic drug. Use: treatment of depression. [Mid-20C. Blend of IMINE + PROPYL + AMINE]

imit. *abbr* **1.** imitation **2.** imitative

im·i·tate /ímmi tàyt/ (**-tat·ed, -tat·ing, -tates**) *vt* **1. MIMIC SOMEBODY** to adopt somebody else's behavior, voice, or manner, sometimes in order to make fun of him or her **2. FOLLOW EXAMPLE OF SOMEBODY OR SOMETHING** to use somebody or something as a model, attempting to copy an existing method, style, or approach **3. BE OR LOOK LIKE SOMETHING** to be or look like something else ○ *a case of life imitating art* **4.** ARTS **COPY STYLE OF ARTISTIC WORK** to reproduce the style of a work of art such as a piece of literature, a painting, or a musical composition [Mid-16C. < Latin *imitat-*, past participle of *imitari*] —**im·i·ta·ble** *adj* —**im·i·ta·tor** *n*

SYNONYMS ***imitate, copy, emulate, mimic, ape***

CORE MEANING: to adopt the behavior of another person

imitate to adopt somebody else's behavior, voice, or manner, often in order to make fun of him or her ○ *"What shall I do, Fiona?" Fiona sneered, imitating Fergus's voice.* ○ *Children learn many skills by imitating their parents.* **copy** to do exactly what somebody else does ○ *Lennie admired George and tried to copy him.* ○ *A puppy will often watch and copy an older dog's actions.* **emulate** to try to equal or surpass somebody who is successful or admired ○ *She has a tough act to follow in attempting to emulate the success of her predecessor.* ○ *He's a truly great president, and one that I would certainly try to emulate.* **mimic** to adopt somebody else's voice, gestures, or appearance, in a deliberate and exaggerated way, especially to amuse people ○ *mimicking the professor's Southern accent* ○ *She whined, mimicking a spoiled child.* **ape** to act like somebody else in an absurd or grotesque way ○ *At home, the lifestyle of the nobles aped that of the royal household.*

im·i·ta·tion /ìmmi táysh'n/ *n* **1. ACT OF IMITATING SOMETHING** the act or an instance of imitating somebody or something, or of using something or somebody as a model **2. COPY OR FAKE** something made to be as much as possible like something else (*often used before a noun*) **3. IMPRESSION OF SOMEBODY** the act of mimicking somebody, or an impression of somebody **4.** MUSIC **REPETITION OF MUSICAL MOTIF** the repetition of a musical idea such as a melody or rhythmic figure in the part for another voice or instrument, often at another pitch and sometimes with variation ■ *adj* **NOT GENUINE** synthetic, intended as a copy of something, or not genuine ○ *imitation leather* —**im·i·ta·tion·al** *adj*

im·i·ta·tive /ímmi tàytiv/ *adj* **1.** designed to be like something else, but usually inferior to the original **2.** involving or practicing imitation **3.** LANGUAGE same as **onomatopoeic** —**im·i·ta·tive·ly** *adv* —**im·i·ta·tive·ness** *n*

im·li /ímmlee/ *n S Asia* in South Asian cuisine, tamarind used as a flavoring [Via Hindi < Sanskrit *amlika*]

im·mac·u·late /i mákyələt/ *adj* **1.** absolutely clean, neat, and free from blemishes ○ *in immaculate condition* **2.** showing faultless perfection ○ *immaculate timing* [15C. < Latin *immaculatus* "without stain" < *macula* "blemish"] —**im·mac·u·late·ly** *adv* —**im·mac·u·late·ness** *n*

Im·mac·u·late Con·cep·tion *n* **1.** in the Roman Catholic Church, the doctrine that the Virgin Mary's soul was free from the stain of original sin from the moment of her soul's conception. The term does not, contrary to popular belief, refer to the conception of Jesus Christ. **2.** in the Roman Catholic Church, the feast of the Immaculate Conception. Date: December 8.

im·ma·nent /ímmənənt/ *adj* **1.** existing within or inherent in something (*formal*) **2.** describes God as existing in and extending into all parts of the created universe [Mid-16C. < late Latin *immanent-*, present participle of *immanere*, literally "dwell within" < Latin *manere* "remain, dwell"] —**im·ma·nence** *n* —**im·ma·nent·ly** *adv*

SPELLCHECK Do not confuse the spelling of ***immanent*** and ***imminent*** ("about to occur"), which sound similar.

im·ma·nent·ism /ímmənən tìzzəm/ *n* the belief that God exists in and extends into all parts of the created universe, including the individual —**im·ma·nent·ist** *adj, n* —**im·ma·nent·is·tic** /ìmmənən tístik/ *adj*

Im·man·u·el /i mánnyoo əl/, **Em·man·u·el** *n* the Messiah referred to in Jewish and Christian scriptures, whom Christians believe to be Jesus Christ [15C. Via late Latin < Greek *Emmanouēl* < Hebrew *'immānū'ēl* "with us is God"]

im·ma·te·ri·al /immə téeree əl/ *adj* **1.** lacking relevance or importance **2.** not made of matter, or not physically real —**im·ma·te·ri·al·i·ty** /immə téeree állətee/ *n* —**im·ma·te·ri·al·ly** *adv*

im·ma·te·ri·al·ism /immə téeree ə lìzzəm/ *n* the metaphysical doctrine that the material world does not exist except as ideas or perceptions in the mind, or that only spirits and nonphysical things exist

im·ma·te·ri·al·ize /immə téeree ə lìz/ (**-ized, -iz·ing, -iz·es**) *vt* to take away the physical substance of something and make it spiritual or intangible

im·ma·ture /immə chóor/ *adj* **1.** NOT FULLY DEVELOPED young, and not fully grown or developed **2.** CHILDISH lacking the wisdom or emotional development usually associated with adults **3.** STYLISTICALLY CRUDE AND IMPERFECT not yet having attained the perfection of a fully developed style ○ *The painting is clearly an immature work.* —**im·ma·ture·ly** *adv* —**im·ma·tur·i·ty** *n*

im·meas·ur·a·ble /i mé<u>zh</u>ərəb'l/ *adj* too large or too much to be measured —**im·meas·ur·a·bly** *adv*

im·me·di·ate /i méedee ət/ *adj* **1.** WITHOUT PAUSE OR DELAY happening or done at first, at once, or without delay ○ *had no immediate comment* **2.** NEAREST nearest in time, space, or relationship ○ *his immediate family* ○ *the immediate future* **3.** CURRENT urgent or pressing, and so needing to be dealt with before anything else ○ *the immediate problem* **4.** HAVING DIRECT EFFECT affecting something directly, without anything intervening ○ *the immediate cause* **5.** PHILOSOPHY KNOWN FROM EXPERIENCE relating to something that is known about from personal experience or by intuition **6.** LOGIC DERIVED FROM SINGLE PREMISE describes an inference derived from a single premise, without any middle term, and often by conversion of a categorical statement. An example is "some cows are brown, therefore some brown things are cows." [14C. Directly or via French < late Latin *immediatus* "not separated" < Latin *mediatus*, past participle of *mediare* (see MEDIATE)] —**im·me·di·a·cy** *n* —**im·me·di·ate·ness** *n*

im·me·di·ate con·stit·u·ent *n* the first level into which a linguistic unit is analyzed, e.g., the subject and predicate as parts of a sentence

im·me·di·ate·ly /i méedee ətlee/ *adv* **1.** AT ONCE without delay or without pausing beforehand **2.** VERY CLOSELY very closely in space or time **3.** DIRECTLY directly, and without anyone or anything in between ■ *conj UK* AS SOON AS as soon as or at the moment that

im·me·mo·ri·al /immə máwree əl/ *adj* so old that it seems always to have existed ○ *have known them since time immemorial* ○ *immemorial customs of the nation* —**im·me·mo·ri·al·ly** *adv*

im·mense /i ménss/ *adj* **1.** exceptionally great in extent or degree ○ *an immense desert* ○ *immense relief* **2.** very good or showing excellence (*slang*) [15C. Via French < Latin *immensus* "not measured" < *mensus*, past participle of *metiri* "measure"] —**im·mense·ness** *n* —**im·men·si·ty** *n*

im·mense·ly /i ménsslee/ *adv* to a huge extent or degree ○ *She was immensely rich.*

im·merse /i múrss/ (**-mersed, -mers·ing, -mers·es**) *v* **1.** *vt* COVER SOMETHING COMPLETELY IN LIQUID to put something into a liquid so that it is entirely below the surface **2. im·merse your·self** *vr* OCCUPY YOURSELF TOTALLY WITH SOMETHING to become completely occupied with something, giving all your time, energy, or concentration to it ○ *immersed herself in her work* **3.** *vt* CHR BAPTIZE SOMEBODY to baptize somebody by lowering the person's head and upper body, or sometimes the whole body, into water [Early 17C. < Latin *immers-*, past participle of *immergere* "plunge into" < *mergere* "plunge"]

im·mer·sion /i múrsh'n, i mú<u>rzh</u>'n/ *n* **1.** COMPLETE INVOLVEMENT involvement in something that completely occupies all the time, energy, or concentration available **2.** EDUC METHOD OF LANGUAGE TEACHING a method of language teaching that involves teachers and students using the foreign language at all times (*often used before a noun*) ○ *an immersion course* **3.** SUBMERSION the placement of something into a liquid so that it is completely covered **4.** CHR BAPTISM BY DIPPING BODY IN WATER the practice of baptism by lowering somebody's head and upper body, or sometimes the whole body, into water **5.** ASTRON PASSAGE OF ASTRONOMICAL OBJECT INTO ECLIPSE the movement of an astronomical object such as the Moon into the shadow of another object, causing an eclipse

im·mer·sion foot *n* MED same as **trench foot**

im·mer·sion heat·er *n* an electric water heater with the heating element completely submerged in the water, especially one that is part of a domestic hot-water tank

im·mer·sion·ism /i múrsh'n ìzzəm, i mú<u>rzh</u>'n-/ *n* in some Christian denominations, the belief that immersion is the only true method of baptism

im·mer·sion suit *n* NAUT same as **survival suit**

im·mesh *vt* same as **enmesh**

im·mi·grant /immigrənt/ *n* **1.** SOMEBODY SETTLING IN COUNTRY a newcomer to a country who has settled there **2.** PLANT OR ANIMAL IN NEW PLACE a plant or animal that establishes itself in a place where it was not found before ■ *adj* SETTLING IN ANOTHER COUNTRY relating to those who have come to settle in another country

im·mi·grate /immi gràyt/ (**-grat·ed, -grat·ing, -grates**) *v* **1.** *vi* COME AND SETTLE IN COUNTRY to enter a new country for the purpose of settling there **2.** *vt* BRING IN PEOPLE AS SETTLERS to bring people into a country and settle them as permanent residents there **3.** *vi* ARRIVE FROM ELSEWHERE to become established in a new environment (*refers to plants and animals*) —**im·mi·gra·tor** *n* —**im·mi·gra·to·ry** /ímmigrə tàwree/ *adj*

im·mi·gra·tion /immi gráysh'n/ *n* **1.** the act of entering a new country to settle permanently **2.** the control point at an airport, seaport, or border crossing where people entering a country must stop to have their passports officially checked —**im·mi·gra·tion·al** *adj*

Im·mi·gra·tion *n* the United States Immigration and Naturalization Service (**INS**) (*informal*)

im·mi·nent /imminənt/ *adj* about to happen, or threatening to happen [Early 16C. < Latin *imminent-*, present participle of *imminere* "hang over" < *minere* "to project"] —**im·mi·nence** *n* —**im·mi·nent·ly** *adv* —**im·mi·nent·ness** *n*

SPELLCHECK See *immanent*

im·mis·ci·ble /i míssəb'l/ *adj* describes two or more liquids that will not mix together to form a single homogeneous substance [Late 17C. < late Latin *immiscibilis* "not subject to mixing" < Latin *miscere* "to mix"] —**im·mis·ci·bil·i·ty** /i mìssə bíllətee/ *n* —**im·mis·ci·bly** *adv*

im·mis·er·ate /i mízzə ràyt/ (**-at·ed, -at·ing, -ates**) *vt* to cause severe economic hardship to a person or a people (*literary*) —**im·mis·er·a·tion** *n*

im·mit·i·ga·ble /i míttigəb'l/ *adj* incapable of being alleviated, weakened, or softened (*formal*) —**im·mit·i·ga·bil·i·ty** /i mìttigə bíllətee/ *n* —**im·mit·i·ga·bly** *adv*

im·mit·tance /i mítt'nss/ *n* the joint concept of electrical admittance and impedance [Mid-20C. Blend of IMPEDANCE + ADMITTANCE]

im·mo·bile /i mṓb'l/ *adj* **1.** without moving ○ *He stood perfectly immobile for a few seconds.* **2.** unable to move or be moved —**im·mo·bil·i·ty** /immō bíllətee, ìmmə-/ *n*

im·mo·bi·lize /i mṓb'l ìz/ (**-lized, -liz·ing, -liz·es**) *vt* **1.** RESTRICT MOVEMENT OF SOMEBODY OR SOMETHING to prevent somebody or something from moving (*often passive*) **2.** PUT MACHINE OUT OF ACTION to make a machine or device stop working, or adjust or damage it so that it cannot be made to work **3.** MED KEEP BROKEN LIMB STILL to rest a joint or keep the parts of a fractured limb fixed in place so that they are unable to move **4.** FIN TAKE MONEY OUT OF CIRCULATION to withdraw money or other capital from circulation to establish a reserve —**im·mo·bi·li·za·tion** /i mṑb'li záysh'n/ *n*

im·mod·er·ate /i móddərət/ *adj* going beyond what is healthy, moral, appropriate, or socially acceptable —**im·mod·er·a·cy** *n* —**im·mod·er·ate·ly** *adv* —**im·mod·er·ate·ness** *n* —**im·mod·er·a·tion** /i mòddə ráysh'n/ *n*

im·mod·est /i móddəst/ *adj* **1.** boasting, or tending to boast a great deal **2.** likely to embarrass, offend, or shock people, especially because of open references to sexual matters or exposure of parts of the body that are normally covered —**im·mod·est·ly** *adv* —**im·mod·es·ty** *n*

im·mo·late /immə làyt/ (**-lat·ed, -lat·ing, -lates**) *vt* to kill a person or an animal, e.g., as a ritual sacrifice, or commit suicide as a protest, especially by burning (*formal*) [Mid-16C. < Latin *immolat-*, present participle of *immolare* "sprinkle with meal" < *mola* "meal, millstone"; from the custom of sprinkling sacrificial victims with meal] —**im·mo·la·tion** /immə láysh'n/ *n* —**im·mo·la·tor** *n*

im·mor·al /i máwrəl/ *adj* contrary to accepted moral principles —**im·mor·al·i·ty** /i maw rállətee/ *n* —**im·mor·al·ly** *adv*

im·mor·al·ist /i máwrəlist/ *n* somebody who behaves immorally or who urges others to behave so

im·mor·tal /i máwrt'l/ *adj* **1.** NEVER DYING able to have eternal life or existence **2.** FAMOUS very famous and likely to be remembered for a long time ■ *n* **1.** FAMOUS PERSON OR THING somebody or something so famous as to be remembered for a long time (*often used in the plural*) **2.** *also* **Im·mor·tal** DEITY a god who lives forever, especially a god of ancient Greece or Rome —**im·mor·tal·i·ty** /i mawr tállətee/ *n* —**im·mor·tal·ly** *adv*

im·mor·tal·ize /i máwrt'l ìz/ (**-ized, -iz·ing, -iz·es**) *vt* **1.** MAKE SOMEBODY'S MEMORY LIVE ON to make somebody or something famous for a very long time, especially as the subject of a work of art such as a painting, novel, or movie **2.** GIVE ETERNAL LIFE TO SOMEBODY to elevate a mortal person to the state of divinity or bestow eternal life on somebody **3.** BIOL CAUSE SOMETHING TO REPRODUCE INDEFINITELY to cause something such as human cells to reproduce indefinitely —**im·mor·tal·i·za·tion** /i màwrt'li záysh'n/ *n*

im·mor·telle /i mawr tél/ *n* PLANTS same as **everlasting** *n* (sense 2) [Mid-19C. < French, shortening of *fleur immortelle* "undying flower"]

im·mo·tile /i mṓt'l/ *adj* describes a plant or animal part that cannot move —**im·mo·til·i·ty** /immō tíllətee/ *n*

im·mov·a·ble /i móovəb'l/ *adj* **1.** UNABLE TO BE MOVED fixed in a permanent position, or incapable of being moved **2.** OF FIXED OPINION sticking firmly to an opinion or decision **3.** ALWAYS OCCURRING ON SAME DATE describes a religious festival that always falls on the same date each year, as does Christmas but not Hanukkah ■ *n* LAW BUILDINGS OR LAND property that consists of land or buildings (*often used in the plural*) —**im·mov·a·bil·i·ty** /i mòovə bíllətee/ *n* —**im·mov·a·ble·ness** *n* —**im·mov·a·bly** *adv*

immun. *abbr* **1.** immunity **2.** immunization **3.** immunology

im·mune /i myóon/ *adj* **1.** SAFE FROM DISEASE protected from getting a disease because of natural resistance, resistance acquired after catching the disease, or resistance conferred by inoculation ○ *immune to smallpox* **2.** RELATING TO DISEASE RESISTANCE relating to or involved in a body's resistance to disease or the creation of this resistance **3.** NOT SUBJECT TO SOMETHING exempt from something that others are subject to or made to endure or perform ○ *immune from prosecution* **4.** NOT AFFECTED BY SOMETHING not sensitive or susceptible to something ○ *immune to flattery* [Late 19C. < Latin *immunis* "exempt from public service" < *munis* "ready for service"]

im·mune com·plex *n* a combination of a disease-causing agent (**antigen**) and its corresponding antibody that plays a role in some types of immune responses and may be associated with autoimmune disease

im·mune re·sponse *n* **1.** the overall activity of the body's immune system following the arrival of a disease-causing agent (**antigen**) **2.** the integrated defense mounted by an organism against a disease-causing agent (**antigen**), including the production of antibodies and white blood cells designed to destroy the antigen or render it harmless

im·mune sys·tem *n* the interacting combination of all the body's ways of recognizing cells, tissues, objects, and organisms that are not part of itself, and initiating the immune response to fight them

im·mu·ni·ty /i myóonətee/ (*plural* **-ties**) *n* **1.** RESISTANCE TO DISEASE a body's ability to resist a disease. Immunity may exist naturally or as a result of inoculation or previous infection. In active immunity, the body itself produces appropriate antibodies and lymphocytes, while in passive immunity, antibodies are introduced from another source, as from mother to fetus. ○ *immunity to smallpox* **2.** FREEDOM FROM RESPONSIBILITY OR PUNISHMENT exemption or protection from something unpleasant, e.g., a duty or penalty, to which others are subject ○ *immunity from deportation* **3.** LAW EXEMPTION FROM PROSECUTION an exemption from prosecution for somebody who has knowledge of possible criminal activity and may be personally culpable, offered in exchange for giving sufficient information to the police or to a grand jury

im·mu·nize /ímmyə nīz/ (**-nized, -niz·ing, -niz·es**) *vt* **1.** to make somebody resistant to a disease, especially by vaccination ○ *people who were immunized against tuberculosis* **2.** give somebody exemption or protection from something that others are subjected to, especially in a criminal matter under investigation —**im·mu·ni·za·tion** /ìmmyəni záysh'n/ *n* —**im·mu·niz·er** *n*

immuno- *prefix* immune, immunity ○ *immunodeficiency* [< IMMUNE]

im·mu·no·as·say /ìmmyənō ássay, i myŏŏ-/ *n* a technique for measuring the amount of antigens and antibodies in tissue —**im·mu·no·as·say·ist** *n*

im·mu·no·bi·ol·o·gy /ìmmyənō bī óllǝjee, i myŏŏ-/ *n* a branch of biology dealing with the effects of the immune system on factors affecting the body, including disease, growth, and genetics —**im·mu·no·bi·o·log·ic** /ìmmyənō bī ə lójjik, i myŏŏ-/ *adj* —**im·mu·no·bi·o·log·i·cal** *adj*

im·mu·no·chem·is·try /ìmmyənō kémmistree, i myŏŏ-/ *n* the study of antibodies using chemical techniques —**im·mu·no·chem·i·cal** *adj*

im·mu·no·com·pe·tence /ìmmyənō kómpət'nss, i myŏŏ-/ *n* the ability of the body to develop an immune response in the presence of a disease-causing agent (**antigen**) —**im·mu·no·com·pe·tent** *adj*

im·mu·no·com·plex /ìmmyənō kóm plèks, i myŏŏnō-/ *n* IMMUNOL same as **immune complex**

im·mu·no·com·pro·mised /ìmmyənō kómprə mīzd, ì myŏŏ-/ *adj* lacking an adequate immune response as a result of disease, exposure to radiation, or treatment with immunosuppressive drugs

im·mu·no·cy·to·chem·is·try /ìmmyənō sītō kémmistree, i myŏŏ-/ *n* a branch of biochemistry that deals with the immunological reactions of cells —**im·mu·no·cy·to·chem·i·cal** *n*

im·mu·no·de·fi·cien·cy /ìmmyənō di físh'nssee, ì myŏŏ-/ (*plural* **-cies**) *n* the inability, either inborn or acquired, of the body to produce an adequate immune response to fight disease —**im·mu·no·de·fi·cient** *adj*

im·mu·no·de·pres·sion /ìmmyənō də présh'n, i myŏŏ-/ *n* MED same as **immunosuppression**

im·mu·no·di·ag·no·sis /ìmmyənō dī əg nóssiss, i myŏŏ-/ (*plural* **-no·ses** /-nō seez/) *n* the diagnosis of disease by studying the antibodies in a sample of blood serum —**im·mu·no·di·ag·nos·tic** /ìmmyənō dī əg nóstik, i myŏŏ-/ *adj*

im·mu·no·e·lec·tro·pho·re·sis /ìmmyənō i lèktrōfə réessiss, i myŏŏ-/ *n* a method of separating and identifying a mixture of antigens using electrophoresis to separate them and an antigen-antibody reaction to identify them —**im·mu·no·e·lec·tro·pho·re·tic** /ìmmyənō i lèktrəfə réttik, i myŏŏ-/ *adj* —**im·mu·no·e·lec·tro·pho·ret·i·cal·ly** *adv*

im·mu·no·fluo·res·cence /ìmmyənō flŏŏ réss'nss, -flaw-, i myŏŏ-/ *n* the labeling of antibodies or disease-causing agents (**antigens**) with a fluorescent dye in order to identify or locate them in a tissue sample —**im·mu·no·fluo·res·cent** *adj*

im·mu·no·ge·net·ics /ìmmyənō jə néttiks, i myŏŏ-/ *n* the study of the genetic basis of the immune system. This study is especially important in organ transplantation, where a close genetic match of tissue lowers the likelihood of organ rejection. (*takes a singular verb*) —**im·mu·no·ge·net·ic** *adj* —**im·mu·no·ge·net·i·cist** /ìmmyənō jə néttəssist, i myŏŏ-/ *n*

im·mu·no·gen·ic /ìmmyənō jénnik, i myŏŏ-/ *adj* creating immunity or an immune response —**im·mu·no·gen·i·cal·ly** *adv* —**im·mu·no·gen·ic·i·ty** /ìmmyənō jə níssətee, i myŏŏ-/ *n*

im·mu·no·glob·u·lin /ìmmyənō glóbbyəlin, i myŏŏ-/ *n* an antibody belonging to a group formed by cells of the immune system and present in the blood. Immunoglobulins are found in blood serum, the respiratory and digestive tracts, and body secretions, and they are grouped into five classes on the basis of their structure and physiological activity.

im·mu·no·he·ma·tol·o·gy /ìmmyənō hemə tóllǝjee, -heemə-, i myŏŏ-/ *n* the discipline concerned with all aspects of immunology relating to the blood, including blood types and blood disorders —**im·mu·no·he·ma·to·log·ic** /ìmmyənō hemətə lójjik, -heemə-, i myŏŏ-/ *adj* —**im·mu·no·he·ma·to·log·i·cal** /-lójjik'l/ *adj*

im·mu·nol·o·gy /ìmmyə nóllǝjee/ *n* the scientific study of the way the immune system works in the body, including allergies, resistance to disease, and acceptance or rejection of foreign tissue —**im·mu·no·log·ic** /ìmmyənə lójjik/ *adj* —**im·mu·no·log·i·cal** *adj* —**im·mu·no·log·i·cal·ly** *adv* —**im·mu·nol·o·gist** *n*

im·mu·no·mod·u·la·tion /ìmmyənō mojə láysh'n, i myŏŏ-/ *n* the modification of some aspect of the immune system as part of a treatment, especially the suppression of the immune system in order to encourage the body to accept a transplanted organ —**im·mu·no·mod·u·la·to·ry** /ìmmyənō mójjələ tàwree, i myŏŏ-/ *adj*

im·mu·no·path·ol·o·gy /ìmmyənō pə thóllǝjee, i myŏŏ-/ *n* the study of disorders of the immune system and the resulting diseases or allergies —**im·mu·no·path·o·log·ic** /ìmmyənō pathə lójjik/ *adj*—**im·mu·no·path·o·log·i·cal** *adj* —**im·mu·no·path·ol·o·gist** *n*

im·mu·no·phar·ma·col·o·gy /ìmmyənō fàarmə kóllǝjee, i myŏŏ-/ *n* the science or study of drugs used to treat allergic diseases and the immune system —**im·mu·no·phar·ma·co·log·ic** /-fàarməkə lójjik/ *adj* —**im·mun·o·phar·ma·co·log·i·cal** *adj* —**im·mun·o·phar·ma·col·o·gist** *n*

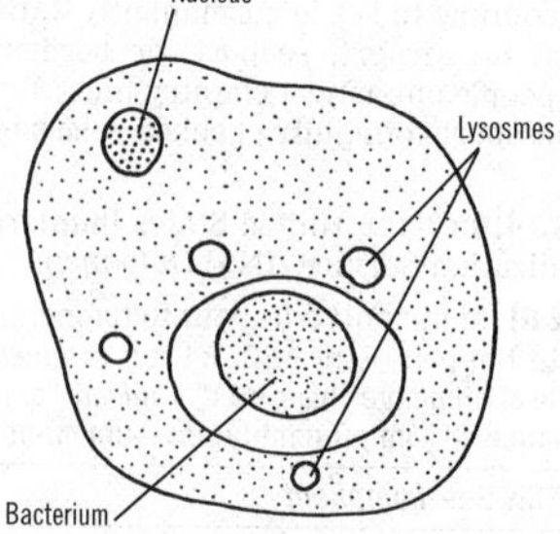

immunoreaction: section of an immune cell ingesting and degrading a disease-causing bacterium

im·mu·no·re·ac·tion /ìmmyənō ree áksh'n, i myŏŏ-/ *n* the reaction between a disease-causing agent (**antigen**) and its specific antibody, either as the body's immune response or as part of a laboratory procedure —**im·mu·no·re·ac·tive** *adj* —**im·mu·no·re·ac·tiv·i·ty** /ìmmyənō ree ak tívvətee, i myŏŏ-/ *n*

im·mu·no·sup·pres·sion /ìmmyənō sə présh'n, i myŏŏ-/ *n* the inhibition of the immune response, usually deliberately by administering drugs to prevent rejection of transplanted organs, but sometimes resulting from disease, as in the case of AIDS —**im·mu·no·sup·pres·sant** *adj, n* —**im·mu·no·sup·pres·sive** *adj, n*

im·mu·no·ther·a·py /ìmmyənō thérrəpee, i myŏŏ-/ *n* treatment of disease or other disorders by strengthening the body's immune system, e.g., by administering antibodies —**im·mu·no·ther·a·peu·tic** /ìmmyənō thèrrə pyóotik, i myŏŏ-/ *adj*

im·mu·no·tox·ic·i·ty /ìmmyənō tok síssətee, i myŏŏ-/ *n* the degree to which something is toxic to the immune system —**im·mu·no·tox·ic** /ìmmyənō tóksik, i myŏŏ-/ *adj* —**im·mu·no·tox·i·cal·ly** *adv*

im·mu·no·tox·i·col·o·gy /ìmmyənō toksi kóllǝjee, i myŏŏ-/ *n* a branch of medicine dealing with the effects of toxic substances on the immune system —**im·mu·no·tox·i·co·log·ic** /-tòksikə lójjik/ *adj* —**im·mu·no·tox·i·co·log·i·cal** *adj* —**im·mu·no·tox·i·col·o·gist** *n*

im·mure /i myŏŏr/ (**-mured, -mur·ing, -mures**) *vt* **1.** IMPRISON SOMEBODY to confine somebody in prison (*literary; usually passive*) **2.** SHUT SOMEBODY AWAY to shut away or seclude somebody (*formal; often passive*) **3.** ENCLOSE SOMETHING to enclose something in a wall or surround something with walls (*archaic*) [Late 16C. Directly or via French < Latin *immurare* "wall in" < *murus* "wall"] —**im·mure·ment** *n*

im·mu·ta·ble /i myóotəb'l/ *adj* not changing or not able to be changed —**im·mu·ta·bil·i·ty** /i myòotə bíllətee/ *n* —**im·mu·ta·ble·ness** *n* —**im·mu·ta·bly** *adv*

IMO *abbr* **1.** ONLINE in my opinion (*used in e-mails or text messages*) **2.** International Meteorological Organization **3.** International Miners' Organization

imp /imp/ *n* **1.** NAUGHTY IMAGINARY BEING a small, mischievous, imaginary being **2.** MISCHIEVOUS CHILD a high-spirited or mischievous child **3.** DEMON a small demon or devil ■ *vt* (**imped, imp·ing, imps**) REPAIR HAWK'S FEATHERS in falconry, to repair the broken wing of a hawk or falcon by grafting on new feathers [Old English *impa* "young shoot, scion," *impian* "to graft" < Greek *emphuein* "implant" < *phuein* "grow"]

IMP *abbr* **1.** imperial **2.** COMPUT interface message processor **3.** CARDS International Match Point

imp. *abbr* **1.** GRAM imperative **2.** GRAM imperfect **3.** imperial **4.** COMM import **5.** important **6.** COMM imported **7.** COMM importer **8.** PUBL imprimatur

Imp. *abbr* GOV **1.** Emperor **2.** Empress [Latin *Imperator* (masculine), *Imperatrix* (feminine)]

im·pact *n* /ím pàkt/ **1.** ACTION OF HITTING the action of one object hitting another **2.** FORCE OF COLLISION the force with which one object hits another **3.** ⚠ STRONG EFFECT the powerful or dramatic effect that something or somebody has ■ *vti* /im pákt/ (**-pact·ed, -pact·ing, -pacts**) **1.** STRIKE SOMETHING to strike something with force **2.** ⚠ HAVE EFFECT ON SOMETHING OR SOMEBODY to have an immediate and strong effect on something or somebody [Early 17C. < Latin *impactus*, past participle of *impingere* (see IMPINGE)] —**im·pac·tion** /im páksh'n/ *n*

USAGE Impact, noun and verb: Many careful writers strongly dislike the verb ***impact*** in any figurative sense whatsoever, as in *The revised budget impacts the university unfavorably* and *The revised budget impacts on the athletic program.* Though the verb in senses extending beyond the infliction of physical force is undeniably common in business, legal, journalistic, and political discourse, anyone who hopes to achieve an effect even faintly literary should avoid it in favor of *affect, change,* or similar verbs. Use of the verb is uncontroversial only in physical senses: *The car impacted the railing.* By the same token, the noun ***impact*** should not be used as a catchall alternative for words like *effect* or *impression*; rather, it should be used to convey the idea of powerful, dramatic consequence: *The sudden rise in prices had a calamitous impact on many economies.*

im·pact ad·he·sive *n* a powerful glue that begins to form a bond as soon as the two coated surfaces are brought together

im·pact·ed /im páktəd/ *adj* **1.** WEDGED SIDEWAYS UNDER THE GUM describes an unerupted tooth wedged sideways against a barrier, usually the root of another tooth, and thus unable to break through the gum **2.** WITH BROKEN ENDS JAMMED TOGETHER describes a bone fracture with the broken ends jammed tightly together by the initial trauma **3.** MED COMPRESSED IN THE INTESTINE TOO TIGHTLY describes feces pressed together so tightly in the intestine that they cannot be eliminated in a bowel movement **4.** DIFFICULT TO MOVE unable to be moved, usually because of being jammed in a narrow space

im·pact print·er *n* a printing device in which ink is pressed onto the paper by the printing element, as it is in a traditional typewriter

im·pact state·ment *n* a written statement outlining the effects of something on a specific person or place ○ *a consumer impact statement*

im·pact zone *n* in surfing, the best and also the most dangerous position on a wave, where the water is about to separate into droplets

im·pair /im páir/ (**-paired, -pair·ing, -pairs**) *vt* to lessen the quality, strength, or effectiveness of something [14C. < Old French *empeirier*, literally "make worse" < Latin *pejor* "worse"] —**im·pair·a·ble** *adj* —**im·pair·er** *n* —**im·pair·ment** *n*

im·paired *adj* with something absent or lessened, either temporarily or permanently (*usually used in combination*) ○ *hearing-impaired*

im·pa·la /im páalə/ (*plural* **-las** or *same*) *n* a large reddish brown antelope with long curved horns that makes spectacular leaps when alarmed. Native to: Africa. Latin name: *Aepyceros melampus.* See illustration on next page [Late 19C. < Zulu]

im·pale /im páyl/ (**-paled, -pal·ing, -pales**), **em·pale** /em páyl/ *vt* **1.** to pierce somebody or something with a pointed object (*often passive*) **2.** to combine two coats of arms on a single shield, divided by a vertical stripe (**pale**) [Mid-16C. Directly or via French < medieval Latin *impalare* "put on a stake" < Latin *palus* "stake"] —**im·pale·ment** *n* —**im·pal·er** *n*

im·pal·pa·ble /im pálpəb'l/ *adj* (*formal*) **1.** not capable

impala

of being perceived by the senses **2.** difficult to understand or grasp [Early 16C. Directly or via French < late Latin *impalpabilis* "not touchable" < *palpare* "touch gently"] —**im·pal·pa·bil·i·ty** /im pàlpə bíllətee/ *n* —**im·pal·pa·bly** *adv*

im·pa·na·tion /impə náysh'n/ *n* according to some denominations of Christianity, the presence of the body and blood of Jesus Christ in bread and wine that has been consecrated for the service of Communion [Mid-16C. < medieval Latin *impanation-* < *impanare* "embody in bread" < Latin *panis* "bread"]

im·pan·el /im pánn'l/ (**-eled, -el·ing, -els**), **em·pan·el** /em-/ *vt* **1.** to draw up a list of people to be selected for jury service **2.** to select a jury from a list of eligible persons [15C. < Anglo-Norman *empaneller* "put on a list" < Old French *panel* "list, jury list" (see PANEL)]

im·part /im paárt/ (**-part·ed, -part·ing, -parts**) *vt* **1.** to communicate information or knowledge **2.** to give something a particular quality [Mid-16C. Via French < Latin *impartire* "give a share in" < *pars* "part"] —**im·par·ta·tion** /im paàr táysh'n/ *n*

im·par·tial /im paársh'l/ *adj* having no direct involvement or interest and not favoring one person or side more than another —**im·par·ti·al·i·ty** /im paàrshee állətee/ *n* —**im·par·tial·ly** *adv* —**im·par·tial·ness** *n*

im·part·i·ble /im paártəb'l/ *adj* not able to be divided, or not to be divided up [Late 16C. < late Latin *impartibilis* "not divisible" < *partire* (see PART)] —**im·part·i·bil·i·ty** /im paàrtə bíllətee/ *n* —**im·part·i·bly** *adv*

im·pass·a·ble /im pássəb'l/ *adj* **1.** impossible to travel on or through, e.g., because of being in bad condition or being blocked by snow, ice, or floodwaters **2.** impossible to solve or overcome ○ *impassable obstacles to peace* —**im·pass·a·bil·i·ty** /im pàssə bíllətee/ *n* —**im·pass·a·ble·ness** *n* —**im·pass·a·bly** *adv*

im·passe /im páss/ *n* **1.** a point at which no further progress can be made or agreement reached ○ *Talks have reached an impasse.* **2.** a road or passage that has no way out or through, e.g., a dead end or a blockage caused by an accident [Mid-19C. < French < *im-* "not" + *passer* (see PASS)]

im·pas·si·ble /im pássəb'l/ *adj* **1.** not susceptible to or not capable of feeling physical pain or injury (*formal*) **2.** not capable of feeling or expressing emotion (*formal or literary*) [14C. Via French < ecclesiastical Latin *impassibilis* "not feeling" < Latin *pass-*, past participle of *pati* "suffer"] —**im·pas·si·bil·i·ty** /im pàssə bíllətee/ *n* —**im·pas·si·ble·ness** *n* —**im·pas·si·bly** *adv*

im·pas·sion /im pásh'n/ (**-sioned, -sion·ing, -sions**) *vt* to arouse strong feelings in somebody (*usually passive*) ○ *a crowd that was impassioned by his oratory* [Late 16C. < Italian *impassionare* < *passione* "passion" < late Latin *passion-* (see PASSION)]

im·pas·sioned /im pásh'nd/ *adj* expressing or revealing strong feelings —**im·pas·sioned·ly** *adv* —**im·pas·sioned·ness** *n*

im·pas·sive /im pássiv/ *adj* **1.** showing no outward sign of emotion, especially on the face **2.** feeling no emotions at all, either positive or negative [Early 17C. < IM-[1] + PASSIVE] —**im·pas·sive·ly** *adv* —**im·pas·sive·ness** *n* —**im·pas·siv·i·ty** /impə sívvətee/ *n*

SYNONYMS ***impassive, apathetic, phlegmatic, stolid, stoic, unmoved***

CORE MEANING: showing no emotional response or interest

impassive showing no outward sign of emotion, especially on the face ○ *the smile that transformed his usually impassive face* ○ *The defendant was impassive as the jury announced its verdict.* **apathetic** not taking any interest in anything, or not bothering to do anything ○ *The political turmoil of the last two years has left voters apathetic.* ○ *A recent report suggests that many people tend to be apathetic about the importance of health and fitness.* **phlegmatic** generally unemotional and difficult to arouse ○ *Although she was disappointed at the news, her response was phlegmatic.* **stolid** solemn, unemotional, and not easily excited or upset ○ *He was a stolid, dignified judge who spoke in slow, deliberate voice.* **stoic** showing admirable patience and endurance in the face of adversity without complaining or getting upset ○ *stoic acceptance of the lack of job security in the industry* **unmoved** having or showing no emotional reaction to something when it would usually be expected ○ *The country's head of state appeared unmoved by widespread international criticism of her policies.* ○ *The cities I had seen left me unmoved; they lacked the color and variety I craved.*

im·pas·to /im pástō, im paástō/ *n* **1.** in art, the technique of applying paint so thickly that brush or knife strokes can be seen **2.** in art, paint applied so thickly that brush or knife strokes can be seen [Late 18C. < Italian, past participle of *impastare* "paint thickly, encrust"]

impatiens

im·pa·tiens /im páysh'nz, -sh'nss/ (*plural same*) *n* a cultivated species of the balsam family, popular as a houseplant and garden plant. Flowers: multicolored. Latin name: *Impatiens balsamina.* [Late 18C. Via modern Latin < Latin, stem *impatient-*; because its capsules tend to burst open when touched]

im·pa·tient /im páysh'nt/ *adj* **1.** ANNOYED AT WAITING annoyed or tending to be annoyed at being kept waiting or by being delayed **2.** EAGER eager to do something immediately, and unwilling to wait **3.** EASILY ANNOYED unable to tolerate a particular thing and easily annoyed by it ○ *He was impatient of formalities.* [14C. Via French < Latin *impatient-*, literally "not enduring" < *pati* "suffer"] —**im·pa·tience** *n* —**im·pa·tient·ly** *adv*

im·peach /im peéch/ (**-peached, -peach·ing, -peach·es**) *vt* **1.** ACCUSE OFFICIAL OF OFFENSE to charge a serving government official with serious misconduct while in office **2.** CAST SOMEBODY OUT OF PUBLIC OFFICE to remove somebody such as a president or a judge from public office because of having committed serious crimes and misdemeanors or because of other gross misconduct (*formal*) **3.** LAW BRING CHARGES AGAINST SOMEBODY to charge somebody with a crime or misdemeanor **4.** DISPARAGE SOMEBODY to question a person's good character (*formal*) **5.** *UK* LAW ACCUSE SOMEBODY OF SERIOUS CRIME to accuse somebody of a crime, especially treason or another crime against the state [14C. Via Old French *empecher* < late Latin *impedicare* "entangle" < *pedica* "snare"] —**im·peach·a·ble** *adj* —**im·peach·er** *n* —**im·peach·ment** *n*

im·pec·ca·ble /im pékəb'l/ *adj* **1.** so perfect or flawless as to be beyond criticism ○ *She had impeccable taste.* **2.** so perfect in character as to be incapable of sinning [Mid-16C. < Latin *impeccabilis* "not liable to sin" < *peccare* "to sin"] —**im·pec·ca·bil·i·ty** /im pèkə bíllətee/ *n* —**im·pec·ca·bly** *adv*

im·pe·cu·ni·ous /impə kyoónee əss/ *adj* having little or no money, and so unable to lead a comfortable life [Late 16C. < IM-[1] + obsolete *pecunious* "wealthy" < Latin *pecunia* (see PECUNIARY)] —**im·pe·cu·ni·os·i·ty** /-kyoònee óssətee/ *n* —**im·pe·cu·ni·ous·ly** *adv* —**im·pe·cu·ni·ous·ness** *n*

im·pe·dance /im peéd'nss/ *n* **1.** PREVENTION OF PROGRESS something that delays or prevents progress, or the preventing of progress (*formal*) **2.** ELEC OPPOSITION TO FLOW OF ALTERNATING CURRENT the opposition in an electrical circuit to the flow of alternating current, consisting of resistance and reactance. Symbol ***Z*** **3.** ACOUSTICS RATIO OF SOUND PRESSURE TO VELOCITY the ratio of the sound pressure in a medium to the velocity of the particles in the medium

im·pede /im peéd/ (**-ped·ed, -ped·ing, -pedes**) *vt* to interfere with the movement, progress, or development of something or somebody [Late 16C. < Latin *impedire* "shackle the feet" < *ped-* "foot"] —**im·ped·er** *n*

SYNONYMS See ***hinder***[1].

im·ped·i·ment /im péddəmənt/ *n* **1.** IMPAIRMENT an impairment, especially one affecting speech **2.** OBSTACLE something that hinders progress **3.** LAW LEGAL OBSTRUCTION the reason a legal contract such as a marriage cannot be entered into [14C. < Latin *impedimentum* "hindrance" < *impedire* (see IMPEDE)] —**im·ped·i·men·tal** /im pèddə mént'l/ *adj* —**im·ped·i·men·ta·ry** /im pèddə méntəree/ *adj*

im·ped·i·men·ta /im pèddə méntə/ *npl* **1.** obstacles, hindrances, or obstructions to progress (*literary*) **2.** equipment and baggage carried by soldiers (*dated*) [Early 17C. < Latin, plural of *impedimentum* (see IMPEDIMENT)]

im·pel /im pél/ (**-pelled, -pel·ling, -pels**) *vt* **1.** to force somebody to do something, or make somebody feel the need to do something ○ *Their behavior impelled me to protest.* **2.** to start or keep something or somebody moving in a particular direction (*formal*) ○ *The boat was impelled toward the shore by the tide.* [15C. < Latin *impellere* "drive toward" < *pellere* "to beat"]

im·pel·ler /im péllər/ *n* the rotating part that transmits motion in a device such as a centrifugal pump, turbine, or blower

im·pend /im pénd/ (**-pend·ed, -pend·ing, -pends**) *vi* **1.** to be threateningly close to happening (*formal*) **2.** to hover or hang above something, usually in a threatening way (*literary*) [Late 16C. < Latin *impendere* "hang over" < *pendere* "hang"] —**im·pend·ence** *n* —**im·pend·en·cy** *n* —**im·pend·ent** *adj*

im·pend·ing /im pénding/ *adj* about to happen

im·pen·e·tra·ble /im pénnətrəb'l/ *adj* **1.** IMPOSSIBLE TO GET IN OR THROUGH not able to be passed through or entered ○ *The woods formed an impenetrable barrier.* **2.** INCOMPREHENSIBLE impossible to understand or discern ○ *impenetrable legal jargon* **3.** CLOSED TO INFLUENCE not open to intellectual or moral influences, impressions, or ideas —**im·pen·e·tra·bil·i·ty** /im pènnətrə bíllətee/ *n* —**im·pen·e·tra·bly** *adv*

im·pen·i·tent /im pénnit'nt/ *adj* having or showing no regret or sorrow for sin or misbehavior ■ *n* an unrepentant person —**im·pen·i·tence** *n* —**im·pen·i·ten·cy** *n* —**im·pen·i·tent·ly** *adv*

im·per·a·tive /im pérrətiv/ *adj* **1.** NECESSARY absolutely necessary or unavoidable ○ *It is imperative that justice is seen to be done.* **2.** COMMANDING forceful and demanding the obedience and respect of others (*formal*) **3.** GRAM USED FOR GIVING ORDERS describes the mood or a form of a verb that expresses a command or request, e.g., the verb form "come" in "Come here!" ■ *n* **1.** PRIORITY something that must be done ○ *Preservation of honor is a moral imperative.* **2.** GRAM WAY OF COMMANDING the mood of a verb used to give an order ○ *when the verb is used in the imperative* **3.** GRAM VERB EXPRESSING COMMAND OR REQUEST a verb in the imperative mood, e.g., "close" in "Please close the door" [15C. < late Latin *imperativus* "specially ordered" < Latin *imperare* "to command" < *parare* "prepare"] —**im·per·a·tive·ly** *adv* —**im·per·a·tive·ness** *n*

im·pe·ra·tor /impə raátər, -raá tàwr/ *n* **1.** ROMAN GENERAL a victorious military commander during the time of the Roman Republic **2.** ROMAN EMPEROR the head of state of the Roman Empire **3.** ABSOLUTE RULER an absolute ruler or commander [Mid-16C. < Latin, "commander" < *imperare* (see IMPERATIVE)] —**im·per·a·to·ri·al** /im pèrrə táwree əl/ *adj*

im·per·cep·ti·ble /impər séptəb'l/ *adj* very slight or gradual ○ *an imperceptible change in temperature* —**im·per·cep·ti·bil·i·ty** /-sèptə bíllətee/ *n* —**im·per·cep·ti·bly** *adv*

im·per·cep·tive /impər séptiv/ *adj* lacking the ability to notice things or to understand somebody or something —**im·per·cep·tive·ly** *adv* —**im·per·cep·tive·ness** *n* —**im·per·cep·tiv·i·ty** /-sep tívvətee/ *n*

imperf. *abbr* **1.** GRAM, BOT imperfect **2.** ANAT, STAMPS imperforate

im·per·fect /im púrfəkt/ *adj* **1. FAULTY** having a fault or defect **2. NOT COMPLETE** lacking a part **3.** BOT **NOT ABLE TO REPRODUCE** describes a flower that lacks either a stamen or a pistil and is therefore unable to reproduce **4.** MUSIC **NOT PERFECT AS INTERVAL** describes a musical interval other than the fourth, fifth, or octave **5.** MUSIC **ENDING ON 5TH NOTE OF SCALE** describes a cadence ending on the fifth note of the scale (**dominant**) rather than on the first note (**tonic**) **6.** GRAM **EXPRESSING INCOMPLETE ACTION** describes a verb form or tense that expresses past action going on but not completed **7.** LAW **UNENFORCEABLE** unable to be enforced ■ *n* GRAM **1. VERB TENSE** a grammatical tense that expresses incomplete or habitual action in the past **2. VERB FORM** a form of a verb used to express the imperfect tense —**im·per·fect·ly** *adv*—**im·per·fect·ness** *n*

im·per·fect fun·gus *n* a fungus that forms only asexual spores (**conidia**). Order: Fungi Imperfecti.

im·per·fec·tion /impər fékshən/ *n* **1.** something that makes a person or thing less than perfect **2.** the possession of faults or defects

SYNONYMS See *flaw*[1].

im·per·fec·tive /impər féktiv/ GRAM *adj* **INDICATING INCOMPLETE ACTION** describes a verb aspect expressing action that is not completed ■ *n* **1. VERB ASPECT** the imperfective aspect of the verb **2. VERB FORM** a verb form belonging to the imperfective aspect —**im·per·fec·tive·ly** *adv*

im·per·fo·rate /im púrfərət/ *adj* **1.** ANAT **PARTIALLY OR COMPLETELY CLOSED** describes a body part lacking an opening of the normal size, especially because of atypical development **2.** STAMPS **WITH NO HOLES** describes a sheet of postage stamps produced without the perforations that allow easy tearing or division ■ *n* STAMPS **STAMP WITHOUT PERFORATIONS** a stamp without perforations around it —**im·per·fo·ra·tion** /im pùrfə ráysh'n/ *n*

im·pe·ri·a plural of **imperium**

im·pe·ri·al /im péeree əl/ *adj* **1. OF EMPIRE OR EMPEROR** involving or relating to an empire or its ruler **2. INDICATING COUNTRY'S AUTHORITY** involving or relating to the authority of a country over colonies or other countries **3. SUPREMELY POWERFUL** holding supreme power ○ *All are subject to the imperial power of the state.* **4. GRAND** very grand or majestic **5. OF UK NONMETRIC MEASURES** in the United Kingdom, belonging or conforming to the nonmetric system of weights and measures that includes the foot, pound, and gallon ■ *n* **1. PAPER SIZE** the largest of the traditional US and UK paper sizes. The US imperial measures 23 x 33 in./584 x 838 mm. The UK imperial measures 22 x 30 in./559 x 762 mm. **2. SMALL BEARD** a tuft or point of hair grown on the chin or below the lower lip. This style was made fashionable by the French emperor Napoleon III. **3. RELATIVE OF EMPEROR OR EMPRESS** somebody belonging to an imperial family (*formal*) **4.** TRANSP **TRUNK FOR LUGGAGE** especially in the past, a chest put onto the top of a coach to store travelers' bags, or the part of a coach's roof where this chest fits **5.** BEVERAGES **LARGE WINE BOTTLE** a wine bottle containing the equivalent of eight standard bottles, used for claret [14C. Via French < Latin *imperialis* < *imperium* (see EMPIRE)] —**im·pe·ri·al·ly** *adv*

im·pe·ri·al gal·lon *n UK* MEASURE same as **gallon** *n* (sense 2)

im·pe·ri·al·ism /im péeree ə lìzzəm/ *n* **1. BELIEF IN EMPIRE-BUILDING** the policy of extending the rule or influence of a country over other countries or colonies **2. DOMINATION BY EMPIRE** the political, military, or economic domination of one country over another **3. TAKEOVER AND DOMINATION** the extension of power or authority over others in the interests of domination ○ *cultural imperialism* —**im·pe·ri·al·ist** *n, adj* —**im·pe·ri·al·is·tic** /im pèeree ə lístik/ *adj* —**im·pe·ri·al·is·ti·cal·ly** *adv*

im·pe·ri·al moth *n* a large moth that has yellow wings and purplish brown markings. Native to: North and South America. Latin name: *Eacles imperialis*. [< its purplish markings, because the color purple was traditionally used for rulers' garments]

Im·pe·ri·al Val·ley /impéeree əl-/ valley in southeastern California, part of a larger valley that extends into Mexico. It is a rich agricultural area. Length: 60 mi./97 km.

im·per·il /im pérrəl/ (**-iled, -il·ing, -ils**) *vt* to put something or somebody in danger —**im·per·il·ment** *n*

im·pe·ri·ous /im péeree əss/ *adj* haughty and domineering [Mid-16C. < Latin *imperiosus* < *imperium* (see EMPIRE)] —**im·pe·ri·ous·ly** *adv* —**im·pe·ri·ous·ness** *n*

im·per·ish·a·ble /im pérrishəb'l/ *adj* **1.** not liable to become spoiled, weak, or damaged through time and wear **2.** not forgotten or ignored over time (*literary*) ○ *The imperishable quality of great literature distinguishes it from humbler writing.* —**im·per·ish·a·bil·i·ty** /im pèrrishə bíllətee/ *n* —**im·per·ish·a·ble·ness** *n* —**im·per·ish·a·bly** *adv*

im·pe·ri·um /im péeree əm/ (*plural* **-ri·a** /-ree ə/) *n* **1. SUPREME POWER** supreme or imperial power (*formal*) **2. EMPIRE** an area controlled by a supreme power (*formal or literary*) **3.** LAW **LEGAL RIGHT TO COMMAND** the use of the power of the state to enforce the law [Mid-17C. < Latin (see EMPIRE)]

im·per·ma·nent /im púrmənənt/ *adj* likely to change, go away, disappear, or fade —**im·per·ma·nence** *n* —**im·per·ma·nen·cy** *n* —**im·per·ma·nent·ly** *adv*

im·per·me·a·ble /im púrmee əb'l/ *adj* not permitting the passage of liquid, gas, or other fluid —**im·per·me·a·bil·i·ty** /im pùrmee ə bíllətee/ *n* —**im·per·me·a·ble·ness** *n* —**im·per·me·a·bly** *adv*

im·per·mis·si·ble /impər míssəb'l/ *adj* not allowed ○ *Such conduct is impermissible.* —**im·per·mis·si·bil·i·ty** /impər mìssə bíllətee/ *n* —**im·per·mis·si·bly** *adv*

im·per·son·al /im púrssən'l, -púrssnəl/ *adj* **1. NOT PERSONALIZED** not referring to individual people or reflecting personalities but focusing on events and facts ○ *an impersonal style of reporting* **2. ANONYMOUS** not considering people as individuals ○ *an impersonal bureaucracy* **3. COLD AND ALIENATING** making somebody feel insignificant and ignored as a person ○ *The service in the restaurant was brisk and impersonal.* **4. LACKING HUMAN TRAITS** having no human characteristics or personality **5.** GRAM **NOT SPECIFIC** describes a clause or construction that includes a personal pronoun that does not refer to a specific person or thing, e.g., "it is raining" or "you shouldn't drink and drive" —**im·per·son·al·i·ty** /im pùrs'n állətee/ *n* —**im·per·son·al·ly** *adv*

im·per·son·al·ize /im púrssən'l ìz/ (**-ized, -iz·ing, -iz·es**) *vt* to make something neutral, lacking in human warmth, or without reference to individuals —**im·per·son·al·i·za·tion** /im pùrssən'li záysh'n/ *n*

im·per·son·ate /im púrss'n àyt/ (**-at·ed, -at·ing, -ates**) *vt* **1.** to mimic the voice, appearance, and manners of somebody else, especially in order to entertain **2.** to pretend to be somebody else, especially illegally in order to deceive [Early 17C. < IM + Latin *persona* "mask worn by an actor, character," after INCORPORATE] —**im·per·son·a·tion** /im pùrss'n áysh'n/ *n* —**im·per·son·a·tor** *n*

im·per·ti·nent /im púrt'nənt/ *adj* **1.** showing a bold or rude lack of respect, especially to a superior **2.** not appropriate or relevant (*formal*) —**im·per·ti·nence** *n* —**im·per·ti·nent·ly** *adv*

im·per·turb·a·ble /impər túrbəb'l/ *adj* not easily worried, distressed, or agitated ○ *The captain's imperturbable manner gave the crew confidence.* —**im·per·turb·a·bil·i·ty** /impər turbə bíllətee/ *n* —**im·per·turb·a·ble·ness** *n* —**im·per·turb·a·bly** *adv*

im·per·vi·ous /im púrvee əss/ *adj* **1.** remaining unmoved and unaffected by other people's opinions, arguments, or suggestions ○ *He was impervious to the growing resentment among the staff.* **2.** not allowing passage into or through something ○ *impervious to damp* [Mid-17C. < Latin *impervius* < *pervius* (see PERVIOUS)] —**im·per·vi·ous·ly** *adv* —**im·per·vi·ous·ness** *n*

im·pe·ti·go /impə tée gō, -tī-/ *n* a contagious infection of the skin caused by staphylococcal and streptococcal bacteria and characterized by blisters that form yellow-brown scabs [14C. < Latin < *impetere* (see IMPETUS)] —**im·pe·tig·i·nous** /impə tíjjənəss/ *adj*

im·pet·u·os·i·ty /im pèchoo óssətee/ (*plural* **-ties**) *n* **1.** a tendency to act rashly **2.** an act performed on the spur of the moment after little or no consideration (*formal*)

im·pet·u·ous /im péchoo əss/ *adj* **1. ACTING IMPULSIVELY** acting on the spur of the moment, without considering the consequences **2. DONE ON IMPULSE** done without thought as a reaction to an emotion or impulse **3. VIOLENT** moving with great force and energy (*literary*) [14C. Via French < late Latin *impetuosus* < *impetus* (see IMPETUS)] —**im·pet·u·ous·ly** *adv* —**im·pet·u·ous·ness** *n*

im·pe·tus /impətəss/ *n* **1.** energy or motivation to accomplish or undertake something **2.** PHYS a force that causes the motion of an object to overcome resistance and maintain its velocity [Mid-17C. < Latin, "assault, force" < *impetere* "assail" < *petere* "seek"]

imp. gal. *abbr* MEASURE imperial gallon

Im·phal /ímfal, im fáal/ capital city of Manipur State in northeastern India. Population: 198,535 (1991).

im·pi·e·ty /im pī ətee/ (*plural* **-ties**) *n* **1. LACK OF RELIGIOUS RESPECT** a lack of due reverence for God or religion **2. UNGODLY ACT** an act that shows a lack of religious respect or devotion **3. LACK OF RESPECT** a lack of respect or dutifulness (*formal*)

im·ping /ím ping/ *n* in falconry, a technique for repairing the broken wing of a hawk or falcon by grafting on new feathers [Old English *impa* "young shoot, scion," *impian* "to graft" < Greek *emphuein* "implant" < *phuein* "grow"]

im·pinge /im pínj/ (**-pinged, -pinge·ing, -ping·es**) *vi* **1.** to affect the limits of something, especially a right or law, often causing some kind of restriction (*formal*) ○ *Members claimed that canceling the ballot impinged on their voting rights.* **2.** to strike or hit something ○ *Loud noise can impinge on the eardrum, causing temporary hearing damage.* [Mid-16C. < Latin *impingere* "drive in forcibly" < *pangere* "drive or fix in"] —**im·pinge·ment** *n* —**im·ping·er** *n*

im·pi·ous /ímpee əs, im pī əss/ *adj* **1.** not showing due reverence for God or something holy **2.** showing a lack of respect for somebody or something (*formal*) —**im·pi·ous·ly** *adv* —**im·pi·ous·ness** *n*

imp·ish /ímpish/ *adj* wicked in a playful way, without causing serious harm —**imp·ish·ly** *adv* —**imp·ish·ness** *n*

im·plac·a·ble /im plákəb'l/ *adj* impossible to pacify or to reduce in strength or force ○ *an implacable foe* ○ *an implacable ice storm* [15C. < Latin *implacabilis* < *placabilis* "easily appeased" < *placare* "to calm"] —**im·plac·a·bil·i·ty** /im plàkə bíllətee/ *n* —**im·plac·a·ble·ness** *n* —**im·plac·a·bly** *adv*

im·plant *v* /im plánt/ (**-plant·ed, -plant·ing, -plants**) **1.** *vt* **ESTABLISH HABITS OR NOTIONS** to fix something deeply in somebody's mind or consciousness as a behavior pattern, thought, or belief **2.** *vt* **INSERT SOMETHING** to fit or set something small into something larger, which then encases it ○ *Gold fillings, implanted in his front teeth, flashed when he smiled.* **3.** *vt* **BURY SOMETHING IN GROUND** to put something in the ground, especially so that it grows **4.** *vt* SURG **EMBED SOMETHING IN BODY** to embed something such as a mechanical device in the body ○ *The hormone pellets are invisibly implanted just below the skin.* **5.** *vi* MED **BECOME EMBEDDED IN WOMB** to become embedded in the lining of the womb (*refers to embryos*) ■ *n* /ím plant/ SURG **SOMETHING INSERTED DURING SURGERY** something inserted or embedded in the tissues or organs of the body during a surgical procedure, e.g., encapsulated drugs or fluid-filled sacs to replace or augment breast tissue —**im·plant·a·ble** *adj* —**im·plant·er** *n*

im·plan·ta·tion /im plan táysh'n/ *n* **1. STATE OR PROCESS OF IMPLANTING** the state of being fixed or embedded in something, or the process of becoming fixed or embedded in something **2.** SURG **SURGICAL INSERTION OF SOMETHING** the insertion or embedding of something into body tissues or organs during a surgical procedure **3.** MED **ATTACHMENT OF EMBRYO** the process by which or stage at which an embryo becomes embedded in the lining of the womb

im·plau·si·ble /im pláwzəb'l/ *adj* hardly likely to be true —**im·plau·si·bil·i·ty** /im plàwzə bíllətee/ *n* —**im·plau·si·bly** *adv*

im·plead /im pléed/ (**-plead·ed, -plead·ing, -pleads**) *vti* to bring a lawsuit against a person or an organization in court —**im·plead·a·ble** *adj*—**im·plead·er** *n*

im·ple·ment *n* /ímpləmənt/ **1. TOOL** a useful piece of equipment, usually a specially shaped object designed to do a particular task ○ *writing implements* **2.** LAW **REQUIREMENT** something needed in order to achieve something else (*formal*) ■ *vt* /ímplə mènt/ (**-ment·ed, -ment·ing, -ments**) **1. CARRY OUT OR FULFILL SOMETHING** to put something into effect or action ○ *The plan has yet to be fully implemented.* **2. GIVE TOOLS TO SOMEBODY** to provide or equip somebody with the tools or other means to do something (*formal*) [15C.

< late Latin *implementum* "filling" < Latin *implere* "fill in" < *plere* "to fill"] —**im·ple·men·tal** /implə mént'l/ *adj* —**im·ple·men·ta·tion** /impləmən táysh'n/ *n* —**im·ple·ment·er** *n*

im·pli·cate /impli kàyt/ (**-cat·ed, -cat·ing, -cates**) *vt* **1. SHOW CONNECTION OF SOMEBODY WITH SOMETHING** to show that somebody or something played a part in or is connected to an activity such as a crime **2. IMPLY SOMETHING** to imply or involve something as a consequence (*formal*) ○ *Do you not see that his words implicate an error on my part?* **3. ENTANGLE OR INTERWEAVE THINGS** to wreathe, twist, or knit things together (*literary*) [15C. < Latin *implicat-*, past participle of *implicare* "entangle" < *plicare* "to fold"] —**im·pli·ca·tive** *adj*

im·pli·ca·tion /impli káysh'n/ *n* **1. INDIRECT SUGGESTION** something that is implied or involved as a natural consequence of something else ○ *It is important to consider the wider implications of making such a decision.* **2. IMPLICIT UNDERSTANDING** the state of implying or being implied, without being plainly expressed **3. INVOLVEMENT** the involvement or entanglement of somebody in something ○ *his implication in the crime* **4.** LOGIC **LOGICAL RELATION** in logic, a relationship between two propositions that holds when both propositions are true and fails when the first is true but the second is false —**im·pli·ca·tion·al** *adj*

im·plic·it /im plíssit/ *adj* **1. IMPLIED** not stated, but understood in what is expressed ○ *Asking us when we would like to start was an implicit acceptance of our terms.* **2. ABSOLUTE** not affected by any doubt or uncertainty ○ *implicit trust* **3. CONTAINED** present as a necessary part of something ○ *Confidentiality is implicit in the relationship between doctor and patient.* **4.** MATH **WITH ONLY DEPENDENT VARIABLES** describes a mathematical function that contains only variables whose value is dependent on the value of the other variables in the function [Late 16C. Directly or via French < Latin *implicitus* "entangled" < *implicare* (see IMPLICATE)] —**im·plic·it·ly** *adv*

USAGE See ***explicit***.

~~**impliment**~~ incorrect spelling of **implement**

im·plode /im plṓd/ (**-plod·ed, -plod·ing, -plodes**) *v* **1.** *vti* to collapse inwardly with force as a result of the external pressure being greater than the internal pressure, or cause something to collapse inwardly **2.** *vi* to suffer from total economic or political collapse e.g., as a result of poor management and financial insolvency ○ *The corporation imploded as a result of gross mismanagement, plummeting stock prices, and indictments for securities fraud.* [Late 19C. < IM + Latin *plodere* "to clap," after EXPLODE]

im·plore /im pláwr/ (**-plored, -plor·ing, -plores**) *vt* **1.** to plead with somebody to do something ○ *The tenants implored their landlord not to sell the building.* **2.** to beg or pray for something (*formal*) [Early 16C. Directly or via French < Latin *implorare* "call upon with tears" < *plorare* "weep"] —**im·plo·ra·tion** /implə ráysh'n, ìm plaw-/ *n* —**im·plo·ra·to·ry** *adj* —**im·plor·er** *n*

im·plor·ing /im pláwring/ *adj* earnestly asking for something ○ *an imploring look* —**im·plor·ing·ly** *adv*

im·plo·sion /im plṓzh'n/ *n* **1.** the violent inward collapse of a vessel or structure resulting from the external pressure being greater than the internal pressure **2.** total economic or political collapse, e.g., as a result of poor management and financial insolvency ○ *the implosion of high-risk stocks* [Late 19C. < IMPLODE]

im·plo·sive /im plṓssiv/ *adj* indicating or relating to violent inward collapse —**im·plo·sive·ly** *adv*

im·ply /im plī́/ (**-plied, -ply·ing, -plies**) *vt* **1.** to make something understood without expressing it directly **2.** to involve something as a necessary part or condition ○ *Such impressive exam results imply good teaching and study methods.* [14C. Via Old French *emplier* < Latin *implicare* (see IMPLICATE)] —**im·plied** *adj*

im·po·lite /impə lī́t/ *adj* not showing proper manners or respect —**im·po·lite·ly** *adv* —**im·po·lite·ness** *n*

im·pol·i·tic /im póllətik/ *adj* likely to be disadvantageous and therefore not advisable ○ *It would be impolitic to refuse.* —**im·pol·i·tic·ly** *adv*

im·pon·der·a·ble /im póndərəb'l/ *adj* not quantifiable in terms of importance or effect ○ *Sheer inspiration remains an imponderable force in cultural and technological developments.* ■ *n* an event, factor, or other matter whose importance or effects cannot be calculated (*often used in the plural*) ○ *just another of life's imponderables* —**im·pon·der·a·bil·i·ty** /im pòndərə bíllətee/ *n* —**im·pon·der·a·ble·ness** *n* —**im·pon·der·a·bly** *adv*

im·port *vt* /im páwrt/ (**-port·ed, -port·ing, -ports**) **1. BRING SOMETHING IN FROM ABROAD** to bring something or cause something to be brought in from another country, usually for commercial or industrial purposes **2. BRING IN SOMETHING FROM OUTSIDE** to introduce something such as knowledge or expertise from an outside source **3. IMPLY SOMETHING** to mean something, often in addition to what is actually expressed (*formal*) **4.** COMPUT **TRANSFER DATA** to transfer data from one location to another in a computer or from one computer to another in a computer network, especially when a change of format is required ■ *n* /im pàwrt/ **1. SOMETHING BROUGHT FROM ABROAD** something that is brought into one country from another, usually for commercial or industrial purposes **2. IDEA OR PERSON BROUGHT IN** an idea, practice, or person introduced from the outside ○ *The new accounting system is an import from the private sector.* **3. IMPORTATION** the bringing in of something from abroad or an outside source ○ *Most governments forbid the import of such goods.* **4. TRUE SIGNIFICANCE** meaning or significance ○ *a foreign-policy decision of great import* [15C. < Latin *importare* "carry in" (in medieval Latin, "imply, be significant") < *portare* "carry"] —**im·port·a·bil·i·ty** /im pàwrtə bíllətee/ *n* —**im·port·a·ble** *adj* —**im·por·ta·tion** /im pawr táysh'n/ *n* —**im·port·er** *n*

im·por·tance /im páwrt'nss/ *n* **1.** value, relevance, or interest ○ *It is difficult to overestimate the importance of this breakthrough.* ○ *The age of the car is of no importance.* **2.** high position, rank, or reputation in society

im·por·tant /im páwrt'nt/ *adj* **1. HAVING VALUE OR SIGNIFICANCE** worthy of note or consideration, especially for its interest, value, or relevance ○ *an important scientific discovery* ○ *an important author* **2. HIGH-RANKING** with high social position or influence among people **3. POMPOUS** seeming to assume more status, significance, or value than is actually due ○ *strode into the room with an important air* [15C. < medieval Latin *important-*, present participle of *importare* (see IMPORT)] —**im·por·tant·ly** *adv*

~~**importent**~~ incorrect spelling of **important**

im·por·tu·nate /im páwrchənət/ *adj* (*formal*) **1.** continually asking for something, especially in a forceful, insistent, or troublesome manner ○ *importunate requests for a loan* **2.** requiring immediate attention and action ○ *importunate requests for medical aid* [Early 16C. < Latin *importunus* (see IMPORTUNE)] —**im·por·tu·na·cy** *n* —**im·por·tu·nate·ly** *adv* —**im·por·tu·nate·ness** *n*

im·por·tune /impər tóon, im páwrchən/ *vt* (**-tuned, -tun·ing, -tunes**) (*formal*) **1. BOTHER SOMEBODY INSISTENTLY** to ask somebody continually, repeatedly, or forcefully for something, especially in a troublesome way **2. MAKE IMMORAL REQUEST OF SOMEBODY** to ask somebody to have sexual relations in exchange for money ■ *adj* **IMPORTUNATE** persistent or pressing [Mid-16C. < French *importuner* or medieval Latin *importunari* < Latin *importunus* "inconvenient, unseasonable" < *Portunus*, god of harbors] —**im·por·tune·ly** *adv* —**im·por·tun·er** *n*

im·por·tu·ni·ty /impər tóonətee/ (*plural* **-ties**) *n* (*formal*) **1.** the fact of being troublesomely demanding or insistent **2.** a demand made repeatedly or insistently

im·pose /im pṓz/ (**-posed, -pos·ing, -pos·es**) *v* **1.** *vt* **LEVY OR ENFORCE SOMETHING** to lay down something compulsory such as a tax or a punishment **2.** *vt* **INSIST ON SOMETHING** to make people agree to something or comply with something by having superior strength or authority ○ *We believe that one country should not try to impose its culture on another.* **3.** *vti* **INCONVENIENCE SOMEBODY** to demand somebody's attention or time in an unreasonable manner ○ *The guests' increasing demands imposed on the family's hospitality.* **4.** *vt* **PASS OFF SOMETHING ON SOMEBODY** to use deceit or fraud to give something to somebody or to persuade somebody to accept something **5.** *vt* PRINTING **ARRANGE PAGES** to order the pages of material such as a book or magazine for printing **6.** *vt* RELIG **LAY ON HANDS** to bless somebody, e.g., in confirmation or ordination, by laying hands on the person's head [15C. < French *imposer* (influenced by *poser* "to put") < Latin *imponere* "place into" < *ponere* "to place"] —**im·pos·a·ble** *adj* —**im·pos·er** *n*

im·pos·ing /im pṓzing/ *adj* large and stately, thus creating an impression of grandeur —**im·pos·ing·ly** *adv*

im·po·si·tion /impə zísh'n/ *n* **1. EXTRA TROUBLE** a request or task, especially a time-consuming one, that is unreasonably expected of somebody **2. ENFORCED DUTY** a tax, fee, or penalty that is imposed on people **3. ESTABLISHMENT OR ENFORCEMENT OF SOMETHING** the official or legal process of laying down something compulsory such as a tax, fee, or penalty **4. DECEPTION** a deception or fraud (*literary*) **5.** PRINTING **ARRANGEMENT OF PAGES** the setting up and ordering of pages for printing **6.** RELIG **BLESSING** the laying of hands on somebody's head in a religious sacrament such as ordination or confirmation

im·pos·si·bil·i·ty /im pòssə bíllətee/ (*plural* **-ties**) *n* **1.** something that cannot exist or cannot be done ○ *Living without water is a physical impossibility.* **2.** the likelihood that something will not happen or cannot be achieved ○ *the impossibility of finding another job close to home*

im·pos·si·ble /im póssəb'l/ *adj* **1. NOT POSSIBLE** not able to exist or be done ○ *an impossible task* **2. TOO DIFFICULT** very difficult to deal with and apparently without a solution ○ *The situation was impossible: I couldn't be honest without offending one of them.* **3. NOT ENDURABLE** unbearably difficult or not possible to endure ○ *The humidity was impossible.* **4. NOT BELIEVABLE** ridiculous or unreasonable, because not able to be true

im·pos·si·bly /im póssəblee/ *adv* **1. EXTREMELY** to an extent that is almost unbelievable ○ *impossibly thin slices* **2. NOT BY ANY MEANS** in a way that could not be done or could not happen **3. INFURIATINGLY** to an infuriating or intolerable degree (*informal*)

im·post[1] /im pṑst/ *n* **1.** a tax or other payment levied on goods brought into a country **2.** the weight a horse must carry, including that of the jockey, in a handicap race [15C. < Italian *imposta*, < past participle of *imporre* "impose" < Latin *imponere* (see IMPOSE)]

im·post[2] /ím pṑst/ *n* the top part of a pillar, column, or wall, which may be decorated or molded and on which a vault or arch rests [Mid-16C. < French < Latin *impostus impositus*, past participle of *imponere* (see IMPOSE)]

im·pos·tor /im póstər/, **im·pos·ter** *n* somebody who makes false claims of identity [Late 16C. Via French *imposteur* < Latin *impositor* < *imponere* (see IMPOSE)]

im·pos·ture /im póschər/ *n* the act of pretending to be somebody else in order to trick people, or an occasion on which this is done [Mid-16C. Via French < late Latin *impostura* "a putting on" < Latin *imponere* (see IMPOSE)]

im·po·tent /ímpət'nt/ *adj* **1.** unable to perform sexual intercourse, usually because erection of the penis cannot be achieved or sustained **2.** without the strength or power to do anything effective or helpful —**im·po·tence** *n* —**im·po·tent·ly** *adv*

im·pound /im pównd/ (**-pound·ed, -pound·ing, -pounds**) *vt* **1. KEEP SOMETHING IN CONFINED PLACE** to lock something such as an illegally parked car in an enclosure or compound **2. TAKE SOMETHING INTO LEGAL CUSTODY** to take goods or possessions into official custody **3. WITHHOLD SOMETHING LEGALLY** to withhold something by legal means, especially funds that the law requires to be spent **4.** CIV ENG **HOLD WATER SUPPLY** to save and collect water in a dam or reservoir [15C. < IM-[2] + POUND[3]] —**im·pound·a·ble** *adj* —**im·pound·age** *n* —**im·pound·er** *n* —**im·pound·ment** *n*

im·pov·er·ish /im póvvərish/ (**-ished, -ish·ing, -ish·es**) *vt* **1. MAKE SOMEBODY OR SOMETHING POOR** to cause somebody or something to be poor or poorer (*often passive*) **2. SPOIL OR REDUCE SOMETHING IN QUALITY** to take away some part or quality belonging to something, leaving it in a worse or weaker condition than before ○ *a vocabulary impoverished by technical jargon* **3. DEPRIVE SOMETHING OF NUTRIENTS** to take away the nutrients and richness from a substance such as soil [15C. < Old French *empoveriss-*, stem of *empov(e)rier* < *povre* (see POOR)] —**im·pov·er·ish·er** *n* —**im·pov·er·ish·ment** *n*

im·prac·ti·ca·ble /im práktikəb'l/ *adj* **1.** impossible to be carried out effectively **2.** not in a fit condition for use —**im·prac·ti·ca·bil·i·ty** /im pràktikə bíllətee/ *n* —**im·prac·ti·ca·ble·ness** *n* —**im·prac·ti·ca·bly** *adv*

USAGE See ***practicable***.

im·prac·ti·cal /im práktik'l/ *adj* **1.** not able to work effectively or be without problems when put into practice **2.** not able to perform practical tasks or deal easily with practical matters ○ *She is a brilliant academic, but completely impractical around the house.* —**im·prac·ti·cal·i·ty** /im pràkti kállətee/ *n* —**im·prac·ti·cal·ly** *adv* —**im·prac·ti·cal·ness** *n*

USAGE See *practicable.*

im·pre·cate /ímprə kàyt/ (**-cat·ed, -cat·ing, -cates**) *vti* to call down harm, especially a curse, on somebody (*formal*) [Early 17C. < Latin *imprecat-*, past participle of *imprecari* < *precari* (see PRAY)] —**im·pre·ca·tor** *n* —**im·pre·ca·to·ry** *adj*

im·pre·ca·tion /ìmprə káysh'n/ *n* (*formal*) **1. CURSE** an oath or curse **2. ACT OF CURSING SOMEBODY** the calling down of harm on somebody **3. ACT OF SWEARING** swearing or blasphemy

im·pre·cise /ìmprə sī́ss/ *adj* not exact or accurate —**im·pre·cise·ly** *adv* —**im·pre·cise·ness** *n* —**im·pre·ci·sion** /-sízh'n/ *n*

im·preg·na·ble /im prégnəb'l/ *adj* **1.** too strong to be captured or entered by force ○ *an impregnable fortress* **2.** unable to be shaken or destroyed by any outside influence ○ *impregnable faith* —**im·preg·na·bil·i·ty** /im prègnə bíllətee/ *n* —**im·preg·na·bly** *adv*

im·preg·nate *vt* /im prég nàyt/ (**-nat·ed, -nat·ing, -nates**) **1. SATURATE MATERIAL** to incorporate a chemical into a porous material such as wood or cloth, especially by soaking it thoroughly with a liquid (*usually passive*) **2. PERMEATE SOMETHING WITH QUALITY** to permeate something with a particular aura or tone, or make something contain a particular quality (*literary*) ○ *This was a major speech impregnated with references to the Constitution and its interpretation.* **3. MAKE FEMALE PREGNANT** to make a woman or female animal pregnant ■ *adj* /im prégnət, -nàyt/ **1. SATURATED** infused or saturated with something **2. PREGNANT** pregnant or fertilized [Early 17C. < late Latin *impregnat-*, past participle of *impregnare* < Latin *praegnas* (see PREGNANT)] —**im·preg·na·tion** /im preg náysh'n/ *n* —**im·preg·na·tor** *n*

im·pre·sa·ri·o /ìmprə sa͡aree ō, -sérree ō/ (*plural* **-os**) *n* **1.** a producer or promoter of commercial entertainment ventures, especially in musical theater **2.** somebody in charge of an opera or ballet company who is responsible for business affairs, contracting artists, and commissioning new works [Mid-18C. < Italian, "somebody who undertakes" < *impresa* "undertaking" < *imprendere* "undertake" < Latin *prendere* "to take"]

im·pre·script·i·ble /ìmprə skríptəb'l/ *adj* impossible to remove or violate ○ *the people's imprescriptible rights* ○ *imprescriptible civil rights* [Late 16C. < medieval Latin *imprescriptibilis* < Latin *praescript-*, past participle of *praescribere* (see PRESCRIBE)] —**im·pre·script·i·bil·i·ty** /ìmprə skriptə bíllətee/ *n* —**im·pre·script·i·bly** *adv*

im·press[1] *v* /im préss/ (**-pressed, -press·ing, -press·es**) **1.** *vti* **AFFECT OR PLEASE SOMEBODY GREATLY** to have a strong, usually favorable effect on the mind or feelings of somebody (*often passive*) ○ *We were very impressed by the way we were treated.* **2.** *vt* **MAKE SOMETHING CLEARLY UNDERSTOOD** to make sure that somebody has a clear and lasting understanding, memory, or mental image of something ○ *She impressed on every child the fact that she expected them to tell the truth.* **3.** *vt* **PRESS SHAPE INTO SOMETHING** to make a pattern, design, or mark on something by pressing or stamping **4.** *vt* ELECTRONICS **APPLY VOLTAGE TO SOMETHING** to apply a voltage to an electronic circuit or device ■ *n* /ìm prèss/ **STAMP** a characteristic mark (*literary*) [14C. < French *empresser* < Latin *impress-*, past participle of *imprimere* "press in" < *premere* "to press"] —**im·press·er** *n* —**im·press·i·bil·i·ty** /im prèssə bíllətee/ *n* —**im·press·i·ble** *adj* —**im·press·i·bly** *adv*

im·press[2] /im préss/ (**-pressed, -press·ing, -press·es**) *vt* **1.** to seize something by force for public use **2.** to compel people to serve in a navy or army, especially by arbitrary means [Late 16C. < IM-[2] + PRESS[2]] —**im·press·ment** *n*

im·pres·sion /im présh'n/ *n* **1. WHAT STAYS IN SOMEBODY'S MIND** a lasting effect, opinion, or mental image of somebody or something ○ *I made a bad impression by arriving late for the interview.* **2. GENERAL IDEA** a belief about or understanding of something ○ *I was under the impression that they were married.* **3. PRESSED-IN SHAPE** a pattern, design, or mark made by something hard being pressed onto something softer ○ *The intruder's boots had left an impression in the mud.* **4. IMITATING OF SOMEBODY** an entertainment in which a performer mimics the way a well-known person speaks and behaves, usually in a humorous or exaggerated way **5. MOLD TAKEN OF TEETH** a mold taken of the teeth and surrounding gums on which dentures, restorations, or dental appliances are constructed **6.** PRINTING, PUBL **COPIES OF BOOK** all the copies of a book printed at one time, or the printing of these **7.** PRINTING, PUBL **COPY OF BOOK** a printed copy of a book [14C. Via French < Latin *impression-* < past participle of *imprimere* "press in" < *premere* "press"] —**im·pres·sion·al** *adj* —**im·pres·sion·al·ly** *adv*

im·pres·sion·a·ble /im présh'nəb'l/ *adj* ready to accept or be impressed by the experiences, opinions, and personalities of other people —**im·pres·sion·a·bil·i·ty** /im prèsh'nə bíllətee/ *n* —**im·pres·sion·a·bly** *adv*

im·pres·sion·ism /im présh'n ìzzəm/, **Im·pres·sion·ism** *n* **1.** a style of painting that concentrates on the general tone and effect produced by a subject, without elaboration of details. Monet and Renoir were practitioners of impressionism. **2.** a style of music, especially of late 19th-century France, characterized by the use of rich harmonies and tones rather than form to express scenes or emotions. Debussy and Ravel were practitioners of impressionism. [Late 19C. < French *impressionisme*]

im·pres·sion·ist /im présh'nist/ *n* **1.** a performer who mimics the way well-known people speak and behave, usually in a humorous or exaggerated way **2.** *also* **Im·pres·sion·ist** an artist or composer whose work is in the style of impressionism, especially one active in France at the end of the 19th century

im·pres·sion·is·tic /im prèsh'n ístik/ *adj* **1.** giving a broad picture or general idea rather than an exact description **2.** relating to or in the style of impressionism or the impressionists in painting or music —**im·pres·sion·is·ti·cal·ly** *adv*

im·pres·sive /im préssiv/ *adj* making a deep and usually favorable impression on the mind or senses —**im·pres·sive·ly** *adv* —**im·pres·sive·ness** *n*

im·prest /im prést/ *n* **1. ADVANCE OF MONEY** an advance payment of money, especially to somebody who is to carry out business for a government **2. LOAN TO DRAW ON** a loan, usually in the form of a petty cash account, that can be drawn on as needed **3. ADVANCE PAYMENT** a payment formerly made in advance to a British soldier or sailor on enlistment [Mid-16C. < IM-[2] + obsolete *prest* "loan" < Old French < *prester* "lend" < Latin *praesto* "at hand"]

im·pri·ma·tur /ìmprə ma͡atər, -ma͡a to͝or/ *n* **1.** authority to do, say, or especially print something (*formal*) **2.** an authorization allowing a book or other work to be published, now usually confined to works sanctioned by the Roman Catholic Church [Mid-17C. < Latin, "let it be printed"]

im·print *n* /ím prìnt/ **1. PRESSED-IN SHAPE** a pattern, design, or mark that is made by pressing something down on or into something else ○ *saw the imprint of a foot on the soil* **2. LASTING EFFECT** an effect that remains and is recognizable for a long time ○ *The years of occupation left their imprint on all the inhabitants.* **3. SPECIAL MARK** a printed or stamped sign on an object, e.g., to indicate its origin **4.** PUBL **PRINTED PUBLICATION DETAILS** the name and address of the publisher and printer as shown in the front of a book ■ *v* /im prínt/ (**-print·ed, -print·ing, -prints**) **1.** *vt* **MARK SOMETHING BY PRESSING** to put a shape or design on something such as the surface of an object using a stamp or printing device **2.** *vt* **MAKE IDEA OR IMAGE PERMANENT** to fix an image, memory, opinion, or idea in a vivid or lasting way ○ *The scene was imprinted on her memory.* **3.** *vi* ZOOL **ESTABLISH SOCIAL ATTACHMENTS** to learn an attraction to members of the same species or substitutes very early in life —**im·print·er** *n*

im·print·ing /im prínting/ *n* a form of rapid learning very early in an animal's social development that results in strong behavioral patterns of attraction to members of its own species, especially parents. Imprinting was first described by Konrad Lorenz in 1937 when he trained young ducks and geese to follow him and regard him as their mother.

im·pris·on /im prízz'n/ (**-oned, -on·ing, -ons**) *vt* to lock somebody up in prison —**im·pris·on·a·ble** *adj* —**im·pris·on·er** *n* —**im·pris·on·ment** *n*

im·prob·a·ble /im próbbəb'l/ *adj* not likely to happen or to be true —**im·prob·a·bil·i·ty** /im pròbbə bíllətee/ *n* —**im·prob·a·ble·ness** *n* —**im·prob·a·bly** *adv*

im·pro·bi·ty /im prṓbətee/ *n* lack of moral scruples or honesty (*formal*)

im·promp·tu /im prómp to͞o/ *adj* **DONE SPONTANEOUSLY** not prepared or planned in advance ○ *an impromptu speech* ■ *adv* **WITHOUT PRIOR PREPARATION** in an unrehearsed way ■ *n* **1. SHORT SOLO PIECE** a short piece of instrumental music whose style gives an impression of improvisation. Such pieces were a highly developed and popular form in the 19th century. **2. SPONTANEOUS OR UNREHEARSED ACT** something done or said without planning [Mid-17C. Via French < Latin *in promptu* "at hand" < *promptus* (see PROMPT)]

im·prop·er /im próppər/ *adj* **1. UNSUITABLE** not appropriate to the context, the nature of the case, or the purpose in view (*formal*) **2. RUDE** not in accordance with accepted good manners or decorum **3. IRREGULAR** not in accordance with the accepted standards of something such as a profession ○ *the improper handling of funds* —**im·prop·er·ly** *adv* —**im·prop·er·ness** *n*

im·prop·er frac·tion *n* a fraction in which the numerator is equal to or greater than the denominator, e.g., 6/4

im·pro·pri·e·ty /ìmprə prī́ ətee/ (*plural* **-ties**) *n* conduct that is not considered correct, moral, or appropriate in a given context

im·prove /im pro͞ov/ (**-proved, -prov·ing, -proves**) *v* **1.** *vti* **MAKE OR BECOME BETTER** to make something better in quality or condition, or become better ○ *His health is improving daily.* **2.** *vt* **INCREASE VALUE OF PROPERTY** to make property such as land or buildings more valuable **3.** *vt* **USE SOMETHING WELL** to make good use of something or employ something to advantage (*formal*) [Early 16C. < Anglo-Norman *emprower* "make a profit" < Old French *prou* "profit" < late Latin *prode* "profitable" < Latin *prodesse* (see PROUD)] —**im·prov·a·bil·i·ty** /im pro͞ovə bíllətee/ *n* —**im·prov·a·ble** *adj* —**im·prov·a·bly** *adv* —**im·prov·er** *n*

improve on, improve upon *vt* to do better or be better than something, especially a previous standard or record ○ *improved on her previous time by four seconds*

im·proved /im pro͞ovd/ *adj* in a better or more valuable condition

im·prove·ment /im pro͞ovmənt/ *n* **1. GETTING OR MAKING BETTER** the process of making something better or of becoming better ○ *an improvement on her past performance* **2. CHANGE OR ADDITION** a change or addition that makes something better **3. CHANGE THAT ADDS VALUE** a change or addition, especially to real estate, that increases value ○ *home improvements* **4. ADVANCE IN VALUE** an increase in value, especially in the value of land or property

im·prov·i·dent /im próvvid'nt/ *adj* **1.** failing to put money aside or give any thought to the future **2.** not sensible, cautious, or wise (*formal*) [15C. < IM-[1] + PROVIDENT, or < late Latin *improvident-*] —**im·prov·i·dence** *n* —**im·prov·i·dent·ly** *adv*

im·pro·vise /ímprə vī̀z/ (**-vised, -vis·ing, -vis·es**) *vti* **1.** to perform or compose something, especially a sketch, play, song, or piece of music, without any preparation or set text to follow **2.** to make a substitute for something out of the materials that happen to be available at the time ○ *If you don't have a hammer, we'll have to improvise.* [Early 19C. Directly or via French < Italian *improvvisare* < Latin *improvisus* "unforeseen" < *providere* (see PROVIDE)] —**im·prov·i·sa·tion** /im pròvvi záysh'n, ìmprəvi-/ *n* —**im·prov·i·sa·tion·al** *adj* —**im·prov·i·sa·tion·al·ly** *adv* —**im·prov·i·sa·to·ri·al** /im pròvvizə táwree əl/ *adj* —**im·prov·i·sa·to·ry** /im próvvizə tàwree, imprə vī́zə-/ *adj* —**im·pro·vis·er** *n*

im·pro·vised ex·plo·sive de·vice *n* a device fabricated or placed in an improvised manner, incorporating lethal, noxious, pyrotechnic, or incendiary materials designed to destroy, incapacitate, harass, or distract. It may incorporate military parts, but is normally constructed from nonmilitary components. [Early 21C.]

im·pru·dent /im pro͞od'nt/ *adj* showing no care, forethought, or judgment —**im·pru·dence** *n* —**im·pru·dent·ly** *adv*

im·pu·dent /ímpyəd'nt/ *adj* showing a lack of respect and excessive boldness [14C. < Latin *impudent-*

< *pudent-* "ashamed," present participle of *pudere* "feel ashamed"] —**im·pu·dence** *n* —**im·pu·dent·ly** *adv*

im·pu·dic·i·ty /impyə díssətee/ *n* lack of modesty or shame (*formal*) [Early 16C. Directly or via French < Latin *impudicitas* < *pudere* "feel ashamed"]

im·pugn /im pyoón/ (**-pugned, -pugn·ing, -pugns**) *vt* to suggest that something cannot be trusted, relied on, or respected ○ *Far be it from me to impugn his motives, but ...* [14C. < Latin *impugnare* "fight against" < *pugnare* "to fight" < *pugnus* "fist"] —**im·pugn·a·ble** *adj* —**im·pugn·er** *n*

im·pulse /ím pùlss/ *n* **1.** SUDDEN URGE a sudden desire, urge, or inclination (*often used before a noun*) ○ *She couldn't resist the impulse to ask him.* **2.** INSTINCTIVE DRIVE an instinctive drive or natural tendency **3.** MOTIVE a motivation or reason for a specific activity **4.** FORCE DRIVING SOMETHING FORWARD a driving force producing a forward motion **5.** FORWARD MOTION the motion produced by a driving force **6.** PHYS FORCE ACTING OVER TIME a measure of momentum arrived at by multiplying the average force acting on a body by the length of time it acts **7.** PHYSIOL NERVE OR MUSCLE SIGNAL a progressive wave of biochemically generated energy that travels along a nerve fiber or muscle and stimulates or inhibits activity [Mid-17C. < Latin *impulsus*, past participle of *impellere* (see IMPEL)]

im·pulse buy·ing *n* the purchase of goods that may be unnecessary, caused by the sudden urge or desire to have them

im·pul·sion /im púlshən/ *n* **1.** ACT OR INSTANCE OF URGING the act of urging or forcing somebody into action, or an instance of this **2.** MOVEMENT OR THRUSTING FORCE a movement that comes from being pushed or thrust, or the force that creates this movement **3.** SUDDEN DESIRE a sudden desire, inclination, or urge

im·pul·sive /im púlssiv/ *adj* **1.** INCLINED TO ACT ON SUDDEN URGES having a tendency to act on sudden urges or desires **2.** SPONTANEOUS based on or motivated by impulse **3.** PHYS COMING IN BURSTS acting or coming in short bursts ○ *an impulsive sound* **4.** ACOUSTICS SHORT AND PERCUSSIVE describes a sound that is of short duration and composed of a wide range of frequencies —**im·pul·sive·ly** *adv* —**im·pul·sive·ness** *n* —**im·pul·siv·i·ty** /im pul sívvətee/ *n*

im·pu·ni·ty /im pyoónətee/ *n* exemption from punishment, harm, or recrimination [Mid-16C. < Latin *impunitas* < *impunis* "without punishment" < *poena* "punishment"]

im·pure /im pyoór/ *adj* **1.** CONTAMINATED unclean because containing something harmful **2.** ADULTERATED combined with something of inferior quality **3.** SINFUL tainted with sin **4.** HAVING MIXED STYLES combining a mixture of styles, or derived from more than one source **5.** MIXED WITH OTHER COLORS describes a color mixed with others —**im·pure·ly** *adv* —**im·pure·ness** *n*

im·pu·ri·ty /im pyoórətee/ (*plural* **-ties**) *n* **1.** LACK OF PURITY the state or quality of being impure **2.** CONTAMINANT a substance that adulterates or contaminates something ○ *drinking water that was found to contain impurities* **3.** SOMETHING ADDED TO SEMICONDUCTOR a small amount of a substance added to a pure semiconductor to control its electrical conductivity

im·pute /im pyoót/ (**-put·ed, -put·ing, -putes**) *vt* **1.** ATTRIBUTE BAD ACTION TO SOMEBODY to attribute a usually undesirable action or event to somebody ○ *"He had married her with that bad past life hidden behind him, and she had no faith left to protest his innocence of the worst that was imputed to him."* (George Eliot, *Middlemarch*; 1872) **2.** ATTRIBUTE BAD QUALITY TO SOMEBODY to attribute a usually undesirable quality to a person, cause, or source ○ *"it was charity to impute some of her unbecoming indifference to the languor of ill-health"* (Jane Austen, *Emma*; 1816) **3.** LAW CHARGE SOMEBODY RESPONSIBLE FOR ANOTHER'S CRIME to bring legal charges against somebody because a person that he or she is responsible for has committed an offense **4.** EXTEND QUALITY TO SOMEBODY ELSE to regard a quality such as righteousness that applies to somebody as also applying to another person associated with him or her [14C. Via French < Latin *imputare* "bring into the reckoning" < *putare* "reckon"] —**im·put·a·ble** *adj* —**im·pu·ta·tion** /ìmpyə táysh'n/ *n* —**im·pu·ta·tive** *adj* —**im·put·er** *n*

IMRT *abbr* MED intensity-modulated radiation therapy

IMS *abbr* INFO SCI information management systems

in[1] /in/ CORE MEANING: a grammatical word indicating that something or somebody is within or inside something ○ (prep) *The dinner's in the oven.* ○ (adv) *I stopped by, but you weren't in.*

1. *prep* INDICATES PLACE indicates that something happens or is situated somewhere ○ *He spent a whole year in Russia.* **2.** *prep* INDICATES STATE indicates a state or condition that something or somebody is experiencing ○ *The banking industry is in a state of flux.* **3.** *prep* AFTER after a period of time that will pass before something happens ○ *She should be well enough to leave in a week or two.* **4.** *prep* DURING indicates that something happens during a period of time ○ *He crossed the desert in 39 days.* **5.** *prep* INDICATES HOW SOMETHING IS EXPRESSED indicates the means of communication used to express something ○ *I managed to write the whole speech in French.* **6.** *prep* INDICATES SUBJECT AREA indicates a subject or field of activity ○ *She graduated with a degree in biology.* **7.** *prep* AS CONSEQUENCE OF while doing something or as a consequence of something ○ *In reaching for a glass he knocked over the ashtray.* **8.** *prep* COVERED BY indicates that something is wrapped or covered by something ○ *The floor was covered in balloons and toys.* **9.** *prep* INDICATES HOW SOMEBODY IS DRESSED indicates that somebody is dressed in a particular way ○ *She was dressed in a beautiful suit.* **10.** *prep* PREGNANT WITH pregnant with offspring ○ *The cows were in calf.* **11.** *adj* FASHIONABLE fashionable or popular ○ *always knew which clubs were in* **12.** *adj, adv* HOLDING POWER OR OFFICE indicates that a party or group has achieved or will achieve power or authority ○ *voted in overwhelmingly* [Old English < Germanic] ◇ **in between** between ○ *Normal light consists of a wave that vibrates up and down, side to side, and every direction in between.* ◇ **in for** indicates that somebody will experience something such as a surprise or a shock ○ *Little did she know what she was in for.* ◇ **in on** having knowledge about or involvement in something ○ *The whole class was in on the plans for the surprise party.* ◇ **in that** introduces an explanation of a statement ○ *She's unusual for a commuter in that she's never late for work.* ◇ **in with** associated with or friendly with ○ *a reporter perhaps too much in with the politicians to be objective* ○ *He's been getting in with a bad crowd.* ◇ **the ins and outs** all the detailed facts and points about something ○ *I don't know all the ins and outs of the matter, but she's leaving.*

USAGE See *into*.

in[2] *abbr* **1.** MEASURE inch, inches **2.** ONLINE India (*used in Internet addresses*) See table at **domain name**

In *symbol* CHEM ELEM indium

IN *abbr* MAIL Indiana

in. *abbr* MEASURE inch, inches

in-[1] *prefix* not ○ *insensitive* ○ *incomplete* [< Latin]

in-[2] *prefix* in, into, toward, within ○ *infighting* ○ *inbound* [< IN[1]]

-in *suffix* an organic chemical or a pharmaceutical ○ *pectin* ○ *botulin* ○ *penicillin* [Alteration of -INE]

in·a·bil·i·ty /ìnnə bíllətee/ *n* a lack of the ability, means, or power to do something ○ *his inability to face the truth*

~~inable~~ incorrect spelling of **enable**

in ab·sen·tia /in əb sénshə/ *adv* in the absence of the person or persons concerned [< Latin, "in absence"]

in·ac·ces·si·ble /ìnnək séssəb'l/ *adj* **1.** DIFFICULT TO GET TO difficult or impossible to gain access to or reach **2.** DIFFICULT TO ACHIEVE difficult or impossible to afford or attain **3.** HARD TO UNDERSTAND difficult or impossible to understand —**in·ac·ces·si·bil·i·ty** /ìnnək sèssə bíllətee/ *n* —**in·ac·ces·si·bly** *adv*

in·ac·cu·ra·cy /in ákyərəssee/ (*plural* **-cies**) *n* **1.** lack of accuracy or correctness **2.** something that is incorrect, especially something that has been measured, calculated, copied, or conveyed incorrectly

SYNONYMS See *mistake*.

in·ac·cu·rate /in ákyərət/ *adj* not accurate or correct —**in·ac·cu·rate·ly** *adv*

in·ac·tion /in áksh'n/ *n* **1.** failure to take action when action is necessary ○ *"But in a nation that demands action, Congress has become the master of inaction."* (National Public Telecomputing Network, *Bush speeches in campaign '92*) **2.** lack of activity, especially laziness or idleness

in·ac·ti·vate /in ákti vàyt/ (**-vat·ed, -vat·ing, -vates**) *vt* to make something inactive or unable to function —**in·ac·ti·va·tion** /in àkti váysh'n/ *n*

in·ac·tive /in áktiv/ *adj* **1.** NOT TAKING ACTION taking no action, or taking no part in an action that others are involved in **2.** NOT BEING USED OR OPERATED not in use, functioning, or operating **3.** LAZY OR SEDENTARY not involving or taking part in physical activity **4.** GEOG DORMANT describes a volcano that is not erupting but is not extinct **5.** MIL NOT IN ACTIVE SERVICE not taking part in, or not being used for, active military service **6.** CHEM INERT having little or no chemical reactivity **7.** CHEM HAVING LOW RADIOACTIVITY having low or no measurable radioactivity **8.** BIOL NOT AFFECTING LIVING THINGS having little if any discernible effect on living things as a result of the loss of some property such as the ability to infect or create antigens **9.** MED NOT DEVELOPING OR SHOWING SYMPTOMS describes a disease that, though present in the body, is not developing or producing any symptoms —**in·ac·tive·ly** *adv* —**in·ac·tive·ness** *n* —**in·ac·tiv·i·ty** /in ak tívvətee/ *n*

in·ad·e·quate /in áddəkwət/ *adj* failing to reach an expected or required level or standard ○ *inadequate supplies of food* —**in·ad·e·qua·cy** *n* —**in·ad·e·quate·ly** *adv*

in·ad·mis·si·ble /ìnnəd míssəb'l/ *adj* not admissible or allowable, especially in a court of law —**in·ad·mis·si·bil·i·ty** /ìnnədmissə bíllətee/ *n* —**in·ad·mis·si·bly** *adv*

in·ad·ver·tent /ìnnəd vúrt'nt/ *adj* **1.** done unintentionally or without thinking **2.** failing to pay enough attention or take enough care [Mid-17C. < IN- + Latin *advertent-*, present participle of *advertere* (see ADVERT[1])] —**in·ad·ver·tence** *n*

in·ad·ver·tent·ly /ìnnəd vúrt'ntlee/ *adv* without intending to or without realizing

in·ad·vis·a·ble /ìnnəd vízəb'l/ *adj* not to be advised or recommended —**in·ad·vis·a·bil·i·ty** /ìnnəd vìzə bíllətee/ *n* —**in·ad·vis·a·bly** *adv*

in ae·ter·num /in ee túrnəm/ *adv* eternally or forever (*formal*) [< Latin, literally "in eternal"]

in·al·ien·a·ble /in áylee ənəb'l/ *adj* not able to be transferred or taken away, e.g., because of being protected by law —**in·al·ien·a·bil·i·ty** /in àylee ənə bíllətee/ *n* —**in·al·ien·a·bly** *adv*

in·al·ter·a·ble /in áwltərəb'l/ *adj* not able to be changed —**in·al·ter·a·bil·i·ty** /in àwltərə bíllətee/ *n* —**in·al·ter·a·bly** *adv*

in·am·o·ra·ta /in àmmə raátə/ (*plural* **-tas**) *n* a woman whom somebody loves or with whom somebody has a romantic relationship (*literary*) [Late 16C. < Italian, form of *inamorato* (see INAMORATO)]

in·am·o·ra·to /in àmmə raátō/ (*plural* **-tos**) *n* a man whom somebody loves or with whom somebody has a romantic relationship [Late 16C. < Italian, past participle of *inamorare* "fall in love" < *amore* "love" < Latin *amor*]

in·ane /i náyn/ *adj* **1.** irritatingly silly or time-wasting **2.** empty, insubstantial, or void [Mid-16C. < Latin *inanis* "empty"] —**in·ane·ly** *adv* —**in·ane·ness** *n*

in·an·i·mate /in ánnimət/ *adj* **1.** DEAD OR INERT not in a physically live state **2.** NOT LIVELY not active, energetic, or lively ○ *"She had relapsed once more into the vacant inanimate creature who had opened the gate to us."* (Wilkie Collins, *The Law and the Lady*; 1875) **3.** RELATING TO NOUNS FOR NONLIVING THINGS belonging to the category of nouns that refer to things and concepts considered to be without life [15C. < late Latin *inanimatus* "lifeless" < Latin *animatus*, past participle of *animare* (see ANIMATE)] —**in·an·i·mate·ly** *adv* —**in·an·i·mate·ness** *n*

in·a·ni·tion /ìnnə nísh'n/ *n* **1.** exhaustion caused by lack of food or water or as a result of disease **2.** lethargy or lack of vitality (*literary*) [14C. < late Latin *inanition-* < Latin *inanis* "empty"]

in·an·i·ty /i nánnətee/ (*plural* **-ties**) *n* **1.** MEANINGLESS QUALITY meaninglessness or senselessness that suggests a lack of understanding or intelligence **2.** SILLINESS silliness or foolishness **3.** SOMETHING INANE something that demonstrates or suggests inanity, e.g., a silly remark

in·ap·pe·tence /in áppət'nss/, **in·ap·pe·ten·cy** /in áppət'nssee/ *n* lack of appetite (*formal*) —**in·ap·pe·tent** *adj*

in·ap·pli·ca·ble /in ápplikəb'l, ìnnə plíkəb'l/ *adj* not applicable, suitable, or relevant —**in·ap·pli·ca·bil·i·ty**

/innəplikə bíllətee, in àpplikə-/ *n* —**in·ap·pli·ca·bly** *adv*

in·ap·po·site /in áppəzit/ *adj* unsuitable or out of place —**in·ap·po·site·ly** *adv* —**in·ap·po·site·ness** *n*

in·ap·pre·cia·ble /innə preéshəb'l/ *adj* too small to be noticed or significant —**in·ap·pre·cia·bly** *adv*

in·ap·pre·cia·tive /innə preéshətiv/ *adj* feeling or showing no appreciation —**in·ap·pre·cia·tive·ly** *adv* —**in·ap·pre·cia·tive·ness** *n*

in·ap·proach·a·ble /innə prṓchəb'l/ *adj* impossible to approach —**in·ap·proach·a·bil·i·ty** /innə prṓchə bíllətee/ *n* —**in·ap·proach·a·bly** *adv*

in·ap·pro·pri·ate /innə prṓpree ət/ *adj* not fitting, timely, or suitable —**in·ap·pro·pri·ate·ly** *adv* —**in·ap·pro·pri·ate·ness** *n*

in·apt /in ápt/ *adj* **1.** not suitable or appropriate **2.** lacking aptitude, capability, or skill —**in·ap·ti·tude** *n* —**in·apt·ly** *adv* —**in·apt·ness** *n*

in·arch /i naárch/ (**-arched, -arch·ing, -arch·es**) *vt* to graft part of one plant onto another without separating it from its parent [Early 17C. < IN-[2] + ARCH[1], because the graft forms an arch between its parent and the new stock]

in·ar·gu·a·ble /in aárgyoo əb'l/ *adj* impossible to deny or take an opposing view about —**in·ar·gu·a·bly** *adv*

in·ar·tic·u·late /in aar tíkyələt/ *adj* **1.** EXPRESSING YOURSELF POORLY not good at choosing the right words or speaking fluently **2.** NOT EFFECTIVELY EXPRESSED not clearly or effectively expressed **3.** NOT UNDERSTANDABLE not understandable as speech or language **4.** NOT SPOKEN ABOUT not expressed, or not able to be expressed in words **5.** UNABLE TO SPEAK lacking the power to speak, especially because of feeling strong emotion **6.** NOT JOINTED describes body parts that have no joints or segments, e.g., the bones of the skull **7.** HAVING SHELL WITHOUT HINGE describes a class of brachiopods that have shells without a hinge and are held together only by muscles and the body wall —**in·ar·tic·u·la·cy** *n* —**in·ar·tic·u·late·ly** *adv* —**in·ar·tic·u·late·ness** *n*

in·ar·tis·tic /in aar tístik/ *adj* **1.** LACKING ARTISTIC SKILL possessing or demonstrating little or no artistic talent **2.** NOT CONFORMING TO RULES OF ART not in accordance with the principles of art **3.** NOT INTERESTED IN ARTS having no appreciation of or sensitivity to the arts —**in·ar·tis·tic·al·ly** *adv*

in·as·much as /innəz múch əz/ *conj* **1.** used to introduce an explanation or reason ○ *"This was an idle and unpractical question, inasmuch as the answer was not forthcoming."* (Henry James, *Confidence*) **2.** used to introduce a comment that limits the extent of something [< IN[1] + AS[1] + MUCH, after French *en tant* "in so much"]

in·at·ten·tion /innə ténsh'n/ *n* failure to take proper care or give enough attention to something

in·at·ten·tive /innə téntiv/ *adj* not paying attention or taking enough care —**in·at·ten·tive·ly** *adv* —**in·at·ten·tive·ness** *n*

in·au·di·ble /in áwdəb'l/ *adj* not loud enough to be heard —**in·au·di·bil·i·ty** /in àwdə bíllətee/ *n* —**in·au·di·bly** *adv*

in·au·gu·ral /i náwgyərəl/ *adj* **1.** RELATING TO INAUGURATION relating to or marking an official beginning, e.g., of a newly elected president's term **2.** FIRST OF SEVERAL being the first of a series ○ *an inaugural meeting* ■ *n* INAUGURATION OR SPEECH an inauguration ceremony, or a speech given at such a ceremony [Late 17C. < French < *inaugurer* "inaugurate" < Latin *inaugurare* (see INAUGURATE)]

in·au·gu·rate /i náwgyə ràyt/ (**-rat·ed, -rat·ing, -rates**) *vt* **1.** SWEAR SOMEBODY FORMALLY INTO OFFICE to install somebody in office with a formal ceremony **2.** OPEN SOMETHING CEREMONIALLY to open or mark the beginning of something with a formal ceremony or dedication **3.** PUT SOMETHING INTO OPERATION to initiate something or put it into operation, especially in a formal or official manner [Late 16C. < Latin *inaugurat-*, past participle of *inaugurare* "predict from birds' flight, install after observing the omens" < *augurari* "predict from omens" < *augur* "augur"] —**in·au·gu·ra·tor** *n* —**in·au·gu·ra·to·ry** *adj*

in·au·gu·ra·tion /i nàwgyə ráysh'n/ *n* **1.** INDUCTION INTO OFFICE the formal act of placing somebody in an official position, especially the President of the United States, or a ceremony held for this purpose **2.** CEREMONIAL OPENING OF SOMETHING a formal ceremony to open or mark the beginning of something such as a new building **3.** PUTTING SOMETHING INTO OPERATION the act of bringing something into service or putting it into operation, or an occasion on which this is done

In·au·gu·ra·tion Day *n* the day in January following a presidential election, on which the inauguration of a new President of the United States takes place

in·aus·pi·cious /in aw spíshəss/ *adj* suggesting that the future is not very promising or that success is unlikely —**in·aus·pi·cious·ly** *adv* —**in·aus·pi·cious·ness** *n*

in·au·then·tic /in aw théntik/ *adj* not authentic or genuine —**in·au·then·tic·i·ty** /in awthən tíssətee/ *n*

in-be·tween *adj, adv* existing or occurring between two states, categories, or points ○ *one of his in-between moods when you don't know what he'll say* ■ *n* somebody or something that exists or happens in-between ○ *the oldest, the youngest, and the in-betweens*

in·board /in báwrd/ *adj* **1.** LOCATED INSIDE BOAT'S HULL describes an engine that is located inside the hull of a boat, not fitted to the outside **2.** HAVING INBOARD ENGINE describes a boat that has an inboard engine ■ *n* BOAT WITH INBOARD MOTOR a boat that has an inboard motor ■ *adv* AWAY FROM SIDES more toward the center of an aircraft or boat than toward the sides or edges

in·born /ín bàwrn/ *adj* inherited from parents or possessed from birth

in·bound[1] /ín bòwnd/ *adj* arriving, incoming, or heading toward an airport, port, or station [Late 19C. < IN-[2] + BOUND[3]]

in·bound[2] /ín bòwnd/ (**-bound·ed, -bound·ing, -bounds**) *vti* in basketball, to put the ball back into play by passing it from out of bounds to a player on the court [Late 20C. Back-formation < INBOUNDS]

in·bounds /ín bòwndz/ *adj* **1.** within the boundaries of the playing area on a sports field **2.** in basketball, involving returning the ball into play ○ *on the ensuing inbounds play*

in·bounds line *n* either of the two broken lines that run the length of a football field

in·box *n* a tray on somebody's desk for papers that have not yet been dealt with

in·breathe /in breéth/ (**-breathed, -breath·ing, -breathes**) *vt* to take something into the airways by breathing in (*technical or literary*)

in·bred /in brèd/ *adj* **1.** INNATE existing naturally, through being possessed from birth or inherited from parents **2.** PRODUCED BY INBREEDING produced by the mating of closely related individuals of a species ■ *n* FORM RESULTING FROM INBREEDING a person or an animal whose health and intelligence are affected because his, her, or its ancestors were too closely related to each other

in·breed /in breéd/ (**-bred** /-brèd/, **-breed·ing, -breeds**) *v* **1.** *vti* to mate closely related individuals of a species with each other, especially over many generations **2.** *vt* to cause something to develop in somebody —**in·breed·er** *n*

in·breed·ing /ín breéding/ *n* the mating of closely related members of a species, especially over many generations. It may be used to enhance desired traits in animals or plants but is avoided in humans as it increases the risk of unwanted inherited characteristics.

in-built *adj* innate or built-in

inc. *abbr* **1.** included **2.** including **3.** inclusive **4.** income **5.** incomplete **6.** *also* **Inc.** BUSINESS incorporated **7.** increase

In·ca /íngkə/ (*plural same or* **-cas**) *n* a member of a Native South American people whose empire, based in Peru and covering the Andean region, lasted from the 12th century until the mid-16th century. The Incas were sophisticated engineers, architects, and artists who had a highly complex social structure. The descendants of the Incas form roughly half of today's population of Peru. [Late 16C. < Quechua, "royal person"] —**In·ca** *adj* —**In·ca·ic** /ing káy ik/ *adj* —**In·can** *adj*

in·cal·cu·la·ble /in kálkyələb'l/ *adj* **1.** too great or numerous to be measured **2.** too uncertain to assess or plan for in advance —**in·cal·cu·la·bil·i·ty** /in kàlkyələ bíllətee/ *n* —**in·cal·cu·la·bly** *adv*

in·ca·les·cent /inkə léss'nt/ *adj* becoming warmer or hotter than before (*technical*) [Mid-17C. < Latin *incalescent-*, present participle of *incalescere* "get hotter" < *calere* "be hot"] —**in·ca·les·cence** *n*

in cam·er·a *adv, adj* **1.** IN PRIVATE in private or in secret **2.** IN CLOSED COURT in a court from which the public is barred **3.** IN JUDGE'S CHAMBERS in a judge's private chambers rather than in open court [< late Latin, "in the chamber"]

in·can·des·cence /inkən déss'nss/ *n* **1.** EMISSION OF LIGHT BY HOT OBJECT the emission of light by an object as a result of its being heated to a high temperature **2.** LIGHT FROM HOT OBJECT the light produced by an object heated to a high temperature **3.** EMOTIONAL INTENSITY intensity of emotion such as anger or romantic passion —**in·can·desce** *vi*

in·can·des·cent /inkən déss'nt/ *adj* **1.** GLOWING WITH HEAT emitting light as a consequence of being heated to a high temperature **2.** GLOWING BRIGHTLY shining or glowing brightly **3.** SHOWING INTENSE EMOTION feeling or displaying intense emotion such as anger or romantic passion [Late 18C. Directly or via French < Latin *incandescent-*, present participle of *incandescere* "glow" < *candescere* "become white" < *candidus* (see CANDID)] —**in·can·des·cent·ly** *adv*

in·can·des·cent lamp *n* an electric lamp that produces light from an electrically heated filament

in·can·ta·tion /in kan táysh'n/ *n* **1.** the ritual chanting or use of supposedly magic words **2.** a set of words spoken or chanted as a supposedly magic spell [14C. Via French < late Latin *incantation-* < Latin *incantare* "to chant" < *cantare* "sing"] —**in·can·ta·tion·al** *adj*

in·ca·pa·ble /in káypəb'l/ *adj* **1.** LACKING NECESSARY ABILITY lacking the ability, character, or strength required to do something ○ *a woman incapable of admitting defeat* **2.** NOT GOOD ENOUGH unable to function or perform adequately ○ *regarded as incapable by most of his coworkers* **3.** IMPOSSIBLE too extreme for something to be possible ○ *damage incapable of repair* **4.** LEGALLY INELIGIBLE legally disqualified or ineligible —**in·ca·pa·bil·i·ty** /in kàypə bíllətee/ *n* —**in·ca·pa·ble·ness** *n* —**in·ca·pa·bly** *adv*

in·ca·pac·i·tant /inkə pássit'nt/ *n* a substance, e.g., tear gas, that can temporarily incapacitate somebody, used especially in riot control and biological warfare

in·ca·pac·i·tate /inkə pássi tàyt/ (**-tat·ed, -tat·ing, -tates**) *vt* **1.** to deprive somebody or something of power, force, or effectiveness **2.** to disqualify somebody or make somebody legally ineligible —**in·ca·pac·i·ta·tion** /inkə passi táysh'n/ *n*

in·ca·pac·i·ty /inkə pássətee/ (*plural* **-ties**) *n* **1.** INABILITY OR INEFFECTIVENESS lack of ability, force, or effectiveness **2.** PHYSICAL OR MENTAL CHALLENGE a physical or mental challenge, making learning or performing basic tasks difficult **3.** LEGAL DISQUALIFICATION a legal or official disqualification

in·cap·su·late *vti* another spelling of **encapsulate**

in-car *adj* installed or provided inside a car

in·car·cer·ate /in kaárssə ràyt/ (**-at·ed, -at·ing, -ates**) *vt* (*formal*) **1.** to put somebody in prison **2.** to place somebody in a place or situation of confinement [Early 16C. < medieval Latin *incarcerat-*, past participle of *incarcerare* < Latin *carcer* "prison"] —**in·car·cer·a·tion** /in kaàrssə ráysh'n/ *n* —**in·car·cer·a·tor** *n*

in·car·di·nate /in kaárd'n àyt/ (**-nat·ed, -nat·ing, -nates**) *vt* **1.** TRANSFER PRIEST to transfer a Roman Catholic priest to a new district under the authority of a different bishop **2.** MAKE PRIEST CARDINAL to promote a member of the Roman Catholic clergy to the position of cardinal **3.** MAKE PRIEST MOST SENIOR to promote a Roman Catholic priest to the position of most senior member of the clergy within an individual church or area [Early 17C. < late Latin *incardinat-*, past participle of *incardinare* "ordain as chief priest" < Latin *cardinalis* (see CARDINAL)] —**in·car·di·na·tion** /in kaàrd'n áysh'n/ *n*

in·car·na·dine /in kaárnə dīn, -din/ (*literary*) *adj* CRIMSON of a crimson or blood-red color ■ *n* CRIMSON COLOR crimson or the color of blood ■ *vt* (**-dined, -din·ing, -dines**) MAKE SOMETHING CRIMSON to tinge or stain something crimson or blood red [Late 16C. Via French < Italian *incarnatino* "carnation," literally "flesh-color" < Latin *carn-* "flesh"]

in·car·nate *adj* /in kaárnət/ **1.** MADE HUMAN having a bodily form, especially a human form **2.** PERSONIFIED being the epitome of something ○ *an adviser who is discretion incarnate* **3.** PINK OR RED describes plant parts that are pink or crimson ■ *vt* /in kaár nàyt/

(-nat·ed, -nat·ing, -nates) 1. SHOW SOMETHING IN HUMAN FORM to give something a bodily form, especially a human form 2. PERSONIFY SOMETHING to be the epitome or personification of something 3. CAUSE SOMETHING TO HAPPEN to bring about something that exists as an idea or theory only [14C. < ecclesiastical Latin *incarnatus*, past participle of *incarnari* "be made flesh" < Latin *carn-* "flesh"] —**in·car·na·tor** /-nàytər/ *n*

in·car·na·tion /in kaar náysh'n/ *n* 1. PERSONIFICATION OF SOMETHING somebody or something personifying, representing, or typifying a quality or idea 2. ONE LIFE IN SERIES OF LIVES one of a succession of lives or periods spent in the body of a particular animal or person 3. MANIFESTATION OF GOD a god's or spirit's appearance in human or animal form

In·car·na·tion *n* in Christianity, God's taking human form as Jesus Christ

in case ➧ **case**[1]

in·cau·tious /in káwshəss/ *adj* careless, rash, or lacking in caution —**in·cau·tion** *n* —**in·cau·tious·ly** *adv* —**in·cau·tious·ness** *n*

in·cen·di·a·rism /in séndee ə rìzzəm/ *n* inflammatory talk or provocative behavior designed or likely to cause civil unrest (*formal*)

in·cen·di·ar·y /in séndee èrree/ *adj* 1. CONTAINING CHEMICALS THAT CAUSE FIRE describes missiles containing highly flammable substances that will cause a fire on impact 2. LIKELY TO CATCH FIRE able to catch fire spontaneously or cause a fire easily 3. INCITING CIVIL UNREST designed or likely to cause civil unrest 4. RELATING TO ARSON relating to or involving the illegal burning of property ■ *n* (*plural* **-ies**) 1. BOMB DESIGNED TO CAUSE FIRE a bomb or missile containing a highly flammable substance such as napalm that is designed to cause a fire on impact 2. SOMEBODY INCITING TROUBLE an instigator of trouble or violence, especially with political motives (*formal*) 3. ARSONIST somebody who illegally sets fire to property [15C. < Latin *incendiarius* < *incendium* "conflagration" < *incendere* (see INCENSE[1])]

in·cense[1] /ín sènss/ *n* 1. SUBSTANCE BURNED FOR ITS SMELL a substance, usually fragrant gum or wood, that gives off a pleasant smell when burned 2. SMOKE FROM INCENSE the smoke or fragrant smell produced when incense is burned 3. FRAGRANCE a pleasant smell 4. PRAISE praise or adulation ■ *v* (**-censed, -cens·ing, -cens·es**) 1. *vti* BURN INCENSE TO GOD to honor a god by burning incense 2. *vt* PERFUME SOMETHING WITH INCENSE to perfume something by burning incense [13C. Via French *encens* < ecclesiastical Latin *incensum*, form of *incensus*, past participle of Latin *incendere* "set fire to" < base of *candere* "to glow"] —**in·cen·sa·tion** /ìn sen sáysh'n/ *n*

in·cense[2] /in sénss/ (**-censed, -cens·ing, -cens·es**) *vt* to make somebody extremely angry [15C. Either < French *encenser* < *encens* "incense," or < ecclesiastical Latin *incensare* < *incensum* (see INCENSE[1])] —**in·cense·ment** *n*

in·cense ce·dar /ín senss-/ *n* 1. a coniferous evergreen tree of the cypress family, with scaly leaves and aromatic wood. Native to: North America, Asia, New Zealand. Genera: *Austrocedrus* or *Calocedrus* or *Libocedrus*. 2. the scented durable wood of the incense cedar. Use: household fragrance, moth repellent, decking, fence posts, pencils.

in·cen·so·ry /ín senssəree, in sénssəree/ (*plural* **-ries**) *n* RELIG same as **censer** [Early 17C. < medieval Latin *incensorium* < ecclesiastical Latin *incensum* (see INCENSE[1])]

in·cen·tive /in séntiv/ *n* something that encourages or motivates somebody to do something ■ *adj* serving to encourage or motivate somebody [Early 17C. < Latin *incentivum* "something that sets the tune" < *incinere* "to sound" < *canere* "sing"] —**in·cen·tive·ly** *adv*

SYNONYMS See *motive*.

in·cen·tiv·ize /in sénti vìz/ (**-ized, -iz·ing, -iz·es**) *vt* to motivate somebody by offering an incentive such as a higher rate of pay (*informal*)

in·cep·tion /in sépsh'n/ *n* 1. the beginning of something (*formal*) 2. *UK* enrollment as a university student, especially one studying for a master's degree or doctorate (*dated formal*) [15C. Directly or via French < Latin *inception-* < *incipere* (see INCIPIENT)]

in·cep·tive /in séptiv/ *adj* 1. INITIAL representing or coming at the beginning of something (*formal*) 2. GRAM EXPRESSING IDEA OF STARTING describes a verb or verb form that, in some languages, indicates the beginning of an action ■ *n* GRAM 1. INCEPTIVE ASPECT the inceptive aspect of verbs 2. INCEPTIVE VERB a verb in the inceptive aspect [Early 17C. < late Latin *inceptivus* < Latin *incipere* (see INCIPIENT)] —**in·cep·tive·ly** *adv*

in·cer·ti·tude /in súrtə tòod/ *n* 1. doubt or uncertainty 2. lack of self-confidence

in·ces·sant /in séss'nt/ *adj* continuing for a long time without stopping [15C. Directly or via French < late Latin *incessant-* < Latin *cessare* (see CEASE)] —**in·ces·san·cy** *n* —**in·ces·sant·ly** *adv*

in·cest /ín sèst/ *n* sexual activity between two people who are considered, for moral or genetic reasons, too closely related to have such a relationship. Incest is regarded as a serious taboo in almost every society, although cultures differ as to the extent to which marriages are allowed between relatives. [13C. < Latin *incestus* < *castus* "pure"]

in·ces·tu·ous /in séschoo əss/ *adj* 1. RELATING TO OR INVOLVING INCEST relating to or involving a sexual relationship between two people who are considered, for moral or genetic reasons, too closely related to have such a relationship 2. GUILTY OF INCEST having had a sexual relationship with somebody considered to be too close a relative 3. UNHEALTHILY CLOSE unhealthily intimate or interconnected, especially so as to exclude the involvement or influence of others ○ *an incestuous friendship* —**in·ces·tu·ous·ly** *adv* —**in·ces·tu·ous·ness** *n*

inch[1] /inch/ *n* 1. UNIT OF LENGTH a unit of length equal to $\frac{1}{12}$ of a foot/2.54 cm. Symbol " 2. SMALL AMOUNT a very small amount, degree, or distance ○ *The committee won't budge an inch on this issue.* 3. AMOUNT OF RAIN OR SNOW a fall of enough rain or snow to cover a surface to a depth of one inch 4. UNIT OF ATMOSPHERIC PRESSURE a unit of atmospheric pressure equal to that needed to maintain a mercury column one inch high in a barometer ■ *vti* (**inched, inch·ing, inch·es**) MOVE SLOWLY to move or cause somebody or something to move very slowly or by small degrees [Pre-12C. < Latin *uncia* "one twelfth" < *unus* "one"]

inch[2] /inch/ *n* in Scotland and Ireland, a small island (*often used in place names*) [15C. < Scottish Gaelic *innis* "island"]

in·cho·ate /in kṓ ət/ *adj* (*formal*) 1. JUST BEGINNING just beginning to develop 2. IMPERFECTLY FORMED only partly formed 3. CHAOTIC lacking structure, order, or organization [Mid-16C. < Latin *inchoatus*, past participle of *inchoare* "begin"] —**in·cho·ate·ly** *adv* —**in·cho·ate·ness** *n* —**in·cho·a·tion** /ìn kō áysh'n/ *n*

in·cho·a·tive /in kṓ ətiv/ *adj, n* GRAM same as **inceptive** *adj* (sense 2), *n*

In·chon /ín chón/, **In·ch'ŏn** city and major port at the mouth of the Han River in northwestern South Korea. In 1950, during the Korean War, it was the site of an amphibious landing by United Nations troops to liberate nearby Seoul. Population: 2,307,618 (1995). Former name **Chemulpo**

inch·worm /ínch wùrm/ *n* the larva of a geometrid moth that has legs only at each end of its body and moves by bringing its rear forward, forming a hump, then moving its front

in·ci·dence /ínssid'nss/ *n* 1. RATE OF OCCURRENCE OF SOMETHING the frequency with which something occurs 2. INSTANCE OR MANNER OF SOMETHING HAPPENING an instance of something happening, or the manner in which it happens 3. IMPACT ON SURFACE the impact that something such as a ray of light or a projectile makes with a surface

USAGE **incidence** or **incidents**? Though pronounced similarly, these two words mean different things and so ought not to be confused. ***Incidents***, a plural noun, means "events, occurrences," as in *Three incidents* [not *incidence*] *of speeding on campus have been reported. Five hundred incidents* [not *incidence*] *of Ebola virus were documented last year.* ***Incidence***, a singular noun, means variously "the rate of occurrence of something happening" and "an instance of something happening and how it happens," as in *studying the annual incidence* [not *incidents*] *of Ebola virus; increased incidence* [not *incidents*] *of poverty.*

in·ci·dent /ínssid'nt/ *n* 1. EVENT something that happens, especially a single event 2. VIOLENT OCCURRENCE a public occurrence, especially a violent one ○ *an incident outside a nightclub* 3. EVENT WITH POTENTIALLY SERIOUS CONSEQUENCES an event that may result in a crisis, especially one involving different countries ■ *adj* 1. RELATED TO SOMETHING accompanying something or occurring as a consequence of it (*formal*) 2. TOUCHING OR STRIKING coming into contact with a surface [15C. Directly or via French < Latin *incident-*, present participle of *incidere* "fall upon" < *cadere* "to fall"]

USAGE See *incidence*.

in·ci·den·tal /ìnssi dént'l/ *adj* 1. RELATED OR ACCOMPANYING related to or accompanying something more important 2. OCCURRING BY CHANCE occurring by chance or without intention 3. OCCASIONAL unimportant or occasional 4. RESULTING FROM SOMETHING occurring as a result of something (*formal*) ■ *n* MINOR ITEM something that is occasional or unimportant, e.g., a minor expense

in·ci·den·tal·ly /ìnssi dént'lee/ *adv* 1. used to introduce additional information such as something that the speaker has just thought of 2. by chance or by accident

in·ci·den·tal mu·sic *n* music that accompanies the action of a movie, play, or television program, as distinct from theme music or songs that feature in a musical

~~incidently~~ incorrect spelling of **incidentally**

in·cin·er·ate /in sínnə ràyt/ (**-at·ed, -at·ing, -ates**) *vti* to burn to ashes, or cause something to burn to ashes, especially in an incinerator [15C. < medieval Latin *incinerat-*, past participle of *incinerare* < Latin *ciner-* "ashes"] —**in·cin·er·a·tion** /in sìnnə ráysh'n/ *n*

in·cin·er·a·tor /in sínnə ràytər/ *n* a furnace for destroying things by burning them, especially one used to burn waste

in·cip·i·ent /in síppee ənt/ *adj* beginning to appear or develop [Mid-17C. < Latin *incipient-*, present participle of *incipere* "undertake" < *capere* "to take"] —**in·cip·i·ence** *n* —**in·cip·i·ent·ly** *adv*

in·ci·pit /ínssipit/ *n* the opening word or words of a medieval manuscript or an early printed book, by which it is often known in the absence of a title [Late 19C. < Latin, "it begins," form of *incipere* (see INCIPIENT)]

in·cise /in sɪ́z/ (**-cised, -cis·ing, -cis·es**) *vt* 1. to cut into something, especially a body part during surgery 2. to carve or engrave a pattern or design into something [Mid-16C. < French *inciser* < Latin *incis-*, past participle of *incidere* "cut into" < *caedere* "to cut"]

in·cised /in sɪ́zd/ *adj* describes a leaf with edges that are deeply and sharply indented

in·ci·sion /in sízh'n/ *n* 1. CUT OR ACT OF CUTTING a cut or the act of cutting, especially when performed by a surgeon 2. LEAF'S INDENTED EDGE a sharp indentation in the edge of a leaf 3. FACT OF BEING INCISIVE the fact or quality of being quick to understand or able to express something clearly

in·ci·sive /in sɪ́ssiv/ *adj* 1. quick to understand, analyze, or act 2. characterized by clear and direct expression —**in·ci·sive·ly** *adv* —**in·ci·sive·ness** *n*

in·ci·sor /in sɪ́zər/ *n* one of the flat sharp-edged teeth in the front of the mouth, used for cutting and tearing food [Late 17C. < medieval Latin *dens incisor* "cutter tooth" < Latin *incis-* (see INCISE)] —**in·ci·sal** *adj*

in·cite /in sɪ́t/ (**-cit·ed, -cit·ing, -cites**) *vt* to stir up feelings in or provoke action by somebody [15C. Via French < Latin *incitare* "urge on" < *citare* (see CITE)] —**in·ci·ta·tion** /in sɪ táysh'n/ *n* —**in·cite·ment** *n* —**in·cit·er** *n*

in·ci·vil·i·ty /ìnssi víllətee/ (*plural* **-ties**) *n* 1. rude or impolite behavior or language 2. a rude or impolite act or remark

incl. *abbr* 1. including 2. inclusive

in·clem·ent /in klémmənt/ *adj* 1. unpleasant in being stormy, rainy, or snowy 2. showing little or no mercy (*formal*) [Mid-16C. Directly or via French < Latin *inclement-* "not clement" < *clement-* "mild"] —**in·clem·en·cy** *n* —**in·clem·ent·ly** *adv*

in·cli·na·tion /ìnkli náysh'n/ *n* 1. WAY SOMEBODY FEELS ABOUT SOMETHING a feeling that pushes somebody to make a particular choice or decision 2. TENDENCY a tendency to do, prefer, or desire something 3. DEVIATION FROM LINE OR PLANE the tilting of something away from a line or surface, or the degree to which it is tilted 4. SLOPE a sloping surface 5. BENDING OF SOMETHING a bending of something, e.g., a bowing of the head 6. MATH ANGLE ON GRAPH the angle between a line on a graph and the positive direction of the x-axis 7. MATH SMALLER ANGLE the smaller angle between two lines or planes 8. ASTRON ANGLE OF ORBIT the angle between a planet's orbit and the apparent orbit of the Sun in relation to Earth **9.** GEOG same as **dip** *n* (sense 12) —**in·cli·na·tion·al** *adj*

in·cline *vti* /in klīn/ (**-clined, -clin·ing, -clines**) **1. BE OR MAKE LIKELY TO ACT** to tend toward a particular belief or course of action, or make somebody tend toward a particular belief or course of action **2. ANGLE OR BE ANGLED** to lie at an angle, or put something at an angle **3. BEND** to bend something, especially the head or body when bowing or nodding, or be bent in this way ■ *n* /ín klīn/ **SLOPE** a slope or sloping surface [14C. Via French < Latin *inclinare* "lean toward" < *clinare* "to lean"] —**in·clin·a·ble** *adj* —**in·clin·er** *n*

in·clined /in klīnd/ *adj* **1. MOTIVATED TO DO SOMETHING** moved or persuaded to do something ○ *I'm not inclined to listen to any more of this.* **2. TALENTED IN PARTICULAR AREA** naturally talented or interested in a particular field or area **3. SLANTED OR FORMING ANGLE** sloping or forming an angle with something else

in·cli·nom·e·ter /ìnklə nómmətər/ *n* **1.** an instrument that measures angles or slopes such as the angle of an aircraft relative to the ground **2.** an instrument used to determine the angle made by the Earth's magnetic field relative to the horizontal plane [Mid-19C. < Latin *inclinare* (see INCLINE)]

in·close *vt* another spelling of **enclose**

in·clo·sure *n* another spelling of **enclosure**

in·clude /in klood/ (**-clud·ed, -clud·ing, -cludes**) *vt* **1.** to have something as a constituent element **2.** to make somebody or something part of a group [15C. < Latin *includere* "enclose" < *claudere* "to shut"] —**in·clud·a·ble** *adj*

USAGE See *comprise.*

in·clud·ed /in kloodəd/ *adj* **1. CONTAINED WITHIN GROUP** forming part of a group or whole **2.** BOT **NOT PROTRUDING** describes the stamens or carpels of a flower that do not protrude beyond the edges of the petals **3.** MATH **LOCATED BETWEEN INTERSECTING LINES** formed by and contained in two intersecting lines

in·clud·ing /in klooding/ *prep* used to introduce examples of people or things forming part of a particular group or whole ○ *It will cost you $65 including sales tax.* ■ *conj* as well as ○ *Discussion of the market analysis – including whether it was skewed in favor of launching the project – went on for an hour.*

in·clu·sion /in kloozh'n/ *n* **1. PRESENCE IN GROUP** the addition of somebody or something to, or the presence of somebody or something in, a group or mixture **2. SOMEBODY OR SOMETHING INCLUDED** somebody or something included in a group or mixture **3.** GEOL **SUBSTANCE INSIDE MINERAL** a solid, liquid, or gas contained within a mineral or rock **4.** BIOL **FOREIGN BODY IN CELL** a nonliving mass in the cytoplasm or nucleus of a cell, e.g., a starch grain or droplet of fat **5.** MATH **RELATION BETWEEN SETS** in mathematics, the relation between two classes or sets when the second is a subset of the first **6.** EDUC **TEACHING CHALLENGED CHILDREN IN REGULAR CLASSES** the practice of educating students with special needs in regular classes for all or nearly all of the day instead of in special education classes [Early 17C. < Latin *inclus-*, past participle of *includere* (see INCLUDE)] —**in·clu·sion·ar·y** *adj*

in·clu·sion bod·y *n* a mass of virus particles inside a cell, formerly used in the diagnosis of some viral infections

in·clu·sive /in kloossiv/ *adj* **1. INCLUDING MANY THINGS** including many things or everything **2. WITHIN PARTICULAR LIMITS** including the numbers, dates, or other series members mentioned immediately before ○ *the period from October 1 to July 31, inclusive* ◊ **exclusive** *adj* (sense 7) **3. INCLUDING PEOPLE OF ALL KINDS** not excluding any group or section of society **4. NONDISCRIMINATORY** describes language that avoids discrimination, limitation, or stereotypes based on gender **5.** GRAM **INCLUDING SPEAKER AND PERSON ADDRESSED** describes a pronoun such as "we" that includes the speaker and the person or persons spoken to **6.** LOGIC **CONTAINING AT LEAST ONE TRUE PROPOSITION** describes a sentence in logic (**disjunction**) containing two propositions of which at least one and possibly both can be true [Late 16C. < medieval Latin *inclusivus* < Latin *inclus-* (see INCLUDE)] —**in·clu·sive·ly** *adv* —**in·clu·sive·ness** *n*

in·co·er·ci·ble /in kō úrssəb'l/ *adj* not giving in to force or pressure from others

in·cog·ni·ta /in kog neetə/ *adj, adv* with the identity disguised or hidden, e.g., under an assumed name (*used to describe a woman or girl*) [Late 17C. < Italian, form of *incognito* "incognito"] —**in·cog·ni·ta** *n*

in·cog·ni·to /in kog neetō/ *adj, adv* **IN DISGUISE** with the identity disguised or hidden, e.g., under an assumed name ■ *n* (*plural* **-tos**) **1. SOMEBODY IN DISGUISE** somebody who acts or travels in disguise so as to be unrecognizable **2. DISGUISE** the character, disguise, or name assumed by somebody who is attempting to be unrecognizable [Mid-17C. Via Italian < Latin *incognitus* "unknown" < *cognoscere* "get to know" (see COGNITION)]

in·co·her·ent /in kō heerənt/ *adj* **1. LACKING CLARITY OR ORGANIZATION** not clearly expressed or well thought out, and consequently difficult to understand **2. UNABLE TO EXPRESS THINGS CLEARLY** unable to express thoughts or feelings clearly or logically **3. NOT COHESIVE** not sticking together as a mass **4.** PHYS **OUT OF PHASE** describes electromagnetic waves that have the same frequency but a random or changing phase —**in·co·her·ence** *n* —**in·co·her·ent·ly** *adv*

in·come /ín kùm/ *n* **1.** the amount of money received over a period of time either as payment for work, goods, or services, or as profit on capital **2.** an act of coming in or flowing in [14C. < Old Norse *innkoma* "arrival"; later < IN–[2] + COME]

in·come bond *n* a bond paying a rate of return in proportion to the issuer's income

in·come tax *n* a tax paid on money made from employment, business, or capital (*hyphenated when used before a noun*)

in·com·ing /in kùmming/ *adj* **1. ARRIVING** arriving, coming in, or entering ○ *incoming flights* **2. TAKING UP NEW JOB** about to take up a new job or position ○ *the incoming president* **3. BEING RECEIVED** being received or taken in ○ *incoming signals* ■ *n* **ARRIVAL** an arrival or entrance (*formal*) ■ **in·com·ings** *npl* **INCOME** sums of money earned or received

in·com·men·su·ra·ble /ìnkə ménssərəb'l, -shərəb'l/ *adj* **1. IMPOSSIBLE TO MEASURE** not able to be compared or measured, especially because of lacking a common quality necessary for a comparison **2.** MATH **HAVING NO COMMON FACTOR** having no common mathematical factor or measure other than 1 ■ *n* **SOMETHING INCOMMENSURABLE** something that cannot be compared or measured, especially a quality or a mathematical value —**in·com·men·su·ra·bil·i·ty** /ìnkə mènssərə bíllətee, -shərə-/ *n* —**in·com·men·su·ra·bly** *adv*

in·com·men·su·rate /ìnkə ménssərət, -ménshə-/ *adj* **1.** not proportionate to or up to the level of something **2.** same as **incommensurable** *adj* (sense 1) —**in·com·men·su·rate·ly** *adv* —**in·com·men·su·rate·ness** *n*

in·com·mode /ìnkə mṓd/ (**-mod·ed, -mod·ing, -modes**) *vt* to cause inconvenience to somebody (*formal*) [Late 16C. Directly or via French < Latin *incommodare* < *commodus* "convenient" (see COMMODE)]

in·com·mo·di·ous /ìnkə mṓdee əss/ *adj* (*formal*) **1.** uncomfortable because lacking in space **2.** causing inconvenience —**in·com·mo·di·ous·ly** *adv*

in·com·mu·ni·ca·ble /ìnkə myoonikəb'l/ *adj* **1. IMPOSSIBLE TO CONVEY** not able to be expressed or conveyed to others **2. IMPOSSIBLE TO PASS ON** not able to be transmitted or passed on to others **3. NOT TALKATIVE** tending not to say much or give much information away —**in·com·mu·ni·ca·bil·i·ty** /ìnkə myoonikə bíllətee/ *n* —**in·com·mu·ni·ca·bly** *adv*

in·com·mu·ni·ca·do /ìnkə myooni kaadō/ *adj* prevented by circumstances or by force from communicating with others [Mid-19C. < Spanish *incomunicado* < *incomunicar* "deprive of communication" < Latin *communicare* (see COMMUNICATE)] —**in·com·mu·ni·ca·do** *adv*

in·com·mu·ni·ca·tive /ìnkə myooni kàytiv, -kətiv/ *adj* unwilling to communicate or provide information —**in·com·mu·ni·ca·tive·ly** *adv* —**in·com·mu·ni·ca·tive·ness** *n*

in·com·mut·a·ble /ìnkə myootəb'l/ *adj* not able to be changed, exchanged for something else, or reduced in severity

in·com·pa·ra·ble /in kómpərəb'l/ *adj* **1.** so excellent, outstanding, or unique as to have no equal **2.** impossible to compare with something else, because there is no basis for a comparison —**in·com·pa·ra·bil·i·ty** /in kòmpərə bíllətee/ *n* —**in·com·pa·ra·bly** *adv*

in·com·pat·i·ble /ìnkəm páttəb'l/ *adj* **1. UNABLE TO COOPERATE OR COEXIST** unable to exist, cooperate, function, or get along with somebody or something else because of basic differences **2.** IMMUNOL **LIKELY TO BE REJECTED BY DONOR** describes a tissue transplant or blood that is rejected by a recipient's immune system **3.** PHARM **NOT SUITABLE FOR USE IN COMBINATION** describes two or more drugs that should not be used together **4.** BOT **NOT ABLE TO BE POLLINATED** describes plants or varieties that cannot be successfully pollinated by or grafted onto each other **5.** LOGIC **CONTRADICTORY** describes two propositions that cannot both be true at the same time **6.** MATH same as **inconsistent** (sense 4) —**in·com·pat·i·bil·i·ty** /ìnkəm patə bíllətee/ *n* —**in·com·pat·i·bly** *adv*

in·com·pe·tent /in kómpət'nt/ *adj* **1. BAD AT DOING SOMETHING** lacking the skills, qualities, or ability to do something properly **2.** LAW **LACKING NECESSARY STATUS** not having the necessary legal status, validity, or powers for the purpose in question ○ *The defendant was found incompetent to stand trial.* **3.** MED **DEFECTIVE** describes a body part such as a muscle that does not function properly ○ *an incompetent cervix* ■ *n* **SOMEBODY BAD AT DOING SOMETHING** somebody who lacks the skills, qualities, or ability to do something properly —**in·com·pe·tence** *n* —**in·com·pe·tent·ly** *adv*

in·com·plete /ìnkəm pleet/ *adj* **1. LACKING PART** lacking something such as a particular part that should be present or available **2. UNFINISHED** not yet finished or fully developed **3. NOT CAUGHT** in football, describes a forward pass that is dropped or not legally caught by an intended receiver ■ *n* **STUDENT'S GRADE INDICATING INSUFFICIENT WORK DONE** a grade that indicates a student has not submitted all the work required to complete a particular course —**in·com·plete·ly** *adv* —**in·com·plete·ness** *n* —**in·com·ple·tion** /-pleesh'n/ *n*

in·com·plete frac·ture *n* a fracture that does not go all the way through a bone

in·com·pli·ant /ìnkəm plī ənt/ *adj* unwilling to be flexible and accommodating, or to comply with something (*formal*) —**in·com·pli·ance** *n*

in·com·pre·hen·si·ble /in kòmpri hénssəb'l/ *adj* impossible or very difficult to understand —**in·com·pre·hen·si·bil·i·ty** /in kòmpri henssə bíllətee/ *n* —**in·com·pre·hen·si·bly** *adv*

in·com·pre·hen·sion /in kòmpri hénshən/ *n* an inability or failure to understand, or a state of bewilderment resulting from this

in·com·pre·hen·sive /in kòmpri hénssiv/ *adj* **1.** limited in scope (*formal*) **2.** unable to understand well —**in·com·pre·hen·sive·ly** *adv* —**in·com·pre·hen·sive·ness** *n*

in·com·press·i·ble /ìnkəm préssəb'l/ *adj* impossible or difficult to compress —**in·com·press·i·bil·i·ty** /ìnkəm pressə bíllətee/ *n*

in·con·ceiv·a·ble /ìnkən seevəb'l/ *adj* **1.** impossible to imagine or to grasp mentally and understand **2.** so unlikely as to be beyond belief or thought impossible ○ *It's inconceivable that she'll accept their terms.* —**in·con·ceiv·a·bly** *adv*

in·con·clu·sive /ìnkən kloossiv/ *adj* not producing a clear-cut result, firm conclusion, or decisive proof of something —**in·con·clu·sive·ly** *adv* —**in·con·clu·sive·ness** *n*

in·con·gru·ent /in kóng groo ənt, ìn kong groo ənt/ *adj* not corresponding in structure or content —**in·con·gru·ence** *n* —**in·con·gru·ent·ly** *adv*

in·con·gru·i·ty /ìnkən groo ətee/ (*plural* **-ties**) *n* **1.** the fact of being incongruous **2.** something that does not seem to fit in with or be appropriate to its context

in·con·gru·ous /in kóng groo əss/ *adj* **1.** unsuitable or out of place in a specific setting or context **2.** not in accord or consistent with something —**in·con·gru·ous·ly** *adv* —**in·con·gru·ous·ness** *n*

in·con·sec·u·tive /ìnkən sékyətiv/ *adj* not following in order one after another —**in·con·sec·u·tive·ly** *adv*

in·con·se·quent /in kónssəkwənt/ *adj* not following as a natural or logical result —**in·con·se·quence** *n* —**in·con·se·quent·ly** *adv*

in·con·se·quen·tial /in kònssə kwénsh'l/ *adj* **1.** of little or no importance **2.** same as **inconsequent** ■ *n* something without importance or significance —**in·con·se·quen·ti·al·i·ty** /in kònssə kwènshee állətee/ *n* —**in·con·se·quen·tial·ly** *adv*

in·con·sid·er·a·ble /ìnkən síddərəb'l/ *adj* **1.** small in size, amount, or value (*often used with "not"*) ○ *It cost $1,500, a not inconsiderable sum.* **2.** so unimportant as to be not worth considering (*formal*) —**in·con·sid·er·a·bly** *adv*

in·con·sid·er·ate /inkən síddərət/ *adj* lacking thought or consideration for other people and their feelings —**in·con·sid·er·ate·ly** *adv* —**in·con·sid·er·ate·ness** *n* —**in·con·sid·er·a·tion** /inkən sidə ráysh'n/ *n*

in·con·sis·ten·cy /inkən sístənssee/ (*plural* **-cies**), **in·con·sis·tence** /inkən sístənss/ *n* **1.** the fact of being inconsistent **2.** something that contradicts something else or that is not in keeping with it

in·con·sis·tent /inkən sístənt/ *adj* **1.** CONTAINING CONFLICTING OR CONTRADICTORY ELEMENTS containing aspects or parts that conflict with or contradict each other ○ *an inconsistent statement* **2.** VARYING AND UNPREDICTABLE unpredictable or unreliable by being likely to behave differently or achieve a different result if a particular situation is repeated ○ *inconsistent performance* **3.** CONFLICTING OR INCOMPATIBLE WITH SOMETHING conflicting with or not corresponding to something such as a rule, principle, or expectation ○ *behavior inconsistent with company policy* **4.** MATH LACKING COMMON VALUES IN EQUATION not having a common set of values for the unknowns in an equation —**in·con·sis·tent·ly** *adv*

in·con·sol·a·ble /inkən sṓləb'l/ *adj* so deeply distressed that nobody can offer any effective comfort —**in·con·sol·a·bly** *adv*

in·con·spic·u·ous /inkən spíkyoo əss/ *adj* not easily seen or noticed —**in·con·spic·u·ous·ly** *adv* —**in·con·spic·u·ous·ness** *n*

in·con·stant /in kónstənt/ *adj* **1.** unfaithful in relationships (*literary*) **2.** likely to change frequently and unpredictably ○ *an inconstant sea breeze* —**in·con·stan·cy** *n* —**in·con·stant·ly** *adv*

in·con·test·a·ble /inkən téstəb'l/ *adj* impossible to question or dispute —**in·con·test·a·bil·i·ty** /inkən testə bíllətee/ *n* —**in·con·test·a·bly** *adv*

in·con·ti·nent /in kóntənənt/ *adj* **1.** UNABLE TO CONTROL BLADDER OR BOWELS unable to control the bladder or bowels and liable to urinate or defecate involuntarily **2.** LACKING SEXUAL CONTROL lacking restraint in sexual matters, or engaging in premarital or extramarital sex **3.** UNRESTRAINED unrestrained and uncontrolled (*literary*) [14C. Directly or via French < Latin *incontinent-* "not holding together" < *continere* (see CONTAIN)] —**in·con·ti·nence** *n* —**in·con·ti·nent·ly** *adv*

in·con·trol·la·ble /inkən trṓləb'l/ *adj* **1.** too strongly felt to be suppressed **2.** too unruly or wild to discipline or control —**in·con·trol·la·bly** *adv*

in·con·tro·vert·i·ble /in kòntrə vúrtəb'l/ *adj* certain, undeniable, and not open to question —**in·con·tro·vert·i·bly** *adv*

in·con·ven·ience /inkən veényənss/ *n* **1.** LACK OF CONVENIENCE the quality or fact of being inconvenient or causing discomfort, difficulty, or annoyance **2.** ANNOYANCE something that causes difficulties or annoyance ■ *vt* (**-ienced, -ienc·ing, -ienc·es**) CAUSE DIFFICULTY TO SOMEBODY to cause somebody difficulties, especially relatively minor or unnecessary ones, or ones involving unwanted extra effort, work, or trouble

in·con·ven·ient /inkən veényənt/ *adj* causing or involving difficulties or unwanted extra effort, work, or trouble —**in·con·ven·ient·ly** *adv*

in·con·vert·i·ble /inkən vúrtəb'l/ *adj* **1.** not exchangeable for gold or silver **2.** not exchangeable for the currency of another country —**in·con·vert·i·bil·i·ty** /inkən vùrtə bíllətee/ *n*

in·con·vinc·i·ble /inkən vínssəb'l/ *adj* impossible or very difficult to convince

in·co·or·di·nate /in kō áwrd'nət/ *adj* lacking coordination —**in·co·or·di·nate·ly** *adv*

in·co·or·di·na·tion /inkō àwrd'n áysh'n/ *n* **1.** an inability to control voluntary muscular movements **2.** a lack of organization or of a consistent approach (*formal*)

in·cor·po·rate *v* /in káwrpə ràyt/ (**-rat·ed, -rat·ing, -rates**) **1.** *vti* JOIN WITH SOMETHING THAT EXISTS to combine something with, or include it within, something already formed, or be combined or included in this way **2.** *vti* MERGE THINGS to combine one thing with another, so as to form a united whole, or be combined in this way **3.** *vti* COMM FORM OR BECOME CORPORATION to form a corporation, or give something the legal form of a corporation **4.** *vt* GIVE REAL FORM TO SOMETHING to give material form to something (*formal*) ■ *adj* /in káwrpərət/ **1.** UNITED merged into a united whole (*formal*) **2.** LAW same as **incorporated** (sense 1) [14C. < late Latin *incorporat-*, past participle of *incorporare* "make into a body" < Latin *corpus* "body"] —**in·cor·po·ra·ble** *adj* —**in·cor·po·ra·tion** /in kàwrpə ráysh'n/ *n* —**in·cor·po·ra·tive** *adj* —**in·cor·po·ra·tor** *n*

in·cor·po·rat·ed /in káwrpə ràytəd/ *adj* **1.** legally established as a corporation **2.** combined or merged into one thing

in·cor·po·re·al /in kawr páwree əl/ *adj* **1.** lacking a physical body or existing solely as a spirit (*formal*) **2.** describes a legal entity that has no material existence of its own but is connected to an actual object such as a patent or copyright —**in·cor·po·re·al·ly** *adv*

in·cor·po·re·i·ty /in kàwrpə reé ətee/ (*plural* **-ties**) *n* **1.** the condition or quality of being incorporeal **2.** something that is incorporeal

in·cor·rect /inkə rékt/ *adj* **1.** wrong, false, or inaccurate **2.** not appropriate, suitable, or proper —**in·cor·rect·ly** *adv* —**in·cor·rect·ness** *n*

in·cor·ri·gi·ble /in káwrijəb'l/ *adj* **1.** IMPOSSIBLE TO CHANGE impossible or very difficult to correct or reform ○ *incorrigible cynics* **2.** UNRULY AND UNMANAGEABLE impossible or very difficult to control or keep in order ■ *n* SOMEBODY OR SOMETHING INCORRIGIBLE somebody or something that is impossible or very difficult to correct or reform [14C. Directly or via French < Latin *incorrigibilis* "not able to be corrected" < *corrigere* (see CORRECT)] —**in·cor·ri·gi·bil·i·ty** /in kàwrijə bíllətee/ *n* —**in·cor·ri·gi·bly** *adv*

in·cor·rupt /inkə rúpt/ *adj* (*formal*) **1.** morally pure and uncorrupted **2.** containing no errors or alterations —**in·cor·rup·tion** *n* —**in·cor·rupt·ly** *adv*

in·cor·rupt·i·ble /inkə rúptəb'l/ *adj* **1.** incapable of being morally corrupted, especially incapable of being bribed or motivated by selfish or base interests **2.** incapable of being affected by decay or decomposition —**in·cor·rupt·i·bil·i·ty** /inkə rùptə bíllətee/ *n* —**in·cor·rupt·i·bly** *adv*

incr. *abbr* **1.** increase **2.** increased **3.** increasing **4.** increment

in·crease *vti* /in kreéss/ (**-creased, -creas·ing, -creas·es**) MAKE OR BECOME LARGER OR GREATER to become, or make something become, larger in number, quantity, or degree ■ *n* /ín kreèss/ **1.** ENLARGEMENT a rise to a greater number, quantity, or degree, or the amount by which something is increased **2.** INCREASING IN SIZE the process of becoming or of making something larger in number, quantity, or degree [14C. Via French < Latin *increscere* < *crescere* "grow"] —**in·creas·a·ble** *adj* —**in·creas·er** *n*

SYNONYMS ***increase, expand, enlarge, extend, augment, intensify, amplify***

CORE MEANING: to make larger or greater

increase to become, or make something become, larger in number, quantity, or degree ○ *Admission prices are to be increased by ten percent next season.* ○ *a world of ever increasing financial pressures* **expand** to become or cause to become larger or more extensive ○ *Wood expands and contracts with temperature and humidity changes.* ○ *The strong economy brought him an excellent opportunity to expand his business.* **enlarge** to increase the size, amount, or extent of something, or become larger ○ *Seating space was enlarged and access provided by vaulted passageways.* ○ *One effect of reading is to modify and enlarge the reader's experience.* **extend** to make larger in terms of length, area, period of time, or other existing limits ○ *Around the same time, both east and west breakwaters were extended.* ○ *The supermarket has extended its range of vegetables to include more exotic varieties.* **augment** (*formal*) to add to something in order to make it larger or more substantial ○ *augment the family income by doing some part-time work* ○ *The municipality needs new recruits to augment the existing police force.* **intensify** to become, or make something become, greater or stronger ○ *As fighting intensified, the capital was said to be without water and food supplies.* ○ *This episode only intensified Rachel's dislike of her sister's fiancé.* **amplify** to become, or make something become, greater in scope, stronger, or louder ○ *The house and shop walls amplify the noise.* ○ *attempting to amplify positive attitudes and reduce negative ones*

---

in·creased /in kreést, íng kreèst/ *adj* larger in number, quantity, or degree

in·creas·ing·ly /in kreéssinglee/ *adv* in a way that increases over time ○ *"As Election Day approaches, there is no front-runner, and the insults and accusations from both sides have been increasingly frequent and bellicose."* (Susan K. Livio, *Election '96: Senate Race*; 1996)

~~**incredable**~~ incorrect spelling of **incredible**

in·cred·i·ble /in kréddəb'l/ *adj* **1.** BEYOND BELIEF impossible or very difficult to believe ○ *I find it incredible that he wasn't nominated.* **2.** AMAZING very surprising ○ *It's incredible how many people turned up.* **3.** MORE THAN THOUGHT POSSIBLE unexpectedly or astonishingly large or great (*informal*) ○ *an incredible amount of food* **4.** EXCELLENT extraordinarily good, talented, or enjoyable (*informal*) ○ *an incredible new band* —**in·cred·i·bil·i·ty** /in krèddə bíllətee/ *n* —**in·cred·i·bly** *adv*

in·cre·du·li·ty /inkrə dóolətee/ *n* a state or feeling of disbelief

in·cred·u·lous /in kréjjələss/ *adj* **1.** unable or unwilling to believe something or completely unconvinced by it **2.** showing or characterized by disbelief —**in·cred·u·lous·ly** *adv* —**in·cred·u·lous·ness** *n*

in·cre·ment /íngkrəmənt/ *n* **1.** INCREASE IN SOMETHING an addition to or increase in the amount or size of something, especially one of a series of small, often regular or planned increases **2.** ACT OF INCREASING the act or process of increasing **3.** MATH SMALL CHANGE IN MATHEMATICAL VALUE a small positive or negative change in the value of a mathematical variable or function [15C. < Latin *incrementum* "growth" < *increscere* (see INCREASE)] —**in·cre·men·tal** /ìngkrə mént'l/ *adj* —**in·cre·men·tal·ly** *adv*

in·cre·men·tal·ism /ìngkrə mént'l ìzzəm/ *n* SOC SCI same as **gradualism** (sense 1)

in·cres·cent /in kréss'nt/ *adj* describes an astronomical object, especially the Moon, that shows a lighted surface area that is increasing in size [Late 16C. < Latin *increscent-*, present participle of *increscere* (see INCREASE)]

in·crim·i·nate /in krímmi nàyt/ (**-nat·ed, -nat·ing, -nates**) *vt* **1.** to prove or make somebody appear to be guilty of a crime or mistake **2.** to accuse somebody of a crime or error (*formal*) [Mid-18C. < late Latin *incriminat-*, past participle of *incriminare* "make criminal" < Latin *crimen* (see CRIME)] —**in·crim·i·na·tion** /in krìmmi náysh'n/ *n* —**in·crim·i·na·to·ry** *adj*

in·cross /in kràwss/ *n* an organism produced through inbreeding within the same strain or breed ■ *vti* (**-crossed, -cross·ing, -cross·es**) to produce an organism by inbreeding within the same strain or breed, or be produced in this way

in-crowd *n* a small, fashionable, and exclusive or influential group, especially one that others want to be part of because of its prestige (*informal*)

in·crust, etc. *v* another spelling of **encrust, etc.**

in·cu·bate /íngkyə bàyt/ (**-bat·ed, -bat·ing, -bates**) *vti* **1.** SIT ON EGGS to keep eggs warm by sitting on them so that the embryos inside can develop and hatch, or be kept warm in this way **2.** KEEP BABY IN INCUBATOR to keep a premature or unwell baby inside a controlled environment in order to keep it alive and assist its growth and development, or be kept in such an environment **3.** GROW MICROORGANISMS IN CONTROLLED ENVIRONMENT to keep cells or microorganisms at a controlled temperature in or on a medium so that they multiply, or be kept in or on such a medium **4.** BUILD UP DISEASE-PRODUCING GERMS to develop an infection, through the reproduction of germs, to the point at which the first signs of a disease appear, or be developed in this way **5.** GRADUALLY BRING SOMETHING INTO BEING to form or develop something such as a plan or an idea slowly and quietly over a period of time, or be formed or developed in this way [Mid-17C. < Latin *incubat-*, past participle of *incubare* "lie down on" < *cubare* "lie down"]

in·cu·ba·tion /íngkyə báysh'n/ *n* **1.** MAINTENANCE OF BABY IN CONTROLLED ENVIRONMENT the keeping of a premature or unwell baby in an environment in which the temperature, humidity, and oxygen levels can be easily controlled **2.** CONTROLLED GROWTH OF MICROORGANISMS the maintenance of cells or microorganisms under a controlled temperature in or on a medium so that they can multiply **3.** GROWTH OF DISEASE-CAUSING MICROORGANISMS the development of an infection inside the body to the point at which the first signs of disease become apparent **4.** GRADUAL DEVELOPMENT the slow development of something, especially through thought and planning **5.** MED same as **incubation period** —**in·cu·ba·tion·al** *adj*

in·cu·ba·tion pe·ri·od *n* the period between the time somebody is infected with a disease and the appearance of its first symptoms

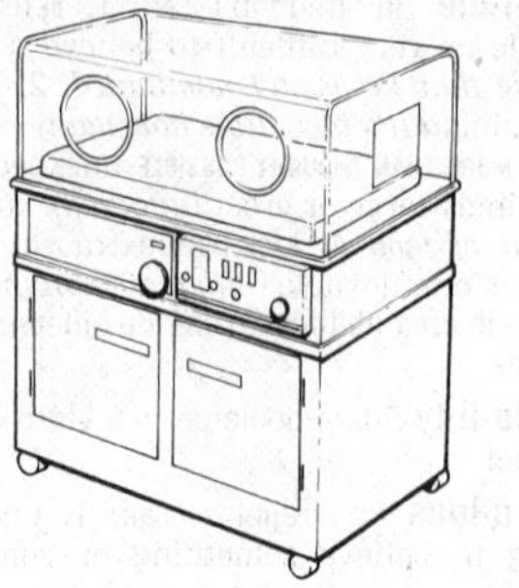

incubator

in·cu·ba·tor /íngkyə bàytər/ *n* **1. HOSPITAL APPARATUS FOR PREMATURE BABIES** a hospital apparatus, usually a transparent box, in which a premature or unwell baby is kept in a controlled environment to protect it from infection and assist its growth and development **2. DEVICE TO NURTURE SOMETHING** an apparatus in which the temperature is kept at a constant level so that eggs can be artificially hatched, or cells and microorganisms can multiply in or on a growth medium **3. SURROUNDINGS FAVORABLE TO PROGRESS** a place, organization, or environment that promotes the growth or development of something **4. COMPANY PROMOTING ENTREPRENEURSHIP FOR STARTUPS** a company or facility that promotes entrepreneurship by offering startup companies, especially in high-tech industries, shared facilities and business advice

in·cu·bus /íngkyəbəss/ (*plural* **-bi** /-bī/ or **-bus·es**) *n* **1.** something that causes somebody much worry or anxiety, especially a nightmare or obsession (*literary*) **2.** in medieval times, a male demon that was believed to have sexual intercourse with women while they were asleep [14C. < late Latin, "nightmare" < Latin *incubare* (see INCUBATE)]

in·cu·des ANAT plural of **incus**

in·cul·cate /in kúl kàyt, ín kul kàyt/ (**-cat·ed, -cat·ing, -cates**) *vt* to fix something firmly in somebody's mind through frequent, forceful repetition [Mid-16C. < Latin *inculcat-*, past participle of *inculcare* "stamp in" < *calcare* (see CAULK)] —**in·cul·ca·tion** /in kul káysh'n/ *n*

in·cul·pa·ble /in kúlpəb'l/ *adj* free of guilt or blame (*formal*) [15C. < late Latin *inculpabilis* < Latin *culpabilis* (see CULPABLE)] —**in·cul·pa·bil·i·ty** /in kùlpə bíllətee/ *n* —**in·cul·pa·ble·ness** *n* —**in·cul·pa·bly** *adv*

in·cul·pate /in kúl pàyt, ín kul pàyt/ (**-pat·ed, -pat·ing, -pates**) *vt* to incriminate somebody, or put the blame for something on somebody (*formal*) [Late 18C. < late Latin *inculpat-*, past participle of *inculpare* "put blame on" < Latin *culpa* "blame, fault"] —**in·cul·pa·tion** /in kul páysh'n/ *n* —**in·cul·pa·to·ry** /in kúlpə tàwree/ *adj*

in·cum·ben·cy /in kúmbənssee/ *n* (*formal*) **1.** the period of time during which somebody occupies an official post **2.** an official post, especially in a church or political organization

in·cum·bent /in kúmbənt/ *n* **SOMEBODY IN OFFICE** somebody currently holding an official post, especially in a church or political organization ○ *Incumbents are generally at a decided advantage in elections.* ■ *adj* **1. OBLIGATORY** necessary as a result of a duty, responsibility, or obligation (*formal*) ○ *It is incumbent on us to observe every stipulation to the letter.* **2. IN OFFICE** currently holding an official post [15C. < Latin *incumbent-*, present participle of *incumbere* "lie in or on" < *-cumbere* "lie down"]

in·cum·ber *vt* another spelling of **encumber**

in·cu·na·ble *n* PRINTING same as **incunabulum**

in·cu·nab·u·la /inkyə nábbyələ/ *npl* the early stages or beginnings of something (*formal*) [Early 19C. < Latin, "swaddling clothes, infancy" < *cunae* "cradle"]

in·cu·nab·u·lum /inkyə nábbyələm/ (*plural* **-la** /-lə/), **in·cu·na·ble** /in kyóonəb'l/ *n* a book printed from movable type before 1501 [Early 19C. < Latin, singular of *incunabula* (see INCUNABULA)]

in·cur /in kúr/ (**-curred, -cur·ring, -curs**) *vt* **1.** to suffer something undesirable such as another person's anger or a financial loss as a result of an action ○ *incur their wrath* **2.** to become burdened with something such as a debt [15C. Via French < Latin *incurrere* "run into" < *currere* "run"] —**in·cur·rence** *n*

in·cur·a·ble /in kyóorəb'l/ *adj* **1. IMPOSSIBLE TO CURE** not possible to cure **2. IMPOSSIBLE TO CHANGE** not possible to change ■ *n* **SOMEBODY OR SOMETHING IMPOSSIBLE TO CURE** a person or animal with an illness or condition that cannot be cured —**in·cur·a·bil·i·ty** /in kyòorə bíllətee/ *n* —**in·cur·a·bly** *adv*

in·cu·ri·ous /in kyóoree əss/ *adj* showing no curiosity about or interest in something —**in·cu·ri·os·i·ty** /in kyòoree óssətee/ *n* —**in·cu·ri·ous·ly** *adv*

in·cur·rent /in kúrrənt, -kúr ənt/ *adj* flowing or running inward into something [Late 16C. < Latin *incurrent-*, present participle of *incurrere* (see INCUR)]

in·cur·sion /in kúrzh'n/ *n* **1.** a brief, hostile, and usually sudden invasion of somebody's territory **2.** the act of flowing, running, or intruding into something, usually with unpleasant or damaging effects (*formal*) [15C. Directly or via French < Latin *incursion-* "a running in" < *incurrere* (see INCUR)] —**in·cur·sive** /in kúrssiv/ *adj*

in·cur·vate *vti* /ín kur vàyt, in kúr vàyt/ (**-vat·ed, -vat·ing, -vates**) same as **incurve** *v* ■ *adj* /in kúr vàyt, in kúrvət/ curved or bending inward [Late 16C. < Latin *incurvat-*, past participle of *incurvare* "bend inward" < *curvus* "curved"]

in·curve /in kúrv/ *vti* (**-curved, -curv·ing, -curves**) to curve inward, or make something do this ■ *n* a curve that bends inward

in·cus /íngkəss/ (*plural* **-cu·des** /-kyòo deézl/) *n* **1.** a small anvil-shaped bone in the middle ear of mammals between the malleus and stapes bones **2.** (*plural same*) METEOROL same as **thunderhead** [Mid-17C. < Latin, "anvil" < *incudere* (see INCUSE)]

in·cuse /in kyóoz/ *adj* **STAMPED INTO COIN AS DESIGN** hammered, stamped, or impressed on a coin as a design ■ *n* **STAMPED-IN COIN DESIGN** a design stamped, hammered, or impressed on a coin ■ *vt* (**-cused, -cus·ing, -cus·es**) **IMPRESS DESIGN ON COIN** to hammer, stamp, or impress a design on a coin [Early 19C. < Latin *incus-*, past participle of *incudere* "hammer on" < *cudere* "to beat" < Indo-European]

IND *abbr* in God's name [Latin *in nomine Dei*]

ind., ind *abbr* **1.** independence **2.** independent **3.** index **4.** GRAM indicative **5.** GRAM indirect **6.** industrial **7.** industry

Ind., Ind *abbr* **1.** India[1] **2.** PEOPLES Indian **3.** Indiana **4.** Indies

in·da·ba /in daábə/ *n S Africa* a political meeting, conference, or consultation, originally held with or among indigenous peoples of South Africa [Early 19C. < Zulu, "discussion"]

in·da·mine /índə meèn/ *n* an organic base that forms blue or green salts. Use: manufacture of dyes.

in·debt·ed /in déttəd/ *adj* **1.** owing money to somebody **2.** obliged or grateful to somebody for something such as assistance or a favor received [13C. Alteration of Old French *endetté*, past participle of *endetter* "put in debt" < *dette* (see DEBT)]

in·debt·ed·ness /in déttədnəss/ *n* **1.** the condition of owing money to somebody or owing somebody thanks **2.** the total amount somebody owes

in·de·cen·cy /in deéss'nssee/ (*plural* **-cies**) *n* **1.** offensiveness according to accepted standards, especially in sexual matters **2.** an act that offends against accepted standards of decency

in·de·cent /in deéss'nt/ *adj* **1.** unacceptable and offensive to accepted standards, especially in sexual matters **2.** inappropriate under the circumstances and disapproved of by others ○ *The funeral was arranged with indecent haste.* —**in·de·cent·ly** *adv*

in·de·cent as·sault *n* a sexual assault on somebody that does not involve rape

in·de·cent ex·po·sure *n* the criminal offense of deliberately displaying part of the body, usually the genitals, to somebody else in public

in·de·cid·u·ous /indi síjjoo əss/ *adj* BOT same as **evergreen** (*technical*)

in·de·ci·pher·a·ble /indi sífərəb'l/ *adj* impossible or very difficult to read or understand —**in·de·ci·pher·a·bil·i·ty** /indi sìfərə bíllətee/ *n* —**in·de·ci·pher·a·bly** *adv*

in·de·ci·sion /indi sízh'n/ *n* the inability to reach a decision, or uncertainty resulting from somebody's inability to reach a decision

in·de·ci·sive /indi síssiv/ *adj* **1.** unable or reluctant to make decisions generally or to come to a decision about something in particular **2.** not producing a clear result, especially a clear victory for somebody —**in·de·ci·sive·ly** *adv* —**in·de·ci·sive·ness** *n*

in·de·clin·a·ble /indi klínəb'l/ *adj* used to describe a noun, adjective, or pronoun existing in one form only without grammatical inflections according to number, case, or gender [15C. Via French < Latin *indeclinabilis* "not declinable" < *declinare* (see DECLINE)]

in·dec·o·rous /in dékərəss/ *adj* somewhat rude or shocking because of being considered socially unacceptable —**in·dec·o·rous·ly** *adv*

in·de·co·rum /indi káwrəm/ *n* **1.** behavior that offends against what is socially acceptable **2.** an indecorous action

in·deed /in deéd/ CORE MEANING: an adverb indicating agreement with or confirmation of something ○ *He is indeed an actor.* ○ *"Do you know that man?" "Indeed I do."*

adv **1. WHAT IS MORE** introduces a statement that strengthens or adds to a point just made ○ *I am willing, indeed eager, to speak on your behalf.* **2. FOR EMPHASIS** gives additional emphasis after a descriptive word or phrase ○ *The news, I learned, was grim indeed.* **3. INDICATES RESPONSE** expresses surprise, curiosity, or disbelief ○ *"He's applied for a job." "Has he indeed?"* [14C. < IN[1] + DEED]

indef. *abbr* GRAM indefinite

in·de·fat·i·ga·ble /indi fáttigəb'l/ *adj* never showing any sign of getting tired or of relaxing an effort [Early 17C. Directly or via French < Latin *indefatigabilis* < *defatigare* "tire out" < *fatigare* "to tire"] —**in·de·fat·i·ga·bil·i·ty** /indi fàttigə bíllətee/ *n* —**in·de·fat·i·ga·bly** *adv*

in·de·fea·si·ble /indi feézəb'l/ *adj* impossible to annul, make void, or forfeit —**in·de·fea·si·bil·i·ty** /indi feèzə bíllətee/ *n* —**in·de·fea·si·bly** *adv*

in·de·fec·ti·ble /indi féktəb'l/ *adj* (*formal*) **1.** not affected by decay or failure **2.** having no fault or imperfection [Mid-17C. IN[1] < obsolete *defectible* "liable to fail" < late Latin *defectibilis* < *defect-* (see DEFECT)] —**in·de·fec·ti·bil·i·ty** /indi fèktə bíllətee/ *n* —**in·de·fec·ti·bly** *adv*

in·de·fen·si·ble /indi fénssəb'l/ *adj* **1. PERMITTING NO EXCUSE** too bad or blameworthy to be in any way justified or excused ○ *indefensible conduct* **2. UNABLE TO BE PROTECTED** incapable of being defended from attack **3. INVALID** not based on fact, proof, or sound reasoning ○ *an indefensible argument* —**in·de·fen·si·bil·i·ty** /indi fènssə bíllətee/ *n* —**in·de·fen·si·bly** *adv*

in·de·fin·a·ble /indi fínəb'l/ *adj* impossible or very difficult to define, describe, or analyze ■ *n* something that is impossible or very difficult to describe, define, or analyze —**in·de·fin·a·bil·i·ty** /indi fìnə bíllətee/ *n* —**in·de·fin·a·bly** *adv*

in·def·i·nite /in déffənət/ *adj* **1. UNLIMITED** not fixed or limited in length, size, duration, or quantity ○ *away for an indefinite period* **2. NOT CLEAR** not clear or not precisely defined or fixed ○ *indefinite plans* **3. VAGUE AND UNCERTAIN** unable or unwilling to give a clear indication of thoughts or plans **4.** BOT **TOO MANY TO COUNT** consisting of units that are too numerous to be counted precisely ○ *indefinite stamens* —**in·def·i·nite·ness** *n*

in·def·i·nite ar·ti·cle *n* a word that designates a noun referring to something that has not been mentioned before and is simply any one of its kind, e.g., "a" or "an" in English ○ *Choose a book and write a review of it.*

in·def·i·nite in·te·gral *n* an integral that when differentiated equals a given function

in·def·i·nite·ly /in déffənətlee/ *adv* **1.** for a length of time that has no fixed or obvious end ○ *postponed indefinitely* **2.** in a general and unspecific or vague and imprecise way ○ *described indefinitely*

in·def·i·nite pro·noun *n* a pronoun that does not refer to a specific person or thing, e.g., "someone," "nothing," or "anything" in English

in·de·his·cent /indi híss'nt/ *adj* describes a fruit that does not open up to release seeds when ripe —**in·de·his·cence** *n*

in·del·i·ble /in délləb'l/ *adj* **1. IMPOSSIBLE TO REMOVE OR ALTER** physically impossible to rub out, wash out, or alter **2. CONTAINING INDELIBLE SUBSTANCE** containing indelible ink or lead ○ *an indelible pencil* **3. UNFORGETTABLE** impossible to remove from the mind or memory and therefore remaining forever ○ *made an indelible impression on us* [15C. Directly or via French < Latin *indelebilis* "not defaceable" < *delere* "blot out"] —**in·del·i·bil·i·ty** /in dèllə bíllətee/ *n* —**in·del·i·bly** *adv*

in·del·i·cate /in déllikət/ *adj* **1.** tactless, crude, or too frank, and therefore causing or likely to cause offense **2.** crude, rough, or coarse in texture or appearance —**in·del·i·ca·cy** *n* —**in·del·i·cate·ly** *adv*

in·dem·ni·fy /in démni fī/ (**-fied, -fy·ing, -fies**) *vt* **1.** to provide somebody with protection, especially financial protection, against possible loss, damage, or liability **2.** to pay compensation to somebody for loss, damage, or liability incurred [Early 17C. < Latin *indemnis* "not injured" < *damnum* "injury"] —**in·dem·ni·fi·ca·tion** /in dèmnifi káysh'n/ *n* —**in·dem·ni·fi·er** *n*

in·dem·ni·ty /in démnətee/ (*plural* **-ties**) *n* **1.** INSURANCE protection or insurance against possible loss, damage, or liability **2.** COMPENSATION a compensation paid for loss, damage, or liability **3.** EXEMPTION FROM PENALTIES legal exemption from penalties or liabilities [15C. Via French < late Latin *indemnitas* "security for damage" < Latin *indemnis* (see INDEMNIFY)]

in·de·mon·stra·ble /indi mónstrəb'l/ *adj* impossible to demonstrate or prove (*formal*) —**in·de·mon·stra·bly** *adv*

in·dene /in deen/ *n* a colorless toxic liquid. Source: coal tar, petroleum. Use: manufacture of synthetic resins. Formula: C_9H_8. [Late 19C. < INDOLE + -ENE]

in·dent[1] *v* /in dént/ (**-dent·ed, -dent·ing, -dents**) **1.** *vti* BEGIN LINE IN FROM MARGIN to start a line or row of text some distance in from the margin **2.** *vt* FORM RECESS IN SOMETHING to form a deep recess in something (*often passive*) **3.** *vt* NOTCH SOMETHING to make jagged, notched, or serrated edges in something **4.** *vt* FIT NOTCHED EDGES TOGETHER to join together two notched pieces of something **5.** *vt* TEAR COPIED DOCUMENT IN HALF to tear a document, especially one containing two copies of the same text, in half along an irregular line **6.** *vt* DRAW UP DOCUMENT IN DUPLICATE to draw up a document in two or more exact copies ■ *n* /ín dènt, in dént/ **1.** SPACE SET IN FROM MARGIN a blank space left between the margin and the beginning of a line or row of text **2.** HIST CERTIFICATE FOR INTEREST ON PUBLIC DEBT a certificate issued by the federal or a state government for the principal or interest on public debt at the end of the American Revolution **3.** LAW same as **indenture** (*archaic*) [14C. Directly or via Anglo-Norman < medieval Latin *indentare* < Latin *in-* "in, into" + *dent-* "tooth"] —**in·dent·er** *n*

ORIGIN Etymologically, English has two separate words ***indent***, although they have converged to a considerable extent. The one meaning "form a recess in" is simply a derivative of *dent*. ***Indent*** "make a jagged edge on" owes its origin to Latin *dent* "tooth." This formed the basis of an Anglo-Latin verb *indentare* that denoted the drawing up of a contract between two parties on two identical documents that were cut along a matching line of notches or "teeth" that could subsequently be rejoined to prove their authenticity. A specific use of such contracts was between master craftsmen and their trainees, who hence became known as *indentured* apprentices.

in·dent[2] *vt* /in dént/ (**-dent·ed, -dent·ing, -dents**) to press something inward to form a dent ■ *n* /ín dènt, in dént/ same as **dent** *n* (sense 1) [14C. < IN-[2] + DENT]

in·den·ta·tion /in den táysh'n/ *n* **1.** NOTCH OR RECESS a notch, recess, or hollowed-out place in something such as an edge, boundary line, or coast **2.** JAGGED EDGE a series of notches or recesses, or the edge formed by this **3.** PRINTING LEAVING OF SPACE AT LINE BEGINNING the leaving of space between the margin and the beginning of a line or row, or the blank space left **4.** ACT OF INDENTING the act of indenting something, or the fact of being indented

in·den·ture /in dénchər/ *n* **1.** CONTRACT WITH APPRENTICE a contract committing an apprentice or servant to serve a master or employer for a specific period of time (*often plural*) **2.** WRITTEN AGREEMENT a written contract or agreement between two or more parties **3.** DUPLICATE DOCUMENT WITH TORN EDGE a document written in duplicate on a single sheet and torn in half so that the edges of the two resulting copies could be matched up to prove their authenticity **4.** AUTHORIZED LIST an official list or inventory that has been authenticated for use as a voucher ■ *vt* CONTRACT SOMEBODY FOR SERVICES to commit somebody to work as an apprentice or servant for a specific period of time by means of indentures —**in·den·tured** *adj* —**in·den·ture·ship** *n*

in·den·tured ser·vant *n* an immigrant to North America between the 17th and 19th centuries who contracted to work for an employer for a number of years in exchange for passage and accommodation

~~**independant**~~ incorrect spelling of **independent**

in·de·pend·ence /ində péndənss/ *n* **1.** freedom from dependence on or control by another person, organization, or state **2.** the date or point in time when a state achieves its political independence ○ *the first elections since independence*

In·de·pend·ence /ində péndənss/ **1.** city in western Missouri, a suburb of Kansas City. It was the home of President Harry S. Truman. Population: 112,301 (2002 estimate). **2.** city in southeastern Kansas, situated 97 mi./156 km southeast of Wichita. Population: 9,521 (2002 estimate).

In·de·pend·ence Day *n* a national holiday marking the signing of the Declaration of Independence in 1776. Date: July 4.

in·de·pend·en·cy /ində péndənssee/ (*plural* **-cies**) *n* **1.** an independent state or territory **2.** same as **independence** (*archaic*)

In·de·pend·en·cy *n* the principle or policy that each local Christian church or congregation should be free of external ecclesiastical control

in·de·pend·ent /ində péndənt/ *adj* **1.** NOT CONTROLLED BY ANOTHER in politics, free from the authority, control, or domination of somebody or something else, especially not controlled by another state or organization and able to self-govern **2.** ABLE TO FUNCTION BY SELF able to operate alone because not dependent on somebody or something else ○ *Each wheel has an independent suspension system.* **3.** SELF-SUPPORTING not forced to rely on another for money or support ○ *financially independent* **4.** SHOWING CONFIDENCE IN SELF capable of thinking or acting without consultation with or guidance from others ○ *an independent thinker* **5.** DONE WITHOUT OBSTRUCTION carried out or operating without interference or influence from interested parties ○ *an independent investigation* **6.** SUFFICIENT TO LIVE ON providing the means on which to live without having to work ○ *independent means* **7.** POL NOT AFFILIATED TO POLITICAL PARTY not belonging to, representing, or supporting any political party **8.** MATH NOT SOLVABLE USING SOLUTION TO ANOTHER describes a system of equations in which no single equation is necessarily solved using a solution to the others **9.** STATS NOT AFFECTING OTHER VARIABLES in statistics, distributed in such a way that the value taken on by one variable leaves all others unaffected **10.** LOGIC NOT DEPENDENT ON AXIOM OR PROPOSITION not proved from another logical axiom or proposition ■ *n* **1.** SOMEBODY OR SOMETHING UNAFFECTED BY OTHERS somebody or something that is free from control, dependence, or interference **2.** POL SOMEBODY POLITICALLY UNAFFILIATED a politician or voter who is not a member, representative, or supporter of any political party —**in·de·pend·ent·ly** *adv*

In·de·pend·ent *n* **1.** somebody who believes that each Christian church or congregation should be free of external ecclesiastical control **2.** POL another spelling of **independent** *n* (sense 2) ■ *adj* another spelling of **independent** *adj* (sense 7)

in·de·pen·dent as·sort·ment *n* in genetics, the principle that genes are inherited independently of one another, although genes close together on the same chromosome have a higher likelihood of being inherited together

in·de·pend·ent clause *n* a clause that can stand on its own as a sentence, e.g., "She'll go on vacation" in the sentence "She'll go on vacation if she can get the money"

in·de·pend·ent coun·sel *n* an attorney appointed by a special panel of three federal judges to investigate, independently of any outside influence, serious allegations of wrongdoing at the federal level

in·de·pend·ent in·ven·tion *n* an invention arrived at independently, even though another group of people may have created the same invention in a different place at a different time

in·de·pend·ent means *npl* money to live on that is gained from sources other than employment, e.g., from investments

in·de·pend·ent var·i·a·ble *n* **1.** the variable in a mathematical statement whose value, when specified, determines the value of another variable or other variables **2.** a variable that is manipulated in an experiment in order to observe the effect on another variable

in-depth *adj* giving careful consideration to all details and aspects of a subject —**in depth** *adv*

in·de·scrib·a·ble /indi skrībəb'l/ *adj* **1.** impossible or very difficult to describe ○ *an indescribable sensation* **2.** so intense or extreme as to defy description ○ *indescribable joy* —**in·de·scrib·a·bil·i·ty** /indi skrībə bíllətee/ *n* —**in·de·scrib·a·bly** *adv*

~~**indespensable**~~ incorrect spelling of **indispensable**

~~**indestructable**~~ incorrect spelling of **indestructible**

in·de·struc·ti·ble /indi strúktəb'l/ *adj* impossible or very difficult to destroy —**in·de·struc·ti·bil·i·ty** /indi strùktə bíllətee/ *n* —**in·de·struc·ti·bly** *adv*

in·de·ter·min·a·ble /indi túrminəb'l/ *adj* **1.** impossible to determine or ascertain exactly **2.** impossible to resolve, answer, or settle —**in·de·ter·min·a·bly** *adv*

in·de·ter·mi·na·cy /indi túrminəssee/ *n* the condition or quality of being indeterminate

in·de·ter·mi·na·cy prin·ci·ple *n* QUANTUM PHYS same as **uncertainty principle**

in·de·ter·mi·nate /indi túrminət/ *adj* **1.** NOT KNOWN EXACTLY not known exactly, or impossible to work out **2.** VAGUE not definite, precise, or clear **3.** UNPREDICTABLE not having a predictable result or outcome **4.** MATH HAVING NO NUMERIC MEANING having no numerical value or meaning, e.g., the expression "0/0" or "0^∞" **5.** MATH WITH UNKNOWN NUMBER OF SOLUTIONS having an infinite number of solutions **6.** BOT GROWING AT TIP continuing to grow at the tip of the main stem instead of terminating in a flower bud —**in·de·ter·mi·nate·ly** *adv* —**in·de·ter·mi·nate·ness** *n* —**in·de·ter·mi·na·tion** /indi turmi náysh'n/ *n*

in·de·ter·mi·nate sen·tence *n* a prison sentence with a date of release that can be varied according to the prisoner's conduct and other factors

in·de·ter·mi·nate vow·el *n* LING same as **schwa**

in·de·ter·min·ism /indi túrmi nìzzəm/ *n* the philosophical theory that human beings have free will and their actions are not always and completely determined by previous events —**in·de·ter·min·ist** *n* —**in·de·ter·min·is·tic** /indi tùrmi nístik/ *adj*

in·dex /ín dèks/ *n* (*plural* **-dex·es** or **-di·ces** /-di seez/) **1.** ALPHABETICAL REFERENCE LIST an alphabetical list of topics, people, or titles, giving the location of where they are mentioned in a text **2.** CATALOG a list of items in a set or collection such as the books in a library, usually including details of where to find them **3.** PUBLICATION LISTING ARTICLES a periodical or book that lists published work alphabetically by subject, title, or author **4.** PRINTING same as **thumb index** **5.** NUMBER EXPRESSING RELATIONSHIP a scale, or a number on it, that expresses the price, value, or level of something in relation to something else or to a base number ○ *the consumer price index* **6.** INDICATOR an indicator or sign of something ○ *One index of the gravity of the situation is the severance of diplomatic relations.* **7.** POINTER a pointer or needle, especially on a piece of scientific equipment **8.** PRINTING CHARACTER a character ☞ used by printers to draw attention to a paragraph, section, or note **9.** MATH same as **exponent** (sense 4) **10.** MATH NUMBER GIVEN AS SUPERSCRIPT a number or variable given as a superscript before a square-root sign showing which root is to be taken **11.** MATH SUBSCRIPT OR SUPERSCRIPT IDENTIFYING ELEMENT a subscript or superscript numeral that identifies an element or range in a set or sequence ■ *v* **1.** *vti* MAKE INDEX FOR SOMETHING to compile an index for something such as a book or computer record **2.** *vt* PUT SOMETHING IN INDEX to enter something such as a name, title, subject, or keyword in an index **3.** *vt* INDICATE SOMETHING to be a sign or indicator of something (*formal*) **4.** *vt* ECON SUBJECT SOMETHING TO INDEXATION to subject a variable such as wages to indexation [Late 16C. < Latin, "forefinger," literally "pointer" < Indo-European, "to show"] —**in·dex·er** *n*

In·dex *n* CHR same as **Index Librorum Prohibitorum**

in·dex·a·tion /in dek sáysh'n/ *n* the linking of wages, pensions, or other remuneration to an index representing the cost of living, so that they are automatically adjusted up or down as that rises or falls

in·dex case *n* the first documented case of an illness in an epidemiologic study

in·dex fin·ger *n* the finger next to the thumb

in·dex fos·sil *n* the fossil of an organism that is specific to a particular geologic age and is used for dating or identifying rocks or rock layers in which it is found

in·dex fund *n* a mutual fund that invests in companies listed in an important stock market index in order to match the market's overall performance

In·dex Li·bro·rum Pro·hib·i·to·rum /in deks li brâwrəm prōhibi tàwrəm/ *n* a list formerly compiled by the Roman Catholic Church of books and publications that Church members were forbidden to read [< Latin, "list of forbidden books."]

in·dex num·ber *n* a number used to indicate the change in a value or quantity such as a price or unemployment, when compared with the level of that value or quantity at an earlier time. The base level is usually arbitrarily set at 100, and the increase or decrease in index numbers over time is often expressed as a percentage change.

in·dex of re·frac·tion *n US* the ratio of the speed of refracted light in a vacuum or reference medium to its speed in the medium under examination. Symbol ***n***. Can term **refractive index**

India

In·di·a[1] /índee ə/ country in South Asia, the second largest in the world by population and the seventh largest by area. It became an independent member of the British Commonwealth in 1947. Language: Hindi, English. Currency: rupee. Capital: New Delhi. Population: 1,049,700,100 (2003). Area: 1,222,243 sq. mi./3,165,596 sq. km. Official name **Republic of India**

In·di·a[2] /índee ə/ *n* a code word for the letter "I," used in international radio communications

In·di·a ink *n* **1.** a black pigment made from lampblack and a binding agent and shaped into cakes or sticks **2.** a liquid black ink made from India ink

In·di·a·man /índee əmən/ (*plural* **-men** /-mən/) *n* a large merchant sailing ship formerly used to transport goods to and from India [Early 18C. < INDIA[1] + MAN "ship," as in *man of war*]

In·di·an /índee ən/ *n* **1.** SOMEBODY FROM INDIA somebody who comes from India or is of Indian descent **2.** ⚠ NATIVE AMERICAN a Native North, South, or Central American (*sometimes considered offensive*) **3.** STATUS INDIAN in Canada, somebody of indigenous ancestry who is neither Inuit nor Metis **4.** NATIVE AMERICAN LANGUAGE a language used by a Native North, South, or Central American people (*sometimes considered offensive*) ■ *adj* **1.** RELATING TO INDIA relating to India, or its peoples, languages, or cultures **2.** RELATING TO NATIVE AMERICANS relating to Native North, South, or Central Americans, or their languages or cultures (*sometimes considered offensive*)

USAGE Initially the term ***Indian*** was applied to the earliest inhabitants of the American continents because Columbus and other early European explorers, having arrived on North America's eastern coast, believed they had reached India by a new route. As a name thus applied in error by conquerors, ***Indian*** may well be regarded as insensitive or even offensive. Some of the people in question prefer to be called *American Indian(s)*, but others prefer the term *Native American(s)*, this last choice being the one least likely to cause offense. The use of ***Indian*** to mean "somebody from India" is perfectly acceptable.

Indiana

In·di·an·a /indee ánnə/ state in the north central United States, bordered by Illinois, Kentucky, Michigan, Ohio, and Lake Michigan. Capital: Indianapolis. Population: 6,951,068 (2002 estimate). Area: 36,420 sq. mi./94,327 sq. km. —**In·di·an·an** *n, adj*

In·di·an a·gent *n* an official in the United States or, formerly, in Canada, acting as a government representative to communities of Native North Americans

In·di·an A·mer·i·can *n* an American of Indian descent

In·di·an·ap·o·lis /indee ə náppələss/ capital of Indiana, in the central part of the state, southwest of Fort Wayne on the White River. It is the largest city in the state. Population: 783,612 (2002 estimate).

In·di·an bread *n* a plant with edible parts, e.g., the breadroot, used by some Native North American peoples as food

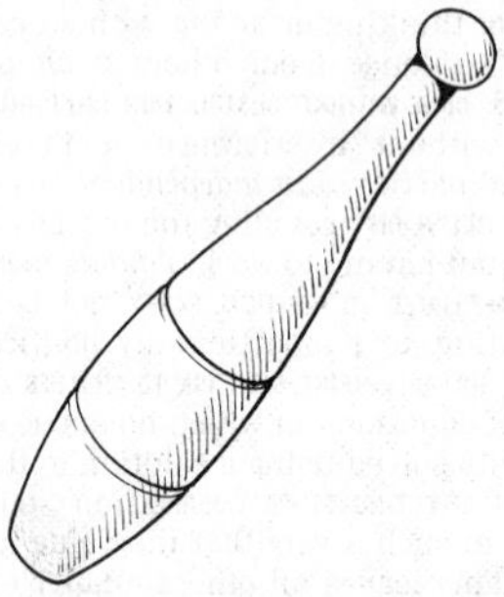

Indian club

In·di·an club *n* a club shaped like an elongated bottle, used in gymnastics and juggling

In·di·an corn *n* same as **corn**[1] *n* (senses 1–2) [< its cultivation by Native Americans]

In·di·an Eng·lish *n* a variety of English spoken in India

WORLD ENGLISH See ***South Asian English***.

In·di·an file *n* an offensive term for single file (*dated*) [< a Native American custom of walking in single file]

In·di·an giv·er *n* an offensive term for somebody who gives something and then asks for its return (*informal*)

In·di·an hemp *n* **1.** PLANTS same as **hemp** (sense 3) **2.** a perennial plant of the dogbane family whose roots can be used as a laxative and emetic. Native to: North America. Latin name: *Apocynum cannabinum*.

In·di·an ink *n UK* same as **India ink**

In·di·an lic·o·rice *n* PLANTS same as **rosary pea**

In·di·an mal·low *n* PLANTS same as **flowering maple**

In·di·an meal *n* FOOD same as **cornmeal**

In·di·an mus·tard *n* PLANTS same as **brown mustard** (sense 2)

In·di·an O·cean /índee ən-/ ocean situated east of Africa, south of Asia, west of Australia, and north of Antarctica. Its greatest known depth is 25,344 ft./7,725 m. Area: 28,360,000 sq. mi./73,440,000 sq. km.

In·di·an paint·brush *n* a wild plant of the figwort family with brightly colored bracts that look like flowers. Native to: North America. Latin name: *Castileja linariaefolia*.

In·di·an peach *n regional* a clingstone peach

REGIONAL NOTE See ***plum peach***.

In·di·an pipe *n* a perennial woodland plant whose single white stem and nodding flower resembles a tobacco pipe. Native to: North America, Asia. Latin name: *Monotropa uniflora*.

In·di·an po·ny *n* a small and rugged horse that is often used in crossbreeding. Native to: western North America.

In·di·an pud·ding *n* a baked pudding made of cornmeal, molasses, milk, and spices

In·di·an red *n* **1.** a red pigment made of iron oxide. Use: paint, cosmetics, polish. **2.** a dark reddish brown color —**In·di·an red** *adj*

In·di·an re·serve *n Can* in Canada, an area of land set aside for a Native North American people whose members are recognized by the government as Status Indians

In·di·an rice *n* PLANTS same as **wild rice**

In·di·an Stan·dard Time *n* the standard time in India, five-and-a-half hours later than Universal Coordinated Time

In·di·an sub·con·ti·nent large region in South Asia, including the countries of Bangladesh, India, and Pakistan

In·di·an sum·mer *n* **1.** a period of mild sunny weather occurring in autumn in the northern hemisphere **2.** a calm or productive and enjoyable period toward the end of somebody's life or the end of a process, period, or activity [Origin ?]

In·di·an Ter·ri·to·ry *n* the territory west of the Mississippi River formally ceded to Native North American peoples for their resettlement in 1834. It gradually diminished in size and was finally incorporated into Oklahoma in 1907.

In·di·an to·bac·co *n* a very poisonous annual plant of the bluebell family that has oval toothed leaves and swollen seed capsules. Flowers: small, purplish. Native to: North America. Latin name: *Lobelia inflata*.

In·di·an tur·nip *n* PLANTS same as **jack-in-the-pulpit**

In·di·an wres·tling *n* a form of wrestling in which one wrestler attempts to force down another's upraised arm or to throw a standing opponent off balance —**In·di·an-wres·tle** *vti*

In·di·a pa·per *n* a thin fine paper originally made in South Asia, used for prints and illustrations

In·di·a rub·ber *n* INDUST same as **rubber**[1] (sense 1) (*dated*)

In·dic /índik/ *n* a large group of languages of South Asia, forming a major division of Indo-Iranian. Native speakers: 700 million. [Mid-19C. Via Latin < Greek *Indikos* < *Indos* "the Indus River"] —**In·dic** *adj*

indic. *abbr* **1.** indicating **2.** GRAM indicative **3.** indicator

in·di·can /índi kàn/ *n* **1.** a substance formed in the intestine by bacterial action and excreted in urine and sweat. Formula: $C_8H_6NO_4SK$. **2.** an off-white crystalline sugar derivative found in plants. Use: original source of indigo dye. [Mid-19C. < Latin *indicum* (see INDIGO)]

in·di·cate /índi kàyt/ (**-cat·ed, -cat·ing, -cates**) *vt* **1.** POINT TO SOMETHING to point something out or point to something **2.** SHOW EXISTENCE OR TRUTH OF SOMETHING to be or provide a sign, signal, or symptom that something exists or is true **3.** REGISTER MEASUREMENT to register a measurement, e.g., of speed or temperature **4.** SHOW WHAT SOMEBODY THINKS OR INTENDS to state or show an opinion, feeling, instruction, or intention, especially briefly or indirectly **5.** SHOW WHAT SHOULD BE DONE to make somebody think that something should be done or used (*usually used in the passive*) ○ *In a case like this, a firm approach is indicated.* **6.** MED SHOW PRESENCE OF DISEASE to point out the presence of, or remedy for, a disease or syndrome [Early 17C. < Latin *indicat-*, past participle of *indicare* "point toward, show" < *dicare* "proclaim"] —**in·di·cant** /índikənt/ *n*

in·di·cat·ed horse·pow·er /índi kaytəd-/ *n* the theoretical power produced by a reciprocating engine such as a steam or internal-combustion engine, calculated as the power produced before reduction due to friction and mechanical movement

in·di·ca·tion /índi káysh'n/ *n* **1.** SIGN OF SOMETHING a sign, signal, or symptom that something exists or is true **2.** ACT OF INDICATING an act of indicating or pointing to something **3.** READING ON INSTRUMENT a reading shown on a measuring instrument **4.** SOMETHING NECESSARY OR DESIRABLE something that is indicated as the right thing to do or use **5.** MED MEDICAL SIGN a medical sign or symptom that shows the presence of a disease or a remedy for it

in·dic·a·tive /in díkətiv/ *adj* **1.** INDICATING EXISTENCE OR TRUTH showing, suggesting, or pointing out that something exists or is true **2.** GRAM RELATING TO BASIC MOOD OF VERBS relating to the basic mood of verbs in ordinary objective statements in languages such as English ■ *n* GRAM **1.** BASIC MOOD OF VERB the basic mood of a verb in languages such as English, used for ordinary objective statements **2.** VERB IN BASIC MOOD a verb in the basic mood used for ordinary objective statements in languages such as English —**in·dic·a·tive·ly** *adv*

in·di·ca·tor /índi kàytər/ *n* **1.** SOMETHING THAT SHOWS WHAT CONDITIONS ARE something observed or calculated that is used to show the presence or state of a condition or trend **2.** MEASURING INSTRUMENT an instrument or gauge that measures something and registers the measurement **3.** SOMETHING GIVING INFORMATION something such as a light, sign, or pointer that gives information, e.g., about which direction to follow **4.** ECOL same as **indicator organism** **5.** CHEM CHEMICAL SHOWING SOMETHING a substance that shows the presence or concentration of a specific material or chemical, e.g., litmus

in·di·ca·tor di·a·gram *n* a graph showing the variation of pressure and volume in a cylinder of a reciprocating engine

in·di·ca·tor or·gan·ism *n* an organism whose presence or absence in an environment indicates conditions such as its oxygen level or the presence of a contaminating substance

in·dic·es plural of **index**

in·di·ci·um /in díshee əm/ (*plural* **-ci·a** /-shee ə/) *n* **1.** a sign indicating the presence or nature of something such as a medical condition **2.** a printed sign on an item of bulk mail showing the postage paid or canceled [Early 17C. < Latin < *indic-*, stem of *index* (see INDEX)]

in·di·co·lite /in díkə līt/ *n* a blue-colored variety of tourmaline. Use: gems. [Early 19C. < Latin *indicum* (see INDIGO)]

in·dict /in dī́t/ (**-dict·ed, -dict·ing, -dicts**) *vt* **1.** to charge somebody formally with commission of a crime **2.** to accuse somebody of wrongdoing [14C. < Anglo-Norman *enditer* < Latin *indict-*, past participle of *indicere* "proclaim," literally "say in" < *dicere* "say"] —**in·dict·ee** /in dī tée/ *n* —**in·dict·er** *n* —**in·dict·or** *n*

in·dict·a·ble /in dī́təb'l/ *adj* **1.** liable to be charged with a criminal offense **2.** making somebody liable to be charged with commission of a crime ○ *an indictable offense*

in·dic·tion /in díksh'n/ *n* a cyclic period of 15 years begun during the reign of Constantine the Great in the later Roman Empire at the end of which property was evaluated for taxation [14C. < Latin *indiction-* "declaration" < *indict-* (see INDICT); from the declaration setting the valuation on which tax was assessed]

in·dict·ment /in dī́tmənt/ *n* **1.** ACCUSATION BEFORE GRAND JURY a formal accusation of a serious crime, presented to a grand jury **2.** ACT OF INDICTING SOMEBODY the act of indicting somebody or the condition of being indicted **3.** STATEMENT OR FACT THAT ACCUSES a statement or indication that something is wrong or somebody is to blame ○ *a stinging indictment of our prison system*

in·die /índee/ (*slang*) *n* a small independent business enterprise, especially one related to music or film ■ *adj* very stylish or in vogue [Early 20C. Shortening of INDEPENDENT]

In·dies ➧ **East Indies, West Indies**

in·dif·fer·ence /in dífərənss, -dífrənss/ *n* **1.** LACK OF INTEREST IN SOMETHING lack of interest, care, or concern **2.** UNIMPORTANCE lack of importance or significance ○ *It's a matter of complete indifference to me whether you go or stay.* **3.** LOW QUALITY ordinariness or lack of quality

in·dif·fer·ent /in dífərənt, -dífrənt/ *adj* **1.** WITHOUT CARE OR INTEREST showing no care or concern for or interest in somebody or something ○ *She was indifferent to their criticism.* **2.** FAVORING NEITHER SIDE without bias or preference for one person, group, or thing rather than another **3.** ONLY AVERAGE average or low in quality **4.** BIOL UNDIFFERENTIATED describes cells or tissues that are not specialized or differentiated **5.** SCI NEUTRAL having no properties that are affected by a process or reaction [14C. Directly or via French < Latin *indifferent-* "making no difference" < *different-* (see DIFFERENT)]

in·dif·fer·ent·ism /in dífərən tìzzəm, -dífrən-/ *n* the belief that variations in doctrine and practice within a religion are unimportant

in·dif·fer·ent·ly /in dífərəntlee, -dífrəntlee/ *adv* **1.** WITHOUT INTEREST without showing interest or concern **2.** NOT WELL in a way that is only average or low in quality **3.** EQUALLY without differences or exceptions (*formal*)

in·di·gence /índijənss/ *n* extreme poverty in which the basic necessities of life are lacking (*formal*)

in·di·gen·ize /in díjjə nīz/ (**-ized, -iz·ing, -iz·es**) *vti* to increase the use of local inhabitants for a task previously done by people from another country, usually the home country of an employing company —**in·di·gen·i·za·tion** /in dìjjəni záysh'n/ *n*

in·dig·e·nous /in díjjənəss/ *adj* **1.** originating in and naturally living, growing, or occurring in a region or country **2.** natural or inborn (*formal*) [Mid-17C. < Latin *indigena*, literally "born in" < *gignere* "beget"] —**in·di·gen·i·ty** /índi jénnətee/ *n* —**in·dig·e·nous·ly** *adv*

SYNONYMS See ***native***.

in·dig·e·nous peo·ple *n* a people who occupy a region at the time of its contact with colonial powers or the outside world

in·di·gent /índijənt/ (*formal*) *adj* lacking the necessities of life, e.g., food, clothing, and shelter ■ *n* an impoverished person [14C. Via French < Latin *indigent-*, present participle of *indigere*, literally "lack in" < *egere* "to need"] —**in·di·gent·ly** *adv*

in·di·gest·i·ble /índi jéstəb'l, ìn dī-/ *adj* difficult or impossible to digest —**in·di·gest·i·bil·i·ty** /índi jèstə bíllətee, ìn dī-/ *n* —**in·di·gest·i·bly** *adv*

in·di·ges·tion /índi jéschən, ìn dī-/ *n* difficulty in digesting food, resulting in such symptoms as belching, heartburn, or stomach pains. Technical name **dyspepsia**

in·di·ges·tive /índi jéstiv, ìn dī-/ *adj* experiencing or resulting from indigestion

in·dig·nant /in dígnənt/ *adj* angry or annoyed at the apparent unfairness or unreasonableness of something [Late 16C. < Latin *indignant-*, present participle of *indignari* "regard as unworthy" < *dignus* "worthy"] —**in·dig·nant·ly** *adv*

in·dig·na·tion /índig náysh'n/ *n* anger because something seems unfair or unreasonable [14C. Directly or via French < Latin *indignation-* < *indignari* (see INDIGNANT)]

SYNONYMS See ***anger***.

in·dig·ni·ty /in dígnətee/ (*plural* **-ties**) *n* a situation that results in a humiliating loss of dignity or self-esteem

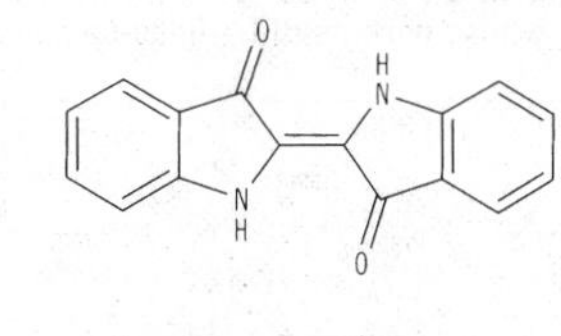

indigo: synthetic indigo

in·di·go /índi gō/ *n* (*plural* **-gos** or **-goes**) **1.** DEEP PURPLISH BLUE COLOR a deep purplish blue color that lies between blue and violet on the visible spectrum **2.** BLUE DYE a blue dye. Source: formerly from plants, but now usually made synthetically. **3.** PLANT YIELDING INDIGO DYE a tropical plant of the pea family with fronds of pointed leaves and flowers, a source of indigo dye. Flowers: red or purple, in spikes. Genus: *Indigofera*. ■ *adj* DEEP PURPLISH BLUE of a deep purplish blue color [Mid-16C. Via Spanish and Portuguese < Latin *indicum* < Greek *indikon* "the Indian substance," form of *Indikos* (see INDIC)]

in·di·go bird /índigō burd/ *n* a songbird, the male of which has deep purplish black feathers. Native to: East Africa. Family: Viduidae.

in·di·go-blue *adj* same as **indigo**

in·di·go snake *n* a large harmless deep-blue snake that preys on small animals. Native to: southern United States, Central and South America. Latin name: *Drymarchon corais*.

in·dig·o·tin /in díggətin, índi gṓt'n/ *n* same as **indigo** *n* (sense 2) [Mid-19C. < INDIGO + *-t-* + -IN]

In·di·o[1] /índee ō/ (*plural* **-os**) *n* a member of an indigenous people in a part of America or East Asia formerly ruled by Spain or Portugal

In·di·o[2] /índee ō/ city in Riverside County, southeastern California, situated southeast of San Bernardino. Population: 54,221 (2002 estimate).

in·di·rect /índi rékt, ìn dī-/ *adj* **1.** NOT IN STRAIGHT LINE not in a direct line, course, or path **2.** NOT IMMEDIATE OR INTENDED not occurring as an immediate or intended effect or consequence **3.** DEVIOUS not obvious or straightforward in approach **4.** INVOLVING INTERMEDIATE STAGES not obtained or proceeding from an immediate or straightforward relationship —**in·di·rect·ly** *adv* —**in·di·rect·ness** *n*

in·di·rect cost *n* a business expense that is not directly connected with a specific product or operation

in·di·rect dis·course *n* GRAM same as **indirect speech**

in·di·rect free kick *n* in soccer, a free kick from which a goal cannot be scored unless the ball touches another player before it passes over the goal line

in·di·rec·tion /índi rékshən, ìn dī-/ *n* **1.** LACK OF DIRECTNESS lack of directness in a path, course, or procedure **2.** AIMLESSNESS lack of a goal or goals **3.** SOMETHING NOT HONEST an approach or action that is devious or deceitful

in·di·rect la·bor *n* work that is not considered in determining costs per unit in producing or manufacturing something, e.g., work done by clerical or maintenance staff

in·di·rect light·ing *n* reflected or diffused light used to avoid glare or shadows

in·di·rect ob·ject *n* the recipient of the action shown by a verb and its direct object, e.g., "the cat" in "She gave the cat a meal"

in·di·rect proof *n* in logic, proof of a conclusion by showing that assuming its negation will lead to a contradiction

in·di·rect ques·tion *n* a question reported in indirect speech, e.g., "He asked why you were not there"

in·di·rect speech *n* a report of something said or written that conveys what was said, but not the exact words in their original form, as in "She said she would join us later"

in·di·rect tax *n* a tax levied on goods or services, instead of directly on companies and individual people —**in·di·rect tax·a·tion** *n*

in·dis·cern·i·ble /índi súrnəb'l/ *adj* impossible to see or understand —**in·dis·cern·i·bil·i·ty** /índi sùrnə bíllətee/ *n* —**in·dis·cern·i·bly** *adv*

in·dis·ci·pline /in díssiplin/ *n* lack of control or discipline

in·dis·creet /índi skréet/ *adj* lacking tact or discretion —**in·dis·creet·ly** *adv* —**in·dis·creet·ness** *n*

SPELLCHECK Do not confuse the spelling of ***indiscreet*** and ***indiscrete*** (= not separated into parts), which sound similar. ***Indiscreet*** is the more common word in general use and means "not tactful or able to keep a secret." ***Indiscrete*** is a much rarer formal or technical word meaning "not consisting of separate parts."

in·dis·crete /índi skréet/ *adj* not divided into parts, or appearing not to consist of separate parts —**in·dis·crete·ly** *adv*

SPELLCHECK See ***indiscreet***

in·dis·cre·tion /índi skrésh'n/ *n* **1.** lack of tact or good judgment **2.** something said or done that is tactless or unwise ○ *apologizing for past indiscretions* —**in·dis·cre·tion·ar·y** *adj*

in·dis·crim·i·nate /ìndi skrímmənət/ *adj* **1.** making no careful distinctions or choices **2.** random, haphazard, or confused —**in·dis·crim·i·nate·ly** *adv* —**in·dis·crim·i·nate·ness** *n* —**in·dis·crim·i·na·tion** /ìndi skrìmmə náysh'n/ *n*

in·dis·crim·i·nat·ing /ìndi skrímmə nàyting/ *adj* lacking discrimination or judgment —**in·dis·crim·i·nat·ing·ly** *adv* —**in·dis·crim·i·na·tive** *adj*

in·dis·pen·sa·ble /ìndi spénssəb'l/ *adj* **1. NECESSARY** necessary, essential, or not to be dispensed with **2. HAVING TO BE FACED** unavoidable, especially as a duty ■ *n* **SOMETHING ESSENTIAL** something that is essential and cannot be dispensed with —**in·dis·pen·sa·bil·i·ty** /ìndi spènssə bíllətee/ *n* —**in·dis·pen·sa·ble·ness** *n* —**in·dis·pen·sa·bly** *adv*

SYNONYMS See *necessary.*

~~indispensible~~ incorrect spelling of **indispensable**

in·dis·pose /ìndi spṓz/ (**-posed, -pos·ing, -pos·es**) *vt* **1. MAKE SOMEBODY UNFIT** to make somebody unfit for something (*formal*) **2. MAKE SOMEBODY AVERSE TO SOMETHING** to make somebody dislike the prospect of something or be unwilling to do something (*formal*) **3. SICKEN SOMEBODY** to make somebody ill

in·dis·posed /ìndi spṓzd/ *adj* (*formal*) **1.** too ill to do something **2.** unwilling to say or do something, especially because of a feeling of annoyance

in·dis·po·si·tion /ìn dispə zísh'n/ *n* (*formal*) **1.** an illness that is not serious **2.** reluctance or unwillingness to do something

in·dis·put·a·ble /ìndi spyóotəb'l/ *adj* impossible to doubt, question, or deny —**in·dis·put·a·bil·i·ty** /ìndi spyòotə bíllətee/ *n* —**in·dis·put·a·ble·ness** *n* —**in·dis·put·a·bly** *adv*

in·dis·sol·u·ble /ìndi sóllyəb'l/ *adj* incapable of being dissolved, broken, or undone —**in·dis·sol·u·bil·i·ty** /ìndi sòllyə bíllətee/ *n* —**in·dis·sol·u·bly** *adv*

in·dis·tinct /ìndi stíngkt/ *adj* **1.** not seen or heard clearly **2.** not clearly remembered, understood, or thought out —**in·dis·tinct·ly** *adv* —**in·dis·tinct·ness** *n*

in·dis·tinc·tive /ìndi stíngktiv/ *adj* with no distinguishing qualities or features —**in·dis·tinc·tive·ly** *adv*

in·dis·tin·guish·a·ble /ìndi stíng gwishəb'l/ *adj* **1.** impossible to tell apart from somebody or something else ○ *His handwriting is indistinguishable from his father's.* **2.** very hard to see, hear, or understand —**in·dis·tin·guish·a·bil·i·ty** /ìndi stìng gwishə bíllətee/ *n* —**in·dis·tin·guish·a·bly** *adv*

in·dite /in dít/ (**-dit·ed, -dit·ing, -dites**) *vt* to write or compose something such as a poem, letter, or speech (*archaic or literary*) [14C. < Old French *enditir*, literally "compose in words in" < Latin *indict-* (see INDICT)]

in·di·um /índee əm/ *n* a soft silvery rare metallic element. Source: zinc and tin ores. Use: alloys, transistors, electroplating. Symbol **In**. See table at **element**

in·di·um phos·phide *n* a brittle metallic solid. Use: manufacture of semiconductors, lasers, solar cells.

in·di·vid·u·al /ìndə víjjoo əl/ *n* **1.** ⚠ **SPECIFIC PERSON** a specific person, distinct from others in a group ○ *belief in the individual's right to self-expression* **2. ANY PERSON** a human being, or a person of a specified type ○ *a panel consisting of four individuals* ○ *a very unfortunate individual* **3. SEPARATE THING** a separate entity or thing **4.** BIOL **SEPARATE ORGANISM** an independent organism separate from a group ○ *The plant part contains the embryo, which gives rise to a new individual.* ■ *adj* **1. SEPARABLE FROM OTHERS** singular and separable from others in a group or class ○ *Each individual bead is hand-sewn.* **2. OF OR FOR ONE PERSON** belonging to, relating to, or intended for one person only **3. VERY DISTINCTIVE** strikingly personal, unusual, or distinctive [15C. < medieval Latin *individualis* < Latin *individuus* "not divisible" < *dividere* "to divide"]

USAGE individual or **person**? In formal general writing, use *person, people,* or another noun in instances where you mean "a human being or one of a specified type": *The faculty has invited several people* [not *individuals*] *from neighboring universities to participate in the symposium. The main character is a unique person* [not *individual*]. In specific professional spheres, especially law enforcement and the criminal justice system, ***individual*** meaning "human being or person" is regularly used, as in *One individual is in custody, charged with armed robbery.* ***Individual*** as a noun meaning "human being" is also acceptable when used in a context contrasting the person with a larger group: *In a true democracy the worth of the individual is of paramount concern* [i.e., the person as a single being is of prime importance as opposed to the masses]; *He is a true individual* [i.e., he has striking personal qualities that make him stand out among the rest].

in·di·vid·u·al·ism /ìndə víjjoo ə lìzzəm/ *n* **1. PURSUIT OF PERSONAL GOALS** the pursuit of personal happiness and independence rather than collective goals or interests **2. PERSONAL TRAIT** a personal peculiarity or trait **3. BELIEF IN IMPORTANCE OF INDIVIDUAL** the belief that society exists for the benefit of individual people, who must not be constrained by government interventions or made subordinate to collective interests

in·di·vid·u·al·ist /ìndə víjjoo əlist/ *n* **1.** somebody of independent thought or behavior **2.** a believer in the philosophy of individualism —**in·di·vid·u·al·is·tic** /ìndə vijoo ə lístik/ *adj* —**in·di·vid·u·al·is·ti·cal·ly** *adv*

in·di·vid·u·al·i·ty /ìndə vìjjoo állətee/ (*plural* **-ties**) *n* **1.** a specific personality, character, or characteristic that distinguishes one person or thing from another **2.** the state or condition of being separate from others

in·di·vid·u·al·ize /ìndə víjjoo ə lìz/ (**-ized, -iz·ing, -iz·es**) *vt* **1. GIVE SOMEBODY OR SOMETHING INDIVIDUAL CHARACTER** to give somebody or something a character that is separate and distinct from other people or things **2. TREAT SOMEBODY OR SOMETHING INDIVIDUALLY** to consider or treat somebody or something specifically, as distinct from other people or things **3. ADAPT SOMETHING TO INDIVIDUAL REQUIREMENTS** to make or modify something to suit a specific person —**in·di·vid·u·al·i·za·tion** /ìndə vijoo əli záysh'n/ *n* —**in·di·vid·u·al·iz·er** *n*

in·di·vid·u·al·ly /ìndə víjjoo əlee/ *adv* as a separate person or entity, not as part of a group or class

in·di·vid·u·al med·ley *n* a swimming race divided into three or four equal parts, in each of which the swimmers must use a particular stroke such as backstroke, crawl, breaststroke, or butterfly stroke

in·di·vid·u·ate /ìndə víjjoo àyt/ (**-at·ed, -at·ing, -ates**) *vt* to make somebody or something separate and distinct from others [Early 17C. < medieval Latin *individuat-*, past participle of *individuare* < Latin *individuus* (see INDIVIDUAL)] —**in·di·vid·u·a·tor** *n*

in·di·vid·u·a·tion /ìndə vìjjoo áysh'n/ *n* **1.** the act or process of making somebody or something separate and distinct from others **2.** in Jungian psychology, the development of the self, achieved by resolving the conflicts arising at life's transitional stages, in particular the transition from adolescence to adulthood. Jung believed this process could not be completed until middle age.

in·di·vis·i·ble /ìndi vízzəb'l/ *adj* **1.** not capable of being separated into parts ○ *"... one nation indivisible, with liberty and justice for all"* (*Pledge of Allegiance*) **2.** not capable of being divided by a given number without leaving a mathematical remainder —**in·di·vis·i·bil·i·ty** /ìndi vizə bíllətee/ *n* —**in·di·vis·i·bly** *adv*

indo- *prefix* a chemical compound derived from indigo ○ *indoxyl* [< INDIGO]

Indo- *prefix* **1.** India ○ *Indo-European* **2.** Indic ○ *Indo-Iranian* [< INDIA[1], INDIC]

In·do-Ca·na·di·an *n* a Canadian who came from India, or whose parents did —**In·do-Ca·na·di·an** *adj*

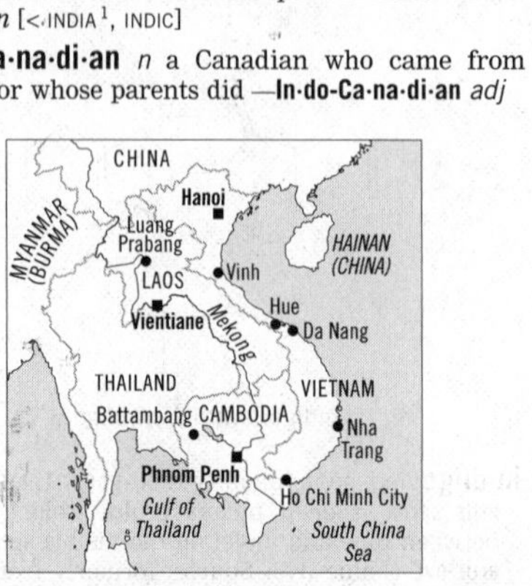

Indochina

In·do·chi·na /ìndō chínə/ peninsula of Southeast Asia that includes Myanmar, Thailand, Cambodia, Vietnam, Laos, and the Malay Peninsula. In a narrower sense it refers only to Cambodia, Laos, and Vietnam. —**In·do·chi·nese** /ìndō chī néez, -néess/ *adj, n*

in·doc·ile /in dóss'l/ *adj* resisting discipline or instruction —**in·do·cil·i·ty** /ìndə síllətee, ìn do-/ *n*

in·doc·tri·nate /in dóktrə nàyt/ (**-nat·ed, -nat·ing, -nates**) *vt* to teach somebody a belief, doctrine, or ideology thoroughly and systematically, especially with the goal of discouraging independent thought or the acceptance of other opinions [Early 17C. < Old French *endoctriner*, literally "teach in" < medieval Latin *doctrinare* "teach" < Latin *doctrina* (see DOCTRINE)] —**in·doc·tri·na·tion** /in dòktrə náysh'n/ *n* —**in·doc·tri·na·tor** *n*

In·do-Eu·ro·pe·an /ìndō yoorə pée ən/ *n* **1. FAMILY OF EUROPEAN AND ASIAN LANGUAGES** a large family of languages spoken from South Asia to Western Europe and the United States, comprising the Balto-Slavonic, Germanic, Italic, Indo-Iranian, Celtic, Greek, Albanian, Armenian, Anatolian, and Tocharian branches. This language family includes many modern languages such as Bangla, English, French, German, Spanish, Russian, Hindi, and Urdu. **2. ANCESTOR OF MODERN INDO-EUROPEAN LANGUAGES** the reconstructed language that is the prehistoric ancestor of modern languages belonging to Indo-European **3. SPEAKER OF INDO-EUROPEAN LANGUAGE** a speaker of a language belonging to Indo-European, especially prehistoric Indo-European —**In·do-Eu·ro·pe·an** *adj*

In·do-I·ra·ni·an *n* a group of languages spoken in northern South Asia and in parts of Southwest Asia, forming a branch of Indo-European and dividing into Indic and Iranian subgroups. Native speakers: 800 million. —**In·do-I·ra·ni·an** *adj*

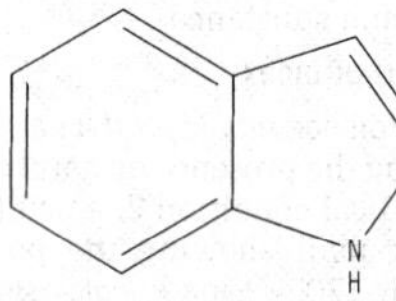

indole

in·dole /ín dōl/, **in·dol** /ín dòl/ *n* a crystalline compound. Source: plants, feces, coal tar. Use: in perfumes, chemical reagent. Formula: C_8H_7N.

in·dole·a·ce·tic ac·id /ìn dōlə seétik-/ *n* a plant hormone that stimulates growth and root formation in cuttings

in·dole·bu·tyr·ic ac·id /ìndōl byoo téerik-/ *n* a synthetic plant hormone that stimulates growth in stems

in·do·lent /índələnt/ *adj* **1.** lethargic and not showing any interest or making any effort **2.** describes a disease or condition that is slow to develop or be healed, and causes no pain [Mid-17C. < late Latin *indolent-* "insensitive to pain" < Latin *dolere* "suffer pain"] —**in·do·lence** *n* —**in·do·lent·ly** *adv*

in·do·meth·a·cin /ìndō méthəssin/ *n* a drug used to relieve pain, fever, and inflammation, especially from arthritis [Mid-20C. < INDOLE + METHYL + ACETIC + -IN]

in·dom·i·ta·ble /in dómmitəb'l/ *adj* brave, determined, and impossible to defeat or frighten [Mid-17C. < late Latin *indomitabilis* "untamable" < Latin *domitare* "to tame"] —**in·dom·i·ta·bil·i·ty** /in dòmmitə bíllətee/ *n* —**in·dom·i·ta·ble·ness** *n* —**in·dom·i·ta·bly** *adv*

In·do·ne·sia /ìndə néezhə, -néeshə/ country in Southeast Asia, the fourth most populous country in the world. It consists of more than 13,670 islands, 6,000 of which are inhabited. Language: Bahasa Indonesia. Currency: rupiah. Capital: Jakarta. Population: 234,893,450 (2003). Area: 735,310 sq. mi./1,904,443 sq. km. Official name **Republic of Indonesia**. See map on next page

In·do·ne·sian /ìndō néezh'n/ *n* **1.** somebody who comes from Indonesia **2.** LANG same as **Bahasa Indonesia** —**In·do·ne·sian** *adj*

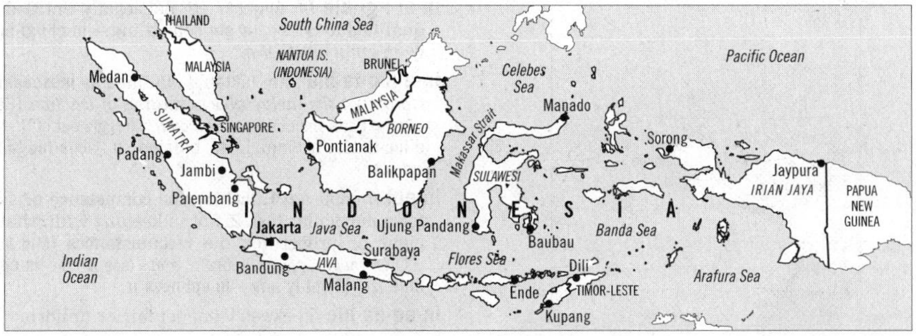

Indonesia

in·door /in dawr/ *adj* situated or done within a building

in·door air qual·i·ty *n* the condition of the air inside buildings, including the extent of pollution caused by smoking, dust, mites, mold spores, radon, and gases and chemicals from materials and appliances

in·door-out·door *adj* designed to be used inside or outside a building

in·doors /in dáwrz/ *adv* into or inside a building

In·do-Pa·cif·ic *n* a large group of languages spoken in New Guinea and the surrounding islands. Native speakers: 3 million. —**In·do-Pa·cif·ic** *adj*

In·dore /in dáwr/ **1.** former state, now part of Madhya Pradesh, central India **2.** city in western Madhya Pradesh, central India. It was the capital of the former state of Indore. Population: 1,639,044 (2001).

in·dorse *vt* another spelling of **endorse**

In·dra /índrə/ *n* in Vedic mythology, a powerful warrior god and the ruler of the sky and weather. He became a subordinate god in later Hindu mythology.

in·draft /ín dràft/ *n* an inward flow or current of air

in·drawn /ín dràwn/ *adj* drawn in or pulled in

in·dri /índree/ *n* a large rare black-and-white lemur with large eyes, silky fur, and a rudimentary tail. Native to: Madagascar. Latin name: *Indri indri.* [Mid-19C. < Malagasy *indry!* "look!" or *indry izy!* "there he is!"]

in·du·bi·ta·ble /in dóobitəb'l/ *adj* obvious or definitely true, and not to be doubted [Early 17C. Directly or via French < Latin *indubitabilis* "not doubtful" < *dubitare* "to doubt"] —**in·du·bi·ta·bil·i·ty** /in dòobitə bíllətee/ *n* —**in·du·bi·ta·bly** *adv*

in·duce /in dóoss, -dyóoss/ (**-duced, -duc·ing, -duc·es**) *vt* **1.** PERSUADE SOMEBODY TO DO SOMETHING to persuade or influence somebody to do or think something **2.** PRODUCE MENTAL OR PHYSICAL STATE to bring about a thought, feeling, or physical condition **3.** HASTEN BIRTH OF BABY to make the process of labor or the birth of a baby start by a medical intervention, usually by administering a drug, before it happens naturally **4.** REASON FROM OBSERVATION to make a statement based on the observation of facts **5.** PRODUCE SOMETHING BY INDUCTION to produce an electric current or a magnetic field by induction [14C. < Latin *inducere* "lead into, persuade" < *ducere* "to lead"]

in·duced drag /in dóost-, -dyóost-/ *n* the drag force created by the lift of an aircraft

in·duce·ment /in dóossmənt, -dyóoss-/ *n* **1.** a prospect or reward that gives somebody a reason for acting in a specific way, especially something that is offered as an incentive **2.** the act of inducing something

SYNONYMS See ***motive.***

in·duc·er /in dóossər/ *n* in genetics, a substance that activates a structural gene within a cell

in·duct /in dúkt/ (**-duct·ed, -duct·ing, -ducts**) *vt* **1.** FORMALLY GIVE SOMEBODY POSITION to install somebody formally into a position or office **2.** EXPOSE SOMEBODY TO NEW IDEAS to introduce somebody to new beliefs, knowledge, or ideas **3.** ENLIST SOMEBODY FOR MILITARY SERVICE to enlist somebody formally for service in the military **4.** PHYS same as **induce** (sense 5) [14C. < Latin *induct-*, past participle of *inducere* (see INDUCE)] —**in·duct·ee** /in dùk tée/ *n*

in·duc·tance /in dúktənss/ *n* **1.** the property of an electric circuit or device whereby an electromotive force is created by a change of current in it or in a circuit near it. Symbol **L 2.** PHYS same as **inductor** (sense 2)

in·duc·tile /in dúkt'l/ *adj* not pliable or yielding (*technical*) —**in·duc·til·i·ty** /in duk tíllətee/ *n*

in·duc·tion /in dúkshən/ *n* **1.** ACT OF INDUCTING SOMEBODY the act or process of inducting somebody into a position or an organization **2.** PROCESS OF INDUCING SOMETHING the process of inducing a state, feeling, or idea **3.** MED PROCESS OF HASTENING BIRTH the act or the process of medically hastening the birth of a baby **4.** LOGIC CONCLUSION BASED ON EVIDENCE a generalization based on observed instances, or the making of such generalizations, in the usual working method of scientists **5.** PHYS CREATION OF ELECTRIC OR MAGNETIC FORCES the process by which electric or magnetic forces are created in a circuit by being in proximity to an electric or magnetic field or a varying current without physical contact **6.** MIL ACT OF ENLISTING SOMEBODY the act of formally enlisting somebody into military service **7.** BIOL PROCESS IN DEVELOPMENT OF EMBRYO the process by which one part of an embryo affects the development of another, e.g., through the diffusion of hormones **8.** CHEM SYNTHESIS OF ENZYME the process by which the production of an enzyme is stimulated by the increased concentration of the substance it acts on **9.** MATH PROCESS OF MATHEMATICAL PROOF a process for proving propositions with variables limited to positive integers by showing that the smallest instance is true and each following instance is derived from the one before —**in·duc·tion·al** *adj*

in·duc·tion coil *n* a transformer that produces an intermittent high-voltage current from a low-voltage direct current by means of several wire windings and, often, a soft iron core

in·duc·tion cook·ing *n* a method of cooking food in metal pans using magnetic energy from induction coils beneath the ceramic cooktop on which the pans are placed

in·duc·tion heat·ing *n* a process for raising the temperature of a metal by inducing an electric current within it

in·duc·tion mo·tor *n* an alternating-current motor in which current is induced into the rotor windings by stationary windings connected directly to the power source

in·duc·tive /in dúktiv/ *adj* **1.** PHYS OF ELECTRIC OR MAGNETIC INDUCTION involving, operating by, or caused by electric or magnetic induction **2.** PSYCHOL PRODUCING MENTAL OR PHYSICAL STATE relating to the process of inducing a feeling, idea, or state **3.** LOGIC REACHING CONCLUSION BASED ON OBSERVATION generalizing to produce a universal claim or principle from observed instances **4.** BIOL AFFECTING ANOTHER EMBRYONIC PART producing an effect on another embryonic part by induction —**in·duc·tive·ly** *adv* —**in·duc·tive·ness** *n*

in·duc·tor /in dúktər/ *n* **1.** AGENT OF INDUCTION somebody or something that inducts somebody or something else **2.** PART OF CIRCUIT GENERATING FORCE a part of an electric circuit, usually a coil, in which an electromotive force is generated by inductance **3.** COMPONENT CAUSING INDUCTANCE an electrical or electronic component designed to cause or work on inductance

in·due *vt* another spelling of **endue**

in·dulge /in dúlj/ (**-dulged, -dulg·ing, -dulg·es**) *v* **1.** *vti* HAVE OR PERMIT TREAT to allow yourself or somebody else to experience something enjoyable **2.** *vi* DRINK ALCOHOL to permit yourself to drink alcohol, especially to excess **3.** *vt* GIVE DEBTOR TIME to allow a debtor time to pay a bill [Early 17C. < Latin *indulgere* "allow space for"] —**in·dulg·er** *n*

in·dulged /in dúljd/ *adj* pampered, spoiled, or catered to

in·dul·gence /in dúljənss/ *n* **1.** YIELDING TO SOMEBODY'S WISH the act of gratifying or yielding to a wish **2.** SOMETHING ALLOWED AS LUXURY something that somebody lets himself or herself or another person have, especially a luxury **3.** TOLERANT ATTITUDE a kind or tolerant attitude toward somebody **4.** REMISSION OF PUNISHMENT FOR SIN in Roman Catholicism, a granting by the pope of partial remission of time to be spent in purgatory or of some other consequence of a sin. In the Middle Ages, a practice of selling indulgences grew up. **5.** BUSINESS PERIOD FOR REPAYMENT time given to a debtor to repay a bill

in·dul·gent /in dúljənt/ *adj* tending to be tolerant and generally allowing people to have what they want —**in·dul·gent·ly** *adv*

in·dult /in dúlt/ *n* a dispensation from the pope that allows a special exception to Roman Catholic Church law [15C. Via French < late Latin *indultum* "grant, concession" < *indulgere* "allow space for"]

in·du·men·tum /ində méntəm, ìndyə-/ (*plural* **-ta** /-tə/ or **-tums**), **in·du·ment** /índəmənt, índyə-/ *n* a covering of hairs on a plant, or of hair, fur, or feathers on an animal [Mid-19C. < Latin, "garment" < *induere* "put on"]

in·du·pli·cate /in dóoplikət, -kàyt/ *adj* describes a bud or leaf that has its edges bent or folded inward, so as to touch but not overlap —**in·du·pli·ca·tion** /in dòopli káysh'n/ *n*

in·du·rate *vti* /ində ràyt/ (**-rat·ed, -rat·ing, -rates**) to make something hard, or become hard (*literary or technical*) ■ *adj* /índərət, in dóorət/ unsympathetic or unfeeling (*literary*) [Mid-16C. < Latin *indurat-*, past participle of *indurare* "make hard" < *durus* "hard"] —**in·du·ra·tive** /in dóorətiv/ *adj*

in·du·ra·tion /ində ráysh'n/ *n* **1.** HARDENING the process of hardening something or of becoming hard (*literary or technical*) **2.** HARDENING OF SEDIMENT the process by which a soft geologic sediment becomes hard **3.** MED HARDNESS IN BODY TISSUE a hardness in body tissue, especially a tumor

In·dus[1] /índəss/ river in Asia. It rises in western Tibet and flows northwest across Jammu and Kashmir and then southwest through Pakistan to the Arabian Sea. Length: 1,800 mi./2,900 km.

In·dus[2] /índəss/ *n* a faint constellation of the southern hemisphere. See illustration at **constellation**

indus. *abbr* **1.** industrial **2.** industry

in·du·si·um /in dóozhee əm, -dóozee-/ (*plural* **-si·a** /-zee ə/) *n* **1.** a membrane on the underside of a fern leaf that protects developing spores **2.** an enveloping protective membrane [Early 18C. < Latin, "tunic" < *induere* "put on"] —**in·du·si·al** *adj*

in·dus·tri·al /in dústree əl/ *adj* **1.** OF INDUSTRY relating to, used in, or created by industry **2.** WITH MANY DEVELOPED INDUSTRIES having a large quantity of highly developed industries **3.** OF INDUSTRY'S WORK FORCE relating to or involving workers in industry ■ *n* MANUFACTURING COMPANY a company or employee engaged in an industry, especially manufacturing ■ **in·dus·tri·als** *npl* STOCK IN INDUSTRIAL COMPANIES the stock and interest-bearing securities of industrial companies —**in·dus·tri·al·ly** *adv*

in·dus·tri·al ac·ci·dent *n* an accident, often causing serious injury, that is job-related in that it usually happens on a work site such as a factory floor or a construction site

in·dus·tri·al ac·tion *n UK* same as **job action**

in·dus·tri·al ar·chae·ol·o·gy *n* the study of sites, buildings, and equipment used by industries in the past

in·dus·tri·al arts *n* a branch of education that develops the skills needed by workers in industry (*takes a singular verb*)

in·dus·tri·al de·sign *n* the art of designing the shape, size, or appearance of manufactured objects

in·dus·tri·al dis·ease *n* a disease affecting people as a result of the work they do

in·dus·tri·al en·gi·neer·ing *n* the study and practice of designing industrial operations

in·dus·tri·al es·pi·o·nage *n* the secret removal, copying, or recording of confidential or valuable information in a company for use by a competitor

in·dus·tri·al es·tate *n UK* a large area of land, usually on the edge of a town, where factories and businesses are concentrated in accordance with local planning regulations

in·dus·tri·al·ism /in dústree ə lìzzəm/ *n* the organization of an economy or a society around extensive manufacturing, rather than around agriculture, the production of handicrafts, or commerce

in·dus·tri·al·ist /in dústree əlist/ *n* an owner or controller of an industrial concern

in·dus·tri·al·ize /in dústree ə lìz/ (**-ized, -iz·ing, -iz·es**) *vti* to adapt a country or group to industrial methods of production and manufacturing, with all the accompanying social changes, or to be adapted in this way —**in·dus·tri·al·i·za·tion** /in dùstree əli záysh'n/ *n*

in·dus·tri·al mel·a·nism *n* the increase in the numbers of animals, especially moths, with dark coloration in places where industries create a lot of black smoke and predators more easily feed on lighter individuals

in·dus·tri·al park *n* a large area of land where factories and businesses are concentrated in accordance with local zoning policy

in·dus·tri·al psy·chol·o·gy *n* the study of human behavior and attitudes in the workplace —**in·dus·tri·al psy·chol·o·gist** *n*

in·dus·tri·al re·la·tions *npl* **1.** the relationship between management and employees in an industrial company **2.** the relations and procedures between employers' organizations and labor unions that are institutionalized in an industrial society

In·dus·tri·al Rev·o·lu·tion *n* the social and economic changes in the United Kingdom, Europe, and the United States that began in the late 18th century and involved widespread adoption of industrial methods of production. The specialization of tasks, the concentration of capital, and the centralization of work forces were important aspects of these changes, which first affected the United Kingdom.

in·dus·tri·al so·ci·ol·o·gy *n* the study of relationships and structures in industrial organizations

in·dus·tri·al-strength *adj* describes materials or chemicals that are strong or of a quality suitable for use in industry

in·dus·tri·al un·ion *n* a labor union made up of workers with different occupations who are all employed in one industry

In·dus·tri·al Work·ers of the World *n* an international labor union with socialist objectives that was founded in the United States in 1905 and lost influence after the 1920s

in·dus·tri·ous /in dústree əss/ *adj* hard-working, conscientious, and energetic —**in·dus·tri·ous·ly** *adv* —**in·dus·tri·ous·ness** *n*

in·dus·try /índəstree/ (*plural* **-tries**) *n* **1.** LARGE-SCALE PRODUCTION organized economic activity connected with the production, manufacture, or construction of a particular product or range of products **2.** WIDESPREAD ACTIVITY an activity that many people are involved in, especially one that has become commercialized or standardized ○ *the counseling industry* **3.** HARD WORK diligent hard work (*formal or literary*) [15C. Directly or via French < Latin *industria* "diligence" < *industrius* "diligent"]

In·dus·try Can·a·da *n* the Canadian government department that is responsible for developing the country's industry and technology, setting telecommunication policy, and promoting investment and trade

in·dus·try-wide *adj* cutting across an entire field of commercial activity

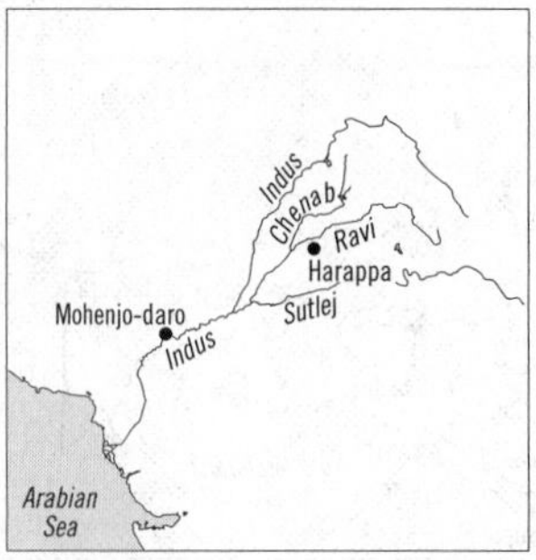

Indus Valley Civilization: map of the Indus River Valley

In·dus Val·ley Civ·i·li·za·tion *n* a Bronze-Age civilization that flourished in the lower Indus River Valley, mainly in present-day Pakistan and northern India, from about 2500 to 1700 B.C. It was the earliest known civilization in South Asia and, with Mesopotamia and Egypt, one of the earliest anywhere in the world.

in·dwell /in dwél/ (**-dwelled, -dwell·ing, -dwells**) *vti* to inhabit, infuse, or abide within a person, community, or place (*formal*) —**in·dwell·er** *n*

-ine *suffix* relating to, made of ○ *crystalline* ○ *murrhine* [Directly or via French < Latin *-inus*, Greek *-inos*]

in·e·bri·ate *vt* /i neébree àyt/ (**-at·ed, -at·ing, -ates**) **1.** MAKE SOMEBODY INTOXICATED to cause somebody to become drunk or intoxicated **2.** EXCITE SOMEBODY to make somebody excited or exhilarated (*formal*) ■ *n* /i neébree ət/ INTOXICATED PERSON a drunk or intoxicated person (*formal*) ■ *adj* /i neébree ət/ INTOXICATED drunk or intoxicated (*formal*) [15C. < Latin *inebriat-*, past participle of *inebriare*, literally "make drunk in" < *ebrius* "drunk"] —**in·e·bri·at·ed** *adj* —**in·e·bri·a·tion** /i neébree áysh'n/ *n* —**in·e·bri·e·ty** /ìnni brí ətee/ *n*

in·ed·i·ble /in éddəb'l/ *adj* unfit for consumption as food —**in·ed·i·bil·i·ty** /in èddə bíllətee/ *n* —**in·ed·i·bly** *adv*

in·ed·it·ed /in éddətəd/ *adj* not having been edited or published

in·ed·u·ca·ble /in éjjəkəb'l/ *adj* considered incapable of being educated (*archaic*) —**in·ed·u·ca·bil·i·ty** /in èjjəkə bíllətee/ *n*

in·ef·fa·ble /in éffəb'l/ *adj* unable to be expressed in words [15C. Directly or via French < Latin *ineffabilis* "unutterable" < *effari* "speak out" < *fari* "speak"] —**in·ef·fa·bil·i·ty** /in èffə bíllətee/ *n* —**in·ef·fa·bly** *adv*

in·ef·face·a·ble /ìnnə fáyssəb'l/ *adj* incapable of being erased or removed (*formal*) —**in·ef·face·a·bil·i·ty** /ìnnə fàyssə bíllətee/ *n* —**in·ef·face·a·bly** *adv*

in·ef·fec·tive /ìnnə féktiv/ *adj* **1.** not producing the desired result or effect **2.** incompetent or inept —**in·ef·fec·tive·ly** *adv* —**in·ef·fec·tive·ness** *n*

in·ef·fec·tu·al /ìnnə fékchoo əl/ *adj* **1.** not competent, decisive, or authoritative enough to achieve desired aims **2.** not able to produce a satisfactory outcome —**in·ef·fec·tu·al·i·ty** /ìnnə fèkchoo állətee/ *n* —**in·ef·fec·tu·al·ly** *adv* —**in·ef·fec·tu·al·ness** *n*

in·ef·fi·ca·cious /in èffi káyshəss/ *adj* not having a positive or useful effect (*formal*) —**in·ef·fi·ca·cious·ly** *adv* —**in·ef·fi·ca·cious·ness** *n* —**in·ef·fi·cac·i·ty** /in èffi kássətee/ *n* —**in·ef·fi·ca·cy** /in éffikəssee/ *n*

in·ef·fi·cient /ìnnə físh'nt/ *adj* performing tasks in a way that is not organized or fails to make the best use of something, especially time —**in·ef·fi·cien·cy** *n* —**in·ef·fi·cient·ly** *adv*

in·e·las·tic /ìnnə lástik/ *adj* **1.** NOT STRETCHY unable to return quickly to its original shape and size after being bent, stretched, or squashed **2.** NOT EASILY CHANGED unable to incorporate changes or adapt to new circumstances easily **3.** PHYS NOT AFFECTING TRANSLATIONAL KINETIC ENERGY describes a collision that does not lead to an overall loss of translational kinetic energy **4.** ECON INSENSITIVE TO PRICE CHANGES describes supply or demand that is not affected by fluctuations in price —**in·e·las·tic·i·ty** /ìnnə lass tíssətee/ *n*

in·el·e·gant /in élləgənt/ *adj* **1.** lacking grace, sophistication, and good taste in appearance or behavior **2.** unnecessarily complicated or long —**in·el·e·gance** *n*

in·el·i·gi·ble /in éllijəb'l/ *adj* not legally entitled or qualified to do, be, or get something —**in·el·i·gi·bil·i·ty** /in èllijə bíllətee/ *n*

in·e·luc·ta·ble /ìnni lúktəb'l/ *adj* same as **inescapable** (*formal*) ○ *the ineluctable casualties of warfare* [Early 17C. < Latin *ineluctabilis* < *eluctari* "struggle out of"] —**in·e·luc·ta·bil·i·ty** /ìnni lùktə bíllətee/ *n* —**in·e·luc·ta·bly** *adv*

in·ept /i népt/ *adj* **1.** lacking the competence or skill for a particular task **2.** not in keeping with what is right or proper for the circumstances [Mid-16C. < Latin *ineptus* "not suitable" < *aptus* (see APT)] —**in·ep·ti·tude** *n* —**in·ept·ly** *adv* —**in·ept·ness** *n*

in·eq·ua·ble /in ékwəb'l/ *adj* not fair or uniform

in·e·qual·i·ty /ìnnə kwóllətee/ (*plural* **-ties**) *n* **1.** DIFFERENCE IN STATUS social or economic disparity between people or groups **2.** LACK OF EQUAL TREATMENT unequal opportunity or treatment based on social, ethnic, racial, or economic disparity **3.** STATE OF BEING UNEQUAL the condition or an instance of not being equal **4.** MATH STATEMENT INDICATING UNEQUAL QUANTITIES a mathematical statement indicating that two quantities are not equal, represented by the symbol <, >, or ≠, meaning less than, greater than, and not equal to. An unconditional inequality is one that is true for all values of a variable, while a conditional inequality is false for some values of a variable. **5.** UNEVENNESS ON SURFACE variability or unevenness on the surface of something

in·eq·ui·ta·ble /in ékwitəb'l/ *adj* showing bias or favoritism —**in·eq·ui·ta·bly** *adv*

in·eq·ui·ty /in ékwetee/ (*plural* **-ties**) *n* **1.** lack of fairness or justice (*formal*) **2.** a situation or action that is not fair

in·eq·ui·valve /in ékwi vàlv, -eékwi-/, **in·eq·ui·valved** /-vàlvd/ *adj* describes a bivalve mollusk whose valves are unequal in size or form

in·e·rad·i·ca·ble /ìnnə ráddikəb'l/ *adj* impossible to get rid of —**in·e·rad·i·ca·bil·i·ty** /ìnnə radikə bíllətee/ *n* —**in·e·rad·i·ca·bly** *adv*

in·er·rant /in érrənt/ *adj* **1.** incapable of making a mistake (*formal*) **2.** containing no mistakes —**in·er·ran·cy** *n*

in·ert /i núrt/ *adj* **1.** MOTIONLESS not moving or not able to move **2.** CHEM, BIOCHEM NONREACTIVE not readily changed by chemical or biological reaction **3.** SLUGGISH OR UNMOTIVATED lacking in energy or motivation [Mid-17C. < Latin *inert-* "having no skill" < *art-* "skill"] —**in·ert·ly** *adv* —**in·ert·ness** *n*

in·ert gas *n* CHEM same as **noble gas**

in·er·tia /i núrshə/ *n* **1.** inability or unwillingness to move or act **2.** PHYS the property of a body by which it remains at rest or continues moving in a straight line unless acted upon by a directional force [Early 18C. < Latin, "lack of skill, inactivity" < *inert-* (see INERT)] —**in·er·tial** *adj* —**in·er·tial·ly** *adv*

in·er·tial con·fine·ment fu·sion *n* nuclear fusion achieved by firing high-energy lasers or particle beams at small pellets, typically containing deuterium and sometimes also tritium

in·er·tial force *n* a force as perceived by an observer in an accelerating or rotating frame of reference, that serves to confirm the validity of Newton's laws of motion, e.g., the perception of being forced backward in an accelerating vehicle

in·er·tial fu·sion *n* PHYS same as **inertial confinement fusion**

in·er·tial guid·ance, **in·er·tial nav·i·ga·tion** *n* navigation by conversion of the accelerations experienced into distances and directions. It is used on aircraft, spacecraft, or missiles that use devices such as gyroscopes, accelerometers, and computers to calculate and adjust course.

in·es·cap·a·ble /ìnnə skáypəb'l/ *adj* impossible to avoid —**in·es·cap·a·bil·i·ty** /ìnnə skaypə bíllətee/ *n* —**in·es·cap·a·bly** *adv*

in es·se /in éssee/ *adj* having actual existence as opposed to potential existence [< Latin, "in existence"]

in·es·sen·tial /ìnnə sénsh'l/ *adj* **1.** NOT ESSENTIAL not absolutely necessary **2.** WITHOUT ESSENCE without substance or being (*literary*) ■ *n* SOMETHING INESSENTIAL something that is unnecessary —**in·es·sen·ti·al·i·ty** /ìnnə senshee állətee/ *n* —**in·es·sen·tial·ly** *adv*

in·es·sive /in éssiv/ *n* in the grammar of languages such as Finnish, a grammatical form (**case**) of nouns and pronouns that indicates the location of something [Late 19C. < Latin *inesse* "be in or at" < *esse* "be"]

in·es·ti·ma·ble /in éstiməb'l/ *adj* **1.** having an extent, magnitude, or amount that is too great to calculate **2.** having a worth that is so great that value cannot be placed upon it —**in·es·ti·ma·bil·i·ty** /in èstimə bíllətee/ *n* —**in·es·ti·ma·bly** *adv*

in·ev·i·ta·ble /in évvitəb'l/ *adj* impossible to avoid or to prevent from happening ■ *n* something that is certain to happen ○ *deciding to accept the inevitable* [15C. < Latin *inevitabilis* "not avoidable" < *evitare* "shun"] —**in·ev·i·ta·bil·i·ty** /in èvvitə bíllətee/ *n* —**in·ev·i·ta·bly** *adv*

~~**inevitible**~~ incorrect spelling of **inevitable**

in·ex·act /ìnnig zákt/ *adj* **1.** not entirely accurate **2.** not thorough or careful —**in·ex·act·i·tude** *n* —**in·ex·act·ly** *adv* —**in·ex·act·ness** *n*

in·ex·cus·a·ble /ìnnik skyóozəb'l/ *adj* impossible to pardon or justify —**in·ex·cus·a·bil·i·ty** /ìnnik skyoozə bíllətee/ *n* —**in·ex·cus·a·ble·ness** *n* —**in·ex·cus·a·bly** *adv*

in·ex·haust·i·ble /ìnnig záwstəb'l/ *adj* **1.** impossible to use up **2.** showing no sign of tiring —**in·ex·haust·i·bil·i·ty** /ìnnig zawstə bíllətee/ *n* —**in·ex·haust·i·ble·ness** *n* —**in·ex·haust·i·bly** *adv*

in·ex·is·tent /ìnnig zíst'nt/ *adj* not in existence

in·ex·o·ra·ble /in éksərəb'l/ *adj* **1.** impossible to stop **2.** not moved by anyone's attempts to plead or persuade (*formal*) [Mid-16C. Via French < Latin *inexorabilis* < *exorare* "prevail upon" < *orare* "pray"] —**in·ex·o·ra·bil·i·ty** /in èksərə bíllətee/ *n* —**in·ex·o·ra·ble·ness** *n* —**in·ex·o·ra·bly** *adv*

in·ex·pe·di·ent /ìnnik spéedee ənt/ *adj* **1.** not convenient or practical **2.** not recommended or prudent (*formal*) —**in·ex·pe·di·ence** *n* —**in·ex·pe·di·ent·ly** *adv*

in·ex·pen·sive /ìnnik spénssiv/ *adj* not costing much money —**in·ex·pen·sive·ly** *adv* —**in·ex·pen·sive·ness** *n*

in·ex·pe·ri·ence /ìnnik spéeree ənss/ *n* **1.** lack of the experience that would lead to an increase in knowledge or skill **2.** lack of sophistication about worldly ways —**in·ex·pe·ri·enced** *adj*

in·ex·pert /in ékspərt/ *adj* lacking in skill or experience —**in·ex·pert·ly** *adv* —**in·ex·pert·ness** *n*

in·ex·pi·a·ble /in ékspee əb'l/ *adj* so bad that it cannot be atoned for (*formal*) [15C. < Latin *inexpiabilis* < *expiare* (see EXPIATE)] —**in·ex·pi·a·ble·ness** *n* —**in·ex·pi·a·bly** *adv*

in·ex·pli·ca·ble /ìnnik splíkəb'l, in éksplikəb'l/, **in·ex·plain·a·ble** /ìnnik spláynəb'l/ *adj* unable to be explained or justified —**in·ex·pli·ca·bil·i·ty** /ìnnik splikə bíllətee, in èksplikə-/ *n* —**in·ex·pli·ca·ble·ness** *n* —**in·ex·pli·ca·bly** *adv*

in·ex·plic·it /ìnnik splíssit/ *adj* not expressed or shown fully, openly, and unambiguously

in·ex·press·i·ble /ìnnik spréssəb'l/ *adj* impossible to put into words —**in·ex·press·i·bil·i·ty** /ìnnik spressə bíllətee/ *n* —**in·ex·press·i·ble·ness** *n* —**in·ex·press·i·bly** *adv*

in·ex·pres·sive /ìnnik spréssiv/ *adj* conveying no feeling —**in·ex·pres·sive·ly** *adv* —**in·ex·pres·sive·ness** *n*

in·ex·pug·na·ble /ìnnik spyóonəb'l/ *adj* (*formal*) **1.** impossible to take by force **2.** impossible to overcome [15C. Via French < Latin *inexpugnabilis* < *expugnare* "fight off" < *pugnare* "to fight"] —**in·ex·pug·na·bil·i·ty** /ìnnik spyoonə bíllətee/ *n* —**in·ex·pug·na·bly** *adv*

in·ex·pun·gi·ble /ìnnik spúnjəb'l/ *adj* impossible to remove or cancel out

in·ex·ten·si·ble /ìnnik sténssəb'l/ *adj* impossible to stretch to a greater length —**in·ex·ten·si·bil·i·ty** /ìnnik stènssə bíllətee/ *n*

in ex·ten·so /ìnnik sténssō/ *adv* at its full length ○ *quote a passage in extenso* [< Latin, "at a stretch"]

in·ex·tin·guish·a·ble /ìnnik stíng gwishəb'l/ *adj* impossible to extinguish or suppress —**in·ex·tin·guish·a·bly** *adv*

in·ex·tir·pa·ble /ìnnik stúrpəb'l/ *adj* impossible to remove or destroy (*formal*) [Early 17C. < Latin *inex(s)tirpabilis* < *ex(s)tirpare* (see EXTIRPATE)] —**in·ex·tir·pa·ble·ness** *n*

in ex·tre·mis /in ik stréemiss/ *adv* in desperate circumstances, especially at the point of death ■ *adj* on the point of death [< Latin, "in the extremes"]

in·ex·tri·ca·ble /in ékstrikəb'l, ìnnik stríkəb'l/ *adj* **1.** IMPOSSIBLE TO ESCAPE FROM impossible to get free from **2.** IMPOSSIBLE TO DISENTANGLE impossible to disentangle or undo **3.** EXTREMELY COMPLEX hopelessly involved or complex [Mid-16C. < Latin *inextricabilis* "that cannot be disentangled" < *extricare* (see EXTRICATE)] —**in·ex·tri·ca·bil·i·ty** /in èkstrikə bíllətee, ìnnik strikə-/ *n* —**in·ex·tri·ca·ble·ness** *n* —**in·ex·tri·ca·bly** *adv*

INF *abbr* intermediate-range nuclear forces

inf. *abbr* **1.** MIL infantry **2.** inferior **3.** BASEBALL infield **4.** BASEBALL infielder **5.** GRAM infinitive **6.** infinity **7.** informal **8.** information **9.** infra

Inf. *abbr* Infantry

in·fal·li·ble /in fálləb'l/ *adj* **1.** NOT ERRING incapable of making a mistake **2.** INCAPABLE OF FAILING certain not to fail **3.** UNERRING IN DOCTRINE incapable of being mistaken in matters of doctrine and dogma [15C. < medieval Latin *infallibilis* < Latin *fallere* "deceive, disappoint"] —**in·fal·li·bil·i·ty** /in fàllə bíllətee/ *n* —**in·fal·li·ble·ness** *n* —**in·fal·li·bly** *adv*

in·fa·mous /ínfəməss/ *adj* **1.** NOTORIOUS having an extremely bad reputation **2.** ABOMINABLE so bad as to earn somebody an extremely bad reputation **3.** LAW PUNISHABLE BY SERIOUS PENALTY formerly, punishable by imprisonment or loss of civil rights —**in·fa·mous·ly** *adv* —**in·fa·mous·ness** *n*

USAGE See *fame*.

in·fa·my /ínfəmee/ (*plural* **-mies**) *n* **1.** NOTORIETY the disgrace to somebody's reputation caused by an infamous act or behavior **2.** SHAMEFUL CONDUCT shameful or criminal conduct or character **3.** EVIL DEED a publicly known infamous act or event **4.** LAW LOSS OF RIGHTS OR IMPRISONMENT formerly, punishment incurred by being convicted of an infamous crime [15C. < French *infamie* < Latin *infamis* "of ill repute," literally "having no fame" < *fama* "fame"]

USAGE See *fame*.

in·fan·cy /ínfənssee/ *n* **1.** BABYHOOD the condition or time of childhood before a baby walks or talks **2.** BEGINNING an early stage of development for an idea, project, or enterprise **3.** TIME OF BEING MINOR the condition or time in which a young person is not legally considered an adult

in·fant /ínfənt/ *n* **1.** BABY a very young child that can neither walk nor talk **2.** LEGAL MINOR a young person legally considered a minor ■ *adj* JUST BEGINNING in an early stage of development [14C. Via French < Latin *infant-* "not speaking" < *fari* "speak"] —**in·fant·hood** *n*

in·fan·ta /in fántə, -fáantə/ (*plural* **-tas**) *n* **1.** the daughter of a Spanish or Portuguese king **2.** the wife of an infante [Late 16C. < Spanish, Portuguese, form of *infante* (see INFANTE)]

in·fan·te /in fán tày, -fáan-/ (*plural* **-tes**) *n* a son, other than the heir to the throne, of a Spanish or Portuguese king, especially the second son [Mid-16C. Via Spanish, Portuguese < Latin *infant-* (see INFANT)]

in·fan·ti·cide /in fántə sīd/ *n* **1.** MURDER OF INFANT the act of killing an infant **2.** KILLING OF BABIES the practice of killing newborn babies **3.** KILLER OF INFANT a killer of an infant —**in·fan·ti·cid·al** /in fàntə sīd'l/ *adj*

in·fan·tile /ínfən tīl/ *adj* **1.** showing a lack of maturity **2.** relating to infants or infancy —**in·fan·til·i·ty** /ìnfən tíllətee/ *n*

in·fan·tile pa·ral·y·sis *n* MED same as **poliomyelitis** (*dated*)

in·fan·til·ism /ínfənt'l ìzzəm, in fánt'l-/ *n* **1.** a condition of mental or physical underdevelopment in which a person fails to mature sexually and emotionally **2.** childish or immature behavior

in·fan·til·ize /ínfənt'l īz, in fánt'l-/ (**-ized, -iz·ing, -iz·es**) *vt* **1.** to make somebody infantile, or keep somebody in an infantile state **2.** to treat somebody as or consider somebody to be infantile —**in·fan·til·i·za·tion** /ìnfənt'li záysh'n, in fànt'li-/ *n*

in·fant mor·tal·i·ty rate *n* the number of deaths during the first year of life per thousand live births

in·fan·try /ínfəntree/ (*plural* **-tries**) *n* **1.** soldiers who are trained to fight on foot, or a unit of such soldiers **2.** a unit of infantry making up a regiment or branch of an army [Late 16C. < French *infanterie* < Italian *infante* "youth, foot soldier" < Latin *infant-* (see INFANT)]

in·fan·try·man /ínfəntrimən/ (*plural* **-men** /-mən/) *n* a soldier in an infantry

in·fant school *n UK* a school, or part of a school, for children between the ages of four or five and seven. This is the first stage of compulsory education in the United Kingdom.

in·farct /in fáarkt, ín faarkt/ *n* an area of tissue that has recently died as a result of the sudden loss of its blood supply, e.g., following blockage of an artery by a blood clot [Late 19C. < modern Latin *infarctus* < the past participle of Latin *infarcire* "cram in" < *farcire* "to stuff"]

in·farc·tion /in fáarkshən, ín faarkshən/ *n* **1.** the formation of an infarct **2.** same as **infarct**

in·fat·u·ate /in fáchoo àyt/ (**-at·ed, -at·ing, -ates**) *vt* to make somebody behave irrationally as a result of a great, often temporary, passion (*usually passive*) [Mid-16C. < Latin *infatuat-*, past participle of *infatuare* "make foolish" < *fatuus* "foolish"] —**in·fat·u·at·ed** *adj* —**in·fat·u·at·ed·ly** *adv*

in·fat·u·a·tion /in fàchoo áysh'n/ *n* **1.** an intense but short-lived and irrational passion for somebody or something **2.** the person or object that somebody is infatuated with

SYNONYMS See *love*.

in·fau·na /in fáwnə/ *npl* organisms that live in tubes or burrows beneath the surface of the sea floor [Early 20C. < IN-[2] + FAUNA] —**in·fau·nal** *adj*

in·fea·si·ble /in féezəb'l/ *adj* not practical or easily achieved —**in·fea·si·bil·i·ty** /in feezə bíllətee/ *n* —**in·fea·si·ble·ness** *n* —**in·fea·si·bly** *adv*

in·fect /in fékt/ (**-fect·ed, -fect·ing, -fects**) *vt* **1.** CAUSE INFECTION IN SOMEBODY to contaminate a person, animal, or organ with a disease-producing agent **2.** CAUSE SOMEBODY TO HAVE COMMUNICABLE DISEASE to give a person or animal a communicable disease **3.** ENTER PERSON OR ANIMAL to invade and live in the body of a person or animal (*refers to microorganisms or endoparasites*) **4.** AFFECT SOMEBODY OR SOMETHING ADVERSELY to corrupt or adversely affect somebody or something **5.** INFLUENCE SOMEBODY'S FEELINGS to communicate an emotion such as enthusiasm or fear to somebody **6.** COMPUT CONTAMINATE COMPUTER to copy to a computer system a computer virus that is capable of damaging the system's programs or data [14C. < Latin *infect-*, past participle of *inficere* "stain," literally "dip in" < *facere* "do"] —**in·fect·ed** *adj* —**in·fec·tor** *n*

in·fec·tion /in fékshən/ *n* **1.** DISEASE a communicable disease **2.** INFECTING OF OTHERS the transmission of infectious microorganisms from one person to another **3.** INFECTING MICROORGANISM an infecting microorganism or agent **4.** STATE OF BEING INFECTED the reproduction and proliferation of microorganisms within the body **5.** TRANSMISSION OF FEELINGS the communication of emotions or attitudes between people **6.** MORAL CORRUPTION something that corrupts somebody morally

in·fec·tious /in fékshəss/ *adj* **1.** COMMUNICABLE describes a disease that is capable of being passed from one person to another **2.** CAUSED BY BACTERIA caused by bacteria, viruses, or other microorganisms **3.** CAUSING INFECTION bringing about infection **4.** AFFECTING FEELINGS OF OTHERS capable of affecting the emotions and attitudes of others ○ *an infectious laugh* —**in·fec·tious·ly** *adv* —**in·fec·tious·ness** *n*

in·fec·tious hep·a·ti·tis *n* MED same as **hepatitis A**

in·fec·tious mon·o·nu·cle·o·sis *n* an acute infectious disease caused by the Epstein-Barr virus, producing fever, swelling of the lymph nodes, sore throat, and increased lymphocytes in the blood

in·fec·tive /in féktiv/ *adj* **1.** capable of producing an infection **2.** capable of affecting the emotions and attitudes of others —**in·fec·tive·ness** *n* —**in·fec·tiv·i·ty** /in fek tívvətee/ *n*

in·fe·lic·i·tous /ìnfə líssitəss/ *adj* inappropriate to the situation or purpose (*formal*) —**in·fe·lic·i·tous·ly** *adv*

in·fe·lic·i·ty /ìnfə líssətee/ (*plural* **-ties**) *n* (*formal*) **1.** the inappropriateness of something, especially an expression, to a particular situation **2.** something inappropriate to a situation or purpose, especially an expression [Early 17C. < Latin *infelicitas* "unhappiness" < *felix* "happy"] —**in·fe·lic·i·tous** *adj*

in·fer /in fúr/ (**-ferred, -fer·ring, -fers**) *v* **1.** *vti* CONCLUDE SOMETHING FROM REASONING to come to a conclusion or form an opinion about something on the basis of evidence or reasoning ○ *I inferred from his behavior that he was no longer interested in setting a good example.* **2.** *vt* INDICATE SOMETHING to lead you necessarily to suppose or conclude something (*formal*) ○ *The steepness of the cliffs would normally* *infer modern erosion.* **3.** *vt* IMPLY SOMETHING to imply or suggest something **4.** *vt* GUESS SOMETHING to make a reasonable guess at something [Early 16C. < Latin *inferre* "bring in" < *ferre* "carry"] —**in·fer·a·ble** *adj* —**in·fer·a·bly** *adv* —**in·fer·rer** *n*

SYNONYMS See ***deduce***.

in·fer·ence /ínfərənss/ *n* **1.** CONCLUSION a conclusion drawn from evidence or reasoning **2.** LOGIC REASONING PROCESS the process of reasoning from a premise to a conclusion **3.** IMPLICATION something that is implied [Late 16C. < medieval Latin *inferentia* < Latin *inferre* (see INFER)] —**in·fer·en·tial** /ìnfə rénsh'l/ *adj* —**in·fer·en·tial·ly** *adv*

in·fe·ri·or /in fēeree ər/ *adj* **1.** LOWER IN STANDING lower or low in rank, standing, or degree **2.** NOT AS GOOD lower in quality or value **3.** MEDIOCRE failing to meet a standard of quality, ability, or achievement **4.** ANAT LOWER IN BODY describes a body part or organ situated beneath another similar part **5.** BOT BELOW CALYX describes a plant ovary located below a calyx **6.** ASTRON BETWEEN EARTH AND SUN orbiting or taking place between Earth and the Sun. Mercury and Venus are designated as inferior planets. **7.** PRINTING PRINTED BELOW LINE written or printed at a slightly lower level than the rest of the characters in a line, e.g., the "2" in "CO_2" ■ *n* **1.** LOWER RANKING PERSON somebody of lower status, rank, or quality **2.** PRINTING SUBSCRIPT CHARACTER a character printed or written below the line [15C. < Latin, "lower" < *inferus* "below"] —**in·fe·ri·or·i·ty** /in fēeree áwrətee/ *n* —**in·fe·ri·or·ly** *adv*

in·fe·ri·or·i·ty com·plex *n* an overdeveloped sense of being inferior to other people. In extreme cases it can manifest itself in either withdrawn or aggressive social behavior.

in·fer·nal /in fúrn'l/ *adj* **1.** VERY ANNOYING extremely annoying or unpleasant **2.** RELATING TO UNDERWORLD relating to hell or the underworld **3.** DIABOLICAL IN NATURE so extreme, wicked, or cruel as to be worthy of hell [14C. < Old French < late Latin *infernus* "lower, the underworld" < Latin *inferus* "below"] —**in·fer·nal·ly** *adv*

in·fer·no /in fúrnō/ (*plural* **-nos**) *n* **1.** a very large fire burning fiercely and uncontrollably, or a place being consumed by a large uncontrollable fire **2.** a place or situation that is reminiscent of hell, e.g., in being hot, fiery, or full of corruption [Mid-19C. Via Italian, "hell" < late Latin *infernus* (see INFERNAL)]

CULTURAL NOTE See ***fire***.

In·fer·no *n* RELIG same as **hell** *n* (sense 1)

CULTURAL NOTE ***The Inferno***, a poem (1307?–20?) by Italian poet Dante Alighieri. The first part of the epic masterpiece *The Divine Comedy*, it describes the poet's journey through Hell with Virgil as his guide. Hell is depicted as funnel-shaped, with a different category of sinner on each of the circular steps, which decrease in size as they descend. The presence of certain historical figures among these sinners, and the punishments they receive, reflect Dante's personal opinions and judgments on past issues and events.

in·fer·tile /in fúrt'l/ *adj* **1.** STERILE physically incapable of conceiving offspring **2.** NOT PRODUCING CROPS incapable of producing crops **3.** NOT FERTILIZED describes an egg that has not been fertilized —**in·fer·tile·ly** *adv* —**in·fer·til·i·ty** /ìn fur tíllətee/ *n*

in·fest /in fést/ (**-fest·ed, -fest·ing, -fests**) *vt* **1.** to overrun a place or site in large numbers and become threatening, harmful, or unpleasant ○ *Their clothing was infested with lice.* **2.** to live as a parasite on or in something [Mid-16C. Directly or via French < Latin *infestare* "to attack" < *infestus* "hostile"] —**in·fes·ta·tion** /ìn fe stáysh'n/ *n* —**in·fest·ed** *adj* —**in·fest·er** *n*

in·fib·u·late /in fíbbyə làyt/ (**-lat·ed, -lat·ing, -lates**) *vt* to close the vagina of a girl or woman partially by stitching it or closing it with a clasp. The clitoris is often removed at the same time. The practice is traditional in some northeastern African cultures, but disapproved of and even outlawed in some countries. [Early 17C. < Latin *infibulat-*, past participle of *infibulare* "fasten with a pin" < *fibula* "brooch"] —**in·fib·u·la·tion** /in fìbbyə láysh'n/ *n*

in·fi·del /ínfid'l, ínfi dèl/ *n* (*disapproving*) **1.** somebody who does not believe in a major religion, especially Christianity or Islam **2.** somebody with no religious belief [15C. Directly or via French < Latin *infidelis* "unbelieving" < *fidelis* "faithful" < *fides* "trust, belief"]

in·fi·del·i·ty /ìnfi déllətee/ (*plural* **-ties**) *n* **1.** UNFAITHFULNESS unfaithfulness or disloyalty, especially to a sexual partner **2.** UNFAITHFUL ACT an act of unfaithfulness or disloyalty, especially to a sexual partner **3.** DISBELIEF absence of religious belief (*disapproving*)

in·field /ín fèeld/ *n* **1.** BASEBALL DIAMOND the area of a baseball field bounded by home plate and the three bases **2.** BASEBALL PLAYERS IN INFIELD the defensive players in the infield considered together. They are the first, second, and third basemen and the shortstop. **3.** AREA WITHIN RACETRACK the area bounded by a racetrack **4.** FARMLAND CLOSE TO FARMHOUSE the farmland close to a farmhouse that is regularly manured and cropped

in·field·er /ín fèeldər/ *n* a defensive baseball player in the infield

in·fight·ing /ín fìting/ *n* **1.** conflict or rivalry between associates or members of the same organization **2.** boxing or fighting at close range —**in·fight·er** *n*

in·fill /ín fìl/ *n* **1.** BUILDING IN SPACES BETWEEN BUILDINGS the development of vacant areas between existing buildings, especially as part of a planned growth or urban renewal program **2.** FILL FOR EMPTY SPACE a substance or material that fills a space ■ *vt* (**-filled, -fill·ing, -fills**) BUILD IN GAPS to build new buildings in vacant areas between existing buildings

in·fil·trate /ín fíl tràyt, ínfil-/ *vti* (**-trat·ed, -trat·ing, -trates**) **1.** ENTER ORGANIZATION TO SPY ON IT to become part of an organization, or enter a place, surreptitiously in order to gather information or influence events, or send agents to do this ○ *Activists were infiltrated into local party organizations.* **2.** ENTER ENEMY TERRITORY SECRETLY to cross into enemy territory without the enemy's knowledge, or send somebody into enemy territory in this way ○ *infiltrate troops behind enemy lines* **3.** CHEM PERMEATE FLUID THROUGH SUBSTANCE to pass through a substance by filtration, or make a liquid or gas pass through a substance by filtration ■ *n* MED FATTY ACCUMULATION a substance that gradually accumulates in tissues and cells, e.g., fat —**in·fil·tra·tion** /ìnfil tráysh'n/ *n* —**in·fil·tra·tive** *adj* —**in·fil·tra·tor** *n*

infin. *abbr* GRAM infinitive

in·fi·nite /ínfənit/ *adj* **1.** NOT MEASURABLE without any finite or measurable limits **2.** EXCEEDINGLY GREAT very great in size, number, degree, or extent ○ *He took infinite pains over it.* **3.** MATH GREATER THAN ANY ASSIGNED VALUE greater in number, size, or scope than any arbitrarily assigned value **4.** MATH WITH UNLIMITED SPATIAL EXTENT having unlimited spatial extent **5.** MATH WITH INDEFINITELY MANY ELEMENTS having an indefinitely extendable number of terms or elements **6.** MATH SUPPORTING ONE-TO-ONE RELATIONSHIP describes a set able to be put into a one-to-one mathematical correspondence with a subset of itself ■ *n* SOMETHING INFINITE something that is infinite, e.g., space [14C. Via French < Latin *infinitus* "not bounded" < *finitus* (see FINITE)] —**in·fi·nite·ly** *adv* —**in·fi·nite·ness** *n*

In·fi·nite *n* same as **God**

in·fi·nite loop *n* a series of instructions in a computer program that repeats endlessly

in·fin·i·tes·i·mal /ìnfini téssəm'l/ *adj* **1.** TINY very small in number, amount, or degree **2.** MATH CLOSE TO ZERO able to assume values arbitrarily close to but greater than zero ■ *n* INFINITESIMAL NUMBER an infinitesimal number or function [Mid-17C. < modern Latin *infinitesimus* "the number in a series corresponding to infinity" < Latin *infinitus* (see INFINITE)] —**in·fin·i·tes·i·mal·ly** *adv*

in·fin·i·tes·i·mal cal·cu·lus *n* MATH same as **calculus** (sense 1)

in·fin·i·tive /in fínnitiv/ *n* a form of a verb with no reference to a specific tense, person, or subject. In English, an infinitive is usually preceded by the word "to," e.g., "to see." [15C. < late Latin *infinitivus* < Latin *infinitus* (see INFINITE)] —**in·fin·i·ti·val** /in fìnni tív'l/ *adj* —**in·fin·i·ti·val·ly** *adv*

in·fin·i·tude /in fínni tòod/ *n* **1.** the infinite nature of something **2.** a very great number, degree, or extent of something [Mid-17C. < Latin *infinitus* (see INFINITE)]

in·fin·i·ty /in fínnətee/ (*plural* **-ties**) *n* **1.** SOMETHING WITHOUT LIMITS limitless time, space, or distance ○ *Beyond the Earth lay infinity.* **2.** SOMETHING TOO GREAT TO COUNT an amount or number so great that it cannot be counted ○ *an infinity of stars* **3.** STATE OF BEING INFINITE the state or quality of being infinite **4.** MATH CONCEPT OF BEING ALWAYS UNLIMITED the concept of being unlimited by always being larger than any imposed value or boundary. For some purposes this may be considered as being the same as one divided by zero. **5.** MATH GEOMETRIC POINT AT INFINITE DISTANCE a part of a geometric figure situated an infinite distance from the observer, e.g., the hypothetical point at which parallel lines meet in Euclidean geometry **6.** OPTICS INFINITELY DISTANT POINT a point sufficiently far from a lens or mirror that the light emitted from it falls in parallel rays on the surface [14C. < French *infinité* < Latin *infinitus* (see INFINITE)]

in·firm /in fúrm/ *adj* **1.** NOT STRONG lacking strength and vitality, especially because of sickness or age **2.** IRRESOLUTE lacking firmness of character or a strong will **3.** CONSTR STRUCTURALLY UNSOUND having a structure that is not strong and undamaged **4.** LAW LEGALLY UNSOUND describes a legal claim that is invalid or not supported ■ *npl* PEOPLE WHO ARE NOT STRONG people who lack strength and vitality, e.g., because of sickness or age (*sometimes considered offensive*) [14C. < Latin *infirmus* < *firmus* "firm"] —**in·firm·ly** *adv* —**in·firm·ness** *n*

SYNONYMS See ***weak***.

in·fir·ma·ry /in fúrmaree/ (*plural* **-ries**) *n* a hospital or area within an institution where sick and injured people are cared for [15C. < medieval Latin *infirmaria* < Latin *infirmus* (see INFIRM)]

in·fir·mi·ty /in fúrmətee/ (*plural* **-ties**) *n* **1.** LACK OF STRENGTH lack of strength and vitality **2.** CHARACTER FLAW a weakness or failing in somebody's character **3.** MINOR ILLNESS any medical condition that causes a lack of strength or vitality

in·fix *vt* /in fíks/ (**-fixed, -fix·ing, -fix·es**) **1.** FIX SOMETHING FIRMLY IN SOMETHING ELSE to insert something into another thing in order to secure it **2.** INSTILL SOMETHING IN MIND to secure something firmly in the mind **3.** GRAM PUT ELEMENT IN WORD to insert a linking element into a word. In the word "acidophilus," the letter "o" is an infix. ■ *n* /ín fìks/ GRAM AFFIX IN MIDDLE an affix inserted into the middle of a word —**in·fix·a·tion** /ìn fik sáysh'n/ *n* —**in·fix·ion** /in fíksh'n/ *n*

infl. *abbr* **1.** inflammable **2.** BOT inflorescence **3.** influence **4.** influenced

in fla·gran·te de·lic·to /in flə gràntee də líktō/, **in fla·gran·te** /in flə grántee/ *adv* **1.** in the act of having sexual relations, especially illicit sexual relations **2.** in the act of committing an offense [< Latin, "in the heat of the crime"]

in·flame /in fláym/ (**-flamed, -flam·ing, -flames**) *v* **1.** *vt* PROVOKE POWERFUL RESPONSE IN SOMEBODY to excite an intense emotion, especially anger or jealousy, in somebody **2.** *vt* MAKE EMOTION STRONGER to make an emotion such as anger or jealousy become more intense **3.** *vti* MAKE TISSUE SWELL AND TURN RED to become, or make body tissue become, red and swollen, in response to injury or infection [14C. Via French < Latin *inflammare* < *flamma* "flame"] —**in·flamed** *adj* —**in·flam·er** *n*

in·flam·ma·ble /in flámməb'l/ *adj* **1.** EASILY SET ON FIRE quickly and easily set on fire and burned **2.** EASILY ROUSED easily made angry or passionate ■ *n* FLAMMABLE ITEM something that is quickly and easily set on fire and burned [Early 17C. < medieval Latin *inflammabilis* "liable to inflammation" < Latin *inflammare* (see INFLAME)] —**in·flam·ma·bil·i·ty** /in flàmmə bíllətee/ *n* —**in·flam·ma·ble·ness** *n* —**in·flam·ma·bly** *adv*

USAGE See ***flammable***.

in·flam·ma·tion /ìnflə máysh'n/ *n* **1.** swelling, redness, heat, and pain produced in an area of the body as a reaction to injury or infection **2.** a heightening or stirring up of emotion

in·flam·ma·to·ry /in flámmə tàwree/ *adj* **1.** liable to arouse strong emotions, especially anger **2.** caused or characterized by inflammation —**in·flam·ma·to·ri·ly** *adv*

in·flam·ma·to·ry bow·el dis·ease *n* a disease causing inflammation of the bowel, typically Crohn's disease or ulcerative colitis

in·flat·a·ble /in fláytəb'l/ *adj* made of expandable material that can be filled with air or gas ■ *n* something such as a boat, mattress, or plaything that has to be filled with air or gas before use

in·flate /in fláyt/ (**-flat·ed, -flat·ing, -flates**) *vti* **1.** EXPAND WITH AIR to fill something such as a ball, mattress, tire, or boat with air or gas to bring it to the proper size, shape, and firmness for use, or to become filled with air or gas **2.** **MAKE SOMETHING APPEAR GREATER** to exaggerate the size or importance of something, or become exaggerated in size or importance **3.** ECON **INCREASE PRICES OR MONEY SUPPLY** to cause inflation in prices or the money supply, or undergo inflation [15C. < Latin *inflat-*, past participle of *inflare* "blow into" < *flare* "to blow"] —**in·fla·tor** *n*

in·flat·ed /in fláytəd/ *adj* **1.** **UNDESERVEDLY GREAT** greater than is justified or normal ○ *an inflated sense of her own importance* **2.** ECON **EXCESSIVELY HIGH** excessively or unusually high **3.** **PRETENTIOUS** exaggerated or pompous in expression **4.** **BLOWN UP** expanded with air or gas —**in·flat·ed·ly** *adv* —**in·flat·ed·ness** *n*

in·fla·tion /in fláysh'n/ *n* **1.** ECON **HIGHER PRICES** an increase in the supply of currency or credit relative to the availability of goods and services, resulting in higher prices and a decrease in the purchasing power of money **2.** **BEING INFLATED** the act of inflating something, or the condition of being inflated **3.** **PROUD CONDITION** the condition of being puffed up with pride **4.** ASTRON **EARLY EXPANSION OF UNIVERSE** a period of rapidly accelerating expansion of the early universe after the big bang

in·fla·tion·ar·y /in fláysh'n èrree/ *adj* relating to or causing economic inflation ○ *inflationary policies*

in·fla·tion·ar·y spi·ral *n* a continuous economic cycle in which higher prices cause higher wages, which in turn cause even higher prices

in·fla·tion·ar·y the·o·ry *n* a theory in cosmology that there was a period of rapid acceleration during the expansion of the early universe after the big bang

in·fla·tion·ism /in fláysh'n ìzzəm/ *n* the advocacy or policy of deliberately causing economic inflation through an increase in the supply of available currency and credit —**in·fla·tion·ist** *adj, n*

in·flect /in flékt/ (**-flect·ed, -flect·ing, -flects**) *v* **1.** *vt* **VARY PITCH OF VOICE** to change the pitch or tone of the voice **2.** *vti* GRAM **CHANGE WORD FORM** to change the form of a word, e.g., to show a change in tense, mood, gender, or number, or be changed in this way **3.** *vt* **DIVERT COURSE OF SOMETHING** to make something turn from a direct line or course [15C. < Latin *inflectere* "bend in" < *flectere* "to bend"] —**in·flect·a·ble** *adj* —**in·flec·tive** *adj* —**in·flec·tor** *n*

in·flect·ed /in fléktəd/ *adj* **1.** changing form, e.g., to reflect tense, mood, gender, or number **2.** modulated or modified in pitch or loudness

USAGE See *accented*.

in·flec·tion /in flékshən/ *n* **1.** **CHANGE IN PITCH** a change in the pitch or tone of the voice **2.** GRAM **WORD CHANGE** a change in the form of a word, often an addition at the end of it, that indicates a particular grammatical function, e.g., the "s" added to most English nouns when they are plural **3.** GRAM **ALTERED FORM OF WORD** an altered form of a word, e.g., one showing a change in tense, mood, gender, or number, or the part of the word that changes in this way **4.** **BENDING** a turning from a straight line or course, or a more general change in direction **5.** MATH same as **inflection point** —**in·flec·tion·al** *adj* —**in·flec·tion·al·ly** *adv* —**in·flec·tion·less** *adj*

in·flec·tion point *n* a point on a curve at which the arc changes from convex to concave or vice versa

in·flexed /in flékst/ *adj* describes a plant part that is bent inward or downward toward the stem [Mid-17C. < Latin *inflex-*, past participle of *inflectere* (see INFLECT)]

in·flex·i·ble /in fléksəb'l/ *adj* **1.** **UNBENDING** adhering firmly to a viewpoint or principle **2.** **IMPOSSIBLE TO CHANGE** firmly established and impossible to change ○ *an inflexible rule* **3.** **RIGID** stiff and bendable only with difficulty —**in·flex·i·bil·i·ty** /in flèksə bíllətee/ *n* —**in·flex·i·ble·ness** *n* —**in·flex·i·bly** *adv*

in·flex·ion *n* GRAM, MATH UK spelling of **inflection**

in·flict /in flíkt/ (**-flict·ed, -flict·ing, -flicts**) *vt* **1.** to be the cause of something harmful or unpleasant such as loss, injury, or damage to somebody or something ○ *Our artillery inflicted heavy casualties on the enemy forces.* **2.** to impose something burdensome or inconvenient on somebody ○ *In that case I won't inflict my company on you any longer.* [Mid-16C. < Latin *inflict-*, past participle of *infligere* "strike upon" < *fligere* "to hit"] —**in·flict·a·ble** *adj* —**in·flict·er** *n* —**in·flic·tion** *n* —**in·flic·tive** *adj*

USAGE See *afflict*.

in-flight *adj* taking place or provided for passengers during an aircraft journey ○ *in-flight entertainment*

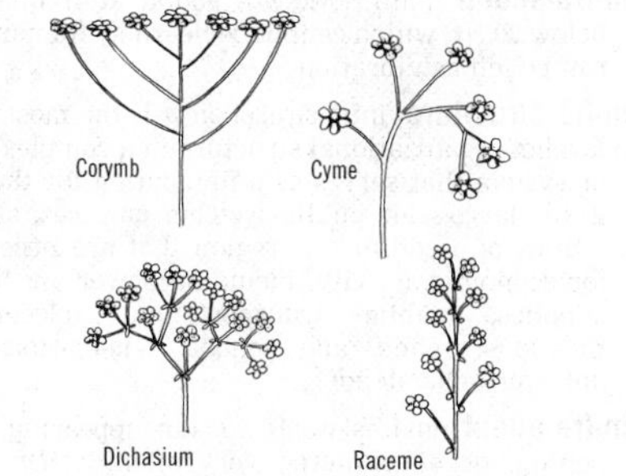

inflorescence

in·flo·res·cence /in flaw réss'nss, ìnflə-/ *n* BOT **1.** **FLOWERING PART OF PLANT** a flowering structure that consists of more than one flower and usually comprises distinct individual flowers **2.** **WAY FLOWERS GROW** the arrangement or manner in which flowers develop on a stalk **3.** **FLOWERING** the budding and flowering of a plant [Mid-18C. < modern Latin *inflorescentia* < Latin *inflorescere* "come into flower" < *flor-* "flower"]

in·flow /ín flō/ *n* **1.** **SOMETHING THAT FLOWS IN** something that flows into a place or container **2.** **INFLUX** an instance or the process of flowing in **3.** **SITE OF INFLOW** the point at which something flows in —**in·flow·ing** *n*

in·flu·ence /ín floo ənss/ *n* **1.** **EFFECT ON SOMETHING** the effect of something on a person, thing, or event ○ *Picasso's influence on the course of 20th-century art* **2.** **POWER TO SWAY** the power that somebody has to affect other people's thinking or actions by means of argument, example, or force of personality ○ *She came under the influence of one of her teachers.* **3.** **SPECIAL ADVANTAGE** the power or authority that comes from wealth, social status, or position **4.** **SOMEBODY WHO CAN SWAY ANOTHER** somebody or something able to affect the course of events or somebody's thinking or action ○ *He's a bad influence on you.* **5.** **STARS' EFFECT ON PEOPLE** in astrology, an emanation that is believed to come from the stars and planets and to affect human characteristics, personality, and actions ■ *vt* (**-enced, -enc·ing, -enc·es**) **1.** **SWAY SOMEBODY** to have an effect on somebody that helps to determine that person's actions, behavior, or way of thinking ○ *What influenced you in your choice of career?* **2.** **AFFECT SOMETHING** to have the power to affect something ○ *the factors that influence a nation's development* [14C. < medieval Latin *influentia* < Latin *influere* "flow in" < *fluere* "to flow"] —**in·flu·ence·a·ble** *adj* —**in·flu·enc·er** *n* ◇ **under the influence** intoxicated by the use of a chemical substance, especially alcohol (*informal*)

~~**influencial**~~ incorrect spelling of **influential**

in·flu·ent /ín floo ənt, in flo͝o ənt/ *n* a stream flowing into a lake or larger river [15C. < Latin *influent-*, present participle of *influere* (see INFLUENCE)]

in·flu·en·tial /in floo énshəl/ *adj* able to have a powerful effect on people and what they do, or on events —**in·flu·en·tial·ly** *adv*

in·flu·en·za /in floo énzə/ *n* **1.** a viral illness producing a high temperature, sore throat, runny nose, headache, dry cough, and muscle pain. The illness is widespread, especially during winter months, and can sometimes be fatal. (*technical*) **2.** a viral disease of domestic animals, usually characterized by fever and respiratory problems [Mid-18C. Via Italian < medieval Latin *influentia* (see INFLUENCE); referring to the supposed influence of the stars] —**in·flu·en·zal** *adj*

in·flux /ín flùks/ *n* **1.** a sudden arrival of a large number of people or things ○ *dealing with the influx of tourists into the city* **2.** a flowing in, especially of a stream or river [Late 16C. < late Latin *influxus* < past participle of Latin *influere* (see INFLUENCE)]

in·fo[1] /ínfō/ *n* same as **information** (*informal*) [Early 20C. Shortening]

info[2] *abbr* ONLINE general use (*used in Internet addresses*) See table at **domain name**

in·fo·bahn /ínfō baan/ *n* ONLINE same as **information superhighway** [Late 20C. Blend of INFORMATION + AUTOBAHN]

in·fold /in fōld/ *v* **1.** *vi* to fold inward **2.** *vt* another spelling of **enfold**

~~**infomation**~~ incorrect spelling of **information**

in·fo·me·di·ar·y /ínfō méedee èrree/ *n* a website providing specialist information for both producers of goods and customers

in·fo·mer·cial /ínfə múrsh'l, ìnfō-/, **in·for·mer·cial** /ìn fawr múrsh'l/ *n* a commercial advertisement on television that is made to appear like a full-length interview or documentary program [Late 20C. Blend of INFORMATION + COMMERCIAL]

in·fo·ne·sia /ínfō néezhə/ *n* inability to remember an item of information or its location, especially on the Internet (*informal*)

in·form /in fáwrm/ (**-formed, -form·ing, -forms**) *v* **1.** *vt* **TELL SOMEBODY** to communicate information or knowledge to somebody ○ *The police informed us of the accident.* **2.** **in·form your·self** *vr* **LEARN ABOUT SOMETHING** to familiarize yourself with a subject **3.** *vi* **GIVE INFORMATION TO POLICE** to give confidential or incriminating information about somebody else's activities, especially to the police **4.** *vt* ARTS **BE ESSENTIAL CHARACTERISTIC OF SOMETHING** to play an essential part in determining the nature, shape, or structure of something ○ *His religious beliefs inform his entire work.* **5.** *vt* **GIVE STRUCTURE TO SOMETHING** to give structure or substance to something (*formal*) ○ *the ethics that inform the profession* [14C. Via French < Latin *informare* "give form to" < *forma* "shape"]

in·for·mal /in fáwrm'l/ *adj* **1.** **FREE OF CEREMONY** relaxed and casual rather than ceremonious and stiff **2.** **UNOFFICIAL** not officially prepared, organized, or sanctioned ○ *The two sides in the conflict held informal talks.* **3.** **CASUAL AND EVERYDAY** suitable for casual or everyday situations ○ *informal dress* **4.** LANGUAGE **COLLOQUIAL** more appropriate in spoken than written form —**in·for·mal·i·ty** /in fawr mállətee/ *n* —**in·for·mal·ly** *adv*

in·for·mal e·con·o·my *n* economic activities organized without government approval, outside mainstream industry and commerce

in·form·ant /in fáwrmənt/ *n* **1.** **SOMEBODY WHO SUPPLIES INFORMATION** somebody who gives information to somebody else **2.** **INFORMER** somebody who gives confidential or incriminating information to the police about somebody else **3.** LING, CULTL ANTHROP **SOMEBODY PROVIDING LANGUAGE INFORMATION** somebody who gives a researcher useful cultural or linguistic information

in for·ma pau·per·is /in fàwrmə páwpəriss/ *adj, adv* not liable for court costs because of being identified as a poor person [Late 16C. < Latin, "in the form of a poor person"]

in·for·mat·ics /ìnfər máttiks/ *n UK* INFO SCI same as **information science** (*takes a singular verb*) [Mid-20C. < INFORMATION, after Russian *informatika*]

in·for·ma·tion /ìnfər máysh'n/ *n* **1.** **KNOWLEDGE** definite knowledge acquired or supplied about something or somebody ○ *a bulletin giving the latest information on the trial* **2.** **GATHERED FACTS** the collected facts and data about a specific subject **3.** a telephone service that supplies telephone numbers to the public on request **4.** **MAKING FACTS KNOWN** the communication of facts and knowledge **5.** COMPUT **ORGANIZED COMPUTER DATA** the meaningful material derived from computer data by organizing it and interpreting it in a specific way **6.** LAW **FORMAL CRIMINAL ACCUSATION** a formal accusation of a crime brought by a prosecutor, as opposed to an indictment brought by a grand jury —**in·for·ma·tion·al** *adj* —**in·for·ma·tion·al·ly** *adv*

SYNONYMS See *knowledge*.

in·for·ma·tion age *n* a period characterized by widespread electronic access to information through the use of computer technology

in·for·ma·tion ap·pli·ance *n* a small portable digital information-processing machine compatible with an electronic network

in·for·ma·tion proc·ess·ing *n* the organization, manipulation, analysis, and distribution of data, nowadays typically carried out by computers

in·for·ma·tion re·triev·al *n* the process of systematically searching for and retrieving stored computerized data

in·for·ma·tion sci·ence *n* the study of the collection, categorization, and distribution of data, particularly computer data

in·for·ma·tion su·per·high·way *n* the worldwide computer network that includes the Internet, private networks, and proprietary online services. It permits the rapid sending of many different forms of data, including voice, video, and text.

in·for·ma·tion tech·nol·o·gy *n* the use of technologies from computing, electronics, and telecommunications to process and distribute information in digital and other forms

in·for·ma·tion the·o·ry *n* the mathematical study of the transmission, reception, storage, and retrieval of information based on the statistical analysis of communication between humans and machines

in·form·a·tive /in fáwrmətiv/ *adj* providing useful information —**in·form·a·tive·ly** *adv* —**in·form·a·tive·ness** *n*

in·formed /in fáwrmd/ *adj* **1.** having sufficient and sufficiently reliable information or knowledge to be able to understand a subject or situation and make appropriate judgments or decisions regarding it ○ *informed citizens* **2.** based on an accurate knowledge and understanding of the situation or subject in question ○ *an informed decision* —**in·form·ed·ly** /in fáwrmədlee/ *adv*

in·formed con·sent *n* agreement by a patient to undergo an operation or medical treatment or take part in a clinical trial after being informed of and having understood the risks involved

in·form·er /in fáwrmər/ *n* **1.** somebody who gives the police or authorities information about criminal activities **2.** somebody or something that provides information about a subject or situation

in·for·mer·cial *n* MEDIA another spelling of **infomercial**

in·fo·tain·ment /infō táynmənt/ *n* television programs that deal with serious issues or current affairs in an entertaining way [Late 20C. Blend of INFORMATION + ENTERTAINMENT] —**in·fo·tain·er** *n*

in·fra /ínfrə/ *adv* used in an explanatory note to refer a reader to a point later in a text, especially in the phrase "vide infra" (*formal*) [Late 19C. < Latin]

infra- *prefix* below, beneath, inferior ○ *infrasonic* ○ *infraclass* [< Latin *infra* "below" < Indo-European]

in·fra·class /ínfrə klàss/ *n* a taxonomic category of organisms that is above an order and below a subclass

in·fra·cos·tal /ínfrə kóst'l/ *adj* lying below the ribs

in·fract /in frákt/ (**-fract·ed, -fract·ing, -fracts**) *vt* to fail to obey or fulfill a law, contract, or agreement [Late 18C. < Latin *infract-*, past participle of *infringere* (see INFRINGE)] —**in·frac·tor** *n*

in·frac·tion /in frákshən/ *n* failure to obey or fulfill a law, contract, or agreement, or an instance of this [15C. Directly and via French < Latin *infraction-* < *infractus* (see INFRACT)]

in·fra dig *adj* below the standard of social behavior that somebody usually maintains (*informal*) [Early 19C. Shortening of Latin *infra dignitatem* "beneath dignity"]

in·fra·hu·man /ínfrə hyóomən/ *adj* in the system of classifying living organisms, belonging to a lower order than human beings

in·fran·gi·ble /in fránjəb'l/ *adj* (*formal*) **1.** unable to be broken or separated into pieces **2.** unable to be disregarded or violated —**in·fran·gi·bil·i·ty** /in frànjə bíllətee/ *n* —**in·fran·gi·ble·ness** *n* —**in·fran·gi·bly** *adv*

in·fra·red /ínfrə réd/ *n* the portion of the invisible electromagnetic spectrum consisting of radiation with wavelengths in the range 750 nm to 1 mm, between light and radio waves ○ *infrared radiation* ■ *adj* using, producing, or affected by infrared radiation [Late 19C. Because it lies below the red end of the visible spectrum]

in·fra·red as·tron·o·my *n* the study of astronomical objects by examining the wavelengths they emit in the infrared range. Infrared sources within our galaxy include cool gas giants and the galactic center.

in·fra·red pho·tog·ra·phy *n* photography with film that is sensitive to infrared radiation, used e.g., in taking pictures at night or in haze and in detecting camouflaged objects

in·fra·son·ic /ínfrə sónnik/ *adj* **1.** relating to sound at frequencies below 20 Hz, which cannot be heard by human beings but can be felt as vibration **2.** using or produced by infrasonic waves or vibrations —**in·fra·son·i·cal·ly** *adv*

in·fra·sound /ínfrə sòwnd/ *n* sound at frequencies below 20 Hz, which cannot be heard by humans but can be felt as vibration

in·fra·struc·ture /ínfrə strùkchər/ *n* **1.** the most basic level of organizational structure in a complex body or system that serves as a foundation for the rest **2.** the large-scale public systems, services, and facilities of a country or region that are necessary for economic activity, including power and water supplies, public transportation, telecommunications, roads, and schools —**in·fra·struc·tur·al** /ínfrə strúkchərəl/ *adj*

in·fre·quent /in fréekwənt/ *adj* not appearing, happening, or encountered very often ○ *Her visits became more infrequent.* —**in·fre·quence** *n* —**in·fre·quen·cy** *n* —**in·fre·quent·ly** *adv*

in·fringe /in frínj/ (**-fringed, -fring·ing, -fring·es**) *v* **1.** *vt* to fail to obey a law or regulation or observe the terms of an agreement **2.** *vti* to take over land, rights, privileges, or activities that belong to somebody else, especially in a minor or gradual way ○ *infringing on our personal freedom* [Mid-16C. < Latin *infringere* "to damage" < *frangere* "to break"] —**in·fringe·ment** *n* —**in·fring·er** *n*

in·fun·dib·u·la ANAT plural of **infundibulum**

in·fun·dib·u·li·form /ìnfən díbbyələ fàwrm/ *adj* describes a flower or other plant part that resembles a funnel in shape

in·fun·dib·u·lum /ìnfən díbbyələm/ (*plural* **-la** /-lə/) *n* a funnel-shaped opening, passage, or structure in vertebrates, e.g., the stalk connecting the pituitary gland to the brain or the opening of a Fallopian tube into the ovary [Mid-16C. < Latin, "funnel" < *infundere* (see INFUSE)] —**in·fun·dib·u·lar** *adj* —**in·fun·dib·u·late** *adj*

in·fu·ri·ate /in fyóoree àyt/ (**-at·ed, -at·ing, -ates**) *vt* to make somebody extremely angry [Mid-17C. < medieval Latin *infuriat-*, past participle of *infuriare* < *furiare* "to anger" < Latin *furia* (see FURY)] —**in·fu·ri·at·ed** *adj* —**in·fu·ri·at·ed·ly** *adv* —**in·fu·ri·at·ing** *adj* —**in·fu·ri·at·ing·ly** *adv* —**in·fu·ri·a·tion** /in fyòoree áysh'n/ *n*

in·fuse /in fyóoz/ (**-fused, -fus·ing, -fus·es**) *v* **1.** *vt* FILL SOMEBODY WITH EMOTION to fill somebody or something with a strong emotion such as hatred, enthusiasm, or desire (*often passive*) **2.** *vt* INTRODUCE SOMETHING INTO SOMEBODY'S MIND to fix an emotion, belief, or quality gradually but firmly in somebody else's mind **3.** *vti* STEEP SOMETHING IN LIQUID to soak tea or herbs in liquid to extract the flavor or another property, or be soaked in this way **4.** *vt* MED GIVE LIQUID USING DRIP FEED to introduce a solution such as saline, sucrose, or glucose using a drip feed into a vein, body cavity, or the intestinal tract in order to treat or feed a patient [15C. < Old French *infuser* < past participle of Latin *infundere* "pour in" < *fundere* "pour"] —**in·fus·er** *n* —**in·fus·i·ble** *adj*

in·fu·sion /in fyóozh'n/ *n* **1.** INTRODUCTION OF SOMETHING NEEDED the addition of a new or necessary quality or element to something ○ *an infusion of private capital into the project* **2.** LIQUID MADE BY INFUSING SOMETHING a liquid that is made by infusing something, e.g., tea **3.** ACT OF INFUSING SOMETHING the act of soaking something in a liquid in order to extract soluble matter **4.** MED ADMINISTERING OF LIQUID THROUGH DRIP FEED the introduction of a solution such as saline, sucrose, or glucose through a drip feed in order to treat or feed a patient **5.** MED LIQUID ADMINISTERED THROUGH DRIP FEED a solution introduced into the body by infusion [14C. Via French < Latin *infusion-* < past participle of *infundere* (see INFUSE)]

-ing[1] *suffix* **1.** forming the present participle of verbs ○ *raining* **2.** forming adjectives from words other than verbs ○ *swashbuckling* [Alteration of *-ende* < Old English]

-ing[2] *suffix* **1.** action or process ○ *rowing* ○ *cooking* **2.** result of (*archaic*) [Old English *-ung, -ing*]

-ing[3] *suffix* somebody or something that has a particular character ○ *gelding* [Old English, "belonging to"]

in·gath·er /ín gàthər/ (**-ered, -er·ing, -ers**) *v* **1.** *vt* to gather in a harvest of something **2.** *vi* to come together or assemble (*formal or literary*) —**in·gath·er·er** *n*

Inge /inj/, **William** (1913–73) US playwright. He is known for his small-town Midwestern dramas such as *Picnic*, which won the Pulitzer Prize in 1953. Full name **Inge, William Motter**

> "Once we find the fruits of success, the taste is nothing like we had anticipated."
> [Attributed to William Inge]

in·gen·ious /in jéenyəss/ *adj* **1.** possessing cleverness and imagination **2.** clever, original, and effective ○ *an ingenious solution* [15C. Via French < Latin *ingeniosus* < *ingenium* "mind"] —**in·gen·ious·ly** *adv* —**in·gen·ious·ness** *n*

USAGE ingenious or **ingenuous**? Though spelled similarly, these two words have different meanings and so should not be used interchangeably. ***Ingenious*** means "inventive" and "cleverly effective," as in *a famed researcher with an ingenious* [not *ingenuous*] *mind; an ingenious* [not *ingenuous*] *marketing strategy.* By contrast, ***ingenuous*** means "innocently unworldly" and "being or seeming to be honest, candid, and direct," as in *an ingenuous* [not *ingenious*] *young child; an ingenuous* [not *ingenious*] *answer to the reporter's hostile question.*

in·gé·nue /áNzhə nòo/ *n* **1.** UNSOPHISTICATED GIRL OR YOUNG WOMAN a girl or young woman who is naive and lacks experience or understanding of life **2.** NAIVE CHARACTER IN DRAMA a character in a play or a movie who is a naive inexperienced young woman **3.** ACTOR IN ROLE OF INGÉNUE an actor, especially a young one, who plays or specializes in playing the role of an ingénue [Mid-19C. Via French < Latin *ingenuus* (see INGENUOUS)]

in·ge·nu·i·ty /ìnjə nóo ətee/ *n* cleverness and originality [Late 16C. < Latin *ingenuitas* < *ingenuus* (see INGENUOUS)]

in·gen·u·ous /in jénnyoo əss/ *adj* **1.** showing innocence and a lack of worldly experience **2.** appearing honest and direct [Late 16C. < Latin *ingenuus* "native, honest" < *gignere* "beget"] —**in·gen·u·ous·ly** *adv* —**in·gen·u·ous·ness** *n*

USAGE See ***ingenious.***

In·ger·soll /íng gər sàwl/, **Robert** (1833–99) US lawyer and orator. He was a noted agnostic, and in his lectures maintained that happiness is the only good. Full name **Ingersoll, Robert Green**. Known as **the Great Agnostic**

> "In nature there are neither rewards nor punishments—there are consequences."
> [Robert Ingersoll, *Some Reasons Why*; 1881]

in·gest /in jést/ (**-gest·ed, -gest·ing, -gests**) *vt* to take food, liquid, or some other substance into the body by swallowing or absorbing it [Early 17C. < Latin *ingest-*, past participle of *ingerere* "carry in" < *gerere* "carry"] —**in·ges·tion** *n* —**in·ges·tive** *adj*

in·ges·ta /in jéstə/ *npl* food or liquid taken into the body by swallowing or absorbing [Early 18C. < Latin < *ingest-* (see INGEST)]

in·gle /íng g'l/ *n* a fireplace, or an open fire burning in a fireplace (*archaic*) [Early 16C. Origin ?]

in·gle·nook /íng g'l nòok/ *n* **1.** a recess for a seat or bench beside a large fireplace **2.** a seat built in an inglenook, especially one of two benches or wing chairs facing each other

In·gle·wood /íng g'l wòod/ city in Los Angeles County, southwestern California, bordering the city of Los Angeles. Population: 114,959 (2002 estimate).

In·glis /íng gliss, íng g'lz/, **Charles** (1734–1816) Irish-born Canadian cleric. He was the Church of England's first colonial bishop (1787–96).

in·glo·ri·ous /in gláwree əss/ *adj* **1.** bringing shame or dishonor **2.** not having received recognition, and so unknown or obscure (*archaic or literary*) [Mid-16C. < Latin *inglorius* < *gloria* "glory"] —**in·glo·ri·ous·ly** *adv* —**in·glo·ri·ous·ness** *n*

in·go·ing /ín gòing/ *adj* in the process of entering, arriving, being received, or taking office

in·got /íng gət/ *n* **1.** a metal casting that is shaped, typically in an oblong, for easy working or for recasting **2.** a mold used for the casting of ingots [14C. Probably < Old English *in* "in" + *gotan*, past participle of *gēotan* "pour"]

in·got i·ron *n* very pure iron that is produced in the same way as steel but using methods that reduce the carbon, manganese, and silicon content

in·graft *vt* BIOL another spelling of **engraft**

in·grain, **en·grain** *vt* /in gráyn/ (**-grained, -grain·ing, -grains**) **IMPRESS SOMETHING IN SOMEBODY'S MIND** to impress a feeling, belief, or experience firmly and indelibly in somebody's mind (*usually passive*) ○ *The sight is still ingrained in my memory.* ■ *adj* /ín gràyn/ **1.** same as **ingrained** (sense 1) **2.** TEXTILES **PREDYED** dyed before being spun or woven ■ *n* /ín gràyn/ TEXTILES **1. PREDYED YARN OR FIBER** yarn or fiber that is dyed before being spun or woven **2. PREDYED RUG OR CARPET** a rug or carpet made of yarn or fiber that is dyed before being spun or woven [15C. < IN[1] + GRAIN in the archaic sense "cochineal, dye"]

in·grained /in gráynd/ *adj* **1. WORKED DEEP INTO SOMETHING** worked into the surface, pores, or fibers of something and very difficult to remove ○ *ingrained dirt* **2. IMPRESSED IN SOMEBODY'S MIND** firmly fixed in somebody's mind and only removed or challenged with difficulty ○ *ingrained attitudes* **3. HABITUAL** long-established or confirmed in a habit or practice ○ *ingrained liar* —**in·grain·ed·ly** /in gráynədlee/ *adv* —**in·grain·ed·ness** /-ədnəss/ *n*

in·grate /in gràyt/ *n* somebody who shows or feels no gratitude ■ *adj* showing or feeling no gratitude [15C. Via French < Latin *ingratus* (see INGRATITUDE)]

in·gra·ti·ate /in gráyshee àyt/ (**-at·ed, -at·ing, -ates**) *vr* **in·gra·ti·ate your·self** to try to win somebody's favor by pleasing him or her, especially in order to gain an advantage ○ *She made blatant attempts to ingratiate herself with top management.* [Early 17C. < Italian *ingraziare* < *in grazia* "into favor" < Latin *gratia* "favor"] —**in·gra·ti·a·tion** /in gràyshee áysh'n/ *n* —**in·gra·ti·a·to·ry** *adj*

in·gra·ti·at·ing /in gráyshee àyting/ *adj* designed to win somebody's approval, especially in order to gain an advantage —**in·gra·ti·at·ing·ly** *adv*

in·grat·i·tude /in gráttə tòod/ *n* failure to express or feel gratitude [14C. Directly or via French < Latin *ingratitudo* < *ingratus* "ungrateful" < *gratus* "grateful"]

~~**ingrediant**~~ incorrect spelling of **ingredient**

in·gre·di·ent /in greédee ənt/ *n* **1.** a component of a mixture, especially an item of food or flavoring included in the recipe for preparing a dish **2.** an element required for a situation, relationship, or plan ○ *What are the ingredients for a happy marriage?* [15C. < Latin *ingredient-*, present participle of *ingredi* "enter" < *gradi* "to step, walk"]

In·gres /áNgrə/, **Jean-Auguste-Dominique** (1780–1867) French artist. He was a leading exemplar of neoclassicism in paintings such as *Grande Odalisque* (1814).

> "Drawing is the true test of art."
> [Jean-Auguste-Dominique Ingres, *Pensées d'Ingres*; 1922]

in·gress /ín grèss/ *n* (*formal*) **1. ENTRY** entry into a place **2. RIGHT OF ENTRY** the right to enter a place **3. ENTRANCE** a way of entering a place [15C. < Latin, "entrance" < *ingredi* (see INGREDIENT)]

in·gres·sive /in gréssiv/ *adj* **1. OF ENTRY** relating to entry into or the entrance to a place **2.** PHON **PRONOUNCED BY INHALING** describes a speech sound that is pronounced by inhaling rather than exhaling **3.** GRAM same as **inceptive** *adj* (sense 2) ■ *n* **1.** GRAM same as **inceptive 2.** PHON **INGRESSIVE SPEECH SOUND** a speech sound pronounced by inhaling —**in·gres·sive·ness** *n*

in-group *n* a group of people who show loyalty and preferential treatment to one another because they share common interests, beliefs, and attitudes

in·grow·ing /ín grōing/ *adj* growing or appearing to grow inward. An ingrowing toenail does not actually grow inward: inflamed tissue around the edge of the nail grows over it.

in·grown /ín grōn/ *adj* **1.** MED **GROWN INTO FLESH** appearing to grow into the flesh ○ *ingrown toenail* **2. NATURAL TO SOMEBODY** having become a natural part of somebody's character over a long period of time **3. INWARD-LOOKING** inward-looking and preoccupied with personal or local interests

in·growth /ín grōth/ *n* **1.** growth or apparent growth into the flesh **2.** something that grows inward, e.g., a hair

in·gui·nal /íng gwən'l/ *adj* located in or affecting the groin [15C. < Latin *inguinalis* < *inguen* "groin"]

in·gulf *vt* another spelling of **engulf**

in·gur·gi·tate /in gúrji tàyt/ (**-tat·ed, -tat·ing, -tates**) *vt* to swallow large amounts of food greedily (*literary*) [Late 16C. < Latin *ingurgitat-*, past participle of *ingurgitare* < *gurges* "gulf"] —**in·gur·gi·ta·tion** /in gùrji táysh'n/ *n*

In·gush /in gŏosh, in gŏosh/ (*plural* **-gush·es** *or same*) *n* a member of a people who live mainly in the Russian provinces of Ingushetia and Chechnya [Early 20C. < Russian *Ingúsh*, former autonomous area] —**In·gush** *adj*

in·hab·it /in hábbit/ (**-it·ed, -it·ing, -its**) *vt* **1.** to live in or occupy a particular place **2.** to be found in or pervade something ○ *the fears that inhabited each waking moment* [14C. Via French < Latin *inhabitare* < *habitare* "possess, dwell" < *habere* "have"] —**in·hab·it·a·bil·i·ty** /in hàbbitə bíllətee/ *n* —**in·hab·it·a·ble** *adj* —**in·hab·i·ta·tion** /in hàbbi táysh'n/ *n* —**in·hab·it·ed** *adj* —**in·hab·it·er** *n*

in·hab·i·tant /in hábbit'nt/ *n* a person or animal that lives in a particular place or area —**in·hab·i·tan·cy** *n*

in·ha·lant /in háylənt/ *adj* breathed in through the nose or mouth as a medicine or for its soothing effect ■ *n* a substance in the form of a vapor or gas that is inhaled, especially as a medicine or for its soothing effect

in·ha·la·tion /ìnhə láysh'n/ *n* **1.** an intake of breath through the nose or mouth into the lungs **2.** a substance in the form of a vapor or gas that is inhaled, especially as a medicine or for its soothing effect [Early 17C. < medieval Latin *inhalation-* < Latin *inhalare* (see INHALE)] —**in·ha·la·tion·al** *adj*

in·ha·la·tion an·thrax *n* a potentially fatal form of anthrax affecting the lungs

in·ha·la·tor /ínhə làytər/ *n* MED **1.** same as **respirator** (sense 1) **2.** same as **inhaler** (sense 1)

in·hale /in háyl/ (**-haled, -hal·ing, -hales**) *vti* to breathe in, or draw a gas, liquid, or solid into the lungs through the nose or mouth [Early 18C. Either back-formation < INHALATION, or < Latin *inhalare* "breathe upon" < *halare* "breathe"]

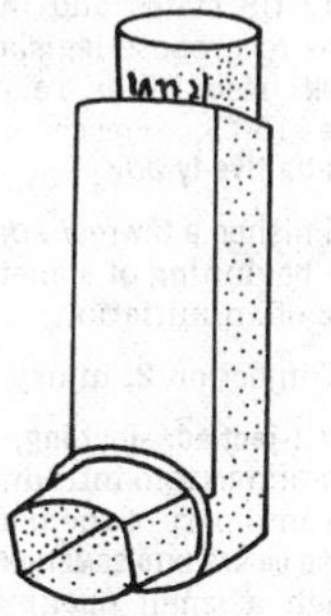

inhaler

in·hal·er /in háylər/ *n* **1.** a small device used for inhaling medicine in the form of a vapor or gas in order to ease a respiratory condition such as asthma or to relieve nasal congestion **2.** somebody who inhales something

in·har·mo·ni·ous /ìn haar mṓnee əss/ *adj* **1. DISCORDANT** lacking harmony, or sounding unpleasant **2. UNHAPPY** characterized by disagreement and conflict **3. CLASHING** not matching in color or style —**in·har·mo·ni·ous·ly** *adv* —**in·har·mo·ni·ous·ness** *n*

in·har·mo·ny /in háarmənee/ *n* lack of harmony, accord, or agreement

in·haul /ín hàwl/, **in·haul·er** /ín hàwlər/ *n* a rope used to haul or hold in a sail

in·here /in heér/ (**-hered, -her·ing, -heres**) *vi* to be a natural and integral part of something (*formal*) [Mid-16C. < Latin *inhaerere* < *haerere* "to stick"]

in·her·ent /in heérənt, -hérrənt/ *adj* part of the very nature of something, and therefore permanently characteristic of it or necessarily involved in it ○ *the risks inherent in investing in the stock market* [Late 16C. < Latin *inhaerent-*, present participle of *inhaerere* (see INHERE)] —**in·her·ence** *n* —**in·her·en·cy** *n* —**in·her·ent·ly** *adv*

in·her·it /in hérrit/ (**-it·ed, -it·ing, -its**) *v* **1.** *vti* **RECEIVE SOMETHING WHEN SOMEBODY DIES** to become the owner of something when somebody dies, in accordance with legal succession or the terms of a will, or as the result of a bequest or legacy **2.** *vt* **RECEIVE CHARACTERISTIC OR QUALITY FROM PARENT** to receive a characteristic or quality as a result of its being passed on genetically **3.** *vt* **GET SOMETHING FROM PREDECESSOR** to take something over from the person or group who previously lived in a place or did a job [14C. Via Old French *enheriter* "make an heir" < late Latin *inhereditare* "inherit" < Latin *heres* "heir"] —**in·her·i·tor** *n*

in·her·it·a·ble /in hérritəb'l/ *adj* **1.** LAW same as **heritable** (sense 1) **2.** describes a characteristic or quality that can be transmitted genetically from parent to offspring —**in·her·it·a·bil·i·ty** /in hèrritə bíllətee/ *n*

in·her·i·tance /in hérrit'nss/ *n* **1.** LAW **INHERITED WEALTH OR TITLE** money, property, or a title that has been inherited or is to be inherited **2.** LAW **OWNERSHIP OR SUCCESSION BY HEREDITY** hereditary ownership of wealth or a title, or the succession to wealth or a title **3.** LAW **RIGHT TO INHERIT** the right of an heir to inherit wealth or a title when an ancestor dies **4. HERITAGE** something that is inherited from the past **5.** GENETICS **TRANSMISSION OF GENETICALLY CONTROLLED CHARACTERISTICS** the transmission of genetically controlled characteristics or qualities from parent to offspring **6.** COMPUT **CREATION OF OBJECT WITH SAME VARIABLES** a feature of computer programming whereby a new object can be created from existing objects and, as a consequence of creation, possess the variables and methods of the parent object

in·her·i·tance tax *n* a tax levied on property received by inheritance or legal succession, calculated according to the value of the property received

in·her·it·ed /in hérrətəd/ *adj* **1.** received by inheritance after the death of the previous owner **2.** controlled by a gene or genes passed on from parent to offspring

in·hib·in /in híbbin/ *n* a hormone secreted by the gonads that inhibits production of follicle-stimulating hormones [Mid-20C. < Latin *inhibere* (see INHIBIT)]

in·hib·it /in híbbit/ (**-it·ed, -it·ing, -its**) *vt* **1. HOLD SOMETHING IN CHECK** to stop something from continuing or developing ○ *Changes in spending patterns are likely to inhibit economic growth.* **2. MAKE SOMEBODY FEEL SELF-CONSCIOUS** to prevent somebody from behaving or speaking freely or unselfconsciously **3.** CHEM **STOP OR RESTRICT CHEMICAL REACTION** to prevent or slow down a chemical reaction **4.** PHYSIOL **INTERFERE WITH BODILY PROCESS OR ORGAN** to slow down or adversely affect a bodily process or the action of an organ **5.** ELECTRONICS **PREVENT SIGNAL OR EVENT** to prevent a specific signal or event from occurring [15C. < Latin *inhibit-*, past participle of *inhibere* "hinder" < *habere* "to hold"] —**in·hib·it·a·ble** *adj* —**in·hib·it·ing** *adj* —**in·hib·i·tive** *adj*

in·hib·it·ed /in híbbitəd/ *adj* unable to behave spontaneously or express feelings openly —**in·hib·it·ed·ly** *adv* —**in·hib·it·ed·ness** *n*

in·hib·it·er *n* another spelling of **inhibitor**

in·hi·bi·tion /ìnnə bísh'n, ìnhə-/ *n* **1. FEELING THAT INHIBITS SOMEBODY** a feeling or belief that prevents somebody from behaving spontaneously or speaking freely **2. SOMETHING THAT INHIBITS** something that inhibits something, or the act of inhibiting something **3.** PSYCHOL **INHIBITED MENTAL STATE** a mental state in which somebody's activity or behavior is stifled or obstructed **4.** PSYCHOL **DIMINISHED RESPONSE TO STIMULUS** in Pavlovian conditioning, the progressive weakening of a response to a stimulus after repeated presentations of the stimulus **5.** CHEM **PREVENTION OF CHEMICAL REACTION** the slowing down or prevention of a chemical reaction **6.** PHYSIOL **OBSTRUCTION OF BODILY PROCESS OR ORGAN** the suppression or blocking of a bodily process or the action of an organ [14C. Via French < Latin *inhibition-* < *inhibere* (see INHIBIT)]

in·hib·i·tor /in híbbitər/, **in·hib·it·er** *n* **1.** CHEM **SUBSTANCE SLOWING CHEMICAL REACTION** a substance that stops or slows a chemical reaction ○ *a rust inhibitor* **2.** BIOCHEM **SUBSTANCE HALTING BIOLOGICAL PROCESS** a substance that prevents the action of an enzyme **3. SOMETHING THAT INHIBITS SOMETHING** somebody or something that inhibits another person or thing —**in·hib·i·to·ry** *adj*

in·hold·er /ín hōldər/ *n* a person who owns private land within the confines of a national park, forest, or refuge, and who is allowed reasonable ingress and egress rights to that property, e.g., in Alaska

in·hold·ing /ín hōlding/ *n* a piece of private land owned by an inholder

in-home *adj* available in somebody's home

in·hos·pi·ta·ble /in ho spíttəb'l, in hóspitəb'l/ *adj* **1.** not welcoming or friendly **2.** harsh and difficult to live or work in ○ *an inhospitable climate* —**in·hos·pi·ta·ble·ness** *n* —**in·hos·pi·ta·bly** *adv* —**in·hos·pi·tal·i·ty** /ìn hospi tállətee/ *n*

in-house *adj* working, carried out, or existing within a company or organization ■ *adv* within a company or organization

in·hu·man /in hyoōmən/ *adj* **1.** VERY CRUEL showing great cruelty and a lack of humanity **2.** UNFEELING giving an impression of being cold and unfeeling **3.** NOT HUMAN not seeming to be human, or not characteristic of human beings —**in·hu·man·ly** *adv* —**in·hu·man·ness** *n*

in·hu·mane /ìn hyoo máyn/ *adj* lacking compassion and causing excessive suffering —**in·hu·mane·ly** *adv* —**in·hu·mane·ness** *n*

in·hu·man·i·ty /ìn hyoo mánnətee/ (*plural* **-ties**) *n* **1.** great cruelty and lack of humanity **2.** an act of great cruelty

in·hume /in hyoōm/ (**-humed, -hum·ing, -humes**) *vt* to bury a dead body (*literary*) [Early 17C. < Latin *inhumare* < *humus* "earth"] —**in·hu·ma·tion** /ìn hyoo máysh'n/ *n* —**in·hum·er** *n*

in·im·i·cal /i nímmik'l/ *adj* (*formal*) **1.** unfavorable to something ○ *activities inimical to the public good* **2.** showing hostility [Early 16C. < late Latin *inimicalis* < Latin *inimicus* "unfriendly" < *amicus* "friend"] —**in·im·i·cal·i·ty** /i nìmmi kállətee/ *n* —**in·im·i·cal·ly** *adv* —**in·im·i·cal·ness** *n*

in·im·i·ta·ble /i nímmitəb'l/ *adj* impossible to imitate, especially because of being unique to a person or group ○ *She carried the speech off in her usual inimitable style.* —**in·im·i·ta·bil·i·ty** /i nìmmitə bíllətee/ *n* —**in·im·i·ta·ble·ness** *n* —**in·im·i·ta·bly** *adv*

in·i·on /ínnee ən/ *n* a projection of the occipital bone that forms a slight lump at the back of the skull just above the neck [Early 19C. < Greek, "nape of the neck"]

in·iq·ui·tous /i níkwitəss/ *adj* immoral, especially in a way that results in great injustice or unfairness —**in·iq·ui·tous·ly** *adv* —**in·iq·ui·tous·ness** *n*

in·iq·ui·ty /i níkwətee/ (*plural* **-ties**) *n* **1.** great injustice or extreme immorality **2.** a grossly immoral act [13C. Via French < Latin *iniquitas* < *iniquus* "unjust" < *aequus* "equal"]

in·i·tial /i nísh'l/ *adj* **1.** COMING AT START coming first, or present at the beginning of an event or process ○ *My initial feeling was one of shock.* **2.** COMING FIRST IN WORD relating to or used as the first letter or letters of a word ■ *n* **1.** FIRST LETTER OF NAME the first letter of the name of a person, place, or organization **2.** PRINTING LARGE ORNATE FIRST LETTER the large and often highly decorative first letter of a verse, paragraph, or page, especially as seen in illuminated manuscripts **3.** BOT PLANT-TISSUE CELL a cell in the growing point (**meristem**) of a plant that gives rise to cells that will develop into different plant tissues ■ **in·i·tials** *npl* FIRST LETTERS OF SOMEBODY'S NAMES the first letter of each of the names of a person, place, or organization, used as an abbreviation or means of identification ■ *vt* (**-tialed, -tial·ing, -tials**) MARK SOMETHING WITH INITIALS to sign or mark a document with initials, especially in order to show approval or give authorization [Early 16C. < Latin *initialis* < *initium* "beginning"] —**in·i·tial·er** *n*

in·i·tial·ism /i nísh'l ìzzəm/ *n* an abbreviation made up of initial letters that are all pronounced separately, e.g., UN for United Nations

in·i·tial·ize /i nísh'l ìz/ (**-ized, -iz·ing, -iz·es**) *vti* to prepare a piece of computer hardware or software for use, often by resetting a memory location to its initial value —**in·i·tial·iz·er** *n*

in·i·tial·ly /i nísh'lee/ *adv* at first or to begin with

in·i·tial pub·lic of·fer·ing *n* a first-time sale of company securities on a stock exchange to public investors

in·i·tial rhyme *n* rhyme used at the start of lines of verse

In·i·tial Teach·ing Al·pha·bet *n* an alphabet of 44 symbols, each representing a single sound in English, used to teach children to read

in·i·ti·ate *vt* /i níshee àyt/ (**-at·ed, -at·ing, -ates**) **1.** MAKE SOMETHING START to cause something, especially an important event or process, to begin ○ *to initiate talks* **2.** TEACH SOMEBODY ABOUT SOMETHING NEW to introduce somebody to a new activity, interest, or area ○ *She initiated me into the joys of snowboarding.* **3.** INTRODUCE SOMEBODY INTO GROUP to allow somebody to take part in a ritual or ceremony in order to become a member of a group, organization, or religion ■ *n* /i níshee ət/ **1.** SOMEBODY INITIATED INTO GROUP somebody who has been recently and ceremonially admitted to a group, organization, or religion **2.** SOMEBODY NEWLY INTRODUCED TO SOMETHING somebody recently introduced to a new activity, interest, or area ■ *adj* /i níshee ət/ **1.** RECENTLY INITIATED belonging or relating to those who have been recently introduced to a new activity, interest, or area **2.** HAVING SECRET OR SPECIAL KNOWLEDGE knowing the secrets of a group, organization, or religion [Mid-16C. < Latin *initiat-*, past participle of *initiare* "begin" < *initium* "beginning"] —**in·i·ti·a·tor** *n*

in·i·ti·at·ed /i níshee àytəd/ *npl* those who know about something that seems difficult or complicated, or who know the secrets of a group, organization, or religion

in·i·ti·a·tion /i nìshee áysh'n/ *n* **1.** ACTION THAT MAKES SOMETHING START action that causes something, especially an important process or event, to begin ○ *the initiation of legal proceedings* **2.** CEREMONY a usually secret or mysterious ceremony by which somebody is admitted to a group, organization, or religion (*sometimes used before nouns*) ○ *initiation rites* **3.** INTRODUCTION TO SOMETHING NEW the introduction of somebody to a new activity, interest, or area [Late 16C. < Latin *initiation-* < *initiat-* (see INITIATE)]

in·i·tia·tive /i níshətiv/ *n* **1.** ABILITY TO ACT ON YOUR OWN the ability to act and make decisions without the help or advice of other people ○ *You'll just have to use your initiative.* **2.** INTRODUCTORY STEP the first step in a process that, once taken, determines subsequent events ○ *decided to take the initiative* **3.** PLAN a plan or strategy designed to deal with a particular problem ○ *a peace initiative* **4.** ADVANTAGEOUS POSITION a favorable position that allows somebody to take preemptive action or control events ○ *lose the initiative* **5.** POL RIGHT TO INTRODUCE NEW LEGISLATION the right to bring a new law or measure before a legislative body **6.** POL PROPOSAL OF LEGISLATION BY CITIZENS a process valid in many US states and in Switzerland that allows citizens to propose legislation by petition ■ *adj* OF INITIATION used in or relating to initiation (*formal*) [Late 18C. < French < Latin *initiat-* (see INITIATE)] —**in·i·tia·tive·ly** *adv*

in·i·ti·a·to·ry /i níshee ə tàwree/ *adj* **1.** occurring at or related to the beginning of something **2.** used in or characteristic of an initiation

inj. *abbr* MED **1.** injection **2.** injury

in·ject /in jékt/ (**-ject·ed, -ject·ing, -jects**) *v* **1.** *vti* PUT FLUID INTO BODY WITH SYRINGE to introduce a drug, vaccine, or other fluid into part of the body using a syringe **2.** *vt* FORCE LIQUID OR GAS INTO SOMETHING to force a liquid or gas through a small opening into a confined space ○ *They injected an insulating foam into the cavity between the walls.* **3.** *vt* ADD SOMETHING TO SITUATION to introduce a particular quality or element into a situation ○ *an attempt to inject a little levity into the proceedings* **4.** *vt* AEROSP PUT ROCKET OR SATELLITE IN ORBIT to put a rocket or satellite into orbit or a spacecraft onto a trajectory to its destination [Late 16C. < Latin *inject-*, past participle of *inicere* "throw in" < *iacere* "to throw"] —**in·ject·a·ble** *adj*

in·jec·tant /in jéktənt/ *n* an injected substance

in·jec·tion /in jékshən/ *n* **1.** INJECTED DOSE OF DRUG a dose of a drug in liquid form that is injected into the body with a syringe **2.** INTRODUCTION OF FLUID WITH SYRINGE the introduction of a fluid into the body by means of a syringe **3.** AUTOMOT SPRAYING OF FUEL INTO ENGINE the process of spraying fuel through a pump into the inlet manifold or cylinder of an internal-combustion engine, eliminating the need for a carburetor **4.** ADDITION OF SOMETHING TO SITUATION the introduction of a particular quality or element into a situation ○ *His playing would benefit from an injection of muscle and soul.* **5.** PROVISION OF MONEY a provision of money for a country, organization, project, or person in financial need ○ *a cash injection* **6.** MATH ONE-TO-ONE MAPPING OF SETS a one-to-one mapping of two algebraic sets such that each element of each set corresponds to only one element of the other set **7.** MANUF INTRODUCTION OF FLUID INTO CAVITY a process for introducing a fluid such as a plastic under pressure into a cavity **8.** AEROSP SENDING OF SATELLITE INTO ORBIT the placing of an artificial satellite into orbit or a space probe onto a trajectory **9.** AEROSP MOMENT OF SATELLITE INSERTION the moment or place at which a satellite or space probe is inserted into its intended orbit or trajectory

in·jec·tion mold·ing *n* a manufacturing process in which heated material (**thermoplastic**) is forced under pressure into a water-cooled mold —**in·jec·tion-mold·ed** *adj*

in-joke *n* a joke that is shared and understood only by a small group of people

in·ju·di·cious /ìn joo díshəss/ *adj* lacking in judgment or discretion —**in·ju·di·cious·ly** *adv* —**in·ju·di·cious·ness** *n*

In·jun /ínjən/ *n* an offensive term for a Native North American (*dated*) [Late 17C. < a pronunciation of INDIAN]

in·junc·tion /in júngkshən/ *n* **1.** COURT ORDER a court order that requires somebody involved in a legal action to do something or refrain from doing something **2.** COMMAND a command or order, especially from somebody in a position of authority **3.** ACT OF ORDERING SOMEBODY the act of ordering somebody to do or not to do something [15C. < late Latin *injunction-* < Latin *injungere* "enjoin" < *jungere* "to join"]

in·jure /ínjər/ (**-jured, -jur·ing, -jures**) *vt* **1.** HURT SOMEBODY OR SOMETHING to cause physical damage to a person, animal, or body part **2.** OFFEND SOMEBODY to cause somebody distress by an unkind action or words **3.** DO LEGAL WRONG TO SOMEBODY to wrong somebody by word or deed in such a way that redress by legal means is available **4.** DAMAGE SOMEBODY'S REPUTATION to damage somebody's reputation, career, or chances of success [15C. Via French < Latin *injuriare* < *injuria* (see INJURY)] —**in·jur·a·ble** *adj* —**in·jur·er** *n*

SYNONYMS See ***harm***.

in·ju·ri·ous /in jŏoree əss/ *adj* **1.** causing harm, hurt, damage, or distress **2.** damaging somebody's reputation, career, or chances of success [15C. Via French < Latin *injuriosus* < *injuria* (see INJURY)] —**in·ju·ri·ous·ly** *adv* —**in·ju·ri·ous·ness** *n*

in·ju·ry /ínjəree/ (*plural* **-ries**) *n* **1.** PHYSICAL DAMAGE physical damage to the body or a body part ○ *They escaped without injury.* **2.** WOUND an instance of physical damage to a body part ○ *a serious back injury* **3.** HARM TO REPUTATION harm caused to somebody's career or reputation by scandal, rumor, or defamation **4.** LAW INFRINGEMENT OF RIGHTS the violation of a person's or group's rights, against which legal action can be taken [14C. Via Anglo-Norman < Latin *injuria* "a wrong" < *injurius* "unjust" < *jus* "justice"]

in·ju·ry time *n* extra time allowed at the end of some games, especially soccer and rugby, to compensate for time spent attending to injured players during the game

~~**injust**~~ incorrect spelling of **unjust**

in·jus·tice /in jústiss/ *n* unfair or unjust treatment of somebody, or an instance of this [14C. Via French < Latin *injustitia* < *injustus* "unjust" < + *justus* "just"]

ink /ingk/ *n* **1.** LIQUID FOR MAKING MARKS a colored liquid or paste used for writing, printing, or drawing **2.** LIQUID EJECTED BY OCTOPUS OR SQUID a dark brown liquid (**sepia**) ejected from a gland (**ink sac**) near the anus by most cephalopods, including the octopus and the squid, to distract predators **3.** PRINT PUBLICITY publicity, especially in the print media (*slang*) ○ *The stunt got him all kinds of ink.* ■ *vt* (**inked, ink·ing, inks**) **1.** WRITE SOMETHING WITH INK to write or draw with ink on a piece of paper or other surface **2.** COVER SURFACE WITH INK to coat something with ink or apply ink to something, usually in preparation for printing **3.** SIGN CONTRACT to put or obtain a signature on a contract or other document (*informal*) [13C. Via Old French *enque* < Greek *enkauston* "purple ink" < *enkaiein* "burn in"; from the process of encaustic painting] —**ink·er** *n*

ink in *vt* to go over the pencil lines of a drawing or design in ink

ink·ber·ry /íngk bèrree/ (*plural* **-ries**) *n* **1.** a black berry from a North American evergreen bush **2.** an evergreen bush that has leathery dark-green leaves and produces black berries. Native to: eastern North America. Latin name: *Ilex glabra.* **3.** BOT same as **pokeweed** [Mid-18C. < the use of the berries for making ink]

ink·blot /íngk blòt/ *n* **1.** a stain or spot of spilled ink **2.** any of the ten abstract patterns resembling an inkblot used in the Rorschach test

ink·blot test *n* PSYCHOL same as **Rorschach test**

ink-cap *n Can, UK* FUNGI same as **inky cap**

ink·horn /íngk hàwrn/ *n* a small portable ink container made from horn or a similar material and used in former times ■ *adj* excessively scholarly in style or language, especially in the use of terms derived from Latin and Greek

in-kind *adj* **1.** in the form of goods or services rather than in cash **2.** giving something that is equivalent to what has been received

ink-jet print·er *n* a printer that prints using particles or droplets of electrically charged ink from a matrix of tiny ink jets

in·kle /íngk'l/ *n* a narrow linen tape. Use: trimmings. [Mid-16C. Origin ?]

in·kling /íngkling/ *n* **1.** a vague idea or suspicion about a fact, event, or person ○ *I had no inkling that he was unhappy.* **2.** an indication of how to go about something ○ *Could you give me some inkling of where to look?* [Early 16C. < obsolete *inkle* "utter in an undertone," origin ?]

ink sac *n* a large gland with an opening close to the anus of most cephalopods, including the octopus and squid, from which ink (**sepia**) is ejected to distract predators

ink·stand /íngk stànd/ *n* **1.** a rack or stand that is kept on a desk and contains bottles of ink, pens, and other writing materials **2.** same as **inkwell**

ink·well /íngk wèl/ *n* a small container for ink, especially one that fits into a hole in a desk

ink·y /íngkee/ (**-i·er, -i·est**) *adj* **1.** consisting of or covered in ink **2.** black or dark blue in color

ink·y cap *n US* a mushroom with a conical cap and gills on the underside that dissolve into an inky black pulp after the spores mature. Species include the common inky cap and the edible shaggymane. Genus: *Coprinus.* Can term **ink-cap**

in·lace *vt* another spelling of **enlace**

in·laid /ín làyd/ *adj* **1.** set into the surface of wood or another material, usually to provide decoration **2.** decorated with an inlaid pattern

in·land /ín lànd, ínlənd/ *adj* **1.** NOT NEAR COAST OR BORDER in or relating to the part of a country that is not near the coast or a border **2.** *UK* WITHIN COUNTRY occurring within a country, rather than between countries ■ *adv* IN OR INTO INLAND PART in or toward the interior of a country ■ *n* INLAND PART the interior of a country

In·land Rev·e·nue *n* in the United Kingdom, a British government department responsible for the collection and administration of direct taxes

In·land Sea /ín lànd-/ arm of the Pacific Ocean in Japan, between the islands of Honshu, Shikoku, and Kyushu. Length: 270 mi./430 km.

in-law *n* a relative by marriage (*informal*)

in-law suite, in-law a·part·ment *n* a self-contained apartment in or attached to a family home in which a parent of advanced years could live independently

in·lay /ín lày/ *vt* (**in·laid** /ín láyd, ín làyd/, **in·lay·ing, in·lays**) **1.** SET SOMETHING INTO SURFACE to set pieces of material such as wood, ivory, or stone into previously cut slots in a surface to form a decorative pattern **2.** DECORATE SOMETHING WITH INLAID DESIGN to decorate something such as a piece of furniture by setting pieces of wood, stone, ivory, or other material into its surface ■ *n* **1.** PIECES OF MATERIAL SET INTO SURFACE pieces of material such as wood, ivory, or stone set into the surface of a piece of furniture to form a decorative pattern **2.** DECORATIVE PATTERN a decorative pattern formed by inlaying **3.** FILLING FOR TOOTH a filling made of gold or porcelain that is inserted into a cavity in a tooth and cemented in position —**in·lay·er** /ín láy ər/ *n*

in·let /ín lèt, ínnlət/ *n* **1.** NARROW OPENING IN COASTLINE a narrow stretch of water reaching inland from a sea or lake **2.** STRETCH OF WATER BETWEEN TWO ISLANDS a narrow stretch of water between two islands **3.** PIECE OF EXTRA FABRIC a piece of fabric put into the seam of a garment to make it bigger or for decoration **4.** PASSAGE OR VALVE an opening through which liquid or gas enters a machine or other device ■ *vt* (**-let, -let·ing, -lets**) HANDICRAFT same as **inlay** [13C. < IN[1] + -LET]

in·li·er /ín lī ər/ *n* a rock formation in which older rocks are completely surrounded by younger rocks [Mid-19C. < IN-[2], after OUTLIER]

in-line *adj* describes a device or machine in which similar parts are located together and in a straight line

in-line skate

in-line skate *n* a roller skate with a boot that has three or four wheels mounted in a single line —**in-line skate** *vi* —**in-line skat·er** *n* —**in-line skat·ing** *n*

~~**inlist**~~ incorrect spelling of **enlist**

in loc. cit. *adv* same as **loc. cit.** [Abbreviation of Latin *in loco citato* "in the place cited"]

in lo·co pa·ren·tis /in lṑkō pə réntiss/ *adv* having or taking on the responsibilities of a parent when dealing with somebody else's child [< Latin, "in the place of a parent"]

in·ly /ínnlee/ *adv* (*literary*) **1.** in an inward way **2.** with deep or intimate understanding

in·ly·ing /ín lī ing/ *adj* situated within a country or region

in·mate /ín màyt/ *n* somebody who is confined to a prison or a psychiatric hospital [Late 16C. < IN[1] + MATE[1] "companion"]

in me·di·as res /in meédee əss ráyss/ *adv* straight in or into the middle of a sequence of events, especially in a literary narrative that has no introduction (*formal*) [< Latin, "into the midst of things"]

in me·mo·ri·am /in mə máwree əm/ *prep, adv* in memory of or in a person's memory (*used in epitaphs and obituaries*) [< Latin]

in·mesh *vt* another spelling of **enmesh**

in-mi·grant *adj* coming from a different part of the same country ■ *n* somebody who travels from a different part of the same country

in-mi·grate *vi* to travel to a place from a different part of the same country —**in-mi·gra·tion** *n*

in·most *adj* same as **innermost** [Old English *innemest* < *inne* "in" + *mest* "most"]

inn /in/ *n* **1.** RESTAURANT a bar or restaurant **2.** HOTEL formerly, a place that provided food and lodging for travelers (*often used in the names of establishments*) **3.** *UK* RESIDENCE FOR STUDENTS formerly, a dormitory for students, especially those studying law [Old English, < Indo-European, "in"]

INN *abbr* PHARM international nonproprietary name

~~**innacurate**~~ incorrect spelling of **inaccurate**

in·nards /ínnərdz/ *npl* (*informal*) **1.** the internal organs of the body, especially the intestines **2.** the internal working parts of a machine or mechanical device [Early 19C. Alteration of INWARDS (plural noun)]

in·nate /i náyt/ *adj* **1.** PRESENT FROM BIRTH relating to qualities that a person or animal is born with **2.** INTEGRAL forming an integral part of something **3.** COMING FROM MIND coming directly from the mind rather than being acquired by experience or from external sources ○ *an innate sense of justice* **4.** BOT JOINED TO FILAMENT BY BASE describes an anther that is joined to the filament by its base only **5.** BIOL ORIGINATING WITHIN THALLUS forming an integral part of the thallus of an organism such as an alga or liverwort [15C. < Latin *innatus,* past participle of *innasci* "be born in" < *nasci* "be born"] —**in·nate·ly** *adv* —**in·nate·ness** *n*

in·nate re·leas·ing mech·a·nism *n* a process within the central nervous system of animals that, in response to specific stimuli, causes the animal to produce instinctive behavior. An example is the way that chicks of some birds peck at the red dot on the adult's beak.

in·ner /ínnər/ *adj* **1.** NEAR OR CLOSER TO CENTER located near or closer to the center of something ○ *the inner suburbs* **2.** BEING OR OCCURRING INSIDE located or happening on the inside of something ○ *an inner door* **3.** OF THE MIND relating to somebody's private feelings or happening in somebody's mind ○ *a quiet exterior that hid an inner confidence* **4.** NOT OBVIOUS needing to be examined closely or thought about in order to be seen or understood ○ *searching for the inner meaning of the text* **5.** PRIVILEGED most privileged or influential ○ *the inner circle* [Old English *innera* < Indo-European, "in"] —**in·ner·ly** *adv* —**in·ner·ness** *n*

in·ner child *n* an adult's conception of himself or herself as a child, often used as a tool in therapeutic processes to explore feelings about the person's childhood

in·ner cir·cle *n* a group of powerful or influential people within a larger group, often those closest to the leader

in·ner cit·y *n* the central or innermost parts of a city, particularly when associated with social problems such as inadequate housing and high levels of crime and unemployment

in·ner-di·rect·ed *adj* guided by personal beliefs rather than by norms imposed by society

in·ner ear *n* the fluid-filled part of the ear, including the cochlea, which is responsible for hearing, and the semicircular canals, which control balance

In·ner Light *n* in Quaker belief, the presence of God as a guiding force within the human soul

in·ner man *n* the soul or the spiritual or intellectual part of a man

In·ner Mon·go·li·a /ínnər-/ ➧ **Nei Monggol**

in·ner·most /ínnər mṑst/ *adj* **1.** most important, private, or personal ○ *innermost thoughts* **2.** taking place or being situated farthest from the outside

in·ner plan·et *n* any of the four planets Mercury, Venus, Earth, or Mars whose orbits lie closest to the Sun and are within the asteroid belt

in·ner prod·uct *n* MATH same as **scalar product**

in·ner sanc·tum *n* a very private place within a building or organization, to which only a few select or privileged people are admitted (*formal*)

in·ner·sole /ínnər sṑl/ *n* a foot-shaped piece of leather, sheepskin, or synthetic material worn inside a shoe or boot to provide a better fit or added warmth

in·ner space *n* **1.** the environment that exists beneath the surface of the sea **2.** somebody's inner spiritual or psychological depths

in·ner·spring /ínnər spring/ *adj* describes a mattress that has many helical springs inside a thick padded cover

in·ner tube *n* a hollow rubber ring filled with compressed air that fits inside a pneumatic tire

in·ner·vate /i núr vàyt, ínnər-/ (**-vat·ed, -vat·ing, -vates**) *vt* **1.** to distribute nerves to an organ or body part **2.** to cause a muscle, organ, or other part of the body to act —**in·ner·va·tion** /ínnər váysh'n/ *n* —**in·ner·va·tion·al** *adj*

in·ner·wear /ínnər wèr/ *n* clothing that is worn next to the skin, e.g., an undershirt or a slip

in·ner wom·an *n* the soul or the spiritual or intellectual part of a woman

In·ness /ínniss/, **George** (1825–94) US artist. He is known for his many landscapes such as *Home of the Heron* (1893).

in·ning /ínning/ *n* each of the divisions of a game of baseball or softball during which each team bats until it makes three outs. Nine innings are standard for baseball and seven for softball, but extra innings are played if the score remains tied. [Old English *innung* < *innian* "put in" < IN[1]]

in·nings /ínningz/ (*plural same*) *n* **1.** PERIOD OF SUCCESS a period of opportunity or success, or a long active life or career **2.** CRICKET TURN AT BATTING the turn of a cricket player or team at batting **3.** CRICKET RUNS SCORED DURING INNINGS the runs scored by a cricket player or team during a turn at batting

in·nit /ínnit/ *contr UK* isn't it (*nonstandard; used as a tag question at the end of a statement*) ○ *Nice weather, innit?*

inn·keep·er /ín keèpər/ *n* an owner or manager of an inn

in·no·cence /ínnəss'nss/ *n* **1. ABSENCE OF GUILT** the state of not being guilty of a crime or offense **2. HARMLESSNESS** harmlessness in intention **3. FREEDOM FROM SIN** freedom from sin or evil **4. LACK OF WORLDLY EXPERIENCE** a lack of experience of the world, especially when this results in a failure to recognize the harmful intentions of other people **5. IGNORANCE** ignorance of the serious consequences of something such as an act or remark **6. CHASTITY** sexual inexperience **7.** LAW **LAWFULNESS** the state of being permitted by law **8.** BOT same as **blue-eyed Mary** [14C. Via French < Latin *innocentia* < *innocent-* (see INNOCENT)] —**in·no·cen·cy** *n*

CULTURAL NOTE ***The Age of Innocence***, a novel (1920) by Edith Wharton. It tells the story of a young man's failure to rise above the repressive social conventions of fashionable New York society in the late 19th century. Newland Archer, a sensitive and intelligent lawyer, falls in love with his wife's cousin, Ellen Olenska, a mysterious sophisticate who has returned from Europe bearing the social stigma of a marital separation. The novel reveals the subtle workings by which his elite tribe reaffirms its mores and thwarts his desire. Martin Scorsese directed a movie adaptation in 1993.

in·no·cent /ínnəss'nt/ *adj* **1. NOT GUILTY** not guilty of a crime or offense **2. WITHIN THE LAW** permitted by or acting within the law ○ *innocent pastimes* **3. HARMLESS IN INTENTION** not intended to cause harm ○ *an innocent remark* **4. UNCORRUPTED** pure and uncorrupted by evil, sin, or experience of the world ○ *an innocent mind* **5. NAIVE** more trusting or naive than most people through lack of experience of life or failure to recognize the motives of others ○ *an innocent young girl caught up in a terrible situation* **6. IGNORANT OF SOMETHING** having very little or no knowledge of something ○ *innocent of the finer points of etiquette* **7. LACKING IN SOMETHING** completely lacking in a particular quality ○ *innocent of any artistic skill* ■ *n* **1. BLAMELESS PERSON** a blameless vulnerable person, especially a very young child **2. NAIVE PERSON** a simple, naive, or inexperienced person [14C. Via French < Latin *innocent-* < *in-* "not" + present participle of *nocere* "harm"] —**in·no·cent·ly** *adv*

In·no·cent III /ínnəss'nt/, (1160?–1216) pope (1198–1216). He exercised considerable power over the European political rulers of the day, launched the Fourth Crusade (1204), and summoned the Fourth Lateran Council (1215).

> "Nothing which happens in the world should escape the notice of the supreme pontiff."
> [Innocent III, *Letter*; 1199]

~~innoculation~~ incorrect spelling of **inoculation**

in·noc·u·ous /i nókyoo əss/ *adj* **1.** not intended to cause offense or provoke a strong reaction and unlikely to do so ○ *an innocuous comment* **2.** harmless in effect ○ *an innocuous white powder* [Late 16C. < Latin *innocuus* < *nocuus* "hurtful" < *nocere* "to harm"] —**in·noc·u·ous·ly** *adv* —**in·noc·u·ous·ness** *n*

in·nom·i·nate /i nómmənət/ *adj* **1.** without a name (*formal*) **2.** same as **anonymous** (senses 1–2) (*literary*) [Mid-17C. < late Latin *innominatus* < *nominatus* "named" < *nominat-* (see NOMINATE)]

in·nom·i·nate ar·ter·y *n* a short artery rising from the arch of the aorta toward the right upper part of the body. It divides to form the right common carotid artery, which supplies blood to the head, and the right subclavian artery, which supplies blood to the right arm.

in·nom·i·nate bone *n* ANAT same as **hipbone** (*technical*) [Because early anatomists could not think of anything it resembled]

in·nom·i·nate vein *n* either of two large veins on opposite sides of the neck that join to form the superior vena cava, one of the two veins taking blood to the heart

in·no·vate /ínnə vàyt/ (**-vat·ed, -vat·ing, -vates**) *vi* to introduce a new way of doing something or a new device [Mid-16C. < Latin *innovat-*, past participle of *innovare* "renew" < *novus* "new"] —**in·no·vat·or** *n* —**in·no·va·to·ry** /ínnəvə tàwree/ *adj*

in·no·va·tion /ìnnə váysh'n/ *n* **1.** the act or process of inventing or introducing something new **2.** a new invention or way of doing something ○ *suspicious of fax machines and other technological innovations* —**in·no·va·tion·al** *adj*

in·no·va·tive /ínnə vàytiv/ *adj* new and original, or taking a new and original approach —**in·no·va·tive·ly** *adv* —**in·no·va·tive·ness** *n*

Inns·bruck /ínz brŏŏk/ city, tourist center, and capital of the Tirol Province, western Austria, situated on the Inn River approximately 85 mi./137 km southwest of Salzburg. Population: 113,826 (2001).

INN stem *n* one of the names selected by the World Health Organization that are the legally required generic names for product labeling for most countries in the world. Most new generic drug names are formed by combining the most appropriate stem with a prefix that may or may not have some medical significance.

In·nu /í nōō/ *n* **1.** a member of an Algonquian people living in northern Quebec and Labrador **2.** the Algonquian language of the Innu people **3.** PEOPLES same as **Mushuau Innu** [< Montagnais, "people"] —**In·nu** *adj*

in·nu·en·do /ìnnyoo éndō/ (*plural* **-does** or **-dos**) *n* **1. HINT OF SOMETHING IMPROPER** an indirect remark or gesture that usually carries a suggestion of impropriety ○ *"'I suppose Mary Garth admires Mr. Lydgate,' said Rosamund, not without a touch of innuendo."* (George Eliot, *Middlemarch*; 1872) **2.** LAW **INTERPRETATION OF POSSIBLY LIBELOUS LANGUAGE** in a legal action for libel or slander, an interpretation of words that are claimed to be libelous where the meaning is not obvious **3.** LAW **GLOSS FOR TECHNICAL LEGAL WORD** an explanation of a technical legal word, usually given in parentheses [Mid-16C. < Latin, "by intimation" < *innuere* "nod to, signify"]

In·nu·it *n, adj* PEOPLES, LANG another spelling of **Inuit**

in·nu·mer·a·ble /i nōōmərəb'l/ *adj* too many to be counted [14C. < Latin *innumerabilis* < *numerus* "number"] —**in·nu·mer·a·bil·i·ty** /i nōōmərə bíllətee/ *n* —**in·nu·mer·a·ble·ness** *n* —**in·nu·mer·a·bly** *adv*

in·nu·mer·ate /i nōōmərət/ *adj* lacking a basic knowledge of mathematics and unable to use numbers in calculation

in·ob·ser·vance /ìnnəb zúrvənss/ *n* **1.** failure to comply with something, especially a rule, law, or custom **2.** lack of heed or attention —**in·ob·ser·vant** *adj* —**in·ob·ser·vant·ly** *adv*

in·ob·tru·sive /ìnnəb trōōssiv/ *adj* same as **unobtrusive**

~~inocence~~ incorrect spelling of **innocence**

in·oc·u·la MED plural of **inoculum**

in·oc·u·lant /i nókyələnt/ *n* MED same as **inoculum**

in·oc·u·late /i nókyə làyt/ (**-lat·ed, -lat·ing, -lates**) *vt* **1.** to inject or introduce a serum, antigen, or a weakened form of a disease-producing pathogen into the body of a person or animal in order to create immunity to the disease ○ *inoculated every child against polio* **2.** to introduce microorganisms into a culture medium [15C. < Latin *inoculat-*, past participle of *inoculare* "graft on a plant part" < *oculus* "bud, eye"] —**in·oc·u·la·bil·i·ty** /i nòkyələ bíllətee/ *n* —**in·oc·u·la·ble** *adj* —**in·oc·u·la·tion** /i nòkyə láysh'n/ *n* —**in·oc·u·la·tive** *adj* —**in·oc·u·la·tor** *n*

in·oc·u·lum /i nókyələm/ (*plural* **-la** /-lə/) *n* material injected into a person or animal to create resistance to a disease [Early 20C. < Latin *inoculare* (see INOCULATE), after COAGULUM]

in·o·dor·ous /in ṓdərəss/ *adj* having no smell

in·of·fen·sive /ìnnə fénssiv/ *adj* not causing harm, annoyance, or offense ○ *the remark was inoffensive enough* —**in·of·fen·sive·ly** *adv* —**in·of·fen·sive·ness** *n*

in·of·fi·cious /ìnnə físhəss/ *adj* violating standards of morality or natural affection, especially failing to give an heir a just, and, in some cases, legally required, share of an inheritance ○ *an inofficious will* —**in·of·fi·cious·ly** *adv* —**in·of·fi·cious·ness** *n*

İn·ö·nü /éenə nyōō/, **Ismet** (1884–1973) Turkish soldier and politician. He was the first premier of the Turkish Republic (1923–37) and its second president (1938–50).

in·op·er·a·ble /in óppərəb'l, -óppr-/ *adj* **1.** describes a medical condition that has advanced to a stage at which surgical intervention would serve no useful purpose **2.** not practical or workable **3.** same as **inoperative** (sense 1) —**in·op·er·a·bil·i·ty** /in òppərə bíllətee, -òppr-/ *n* —**in·op·er·a·ble·ness** *n* —**in·op·er·a·bly** *adv*

in·op·er·a·tive /in óppərətiv, -óppr-/ *adj* **1.** not functioning properly or as usual **2.** not effective or no longer valid or able to be enforced —**in·op·er·a·tive·ly** *adv* —**in·op·er·a·tive·ness** *n*

in·op·por·tune /in òppər tōōn/ *adj* happening at a bad moment or an inconvenient time —**in·op·por·tune·ly** *adv* —**in·op·por·tune·ness** *n* —**in·op·por·tu·ni·ty** *n*

in·or·di·nate /in áwrd'nət/ *adj* **1.** beyond reasonable limits in amount or degree ○ *"capable of expressing an inordinate degree of unreason"* (Henry James, *Roderick Hudson*; 1876) **2.** showing a lack of restraint or control (*archaic or literary*) [14C. < Latin *inordinatus* "out of order" < *ordo* "order"] —**in·or·di·na·cy** *n* —**in·or·di·nate·ly** *adv* —**in·or·di·nate·ness** *n*

in·or·gan·ic /ìn awr gánnik/ *adj* **1.** composed of minerals rather than living material **2.** describes chemical compounds that contain no carbon, excluding the oxides of carbon, carbon disulfide, cyanides, and their associated acids and salts —**in·or·gan·i·cal·ly** *adv*

in·or·gan·ic chem·is·try *n* the branch of chemistry relating to inorganic compounds

in·os·cu·late /in óskyə làyt/ (**-lat·ed, -lat·ing, -lates**) *vti* to join and blend with something else, or join or blend one thing with another [Late 17C. < IN-[2] + Latin *osculat-*, past participle of *osculare* "provide with a mouth" < *osculum* "little mouth" < *os* "mouth"] —**in·os·cu·la·tion** /in òskyə láysh'n/ *n*

in·o·sine /ínnə seen/ *n* an organic compound (**nucleoside**) involved in the formation of purines and energy metabolism. Use: sports supplement, transplant management.

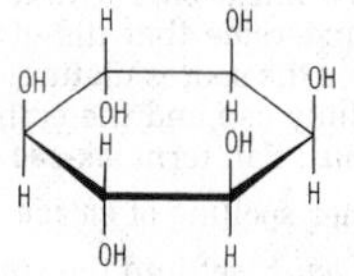

inositol

in·o·si·tol /i nṓssə tàwl, -tōl/ *n* a cyclic alcohol that is a component of cell membranes and a precursor of various messenger molecules. Formula: $C_6H_{12}O_6$. [Late 19C. < Greek *in-* "sinew" + -OSE[2] + -ITE[1] + -OL[1]]

in·o·trop·ic /èenə tróppik, -trṓpik, ìnə-/ *adj* having an effect on the force of muscular contraction ○ *an inotropic drug* [Early 20C. < Greek *in-* "sinew"]

in·pa·tient /ín pàysh'nt/ *n* somebody receiving medical treatment that requires a hospital stay ■ *adj* relating to, designed for, or used by inpatients

in per·pe·tu·um /in pər péttoo əm/ *adv* LAW same as **forever** (sense 1) [< Latin]

in per·so·nam /in pər sṓnəm/ *adj, adv* made about or directed at a person rather than at property [< Latin, "against a person"]

in pet·to /in péttō/ *adj* not disclosing publicly the name of a cardinal appointed by the pope [Late 17C. < Italian, "in the breast"]

in·phase /ín fàyz/ *adj* of the same electrical phase

INPO *abbr* ONLINE in no particular order (*used in e-mails or text messages*)

in pos·se /in pó say/ *adj* potentially rather than in reality (*formal*) [< Latin]

in·pour·ing /ín pàwring/ *n* a sudden flowing in of a large amount of something

in-proc·ess *adj* **1.** in the process of happening **2.** in the process of being manufactured

in pro·pri·a per·so·na /in prṓpree ə pər sṓnə/ *adv* in person, especially when unrepresented by a lawyer [< Latin, "in your own person"]

in·put /ín pŏŏt/ *n* **1. CONTRIBUTION** a contribution to something, especially comments or suggestions made to a group **2. SOMETHING GOING IN** something that enters a process or situation from the outside and is then acted upon or integrated ○ *dollar input* ○ *sensory input* **3.** ELECTRONICS **ELECTRICITY THAT DRIVES SOMETHING** power, electrical energy, or an electric signal that enters a device and is usually recovered in the form of work or some other output effect **4.** COMPUT **DATA ENTERED INTO COMPUTER** data entered into a computer for processing **5.** COMPUT **COMPUTER TERMINAL** a terminal or connection where data enters a computer ■ *v* (**-put·ted** or **-put, -put·ting, -puts**) **1.** *vt* **CONTRIBUTE INFORMATION** to provide information to help somebody make a decision (*informal*) **2. ENTER DATA** to enter data into a computer —**in·put·ter** *n*

in·put/out·put *n* hardware or software that controls the passage of information into and out of a computer or computer component

in·quest /ín kwèst/ *n* **1.** an official inquiry in front of a magistrate, coroner, or jury into the facts of a case such as a sudden unexpected death **2.** an investigation of the facts of a situation, particularly one that had an undesired outcome (*literary*) [14C. Via French < Latin *inquesta* < *inquirere* "inquire"]

in·qui·e·tude /in kwī́ ə to͞od/ *n* a worried or restless state of mind (*literary*) [15C. < late Latin *inquietudo* < Latin *quietus* "quiet"]

in·qui·line /ínkwə lī̀n, ínkwəlin/ *n* an animal that lives in the nest or home of another species [Mid-17C. < Latin *inquilinus* "tenant, lodger" < *incolere* "inhabit" < *colere* "dwell"]

in·quire /in kwī́r/ (**-quired, -quir·ing, -quires**), **en·quire** /en-/ *v* **1.** *vti* to ask a question ○ *inquire about a job* ○ *May I inquire to whom I have the honor of speaking?* **2.** *vi* to try to discover the facts of a case [13C. Via French < Latin *inquirere* "inquire into" < *quaerere* "seek"] —**in·quir·er** *n*

in·quir·ing /in kwī́ring/, **en·quir·ing** /en-/ *adj* **1.** eager to learn new things **2.** appearing to want to know or learn something ○ *an inquiring glance from the attendant* —**in·quir·ing·ly** *adv*

in·quir·y /in kwī́ree, ínkwəree/ (*plural* **-ies**), **en·quir·y** /en kwī́ree, énkwəree/ *n* **1.** a formal investigation to determine the facts of a case **2.** a request for information

in·qui·si·tion /ìnkwə zísh'n/ *n* **1.** a succession of detailed and relentless questions **2.** an inquiry or investigation that is harsh or unfair [14C. Via French < Latin *inquisition-* < *inquirere* (see INQUIRE)] —**in·qui·si·tion·al** *adj* —**in·qui·si·tion·ist** *n*

In·qui·si·tion *n* a former organization in the Roman Catholic Church established to find, question, and sentence those who did not hold orthodox religious beliefs. The Spanish Inquisition lasted until the 19th century and was known for its harsh punishments and use of torture.

in·quis·i·tive /in kwízzətiv/ *adj* **1.** eager for knowledge **2.** too curious about other people's business [14C. Via French < late Latin *inquisitivus* < Latin *inquirere* (see INQUIRE)] —**in·quis·i·tive·ly** *adv* —**in·quis·i·tive·ness** *n*

in·quis·i·tor /in kwízzitər/ *n* **1.** somebody who relentlessly asks searching or hostile questions **2.** *also* **In·quis·i·tor** an official working for the Inquisition [Early 16C. Via French < Latin < *inquirere* (see INQUIRE)]

in·quis·i·to·ri·al /in kwìzzə táwree əl/ *adj* **1.** resembling a formal inquiry, especially in using rigorous or relentless questioning **2.** describes a trial in which one person is both judge and prosecutor —**in·quis·i·to·ri·al·ly** *adv*

in re /-rée, -ráy/ *prep* with regard to [< Latin, "in the matter of"]

in rem /-rém/ *adj* describes something such as a law or right made about or directed at property rather than a person [< Latin, "against a thing"]

in-res·i·dence *adj* officially connected with a university or other institution, often as a teacher or lecturer, but allowed time for original creative work (*used in combination*) ○ *She completed her book while serving as poet-in-residence at a small college.*

I.N.R.I. *abbr* Jesus of Nazareth, king of the Jews (*used as an inscription over the head of the crucified Jesus Christ*) [Latin *Iesus Nazarenus Rex Iudaeorum*]

in·ro /ín rṑ/ (*plural same*) *n* a small ornamented box worn hanging from the sash of a kimono with compartments for holding cosmetics, perfumes, and medicines [Early 17C. < Japanese *inrō* < *in* "seal" + *rō* "basket"]

in·road /ín rṑd/ *n* **1.** a gradual encroachment on something (*usually used in the plural*) ○ *Young companies using electronic sales methods have made inroads into traditional markets.* **2.** a sudden attack on an enemy camp (*archaic*) [Mid-16C. < IN[1] + ROAD in the obsolete sense "a riding, raid"]

in·rush /ín rùsh/ *n* a sudden flooding or flowing in

INS *abbr* **1.** GOV Immigration and Naturalization Service **2.** NAVIG inertial navigation system **3.** MEDIA International News Service

ins. *abbr* **1.** MEASURE inches **2.** inscription **3.** *also* **Ins.** inspector **4.** insulation **5.** insurance

in·sal·i·vate /in sállə vàyt/ (**-vat·ed, -vat·ing, -vates**) *vt* to mix food with saliva in the process of chewing —**in·sal·i·va·tion** /in sàllə váysh'n/ *n*

in·sa·lu·bri·ous /in sə lo͞obree əss/ *adj* not pleasant, healthy, or wholesome —**in·sa·lu·bri·ous·ly** *adv* —**in·sa·lu·bri·ty** *n*

in·sane /in sáyn/ *adj* **1. LEGALLY CONSIDERED AS PSYCHIATRICALLY DISORDERED** considered legally incompetent or irresponsible because of a psychiatric disorder **2. LACKING REASONABLE THOUGHT** showing a complete lack of reason or foresight (*informal*) ■ *npl* **PEOPLE LEGALLY CONSIDERED AS PSYCHIATRICALLY DISORDERED** people who are considered legally incompetent or irresponsible because of a psychiatric disorder (*dated*) [Mid-16C. < Latin *insanus* < *sanus* "healthy, sane"] —**in·sane·ly** *adv* —**in·sane·ness** *n*

in·san·i·tar·y /in sánnə tèrree/ *adj* dirty or unhygienic and thus likely to cause disease —**in·san·i·ta·tion** /in sànnə táysh'n/ *n*

in·san·i·ty /in sánnətee/ (*plural* **-ties**) *n* **1.** extreme foolishness, or an act that demonstrates such foolishness **2.** legal incompetence or irresponsibility that results from a psychiatric disorder

in·sa·tia·ble /in sáyshəb'l/ *adj* always needing more and impossible to satisfy [15C. < Old French *insaciable* < Latin *satiare* (see SATIATE)] —**in·sa·tia·bil·i·ty** /in sàyshə bíllətee/ *n* —**in·sa·tia·ble·ness** *n* —**in·sa·tia·bly** *adv*

in·sa·ti·ate /in sáyshee ət/ *adj* same as **insatiable** (*literary*) [15C. < Latin *insatiatus* < *satiatus*, past participle of *satiare* (see SATIATE)] —**in·sa·ti·ate·ly** *adv* —**in·sa·ti·ate·ness** *n*

in·scape /ín skàyp/ *n* the distinctive and essential inner quality of something, especially a natural object or a scene in nature [Mid-19C. Probably after LANDSCAPE]

in·scribe /in skrī́b/ (**-scribed, -scrib·ing, -scribes**) *vt* **1. PUT WRITING ON SOMETHING** to write, print, or engrave words or letters on a surface **2. WRITE SOMETHING ON LIST** to add a name to a list or book **3. WRITE DEDICATION ON SOMETHING** to write a signed message to somebody in a book or on a photograph, often when presenting it as a gift **4.** MATH **DRAW GEOMETRIC FIGURE WITHIN ANOTHER** to draw a geometric figure within another so that all of the second figure lies within the first and touches it at as many points as possible ○ *inscribe a circle within a square* [15C. < Latin *inscribere* "write on" < *scribere* "write"] —**in·scrib·a·ble** *adj* —**in·scrib·er** *n*

in·scrip·tion /in skrípsh'n/ *n* **1.** a sequence of words or letters written, printed, or engraved on a surface **2.** a signed message written in a book or on a photograph, often when it is being presented as a gift [14C. < Latin *inscription-* < past participle of *inscribere* (see INSCRIBE)] —**in·scrip·tion·al** *adj*

in·scrip·tive /in skríptiv/ *adj* relating to or constituting an inscription —**in·scrip·tive·ly** *adv*

in·scru·ta·ble /in skro͞otəb'l/ *adj* not expressing anything clearly and thus hard to interpret ○ *his inscrutable expression* [15C. Via French < ecclesiastical Latin *inscrutabilis* < Latin *scrutari* "investigate"] —**in·scru·ta·bil·i·ty** /in skro͞otə bíllətee/ *n* —**in·scru·ta·ble·ness** *n* —**in·scru·ta·bly** *adv*

in·seam /ín sèem/ *n* **1.** the inner seam of a pair of pants, from the crotch to the bottom of the pant leg **2.** the measurement of a pant leg's inner seam

in·sect /ín sèkt/ *n* **1. SMALL SIX-LEGGED ANIMAL** an air-breathing invertebrate animal (**arthropod**) with a body that has well-defined segments, including a head, thorax, abdomen, two antennae, three pairs of legs, and usually two sets of wings. There are more than a million species of insects including flies, crickets, bees, beetles, and gnats. Class: Insecta. **2. SOMETHING LIKE INSECT** a small animal that resembles an insect, e.g., a spider or centipede (*not in technical use*) **3. CONTEMPTIBLE PERSON** somebody viewed with contempt, especially somebody regarded as unimportant (*insult*) [Early 17C. < Latin *insectum* < *insecare* "cut up" < *secare* "to cut"] —**in·sect·an** /in séktən/ *adj*

in·sec·tar·i·um /in sek térree əm/ (*plural* **-i·ums** or **-i·a** /-ee ə/), **in·sec·ta·ry** /in séktəree, in séktəree/ (*plural* **-ries**) *n* a place for breeding or observing insects

in·sec·ti·cide /in sékti sī̀d/ *n* a chemical substance used to kill insects —**in·sec·ti·cid·al** /in sèkti sī́d'l/ *adj* —**in·sec·ti·cid·al·ly** *adv*

in·sec·ti·vore /in sékti vàwr/ *n* **1.** a small nocturnal mammal that feeds primarily on insects. Moles, shrews, and hedgehogs are all insectivores. **2.** any plant or animal that feeds primarily on insects [Mid-19C. < modern Latin *Insectivora* "insect-eaters" < Latin *insectum* (see INSECT)] —**in·sec·tiv·o·rous** /in sek tívvərəss/ *adj*

in·se·cure /in sə kyo͝or/ *adj* **1. NOT CONFIDENT** anxious and lacking in self-confidence **2. NOT SAFE** unsafe and unprotected ○ *insecure premises that are vulnerable to thieves* **3. UNSTABLE** not firm or steady ○ *an insecure walkway* ○ *an insecure grip on his hand* —**in·se·cure·ly** *adv* —**in·se·cure·ness** *n*

in·se·cu·ri·ty /in sə kyo͝orətee/ (*plural* **-ties**) *n* **1. INSECURE CONDITION** the state of being unsafe or insecure **2. UNSAFE FEELING** a state of mind characterized by self-doubt and vulnerability **3. INSECURE PHENOMENON** an instance or cause of being insecure

in·sel·berg /ínss'l bùrg/ *n* an isolated hill or mountain, often heavily eroded on its lower slopes, rising abruptly from a plain [Early 20C. < German, "island mountain"]

in·sem·i·nate /in sémmi nàyt/ (**-nat·ed, -nat·ing, -nates**) *vt* to insert sperm into the reproductive tract of a female [Early 17C. < Latin *inseminat-*, past participle of *inseminare* "implant" < *semen* "seed"] —**in·sem·i·na·tion** /in sèmmi náysh'n/ *n*

in·sen·sate /in sén sàyt/ *adj* **1. WITHOUT FEELING** inanimate and thus unable to feel anything **2. COLD AND HEARTLESS** entirely lacking in sympathetic feeling or human kindness (*formal*) **3. THOUGHTLESS** lacking in common sense or reasonable thought (*formal*) [15C. < ecclesiastical Latin *insensatus* < late Latin *sensatus* "equipped with senses" < Latin *sensus* (see SENSE)] —**in·sen·sate·ly** *adv* —**in·sen·sate·ness** *n*

in·sen·si·ble /in sénssəb'l/ *adj* **1.** same as **insensate** (sense 1) **2. NOT CONSCIOUS** without feeling or consciousness **3. NOT AWARE OR RESPONSIVE** unaware of or unresponsive to something **4. UNNOTICEABLE** so small or gradual as to be almost imperceptible ○ *an insensible shift in emphasis* [14C. Via French < Latin *insensibilis* "imperceptible" < *sensus* (see SENSE)] —**in·sen·si·bil·i·ty** /in sènssə bíllətee/ *n* —**in·sen·si·ble·ness** *n* —**in·sen·si·bly** *adv*

in·sen·si·tive /in sénssətiv/ *adj* **1. THOUGHTLESS** insufficiently aware of other people's feelings and unable to respond to them appropriately **2. NOT REACTING PHYSICALLY** not responsive to a physical stimulus such as touch or sound **3. INDIFFERENT AND UNRESPONSIVE** indifferent to the importance of something and therefore not responding to it —**in·sen·si·tive·ly** *adv* —**in·sen·si·tive·ness** *n* —**in·sen·si·tiv·i·ty** /in sènssə tívvətee/ *n*

in·sen·tient /in sénshənt/ *adj* without life, consciousness, or perception —**in·sen·tience** *n*

in·sep·a·ra·ble /in séppərəb'l, -séppre-/ *adj* **1.** sharing a close friendship and always seen or found together ○ *The two girls became inseparable.* **2.** so closely linked as to be impossible to consider separately ○ *Reading and the ability to spell will seem inseparable.* —**in·sep·a·ra·bil·i·ty** /in sèppərə bíllətee, -sèppre-/ *n* —**in·sep·a·ra·ble·ness** *n* —**in·sep·a·ra·bly** *adv*

in·sert *vt* /in súrt/ (**-sert·ed, -sert·ing, -serts**) **1. PLACE SOMETHING INSIDE SOMETHING** to put something inside or into something else ○ *Insert the screws in the holes already drilled.* **2. ADD SOMETHING TO SOMETHING** to add new material to the body of something, especially a text ■ *n* /ín sùrt/ **1. ADVERTISING SUPPLEMENT IN MAGAZINE** a supplement in the form of a single sheet or booklet placed inside a magazine or newspaper, usually as advertising **2. ADDED PART** a piece of fabric, usually contrasting, that is sewn into a main piece [15C. < Latin *insert-*, past participle of *inserere* < *serere* "join"] —**in·sert·a·ble** *adj* —**in·sert·er** *n*

in·ser·tion /in súrsh'n/ *n* **1. ADDITION** the act of putting something into something else **2. SOMETHING ADDED** material that is inserted into a text **3. ATTACHMENT POINT** the point of attachment of something, e.g., the point at which a leaf is joined to its stem or a muscle to a bone it moves **4.** GENETICS **INSERTED GENETIC MATERIAL** a segment of DNA that is inserted into a gene sequence **5.** AEROSP same as **injection** (senses 8–9) —**in·ser·tion·al** *adj*

in·ser·tion stitch *n* an embroidery stitch that joins two pieces of fabric together and decorates the gap between them

in·serv·ice *adj* **1.** taking place while somebody is employed full time ○ *in-service training* **2.** working as a full-time employee

in·ses·so·ri·al /in se sáwree əl/ *adj* used to describe birds that are adapted, or have feet that are adapted, for perching [Mid-19C. < modern Latin *Insessores*, former order name < past participle of Latin *insidere* (see INSIDIOUS)]

in·set *vt* /in sét/ (**-set, -set·ting, -sets**) **PLACE SMALLER THING IN LARGER THING** to insert something into a larger thing, e.g., a gem in a ring or a small map in the corner of a larger map ■ *n* /ín sèt/ **1. THING PLACED IN SOMETHING LARGER** something inserted into a larger thing ○ *a map of the state with city maps as insets* **2.** GEOG **CHANNEL** a place where something flows in, especially the tide

in·shal·lah /in shállə/, **in·sh'al·lah** *interj* an expression meaning "if God wills," used to suggest that something in the future is uncertain [Mid-19C. < Arabic *in šā 'Allāh*]

in·shore *adj* /ín shàwr/ near or toward the coast ○ *inshore waters* ■ *adv* /in sháwr/ toward the coast from the direction of the sea

in·shrine *vt* another spelling of **enshrine**

in·side /in sīd, ín sīd/ CORE MEANING: a grammatical word indicating the interior part of something, or the part that is enclosed by or surrounded with something ○ (adv) *I opened the door and looked inside.* ○ (adj) *his inside jacket pocket* ○ (n) *I looked around the room, gnawing the inside of my cheek nervously.* ○ (prep) *The jewels are kept inside a locked box.*

1. *adj, prep* **WITHIN ORGANIZATION** happening or coming from within an organization ○ *They had inside knowledge about the takeover bid.* ○ *things that were going on inside the committee* **2.** *adv, prep* **RELATING TO INNER FEELINGS** indicating emotions that are not expressed ○ *She doesn't like to look inside and face up to what she's really like.* ○ *Seeing her like that had snapped something inside him.* **3.** *prep* **WITHIN PARTICULAR TIME** done in a period of time less than the one stated (*informal*) ○ *We managed to completely redecorate the room inside seven hours.* **4.** *adj* **AT EDGE OF ROAD** farthest from the center of a road **5.** *adj* SPORTS **NEARER TO CENTER OF PLAYING AREA** in soccer, field hockey, and other sports, describes a position nearer to the center of the field than another of the same name ○ *inside right* **6.** *adv* **IN PRISON** serving time in prison (*informal*) ○ *He was inside for three years.* **7.** *n* **INNER EDGE** the part of a road or path farthest from the center ○ *was forced to pass him on the inside* **8.** *n* **PRIVILEGED ACCESS** a position that gives access to privileged information ○ *information from someone on the inside* **9.** *npl* **in·sides** ANAT **INTERNAL ORGANS** the internal organs of the body, especially the stomach and bowels (*informal*) ◇ **inside of** within a particular period of time (*informal*) ◇ **inside out** with the part that is normally inside facing out ◇ **know something inside out** to know something extremely well

USAGE inside, inside of, or **within**? Though the idiomatic expressions ***inside*** and ***inside of*** in the sense "within a given amount of time" are used in informal writing and conversation (*We'll be finished inside of a month*), the usage may be regarded as inappropriate to formal writing. Therefore, the safest choice is ***within***, as in *We'll be finished within a month.*

in·side ad·dress *n* the name, title, and street address of the person to whom a business letter is written, as it appears on the letter above the salutation

in·side in·for·ma·tion *n* something secret or confidential known only to somebody who holds a position within a corporation or other organization

in·side job *n* a crime carried out by or with the help of somebody who works for the person or organization affected (*informal*)

In·side Pas·sage /in sīd pássij/ natural protected waterway along the northwestern coast of North America from Seattle, Washington, to Skagway, Alaska. It is an important year-round shipping lane made up of a series of straits sheltered from the Pacific Ocean by islands. Length: 950 mi./1,530 km.

in·sid·er /in sīdər/ *n* a member of a group who knows all about its inner workings

in·sid·er trad·ing, in·sid·er deal·ing *n* profitable trading in securities that is done using access to privileged information. Such trading is usually illegal.

in·side track *n* **1.** the lane of an oval racetrack nearest the center and thus shorter than the outer lanes **2.** an advantageous position

in·sid·i·ous /in síddee əss/ *adj* slowly and subtly harmful or destructive ○ *an insidious evil* [Mid-16C. < Latin *insidiosus* < *insidiae* "ambush" < *insidere* "sit on, lie in wait" < *sedere* "sit"] —**in·sid·i·ous·ly** *adv* —**in·sid·i·ous·ness** *n*

USAGE insidious or **invidious**? Though these words are spelled similarly and both have negative meanings, they are not interchangeable. ***Insidious***, which comes from a Latin word meaning "ambush," means "slowly and subtly harmful": *the insidious effects of poverty*; *The candidate launched an insidious whispering campaign against his opponent.* ***Invidious***, which comes from another Latin word meaning "looking at with malice," means "causing another person to feel resentment because of unfair treatment," "feeling envious," and "slighting and discriminatory to another person": *A judge should not hold membership of an organization that practices invidious discrimination on the basis of race, sex, religion, or national origin.*

in·sight /ín sīt/ *n* **1. PERCEPTIVENESS** the ability to see clearly and intuitively into the nature of a complex person, situation, or subject **2. CLEAR PERCEPTION** a clear perception of something ○ *thanked him for his remark and told him it was an interesting insight* **3. SELF-AWARENESS** the ability of somebody to understand and find solutions to his or her personal problems **4. PERCEPTION THAT HALLUCINATIONS ARE NOT REAL** the perception, lacking in some psychiatric disorders such as schizophrenia, that symptoms such as delusions and hallucinations are not objective —**in·sight·ful** /in sítf'l, in sítf'l/ *adj* —**in·sight·ful·ly** *adv* —**in·sight·ful·ness** *n*

in·sight med·i·ta·tion *n* BUDDHISM same as **vipassana**

in·sig·ne /in sígnee/ *n* same as **insignia** (*formal; only used in the singular*) [Late 18C. < Latin, singular of *insignia* (see INSIGNIA)]

in·sig·ni·a /in sígnee ə/ (*plural same* or **-as**) *n* **1.** a badge of authority or membership of a group **2.** an identifying mark or sign [Mid-17C. < Latin (plural) < *insignis* "marked" < *signum* "sign"]

in·sig·nif·i·cant /in sig nífikənt/ *adj* **1. WITHOUT IMPORTANCE** too small and unimportant to be relevant ○ *statistically insignificant* **2. WITHOUT MEANING** having little or no meaning **3. POWERLESS** lacking in power or status —**in·sig·nif·i·cance** *n* —**in·sig·nif·i·cant·ly** *adv*

in·sin·cere /in sin séer/ *adj* not genuine and not reflecting true feelings —**in·sin·cere·ly** *adv* —**in·sin·cer·i·ty** /in sin sérrətee/ *n*

in·sin·u·ate /in sínnyoo àyt/ (**-at·ed, -at·ing, -ates**) *v* **1.** *vti* to hint at something unpleasant or suggest it indirectly and gradually **2. in·sin·u·ate your·self** *vr* to introduce yourself gradually or cunningly into a position, especially a place of confidence or favor [Early 16C. < Latin *insinuat-*, past participle of *insinuare* < *sinus* "curve"] —**in·sin·u·at·ing·ly** *adv* —**in·sin·u·a·tive** *adj* —**in·sin·u·a·tor** *n*

in·sin·u·at·ing /in sínn yoo àyting/ *adj* **1.** hinting at or implying something unpleasant **2.** trying gradually or cunningly to gain influence or favor

in·sin·u·a·tion /in sìnnyoo áysh'n/ *n* **1.** something unpleasant artfully and indirectly suggested to another person **2.** the act of hinting at something unpleasant or suggesting something indirectly and gradually

in·sip·id /in síppid/ *adj* **1.** dull because lacking in character and lively qualities **2.** bland and without flavor [Early 17C. Directly or via French < late Latin *insipidus* "tasteless" < *sapidus* "having a flavor"] —**in·si·pid·i·ty** /inssi píddətee/ *n* —**in·sip·id·ly** *adv* —**in·sip·id·ness** *n*

in·sist /in síst/ (**-sist·ed, -sist·ing, -sists**) *vti* **1.** to state or demand something firmly in spite of disagreement or resistance from others ○ *She insisted that he was wrong.* ○ *Please, you must take it, I insist!* **2.** to state or require something firmly and steadfastly ○ *They insist on punctuality.* ○ *He insisted there was nothing to worry about.* [Late 16C. < Latin *insistere* "persist" < *sistere* "to stand"]

~~**insistant**~~ incorrect spelling of **insistent**

in·sis·tent /in sístənt/ *adj* **1.** persistent in maintaining or demanding something ○ *She was most insistent.* **2.** persistently calling for or compelling attention ○ *insistent pleas* —**in·sis·tence** *n* —**in·sis·ten·cy** *n* —**in·sis·tent·ly** *adv*

in si·tu /in sítoo, -sée-/ *adv, adj* in its natural or original place ○ *a useful tool for studying cell proliferation in situ under normal and pathological conditions* [< Latin]

in·snare *vt* another spelling of **ensnare**

in·so·bri·e·ty /ìn sō brī́ ətee/ *n* lack of moderation, especially in drinking alcohol

in·so·far as /ìn sō fáar-/ *conj* used to introduce a statement that explains or qualifies a previous statement

in·so·late /ín sō làyt/ (**-lat·ed, -lat·ing, -lates**) *vt* to expose something to sunlight (*technical*) [Early 17C. < Latin *insolat-*, past participle of *insolare* < *sol* "sun"]

in·so·la·tion /ìn sō láysh'n/ *n* **1.** exposure of something to sunlight **2.** ASTRON the rate of solar radiation received per unit area **3.** MED same as **sunstroke** (*technical*)

in·sole /ín sōl/ *n* **1.** the inner lining of a shoe **2.** a thin removable liner placed inside a shoe to make it warmer or more comfortable or to prevent the buildup of odor

in·so·lent /ínssələnt/ *adj* showing an aggressive lack of respect in speech or behavior [14C. < Latin *insolent-* "unusual, arrogant" < *solere* "be accustomed"] —**in·so·lence** *n* —**in·so·lent·ly** *adv*

in·sol·u·bi·lize /in sóllyəbə līz/ (**-lized, -liz·ing, -liz·es**) *vt* to make something incapable of being dissolved in a liquid —**in·sol·u·bi·li·za·tion** /in sòllyəbəli záysh'n/ *n*

in·sol·u·ble /in sóllyəb'l/ *adj* **1.** incapable of being dissolved in a liquid **2.** not able to be solved —**in·sol·u·bil·i·ty** /in sòllyə bíllətee/ *n* —**in·sol·u·ble·ness** *n* —**in·sol·u·bly** *adv*

in·solv·a·ble /in sólvəb'l/ *adj* same as **insoluble** (sense 2) —**in·solv·a·bil·i·ty** /in sòlvə bíllətee/ *n*

in·sol·vent /in sólvənt/ *adj* **1. BANKRUPT** unable to pay debts **2. OF BANKRUPTCY** relating to people or businesses that are bankrupt ■ *n* **BANKRUPT PERSON** somebody who is unable to pay any debts —**in·sol·ven·cy** *n*

in·som·ni·a /in sómnee ə/ *n* inability to fall asleep or to remain asleep long enough to feel rested, especially when this is a problem that continues over time [Early 17C. < Latin < *insomnis* "sleepless" < *somnus* "sleep"] —**in·som·ni·ac** *adj, n*

in·so·much as /ìn sō múch-/ *conj* used to introduce an explanation or reason

in·so·much that *conj* used to indicate the extent to which something is true or is the case

in·sou·ci·ance /in sóossee ənss/ *n* cheerful lack of anxiety or concern [Early 19C. < French < *soucier* "to care" < Latin *sollicitare* (see SOLICIT)] —**in·sou·ci·ant** *adj* —**in·sou·ci·ant·ly** *adv*

in·soul *vt* another spelling of **ensoul**

insp. *abbr* **1.** inspected **2.** *also* **Insp.** inspector

in·spect /in spékt/ (**-spect·ed, -spect·ing, -spects**) *vt* **1.** to examine something carefully in order to judge its quality or correctness ○ *She took the cheese out of the refrigerator and inspected it for mold.* **2.** to examine or review something officially ○ *The barracks is inspected every day.* [Early 17C. < Latin *inspect-*, past participle of *inspicere* < *specere* "look at"] —**in·spect·a·ble** *adj* —**in·spec·tive** *adj*

in·spec·tion /in spéksh'n/ *n* **1.** a critical examination of somebody or something aimed at forming a judgment or evaluation **2.** an official authoritative examination ○ *a motor vehicle inspection*

in·spec·tion arms *n* a position in which a rifle is held diagonally in front of the body with the muzzle pointing upward to the left and the rifle chamber open for inspection

in·spec·tor /in spéktər/ *n* **1.** an official who examines something in order to judge its quality or compliance with rules or the law **2.** a British police officer of a rank above sergeant or a Royal Canadian Mounted Police officer of a rank above corps sergeant major —**in·spec·to·ral** *adj* —**in·spec·to·ri·al** /in spek táwree əl/ *adj* —**in·spec·tor·ship** *n*

in·spec·tor·ate /in spéktərət/ *n* **1. GROUP OF INSPECTORS** a group or department of inspectors **2. INSPECTOR'S DISTRICT** an area supervised by an inspector **3. INSPECTOR'S DUTIES** the office or duties of an inspector

in·spec·tor gen·er·al (*plural* **in·spec·tors gen·er·al**) *n* **1.** an official who is the head of an inspectorate **2.** a military officer who investigates and reports on organizational matters

in·sphere *vt* another spelling of **ensphere**

in·spi·ra·tion /inspə ráysh'n/ *n* **1. STIMULATION TO DO CREATIVE WORK** stimulation for the human mind to creative thought or to the making of art ○ *found inspiration in the landscape around her* **2. SOMEBODY OR SOMETHING THAT INSPIRES** somebody or something that inspires somebody to creative thought or to the making of art ○ *His book is an inspiration to all would-be travelers.* **3. CREATIVENESS** the quality of being stimulated to creative thought or activity, or the manifestation of this ○ *a moment of inspiration* **4. GOOD IDEA** a sudden brilliant idea **5. DIVINE INFLUENCE** divine guidance and influence on human beings **6.** PHYSIOL **BREATHING IN** the drawing of air into the lungs [14C. Via French < late Latin *inspiration-* < Latin *inspirare* (see INSPIRE)] —**in·spi·ra·tion·al** *adj*

in·spi·ra·tor /ínspi ràytər/ *n* a device for drawing in a gas or vapor [Late 19C. < INSPIRE]

in·spir·a·to·ry /in spírə tàwree/ *adj* relating to the process of breathing in, or used in breathing in [Late 18C. < INSPIRE]

in·spire /in spír/ (**-spired, -spir·ing, -spires**) *v* **1.** *vti* **STIMULATE SOMEBODY TO DO SOMETHING** to encourage somebody to greater effort, enthusiasm, or creativity ○ *a speech that inspired a generation* **2.** *vt* **PROVOKE PARTICULAR FEELING** to arouse a particular feeling in somebody ○ *inspires optimism* **3.** *vt* **CAUSE CREATIVE ACTIVITY** to stimulate somebody to do something, especially creative or artistic work ○ *inspired him to write a song* **4.** *vti* PHYSIOL **BREATHE IN** to inhale air or a gas into the lungs [14C. Via French < Latin *inspirare* < *spirare* "breathe"] —**in·spir·a·ble** *adj* —**in·spir·er** *n*

in·spired /in spírd/ *adj* **1.** brilliant and creative ○ *an inspired rendition of a classic song* ○ *She was an inspired teacher.* **2.** based on a particular motive or example (*usually used in combination*) ○ *cubist-inspired dreamscapes*

in·spir·ing /in spíring/ *adj* making somebody feel more enthusiastic, confident, or stimulated —**in·spir·ing·ly** *adv*

in·spir·it /in spírrit/ (**-it·ed, -it·ing, -its**) *vt* to give energy or courage to somebody (*archaic or literary*) —**in·spir·it·ing** *adj*

in·spis·sate /in spí sàyt, ínspi sàyt/ (**-sat·ed, -sat·ing, -sates**) *vti* to become thicker in consistency, or cause something to thicken, especially by boiling or evaporation [Early 17C. < Latin *inspissat-*, past participle of *inspissare* "thicken" < *spissus* "thick"] —**in·spis·sa·tion** /ínspi sáysh'n/ *n* —**in·spis·sa·tor** /in spí sàytər, ínspi sàytər/ *n*

inst. *abbr* **1.** instant **2.** instantaneous **3.** institute **4.** institution **5.** institutional

Inst. *abbr* **1.** Institute **2.** Institution

in·sta·bil·i·ty /ìnstə bíllətee/ *n* **1.** the quality of being unstable, erratic, or unpredictable **2.** a lack of steadiness or firmness

~~**instalation**~~ incorrect spelling of **installation**

in·stall /in stáwl/, **in·stal** *v* (**-stalled, -stall·ing, -stalls**) **1.** *vt* **FIT OR CONNECT SOMETHING** to put machinery or equipment into place and make it ready for use **2.** *vt* COMPUT **LOAD SOFTWARE** to load software onto a computer **3.** *vt* **PLACE SOMEBODY IN JOB** to appoint somebody to a particular position or to induct somebody formally into office **4. in·stall your·self** *vr* **SETTLE IN** to settle yourself comfortably somewhere ■ *n* COMPUT **ACT OF LOADING SOFTWARE** the act of loading software onto a computer ○*"I opted for the full install, which can involve anything up to 72Mb of space."* (*Internet Magazine*; November 1998) [15C. Directly or via French < medieval Latin *installare* "place in office" < *stallum* "stall"] —**in·stall·er** *n*

in·stal·la·tion /ìnstə láysh'n/ *n* **1. ACT OF INSTALLING EQUIPMENT** the process of putting a piece of equipment or machinery in place and making it ready for use **2. PLACE WITH EQUIPMENT** a place housing equipment or machinery for a particular use ○ *a communications installation* **3. SOMETHING THAT HAS BEEN INSTALLED** a piece of equipment or system that has been put in place and made ready for use **4.** MIL **MILITARY BASE** a military base or camp ○ *on the grounds of a navy installation* **5. APPOINTING OF SOMEBODY TO POSITION** the act of appointing somebody to a particular position or of inducting somebody formally into office **6.** ARTS **ART EXHIBIT** an artwork assembled by an artist that involves the arrangement of three-dimensional objects or the use of paint and other media directly on the walls or floors of the exhibition space ○ *an installation using video monitors and empty bottles*

in·stal·la·tion pro·gram *n* a computer program used in installing applications or hardware

in·stall·ment /in stáwlmənt/, **in·stal·ment** *n* **1.** one of a series of sums of money paid at regular intervals to settle a debt **2.** one of the parts of something that appears or is presented at intervals ○ *published in installments* ○*"The working documents now circulating are but the latest installment of a debate that first surfaced in the 1970s."* (Art Weissman, *Pulse of the People*; 1997) [Mid-18C. < Anglo-Norman *estallment* < Old French *estaler* "to fix, place"]

in·stall·ment plan *n* a system for buying merchandise involving a series of payments at regular intervals instead of a single lump sum

in·stal·ment *n* another spelling of **installment**

in·stance /ínstənss/ *n* **1. ILLUSTRATION** an example of a particular situation or event ○ *cited several instances of plagiarism* **2. EVENT** an occurrence of something ○ *We can overlook it in this instance.* **3.** LAW **LEGAL ACTION** a legal proceeding or lawsuit ■ *vt* (**-stanced, -stanc·ing, -stanc·es**) **1. GIVE SOMETHING AS EXAMPLE** to offer something as an example **2. SERVE AS EXAMPLE** to serve as an example of something [14C. Via French < Latin *instantia* < *instant-* (see INSTANT)] ◇ **for instance** as an example ◇ **in the first instance** used to indicate something that is or happens first, before other events or stages (*formal*)

in·stant /ínstənt/ *adj* **1. IMMEDIATE** happening immediately, without delay or effort ○ *an instant dislike* **2.** FOOD **QUICK TO PREPARE** describes food that is quickly and easily prepared, often premixed, precooked, or powdered ○ *instant cocoa* **3. URGENT AND PRESSING** requiring immediate attention or an immediate response ○ *an instant need for help* **4. CURRENT** present or current **5. OF THIS MONTH** happening in the current month (*archaic*) ○ *your letter of the 13th instant* ■ *n* **1. SHORT TIME** an extremely brief period of time ○ *for an instant* **2. MOMENT IN TIME** a particular moment in time ○ *Liftoff occurs the instant the bolts are released.* **3.** FOOD **QUICKLY PREPARED PRODUCT** a quickly prepared item of food or drink [15C. Via French < Latin *instant-*, present participle of *instare* "be present" < *stare* "to stand"]

in·stan·ta·ne·ous /ìnstən táynee əss/ *adj* **1.** occurring immediately or almost immediately **2.** indicating the value of something at a given moment in time, expressed as the average value of a varying quantity over an infinitesimally small time interval ○ *instantaneous velocity* [Mid-17C. < medieval Latin *instantaneus* < Latin *instant-* (see INSTANT)] —**in·stan·ta·ne·i·ty** /in stàntə née ətee, ìnstəntə-/ *n* —**in·stan·ta·ne·ous·ly** *adv* —**in·stan·ta·ne·ous·ness** *n*

in·stan·ter /in stántər/ *adv* without delay [Late 17C. Via medieval Latin < Latin *instant-* "present" (see INSTANT)]

in·stan·ti·ate /in stánshee àyt/ (**-at·ed, -at·ing, -ates**) *vt* to provide an example to support or explain something [Mid-20C. < INSTANCE]

in·stant·ly /ínstəntlee/ *adv* **1. IMMEDIATELY** immediately and without delay **2. URGENTLY** urgently or insistently (*archaic*) ■ *conj* **AS SOON AS** immediately after ○ *I phoned instantly I heard you were back.*

in·stant mes·sag·ing *n* a system for real-time text messaging on the Internet

in·stan·ton /in stánton/ *n* in theoretical cosmology, a mathematical solution, one form of which implies that the universe began as a pea-sized structure of space, time, matter, and energy before the big bang

in·stant-on *adj* including a device or technology that allows for a rapid startup, so eliminating the need for a warm-up period

in·stant re·play *n* a playing back of a videotape in slow motion, usually to show the movement of a ball or player in a sport shown on television

in·star /ín staar/ *n* in the life cycle of an arthropod such as an insect, a stage between two successive molts [Late 19C. < Latin, "form, image"]

in·state /in stáyt/ (**-stat·ed, -stat·ing, -states**) *vt* to establish somebody in office —**in·state·ment** *n*

in sta·tu quo /in stàttoo kwṓ, -stày-/ *adv* in the same state (*formal*) [< Latin *in statu quo ante* "in the (same) state as before"]

in·stau·ra·tion /ìn staw ráysh'n/ *n* (*formal*) **1.** the restoration of something that has lapsed or fallen into decay **2.** the founding or establishment of something [Early 17C. < Latin *instauration-* < *instaurare* "renew"]

in·stead /in stéd/ *adv* as a replacement or substitute for something [13C. < IN[1] + STEAD "place"] ◇ **instead of** as an alternative to or substitute for something

in·step /ín stèp/ *n* **1.** the arched middle portion of the human foot between the ankle and toes, especially its upper surface **2.** the part of a shoe that covers the middle portion of the foot [15C. Origin ?]

in·sti·gate /ínsti gàyt/ (**-gat·ed, -gat·ing, -gates**) *vt* **1.** to cause a process to start **2.** to cause trouble, especially by urging somebody to do something destructive or wrong [Mid-16C. < Latin *instigat-*, past participle of *instigare* < *stigare* "prick, incite"] —**in·sti·ga·tion** /ìnsti gáysh'n/ *n* —**in·sti·ga·tor** *n*

in·still /in stíl/ (**-stilled, -still·ing, -stills**), **in·stil** (**-stilled, -still·ing, -stils**) *vt* **1.** to impress ideas, principles, or teachings gradually on somebody's mind ○ *tried to instill self-respect in my students* **2.** to pour medicine or another liquid into something drop by drop [15C. < Latin *instillare* < *stilla* "drop"] —**in·stil·la·tion** /ìnsti láysh'n/ *n*

in·stinct /ín stìngkt/ *n* **1. STRONG NATURAL IMPULSE** a powerful impulse that feels natural rather than reasoned ○ *followed his instincts and took to his heels* **2. BIOLOGICAL DRIVE** an inborn pattern of behavior characteristic of a species and shaped by biological necessities such as survival and reproduction ○ *the survival instinct* **3. KNACK** a natural gift or skill ○ *an instinct for putting people at ease* ■ *adj* **FILLED** completely filled or imbued with something (*formal*) ○ *a look instinct with compassion* [15C. < Latin *instinctus* "impulse" < *instinguere* "incite" < *stinguere* "to sting"] —**in·stinc·tu·al** /in stíngkchoo əl/ *adj*

in·stinc·tive /in stíngktiv/ *adj* **1.** relating to, prompted by, or based on a strong natural impulse ○ *an instinctive fear of water* **2.** having a particular quality or skill spontaneously and without effort or instruction ○ *an instinctive feel for color* ○ *an instinctive cook* —**in·stinc·tive·ly** *adv* —**in·stinc·tive·ness** *n*

in·sti·tute /ínsti tòot/ *n* **1. ORGANIZATION WITH SPECIALIZED GOAL** an organization for promoting something such as art, science, or the well-being of a group **2. PLACE FOR ADVANCED STUDY** an educational institution, especially one concerned with technical subjects **3. PRINCIPLE** an established principle or rule **4. SEMINAR** a short intensive teaching or study program ■ **in·sti·tutes** *npl* LAW **LAW SUMMARY** a summary of laws ■ *vt* (**-tut·ed, -tut·ing, -tutes**) **1. START SOMETHING** to start or initiate something in an official or formal way ○ *institute legal proceedings* **2. SET SOMETHING UP** to set up or establish something ○ *institute a literary prize* **3. APPOINT SOMEBODY** to appoint somebody to an office, especially a religious one [14C. < Latin *institut-*, past participle of *instituere* "establish" < *statuere* "set up" < *stare* "to stand"] —**in·sti·tut·er** *n*

in·sti·tu·tion /ìnsti tóosh'n/ *n* **1. IMPORTANT ORGANIZATION** a large organization that is influential in the community, e.g., a college, hospital, or bank **2. ESTABLISHED PRACTICE** an established law, custom, or practice ○ *the institution of marriage* **3. STARTING OF SOMETHING** the act of initiating or establishing something **4. LONG-ESTABLISHED PERSON OR THING** somebody or something that has been well known and established in a place for a long time (*informal*) **5. PLACE OF CARE OR CONFINEMENT** a place where people who are, e.g., mentally or physically challenged are cared for —**in·sti·tu·tion·al** *adj* —**in·sti·tu·tion·al·ly** *adv*

in·sti·tu·tion·al·ism /ìnsti tóoshən'l ìzzəm/ *n* a belief in the merits of established customs and systems —**in·sti·tu·tion·al·ist** *n*

in·sti·tu·tion·al·ize /ìnsti tóoshən'l ìz, -tóoshnəl-/ (**-ized, -iz·ing, -iz·es**) *vt* **1. PUT SOMEBODY INTO INSTITUTION** to put somebody into an institution such as an alcohol or drug-treatment facility, a psychiatric hospital, or a prison **2. ESTABLISH SOMETHING AS USUAL** to make something an established custom or an accepted part of the structure of a large organization or society **3.** MAKE SOMETHING INTO OR LIKE INSTITUTION to convert something into an institution, or make something resemble an institution —**in·sti·tu·tion·al·i·za·tion** /ìnsti to͞oshən'li záysh'n, -to͞oshnəli-/ *n*

in·sti·tu·tion·al·ized /ìnstə to͞oshən'l ìzd, -to͞oshnə lìzd/ *adj* **1.** having become an established custom or an accepted part of the structure of a large organization or society because of having existed for so long **2.** lacking the will or ability to think and act independently because of having spent a long time in an institution such as a psychiatric hospital or prison

in·sti·tu·tive /ínsti to͞otiv/ *adj* serving to establish or being established

in-store *adj* happening, available, or situated within a large store such as a supermarket or department store ○ *an in-store bakery*

instr. *abbr* **1.** instruction **2.** EDUC instructor **3.** instrument **4.** GRAM, MUSIC instrumental

in·struct /in strúkt/ (**-struct·ed, -struct·ing, -structs**) *v* **1.** *vti* TRAIN SOMEBODY to teach somebody a subject or how to do something **2.** *vt* DIRECT SOMEBODY to tell somebody to do something, especially with authority or as an order **3.** *vt* GIVE SOMEBODY INFORMATION to inform somebody about something, especially in a formal or official manner ○ *The judge instructed the jurors that they could consider a lesser charge.* **4.** *vt* LAW BRIEF JURY AT END OF CASE to give information as a judge to a jury at the end of a case in order to explain the applicable points of law and summarize what has to be proved **5.** *vt UK* OBTAIN LEGAL REPRESENTATION to ask or authorize a lawyer to act on your behalf and supply him or her with relevant information [15C. < Latin *instruct-*, past participle of *instruere* "prepare, equip" < *struere* "build"]

SYNONYMS See ***teach***.

in·struc·tion /in strúkshən/ *n* **1.** STATEMENT OF COMMAND a spoken or written statement of what must be done, especially delivered formally, with official authority, or as an order ○ *got instructions to cooperate fully* **2.** TEACHING OR THINGS TAUGHT teaching in a particular subject or skill, or the facts or skills taught ○ *driving instruction* **3.** TEACHING PROCESS OR PROFESSION the act, process, or profession of teaching **4.** COMPUT COMPUTER COMMAND a code that tells a computer to perform a specific operation ■ **in·struc·tions** *npl* **1.** LIST OF THINGS TO DO printed information about how to do, make, assemble, use, or operate something ○ *instructions for setting up your e-mail* **2.** LAW JUDGE'S SUMMARY the information given by a judge to a jury at the end of a case that explains the applicable points of law and summarizes what has to be proved —**in·struc·tion·al** *adj* —**in·struc·tion·al·ly** *adv*

in·struc·tive /in strúktiv/ *adj* providing useful information or insight into something —**in·struc·tive·ly** *adv* —**in·struc·tive·ness** *n*

in·struc·tor /in strúktər/ *n* **1.** somebody who teaches something such as a sport or a practical skill ○ *a ski instructor* **2.** a university, college, or community college teacher of the lowest rank —**in·struc·tor·ship** *n*

in·stru·ment *n* /ínstrəmənt/ **1.** TOOL a tool or mechanical device, especially one used for precision work in science, medicine, or technology **2.** MUSIC OBJECT THAT PRODUCES MUSIC an object used to produce music, e.g., a flute, guitar, or drum **3.** MEASURE MEASURING DEVICE a device that measures or controls something, e.g., a speedometer or voltmeter **4.** MEANS OF DOING SOMETHING somebody or something used as a means of achieving a desired result or accomplishing a particular purpose ○ *They view standardized testing as an instrument for improving the schools.* **5.** OBJECT USED FOR PURPOSE an object that has been or could be used for a purpose ○ *hit by a blunt instrument* **6.** LAW DOCUMENT a legal document (*formal*) ■ *vt* /ínstrə mènt/ (**-ment·ed, -ment·ing, -ments**) **1.** MUSIC ARRANGE MUSIC to write or arrange a piece of music for performance on musical instruments **2.** MEASURE SUPPLY WITH MEASURING DEVICES to equip something with instruments for measurement or control [13C. Via French < Latin *instrumentum* < *instruere* "prepare" (see INSTRUCT)]

in·stru·men·tal /ìnstrə mént'l/ *adj* **1.** MAKING SOMETHING HAPPEN playing an important part in achieving a result or accomplishing a purpose ○ *She was instrumental in getting the legislation passed.* **2.** MUSIC FOR INSTRUMENTS, NOT VOICES performed on a musical instrument or instruments, not with the voice **3.** CONNECTED WITH INSTRUMENTS done with or produced by an instrument or instruments ○ *instrumental readings* **4.** GRAM INDICATING MEANS OF DOING SOMETHING describes a noun case that indicates that something is used for a purpose or is the means by which something is done **5.** PHILOSOPHY OF INSTRUMENTALISM relating to instrumentalism ■ *n* **1.** MUSIC MUSIC PLAYED BY INSTRUMENTS a piece of music that is performed on a musical instrument or instruments, not with the voice **2.** GRAM NOUN FORM INDICATING MEANS the instrumental case, or a noun in the instrumental case —**in·stru·men·tal·ly** *adv*

in·stru·men·tal·ism /ìnstrə mént'l ìzzəm/ *n* the belief that theories are useful tools for making predictions but cannot be literally true or false

in·stru·men·tal·ist /ìnstrə mént'list/ *n* **1.** MUSIC PLAYER OF INSTRUMENT somebody who plays a musical instrument **2.** PHILOSOPHY PROPONENT OF INSTRUMENTALISM a supporter or advocate of instrumentalism ■ *adj* PHILOSOPHY ADVOCATING INSTRUMENTALISM supporting or advocating instrumentalism

in·stru·men·tal·i·ty /ìnstrəmən tállətee, -men-/ (*plural* **-ties**) *n* (*formal*) **1.** QUALITY OF BEING INSTRUMENTAL the quality or state of being instrumental **2.** ACTION OR USE interventionist action ○ *"But for her instrumentality, the fatal knowledge would not have been imparted."* (Elizabeth Gaskell, *Some Passages from the History of the Chomley Family*; 1865) **3.** POL SECTION a subsidiary branch of a department or agency ○ *Every department, agency, and instrumentality of the federal government is so authorized.*

in·stru·men·tal learn·ing *n* a form of learning that takes place as a direct consequence of a reward or pleasant outcome for the learner

in·stru·men·ta·tion /ìnstrəmən táysh'n, -men-/ *n* **1.** MUSIC ARRANGEMENT FOR MUSICAL INSTRUMENTS the composition or arrangement of music for performance, in which a combination of musical instruments is specified **2.** MUSIC MUSICAL INSTRUMENTS USED the instruments that are used to perform a piece of music **3.** EQUIPMENT FOR CONTROL OR OPERATION a set of instruments used for a specific purpose such as operating a machine or controlling an aircraft **4.** USE OF INSTRUMENTS the use of instruments as tools or for measurement or control **5.** MAKING OF INSTRUMENTS the design, development, or manufacture of instruments for use in science, medicine, technology, or industry **6.** MEANS the means or agency through which something is done (*formal*)

in·stru·ment board *n* TECH same as **instrument panel**

in·stru·ment fly·ing *n* the flying of an aircraft using only information obtained from instruments rather than from what the pilot can see out of the window

in·stru·ment land·ing *n* the landing of an aircraft while relying on information obtained from instruments rather than from what the pilot can see out of the window

in·stru·ment pan·el *n* a set of instruments mounted at the front of a machine or in front of somebody driving or steering a motor vehicle, aircraft, or ship

in·sub·or·di·nate /ìn sə báwrd'nət/ *adj* refusing to obey orders or submit to authority ■ *n* somebody who refuses to obey orders or submit to authority —**in·sub·or·di·na·tion** /ìn sə bawrd'n áysh'n/ *n*

in·sub·stan·tial /ìn səb stánsh'l/ *adj* **1.** not very large, solid, or strong **2.** not existing in reality ○ *an insubstantial apparition* —**in·sub·stan·ti·al·i·ty** /ìn səb stanshee állətee/ *n* —**in·sub·stan·tial·ly** *adv*

in·suf·fer·a·ble /in súffərəb'l/ *adj* so annoying, unpleasant, or uncomfortable as to be unbearable —**in·suf·fer·a·bly** *adv*

in·suf·fi·cien·cy /ìn sə físh'nssee/ (*plural* **-cies**) *n* **1.** NOT ENOUGH a smaller number or lesser amount than is needed ○ *an insufficiency of provisions for a long cruise* **2.** MED UNFITNESS OR FAILURE the inability or failure to perform competently, adequately, or as usual ○ *cardiac insufficiency* **3.** FAILURE TO MEASURE UP a failure to meet a standard or requirement ○ *felt his own insufficiency for the task*

in·suf·fi·cient /ìn sə físh'nt/ *adj* not enough in amount or quality to satisfy a purpose or standard ○ *insufficient evidence* —**in·suf·fi·cient·ly** *adv*

in·suf·flate /ínssə flàyt, in sú flàyt/ (**-flat·ed, -flat·ing, -flates**) *vt* **1.** to blow or breathe into something (*formal*) **2.** to blow something such as air, powder, or gas into the lungs or another body cavity in the course of medical treatment [Late 17C. < Latin *insufflat-*, past participle of *insufflare* < *sufflare* "blow up"] —**in·suf·fla·tion** /ìnssə fláysh'n/ *n* —**in·suf·fla·tor** *n*

in·su·lar /ínssələr, ínssyə-/ *adj* **1.** LIMITED IN OUTLOOK concerned only with local matters and not interested in new ideas or different cultures **2.** NOT CLOSE TO OTHERS physically or emotionally removed from others **3.** OF ISLANDS relating to or originating in an island **4.** ANAT OF ISLANDS OF CELLS relating to a collection of cells or tissue reminiscent of an island [Mid-16C. Via French < late Latin *insularis* < Latin *insula* "island"] —**in·su·lar·i·ty** /ìnssə lárrətee, ìnssyə-/ *n*

in·su·late /ínsə làyt, ínsyə-/ (**-lat·ed, -lat·ing, -lates**) *vt* **1.** to protect or isolate somebody from something, especially from something unpleasant or undesirable **2.** to prevent or reduce the passage of heat, electricity, or sound into, from, or through something, especially by surrounding it with some material [Mid-16C < Latin *insula* "island"] —**in·su·lant** *n*

in·su·lat·ing tape *n Can, UK* ELEC a thin strip of adhesive material that can be wrapped round bare wires or electrical connections to stop electricity from passing from them to somebody or something that touches them. US term **friction tape**

in·su·la·tion /ìnssə láysh'n, ìnssyə-/ *n* **1.** MATERIAL THAT INSULATES material that prevents or reduces the passage of heat, electricity, or sound, e.g., a special fabric or a layer of air **2.** PREVENTION OF CONDUCTION the act of covering or surrounding something to prevent or reduce the passage of heat, electricity, or sound **3.** PROTECTION protection or isolation from something undesirable or unpleasant —**in·su·la·tive** /ínsə làytiv, ínsyə-/ *adj*

in·su·la·tor /ínssə làytər, ínssyə-/ *n* a material or device that prevents or reduces the passage of heat, electricity, or sound

in·su·lin /ínssəlin/ *n* a hormone produced in the pancreas that regulates the level of glucose in the blood [Early 20C. < Latin *insula* "island," after the ISLETS OF LANGERHANS]

in·su·lin shock, **in·su·lin re·ac·tion** *n* a severe drop in blood sugar resulting from an excess of insulin and marked by sweating, dizziness, trembling, and eventual coma

in·sult *v* /in súlt/ (**-sult·ed, -sult·ing, -sults**) **1.** *vti* BE OFFENSIVE TO SOMEBODY to say or do something rude or insensitive that offends somebody **2.** *vt* SHOW CONTEMPT FOR SOMEBODY OR SOMETHING to say or do something that suggests a low opinion of somebody or something ○ *Don't insult me by offering me pity.* ■ *n* /ín sùlt/ **1.** OFFENSIVE WORDS OR ACTION a remark or action that offends somebody, usually because it is rude or insensitive **2.** SOMETHING SHOWING CONTEMPT a remark or action that suggests a low opinion of somebody or something ○ *The article is an insult to the intelligence of the reader.* ○ *The fee they offered was an insult.* **3.** MED INJURY OR CAUSE OF INJURY an injury or trauma to the body, or something that causes such harm [Mid-16C. Via French < Latin *insultare*, literally "keep jumping on" < *salire* "to jump"] —**in·sult·er** *n*

USAGE Insults English has insulting words for most races and cultures with which its speakers have come into extended contact, and for so-called minority groups within English-speaking societies, even though such groups can and do constitute demographic majorities in many regions. When the people insulted are English speakers, the insulting words can and often do become part of their own vocabulary. Those insulted will generally avoid using these terms in interaction with their insulters, since to do so would be to endorse the insulters' view of them. However, among themselves they may well deliberately adopt an insult in order to subvert it or rob it of its power. For instance, Australian Aboriginals reportedly are not averse to using terms like *Abo* and *blackfella* when talking with one another, even though they are highly offensive when applied to them by non-Aboriginals. Similarly, other groups may defy their detractors by adopting the insults directed at them: gay people may refer to themselves, polemically, as *queer*, as in *Queer Nation*; and some feminists have struck back against ageist putdowns by reclaiming *crone* and making it their own.

in·sult·ing /in súlting/ *adj* causing offense by being rude or insensitive or by suggesting a low opinion of somebody or something —**in·sult·ing·ly** *adv*

in·su·per·a·ble /in so͞opərəb'l/ *adj* impossible to overcome, get rid of, or deal with successfully ○ *battling insuperable odds* [14C. Directly or via French < Latin *insuperabilis* < *superare* "to overcome" < *super* "above"] —**in·su·per·a·bly** *adv*

in·sup·port·a·ble /inssə páwrtəb'l/ *adj* **1.** too great, unpleasant, or difficult to bear ○ *insupportable heat* **2.** impossible to justify or defend ○ *an insupportable claim* —**in·sup·port·a·bly** *adv*

in·sur·ance /in sho͝orənss/ *n* **1. FINANCIAL PROTECTION AGAINST LOSS OR HARM** an arrangement by which a company gives customers financial protection against loss or harm such as theft or illness in return for payment (**premium**) **2. MONEY PAID BY INSURANCE COMPANY** the sum of money that an insurance company pays or agrees to pay if a specific undesirable event occurs **3. PREMIUM** the payment made to obtain insurance ○ *My car insurance has gone up again.* **4. INSURANCE BUSINESS** the commercial business of providing insurance **5. MEANS OF PROTECTION** an act, measure, or provision that gives protection against an undesirable event or risk ○ *provided a map as insurance against getting lost* ■ *adj* SPORTS **PREVENTING OF OPPONENT FROM TYING GAME** in some sports, relating to an act of scoring that increases a team's lead to the extent that the other side cannot tie the game in a single play [15C. < Old French *enseürance* < *enseürer* (see ENSURE)]

PRONUNCIATION The correct pronunciation of ***insurance*** places primary stress on the second syllable /in sho͝orənss/, not on the first syllable /ín sho͝orənss/.

in·sur·ance pol·i·cy *n* a written contract between an insurance company and a person or organization requiring insurance against loss or harm

in·sure /in sho͝or/ (**-sured, -sur·ing, -sures**) *v* **1.** *vti* to agree formally that, for a sum of money paid to a company, the company will pay compensation or costs if a particular harm or loss occurs to somebody or something ○ *insured the ring for $5,000* **2.** *vi* to get protection from something undesirable that might happen, usually by making contingency plans or taking precautionary or preventive measures **3.** *vt* another spelling of **ensure** [15C. Variant of ENSURE] —**in·sur·a·ble** *adj* —**in·sured** *adj, n*

USAGE See ***assure***.

~~**insurence**~~ incorrect spelling of **insurance**

in·sur·er /in sho͝orər/ *n* a person or company providing insurance

in·sur·gent /in súrjənt/ *n* **1. REBEL** somebody who rebels against authority or leadership, especially somebody who belongs to a group involved in an uprising **2. POLITICAL REBEL** a member of a political party who rebels against the party leaders or policies ■ *adj* **REBELLIOUS** rebelling against authority or leadership, especially against a government or ruler of a country [Mid-18C. < Latin *insurgent-*, present participle of *insurgere* "rise up" < *surgere* "to rise"] —**in·sur·gence** *n* —**in·sur·gen·cy** *n*

in·sur·mount·a·ble /in sər mówntəb'l/ *adj* impossible to overcome or deal with successfully —**in·sur·mount·a·bil·i·ty** /in sər mowntə bíllətee/ *n* —**in·sur·mount·a·bly** *adv*

in·sur·rec·tion /inssə rékshən/ *n* a rebellion against the government or rulers of a country, often involving armed conflict [15C. < Latin *insurrection-* < past participle of *insurgere* "rise up"] —**in·sur·rec·tion·al** *adj* —**in·sur·rec·tion·ar·y** *n, adj* —**in·sur·rec·tion·ist** *n, adj*

in·sus·cep·ti·ble /in sə séptəb'l/ *adj* **1.** not likely to be affected or influenced by something **2.** not able to undergo a particular process —**in·sus·cep·ti·bil·i·ty** /in sə septə bíllətee/ *n* —**in·sus·cep·ti·bly** *adv*

in·swing·er /ín swìngər/ *n* in soccer, a ball kicked, particularly from a corner, that curves through the air toward the goal

int *abbr* ONLINE international organization (*used in Internet addresses*) See table at **domain name**

int. *abbr* **1.** intelligence **2.** intercept **3.** BANKING interest **4.** interim **5.** interior **6.** GRAM interjection **7.** intermediate **8.** internal **9.** international **10.** interpreter **11.** MATH intersection **12.** interval **13.** interview **14.** GRAM intransitive **15.** MUSIC introit

Int. *abbr* International

in·tact /in tákt/ *adj* **1. NOT DAMAGED** whole and undamaged ○ *found the ancient tomb intact* **2. COMPLETE** not having any missing parts ○ *kept the collection intact* **3.** ANAT **WITHOUT ANY REMOVED PARTS** having all body parts in place and undamaged [15C. < Latin *intactus* "untouched" < *tangere* "to touch"] —**in·tact·ness** *n*

Barnaby's

intaglio: Ancient Egyptian granite carving

in·ta·glio /in tállyō, in taályō/ (*plural* **-glios**) *n* **1. HOLLOWED-OUT DESIGN** a carving made by cutting a hollowed-out design in material such as stone **2. CARVING OF INTAGLIOS** the process or art of carving hollowed-out designs in material such as stone **3. CARVED GEM** a gem in which a hollowed-out design has been carved **4.** PRINTING **PRINTING WITH INCISED PLATES** a printing technique such as engraving or etching in which the design is cut into the plate instead of protruding from it **5.** PRINTING **INCISED PRINTING PLATE** a printing plate into which a design is cut [Mid-17C. < Italian < *intagliare* "engrave" < *tagliare* "to cut"]

in·take /ín tàyk/ *n* **1. AMOUNT TAKEN IN** an amount taken in or consumed ○ *increase your intake of fluids* **2. TAKING IN OF SOMETHING** the process of taking in a substance, especially by eating or drinking **3. OPENING THROUGH WHICH FLUID PASSES** an opening through which fluid enters a duct or contained area ○ *the fuel intake* **4. PEOPLE ADMITTED** the number of people admitted to a place or organization at a particular time, or the people themselves

in·tan·gi·ble /in tánjəb'l/ *adj* **1. NONMATERIAL** lacking material qualities, and so not able to be touched or seen ○ *intangible benefits* **2. HARD TO DESCRIBE** difficult to define or describe clearly, but nonetheless perceived ○ *an intangible quality of serenity in the music* ■ *n* **SOMETHING UNQUANTIFIABLE** an unquantifiable quality or asset ○ *such intangibles as duty* —**in·tan·gi·bil·i·ty** /in tànjə bíllətee/ *n* —**in·tan·gi·bly** *adv*

in·tan·gi·ble as·set *n* a business asset such as a company's customer goodwill that is of value although it is not directly quantifiable in terms of goods produced or sold

Massimo Listri/Corbis

intarsia: panel (1506) in the Palazzo Ducale, Mantua, Italy

in·tar·si·a /in taársee ə/ *n* **1. WOOD INLAY** wood inlay using different colors of wood, commonly used in furniture in the Italian Renaissance **2.** HANDICRAFT **WAY OF KNITTING** a method of knitting with two or more colored yarns in which the pattern can be seen from both sides of the finished piece **3.** HANDICRAFT **MAKING OF INTARSIAS** the art or process of making intarsias, e.g., for wall panels [Mid-19C. < German, alteration of Italian *intarsio* < Arabic *tarṣī*]

in·te·ger /íntəjər/ *n* **1.** a positive or negative whole number or zero **2.** a whole unit or entity (*technical*) [Early 16C. < Latin, "whole"]

in·te·gral /íntəgrəl, in téggrəl/ *adj* **1. NECESSARY OR CONSTITUENT** forming an essential part of something ○ *Adequate funding is integral to the success of the venture.* ○ *Mealtimes are an integral part of family life.* **2. MADE UP OF PARTS** composed of parts that together make a whole **3. COMPLETE** having no missing parts **4.** MATH **OF INTEGER** relating to an integer **5.** MATH **RELATING TO INTEGRALS** relating to definite integrals, indefinite integrals, or integration ■ *n* MATH **1.** same as **definite integral 2.** same as **indefinite integral** [Mid-16C. < late Latin *integralis* < Latin *integer* "whole"] —**in·te·gral·ly** *adv*

in·te·gral cal·cu·lus *n* a branch of mathematics dealing with integrals and differential equations, used to determine areas, volumes, and lengths, and in many areas of applied mathematics

in·te·grand /íntə grànd/ *n* a mathematical function or equation to be integrated [Late 19C. < Latin *integrandus* "to be integrated" < *integrare* (see INTEGRATE)]

in·te·grant /íntəgrənt/ (*formal*) *adj* part of a whole ■ *n* an integral part of something

in·te·grate /íntə gràyt/ (**-grat·ed, -grat·ing, -grates**) *v* **1.** *vt* **MAKE SOMETHING OPEN TO ALL** to make a group, community, place, or organization and its opportunities available to everyone, regardless of race, ethnicity, religion, gender, or social class **2.** *vti* **FIT IN WITH GROUP** to become an accepted member of a group and its activities, or help somebody do this ○ *integrating newcomers into the community* **3.** *vti* **MAKE INTO WHOLE** to join two or more objects or make something part of a larger whole, or be joined or made part of a larger whole ○ *integrating light rail into the regional transportation plan* **4.** *vt* MATH **FIND MATHEMATICAL INTEGRAL OF SOMETHING** to find the definite or indefinite integral of a function or equation [Mid-17C. < Latin *integrat-*, past participle of *integrare* "make whole" < *integer* "whole"] —**in·te·gra·bil·i·ty** /íntəgrə bíllətee/ *n* —**in·te·gra·ble** *adj* —**in·te·gra·tive** *adj*

in·te·grat·ed /íntə gràytəd/ *adj* **1. COMBINED OR COMPOSITE** made up of aspects or parts that work well together ○ *an integrated communications system* **2. COMBINING DISSIMILAR THINGS** bringing together processes or functions that are normally separate **3. OPEN TO ALL PEOPLE** open to everyone, regardless of race, ethnicity, religion, gender, or social class

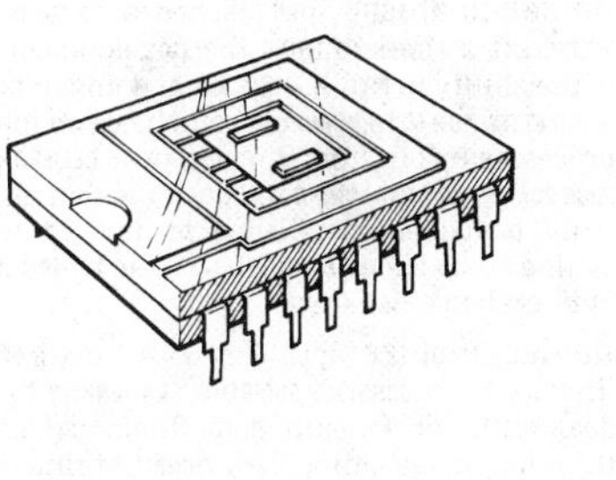

integrated circuit

in·te·grat·ed cir·cuit *n* a tiny complex of electronic components contained on a thin chip or wafer of semiconducting material —**in·te·grat·ed cir·cuit·ry** *n*

in·te·gra·tion /íntə gráysh'n/ *n* **1. EQUAL ACCESS FOR ALL** the process of opening a group, community, place, or organization to all, regardless of race, ethnicity, religion, gender, or social class **2. ACCEPTANCE INTO COMMUNITY** the process of becoming an accepted member of a group or community **3. COMBINATION** a combination of parts or objects that work together well **4.** MATH **MATHEMATICAL OPERATION** the mathematical process of finding the solution of a differential equation or a function whose differential equation is known **5.** PSYCHOL **ORGANIZATION OF PERSONALITY TRAITS** the process of coordinating separate personality elements into a balanced whole or producing behavior compatible with somebody's environment

in·te·gra·tion·ist /íntə gráysh'nist/ *n* a supporter or activist who works to promote or maintain integration ■ *adj* supporting, promoting, or maintaining integration

in·te·gra·tor /íntə gràytər/ *n* **1.** a computer component that performs numerical integration to solve differential equations **2.** somebody or something that brings about integration

in·teg·rin /in téggrin/ *n* a cell-surface receptor that is a glycoprotein involved in homeostasis, wound healing, and immune defense mechanisms [Late 20C. < INTEGRATE]

in·teg·ri·ty /in téggrətee/ *n* **1. POSSESSION OF FIRM PRINCIPLES** the quality of possessing and steadfastly adhering to high moral principles or professional standards **2. COMPLETENESS** the state of being complete or undivided (*formal*) ○ *the territorial integrity of the nation* **3. WHOLENESS** the state of being sound or undamaged (*formal*) ○ *public confidence in the integrity of the voting process* [15C. Via French < Latin *integritas* < *integer* "whole"]

in·teg·u·ment /in téggyəmənt/ *n* an outer protective layer or part of an animal or plant, e.g., a shell, rind, husk, or skin [Early 17C. < Latin *integumentum* < *integere* "cover up" < *tegere* "to cover"] —**in·teg·u·men·tal** /in tèggyə mént'l/ *adj* —**in·teg·u·men·ta·ry** /-méntəree, -méntree/ *adj*

~~intelectual~~ incorrect spelling of **intellectual**

~~inteligence~~ incorrect spelling of **intelligence**

in·tel·lect /ínt'l èkt/ *n* **1.** somebody's ability to think, reason, and understand ○ *appeals to the intellect rather than the emotions* ○ *a highly developed intellect* **2.** a very intelligent and knowledgeable person ○ *some of the greatest intellects of the period* [14C. Via French < Latin *intellectus* < past participle of *intellegere* (see INTELLIGENT)]

in·tel·lec·tion /ínt'l éksh'n/ *n* (*formal*) **1.** thinking, reasoning, or other mental activity **2.** a thought or an idea —**in·tel·lec·tive** *adj*

in·tel·lec·tu·al /ínt'l ékchoo əl/ *adj* **1. RELATING TO THOUGHT PROCESS** relating to or involving the mental processes of abstract thinking and reasoning rather than the emotions **2. INTELLIGENT AND KNOWLEDGEABLE** having a highly developed ability to think, reason, and understand, especially in combination with wide knowledge **3. FOR INTELLIGENT PEOPLE** intended for, appealing to, or done by intelligent people ○ *intellectual pursuits* ■ *n* **INTELLIGENT PERSON** somebody with a highly developed ability to reason and understand, especially if also well educated and interested in the arts or sciences or enjoying activities involving serious mental effort [15C. Via French < late Latin *intellectualis* < Latin *intellectus* (see INTELLECT)] —**in·tel·lec·tu·al·i·ty** /ínt'l ekchoo állətee/ *n* —**in·tel·lec·tu·al·ly** *adv*

in·tel·lec·tu·al·ism /ínt'l ékchoo ə lìzzəm/ *n* **1. DEVELOPMENT OF POWER TO THINK** the development and use of the ability to think, reason, and understand **2. TOO MUCH ATTENTION TO THINKING** overemphasis on intellectual processes or pursuits **3.** PHILOSOPHY **BELIEF THAT KNOWLEDGE COMES FROM REASONING** the doctrine that all that can truly be called knowledge is derived from reasoning —**in·tel·lec·tu·al·ist** *n* —**in·tel·lec·tu·al·is·tic** /ínt'l ekchoo ə lístik/ *adj*

in·tel·lec·tu·al·ize /ínt'l ékchoo ə lìz/ (**-ized, -iz·ing, -iz·es**) *v* **1.** *vti* **CONSIDER SOMETHING RATIONALLY** to analyze, deal with, or explain something exclusively by thinking or reasoning **2.** *vi* **THINK** to think or reason **3.** *vti* **MAKE OR BECOME INTELLECTUAL** to make somebody or something intellectual, or become intellectual ○ *intellectualized poetry* **4.** *vt* PSYCHOL **REASON AWAY PROBLEMS** to protect yourself unconsciously from the emotional stress that would come from dealing with fears or problems by reasoning them away —**in·tel·lec·tu·al·i·za·tion** /ínt'l ekchoo əli záysh'n/ *n*

in·tel·lec·tu·al prop·er·ty *n* original creative work manifested in a tangible form that can be legally protected, e.g., by a patent, trademark, or copyright

in·tel·li·gence /in téllijənss/ *n* **1. ABILITY TO THINK AND LEARN** the ability to learn facts and skills and apply them, especially when this ability is highly developed **2. SECRET INFORMATION** information about secret plans or activities, especially those of foreign governments, the armed forces, business competitors, or criminals **3. GATHERING OF SECRET INFORMATION** the collection of secret military or political information **4. PEOPLE GATHERING SECRET INFORMATION** an organization that gathers information about the secret plans or activities of an adversary or potential adversary, or the people involved in gathering such information **5. INTELLIGENT SPIRIT** an entity capable of rational thought, especially one that does not have a physical form [14C. Via French < Latin *intelligentia* < *intelligent-* (see INTELLIGENT)]

in·tel·li·gence quo·tient *n* PSYCHOL, EDUC full form of **IQ**

in·tel·li·genc·er /in téllijənssər/ *n* somebody who supplies or gathers information, especially about secret plans or activities (*archaic*)

in·tel·li·gent /in téllijənt/ *adj* **1. MENTALLY ABLE** having intelligence, especially to a highly developed degree **2. SENSIBLE OR RATIONAL** showing or resulting from an ability to think and understand things clearly and logically ○ *an intelligent solution* **3.** COMPUT **ABLE TO STORE AND PROCESS DATA** having a built-in electronic processing and data storage ability ○ *an intelligent terminal* **4.** COMPUT **SELF-REGULATING** programmed to be able to adjust to changes in the environment and make deductions from information being processed ○ *an intelligent building* [Early 16C. < Latin *intelligent-*, present participle of *intellegere* "perceive, discern" < *inter-* "between" + *legere* "choose, read"] —**in·tel·li·gent·ly** *adv*

SYNONYMS ***intelligent, bright, quick, smart, clever, able, gifted***

CORE MEANING: having the ability to learn and understand easily

intelligent having a highly developed ability to learn facts and skills and apply them ○ *a highly intelligent group of engineers* ○ *We're looking for trainees who are intelligent, inquisitive, and passionate about their work.* **bright** showing an ability to think, learn, or respond quickly, especially used of younger people ○ *He's a bright and unusually focused little boy.* ○ *lucky to work with some of the real comers and bright young people* **quick** alert, perceptive, and able to respond quickly ○ *She's quick: you'll only need to explain it to her once.* **smart** showing intelligence and mental alertness ○ *too smart to be taken in by the hype* ○ *He's smart, but it was a mistake for him not to take advice.* **clever** having sharp mental abilities, sometimes suggesting showy or superficial cleverness ○ *As a bridge player, he's very clever at anticipating his opponents' moves.* ○ *her clever exploitation of Hollywood's publicity machine* **able** capable or talented ○ *an exceptionally able manager who gets results from his team* **gifted** talented, especially artistically or creatively, also used in educational circles of children who are exceptionally intelligent ○ *acclaimed as an exceptionally gifted pianist from the time of his first solo recital* ○ *took on the challenge of teaching the gifted students*

in·tel·li·gent·si·a /in tèlli jéntsee ə/ *n* the most intelligent, intellectual, or highly educated members of a society or community, especially those who are interested in the arts, literature, philosophy, and politics [Early 20C. Via Russian *intelligentsiya* < Latin *intelligentia* (see INTELLIGENCE)]

in·tel·li·gi·ble /in téllijəb'l/ *adj* **1.** capable of being understood ○ *His speech was barely intelligible.* **2.** PHILOSOPHY perceptible only by the mind, not the senses [14C. Via French < Latin *intelligibilis* < *intellegere* (see INTELLIGENT)] —**in·tel·li·gi·bil·i·ty** /in tèllijə bíllətee/ *n* —**in·tel·li·gi·bly** *adv*

In·tel·sat /ín tel sàt/, **INTELSAT** *n* **1.** an international organization that owns the communications satellites that orbit Earth and whose members include the telecommunications agencies of most countries. Full form **International Telecommunications Satellite Organization 2.** a telecommunications satellite launched by Intelsat

in·tem·per·ate /in témpərət, -prət/ *adj* **1. LACKING SELF-CONTROL** having or showing a lack of self-control, especially in expressing feelings or satisfying physical desires **2. DRINKING TO EXCESS** drinking too much alcohol, especially frequently **3.** METEOROL **TOO HOT OR COLD** extremely or unpleasantly hot or cold (*formal*) —**in·tem·per·ance** *n* —**in·tem·per·ate·ly** *adv*

in·tend /in ténd/ (**-tend·ed, -tend·ing, -tends**) *vt* **1. MEAN TO DO SOMETHING** to have something in mind as a plan ○ *I really intended to write, but I didn't have time.* **2. DO OR SAY SOMETHING FOR PURPOSE** to do, say, or produce something with a particular purpose, use, target, or group of people in mind ○ *a dictionary intended for schoolchildren* **3. MEAN SOMETHING** to signify or indicate something through speech or behavior ○ *a exchange intended to cement cultural ties* [14C. Via French < Latin *intendere* < *in-* "toward" + *tendere* "to stretch"]

in·ten·dant /in téndənt/ *n* an official or administrator in some countries, especially currently in parts of Latin America and formerly in France, Spain, and Portugal [Mid-17C. < French < Latin *intendent-*, present participle of *intendere* (see INTEND)] —**in·ten·dance** *n*

in·tend·ed /in téndəd/ *adj* **1. ENVISIONED** aimed at or designed for somebody or something ○ *our intended destination* **2. PLANNED** planned for the future ○ *an intended visit* **3. DELIBERATE** said or done deliberately ○ *an intended insult* ■ *n* **FUTURE HUSBAND OR WIFE** the person to whom somebody is engaged to be married (*dated or humorous*) ○ *He cherished the letter from his intended.*

in·tend·ing /in ténding/ *adj* planning or having in mind to be a particular thing ○ *an intending candidate*

in·tend·ment /in téndmənt/ *n* the meaning of something, especially a word or term, according to law

intens. *abbr* **1.** intensify **2.** intensive

in·tense /in ténss/ *adj* **1. EXTREME** great, strong, or extreme in a way that can be felt ○ *intense heat* **2. EFFORTFUL OR ACTIVE** involving great effort or much activity ○ *showed intense dedication to the task* **3. CONCENTRATED** narrowly focused or concentrated ○ *an intense stare* **4. PASSIONATE** feeling or showing strong and deeply felt emotions in a serious way ○ *a very intense young student* **5. THRILLING** extremely exciting or pleasing (*informal*) [15C. Via French < Latin *intensus*, past participle of *intendere* (see INTEND)] —**in·tense·ly** *adv* —**in·tense·ness** *n*

in·ten·si·fi·er /in ténssə fìər/ *n* **1.** *Can, UK* GRAM same as **intensive** *n* (sense 2) **2.** somebody or something that makes something larger, sharper, or stronger

in·ten·si·fy /in ténssə fì/ (**-fied, -fy·ing, -fies**) *vti* **1.** to become, or make something become, greater or stronger ○ *intensifying rumors of his resignation* **2.** to do something with greater effort or more activity, or become more concentrated ○ *intensified the search* —**in·ten·si·fi·ca·tion** /in tènssəfi káysh'n/ *n*

SYNONYMS See ***increase***.

in·ten·sion /in ténshən/ *n* **1.** LOGIC the meaning of an expression as opposed to what it refers to. The intension of the word "human" is the property of being human, whereas it has as its reference, or extension, human beings as a group. **2.** same as **intensity** (sense 1) (*formal*) [Early 17C. < Latin *intension-* < *intensus* (see INTENSE)] —**in·ten·sion·al** *adj* —**in·ten·sion·al·ly** *adv*

in·ten·sion·al ob·ject *n* in logic, a concept, property, or proposition, as opposed to an individual, set, or truth value, which are the extensional counterparts of intensional objects

in·ten·si·ty /in ténssətee/ (*plural* **-ties**) *n* **1. QUALITY OF BEING INTENSE** the strength, power, force, or concentration of something ○ *The pain increased in intensity.* **2. INTENSE MANNER** a passionate and serious attitude or quality ○ *a rare emotional intensity in her work* **3.** PHYS **MAGNITUDE OF ENERGY** the strength of a source of energy such as light, electricity, or sound per unit area, mass, or time

in·ten·sive /in ténssiv/ *adj* **1. CONCENTRATED** involving concentrated effort, usually in order to achieve something in a comparatively short time ○ *an intensive course in German* **2.** AGRIC **INCREASING AGRICULTURAL PRODUCTION** relating to a form of agriculture in which scientific and technological methods such as the use of chemicals that boost growth or crop yields are used to increase productivity **3. MAKING HEAVY USE OF SOMETHING** requiring or using a great deal of a particular thing (*often used in combination*) ○ *capital-intensive* **4.** GRAM **INDICATING HOW MUCH** describes a word or phrase, e.g., "extremely," that emphasizes or intensifies the word that it modifies ■ *n* **1. QUICK COURSE WITH MUCH INFORMATION** a course or workshop in which a great deal of information is absorbed in a very short time (*informal*) ○ *She's taken several intensives in personnel management.* **2.** *US* GRAM **WORD INDICATING HOW MUCH** a word or phrase, e.g., "extremely," that emphasizes or intensifies the word that it modifies. Can term **intensifier** —**in·ten·sive·ly** *adv* —**in·ten·sive·ness** *n*

in·ten·sive care *n* **1.** HEALTH SERVICES same as **intensive care unit 2.** MED the monitoring, care, and treatment in a hospital of patients who are seriously ill or injured, especially by the use of specialist equipment such as that aiding breathing ○ *needed intensive care after the accident* ◊ **critical care**

in·ten·sive care u·nit *n* the department of a hospital that is designed and equipped for the monitoring, care, and treatment of seriously ill or injured patients

in·tent /in tént/ *n* **1. PLAN OR PURPOSE** something planned, or the purpose that accompanies a plan ○ *"My intent is to use our attractive domestic market as the basis of a muscular free trade policy that will strengthen*

America's global economic reach..." (National Public Telecomputing Network, *George H. W. Bush speeches in campaign '92*; 1992) **2.** LAW **STATE OF MIND** somebody's state of mind when deliberately committing or planning to commit an illegal act **3. CONNOTATION** the meaning or significance of something, especially when not explicitly expressed ■ *adj* **1. WITH FIXED ATTENTION** having full attention or effort concentrated or focused on one thing ○ *Intent on her work, she lost track of the time.* **2. DETERMINED** showing great determination to do something ○ *They are intent on leaving early.* [13C. < Old French *entent* < Latin *intendere* (see INTEND)] —**in·tent·ly** *adv* —**in·tent·ness** *n* ◇ **to all intents and purposes** in effect, although not actually

in·ten·tion /in ténsh'n/ *n* **1. AIM OR OBJECTIVE** something that somebody plans to do ○ *State your intentions.* **2. QUALITY OF PURPOSEFULNESS** the quality or state of having a purpose in mind ○ *She acted without intention.* ■ **in·ten·tions** *npl* **SOMEBODY'S MARRIAGE PLANS** somebody's plans with respect to marriage (*dated*) [14C. Via French < Latin *intention-* < *intendere* (see INTEND)]

in·ten·tion·al /in ténshən'l, -ténshnəl/ *adj* **1.** done on purpose, not by accident **2.** PHILOSOPHY involving thoughts such as beliefs or desires about different kinds of objects, including those that have no actual existence —**in·ten·tion·al·i·ty** /in tènshə nállətee/ *n* —**in·ten·tion·al·ly** *adv*

in·ter /in túr/ (**-terred, -ter·ring, -ters**) *vt* to bury the remains of a corpse in a grave or tomb [15C. < Old French *enterer* < Latin *terra* "earth"]

inter. *abbr* intermediate

inter- *prefix* **1.** between, among ○ *interlinear* ○ *interstate* ○ *intercut* **2.** mutual, reciprocal ○ *interchange* **3.** involving two or more groups ○ *international* [Directly or via French *entre* < Latin *inter* "between, among" < Indo-European, "more in"]

in·ter·Af·ri·can *adj*
in·ter·a·gen·cy *adj*
in·ter·al·lied *adj*
in·ter·a·tom·ic *adj*
in·ter·bor·ough *adj*
in·ter·branch *adj*
in·ter·cell *adj*
in·ter·cel·lu·lar *adj*
in·ter·chro·mo·so·mal *adj*
in·ter·church *adj*
in·ter·cit·y *adj*
in·ter·class *adj*
in·ter·club *adj*
in·ter·coast·al *adj*
in·ter·col·le·giate *adj*
in·ter·com·mu·nal *adj*
in·ter·com·mu·ni·ty *adj*
in·ter·com·pa·ny *adj*
in·ter·cor·po·rate *adj*
in·ter·cor·ti·cal *adj*
in·ter·coun·try *adj*
in·ter·coun·ty *adj*
in·ter·cul·tur·al *adj*
in·ter·cul·tur·al·ly *adv*
in·ter·cul·ture *adj*
in·ter·de·nom·i·na·tion·al *adj*
in·ter·de·part·men·tal *adj*
in·ter·de·part·men·tal·ly *adv*
in·ter·dis·ci·pli·nar·y *adj*
in·ter·dis·trict *adj*
in·ter·di·vi·sion·al *adj*
in·ter·do·min·ion *adj*
in·ter·eth·nic *adj*
in·ter·fac·ul·ty *adj*
in·ter·faith *adj*
in·ter·fa·mil·ial *adj*
in·ter·fam·i·ly *adj*
in·ter·fi·ber *adj*
in·ter·firm *adj*
in·ter·fold *vt*
in·ter·fra·ter·ni·ty *adj*
in·ter·gang *adj*
in·ter·gen·er·a·tion·al *adj*
in·ter·gov·ern·men·tal *adj*
in·ter·gov·ern·men·tal·ly *adv*
in·ter·gran·u·lar *adj*
in·ter·group *adj*
in·ter·in·dus·try *adj*
in·ter·in·sti·tu·tion·al *adj*
in·ter·is·land *adj*
in·ter·ju·ris·dic·tion·al *adj*
in·ter·lend *vt*
in·ter·lob·u·lar *adj*
in·ter·mi·gra·tion *n*
in·ter·mo·lec·u·lar *adj*
in·ter·mo·lec·u·lar·ly *adv*
in·ter·o·ce·an·ic *adj*
in·ter·of·fice *adj*
in·ter·or·bi·tal *adj*
in·ter·os·cu·la·tion *n*
in·ter·par·ish *adj*
in·ter·par·ti·cle *adj*
in·ter·par·ty *adj*
in·ter·pen·e·tra·ble *adj*
in·ter·pen·e·trate *vti*
in·ter·pen·e·tra·tion *n*
in·ter·plan·e·tar·y *adj*
in·ter·pop·u·la·tion *adj*
in·ter·pro·fes·sion·al *adj*
in·ter·pro·vin·cial *adj*
in·ter·ra·cial *adj*
in·ter·ra·cial·ly *adv*
in·ter·re·gion·al *adj*
in·ter·re·li·gious *adj*
in·ter·re·nal *adj*
in·ter·scho·las·tic *adj*
in·ter·scho·las·ti·cal·ly *adv*
in·ter·school *adj*
in·ter·seg·men·tal *adj*
in·ter·sen·so·ry *adj*
in·ter·so·ci·e·tal *adj*
in·ter·so·ci·e·ty *adj*
in·ter·strat·i·fi·ca·tion *n*
in·ter·strat·i·fy *vt*
in·ter·sys·tem *adj*
in·ter·ter·ri·to·ri·al *adj*
in·ter·trib·al *adj*
in·ter·trib·al·ly *adv*
in·ter·un·ion *adj*
in·ter·u·ni·ver·si·ty *adj*
in·ter·ur·ban *adj*
in·ter·var·si·ty *adj*
in·ter·vil·lage *adj*
in·ter·war *adj*

in·ter·a·bang *n* PRINTING another spelling of **interrobang**

in·ter·act /ìntər ákt/ (**-act·ed, -act·ing, -acts**) *vi* **1.** to be or become involved in communication, social activity, or work with somebody else or one another **2.** to have an effect on somebody or something else or on one another —**in·ter·ac·tant** *n*

in·ter·ac·tion /ìntər ákshən/ *n* **1. COMMUNICATION OR COLLABORATION** communication between or joint activity involving two or more people **2. RECIPROCAL ACTION** the combined or reciprocal action of two or more things that have an effect on each other and work together **3.** PHYS **FORCE BETWEEN ELEMENTARY PARTICLES** one of the four fundamental forces, gravitational, electromagnetic, strong, and weak, that act between elementary particles

in·ter·ac·tion·ism /ìntər ákshə nìzzəm/ *n* in Western metaphysics, the theory that the mind and the body act on each other

in·ter·ac·tive /ìntər áktiv/ *adj* **1. COMMUNICATING OR COLLABORATING** involving the communication or collaboration of people or things **2.** COMPUT **WITH USER-MACHINE COMMUNICATION** allowing or involving the exchange of information or instructions between a person and a machine such as a computer or a television **3.** COMPUT **OPERATOR-CONTROLLED** operating on instructions entered by somebody at a keyboard or other input device —**in·ter·ac·tive·ly** *adv* —**in·ter·ac·tiv·i·ty** /ìntər ak tívvətee/ *n*

in·ter a·li·a /ìntər áylee ə, -áalee ə/ *adv* among other things [< Latin]

in·ter a·li·os /-áylee òss, -áalee-/ *adv* among other people [< Latin]

in·ter-A·mer·i·can *adj* involving two or more countries of North, Central, or South America

in·ter·au·ric·u·lar /ìntər aw ríkyələr/ *adj* **1. BETWEEN UPPER CHAMBERS OF HEART** situated or occurring in the area lying between the right and left upper chambers (**auricles**) of the heart **2. BETWEEN EARS** situated or occurring in the area lying between the ears **3.** PHYSIOL **INVOLVING TWO EARS** involving a physiological or acoustic relationship between the two ears

in·ter·bank /ìntər bángk/ *adj* between, connecting, or involving two or more banks

in·ter·breed /ìntər bre͞ed/ (**-bred** /-bréd/, **-breed·ing, -breeds**) *vti* **1.** to produce offspring by mating with a member of a different breed or species, or mate an animal of one breed or species with one of another **2.** to breed within a closed population or narrow range of types, or make something breed in this way

in·ter·bro·ker deal·er /ìntər brṓkər-/ *n* a broker whose job is to make stock exchange dealings between other brokers easier

in·ter·ca·lar·y /in túrkə lèrree, ìntər kállərree/ *adj* **1. INSERTED INTO CALENDAR** added to the calendar year to keep calendar years concurrent with solar years. In the Gregorian calendar February 29 is an intercalary day in leap years. **2. INDICATING YEAR WITH ADDITION** describes a year to which an intercalary day or month has been added. A leap year is an intercalary year. **3. INSERTED OR INTRODUCED** inserted between other parts (*formal*) **4.** BOT **GROWING IN INTERNODE** describes a meristem that grows in the internode of a stem [Early 17C. < Latin *intercalarius* < *intercalare* (see INTERCALATE)]

in·ter·ca·late /in túrkə làyt/ (**-lat·ed, -lat·ing, -lates**) *v* **1.** *vt* to insert an extra day or month into a calendar year in order to keep it consistent with the solar year **2.** *vti* to place something into something else, inserting it between other parts, or be placed between other parts (*formal*) [Early 17C. < Latin *intercalat-*, past participle of *intercalare* < *calare* "proclaim"] —**in·ter·ca·la·tion** /in tùrkə láysh'n/ *n* —**in·ter·ca·la·tive** *adj*

in·ter·cede /ìntər se͞ed/ (**-ced·ed, -ced·ing, -cedes**) *vi* **1. PLEAD FOR SOMEBODY** to plead with somebody in authority on behalf of somebody else, especially somebody who is to be punished for something **2. SPEAK FOR SOMEBODY** to speak in support of somebody involved in a dispute **3. MEDIATE IN DISPUTE** to attempt to settle a dispute between other people [Late 16C. < Latin *intercedere* < *cedere* "give way"] —**in·ter·ced·er** *n*

in·ter·cept *v* /ìntər sépt/ (**-cept·ed, -cept·ing, -cepts**) **1.** *vti* **INTERRUPT PROGRESS OF SOMEBODY OR SOMETHING** to prevent people or objects from reaching their destination or target by stopping, diverting, or seizing them ○ *intercepting their communications* **2.** *vt* **GET BALL** in sports, to gain possession of a ball intended for an opponent **3.** *vt* MATH **MARK EXTENT OF SOMETHING** to include part of a curve, surface, or solid between two points or lines ■ *n* /ìntər sèpt/ **1. ACT OF INTERCEPTING** the intercepting of something, especially a radio transmission, missile, or aircraft **2.** MATH **DISTANCE FROM ORIGIN TO AXIS CROSSING** the distance from the origin of a coordinate system to the point where a curve or surface crosses an axis **3.** ASTRON **DIFFERENCE BETWEEN CALCULATED AND OBSERVED ALTITUDE** the difference between the calculated and observed altitude of an astronomical object [15C. < Latin *intercept-*, past participle of *intercipere* < *capere* "seize"] —**in·ter·cep·tive** *adj*

in·ter·cept·er *n* AIR FORCE, ARMS another spelling of **interceptor**

in·ter·cep·tion /ìntər sépshən/ *n* **1.** the act or an instance of intercepting somebody or something **2.** something intercepted, especially a passed ball that is intercepted by an opponent while it is in the air

in·ter·cep·tor /ìntər séptər/, **in·ter·cept·er** *n* **1.** AIR FORCE **FAST FIGHTER PLANE** a fast, very maneuverable fighter plane designed to intercept enemy aircraft **2.** ARMS **GUIDED MISSILE** a guided missile designed to intercept enemy missiles or spacecraft **3. INTERCEPTING PERSON OR THING** somebody or something that intercepts

in·ter·ces·sion /ìntər sésh'n/ *n* **1. INTERCEDING** the action of pleading on somebody's behalf **2. ATTEMPT TO RESOLVE CONFLICT** the action of attempting to settle a dispute **3. PRAYER OR PETITION** a prayer to God, a god, or a saint on behalf of somebody or something [15C. Via French < Latin *intercession-* < *intercedere* (see INTERCEDE)] —**in·ter·ces·sion·al** *adj* —**in·ter·ces·sor** *n* —**in·ter·ces·so·ry** *adj*

in·ter·change *v* /ìntər cháynj/ (**-changed, -chang·ing, -chang·es**) **1.** *vti* **SWITCH OR SWAP PLACES** to put each of two things in the place of the other, or change places with something else **2.** *vti* **ALTERNATE OR FOLLOW EACH OTHER** to arrange things alternately in a series, or be arranged in this way **3.** *vt* **EXCHANGE THINGS** to give something to somebody and receive a similar thing from them in return ■ *n* /íntər chàynj/ **1. EXCHANGE OF THINGS** an exchange of things, especially ideas, opinions, or information, among people **2. ALTERNATION** the action of alternating or changing places **3.** ROADS **ROAD INTERSECTION** a major road junction where vehicles can, by means of access roads, bridges, and underpasses, change from one road to another without stopping or crossing other traffic **4.** TRANSP **PLACE WHERE PASSENGERS CHANGE TRANSPORTATION** a place where passengers can change from one train or bus to another or between trains and buses [14C. < Old French *entrechangier* < *entre* (see INTER-) + *changier* (see CHANGE)] —**in·ter·change·a·bil·i·ty** /ìntər chàynjə bíllətee/ *n* —**in·ter·change·a·ble** *adj* —**in·ter·change·a·bly** *adv* —**in·ter·chang·er** *n*

in·ter·change fee *n* a fee paid by one bank to another to cover cardholder costs until payment is made

in·ter·co·lum·ni·a·tion /ìntər kə lumnee áysh'n/ *n* in architecture, a system used to space columns in a colonnade, based on the use of their diameters as a measurement

in·ter·com /íntər kòm/ *n* a system or device that allows people in different parts of a building, aircraft, or ship to speak to each other [Mid-20C. Shortening of *intercommunication system*]

in·ter·com·mu·ni·cate /ìntər kə myo͞oni kàyt/ (**-cat·ed, -cat·ing, -cates**) *vi* **1.** to communicate with each other **2.** to be connected to something else or each other, especially to another room by means of a door in the dividing wall ○ *intercommunicating hotel rooms* —**in·ter·com·mu·ni·ca·tion** /-myo͞oni káysh'n/ *n* —**in·ter·com·mu·ni·ca·tive** /-kàytiv/ *adj* —**in·ter·com·mu·ni·ca·tor** *n*

in·ter·com·mun·ion /ìntər kə myo͞onyən/ *n* **1.** an arrangement between different Christian denominations enabling members to receive the Communion at each other's services **2.** a close relationship between people or groups, especially one that involves mutual participation or action

in·ter·con·nect /ìntər kə nékt/ (**-nect·ed, -nect·ing, -nects**) *vti* **1.** to be joined to something else or to a number of joined things, or make something part of such a network (*often passive*) ○ *The rooms are interconnected to form a suite.* **2.** to show a relationship between two or more things, or be related —**in·ter·con·nect·i·ble** *adj* —**in·ter·con·nec·tion** *n*

in·ter·con·nec·tive /ìntər kə néktiv/ *adj* connecting or capable of connecting with something else or with each other —**in·ter·con·nec·tiv·i·ty** /ìntər kə nék tívvətee/ *n*

in·ter·con·ti·nen·tal /intər kontə nént'l/ *adj* **1.** involving or occurring between two or more continents **2.** going from one continent to another —**in·ter·con·ti·nen·tal·ly** *adv*

in·ter·con·ti·nen·tal bal·lis·tic mis·sile *n* a ballistic missile with a range of 3,000 to 8,000 nautical miles

in·ter·con·ver·sion /intərkən vúrzh'n/ *n* the mutual conversion or two or more things, e.g., heat into work, as in an engine, and work into heat —**in·ter·con·vert** *vt* —**in·ter·con·vert·i·bil·i·ty** /intərkən vurtə bíllətee/ *n* —**in·ter·con·vert·i·ble** *adj*

in·ter·cool·er /íntər kòolər/ *n* a heat exchanger that cools a fluid between successive stages of compression or chemical reaction

in·ter·cos·tal /intər kóst'l/ *adj* situated or occurring between the ribs ○ *an intercostal nerve* [Late 16C. < INTER- + Latin *costa* "side, rib"]

in·ter·course /íntər kàwrss/ *n* **1.** same as **sexual intercourse 2.** exchanges between people or groups, especially conversation or social activity (*formal*) [15C. Via Old French *entrecours* "commerce" < Latin *intercursus* "running between" < *currere* "to run"]

in·ter·crop /intər króp/ (**-cropped, -crop·ping, -crops**) *vti* to grow different crops in the same field, usually in alternate rows, or plant a crop between the rows of another crop —**in·ter·crop** /íntər kròp/ *n*

in·ter·crop·ping /íntər kròpping/ *n* the growing of two or more crops with different characteristics and requirements at the same time on the same plot of land

in·ter·cur·rent /intər kúrrənt, -kúr ənt/ *adj* **1.** occurring during and changing the course of an already existing disease ○ *treating an intercurrent infection* **2.** occurring at the same time as something else or during the period between two other events (*formal*) [Early 17C. < Latin *intercurrent-*, present participle of *intercurrere* "run between" < *currere* "to run"] —**in·ter·cur·rence** *n* —**in·ter·cur·rent·ly** *adv*

in·ter·cut /intər kút/ (**-cut, -cut·ting, -cuts**) *vt* to alternate scenes or shots of a movie, usually to show different events taking place at the same time

in·ter·den·tal /intər dént'l/ *adj* **1.** BETWEEN THE TEETH existing between or designed for use between the teeth **2.** WITH TONGUE BETWEEN TEETH describes a speech sound that is made by placing the tip of the tongue between the teeth ■ *n* SOUND MADE WITH TONGUE BETWEEN TEETH a sound made by putting the tip of the tongue between the teeth —**in·ter·den·tal·ly** *adv*

in·ter·de·pend·ent /intər di péndənt/ *adj* **1.** unable to exist or survive without each other ○ *interdependent organisms* **2.** relying on mutual assistance, support, cooperation, or interaction among constituent parts or members —**in·ter·de·pend** *vi* —**in·ter·de·pend·ence** *n* —**in·ter·de·pend·ent·ly** *adv*

in·ter·dict *n* /íntər dìkt/ **1.** PROHIBITIVE ORDER a court order that prohibits something **2.** EXCLUSION FROM CHURCH SACRAMENTS a ban imposed by a pope, church council, or bishop that excludes a person, group, or nation from the sacraments of the Roman Catholic Church. In the past, the interdict was used to enforce obedience. ■ *vt* /intər díkt/ (**-dict·ed, -dict·ing, -dicts**) **1.** BAN SOMEBODY OR SOMETHING BY LAW to prohibit something or forbid somebody from doing something, especially in accordance with civil or ecclesiastical law **2.** PREVENT ILLEGAL ENTRY to prevent somebody or something from entering a country illegally ○ *Patrols will be increased along the border to interdict smugglers.* **3.** KEEP ENEMY OUT OF AREA to keep an enemy from using an area by troop movements or other means [13C. Via French < Latin *interdictum* < *interdicere* "prohibit" < *dicere* "speak"] —**in·ter·dic·tion** *n* —**in·ter·dic·tor** *n* —**in·ter·dic·to·ry** *adj*

in·ter·dig·i·tal /intər díjjit'l/ *adj* **1.** arranged in the form of two series of parallel strips that fit together like the fingers of clasped hands **2.** situated between the fingers or toes —**in·ter·dig·i·tal·ly** *adv*

in·ter·dig·i·tate /intər díjji tàyt/ (**-tat·ed, -tat·ing, -tates**) *vti* to fit together like the fingers of clasped hands, or place or hold objects together in such a pattern —**in·ter·dig·i·ta·tion** /intər diji táysh'n/ *n*

in·ter·dine /intər dín/ (**-dined, -din·ing, -dines**) *vi S Asia* to eat a meal with somebody belonging to a different religion or caste

in·ter·est /íntrəst/ *n* **1.** CURIOSITY OR CONCERN a feeling of curiosity or concern about something that makes the attention turn toward it ○ *an interest in art* **2.** QUALITY THAT ATTRACTS ATTENTION a power, quality, or aspect of something that attracts attention, concern, or curiosity ○ *It's of no interest to me.* **3.** ENJOYABLE THING something that somebody enjoys doing (*often used in the plural*) ○ *My leisure interests include sailing, music, reading, and walking.* **4.** BENEFIT OR ADVANTAGE the good, benefit, or advantage of somebody or something ○ *in the interests of peace* **5.** INVOLVEMENT somebody's involvement with something that makes its progress or success important to him or her ○ *took a personal interest in the progress of the project* **6.** BORROWING CHARGE OR PAYMENT a charge made for a loan or credit facility, or a payment made by a bank or other financial institution for the use of money deposited in an account **7.** SHARE IN SOMETHING a legal right to claim a share in something, especially in a business or property, or the business or property itself **8.** CONNECTION a personal or commercial connection with something or somebody, especially when this prevents somebody from being objective or impartial ○ *had to declare a conflict of interest* ■ **in·ter·ests** *npl* INFLUENTIAL GROUP a group of people in business or society who have the same objectives or support the same cause, especially a powerful or influential group ■ *vt* (**-est·ed, -est·ing, -ests**) **1.** GET SOMEBODY'S ATTENTION to attract or hold somebody's attention or arouse somebody's curiosity or concern ○ *It may interest you to know that the building used to be a mortuary.* **2.** MAKE SOMEBODY WANT SOMETHING to make somebody want to have or buy something, do something, or become involved with something ○ *I tried to interest him in helping with the preparations.* [15C. Alteration of Anglo-Norman *interesse* < medieval Latin, "compensation for loss" < Latin, "differ, be important," by association with Old French *interest* "damage, loss" < Latin, "it matters"]

in·ter·est·ed /íntrəstəd/ *adj* **1.** CURIOUS OR CONCERNED paying attention to something or devoting time to something because of curiosity, concern, or enjoyment **2.** WANTING SOMETHING involved or wanting to be involved in something ○ *interested parties* **3.** AFFECTED OR INVOLVED having a legal right or share in something or a personal or commercial connection with something —**in·ter·est·ed·ly** *adv* —**in·ter·est·ed·ness** *n*

in·ter·est group *n* **1.** a group of people who act or work together in support of a cause **2.** a group of people who share an interest in something such as a subject of study

in·ter·est·ing /íntrəsting/ *adj* **1.** arousing curiosity, attracting or holding attention, or provoking thought **2.** enjoyable because of being varied, challenging, stimulating, or exciting —**in·ter·est·ing·ly** *adv*

in·ter·face *n* /íntər fàyss/ **1.** COMMON BOUNDARY the surface, place, or point where two things touch each other or meet **2.** BOUNDARY BETWEEN THINGS a common boundary between objects or different phases of a substance ○ *an oil-water interface* **3.** POINT OF INTERACTION the place, situation, or way in which two things or people act together or affect each other, or the point of connection between things **4.** COMPUT BOUNDARY ACROSS WHICH DATA PASSES a common boundary shared by two devices, or by a person and a device, across which data or information flows, e.g., the screen of a computer **5.** COMPUT LINKING SOFTWARE software that links a computer with another device, or the set of commands, messages, images, and other features allowing communication between computer and user **6.** ELECTRONICS LINKING DEVICE an electronic device or circuit or other point of physical contact between two pieces of equipment ■ *vti* /íntər fàyss, ìntər fáyss/ (**-faced, -fac·ing, -fac·es**) **1.** HAVE OR GIVE COMMON BOUNDARY to touch or meet at a surface, place, or point, or make things join in this way **2.** INTERACT to act together or affect each other, or make things or people interact **3.** SERVE AS INTERFACE to connect two or more pieces of equipment, or be connected —**in·ter·fa·cial** /intər fáysh'l/ *adj* —**in·ter·fa·cial·ly** *adv*

in·ter·fac·ing /íntər fàyssing/ *n* a fabric that is used to stiffen or support collars, cuffs, or other parts of a garment

~~**interferance**~~ incorrect spelling of **interference**

in·ter·fere /intər féer/ (**-fered, -fer·ing, -feres**) *vi* **1.** HAVE UNDESIRABLE EFFECT to delay, hinder, or obstruct the natural or desired course of something ○ *The weather interfered with our plans.* **2.** MEDDLE IN OTHER PEOPLE'S AFFAIRS to participate in the affairs of others, especially by offering unwanted or unhelpful advice or by trying to resolve other people's disputes ○ *It's not advisable to interfere in a private quarrel.* **3.** OBSTRUCT ILLEGALLY to obstruct, block, or hinder illegally an opponent in a sport ○ *a 15-yard penalty for interfering with the pass* **4.** PHYS AFFECT DISPLACEMENT OR AMPLITUDE to act together to increase, decrease, or cancel out displacement or amplitude **5.** COMMUNICATION, ELECTRONICS CAUSE INTERFERENCE to cause electronic interference **6.** HIT HOOF AGAINST LEG to hit one hoof against the opposite hoof or leg while walking (*refers to horses*) [15C. < Old French *s'entreferir* "strike each other" < Latin *ferire* "to strike"] —**in·ter·fer·er** *n*

in·ter·fer·ence /intər féerənss/ *n* **1.** HINDRANCE hindrance or obstruction that prevents a natural or desired outcome **2.** MEDDLING IN OTHER PEOPLE'S AFFAIRS involvement in something without any invitation or justification ○ *He deeply resented any interference in his private life.* **3.** SPORTS ILLEGAL OBSTRUCTING in some sports, the illegal blocking, hindering, or obstruction of an opposing player **4.** FOOTBALL LEGAL BLOCKING in football, the legal blocking of defensive players to protect and make way for the player carrying the ball **5.** COMMUNICATION, ELECTRONICS SIGNAL THAT INTERFERES an unwanted signal that disrupts radio, telephone, or television reception **6.** PHYS PROCESS OF WAVE INTERACTION a process in light-wave transmission in which two or more waves are superimposed in such a way that they produce higher peaks, lower troughs, or a new wave pattern —**in·ter·fer·en·tial** /intərfə rénshəl/ *adj* ◇ **run interference 1.** in football, to carry out legal blocking of defensive players to protect and make way for the player carrying the ball **2.** to contribute help or support to somebody or something, especially by preventing others from acting as a hindrance (*informal*)

in·ter·fer·ing /intər féering/ *adj* deliberately becoming involved in other people's affairs in a way that is neither needed nor welcome —**in·ter·fer·ing·ly** *adv*

in·ter·fe·rom·e·ter /intərfə rómmətər/ *n* a device that uses an interference pattern to determine wave frequency, length, or velocity —**in·ter·fer·o·met·ric** /intər feerə méttrik/ *adj* —**in·ter·fer·o·met·ri·cal·ly** *adv* —**in·ter·fe·rom·e·try** *n*

in·ter·fer·on /intər féer òn/ *n* a protein produced by cells in response to virus infection that inhibits viral replication [Mid-20C. < INTERFERE]

in·ter·fer·tile /intər fúrt'l/ *adj* able to interbreed with other species or subspecies and produce viable offspring —**in·ter·fer·til·i·ty** /intər fər tíllətee/ *n*

in·ter·file /intər fíl/ (**-filed, -fil·ing, -files**) *vt* to put an item or items among similar items in a file

in·ter·flow /intər flṓ/ (**-flowed, -flow·ing, -flows**) *vi* to merge into a single stream

in·ter·flu·ent /intər flóo ənt/ *adj* **1.** merging into a single stream **2.** flowing between things or places [Mid-17C. < Latin *interfluent-*, present participle of *interfluere* "flow together" < *fluere* "to flow"]

in·ter·fluve /intər flóov/ *n* **1.** the ridge line separating two drainage basins **2.** a line joining points on one side of which water will flow to one river while on the other side water will flow to another river [Early 20C. Back-formation < *interfluvial*] —**in·ter·flu·vi·al** *adj*

in·ter·fuse /intər fyóoz/ (**-fused, -fus·ing, -fuses**) *vti* to mingle, blend, or fuse thoroughly, or mix two or more things in this way (*literary*) [Late 16C. < Latin *interfus-*, past participle of *interfundere* "pour together" < *fundere* "pour"] —**in·ter·fu·sion** *n*

in·ter·ga·lac·tic /intərgə láktik/ *adj* situated, happening, or moving between galaxies, or involving two or more galaxies —**in·ter·ga·lac·ti·cal·ly** *adv*

in·ter·gla·cial /intər gláysh'l/ *n* a period of warmer climate separating two periods of glaciation and displaying a characteristic sequence of changes in vegetation. The term is used especially for several such periods that occurred during the Pleistocene epoch, lasting from 1.8 million to 10,000 years ago. —**in·ter·gla·cial** *adj*

In·ter·gov·ern·men·tal Pan·el on Cli·mate Change *n* an international body set up in 1988 to assess the scientific, technical, and socio-economic information relating to human-induced climate change

in·ter·grade /intər gráyd/ *vi* (**-grad·ed, -grad·ing, -grades**) CHANGE BY STAGES to be transformed from one form to another through a series of stages or forms that involve partial transitions ■ *n* 1. TRANSITIONAL FORM a transitional form or stage 2. TRANSITIONAL SOIL HORIZON a transitional soil horizon between two distinctive soils —**in·ter·gra·da·tion** /-grə dáysh'n/ *n* —**in·ter·gra·di·ent** /intər gráydee ənt/ *adj*

in·ter·growth /intər grōth/ *n* growth of one thing into or within another thing, or among other things, or the result of such growth

in·ter·im /intərim/ *adj* 1. HAVING TEMPORARY EFFECT serving as a temporary measure until something more complete and permanent can be established 2. HOLDING TEMPORARY OFFICE serving temporarily until a permanent replacement can be elected or appointed ■ *n* INTERVENING TIME a period of time between two occurrences or periods ○ *in the interim* [Mid-16C. < Latin, "meanwhile"]

in·ter·i·on·ic /intər ī ónnik/ *adj* situated between or involving two or more ions

in·te·ri·or /in teéree ər/ *n* 1. INSIDE PART the inside of something ○ *The interior of the church was dark.* 2. INSIDE OF BUILDING OR ROOM the inside of a building or room considered especially with regard to its decoration and furnishing 3. PART FARTHEST IN FROM EDGE the part of something that is far or farthest from its edge, boundary, or surface, especially the part of a country or continent that is remote or farthest from the coast 4. PICTURE OF INSIDE OF ROOM a painting or photograph of the inside of a room 5. INSIDE SET OR SCENE a setting or actual location that represents the inside of a building, or a scene filmed inside a building 6. POL another spelling of **Interior** ■ *adj* 1. LOCATED INSIDE located in, suitable for, or occurring inside something 2. CENTRAL remote or farthest from the edge, boundary, or surface of something, especially from the coast of a country or continent 3. OCCURRING IN MIND taking place within somebody's mind and usually not expressed out loud 4. POL another spelling of **Interior** [15C. Directly or via French < Latin, literally "more in the midst of" < *inter* (see INTER-)] —**in·te·ri·or·i·ty** /in teéree áwrətee/ *n* —**in·te·ri·or·ly** *adv*

In·te·ri·or *n* in the United States and some other countries, the domestic affairs of the nation, especially as opposed to its foreign affairs ■ *adj* relating to the domestic affairs of a country, especially as opposed to its foreign affairs

in·te·ri·or an·gle *n* 1. the angle formed between two adjacent sides of a polygon and lying in its interior. The sum of the interior angles of any polygon is equal to the number of its sides minus two and multiplied by 180°. 2. any of the four angles formed in the area between two parallel lines by a third line that intersects them (**transversal**)

in·te·ri·or ar·rang·er *n* somebody whose business is to change the appearance of a house or room, using and rearranging furnishings and accessories that are already there

in·te·ri·or dec·o·ra·tion *n* 1. DECORATIONS AND FURNISHINGS the way that a room or building is decorated and furnished 2. PLANNING OF DECORATION the art or process of planning the decoration and furnishings of a room or building 3. *UK* WALLPAPERING AND PAINTING the skill or trade of somebody who specializes in wallpapering and painting interiors —**in·te·ri·or dec·o·ra·tor** *n*

in·te·ri·or de·sign *n UK* same as **interior decoration** —**in·te·ri·or de·sign·er** *n*

in·te·ri·or mon·o·logue *n* an extended passage in a story or novel that expresses what a character is thinking and feeling

In·te·ri·or Sa·lish (*plural same*) *n* a member of a Native North American people who formerly lived in British Columbia, northern Washington, northern Idaho, and western Montana and now live on a reservation in Montana —**In·te·ri·or Sa·lish** *adj*

in·te·ri·or-sprung *adj UK* FURNITURE same as **innerspring**

in·ter·ject /intər jékt/ (**-ject·ed, -ject·ing, -jects**) *vti* to say or insert something in a way that interrupts what is being said or discussed [Late 16C. < Latin *interject-*, past participle of *interjicere* "interpose," literally "throw between" < *jacere* "to throw"] —**in·ter·jec·tor** *n* —**in·ter·jec·to·ry** *adj*

in·ter·jec·tion /intər jékshən/ *n* 1. a sound, word, or phrase that expresses a strong emotion such as pain or surprise but otherwise has no meaning 2. something said loudly and abruptly, or something inserted in a text, especially something that interrupts what is being said or discussed —**in·ter·jec·tion·al** *adj* —**in·ter·jec·tion·al·ly** *adv*

in·ter·ki·ne·sis /intər ki neéssiss, -kī-/ *n* the period of rest between meiotic cell divisions, similar to the interphase stage in mitosis

in·ter·lace /intər láyss/ (**-laced, -lac·ing, -lac·es**) *v* 1. *vti* to join or interweave two or more things together, often in an intricate pattern, or be joined or interwoven in this way 2. *vt* to break up the flow or relieve the monotony of something by occasionally inserting something different, e.g., jokes in a serious talk [14C. < Old French *entrelacier* "lace together" < *lacier* "to lace"] —**in·ter·lace·ment** *n*

in·ter·laced scan·ning *n* a technique used in television and computer monitors in which high vertical resolution is achieved by scanning all odd- and then all even-numbered lines

in·ter·lan·guage /intər làng gwidj/ *n* a form of language produced by learners of a second or foreign language, combining features of two or more languages

in·ter·lard /intər laárd/ (**-lard·ed, -lard·ing, -lards**) *vt* to vary, punctuate, or interrupt speech or writing by interspersing contrasting material [Mid-16C. < French *entrelarder* "mix with layers of fat" < *larde* "lard"]

in·ter·lay *vt* /intər láy/ (**-laid** /-láyd/, **-lay·ing, -lays**) to layer something with something else ■ *n* /intər lày/ something laid between two surfaces

in·ter·leaf /intər leéf/ (*plural* **-leaves** /-leévz/) *n* an extra sheet or page, usually a blank one, inserted into a book

in·ter·leave /intər leév/ (**-leaved, -leav·ing, -leaves**) *vt* to add extra sheets or pages, usually blank ones, between the pages of a book, e.g., to allow for notes or to protect illustrations [Mid-17C. < INTER- + LEAF]

in·ter·leaves plural of **interleaf**

in·ter·leu·kin /intər loókin/ *n* a chemical found in white blood cells that stimulates them to fight infection [Late 20C. < INTER- + LEUKOCYTE + -IN]

in·ter·leu·kin-1 *n* an interleukin that stimulates the production of other factors that activate the immune system

in·ter·leu·kin-2 *n* an interleukin that stimulates T-cells and is used in the treatment of cancer

in·ter·li·brar·y loan /intər lī̀b rerree-/ *n* 1. BOOK-BORROWING SYSTEM a system by which libraries and library users can borrow books from other libraries 2. BORROWING OF BOOK a borrowing of a book through an interlibrary loan system 3. BOOK BORROWED a book borrowed through an interlibrary loan system

in·ter·line[1] /intər lī́n/ (**-lined, -lin·ing, -lines**) *vt* to write or print words between the lines of writing or printing in a text or document [15C. < medieval Latin *interlineare* < Latin *linea* (see LINE[1])] —**in·ter·lin·e·a·tion** /intər linee áysh'n/ *n*

in·ter·line[2] /intər lī́n/ (**-lined, -lin·ing, -lines**) *vt* to put an extra lining between the fabric and the lining of a curtain or piece of clothing [15C. < INTER- + LINE[2]]

in·ter·lin·e·ar /intər línnee ər/, **in·ter·lin·e·al** /intər línnee əl/ *adj* 1. inserted between the lines of a text or document 2. written or printed with different versions of the same text on alternate or succeeding lines [14C. < medieval Latin *interlinearis* < Latin *linea* (see LINE[1])] —**in·ter·lin·e·ar·ly** *adv*

In·ter·lin·gua /intər líng gwə/ *n* an artificial language designed to facilitate international communication, based on the common features of living Latinate languages [Early 20C. < INTER- + Latin *lingua* "tongue, language"]

in·ter·lin·ing /intər lī̀ning/ *n* an extra lining inserted between the fabric and lining of a curtain or piece of clothing to make it thicker or warmer, or the fabric used for this

in·ter·link /intər língk/ (**-linked, -link·ing, -links**) *vti* to connect something with something else in several ways, or be connected together in several ways

in·ter·lock /intər lòk/ *vti* (**-locked, -lock·ing, -locks**) 1. FIT TOGETHER CLOSELY to fit things together closely, especially by means of parts that mesh, hook, or dovetail, or be fitted together in this way 2. OPERATE AS UNIT to connect parts in such a way that all move or operate if one does, or be connected in this way ■ *n* 1. MECH ENG CONNECTING AND COORDINATING DEVICE a device that connects parts of something such as a machine in a way that coordinates their action 2. CLOSE CONNECTION a close connection by means of parts that fit or fasten together closely and firmly 3. TEXTILES TIGHTLY KNITTED FABRIC a fabric made with tightly knitted stitches 4. HANDICRAFT CANVAS FOR NEEDLEPOINT canvas used for needlepoint that has the warp and weft threads knotted together to prevent movement 5. COMPUT COMPUTER SECURITY DEVICE a security device designed to prevent unauthorized use of a computer, e.g., a password system ■ *adj* TIGHTLY KNITTED knitted with close, tight stitches

in·ter·lock·ing di·rec·tor·ates *npl* boards of directors that have enough members in common to place the companies that they oversee under the same control

in·ter·loc·u·tor /intər lókyətər/ *n* 1. a participant in a discussion or conversation (*formal*) 2. a performer in a minstrel show who acted as the master of ceremonies and stood in the middle and bantered with the end men [Early 16C. < modern Latin < Latin *interlocut-*, form of *interloqui* "to interrupt"]

in·ter·loc·u·to·ry /intər lókyə tàwree/ *adj* 1. issued provisionally during a lawsuit ○ *an interlocutory decree* 2. involving or characteristic of conversation or discussion (*formal*)

in·ter·lop·er /intər lōpər/ *n* 1. an intruder into a place, gathering, or situation 2. somebody who interferes in other people's affairs, especially for selfish reasons [Late 16C. After archaic *landloper* "vagabond" < Middle Dutch *landlooper* "land-runner" < *loopen* "to run"] —**in·ter·lope** *vi*

in·ter·lude /intər lood/ *n* 1. a relatively short period of time between two longer periods, during which something happens that is different from what has happened before and what follows 2. a short play, piece of music, or other entertainment performed during a break in the performance of a long work [14C. < medieval Latin *interludium* "in-between-play" (because originally performed between the acts of a medieval mystery play) < Latin *ludus* "play"]

in·ter·mar·riage /intər márrij/ *n* 1. marriage between members of different religious, social, or racial groups, or an instance of this 2. marriage between members of the same people, clan, or other kinship group, or an instance of this

in·ter·mar·ry /intər márree/ (**-ried, -ry·ing, -ries**) *vi* 1. to marry a member of a different religious, social, or racial group 2. to marry a member of the same people, clan, or other kinship group

in·ter·me·di·ar·y /intər meédee èrree/ *n* (*plural* **-ies**) 1. GO-BETWEEN somebody who carries messages between people, or tries to help them reach an agreement 2. MEANS OR MEDIUM something that functions as a means or medium for bringing something about ■ *adj* 1. MEDIATING acting as a messenger or mediator between two or more people or groups 2. LYING IN BETWEEN lying or occurring between two different forms, states, points, or extremes [Late 18C. < French *intermédiaire* < Latin *intermedius* (see INTERMEDIATE[1])]

in·ter·me·di·ate[1] /intər meédee ət/ *adj* 1. BEING IN BETWEEN lying or occurring between two different forms, states, points, or extremes ○ *an intermediate course* 2. GEOL CONTAINING BETWEEN 55% AND 66% SILICA describes an igneous rock with a silica content of between 55 percent and 66 percent ■ *n* 1. SOMETHING BETWEEN TWO OTHER THINGS something that lies or occurs between two different forms, states, points, or extremes 2. same as **intermediary** *n* (sense 1) 3. CHEM CHEMICAL FOR FURTHER REACTIONS a chemical compound that is formed during a chemical reaction and is used in another reaction to obtain another compound 4. CHEM SHORT-LIVED CHEMICAL COMPONENT a molecule, ion, or free radical that exists for a short time during a chemical reaction [15C. Directly or via French < medieval Latin *intermediatus* < Latin *intermedius* < *medius* "middle"] —**in·ter·me·di·ate·ly** *adv* —**in·ter·me·di·ate·ness** *n*

in·ter·me·di·ate[2] /intər meédee àyt/ (**-at·ed, -at·ing, -ates**) *vi* to act as a go-between or mediator between two or more people or groups [Early 16C. < INTER- + MEDIATE] —**in·ter·me·di·a·tion** /intər meedee áysh'n/ *n* —**in·ter·me·di·a·tor** *n*

in·ter·me·di·ate-act·ing *adj* having a period of therapeutic activity that is between that of long-acting and short-acting drugs

in·ter·me·di·ate bulk con·tain·er *n* a portable container for transporting liquids or solids that holds 132 to 264 gallons/500 to 1,000 liters or 1,100 to 3,300 lb./500 to 1,500 kg. It is intermediate in size between a drum and a tanker load.

in·ter·me·di·ate fre·quen·cy *n* the frequency that an incoming signal is changed to in a heterodyne receiver prior to amplification

in·ter·me·di·ate host *n* an animal that is the host for an immature parasite, which then moves on to a different host before reproducing

in·ter·me·di·ate-lev·el waste *n* radioactive waste from reactors and processing plants that is solidified, mixed with concrete, and stored in drums. These drums are then placed for long-term storage in waste repositories.

in·ter·me·di·ate-range bal·lis·tic mis·sile *n* a ballistic missile that has a range of 750 to 1,000 mi./1,200 to 1,600 km

in·ter·me·di·ate school *n* EDUC same as **junior high, middle school**

in·ter·me·di·ate vec·tor bo·son *n* an elementary particle that transmits weak interactions between other elementary particles. The three postulated intermediate vector bosons, the W^+, W^-, and Z^0 particles, have all been observed.

in·ter·me·din /intər meéd'n/ *n* PHYSIOL same as **melanocyte-stimulating hormone** [Mid-20C. < modern Latin *(pars) intermedia* "intermediate (part) (of the pituitary)" < Latin *intermedius* (see INTERMEDIATE 1)]

in·ter·ment /in túrmənt/ *n* the burial of a corpse, usually accompanied by a funeral ceremony

in·ter·mer·cial *n* ONLINE same as **interstitial** [Late 20C. < INTER- + COMMERCIAL]

in·ter·mesh /intər mésh/ (**-meshed, -mesh·ing, -mesh·es**) *vti* to engage or mesh with one another, or cause something such as the teeth of gears to do so

in·ter·me·tal·lic /intərmə tállik/ *adj* consisting of two or more metals in specific proportions

in·ter·mez·zo /intər mét sō/ (*plural* **-zos** or **-zi** /-métsee/) *n* **1.** a short piece of music that is performed between longer movements of an extended musical composition **2.** a short musical composition, usually for solo piano **3.** ARTS same as **interlude** (sense 2) [Late 18C. Via Italian < Latin *intermedius* (see INTERMEDIATE 1)]

in·ter·mi·na·ble /in túrminəb'l/ *adj* so long and boring or frustrating as to seem endless ○ *interminable delays* [14C. Directly or via French < late Latin *interminabilis* "unending" < Latin *terminare* (see TERMINATE)] —**in·ter·mi·na·bil·i·ty** /in tùrmənə bíllətee/ *n* —**in·ter·mi·na·bly** *adv*

in·ter·min·gle /intər míng g'l/ (**-gled, -gling, -gles**) *vti* to mix something together with something else, or become mixed together ○ *The scents of jasmine and honeysuckle intermingled.*

in·ter·mis·sion /intər mísh'n/ *n* **1.** a break between parts of a musical or theatrical performance or in the showing of a movie in a movie theater **2.** a pause in, or temporary discontinuation of, an activity [15C. Directly or via French < Latin *intermission-* < *intermiss-*, past participle of *intermittere* (see INTERMIT)]

in·ter·mit /intər mít/ (**-mit·ted, -mit·ting, -mits**) *vti* (*formal*) **1.** to discontinue doing something temporarily, or be discontinued temporarily **2.** to stop for a short time or for short intervals, or cause something to stop in this way [Mid-16C. < Latin *intermittere* "interrupt," literally "send between" < *mittere* "send"] —**in·ter·mit·ter** *n* —**in·ter·mit·ting·ly** *adv*

in·ter·mit·tent /intər mítt'nt/ *adj* occurring at irregular intervals [Mid-16C. < Latin *intermittent-*, present participle of *intermittere* (see INTERMIT)] —**in·ter·mit·tence** *n* —**in·ter·mit·tent·ly** *adv*

SYNONYMS See *periodic.*

in·ter·mit·tent clau·di·ca·tion *n* a cramping pain, induced by exercise and relieved by rest, that is caused by inadequate blood supply to the affected muscles, usually the calves

in·ter·mit·tent cur·rent *n* a unidirectional current that is interrupted periodically

in·ter·mit·tent fe·ver *n* a fever that rises and falls and then returns, occurring in diseases such as malaria

in·ter·mix /intər míks/ (**-mixed, -mix·ing, -mix·es**) *vti* same as **intermingle** —**in·ter·mix·a·ble** *adj*

in·ter·mod·al /intər mṓd'l/ *adj* describes containers designed to be transferred from one means of transportation to another while in transit, e.g., from a train to a ship to a truck ■ *n* a container for freight that can be transferred from one mode of transportation to another during shipment without being unpacked

in·ter·mod·u·la·tion /intər mojə láysh'n/ *n* the undesired interaction of electronic signals of different frequencies transmitted within a nonlinear system, resulting in distortion

in·ter·mon·tane /intər món tàyn/ *adj* describes basins that lie between two mountain ranges and often fill up with sediment washed down from them

in·ter·mu·ral /intər myŏŏrəl/ *adj* involving participants from two or more educational institutions, athletic clubs, or other groups

in·tern /íntərn/ *n also* **in·terne 1.** JUNIOR DOCTOR IN HOSPITAL a doctor who has recently graduated from medical school and is receiving practical supervised training in a hospital **2.** TRAINEE an assistant or trainee working to gain practical experience in an occupation ■ *v* (**-terned, -tern·ing, -terns**) **1.** *vi* WORK AS TRAINEE to work as a trainee gaining practical experience, e.g., as a junior doctor in a hospital **2.** /in tùrn, in túrn/ *vt* DETAIN SOMEBODY to detain somebody in confinement as being a security threat [Mid-19C. < French *interne* (noun), *interner* (verb) < Latin *internus* (see INTERNAL)] —**in·tern·ment** /in túrnmənt/ *n* —**in·tern·ship** *n*

in·ter·nal /in túrn'l/ *adj* **1.** LOCATED INSIDE located within or affecting the inside of something, especially the inside of the body ○ *internal organs* **2.** INTENDED FOR USE INSIDE effective when used or suitable for use inside something, especially inside the body **3.** SELF-CONTAINED OR SELF-GENERATING existing, evident in, or arising from the nature, structure, or qualities that somebody or something has ○ *internal cohesion* **4.** OCCURRING WITHIN COUNTRY originating, operating, or located within a country's borders ○ *internal affairs* **5.** MENTAL involving or existing within the mind or spirit ○ *internal conflict* **6.** OCCURRING WITHIN ORGANIZATION working at or carried out within an organization or institution ○ *internal e-mail* [15C. Directly or via French < medieval Latin *internalis* < Latin *internus* "inward, within" < *inter* (see INTER-)] —**in·ter·nal·i·ty** /intər nállətee/ *n* —**in·ter·nal·ly** *adv* —**in·ter·nal·ness** *n*

in·ter·nal clock *n* **1.** a clock within a machine such as a computer, that may control some of the functions of the machine **2.** BIOL same as **biological clock**

in·ter·nal-com·bus·tion en·gine *n* an engine in which fuel is burned in combustion chambers within the engine, instead of in an external furnace, and in which the energy released moves one or more pistons

in·ter·nal en·er·gy *n* the total kinetic energy of the atoms and molecules of a system plus the potential energy of their mutual interaction. An increase in internal energy manifests as a rise in temperature or a change in phase. Symbol ***U***

in·ter·nal·ize /in túrn'l ìz/ (**-ized, -iz·ing, -iz·es**) *vt* **1.** to adopt the beliefs, values, and attitudes of others, either consciously or unconsciously **2.** to deal with an emotion or conflict by thinking about it rather than expressing it openly —**in·ter·nal·i·za·tion** /in tùrn'li záysh'n/ *n*

in·ter·nal med·i·cine *n* the branch of medicine concerned with the diagnosis and nonsurgical treatment of diseases affecting the internal organs, and with preventive medicine

in·ter·nal re·sis·tance *n* the resistance within a source of electric current, e.g., a cell or generator

in·ter·nal res·pi·ra·tion *n* the metabolic use of oxygen by a cell to produce energy, resulting in the release of carbon dioxide

In·ter·nal Rev·e·nue Ser·vice *n* the division of the US Department of the Treasury responsible for the collection of income, excise, and other taxes and the enforcement of the tax laws

in·ter·nal rhyme *n* a rhyme in which one of the rhyming words is within the line of poetry and the other is at the end of the same line or within the next line

in·ter·nal se·cre·tion *n* a secretion, especially a hormone, that is absorbed into the blood directly after production

in·ter·nal wave *n* a waveform that develops below the surface of a body of water where two water masses with different densities meet. An internal wave can develop in an estuary where salt water lies underneath less dense river water.

in·ter·na·tion·al /intər náshən'l, -náshnəl/ *adj* **1.** INVOLVING SEVERAL COUNTRIES involving two or more countries or their citizens **2.** CROSSING NATIONAL BOUNDARIES extending beyond or across national boundaries **3.** OF RELATIONS AMONG NATIONS dealing with or concerned with relations among nations ○ *the university's international studies department* ■ *n* **1.** INTERNATIONAL ORGANIZATION an organization that has offices or branches in two or more countries **2.** MEMBER OF INTERNATIONAL TEAM a member of a team representing his or her country in an international event —**in·ter·na·tion·al·i·ty** /intər nashə nállətee/ *n* —**in·ter·na·tion·al·ly** *adv*

In·ter·na·tion·al *n* any of four international Socialist, Communist, or Anarchist organizations formed in 1864, 1889, 1919, and 1938 respectively

In·ter·na·tion·al A·tom·ic Time *n* a precisely determined system of measuring time in which a second is defined in terms of atomic events that are known to a high degree of accuracy

in·ter·na·tion·al bac·ca·lau·re·ate *n* a set of examinations in various subjects taken at the end of secondary education and accepted in many countries as a qualification for admission to a college or university

In·ter·na·tion·al Bank for Re·con·struc·tion and De·vel·op·ment *n* BANKING same as **World Bank**

In·ter·na·tion·al Bri·gade *n* a Communist and Socialist force of volunteers from different countries that fought on the Republican side during the Spanish Civil War

in·ter·na·tion·al can·dle *n* a former unit of luminous intensity, now replaced by the candela

In·ter·na·tion·al Court of Jus·tice *n* the chief judicial body of the United Nations, empowered to resolve international disputes between member nations who submit a case to the court

In·ter·na·tion·al Crim·i·nal Po·lice Or·gan·i·za·tion *n* full form of **Interpol**

In·ter·na·tion·al Date Line *n* an internationally agreed imaginary line running roughly along the 180° meridian of longitude, to the east of which the date is one day earlier than to the west

In·ter·na·tion·al De·vel·op·ment As·so·ci·a·tion *n* a specialized agency of the United Nations that provides credit to nations on easier terms than the World Bank

In·ter·na·tion·ale /intər nashə nál/ *n* a revolutionary Socialist song written in France in 1871 and adopted as the anthem of the First, Second, and Third Internationals. A Russian version was the national anthem of the Soviet Union until 1944. [Early 20C. < French *(chanson) internationale* "international (song)"]

In·ter·na·tion·al Fi·nance Cor·po·ra·tion *n* a specialized agency of the United Nations that is affiliated with the World Bank and promotes private enterprise in developing nations by providing risk capital

In·ter·na·tion·al Goth·ic *n* a style of painting and other visual art that emerged in Europe with the increasing exchange of ideas and techniques among European artists toward the end of the 14th century

In·ter·na·tion·al Grand·mas·ter *n* a chess player of the highest rank awarded to a participant in international competitions

in·ter·na·tion·al·ism /intər náshən'l ìzzəm, -náshnəlizzəm/ *n* **1.** COOPERATION BETWEEN COUNTRIES a policy or spirit of cooperation and mutual understanding between countries **2.** INTEREST IN OTHER COUNTRIES a willingness to understand and respect the concerns, attitudes, and ways of life of other countries **3.** INTERNATIONAL CHARACTER OR QUALITY the international character or quality of somebody or something

in·ter·na·tion·al·ist /intər náshən'list, -náshnəlist/ *n* **1.** ADVOCATE OF INTERNATIONAL COOPERATION a supporter or advocate of greater cooperation and understanding between countries **2.** SOMEBODY INTERESTED IN OTHER COUNTRIES somebody who is interested in other countries and understands and respects their peoples and cultures **3.** SPORTS same as **international** *n* (sense 2) ■ *adj* FAVORING INTERNATIONAL COOPERATION favoring greater cooperation and understanding between countries

in·ter·na·tion·al·ize /intər náshən'l ī̀z, -náshnə lī̀z/ (**-ized, -iz·ing, -iz·es**) *vt* **1.** to make something international in character, structure, or outlook **2.** to place something under the protection or control of several countries instead of one country —**in·ter·na·tion·al·i·za·tion** /intər nashən'li záysh'n, -nàshnəli záysh'n/ *n*

in·ter·na·tion·al law *n* the accepted rules that govern countries in their relations with other countries

In·ter·na·tion·al Mas·ter *n* a chess player of a rank in international competitions that is below International Grandmaster

In·ter·na·tion·al Mon·e·tar·y Fund *n* a specialized agency of the United Nations that seeks to promote international monetary cooperation and the stabilization of national currencies and help nations resolve balance of payment problems

In·ter·na·tion·al Morse code *n* the form of Morse code used internationally

in·ter·na·tion·al non·pro·pri·e·tar·y name *n* each of 8,000 names selected by the World Health Organization that are the legally required generic names for pharmaceutical product labeling for most countries in the world

In·ter·na·tion·al Or·gan·i·za·tion for Stan·dard·i·za·tion *n* SCI ♦ **ISO**[2]

In·ter·na·tion·al Pho·net·ic Al·pha·bet *n* a system of letters and marks, mostly based on the letters of the Roman alphabet, used internationally to represent speech sounds

In·ter·na·tion·al Prac·ti·cal Tem·per·a·ture Scale *n* a scientific temperature scale, expressed in degrees Celsius, that has eleven fixed temperature reference points, including the boiling point of oxygen and the freezing point of gold

in·ter·na·tion·al re·la·tions *npl* political and other dealings between two or more countries ■ *n* the branch of political science that studies the relations between countries (*takes a singular verb*)

International Style: studio building (1925) at the Bauhaus, Dessau, Germany

In·ter·na·tion·al Style *n* **1.** ART same as **International Gothic 2.** an early 20th-century architectural style in the United States and Europe that favored the use of simple geometric lines, spacious interiors, and materials such as steel and reinforced concrete

In·ter·na·tion·al Sys·tem (of U·nits) *n* an internationally accepted system of units of measurement used for scientific work. The basic units are the meter, kilogram, second, kelvin, mole, ampere, and candela, these being the basic quantities of length, mass, time, temperature, amount of substance, electric current, and luminous intensity.

in·ter·na·tion·al u·nit *n* the amount of a hormone or vitamin required to produce a specific response

in·ter·naut /intər nàwt/ *n* somebody who surfs the Internet [Late 20C. Blend of INTERNET + ASTRONAUT]

in·terne *n* another spelling of **intern**

in·ter·nec·ine /intər né sèen, -nèe sèen/ *adj* **1.** relating to or involving conflict within a group or organization ○ *an internecine feud* **2.** damaging or injuring participants on both sides of a conflict [Mid-17C. < Latin *internecinus* "deadly" < *internecare* "exterminate," literally "kill completely" < *necare* "kill" < *nex* "death"]

ORIGIN The original meaning of ***internecine*** is "involving great slaughter." Its modern meaning of "involving conflict within a group," which can be traced back to the 18th century (Samuel Johnson in his *Dictionary* (1755) defined it as "endeavoring mutual destruction"), arose from the standard interpretation of *inter-* as "among, between," but in fact in the case of Latin *internecinus* it was being used simply to add emphasis.

in·tern·ee /intər née/ *n* an inmate of a prison, prisoner-of-war camp, or other similar place, especially during a war

in·ter·ne·sia /intər neézhə/ *n* an inability to remember either the location of or information contained in a website (*informal*) [Blend of INTERNET + AMNESIA]

In·ter·net /intər nèt/ *n* a network that links computer networks all over the world by satellite and telephone, connecting users with service networks such as e-mail and the World Wide Web

In·ter·net bank·ing *n* a system of banking in which customers can view their account details, pay bills, and transfer money by means of the Internet

In·ter·net ca·fé *n* ONLINE same as **cybercafé** (sense 1)

In·ter·net ho·tel *n* a business that provides Internet and server facilities for other businesses

In·ter·net pro·to·col *n* the standard that controls the routing and structure of data transmitted over the Internet

In·ter·net re·lay chat *n* ONLINE full form of **IRC**

In·ter·net ser·vice pro·vid·er *n* a business that provides access to the Internet, usually for a monthly fee. Some large providers offer users a wide range of news, information, and entertainment services.

In·ter·net store·front *n* ONLINE, COMM same as **storefront** *n* (sense 3)

in·ter·neu·ron /intər nóor òn/ *n* a short nerve cell in the central nervous system that connects nerve cells such as sensory and motor nerve cells in a reflex arc —**in·ter·neu·ro·nal** /intər nóorən'l, ìntər nòo rṓn'l/ *adj*

in·ter·nist /in túrnist/ *n* a doctor who specializes in the diagnosis, prevention, and nonsurgical treatment of diseases affecting the internal organs [Early 20C. < INTERNAL + -IST]

in·ter·node /intər nṑd/ *n* **1.** the part of a plant stem between two nodes **2.** the part of the axon of a nerve cell that lies between the nodes of Ranvier and is covered by the myelin sheath [Mid-17C. < Latin *internodium* < *nodus* "knot"] —**in·ter·nod·al** /intər nṓd'l/ *adj*

in·ter nos /intər nṓss/ *adv* between or among ourselves (*formal or humorous*) [< Latin]

in·ter·nun·cial /intər núnshəl/ *adj* **1.** describes nerve cells that connect one nerve cell to another **2.** acting as or connected with an internuncio of the Roman Catholic Church —**in·ter·nun·cial·ly** *adv*

in·ter·nun·ci·o /intər núnssee ṑ/ (*plural* **-os**) *n* **1.** a diplomatic representative of the pope of a rank below a nuncio **2.** a messenger or go-between (*formal*) [Mid-17C. Via Italian *internunzio* < Latin *internuntius* "intermediate messenger" < *nuntius* "messenger"]

in·ter·op·er·a·bil·i·ty /intər óppərə bíllətee/ *n* the ability of the component parts of a system to operate successfully together —**in·ter·op·er·a·ble** /-óppərəb'l, -óppr-/ *adj*

in·ter·pel·late /in túrpə làyt, ìntər pé làyt/ (**-lat·ed, -lat·ing, -lates**) *vt* in European legislatures, to interrupt a parliamentary debate by asking a question on an aspect of government policy [Late 19C. < Latin *interpellat-*, past participle of *interpellare* "thrust yourself between" < variant of *pellere* "beat"]

in·ter·per·son·al /intər púrssən'l, -púrssnəl/ *adj* concerning or involving relationships between people —**in·ter·per·son·al·ly** *adv*

in·ter·pha·lan·ge·al /intərfə lánjee əl/ *adj* situated between the bones of the fingers or toes

in·ter·phase /intər fàyz/ *n* the period during which a cell is not actively dividing, when other activities such as DNA synthesis take place

in·ter·play /intər plày/ *n* the way in which people or things repeatedly act on and react to each other

in·ter·plead /intər pléed/ (**-plead·ed** or **-pled** /-pléd/, **-plead·ing, -pleads**) *vi* to go to trial to resolve which of several claimants has the right to claim money or property held by a third party [Mid-16C. < Anglo-Norman *enterpleder* "plead together" < *pleder* (see PLEAD)]

in·ter·plead·er /intər pléedər/ *n* a trial to resolve which of several claimants can sue for money or property held by a third party, instituted by the third party to avoid several proceedings

In·ter·pol /intər pàwl/ *n* an association of national police forces that promotes cooperation and mutual assistance in apprehending international criminals and criminals who flee abroad to avoid justice. The headquarters of Interpol is in Paris. Full form **International Criminal Police Organization**

in·ter·po·late /in túrpə làyt/ (**-lat·ed, -lat·ing, -lates**) *v* **1.** *vt* INSERT SOMETHING INTO SOMETHING ELSE to add one thing, often an unnecessary item, between the existing parts of something else **2.** *vt* ALTER TEXT to alter or deliberately falsify a text by adding a comment or extra words to it **3.** *vti* INTERRUPT BY SAYING SOMETHING to say something that interrupts what somebody else is saying **4.** *vt* MATH ESTIMATE VALUE OF MATHEMATICAL FUNCTION to estimate the value of a mathematical function that lies between known values, often by means of a graph [Early 17C. < Latin *interpolat-*, past participle of *interpolare* "polish up"] —**in·ter·po·la·tion** /in tùrpə láysh'n/ *n* —**in·ter·po·la·tive** /in túrpə làytiv/ *adj* —**in·ter·po·la·tor** *n*

in·ter·pose /intər pṓz/ (**-posed, -pos·ing, -pos·es**) *v* **1.** *vti* INTERRUPT BY SAYING SOMETHING to say something that interrupts what somebody else is saying **2.** *vt* PLACE SOMETHING BETWEEN PEOPLE OR THINGS to place yourself or something else between two people or things **3.** *vti* INTERVENE WITH SOMETHING to intervene or interfere in a situation such as a dispute [Late 16C. < French *interposer*, alteration (influenced by *poser* "to place") of Latin *interponere* "place between" < *ponere* "to place"] —**in·ter·pos·a·ble** *adj* —**in·ter·pos·al** *n* —**in·ter·pos·er** *n* —**in·ter·po·si·tion** /intərpə zísh'n/ *n*

~~**interpratation**~~ incorrect spelling of **interpretation**

in·ter·pret /in túrprət/ (**-pret·ed, -pret·ing, -prets**) *v* **1.** *vt* FIND MEANING OF SOMETHING to establish or explain the meaning or significance of something **2.** *vt* ASCRIBE MEANING TO SOMETHING to ascribe a particular meaning or significance to something ○ *I interpreted his gesture as an invitation.* **3.** *vt* PERFORM SOMETHING IN PARTICULAR WAY to perform something such as a play or piece of music in a way that conveys particular ideas or feelings about it **4.** *vti* TRANSLATE SOMETHING to translate what is said in one language into another so that speakers of different languages can communicate **5.** *vt* EXECUTE COMPUTER PROGRAM to convert instructions in a computer program written in a high-level language into machine language and execute them, one instruction at a time [14C. Directly or via French < Latin *interpretari* "explain" < *interpret-*, stem of *interpres* "broker"] —**in·ter·pret·a·bil·i·ty** /in tùrprətə bíllətee/ *n* —**in·ter·pret·a·ble** *adj* —**in·ter·pret·a·bly** *adv*

in·ter·pre·ta·tion /in tùrprə táysh'n/ *n* **1.** ESTABLISHMENT OF MEANING an explanation or establishment of the meaning or significance of something **2.** ASCRIPTION OF PARTICULAR MEANING an ascription of a particular meaning or significance to something **3.** PERFORMANCE OF SOMETHING the way in which an artistic work such as a play or piece of music is performed in order to convey a specific understanding of the work **4.** TRANSLATION the oral translation of what is said in one language into another, so that speakers of different languages can communicate —**in·ter·pre·ta·tion·al** *adj*

in·ter·pre·ta·tive *adj* same as **interpretive** —**in·ter·pre·ta·tive·ly** *adv*

in·ter·pret·er /in túrprətər/ *n* **1.** TRANSLATOR somebody who carries out oral translation from one language to another **2.** PERFORMER EXPRESSING PARTICULAR IDEAS somebody who performs something such as a play or piece of music in a way that expresses particular ideas or feelings about it **3.** PROGRAM EXECUTING INSTRUCTIONS a computer program that translates instructions in a program written in a high-level computer language into machine language and executes them —**in·ter·pre·ter·ship** *n*

in·ter·pre·tive /in túrprətiv/, **in·ter·pre·ta·tive** /-tàytiv/ *adj* relating to, involving, or providing an interpretation or explanation of something —**in·ter·pre·tive·ly** *adv*

in·ter·pu·pil·lar·y /intər pyóop'l èrree/ *adj* between the pupils of the eyes

in·ter·quar·tile range /intər kwàwr tīl-, -kwàwrt'l-/ *n* a measure of the spread of a group of values equal to the difference between the upper limit for the lower quarter and the lower limit for the upper quarter

in·ter·reg·num /íntər régnəm/ (*plural* **-nums** or **-na** /-nə/) *n* **1. TIME BETWEEN ONE REIGN AND NEXT** the period of time between the end of one reign or regime and the beginning of the next **2. TIME WITHOUT GOVERNMENT OR CONTROL** a period of time during which there is no government, control, or authority **3. INTERRUPTION** a pause or gap in any continuous activity or series [Late 16C. < Latin, "period between kingships" < *regnum* "kingship"] —**in·ter·reg·nal** *adj*

in·ter·re·late /íntəri láyt/ (**-lat·ed, -lat·ing, -lates**) *vti* to have a relationship in which each person or thing depends on or is affected by the others, or cause persons or things to have such a relationship —**in·ter·re·la·tion** *n* —**in·ter·re·la·tion·ship** *n*

in·ter·re·lat·ed /íntərə láytəd/ *adj* in a relationship in which each depends on or is affected by the other or others

in·ter·ro·bang /in térrə bàng/, **in·ter·a·bang** *n* a punctuation mark in the form of a question mark over the top of an exclamation point. It is used at the end of, or sometimes in place of, an utterance that is both question and exclamation, especially to indicate an emphatic rhetorical question or disbelief. [Mid-20C. Blend of INTERROGATION POINT + BANG[1] (printers' slang for an exclamation point)]

interrog. *abbr* **1.** interrogate **2.** interrogation **3.** GRAM interrogative

in·ter·ro·gate /in térrə gàyt/ (**-gat·ed, -gat·ing, -gates**) *vt* **1.** to question somebody thoroughly, often in an aggressive or threatening manner and especially as part of a formal investigation, e.g., in a police station or courtroom **2.** to transmit a request to a program or device for information, e.g., to a printer for the status of a print job or to a database for specific data [15C. < Latin *interrogat-*, past participle of *interrogare*, literally "ask in the presence of" < *rogare* "ask"] —**in·ter·ro·ga·tee** /in tèrrə gay tée/ *n* —**in·ter·ro·ga·tor** *n*

SYNONYMS See ***question***.

in·ter·ro·ga·tion /in tèrrə gáysh'n/ *n* **1. THOROUGH QUESTIONING** the act or process of questioning somebody closely, often in an aggressive manner, especially as part of an official investigation or trial **2. QUESTION** a question or query (*formal*) **3.** COMPUT **TRANSMISSION OF SIGNAL TO COMPUTER** the transmission of a signal to a device or program that triggers a response —**in·ter·ro·ga·tion·al** *adj*

in·ter·ro·ga·tion point, **in·ter·ro·ga·tion mark** *n* same as **question mark**

in·ter·rog·a·tive /íntə róggətiv/ *adj* **1. QUESTIONING** questioning or seeming to question somebody or something **2. USED TO ASK QUESTION** consisting of or used in asking a question ○ *an interrogative pronoun* ■ *n* **1. WORD USED TO ASK QUESTION** a word or particle that is used to form a question, e.g., "who," "what," or "where" **2. FORM OF QUESTION** the form of a sentence that is used to ask a question —**in·ter·rog·a·tive·ly** *adv*

in·ter·rog·a·to·ry /íntə róggə tàwree/ *adj* **ASKING QUESTION** asking a question, used to ask a question, or in the form of a question (*formal*) ■ *n* (*plural* **-ries**) **1. QUESTION** a question or series of questions **2. FORMAL WRITTEN QUESTION** a formal written question asked during a legal proceeding and usually answered under oath —**in·ter·rog·a·to·ri·ly** *adv*

in·ter·ro·gee /in tèrrə gée, -térrə gee/ *n* somebody who is interrogated [Mid-20C. < INTERROGATE]

in·ter·rupt /íntə rúpt/ *v* (**-rupt·ed, -rupt·ing, -rupts**) **1.** *vti* **HALT SPEAKER OR SPEAKER'S UTTERANCE** to halt the flow of a speaker or of a speaker's utterance with a question or remark **2.** *vti* **DISTURB SOMEBODY OR SOMEBODY'S WORK** to disturb somebody who is busy doing something, causing him or her to stop **3.** *vt* **CAUSE SOMETHING TO STOP** to cause a break in the flow of something or put a temporary stop to something **4.** *vt* **TAKE A BREAK FROM SOMETHING** to discontinue doing something temporarily **5.** *vt* **OBSTRUCT VIEW** to block a view ■ *n* COMPUT **1. SIGNAL TO SUSPEND OPERATION** a signal to a computer processor to suspend the currently running operation while it either performs the instruction specified by the signal or saves it in a queue to perform later **2. CIRCUIT SENDING SIGNAL INTERRUPTING COMPUTER PROCESS** the circuit that conveys a signal to suspend a computer operation [14C. < Latin *interrupt-*, past participle of *interrumpere* "break apart" < *rumpere* "to break"] —**in·ter·rupt·er** *n* —**in·ter·rupt·i·ble** *adj* —**in·ter·rup·tive** *adj* —**in·ter·rup·tive·ly** *adv*

in·ter·rupt·ed ca·dence /íntə ruptəd-/ *n* in music, a cadence that does not end with the expected chord of the tonic but moves from the dominant to the submediant or subdominant

in·ter·rupt·ed screw *n* a screw whose thread is broken in one or more places by a lengthwise slot that enables a partial turn to lock or unlock the screw

in·ter·rup·tion /íntə rúpshən/ *n* **1.** the act of interrupting somebody, or something that interrupts somebody who is saying or doing something **2.** a pause, break, or temporary halt in an ongoing activity or process

in·ter se /íntər sáy, -sée/ *adv, adj* between or among themselves [< Latin]

in·ter·sect /íntər sékt/ (**-sect·ed, -sect·ing, -sects**) *v* **1.** *vti* **CROSS** to cross something, or cross each other **2.** *vt* **GO THROUGH SOMETHING** to follow a path across or through something **3.** *vti* **OVERLAP** to overlap or have things in common with something or each other **4.** *vti* **HAVE POINTS IN COMMON** to overlap a figure or figures geometrically so as to have a point or set of points in common, or overlap each other in this way [Early 17C. < Latin *intersect-*, past participle of *intersecare* "cut between" < *secare* "to cut"]

in·ter·sec·tion /íntər sékshən/ *n* **1. ACT OF INTERSECTING** the act or fact of intersecting **2. CROSSROADS** a place where two roads or paths cross each other **3. CROSSING POINT** the place or point where two things cross each other **4. OVERLAPPING** an overlapping between two things such as different personal interests or political positions **5.** MATH **COMMON POINT** a point or set of points common to two or more intersecting geometric figures **6.** MATH **SET OF COMMON ELEMENTS** a set that consists of all of the elements common to two or more other sets, thus being the largest set contained in all of the others —**in·ter·sec·tion·al** *adj*

in·ter·ser·vice /íntər súrviss/ *adj* occurring among the various branches of the armed forces

in·ter·ses·sion /íntər sèsh'n/ *n* a period of time, usually about a month, between two college or university semesters or terms, during which students sometimes undertake special projects or attend special classes —**in·ter·ses·sion·al** /íntər séshən'l, -séshnəl/ *adj*

in·ter·sex /íntər sèks/ *n* an organism with characteristics of both sexes

in·ter·sex·u·al /íntər sékshoo əl, -séksh'l/ *adj* **1.** occurring between males and females or affecting their relations **2.** having characteristics of both sexes —**in·ter·sex·u·al·ism** *n* —**in·ter·sex·u·al·i·ty** /íntər sekshoo állətee/ *n* —**in·ter·sex·u·al·ly** *adv*

in·ter·space *n* /íntər spàyss/ **SPACE OR INTERVAL** a space or interval of time between two things ■ *vt* /íntər spáyss/ (**-spaced, -spac·ing, -spac·es**) **1. PUT SOMETHING BETWEEN TWO THINGS** to put something in the spaces or gaps between things **2. INSERT SPACES BETWEEN TWO THINGS** to put spaces or breaks between things —**in·ter·spa·tial** /íntər spáysh'l/ *adj* —**in·ter·spa·tial·ly** *adv*

in·ter·spe·cif·ic /íntər spə síffik/ *adj* **1.** created by crossing different species **2.** occurring between or involving different species

in·ter·sperse /íntər spúrss/ (**-spersed, -spers·ing, -spers·es**) *vt* **1.** to break up the continuity or flow of something with something else **2.** to put or insert something here and there among or in something else [Mid-16C. < Latin *interspers-*, past participle of *interspergere* "scatter between" < *spargere* "scatter"] —**in·ter·spers·ed·ly** /-ədlee/ *adv* —**in·ter·sper·sion** *n*

in·ter·sta·di·al /íntər stáydee əl/ *adj* relating to a short period of relatively warmer climate within an ice age [Early 20C. < INTER- + Latin *stadium* "stage"]

in·ter·state /íntər stàyt/ *adj* occurring between, connecting, or involving two or more states ■ *n* a limited-access road that forms part of the federally funded system of highways connecting the major cities of the United States

in·ter·sta·tion /íntər stáysh'n/ *adj* occurring between or connecting stations

in·ter·stel·lar /íntər stéllər/ *adj* situated, happening, or moving between stars, or involving two or more stars

in·ter·ster·ile /íntər stérrəl/ *adj* not capable of interbreeding —**in·ter·ster·il·i·ty** /íntər stə rìllətee/ *n*

in·ter·stice /in túrstiss/ *n* **1. SMALL SPACE** a small opening, crack, or gap between two things **2. SPACE IN CRYSTAL LATTICE** a gap between neighboring atoms in the lattice of a crystal **3. SPACE IN BODY TISSUE** a small space in a tissue or between parts of the body [15C. Via French < Latin *interstitium* < *intersistere*, literally "stand still in the middle" < *sistere* "cause to stand" < *stare* "to stand"]

in·ter·sti·tial /íntər stísh'l/ *adj* **1. RELATING TO GAPS** forming, situated in, or relating to one or more small openings, gaps, or cracks **2.** GEOL **OCCURRING BETWEEN OTHER MINERALS** located in the pores or between the crystals of a rock **3.** CHEM **OF COMPOUND CONTAINING METALS AND NONMETALS** relating to a compound, e.g., a carbide, in which ions or atoms of a nonmetal occupy positions in a metal lattice. Interstitial compounds generally have metallic characteristics. **4.** PHYSIOL **OCCURRING BETWEEN TISSUES** lying between parts of an organ or between groups of cells or tissues. The interstitial cells between mammalian testicles are responsible for secreting male sex hormones. ■ *n* ONLINE **UNSOLICITED ADVERTISEMENT ON INTERNET** an unsolicited advertisement on the World Wide Web that briefly precedes a selected page —**in·ter·sti·tial·ly** *adv*

in·ter·tes·ta·men·tal /íntər testə mént'l/ *adj* during, from, or relating to the period between the composition of the last books of the Hebrew Scriptures, called the Old Testament by Christians, and the first books of the New Testament of the Bible

in·ter·text·u·al·i·ty /íntər tekschoo állətee/ *n* the relationship that exists between different texts, especially literary texts, or the reference in one text to others —**in·ter·text·u·al** /íntər tékschoo əl/ *adj* —**in·ter·text·u·al·ly** *adv*

in·ter·tex·ture /íntər tékschər/ *n* **1.** an object or material that has been made by interweaving two or more things **2.** an act of interweaving two or more things, or the fact of being interwoven

in·ter·tid·al /íntər tī́d'l/ *adj* occurring within, or forming, the area between the high and low tide levels in a coastal zone —**in·ter·tid·al·ly** *adv*

in·ter·tri·go /íntər trī́gō/ *n* the inflammation of two skin surfaces that are in constant contact, caused by friction or sweat [Early 18C. < Latin, "chafing of the skin" < assumed *interterere* "rub together" < *terere* "to rub"]

in·ter·trop·i·cal /íntər tróppik'l/ *adj* located or occurring between the Tropic of Capricorn and Tropic of Cancer

in·ter·twine /íntər twī́n/ (**-twined, -twin·ing, -twines**) *vti* **1.** to twist two or more things closely together or around and through each other, or be or become twisted in this way **2.** to become closely and intricately linked with each other, or link something closely and intricately with something else ○ *Their lives had intertwined.* —**in·ter·twine·ment** *n*

in·ter·twist /íntər twíst/ (**-twist·ed, -twist·ing, -twists**) *vti* same as **intertwine** (sense 1)

~~**interupt**~~ incorrect spelling of **interrupt**

in·ter·val /íntərvəl/ *n* **1. INTERVENING PERIOD OF TIME** a period of time between one event and the next **2. INTERVENING DISTANCE** the distance between one thing and another **3.** *UK* THEATER same as **intermission** (sense 1) **4.** MUSIC **DIFFERENCE IN MUSICAL PITCH** the musical distance between the pitches of two notes **5.** MATH **ALL NUMBERS BETWEEN TWO NUMBERS** a set containing all the real numbers or points between two real numbers or points, which are called the endpoints. If the set includes the endpoints it is a closed interval, and if it excludes the endpoints it is an open interval. [14C. Via French < Latin *intervallum* "space between ramparts" < *vallum* "rampart"] —**in·ter·val·lic** /íntər vállik/ *adj* ◇ **at intervals 1.** at different points in time **2.** at various locations

in·ter·vale /íntərvəl/ *n* in New England and the Maritime Provinces of Canada, a piece of low-lying land between hills or along a river [Mid-17C. Blend of INTERVAL + VALE[1]]

in·ter·val·om·e·ter /íntərvə lómmətər/ *n* a device that is designed to activate a mechanism automatically at regular intervals, especially one that operates a camera shutter [Mid-20C. < INTERVAL]

in·ter·val train·ing *n* a method of training, especially in athletics, that involves alternating between aerobic and nonaerobic exercise in the same session

in·ter·vene /íntər véen/ (**-vened, -ven·ing, -venes**) *vi* **1. BECOME INVOLVED IN SITUATION** to involve yourself deliberately in a situation, especially in a conflict or dispute, in order to influence what is happening and, most often, to prevent undesirable consequences ○ *The referee had to intervene to stop the fight.* **2.** HAVE PREVENTIVE OR DELAYING EFFECT to occur or take effect in such a way as to stop or delay something ○ *The weather intervened before the contest could get under way.* **3.** ELAPSE to elapse between one point in time and another **4.** BREAK INTO CONVERSATION to break into a conversation or discussion **5.** BE SITUATED IN BETWEEN to be located between two things **6.** LAW ENTER LAWSUIT to enter a lawsuit as a third party in order to protect your own interests **7.** ECON ACT TO MANIPULATE ECONOMIC MARKETS to take economic action that is designed to counter a trend in a market, especially in order to stabilize a country's currency [Late 16C. < Latin *intervenire* "come between" < *venire* "come"]

in·ter·ven·er *n* another spelling of **intervenor**

in·ter·ven·ing /intər veéning/ *adj* occurring, coming, or standing between two things

in·ter·ve·nor /intər veénər/ *n* **1.** somebody who intervenes in something **2.** a party that enters a lawsuit as a third party in order to protect its interests

in·ter·ven·tion /intər vénshən/ *n* **1.** the act of intervening, especially a deliberate entry into a situation or dispute in order to influence events or prevent undesirable consequences **2.** economic action that is designed to counter a trend in a market, especially in order to stabilize a country's currency —**in·ter·ven·tion·al** *adj*

in·ter·ven·tion·ism /intər vénshə nìzzəm/ *n* **1.** political interference or military involvement by one country in the affairs of another **2.** action by a government to influence and improve the country's economic situation or some aspect of it —**in·ter·ven·tion·ist** *n, adj*

in·ter·ven·tric·u·lar /intər ven tríkyələr/ *adj* situated or occurring between the ventricles of the heart

in·ter·ver·te·bral /intər vúrtəbrəl/ *adj* situated or occurring between the vertebrae of the backbone —**in·ter·ver·te·bral·ly** *adv*

in·ter·ver·te·bral disk *n* one of the flexible plates of cartilage connecting adjacent vertebrae of the backbone that impart flexibility and act as shock absorbers to protect the spinal cord from impact, e.g., when running

in·ter·view /íntər vyoō/ *n* **1.** MEETING FOR ASKING QUESTIONS a meeting during which somebody is asked questions, e.g., by a prospective employer, a journalist, or a researcher **2.** RECORD OF INTERVIEW a transcript, report on, or recording of an interview **3.** SOMEBODY IN INTERVIEW somebody who is asked to be interviewed (*informal*) ■ *v* (**-viewed, -view·ing, -views**) **1.** *vt* ASK SOMEBODY QUESTIONS to ask somebody a series of questions in an interview **2.** *vi* PERFORM IN INTERVIEW to speak and answer in a particular way in an interview ○ *She always interviews well.* [Early 16C. < obsolete French *entrevue* < *entrevoir* "see each other" < *voir* "see" < Latin *videre*] —**in·ter·view·ee** /intər vyoo eé/ *n* —**in·ter·view·er** *n*

in·ter vi·vos /intər veé vōss, -vī-/ *adv, adj* from one living person to another ○ *an inter vivos gift* [< Latin, "between the living"]

in·ter·vo·cal·ic /intər vō kállik/ *adj* describes a speech sound occurring or inserted between vowels, e.g., between one word that ends with a vowel and another word that starts with a vowel —**in·ter·vo·cal·i·cal·ly** *adv*

in·ter·weave /intər weév/ (**-wove** /-wṓv/, **-woven** /-wṓvən/, **-weav·ing, -weaves**) *vti* **1.** to weave something into or with something else, or be woven together, into, or with something else **2.** to combine one thing with another, or be combined with something else

in·ter·zone /intər zṓn/ *adj* between zones ■ *n* an intermediate zone —**in·ter·zon·al** *adj*

in·tes·tate /in té stàyt, in téstət/ *adj* **1.** LEAVING NO LEGALLY VALID WILL not having made a legally valid will **2.** NOT WILLED TO SOMEBODY not having been assigned to somebody in a legally valid will ■ *n* SOMEBODY LEAVING NO LEGALLY VALID WILL somebody who has died without having made a legally valid will [14C. Directly or via French < Latin *intestatus* "not having made a will" < *testari* "make a will" < *testis* "witness"] —**in·tes·ta·cy** /in téstəssee/ *n*

in·tes·ti·nal /in téstən'l/ *adj* **1.** found in or affecting the intestines **2.** characteristic of, forming part of, or relating to the intestines —**in·tes·ti·nal·ly** *adv*

in·tes·ti·nal flo·ra *npl* bacteria present in a healthy intestine that complete digestion, synthesize vitamin K, and create an acid environment that prevents infection by harmful bacteria

in·tes·ti·nal for·ti·tude *n* courage and perseverance (*humorous*)

in·tes·tine /in téstin/ *n* the part of the digestive system between the stomach and the anus or cloaca that digests and absorbs food. In mammals, the small intestine digests and absorbs food from the stomach, and the large intestine then absorbs most of the remaining water in the food. (*often used in the plural*) [15C. Via French < Latin *intestinus* "internal" < *intus* "within"]

in·thrall *vt* another spelling of **enthrall**

in·throne *vt* POL, RELIG another spelling of **enthrone**

in·ti·fa·da /inti faádə/ *n* the Palestinian uprising in the West Bank and Gaza Strip that started in 1987 in protest against the continued Israeli occupation [Late 20C. < Arabic *intifāḍa* "a shaking off"]

in·ti·ma·cy /íntəməssee/ (*plural* **-cies**) *n* **1.** CLOSE RELATIONSHIP a close personal relationship **2.** QUIET ATMOSPHERE a quiet and private atmosphere **3.** DETAILED KNOWLEDGE a detailed knowledge resulting from a close or long association or study **4.** PRIVATE UTTERANCE OR ACTION a private and personal utterance or action **5.** SEXUAL ACT a sexual act or sexual intercourse (*often used euphemistically*)

in·ti·mate[1] /íntəmət/ *adj* **1.** CLOSE having, involving, or resulting from a close personal relationship **2.** COZY quiet and private or secluded, enabling people to feel relaxed with each other **3.** PRIVATE AND PERSONAL so private and personal as to be kept secret or discussed only with a close friend or relative **4.** SEXUAL involving or having a sexual relationship (*often used euphemistically*) **5.** CLOSELY CONNECTED very close because of the influence of one thing on another ○ *the intimate connection between power and corruption* **6.** THOROUGH very great and detailed as a result of extensive study or close experience ○ *an intimate knowledge of the workings of government* **7.** WORN NEXT TO SKIN intended to be worn next to the skin or in a private setting ○ *intimate apparel* **8.** INNERMOST relating to or involving the innermost nature of something ■ *n* CLOSE FRIEND a close personal friend [Early 17C. < late Latin *intimatus*, past participle of *intimare* (see INTIMATE[2])] —**in·ti·mate·ly** *adv* —**in·ti·mate·ness** *n*

in·ti·mate[2] /íntə màyt/ (**-mat·ed, -mat·ing, -mates**) *vt* **1.** to hint at something or let something be known in a quiet, indirect, or subtle way **2.** to announce something formally [Early 16C. < late Latin *intimat-*, past participle of *intimare* "make known" < *intimus* "innermost"] —**in·ti·mat·er** *n* —**in·ti·ma·tion** /intə máysh'n/ *n*

in·time /aN teém/ *adj* small, quiet, and private or secluded [Early 17C. Via French, "intimate" < Latin *intimus* "innermost"]

in·tim·i·date /in tímmə dàyt/ (**-dat·ed, -dat·ing, -dates**) *vt* **1.** to frighten somebody into doing or not doing something, e.g., by means of violence or blackmail **2.** to create a feeling of fear, awe, or inadequacy in another person [Mid-17C. < medieval Latin *intimidat-*, past participle of *intimidare* "put in fear" < Latin *timidus* "fearful"] —**in·tim·i·da·tion** /in tìmmə dáysh'n/ *n* —**in·tim·i·dat·or** *n* —**in·tim·i·da·to·ry** /in tímmədə tàwree/ *adj*

in·tim·i·dat·ing /in tímmi dàyting/ *adj* instilling fear, awe, or a sense of inadequacy —**in·tim·i·dat·ing·ly** *adv*

in·tinc·tion /in tíngksh'n/ *n* in a Christian religious service of Communion, the act of dipping the consecrated bread into the consecrated wine so that somebody taking Communion receives both [Late 19C. < late Latin *intinction-* < Latin *intingere* "dip in" < *tingere* "moisten"]

in·tine /in teén/ *n* the inner wall of a pollen grain or spore [Mid-19C. Alteration of Latin *intimus* "innermost"]

intl. *abbr* international

in·to *stressed* /íntoo/; *unstressed* /íntə/ CORE MEANING: a preposition indicating that somebody or something moves inside something, either physically or figuratively ○ *I released the balloon into the air.* ○ *in case you get into difficulties* ○ *I decided to go into the army.* ○ *When did you go into partnership with them?*

prep **1.** INDICATES MOVEMENT TO INSIDE indicates that something or somebody moves or is moved from outside to inside or toward the inner part of something ○ *came into the house* **2.** INDICATES MOVEMENT TO MIDST OF SOMETHING indicates that something or somebody moves to the middle of something and becomes part of it or is surrounded by it ○ *leaped into the water* **3.** INDICATES ENTRY indicates entering a state, career, or period of time ○ *burst into action* ○ *went into marketing* **4.** INDICATES ACCIDENTAL CONTACT indicates coming up against something accidentally ○ *bumped into them* **5.** INDICATES CHANGE indicates becoming a new entity, shape, or form as a result of a change or transformation ○ *turned into a frog* **6.** INDICATES RESULT indicates a situation resulting from somebody's persuasion ○ *talked me into going* **7.** INDICATES RESULT OF DIVIDING indicates the number or nature of the smaller parts that are left when something is divided ○ *divided the cake into six* **8.** MATH INDICATES DIVISION placed before a number being divided by another number to indicate the process of division ○ *9 into 63 equals 7.* **9.** ENTHUSIASTIC ABOUT indicates interest in or enthusiasm about something (*informal*) ○ *really into tennis* [Old English *in(n)tō* < IN[1] + TO[1]]

USAGE in, into, or **in to**? In formal written English, the preposition for inward movement is ***into***, not ***in***: *She came into* [not *in*] *the room. We welcomed him into* [not *in*] *the family.* It is sometimes acceptable to use either ***in*** or ***into***, but the latter is usually preferable in formal English: *He put it into* [or *in*] *his pocket.* Using ***in*** for ***into*** can be misleading, as in *She jumped in the pool.* (Did she jump into the pool, or was she already standing in the pool when she jumped?) Do not confuse ***into*** with ***in to*** – the preposition ***into*** is never written as two separate words; when the separate words ***in*** and ***to*** occur side by side, they should not be joined together: *I went into* [not *in to*] *the house. I went in to* [not *into*] *get my jacket.* See ***onto***.

---

in·tol·er·a·ble /in tóllərəb'l/ *adj* **1.** so bad, difficult, or painful that it cannot be endured ○ *The pain was intolerable.* **2.** very unpleasant or annoying —**in·tol·er·a·bil·i·ty** /in tòllərə bíllətee/ *n* —**in·tol·er·a·bly** *adv*

in·tol·er·ance /in tóllərənss/ *n* **1.** REFUSAL TO ACCEPT DIFFERENCES unwillingness or refusal to accept people who are different from you, or views, beliefs, or lifestyles that differ from your own ○ *racial intolerance* **2.** STATE OF BEING INTOLERANT the state of being easily annoyed ○ *her intolerance of noise* **3.** ALLERGIC SENSITIVITY the inability to eat or drink a particular food, ingredient, or substance, or to take a particular drug, without having an allergic reaction or getting sick ○ *lactose intolerance* **4.** UNFITNESS FOR SOMETHING unable to thrive or survive in a particular environment

in·tol·er·ant /in tóllərənt/ *adj* **1.** REFUSING TO ACCEPT DIFFERENCES showing an unwillingness or refusal to accept people who are different from you, or views, beliefs, or lifestyles that differ from your own ○ *an intolerant society* **2.** EASILY ANNOYED easily angered or annoyed ○ *He is rather intolerant of vague ideas and vague people.* **3.** ALLERGIC TO SOMETHING unable to eat or drink a particular food, ingredient, or substance, or to take a particular drug without having an allergic reaction or getting sick **4.** UNFITTED TO SOMETHING unable to thrive or survive in a particular environment ○ *a plant intolerant of dry conditions* —**in·tol·er·ant·ly** *adv*

~~**intolerent**~~ incorrect spelling of **intolerant**

in·to·nate /íntə nàyt/ (**-nat·ed, -nat·ing, -nates**) *v* **1.** *vt* SAY SOMETHING IN PARTICULAR WAY to say something with a particular tone of voice ○ *The way she intonated the word "society" indicated her deep contempt for what it represented.* **2.** *vi* PHON SPEAK WITH VARYING PITCH to speak with the rising and falling pitch that is characteristic of ordinary speech **3.** *vt* PHON PRONOUNCE CONSONANT WITH VOICING to pronounce a consonant with a vibration of the vocal cords, as English speakers do when they pronounce the consonant "v" as opposed to the consonant "f" [Late 18C. < medieval Latin *intonat-*, past participle of *intonare* (see INTONE)]

in·to·na·tion /intə náysh'n/ *n* **1.** PITCH OF VOICE the rising or falling pitch of the voice when somebody says a word or syllable, or the rising and falling pattern of speech generally **2.** INTONING a saying or chanting of something in a solemn or serious way, or something said or chanted in this way **3.** MUSIC ACCURACY OF PITCH accuracy of pitch in performing music **4.** MUSIC BEGINNING OF GREGORIAN CHANT the opening phrase of a

Gregorian chant, sung by a soloist or just a few members of the choir —**in·to·na·tion·al** *adj*

in·to·na·tion con·tour, in·to·na·tion pat·tern *n* the pattern of rising and falling pitch in speech that helps to distinguish between questions, statements, and other types of speech

in·tone /in tṓn/ (**-toned, -ton·ing, -tones**) *vt* **1.** to say something, especially in a slow and serious or solemn way **2.** to sing the opening phrase of a Gregorian chant [14C. Directly or via French < medieval Latin *intonare* "(sing) in tone" < Latin *tonus* "tone" < Greek *tonos*]

in to·to /in tṓtō/ *adv* in its entirety or as a whole ○ *considering his published works in toto* [< Latin]

in·tox·i·cant /in tóksikənt/ *n* something that causes physical or psychological intoxication, e.g., an alcoholic beverage or great power ■ *adj* capable of making somebody intoxicated

in·tox·i·cate /in tóksi kàyt/ (**-cat·ed, -cat·ing, -cates**) *v* **1.** *vt* to make somebody drunk with alcohol or stupefied with drugs or other substances **2.** *vt* to make somebody intensely excited or overjoyed, often so much so that the person becomes irrational **3.** *vti* MED same as **poison** *v* (sense 2) (*technical*) [15C. < medieval Latin *intoxicat-*, past participle of *intoxicare* "to poison" < Latin *toxicum* "poison" < Greek *toxicon*] —**in·tox·i·cat·ed** *adj* —**in·tox·i·ca·tion** /in tòksi káysh'n/ *n*

in·tox·i·cat·ing /in tóksi kàyting/ *adj* **1.** capable of making somebody drunk or stupefied (*formal*) **2.** capable of making somebody intensely excited or overjoyed, often so much so that the person becomes irrational —**in·tox·i·cat·ing·ly** *adv*

intr. *abbr* GRAM intransitive

intra- *prefix* within or inside ○ *intranasal* [Directly or via modern Latin, "on the inside" < Latin *intra* < Indo-European]

in·tra·ar·te·ri·al *adj* within or introduced into an artery or arteries —**in·tra·ar·te·ri·al·ly** *adv*

in·tra·ar·tic·u·lar *adj* within or introduced into a joint of the body

in·tra·a·tom·ic *adj* existing or occurring within an atom or atoms, rather than between atoms

in·tra·car·di·ac /intrə kaárdee àk/, **in·tra·car·di·al** /-kaárdee əl/ *adj* within or introduced into the heart —**in·tra·car·di·al·ly** *adv*

in·tra·cel·lu·lar /intrə séllyələr/ *adj* within a cell or cells —**in·tra·cel·lu·lar·ly** *adv*

in·tra·cer·e·bral /intrə sə reébrəl, -sérrə-/ *adj* existing or taking place inside the main part of the brain or cerebrum —**in·tra·cer·e·bral·ly** *adv*

In·tra·coast·al Wa·ter·way /intrə kṓst'l-/ system of protected waterways, including rivers, bays, coastal sounds, and canals, in the eastern and southeastern United States, made up of the Atlantic Intracoastal Waterway and the Gulf Intracoastal Waterway. Length: 2,485 mi./4,000 km.

in·tra·com·pa·ny /intrə kúmpənee/ *adj* within the same company or between employees or divisions of the same company

in·tra·cra·ni·al /intrə kráynee əl/ *adj* within or introduced into the skull —**in·tra·cra·ni·al·ly** *adv*

in·trac·ta·ble /in tráktəb'l/ *adj* **1.** DIFFICULT TO DEAL WITH difficult to deal with or solve ○ *an intractable problem* **2.** DIFFICULT TO MANIPULATE difficult to shape or manipulate **3.** STRONG-WILLED AND RESISTANT TO OUTSIDE INFLUENCE stubbornly refusing to be controlled or submit to discipline ○ *Persuasion was tried, but she proved intractable.* —**in·trac·ta·bil·i·ty** /in tràktə bíllətee/ *n* —**in·trac·ta·bly** *adv*

SYNONYMS See *unruly*.

in·tra·cu·ta·ne·ous /intrə kyoo táynee əss/ *adj* ANAT same as **intradermal** —**in·tra·cu·ta·ne·ous·ly** *adv*

in·tra·der·mal /intrə dúrm'l/ *adj* within or introduced between the layers of the skin —**in·tra·der·mal·ly** *adv*

in·tra·der·mal test *n* a test for immunity or allergic sensitivity involving the injection of small amounts of a test material into the skin through a fine needle

in·tra·der·mic /intrə dúrmik/ *adj* ANAT same as **intradermal**

in·tra·dos /íntrə dòss, -dŏss, in tráy-/ (*plural same* or **-dos·es**) *n* the inner curve of an architectural arch [Late 18C. < French < Latin *intra* "within" + French *dos* "back" (< Latin *dorsum*)]

in·tra·gen·ic /intrə jénnik/ *adj* located or occurring within the same gene

in·tra·lin·gual /intrə líng gwəl/ *adj* occurring within a single language

in·tra·mo·lec·u·lar /intrə mə lékyələr/ *adj* existing or occurring within a single molecule —**in·tra·mo·lec·u·lar·ly** *adv*

in·tra·mu·ral /intrə myoórəl/ *adj* **1.** occurring within, or involving members of, a single school, college, or institution **2.** within the tissue of the wall of a blood vessel or another hollow body part —**in·tra·mu·ral·ly** *adv*

in·tra·mus·cu·lar /intrə múskyələr/ *adj* within or into the substance of a muscle —**in·tra·mus·cu·lar·ly** *adv*

in·tra·na·sal /intrə náyz'l/ *adj* within or introduced into the nose —**in·tra·na·sal·ly** *adv*

in·tra·net /íntrə nèt/ *n* a network of computers, especially one using World Wide Web conventions, accessible only to authorized users such as those within a company

intrans. *abbr* GRAM intransitive

in·tran·si·gent /in tránssəjənt, -zəjənt/ *adj* stubbornly or unreasonably refusing even to consider changing a decision or attitude ■ *n* somebody who refuses to compromise or change an attitude or decision, especially in politics [Late 19C. < French < Spanish *los intransigentes*, a political party (literally "the uncompromising ones") < *transigir* "to compromise" < Latin *transigere* (see TRANSACTION)] —**in·tran·si·gence** *n* —**in·tran·si·gent·ly** *adv*

in·tran·si·tive /in tránssətiv, -tránz-/ *adj* describes a verb, or the use of a verb, without a direct object, e.g., the verb "die" in the sentence "He was slowly dying" ■ *n* a verb that does not take a direct object —**in·tran·si·tive·ly** *adv*

in·tra·nu·cle·ar /intrə nóoklee ər/ *adj* **1.** existing or occurring within the nucleus of an atom **2.** existing or occurring within the nucleus of a cell

in·tra·oc·u·lar /intrə ókyələr/ *adj* within or introduced into the inside of the eyeball —**in·tra·oc·u·lar·ly** *adv*

in·tra·pe·ri·to·ne·al /intrə perit'n eé əl/ *adj* within or introduced into the peritoneal cavity —**in·tra·pe·ri·to·ne·al·ly** *adv*

in·tra·per·son·al /intrə púrssən'l, -púrssnəl/ *adj* relating to the internal aspects of a person, especially emotions —**in·tra·per·son·al·ly** *adv*

in·tra·pre·neur /intrə prə núr, -noór/ *n* an employee with a flair for innovation and risk-taking who is given unusual freedom to develop products or subsidiary businesses within a company [Late 20C. < INTRA- + ENTREPRENEUR] —**in·tra·pre·neur·i·al** *adj*

in·tra·psy·chic /intrə síkik/ *adj* existing or occurring within the mind —**in·tra·psy·chi·cal·ly** *adv*

in·tra·spe·cif·ic /intrə spə síffik/, **in·tra·spe·cies** /-speé sheez, -seez/ *adj* existing within a single species or confined to members of one species

in·tra·state /intrə stáyt/ *adj* existing or occurring within the boundaries of a single state

in·tra·u·ter·ine /intrə yóotərin, -rīn/ *adj* existing, occurring, or designed to be used inside the womb

in·tra·u·ter·ine de·vice *n* a plastic or metal device that is inserted into the cavity of the womb in order to prevent pregnancy

in·tra·vas·cu·lar /intrə váskyələr/ *adj* situated or occurring within blood vessels or within a similar system of fluid-bearing vessels in plants —**in·tra·vas·cu·lar·ly** *adv*

in·tra·ve·nous /intrə veénəss/ *adj* **1.** existing or occurring inside a vein, or administered into a vein **2.** used in administering fluids or medicines into the veins —**in·tra·ve·nous·ly** *adv*

in·tra·ven·tric·u·lar /intrə ven tríkyələr/ *adj* within or introduced into a ventricle such as one in the heart or brain —**in·tra·ven·tric·u·lar·ly** *adv*

in·tra·vi·tal /intrə vít'l/, **in·tra·vi·tam** /-veé tàm, -weé taám/ *adj* occurring in or used on a living cell or organism [Late 19C. < modern Latin *intra vitam* "within life"] —**in·tra·vi·tal·ly** *adv*

in-tray *n* same as **in-box**

in·tra·zo·nal /intrə zṓn'l/ *adj* describes a soil that has a well-developed and differentiated set of soil characteristics (**profile**), determined by the nature of the parent material and age of the soil

in·treat /in treét/ *vti* to entreat somebody (*archaic*)

in·trench *vti* CONSTR, POL another spelling of **entrench**

in·trep·id /in tréppid/ *adj* courageous and bold [Late 17C. Directly or via French < Latin *intrepidus* "not agitated" < *trepidus* "agitated"] —**in·tre·pid·i·ty** /intrə píddətee/ *n* —**in·trep·id·ly** *adv*

~~**intrest**~~ incorrect spelling of **interest**

in·tri·ca·cy /íntrikəssee/ (*plural* **-cies**) *n* **1.** the character of something that has many aspects or parts arranged together in a particularly complex or artful way ○ *a carving of incredible intricacy* **2.** one of the parts or details making up a complex and often puzzling whole (*often used in the plural*) ○ *We had difficulty following the intricacies of the plot.*

in·tri·cate /íntrikət/ *adj* **1.** containing many details or small parts that are combined in a particularly complex or skillful way **2.** complex and difficult to understand or resolve, through having many interrelated elements, parts, or factors [15C. < Latin *intricatus*, past participle of *intricare* "entangle" < *tricae* "impediments, tricks"] —**in·tri·cate·ly** *adv*

in·trigue *v* /in treég/ (**-trigued, -trigu·ing, -trigues**) **1.** *vt* INTEREST SOMEBODY to make somebody greatly interested or curious **2.** *vi* SCHEME to scheme or use underhanded methods to achieve something **3.** *vi* HAVE SECRET LOVER to carry on a secret love affair (*archaic*) ■ *n* /in treég, in treég/ **1.** SECRET PLOTTING secret scheming or plotting **2.** SECRET PLOT a secret scheme or plot [Early 17C. Via French < Italian *intrigo* < *intrigare* "entangle" < Latin *intricare* (see INTRICATE)] —**in·trigu·er** *n* —**in·trigu·ing** *adj* —**in·trigu·ing·ly** *adv*

in·trin·sic /in trínzik, -sik/, **in·trin·si·cal** /-zik'l, -sik'l/ *adj* **1.** BASIC AND ESSENTIAL belonging to something as one of the basic and essential features that make it what it is ○ *an intrinsic part of the plan* **2.** OF ITSELF by or in itself, rather than because of its associations or consequences ○ *has no intrinsic value* **3.** ANAT FOUND IN BODY PART occurring wholly within or belonging wholly to a part of the body such as an organ [15C. Via French < late Latin *intrinsecus* "inward" < assumed Latin *intrim* "within"] —**in·trin·si·cal·ly** *adv*

in·trin·sic fac·tor *n* a protein produced in the stomach that promotes the absorption of vitamin B_{12} in the small intestine. Insufficient intrinsic factor results in pernicious anemia.

in·trin·sic sem·i·con·duc·tor *n* a semiconductor of very high purity in which the density of charge carriers is that of the material itself and is not modified by the presence of impurities

in·tro /íntrō/ *n* an introduction, especially the opening few bars of a piece of pop music (*informal*) [Early 19C. Shortening]

intro. *abbr* **1.** introduction **2.** introductory

intro- *prefix* **1.** in, into ○ *intromission* **2.** inward ○ *introvert* [< Latin *intro* "to the inside"]

introd. *abbr* **1.** introduction **2.** introductory

in·tro·duce /intrə dóoss/ (**-duced, -duc·ing, -duc·es**) *v* **1.** *vt* PRESENT SOMEBODY TO SOMEBODY to make yourself or another person known to somebody else by saying who you are or who the other person is, as a way of beginning an acquaintance **2.** *vt* BRING IN SOMETHING NEW to bring something to a place, into existence, or into operation for the first time **3.** *vt* CAUSE SOMEBODY TO EXPERIENCE SOMETHING NEW to make somebody aware of something for the first time, or give somebody a first experience of something **4.** *vt* PREFACE SOMETHING WITH SOMETHING ELSE to begin an action with a preface of some sort, especially one designed to get people's attention **5.** *vt* TALK ABOUT SOMETHING NEW to mention a matter for the first time **6.** *vt* GIVE AUDIENCE FORETASTE to tell an audience a little about what or whom they are going to see or hear **7.** *vt* POL PRESENT LEGISLATION FORMALLY to present proposed legislation formally to an assembly, so that it can be debated and voted on **8.** *vt* INSERT SOMETHING INTO SOMETHING ELSE to insert one thing into another **9.** BOT, ZOOL BRING IN NEW SPECIES to place or establish an individual or species of plant or animal in a new habitat or environment [15C. Either < Latin *introducere* "lead in" < *ducere* "to lead," or back-formation < INTRODUCTION] —**in·tro·duc·er** *n*

in·tro·duc·tion /intrə dúkshən/ *n* **1.** EXPLANATORY SECTION AT BEGINNING a section at the beginning of a book or other piece of writing that summarizes what it is about or sets the scene **2.** SOMETHING GIVING BASIC FACTS a book or course of study that gives somebody basic facts or skills in a field **3.** BEGINNING OF PIECE OF MUSIC the opening passage or movement of a piece of music **4.** PRESENTATION OF SOMEBODY TO SOMEBODY the act of formally presenting somebody or yourself to another person in order to make that person's acquaintance **5.** PRESENTATION the act of presenting somebody or something to an audience, assembly, or other group **6.** FIRST EXPERIENCE somebody's first experience of something **7.** BRINGING IN SOMETHING NEW the act of bringing something to a place, into existence, or into operation for the first time **8.** SOMETHING BROUGHT IN something recently brought from elsewhere, into existence, or into operation **9.** INSERTION the insertion of something somewhere [14C. Directly or via French < Latin *introduction-* < *introduct-*, past participle of *introducere* (see INTRODUCE)]

in·tro·duc·to·ry /intrə dúktəree/ *adj* **1.** GIVING FORETASTE preparing for what is to be communicated or done later by means of a brief summary or by providing information necessary to understand it ○ *an introductory chapter* **2.** PROVIDING BASICS providing the basic facts or skills ○ *an introductory course* **3.** INITIAL made or used when something begins or is first introduced ○ *an introductory price* [14C. Directly or via French < late Latin *introductorius* < *introduct-* (see INTRODUCTION)]

in·tro·gres·sion /intrə grésh'n/ *n* the incorporation of genes from one species into the gene pool of another as a result of hybridization [Mid-17C. < INTRO- + *-gression* "going," as in PROGRESSION] —**in·tro·gres·sant** *adj* —**in·tro·gres·sive** *adj*

in·tro·it /ín tròyt, -trō it, in trṓ it/, **In·tro·it** *n* **1.** the part of the Roman Catholic Mass consisting of psalm verses and the Gloria Patri, said or sung when the priest first approaches the altar **2.** a psalm or hymn sung as the minister enters the church at the beginning of the Anglican service of Communion [15C. Via French < medieval Latin *introitus* < Latin, "entrance," past participle of *introire* "go in" < *ire* "go"]

in·tro·jec·tion /intrə jéksh'n/ *n* the unconscious adoption by somebody of the values or attitudes of another person, whom he or she wants to impress or be accepted by [Mid-19C. < INTRO- + *-jection* as in PROJECTION] —**in·tro·ject** /-jékt/ *vt*

in·tro·mis·sion /intrə mísh'n/ *n* the insertion or admission of something into something else (*formal*) [Mid-16C. Directly or via French < medieval Latin *intromission-* < Latin *intromittere* "send in" < *mittere* "send"]

in·tron /ín tròn/ *n* a section of DNA that is not expressed in the gene product [Late 20C. < INTRAGENIC]

in·trorse /ín tràwrss, in tráwrss/ *adj* pointing and opening inward, as the anthers of some flowers do, releasing pollen toward the center of the flower [Mid-19C. < Latin *introrsus*, contraction of *introversus* < *versus*, past participle of *vertere* "turn"] —**in·trorse·ly** *adv*

in·tro·spect /intrə spékt, íntrə spèkt/ (**-spect·ed, -spect·ing, -spects**) *vi* to undertake a detailed mental examination of your own feelings, thoughts, and motives [Late 17C. < Latin *introspectare* "look into repeatedly" or its source Latin *introspect-*, past participle of *introspicere* "look into" < *specere* "to look"]

in·tro·spec·tion /intrə spéksh'n/ *n* the detailed mental examination of your own feelings, thoughts, and motives

in·tro·spec·tion·ism /intrə spékshə nìzzəm/ *n UK* PSYCHOL same as **introspective psychology** —**in·tro·spec·tion·is·tic** /intrə speksh'n ístik/ *adj*

in·tro·spec·tive /intrə spéktiv/ *adj* involving, or frequently undertaking, a deep and candid examination of your own feelings, thoughts, and motives —**in·tro·spec·tive·ly** *adv*

in·tro·spec·tive psy·chol·o·gy *n* a school of psychology concentrating on the study of immediate subjective experience

in·tro·ver·sion /intrə vúrzh'n, -sh'n/ *n* **1.** the tendency to be self-absorbed and uninterested in other people and the world around **2.** a turning inward of a hollow organ such as the womb into itself [Mid-17C. < INTROVERT]

in·tro·vert *n* /íntrə vùrt/ **1.** RESERVED PERSON a shy person who tends not to socialize much **2.** SOMEBODY FOCUSING ON OWN SELF somebody whose feelings and thoughts are directed inward ■ *vt* /íntrə vùrt, intrə vúrt/ (**-vert·ed, -vert·ing, -verts**) **1.** TURN INWARD to direct or turn something inward or in on itself **2.** PSYCHOL THINK ONLY ABOUT SELF to direct your mind inward and examine or dwell on personal thoughts, feelings, and motives ■ *adj* PSYCHOL, MED same as **introverted** [Mid-17C. < modern Latin *introvertere* "turn in" < Latin *vertere* "to turn"]

in·tro·vert·ed /íntrə vùrtəd, íntrə vúrtəd/ *adj* **1.** SHY tending to be shy and quiet or ill at ease in a group **2.** INTERESTED IN SELF self-absorbed and uninterested in other people and the world around **3.** MED TURNED INTO ITSELF turned into itself or pulled back inside a larger part

in·trude /in tróod/ (**-trud·ed, -trud·ing, -trudes**) *v* **1.** *vi* INVADE SOMEBODY'S PRIVACY to disturb somebody's peace or privacy by going or being somewhere uninvited **2.** *vi* HAVE UNWELCOME EFFECT to be an unwelcome presence in, or make an unwelcome entry into, something ○ *The noise of large machinery intruded on the quiet afternoon.* **3.** *vti* GEOL MOVE INTO ROCK FORMATION to move in a molten state into a preexisting rock formation, or force molten rock into a preexisting rock formation [15C. Partly < Latin *intrudere* "thrust in" < *trudere* "to thrust"; partly < INTRUSION]

in·trud·er /in tróodər/ *n* **1.** an illegal entrant into a building or property, usually in order to commit a crime **2.** somebody who is present where he or she is not welcome

in·tru·sion /in tróozh'n/ *n* **1.** DISTURBANCE a disturbance of somebody's peace or privacy by an unwelcome arrival or presence **2.** SOMETHING UNWELCOME an unwelcome presence or effect that disturbs or upsets something **3.** CRIME UNLAWFUL ENTRY an illegal entry into a place, often by force, in order to commit a crime (*formal*) **4.** GEOL INTRUDED ROCK a body of igneous rock that has moved while molten into older solid rocks with subsequent alteration of those rocks **5.** GEOL MOVEMENT OF MOLTEN ROCK the movement of molten rock (**magma**) into preexisting rock [14C. Directly or via French < medieval Latin *intrusion-* < Latin *intrus-*, past participle of *intrudere* (see INTRUDE)]

in·tru·sive /in tróossiv/ *adj* **1.** APPEARING WHERE UNWELCOME forcing itself or yourself into a situation or on people's attention in an unwelcome or inappropriate way **2.** CAUSING UNINVITED DISTURBANCE causing an uninvited and unwarranted disturbance of somebody's peace and privacy **3.** GEOL FORMED BY INTRUSION describes a rock formed by having moved while in a molten state into preexisting rocks **4.** PHON OF CONNECTING SPEECH SOUND describes a speech sound that is introduced between two words only to facilitate more fluent pronunciation —**in·tru·sive·ly** *adv* —**in·tru·sive·ness** *n*

in·trust *vt* another spelling of **entrust**

in·tu·bate /íntoo bàyt/ (**-bat·ed, -bat·ing, -bates**) *v* **1.** *vti* to insert a tube through the vocal cords and into the windpipe in order to provide a patient's lungs with oxygen, usually during surgery under anesthesia **2.** *vt* to treat a patient by inserting a tube into the windpipe so that oxygen can be supplied to the lungs [Late 19C. < IN-[2] + Latin *tuba* "tube"] —**in·tu·ba·tion** /íntoo báysh'n/ *n*

in·tu·it /in tóo it/ (**-it·ed, -it·ing, -its**) *vt* to be aware of or know something without having to think about it or learn it [Mid-19C. Back-formation < INTUITION]

in·tu·i·tion /íntoo ísh'n/ *n* **1.** INSTINCTIVE KNOWLEDGE the state of being aware of or knowing something without having to discover or perceive it, or the ability to do this **2.** INSTINCTIVE BELIEF something known or believed instinctively, without actual evidence for it **3.** PHILOSOPHY IMMEDIATE KNOWLEDGE immediate knowledge of something [15C. Directly or via French < late Latin *intuition-* "consideration" < Latin *intueri* "look upon" < *tueri* "to look"] —**in·tu·i·tion·al** *adj*

in·tu·i·tion·ism /ín too ísh'n ìzzəm/ *n* **1.** PHILOSOPHY DOCTRINE OF INTUITIVE PERCEPTION the doctrine that asserts that a perceived object is intuitively known to be real **2.** ETHICS ETHICAL PRINCIPLES UNDERSTOOD THROUGH INTUITION the doctrine that knowledge of goodness or obligation and the principles governing them can be discerned through intuition **3.** LOGIC, MATH MATHEMATICAL THEORY a theory in the foundation of mathematics that holds that only proofs constrained by specific restrictions are permitted

in·tu·i·tive /in tóo itiv/ *adj* **1.** known directly and instinctively, without being discovered or consciously perceived **2.** knowing things instinctively —**in·tu·i·tive·ly** *adv* —**in·tu·i·tive·ness** *n*

in·tu·mesce /íntoo méss/ (**-mesced, -mesc·ing, -mesc·es**) *vi* to become enlarged or swollen as a result of increased flow of blood or other fluids [Late 18C. < Latin *intumescere* "swell up" < *tumescere* (see TUMESCENT)] —**in·tu·mes·cence** *n*

in·tus·sus·cept /intəssə sépt/ (**-cept·ed, -cept·ing, -cepts**) *vti* to cause part of a tubular structure to slide partially into itself, e.g., as part of the intestine sometimes does [Early 19C. Back-formation < INTUSSUSCEPTION] —**in·tus·sus·cep·tive** *adj*

in·tus·sus·cep·tion /intəssə sépshən/ *n* **1.** MED a sliding of a portion of a tubular organ into another portion, especially a condition of the bowel in which this happens, creating swelling that leads to obstruction **2.** BIOL the growth of the surface area of a cell wall by the incorporation of new particles into the wall [Early 18C. Directly or via French < modern Latin *intussusception-* < Latin *intus* "within" + *susception-* "undertaking" < *suscept-*, past participle of *suscipere* (see SUSCEPTIBLE)]

in·twine *vti* another spelling of **entwine**

in·twist *vt* another spelling of **entwist**

~~inuendo~~ incorrect spelling of **innuendo**

In·u·it /ínnoo it, -yoo-/ (*plural same* or **-its**), **In·nu·it** *n* **1.** a member of an aboriginal people who live in the coastal Canadian Arctic, in Alaska, and in Greenland. The Inuit are related to the Yupik of Alaska and northeastern Siberia. **2.** a language of the Inuit, forming one branch of Eskimo-Aleut. Native speakers: 60,000. [Mid-18C. < Inuit, plural of *inuk* "person"] —**In·u·it** *adj*

USAGE The Inuit Circumpolar Conference, held in 1977 in Barrow, Alaska, chose officially to replace the term *Eskimo* with ***Inuit*** (which means "the real people"). *Eskimo* nonetheless remains in common use, appearing even in academic contexts. Because some may find *Eskimo* offensive, care should be exercised in using this word.

in·uk·shuk /i nóok shòok/ *n Can* rocks piled up to look like a person from a distance, used as a marker or guidepost by the Inuit [< Inuit "like a man"]

I·nuk·ti·tut /i nóokti tòot/ *n* a language of the Inuit people, especially those in the eastern Arctic [Late 20C. < Inuit, "the Inuit way"] —**I·nuk·ti·tut** *adj*

in·u·lase /ínnyə làyss, -làyz/ *n* an enzyme that brings about the breakdown of inulin [Late 19C. < INULIN]

in·u·lin /ínnyəlin/ *n* a fructose polysaccharide that is a food reserve found in the roots and tubers of various plants [Early 19C. < Latin *inula* "elecampane"]

in·un·date /ínnən dàyt/ (**-dat·ed, -dat·ing, -dates**) *vt* **1.** to overwhelm somebody with a huge quantity of things that must be dealt with **2.** to flood a place with water [Late 16C. Back-formation < INUNDATION]

in·un·da·tion /innən dáysh'n/ *n* **1.** an accumulation of an overwhelming amount of things that somebody has to deal with **2.** a flood of water (*formal*) [15C. Directly or via French < Latin *inundation-* < *inundare* "flow onto" < *unda* "wave"]

In·u·pi·aq /i nóopee àk/, **In·u·pik** /i nóopik/ *n* a language of the Inuit people who live in northern Alaska [Mid-20C. < Inuit < *inuk* "person" + *piaq* "genuine"] —**In·u·pi·aq** *adj*

In·u·pi·at /i nóopee àat/ (*plural same*) *n* a member of an Inuit people who live along the Beaufort Sea and Chukchi coast of the Arctic Ocean [Late 20C. < Inuit (plural) < *inuk* "person" + *piaq* "genuine"]

In·u·pik *n, adj* LANG another spelling of **Inupiaq**

in·ur·bane /in ur báyn/ *adj* lacking good manners or sophistication

in·ure /i nóor, -nyóor/ (**-ured, -ur·ing, -ures**), **en·ure** *v* **1.** *vt* to make somebody used to something unpleasant over a period of time, so that he or she no longer is bothered or upset by it **2.** *vi* to come into legal operation or effect [15C. < assumed Anglo-Norman *eneurer* "accustom by use" < assumed *eure* "use" < Latin *opera* "work"] —**in·ure·ment** *n*

in·urn /in úrn/ (**-urned, -urn·ing, -urns**) *vt* **1.** to place a cremated body's ashes in an urn **2.** to put a dead body in a grave (*formal*) —**in·urn·ment** *n*

in u·ter·o /in yóotərō/ *adv, adj* in, or while still inside, a woman's uterus [< Latin]

inv. *abbr* **1.** MATH, GRAM invariable **2.** invented **3.** invention **4.** inventor **5.** COMM invoice

in vac·u·o /in vákyoo ō/ *adv* **1.** in a vacuum **2.** in isolation, without considering any legal evidence [< Latin]

in·vade /in váyd/ (**-vad·ed, -vad·ing, -vades**) *v* **1.** *vti* ENTER COUNTRY BY MILITARY FORCE to enter a country by force with or as an army, especially in order to conquer it **2.** *vt* ENTER AND SPREAD THROUGH SOMETHING to enter and spread throughout something completely **3.** *vt* GO SOMEWHERE IN NUMBERS to enter or be present in a place in great numbers ○ *The town has been invaded by tourists.* **4.** *vt* SPOIL SOMETHING to spoil something by interfering with or in it, interrupting it, or reducing it ○ *invading our privacy* **5.** *vti* MED CAUSE DISEASE to enter and spread gradually throughout a part of the body, causing harm or damage **6.** *vti* BOT GROW RAPIDLY AND HARMFULLY to become established and spread rapidly in an area, crowding out the preexisting plants [15C. Directly or via French < Latin *invadere* "go in" < *vadere* "to go"] —**in·vad·er** *n*

in·vag·i·nate /in vájjə nàyt/ (**-nat·ed, -nat·ing, -nates**) *vti* to push the wall of a cavity or hollow organ into itself, or one section of a hollow organ into another, or be pushed in this way [Mid-17C. Back-formation < INVAGINATION]

in·vag·i·na·tion /in vàjjə náysh'n/ *n* **1.** MED PUSHING SOMETHING INSIDE ITSELF the pushing of something into itself or partially inside out, like a glove finger pushed into itself, or the condition of something that results from this **2.** MED INVAGINATED ORGAN a hollow organ or body part that has been pushed back inside itself **3.** BIOL INFOLDING OF CELL STRUCTURE the process of folding a portion of a cell structure inward, e.g., when the cell membrane turns inward during phagocytosis **4.** BIOL FORMING OF HOLLOW GROWTH INSIDE the pushing inward of a layer of cells to produce a hollow ingrowth in something, e.g., when the wall of the blastula forms the gastrula [Mid-17C. < modern Latin *invagination-* < medieval Latin *invaginare* "sheathe" < Latin *vagina* "sheath"]

in·va·lid[1] /in vállid/ *adj* **1.** not acceptable or correct through being based on a mistake or employing flawed reasoning **2.** not legally binding or enforceable [Mid-16C. < Latin *invalidus* "not strong" < *validus* (see VALID)] —**in·va·lid·ly** *adv*

in·va·lid[2] /ínvəlid/ *n* **1.** SOMEBODY WITH PERSISTENT DISEASE a patient who has been affected by a disease or medical disorder over a long period **2.** OFFENSIVE TERM an offensive term for somebody who is physically challenged (*dated*) ■ *adj* **1.** AFFECTED BY PERSISTENT DISEASE having a persistent disease or medical disorder **2.** FOR SOMEBODY WITH PERSISTENT LONG-TERM DISEASE intended for somebody who has a persistent long-term disease or medical disorder ■ *vt* (**-lid·ed, -lid·ing, -lids**) CAUSE SOMEBODY TO BE INVALID to cause somebody to have a persistent long-term disease or medical disorder [Mid-17C. < INVALID[1]]

in·val·i·date /in vállə dàyt/ (**-dat·ed, -dat·ing, -dates**) *vt* **1.** to deprive something of its legal force or value **2.** to prove that something is wrong or make something worthless —**in·val·i·da·tion** /in vàllə dáysh'n/ *n*

SYNONYMS See *nullify.*

in·va·lid·ism /ínvələ dìzzəm/ *n* persistent illness or medical disorder

in·va·lid·i·ty /ìnvə líddətee/ *n* **1.** a lack of soundness or accuracy that results from an error in reasoning **2.** LAW the condition of not being legally binding or enforceable

in·val·u·a·ble /in vállyoo əb'l/ *adj* extremely useful or valuable —**in·val·u·a·bly** *adv*

in·var·i·a·ble /in vérree əb'l/ *adj* never changing or varying ■ *n* a mathematical quantity that is a constant —**in·var·i·a·bil·i·ty** /in vèree ə bíllətee/ *n*

in·var·i·a·bly /in vérree əblee/ *adv* always or almost always

in·var·i·ant /in vérree ənt/ *adj* **1.** same as **invariable 2.** MATH describes a quantity or set of quantities that is not changed by a designated mathematical operation such as the transformation of coordinates ■ *n* MATH a relationship that is not changed by a designated mathematical operation such as the transformation of coordinates —**in·var·i·ance** *n*

in·va·sion /in váyzh'n/ *n* **1.** ATTEMPT TO CONQUER a hostile entry by an armed force into a country's territory, especially with the intention of conquering it **2.** ARRIVAL IN LARGE NUMBERS the arrival of large numbers of people or things at one time ○ *an invasion of tourists* **3.** SPOILING a spoiling of something by interfering with it or taking some of it away **4.** SPREAD OF SOMETHING HARMFUL the arrival or spread of something that causes damage or harm **5.** MED SPREAD OF DISEASE the spread of disease-causing organisms or malignant cells in the body **6.** BOT AGGRESSIVE SPREAD OF PLANT the aggressive spread of a plant species in an area, stifling the growth of preexisting species [15C. Directly or via French < late Latin *invasion-* < Latin *invas-*, past participle of *invadere* (see INVADE)]

in·va·sive /in váyssiv/ *adj* **1.** MED ATTACKING ADJACENT TISSUE having or showing a tendency to spread from the point of origin to adjacent tissue, as some cancers do **2.** SURG INTO PATIENT'S BODY done by inserting something into or operating on the body through an incision or a natural orifice **3.** INTRUDING involving an intrusion or infringement, e.g., of somebody's privacy or rights **4.** BOT GROWING AGGRESSIVELY growing aggressively in an area and stifling the growth of preexisting plants **5.** MIL ATTACKING involving or mounting a military attack on a territory, especially with a view to conquering it —**in·va·sive·ly** *adv* —**in·va·sive·ness** *n*

in·vec·tive /in véktiv/ (*formal*) *n* abusive or violent language used to attack, blame, or denounce somebody ■ *adj* using abusive language [15C. Directly or via French < late Latin *invectivus* "abusive" < Latin *invehere* "carry in" < *vehere* "carry"]

in·veigh /in váy/ (**-veighed, -veigh·ing, -veighs**) *vi* to speak angrily in criticism of or protest at something [15C. < Latin *invehere* (see INVECTIVE)]

in·vei·gle /in váyg'l, -veeg'l/ (**-gled, -gling, -gles**) *vt* **1.** to charm or entice somebody into doing something that he or she would not otherwise have done ○ *They inveigled me into driving them to school.* **2.** to obtain something by persuading somebody to give it ○ *She inveigled an introduction to him.* [15C. < Anglo-Norman *envegler*, alteration of French *aveugler* "deprive of sight" < assumed Vulgar Latin *aboculus* "without an eye" < Latin *oculus* "eye"]

in·vent /in vént/ (**-vent·ed, -vent·ing, -vents**) *vt* **1.** to be the first to think of, make, or use something **2.** to make up something false such as a false excuse ○ *invented a reason for being late* [15C. < Latin *invent-*, past participle of *invenire* "come upon" < *venire* "come"]

in·ven·tion /in vénshən/ *n* **1.** CREATED THING a thing that somebody has created, especially a device or process **2.** ACT OF CREATING the creation of something new **3.** LIE a lie, or the telling of lies (*often used euphemistically*) **4.** CREATIVE ABILITY the talent to create new things **5.** MUSIC SHORT INSTRUMENTAL WORK a short instrumental work, usually for keyboard, that has two or three parts and employs the technique of counterpoint

in·ven·tive /in véntiv/ *adj* **1.** SKILLED AT INVENTING good at creating new things **2.** DISPLAYING CREATIVITY displaying creativity or imagination in its design ○ *an inventive solution to a long-standing problem* **3.** INVOLVED IN INVENTION involved in or concerned with invention —**in·ven·tive·ly** *adv* —**in·ven·tive·ness** *n*

in·ven·tor /in véntər/ *n* somebody who invents something

in·ven·to·ry /ínvən tàwree/ *n* (*plural* **-ries**) **1.** COMM STOCK OF GOODS the merchandise or stock that a store or company has on hand **2.** MAKING OF INVENTORY the act or process of making an inventory, or the period of time when this is done **3.** LIST OF ITEMS a list of things, especially items of property, assets, or other resources **4.** ACCT RECORD OF ASSETS a record of a business's current assets, including property owned, merchandise on hand, and the value of work in progress and work completed but not sold ■ *vt* (**-ried, -ry·ing, -ries**) MAKE INVENTORY OF SOMETHING to make a list of items, or enter a specific item in an inventory [15C. < medieval Latin *inventorium*, alteration of late Latin *inventarium* "list of what is found" < Latin *invenire* (see INVENT)]

in·ve·rac·i·ty /ìnvə rássətee/ (*plural* **-ties**) *n* a lie, or the telling of lies

in·ver·ness /ìnvər néss/ *n* a long overcoat with a rounded collar and a detachable cape [Mid-19C. After INVERNESS]

In·ver·ness /ìnvər néss/ city in northern Scotland, at the northeastern end of the Caledonian Canal. Population: 63,850 (1993).

in·verse *adj* /in vúrss, ín vùrss/ **1.** OPPOSITE OR REVERSING opposite to or reversing something **2.** MATH INVOLVING OPPOSITELY AFFECTED VARIABLES involving two variables that are in a mathematical relationship where, when one increases, the other decreases and vice versa ■ *n* /ín vùrss, in vúrss/ **1.** OPPOSITE something that is a total opposite **2.** MATH ELEMENT OF SET either of two elements of a set that when added together give 0, one being the negative of the other, e.g., 7 and –7 **3.** MATH same as **inverse function 4.** LOGIC OPPOSITE LOGICAL PROPOSITION a logical proposition in which both the subject and the predicate are the opposite of another proposition [15C. < Latin *inversus*, past participle of *invertere* "turn upside down," literally "turn in" < *vertere* "to turn"] —**in·verse·ly** *adv*

in·verse func·tion *n* a mathematical operation or function that exactly reverses another operation or function. Addition and subtraction are inverse functions.

in·verse·ly pro·por·tion·al *adj* **1.** opposite in size, degree, or rate of development **2.** involving a mathematical relationship in which an increase in one variable by a given factor brings about a decrease by the same factor in another

in·verse square law *n* a law in physics stating that the magnitude of a physical quantity varies inversely with the square of its distance from its source

in·ver·sion /in vúrzh'n, -sh'n/ *n* **1.** REVERSAL a reversing of the order, arrangement, or position of something **2.** REVERSED STATE OR THING a state in which the order, arrangement, or position of something is reversed, or something in such a state **3.** METEOROL TEMPERATURE INCREASE WITH ALTITUDE a stable atmospheric condition in which air temperature increases vertically upward through a layer **4.** MATH INVERTED RATIO the transformation of a mathematical proportion by inverting the ratio and order of its terms **5.** MUSIC CHANGING OF INTERVAL BY OCTAVE a raising of the lower note of an interval, or a lowering of the upper note, by an octave **6.** MUSIC MOVING OF CHORD TONE a moving of the root tone of a chord to a position other than the lowest **7.** MUSIC REVERSING OF MELODY INTERVALS a converting of all the intervals in a melody from ascending to descending and vice versa **8.** GRAM same as **anastrophe 9.** CHEM PRODUCTION OF OPPOSITE OPTICAL ACTIVITY a chemical reaction in which an optically active compound gives a product with opposite optical configuration **10.** GENETICS CHROMOSOMAL MUTATION a chromosomal mutation in which a block of genes in a segment is in reverse order **11.** MED INVERTING OF ORGAN atypical positioning of an organ, especially the turning inward or inside out of an organ —**in·ver·sive** *adj*

in·vert *vt* /in vúrt/ (**-vert·ed, -vert·ing, -verts**) **1.** REVERSE ARRANGEMENT OF SOMETHING to reverse the order, position, or arrangement of something **2.** CHANGE SOMETHING TO OPPOSITE to change something to its opposite or contrary **3.** MUSIC ALTER POSITION OF NOTES to change the position or arrangement of the musical notes in an interval, chord, or melody to produce inversion **4.** CHEM CHANGE OPTICAL CONFIGURATION to convert an optically active isomer into an isomer with the opposite configuration **5.** LOGIC CONVERT LOGICAL PROPOSITION to negate both the subject and predicate of a logical proposition ■ *n* /ín vùrt/ CHEM PRODUCT OF INVERSION a substance obtained by optical inversion ■ *adj* /ín vùrt/ CHEM OPTICALLY INVERTED subjected to optical inversion [Mid-16C. < Latin *invertere* (see INVERSE)] —**in·vert·i·bil·i·ty** /in vùrtə bíllətee/ *n* —**in·vert·i·ble** *adj*

in·ver·tase /in vúr tàyss, -tàyz, ínvər-/ *n* an enzyme that hydrolyzes sucrose

in·ver·te·brate /in vúrtəbrət, -bràyt/ *n* ANIMAL WITHOUT BACKBONE an animal that does not have a backbone, e.g., an insect or worm ■ *adj* **1.** WITH NO BACKBONE lacking a backbone or spinal column **2.** OF INVERTEBRATES relating to or consisting of animals that lack backbones ○ *invertebrate biology*

in·vert·ed /in vúrtəd/ *adj* **1.** REVERSED turned upside down, inside out, or backward **2.** MUSIC WITH FUNDAMENTAL NOTE REPOSITIONED modified so that the fundamental note of the chord is not the lowest note of the chord **3.** MUSIC WITH NOTES IN MIRROR IMAGE with the musical notes so arranged that every ascending interval is made descending and vice versa

in·vert·ed com·ma *n UK* same as **quotation mark**

in·vert·ed mor·dent *n* a musical ornament consisting of two notes of the same pitch separated by a third note one step above the others

in·vert·ed pleat *n* a flat symmetrical pleat formed by folding the fabric to the front on each side of the section being pleated

in·vert·er /in vúrtər/ *n* **1.** somebody or something that inverts or causes an inversion **2.** a device that changes direct current into alternating current and is commonly used on boats to operate devices such as radios from batteries

in·vert sug·ar /ín vurt-/ *n* a mixture of glucose and fructose. Source: optical inversion of sucrose, fruits, honey. Use: in the food industry.

in·vest /in vést/ (**-vest·ed, -vest·ing, -vests**) *v* **1.** *vti* **BUY STOCKS OR BONDS** to use money to buy or participate in a business enterprise that offers the possibility of profit, especially by buying stocks or bonds **2.** *vti* **DEPOSIT MONEY IN BANK** to deposit money in a bank or other financial institution in an account that pays interest **3.** *vti* **SPEND MONEY ON PROJECT** to spend money on something in the hope of a future return or benefit **4.** *vt* **CONTRIBUTE EFFORT TO SOMETHING** to contribute time, energy, or effort to an activity, project, or undertaking in the expectation of a benefit ○ *investing all their energy into fundraising* **5.** *vt* **GIVE SOMETHING PARTICULAR QUALITY** to provide somebody or something with a particular quality or characteristic (*often passive*) ○ *He endeavored to ensure that the occasion was invested with a suitable grandeur.* **6.** *vt* **CONFER SOMETHING ON SOMEBODY** to confer something such as a power or right on a person or group ○ *invests the directors with unprecedented power* **7.** *vi* **MAKE PURCHASE** to use money to buy something, especially something that somebody should be able to use for a relatively long time (*informal*) ○ *It's time this family invested in a new car.* **8.** *vt* **INSTALL SOMEBODY IN OFFICIAL ROLE** to install somebody formally or ceremoniously in an official position (*formal*) ○ *was invested as queen of the carnival* **9.** *vt* **ADORN SOMEBODY OR SOMETHING** to dress, clothe, or cover somebody or something with a garment or other covering (*literary*) **10.** *vt* **BESIEGE SOMETHING** to lay siege to a place (*archaic*) [Mid-16C. Directly or via French < Latin *investire* "clothe (in)" < *vestis* "clothing"] —**in·vest·a·ble** *adj*

in·ves·ti·gate /in vésti gàyt/ (**-gat·ed, -gat·ing, -gates**) *v* **1.** *vti* to carry out a detailed examination or inquiry, especially officially, in order to find out about something or somebody ○ *The local police are investigating a murder.* **2.** *vi* to take a look or go and see what has happened ○ *We heard noises downstairs, so Fred went down to investigate.* [Early 16C. < Latin *investigat-*, past participle of *investigare*, literally "look into for traces" < *vestigium* "footprint"] —**in·ves·ti·ga·ble** *adj*

in·ves·ti·ga·tion /in vèsti gáysh'n/ *n* an examination or inquiry into something, especially a detailed one that is undertaken officially, or the act of undertaking an examination [15C. Directly or via French < Latin *investigat-*, past participle of *investigare* (see INVESTIGATE)] —**in·ves·ti·ga·tion·al** *adj*

in·ves·ti·ga·tive /in vésti gàytiv/ *adj* **1.** responsible for or specializing in investigating **2.** used in or relating to investigation ○ *investigative techniques*

in·ves·ti·ga·tor /in vésti gàytər/ *n* somebody who seeks facts about somebody or something on a professional basis, especially somebody who investigates crimes or prepares official or confidential reports

in·ves·ti·ga·to·ry /in véstigə tàwree/ *adj* same as **investigative**

in·ves·ti·ture /in véstə choòr, -chər/ *n* **1.** the formal installation of somebody in a position or role, especially an official one, or a ceremony held to mark this **2.** the appointment of bishops in the Roman Catholic Church by a civil ruler instead of by the Church [14C. < medieval Latin *investitura* < Latin *investire* "clothe" (see INVEST); because the person is clothed in the insignia of the position]

in·vest·ment /in véstmənt/ *n* **1. USE OF MONEY FOR FUTURE PROFIT** the outlay of money, e.g., by depositing it in a bank or by buying stock in a company, with the object of making a profit **2. MONEY INVESTED** an amount of money invested in something for the purpose of making a profit **3. SOMETHING IN WHICH MONEY IS INVESTED** something, e.g., a company, endeavor, or property, that money is invested in with the goal of making a profit **4. CONTRIBUTION TO ACTIVITY** a contribution of something such as time, energy, or effort to an activity, project, or undertaking, in the expectation of a benefit **5. PURCHASE** a purchase, especially something that somebody should be able to use for a relatively long time (*informal*) **6. INVESTITURE** the formal or ceremonial installation of somebody in a role or position, especially an official one (*formal*) **7.** MIL **SIEGE** a siege or besieging (*archaic*) **8.** BIOL **OUTER LAYERS OF ORGANISM** the outer layers of an animal or organ

in·vest·ment an·a·lyst *n* a researcher employed by a financial institution to research investments

in·vest·ment bank *n* a bank that offers financial services such as trading securities, raising capital, and managing corporate mergers and acquisitions

in·vest·ment com·pa·ny *n* a company that holds securities in other companies purely for investment

in·vest·ment trust *n* a financial enterprise whose business is to invest the capital subscribed by its member shareholders in securities

in·ves·tor /in véstər/ *n* a person, company, or other organization that has money invested in something, especially one that holds stock in publicly owned corporations

in·vet·er·ate /in véttərət/ *adj* **1.** fixed in a habit or practice, especially a bad one **2.** firmly established and of long standing [14C. < Latin *inveteratus*, past participle of *inveterare* "become old" < *veter-* "old"] —**in·vet·er·a·cy** *n* —**in·vet·er·ate·ly** *adv* —**in·vet·er·ate·ness** *n*

in·vi·a·ble /in ví əb'l/ *adj* unable to survive, especially financially or biologically —**in·vi·a·bil·i·ty** /in ví ə bíllətee/ *n* —**in·vi·a·ble·ness** *n* —**in·vi·a·bly** *adv*

in·vid·i·ous /in víddee əss/ *adj* **1.** making or implying an unfair distinction ○ *an invidious comparison* **2.** unpleasant because producing or likely to produce jealousy, resentment, or hatred in other people ○ *placed in the invidious position of appearing to criticize from the sidelines* [Early 17C. < Latin *invidiosus* < *invidia* "ill will," literally "looking at" < *videre* "to look"] —**in·vid·i·ous·ly** *adv* —**in·vid·i·ous·ness** *n*

USAGE See ***insidious***.

in·vig·i·late /in víjjə làyt/ (**-lat·ed, -lat·ing, -lates**) *vti UK* EDUC same as **proctor** *v* [Mid-16C. < Latin *invigilat-*, past participle of *invigilare* "to watch" < *vigil* "awake"] —**in·vig·i·la·tion** /in vìjjə láysh'n/ *n*

in·vig·i·la·tor /in víjjə làytər/ *n UK* EDUC same as **proctor** *n* (sense 1)

in·vig·or·ate /in víggə ràyt/ (**-at·ed, -at·ing, -ates**) *vt* to fill somebody or something with energy or life [Mid-17C. Probably < *invigor* < Old French *envigourer* < Latin *vigor* "vigor"] —**in·vig·or·a·tion** /in vìggə ráysh'n/ *n* —**in·vig·o·ra·tive** *adj* —**in·vig·o·ra·tive·ly** *adv* —**in·vig·or·a·tor** *n*

in·vig·or·at·ing /in víggə ràyting/ *adj* filling somebody or something with energy or life —**in·vig·or·at·ing·ly** *adv*

in·vin·ci·ble /in vínssəb'l/ *adj* **1. UNBEATABLE** too strong or skillful to ever be defeated **2. TOO DIFFICULT TO OVERCOME** so great or difficult as to be impossible to overcome **3. DEEP-ROOTED** too deep-rooted or ingrained to be altered [15C. Directly or via French < Latin *invincibilis* < *vincibilis* "conquerable"] —**in·vin·ci·bil·i·ty** /in vìnssə bíllətee/ *n* —**in·vin·ci·ble·ness** *n* —**in·vin·ci·bly** *adv*

in·vi·o·la·ble /in ví ələb'l/ *adj* **1.** secure from being infringed, breached, or broken ○ *The old traditions are no longer inviolable.* **2.** secure from violence or attack ○ *The monarch's person is inviolable.* [15C. Directly or via French < Latin *inviolabilis* < *violabilis* "that may be injured"] —**in·vi·o·la·bil·i·ty** /in ví ələ bíllətee/ *n* —**in·vi·o·la·ble·ness** *n* —**in·vi·o·la·bly** *adv*

in·vi·o·late /in ví ələt/ *adj* **1.** not subject to change, damage, or destruction **2.** kept pure, untouched, or unblemished [15C. < Latin *inviolatus* < *violat-*, past participle of *violare* "injure, treat violently"] —**in·vi·o·la·cy** *n* —**in·vi·o·late·ly** *adv* —**in·vi·o·late·ness** *n*

in·vis·i·ble /in vízzəb'l/ *adj* **1. IMPOSSIBLE TO SEE** not able to be seen with the eyes **2. HIDDEN** hidden from view **3. MADE TRANSPARENT MAGICALLY** impossible to see as a result of magic or pseudoscientific processes **4. NOT EASILY NOTICED** not readily noticed or detected **5. UNRECORDED STATISTICALLY** not reflected, recorded, or reported in economic statistics ○ *invisible earnings* ■ *n* **1. ITEM NOT IN FINANCIAL STATEMENT** an item not reported in a company's financial statement **2. INVISIBLE PERSON OR THING** somebody or something that is invisible ■ **in·vis·i·bles** *npl* ECON **NONPHYSICAL EXPORTS AND IMPORTS** exports and imports such as financial and leisure services, as opposed to physical goods —**in·vis·i·bil·i·ty** /in vìzzə bíllətee/ *n* —**in·vis·i·ble·ness** *n* —**in·vis·i·bly** *adv*

in·vis·i·ble ink *n* a liquid used to write something that cannot be seen until the paper is treated in some way, e.g., with heat

in·vi·ta·tion /ìnvi táysh'n/ *n* **1. OFFER** an offer to come or go somewhere, especially one promising pleasure or hospitality, or the making of such an offer **2. WRITTEN NOTE** a note or printed card that contains an invitation **3. ENCOURAGEMENT** encouragement to do something ■ *adj UK* same as **invitational** *adj* (sense 1)

in·vi·ta·tion·al /ìnvi táyshən'l, -shnəl/ *adj* **1. OPEN ONLY TO THOSE INVITED** open only to people who have been invited **2. REQUESTED** asked for or requested ■ *n* **EVENT FOR INVITED PEOPLE** an event, especially a sports tournament, that is open only to people who have been invited to participate

in·vi·ta·to·ry /in vítə tàwree/ *adj* inviting or encouraging something

in·vite *vt* /in vít/ (**-vit·ed, -vit·ing, -vites**) **1. ASK SOMEBODY TO PARTICIPATE** to ask somebody politely to come or go somewhere, or ask somebody to do something **2. REQUEST SOMETHING** to ask for something or say that something would be welcome ○ *She invited questions from the audience.* **3. PROVOKE SOMETHING** to encourage or provoke something that might not have happened otherwise ○ *an attitude that invites disaster* ■ *n* /ín vìt/ same as **invitation** (*informal*) [Mid-16C. Directly or via French < Latin *invitare*] —**in·vi·tee** /in vì teé/ *n* —**in·vit·er** *n*

in·vit·ing /in víting/ *adj* suggesting or offering pleasure or enjoyment ○ *Inviting smells were coming from the kitchen.* —**in·vit·ing·ly** *adv* —**in·vit·ing·ness** *n*

in vi·tro /in veétrō/ *adj, adv* in an artificial environment rather than inside a living organism, e.g., in a test tube [< Latin, "in glass."]

in vi·tro fer·til·i·za·tion *n* fertilization of an ovum by sperm outside the body when normal conception is not achievable because of a woman's low fertility. After five days, this is followed by implantation in the womb.

in vi·vo /in veévō/ *adj, adv* existing or carried out inside a living organism, e.g., in a test or experiment [< Latin, "in the living"]

in·vo·ca·tion /ìnvə káysh'n/ *n* **1. CALLING UPON HIGHER POWER** a calling upon a greater power such as God or a spirit for help **2. PRAYER** a short prayer forming part of a religious service **3. QUOTING OF SOMETHING AS REASON** the act of calling upon or quoting something such as a law as a reason or justification **4. INCANTATION SUPPOSEDLY SUMMONING DEMON** a casting of a spell in an attempt to make an evil spirit appear, or the spell itself —**in·vo·ca·tion·al** *adj* —**in·voc·a·to·ry** /in vókə tàwree/ *adj*

in·voice /ín vòyss/ *n* **1. REQUEST FOR PAYMENT** a written record of goods or services provided and the amount charged for them, sent to a customer or employer as a request for payment **2. SHIPMENT OF GOODS** a shipment of goods that is recorded on an invoice ■ *vt* (**-voiced, -voic·ing, -voic·es**) **SEND INVOICE TO SOMEBODY** to send somebody an invoice for payment [Mid-16C. Originally plural of obsolete *invoy* < obsolete French *envoy* < *envoyer* (see ENVOY)]

in·voke /in vók/ (**-voked, -vok·ing, -vokes**) *vt* **1. CALL UPON GREATER POWER** to call upon a greater power such as God or a spirit for help **2. QUOTE SOMETHING IN SUPPORT** to quote, rely on, or use something such as a law in support of an argument or case **3. ASK FOR SOMETHING** to ask or appeal for something **4. ATTEMPT TO SUMMON DEMON** to call upon an evil spirit to appear, e.g., by casting a spell **5. AROUSE SOMETHING** to create or arouse an idea, emotion, or image [15C. Via French < Latin *invocare* "call upon" < *vocare* "to call"] —**in·vok·er** *n*

in·vo·lu·cra PHYSIOL, BOT plural of **involucrum**

in·vo·lu·cre /ínvə loòkər, ìnvə loòkər/ *n* a ring of modified leaves beneath a flower or flower cluster, e.g., in a dandelion or daisy flower [Late 16C. Directly or via French < Latin *involucrum* "wrapper" < *involvere* "roll into" < *volvere* "to roll"] —**in·vo·lu·cral** /ìnvə loòkrəl/ *adj* —**in·vo·lu·crate** /ìnvə loò kràyt, -loòkrət/ *adj*

in·vo·lu·crum /ìnvə loòkrəm/ (*plural* **-cra** /-krə/) *n* **1.** a growth of new bone that forms around a mass of dead or infected bone **2.** BOT same as **involucre** [Late 17C. < Latin (see INVOLUCRE)]

in·vol·un·tar·i·ly /in vóllən tèrrəlee/ *adv* without wanting or intending to

in·vol·un·tar·y /in vóllən tèrree/ *adj* **1.** required or exacted against somebody's will or wishes **2.** spontaneous or automatic, and not controlled or controllable by the mind —**in·vol·un·tar·i·ness** *n*

in·vol·un·tar·y man·slaugh·ter *n* the unintentional and unlawful killing of one person by another in an act that the killer knew was dangerous or could be a threat to the lives of others

in·vol·un·tar·y mus·cle *n* a muscle that acts independently of the will, especially in reflex functions

in·vo·lute *adj* /ínvə lòot/ **1.** *also* **in·vo·lut·ed** /ínvə lóotəd/ COMPLEX complicated or intricate **2.** *also* **in·vo·lut·ed** ROLLING INWARD having petals or leaves that roll inward at the edges **3.** TIGHTLY WHORLED describes a shell whose axis is hidden by tight whorls ■ *n* /ínvə lòot/ TYPE OF CURVE a curve traced by the end of a taut thread that cannot be extended as it is wound upon or unwound from another curve ■ *vi* /ínvə lòot/ (**-lut·ed, -lut·ing, -lutes**) BECOME INVOLUTE to become complex or inwardly rolled, whorled, or curved [Mid-17C. < Latin *involutus* "intricate," past participle of *involvere* (see INVOLVE)] —**in·vo·lute·ly** *adv*

in·vo·lu·tion /ínvə lóosh'n/ *n* **1.** COMPLICATION an act of making something complicated or intricate, or the condition of being complicated or intricate **2.** SOMETHING COMPLEX something complicated or intricate **3.** INVOLUTE PART an involute part or structure **4.** PHYSIOL DECLINE IN FUNCTION a decline or degeneration in the physiological function of an organ **5.** PHYSIOL DECREASE IN SIZE a return to normal size of a body or body part after expansion **6.** MATH RAISING OF QUANTITY TO POWER the algebraic operation of raising a number, variable, or expression to a specified positive integral power, x^n **7.** GRAM COMPLEX GRAMMATICAL STRUCTURE a complicated grammatical construction **8.** BIOL DEVELOPMENTAL PROCESS FORMING TUBE the process by which some cells grow inward over the edge of an organ or part until they rejoin the structure to form a tube. The bladder is formed by involution. —**in·vo·lu·tion·al** *adj*

in·volve /in vólv/ (**-volved, -volv·ing, -volves**) *vt* **1.** CONTAIN SOMETHING to contain or include something as a necessary element **2.** CONCERN SOMEBODY to be a matter that concerns or affects somebody **3.** CAUSE SOMEBODY TO PARTICIPATE to make somebody part of, or make somebody take part in, an event or ongoing process **4.** IMPLICATE SOMEBODY to connect somebody with something, especially something disreputable **5.** ENGROSS SOMEBODY to take up somebody's whole attention **6.** COMPLICATE SOMETHING to make something complicated or difficult to follow (*often passive*) **7.** ENCLOSE SOMETHING to envelop something (*literary; often passive*) [Late 14C. < Latin *involvere* "enfold" < *volvere* "to roll"] —**in·volve·ment** *n* —**in·volv·er** *n* —**in·volv·ing** *adj*

in·volved /in vólvd/ *adj* **1.** COMPLICATED complicated or difficult to follow **2.** CONNECTED connected with or participating in something **3.** IN RELATIONSHIP participating in a romantic or sexual relationship —**in·volv·ed·ly** /in vólvədlee/ *adv*

in·vul·ner·a·ble /in vúlnərəb'l/ *adj* **1.** not able to be wounded, damaged, hurt, or affected ○ *invulnerable to criticism* **2.** not able to be successfully attacked —**in·vul·ner·a·bil·i·ty** /in vùlnərə bílləteee/ *n* —**in·vul·ner·a·ble·ness** *n* —**in·vul·ner·a·bly** *adv*

in·ward /ínnwərd/ *adj* **1.** INSIDE situated within something **2.** OF MIND OR SPIRIT relating to or existing in the mind or spirit **3.** TOWARD INSIDE moving toward the inside or center of something ■ *adv also* **in·wards** /-wərdz/ **1.** TOWARD INSIDE toward the inside or center of something **2.** TOWARD MIND toward the mind or spirit ■ *n* THE INSIDE the inner part of something (*literary archaic*) ○ *"To kiss the tender inward of thy hand"* (William Shakespeare, *Sonnets*; 1609) —**in·ward·ness** *n*

In·ward Light *n* CHR same as **Inner Light**

in·ward-look·ing *adj* not concerned with other people or with what is happening in the wider world

in·ward·ly /ínnwərdlee/ *adv* **1.** to yourself, or without outward expression ○ *He raged inwardly at the injustice.* **2.** on or to the inside

in·wards *adv* same as **inward**

in·weave /in wéev/ (**-wove** /-wṓv/, **-wo·ven** /-wṓvən/, **-weav·ing, -weaves**) *vt* to weave something into a fabric or design

in·wind *vt* another spelling of **enwind**

in·wrap *vt* another spelling of **enwrap**

in·wreathe *vt* another spelling of **enwreathe**

in-your-face *adj* (*informal*) **1.** expressing opinions in a forceful, sometimes aggressive, way ○ *Her approach is a little too in-your-face for me.* **2.** direct or provocative in a way that is designed to attract attention ○ *an in-your-face ad campaign*

io *abbr* ONLINE British Indian Ocean Territory (*used in Internet addresses*) See table at **domain name**

I·o /ī ō, ée ō/ *n* **1.** in Greek mythology, the daughter of the river god Inachus, turned into a heifer by the god Zeus to protect her from the jealousy of his wife Hera **2.** a large volcanically active satellite of Jupiter [Via Latin < Greek *Iō*]

I/O *abbr* COMPUT input/output

IOC *abbr* International Olympic Committee

iod- *prefix* same as **iodo-** (*used before vowels*)

i·o·date /ī ə dàyt/ *n* a salt of iodic acid, e.g., sodium or potassium iodate. Use: in medicine. [Early 19C. < IODIC ACID]

i·od·ic /ī óddik/ *adj* relating to, containing, or caused by iodine, especially with a valence of five

i·od·ic ac·id *n* a colorless or white crystalline solid that is soluble in water. Use: in analytic chemistry, disinfectant, deodorant, antiseptic. Formula: HIO_3.

i·o·dide /ī ə dīd/ *n* a salt of hydriodic acid that contains the univalent anion ion I^-. Metallic iodides such as silver, sodium, or potassium iodide are used in photography and in iodized table salt.

i·o·di·nate /ī ədi nàyt/ (**-nat·ed, -nat·ing, -nates**) *vt* to treat something with iodine or an iodine compound, or add or substitute iodine atoms to or in an organic compound —**i·o·di·na·tion** /ī ədi náysh'n/ *n*

i·o·dine /ī ə dīn, -din, -deen/ *n* **1.** a poisonous, dark gray to purple-black, lustrous, nonmetallic crystalline element in the halogen family. Source: brine. Use: germicide, antiseptic, preparation of dyes, pharmaceuticals, tinctures, isotopes in medicine and industry. Symbol **I**. See table at **element** **2.** a mixture of iodine solution and potassium iodide in alcohol. Use: topical antiseptic. [Early 19C. < French *iode* < Greek *iōdēs* "violet-colored" < *ion* "violet"] —**i·o·dous** /ī ōdəss, ī ədəss/ *adj*

i·o·dize /ī ə dīz/ (**-dized, -diz·ing, -diz·es**) *vt* to treat or combine something with iodine or an iodine compound —**i·o·di·za·tion** /ī ədi záysh'n/ *n* —**i·o·diz·er** *n*

iodo- *prefix* iodine ○ *iodophor* [< French *iode* (see IODINE)]

i·o·do·form /ī ōdə fàwrm, -óddə-/ *n* a yellow volatile crystalline compound with a penetrating odor. Use: antiseptic, in ointments for minor skin diseases. Formula: CHI_3. [Mid-19C. < IODO- + FORMYL]

i·o·dom·e·try /ī ə dómmətree/ *n* an analytic process involving the liberation of or reaction with iodine by a substance in order to determine the quantity of the substance present in the sample being analyzed [Late 19C. < IODO- + -METRY]

i·o·do·phor /ī ōdə fàwr/ *n* a substance consisting of iodine and a surface-active agent in solution that slowly releases elemental iodine. Use: disinfectant. [Mid-20C. < IODO- + *-phor*, variant of -PHORE]

i·o·dop·sin /ī ə dópsin/ *n* a photosensitive violet pigment in the retinal cones of the eye [Mid-20C. < Greek *iōdēs* (see IODINE) + OPSIN, after *rhodopsin*]

i·o·lite /ī ə līt/ *n* MINERALS same as **cordierite** [Early 19C. < Greek *ion* "violet"]

I·o moth *n* a large yellow moth with a large spot resembling an eye on each of its hind wings. Native to: North America. Latin name: *Automeris io*. [After IO (sense 1)]

i·on /ī ən, ī òn/ *n* an atom or group of atoms that has acquired an electric charge by losing or gaining one or more electrons [Mid-19C. < Greek, "moving thing" < present participle of *ienai* "go"; because an ion moves toward the electrode of opposite charge]

-ion *suffix* **1.** action or process ○ *eruption* ○ *erosion* **2.** result of an action or process ○ *abrasion* **3.** condition, state ○ *elation* [Via French < Latin *-ion-*]

I·o·na /ī ṓnə/ low-lying island off the southwestern tip of Mull, in the Inner Hebrides, western Scotland. Population: 90. Area: 3.28 sq. mi./8.5 sq. km.

i·on en·gine *n* a hypothetical rocket engine that derives its thrust from the electrostatic acceleration of a stream of positive ions. Because the engine does not provide enough thrust to escape the Earth's gravity, it could be used only in space.

Popperfoto
Eugene Ionesco

Io·nes·co /ée ə néskō/, **Eugène** (1912–94) Romanian-born French dramatist. He was one of the chief exponents of the Theater of the Absurd. His plays include *The Chairs* (1952) and *Rhinoceros* (1959).

> "It's as we speak that we find our ideas, our words, ourselves too, in our words, and the city, the gardens, perhaps everything comes back and we're not orphans anymore."
> [Eugène Ionesco, *The Chairs*; 1952]

i·on ex·change *n* the interchange of ions of the same charge between a solution and a solid in contact with it —**i·on ex·chang·er** *n*

I·o·ni·a /ī ṓnee ə/ region of ancient western Asia Minor on the Aegean coast that was colonized by the Greeks around 1000 B.C. —**I·o·ni·an** *adj, n*

I·o·ni·an Is·lands /ī ṓnee ən-/ group of seven Greek islands in the Ionian and Mediterranean seas. Corfu is the capital and largest city in the islands. Population: 191,003 (1991). Area: 868 sq. mi./2,250 sq. km.

I·o·ni·an mode *n* a medieval scale of notes that consists of the eight notes of the diatonic scale rising from G to G, corresponding to the modern C major scale

I·o·ni·an Sea part of the Mediterranean Sea, situated between the southeastern coast of Italy and western Greece

i·on·ic /ī ónnik/ *adj* relating to or containing matter in the form of charged atoms or groups of atoms [Late 19C. < ION]

I·on·ic /ī ónnik/ *n* **1.** IONIAN DIALECT an extinct dialect of Ancient Greek that was spoken mainly in Ionia **2.** METRICAL FOOT in classical poetry, a metrical foot of two long syllables followed by two short ones (**greater Ionic**), or two short syllables followed by two long ones (**lesser Ionic**) ■ *adj* **1.** OF ARCHITECTURAL ORDER relating to or typical of the order of architecture characterized by fluted columns and capitals with spiral scroll-shaped ornaments **2.** IN IONIC METER relating to, typical of, or expressed in Ionic meter [Early 17C. < Greek *Iōnikos* "of Ionia"]

I·on·ic or·der *n* one of the five classical orders of architecture, characterized by fluted columns and capitals with spiral scroll-shaped ornaments

i·on·ic pro·pul·sion *n* motion produced in reaction to the expulsion of a stream of accelerated ions

i·on·ics /ī ónniks/ *n* the study of the development and behavior of solid electrolytes (*takes a singular verb*)

i·on im·plan·ta·tion *n* the use of a stream of electrically accelerated ions to implant impurities on or near the surface of the substrate during the manufacture of a semiconductor

i·on·i·za·tion /ī əni záysh'n/ *n* a process in which an atom or molecule loses or gains electrons, acquiring an electric charge or changing an existing charge

i·on·i·za·tion cham·ber *n* a device used to detect and measure ionizing radiation, consisting of a gas-filled tube with electrodes at each end between which a voltage is maintained. Radiation that ionizes gas molecules in the tube causes a current between the electrodes, the strength of which is a function of the radiation's intensity.

i·on·i·za·tion po·ten·tial *n* the energy needed to

remove an electron from an atom or molecule and move it an infinite distance away

i·on·ize /ī́ ə nīz/ (**-ized, -iz·ing, -iz·es**) *vti* to undergo ionization, or cause something to undergo ionization —**i·on·iz·a·ble** *adj*

i·o·none /ī́ ə nōn/ *n* a yellow liquid smelling of violets. Source: plants. Use: manufacture of perfumes. Formula: $C_{13}H_{20}O$. [Late 19C. < Greek *ion* "violet"]

i·on·o·phore /ī ónnə fàwr/ *n* a molecule found in lipid membranes that helps transport ions across the membrane [Mid-20C. < ION]

i·on·o·sphere /ī ónnə sfeer/ *n* four layers of the Earth's upper atmosphere in which incoming ionizing radiation from space creates ions and free electrons that can reflect radio signals, enabling their transmission around the world [Early 20C. < ION] —**i·on·o·spher·ic** /ī ònnə sféerik, -sférrik/ *adj* —**i·on·o·spher·i·cal·ly** *adv*

i·on·o·spher·ic wave *n* MEDIA same as **sky wave**

i·on pro·pul·sion *n* AEROSP same as **ionic propulsion**

i·on rock·et *n* a rocket powered by an ion engine

i·on·to·pho·re·sis /ī òntəfə réessiss/ *n* the movement of ions through biological material under the influence of an electric current [Early 20C. < Greek *iont-*, present participle of *ienai* "go"] —**i·on·to·pho·ret·ic** /-fə réttik/ *adj* —**i·on·to·pho·ret·i·cal·ly** *adv*

i·on trap *n* a technique for deflecting the ions in the electron beam in a cathode-ray tube to prevent damage to the phosphor caused by the ions bombarding the screen. Typically, a magnet is used to deflect the beam through a tiny opening in the electron gun while the heavier ions are deflected less and remain trapped in the gun.

IOOF *abbr* Independent Order of Odd Fellows

i·o·ta /ī ṓtə/ *n* **1.** the ninth letter of the Greek alphabet, represented in the English alphabet as "i." See table at **alphabet 2.** a very small amount of something ○ *anyone with an iota of sense* [Early 17C. Via Latin < Greek *iōta* < Semitic]

i·o·ta·cism /ī ṓtə sìzzəm/ *n* the tendency in speakers of modern Greek to use the sound of iota in place of the sound of other vowel characters such as eta or upsilon [Mid-17C. Via Latin < Greek *iōtakismos* < *iōta* (see IOTA)]

IOU *n* a written acknowledgment of a debt between the writer and somebody else [Representation of *I owe you*]

IOW *abbr* in other words (*used in e-mails or text messages*)

Iowa

I·o·wa /ī́ əwə/ **1.** state in the north central United States bordered by Illinois, Minnesota, Missouri, Nebraska, South Dakota, and Wisconsin. Capital: Des Moines. Population: 2,936,760 (2002 estimate). Area: 56,276 sq. mi./145,754 sq. km. **2.** river in Iowa that flows southeastward and empties into the Mississippi River. Length: 330 mi./530 km. —**I·o·wan** *n, adj*

I·o·wa Cit·y city in eastern Iowa, on the eastern bank of the Iowa River, northwest of Davenport and southeast of Cedar Rapids. Population: 63,816 (2002 estimate).

IP *abbr* **1.** ONLINE image processing **2.** BASEBALL innings pitched **3.** ONLINE Internet protocol

IPA, I.P.A. *abbr* PHON International Phonetic Alphabet

IPCC *abbr* ENVIRON Intergovernmental Panel on Climate Change

ip·e·cac /íppi kàk/, **ip·e·cac·u·an·ha** /íppi kakyoo ánnə/ *n* **1.** an emetic made from dried roots **2.** a bush, the roots of which are a source of ipecac. Native to: South America. Latin name: *Cephaelis ipecacuanha.* [Early 17C. Via Portuguese < Tupi *ipe-kaâ-guéne* "low plant causing vomit"]

Iph·i·ge·ni·a /ìffijə nī́ ə, -née ə/ *n* in Greek mythology, a daughter of Agamemnon, who was prepared to sacrifice her to Artemis in order to gain favorable winds for the Greek fleet to sail for Troy. Differing versions of the myth give different accounts of her fate.

IPL *abbr* COMPUT initial program load

ipm *abbr* MEASURE inches per minute

IPO *abbr* FIN initial public offering

I·poh /éepō/ city and capital of Perak State, western Malaysia. Population: 382,853 (1996).

ip·pon /i pón/ *n* a winning point awarded in judo or karate for perfect technique [Mid-20C. < Japanese]

IPR *abbr* LAW intellectual property rights

i·pro·ni·a·zid /ìprə nī́ əzid/ *n* a synthetic drug. Use: antidepressant and, formerly, to treat tuberculosis. [Mid-20C. Blend of ISOPROPYL + ISONIAZID]

ips *abbr* inches per second

ip·sa·tive /ípsətiv/ *adj* using yourself as the norm against which to measure something, e.g., your present performance against your past performance rather than the performance of others [Mid-20C. < Latin *ipse* "self"]

ip·se dix·it /ípsee díksit/ *n* something asserted dogmatically and without proof [Late 16C. < Latin, "he himself said it"]

ip·si·lat·er·al /ìpsə láttərəl/ *adj* being on or affecting the same side of the body [Early 20C. < Latin *ipse* "same"] —**ip·si·lat·er·al·ly** *adv*

ip·sis·si·ma ver·ba /ip sìssəmə vúrbə/ *npl* the precise words used in something that is quoted [< Latin, "the very words"]

ip·so fac·to /ìpsō fáktō/ *adv* as the result of a particular fact [< Latin, "by the fact itself"]

ip·so ju·re /ìpsō jŏŏree, -yŏŏree/ *adv* by reason of a particular law [< Latin, "by the law itself"]

Ips·wich /ípswich/ **1.** city in Queensland, eastern Australia, just outside Brisbane. Population: 128,967 (2002 estimate). **2.** town in northeastern Massachusetts, on the Ipswich River, northwest of Gloucester and south of Newburyport. Population: 13,278 (2002 estimate).

iq *abbr* Iraq (*used in Internet addresses*) See table at **domain name**

IQ, I.Q. *n* a measure of somebody's intelligence, obtained through a series of aptitude tests concentrating on different aspects of intellectual functioning. An IQ score of 100 represents "average" intelligence. Full form **intelligence quotient**

i.q. *abbr* the same as [Latin *idem quod*]

I·qal·u·it /i kálloo it/ capital city of Nunavut, Canada, located on the southeastern coast of Baffin Island. Population: 5,236 (2001).

Iq·bal /ík bal/, **Sir Muhammad** (1875–1938) Indian philosopher, poet, and political leader. He became president of the Muslim League in 1930, and his separatist political philosophy underpinned the eventual formation of Pakistan.

I·qui·que /ee kée kày/ seaport, city, and capital of Tarapacá Region, northern Chile, situated 130 mi./209 km south of the Peruvian border. Population: 177,892 (1998).

I·qui·tos /ee kée tŏss/ city and river port in northeastern Peru, situated on the upper Amazon River, 1,268 mi./2,040 km overland northeast of Lima. Population: 334,013 (1998).

ir *abbr* Iran (*used in Internet addresses*) See table at **domain name**

Ir *symbol* CHEM ELEM iridium

IR *abbr* **1.** COMPUT information retrieval **2.** PHYS infrared (radiation) **3.** SPORTS inside right **4.** international registration

Ir. *abbr* **1.** Ireland **2.** Irish

ir- *prefix* (*used before r*) **1.** same as **in-**[1] **2.** same as **in-**[2]

IRA[1] *n* an organization of Irish nationalists originally set up to strive for an independent Ireland by force of arms and still dedicated to achieving the unity of the island of Ireland. Full form **Irish Republican Army**

IRA[2] /ī́rə/ *n* a plan that permits working people to invest money for retirement and pay no tax on the amount invested either at the time of investment or after retirement. Full form **Individual Retirement Account**

i·ra·de /ee ráadee/ *n* a written decree of a Muslim ruler, especially, formerly, the sultan of Turkey [Late 19C. < Arabic *irādah* "will, desire"]

Iran

I·ran /i rán, i raan/ country in Southwest Asia, located south of the Caspian Sea, northeast of the Persian Gulf, and north of the Gulf of Oman. Language: Farsi. Currency: Iranian rial. Capital: Tehran. Population: 68,278,826 (2003). Area: 636,300 sq. mi./1,648,000 sq. km. Official name **Islamic Republic of Iran.** Former name **Persia**

I·ra·ni·an /i ráynee ən/ *n* **1.** somebody who comes from Iran **2.** a group of languages spoken in the region northeast of the Persian Gulf, a subgroup of the Indo-Iranian branch of Indo-European. Native speakers: 70 million. —**I·ra·ni·an** *adj*

Iran-Iraq War *n* the war fought between Iran and Iraq that lasted from 1980 to 1988, following the invasion of border territory in Iran by Iraq

Iraq

I·raq /i rák, i raak/ country in Southwest Asia, bordered by Turkey, Iran, Saudi Arabia, Kuwait, the Persian Gulf, Jordan, and Syria. Language: Arabic. Currency: Iraqi dinar. Capital: Baghdad. Population: 24,683,313 (2003). Area: 169,235 sq. mi./438,317 sq. km. Official name **Republic of Iraq**

I·ra·qi /i rákee, i raakee/ *n* **1.** somebody who comes from Iraq **2.** the modern dialect of Arabic spoken in Iraq —**I·ra·qi** *adj*

I·raq War, I·raqi War *n* ➧ **Gulf War** (sense 2)

i·ras·ci·ble /i rássəb'l/ *adj* **1.** easily provoked to anger or outbursts of temper **2.** showing or typical of anger ○ *an irascible gesture* [Mid-16C. Via French < Latin *irascibilis* "quick to anger" < *irasci* "grow angry" < *ira* "anger"] —**i·ras·ci·bil·i·ty** /i ràssə bíllətee/ *n* —**i·ras·ci·ble·ness** *n* —**i·ras·ci·bly** *adv*

i·rate /ī ráyt/ *adj* **1.** feeling great anger **2.** showing or typical of great anger ○ *an irate phone call* [Mid-19C. < Latin *iratus*, past participle of *irasci* "grow angry"] —**i·rate·ly** *adv* —**i·rate·ness** *n*

~~irational~~ incorrect spelling of **irrational**

Ir·a·wad·i GEOG another spelling of **Irrawaddy**

IRBM *abbr* intermediate-range ballistic missile

IRC *n* an Internet facility that enables two or more

people to participate in real-time online discussions. Full form **Internet relay chat**

ire /īr/ *n* strong anger (*literary*) [13C. Via French < Latin *ira* "anger"] —**ire·ful** *adj*

SYNONYMS See *anger*.

Ireland

Ire·land /írlənd/ **1.** island in northwestern Europe, in the North Atlantic Ocean, west of Great Britain. It comprises the Republic of Ireland and the British province of Northern Ireland. Area: 32,598 sq. mi./84,429 sq. km. **2.** country occupying the southern, central, and northwestern parts of the island of Ireland. Language: English, Irish Gaelic. Currency: euro. Capital: Dublin. Population: 3,924,410 (2003). Area: 27,133 sq. mi./70,273 sq. km. Official name **Republic of Ireland**. Gaelic name **Éire**

Ire·land, North·ern ▸ **Northern Ireland**

i·ren·ic /ī rénnik, -réenik/, **i·ren·i·cal** /ī rénnik'l, -réenik'l/ *adj* promoting or intended to promote peace (*literary*) [Mid-19C. < Greek *eirēnikos* "peaceable" < *eirēnē* "peace"] —**i·ren·i·cal·ly** *adv*

i·ren·ics /ī rénniks, ī reeniks/ *n* a branch of theology that seeks to promote unity between different churches and religious groups (*takes a singular verb*)

I·ri·an Jay·a /irree aan jī ə/ province of Indonesia, consisting of the western half of the island of New Guinea and including islands off its northern and northwestern coasts. Capital: Jayapura. Population: 1,560,000 (1989). Area: 162,928 sq. mi./421,981 sq. km. Former name **West New Guinea** (1828–1962), **West Irian** (1963–72)

irid- *prefix* same as **irido-** (*used before vowels*)

ir·i·da·ceous /irri dáyshəss/ *adj* relating or belonging to the family of flowering plants that includes the iris and crocus. Family: Iridaceae.

ir·i·dec·to·my /irri déktəmee/ (*plural* **-mies**) *n* the surgical removal of part of the iris of the eye

ir·i·des·cent /irri déss'nt/ *adj* **1.** having rainbow colors that appear to move and change as the angle at which they are seen changes **2.** having a lustrous or brilliant appearance —**ir·i·des·cence** *n* —**ir·i·des·cent·ly** *adv*

i·rid·ic[1] /i ríddik, ī-/ *adj* relating to, involving, or containing the element iridium [Mid-19C. < IRIDIUM]

i·rid·ic[2] /i ríddik, ī-/ *adj* relating to or typical of the iris of the eye [Late 19C. < Latin *irid-*, stem of *iris* "iris (of the eye)"]

i·rid·i·um /i ríddee əm/ *n* a brittle, corrosion-resistant, silver-white metallic element. Use: alloys for pen nibs, jewelry, watch and compass pivot bearings, surgical instruments, electrical contacts, chemical crucibles. Symbol **Ir**. See table at **element** [Early 19C. < Latin *irid-*, stem of *iris* "rainbow"]

irido- *prefix* **1.** iris ○ *iridotomy* ○ *iridaceous* **2.** rainbow ○ *iridescent* **3.** iridium ○ *iridosmine* [Via Latin < Greek *irid-*, stem of *iris* "rainbow, iris (of the eye)"]

ir·i·dol·o·gy /irri dóllәjee/ *n* a technique in alternative medicine by which diagnosis of various bodily disorders is claimed to be possible by examination of the fine structure of the iris of the eye —**ir·i·dol·o·gist** *n*

ir·i·dos·mine /irri dóz meen/, **ir·i·dos·mi·um** /-dózmee əm/ *n* an ore and natural alloy of iridium and osmium in which the osmium content exceeds 35 percent, with traces of platinum, rhodium, ruthenium, iron, and copper [Early 19C. Blend of IRIDIUM + OSMIUM]

ir·i·dot·o·my /irri dóttəmee/ (*plural* **-mies**) *n* a surgical operation in which the iris of the eye is cut into, nowadays using a laser

WORLD ENGLISH ***Irish English*** is the variety of English used in Ireland since at least the 16th century. For some observers, the terms *Irish English*, *Anglo-Irish*, and *Hiberno-English* mean much the same; for others, the term Irish English refers to English throughout Ireland, Anglo-Irish refers to a variety that originated among settlers from England (and has been especially associated with a Dublin elite), and Hiberno-English refers to usage markedly influenced by Irish Gaelic. All commentators agree, however, that it is difficult to draw a clear line between the various kinds of Irish English. Northern Irish English is generally regarded as a distinct variety of Irish English (but is not usually contrasted with a "Southern Irish English"). Within Northern Ireland, the variety Ulster Scots derives from the settlement (or as it was called at the time, "plantation") of Scottish Protestants in the North from the early 17th century onward.

In Irish English *r* is generally pronounced in words such as *art, door,* and *worker,* with the tip of the tongue curled back and raised. The *wh* in words like *why* and *what* is pronounced as /hw/, so that *whales* and *Wales* are clearly distinguished. Words like *three* and *those* are commonly pronounced like "tree" and "dose," and words like *leave* and *tea* as "lave" and "tay." There are distinctive grammatical forms influenced by Irish Gaelic. First, forms like these are used for emphasis and increased focus: *It's a fine man he is, It was to help her I went,* and *It's himself was the best player.* Second is the use of *after* and *-ing* to mark an action just completed: *She's after helping them this very morning.* The third is the omission of *yes* and *no* in answers: *Did you come yesterday? – I did; Can you see him now? – We can.* Vocabulary adapted from Gaelic includes the now internationally current *banshee* (from *bean sidhe* "fairy woman"), *colleen* ("young woman," from *cailin*), *shillelagh* (a thick stick, from the town of the same name); and *whiskey* or *whisky* (both originally from Gaelic *uisge beatha* "water of life").

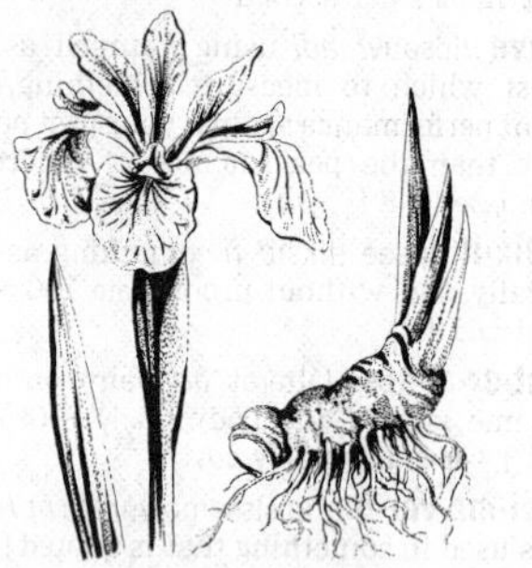
iris (sense 2)

i·ris /íriss/ *n* **1.** PART OF EYE the colored part of the eye that consists of a muscular diaphragm surrounding the pupil and regulates the light entering the eye by expanding and contracting the pupil **2.** FLOWERING PLANT a plant with long sword-shaped leaves. Flowers: many-colored. Genus: *Iris.* **3.** same as **rainbow** *n* (sense 1) (*literary*) **4.** RAINBOW SHOW OF COLORS a show of colors of various hues, like a rainbow **5.** PHOTOGRAPHY same as **iris diaphragm** [15C. Via Latin < Greek, "rainbow, iris (of the eye)"]
iris in *vi* to open up the iris diaphragm of a camera gradually in order to expand the picture area
iris out *vi* to close the iris diaphragm of a camera gradually in order to contract the picture area until the image darkens completely. Irising out was formerly a common way to end a film or sequence.

i·ris di·a·phragm *n* a diaphragm consisting of adjustable thin plates that control the size of an aperture, especially one used in a camera to control the amount of light allowed to enter

I·rish /írish/ *adj* **1.** OF IRELAND relating to the island or country of Ireland **2.** OF IRISH GAELIC relating to the Irish Gaelic language **3.** OF ENGLISH DIALECT OF IRELAND relating to the dialect of English spoken in Ireland ■ *n* LANG same as **Irish Gaelic** ■ *npl* PEOPLE FROM IRELAND people who come from Ireland [13C. < Old English *Īr(as)* "inhabitants of Ireland," probably < Old Irish *Ériu* "Ireland"] —**I·rish·ness** *n*

LANGUAGE HERITAGE See *Celtic.*

I·rish cof·fee *n* a hot drink of sweetened coffee containing Irish whiskey and topped with cream

I·rish elk *n* an extinct giant deer with large antlers that lived in the Pleistocene epoch. Native to: Europe, Asia. Genus: *Megaloceros.*

I·rish Eng·lish *n* the variety of English spoken in Ireland —**I·rish Eng·lish** *adj*

I·rish Gael·ic *n* an official language of the Republic of Ireland, spoken mainly in the west of the country, belonging to the Celtic branch of Indo-European. Native speakers: 5,000. Other speakers: 1 million. —**I·rish Gael·ic** *adj*

I·rish harp *n* a small diatonic harp constructed with a hollowed willow soundbox

I·rish·ism /íri shìzzəm/ *n* an expression or custom common among the Irish

I·rish·man /írishmən/ (*plural* **-men** /-mən/) *n* a man who comes from Ireland

I·rish moss *n* an edible red seaweed from which a complex carbohydrate food additive (**carrageenan**) is obtained. Native to: coasts of Europe and North America. Latin name: *Chondrus crispus.*

I·rish po·ta·to *n* FOOD same as **potato** (sense 1)

I·rish Re·pub·li·can Ar·my *n* POL, MIL full form of **IRA**

I·rish Sea /írish-/ body of water situated between Great Britain and Ireland, connecting to the North Atlantic Ocean to the south through St. George's Channel and to the north through the North Channel. Area: 39,000 sq. mi./100,000 sq. km.

Irish setter

I·rish set·ter *n* a setter with a silky reddish coat, belonging to a breed originating in Ireland

I·rish stew *n* a stew of lamb or mutton, potatoes, and onions

I·rish ter·ri·er *n* a terrier with a wiry reddish coat, belonging to a breed originating in Ireland

I·rish Trav·el·ler, I·rish Trav·el·er *n* a descendant of nomadic Irish traders and craftspersons who immigrated to the United States in the mid-19th century and who maintain an itinerant lifestyle and speak a language derived from Gaelic

I·rish whis·key *n* whiskey made in Ireland, principally from barley

Irish wolfhound

I·rish wolf·hound *n* a large powerful dog with a rough shaggy coat, belonging to a breed developed in Ireland. The Irish wolfhound is the tallest breed of dog in the world.

I·rish·wom·an /írish wŏŏmmən/ (*plural* **-wom·en** /-wìmmin/) *n* a woman who comes from Ireland

i·ri·tis /ī ríttiss/ *n* inflammation of the iris of the eye [Early 19C. < IRIS] —**i·rit·ic** /ī ríttik/ *adj*

irk /urk/ (**irked, irk·ing, irks**) *vt* to annoy somebody slightly, especially by being tedious [14C. Perhaps < Old Norse *yrkja* "to work"; originally N English, "grow weary or vexed"]

SYNONYMS See ***annoy*** and ***bother***.

irk·some /úrksəm/ *adj* slightly annoying, especially because of being tedious —**irk·some·ly** *adv*—**irk·some·ness** *n*

Ir·kutsk /ur kŏŏtsk, eer-/ city in southern Siberian Russia and capital of Irkutsk Oblast. It is situated on the Angara River, 45 mi./72 km from the southwestern shore of Lake Baikal. Population: 668,449 (1995).

IRO *abbr* **1.** INTERNAT REL, HIST International Refugee Organization **2.** international relief organization

i·ro·ko /i rṓkō/ (*plural* **-kos**) *n* **1.** a hard brown African wood often used instead of teak **2.** a hardwood tree that produces iroko. Native to: tropical Africa. Genus: *Chlorophora*. [Late 19C. < Yoruba]

i·ron /ī́rn/ *n* **1. METALLIC ELEMENT** a heavy, magnetic, malleable, ductile, lustrous, silvery white metallic element that is present in very small quantities in the blood and is the fourth most abundant element in the Earth's crust. Source: hematite, limonite, magnetite. Use: engineering and structural products. Symbol **Fe**. See table at **element 2. HEATED TOOL** a tool made of iron or steel, usually heated before and during use ○ *a soldering iron* **3. CLOTHES PRESSER** a small electrical appliance with a flat metal base that is heated and used to press clothes **4. HARSH CHARACTER** a strong, unyielding, or hard aspect of somebody's nature ○ *a will of iron* **5. METAL-HEADED GOLF CLUB** any golf club with a metal head, differentiated by numbers that indicate different angles of the face and lengths of the shaft **6. COMPUTER HARDWARE** computer hardware, especially older and larger mainframes (*slang*) ○ *a company with some big iron* **7. HANDGUN** a handgun, especially a revolver (*dated slang*) ○ *a shooting iron* **8.** RIDING same as **stirrup** (sense 1) ■ **i·rons** *npl* **RESTRAINTS FOR ARMS OR LEGS** manacles or fetters for restraining the arms or legs ■ *adj* **1. MADE OF IRON** relating to or made of iron **2. VERY STRONG** very strong or hard **3. TOUGH** very robust or tough **4. UNYIELDING** very determined, unyielding, or cruel ■ *v* (**i·roned, i·ron·ing, i·rons**) **1.** *vti* **PRESS CLOTHES** to press clothes or other fabrics with an iron to remove wrinkles **2.** *vt* **COVER SOMETHING WITH IRON** to cover or clad something with iron [Old English *īren* < Germanic] —**i·ron·ness** *n* ◇ **have several irons in the fire** to be involved in several different activities at the same time ◇ **pump iron** to do weightlifting exercises for bodybuilding or fitness (*slang*) ◇ **strike while the iron is hot** to act while circumstances are favorable for a successful outcome

iron out *vt* **1.** to smooth away wrinkles in a garment or fabric using an iron **2.** to settle a dispute or resolve a problem by removing difficulties

i·ron age *n* in classical mythology, an era regarded as the third and last step in humankind's degeneration from the golden age

I·ron Age *n* the period following the Bronze Age, beginning around 1500 B.C. in Southwest Asia, during which iron was increasingly used in making tools and weapons

i·ron blue *n* an insoluble compound. Use: in fertilizers, as a blue pigment in paint, ink, and paper dyeing. Formula: $Fe_7C_{18}N_{18}{\cdot}10H_2O$.

i·ron·bound /ī́rn bòwnd/ *adj* **1. DECORATED WITH IRON** wrapped or decorated with iron bands **2. HARSH** stern or unyielding **3. RUGGED** edged or enclosed with rocks (*literary*) ○ *an ironbound coast*

i·ron·clad /ī́rn klàd/ *adj* **1. COVERED OR PROTECTED WITH IRON** covered with iron, especially as a protection or armor **2. STRONG** strong, firm, or unyielding **3. IRREFUTABLE** not capable of being attacked or refuted ○ *an ironclad agreement* ■ *n* **ARMORED SHIP** a 19th-century wooden warship armored with metal plates

I·ron Cross *n* the highest German military decoration, instituted in Prussia in 1813 and awarded during World Wars I and II

i·ron cur·tain *n* an impenetrable barrier to understanding, awareness, or agreement

I·ron Cur·tain *n* **1.** the militarized border between the Communist bloc and Western Europe during the Cold War. The Iron Curtain existed from the end of World War II until the fall of Eastern European Communist governments between 1989 and 1991. ○ *"From Stettin in the Baltic to Trieste in the Adriatic, an iron curtain has descended across the continent."* (Sir Winston Churchill, *Fulton, Missouri, Speech*; 1946) **2.** the policy of isolation that prevented freedom of travel and communication between Western and Eastern Europe during the Cold War

i·ron gray *adj* of a dark greenish gray color —**i·ron gray** *n*

i·ron hand *n* strict, harsh, or despotic control —**i·ron·hand·ed** /ī́rn hándəd/ *adj* —**i·ron·hand·ed·ness** *n*

i·ron horse *n* a steam-powered railroad locomotive (*archaic*)

i·ron·ic /ī rónnik/, **i·ron·i·cal** /ī rónnik'l/ *adj* **1.** deliberately stating the opposite of the truth, often with the intention or result of being amusing **2.** ⚠ involving a surprising or apparently contradictory fact —**i·ron·i·cal·ly** *adv* —**i·ron·i·cal·ness** *n*

USAGE Is it really **irony** or is it merely coincidence? When you use ***irony, ironic,*** and ***ironically,*** be sure that you use them in contexts associated with stark incongruity, inconsistency, or even folly, and not in contexts associated with things merely coincidental or improbable. This use of ***ironically*** is inappropriate, and *coincidentally* is the better choice: *Ironically, both the defense counsel and the prosecutor graduated from Yale Law School.* Appropriate use of irony requires an incongruity between what is expected and what has happened in fact: *Ironically, because they lacked sophisticated computers they developed efficient algorithms that can now add to the power of supercomputers.*

SYNONYMS See ***sarcastic***.

i·ron·ing /ī́rning/ *n* **1.** the act of pressing clothes or other fabrics to remove wrinkles **2.** clothes that have been ironed or have to be ironed

i·ron·ing board *n* a covered, often padded board on legs on which clothes are ironed

i·ron·ize /ī́rə nīz/ (**-ized, -iz·ing, -iz·es**) *v* **1.** *vi* to use irony or be ironic **2.** *vt* to give something an ironic tone or make something ironic in nature

i·ron lung *n* an airtight metal cylinder encasing a patient up to the neck, formerly used to provide help in breathing by alternating air pressure within the cylinder

i·ron maid·en *n* a medieval instrument of torture consisting of a hinged box shaped like a human body and lined with spikes that impale somebody placed inside as it is closed

i·ron·man /ī́rn màn/ (*plural* **-men** /-mèn/) *n* **1.** *also* **I·ron·man** a triathlon for men and women that includes competitions in, e.g., bicycling, swimming, and running **2.** *US* a man athlete with great endurance who takes part in a triathlon or ironman competition

i·ron·mon·ger /ī́rn mùng gər, -mòng-/ *n UK* a dealer in tools and other articles made chiefly of metal —**i·ron·mon·ger·y** *n*

i·ron ox·ide *n* any natural or synthetic compound of iron and oxygen

i·ron pan *n* a hard layer below the surface of sand or gravel in which iron salts from percolating water have precipitated, cementing the grains of the material together

i·ron·per·son /ī́rn pùrss'n/ (*plural* **-per·sons** or **-peo·ple** /-peep'l/) *n* an athlete with great endurance who takes part in a triathlon or ironman competition

i·ron py·rites /ī̀rn pī rī́ts/ *n* MINERALS same as **pyrite**

i·ron ra·tion *n US* food designed to be used in an emergency, especially by military personnel. Can term **iron rations**

i·ron·side /ī́rn sīd/ *n* a man of great physical strength or endurance

i·ron·sides /ī́rn sīdz/ (*plural same*) *n* same as **ironside**

i·ron·stone /ī́rn stōn/ *n* **1.** any sedimentary rock that contains a large amount of iron ore **2.** a hard and durable variety of white pottery

i·ron·weed /ī́rn weed/ *n* a weed with a strong stem. Flowers: purplish. Native to: North America. Genus: *Vernonia*.

i·ron-willed *adj* extremely strong-willed

i·ron·wom·an /ī́rn wŏŏmmən/ (*plural* **-wom·en** /-wìmmin/) *n* a woman athlete with great endurance who takes part in a triathlon or ironman competition

i·ron·wood /ī́rn wŏŏd/ (*plural* **-woods** or *same*) *n* **1.** a tree with very hard timber, e.g., a hornbeam **2.** the very hard wood of an ironwood tree

i·ron·work /ī́rn wùrk/ *n* something made of iron, e.g., a gate, especially when it is decorative

i·ron·work·er /ī́rn wùrkər/ *n* **1.** somebody employed in an ironworks **2.** a maker of ironwork

i·ron·works /ī́rn wùrks/ (*plural same*) *n* a factory where iron is smelted or large metal goods are made

i·ro·ny /ī́rənee/ (*plural* **-nies**) *n* **1. HUMOR BASED ON OPPOSITES** humor based on using words to suggest the opposite of their literal meaning **2. SOMETHING HUMOROUS BASED ON CONTRADICTION** something said or written that uses humor based on words suggesting the opposite of their literal meaning **3. INCONGRUITY** incongruity between what actually happens and what might be expected to happen, especially when this disparity seems absurd or laughable **4. INCONGRUOUS THING** something that happens that is incongruous with what might be expected to happen, especially when this seems absurd or laughable **5.** THEATER same as **dramatic irony 6.** PHILOSOPHY same as **Socratic irony** [Early 16C. Via Latin *ironia* < Greek *eirōneia* "pretended ignorance" < *eirōn* "dissembler"]

USAGE See ***ironic***.

Ir·o·quoi·an /ìrrə kwóy ən/ *n* **1.** a family of languages spoken by Iroquois peoples of eastern North America **2.** a member of a Native North American people who speaks an Iroquoian language —**Ir·o·quoi·an** *adj*

Ir·o·quois /írrə kwòy/ (*plural same*) *n* a member of a former confederacy of six Native North American peoples, the Mohawk, Oneida, Seneca, Onondaga, Cayuga, and Tuscarora. Originally settled along the Hudson River Valley, many Iroquois now live in urban areas. [Mid-17C. Via French < Algonquian] —**Ir·o·quois** *adj*

ir·ra·di·ant /i ráydee ənt/ *adj* radiating light or shining brightly [Early 16C. < Latin *irradiant-*, present participle of *irradiare* (see IRRADIATE)]

ir·ra·di·ate /i ráydee àyt/ (**-at·ed, -at·ing, -ates**) *v* **1.** *vt* **EXPOSE SOMEBODY OR SOMETHING TO RADIATION** to expose somebody to or treat somebody or something with radiation or streams of particles **2.** *vt* **PRESERVE FOOD** to treat food with electromagnetic radiation to kill microorganisms and slow down the process of ripening and gradual deterioration or rotting **3.** *vt* **LIGHT SOMETHING UP** to make something brighter by shining light onto it **4.** *vt* **MAKE SOMETHING INTELLIGIBLE** to make something intellectually clear **5.** *vti* PHYS same as **radiate** *v* (sense 1) [Early 17C. < Latin *irradiat-*, past participle of *irradiare* "illumine" < *radius* "ray"] —**ir·ra·di·a·tive** *adj* —**ir·ra·di·a·tor** *n*

ir·ra·di·a·tion /i ràydee áysh'n/ *n* **1. IRRADIATING** the act of irradiating somebody or something, or the state of being irradiated **2. LIGHTING EFFECT** the visual effect by which a brightly lit thing appears larger against a dark background **3. MEDICAL RADIATION** the medical use of radiation, e.g., X-rays, gamma rays, or neutrons

ir·rad·i·ca·ble /i ráddikəb'l/ *adj* incapable of being eradicated [Early 18C. < medieval Latin *irradicabilis* < Latin *radicare* "take root," wrongly understood as "root out"] —**ir·rad·i·ca·bly** *adv*

ir·ra·tion·al /i rásh'n'l, i ráshnəl/ *adj* **1. LACKING IN REASON** contrary to or lacking in reason or logic **2. LACKING LOGICAL THOUGHT** unable to think logically **3. UNABLE TO THINK CLEARLY** lacking the normal ability to think clearly, especially because of shock or injury to the brain **4.** MATH **CONTAINING IRRATIONAL NUMBER** describes a mathematical expression that contains an irrational number **5.** LITERAT **CONTAINING METRIC IRREGULARITY** describes an irregularity in the meter of a classical poem, usually where there is a long foot instead of a short one ■ *n* **1. IRRATIONAL PERSON** an unclear or illogical thinker **2.** MATH same as **irrational number** [15C. < Latin *irrationalis* < *rationalis* (see RATIONAL)] —**ir·ra·tion·al·i·ty** /i ràsh'n állətee/ *n* —**ir·ra·tion·al·ly** *adv* —**ir·ra·tion·al·ness** *n*

ir·ra·tion·al·ism /i rásh'n'l ìzzəm, i ráshnə lìzzəm/ *n* **1.** the state of lacking reason or logic **2.** the belief that feelings and intuition are more important than reason —**ir·ra·tion·al·is·tic** /i ràshən'l ístik, i ràshnə lístik/ *adj*

ir·ra·tion·al num·ber *n* any real number that cannot be expressed as the exact ratio of two integers, e.g., ⁻2; and π

Ir·ra·wad·dy /ìrrə wóddee/, **Ir·a·wad·i** principal river of Myanmar. Length: 1,300 mi./2,100 km.

ir·real /i reé əl/ *adj* illusory or not actually existing (*literary*) —**ir·re·al·i·ty** /ìrree állətee/ *n*

ir·re·claim·a·ble /ìrri kláymәb'l/ *adj* not able to be reclaimed ○ *an irreclaimable desert* ○ *irreclaimable damages* —**ir·re·claim·a·bil·i·ty** /ìrri klaymə bíllətee/ *n* —**ir·re·claim·a·ble·ness** *n* —**ir·re·claim·a·bly** *adv*

ir·rec·on·cil·a·ble /i rèkən sīləb'l, i rékən sīləb'l/ *adj* **1. INCOMPATIBLE** not capable of being made to agree or coexist with something else **2. UNRESOLVABLE** incapable of being resolved **3. IMPLACABLE** determinedly hostile and unwilling to accept compromise —**ir·rec·on·cil·a·bil·i·ty** /i rèkən sīlə bíllətee/ *n* —**ir·rec·on·cil·a·bly** *adv*

ir·re·cov·er·a·ble /ìrri kúvvərəb'l/ *adj* **1.** impossible to get back or regain **2.** impossible to repair or remedy —**ir·re·cov·er·a·ble·ness** *n* —**ir·re·cov·er·a·bly** *adv*

ir·re·deem·a·ble /ìrri deémәb'l/ *adj* **1. WITHOUT HOPE OF IMPROVEMENT** not able to be improved, corrected, or made good **2. NOT REPAIRABLE** impossible to repair **3.** CHR **INCAPABLE OF REDEMPTION** refusing to reform and unable to be saved **4.** FIN **UNABLE TO BE PAID OFF** not having a fixed date for repayment of the principal ○ *an irredeemable bond* **5.** FIN **NOT CONVERTIBLE INTO COINS** unable to be converted into coins —**ir·re·deem·a·bil·i·ty** /ìrri deemə bíllətee/ *n* —**ir·re·deem·a·bly** *adv*

ir·re·den·ta /ìrri déntə/ *n* a territory that was once part of one country but is now ruled by another and is subject to claims that it should be returned to its former country [Early 20C. < Italian *(Italia) irredenta* (see IRREDENTIST)]

ir·re·den·tist /ìrri déntist/ *n* a member of a group of people who support the return to their country of territories that used to belong to it but are now under foreign rule [Early 20C. < IRREDENTIST] —**ir·re·den·tism** *n*

Ir·re·den·tist /ìrri déntist/ *n* a member of a former Italian organization that advocated the adding to Italy of Italian-speaking territories that were under foreign control [Late 19C. < Italian *irredentista* < *(Italia) irredenta* "unrecovered (Italy)" < *redento* "redeemed" < Latin *redemptus*, past participle of *redimere* (see REDEEM)]

ir·re·duc·i·ble /ìrri dóossəb'l/ *adj* **1. INCAPABLE OF BEING DECREASED** not able to be made smaller **2. INCAPABLE OF SIMPLIFICATION** not able to be simplified, or simplified further **3. IMPOSSIBLE TO FACTOR INTO LESSER POLYNOMIALS** in mathematics, used to describe a polynomial that cannot be factored into two polynomials of a lesser degree **4. IMPOSSIBLE TO REDUCE TO RATIONAL EXPRESSION** in mathematics, used to describe a radical that cannot be reduced to a rational expression —**ir·re·duc·i·bil·i·ty** /ìrri doossə bíllətee/ *n* —**ir·re·duc·i·ble·ness** *n* —**ir·re·duc·i·bly** *adv*

ir·re·flex·ive /ìrri fléksiv/ *adj* describes a relation in which, if a has the relation to b, then b does not have the relation to a

ir·re·form·a·ble /ìrri fáwrmәb'l/ *adj* **1.** incapable of being reformed **2.** impossible to revise or alter —**ir·re·form·a·bil·i·ty** /ìrri fàwrmə bíllətee/ *n*

ir·re·fran·gi·ble /ìrrə fránjəb'l/ *adj* **1. INCAPABLE OF BEING DISOBEYED** impossible to disobey or violate (*formal*) **2. INCAPABLE OF BEING BROKEN** impossible to break or smash (*formal*) **3. INCAPABLE OF BEING REFRACTED** describes visible light or other radiation that cannot be refracted —**ir·re·fran·gi·bil·i·ty** /ìrrə franjə bíllətee/ *n* —**ir·re·fran·gi·bly** *adv*

ir·ref·u·ta·ble /ìrrə fyoótəb'l, i réffyə-/ *adj* impossible to refute or disprove [Early 17C. < late Latin *irrefutabilis* < Latin *refutare* "refute"] —**ir·ref·u·ta·bil·i·ty** /ìrrə fyootə bíllətee, i rèffyə-/ *n* —**ir·ref·u·ta·bly** *adv*

ir·re·gard·less /ìrri gaárdləss/ *adv* ⚠ same as **regardless** (*nonstandard*) [Early 20C. Probably blend of IRRESPECTIVE + REGARDLESS]

USAGE Since the prefix *ir-* means "not" (as it does in *irrespective*), and the suffix *-less* means "without," ***irregardless*** is a double negative and is regarded as nonstandard. As such, it is to be avoided, in favor of *irrespective* or *regardless.*

ir·reg·u·lar /i réggyələr/ *adj* **1. NOT OF UNIFORM APPEARANCE** not even, uniform, or symmetrical in appearance **2. OCCURRING AT ODD INTERVALS** not occurring at equally spaced intervals of time **3. NONCONFORMING** not conforming to common practices **4. BEHAVING UNACCEPTABLY** not conforming to accepted rules or standards of behavior **5. UNAUTHORIZED** not conforming to law or social conventions **6.** MIL **UNOFFICIAL** not forming part of an official military body **7.** GRAM **NOT FORMED BY USUAL GRAMMATICAL RULES** not following the usual rules of word formation ○ *an irregular verb* **8. CONSTIPATED** not having a regular daily bowel movement (*euphemistic*) **9. SUBSTANDARD** not meeting the manufacturer's standards for goods but still salable **10.** BOT **HAVING ASYMMETRICAL PARTS** describes a plant that does not have symmetrical parts ■ *n* **1.** MIL **SOLDIER NOT PART OF REGULAR FORCES** a soldier who is not part of an official military body **2. SUBSTANDARD ITEM** an item of merchandise that does not meet the manufacturer's standards but is still salable (*often used in the plural*) [15C. Via French < medieval Latin *irregularis* "breaking a rule" < Latin *regularis* (see REGULAR)] —**ir·reg·u·lar·ly** *adv*

ir·reg·u·lar·i·ty /i règgyə lárrətee/ (*plural* **-ties**) *n* **1. BEING IRREGULAR** the state of being irregular **2. IRREGULAR THING** something irregular, e.g., a bump in a road **3. UNAUTHORIZED THING** something unauthorized or unacceptable by usual standards **4. CONSTIPATION** the state of not having a regular daily bowel movement (*euphemistic*)

ir·rel·a·tive /i réllətiv/ *adj* **1.** not related or connected **2.** not relevant

ir·rel·e·vant /i rélləvənt/ *adj* not relevant or important —**ir·rel·e·vance** *n* —**ir·rel·e·van·cy** *n* —**ir·rel·e·vant·ly** *adv*

~~**irrelevent**~~ incorrect spelling of **irrelevant**

ir·re·lig·ious /ìrri líjjəss/ *adj* **1.** lacking in any religious faith **2.** opposed to religion —**ir·re·lig·ious·ly** *adv* —**ir·re·lig·ious·ness** *n*

ir·re·me·di·a·ble /ìrri meédee əb'l/ *adj* impossible to remedy or make right [Mid-16C. < Latin *irremediabilis* < *remediare* "to cure"] —**ir·re·me·di·a·bly** *adv*

ir·re·mis·si·ble /ìrri míssəb'l/ *adj* **1.** not able to be pardoned or excused **2.** not able to be avoided or postponed [15C. Directly or via French < ecclesiastical Latin *irremissibilis* "unpardonable" < Latin *remiss-*, past participle of *remittere* (see REMIT)] —**ir·re·mis·si·bil·i·ty** /ìrri missə bíllətee/ *n* —**ir·re·mis·si·bly** *adv*

ir·re·mov·a·ble /ìrri moóvəb'l/ *adj* incapable of being removed —**ir·re·mov·a·bil·i·ty** /ìrri moovə bíllətee/ *n* —**ir·re·mov·a·bly** *adv*

ir·rep·a·ra·ble /i réppərəb'l/ *adj* not able to be repaired or fixed ○ *did irreparable damage to the computer* [15C. Directly or via French < Latin *irreparabilis* "not to be recovered" < *reparare* (see REPAIR [1])] —**ir·rep·a·ra·bil·i·ty** /i rèppərə bíllətee/ *n*—**ir·rep·a·ra·ble·ness** *n*—**ir·rep·a·ra·bly** *adv*

ir·re·peal·a·ble /ìrri peéləb'l/ *adj* not able to be repealed —**ir·re·peal·a·bil·i·ty** /ìrri peelə bíllətee/ *n* —**ir·re·peal·a·bly** *adv*

ir·re·place·a·ble /ìrri pláyssəb'l/ *adj* not able to be replaced —**ir·re·place·a·bil·i·ty** /ìrri playssə bíllətee/ *n* —**ir·re·place·a·ble·ness** *n* —**ir·re·place·a·bly** *adv*

ir·rep·re·hen·si·ble /i rèppri hénssəb'l/ *adj* deserving no censure

ir·re·press·i·ble /ìrri préssəb'l/ *adj* not able to be controlled ○ *irrepressible high spirits* —**ir·re·press·i·bil·i·ty** /ìrri pressə bíllətee/ *n* —**ir·re·press·i·ble·ness** *n* —**ir·re·press·i·bly** *adv*

ir·re·proach·a·ble /ìrri próchəb'l/ *adj* not incurring any reproach or criticism [Mid-17C. < French *irréprochable* < *réprochable* "reproachable"] —**ir·re·proach·a·bil·i·ty** /ìrri prōchə bíllətee/ *n*—**ir·re·proach·a·ble·ness** *n* —**ir·re·proach·a·bly** *adv*

ir·re·pro·duc·i·ble /i reeprə dóossəb'l/ *adj* impossible to reproduce —**ir·re·pro·duc·i·bil·i·ty** /i reeprə doossə bíllətee/ *n*

~~**irresistable**~~ incorrect spelling of **irresistible**

ir·re·sis·ti·ble /ìrri zístəb'l/ *adj* **1.** not able to be resisted or successfully opposed **2.** so desirable as to be very difficult to resist [Late 16C. < medieval Latin *irresistibilis* < Latin *resistere* "resist"] —**ir·re·sis·ti·bil·i·ty** /ìrri zistə bíllətee/ *n* —**ir·re·sis·ti·ble·ness** *n* —**ir·re·sis·ti·bly** *adv*

ir·re·sol·u·ble /ìrri zóllyəb'l/ *adj* incapable of being solved, reconciled, or explained [Mid-17C. < Latin *irresolubilis* "indissoluble" < *resolvere* "melt"] —**ir·re·sol·u·bil·i·ty** /ìrri zolyə bíllətee/ *n* —**ir·re·sol·u·bly** *adv*

ir·res·o·lute /i rézzə loót/ *adj* unsure and unable to make decisions —**ir·res·o·lute·ly** *adv* —**ir·res·o·lute·ness** *n* —**ir·res·o·lu·tion** /i rèzzə loósh'n/ *n*

ir·re·solv·a·ble /ìrri zólvəb'l/ *adj* **1.** not able to be broken down into different parts **2.** not able to be solved —**ir·re·solv·a·bil·i·ty** /ìrri zolvə bíllətee/ *n* —**ir·re·solv·a·bly** *adv*

ir·re·spec·tive /ìrri spéktiv/ —**ir·re·spec·tive·ly** *adv* ◇ **irrespective of** without taking something into account ○ *We have to work together irrespective of our differences.*

USAGE See *irregardless.*

ir·re·spon·si·ble /ìrri spónssəb'l/ *adj* **1. NOT CARING** not having or showing any care for the consequences of personal actions **2. INCAPABLE OF RESPONSIBILITY** not legally capable of assuming responsibility for personal actions ■ *n* **IRRESPONSIBLE PERSON** somebody who behaves irresponsibly —**ir·re·spon·si·bil·i·ty** /ìrri spònssə bíllətee/ *n* —**ir·re·spon·si·ble·ness** *n* —**ir·re·spon·si·bly** *adv*

ir·re·spon·sive /ìrri spónssiv/ *adj* not responding quickly or favorably —**ir·re·spon·sive·ly** *adv* —**ir·re·spon·sive·ness** *n*

ir·re·triev·a·ble /ìrri treévəb'l/ *adj* **1.** impossible to find or recover **2.** impossible to repair or fix —**ir·re·triev·a·bil·i·ty** /ìrri treevə bíllətee/ *n* —**ir·re·triev·a·ble·ness** *n* —**ir·re·triev·a·bly** *adv*

~~**irrevelant**~~ incorrect spelling of **irrelevant**

~~**irreverant**~~ incorrect spelling of **irreverent**

ir·rev·er·ent /i révvərənt/ *adj* lacking in respect [Mid-16C. < Latin *irreverent-* < present participle of *revereri* (see REVERE)] —**ir·rev·er·ence** *n* —**ir·rev·er·ent·ly** *adv*

ir·re·vers·i·ble /ìrri vúrssəb'l/ *adj* impossible to reverse or undo —**ir·re·vers·i·bil·i·ty** /ìrri vurssə bíllətee/ *n* —**ir·re·vers·i·ble·ness** *n* —**ir·re·vers·i·bly** *adv*

ir·rev·o·ca·ble /i révvəkəb'l/ *adj* impossible to revoke, undo, or change [14C. Directly or via French < Latin *irrevocabilis* "that cannot be recalled" < *revocare* (see REVOKE)] —**ir·rev·o·ca·bil·i·ty** /i rèvvəkə bíllətee/ *n* —**ir·rev·o·ca·ble·ness** *n* —**ir·rev·o·ca·bly** *adv*

ir·ri·gate /írri gàyt/ (**-gat·ed, -gat·ing, -gates**) *vt* **1.** AGRIC **SUPPLY AREA WITH WATER** to bring a supply of water to a dry area, especially in order to help crops to grow **2.** MED **WASH OUT WOUND** to make water or liquid medication flow through or over a body part or wound in order to cleanse it **3. REFRESH SOMETHING** to make something fresh [Early 17C. < Latin *irrigat-*, past participle of *irrigare*, literally "to water in" < *rigare* "to water"] —**ir·ri·ga·ble** *adj*—**ir·ri·ga·tion** /ìrri gáysh'n/ *n*—**ir·ri·ga·tion·al** *adj*—**ir·ri·ga·tive** *adj*—**ir·ri·ga·tor** *n*

ir·ri·ta·ble /írritəb'l/ *adj* **1. EASILY ANNOYED** easily annoyed or exasperated **2.** MED **SENSITIVE** extremely sensitive, especially to inflammation **3.** BIOL **RESPONSIVE TO STIMULI** describes an organism that is able to respond to stimuli [Mid-17C. < Latin *irritabilis* "easily enraged" < *irritare* "provoke"] —**ir·ri·ta·bil·i·ty** /ìrritə bíllətee/ *n* —**ir·ri·ta·ble·ness** *n* —**ir·ri·ta·bly** *adv*

ir·ri·ta·ble bow·el syn·drome *n* a condition of the bowel in which there is recurrent pain with constipation or diarrhea or alternating attacks of these

ir·ri·tant /írritənt/ *adj* causing irritation, especially physical irritation [Early 17C. < Latin *irritant-*, present participle of *irritare* "provoke"] —**ir·ri·tan·cy** *n* —**ir·ri·tant** *n*

ir·ri·tate /írri tàyt/ (**-tat·ed, -tat·ing, -tates**) *v* **1.** *vti* **ANNOY SOMEBODY** to cause somebody to feel annoyance or exasperation, or cause annoyance or exasperation **2.** *vt* MED **INFLAME BODY PART** to stimulate a body part excessively, causing a painful reaction such as inflammation **3.** *vt* BIOL **STIMULATE ORGANISM** to stimulate an organism in a way that provokes a response [Mid-16C. < Latin *irritat-*, past participle of *irritare* "provoke"] —**ir·ri·tat·ing** *adj* —**ir·ri·tat·ing·ly** *adv* —**ir·ri·ta·tive** *adj* —**ir·ri·ta·tor** *n*

SYNONYMS See *annoy.*

ir·ri·ta·tion /ìrri táysh'n/ *n* **1. ANNOYANCE** a feeling of impatience or exasperation **2. ACT OF ANNOYING** the act of causing annoyance or exasperation **3. SOMEBODY OR SOMETHING ANNOYING** somebody or something that causes annoyance or exasperation **4.** MED **REACTION TO**

IRRITANT a painful reaction, especially an inflammation, caused by an irritant **5.** MED **INFLAMING** the act of causing a painful reaction, especially an inflammation

SYNONYMS See *anger.*

ir·rupt /i rúpt/ (**-rupt·ed, -rupt·ing, -rupts**) *vi* **1.** to enter suddenly or violently **2.** to increase suddenly and rapidly, e.g., in number [Mid-19C. < Latin *irrupt-*, past participle of *irrumpere* "break into a place" < *rumpere* "to break"]

ir·rup·tion /i rúpshən/ *n* **1.** a sudden, often violent appearance of something ○ *the irruption of violence in everyday life* **2.** a very rapid and pervasive increase in the numbers of something, e.g., predators (*technical*) ○ *irruption of High Plains coyotes and other mammal predators*

ir·rup·tive /i rúptiv/ *adj* **1.** entering or likely to enter suddenly or violently **2.** describes igneous rock that is injected forcibly into preexisting rock formations —**ir·rup·tive·ly** *adv*

IRS *abbr* GOV Internal Revenue Service

Ir·tysh ♦ **Ob'-Irtysh**

Ir·vine /úr vīn/ city in southwestern California, situated directly southeast of Santa Ana. Population: 162,122 (2002 estimate).

Cook Neilson

John Irving

Ir·ving /úrving/, **John** (*b.* 1942) US novelist. His works include *The World According to Garp* (1978) and *The Hotel New Hampshire* (1981).

Ir·ving, Washington (1783–1859) US writer. The first US author to achieve international renown, he is best known for *The Sketch Book* (1819–20), which includes the stories "Rip Van Winkle" and "The Legend of Sleepy Hollow."

> "For what is history, but...huge libel on human nature, to which we industriously add page after page, volume after volume, as if we were holding up a monument to the honor, rather than the infamy of our species."
> [Washington Irving, *A History of New York*; 1809]

Ir·ving·ton /úrvingtən/ **1.** township in northeastern New Jersey, adjoining southwestern Newark. Population: 60,516 (2002 estimate). **2.** village in Westchester County, New York, situated on the Hudson River 22 mi./35 km north of New York City

Ir·win /úrwin/, **Bill** (*b.* 1940) US actor and director. His performances often combine aspects of vaudeville, clowning, and satire.

is[1] 3rd person singular present of **be**[1]

is[2] *abbr* ONLINE Iceland (*used in Internet addresses*) See table at **domain name**

IS *abbr* COMPUT information services

is. *abbr* GEOG **1.** island **2.** isle

Is. *abbr* **1.** BIBLE Isaiah **2.** GEOG Island (*used in place names*) **3.** GEOG Isle (*used in place names*)

is- *prefix* same as **iso-** (*used before vowels*)

ISA *abbr* AEROSP International Standard Atmosphere

Isa. *abbr* BIBLE Isaiah

I·saac /īzək/ *n* in the Bible, the son of Abraham and Sarah, who was offered by his father as a sacrifice to God, but was saved at the last moment by divine intervention. He was the father of Jacob and Esau. (Genesis 21–28)

Is·a·bel·la I /ìzzə béllə/ (1451–1504) queen of Castile and León. The heir to the crown of Castile and León, she married Ferdinand of Aragón (1469), bringing about the unification of Spain. As queen of Castile and León (1474–1504), she supported the Inquisition, expelled the Jews from Spain, and defeated Granada, the last Moorish kingdom in Spain. She sponsored Christopher Columbus's voyages. Known as **Isabella the Catholic**

Is·a·bel·la II (1830–1904) queen of Spain. She ruled from 1833 until she was deposed in 1868. Her reign was marked by political turmoil and insurrection.

is·a·gog·ics /īssə gójjiks/ *n* introductory studies, especially of the Bible in its literary and historical contexts (*takes a singular verb*) [Mid-19C. < *isagogic* "introductory," via Latin < Greek *eisagōgikos* < *eisagōgē* "introduction" < *eis* "into" + *agein* "to lead"] —**is·a·gog·ic** *adj*

I·sa·iah /ī záy ə, ī zī ə/ *n* **1.** in the Bible, a Hebrew prophet who lived in the latter half of the 8th century B.C. He was the earliest of the major prophets. **2.** a book of the Bible that contains prophecies and apocalyptic material, traditionally attributed to Isaiah. See table at **Bible**

is·al·o·bar /ī sállə baar/ *n* a contour line on a weather chart joining places where equal changes in atmospheric pressure occur during a given time interval [Early 20C. < IS- + ALLO- + Greek *baros* "weight," after ISOBAR]

i·sa·tin /īssət'n/ *n* a water-soluble compound related to indigo and indole that crystallizes as orange needles. Use: manufacture of vat dyes. Formula: $C_8H_5NO_2$. [Mid-19C. < Greek *isatis* "woad"] —**i·sa·tin·ic** /īssə tínnik/ *adj*

ISBN *abbr* PUBL International Standard Book Number

is·chae·mi·a *n* MED UK spelling of **ischemia**

is·che·mi·a /i skeémee ə/ *n* an inadequate supply of blood to a part of the body, caused by partial or total blockage of an artery [Late 19C. < modern Latin < Greek *iskhaimos* "stopping blood" < *iskhein* "to hold" + *haima* "blood"] —**is·che·mic** *adj*

Is·chi·a /iskee ə/ island in west central Italy, situated in the Tyrrhenian Sea between the Gulf of Gaeta and the Bay of Naples. Its highest point is Mount Epomeo, 2,589 ft./789 m. Population: 18,253 (2001). Area: 18 sq. mi./47 sq. km.

is·chi·um /iskee əm/ (*plural* **-chi·a** /-kee ə/) *n* the lowest and rearmost of the three bones that make up each half of the pelvis [Early 17C. Via Latin < Greek *iskhion* "hip joint"] —**is·chi·al** *adj*

ISDN *n* a digital telephone network that can transmit both voice and data messages ○ *an ISDN line* Full form **Integrated Services Digital Network**

-ise *suffix UK* another spelling of **-ize**

is·en·trope /īss'n trōp, īz'n-/ *n* a line on a graph or chart linking points of equal entropy [Back-formation < ISENTROPIC]

is·en·tro·pic /īss'n tróppik, īss'n trōpik, īz'n-/ *adj* **1.** describes a reaction or process that takes place without a change in entropy **2.** relating to an isentrope —**is·en·tro·pi·cal·ly** *adv*

I·seult *n* ♦ **Tristan and Iseult**

Is·fa·han ♦ **Esfahan**

-ish *suffix* **1.** characteristic of, like, tending to ○ *churlish* ○ *babyish* ○ *bookish* **2.** of or relating to, from ○ *Gaulish* **3.** somewhat, approximately ○ *bluish* ○ *latish* [Old English *-isc* < Germanic]

Ish·er·wood /ishər wŏŏd/, **Christopher** (1904–86) British-born US writer. He described prewar Berlin in two volumes of short stories, *Mr. Norris Changes Trains* (1935) and *Goodbye to Berlin* (1939). Full name **Isherwood, Christopher William Bradshaw**

> "I am a camera with its shutter open, quite passive, recording, not thinking."
> [Christopher Isherwood, "Berlin Diary," *Goodbye to Berlin*; 1939]

Ish·i·gu·ro /ishee góorō/, **Kazuo** (*b.* 1954) Japanese-born British novelist. He won the British Booker Prize for *The Remains of the Day* (1989).

Ish·ma·el /ishmee əl, ish màyl/ *n* **1.** in the Bible, the son of Abraham, expelled into the desert after the birth of his brother Isaac, who was the forebear of twelve desert tribes. Muslims, who call him Ismail, regard themselves as his descendants. (Genesis 16–21) **2.** same as **outcast** (*literary*)

Ish·ma·el·ite /ishmee ə līt, ish mayə līt/ *n* **1.** in the Bible, a descendant of Abraham's son Ishmael **2.** same as **outcast** (*literary*) —**Ish·ma·el·it·ish** *adj* —**Ish·ma·el·it·ism** *n*

Ish·tar /ish taar/ *n* in Babylonian and Assyrian mythology, the queen of heaven and goddess of fertility. Tammuz was her consort. She was worshiped throughout Southwest Asia under various names, including the Phoenician Astarte.

i·sin·glass /īz'n glàss, īzing-/ *n* **1.** a transparent or translucent gelatin made from the air bladders of various fish, especially the sturgeon. Use: clarifying agent, in adhesives and jellies. **2.** MINERALS same as **mica** [Mid-16C. < obsolete early Dutch *huysenblas* "sturgeon's bladder" < *huysen* "sturgeon" + *blas* "bladder"]

I·sis[1] /īsiss/ *n* in Egyptian mythology, the goddess of fertility, generally depicted wearing a cow's horns bearing a golden disk representing the sun. She was the wife of her brother Osiris and the mother of Horus.

I·sis[2] /īssəss/ alternative name for the Thames River around Oxford, England

Is·ken·de·run /iss kèndə róon/, **Is·ken·de·ron** /-rón/ city in southern Turkey, on the southeastern shore of the Gulf of Iskenderun, situated approximately 60 mi./96 km southeast of Adana. Population: 154,807 (1990).

isl. *abbr* GEOG **1.** island **2.** isle

Is·la de Cu·le·bra /eésslə day-/ ♦ **Culebra**

Is·la de Vi·e·ques ♦ **Vieques**

Is·lam /iss laam, iz-, íz laam, íss-/ *n* **1.** a monotheistic religion based on the word of God as revealed to Muhammad during the 7th century **2.** Muslim people, their culture, or their countries considered collectively [Early 17C. < Arabic *islām* "submission (to God)" < base of *aslāma* "he surrendered"] —**Is·lam·ic** /iss laamik, iz-/ *adj*

Is·lam·a·bad /iz laammə bàd/, **Is·lām·ā·bād** city and capital of Pakistan, situated northeast of Rawalpindi. Population: 791,085 (1998).

Is·lam·ic Ji·had *n* an Islamic fundamentalist organization committed to the introduction of an Islamic Palestinian state by armed opposition to Israel. It also opposes pro-Western Arab governments.

Is·lam·ism /íssla mìzzəm, ízz-/ *n* **1.** a conservative Islamic political movement **2.** the religion or principles of Islam —**Is·lam·ist** *adj, n*

Is·lam·ize /íssla mīz, ízzla-/ (**-ized, -iz·ing, -iz·es**) *vt* **1.** to convert people or countries to Islam **2.** to cause people, institutions, or countries to follow Islamic law —**Is·lam·i·za·tion** /ìsslami záysh'n, ìzzlami-/ *n*

is·land /īlənd/ *n* **1.** PIECE OF LAND SURROUNDED BY WATER an area of land, smaller than a continent, that is completely surrounded by water (*often used in place names*) **2.** SOMETHING LIKE ISLAND something that is like an island because it is isolated or surrounded by something different ○ *"No man is an island, entire of itself."* (John Donne, *Devotions upon Emergent Occasions*; 1624) **3.** ANAT ISOLATED BODY PART a body part or group of cells that is different in construction from its surroundings ■ *vt* (**-land·ed, -land·ing, -lands**) **1.** MAKE SOMETHING INTO ISLAND to form something into an island **2.** ISOLATE SOMEBODY to cause somebody to feel isolated, e.g., from contact with peers or colleagues **3.** FILL OCEAN WITH ISLANDS to provide a body of water with islands (*literary*) ○ *the many-islanded Aegean* **4.** UTIL ISOLATE ELECTRIC GRID SECTORS to isolate separate sectors of an electrical grid via widespread defensive blackouts to avoid permanent damage to utility equipment during periods of unusually heavy peak use and power failures [Old English *īegland* < *īeg* "island" (< Indo-European, "water") + LAND; spelling influenced by ISLE] —**is·land·er** *n*

is·land arc *n* an arc-shaped chain of islands, usually found in an area of volcanic or seismic activity

is·land-hop *vi* to travel from island to island within the same chain, especially as part of a vacation (*informal*)

is·lands of Lang·er·hans *npl* ANAT same as **islets of Langerhans**

Is·lands of the Bless·ed *npl* MYTHOL same as **Hesperides** (sense 2)

Is·lay /īlə, ī lay/ southernmost island of the Inner Hebrides, western Scotland. Population: 3,500. Area: 236 sq. mi./610 sq. km.

isle /īl/ *n* an island, often a small one (*literary*) [13C. Via Old French *ile, isle* < Latin *insula*]

SPELLCHECK See *aisle.*

Isle of Man /īl əv mán/ self-governing Crown dependency of the United Kingdom, lying in the Irish Sea midway between Northern Ireland and England. Language: English, Manx. Capital: Douglas. Population: 74,261 (2003). Area: 221 sq. mi./572 sq. km.

Isle of Wight /-wīt/ largest offshore island of England, off the southern coast, in the English Channel. It is a separate county and Newport is the administrative center. Population: 132,731 (2001). Area: 147 sq. mi./381 sq. km.

Isle Roy·ale Na·tion·al Park /-ròy əl-/ national park in Northwestern Michigan, on Isle Royale and extending on to islands in Lake Superior. Area: 893 sq. mi./2,314 sq. km.

is·let /īlət/ *n* a small isle or island

is·lets of Lang·er·hans /-laángər haàns/ *npl* clusters of endocrine cells found in the pancreas that secrete insulin and glucagon

Is·lip /īzlip/ town in Suffolk County, southeastern New York, situated on Long Island. Population: 18,924 (1996).

ism /ízzəm/ *n* a movement, doctrine, or system of belief (*informal*) [Late 17C. < -ISM]

-ism *suffix* **1.** action, process ○ *mesmerism* ○ *volcanism* **2.** characteristic behavior or manner ○ *despotism* **3.** state, condition ○ *conservatism* ○ *gangsterism* **4.** unusual or unhealthy state ○ *caffeinism* **5.** doctrine, system of beliefs ○ *defeatism* ○ *Calvinism* **6.** prejudice ○ *sexism* **7.** distinctive feature or trait ○ *Southernism* ○ *vulgarism* [Via French < Latin *-ismus* < Greek *-ismos*]

Is·ma·i·li /izmə eélee, iz maa-, issmə-, iss maa-/ *n* a member of a branch of Shiite Muslims whose members believe that Ismail, son of the sixth imam, was the true seventh imam [Mid-19C. < Arabic < *'Ismā'īl*, proper name] —**Is·ma·i·li** *adj*

Is·ma·i·liy·ya /izmə eélee ə/ city in northeastern Egypt, situated on Lake Timsah. It is the halfway station on the Suez Canal. Population: 255,000 (1992).

Is·ma·il Sa·man·i Peak /issmə eél sə maánee-/ mountain situated in central Tajikistan, and the highest peak in the country. Height: 24,590 ft./7,495 m. Former name **Garmo Peak** (until 1933), **Stalin Peak** (1933–62), **Communism Peak** (1962–98)

is·n't /ízz'nt/ *contr* is not ○ *It isn't ready yet.*

ISO[1] *abbr* in search of

ISO[2] *n* an international organization established in 1947 to standardize such things as units of measurement and the meanings of technical terms [< Greek *isos* "equal" (not an abbreviation of *International Standards Organization*)]

iso- *prefix* **1.** equal, uniform ○ *isoelectric* ○ *isogloss* **2.** isomeric ○ *isooctane* **3.** of or for different members of the same species ○ *isoagglutination* [< Greek *isos* "equal"]

i·so·ag·glu·ti·na·tion /ìssō əgloot'n áysh'n/ *n* the agglutination of red blood cells in one individual induced by antibodies in the serum of another individual of the same species —**i·so·ag·glu·ti·na·tive** /-əgloót'n àytiv/ *adj*

i·so·ag·glu·ti·nin /ìssō ə gloót'nin/ *n* an antibody from one individual that causes the clumping together (agglutination) of red blood cells in another individual of the same species but of a different blood group

i·so·bar /íssə baàr/ *n* **1.** a line drawn on a weather map that connects places with equal atmospheric pressure. Isobars are often used collectively to indicate the movement or formation of weather systems. **2.** one of two or more atoms or elements that have the same mass number but different atomic numbers [Mid-19C. < Greek *isobaros* "of equal weight"] —**i·so·bar·ism** *n*

i·so·bar·ic /ìssə bárrik/ *adj* **1.** having constant or equal atmospheric pressure **2.** relating to isobars

i·so·bar·ic spin *n* PHYS same as **isospin**

i·so·bath /íssō bàth/ *n* a line on a map of the sea that connects points that are at the same depth [Late 19C. < ISO- + Greek *bathos* "depth"] —**i·so·bath·ic** /ìssō báthik/ *adj*

i·so·bu·tane /ìssō byoō tàyn/ *n* a colorless gaseous hydrocarbon that is an isomer of butane. Use: fuel, refrigerant. Formula: C_4H_{10}.

i·so·car·box·a·zid /ìssō kaar bóksəzid/ *n* a drug that is a monoamine oxidase inhibitor. Use: antidepressant, treatment of agoraphobia. [Mid-20C. < ISO- + contraction of CARBONYL + OX- + HYDRAZIDE]

~~isoceles~~ incorrect spelling of **isosceles**

i·so·cheim /íssə kīm/, **i·so·chime** *n* a line on a weather map connecting places that have the same average temperature in winter [Mid-19C. < ISO- + Greek *kheima* "winter weather"] —**i·so·cheim·al** /ìssə kīm'l/ *adj* —**i·so·cheim·e·nal** /ìssə kīmən'l/ *adj*

i·so·chro·mat·ic /ìssə krō máttik/ *adj* **1.** OPTICS same as **orthochromatic 2.** having the same color or wavelength of light

i·soch·ro·nous /ī sókrənəss/, **i·soch·ro·nal** /-krən'l/ *adj* **1.** having the same frequency or periodicity **2.** measured or occurring at the same time, or lasting for the same length of time —**i·soch·ro·nous·ly** *adv*

i·soch·ro·ous /ī sókrō əss/ *adj* having the same color throughout [Mid-19C. < ISO- + Greek *khrōs* "color"]

i·so·cli·nal /ìssə klīn'l/ *adj* **1.** having the same inclination or slope **2.** GEOL having the sides of a geologic fold parallel to one another ■ *n* **1.** GEOL same as **isocline** (sense 1) **2.** MAPS same as **isoclinic line**

i·so·cline /íssə klīn/ *n* **1.** a geologic fold with rock beds that slope in the same direction **2.** MAPS same as **isoclinic line** [Late 19C. < Greek *isoklinēs* "equally balanced," literally "leaning equally" < *klinein* "to lean"]

i·so·clin·ic /ìssə klínnik/ *adj* same as **isoclinal**

i·so·clin·ic line *n* a line on a map connecting points on the Earth's surface that have the same magnetic dip

i·so·cy·a·nate /ìssə sí ə nàyt/ *n* a chemical compound containing the chemical group -NCO. Use: in resins, adhesives.

i·so·cy·a·nide /ìssə sí ə nīd/ *n* a colorless liquid with a pungent odor that contains the chemical group -NC

i·so·di·a·met·ric /ìssō dī ə méttrik/ *adj* having diameters or axes of equal length

i·so·dose /íssə dōss/ *n* a dose of radiation of equal intensity applied to more than one part of the body as a medical treatment

i·so·dy·nam·ic /ìssō dī námmik/ *adj* **1.** having the same strength or intensity **2.** connecting points on a map of the Earth's surface that have the same magnetic intensity

i·so·e·lec·tric /ìssō i léktrik/ *adj* having exactly the same electric potential

i·so·e·lec·tric point *n* the pH value at which the electric force on a molecule in a solution is zero

i·so·e·lec·tron·ic /ìssō i lek trónnik/ *adj* having the same number of electrons or the same outer atomic structure —**i·so·e·lec·tron·i·cal·ly** *adv*

i·so·en·zyme /ìssō én zīm/ *n* one of two or more enzymes that are different chemically but function in the same way —**i·so·en·zy·mat·ic** /-enzə máttik/ *adj* —**i·so·en·zy·mic** /-en zímmik/ *adj*

i·so·fla·vone /ìssō fláy vōn/ *n* an isoflavonoid, e.g., genistein

i·so·flav·o·noid /ìssō fláyvə nòyd/ *n* a flavonoid belonging to a group that occurs in legumes, especially soy bean, and is converted by bacteria in the intestines into substances having activity similar to that of estrogen

i·so·ga·mete /ìssō gá meét, -gə meét/ *n* a gamete physically identical to another with which it unites to form a zygote —**i·so·ga·met·ic** /-gə méttik/ *adj*

i·sog·a·my /ī sóggəmee/ *n* the fusion of isogametes in some algae and fungi during reproduction

i·so·ge·ne·ic /ìssōjə neé ik/ *adj* IMMUNOL same as **syngeneic** [Mid-20C. Alteration of ISOGENIC]

i·so·gen·ic /ìssə jénnik/ *adj* having identical genes

i·sog·e·nous /ī sójjənəss/ *adj* **1.** describes organs or parts of the body that have the same or a similar origin **2.** GENETICS same as **isogenic** —**i·sog·e·ny** *n*

i·so·gloss /íssə glòss/ *n* a line on a language map that surrounds an area within which a linguistic usage such as a dialectal word is found [Early 20C. < ISO- + Greek *glossa* "language"] —**i·so·gloss·al** /ìssə glóss'l/ *adj* —**i·so·glos·sic** /-glóssik/ *adj* —**i·so·glot·tal** /-glótt'l/ *adj* —**i·so·glot·tic** /-glóttik/ *adj*

i·so·gon /íssə gòn/ *n* a polygon whose angles are all equal [Late 17C. < Greek *isogōnios* "equiangular"]

i·sog·o·nal /ī sóggən'l/ *adj, n* MATH, PHYS same as **isogonic**

i·sog·o·nal line *n* MAPS same as **isogonic line**

i·so·gone /íssə gōn/ *n* MAPS same as **isogonic line** [Alteration of ISOGON]

i·so·gon·ic /ìssə gónnik/ *adj* MATH having equal angles ■ *n* MAPS same as **isogonic line** [Mid-19C. < Greek *isogōnios* "equiangular"]

i·so·gon·ic line *n* a line on a map of the Earth's surface connecting points at which a compass would give the same deviation from true north

i·so·graft /íssə gràft/ *n* a tissue graft taken from an individual genetically identical to the recipient of the graft, e.g., from an identical twin

i·so·gram /íssə gràm/ *n* MAPS, METEOROL same as **isoline**

i·so·hel /íssə hèl/ *n* a line on a map connecting places that receive the same number of hours of sunshine in the course of a year [Early 20C. < ISO- + Greek *hēlios* "sun"]

i·so·hy·et /ìssə hī ət/ *n* a line on a map connecting places that receive the same amount of rainfall in the course of a year [Late 19C. < ISO- + Greek *huetos* "rain"] —**i·so·hy·et·al** *adj*

i·so·la·ni /ìssō laánee/ (*plural* **-nis**) *n* CHESS same as **isolated pawn**

i·so·late *vt* /íssə làyt/ (**-lat·ed, -lat·ing, -lates**) **1.** SEPARATE SOMEBODY OR SOMETHING FROM OTHERS to separate somebody or something from others of the same type **2.** CUT PLACE OFF to make a place unreachable from the surrounding area ○ *Heavy snowfalls have temporarily isolated the town.* **3.** FIND CAUSE OF SOMETHING to discover which of a number of possible causes or factors is responsible for a specific phenomenon or problem ○ *He isolated a bug in the software as the cause of the failure.* **4.** MED QUARANTINE SOMEBODY to keep somebody who is infected away from other people in order to prevent the spread of a contagious disease **5.** BIOL SEPARATE OUT VIRUS to separate out a chemical or biological material such as a virus or bacterium in order to identify and study it **6.** ELECTRONICS INSULATE ELECTRONIC DEVICE to prevent a circuit or device from interacting with another or with an outside stimulus ■ *n* /íssələt, -làyt/ **1.** LONE PERSON OR GROUP a person or group separated or cut off from others **2.** BIOL, CHEM MICROORGANISM GROWN IN LABORATORY a sample of biological material, especially a microorganism, that has been cultured for study **3.** FITNESS NUTRITIONAL PRODUCT cultured biological material prepared for use as a nutritional supplement ○ *whey protein isolate* **4.** LING ONLY LANGUAGE OF FAMILY a language that is the only known surviving member of its language family [Early 19C. Back-formation < ISOLATED < French *isolé* < late Latin *insulatus* "made into an island" < Latin *insula* "island"] —**i·so·la·ble** *adj* —**i·so·lat·a·ble** *adj* —**i·so·la·tor** *n*

i·so·lat·ed /íssə làytəd/ *adj* **1.** REMOTE far away from other inhabited areas or buildings **2.** ALONE OR LONELY not having enough social contact, friends, or support **3.** RARE happening rarely or only once and unlikely to prove a continuing problem ○ *an isolated incident* [Mid-18C. See ISOLATE]

i·so·lat·ed pawn *n* in chess, a pawn that is not supported by other pawns of the same color on adjacent files

i·so·lat·ing /íssə làyting/ *adj* LING same as **analytic** (sense 5)

i·so·la·tion /ìssə láysh'n/ *n* **1.** the process of separating somebody or something from others, or the fact of being alone and separated from others **2.** remoteness from other inhabited areas or buildings ◇ **in isolation 1.** separate from other related factors or things ○ *We have to look at the problem in isolation.* **2.** alone and physically separated from other people

i·so·la·tion·ism /ìssə láysh'n ìzzəm/ *n* **1.** a government policy based on the belief that national interests are best served by avoiding economic and political alliances with other countries **2.** electronic ambient music that is generally produced without beats, creating a soothing ambience with unusual sounds —**i·so·la·tion·ist** *n, adj*

i·so·la·tive /īssə làytiv/ *adj* **1.** describes a sound change that occurs in all phonetic environments **2.** causing somebody or something to be separated or cut off

I·sol·de *n* ➧ **Tristan and Iseult**

i·so·lec·i·thal /īssə léssithəl/ *adj* describes the eggs of mammals and some other vertebrates in which the yolk is evenly distributed throughout the egg

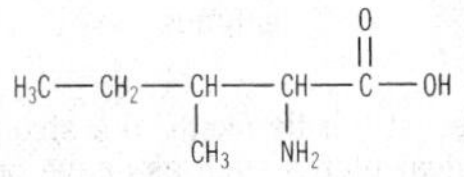

isoleucine

i·so·leu·cine /īssə lóoss'n/ *n* an amino acid that is an isomer of leucine and is found in most proteins. Formula: $C_6H_{13}NO_2$.

i·so·lex /īssə lèks/ *n* a line on a language map that surrounds an area within which a particular word is used [Early 20C. < ISO- + Greek *lexis* "word"]

i·so·line /īssō līn/ *n US* a line on a map connecting points with the same value for variables such as temperature or air pressure. Can term **isopleth**

i·so·lo·gous /ī sólləgəss/ *adj* describes two organic compounds that have the same molecular structure but different atoms of the same valence [Mid-19C. < ISO- + Greek *logos* "ratio"]

i·so·mag·net·ic /īssō mag néttik/ *n* a line on a map connecting points of the same magnetic force —**i·so·mag·net·ic** *adj*

i·so·mag·net·ic line *n* MAPS, PHYS same as **isomagnetic**

i·so·mer /īssəmər/ *n* **1.** each of two or more molecules that have the same number of atoms but have different chemical structures and therefore different properties **2.** each of two or more nuclides that have the same mass number and atomic number but different energy states and half-lives [Mid-19C. < Greek *isomerēs* "sharing equally"] —**i·so·mer·ic** /īssə mérrik/ *adj*

i·som·er·ase /ī sómmə ràyss, -ràyz/ *n* an enzyme that converts one isomer into another

i·som·er·ism /ī sómmə rizzəm/ *n* **1.** the existence of two or more molecules that are isomers **2.** the existence of two or more nuclides that are isomers

i·som·er·ize /ī sómmə rīz/ (**-ized, -iz·ing, -iz·es**) *vti* to change something into an isomer, or become an isomer —**i·som·er·i·za·tion** /ī sòmmərī záysh'n/ *n*

i·som·er·ous /ī sómmərəss/ *adj* having physical parts that are similar in number, markings, or other characteristics

i·so·met·ric /īssə méttrik/, **i·so·met·ri·cal** /-méttrik'l/ *adj* **1.** PHYSIOL **INVOLVING PUSHING MUSCLES AGAINST SOMETHING** describes exercises in which muscles are put under tension but not allowed to contract **2. EQUAL** equal in dimension or measurement **3.** CRYSTALS **WITH THREE EQUAL AXES** describes a crystalline system that has three equal axes at right angles to one another **4.** LITERAT **WITH LINES OF SAME LENGTH** having the same number of metrical feet in each line of poetry **5.** ENG **PROJECTED AT SAME ANGLE TO AXES** projected so that the plane of projection of a three-dimensional drawing is at an equal angle to each of the three axes of the object drawn [Mid-19C. < Greek *isometria* "equality of measure"] —**i·so·met·ri·cal·ly** *adv*

i·so·met·rics /īssə méttriks/ *n* a form of exercise in which the muscles are pushed against something fixed or against other muscles to strengthen them (*takes a singular or plural verb*)

i·so·me·tro·pi·a /īssōmə trṓpee ə/ *n* the condition of equal refraction of light by both eyes [< Greek *isometros* "of equal measure"]

i·som·e·try /ī sómmətree/ (*plural* **-tries**) *n* **1.** equality of measure **2.** a geometric transformation in which the distance between any two points is preserved, e.g., the rotation of a plane

i·so·morph /īssə màwrf/ *n* a substance or organism that exhibits similarity in form or appearance to others **(isomorphism)**

i·so·mor·phic /īssə máwrfik/ *adj* **1.** having the same form or appearance as another organism or the same organism at a different stage in its life cycle **2.** describes mathematical sets with a one-to-one correspondence so that an operation such as addition or multiplication in one produces the same result as the analogous operation in the other **3.** CHEM same as **isomorphous** —**i·so·mor·phi·cal·ly** *adv*

i·so·mor·phism /īssə máwr fìzzəm/ *n* **1.** BIOL **SIMILARITY IN ORGANISMS** similarity in form or appearance between organisms of different ancestry or between different stages in the life cycle of the same organism **2.** MATH **CORRESPONDENCE BETWEEN SETS** a one-to-one correspondence between sets so that an operation such as addition or multiplication in one produces the same result as the analogous operation in the other **3.** CHEM **SIMILARITY BETWEEN CHEMICALS** similarity in crystalline form between chemicals

i·so·mor·phous /īssə máwrfəss/ *adj* describes a chemical compound that is able to crystallize in a form similar to another chemical compound

i·so·ni·a·zid /īssə nī́ əzid/ *n* a colorless crystalline compound. Use: to treat tuberculosis. Formula: $C_6H_7N_3O$. [Mid-20C. < ISO- + contraction of *nicotinic* + HYDRAZIDE]

i·so·oc·tane /īssō ók tàyn/ *n* a flammable isomer of octane. Use: determination of the octane number of fuel. Formula: $(CH_3)_3CCH_2$.

i·so·pach /īssə pàk/ *n* a line on a map of the Earth's surface connecting points where a rock stratum has equal thickness [Early 20C. < ISO- + Greek *pakhus* "thick"]

i·so·phone /īssə fōn/ *n* a line on a language map surrounding an area within which a specific pronunciation is used

i·so·pi·es·tic /īssō pī éstik/ *adj* METEOROL, PHYS same as **isobaric** [< ISO- + Greek *piezein* "to squeeze"] —**i·so·pi·es·ti·cal·ly** *adv*

i·so·pleth /īssə plèth/ *n Can, UK* MAPS, METEOROL same as **isoline** [Early 20C. < Greek *isoplēthēs* "equal in quantity"] —**i·so·pleth·ic** /īssə pléthik/ *adj*

i·so·pod /īssə pòd/ *n* a small invertebrate animal with a flattened body and seven pairs of legs. Sow bugs are isopods, but most isopods are sea animals. Order: Isopoda. [Mid-19C. < modern Latin *Isopoda*, literally "equal foot" < Greek *pod-* "foot"] —**i·sop·o·dan** /ī sóppəd'n/ *adj* —**i·sop·o·dous** /ī sóppədəss/ *adj*

i·so·pre·na·line /īssə prénn'lin, -prénn'l èen/ *n UK* PHARM same as **isoproterenol** [Mid-20C. Contraction of *N-isopropylnoradrenaline*]

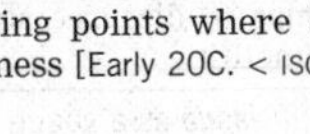

isoprene

i·so·prene /īssə prèen/ *n* a colorless flammable liquid hydrocarbon. Use: manufacture of synthetic rubber. Formula: C_5H_8. [Mid-19C. < ISO- + contraction of *prophylene*]

i·so·pro·pa·nol /īssə prṓpə nàwl/ *n* CHEM same as **isopropyl alcohol**

i·so·pro·pyl /īssə prṓp'l/ *n* a chemical radical isomer of propyl. Formula: C_3H_7.

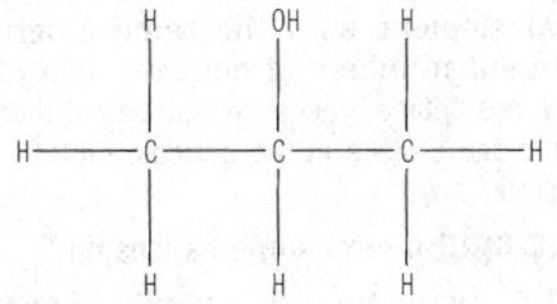

isopropyl alcohol

i·so·pro·pyl al·co·hol *n* a colorless flammable alcohol. Use: antifreeze, rubbing alcohol, solvent. Formula: C_3H_8O.

i·so·pro·ter·e·nol /īssəprō térrə nàwl/ *n* a drug that dilates the bronchial tubes. Use: treatment of asthma. [Mid-20C. Contraction of *N-isopropylarterenol*]

ISO rat·ing *n* a measure of the sensitivity to light of a material such as photographic film or paper

i·so·rhy·thm /īssə rìthəm/ *n* a technique of musical composition of the 14th and 15th centuries that uses a repeated rhythmic pattern —**i·so·rhyth·mic** /īssə rìthmik/ *adj*

i·sos·ce·les /ī sóssə lèez/ *adj* **1.** describes a triangle in which two of the three sides are of equal length **2.** describes a trapezoid in which the two nonparallel sides are of equal length [Mid-16C. Via late Latin < Greek *isoskelēs* "equally legged"]

i·so·seis·mal /īssə sī́zməl/, **i·so·seis·mic** /-sī́zmik/ *adj* relating to or showing equal strength of earthquake shock ■ *n* a line on a map connecting points of equal strength of earthquake shock

i·sos·mot·ic /īs oz móttik/ *adj US* relating to or exerting equal osmotic pressure. Can term **isotonic** —**i·sos·mot·i·cal·ly** *adv*

i·so·spin /īssə spìn/ *n* a quantum characteristic of baryons and mesons that relates to the number of different values of electric charge they can have. Symbol ***I*** [Mid-20C. Contraction of ISOBARIC SPIN, ISOTOPIC SPIN]

i·sos·ta·sy /ī sóstəssee/ *n* a state of equilibrium between forces such as accumulated ice pushing down on a section of the Earth's surface and those pushing up from below [Late 19C. < ISO- + Greek *stasis* "stoppage"] —**i·so·stat·ic** /īssə státtik/ *adj* —**i·so·stat·i·cal·ly** *adv*

i·so·stat·ic ad·just·ment *n* a slow uplifting of the Earth's surface resulting from the removal of a load, as occurs after the melting of a glacier

i·so·tach /īssə tàk/ *n* a line on a weather map connecting points where the wind speed is equal [Mid-20C. < ISO- + Greek *takhos* "speed"]

i·so·tac·tic /īssə táktik/ *adj* describes a polymer whose constituent molecules give it a repetitive spatial structure [Mid-20C. < ISO- + Greek *taktos* "ordered"]

i·so·there /īssə thèer/ *n* a line on a weather map connecting places that have the same average temperature in summer [Mid-19C. < French *isothère* < Greek *isos* "equal" + *theros* "summer"]

i·so·therm /īssə thùrm/ *n* **1.** a line drawn on a weather map that connects places with the same temperature **2.** a line on a graph showing the relationship between variables, especially pressure and volume, at a constant temperature [Mid-19C. < French *isotherme*, literally "equal heat" < Greek *thermē* "heat" or *thermos* "hot"] —**i·so·ther·mal** /īssə thúrməl/ *adj* —**i·so·ther·mal·ly** *adv*

i·so·thi·o·cy·a·nate /īssō thī ō sī́ ə nàyt/ *n* a chemical compound containing the chemical group -NCS

i·so·tone /īssə tōn/ *n* each of two or more atoms with the same number of neutrons but different atomic numbers

i·so·ton·ic /īssə tónnik/ *adj* **1.** PHYSIOL relating to the contraction and shortening of a muscle under relatively constant tension, e.g., in weightlifting **2.** *Can, UK* CHEM same as **isosmotic** **3.** PHYSIOL specially formulated to supply the body's chemical needs in situations in which minerals and fluids are used up by the body, e.g., during vigorous exercise ○ *isotonic drinks* —**i·so·ton·i·cal·ly** *adv* —**i·so·to·nic·i·ty** /ìssə tō níssətee/ *n*

i·so·tope /íssə tōp/ *n* each of two or more forms of a chemical element with the same atomic number but different numbers of neutrons [Early 20C. < ISO- + Greek *topos* "place"; because isotopes of the same name occupy the same place in the periodic table] —**i·so·top·ic** /ìssə tóppik/ *adj*

i·so·top·ic spin *n* PHYS same as **isospin**

i·so·tro·pic /ìssə tróppik, -trṓpik/, **i·so·tro·pous** /ī sóttrəpəss/ *adj* having physical properties that do not vary with direction [Mid-19C. < ISO- + Greek *tropos* "turn"] —**i·so·trop·i·cal·ly** *adv* —**i·so·trop·ism** /ī sóttrə pìzzəm/ *n* —**i·so·tro·py** /ī sóttrəpee/ *n*

i·so·zyme /íssə zīm/ *n UK* BIOCHEM same as **isoenzyme** [Mid-20C. < ISO- + shortening of ENZYME]

ISP *abbr* ONLINE Internet service provider

i-spin *n* QUANTUM PHYS same as **isospin**

I-spy *n* a children's guessing game in which players try to guess which thing in visual range another player has in mind, having been given the first letter of the word

Israel

Is·ra·el /ízree əl/ country in Southwest Asia formed in 1948 as a Jewish state in the historic region of Palestine, on the eastern shore of the Mediterranean Sea. Language: Hebrew, Arabic. Currency: shekel. Capital: Jerusalem. Population: 6,116,533 (2003). Area: 8,473 sq. mi./21,946 sq. km. Official name **State of Israel** —**Is·rae·li** /iz ráylee/ *n, adj*

Is·ra·el·ite /ízzree ə līt/ *n* **1.** a member of the ancient Hebrew people descended from the patriarch Jacob **2.** somebody who came from the ancient kingdom of Israel —**Is·ra·el·it·ic** /ìzzree ə líttik/ *adj*

Is·ra·fil /ízzrə feel/, **Is·ra·feel**, **Is·ra·fel** *n* according to the Koran, the archangel who will herald the end of the world by sounding a trumpet on the Day of Judgment [< Hebrew, "God heals"]

~~**Isreal**~~ incorrect spelling of **Israel**

ISS *abbr* AEROSP International Space Station

Is·sa·char /íssə kaar/ *n* **1.** in the Bible, a son of Jacob and Leah **2.** one of the twelve tribes of Israel, descended from Issachar [Via late Latin < Greek < Hebrew *Yiśśākhār*]

is·sei /ee sáy/ (*plural same*), **Is·sei** *n* a Japanese immigrant to the United States or Canada [Early 20C. < Japanese, "first generation"]

Is·si·go·nis /issi gṓniss/, **Sir Alec** (1906–88) Palestinian-born British car designer. He is best known for designing the Morris Minor (1948) and the Mini (1959). Full name **Issigonis, Sir Alexander Arnold Constantine**

ISSN *abbr* PUBL International Standard Serial Number

is·su·ant /íshoo ənt/ *adj* in heraldry, displaying an animal rising up from something with only its upper body showing

is·sue /íshoo/ *n* **1.** SUBJECT OF CONCERN something for discussion or of general concern ○ *I want to raise several issues at the meeting.* **2.** MAIN SUBJECT the central or most important topic in a discussion or debate ○ *The real issue is education.* **3.** LAW LEGAL MATTER IN DISPUTE a legal matter in a dispute between two parties **4.** ALLOTTING OF SOMETHING the distribution of something by an official body ○ *the issue of parking permits* **5.** PUBL COPY OF PUBLICATION a copy of a magazine or newspaper published on a particular date **6.** COMM OFFICIAL RELEASE OF SOMETHING a set of things such as new stamps or bonds that are made available for sale by an official body at a particular time **7.** FIN STOCK MADE AVAILABLE a series of items such as stock in a company that becomes available at the same time **8.** OFFICIAL ALLOTMENT something officially distributed or supplied, or an amount of something officially distributed or supplied ○ *government issue rations* **9.** LAW PROGENY somebody's offspring ○ *died without issue* **10.** ⚠ PROBLEM OR DIFFICULTY a source of conflict, misgiving, or emotional distress (*informal*) ○ *had issues with some of her suggestions* **11.** FINAL OUTCOME a final outcome or conclusion of a matter that is usually a solution to a problem or difficulty (*dated*) ○ *Let's bring our differences to an issue.* **12.** SOURCE OF FLOW a place from which something flows **13.** MED DISCHARGE FROM WOUND pus or blood coming from an open wound or ulcer **14.** LAW PROFIT FROM PROPERTY profits made from owning land or buildings ■ *v* (**-sued, -su·ing, -sues**) **1.** *vt* SUPPLY SOMETHING to supply or distribute something officially **2.** *vt* ANNOUNCE SOMETHING PUBLICLY to make public something such as a bulletin, statement, or warning, or deliver it officially to somebody ○ *The mayor's office issued a press release.* **3.** *vt* PUBL PUBLISH SOMETHING to publish something such as a newspaper, magazine, or book **4.** *vt* COMM RELEASE SOMETHING FOR SALE to make a set of things such as new stamps or bonds available for sale at a particular time **5.** *vi* ORIGINATE to emerge or come out from somewhere ○ *Smoke issued from the burning building.* **6.** *vi* ARISE FROM CONDITION to result from or be produced by a particular thing or situation ○ *Our conclusions issue from analysis of the data.* **7.** *vi* FIN ADD UP AS GAIN to accrue in the form of interest or profit [13C. < Old French < Latin *exitus*, past participle of *exire* (see EXIT)] —**is·su·a·ble** *adj* —**is·su·ance** *n* —**is·sue·less** *adj* —**is·su·er** *n* ◇ **at issue** under discussion or to be decided ◇ **take issue with somebody** *or* **something** to disagree strongly with somebody about something

USAGE Avoid using ***issue*** as a vague substitute for more precise expressions such as *problem, difficulty,* or *point of disagreement*, as in *She has some issues with your presentation of the facts.* Say instead: *She has some problems...* The euphemistic use of *issues* to denote intentionally unstated problems, typically emotional or mental problems, should also be avoided, as in *He has issues with his weight.*

SYNONYMS See ***disagree, subject.***

is·sue price *n* the price of new securities when they are first offered to the public

Is·syk-Kul /issik kŏŏl/ lake in northeastern Kyrgyzstan. It has a maximum depth of 2,300 ft./700 m. Area: 2,360 sq. mi./6,100 sq. km.

IST *abbr* **1.** COMPUT information sciences technology **2.** MED insulin shock therapy

-ist *suffix* **1.** practicing a particular skill or profession ○ *psychologist* ○ *etymologist* **2.** following a particular belief or school of thought ○ *idealist* ○ *Socialist* **3.** somebody who plays a particular instrument ○ *oboist* **4.** somebody who is prejudiced against a particular social grouping ○ *racist* ○ *sexist* [Directly or via French < Latin *-ista* < Greek *-istēs*] —**-istic** *suffix*

Is·tan·bul /iss tan bŏŏl, -taan-/, **İs·tan·bul** largest city in Turkey, situated in the northwest of the country on the Bosporus. Population: 9,451,000 (2000). Former name **Byzantium** (c.600 B.C.-A.D. 330), **Constantinople** (330–1930)

isth·mi GEOG plural of **isthmus**

isth·mi·an /íssmee ən/ *adj* **1.** relating to an isthmus of land **2.** ANAT same as **isthmic** ■ *n* somebody who lives on or comes from an isthmus

Isth·mi·an *adj* relating to the Isthmus of Panama or the Isthmus of Corinth

Isth·mi·an Games *npl* a sports festival held in ancient Greece on the Isthmus of Corinth that included horseracing and chariot racing

isth·mic /íssmik/ *adj* relating to an isthmus in the body ○ *an isthmic constriction*

isth·mus /íssməss/ (*plural* **-mus·es** or **-mi** /-mī/) *n* **1.** a narrow strip of land that joins two larger areas of land ○ *The isthmus connects North and South America.* **2.** a narrow connection or passage between parts of the body [Mid-16C. Via Latin < Greek *isthmos* "island"] —**isth·moid** /iss mòyd/ *adj*

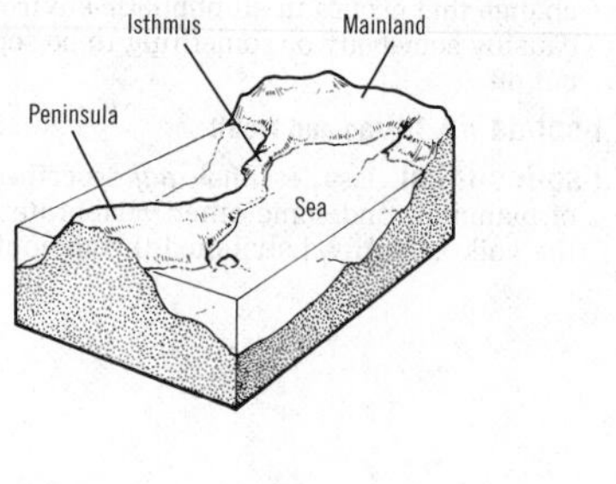

isthmus

is·tle /ísslee, íst-/, **ix·tle** /íkstli/ *n* a strong fiber from some tropical plants such as agave or yucca. Use: rope, baskets, carpets. [Mid-19C. Via American Spanish *ixtle* < Nahuatl *ixtli*]

Is·tri·a /ístree ə/ peninsula in northwestern Croatia and southwestern Slovenia, projecting into the Adriatic Sea. Area: 1,500 sq. mi./3,885 sq. km.

ISV *abbr* SCI International Scientific Vocabulary

it[1] /it/ CORE MEANING: a pronoun used to refer to an object or an animal, and sometimes a baby ○ *It's a lovely baby.* ○ *They've had the dog a week, and they still haven't thought of a name for it.*

1. *pron* INDICATING SPECIFIC SITUATION used to refer to a situation just described, or to an unspecified or implied situation ○ *He's very upset, but he won't talk about it.* **2.** *pron* INDICATING POINT OF VIEW used to indicate feelings or a viewpoint on a particular situation ○ *It's strange how things turn out.* **3.** *pron* INDICATING SOMETHING REPORTED used in the formation of passive sentences reporting a situation ○ *It was reported that several people had been arrested.* **4.** *pron* INDICATING WEATHER used as the subject of verbs such as "be," "get," "seem," and "feel" in order to describe something about the environment such as the temperature or the weather ○ *It's cold and rainy.* **5.** *pron* INDICATING TIME used to state the time, e.g., the time of day, the month, the year, or the season ○ *It's six o'clock.* **6.** *pron* INDICATING DESCRIPTION OF EXPERIENCE used to refer to life or a particular experience ○ *What's it like being famous?* **7.** *pron* EMPHASIZING FOLLOWING CLAUSE used to draw attention to the person, thing, or clause that immediately follows ○ *It's you who are always complaining!* ○ *It isn't that I don't care.* **8.** *pron* INDICATING CRISIS the crucial or ultimate point, the perfect situation, person, or thing, or the death or end of somebody or something ○ *When the car turned over I really thought that was it.* **9.** *pron* ATTRACTIVE OR SELLING QUALITY a quality considered by somebody to be the most important, e.g., talent, charm, sex appeal, or profitability (*informal*) ○ *You either have it or you don't.* **10.** *pron* SEX sexual intercourse (*slang*) **11.** *n* LEISURE PLAYER IN CHILDREN'S GAMES in children's informal games, the player who must do something to the others, e.g., run after and touch them in the game of tag ○ *You're it!* [Old English *hit* < Germanic]

it[2] *abbr* ONLINE Italy (*used in Internet addresses*) See table at **domain name**

IT *abbr* COMPUT information technology

It. *abbr* Italian

ITA, I.T.A. *abbr* EDUC initial teaching alphabet

ital. *abbr* PUBL **1.** italic **2.** italics

Ital. *abbr* **1.** Italian **2.** Italy

I·tal·ian /i tállyən/ *n* **1.** somebody who comes from Italy **2.** the official language of Italy and an official language of Switzerland, a Romance language belonging to the Italic branch of Indo-European. Native speakers: 60 million. Other speakers: 60 million. See panel on next page [14C. < Italian *italiano* "of Italy" < *Italia* "Italy"] —**I·tal·ian** *adj*

I·tal·ian·ate /i tállyə nàyt/ *adj* expressed, done, or made in an Italian style or character

I·tal·ian dress·ing *n* a salad dressing typically made with oil and vinegar, garlic, and oregano

I·tal·ian·esque /i tàllyə nésk/ *adj* same as **Italianate**

I·tal·ian·ism /i tállyə nìzzəm/ *n* something that comes from or is characteristic of Italy, e.g., a word or phrase that is derived from Italian

LANGUAGE HERITAGE ***Italian*** Much of English is made up of words from other languages, and Italian is a very important contributor, especially to music, the other arts, and cuisine. Many music terms are direct borrowings from Italian, while others came into English via Italian from other languages. These words traverse the broad landscape of music, occupying numerous subcategories. A few representative examples are these: directions, ***agitato, con sordino, grandioso, lentissimo, vivace***; composition, ***capriccio, concerto, fantasia, intermezzo, operetta***; performers and singing-voice ranges, ***alto, basso, diva, contralto, soprano***; and instruments, ***ocarina, piano, timpani, violin, violoncello***. The word ***segue***, originally restricted in use to music, has extended its meanings over time. Dating from the mid-18th century, this Italian borrowing goes back to Latin *sequi* "follow."

To the other arts Italian has contributed words like ***fresco, tarantella, galleria, cameo***, and ***literati***. To cuisine, Italian's prolific contributions are evidenced by these representative examples: ***antipasto, calamari, cappuccino, espresso, gnocchi, maraschino, mozzarella, pasta*** (and the words for all its shapes and varieties), ***pizza, spumoni, zabaglione***, and ***zucchini***. The word ***tetrazzini***, as in *chicken tetrazzini*, is an eponym based on the surname of the Italian opera diva Luisa Tetrazzini (1874–1940).

Italian has also contributed various miscellaneous words to English, for example, ***ghetto, regatta, rialto*** (from the marketplace district of Venice so named), ***trattoria***, the soccer term ***catenaccio, paparazzo*** (first recorded in English in the mid-20th century, from the surname of a photographer in the 1959 Federico Fellini film *La Dolce Vita*), and the interjection ***ciao***, used in English especially to say "goodbye," Italian dialect for "(I am your) slave."

Italian has been the transport language of many émigrés with origins in other languages. For example, ***tariff***, first recorded in English in the late 16th century, arrived via Italian *tariffa*, which goes back to Arabic *ta'rif* "notification, inventory of fees to be paid." ***Graffito***, the plural of which is ***graffiti***, is first recorded in English in the mid-19th century. ***Graffito*** is a direct borrowing from Italian and in that language it means "scribbling."

Some English words transported to English by Italian but having other roots have undergone alterations to the extent that their Italian and ultimate ancestral connections may not be readily apparent at first glance. Such is the case with ***garble***, especially interesting because it underwent major spelling and meaning changes over the centuries. First recorded in English in the 15th century, ***garble*** is traced to Italian *garbellare* "to sift," then to Arabic *ġarbala* "to select," from late Latin *cribellum* "small sieve," from Latin *cribrum* "sieve." ***Garble*** is rooted in Mediterranean commerce, where as a verb it meant "to sift or cull refuse from spices," later coming to mean "to pick and choose the best." Now its most common meaning is just the opposite: "to confuse a message or information so that it is misleading or unintelligible."

I·tal·ian·ize /i tállyə nīz/ (**-ized, -iz·ing, -iz·es**) *vti* to make something Italian in character, or become Italian in character —**I·tal·ian·i·za·tion** /i tàllyəni záysh'n/ *n*

I·tal·ian sand·wich *n Northeast US* FOOD same as **submarine**

I·tal·ian sixth *n* a three-note chord consisting of an augmented sixth chord and a major third above the root of the chord, used for modulation and for providing color

I·tal·ian son·net *n* LITERAT same as **Petrarchan sonnet**

i·tal·ic /i tállik/ *adj* **1. WITH PRINTED LETTERS SLOPING TO RIGHT** printed in or using letters that slope to the right. Italic letters are sometimes used in book titles or to show emphasis in text. **2. WITH HANDWRITTEN LETTERS SLOPING TO RIGHT** handwritten in letters that slope to the right ■ *n* **ITALIC LETTER** a printed letter that slopes to the right, or a font that uses such letters (*often used in the plural*) [Early 17C. < ITALIC; from its introduction by an Italian printer in 1501]

I·tal·ic /i tállik/ *n* **BRANCH OF INDO-EUROPEAN LANGUAGE FAMILY** a branch of the Indo-European language family that includes many former languages of Italy, including Latin and Umbrian ■ *adj* **1. OF ITALIC** relating to the language family Italic **2. ANCIENT ITALIAN** relating to ancient Italy [15C. Via Latin < Greek *Italikos* < *Italia* "Italy"]

I·tal·i·cism /i tálli sìzzəm/ *n* a word or phrase that is borrowed from Italian

i·tal·i·cize /i tálli sīz/ (**-cized, -ciz·ing, -ciz·es**) *vt* to print a word, letter, or document in italics, or change words to an italic font —**i·tal·i·ci·za·tion** /i tàllissi záysh'n/ *n* —**i·tal·i·cized** *adj*

Italo- *prefix* Italy or Italian ○ *Italo-American* [< ITALIAN]

I·tal·o·phile /i tállō fīl/ *n* somebody who loves Italy and the Italian people, culture, or language —**I·tal·o·phil·i·a** /i tàllō fíllee ə/ *n*

Italy

It·a·ly /ítt'lee/ country in southern Europe. Its mainland area projects as a peninsula into the Mediterranean Sea, and it includes, among others, the islands of Elba, Sicily, and Sardinia. Language: Italian. Currency: euro. Capital: Rome. Population: 57,998,353 (2003). Area: 116,341 sq. mi./301,323 sq. km. Official name **Italian Republic**

I·ta·nag·ar /èetə núggər/ capital of Arunachal Pradesh State in northeastern India. Population: 17,300 (1991).

I·tar Tass /èe taar táss/, **I·TAR-Tass** *n* a Russian news agency founded in 1992 to replace Tass, the news agency of the former Soviet Union [Late 20C. < Russian < acronym < *Informatsionnoe telegrafnoe agentsvo Rossii* "Information Telegraph Agency of Russia" + TASS]

itch /ich/ *v* (**itched, itch·ing, itch·es**) **1.** *vti* **WANT TO SCRATCH** to have an irritating sensation on the body that provokes a desire to scratch the skin, or produce or cause somebody to feel such a sensation **2.** *vi* **BE ANXIOUS TO DO SOMETHING** to be very eager or impatient to do something **3.** *vt* **SCRATCH ITCHY SKIN** to scratch the skin where it itches (*nonstandard*) ■ *n* **1. FEELING OF WANTING TO SCRATCH** an irritating sensation in the body that provokes a desire to scratch the skin **2. LONGING FOR SOMETHING** a restless or uneasy desire for something **3.** MED **ITCHY SKIN DISORDER** a skin disorder that causes the skin to itch, e.g., scabies [Old English *giccan* < Germanic] —**itch·i·ness** *n* —**itch·ing** *n* —**itch·y** *adj*

itch mite *n* a tiny parasite that burrows into the skin and causes the disease scabies in humans. Latin name: *Sarcoptes scabiei*.

it'd /íttəd/ *contr* **1.** it had **2.** it would

-ite[1] *suffix* **1.** mineral, rock, ore, soil, fossil ○ *carnotite* ○ *nummulite* **2.** descendant or follower of ○ *Hamite* ○ *Hussite* **3.** native or resident of ○ *Israelite* ○ *urbanite* **4.** organ, body part, cell, protozoan ○ *sporozoite* **5.** commercial product, explosive ○ *cordite* **6.** product of a chemical process ○ *evaporite* [Via French and Latin < Greek *-itēs*]

-ite[2] *suffix* salt or ester of an acid with a name ending in *-ous* ○ *phosphite* [Alteration of -ATE]

i·tem /ītəm/ *n* **1. ONE IN COLLECTION** a single thing in a group or collection of things **2. ONE IN LIST** a single thing in a list of things **3. BROADCAST OR PUBLISHED REPORT** a piece of information in a news report, e.g., in a newspaper or on television **4.** ACCT **BOOKKEEPING ENTRY** an entry in a set of financial accounts **5. COUPLE IN RELATIONSHIP** a couple who are linked in a romantic or sexual relationship (*informal*) ■ *adv* **INTRODUCING LISTED ITEM** used to introduce an item in a list [Late 16C. < Latin, "likewise" < *ita* "thus, so"]

i·tem·ize /ītə mīz/ (**-ized, -iz·ing, -iz·es**) *v* **1.** *vt* to list individually all the things that make up a set or whole ○ *an itemized bill* **2.** *vi* to list separately on a tax return all deductions from taxable income ○ *Unless you want to itemize, you can use the easier, shorter tax form.* —**i·tem·i·za·tion** /ītəmi záysh'n/ *n* —**i·tem·iz·er** *n*

it·er·ance /íttərənss/ *n* same as **iteration** (sense 1) [Early 17C. < Latin *iterare* (see ITERATE)]

it·er·ant /íttərənt/ *adj* marked by repetition or recurrence [Early 17C. < Latin *iterant-*, present participle of *iterare* (see ITERATE)]

it·er·ate /íttə ràyt/ (**-at·ed, -at·ing, -ates**) *vt* to say or do the same thing again [Mid-16C. < Latin *iterat-*, past participle of *iterare* "repeat" < *iterum* "again"]

it·er·a·tion /ìttə ráysh'n/ *n* **1. REPETITION** an instance or the act of doing something again **2.** MATH **STEP-BY-STEP PROCESS** a process of achieving a desired result by repeating a sequence of steps and successively getting closer to that result **3.** COMPUT **REPETITION OF STEPS** the repetition of a sequence of instructions in a computer program until a result is achieved **4. NEW VERSION OF SOMETHING** a different version of something, especially a new version of existing computer hardware or software

it·er·a·tive /íttə ràytiv, -rətiv/ *adj* **1.** MATH, LOGIC same as **recursive** (sense 2) **2.** COMPUT using repeated routines in a loop as part of a computer program **3.** GRAM, LING same as **frequentative 4.** repeating again and again —**it·er·a·tive·ly** *adv*

Ith·a·ca /íthəkə/ **1.** island in western Greece, the traditional site of the legendary kingdom of Odysseus. Population: 1,715 (1991). Area: 37 sq. mi./96 sq. km. **2.** city in south central New York, south of Cayuga Lake and northwest of Binghamton. Population: 29,974 (2002 estimate).

ith·y·phal·lic /ìthə fállik/ *adj* **1. SHOWING ERECT PENIS IN ART** in sculpture, painting, or other art, having or showing an erect penis **2. IN METER USED IN BACCHIC HYMNS** relating to or composed in the meter used in hymns to the ancient Greek god Bacchus ■ *n* **POEM** a poem composed in ithyphallic meter [Early 17C. < late Latin *ithyphallicus* < Greek *ithuphallos* "phallus carried in procession at festivals of Bacchus," literally "straight phallus"]

i·tin·er·ant /ī tínnərənt/ *adj* traveling from place to place, especially to find work or as part of your work [Late 16C. < late Latin *itinerant-*, present participle of *itinerari* "journey" < Latin *itiner-* "way, road, journey"] —**i·tin·er·an·cy** *n* —**i·tin·er·ant** *n* —**i·tin·er·ant·ly** *adv*

i·tin·er·ar·y /ī tínnə rèrree/ *n* (*plural* **-ies**) **1. LIST OF PLACES TO BE VISITED** a plan for a journey listing different places in the order in which they are to be visited **2. RECORD OF JOURNEY** a written record of a journey to visit different places **3. GUIDEBOOK** a guidebook for travelers ■ *adj* **INTENDED FOR TRAVELING** intended or used for the purpose of traveling [15C. < late Latin *itinerarius* < Latin *itiner-* "way, road, journey"]

i·tin·er·ate /ī tínnə ràyt/ (**-at·ed, -at·ing, -ates**) *vi* to move from place to place on a circuit (*refers to judges or preachers*) [Early 17C. < late Latin *itinerat-*, past participle of *itinerari* (see ITINERANT)] —**i·tin·er·a·tion** /ī tìnnə ráysh'n/ *n*

-itis *suffix* **1.** inflammation, disease ○ *retinitis* **2.** excessive interest in ○ *spectatoritis* [< Greek]

it'll /ítt'l/ *contr* it will ○ *It'll be so good to see you.*

I·to Ja·ku·chu /èetō ja kōō chōō/ (1716?–1800) Japanese artist. He is known for his meticulously detailed paintings of birds, flowers, and fish.

-itol *suffix* polyhydric alcohol ○ *inositol* [< -ITE[1] + -OL[1]]

its /its/ *adj* used to indicate that something belongs or relates to something ○ *The park changed its policy.* [Late 16C. < IT[1] + -'S (possessive)]

USAGE its or it's? The possessive form of the pronoun *it* is *its*, even though it does not have an apostrophe before the *s*. *The cat is licking its* [not *it's*] *paws.* ***It's*** is a contraction for *it is* or *it has*. *It's* [not *Its*] *going to rain tonight. It's* [not *Its*] *been rebuilt.*

it's /its/ *contr* **1.** it has ○ *It's begun to rain.* **2.** it is ○ *It's perfect.*

it·self /it sélf/ CORE MEANING: a reflexive pronoun used to refer back to the subject of a verb or for emphasis *pron* **1. USED TO REFER BACK TO SOMETHING** used to refer back to the subject of a verb when it is an object, animal, or abstract thing ○ *His ignorance finally revealed itself.* **2. USED TO EMPHASIZE SOMETHING** used to emphasize the thing that is referred to ○ *The house itself was cheap compared to the land.* **3. ITS NORMAL SELF** the way it usually feels or behaves ○ *The dog's not itself since we moved to the city.*

it·sy-bit·sy /ítsee bítsee/ *adj* extremely small (*informal*) [Alteration of LITTLE + BIT[1]]

it·ty-bit·ty /ítti-/ *adj* same as **itsy-bitsy** (*informal*) [Alteration of LITTLE + BIT[1]]

ITU *abbr* **1.** MED intensive therapy unit **2.** International Telecommunication Union

I·tur·bi·de /ee toor bee day/, **Agustín de** (1783–1824) Mexican army general and national leader. A leader of Mexico's independence movement, he declared himself emperor (1822–23), but was forced to abdicate and was executed.

ITV *abbr* instructional television

IU *abbr* **1.** IMMUNOL immunizing unit **2.** PHARM international unit

IUD *abbr* intrauterine device

-ium *suffix* chemical element, radical, or ion ○ *californium* [< modern Latin, alteration of Latin *-um*]

IV[1] *abbr* MED **1.** intravenous **2.** intravenously

IV[2] /ī veé/ (*plural* **IVs** or **IV's**) *n* **1.** the injection of quantities of a therapeutic fluid such as blood, plasma, saline, or glucose directly into somebody's vein at an adjustable rate **2.** the equipment used to administer an IV [Mid-20C. < INTRAVENOUS]

I·van III /ívən/, **grand duke of Moscow** (1440–1505) In the course of his reign (1462–1505), he declared himself sovereign of all Russia (1472) and greatly expanded his empire. He also ended Moscow's subjection to the Tatars (1480). Known as **Ivan the Great**

I·van IV, tsar of Russia (1530–84) The grand duke of Moscow, he became the first tsar of Russia (1547–84). He expanded his empire into the Urals and Siberia and instigated major internal reforms, but is mainly remembered in history for the extreme despotism of his last 20 years. Known as **Ivan the Terrible**

> "Did I ascend the throne by robbery or armed bloodshed? I was born to rule by the grace of God; and I do not even remember my father bequeathing the kingdom to me and blessing me—I grew up upon the throne."
> [Ivan IV, *Letter to Prince Kurbsky*; September 1577]

I·va·no·vo /i vaánəvə/ city in central Russia, situated approximately 145 mi./233 km northeast of Moscow. Population: 504,005 (1995).

I've /īv/ *contr* I have

-ive *suffix* tending to or performing ○ *illustrative* [Via French < Latin *-ivus*]

Ives /īvz/, **Charles E.** (1874–1954) US composer. He was an early proponent of modernism in works such as *Three Places in New England* (1903–14), combining and distorting fragments of marches, hymns, and popular songs. Full name **Ives, Charles Edward**

> "Music is one of the ways God has of beating in on man."
> [Charles E. Ives, "Epitaph for David Twitchell"; 1924]

Ives, James Merritt (1824–95) US lithographer. He was a partner in the New York lithographic firm Currier & Ives, famous for its colored prints of 19th-century social and domestic life.

IVF *abbr* MED in vitro fertilization

i·vied /íveed/ *adj* covered or overgrown with ivy

i·vo·ry /ívəree/ *n* (*plural* **-ries**) **1.** MATERIAL OF ELEPHANT'S TUSKS a hard cream-colored substance (**dentine**) that forms the tusks of animals such as the elephant, walrus, and sperm whale and was formerly used to carve small decorative objects **2.** SOMETHING MADE OF IVORY an object made of ivory, e.g., a figurine of a person or animal **3.** COLORS CREAMY WHITE a creamy white color, like that of an elephant's tusk ■ **i·vo·ries** *npl* **1.** PIANO KEYS the keys of a piano (*informal*) **2.** TEETH a person's teeth (*slang*) **3.** DICE dice for gambling or playing games (*slang*) [13C. Via Old French *ivurie* < Latin *ebur*] —**i·vo·ry** *adj*

i·vo·ry black *n* a black pigment made from burned ivory

I·vo·ry Coast /ívəree-/ English name for **Côte d'Ivoire**

i·vo·ry nut *n* the white nut of the ivory palm, whose kernel is used to make buttons or other small items

i·vo·ry palm, **i·vo·ry-nut palm** *n* a low-growing palm tree that yields ivory nuts. Native to: Brazil, Peru. Latin name: *Phytelephas macrocarpa*.

i·vo·ry tow·er *n* a state or situation in which somebody is sheltered from the practicalities or difficulties of ordinary life [Translation of French *tour d'ivoire*] —**i·vo·ry-tow·ered** *adj*

ivy

i·vy /ívee/ (*plural* **i·vies** or *same*) *n* **1.** EVERGREEN CLIMBING PLANT an evergreen climbing plant with woody stems and green, green-and-yellow, or green-and-white leaves that grows easily on walls or trees or along the ground. Genus: *Hedera*. **2.** PLANT SIMILAR TO IVY a climbing plant that resembles the true ivy, e.g., Boston ivy, Japanese ivy, poison ivy, or ground ivy **3.** *regional* MOUNTAIN LAUREL the mountain laurel, an evergreen bush with leathery poisonous leaves [Old English *īfig* < Germanic]

REGIONAL NOTE In the sense "mountain laurel," *ivy* is used mainly in Appalachia, from Virginia and Kentucky to the Carolinas and Georgia, but also in New England, notably Connecticut and Massachusetts.

I·vy League *n* a group of prestigious and respected universities in the northeastern United States consisting of Brown, Columbia, Cornell, Dartmouth, Harvard, Princeton, the University of Pennsylvania, and Yale [< the presumption that the universities' buildings were ivy-clad on account of their great age] —**I·vy League** *adj* —**I·vy Leagu·er** *n*

I·wo /eewō/ city in southwestern Nigeria, just north of Ibadan. Population: 353,000 (1995).

I·wo Ji·ma /eewə jeemə, eewō-/ largest of the Volcano Islands of Japan, in the western Pacific Ocean, east of Taiwan. It was the scene of heavy fighting during World War II when US Marines invaded and captured the Japanese air base there in February and March 1945. Area: 12 sq. mi./36 sq. km.

IWW *abbr* Industrial Workers of the World

Ix·i·on /íksee òn, íksee ən/ *n* in Greek mythology, a king of Thessaly who was bound to a perpetually turning wheel by Zeus as punishment for making sexual advances to Hera

Ix·ta·cal·co /eesta kálkō/ industrial city in south central Mexico, situated directly south of Mexico City. Population: 430,914 (2000).

ix·tle *n* TEXTILES another spelling of **istle**

I·yar /ee yaar/ *n* in the Jewish calendar, the second month of the religious year, lasting 29 days and falling about the same time as April to May. See table at **calendar** [Mid-18C. < Hebrew *iyyār*]

-ize *suffix* **1.** to cause to be, make ○ *formalize* **2.** to treat with or as ○ *oxidize* ○ *lionize* **3.** to become, become like ○ *crystallize* **4.** to engage in ○ *extemporize* [Via Old French *-iser* < Latin *-izare* < Greek *-izein*] —**-ization** *suffix*

I·zet·beg·o·vic /íz et béggəvich/, **Alija** (1925–2003) president of Bosnia and Herzegovina (1990–96), and Muslim representative in the three-member collective presidency of the republic of Bosnia and Herzegovina (1996–2000)

I·zhevsk /ee zhéfsk/ city and capital of Udmurtia, eastern Russia, located on the Izh River. Population: 787,340 (1995).

Iz·mir /iz meer/, **İz·mir** city and seaport in western Turkey. Population: 2,130,359 (1997). Former name **Smyrna**

Iz·mit /iz mít/, **İz·mit** city in northwestern Turkey, on the Gulf of Izmit. Population: 210,068 (1997).

iz·zat /ízzət/ *n S Asia* the honor or reputation of a person, organization, or institution [Mid-19C. < Persian and Urdu < Arabic *izza* "glory"]

Jj

j[1] /jay/ (*plural* **j's**), **J** (*plural* **J's** or **Js**) *n* **1.** the tenth letter of the English alphabet, representing a consonant sound **2.** a written representation of the letter "J"

j[2] *symbol* **1.** ELEC electric current density **2.** MATH the imaginary number $\sqrt{-1}$

j[3] *abbr* **1.** CARDS jack **2.** PHYS joule **3.** MEDIA journal **4.** LAW judge **5.** LAW justice

J[1] /jay/ (*plural* **J's** or **Js**) *n* **1.** something shaped like a letter "J" **2.** a marijuana cigarette (*slang*)

J[2] *symbol* ELEC electric current density

J[3] *symbol* PHYS joule

J. *abbr* **1.** CARDS jack **2.** MEDIA journal **3.** LAW judge **4.** LAW justice

JA *abbr* **1.** BANKING joint account **2.** LAW *also* **J.A.** Judge Advocate **3.** COMM Junior Achievement

Ja. *abbr* January

jab /jab/ *vti* (**jabbed, jab·bing, jabs**) **1. PUNCH SHARPLY** to make a short punching movement, or push something with a short punching movement **2. MAKE SHORT FAST PUNCH** to make a short fast punch at an opponent, e.g., in boxing ■ *n* **1. PUNCHING MOVEMENT** a short sharp punching movement **2. SHORT SHARP PUNCH** a short sharp punch, as used in boxing **3.** *UK* MED same as **shot**[1] (sense 15) (*informal*) [Early 19C. Variant of *job* "pierce, thrust," an imitation of the sound of a brief forcible action]

Jab·al·pur /jùbb'l poór/ city in central India. It is a major commercial center. Population: 1,117,200 (2001). Former name **Jubbulpore**

jab·ber /jábbər/ *vti* (**-bered, -ber·ing, -bers**) to talk, or say something, rapidly and excitedly, so that what is said is often incomprehensible ■ *n* rapid speech that is incomprehensible [15C. Probably an imitation of the sound] —**jab·ber·er** *n*

jab·ber·wock·y /jábbər wòkee/ *n* speech or writing that is meaningless or intended as humorous nonsense [Early 20C. < "Jabberwocky," nonsense poem by Lewis Carroll]

jabiru

jab·i·ru /jàbbə roó, jábbə roó/ (*plural* **-rus** or *same*) *n* **1.** a large tropical stork with white feathers and a naked head. Native to: Central and South America. Latin name: *Jabiru mycteria*. **2.** a large black-and-white stork. Native to: India to Australia. Latin name: *Ephippiorhynchus asiaticus*. [Late 18C. < Tupi-Guarani *jabirú* "swollen-necked"; < the large neck of the tropical storks]

Jab·i·ru /jábbirə/ town in the Northern Territory, Australia, inside Kakadu National Park. It is a mining town and tourist resort. Population: 1,171 (2002 estimate).

jab jab /jáb jab/ *n Carib* a devil as represented by somebody in costume at a carnival [Via French Creole < French *diable* "devil"]

jab·o·ran·di /jàbbə rándee/ (*plural* **-dis** or *same*) *n* **1.** dried leaves that yield the drug pilocarpine **2.** a bush of the rue family whose leaves yield pilocarpine. Native to: tropical America. Genus: *Pilocarpus*. [Early 17C. Via Portuguese < Tupi-Guarani *jaburandi* "somebody who spits"; from the increased saliva of those who chew the leaves]

ja·bot /zha bō, jábbō/ (*plural* **-bots**) *n* **1.** an edging of ruffles at the upper front of a blouse or dress **2.** formerly, a set of ruffles attached to the neckband and falling in tiers down the front of a man's shirt [Early 19C. < French, "bird's crop, shirt frill"]

ja·bot·i·ca·ba /jə bòtti kaábə/ (*plural* **-bas** or *same*) *n* a Brazilian evergreen tree of the myrtle family cultivated for its clusters of fruit. Latin name: *Myrciaria cauliflora*. [Early 17C. Via Portuguese < Tupi *iauoti'kaua*]

ja·cal /hə kaál/ *n Hispanic* in the southwestern United States and Mexico, a thatched hut that has walls made of stakes driven into the ground and daubed with mud [Mid-19C. Via Mexican Spanish < Nahuatl *xacalli*, contraction of *xamitl calli* "adobe house"]

jacamar

jac·a·mar /jákə maár/ (*plural* **-mars** or *same*) *n* a bird with a very long beak and iridescent blue or green feathers that lays its eggs in holes in earth banks. Native to: South and Central America. Family: Galbulidae. [Early 19C. < French]

jacana

ja·ca·na /zhaà kə naá/ (*plural* **-nas** or *same*) *n* a water bird with short rounded wings and tail and long toes that enable it to walk on floating plants. Male jacanas incubate the eggs and raise the young birds. Native to: tropics, subtropics. Family: Jacanidae. [Mid-18C. Via Portuguese < Tupi-Guarani *jasanã*]

jac·a·ran·da /jàkə rándə/ (*plural* **-das** or *same*) *n* **1.** a pleasant smelling wood. Use: cabinetry, veneers, carving. **2.** a widely cultivated tree or bush with ferny leaves and purple flowers that produces jacaranda. Native to: tropical America. Genus: *Jacaranda*. [Mid-18C. Via Portuguese < Tupi-Guarani *jakara'na*]

ja·cinth /jáyssinth/ *n* a reddish variety of zircon. Use: gems. [13C. < Old French *iacinte* or medieval Latin *iacintus*, alteration of Latin *hyacinthus* "blue stone"]

jack[1] /jak/ *n* **1. LIFTING DEVICE** a portable device that uses a mechanical or hydraulic lifting system to raise heavy objects, especially cars, a short distance **2. PLAYING CARD** a playing card ranking between a ten and a queen, with a picture of a young man on it **3. ELECTRICAL SOCKET** a female socket designed to receive a male plug in order to complete a circuit **4. OBJECT USED IN JACKS** a small, usually metal object with six points that is used in the game of jacks **5. TARGET BALL USED IN LAWN BOWLING** in lawn bowling, a small, usually white ball that players aim at **6. MALE ANIMAL** the male of various animals, especially the donkey **7.** same as **jackrabbit 8. TROPICAL FISH** a warm-water ocean fish that has a forked tail. Genus: *Caranx*. **9.** same as **applejack 10. FLAG ON SHIP** a small flag displayed to indicate the nationality of a ship **11.** NAUT **BRACE ON MAST** either one of a pair of wooden braces (**crosstrees**) at the head of a topgallant mast used to hold the mast stays away from the mast **12. LABORER** a laborer or somebody who does odd jobs (*usually used in combination*) **13. DEVICE THAT TURNS SPIT** a device that mechanically turns a spit over an open fire **14.** same as **money** (*slang*) **15. NOTHING AT ALL** anything or nothing at all (*slang*) ○ *He doesn't know jack about plumbing.* **16.** NAVY same as **jack-tar** (*dated informal*) ■ *v* (**jacked, jack·ing, jacks**) **1.** *vt* **RAISE SOMETHING WITH JACK** to raise a heavy object a short distance using a jack **2.** *vti* HUNTING **HUNT AT NIGHT WITH LIGHT** to hunt or fish for game at night using a jacklight as a lure **3.** *vt* CRIME **ROB SOMEBODY** to steal something, especially a car, from somebody (*slang*) **4.** *vt* **PRY SOMETHING OPEN** to open something by prying it apart (*slang*) [14C. < the name *Jack*, nickname for *John*, often implying "ordinary" or "small"] ◇ **jack shit** an offensive term meaning anything or nothing at all (*slang*)

jack around *v* **1.** *vi* to waste time, loaf, or act irresponsibly (*slang*) ○ *Stop jacking around and get to work!* **2.** *vt* to make things difficult for somebody, especially by teasing, bullying, or unfair treatment

jack in *or* **into** *vt* to connect somebody or something electronically to something (*slang*) ○ *We're jacked into the Internet.*

jack off *vti* a highly offensive term meaning to masturbate, or masturbate somebody (*taboo*)

jack up *v* **1.** *vt* **LIFT SOMETHING WITH JACK** to use a jack to lift a heavy object, especially a motor vehicle, off the ground **2.** *vt* **INCREASE AMOUNT OF SOMETHING** to increase something, especially a price or salary, often to an unreasonably high level **3.** *vti* **INJECT ILLEGAL DRUGS** to inject a drug, especially heroin, intravenously (*slang*)

jack[2] /jak/ *n* TREES another spelling of **jak**

Jack /jak/ *n* used to address a man who is a stranger ○ *Hey, Jack, what time is it?* [< the name *Jack*, nickname for *John*]

jack·al /ják'l/ (*plural* **-als** or *same*) *n* **1.** a wild animal resembling a dog, with long legs, large ears, and a bushy tail, that often hunts in packs and feeds on small game, fruit, and the carcasses of dead animals. Native to: Africa, South Asia. Genus: *Canis*. See illustration on next page **2.** somebody who works with accomplices to deceive people, especially to swindle them [Early 17C. Via Turkish < Persian *šagāl*]

jackal

jack·a·napes /jákə nàyps/ (*plural same*) *n* (*dated*) **1.** an impudent, self-centered person **2.** a child who behaves mischievously or impertinently [Early 16C. Originally *Jack Napes*, origin ?]

jack·ass /ják àss/ *n* **1.** a male donkey or ass **2.** an offensive term that deliberately insults somebody's intelligence (*slang insult*) [Early 18C. < the name *Jack*]

jack bean *n* a climbing plant of the pea family with purple clustering flowers. Use: forage. Native to: tropical America, southern United States. Latin name: *Canavalia ensiformis*.

jack·boot /ják bo͝ot/ *n* **1.** a sturdy long black leather boot that comes up to, or over, the knee, worn especially by the military in Nazi Germany **2.** military or other rule that is characterized by cruelty, oppression, or arbitrary aggression [Late 17C. Origin ?]

jack cheese *n* FOOD same as **Monterey Jack**

jack cre·val·le (*plural same* or **jack cre·val·les**) *n* a spiny-finned, game fish. Native to: western Florida coast. Latin name: *Caranx hippos*.

jack·daw /ják dàw/ *n* a medium-sized noisy bird of the crow family known for stealing things, especially shiny objects. Native to: Europe, Asia. Latin name: *Corvus monedula*. [Mid-16C. < the name *Jack*]

jacked /jakt/ *adj* highly stimulated and wide awake (*slang*) ○ *jacked on coffee*

jack·et /jákət/ *n* **1.** SHORT COAT a short, usually hip-length or waist-length coat, sometimes forming part of a suit **2.** PROTECTIVE CLOTHING something that is worn on the upper part of the body for protection or support ○ *a life jacket* **3.** same as **dust jacket 4.** RECORD COVER a decorated protective cover for a record or CD that usually lists the performers and contents **5.** POTATO SKIN the outer skin of an unpeeled cooked potato, especially a baked one **6.** FLOPPY DISK CASING the casing of a floppy disk **7.** FOLDER a strong envelope or folder for holding papers or documents **8.** BOILER COVER a cover or outer casing designed to insulate a boiler **9.** OUTER CASING OF PIPE an outer casing around a pipe that can be filled with steam or hot water to keep the contents of the pipe warm **10.** OUTER CASING OF BULLET an outer casing on some bullets and other types of ammunition ■ *vt* (**-et·ed, -et·ing, -ets**) PUT JACKET ON SOMEBODY OR SOMETHING to put a jacket on somebody or something such as a book or record [15C. < French *jaquet*, diminutive of Old French *jacque* "tunic" < *jacques* "peasant" < the name *Jacques*]

jack·fish /ják fish/ (*plural same* or **-fish·es**) *n* a pike, especially a young or small one [Late 16C. < JACK[1] implying "small"]

Jack Frost *n* a personification of frost, very cold wintry weather, or the effects that frost or cold weather can produce

jack·fruit /ják fro͞ot/ (*plural same* or **-fruits**) *n* **1.** FOOD same as **jak 2.** a tree that produces jaks and fine-grained yellowish wood. Native to: tropical Asia. Latin name: *Artocarpus heterophyllus*. [Mid-19C. < variant of JAK]

jack·ham·mer /ják hàmmər/ *n* a handheld power tool, usually powered by compressed air and used for splitting or drilling rock, or for breaking up paved areas [< JACK[1] implying "small"] —**jack·ham·mer** *vti*

Jack·ie-O /jàkee ṓ/ *adj* describes a fashion style associated with Jacqueline Kennedy Onassis ○ *a neat little Jackie-O pillbox*

jack-in-the-box (*plural* **jacks-in-the-box** or **jack-in-the-box·es**) *n* a child's toy consisting of a puppet on a spring inside a box. The puppet jumps out when a mechanism is triggered to open the lid.

jack-in-the-pul·pit *n* a woodland plant with tiny flowers in a thick spike surrounded by a sheath. Native to: eastern North America. Latin name: *Arisaema triphyllum*.

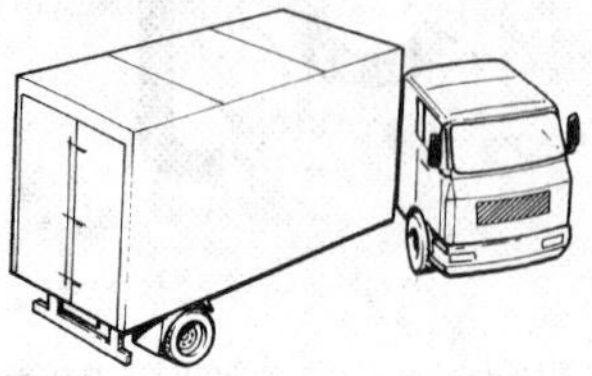

jackknife: a jackknifed truck

jack·knife /ják nīf/ *n* (*plural* **-knives** /-nīvz/) **1.** POCKETKNIFE a large pocketknife **2.** DIVE a dive in which the diver jumps, bends the body at the waist while keeping the legs together and straight, then straightens out to enter the water headfirst ■ *v* (**-knifed, -knif·ing, -knifes**) **1.** *vti* BEND DOUBLE to bend, or bend something, double or into an acute angle **2.** *vi* TRANSP LOSE CONTROL OF TRUCK TRAILER to lose control of the trailer of a tractor-trailer as a result of sudden braking or swerving at speed, or for the trailer to go out of control, so that it swings around violently and ends up at an acute angle to the cab ○ *The truck struck a patch of ice and jackknifed.* **3.** *vi* SWIMMING DO JACKKNIFE DIVE to perform a jackknife dive [Early 18C. Origin ?]

jack·leg /ják lèg/ *adj* **1.** *Southern US* INCOMPETENT incompetent or untrained **2.** *Southern US* UNSCRUPULOUS unscrupulous and untrustworthy **3.** TEMPORARY intended or made for temporary use and usually of inferior quality ■ *n Southern US* INCOMPETENT PERSON an incompetent or untrustworthy person [Mid-17C. < JACK[1] + *-leg*, as in BLACKLEG]

jack·light /ják līt/ *n* a light used for fishing or hunting at night, usually illegally ■ *vi* (**-lit** or **-light·ed, -lit** /-lit/, **-light·ing, -lights**) to hunt or fish at night using a jacklight [Late 19C. < JACK[1] "old type of oil lamp on a pole"]

jack mack·er·el *n* a torpedo-shaped fish of the jack family, with a body that is bluish green on top and silvery underneath. Native to: Pacific coastal waters. Latin name: *Trachurus symmetricus*.

jack-of-all-trades (*plural* **jacks-of-all-trades**) *n* somebody who can do many types of work

jack-o'-lan·tern *n* a lantern made from a hollowed-out pumpkin that has facial features cut out of it, used as a Halloween decoration

jack pine *n* a pine tree with short needles arranged in pairs and curving cones, whose timber is used for paper pulp. Native to: northern North America. Latin name: *Pinus banksiana*.

jack plane *n* a large carpentry plane used for rough planing of wood and other surfaces [< JACK[1] implying "instrument"]

jack·pot /ják pòt/ *n* **1.** an amount of money won in a competition or lottery or as a payout from a slot machine or other kind of gambling machine **2.** an accumulated stake in a poker game that can be competed for only by players holding a pair of jacks or a better hand [Late 19C. < a pair of jacks being the least required to compete for the pot in poker] ◇ **hit the jackpot** to achieve great success, especially financially

jack·rab·bit /ják ràbbit/, **jack rab·bit** *n* a large hare with long hind legs and extremely long ears. Native to: prairies of western North America. Genus: *Lepus*. [< JACKASS, because of its long ears]

jack·rab·bit start *n* a fast acceleration of a motor vehicle from a stationary position (*informal*)

Jack Rob·in·son [Origin ?] ◇ **before you can** *or* **could say Jack Robinson** *UK* without the slightest delay or hesitation (*informal*)

Jack Rus·sell, Jack Rus·sell ter·ri·er *n* a small terrier with short legs and a white coat with patchy markings in black, brown, or tan, or a combination of these colors [Early 20C. After John *(Jack) Russell* (1795–1883), British cleric]

jacks /jaks/ *n* a game involving picking up small metal or plastic pieces in sequence between bouncing or throwing and catching a ball (*takes a singular verb*) [Early 19C. Shortening of JACKSTONES]

jack·screw /ják skro͞o/ *n* MECH ENG same as **screw jack**

jack·shaft /ják shàft/ *n* a short shaft that transmits power from a motor or engine to a machine

jack·smelt /ják smèlt/ (*plural* **-smelts** or *same*) *n* a commercially important fish of the silverside family. Native to: northern American Pacific coast. Latin name: *Atherinopsis californiensis*.

Jack·son /jáks'n/ city and capital of Mississippi, situated on the Pearl River in the central part of the state. An important telecommunications, transportation, and commercial center, it is home to Jackson State University. Population: 180,881 (2002 estimate).

Library of Congress

Andrew Jackson

Jack·son, Andrew (1767–1845) 7th president of the United States. His army defeated the British at New Orleans during the War of 1812. As Democratic president (1829–37), he opposed the Bank of America and greatly strengthened the presidency. Known as **Old Hickory**. See table at **president**

> "There are no necessary evils in government. Its evils exist only in its abuses."
> [Andrew Jackson, *Veto of the Bank Bill*; July 10, 1832]

Jack·son, Glenda (*b.* 1936) British actor and politician. She played in numerous Royal Shakespeare Company productions and in movies, winning two Academy Awards, before becoming a Labour Member of Parliament (1992).

> "My mother polishes them to an inch of their lives until the metal shows. That sums up the Academy Awards—all glitter on the outside and base metal coming through. Nice presents for a day. But they don't make you any better."
> [Glenda Jackson, *People*; March 18, 1985]

Jack·son, Jesse (*b.* 1941) US civil rights leader, minister, and politician. He was closely associated with civil rights leader Martin Luther King and the Southern Christian Leadership Conference in the 1960s, and later twice ran for the Democratic presidential nomination (1984, 1988) at the head of his own political organization, the Rainbow Coalition. Full name **Jackson, Jesse Louis**

> "We are all precious in God's sight—the real rainbow coalition."
> [Jesse Jackson, *Speech to the Democratic National Convention*; July 19, 1988]

> "The great temptation in these difficult days of racial polarization and economic injustice is to make political arguments black and white and miss the moral imperative of wrong and right. Vanity asks, 'Is it popular?' Politics asks 'Will it win?' Morality and conscience ask, 'Is it right?'"
> [Jesse Jackson, *Speech to the Democratic National Convention*; July 14, 1992]

Jack·son, Mahalia (1911–72) US singer. She helped to popularize gospel music during the 1940s and 1950s.

> "Blues are the songs of despair, but gospel songs are the songs of hope."
> [Mahalia Jackson, *Movin' On Up*; 1966]

Jack·son, Robert Houghwout (1892–1954) US Supreme Court associate justice (1941–54). He was also chief US prosecutor at the Nuremberg war crimes trials (1945–46).

Library of Congress

Stonewall Jackson

Jack·son, Stonewall (1824–63) US Confederate army general. He was one of the most successful Confederate commanders during the Civil War. Born **Jackson, Thomas Jonathan**

> "Always mystify, mislead, and surprise the enemy, if possible."
> [Stonewall Jackson, *Motto*; 1860s]

> "Let us cross over the river, and rest under the trees."
> [Stonewall Jackson, last words after having been shot accidentally by his own troops earlier in the month; May 10, 1863]

Jack·son Day *n* a legal holiday celebrated in Louisiana marking Andrew Jackson's victory over the British in the Battle of New Orleans in 1815. Date: January 8.

Jack·son Hole /jáksən hōl/ valley in northwestern Wyoming, east of the Teton Range and extending into Grand Teton National Park. Length: 50 mi./80 km.

Jack·so·ni·an /jak sṓnee ən/ *adj* relating to Andrew Jackson or to his presidential term or policies, especially his advocacy of greater public involvement in politics —**Jack·so·ni·an** *n* —**Jack·so·ni·an·ism** *n*

Jack·son·ville /jáks'n vil/ city in northeastern Florida. It is a major commercial and cultural center. Population: 762,461 (2002 estimate).

jack·stay /ják stày/ *n* **1.** a rod attached to a horizontal beam (**yard**) on a mast, used for securing a sail **2.** a support for the ring (**parrel**) that holds a boom to a mast

jack·stone /ják stōn/ *n* a small piece of metal or plastic used in the game of jacks

jack·stones /ják stōnz/ *n* LEISURE same as **jacks** (*takes a singular verb*) [Early 19C. < JACK[1] implying "small"]

jack·straw /ják stràw/ *n* a small thin stick used in the game of jackstraws [Early 19C. < JACK[1] implying "small"]

jack·straws /ják stràwz/ *n* a game that involves trying to remove small thin sticks from a pile one at a time without disturbing the rest of the pile (*takes a singular verb*)

jack-tar *n* same as **sailor** (sense 1) (*dated informal*) [< the name *Jack* implying "Everyman" + TAR[2] "sailor"]

Jack the Rip·per /jàk t͟hə ríppər/ (*fl* 1880s) British murderer. He was the notorious unknown killer of at least five prostitutes in London's East End between August and November 1888.

jack-up, jack-up rig *n* an offshore oil rig with a floating hull and retractable legs that can be lowered to the seabed for support

Ja·cob /jáykəb/ *n* in the Bible, the second son of Isaac and Rebekah, and the grandson of Abraham. He tricked his older brother, Esau, out of his father's blessing, and had a vision of ascent into heaven that came to be called "Jacob's ladder" (Genesis 25–35).

Jac·o·be·an /jàkə beé ən, jàykə-/ *adj* **1.** OF JAMES I relating to King James I or to the period of his English reign, from 1603 to 1625 **2.** OF ARTISTIC STYLE in the style of furniture, architecture, or drama fashionable during the reign of King James I ■ *n* CONTEMPORARY OF JAMES I somebody, especially a prominent person, who lived during the reign of King James I of England [Late 18C. < ecclesiastical Latin *Jacobus* "James"]

Jac·o·be·an lil·y *n* a cultivated plant of the amaryllis family. Flowers: bright red. Native to: Mexico. Latin name: *Sprekelia formosissima*. [After St. JAMES[1]]

Jac·o·bin /jákəbin/ *n* **1.** HIST FRENCH REVOLUTIONARY EXTREMIST a member of a group of left-wing extremists founded during the French Revolution. In 1793, they overthrew the more moderate republicans, the Girondists, and this allowed Robespierre, the leader of the group, to adopt revolutionary measures and begin the Reign of Terror. **2.** POL LEFT-WING EXTREMIST a political radical, especially one who holds extreme left-wing views **3.** CHR FRIAR a French Dominican friar ■ *adj* HIST OF FRENCH JACOBINS relating to the Jacobins of the French Revolution or to their policies [14C. < Old French < ecclesiastical Latin *Jacobus*; because the Jacobin friars were established at the church of St. Jacques in Paris] —**Jac·o·bin·i·cal** /jàkə bínnik'l/ *adj* —**Jac·o·bin·ism** *n*

Jac·o·bite /jákə bìt/ *n* **1.** a supporter of King James II of England and his descendants in the Stuart claim to the British throne **2.** a member of any of the Monophysite churches, especially of Syria [Late 17C. < ecclesiastical Latin *Jacobus* "James"] —**Jac·o·bite** *adj* —**Jac·o·bit·ism** *n*

Ja·cob·sen /jáykəbssən/, **Josephine** (1908–2003) Canadian-born US poet. She served as poetry consultant to the Library of Congress from 1971 to 1973 and published many volumes of poetry, including *The Shade-Seller* (1974).

Ja·cob's lad·der *n* **1.** a wild or garden plant with leaves divided into several leaflets in an arrangement similar to a ladder. Flowers: blue, white. Native to: North America. Genus: *Polemonium*. **2.** a ladder, used especially on ships, whose rungs are held together by ropes or chains, thus allowing it to be rolled up and stored in a small space [< Jacob's vision of a ladder reaching to heaven in the Bible (Genesis 28:12)]

Ja·cob's staff *n* a medieval instrument for measuring distance [< the pilgrim's staff that is a symbol of St. James (ecclesiastical Latin *Jacobus*), or the staff of Jacob in the Bible (Genesis 30:10)]

jac·o·net /jákə nèt/ *n* a cotton fabric that is like muslin but slightly heavier. Use: clothing, bandages. [Mid-18C. Anglicization of *Jagannāth(purī)* in India]

jac·quard /ják aàrd, jə kaárd/ *n* **1.** PATTERNED MATERIAL a fabric that has been woven with an intricate pattern **2.** WEAVING TECHNIQUE a technique for producing intricate patterns in material by means of punched cards that give instructions to use or withhold various colors of thread **3.** LOOM ATTACHMENT a loom attachment with punched cards that makes jacquard patterns **4.** same as **jacquard loom** [Mid-19C. After J. M. JACQUARD]

Jac·quard /jə kaárd/, **Joseph Marie** (1752–1834) French inventor. His invention of the jacquard loom (1801–08), the first mechanical loom for weaving complex patterns, was an inspiration for modern computer programming.

jac·quard loom *n* a loom with an attachment for making jacquard patterns

Jacques-Car·tier /z͟haàk kaàr tyáy/ river in southern Quebec, Canada that flows south into the St. Lawrence River just south of Quebec City. Length: 70 mi./113 km.

Jacques-Car·tier, Mount mountain in Quebec, Canada, on the northern tip of the Gaspé Peninsula. It is Quebec's second highest point. Height: 4,160 ft./1,268 m.

jac·ti·ta·tion /jàktə táysh'n/ *n* **1.** MED UNCONTROLLED THRASHING violent and uncontrollable movements of the body and limbs, usually brought on by extremely high temperature, or occasionally by psychiatric disorders **2.** HARMFUL LIE in law, a false boast or claim, especially one that is intended to harm another **3.** BOASTING the act of boasting or exaggerating (*literary*) [Mid-17C. < medieval Latin *jactitation-* < Latin *jactitare* "bring forward in public, boast" < *jacere* "throw"]

Ja·cuz·zi /jə koózee/ *tdmk* a trademark for a whirlpool bath with a system of underwater jets that deliver water under pressure in order to massage and invigorate the body

jade[1] /jayd/ *n* **1.** a semiprecious stone made of either nephrite or jadeite, varying in color from a deep green through yellow and brown to white. Use: ornaments, jewelry. **2.** objects made of jade, collectively ○ *a collector of jade* **3.** COLORS same as **jade green** [Late 16C. Via French *l'ejade* < Spanish *piedra de ijada* "stone of the flanks" < Latin *ilia* "flanks"] —**jade** *adj*

ORIGIN Despite the close association of ***jade*** with China and Japan, its name has no Asian connections. A derivative of Latin *ilia* "flanks," the part of the body where the kidneys are situated, passed into Spanish as *ijada*. It was thought that jade could cure pain in the renal area, so the Spanish called it *piedra de ijada*, literally "stone of the flanks," eventually reduced to *ijada*. In French it became *ejade*. Subsequently *l'ejade* "the jade" became *le jade*, from which English ***jade*** is derived. (The alternative name for one of the types of ***jade***, *nephrite*, is based on the same idea: it comes from Greek *nephros* "kidney.")

jade[2] /jayd/ *n* (*archaic*) **1.** an old horse, especially one that is worn out through overwork **2.** an offensive term for a woman that deliberately insults her temperament or morality [14C. Origin ?]

jad·ed /jáydəd/ *adj* **1.** no longer interested in something, often because of having been overexposed to it **2.** exhausted, especially through overwork —**jad·ed·ly** *adv* —**jad·ed·ness** *n*

jade green *n* a pale milky green color, like that of some types of jade —**jade-green** *adj*

jade·ite /jáy dìt/ *n* a usually greenish pyroxene mineral consisting of sodium aluminum silicate. Source: metamorphic rocks. Use: ornaments, jewelry. —**ja·dit·ic** /jay díttik/ *adj*

jade plant *n* a plant with thick fleshy leaves the color of jade, popular as a houseplant. Native to: southern Africa, Asia. Latin name: *Crassula argentea*.

j'a·doube /z͟ha doób, z͟haa-/ *interj* an expression used by a chess player who is about to adjust a piece on the board, to ensure that this will not be counted as an official move [Early 19C. < French, "I dub" (touch on the shoulder)]

jae·ger /yáygər/ *n* **1.** a brownish or grayish predatory seabird with narrow wings. Native to: northern Pacific and Atlantic. Genus: *Stercorarius*. **2.** a hunter, especially in Germany and Switzerland [Mid-19C. < German *Jäger* "huntsman" < *jagen* "hunt, pursue"]

Ja·én /ha áyn/ capital city of Jaén Province in southern Spain. It is an industrial center. Population: 110,467 (2002).

Jaff·na /jaáfnə/ port and capital city of Northern Province, in northern Sri Lanka. Population: 129,000 (1990 estimate).

jag[1] /jag/ *n* JAGGED PROJECTION a sharp projection, especially of rock ■ *v* (**jag·ged, jag·ging, jags**) **1.** *vt* CUT SOMETHING UNEVENLY to cut notches in something, or cut something unevenly **2.** *vi* ZIGZAG to zigzag or move in jerks (*informal*) [14C. Origin ?]

jag[2] /jag/ *n* **1.** PERIOD OF INTOXICATION a period of intoxication by drugs or alcohol (*informal*) **2.** DRUNKEN STATE the state of being intoxicated from drugs or alcohol (*informal*) **3.** BINGE a period of time spent doing something in an uncontrolled or excessive way (*informal*) ○ *a crying jag* **4.** *US regional, Can* QUANTITY OF GRAIN OR WOOD the quantity of grain or wood transported in one delivery [Late 16C. Origin ?]

J.A.G., JAG *abbr* LAW, MIL Judge Advocate General

Ja·gan /yaágən/, **Cheddi** (1918–97) Guyanan politician. As the first prime minister of British Guiana (1961–69), he was instrumental in gaining Guyana's independence (1966), and later served as president (1992–97).

Ja·gan·nath /júggə naàt, -nàwt/, **Jag·ga·nath, Ja·gan·na·tha** /júggə naáthə/ *n* HINDUISM same as **Juggernaut** [Mid-17C. Earlier form of JUGGERNAUT]

Jag·de·o /jágdee ō/, **Bharrat** (*b.* 1964) president of Guyana (1999–). A member of the Progressive People's Party, he also served as the country's finance minister (1995–99).

Jag·ga·nath *n* HINDUISM another spelling of **Jagannath**

jag·ged /jággəd/ *adj* **1.** having sharp protruding parts or points ○ *jagged peaks of the distant mountains* **2.** having rough and uneven edges or surfaces ○ *a hastily drawn, jagged portrait* —**jag·ged·ly** *adv* —**jag·ged·ness** *n*

Mick Jagger

Jag·ger /jággər/, **Mick** (*b.* 1943) British rock musician and songwriter. He founded, with Keith Richards, the Rolling Stones, and wrote many of their hits, including "Satisfaction" (1965). He was knighted in 2003. Full name **Jagger, Sir Michael Phillip**

> "The only true performance is the one which attains madness."
> [Mick Jagger. Quoted in *The Wit and Wisdom of Rock and Roll*, Maxim Jabukowski (ed.); 1983]

jag·ger·y /jággəree/ *n* unrefined brown sugar, made from sugar cane or the sap of the date palm [Late 16C. Via Portuguese < Sanskrit *śarkarā* "sugar"]

jag·gies /jággeez/ *npl* on a computer screen, the jagged or stepped edges of curves or diagonal lines caused by the image being formed of tiny rectangular pixels

jag·gy /jággee/ (**-gi·er, -gi·est**) *adj* same as **jagged** (*informal*)

ja·gir /jaá geér/ *n S Asia* a district where public revenues or payments-in-kind have been granted to a person or group [Early 17C. Via Urdu < Persian *jāgīr* < *jā* "place" + *gīr* "holding"]

jaguar

jag·uar /jág waar/ *n* a large cat related to the leopard but with a shorter tail and black spots inside black rings on its tawny coat. Native to: southern North America, Central America, northern South America. Latin name: *Panthera onca*. [Early 17C. Via Portuguese < Tupi *jaguara*, Guarani *yaguará* "carnivorous animal"]

jag·ua·run·di /jàggwə rúndee, jaàgwə-/, **jag·ua·ron·di** /-róndee/ *n* a small slender cat that has a brownish, grayish, or reddish coat and small ears. Native to: Central and South America, occasionally southwestern United States. Latin name: *Felis yagouaroundi*. [Mid-19C. < Portuguese < *jaguar* (see JAGUAR) + Tupi-Guarani *undi* "dark"]

Jah /jaa/ *n* God, especially in Rastafarianism [Mid-16C. < Hebrew *Yāh*, shortening of *Yahweh* "Jehovah"]

Jah·veh, Jah·weh *n* RELIG another spelling of **Yahweh**

jai a·lai /hī́ lī, hī́ ə lī/ *n* a Latin American game similar to handball, played with baskets fastened to the arm for catching and throwing the ball [Early 20C. < Spanish < Basque *jai* "festival" + *alai* "merry"]

jail /jayl/ *n* **1.** PLACE WHERE CRIMINALS ARE KEPT a secure place for keeping people found guilty of minor crimes or awaiting legal judgment **2.** LIFE AS PRISONER the state of being kept in a jail ○ *sentenced to three years' jail* ■ *vt* (**jailed, jail·ing, jails**) **1.** SEND SOMEBODY TO JAIL to sentence somebody to spend time in a jail ○ *The judge jailed her for three months.* **2.** LOCK SOMEBODY IN JAIL to keep somebody in a jail or other secure place ○ *prisoners who were jailed in a dungeon* [13C. Via Old French *jaiole* < Latin *caveola*, diminutive of *cavea* "cage"]

jail·bait /jáyl bàyt/ *n* an offensive term for a minor under the age of consent who is sexually desirable to somebody older (*slang*)

jail·bird /jáyl bùrd/ *n* a current or former prisoner, especially somebody with more than one experience of prison (*slang*)

jail·break /jáyl bràyk/ *n* a forceful escape from jail or prison

jail·er /jáylər/, **jail·or** *n* a supervisor or employee who is in charge of prisoners in a jail

jail·house /jáyl hòwss/ *n* same as **jail** *n* (sense 1) (*informal*)

jail·house law·yer *n* a prisoner who has studied law while serving time in order to represent himself or herself in legal proceedings or assist other prisoners with their legal defense

jail·or *n* another spelling of **jailer**

Jain /jīn/, **Jai·na** /jī́nə/ *n* a believer in or follower of Jainism [Late 18C. < Hindi < Sanskrit *jaina* "of a conqueror"]

Jain·ism /jī́n ìzzəm/ *n* an ancient branch of Hinduism that rejects the notion of a supreme being and advocates a deep respect for all living things —**Jain·ist** *adj*

Jai·pur /jī poŏr/ capital city of Rajasthan State, northern India. It is a major commercial, manufacturing, and tourist center. Population: 2,324,319 (2001).

jak /jak/, **jack** *n* a large greenish bulbous fruit produced by the jackfruit tree. It can weigh up to 60 lb./27 kg and has highly nutritious seeds. [Late 16C. Via Portuguese *jaca* < Malayalam *cakka*]

Ja·kar·ta /jə kaártə/ capital and largest city of Indonesia, located in the center of the country, on the northwestern coast of the island of Java. Population: 8,389,443 (2000 estimate). Former name **Batavia**

jake leg /jáyk-/ *n* permanent inability to move, caused by drinking contaminated or improperly distilled alcoholic drink [< *jake* "alcoholic drink made from Jamaica ginger," contraction of JAMAICA]

jakes /jayks/ (*plural* **jakes·es** or *same*) *n* an outhouse [Mid-16C. Origin ?]

Ja·lal·a·bad /jə laálə baád/, **Ja·lāl·ā·bād** city in eastern Afghanistan, on the Kabul River. Population: 60,000 (1993).

Ja·lan·dhar ♦ **Jullundur**

jal·ap /jálləp, jaáləp/ *n* a twining plant of the convolvulus family, the dried tubers of which have a purgative effect. Native to: Mexico. Latin name: *Ipomoea purga*. [Mid-17C. Via French < abbreviation of Spanish *purga de Jalapa*, after *Jalapa*, Mexican city]

ja·la·pe·ño /haàlə páynyō/ (*plural* **-ños**), **ja·la·pe·ño pep·per** *n* a small hot pepper that is picked when green and is used extensively in Mexican cooking. Latin name: *Capsicum annuum*. [Mid-20C. < Mexican Spanish]

ja·le·bi /jə láybee/ (*plural* **-bis**) *n* in Indian cuisine, a dessert made of batter deep-fried in a coil shape and served in syrup [Mid-19C. < Hindi]

Ja·lis·co /hə leéskō/ state in western Mexico. Capital: Guadalajara. Population: 6,322,002 (2000). Area: 30,266 sq. mi./78,390 sq. km.

ja·lop·y /jə lóppee/ (*plural* **-ies**) *n* a rickety or battered old car (*dated informal*) [Early 20C. Origin ?]

jalousie

jal·ou·sie /jálləssee/ *n* a shutter or window covering consisting of a set of angled parallel slats that can be opened to various degrees to control the amount of light or air passing through [Mid-18C. < French, literally "jealousy"]

jam[1] /jam/ *v* (**jammed, jam·ming, jams**) **1.** *vt* PUSH SOMETHING IN FORCIBLY to push something into a tight space with force ○ *jammed the clothes into the hamper* **2.** *vt* FILL SOMETHING UP to fill a place with people or things pressed closely together ○ *The fans jammed the streets to see their heroes.* ○ *jammed the refrigerator with delicacies* **3.** *vti* STOP SOMETHING WORKING to cause a piece of machinery or equipment to stick or stop working, or to become stuck or stop working ○ *The photocopier jammed.* **4.** *vt* BLOCK SOMETHING UP to block up something that functions as an exit, passage, or means of escape ○ *Leaves had jammed the gutters.* **5.** *vt* INTERFERE WITH BROADCASTING SIGNALS to block a radio or TV signal, usually by broadcasting other signals on the same frequency **6.** *vt* OVERWHELM SWITCHBOARD to overwhelm a switchboard with telephone calls **7.** *vt* PUT ON BRAKES HARD to apply the brakes of a vehicle suddenly and hard ○ *jammed on the brakes* **8.** *vt* RECORDING MAKE TAPE IMPOSSIBLE TO COPY to put a blocking device on something, especially a prerecorded videotape, in order to prevent it from being copied **9.** *vt* CRUSH PART OF BODY to injure a part of the body, especially by squeezing or mashing it ○ *I jammed my finger in the door.* **10.** *vi* MUSIC IMPROVISE MUSIC TOGETHER to play music, especially jazz, rock, or pop, in an improvised way, often in a group ■ *n* **1.** same as **traffic jam 2.** DIFFICULT SITUATION a difficult, awkward, or embarrassing situation (*informal*) ○ *I can lend you some money if you're in a jam.* **3.** STOPPAGE an instance of something being blocked or prevented from functioning ○ *a paper jam in the printer* **4.** SIGNAL BLOCKAGE a blockage of radio or television signals [Early 18C. Origin ?] —**jam·mer** *n*

jam[2] /jam/ *n* a spread made from fruit boiled with sugar [Mid-18C. Origin ?]

Jam. *abbr* **1.** Jamaica **2.** BIBLE James

JAMA *abbr* Journal of the American Medical Association

jam·a·dar /júmmə daár/, **jem·a·dar** /jémmə daar/ *n S Asia* **1.** a junior officer in the Indian police force **2.** a minor official [Mid-18C. Via Urdu < Persian < Arabic *jamā'at* "muster" + Persian *dār* "holding, holder"]

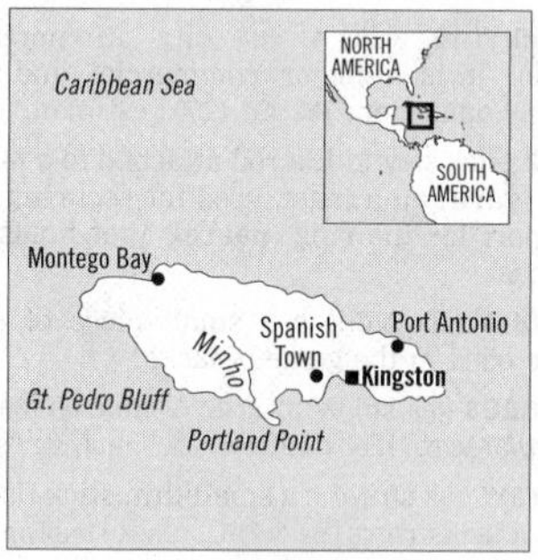

Jamaica

Ja·mai·ca /jə máykə/ island country situated south of Cuba in the northern Caribbean Sea. It is the third largest island of the Greater Antilles. It became an independent member of the British Commonwealth in 1962. Language: English. Currency: Jamaican dollar. Capital: Kingston. Population: 2,695,867 (2003). Area: 4,244 sq. mi./10,991 sq. km. —**Ja·mai·can** *n, adj*

Ja·mai·ca pep·per *n* FOOD same as **allspice** (sense 1)

Ja·mai·ca rum *n* a slowly fermented rum that has a dark color and a strong flavor

jamb /jam/, **jambe** *n* **1.** either of the upright parts of a door or window frame or the sides of a fireplace **2.** the inside vertical face of an opening [14C. Via Italian *gamba* or Old French *jambe* "leg" < Greek *kampē* "bend, joint"]

jam·ba·lay·a /jùmbə lī́ ə/ *n* a Creole dish of rice with a mixture of fish and meat such as shrimp, chicken, ham, and spicy sausage [Late 19C. Via Louisiana French < Provençal *jambalaia* "stewed mixture of rice and fowl"]

jambe *n* CONSTR another spelling of **jamb**

Jam·bi /jaámbee/ city and port in western Indonesia,

on the island of Sumatra. It is the capital of Jambi Province. Population: 427,095 (1997).

jam·bo·ree /jàmbə rée/ *n* **1.** a large-scale planned celebration with various events and entertainments **2.** a large gathering of members of the Boy Scouts, often on an international scale [Mid-19C. Origin ?]

James[1] /jaymz/ *n* a book of the Bible, originally a letter and traditionally attributed to James, a brother of Jesus Christ. See table at **Bible**

James[2] /jaymz/ river in western Virginia, formed at Iron Gate by the joining of the Cowpasture and Jackson rivers, that flows into the Chesapeake Bay. Length: 340 mi./547 km.

James[1], **St.** (*fl* A.D. 1st century) One of the 12 apostles of Jesus Christ, he was a member of the inner circle of Jesus Christ's disciples. He was the son of Zebedee and Salome and the brother of St. John. (Matthew 4:21). Known as **St. James the Great**

James[2], **St.** (*fl* A.D. 1st century) He was a relative of Jesus Christ, and is identified in the Bible as a leader of the early Christian Church in Jerusalem. (Mark 6:3). Known as **St. James the Just**

James[3], **St.** (*d.* A.D. 62?) One of the 12 apostles of Jesus Christ, he was the son of Alphaeus. (Matthew 10:3). Known as **St. James the Less**

James I[1] (1208–76) king of Aragón. During his reign (1213–76), he captured the Balearic Islands (1229–35) and Valencia (1238) from the Moors. Known as **James the Conqueror**

James I[2] (1566–1625) king of England, Scotland, and Ireland. He was king of Scotland as James VI (1567–1625), and succeeded to the English throne in 1603. He authorized the King James Bible.

> "The state of monarchy is the supremest thing upon earth: for kings are not only god's lieutenants upon earth, and sit upon God's throne, but even by God himself they are called gods."
> [James I, *Speech to the British Parliament*; March 21, 1609]

James II (1633–1701) king of England, Scotland, and Ireland. His Roman Catholicism occasioned political conflict before and during his reign (1685–88), and he was deposed in the Revolution of 1688–89 by his nephew and son-in-law William III.

James, Henry (1843–1916) US-born writer. He described the collision of American innocence and European worldliness in novels such as *The Portrait of a Lady* (1881) and *The Golden Bowl* (1904). He was the brother of William James. See Cultural note at **ambassador, portrait**

> "The Story is just the spoiled child of art."
> [Henry James, *The Ambassadors*; 1903]

> "Experience is never limited, and it is never complete; it is an immense sensibility, a kind of huge spider web of the finest silken threads suspended in the chamber of consciousness, and catching every airborne particle in its tissue."
> [Henry James, "The Art of Fiction," *Partial Portraits*; 1888]

James, Jesse (1847–82) US outlaw. He robbed banks and trains between Missouri and Texas, and was killed in a shootout. Full name **James, Jesse Woodson**

P. D. James

James, P. D., Baroness James of Holland Park (*b.* 1920) British novelist. Her bestselling crime novels include *The Black Tower* (1975) and *Original Sin* (1994). Full name **James, Phyllis Dorothy**

> "I had an interest in death from an early age. It fascinated me. When I heard 'Humpty Dumpty sat on a wall,' I thought, 'Did he fall or was he pushed?'"
> [P. D. James, *Paris Review*; 1995]

> "What the detective story is about is not murder but the restoration of order."
> [P. D. James, *Face*; December 12, 1986]

James, William (1842–1910) US philosopher and psychologist. The brother of Henry James, he developed the philosophy of pragmatism, and encouraged an empirical approach to psychology.

> "Man, biologically considered, and whatever else he may be into the bargain, is simply the most formidable of all the beasts of prey, and, indeed, the only one that preys systematically on its own species."
> [William James, *Atlantic Monthly*; December 1904]

James Bay southern extension of Hudson Bay, between western Quebec and northeastern Ontario, Canada. Area: 12,355 sq. mi./32,000 sq. km.

James·i·an /jáymzee ən/ *adj* relating to or characteristic of Henry James or his literary style, e.g., in containing long complex sentences, or describing emotional states and relationships in minute detail

James·town /jáymz tòwn/ **1.** city in southwestern New York, east of Lake Chautauqua and southwest of Buffalo. Population: 31,033 (2002 estimate). **2.** former village in southeastern Virginia, established on May 14, 1607 by the London Company as the first permanent English settlement in America

James·town Is·land island, once a peninsula, in eastern Virginia, on the James River. It was the site of Jamestown village.

James VI ♦ **James I**[2]

jam·mies /jámmeez/ *npl* same as **pajamas**[2] (sense 1) (*informal; often used by or to children*) [Late 20C. Shortening and alteration]

jam·min' /jámmin/ *adj* excellent or first-rate (*slang*)

Jam·mu and Kash·mir /jùmmoo-/ state in northern India. It is the section of the disputed territory of Kashmir that is under Indian administration. Capital: Srinagar. Population: 10,069,917 (2001). Area: 39,145 sq. mi./101,387 sq. km.

jam-packed *adj* full to capacity or very crowded (*informal*) ○ *The square was jam-packed with tourists.*

jam ses·sion *n* a period of time spent making improvised music, especially jazz, rock, or pop music, as practice, for fun, or to experiment with new songs or techniques

Jam·shed·pur /jaàm shed póor/ city in eastern India, on the Subarnarekha River, in Bihar State. Population: 1,101,804 (2001).

Jan. *abbr* CALENDAR January

Ja·ná·ček /yaànə chèk/, **Leoš** (1854–1928) Czech composer. His music was influenced by traditional Czech folk songs, and includes the operas *Jenufa* (1904) and *The Cunning Little Vixen* (1924).

Jane Doe /jàyn dṓ/ *n* **1.** a woman or girl, especially one who is involved in legal proceedings and whose identity is not known or is being protected **2.** an average woman affected by everyday events [After JOHN DOE]

Jane·ite /jáyn ìt/ *n* an expert on or admirer of the life and works of the English novelist, Jane Austen [Late 19C. < the name *Jane*]

Janes·ville /jáynz vìl/ city in southern Wisconsin. It is the seat of Rock County. Population: 60,921 (2002 estimate).

jan·gle /jáng g'l/ *vti* (**-gled, -gling, -gles**) **1.** MAKE METALLIC SOUND to make a harsh metallic noise, or cause something made of metal to make such a noise ○ *heard his keys jangling* **2.** IRRITATE SOMEBODY'S NERVES to put somebody's nerves on edge, or be tense and on edge ○ *The shock jangled her nerves.* ■ *n* **1.** METALLIC SOUND a harsh metallic noise **2.** ARGUMENT a disagreement or quarrel (*dated*) [13C. < Old French *jangler* "to chatter"] —**jan·gly** *adj*

Jang·lish /jáng glísh/ *n* LANG same as **Japlish** [Late 20C. Blend of JAPANESE + ENGLISH] —**Jang·lish** *adj*

jan·is·sar·y /jánnə sèrree/ (*plural* **-ies**), **jan·i·zar·y** /-zèrree/ *n* **1.** a member of the Turkish sultan's elite personal guard from the 14th century until 1826. Janissaries were recruited from Christians in the Balkans and disbanded as part of 19th-century reforms. **2.** a loyal follower or supporter [Early 16C. Via French *janissaire* < Turkish *yeniçeri* "new troops"]

jan·i·tor /jánnətər/ *n N Am, Scotland* somebody whose job is to look after the cleaning and maintenance of a building, especially a school or an apartment building [Mid-16C. < Latin, "door person" < *janua* "door"] —**jan·i·to·ri·al** /jànnə táwree əl/ *adj*

ja·ni·tor's in·sur·ance *n* INSUR same as **corporate-owned life insurance** (*slang*)

jan·i·zar·y *n* same as **janissary**

Jan May·en /yaan mī́ ən/ uninhabited island of Norway, lying between Norway and Greenland in the Arctic Ocean. Area: 144 mi./373 km. Length: 39 mi./63 km.

Jan·sen /jánssən/, **Cornelis** (1585–1638) Flemish theologian. He was the founder of the Roman Catholic reform movement known as Jansenism. His posthumous work *Augustinus* (1640) was condemned as heretical.

Jan·sen·ism /jánssən ìzzəm/ *n* a Roman Catholic reform movement of the 17th and 18th centuries based on the theological views of Cornelis Jansen, who maintained that there can be no good act without divine will or the grace of God —**Jan·sen·ist** *n*

jan·sky /jánskee/ (*plural* **-skys**) *n* a unit used to indicate the strength of radio sources in astronomy, equal to 10^{-26} watts per square meter per hertz. Symbol **Jy** [Mid-20C. After Karl JANSKY]

Jan·sky /jánskee/, **Karl** (1905–50) US engineer. He discovered radio waves in outer space (1931), thus laying the foundation of radio astronomy. Full name **Jansky, Karl Guthe**

Jan·u·ar·y /jánnyoo èrree/ (*plural* **-ys**) *n* in the Gregorian calendar, the first month of the year, lasting 31 days. See table at **calendar** [Pre-12C. < Latin *Januarius (mensis)* "month of Janus"]

Ja·nus /jáynəss/ *n* **1.** in Roman mythology, the god of beginnings, of the past and the future, of gates, doorways, and bridges, and of peace, traditionally depicted as having two faces. Unusually, he has no Greek counterpart. **2.** a small irregularly shaped satellite of Saturn, discovered in 1978

Ja·nus-faced *adj* insincere or hypocritical (*literary*)

JAP /jap/ *n* an offensive term for a Jewish girl or woman that deliberately insults her ethnic background, upbringing, and character (*slang*) Full form **Jewish American Princess**

ja·pan /jə pán/ *n* **1.** BLACK VARNISH a lacquer that, when used to coat wood or metal, gives a glossy black finish **2.** VARNISHED OBJECTS decorative work that has been coated with japan or a similar kind of varnish ■ *vt* (**-panned, -pan·ning, -pans**) APPLY JAPAN TO SOMETHING to varnish an object with japan [Late 17C. After JAPAN]

Japan

Ja·pan /jə pán/ country in East Asia, comprising four large islands, Hokkaido, Honshu, Shikoku, and Kyushu, and more than 1,000 lesser adjacent islands. Language: Japanese. Currency: yen. Capital: Tokyo. Population: 127,214,500 (2003). Area: 145,884 sq. mi./377,837 sq. km.

Ja·pan, Sea of sea between Korea and Japan that has been the subject of a dispute between the two countries. Area: 389,200 sq. mi./1,008,000 sq. km.

LANGUAGE HERITAGE ***Japanese*** Much of English is made up of words from other languages, and Japanese is an important contributor in this respect. A good many English words are borrowings directly and solely from Japanese, and they span various subjects, with words relating to cuisine especially prolific: ***hijiki, miso, mizuma, nori, sake, sashimi, shiitake, sukiyaki, sushi, tamari, tempura, udon,*** and ***wasabi.*** Others are: in the decorative arts, ***ikebana, makimono,*** and ***origami***; in furnishings, ***tatami***; in music, ***koto***; in clothing, ***kimono*** and ***netsuke***; in religion, ***satori*** and ***torii***; in meteorology, ***tsunami***; in business, ***kanban*** and ***keiretsu***; in botany, ***kudzu***; and in the military and the martial arts, ***hara-kiri, karate, kata,*** and ***samurai.***

Another direct borrowing solely from Japanese is the well-known ***kamikaze,*** which has taken on extended senses in English that distance themselves from the word's language and culture of origin. ***Kamikaze,*** first recorded in English in the late 19th century, means "divine wind." This word originally referred to a typhoon that saved Japan by destroying the Mongol navy in 1281.

But many other borrowings, though entering English via Japanese, are ultimately of Chinese origin, and they too span various subjects. An example is ***futon,*** first recorded in English in the late 19th century. It came into English directly from Japanese, in which the word means "bedclothes," but its constituent elements, *fu* "quilt" and *ton* "round," derive from Middle Chinese *phu* and *thuan.* Still others of ultimate Chinese origin are: in cuisine, ***daikon*** and ***tofu***; in the arts, ***haiku, kabuki, No,*** and ***samisen***; in botany and horticulture, ***bonsai*** and ***gingko***; in business, ***tycoon***; in entertainment, ***geisha***; in religion, ***Shinto***; in furniture and the decorative arts, ***shoji***; in clothing, ***zori***; in games, ***shogi***; and in the military and martial arts, ***aikido, banzai, Bushido, dan, judo, jujitsu, ninja, sensei, seppuku,*** and ***shogun.***

Japanese has also been just one of several stops that words have made en route from their languages of origin. An example is ***soy,*** which made its way into English via Dutch, Malay, and Japanese, ultimately from Chinese *jiàngyoú* "soy bean oil."

In terms of relatively modern in- and out-migrations involving Japanese and English, the Japanese language has taken in some English terms, modified them, and then, as a result of globalized pop culture, passed them back to English in a transformed state. An example is ***anime,*** a Japanese style of animated cartoon. This Japanese word is a shortening of *animeshon,* a Japanese version of English *animation.* ***Anime*** then entered English in the late 20th century. Sometimes Japanese partially Anglicizes terms. An example is ***karaoke,*** a combination of Japanese *kara* "empty," and *oke,* a shortening of the loanword *okesutora* "orchestra," coming from English *orchestra.*

Ja·pan clo·ver *n* an annual plant grown as a forage crop. Native to: China, Japan, now widely grown in the southeastern United States. Latin name: *Lespedeza striata.*

Ja·pan Cur·rent ▸ **Kuroshio**

Jap·a·nese /jàppə neéz, -neéss/ (*plural same*) *n* **1.** somebody who comes from Japan **2.** the official language of Japan, also spoken in parts of Brazil and North America. Its linguistic affiliations are disputed. Native speakers: 126 million. —**Jap·a·nese** *adj*

Jap·a·nese an·drom·e·da *n* a cultivated ornamental bush. Flowers: bell-shaped, early blooming. Native to: Asia. Latin name: *Pieris japonica.*

Jap·a·nese bee·tle *n* a shiny green-and-brown scarab beetle that was accidentally introduced into the eastern United States where it is now a serious pest of cereal crops

Jap·a·nese ce·dar *n US* an evergreen coniferous tree with a narrow conical crown, widely grown as an ornamental and for timber. Native to: China, Japan. Latin name: *Cryptomeria japonica.* Can term **cryptomeria**

Jap·a·nese clo·ver *n* PLANTS same as **Japan clover**

Jap·a·nese gar·den *n* a garden designed according to formal Japanese rules, distinguished by its use of foliage plants, rocks, sand, and wooden garden paths, bridges, and pavilions

Jap·a·nese i·ris *n* a cultivated ornamental plant. Flowers: reddish purple, large-petaled. Native to: Asia. Latin name: *Iris ensata.*

Jap·a·nese knot·weed *n* a tall fast-growing perennial plant with reddish brown bamboo-like stems, originally an ornamental, but now considered an invasive weed in many countries. Flowers: creamy white, in clusters. Native to: East Asia. Latin name: *Fallopia japonica.*

Jap·a·nese ma·ple *n* a tree widely cultivated for its attractive deeply lobed leaves and purple flowers. Native to: Asia. Latin name: *Acer palmatum.*

Jap·a·nese mil·let *n* a coarse annual grass that has edible seeds and is grown for fodder. Native to: Asia. Latin name: *Echinochloa frumentacea.*

Jap·a·nese per·sim·mon *n* **1.** a red or orange fruit that is bitter when unripe **2.** a tree that produces Japanese persimmons. Native to: Asia. Latin name: *Diospyros kaki.*

Jap·a·nese plum *n* **1.** a yellow or red fruit, often pickled or dried **2.** a tree that produces Japanese plums. Native to: Asia. Latin name: *Prunus salicina.*

Jap·a·nese quince *n* **1.** an aromatic round white, yellow, or green fruit that is hard and acidic when raw but is edible after processing **2.** an ornamental bush of the rose family that produces Japanese quinces and is cultivated for its bright red or pink flowers. Native to: Asia. Latin name: *Chaenomeles japonica.*

Jap·a·nese rad·ish *n* FOOD same as **daikon**

Jap·a·nese um·brel·la pine *n* a coniferous tree widely grown for ornament, with needles arranged in whorls like the ribs of an umbrella. Native to: central Japan. Latin name: *Sciadopitys verticillata.*

Ja·pan wax, Ja·pan tal·low *n* a hard yellow wax obtained from some berries. Use: candles, matches, soap, polish, food packaging, as a substitute for beeswax.

jape /jayp/ (*archaic or literary*) *n* a joke or an act of mischief ■ *vti* (**japed, jap·ing, japes**) to joke, trick, or make fun of something [14C. < Old French *japer* "yelp," influenced by *gaber* "mock"] —**jap·er** *n* —**jap·er·y** *n*

Ja·pheth /jáyfith/ *n* in the Bible, the third son of Noah and brother of Shem and Ham. He was traditionally regarded as the ancestor of a number of non-Semitic peoples of the Mediterranean (Genesis 10:1–5).

Jap·lish /jápplish/ *n* Japanese with many adoptions of English words, phrases, and idioms [Mid-20C. Blend of JAPANESE + ENGLISH] —**Jap·lish** *adj*

ja·pon·i·ca /jə pónnikə/ *n* PLANTS **1.** same as **Japanese quince 2.** same as **camellia** (sense 1) [Early 19C. < modern Latin, form of *Japonicus* "of Japan"]

Jaques-Dal·croze /zhàk dal krṓz/, **Émile** (1865–1950) Swiss music teacher and composer. He was the originator of eurythmics.

jar[1] /jaar/ *n* **1.** a cylindrical container, usually one that has a wide mouth and a lid but no spout, typically made of glass, plastic, or earthenware ○ *pickle jars* **2.** the amount a jar holds, or the contents of a jar [Late 16C. Via French < Arabic *jarra*] —**jar·ful** *n*

jar[2] /jaar/ *v* (**jarred, jar·ring, jars**) **1.** *vt* SHAKE SOMETHING ABRUPTLY to give something an abrupt shake or shock especially so as to cause it to start vibrating ○ *The tremor jarred us awake.* **2.** *vti* HAVE DISTURBING EFFECT ON SOMEBODY to have an irritating, unsettling, or unpleasantly disturbing effect on somebody or something ○ *That constant drilling really jars my nerves.* **3.** *vi* CLASH to look or seem bad or inappropriate in the context of something else **4.** *vti* GRATE to make a harsh grating noise, or cause something to make such a noise ■ *n* **1.** PHYSICAL JOLT an act of knocking against something with a sudden blow **2.** GRATING SOUND a harsh grating noise [15C. Probably an imitation of a discordant sound] —**jar·ring** *adj* —**jar·ring·ly** *adv*

jar·di·nière /jaard'n éer, jaard'n éer, jaard'n yér, jaard'n yèr/ *n* a large, usually decorative flower pot or other holder for plants [Mid-19C. < French, "woman gardener"]

jar·gon[1] /jaar gən/ *n* **1.** language that is used by a group, profession, or culture, especially when the words and phrases are not understood or used by other people ○ *typesetters' jargon* **2.** pretentious or meaningless language (*disapproving*) ○ *Cut the jargon and get to your point.* **3.** LING same as **pidgin** [14C. < Old French *jargoun*] —**jar·gon·is·tic** /jaargə nístik/ *adj*

USAGE The term ***jargon*** is applied chiefly to the words and phrases that are used and understood by people within a specific profession or field of study but not by others, as in *medical jargon, business jargon,* or *computer jargon.* Examples of Internet ***jargon*** include *secure server, netiquette, spamming,* and *viral marketing.* ***Jargon*** is an indispensable means of communication within its own sphere, but it is criticized when used unnecessarily in everyday contexts, or to impress, intimidate, or confuse outsiders.

SYNONYMS ***jargon, vocabulary, terminology, slang, idiom, argot, parlance, lingo, -speak, -ese***

CORE MEANING: language used by a particular group of people

jargon language that is used by a group, profession, or culture, especially when the words and phrases are not understood or used by other people. ○ *technical jargon* ○ *The opportunity is staring us in the face to generate a billion-dollar "tourism product" – to use that awful jargon.* **vocabulary** the set of words associated with a subject or area of activity, or used by an individual person ○ *the fashionable vocabulary of the times* ○ *Ongoing scientific, technological, and social changes generate a stream of new vocabulary.* **terminology** the expressions and words, or a set of expressions and words, used by people involved in a specialized activity or field of work ○ *commercial and financial terminology* ○ *Of the world's 53 subspecies of Asian hornbills, only nine, in the terminology of a recent conference on the status of these birds, are "stable."* **slang** words, expressions, and usages that are casual, vivid, racy, or playful replacements for standard ones, are often short-lived, and are usually considered unsuitable for formal contexts ○ *Bean is a slang word for head.* ○ *He used vulgar slang that is not appropriate for someone in his high position.* **idiom** the style of expression of a specific person or group ○ *This time the writer has failed to capture the American idiom.* ○ *I don't think there will be much difference in the central thrust of their politics; the idiom might change, but not the substance.* **argot** the special language used by a particular group of people ○ *teenage argot* ○ *the argot of the diplomatic community* **parlance** the style of speech or writing used by people in a specific context or profession ○ *Now accepted in common parlance, the computer term "WYSIWYG" stands for What You See Is What You Get.* ○ *Uptown is, in a real estate agent's parlance, a "desirable part of the city."* **lingo** (*informal*) a foreign language, or a specialized set of terms requiring to be learned like a language ○ *My wife picked up the lingo as soon as we moved here.* ○ *An expert can help translate the complicated lingo of lawyers into plain English.* **-speak** (*disapproving*) a suffix added to nouns to describe the language used by a particular group of people or in a particular context ○ *I'm not put off by people using tech-speak.* ○ *The 40-page document is salted with politician-speak.* **-ese** (*disapproving*) a suffix added to nouns to describe the style of language associated with a particular group of people ○ *No matter what the government has to announce, it always seems to come out in a strangulated officialese.*

jar·gon[2] /jaar gón/, **jar·goon** /-goon/ *n* a colorless, pale, or smoky zircon [Mid-18C. Via French < Italian *giargone* < Persian *zargūn* "gold-colored"]

jar·gon·ize /jaargə nīz/ (**-ized, -iz·ing, -iz·es**) *v* **1.** *vt* to convert ordinary language into jargon **2.** *vi* to talk in jargon

jar·goon *n* MINERALS same as **jargon**[2]

jar·head /jaar hèd/ *n* a US Marine (*slang*) [Origin ?]

jarl /yaarl/ *n* formerly, a chieftain or nobleman in Scandinavia [Early 19C. < Old Norse *jarl* "earl"] —**jarl·dom** *n*

ja·ro·site /járrə sīt/ *n* a yellow to brown mineral consisting of hydrous iron potassium sulfate [Mid-19C. After the *Jarosa* ravine, S Spain]

jar·rah /járrə/ *n* **1.** a dark reddish hardwood. Use: flooring, building. **2.** a tree that yields jarrah. Native to: southwestern Australia. Latin name: *Eucalyptus marginata.* [Mid-19C. < Aboriginal *djarryl, jerrhyl*]

Jar·rell /jə rél/, **Randall** (1914–65) US poet and critic. A soldier during World War II, he is noted especially for poems based on his wartime experiences, collected in *Little Friend, Little Friend* (1945) and *Losses*

(1948). His criticism collections include *Poetry and the Age* (1953).

> "From my mother's sleep I fell into the State, / And I hunched in its belly till my wet fur froze. / Six miles from earth, loosed from its dream of life, / I woke to black flak and the nightmare fighters. / When I died they washed me out of the turret with a hose."
> [Randall Jarrell, "The Death of the Ball Turret Gunner"; 1945]

Ja·ru·zel·ski /yàrroo zhélskee/, **Wojciech** (*b.* 1923) Polish politician and general. As Communist head of state (1981–89) and president (1989–90) of Poland, he resisted liberal reforms, but in 1990 was defeated by Lech Walesa in free elections. Full name **Jaruzelski, Wojciech Witold**

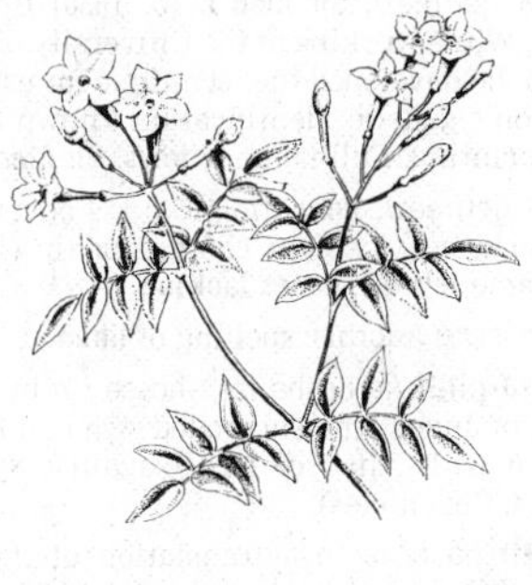

jasmine

jas·mine /jázmin/ (*plural same* or **-mines**), **jes·sa·mine** /jéssəmin/ *n* **1.** a climbing plant often grown as a house or garden plant. Flowers: fragrant white, yellow, or red. Use: perfumes. Native to: tropics, subtropics. Genus: *Jasminum*. **2.** a perfume made from the oil of a variety of jasmine **3.** PLANTS same as **Carolina jasmine** [Mid-16C. Via French *jasmin, jessemin* < Persian *yāsaman*]

jas·mine tea *n* a black tea flavored with jasmine blossoms

Ja·son /jáyss'n/ *n* in Greek mythology, a prince who led a group of heroes on his ship, the *Argo*, on a quest to obtain the Golden Fleece and bring it back to Greece

jas·pé /zha spáy/ *adj* describes fabric that is streaked or veined with different colors like jasper [Mid-19C. < French, past participle of *jasper* "to marble"]

jas·per /jáspər/ *n* **1.** a red, iron-bearing chalcedony. Use: jewelry, ornaments. **2.** CERAMICS same as **jasperware** [13C. Via Anglo-Norman *jaspre* < Latin *iaspid-* < Greek *íaspis* "jasper" < Semitic]

Jas·per Na·tion·al Park /jàspər-/ national park in western Alberta, Canada, in the Rocky Mountains. Area: 4,209 sq. mi./10,900 sq. km.

jas·per·ware /jáspər wèr/ *n* an ornamental porcelain invented by Josiah Wedgwood in 1775. It usually has raised classical motifs in white on backgrounds of various colors that are created by staining the porcelain with metallic oxides.

Jat /jaat/ *n* a member of an Indo-European people living in the Punjab, northwestern India, and Pakistan [Early 17C. < Hindi *Jāt*]

jath·a /játtə/ *n S Asia* a parade of people, especially Sikhs, carrying weapons [Early 20C. < Punjabi]

ja·to /jáytō/, **JATO** *n* an auxiliary jet or rocket designed to aid the combined thrust of aircraft jet engines during takeoff. Full form **jet-assisted takeoff**

jaun·dice /jáwndiss/ *n* **1.** ILLNESS CAUSING YELLOW SKIN a medical condition in which there is yellowing of the whites of the eyes, skin, and mucous membranes, caused by bile pigments in the blood. It is a symptom of liver diseases such as hepatitis and cirrhosis, or of a blocked bile duct, and sometimes occurs temporarily in new-born babies whose livers are slightly immature. Technical name **icterus 2.** CYNICAL STATE OF MIND an attitude that is characterized by cynical hostility, resentment, or suspicion ■ *vt* (**-diced, -dic·ing, -dic·es**) **1.** MAKE SOMEBODY CYNICAL to alter somebody's attitude for the worse, especially when it results in cynical hostility, resentment, or suspicion **2.** AFFECT SOMEBODY WITH JAUNDICE to affect somebody with jaundice, as a symptom of liver disease [14C. < Old French *jaunice* < *jaune* "yellow"] —**jaun·diced** *adj*

jaunt /jawnt/ *n* a trip, especially a short one taken for fun or pleasure ■ *vi* (**jaunt·ed, jaunt·ing, jaunts**) to go on a short trip, especially for fun or pleasure [Late 16C. Origin ?]

jaunt·ing car /jáwnting-/ *n* a lightweight two-wheeled open vehicle pulled by a single horse with lengthwise seats positioned so that passengers either face each other or sit back-to-back. It was formerly widely used in Ireland.

jaun·ty /jáwntee/ (**-ti·er, -ti·est**) *adj* **1.** happy, carefree, and confident **2.** perky and casually fashionable [Mid-17C. < French *gentil* "polite, kind"] —**jaun·ti·ly** *adv* —**jaun·ti·ness** *n*

Jau·rès /zho réss/, **Jean** (1859–1914) French politician and newspaper editor. Cofounder and editor of the newspaper *L'Humanité* (1904), he also helped to found the French Socialist Party (1905).

Jav. *abbr* **1.** PEOPLES, LANG Javanese **2.** *also* **jav.** TRACK AND FIELD javelin

ja·va /jaávə/ *n* coffee, especially brewed coffee as opposed to instant coffee (*informal*) [Early 20C. < JAVA[2]]

Ja·va[1] /jaávə/ island in Southeast Asia, the most populous island in Indonesia. Population: 101,742,117 (2000 estimate). Area: 51,755 sq. mi./134,045 sq. km.

Ja·va[2] /jaávə, jávvə/ *n* a variety of rich coffee grown on Java and the surrounding islands [Mid-19C. After JAVA[1]]

Ja·va[3] /jaávə/ *tdmk* a trademark for a high-level computer programming language that allows small application programs to be downloaded from a server to a client along with the data that each program processes

Ja·va man *n* a fossil human being found in Java and elsewhere in Indonesia, assumed to be from the Paleolithic Age. The body and limbs of Java man are very similar to those of Homo sapiens, but the brain and skull are smaller. [< JAVA[1]]

Jav·a·nese /jaàvə neéz, -neéss/ (*plural same*) *n* **1.** somebody who comes from Java **2.** a language spoken on Java, belonging to the Western branch of Austronesian. Native speakers: 70 million. [Early 18C. < JAVA[1]] —**Jav·a·nese** *adj*

Ja·va Sea /jaàvə-/ arm of the southern Pacific Ocean bordered by Borneo, Sulawesi, Java, and Sumatra. Area: 120,000 sq. mi./310,000 sq. km.

jave·lin /jávvlən, -vələn/ *n* **1.** a long thin piece of wood, plastic, or metal with a pointed end, used as a weapon or thrown in field competitions **2.** a track-and-field event in which the contestants compete to throw a javelin as far as possible [15C. < Middle French *javeline*, diminutive of Old French *javelot*]

ja·ve·li·na /haàvə leénə/ *n* ZOOL same as **peccary** [Early 19C. < Spanish *jabalina*, form of *jabalí* "wild boar" < Arabic *jabalīy*]

Ja·velle wa·ter /jə vèl-, zhə vèl-/, **Ja·vel wa·ter** *n* a solution of sodium hypochlorite. Use: bleach, disinfectant. Formula: NaOCl. [Early 19C. After a village on the outskirts of Paris]

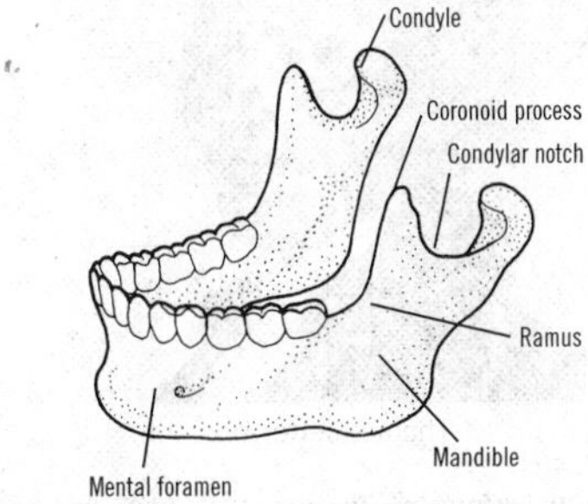

jaw

jaw /jaw/ *n* **1.** BONE IN WHICH TEETH ARE SET either of the upper or lower bones that anchor the teeth and form the structural basis of the mouth in vertebrates. In humans and other higher vertebrates, the upper jaw is known as the maxilla and the lower is the mandible. **2.** INVERTEBRATE BITING PART an invertebrate body part with a function or structure similar to a vertebrate jaw **3.** GRIPPING PART either of two hinged parts of a tool or machine used to grip objects securely **4.** FACE PART the lower, mobile part of the human face ○ *a strong square jaw* **5.** IMPUDENCE cocky or impudent talk (*slang*) **6.** LONG TALK a long conversation or discussion (*slang*) **7.** MORALIZING TALK a moralizing talk or lecture (*slang*) ■ **jaws** *npl* **1.** GEOG NATURAL ENTRANCE a narrow opening in something such as a cave, gorge, canyon, or other natural feature **2.** DANGEROUS PLACE a situation that is dangerously close to something horrible or frightening ■ *vi* (**jawed, jaw·ing, jaws**) TALK AT LENGTH to talk or gossip, usually at length (*slang*) ○ *Quit your jawing about travel arrangements and let's get going.* [14C. Origin ?] —**jawed** *adj* —**jaw·less** *adj*

Ja·wa·ra /jaáwərə/, **Sir Dawda** (*b.* 1924) Gambian politician. He was the first prime minister (1963–70) and president (1970–94) of the Gambia. Full name **Jawara, Sir Dawda Kairaba**

jaw·bone /jáw bōn/ *n* a bone in the jaw, especially the lower jaw ■ *vt* (**-boned, -bon·ing, -bones**) to coerce somebody to comply with something by using the authority of high office (*informal*) —**jaw·bon·er** *n*

jaw·break·er /jáw bràykər/ *n* **1.** FOOD HARD CANDY a large round hard piece of candy (*informal*) **2.** CRUSHING MACHINE a machine that crushes rocks using powerful jaws **3.** UNPRONOUNCEABLE WORD a long word that is difficult to pronounce (*informal*)

jaw·line /jáw līn/ *n* the shape of somebody's lower jaw

Jaws of Life *tdmk* a trademark for a pneumatically operated device resembling pincers that is inserted into a severely damaged motor vehicle and then opened in order to pry the vehicle apart and access people trapped inside

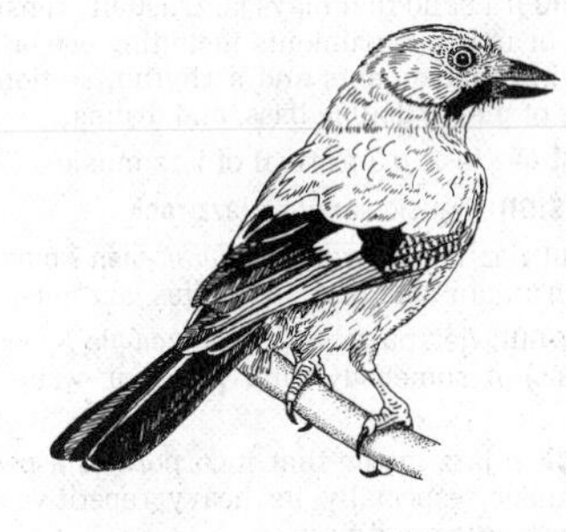

jay

jay[1] /jay/ *n* **1.** a noisy, often brightly colored bird of the crow family, known for its intelligence. Family: Corvidae. **2.** a heedless or chattering person (*informal*) [13C. Via French < Latin *gaius*]

jay[2] /jay/ *n* a marijuana cigarette (*slang*) [Late 20C. Probably representing pronunciation of *J*, abbreviation of JOINT]

Jay /jay/, **John** (1745–1829) first chief justice of the US Supreme Court (1789–95). He also served as president of the Second Continental Congress (1778–79) and negotiated the Treaty of Paris (1783) that ended the American Revolution.

jay·bird /jáy bùrd/ *n regional* BIRDS same as **jay**[1] (sense 1)

Jay·cee /jày seé/ *n* in North America, Australia, and New Zealand, a member of a junior chamber of commerce, an organization for young people that promotes leadership and business skills [Mid-20C. < the initial letters of *Junior Chamber*]

Jay·hawk·er /jáy hàwkər/ *n* somebody who comes from Kansas (*informal*) [Mid-19C. < *jayhawk*, fictitious bird of Kansas]

Jay·hawk·er State *n* a nickname for Kansas

jay·vee /jày veé/ *n* **1.** SPORTS same as **junior varsity 2.** a member of a junior varsity team

jay·walk /jáy wàwk/ (**-walked, -walk·ing, -walks**) *vi* to cross a street anywhere other than at a designated crossing place. It is a violation of the law in some places, though prosecutions are rarely brought. [Early 20C. < JAY[1] (sense 2)] —**jay·walk·er** *n* —**jay·walk·ing** *n*

jazz /jaz/ *n* **1.** SYNCOPATED POPULAR MUSIC popular music that originated among Black people in New Orleans in the late 19th century and is characterized by syncopated rhythms and improvisation. Jazz originally drew on ragtime, gospel, Black spiritual songs, West African rhythms, and European harmonies. **2.** STUFF unnamed related things or belongings (*slang*) ○ *a new motorcycle and all the jazz that comes with it* **3.** BLATHER information or ideas regarded as untrue, misconceived, or misleading (*slang*) ○ *Don't be fooled if she starts giving you that jazz about being broke.* **4.** LIVELINESS animated enthusiasm or vivacity (*slang*) ■ *v* (**jazzed, jazz·ing, jazz·es**) **1.** *vi* LISTEN TO JAZZ to play or dance to jazz music **2.** *vi* EXAGGERATE to engage in exaggeration (*slang*) **3.** *vt* LIE TO SOMEBODY to tell lies or a lie to somebody (*slang*) ○ *Stop jazzing me and tell me where you really were!* [Early 20C. Origin ?] —**jazz·er** *n*

ORIGIN The term ***jazz*** originated in the southern United States (it is first recorded in 1909, applied to a type of ragtime dance), and it is tempting to speculate that its ancestor crossed the Atlantic on the slave ships from Africa. In the absence of any certain origin, various colorful theories have been put forward – for example, that ***jazz*** came from the nickname of a certain Jasbo Brown, an itinerant musician along the banks of the Mississippi ("Jasbo" perhaps being an alteration of "Jasper").

jazz up *vt* **1.** to make somebody or something more interesting or decorative (*informal*) ○ *jazzed up his wardrobe with some Hawaiian shirts* **2.** to make a piece of music more lively, especially by quickening the tempo or adding improvisations

jazz age *n* the era that immediately followed World War I and lasted until the beginning of the Depression, during which jazz increased in popularity. It was a reaction to the austerity and hardship of the war and was characterized by extravagance and hedonism.

jazz band *n* a band that plays jazz, usually consisting of five or more instruments including one or more solo wind instruments and a rhythm section consisting of piano, double bass, and drums

jazz·fest /jáz fèst/ *n* a festival of jazz music

jazz-fu·sion *n* MUSIC same as **jazz-rock**

jazz·man /jáz màn, jázmən/ (*plural* **-men** /-mən, jáz mèn/) *n* a man who plays or writes jazz music

jazz·per·son /jáz pùrss'n/ (*plural* **-peo·ple** /-pèep'l/ or **-per·sons**) *n* somebody who plays or writes jazz music

jazz-rock *n* jazz music that incorporates aspects of rock music, especially its heavy repetitive beats and electronic amplification

jazz·wom·an /jáz wòomman/ (*plural* **-wom·en** /-wìmmin/) *n* a woman who plays or writes jazz music

jazz·y /jázzee/ (**-i·er, -i·est**) *adj* **1.** SHOWY showy, bright, and colorful (*slang*) **2.** JAZZED UP TO APPEAL made more lively or exaggerated for the sake of appeal (*slang*) **3.** LIKE JAZZ in the style of jazz music, especially with the syncopated rhythms of jazz —**jazz·i·ly** *adv* —**jazz·i·ness** *n*

Jb. *abbr* BIBLE Job

J-bar *n* a metal bar that is suspended from an overhead cable, used to tow a single skier up a slope ○ *rode to the summit on the J-bar* [< its shape]

JC *abbr* EDUC junior college

J.C. *abbr* **1.** Jesus Christ **2.** Julius Caesar

JCC *abbr* JUDAISM Jewish Community Center

JCL *n* a powerful computer language for writing a script used to control the execution of programs in batch processing systems. Full form **job control language**

J.C.S., JCS *abbr* MIL Joint Chiefs of Staff

jct. *abbr* junction

JD *abbr* **1.** EDUC, LAW Juris Doctor **2.** GOV Justice Department **3.** *also* **J.D.** CRIME juvenile delinquent

JDL *abbr* JUDAISM Jewish Defense League

Jdt. *abbr* BIBLE Judith

je *abbr* ONLINE Jersey (*used in Internet addresses*) See table at **domain name**

jeal·ous /jélləss/ *adj* **1.** ENVIOUS feeling bitter and unhappy because of another's advantages, possessions, or luck **2.** SUSPICIOUS OF RIVALS feeling suspicious about a rival's or competitor's influence, especially in regard to a loved one **3.** WATCHFUL possessively watchful of something ○ *keeps a jealous watch on his research* **4.** DEMANDING LOYALTY demanding exclusive loyalty or adherence (*archaic*) ○ *a jealous god* [13C. Via Old French *gelos* < Latin *zelosus* < Greek *zēlos* "jealousy, enthusiasm"] —**jeal·ous·ly** *adv* —**jeal·ous·ness** *n*

jeal·ous·y /jélləssee/ *n* **1.** jealous feelings or behavior **2.** (*plural* **jeal·ous·ies**) an instance of feeling jealous ○ *a man of many jealousies*

jean /jeen/ *n* a strong twill cotton. Use: work clothes, uniforms, overalls, jeans. ○ *a jean jacket* [15C. Via Old French *Janne* < medieval Latin *Janua* "Genoa"]

jeans /jeenz/ *npl* casual pants with raised seams, made from denim, jean, or another strong fabric

je·bel /jébb'l/, **dje·bel, ge·bel** *n* in Southwest Asia or North Africa, a hill or mountain (*often used in place names*) [Mid-19C. < Arabic *jabal* "mountain"]

Jed·da ♦ **Jiddah**

jeep /jeep/ *n* a vehicle developed by the military in World War II with four-wheel drive, for use on poor roads or open terrain [Mid-20C. < *GP*, abbreviation of *general purpose*]

Jeep /jeep/ *tdmk* a trademark for a four-wheel-drive vehicle suitable for rough terrain

jeep·ers /jéepərz/, **jeep·ers creep·ers** *interj* used to express surprise (*dated informal*) [Early 20C. Alteration of *Jesus*]

jeep·ney /jéepnee/ (*plural* **-neys**) *n* a jeep or similar vehicle that has been converted into a jitney, used in the Philippines as a form of public transportation [Mid-20C. Blend of JEEP + JITNEY]

jeep sa·fa·ri *n* an organized group sightseeing tour or excursion in a Jeep or other four-wheel-drive vehicle

jeer /jeer/ *vti* (**jeered, jeer·ing, jeers**) to shout or laugh at somebody or something in a mocking or scornful way ■ *n* a mocking or scornful shout or laugh [Mid-16C. Origin ?] —**jeer·er** *n* —**jeer·ing·ly** *adv*

Jeeves /jeevz/ *n* a useful and reliable person who provides ready solutions to problems (*informal*) [Mid-20C. < a character in the novels of P. G. WODEHOUSE]

jeez /jeez/ *interj* used to express surprise, enthusiasm, or annoyance (*slang*) [Early 20C. Shortening of *Jesus*]

je·fe /háy fay/ *n Hispanic* **1.** a military or political leader, especially in a Spanish-speaking country **2.** a work supervisor or boss [< Spanish, "chief"]

Jef·fers /jéffərz/, **Robinson** (1887–1962) US poet. His verse expresses contempt for human society. His work includes a successful adaptation of the ancient Greek myth *Medea* (1946). Full name **Jeffers, John Robinson**

> "But for my children, I would have them keep their distance from the thickening center; corruption/Never has been compulsory, when the cities lie at the monster's feet there are left the mountains."
> [Robinson Jeffers, "Shine, Perishing Republic," *Taman and Other Poems*; 1924]

Library of Congress

Thomas Jefferson

Jef·fer·son /jéffərss'n/, **Thomas** (1743–1826) 3rd president of the United States. He was the author of the Declaration of Independence. As Democratic Republican president (1801–09), he strengthened the executive branch of government. See table at **president**

> "We hold these truths to be self-evident: that all men are created equal; that they are endowed by their Creator with certain unalienable rights; that among these are life, liberty, and the pursuit of happiness."
> [Thomas Jefferson, *Declaration of Independence*; July 4, 1776]

> "Sometimes it is said that man cannot be trusted with the government of himself. Can he, then, be trusted with the government of others? Or have we found angels in the forms of kings to govern him? Let history answer this question."
> [Thomas Jefferson, *First Inaugural Address*; March 4, 1801]

Jef·fer·son Cit·y capital of Missouri and county seat of Cole County, situated in the central part of the state on the Missouri River, southeast of Columbia. Population: 39,079 (2002 estimate).

Jef·fer·son Day *n* a public holiday in Alabama marking the birth of Thomas Jefferson. Date: April 13.

Jeff·reys /jéffreez/, **Sir Alec J.** (*b.* 1950) British geneticist. While working at the University of Leicester in 1984, he developed the technique for establishing a person's genetic identification known as genetic fingerprinting. Full name **Jeffreys, Sir Alec John**

Jef·fries /jéffreez/, **Jim** (1875–1953) US boxer. He held the world heavyweight championship (1899–1905). Full name **Jeffries, James Jackson**

je·had *n* ISLAM another spelling of **jihad**

Je·hosh·a·phat /jə hóshə fàt, -hóssə-/ *n* in the Bible, a king of Judea who succeeded Asa and formed an alliance with Ahab of Israel against Syria. (1, 2 Kings; 2 Chronicles).

Je·ho·vah /jə hṓvə/ *n* a translation of the Hebrew name of God used in the Bible [Mid-16C. < medieval Latin *Iehoua*, mistaken transliteration of *YHWH*, the name too sacred to pronounce, using the vowel points of Hebrew *ădōnāy* "my lord"]

Je·ho·vah's Wit·ness *n* a member of a religious group that believes in the imminence of Jesus Christ's personal reign on Earth and rejects secular law where it appears to conflict with the divine. Jehovah's Witnesses reject the doctrine of the Trinity.

Je·ho·vist /jə hṓvist/ *n* **1.** BIBLE same as **Yahwist** **2.** somebody who believes that the Hebrew word "YHVH" in the Bible was pronounced "Jehovah" —**Je·ho·vism** *n* —**Je·ho·vis·tic** /jə hō vístik, jèehō vístik/ *adj*

je·june /jə jóon/ *adj* **1.** BORING uninteresting and intellectually undemanding **2.** CHILDISH lacking maturity or sophistication ○ *jejune chatter about concepts beyond their understanding* **3.** WITHOUT PROPER NOURISHMENT lacking or not providing proper nourishment **4.** BARREN not fertile [Early 17C. < Latin *jejunus* "fasting, meager"] —**je·june·ly** *adv* —**je·june·ness** *n*

je·jun·os·to·my /jə jòo nóstəmee/ (*plural* **-mies**) *n* **1.** a surgical operation that creates access from the outside of the body into the middle part of the small intestine (**jejunum**) so that nourishment can be directly introduced **2.** the opening formed in a jejunostomy

je·ju·num /jə jóonəm/ *n* the section of the small intestine situated between the duodenum and the ileum, whose main function is the absorption of nutrients from digested food [Mid-16C. < modern Latin < Latin *jejunus* "fasting," because usually empty after death] —**je·ju·nal** *adj*

Je·kyll and Hyde /jèk'l ən hī́d/ (*plural* **Je·kyll and Hydes**) *n* somebody who has two distinct personalities, one good and the other evil [Late 19C. < *The Strange Case of Dr. Jekyll and Mr. Hyde* (1886), by R. L. Stevenson]

jell /jel/ (**jelled, jell·ing, jells**) *v* **1.** *vti* SOLIDIFY to become set or firm, or cause a substance to become set or firm **2.** *vti* TAKE SHAPE to become fixed or more definite in shape or form, or cause something to become fixed or more definite in shape or form **3.** *vi* GET ON WELL TOGETHER to bond in a way that gives rise to mutual cooperation ○ *"It's fun being with a bunch of guys who are fighting through adversity and jelling together."* (*The Philadelphia Inquirer*; 1997) [Mid-18C. Back-formation < JELLY]

jel·la·ba /jélləbə, jə láabə/, **djel·la·ba** *n* a unisex long, loose, sleeved garment with a hood, worn in Morocco and other parts of North Africa [Early 19C. < Moroccan Arabic *jellāb(a)*]

jel·li·fy /jéllə fī/ (**-fied, -fy·ing, -fies**) *vti* to turn into jelly, or cause a substance to turn into jelly —**jel·li·fi·ca·tion** /jèlləfi káysh'n/ *n*

Jell-O /jéllō/ *tdmk* a trademark for a gelatin-based dessert

jel·ly /jéllee/ *n* **1.** FRUIT PRESERVE a fruit preserve that is made by boiling fruit juice, sugar, and sometimes pectin until it has a semisolid consistency **2.** THICKENED MEAT STOCK a semisolid food made from gelatin boiled with meat stock ○ *calf's foot jelly* **3.** SEMISOLID SUBSTANCE a substance that has the consistency of jelly, especially a pharmaceutical preparation ■ *vti* (**-lied, -ly·ing, -lies**) THICKEN to set into a jelly, or cause something to set into a jelly [14C < Old French *gelee* "frost, jelly" < Latin *gelare* "freeze"] —**jel·ly·like** *adj* ◇ **turn to jelly** to feel shaky because of extreme fear, nervousness, or exhaustion (*informal*)

jel·ly·bean /jéllee been/ *n* a small bean-shaped fruit candy with a hard coating and a soft jelly center

jel·ly·fish /jéllee fish/ (*plural* **-fish·es** or *same*) *n* **1.** STINGING SEA ANIMAL an invertebrate sea animal that, in its reproductive stage, has a nearly transparent body shaped like an umbrella with trailing tentacles bearing stinging cells. Phylum: Coelenterata. **2.** SEA ANIMAL LIKE JELLYFISH an invertebrate sea animal that looks similar to a true jellyfish **3.** WEAK PERSON a weak or indecisive person (*informal*) ○ *I'm afraid I'm just a jellyfish when it comes to making decisions.*

jel·ly fun·gus *n* a fungus that grows on trees and has a gelatinous fruiting body. Order: Tremellales.

jel·ly roll *n* a long cylindrical cake made by rolling up a thin rectangle of light sponge spread with jelly

~~**jelous**~~ incorrect spelling of **jealous**

jem·a·dar *n S Asia* PUBLIC ADMIN another spelling of **jamadar**

jem·my /jémmee/ *UK n* (*plural* **-mies**) same as **jimmy** *n* (sense 1) ■ *vt* (**-mied, -my·ing, -mies**) same as **jimmy** [Early 19C. < *Jemmy*, familiar form of the name *James*]

je ne sais quoi /zhō nə say kwaá/ *n* an indefinable quality that makes somebody or something more attractive or interesting [Mid-17C. < French, "I do not know what"]

Jen·kins /jéngkinz/, **Roy, Baron Jenkins of Hillhead** (1920–2003) British politician. After serving as a minister in two British Labour governments, he cofounded the Social Democratic Party (1981). He was the president of the European Commission (1977–81). Full name **Jenkins, Roy Harris**

> "There are always great dangers in letting the best be the enemy of the good."
> [Roy Jenkins, *Speech to the British Parliament*; 1975]

Jen·ner /jénnər/, **Bruce** (*b.* 1949) US athlete. He won the gold medal in the decathlon at the 1976 Olympic games.

Jen·ner, Edward (1749–1823) British physician. He discovered the vaccine against smallpox.

> "The deviation of man from the state in which he was originally placed by nature seems to have proved to him a prolific source of diseases."
> [Attributed to Edward Jenner]

jen·net /jénnit/, **gen·et** *n* **1.** a female donkey **2.** a small Spanish riding horse [15C. Via French *genet* < Spanish Arabic *Genētī* "light horseman"]

jen·ny /jénnee/ (*plural* **-nies**) *n* **1.** DONKEY a female donkey **2.** BIRD a female bird (*often used before a noun*) ○ *a jenny wren* **3.** MARINE BIOL CRAB a female crab **4.** MANUF same as **spinning jenny** [Early 17C. < the name *Jenny*, diminutive of *Jane* and *Jennifer*]

Je·no·lan Caves /jə nṓlən-/ cave system in southeastern New South Wales, Australia. Located in the Blue Mountains National Park, the limestone cave system is a major tourist attraction.

jeop·ard·ize /jéppər dīz/ (**-ized, -iz·ing, -iz·es**) *vt* to put somebody or something at risk of being lost, harmed, killed, or destroyed ○ *jeopardizing the entire mission through their indiscretion*

jeop·ard·y /jéppərdee/ *n* **1.** the risk of loss, harm, death, or destruction ○ *The entire project is in jeopardy.* **2.** the risk of being convicted when put on trial for a crime [14C. < Old French *jeu* (< Latin *jocus* "pastime") + *parti* (past participle of *partir* "divide"), literally "even or divided game"]

~~**jepardy**~~ incorrect spelling of **jeopardy**

Jer. *abbr* **1.** BIBLE Jeremiah **2.** Jersey **3.** Jerusalem

jerboa

jer·bo·a /jər bṓ ə/ *n* **1.** a small nocturnal rodent that has large ears, a long tufted tail, and long hind legs adapted for leaping. Native to: dry regions of Asia and Africa. Family: Dipodidae. **2.** a small marsupial with long hind legs and a long bushy tail. Native to: central desert areas of Australia. Genus: *Antechinomys*. [Mid-17C. Via modern Latin < Arabic *yarbū'(a)*, *jarbū*]

jer·e·mi·ad /jèrrə mī əd/ *n* a long recitation of mournful complaints (*formal*) [Late 18C. < French *jérémiade* < *Jérémie* "Jeremiah"]

Jer·e·mi·ah /jèrrə mī ə/ *n* **1.** HEBREW PROPHET in the Bible, a Hebrew prophet who lived in Judah in the 7th and 6th centuries B.C. and was persecuted for prophesying the fall of Judah and Jerusalem and the Israelites' captivity in Babylon **2.** BOOK OF BIBLE the book of the Bible that contains the prophecies traditionally attributed to Jeremiah. See table at **Bible 3.** NEGATIVE PERSON somebody with a gloomy attitude toward the present and future

Je·rez de la Fron·te·ra /he rèss də laa frun térrə/ city in southwestern Spain, in Cádiz Province, Andalusia. It is the world's sherry capital. Population: 187,087 (2002).

Jer·i·cho /jérrikō/ town in the West Bank, in the Jordan Valley. It is regarded as the world's oldest town, with remains dating back to 8000 B.C. and, according to the Bible, was destroyed by Joshua after he led the Israelites back from captivity in Egypt (Joshua 3–8). Population: 14,744 (1997).

jer·id /jə reéd/ *n* a javelin used by Persian, Turkish, and Arabian horsemen, especially during the time of the Ottoman Empire [Mid-17C. < Arabic *jarīd* "palm branch stripped of its leaves, javelin"]

jerk[1] /jurk/ *v* (**jerked, jerk·ing, jerks**) **1.** *vt* YANK SOMEBODY OR SOMETHING to pull somebody or something with a sudden strong movement ○ *He jerked her back from in front of the speeding car.* **2.** *vti* MOVE JOLTINGLY to proceed with bumps and jolts, or cause somebody or something to do this ○ *The car jerked forward.* **3.** *vi* MOVE IN SPASM to move in response to muscular spasms (*refers to parts of the body*) **4.** *vt* SAY SOMETHING ABRUPTLY to utter words or sounds suddenly and forcefully, e.g., from excitement **5.** *vt* MAKE ICE CREAM REFRESHMENTS to prepare and serve ice cream sodas, sundaes, and other refreshments at a soda fountain ■ *n* **1.** SUDDEN YANK a sudden strong pulling movement ○ *giving the door a jerk* **2.** JOLTING MOTION a bumping or jolting motion ○ *moving in jerks* **3.** TWITCH a spasmodic movement in a muscle **4.** OFFENSIVE TERM an offensive term for somebody who is regarded as behaving foolishly (*slang insult*) **5.** OVERHEAD LIFT IN WEIGHTLIFTING a lift in weightlifting in which a barbell is thrust from shoulder height to above the head ■ **jerks** *npl* SPASMODIC MOVEMENTS involuntary muscular movements often caused by nervousness or excitement [Mid-16C. Origin ?] —**jerk·er** *n*
jerk around *vt* to encourage somebody to have unrealistic expectations by providing dishonest or misleading information (*slang*) ○ *You've jerked me around long enough.*
jerk off *vti* a highly offensive term meaning to masturbate, or masturbate somebody (*taboo*)

jerk[2] /jurk/ *vt* (**jerked, jerk·ing, jerks**) PRESERVE MEAT IN STRIPS to preserve meat by cutting it into long thin strips and drying or smoking it ■ *adj* **1.** STRONGLY FLAVORED AND SPICY made with strongly flavored spices, including hot peppers and allspice, as a marinade or rub for grilled meats **2.** SPICY AND GRILLED marinated in a jerk sauce and grilled [Early 18C. Via American Spanish *charquear* < Quechua *echarquini* "prepare dried meat"]

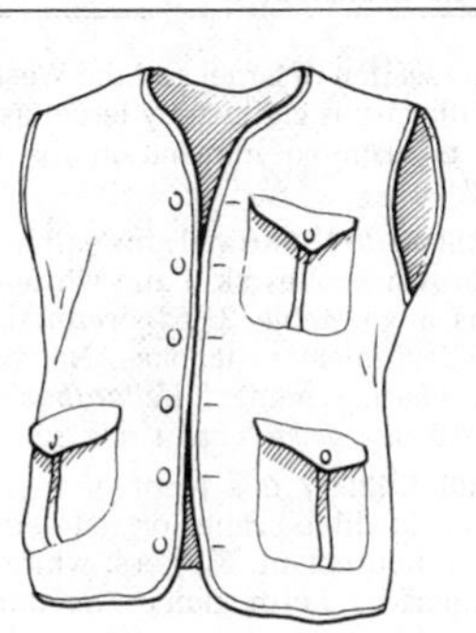

jerkin

jer·kin /júrkin/ *n* **1.** a sleeveless coat or jacket worn by men or women **2.** a man's close-fitting sleeveless tunic, often made of leather, worn in the 16th and 17th centuries [Early 16C. Origin ?]

jerk·wa·ter /júrk wàwtər/ *adj* **1.** remote from population centers and considered insignificant and backward **2.** lacking consequence or significance [< supplying water to early trains in remote places with a bucket on a rope]

jerk·y[1] /júrkee/ (**-i·er, -i·est**) *adj* **1.** moving irregularly with sudden stops and starts **2.** lacking good sense or reason (*informal*) [Mid-19C. < JERK[1]] —**jerk·i·ly** *adv* —**jerk·i·ness** *n*

jerk·y[2] /júrkee/ *n* meat cut into thin strips and dried or smoked [Mid-19C. Alteration of CHARQUI]

REGIONAL NOTE ***Jerky*** is a Western term, used from the Dakotas and Texas to the Pacific states, and now generalized as a commercial snack food.

jer·o·bo·am /jèrrə bṓ əm/ *n* **1.** a large wine or champagne bottle holding the equivalent of four standard wine bottles, 108 fl. oz/3 liters **2.** a large Bordeaux wine bottle equivalent to six bottles, 162 fl oz/4.5 liters [Early 19C. After *Jeroboam* "a mighty man of valor" (I Kings 11:28)]

Jer·o·bo·am I /jèrrə bṓ əm/ (*fl* 10th century B.C.) king of Israel. According to the Bible (1, 2 Kings; 2 Chronicles), he was the first king of the ten northern tribes of Israel (922–901 B.C.).

Jer·o·bo·am II (*fl* 8th century B.C.) king of Israel. According to the Bible (2 Kings 13–15), he reigned from 786 to 746 B.C.

Je·rome /jə rṓm/, **St.** (347?–419?) Croatian-born monk and scholar. He translated the Vulgate, the first translation of the Bible from Hebrew into Latin. Born **Eusebius Hieronymus**

Je·rome, Jerome K. (1859–1927) British novelist. He is best known for his humorous novel *Three Men in a Boat* (1889). Full name **Jerome, Jerome Klapka**

Jer·ry /jérree/ (*plural* **-ries**) *n UK* an offensive term for a German person, especially a German soldier in World War II (*dated slang insult*) [Early 20C. Alteration of GERMAN]

jer·ry·build /jérree bìld/ *vt* to build something as quickly and cheaply as possible, with little regard for quality [Mid-19C. Origin ?] —**jer·ry·build·er** *n* —**jer·ry·build·ing** *n* —**jer·ry·built** *adj*

jer·ry can *n* a flat-sided can with a capacity of approximately 5 gal./19 liters of liquid, originally of German design and used in World War II [< alteration of GERMAN]

jer·sey /júrzee/ (*plural* **-seys**) *n* **1.** a knitted fabric, usually made with a plain or stocking stitch. Use: clothing. **2.** a knitted woolen pullover [Late 16C. After JERSEY[1]]

Jer·sey[1] /júrzee/ largest and southernmost of the Channel Islands in the English Channel, a dependency of the British crown. Language: English, French. Capital: St. Helier. Population: 89,361 (2001). Area: 45 sq. mi./116 sq. km.

Jer·sey[2] /júrzee/ (*plural* **-seys**) *n* a pale brown dairy cow that produces particularly creamy milk, belonging to a breed originating on the island of Jersey [Mid-19C. After JERSEY[1]]

Jer·sey Cit·y city and port in northeastern New Jersey. It is an industrial center. Population: 240,100 (2002 estimate).

Je·ru·sa·lem /jə roóssələm, -roózə-/ historic city lying at the intersection of Israel and the West Bank. The whole of the city is claimed by Israel as its capital, but this is disputed internationally. Population: 633,700 (1999).

Je·ru·sa·lem ar·ti·choke *n* **1.** an edible tuber with reddish brown knobby skin and white flesh, eaten cooked as a vegetable **2.** a perennial plant that produces Jerusalem artichokes. Native to: North America. Latin name: *Helianthus tuberosus.* [< Italian *girasole* < *girare* "turn" + *sole* "sun"]

Je·ru·sa·lem cher·ry *n* a plant of the nightshade family with inedible orange or red berries, widely grown as a houseplant. Flowers: white. Native to: South America. Latin name: *Solanum pseudocapsicum.*

Je·ru·sa·lem cross *n* a cross with equal arms each ending in a short bar at right angles and having a small cross in each of the four angles made by the main arms [Adopted by the Christian kings of Jerusalem (1099–1291)]

Je·ru·sa·lem oak *n* a strong-smelling plant of the goosefoot family that grows as a weed. Flowers: white. Native to: northern United States, Canada. Latin name: *Chenopodium botrys.*

Je·ru·sa·lem thorn *n* a thorny leguminous bush. Flowers: yellow, in long clusters. Native to: tropical America. Latin name: *Parkinsonia aculeata.*

Je·ru·sa·lem Ver·sion *n* a modern version of the Bible produced from original language documents such as the Dead Sea Scrolls and containing the complete canon of biblical scripture, published in 1966

Jer·vis Bay /jaárvəss-/ harbor in southeastern Australia, on the eastern coast of New South Wales. The headland on its southern side is part of the Australian Capital Territory. Area: 60 sq. mi./160 sq. km.

jess /jess/ *n* a short strap with a ring for attaching a leash, fastened around one of the legs of a falcon or other trained bird of prey ■ *vt* (**jessed, jess·ing, jess·es**) to put a jess on a bird [14C. < Old French *ges*, form of *get* "act of throwing" < Latin *jactus* < *jacere* "to throw"]

jes·sa·mine *n* PLANTS same as **jasmine**

Jes·sel·ton /jéss'ltən/ former name for **Kota Kinabalu**

jest /jest/ *n* **1.** PLAYFUL JOKE something done or said in a playful joking manner (*literary*) ○ *Forgive my little jest.* **2.** SOMETHING JOKED ABOUT an object of scorn or derision (*archaic*) ■ *vti* (**jest·ed, jest·ing, jests**) JOKE PLAYFULLY to act, write, or speak in a playfully joking manner about something (*literary*) [13C. Via Old French *geste* "romantic exploit" < Latin *gestus* < *gerere* "behave, perform"] —**jest·ing·ly** *adv* ◇ **in jest** as a joke

jest·er /jéstər/ *n* **1.** an entertainer employed at a medieval court to amuse the monarch and guests **2.** somebody who likes fun or making jokes

Jes·u·it /jézhoo it, jézzoo-/ *n* **1.** MEMBER OF ROMAN CATHOLIC RELIGIOUS ORDER a member of the Society of Jesus, a Roman Catholic religious order engaged in missionary and educational work worldwide. The order was founded by Saint Ignatius Loyola in 1534 with the objective of defending Catholicism against the Reformation. **2.** *also* **jes·u·it** OFFENSIVE TERM an offensive term for somebody regarded as crafty or scheming, especially somebody who uses deliberately ambiguous or confusing words to deceive others (*insult*) ■ *adj* OF JESUITS relating to or belonging to the members of the Society of Jesus ○ *a Jesuit priest* [Mid-16C. < French *jésuite* or modern Latin *Jesuita* "follower of Jesus Christ" < *Jesus*] —**Jes·u·it·ic** /jèzhoo íttik, jèzzoo-/ *adj* —**Jes·u·it·i·cal** *adj* —**Jes·u·it·i·cal·ly** *adv* —**Jes·u·it·ism** *n* —**Jes·u·it·ry** *n*

Je·sus Christ /jeézəss-/, **Je·sus** *n* **1.** FOUNDER OF CHRISTIANITY a Jewish religious teacher who lived from about 4 B.C. to A.D. 33. His life and teachings form the basis of Christianity. **2.** HUMAN EMBODIMENT OF DIVINE in Christian Science, the highest human embodiment of the divine idea ■ *interj* OFFENSIVE TERM an offensive term expressing frustration or dismay (*slang*)

Je·sus freak *n* an offensive term for somebody who belongs to a youthful evangelical Christian group that is contemporary in tone (*slang*)

jet[1] /jet/ *n* **1.** PRESSURIZED STREAM OF FLUID a thin concentrated stream of liquid, air, or gas that is forced under pressure from a small nozzle or opening **2.** HOLE THROUGH WHICH FLUID IS FORCED a small nozzle or opening for letting out a stream of liquid, air, or gas **3.** AVIAT AIRCRAFT an aircraft powered by jet engines (*often used before a noun*) ○ *a jet landing strip* **4.** AVIAT same as **jet engine** (*often used before a noun*) ○ *using jet technology* ■ *v* (**jet·ted, jet·ting, jets**) **1.** *vi* AVIAT TRAVEL BY AIR to travel by air, especially by modern passenger aircraft ○ *always jetting off to business meetings* **2.** *vti* FLOW FORCEFULLY IN THIN STREAM to be emitted forcefully in a thin concentrated stream, or emit something in this way ○ *Water jetted from the broken pipe.* [Late 16C. Via Old French *jeter* "to throw" < Latin *jacere*]

ORIGIN *Jet* was originally used in English to mean "to protrude, stick out." This sense is best preserved in the related *jetty* "projecting pier," while the underlying meaning "to throw" is still present in the related *jettison* "throw something overboard." *Jet* began to be used for "to spurt out in a forceful stream" in the 17th century. The notion of using such a stream to create forward motion was first encapsulated in the term "jet propulsion" in the mid-19th century, but it did not take concrete form for nearly a hundred years (the term *jet engine* is not recorded until 1943). Other English words descended from Latin *jacere* "to throw," include *abject, dejected, ejaculate, eject, inject, interject, jettison, jetty*[1], *object, project, reject, subject,* and *trajectory.*

jet[2] /jet/ *n* **1.** a dense black variety of the mineral lignite. Use: jewelry, ornaments. **2.** COLORS same as **jet black** [14C. Via Old French *jaiet* < Latin *gagates* < Greek *Gagatēs*, after *Gagai*, town in Asia Minor] —**jet** *adj*

jet black *n* a very dark black color —**jet-black** *adj*

jet boat *n* a boat powered by an engine that produces a pressurized stream of water directed backward —**jet boat·ing** *n*

jet·bridge /jét brìj/ *n* AVIAT same as **loading bridge**

je·té /zhə táy/ *n* a ballet leap from one leg to the other in which one leg is stretched forward and the other backward [Mid-19C. < French, past participle of *jeter* "throw"]

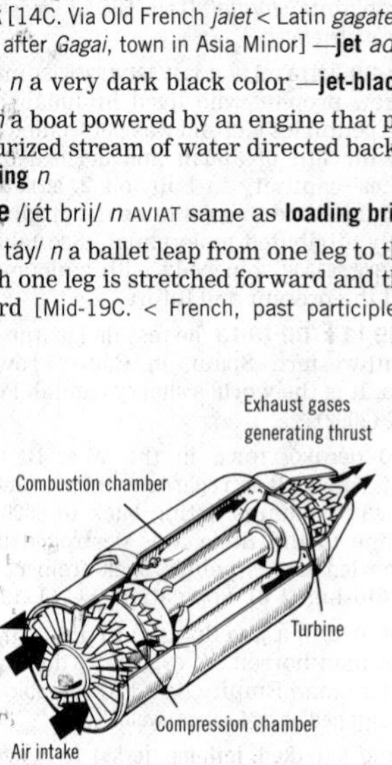

jet engine: cutaway view

jet en·gine *n* an engine, especially one used to propel an aircraft, that produces forward thrust by means of a rearward discharge of fluid, usually combustion gases

jet fight·er *n* a fighter plane that is powered by a jet engine or engines

jet·foil /jét fòyl/ *n* a passenger-carrying jet-powered hydrofoil

jet lag *n* an internal physical disturbance experienced by air travelers on flights across different time zones. It affects the body's internal clock, disrupting sleeping patterns, eating schedules, and body temperature. —**jet-lagged** *adj*

jet·lin·er /jét lìnər/ *n* a large passenger airplane powered by jet engines [Mid-20C. Blend of JET[1] + AIRLINER]

jet·pack /jét pàk/ *n* a device fitted with pressurized metal containers that let out jets of gas, worn by astronauts on their backs to enable them to move around in space outside a spacecraft

jet plane *n* an airplane powered by jet engines

jet-pro·pelled *adj* powered by means of engines that use jet propulsion

jet pro·pul·sion *n* forward thrust that results from the rearward discharge of a jet of fluid, especially a jet engine's combustion gases —**jet-pro·pelled** *adj*

jet·sam /jétsəm/ *n* **1.** cargo or equipment that either sinks or is washed ashore after being thrown overboard to lighten the load of a ship in distress **2.** things that have been discarded as useless or unwanted [Late 16C. Contraction of JETTISON]

jet set *n* wealthy people who travel internationally on a regular basis, especially in pursuit of pleasure (*informal*) —**jet-set·ter** *n* —**jet-set·ting** *n*

Jet Ski *tdmk* a trademark for a jet-propelled personal watercraft

jet stream *n* **1.** a strong permanent high-altitude wind current that moves east in a meandering pattern, affecting the development and movement of weather systems **2.** a flow of exhaust gases produced by a jet engine

jet·ti·son /jéttiss'n/ *vt* (**-soned, -son·ing, -sons**) **1.** REJECT SOMETHING to discard or abandon something such as an idea or project ○ *plans that had to be jettisoned* **2.** THROW SOMETHING OVERBOARD to throw something from a ship, aircraft, or vehicle ■ *n* **1.** REJECTION the discarding or abandoning of something **2.** SHIPPING SHIP'S DISCARDED CARGO the cargo and equipment thrown from a distressed ship to lighten it [15C. < Anglo-Norman *getteson* "throwing cargo overboard" (to lighten a ship) < Latin *jectare* "throw about"] —**jet·ti·son·a·ble** *adj*

jet·ty[1] /jéttee/ (*plural* **-ties**) *n* **1.** a landing pier **2.** a wall or other barrier built out into a body of water to shelter a harbor, protect a shoreline from erosion, or redirect water currents [15C. < Old French *jetee* "something thrown (up as a breakwater)" < *jeter* (see JET[1])]

jet·ty[2] /jéttee/ *adj* **1.** of a jet-black color **2.** similar to or made of jet

Jet·way /jét wày/ *tdmk* a trademark for an enclosed telescoping walkway between an airplane and a terminal building, through which passengers can embark and disembark

jeu d'e·sprit /zhōō de spreé/ (*plural* **jeux d'e·sprit** /*pronunc. same*/) *n* a witticism, especially one that appears in a work of literature [Early 18C. < French, "game of spirit or wit"]

jeu·nesse do·rée /zhoo nèss daw ráy/ *n* young people who enjoy wealth and privilege (*literary*) [Mid-19C. < French, "gilded youth"]

Jev·ons /jévv'nz/, **William** (1835–82) British economist and mathematician. He introduced the theory of marginal utility and pioneered the use of mathematics in economics. Full name **Jevons, William Stanley**

> "It is clear that Economics, if it is to be a science at all, must be a mathematical science."
> [William Jevons, *Theory of Political Economy*; 1871]

Jew /joo/ *n* **1.** BELIEVER IN JUDAISM somebody whose religion is Judaism **2.** MEMBER OF SEMITIC PEOPLE a member of a Semitic people descended from the ancient Hebrews, sharing cultural and religious ties based on Judaism **3.** SOMEBODY FROM ANCIENT JUDEA somebody who lived or was born in ancient Judea [Pre-12C. Via Old French *giu* < Latin *Judaeus*, Greek *Ioudaios* < Hebrew *yĕhūḏī* < *yĕhūḏāh* "Judah," son of the patriarch Jacob, and the tribe descended from him]

jew·el /jōō əl/ *n* **1.** PERSONAL ORNAMENT an item, worn as an ornament, made of a gemstone placed in a setting of gold, silver, or other metal, e.g., a ring, necklace, or bracelet ○ *She wore her best jewels to the ball.* **2.** GEMSTONE a precious stone, e.g., a diamond or sapphire **3.** WATCH BEARING a small crystal or precious stone used as a bearing in a watch **4.** PRIZED EXAMPLE a fine example of a particular type of person or thing ○ *Her new teacher's such a jewel!* ■ *vt* (**-eled, -el·ing, -els**) ADORN SOMETHING WITH JEWELS to equip or decorate something with jewels [13C. < Anglo-Norman *juel* < *jeu* "game" < Latin *jocus*] ◇ **the jewel in the crown** the best or most outstanding example of something

jew·el bee·tle *n* a beetle with an iridescent body that gives it a superficial resemblance to a gemstone. Native to: Australia. Family: Buprestidae.

jew·el box, jew·el case *n* a hinged plastic case in which a CD is sold and stored

jew·el·er /jōō ələr/, **jew·el·ler** *n* somebody who makes, sells, or repairs jewelry

~~**jewelery**~~ incorrect spelling of **jewelry**

jew·el·fish /jōō əl fish/ (*plural* **-fish·es** or *same*) *n* a brightly colored fish that is popular as an aquarium fish. Native to: Africa. Latin name: *Hemichromis bimaculatus.* [< its speckling of emerald green or sapphire]

jew·el·ler *n* OCCUPATIONS another spelling of **jeweler**

jew·el·ler's rouge *n Can, UK* metal polish in the form of finely ground ferric oxide. US term **crocus**

jew·el·ler·y *n* CLOTHING Can, UK spelling of **jewelry**

jew·el·ry /jóo əlree, jóolree/ *n* items worn as ornaments, e.g., necklaces, bracelets, earrings, or rings (*often used before a noun*) ○ *a jewelry box*

jew·el·weed /jóo əl wèed/ (*plural* **-weeds** or *same*) *n* a plant with seed pods that burst open to the touch when mature. Flowers: spurred, yellow, orange, white. Native to: North America. Genus: *Impatiens.* [< the earring shape of the flowers and the silver sheen of the underside of the leaf]

Jew·ess /jóo əss/ *n* a highly offensive term for a Jewish woman or girl (*dated taboo*)

Jew·ett /jóo it/, **Sarah Orne** (1849–1909) US writer. Her novels and short stories, set on the coast of her native Maine, are leading examples of the regional literature of her time.

> "In the life of each of us, I said to myself, there is a place remote and islanded, and given to endless regret or secret happiness."
> [Sarah Orne Jewett, *The Country of the Pointed Firs*; 1896]

jew·fish /jóo fìsh/ (*plural* **-fish·es** or *same*) *n* an offensive term for a goliath grouper (*offensive*) [Probably because approved by Jewish dietary law]

Jew·ish /jóo ish/ *adj* **1.** relating to or practicing Judaism **2.** relating to or belonging to a people descended from the ancient Hebrews —**Jew·ish·ly** *adv* —**Jew·ish·ness** *n*

Jew·ish cal·en·dar *n* the lunar calendar of the Jewish religious year. It has 12 months, with 13 in leap years, and dates from 3761 B.C., considered the year of Creation.

Jew·ry /jóoree/ *n* **1.** Jews in general **2.** JUDAISM same as **Judaism**

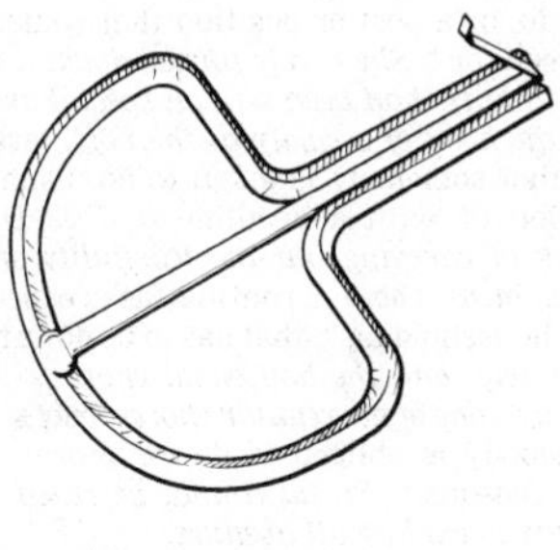

jew's harp

jew's harp *n* a small musical instrument held between the teeth and played by plucking a protruding metal tongue. It has a soft twanging sound. [Origin ?]

Jez·e·bel /jézzə bèl/ *n* **1.** in the Bible, a Phoenician princess and wife of King Ahab, who lived in the 9th century B.C. **2.** *also* **jez·e·bel** an offensive term for a woman regarded as sexually immoral or manipulative (*insult*)

JFF *abbr* ONLINE just for fun (*used in e-mails or text messages*)

JFK *abbr* **1.** John Fitzgerald Kennedy **2.** TRAVEL John Fitzgerald Kennedy International Airport

jg, **j.g.** *abbr* MIL junior grade

Jhan·si /jáanssee/, **Jhān·si** capital city of Jhansi District, central India, in Uttar Pradesh State. Population: 463,281 (2001).

Jhar·khand /jàar kaánd/ state in northeastern India. Capital: Ranchi. Population: 26,909,428 (2000). Area: 30,780 sq. mi./79,714 sq. km.

Jhe·lum /jéeləm/ river in northwestern India and northeastern Pakistan. It runs through the Indian city of Srinagar. Length: 480 mi./772 km.

JHVH, **JHWH** *n* BIBLE another spelling of **YHWH**

Jiang Qing /jyaáng chíng/, **Chiang Ch'ing** (1914–91) Chinese political activist. She was the third wife of Mao Zedong and was one of the prime movers of China's Cultural Revolution (1966–76). Born **Li Yunheshe**

Jiang·su /jyaáng sóo/ province in eastern China, bordering on the Yellow Sea. Capital: Nanjing. Population: 71,100,000 (1997). Area: 39,614 sq. mi./102,600 sq. km.

Jiang·xi /jyaáng shée/ inland province in southeastern China. Capital: Nanchang. Population: 41,050,000 (1997). Area: 63,630 sq. mi./164,800 sq. km.

Jiang Ze·min /jyaáng zöy méen/ (*b.* 1926) president of the People's Republic of China (1993–2003). He introduced many economic reforms after succeeding Deng Xiaoping in 1993. He retired as Communist Party secretary in 2002, but remained influential as head of the Central Military Commission.

> "History shows that anything conducive to our national stability is good."
> [Jiang Zemin, *Times (London)*; May 14, 1994]

jiao /jow/ (*plural same*) *n* a subunit of Chinese currency. See table at **currency** [Mid-20C. < Chinese *jiăo*]

jib[1] /jib/ *n* a small triangular sail in front of the main or only mast on a sailing ship or sailboat [Mid-17C. Origin ?]

jib[2] /jib/ *n* the projecting arm of a crane [Mid-18C. Origin ?]

jib[3] /jib/ (**jibbed, jib·bing, jibs**) *vi* **1.** to stop and refuse to move on (*refers to animals*) **2.** to be reluctant to do something [Early 19C. Origin ?] —**jib·ber** *n*

jib boom, **jib·boom** /jíb bóom/ *n* an extension of the spar that sticks out from the front of a sailing ship (**bowsprit**) and supports the jib

jibe[1] /jīb/, **gybe** SAILING *vti* (**jibed, jib·ing, jibes; gybed, gyb·ing, gybes**) **1.** SWING ACROSS BOAT to make a fore-and-aft-sail swing across from one side of the boat to the other when sailing with the wind behind, or to swing across in this way **2.** CHANGE DIRECTION IN SAILING BOAT to make a fore-and-aft rigged boat change direction by turning the stern across a following wind, or change direction by turning in this way ■ *n* SAIL SHIFT OR DIRECTION CHANGE a sudden shift of a sail back and forth or change in the direction a ship is sailing [Late 17C. < Dutch *gijben*]

jibe[2] /jīb/ (**jibed, jib·ing, jibes**) *vi* to conform or agree with somebody or something or with one another (*informal*) ○ *His story doesn't jibe with reality.* [Early 19C. Origin ?]

jibe[3] /jīb/ *n, vti* another spelling of **gibe**

jib·sheet /jíbsheet/ *n* the rope that controls the angle of the jib to the wind

JIC *abbr* ONLINE just in case (*used in e-mails or text messages*)

ji·ca·ma /héekəmə/ *n* **1.** a starchy tuberous root eaten raw in salads or cooked as a vegetable **2.** the tropical plant of the pea family that produces the jicama root. Latin name: *Pachyrhizus erosus.* [Early 17C. Via Mexican Spanish < Nahuatl *xicama*]

Ji·car·il·la /hèekə réeyə/ (*plural same* or **-las**) *n* a member of an Apache people who lived in central and southwestern North America and now live in northern New Mexico [Mid-19C. < Mexican Spanish, "small calabash tree" < *jicara* "calabash tree" < Nahuatl *xicalli* "container made from the fruit of the calabash tree"] —**Ji·car·il·la** *adj*

Jid·dah /jíddə/, **Jed·da** /jéddə/ city and port in western Saudi Arabia, on the Red Sea, in Al Hijaz State. Population: 1,490,000 (1995).

jif·fy /jíffee/, **jiff** /jif/ *n* the shortest possible length of time (*informal*) ○ *I'll be with you in a jiffy.* [Late 18C. Origin ?]

Jif·fy /jíffee/ *tdmk* a trademark for a padded mailing envelope

jig /jig/ *n* **1.** DANCE LIVELY DANCE a folk dance in triple time, especially one with kicking or jumping steps ○ *an Irish jig* **2.** MUSIC DANCING MUSIC the music for a jig **3.** WOODWORK, MANUF DEVICE FOR HOLDING PIECE OF WORK the part of a woodworking or metalworking machine that holds the object to be worked on and guides the cutting or drilling tool **4.** FISHING WIGGLY FISHING LURE a fishing lure made to attract a fish's attention through its motion as it is jerked around in the water **5.** MIN EXTRACT MINERAL-WASHING DEVICE a device that cleans and separates coal or other excavated minerals from waste material by shaking and washing ■ *v* (**jigged, jig·ging, jigs**) **1.** *vti* JERK AROUND QUICKLY to move around in a quick jerky way, or cause somebody or something to do this **2.** *vi* DANCE JIG to engage in dancing a jig **3.** *vt* WOODWORK, MANUF CUT WOOD GUIDED BY JIG to cut or drill a piece of work using a jig as a guide **4.** *vti* FISHING FISH WITH JIG to fish, or catch a fish, using a jig **5.** *vt* MIN EXTRACT CLEAN MINERALS WITH JIG to wash and separate coal or other excavated minerals with a jig [Mid-16C. Origin ?] ◇ **the jig is up** it is all finished (*informal*)

jig·ger[1] /jíggər/ *n* **1.** MEASURE, BEVERAGES MEASURE FOR ALCOHOLIC SPIRITS a measure used for alcoholic spirits, equal to approximately 1.5 fl oz **2.** BEVERAGES GLASS OF ALCOHOLIC SPIRITS a small glass of alcoholic spirits containing approximately 1.5 fl oz **3.** MANUF JIG OPERATOR somebody who operates a mechanical jig **4.** SOMETHING OR OTHER an object whose name is not known or cannot be recalled (*informal*) **5.** *Can* FISHING FISHING LINE a short line attached to an unbaited hook, used to catch squid or cod by a jerking motion **6.** SAILING SAIL AT STERN a small sail near the stern of a small sailboat **7.** SAILING same as **jiggermast** **8.** MECH ENG DEVICE WITH JERKING MOTION a mechanical device that operates with a jerking movement, e.g., a drill **9.** FISHING same as **jig** *n* (sense 4) [Early 18C. <JIG]

jig·ger[2] /jíggər/ *n* INSECTS same as **chigoe** (sense 1) [Late 18C. Alteration of CHIGGER]

jig·ger·mast /jíggər màst/ *n* **1.** the shorter mast near the stern of a small sailboat **2.** the mast nearest the stern on a four-masted sailing ship

jig·ger·y-pok·er·y /jìggəree pṓkəree/ *n* devious, deceitful, or dishonest behavior (*informal*) ○ *All this ridiculous jiggery-pokery going on behind my back!* [Late 19C. Origin ?]

jig·ging grounds /jígging gròwndz/ *n Can* an area of shallow water where fish or squid can be caught using a jigger

jig·gle /jígg'l/ *vti* (**-gled, -gling, -gles**) to move with small rapid movements in any direction, or cause something to do this ○ *He jiggled the ball before catching it.* ■ *n* a series of small rapid movements in any direction ○ *giving the key a quick jiggle in the lock* [Mid-19C. Blend of JIG + JOGGLE] —**jig·gly** *adj*

jig·gy /jíggee/ *n* money or wealth (*slang*) ◇ **get jiggy with it** to become excited about or involved in something

jig·saw /jíg sàw/ *n* **1.** HOBBIES same as **jigsaw puzzle** **2.** WOODWORK POWER SAW FOR CURVES a machine saw with a narrow blade, used for cutting curves and shapes ■ *vt* (**-sawed, -sawed** or **-sawn** /-sàwn/, **-saw·ing, -saws**) WOODWORK CUT SOMETHING WITH JIGSAW to cut or shape something using a jigsaw ■ *adj* COMPLEX IN STRUCTURE having many interrelating parts that form a complex whole ○ *the jigsaw nature of politics*

jig·saw puz·zle *n* **1.** a puzzle in the form of interlocking irregularly shaped pieces that make a picture when fitted together **2.** something made up of many interconnecting parts whose relation to each other is difficult to understand ○ *help the police to figure out this jigsaw puzzle of a crime*

ji·had /ji haád/, **je·had** *n* **1.** a campaign waged by Muslims in defense of the Islamic faith against people, organizations, or countries regarded as hostile to Islam **2.** a relentless campaign against somebody or something [Mid-19C. < Arabic *jihād* "effort"] —**ji·had·ist** *n*

Ji·lin /jéelín/ province in northeastern China. The southeast of the province borders Russia and North Korea. Capital: Changchun. Population: 1,420,000 (1995). Area: 72,200 sq. mi./187,000 sq. km.

jill *n* ZOOL another spelling of **gill**[3]

jil·lion /jíllyən/ *n* a number or amount too great to specify (*informal*) [Mid-20C. After BILLION]

jilt /jilt/ *vt* (**jilt·ed, jilt·ing, jilts**) to abruptly break off a romantic or sexual relationship with somebody ■ *n* somebody who abruptly breaks off a romantic or sexual relationship with somebody else [Mid-17C. Origin ?]

Jim Crow /jìm krṓ/, **jim crow** *n* **1.** *also* **jim crow** *or* **Jim Crow·ism** /jìm krō ìzzəm/ *or* **jim crow·ism** RACIAL DISCRIMINATION the practice of discriminating against Black people, especially by operating systems of public segregation (*informal*) **2.** TABOO TERM a highly offensive term for a Black person (*taboo*) ■ *adj* DISCRIMINATING AGAINST BLACK PEOPLE discriminating against or intended to discriminate against Black people (*informal*) ○ *Jim Crow segregation laws* ○ *Jim Crow racial attitudes* [Mid-19C. After a Black character in a plantation song]

jim·dan·dy /jìm dándee/ (*informal*) *adj* exceptionally good ■ *n* (*plural* **jim·dan·dies**) something that is exceptionally good of its kind [Late 19C. < *Jim*, familiar form of the name *James* + DANDY]

jim·jams /jím jàmz/ *npl* (*informal*) **1.** an attack of delirium tremens **2.** an attack of nervous anxiety [Late 19C. Plural of obsolete *jimjam* "trivial article, knick-knack"]

jim·mies /jímmeez/ *npl* small pieces of chocolate or candy sprinkled on top of ice cream

jim·my /jímmee/ *n* (*plural* **-mies**) **1. LEVER FOR PRYING SOMETHING OPEN** a short crowbar used as a lever, usually for prying things open **2.** MARINE BIOL **MALE CRAB** a male crab ■ *vt* (**-mied, -my·ing, -mies**) **OPEN SOMETHING WITH JIMMY** to force something open using a jimmy [Mid-19C. Alteration of JEMMY]

jim·son·weed /jímss'n weed/ *n* a tall poisonous weed of the nightshade family with foul-smelling foliage and spiny capsule fruits. Flowers: large, white, purple, trumpet-shaped. Latin name: *Datura stramonium*. [Late 17C. Alteration of JAMESTOWN, Virginia]

Ji·nan /jée naán/, **Chi-nan** city and capital of Shandong Province on the Huang He, eastern China. Population: 3,470,000 (1995).

jin·gle /jíng g'l/ *n* **1. METALLIC TINKLE** a light musical noise like that of small bells or pieces of metal being shaken together **2. TUNE FOR ADVERTISING SOMETHING** a catchy tune or verse, usually one that is played repeatedly to advertise something ■ *v* (**-gled, -gling, -gles**) **1.** *vti* **MAKE TINKLING SOUND** to make a light musical noise like that of small bells or pieces of metal being shaken together, or cause something to make this sound ○ *He jingled the coins in his pocket.* **2.** *vi* **HAVE EASILY REMEMBERED SOUND** to have a sound or rhyme that is catchy or repetitious [14C. An imitation of the sound] —**jin·gly** *adj*

jin·go /jíng gō/ (*plural* **-goes**) *n* an extreme patriot, especially somebody who advocates hostility toward other countries [Late 17C. Origin ?] —**jin·go·ish** *adj* ◇ **by jingo** used to express surprise or annoyance (*dated informal*)

jin·go·ism /jíng gō ìzzəm/ *n* extreme patriotism expressing itself especially in hostility toward other countries —**jin·go·ist** *adj, n* —**jin·go·is·tic** /jìng gō ístik/ *adj* —**jin·go·is·ti·cal·ly** *adv*

ORIGIN The context of the coining of ***jingoism*** was British foreign policy of the late 1870s. The prime minister, Benjamin Disraeli, favored sending gunboats to halt the advance of the Russian fleet out of their own waters into the Mediterranean. This gave rise to a music-hall song, written in 1878 by G. W. Hunt, the refrain of which went: "We don't want to fight, yet by Jingo! if we do, We've got the ships, we've got the men, and got the money too." Opponents of the policy picked up on the word *jingo* and used it as an icon of blind patriotism.

Jin·ja /jínjə/ city in southeastern Uganda, in the Eastern Region, on Lake Victoria. Population: 60,979 (1991).

jink /jingk/ *vi* (**jinked, jink·ing, jinks**) to make a quick sideways movement in order to evade somebody or something ■ *n* a quick evasive movement or maneuver [Late 17C. Origin ?]

Jin·nah /jínnə/, **Muhammad Ali** (1876–1948) South Asian lawyer and politician. He became president of the Muslim League in India in 1935. His campaign for a separate Muslim state resulted in the creation of Pakistan in 1947, when he became the state's first president and governor-general.

> "Muslims are a thousandfold more keen to get their independence than Hindus. But what do Hindus want? They want to remain the slave of the English but at the same time want us to become their slaves. They want the Muslims to be doubly enslaved."
> [Muhammad Ali Jinnah, *Speech, Peshawar, Pakistan*; November 1945]

jin·ni /jínnee/ (*plural* **jinn** /jin/), **djin·ni** (*plural* **djinn**) *n* in Islamic folklore, a spirit that can take on various human and animal forms and makes mischievous use of its supernatural powers [Early 19C. < Arabic *jinnī*]

Jin Nong /jìn náwng/ (1687–1764?) Chinese artist. He frequently incorporated calligraphy into his paintings, which are often of fruits and plants.

jin·rik·sha /jin ríkshə/, **jin·rick·sha** *n* VEHICLES same as **rickshaw** (sense 1) [Late 19C. < Japanese, < *jin* "man" + *riki* "strength" + *sha* "vehicle"]

jinx /jingks/ *n* an unseen force, a person, or something such as a curse that is thought to bring bad luck ○ *There must be a jinx on this expedition.* ■ *vt* (**jinxed, jinx·ing, jinx·es**) to make somebody or something likely to be unsuccessful or ineffective as a result of bad luck ○ *the feeling that they had been jinxed in some way* [Early 20C. Probably < *jynx* "wryneck," from the bird's use in witchcraft] —**jinxed** *adj*

ji·pi·ja·pa /heepee haápə/ *n* a plant without a stem that resembles a palm and has large leaves that are used to make panama hats. Native to: Central and South America. Latin name: *Carludovica palmata*. [Mid-19C. After *Jipijapa*, town in Ecuador]

JIT *abbr* MANAGEMT just-in-time

jit·ney /jítnee/ (*plural* **-neys**) *n* a small bus that takes passengers on a regular route for a small fare [Early 20C. Origin ?]

jit·ter /jíttər/ *vi* (**-tered, -ter·ing, -ters**) **BEHAVE NERVOUSLY** to behave in a nervous or restless way (*informal*) ■ *n* ELEC ENG **1. RAPID SIGNAL FLUCTUATION** an undesired rapid movement of electrical signals or images, e.g., on a television or oscilloscope screen, because of circuit instability or faulty components **2. DISTORTION IN DIGITIZED INFORMATION** a distortion in digitally transmitted or recorded sound or images, caused when two devices such as the recording and playback devices of audio recordings are not perfectly synchronized ■ **jit·ters** *npl* **NERVOUS ATTACK** feelings of nervousness or agitation (*informal*) ○ *He's got the jitters about his interview tomorrow.* [Early 20C. Origin ?]

jit·ter·bug /jíttər bùg/ *n* **1.** an energetic 1940s jazz dance for couples **2.** somebody who dances the jitterbug [Mid-20C. Origin ?] —**jit·ter·bug** *vi*

jit·ter·y /jíttəree/ *adj* **1.** feeling nervous or agitated **2.** making rapid jumpy movements —**jit·ter·i·ness** *n*

jiu·jit·su *n* MARTIAL ARTS another spelling of **jujitsu**

Ji·va·ro /heevə rō/ (*plural same or* **-ros**) *n* **1.** a member of a Native South American people living in the tropical forests of Ecuador and northeastern Peru. Their ancestors were noted for their ritual of shrinking and preserving the heads of enemies they had killed. **2.** a language spoken by the Jivaro people, belonging to the Equatorial branch of Andean-Equatorial. Native speakers: 20,000. [Mid-19C. < Spanish *jíbaro*] —**Ji·va·ro** *adj*

jive /jīv/ *n* **1.** DANCE **LIVELY DANCING STYLE** an uninhibited dance, often with a man swinging and throwing a woman, originally to jazz music and later to rock and roll **2. JAZZ MUSIC** jazz or swing music, especially that of the 1930s and 1940s **3.** LANGUAGE **JAZZ JARGON** the terminology and slang used by jazz musicians (*slang*) **4. INSINCERE TALK** smooth talk that is often deceptive or insincere (*slang*) ■ *v* (**jived, jiv·ing, jives**) **1.** *vi* **DANCE JIVE** to engage in dancing the jive **2.** *vi* LANGUAGE **TALK JIVE** to use the terminology and slang of jazz musicians (*slang*) **3.** *vti* **FLATTER** to flatter or deceive somebody with smooth or insincere talk (*slang*) ○ *I know when you're jiving me.* ■ *adj* **INSINCERE** lacking sincerity or honesty (*slang*) ○ *His comments are so jive!* [Early 20C. Origin ?] —**jiv·er** *n*

JJ, JJ. *abbr* **1.** BIBLE Judges **2.** LAW Justices

Jl. *abbr* **1.** BIBLE Joel **2.** PUBL journal **3.** CALENDAR July

jm *abbr* ONLINE Jamaica (*used in Internet addresses*) See table at **domain name**

Jm. *abbr* BIBLE James

Jn. *abbr* BIBLE John

j.n.d. *abbr* PSYCHOL just noticeable difference

jnr., **Jnr.** *abbr* junior

jnt. *abbr* joint

jo *abbr* ONLINE Jordan (*used in Internet addresses*) See table at **domain name**

Jo. *abbr* BIBLE Joel

Joan of Arc /jōn əv aárk/, **St.** (1412–31) French patriot and saint. She led the French to victory against the English, but was captured and burned at the stake as a heretic. She is the patron saint of France.

> "If I said that God did not send me, I should condemn myself; truly God did send me."
> [Attributed to Joan of Arc, *Remark at her trial*; February-May 1431]

João Pes·so·a /zhwóng pe sṓ ə/ capital city of Paraíba State, in northeastern Brazil. It is an important trade center. Population: 549,363 (1996). Former name **Parahyba**

job /job/ *n* **1. PAID OCCUPATION** an activity such as a trade or profession that somebody does regularly for pay, or a paid position doing this ○ *She's got a new job.* **2. TASK** something that remains to be done or dealt with ○ *I have a couple jobs to do this afternoon.* ○ *several jobs around the house* **3. ASSIGNMENT** an individual piece of work of a particular nature ○ *We managed to complete the job in under a week.* **4. FUNCTION** the role that somebody or something fulfills ○ *It's her job to look after the finances.* **5. DIFFICULTY** something that is difficult to accomplish ○ *I had quite a job getting it to start.* **6. QUALITY OF WORK DONE** a completed piece of work of a particular quality ○ *They did a very good job on the exterior.* **7. PARTICULAR KIND OF OBJECT** a particular kind of object, especially a manufactured item (*informal*) ○ *one of those big four-wheel-drive jobs* **8. CRIME** a criminal act, especially a robbery (*informal*) ○ *a bank job* **9.** COMPUT **PROGRAMMING TASK** a computer programming task run as a single application or unit ■ *v* (**jobbed, job·bing, jobs**) **1.** *vi* **WORK OCCASIONALLY** to take occasional or casual work ○ *He jobs as a gardener from time to time.* **2.** *vti* **DEAL IN WHOLESALE MERCHANDISE** to buy and sell merchandise as a wholesaler or agent **3.** *vt* **DISTRIBUTE WORK TO OTHERS** to subcontract portions of contract work to others ○ *job out the plumbing work on the house* **4.** *vi* **PROFIT FROM PUBLIC OFFICE** to make a private gain from working in a public position [Mid-16C. Origin ?] ◇ **good job** used for telling somebody that they have done something correctly or well (*informal*) ◇ **make the best of a bad job** to get the best result possible from an unfavorable situation ◇ **on the job** engaged in working

SYNONYMS ***job, assignment, task, chore, duty***

CORE MEANING: a piece of work to be done

job an activity that somebody regularly does for pay ○ *He had managed to get himself a job on a building site.* ○ *Omar said he would make himself useful doing odd jobs.* **assignment** a piece of work that somebody is given to do, or a post or position that somebody has been chosen for ○ *She rarely turned down a modeling assignment.* ○ *He had been sent on special assignment to assist the head of security at the port.* **task** a piece of work that somebody is given to do, usually short in duration or with a deadline ○ *R & D has the main task of carrying out the feasibility study and the development.* **chore** a routine task, especially an ordinary household task, that has to be done regularly ○ *ask for help with the household chores* ○ *Cleaning the shoes was one of my regular chores.* **duty** something that somebody is obliged to do for moral, legal, or religious reasons ○ *Fraud cannot be ruled out – we have a duty to explore all avenues.*

Job /jōb/ *n* **1.** in the Bible, a righteous man whose faith withstood severe testing by God ○ *have the patience of Job* **2.** a book of the Bible that describes Job's afflictions and eventual reward. See table at **Bible**

job ac·tion *n* a short-term action by workers, e.g., a slowdown, to achieve demands or protest policies

job·ber /jóbbər/ *n* **1.** somebody who does piecework or work on a job by job basis **2.** a wholesaler to retailers

job·ber·y /jóbbəree/ *n* the corrupt practice of making private gains from public office, or an instance of this

Job Corps *n* a US government training program for young people to enable them to obtain employment

job de·scrip·tion *n* an official written description of the responsibilities and requirements of a specific job, often one agreed between employer and employee

job·hold·er /jób hōldər/ *n* a holder of a regular job

job-hop *vi* to change jobs frequently, especially in working for different companies (*informal*) —**job-hop·per** *n* —**job-hop·ping** *n*

job-hunt *vi* to look for a job (*informal*) —**job hunt·er** *n*

job·less /jóbbləss/ *adj* without a job ■ *npl* unemployed people considered collectively —**job·less·ness** *n*

job lot *n* a miscellaneous collection of articles, especially ones that are bought or sold together ○ *I bought it as a job lot.*

job-re·lat·ed ill·ness *n* MED same as **industrial disease**

Jobs /jobz/, **Steve** (*b.* 1955) US entrepreneur. He cofounded Apple Computer Company (1976), which produced the first user-friendly home computer. Full name **Jobs, Steven Paul**

> "Do you want to spend the rest of your life selling sugared water or do you want the chance to change the world?"
> [Steve Jobs, *Fortune*; September 14, 1987]

Job's com·fort·er /jōbz-/ *n* somebody who, though appearing or intending to comfort a distressed person, only succeeds in worsening the situation [< the friends who came to "comfort" Job in his affliction (Job 5:17)]

job·seek·er /jób seekər/ *n* somebody who is actively looking for employment —**job·seek·ing** *n*

job-shar·ing *n* the system of dividing up the responsibilities of a single full-time job between two or more part-time workers —**job-share** *n, vi* —**job-shar·er** *n*

Job's tears /jōbz-/ *n* (*plural same*) a grass plant with sword-shaped leaves and hard white spherical seeds that are used as beads. Native to: tropical Asia. Latin name: *Coix lacryma-jobi.* ■ *npl* the hard white seeds of Job's tears, used as beads and, in East Asia, as a cereal [< its round shiny leaves]

Jo·cas·ta /jə kástə/ *n* in Greek mythology, the wife of Laius, king of Thebes, and later of their son Oedipus

jock[1] /jok/ *n* (*informal*) **1.** same as **jockey** *n* (sense 1) **2.** same as **DJ** (sense 1) [Late 18C. Shortening]

jock[2] /jok/ *n* (*informal*) **1.** an athlete, especially a male athlete in college **2.** same as **jockstrap** **3.** a man with macho attitudes [Mid-20C. Shortening of JOCKSTRAP]

jock·ey /jókee/ *n* (*plural* **-eys**) **1. RIDER OF RACEHORSES** a rider of racehorses, especially professionally **2. OPERATOR** somebody whose work involves the use or operation of a particular device, vehicle, or object (*informal*) ○ *We desk jockeys need to get out and exercise more.* ■ *v* (**-eyed, -ey·ing, -eys**) **1.** *vti* **RIDE RACEHORSE** to ride a racehorse, especially as a professional jockey **2.** *vi* **TRY TO GAIN ADVANTAGE** to maneuver in order to gain an advantage ○ *Watch them all jockeying for promotion.* **3.** *vt* **MANIPULATE SOMEBODY** to trick somebody, usually for personal gain ○ *She has been jockeyed into doing work for which he gets the credit.* **4.** *vti* **SKILLFULLY CHANGE POSITIONS** to change position using skillful maneuvers, or change the position of something in this way ○ *jockey a motorcycle through traffic* [Late 16C. < familiar form of the Scottish personal name *Jock*]

Jock·ey /jókee/ *tdmk* a trademark for underwear

jock·ey box *n regional* the glove compartment in a vehicle's dashboard

REGIONAL NOTE The term ***jockey box*** is a Western usage, especially of the Upper Rocky Mountain states, but is found as far south as Texas.

jock·ey park·ing *n* TRANSP same as **valet parking**

jock itch *n* a fungal infection of the skin in the groin area, especially in men and boys. Technical name **tinea cruris**

jock·strap /jók stràp/ *n* an elasticized belt with a pouch at the front, worn by sportsmen to support their genitals or to keep a protective cup in place [Late 19C. < slang *jock* "genitals," origin ?]

jo·cose /jō kṓss/ *adj* (*literary*) **1.** with a playful joking disposition **2.** playfully humorous in style [Late 17C. < Latin *jocosus* "full of joking" < *jocus* "joke"] —**jo·cose·ly** *adv* —**jo·cose·ness** *n* —**jo·cos·i·ty** /jō kóssətee/ *n*

joc·u·lar /jókyələr/ *adj* **1.** with a playful joking disposition **2.** intended to be funny [Early 17C. < Latin *jocularis* "of a little joke" < *jocus* "joke"] —**joc·u·lar·i·ty** /jòkyə lérrətee/ *n* —**joc·u·lar·ly** *adv*

joc·und /jókənd/ *adj* cheerful and full of good humor (*literary*) [14C. Via Old French *jocond* (influenced by Latin *jocus* "joke") < Latin *jucundus* < *juvare* "please, help"] —**jo·cun·di·ty** /jə kúndətee/ *n* —**joc·und·ly** *adv*

Jodh·pur /jód po͝or/ city in northwestern India, in the state of Rajasthan. Population: 666,279 (1991).

jodh·purs /jódpərz/ *npl* riding breeches that are wide at the hip and narrow around the calves, often with reinforced patches at the knee and thigh where the rider's legs grip the horse [Late 19C. After JODHPUR]

Jo·do·in /zhō dwáN/, **Claude** (1913–75) Canadian labor leader. He was the first president of the Canadian Labour Congress (1956–66).

Joe /jō/, **joe** *n* an ordinary man (*informal*) [Late 18C. Familiar form of the name *Joseph*]

Joe Bloggs /jō blógz/ *n UK* same as **Joe Blow** (*informal*)

Joe Blow *n* the average man in the street (*informal*)

joe·boat /jṓ bṑt/ *n regional* a small rowboat [Origin ?]

REGIONAL NOTE The term ***joeboat*** is a Lower Ohio Valley usage, found especially in Kentucky.

joe job *n* (*informal*) **1.** *Can* a boring or menial task **2.** ONLINE same as **spoof** *n* (sense 3)

Jo·el /jṓ əl, jōl/ *n* **1.** in the Bible, a Hebrew prophet who lived in the 6th century B.C. **2.** a book of the Bible that contains the prophecies traditionally attributed to Joel, dating from the years following the Israelites' Babylonian exile. See table at **Bible**

joe-pye weed /jō pī́-/ *n* a tall perennial plant with whorled leaves. Flowers: small, pink or purple, in clusters. Native to: North America. Latin name: *Eupatorium maculatum* or *Eupatorium purpureum.* [Early 19C. After *Joe Pye*, Native American turned into this plant according to a traditional story]

Joe Six-Pack *n* the ordinary working man (*slang*) [Because such a man supposedly buys six-packs of beer]

jo·ey /jṓ ee/ *n* a young animal, especially a kangaroo still young enough to be carried in its mother's pouch [Mid-19C. < Aboriginal *joè*]

Jof·frey /jóffree/, **Robert** (1930–88) US choreographer and ballet dancer. He founded the Joffrey Ballet (1954), and is known for his imaginative experimental works. Born **Khan, Abdulla Jaffa Anver Bey**

jog[1] /jog/ *v* (**jogged, jog·ging, jogs**) **1.** *vi* **TROT** to run at a slow steady pace ○ *He jogged across the road to the shop.* **2.** *vi* **RUN FOR EXERCISE** to run at a slow steady pace as a fitness exercise ○ *She jogs around the park every morning.* **3.** *vt* **NUDGE SOMETHING** to give a light push or shake to something ○ *A hand jogged his elbow and he turned.* **4.** *vi* **GO SLOWLY BUT STEADILY** to move along at a slow steady pace ○ *The little steam train jogged along the track.* **5.** *vi* **PLOD** to progress at a slow dull pace ○ *How are things? – Oh, you know: jogging along.* **6.** *vt* **REMIND SOMEBODY** to cause somebody to remember something ○ *thought the photo might have jogged your memory* ■ *n* **1. SPELL OF RUNNING** a spell of slow steady running for exercise ○ *I'm going for a quick jog.* **2. SLOW SPEED** a slow steady pace or motion ○ *moving along at a jog* **3. NUDGE** a light push or shake **4. REMINDER** something that reminds somebody ○ *a hint that might give your memory a jog* [Mid-16C. Origin ?]

jog[2] /jog/ *n* a sharp turn or angle ○ *We took a jog to the left.* ■ *vi* (**jogged, jog·ging, jogs**) to make a sharp turn or angle ○ *The path jogs toward the south.* [Early 18C. Origin ?]

jog·ger /jóggər/ *n* somebody who runs at a moderate pace, often over long distances, for exercise ■ **jog·gers** *npl* loose-fitting pants with an elasticized waist and ankles, used for jogging

jog·ging /jógging/ *n* a fitness or recreational activity that involves running at a moderate pace, often over long distances

jog·gle /jógg'l/ *n* **1. SHAKING ACTION** a gentle shaking motion or action **2. MASONRY JOINT** a joint between two pieces of masonry or concrete, in which a projection on one fits into a recess of the other ■ *v* (**-gled, -gling, -gles**) **1.** *vti* **SHAKE** to shake something gently, or be shaken ○ *The table joggled and my soda spilled all over.* **2.** *vt* **FIX MASONRY WITH JOGGLE** to join pieces of masonry or concrete with a joggle [Early 18C. Origin ?]

Jog·ja·kar·ta /jòg jə kaártə/ city in southwestern Indonesia, on the island of Java. Population: 477,073 (1997).

jog trot *n* **1.** a slow steady running pace **2.** a dull steady pace of life ○ *things going on at a jog trot*

Jo·han·nes·burg /jō haánnəss bùrg/ city in northeastern South Africa, and the capital of Gauteng Province. It originally developed as the center of a gold mining region. Population: 3,225,796 (2001).

Jo·han·nine /jō hán nīn/ *adj* relating to the apostle John or to the books of the Bible attributed to him [Mid-19C. < late Latin *Joannes* "John"]

Jo·har·i win·dow /jō hàree-/ *n* a graphical representation of how people give and receive information, used to help people understand interpersonal communication [late 20C. After the first names of Joseph Luft and Harry Ingham, inventors of the system]

john /jon/ *n* **1.** same as **toilet** (sense 1) (*informal*) **2.** a man who is a prostitute's customer (*slang*) [Early 20C. < the name *John*]

John /jon/ *n* **1.** a book of the Bible, the fourth of the gospels in which the life and teachings of Jesus Christ are described, traditionally attributed to St. John. **2.** a name for three books of the Bible, originally written as letters and traditionally attributed to St. John. ▶ see table at **Bible**

John /jon/, **St.** (*d.* 101?) one of the 12 apostles of Jesus Christ. He helped organize the early church throughout Palestine and Asia Minor. By tradition he is the author of the fourth Gospel, three Epistles, and Revelations in the Bible.

John (1167–1216) king of England. The youngest son of Henry II, he succeeded his brother Richard I as king (1199–1216). He was forced to issue the Magna Carta in 1215 after demands by the barons of England for constitutional reform. Known as **John Lackland**

John II (1319–64) king of France. He came to the throne in 1350. He was captured by the English (1356) but allowed to return to France to raise a ransom. Failing to do so, he returned to captivity. Known as **John the Good**

John VI (1769–1826) king of Portugal. He fled to Brazil following Napoleon's invasion of Portugal (1807), became king in 1816, and returned to Portugal in 1821. He granted Brazil independence (1822).

John (of Gaunt) /-gáwnt/, **Duke of Lancaster** (1340–99) English soldier and politician. The fourth son of Edward III, he fought the French and Spanish during the Hundred Years' War. In England, he acted as a peacemaker during the reign of his nephew Richard II.

John (the Bap·tist), St. (8? B.C.–A.D. 27?) Judean prophet. He is described in the gospels as the cousin and precursor of Jesus Christ. He was beheaded at the behest of Salome.

John, Augustus (1878–1961) British painter. The brother of Gwen John, he is known for his portraits of contemporary figures. Full name **John, Augustus Edwin**

John, Sir Elton (*b.* 1947) British rock singer and pianist. His partnership with lyricist Bernie Taupin produced a string of international hits. His songs include "Can You Feel the Love Tonight" (1994) and "Candle in the Wind," which was revised and reissued in commemoration of Princess Diana in 1997 and became the bestselling single of all time. Born **Dwight, Reginald**. Full name **John, Sir Elton Hercules**

John, Gwen (1876–1939) British painter. The sister of Augustus John, many of her works are portraits of women.

John Bar·ley·corn /-baárlee kàwrn/ *n* the personification of alcoholic drink (*literary or humorous*)

John Birch So·ci·e·ty /-búrch-/ *n* a right-wing political organization formed in the United States to combat Communism

john·boat /jón bṑt/ *n* a narrow boat with a flat bottom and squared-off ends that is paddled or poled in shallow waterways [Early 20C. < the name *John*]

John Bull *n* **1.** the personification of England and the English people **2.** an Englishman, especially one regarded as embodying Englishness [Late 18C. After a character in *Law is a Bottomless Pit* (1712), by J. Arbuthnot] —**John Bull·ish** *adj*

john-crow *n Carib* same as **black vulture** (sense 1)

John Doe /-dṓ/ *n* **1.** an average man affected by everyday events (*informal*) **2.** a man or boy in a legal proceeding whose identity is either not known or not revealed

John Do·ry /-dáwree/ *n* a deep-sea fish with a large flat olive-yellow body, long dorsal spines, and large jaws. Native to: eastern Atlantic, Mediterranean. Latin name: *Zeus faber.*

Joh·ne's dis·ease /yṓnəz-/ *n* a chronic disease of sheep, cattle, and other domestic animals, with symptoms of diarrhea and loss of weight, caused by a bacterium that is related to the tuberculosis bacterium [Early 20C. After H. A. *Johne* (1839–1910), German veterinary surgeon]

John Han·cock /-háng kòk/ *n* somebody's signature (*informal*) [After the first person to sign the US Declaration of Independence]

John Hen·ry /-hénnree/ *n* **1.** in US folklore, an African American hero renowned for his great strength. He died after beating a steam drill in a contest of endurance. **2.** somebody's signature (*informal*) [Partly after JOHN HANCOCK]

john·ny /jónnee/ (*plural* **-nies**) *n* a short gown that ties at the back, worn in hospitals by patients [Late 17C. < *Johnny*, familiar form of the name *John*]

John·ny Ap·ple·seed /-ápp'l seed/ ➧ **Chapman, John**

john·ny·cake /jónnee kàyk/ *n Can, Northeast US* a flat corn bread either baked or fried on a griddle [Mid-18C. Probably < *Johnny*, familiar form of the name *John*]

John·ny Ca·nuck *n Can* a personification of Canada, in the form of a strong clean-cut young man, often a lumberjack

John·ny-come-late·ly (*plural* **John·ny-come-late·lies** or **John·nies-come-late·ly**) *n* a recent arrival at a place, group, position, or point of view (*informal*) ○ *these Johnny-come-latelies and their "new" ideas*

John·ny-jump-up *n* a common pansy grown in flower beds. Flowers: small, multicolored. Native to: North America. Latin name: *Viola tricolor*.

John·ny-on-the-spot *n* somebody who is always ready to help (*dated informal*)

John·ny Reb *n* a Confederate soldier in the Civil War (*informal*) [Mid-19C. Shortening of *Johnny Rebel*]

John o'Groats /jòn ə grṓts/ tourist village on the northeastern tip of Scotland. The distance between John o'Groats and Land's End in Cornwall is the longest between two places in mainland Great Britain, 873 mi./1,405 km.

John Paul I, Pope (1912–78) He died 34 days after becoming pope in 1978. Born **Luciani, Albino**

John Paul II, Pope (*b.* 1920) In 1978 he became both the first ever Polish-born pope and the first non-Italian pope since 1523. Born **Wojtyła, Karol**

> "Love is never defeated, and I could add, the history of Ireland proves it."
> [John Paul II, *Speech, Galway*; September 30, 1979]

Johns /jonz/, **Jasper** (*b.* 1930) US artist. His work was an important influence on pop art, and features such imagery as the US flag.

> "Sometimes I see it and then paint it. Other times I paint it and then see it. Both are impure situations, and I prefer neither."
> [Jasper Johns. Quoted in *Sixteen Americans*, Dorothy C. Miller (ed.); 1959]

Popperfoto
Amy Johnson

John·son /jónss'n/, **Amy** (1903–41) British aviator. She made record solo flights to Australia (1930), Tokyo (1931), and the Cape of Good Hope and back (1936), and flew the Atlantic in 1933 with her husband. She was killed in an air crash.

> "Had I been a man I might have explored the Poles or climbed Mount Everest, but as it was my spirit found outlet in the air."
> [Amy Johnson. Quoted in *Myself When Young*, Margot Asquith (ed.); 1938]

Corbis
Andrew Johnson

John·son, Andrew (1808–75) 17th president of the United States (1865–69). A Democrat, he was Abraham Lincoln's vice president (1865), and succeeded to the presidency after Lincoln's assassination in April 1865. As president, he withstood an impeachment by Republicans opposed to his conciliatory Reconstruction policies. See table at **president**

> "The only safety of the nation lies in a generous and expansive plan of conciliation."
> [Andrew Johnson. Quoted in *The Critical Year: A Study of Andrew Johnson*, Howard K. Beale; 1930]

John·son, Claudia Alta Taylor (*b.* 1912) US first lady (1963–69). She took an active interest in ecological issues and in her husband's war-on-poverty program. Known as **Lady Bird**

John·son, Jack (1878–1946) US boxer. He became the first African American to win the world heavyweight boxing championship (1908). Full name **Johnson, John Arthur**

> "It was not the fights but the fights to get those fights that proved the hardest part of the struggle. It was my color."
> [Jack Johnson. Quoted in *World's Great Men of Color*, Joel Augustus Rogers; 1947]

John·son, James Weldon (1871–1938) US poet and writer. He is best known for his novel *The Autobiography of an Ex-Colored Man* (1912).

> "Sing a song full of the faith that the dark past has taught us, / Sing a song full of hope that the present has brought us, / Facing the rising sun of our new day begun, / Let us march on till victory is won."
> [James Weldon Johnson, *Lift Every Voice and Sing*; 1900]

The White House
Lyndon B. Johnson and Lady Bird Johnson

John·son, Lyndon B. (1908–73) 36th president of the United States. A Democrat, he was John F. Kennedy's vice president and became president when Kennedy was assassinated, winning a full term the following year. During his presidency (1963–69), increased US involvement in the Vietnam War made him unpopular, and diverted attention from his program of social reform, the "Great Society." See table at **president**. Full name **Johnson, Lyndon Baines**. Known as **L.B.J.**

> "It is a common failing of totalitarian regimes that they cannot really understand the nature of our democracy. They mistake dissent for disloyalty. They mistake restlessness for a rejection of policy...They mistake individual speeches for public policy."
> [Lyndon B. Johnson, *Speech, San Antonio, Texas*; September 29, 1967]

John·son, Magic (*b.* 1959) US basketball player. He played guard for the Los Angeles Lakers (1979–91, 92, 96), and is regarded as one of the greatest players of the game. Born **Johnson, Earvin, Jr.**

John·son, Philip (*b.* 1906) US architect. His eclectic designs include the AT&T headquarters (1984) in New York City. Full name **Johnson, Philip Cortelyou**

> "Architecture is the art of how to waste space."
> [Philip Johnson, *New York Times*; December 27, 1964]

John·son, Richard Mentor (1781–1850) vice president of the United States (1837–41). He was a vice president in Martin van Buren's Democratic administration.

John·son, Robert (1911–38) US blues singer and guitarist. His songs influenced Chicago blues and 1960s rock.

John·son, Samuel (1709–84) British critic, poet, and lexicographer. His works include his *Dictionary of the English Language* (1755) and *Lives of the Poets* (1779–81). He founded two periodicals, *The Rambler* (1750–52) and *The Idler* (1758–60), and his witty conversation is recorded in James Boswell's biography of him. —**John·so·ni·an** /jon sṓnee ən/ *adj*

> "I am not yet so lost in lexicography as to forget that words are daughters of earth..."
> [Samuel Johnson. Preface, *A Dictionary of the English Language*; 1755]

> "Language is the dress of thought."
> [Samuel Johnson, "Cowley," *Lives of the English Poets*; 1779–81]

John·son, Thomas (1732–1819) US Supreme Court associate justice (1791–93)

John·son, Walter (1887–1946) US baseball player. One of the greatest major league pitchers, he was elected to the Baseball Hall of Fame (1936). Known as **the Big Train**. Full name **Johnson, Walter Perry**

John·son grass *n* a coarse perennial variety of sorghum often grown as forage. Native to: Mediterranean. Latin name: *Sorghum halepense*. [After William *Johnson*, an Alabama planter]

John·ston /jónstən/ town in northeastern Rhode Island, west of Providence. Population: 29,023 (2002 estimate).

John·ston, Albert Sidney (1803–62) US Confederate army general. He led the Confederate army at the battle of Shiloh, in which he was killed.

John·ston, Joseph Eggleston (1807–91) US Confederate army general. He helped to win the First Battle of Bull Run (1861), but was unsuccessful in defending Vicksburg (1862) and Atlanta (1864).

Johns·town /jónz tòwn/ city in south central Pennsylvania, in Cambria County. It is a manufacturing center. Population: 23,231 (2002 estimate).

Jo·hor Strait /jə hàwr-/ narrow strait running between Singapore and Malaysia

joie de vi·vre /zhwaà də veévrə/ *n* energy and love of life [Late 19C. < French, "joy of living"]

join /joyn/ *v* (**joined, join·ing, joins**) **1.** *vti* BRING OR COME TOGETHER to meet, or make two or more things meet, and become linked or united **2.** *vt* FIX THINGS TOGETHER to put or fix two or more things together ○ *Join the wing to the body with glue.* **3.** *vt* MAKE CONNECTION BETWEEN THINGS to establish a connection between two or more things, e.g., by drawing a line between them ○ *join the dots* **4.** *vti* BECOME PART OF GROUP to become a member of something such as a club, social group, company, team, or other organization ○ *I've joined the Mountaineering Club.* **5.** *vt* DO SAME AS SOMEBODY to agree to do the same as somebody ○ *I'm sure my colleagues will want to join me in thanking you for your visit today.* **6.** *vt* UNITE PEOPLE IN PARTNERSHIP to bring two or more people into a partnership such as a marriage **7.** *vt* MEET SOMEBODY to go to meet somebody ○ *I'll join you later.* **8.** *vt* SHARE SOMEBODY'S COMPANY to enter into the company of another person ○ *Do you mind if I join you?* **9.** *vti* BE ADJACENT to be next to something or to each other ○ *This room joins the bathroom.* ■ *n* JOINT a place where two or more things have been joined ○ *You can hardly see the join.* [13C. Via Old French *joign-*, present stem of *joindre* < Latin *jungere* "join"] —**join·a·ble** *adj*

ORIGIN The Indo-European word from which *join* is ultimately derived is also the ancestor of English *adjust, conjugal, jostle, joust, jugular, juxtapose, subjugate, yoga, yoke,* and *zygo-*.

join in *vti* to take part in an activity along with other people ○ *Can I join in?*
join up *vi* to enlist as a member of one of the armed forces, especially at the outbreak of hostilities

join·der /jóyndər/ *n* **1. ACT OF JOINING** a joining or bringing together of two things (*formal*) **2. JOINING OF LEGAL PARTIES** a joining of two parties in a single lawsuit **3. COMBINING OF LEGAL PROCEEDINGS** a joining of two causes of action or two defenses in a single lawsuit **4. ACCEPTANCE OF ISSUE IN LAWSUIT** a formal acceptance of an issue offered in a lawsuit [Early 17C. < Anglo Norman < Old French *joindre* "to join" (see JOIN)]

join·er /jóynər/ *n* **1.** somebody who makes wooden components for buildings, especially finished woodwork **2.** somebody who readily joins clubs, societies, or organizations (*informal*)

join·er·y /jóynəree/ *n* **1.** the visible finished woodwork in a building, e.g., door frames and window frames **2.** the work of a joiner, or the techniques that a joiner uses

joint /joynt/ *n* **1. JUNCTION BETWEEN BONES** a part of the body where bones are connected, e.g., the knee, elbow, or skull. Many joints have supporting ligaments, protective cartilage, and a particular range of movement, while others such as those between the bones of the vault of the skull are immobile. **2.** ZOOL **JUNCTION BETWEEN SEGMENTS OF INVERTEBRATE BODY** any of the points of connection between movable segments of the body in an insect, spider, crab, or other invertebrate **3.** BOT **DIVIDING POINT ON PLANT STEM** the place on a plant stem from which a leaf or branch grows **4.** GEOL **CRACK IN ROCK** a crack or fissure in rock, without any looseness or displacement of the surrounding mass **5.** PUBL **HINGE OF BOOK COVER** either of the creases between the spine and the front and back covers of a book, especially a hardback **6. PLACE WHERE PARTS ARE JOINED** the place where parts or pieces of something are joined together **7. PIECE OF MEAT** a large piece of meat prepared and cooked for several people, especially one that is roasted **8. BAR OR NIGHTCLUB** a place of entertainment, e.g., a nightclub, especially one considered cheap or disreputable (*slang*) **9. PRISON** a prison or similar penal institution (*slang*) **10. PLACE** a building or dwelling of any kind (*slang*) **11. MARIJUANA CIGARETTE** a cigarette containing marijuana (*slang*) **12. TABOO TERM** a highly offensive term for a penis (*taboo slang*) ■ *adj* **1. DONE TOGETHER** done or produced together with others ○ *A joint statement was issued by the three party leaders.* **2. SHARING SAME ROLE** sharing the same role or position with another person or body ○ *My brother and I were appointed joint executors of her will.* **3. OWNED IN COMMON** owned in common by two or more people or concerns ○ *joint assets* **4. COMBINED** existing and operating in combination ○ *the joint ravages of the weather and pollution* ■ *v* (**joint·ed, joint·ing, joints**) **1.** *vt* **FIT PARTS TOGETHER** to fit or put parts together by means of a joint **2.** *vt* **DIVIDE CARCASS INTO PIECES** to cut a carcass into pieces of meat for cooking **3.** *vt* **PLANE EDGE OF BOARD** to plane and shape the edge of a board so that it fits with another edge to form a joint **4.** *vi* **FORM JOINTS DURING GROWTH** to form joints in the stem during the growth process (*refers to cereal plants*) [13C. < French, past participle of *joindre* (see JOIN)] —**joint·ed** *adj* —**joint·ing** *n* ◇ **out of joint 1.** dislocated or painfully displaced **2.** disturbed or disrupted, usually as a result of some major change or upheaval

joint ac·count *n* a bank account held in the names of more than one person, typically spouses or partners

Joint Chiefs of Staff *npl* the most important military advisory group to the president of the United States, consisting of the Chiefs of Staff of the Army and Air Force, the commandant of the Marine Corps, and the Chief of Naval Operations

joint de·fense *n* in legal proceedings, a defense strategy in which two or more defendants join and cooperate with one another, their attorneys working together and sharing information. Such defendants can assert attorney-client privilege not only with respect to statements made in confidence to their own attorneys, but also to attorneys of codefendants.

joint·er /jóyntər/ *n* **1.** a tool for pointing the mortar in brickwork or stonework after it has been laid **2.** a long plane used to shape the edges of planks into joints

joint grass *n* a creeping grass that roots at the nodes, or joints, in the stem and is used to bind loose soil and as a fodder grass. Latin name: *Paspalum distichum.*

joint·ly /jóyntlee/ *adv* in conjunction with, or in cooperation with, a person or organization ○ *The copyright is jointly owned by the composer and the publisher.*

joint res·o·lu·tion *n* a resolution passed by both Houses of Congress or both houses of any bicameral legislative body, that will become law when it is signed by the chief executive

join·tress /jóyntrəss/ *n* a woman on whom property has been settled by her husband at the time of their marriage

joint stock *n* stock held jointly, especially in a joint-stock company, a commercial enterprise whose capital is in shares that individual holders may transfer without the consent of the whole body

join·ture /jóynchər/ *n* an estate or property settled by a husband on his wife at the time of their marriage, to take effect in the event of his death

joint ven·ture *n* **1. JOINTLY UNDERTAKEN BUSINESS ENTERPRISE** a business enterprise jointly undertaken by two or more companies, who share the initial investment, risks, and profits **2.** CRIME, LAW **ILLEGAL ACTION BY TWO PARTIES** an illegal or criminal action that is undertaken by two or more parties ■ *vi* **GO INTO BUSINESS WITH OTHERS** to enter into a business enterprise jointly with another or others (*informal*) —**joint ven·tur·ing** *n*

joint·worm /jóynt wùrm/ *n* the larva of some wasps that forms a weakening swelling at the stem joint of a cereal plant. Family: Eurytomidae.

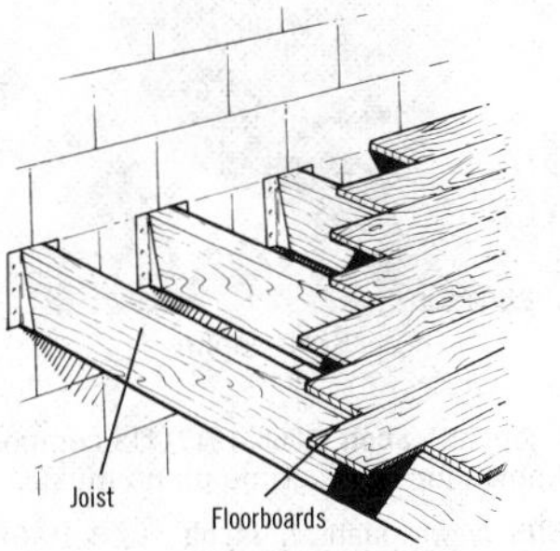

joist

joist /joyst/ *n* any of the parallel beams of wood, metal, or concrete that support a floor, roof, or ceiling [14C. < Old French *giste* "beam supporting a bridge" < Latin *jacere* "lie down"]

jo·jo·ba /hə hṓbə, hō-/ (*plural* **-bas**) *n* **1.** a waxy oil derived from the seeds of a desert tree. Use: shampoos, cosmetics. (*often used before a noun*) **2.** a desert bush or small tree whose seeds yield jojoba. Native to: southwestern North America. Latin name: *Simmondsia chinensis.* [Early 20C. Via Mexican Spanish < a Native American language]

joke /jōk/ *n* **1. FUNNY STORY** a story, anecdote, or wordplay that is intended to amuse **2. CAUSE OF AMUSEMENT** anything said or done to make people laugh ○ *dressed up the dog in a hat and sunglasses as a joke* **3. SOMETHING INADEQUATE** somebody or something that is laughably inadequate or absurd (*slang*) ○ *The surroundings were pleasant enough but the food was a joke.* ■ *v* (**joked, jok·ing, jokes**) **1.** *vti* **MAKE JOKES** to tell funny stories or say or do things to make somebody laugh **2.** *vi* **NOT TO BE SERIOUS** to be trying to be amusing, rather than serious or in earnest ○ *We knew he was only joking.* [Late 17C. < Latin *jocus* "jest, wordplay"] ◇ **be no joke** to be a serious or difficult matter (*informal*) ○ *It's no joke driving to work in the rush hour every day.*

jok·er /jṓkər/ *n* **1. TELLER OR PLAYER OF JOKES** a frequent teller or player of jokes **2. CARD BEARING PICTURE OF JESTER** an extra playing card in a deck, bearing a picture of a jester, that in some games can be substituted for other cards **3. AMUSING ECCENTRIC PERSON** an amusing, entertaining, or entertainingly eccentric person (*slang*) **4. THOUGHTLESS OR INCONSIDERATE PERSON** somebody whose thoughtless or inconsiderate action is highly annoying (*slang*) ○ *I'm looking for the joker who double-parked outside my front door.* **5.** LAW, POL **DISABLING CLAUSE** a clause or phrase surreptitiously slipped into a legislative bill or legal contract with the purpose of compromising its effect or making it unworkable ◇ **the joker in the deck** an unpredictable element that makes planning or projections difficult (*slang*)

jok·ey /jṓkee/ (**-i·er, -i·est**), **jok·y** *adj* good-humored and amusing, or full of jokes —**jok·i·ly** *adv* —**jok·i·ness** *n*

jok·ing·ly /jṓkinglee/ *adv* with the intention of making a joke rather than a serious comment or suggestion

jok·y *adj* another spelling of **jokey**

jol·ie laide /zhàwlee léd/ (*plural* **jol·ies laides** /*pronunc. same*/) *n* a woman whose facial features are not pretty in conventional terms, but nevertheless have a distinctive harmony or charm [< French < *jolie* "pretty" + *laide* "ugly"]

Jo·li·et /jṑlee ét/ city in northeastern Illinois, southeast of Aurora and southwest of Chicago. Population: 118,423 (2002 estimate).

Jo·liot-Cu·rie /zhàwlyō kyŏor ee/, **Frédéric** (1900–58) French physicist. Together with his wife, Irène Joliot-Curie (the daughter of Marie and Pierre Curie), he produced the first radioisotope artificially. They were joint winners of the Nobel Prize in chemistry (1935). Born **Joliot, Jean-Frédéric**

Jo·liot-Cu·rie, Irène (1897–1956) French physicist. Together with her husband, Frédéric Joliot-Curie, she produced the first radioisotope artificially. They were joint winners of the Nobel Prize in chemistry (1935). Born **Curie, Irène**

Jol·li·et /jṑlee ét/, **Jo·li·et, Louis** (1645–1700) French-Canadian explorer. With Father Jacques Marquette he charted the upper reaches of the Mississippi River (1673).

jol·li·fi·ca·tion /jòllifi káysh'n/ *n* the activities of people who are enthusiastically celebrating something in a happy, friendly way

jol·li·fy /jólli fī/ (**-fied, -fy·ing, -fies**) *vt* to make somebody cheerful, or create a festive atmosphere in something

jol·li·ty /jóllətee/ *n* cheerful, joking, or celebratory behavior [13C. < Old French *jolite* < *joli* "merry, pleasant"]

jol·ly /jóllee/ *adj* (**-li·er, -li·est**) **1. FRIENDLY AND CHEERFUL** friendly and cheerful, especially in a hearty or exuberant way ○ *a jolly pink-cheeked woman* **2. HAPPY** happily festive in tone or mood (*dated*) **3.** *UK* **ENJOYABLE** bringing pleasure or enjoyment (*dated informal*) ○ *A picnic would be jolly.* ■ *adv UK* **VERY** used to emphasize the extent to which something is good or bad (*dated informal*) ○ *Jolly nice of you to come.* [13C. < Old French *joli* "merry, pleasant"] ◇ **get your jollies** to get pleasure out of something (*slang*)
jolly along *vt* to keep somebody happy or cooperative by using flattery or encouragement (*informal*)

jol·ly·boat /jóllee bṓt/ *n* a small boat carried on a larger ship, often one kept hoisted at the stern of the ship [Late 17C. Origin ?]

Jolly Roger

Jol·ly Rog·er *n* the flag traditionally flown by a pirate ship, depicting a white skull and crossbones against a black background [Late 18C. Origin ?]

Jol·son /jólss'n/, **Al** (1886–1950) Russian-born US entertainer. He was known for his minstrel-style singing in blackface makeup. He starred in the first talking movie, *The Jazz Singer* (1927). Born **Yoelson, Asa**

"You ain't heard nothin' yet, folks."
[Al Jolson, *The Jazz Singer*; 1927]

jolt /jōlt/ *v* (**jolt·ed, jolt·ing, jolts**) **1.** *vti* SHAKE OR JERK VIOLENTLY to shake or jerk suddenly and violently, or make somebody or something shake or jerk suddenly and violently, especially as a result of a sudden movement **2.** *vt* STARTLE SOMEBODY INTO REALITY to startle somebody out of a daydream, fantasy, or other state of semiawareness **3.** *vi* BUMP UP AND DOWN to bump up and down or shake from side to side while moving ■ *n* **1.** SHOCK OR REMINDER an emotional shock or a sharp reminder **2.** VIOLENT MOVEMENT a sudden violent movement or blow ○ *The train moved off again with a series of jolts.* [Late 16C. Origin ?] —**jolt·ing·ly** *adv* —**jolt·y** *adj*

Jon. *abbr* BIBLE Jonah

Jo·nah[1] /jṓnə/ *n* **1.** in the Bible, a Hebrew prophet of the 8th century B.C. who was swallowed by a great fish and vomited out three days later, unharmed **2.** a book of the Bible that tells the story of Jonah, whose preaching caused the Assyrians to repent their wickedness. See table at **Bible**

Jo·nah[2] /jṓnə/ *n* somebody who brings bad luck [Late 16C. < JONAH[1]] —**Jo·nah·esque** /jṑnə ésk/ *adj*

Jon·a·than[1] /jónnəthən/ *n* **1.** a North American variety of red-skinned dessert apple **2.** a citizen or resident of New England, especially in the early to mid-19th century (*humorous or archaic*) [Late 18C. After *Jonathan* Trumbull, 18C governor of Connecticut]

Jon·a·than[2] /jónnəthən/ *n* in the Bible, the eldest son of King Saul and close friend of David, who was killed in battle against the Philistines (1 Samuel 13–2 Samuel 21)

jones /jōnz/ *n* **1.** ADDICTION an addiction, especially a heroin addiction (*slang*) **2.** WITHDRAWAL drug withdrawal symptoms, especially from heroin (*slang*) **3.** HABITUAL CRAVING an all-consuming craving or desire for something (*slang*) **4.** *also* **Jones** TABOO TERM a highly offensive term for a penis (*taboo*) [Late 20C. Origin ?]

Jones /jōnz/, **Bobby** (1902–71) US amateur golfer. He won several major tournaments (1923–29) and the Grand Slam (1930). Full name **Jones, Robert Tyre, Jr.**

Jones, Inigo (1573–1652) English architect and stage designer. He introduced the Palladian style into English architecture. His designs include the Queen's House at Greenwich, England (1616–35).

Jones, James (1921–77) US writer. He is known for his war novel *From Here to Eternity* (1951).

Jones, James Earl (*b.* 1931) US actor. After a successful stage, movie, and television career, he become well known as the distinctive voice of Darth Vader in the *Star Wars* movies (1977–83).

Jones, John Paul (1747–92) Scottish-born US naval officer. He captured or destroyed many British ships during the Revolution.

Jones·bor·o /jṓnzbərə/ city in northeastern Arkansas, northwest of West Memphis. Population: 56,888 (2002 estimate).

Jone·ses /jṓnzəz/ *npl* neighbors, especially somebody's next-door neighbors [Late 19C. < *Jones*, common British surname]

jon·gleur /zhawN glúr/ *n* a wandering minstrel of medieval times who traveled around singing the compositions of troubadours or reciting epic poems in noble households or royal courts [Late 18C. Via French < Latin *joculator* "jester" < *jocus* "joke"]

Jön·kö·ping /yṓn chŏ ping/ city and capital of Jönköping County, in southern Sweden. Population: 115,897 (1998).

Jon·quière /zhōn kyér/ city in eastern Canada, in Chicoutimi County, southern Quebec Province. Population: 54,842 (2002).

jonquil

jon·quil /jóngkwəl/ *n* a variety of narcissus. Flowers: small, fragrant, yellow. Native to: southern Europe. Latin name: *Narcissus jonquilla.* [Early 17C. Via modern Latin *jonquilla* or French *jonquille* < Spanish *junquillo* "little rush" < *junco* "rush"] —**jon·quil** *adj*

Jon·son /jónssən/, **Ben** (1572–1637) English playwright and poet. His plays include brilliant comedies such as *Volpone* (1606) as well as classical tragedies. James I appointed him poet laureate in 1616. Full name **Jonson, Benjamin**

"Helter skelter, hang sorrow, care'll kill a cat, up-tails all, and a louse for the hangman."
[Ben Jonson, *Every Man in His Humour*; 1598]

Jop·lin /jóplin/, **Janis** (1943–70) US rock singer. She is known for her raw and emotionally charged renditions of rock and blues songs.

Corbis-Bettmann

Scott Joplin

Jop·lin /jópplin/, **Scott** (1868–1917) US composer. He is best known for his ragtime piano music.

Jor·daens /yawr daánss/, **Jacob** (1593–1678) Flemish painter. His large baroque works feature subjects such as banquets, revelry, and genre scenes.

Jordan

Jor·dan /jáwrd'n/ **1.** country in Southwest Asia, bordered by Syria, Iraq, Saudi Arabia, the Gulf of Aqaba, Israel, and the West Bank. Language: Arabic. Currency: Jordanian dinar. Capital: Amman. Population: 5,460,265 (2003). Area: 34,578 sq. mi./89,556 sq. km. Official name **Hashemite Kingdom of Jordan 2.** river in Southwest Asia that rises in the Anti-Lebanon Mountains of Lebanon and flows south through the Sea of Galilee before emptying into the Dead Sea. Length: 200 mi./320 km. —**Jor·da·nian** /jawr dáynee ən/ *adj, n*

Jor·dan, Barbara Charline (1936–96) US politician. The first African American woman to win a seat in the Texas Senate (1966), she served as a member of the United States House of Representatives (1972–78) and was renowned for her eloquent speeches against racism.

Jor·dan, Michael (*b.* 1963) US basketball player. He played for the Chicago Bulls from 1984 to 1993, and again from 1995 to 1998. He is considered by many to be the greatest player in basketball history. Known as **Air Jordan**

"Talent wins games, but teamwork and intelligence win championships."
[Michael Jordan, *I Can't Accept Not Trying*; 1994]

Jor·dan al·mond *n* **1.** a large Spanish variety of almond chiefly cultivated around and exported from Málaga **2.** a Jordan almond or other almond with a hard sugar coating [15C. < alteration of French or Spanish *jardin* "garden"]

Jor·dan curve *n* in mathematics, any simple closed curve, e.g., a circle or an ellipse [Early 20C. After M. E. C. *Jordan* (1838–1922), French mathematician]

Jor·dan curve the·o·rem *n* in geometry, a theorem holding that every simple closed curve divides a plane into two regions and serves as their boundary

Jo·seph /jṓzəf/ *n* in the Bible, the son of Jacob and Rachel, sold into slavery in Egypt by his jealous brothers

Jo·seph /jṓzəf/ **1.** ♦ **Akiba ben Joseph 2.** ♦ **Saadia ben Joseph**

Jo·seph, St. (*fl* 1st century B.C.) According to the Bible, he was a carpenter of Nazareth and the husband of Mary, the mother of Jesus Christ

Jo·seph (1840?–1904) Nez Percé leader. He resisted white encroachment in the western United States. Born **In-mut-too-yah-lat-lat** ("thunder coming up from the water over the land"). Known as **Chief Joseph**

"The earth is the mother of all people, and all people should have equal rights upon it. You might as well expect the rivers to run backward as that any man who was born a free man should be contented when penned up and denied liberty."
[Joseph, "An Indian's View of Indian Affairs," *North American Review*; 1879]

Jo·seph II (1741–90) Holy Roman Emperor. He was the son of Francis I and Maria Theresa. As emperor (1765–90), he saw his reforms frustrated by insurrection and the distractions of war.

Jo·seph Bo·na·parte Gulf /jṓsəf bṓnə paart-/ inlet of the Timor Sea on the northern coast of Australia, extending from Western Australia into the Northern Territory. It is 200 mi./320 km wide.

Jo·sé·phine /jṓzə feén/, **Empress of the French** (1763–1814) She married the future Napoleon I in 1796 and was empress from 1804 until the childless marriage was dissolved in 1809. Born **Pagerie, Marie Joséphine Rose Tascher de la**

Jo·seph of Ar·i·ma·the·a /-àrrə mə theé ə/, **St.** (*fl* A.D. 1st century) According to the Bible, he asked Pontius Pilate for the body of Jesus Christ, and buried it in his own tomb (Matthew 27)

Jo·seph·son ef·fect /jṓzəfs'n-/ *n* the passage of an electric current through a thin insulating layer between two superconducting metals [Late 20C. After Brian David *Josephson* (b. 1940), British physicist]

Jo·seph·son junc·tion *n* in electrical or electronic circuits, a junction that utilizes the Josephson effect, consisting of two superconducting materials separated by a thin insulating layer. In a computer memory, a Josephson junction acts as a high-speed switch.

Jo·se·phus /jō seéfəss/, **Flavius** (A.D. 37?–100?) Jewish historian and general. His works include a history of the Jewish revolt against Rome (A.D. 66) and a history of the Jews. Born **Matthias, Joseph Ben**

josh /josh/ (**joshed, josh·ing, josh·es**) *v* (*informal*) **1.** *vti* to make fun of somebody in a friendly, good-humored way **2.** *vi* to joke or indulge in banter with somebody [Mid-19C. Origin ?] —**josh·er** *n* —**josh·ing·ly** *adv*

Josh. *abbr* BIBLE Joshua

Josh·u·a /jóshoo ə/ *n* **1.** in the Bible, Moses' successor as leader of the Israelites **2.** a book of the Bible that describes the Hebrew invasion and partition of Canaan under Joshua's command. See table at **Bible**

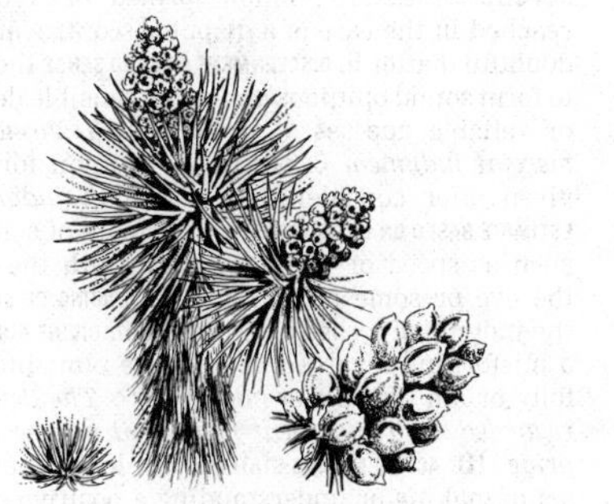

Joshua tree

Josh·u·a tree *n* a small tree-shaped yucca with sword-shaped leaves. Flowers: white, in clusters. Native to: deserts of southwestern United States. Latin name: *Yucca brevifolia*. [Mid-19C. Probably after JOSHUA, because the tree's branching shape resembles somebody brandishing a spear (Joshua 8:18)]

Josh·u·a Tree Na·tion·al Park /jòshoo ə tree-/ national park, in southern California, established in 1994. It comprises parts of the Mojave and Sonoran deserts. Area: 1,590 sq. mi./4,120 sq. km.

Jo·si·ah /jō sī́ ə/, **king of Judah** (648?–609 B.C.) He is credited in the Bible with restoring the worship of Yahweh, and was killed by the Assyrians at the Battle of Megiddo

joss /joss/ *n* an image or statue representing a Chinese deity [Early 18C. Via Javanese *dejos* < Portuguese *deus* "god" < Latin]

joss house *n* a Chinese shrine or temple containing images or statues of deities

joss stick *n* incense in the form of a stick of dried paste

jos·tle /jóss'l/ (**-tled, -tling, -tles**) *vti* to knock or bump against somebody, or push or elbow somebody deliberately, sometimes as an expression of aggression or hostility ○ *We managed to jostle our way to the front.* [Mid-16C. < JOUST] —**jos·tler** *n*

jot /jot/ *vt* (**jot·ted, jot·ting, jots**) to write something down hastily for later reference ○ *jotted down the title in her notebook* ■ *n* a very small amount [15C. Via Latin < Greek *iōta* (see IOTA)]

jo·ta /khṓtə/ *n* a fast Spanish dance performed with castanets in 3/4 time, usually to voice and guitar accompaniment. It is the traditional dance of Aragón. [Mid-19C. < Spanish]

jot·ting /jótting/ *n* a hastily written note, comment, or observation

Jo·tun /jṓ tùn/, **Jo·tunn** *n* in Norse mythology, a member of a race of giants with supernatural powers

Jo·tun·heim /jṓtun hìm/ *n* in Norse mythology, the home of the giants [< Old Norse *Jotunheimar*]

Jo·tunn *n* MYTHOL another spelling of **Jotun**

jou·al /zhōo ál, -aál/ *n Can* a mainly urban dialect of Canadian French containing many English words, also spoken in parts of Maine [Mid-20C. Via dialectal Canadian French < French *cheval* "horse"]

joule /jool/ *n* the International System unit of energy or work, equal to the work done when the application point of a one newton force moves one meter in the direction of application. Symbol **J** [Late 19C. After James *Joule* (1818–89), British physicist]

Joule ef·fect /jóol-/ *n* an increase in heat resulting from the passage of a current through a conductor

jounce /jownss/ *vti* (**jounced, jounc·ing, jounc·es**) to bounce up and down and rock from side to side while moving, or make somebody or something move in this way ■ *n* a jolting, swaying, bouncing, or rocking movement [15C. Origin ?] —**jounc·y** *adj*

jour. *abbr* **1.** journal **2.** journalist **3.** journeyman

jour·nal /júrn'l/ *n* **1. MAGAZINE OR PERIODICAL** a magazine or periodical, especially one published by a specialist or professional body for its members, containing information and contributions relevant to their area of activity ○ *a medical journal* **2. DIARY** somebody's written daily record of personal experiences **3. PRELIMINARY RECORD OF FINANCIAL TRANSACTIONS** a book for recording daily transactions, especially in double entry bookkeeping, using a formulaic style to ensure their correct entry in a ledger **4. OFFICIAL RECORD** the official daily record of proceedings kept by an association or body, especially a legislative body or parliament **5.** MECH ENG **SECTION OF SHAFT** a cylindrical section of a shaft designed to rotate inside a bearing [14C. Via French, "daily" < late Latin *diurnalis* (see DIURNAL)]

jour·nal box *n* the metal housing of a journal and its bearing. It often serves as a place for lubricant.

jour·nal·ese /jùrn'l éez/ *n* the style of writing supposedly associated with journalists, marked by the use of formulaic expressions (*disapproving*)

jour·nal·ism /júrn'l ìzzəm/ *n* **1.** the profession of gathering, editing, and publishing news reports and related articles for newspapers, magazines, television, or radio **2.** writing or reporting for the media as a literary genre or style

jour·nal·ist /júrn'list/ *n* a writer or editor for a newspaper or magazine or for television or radio

jour·nal·is·tic /jùrn'l ístik/ *adj* relating to journalism, or similar in style to journalism —**jour·nal·is·ti·cal·ly** *adv*

jour·nal·ize /júrn'lìz/ (**-ized, -iz·ing, -iz·es**) *vti* to keep a journal, or record something in a journal —**jour·nal·i·za·tion** /jùrn'li záysh'n/ *n* —**jour·nal·iz·er** *n*

~~**journel**~~ incorrect spelling of **journal**

jour·ney /júrnee/ *n* (*plural* **-neys**) **1. TRIP SOMEWHERE** a trip or expedition from one place to another **2. PROCESS OF DEVELOPMENT** a gradual passing from one state to another regarded as more advanced, e.g., from innocence to mature awareness ○ *a spiritual journey* ■ *vi* (**-neyed, -ney·ing, -neys**) **TRAVEL SOMEWHERE** to travel to a place or over a particular distance ○ *We are journeying into the unknown.* [12C. Via Old French *journee* "day, day's work or travel" < Latin *diurnum* "daily portion" < *diurnus* (see DIURNAL)] —**jour·ney·er** *n*

jour·ney cake *n Northeast US* COOK same as **johnnycake**

jour·ney·man /júrnimən/ (*plural* **-men** /-mən/) *n* (*often used before a noun*) **1.** a competent and reliable but unexceptional performer or exponent of something ○ *a good journeyman violinist* **2.** an artisan who has completed an apprenticeship and is fully trained and qualified but still works for an employer ○ *a journeyman electrician* [15C. Literally, somebody qualified to work for a daily wage rather than as an apprentice]

jour·no /júrnō/ (*plural* **-nos**) *n UK* same as **journalist** (*informal*) [Mid-20C. Contraction]

joust /jowst/ *n* **MEDIEVAL TOURNAMENT** a form of combat in medieval times held between two mounted knights in full armor who charged at and tried to unseat each other with a lance ■ *vi* (**joust·ed, joust·ing, jousts**) **1. ENGAGE IN JOUST** to take part in a joust **2. ENGAGE IN CONTEST** to take part in a contest against others ○ *candidates jousting for ninety minutes in a televised debate* [13C. < Old French *jouster* "bring together" < Latin *juxta* "close, beside"] —**joust·er** *n*

J'Ou·vert /jòo váy/ *n Carib* the Monday that is the eve of Mardi Gras, when the festivities begin [< French *jour ouvert* "the day having been opened"]

Jove /jōv/ *n* the Roman god Jupiter [14C. < Latin *Jov-*] —**Jo·vi·an** *adj* ◇ **by Jove** used to convey surprise, or to emphasize a conviction (*dated informal*)

jo·vi·al /jṓvee əl/ *adj* cheerful in mood or disposition [Late 16C. Via French < Latin *jovialis* < *Jov-* "Jove"] —**jo·vi·al·i·ty** /jṑvee állətee/ *n* —**jo·vi·al·ly** *adv* —**jo·vi·al·ness** *n*

Jo·vi·an plan·et *n* any one of the four major planets, Jupiter, Uranus, Saturn, or Neptune

jo·war /jə waár/ *n S Asia* PLANTS same as **sorghum** (sense 1) [Early 19C. < Hindi *jauār*]

jowl[1] /jowl/ *n* **1.** the jaw, especially the lower jaw **2.** a cheek, especially a prominent one [Old English *ceafl* < Germanic]

jowl[2] /jowl/ *n* **1.** a flaccid plump fold of flesh under somebody's chin **2.** a dewlap under the neck of cattle or a wattle on the neck of a bird [Old English *ceole* < Germanic]

jowl·y /jówlee/ (**-i·er, -i·est**) *adj* with a fold of flesh hanging under the neck —**jowl·i·ness** *n*

joy /joy/ *n* **1. GREAT HAPPINESS** feelings of great happiness or pleasure, especially of an elevated or spiritual kind **2. SOMETHING THAT BRINGS HAPPINESS** a pleasurable aspect of something or source of happiness ○ *His little granddaughter was a great joy to him.* ■ *vi* (**joyed, joy·ing, joys**) **ENJOY SOMETHING** to delight in something (*literary or archaic*) [12C. < French *joie* < Latin *gaudere* "rejoice"]

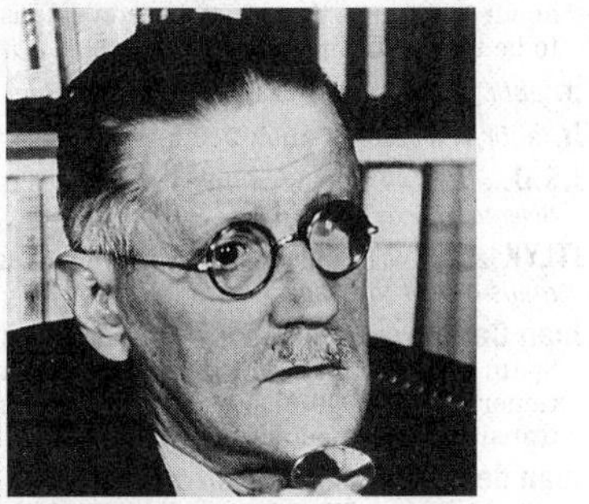
AKG London

James Joyce

Joyce /joyss/, **James** (1882–1941) Irish novelist. His innovative techniques, as demonstrated in *Ulysses* (1922) and *Finnegans Wake* (1939), make him one of the most influential modern writers. Full name **Joyce, James Augustine Aloysius**

> "The mystery of æsthetic like that of material creation is accomplished. The artist, like the God of the creation, remains within or behind or beyond or above his handiwork, invisible, refined out of existence, indifferent, paring his fingernails."
> [James Joyce, *A Portrait of the Artist as a Young Man*; 1916]

> "Every life is many days, day after day. We walk through ourselves, meeting robbers, ghosts, giants, old men, young men, wives, widows, brothers-in-love. But always meeting ourselves."
> [James Joyce, *Ulysses*; 1922]

Joyce, William (1900–46) British traitor. He was found guilty of treason and hanged for broadcasting Nazi propaganda to Britain during World War II. Known as **Lord Haw-Haw**

joy·ful /jóyf'l/ *adj* **1.** full of joy, or feeling or expressing joy **2.** bringing or causing joy —**joy·ful·ly** *adv* —**joy·ful·ness** *n*

joy·less /jóyləss/ *adj* lacking in warmth or happiness —**joy·less·ly** *adv* —**joy·less·ness** *n*

Joy·ner-Ker·see /jòynər kúrzee/, **Jackie** (*b.* 1962) US track and field champion. She won Olympic gold medals in the heptathlon (1988 and 1992). Born **Joyner, Jacqueline**

joy·ous /jóy əss/ *adj* **1.** full of joy, especially of a fervent and unrestrained nature **2.** making people happy or joyful —**joy·ous·ly** *adv* —**joy·ous·ness** *n*

joy·pad /jóy pàd/ *n* a handheld control mechanism for a computer game

joy·pop /jóy pòp/ (**-popped, -pop·ping, -pops**) *vi* to take illicit drugs occasionally rather than habitually (*slang*) —**joy·pop·per** *n*

joy·rid·ing /jóy rìding/ *n* a crime that involves stealing a car and driving it dangerously at high speed —**joy·ride** *n, vi* —**joy·rid·er** *n*

joy·stick /jóy stìk/ *n* **1.** the control lever of an aircraft or of a small motor-powered vehicle **2.** a hand-held control stick that allows a player to control the movements of a cursor on a computer screen or a symbol in a video game

jp *abbr* ONLINE Japan (*used in Internet addresses*) See table at **domain name**

J.P., JP *n* somebody appointed to judge minor criminal cases, perform marriages, administer oaths, and refer cases to higher courts. Full form **justice of the peace**

J par·ti·cle *n* PHYS same as **J/psi particle**

jpeg /jáy pèg/ *abbr* a file extension for a JPEG file. Full form **Joint Photographic Experts Group**

JPEG /jáy pèg/ *n* a format for encoding high-resolution graphic images as computer files for storage and transmission. Full form **Joint Photographic Experts Group**

jpg *abbr* a file extension for a JPEG file. Full form **Joint Photographic (Experts) Group**

Jpn. *abbr* **1.** Japan **2.** Japanese

J/psi par·ti·cle /jày sī-, -psī-/ *n* an unstable elementary particle of the meson group. It has a large mass, about 6,000 times that of an electron, and is thought to be formed from charmed quarks.

jr. *abbr* junior

Jr. *abbr* **1.** BIBLE Jeremiah **2.** Junior

J.S.D. *abbr* LAW Doctor of Juristic Science [Latin *Juris Scientiae Doctor*]

JTLYK *abbr* ONLINE just to let you know (*used in e-mails or text messages*)

Juan Car·los /waan kaarlōss, hwaan-/ (*b.* 1938) king of Spain. He became king following the death of General Franco (1975), presiding over Spain's rapid transition to democracy.

Juan de Fu·ca, Strait of /waan də fo͞okə/ body of water lying between Washington State and Vancouver Island, Canada, connecting the Strait of Georgia and Puget Sound to the Pacific Ocean. Length: 99 mi./160 km.

Juá·rez /waar ez, hwaar-/, **Benito Pablo** (1806–72) Mexican president and national hero. He fought against the government of General Antonio López de Santa Anna and served as president of Mexico (1861–63 and 1867–72).

ju·ba /jo͞obə/ *n* formerly in the southern United States, a lively rustic dance with much clapping and thigh-slapping, the word "juba" being repeated as a refrain [Mid-19C. Origin ?]

Ju·ba /jo͞obə/ city in southern Sudan on the White Nile River. Population: 114,980 (1993).

Jub·bul·pore /júbb'l pàwr/ former name for **Jabalpur**

ju·bi·lant /jo͞obilənt/ *adj* feeling or expressing great delight over a success, achievement, or victory [Mid-17C. < Latin *jubilant-*, present participle of *jubilare* "call out, shout for joy"] —**ju·bi·lant·ly** *adv*

Ju·bi·la·te /jo͞obə láytee, yo͞obə-/ *n* Psalm 100, which is sung as a canticle in the Roman Catholic and Anglican churches. In the Latin version, it begins "Jubilate Deo," meaning "Rejoice in the Lord."

ju·bi·la·tion /jo͞obə láysh'n/ *n* uninhibited rejoicing in the celebration of a victory or success [14C. < Latin *jubilation-* < *jubilat-*, past participle of *jubilare* "call out, shout for joy"]

ju·bi·lee /jo͞obə lee, jo͞obə lée/ *n* **1.** SPECIAL ANNIVERSARY a significant anniversary of an important event such as a wedding **2.** JOYFUL TIME a time or season of celebration **3.** YEAR OF INDULGENCE SET BY POPE in the Roman Catholic Church, a period set by the pope, traditionally every 25 years, in which forgiveness of sins is granted in return for acts of piety or repentance **4.** JEWISH YEAR OF RESTITUTION in Jewish history, a year of restoration or restitution that was proclaimed every 50 years by a countrywide blast of trumpets. During the period, land was left uncultivated, slaves were emancipated, and land that had been sold reverted to its former owner. [14C. Via French *jubilé* < Latin *jubilaeus (annus)* "(year) of jubilee" < ecclesiastical Greek *iōbēlos* < Hebrew *yōbēl* "ram"; from the ram's horn with which the year of jubilee was proclaimed]

Jub·ran /jo͝o braan/ ♦ **Gibran, Khalil**

Jud. *abbr* BIBLE **1.** Judges **2.** Judith

Judaeo- *prefix* another spelling of **Judeo-**

Ju·dah ♦ **Judea**

Ju·da·ic /joo dáy ik/, **Ju·da·i·cal** /-ik'l/ *adj* belonging to or relating to Judaism or Jews [15C. Via Latin *Judaicus* < Greek *Ioudaikos* < *Ioudaios* (see JEW)] —**Ju·da·i·cal·ly** *adv*

Ju·da·i·ca /joo dáy ikə/ *npl* the Jewish religion, customs, and culture, or artifacts and historical and literary materials that relate to them [Early 20C. < Latin, form of *Judaicus* (see JUDAIC)]

Ju·da·i·cal *adj* JUDAISM same as **Judaic**

Ju·da·ism /jo͞odee ìzzəm/ *n* **1.** the religion of the Jews, which has its basis in the Bible and the Talmud. In Judaism, God is the creator of everything and the source of all goodness. **2.** Jewish religious practices, customs, and culture as a way of life [14C. Via ecclesiastical Latin < Greek *Ioudaismos* < *Ioudaios* (see JEW)] —**Ju·da·is·tic** /jo͞odee ístik/ *adj*

Ju·da·ize /jo͞o dee ìz/ (**-ized, -iz·ing, -iz·es**) *v* **1.** *vi* to adopt the Jewish religion and Jewish cultural practices **2.** *vt* to give something a Jewish character [Late 16C. Via ecclesiastical Latin < Greek *ioudaizein* < *Ioudaios* (see JEW)] —**Ju·da·i·za·tion** /jo͞odee i záysh'n/ *n*

ju·das /jo͞odəss/ *n* a peephole or very small window, e.g., in a door [Mid-19C. After JUDAS]

Ju·das /jo͞odəss/ *n* **1.** BIBLE same as **Judas Iscariot 2.** a traitor, especially somebody who betrays a close friend or a cause or belief (*literary*)

ju·das hole *n* same as **judas**

Ju·das Is·car·i·ot /-i skárree ət/ *n* one of Jesus Christ's disciples, who betrayed him by identifying him with a kiss to the Jewish leaders in exchange for thirty pieces of silver (Luke 22)

Ju·das tree *n* a leguminous tree whose purplish red flowers come out before the leaves. Native to: Europe, Asia. Latin name: *Cercis siliquastrum*. [Mid-17C. After JUDAS; from the popular notion that he hanged himself from this tree]

jud·der /júddər/ *vi* (**-dered, -der·ing, -ders**) to shake or vibrate violently and rapidly, or to move while shaking ■ *n* a violent, rapid vibration or shaking motion [Mid-20C. An imitation of the sound]

Jude /jood/ *n* a book of the Bible, originally a letter, probably written in the late 1st century A.D., and traditionally attributed to St. Jude. See table at **Bible**

Jude /jood/, **St.** (*fl* A.D. 1st century) one of the 12 apostles of Jesus Christ. He is traditionally believed to have been martyred in Persia with St. Simon.

Ju·de·a /joo dée ə/, **Ju·dae·a**, **Ju·dah** /jo͞odə/ region in Southwest Asia, incorporating parts of Israel and the West Bank

Judeo- *prefix* Jewish, Judaism ○ *Judeo-Christian* [< Latin *Judaeus* (see JEW)]

Ju·de·o-Chris·ti·an /joo dày ō-/ *adj* in the shared tradition of Judaism and Christianity, or combining their common beliefs

Ju·de·o-Span·ish, **Ju·dez·mo** /joo déz mō/ *n, adj* LANGUAGE same as **Ladino** (sense 1)

Judg. *abbr* BIBLE Judges

judge /juj/ *n* **1.** LAW A SENIOR OFFICIAL IN COURT OF LAW a high-ranking court officer, formerly a lawyer, who supervises court trials, instructs juries, and pronounces sentence **2.** ADJUDICATOR a person, sometimes one of several, appointed to assess entries or performances in a competition and decide who wins **3.** SOMEBODY GIVING INFORMED OPINION somebody who can give an informed opinion on something ○ *a good judge of character* **4.** JEWISH WARRIOR LEADER in Jewish history, any of a succession of warrior leaders who each temporarily held supreme power in Israel between Joshua's death and Saul's succession ■ *v* (**judged, judg·ing, judg·es**) **1.** *vt* DECIDE LEGAL CASE to act as the judge of a legal case **2.** *vti* BE JUDGE IN CONTEST to act as a judge in a competition or, as an adjudicator, pronounce officially on the entries **3.** *vti* ASSESS to assess the quality of something or estimate probabilities ○ *Each proposal has to be judged on its own merits.* **4.** *vt* FORM OPINION OF SOMEBODY OR SOMETHING to form an opinion of somebody or something, especially after thought or consideration ○ *She was judged to have the best qualifications.* **5.** *vti* ESTIMATE to measure by guesswork, using the eye or some other sense as a rough guide ○ *You can't always judge people's ages by their voices.* **6.** *vt* CONDEMN SOMEBODY to criticize or condemn somebody on moral grounds [12C. Via Old French *juge* < Latin *judex* "somebody who speaks the law" < *jus* "law, right"] —**judg·er** *n*

judge ad·vo·cate *n* a military officer-lawyer who advises commanders on points of law, especially the Uniform Code of Military Justice, and who may function as defense counsel or prosecutor at courts-martial

judge·ment *n* another spelling of **judgment**

Judg·es /jújəz/ *n* a book of the Bible that tells the story of the Israelites from Joshua's death in the 13th century B.C. to Samuel's birth in the 11th century B.C. (*takes a singular verb*) See table at **Bible**

judg·ment /júj mənt/, **judge·ment** *n* **1.** LEGAL VERDICT the decision arrived at and pronounced by a court of law **2.** OBLIGATION RESULTING FROM VERDICT an obligation, e.g., a debt, that arises as a result of a court's verdict, or a document setting out an obligation of this kind **3.** DECISION OF JUDGE the decision reached by one or more judges in a contest ○ *The judgment of the panel must be regarded as final.* **4.** DECISION ON DISPUTED MATTER an opinion formed or a decision reached in the case of a disputed, controversial, or doubtful matter **5.** DISCERNMENT OR GOOD SENSE the ability to form sound opinions and make sensible decisions or reliable guesses ○ *someone with shrewd commercial judgment* **6.** OPINION an opinion formed or given after consideration ○ *a snap judgment* **7.** ESTIMATE BASED ON OBSERVATION an estimate of something such as speed or distance, made with the help of the eye or some other sense **8.** JUDGING OF SOMETHING the judging of a case or a contest **9.** DIVINE PUNISHMENT a misfortune regarded as a divine punishment for folly or sin (*archaic or humorous*) ○ *The defeat was regarded as a judgment from God on the leader's pride.* **10.** ACT OF MAKING STATEMENT in logic, the mental act of making or understanding a positive or negative proposition about something, e.g., in "a chihuahua is a dog" or "a lobster is not an insect" [13C. < Old French *jugement* < *jugier* "to judge" < Latin *judicare* (see JUDICATURE)]

Judg·ment *n* **1.** in Roman Catholic belief, God's decision at the instant of somebody's death on whether the soul is to be saved or damned **2.** RELIG same as **Last Judgment**

judg·men·tal /juj mént'l/ *adj* tending to judge or criticize the conduct of other people —**judg·men·tal·ly** *adv*

judg·ment call *n* a decision that must be made on the basis of personal judgment, as neither alternative is clearly right or wrong

Judg·ment Day *n* in Jewish, Christian, and Islamic traditions, the day at the end of the world when God delivers his final judgment on humankind

ju·di·ca·ble /jo͞odikəb'l/ *adj* capable of being or liable to be tried in a court of law [Mid-17C. < late Latin *judicabilis* < Latin *judicare* (see JUDICATURE)]

ju·di·ca·to·ry /jo͞odikə tàwree/ *adj also* **ju·di·ca·to·rial** /jo͞odikə táwree əl/ relating to a legal system or to judges or judgment ■ *n* (*plural* **-ries**) a system of administering justice (*formal*) [Late 16C. < Latin *judicare* (see JUDICATURE)]

ju·di·ca·ture /jo͞odikə cho͝or/ *n* **1.** ADMINISTERING OF JUSTICE the dispensation of justice **2.** JUDGE'S OFFICE the power or office of a judge, or a judge's tenure of office **3.** JUDGE'S AREA OF AUTHORITY the area of authority of a judge or a court of law **4.** BODY OF JUDGES a body of judges or of people holding judicial power **5.** SYSTEM OF LAW COURTS a law court, or a system of law courts [Mid-16C. < medieval Latin *judicatura* < Latin *judicare* "to judge" < *judex* (see JUDGE)]

ju·di·cial /joo dísh'l/ *adj* **1.** RELATING TO JUDGES relating or belonging to a body of judges or to the system that administers justice **2.** RELATING TO COURT JUDGMENTS relating to judges in performance of their duties or to judgment in a court of law **3.** ENFORCED BY LAW COURT enforced or sanctioned by a court of law **4.** APPROPRIATE TO JUDGES appropriate to a judge or expected of a judge [14C. < Latin *judicialis* < *judicium* "legal proceedings" < *judex* (see JUDGE)] —**ju·di·cial·ly** *adv*

ju·di·cial ac·tiv·ism *n* the doctrine that the judicial branch, especially the federal courts, may interpret the Constitution by deviating from legal precedent as a means of effecting legal and social change

ju·di·cial re·view *n* **1.** a reassessment or re-examination by judges of a decision or proceeding by a lower court or a government department **2.** a constitutional right of the court system in some countries to review and cancel government legislation that is held to have been passed illegally

ju·di·cial sep·a·ra·tion *n* LAW same as **legal separation**

ju·di·ci·ar·y /joo díshee èrree/ *n* (*plural* **-ies**) **1.** GOVERNMENT BRANCH DISPENSING JUSTICE the branch of a country's central administration that is concerned with dispensing justice **2.** COURT SYSTEM a country's system of law courts **3.** JUDGES IN GENERAL a country's body of judges ■ *adj* RELATING TO JUDGES relating to courts, judges, and judgment [15C. < Latin *judiciarius* < *judicium* (see JUDICIAL)]

ju·di·cious /joo díshəss/ *adj* showing wisdom, good sense, or discretion, often with the underlying objective of avoiding trouble or waste ○ *a little judicious pruning* [Late 16C. < French *judicieux* < Latin *judicium* (see JUDICIAL)] —**ju·di·cious·ly** *adv* —**ju·di·cious·ness** *n*

Ju·dith /jóodəth/ *n* **1.** in the Bible, a Jewish woman who saved the city of Bethulia by beheading the general Holofernes **2.** a book of the Roman Catholic Bible and the Protestant Apocrypha that describes Judith's heroism in saving her people. See table at **Bible**

Barnaby's

judo

ju·do /jóodō/ *n* a Japanese martial art in which opponents use balance and body weight, with minimal physical effort, to throw each other or hold each other in a lock. Judo was developed from jujitsu, a samurai art, by Jigoro Kano (1860–1938). [Late 19C. < Japanese *jūdō* < *jū*"gentle" (< Middle Chinese *nʸuw*) + *dō*"way" (< Middle Chinese *daw*)] —**ju·do·ist** *n*

ju·do·gi /jóodō gèe/ *n* the costume worn by participants in judo, made of thick white cotton and consisting of a loose jacket secured by a belt and loose pants. The color of belt indicates the participant's grade, from the white belt worn by a beginner through various colors to black belt, the highest grade. [Mid-20C. < Japanese]

ju·do·ka /jóodōkə/ (*plural* **-kas** *or same*) *n* an expert or practitioner in the art of judo [Mid-20C. < Japanese]

Ju·dy /jóodee/ *n* the wife of Punch in a traditional Punch-and-Judy puppet show

jug[1] /jug/ *n* **1. LARGE CONTAINER FOR LIQUIDS** a large container for liquids, typically of earthenware or glass, with a handle and a narrow mouth usually closed with a cork **2. LIQUID CONTAINED IN JUG** the quantity of liquid held in a jug **3. PRISON** prison or jail (*humorous*) **4. OFFENSIVE TERM** an offensive term for a woman's breast (*slang*) ■ *vt* (**jugged, jug·ging, jugs**) **STEW MEAT IN EARTHENWARE POT** to stew meat in a deep earthenware pot [15C. Origin ?]

jug[2] /jug/ (**jugged, jug·ging, jugs**), **jug-jug** *vi* to make a call that sounds like "jug" or "jug-jug," as the nightingale and some other birds do [Early 16C. An imitation of the sound]

ju·gate /jóo gàyt, jóogət/ *adj* **1.** describes leaves that consist of paired leaflets attached to a single leaf stalk **2.** describes heads or busts on coins that are superimposed in profile one on another [Late 19C. < Latin *jugatus*, past participle of *jugare* "join together"]

jug band *n* a blues or jazz band featuring jugs as instruments, played by blowing across their rims

jug-eared *adj* an offensive term meaning having large ears that stick out (*informal*)

Ju·gend·stil /yóogənd shtèel/ *n* the equivalent in Germany and Austria of art nouveau, a style of design that influenced all the visual arts in Europe during the late 19th and early 20th centuries. It is characterized by curvilinearity and the stylization of forms. [Early 20C. < German < *Jugend* "youth" (title of a magazine) + *Stil* "style"]

jug·ful /júg fòol/ (*plural* **-fuls**) *n* MEASURE same as **jug**[1] *n* (sense 2) ○ *I found I was drinking jugfuls of water every day and still feeling thirsty.*

jug·ger·naut /júggər nàwt/ *n* **1.** a force that is relentlessly destructive, crushing, and insensitive **2.** *UK* a very large long truck for transporting goods in bulk [Mid-19C. < JUGGERNAUT]

ORIGIN It used to be said, apocryphally, that worshipers of Krishna threw themselves under the wheels of the ***Juggernaut*** wagon in an access of religious ecstasy, so ***juggernaut*** came to be used metaphorically in English for an irresistible crushing force. The British application to large trucks did not become firmly established until the late 1960s.

Jug·ger·naut /júggər nawt/ *n* in Hinduism, a form of the god Krishna. During a festival held each year in his honor, his statue is pulled through the Indian town of Puri on a huge chariot. [Early 19C < Sanskrit *Jagannātha* "protector of the world"]

jug·gle /júgg'l/ (**-gled, -gling, -gles**) *v* **1.** *vti* **KEEP SEVERAL OBJECTS IN AIR** to keep several objects in motion in the air at the same time by throwing them and catching them in quick succession **2.** *vt* **HAVE DIFFICULTY HOLDING SOMETHING** to keep adjusting your grip or stance in order to balance objects being held ○ *I was juggling coffee and a plate of sandwiches in one hand.* **3.** *vt* **FIT THINGS INTO SCHEDULE** to try to make something fit into a satisfactory pattern or schedule by careful arranging ○ *parents juggling careers and family life* **4.** *vt* **REARRANGE DATA** to manipulate data in order to deceive ○ *juggling the company's books* [14C. Back-formation < JUGGLER] —**jug·gler·y** *n*

Corbis/Hulton-Deutsch Collection

juggler

jug·gler /júgglər, júgg'lər/ *n* a professional entertainer who juggles [Pre-12C. Via Old French *jogler* < Latin *joculator* "jester" < *jocus* "joke"]

jug·gling act *n* **1.** a skillful or precarious attempt to perform a variety of tasks at the same time **2.** a performance by a juggler

jug-jug *vi* BIRDS same as **jug**[2]

jug·u·lar /júggyələr/ *n* ANAT same as **jugular vein** ■ *adj* **1.** relating to or situated close to the neck or throat **2.** describes a fish that has pelvic fins in front of the pectoral fins [Late 16C. < late Latin *jugularis* < Latin *jugulum* "collarbone, throat" < *jugum* "yoke"] ◇ **go for the jugular** to make an attack that is intended to be highly destructive and conclusive (*informal*)

jug·u·lar vein *n* any one of four pairs of veins in the neck that drain blood from the head. A larger internal vein is flanked by an external vein on each side of the neck.

ju·gum /jóogəm/ *n* **1.** a lobe that sticks out from the base of the forewing of some insects in order to couple it with the hind wing during flight **2.** a pair of opposed leaflets in a compound leaf [Mid-19C. < Latin, "yoke"]

Ju·gur·tha /jə gúrthə/ (160–104 B.C.) king of Numidia. He tried to free his northern African kingdom from Roman rule.

jug wine *n* a modest, inexpensive wine packaged and sold in a large bottle

juice /jooss/ *n* **1. LIQUID FROM FRUIT OR VEGETABLES** the extractable liquid that is contained in fruit or vegetables, or a drink made from this liquid ○ *lemon juice* **2. LIQUID FROM COOKING MEAT** the liquid that comes from a piece of meat when it is roasted or otherwise cooked **3. POWER** electric power (*informal*) **4. BODILY FLUID** a natural fluid or secretion of the body ○ *gastric juices* **5. LIQUID EXTRACT** any liquid extract or essence, especially from biological material ○ *Pure penicillin was isolated from mold juice.* **6. MONEY OR INFLUENCE** money or influence gained from or used in corrupt or criminal activities (*slang*) **7. ALCOHOL** alcoholic drink (*slang*) **8. LOAN OR INTEREST** money lent at an extortionate rate of interest, or the interest extorted (*slang*) ■ *vt* (**juiced, juic·ing, juic·es**) **TAKE JUICE FROM SOMETHING** to extract the juice from a fruit or vegetable [13C. Via French *jus* < Latin, "broth, sauce, vegetable juice"] ◇ **stew in your own juice** *or* **juices** to have to suffer the consequences of your actions without any help from others

juice up *vt* to make something or somebody more lively, exciting, or interesting (*slang*) ○ *juice the party up by bringing in a live band*

juice bar *n* a café serving freshly prepared fruit juices and other healthy food and drinks

juice box *n* a small box of fruit juice for one person that is sold with a straw attached to it

juiced /joost/ *adj* **1. WITH JUICE REMOVED** having had the juice extracted **2. HAVING PARTICULAR JUICE** containing juice of a particular kind or quality (*usually used in combination*) **3. INTOXICATED** drunk (*dated slang*)

juice ex·tract·or *n UK* HOUSEHOLD same as **juicer** (sense 1)

juice·head /jóoss hèd/ *n* a heavy drinker or an alcoholic (*slang*)

juic·er /jóossər/ *n* **1.** a kitchen appliance, usually electrically powered, for extracting the juice from fruit or vegetables **2.** an alcoholic or habitual drunkard (*slang*)

juic·y /jóossee/ (**-i·er, -i·est**) *adj* **1. SUCCULENT** containing a lot of juice **2. PROVIDING INTEREST** repaying effort by providing plenty of stimulation and food for thought ○ *I like getting my teeth into a nice juicy problem.* **3. TITILLATING** containing scenes or details that evoke interest because of their sensational nature (*informal*) **4. LUCRATIVE** extremely profitable or productive (*informal*) —**juic·i·ly** *adv* —**juic·i·ness** *n*

ju·jit·su /joo jítsoo/, **jiu·jit·su** *n* a Japanese system of unarmed fighting devised by the samurai, or the martial art based on it. Judo, aikido, and karate are all developments of jujitsu. [Late 19C. < Japanese *jūjutsu* < *jū* "gentle" (< Middle Chinese *nʸuw*) + *jitsu* "arts" (< Middle Chinese *zhwit*)]

ju·ju /jóojoo/ *n* **1. OBJECT WITH SUPPOSED MAGICAL POWERS** an object revered among some West African peoples for the magical powers that it is thought to possess **2. SUPPOSED MAGIC POWER OF JUJU** the magical or supernatural power associated with a juju **3. SPELL EFFECTED BY JUJU** a spell put on something or somebody by means of a juju [Early 17C. < Hausa] —**ju·ju·ism** *n*

ju·jube /jóo jòob/ *n* **1. DARK-RED FRUIT** a plum-shaped dark-red fruit that is sometimes dried like a date **2. TREE WITH RED FRUITS** a tree that produces jujubes. Native to: Asia. Latin name: *Ziziphus jujuba*. **3. CHEWY CANDY** a chewy, usually fruit-flavored, candy made of gum or gelatin [14C. Directly or via French < medieval Latin *jujuba* < Greek *ziziphos*]

juke /jook/ *vti* (**juked, juk·ing, jukes**) to move deceptively in a competitive sport so as to induce an opponent to move in a way that brings about an advantage (*slang*) ■ *n* a jukebox (*dated slang*) [Mid-20C. Probably < Gullah, "disorderly, wicked" < a W African language]

juke·box /jóok bòks/ *n* a coin-operated machine that automatically plays selected records or compact disks

juke joint *n* a roadhouse where music is played on a jukebox for dancing (*informal*) [Mid-20C. < slang *juke* "roadhouse, brothel," probably < Gullah, "disorderly, wicked" < a W African language]

Jul. *abbr* CALENDAR July

ju·lep /jóoləp/ *n* BEVERAGES same as **mint julep** [14C. Via French or medieval Latin < Persian *gulāb* "rose water"]

Jul·ian /jóolyən/ *adj* **1.** relating to or associated with Julius Caesar **2.** relating to or reckoned according to the Julian calendar [Late 16C. < Latin *Julianus* < *Julius*]

Ju·li·an·a /jóolee ánnə/ (1909–2004) queen of the Netherlands. She reigned as the queen of the Netherlands from 1948 to 1980, and abdicated in favor of her eldest daughter Beatrix.

Jul·ian cal·en·dar *n* the twelve-month solar calendar introduced by Julius Caesar in 46 B.C., consisting of 365 days, with an extra day every four years. It was replaced by the Gregorian calendar in 1582.

Jul·ian date *n* in computer programming, a date expressed as the number of days since January 1 of the current year

ju·li·enne /jóolee èn, zhóolee-/ *adj* **CUT THINLY** describes food, usually vegetables, cut into long thin matchstick strips ■ *n* **CLEAR SOUP WITH VEGETABLE STRIPS** a clear soup containing vegetables cut into thin matchstick strips ■ *vt* (**-enned, -en·ning, -ennes**) **CUT VEGETABLES THINLY** to cut vegetables into thin matchstick strips [Early 18C. < French < *Jules* or *Julien*, proper names]

Ju·li·et /jóolee ət/ *n* **1.** a small inner natural satellite of Uranus, discovered in 1986 by the spacecraft Voyager 2. It is 52 mi./84 km in diameter. **2.** a code word for the letter "J," used in international radio communications

Ju·li·et cap *n* a round close-fitting crocheted net cap for women, sometimes set with pearls. It was fashionable in the 1920s, 1930s, and 1950s for brides and bridesmaids. [Early 20C. < the heroine of Shakespeare's *Romeo and Juliet*]

Ju·lius II /jo͝olyəss/, **Pope** (1443–1513) Becoming pope in 1503, he was a powerful ruler and lavish patron of the arts, commissioning Donato Bramante's design for St. Peter's in Rome and Michelangelo's frescoes for the Sistine Chapel in the Vatican.

Jul·lun·dur /júlləndər/ city in northwestern India, a major industrial center. Population: 709,255 (2001).

Ju·ly /joo lī́/ (*plural* **-lies**) *n* in the Gregorian calendar, the seventh month of the year, lasting 31 days. See table at **calendar** [12C. Via Anglo-Norman < Latin *Julius*, after *Julius* CAESAR]

Ju·ma·da /jo͝o maádaa/ *n* in the Islamic calendar, either the fifth or the sixth month in the year. See table at **calendar** [Late 18C. < Arabic *jumādā* < *jamada* "freeze"]

ju·mar /jo͝omər/ *n also* **ju·mar clamp** a clip or clamp used in rock climbing or ice climbing that runs freely up a slack rope but tightens around the rope in response to weight applied from below ■ *vi* (**-mared, -mar·ing, -mars**) to climb using jumar clamps [Mid-20C. Origin ?]

jum·bie /júmbee/ *n Carib* PARANORMAL same as **duppy** [Late 19C. < Kongo *zumbi* "fetish"]

jum·ble /júmb'l/ *vti* (**-bled, -bling, -bles**) **1.** PUT THINGS OUT OF ORDER to mix things together indiscriminately so that they are no longer neat or ordered, or become mixed together in this way **2.** CONFUSE THINGS to mix things up in the mind, or become mixed up ■ *n* **1.** MUDDLED MASS an untidy or disorganized mass of objects, images, or ideas ○ *His thoughts were all in a jumble.* **2.** *UK* same as **rummage** *n* (sense 2) [Early 16C. Origin ?]

jum·ble sale *n UK* same as **rummage sale**

jum·bo /júmbō/ *n* **1.** something or somebody that is extra large (*often used before a noun*) ○ *a jumbo helping* **2.** AVIAT same as **jumbo jet** [Early 19C. < the name of a very large elephant at London Zoo, later sold to Barnum and Bailey circus]

jum·bo jet *n* a large wide-bodied commercial aircraft capable of carrying several hundred passengers

Jum·na /júmnə/ former name for **Yamuna**

jump /jump/ *v* (**jumped, jump·ing, jumps**) **1.** *vi* LEAVE SURFACE WITH BOTH FEET to bend the knees and push the whole body quickly up off a surface or the ground **2.** *vt* GET OVER SOMETHING to pass from one side of something to the other by jumping ○ *jump the fence* **3.** *vti* JUMP AS SPORTING SKILL in various sports such as riding and skiing, to perform a movement in which the whole body leaves the ground to travel over something ○ *Make sure you have your skis parallel before you attempt to jump.* **4.** *vi* MOVE QUICKLY to move quickly in a particular direction ○ *Jump in and I'll give you a lift home.* **5.** *vi* OBEY SOMEBODY IMMEDIATELY to carry out orders immediately (*informal*) ○ *When she speaks, you jump.* **6.** *vi* RISE SUDDENLY to rise or increase suddenly by a large amount ○ *The Nikkei Index jumped 35 points.* **7.** *vt* AMBUSH SOMEBODY to ambush somebody by attacking unexpectedly (*informal*) ○ *The guy jumped me.* **8.** *vi* MAKE PARACHUTE DESCENT to make a descent by parachute from an aircraft **9.** *vi* MOVE JERKILY to move in a jerky way that suggests a mechanical or electrical fault ○ *Interference was making the picture jump.* **10.** *vi* START IN SURPRISE to give a start of surprise or fright ○ *The noise made me jump.* **11.** *vti* LEAVE TRACK to come off the track accidentally (*refers to trains*) **12.** *vt* VIOLATE ENGAGEMENT BY LEAVING to abscond or desert in violation of an engagement, contract, or undertaking ○ *jumped bail* **13.** *vti* OMIT SOMETHING to omit the intervening parts of something, especially passages of a text, sometimes inadvertently **14.** *vi* MAKE MENTAL LEAP to make an illogical mental leap ○ *His mind keeps jumping from one thing to another.* **15.** *vt* USURP OWNERSHIP to usurp ownership of a piece of land, especially a mining claim, on the grounds that the owner has abandoned it or not fulfilled the conditions of ownership ○ *jump a claim* **16.** *vti* RAISE BID to raise a partner's bid to indicate a strong hand **17.** *vt* PASS PIECE OVER OPPONENT'S PIECE in checkers, to capture an opponent's playing piece by passing a piece over it into an empty square **18.** *vt* START BEFORE PERMITTED to fail to stop at a red traffic light, or to start moving before a red light changes green or a starter's gun fires (*informal*) **19.** *vt* BOARD TRAIN ILLEGALLY to board a train surreptitiously with the intention of traveling on it without paying (*informal*) **20.** *vt* OFFENSIVE TERM an offensive term meaning to have sexual intercourse with a woman (*slang*) ■ *n* **1.** JUMPING MOVEMENT a jumping movement or the distance jumped ○ *a winning jump of 26 feet* **2.** OBSTACLE OR APPARATUS USED IN JUMPING a specially constructed obstacle or other piece of apparatus for use in competitive jumping, e.g., a fence in steeplechasing or a platform from which skiers take off **3.** LEAP OF PARTICULAR DISTANCE IN SPORTS in field events, a leap of a particular distance or height, or the action of attempting or completing such a leap **4.** SUDDEN RISE a sudden steep rise or increase in an amount ○ *a jump in property prices* **5.** START OF SURPRISE an involuntary movement made when startled **6.** SUDDEN TRANSITION a sudden transition or change of direction, representing a break in continuity or logical progression **7.** PARACHUTE DESCENT a descent by parachute from an aircraft **8.** CARDS same as **jump bid** **9.** JUMP OVER OPPONENT'S PIECE in checkers, the move of jumping an opponent's piece and capturing it **10.** DISCONTINUOUS NUMERIC INCREASE in mathematics, a point at which a function or a curve undergoes a sudden or major transition [Early 16C. Origin ?] —**jump·a·ble** *adj* ◇ **jump to it** to hurry up and carry out orders or instructions (*informal*) ◇ **take a running jump** *UK* used dismissively as a blunt refusal or an instruction to go away (*informal*)

jump at *vt* to accept a chance or opportunity eagerly ○ *would jump at the chance*

jump on *vt* to make a sudden physical or verbal attack on somebody (*informal*) ○ *jumped on the students for missing easy questions*

jump up *vi* to get to your feet immediately

jump ball *n* in basketball, a restarting of play, in which the referee throws the ball up high between two opponents who each try to tip it toward a team member

jump bid *n* in bridge, a bid of one more than is necessary to raise the existing bid

jump boot *n* a boot worn by a paratrooper

jump cut *n* in movies and television, a sudden abrupt change from one sequence to another

jump·er[1] /júmpər/ *n* **1.** a sleeveless dress designed for wearing over a blouse or sweater ○ *She was wearing a plaid jumper with a long-sleeved white blouse.* **2.** *UK* CLOTHING same as **sweater** (sense 1) [Mid-17C. Probably < *jump* "man's short coat," alteration of *jupe*, via French < Arabic *jubba*]

jump·er[2] /júmpər/ *n* **1.** PERSON OR ANIMAL THAT JUMPS a person or animal that jumps or is trained to jump competitively **2.** JUMP SHOT a jump shot in basketball (*informal*) **3.** WIRE FOR MAKING CONNECTION a short length of wire for making an electrical connection or for short-circuiting a portion of circuit [Early 17C. < JUMP]

jump·er ca·bles *npl* a pair of electric cables used to start the engine of a vehicle that has a dead battery by connection to a live battery

jump·ers /júmpərz/ *npl* a child's one-piece playsuit made of pants and a bibbed top or bodice

jump·ing bean /júmping-/ *n* a seed of some Mexican bushes when it contains the larva of a small moth. The larva feeds on the seed pulp, making the seed move jerkily. The movements intensify if the seed is warmed, e.g., in the palm of the hand.

jump·ing gene *n* GENETICS same as **transposon**

jump·ing jack *n* **1.** a warm-up exercise in which the legs are flung apart while the hands are clapped or swung above the head **2.** a flat wooden or cardboard puppet whose limbs are worked by a string or a sliding stick

jump·ing mouse *n* a rodent that looks like a mouse but has long hind legs and a long tail. Native to: northern temperate regions. Family: Zapodidae.

jump·ing-off place *n* a very remote place, especially a point at the edge of civilization beyond which lies the wilderness

jump·ing-off point *n* **1.** a place from which to begin a trip **2.** a basis on which to begin an enterprise or a discussion **3.** same as **jumping-off place**

jump·ing plant louse *n* a small insect that is a weak flier but has enlarged hind legs for jumping. Found worldwide, it feeds on the sap of plants. Family: Psyllidae.

jump·ing spi·der *n* a spider that fixes on its prey using an enlarged central pair of eyes, then pounces by rapidly extending its legs. The jumping is a result of a sudden increase in blood pressure, which causes the legs to extend rapidly, and the spiders can achieve distances of several inches. Family: Salticidae.

jump jet *n* a fixed-wing jet aircraft that takes off and lands vertically

jump leads *npl UK* ELEC ENG same as **jumper cables**

jump·mas·ter /júmp màstər/ *n* somebody who oversees military paratroopers or civilian parachutists and decides when they will jump from an aircraft

jump-off *n* **1.** the start of something such as a race or a military attack **2.** a final extra round of a jumping competition, e.g., one in horseback riding in which all the riders who have had clear rounds compete against the clock —**jump off** *vi*

jump pass *n* in basketball, a pass that one player makes to another while in mid-jump

jump rope *n US* a rope that is swung around and jumped over in children's games and adult exercises. Can term **skipping rope**

jump seat *n* a folding seat between the front and back seats of a limousine or similarly large vehicle, or a seat like this for temporary use in an aircraft or train

jump shot *n* in basketball, a shot made with one or both hands by a player who is at the highest point of a jump —**jump shoot·er** *n*

jump-start *vt* to start a motor vehicle by attaching it to an external battery using jumper cables ■ *n* a jump-starting of a motor vehicle

jump·sta·tion /júmp stàysh'n/ *n* a website whose primary function is to provide links to other websites, especially those relating to a particular subject

jump suit, jump·suit /júmp so͞ot/ *n* **1.** a woman's casual one-piece suit combining top and pants **2.** a protective zippered one-piece suit combining long pants and jacket, worn by a parachutist when jumping

jump·y /júmpee/ (**-i·er, -i·est**) *adj* **1.** very nervous or anxious **2.** moving jerkily or erratically —**jump·i·ly** *adv* —**jump·i·ness** *n*

jun. *abbr* junior

Jun. *abbr* June

Ju·na·gadh /joo naá gaád/, **Jū·nā·gadh** city in Gujarat State, western India. Population: 252,138 (2001).

jun·co /júngkō/ (*plural* **-cos**) *n* a small finch with grayish feathers, a pink beak, and white outer tail feathers. Native to: North America. Genus: *Junco*. [Early 18C. Via Spanish < Latin *juncus* "rush (plant)"]

junc·tion /júngkshən/ *n* **1.** PLACE WHERE THINGS JOIN a place where two or more structures such as roads or railroad routes meet or cross **2.** ELECTRICAL CONNECTION a connection between electrical wires or cables **3.** PHYS LAYER BETWEEN METALS a layer of metal separating two metals with different properties and serving as a contact between them, especially in a thermocouple **4.** ELECTRONICS SEMICONDUCTOR CONTACT a point in a semiconductor device at which regions with different electrical properties come into contact with each other **5.** STATE OR ACT OF JOINING the joining of things, or their joined state [Early 18C. < Latin *junction-* < *jungere* "join"] —**junc·tion·al** *adj*

junc·tion box *n* an enclosed and protected box inside which electrical circuits are interconnected or branched for distribution

Junc·tion Cit·y /júngksh'n-/ city in north central Kansas, at the junction of the Republican and Smoky Hill rivers. Population: 17,753 (2002 estimate).

junc·ture /júngkchər/ *n* **1.** POINT IN TIME a point in time, especially an important or critical one **2.** JOINING PLACE a place where two or more things join (*formal*) **3.**

JOINING OF THINGS the joining of one thing with another, or their joined state (*formal*) **4.** LING **BREAK BETWEEN WORDS** the break between one spoken word and another, or the pronunciation features that help a listener to recognize the break, distinguishing between groups of words such as "gray day" and "grade A" [14C. < Latin *junctura* "joint" < *jungere* "join"]

June /joon/ *n* in the Gregorian calendar, the sixth month of the year, lasting 30 days. See table at **calendar** [Pre-12C. Via French *juin* < Latin *(mensis) junius* "(month) of Juno"]

Ju·neau /jŏŏ nō/ port and capital city of the state of Alaska, on the Gastineau Channel, opposite Douglas Island. Population: 30,751 (2002 estimate).

June bee·tle *n* INSECTS same as **June bug**

June·ber·ry /jŏŏn bèrree/ (*plural* **-ries**) *n* TREES, FOOD same as **serviceberry** [Mid-19C. < the month when it blooms]

June bug *n* a large brown flying beetle that is seen in late spring and feeds on leaves. Native to: North America. Subfamily: Melolonthinae.

June·teenth /jŏŏn teénth/ *n* a holiday commemorating the day on which slaves in Texas learned of the Emancipation Proclamation, which granted them freedom. Date: June 19. [Blend of JUNE + NINETEENTH]

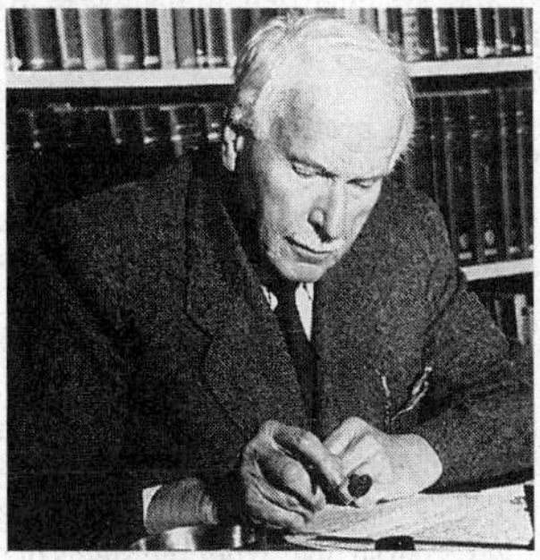

Carl Gustav Jung

Jung /yŏŏng/, **Carl Gustav** (1875–1961) Swiss psychiatrist. He broadened Freud's interpretation of the unconscious, and introduced the concepts of introvert and extrovert types and the collective unconscious. —**Jung·i·an** *adj, n*

> "Every form of addiction is bad, no matter whether the narcotic be alcohol or morphine or idealism."
> [Carl Gustav Jung, *Memories, Dreams, Reflections*; 1962]

Jung Chang /yŏŏng cháng/ (*b.* 1952) Chinese-born US author. She wrote *Wild Swans* (1991), an account of her family's experience in Communist China.

> "Gentleness was considered 'bourgeois'...Over the years of the Cultural Revolution, I was to witness people being attacked for saying 'thank you' too often, which was branded as 'bourgeois hypocrisy.'"
> [Jung Chang, *Wild Swans*; 1991]

Jung·frau /yŏŏng frŏw/ mountain in southern Switzerland. Height: 13,642 ft./4,158 m.

Jung·gar Pen·di /jŏŏng gaăr péndi/, **Dzun·gar·ia** /zŏŏng gérree ə, dzŏŏng-/ region in Northwestern China, west of the Republic of Mongolia and east of Kazakhstan, in Xinjiang Uygur Autonomous Region

jun·gle /júng g'l/ *n* **1.** **TROPICAL FOREST** an area of tropical rain forest covered with vegetation so dense that it is largely impenetrable **2.** **THICKLY COVERED AREA** any area covered with dense vegetation **3.** **TANGLE** a tangled or confused mass **4.** **COMPLEX MATTER** a frustratingly or impenetrably complex system **5.** **HARSH PLACE** a harsh environment characterized by fierce competitiveness or struggle for survival **6.** **HOBO CAMP** a place where homeless people camp (*dated slang*) [Late 18C. Via Hindi *jangal* "wasteland" < Sanskrit *jāṅgala* "dry"]

jun·gle fe·ver *n* a severe form of malaria common in tropical regions, especially Southeast Asia

jun·gle fowl (*plural* **jun·gle fowls** or *same*) *n* a wild bird related to pheasants that is thought to be the ancestor of the modern domestic fowl. Native to: Asia. Genus: *Gallus.*

jun·gle gym *n* a framework of interlocking metal, wooden, or plastic bars on which children can climb

jun·ior /jŏŏnyər/ *adj* **1.** **RELATING TO YOUTH OR CHILDHOOD** relating to youth, childhood, or children **2.** *also* **Ju·nior** **YOUNGER** younger in age, used especially when referring to the younger of two family members such as father and son who share the same name **3.** **LOW IN RANK** of relatively low rank or little experience **4.** **SMALLER** smaller than the standard or expected size **5.** **OF THIRD-YEAR STUDENTS** relating to or involving students in the third year of high school or college **6.** *UK* **FOR CHILDREN BETWEEN 7 AND 11** relating to or involving schoolchildren between the ages of 7 and 11 ○ *junior school* **7.** BOXING **BOXING WEIGHT CATEGORY** in boxing, used to describe a competitive category that has a slightly lower weight limit than the standard category ○ *junior middleweight* ■ *n* **1.** **YOUNGER PERSON** somebody who is younger than another being referred to ○ *My sister is three years my junior.* **2.** **LOW-RANKING PERSON** somebody of relatively low rank or little experience **3.** **CHILD** a young person, especially somebody younger than a teenager **4.** *also* **Jun·ior** **WAY OF ADDRESSING BOY** a form of address used for a boy or young man, affectionately to the son in a family or condescendingly to a stranger (*informal; sometimes offensive*) **5.** **THIRD-YEAR STUDENT** a student in the third year of high school or college **6.** CLOTHING **CLOTHING SIZE** a range of clothing sizes for teenage girls and slender women **7.** *UK* **JUNIOR-SCHOOL STUDENT** a pupil in a junior school [13C. < Latin, "younger" < *juvenis* "young"]

jun·ior col·lege *n* a college offering students a two-year course of study that either terminates in an associate degree or corresponds to the first two years at a four-year college

jun·ior high, **jun·ior high school** *n* a school that is intermediate between elementary school and high school, embracing grades six or seven through eight or nine. School districts often replace junior high schools with middle schools when demographic factors increase the number of younger students.

jun·ior miss *n* a girl or young woman in her teenage years (*dated*)

jun·ior var·si·ty *n* a high-school or college sports team that competes at a level below varsity

juniper

ju·ni·per /jŏŏnipər/ *n* **1.** an evergreen tree or bush with small purple cones resembling berries that are used in cooking and yield juniper oil. Genus: *Juniperus.* **2.** the oil from juniper berries. Use: to flavor gin. [14C. < Latin *juniperus*]

ju·ni·per tar, **ju·ni·per tar oil** *n* an oily brown substance. Source: wood of a species of juniper. Use: antiseptic soaps, pharmaceuticals.

junk[1] /jungk/ *n* **1.** **USED GOODS FOR SALE** secondhand goods offered for sale (*informal*) **2.** **RUBBISH** discarded things, or things regarded as worthless or causing clutter (*informal*) **3.** **CHEAP STUFF** cheap and poorly made goods (*informal*) **4.** **NONSENSE** meaningless or worthless talk (*informal*) **5.** **HEROIN** narcotics, especially heroin (*slang*) ■ *vt* (**junked, junk·ing, junks**) **DISCARD SOMETHING** to get rid of something as useless (*informal*) [14C. Origin ?]

junk[2] /jungk/ *n* a flat-bottomed sailing boat, popular in Chinese waters, that is high at the stern and has squarish sails, each supported on several battens [Mid-16C. Via Portuguese *junco* or Dutch *jonk* < Malay *jong*]

junk bond *n* an investment bond that offers the possibility of a high return but at a high risk

junk

junk·er /júngkər/ *n* an old vehicle in a very bad state of repair (*slang*) [< JUNK[1]]

Jun·ker /yŏŏngkər/ *n* **1.** an aristocratic landowner in Prussia, with great political power **2.** an offensive term for a German army officer or official regarded as arrogant and dictatorial [Mid-16C. < German *Junker* "young lord"] —**Jun·ker·dom** *n* —**Jun·ker·ism** *n*

jun·ket /júngkət/ *n* **1.** **EXPENSE-PAID TRIP** a trip taken at somebody else's expense, especially one taken by a politician at public expense **2.** **ENTERTAINMENT** an outing, excursion, or party of any kind **3.** **SET MILK DESSERT** a dessert made from milk that has been set with rennet ■ *v* (**-ket·ed, -ket·ing, -kets**) **1.** *vti* **HOLD PARTY** to hold a party or entertain somebody with a party **2.** *vi* **HAVE EXPENSE-PAID TRIP** to go on an expense-paid trip, especially one paid for with public money [14C. < French *jonquette* < *jonc* "rush (plant)" < Latin *juncus*] —**jun·ket·er** *n*

junk food *n* food that does not form part of a well-balanced diet, especially highly processed, high-fat snack items eaten in place of or in addition to regular meals

junk·ie /júngkee/, **junk·y** (*plural* **-ies**) *n* **1.** a drug addict, especially somebody addicted to heroin (*slang*) **2.** somebody whose interest in or liking for something resembles an addiction (*informal*) ○ *a baseball junkie*

junk mail *n* unsolicited mail, especially advertising material

junk shop *n* **1.** a store selling a variety of secondhand goods **2.** a second-rate antique store

junk·y[1] /júngkee/ (**-i·er, -i·est**) *adj* of very low quality or very little value (*informal*) [Mid-20C. < JUNK[1]]

junk·y[2] *n* another spelling of **junkie**

junk·yard /júngk yaărd/ *n* a place where junk is collected before being sold or processed

junk·yard dog *n* a particularly vicious and combative dog, especially one chained up (*slang*)

Ju·no /jŏŏnō/ (*plural* **-nos**) *n* **1.** in Roman mythology, the queen of the gods and wife of Jupiter. Greek equivalent **Hera** **2.** a woman of queenly bearing and imposing beauty —**Ju·no·esque** /jŏŏnō ésk/ *adj*

jun·ta /hŏŏntə, júntə/ (*plural* **-tas**) *n* **1.** **NEW RULERS AFTER COUP** a group of military officers who have taken control of a country following a coup d'état (*takes a singular or plural verb*) **2.** **SECRET GROUP** a small group of people, especially one secretly assembled for a common goal (*takes a singular or plural verb*) **3.** **LATIN AMERICAN GOVERNMENT BODY** in some parts of Central and South America, a council or other legislative body within the government [Early 17C. < Spanish or Portuguese < Latin *jungere* "join"]

jun·to /júntō/ *n* POL same as **junta** (sense 2) [Early 17C. Alteration]

ju·pa /jŏŏpə/ *n Carib* BUILDINGS same as **ajoupa**

Ju·pi·ter /jŏŏpitər/ *n* **1.** in Roman mythology, the king of the gods. Greek equivalent **Zeus** **2.** the largest planet in the solar system, fifth in order from the Sun [12C. < Latin < *Jov-* "Jove" + *pater* "father"]

Jup·pé /zhoo páy/, **Alain** (*b.* 1945) French politician. He was prime minister of France from 1995 to 1997. Full name **Juppé, Alain Marie**

Ju·ra /zhŏŏrə/ department in east central France, in the province of Franche-Comté. Area: 1,930 sq. mi./4,999 sq. km.

ju·ral /jŏŏrəl/ *adj* **1.** relating to law or the administration of justice **2.** relating to rights or obligations (*formal*) [Mid-17C. < Latin *jur-* "law"] —**ju·ral·ly** *adv*

Ju·ra Moun·tains /zhoōrə-/ mountain range situated on the border between France and Switzerland. The highest point is Crêt de la Neige, 5,636 ft./1,718 m. Length: 200 mi./320 km.

Ju·ras·sic /jōō rássik/ *n* the period of geologic time, 206 million years to 144 million years ago, during which dinosaurs flourished and birds and mammals first appeared. It is the middle period of the Mesozoic era. See table at [Mid-19C. < French *Jurassique* < *Jura* "Jura"] —**Ju·ras·sic** *adj*

ju·rat /joŏr àt/ *n* **1.** a closing statement on an affidavit, giving details of the parties to it, the witnesses, and the place and time of signing **2.** a magistrate in France or the Channel Islands [15C. < medieval Latin *juratus* "sworn man" < Latin *jurare* (see JURY)]

ju·rid·i·cal /jōō ríddik'l/, **ju·rid·ic** /-ríddik/ *adj* relating to judges, to the administration of the law, or to law in general —**ju·rid·i·cal·ly** *adv*

ju·rid·i·cal days *npl* days on which law courts are in session

ju·ris·con·sult /joŏriss kón sùlt, -kən súlt/ *n* an expert in law who gives advice on legal matters, especially in relation to public or international law [Early 17C. < Latin *jurisconsultus* "skilled in law"]

ju·ris·dic·tion /joŏriss díksh'n/ *n* **1.** LEGAL AUTHORITY the authority to enforce laws or pronounce legal judgments **2.** RANGE OF LEGAL AUTHORITY the area over which legal authority extends **3.** AUTHORITY power or authority generally [13C. Via French < Latin *jurisdiction-* < *jur-* "law" + *diction-* "saying"] —**ju·ris·dic·tion·al** *adj* —**ju·ris·dic·tion·al·ly** *adv* —**ju·ris·dic·tive** *adj*

ju·ris·pru·dence /joŏriss proōd'nss/ *n* **1.** THEORY OF LAW the philosophy or science of law **2.** LEGAL SYSTEM a system of law, or the body of laws applied in a particular country or state **3.** BRANCH OF LAW a branch of law, or the law as it applies to a particular area of life [Early 17C. < late Latin *jurisprudentia* < Latin *jur-* "law" + *prudentia* "skill"] —**ju·ris·pru·den·tial** /joŏriss proo dénsh'l/ *adj* —**ju·ris·pru·den·tial·ly** *adv*

ju·rist /joŏrist/ *n* an expert in the science or philosophy of law, especially a judge or legal scholar [15C. Directly or via French < medieval Latin *jurista* < Latin *jur-* "law"] —**ju·ris·tic** /joor ístik/ *adj* —**ju·ris·ti·cal** *adj* —**ju·ris·ti·cal·ly** *adv*

ju·ror /joŏrər/ *n* **1.** a member of a jury, especially in a court of law **2.** somebody who swears an oath such as an oath of allegiance (*formal or literary*) [14C. Via Anglo-Norman *jurour*, Old French *jureor* < Latin *jurator* < *jurare* (see JURY)]

ju·ry /joŏree/ (*plural* **-ries**) *n* **1.** a group of people, usually twelve people, chosen to give a verdict on a legal case that is presented before them in a court of law **2.** a group of people who judge a competition [14C. < Anglo-Norman, Old French *juree* "oath, inquest" < Latin *jurare* "swear" < *jur-* "law"] ◇ **the jury is out** no conclusion has yet been drawn or no decision made about something disputed ○ *The jury is still out on whether the ban will limit pollution.*

ju·ry box *n* the part of a court where the jury sits

ju·ry du·ty *n* service as a member of a jury in a court of law

ju·ry·man /joŏreemən/ (*plural* **-men** /-mən/) *n* a man who is on a jury in a court of law

ju·ry nul·li·fi·ca·tion *n* the process whereby a jury in a criminal case effectively nullifies a law by acquitting a defendant regardless of the weight of evidence against him or her

ju·ry-rig *vt* to build something in a makeshift way or fit something out, especially a boat, with makeshift equipment

ju·ry ser·vice *n UK* LAW same as **jury duty**

ju·ry·wom·an /joŏree wŏŏmmən/ (*plural* **-wom·en** /-wìmmin/) *n* a woman who is on a jury in a court of law

jus gen·ti·um /yoŏss géntee əm/ *n* international law (*technical*) [< Latin, "law of nations"]

jus san·gui·nis /yoŏss sáng gwənəss/ *n* the principle in law according to which children's citizenship is determined by the citizenship of their parents [< Latin, "right of blood"]

jus·sive /jússiv/ *adj* GRAM same as **imperative** *adj* (sense 3) [Mid-19C. < Latin *juss-*, past participle of *jubere* "command"]

jus so·li /yoŏss sō lee/ *n* the principle in law according to which children's citizenship is determined by the place of their birth [< Latin, "right of soil"]

just /just/ *adv* **1.** IN IMMEDIATE PAST a very short time ago ○ *The train just left.* **2.** AT THIS MOMENT indicating that somebody will begin doing something or something will start happening now (*used also with "about to" and "going to"*) ○ *I'll just go and get it.* ○ *I was just about to tell you.* **3.** ONLY only or merely the thing, amount, or situation mentioned ○ *This is just a warning.* **4.** BARELY by only a small degree or margin ○ *I arrived just in time.* **5.** USED FOR EMPHASIS used to emphasize a statement, usually in order to express an emotion ○ *It's just plain wrong.* **6.** EXACTLY precisely the thing, amount, or situation mentioned ○ *It's just what you need.* ■ *adj* **1.** FAIR AND IMPARTIAL acting with fairness and impartiality **2.** MORALLY CORRECT done, pursued, or given in accordance with what is morally right **3.** REASONABLE valid or reasonable [14C. Via French < Latin *justus* < *jus* "law, right"] —**just·ly** *adv* —**just·ness** *n* ◇ **just about** used to indicate that something is the case, but only by a very small degree or amount ○ *I can just about reach it.* ○ *These days, you can travel just about anywhere.* ◇ **just a moment** *or* **second** *or* **minute** used to ask someone to wait for a short time ◇ **just like that** without great effort, trouble, or inconvenience ○ *I can't move to another country just like that.* ◇ **just now 1.** a very short time ago **2.** at this very moment ◇ **just so 1.** used to express agreement with or confirmation of a statement that has just been made **2.** done or arranged precisely ○ *They wanted the room decorated just so.*

just-folks *adj* friendly and informal or unpretentious (*informal*) ○ *has a just-folks attitude*

jus·tice /jústiss/ *n* **1.** FAIRNESS fairness or reasonableness, especially in the way people are treated or decisions are made **2.** SYSTEM OR APPLICATION OF LAW the legal system, or the act of applying or upholding the law **3.** VALIDITY validity in law **4.** GOOD REASON sound or good reason **5.** JUDGE a judge, especially of a higher court [12C. Via French < Latin *justitia* < *justus* (see JUST)] ◇ **bring somebody to justice** to arrest somebody to be tried in a court of law ◇ **do justice to somebody** *or* **something 1.** to deal with somebody *or* something fairly **2.** to convey the true qualities, especially the merits, of somebody *or* something ◇ **do yourself justice** to display your own abilities fully or perform to your full potential (*often used in the negative*)

Jus·tice /jústiss/ village in northeastern Illinois, southeast of Downers Grove. It is a western suburb of Chicago. Population: 12,297 (2002 estimate).

Jus·tice Can·a·da *n* GOV same as **Department of Justice Canada**

jus·tice of the peace *n* full form of **J.P.**

jus·ti·ci·a·ble /ju stíshəb'l/ *adj* **1.** able or required to be tried in a court of law **2.** able to be settled by applying the principles of law —**jus·ti·ci·a·bil·i·ty** /ju stìshə bíllətee/ *n*

jus·ti·ci·ar·y /ju stíshee èrree/ *adj* relating to the administration of law

jus·ti·fi·a·ble /jústi fī əb'l, jùsti fī əb'l/ *adj* capable of being shown as reasonable or merited according to accepted standards —**jus·ti·fi·a·bil·i·ty** /jùsti fī ə bíllətee/ *n* —**jus·ti·fi·a·ble·ness** *n* —**jus·ti·fi·a·bly** *adv*

jus·ti·fi·a·ble hom·i·cide *n* killing that is deemed to be lawful, especially because it is carried out in self-defense or as the only way to prevent a crime

jus·ti·fi·ca·tion /jùstifi káysh'n/ *n* **1.** SOMETHING THAT JUSTIFIES something, e.g., a reason or circumstance, that justifies an action or attitude **2.** GIVING OF REASONS FOR SOMETHING the act of justifying something **3.** ALIGNMENT OF MARGINS adjustment of the lengths of spaces between and within words in text in order to make both left and right margins align **4.** CHRISTIAN DOCTRINE the Christian belief that people are absolved from all sin if they believe in Jesus Christ [14C. Directly or via French < late Latin *justification-* < *justificare* (see JUSTIFY)]

jus·tif·i·ca·to·ry /ju stífikə tàwree/, **jus·ti·fi·ca·tive** /jústifi kàytiv/ *adj* serving or acting to justify something [Late 16C. < medieval Latin *justificatorius* < late Latin *justificare* (see JUSTIFY)]

jus·ti·fied /jústi fīd/ *adj* **1.** WITH GOOD REASON having an acceptable reason for the action taken ○ *was justified in not waiting* **2.** ACCEPTABLE acceptable or reasonable in the circumstances ○ *a justified faith in her* **3.** PRINTING WITH MARGINS ALIGNED in printing, with both left and right margins aligned

jus·ti·fy /jústi fī/ (**-fied, -fy·ing, -fies**) *vt* **1.** MAKE SOMETHING SEEM REASONABLE to serve as an acceptable reason or excuse for something (*often passive*) **2.** GIVE SOMEBODY REASON to give somebody an acceptable reason for taking a particular action (*often passive*) **3.** EXPLAIN SOMETHING to give a reason or explanation why something was done **4.** PRINTING PRINT TEXT WITH MARGINS ALIGNED to adjust the lengths of spaces between and within words in text in order to make both the left and right margins align **5.** CHR FREE SOMEBODY FROM SIN in Christianity, to free somebody from sinfulness through faith in Jesus Christ or by the grace of Jesus Christ (*refers to God*) **6.** LAW GIVE LEGAL REASON FOR SOMETHING to provide a good reason in law for something, especially for committing the offense that is the subject of a criminal charge [14C. Via French *justifier* < late Latin *justificare* "act justly, justify" < Latin *justus* (see JUST)]

Jus·tin·i·an I /ju stínnee ən/ (483–565) Roman emperor. During his reign (527–65), he restored Byzantine power in Rome, northern Italy, and Spain. He revised and systematized Roman law. Known as **Justinian the Great**

> "Justice is the constant and perpetual wish to render to everyone his due."
> [Justinian I, *Institutes*; 533?]

just-in-time *n* a manufacturing and stock-control system in which goods are produced and delivered as they are required. It is designed to eliminate waste and avoid the need for large inventories.

jut /jut/ *vti* (**jut·ted, jut·ting, juts**) to stick out, or make something stick out, especially beyond the surface or edge of something ■ *n* something that sticks out [Mid-16C. Alteration of JET[1]] —**jut·ting** *adj*

jute /joot/ *n* **1.** coarse fiber from the stems of an Asian plant. Use: sacking, rope. **2.** either of two main species of plant from which jute is produced. Native to: Asia. Genus: *Corchorus*. [Mid-18C. Via Bangla *jhuṭo* < Sanskrit *jūṭaḥ* "matted hair"]

Jute /joot/ *n* a member of a Germanic people from around the Rhine estuary who invaded southeastern England during the fifth century A.D. They settled in Kent and the Isle of Wight, where they soon became the dominant people. [Pre-12C. < Latin *Jutae* < Germanic]

Jut·land /júttlənd/ peninsula in northern Europe, containing all of mainland Denmark. The base of the peninsula is part of Germany. Length: 210 mi./338 km.

Ju·ve·nal /joōvən'l/ (A.D. 65?–128?) Roman satirist. His sixteen extant *Satires*, which were famously translated into English by John Dryden, attack the follies and vices of Roman imperial society. Full name **Juvenalis, Decimus Junius**

> "The people long eagerly for just two things—bread and circuses."
> [Juvenal, *Satires*; 98?–128?]

ju·ve·nes·cent /joōvə néss'nt/ *adj* (*literary*) **1.** youthful or young-looking **2.** growing out of infancy and into childhood [Early 19C. < Latin *juvenescent-*, present participle of *juvenescere* "grow up"] —**ju·ve·nes·cence** *n*

ju·ve·nile /joōvən'l/ *adj* **1.** YOUTHFUL young or youthful **2.** RELATING TO YOUNG PEOPLE relating to, intended for, or suitable for young people ○ *a juvenile court* **3.** IMMATURE immature or childish ○ *juvenile behavior* **4.** NOT YET MATURE describes a plant or animal that has not yet reached maturity **5.** SEXUALLY IMMATURE describes a bird that has developed contour feathers but is not yet sexually mature **6.** FROM WITHIN EARTH describes water or gas that has risen to the Earth's surface for the first time ■ *n* **1.** YOUNGSTER a young person **2.** IMMATURE ANIMAL OR PLANT an animal or plant that has not yet reached maturity **3.** ACTOR SUITED TO YOUTHFUL PARTS an actor who plays youthful roles **4.** BOOK FOR CHILDREN a book intended to be read by young people [Early 17C. < Latin *juvenilis* < *juvenis* "young"] —**ju·ve·nile·ly** *adv* —**ju·ve·nile·ness** *n*

ju·ve·nile de·lin·quent *n* a young person who habitually breaks the law, especially somebody repeatedly charged with vandalism or other antisocial behavior —**ju·ve·nile de·lin·quen·cy** *n*

ju·ve·nile hor·mone *n* a hormone present in insect larvae that regulates the form of the larva after each molt. The levels of it eventually fall to allow the larva to be transformed into the adult insect.

ju·ve·nil·i·a /jóovə níllee ə, jóovə níllyə/ *npl* works produced in a writer's, artist's, or composer's youth, especially before a mature style has developed [Early 17C. < Latin, form of *juvenilis* (see JUVENILE)]

ju·ve·nil·i·ty /jóovə níllətee/ *n* **1. JUVENILE QUALITY** juvenile quality or state **2. IMMATURITY** foolishly immature behavior **3. ACT OF IMMATURITY** an act of foolishly immature behavior (*often used in the plural*)

jux·ta·pose /jùkstə pṓz/ (**-posed, -pos·ing, -pos·es**) *vt* to place two or more things together, especially in order to suggest a link between them or emphasize the contrast between them [Mid-19C. < French *juxtaposer* < Latin *juxta* "close" + French *poser* (see POSE [1])] —**jux·ta·po·si·tion** /jùkstəpə zísh'n/ *n* —**jux·ta·po·si·tion·al** *adj*

JV *abbr* **1.** COMM joint venture **2.** junior varsity

J.W.V. *abbr* Jewish War Veterans

Jy *symbol* MEASURE jansky

Jy·ais·tha /jī ástə/ *n* in the Hindu calendar, the third month of the year, lasting 31 days and falling about the same time as May to June. See table at **calendar**

K k

k[1] /kay/ (*plural* **k's**), **K** (*plural* **K's** or **Ks**) *n* **1.** the 11th letter of the English alphabet, representing a consonant sound **2.** a written representation of the letter "k"

k[2] *abbr* **1.** MEASURE karat **2.** MEASURE kilo- **3.** POL knight **4.** HANDICRAFT knit **5.** NAUT knot

K[1] /kay/ (*plural* **K's** or **Ks**) *n* **1.** something shaped like a letter "K" **2.** MEASURE same as **kilometer** (*informal*) **3.** one thousand dollars (*informal*)

K[2] *symbol* **1.** PHYS kaon **2.** PHYS kelvin **3.** PHYS kinetic energy **4.** CHEM ELEM potassium **5.** BASEBALL strikeout

K[3] *abbr* **1.** COMPUT kilobyte **2.** MEASURE kilometer **3.** EDUC kindergarten **4.** CARDS, CHESS king **5.** POL knight **6.** MUSIC Köchel (*preceding a number in Köchel's catalogue of Mozart's works*)

K-1 *n* a sport in which competitors utilize standing techniques from sports such as karate, kick-boxing, kung fu, and tae kwon do to determine the world's strongest martial artist [< K[1] (sense 1) as the initial letter of KARATE, KUNG FU, and other martial arts + ONE, because of the event's single weight class]

K2 /kày to͞o/ second highest mountain in the world. It is situated in the Karakorum Range in the western part of the Himalayan system on the border between China and the disputed territory of Jammu and Kashmir. Height: 28,251 ft./8,611 m.

K-12 /kày twélv/ *n* the school system from kindergarten through twelfth grade ○ *a need for K-12 funding* [Representation of *kindergarten through twelfth grade*]

ka[1] /kaa/ *n* in ancient Egypt, the soul of a dead person, said to be able to reside in a statue of that person after death [Late 19C. < Egyptian]

ka[2] *symbol* ELECTRONICS cathode

Kaa·ba /kaábə/ *n* a square building inside the great mosque in Mecca, containing a sacred stone (**Black Stone**) said to have been given by God. It is the most holy site in the Islamic religion. [Early 17C. < Arabic, "the square house"]

ka·bab *n* FOOD another spelling of **kebab**

Ka·bar·di·an /kə baárdee ən, -baárdyən/ *n* **1.** a member of a people who live to the north of the Caucasus Mountains in southern European Russia **2.** a language spoken to the north of the Caucasus Mountains in southern European Russia, belonging to the Abkhaz-Adyghean group of Caucasian languages. Native speakers: 300,000. [Late 19C. < Russian *Kabarda*, place name] —**Ka·bar·di·an** *adj*

Kab·ba·lah /kábbələ, kə baálə/, **Kab·ba·la**, **Qa·ba·lah**, **Ca·ba·la**, **Cab·ba·la** *n* **1.** a body of mystical Jewish teachings based on an interpretation of the Hebrew scriptures as containing hidden meanings **2.** a set of secret or mystical beliefs [Early 16C. Via medieval Latin < Rabbinic Hebrew *qabbālāh* "tradition" < *qibbēl* "receive"] —**Kab·bal·ism** /kábbə lìzzəm/ *n* —**Kab·bal·ist** /-list/ *n* —**Kab·bal·is·tic** /kàbbə lístik/ *adj* —**Kab·bal·is·ti·cal·ly** *adv*

Kab·i·nett /kàbbee nét/ *n* the lowest grade of high-quality German table wine, typically dry to medium dry [Early 20C. < German *Kabinettwein* "cabinet wine"; because it was kept in a special cellar]

ka·bob *n* FOOD same as **kebab**

ka·bu·ki /kə bo͞okee/ *n* traditional Japanese drama in which male actors play both male and female parts [Late 19C. < Japanese < *ka* "song" (< Middle Chinese) + *bu* "dance" (< Middle Chinese *muə*) + *ki* "art" (< Middle Chinese *khi*)]

Barnaby's

kabuki

Ka·bul /kaá bo͝ol, kə bo͞ol/ capital city of Afghanistan, located in the center of the country. Population: 700,000 (1993).

Ka·byle /kə bíl/ (*plural* **-byles** or *same*) *n* **1.** a member of a Berber people who live in northeastern Algeria **2.** a Berber language spoken in northeastern Algeria. Native speakers: 3 million. [Mid-18C. Probably < Arabic *kabā'il* "tribes"] —**Ka·byle** *adj*

ka·chi·na /kə cheénə/ (*plural* **-nas**) *n* **1.** any of the spirits believed by the Native North American Hopi people to be the ancestors of human beings **2.** a representation of a kachina, usually either a carved wooden doll or a costumed performer in a ceremonial dance [Late 19C. < Hopi *katsina* "supernatural being"]

ka·dai·tcha *n* CULTL ANTHROP same as **kurdaitcha**

Ká·dár /kaád aar/, **János** (1912–89) prime minister of Hungary (1956–58, 1961–65). He formed a pro-Soviet government in Hungary after the Soviet Union crushed the 1956 Hungarian uprising, and exercised supreme power until 1988. Born **Csermanck, János**

Kad·dish /kaádish/ (*plural* **-dish·im** /-díshim/) *n* a prayer recited at the close of the sections of Jewish religious services, and by close relatives of a deceased person at times of mourning and anniversaries of the death [Early 17C. < Aramaic *qaddīš* "holy"]

ka·doo·ment /kə do͞o mènt/ *n Carib* serious trouble or difficulty [< English dialect *ka* "look" (contraction) + *dooment* "commotion, disturbance" (< DO)]

Ka·du·na /kə do͞onə/ capital of Kaduna State, north central Nigeria, situated about 90 mi./145 km north of the national capital, Abuja. Population: 333,600 (1995).

kaf·fee·klatsch /káwffee klàch, kóffee klach/, **kaf·fee klatch** *n* LEISURE same as **coffee klatch** [Late 19C. < German < *Kaffee* "coffee" + *Klatsch* "gossip"]

Kaf·fir /káffər/, **Kaf·ir** *n* **1.** *S Africa* a highly offensive term for a Black African person (*taboo*) **2.** an offensive term for somebody who is not a Muslim (*slang*) **3.** LANG same as **Xhosa** (sense 2) (*dated*) [Mid-16C. < Arabic *kāfir* "unbeliever, infidel"] —**Kaf·fir** *adj*

kaf·fir corn, **kaf·ir corn** *n S Africa* a type of sorghum cultivated for its grain. Use: making beer, animal feed. (*sometimes considered offensive*)

kaf·fi·yeh /kə feé ə, kaa-/, **kef·fi·yeh** *n* a cotton headdress fastened by a band and worn by some Arab men [Early 19C. < Arabic *kūfiyya*]

Kaf·ir *n* another spelling of **Kaffir**

Kaf·i·ri /káffəree/ *n* a language of northeastern Pakistan and Afghanistan, belonging to the Dardic branch of Indic [Early 20C. < Arabic *kāfir* "unbeliever, infidel"] —**Kaf·i·ri** *adj*

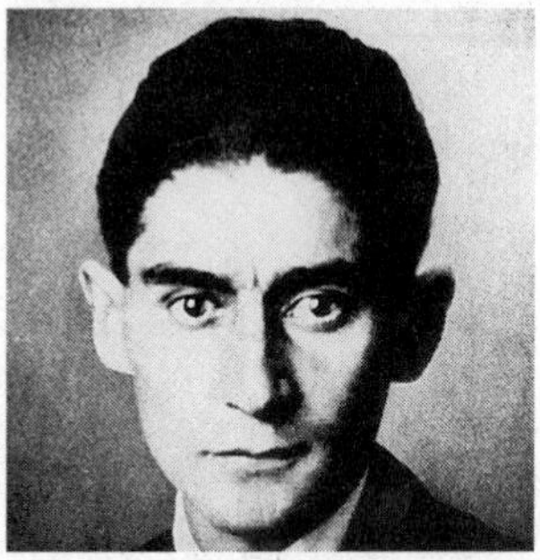

AKG London

Franz Kafka

Kaf·ka /kaáfkə/, **Franz** (1883–1924) Austrian (Czech) novelist. His dreamlike works such as *The Trial* (1925) and *The Castle* (1926) are full of oppression and despair. See Cultural note at **metamorphosis, trial**

> "Gregory Samsa woke from uneasy dreams
> one morning to find himself changed into
> a giant bug."
> [Franz Kafka, "The Metamorphosis," *Franz Kafka: Stories 1904–24*; 1981]

Kaf·ka·esque /kaáfkə ésk/ *adj* **1.** relating to or characteristic of the work of Franz Kafka **2.** overly complex in a seemingly pointless, impersonal, and often disturbing way

kaf·tan *n* CLOTHING another spelling of **caftan**

Ka·fu·e /kaa fo͞o ay/ river in central Zambia, a tributary of the Zambezi. It rises near Zambia's northern border with the Democratic Republic of the Congo. Length: 590 mi./950 km.

Ka·go·shi·ma /kaágō sheémə/ seaport and capital of Kagoshima Prefecture on the southern coast of Kyushu, Japan. Population: 544,840 (2002).

ka·gu /kaá go͞o/ *n* a large grayish flightless bird. Native to: New Caledonia. Latin name: *Rhynochetos jubatus*. [Mid-19C. < Melanesian]

~~**kahki**~~ incorrect spelling of **khaki**

Ka·hi·wa Wa·ter·fall /kə heéwə-/ falls located on the island of Molokai, Hawaii, United States. Height: 1,748 ft./533 m.

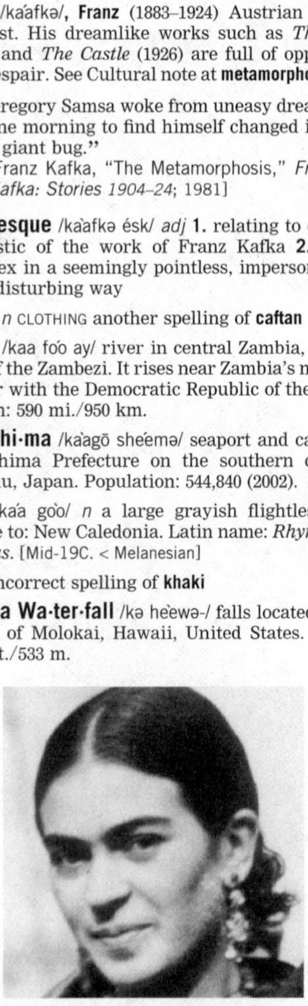

AKG London

Frida Kahlo: photographed in 1930 by Edward Weston

Kah·lo /kaálō/, **Frida** (1907–54) Mexican painter. She is known for her idiosyncratic self-portraits that incorporate features and subject matter inspired by

Mexican folk art and her personal life. She was married to the Mexican painter Diego Rivera.

Kahn /kaan/, **Louis I.** (1901–74) Estonian-born US architect and teacher. He combined functionalism with a strong sense of aesthetics to create bold designs, often in brick and concrete, like his last work, the Yale Center for British Art, New Haven, Connecticut (completed 1977). Full name **Kahn, Louis Isadore**

Ka·hu·lu·i /kaáhoo lóo ee/ community in Maui County, Hawaii, on the northern coast of Maui. Population: 16,889 (1996).

ka·hu·na /kə hóonə/ *n* **1.** a Hawaiian priest or traditional healer **2.** an important or influential person (*informal*) ○ *the big kahuna* [Late 19C. < Hawaiian]

kai·ak *n* CANOEING another spelling of **kayak**

Kai·e·teur Falls /kī ə tóor-/ falls in central Guyana, on the Potaro branch of the Essequibo River. Height: 740 ft./225 m.

kaif *n* DRUGS same as **kif**

Kai·feng /kī fúng/ city in northern China, in the Huang He valley of northern Henan Province. Population: 508,224 (1991).

Kai·kou·ra Rang·es /kī kóorə-/ twin mountain ranges near the northeastern coast of the South Island, New Zealand. The highest point is Tapuaenuku, 9,465 ft./2,885 m.

Kai·lu·a /kī lóo ə/ community in Honolulu County, Hawaii, on the southeastern coast of Oahu. Population: 36,818 (1990).

kai·nite /kī nìt, káy-/ *n* a variously colored mixed sulfate and chloride mineral containing potassium and magnesium. Use: source of potassium, fertilizer. [Mid-19C. < German *Kainit* < Greek *kainos* "new"]

Kai·pa·ra Har·bour /kī paà raa-/ wide harbor on the northwestern coast of the North Island, New Zealand. Area: 201 sq. mi./520 sq. km.

Kair·ouan /kər waán/ city in northern Tunisia. Called "the City of a Hundred Mosques," it is one of the holiest Muslim cities. Population: 110,280 (1999).

kai·ser /kīzər/ *n* formerly, a German, Austrian, or Austro-Hungarian emperor, especially the German emperor Wilhelm II, who ruled Germany during World War I [Early 19C. < German, via Germanic < Greek *kaisar* < Latin *Caesar*, family name of Gaius Julius CAESAR] —**kai·ser·dom** *n*

Kai·ser /kīzər/, **Henry J.** (1882–1967) US industrialist. He was involved in the construction, shipbuilding, automobile, steel, aluminum, and chemical industries. Full name **Kaiser, Henry John**

kai·ser·in /kīzərin/ *n* a German empress, or the wife of a German emperor [Late 19C. < German, form of *kaiser* (see KAISER)]

kai·ser roll /kīzər-/ *n* a crusty round roll, often sprinkled with poppy or sesame seeds, made by folding corners of a square inward so that their points meet

kai·zen /kī zén/ *n* a Japanese business philosophy advocating the need for continuous improvement in somebody's personal and professional life [Late 20C. < Japanese, "improvement"]

ka·jal /kaá yəl/ *n S Asia* lampblack or other black powder, worn as eye makeup or to make a mark on the forehead by some women and children in or from South Asia [< Hindi]

ka·ka /kaákə/ *n* a parrot with a long gray beak and greenish brown feathers. Native to: New Zealand. Latin name: *Nestor meridionalis*. [Late 18C. < Maori]

Ka·ka·du Na·tion·al Park /kaákə doo-/ national park in the Northern Territory, Australia. Area: 7,722 sq. mi./20,000 sq. km.

ka·ka·po /kaákə pō/ (*plural* **-pos**) *n* a large flightless nocturnal parrot with green feathers, now extremely rare. Native to: New Zealand. Latin name: *Strigops habroptilus*. [Mid-19C. < Maori]

kakapo

ka·ke·mo·no /kaákə mṓ nō/ (*plural* **-nos**) *n* a Japanese wall hanging in the form of a tall narrow scroll, weighted at the base with a roller and decorated with a painting or with a text in ornamental handwriting [Late 19C. < Japanese < *kake-* "hang" + *mono* "thing"]

ka·ki /kaákee/ *n* TREES, FOOD same as **Japanese persimmon** [Early 18C. < Japanese]

kak·is·toc·ra·cy /kàkə stókrəssee/ (*plural* **-cies**) *n* government by the most unscrupulous or unsuitable people, or a state governed by such people [Early 19C. < Greek *kakistos* "worst"]

ka·la-a·zar /kaálə ə zaár/ *n* a severe, often fatal tropical fever caused by a parasite that enters the body via a sand fly bite. Symptoms include acute anemia, weight loss, and an enlarged liver and spleen. [Late 19C. < Assamese < *kala* "black" + *āzār* "disease"]

Ka·la·chak·ra /kaálə chùkrə/ *n* a mandala, traditionally constructed out of grains of sand, depicting Buddhist deities in a portrayal of time. The mandala is destroyed shortly after construction to illustrate the Buddhist teaching of impermanence.

Ka·la·ha·ri De·sert /kaálə haáree-/ arid and semiarid region in southern Africa. It occupies much of Botswana and parts of Namibia and South Africa. Area: 100,000 sq. mi./260,000 sq. km.

Kal·a·ma·zoo /kàllə mə zóo/ city on the Kalamazoo River in southwestern Michigan. A manufacturing center, it is home to Kalamazoo College and Western Michigan University. Population: 75,858 (2002 estimate).

kal·an·cho·e /kàllən kṓ ee/ *n* a cultivated succulent plant often grown as a potted plant for its shiny leaves. Flowers: small, bright red, pink, or white, in clusters. Native to: tropical Africa. Genus: *Kalanchoe*. [Mid-19C. Via modern Latin < French < Chinese *gāláncài*]

kal·an·su·wa /kàllən sóowə/ *n* a white turban wrapped around a conical or spherical hat, worn by some Muslim spiritual leaders [< Arabic]

Ka·lash·ni·kov /kə laáshni kàwf/ *n* a Russian-manufactured semiautomatic assault rifle widely used as a weapon by terrorists and paramilitary organizations [Late 20C. < Russian, after M. T. *Kalashnikov* (b. 1919), Russian weapons designer]

Ka·lat /kə laát/, **Ka·lāt** town in western Pakistan, principal town of the Kalat region, in Baluchistan Province. Population: 11,000 (1981 estimate).

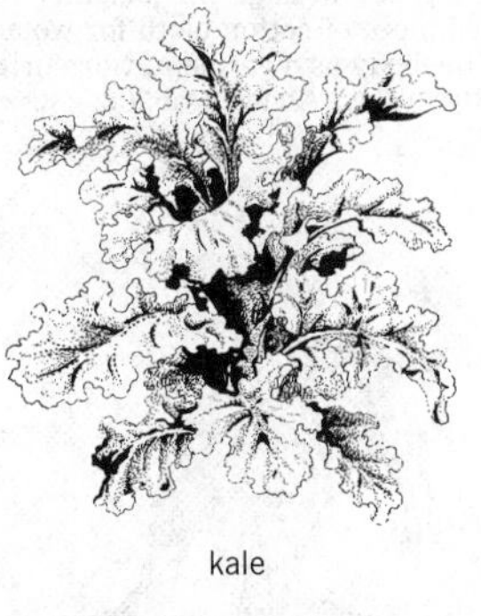

kale

kale /kayl/ *n* **1.** a hardy cabbage with dark green curly leaves and no heart. Latin name: *Brassica oleracea acephala*. **2.** same as **money** (*slang*) [14C. Scottish variant of COLE]

ka·lei·do·scope /kə līdə skōp/ *n* **1.** OPTICAL TOY an optical toy consisting of a cylinder with mirrors and colored shapes inside that create shifting symmetrical patterns when the end is rotated **2.** COMPLEX SCENE OR PATTERN a complex, colorful, and shifting pattern or scene **3.** COMPLEX SET OF EVENTS a complex set of events or circumstances [Early 19C. < Greek *kalos* "beautiful" + *eidos* "form"] —**ka·lei·do·scop·ic** /kə līdə skóppik/ *adj* —**ka·lei·do·scop·i·cal·ly** *adv*

kal·ends *npl* CALENDAR another spelling of **calends**

Kale·yard School *n* a group of Scottish writers, active in the late 19th and early 20th centuries, who wrote romantic portrayals of life in the Scottish Lowlands [*Kaleyard* "kitchen garden" < KALE; from their portrayal of local town life]

Kal·goor·lie-Boul·der /kal góorlee-/ city in southern Western Australia, a gold mining center. Population: 29,506 (2002 estimate).

Ka·li /kaálee/ *n* a Hindu goddess of destruction, one of the manifestations of the wife of the god Shiva, who destroys in order to recreate. She is depicted with wild red eyes, wears a necklace of severed heads, and wields a bloody sword. [< Sanskrit]

Ka·li·da·sa /kùlli daássə/ (*fl* A.D. 5th century) Indian poet and dramatist. He is best known for his verse drama *Sakuntala*.

~~**kaliedoscope**~~ incorrect spelling of **kaleidoscope**

ka·lif, etc. ISLAM another spelling of **caliph, etc.**

Ka·li·man·tan /kàllə mán tàn/ region of Indonesia covering the eastern, southern, southwestern, and central portions of Borneo. Population: 3,102,500 (1999). Area: 14,541 sq. mi./37,660 sq. km.

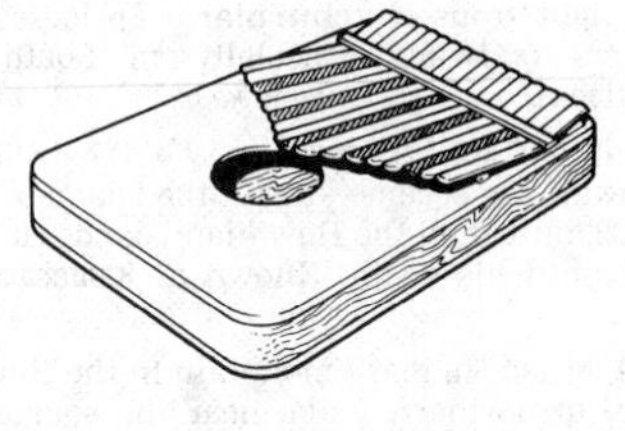

kalimba

ka·lim·ba /kə límbə/ *n* an African instrument consisting of a soundboard with tuned metal or bamboo bars of varying lengths that are plucked to give sound [Mid-20C. < Bantu]

Ka·li·nin /kə leénin/ former name for **Tver** (1933–90)

Ka·li·nin·grad /kə leénin gràd/ city in western Russia, on the Pregolya River. It is the capital of Kaliningrad Oblast. Population: 512,508 (1995). Former name **Königsberg** (until 1946)

Ka·li Yu·ga /kaálee yóogə, kùllee-/ *n* in Hindu philosophy, the age of decadence. It is the fourth and last age in the Hindu cycle of the world. [< Sanskrit]

kal·li·kre·in /kàllə kreé in, kə líkree ən/ *n* an enzyme present in blood, urine, and body tissue that, when activated, dilates blood vessels [Mid-20C. < Greek *kallikreas* "pancreas"]

Kal·mar /kaál maàr/ port and city in southern Sweden, the capital of Kalmar County. It is situated on Kalmarsund opposite the island of Öland. Population: 56,863 (1994).

kal·mi·a /kálmee ə, kálmyə/ *n* an evergreen bush that belongs to the heath family and has poisonous leaves. Native to: North America. Genus: *Kalmia*. [Mid-18C. < modern Latin, after Pehr *Kalm* (1716–79), Swedish botanist]

Kal·myck /kál mìk, kàl mík/ (*plural* **-mycks** or *same*), **Kal·muk** /kál mùk, kàl múk/ (*plural* **-muks** or *same*) *n* **1.** a member of a people who live in southwestern Russia. They migrated from northeastern China during the 17th century. **2.** a language spoken by the Kalmyck people, belonging to the Mongolian branch of Altaic. Native speakers: 150,000. [Early 17C. < Russian *Kalmyk*] —**Kal·myck** *adj*

kal·pa /kálpə, kúlpə/ *n* in Hindu philosophy, an immeasurably long period of time. Its length is variable, sometimes described as one complete cycle of the world (**yuga**), sometimes as 1,000 cycles. [Late 18C. < Sanskrit]

kal·pak *n* CLOTHING another spelling of **calpac**

Ka·lu·za /kə lóozə/, **Theodor F. E.** (1885–1945) German mathematician. In 1919 he suggested the existence of a fourth spatial dimension to unify electromagnetism with gravity. Full name **Kaluza, Theodor Franz Eduard**

ka·ma /kaámə/ *n* sexual pleasure as the third of the four Hindu goals of life [< Sanskrit *kāma* "love, desire"]

kam·a·cite /kámmə sīt/ *n* an alloy of nickel and iron. Source: meteorites. [Late 19C. < Greek *kamak-* "vine pole"]

Ka·ma·ku·ra /kaámə kóorə/ city on southeastern Honshu Island, Japan, on Sagami Bay, in Kanagawa Prefecture. Population: 169,714 (2002).

ka·ma·la /kaáməla, kámmələ/ *n* **1.** a powder obtained from the seeds of a spurge. Use: dye, formerly to treat worm infestations. **2.** a tree belonging to the spurge family whose seeds yield kamala. Native to: South and Southeast Asia. Latin name: *Mallotus philippinensis*. [Early 19C. < Sanskrit, probably < Dravidian]

Ka·ma Su·tra /kaámə sóotrə/ *n* an ancient Sanskrit text giving instruction on the art of lovemaking [Late 19C. < Sanskrit < *kāma* "love, desire" + *sūtra* "precept"]

Kam·chat·ka Pen·in·su·la /kam chàt kə-/ large peninsula of eastern Russia that separates the Sea of Okhotsk from the Bering Sea and the Pacific Ocean. Area: 200,001 sq. mi./518,000 sq. km.

kame /kaym/ *n* a ridge of sand and gravel left by a melting glacier [Late 18C. < Scottish form of COMB]

ka·meez /kə méez/ (*plural same* or **-meez·es**) *n* a long garment like a tunic, often worn by men and women over tight trousers (**churidars**) or loose pleated trousers (**salwar**), especially in South Asian countries [Early 19C. < Arabic *kamīs*]

Ka·me·ha·me·ha I /kə mày ə máy ə/ (1758–1819) king of Hawaii. He became king of the island of Hawaii in 1782, united all the Hawaiian islands (1810), and ruled until his death. Known as **Kamehameha the Great**

Ka·met, Mount /kú màyt/ mountain in the Himalayan range, in northern India, near the source of the Jumna River. Height: 25,446 ft./7,756 m.

ka·mi·ka·ze /kaámi kaázee/ *n* **1.** JAPANESE SUICIDE PILOT a World War II Japanese pilot trained for the suicide mission of flying an aircraft packed with explosives into an enemy target, often a ship (*often used before a noun*) **2.** JAPANESE AIRCRAFT an aircraft used by a kamikaze, especially one designed specifically for suicide crashes (*often used before a noun*) **3.** RECKLESS PERSON a reckless person, often somebody whose actions seem self-defeating or self-destructive (*informal*) ■ *adj* RECKLESS reckless, especially in seeming to invite failure or self-destruction (*informal*) [Late 19C. < Japanese < *kami* "divine" + *kaze* "wind"]

Kam·i·la·roi /kámmələ ròy/ (*plural same*) *n* **1.** a member of a group of Australian Aboriginal peoples living in northeastern New South Wales **2.** the language of the Kamilaroi people, now extinct [Mid-19C. < Kamilaroi]

Kam·loops /kám loops/ city in southern British Columbia, Canada. It is a transportation and commercial hub. Population: 67,952 (2001).

Kam·pa·la /kaam paálə/ capital city of Uganda, situated in the southern part of the country, near Lake Victoria. Population: 773,463 (1991 estimate).

Kam·pu·che·a /kàmpoo chée ə/ former name for **Cambodia** (1976–89) —**Kam·pu·che·an** *n, adj*

Kam·tok /kám tòk/ *n* an English-based pidgin language used in Cameroon [Late 20C. < shortening of CAMEROON + *tok*, alteration of TALK]

ka·na /kaánə/ *n* **1.** either of two systems of symbols representing syllables, used in writing Japanese **2.** a syllabic symbol used in kana [Early 18C. < Japanese]

Ka·nak /kə naák/ *n* somebody who comes from the French overseas territory of New Caledonia in the South Pacific and supports independence from France [Early 20C. < French *canaque*] —**Ka·nak** *adj*

Ka·na·ka /kə naákə, -nákə/ *n* somebody who comes from Hawaii, especially somebody of Polynesian descent [Mid-19C. < Hawaiian, "person"] —**Ka·na·ka** *adj*

kan·a·my·cin /kànnə míss'n/ *n* an antibiotic obtained from a soil bacterium. Use: treatment of infections resistant to other antibiotics. [Mid-20C. < modern Latin *kanamyceticus*, bacterium species name]

Ka·nan·ga /kə naáng gə/ city in the southern Democratic Republic of the Congo, capital of Kasai-Occidental Region. Population: 393,030 (1994). Former name **Luluabourg**

Ka·na·wha /kə naáwə/ river mainly in west central West Virginia. It rises in northwestern North Carolina and joins the Ohio River at Point Pleasant. Length: 97 mi./160 km.

Ka·na·za·wa /kaánə zaáwə/ city and seaport in northern Honshu, Japan. Population: 438,272 (2000).

kan·ban /kaán baán/ *n* **1.** in the just-in-time manufacturing and stock-control system, a card bearing an order for goods, sent to a manufacturer or supplier **2.** MANUF same as **just-in-time** [Late 20C. < Japanese, "sign"]

Kan·chen·jun·ga /kùnchən júng gə, -jóong-/ third highest mountain in the world, in the Himalayan system, on the border between Nepal and India. Height: 28,209 ft./8,598 m.

Kan·da·har /kaándə haár, kùndə-/ city in southern Afghanistan. It is the capital of Kandahar Province and the country's commercial center. Population: 225,500 (1988 estimate).

Wassily Kandinsky: photographed at the Bauhaus, Dessau, Germany (1930?)

Kan·din·sky /kan dínskee/, **Wassily** (1866–1944) Russian painter. One of the earliest exponents of pure abstraction in art, he wrote *Concerning the Spiritual in Art* (1912), the first treatise on this subject. He taught at the Bauhaus school of design in Weimar and Dessau, Germany (1922–33).

> "Violet is red withdrawn from humanity by blue."
> [Attributed to Wassily Kandinsky]

K&R in·dus·try *n* a global business composed of legitimate personal security companies offering kidnap-and-ransom insurance and relevant negotiating skills and ransom payments

Kan·dy /kándee/ city in central Sri Lanka and the capital of Central Province. Population: 104,000 (1990 estimate).

Ka·ne·o·he /kaà nee ō hee/ community in Honolulu County, Hawaii, on the southeastern coast of Oahu. Population: 35,448 (1996).

kan·ga /káng gə/, **khan·ga** *n* a brightly colored and decorated piece of cotton cloth for women to wrap around the body as a garment, worn originally and especially in East Africa [Mid-20C. < Kiswahili]

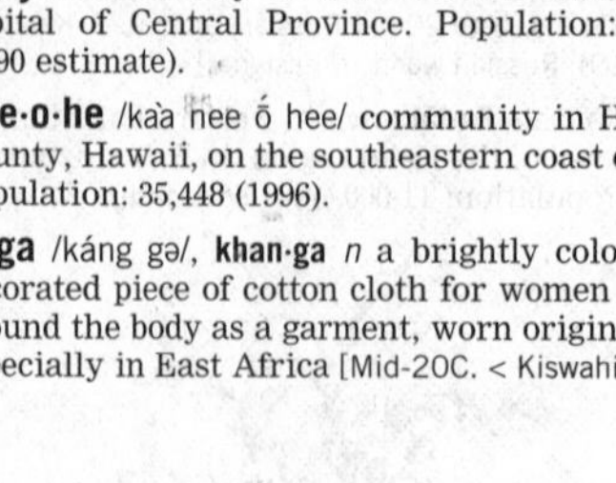

kangaroo

kan·ga·roo /kàng gə róo/ (*plural* **-roos**) *n* a large leaping marsupial with powerful hind legs, short forelegs, and a long tail. Native to: Australia, New Guinea. Family: Macropodidae. [Late 18C. < Aboriginal]

kan·ga·roo court *n* an unofficial or mock court set up spontaneously for the purpose of delivering a judgment arrived at in advance, usually one in which a disloyal associate's fate is decided

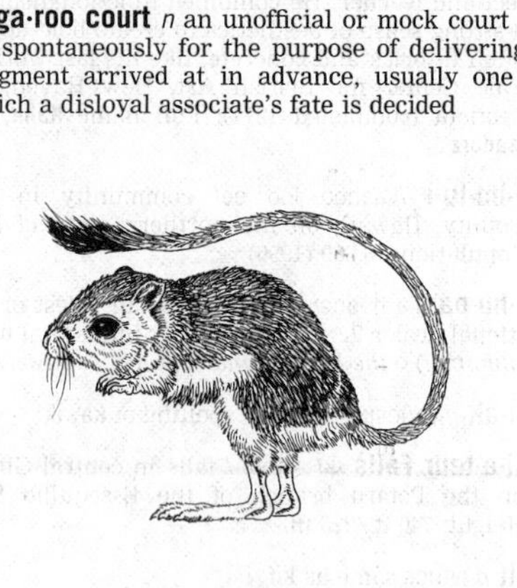

kangaroo rat

kan·ga·roo rat *n* a small nocturnal jumping rodent with a long tail and long hind limbs. Native to: deserts of the United States and Mexico. Genus: *Dipodomys*.

kan·ga·roo vine *n* a climbing vine with shiny green or mottled leaves. Native to: Australia. Latin name: *Cissus antarctica*.

kan·ji /kaánjee/ (*plural same* or **-jis**) *n* **1.** a writing system for Japanese that uses pictorial characters based largely on Chinese ideograms **2.** a character used in kanji [Early 20C. < Japanese < *kan* "Chinese" + *ji* "letter, character"]

Kan·ka·kee /kàngkə kée/ city in northeastern Illinois, on the Kankakee River, northeast of Urbana and southwest of Chicago. Population: 27,168 (2002 estimate).

Kan·na·da /kaánədə/ *n* a Dravidian language spoken in some states of southern India. Native speakers: 44 million. [Mid-19C. < Kannada *Kannaḍa*] —**Kan·na·da** *adj*

LANGUAGE HERITAGE See ***Dravidian***.

Kan·na·di·ga /kùnnə déegə/ *n* a member of a people living in the southern Indian state of Karnataka [< Kannada] —**Kan·na·di·ga** *adj*

Ka·no /kaánō/ capital of Kano State, northern Nigeria. Population: 657,300 (1995).

Ka·no Ma·sa·no·bu /kaánō masə nṓboo/ (1453–90) Japanese artist. He founded the school of painting named Kano for him and based his style on that of Chinese ink painting.

Ka·no Mo·to·no·bu /-mōtō nṓboo/ (1476–1539) Japanese artist. He continued the style of his father Kano Masanobu, and introduced a firm brush line.

Kan·pur /kaán poor, kaan póor/, **Kān·pur** city in Uttar Pradesh State, northern India, on the Ganges River. Population: 2,690,486 (2001).

Kans. *abbr* Kansas

Kan·sa /kánzə, kánssə/ (*plural* **-sas** or *same*) *n* **1.** a member of a Native North American people who lived in central and eastern Kansas and now live mainly in eastern Oklahoma **2.** the Siouan language of the Kansa people [Early 18C. < Algonquian] —**Kan·sa** *adj*

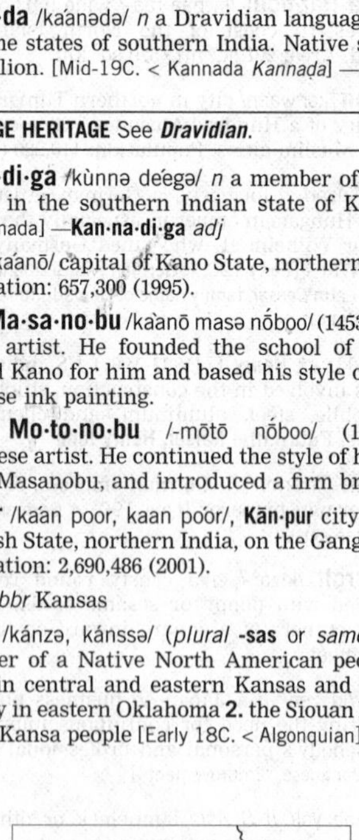

Kansas

Kan·sas /kánzəss/ state in the western part of the central United States, bordered by Colorado, Missouri, Nebraska, and Oklahoma. Capital: Topeka. Population: 2,715,884 (2002 estimate). Area: 82,282 sq. mi./213,109 sq. km. See map on previous page —**Kan·san** *n, adj*

Kan·sas Cit·y 1. city in northeastern Kansas. It is directly across the Missouri River from Kansas City, Missouri. Population: 146,978 (2002 estimate). **2.** largest city in Missouri, situated in the western part of the state, on both banks of the Missouri River at its confluence with the Kansas River. Located near the geographic center of the United States, it is a major Midwestern transportation and commercial hub. Population: 443,471 (2002 estimate).

Kan·sas Cit·y jazz *n* a style of big band jazz music characterized by blues motifs and a relaxed beat

Kant /kant, kaant/, **Immanuel** (1724–1804) German philosopher. He is a seminal figure in Western philosophy whose major work is *Critique of Pure Reason* (1781). —**Kant·i·an** *adj* —**Kant·i·an·ism** *n*

> "Happiness is not an ideal of reason but of imagination."
> [Immanuel Kant, *Fundamental Principles of Metaphysics*; 1785]

kan·zu /kán zoo/ *n* a long garment resembling a robe, usually white and with long sleeves, worn by some men in East Africa [Early 20C. < Kiswahili]

Kao·hsiung /kòw shyóong/ city in southwestern Taiwan, on the Taiwan Strait. It is the largest port on the island. Population: 1,462,302 (1999).

kao·li·ang /kòwlee áng/ *n* **1.** a type of sorghum cultivated in China for its grain. Use: food grain, making liquor. Latin name: *Sorghum bicolor*. **2.** a strong alcoholic beverage made from the stalks of kaoliang [Early 20C. < Chinese *gāoliang* < *gāo* "high" + *liáng* "fine grain"]

ka·o·lin /káy əlin/, **ka·o·line** *n* a fine white clay. Use: porcelain, ceramics, medicines. [Early 18C. < Chinese *gāolǐng*, literally "high hill," hill in Jiangxi province]

ka·o·lin·ite /káy əli nīt/ *n* a white or gray aluminosilicate clay mineral. Source: kaolin, altered feldspars. Formula: $Al_2Si_2O_5(OH)_4$. —**ka·o·lin·it·ic** /kày əli níttik/ *adj*

ka·on /káy òn/ *n* an unstable elementary particle produced as a result of high-energy particle collision. It occurs in both charged and neutral forms and helps to hold protons and neutrons together inside a nucleus. Symbol **K** [Mid-20C. Contraction of K-MESON]

ka·pell·meis·ter /kə pél mīstər/ *n* **1.** the director of a choir **2.** formerly, the director of the orchestra, choir, or opera in the household of a German prince [Mid-19C. < German < *Kappelle* "court orchestra" + *Meister* "master"]

kaph /kaaf/ *n* the 11th letter of the Hebrew alphabet, represented in the English alphabet as "k" or, at the end of a word, as "kh." See table at **alphabet** [Early 19C. < Hebrew, "palm of the hand"]

ka·pok /káy pòk/ *n* a silky fiber obtained from the seed covering of a tropical tree. Use: stuffing and padding material. [Mid-18C. < Malay]

ka·pok bush *n* a small deciduous tree. Flowers: bright yellow. Native to: Australia. Genus: *Cochlospermum*.

Ka·po·si's sar·co·ma /kə pósseez-/ *n* a cancer of connective tissue that causes purplish red patches on the skin, most commonly found in equatorial Africa and in AIDS patients [Late 19C. After M. K. *Kaposi* (1837–1902), Hungarian dermatologist]

kap·pa /káppə/ *n* the tenth letter in the Greek alphabet, represented in the English alphabet as "k." See table at **alphabet** [15C. < Greek]

Kap·row /káp rō/, **Allan** (*b.* 1927) US artist. His *18 Happenings in 6 Parts* (1959) established the happening as a new art form.

ka·put /kaa póot, -póot, kə-/ *adj* broken, incapacitated, or not functioning (*informal*) [Late 19C. Via German *kaputt* < French (*être*) *capot* "(be) without tricks in the game of piquet"]

kar·a·bi·ner *n* CLIMBING another spelling of **carabiner**

Ka·ra·chay-Cher·kes·sia /kàrrə chī chər késsyə/ autonomous republic in southwestern European Russia, bordering Georgia. Capital: Cherkessk. Population: 436,000 (1997). Area: 5,440 sq. mi./14,100 sq. km.

Ka·ra·chi /kə ráachee/ seaport and largest city of Pakistan, located in the south of the country. Population: 9,269,265 (1998).

Ka·ra·dzic /káarə jiich/, **Radovan** (*b.* 1945) Bosnian Serb leader (1992–96). He was indicted by the International War Crimes Tribunal (1995) for genocide and crimes against humanity for actions during his time as president of the self-declared Bosnian Serb Republic during the civil war in Bosnia and Herzegovina.

Kar·a·ism /kárrə ìzzəm/ *n* the system of beliefs of a Jewish denomination founded in the 8th century whose members accept the Bible as the sole source of religious law and reject rabbinical interpretations [Late 19C. < Hebrew *qərāīm* "Karaites" < *qārā'* "to read"] —**Kar·a·ite** *n*

Hulton-Deutsch Collection/Corbis

Herbert von Karajan

Ka·ra·jan /káarə yaan/, **Herbert von** (1908–89) Austrian conductor. He was the music director of the Berlin Philharmonic Orchestra (1955–89) and director of the Vienna State Opera (1955–64).

Ka·ra-Kal·pak /kàrrə kál pàk/ (*plural* **Ka·ra-Kal·paks** or *same*) *n* **1.** a member of a people who live mainly in northwestern Uzbekistan **2.** a Turkic language spoken by the Kara-Kalpak people. Native speakers: 300,000. [Early 18C. < Kirghiz < *kara* "black" + *kalpak* "cap"] —**Ka·ra-Kal·pak** *adj*

Charles & Josette Lenars/Corbis

Karakoram Range: view of the Sind Valley

Ka·ra·ko·ram Range /kàrrə káwrəm-/ mountain range in the western Himalayan system, in south central Asia. Its highest peak is K2, 28,250 ft./8,611 m.

kar·a·kul /kárrəkəl/, **car·a·cul** *n* **1.** a soft curly black wool from central Asian lambs. Use: fur coats. **2.** a hardy sheep from central Asia, the lambs of which provide karakul [Mid-19C. < Russian, after an oasis in Uzbekistan and Kara Kul in Tajikistan]

Ka·ra Kul /kàrrə kóol/ dual lake system in eastern Tajikistan, on the Pamir plateau near the border with China. The two lakes are called Great Kara Kul and Little Kara Kul. Area: 140 sq. mi./363 sq. km. Depth: 780 ft./238 m.

Ka·ra·man·lis /kàrrə man léess/, **Constantine** (1907–98) prime minister (1955–63, 1974–80) and president (1980–85, 1990–95) of Greece. He supervised Greece's transition from military to civilian rule in the 1970s.

Ka·ra·man·lis, Kostas (*b.* 1956) prime minister of Greece (2004–). The son of Constantine Karamanlis, he represents the conservative New Democracy Party.

kar·a·o·ke /kàrree ókee/ *n* a form of entertainment in which amateur singers sing popular songs accompanied by prerecorded music from a machine that may also display the words on a video screen [Late 20C. < Japanese < *kara* "empty" + *oke*, shortening of *ōkesutora* "orchestra" < English ORCHESTRA]

Ka·ra Sea /káarə-/ sea bordering the northwestern coast of Siberian Russia. It is an arm of the Arctic Ocean. Area: 300,001 sq. mi./777,000 sq. km.

kar·at /kárrət/ *n* a unit of proportion of gold in an alloy equal to 1/24 part of pure gold [Variant of CARAT]

Barnaby's

karate

ka·ra·te /kə ráatee/ *n* a traditional Japanese form of unarmed combat, now widely popular as a sport, in which fast blows or kicks are used [Mid-20C. < Japanese < *kara* "empty" + *te* "hand"] —**ka·ra·te·ist** *n*

ka·ra·te·ka /kə ráatə kàa/ *n* somebody who practices or is an expert in karate [< Japanese, "karate person"]

Kar·ba·la /káarbələ/, **Kar·ba·lā'** city in central Iraq, on the edge of the Syrian Desert. Population: 296,705 (1987).

Ka·re·li·a /kə réelee ə, -lyə/ **1.** autonomous republic in the northwestern part of the Russian Federation. It is mainly covered by forest and has considerable mineral wealth. Language: Finnish, Russian. Currency: ruble. Capital: Petrozavodsk. Population: 766,400 (2000). Area: 69,690 sq. mi./180,500 sq. km. Official name **Republic of Karelia 2.** historic region on the border between Finland and Russia in northeastern Europe, now divided between a Finnish province and the Republic of Karelia

Ka·re·li·an /kə réelee ən, -lyən/ *n* **1.** a dialect of Finnish spoken in Karelia. Native speakers: 120,000. **2.** somebody who comes from Karelia —**Ka·re·li·an** *adj*

Ka·ren /kə réen, kə rén/ (*plural* **-rens** or *same*) *n* **1.** a member of a people who live mainly in southern and eastern Myanmar **2.** a Tibeto-Burman language spoken in southern and eastern Myanmar. Native speakers: 2 million. [Mid-18C. < Burmese *ka-reng* "wild, unclean man"] —**Ka·ren** *adj*

Ka·ri·ba, Lake /kə réebə/ artificial lake on the border between Zambia and Zimbabwe, southern Africa. It was created by building the Kariba Dam across the Zambezi River. Area: 2,050 sq. mi./5,310 sq. km.

Karl-Marx-Stadt /káarl máarks shtàat/ former name for **Chemnitz** (1953–90)

Kar·loff /káar làwf/, **Boris** (1887–1969) British actor. He appeared in numerous US horror films, notably as the monster in *Frankenstein* (1931). Born **Pratt, William Henry**

> "The monster was indeed the best friend I could ever have."
> [Boris Karloff. Quoted in *Connoisseur*; January 1991]

Kar·lo·vy Va·ry /káarləvee váaree/ city in the northwestern Czech Republic, situated on the Ohře River, west of Prague. Population: 55,000 (1997).

Karls·ru·he /káarlz ròo ə/ industrial and university city in Baden-Württemberg State, southwestern Germany. Population: 277,011 (1997).

kar·ma /káarmə/ *n* **1.** ACTIONS DETERMINING FUTURE STATE in Hindu and Buddhist philosophy, the quality of somebody's current and future lives as determined by that person's behavior in this and in previous lives **2.** ATMOSPHERE the atmosphere radiated by a place, situation, person, or object (*informal*) **3.** DESTINY destiny or fate [Early 19C. < Sanskrit *karman* "fate, action"] —**kar·mic** *adj*

Kar·nak /káar nàk/ village in eastern Egypt, on the Nile River, occupying part of the site of ancient Thebes

Kar·nat·ak /kər náatək/ *adj* relating to the linguistic region in south central India between the Eastern

Ghats and the Coromandel coast, now part of Madras state [Early 19C, < KARNATAKA (see CARNATIC)]

Kar·na·ta·ka /kər naátəkə/, **Kar·nā·ta·ka** state in southern India. Capital: Bangalore. Language: Kannada. Population: 52,733,958 (2001). Area: 74,051 sq. mi./ 191,791 sq. km.

Kar·na·tak mu·sic /kər naátək-/, **Kar·nat·ic mu·sic** /-tik-/ *n* the classical music of southern India, which often accompanies dance

Kar·nat·ic *adj* GEOG same as **Karnatak**

Kar·ok /kə rók/ (*plural* **-oks** or *same*) *n* **1.** a member of a Native North American people living mainly in northwestern California **2.** the Hokan language of the Karok people [Mid-19C. < Karok *karuk* "upstream"] —**Kar·ok** *adj*

Ka·roo /kə ro͞o/, **Kar·roo** semidesert plateau region in Western Cape Province, South Africa. Area: 100,000 sq. mi./259,000 sq. km.

kar·oss /kə róss/ *n* a blanket made of animal skins, used in southern Africa as either a cloak or a mattress [Mid-18C. < Afrikaans *karos*]

Kar·roo ◆ **Karoo**

karst /kaarst/ *n* a limestone landscape, characterized by caves, fissures, and underground streams [Late 19C. < German *der Karst*, plateau region in Slovenia] —**karst·ic** *adj*

kart /kaart/ *n* a small low engine-powered vehicle, like a miniature racing car, used in racing [Mid-20C. Alteration of CART] —**kart·ing** *n*

Kart·ti·ka /kaártəkə/, **Kar·ti·ka** *n* in the Hindu calendar, the eighth month of the year, lasting 30 days. Date: October to November. See table at **calendar**

Kart·ve·lian /kaart veélyən/ *n* a family of languages including Georgian, spoken in the region south of the Caucasus Mountains. They are unrelated to the North Caucasian languages. Native speakers: 4 million. [< Georgian *Kartvelebi* "Georgians"] —**Kart·ve·lian** *adj*

karyo- *prefix* cell nucleus ○ *karyoplasm* [Via modern Latin < Greek *karuon* "kernel"]

kar·y·og·a·my /kàrree óggəmee/ *n* the fusion of cell nuclei that occurs during fertilization —**kar·y·o·gam·ic** /kèrree ə gámmik/ *adj*

kar·y·o·gram /kárree ə gràm/ *n* a photograph or diagram of the chromosomes of a cell in sequence

kar·y·o·ki·ne·sis /kàrree ōkə neéssəss/ *n* BIOL same as **mitosis** —**kar·y·o·ki·net·ic** /kàree ōkə nétik, -ōkī nétik/ *adj*

kar·y·ol·o·gy /kàrree óllәjee/ *n* the study of cell nuclei, especially with reference to chromosomes —**kar·y·o·log·ic** /kàrree ə lójjik/ *adj* —**kar·y·o·log·i·cal** *adj* —**kar·y·ol·o·gist** *n*

kar·y·o·lymph /kárree ə lìmf/ *n* BIOL same as **nuclear sap**

kar·y·o·plasm /kárree ə plàzzəm/ *n* BIOL same as **nucleoplasm** —**kar·y·o·plas·mic** /kàrree ə plázmik/ *adj*

kar·y·o·some /kárree ə sȍm/ *n* a thickened mass of chromatin in a cell nucleus

kar·y·o·type /kárree ə tīp/ *n* **1.** CHARACTERISTICS OF CELL CHROMOSOMES the appearance and characteristics of the chromosomes of a cell, especially size, number, and form **2.** PHOTOMICROGRAPH OF CELL CHROMOSOMES a photomicrograph in which a cell's chromosomes are arranged according to size and classification ■ *vt* (**-typed, -typ·ing, -types**) FIND KARYOTYPE OF CELL to determine the karyotype of a cell —**kar·y·o·typ·ic** /kàrree ə típpik/ *adj* —**kar·y·o·typ·i·cal** *adj* —**kar·y·o·typ·i·cal·ly** *adv*

Kar·zai /kaar zí/, **Hamid** (*b.* 1955?) prime minister of Afghanistan. He was deputy foreign minister (1992–94) and chairman of the Interim Administration of Afghanistan (2001–02) before becoming prime minister in 2002.

kas·bah *n* another spelling of **casbah** [Mid-18C. Via French < form of Arabic *ḳaṣaba* "fortress"]

ka·sha /kaáshə/ *n* **1.** a dish of cooked buckwheat resembling oatmeal, originally from eastern Europe **2.** the buckwheat from which kasha is made [Early 19C. < Russian]

Kash·mir /kásh meér, kázh-, kash meér/ **1.** disputed territory in the northern part of South Asia. All of the territory is claimed by India and Pakistan, and part of the territory is claimed by China. Area: 85,806 sq. mi./222,236 sq. km. **2.** ◆ **Azad Kashmir**

Kash·mir·i /kash meéree, kazh-/ *n* **1.** somebody who comes from Kashmir **2.** the Dardic official state language of Kashmir, also spoken in neighboring areas. Native speakers: 5 million. —**Kash·mir·i** *adj*

kash·ruth /kaáshrəth, kaash ro͝ot/, **kash·rut** *n* **1.** the body of Jewish laws that relate to the preparation and fitness of foods and to items such as textiles and ritual scrolls to be used by Jewish people **2.** the fitness of an item for use by Jews, as determined by reference to kashruth [Early 20C. < Hebrew, "fitness"]

Kas·kas·ki·a[1] /kəss káskee ə/ (*plural* **-as** or *same*) *n* a member of a Native North American people, one of the six peoples who formed the Illinois Confederacy —**Kas·kas·ki·a** *adj*

Kas·kas·ki·a[2] /kəss káskee ə/ river in Illinois. It flows southwestward into the Mississippi River. Length: 320 mi./515 km.

Kas·pa·rov /káspə ràwf/, **Garry** (*b.* 1963) Azerbaijani chess player. He became world champion following his defeat of Anatoly Karpov in 1985. Full name **Kasparov, Garry Kimovich**. Born **Weinstein, Garri**

Kas·sa·la /kə saálə/, **Kas·sa·lā** city in northeastern Sudan. Population: 234,270 (1993).

Kas·sel /káss'l/, **Cas·sel** industrial city in west central Germany. It is known for its exhibitions of contemporary art that have been held there every four years since 1955. Population: 201,789 (1997).

ka·ta /kaá taà/ *n* a sequence of movements in some martial arts such as karate, used either for training or to demonstrate technique [Mid-20C. < Japanese, "model, pattern"]

kat·a·bat·ic /kàttə báttik/ *adj* describes a wind that moves down a slope as a result of the cooling of air at higher altitudes [Late 19C. < Greek *katabatikos* < *katabainein* "go down"]

ka·tab·o·lism *n* BIOCHEM another spelling of **catabolism**

Ka·tah·din, Mount /kə taád'n/ mountain in northern Maine, in Baxter State Park. Height: 5,267 ft./1,605 m.

ka·ta·ka·na /kaàtə kaánə/ *n* a set of angular symbols representing syllables used in Japanese writing mainly for transliterating non-Japanese words [Early 18C. < Japanese < *kata* "side" + *kana*, syllabic writing system]

Kath·ak /kúttək/ *n* a form of classical dance from northern India that tells a story and is marked by fast footwork and pirouettes [Mid-20C. < Sanskrit *kathaka* "storyteller" < *kathā* "story"]

Kath·a·ka·li /kaàtə kaálee/ *n* a stylized form of drama from Kerala, southern India, that interprets stories from Hindu classical literature by combining dance and mime [Early 20C. < Malayalam < Sanskrit *kathā* "story" + Malayalam *kaḷi* "play"]

Ka·tha·rev·ou·sa /kaàthə révvoo saà/ *n* a form of modern Greek, used in literature as opposed to everyday speech and writing, that employs some of the features of classical Greek. ◊ **Demotic** (sense 1) [Early 20C. < Greek *kathareuousa* < *katharos* "pure"]

Kath·man·du /kàt man do͞o/, **Kat·man·du** capital city of Nepal, located in the central part of the country. It is situated about 55 mi./89 km from the border with India. Population: 533,000 (1995).

Kat·mai, Mount /kát mī/ volcano in southwestern Alaska, in Katmai National Park and Preserve. Height: 6,716 ft./2,047 m.

Kat·mai Na·tion·al Park and Pre·serve national park in southwestern Alaska, on the Alaska Peninsula. Area: 6,396 sq. mi./16,565 sq. km.

Kat·man·du another spelling of **Kathmandu**

Ka·to·wi·ce /kaàtə veétsə/ city in southern Poland. It is an important mining and industrial center. Population: 349,000 (1997).

Kat·si·na /kaat seénə/ city in northern Nigeria, the capital of Katsina State. Population: 201,500 (1995).

Kat·te·gat /káttə gàt/ strait between the southwestern coast of Sweden and the eastern coast of the Jutland peninsula, Denmark. Length: 140 mi./225 km.

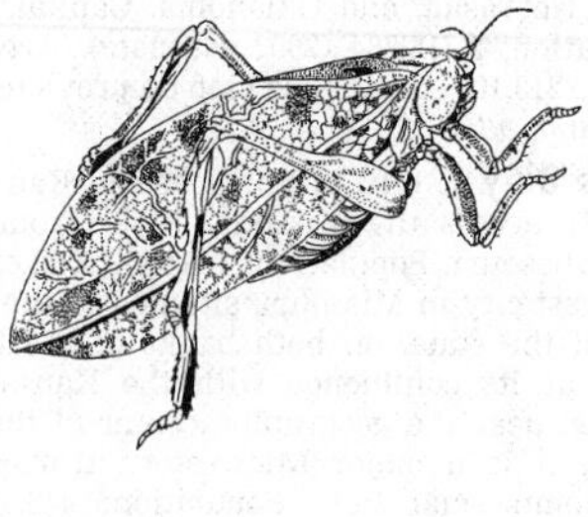

katydid

ka·ty·did /káytee dìd/ *n* a large green grasshopper with very long antennae. Native to: North America. Family: Tettigoniidae. [Late 18C. An imitation of the sound produced when the male rubs its front wings together]

Ka·tyn For·est /ka teén-/ forest in western European Russia, near Smolensk, where the mass grave of thousands of Polish army officers murdered by Soviet security services was discovered in 1943

katz·en·jam·mer /kátsən jàmər/ *n* (*dated informal*) **1.** MED same as **hangover 2.** a bewildered or discouraged state **3.** a loud and confused noise [Mid-19C. < German < *Katze* "cat" + *Jammer* "distress"]

Kau·ai /ków wī/ fourth largest island in Hawaii, the northernmost of the main islands. Population: 59,946 (2002 estimate). Area: 552 sq. mi./1,430 sq. km.

Kauff·man /kówfmən/, **Angelica** (1741–1807) Swiss painter. Her essentially rococo paintings, often of historical or mythological subjects, incorporated aspects of neoclassicism. She was a founding member of the Royal Academy in London. Full name **Kauffman, Maria Ann Angelica**

Kauf·man, Mount /káwfmən/ former name for **Lenin Peak**

Kauf·man /káwfmən/, **George S.** (1889–1961) US playwright and director. He cowrote many Broadway comedies such as *Animal Crackers* (1928), *Stage Door* (1936), and *The Man Who Came to Dinner* (1939). Full name **Kaufman, George Simon**

> "Satire is what closes Saturday night."
> [George S. Kaufman. Quoted in *George S. Kaufman and His Friends*, Scott Meredith; 1974]

Kau·nas /kównəss/ industrial city in central Lithuania, situated about 60 mi./100 km west of Vilnius. Population: 412,610 (2000).

Ka·un·da /kaa o͞ondə/, **Kenneth** (*b.* 1924) Zambian politician. He was Zambia's first president after independence (1964–91). Full name **Kaunda, Kenneth David**

> "I pray the Good Lord to give us courage to recognize our weaknesses and to give us wisdom to recognize the truth and, having recognized that truth, moral power to get committed to it through thick and thin."
> [Kenneth Kaunda. Quoted in *Kenneth Kaunda*, Philip Brownrigg; 1989]

kau·ri /kówree/ *n* **1.** a strong light-colored wood distinguished by fine speckling. Use: cabinetwork, boats, carving. **2.** an evergreen tree that yields kauri. Native to: New Zealand. Latin name: *Agathis australis*. **3.** INDUST same as **kauri gum** [Early 19C. < Maori]

kau·ri gum, **kau·ri res·in** *n* the brittle resin of the kauri tree that is usually found in fossilized form. Use: varnishes.

ka·va /kaávə/ *n* **1.** HERBAL REMEDY an herbal medicine made from the dried roots and rhizome of a bush of the pepper family. Use: to relieve anxiety, improve sleep. **2.** DRINK a narcotic drink made from the roots of a bush of the pepper family **3.** POLYNESIAN BUSH a bush of the pepper family whose root and rhizome are the source of kava. Flowers: small, clustered in spikes. Native to: Polynesia. Latin name: *Piper methysticum*. [Late 18C. < Polynesian, "bitter"]

Ka·va·rat·ti /kùvvə rúttee/ island and capital of the Union Territory of Lakshadweep, southwestern India. Population: 10,113 (2001).

Kā·ve·ri another spelling of **Cauvery**

Kaw /kaw/ *n* (*plural same* or **Kaws** /kaws/), *adj* PEOPLES, LANG same as **Kansa**

Ka·wa·ba·ta /kaàwə baàtə/, **Yasunari** (1899–1972) Japanese novelist. His works include *Snow Country* (1956) and *Thousand Cranes* (1959). He was the first Japanese writer to be awarded the Nobel Prize in literature (1968).

Ka·wa·gu·chi /kaàwə goòchee/ city in southeastern Honshu, Japan, north of Tokyo in Saitama Prefecture. Population: 463,879 (2002).

Ka·wa·sa·ki /kaàwə saàkee/ city in east central Honshu, Japan, south of Tokyo, beside Tokyo Bay in Kanagawa Prefecture. Population: 1,245,780 (2002).

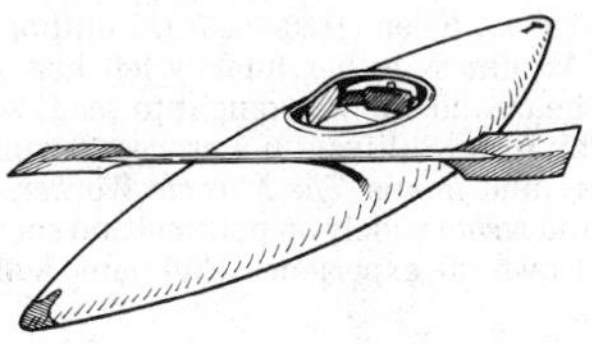

kayak

kay·ak /kī àk/, **kai·ak** *n* **1.** a lightweight plastic or fiberglass covered canoe propelled by a double-bladed paddle, used for leisure and in competitive sport **2.** a traditional Inuit boat that is narrow and pointed and consists of a light frame covered with skins. It is propelled by one or two people using double-bladed paddles. [Mid-18C. < Inuit *qayaq*] —**kay·ak** *vti* —**kay·ak·er** *n* —**kay·ak·ing** *n*

kay·o /kày ṓ/ (*slang*) *n* (*plural* **-os**) a knockout, especially in boxing ■ *vt* (**-oed, -o·ing, -os**) to knock somebody out, especially in boxing [Early 20C. < the pronunciation of KO]

Kay·se·ri /kīzə reè/ city in central Turkey, near Mount Argaeus. It is the capital of Kayseri Province. Population: 475,657 (1997).

ka·za·chok /kaàzə cháwk/ *n* a Ukrainian and Russian folk dance in which high kicks are made from a squatting position [Early 20C. < Russian, diminutive of *kazak* "Cossack"]

Ka·zakh /kaà zaàk, kə zaàk/, **Ka·zak** *n* **1.** a member of a people of Central Asia living mainly in Kazakhstan **2.** the Turkic official language of Kazakhstan, also spoken in Mongolia, China, and Afghanistan. Native speakers: 8 million. [Mid-19C. Via Russian < Kazakh *kazak*] —**Ka·zakh** *adj*

Kazakhstan

Ka·zakh·stan /kaà zaak staàn, kə zaàk-/ country in Central Asia, bordered by Russia, China, Kyrgyzstan, Uzbekistan, Turkmenistan, and the Caspian Sea. Language: Kazakh. Currency: tenge. Capital: Astana. Population: 16,763,795 (2003). Area: 1,049,200 sq. mi./2,717,300 sq. km. Official name **Republic of Kazakhstan**

Ka·zan /kə zaàn/, **Elia** (1909–2003) Turkish-born US stage and movie director and novelist. He won Academy Awards for directing *Gentleman's Agreement* (1947) and *On the Waterfront* (1954). Born **Kazanjoglous, Elia**

Ka·zant·za·kis /kaàz'n zaàkiss/, **Nikos** (1883–1957) Greek writer. His novels include *Zorba the Greek* (1943) and *The Last Temptation of Christ* (1951).

ka·zat·sky /kə zaàtskee/ (*plural* **-skies**), **ka·zat·ske** *n* DANCE same as **kazachok**

Kaz·bek /kaàz bèk/ peak on the border of Russia and Georgia in the Caucasus Mountains. Height: 16,526 ft./5,037 m.

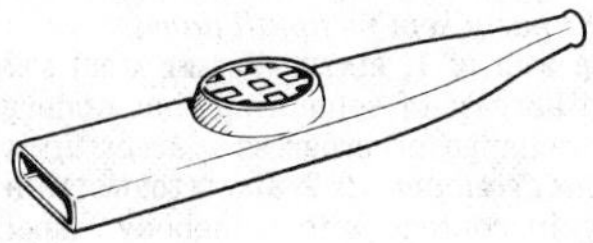

kazoo

ka·zoo /kə zoó/ (*plural* **-zoos**) *n* a toy instrument that makes a buzzing sound, consisting of a tube with a mouthpiece and a hole covered by a thin diaphragm [Late 19C. An imitation of its sound]

KB *abbr* **1.** COMPUT kilobyte **2.** CHESS king's bishop

KBP *abbr* CHESS king's bishop's pawn

kbyte /káy bīt/ *abbr* COMPUT kilobyte

kc *abbr* PHYS kilocycle

K.C. *abbr* **1.** Kansas City **2.** Kennel Club **3.** LAW King's Counsel **4.** RELIG Knight of Columbus

kcal *abbr* MEASURE kilocalorie

ke *abbr* ONLINE Kenya (*used in Internet addresses*) See table at **domain name**

ke·a /keè ə/ *n* a large parrot with brownish green feathers. Native to: mountainous regions of New Zealand. Latin name: *Nestor notabilis*. [Mid-19C. < Maori]

Kean /keen/, **Edmund** (1787–1833) British actor. He was noted for his tragic Shakespearean roles, principally Richard III, Hamlet, Othello, Iago, and Macbeth.

Keat·ing /keèting/, **Paul** (*b.* 1944) Australian politician. He was Labor prime minister of Australia (1991–96). Full name **Keating, Paul John**. See table at **prime minister**

> "Good economics is good politics."
> [Paul Keating, *Sydney Morning Herald*; August 27, 1988]

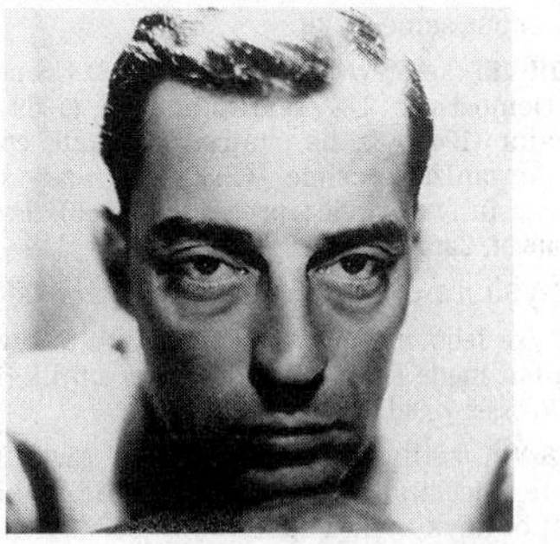

Buster Keaton

Kea·ton /keèt'n/, **Buster** (1895–1966) US silent movie actor and director. He was a deadpan acrobatic clown in many classic silent movies such as *The Navigator* (1924) and *The General* (1927). Born **Keaton, Joseph Francis**

Keats /keets/, **John** (1795–1821) British poet. His lyrical intensity made him one of the most influential of the romantic poets. His great odes were collected in *Lamia, Isabella, The Eve of St. Agnes, and Other Poems* (1820). See Cultural note at **nightingale, urn** —**Keats·i·an** *adj*

> "'Beauty is truth, truth beauty,'—that is all / Ye know on earth, and all ye need to know."
> [John Keats, "Ode on a Grecian Urn"; 1820]

> "Now more than ever seems it rich to die, / To cease upon the midnight with no pain, / While thou art pouring forth thy soul abroad / In such an ecstasy!"
> [John Keats, "Ode to a Nightingale"; 1820]

ke·bab /kə bób/, **ka·bob, ka·bab** *n* a selection of small pieces of tender food such as poultry, meat, seafood, or vegetables threaded onto a stick and grilled [Late 17C. < Arabic *kabāb*]

Kech·ua *n, adj* PEOPLES, LANG another spelling of **Quechua**

Ke·dah /kéddə/ state in northwestern Malaysia, on the Malay Peninsula. Capital: Alur Setar. Area: 3,639 sq. mi./9,426 sq. km.

kedge /kej/ *vti* (**kedged, kedg·ing, kedg·es**) to move a vessel by pulling on a rope or cable attached to a light anchor, or be moved in this way ■ *n also* **kedge an·chor** a light anchor, especially one that is lodged some distance from a vessel so that the vessel can be pulled toward it [15C. Origin ?]

ked·ger·ee /kéjjə reè, kèjjə reè/ *n* **1.** a dish of British origin consisting of rice with flaked smoked fish and hard-boiled eggs **2.** a spicy dish of South Asian origin made from lentils, rice, and sometimes fish [Mid-17C. < Hindi *khicṛī*]

keel /keel/ *n* **1.** NAUT **SHIP'S STRUCTURAL ELEMENT** the main structural element of a ship, stretching along the center line of its bottom from the bow to the stern. It sometimes extends farther downward into the water to provide extra stability. **2.** AVIAT **AIRCRAFT'S STRUCTURAL ELEMENT** a structure that looks or acts like a ship's keel, e.g., the main structural element of an aircraft's fuselage **3.** BIRDS **PART OF BIRD'S BREASTBONE** a ridge-shaped part in the breastbone of a bird to which the flight muscles are anchored. Technical name **carina 4.** BIOL **PART LIKE RIDGE** any ridge-shaped part of an organism **5.** same as **ship** (*literary*) ■ *vti* (**keeled, keel·ing, keels**) NAUT **CAPSIZE** to capsize a vessel, or capsize [14C. < Old Norse *kjǫlr*] ◇ **on an even keel** in a stable steady condition

keel over *v* **1.** *vi* to collapse or fall over, often through exhaustion or illness (*informal*) **2.** *vti* NAUT same as **keel**

keel·age /keèlij/ *n* a docking fee for merchant ships, charged by a port

keel·boat /keèl bṓt/ *n* a covered riverboat with a keel and shallow draft but no sail, propelled by rowing, poling, or towing, and used for transporting freight

keel·haul /keèl hàwl/ (**-hauled, -haul·ing, -hauls**) *vt* **1.** to drag somebody on a rope from one side of a vessel to the other under the keel as a form of punishment **2.** to reprimand somebody severely (*informal*) [Mid-17C. < Dutch *kielhalen*]

keel·son /keèlssən, kélssən/, **kel·son** /kélssən/ *n* a metal or wooden beam attached to the upper side of a boat's keel to reinforce it [13C. Probably < Old Norse *kjölsvīn* or Low German *kielsvīn*]

kee·ma /keèmə/ *n* S Asia in South Indian cooking, ground meat [Late 20C. < Hindi]

keen[1] /keen/ *adj* **1.** **SENSITIVE** finely tuned and able to sense minor differences, distinctions, or details ○ *a keen sense of smell* **2.** **INTENSE** intense and lively ○ *keen competition* **3.** **SHARP** having a sharp cutting edge (*literary*) ○ *a keen razor* **4.** **BITING** cold and penetrating ○ *a keen wind* **5.** **ACUTE** quick to understand things ○ *a keen mind* **6.** **ENTHUSIASTIC** eager and willing to do something ○ *not very keen on the idea* **7.** **VERY GOOD** fine or very good (*slang dated*) ○ *a keen new bike* [Old English *cēne* "brave, clever" < Germanic] —**keen·ly** *adv* —**keen·ness** *n*

keen[2] /keen/ *vi* (**keened, keen·ing, keens**) to cry out or wail in grief, especially while lamenting the dead ■ *n* a lamentation for a dead person (*literary*) [Early 19C. < Irish *caoinin* "I wail"] —**keen·er** *n*

Keene /keen/ city in southwestern New Hampshire. Population: 22,714 (2002 estimate).

~~**keeness**~~ incorrect spelling of **keenness**

keep /keep/ *v* (**kept** /kept/, **keep·ing, keeps**) **1.** *vti* **POSSESS SOMETHING** to hold or maintain something in your possession ○ *The sample is yours to keep.* **2.** *vt* **MAINTAIN CONDITION OF SOMETHING** to maintain somebody or something in a particular place or condition ○ *Keep your arm up.* **3.** *vt* **STORE SOMETHING** to store something in a place when it is not in use ○ *kept the keys in a drawer* **4.** *vti* **CONTINUE** to cause somebody or something to continue in a particular way or activity, or continue in a particular way ○ *kept working* **5.** *vt* **SAFEGUARD INFORMATION** to refrain from telling a secret or giving other information ○ *keep* *a secret* **6.** *vt* **SAVE SOMETHING** to save something for later use or withhold something from use ○ *kept some in reserve* **7.** *vt* **BE TRUE TO SOMETHING** to fulfill a promise or other verbal commitment ○ *kept his word* **8.** *vt* **FULFILL RELIGIOUS DUTY** to observe a religious obligation ○ *keep kosher* ○ *keep the Sabbath* **9.** *vt* **MAINTAIN RECORD** to create or maintain something as a written record ○ *keep a diary* **10.** *vi* **STAY** to remain in a particular condition ○ *keep warm* **11.** *vi* **MAINTAIN COURSE** to follow a particular course or direction **12.** *vi* **NOT SPOIL** to remain fresh or in a usable condition ○ *That fish won't keep in this hot weather.* **13.** *vi* **DO SOMETHING REPEATEDLY** to repeat an action a number of times **14.** *vi* **NOT REQUIRE ATTENTION** to be able to be postponed ○ *The dusting will keep until tomorrow.* **15.** *vt* **HAVE SOMETHING FOR SALE** to have something in stock in order to sell it ○ *keep a large selection of scarves* **16.** *vt* **DETAIN SOMEBODY** to make somebody wait or prevent somebody from going ○ *I won't keep you a moment.* **17.** *vt* **LOOK AFTER SOMEBODY OR SOMETHING** to take care of a person or animal, providing what is required to live ○ *keep pets* **18.** *vt* **HAVE ANIMAL AS LIVESTOCK** to raise an animal for profit ○ *keep cattle* **19.** *vt* **EMPLOY SOMEBODY** to employ somebody, especially in a household ○ *keep servants* **20.** *vt* **RUN BUSINESS OR HOUSEHOLD** to maintain a business, house, or other establishment ○ *keeps house for the ambassador* **21.** *vt* **SUPPORT SOMEBODY FINANCIALLY** to provide financially for a spouse or lover (*dated*) **22.** *vt Malaysia* **PUT SOMETHING AWAY** to put something in the place where it is normally stored or kept ready for use ○ *I must just keep these papers in my desk before I leave.* ■ *n* **1.** **MAINTENANCE** food and lodging, or whatever somebody needs to live ○ *work for your keep* **2.** **CASTLE PART** a stronghold or the innermost fortified part of a castle [Old English *cēpan* "take, observe," origin ?] ◇ **for keeps** permanently or forever (*informal*) ◇ **keep something to yourself** to refrain from revealing something ◇ **keep (yourself) to yourself** to avoid mixing or communicating with other people

keep at *vt* **1.** to persevere with something, especially something difficult or strenuous **2.** to persist in asking somebody to do something (*informal*) ○ *kept at me to put in longer hours*

keep away *v* **1.** *vt* to prevent somebody or something from going near somebody or something **2.** *vi* to avoid going near somebody or something

keep back *vt* **1.** **RESTRAIN SOMETHING** to restrain or confine something to a limit **2.** **NOT TELL SOMETHING** to refrain from telling or revealing something **3.** **WITHHOLD SOMETHING FOR LATER USE** to hold something in reserve for later use or for another purpose

keep down *v* **1.** *vt* **OPPRESS SOMEBODY OR SOMETHING** to maintain somebody or something in an inferior position or in a state of oppression **2.** *vt* **MAINTAIN SOMETHING AT LOW LEVEL** to maintain something at a low level, position, or number ○ *Keep the costs down.* **3.** *vi* **STAY LOW** to stay in a place or position where you cannot be seen **4.** *vt* **NOT VOMIT SOMETHING** to hold food or drink in your stomach without vomiting ○ *He hasn't been able to keep anything down since the operation.*

keep from *vt* **1.** **HIDE SOMETHING FROM SOMEBODY** to refrain from disclosing something to somebody **2.** **RESTRAIN SOMEBODY** to prevent somebody from doing something **3.** **SAFEGUARD SOMEBODY** to protect somebody from something ○ *kept us from harm*

keep in *vt* to repress something that you feel

keep off *vt* **1.** **PREVENT SOMEBODY OR SOMETHING FROM TOUCHING** to prevent somebody or something from having direct contact with somebody or something else **2.** **NOT TOUCH SOMEBODY OR SOMETHING** to refrain from direct contact with something or somebody ○ *Keep off the grass!* **3.** **NOT CONSUME SOMETHING** to prevent somebody from consuming something, or refrain from consuming something ○ *kept off caffeine* **4.** **NOT TALK ABOUT SOMETHING** to prevent somebody from discussing something, or refrain from discussing something ○ *kept off the topic of money*

keep on *v* **1.** *vi* **CONTINUE** to continue doing something ○ *kept on teasing the dog* **2.** *vt* **NOT TAKE SOMETHING OFF** to continue wearing something **3.** *vt* **NOT DISMISS SOMEBODY** to continue to employ somebody **4.** *vi UK* **PERSIST IN TALKING ABOUT SOMETHING** to talk repetitively or continuously about one thing in a way that makes others bored or annoyed (*informal*)

keep out *vti* to prevent somebody from entering a place, or refrain from entering a place

keep out of *vti* **1.** to prevent somebody or something from exposure to something, or avoid exposure to something ○ *keep it out of the rain* **2.** to prevent somebody from becoming involved in something, or avoid becoming involved in something ○ *Keep out of her way.*

keep to *vt* to adhere without deviation to a plan, course, or subject

keep up *v* **1.** *vt* **MAINTAIN PRESENT LEVEL OF SOMETHING** to maintain something at its present level ○ *Keep up the good work.* ○ *That's excellent. Keep it up.* **2.** *vi* **STAY EVEN** to go as fast or make the same progress as somebody else **3.** *vt* **MAINTAIN SOMETHING IN GOOD CONDITION** to make sure that something stays in good condition ○ *has a beautiful home but doesn't really keep it up* **4.** *vt* **NOT LET SOMEBODY GO TO BED** to prevent somebody from sleeping or going to bed at night ○ *The music from the party kept us up till dawn.*

keep up with *vt* **1.** **REMAIN INFORMED ABOUT SOMETHING** to remain abreast of something that undergoes continuous change or progress ○ *keeps up with technological developments* **2.** **STAY IN CONTACT WITH SOMEBODY** to stay in contact with somebody, especially by letter ○ *I still keep up with a few friends from school.* **3.** **CONTINUE MAKING PAYMENTS** to remain current in making scheduled payments

keep·a·way *n* LEISURE same as **monkey in the middle**

keep·er /keépər/ *n* **1.** **CARETAKER** somebody in charge of a building or small business (*usually used in combination*) ○ *a lighthouse keeper* **2.** **WARDEN** somebody whose job is to take care of or protect animals **3.** **PRISON GUARD** somebody who is responsible for guarding other people, especially in a prison **4.** **SOMEBODY MAINTAINING SOMETHING** somebody who keeps or maintains something ○ *a good record keeper* **5.** **SOMETHING WORTH KEEPING** something that is worth keeping, especially a fish that is large enough to be legally caught and retained (*informal*) **6.** FOOTBALL **PLAY IN FOOTBALL** in football, a play in which the quarterback runs toward the goal with the ball **7.** SPORTS same as **goalkeeper** (*informal*) **8.** PHYS **BAR ACROSS MAGNET'S POLES** an iron or steel bar placed across the poles of a permanent horseshoe magnet when it is not in use, to close the magnetic circuit and prevent demagnetization

keep·ing /keéping/ *n* **1.** the act of looking after or caring for somebody or something **2.** somebody's charge, custody, or possession ○ *in his keeping* ◇ **in keeping with** consistent with or suitable for something ◇ **out of keeping with** not consistent with or suitable for something

keep·sake /keép sàyk/ *n* a small item or gift kept because it evokes memories of somebody or something [Late 18C. Because kept "for the sake of" the giver]

kees·hond /káyss hàwnt, -hònd/ (*plural* **-honds** or **-honden** /-hàwndən/) *n* a dog with a dense shaggy blackish gray coat and a tightly curled tail, belonging to a breed developed in the Netherlands [Early 20C. < Dutch, "Kees dog" < *Kees*, pet form of *Cornelis* "Cornelius"]

kees·ter *n* ANAT another spelling of **keister**

kef *n* DRUGS same as **kif**

Ke·fau·ver /keé fàwvər/, **Estes** (1903–63) US politician. A Democratic US representative (1939–49) and senator (1949–63), he chaired a Senate committee on organized crime (1950–51), and ran unsuccessfully for vice president (1956). Full name **Kefauver, Carey Estes**

kef·fi·yeh *n* CLOTHING another spelling of **kaffiyeh**

ke·fir /ke feér/ *n* a creamy drink with a low alcohol content made from fermented cow's milk [Late 19C. Via Russian < Old Turkic *köpür* "milk"]

Kef·la·vik /kéfflə veék, kyébblə veék/ town in southwestern Iceland, situated about 22 mi./35 km southwest of Reykjavik. Population: 7,637 (1996).

keg /keg/ *n* **1.** **SMALL BARREL** a small barrel used for storing liquids **2.** **BEER BARREL** an aluminum barrel that is used for storing and transporting beer **3.** **CONTENTS OF KEG** the amount that a keg can hold **4.** **NAIL WEIGHT UNIT** a unit of weight used for nails, equivalent to 100 lb./45.5kg ■ *vt* (**kegged, keg·ging, kegs**) **STORE BEER IN BARREL** to put or store beer in a small barrel [Early 17C. Alteration of *cag* < Old Norse *kaggi*]

keg·ger /kéggər/ *n* a party at which beer is served from kegs (*slang*)

keg·ler /kégglər/ *n* a participant in the sport of bowling (*informal*) [Mid-20C. < German < *kegeln* "to bowl"]

Keil·lor /keélər/, **Garrison** (*b.* 1942) US humorist, broadcaster, and essayist. He is the popular radio host of *A Prairie Home Companion*, which airs on NPR weekly.

kei·ret·su /kay rétsoo/ (*plural same*) *n* in Japan, a conglomerate headed by a major Japanese bank or made up of companies with a common supply chain linking wholesalers and retailers [< Japanese]

keis·ter /keéstər/, **kees·ter** *n* the buttocks (*slang humorous*) [Late 19C. Origin ?]

Kei·tel /kít'l/, **Wilhelm** (1882–1946) German field marshal. Hitler's chief military adviser during World War II, he was executed for war crimes in 1946.

Ke·jim·ku·jik Na·tion·al Park /kèjjim kŏŏjik-/ national park and wildlife preserve in southern Nova Scotia, Canada, established in 1974. Area: 156 sq. mi./403 sq. km.

Ke·ku·lé for·mu·la /kékyə lay-/ *n* the representation of a benzene molecule as a hexagonal ring with alternating single and double bonds linking six carbon atoms, each linked to one hydrogen atom at the vertices [Mid-20C. After Friedrich August *Kekulé* (1829–96), German physicist]

Kel·ler /kéllər/, **Helen** (1880–1968) US author and lecturer. An illness in her infancy left her unable to see or hear, and she was taught to read, write, and speak by Anne Sullivan in a process dramatized in the play and movie *The Miracle Worker*. She lectured and wrote widely on political and social issues and her own life experience. Full name **Keller, Helen Adams**

> "We could never learn to be brave and patient, if there were only joy in the world."
> [Helen Keller, *Atlantic Monthly*; May 1890]

Kel·logg /kél àwg/, **John** (1852–1943) US surgeon and food manufacturer. During the 1890s he and his brother William developed the process for making cornflakes. Full name **Kellogg, John Harvey**

Kel·ly /kéllee/, **Gene** (1912–96) US movie actor, dancer, and director. He is best known for starring in and codirecting *Singin' in the Rain* (1952). Full name **Kelly, Eugene Curran**

> "You learn to use the camera as part of the choreography. Film dancing will always be a problem because the eye of the camera is coldly realistic, demanding that everything looks natural, and dancing is unrealistic."
> [Gene Kelly. Quoted in *The Films of Gene Kelly*, Tony Thomas; 1991]

Kel·ly, Grace (1929–82) US movie actor. She starred in motion pictures such as *High Noon* (1952) and *Rear Window* (1954) before retiring in 1956 to marry Prince Rainier III of Monaco. Full name **Kelly, Grace Patricia**

kel·ly green /kèllee-/ *adj* of a bright green color [Because green is associated with Ireland, where the surname *Kelly* is common] —**kel·ly green** *n*

ke·loid /keé lòyd/ *n* an area of raised pink or red fibrous scar tissue at the edges of a wound or incision [Mid-19C. < French *kéloïde* < Greek *khēlē* "crab claw"] —**ke·loid·al** /kee lóyd'l/ *adj*

Ke·low·na /kə lṓnə/ city in south central British Columbia, Canada, 60 mi./97 km north of the US border. Population: 108,330 (2001).

kelp /kelp/ *n* **1.** a brown seaweed with thick broad fronds. Order: Laminariales. **2.** the ash from kelp or other seaweeds. Use: source of potash and iodine. [14C. Origin ?]

kel·pie[1] /kélpee/, **kel·py** (*plural* **-pies**) *n* in Scottish folklore, a malicious water spirit that takes the form of a horse and lures people to death by drowning [Late 17C. Origin ?]

kel·pie[2] /kélpee/ *n* a smooth-haired dog belonging to a breed of sheepdog. Native to: Australia. [Early 20C. After *King's Kelpie*, the female dog that founded the breed]

kel·py *n* another spelling of **kelpie**[1]

Kel·sey /kélssee/, **Henry** (1667?–1724) English explorer. He trekked across the Canadian plains from Hudson Bay to present-day Alberta (1690–92).

kel·son *n* NAUT same as **keelson**

Kelt *n* PEOPLES another spelling of **Celt**

kel·vin /kélvin/ *n* the SI unit of absolute temperature, equal to 1/273.16 of the absolute temperature of the triple point of water, equivalent to one degree Celsius. A temperature in kelvin may be converted to Celsius by subtracting 273.16. Symbol **K** ■ *adj* relating to or measured on the Kelvin scale [Early 20C. After William Thomson, 1st Baron KELVIN]

Kel·vin /kélvin/, **William Thomson, 1st Baron** (1824–1907) British physicist. He did pioneering work in thermodynamics and electricity, and devised the absolute temperature scale. His work helped develop the law of the conservation of energy. Full name **Kelvin of Largs, William Thomson, 1st Baron**

Kel·vin scale *n* a temperature scale on which zero is the lowest possible temperature and the triple point of water is defined as 273.16K. It is based on heat transfer between two sections of a reversible heat engine.

Ke·me·ro·vo /kèmmə rṓvə/ city in southern Siberian Russia, on the Tom' River. It is the capital city of Kemerovo Oblast. Population: 538,193 (1995).

kemp /kemp/ *n* a short coarse hair or fiber [14C. < Old Norse *kampr* "beard, whisker"]

Kem·pe /kémpə/, **Rudolf** (1910–76) German conductor. He is known for his interpretations of Richard Strauss and Richard Wagner. He conducted the Royal Philharmonic Orchestra, London, England (1961–75).

Kemp's ri·d·ley /kèmps-/ *n* a small endangered ocean turtle with a drab grayish green back and a prominent beak. Native to: Gulf of Mexico, Atlantic Ocean. Latin name: *Lepidochelys kempii.* [After Richard M. *Kemp*, who found a specimen in Key West, Florida, in 1880 and sent it to Harvard for identification]

kempt /kempt/ *adj* neat in appearance and well taken care of (*archaic*) [Old English *cemd*, past participle of *cemban* "comb" < Germanic]

ken /ken/ *n* somebody's knowledge or understanding ○ *It's beyond my ken.* ■ *vti* (**kenned** or **kent** /kent/, **ken·ning, kens**) *Scotland* same as **know** [Old English *cennan* "make known" < Indo-European]

Ken. *abbr* Kentucky

Ke·nai Fjords Na·tion·al Park /kéenī-/ national park on the Kenai Peninsula, in southern Alaska, established in 1980. Area: 1,045 sq. mi./2,710 sq. km.

Ken·dal green /kénd'l-/ *n* **1.** a light grayish green coarse thick woolen cloth similar to tweed **2.** a light grayish green color —**Ken·dal green** *adj*

Ken·dall /kénd'l/, **Edward Calvin** (1886–1972) US biochemist. He won the Nobel Prize in physiology or medicine (1950) for his research on hormones such as cortisone.

kendo

ken·do /kéndō/ *n* a Japanese martial art in which people fence using bamboo sticks instead of swords [Early 20C. < Japanese, "way of the sword"]

Ken·drew /kéndroo/, **Sir John** (1917–97) British molecular biologist. He won a joint Nobel Prize in chemistry (1962) for his work on determining the structure of proteins. Full name **Kendrew, Sir John Cowdery**

Ke·neal·ly /kə náll ee/, **Thomas** (*b.* 1935) Australian novelist. His book *Schindler's Ark* (1982) won the British Booker Prize and was made into a movie, *Schindler's List* (1993), by Stephen Spielberg. Full name **Keneally, Thomas Michael**. See Cultural note at **ark**

Ken·ne·bec /kénnə bèk/ river in western Maine that flows south from Moosehead Lake to the Atlantic Ocean. Length: 164 mi./264 km.

Ken·ne·bunk·port /kènnə búngk pàwrt/ resort town in southeastern Maine, on the Atlantic coast at the mouth of the Kennebunk River. Population: 3,869 (2002 estimate).

Ken·ne·dy, Cape /kénnədee/ former name for **Canaveral, Cape** (1963–73)

Ken·ne·dy, Mount /kénnədee/ mountain in the St. Elias Range in southwestern Yukon Territory, Canada. Height: 13,904 ft./4,238 m.

Ken·ne·dy, Anthony M. (*b.* 1936) associate justice of the US Supreme Court (1988–). He was nominated to the Supreme Court by President Ronald Reagan. Full name **Anthony McLeod Kennedy**

Ken·ne·dy, Edward M. (*b.* 1932) US politician. He became a US senator in 1962 and unsuccessfully ran for the Democratic presidential nomination in 1980. John F. Kennedy and Robert F. Kennedy were his brothers. Full name **Kennedy, Edward Moore**. Known as **Ted Kennedy**

> "I even opposed the death penalty for the man who killed my brother."
> [Edward M. Kennedy, *Washington Post*; April 29, 1990]

Jackie Kennedy

Ken·ne·dy, Jackie (1929–94) US first lady. She married John F. Kennedy in 1953 and as first lady (1961–63) became an international celebrity and style-setter. Her great dignity after her husband's assassination increased public admiration for her. She married Greek shipping magnate Aristotle Onassis in 1968, and, after his death in 1975, worked in publishing in New York and continued her lifelong patronage and promotion of the arts. Born **Bouvier, Jacqueline Lee**. Full name **Kennedy-Onassis, Jacqueline Lee**

John F. Kennedy

Ken·ne·dy, John F. (1917–63) 35th president of the United States. The youngest man elected president (1960), he promoted civil rights, established the Peace Corps, and in 1962 forced Nikita Khrushchev to remove Soviet ballistic missiles from Cuba. He was assassinated in Dallas, Texas, on November 22, 1963. Full name **Kennedy, John Fitzgerald**. Known as **Jack Kennedy**. See table at **president**

> "And so, my fellow Americans: ask not what your country can do for you—ask what you can do for your country. My fellow citizens of the world: ask not what America will do for you, but what together we can do for the freedom of man."
> [John F. Kennedy, *Inaugural address as president of the United States*; January 20, 1961]

Ken·ne·dy, Joseph P. (1888–1969) US business executive and government official. He was the father of John F., Robert F., and Edward M. Kennedy. He was ambassador to the United Kingdom (1938–40). Full name **Kennedy, Joseph Patrick**

Ken·ne·dy, Robert F. (1925–68) US attorney general (1961–64) during the Democratic administration of his brother John F. Kennedy. He was assassinated during his own presidential campaign. Full name **Kennedy, Robert Francis**. Known as **Bobby Kennedy**

> "Some men see things as they are and say why? I dream things that never were and say 'Why not?'"
> [Robert F. Kennedy, *Esquire*; 1969]

Ken·ne·dy, William (*b.* 1928) US writer. He won a Pulitzer Prize for his novel *Ironweed* (1983).

> "I don't hold no grudges more'n five years."
> [William Kennedy, *Ironweed*; 1983]

ken·nel /kénn'l/ *n* **1.** *UK* same as **doghouse** **2.** BOARDING OR BREEDING PLACE a place where dogs are bred and trained and where people can leave their dogs while they are away **3.** PACK OF DOGS a pack of hounds or dogs ■ *vti* (**-neled, -nel·ing, -nels**) PUT OR STAY IN KENNEL to put a dog into a kennel, or stay in a kennel [14C. < assumed Anglo-Norman *kenil* < Latin *canis* "dog"]

Ken·nel·ly-Heav·i·side lay·er /kènn'lee hévvee sīd-/ *n* PHYS same as **E region** [Early 20C. After Arthur Edwin *Kennelly* (1861–1939), US electrical engineer, and Oliver *Heaviside* (1850–1925), British physicist]

Ken·neth I /kénnith/ (*fl* A.D. mid-9th century) king of Scotland. Around 846 he united the kingdoms of the Scots and the Picts, becoming the first king of Scotland. Known as **Kenneth MacAlpin**

ke·no /kéenō/ *n* a game of chance in which players wager on a set of numbers to be drawn at random [Early 19C. Alteration of French *quine* "set of five winning numbers" < Latin *quini* "five each" < *quinque* "five"]

Ke·no·sha /kə nṓshə/ industrial city in southeastern Wisconsin, on Lake Michigan. Population: 92,513 (2002 estimate).

ke·no·sis /kə nṓssiss/ *n* according to Christian belief, Jesus Christ's act of partly giving up his divine status in order to become a man, as recorded in the Bible (Philippians 2:6–7) [Late 19C. < Greek *kenōsis* "an emptying" < *heauton ekenōse* "emptied himself," phrase in Philippians 2:7] —**ke·not·ic** /kə nóttik/ *adj*

Ken·sett /kénssət/, **John Frederick** (1816–72) US artist. Noted for his detailed landscapes, he was a member of the Hudson River School.

kent *Scotland* past participle, past tense of **ken**

Kent /kent/ county in the southeastern corner of England, and a former Anglo-Saxon kingdom. It contains the ports of Dover and Sheerness, and the terminus of the Channel Tunnel. Maidstone is the administrative center. Population: 1,329,718 (2001). Area: 1,441 sq. mi./3,731 sq. km. —**Ken·tish** *adj*

Kent, Rockwell (1882–1971) US artist. He is known for his stark woodcut illustrations and landscape paintings.

Kent, William (1685–1748) English architect and landscape designer. He promoted the Palladian style in architecture and an informal style in garden design.

ken·te /kén tay/, **ken·te cloth** *n* a handwoven cloth from Ghana, usually with complex designs of very bright colors, traditionally worn on important ceremonial and religious occasions [Mid-20C. < Twi, "cloth"]

kent·ledge /kéntlij/ *n* scrap iron or other heavy material used as permanent ballast on ships [Early 17C. < Old French *quintelage* "ballast" < *quintal* (see QUINTAL)]

Kentucky

Ken·tuck·y /ken túkee/ **1.** state in the east central United States, bordered by Illinois, Indiana, Missouri, Ohio, Tennessee, Virginia, and West Virginia. Capital: Frankfort. Population: 5,092,891 (2002 estimate). Area: 40,411 sq. mi./104,664 sq. km. **2.** river in central Kentucky that flows northwestward to join the Ohio River at Carrollton. Length: 259 mi./417 km. —**Ken·tuck·i·an** *n, adj*

Ken·tuck·y blue·grass *n* a grass widely used for pastureland and lawns. Native to: Africa, Europe, Asia, naturalized in North America. Latin name: *Poa pratensis.*

Ken·tuck·y cof·fee tree *n* a deciduous leguminous tree with compound leaves, brown pods, and pulpy seeds that were formerly a coffee substitute. Native to: eastern North America. Latin name: *Gymnocladus dioica.*

Ken·tuck·y Der·by *n* a race for three-year-old horses that has been run annually since 1875 at Churchill Downs in Louisville, Kentucky. It is held on the first Saturday in May.

Ken·tuck·y ri·fle *n* a muzzle-loading rifle developed in the 18th century and widely used on the American frontier

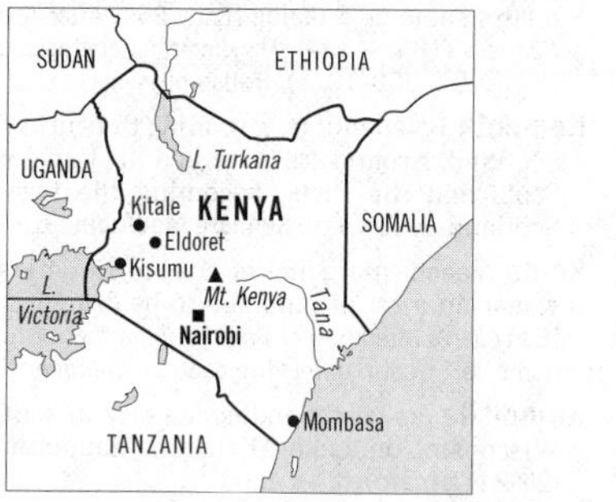

Kenya

Ken·ya /kénnyə/ country in eastern Africa. It became an independent member of the British Commonwealth in 1963. Language: English, Swahili. Currency: Kenyan shilling. Capital: Nairobi. Population: 31,639,091 (2003). Area: 224,961 sq. mi./582,646 sq. km. Official name **Republic of Kenya** —**Ken·yan** *n, adj*

Ken·ya, Mount extinct volcano in central Kenya, the second highest mountain in Africa. Height: 17,057 ft./5,199 m.

Ken·yat·ta /ken yaátə/, **Jomo** (1891–1978) Kenyan politician. Following the outbreak of the Mau Mau uprising during Kenya's colonial period, he was imprisoned (1951–61). After independence he became Kenya's first prime minister (1963–64) and president (1964–78). Born **Kamau wa Ngengi**

> "The African is conditioned, by the cultural and social institutions of centuries, to a freedom of which Europe has little conception, and it is not in his nature to accept serfdom forever."
> [Jomo Kenyatta, *Facing Mount Kenya*; 1938]

Keogh plan /keé ō-/ *n* a retirement plan for the self-employed and their employees [Late 20C. After Eugene James *Keogh* (d. 1989), US politician]

Ke·o·kuk /keé ə kùk/ city in southeastern Iowa, on the Mississippi River. Population: 11,029 (2002 estimate).

keph·a·lin *n* BIOL another spelling of **cephalin**

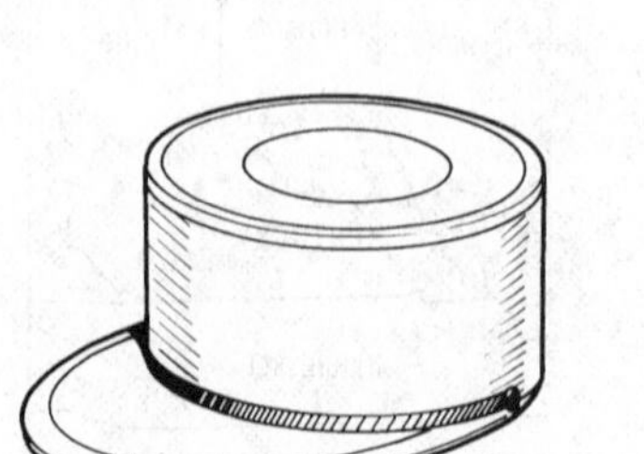
kepi

ke·pi /káypee, képpee/ (*plural* **-pis**) *n* a French military hat with a round flat top and a visor [Mid-19C. Via French *képi* < Swiss German *Käppi* "little cap"]

Kep·ler /képplər/ *n* crater on the Moon in Oceanus Procellarum, 20 mi./32 km in diameter [After Johannes KEPLER]

Kep·ler /képplər/, **Johannes** (1571–1630) German astronomer. His three laws of planetary motion include his finding that the planets move around the Sun in elliptical orbits.

> "Where there is matter, there is geometry."
> [Johannes Kepler. Quoted in *Solid Shape*, J. Koenderink; 1990]

Kep·ler's laws *npl* three mathematical statements that describe the movement of the planets in their orbits around the Sun. The first two laws were published in 1609 and the third a decade later.

kept /kept/ past participle, past tense of **keep** ■ *adj* supported financially by a lover, especially a married one

Ker·a·la /kérrələ/ state in southwestern India. Capital: Trivandrum. Language: Malayalam. Population: 31,838,619 (2001). Area: 15,005 sq. mi./38,864 sq. km. —**Ker·a·lite** *adj, n*

kerat- *prefix* same as **kerato-** (*used before vowels*)

ker·a·tec·to·my /kèrrə téktəmee/ *n* the surgical removal of part of the cornea

ker·a·tin /kérrətin/ *n* a fibrous insoluble protein that is the main structural element in hair, nails, feathers, and hooves [Mid-19C. < Greek *kerat-* "horn"] —**ke·rat·i·nous** /ke rátt'nəss/ *adj*

ker·a·tin·i·za·tion /kèrrətəni záysh'n/ *n* the deposition of keratin in skin cells, e.g., in hair and nails, giving them the texture of horn

ker·a·tin·ize /kérrəti nīz/ (**-ized, -iz·ing, -iz·es**) *vti* to convert something into keratin, or become keratin

ker·a·ti·tis /kèrrə tītiss/ *n* the inflammation and swelling of the cornea

kerato- *prefix* **1.** horny tissue ○ *keratose* **2.** cornea ○ *keratoplasty* [< Greek *kerat-* "horn" < Indo-European]

ker·a·toid /kérrə tòyd/ *adj* like horn in texture or appearance

ker·a·to·mi·leu·sis /kèrrətō mī lóossis/ *n* eye surgery to change the shape of a cornea that refracts light wrongly [Late 20C. < KERATO- + Greek *smileusis* "carving"]

ker·a·top·a·thy /kèrrə tóppəthee/ *n* a non-inflammatory disorder of the cornea

ker·a·to·plas·ty /kérrətō plàstee/ (*plural* **-ties**) *n* plastic surgery on the cornea, especially corneal grafting —**ker·a·to·plas·tic** /kèrrətō plástik/ *adj*

ker·a·tose /kérrə tōss/ *adj* describes sponges that have a horny skeleton

ker·a·to·sis /kèrrə tóssiss/ (*plural* **-to·ses** /-tó seez/) *n* **1.** the growth of hard horny tissue on the skin **2.** a horny growth on the skin —**ker·a·tot·ic** /-tóttik/ *adj*

ker·a·tot·o·my /kèrrə tóttəmee/ (*plural* **-mies**) *n* a surgical cutting of the cornea

kerb *n* UK spelling of **curb** *n* (sense 1) ■ *vt* (**kerbed, kerb·ing, kerbs**) UK spelling of **curb** *v* (sense 2)

kerb·side *n* UK spelling of **curbside**

kerb·stone *n* UK spelling of **curbstone**

Kerch /kurch/ seaport in southern Ukraine, on the east of the Crimean Peninsula. Population: 175,000 (1996).

ker·chief /kúrchif, -cheef/ *n* a square scarf for women, worn around the neck or as a headscarf [13C. < Anglo-Norman *courchef* or Old French *cuevre-chef*, literally "cover-head"] —**ker·chiefed** *adj*

Ke·ren·sky /kə rénskee/, **Aleksandr Fyodorovich** (1881–1970) Russian revolutionary leader. He was the head of the 1917 provisional government of Russia from July until the Bolshevik takeover in November 1917.

kerf /kurf/ *n* a cut or the width of a cut made by an ax, saw, or cutting tool [Old English *cerf* < W Germanic]

ker·fuf·fle /kər fúff'l/ *n UK* a noisy disturbance or commotion (*informal*) ○ *"But [the group] didn't want to litigate, and it didn't want to walk away either. Instead it put out a press release and posted the details of the kerfuffle on the Web."* (Brendan Miniter *Wall Street Journal*; October 31, 2003) [Early 19C. Origin ?]

Ker·gue·len Is·lands /kúrgələn-/ island group in the southern Indian Ocean, consisting of one main island and about 300 smaller islands and islets. Area: 2,300 sq. mi./6,000 sq. km.

Ker·ma·dec Is·lands /kər máddək-/ island group in the southern Pacific Ocean, a dependency of New Zealand. Area: 11 sq. mi./29 sq. km.

Ker·man /kur maán/, **Ker·mān** city in southeastern Iran, the capital of Kerman Province. Population: 384,991 (1996).

ker·mes /kúr meez, kúrməss/ (*plural same*) *n* **1.** a purplish red dye obtained from the dried bodies of female scale insects of the genus *Kermes*, or the dried bodies of these insects **2.** TREES same as **kermes oak** [Late 16C. Via French < Arabic *ḳirmiz* "kermes beetle"]

ker·mes oak *n* a small evergreen oak tree that provides a habitat for the scale insects used to make kermes. Native to: Europe, Asia. Latin name: *Quercus coccifera.*

ker·mis /kúrmiss/, **kir·mess, ker·mess** *n* **1.** in former times, an annual country fair held in the Netherlands and northern Germany **2.** a festival or fair held to collect money for charity [Late 16C. < Dutch, "mass on the anniversary of the church's dedication" < *kerk* "church" + *misse* "mass"]

kern[1] /kurn/ *n* PART OF CHARACTER the part of a typographical character that projects beyond its body ■ *v* (**kerned, kern·ing, kerns**) **1.** *vti* BRING PRINTING TYPE TOGETHER to eliminate white space between adjacent printed letters that may appear too widely separated on a line **2.** *vt* OVERLAP ADJACENT CHARACTERS to join adjacent printed characters, or make them overlap [Late 17C. Via French *carne* "corner" < Latin *cardin-* "hinge"]

kern[2] /kurn/, **kerne** *n* a medieval Irish or Scottish light infantryman [14C. < Irish *ceithearn*]

Kern /kurn/, **Jerome** (1885–1945) US composer. He wrote numerous Broadway musicals, including *Show Boat* (1927). His songs include "Ol' Man River" and "Smoke Gets in Your Eyes." Full name **Kern, Jerome David**

> "Irving Berlin *is* American music."
> [Jerome Kern. Quoted in *Guardian (London)*; September 25, 1989]

kerne *n* MIL, HIST another spelling of **kern**[2]

ker·nel /kúrn'l/ *n* **1.** EDIBLE CORE the edible content of a nut or fruit stone **2.** CEREAL GRAIN the grain of a cereal that contains a seed and husk **3.** CENTRAL PART the central or most important part of something ○ *a kernel of self-belief that never wavered* **4.** PHYS ATOM STRIPPED OF ITS ELECTRONS a positively charged atomic nucleus that has lost its valence electrons **5.** COMPUT KEY PORTION OF OPERATING SYSTEM the core of a computer's operating system that resides in the memory and performs essential functions such as controlling memory and files and allocating system resources [Old English *cyrnel* "little seed" < CORN[1]]

SPELLCHECK See ***colonel.***

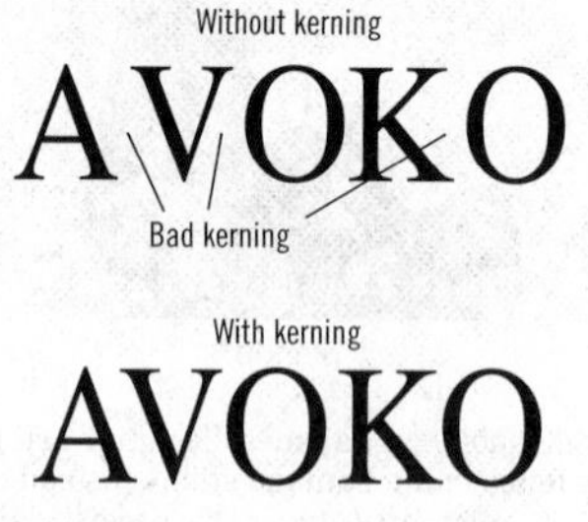

kerning

kern·ing /kúrning/ *n* the addition or removal of space between individual characters in a piece of typeset text to improve its appearance or alter its fit [Late 17C. < KERN[1]]

kern·ite /kúr nīt/ *n* a colorless or white crystalline mineral consisting of hydrated sodium borate. Use: source of borax and other boron compounds. [Early 20C. After *Kern* County, California]

ker·o·gen /kérrəjən/ *n* a fossilized insoluble organic material found in some sedimentary rocks such as oil shales, yielding petroleum products when heated [Early 20C. < Greek *kēros* "wax"]

ker·o·sene /kérrə seen, kèrrə seén/, **ker·o·sine** *n* a colorless flammable oil distilled from petroleum. Use: fuel for jet engines, heating, cooking, and lighting. [Mid-19C. < Greek *kēros* "wax"]

Ker·ou·ac /kérrə wàk/, **Jack** (1922–69) US novelist. He was a leading figure in the 1950s Beat Generation, and his best-known novel is *On the Road* (1957). Full name **Kerouac, Jean Louis**. See Cultural note at **road**

> "Because the only people for me are the mad ones...the ones who never yawn or say a commonplace thing, but burn, burn, burn, like fabulous yellow roman candles exploding like spiders across the stars and in the middle you see the blue centerlight pop and everybody goes 'Awww!'"
> [Jack Kerouac, *On the Road*; 1957]

ker·plunk /kər plúngk/ *adv, interj* used to imitate the sound made by something heavy falling suddenly (*informal*) [Early 20C. An imitation of the sound.]

Kerr ef·fect /káar-, kúr-/ *n* **1.** the property of some transparent substances that makes them refract doubly when placed in an electric field **2.** the elliptical polarization of plane-polarized or unpolarized light when reflected from the polished pole of a magnetized material [Early 20C. After John *Kerr* (1824–1907), Scottish physicist]

Ker·ry[1] /kérree/ (*plural* **-ries**) *n* a small black bull or dairy cow belonging to a breed that originated in Ireland [Mid-19C. After KERRY[2]]

Ker·ry[2] /kérree/ county in Munster Province, southwestern Republic of Ireland. Population: 126,130 (2002). Area: 1,815 sq. mi./4,701 sq. km.

Ker·ry, John (*b.* 1943) US politician. He has served as Democratic US senator from Massachusetts (1984–) and is the Democratic presidential candidate in 2004. A much-decorated Vietnam veteran, he co-founded Vietnam Veterans of America. Full name **Kerry, John Forbes**

Ker·ry blue ter·ri·er, **Ker·ry blue** *n* a terrier with a dense but soft wavy bluish gray coat, belonging to a breed originating in Ireland [Early 20C. After KERRY[2]]

ker·sey /kúrzee/ *n* a smooth woolen fabric. Use: coats. [14C. After *Kersey*, village in Suffolk, England]

ker·sey·mere /kúrzee meer/ *n* a fine soft woolen cloth with a fancy twill weave [Late 18C. Alteration of *cassimere*, "woolen fabric," alteration of CASHMERE, after KERSEY]

Ker·tész /kər tésh/, **André** (1894–1985) Hungarian-born US photographer. One of the founders of photojournalism, he is known for his realistic and sensitive scenes of everyday life.

ke·ryg·ma /kə rígmə/ *n* the proclamation of Jesus Christ's teachings, especially as taught in the Gospels [Late 19C. < Greek *kērugma* < *kērussein* "proclaim"] —**ker·yg·mat·ic** /kèrrig máttik/ *adj*

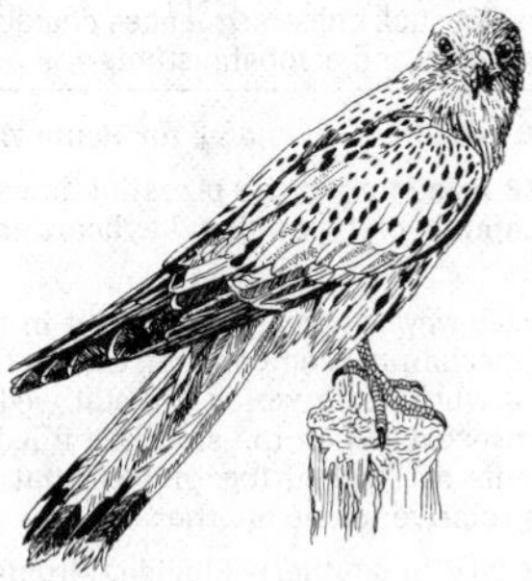

kestrel

kes·trel /késtrəl/ *n* a small falcon that hovers before swooping on its prey of small mammals. Genus: *Falco*. [14C. Probably < French dialect *casserelle* < French *crécerelle* "rattle" < Latin *crepitacillum* "small rattle" < *crepitare* "to rattle"]

ket- *prefix* same as **keto-** (*used before vowels*)

ke·ta·mine /kéttə meen/ *n* a white crystalline powder. Use: general anesthetic in human and veterinary medicine. Formula: $C_{13}H_{16}ClNO$.

ketch /kech/ *n* a small fore-and-aft rigged sailboat with two masts, the forward mast taller than the other [Mid-17C. Probably < CATCH]

ketch·up /kéchəp/, **catch·up** /káchəp, kéchəp/, **cat·sup** /kátsəp, káchəp, kéchəp/ *n* a thick sauce, made with tomatoes, that is served cold as a condiment [Late 17C. Probably via Malay *kēchap* "fish sauce" < Chinese (Cantonese) *k'ē chap* "sauce"]

ke·tene /kee teen/ *n* a strong-smelling colorless highly reactive toxic gas. Use: agent to attach an acetyl group to an organic compound. Formula: C_2H_2O. [Early 20C. < KETONE]

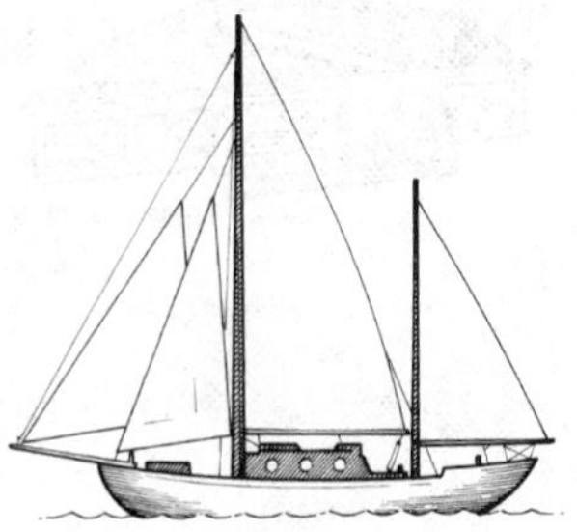

ketch

keto- *prefix* containing a ketone or ketone group ○ *ketonuria* [< KETONE]

ke·to form /keetō-/ *n* one of two interconvertible forms of an organic compound, having a carbonyl group attached to two alkyl groups

ke·to·gen·e·sis /keetō jénnəssiss/ *n* the formation or stimulation of the production of ketone bodies, as can happen in diabetes —**ke·to·gen·ic** *adj*

ke·tone /kee tōn/ *n* an organic compound containing a carbon atom connected to an oxygen atom by a double bond and to two carbon atoms. The simplest ketone is acetone, an important industrial solvent. ■ *adj* relating to the chemical group comprising a carbon atom connected to an oxygen atom by a double bond and to two carbon atoms [Mid-19C. < German *Keton*, alteration of *Aketon* "acetone"] —**ke·ton·ic** /kee tónnik/ *adj*

ke·tone bod·y *n* a mixture of ketones produced when body fat is broken down. The concentration of ketone bodies in blood and urine increases in starvation, diabetes, and pregnancy.

ke·tone group *n* the carbonyl group, containing carbon atoms doubly bonded to an oxygen atom and linked to the carbon atoms of two other organic groups, a characteristic of all ketones

ke·to·nu·ri·a /keetō nóoree ə/ *n* the presence of ketones in the urine, a warning sign of severe and uncontrolled diabetes

ke·tose /kee tōss/ *n* a carbohydrate that contains a ketone group

ke·to·sis /kee tóssiss/ *n* the condition resulting from overproduction of ketone bodies —**ke·tot·ic** /-tóttik/ *adj*

ke·tox·ime /kee tók seem/ *n* an organic compound containing a nitrogen atom bonded to a hydroxyl group and a carbon atom, which is bonded to two ketones. It is produced by the reaction between hydroxylamine and a ketone.

ket·tle /kétt'l/ *n* **1.** HOUSEHOLD same as **teakettle 2.** a metal pot used for cooking, usually one with a lid ○ *a fish kettle* **3.** GEOL a steep-sided basin, often a lake or swamp, in a glacial drift deposit, caused by the melting of an ice mass left behind as the glacier retreated [Old English *cetel*, via Germanic < Latin *catillus* "small cooking pot"] ◇ **a different kettle of fish** a different situation or person to be dealt with ◇ **a pretty** *or* **fine kettle of fish** an undesirable situation, usually one caused by somebody's negligence or incompetence

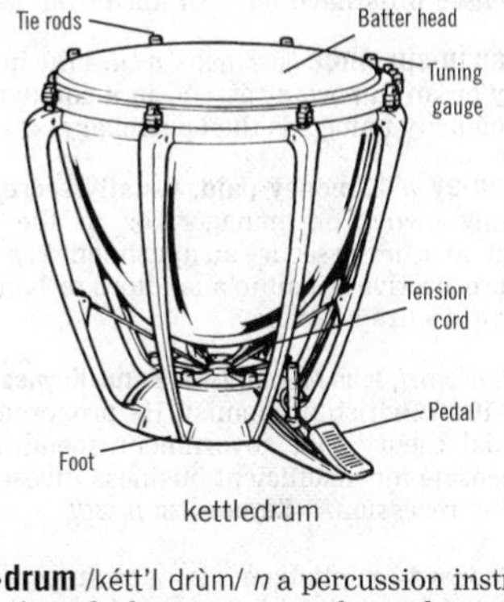

kettledrum

ket·tle·drum /kétt'l drùm/ *n* a percussion instrument consisting of a large copper or brass drum covered with a parchment skin that can be adjusted to alter the pitch. Pitch is altered by screws and pedals that increase or decrease the skin's tension. —**ket·tle·drum·mer** *n*

ket·tle hole *n* GEOL same as **kettle** (sense 3)

keV *abbr* kilo-electron volt

kev·el[1] /kévv'l/ *n* a sturdy bitt or bollard for securing the heavier cables on a ship [13C. Via Old N French *keville* "pin, peg" < Latin *clavicula* "small key"]

kev·el[2] /kévv'l/ *n* a two-headed hammer, one head with a sharp edge, the other with a point, used for breaking up or shaping stone [Origin ?]

Kev·lar /kév laar/ *tdmk* a trademark for a reinforcing material used in tires and bulletproof vests

Ke·wa·nee /ki waanee/ city in northwestern Illinois, northwest of Peoria and southeast of Moline. Population: 12,797 (2002 estimate).

kew·pie /kyoopee/ *n* a plump doll with rosy cheeks and a curl of hair on its head [Early 20C. Originally a trademark]

key[1] /kee/ *n* (*plural* **keys**) **1. INSTRUMENT FOR LOCKING** a metal bar with notches or grooves that, when inserted into a lock and turned, operates the lock's mechanism **2. DOOR OR LOCK OPENER** a device that operates a door or lock, e.g., a plastic card with an encoded magnetic strip **3.** MUSIC **INSTRUMENT FEATURE** the levers on a keyboard instrument that sound a note when pressed, or the metal buttons on a woodwind instrument that alter a note's pitch **4.** MUSIC **MUSICAL SCALE** a system of related notes in a scale beginning on a particular note ○ *in the key of E* **5. INSTRUMENT FOR WINDING UP** a fitted tool that is turned repeatedly to wind up, set, or calibrate a mechanism **6. MEANS** a way or means of achieving something ○ *Continuity of effort is the key to success.* **7. IMPORTANT ASPECT** the aspect of something that, once understood, provides a full understanding or explanation of the whole ○ *The key to this riddle lies in the subtle meanings of the words used.* **8. STRATEGIC PLACE** a place that is strategically vital in gaining access to or controlling a larger area ○ *Istanbul is the key to the Bosporus.* **9. LIST OF ANSWERS** a list of the answers to a test or exercise **10. KEYBOARD BUTTON** a button on a typewriter's or computer's keyboard or keypad that performs an operation when pressed **11.** ELEC ENG **DEVICE FOR OPERATING CIRCUITS** a small manual device for opening, closing, or switching circuits ○ *a telegraph key* **12.** BASKETBALL **AREA AT END OF BASKETBALL COURT** the area at the ends of a basketball court between the base line and the foul line **13.** MUSIC **MAIN NOTE OF SCALE** the note on which a musical scale begins **14.** MUSIC **TONAL CENTER** the relationship between the notes of a scale and the scale's main note **15.** ARTS **MOOD OF ART WORK** the general mood or style of a work of art, literature, or music **16. PITCH OR QUALITY** the pitch or quality of an expressive sound, especially the voice ○ *answered in thoughtful key* **17.** MAPS **EXPLANATORY LIST** an explanatory list of the symbols or abbreviations used on a map or diagram **18.** COMMUNICATION **CRYPTOGRAPHIC FEATURE** in cryptography, the sequence of symbols or characters that defines the makeup of an encoding mechanism **19.** ARTS **EXPLANATORY TEXT** a text that provides additional information on or an explanation of a work of literature, art, or music **20.** ENG **METAL PIN** a metal wedge or pin used to lock together two structural or mechanical components such as a shaft and a hub to prevent movement relative to each other **21.** COMPUT **DATABASE FEATURE** a field in a database record that uniquely identifies that record **22.** ARCHIT same as **keystone** (sense 1) **23.** BIOL **OUTLINE OF CHARACTERISTICS** an outline of the characteristics of an organism, used for taxonomic identification **24.** PHOTOGRAPHY, ART **IMAGE FEATURE** the tonal value of an image with regard to lightness, darkness, or color intensity **25.** CONSTR **SURFACE PREPARATION** the process of preparing a surface, usually by making it rough or grooved, so that paint or some other finish will stick to it **26. WINGED FRUIT** a dry winged fruit like that of an ash or sycamore tree, usually growing in bunches. Technical name **samara** ■ *adj* **CRUCIAL** vital in achieving understanding or success ○ *the key points in the report* ■ *v* (**keyed, key·ing, keys**) **1.** *vti* COMPUT **TYPE** to use the keyboard of a computer, or input data using it ○ *keyed for a solid hour* **2.** *vt* **LOCK SOMETHING** to lock or adjust something with a key **3.** *vt* **PROVIDE SOMETHING WITH EXPLANATION** to provide something with an explanatory list or text **4.** *vt* MUSIC **REGULATE INSTRUMENT'S PITCH** to regulate the pitch of a musical instrument **5.** *vt* **ADAPT SOMETHING** to bring something in line with or make something consistent with something else

(*often passive*) ○ *We want these ads keyed to an upscale clientele.* **6.** *vt* PRINTING **MARK SOMETHING FOR CORRECT REPRODUCTION** to mark artwork, or anything to be reproduced, with symbols that will allow different parts to be correctly aligned for reproduction **7.** *vt* CONSTR **LOCK ARCH WITH KEYSTONE** to provide an arch with a keystone **8.** *vt* BIOL **IDENTIFY SOMETHING** to identify an organism or specimen [Old English *cæg*, origin ?]
key in *vt* to enter data such as a password or PIN by typing on a keyboard or keypad
key up *vt* to make somebody nervous, tense, or excited (*informal; often used in the passive*)

key[2] /kee/ *n* a small low island of sand or coral, especially in the Gulf of Mexico or the Caribbean [Late 17C. < Old French *kay*, probably < Celtic]

key[3] /kee/ *n US* a kilogram of marijuana, heroin, or cocaine (*slang*) [Mid-20C. Shortening of KILOGRAM]

Key /kee/, **Francis Scott** (1779–1843) US poet and lawyer. He wrote the lyrics to "The Star Spangled Banner" (1814), adopted as the US national anthem in 1931.

> "'Tis the star-spangled banner; O long may it wave / O'er the land of the free and the home of the brave!"
> [Francis Scott Key, "The Star-Spangled Banner"; September 14,1814]

key·board /keé bàwrd/ *n* **1. SET OF KEYS** an array of keys in a row or rows used for operating something such as a computer or musical instrument **2. MUSICAL INSTRUMENT** a musical instrument with a keyboard, especially an electronic instrument ■ **key·boards** *npl* **MUSICAL INSTRUMENT WITH MULTIPLE KEYBOARDS** an electronic musical instrument with a tier of two or more keyboards ■ *adj vti* (**-board·ed, -board·ing, -boards**) **INPUT DATA** to enter information into a computer using a keyboard

key·board·er /keé bàwrdər/ *n* an operator of the keyboard of a computer or typesetting machine

key·board in·stru·ment *n* a musical instrument with a keyboard or keyboards, especially one with a horizontal keyboard, a soundboard, and strings, e.g., a piano

key·board·ist /keé bàwrdist/ *n* a musician who plays a keyboard instrument

key card *n* a card, usually made of plastic with an encoded magnetic strip, giving access to a door or mechanism

key·chain drive /keé chayn-/ *n* COMPUT a small plastic device functioning as a disk drive, key-sized, containing memory chips that retain their contents without electrical power and that have a capacity of 16 megabytes and 2 gigabytes of data. On the end is a standard USB connector that fits into USB ports. [Early 21C.]

key club *n* **1.** a private nightclub, restaurant, or country club in which each member is given a key to enter in return for a set membership fee **2.** *US* an organization for high-school students who participate in community service projects

key da·ta·base *n* a database that holds all keys used by a certificate authority

key deer *n* a small white-tailed deer that is nearly extinct and survives only in game preserves. Native to: Florida Keys. Latin name: *Odocoileus virginianus clavium*.

keyed up *adj* in a state of nervousness, tension, or excitement (*informal*)

key es·crow *n* a system for encrypting computer data in which the decoding key is held by a third party

key fruit *n* BOT same as **key**[1] *n* (sense 26)

key grip *n* the chief mover of equipment in a film or stage crew

key·hole /keé hòl/ *n* **1.** the small hole in a lock into which a key fits **2.** *US* BASKETBALL same as **key**[1] *n* (sense 12)

key·hole saw *n* a handsaw with a stiff narrow pointed fine-toothed blade, used to make small-radius curved and internal cuts

key·hole sur·ger·y *n* surgery performed using instruments that can be introduced into the body through a very small hole and manipulated externally, thus avoiding the need for major incisions

Key Lar·go /-laárgō/ one of the largest of the Florida Keys, in southeastern Florida, at Biscayne Bay. Length: 30 mi./48 km.

Virginal (*c.* 1570)

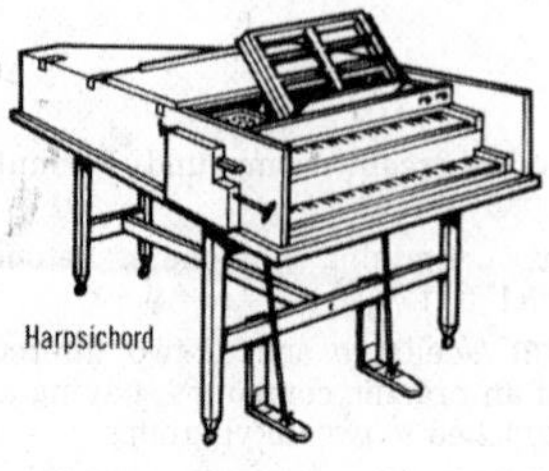

Harpsichord

Celesta

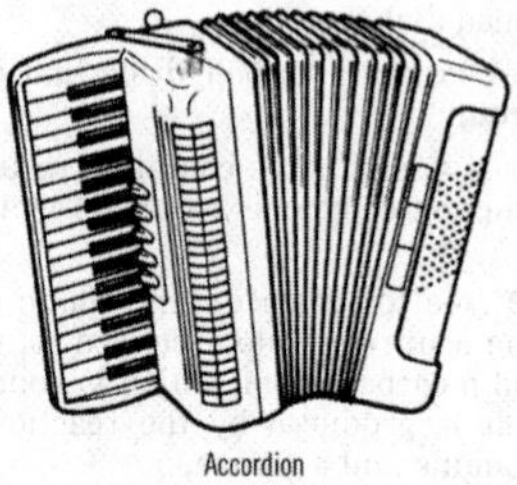

Accordion

keyboard: instruments with keyboards

key light *n* the main studio or stage light that sets the overall level of light intensity for something that is being filmed, videotaped, or photographed

key lime, Key lime *n* a small tart lime grown in the Florida Keys and Caribbean islands

key lime pie *n* a pie made from thickened sweetened condensed milk flavored with juice from key limes

key·man in·sur·ance /keé man-/ *n US* a life insurance policy on an important person in a company, with the company named as the beneficiary

key mon·ey *n* **1.** money paid, usually secretly, to a building owner or manager, or to the current tenant, in order to secure an apartment **2.** a fee paid by a prospective tenant to a landlord or landlady in order to secure a tenancy

Keynes /kaynz/, **John Maynard, 1st Baron Keynes of Tilton** (1883–1946) British economist. He proposed the influential theory that government spending must compensate for insufficient business investment in times of recession. —**Keynes·i·an** *n, adj*

> "Modern capitalism is absolutely irreligious, without internal union, without much public spirit, often, though not always, a mere congeries of possessors and pursuers."
> [John Maynard Keynes, *Essays in Persuasion*; 1925]

Keynes·i·an·ism /káynzee ən ìzzəm/ *n* the theory that government spending must compensate for insufficient business investment in times of recession

key·note /keé nòt/ *n* **1. MAIN THEME** the central or most important point or theme of something **2.** MUSIC same as **tonic** *n* (sense 5) ■ *adj* **MOST IMPORTANT** containing or outlining the most important themes or policies ■ *v* (**-not·ed, -not·ing, -notes**) **1.** *vti* **DELIVER KEYNOTE SPEECH** to deliver the most important speech at a convention or meeting **2.** *vt* **NOTE IMPORTANT POINTS** to outline an important policy in a speech or report

key·note ad·dress *n* same as **keynote speech**

key·not·er /keé nòtər/, **key·note speak·er** *n* a speaker who delivers the most important speech at a conference or political convention

key·note speech, key·note ad·dress *n* the most important speech at a conference or political convention

key·pad /keé pàd/ *n* **1.** a small keyboard, e.g., on a calculator or television remote control, usually with numbers on the keys **2.** the part of a computer keyboard in which the number and command keys are grouped

key·pal /keé pàl/ *n US* somebody with whom regular e-mail is exchanged [Late 20C. After PEN PAL]

key·punch /keé pùnch/ *n* a machine, operated by keyboard, that punches holes in cards or paper for use in a data-processing system, now largely obsolete ■ *vti* to use a keypunch to punch holes in a card or paper tape for data entry into a computer —**key·punch·er** *n*

key ring *n* a metal ring used for keeping keys together, often with a decorative or identifying attachment

key sig·na·ture *n* a group of sharps or flats printed on the staffs at the beginning of a piece of music to show the key in which it is to be played

key·stone /keé stòn/ *n* **1.** the wedge-shaped stone at the highest point of an arch that locks the others in place **2.** something on which other interrelated things depend ○ *Alliances are the keystone of a country's security.*

CULTURAL NOTE ***The Keystone Kops***, a group of comic characters who appeared in a number of silent movies (1880–1960) by Mack Sennett. A bumbling police squad dressed in oversized uniforms, the Kops usually featured in slapstick chase sequences characterized by superb sight gags and acrobatic stunts.

Key·stone State *n* a nickname for Pennsylvania

key·stroke /keé stròk/ *n* the pressing down of a key on a computer or typewriter keyboard, activating it

key·way /keé wày/ *n* a longitudinal slot in two structural or mechanical components, e.g., in the hub or shaft of a wheel, into which a metal wedge or pin can be inserted. When the slots are filled, the two components are locked together so that they will not turn relative to one another.

Key West city in southern Florida, situated on the island of the same name. It is a port and a resort. Population: 25,273 (2002 estimate).

key·word /keé wùrd/ *n* **1. REFERENCE POINT** a word used as a reference point for further information or as an indication of the contents of a document **2. CODE WORD** a word that is used as a key to a code **3.** COMPUT **WORD WITH A SPECIAL MEANING TO A COMPUTER** a sequence of letters and numbers, often in the form of a common word, with special significance to a computer database or a programming or command language

kg[1] *symbol* MEASURE kilogram

kg[2] *abbr* ONLINE Kyrgyzstan (*used in Internet addresses*) See table at **domain name**

KGB *n* the secret police of the former Soviet Union [< Russian, abbreviation of *Komitet Gosudarstvennoĭ Bezopasnosti* "Committee of State Security"]

kgf *symbol* MEASURE kilogram-force

kh *abbr* ONLINE Cambodia (*used in Internet addresses*) See table at **domain name**

Kha·ba·rovsk /kə baárəfsk/ city in eastern Russia,

the administrative center of Khabarovsk Territory. Population: 774,762 (1995).

khad·dar /kaádər/, **kha·di** /kaádee/ *n* a cotton cloth from South Asia that has a plain weave [Early 20C. < Punjabi *khaddar* or Hindi *khādar*]

Kha·kas·sia /kə kaássi ə/ autonomous republic in south-central Siberia, Russia. Capital: Abakan. Population: 584,000 (1994). Area: 23,899 sq. mi./61,900 sq. km.

khak·i /kákee, kaákee/ *n* **1. BROWNISH YELLOW** a dull brownish yellow color **2. BEIGE CLOTH** a tough pale brown fabric. Use: military uniforms. ■ **khak·is** *npl US* **PANTS OR UNIFORM** a pair of pants or a uniform made of khaki or fabric of a khaki color [Mid-19C. < Urdu *kakī* "dust-colored" < Persian *kāk* "dust"] —**khak·i** *adj*

kha·lif, etc. ISLAM another spelling of **caliph, etc.**

Khal·sa /kaálssə/ *n* a strict Sikh religious order founded in 1699 by Guru Gobind Singh [Late 18C. Via Urdu < Arabic *kāliṣ* "pure"]

Kha·me·nei /kaá me neé/, **Ali, Ayatollah** (*b.* 1939) supreme spiritual leader of Iran (1989–). A former deputy defense minister and Revolutionary Guard commander, he served as president (1981–89) before he was chosen to succeed Ayatollah Khomeini.

kham·sin /kam seén/ *n* a dry dusty hot southerly wind that blows from the Sahara across Egypt and over the Red Sea from March to May [Late 17C. < Arabic *kamāsīn* < *kamsīn* "fifty"; because it blows for about fifty days]

khan[1] /kaan, kan/ *n* **1.** formerly in parts of Asia, a medieval title used by Mongol and Turkish rulers (*usually added to a name*) ○ *Genghis Khan* **2.** in Central Asian countries, a title of respect taken by some dignitaries ○ *the Aga Khan* [14C. Via Old French *chan* or medieval Latin *ca(a)nus* < Turkic *kān* "lord, ruler"]

khan[2] /kaan, kan/ *n* in Turkey and some Central Asian countries, an inn [14C. < Persian *kān*]

Imran Khan

Khan /kaan/, **Imran** (*b.* 1952) Pakistan cricketer. He was four times captain of Pakistan's national team between 1982 and his retirement from cricket in 1992, and also played for Sussex and Worcestershire. Full name **Niazi, Imran Ahmad Khan**

khan·a /kaánə/ *n S Asia* **1.** same as **food 2.** same as **meal**[1] [Early 19C. < Hindi]

khan·ate /kaá nàyt/ *n* **1.** the territory governed by a medieval Chinese emperor or a Mongolian or Turkish khan **2.** the position or rank of a khan

khan·ga CLOTHING another spelling of **kanga**

khap·ra bee·tle /kaáprə-/ *n* a beetle that is a pest of grain. Native to: Southeast Asia but now common elsewhere. Latin name: *Trogoderma granarium.* [Via Hindi < Sanskrit *khapara* "thief"]

kha·rif /kə reéf/ *n S Asia* a crop that is harvested at the beginning of winter [Early 19C. Via Persian or Urdu < Arabic *karīf* "autumn"]

Khar·kiv /kaárkiv, khaár-/ second largest city in Ukraine, capital of Kharkiv Oblast. It is situated about 260 mi./418 km east of Kiev. Population: 1,494,235 (1999). Former name **Kharkov**

Khar·toum /kaar toóm/ capital city of Sudan and of Khartoum Province. It is situated just south of the confluence of the Blue Nile and White Nile rivers. Population: 924,505 (1993).

khat /kaat/ *n* **1.** fresh leaves and twigs that act as a stimulant when chewed or brewed as tea **2.** an evergreen bush whose leaves and twigs are used as khat. Native to: Arabia, Africa. Latin name: *Catha edulis.* [Mid-19C. < Arabic *kāt*]

Kha·ta·mi /kaá taa meé, khaá-/, **Mohammad** (*b.* 1943) president of Iran (1997–) and cleric. He entered parliament after the Iranian Revolution (1979) and held several government posts including minister of culture and Islamic guidance (1989–92). He has gained a reputation as a moderate and has pursued closer ties with the West.

khe·dive /kə deév/ *n* the title of the Turkish viceroys who governed Egypt from 1867 to 1914 while it was under Turkish rule [Mid-19C. Via French < Ottoman Turkish *kedīv* < Persian *kadīw* "prince" < *kudā* "god"] —**khe·di·val** *adj* —**khe·di·vate** *n*

khi *n* another spelling of **chi**[1]

khich·ri /kíchree/ *n* a South Asian dish made from rice, pulses, onions, and spices [< Hindi *khicṛī*, < Sanskrit *khiccā* "dish of boiled rice and sesame"]

khir /keer/ *n* in South Asian cuisine, a sweet rice pudding [< Hindi]

Khmer[1] /kmer, kə mér/ (*plural same* or **Khmers**) *n* **1. MEMBER OF CAMBODIAN PEOPLE** a member of the most populous people in Cambodia **2. INHABITANT OF ANCIENT KINGDOM** an inhabitant of an ancient kingdom that flourished in the Mekong valley between the 9th and 13th centuries **3. OFFICIAL LANGUAGE OF CAMBODIA** the official language of Cambodia, belonging to Mon-Khmer. Native speakers: 5 million. [Late 19C. < Khmer] —**Khmer** *adj*

Khmer[2] /kmer, kə mér/ ancient kingdom that flourished in the Mekong valley, Southeast Asia, between the 9th and 13th centuries. Its capital was the city of Angkor situated in the northwestern part of modern-day Cambodia.

Khmer Re·pub·lic former name for **Cambodia** (1970–75)

Khmer Rouge /-r\ roózh, kə mèr-/ *n* the Cambodian Communist party that seized power in the civil war of 1975 and controlled the country until 1979 [< Khmer *Khmer* "Cambodia" + French *rouge* "red"]

Khoi·khoi /kóy kòy/ (*plural same* or **-khois**) *n* **1.** a member of a formerly nomadic people now living mainly in Namibia **2.** *also* **Khoi Khoi** a language spoken in Namibia and some parts of western South Africa, belonging to Khoisan and characterized by the use of click consonants. Native speakers: 55,000. [Late 18C. < Nama, "men of men"] —**Khoi·khoi** *adj*

Khoi·san /kóy saán/, **Khoi-San** *n* a family of African languages spoken in parts of Namibia and Botswana and notable for the use of click consonants [Mid-20C. Blend of KHOIKHOI + SAN[2]]

Kho·mei·ni /kō máynee/, **Ruhollah, Ayatollah** (1900?–89) Iranian Shiite head of state. He led an Islamic revolution that overthrew the shah (1979) and introduced a constitution and administration based on strict interpretation of Islamic law.

> "Islam is the religion of militant individuals who are committed to truth and justice. It is the religion of those who desire freedom and independence. It is the school of those who struggle against imperialism."
> [Ruhollah Khomeini, "Islamic Government," *Islam and Revolution*; 1985]

khoum /koom, koóm/, **khum** *n* a subunit of Mauritanian currency. See table at **currency** [Late 20C. < Arabic *kums* "one-fifth"]

Khru·shchev /kroósh chef, -chawf/, **Nikita** (1894–1971) premier of the USSR (1958–64). In 1953, after Stalin's death, he became first secretary of the Communist Party, and embarked on a program of de-Stalinization. He was ousted in 1964. Full name **Khrushchev, Nikita Sergeyevich**

> "Whether you like it or not, history is on our side. We will bury you."
> [Nikita Khrushchev, *Speech in Moscow to Western diplomats*; November 18, 1956]

Khul·na /koólnə/ city and river port in southwestern Bangladesh. It is situated about 90 mi./145 km southwest of Dhaka. Population: 601,051 (1991).

khum *n* MONEY another spelling of **khoum**

khus·khus /kúskəss/, **khus-khus** *n S Asia* PLANTS same as **vetiver** [Early 19C. < Urdu, Persian *kaskas*]

Khyber Pass

Khy·ber Pass /kíbər-/ mountain pass in western Asia, the most important pass connecting Afghanistan and Pakistan

KHYF *abbr* ONLINE know how you feel (*used in e-mails or text messages*)

kHz *abbr* MEASURE kilohertz

ki *abbr* ONLINE Kiribati (*used in Internet addresses*) See table at **domain name**

KIA[1] *n US* a member of the armed forces who is reported killed while on active service. Full form **killed in action**

KIA[2] *abbr US* ONLINE know-it-all (*used in emails*)

Ki·am·a /kī ámmə/ coastal town in southeastern New South Wales, Australia, an administrative center and tourist resort. Population: 20,139 (2002 estimate).

ki·ang /kee aáng/ *n* a large wild ass. Native to: Tibetan plateau, Himalayan region. Latin name: *Equus hemionus kiang.* [Mid-19C. < Tibetan *kyang*]

Ki·ba·ki /kə baákee/, **Mwai** (*b.* 1931) president of Kenya. A trained economist and experienced politician, he founded the Democratic Party in 1991 and contested the presidential elections as its candidate in 1992 and 1997 before being elected in 2002.

kib·be /kíbbə/ *n* a dish made with ground lamb, pine nuts, and spices, of Southwest Asian origin [Mid-20C. < Arabic *kubbah*]

kib·ble /kíbb'l/ *n* meal that has been ground into small pieces and then formed into pellets, especially for pet food ■ *vt* (**-bled, -bling, -bles**) to grind something such as grain into small pieces [Late 18C. Origin ?]

kib·butz /ki boóts, -boóts/ (*plural* **-but·zim** /-boót seém, -boót-/) *n* a communal farm or factory in Israel run collectively and dedicated to the principle that production work and domestic work are of equal value [Mid-20C. < modern Hebrew *qibbūs* "gathering"]

kib·butz·nik /ki boótsnik, -boóts-/ *n* somebody who lives and works on a kibbutz

kibe /kīb/ *n* a chapped or swollen area of skin, usually on the heel and often ulcerated, caused by exposure to cold [14C. Origin ?]

Ki·bei /kee báy/ (*plural same*) *n US* somebody born in the United States of Japanese parents and educated in Japan [< Japanese, literally "go home"]

ki·bit·ka /ki bítkə/ *n* **1. RUSSIAN SLED** a covered sled or wagon in Russia **2. TATAR TENT** a tent made of felt used by the Tatars **3. TATAR FAMILY** a family of Tatars [Late 18C. < Russian]

kib·itz /kíbbits/ (**-itzed, -itz·ing, -itz·es**) *vi* (*informal*) **1.** to interfere or give unwanted advice, especially when watching a card game **2.** same as **chat** [Early 20C. Via Yiddish < German *kiebitsen*] —**kib·itz·er** *n*

kib·lah /kíbblə/ *n* the direction of Mecca that Muslims must face when praying [Mid-17C. < Arabic *kibla* "that which is opposite"]

ki·bosh /kī bòsh, ki bósh/ (**-boshed, -bosh·ing, -bosh·es**) *vt* to put a stop to something (*informal*) [Mid-19C. Origin ?] ◇ **put the kibosh on something** to prevent something from happening or from being successful (*informal*)

kick /kik/ *v* (**kicked, kick·ing, kicks**) **1.** *vti* **STRIKE WITH FOOT** to strike something or somebody with the foot **2.** *vti* **MOVE WITH FOOT** to make something move by striking it with the foot ○ *kick a ball around* **3.** *vti* **MAKE THRASHING MOVEMENT** to make a thrashing movement with the legs, e.g., when fighting or swimming ○ *Hold onto the side of the pool and kick your legs as* *hard as you can.* **4.** *vti* **RAISE LEG HIGH** to raise the leg up high in a swift movement, e.g., in a dance **5.** *vi* ARMS **RECOIL** to recoil when fired (*refers to firearms*) **6.** *vti* **SCORE GOAL** in various football games, to score a field goal by kicking **7.** *vr* **BLAME YOURSELF** to be irritated with yourself (*informal*) ○ *I'm kicking myself for missing the deadline.* ■ *n* **1. FOOT MOVEMENT** a blow with the foot **2. LEG MOVEMENT** a thrashing movement with the leg ○ *a swimming kick* **3. RAISING OF LEG** a swift lift of the leg, e.g., in a dance ○ *a high kick* **4. KICKING OF BALL** the striking of a ball with the foot ○ *opted for a kick instead of a pass* **5. PLEASURE** an exciting, pleasurable, or satisfying feeling (*informal*) ○ *She really gets a kick out of appearing on stage.* **6. STIMULANT EFFECT** a sudden stimulant effect, especially one produced by alcohol (*informal*) **7. POWER** power or strength (*informal*) ○ *That sauce has quite a kick to it.* **8. TEMPORARY INTEREST** a temporary interest, especially a strongly absorbing interest (*informal*) ○ *They're on some kind of a health food kick right now.* **9.** ARMS **RECOIL OF GUN** the backward thrust of a gun when it is fired [14C. Origin ?] —**kick·a·ble** *adj* ◇ **a kick in the pants** a reprimand given to somebody who is not showing enough enthusiasm or effort (*informal*) ◇ **a kick in the teeth** an insult (*informal*) ◇ **kick somebody upstairs** to promote somebody to a seemingly higher position that is actually less important or influential (*informal*)

kick against *vt* to show disapproval or resentment of a rule or institution by not complying or cooperating with it (*informal*) ○ *He kicked against the restrictions.*

kick around *v* **1.** *vt* **MISTREAT SOMEBODY** to treat somebody badly and unfairly (*informal*) **2.** *vt* **DISCUSS SOMETHING** to discuss a topic or range of topics in an informal way (*informal*) **3.** *vti* **TRAVEL AIMLESSLY** to travel around a place without any fixed plans **4.** *vi* **REMAIN UNNOTICED** to remain forgotten or neglected (*informal*)

kick back *v* **1.** *vti* **PAY BRIBE** to pay money illegally in order to gain concessions or favors (*informal*) **2.** *vi* **REACT SUDDENLY** to react strongly and violently (*informal*) **3.** *vi* ARMS **UNDERGO RECOIL** to recoil when fired (*refers to firearms*) **4.** *vi US* **RELAX** to relax comfortably (*informal*)

kick in *v* **1.** *vi* to start to take effect or come into operation (*informal*) ○ *I'll feel better once the antibiotics kick in.* **2.** *vti* to contribute toward the cost of something (*informal*) **3.** *vi US* same as **die**[1] (*slang*)

kick off *v* **1.** *vi* **START PLAY** in football, to start play by kicking the ball to the receiving team **2.** *vti* **BEGIN** to start something, or begin (*informal*) ○ *Let's kick off tonight's show with our first guest.* **3.** *vi US* same as **die**[1] (*slang*)

kick out *vt* to throw somebody out or send somebody away (*informal*)

kick over *vi US* to turn over or begin to fire (*slang; refers to engines*)

kick up *v* (*informal*) **1.** *vt* to cause or instigate something, usually something undesirable ○ *kicked up a fuss* **2.** *vi US* to misbehave or malfunction

Kick·a·poo /kíkə po͞o/ (*plural same* or **-poos**), **Kik·a·poo** *n* **1.** a member of a Native North American people who lived in southwestern Wisconsin and now live in Kansas, Oklahoma, and Texas **2.** the Algonquian language of the Kickapoo people. Native speakers: 4,000. [Late 17C. < Kickapoo *kiikaapoa*] —**Kick·a·poo** *adj*

kick-ass *adj* an offensive term meaning forceful, aggressive, or ruthless (*taboo*)

kick·back /kík bàk/ *n* (*informal*) **1.** a sum of money paid illegally in order to gain concessions or favors **2.** a strong or violent reaction

kick·ball /kík bàwl/ *n* a children's game similar to baseball but using a large inflated ball that is kicked instead of batted

kick·board /kík bàwrd/ *n* a small buoyant board held by a swimmer in order to stay afloat while practicing kicking techniques

kick·box·ing /kík bòksing/ *n* a form of boxing that involves kicking as well as punching —**kick·box·er** *n*

kick·er /kíkər/ *n* **1. SOMEBODY WHO KICKS** somebody who kicks, especially a football player whose job on the team is to kick the ball **2. CATCH** a disadvantage that is often hidden or unexpected (*informal*) ○ *The price isn't bad, but the kicker is that he wants it all in cash.* **3.** *US* **AUTOMATIC INCREASE** an increase that makes something such as a pension or labor contract more valuable **4. SOMETHING THAT KICKS** something, especially a firearm, that kicks or recoils

kick·ing /kíking/ *adj* excellent, exciting, or very enjoyable (*slang*)

kick·off /kík àwf, -òf/ *n* **1. START OF GAME** in football, the kicking of the ball at the beginning of a game or half, or after a touchdown or field goal **2. START OF MATCH** in soccer, the place kick from the center spot that begins the match **3. STARTING TIME** the time at which a soccer match is due to start **4. START OF SOMETHING** the start of something, or the time when something starts (*informal*)

kick plate *n* a metal plate attached to a door at foot level to protect it

kick pleat *n* an inverted pleat at the lower back of a straight skirt to prevent the wearer from being hampered when walking

kick scoot·er *n* VEHICLES same as **micro scooter**

kick·shaw /kík shàw/ *n* (*archaic*) **1.** a trinket of little value **2.** an exotic food delicacy [Late 16C. < French *quelque chose* "something"]

kick·sin' /kíksin/ *n Carib* playing around and not acting serious (*informal*)

kick·stand /kík stànd/ *n* a pivoting metal bar on a bicycle or motorcycle that can be pushed down into contact with the ground to keep the vehicle upright when it is stationary [Mid-20C. Because raised and lowered with the foot]

kick-start *vt* **1. START MOTORCYCLE** to start the engine on a motorcycle by stepping down hard on the kick-starter **2. START SOMETHING QUICKLY** to quickly start or give new life to a process or activity ○ *policies designed to kick-start an ailing economy* ■ *n* **1.** MOTORCYCLES same as **kick-starter 2. SOMETHING THAT GIVES QUICK START** something that quickly starts or gives new life to a process or activity (*informal*) ○ *a development package to give the museum a $100,000 kick-start*

kick-start·er *n* the pedal on a motorcycle that starts the engine when it is kicked downward

kick turn *n* in skiing, a standing 180-degree turn made by swiveling each ski separately

kick·up /kík ùp/ *n US* a noisy commotion or protest (*informal*)

kick wheel *n* a mechanical potter's wheel that is turned by a foot-operated treadle

kick·y /kíkee/ (**-i·er, -i·est**) *adj* thrilling and unusual (*slang*)

kid[1] /kid/ *n* **1. CHILD** a young child (*informal*) **2. YOUTH** a young person (*informal*) **3. TERM OF ADDRESS** used as a term of address (*informal*) ○ *Here's looking at you, kid.* **4. YOUNG GOAT** a young goat, antelope, or similar animal **5. SOFT LEATHER** soft leather made from the skin of a young goat ■ *adj* **YOUNGER** younger, especially of two siblings (*informal*) ○ *my kid sister* ■ *vti* (**kid·ded, kid·ding, kids**) **BEAR YOUNG** to give birth to a kid or kids (*refers to goats*) [12C. < Old Norse *kið*]

SYNONYMS See ***youth***.

kid[2] /kid/ (**kid·ded, kid·ding, kids**) *v* **1.** *vti* to tell somebody something that is not true, especially as a joke or tease **2.** *vt* to deceive or mislead another person or yourself (*informal*) ○ *Don't kid yourself.* [Late 16C. < KID[1]] —**kid·der** *n*

Kidd /kid/, **William** (1645?–1701) Scottish-born American pirate. He was commissioned to suppress piracy in the Indian Ocean (1695), but made his own attacks on merchant vessels (1697–99) and was later hanged. Known as **Captain Kidd**

Kid·der·min·ster /kíddər mìnstər/, **Kid·der·min·ster car·pet** *n* a type of ingrain carpet originally made in Kidderminster in west central England

kid·die /kíddee/, **kid·dy** (*plural* **-dies**) *n* a small child (*informal*)

kid·do /kíddō/ (*plural* **-dos** or **-does**) *n* **1.** used as a term of address, especially to a young person (*informal*) **2.** a child, young person, or friend (*slang*)

Kid·dush /kíddəsh, ki do͝osh/ (*plural* **-dush·im** /ki do͝o sheēm/), **kid·dush** (*plural* **-dush·im**) *n* **1.** in Judaism, a special blessing, usually for wine, said before a meal on the eve of the Sabbath or a holiday in order to consecrate the festival **2.** a reception following the recitation of the Kiddush for the congregants, at which drinks and snacks are served [Mid-18C. < Hebrew *qiddūš* "sanctification"]

kid·dy *n* another spelling of **kiddie** (*informal*)

kid glove *n* a glove of soft leather made from the skin of a young goat ◇ **handle** *or* **treat somebody** *or* **something with kid gloves** to use great care or delicacy when dealing with somebody or something

kid·glove /kíd glùv/ *adj* displaying tact and sensitivity

kid·lit /kíd lìt/ *n* literature for children (*informal*) [Late 20C. < KID[1] + *lit* shortening of LITERATURE]

kid·nap /kíd nàp/ (**-napped** or **-naped, -nap·ping** or **-nap·ing, -naps**) *vti* to take somebody away by force and hold him or her prisoner, usually for ransom [Mid-17C. < KID[1] + *nap* "to steal," origin ?] —**kid·nap·per** *n*

kid·nap·ping /kíd nàpping/, **kid·nap·ing** *n* the action or crime of forcefully taking away and holding somebody prisoner, usually for ransom

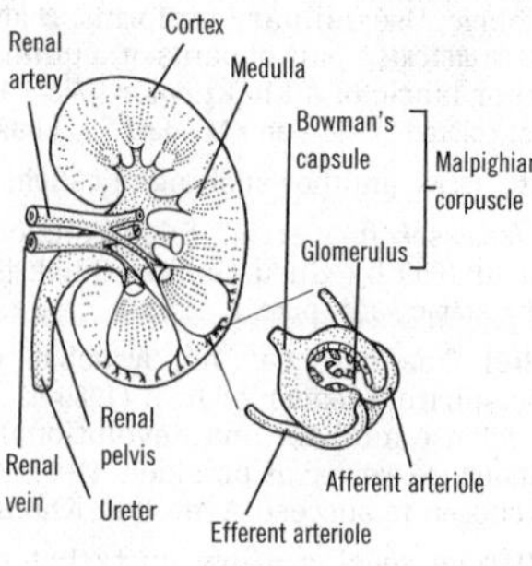

kidney

kid·ney /kídnee/ (*plural* **-neys**) *n* **1. WASTE-REMOVING VERTEBRATE ORGAN** either of a pair of organs in the abdomen of vertebrates that filter waste liquid resulting from metabolism of the blood, which is subsequently excreted as urine **2. INVERTEBRATE ORGAN** the organ in invertebrates that filters waste material for excretion **3. ANIMAL KIDNEY AS FOOD** the kidney of a pig, calf, ox, or lamb, eaten as meat **4. KIND** a kind, type, or disposition (*dated*) ○ *a person of a very different kidney* [14C. Origin ?]

kid·ney bean *n* **1.** a small, kidney-shaped, usually dark red, edible bean **2.** a widely cultivated annual plant that produces kidney beans. Latin name: *Phaseolus vulgaris.*

kid·ney dish, **kid·ney tray** *n* a shallow kidney-shaped container used in hospitals and doctors' offices to hold soiled dressings, fluids, needles, or the instruments needed for a minor procedure

kid·ney-shaped *adj* in the shape of an oval with a concavity in one side ○ *a kidney-shaped swimming pool*

kid·ney stone *n* a small hard mass that forms in the kidney, consisting mainly of phosphates, oxalates, and urates

kid·skin /kíd skìn/ *n* same as **kid**[1] *n* (sense 5)

kid stuff *n* (*informal*) **1.** something considered suitable only for children or immature people **2.** something that is very easy or very boring

kid·ult /kíddult/ *n* an adult who enjoys entertainment such as films or computer games intended mainly for children (*slang*) [Mid-20C. Blend of KID[1] + ADULT]

kid·vid /kíd vìd/ *n US* a video for children (*informal*)

Kiel /keel/ city and seaport in north central Germany, the capital of the state of Schleswig-Holstein, situated north of Hamburg. Population: 246,586 (1997).

kiel·ba·sa /kil baássa, keel-/ *n* a spicy smoked Polish sausage [Mid-20C. Via Polish < Turkic *kūl bastī* "roast pressed meat"]

Kiel Ca·nal canal in northwestern Germany connecting the North and Baltic seas. Length: 61 mi./98 km.

kier /keer/ *n* a vat in which yarn or cloth is bleached or dyed [Late 16C. < Old Norse *ker* "tub"]

Kier·ke·gaard /keérkə gaàrd/, **Søren** (1813–55) Danish philosopher. His religious philosophy is concerned with individual existence, choice, and commitment, and has profoundly influenced theology and the existential philosophers. His books include *The Concept of Irony* (1841) and *Either/Or* (1843). Full name **Kierkegaard, Søren Aabye**

kie·ser·ite /keézə rìt/ *n* a white-to-yellow crystalline hydrated magnesium sulfate mineral. Source: salt residues. [Mid-19C. After Dietrich *Kieser* (1779–1862), German physician]

Ki·ev /keé ev/ capital and largest city of Ukraine, located in the north central part of the country. Population: 2,600,000 (1998).

kif /kif, keef/, **kef** /kef, keef, kayf/, **kaif** /kayf/ *n* marijuana, especially in North Africa [Early 19C. < Arabic *kayf, kef* "pleasure"]

Ki·ga·li /ki gaálee/ capital city of Rwanda, situated on a plateau in the center of the country, just south of the equator. Population: 286,000 (1995).

kike /kīk/ *n* a highly offensive taboo term for a Jew (*taboo*) [Early 20C. Origin ?]

Ki·kon·go /kee kóng gō/ *n* LANG same as **Kongo**[1] (sense 2) [Late 19C. < Kongo] —**Ki·kon·go** *adj*

ki·ku·mon /kíkə mòn, keékə-/ *n* the emblem of the Japanese imperial family, in the form of a chrysanthemum [< Japanese]

Ki·ku·yu /ki kóoyoo/ (*plural same* or **-yus**) *n* **1.** a member of a people living mainly in highland Kenya, especially around Mount Kenya **2.** a Benue-Congo language spoken in parts of Kenya. Native speakers: 5 million. [Mid-19C. < Bantu] —**Ki·ku·yu** *adj*

Ki·lau·e·a /keè low áy ə/ the world's most active volcano, on central Hawaii Island, situated in Hawaii Volcanoes National Park. Height: 4,090 ft./1,247 m.

Kil·dare /kil dér/ county in the province of Leinster, eastern Republic of Ireland. The county town is Naas. Population: 134,992 (2002). Area: 654 sq. mi./1,694 sq. km.

kil·der·kin /kíldərkin/ *n* **1.** an obsolete British measurement for liquids, equivalent to about 18 gallons or 68 liters **2.** a cask with a capacity of one kilderkin [14C. < Middle Dutch *kinderkin* "small quintal"]

ki·lim /kee leèm, kíllim/ *n* a woven rug with richly colored geometric patterns, made in Southwest Asia [Late 19C. Via Turkish < Persian *gelīm*]

Mount Kilimanjaro: view from Amboseli National Park

Kil·i·man·ja·ro, Mount /kìllәmən jaárō/ the highest mountain in Africa, located in northeastern Tanzania. Height: 19,340 ft./5,895 m.

Kil·ken·ny /kil kénnee/ county in the province of Leinster, eastern Republic of Ireland. The county town is Kilkenny. Population: 75,336 (2002). Area: 796 sq. mi./2,062 sq. km.

kill[1] /kil/ *v* (**killed, kill·ing, kills**) **1.** *vti* CAUSE SOMETHING LIVING TO DIE to cause the death of a person, animal, or other organism ○ *They were killed in a car accident.* **2.** *vt* RUIN SOMETHING to cause something to end or be ruined ○ *The remark killed the conversation.* **3.** *vt* OVERPOWER SOMETHING SUBTLE OR LESS STRONG to destroy or severely damage an essential, often delicate quality in something by superimposing something stronger ○ *Her perfume killed the scent of the roses.* **4.** *vt* BLOCK PLAN to prevent a proposal such as the passing of a congressional bill from going through ○ *The bill was killed in the Appropriations Committee.* **5.** *vt* HURT PART OF SOMEBODY'S BODY to cause severe physical pain or discomfort to somebody (*informal*) ○ *My feet are killing me!* **6.** *vt* TIRE SOMEBODY OUT to exhaust somebody completely (*informal*) ○ *These stairs kill me every time.* **7. kill your·self** *vr* OVEREXERT YOURSELF to push yourself too hard (*informal; often used ironically*) ○ *She was killing herself to get the job done on time.* **8.** *vt* TURN SOMETHING OFF to disconnect the power to something electrical or mechanical so that it stops working (*informal*) ○ *Kill the engine.* **9.** *vt* MAKE TIME PASS to use up spare time in some activity (*informal*) ○ *We had a couple of hours to kill before going to the airport.* **10.** *vti* BOWL SOMEBODY OVER to have an overpowering effect on somebody, e.g., causing extreme admiration, helpless laughter, or utter amazement (*informal*) ○ *dressed to kill* **11.** *vt* DRINK ALL OF SOMETHING to finish off a bottle of something, usually an alcoholic beverage (*slang*) **12.** *vt* SOCCER CONTROL BALL in soccer, to bring a fast-moving ball under instant control **13.** *vt* RACKET GAMES MAKE BALL UNRETURNABLE in racket games, to hit the ball so hard, with such skill, or in such a direction that your opponent has no chance of returning it **14.** *vt* US FOOTBALL MAKE BALL DEAD in football, to stop the ball so that it is no longer in play (*informal*) **15.** *vt* US HIT BALL HARD to hit a ball very hard **16.** *vt* PUBL CUT TEXT to delete a piece of text from a publication or remove a particular amount from a text (*slang*) ○ *We had to kill half a column to make space for the ad.* ■ *n* **1.** KILLING the moment or an act of killing an animal, especially prey or game, or the bull at the end of a bullfight **2.** HUNTING PREY the prey killed by an animal or human being **3.** MIL DESTRUCTION OF ENEMY VEHICLE the destroying of an enemy vehicle such as a plane, ship, or tank (*slang*) [13C. < assumed Old English *cyllan* < Germanic] ◇ **be in at the kill** to be present at the end of something or the achievement of an aim, especially when you have worked to cause it

SYNONYMS ***kill, murder, assassinate, execute, put to death, slaughter, slay, put down, put to sleep, take somebody's life***

CORE MEANING: to deprive of life

kill to cause the death of a person, animal, or other organism ○ *Floods have killed at least three people and forced hundreds from their homes.* ○ *a resolution asking countries not to kill whales for scientific purposes* ○ *A severe frost killed all the seedlings.* **murder** to kill another person deliberately and not in self-defense or with any other extenuating circumstance recognized by law ○ *She was found guilty of murdering a nursing colleague.* **assassinate** to kill somebody, especially a political leader or other public figure, by a sudden violent attack ○ *A police spokesperson told reporters a plot to assassinate the pontiff had been foiled.* **execute** to kill somebody as part of a legal or extralegal process ○ *Cromwell ordered the Abbot of Reading to be tried and executed immediately.* **put to death** to kill somebody, especially in accordance with a legal death sentence ○ *put to death for treason* **slaughter** to kill a person or large numbers of people brutally, or to kill farm animals for food ○ *accused of slaughtering hundreds of unarmed protesters* ○ *cattle sent to be slaughtered at two years old* **slay** (*formal or literary*) to kill a person or animal ○ *Cain plotted to slay his brother Abel.* **put down** *or* **put to sleep** to kill an animal in a humane way, especially because it is ill, injured, or in pain ○ *Some of the animals were beyond help and had to be put down.* ○ *I think I'll have to have my poor old dog put to sleep.* **take somebody's life** to kill a person or yourself ○ *They were accused of taking the lives of hundreds of innocent women and children.* ○ *The verdict of the inquiry into his death was that he had taken his own life.*

kill off *vt* **1.** to destroy something or somebody utterly, especially the remaining members of a group of people or animals ○ *The spray killed off all the aphids.* **2.** to write in the death of a character, especially in a serial or soap opera

kill[2] /kil/ *n regional* a stream, channel, or waterway [Mid-17C. < Dutch *kil* "channel"]

REGIONAL NOTE The term ***kill*** meaning "waterway" endures today mainly in place names in New York State (*Catskill* and *Peekskill*) and New Jersey (*Paulins Kill*).

Kil·lar·ney /ki laárnee/ town and tourist center in the southwestern Republic of Ireland, situated by the Lakes of Killarney. Population: 12,087 (2002).

kill·deer /kíl deèr/ (*plural same* or **-deers**) *n* a bird with brown and white feathers, two black breast bands, and a distinctive noisy cry. Native to: North America. Latin name: *Charadrius vociferus*. [Mid-18C. An imitation of its call]

kill·er /kíllər/ *n* **1.** SOMEBODY OR SOMETHING THAT KILLS a person or animal that kills others intentionally, especially one that does this more than once (*often used before a noun*) ○ *a killer crocodile* **2.** SOMETHING VERY DIFFICULT something that is very demanding or difficult (*informal*) ○ *This aerobics class is a killer.* **3.** DESTRUCTIVE PERSON OR THING somebody or something that destroys or is fatal ○ *A killer storm hit the nation on Sunday.* ○ *a cancer that is still a major killer* **4.** EXCEPTIONAL THING something that is excellent or exceptional (*slang*) ■ *adj* EXCEPTIONAL excellent or exceptional (*slang*) ○ *a killer performance*

kill·er app *n* a highly popular computer application, seen as definitive (*slang*)

kill·er bee *n* INSECTS same as **Africanized bee** (*informal*)

kill·er cell, kill·er T cell *n* a T cell that is part of the body's immune system and attacks cells having specific antigens on their surface such as cancer cells and those infected with a virus

kill·er in·stinct *n* **1.** a tendency, capacity, or urge to kill **2.** an overpowering drive to succeed, e.g., in business deals or sports, whatever the cost may be to other people

kill·er T cell *n* ANAT same as **killer cell**

killer whale

kill·er whale *n* a black-and-white toothed whale. It grows up to 25 ft./7.62 m long, has a tall dorsal fin, and feeds mainly on fish and squid. Native to: colder seas. Latin name: *Orcinus orca*.

kill fee *n* US a payment made to a writer, photographer, artist, or illustrator by a publisher who has decided not to publish the contracted work

kill·file /kíll fīl/ *n* a list on an Internet newsreader of authors, subjects, or threads that the user is not interested in, enabling messages or articles relating to the persons or topics listed to be filtered out ■ *v* to add somebody's name to a killfile in order to block any e-mail from that sender

kil·lick /kíllik/, **kil·lock** /kíllək/ *n* a small anchor, especially one made of a heavy stone [Early 17C. Origin ?]

kil·li·fish /kíllee fish/ (*plural* **-fish·es** or *same*) *n* a freshwater fish about the size of a minnow, kept in aquariums or used as bait and in mosquito control. Family: Cyprinodontidae. [Early 19C. Origin ?]

kill·ing /kílling/ *n* **1.** SLAYING the act of causing the death of a person or animal **2.** QUICK PROFIT a large and quick profit (*informal*) ○ *made a killing on the hog futures market* ■ *adj* **1.** EXHAUSTING totally exhausting **2.** FATAL causing or resulting in death ○ *We expect a killing frost tonight.* **3.** GIVING PLEASURE providing extreme pleasure or very good (*slang*) **4.** INTENSE very intense (*slang*) —**kill·ing·ly** *adv*

kill·ing fields *npl* the site of mass slaughter, e.g., of civilians

CULTURAL NOTE ***The Killing Fields***, a movie (1984) by British director Roland Joffe. Through the true story of US journalist Sydney Schanberg's attempts to trace the Cambodian aide he was forced to leave behind after the fall of Phnom Penh in 1975, Joffe portrays the atrocities perpetrated on the Cambodian people by the Khmer Rouge regime between 1975 and 1978. References such as "the killing fields of Bosnia" clearly take their linguistic cues from this movie title.

kill·joy /kíl jòy/ *n* somebody whose behavior prevents other people from having a good time

kil·lock *n* NAUT same as **killick**

kill shot *n* US in racket games, a shot that is hit so hard or accurately that it cannot be returned

Kil·mer /kílmər/, **Joyce** (1886–1918) US poet. He is known for the title poem of his collection *Trees and Other Poems* (1914). He was killed in World War I. Full name **Kilmer, Alfred Joyce**

> "I think that I shall never see / A poem lovely as a tree."
> [Joyce Kilmer, "Trees," *Trees and Other Poems*; 1914]

kiln /kiln/ *n* **1.** INDUSTRIAL OVEN a specialized oven or furnace used for industrial processes such as firing clay for pottery or bricks and for drying materials such as hops or timber. See illustration on next page **2.** *regional* AGRIC PILE OF VEGETABLES a heap of vegetables, usually potatoes, covered with earth and mulch and sometimes stored in a shed ■ *vt* (**kilned, kiln·ing, kilns**) PROCESS SOMETHING IN KILN to dry, fire, or bake something in a kiln [Pre-12C. < Latin *culina* < *coquere* "to cook"]

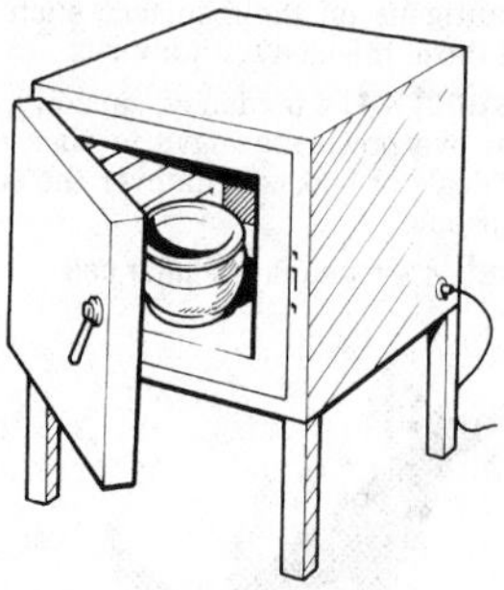

kiln: pottery kiln

REGIONAL NOTE See *bank*².

ki·lo /kéelō/ *n* **1.** MEASURE same as **kilogram 2.** a code word for the letter "K," used in international radio communications [Mid-19C. Shortening]

kilo- *prefix* **1.** a thousand (10^3) ○ *kilogram* Symbol **k 2.** in the binary system, a thousand (2^{10}) ○ *kilobyte* [Via French < Greek *khilioi* "thousand"]

kil·o·bit /kíllə bìt/ *n* 1,024 bits

kil·o·byte /kíllə bìt/ *n* a unit of computer data or storage space equivalent to 1,024 bytes

kil·o·cal·o·rie /kíllə kàlləree, -kàllree/ *n* PHYS, MEASURE same as **calorie** (sense 2)

kil·o·cy·cle /kíllə sìk'l/ *n* MEASURE same as **kilohertz**

kil·o·e·lec·tron·volt /kìllō i lék tron vòlt/ *n* one thousand electron volts

kil·o·gram /kíllə gràm/ *n* the basic unit of mass in the SI system, equal to 1,000 grams or 2.2046 lbs. Symbol **kg**

kil·o·gram-me·ter *n* a unit of energy measuring how much work a kilogram force does across a distance of one meter in the direction of the applied force

kil·o·hertz /kíllə hùrts/ *n* 1,000 hertz

kil·o·joule /kíllə jòol/ *n* 1,000 joules

ki·lom·e·ter /ki lómmətər/ *n* 0.621 miles/1,000 meters

kil·o·par·sec /kíllə paar sek/ *n* 1,000 parsecs

kil·o·ton /kíllə tùn/ *n* **1.** 1,000 tons **2.** an explosive force equal to 1,000 tons of TNT

kil·o·volt /kíllə vòlt/ *n* 1,000 volts

kil·o·watt /kíllə wòt/ *n* 1,000 watts

kil·o·watt-hour *n* a unit of energy equal to the work done by one kilowatt in one hour

kilt /kilt/ *n* a knee-length wraparound tartan garment that is part of the traditional Scottish highland dress for men and is also worn by women and girls [Mid-18C. < dialect *kilt* "tuck up, gird" < N Germanic] —**kilt·ed** *adj*

kil·ter /kíltər/ *n* good working order or condition ○ *The well pump is out of kilter.* [Mid-17C. Variant of *kelter*, origin ?]

Kim·ber·ley¹ /kímbər lee/ capital of Northern Cape Province in central South Africa. It is located in a diamond-mining region. Population: 167,060 (1991).

Kim·ber·ley², **Kim·ber·leys** /kímbər leez/ plateau region of northwestern Western Australia, near the border with the Northern Territory. The highest point is Mount Hann, 2,545 ft./776 m. Area: 140,000 sq. mi./360,000 sq. km.

kim·ber·lite /kímbər lìt/ *n* a form of igneous rock, found especially in South Africa, composed mainly of peridotite and often containing diamonds [Late 19C. After *Kimberley*, town in South Africa]

kim·chi /kímchee/ *n* a pickle made with vegetables such as cabbage and white radish seasoned with chili, garlic, and ginger, regarded as the national dish of Korea [Late 19C. < Korean *kimch'i*]

Kim Il Sung /kìm il súng/ (1912–94) North Korean premier (1948–72) and president (1972–94) of North Korea. He encouraged a personality cult around himself and tried to extend Communist rule into South Korea, leading to the Korean War (1950–53). Born **Kim Song Ju**

Kim Jong Il /kìm jong íl/ (*b.* 1941) North Korean head of state. He took over several major posts after the death of his father Kim Il Sung in 1994 but it was not until 1998 that he was officially made head of state. In 2000 he signed an agreement with the president of South Korea to work toward the reunification of the Korean peninsula.

kimono

ki·mo·no /kə mṓnə, -mṓnō/ (*plural* **-nos**) *n* **1.** a loose floor-length traditional Japanese garment that has wide sleeves, wraps in front, and is fastened with a sash **2.** a western garment, especially a robe, similar to the Japanese kimono [Late 19C. < Japanese < *ki* "wear" + *mono* "thing"] —**ki·mo·noed** *adj*

kin /kin/ *n* **1.** FAMILY GROUP somebody's relatives as a group (*takes a plural verb*) **2.** BLOOD RELATION somebody related by blood ○ *He's not kin but we consider him one of the family.* **3.** GROUP OR CLASS a member of a group that shares characteristics with another group ○ *the starfish and its kin the sea urchin* ■ *adj* RELATED related to somebody ○ *I'm kin to them through my grandmother.* [Old English *cyn(n)* < Indo-European]

-kin *suffix* little, dear ○ *limpkin* [Probably < Middle Dutch *-ki(j)n*]

ki·na /kéenə/ *n* the main unit of Papua New Guinean currency. See table at **currency** [Late 20C. < Tok Pisin]

Ki·na·ba·lu, Mount /kìnnəbə lóo/ mountain in Malaysia in the state of Sabah, in northern Borneo. It lies in Kinabalu National Park. Height: 13,455 ft./4,101 m.

ki·nase /kí nàyss, -nàyz/ *n* an enzyme that catalyzes the transfer of a phosphate group from ATP [Early 20C. < KINETIC]

kin·cob /kín kòb, kíng-/ *n* a South Asian silk fabric embroidered with gold or silver thread [Early 18C. < Urdu, Persian *kamkāb* "gold or silver brocade," alteration of *kamkā* "damask silk" < Chinese, "gold flower"]

kind¹ /kīnd/ *adj* **1.** COMPASSIONATE having a generous warm compassionate nature **2.** GENEROUS showing generosity or compassion ○ *a kind act* **3.** AGREEABLE OR SAFE not harsh, unpleasant, or likely to have destructive effects ○ *a detergent that is kind to the environment* **4.** CARING showing courtesy or caring about somebody (*formal*) ○ *my kindest regards to your family* [Old English *gecynde* "innate, natural" < Germanic]

kind² /kīnd/ *n* **1.** ⚠ GROUP OF INDIVIDUALS THAT SHARE FEATURES a group of individuals or items connected by shared characteristics ○ *What kind of fruit is this?* **2.** SOMETHING INFERIOR an example of something, especially if it is seen as inferior or doubtful ○ *Well, you could say it's a kind of tool, but how would you use it?* **3.** ESSENCE OF SOMETHING the primary character of something that determines the class to which it belongs [Old English *cynde* < Germanic] ◇ **in kind 1.** with goods or services, not with money **2.** with something of the same sort that was given ○ *If they attack us, they'll be paid back in kind.* ◇ **kind of** rather, to some extent, or in a way (*informal*) ○ *She seemed kind of upset when I talked to her.* ◇ **of a kind 1.** like something else in some respects but not enough to be satisfactory **2.** alike, or belonging to the same sort ○ *She's one of a kind, is Sarah.*

USAGE When *kind of* is followed by a plural word, there is a temptation to precede the whole phrase with a corresponding plural such as *these* or *those*, so that *this kind of thing* becomes *these kind of things.* Such expressions (and ones on the same pattern using *sort* or *type*) are ungrammatical. *These kinds of things* or *things of this kind* is to be preferred.

SYNONYMS See *type*.

kin·da /kíndə/ *contr* kind of (*nonstandard*) ○ *It's kinda strange.*

kin·der·gar·ten /kíndər gaart'n, -gaard'n/ *n* a school or class for young children, usually between the ages of four and six, immediately before they begin formal education [Mid-19C. < German, "children's garden"] —**kin·der·gart·ner** *n*

kind·heart·ed /kīnd háartəd/ *adj* **1.** sympathetic and kind ○ *She's too kindhearted to be angry with you for long.* **2.** showing or arising from a sympathetic and generous nature ○ *a kindhearted gesture* —**kind·heart·ed·ly** *adv* —**kind·heart·ed·ness** *n*

Kin·di /kíndee/, **al-** (A.D. 801?–873?) Arabian Islamic philosopher. He translated the work of Aristotle into Arabic and formulated the theology of the Mutazilites.

kin·dle¹ /kínd'l/ (**-dled, -dling, -dles**) *vti* **1.** START BURNING to set something alight, or begin to burn **2.** BRIGHTEN OR GLOW to begin to glow, or make something begin to glow **3.** IGNITE EMOTION OR INTEREST to become aroused, or arouse feelings or interest ○ *The program kindled his interest in antiquarian books.* [12C. < Old Norse *kynda*; influenced by Old Norse *kyndill* "torch, candle"] —**kin·dler** *n*

kin·dle² /kínd'l/ *n* a brood or a litter, e.g., of kittens ■ *vi* (**-dled, -dling, -dles**) to give birth, especially to baby rabbits [13C. Probably < KIND²]

kin·dling /kíndling/ *n* **1.** FIRE-LIGHTING MATERIAL something used to start a fire because it burns easily, e.g., a bunch of small dry twigs **2.** MAKING SOMETHING BURN the act of making something start to burn **3.** STIRRING UP OF EMOTION the arousal of somebody's interest or feelings

kind·ly /kíndlee/ *adj* (**-li·er, -li·est**) **1.** FRIENDLY AND GENEROUS BY NATURE sympathetic and kind **2.** SHOWING SYMPATHY arising from or showing a sympathetic and generous nature **3.** PLEASANT pleasant, mild, or comfortable ■ *adv* **1.** ⚠ PLEASE used in polite requests ○ *Kindly take your seats.* **2.** IN KIND WAY showing kindness and considerateness ○ *He kindly accompanied me home.* **3.** TOLERANTLY with tolerance and patience ○ *She kindly disregarded their lack of skill during the first few days.* —**kind·li·ness** *n*

USAGE *Kindly* is not restricted just to *kindness* as such but may also mean, approximately, "please." In either case, it should modify the action or thing wished for, not another part of the sentence. The intention of, for example, *May we kindly request that patrons take their seats,* is to encourage patrons to be so kind as to sit down. Thus the sentence should be reworded as *May we request that patrons kindly take their seats.*

kind·ness /kíndnəss/ *n* **1.** the practice of being or the tendency to be sympathetic and compassionate **2.** an act that shows consideration and caring ○ *How can we thank you for your many kindnesses?*

kin·dred /kíndrəd/ *adj* **1.** SIMILAR TO SOMEBODY OR SOMETHING close to somebody or something else because of similar qualities or interests ○ *the kindred relationship between neuroscience and neurology* **2.** OF SAME FAMILY related to somebody by blood (*formal*) ○ *the search for someone kindred to him* ■ *n* **1.** AFFINITY closeness to somebody that is based on something other than a blood relationship, e.g., on similarity of character or interests ○ *a sense of kindred between the two candidates* **2.** FAMILY RELATIONSHIP relationship by blood or, less strictly, by marriage ○ *occasions that reinforce the ties of kindred* **3.** SOMEBODY'S FAMILY somebody's relatives as a group (*takes a plural verb*) **4.** CLAN a family or group of closely related families, e.g., in the Celtic kin-based social system [12C. < KIN + Old English *rǣden* "condition"] —**kin·dred·ness** *n* —**kin·dred·ship** *n*

kin·dred spir·it *n* somebody who resembles somebody else in character, interests, and temperament

kine /kīn/ *npl* cows or cattle (*archaic*) [Old English *cȳna*, form of the plural of *cū* (see cow¹)]

kin·e·mat·ics /kìnnə máttiks/ *n* a branch of physics that deals with the motion of a body or system without reference to force and mass (*takes a singular verb*) [Mid-19C. < Greek *kinēmat-* "motion"] —**kin·e·mat·ic** *adj* —**kin·e·mat·i·cal·ly** *adv*

kin·e·scope /kínnə skòp/ *US n* **1.** RECORDED TELEVISION PROGRAM a film of a transmitted television program **2.** PICTURE TUBE a cathode ray tube in a television ■ *vt* (**-scoped, -scop·ing, -scopes**) FILM TELEVISION PROGRAM to make a film of a transmitted television program [Mid-20C. Originally a trademark]

ki·ne·sics /ki néessiks, kī-, -néeziks/ *n* the study of the ways in which people use body movements such as shrugging to communicate without speaking (*takes a singular verb*) [Mid-20C. < Greek *kinēsis* (see KINESIS)]

ki·ne·sin /kī néessin/ *n* a protein that uses chemical energy from ATP to create movement within cells, e.g., separating chromosomes during division and transporting neurotransmitters inside nerve cells

ki·ne·si·ol·o·gy /ki nèessee óllǝjee, -nèezee-/ *n* **1.** the study of the mechanics of motion with respect to human anatomy **2.** in alternative medicine, a system of muscle testing that reveals and corrects musculoskeletal imbalances and identifies food sensitivities [Late 19C. < Greek *kinēsis* (see KINESIS)] —**ki·ne·si·ol·o·gist** *n*

ki·ne·sis /ki néessiss, kī-/ *n* the movement of a cell or organism in response to a stimulus such as light. Such movement can be in any direction and its rate depends on the intensity of stimulation. [Early 20C. < Greek *kinēsis* "movement" < *kinein* "to move"]

-kinesis *suffix* **1.** motion, activity ○ *psychokinesis* **2.** cell division ○ *diakinesis* [< Greek *kinēsis* (see KINESIS)]

kin·es·the·sia /kìnnǝss théezhǝ/, **kin·es·the·sis** /-théessiss/ *n* the perception or sensing of the motion, weight, or position of the body as muscles, tendons, and joints move [Late 19C. < Greek *kinein* "to move" + *aisthēsis* "sensation"] —**kin·es·thet·ic** /kìnnǝss théttik/ *adj* —**kin·es·thet·i·cal·ly** *adv*

kin·e·the·od·o·lite /kìnnǝ thee ódd'l ìt/ *n* an optical instrument that contains a movie camera and provides continuous footage of a moving target such as a missile or satellite along with its altitude and trajectory [Mid-20C. < KINESIS]

ki·net·ic /ki néttik, kī-/ *adj* relating to, caused by, or producing motion [Mid-19C. < Greek *kinētikos* "for putting in motion" < *kinein* "to move"]

ki·net·ic art *n* art, especially sculpture, with parts that move, e.g., when blown by the wind or activated by electricity —**ki·net·ic art·ist** *n*

ki·net·ic en·er·gy *n* the energy that a body or system has because of its motion. Symbol *T*, E_k

ki·net·ics /ki néttiks, kī-/ *n* (*takes a singular verb*) **1.** PHYS same as **dynamics 2.** the branch of chemistry that studies rates of reactions

ki·net·ic the·o·ry *n* a theory of the behavior of gases that assumes heat is a process of energy transfer and the internal energy of a gas is the total energy of its particles

kineto- *prefix* motion, movement ○ *kinetosome* [< Greek *kinetos* "moving" < *kinein* "to move"]

ki·net·o·plast /ki néttǝ plàst/ *n* a small cell body outside the nucleus and near the base of the flagellum in some protozoans

ki·net·o·some /ki néttǝ sōm/ *n* BIOL same as **basal body**

kin·folk /kín fōk/ *npl* somebody's relatives

king /king/ *n* **1.** MALE SOVEREIGN a man or boy who rules as a monarch over an independent state **2.** CHIEF a ruler of a group ○ *Jupiter was king of the Roman gods.* **3.** BEST EXAMPLE any animal considered as the best, strongest, or biggest of its kind ○ *The lion is variously called the king of beasts or the king of the jungle.* **4.** PREEMINENT MAN the principal man or preeminent male figure in a field ○ *king of the talk shows* **5.** HIGH FACE CARD a card in each suit of a deck that carries the picture of a king **6.** PRINCIPAL CHESS PIECE the most important piece in chess, whose capture wins the game **7.** CROWNED PIECE IN CHECKERS a piece in the game of checkers that has reached the far side of the board and has been crowned, and may therefore move in any direction ■ *vt* (**kinged, king·ing, kings**) **1.** CROWN PIECE IN CHECKERS to make a piece into a king in the game of checkers **2.** CROWN SOMEBODY KING to make somebody a king [Old English *cyning* < Germanic] —**king·ship** *n*

King *n* in Christianity, God or Jesus Christ

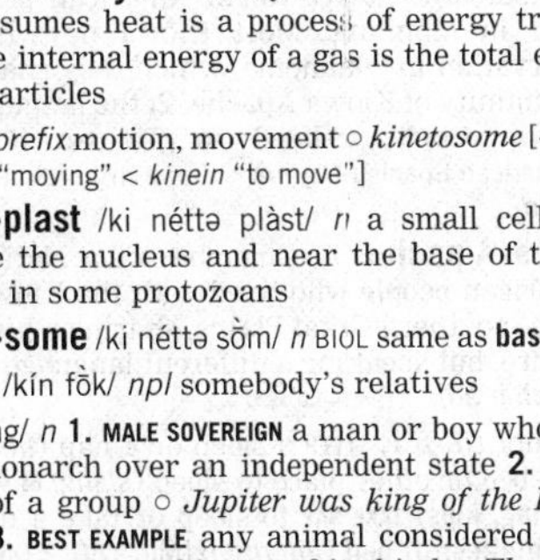

Express Newspapers

B. B. King

King /king/, **B. B.** (*b.* 1925) US blues musician. He led a blues revival in the 1960s and his rhythm-and-blues hits include "The Thrill is Gone" (1970) and the album *Live at Cook County Jail* (1971). Born **King, Riley B.**

> "Being a blues singer is like being Black two times."
> [B. B. King. Quoted in *The Wit and Wisdom of Rock and Roll*, Maxim Jabukowski (ed.); 1983]

Popperfoto

Billie Jean King

King, Billie Jean (*b.* 1943) US tennis player. Between 1961 and 1979 she won a record 20 Wimbledon titles. She also won numerous other titles in the United States, France, and Australia. She became the first president of the Women's Tennis Association in 1974. Born **Moffat, Billie Jean**

> "It's really impossible for athletes to grow up. As long as you're playing, no one will let you."
> [Billie Jean King, *Billie Jean*; 1982]

King, Coretta Scott (*b.* 1927) US civil rights leader. The widow of Martin Luther King, Jr., she has continued her husband's civil rights advocacy and activism.

King, Mackenzie (1874–1950) prime minister of Canada. He became leader of the Liberal Party in 1919, and served three terms as prime minister (1921–26, 1926–30, 1935–48). Full name **King, William Lyon Mackenzie**. See table at **prime minister**

AKG London

Martin Luther King, Jr.

King, Martin Luther, Jr. (1929–68) US civil rights leader and minister. His nonviolent demonstrations against racial inequality led to civil rights legislation. He was awarded the Nobel Peace Prize (1964) and was assassinated four years later in Memphis, Tennessee.

> "I have a dream that my four little children will one day live in a nation where they will not be judged by the color of their skin but by the content of their character."
> [Martin Luther King, Jr., *Speech at the Civil Rights March on Washington, D.C.*; August 28, 1963]

> "A riot is at bottom the language of the unheard."
> [Martin Luther King, Jr., *Where Do We Go From Here?*; 1967]

King, Stephen (*b.* 1947) US writer. His horror stories such as *Carrie* (1973) and *Needful Things* (1991) have sold more than 100 million copies worldwide, and many have been made into motion pictures. Full name **King, Stephen Edwin**

King, Thomas J. (1921–2000) US embryologist. His research on frog embryos with Robert Briggs at the Institute for Cancer Research in Philadelphia led to the creation of the first amphibian clones in 1951.

King, William Rufus de Vane (1786–1853) vice president of the United States (1853). He died six weeks after taking up office as vice president in the Democratic administration of Franklin Pierce.

king·bird /kíng bùrd/ (*plural same* or **-birds**) *n* a large songbird. Native to: Americas. Genus: *Tyrannus.*

king·bolt /kíng bōlt/ *n* a vertical bolt that joins the body of a carriage, wagon, or railroad car to the front axle

King Charles span·iel *n* **1.** a small spaniel of a breed with a markedly domed head, snub nose, bulging eyes, floppy ears, and a tan or black coat with white patches **2.** a slightly larger breed of spaniel that has a longer nose [Late 19C. After CHARLES II, who was partial to the breed]

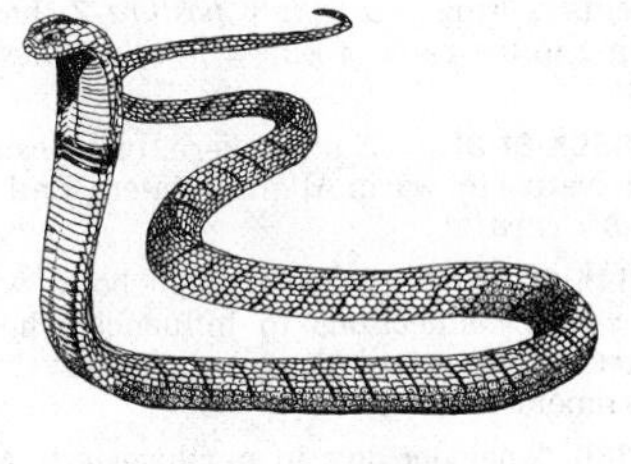

king cobra

king co·bra *n* a very large poisonous cobra that eats other reptiles and can reach a length of 18 ft./5.5 m. Native to: Southeast Asia. Latin name: *Ophiophagus hannah*.

King Coun·try /kìng-/ region in the west of the North Island, New Zealand, lying south of the Waikato region between the western coast and Lake Taupo

king crab *n* **1.** a very large edible crab caught commercially and prized for its flesh. Native to: coastal waters of the North Pacific and Japan. Latin name: *Paralithoides camtschaticus.* **2.** MARINE BIOL same as **horseshoe crab**

king·cup /kíng kùp/ *n UK* a plant of the buttercup family, especially a marsh marigold. Flowers: yellow. Native to: wetlands of Europe, North America. Family: Ranunculaceae.

king·dom /kíngdǝm/ *n* **1.** MONARCH'S TERRITORY a state or people ruled over by a king or queen **2.** SPHERE OF ACTIVITY a realm or area of activity in which a particular thing is thought to dominate ○ *the kingdom of professional tennis* **3.** HIGHEST CLASSIFICATION FOR NATURAL THINGS each of the three groups, animal, vegetable, and mineral, into which natural organisms and objects are traditionally, as opposed to scientifically, divided

king·dom come *n* **1.** the next world or the state after death **2.** the point at which the world comes to an end (*informal*) [Late 18C. < *Thy kingdom come* (in the Lord's Prayer (Matthew 6:10)) "may Thy kingdom come"]

king·fish /kíng fish/ (*plural* **-fish·es** or *same*) *n* **1.** LARGE GAME FISH a large game fish. Native to: warm Atlantic coastal waters. Genus: *Menticirrhus.* **2.** *US* FISH same as **king mackerel 3.** KINGFISH AS FOOD the flesh of a kingfish as food **4.** FISH same as **opah 5.** *US* POWERFUL MAN somebody very powerful, especially a man who has no challengers to his authority (*slang*) ○ *He's the kingfish in this two-bit town.*

kingfisher

king·fish·er /kíng fìshər/ *n* a brightly colored bird that usually has a short tail, a long strong beak, and sometimes a crest. It feeds on fish, insects, and other prey. Native to: mainly tropical, subtropical regions worldwide. Family: Alcedinidae. See illustration on previous page [15C. Originally *king's fisher*]

King Is·land island off the northwestern coast of Tasmania, Australia. It is known for its dairy produce. Population: 1,689 (2002 estimate). Area: 424 sq. mi./1,098 sq. km.

King James Bi·ble, **King James Ver·sion** *n* a version of the Bible published in England in 1611 and authorized by James I for use in the Church of England

king·let /kínglət/ *n* **1.** a small gray bird that has a black-edged yellow or reddish crown and feeds on insects. Native to: North America. Genus: *Regulus*. **2.** a minor king, especially of a contemptibly small or unimportant kingdom (*insult*)

king·ly /kínglee/ (**-li·er, -li·est**) *adj* **1.** stately and grand, as befits a king ○ *a kingly posture* **2.** having or relating to the rank of king ○ *kingly duties* —**king·li·ness** *n*

king mack·er·el *n US* a mackerel often caught for sport. Native to: warm Atlantic waters. Latin name: *Scomber cavalla*.

king·mak·er /kíng màykər/ *n* somebody with the power and connections to influence who is appointed to important positions, usually within a government

King·man /kíngmən/ city in northwestern Arizona, east of Bullhead City. Population: 22,092 (2002 estimate).

king-of-arms (*plural* **kings-of-arms**) *n UK* each of the principal heralds in the British colleges of arms

king of kings, **King of Kings** *n* **1.** in Christianity, God or Jesus Christ **2.** a male monarch who rules over other, subordinate kings

king of the hill *n US* a game in which a child stands on a piece of high ground and keeps other children from taking it over

King Peak mountain in the St. Elias Range of southwestern Yukon Territory, Canada. Height: 16,972 ft./5,173 m.

king pen·guin *n* a large penguin. Native to: Antarctic. Latin name: *Aptenodytes patagonica*.

king·pin /kíng pìn/ *n* **1.** LEADER the most important person in a group or place (*informal*) **2.** PART OF AXLE a pivot pin that secures an axle to an axle beam and allows a vehicle to be steered **3.** FRONT PIN IN BOWLING the pin at the apex of a layout of the pins in bowling, which must be struck at a specific angle if all the pins are to be knocked down

king post *n* a vertical post that joins the apex of a triangular roof truss to the crossbeam

Kings /kingz/ *n* either of two books of the Bible that relate the histories of Israel and the kings of Judah (*takes a singular verb*) See table at **Bible**

king salm·on *n* FISH same as **Chinook salmon**

King's Bench *n UK* a division of the High Court of Justice in England (*used when the reigning monarch is a man or boy*)

Kings Can·yon /kingz-/ canyon in central Australia, near Alice Springs in the Northern Territory

Kings Can·yon Na·tion·al Park national park in the Sierra Nevadas in east central California. Its main features are deep canyons, the Kings River, and a grove of giant sequoia trees. Area: 722 sq. mi./1,869 sq. km.

King's Coun·sel *n UK* a senior barrister in England (*used when the reigning monarch is a man or boy*)

King's Daught·ers *npl* a group of young, single women who, from 1663 and 1673, emigrated to Quebec at the behest of Louis XIV to marry French soldiers garrisoned there. Regarded as founding mothers of French culture in Canada, the young women were trained by nuns in domestic skills and were given the right of interviewing prospective husbands and refusing marriage proposals.

King's Eng·lish *n* standard written or spoken English, especially British English, considered as the most correct form of the language (*used when the reigning monarch is a man or boy*)

King's ev·i·dence *n* in English law, evidence for the prosecution given by somebody who took part in a crime, usually in exchange for leniency (*used when the reigning monarch is a man or boy*)

king-size, **king-sized** *adj* **1.** EXTRA BIG larger, wider, or longer than the standard version of the same thing **2.** FULL-SIZE describes an extra-large size of bed, 76 in. x 80 in., or bedding made to fit this size of bed **3.** VERY GREAT very great in intensity, scope, or difficulty (*informal*) ○ *a king-size job to finish this weekend*

King's Lynn /kìngz lín/ historic town in Norfolk, eastern England. Population: 41,281 (1991).

king snake *n* a nonpoisonous constricting snake that ranges from 2 ft./0.6 m to 6 ft./1.8 m in length and preys on small animals and other snakes. Native to: North America. Genus: *Lampropeltis*.

king's ran·som *n* an enormous sum of money

King·ston /kíngstən/ **1.** largest city, chief seaport, and capital of Jamaica, situated on the southeastern coast of the island at the foot of the Blue Mountains. Population: 538,100 (1995). **2.** city on Lake Ontario, at the mouth of the St. Lawrence River, in southeastern Ontario Province, Canada. Population: 108,158 (2001). **3.** city in eastern New York, on the Hudson River, in the Catskill Mountain foothills. Population: 23,347 (2002 estimate).

King·ston-up·on-Hull ➧ **Hull** (sense 1)

Kings·town /kíngz tòwn/ capital and principal port of St. Vincent and the Grenadines, on the southwestern coast of St. Vincent Island. It is the site of the oldest botanical garden in the western hemisphere, established in 1763. Population: 16,130 (1995).

King·wa·na /kìng waánə/ *n* a Bantu language related to Kiswahili, spoken in the Democratic Republic of the Congo and widely used as a lingua franca —**King·wa·na** *adj*

king·wood /kíng wòod/ *n* **1.** a hard fine-grained purplish wood. Use: cabinetwork. **2.** the leguminous tree that yields kingwood. Native to: Brazil. Latin name: *Dalbergia cearensis*.

ki·nin /kínin/ *n* **1.** a polypeptide that causes dilation in blood vessels and contraction of smooth muscle **2.** BIOCHEM same as **cytokinin** [Mid-20C. Origin ?]

kink /kingk/ *n* **1.** TIGHT COIL a tight twist or coil in an otherwise straight section of something such as rope, string, or wire **2.** MINOR DIFFICULTY a slight difficulty or holdup in the progress of something (*informal*) **3.** MUSCULAR SPASM a sudden spasm in a muscle, especially a crick in the neck (*informal*) **4.** ECCENTRICITY something that is eccentric or peculiar in somebody's personality or behavior **5.** *US* ODD IDEA a quirky odd idea or impulse (*informal*) ○ *She got a kink in her head to swim across the Chesapeake Bay alone.* **6.** SEXUAL ODDITY an unusual sexual practice, especially one that might be considered deviant (*slang*) ■ *vti* (**kinked, kink·ing, kinks**) MAKE OR BECOME TWISTED to put a kink in something, or develop a kink [Late 17C. < Low German *kinke* "twist in a rope"]

kink·a·jou /kíngkə jòo/ (*plural* **-jous** or *same*) *n* a tree-dwelling fruit-eating mammal related to the raccoon that has a long prehensile tail, brownish fur, and large eyes. Native to: Central and South America. Latin name: *Potos flavus*. [Late 18C. Via French *quincajou* "wolverine" probably < a blend of Montagnais *kwa:hkwa:če:w* and Ojibwa *gwiingwa'aage*]

kink·y /kíngkee/ (**-i·er, -i·est**) *adj* **1.** SEXUALLY DEVIANT being or engaging in unusual sexual practices that may be considered deviant (*slang*) **2.** SEXUALLY PROVOCATIVE intended to be provocative or sexually alluring, usually by being deliberately unusual or bizarre (*slang*) **3.** ECCENTRIC behaving in an unusual, idiosyncratic way (*informal*) **4.** TIGHTLY COILED full of tight coils ○ *kinky copper wire* —**kink·i·ly** *adv* —**kink·i·ness** *n*

kin·ni·kin·nick /kìnnikə ník/ *n* **1.** a mixture of dried leaves, bark, and sometimes tobacco, formerly smoked by some Native Americans **2.** a plant used for making kinnikinnick, e.g., sumac or dogwood [Late 18C. < Unami *kələkkəníkkan* "receptacle for mixing"]

ki·no /keénō/ (*plural* **-nos**) *n* a red substance resembling resin, obtained by tapping several unrelated tropical trees. Use: locally, as an astringent and in tanning. [Early 19C. < a W African language, related to Mandingo *keno*, type of gum]

Ki·no /keénō/, **Eusebio Francisco** (1645–1711) Italian Jesuit missionary and explorer. He explored and mapped parts of Mexico and what is now the southwestern United States.

kin se·lec·tion *n* natural selection that favors self-sacrificing behavior toward relatives because, even if the individual dies, those relatives that survive will carry some of its genes

Kin·sey /kínzee/, **Alfred** (1894–1956) US biologist. He is best known for his studies of male (1948) and female (1953) sexuality (the *Kinsey Reports*). Full name **Kinsey, Alfred Charles**

kins·folk /kínz fōk/ *npl* somebody's relatives

Kin·sha·sa /kin shaássə/ capital of the Democratic Republic of the Congo, situated on the southern bank of the Congo River. Population: 4,655,313 (1994). Former name **Léopoldville** (until 1966)

kin·ship /kín shìp/ *n* **1.** relationship by blood or marriage to another or others **2.** relationship through common characteristics or a common origin ○ *kinship between Italic and Celtic languages*

kins·man /kínzmən/ (*plural* **-men** /-mən/) *n* a man or boy who is somebody's relative [12C. < Old English *cynnes* "kin's"]

Kin·ston /kínstən/ city in North Carolina, near the Atlantic Ocean. Population: 23,238 (2002 estimate).

kins·wom·an /kínz wòommən/ (*plural* **-wom·en** /-wìmmin/) *n* a woman or girl who is somebody's relative [14C. After KINSMAN]

Kin·tyre /kin tír/ peninsula of western Scotland, between the Firth of Clyde and the Atlantic Ocean. The Mull of Kintyre is its southernmost tip. Length: 40 mi./64 km.

ki·osk /keé òsk, kee ósk/ *n* **1.** SMALL ROOFED STREET BOOTH a small permanent or temporary structure on a sidewalk that sells items such as newspapers and candy **2.** SMALL STRUCTURE FOR ADVERTISING a cylindrical structure that stands at an intersection of walkways or sidewalks or on the street, used to post advertisements and announcements of events **3.** SW ASIAN GAZEBO formerly in Southwest Asia, a small open pavilion, especially in a garden [Early 17C. Via French < Turkish *köşk* "villa" < Persian *kūšk* "villa, palace"]

Ki·o·wa /kí ə wàw, -ə waá/ (*plural same* or **-was**) *n* **1.** a member of a Native North American people who lived in Montana. Most Kiowa now live on a reservation in Oklahoma, which they share with a community of Kiowa Apache. **2.** the language of the Kiowa people, related to Tanoan [Early 19C. < American Spanish *Caygua* < Kiowa *kygú* (plural)] —**Ki·o·wa** *adj*

Ki·o·wa A·pach·e *n* a member of a Native North American people who lived with the Kiowa people on the southern Great Plains, sharing a history and culture, but speaking a different language —**Ki·o·wa A·pach·e** *adj*

kip[1] /kip/ *UK n* **1.** SLEEP a sleep or a nap (*informal*) **2.** BED a bed or other place to sleep (*slang*) ■ *vi* (**kipped, kip·ping, kips**) TAKE NAP to sleep or take a nap, often in a makeshift bed (*informal*) [Mid-18C. < Danish *kippe* "cheap inn"]

kip[2] /kip/ *n* a unit of weight equivalent to 1,000 lb./455 kg [Early 20C. Contraction < KILO- + POUND[2]]

kip[3] /kip/ (*plural same*) *n* the main unit of currency of Laos. See table at **currency** [Mid-20C. < Thai]

kip[4] /kip/ *n* a hide taken from an immature animal, especially a calf or a lamb [14C. < Middle Dutch or Middle Low German, "bundle (of hides)"]

Kip·ling /kíppling/, **Rudyard** (1865–1936) British writer and poet. His books, many with Indian settings, include *The Jungle Books* (1894, 1895) and *Kim* (1901). He won the Nobel Prize in literature (1907).

> "Oh, East is East, and West is West, and never the twain shall meet / Till Earth and Sky stand presently at God's great Judgment Seat..."
> [Rudyard Kipling, "The Ballads of East and West"; 1892]

> "The Devil whoops, as he whooped of old: 'It's clever, but is it Art?'"
> [Rudyard Kipling, "The Conundrum of the Workshops"; 1892]

kip·pa /kì paá/ (*plural* **-pot** /-pót/ or **-poth** /-pót/) *n* the skullcap worn by Jewish men and boys for prayer and by Orthodox Jewish men at all times [Mid-20C. < modern Hebrew *kippāh*]

kip·per /kíppər/ *n* **1.** SMOKED HERRING a fish, usually a herring, that has been cleaned, split open, and then salted and smoked **2.** SALMON a male salmon during the spawning season ■ *vt* (**-pered, -per·ing, -pers**)

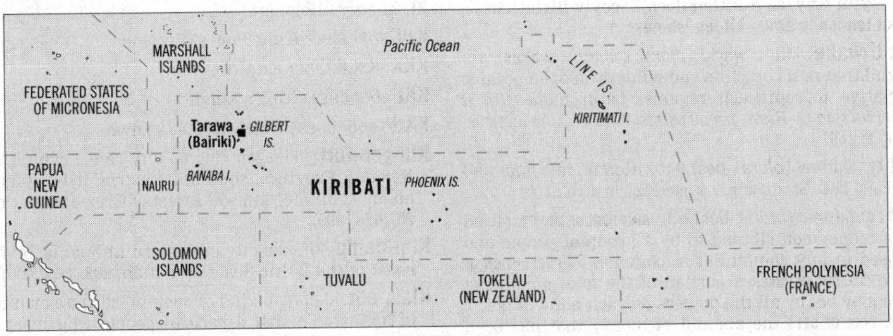

Kiribati

SMOKE FISH to cure fresh fish, especially herring, by salting and smoking it (*usually passive*) [Old English *cypera* "spawning salmon," origin ?] —**kip·per·er** *n*

kip·pot, kip·poth JUDAISM, CLOTHING plural of **kippa**

kir /keer/, **Kir** *n* an alcoholic drink made by adding cassis to dry white wine [Mid-20C. After Canon Félix *Kir* (1876–1968), mayor of Dijon, France]

Kirch·hoff /ke͡er kàwf, kírk hàwf/, **Gustav** (1824–87) German physicist. With Robert Bunsen, he invented spectroscopy and discovered cesium and rubidium (1860). He formulated Kirchhoff's laws of electrical networks. Full name **Kirchhoff, Gustav Robert**

Kirch·ner /ke͡erknər/, **Nestor** (*b.* 1950) president of Argentina (2003–). A lawyer by training, he was governor of Santa Cruz until becoming president by default when former president Carlos Menem withdrew on the eve of the election.

Kir·ghiz, Kir·giz *n, adj* PEOPLES, LANG another spelling of **Kyrgyz**

Ki·ri·ba·ti /ke͡erə ba͡atee/ independent state in the west central Pacific Ocean, part of Micronesia. It became an independent member of the British Commonwealth in 1979. Language: English. Currency: Australian dollar. Capital: Tarawa. Population: 98,594 (2003). Area: 313 sq. mi./811 sq. km. Official name **Republic of Kiribati**

kir·i·ga·mi /ke͡eri ga͡amee/ *n* the art of folding and cutting paper into ornamental shapes [< Japanese < *kiri* "cut" + *gami* "paper"]

Kir·i·ti·ma·ti /kìrrətee ma͡atee/ island forming part of Kiribati Republic. It is the largest atoll in the Pacific Ocean. Population: 2,537 (1990). Area: 235 sq. mi./609 sq. km.

kirk /kurk/ *n Scotland* same as **church** [12C. < Old Norse *kirkja* < Old English *cir(i)ce* (see CHURCH)]

Kirk *n Scotland* the Church of Scotland, the largest presbyterian church in Scotland

Kirk·land Lake /kùrklənd-/ town in northern Ontario, Canada, a former gold mining center

Kirk·wall /kúrk wàwl/ capital and largest town of the Orkney Islands, northeastern Scotland, on the northern coast of Mainland Island. Population: 6,469 (1991).

Kir·li·an pho·tog·ra·phy /ke͡erlee ən-/ *n* a photographic process that records the radiation emitted by, or the aura surrounding, an object in a high-frequency electric field [Late 20C. After Semyon D. *Kirlian* 1900–80 and Valentina K. *Kirlian* d. 1971, Russian technicians]

Kir·man /keer ma͡an/ *n* a Persian carpet or rug of a type characterized by soft colors and naturalistic designs [Late 19C. After a province in Iran]

kir·mess *n* LEISURE, HIST same as **kermis**

Ki·rov /ke͡e ràwf/ city in northeastern European Russia, capital of Kirov Oblast. Population: 633,395 (1995). Former name **Vyatka** (1780–1934)

Ki·ro·vo·hrad /ki rṓvə hràd/ city in central Ukraine, situated southeast of Kiev. Population: 270,000 (1998).

kirsch /keersh/, **kirsch·was·ser** /ke͡ersh va͡assər/ *n* a clear brandy distilled from black cherries, especially in Germany and France [Early 19C. < German, shortening of *Kirschwasser* "cherry-water" < *Kirsche* "cherry" < assumed Vulgar Latin *cerasia*]

kir·tle /kúrt'l/ *n* **1.** a long gown or skirt worn by women from the Middle Ages to the 17th century **2.** a long tunic or coat worn by men until the 16th century [Old English *cyrtel* "short coat" < Germanic < Latin *curtus* "short, cut short"]

Ki·ru·na /ke͡erə na͡a/ city in Norrbotten County, northern Sweden, a region rich in high-quality iron ore. Population: 26,217 (1994).

Ki·run·di /ki ro͝ondee/ *n* a Bantu language that is the official language of Burundi —**Ki·run·di** *adj*

Ki·san·ga·ni /ke͡e ssaan ga͡anee/ capital of Orientale Region, in the northern Democratic Republic of the Congo. Population: 417,517 (1994).

Kish·i·nev /kíshi nèf/ former name for **Chişinău**

kish·ke /kíshkə/ *n* a Jewish dish consisting of a chicken's or cow's intestine stuffed with flour meal, onion, and fat, and then boiled and roasted [Mid-20C. < Yiddish < Slavic]

kis·ka·dee /kískə de͡e/, **kes·ka·dee** *n* a bird of the flycatcher family that has a yellow breast and a black head with a white stripe. Native to: tropical America. Family: Tyrannidae. [Late 19C. An imitation of its call]

Kis·ka Is·land /kískə-/ island in the Aleutian Islands, southwestern Alaska, the largest and westernmost of the Rat Islands. Area: 110 sq. mi./285 sq. km.

Kis·lev /kísslәf/ *n* in the Jewish calendar, the ninth month of the religious year, lasting either 29 or 30 days and falling about the same time as November to December. See table at **calendar** [< Hebrew *Kislēw*]

kis·met /kíz mèt, -mət/ *n* **1.** fate or destiny **2.** in Islam, the will of Allah [Mid-19C. Via Turkish < Persian *ķismat* < Arabic *ķisma(t)* "lot, portion" < *ķasama* "he divided"]

kiss /kiss/ *v* (**kissed, kiss·ing, kiss·es**) **1.** *vti* CARESS WITH LIPS to touch somebody or something with the lips, either gently or passionately **2.** *vti* TOUCH BALL GENTLY in cue games, to come into very light contact while passing each other, or touch another ball gently while passing it (*refers to balls*) **3.** *vt US* SIDESWIPE SOMETHING to clip or brush against an object while in a moving vehicle (*informal*) **4.** *vt* TOUCH SOMETHING GENTLY to touch or brush against something lightly (*usually passive*) ○ *oranges kissed by the California sun* ■ *n* **1.** CARESS DONE WITH LIPS a gentle or passionate touch with the lips **2.** GENTLE PASSING TOUCH a very light, almost imperceptible touch in passing ○ *She felt the kiss of the evening breeze on her skin.* **3.** FOOD SMALL PIECE OF CANDY a very small piece of soft candy, sometimes individually wrapped in foil [Old English *cyssan* (verb) < *coss* (noun) < Germanic] —**kiss·a·ble** *adj* ◇ **the kiss of death** something that is certain to destroy or ruin something

kiss off *v* (*slang*) **1.** *vt* REJECT SOMEBODY OR SOMETHING to reject somebody or something abruptly ○ *The boss kissed off that idea fast.* **2.** *vt* BE FORCED TO YIELD SOMETHING to be compelled to give something up ○ *We had to kiss the trip off for lack of money.* **3.** *vi* GO AWAY to leave immediately or leave somebody alone

kiss up to *vt* to try to please or win the favor of somebody by behaving in an obsequious or sycophantic manner (*slang*)

kiss and tell *n* a book, article, or broadcast interview in which the author or interviewee publicly relates past sexual intimacy with somebody

kiss-and-tell *adj* revealing an earlier sexual experience with somebody else, especially when the information, considered to be confidential, is made public (*informal*)

kiss curl *n UK* same as **spit curl**

kiss·er /kíssər/ *n* **1.** somebody who kisses ○ *not much of a kisser* **2.** somebody's mouth (*slang*)

Kis·sim·mee /kíssi me͡e/ river in central Florida that runs south into Lake Okeechobee. Length: 140 mi./225 km.

kiss·ing ball /kíssing bàwl/ *n US* mistletoe arranged in a ball shape, decorated with ribbons, and hung, e.g., in a hall or doorway during the Christmas season

kiss·ing bug *n* same as **conenose**

kiss·ing cous·in *n* **1.** somebody who is distantly related but can be kissed on meeting **2.** something closely related in kind to something else ○ *XML and its kissing cousin HTML*

kiss·ing dis·ease *n* same as **infectious mononucleosis** (*informal*)

Kis·sin·ger /kíssinjər/, **Henry** (*b.* 1923) German-born US secretary of state (1973–77). National security adviser and then secretary of state under US presidents Nixon and Ford, he helped to negotiate an end to the Vietnam War, for which he shared the Nobel Peace Prize (1973). His shuttle diplomacy was aimed at bringing peace between Israel and the Arab states. Full name **Kissinger, Henry Alfred**

> "The conventional army loses if it does not win. The guerrilla wins if he does not lose."
> [Henry Kissinger, "The Vietnam Negotiations," *Foreign Affairs*; January 1969]

kiss of death *n* something or somebody whose presence will bring failure or disaster to something [< the Bible passage (Mark 14:44–46) in which Judas kissed Jesus Christ, thereby betraying him]

kiss of life *n* (*informal*) **1.** mouth-to-mouth resuscitation **2.** something that revives or restores an enterprise or, less commonly, somebody's spirits

kiss of peace *n* a gesture, usually either a kiss or handshake, used as a sign of Christian fellowship during Communion

kist *n* ARCHAEOL another spelling of **cist**

Ki·su·mu /ki so͞omoo/ city in southwestern Kenya, on Lake Victoria, a port and capital of Nyanza Province. Population: 185,100 (1989).

Ki·swa·hi·li /ke͡e swaa he͡elee/ *n* the Bantu national language of Tanzania and Kenya, widely used in Uganda, the Democratic Republic of the Congo, and neighboring countries. Native speakers: 2 million. Other speakers: 20 million. [Mid-19C. < Bantu < *ki-*, prefix + *Swahili* (see SWAHILI)] —**Ki·swa·hi·li** *adj*

kit /kit/ *n* **1.** SET OF THINGS FOR USE TOGETHER a set of articles, tools, or equipment used for a particular purpose **2.** CONTAINER FOR SET the container for a set of things ○ *a sewing kit* **3.** SPECIAL CLOTHING AND EQUIPMENT a special set of clothing and equipment assembled for a member of the armed forces or a sportsperson **4.** SET OF PARTS FOR ASSEMBLING a set of parts ready to be put together ○ *a model of a fire engine made from a kit* [14C. < Dutch *kitte* "tankard, jug"]

kit out *vt UK* to provide somebody with the clothes, and sometimes also the equipment, needed to do something

Ki·ta·kyu·shu /ke͡etaa kyo͞oshoo/, **Ki·ta·kyū·shū** industrial city at the northern tip of Kyushu Island, in Fukuoka Prefecture, Japan. Population: 999,806 (2002).

Ki·ta·sa·to Shi·ba·sa·bu·ro /ke͡e taa sa͡atō she͡e baassə bo͡orō/ (1852–1931) Japanese bacteriologist. He isolated the bacteria that cause tetanus, anthrax, dysentery, and bubonic plague.

kit bag *n* a canvas bag, usually cylindrical, for holding military gear, or a similar bag used by civilians, carried on the shoulder

kitch·en /kíchən/ *n* a room or part of a room or building in which food is prepared and cooked [Pre-12C. < Latin *coquina* < *coquere* "to cook"]

kitch·en cab·i·net *n* an informal unelected group of advisers to a head of government who are often believed to have more influence than the official cabinet

Kitch·e·ner /kíchənər/ industrial city located southwest of Toronto in southern Ontario, Canada. Population: 387,319 (2001).

Kitch·e·ner, Herbert, 1st Baron Kitchener of Khartoum and 1st Earl of Broome (1850–1916) British field marshal and politician. After successful campaigns in Sudan and South Africa, he became Britain's war secretary during World War I (1914–16). He was lost with HMS *Hampshire*, mined near the Orkney

Islands. Full name **Kitchener, Horatio Herbert**. Known as **Lord Kitchener**

kitch·en·ette /kìchə nét/ *n* a very small room, or part of another room, equipped and furnished as a kitchen

kitch·en gar·den *n* a garden in which vegetables, herbs, and sometimes fruit are grown for the use of a household

kitch·en mid·den *n* an area of an archaeological site that contains domestic refuse such as food waste, broken pottery, and pieces of other household artefacts, indicating long-term human occupation

kitch·en po·lice *npl US* enlisted soldiers assigned to work in a kitchen, usually as a punishment

kitch·en-sink *adj* describes a type of drama, or less commonly a type of novel or movie, that deals with the tribulations of domestic life in an unglamorous way

kitch·en·ware /kíchən wèr/ *n* utensils used in the kitchen, including pots and pans, mixing bowls, cutting boards, knives, spoons, and gadgets

kite /kīt/ *n* **1. TOY FOR FLYING** a light framework covered in a thin light material, flown for fun in the wind at the end of a long string **2. SMALL HAWK** a small slim hawk with long pointed wings and a forked tail. Family: Accipitridae. **3. LIGHT SAIL** a light sail used in addition to a sailing ship's standard sails **4. FAKE FINANCIAL TRANSACTION** a negotiable bill, e.g., a check, that is fraudulently used to sustain credit by representing a fictitious monetary transaction (*slang*) **5. BAD CHECK** a check that is fraudulently written against an account containing insufficient funds and dated so as to allow the perpetrator to take advantage of the time lag required for clearing ■ *v* **(kit·ed, kit·ing, kites) 1.** *vti* **PASS BAD CHECKS** to write and pass bad checks in order to sustain credit on a temporary basis, all the time using to advantage the period between writing them and their clearing (*slang*) **2.** *vi* **GLIDE AS IF FLYING** to glide and soar like a kite ■ *n* **LIGHTWEIGHT SAIL FOR KITEBOARDERS AND KITESURFERS** a large, often crescent-shaped, wind-catching device, like a large toy kite or a small parachute, with a harness, used by participants in kiteboarding or kitesurfing to provide propulsion and lift [< Old English *cȳta* "kite (bird)," ultimately an imitation of its call] —**kit·er** *n* ◇ **fly a kite** (*slang*) **1.** to do something or speak about something in order to test public opinion on it **2.** to issue a fraudulent financial document such as a check without having enough funds to cover it ◇ **high as a kite** (*informal*) **1.** extremely excited or elated **2.** extremely intoxicated or drug-affected

kite·board·ing /kīt bàwrding/ *n* **1.** a sport in which the participants ride on skateboards or snowboards with a kite attached to their bodies to give propulsion and lift **2.** EXTREME SPORTS same as **kitesurfing** —**kite·board·er** *n*

kite·surf·ing /kīt sùrfing/ *n* a water sport in which the participants ride on surfboards with a kite attached to their bodies to give propulsion and lift —**kite·surf·er** *n*

kit fox *n* a small slender fox that has large ears. Native to: western United States. Latin name: *Vulpes macrotis*. [Early 19C. Origin ?]

kith /kith/ *n* somebody's friends and acquaintances (*dated; takes a plural verb*) [14C. < Old English *cȳþ(þ)* "knowledge, friends" < Germanic] ◇ **kith and kin** somebody's friends and relatives

ki·tha·ra *n* MUSIC another spelling of **cithara**

Kit·i·mat /kíttə màt/ town and seaport on Douglas Channel in western British Columbia, Canada. Population: 10,233 (2001).

kitsch /kich/ *n* **1.** sentimentality, tastelessness, or ostentation in any of the arts ○ *The book jackets were pure kitsch.* **2.** collectively, decorative items that are regarded as tasteless, sentimental, or ostentatious in style ○ *tourist shops full of kitsch* [Early 20C. < German < *kitschen* "throw together"] —**kitsch·y** *adj*

kit·ten /kítt'n/ *n* the young of a cat ■ *vi* **(-tened, -ten·ing, -tens)** to give birth to young cats [14C. < Old French *chitoun*, diminutive of *chat* "cat"] ◇ **have kittens** to become angry, excited, or nervous about something (*informal*)

kit·ten heel *n* (*usually pl*) **1.** a low heel on a woman's shoe **2.** a woman's shoe with a low heel

kit·ten·ish /kítt'nish/ *adj* **1.** behaving in a lively and playful way, as a kitten does **2.** coyly flirtatious —**kit·ten·ish·ly** *adv* —**kit·ten·ish·ness** *n*

kit·ti·wake /kíttee wàyk/ (*plural same* or **-wakes**) *n* a gull that nests on cliffs and winters on open oceans. Native to: northern regions. Latin name: *Rissa tridactyla* or *Rissa brevirostris*. [Mid-17C. An imitation of its call]

kit·ty[1] /kíttee/ (*plural* **-ties**) *n* a kitten or cat (*informal*) [Early 18C. Shortening and alteration of KITTEN]

kit·ty[2] /kíttee/ (*plural* **-ties**) *n* **1. JOINT POOL OF MONEY** a fund of money contributed to by a group of people and used to buy something in common **2. PROPORTION OF OVERALL POT IN POKER** a portion of the total amount of money bet by all the players on each hand of poker **3. POOL OF BETS** the amount of money that has been bet by the players in a game **4.** *US* CARDS same as **widow** *n* (sense 4) [Early 19C. Originally "prison." Origin ?]

kit·ty-cor·nered, kit·ty-cor·ner *adv, adj* same as **cater-cornered**

Kit·ty Hawk /kíttee hàwk/ town in northeastern North Carolina, on the Atlantic Ocean. On nearby Kill Devil Hill, the Wright brothers engaged in successful glider and airplane experiments between 1900 and 1903. It is the site of the Wright Brothers National Memorial. Population: 3,171 (2002 estimate).

Ki·twe /kée twày/ copper-mining city in north central Zambia, north of Lusaka. Population: 338,207 (1990).

ki·va /kéevə/ *n* an underground or partly underground chamber, usually with a hole at the top that lets in daylight, used by the men in a Pueblo community for ceremonial or formal meetings [Late 19C. < Hopi *kíva*]

Ki·vu, Lake /kéevoo/ freshwater lake in the Great Rift Valley of Africa, between western Rwanda and the eastern Democratic Republic of the Congo. Area: 1,040 sq. mi./2,700 sq. km.

Ki·wa·nis /ki wáaniss/ *npl* a North American-based association of men's clubs that encourages community service

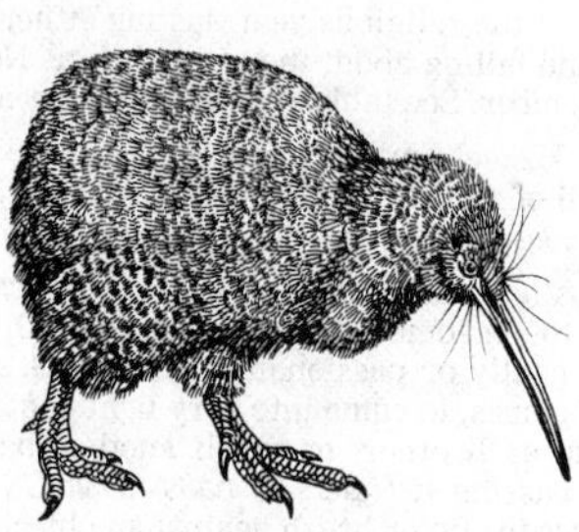

kiwi

ki·wi /kéewee/ *n* (*plural same* or **-wis**) **1. FLIGHTLESS BIRD** a nocturnal flightless bird with a long slender beak and shaggy feathers. Native to: New Zealand. Genus: *Apteryx*. **2.** *also* **Ki·wi SOMEBODY FROM NEW ZEALAND** somebody who comes from New Zealand (*informal*) **3.** FOOD same as **kiwi fruit 4. CHINESE VINE WITH EDIBLE FRUIT** a vine that produces kiwi fruit. Native to: China. Latin name: *Actinidia chinensis*. ■ *adj* **OF NEW ZEALAND** relating to New Zealand or its people (*informal*) [Mid-19C. < Maori, an imitation of the bird's call]

kiwi fruit

ki·wi fruit *n* the fruit of the kiwi plant, which has a greenish brown fuzzy skin and sweet green pulp

kj, kJ *abbr* kilojoule

KJV *abbr* BIBLE King James' Version

KKK, K.K.K. *abbr* Ku Klux Klan

KKt *abbr* CHESS king's knight

KKtP *abbr* CHESS king's knight's pawn

Kla·gen·furt /kláagən fòort/ city and capital of Kärnten Province, southern Austria. It is situated about 62 mi./100 km southwest of Graz. Population: 90,765 (1999).

Klai·pe·da /klīpidə/ city in western Lithuania, on the coast of the Baltic Sea. Population: 202,480 (2000).

Klam·ath /klámməth/ (*plural same* or **-aths**) *n* a member of a Native North American people who lived in Oregon and northern California, in part of the Cascade Range [Early 19C. < Chinook *Łámaƚ*] —**Klam·ath** *adj*

Klam·ath River /klàmməth-/ river in the states of Oregon and California, flowing from Upper Klamath Lake into the Pacific Ocean. Length: 250 mi./400 km.

Klan /klan/ *n* POL same as **Ku Klux Klan** (*informal*) —**Klan·ism** *n*

Klans·man /klánzmən/ (*plural* **-men** /-mən/) *n* a member of the Ku Klux Klan, especially a man

Klans·wom·an /klánz wòomən/ (*plural* **-wom·en** /-wìmmin/) *n* a woman who is a member of the Ku Klux Klan

klatch /klach/ *n regional* same as **coffee klatch**

REGIONAL NOTE ***Klatch*** and its fuller forms *coffee klatch* and *kaffeeklatsch* are fairly widespread, but centered in German settlements of the Upper Midwest and the western Great Lakes regions.

klav·ern /klávvərn/ *n* a local unit of the Ku Klux Klan [Early 20C. Blend of KLAN + CAVERN]

Klax·on /kláksən/ *tdmk* a trademark for a loud electric horn

Klee /klay/, **Paul** (1879–1940) Swiss painter. His imaginative and often witty works, some inspired by children's paintings and drawings, had a great influence on modern art.

> "Art does not reproduce the visible; rather, it makes visible."
> [Paul Klee, "Creative Credo (1920)," *Inward Vision*; 1958]

Kleen·ex /klée nèks/ *tdmk* a trademark for a soft facial tissue

Klein /klīn/, **A. M.** (1909–72) Canadian poet and novelist. His works are concerned with Jewish culture and history. Full name **Klein, Abraham Moses**

Calvin Klein

Klein, Calvin (*b.* 1942) US fashion designer. After establishing his own company in 1968, he became known for his understated sophisticated designs. Full name **Klein, Calvin Richard**

Klein, Melanie (1882–1960) Austrian psychoanalyst. She pioneered studies in child psychoanalysis using free-play therapy. She moved to England in 1926.

Klein bot·tle /klīn-/ *n* a one-sided surface formed by inserting the small open end of a tapered tube through the side of the tube and upward until it is contiguous with the larger end [Mid-20C. After Felix *Klein* (1849–1925), German mathematician]

Klem·per·er /klémpərər/, **Otto** (1885–1973) German conductor. Noted for his interpretations of Beethoven, Mozart, and Mahler, he moved to the United States in 1933, where he conducted the Los Angeles Symphony Orchestra. From 1959, he conducted the Philharmonia Orchestra of London.

klepht /kleft/ *n* any of the Greeks who resisted Turkish rule in Greece from 1456 to 1832 and who lived in the mountains as outlaws and brigands [Early 19C. < modern Greek *klephtēs* "thief," later form of Greek *kleptēs*] —**kleph·tic** *adj*

klep·to·ma·ni·ac /klèptə máynee àk/ *n* somebody with an obsessive urge to steal, especially when there is no economic necessity —**klep·to·ma·ni·a** *n* —**klep·to·ma·ni·a·cal** /klèptəmə nī́ ək'l/ *adj*

Klerk ♦ **de Klerk, F. W.**

klez·mer /klézmər/ *n* a traditional style of Jewish ensemble music with roots in Eastern Europe that features vocals and various instruments, especially the violin and the clarinet. It has had an influence on American popular music. [Mid-20C. Via Yiddish < Hebrew *kĕlēy zemer* "musical instruments"]

klick /klik/ *n* same as **kilometer** (*informal*) [Mid-20C. Origin ?]

klieg light /kleég-/ *n* a powerful carbon-arc light formerly used in making movies [Early 20C. After John H. *Kliegl* (1869–1959) and Anton T. *Kliegl* (1872–1927), German-born US inventors]

Klimt /klimt/, **Gustav** (1862–1918) Austrian painter. Founder of the Vienna Secession school of painting (1897), he created richly decorated portraits of women.

Kline /klīn/, **Franz** (1910–62) US artist. He is known for his abstract expressionist paintings, which consist of large black forms on a white background. Full name **Kline, Franz Josef**

klip·spring·er /klíp sprìngər/ *n* a small agile antelope with large ears. Native to: mountainous regions of Africa. Latin name: *Oreotragus oreotragus*. [Late 18C. < Afrikaans, "cliff-springer"]

Klon·dike /klón dīk/ region of northwestern Yukon Territory, Canada, named for the Klondike River, which traverses it. After 1897, it was the site of a decade-long gold rush in which 30,000 prospectors streamed into the area. Gold was mined there until the mid-1960s.

Klu·a·ne Na·tion·al Park Re·serve /kloo áanee-/ national park in southwestern Yukon Territory, Canada. It includes Canada's highest peak, Mt. Logan. Area: 8,494 sq. mi./22,000 sq. km.

kludge /klooj/, **kluge** (*slang*) *n* a makeshift combination of hardware and software put together to solve a computing problem that is effective but not suitable for manufacture ■ *vt* (**kludged, kludg·ing, kludges; kluged, klug·ing, kluges**) to solve a computing problem using a makeshift combination of hardware and software [Mid-20C. After BOTCH, FUDGE] —**kludg·y** *adj*

klutz /kluts/ *n* (*slang insult*) **1.** an offensive term that deliberately insults somebody's physical coordination or social skills **2.** an offensive term that deliberately insults somebody's intelligence [Mid-20C. Via Yiddish *klots* "wooden beam" < German *Klotz* "clod"] —**klutz·i·ness** *n* —**klutz·y** *adj*

kly·stron /klī́ stròn/ *n* an electron tube that uses an electric field to generate and amplify microwaves [Mid-20C. < Greek *klus-*, stem of *kluzein* "wash over"]

km *abbr* **1.** ONLINE Comoros (*used in Internet addresses*) See table at **domain name 2.** kilometer

K-mes·on *n* PHYS same as **kaon**

km/h, **kmph** *abbr* kilometers per hour

kmps *abbr* kilometers per second

kn, **kn.** *abbr* **1.** NAUT knot **2.** MONEY krona **3.** MONEY krone **4.** ONLINE St. Kitts and Nevis. (*used in Internet addresses*) See table at **domain name**

KN *abbr* CHESS king's knight

knack /nak/ *n* **1.** an easy and smart way of doing something or handling a problem ○ *I can't get the knack of this software.* **2.** a particular skill, especially one that might be innate or intuitive and therefore difficult to teach ○ *You certainly have a knack with children.* [14C. Origin ?]

SYNONYMS See *talent*.

knack·er /nákər/ *UK n* **1.** SOMEBODY WHO KILLS HORSES somebody who buys and slaughters old, worn-out, or injured horses for their body parts such as their flesh and hide **2.** DEMOLITION MERCHANT somebody who buys and demolishes unwanted buildings and sells their materials for scrap ■ *vt* TIRE SOMEBODY OUT to exhaust somebody completely (*slang*) [Early 19C. Originally "saddler, harness maker," origin ?] —**knack·ered** *adj*

knack·wurst /naák wùrst, -wòorst/, **knock·wurst** /nók-/ *n* a spicy smoked European sausage similar to a frankfurter but shorter and thicker [Mid-20C. < German, "crack-sausage" (because its skin cracks open when bitten) < *knacken* "to crack"]

knap /nap/ (**knapped, knap·ping, knaps**) *vt* to chisel or hammer something such as a stone so that it breaks into flakes [15C. Probably < Low German or Dutch *knappen* "to crack," an imitation of the sound of breaking stone] —**knap·per** *n*

knap·sack /náp sàk/ *n* a cloth or leather bag with shoulder straps, designed for carrying personal items and supplies on a hiker's back [Early 17C. < Low German < *knappen* "bite, eat" + *Sack* "sack"]

knapweed

knap·weed /náp weèd/ (*plural* **-weeds** or *same*) *n* a thistle plant. Flowers: purple, grouped in a head. Native to: Europe, Asia. Latin name: *Centaurea nigra*. [Early 16C. Alteration of *knopweed* < variant of KNOB; from the shape of its cluster of flowers]

knar /naar/ *n* a knot on a tree or in wood [13C. Origin ?] —**knarred** *adj* —**knarr·y** *adj*

knave /nayv/ *n* **1.** a man who is considered dishonest and deceitful (*archaic*) **2.** a man who works as a servant (*archaic*) **3.** CARDS same as **jack**[1] *n* (sense 2) [Old English *cnafa* "boy, male servant" < Germanic] —**knav·er·y** *n* —**knav·ish** *adj* —**knav·ish·ly** *adv* —**knav·ish·ness** *n*

knead /need/ (**knead·ed, knead·ing, kneads**) *v* **1.** *vti* WORK DOUGH UNTIL SMOOTH to fold, press, and stretch a soft substance such as dough or clay, working it into a smooth uniform mass **2.** *vt* MASSAGE MUSCLES to rub, squeeze, or press a part of the body with the hands, e.g., in order to relax the muscles **3.** *vt* SHAPE SOMETHING WITH HANDS to make or shape something out of a soft substance by kneading it [Old English *cnedan* < W Germanic] —**knead·a·ble** *adj* —**knead·er** *n*

USAGE knead or **need**? Do not confuse the spelling of ***knead*** and ***need***, which sound similar. ***Knead*** is a verb meaning "to work dough" or "to massage muscles." ***Need***, the more frequent of the two words, is a verb or noun referring to something that is required: *I need your help. There's no need to panic.*

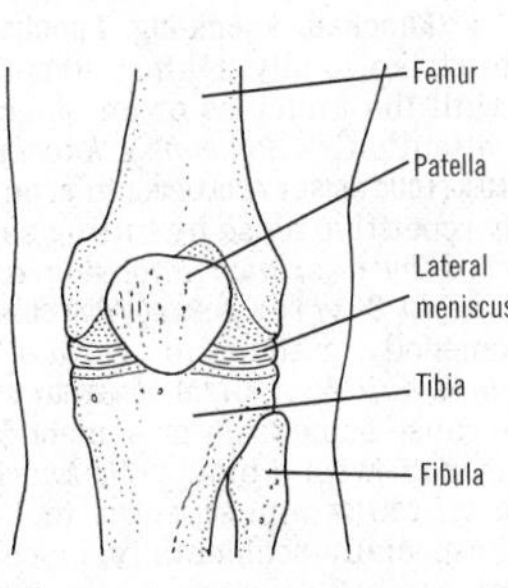

knee

knee /nee/ *n* **1.** MIDDLE JOINT OF HUMAN LEG the joint of the human leg between the thigh and the lower leg, where the femur and the tibia meet, covered in front by the kneecap (**patella**) **2.** AREA AROUND KNEE JOINT the general area surrounding the knee joint **3.** UPPER LEG the upper surface of the thigh of somebody sitting down ○ *Come and sit on my knee.* **4.** PART OF CLOTHING the part of a piece of clothing, especially pants, that fits around the knee **5.** LEG JOINT IN ANIMALS the joint between the upper and lower parts of the hind legs in four-legged vertebrates and of the legs in birds **6.** GROWTH FROM ROOT a woody outgrowth from the roots of some trees that grow in saturated soils or standing water, which protrudes above the surface and enables them to breathe **7.** OBJECT LIKE KNEE something that resembles the human knee, e.g., a bent pipe ■ *vt* (**kneed, knee·ing, knees**) HIT SOMEBODY WITH KNEE to strike somebody with the uplifted knee [Old English *cnēow* < Indo-European, "to bend"] ◇ **bring somebody to his** *or* **her knees** to reduce somebody to a state of abject weakness and vulnerability, or force somebody to admit defeat

knee ac·tion *n* front-wheel suspension in an automobile that allows each wheel to move independently in a vertical direction

knee breech·es *npl* CLOTHING same as **breeches** (sense 1)

knee·cap /neé kàp/ *n* **1.** a flat triangular bone located at the front of the knee. It protects the knee joint. Technical name **patella 2.** same as **kneepad** ■ *vt* (**-capped, -cap·ping, -caps**) to shoot somebody deliberately in the knees as a punishment, in order to cause lasting difficulty in standing or walking (*informal*)

knee-deep *adj* **1.** IN AS HIGH AS KNEES standing or sunk in something that reaches up to the knees ○ *be knee-deep in mud* **2.** AS HIGH AS KNEES reaching up to the knees ○ *The river was only knee-deep.* **3.** EXTREMELY INVOLVED IN SOMETHING completely occupied by or entangled in something ○ *knee-deep in paperwork*

knee-high *adj* reaching up to the knees ■ *n* a sock or stocking that comes up as high as the knee

knee·hole /neé hōl/ *n* a hole made for the knees in a desk or other piece of furniture

knee jerk *n* an involuntary contraction of the thigh muscle that produces a sudden extension of the leg, usually in response to a light rap on the tendon below the kneecap

knee-jerk *adj* (*informal*) **1.** given or occurring immediately and automatically, without thought, and usually expressing habitual attitude or prejudice ○ *a knee-jerk opinion* **2.** tending to respond in a predictable and often unthinking way to a situation ○ *a knee-jerk political hack*

kneel /neel/ (**knelt** /nelt/ or **kneeled, kneel·ing, kneels**) *vi* to rest on, or get down on, one or both knees [Old English *cnēowlian* < *cnēow* (see KNEE)]

knee-length *adj* reaching up to or down to the knee ○ *a knee-length skirt* ○ *knee-length boots*

kneel·er /neélər/ *n* CHR, FURNITURE, GARDENING same as **hassock** (sense 2)

knee·pad /neé pàd/ *n* a covering that protects the knee from injury, especially during sports

knee·pan /neé pàn/ *n* ANAT same as **kneecap** *n* (sense 1)

knee sock *n* a sock that reaches to the knee

knell /nel/ *n* **1.** SLOW BELL RING the sound of a bell rung slowly, associated with solemnity or mourning, used to announce a death or funeral **2.** OMINOUS SIGNAL something that signals death, disaster, or the end of something (*literary*) ■ *v* (**knelled, knell·ing, knells**) **1.** *vti* RING BELL to ring a bell slowly, or produce a slow ringing sound, especially as a sign of mourning or to announce a death or funeral **2.** *vt* SIGNAL SOMETHING OMINOUS to announce or signal something such as a death, disaster, or the end of something (*literary*) [Old English *cnyll* < *cnyllan* "to strike" < Indo-European]

knelt past participle, past tense of **kneel**

Knes·set /knéssət/, **Knes·seth** *n* the parliamentary legislature of Israel. It has one legislative chamber with supreme authority. [Mid-20C. < Hebrew, "gathering"]

knew past tense of **know**

Knick·er·bock·er /níkər bòkər/ *n US* **1.** somebody descended from the early Dutch settlers of New York **2.** somebody who comes from the state of New York (*informal*) [Early 19C. After Diedrich *Knickerbocker*, fictitious author of Washington Irving's *History of New York*]

knick·er·bock·ers /níkər bòkərz/ *npl* loose-fitting short breeches gathered at or just below the knee [Mid-19C. Origin ?]

knick·ers /níkərz/ *npl* **1.** CLOTHING same as **knickerbockers 2.** *UK* women's or girl's underpants [Late 19C. Shortening of KNICKERBOCKERS]

knick·knack /ník nàk/, **nick·nack** *n* a small decorative ornament or object [Late 16C. < reduplication of KNACK]

knick·point /ník pòynt/ *n* a point along a river's length at which it suddenly begins to flow in a steeper course [Early 20C. Partial translation of German *Knickpunkt* < *Knick* "bend" + *Punkt* "point"]

knife /nīf/ *n* (*plural* **knives** /nīvz/) **1.** TOOL FOR CUTTING a tool, usually with a sharp blade and a handle, used for cutting, slicing, or spreading **2.** STABBING WEAPON a knife with a handle and a sharpened blade specifically made to be a weapon ■ *v* (**knifed, knif·ing, knifes**) **1.** *vt* STAB SOMEBODY to stab or cut somebody with a knife **2.** *vi* MOVE WITH SWIFT SMOOTH MOTION to move quickly, forcefully, and cleanly through something ○ *The hawk knifed through the air.* [Old English *cnīf* < Germanic] —**knife·like** *adj* —**knif·er** *n* ◇ **twist** *or* **turn the knife (in the wound)** to try to make a difficult or painful situation even worse for somebody ◇ **under the knife** undergoing surgery (*informal*)

knife-edge *n* **1.** CRITICAL TIME IN SITUATION a decisive and precarious point at which a situation is finely balanced between different possibilities or outcomes ○ *with the future of the project on a knife-edge* **2.** KNIFE'S CUTTING EDGE the cutting edge of the blade of a knife **3.** OBJECT LIKE EDGE OF KNIFE an object that is sharp, thin, and narrow **4.** TECH FULCRUM FOR PRECISE INSTRUMENT a metal wedge whose narrow edge is used as a fulcrum for a scale beam or a lever in a precision instrument

knife·point /nīf pòynt/ ◇ **at knifepoint** while being threatened with a knife

knight /nīt/ *n* **1.** HIST MEDIEVAL SOLDIER OF HIGH RANK in late medieval Europe, a noble in the military, promoted by the king after serving as a page and squire **2.** HIST MEDIEVAL MOUNTED SOLDIER OF LOW RANK in early medieval Europe, a tenant of a feudal lord who was required to serve as a soldier on horseback **3.** POL MAN WITH TITLE "SIR" a man who holds a nonhereditary title conferred by a ruler for personal achievement or public service. A British knight has the title "Sir" before his name. **4.** MEMBER OF BROTHERHOOD a man who belongs to a special group or organization, especially a religious or secret brotherhood **5.** CHAMPION OF CAUSE a fervent supporter or defender of a cause or belief **6.** PROTECTOR OF WOMAN a man who is protective of and devoted to a woman **7.** CHESS HORSE'S HEAD CHESS PIECE a chess piece shaped like a horse's head that moves two squares horizontally and one vertically or two vertically and one horizontally. Symbol **N** ■ *vt* (**knight·ed, knight·ing, knights**) MAKE MAN KNIGHT to bestow a knighthood on a man [Old English *cniht* "boy, male attendant" < Germanic] ◇ **a knight in shining armor** a man who gallantly comes to the rescue of somebody in danger or difficulty

knight bach·e·lor (*plural* **knights bach·e·lors** or **knights bach·e·lor**) *n* a British knight who is not a member of a specific order of knighthood

knight-er·rant (*plural* **knights-er·rant**) *n* **1.** a medieval knight who traveled around looking for adventure **2.** a man preoccupied with ideas of adventure and romance —**knight-er·rant·ry** *n*

knight·head /nīt hèd/ *n* either of two upright timbers supporting the inner end of the bowsprit of a sailing ship, to which mooring cables or ropes are sometimes attached [Early 18C. Because it often had a carving of a man's head]

knight·hood /nīt hŏŏd/ *n* **1.** POSITION OF KNIGHT the rank, title, or occupation of a knight **2.** CHIVALRY AND HONOR the qualities of chivalry, bravery, and honor, thought to be characteristic of a knight **3.** KNIGHTS knights considered as a group

knight·ly /nītlee/ (**-li·er, -li·est**) *adj* relating to knights, or characteristic of a knight, especially in being noble and chivalrous —**knight·li·ness** *n*

Knight of Co·lum·bus *n* a member of a benevolent and fraternal organization of Roman Catholic men, founded in 1882 [Late 19C. After Christopher COLUMBUS]

Knight of Pyth·i·as /-píthee əss/ *n* a member of a benevolent and fraternal organization for men, founded in the 1860s [After a man from Syracuse in the 4C B.C. who, according to legend, was sentenced to death, bailed by his friend Damon who was to be executed in his place, returned just in time to prevent this, and was then reprieved]

Knight of the Mac·ca·bees *n* a member of a benevolent organization, founded in Canada in 1878

Knights of the Round Ta·ble *npl* an order of knights said to have been created by King Arthur that figures prominently in Arthurian legends and chivalric poems [Because the knights sat at a round table, where no one could be seated in a position of superiority]

Knight Tem·plar (*plural* **Knights Tem·plar**) *n* **1.** a member of a Christian military order that was founded in Jerusalem in 1119 to protect pilgrims after the First Crusade of 1096. The order grew wealthy and influential from banking activities before being suppressed by the pope in 1312. **2.** a member of a Masonic order in the United States

knish /kə nísh/ *n* a piece of dough filled with meat, cheese, or potato and eaten as a snack or appetizer, especially in Jewish-American cooking [Mid-20C. Via Yiddish < Russian]

knit /nit/ *v* (**knit·ted** or **knit, knit·ting, knits**) **1.** *vti* INTERLOCK YARN LOOPS to interlock loops of yarn, using either long needles or a machine, or make a garment or other item by this method **2.** *vti* USE PLAIN STITCH to use a basic plain stitch that forms a flat vertical loop on the front of a piece of knitting ○ *Knit one, purl one.* **3.** *vti* UNITE to bring people or things together in a close association, or come together in this way **4.** *vi* MED BECOME HEALED to grow together again after a fracture (*refers to a bone*) **5.** *vti* BRING BROWS CLOSER TOGETHER to draw the brows together in a frown, or be drawn together in a frown ■ *n* **1.** SOMETHING MADE BY KNITTING a knitted garment or fabric **2.** WAY OF KNITTING a method or style of knitting a garment or fabric **3.** PLAIN STITCH a basic knitting stitch that forms a flat vertical loop on the front of something being knitted [Old English *cnyttan* "tie in knots" < Germanic] —**knit·ta·ble** *adj* —**knit·ter** *n*

SPELLCHECK knit or **nit**? Do not confuse the spelling of ***knit*** and ***nit***, which sound similar. ***Knit*** is chiefly used as a verb, meaning "to interlock loops of yarn" or "to join" or "to bring together," as in *knit a scarf, when the bones have knitted together, knitting his brow.* ***Knit*** is also occasionally used as a noun, referring to something knitted. The word ***nit*** is only used as a noun denoting an egg of a louse, or as an offensive term.

---

knit·ting /nítting/ *n* **1.** the act or process of making knitted items or fabric by hand-held needles or by machine **2.** an item that is in the process of being knitted

knit·ting nee·dle *n* a long slim rod with a dull point, used in pairs in knitting

knit·wear /nít wèr/ *n* garments made from knitted fabric

knives plural of **knife**

knob /nob/ *n* **1.** ROUNDED HANDLE OR DIAL a rounded projecting part attached to a door, drawer, appliance, or other object, used as a handle or a dial or switch **2.** ROUNDED PROJECTION any rounded lump or part projecting from the surface of something **3.** HILL a rounded hill [14C. < Middle Low German *knobbe* "knot, knob, bud"] —**knobbed** *adj*

knob·by /nóbbee/ (**-bi·er, -bi·est**) *adj* having small hard rounded parts sticking out from the surface [Mid-17C. < *knobbe* "small knob" < KNOB]

knob·ker·rie /nób kèrree/, **knob·stick** /nób stìk/ *n* a short wooden stick with a knob at one end, used by some South African peoples as a weapon [Mid-19C. < KNOB + *kierie* "club" (< Nama), after Afrikaans *knopkierie*]

knock /nok/ *v* (**knocked, knock·ing, knocks**) **1.** *vi* HIT REPEATEDLY to strike loudly against something such as a door with the knuckles or an object in order to attract attention ○ *Someone's knocking at the door.* **2.** *vi* MAKE LOUD NOISE BY COLLIDING to produce a loud and usually repetitive noise by hitting something ○ *was disturbed by a branch knocking against the window all night* **3.** *vt* DEAL SOMEBODY OR SOMETHING BLOW to strike somebody or something with a hard blow ○ *knocked in a nail* **4.** *vt* AFFECT SOMEBODY OR SOMETHING WITH BLOW to cause something or somebody to be in a particular state with a blow ○ *He knocked me off balance.* **5.** *vti* COLLIDE WITH SOMETHING to hit against something, especially accidentally, or cause something to hit against something else ○ *The glass broke when I knocked it against the table.* **6.** *vt* MAKE SOMETHING BY STRIKING to produce something, especially a hole, by means of repeated blows ○ *knocked a hole in the partition* **7.** *vt* CRITICIZE SOMEBODY OR SOMETHING to criticize or find fault with somebody or something (*slang*) ○ *Don't knock it until you've tried it.* **8.** *vi* AUTOMOT PRODUCE REPEATED RAPPING SOUND to make a regular rapping noise that is usually caused by faulty fuel combustion (*refers to a vehicle or its engine*) **9.** *vi* CARDS END CARD GAME to end a game, especially gin rummy, by striking the table before laying down a hand in which those cards not in sets total less than a specific amount ■ *n* **1.** BLOW OR COLLISION a blow struck against somebody or something, or a collision with somebody or something **2.** SOUND OF KNOCKING the sound made by a person or object hitting something, especially repeatedly **3.** BAD EXPERIENCE a painful, damaging, or distressing experience (*informal*) **4.** CRITICISM a disparaging or critical comment about somebody or something (*slang*) **5.** AUTOMOT REPEATED RAPPING SOUND IN ENGINE a regular rapping noise made by an engine, usually caused by faulty fuel combustion [Old English *cnocian*, ultimately an imitation of the sound] ◇ **knock it off** used to demand that somebody stop doing or saying something (*slang*) ◇ **knock somebody dead** to amaze and delight somebody with the quality of a performance (*informal*)

knock about *v* same as **knock around**

knock around *v* (*informal*) **1.** *vt* BEAT SOMEBODY to abuse somebody physically **2.** *vti* TRAVEL AROUND to travel to different places, or to different places within an area, especially without a specific itinerary **3.** *vi* HAVE RELAXING TIME to relax by doing nothing in particular **4.** *vi* SPEND TIME to spend time habitually in the company of somebody **5.** *vt* DISCUSS SOMETHING SPECULATIVELY to discuss something casually in order to hear different views **6.** *vt* KICK BALL AROUND to kick, hit, or throw a ball in an informal game

knock back *vt* (*informal*) **1.** to drink something, especially alcohol, very quickly **2.** to cost somebody a large amount of money ○ *The repairs knocked me back $500.*

knock down *vt* **1.** MAKE SOMEBODY OR SOMETHING FALL to cause somebody or something to fall to the ground by striking or pushing **2.** DISMANTLE SOMETHING to take something apart for shipping or storage **3.** PRONOUNCE SOMETHING SOLD to show that something has been sold at an auction by striking a surface with a gavel **4.** CUT PRICE OF SOMETHING to reduce the price of something (*informal*) ○ *furniture knocked down by 50%* **5.** MAKE SOMEBODY CUT PRICE to persuade somebody to reduce the price of something ○ *He wanted $75 but I knocked him down to $60.* **6.** *US* FIN EARN to earn a particular amount of money as salary or wages (*informal*) **7.** BASKETBALL MAKE BASKET in basketball, to score a basket (*informal*)

knock off *v* **1.** *vti* STOP WORKING to finish work at the end of the day, or stop working or doing something in order to take a break (*informal*) **2.** *vt* CUT PRICE to decrease the price of something by a particular amount **3.** *vt* DEDUCT AMOUNT OR POINTS to deduct something from something, especially an amount from a price or a number of points from a score or total **4.** *vt* PRODUCE SOMETHING WITH EASE OR SPEED to make or deal with something easily and quickly (*informal*) ○ *knocks off six or seven articles a month* **5.** *vt* CRIME KILL SOMEBODY to kill somebody, especially intentionally (*slang*) **6.** *vt* CRIME ROB PLACE to rob a bank, store, or other business (*slang*) **7.** *vt* COMM MAKE CHEAP COPY OF PRODUCT to produce a inexpensive, sometimes illegal copy of a well-known product (*slang*) **8.** *vt* PLAGIARIZE SOMETHING to copy somebody else's work (*slang*)

knock out *vt* **1.** DEFEAT OPPOSING BOXER WITH PUNCH in boxing, to knock an opponent down for a count of ten, thus winning the match **2.** MAKE SOMEBODY UNCONSCIOUS BY HITTING to cause somebody to lose consciousness by striking him or her **3.** STUPEFY SOMEBODY WITH DRUGS OR ALCOHOL to cause somebody to lose consciousness or fall asleep by means of drugs or alcohol **4.** ELIMINATE OPPONENT FROM TOURNAMENT to eliminate an opponent or team from a competition by winning a match or game **5.** MAKE SOMETHING USELESS to destroy something, or make something inoperable ○ *The storm knocked out our electricity.* **6.** TIRE SOMEBODY OUT to exhaust somebody completely (*informal*) **7.** PRODUCE SOMETHING WITH EASE OR SPEED to make or do something easily or quickly (*informal*) **8.** BASEBALL REPLACE PITCHER to cause a baseball pitcher's removal from a game by getting several hits **9.** PLEASE OR IMPRESS SOMEBODY GREATLY to overwhelm somebody with excitement or pleasure (*informal*) ○ *That music really knocks me out.*

knock over *vt* (*informal*) **1.** to overwhelm somebody with amazement or shock **2.** to rob a bank, store, or other business

knock together *vt* to make something quickly, without much preparation, and often with little care (*informal*)

knock up *vt* an offensive term meaning to make a woman pregnant (*slang*)

knock·a·bout /nókə bòwt/ *n* **1.** SMALL SAILBOAT a small sailboat with a mainsail, jib, and keel but no bowsprit **2.** *UK* INFORMAL GAME an informal ball game, especially an informal game of soccer (*informal*) ■ *adj* **1.** USING SLAPSTICK characterized by boisterous physical activity **2.** STURDY AND INFORMAL suitable for rough or casual activities

knock·down /nók dòwn/ *n* **1.** OVERWHELMING BLOW a powerful emotional or physical blow **2.** PRICE DROP a reduction in the price of something **3.** EASILY DISASSEMBLED OBJECT something that is made so that it can be taken apart easily, e.g., a piece of furniture ■ *adj* **1.** VERY POWERFUL having an overwhelmingly powerful or very damaging effect ○ *a knockdown blow* **2.** EASILY DISASSEMBLED made to be taken apart easily **3.** DISCOUNTED for sale at a reduced or very low price ○ *a knockdown price*

knock·down-drag·out /-drág òwt/, **knock-down-drag-out** *adj* fought violently or argued bitterly and without mercy —**knock·down-drag·out** *n*

knock·er /nókər/ *n* **1.** FIXTURE FOR KNOCKING ON DOOR a metal fixture attached with hinges to the door of a house, used for knocking on the door **2.** CRITIC a carping or unfair critic (*informal*) ■ **knock·ers** *npl* OFFENSIVE TERM an offensive term for a woman's breasts (*slang*)

knock-knee *n* a condition in which the legs are permanently bent so that the knees are close together and the ankles are spread far apart ■ **knock-knees** *npl* the knees of somebody with knock-knee —**knock-kneed** *adj*

knock·off /nók àwf, -òf/ *n* an inexpensive, sometimes illegal copy of a piece of well-known or popular merchandise (*informal*)

knock-on *n* in rugby, an illegal use of the hand or arm to move the ball forward

knock·out /nók òwt/ *n* **1.** PUNCH WINNING BOXING MATCH in boxing, a punch that knocks an opponent down for a count of ten and so wins a contest **2.** BLOW CAUSING UNCONSCIOUSNESS a blow that knocks somebody unconscious **3.** WIN BY KNOCKOUT a victory in a boxing match by a knockout **4.** SOMEBODY OR SOMETHING STUNNING somebody or something extremely attractive, good-looking, or enjoyable (*informal*)

knock·out drops *npl* a solution, usually containing chloral hydrate, secretly put in a drink to render the drinker unconscious (*informal*)

knock·wurst *n* FOOD same as **knackwurst**

~~**knoledge**~~ incorrect spelling of **knowledge**

knoll[1] /nōl/ *n* a small rounded hill or mound [Old English *cnoll* < Germanic] —**knoll·y** *adj*

knoll[2] /nōl/ *n, vti* (**knolled, knoll·ing, knolls**) same as **knell** (*archaic*) [14C. Ultimately < Germanic]

knop /nop/ *n* a small decorative knob [14C. < Middle Low German or Middle Dutch *knoppe* "knob, knot"] —**knopped** *adj*

Knos·sos /nóssəss, knóssəss/ ruined city in northern Crete, the center of the Minoan civilization from about 3000 B.C. to 1100 B.C.

knot[1] /not/ *n* **1.** OBJECT MADE BY TYING a usually hard, lump-shaped object formed when a strand of something such as string or rope is interlaced with itself or another strand and pulled tight **2.** WAY OF TYING a way of joining or securing lengths of rope, thread, or other strands by tying the material together or around itself **3.** TANGLED MASS a tightly tangled mass of strands that are hard to separate **4.** TIGHT GROUP a number of people or things grouped closely together **5.** TENSE FEELING a feeling of tightness or anxiety ○ *a knot in my stomach* **6.** CLOSE EMOTIONAL TIE a deep bond, especially marriage **7.** DECORATION a piece of material such as ribbon or braid tied in a knot or bow and used as a decoration **8.** PROBLEM a difficult or complex problem **9.** LUMP ON TREE a lump on a tree trunk or branch **10.** HARD PATCH ON TREE a hard patch on a tree out of which a branch or stem grows **11.** WOODWORK DARK WHORL IN LUMBER a hard dark colored patch in cut wood at a point where a branch or stem formerly grew out of the tree **12.** MED LUMP IN BODY a node, ganglion, lump, or swelling in the body **13.** MEASURE UNIT OF SPEED a unit of measurement for the speed at which a ship or aircraft travels, equivalent to one nautical mile per hour, approximately 1.15 statute mph/1.85 kph. Symbol **kn** **14.** NAUT INDICATOR MEASURING SHIP'S SPEED a division on a log line used for calculating the speed of a ship **15.** NAUT, MEASURE same as **nautical mile** ■ *v* (**knot·ted, knot·ting, knots**) **1.** *vti* MAKE KNOT to tie something in a knot, or be tied with a knot **2.** *vti* ENTANGLE to tangle something, or become tangled **3.** *vt* MAKE SOMETHING WITH PATTERN OF KNOTS to produce something such as a piece of macramé that consists of a pattern of decorative knots **4.** *vti* BECOME TENSE to become tight or tense with anxiety or fear, or cause something to become so ○ *My stomach knotted up.* [Old English *cnotta* < Germanic, "round lump"] —**knot·ter** *n* ◇ **tie somebody (up) in knots** to confuse somebody completely, especially in trying to explain something ◇ **tie the knot** to get married (*informal*)

USAGE knot or **not**? Do not confuse the spelling of ***knot*** and ***not***, which sound similar. ***Knot*** is a verb or noun referring to the tying of rope, thread, etc.; as a noun it also denotes a round patch on wood, a measure of speed, or a tight group of people. ***Not*** is an adverb used to form a negative: *I hope not. Not all children like ice cream.*

knot[2] /not/ *n* a small migratory sandpiper. Native to: Arctic. Latin name: *Calidris canutus* or *Calidris tenuirostris*. [15C. Origin ?]

knot gar·den *n* an herb or flower garden that has its plants arranged in an intricate pattern and sometimes also has trees and bushes trimmed in decorative designs

knot·grass /nót gràss/ (*plural* **-grass·es** or *same*) *n* a creeping plant with small pink flowers and prominent nodes on its stems, considered a troublesome weed. Native to: Europe. Latin name: *Polygonum aviculare*. [Early 16C. < its knotted stem]

knot·hole /nót hōl/ *n* a hole in wood where a knot has fallen out or been removed

knot·ted /nóttəd/ *adj* **1.** tied in a knot, tangled up in knots, or made using decorative knots **2.** WOODWORK same as **knotty** (sense 2) **3.** BOT describes a plant that has stems with swellings resembling knots

knot·ty /nóttee/ (**-ti·er, -ti·est**) *adj* **1.** PUZZLING OR COMPLEX very difficult to understand or solve **2.** MARKED WITH KNOTS used to describe wood that contains or is marked with many knots **3.** FULL OF KNOTS full of tied or tangled knots —**knot·ti·ly** *adv* —**knot·ti·ness** *n*

knot·ty pine *n* pine wood that has many knots in it. Use: paneling, furniture.

knot·weed /nót wèed/ (*plural* **-weeds** or *same*) *n* PLANTS same as **knotgrass**

knout /nowt/ *n* a leather whip used for flogging ■ *vt* (**knout·ed, knout·ing, knouts**) to flog somebody using a knout [Mid-17C. Via French < Russian *knut* < Old Norse *knútr* "knot"]

know /nō/ (**knew** /noo/, **known** /nōn/, **know·ing, knows**) *v* **1.** *vti* HOLD INFORMATION IN MIND to have information firmly in the mind or committed to memory ○ *They know the names of all the US presidents.* **2.** *vti* BE CERTAIN ABOUT SOMETHING to believe firmly in the truth or certainty of something ○ *I know she wouldn't be late without a good reason.* **3.** *vti* REALIZE SOMETHING to be or become aware of something ○ *I didn't know you cared.* **4.** *vt* COMPREHEND SOMETHING to have a thorough understanding of something through experience or study ○ *know computers* **5.** *vt* HAVE ENCOUNTERED SOMEBODY OR SOMETHING BEFORE to be acquainted, associated, or familiar with somebody or something ○ *I have known John for years.* **6.** *vt* RECOGNIZE DIFFERENCES to be able to perceive the differences or distinctions between things or people ○ *old enough to know right from wrong* **7.** *vt* IDENTIFY SOMEBODY OR SOMETHING BY CHARACTERISTIC to recognize somebody or something by a distinguishing characteristic or attribute ○ *I'd know him anywhere by his peculiar laugh.* **8.** *vt* HAVE SEX WITH SOMEBODY to engage in sexual intercourse with somebody (*archaic*) [Old English *cnāwan* < Indo-European] —**know·a·ble** *adj* —**know·er** *n* ◇ **in the know** possessing information that is secret or known only to a small group of people ◇ **know something back to front** *UK* same as **know something backward and forward** ◇ **know something backward and forward** to be completely familiar with all the details of or facts about something ◇ **know something backwards** *UK* same as **know something backward and forward** ◇ **not know where to put yourself** to feel acutely embarrassed (*informal*) ◇ **you know** used to fill a pause, add emphasis to a statement, or elicit a response from a listener (*informal*) ◇ **you never know** used to indicate that the outcome of events is uncertain and it is possible that something that seems unlikely could happen

SPELLCHECK know or **no**? Do not confuse the spelling of ***know*** and ***no***, which sound similar. ***Know*** is chiefly used as a verb, meaning "to have in the mind" (as in *know what to do next*), or as a noun in the phrase *in the know*. The word ***no*** indicates a negative response or a lack of something: *No, I won't! There's no coffee left in the pot.*

know-all *n UK* same as **know-it-all** (*informal*)

know-how *n* the practical skill and knowledge necessary to do something (*informal*)

know·ing /nō ing/ *adj* **1.** INDICATING PRIVATE KNOWLEDGE suggesting that somebody knows a secret or something that others are unaware of ○ *a knowing smile* **2.** ASTUTE aware of things and able to act cleverly and judge shrewdly **3.** SHOWING INTELLIGENCE having knowledge, information, or understanding **4.** INTENTIONAL done on purpose —**know·ing·ly** *adv* —**know·ing·ness** *n*

know-it-all *n* somebody who professes to know more or better than anyone else about everything (*informal*)

knowl·edg·a·ble *adj* another spelling of **knowledgeable**

knowl·edge /nóllij/ *n* **1.** INFORMATION IN MIND general awareness or possession of information, facts, ideas, truths, or principles ○ *Her knowledge and interests are extensive.* **2.** SPECIFIC INFORMATION clear awareness or explicit information, e.g., of a situation or fact ○ *I believe they have knowledge of the circumstances.* **3.** ALL THAT CAN BE KNOWN all the information, facts, truths, and principles learned throughout time ○ *With all our knowledge, we still haven't found a cure for the common cold.* **4.** LEARNING THROUGH EXPERIENCE OR STUDY familiarity or understanding gained through experience or study ○ *knowledge of nuclear physics* **5.** COMMUNICATION TRANSMISSION OF INFORMATION information services and the storage and transmission of information, especially within a large organization **6.** INTERCOURSE sexual intercourse (*archaic*) [14C. Probably < obsolete *knowledge* "acknowledge" < KNOW + Old English *-lǣcan* < *-lāc* "practice"]

SYNONYMS ***knowledge, erudition, information, learning, scholarship, wisdom***

CORE MEANING: general awareness or possession of information, facts, ideas, truths, or principles

knowledge awareness of information, either general or specific ○ *They had a lifetime of experience and involvement with primary schools, and were able to distill that lifetime's knowledge very rapidly.* **erudition** knowledge acquired through study and reading ○ *A master storyteller, he draws together elements of classical erudition.* **information** the collected facts and data about a specific subject. ○ *The organization provides the public with information about alcohol to help them make informed choices.* ○ *the increasing use of the media as a source of information* **learning** knowledge or skill gained through education ○ *A man of obvious learning with a great admiration for classical civilization.* **scholarship** academic learning or achievement ○ *a multi-volume work of scholarship that took more than a decade to complete* **wisdom** accumulated knowledge of life or of a sphere of activity that has been gained through experience ○ *We admired the wisdom she showed in refusing to agree to their requests too readily.* ○ *another health report challenging the conventional wisdom about high blood pressure*

knowl·edge·a·ble /nóllijəb'l/, **knowl·edg·a·ble** *adj* possessing or showing a great deal of knowledge, awareness, or intelligence —**knowl·edge·a·bil·i·ty** /nòllijə billətee/ *n* —**knowl·edge·a·ble·ness** *n* —**knowl·edge·a·bly** *adv*

knowl·edge base *n* **1.** the computerized data in an expert system required for solving problems in a specific area **2.** the facts required for solving problems

knowl·edge in·dus·try *n* businesses that specialize primarily in data processing or the development and use of information technology

knowl·edge man·age·ment *n* the organization of intellectual resources and information systems within a business environment

know·ledge trans·fer *n* the communication of specialized knowledge developed in part of an organization to a wider group such as another part of the organization or business customers

knowl·edge work·er *n* somebody working in an industry such as management consultancy or computer programming that produces information rather than goods

~~**knowlegable**~~ incorrect spelling of **knowledgeable**

known /nōn/ past participle of **know** ■ *adj* **1.** AC-

KNOWLEDGED generally recognized as or proven to be something ○ *a known criminal* **2.** FAMILIAR belonging to an established body of knowledge ○ *the limits of the known universe* ■ *n* CERTAINTY a fact or piece of information that is certain ○ *separate the knowns from the unknowns*

know-noth·ing *n* **1.** an ignorant or uninformed person (*often used before a noun*) **2.** a believer in the impossibility of knowing anything for certain, especially the existence of God —**know-noth·ing·ism** *n*

Know-Noth·ing *n* a member of a US political party of the 1850s that opposed the participation of immigrants and Roman Catholics in political affairs, and whose members denied knowledge of the party —**Know-Noth·ing·ism** *n*

Knox /noks/, **Henry** (1750–1806) American Revolutionary soldier. During the Revolution he commanded the American artillery. He served as Secretary of War (1785–94).

Knox, John (1513?–72) Scottish religious reformer. He was chaplain to Edward VI of England. He helped to found the Presbyterian Church of Scotland (1560), and opposed the rule of the Roman Catholic Mary, Queen of Scots.

> "A man with God is always in the majority."
> [John Knox, *Inscription on Reformation monument, Geneva, Switzerland*; 16th century]

Knox·ville /nóks vìl, -vəl/ city and county seat of Knox County in eastern Tennessee, situated on the Tennessee River, northeast of Chattanooga. It is an industrial center and home to the University of Tennessee. Population: 173,661 (2002 estimate).

Knt *abbr* CHESS knight

knuck·le /núk'l/ *n* **1.** FINGER JOINT a joint of a finger, especially a joint connecting a finger to the hand **2.** ROUNDED PROJECTION WHEN FIST IS MADE one of the rounded projections above a knuckle that appears on the back of a hand when a fist is made (*often used in the plural*) **3.** FOOD PIECE OF MEAT NEAR KNEE a cut of meat consisting of the lower joint from the hind leg of a calf, pig, or lamb **4.** MECH ENG HINGE PIVOT the cylindrical part of a hinge through which the pin passes **5.** MECH ENG same as **knuckle joint** (sense 2) ■ **knuck·les** *npl* ARMS same as **brass knuckles** ■ *v* (**-led, -ling, -les**) **1.** *vt* APPLY KNUCKLES TO SOMETHING to rub, hit, or press something with the knuckles ○ *knuckled her eyes in disbelief* **2.** *vi* LEISURE HAVE KNUCKLES ON GROUND PLAYING MARBLES to have the knuckles on the ground when shooting a marble with the thumb pressed into the bent forefinger [14C. < Middle Low German *knökel* "small bone" < Germanic] —**knuck·ly** *adj*
knuckle down *vi* to work hard and conscientiously at something (*informal*)
knuckle under *vi* to give in to force or pressure

knuck·le·ball /núk'l bàwl/ *n* in baseball, a slow pitch with little spin and an unpredictable flight, produced by releasing the ball from the knuckles and the thumb or the tips of two or three fingers —**knuck·le·ball·er** *n*

knuck·le·bone /núk'l bṓn/ *n* a knobby bone forming part of a joint in the human finger (*informal*)

knuck·le-dust·er *n UK* ARMS same as **brass knuckles**

knuck·le·head /núk'l hèd/ *n* an offensive term that deliberately insults somebody's intelligence or consideration for others (*slang insult*) —**knuck·le·head·ed** /nùk'l héddəd/ *adj*

knuck·le joint *n* **1.** a joint of the human finger **2.** a hinge with a pin that fastens the ends of two rods together, allowing movement in one plane only

knuck·ler /núklər/ *n* BASEBALL same as **knuckleball**

knuck·le sand·wich *n* a blow with the fist to the mouth (*slang*)

knur /nur/ *n* a bump or knot on a tree trunk or in wood [15C. Origin ?]

knurl /nurl/ *n* **1.** BUMP OR KNOB a small hard knob or protuberance **2.** RIDGE USED FOR GRIPPING a ridge, especially one in a series that runs along the edge of something such as a thumbscrew that makes it easier to grip ■ *vt* (**knurled, knurl·ing, knurls**) MAKE SOMETHING RIDGED to put ridges on something, especially to make it easier to grip [Early 17C. Probably < KNUR] —**knurl·y** *adj*

Knut another spelling of **Canute**

KO /kay ṓ/ (*informal*) *n* (*plural* **KO's**) a knockout, especially in boxing ■ *vt* (**KO'd, KO'ing, KO's**) to knock somebody out, especially in boxing [Early 20C. < the initial letters of *knock out*]

ko·a /kṓ ə/ (*plural* **-as** or *same*) *n* a tree with gray bark that yields a valuable reddish to yellowish brown hardwood used in furniture-making. Native to: Hawaii. Latin name: *Acacia koa*. [Early 19C. < Hawaiian]

koala

ko·a·la /kō áalə/, **ko·a·la bear** *n* a marsupial that resembles a small bear and has gray fur, a round face, and large ears. It lives in eucalyptus trees, feeding almost exclusively on their leaves. Native to: Australia. Latin name: *Phascolarctos cinereus*. [Late 18C. < Dharuk *kūl(l)a*]

ko·an /kṓ àan/ (*plural* **-ans** or *same*) *n* a Zen Buddhist riddle used to focus the mind during meditation and to develop intuitive thinking [Mid-20C. Via Japanese < Chinese *gōngàn* "official business"]

Ko·be /kṓbee, kṓ bày/, **Kō·be** capital of Hyogo Prefecture, and seaport on Osaka Bay, southern Honshu Island, Japan. Population: 1,478,380 (2002).

Ko·blenz /kṓ blènts/ city in the Rhineland-Palatinate, west central Germany, south of Bonn. Population: 109,550 (1997).

ko·bo /kṓ bō/ (*plural same* or **-bos**) *n* a subunit of Nigerian currency. See table at **currency** [Late 20C. < Nigerian English, alteration of COPPER [1]]

ko·bold /kṓ bàwld/ *n* in German folklore, a mischievous elf that lives in houses or a gnome that haunts underground places, especially mines [Mid-19C. < German, variant of *Kobalt* (see COBALT)]

Ko·buk Val·ley Na·tion·al Park /kṑ búk-/ national park located entirely north of the Arctic Circle in northwestern Alaska. Area: 2,735 sq. mi./7,085 sq. km.

Koch /kawk, kawkh/, **Robert** (1843–1910) German bacteriologist. He discovered the tuberculosis bacillus (1882) and the cholera bacillus (1883). He was awarded the Nobel Prize in physiology or medicine (1905).

Ko·dály /kō dī́/, **Zoltán** (1882–1967) Hungarian composer. His works are influenced by the folk songs he collected. He developed an influential system of music education for children.

Ko·di·ak[1] /kṓdee àk/ city in southern Alaska, on northeastern Kodiak Island, south of Anchorage. Population: 6,441 (2002 estimate).

Ko·di·ak[2] /kṓdee àk/ (*plural* **-aks** or *same*), **Ko·di·ak bear** *n* a brown bear that can grow to a very large size. Native to: coastal areas and nearby islands of Alaska and British Columbia. Latin name: *Ursus middendorffi*. [Late 19C. After KODIAK ISLAND]

Ko·di·ak Is·land /kōdee ak ī́lənd/ island in the Gulf of Alaska, southwestern Alaska, noted for its bears and marine life. Area: 3,465 sq. mi./8,974 sq. km.

Koest·ler /kúrstlər/, **Arthur** (1905–83) Hungarian-born British writer. He is best known for his novel *Darkness at Noon* (1941), which reflects his disenchantment with the Soviet Communist regime.

> "God seems to have left the receiver off the hook, and time is running out."
> [Arthur Koestler, *The Ghost in the Machine*; 1967]

Ko·et·su Hon'A·mi /ko ètsoo hō nа́amee/ (1558–1637) Japanese artist. A founder member of the revivalist Rimpa school, he was noted for his paintings, calligraphy, pottery, and patronage of the arts.

K of C *abbr US* CHR Knight of Columbus

K of P *abbr US* Knight of Pythias

ko·hen *n* JUDAISM another spelling of **cohen**

Ko·hi·ma /kō héemə/ capital of Nagaland State in northeastern India. Population: 67,200 (1991).

kohl /kōl/ *n* especially in South Asia and North Africa, a chemical preparation used by women to darken the rims of their eyelids. It usually consists of powdered antimony sulfide or lead sulfide. [Late 18C. < Arabic *kuḥl*]

Kohl /kōl/, **Helmut** (*b.* 1930) chancellor of the Federal Republic of Germany (1982–98). As Christian Democratic chancellor, he played the leading role in German reunification (1990).

> "Only through resolute commitment to the realization of European unification can we obviate a relapse into the destructive nationalism of the past."
> [Helmut Kohl, *Speech to the Bundestag, Bonn*; June 17, 1992]

> "The policy of European integration is in reality a question of war and peace in the 21st century."
> [Helmut Kohl, *Speech at Louvrain University*; February 2, 1996]

kohlrabi

kohl·ra·bi /kōl ráabee, -rábbee/ *n* **1.** (*plural* **kohl·ra·bies**) a swollen turnip-shaped stem of a plant, eaten as a vegetable **2.** a plant of the cabbage family whose swollen stems are kohlrabies. Latin name: *Brassica oleracea* var. *gongylodes*. [Early 19C. Via German < plural of Italian *cavolo rapa* < medieval Latin *caulorapa* < Latin *caulis* "cabbage" + *rapa* "turnip"]

koi /koy/ (*plural same*), **koi carp** *n* a carp with red-gold or white coloring, kept as an aquarium or ornamental pond fish. Native to: Japan, temperate regions of East Asia. Latin name: *Cyprinus carpio*. [Early 18C. < Japanese]

koi·ne /koy náy, kóynee/ *n* **1.** LANGUAGE same as **lingua franca** (sense 1) **2.** a dialect or regional variant of a language that becomes the standard language for a wider population of speakers [Late 19C. < KOINE]

Koi·ne /koy náy, kóynee/ *n* the form of Greek, mostly derived from the Attic dialect, that became the standard language for Greek-speaking people during the Hellenistic period [Late 19C. < Greek *koinē* "common"] —**Koi·ne** *adj*

Koi·zu·mi /koy zóomee/, **Junichiro** (*b.* 1942) Japanese prime minister. A member of the Liberal Democratic Party, he was elected to the Lower House in 1972 and took up ministerial office in 1988. He was elected prime minister in 2001.

ko·kan·ee /kō kánnee/ (*plural* **-ees** or *same*), **ko·kan·ee salmon** *n* a small nonmigratory sockeye salmon. Native to: landlocked lakes from western North America to Siberia and Japan. Latin name: *Oncorhynchus nerka kennerlyi*. [Late 19C. < Salish *kəknǽxʷ*]

Ko·ko·mo /kṓkə mō/ industrial city in north central Indiana, on Wildcat Creek, directly north of Indianapolis. Population: 45,956 (2002 estimate).

Ko·ko Nor /kṓkō náwr/ GEOG ➧ **Qinghai Hu**

Ko·kosch·ka /kə káwshkə/, **Oskar** (1886–1980) Austrian-born painter and writer. He is best known for his expressionist portraits and landscapes. He lived in Britain (1938–53) before settling in Switzerland.

kok-sa·ghyz /kṓksə géez/ (*plural* **kok-sa·ghyz·es**), **kok-sa·gyz** (*plural* **kok-sa·gyz·es**) *n* a dandelion with fleshy roots that are a source of rubber. Native to: central

Asia. Latin name: *Taraxacum kok-saghyz.* [< Russian *kok-sagyz* < Turkic *kök* "root" + *sagiz* "gum, resin"]

ko·ku·jo /kṓkoo jṑ/ (*plural same*) *n* in Okinawa, an offensive term for a young Okinawan woman who dates African American men who are members of the armed forces [< Japanese, perhaps < alteration of COCOA + *jo* "woman"]

ko·la *n* TREES another spelling of **cola**[1] (sense 2)

Ko·la Pen·in·su·la /kṓlə-/ peninsula in northwestern European Russia, between the Barents Sea and the White Sea. Area: 40,000 sq. mi./100,000 sq. km.

Ko·lar Gold Fields /kō laar-/ city in southern Karnataka State, southern India, near Bangalore. Population: 156,398 (1991).

Kol·ha·pur /kṓl haa poor/ city in Maharashtra State, southwestern India. Population: 497,554 (2001).

ko·lin·sky /kə línskee/ (*plural* **-skies**) *n* **1.** the dark tawny fur of a weasel **2.** a weasel whose fur is kolinsky. Native to: northern Europe and Asia. Latin name: *Mustela sibirica.* [Mid-19C. < Russian *kolinskiĭ* "of Kola" (port in NW Russia)]

Kol·ka·ta /kol káttə/ capital of Bangla State and one of India's largest cities. It is a major commercial and industrial city and port, situated on the Hoogly River, an arm of the Ganges about 60 mi./100 km from its mouth at the Bay of Bengal. Population: 4,580,544 (2001). Former name **Calcutta**

kol·khoz /kol káwz/ (*plural* **-khoz·es** or *same* or **-khoz·y** /kol káwzee/), **kol·koz** (*plural* **-koz·es** or *same* or **-koz·y**) *n* a collective farm in the former Soviet Union [Early 20C. < Russian < *kol(lektivnoe) khoz(yaĭstvo)* "collective farm"]

kol·khoz·nik /kol káwznik/ *n* a worker on a collective farm in the former Soviet Union

kol·koz *n* AGRIC another spelling of **kolkhoz**

Kol Nid·re /kōl ní dràỳ, kàwl nee dráỳ/ *n* in Judaism, the prayer recited at the opening of the service on the eve of Yom Kippur. It asks that all unfulfilled vows to God be nullified and that all transgressions be forgiven. [Late 19C. < Aramaic *kol nidrē* "all the vows," its opening words]

ko·lo /kṓlō/ (*plural* **-los**) *n* a Serbian folk dance in which one or more dancers perform inside a circle of other dancers [Late 18C. < Serbo-Croatian, "wheel"]

Ko·lon·ia /kə lṓnee ə/ largest town in the Federated States of Micronesia, and capital of Pohnpei island state. Population: 6,600 (1994).

Ko·ly·ma Range /kə leémə-/ mountain range in northeastern Siberian Russia. Length: 1,300 mi./2,100 km.

kom·a·tik /kómmətik, kō máttik/ *n* an Inuit sled with wooden crossbars tied to the runners with rawhide [Early 19C. < Inuit *qamutik*]

kom·bu /kóm bòo/ *n* a kelp sold dried. Use: in Japanese cooking. [Late 19C. < Japanese]

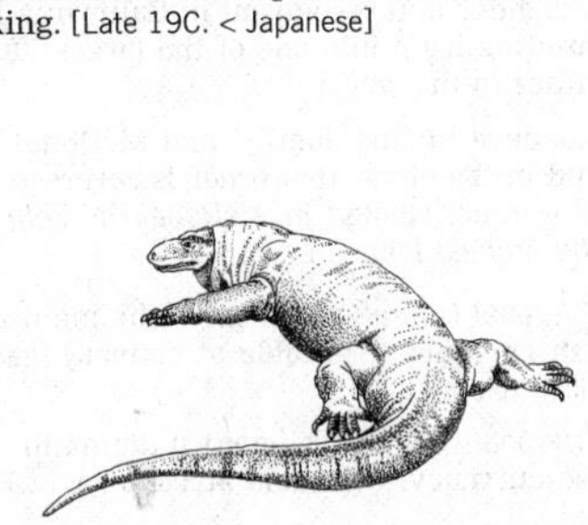

Komodo dragon

Ko·mo·do drag·on /kə mṑdō-/, **Ko·mo·do liz·ard** *n* a large monitor lizard, growing to a length of 10 ft./3 m. Native to: island of Komodo, east of Java. Latin name: *Varanus komodoensis.* [After an island east of Java]

Kom·so·mol /kómssə màwl, kòmssə máwl/ *n* a Communist organization for young people in the former Soviet Union [Mid-20C. < Russian < *Kommunisticheskiĭ Soyuz Molodëzhi* "Communist Union of Youth"]

Kom·so·molsk /kòmssə máwlsk/ city in far eastern Russia, on the Amur River. Population: 355,634 (1995).

Kon·go[1] /kóng gō/ (*plural* **-gos** or *same*) *n* **1.** a member of a people who live along the lower Congo River in west central Africa **2.** the Bantu language spoken by the Kongo people in southern Congo and northern Angola. Native speakers: 7 million. Other speakers: 2 million. [Mid-19C. < Kongo] —**Kon·go** *adj*

Kon·go[2] /kóng gō/ former kingdom in central Africa that flourished between the 14th and 16th centuries in the area between present-day Gabon and northern Angola

Kö·nigs·berg /kṓnigz bùrg/ former name for **Kaliningrad**

Kon·ka·ni /kóngkənee/ *n* a dialect of Marathi spoken in coastal Maharashtra in western India [Late 19C. < Marathi *kōkṇī*] —**Kon·ka·ni** *adj*

Koo /koo/, **Vi Kyuin Wellington** (1888–1985) Chinese and Taiwanese politician and diplomat. He represented China at the United Nations (1946), and followed the Chinese Nationalist government when it retreated to Taiwan. Born **Ku Wei-chun**

koo·doo *n* ZOOL another spelling of **kudu**

kook /kook/ *n* **1.** an offensive term for somebody whose behavior is regarded as unpleasantly eccentric (*slang insult*) **2.** a snowboarder who is a beginner or inexperienced (*slang*) [Mid-20C. Probably shortening of CUCKOO]

kookaburra

kook·a·bur·ra /kóokə bùrrə/ (*plural* **-ras** or *same*) *n* a large bird of the kingfisher family with a loud call that sounds like laughter. Native to: Australia and nearby islands. Latin name: *Dacelo novaeguineae* or *Dacelo leachii.* [Mid-19C. < Wiradhuri *gugubarra*]

kook·y /kóokee/ (**-i·er, -i·est**) *adj* an offensive term meaning thought to be unpleasantly eccentric (*slang insult*) —**kook·i·ly** *adv* —**kook·i·ness** *n*

Koo·ning ➧ **de Kooning, Willem**

Koons /koonz/, **Jeff** (*b.* 1955) US artist. He transforms everyday and often kitsch objects into works of art. His controversial *Made in Heaven* series (1989–91) deliberately challenges the boundaries between pornography and art.

Koo·te·nai *n, adj* PEOPLES, LANG another spelling of **Kutenai**

Koo·te·nay[1] /kóot'n àỳ/, **Koo·te·nai** river of the northwestern United States and southwestern Canada. It rises in the Rocky Mountains of southeastern British Columbia, flows into the United States, then reenters Canada through Kootenay Lake and joins the Columbia River. Length: 407 mi./655 km.

Koo·te·nay[2] *n, adj* PEOPLES, LANG another spelling of **Kutenai**

Koo·te·nay Na·tion·al Park national park in the Rocky Mountains of southeastern British Columbia, Canada. Area: 543 sq. mi./1,406 sq. km.

kop /kop/ *n S Africa* a prominent crest of a hill [Mid-19C. Via Afrikaans < Dutch, "head"]

ko·pek /kṓ pèk/, **ko·peck, co·peck** *n* a subunit of Russian currency. See table at **currency** [Early 17C. < Russian *kopeika*, literally "little lance"; from the figure of a tsar bearing a lance on the coin]

ko·piy·ka /kō peékə/ *n* a subunit of currency in the Ukraine. See table at **currency** [< Ukrainian]

kop·pa /kóppə/ *n* the 17th letter of the ancient Greek alphabet, later adopted by the Romans as the letter "q." See table at **alphabet** [Late 19C. < Greek]

Kor. *abbr* **1.** Korea **2.** PEOPLES, LANG Korean

Ko·ran /kə raán, kaw-/, **Qur·'an** *n* the sacred text of Islam, believed by Muslims to record the revelations of God to Muhammad [Early 17C. < Arabic *ḳur'ān* "recitation" < *ḳara'a* "recite"] —**Ko·ran·ic** /kə raánik, -ránnik, kaw-/ *adj*

Kor·do·fan /kàwrdə faán/ former province in central Sudan

Kor·do·fan·i·an /kàwrdə fánnee ən/ *n* AFRICAN LANGUAGE GROUP a small group of languages spoken in southern Sudan that may be distinct from other African languages or a branch of Niger-Congo ■ *adj* **1.** OF KORDOFANIAN relating to Kordofanian **2.** OF KORDOFAN relating to Kordofan, central Sudan

Ko·re·a /kə reé ə, kō-/ peninsula in East Asia, divided since 1948 into the Democratic People's Republic of Korea (North Korea) and the Republic of Korea (South Korea). Area: 84,868 sq. mi./219,806 sq. km.

Ko·re·a, North ➧ **North Korea**

Ko·re·a, South ➧ **South Korea**

Ko·re·an /kə reé ən/ *n* **1.** somebody who comes from North or South Korea **2.** the Altaic official language of North and South Korea, also spoken in China, Japan, and Asia of the former Soviet Union. Native speakers: 60 million. Other speakers: 60 million. —**Ko·re·an** *adj*

Ko·re·an War *n* a war that lasted from 1950 to 1953 between North Korea, and its ally China, and South Korea, supported by United Nations troops, especially from the United States

Kō·rin /kṓrin/ (1658?–1716) Japanese artist. He is known for his bird, flower, and landscape paintings.

kor·ma /káwrmə/ (*plural* **-mas**), **qor·ma** *n* in South Asian cuisine, a mildly spiced dish of meat, seafood, or vegetables cooked in a cream or yogurt sauce [Late 19C. < Urdu *ḳormā*]

Korn·berg /káwrn bùrg/, **Arthur** (*b.* 1918) US biochemist. He shared the Nobel Prize in physiology or medicine (1959) with Severo Ochoa for his research on DNA and its replication.

Ko·ror /kə ráwr/ island and administrative center of the Republic of Palau, in the western Pacific Ocean. Population: 11,552 (1997). Area: 8.1 sq. mi./21 sq. km.

ko·ru·na /káwrə naa/ (*plural* **-run** or **-ru·nas**) *n* the main unit of Czech and Slovak currency. See table at **currency** [Early 20C. < Czech, "crown"]

Kos another spelling of **Cos**

Kos·ci·usz·ko, Mount /kòssee úskō/ highest mountain in Australia, located in the Snowy Mountains in southeastern New South Wales. Height: 7,310 ft./2,228 m. Former name **Kosciusko**

Koś·ci·usz·ko /kòssee úskō/, **Thaddeus** (1746–1817) Polish soldier and revolutionary. He served with George Washington in the American Revolution, and in 1794 led a revolt for Polish independence. Born **Kościusko, Tadeusz Andrzej Bonawentura**

ko·sher /kṓshər/ *adj* **1.** RITUALLY PURE describes food that has been prepared so that it is fit and suitable under Jewish law **2.** PREPARING OR SELLING KOSHER FOOD preparing or selling foods that are fit and suitable under Jewish law **3.** LAWFUL OR PROPER allowed by law, or regarded as correct or proper (*informal*) ○ *Something's not kosher about his handling of the situation.* **4.** REAL genuine, not false or fake (*informal*) ■ *vt* (**-shered, -sher·ing, -shers**) PREPARE KOSHER FOOD to prepare food in a way that is fit and suitable under Jewish law [Mid-19C. < Hebrew *kāšēr* "fit, proper"]

Ko·so·vo /káwssə vṑ/ former autonomous province in southwestern Serbia, in the Federal Republic of Yugoslavia. The administrative center is Priština. Large numbers of the majority Albanian population were displaced by a Serbian program of ethnic cleansing. Since 1999 Kosovo has become a United Nations supervised region. Population: 1,956,196 (1991). Area: 4,203 sq. mi./10,887 sq. km. Albanian name **Kosova** —**Ko·so·van** *n, adj* —**Ko·so·var** /-vaar/ *n, adj*

Kos·suth /kóss ooth, káw shoot/, **Lajos** (1802–94) Hungarian politician and nationalist. A leader of the Hungarian Revolution (1848), he was appointed provisional governor of Hungary (1849) but was deposed shortly afterward.

Ko·suth /kóssooth/, **Joseph** (*b.* 1945) US conceptual artist. His installations such as *One and Three Chairs* (1965) challenge the aesthetic value of art and emphasize its concept and meaning.

> "Being an artist now means to question the nature of art."
> [Joseph Kosuth. Quoted in *Arte Povera*, Germano Celant; 1968]

Ko·sy·gin /kə se̅e̅gin/, **Aleksey** (1904–80) Soviet premier. In this capacity, he was chairman of the Council of Ministers of the Soviet Union (1964–80). Full name **Kosygin, Aleksey Nikolayevich**

Ko·ta Baha·ru /kṓtə baá ro͞o/ city on the northeastern coast of the Malay Peninsula, Malaysia, and capital of Kelantan State. Population: 219,582 (1996).

Ko·ta Kin·a·ba·lu /kṓtə kinəbə lo͞o/ city in eastern Malaysia. It is the capital of Sabah State, on the South China Sea. Population: 76,120 (1996). Former name **Jesselton** (until 1968)

ko·to /kṓtō/ (*plural* **-tos**) *n* a Japanese musical instrument resembling a zither, with strings stretched over a convex wooden sounding board. It is plucked using three picks worn on the thumb, index finger, and middle finger. [Late 18C. < Japanese]

Kou·fax /kṓ faks/, **Sandy** (*b.* 1935) US baseball player. He pitched for the Brooklyn (later Los Angeles) Dodgers (1955–66), and won the Cy Young Award (1963, 1965, 1966). Full name **Koufax, Sanford**

kou·miss, **kou·mis** *n* FOOD another spelling of **kumiss**

kou·prey /ko͞o prày/ (*plural* **-preys** or *same*) *n* an endangered species of wild ox with a blackish brown body and white markings on its back and feet. Native to: Cambodia, Vietnam. Latin name: *Bos sauveli*. [Mid-20C. < Khmer]

Kous·se·vitz·ky /ko͞ossə vítskee/, **Serge** (1874–1951) Russian-born US conductor. He conducted the Boston Symphony Orchestra (1924–49). Full name **Koussevitzky, Serge Alexandrovitch**

> "When my stick touches the air, you play."
> [Attributed to Serge Koussevitzky]

Kow·loon /kòw lo͞on/ city in Hong Kong Special Administrative Region, southeastern China, on the northern side of Hong Kong harbor. Population: 2,030,683 (1991).

kow·tow /kòw tów, ków tòw/ *vi* (**-towed, -tow·ing, -tows**) **1.** BE SERVILE to behave in an extremely submissive way in order to please somebody in a position of authority **2.** KNEEL TO SHOW RESPECT formerly, in China, to kneel and touch the forehead to the ground in order to show respect, awe, or submission ■ *n* **1.** SERVILE ACT an extremely submissive act aimed at pleasing somebody in a position of authority **2.** ACT OF KNEELING TO SHOW RESPECT a show of respect or worship made by kneeling and touching the forehead to the ground [Early 19C. < Chinese *kòutóu* "strike (the) head"] —**kow·tow·er** *n*

Ko·zhi·kode /kṓz̲h̲i kṓd/ city and seaport in Kerala State, southwestern India. It has been an important textile center since the 16th century. Population: 419,531 (1991).

kp *abbr* ONLINE North Korea (*used in Internet addresses*) See table at **domain name**

KP[1] (*plural* **KPs** or **KP's**) *n* MIL same as **kitchen police**

KP[2] *abbr* **1.** CHESS king's pawn **2.** Knight of Pythias

K.P. *abbr US* Knight of Pythias

kph, **k.p.h.** *abbr* MEASURE kilometers per hour

kr *abbr* ONLINE South Korea (*used in Internet addresses*) See table at **domain name**

Kr *symbol* CHEM ELEM krypton

KR *symbol* CHESS king's rook

kr. *abbr* MONEY **1.** krona **2.** króna **3.** krone

kraal /kraal/ *n S Africa* **1.** a traditional rural village, usually consisting of a number of huts surrounded by a stockade **2.** a pen or other enclosure for livestock, especially cattle [Mid-18C. Via Afrikaans < Portuguese *curral* < Nama]

Krafft-E·bing /kràft ébbing/, **Richard, Freiherr von** (1840–1902) German neuropsychologist. He is known for his pioneering studies into sexual psychopathology. His major work is *Psychopathia Sexualis* (1886).

kraft /kraft/, **kraft pa·per** *n* tough, usually brown paper made from chemically treated wood pulp. Use: bags, wrapping paper. [Early 20C. < Swedish, shortening of *kraftpapper* "strength paper"]

krait /krīt/ *n* an extremely poisonous snake with brightly colored bands on its back. Native to: Southeast Asia. Genus: *Bungarus*. [Late 19C. < Hindi *karait*]

Kra·ji·na /krī e̅e̅nə/ region of central Croatia on the border with Bosnia and Herzegovina. Its predominantly Serbian population opposed Croatia's secession from Yugoslavia, declaring the Serbian Republic of Krajina in 1991. It fell to Croatian forces in 1995.

Kra·ka·tau /kràkə tów/, **Kra·ka·to·a** /-tṓ ə/ **1.** small volcanic island in southwestern Indonesia, in the Sunda Strait between Java and Sumatra. Area: 5.8 sq. mi./15 sq. km. **2.** volcano on the island of Krakatau, whose eruption in 1883 destroyed most of the island and caused thousands of deaths. Height: 2,667 ft./813 m.

kra·ken /kraákən/ *n* in Norwegian folklore, a huge sea monster shaped like a giant squid. Norwegian fishermen have periodically reported sightings since the 16th century. [Mid-18C. < Norwegian]

Kra·ków /kraá kòw, krá kòw/, **Cra·cow** university city on the Vistula River in southern Poland. Its medieval architecture attracts many tourists, but it is also an important industrial center. Population: 740,500 (1997).

kram /kram/ *n regional* articles of little value [< German *Kram* "rubbish" or Norwegian *kram* "junk"]

REGIONAL NOTE ***Kram*** is a Wisconsin word, of German origin.

Kra·mer /kráymər/, **Jack** (*b.* 1921) US tennis player. He won the US singles championship (1946, 1947) and the Wimbledon men's singles championships (1947). Full name **Kramer, John Albert**

Kra·mer, Larry (*b.* 1935) US writer and AIDS activist. His works include the play *The Normal Heart* (1985). He is the founder of ACT UP (AIDS Coalition to Unleash Power).

Kras·ner /kráznər/, **Lee** (1908–84) US artist. She was one of the abstract expressionists, and was married to Jackson Pollock.

Kras·no·dar /kràssnə daár/ city and port in southwestern Russia. It is the administrative center of Krasnodar Territory. Population: 761,681 (1995). Former name **Yekaterinodar** (until 1922)

Kras·no·yarsk /kràssnə yaársk/ city in southern Siberian Russia. It is the administrative center of Krasnoyarsk Territory. Population: 1,122,874 (1995).

krater

kra·ter /kráytər/, **cra·ter** *n* in ancient Greece, a large two-handled bowl, used to mix wine with water [Mid-18C. < Greek *kratēr* "mixing bowl"]

K ra·tion *n* an emergency food ration consisting of one prepared meal, supplied to US soldiers fighting in World War II [Mid-20C. After Ancel Benjamin *Keys* (b. 1904), US physiologist]

kraut /krowt/ *n US* FOOD same as **sauerkraut** [Mid-19C. < German, "vegetable, cabbage"]

Kraut /krowt/ *n* an offensive term for a German (*slang*) [Early 20C. < German, "vegetable, cabbage"] —**Kraut** *adj*

Krebs /krebz/, **Sir Hans** (1900–81) German-born British biochemist. He discovered the citric acid cycle (**Krebs cycle**), for which he shared the Nobel Prize in physiology or medicine (1953) with Fritz Albert Lipmann. Full name **Krebs, Sir Hans Adolf**

Krebs cy·cle /krébz-/ *n* a sequence of biochemical reactions occurring in cells that is part of the metabolism of carbohydrates to produce energy

Krei·sler /krī́sslər/, **Fritz** (1875–1962) Austrian-born US violinist and composer. He was one of the most noted violinists of his generation, and wrote numerous pieces for the violin.

krem·lin /krémmlin/ *n* a fortress or citadel in a Russian city [Mid-17C. Via French < Russian *kreml* "citadel"]

Krem·lin *n* **1.** the walled citadel in Moscow in which cathedrals, palaces, and the offices of the Russian government are located. The outer walls date back to the 15th century. **2.** the government of the former Soviet Union

Krem·lin·ol·o·gy /krèmmlə nóllәjee/ *n* the study of the government and policies of the former Soviet Union —**Krem·lin·o·log·i·cal** /-nə lójjik'l/ *adj* —**Krem·lin·ol·o·gist** *n*

krep·lach /krépplə*kh*/ *npl* a Jewish dish consisting of triangles or squares of pasta filled with liver or meat that are boiled and served in soup [Late 19C. < Yiddish *kreplech*, plural of *krepel* < German dialect *Kräppel* "fried pastry"]

kreut·zer /króytsər/, **kreu·zer** *n* a small silver or copper coin used in Germany, Austria, and Hungary between the 13th and the mid-19th centuries [Mid-16C. < German *Kreuzer* < *Kreuz* "cross"; after medieval Latin *denarius crucigerus* "cross-bearing penny"]

krill /kril/ (*plural same*) *n* a tiny ocean crustacean resembling a shrimp that is the primary food of baleen whales and other animals that filter their food from seawater. Order: Euphausiacea. [Early 20C. < Norwegian *kril* "small fry of fish"]

krim·mer /krímmər/ *n* pale fur made from the soft curly wool of lambs from the Crimean Peninsula [Mid-19C. < German < *Krim* "Crimea"]

Kri·o /kre̅e̅ ō/ (*plural* **-os**) *n* **1.** a creole language spoken in Sierra Leone, based on English and with a strong Yoruba influence. Native speakers: 50,000. Other speakers: 200,000. **2.** somebody who speaks Krio [Mid-20C. Probably alteration of CREOLE] —**Kri·o** *adj*

kris /kreess/ *n* a Malay and Indonesian dagger with a wavy two-edged blade [Late 16C. < Malay *keris*]

Krish·na /kríshnə/ *n* in Hinduism, the eighth incarnation of the god Vishnu, often depicted as a young cowherd [< Sanskrit *kṛṣṇa*] —**Krish·na·ism** *n*

Krish·na Ja·yan·ti /-jī úntee/ *n* a Hindu festival celebrating Krishna's birthday. Date: late Sravana. [*Jayanti* < Hindi, "birthday"]

Kriss Kring·le /kriss kríng g'l/ *n* same as **Santa Claus** (*humorous or literary*) [Mid-19C. Alteration of German dialect *Christkindl* "Christmas child, Christmas present"]

Kri·ste·va /kri stáyvə/, **Julia** (*b.* 1941) Bulgarian-born French psychoanalyst, linguist, and writer. Her early works on linguistics and semiotics appeared in the journal *Tel Quel*, an important forum for post-structuralist pioneers. Her training as a psychoanalyst, completed in 1979, has influenced her later works, including *Desire and Language: A Semiotic Approach to Literature and Art* (1980).

Kri·voy Rog /kri vòy ráwk/, **Kri·voi Rog** city and major iron-producing center in south central Ukraine. Population: 715,000 (1998).

KRL *abbr* COMPUT knowledge representation language

Kroc /krok/, **Ray** (1902–84) US restaurateur. He started out as a milk shake salesman before buying the rights to a drive-in restaurant in California in 1955 and building it up into one of the largest fast-food companies in the world.

> "I believe in God, family, and McDonald's and in the office, that order is reversed."
> [Ray Kroc. Quoted in *McDonald's: Behind the Arches*, John F. Love; 1986]

kro·na[1] /krṓnə/ (*plural* **-nor** /-nər/) *n* the main unit of Swedish currency. See table at **currency** [Late 19C. < Swedish, "crown"]

kro·na[2] /krṓnə/ (*plural* **-nur** /-nər/) *n* the main unit of Faroese currency. See table at **currency** [< Faroese, "crown"]

kró·na /krṓnə/ (*plural* **-nur** /krṓnər/), **kro·na** *n* the main unit of Icelandic currency. See table at **currency** [Late 19C. < Icelandic, "crown"]

kro·ne /krṓnə/ (*plural* **-ner** /-nər/) *n* **1.** the main unit of currency in Denmark **2.** the main unit of currency in Norway ▶ See table at **currency** [Late 19C. < Danish, German, "crown"]

Kro·neck·er del·ta /krṓ nèkər-/ *n* a mathematical function of two variables that takes on only two values, 0 when the variables are unequal, and 1 when the variables are equal [Early 20C. After Leopold *Kronecker* (1823–91), German mathematician]

kro·ner MONEY plural of **krone**

kro·nor MONEY plural of **krona**[1]

Kron·stadt /krṓn shtàt/, **Kron·shtadt** military port on Kotlin Island in the Gulf of Finland, situated in northwestern European Russia. It was founded by Peter I. Population: 40,525 (1995).

kro·nur MONEY plural of **krona**[2]

kró·nur MONEY plural of **króna**

kroon /kroon/ (*plural* **kroons** or **kroon·i** /kroōnee/) *n* the main unit of Estonian currency. See table at **currency** [Early 20C. < Estonian, "crown"]

Kro·pot·kin /krə pótkin/, **Pyotr Alekseyevich, Prince** (1842–1921) Russian revolutionary. He was a leading theorist of the anarchist movement. He devoted himself to life as a revolutionary, advocating the abolition of governments and the founding of a society based on mutual trust.

Kro·to /krṓtō/, **Sir Harold Walter** (*b.* 1939) British chemist. Together with Richard Smalley and Robert Curl, he discovered the family of carbon molecules called fullerenes, and shared the Nobel Prize in chemistry (1996).

krou·žek /kroō zhèk/ *n* in Czech, a mark (°) placed over the letter u to indicate the vowel is long. See table at **diacritic** [< Czech]

Kru /kroo/ (*plural same* or **Krus**) *n* **1.** a member of an African people inhabiting mainly the coastal regions of Liberia and Côte d'Ivoire **2.** the language of the Kru people, belonging to the Kwa group of Niger-Congo languages. Kru has a large number of different dialects. [Mid-19C. < Kru]

Kru·ger /kroōgər/, **Paul** (1825–1904) South African soldier and politician. During his period as president of the Transvaal, South Africa (1883–1902), his discriminatory policies directed at non-Boers led to the Second Boer War (1899–1902). Full name **Kruger, Stephanus Johannes Paulus**

Kru·ger Na·tion·al Park national park in northeastern South Africa, bordering Mozambique, established in 1926. Area: 7,523 sq. mi./19,485 sq. km.

Kru·ger·rand /kroōgə rànd, -raànd/ *n* a South African gold coin weighing one ounce, intended mostly to be purchased as an investment [Mid-20C. After Paul KRUGER]

Kru·gers·dorp /kroōgərz dàwrp/ city in Gauteng Province, northeastern South Africa, near Johannesburg. Population: 93,000 (1991 estimate).

krul·ler *n US* FOOD another spelling of **cruller**

krum·horn *n* MUSIC another spelling of **crumhorn**

krumm·holz /kroōm hòlts/ (*plural same*) *n* **1.** stunted trees that grow just above the timberline on a mountain **2.** a high-altitude zone in which krummholz grows [Early 20C. < German, "crooked wood"]

krumm·horn *n* MUSIC another spelling of **crumhorn**

Krutch /kruch/, **Joseph Wood** (1893–1970) US critic and naturalist. He is known for his literary biographies and nature writings.

> "The impulse to mar and to destroy is as ancient and almost as nearly universal as the impulse to create. The one is an easier way than the other of demonstrating power."
> [Joseph Wood Krutch, *The Best of Two Worlds*; 1950]

kryp·ton /kríp tòn/ *n* a colorless inert gaseous element, constituting one millionth by volume of the atmosphere. Use: fluorescent lamps, lasers. Symbol **Kr**. See table at **element** [Late 19C. < Greek *krupton* "hidden"]

KS *abbr* **1.** Kansas **2.** MED Kaposi's sarcoma

K se·lec·tion *n* a process of natural selection that leads to a lowering of the birthrate when the population of a species approaches the maximum number that the environment can sustain [< *K*, the constant for carrying capacity in the population growth equation]

Ksha·tri·ya /ksháttree ə, kə sháttree ə/ *n* **1.** the second of the four Hindu castes, originally a royal and warrior caste. In modern times its members are professionals, administrators, or military personnel. **2.** a member of a Kshatriya caste [Late 18C. < Sanskrit *kṣatriya* < *kṣatra* "rule"]

kt *abbr* PHYS kiloton

Kt *abbr* MEASURE karat

kt. *abbr* **1.** CHESS knight **2.** MEASURE knot

K.T. *abbr* HIST, CHR Knight Templar

Kua·la Lum·pur /kwaálə loōm poōr/ capital of Malaysia, located on the southern Malay Peninsula. Population: 1,297,526 (2000).

Ku·blai Khan /koōblī kaán/ (1215–94) Mongol leader and emperor of China. He completed the conquest of China begun by his grandfather Genghis Khan, and founded the Yuan dynasty (1279).

Ku·brick /kyoōbrik/, **Stanley** (1928–99) US movie director. His varied movies include *Lolita* (1962), *Dr. Strangelove* (1964), *2001: A Space Odyssey* (1968), and *Eyes Wide Shut* (1999).

> "The great nations have always acted like gangsters, and the small nations like prostitutes."
> [Stanley Kubrick, *Guardian (London)*; June 5, 1963]

> "The very meaninglessness of life forces man to create his own meaning. If it can be written or thought, it can be filmed."
> [Stanley Kubrick, *Halliwell's Filmgoer's and Video Viewer's Companion*; 1999]

ku·chen /koōkən, koōkhən/ (*plural same*) *n* a cake that has been raised with yeast [Mid-19C. < German, "cake"]

ku·dos /koō dṓz, koō dṑss/ *n* praise, credit, or glory for an achievement (*takes a singular verb*) [Late 18C. < Greek, "praise, renown"]

USAGE Careful writers and speakers avoid the form *kudo*, created in the erroneous belief that ***kudos*** is a plural.

ku·du /koō doō/ (*plural* **-dus** or *same*), **koo·doo** (*plural* **-doos** or *same*) *n* a large antelope, the male of which has long spiraling horns. Native to: Africa. Latin name: *Tragelaphus strepsiceros* or *Tragelaphus imberbis*. [Late 18C. Via Afrikaans *koedoe* < Xhosa *i-qudu*]

kud·zu /kúd zoō/ *n* a hardy vine that has compound leaves and purplish flowers, and roots that contain a nourishing starch used medicinally. It is an invasive weed in the southeastern United States. Native to: eastern Asia. Latin name: *Pueraria lobata*. [Late 19C. < Japanese *kuzu*]

Kuf·far ISLAM plural of **Kaffir** (sense 2) (*slang offensive*)

Ku·fic /koōfik/, **Cu·fic** *adj* having an early angular style of Arabic writing used for Koranic manuscripts and inscriptions ■ *n* the Arabic alphabet written in Kufic script [Early 18C. After *Kufa*, ancient city south of Baghdad]

Ku·fuor /koō fwáwr/, **John** (*b.* 1938) president of Ghana (2001–). Leader of the New Patriotic Party, he served as deputy foreign minister and minister for local government before his election as president. Full name **Kufuor, John Kofi Agyekum**

ku·gel /koōg'l/ *n* in Jewish cooking, a casserole often made of noodles or potatoes [Mid-19C. < Yiddish, "ball" < Middle High German; probably from its traditional mound shape]

Kui·per belt /kīpər-/ *n* a ring of small astronomical objects orbiting through the outer solar system, beyond the farthest planets, Neptune and Pluto. It is believed that the Kuiper belt is a source of comets. [After Gerald Peter (Gerrit Pieter) *Kuiper* (1905–73), Dutch-born US astronomer]

Ku Klux Klan /koō klùks klán/ *n* **1.** a terrorist secret society organized in the South after the Civil War that used violence and murder to promote its white supremacist beliefs **2.** a white supremacist organization founded in Georgia in 1915. Its secret membership, supremacist views, and terrorist methods are similar to those of the 19th-century Ku Klux Klan. [Mid-19C. Origin ?]

kuk·ri /koōkree/ *n* a large knife with a sharp curved blade that gets broader toward the point, used by the Gurkhas in Nepal for hunting and fighting [Early 19C. < Nepali *khukuri*]

ku·ku·i nut /koo koō ee-/ *n Hawaii* the nut from the candlenut tree [< Hawaiian]

ku·lak /koo laák, -lák/ *n* a wealthy landowning peasant in Russia during the time between the emancipation of the serfs and the Stalinist era [Late 19C. Via Russian, "fist, tight-fisted person" < Turkic *kol* "hand"]

kul·cha /koōlchə/ *n* in South Asian cuisine, bread made with flour, milk, yeast, and butter, baked in small rounds and usually stuffed with meat or vegetables [< Persian *kulīka*]

kul·fi /koōlfee/ (*plural* **-fis**) *n* in South Asian cuisine, a rich ice cream [< Hindi *kulfī*]

Kul·tur /koōl toōr/ *n* **1.** culture or civilization in general **2.** German culture, regarded as superior and used as a vehicle of German imperialism during the period of the German Empire and under the Nazi regime [Early 20C. Via German < Latin *cultura* or French *culture* "culture"]

Kul·tur·kampf /koōl toōr kaàmpf/ *n* **1.** the struggle between the German government under Bismarck and the Roman Catholic Church over control of education, marriage, and Church appointments. It lasted from 1871 to 1887 and ended in compromise. **2.** a struggle between religious authorities and a government [Late 19C. < German < *Kultur* "culture" + *Kampf* "struggle"]

Ku·ma·mo·to /koōmə mṓtō/ city on the west of Kyushu Island, Japan, the capital city of Kumamoto Prefecture. Population: 653,835 (2002).

Ku·ma·ra·tun·ga /koo maárə toōng gə/, **Chandrika** (*b.* 1945) Sri Lankan politician. The daughter of S.W.R.D. Bandaranaike, she was elected president of Sri Lanka in 1994. Full name **Kumaratunga, Chandrika Bandaranaike**

Ku·ma·si /koo maássee/ capital of the Ashanti Region, central Ghana. It is situated northwest of Accra. Population: 399,300 (1990 estimate). Former name **Coomassie**

Ku·min /koōmin/, **Maxine** (*b.* 1925) US writer of poetry, fiction, and essays. Her collection *Up Country: Poems of New England* (1972) won the 1973 Pulitzer Prize for poetry.

ku·miss /koo míss, koōmiss/, **kou·miss**, **kou·mis** *n* slightly alcoholic, fermented, and sour-tasting milk from a mare or camel, drunk by some of the peoples of central and western Asia [Late 16C. Via French *koumis*, German *Kumiss*, Polish and Russian *kumys* < Tatar *kumiz*]

kum·kum /koōm koōm/ *n S Asia* a red round decorative mark worn on the forehead by Hindu women and girls, but traditionally not by widows [Mid-20C. < Sanskrit *kuṅkuma* "saffron"]

küm·mel /kímm'l/, **kum·mel** *n* a colorless liqueur or cordial that is flavored with cumin and caraway seeds and is made primarily in the Baltic region [Mid-19C. < German, "caraway seed" < Old High German *kumīn* "cumin"]

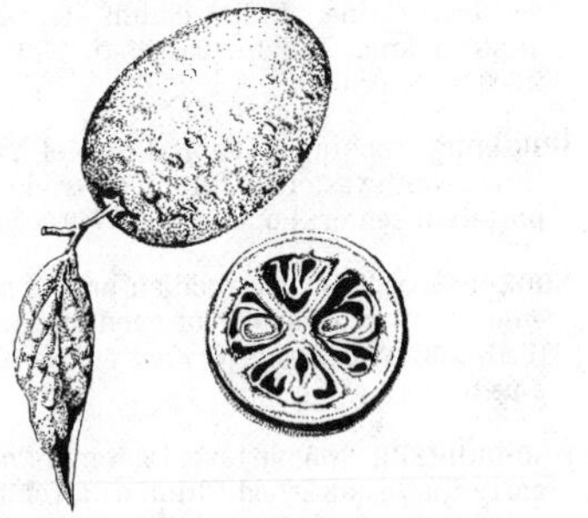

kumquat

kum·quat /kúm kwòt/, **cum·quat** *n* **1.** a small oval orange fruit, related to citrus fruits, with sweet skin and tart flesh, eaten whole or preserved **2.** an evergreen tree related to citrus species that produces kumquats. Native to: China. Genus: *Fortunella*. [Late 17C. < Chinese (Cantonese) *kam kwat* "gold orange"]

ku·na /koōnə/ (*plural* **-ne** /-này/) *n* the main unit of Croatian currency. See table at **currency** [Late 20C. < Serbo-Croatian]

Ku·na *n, adj* LANG another spelling of **Cuna**

kun·da·li·ni /koōndə leénee, kùndə-/ *n* vital energy that Hindus believe lies dormant at the base of the spine until it is called into action, e.g., through yoga, to be used in seeking enlightenment [Late 19C. < Sanskrit *kuṇḍalinī*, literally "snake"; because likened to a coiled snake]

Kun·de·ra /kən dérrə/, **Milan** (*b.* 1929) Czech writer. His novels include *The Joke* (1967) and *The Unbearable Lightness of Being* (1984). He moved to France in 1975.

> "The struggle of man against power is the struggle of memory against forgetting."

[Milan Kundera, *The Book of Laughter and Forgetting*; 1982]

"Mankind's true moral test, its fundamental test (which lies deeply buried from view) consists of its attitudes toward those who are at its mercy: animals."
[Milan Kundera, *The Unbearable Lightness of Being*; 1984]

kun·di·man /kóondee màn/ *n Philippines* a love song [< Tagalog]

ku·ne MONEY plural of **kuna**

Kung /kŏong/ (*plural same*), **!Kung** *n* **1.** a member of a San people who live in eastern Namibia and western Botswana **2.** the Khoisan language of the Kung people [Early 20C. < Khoikhoi *!Kung*, literally "people"] —**Kung** *adj*

UPI/Corbis-Bettmann

kung fu

kung fu /kùng fóo, kŏong-/ *n* a Chinese form of self-defense in which fluid, circular movements of the arms and legs are used to attack an opponent [Late 19C. < Chinese *gongfu*, literally "merit master"]

Ku·nitz /kyóonits/, **Stanley** (*b.* 1905) US poet. His *Selected Poems 1928–58* (1958) won the 1959 Pulitzer Prize for poetry. He was named US poet laureate in 2000.

Kun·lun Moun·tains /kŏon lŏon-/ mountain range in western China. India claims territory in the western area. Height: 25,338 ft./7,723 m. Length: 2,000 mi./3,000 km.

Kun·ming /kŏon míng/ capital city of Yunnan Province, southwestern China, a trade and transportation center. Population: 1,740,000 (1995).

kunz·ite /kŏont sìt/ *n* a reddish purple semiprecious stone that is a variety of spodumene. Use: gems. [Early 20C. After George F. *Kunz* (1856–1932), US gem expert]

Kuo·min·tang /kwōmin táng, kwàwmin-/ *n* the political party that established China as a republic in 1911, ruled China from 1928 to 1947 until defeated by the Communists, and then withdrew to rule in Taiwan [Early 20C. < Chinese *guómíndǎng* "national people's party"]

Ku·ra /kŏo rá/ river in Transcaucasia, flowing through Turkey, Georgia, and Azerbaijan, and emptying into the Caspian Sea. Length: 940 mi./1,500 km.

kur·cha·tov·i·um /kùrchə tŏvee əm/ *n* the name given to the element rutherfordium in the former Soviet Union [Mid-20C. After I. V. *Kurchatov* (1903–60), Russian nuclear physicist]

Kurd /kurd/ *n* a member of a largely Muslim people who live in Southwest Asia, in an area comprising parts of Iraq, Turkey, and Iran [Early 17C. < Kurdish]

kur·dai·tcha /kər dícha/, **ka·dai·tcha** /kə dícha/ *n* among Aboriginal peoples of central Australia, a sorcerer who was responsible for avenging the death of a kinsman [Late 19C. < Aboriginal]

Kurd·ish /kúrdish/ *n* an Iranian language spoken in Turkey, Iraq, Iran, Armenia, and Syria, belonging to the Indo-Iranian branch of Indo-European languages. Native speakers: 10 million. ■ *adj* relating to the Kurds, or their language or culture

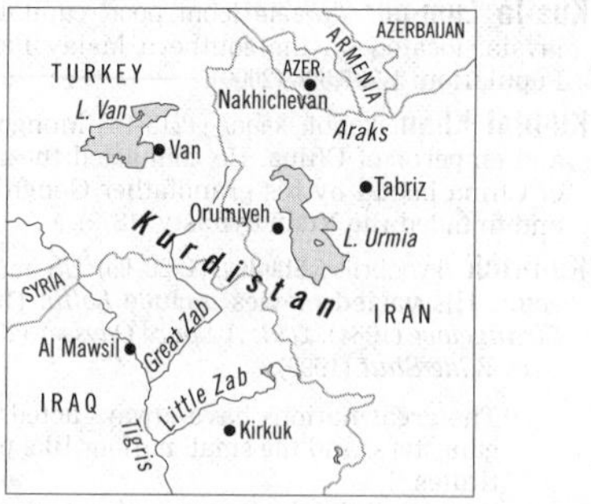

Kurdistan

Kurd·i·stan /kúrdə stàn/, **Kurd·i·stān** region in Southwest Asia, encompassing parts of Turkey, Iraq, Iran, Armenia, and Syria, considered the homeland of the Kurdish people. Population: 26,000,000 (early 1990s).

kur·gan /koor gáan, -gán/ *n* a burial mound built by a prehistoric culture of eastern Europe and northern Iran [Late 19C. < Russian]

Ku·ril Is·lands /kóoril-/, **Ku·rile Is·lands** island chain extending from northeastern Hokkaido in Japan to southern Kamchatka Peninsula in Russia. The islands were settled by Russians and Japanese in the 18th century, and are the subject of dispute between the two countries. Population: 25,000 (1990). Area: 6,020 sq. mi./15,590 sq. km.

Ku·ro·sa·wa /kóorə sáawə/, **Akira** (1910–98) Japanese movie director. He is known for such classic movies as *Rashomon* (1950) and *The Seven Samurai* (1954).

Ku·ro·shi·o /kŏo rōshee ō/ warm current in the Pacific Ocean, flowing from the Philippines northeastward along the eastern coast of Japan

kur·ra·jong /kúr ə jàwng, kúrrə-/ *n* a tree that has yellowish or red bell-shaped flowers and yields a tough fiber. Native to: eastern Australia. Latin name: *Brachychiton populneum.* [Early 19C. < Aboriginal]

Kursk /koorsk/ city in western Russia, the capital of Kursk Oblast, and a mining center. Population: 578,671 (1995).

kur·ta /kóortə/ *n* a long loose collarless shirt worn by some men and women in or from South Asia [Early 20C. < Urdu, Persian *kurtah*]

kur·to·sis /kər tŏssiss/ (*plural* **-to·ses** /-tō seez/) *n* in statistics, a measure of the extent to which a frequency distribution is concentrated about its mean [Early 20C. < Greek *kurtōsis* "curvature" < *kurtos* "bent"]

ku·ru /kŏo roo/ *n* a fatal degenerative disease of the central nervous system similar to Creutzfeldt-Jakob disease that affects some peoples in New Guinea. It is believed to derive from the practice of eating the brains of an ancestor. [Mid-20C. < a dialect of New Guinea, "trembling"]

Kusch /kóosh/, **Polykarp** (1911–93) German-born US physicist. He established the magnetic moment of the electron and shared a Nobel Prize in physics (1955).

Kush *n* BIBLE another spelling of **Cush**

Kus·ko·kwim /kúskə kwìm/ river in southwestern Alaska, rising in the Alaska Range and flowing into the Bering Sea. Length: 724 mi./1,170 km.

Kutch, Rann of ◆ **Rann of Kutch**

Ku·te·nai /kóot'n ày, -ee/ (*plural same* or **-nais**), **Koo·te·nai, Koo·te·nay** (*plural same* or **-nays**) *n* **1.** a member of a Native North American people living mainly in Montana, Idaho, and British Columbia **2.** the language of the Kutenai people, which has no known linguistic affiliations. Native speakers: 200. [Early 19C. < Blackfoot *Kotonáai-*] —**Ku·te·nai** *adj*

Ku·wait /koo wáyt/ country in Southwest Asia, at the northwestern tip of the Persian Gulf. It is bordered by Iraq and Saudi Arabia. Language: Arabic. Currency: Kuwaiti dinar. Capital: Kuwait City. Population: 2,183,161 (2003). Area: 6,880 sq. mi./17,818 sq. km. Official name **State of Kuwait** —**Ku·wait·i** *n, adj*

Ku·wait Cit·y capital of Kuwait, in the east of the country, on Kuwait Bay. Population: 28,259 (1995).

Kuz·nets /kóoznits/, **Simon** (1901–85) Russian-born US economist. He developed the concept of the gross national product (GNP), for which he received the Nobel Prize in economics (1971).

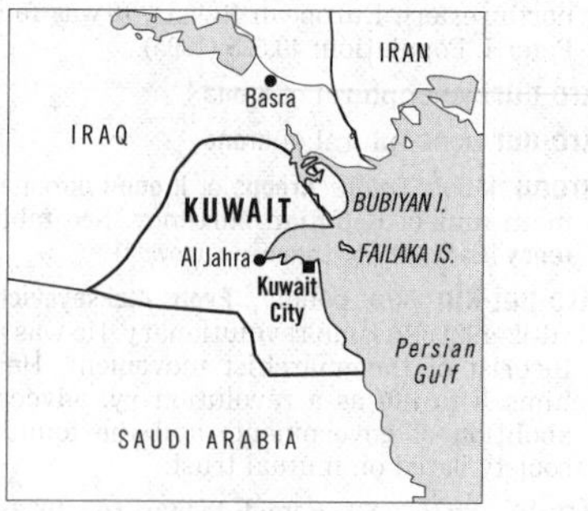

Kuwait

kV, kv *abbr* MEASURE kilovolt

kvass /kə váass, kfaass/, **kvas, quass** *n* an alcoholic drink similar to beer, made in Russia and eastern European countries from rye or barley or from stale bread [Mid-16C. < Russian *kvas*]

kvetch /kvech/ (*informal*) *vi* (**kvetched, kvetch·ing, kvetch·es**) COMPLAIN INCESSANTLY to grumble and complain about things all the time ■ *n* **1.** SOMEBODY INCESSANTLY COMPLAINING a constant grumbler or complainer **2.** COMPLAINT a complaint about something [Mid-20C. Via Yiddish *kvetsh* (noun), *kvetshn* (verb) < German *Quetsche* "crusher," *quetschen* "to crush"]

kw *abbr* **1.** *also* **KW** MEASURE kilowatt **2.** Kuwait (*used in Internet addresses*) See table at **domain name**

Kwa /kwaa/ *n* a group of languages in the Niger-Congo family that are spoken in West Africa, and include Yoruba and Ibo [Mid-19C. < Kwa] —**Kwa** *adj*

kwa·cha /kwáachə/ *n* the main unit of currency in Malawi and Zambia. See table at **currency** [Mid-20C. < Bantu, "dawn"]

Kwa·ki·utl /kwàakee óot'l/ (*plural same* or **-utls**) *n* **1.** a member of a Native North American people who live on Vancouver Island and on the adjacent coast of British Columbia **2.** the Wakashan language of the Kwakiutl people [Mid-19C. < Kwakiutl *Kwágu*ł] —**Kwa·ki·utl** *adj*

kwa·li /kwáalee/ (*plural* **-lis**) *n Malaysia* same as **wok** [< Malay]

Kwang·ju /kwàang jóo/ city in southwestern South Korea. It is the capital of South Chŏlla Province. Population: 1,334,000 (1998 estimate).

kwan·za /kwáanzə/ (*plural* **-zas** or *same*) *n* the main unit of Angolan currency. See table at **currency** [Late 20C. < Bantu]

Kwan·zaa /kwáanzə/, **Kwan·za** *n* a cultural and harvest festival celebrated by African Americans. Date: December 26 to January 1. [Late 20C. < Kiswahili, literally "first"]

kwa·shi·or·kor /kwàashee áwr kàwr/ *n* malnutrition in children caused by inadequate intake of protein, common in impoverished African children weaned onto a cornmeal diet [Mid-20C. < a name in Ghana, "red boy"; from the symptomatic reddening of the hair]

Kwas·niew·ski /kvàsh nyéfski/, **Aleksander** (*b.* 1954) Polish politician. A founding member of the Democratic Left Alliance, he has twice been elected president (1995 and 2000).

Kwa·Zu·lu /kwaa zóoloo/ former homeland in South Africa, part of the province of KwaZulu-Natal since 1994

Kwa·Zu·lu-Na·tal province in South Africa, in the southeastern part of the country. Capital: Pietermaritzburg. Population: 9,426,018 (2001). Area: 35,560 sq. mi./92,100 sq. km.

kWh, kW-hr *abbr* MEASURE kilowatt-hour

KWIC /kwik/ *abbr* COMPUT, LING key word in context

KWIM *abbr* know what I mean (*used in e-mails or text messages*)

KWOC *abbr* COMPUT key word out of context

kwy·ji·bo /kwí jee bō/ (*plural* **-bos**) *n* an offensive term for a person who is regarded as being big, clumsy, stupid, and resembling an ape (*slang*) [Late 20C. From its use during a Scrabble game on an episode of the television sitcom "The Simpsons"]

ky *abbr* Cayman Islands (*used in Internet addresses*) See table at **domain name**

KY, **Ky.** *abbr* Kentucky

ky·ack /kī̀ àk/ *n US* a double packsack designed to be slung across a packsaddle, with one sack on either side of the saddle [Early 20C. Origin ?]

ky·a·nite /kī́ ə nīt/, **cy·a·nite** /sī́ ə-/ *n* a bluish aluminosilicate mineral found as thin-bladed crystals or in masses. Source: metamorphic rocks. Use: gems, refractory. [Late 18C. < Greek *kuan(e)os* "dark blue"]

ky·a·nize /kī́ ə nīz/ (**-nized, -niz·ing, -niz·es**) *vt* to preserve wood against decay by treating it with a corrosive sublimate [Mid-19C. After J. H. *Kyan* (1774–1850), Irish inventor]

kyat /chaʹ/ *n* the main unit of currency in Myanmar. See table at **currency** [Mid-20C. < Burmese]

Kyd /kid/, **Thomas** (1558–94) English playwright. His best known work is *The Spanish Tragedy* (1580?), which established the genre of revenge tragedy.

KYFC *abbr* ONLINE keep your fingers crossed (*used in e-mails or text messages*)

ky·lix /kī́liks, kíliks/ (*plural* **-li·ces** /-lə seez/) *n* in ancient Greece, a shallow two-handled cup, often with a footed stem [Mid-19C. < Greek *kulix*]

ky·mo·graph /kī́mə gràf/ *n* a device for recording variations in motion or pressure, e.g., of blood, consisting typically of a stylus and a rotating drum [Mid-19C. < Greek *kuma* "wave"] —**ky·mo·graph·ic** /kìmə gráffik/ *adj* —**ky·mog·ra·phy** /kī mógrəfee/ *n*

Kyo·to /kee ṓtō, kyṓtō/ city on southern Honshu Island, Japan. It is a manufacturing center and capital of Kyoto Urban Prefecture. Population: 1,387,264 (2002).

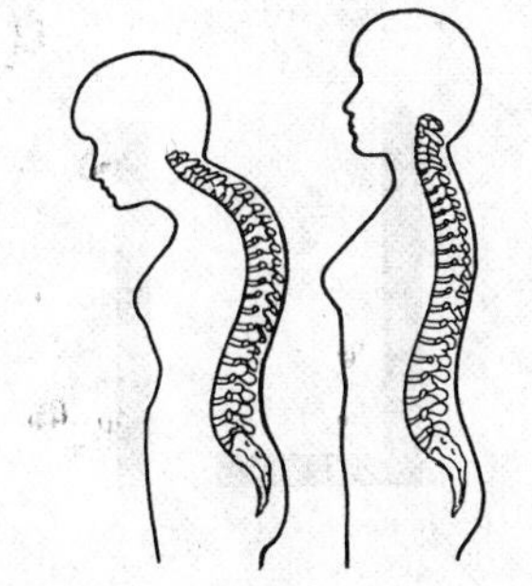

kyphosis

ky·pho·sis /kī fóssiss/ *n* a permanent curving of the spine that makes somebody look hunched over [Mid-19C. < Greek *kuphōsis* < *kuphos* "bent"] —**ky·phot·ic** /kī fóttik/ *adj*

Kyp·ri·a·nou /kìppree áanoo/, **Spyros** (1932–2002) president of Cyprus (1977–88). He succeeded Archbishop Makarios as president.

Kyr·gyz /keer geéz/ (*plural same*), **Kir·ghiz**, **Kir·giz** *n* **1.** a member of a people living in Kyrgyzstan and Siberia **2.** the Turkic language of the Kyrgyz —**Kyr·gyz** *adj*

Kyrg·yz·stan /keérgi stàn/ country in Central Asia, bordered by Kazakhstan, China, Tajikistan, and Uzbekistan. Language: Kyrgyz, Russian. Currency: som. Capital: Bishkek. Population: 4,892,808 (2003). Area: 76,640 sq. mi./198,500 sq. km. Official name **Kyrgyz Republic**

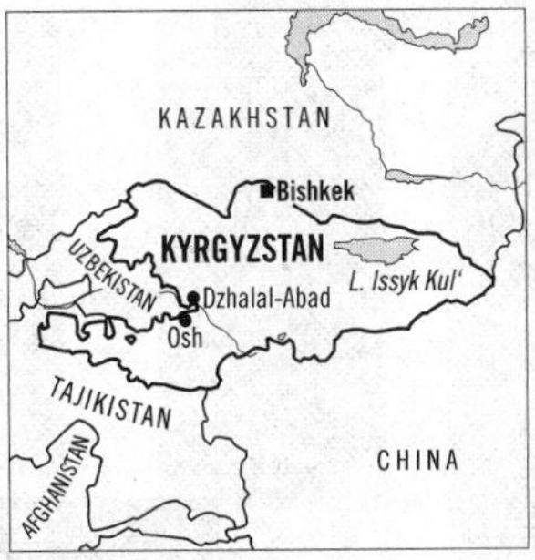

Kyrgyzstan

Kyr·i·e /keéree ày/, **Kyr·i·e e·le·i·son** /keéree ay ə láy sòn, -ə láyss'n/ *n* **1.** a form of prayer that begins with the words "Lord, have mercy," used in the Roman Catholic, Greek Orthodox, and Anglican churches **2.** a musical setting for the Kyrie, often forming part of a sung Mass [< medieval Latin *Kyrie eleison* < Greek *Kuriē eleēson* "Lord, have mercy"]

Kyu·shu /kee óoshoo, kyóoshoo/, **Kyū·shū** southernmost of the four major islands of Japan. Population: 13,269,000 (1990). Area: 14,114 sq. mi./36,554 sq. km.

kz *abbr* ONLINE Kazakhstan (*used in Internet addresses*) See table at **domain name**

Ll

l[1] /el/ (*plural* **l's**), **L** (*plural* **L's** or **Ls**) *n* **1.** 12TH LETTER OF ENGLISH ALPHABET the 12th letter of the English alphabet, representing a consonant sound **2.** LETTER "L" WRITTEN a written representation of the letter "L" **3.** ROMAN NUMERAL FOR 50 the Roman numeral for 50

l[2] *abbr* MEASURE liter

L[1] /el/ (*plural* **L's** or **Ls**) *n* something shaped like a letter "L"

L[2] *symbol* **1.** PHYS angular momentum **2.** PHYS inductance (sense 1) **3.** PHYS latent heat **4.** PHYS luminance **5.** ASTRON luminosity

L[3] *abbr* **1.** large **2.** ANCIENT HIST, LANG Latin

l. *abbr* **1.** GEOG latitude **2.** law **3.** left **4.** length **5.** AVIAT lift **6.** line **7.** MONEY lira

L. *abbr* **1.** MAPS Lake **2.** large **3.** ANCIENT HIST, LANG Latin **4.** SPORTS League

L8R *abbr* ONLINE later (*used in e-mails or text messages*)

la[1] /laa, law/ *interj US* used to show surprise or to emphasize what is being said [Late 16C. Natural exclamation]

la[2] /laa/, **lah** *n* a syllable that represents the sixth note in a musical scale when singing solfeggio. In fixed solfeggio it represents the note A. [14C. < medieval Latin, originally a syllable sung to this note in a hymn to St. John the Baptist]

la[3] *abbr* ONLINE Laos (*used in Internet addresses*) See table at **domain name**

La *symbol* CHEM ELEM lanthanum

LA *abbr* **1.** *also* **L.A.** Los Angeles **2.** Louisiana

La. *abbr* Louisiana

laa·ger /laágər/, **la·ger** *n* a camp protected by a circle of wagons or other vehicles, formerly used by the Boers in South Africa ■ *vti* (**-gered, -ger·ing, -gers**) to form wagons or other vehicles into a circle to make a protected camp [Mid-19C. Alteration of obsolete Afrikaans *lager*]

La Ar·gen·ti·na /la aarjən teénə/ (1890?–1936) Argentine-born Spanish dancer. She reestablished Spanish dancing as a popular art form in the 20th century. Born **Mercé, Antonia**

laa·ri /laáree/ (*plural same* or **-ris**), **la·ri** *n* a subunit of currency in the Maldives. See table at **currency** [Late 20C. Via Divehi < Persian *lārī*, after *Lār*, town north of the Persian Gulf]

lab /lab/ *n* same as **laboratory** (*informal*) [Late 19C. Shortening]

Lab. *abbr* Labrador

La·ban /laábən/, **Rudolf von** (1879–1958) Hungarian dancer and choreographer. He devised a method of notating dance movements and founded several dance schools.

la·ba·no·ta·tion /laàbə nō táysh'n/ *n* a method of notating dance movements in detail, including the placement of the dancer's body, direction of movement, tempo, and dynamics [Mid-20C. Blend of LABAN + NOTATION]

lab·a·rum /lábbərəm/ (*plural* **-ra** /-rə/) *n* a military banner carried before Roman emperors, especially one with Christian symbols that was carried in front of Constantine the Great as a sign of his conversion to Christianity [Early 17C. < late Latin]

la·basse /la báss/ *n Carib* a garbage dump [Late 20C. < French *la basse* "the flatlands, the shoal, the swampland," after an area near Port-of-Spain, Trinidad, where garbage is dumped]

lab·da·num /lábdənəm/, **lad·a·num** /ládd'nəm/ *n* a bitter resinous gum extracted from various rockroses. Use: flavorings, perfumes. [Early 16C. < medieval Latin, alteration of Latin *ladanum* < Greek *lēdanon* < *lēdon* "mastic"]

la·bel /láyb'l/ *n* **1.** INFORMATIVE ITEM ATTACHED TO SOMETHING a piece of paper, fabric, or plastic attached to something to give instructions about it or identify it **2.** DESCRIPTIVE WORD OR PHRASE a word or phrase used to describe a person or group **3.** NAME OF RECORD COMPANY the name of a record company, especially when displayed on a record, CD, or cassette **4.** BRAND a brand name of some items of fashion ○ *always wore designer labels* **5.** IDENTIFIER FOR PART OF COMPUTER PROGRAM a number or word that acts as a unique identifier for a part of a computer program **6.** CHEMICAL IDENTIFIER a substance, usually a radioactive isotope or dye, that can be traced to identify a compound as it undergoes a chemical reaction or assimilation **7.** HERALDIC DESIGN a figure on a heraldic shield consisting of a horizontal band with pendants and identifying the person to whom it belongs as an eldest son ■ *vt* (**-beled** or **-belled, -bel·ing** or **-bel·ling, -bels**) **1.** PUT LABEL ON SOMETHING to attach a label to something as identification or to give instructions **2.** USE DESCRIPTIVE WORD FOR SOMETHING to describe somebody or something using a particular word or phrase ○ *resents being labeled as a troublemaker* **3.** ATTACH CHEMICAL LABEL TO SOMETHING to make a chemical substance identifiable with a marker such as a radioactive isotope or dye [13C. < Old French, "ribbon, fillet"] —**la·bel·er** *n*

la·bel·lum /lə béllәm/ (*plural* **-la** /-lə/) *n* **1.** the petal of an orchid that is its lowest and largest and forms a lip **2.** the lobe at the end of an insect's proboscis that it uses for feeding on liquids [Early 19C. < Latin, "small lip" < *labrum* "lip"]

la·bi·a ANAT plural of **labium**

la·bi·al /láybee əl/ *adj* **1.** INVOLVING LIPS OR LABIA in, on, close to, or involving the lips or the labia **2.** PRONOUNCED WITH LIPS CLOSED pronounced with the lips closed or nearly closed as, e.g., in the sounds "b" and "p" **3.** SOUNDED BY MOVING AIR ACROSS EDGE describes an instrument or organ pipe that produces sound by the movement of air across a sharp edge ■ *n* **1.** SOUND PRONOUNCED WITH LIPS CLOSED a speech sound pronounced with the lips closed or nearly closed as, e.g., in "b" and "p" **2.** MUSICAL INSTRUMENT an instrument or organ pipe in which sound is produced by the movement of air across a sharp edge [Late 16C. < medieval Latin *labialis* < Latin *labia* "lips"] —**la·bi·al·ly** *adv*

la·bi·al·ize /láybee ə līz/ (**-ized, -iz·ing, -iz·es**) *vt* to pronounce a sound with the lips rounded —**la·bi·al·i·za·tion** /làybee əli záysh'n/ *n*

la·bi·a ma·jo·ra /làybee ə mə jáwrə/ *npl* the two thick outer folds of skin that surround the clitoris, the opening of the urethra, and the opening of the vagina of women and girls [< modern Latin, "larger lips"]

la·bi·a mi·no·ra /làybee ə mə náwrə/ *npl* the two small folds of skin that lie immediately inside the labia majora of women and girls and join at the front to form the hood of the clitoris [< modern Latin, "smaller lips"]

la·bi·ate /láybee ət, -àyt/ *adj* **1.** WITH DIVIDED SET OF PETALS describes a flower such as a snapdragon that has its set of petals (**corolla**) divided into two unequal and overlapping parts **2.** OF MINT FAMILY belonging to the mint family ■ *n UK* PLANT OF MINT FAMILY a plant of the mint family. Family: Labiatae. [Early 18C. < modern Latin *labiatus* < Latin *labium* "lip"]

la·bile /láyb'l, -bīl/ *adj* **1.** liable to change **2.** readily or frequently undergoing chemical or physical change ○ *a labile compound* [15C. < late Latin *labilis* "prone to slip" < Latin *labi* "to fall"]

labio- *prefix* lips, labial ○ *labiodental* [< Latin *labium* "lip"]

la·bi·o·den·tal /làybee ō dént'l/ *adj* pronounced with the upper teeth resting on the inside of the lower lip, as in the sounds "f" and "v" —**la·bi·o·den·tal** *n*

la·bi·o·na·sal /làybee ō náyz'l/ *adj* pronounced with the lips closed and the air being pushed through the nose, as in the sound "m" —**la·bi·o·na·sal** *n*

la·bi·o·ve·lar /làybee ō veélər/ *adj* pronounced by constricting the back of the mouth and closing the lips, as in the sound "kw" —**la·bi·o·ve·lar** *n*

la·bi·um /láybee əm/ (*plural* **-bi·a** /-bee ə/) *n* **1.** FOLD AROUND WOMEN'S GENITALIA a fold that surrounds a woman's or girl's genital organs. There are two inner (**labia minora**) and two outer (**labia majora**) folds. **2.** MOUTHPART OF INSECT a mouthpart of some insects, formed from a fused pair of appendages **3.** LIP OF FLOWER the lower lip of the corolla of a labiate flower **4.** PART LIKE LIP any part that looks or functions like a lip [Late 16C. < Latin, "lip"]

lab·lab /láb làb/ *n* BOT same as **hyacinth bean** [Early 19C. < Arabic *lablāb*]

la·bor /láybər/ *n* **1.** WORKERS COLLECTIVELY the workers, especially manual workers, in a country, company, or industry considered as a group (*often used before a noun*) ○ *labor relations* **2.** SUPPLY OF WORK the supply of work or workers for a particular job, industry, or employer ○ *outlawed child labor* **3.** LABOR UNIONS COLLECTIVELY labor unions collectively and the movement that built and supported them **4.** PHYSICAL WORK work done using the strength of the body ○ *forced into hard labor* **5.** PARTICULAR PIECE OF WORK a piece of work of a particular type, especially a difficult or long one (*often used in the plural*) ○ *a labor of love* ○ *the labors of Hercules* **6.** PROCESS OF CHILDBIRTH the process of giving birth to a baby from when the contractions start to the baby's delivery, or the time taken for this process (*often used before a noun*) ○ *labor pains* ■ *v* (**-bored, -bor·ing, -bors**) **1.** *vi* WORK HARD to work hard, especially at physical work ○ *labored all day in the hot sun* **2.** *vi* STRUGGLE TO DO SOMETHING to struggle to do something very difficult or very tiring ○ *labored over the exam* **3.** *vi* MOVE WITH DIFFICULTY to move with difficulty or great effort ○ *labored up to the summit* **4.** *vi* OPERATE WITH DIFFICULTY to have difficulty in running or functioning smoothly, e.g., because of being overloaded or defective (*refers to engines or machines*) **5.** *vt* OVEREMPHASIZE SOMETHING to continue trying to express or emphasize something when it is unnecessary ○ *Don't labor the point.* **6.** *vi* GIVE BIRTH to be in the process of giving birth to a baby **7.** *vi* PITCH AND ROLL to pitch and roll heavily at sea (*refers to boats*) [14C. Via French < Latin, "toil, pain"]
◇ **a labor of love** something demanding or difficult that is done just for pleasure rather than for money

CULTURAL NOTE ***Love's Labour's Lost***, a play by English dramatist William Shakespeare (1594–95). Ferdinand, king of Navarre, and three of his lords agree to forgo the company of women in order to devote themselves to study. The arrival of the Princess of France and three of her ladies upsets their plans, giving rise to lively comedy and witty and poetic dialogue.

SYNONYMS See *work*.

labor under *vt* to be at a disadvantage because of believing something to be true that is not ○ *She had been laboring under the misconception that the problem was solved.*

lab·o·ra·to·ry /lábbrə tàwree/ (*plural* **-ries**) *n* **1. PLACE FOR SCIENTIFIC RESEARCH** a place where research and testing is carried out **2. ROOM FOR TEACHING SCIENCE** a room or place with appropriate equipment for teaching science or doing scientific work **3. ACADEMIC PERIOD FOR DOING SCIENCE** a period in school when students work in a laboratory [Early 17C. < medieval Latin *laboratorium* "place for work" < Latin *laborare* "to work" < *labor* "toil"]

la·bor camp *n* a prison where the prisoners have to do hard physical work under a harsh, typically cruel, regime

La·bor Day *n* **1.** a national holiday in the United States and Canada honoring working people. Date: 1st Monday in September. **2.** CALENDAR same as **May Day** (sense 2)

la·bored /láybərd/ *adj* **1.** done with obvious effort or difficulty ○ *labored breathing* **2.** lacking natural ease and grace ○ *a labored speaker*

la·bor·er /láybərər/ *n* somebody who works at a job that requires physical strength and stamina

la·bor force *n* HR same as **work force**

la·bor-in·ten·sive *adj* involving a relatively high number of workers or greater costs for labor than for other areas such as materials, machines, or design ○ *a labor-intensive industry*

la·bo·ri·ous /lə báwree əss/ *adj* **1.** requiring much unwelcome, often tedious effort **2.** showing signs of effort or difficulty rather than naturalness or fluency, especially in speech or writing —**la·bo·ri·ous·ly** *adv* —**la·bo·ri·ous·ness** *n*

SYNONYMS See *hard*.

la·bor·ite /láybə rìt/ *n US* a member or supporter of a labor union or the labor movement

la·bor of love *n* something demanding or difficult done for pleasure rather than money

la·bor·sav·ing /láybər sàyving/ *adj* designed or made to require less physical effort

la·bor un·ion *n* an organization of wage earners that is set up to serve and advance its members' interests in terms of wages, benefits, and working hours and conditions

la·bour *n, vti* Can, UK spelling of **labor**

La·bour *n UK* POL same as **Labour Party** (*takes singular or plural verb*) ■ *adj* supporting, belonging to, or associated with the Labour Party in the United Kingdom or New Zealand

La·bour Par·ty *n* **1.** a British political party founded in 1900 to support the rights and interests of working people **2.** a party with similar objectives in another country such as New Zealand

la·bra ZOOL plural of **labrum**

Lab·ra·dor[1] /lábbrə dàwr/ *n* a large dog with a short thick black, brown, or yellow coat, belonging to a breed originally developed to fetch killed or injured game during a hunt. Labradors were first bred in Newfoundland. [Early 20C. After LABRADOR[2]]

Lab·ra·dor[2] /lábbrə dàwr/ mainland portion of Newfoundland, eastern Canada, on the Labrador Sea. It abuts Quebec to the west and south and the Atlantic Ocean on the east. Area: 114,618 sq. mi./296,860 sq. km.

Lab·ra·dor Cur·rent cold ocean current that flows south past western Greenland and eastern Labrador and Newfoundland, Canada, to join the Gulf Stream

lab·ra·dor·ite /lábbrə daw rìt/ *n* a variety of plagioclase feldspar, the color of which shifts between blue and green depending on the angle it is seen from [After LABRADOR[2]]

Lab·ra·dor Pen·in·su·la large peninsula in eastern Canada, including much of Quebec and the mainland portion of Newfoundland. Area: 625,100 sq. mi./1,619,000 sq. km.

Lab·ra·dor re·triev·er *n* BREED same as **Labrador**[1]

Lab·ra·dor Sea arm of the Atlantic Ocean that separates Labrador in eastern Canada from Greenland and the Atlantic Ocean. It is about 550 mi./900 km wide.

Lab·ra·dor tea *n* a low-growing evergreen bush with bell-shaped flowers and leaves that are used in making a tea. Native to: northern North America. Latin name: *Ledum groenlandicum*.

~~**labratory**~~ incorrect spelling of **laboratory**

labret

la·bret /láybrət/ *n* an ornament made of bone, shell, steel, or other material that is worn pierced through the lower lip or in the skin just below the lower lip. They are worn by some peoples in East Africa and South America and by people elsewhere who engage in body piercing. [Mid-19C. < Latin *labrum* "lip"]

la·brum /láybrəm, láb-/ (*plural* **-bra** /-brə/) *n* a projecting upper mouthpart of some arthropods [Early 18C. < Latin, "lip"]

La·bu·an /lə bóo ən, laá boo aán/ island in Malaysia, off the northern coast of Borneo, northeast of Singapore. Population: 54,307 (1991). Area: 40 sq. mi./100 sq. km.

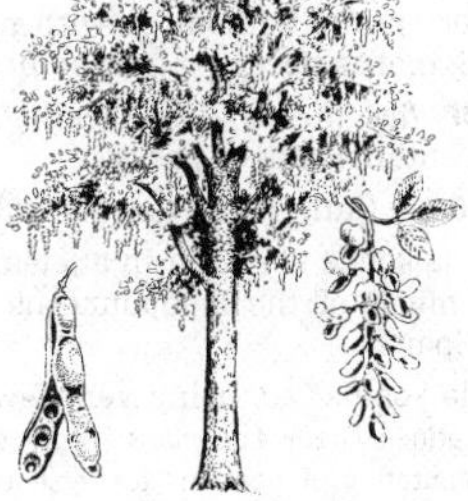
laburnum

la·bur·num /lə búrnəm/ *n* a tree with poisonous leaves, bark, and seeds. Flowers: yellow, drooping. Native to: Europe, Asia. Genus: *Laburnum*. [Mid-16C. < Latin]

lab·y·rinth /lábbə rìnth/ *n* **1. CONFUSING NETWORK** a place with a lot of crisscrossing or complicated passages, tunnels, or paths in which it would be easy to become lost **2. SOMETHING VERY COMPLICATED** something that is made up of many different parts that is complicated and hard to understand ○ *a labyrinth of insurance regulations* **3.** ANAT **SET OF CONNECTED TUBES** a structure consisting of connected cavities or canals, especially the inside of the ear [14C. Directly or via French < Latin *labyrinthus* < Greek *laburinthos*]

Lab·y·rinth *n* in Greek mythology, the maze designed by Daedalus for King Minos of Crete to confine the Minotaur

lab·y·rinth fish *n* a fish with a specialized labyrinthine breathing organ that allows it to breathe air out of water. Family: Anabantidae.

lab·y·rin·thine /làbbə rínthin, -theen, -thīn/, **lab·y·rin·thi·an** /-rínthee ən/ *adj* **1.** consisting of or resembling a labyrinth of passages or paths ○ *a labyrinthine maze of backstreets* **2.** extremely complicated and therefore difficult to understand

lab·y·rin·thi·tis /làbbərin thítiss/ *n* an illness in which the inner ear becomes inflamed, causing a loss of balance and nausea

lab·y·rin·tho·dont /làbbə rínthə dònt/ *n* an extinct amphibian resembling the crocodile that lived in the Late Paleozoic and Early Mesozoic eras. Order: Labyrinthodontia. [Mid-19C. < modern Latin *Labyrinthodontia*, literally "labyrinth-toothed" < Greek *laburinthos* "labyrinth"]

lac[1] /lak/ *n* a resinous substance secreted by some insects (**lac insects**). Use: formerly, source of shellac. [15C. Via Portuguese *lac(c)a* < Persian *lāk*, Hindi *lākh* < Sanskrit *lākṣā* "red dye"]

lac[2] *n* MEASURE another spelling of **lakh**

La·can /lə kaán, laa kaáN/, **Jacques** (1901–81) French psychoanalyst. A lifelong advocate of a traditional Freudian approach to psychoanalysis, he published a notoriously difficult collection of papers, *Escrits* (1966), that has had considerable influence on linguistics, critical theory, and psychology. Full name **Lacan, Jacques Marie Émile** —**La·ca·ni·an** /lə káynee ən/ *n, adj* —**La·ca·ni·an·ism** *n*

> "How can we be sure that we are not impostors?"
> [Jacques Lacan, *The Four Fundamental Concepts of Psychoanalysis*; 1977]

lac·co·lith /lákə lìth/ *n* a massive intrusion of igneous rock between beds of sedimentary rock, creating a dome-shaped structure [Late 19C. < Greek *lakkos* "pond, pit"] —**lac·co·lith·ic** /làkə líthik/ *adj*

lace

lace /layss/ *n* **1. DELICATE FABRIC WITH PATTERNED HOLES** a delicate fabric made by weaving cotton, silk, or a synthetic yarn in a pattern that leaves small holes between the threads (*often used before a noun*) ○ *a lace shawl* **2. CORD USED TO TIE EDGES TOGETHER** a long cord that is used to tie two parts of a garment, shoe, or boot together and is threaded through holes or round hooks **3. BRAID ON MILITARY UNIFORMS** ornamental gold or silver braid used on military officers' uniforms and hats ■ *vt* (**laced, lac·ing, lac·es**) **1. FASTEN SOMETHING WITH LACES** to tie the edges of something with holes or hooks together by threading laces through the holes or around the hooks, pulling the edges close, and knotting the laces **2. PASS LACE THROUGH HOLES** to thread a lace or cord through holes or around hooks **3. ADD ALCOHOL TO DRINK** to add a small amount of alcohol or a drug to a drink or to food ○ *eggnog laced with rum* **4. ADD SMALL AMOUNT TO SOMETHING** to add an amount of something to something else to enhance it ○ *an intelligent article laced with wit* **5. STREAK SOMETHING WITH DIFFERENT COLOR** to mark something with streaks of a different color **6. INTERTWINE SOMETHING** to intertwine something with something else ○ *laced her fingers together* **7. ADD LACE TO SOMETHING** to decorate or trim something with lace **8. BEAT SOMEBODY** to beat or thrash somebody (*informal*) [12C. < Old French *laz* "net, string" < Latin *laqueus* "noose"]

lace into *vt* **1.** to fasten a corset or close-fitting garment around somebody by lacing it up **2.** to attack somebody verbally or physically (*informal*)

lace up *vt* to fasten or tighten the laces of something such as a boot or corset

lace bug *n* a small bug with a delicate lacy vein pattern on its wings. Family: Tingitidae.

Lac·e·dae·mo·ni·an /làssədə mṓnee ən/ *adj* relating to the ancient Greek city of Sparta [Mid-16C. < Latin *Lacedaemonius*, Greek *Lakedaimonios* "of Lacedaemon (an ancient region)"] —**Lac·e·dae·mo·ni·an** *n*

lace pil·low *n* HANDICRAFT same as **cushion** *n* (sense 6)

lac·er·ate *vt* /lássə ràyt/ (**-at·ed, -at·ing, -ates**) **1. CUT SKIN JAGGEDLY** to cut or gash the skin so that the wound is deep with irregular edges **2. CAUSE SOMEBODY DEEP DISTRESS** to distress somebody deeply or agonizingly ■ *adj* /lássərət, -ràyt/ **WITH JAGGED EDGES** describes leaves or petals that have jagged or irregular edges [15C.

< Latin *lacerat-*, past participle of *lacerare* "tear to pieces" < *lacer* "torn"] —**lac·er·a·tion** /lássə ráysh'n/ *n*

lac·er·at·ing /lássə ràyting/ *adj* **1.** causing intense emotional or physical distress ○ *lacerating criticism* ○ *lacerating pain* **2.** cutting or gashing the skin in a way that leaves a deep jagged wound

La·cer·ta /lə súrtə/ *n* a small constellation of the northern hemisphere. See illustration at **constellation** [Late 18C. < Latin, "lizard"]

la·cer·tid /lə súrtid/ *n* a lizard with rough irregular scales and bony plates on its skull, e.g., the common wall lizard or green lizard. Family: Lacertidae. [Late 19C. < Latin *lacerta* "lizard"]

lace-up *n* a shoe or boot that fastens with laces —**lace-up** *adj*

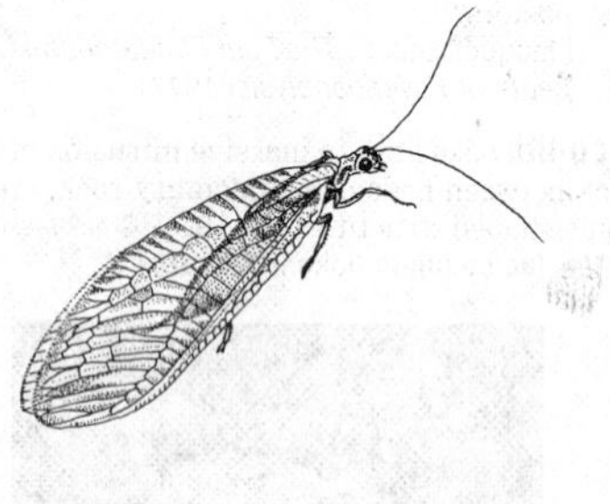

lacewing

lace·wing /láyss wìng/ *n* an insect with transparent wings and long antennae whose larvae feed on aphids and other insect pests. There are several species of lacewing, including the green lacewing and the brown lacewing. Superfamily: Hemerobioidea. [< the fine network of veins in its wings, likened to lace]

La·chaise /lə sháyz/, **Gaston** (1882–1935) French-born US sculptor. He is known for his large representations of nude figures such as *Standing Woman* (1930–33) and portrait busts.

lach·es /láchəz, láychəz/ *n* negligence or delay in doing something, especially in pursuing a legal claim [14C. < Anglo-Norman *laches(se)* "negligence" < Old French *lasche* "lazy" < Latin *laxus* "loose"]

Lach·e·sis /lákəssiss/ *n* in Greek mythology, one of the three Fates who influenced human destiny. She determined the extent of the thread of life that was spun and cut by the other two.

La·chine /lə sheén/ city in southern Quebec Province, Canada, on Montreal Island in the St. Lawrence River. Population: 40,222 (2002).

Lach·lan /laáklən/ river in south central New South Wales, Australia. Length: 922 mi./1,484 km.

lach·ry·mal /lákrəməl/ *adj* **1.** relating to tears or weeping (*literary*) **2.** ANAT same as **lacrimal** [Variant of LACRIMAL]

lach·ry·ma·tion, etc. *n* PHYSIOL another spelling of **lacrimation, etc.**

lach·ry·ma·to·ry /lákrəmə tàwree/ *n* (*plural* **-ries**) a small bottle of a kind found in ancient tombs, thought in the past to have contained the tears of mourners ■ *adj* PHYSIOL same as **lacrimatory** [Mid 17C. < Latin *lacrima* "tear," after *chrismatory* "vessel for the chrism"]

lach·ry·mose /lákrə mòss/ *adj* (*literary*) **1.** crying or tending to cry easily and often **2.** so sad as to make people cry [Early 18C. < Latin *lacrimosus* < *lacrima* "tear"] —**lach·ry·mose·ly** *adv* —**lach·ry·mos·i·ty** /lákrə mόssətee/ *n*

lac·ing /láyssing/ *n* **1.** LACE THAT FASTENS a lace that is used to fasten something **2.** ALCOHOL ADDED TO DRINK a small amount of alcohol or a drug added to a drink or to food **3.** BEATING a beating or thrashing (*informal*)

la·cin·i·ate /lə sínnee ət, -àyt/, **la·cin·i·at·ed** /-àytəd/ *adj* describes a leaf that has a fringed, jagged, or lobed border [Mid-17C. < Latin *lacinia* "fringe"] —**la·cin·i·a·tion** /lə sìnnee áysh'n/ *n*

lac in·sect *n* an insect, the female of which secretes a substance (**lac**) that was formerly used to make shellac. Native to: South Asia. Latin name: *Laccifer lacca.*

lack /lak/ *n* **1.** SHORTAGE a complete absence of a particular thing ○ *Lack of sleep makes it difficult to concentrate.* **2.** SOMETHING ABSENT something that is needed but is in short supply or missing ■ *vt* (**lacked, lack·ing, lacks**) **1.** NOT HAVE SOMETHING not to have something that is needed ○ *The project lacked funding.* **2.** NOT HAVE ENOUGH OF SOMETHING to have too little of something ○ *What he lacks in patience, he makes up for in drive.* [13C. Probably < assumed Old English *lac* < Germanic]

SYNONYMS *lack, shortage, deficiency, deficit, want, dearth*

CORE MEANING: an insufficiency or absence of something

lack a complete absence of a particular thing ○ *public lack of confidence in the media's objectivity* ○ *The conditions are substandard and overcrowded, and there is a total lack of the most basic amenities.* **shortage** an absence of something that is needed or required ○ *a shortage of skilled labor* ○ *The drought is likely to cause severe food shortages.* **deficiency** an inadequate supply of something necessary, especially a nutrient, or a weakness in the provision or performance of something ○ *A diet of fast food and snacks can lead to nutritional deficiencies.* ○ *We accept responsibility for any deficiencies in our safety procedures.* **deficit** the amount by which a total is less than it should be ○ *How does the administration intend to cut the budget deficit without raising taxes?* ○ *rallied from a 2-goal deficit to win the game* **want** *or* **dearth** an absence or scarcity of something ○ *exhausted from overwork and want of sleep* ○ *There's a real dearth of data for the high-seas fisheries.*

lack·a·dai·si·cal /làkə dáyzik'l/ *adj* without much enthusiasm, energy, or effort [Mid-18C. < *lackadaisy* "alas," alteration of LACKADAY] —**lack·a·dai·si·cal·ly** *adv*

lack·a·day /lákə dày/ *interj* used to express regret, disapproval, or dismay (*archaic*) [Late 17C. Shortening of *alack-a-day* < ALACK]

lack·ey /lákee/ (*plural* **-eys**) *n* **1.** somebody who is excessively willing to obey another's orders **2.** a man servant, especially a footman or valet who wears a uniform (*archaic*) [Early 16C. < French *laquais*]

lack·ing /láking/ *adj* without or with not enough of something that is needed ○ *lacking in good taste*

lack·lus·ter /lák lùstər/ *adj* lacking energy, excitement, enthusiasm, or passion

lack·lus·tre *adj* Can, UK spelling of **lackluster**

La·co·ni·a /lə kṓnee ə/ region in ancient Greece that occupied much of the Peloponnesus. The capital city was Sparta.

la·con·ic /lə kónnik/ *adj* using very few words [Mid-16C. Via Latin < Greek *Lakōnikos* "of Laconia, Spartan"; from the reputation of Spartans for terseness] —**la·con·i·cal·ly** *adv*

lac·o·nism /lákə nìzzəm/, **la·con·i·cism** /lə kónni sìzzəm/ *n* **1.** the use of very few words **2.** something that is said in few words but is full of meaning [Late 16C. < Greek *lakōnismos* "imitation of Spartan manners" < *Lakōn* "Laconia"]

La Co·ru·ña /laà kō roónyə/ city, port, and capital of La Coruña Province, in the autonomous region of Galicia, northwestern Spain. Population: 236,371 (2002).

lac·quer /lákər/ *n* **1.** a hard, glossy, clear or colored coating made up of resins or cellulose derivatives and a plasticizer in a volatile solvent **2.** a varnish made from the sap of an eastern Asian tree. Use: protective coating, especially for wood. **3.** HAIR same as **hair spray** (*dated*) [Late 16C. < obsolete French *lacre* "sealing wax," alteration of Portuguese *la(c)ca* (see LAC[1])] —**lac·quer** *vt* —**lac·quer·er** *n*

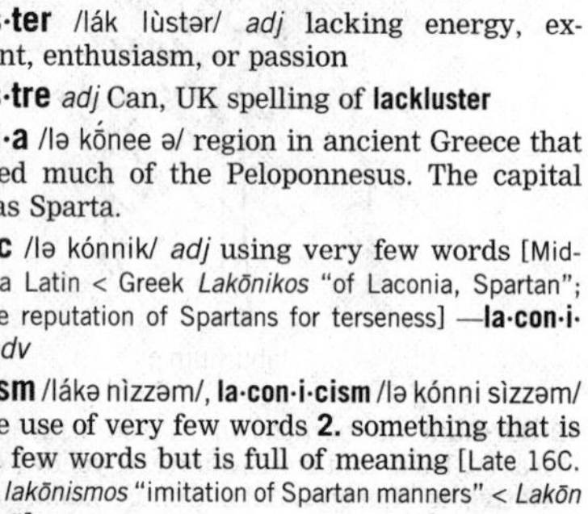

AKG London

lacquerware: Japanese lacquered box (1890)

lac·quer·ware /lákər wèr/, **lac·quer·work** /-wùrk/ *n* ornamental objects, usually of wood, that have been coated with lacquer and sometimes inlaid

lac·ri·mal /lákrəməl/ *adj* **1.** relating to the glands that produce tears, or the ducts through which they drain **2.** LITERAT same as **lachrymal** (sense 1) [15C. < medieval Latin *lacrimalis* < Latin *lacrima* "tear"]

lac·ri·mal duct *n* the passage carrying tears into the nose

lac·ri·mal gland *n* a gland in the outer corner of the eye that produces tears

lac·ri·ma·tion /làkrə máysh'n/, **lach·ry·ma·tion** *n* the production of tears in the eyes, especially excessive production as in crying or in reaction to a foreign body [Late 16C. < Latin *lacrimation-* < *lacrimat-*, past participle of *lacrimare* "shed tears" < *lacrima* "tear"]

lac·ri·ma·tor /lákrə màytər/, **lach·ry·ma·tor** *n* a substance that makes tears form in the eyes, e.g., tear gas [Early 20C. < Latin *lacrimat-* (see LACRIMATION)]

lac·ri·ma·to·ry /lákrəmə tàwree/ *adj* causing the eyes to produce tears [Mid 19C. Variant of LACHRYMATORY]

Popperfoto

lacrosse

la·crosse /lə kráwss/ *n* a sport in which two teams of ten players use sticks with a net pouch (**crosse**) at one end to throw and catch a small hard rubber ball. The objective is to score a goal by throwing the ball into the opposing team's goal net. Lacrosse was originated by Native North Americans. (*often used before a noun*) ○ *a lacrosse stick* [Early 18C. < Canadian French *(jeu de) la crosse* "(game of) the hooked stick" < Germanic]

La Crosse /lə kráwss/ city in western Wisconsin, situated at the junction of the Mississippi, Black, and La Crosse rivers. Population: 51,209 (2002 estimate).

lact- *prefix* same as **lacto-** (*used before vowels*)

lac·tal·bu·min /làk tal byoómən/ *n* a milk protein that contains all the essential amino acids

lac·tase /lák tàyss, -tàyz/ *n* an intestinal enzyme that breaks down lactose into glucose and galactose [Late 19C. < LACTOSE]

lac·tate[1] /lák tàyt/ (**-tat·ed, -tat·ing, -tates**) *vi* to produce milk in the body (*refers to female mammals*) [Late 19C. Back-formation < LACTATION]

lac·tate[2] /lák tàyt/ *n* a chemical compound that is a salt or ester of lactic acid [Late 18C. < LACTIC]

lac·ta·tion /lak táysh'n/ *n* **1.** the production of milk by the mammary glands **2.** the period during which milk is produced by the mammary glands [Mid-17C. Directly or via French < late Latin *lactation-* < Latin *lactare* "suckle" < *lact-* "milk"] —**lac·ta·tion·al** *adj*

lac·te·al /láktee əl/ *adj* **1.** OF MILK relating to milk or milk production **2.** ANAT CARRYING MILKY FLUID carrying or containing a milky fluid (**chyle**) ○ *a lacteal vessel* ■ *n* ANAT LYMPHATIC VESSEL a lymphatic vessel that originates in the small intestine and carries a milky fluid (**chyle**) to the thoracic duct [Mid-17C. < Latin *lacteus* "of milk" < *lact-* "milk"] —**lac·te·al·ly** *adv*

lac·tes·cent /lak téss'nt/ *adj* **1.** describes plants and insects that secrete a milky substance **2.** looking like milk, or becoming milky [Mid-17C. < Latin *lactescent-*, present participle of *lactescere* "turn to milk" < *lactere* "be milky" < *lact-* "milk"] —**lac·tes·cence** *n*

lac·tic /láktik/ *adj* relating to or derived from milk [Late 18C. < Latin *lact-* "milk"]

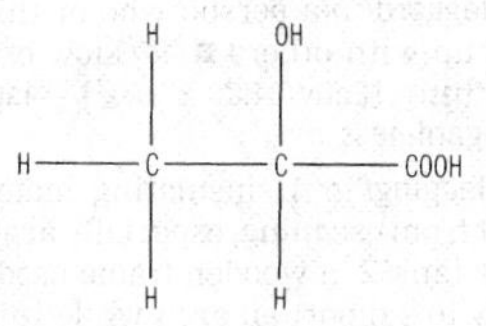

lactic acid

lac·tic ac·id *n* a colorless organic acid produced by muscles and found in sour milk. Use: preservative, in dyeing, manufacture of adhesives and pharmaceuticals. Formula: $C_3H_6O_3$.

lac·tif·er·ous /lak tíffərəss/ *adj* **1.** describes a body part that carries or produces milk, or is capable of producing milk ○ *a lactiferous duct* **2.** describes a plant that produces a milky juice (**latex**) [Late 17C. < Latin *lact-* "milk"] —**lac·tif·er·ous·ness** *n*

lacto- *prefix* **1.** milk ○ *lactometer* **2.** lactic acid ○ *lactobacillus* **3.** lactose ○ *lactase* [< Latin *lact-* "milk"]

lac·to·ba·cil·lus /làktō bə sílləss/ (*plural* **-li** /-lī/) *n* a rod-shaped bacterium that produces lactic acid through fermentation. Genus: *Lactobacillus.*

lac·to·fla·vin /làktə fláyvin/ *n* BIOCHEM same as **riboflavin**

lac·to·gen·ic /làktə jénnik/ *adj* causing the mammary glands to produce milk

lac·to·glob·u·lin /làktō glóbbyəlin/ *n* one of a group of globular proteins that occur in milk

lac·tom·e·ter /lak tómmətər/ *n* an instrument that is used to measure the density of milk. It is a kind of hydrometer.

lac·tone /lák tōn/ *n* a chemical compound belonging to a group derived from hydroxy acids, often occurring as the odor-bearing component of a plant product —**lac·ton·ic** /lak tónnik/ *adj*

lac·to·pro·tein /làktō prṓ teen/ *n* a protein that is present in milk

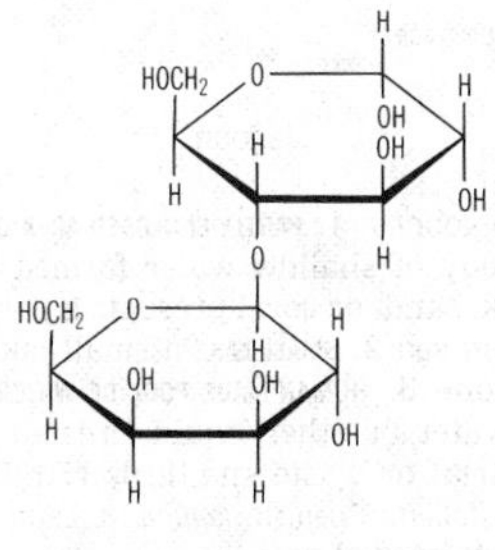

lactose

lac·tose /lák tōss, -tōz/ *n* **1.** a sugar (**disaccharide**) composed of glucose and galactose. Source: milk. Formula: $C_{12}H_{22}O_{11}$. **2.** a white crystalline form of lactose. Source: whey. Use: in food products and pharmaceuticals. Formula: $C_{12}H_{22}O_{11}$.

lac·tose in·tol·er·ance *n* a condition resulting from low activity or absence of the enzyme lactase, which is responsible for the digestion of milk sugar. It is common in people of Asian and African descent.

lac·to·veg·e·tar·i·an /làktō vejə térree ən/ *n* somebody who eats vegetables, grains, fruit, nuts, and milk products but not meat or eggs

lac·tu·lose /láktyə lōss, -lōz/ *n* a synthetic sugar that is broken down by bacteria in the colon into products that draw water and ammonia into the colon. Use: treatment of constipation and symptoms of liver disease. [Mid-20C. < LACTO-, probably after CELLULOSE]

la·cu·na /lə kyṓnə, -kṓnə/ (*plural* **-nae** /-nee/ or **-nas**) *n* **1.** a gap or place where something is missing, e.g., in a manuscript or a line of argument (*literary*) **2.** ANAT a small cavity, e.g., in bone or cartilage [Mid-17C. < Latin, "hole" < *lacus* "pond"] —**la·cu·nal** *adj*

la·cu·nar /lə kyṓnər, -kṓnər/ *n* **1.** CEILING WITH SUNKEN PANELS a ceiling that has sunken panels in it **2.** SUNKEN PANEL IN CEILING a decorative sunken panel in a ceiling ■ *adj* OF BODILY CAVITIES relating to pits or cavities in tissue, e.g., in bone or cartilage, especially ones that are atypical [Late 17C. < Latin < *lacuna* (see LACUNA)]

la·cus·trine /lə kústrən/ *adj* **1.** relating to lakes **2.** growing, living, or formed in or at the edge of a lake [Early 19C. < Latin *lacus* "lake"]

lac·y /láyssee/ (**-i·er, -i·est**) *adj* **1.** made of or decorated with lace **2.** having the appearance of lace ○ *lacy clouds* —**lac·i·ness** *n*

lad /lad/ *n* **1.** a boy or young man **2.** a man of any age (*informal*) [13C. Origin ?]

La·dakh /lə dáak/ dry mountainous region of NW India, Pakistan, and China. It is one of the highest inhabited regions of the world.

La·da·khi /lə dáakee/ *n* **1.** somebody who was born or raised in Ladakh **2.** the form of Tibetan spoken in Ladakh [Mid-19C. < Tibetan] —**La·da·khi** *adj*

lad·a·num *n* INDUST same as **labdanum**

lad·der /láddər/ *n* **1.** DEVICE WITH RUNGS TO CLIMB ON a portable piece of equipment with rungs attached to sides made of metal, wood, or rope, used for climbing up or down **2.** PATH TO ADVANCEMENT a series of hierarchical levels on which somebody moves up or down within an organization or society ○ *working her way up the corporate ladder* **3.** LIST OF RANKED PLAYERS a list of contestants in an ongoing sports or games competition, arranged according to ability [Old English *hlǣd(d)er* < Indo-European, "to lean"]

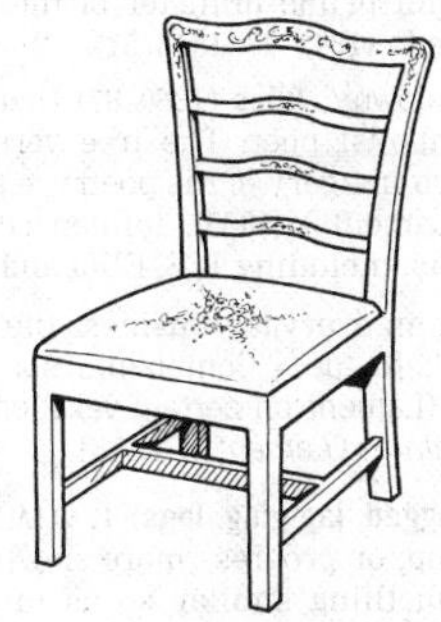

ladder-back

lad·der-back *n* **1.** a chair with a back formed by horizontal slats between the two vertical parts that form the sides **2.** the tall back of a ladder-back chair —**lad·der-back** *adj*

lad·der tour·na·ment *n* a tournament based on a list of ranked players in a game or sport, in which each player may challenge any other player who is ranked one or two positions higher

lad·der truck *n* EMERGENCIES same as **hook-and-ladder truck**

lad·die /láddee/ *n UK* a boy or young man (*informal*)

lad·du /lúddoo/, **lad·doo** (*plural* **-doos**), **lad·oo** (*plural* **-oos**) *n* in South Asian cuisine, a dessert made by frying a mixture of flour, sugar, and shortening, and then shaping it into a ball [< Hindi *laḍḍū*]

lade /layd/ (**lad·ed, lad·en** /láyd'n/ or **lad·ed, lad·ing, lades**) *v* **1.** *vti* PUT CARGO ON SHIP to take on cargo or freight, or load a ship with cargo or freight **2.** *vti* REMOVE LIQUID WITH LADLE to remove a measure of liquid using a ladle **3.** *vt* BURDEN SOMETHING OR SOMEBODY to place a load on something or a heavy burden on somebody (*dated*) [Old English *hladan* < Germanic]

la-de-da *adj* another spelling of **la-di-da**

~~ladel~~ incorrect spelling of **ladle**

lad·en /láyd'n/ past participle of **lade** ■ *adj* **1.** carrying a load, usually a heavy load (*often used in combination*) ○ *He was laden down with shopping bags.* ○ *fruit-laden boughs* **2.** weighed down by a problem or an unpleasant feeling such as doubt or unhappiness ○ *laden with guilt*

La·den ➧ **Bin Laden, Osama**

la-di-da /laa dee dáa/, **lah-di-dah, la-de-da** *adj* speaking or behaving in a way that is affectedly upper-class (*informal*) [Late 19C. An imitation of affected pronunciation]

la·dies /láydeez/ *n UK* same as **ladies room** (*informal; takes a singular verb*)

la·dies' man, la·dy's man *n* a man who enjoys being with women and flirting with them (*informal*)

la·dies room, la·dies' room *n* a women's restroom

La·din /lə deén/ *n* a language spoken in some valleys in northern Italy, belonging to the Rhaeto-Romance subgroup of Romance languages. Native speakers: 25,000. [Mid-19C. Via Rhaeto-Romance < Latin *Latinus* (see LATIN)] —**La·din** *adj*

lad·ing /láyding/ *n* freight or cargo being transported from one place to another

La·di·no /lə deénō/ (*plural* **-nos**) *n* **1.** a language based on Spanish with Hebrew elements, spoken by some Sephardic Jews. It is usually written in a form of Hebrew script. **2.** *also* **la·di·no** somebody of partially Spanish or indigenous ancestry in Central America who speaks Spanish [Late 19C. Via Spanish < Latin *Latinus* (see LATIN)] —**La·di·no** *adj*

la·di·no clo·ver /lə deénō-/ *n* a large variety of white clover grown as forage. Native to: North America. [Via Italian < Latin *Latinus* (see LATIN)]

la·dle /láyd'l/ *n* a spoon with a long handle and a deep bowl, used to serve soup and other liquids ■ *vt* (**-dled, -dling, -dles**) to serve food such as soup onto a plate using a ladle [Old English *hlædel* < *hladan* (see LADE)]

ladle out *vt* to give out generous or overgenerous amounts of something, especially something intangible (*informal*) ○ *ladled out praise*

La·do·ga, Lake /láadəgə/ largest lake in Europe, in northwestern Russia, northeast of St. Petersburg. Its outlet is the Neva River, which connects it with the Gulf of Finland. Area: 7,100 sq. mi./18,390 sq. km.

lad·oo *n* FOOD another spelling of **laddu**

la·dy /láydee/ (*plural* **-dies**) *n* **1.** WOMAN a woman, especially when addressed as part of a group ○ *Ladies and gentlemen, please take your seats.* **2.** REFINED WOMAN a woman of refined family background or upbringing **3.** POLITE DIGNIFIED WOMAN a woman who behaves very politely and with dignity **4.** WIFE OR USUAL WOMAN COMPANION a man's wife or usual woman companion (*informal*) **5.** WOMAN FEUDAL SUPERIOR in medieval Europe, a woman who was a powerful land or property owner with authority over an area, castle, or community such as a manor **6.** DRUGS same as **cocaine** (*slang*) [Old English *hlǣfdīge* "bread-kneader" < *hlāf* "bread," earlier form of LOAF[1]]

La·dy *n UK* **1.** TITLE FOR WOMAN used as an alternative title for a marchioness, countess, viscountess, or baroness **2.** COURTESY TITLE FOR WOMAN used as a courtesy title for the daughter of an earl, marquess, or duke **3.** FORM OF ADDRESS FOR WOMAN used as a form of address for the wife of a viscount, earl, marquess, baron, baronet, or knight, and the daughter of a duke, marquess, or earl

la·dy bee·tle *n US* INSECTS same as **ladybug**

la·dy·bird /láydee bùrd/ *n UK* same as **ladybug**

la·dy·bird bee·tle *n US* INSECTS same as **ladybug**

La·dy Boun·ti·ful *n* a woman who makes generous and well-publicized charitable donations

la·dy·bug /láydee bùg/ *n* a small round flying beetle that has red or orange outer wings with black spots. It eats aphids and other insects. Family: Coccinellidae. [Late 17C. After *(Our) Lady*, the mother of Jesus Christ]

La·dy Chap·el, la·dy chap·el *n* a chapel dedicated to Mary, mother of Jesus Christ, that is inside a cathedral or church

La·dy Day *n UK* the feast of the Annunciation. Date: March 25.

la·dy·fin·ger /láydee fìng gər/ *n* a small finger-shaped sponge cake, several of which are often used to surround molded desserts

la·dy·fish /láydee fìsh/ (*plural same* or **-fish·es**) *n* **1.** a large silvery ocean fish, related to the tarpon and prized as a game fish. Native to: tropics. Latin name: *Elops saurus.* **2.** *US* FISH same as **bonefish**

la·dy friend *n* a man's woman companion (*informal; sometimes considered offensive*)

la·dy-in-wait·ing (*plural* **la·dies-in-wait·ing**) *n* a woman who is an attendant for a queen or princess

la·dy-kill·er *n* a man who is extremely attractive to women (*informal*)

la·dy·like /láydee lìk/ *adj* behaving or done in a polite and dignified way ○ *not a very ladylike thing to whine* —**la·dy·like·ness** *n*

la·dy·love /láydee lùv/ *n* a woman that a man is in love with (*dated*)

la·dy luck, La·dy Luck *n* luck or good fortune personified as a woman (*informal; sometimes considered offensive*)

la·dy of the eve·ning *n* same as **prostitute** (*dated*)

La·dy of the Lake *n* in Arthurian legend, a supernatural woman, sometimes considered to be the same person as Vivian, the lover of Merlin

la·dy of the night *n UK* same as **prostitute** (*dated*)

La·dy·ship /láydee ship/, **la·dy·ship** *n* a title used when addressing or referring to a woman with the title of "Lady"

la·dy slip·per *n* PLANTS same as **lady's slipper**

la·dy's maid *n UK* a woman who serves another woman, looking after her and her clothes and accessories

la·dy's man *n* same as **ladies' man**

La·dy·smith /láydee smìth/ town in KwaZulu-Natal Province, eastern South Africa. It was the scene of a famous siege (1899–1900) during the Boer War. Population: 25,102 (1985).

lady's slipper

la·dy's slip·per, la·dy slip·per *n* a wild orchid. Flowers: various colors, including pink, purple, yellow, resembling slippers. Native to: North America. Genus: *Cypripedium*.

la·dy's smock *n* PLANTS same as **cuckooflower**

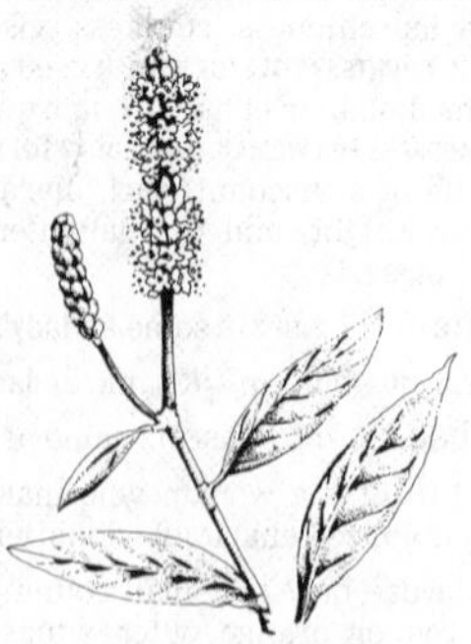

lady's thumb

la·dy's thumb *n* an annual weedy plant that has long leaves with a dark spot resembling a thumbprint. Flowers: pink or purplish, in spikes. Native to: Europe, Asia. Latin name: *Polygonum persicaria*.

La·ën·nec /la énnek/, **René** (1781–1826) French physician. He invented the stethoscope, and was a pioneer of thoracic medicine.

La·er·tes /lay úrteez, -érteez/ *n* in Greek mythology, the father of Odysseus

laevo- *prefix* UK spelling of **levo-**

lae·vo·ro·ta·to·ry *adj* OPTICS UK spelling of **levorotatory**

La Farge /lə faarzh/, **John** (1835–1910) US artist and critic. He is known for his landscapes, murals, and work in stained glass.

La·fay·ette /làffee ét/ **1.** city in west central Indiana, situated on the Wabash River, southwest of Kokomo. Population: 60,594 (2002 estimate). **2.** city in southern Louisiana, situated north of Abbeville and southwest of Baton Rouge. Population: 111,272 (2002 estimate).

La·fay·ette, Marie Joseph Paul Yves Roch Gilbert du Motier, Marquis de (1757–1834) French soldier and politician. He fought against the British in the American Revolution, and then took part in the French Revolution. He became a member of the French post-revolutionary government.

La Fa·yette /laa faa yét/, **Marie Madeleine, Comtesse de** (1634–93) French novelist. She wrote the romances *Zaïde* (1670) and *La princesse de Clèves* (1678). Known as **La Fayette, Madame de**

laff /laf/ *n* same as **laugh** (*nonstandard; often used ironically*) ○ *a lot of tasteless laffs* [Late 20C. Respelling]

Laf·fer curve /láffər-/ *n* a graph summarizing the fact that tax revenues are low for very high and for very low tax rates, thus demonstrating that raising tax rates beyond an optimum point will discourage investment and decrease tax revenues [Late 20C. After Arthur B. *Laffer* (b. 1942–), US economist]

Laf·fite /lə féet/, **Jean** (1780?–1825?) French-born US pirate. He helped defend New Orleans against Britain in the War of 1812.

La Fol·lette /lə fóllət/, **Robert Marion** (1855–1925) US senator. He led the progressive wing of the Republican Party, often opposing the leadership in the cause of reform.

La·fon·taine /lə fon táyn/, **Sir Louis Hippolyte** (1807–64) Canadian politician. He is credited with launching responsible government and was, with Robert Baldwin, joint prime minister of the united province of Canada (1842–43, 1848–51).

La·forgue /la fáwrg/, **Jules** (1860–87) Uruguayan-born French symbolist poet. The free verse and strikingly modern imagery of his poetry, e.g., "Les Complaintes" (Laments) (1885), influenced many 20th-century poets, including T. S. Eliot and Ezra Pound.

> "O what an everyday business life is!"
> [Jules Laforgue, "Complainte sur certains ennuis (Lament on certain vexations)", *Les Complaintes (Laments)*; 1885]

lag[1] /lag/ *v* (**lagged, lag·ging, lags**) **1.** *vi* FALL BEHIND OTHERS to go, develop, or progress more slowly than somebody or something similar so as to fall back or fall behind **2.** *vi* SLACKEN to decrease in strength or intensity ○ *Interest in the scandal has never lagged.* **3.** *vi* DECIDE ORDER OF PLAY in pool or billiards, to decide who is to play first by having each player rebound a ball from the top cushion as close as possible to the hand rail **4.** *vt* TOSS SOMETHING AT TARGET to pitch or shoot something such as a coin or marble at a target ■ *n* **1.** POSITION OF HAVING FALLEN BEHIND the condition or an instance of having fallen behind **2.** PERIOD BETWEEN EVENTS a period of time between one event and a related event **3.** LAGGING IN BILLIARDS in pool, billiards, or some other game, an act or instance of lagging [Early 16C. Origin ?]

lag[2] /lag/ *vt* (**lagged, lag·ging, lags**) to insulate something such as a pipe or hot water tank with lagging to prevent freezing or heat escaping ■ *n* a strip of wood, e.g., a stave of a barrel or a lath [Late 17C. Probably < N Germanic]

lag·an /lággən/, **li·gan** /lígən/ *n* cargo or wreckage lying on the sea bed, often with a buoy attached so that it can be recovered [Mid-16C. < Old French]

Lag b'O·mer /laag bómər/ *n* a minor Jewish festival marking the day on which some of the restrictions on activities imposed during the Omer are lifted. Date: 18th day of Iyar, 33rd day of the Omer. [< Hebrew < *lāg* "thirty-third" (pronunciation of the letters LG that symbolize this number) + *bā* "in the" + *ōmer* "Omer"]

la·ger[1] /laagər/ *n* a light-colored beer made with a low proportion of hops, usually stored for a period after brewing [Mid-19C. Shortened < German *Lager-Bier* < *Lager* "storehouse" + *Bier* "beer"]

la·ger[2] *n, vti* MIL another spelling of **laager**

La·ger·kvist /laagər kvìst/, **Pär** (1891–1974) Swedish novelist, poet, and playwright. He won a Nobel Prize in literature (1951). Full name **Lagerkvist, Pä Fabien**

la·ger lout *n UK* a young man who is perceived as behaving violently or disruptively, usually as a result of drinking alcohol (*informal insult*)

lag·gard /lággərd/ *n* a person who or thing that does not keep up with others ■ *adj* slow or reluctant to do something [Early 18C. < LAG[1]] —**lag·gard·ly** *adv, adj* —**lag·gard·ness** *n*

lag·ging /lágging/ *n* **1.** insulating material used to keep heat from escaping, especially around a pipe or hot water tank **2.** a wooden frame used in building, especially to support an arch while it is being built [Mid-19C. < LAG[2]]

lag·ging in·di·ca·tor, lag·ging ec·o·nom·ic in·di·ca·tor *n US* an economic statistic that typically reflects how the economy was rather than how it is or will be

la·gniappe /lan yáp, lán yàp/ *n* **1.** *Southern US, Carib* a small present given by a store to a customer who has just purchased something **2.** *Southern US* an unexpected bonus or extra ○ *"You have earned your claim for a little lagniappe like mail, meals, electricity, and life-support systems."* (Dave Lesar *Wall Street Journal*; October 17, 2003) [Mid-19C. Via Louisiana French < American Spanish *la ñapa* "the gift" < Quechua *yapay* "give more"]

REGIONAL NOTE ***Lagniappe*** is primarily a Louisiana French term, although it is derived from American Spanish and Quechua. Although it has scattered usage to the east and west, it is most common in the New Orleans area, and across Lower Mississippi and East Texas.

lag·o·morph /lággə màwrf/ *n* a plant-eating mammal with two pairs of incisors in the upper jaw specifically adapted for gnawing. Rabbits, hares, and pikas are lagomorphs. Order: Lagomorpha. [Late 19C. < modern Latin *Lagomorpha* < Greek *lagōs* "hare" + *morphē* "shape"] —**lag·o·mor·phic** /làggə máwrfik/ *adj* —**lag·o·mor·phous** /làggə máwrfəss/ *adj*

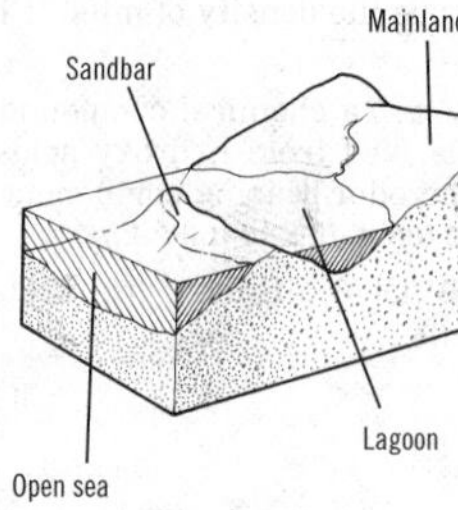

lagoon

la·goon /lə góon/ *n* **1.** PARTLY-ENCLOSED AREA OF SEAWATER a coastal body of shallow water formed where low-lying rock, sand, or coral presents a partial barrier to the open sea **2.** SMALL LAKE a small lake adjoining a larger one **3.** HUMAN-MADE POOL OF WATER a shallow body of water or other liquid, created by or near an industrial or waste site [Early 17C. Directly or via French < Italian, Spanish *laguna* < Latin *lacuna* (see LACUNA)] —**la·goon·al** *adj*

La·gos /láy gòss/ largest city, chief port, and former capital of Nigeria. Population: 1,484,000 (1995).

La·gos Es·co·bar /laagoss éskō baar/, **Ricardo** (*b.* 1938) president of Chile. After a period of exile in the United States during the rule of General Pinochet, he returned to found the Party for Democracy (1987). He served as minister of education (1990–92) and minister of public works (1994–96) before winning the 2000 presidential elections.

La·grange /lə graanj/, **Joseph Louis, comte de l'Empire** (1736–1813) Italian-born French mathematician and astronomer. The author of *Mécanique analytique* (*Analytical Mechanics*) (1788), he pioneered many concepts in mechanics, algebra, and number theory.

> "When we ask advice, we are usually looking for an accomplice."
> [Attributed to Joseph Louis Lagrange]

La Grange /lə gráynj/ village in northeastern Illinois, northeast of Downers Grove. It is a western suburb of Chicago. Population: 15,584 (2002 estimate).

La Guar·di·a /lə gwaardee ə/, **Fiorello Henry** (1882–1947) US politician. He was a popular, and populist, reforming mayor of New York City from 1933 to 1945. Known as **the Little Flower**

> "When I make a mistake, it's a beaut!"
> [Fiorello LaGuardia, remarks about an unacceptable judicial appointment of his, quoted in *Patience and Fortitude*, William Manners; 1976]

La·gu·na Beach /lə go͞onə-/ city in Orange County, southwestern California, situated 27 mi./43 km southeast of Long Beach. Population: 24,269 (2002 estimate).

La·gu·na Hills city in Orange County, southwestern California. Population: 33,627 (2002 estimate).

La·gu·na Ni·guel /-nee gèl/ city in Orange County, southwestern California. Population: 63,057 (2002 estimate).

lah[1] *n* MUSIC another spelling of **la**[1]

lah[2] /laa/ *adv Malaysia, Singapore* added to something said to indicate informality and intimacy (*informal*)

La Ha·bra /lə haábrə/ city in Orange County, southwestern California, situated 19 mi./31 km northeast of Long Beach. Population: 59,984 (2002 estimate).

la·har /laá haar/ *n* a landslide or mudflow of volcanic debris, especially after a heavy rainfall [Early 20C. < Javanese]

lah-di-dah *adj* another spelling of **la-di-da** (*informal*)

Lah·nda /laándə/ *n* a language spoken in Pakistan, related to Punjabi. It belongs to the Indic branch of the Indo-European family of languages. [Early 20C. < Punjabi *lahandā* "western"] —**Lah·nda** *adj*

La·hore /lə háwr/ city and capital of Punjab Province, northeastern Pakistan, about 160 mi./257 km southeast of Islamabad. Population: 5,063,499 (1998).

Lah·ti /laátee/ industrial city in southern Finland, north of Helsinki. Population: 96,666 (2000).

LAIA *abbr* COMM Latin American Integration Association

la·ic /láy ik/, **la·i·cal** /láy ik'l/ *adj* relating to or involving followers of a religion who are not clergy [Mid-16C. Via late Latin < Greek *laikos* "of the people" < *laos* "people"] —**la·i·cal·ly** *adv*

la·i·cize /láy i sīz/ (**-cized, -ciz·ing, -ciz·es**) *vt* to remove something from control or governance by the church or the clergy and give control of it to the lay community —**la·i·ci·za·tion** /lày issi záysh'n/ *n*

laid past participle, past tense of **lay**[1]

laid-back *adj* very relaxed, easygoing, and unworried (*informal*) —**laid-back·ness** *n*

laid pa·per *n* a paper with a watermark of fine lines on it that are produced in the manufacturing process

Lai·lat al-Ba·raah /láylat al bə raá/, **Lai·lat ul-Ba·raah** /-o͝ol-/ *n* an Islamic festival, the Night of Repentance, marking the night when God sets each person's path for the coming year and all who repent their sins are granted forgiveness. Date: 15th of Sha'ban.

Lai·lat al-Mi·raj /-al mi raáj/, **Lai·lat ul-Mi·raj** /-o͝ol-/ *n* an Islamic festival, the Night of Ascent, marking the ascent of Muhammad to heaven. Date: 27th of Rajab. [< Arabic, "night of the ascent"]

Lai·lat al-Qa·dr /-al kaádər/, **Lai·lat ul-Qa·dr** /-o͝ol-/ *n* an Islamic festival, the Night of Power, marking the sending down of the Koran to Muhammad. Date: 27th of Ramadan. [< Arabic, "night of the power"]

Laing /lang/, **R. D.** (1927–89) British psychiatrist. His radical views on schizophrenia were set out in *The Divided Self* (1960). Other books include *The Politics of Experience* (1967) and *The Politics of the Family* (1969). Full name **Laing, Ronald David**

> "Children do not give up their innate imagination, curiosity, dreaminess easily. You have to love them to get them to do that."
> [R. D. Laing, *The Politics of Experience*; 1967]

lair /ler/ *n* **1. WILD ANIMAL'S DEN** a place where a wild animal rests or sleeps **2. PLACE TO BE ALONE IN** a retreat or hideaway (*informal*) ■ *vti* (**laired, lair·ing, lairs**) **RETURN TO LAIR** to go to a lair, or take or drive an animal to a lair [Old English *leger* "act of lying, bed" < Indo-European]

laird /lerd/ *n Scotland* an owner of land, especially a large estate [14C. Variant of LORD]

lais·ser-faire *n* another spelling of **laissez-faire**

lais·ser-pas·ser *n* another spelling of **laissez-passer**

lais·sez-faire /lè say fér, lè zay-/, **lais·ser-faire** *n* **1.** the principle that the economy works best if private industry is not regulated and markets are free **2.** refusal to interfere in other people's affairs, or the practice of letting people do as they wish [< French, "allow to do"]

lais·sez-pas·ser /lè say paa sáy/, **lais·ser-pas·ser** *n* a document that permits the holder to travel freely, especially one given in lieu of a passport [< French, "allow to pass"]

la·i·ty /láy ətee/ *npl* **1.** the followers of a religion who are not clergy **2.** all the people who are not members of a specific profession, as distinguished from those who are members [15C. < LAY[2]]

La·ius /láy əss, lī́ əss/ *n* in Greek mythology, a king of Thebes mistakenly killed by his son Oedipus

WORLD'S LARGEST LAKES

	Lake	Area	Location
1	Caspian Sea	143,000 sq. mi. / 370,000 sq. km	Europe/Asia
2	Lake Superior	31,700 sq. mi. / 82,100 sq. km	North America
3	Lake Victoria	26,830 sq. mi. / 69,490 sq. km	Africa
4	Lake Huron	23,000 sq. mi. / 59,600 sq. km	North America
5	Lake Michigan	22,300 sq. mi. / 57,800 sq. km	North America
6	Lake Tanganyika	12,700 sq. mi. / 32,900 sq. km	Africa
7	Great Bear Lake	12,270 sq. mi. / 31,790 sq. km	North America
8	Lake Baikal	12,200 sq. mi. / 31,500 sq. km	Asia
9	Aral Sea	12,050 sq. mi. / 31,220 sq. km	Asia
10	Lake Nyasa	8,683 sq. mi. / 22,490 sq. km	Africa

lake[1] /layk/ *n* **1. INLAND BODY OF WATER** a large body of water surrounded by land **2. POOL OF LIQUID** a large pool of liquid that has collected or spilled somewhere ○ *A lake of hot grease covered the floor by the stove.* **3. SURPLUS OF LIQUID PRODUCT** a large surplus of a liquid product, e.g., milk or wine, that is stored and not sold in order to prevent prices from becoming too low, especially in the European Union (*informal; usually used in combination*) ○ *a wine lake* [Pre-12C. Directly or via French < Latin *lacus* "pond"]

CULTURAL NOTE ***The Lady of the Lake***, a poem (1810) by Scottish writer Sir Walter Scott. Set in early 16th-century Scotland, it describes the eventful courtship of Ellen, daughter of outlawed chieftain James of Douglas, who lives at Loch Katrine (the lake of the title). Regarded as one of Scott's finest works, it is admired for its satisfying plot, strong characterization, and charming songs."Hail to the Chief who in triumph advances!", canto II, stanza 19, is a famed line in this work.

lake[2] /layk/ *n* **1.** a bright translucent pigment of various colors, made by combining an organic dye with a metallic hydroxide or other inorganic substance **2.** a red pigment made by combining cochineal with a metallic compound [Early 17C. Variant of LAC[1]]

Lake Clark Na·tion·al Park and Pre·serve /làyk klaark-/ national park and preserve in southern Alaska, established in 1980. Area: 6,300 sq. mi./16,310 sq. km.

Lake Dis·trict region of mountains and lakes in Cumbria, northwestern England. The district extends about 30 mi./50 km from north to south and 25 mi./40 km from east to west.

lake dwell·ing *n* a home or settlement built on a platform supported by wooden posts over or by a shallow lake or river edge, especially in prehistoric times —**lake dwell·er** *n*

lake ef·fect *n* the effect that a large lake such as any of the Great Lakes has on the local weather

Lake For·est city in northeastern Illinois, situated beside Lake Michigan 30 mi./50 km north of Chicago. Population: 20,723 (2002 estimate).

lake·front /láyk frùnt/ *n* the land along the shores of a lake

Lake George historic village and county seat of Warren County, in eastern New York State, situated on the southern end of Lake George, 40 mi./64 km northeast of Amsterdam. Population: 3,575 (2002 estimate).

Lake Hav·a·su City /-hàvvə so͞o-/ city in Mohave County, Arizona, situated on Lake Havasu on the Colorado River, bordering California. Population: 46,407 (2002 estimate).

lake her·ring *n* a fish related to the whitefish. Native to: Great Lakes. Latin name: *Coregonus artedii*.

Lakeland terrier

Lake·land ter·ri·er /láyklənd-/ *n* a wirehaired terrier with a black and tan coat, belonging to a breed originally developed in England for foxhunting [Early 20C. After *Lakeland* "the Lake District," NW England]

Lake Mac·quar·ie /-mə kwaáree/ city in eastern New South Wales, Australia. Population: 188,717 (2002 estimate).

Lake of the Woods lake in central North America, on the border between the United States and Canada. It includes hundreds of wooded islands. Area: 1,695 sq. mi./4,390 sq. km.

Lake Pla·cid /-plássid/ village in the Adirondack Mountains, northeastern New York. A popular vacation spot, it hosted the Winter Olympics in 1932 and 1980. Population: 2,674 (2002 estimate).

Lake Po·ets *npl* the poets Wordsworth, Coleridge, and Southey, who lived in the Lake District in northwestern England in the early 19th century

lak·er /láykər/ *n* **1.** a boat or ship that is used on lakes rather than the sea **2.** a fish living in a lake rather than the sea, e.g., a lake trout [Late 18C. < LAKE[1]]

lake·shore /láyk shàwr/ *n* land lying next to a lake

lake·side /láyk sīd/ *n* same as **lakefront**

lake trout *n* **1.** a fish of the salmon family. Native to: deep North American lakes. Latin name: *Salvelinus namayacush*. **2.** *UK* FISH same as **brown trout**

Lake Worth /-wúrth/ city in Palm Beach County, southeastern Florida, situated on Lake Worth, 6 mi./10 km south of West Palm Beach. Population: 35,575 (2002 estimate).

lakh /laak/ (*plural* **lakhs** or *same*), **lac** (*plural* **lacs** or *same*) *n S Asia* the number 100,000, used especially for referring to sums of rupees [Early 17C. Via Hindi *lākh* < Sanskrit *lakṣam* "mark, 100,000"]

La·ko·ta /lə kṓtə/ (*plural* **-tas** or *same*) *n* PEOPLES, LANG same as **Teton**[1] [Mid-19C. < Teton *lakhóta*] —**La·ko·ta** *adj*

laks /laks/ *n US* same as **lox**[1]

lak·sa /láksə/ *n* a Malaysian or Singaporean rice noodle, slightly thicker than spaghetti, often served in a spicy fish sauce or soup [< Malay]

Lak·shad·weep /laak shaád weép, lùkshəd weép/ Union Territory of southwestern India, comprising an archipelago of 36 islands in the Arabian Sea. Capital: Kavaratti Island. Population: 60,595 (2001). Area: 12.4 sq. mi./32 sq. km.

Lak·shmi /lúkshmee/, **Lak·smi** *n* in Hinduism, the goddess of prosperity, wealth, and royalty, and wife of the god Vishnu

la·ky /láykee/ *adj* of a color similar to a red form of the pigment lake [Mid-19C. < LAKE[2]]

La·la /laá laá/ *n S Asia* a title equivalent to "Mr.," used before men's names [< Hindi]

La-La /laá laá/ *n* used as a nickname for Los Angeles (*slang; often used humorously*) ○ *moving to La-La* [< doubling of LA]

la-la land *n* (*slang*) **1.** a state of mind divorced from reality **2.** a place where people live shallow, frivolous lives [< LA-LA]

la·lang /laá laang/ *n* a tall coarse tropical grass. Native to: Malay Archipelago. Latin name: *Imperata arundinacea*. [Late 18C. < Malay]

la·la·pa·loo·za *n* same as **lollapalooza** (*informal*)

-lalia *suffix* speech, speech disorder ○ *echolalia* [< Greek *lalia* "talk" < *lalein* "to talk"]

La·lique glass /lə leék-/ *n* ornamental frosted glassware decorated with bas-relief figures, fruits, and flowers, designed by the French Art Nouveau craftsperson René Lalique (1860–1945)

Lal·lans /lállənz/, **Lal·lan** /lállən/ *adj* relating to the Lowlands of Scotland, or any dialect of Scots spoken there [Early 18C. < a pronunciation of LOWLAND]

lal·la·pa·loo·za *n* same as **lollapalooza** (*informal*)

lal·la·tion /la láysh'n/ *n* a mispronunciation of "r," especially one that sounds like "l" [Mid-17C. < Latin *lallation-* < *lallare* "sing a lullaby"]

lal·ly·gag *vi* another spelling of **lollygag**

lam /lam/ (*informal*) *v* (**lammed, lam·ming, lams**) **1.** *vti* HIT HARD to hit somebody or something hard ○ *lammed into him with her fists* **2.** *vi* SPEAK ANGRILY to speak angrily to somebody ○ *lammed into me for being late* **3.** *vi* ESCAPE HASTILY to escape or run away, especially from the law ■ *n* HASTY ESCAPE a hasty escape, especially to avoid arrest [Late 16C. Origin ?] ◇ **on the lam** making a hasty escape, especially from the law (*informal*)

la·ma /laámə/ *n* **1.** a Tibetan or Mongolian Buddhist monk **2.** in Buddhism, a title used for those people who are believed to be the reincarnations of a bodhisattva [Mid-17C. Representing the pronunciation of Tibetan *bla-ma*]

La·ma·ism /laámə ìzzəm/ *n* a form of Mahayana Buddhism practiced in Tibet and Mongolia that has non-Buddhist elements from South Asia and from an older nature-worshipping religion. Its monks (**lamas**) are led by the Dalai Lama, a temporal as well as spiritual ruler. —**La·ma·ist** *n, adj* —**La·ma·is·tic** /laámə ístik/ *adj*

La Man·cha /laa maánchə/ historic region occupying a high barren plateau in south central Spain. Miguel de Cervantes set his Novel *Don Quixote* (1605–15) there.

La·mar /lə maár/, **Lucius Quintus Cincinnatus** (1825–93) associate justice of the US Supreme Court (1888–93). He was a strong advocate of states' rights.

La·marck /lə maárk/, **Jean-Baptiste Pierre Antoine de Monet, Chevalier de** (1744–1829) French naturalist and evolutionist. His theory that evolution proceeded by the inheritance of acquired characteristics was superseded by Darwin's theory of natural selection. —**La·marck·i·an** *adj, n*

La·marck·ism /lə maár kizzəm/ *n* the evolutionary theory of Jean Baptiste Lamarck that holds that evolution proceeds through the inheritance of characteristics acquired by individual organisms

La·marr /lə maár/, **Hedy** (1914–2000) Austrian-born US movie actor. She starred in movies in the 1930s and 1940s, including *Samson and Delilah* (1949) and, with co-inventor George Antheil (1900–59), patented a secret communication system for military use, which was a forerunner of cellular phone technology. Born **Kiesler, Hedwig Eva Maria**

la·ma·ser·y /laámə sèrree/ (*plural* **-ies**) *n* a Tibetan or Mongolian monastery of lamas [Mid-19C. < French *lamaserie* "lama dwelling" < *lama* "lama" < Tibetan *bla-ma*]

La Mau·ri·cie Na·tion·al Park /laa màwri seé-/ national park situated due west of Quebec City, in the Laurentian Mountains, in southern Quebec, Canada. Area: 207 sq. mi./536 sq. km.

La·maze /lə maáz/ *n* a method of natural childbirth by which a woman is physically and psychologically prepared through prenatal training. Lamaze encourages the use of controlled breathing and the participation of the woman's partner during the process of childbirth. [Mid-20C. After Fernand *Lamaze* (1890–1957), French physician]

lamb /lam/ *n* **1.** YOUNG SHEEP an immature sheep, especially one under a year old and without permanent teeth **2.** MEAT OF LAMB the meat of an immature sheep that is under a year old **3.** CLOTHING same as **lambskin** (sense 1) **4.** SOMEBODY MEEK AND MILD a gentle and innocent person, especially a baby or small child **5.** SOMEBODY EASILY DECEIVED somebody who is easily cheated, especially financially ■ *vti* (**lambed, lamb·ing, lambs**) BEAR LAMB to give birth to a lamb [Old English < Germanic] ◇ **like a lamb to the slaughter** going to face something unpleasant, difficult, or dangerous calmly and without resistance

Lamb /lam/, **Charles** (1775–1834) British essayist. He was a prose stylist of great clarity whose books include *Essays of Elia* (1823). Pseudonym **Elia**

> "I love to lose myself in other men's minds. When I am not walking, I am reading; I cannot sit and think. Books think for me."
> [Charles Lamb, "Detached Thoughts on Books and Reading," *Last Essays of Elia*; 1833]

Lam·ba /lámbə, laámbə/ *n* a language spoken in Benin, belonging to the Gur branch of Niger-Congo. Native speakers: 29,000. [Early 20C. < Bantu] —**Lam·ba** *adj*

lam·ba·da /lam baádə/ *n* **1.** a fast rhythmic dance of Brazilian origin in which partners hold each other close and gyrate their hips **2.** the music for a lambada [Late 20C. < Brazilian Portuguese, "a beating"]

Lam·ba·ré·né /làmbə reénee, lóNbə ráy nay/ capital of Moyen-Ogooué Region, western Gabon. Population: 42,316 (1993).

lam·baste /lam báyst/ (**-bast·ed, -bast·ing, -bastes**), **lam·bast** /-bást/ (**-bast·ed, -bast·ing, -basts**) *vt* **1.** to criticize somebody or something severely **2.** to beat or whip somebody [Mid-17C. < LAM + BASTE[3]]

lamb·da /lámdə/ *n* **1.** the 11th letter of the Greek alphabet, represented in the English alphabet as "l." See table at **alphabet 2.** the point of junction at the center of the back of the cranium between the rear plate of the cranium (**occipital bone**) and the two upper plates (**parietal bones**). This junction is said to resemble the Greek capital letter lambda. [Early 17C. < Greek]

lamb·da cal·cu·lus *n* a descriptive theory of mathematical functions and the way they combine, used as the basis for some high-level computer programming languages

lamb·da·cism /lámdə sìzzəm/ *n* the erroneous substitution of "l" for "r" in speech [Mid-17C. Via late Latin < Greek *lambdakismos* < *lambda* "lambda"]

lamb·da hy·per·on *n* a short-lived elementary particle that has a mass approximately 1.1 times that of the proton and zero electric charge

lamb·doid /lám dòyd/, **lamb·doid·al** /lam dóyd'l/ *adj* describes the suture that joins bones at the back of the skull, shaped like the Greek capitalized lambda

lam·bent /lámbənt/ *adj* **1.** GLEAMING softly gleaming or glowing (*literary*) **2.** PLAYING OVER SURFACE flickering or playing as a flame over a surface without burning it (*literary*) **3.** BRILLIANTLY LIGHT having a light but brilliant touch ○ *lambent wit* [Mid-17C. < Latin *lambent-*, present participle of *lambere* "lick"] —**lam·ben·cy** *n* —**lam·bent·ly** *adv*

lam·bert /lámbərt/ *n* an SI unit of surface brightness (**luminance**) equivalent to one lumen per square centimeter [Late 19C. After Johann Heinrich *Lambert* (1728–77), German scientist]

Lam·beth walk /làmbəth-/, **Lam·beth Walk** *n* a lively ballroom dance originating in England during the 1930s [Mid-19C. After a street in *Lambeth*, borough in S London]

lam·bie /lámbee/ *n Carib* tenderized conch flesh used for food [Late 20C. < French *lambi* "sea mollusk"]

lamb·ing /lámming/ *n* **1.** the birth of lambs, or the season when they are born **2.** the work of helping ewes give birth to lambs

lamb·kill /lám kil/ (*plural* **-kills** or *same*) *n US* PLANTS same as **sheep laurel**

lamb·kin /lámkin/ *n* **1.** a baby lamb **2.** used as a term of endearment for a baby or small child

Lamb of God *n* Jesus Christ, seen as a sacrifice whose crucifixion and resurrection redeemed humankind

lam·bre·quin /lámbrəkin, -bər-/ *n* **1.** HOUSEHOLD ORNAMENTAL HANGING a decorative strip of drapery, hung along the top of a doorway, window, shelf, or mantelpiece **2.** HIST SCARF ATTACHED TO KNIGHT'S HELMET a veil, scarf, or piece of drapery attached to a knight's helmet to protect it from heat and rust **3.** HERALDRY same as **mantling 4.** CERAMICS ORNAMENTAL BORDER ON VASE a decorative border near the top of a vase [Early 18C. Via French < assumed Dutch, "small veil" < *lamper* "veil"]

Lam·brus·co /lam bróoskō/ *n* a sparkling wine, typically red and sweet, from the Emilia-Romagna district in northern Italy [Mid-20C. Via Italian < Latin *labruscum* "fruit of the wild grape Vitis labrusca" < *labrusca* "wild vine"]

lamb's fry *n UK* lamb's testicles or internal organs, traditionally sold skinned and ready for cooking by frying [< FRY[1] "internal part of an animal"]

lamb·skin /lám skìn/ *n* **1.** the woolly pelt of a lamb. Use: making or trimming winter clothing. **2.** the hide of a lamb, prepared as leather

lamb's let·tuce *n UK* same as **corn salad** [Translation of Latin *lactuca agnina*]

lamb's quar·ters *n US* PLANTS same as **pigweed** (sense 2)

lambs·wool /lámz wòol/, **lamb's wool** *n* fine soft wool sheared from a year-old lamb. Use: knitwear.

Lamb·ton /lámtən/, **John George, 1st Earl of Durham** (1792–1840) British colonial administrator. He served briefly as governor-general of Canada (1838). His report on the status of Canada paved the way for eventual self-government.

lame[1] /laym/ *adj* (**lam·er, lam·est**) **1.** WALKING UNEVENLY walking unevenly because of a leg injury or motion impairment (*offensive when used of a person*) **2.** DISABLED injured or with impaired strength or motion (*offensive when used of a person*) **3.** UNCONVINCING inadequate, unconvincing, or unsatisfactory (*offensive in some contexts*) **4.** INEFFECTIVE ineffectual or inept (*offensive in some contexts*) **5.** BORING AND OLD-FASHIONED boring, old-fashioned, and neither street-wise nor having street credibility (*slang; sometimes considered offensive*) ■ *vt* (**lamed, lam·ing, lames**) DISABLE PERSON OR ANIMAL to cause a person or animal to be unable to walk evenly because of injury or impairment (*offensive when used of a person*) [Old English *lama* < Germanic, "weak-limbed" < Indo-European, "break by hitting"] —**lame·ness** *n*

lame[2] /laym/ *n* a thin plate of metal, especially one of the overlapping metal plates of which medieval armor was made from the mid-14th century [Late 16C. < French (see LAMÉ)]

la·mé /la máy/ *n* a fabric with gold or silver threads interwoven with silk, wool, or cotton [Early 20C. < French, "worked with silver and gold thread" < *lame* "thin metal plate" < Latin *lamina* "thin plate or layer"]

lame·brain /láym bràyn/ *n* an offensive term that deliberately insults somebody's intelligence (*slang insult*) —**lame·brained** *adj*

la·medh /laá mèd/, **la·med** *n* the 12th letter of the Hebrew alphabet, represented in the English alphabet as "l." See table at **alphabet** [Mid-17C. < Hebrew *lāmēdh*]

lame duck *n* **1.** POL OUTGOING OFFICEHOLDER an elected officeholder left seemingly powerless after a successor has been elected but has hot yet taken office

2. *US* POL **OFFICEHOLDER NOT RUNNING FOR REELECTION** an elected official who either will not or may not legally run for another term in office and has reduced power or effectiveness **3. SOMEBODY OR SOMETHING WEAK** a person or thing considered as weak, inadequate, or unfortunate (*offensive when used of a person*)

la·mel·la /lə méllə/ (*plural* **-lae** /-lee/) *n* **1.** ANAT **THIN PIECE OF BONE** any thin flat structure of bone or tissue **2.** FUNGI **PART OF FUNGUS** a gill of a fungus **3.** BIOL **MEMBRANE LAYER** a membrane layer in a plant chloroplast **4.** CONSTR **VAULT FRAMEWORK** a structural part of wood, metal, or reinforced concrete that is crisscrossed to form a vault [Late 17C. < Latin, "small thin plate" < *lamina* "thin plate or layer"] —**la·mel·lar** *adj* —**la·mel·lar·ly** *adv* —**la·mel·late** /lə mé làyt, lə méllət, lámmə làyt/ *adj*

lamelli- *prefix* lamella ○ *lamelliform* [< LAMELLA]

la·mel·li·branch /lə mélli brángk/ *n* ZOOL same as **bivalve** [Mid-19C. < modern Latin *Lamellibranchia* < Latin *lamella* (see LAMELLA) + Greek *bragkhia* "gills"] —**la·mel·li·branch·i·ate** /lə mèlli brángkee ət, -kee àyt/ *adj, n*

la·mel·li·corn /lə mélli kàwrn/ *adj* describes a beetle that has antennae composed of layered segments, e.g., a dung beetle [Mid-19C. < modern Latin *Lamellicornia* < Latin *lamella* (see LAMELLA) + *cornu* "horn"] —**la·mel·li·corn** *n*

la·mel·li·form /lə mélli fàwrm/ *adj* shaped like a thin plate or scale

lame·ly /láymlee/ *adv* inadequately, unconvincingly, or ineptly

la·ment /lə mént/ *vti* (**-ment·ed, -ment·ing, -ments**) **1. EXPRESS SADNESS** to express grief or sorrow about something **2. EXPRESS REGRET** to express regret, annoyance, or disappointment about something ○ *She was lamenting the lack of funding for her project.* ■ *n* **1. EXPRESSION OF SADNESS** an expression of grief or sorrow **2. EXPRESSION OF REGRET** an expression of regret, annoyance, or disappointment **3. WORK LAMENTING DEATH** a song or poem of mourning [Mid-16C. Directly or via French < Latin *lamentari* < *lamenta* "laments"] —**lam·en·ta·tion** /làmmən táysh'n/ *n* —**la·ment·ed** *adj* —**la·ment·er** *n* —**la·ment·ing·ly** *adv*

la·men·ta·ble /lə méntəb'l, lámməntəb'l/ *adj* **1.** unsatisfactory, pitiful, or deplorable **2.** sad and mournful (*literary*) —**la·men·ta·ble·ness** *n* —**lam·en·ta·bly** *adv*

Lam·en·ta·tions /làmmən táysh'nz/ *n* a book of the Bible written in the form of elegies, traditionally attributed to Jeremiah (*takes a singular verb*) See table at **Bible**

La Me·sa /lə máyssə/ city in San Diego County, southwestern California, situated 8 mi./13 km east of San Diego. Population: 54,966 (2002 estimate).

la·mi·a /láymee ə/ (*plural* **-mi·as** or **-mi·ae** /-mee ee/) *n* in classical mythology, a blood-sucking witch who takes the form of a serpent to threaten children [14C. Via Latin < Greek, mythical monster]

La Mig·ra /laa méegrə/ *n Hispanic* the US immigration and border patrol services, especially along the US-Mexico border [< Mexican Spanish < shortening of *Instituto Nacional de Migración* "National Institute of Migration"]

lam·i·na /lámmənə/ (*plural* **-nae** /-nee/ or **-nas**) *n* **1. THIN LAYER** a thin plate, layer, or flake **2.** BOT **LEAF BLADE** the blade or flat part of a leaf **3.** ZOOL **PROTECTIVE PLATE INSIDE HOOF** in hoofed mammals, any of the parallel layers of sensitive tissue just inside the hard exterior of the hoof [Mid-17C. < Latin, "thin plate or layer, leaf"]

lam·i·nal /lámmən'l/ *adj* describes speech sounds articulated using the blade or flat part of the tongue

lam·i·nar flow /làmmənər-/ *n* a flow in a liquid or gas in which neighboring layers do not mix but flow at different velocities

lam·i·nar·i·a /làmmə nérree ə/ *n* a large brown seaweed (**kelp**) that has broad flat fronds. Genus: *Laminaria*. [Mid-19C. < modern Latin *Laminaria* < Latin *lamina* "thin plate or layer"]

lam·i·nar·in /làmmə nérrin/ *n* a carbohydrate occurring in brown algae [Mid-20C. < modern Latin *Laminaria* (see LAMINARIA)]

lam·i·nate *v* /lámmə nàyt/ (**-nat·ed, -nat·ing, -nates**) **1.** *vt* **COVER SOMETHING WITH THIN LAYER** to cover something with a thin sheet of protective material such as plastic or metal **2.** *vt* **BOND LAYERS TOGETHER** to bond sheets or layers together so as to produce a strong and durable composite material ○ *Wood veneers were laminated to produce a cheap and durable alternative to expensive hardwoods for furniture-making.* **3.** *vt* **FORM METAL INTO THIN LAYERS** to roll or beat metal into thin sheets **4.** *vti* **SEPARATE INTO LAYERS** to split something into thin layers, or be split into thin layers ■ *n* /lámmə nàyt, -nit/ **MATERIAL MADE UP OF BONDED LAYERS** a product composed of layers or sheets bonded together ■ *adj* /lámmə nit, -nàyt/ **IN LAYERS** composed of or with layers —**lam·in·a·ble** *adj* —**lam·i·nat·ed** *adj* —**lam·i·na·tor** *n*

lam·i·na·tion /làmmə náysh'n/ *n* **1. PROCESS OF BONDING LAYERS** the bonding together of thin layers of materials to form a composite material **2. FORMATION OF LAYERS** the formation of layers in something **3. THINLY LAYERED STRUCTURE** a structure composed of thin layers **4. THIN LAYER** a thin layer in something (*technical*) **5.** ELEC ENG **THIN STEEL PLATE IN TRANSFORMER CORE** one of a number of thin steel or iron plates that are held together to form a transformer core

lam·i·nec·to·my /làmmə néktəmee/ (*plural* **-mies**) *n* a surgical operation to remove one or more sides of the rear arches of a spinal vertebra and gain access to the spinal cord or spinal nerve roots

Lam·ing·ton Na·tion·al Park /lámmingtən-/ national park in southeastern Queensland, Australia

Lam·ing·ton Pla·teau high mountain plateau situated in the Macpherson Range, Lamington National Park, Queensland, Australia

lam·i·ni·tis /làmmə nítiss/ *n* inflammation of the sensitive plates of tissue in a hoof, especially a horse's hoof, usually causing lameness. It is one of the most serious equine hoof diseases.

La Mi·ra·da /laa mə raadə/ city in Los Angeles County, southwestern California, situated 13 mi./21 km southeast of Los Angeles. Population: 48,478 (2002 estimate).

Lam·mas /lámməss/ *n* **1.** formerly, a Christian religious feast marking St. Peter's deliverance from prison. Date: August 1. **2.** a day formerly celebrated in England as a harvest festival. Date: August 1. [Old English *hlāfmæsse* < earlier forms of LOAF[1] + MASS; by association with LAMB]

lam·mer·gei·er /lámmər gī ər/, **lam·mer·gey·er** *n* a large vulture with dark wings and dark feathers that resemble a beard around its beak. It drops bones on rocks to break them in order to obtain marrow. Native to: mountains of southern Europe, Africa, Asia. Latin name: *Gypaetus barbatus*. [Early 19C. < German *Lämmergeier* "lambs' vulture"; because it commonly feeds on their carcasses]

lamp /lamp/ *n* **1. ELECTRIC LIGHT** a device that produces electric light **2. DEVICE PRODUCING LIGHT** a device that burns oil, gas, or wax to produce light **3. RADIATION SOURCE** a device that supplies ultraviolet light or infrared heat radiation, especially for medical or cosmetic treatment ○ *a sun lamp* **4. SOURCE OF ENLIGHTENMENT** a source of enlightenment or inspiration (*literary*) [12C. Via French *lampe* < Latin *lampas* < Greek, "torch" < *lampein* "to shine"]

lam·pas /lámpəss/ *n* an ornately patterned fabric resembling damask. Use: upholstery. [Mid-19C. < French]

lamp·black /lámp blàk/ *n* a fine powdery form of carbon that is deposited when oils containing carbon are burned. Use: pigment, printing ink, in electrodes.

lamp·brush chro·mo·some /lámp brush-/ *n* an enlarged chromosome covered with fine loops of chromatin, observed during the early part of reproductive division (**meiosis**) [Because it resembles a brush for the inside of a glass lampshade]

lamp chim·ney *n* a glass cover that is placed over the wick of an oil or kerosene lamp to protect and control the flame

Lam·pe·du·sa /làmpee doozə/, **Giuseppe Tomasi di** (1896–1957) Italian author. A member of the Sicilian aristocracy, he wrote only one novel, *Il Gattopardo* (1958), translated into English as *The Leopard* (1960), which was published posthumously to critical acclaim. See Cultural note at **leopard**

lam·per eel /lámpər-/ *n* FISH same as **lamprey** [Early 16C. Probably < variant of LAMPREY]

lamp glass *n* HOUSEHOLD same as **lamp chimney**

lam·pi·on /lámpee ən/ *n* a small oil lamp, usually with a tinted glass chimney, formerly popular as a carriage light [Mid-19C. Via French < Italian *lampione* "large lamp" < *lampa* "lamp" < French *lampe* (see LAMP)]

lamp·light /lámp līt/ *n* the light cast by a lamp —**lamp·lit** *adj*

lamp·light·er /lámp lītər/ *n* **1.** formerly, an employee who lit gas streetlamps **2.** a device used to light lamps

Lamp·man /lámpmən/, **Archibald** (1861–99) Canadian poet. He was best known for his nature poems.

lamp oil *n* **1.** oil suitable as lamp fuel **2.** *regional* same as **kerosene**

lam·poon /lam poon/ *n* a piece of satirical writing or verse ridiculing somebody or something ■ *vt* (**-pooned, -poon·ing, -poons**) to use ridicule as a way of satirizing somebody or something in a piece of writing [Mid-17C. < French *lampon*] —**lam·poon·er** *n* —**lam·poon·er·y** *n* —**lam·poon·ist** *n*

lamp·post /lámp pōst/ *n* **1.** a post or pillar that supports a streetlight **2.** *Malaysia* an unwanted single person with a couple or a group otherwise made up of couples (*informal*) ○ *I don't want to play lamppost.*

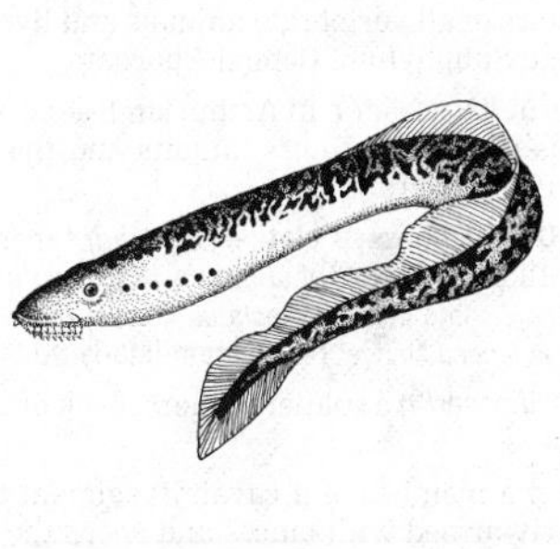

lamprey

lam·prey /lámpree/ (*plural* **-preys**), **lam·prey eel** *n* a freshwater jawless fish with a round sucking mouth for attaching itself to other fish and, in the case of adults, feeding parasitically on their blood. Family: Petromyzontidae. [13C. Via Old French *lampreie* < medieval Latin *lampreda*]

lam·pro·phyre /lámprə fīr/ *n* an igneous rock that occurs mainly as an intrusion or dike containing large crystals, especially of biotite and mica [Late 19C. < German *lamprophyr*, literally "shining purple" < Greek *(por)phureos* "purple"]

lamp·shade /lámp shàyd/ *n* a cover, typically decorative, used to moderate and direct artificial light from a lamp

lamp·shell /lámp shél/ *n* MARINE BIOL same as **brachiopod** [< its resemblance to an ancient oil lamp and its wick]

lamp·work·ing /lámp wùrking/ *n* the process or technique of forming glass items made of rods and tubes by heating them with an oxygen-gas flame

La·mut /lə moot/ *n* a language spoken in parts of eastern Siberia, belonging to the Tungusic branch of Altaic. Native speakers: 12,000. [Early 18C. Via Russian < Evenki, "those living by the sea" < *lamu* "sea"] —**La·mut** *adj*

LAN /lan/ *abbr* COMPUT local area network

la·nai /lə nī/ (*plural* **-nais**) *n* in Hawaii, an open roofed porch or veranda, often used as a living room [Early 19C. < Hawaiian]

la·nate /láy nàyt/ *adj* covered with or consisting of woolly hairs [Mid-18C. < Latin *lanatus* < *lana* "wool"]

lan·ça·do /làn saadō/ (*plural* **-dos**) *n* a collection point in the interior of Africa for Portuguese trade, from the 16th century onward, that linked African economies to the commercial centers on the Atlantic coast [< Portuguese, "launching point"]

Lan·ca·shire /lángkə sheer, -shər/ coastal county in northwestern England. Population: 1,134,974 (2001). Area: 1,183 sq. mi./2,896 sq. km.

Lan·cas·ter /lángkəstər/ historic city in the county of Lancashire, northwestern England. Population: 133,914 (2001).

Lan·cas·ter /láng kàstər/, **Burt** (1913–94) US actor. His movies include *From Here to Eternity* (1953), *Elmer*

Gantry (1960), *The Swimmer* (1968), and *Local Hero* (1983). Full name **Lancaster, Burton Stephen**

Lan·cas·tri·an /lang kástree ən/ *adj* **1.** relating to Lancashire or Lancaster in England **2.** belonging to or supporting the royal house of Lancaster, especially during the 15th-century Wars of the Roses —**Lan·cas·tri·an** *n*

lance /lanss/ *n* **1.** CAVALRY SPEAR a long weapon with a metal point carried by cavalry in battle **2.** HUNTING SPEAR FOR HUNTING OR FISHING a long pointed spear used in hunting or fishing **3.** METALL METAL-PIERCING DEVICE a thin metal tube or pipe through which a stream of oxygen is directed at a heated metal surface in order to pierce it ■ *vt* (**lanced, lanc·ing, lanc·es**) MED PIERCE WITH SHARP INSTRUMENT to pierce flesh with a sharp instrument to let out pus ○ *lance a blister* [13C. Via French < Latin *lancea*]

lance cor·po·ral *n* **1.** a noncommissioned officer in the US Marine Corps of a rank above private first class **2.** a British Army or British Royal Marines noncommissioned officer of a rank above private [< obsolete *lancepesade* "officer of the lowest rank," via French < Old Italian *lancia spezzata* "broken lance"]

lance·let /lánsslət/ *n* a small slender translucent animal living in the ocean that is related to the ancestors of all vertebrate animals and lives buried in sand. Subphylum: Cephalochordata.

Lan·ce·lot /lánssəlot/ *n* in Arthurian legend, the most famous of King Arthur's knights and the lover of Queen Guinevere

lan·ce·o·late /lánssee ələt, -ə làyt/ *adj* tapering to a point like the head of a lance ○ *lanceolate leaves* [Mid-18C. < late Latin *lanceolatus* < Latin *lanceola* "small lance" < *lancea* "lance"] —**lan·ce·o·late·ly** *adv*

lanc·er /lánssər/ *n* a soldier on horseback armed with a lance

Lancer *n* a member of a cavalry regiment that was formerly armed with lances and keeps the title

lanc·ers /lánssərz/ *n* (*takes a singular verb*) **1.** a square dance for 8 or 16 couples, originally a 19th-century quadrille **2.** the music for a lancers

lance ser·geant *n* a noncommissioned officer in some regiments of the British Army of a rank equivalent to corporal

lan·cet /lánssət/ *n* **1.** SURG same as **scalpel 2.** ARCHIT same as **lancet arch 3.** ARCHIT same as **lancet window**

lan·cet arch *n* a narrow arch that comes steeply to a point, typical in Gothic architecture

lanc·et·ed /lánssətəd/ *adj* **1.** built with lancet arches or lancet windows, as in Gothic architecture **2.** having an arched, steeply pointed top

lan·cet fish *n* a long-bodied carnivorous deep-sea fish with a long dorsal fin and sharp teeth. Latin name: *Alepisauridae*. [< the sharpness of the fins]

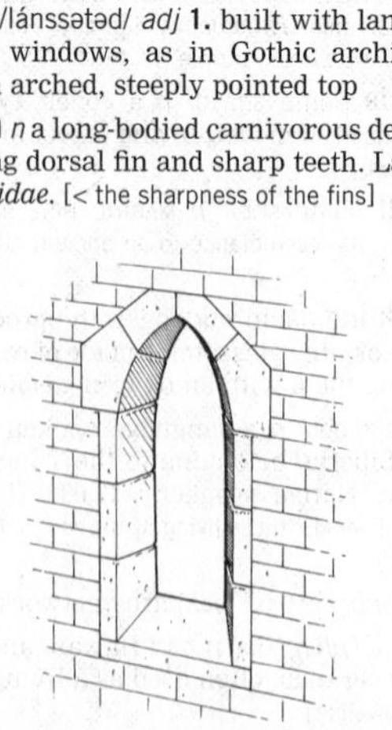

lancet window

lan·cet win·dow *n* a window formed as one or more slender pointed arches

lance·wood /lánss wŏŏd/ (*plural* **-woods** or *same*) *n* **1.** a tough flexible wood. Use: fishing rods, bows, cabinetmaking. **2.** a tree that yields lancewood. Native to: tropical America, Caribbean. Latin name: *Oxandra lanceolata*.

Lan-chou another spelling of **Lanzhou**

lan·ci·form /lánssə fàwrm/ *adj* shaped like a lance

land /land/ *n* **1.** SOLID EARTH the solid part of the Earth's surface not covered by a body of water **2.** PART OF EARTH a part of the Earth's surface of a particular kind or that is used for a particular purpose ○ *low-lying land* ○ *agricultural land* **3.** COUNTRYSIDE ground used for agriculture, or rural or agricultural areas as distinguished from villages, towns, or cities ○ *He had worked on the land all his life.* **4.** OWNED GROUND an area of ground that somebody owns ○ *public land* ○ *What are you doing on my land?* **5.** HOMELAND a territory, country, or nation inhabited by those who regard it as their home ○ *her native land* **6.** IMAGINED PLACE an imagined place ○ *She's living in the land of make-believe.* **7.** SMOOTH PARTS OF GROOVED AREA the unindented parts of a grooved surface, e.g., a ridge between grooves in the bore of a rifle **8.** UNFURROWED SOIL the parts of the ground between furrows in a plowed field ■ *v* (**land·ed, land·ing, lands**) **1.** *vi* ARRIVE BY PLANE to arrive by aircraft ○ *We land at 8:43.* **2.** *vti* SET DOWN AIRCRAFT to come down onto solid ground or water, or bring an aircraft down onto solid ground or water, especially at an airport ○ *The Baltimore plane landed five minutes ago.* **3.** *vti* GO OR PUT SOMETHING ASHORE to arrive on shore from a ship, or put something ashore from a ship ○ *We decided to land and explore the port.* **4.** *vi* COME DOWN THROUGH AIR to come down from a height ○ *The ball shot up and landed on the roof.* **5.** *vt* OBTAIN SOMETHING to win, obtain, secure, or be awarded something desired ○ *He finally landed the job he wanted.* **6.** *vt* STRIKE BLOW to deliver a blow that hits somebody or something ○ *She landed a blow on his head.* **7.** *vti* END UP SOMEWHERE UNPLEASANT to end up in an undesirable place or situation, or cause somebody or something to end up in an undesirable place or situation ○ *It could land him in jail.* **8.** *vi* APPEAR UNEXPECTEDLY to appear in an undesired and unexpected way ○ *One problem after another landed in our lap.* **9.** *vt* CATCH AND BRING IN FISH to catch a fish and get it onto a boat or solid ground [Old English, < Germanic, "particular (enclosed) area"] ◇ **back to the land** relating to moving from a city to a rural area and taking up a simple life ◇ **be in the land of the living** to be alive or awake (*humorous*) ◇ **find out** *or* **see how the land lies** to assess a situation before taking action

land on *vt US* to criticize somebody severely

land up *vi* to finally get to a place or situation after a series of events or circumstances (*informal*) ○ *land up on the streets*

land with *vt UK* to give somebody something to do or deal with, especially because no one else wants to do it (*informal*) ○ *I was landed with the bill.*

Land /land/, **Edwin Herbert** (1909–91) US inventor and entrepreneur. He invented the Polaroid Land camera (1947) and founded and headed a major corporation for its development (1937–82).

> "Anything worth doing is worth doing to excess."
> [Attributed to Edwin Herbert Land]

land a·gent *n* in the 19th and early 20th centuries, an agent who arranged the sale or settlement of North American public lands

lan·dau /lán dòw/ (*plural* **-daus**) *n* a four-wheeled horse-drawn carriage with a top that may be let down or folded back and a raised seat for the driver [Mid-18C. After *Landau*, town in Bavaria, Germany]

lan·dau·let /làndə lét/, **lan·dau·lette** *n* **1.** a small horse-drawn landau **2.** an automobile that has a convertible top for the back seat, while the front seat is either roofed or open

land bank *n* a bank that issues loans using the borrower's property as security

land-based *adj* **1.** existing on or operating from land, rather than from the sea or the sky ○ *land-based missiles* **2.** existing in a physical location rather than as a website ○ *a land-based bookstore*

land bridge *n* a tract of land that connects continents, permitting the passage of people and animals

land crab *n* any crab that lives mainly on land and breeds in the sea

land·ed /lándəd/ *adj* **1.** OWNING LAND possessing land, especially a large rural property **2.** CONSISTING OF LAND consisting of a large area of land **3.** *Can* OFFICIALLY RESIDENT OF CANADA in Canada, given official status as a resident prior to being granted citizenship

land·er /lándər/ *n* a spacecraft designed to land on the surface of the Moon or a planet

land·fall /lánd fàwl/ *n* **1.** an arrival on or a sighting of land, especially after a long journey by sea **2.** the first land that somebody reaches after a long journey, especially by sea

land·fill /lánd fil/ *n* **1.** AREA CONTAINING BURIED WASTE a site where waste material has been buried **2.** BURIAL OF WASTE MATERIAL the disposal of waste material or refuse by burying it in natural or excavated holes or depressions **3.** BURIED WASTE MATERIAL waste material or refuse buried under the soil for landscaping or as a means of safe and sanitary waste disposal

land·fill gas *n* a gas that is generated by the decomposition of organic material in a landfill site, e.g., methane

land·form /lánd fàwrm/ *n* a natural physical feature of the Earth's surface, e.g., a valley, mountain, or plain

land·grab·ber /lánd gràbbər/ *n US* somebody who seizes land unfairly or illegally —**land·grab** *n*

land grant *n* a grant of public land, especially for the establishment of a state university

land·grave /lánd gràyv/ *n* **1.** in Germany, from the 13th century to 1806, a count who had jurisdiction over a region **2.** a title given to some princes in central Germany after 1806 [Early 16C. < Middle Low German < *land* "land" + *grave* "count"]

land·hold·er /lánd hōldər/ *n* the owner or occupant of a piece of land —**land·hold·ing** *n, adj*

land·ing /lánding/ *n* **1.** ACT OF COMING TO GROUND the act of reaching, touching, or alighting on the ground, e.g., after a jump or fall **2.** ARRIVAL ON LAND an arrival on the ground after having been in the air or at sea **3.** PLACE FOR LOADING OR UNLOADING a place for loading or unloading passengers or goods, especially from a ship ○ *There are good landings at most of the villages along the coast.* **4.** LEVEL AREA BETWEEN STAIRS a platform between flights of stairs or the floor at the top or foot of a flight of stairs

land·ing beam *n* a radio beam emitted by a beacon at a landing field that enables incoming aircraft to make a landing

land·ing craft *n* a low open flat-bottomed boat designed for landing troops and equipment on shore from a ship

land·ing field *n* a place where aircraft can land and take off

land·ing gear *n* the wheels or floats and related mechanisms that are used by an aircraft or spacecraft when taking off and landing

land·ing net *n* a net like a bag fitted on a frame that is used by anglers to scoop up a hooked fish

land·ing pad *n* AVIAT same as **helipad**

land·ing speed *n* the minimum speed at which an aircraft has to be flying in order to land safely

land·ing stage *n* a floating or fixed wooden platform, used for loading or unloading passengers and goods from a boat

land·ing strip *n* AVIAT same as **airstrip**

land·la·dy /lánd làydee/ (*plural* **-dies**) *n* **1.** a woman who owns property that she rents to tenants **2.** a woman who owns or runs a place offering accommodations, e.g., a rental house, apartment, or duplex

land·less /lándləss/ *adj* not owning any land —**land·less·ness** *n*

land·line /lánd līn/ *n* **1.** a telecommunications cable laid overland **2.** a telephone that is not a cell phone or satellite phone

land·locked /lánd lòkt/ *adj* **1.** closed in completely or almost completely by land **2.** adapted to life in a freshwater environment, with no access to the ocean, though being a species historically found in the ocean

land·lord /lánd làwrd/ *n* **1.** a person or organization that owns property that is rented to tenants **2.** a man who owns or runs a place offering accommodations, e.g., a rental house, apartment, or duplex

land·lub·ber /lánd lùbbər/ *n* somebody who is clumsy aboard a ship due to lack of experience at sea —**land·lub·ber·ly** *adj*

land·mark /lánd maàrk/ *n* **1.** SOMETHING PROMINENT THAT IDENTIFIES LOCATION a prominent structure or geographic feature that identifies a location and serves as a guide to finding it **2.** IMPORTANT NEW DEVELOPMENT an event, idea, or item that represents a significant or historic development **3.** SOMETHING PRESERVED FOR HISTORIC IMPORTANCE a structure or site identified and preserved because of its historical significance **4.** BOUNDARY MARKER a conspicuous object, e.g., a tree or stone, that is recognized as marking the boundary of a piece of land ■ *adj* HIGHLY SIGNIFICANT marking a significant change or turning point in something, especially the law ○ *a landmark ruling*

land·mass /lánd màss/ *n* a very large unbroken area of land, e.g., a continent or large island

land·mine /lánd mīn/ *n* **1.** an explosive mine that is laid just under the surface of the ground and detonates if disturbed by pressure or the proximity of something such as metal **2.** a trap that is difficult to see (*informal*) ○ *That process seems simple, but it's loaded with landmines.*

Land of En·chant·ment *n* a nickname for New Mexico

land of·fice *n* a government office that administers and records sales and transfers of public land

land-of·fice bus·i·ness *n* a highly successful trade in something (*informal*) [< the offices established in western US territories for selling land to settlers quickly and cheaply]

land of milk and hon·ey *n* **1.** in the Bible, a land of prosperity and plenty promised by God to the Israelites **2.** a rich and fertile area or region of plenty (*literary*)

land of Nod *n* an imaginary place where people who are sleeping are said to be (*informal humorous*) [Pun, after a place mentioned in *Genesis* 4:16]

Lan·don /lándən/, **Alfred Mossman** (1887–1987) US politician. As the Republican candidate he lost the presidential election to Franklin D. Roosevelt in 1936.

land·own·er /lánd ōnər/ *n* an owner of land —**land·own·er·ship** *n* —**land·own·ing** *n, adj*

land-poor *adj* owning a large area of unprofitable land while lacking the money needed for its improvement

land·rail /lánd ràyl/ *n* BIRDS same as **corncrake** [< RAIL[3]]

land·scape /lánd skàyp/ *n* **1.** VISUALLY DISTINCT SCENERY an expanse of scenery of a particular type, especially as much as can be seen by the eye **2.** PAINTING OF VIEW a painting, drawing, or photograph of scenery, especially rural scenery **3.** ART OF PAINTING OR DRAWING SCENERY the branch of art dealing with the painting, drawing, or photographing of scenery **4.** GENERAL SITUATION OF ACTIVITY the general situation providing the background to a particular type of activity ○ *the economic landscape* **5.** RANGE OF MENTAL CONCERNS any characteristic group of intellectual or imaginative features (*literary*) ■ *adj* PRINTED WITH LONG SIDES HORIZONTAL photographed or printed so that the long sides of a picture or the lines of text are parallel to the long sides of a rectangular page ■ *vt* (**-scaped, -scap·ing, -scapes**) MAKE LAND LOOK BETTER to enhance the appearance of land by altering its contours and planting trees and shrubs for aesthetic effect (*often passive*) ○ *The property was beautifully landscaped.* [Late 16C. < Dutch *landschap*, literally "condition of being land" < *land* "land"]

land·scape ar·chi·tect *n* somebody who plans and designs environments, especially with the idea of making new buildings, roads, and other structures compatible with their natural surroundings —**land·scape ar·chi·tec·ture** *n*

land·scape gar·den·er *n* a designer of grounds and gardens —**land·scape gar·den·ing** *n*

land·scap·er /lánd skàypər/ *n* a designer of grounds or gardens

land·scap·ing /lánd skàyping/ *n* **1.** the enhancement of the appearance of land, especially around buildings, by altering its contours and planting trees, shrubs, and flowers **2.** the profession of designing or creating gardens by combining plants and other features to produce a pleasing overall effect

land·scap·ist /lánd skàypist/ *n* an artist who specializes in painting landscapes

Land's End /làndz énd/ cliff and headland in Cornwall, England that forms the extreme southwestern tip of Great Britain

land·shark /lánd shaárk/ *n* an unethical dealer in land (*informal insult*)

land·side /lánd sīd/ *n* the flat part of a plow that faces unbroken land as it moves

lands·knecht /laánts kə nékht/ *n* a mercenary foot soldier in Europe during the 16th century, especially a German pikeman [Early 17C. < German, "servant of the country"]

lands·leit JUDAISM plural of **landsman**[2]

land·slide /lánd slīd/ *n* **1.** SUDDEN COLLAPSE OF LAND the collapse of part of a mountainside or cliff so that it descends in a disintegrating mass of rocks and earth **2.** MASS OF LOOSENED ROCK AND EARTH a disintegrating mass of rock and earth that suddenly descends from a mountainside or cliff **3.** CONSPICUOUS TRIUMPH an overwhelming victory, especially in an election

lands·man[1] /lándzmən/ (*plural* **-men** /-mən/) *n* somebody who lives and works on land rather than at sea

lands·man[2] /laántsmən/ (*plural* **-leit** /-līt/) *n* a fellow Jew, usually one from the same district or area, originally in Eastern Europe [Mid-20C. Via Yiddish < Middle High German *lantsman* "man from the (same) country"]

Land·stei·ner /lánd stīnər/, **Karl** (1868–1943) Austrian pathologist. He was responsible for developing the ABO blood group classification system and was awarded the Nobel Prize in physiology or medicine (1930).

Land·sturm /laánt shtoȯrm/ *n* **1.** in some European countries, a general draft of people for conscription into the armed forces **2.** in some European countries, a military force of people drafted from the general population [Early 19C. < German, "land storm"]

Land·tag /laánt taák/ *n* the legislative assembly of a German or Austrian state [Late 16C. < German, literally "land day"]

land·ward /lándwərd/ *adj* facing toward the land ■ *adv also* **land·wards** /-wərdz/ in the direction of land

Land·wehr /laánt vèr/ *n* in German-speaking countries, a reserve military force [Early 19C. < German, "national defense"]

land yacht *n* a wind-driven vehicle resembling a boat with a mast, sails, and three wheels, for use on beaches or other hard surfaces

lane /layn/ *n* **1.** NARROW STREET a narrow path, road or street, typically in older town areas or in the countryside, often enclosed by walls or hedges **2.** TRACK INTO WHICH ROAD IS DIVIDED a division of a road, street, or highway wide enough for a single line of motor vehicles **3.** STRIP OF FLOOR IN BOWLING ALLEY the long strip of polished wooden flooring along which balls are rolled in a bowling alley **4.** TRACK ASSIGNED TO RACER a track assigned to a competitive runner on a racing track or a swimmer in a swimming pool **5.** AVIAT same as **air lane 6.** DIVISION OF BASKETBALL COURT an area of a basketball court extending from the free-throw line to just below the basket **7.** SHIPPING ROUTE a route assigned to a ship on a journey, especially through a congested area of sea [Old English < W Germanic] ◇ **in the fast lane** at a fast, hectic, or stressful pace associated with success and achievement

Popperfoto

Fritz Lang

Lang /lang/, **Fritz** (1890–1976) Austrian-born US movie director. He made many Hollywood movies, but is best known for the silent film *Metropolis* (1927) and the German-language film *M* (1931).

lang. *abbr* language

Lange /lang/ /lang/, **Dorothea** (1895–1965) US photographer. Her haunting documentary photographs of the Depression and migrant workers in the southern states were published as *An American Exodus* (1939), a pioneering work of documentary photography.

> "The camera is an instrument that teaches people how to see without a camera."
> [Dorothea Lange. Quoted in *Los Angeles Times*; August 13, 1978]

Lan·gi *n* PEOPLES, LANG same as **Lango**

lang·lauf /laáng lȯwf/ *n* **1.** SKIING same as **cross-country skiing 2.** a contest in cross-country skiing [Early 20C. < German < *lang* "long" + *Lauf* "a run" (< Germanic)] —**lang·lauf·er** *n*

lang·ley /lánglee/ (*plural* **-leys**) *n* a unit of solar radiation equivalent to one calorie per square centimeter [Mid-20C. After Samuel P. LANGLEY]

Lang·ley /lánglee/, **Samuel Pierpont** (1834–1906) US aviation pioneer. In 1896 he successfully launched two uncrewed aircraft.

Lang·muir /láng myoȯr/, **Irving** (1881–1957) US chemist. He received a Nobel Prize in chemistry (1932) for his research on surface reactions of solids.

Lan·go /laáng gō/ (*plural* **-gos** or *same*), **Lan·gi** /-gee/ (*plural* **-gis** or *same*) *n* **1.** a member of a Nilotic people who live in northern Uganda **2.** the language of the Lango people, belonging to the Chari-Nile branch of Nilo-Saharan. Native speakers: 500,000. [Early 20C. < Nilotic] —**Lan·go** *adj*

Lan·go·bard /láng gə baárd/ *n* PEOPLES same as **Lombard** (sense 2) [Late 18C. < late Latin *Langobardus* "Lombard"]

Lan·go·bar·dic /làng gə baárdik, -gō-/ *n* a dialect of Old High German spoken by the ancient Lombards —**Lan·go·bar·dic** *adj*

lan·gouste /laaN góost/ *n* ZOOL, MARINE BIOL same as **spiny lobster** [Mid-20C. Via French < Old Provençal *lagosta* < Latin *locusta* "locust, crustacean"]

lan·gous·tine /laáng goo stéen, laáng goo stèen/ *n* a large prawn or small lobster. Native to: North Atlantic. [Mid-20C. < French < *langouste* (see LANGOUSTE)]

lan·grage /lángrij/, **lan·gridge** *n* shot consisting of a case filled with fragments of iron, formerly used for tearing the sails and rigging of enemy ships [Mid-18C. Origin ?]

Lan·gre·nus /lan gréenəss/ *n* a plain on the Moon with a complex central peak located on the eastern edge of the Mare Fecunditatis, 82 mi./132 km in diameter

lan·gridge *n* ARMS another spelling of **langrage**

Lang·try /lángtree/, **Lillie** (1853–1929) British actress. She was the first woman of high social standing to go on the stage in Great Britain. She became the mistress of the Prince of Wales (later Edward VII). Born **Le Breton, Emilie Charlotte**

lan·guage /láng gwij/ *n* **1.** COMMUNICATION WITH WORDS the human use of spoken or written words as a communication system **2.** SPEECH OF GROUP the speech of a country, region, or group of people, including its vocabulary, syntax, and grammar **3.** SYSTEM OF COMMUNICATION a system of communication with its own set of conventions or special words ○ *sign language* **4.** NONVERBAL COMMUNICATION BETWEEN ANIMALS a nonverbal form of communication used by birds and animals **5.** NONVERBAL COMMUNICATION BETWEEN HUMANS the use of signs, gestures, or inarticulate sounds to communicate something **6.** SPECIALIST VOCABULARY the forms of expression used by those in a particular group or sphere of activity **7.** STYLE OF VERBAL EXPRESSION the verbal style by which people express themselves ○ *the language of diplomacy* **8.** COMPUT same as **programming language** [13C. < French *langage* < *langue* "tongue" < Latin *lingua*] ◇ **speak the same language** to have values and interests in common with somebody so that it is possible to communicate effectively

SYNONYMS ***language, tongue, speech, dialect, idiolect***

CORE MEANING: communication by words

language the human use of spoken or written words as a communication system, or the speech of a country, region, or group ○ *a full account of how we use language to communicate* ○ *Persian was for centuries the official language of much of the Indian subcontinent.* **tongue** a language used by a specific country, nation, or community ○ *students whose mother tongue is not English* ○ *Neither of them could speak the other's native tongue.* **speech** spoken language, especially as distinct from the written language ○ *The natural communication system for humans is speech, not typing messages on keyboards.* ○ *a writer trying to capture the patterns of speech of traditional village life* **dialect** a regional variety of a language, or a form of a language spoken by members of a specific social class or profession ○ *a dialect poem of 1730* ○ *A kill is a waterway in the local dialect.* **idiolect** an individual person's vocabulary and unique way of using language ○ *the distinct idiolect of each member of the family* ○ *With its phantasmagoric idiolect and cruel humor, this is a quite extraordinary book.*

lan·guage arts *npl* a range of skills taught in school that are designed to give students proficiency in using language

lan·guage lab·o·ra·to·ry *n* a room equipped with audio or multimedia equipment for use in learning languages

lan·guage po·lice *npl* people who try to set limits on written language considered offensive, discriminatory, or inappropriate (*informal disapproving*)

langue /laangg, laaNg/ *n* language regarded as a communication system and the common property of a speech community (*technical*) [Early 20C. < French (see LANGUAGE)]

langue de chat /laángg də sha̋a, laáNg də sha̋a/ (*plural* **langues de chat** /laángg də sha̋a/) *n* a small narrow flat cookie often coated with chocolate [< French, "cat's tongue"]

langue d'oc /laáNg dáwk/ *n* the group of French dialects, usually considered to include Provençal, spoken in southern parts of medieval France [< French, "language of 'oc'"; from the use of *oc* (< Latin *hoc*) for "yes"]

Lan·gue·doc /laáNg dáwk/ historical region and former province in southern France, stretching from the Pyrenees eastward along the Mediterranean coast to the Rhône River

langue d'oïl /laáNg dóyl/ *n* the group of French dialects spoken in the northern part of medieval France [< French, "language of 'oïl'"; from the use of *oïl* (< Latin *hoc ille*) for "yes"]

lan·guet /láng gwət, lang gwét/ *n* something, e.g., a part in a machine or instrument, that is shaped like a tongue (*technical*) [14C. < Old French *languete* "small tongue" < *langue* (see LANGUAGE)]

lan·guid /láng gwid/ *adj* **1.** lacking vigor and energy ○ *a languid gesture* **2.** moving slowly ○ *a languid afternoon breeze* [Late 16C. Directly or via French < Latin *languidus* < *languere* "be weak"] —**lan·guid·ly** *adv* —**lan·guid·ness** *n*

lan·guish /láng gwish/ (**-guished, -guish·ing, -guish·es**) *vi* **1. BE NEGLECTED OR DEPRIVED** to undergo hardship as a result of being deprived of something, typically attention, independence, or freedom **2. BECOME LESS SUCCESSFUL** to decline steadily, becoming less vital, strong, or successful **3. PINE** to long for something that is being denied [14C. < Old French *languiss-*, stem of *languir* < Latin *languere* "be weak or faint"] —**lan·guish·er** *n* —**lan·guish·ing** *n, adj* —**lan·guish·ing·ly** *adv* —**lan·guish·ment** *n*

lan·guor /láng gər, lánggər/ *n* **1. TIREDNESS** a pleasant feeling of weariness or weakness **2. LISTLESSNESS IN SPEECH OR BEHAVIOR** listlessness and indifference in speech or behavior **3. HEAVINESS IN ATMOSPHERE** an oppressive heaviness or sultriness in the air [13C. Via French < Latin < *languere* "be weak or faint"]

lan·guor·ous /láng gərəss, lánggərəss/ *adj* **1.** listless and indifferent **2.** moving slowly ○ *They performed a languorous dance of infinite restraint.* —**lan·guor·ous·ly** *adv* —**lan·guor·ous·ness** *n*

lan·gur /lan go͝or/ *n* a slender, leaf-eating monkey with a long tail, bushy eyebrows, and a chin tuft. Native to: Southeast Asia. Genus: *Presbytis.* [Early 19C. < Hindi *langūr* < Sanskrit *lāṅgūla* "having a tail"]

lan·iard *n* MIL, CLOTHING, NAUT, ARMS another spelling of **lanyard**

la·ni·a·ry /láynee érree/ *adj* describes a tooth adapted for tearing food [Early 19C. < Latin *laniarius* "of a butcher" < *lanius* "butcher" < *laniare* "to tear"] —**la·ni·a·ry** *n*

La·nier /lə néer/, **Sidney** (1842–81) US poet and lecturer. He is known for his melodic poems.

"Oh, might I through these tears / But glimpse some hill my Georgia high uprears, / Where white the quartz and pink the pebble shine, / The hickory heavenward strives, the muscadine / Swings o'er the slope, the oak's far-falling shade / Darkens the dogwood in the bottom glade."

[Sidney Lanier, "From the Flats," *Sidney Lanier: Poems and Letters*; 1960]

la·nif·er·ous /lə nífərəss/ *adj* wool-bearing or wool-covered [Mid-17C. < Latin *lanifer* < *lana* "wool"]

la·ni·ger·ous /lə níjjərəss/ *adj* same as **laniferous** [Early 17C. < Latin *laniger* < *lana* (see LANIFEROUS)]

lank /langk/ *adj* **1.** limp and straight ○ *lank hair* **2.** long and slender [Old English *hlanc* "lean" < Germanic, "flexible"] —**lank·ly** *adv* —**lank·ness** *n*

lank·y /lángkee/ (**-i·er, -i·est**) *adj* tall and thin in a bony, ungracefully angular way —**lank·i·ly** *adv* —**lank·i·ness** *n*

lan·ner /lánnər/ (*plural* **-ners** or *same*) *n* a large falcon, the female of which is used especially in falconry. Native to: Africa, Middle East, Mediterranean. Latin name: *Falco biarmicus.* [13C. < French *lanier*]

lan·ner·et /lánnə rèt, lànnə rét/ (*plural* **-ets** or *same*) *n* a male lanner, smaller than the female and used in falconry

lan·o·lin /lánn'lin/, **lan·o·line** /-l een/ *n* a fat extracted from sheep's wool. Use: in skin ointments. [Late 19C. < Latin *lana* "wool" + *oleum* "oil"]

lans·for·dite /lánssfər dìt/ *n* a crystallized hydrate of magnesium carbonate occurring as stalactites [Late 19C. After *Lansford*, Pennsylvania]

Lan·sing /lánssing/ **1.** capital of Michigan, a manufacturing city in the south central part of the state. Population: 118,588 (2002 estimate). **2.** village in northeastern Illinois, on the Illinois-Indiana border south of Calumet City. It is a southern suburb of Chicago. Population: 28,156 (2002 estimate).

lan·ta·na /lan tánnə/ (*plural* **-nas** or *same*) *n* an ornamental evergreen bush of the vervain family. Native to: tropical America. Genus: *Lantana.* [Late 18C. Via modern Latin < Italian dialect, "wayfaring tree," which it resembles]

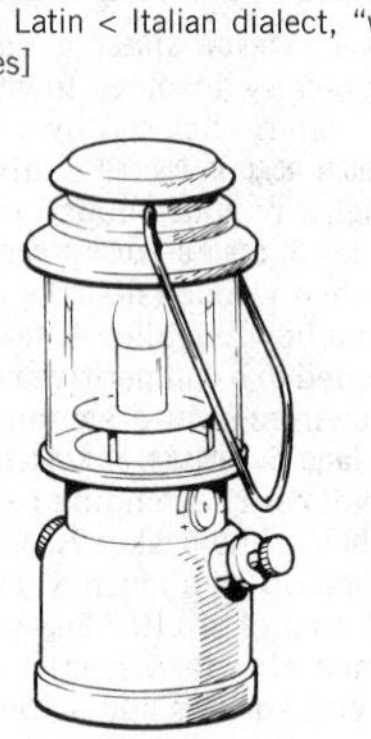

lantern

lan·tern /lántərn/ *n* **1. PORTABLE LAMP** a portable case with transparent or translucent sides that protects and holds a lamp **2. LIGHTHOUSE ROOM** a room containing the large lamp at the top of a lighthouse **3. STRUCTURE WITH WINDOWS** a structure with windows on all sides, resembling a lantern, e.g., one at the top of a dome [13C. Via French < Latin *lanterna* < Greek *lamptēr* "torch, lamp" < *lampein* "to shine"]

lan·tern fish *n* a small bony deep-sea fish with rows of luminous spots along its body. Family: Myctophidae.

lan·tern fly *n* a tropical insect with an elongated head that resembles a lantern and was formerly thought to emit light. Family: Fulgoridae.

lan·tern jaw *n* a long bony lower jaw, typically projecting beyond the upper jaw —**lan·tern-jawed** *adj*

lan·tern pin·ion *n* a gearwheel used in clocks and watches that has two circular disks connected by cylindrical pins

lan·tern slide *n* a transparent slide, typically made of glass, for projection onto a screen by a slide projector or magic lantern

lan·tha·nide /lánthə nìd/ *n* an element of the lanthanide series of rare earths [Early 20C. < LANTHANUM]

lan·tha·nide se·ries *n* a group of the rare earths that range from lanthanum at atomic number 57 to lutetium at atomic number 71

lan·tha·num /lánthənəm/ *n* a silvery ductile metallic element resembling aluminum that belongs to the rare-earth group. Source: monazite, bastnaesite. Use: glass manufacture. Symbol **La**. See table at **element** [Mid-19C. < Greek *lanthanein* "lie hidden"; because it was discovered hidden in cerium oxide]

la·nu·go /lə no͝ogō/ (*plural* **-gos** or *same*) *n* a covering of soft downy hairs, especially those on a developing human fetus or newborn infant [15C. < Latin < *lana* "wool"] —**la·nu·gi·nous** /lə no͝ojənəss/ *adj*

La·nús /laa no͝oss/ city in Buenos Aires Province, eastern Argentina. It is a suburb of Buenos Aires. Population: 468,561 (1991).

lan·yard /lánnyərd/, **lan·iard** *n* **1. CORD WORN AROUND NECK** a cord worn around the neck by military and naval personnel or by Boy Scouts and Girl Scouts for carrying something such as a whistle or pocket-knife **2. SHORT ROPE ABOARD SHIP** a short rope or cord used to hold or fasten something on a ship **3. CORD FOR FIRING CANNON** a cord tied to the breech mechanism of a cannon and used to fire it [14C. < French *lanière* "strap"; influenced by YARD[1] "spar"]

Lan·za·rot·e /lànzə róttee/ easternmost island of the Canary Islands, Las Palmas Province, Spain, situated northeast of Grand Canary in the Atlantic Ocean. Population: 96,781 (2002). Area: 311 sq. mi./805 sq. km.

Lan·zhou /laán jṓ/, **Lan-chou**, **Lan·chow** capital of Gansu Province and a major transport and industrial centre on the Huang He (Yellow River), northern China. Population: 1,194,640 (1990).

Lao /low/ (*plural same*) *n* **1.** a member of a people of Laos and northeastern Thailand **2.** the language of the Lao and the official language of Laos, belonging to the Tai group of languages and closely related to Thai. Lao is spoken by about 3,000,000 people. [Mid-20C. < Lao] —**Lao** *adj*

La·oag /laa wa̋ag/ city in the northwestern part of Luzon island in the northern Philippines. Population: 83,756 (1990).

La·oc·o·ön /lay ókō òn/, **La·oc·o·on** *n* in Greek mythology, a Trojan priest of Apollo who warned the Trojans about the Wooden Horse and was killed along with his two sons by sea serpents after he gave his warning

la·od·i·ce·an /lay òddə sée ən/, **La·od·i·ce·an** *adj* lacking in religious or political commitment ■ *n* somebody who has lukewarm or indifferent views, especially about religion or politics [Early 17C. < Latin *Laodicea*, city in modern-day Turkey, whose Christians were rebuked for indifference (*Rev.* 3:16)]

Laois /leesh/, **Leix** county in Leinster Province, Republic of Ireland. The county town is Port Laoise. Population: 52,945 (2002). Area: 664 sq. mi./1,720 sq. km.

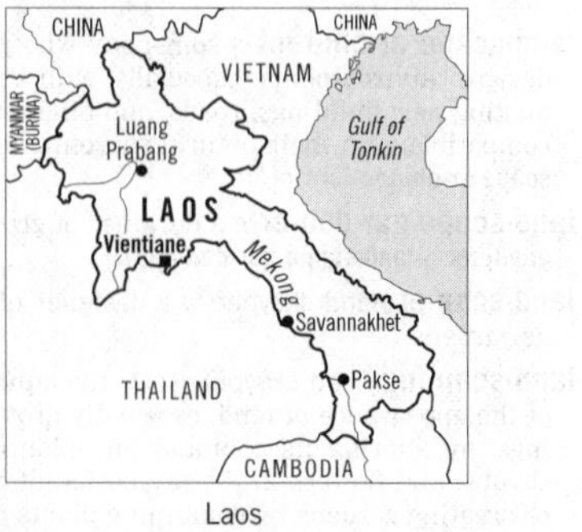

Laos

Laos /lowss/ independent state of Southeast Asia, bordered by China, Vietnam, Cambodia, Thailand, and Myanmar. It is the only landlocked nation in Southeast Asia. Language: Lao. Currency: kip. Capital: Vientiane. Population: 5,921,545 (2003). Area: 91,430 sq. mi./236,800 sq. km. Official name **Lao People's Democratic Republic** —**La·o·tian** /lay ṓsh'n, lówsh'n/ *n, adj*

Lao-tzu /lòw dzóo/ (570?–490? B.C.) Chinese philosopher. He is credited with originating Taoism, described in the seminal *Tao-te Ching*. Known as **Master Lao**

lap[1] /lap/ *n* **1.** TOP OF SOMEBODY'S THIGHS WHEN SITTING the level area provided by the upper surface of the thighs of somebody who is seated **2.** PART OF CLOTHING RESTING ON THIGHS the part of a garment that hangs loosely across the thighs of somebody seated **3.** VALLEY a hollow in the contours of land, especially the gap between hills [Old English *læppa* "flap of a garment, lobe" < Germanic] —**lap·ful** *n* ◇ **drop in** *or* **into your lap** to be given as something welcome and unexpected ◇ **drop something in somebody's lap** to become or make something somebody's responsibility ◇ **in the lap of luxury** in great luxury and comfort ◇ **in the lap of the gods** beyond human control or influence

lap[2] /lap/ *n* **1.** ONE CIRCUIT OF TRACK a single circuit of a racetrack or running track or one length of a swimming pool **2.** STAGE a phase in an extended project, enterprise, or journey **3.** OVERLAPPING PART an overlapping part of something **4.** LENGTH GOING ONCE AROUND REEL a length of fabric, thread, or rope that goes once around a roller, drum, or reel **5.** POLISHING DISK a rotating disk for cutting or polishing something such as glass or gemstones ■ *v* (**lapped, lap·ping, laps**) **1.** *vt* PASS COMPETITORS BY COMPLETE CIRCUIT to overtake a competitor on a racetrack or running track after having completed at least one circuit more than he or she has **2.** *vi* COMPLETE ONE TRACK CIRCUIT to run one complete circuit around a track or to swim one length of a swimming pool **3.** *vt* WRAP SOMEBODY IN SOMETHING to enfold or enwrap somebody in something (*literary; often passive*) **4.** *vti* OVERLAP to overlap something (*literary*) **5.** *vt* POLISH OR CUT HARD SURFACES to polish or cut something hard such as glass, metal, or gemstones **6.** *vt* FORM FIBERS INTO BAND to arrange fibers so that they lie one against the other and form a band [14C. < LAP[1]] —**lap·per** *n*

lap[3] /lap/ *vti* (**lapped, lap·ping, laps**) **1.** DRINK SOMETHING WITH TONGUE to drink a liquid by scooping it into the mouth with the tongue (*refers to animals*) **2.** WASH GENTLY AGAINST SURFACE to flow or splash gently against a surface ■ *n* **1.** PROCESS OF DRINKING SOMETHING WITH TONGUE the action of drinking liquid by scooping small amounts of it into the mouth with the tongue **2.** SOUND OF MOVING LIQUID the sound of a liquid gently flowing or splashing against something [Old English *lapian* < Germanic] —**lap·per** *n*

lap up *v* **1.** *vti* same as **lap**[3] *v* (sense 1) **2.** *vt* to drink or eat something enthusiastically **3.** *vt* to enjoy something eagerly and uncritically

La Pal·ma /lə paálmə/ **1.** city in Orange County, southwestern California, situated 16 mi./26 km southeast of Los Angeles. Population: 15,774 (2002 estimate). **2.** town, port, and capital of Darién Province, eastern Panama, situated on an inlet of the Gulf of Panama 100 mi./161 km southeast of Panama City. Population: 1,634 (1980). **3.** one of the Canary Islands, Spain, situated off the north coast of Africa. Population: 78,800 (2001). Area: 273 sq. mi./708 sq. km.

lap·a·ro·scope /láppərə skŏp/ *n* an instrument in the shape of a tube that is inserted through the abdominal wall to give an examining doctor a view of the internal organs

lap·a·ros·co·py /làppə róskəpee/ (*plural* **-pies**) *n* examination of the internal organs of the abdomen using a laparoscope [Mid-19C. < Greek *lapara* "flank"] —**lap·a·ro·scop·ic** /làppərə skóppik/ *adj* —**lap·a·ros·co·pist** *n*

lap·a·rot·o·my /làppə róttəmee/ (*plural* **-mies**) *n* a surgical incision through the abdominal wall made to allow investigation of an abdominal organ or diagnosis of an abdominal disorder [Mid-19C. < Greek *lapara* "flank"]

La Paz /lə páz, laa páss/ **1.** capital city of Bolivia, located in the western part of the country. Population: 1,004,440 (2000). **2.** capital of Baja California Sur State, in western Mexico. Population: 170,366 (2000).

lap belt *n* a safety belt that is fitted to the seat of a motor vehicle and fastens across the lap

lap·board /láp bàwrd/ *n* a thin flat board that is laid across the knees to serve as a table or writing surface

lap-chart *n* a record of each lap made by a motor vehicle in a race, showing each vehicle's exact position

lap dan·cer *n* a stripteaser who dances erotically close to or in the lap of a customer —**lap danc·ing** *n*

lap desk *n* a portable writing surface that fits over or on somebody's lap

lap·dog /láp dàwg, -dòg/ *n* **1.** a small gentle-natured dog **2.** somebody who unthinkingly obeys somebody else's command, especially in an organization or institution

la·pel /lə pél/ *n* either of the two folded-back front edges of a jacket that are continuous with the collar [Mid-17C. < LAP[1] "part of a garment that projects"] —**la·pelled** *adj*

lap·i·dar·y /láppi dèrree/ *adj* **1.** ENGRAVED ON STONE engraved in stone or on a gemstone **2.** OF GEMSTONES relating to the art of cutting or engraving gemstones **3.** DIGNIFIED AND ELEGANT careful, elegant, and dignified in style (*formal*) ■ *n* (*plural* **-ies**) CUTTER OF PRECIOUS STONES an expert cutter, polisher, or engraver of gemstones [14C. < Latin *lapidarius* "of stone" < *lapid-* "stone"]

lap·i·date /láppi dàyt/ (**-dated, -dat·ing, -dates**) *vt* (*literary*) **1.** to throw stones at somebody **2.** to stone somebody to death, especially as a punishment for wrongdoing [Early 17C. < Latin *lapidat-*, past participle of *lapidare* < *lapid-* "stone"] —**lap·i·da·tion** /làppi dáysh'n/ *n*

la·pil·lus /lə pílləss/ (*plural* **-li** /-lī/) *n* a small fragment of lava thrown from a volcano [Mid-18C. < Latin, "small stone" < *lapis* "stone"]

la·pis laz·u·li /làppiss lázzyə lī, -lázhə-, -lázzyəlee/ *n* a deep blue semiprecious stone containing lazurite. Use: jewelry. ■ *adj* of the same deep brilliant blue as lapis lazuli [< Latin *lapis* "stone" + medieval Latin *lazuli* "of lapis lazuli" < Persian *lāžward* "lapis lazuli"]

Lap·ith /láppith/ (*plural* **-iths** or **-i·thae** /-pithee/) *n* in Greek mythology, a member of a people of Thessaly who fought the drunken centaurs at the wedding of their king, Pirithous. The contest of the Lapiths and centaurs was a frequent theme in Greek sculpture. [Early 17C. Via Latin < Greek *Lapithai* (plural)]

lap joint, lapped joint /lápt-/ *n* a joint made by overlapping the ends of two parts or pieces and fastening them together —**lap-joint·ed** *adj*

La·place /laa pláss/, **Pierre Simon, Marquis de** (1749–1827) French astronomer and mathematician. He used Newton's theory of gravitation to account for the movement of planets in the solar system.

Lap·land /lápplənd/ region largely within the Arctic Circle, extending across the northern parts of Norway, Sweden, Finland, and the Kola Peninsula of Russia —**Lap·lan·der** *n*

La Pla·ta /laa plaá taa/ city and capital of Buenos Aires Province, eastern Argentina. Population: 676,128 (1991).

Lapp /lap/ *n* **1.** an offensive term for a member of the Saami people of northern Europe **2.** an offensive term for the language of the Saami people [Late 16C. < Swedish] —**Lapp** *adj*

lapped joint *n* CONSTR same as **lap joint**

lap·pet /láppət/ *n* **1.** a loose fold or flap of fabric on a garment **2.** a lobe or hanging flap of flesh, e.g., a cow's dewlap or the wattle on a bird's head [15C. < LAP[1]]

lap·pet moth *n* a large purplish brown moth whose furry larvae have flaps along their sides. Latin name: *Gastropacha quercifolia*.

lap pool *n* a pool designed for swimming laps, sometimes with a pump to create a current against which to swim

lap robe *n* a small rug that wraps around the knees

lapse /laps/ *n* **1.** ERROR a momentary fault or failure in behavior or morality **2.** GAP IN CONTINUITY a break in the continuity of something **3.** PERIOD a passage of time **4.** LAW FAILURE TO ACT IN TIME a failure to exercise a right within a specific period of time, e.g., the failure to buy a property before the termination of an option to buy ■ *vi* (**lapsed, laps·ing, laps·es**) **1.** GRADUALLY COME TO STOP to come to an end or stop doing something gradually **2.** DECLINE to decline in value, quality, or conduct ○ *Their standards have lapsed.* **3.** LOSE SIGNIFICANCE to decline gradually, becoming less important **4.** LAW BECOME VOID to become null and void through disuse, negligence, or death **5.** same as **elapse** [14C. < Latin *lapsus* "falling, failure" < past participle of *labi* "fall"] —**laps·a·ble** *adj* —**laps·er** *n* ◇ **a lapse from grace** a failure in moral conduct or religious belief

lapse into *vi* **1.** to revert to a previous state, especially of quiet or inactivity **2.** to revert to a previous habit or way of life, often an undesirable one

lapsed /lapst/ *adj* **1.** no longer committed to something, especially religious faith or observance **2.** expired or terminated

lapse rate *n* the rate at which the temperature of the atmosphere falls as altitude increases

lap·strake /láp stràyk/ *adj* NAUT same as **clinker-built** ■ *n* a boat built with overlapping planks [Late 18C. < LAP[2] + STRAKE]

Lap·tev Sea /làptef-/ section of the Arctic Ocean, situated off the northern coast of Siberian Russia

lap·top /láp tòp/ *n* a small portable personal computer, often battery operated, usually consisting of a case that opens to reveal a screen in the upper part and a keyboard in the lower part

La Pu·en·te /laà pŏŏ èntee/ city in Los Angeles County, southwestern California, situated northeast of Long Beach. Population: 42,007 (2002 estimate).

La·pu·tan /lə pyóot'n/ *adj* concentrating on absurdly impractical ideas or projects, often to the exclusion of things that need to be done [Mid-19C. < *Laputa*, island in *Gulliver's Travels* (1726) by Jonathan Swift whose people were like this]

lap·ware /láp wèr/ *n* software for children that includes simple text and animation for telling stories

lap·wing /láp wìng/ (*plural* **-wings** or *same*) *n* a long-legged bird that is noted for its shrill cry and erratic flight. Genus: *Vanellus*. [Old English *hleapewince* < LEAP + Germanic ancestor of WINK meaning "move from side to side"; altered by association with LAP[1], WING]

~~**laquer**~~ incorrect spelling of **lacquer**

La Quin·ta /laa kwíntə/ city in Riverside County, southern California. Population: 30,043 (2002 estimate).

lar /laar/ (*plural* **lar·es** /lérreez, laáreez/) *n* in ancient Rome, a protective god or a statue of a protective god in a household [Late 16C. < Latin]

Lar·a·mie /lárrəmee/ city in Albany County, southeastern Wyoming. It is the site of the University of Wyoming. Population: 26,885 (2002 estimate).

La Ra·za /laa raá saa/ *n Hispanic* Mexicans, Mexican Americans, or Spanish-speaking people of the Americas, considered as a group [< American Spanish, "the race or breed"]

lar·board /laár bàwrd, -bərd/ *n* the port or left side of a vessel (*dated*) [Late 16C. Alteration of *ladeboard* "loading side"]

~~**larceency**~~ incorrect spelling of **larceny**

lar·ce·ny /laárssənee/ *n* the unlawful taking and removal of another person's property [15C. < Anglo-Norman < Old French *larcin* < Latin *latrocinium* "theft" < *latro* "thief" < Greek *latron* "pay, wages"] —**lar·ce·ner** *n* —**lar·ce·nist** *n* —**lar·ce·nous** *adj* —**lar·ce·nous·ly** *adv*

larch /laarch/ (*plural* **larch·es** or *same*) *n* **1.** a deciduous tree of the pine family with clusters of needle-shaped leaves and erect cones. Genus: *Larix*. **2.** the durable wood of a larch tree [Mid-16C. < Middle High German *larche* < Latin *larix*]

lard /laard/ *n* WHITE COOKING FAT white, slightly soft, pork fat. Use: cooking, in ointments and perfumes. ■ *v* (**lard·ed, lard·ing, lards**) **1.** *vti* ADD LARD TO MEAT BEFORE COOKING to thread strips of fat or fatty bacon through holes made in a lean cut of meat to keep the meat moist while cooking **2.** *vt* INCLUDE EXTRA WORDS IN TEXT to include an unnecessary or undesirable amount of additional material in a speech or piece of writing ○ *larded with quotations* [14C. < French, "bacon" < Latin *lar(i)dum*]

lard·ass /laárd àss/ *n* an offensive term that deliberately insults somebody's body weight (*slang insult*)

lar·der /laárdər/ *n* **1.** a cool place, especially a small room or large cupboard, used for storing food **2.** a supply of food [13C. < Anglo-Norman < Old French *lard* (see LARD)]

lard·ing nee·dle /laárding-/ *n* a long thick metal needle that grips one end of a strip of fat to allow it to be threaded through lean meat to keep it moist while cooking

Lard·ner /laárdnər/, **Ring** (1885–1933) US humorist and writer. He is known for his satirical short stories, particularly the baseball stories collected in the volume *You Know Me, Al* (1914). Full name **Lardner, Ringgold Wilmer**

> "How do you look when I'm sober?"
> [Ring Lardner. Quoted in *Ring*, J. Yardley; 1977]

La·re·do /lə ráydō/ city in southern Texas, on the border with Mexico. Population: 191,538 (2002 estimate).

lar·es and pe·nates /lèrreez ən pə náyteez/ *npl* **1.** in ancient Roman religion, the household deities. The lares were believed to protect the household from danger, while the penates were believed to bring wealth. **2.** a family's treasured or valuable possessions (*dated*) [Late 16C. < Latin]

large /laarj/ (**larg·er, larg·est**) *adj* **1.** VERY BIG comparatively big in size, number, or quantity, or bigger in size, number, or quantity than is usual or expected **2.** OF TALL HEAVY BUILD tall and well-built, heavy set, broad, or overweight **3.** IMPORTANT significant or general in scope, extent, or effect ○ *a large view of the subject* **4.** GENEROUS generous in spirit or attitude **5.** FAVORABLE FOR SAILING describes a wind that is blowing in a favorable direction ○ *a large wind* [12C. Via French < Latin *larga*, form of *largus* "abundant"] —**large·ness** *n* ◇ **at large 1.** as a widely based and general group of people **2.** escaped or free and possibly dangerous ◇ **by and large** speaking generally ◇ **live large** to live in an extravagant way (*informal*)

large cal·o·rie *n* MEASURE same as **calorie**

large cap *adj* relating to a company with a large amount of share capital, especially when considered as one of a group of such companies on a stock market [< shortening of *capitalization*]

large-heart·ed *adj* generous, kind, or understanding —**large-heart·ed·ness** *n*

large in·tes·tine *n* the end section of the alimentary canal reaching from ileum to anus and consisting of the cecum, colon, and rectum. Its function is to extract water and form feces.

large·ly /laárjlee/ *adv* **1.** for the most part **2.** on a big or grand scale

large-mind·ed *adj* characterized by a liberal attitude —**large-mind·ed·ly** *adv* —**large-mind·ed·ness** *n*

large·mouth bass /laárj mowth báss/ *n* a large blackish-green freshwater bass with a large mouth extending behind the eye that is popular as a game fish. Native to: North America. Latin name: *Micropterus salmoides*.

large-print *adj* set in type that is bigger than normal for the benefit of partially sighted readers ○ *a large-print book*

larg·er-than-life *adj* very confident, impressive, flamboyant, and likely to attract attention (*not hyphenated when used after a verb*)

large-scale *adj* **1.** comparatively big in size and showing a lot of detail **2.** extensive in scope or scale

large-scale in·te·gra·tion *n* the process of integrating a large number of circuits, often several thousand, on a silicon chip

lar·gesse /laar jéss/, **lar·gess** *n* **1.** GENEROSITY the generous giving of gifts, money, or favors **2.** GIFTS the gifts, money, or favors given as a result of somebody's generosity **3.** LIBERALITY generosity or liberality, especially in spirit or attitude [13C. < French < Latin *largus* "abundant"]

large-toothed as·pen *n* a deciduous tree that has leaves with indentations like teeth. Native to: eastern North America. Latin name: *Populus grandidentanta*.

lar·ghet·to /laar géttō/ *adv* at a fairly slow tempo, but slightly faster than largo (*used as a musical direction*) ■ *n* (*plural* **-tos**) a larghetto movement or musical piece [Early 18C. < Italian, "little largo" < *largo* "broad"] —**lar·ghet·to** *adj*

larg·ish /laárjish/ *adj* quite big, rather than enormous

lar·go /laárgō/ *adv* at a fairly slow and broad tempo, more slowly than lento but faster than grave (*used as a musical direction*) ■ *n* (*plural* **-gos**) a largo movement or musical piece [Late 17C. < Italian, "broad"] —**lar·go** *adj*

la·ri[1] /laáree/ (*plural same or* **-ris**) *n* the main unit of Georgian currency. See table at **currency** [Late 20C. < Georgian]

la·ri[2] /laáree/ *n* MONEY another spelling of **laari**

lar·i·at /lárree ət/ *n* **1.** AGRIC same as **lasso 2.** a tethering rope, especially one used to hold a grazing animal in one place [Mid-19C. < Spanish *la reata* "the rope" < *reatar* "tie again" < Latin *aptare* "adjust"]

La·ris·sa /lə ríssə/ *n* a small inner natural satellite of Neptune, discovered in 1989 by Voyager 2. It is irregular in shape and has a maximum dimension of approximately 210 km (130 mi.).

lark

lark[1] /laark/ *n* a small songbird with brownish feathers, noted for its song. Native to: worldwide. Family: Alaudidae. [Old English *lāferce, læwerce* < W Germanic]

lark[2] /laark/ *n* **1.** MISCHIEVOUS ADVENTURE adventurous or risky fun ○ *did it for a lark* **2.** AMUSING PRANK a good-humored prank ■ *vi* (**larked, lark·ing, larks**) ACT MISCHIEVOUSLY to behave in a mischievous, annoying, or irresponsible manner [Early 19C. Origin ?] —**lark·ish** *adj* —**lark·ish·ness** *n* —**lark·y** *adj*

lark bunt·ing *n* a small songbird related to the finch and sparrow with a black or brown body, white wing patch, and a large pale beak. Native to: south central Canada and central United States. Family: Fringillidae.

Lar·kin /laárkin/, **Philip** (1922–85) British poet and jazz critic. He worked as a librarian at Hull University. His works include *The Whitsun Weddings* (1964) and *High Windows* (1974). Full name **Larkin, Philip Arthur**

> "Nothing, like something, happens anywhere."
> [Philip Larkin, "I Remember, I Remember," *Philip Larkin Collected Poems*; 1988]

lark·spur /laárk spùr/ *n* a delphinium plant. Flowers: pink, white, or blue, in spikes. Native to: cool regions worldwide. Genus: *Delphinium*. [Late 16C. < the resemblance of the spurred flowers to the lark's long hind claws]

Lark·spur /laárk spùr/ city in Marin County, western California, situated approximately 280 mi./725 km northwest of San Francisco. Population: 11,931 (2002 estimate).

La Ro·chelle /laà rə shél/ seaport, tourist center, and capital of Charente-Maritime Department, Poitou-Charentes Region, western France. Population: 76,584 (1999).

lar·ri·gan /lárrigən/ *n* a knee-high boot with the leg part made of oiled leather, worn especially by lumberjacks, trappers, and woodsmen [Late 19C. Origin ?]

lar·rup /lárrəp/ *vt* (**-ruped, -rup·ing, -rups**) to beat or flog a person or animal ■ *n* a blow, especially one delivered with a lot of force [Early 19C. Origin ?] —**lar·ru·per** *n*

Lar·son /laárss'n/, **Gary** (*b.* 1950) US cartoonist. His popular comic strip *The Far Side* (1980–95) is characterized by whimsical, absurd, and macabre animal and insect characters.

lar·va /laárvə/ (*plural* **-vae** /-vee/ *or* **-vas**) *n* **1.** the wingless immature worm-shaped form of many insects that develops into a pupa or chrysalis before becoming an adult insect **2.** the immature, early-stage form of frogs and other animals that undergo marked changes during metamorphosis [Mid-17C. < Latin, "ghost"] —**lar·val** *adj*

lar·vi·cide /laárvə sīd/ *n* a chemical used to kill larvae —**lar·vi·cid·al** /laárvə sīd'l/ *adj*

laryng- *prefix* same as **laryngo-** (*used before vowels*)

la·ryn·ge·al /lə rínjee əl, làrrən jée əl, lə rínjəl/ *adj* **1.** RELATING TO LARYNX belonging to, relating to, situated in, or affecting the larynx **2.** PRODUCED AT LARYNX describes a speech sound produced in the region of the larynx ■ *n* PHON CONSONANT a sound made in the region of the larynx, especially a sound similar to "/h/" that some linguists believe was used by speakers of Proto-Indo-European [Late 18C. < modern Latin *laryngeus* < *laryng-* (see LARYNGO-)] —**la·ryn·ge·al·ly** *adv*

lar·yn·gec·to·my /làrrən jéktəmee/ (*plural* **-mies**) *n* the surgical removal of all or part of the larynx

la·ryn·ges ANAT plural of **larynx**

lar·yn·gi·tis /làrrən jītiss/ *n* inflammation of the larynx, usually accompanied by hoarseness and coughing —**lar·yn·git·ic** /-jíttik/ *adj*

laryngo- *prefix* larynx ○ *laryngotomy* [Via modern Latin *laryng-* < Greek *larugg-*, stem of *larugx*]

lar·yn·gol·o·gy /làrrəng góllәjee/ *n* a branch of medicine dealing with diseases and conditions of the larynx and vocal cords —**lar·yn·go·log·ic** /lə rìng gə lójjik/ *adj* —**lar·yn·go·log·i·cal·ly** *adv* —**lar·yn·gol·o·gist** *n*

la·ryn·go·phar·ynx /lə rìng gō fárringks/ (*plural* **-pha·ryn·ges** /-fə rínjeez/ *or* **-phar·ynx·es**) *n* the part of the throat immediately behind the voice box or larynx, and extending downward to the top of the gullet or esophagus

la·ryn·go·scope /lə ríng gə skōp/ *n* a medical instrument consisting of a short metal or plastic tube fitted with a tiny light bulb, used when examining the larynx. Its most common use is for viewing the entrance to the larynx when inserting a breathing tube during surgery.

lar·yn·gos·co·py /làrrəng góskəpee/ (*plural* **-pies**) *n* an examination of the entrance to, or interior of, the larynx, for the purpose of diagnosis or to facilitate the passage of a tube through the larynx —**la·ryn·go·scop·ic** /lə rìng gə skóppik/ *adj* —**la·ryn·go·scop·i·cal·ly** *adv* —**lar·yn·gos·co·pist** *n*

lar·yn·got·o·my /làrrəng góttəmee/ (*plural* **-mies**) *n* a surgical procedure in which an incision is made in the larynx

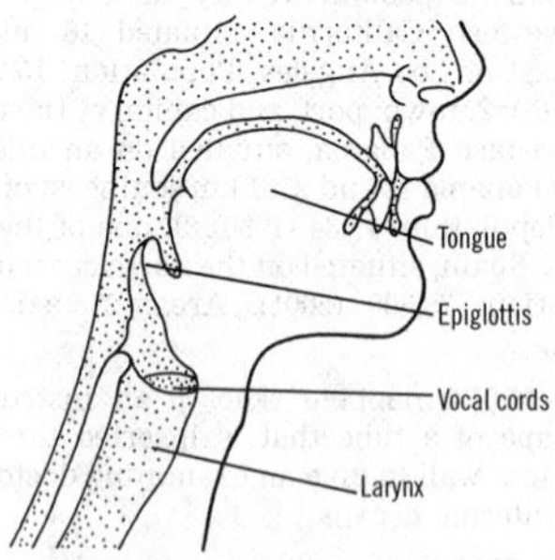

larynx

lar·ynx /lárringks/ (*plural* **la·ryn·ges** /lə rín jeez/ *or* **lar·ynx·es**) *n* the cartilaginous box-shaped part of the respiratory tract between the level of the root of the tongue and the top of the trachea. In humans and some other air-breathing vertebrates it is the organ of voice production, containing the vocal cords. [Late 16C. Via modern Latin < Greek *larugx*]

la·sa·gna /lə zaányə/ (*plural* **-gnas** *or* **-gne**), **la·sa·gne** (*plural* **-gnes** *or same*) *n* **1.** a dish of Italian origin consisting of alternate layers of pasta sheets and filling, especially alternating pasta, tomato sauce, cheese, and usually ground meat, baked in the oven. Various other sauces or fillings may also be used. **2.** thin flat sheets of fresh or dried pasta, which are generally layered with sauces or other ingredients, then baked [Mid-19C. < Italian, < Latin *lasanum* "cooking vessel"]

La Salle /lə sál/ industrial city in La Salle County,

north central Illinois, 51 mi./82 km northeast of Peoria. Population: 9,646 (2002 estimate).

La Salle /lə sál, laa-/, **René-Robert Cavelier, Sieur de** (1643–87) French explorer. He navigated the Mississippi River to its mouth, and tried to colonize the area for France.

las·car /láskər/, **Las·car** *n* a South or Southeast Asian sailor, army servant, or artilleryman (*dated*) [Early 17C. < Persian, Urdu *laškarī* "soldier" < *laškar* "army, camp"]

Las Ca·sas /laass kaássəss/, **Bartolomé de** (1474–1566) Spanish missionary. He was the first person to be ordained as a priest in the Americas (1512). Known as **the Apostle of the Indians**

Las·caux /la skṓ/ site of an underground cave, called Grotte de Lascaux, in southwestern France, that contains outstanding examples of Stone Age art

las·civ·i·ous /lə sívvee əss/ *adj* **1.** showing a desire for, or unseemly interest in, sex **2.** provoking lust [15C. < late Latin *lasciviosus* < Latin *lascivus* "lustful"] —**las·civ·i·ous·ly** *adv* —**las·civ·i·ous·ness** *n*

Las Cru·ces /laass kroóssiss/ city in southern New Mexico, situated north of El Paso, Texas, and Juárez, Mexico. Population: 75,015 (2002 estimate).

lase /layz/ (**lased, las·ing, las·es**) *vi* to emit the type of single-wavelength radiation produced by a laser [Mid-20C. Back-formation < LASER]

LASEK /láyzek/ *n* laser surgery performed to correct nearsightedness, farsightedness, or astigmatism by making a flap in the topmost layer of the cornea before reshaping the tissue underneath [Acronym < *laser epithelial keratomileusis*]

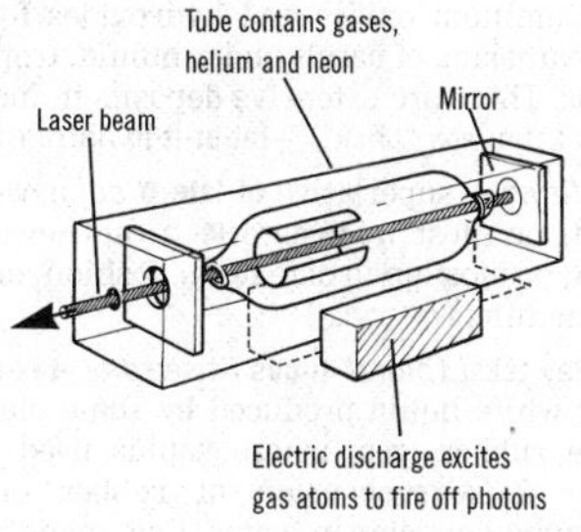

laser

la·ser /láyzər/ *n* a device that utilizes the ability of some substances to absorb electromagnetic energy and re-radiate it as a highly focused beam of synchronized single-wavelength radiation [Mid-20C. Acronym < *light amplification by stimulated emission of radiation*]

la·ser disk *n* COMPUT same as **optical disk**

la·ser dop·pler flow·me·ter *n* an instrument that measures blood flow through the arteries and veins, used to help detect narrowing of the arteries and the presence of blood clots —**la·ser dop·pler flow·met·ry** *n*

la·ser print·er *n* a computer printer using a focused laser beam to place an image on a photosensitive drum, which uses electrostatic charge to print the image

las·er sur·ger·y *n* surgery performed using a laser to remove exact amounts of tissue without harming surrounding tissue, e.g., to improve eyesight or remove skin blemishes

la·ser vi·sa *n* a visa for Mexican nationals entering the United States, similar to a credit card (*informal*)

la·ser weld·ing *n* the process of using a laser to join tissues together in order to seal up wounds

lash[1] /lash/ *n* **1.** STROKE WITH WHIP a stroke with a whip or some other long flexible object, often one of several given as a punishment **2.** same as **eyelash** **3.** MOVEMENT LIKE WHIP a movement like that of a whip being cracked ○ *The lion gave a lash of its tail.* **4.** END OF WHIP the flexible end of a whip **5.** SEVERE SCOLDING a severe reproof or verbal attack ○ *He felt the full lash of his father's tongue.* **6.** IMPACT OF SOMETHING a strong or powerful, often continuous, impact of something, especially a natural element, against a surface ○ *the lash of waves onto the beach* ■ *v* (**lashed, lash·ing, lash·es**) **1.** *vti* SMASH ONTO SOMETHING to have a strong or powerful, often continuous, impact on a surface ○ *Heavy seas lashed the shore.* **2.** *vti* CRITICIZE SOMEBODY to criticize somebody or something severely ○ *She lashed into her critics.* **3.** *vt* WHIP SOMEBODY to hit somebody or something with a whip or an object like a whip, often repeatedly as a form of punishment ○ *Prisoners were lashed severely.* **4.** *vti* FLICK TO AND FRO to flick something from side to side sharply so that it moves like a whip, or move in this way ○ *The cat lashed its tail angrily.* **5.** *vt* INCITE PEOPLE to encourage somebody, especially a crowd of people, to feel a strong emotion such as anger ○ *The fans had lashed themselves into a fever of enthusiasm.* —**lash·er** *n*

lash out *vi* **1.** to attack somebody verbally and suddenly **2.** to start suddenly to attack somebody with uncontrolled movements

lash[2] /lash/ (**lashed, lash·ing, lash·es**) *vt* to tie something tightly or securely to another object [15C. Origin ?] —**lash·er** *n*

lash·ing[1] /láshing/ *n* **1.** FLOGGING a beating with a whip or something resembling a whip **2.** SEVERE SCOLDING a severe rebuke or critical attack ■ **lash·ings** *npl UK* LARGE QUANTITY generous or plentiful amounts of something [15C. < LASH[1]]

lash·ing[2] /láshing/ *n* rope or cord used for securing things [Mid-17C. < LASH[2]]

LASIK /láyzik/ *n* laser surgery performed to correct nearsightedness, farsightedness, or astigmatism by cutting a flap in the cornea and removing tissue underneath [Acronym < *laser-assisted in situ keratomileusis*]

Las·kin /láskin/, **Bora** (1912–84) Canadian lawyer and judge. He served as chief justice of Canada (1973–84).

Las Pal·mas /laass paálməss/ city, seaport, and capital of Las Palmas Province, northeastern Grand Canary Island, Spain. Population: 352,641 (1998).

La Spe·zia /laa speétsee ə/ naval base, port city, and capital of La Spezia Province, Liguria Region, northwestern Italy. Population: 91,391 (2001).

lass /lass/ *n* **1.** a girl or young woman (*sometimes considered offensive*) **2.** a girlfriend or sweetheart [14C. Probably related to Old Norse *laskura* "unmarried"]

Las·sa fe·ver /laássə-/ *n* an infectious, often fatal, viral disease of West Africa marked by high fever, muscle pain, ulcers of the mucous membranes, headaches, hemorrhaging, and heart and kidney failure [Late 20C. After a village in Nigeria]

Las·sen Vol·can·ic Na·tion·al Park /láss'n-/ national park in Northeastern California, established in 1907. Its main feature is the volcanic Lassen Peak, 10,457 ft./3,187 m high. Area: 166 sq. mi./430 sq. km.

las·si /lássee/ *n* a South Asian drink consisting of flavored yogurt or buttermilk diluted with water [Late 20C. < Hindi]

las·sie /lássee/ *n N England, Scotland* a girl or young woman (*informal; sometimes considered offensive*)

las·si·tude /lássi tood/ *n* a state of weariness accompanied by listlessness or apathy [15C. Via French < Latin *lassitudo* < *lassus* "weary"]

las·so /lássō, la soó/ *n* (*plural* **-sos**) a long stiff piece of rope or cord with a sliding noose at one end, used especially for catching horses and cattle ■ *vt* (**-soed, -soing, -sos**) to use a lasso or other length of rope to catch a horse, cow, or other animal [Mid-18C. Representing the American Spanish pronunciation of Spanish *lazo* < Latin *laqueus* "noose"] —**las·so·er** *n*

last[1] /last/ CORE MEANING: a grammatical word indicating that something is the most recent or final of all ○ (adj) *She was married last April.* ○ (adj) *Johnny turned and took a last look at the band.* ○ (adv) *Allow me to apologize for the uncomfortable circumstances under which we last met.* ○ (adv) *He got to the meeting last.* ○ (pron) *Her new album's even better than the last.*

1. *adj, pron* MOST RECENT occurring most recently ○ (adj) *I saw him last Tuesday.* ○ (pron) *This flood may turn out to be even worse than the last.* **2.** *adj, pron* AFTER ALL OTHERS being or occurring after all the others ○ (adj) *He is believed to be the last person to see her before she left.* ○ (pron) *Your first complaint may well be your last.* **3.** *adj, pron* ONLY REMAINING the final or only person, thing, or part remaining ○ (adj) *This machine just ate my last dollar!* ○ (pron) *Here – finish up the last of the cake.* **4.** *adj, pron* LEAST SUITABLE least suitable, appropriate, or likely ○ (adj) *She's the last person we want on this project.* ○ (pron) *I am the last to criticize you in any way.* **5.** *adj* RELATING TO END relating to the end of somebody's life **6.** *adv* MOST RECENTLY on the most recent occasion ○ *When I last spoke to them they sounded fine.* **7.** *adv* AFTER ALL OTHERS after all the others in a series or order **8.** *adv* FINALLY as the final point ○ *Last, I'd like to mention all the people who helped to make this evening a success.* **9.** *n* FINAL MOMENT the final moment, especially of life ○ *She remained cheerful to the last.* [Old English *latost* (adverb) "after all the others" < Germanic] ◇ **at last** finally or in the end ○ *I've found you at last – I've been looking everywhere.* ◇ **at long last** eventually, after a long delay or many difficulties ○ *They fought the case for years and at long last got some compensation.* ◇ **breathe your last** same as **die**[1] (sense 1) (*literary*) ○ *I was by her side when she breathed her last.* ◇ **every last** everything without exception ○ *They ate it up, every last piece of it.* ◇ **last but not least** the final thing to be mentioned but important nevertheless ○ *And of course, last but not least, we thank the staff of customer relations.* ◇ **the last of 1.** the last remaining person, thing, or part of something, or the last in a sequence ○ *That's the last of the bread – I'll get some more tomorrow.* **2.** somebody's final contact with or news of somebody or something ○ *You haven't heard the last of this – I'm going to complain.*

CULTURAL NOTE ***The Last of the Mohicans***, a novel (1826) by writer James Fenimore Cooper. The most popular of Cooper's evocative accounts of frontier life, it is set in mid-18th-century North America during the wars between Britain and France. It describes the attempts of frontiersman Hawkeye and his Mahican companions, Chingachook and Uncas, the last of their people, to protect a British family from the French and their Huron allies.

last[2] /last/ (**last·ed, last·ing, lasts**) *vti* to continue to be used or available for a period of time ○ *The provisions lasted for ten days.* ○ *The fruit lasted us a week.* [Old English *læstan* "last, follow" < Germanic]

last out *vt* **1.** to be an adequate supply for a particular length of time ○ *I think we've got enough food to last out the week.* **2.** to survive for a particular length of time ○ *The vet said she didn't think Prince would last out the night.*

last[3] /last/ *n* a wooden or metal block shaped like a human foot that a shoemaker or cobbler uses for making and repairing footwear [Old English *læste* < *lāst* "sole of the foot, footprint" < Germanic, "follow"]

last-born *adj* youngest in a family

last call *n* a bartender's request for last drink orders before closing time (*informal*)

last-ditch *adj* done or taken when all other options have been exhausted

Last Fron·tier *n* a nickname for Alaska

last-gasp *adj* done as a last measure when all other options have failed and time is running out

last hur·rah *n* a final appearance, performance, or effort [Mid-20C. < *The Last Hurrah*, novel by Edwin O'Connor (1918–68)]

last-in, first-out *n* a method of accounting in which it is assumed that the most recently purchased items in an inventory are the first to be sold

last·ing /lásting/ *adj* continuing for a very long time or indefinitely ■ *n* a strong durable twill fabric. Use: shoe uppers. [14C. < LAST[2]] —**last·ing·ly** *adv* —**last·ing·ness** *n*

Last Judg·ment *n* in Jewish, Islamic, and Christian traditions, God's final judgment of humankind, which is to take place at the end of the world

last·ly /lástlee/ *adv* as the final thing at the end of a series [14C. < LAST[1]]

last min·ute *n* the latest time that it is possible to do something and still be in time —**last-min·ute** *adj*

last name *n* same as **surname**

last or·ders *npl, interj UK* the final opportunity to buy drinks before a pub, bar, or other place selling alcohol closes

last re·sort *n* something tried or done when everything else has failed

last rites *npl* **1.** in the Roman Catholic Church, religious rites performed for somebody who is close to death **2.** in Christianity, religious rites accompanying a burial or funeral

last spike *n* the final section completing a rail line, symbolized by the final spike driven to secure the rails

last straw *n* a minor annoyance that, because it comes at the end of a series of other misfortunes, makes a situation unbearable [< the fable of the camel whose back was broken by the last straw added to its load]

Last Sup·per *n* the last meal that Jesus Christ ate with his disciples before his crucifixion, commemorated by Christians in the Communion ceremony

last time *adv Malaysia, Singapore* during or at an earlier period, but no longer ○ *Last time I lived in Ipoh.* [Probably translation < Chinese]

last word *n* **1.** FINAL REMARK IN DISCUSSION the final thing to be said, especially at the end of an argument, disagreement, or discussion **2.** ULTIMATE DECISION the final decision on something **3.** BEST the best of its kind ○ *the last word in convenience* ■ **last words** *npl* DYING STATEMENT the final remarks spoken by somebody who is dying, often thought to be very personal and sometimes of great significance

Las Ve·gas /laass váygəss/ city in southern Nevada, a center for tourism and gambling. It is famous for the extravagant neon-lighted resort hotels, casinos, and bars that line its main street, known as "The Strip." Population: 508,604 (2002 estimate).

lat[1] /laat/ (*plural* **lat·i** /láttee/ or **lats**) *n* the main unit of Latvian currency. See table at **currency** [Late 20C. < Latvian, shortening of *Latvija* "Latvia"]

lat[2] /lat/ *n* ANAT same as **latissimus dorsi** (*informal*) [Shortening]

lat. *abbr* GEOG latitude

Lat. *abbr* **1.** LANG Latin **2.** Latvia **3.** PEOPLES, LANG Latvian

Lat·a·ki·a /làttə kée ə/ city and seaport, capital of Latakia Governorate, northwestern Syria. Population: 311,784 (1994).

latch /lach/ *n* **1.** DEVICE FOR KEEPING DOORS SHUT a device for holding a door, gate, or other opening closed consisting of a movable bar that drops into a hole or notch **2.** DOOR LOCK a door lock that needs a key to be opened from the outside but not the inside ■ *vt* (**latched, latch·ing, latch·es**) FASTEN SOMETHING WITH LATCH to close or lock something with a latch [Old English *læccan* "to grasp" < Indo-European]

latch onto *vt* (*informal*) **1.** GET to get hold of something **2.** REMAIN CONSTANTLY IN SOMEBODY'S COMPANY to remain constantly in somebody's company even if the person would prefer other company or solitude **3.** BECOME ENTHUSIASTIC ABOUT SOMETHING to adopt something enthusiastically ○ *latched onto the idea*

latch·et /láchət/ *n* a leather thong for tying a shoe or sandal (*archaic*) [14C. < Old French *lachet* "little string" < *laz* (see LACE)]

latch·key /lách kèe/ (*plural* **-keys**) *n* a key for lifting a latch, especially one on an outside door or gate

latch·key child, latch·key kid *n* a child who returns from school to an empty home because the adults in the family are still at work

latch·string /lách strìng/ *n* a string attached to a latch and passed through a hole in a door to allow somebody to open it from the other side

late /layt/ *adj* **1.** AFTER EXPECTED TIME happening or arriving after an expected or arranged time ○ *Hurry up or we'll be late!* **2.** AFTER USUAL TIME happening or done after the normal or usual time ○ *a late lunch* **3.** NEAR END OF PERIOD near the end of a particular period of time ○ *The meeting is scheduled for late morning.* **4.** INTO NIGHT well into the evening or night ○ *It's late – time for bed.* **5.** ⚠ DEAD having died, especially fairly recently ○ *my late grandfather* **6.** UP UNTIL RECENTLY having recently done something, lived somewhere, or belonged to a group or organization but no longer doing so ○ *That reporter, late of the European bureau, is now moving to Southeast Asia.* **7.** DONE TOWARD END OF CAREER produced near the end of somebody's career or life ○ *a late Degas* ■ *adv* (**lat·er, lat·est**) **1.** NOT ON TIME after an expected or arranged time ○ *He arrived late.* **2.** BEYOND USUAL TIME after the usual or normal time ○ *She had to work late.* **3.** NEAR END OF PERIOD toward the end of a period of time ○ *These birds tend to nest late in the year.* **4.** WELL INTO EVENING at or until a point well into the evening or night ○ *Their flight is due late on Friday.* **5.** RECENTLY relatively recently ○ *She didn't pack her bags until as late as yesterday.* [Old English *læt* < Indo-European, "let go"] —**late·ness** *n* ◇ **of late** recently

USAGE late meaning "deceased": In obituaries or death announcements the person in question is hardly ever described as *the late...* Nor is it usual for somebody who died centuries ago to be described in that way. The purpose of ***late*** is to serve as a reminder that the person in question is no longer living. In an obituary, that much is obvious, so ***late*** is not needed. Nor is it needed in historical contexts, except to indicate that somebody was dead by a particular time: *By 1800 Thomas Jefferson's late wife, Martha....*

SYNONYMS See ***dead***.

late blight *n* a disease of potatoes, caused by a fungus, in which both tubers and foliage decay

late·com·er /láyt kùmmər/ *n* **1.** somebody who arrives late for an event **2.** somebody who has recently become involved with or interested in something ○ *a latecomer to Bach*

late de·vel·op·er *n* a child whose potential in some or all aspects of school work develops later than is the case for the majority of his or her contemporaries

la·teen /lə téen, la-/ *adj* describes a triangular sail hung on a yard attached to a small mast, or a ship with such a sail [Mid-16C. < French *(voile) latine* "Latin (sail)" < Latin *Latinus* (see LATIN); because it was used in the Mediterranean]

la·teen-rigged *adj* using a lateen sail

late Greek *n* the form of Greek used between the 3rd and the 9th centuries A.D.

late He·brew *n* the form of Hebrew used between the 12th and the 18th centuries A.D.

late Lat·in *n* the written form of Latin used between the 3rd and the 7th centuries A.D.

late·ly /láytlee/ *adv* within the last few days or weeks, or not too long ago

lat·en /láyt'n/ (**-ened, -en·ing, -ens**) *vti* to grow late, or make something late (*literary*)

la·ten·cy pe·ri·od *n* PSYCHOANAL same as **latent period**

La Tène /la tén/ *adj* relating to an Iron-Age culture that flourished in Europe between the 5th and the 1st centuries B.C. [Late 19C. After a district in Switzerland]

late-night *adj* **1.** done or happening at or until a late hour of the night ○ *late-night television* **2.** open for business at a late hour of the night ○ *a late-night club*

la·tent /láyt'nt/ *adj* **1.** HIDDEN present or existing, but in an underdeveloped or unexpressed form **2.** BIOL DORMANT dormant or undeveloped but able to develop normally under suitable conditions **3.** PSYCHOANAL PRESENT BUT UNEXPRESSED present in the unconscious but not consciously expressed [Early 17C. < Latin *latent-*, present participle of *latere* "be hidden"] —**la·ten·cy** /láyt'nssee/ *n*

la·tent con·tent *n* in psychoanalysis, the content of a dream that is hidden or repressed, and is represented in symbols

la·tent heat *n* the heat that is absorbed or emitted when a substance undergoes a physical phase change but that does not make the substance change temperature. Symbol *L*

la·tent im·age *n* the invisible image recorded on light-sensitive materials such as photographic film or paper but not yet developed

la·tent pe·ri·od *n* **1.** MED DISEASE INCUBATION PERIOD the incubation period of a disease **2.** PHYSIOL TIME BETWEEN STIMULUS AND RESPONSE the interval between the application of a stimulus and the start of a response **3.** PSYCHOANAL THEORETICAL CHILDHOOD DEVELOPMENTAL STAGE in Freudian theory, a period between five or six years of age and adolescence when sexual interest is suppressed

la·tent print *n* a fingerprint that is left at a crime scene and remains invisible until chemically treated

lat·er /láytər/ comparative of **late** ■ *adv* after a particular period of time, the present time, or the time being discussed ■ *interj* used to say goodbye for now (*informal*)

lat·er·al /láttərəl/ *adj* **1.** AT SIDE relating to, located at, or affecting the side **2.** SIDEWAYS IN CAREER, RATHER THAN UP involving transfer to a position in an organization or career that has the same status or pay as the previous one **3.** PHON PRODUCED WITH INCOMPLETE OBSTRUCTION OF AIR describes a speech sound produced with the tip of the tongue touching the alveolar ridge so that air moves around one or both sides of the tongue. The only lateral sound in English is /l/. **4.** GENETICS same as **horizontal** *adj* (sense 7) ■ *n* **1.** PART AT SIDE a part, appendage, movement, or object at the side of something **2.** PHON LATERAL CONSONANT a lateral speech sound, e.g., /l/ in English **3.** FOOTBALL SIDEWAYS OR BACKWARD FOOTBALL PASS in football, a sideways or backward pass ■ *vti* (**-aled, -al·ing, -als**) FOOTBALL PASS BALL SIDEWAYS in football, to pass the ball sideways or backward [15C. < Latin *lateralis* < *later-* "side"] —**lat·er·al·ly** *adv*

lat·er·al bud *n* a bud that develops in the angle between a leaf and a stem

lat·er·al·i·za·tion /làttərəli záysh'n/ *n* the localization of the control center for a specific function, e.g., speech, on the right or left side of the brain

lat·er·al line *n* a line of sensory pores along the head and sides of fish and some amphibians that detect pressure, current variations, and vibrations

lat·er·al think·ing *n* a way of solving problems by unconventional or apparently illogical means rather than by a traditionally logical approach

lat·er·ite /láttə rìt/ *n* a reddish mixture of clayey iron and aluminum oxides and hydroxides formed by the weathering of basalt under humid, tropical conditions. There are extensive deposits in India. [Early 19C. < Latin *later* "brick"] —**lat·er·it·ic** /làttə ríttik/ *adj*

lat·est /láytəst/ superlative of **late** ■ *adj* newest, most recent, or most up-to-date ■ *n* the newest, most recent, or most up-to-date news, fashion, or version of something (*informal*)

la·tex /láy tèks/ (*plural* **-ti·ces** /-tisèez/ or **-tex·es**) *n* **1.** a milky white liquid produced by some plants such as the rubber tree, whose sap is used to make rubber **2.** a suspension of rubber or plastic (**polymer**) particles in water. Use: manufacture of emulsion paints, adhesives, other products. [Mid-17C. < Latin, "liquid"]

la·tex paint *n* paint that contains latex as a binder

lath /lath/ *n* **1.** WOODEN STRIP USED IN FRAMEWORK one of the thin strips of wood used to form a framework to support plaster, tiles, or slates **2.** SUPPORT FOR PLASTERING a sheet of metal or a framework of wire mesh used as a support for plasterwork **3.** THIN STRIP OF WOOD a thin strip of wood, especially one used in the building trades ■ *vt* (**lathed, lath·ing, laths**) ATTACH LATHS TO SURFACE to attach or nail laths to a surface before plastering, tiling, or fixing slates [Old English *lætt* < Germanic]

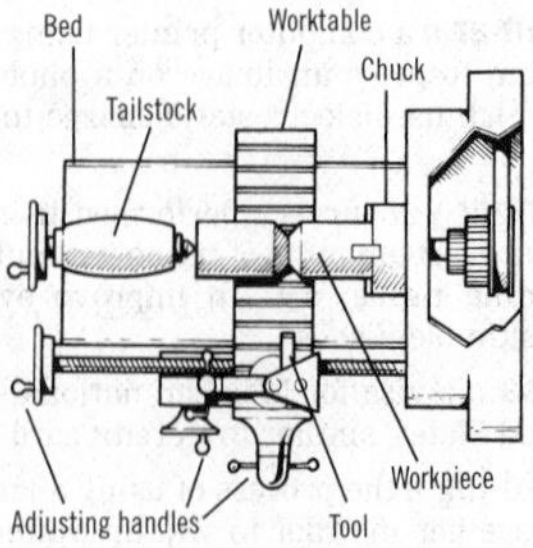

lathe

lathe /layth/ *n* a machine for working wood or metal, in which the piece being worked is held and rotated while a cutting tool is applied to it ■ *vt* (**lathed, lath·ing, lathes**) to shape wood or metal using a lathe [14C. Probably < Old Danish *lad* "stand, framework"]

lath·er /láthər/ *n* **1.** SOAPY FROTH foam that is produced by soap or detergent used with water **2.** SWEATY FROTH white foam produced during periods of extremely heavy sweating, especially by horses **3.** AGITATED STATE a state of agitation or nervous anxiety (*informal*) ■ *v* (**-ered, -er·ing, -ers**) **1.** *vti* CREATE LATHER to produce a lather using a soap or detergent, or cause something to produce a lather **2.** *vt* PUT LATHER ON SOMETHING to coat something with soapy lather [Old English *lēaþor* < Indo-European, "to wash"] —**lath·er·y** *adj*

la·thi /laätee/ (*plural* **-this**) *n S Asia* in South Asia, a long heavy stick used as a weapon, especially by police [Mid-19C. < Hindi *lāṭhī*]

lath·y·rism /láthə rìzzəm/ *n* a neurological disease of humans and domestic animals, caused by eating some types of legumes and characterized by lack of strength in the legs or inability to move the legs. The legumes responsible for the disease are of the genus *Lathyrus*. [Late 19C. < modern Latin *Lathyrus* < Greek *lathuros*, species of vetch]

lat·i MONEY plural of **lat**[1]

la·ti·ces INDUST plural of **latex**

la·tic·i·fer /la tíssəfər/ *n* a duct in some plants that produces latex [Early 20C. < Latin *latici-*, stem of *latex* "liquid"] —**lat·i·cif·er·ous** /làtti síffərəss/ *adj*

lat·i·fun·di·um /làttə fúndee əm/ (*plural* **-di·a** /-dee ə/) *n* in ancient Rome, an agricultural estate, especially one that was worked by slaves [Mid-17C. < Latin < *latus* "broad" + *fundus* "landed estate"]

lat·i·go /láttə gṑ, laätə gṑ/ (*plural* **-gos** or **-goes**) *n* a strap for tightening the girth on a western saddle [Late 19C. < Spanish, "strap"]

Lat·in /látt'n/ *n* **1.** ANCIENT ROMAN LANGUAGE the extinct Indo-European language of ancient Rome and its empire, adopted in medieval Europe as the language of education, culture, religion, and government. The Romance languages developed from Vulgar Latin, and its prominence during medieval times led to Latin-derived words entering the vocabularies of other European languages. **2.** SOMEBODY FROM ANCIENT LATIUM somebody who came from ancient Latium in west central Italy **3.** SOMEBODY SPEAKING ROMANCE LANGUAGE somebody who speaks a language derived from Latin, especially somebody living in Latin America or southern Europe ■ *adj* **1.** OF LATIN relating to Latin **2.** OF PEOPLE SPEAKING ROMANCE LANGUAGES relating to a people using a language derived from Latin, especially a people living in Latin America or in southern Europe **3.** OF ROMAN CATHOLIC CHURCH belonging or relating to the Roman Catholic Church **4.** WRITTEN IN ROMAN ALPHABET written in or relating to the Roman alphabet [Pre-12C. < Latin *Latinus* "of the people of Latium, Roman" < *Latium*, ancient region in Italy]

Lat·i·na /lə teénə/ *n Hispanic* a woman or girl of Latin American descent who comes from the United States [Mid-20C. < American Spanish, form of *Latino* (see LATINO)]

USAGE See ***Anglo*** and ***Hispanic***.

Lat·in al·pha·bet *n* LANGUAGE same as **Roman alphabet**

Lat·in A·mer·i·ca *n* **1.** the entire western hemisphere south of the United States **2.** the countries of the Americas that developed from the colonies of Spain, Portugal, and France —**La·tin-A·mer·i·can** *adj, n*

Lat·in A·mer·i·can In·te·gra·tion As·so·ci·a·tion *n* a trade association formed by Argentina, Bolivia, Brazil, Chile, Columbia, Ecuador, Mexico, Paraguay, Peru, Uruguay, and Venezuela in 1980

Lat·in A·mer·i·can·ist *n* an expert in or student of Latin America, especially its history or culture

Lat·in·ate /látt'n àyt/ *adj* derived from, relating to, or characteristic of Latin

Lat·in Church *n* CHR same as **Roman Catholic Church**

Lat·in cross *n* an upright cross in which the lowest limb is longer than the other three, often associated with Christianity

Lat·in·ism /látt'n ìzzəm/ *n* a word or phrase borrowed from Latin

Lat·in·ist /látt'nist/ *n* an expert in or student of Latin

La·tin·i·ty /lə tínnətee/ *n* a style or level of expertise in using Latin

Lat·in·ize /látt'n ìz/ (**-ized, -iz·ing, -iz·es**) *vt* **1.** TRANSLATE SOMETHING INTO LATIN to translate something into Latin, or give a Latin form to something such as a name **2.** TRANSCRIBE SOMETHING INTO ROMAN ALPHABET to transcribe words into the Roman alphabet from another alphabet **3.** MAKE SOMETHING LIKE ROMAN CATHOLIC CHURCH to cause something to resemble the practices of the Roman Catholic Church **4.** ANCIENT HIST MAKE PEOPLE MORE ROMAN to make people adapt to Roman customs and styles —**Lat·in·i·za·tion** /làtt'ni záysh'n/ *n* —**Lat·in·iz·er** *n*

LANGUAGE HERITAGE ***Latin*** Much of English is made up of words from other languages, and a large proportion come from Latin, the extinct language of ancient Rome and its empire, inherited either directly, or indirectly through French (a Romance language developed from Latin). After it ceased to be a living first language, Latin nevertheless survived as the language of the Christian church and of scholarship, including science, where modern Latin still provides the taxonomic names for plants and animals. Latin has therefore been available as a source of new words for English throughout the history of the language.

Migrants direct from Latin tend to be more formal and technical than those that made their way into English through French, though many everyday words are still of immediate Latin origin (for example, ***curve***, ***except***, ***motor***, ***persuade***, ***produce***, and ***silent***). Words that came into English from Latin via French include ***absent***, ***benign***, ***card***, ***human***, ***legal***, and ***patient***. The picture is further complicated by the similarity of related French and Latin forms, making either language the possible source of words such as ***addition***, ***canine***, ***normal***, ***succeed***, and ***valid***; moreover English words from French were often Latinized after their adoption, for example, ***ocular*** (directly from French *oculaire* but now reformed as if from its source late Latin *ocularis*), and ***serious*** (directly from French *sérieux* but now as if from late Latin *seriosus*, from Latin *serius*). ("Latin" alone usually refers to classical Latin, used between the end of the first century B.C. and the third century A.D.: later periods are specified as "late Latin," "modern Latin," etc., as appropriate.)

One large class of words clearly identifiable as being of Latin origin is that of verbs ending in *-ate* (***deviate***, ***generate***, ***liberate***, ***vibrate***, etc.). Latin is a highly inflected language, with numerous different forms for the same word, and English tends to borrow such verbs from their past participles, whereas in French they have usually developed from the infinitive; for example, ***elevate*** comes from *elevat-*, the past participle form of the Latin infinitive *elevare*, from which the equivalent French verb *élever* derives. Adjectives in *-ose* are also usually from Latin, and mostly late arrivals (early Latin words in *-osus* are usually Anglicized as *-ous*), for example, ***bellicose*** (15th century) and ***religiose*** (mid-19th). Certain types of irregular plurals are also telltale signs of Latin migrant nouns: *-ae* for nouns in *-a* (***formula***, plural ***formulae*** alongside ***formulas***), *-i* for nouns in *-us* (***stimulus***, plural ***stimuli***), *-a* for nouns in *-um* (***ovum***, plural ***ova***), a change of *-sis* to *-ses* (***emphasis***, plural ***emphases*** – though some words of this form may be directly from Greek), and in some technical words changes of *-x* to *-c-* or *-g-* (***calyx***, plural ***calyces*** alongside ***calyxes***, ***larynx***, plural ***larynges*** alongside ***larynxes***). These irregular plurals have often caused difficulty and change in English: see, for example, ***agenda***, ***data***, and ***media***; others have maintained their plural status, for example, ***impedimenta***, ***memorabilia***, and ***viscera***.

Some Latin words have changed grammatical status in the voyage into English: ***alibi***, for example, was an adverb meaning "elsewhere" in Latin and for the first century of its use in English, but during the late 18th century the adverbial use became obsolete and the current noun use took over; ***tandem*** was also an adverb, meaning "at length," but was humorously applied to a vehicle; ***veto*** meant "I forbid" in Latin, but in English became a noun and a fully inflected verb.

Up to the time of the Reformation, in the early 16th century, the main category of Latin words entering English belonged to the Christian church; from the late 16th century emphasis changed to scholarly and legal terms, and there was a conscious attempt to elevate and improve the English language and create a Latinate formal and literary stratum. Latin phrases and tags were introduced (including ***a fortiori***, ***caveat emptor***, ***cui bono***, and ***ne plus ultra***). ***Exempli gratia*** arrived in the mid-17th century, was abbreviated to ***e.g.*** before the century was out, and its Latin origin receded into the background. Latin alternatives to older English words were advocated, for example, ***terminate*** (late 16th century) instead of "end" or "finish"; some found a regular useful place in the language, but others, for example ***sequacious***, were always formal and are now often archaic. The vocabulary of science remains, however, resolutely Latinate, though English is now the usual vehicle of scientific publication. Chemical elements are given Latin forms, for example, ***aluminum*** (early 19th century) and ***lutetium*** (early 20th); anatomical terms often derive from Latin, as in the ***hippocampus***, ***medulla oblongata***, and ***pia mater*** of the brain. Although the main waves of migration were over, the 20th century continued to receive Latin words in technical areas: in psychoanalysis, for example, ***ego*** and ***id***, and in the same field of human observation ***gravitas***, ***libido***, and ***persona***; in phonetics ***fortis*** and ***lenis*** consonants; in biology ***mutant*** and ***predator***; and in ***academia*** (mid-20th century) ***curriculum vitae***. In addition Latin elements have continued to be combined with others to create new terms, for example, in the late 20th century in ***lentivirus*** (from *lentus* "slow") and ***nutraceutical*** (another word for "functional food," from *nutrire* "nourish").

Lat·in-Jazz *n* a form of jazz music that is a mixture of Afro-Cuban music and Fusion

La·ti·no /lə teénō/ (*plural* **-nos**) *n Hispanic* **1.** somebody who comes from a country of Latin America **2.** somebody of Latin American descent who comes from the United States [Mid-20C. Via American Spanish < Spanish, "Latin, a Latin" < Latin *Latinus* (see LATIN)]

USAGE See ***Anglo*** and ***Hispanic***.

Lat·in Quar·ter *n* an area in central Paris on the Left Bank, noted for educational and cultural pursuits

lat·ish /láytish/ *adj* fairly late, or later than is desirable or expected ○ *a latish supper* ■ *adv* at a fairly late time, or later than is desirable or expected ○ *They arrived latish.*

la·tis·si·mus dor·si /la tìssəməss dáwr sì/ (*plural* **la·tis·si·mi dor·si** /-mī-/) *n* either of the two broad triangular muscles along the sides of the back [Shortening of modern Latin *musculus latissimus dorsi* "broadest muscle of the back"]

lat·i·tude /láttə to͞od/ *n* **1.** IMAGINARY LINE AROUND EARTH an imaginary line joining points on Earth's surface that are all of equal distance north or south of the equator **2.** AREA OF EARTH'S SURFACE a region of the Earth's surface near a particular latitude (*often used in the plural*) ○ *snow showers in the northerly latitudes* **3.** ROOM TO MANEUVER enough scope or leeway for some freedom of choice, action, or thinking ○ *It's a very creative job, allowing me a great deal of latitude.* **4.** PHOTOGRAPHY DEGREE OF TOLERANCE OF EXPOSURE ERROR the degree of overexposure or underexposure that light-sensitive material can accommodate and still provide an acceptable image [14C. < Latin *latitudo* "breadth" < *latus* "broad"] —**lat·i·tu·din·al** /làttə to͞od'nəl/ *adj* —**lat·i·tu·di·nal·ly** *adv*

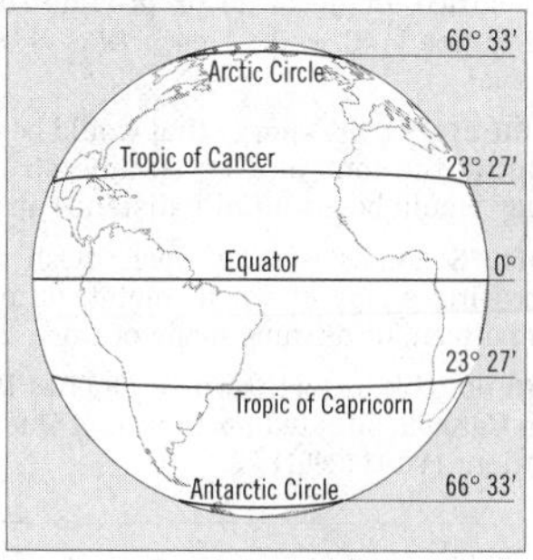

latitude

lat·i·tu·di·nar·i·an /làttə tood'n érree ən/ *adj* allowing some freedom in attitude, beliefs, behavior, or interpretation, especially in religious matters [Mid-17C. < Latin *latitudin-*, stem of *latitudo* (see LATITUDE)] —**lat·i·tu·di·nar·i·an** *n*

lat·ke /látkə/ *n* a fried flat cake of grated potato with beaten egg. It is an Eastern European and particularly a Jewish specialty. [Early 20C. Via Yiddish < Russian *latka* "earthenware cooking vessel"]

La·to·na /lə tṓnə/ *n* in Roman mythology, the mother of Apollo and Diana by Jupiter. Greek equivalent **Leto**

lat·o·sol /láttə sàwl/ *n* a soil variety that is common in tropical or subtropical regions and is rich in iron and aluminum [Mid-20C. < LATERITE + Latin *solum* "ground"]

La Tour /lə to͝or/, **Georges de** (1593–1652) French painter. The simplicity of his religious paintings, often depicting a candlelit scene, differentiates him from his contemporary baroque painters.

la·trine /lə treén/ *n* a toilet, especially a communal one on a military base [13C. < Latin *latrina*, contraction of *lavatrina* < *lavare* "to wash"]

La·trobe /lə trṓb/, **Benjamin Henry** (1764–1820) British-born US architect. He designed and rebuilt part of the Capitol building in Washington, D.C. (1803 and 1814).

-latry *suffix* worship ○ *iconolatry* [< Greek *latreia*]

lat·te /laá tay/ *n* an espresso coffee with frothy steamed milk [< Italian, "milk"]

lat·ter /láttər/ *n* **SECOND OF TWO** the second of two people or things that have been mentioned, or that are being considered or referred to ○ *She went out with Joe and Sam, eventually marrying the latter.* ■ *adj* **1. CLOSING** near or relatively near the end of something ○ *spent the latter part of the day relaxing by the pool* **2. LATER** more recent, or more advanced in time ○ *In his latter years he became very forgetful.* [Old English *lætra* (adjective), *lator* (adverb), comparatives of *læt* (see LATE)]

lat·ter-day *adj* resembling a particular person or type of person from the past ○ *thought of himself as a latter-day Roosevelt*

Lat·ter-Day Saint *n* a member of the Church of Jesus Christ of Latter-Day Saints, founded by Joseph Smith in 1830 and centered in Salt Lake City, Utah

lat·ter·ly /láttərlee/ *adv* recently or in the most recent period ○ *He was quite ill for a while, but latterly seems to have returned to normal.*

lat·ter·math /láttər màth/ *n regional* a second crop or growth of grass in the same season, after the first harvest or mowing [Mid-16C. < LATTER + obsolete *math* "mowing"]

lat·tice /láttiss/ *n* **1. CRISSCROSS FRAMEWORK** an interwoven open-mesh frame made by crisscrossing strips of wood, metal, or plastic to form a pattern **2. SOMETHING MADE FROM LATTICE** something, e.g., a door, gate, or fence, that is made from or consists of a lattice **3. INTERWOVEN FORM** a representation of a lattice framework, especially a heraldic one **4. ARRANGEMENT OF POINTS** a regular geometric arrangement of points or objects such as the atoms in a crystal ■ *vti* (**-ticed, -tic·ing, -tices**) **PROVIDE LATTICE** to interweave strips to form a lattice, or decorate or provide something with a lattice [14C. < Old French *lattis* < *latte* "lath" < Germanic]

lat·tice en·er·gy *n* the energy that would be required to separate the ions of a crystalline structure so that they would be an infinite distance apart

lat·tice·work /láttiss wùrk/ *n* open mesh made by crisscrossing strips of wood, metal, or plastic to form a pattern, or a frame made of this

La Tuque /lə to͞ok/ resort town in Québec Province, eastern Canada, situated northwest of Québec City. Population: 11,298 (2001).

Latvia

Lat·vi·a /laátvee ə/ country bordering the Baltic Sea in northeastern Europe. It is one of the Baltic States and became a member of the European Union in 2004. Language: Latvian. Currency: lat. Capital: Riga. Population: 2,348,784 (2003). Area: 24,600 sq. mi./63,700 sq. km. Official name **Republic of Latvia**

Lat·vi·an /látvee ən/ *n* **1.** somebody who comes from Latvia **2.** the official Balto-Slavic language of Latvia, also spoken in western European Russia. Native speakers: 3 million. —**Lat·vi·an** *adj*

laud /lawd/ *vt* (**laud·ed, laud·ing, lauds**) **PRAISE SOMEBODY** to glorify somebody, or praise somebody highly ■ *n* **1. GREAT PRAISE** high praise, acclaim, or glorification (*literary*) **2.** MUSIC **SONG OF PRAISE** a hymn of praise or glorification **3.** CHR **FIRST PRAYER OF DAY** in the Roman Catholic Church, the first prayer of the seven separate hours (**canonical hours**) that are set aside for prayer each day (*often used in the plural*) [14C. Noun via French < Latin *laud-* "praise"; verb < Latin *laudere* "to praise" < *laud-*] —**laud·a·to·ry** /láwdə tàwree/ *adj* —**laud·er** *n*

Lau·da /lówdə/, **Niki** (*b.* 1949) Austrian racecar driver. He became Grand Prix world champion in 1975, 1977, and 1984, despite a near-fatal crash in 1976. Full name **Lauda, Nikolas Andreas**

laud·a·ble /láwdəb'l/ *adj* admirable and worthy of praise —**laud·a·bil·i·ty** /làwdə bílləteel *n* —**laud·a·ble·ness** *n* —**laud·a·bly** *adv*

lau·da·num /láwd'nəm/ *n* a solution of opium in alcohol. Use: formerly, for pain relief. [Mid-16C. Origin ?]

laud·a·to·ry /láwdə tàwree/, **laud·a·tive** /-tiv/ *adj* expressing praise or admiration

Laud·er /láwdər/, **Estée** (*b.* 1908) US entrepreneur. She began working in the cosmetics industry selling a face cream in New York department stores before going on to found one of the world's largest cosmetics businesses (1946).

> "For most women...a half-boudoir, half-boardroom image is the image that works best, and neither is stronger than the other."
> [Estée Lauder, *Estée, a Success Story*; 1985]

Lau·der·dale Lakes /láwdər dàyl-/ city in Broward County, southeastern Florida. Population: 31,665 (2002 estimate).

laugh /laf/ *v* (**laughed, laugh·ing, laughs**) **1.** *vti* **MAKE SOUNDS EXPRESSING AMUSEMENT** to make sounds from the throat while breathing out in short bursts or gasps as a way of expressing amusement **2.** *vt* **BRING SOMEBODY TO STATE BY LAUGHING** to cause somebody or yourself to be in a particular state by laughing ○ *We both laughed ourselves silly.* **3.** *vi* **MOCK** to show mockery for somebody or something ○ *They laughed when I said I'd enter the tournament, but I won it.* **4.** *vi* **SHOW CONTEMPT** to express amusement, contempt, or disrespect for something ○ *laugh in the face of adversity* ○ *She has the ability to laugh at her own mistakes.* **5.** *vi* **MAKE NOISE LIKE LAUGHTER** to make a noise that sounds like somebody laughing (*refers to some birds and mammals*) ■ *n* **1. SOUND MADE WHEN LAUGHING** a series of sounds made when somebody laughs **2. SOMETHING FUNNY OR ENJOYABLE** a time of great fun and enjoyment, or something that gives fun and enjoyment (*informal*) ○ *had a real laugh with Bob and Patty* **3. SOMEBODY FUNNY** a funny or entertaining person ○ *You'll like him; he's a real laugh.* [Old English *hlæhhan* < Indo-European] —**laugh·er** *n* ◇ **have the last laugh** to be proved right or successful after being treated with disbelief, lack of confidence, or scorn

laugh down *vt* to reject something with contemptuous laughter ○ *The entire committee laughed down the new design.*

laugh off *vt* to trivialize or treat as amusing something serious or important ○ *Later we laughed the incident off as just a silly mistake.*

laugh·a·ble /láffəb'l/ *adj* so inadequate as to cause laughter or ridicule —**laugh·a·ble·ness** *n* —**laugh·a·bly** *adv*

laugh·ing gas /láffing-/ *n* CHEM same as **nitrous oxide** (*not in technical use*)

laugh·ing gull *n* a common black-headed gull with a high-pitched song resembling a human laugh. Native to: eastern North America to northern South America. Latin name: *Larus atricilla.*

laugh·ing jack·ass *n* BIRDS same as **kookaburra** (*dated*)

laugh·ing·ly /láffinglee/ *adv* with laughter that shows amusement or contempt at something or somebody funny or ridiculous ○ *She laughingly dismissed this idea and changed the subject.*

laugh·ing·stock /láffing stòk/ *n* somebody whose behavior has made him or her an object of ridicule or fun

laugh·ing thrush *n* a bird that makes a laughing call, often in groups, and usually has dark gray or brown plumage. Native to: South and Southeast Asia. Genus: *Garrulax.*

laugh lines *npl* wrinkles on the face at the outer corners of the eyes, associated with laughing or smiling

laugh·ter /láftər/ *n* **1.** the sound or an act of laughing **2.** happiness or fun expressed by laughing [Old English *hleahtor* < Germanic]

Laugh·ton /láwt'n/, **Charles** (1899–1962) British-born US actor. He acted on stage and screen, winning an Academy Award for *The Private Life of Henry VIII* (1933).

laugh track *n* a recording of laughter added to the soundtrack of a radio or television program

launce /lawnss/ *n* FISH same as **sand lance** [Early 17C. Variant of LANCE]

Launce·ston /láwnstən/ city and port in northern Tasmania, Australia, situated where the North Esk and South Esk rivers join to form the Tamar River. Population: 62,417 (2002 estimate).

launch[1] /lawnch/ *vt* (**launched, launch·ing, launch·es**) **1. FIRE ROCKET INTO AIR** to send a rocket, missile, or spacecraft into the air or the upper atmosphere **2. PUT CRAFT TO SEA** to push or put a vessel into the water so that it is ready to sail **3. LAUNCH SHIP FOR FIRST TIME** to send a newly built vessel into the water for the first time, usually with a special ceremony **4. BEGIN CAMPAIGN** to begin an attack, campaign, investigation, or other carefully planned activity ○ *The police have launched an investigation.* **5. PUT PRODUCT ON SALE** to put a new product on sale to the public and begin promoting it **6. THROW SOMETHING WITH GREAT FORCE** to throw or propel something, especially forcefully **7. START PROGRAM** to start a computer program ■ *n* **1. START OF ACTIVITY** the start of something, especially a carefully planned activity such as a military offensive, an investigation, or a campaign **2. EVENT TO PRESENT NEW PRODUCT** an occasion, e.g., a party, at which a new product is launched ○ *the launch of her new book* **3. TIME WHEN ROCKET IS LAUNCHED** the occasion when a rocket, missile, or spacecraft is launched **4. TIME WHEN SHIP IS LAUNCHED** the occasion when a boat or ship is launched, especially for the first time [14C. < Anglo-Norman *launcher*, variant of Old French *lancier* "pierce" < *lance* (see LANCE)]

launch into *vt* to begin an activity suddenly and enthusiastically ○ *The professor launched into yet another of his theories about how dinosaurs became extinct.*

launch[2] /lawnch/ *n* **1. LARGE MOTORBOAT** a large powerful motorboat **2. SMALL MOTORBOAT ON LARGE SHIP** a small motorboat carried on a large ship **3. LARGEST BOAT ON OLD WARSHIP** the largest boat formerly carried by a man-of-war [Late 17C. < Spanish *lancha* "pinnace"]

launch com·plex *n* a site containing the people and equipment needed for a rocket, missile, or spacecraft launch

launch·er /láwnchər/ *n* a device or platform for firing something such as a rocket or missile

launch pad, **launch·ing pad** /láwnching-/ *n* **1.** a platform, usually in a launch complex, from which a rocket, missile, or spacecraft is launched **2.** a starting point from which great or successful progress is made, e.g., in somebody's career

launch par·ty *n* a party held to celebrate and to introduce a new book, author, book publisher, or retailer

launch ve·hi·cle *n* a rocket that is used to launch a spacecraft or satellite into space

launch win·dow *n* the restricted period during which a rocket or other projectile can be successfully launched

laun·der /láwndər/ *v* (**-dered, -der·ing, -ders**) **1.** *vt* **MAKE MONEY APPEAR LEGAL** to pass illegally acquired money through a legitimate business or bank account in order to disguise its illegal origins **2.** *vt* **WASH AND IRON SOMETHING** to wash dirty clothes or linen and, often, iron them as well **3.** *vi* **BE WASHABLE** to be able to be washed ○ *It's a beautiful fabric, but I doubt that it would launder well.* ■ *n* MIN EXTRACT **TROUGH FOR WASHING**

ORE a trough used for washing ore [Late 16C. < contraction of obsolete *lavender* "washer of linen" < Old French *lavandier* < Latin *lavare* "to wash"] —**laun·der·a·ble** *adj* —**laun·der·er** *n*

laun·der·ette /làwndə rét/ *n* a laundry, usually self-service, containing coin-operated washing and drying machines

laun·dress /láwndrəss/ *n* a woman who does washing and ironing, especially one who does other people's washing and ironing as a way of earning a living (*dated*) [Mid-16C. < obsolete *launder* (see LAUNDER)]

Laun·dro·mat /láwndrə màt/ *tdmk* a service mark for a self-service coin-operated commercial laundry

laun·dry /láwndree/ (*plural* **-dries**) *n* **1. DIRTY WASH** dirty clothes or linen put aside to be washed and ironed **2. CLEAN WASH** freshly washed clothes or linen **3. WASHING AND IRONING PLACE** a place, especially a commercial establishment or a communal room in a building, where clothes and linen can be washed and ironed [Early 16C. Contraction of obsolete *lavendry* < Old French *lavanderie* < Latin *lavare* "to wash"]

laun·dry bas·ket *n* a wicker or plastic container used for carrying clothes that are to be washed or that have just been washed or dried

laun·dry de·ter·gent *n* detergent in powder or liquid form, used for washing clothes

laun·dry list *n* a lengthy list of items, usually things wanted or needed

laun·dry·man /láwndreemən/ (*plural* **-men** /-mən/) *n* **1.** somebody whose job involves working in a laundry or cleaners **2.** a man whose job involves collecting dirty washing and delivering it back after it has been washed and ironed or cleaned (*dated*)

laun·dry·wom·an /láwndree wòommən/ (*plural* **-wom·en** /-wìmmin/) *n* a woman whose job involves working in a laundry or cleaners

Laun·fal /láwnfəl/ *n* in Arthurian legend, one of the knights at the court

Laur·a·sia /law ráyzhə, -shə/ northern part of the ancient supercontinent of Pangaea, an ancient landmass thought to include what would become North America, Greenland, northern and central Europe, and most of Asia

lau·re·ate /láwree ət/ *n* **1. AWARD WINNER** a recipient of a prize or honor for outstanding achievement in the arts or sciences **2.** LITERAT same as **poet laureate** ■ *adj* **1. DESERVING HONOR** deserving honor or distinction **2. CROWNED WITH LAUREL** crowned with laurel as a sign of honor (*literary*) **3. MADE OF LAUREL** made of laurel leaves or branches (*literary*) [14C. < Latin *laureatus* < *laurus* "bay tree"] —**lau·re·ate·ship** *n*

lau·rel /láwrəl/ *n* **1.** PLANTS same as **bay**[4] (sense 1) **2. TREE OR BUSH RESEMBLING BAY** a tree or bush whose leaves, aroma, or berries are similar to those of the bay, e.g., the mountain laurel and cherry laurel **3. WREATH OF LEAVES** a wreath of woven bay leaves used as a mark of honor or victory in ancient times, e.g., to crown the winners of sports events ■ **lau·rels** *npl* **HONORS FOR ACHIEVEMENT** honors won for an achievement ■ *vt* (**-reled** or **-relled, -rel·ing** or **-rel·ling, -rels**) **1. GIVE SOMEBODY AWARD** to honor somebody with an award or prize **2. CROWN SOMEBODY WITH BAY** to crown somebody with a wreath of bay as a sign of honor (*literary*) [14C. Via Old French *lorier* < Latin *laureola* "small bay branch" < *laurus* "bay tree"] ◇ **look to your laurels** to be careful not to lose a successful or winning position because of a better performance by somebody else ◇ **rest on your laurels** to be satisfied with your success and do nothing to improve on it

REGIONAL NOTE The term ***laurel*** identifies three different trees in the eastern United States. From Massachusetts and Pennsylvania through Tennessee to Florida and westward to Mississippi, it may mean "magnolia." In the eastern states, it may mean "mountain laurel." In the Upper South, especially North Carolina, it may mean "rhododendron."

Lau·rel /láwrəl/ city in west central Maryland, on the Patuxent River, southwest of Baltimore and northeast of Washington, D.C. Population: 20,590 (2002 estimate).

Laurel and Hardy

Lau·rel, Stan (1890–1965) British-born US comedian. His partnership with Oliver Hardy was the first Hollywood movie comedy duo. Laurel was the "thin one" whose clumsiness was always getting them into trouble. Born **Jefferson, Arthur Stanley**

> "Another nice mess you've gotten me into."
> [Stan Laurel, line in the movie *Another Fine Mess*; 1930]

Lau·rence /láwrənss/, **Margaret** (1926–87) Canadian writer. Her novels, set in western Canada, are characterized by strong-minded women. Born **Wemyss, Jean Margaret**

Lau·rens /láwrənz/, **Henry** (1724–92) American patriot. He led the Continental Congress (1777–78) and fought against the British in the American Revolution.

Lau·ren·tian Moun·tains /law rènshən-/ range that runs north of the St. Lawrence River in southern Quebec Province, Canada. Height: 3,905 ft./1,190 m.

Lau·ren·tian Pla·teau ➧ **Canadian Shield**

lau·ric ac·id /làwrik-/ *n* a crystalline fatty acid. Source: coconut, laurel oils. Use: manufacture of soaps, insecticides, cosmetics, lauryl alcohol. Formula: $C_{12}H_{24}O_2$. [Late 19C. < Latin *laurus* "bay tree"]

Lau·ri·er /láwree ày/, **Sir Wilfrid** (1841–1919) Canadian lawyer, journalist, and politician. He served as prime minister of Canada (1896–1911). See table at **prime minister**

> "I am a subject of the British Crown, but whenever I have to choose between the interests of England and Canada it is manifest to me that the interests of my country are identical with those of the United States of America."
> [Sir Wilfrid Laurier, *Speech, Boston, Massachusetts*; November 17, 1891]

lau·ryl al·co·hol /làwrəl-/ *n* a crystalline solid that is insoluble in water. Use: manufacture of detergents. Formula: $C_{12}H_{27}O$. [Early 20C. < shortening of *lauric* (see LAURIC ACID)]

Lau·sanne /lō záan, -zán/ capital of Vaud Canton, western Switzerland, on Lake Geneva. Population: 114,161 (1998).

Laut·er·bur /lówtər bòor/, **Paul C.** (*b.* 1929) US chemist and biomedical scientist. He and Sir Peter Mansfield of the United Kingdom shared the 2003 Nobel Prize in physiology or medicine for their work in magnetic resonance imaging.

lav /lav/ *n UK* same as **lavatory** (sense 2) (*informal*) [Early 20C. Shortening]

la·va /laávə, lávvə/ *n* **1.** molten rock that originates in the Earth's mantle and flows from a volcano or a fissure on land or the ocean floor **2.** rock formed from solidified lava, typically full of small air holes caused by escaping volcanic gases [Mid-18C. < Italian (originally Neapolitan)]

la·va·bo /le váy bō, lə vaá bō/ (*plural* **-boes**) *n* **1. BASIN ATTACHED TO WALL** a basin with a water tank above attached to a wall, often used as a planter **2.** *also* **La·va·bo RELIGIOUS RITUAL** a priest's ritual washing of the hands and reciting from the Psalms during the Communion service in some Christian churches **3. PLACE FOR WASHING** a place for washing in a monastery [Mid-18C. < Latin, "I will wash," form of *lavare* "to wash"]

lav·age /lə vaázh, lávvij/ *n* the washing out of a hollow body organ such as the stomach using a flow of water [Late 18C. < French *laver* "to wash" < Latin *lavare*]

La·val /lə vál/ city in le-Jésus County, southern Québec, Canada, situated on le-Jésus just north of Montreal. Population: 343,005 (2001).

La·val, Francois-Xavier de Montmorency (1623–1708) French-born Canadian cleric. He was the first Roman Catholic bishop of Quebec (1674–88).

la·va-la·va *n* a rectangular piece of printed cotton worn wrapped around the waist by the people of Samoa and other parts of Polynesia [Late 19C. < Samoan]

lav·a·liere /làvvə leér, laàvə-/ *n* a pendant on a chain worn around the neck ■ *vt* (**-liered, -lier·ing, -lieres**) to give a lavaliere, especially one with the emblem of a fraternity, usually to a sweetheart as a symbol of attachment [Late 19C. After Louise de *la Valière*, lover of Louis XIV of France] —**lav·a·liered** *adj*

la·va sled·ding *n* in Hawaii, the traditional sport of riding a 50-lb., 12-ft.-long wooden sled made of hardwood, crafted like a narrow ladder, down volcanic slopes. Riders can reach speeds of 50 mph. (*regional*)

lav·a·te·ra /làvvə teérə, lə vaátərə/ (*plural* **-ras** or *same*) *n* a plant or bush that is a type of mallow. Native to: Europe, naturalized in California. Genus: *Lavatera*. [Mid-18C. < modern Latin, after the brothers *Lavater*, 17 and 18C Swiss doctors and naturalists]

lav·a·to·ry /lávvə tàwree/ (*plural* **-ries**) *n* **1.** a room or building with washing and toilet facilities **2.** a toilet, or a small room containing a toilet [14C. < late Latin *lavatorium* < Latin *lavare* "to wash"] —**lav·a·to·ri·al** /làvvə táwree əl/ *adj*

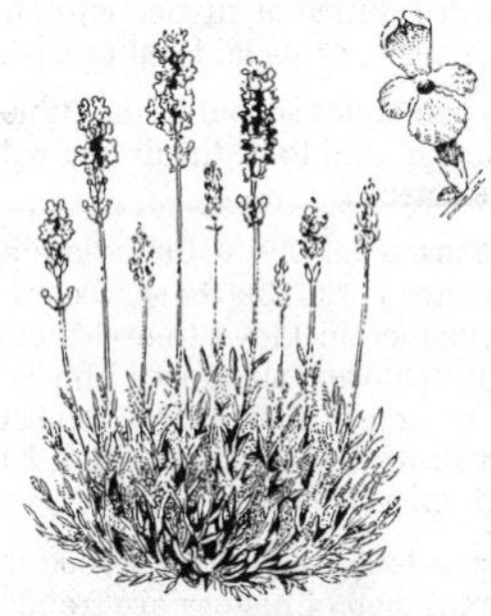
lavender

lav·en·der /lávvəndər/ *n* **1. FRAGRANT PLANT** a low-growing aromatic bush with very thin gray leaves. Flowers: fragrant, bluish-purple, in clusters. Native to: Mediterranean region. Latin name: *Lavendula officinalis*. **2. FLOWERS AND LEAVES** the dried flowers and leaves of the lavender plant. Use: essential oil, perfume for clothes, linen, toiletries. **3. PALE PURPLE COLOR** a pale bluish purple color [14C. Via Anglo-Norman *lavendre* < medieval Latin *lavendula*] —**lav·en·der** *adj*

lav·en·der wa·ter *n* perfume or toilet water made from the flowers of the lavender plant

la·ver[1] /láyvər/ *n* **1.** a large basin for ritual washing in the temple in Jerusalem and in modern synagogues **2.** a basin to wash in (*archaic*) [14C. Via Old French *laveor* < late Latin *lavatorium* (see LAVATORY)]

la·ver[2] /láyvər/ *n* a dried edible seaweed of the red algae family. Genus: *Porphyra*. [12C. < Latin]

La·ver /láyvər/, **Rod** (*b.* 1938) Australian tennis player. He is the only man to have won the tennis grand slam twice (1962 and 1969). Full name **Laver, Rodney George**

La Vé·ren·drye /la vè raaN dreé/, **Sieur Pierre Gaultier de Varennes de** (1685–1749) Canadian explorer and fur trader. He explored and established forts in western Canada and the United States from 1731.

lav·ish /lávvish/ *adj* **1. ABUNDANT** given or produced in abundance or to excess **2. GENEROUS** giving or spending generously or to excess ■ *vt* (**-ished, -ish·ing, -ish·es**) **BE EXTRAVAGANT WITH SOMETHING** to give or spend something generously or to excess ○ *lavished attention on the child* [15C. < Old French *lavasse* "torrential rain" < *laver* "pour" < Latin *lavare* "to wash"] —**lav·ish·er** *n* —**lav·ish·ly** *adv* —**lav·ish·ness** *n*

La·voi·sier /lə vwaá zyày, laa vwaa zyáy/, **Antoine Laurent** (1743–94) French chemist. He disproved the phlogiston theory of combustion and published the first proper table of the chemical elements. He was guillotined during the Reign of Terror.

law /law/ *n* **1. BINDING OR ENFORCEABLE RULE** a rule of conduct or procedure recognized by a community as binding or enforceable by authority **2. PIECE OF LEGISLATION** an act passed by a legislature or similar body **3. LEGAL SYSTEM** the body or system of rules recognized by a community that are enforceable by established process ○ *You are forbidden by law to enter the premises.* **4. CONTROL OR AUTHORITY** the control or authority resulting from the observance and enforcement of a community's system of rules ○ *Nobody is above the law.* **5. BRANCH OF KNOWLEDGE** the branch of knowledge or study concerned with the rules of a community and their enforcement ○ *went to school to study law* **6. AREA OF LAW** the body of law relating to a particular subject or area **7.** SOC SCI same as **common law 8. LAWYERS** the legal profession **9. LEGAL ACTION** legal action or proceedings **10. LAW ENFORCEMENT AGENT OR AGENCY** a person or organization responsible for enforcing the law, especially the police **11. GENERAL RULE OR PRINCIPLE** a general rule or principle that is thought to be true or held to be binding **12. STATEMENT OF SCIENTIFIC TRUTH** a statement of a scientific fact or phenomenon that is invariable under given conditions ○ *the laws of physics* **13. MATHEMATICAL PRINCIPLE** a general relationship that is assumed or proved to exist between mathematical expressions [Pre-12C. < Old Norse *lög* "laws" < *lag* "something set down" < Germanic, "put"] ◇ **be a law unto yourself** to refuse to obey the rules, conventions, or suggestions made or upheld by others ◇ **lay down the law** to express an opinion in an overbearing or dogmatic way ◇ **take the law into your own hands** to try to obtain revenge or justice without involving the police, courts, or usual legal procedures

Law *n* **1.** the principles set out in the Bible, especially the Pentateuch, said to be the divine will **2.** JUDAISM same as **Pentateuch**

Law /law/, **Bonar** (1858–1923) Canadian-born British prime minister (1922–23). He served as Chancellor of the Exchequer in Lloyd George's coalition government (1916–18) and succeeded him as prime minister. He resigned after seven months in office because of ill health. Full name **Law, Andrew Bonar**. See table at **prime minister**

> "If I am a great man, then a good many of the great men of history are frauds."
> [Attributed to Bonar Law]

law-a·bid·ing *adj* voluntarily and habitually obeying the law

law and or·der *n* **1.** the strict enforcement of the law (*hyphenated when used before a noun*) ○ *law-and-order issues* **2.** the stability created by the observance and enforcement of the law within a community

law·break·er /láw bràykər/ *n* somebody who breaks the law —**law·break·ing** *n, adj*

law clerk *n* somebody, often a student or novice lawyer, who works as an assistant to a judge or lawyer

law court *n* a court where legal cases are heard

law en·force·ment *n* an officer or agency responsible for enforcing the law ○ *Law enforcement is at the scene of the crime.*

law·ful /láwf'l/ *adj* permitted or recognized by law —**law·ful·ly** *adv* —**law·ful·ness** *n*

SYNONYMS See *legal.*

law·giv·er /láw gìvvər/ *n* **1.** a giver of a code of laws to a people **2.** LAW same as **lawmaker** —**law·giv·ing** *n*

law·less /láwləss/ *adj* **1. UNREGULATED** uncontrolled or unregulated ○ *a disorderly and lawless gathering* **2. AGAINST LAW** contrary to the law ○ *lawless conduct* **3. WITHOUT LAW** having no laws ○ *a lawless society* —**law·less·ly** *adv* —**law·less·ness** *n*

law·mak·er /láw màykər/ *n* a drafter and enactor of laws —**law·mak·ing** *n, adj*

law·man /láw màn, -mən/ (*plural* **-men** /-mèn, -mən/) *n* an officer, especially a man, responsible for enforcing the law, e.g., a sheriff

law mer·chant *n* the principles and rules governing commercial transactions, which originated in English common law and are codified in US law

lawn[1] /lawn/ *n* an area of closely mowed grass, sometimes part of a yard [Mid-16C. Alteration of obsolete *laund* "woodland clearing, pasture" < Old French *launde* "wooded district, heath" < Celtic]

lawn[2] /lawn/ *n* a fine light cotton or cotton-and-polyester fabric. Use: clothing, household linen. [15C. After *Laon*, town in France] —**lawn·y** *adj*

lawn bowl·ing *n* a game played on a lawn in which the players roll balls toward a smaller target ball, trying to come as close as possible

Lawn·dale /láwn dàyl/ city in Los Angeles County, southwestern California, situated east of Manhattan Beach. Population: 32,388 (2002 estimate).

lawn mow·er *n* a machine, often power-operated, that cuts grass with rotating blades

lawn par·ty *n* LEISURE same as **garden party**

lawn ten·nis *n* a game for two or four players played on a hard or grass court of standard dimensions in which the players hit balls with rackets across a central net

law of av·er·ag·es *n* **1.** the principle that over the long term laws of probability will influence all events that are subject to them **2.** the unscientific but reasonable assumption that things are bound to change some time

law of di·min·ish·ing re·turns *n* the principle that a continual increase in effort or investment does not lead to a continual increase in output or results

law of ef·fect *n* the theory that behavior that is rewarded is more likely to be repeated than behavior that is not rewarded. This theory was put forward by the US psychologist Edward Lee Thorndike.

Law of In·de·pend·ent As·sort·ment *n* one of Mendel's laws stating that during meiosis, the alleles of a gene segregate independently of the alleles of other genes, so that the inheritance of an allele of one gene does not influence the inheritance of an allele of another gene. In practice, genes that are close together on a chromosome may be inherited together.

law of large num·bers *n* the principle that a large sample is more likely than a smaller sample to have the characteristics of the whole

Law of Mos·es *n* RELIG same as **Mosaic Law**

law of na·tions *n* LAW same as **international law**

law of na·ture *n* a broadly applicable principle relating to natural phenomena

law of par·si·mo·ny *n* SCI same as **Ockham's razor**

Law of Seg·re·ga·tion *n* one of Mendel's Laws stating that during meiosis, the alleles of a gene pair segregate, each going to a separate gamete

law of sup·ply and de·mand *n* the economic principle that the price charged for a product is determined by the level of demand and the quantity available

law of the jun·gle *n* aggressive or competitive behavior based on the principle that self-interest and survival are of prime importance

law of the sea *n* the international rules that govern the use of the oceans, derived from custom, treaties, and judicial decisions

law of war *n* a rule or body of rules that governs the rights and duties of those engaged in international war

law·per·son /láw pùrss'n/ (*plural* **-peo·ple** /-pèep'l/ or **-per·sons**) *n* an officer responsible for enforcing the law, e.g., a sheriff

Law·rence /láwrənss/ **1.** city in eastern Kansas, on the Kansas River, west of Kansas City and east of Topeka. It is home to the University of Kansas. Population: 81,604 (2002 estimate). **2.** city in northeastern Massachusetts, on the north bank of the Merrimack River, southwest of Haverhill and northeast of Lowell. Population: 72,451 (2002 estimate).

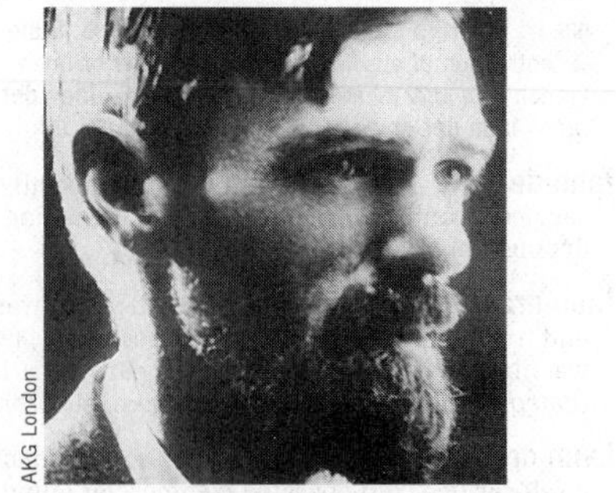

AKG London

D. H. Lawrence

Law·rence, D. H. (1885–1930) British writer. His novels include *Sons and Lovers* (1913), *Women in Love* (1921), and *Lady Chatterley's Lover* (1928). Full name **Lawrence, David Herbert**

> "Some things can't be ravished. You can't ravish a tin of sardines."
> [D. H. Lawrence, *Lady Chatterley's Lover*; 1928]

> "Why doesn't the past decently bury itself, instead of sitting and waiting to be admitted by the present?"
> [D. H. Lawrence, *St. Mawr*; 1925]

Law·rence, Gertrude (1898–1952) British actor. She starred in comedies and musical revues in London and New York, including *Private Lives* (1931) and several other plays by her friend, Sir Noel Coward, as well as in the musical *The King and I* (1951). Born **Klasen, Gertrud Alexandra Dagmar Lawrence**

Law·rence, Jacob Armstead (1917–2000) US artist. His paintings such as *The Migration of the Negro* (1940–41) explore the African American experience in US history.

Law·rence, T. E. (1888–1935) British soldier and author. Stationed in Cairo at the start of World War I, he joined and later led the Arab revolt against the Turks (1916–18). His work *The Seven Pillars of Wisdom* (1926) is based on his travels in North Africa and Southwest Asia. Full name **Lawrence, Thomas Edward**. Known as **Lawrence of Arabia**

> "All men dream: but not equally. Those who dream by night...wake in the day to find that it was vanity: but the dreamers of the day are dangerous men, for they may act their dream with open eyes, to make it possible."
> [T. E. Lawrence, *Seven Pillars of Wisdom*; 1926]

law·ren·ci·um /law rénssee əm/ *n* a short-lived radioactive metallic element. Source: produced artificially from californium and other elements. Symbol **Lr**. See table at **element** [Mid-20C. After Ernest O. *Lawrence* (1901–58), US physicist]

law·suit /láw soot/ *n* a legal action brought between two private parties in a court of law

law·wom·an /láw wòommən/ (*plural* **-wom·en** /-wimmin/) *n* a woman officer responsible for enforcing the law, e.g., a sheriff

law·yer /láwyər/ *n* a qualified professional adviser on legal matters who can represent clients in court —**law·yer·like** *adj* —**law·yer·ly** *adj*

lawyer up *vi US* to ask to be represented by a lawyer, especially when being questioned by the police (*slang*)

law·yered /láwyərd/ *adj US* having or being represented by a lawyer (*informal*)

law·yer·ing /láwyəring/ *n US* the work done by a lawyer, or the law profession

lax /laks/ *adj* **1. NOT STRICT** not strict or careful enough **2. NOT TENSE** not tight or tense **3.** PHYSIOL **WITH TENDENCY TO DIARRHEA** describes a bowel that is not easily controlled and produces loose feces **4.** PHON **PRONOUNCED WITH RELAXED MUSCLES** pronounced with the muscles of the jaw relaxed rather than tense, as is the "a" in "hat" [14C. < Latin *laxus* "loose"] —**lax·ly** *adv* —**lax·ness** *n*

lax·a·tion /lak sáysh'n/ *n* the action of making something loose, or the process of becoming loose

lax·a·tive /láksətiv/ *n* a drug or other substance that promotes bowel movements, either by irritating the lower colon or by bulking the stool [14C. < Old French *laxatif* < medieval Latin *laxativus* "loosening" < Latin *laxare* "loosen" < *laxus* "loose"] —**lax·a·tive** *adj*

lax·i·ty /láksətee/ *n* the condition or fact of being not strict or careful enough

lay[1] /lay/ *v* (**laid** /layd/, **lay·ing**, **lays**) **1.** *vt* **SET SOMETHING DOWN** to put something down, often carefully, in a horizontal position ○ *I laid the files on my desk.* **2.** *vt* **PUT IN RESTING POSITION** to place somebody or something in a position of rest ○ *It was time to lay the baby down for a nap.* **3.** *vt* **BURY SOMEBODY** to bury somebody or something in the ground ○ *They laid him in the family plot.* **4.** *vt* **PLACE SOMETHING ON SURFACE** to arrange, place, or spread something on, over, or along a surface ○ *They are laying the carpet tomorrow.* **5.** *vt* **PRESS SOMETHING DOWN FLAT** to smooth something down or make something lie flat ○ *The cat laid back its ears.* **6.** *vt* **ARRANGE THINGS ON TABLE** to prepare a table for a meal by setting out the required items ○ *lay the table for lunch* **7.** *vt* **ARRANGE FUEL FOR FIRE** to prepare a fire by arranging fuel, usually in a grate **8.** *vt* **IMPOSE SOMETHING** to impose something as a burden, duty, or penalty ○ *lay a tariff on imported products* **9.** *vt* **ATTRIBUTE SOMETHING** to impute or attribute something ○ *He laid the blame on me.* **10.** *vt* **BRING SOMETHING TO BEAR** to use something to bring about a desired outcome ○ *laid emphasis on the fact that we must study to excel* **11.** *vti* **BET** to place a bet with somebody on something **12.** *vt* **DEVISE SOMETHING** to devise, organize, or prepare something ○ *lay a trap* **13.** *vt* **MAKE PREPARATIONS** to prepare something as a basis **14.** *vti* **PRODUCE EGGS** to produce or deposit eggs ○ *All the hens are laying.* **15.** *vi* **PUT EFFORT INTO SOMETHING** to apply effort vigorously to a task ○ *The rowing team laid to their oars.* **16.** *vi* **BE IN OR GO TO POSITION** to put a boat in a particular position, or move in a particular direction **17.** *vi* **LIE DOWN** to be in or adopt a lying position (*nonstandard*) ○ *Lay down on the sofa and have a rest.* **18.** *vt* **OFFENSIVE TERM** an offensive term meaning to have sexual intercourse with somebody (*slang*) **19.** *vt* **ARRANGE STRANDS OF ROPE** to twist strands together to make a rope or cable **20.** *vt* **PUT CANNON IN POSITION** to establish the direction and elevation of a cannon or a battery of cannon **21.** *vt* **TREAT HEDGE TO KEEP IT THICK** to make partial cuts through some of the branches of a hedge, bending them over horizontally and pegging them to the ground to keep the hedge thick and dense ○ *hedge laying* ■ *n* **1. WAY SOMETHING LIES** the way or position in which something lies ○ *wanted to inspect the lay of the property* **2. OFFENSIVE TERM** an offensive term for a partner in sexual intercourse (*slang*) **3. OFFENSIVE TERM** an offensive term for sexual intercourse (*slang*) **4. TWIST OF ROPE OR CABLE STRANDS** the arrangement of strands in a rope or cable, determined by the number, length, angle, and direction of twist **5.** *US* **TERMS OF EMPLOYMENT** terms of employment or purchase **6. SHARE OF PROCEEDS** a share in the proceeds of a whaling expedition [Old English *lecgan* < Germanic, "put"] ◇ **be laid low** to become ill or incapacitated ◇ **lay it on (thick)** to exaggerate greatly, especially in order to flatter somebody ◇ **lay yourself open to something** to put yourself in a position that will make you liable to be blamed, criticized, or attacked

USAGE lay or **lie**? The verb ***lay*** is mainly transitive: it needs an object, as in *Lay the blanket across the bed.* ***Lay*** is sometimes used without an object in place of the intransitive verb ***lie***, but this is unacceptable in standard English: *Lie* [not *Lay*] *down on the bed. The letter was lying* [not *laying*] *on the table.* Confusion may arise because ***lay*** is the past tense of the verb ***lie***: *I lay down on the bed.* The past tense of the verb ***lay*** is *laid*: *I laid* [not *lay*] *the blanket across the bed.*

lay aside *vt* **1.** to give up on or abandon something ○ *"Be not the first by whom the new are tried, nor the last to lay the old aside."* (Alexander Pope, *An Essay on Criticism*; 1711) **2.** to put something away for the future

lay away *vt* **1.** to put something away for the future **2.** to set merchandise aside for future delivery

lay before *vt* to present something for consideration by somebody

lay by *vt* to set something aside for the future

lay down *v* **1.** *vt* **SURRENDER SOMETHING** to put down, surrender, or sacrifice something **2.** *vt* **DECIDE ON RULE** to formulate a rule or principle **3.** *vt* **STORE SOMETHING FOR FUTURE** to acquire and store something for future use **4.** *vt* **PLACE BET** to place money as a bet **5.** *vt* **DELIVER MILITARY FIRE** to deliver a concentration of military fire **6.** *vi* **LIE DOWN** to lie down in a horizontal position (*nonstandard*)

lay in *vt* to acquire and store something for future use

lay into *vt* **1.** to attack somebody forcefully with blows **2.** to attack somebody forcefully with words (*informal*)

lay off *v* **1.** *vt* **TERMINATE EMPLOYMENT OF SOMEBODY** to stop employing somebody when there is insufficient work to be done **2.** *vti* **STOP DOING SOMETHING** to stop doing or using something (*informal*) **3.** *vti* **STOP IRRITATING SOMEBODY** to stop bothering somebody (*informal*) **4.** *vt* **MEASURE OR MARK SOMETHING OFF** to measure off a distance or mark out the boundaries of something **5.** *vt* **REDUCE RISK ON BET** to reduce risk as a bookmaker by placing all or part of a bet with another bookmaker

lay on *vt* **1. APPLY SOMETHING** to apply something by spreading it **2. USE SOMETHING TO EXCESS** to apply, administer, or use something in an exaggerated manner **3. PROVIDE SOMETHING SPECIAL** to provide or arrange something, often in an elaborate or extravagant manner

lay out *vt* **1. SPREAD SOMETHING OUT FOR DISPLAY** to arrange things or spread things out for display **2. PLAN OR DESIGN SOMETHING** to plan or design something in detail **3. PREPARE SOMEBODY FOR BURIAL** to prepare a body for burial **4. MAKE SOMEBODY UNCONSCIOUS** to knock somebody unconscious (*informal*) **5. SPEND MONEY** to spend money, especially in large quantities

lay over *vi* to make a brief stop during a journey

lay to *vi* to make a ship or boat stop, e.g., by turning a sailing vessel into the wind

lay up *vt* **1. STORE SOMETHING FOR FUTURE** to store something for future use **2. CONFINE SOMEBODY WITH INJURY OR ILLNESS** to prevent somebody from leading a normal active life, usually temporarily because of injury or illness (*usually passive*) ○ *He was laid up with a bad back.* **3. STOP USING SHIP OR BOAT** to take a ship or boat out of service, usually temporarily, e.g., by moving it to a dry dock for maintenance or repairs

lay[2] /lay/ *adj* **1.** belonging to or involving the people of a church who are not members of the clergy **2.** without expertise or professional training in a specific field [14C. < Old French *lai* < late Latin *laicus* (see LAIC)]

lay[3] /lay/ *n* **1.** a short narrative poem that is sung **2.** a medieval lyric or narrative song [13C. < Old French *lai*]

lay[4] /lay/ past tense of **lie**[1]

lay·a·bout /láy ə bòwt/ *n* somebody regarded as lazy and given to loafing around and doing no work (*informal insult*)

lay at·tend·ant *n* in Buddhist monasteries, somebody who is responsible for taking care of tasks that the monks are forbidden to undertake

lay·a·way /láy ə wày/ *n* a method of purchasing something in which the purchaser pays a deposit and the seller keeps the goods until full payment is made

lay·back /láy bàk/ *n* a way of climbing a vertical crack in a rock by leaning back and pulling on one side of the crack and pushing against the other side with the feet

lay broth·er *n* in a Christian religious order, a man who has taken vows, but does not take part in the full liturgical program and serves as an ancillary or manual worker

lay-by (*plural* **lay-bys**) *n UK* a short strip of ground alongside a main road where vehicles can stop for a short time

lay days *npl* the time allowed in port for a ship to load or unload its cargo without extra payment

lay-down *n US* an easy target or victim (*slang*)

lay·er /láy ər/ *n* **1. FLAT COVERING OVER OR BETWEEN OTHERS** a single thickness of something that lies over or under something or between other similar thicknesses **2. SOMEBODY WHO LAYS SOMETHING** somebody whose work is laying something such as tile or brick (*usually used in combination*) ○ *a bricklayer* **3. LAYING HEN** a hen that lays eggs **4.** GARDENING **ROOTED PLANT SHOOT** a branch or shoot that has been bent over and covered with soil to make it take root and grow into a new plant ■ *v* (**-ered, -er·ing, -ers**) **1.** *vti* **MAKE LAYERS OF SOMETHING** to apply or arrange things as separate thicknesses, or form into separate thicknesses **2.** *vt* **CUT HAIR IN DIFFERENT LENGTHS** to cut somebody's hair in overlapping sections of different lengths, usually in order to give shape to a hairstyle **3.** *vti* GARDENING **PROPAGATE PLANT BY ROOTING SHOOTS** to bend a branch or shoot over and cover it with soil to make it take root as a new plant, or take root as a result of this procedure

lay·er cake *n* a cake, usually frosted, that consists of two or more layers sandwiched together with frosting, cream, jam, or other filling. The layers may be baked separately or cut horizontally.

lay·er·ing /láy əring/ *n* a method of propagating plants by covering a branch or shoot with soil so that it takes root while still attached to the parent plant

lay·ette /lay ét/ *n* a complete set of clothing and accessories for a newborn baby [Mid-19C. < French, literally "small drawer" < Old French *laie* "drawer, box" < Middle Dutch *laege* < Germanic, "load"]

lay fig·ure *n* **1.** a jointed model of the human body used by artists **2.** a submissive or insignificant person

lay·ing on of hands /làying-/ *n* a blessing involving placing the hands on somebody, especially on somebody's head, in a religious ceremony such as ordination or in faith healing

lay·man /láymən/ (*plural* **-men** /-mən/) *n* **1.** somebody, especially a man, who is not trained or expert in a specific area ○ *a law book for the layman* **2.** somebody, especially a man, who does not belong to the clergy

lay·off /láy àwf, -òf/ *n* **1.** a dismissal of employees because of lack of work to be done **2.** the time during which employees are out of work

lay of the land *n* the general appearance or state of an area or situation presenting itself to somebody (*informal*)

lay·out /láy òwt/ *n* **1. WAY THINGS ARE ARRANGED** the way component parts or individual items are arranged **2. DESIGN SHOWING POSITIONS** a design or plan showing the way things are arranged **3. DESIGN OF PRINTED MATTER** the design or arrangement of printed material such as an advertisement or the pages of a book **4. PAGE SHOWING DESIGN** a page or pages showing the design for printed material **5. DESIGNING OF PRINTED MATERIAL** the art of designing printed material **6. ESTABLISHMENT** a residence, business establishment, or other property, especially one that is large or elaborate ○ *a new high-tech manufacturing layout* **7. SET OF TOOLS** a set or kit of tools (*dated*) **8.** GYMNASTICS **GYMNASTIC POSITION** a position in the air in which the performer's body is straight with the arms extended

lay·o·ver /láy ồvər/ *n* a brief stop during a journey

lay·per·son /láy pùrss'n/ (*plural* **-peo·ple** /-peep'l/) *n* **1.** somebody who is not trained or expert in a specific area **2.** somebody who does not belong to the clergy

lay read·er *n* a lay member of a church, especially an Anglican church or the Roman Catholic Church, who is authorized to read some parts of the service

Lay·ton /láyt'n/, **Irving** (*b.* 1912) Romanian-born Canadian poet. Born **Israel Lazarovitch**

lay-up *n* in basketball, a shot made close to the basket, usually made one-handed and by bouncing the ball off the backboard

lay·wom·an /láy wòommən/ (*plural* **-wom·en** /-wìmmin/) *n* **1.** a woman who is not trained in a specific profession **2.** a woman who does not belong to the clergy

la·zar /lázzər, láyzər/ *n* a poor and sick person, especially somebody affected by leprosy (*archaic*) [13C. < medieval Latin *lazarus*, after *Lazarus*, a beggar in the Bible (Luke 16:20)]

laz·a·ret·to /làzzə réttō/ (*plural* **-tos**), **laz·a·ret** /-rét/, **laz·a·rette** *n* **1. QUARANTINE FACILITY** a building or ship used to hold people during a period of quarantine **2. SHIP'S STORAGE SPACE** a storage space below deck near the stern of a ship **3. HOSPITAL FOR CONTAGIOUS DISEASES** a hospital for the treatment of contagious diseases such as leprosy, especially in former times [Mid-16C. < Italian *lazzaretto*, blend of *lazzaro* "leper" (< medieval Latin *lazarus*; see LAZAR) + *Nazareto*, hospital in Venice, after Santa Maria di *Nazaret* "St. Mary of Nazareth"]

Laz·a·rus /lázzərəss/ *n* in the Bible, a friend of Jesus Christ and the brother of Mary and Martha who died but was brought to life again by Jesus

Laz·a·rus /lázzərəss/, **Emma** (1849–87) US writer. She wrote the poem "The New Colossus" (1883) as an ode to the Statue of Liberty.

> "Give me your tired, your poor, / Your huddled masses yearning to breathe free..."
> [Emma Lazarus, "The New Colossus"; 1883]

laze /layz/ (**lazed, laz·ing, laz·es**) *v* **1.** *vi* to relax and do no work ○ *I just lazed in the shade with a book.* **2.** *vt* to pass time idly ○ *laze the day away* [Late 16C. Back-formation < LAZY]

laze around *vti* to relax, doing nothing that requires effort

laz·u·lite /lázzyə lìt, lá<u>zh</u>ə-/ *n* a blue glassy rare phosphate mineral containing aluminum, iron, and magnesium. Use: gems. [Early 19C. < LAPIS LAZULI]

laz·u·rite /lázzyə rìt, lá<u>zh</u>ə-/ *n* a deep violet blue or greenish blue rare aluminosilicate mineral that contains sodium and is the main constituent of lapis lazuli [Late 19C. < medieval Latin *lazur* < Arabic *lāžward* "lapis lazuli"]

la·zy /láyzee/ (**-zi·er, -zi·est**) *adj* **1. NOT WANTING TO WORK** unwilling to do any work or make an effort **2. CONDUCIVE TO IDLENESS** contributing to an unwillingness to work or make an effort ○ *a lazy spring day* **3. SLOW** moving slowly ○ *a lazy river* **4. SLOPING** shown as a brand on livestock as a letter or number rotated 90 degrees from an upright position ○ *a lazy H* [Mid-16C. Origin ?] —**la·zi·ly** *adv* —**la·zi·ness** *n*

la·zy·bones /láyzee bōnz/ (*plural same*) *n* somebody who is regarded as lazy or without ambition (*informal*)

la·zy dai·sy stitch *n* in embroidery, a single unattached chain stitch, often worked in a circle to resemble the petals of a flower

la·zy eye *n* **1.** an eye disorder in which vision is impaired for no apparent reason, or an eye affected by this disorder (*not in technical use*) Technical name **amblyopia 2.** a disorder in which the eyes appear to be looking in different directions, or an eye affected by this disorder

la·zy Su·san /-sóoz'n/ *n* a revolving tray holding a selection of items such as cheeses or sauces, usually placed in the middle of a dining table

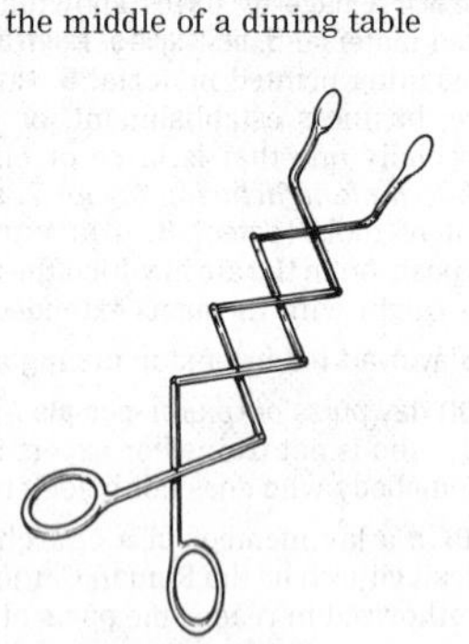

lazy tongs

la·zy tongs *npl* tongs that can be used to grasp objects at a distance, usually by bringing together the handles to extend the jointed arms

lb *abbr* ONLINE Lebanon (*used in Internet addresses*) See table at **domain name**

LB *abbr* FOOTBALL linebacker

lb. *abbr* MEASURE pound or pounds (*of weight*)

L-band *n* the range of frequencies of electromagnetic waves from 390 megahertz to 1550 megahertz, used for radar. Other bands in the microwave spectrum used for radar are designated S, X, and K.

LBD *abbr* CLOTHING little black dress

LBJ *abbr* Lyndon Baines Johnson

LBO *abbr* BUSINESS leveraged buyout

lbs. *abbr* MEASURE pounds

lc *abbr* **1.** PRINTING lowercase **2.** St. Lucia. (*used in Internet addresses*) See table at **domain name**

LC *abbr* **1.** MIL Lance Corporal **2.** NAVY landing craft **3.** *also* **L.C.** LIBRARIES Library of Congress

l.c. *abbr* **1.** loco citato **2.** PRINTING lowercase

l/c, L/C *abbr* letter of credit

LCD *abbr* COMPUT liquid-crystal display

l.c.d. *abbr* MATH least common denominator

l'chaim /lə <u>kh</u>ī́ im/, **le·ha·yim, le·cha·yim** *interj* a word used to express good wishes just before drinking an alcoholic drink ■ *n* a small drink of alcohol used to toast somebody or something [Mid 20C. < Hebrew *lĕḥayyīm* "to life"]

LCL *abbr* COMM, TRANSP **1.** less-than-carload lot **2.** less-than-container load

lcm *abbr* MATH least common multiple

LCM *abbr* NAVY landing craft, mechanized

LCSW *abbr* SOC WELFARE Licensed Clinical Social Worker

LCT *abbr Can* FIN large corporations tax

LD *abbr* **1.** EDUC learning disability **2.** EDUC learning-disabled **3.** PHARM lethal dose

ld. *abbr* **1.** PRINTING lead **2.** load

Ld. *abbr* **1.** COMM Limited (company) **2.** Lord

LD50 /èl dee fíftee/ *n* a toxicological test in which the dose that kills 50 percent of a group of test animals is calculated. This test has been criticized by animal protection organizations and by many scientists, but it is still used.

LDC *abbr* ECON less-developed country

LDL *abbr* BIOCHEM low-density lipoprotein

L-do·pa *n* a natural substance that stimulates the production of dopamine in the brain. Use: treatment of Parkinson's disease. [Mid-20C. < abbreviation of LEVO-ROTATORY + acronym < DI-[1] + OXY- + PHENYL + ALANINE]

LDR *abbr* ONLINE long-distance relationship

LDS[1] *abbr* Latter-Day Saints

LDS[2] *abbr* CHR praise be to God forever [Latin *laus Deo semper*]

lea /lee, lay/ *n* **1.** a grassy field or meadow (*literary*) **2.** a field sown with grass [Old English *lēah* "meadow, clearing" < Indo-European]

lea. *abbr* **1.** MEASURE league **2.** leather

leach[1] /leech/ *v* (**leached, leach·ing, leach·es**) **1.** *vti* **DRAIN AWAY** to drain away from soil when dissolved in rainwater, or lose a mineral or chemical dissolved in rainwater ○ *herbicides that leached into the ground water* **2.** *vt* **REMOVE SOMETHING BY DISSOLUTION** to remove soluble components from a solid mixture by the use of a solvent **3.** *vi* **LOSE SOLUBLE MATERIAL** to lose soluble material by dissolution ■ *n* **1. CONTAINER USED IN LEACHING** a porous container used to hold a solid mixture through which a solvent is run in order to remove soluble components **2. MIXTURE USED IN LEACHING** a solid mixture through which a solvent is run in order to remove soluble components **3. LIQUID CONTAINING LEACHED SUBSTANCE** a solution containing a substance leached from a solid mixture [Old English *leccan* < Germanic] —**leach·a·bil·i·ty** /leèchə bíllətee/ *n* —**leach·er** *n*

leach[2] *n* NAUT another spelling of **leech**[2]

Leach /leech/, **Bernard** (1887–1979) British potter. He revived the art of handmade pottery in Britain, setting up the Leach pottery in St. Ives, Cornwall (1920). Full name **Leach, Bernard Howell**

> "There can be no fullness or complete realization of utility without beauty, refinement and charm, for the simple reason that their absence must...be intolerable to both maker and consumer."
> [Bernard Leach, *The Potter's Book*; 1940]

leach·ate /leè chàyt/ *n* **1.** a liquid containing soluble material removed from a solid mixture through which the liquid has passed **2.** the liquid produced in a landfill from the decomposition of waste within the landfill

Lea·cock /leè kòk/, **Stephen** (1869–1944) British-born Canadian writer. He is best known for his satirical short stories and essays, collected in volumes including *Literary Lapses* (1910). Full name **Leacock, Stephen Butler**

> "Advertising may be described as the science of arresting human intelligence long enough to get money from it."
> [Stephen Leacock, "The Perfect Salesman," *The Garden of Folly*; 1924]

lead[1] /leed/ *v* (**led** /led/, **lead·ing, leads**) **1.** *vti* **GUIDE SOMEBODY** to show the way to others, usually by going ahead of them ○ *He led us down the mountain.* **2.** *vti* **BE THE WAY SOMEWHERE** to be the route or direction that goes to a particular place or in a particular direction ○ *That street leads to the school.* **3.** *vt* **BRING SOMEBODY OR SOMETHING** to bring a person or animal along with physical guidance, e.g., by holding the person's hand or pulling a horse's reins **4.** *vt* **COMMAND OTHERS** to control, direct, or command others ○ *He led an infantry division during the Korean War.* **5.** *vt* **BE IN CHARGE OF SOMETHING** to have a principal part or guiding role in something **6.** *vt* **BE BETTER THAN OTHERS** to be more successful than and an example to others ○ *a city that leads the nation in the fight against crime* **7.** *vti* **BE AHEAD OF OTHERS** to be ahead in a race or competition ○ *is leading in the election* **8.** *vt* **INFLUENCE SOMEBODY TO DO SOMETHING** to cause somebody to think or act in a particular way ○ *I was led to believe the house had been sold.* **9.** *vi* **RESULT IN SOMETHING** to bring about a particular outcome ○ *Her hard work ultimately led to stardom.* **10.** *vt* **LIVE LIFE** to go through life or spend time in a particular way ○ *We all lead very busy lives.* **11.** *vt* **BE AT START OF SOMETHING** to be at the beginning or front of something ○ *Your name leads the waiting list.* **12.** *vt* **BE PRINCIPAL MUSICIAN IN ORCHESTRA** to be the principal performer of an orchestra or of a section of an orchestra **13.** *vti* DANCE **GUIDE DANCE PARTNER** to guide a partner in a ballroom dance **14.** *vt* **ASK WITNESS LEADING QUESTION** to suggest to a witness an answer to a question by phrasing the question in a way that will elicit the desired response **15.** *vt* **CHANNEL OR CONVEY SOMETHING** to guide something through a passage such as a conduit or channel **16.** *vti* **PUT DOWN FIRST CARD** to play the first card in a trick in a card game, often requiring others to play a card of the same suit if they can ○ *lead trumps* **17.** *vi* **AIM FIRST BLOW** to direct the first of a series of punches **18.** *vi* **LEAVE BASE EARLY** in baseball, to leave a base as a runner before a pitch **19.** *vt* **AIM AHEAD OF SOMETHING** to aim something such as a missile or ball at a point in front of a moving target to allow for the time of flight ■ *n* **1. FRONT POSITION OR PRINCIPAL ROLE** the front position, first place, or principal role ○ *The President took the lead in condemning the attacks.* **2. FORWARD POSITION** a position ahead of all competitors ○ *Which party has the lead in the opinion polls?* **3. FRONT RUNNER** somebody or something ahead of all competitors **4. DISTANCE BETWEEN FIRST AND SECOND** the margin by which somebody or something is ahead of all competitors ○ *She had a narrow lead as the runners entered the last lap.* **5. STARRING ROLE** a principal role in a play, motion picture, or show ○ *He will play the male lead in the movie version.* **6. SOMEBODY WITH STARRING ROLE** somebody who has a principal role in a play, motion picture, or show **7. ROLE OF TAKING INITIATIVE** the role of somebody who directs or guides others ○ *take the lead in a discussion* **8. PRECEDENT** an example or precedent ○ *follow his lead* **9. TIP OR CLUE** a piece of helpful or useful information ○ *The police are following up a number of leads.* **10.** MEDIA **INTRODUCTION TO NEWS ITEM** an introduction to a news story **11.** MEDIA **HEADLINE ITEM** the most important story in a newspaper or news broadcast ○ *The conflict should make the lead in all tomorrow's papers.* **12.** CARDS **FIRST CARD PLAYED** the first card played in a trick in a game **13.** CARDS **RIGHT TO PUT DOWN FIRST CARD** the right to play a card first in a trick in a game **14.** *UK* **DOG'S LEASH** a leash for an animal, especially a dog. Same as **leash** *n* (sense 1). Can term **leash 15.** *UK* ELEC **WIRE CONDUCTING ELECTRICITY** an insulated electrical conductor used to connect two points in a circuit, e.g., a cable connecting an appliance to a source of electricity **16.** GEOL **WATER CHANNEL THROUGH ICE** a water channel through an ice field **17.** NAUT **DIRECTION OF ROPE** the direction in which a rope runs **18.** BASEBALL **POSITION OF BASE RUNNER** a position taken by a runner off one base of a baseball diamond toward another **19.** BOXING **PUNCH** an attacking punch **20.** MIL **DISTANCE AHEAD OF MOVING TARGET** the distance a missile, ball, or other projectile is aimed in front of a moving target to allow for the time of flight **21.** GEOL same as **lode** (sense 1) [Old English *lǣdan* < Germanic]

USAGE lead or **led**? ***Led***, the past tense and past participle of the verb ***lead***, "to guide, command, be in charge," etc., is the correct choice in sentences like this: *The captain led* [not *lead*] *the troops into battle.* There is also a noun spelled ***lead***, pronounced like ***led***, that means "a heavy metallic element": *found a high degree of lead* [not *led*] *in the paint.*

SYNONYMS See *guide*.

lead off *v* **1.** *vi* to begin doing something **2.** *vt* to be the first batter in a baseball or softball lineup or inning

lead on *vt* **1.** to lure somebody with an offer or promise that is later withdrawn **2.** to persuade somebody to do something foolish or wrong ○ *She doesn't let the older kids lead her on.*

lead up to *vt* **1.** to prepare the way for something **2.** to approach a subject gradually or indirectly

lead[2] /led/ *n* **1.** CHEMICAL ELEMENT a heavy bluish gray metallic element that bends easily. Source: galena, cerussite. Use: car batteries, pipes, solder, radiation shields. Symbol **Pb**. See table at **element 2.** GRAPHITE IN PENCIL a long thin stick of graphite used in a pencil for writing or drawing **3.** DEVICE FOR MEASURING DEPTH a weight on the end of a line used to measure the depth of water **4.** WEIGHT FOR FISHING LINE a lead weight used on a fishing line **5.** AMMUNITION FOR GUNS bullets or shot for firearms (*informal*) **6.** STRIP BETWEEN LINES OF TYPE in traditional hot-metal printing, a thin strip of metal between lines of type that creates the space between lines on the printed page ■ **leads** *npl* LEAD STRIPS BETWEEN GLASS PANES strips of lead used to hold the small glass panes in place in a decorative window or art object ■ *vt* (**lead·ed, lead·ing, leads**) **1.** PUT LEAD OVER SOMETHING to cover, fill, or weight something with lead **2.** INSERT STRIP BETWEEN LINES OF TYPE to put a thin strip of metal between lines of type to create a space on the printed page **3.** SECURE GLASS USING LEADS to hold small panes of glass together with strips of lead [Old English *lēad* < W Germanic] —**lead·less** *adj* —**lead·y** *adj*

lead ac·e·tate /lèd-/ *n* a poisonous crystalline compound. Use: manufacture of paints, varnishes, mordant in dyeing, printing cottons. Formula: $Pb(C_2H_3O_2)_2 \cdot 3H_2O$.

lead ar·se·nate /lèd-/ *n* a poisonous crystalline compound. Use: insecticide. Formula: $Pb_3(AsO_4)_2$.

lead az·ide /lèd-/ *n* a colorless crystalline compound. Use: detonator in explosives. Formula: $Pb(N_3)_2$.

lead bal·loon /lèd-/ *n* a total failure ○ *went over like a lead balloon*

Lead·bel·ly /léd bèllee/ (1888–1949) US singer and guitarist. His work influenced folk, jazz, and popular music. Born **Ledbetter, Huddie William**

lead car·bon·ate /lèd-/ *n* a poisonous white solid. Use: pigment in paints. Formula: $PbCO_3$.

lead chro·mate /lèd-/ *n* a poisonous yellow crystalline substance. Use: pigment. Formula: $PbCrO_4$.

lead crys·tal /lèd-/ *n* glass containing a high proportion of lead, used to make decorative items, especially tableware

lead di·ox·ide /lèd-/ *n* a poisonous brown crystalline compound. Use: batteries, explosives, textile dyeing. Formula: PbO_2.

lead·ed /léddəd/ *adj* **1.** containing or treated with lead or a compound of lead **2.** containing many small panes of glass held together with strips of lead

lead·en /lédd'n/ *adj* **1.** DULL AND GRAY of a dull gray color, like lead ○ *leaden skies* **2.** TIRED AND HEAVY tired, heavy, and hard to move ○ *My legs felt stiff and leaden from miles of walking.* **3.** SLOW sluggish or labored ○ *a leaden pace* **4.** LIFELESS lacking spirit or vitality ○ *leaden prose* **5.** OF LEAD made of lead —**lead·en·ly** *adv* —**lead·en·ness** *n*

lead·er /leédər/ *n* **1.** SOMEBODY WHOM PEOPLE FOLLOW somebody who guides or directs others **2.** SOMEBODY OR SOMETHING IN LEAD somebody or something in front of all others, e.g., in a race or procession **3.** SOMEBODY IN CHARGE OF OTHERS the head of a nation, political party, legislative body, or military unit **4.** MUSIC MUSICAL CONDUCTOR a conductor of a band or group **5.** *UK* MUSIC PRINCIPAL MUSICIAN the principal performer of an orchestra or of a section of an orchestra **6.** *also* **lead·ing ar·ti·cle** *UK* MEDIA ARTICLE EXPRESSING EDITORIAL OPINION a newspaper article expressing the opinion of the editor **7.** MARKETING same as **loss leader 8.** BOT MAIN STEM the main growing shoot of a tree or bush **9.** RECORDING BLANK END OF TAPE a short strip of blank film or recording tape at the beginning or end of a reel, used for threading **10.** FISHING LINE CONNECTING HOOK a short length of nylon or other material attached to a fishing line and used to connect a lure or hook **11.** FISHING LINE AT END OF FISHING LINE a short length of heavy fishing line or wire tied to the end of the main line to prevent sharp-toothed fish from breaking off the hook ■ **lead·ers** *npl* PRINTING GUIDE IN PRINTED MATTER dots or dashes in printed material used to guide the eye across a page

lead·er·ship /leédər shìp/ *n* **1.** ABILITY TO LEAD the ability to guide, direct, or influence people **2.** GUIDANCE guidance or direction **3.** LEADERS a group of leaders (*takes a singular or plural verb*) **4.** OFFICE OR POSITION OF LEADER the office or position of the head of a political party or other body of people

lead-free /léd-/ *adj* containing no lead or harmful compounds of lead ○ *lead-free paint*

lead glass /léd-/ *n* glass that contains a high proportion of lead oxide. Use: decorative objects, optical components.

lead-in /leéd-/ *n* **1.** an introduction to something such as an item on television or a topic for discussion **2.** a wire that connects an outside antenna with a transmitter or receiver

lead·ing[1] /leéding/ *adj* **1.** most important or well known **2.** ahead of all others, e.g., in a race or procession [Late 16C. < LEAD[1]]

lead·ing[2] /lédding/ *n* **1.** lead strips around small panes in windows or art objects **2.** the spacing between lines of type in traditional hot metal printing [Early 19C. < LEAD[2]]

lead·ing ec·o·nom·ic in·di·ca·tor /leéding-/ *n* an economic variable that tends to show the direction of future economic activity

lead·ing edge /leéding-/ *n* **1.** MOST ADVANCED POSITION the forefront of development in technology, science, or some other field (*hyphenated when used before a noun*) ○ *at the leading edge of technology* **2.** FRONT EDGE the forward edge of an aircraft wing, propeller, or airfoil **3.** INNER EDGE OF CURTAIN the vertical edge of a curtain that faces the middle of the window

lead·ing la·dy /leéding-/ *n* the actor who has the principal female role in a play or motion picture

lead·ing light /leéding-/ *n* an influential or exemplary person in a field of endeavor

lead·ing man /leéding-/ *n* **1.** the actor who has the principal male role in a play or motion picture **2.** a man who is at the forefront of a specific sphere or activity, especially in politics or business

lead·ing note /leéding-/ *n UK* same as **leading tone**

lead·ing ques·tion /leéding-/ *n* a question asked in a way that prompts the desired answer, e.g., "Do you think the government should be wasting taxpayers' money on such a venture?"

lead·ing tone /leéding-/ *n* the seventh tone of the diatonic scale

lead·ing wo·man /leéding-/ *n* **1.** a woman who is at the forefront of a specific sphere or activity, especially in politics or business **2.** ARTS same as **leading lady**

lead line /léd-/ *n* a line, weighted at one end, used to measure the depth of water. The line is usually marked at intervals to make measurement easier.

lead mon·ox·ide /lèd-/ *n* a poisonous yellow or reddish yellow lead compound. Use: manufacture of storage batteries, pottery, glass, rubber, pigment in paints. Formula: PbO.

lead-off /leéd àwf, -òf/ *n* the first move or action in a series, or somebody who begins something

lead ox·ide /lèd-/ *n* an oxide of lead, e.g., litharge or red lead

lead·plant /léd plànt/ *n* a bush with hairy grayish leaves, thought by early miners to indicate the presence of lead. Native to: North America. Latin name: *Amorpha canescens.*

lead poi·son·ing /lèd-/ *n* **1.** poisoning from the absorption of lead into the body, which over time can cause damage to the nervous system, brain, liver, and gastrointestinal tract **2.** injury or death from a bullet wound (*slang*)

lead screw /leéd-/ *n* a threaded shaft that controls the movement of a machine part such as the tool carriage of a lathe

leads·man /lédzmən/ (*plural* **-men** /-mən/) *n* somebody on a boat who uses a lead line to measure the depth of water

lead tet·ra·eth·yl /lèd-/ *n* CHEM same as **tetraethyl lead**

lead time /leéd-/ *n* **1.** the length of time in advance of a deadline that somebody must know or have something **2.** the time needed to do something measured from start to finish, e.g., from design to production or from placing an order to delivery of the goods ○ *How much lead time do you need?*

lead-up /leéd-/ *n* the period of time or series of events that precede an important event or occasion ○ *in the lead-up to the election*

Lead·ville /léd vìl/ city and county seat of Lake County, central Colorado, situated in the Rocky Mountains, southwest of Denver. Population: 2,723 (2002 estimate).

lead·wort /léd wùrt, -wàwrt/ *n* an evergreen garden plant. Flowers: blue, white, red, in spikes. Native to: tropics. Genus: *Plumbago.*

leaf /leef/ *n* (*plural* **leaves** /leevz/) **1.** PLANT PART a flat green part that grows in various shapes from the stems or branches of a plant or tree and whose main function is photosynthesis. See illustration on next page **2.** FOLIAGE the foliage of a plant or tree, or the time when a plant or tree has leaves ○ *when the trees are in leaf* **3.** LEAVES AS CROP a crop in the form of leaves **4.** PAPER IN BOOK a sheet of paper in a book **5.** VERY THIN METAL FOIL a very thin sheet of metal such as gold or silver used to decorate an object **6.** PART OF TABLE TOP a hinged or removable section of a table top **7.** PART OF DOOR a hinged or sliding section of a door, shutter, or gate **8.** PART OF SPRING IN VEHICLE one of the metal strips that form a spring in a vehicle suspension system (**leaf spring**) ■ *vi* (**leafed, leaf·ing, leafs**) GROW LEAVES to put out new leaves [Old English *lēaf* < Germanic] —**leaf·less** *adj* ◇ **take a leaf out of somebody's book** to follow somebody else's usually good example ◇ **turn over a new leaf** to start to behave in a more acceptable way

leaf through *vt* to turn the pages of a book or magazine quickly and casually

leaf·age /leéfij/ *n* leaves or foliage

leaf bee·tle *n* a beetle that feeds on the leaves of plants and can be destructive to cultivated crops, e.g., the Colorado potato beetle or the flea beetle. Family: Chrysomelidae.

leaf·bird /leéf bùrd/ *n* a bird with bold black and green or yellow markings. Native to: forests of Southeast Asia. Family: Aegithinidae.

leaf but·ter·fly *n* a butterfly that resembles a leaf. Native to: South and Southeast Asia. Genus: *Kallima.*

leaf curl *n* a disease of plants that causes the leaves to curl

leaf·cut·ter ant /leéf kùttər-/ *n* an ant that cuts leaves into pieces to use as fertilizer for the fungi it grows in its nest for food. Native to: tropical America. Genus: *Atta.*

leaf fat *n* the dense layers of fat surrounding the kidneys, especially a hog's kidneys, often used for making lard

leaf·hop·per /leéf hòppər/ *n* a slender spindle-shaped leaping insect that sucks the sap from plants and spreads plant diseases. Native to: worldwide. Family: Cicadellidae.

leaf in·sect *n* an insect with a flat body that resembles a leaf in shape and color. Native to: South Asia. Family: Phyllidae.

leaf lard *n* a high-quality lard made from the fat surrounding the kidneys of hogs (**leaf fat**)

leaf·let /leéflət/ *n* **1.** FREE PRINTED MATERIAL a sheet of printed paper, usually folded, that is distributed free as part of an advertising or information campaign **2.** SMALL LEAF a small or young leaf **3.** PART OF LEAF a division of a compound leaf ■ *vti* (**-let·ed** or **-let·ted, -let·ing** or **-let·ting, -lets**) DISTRIBUTE LEAFLETS to distribute leaflets in a particular place or to a particular group of people

leaf·le·teer /leéflə teér/, **leaf·le·ter** /leéflətər/ *n* somebody who writes or distributes leaflets

leaf min·er *n* an insect of a type whose larvae tunnel into and feed on leaf tissue, including several species of very small moths and a species of fly. Family: Agromyzidae.

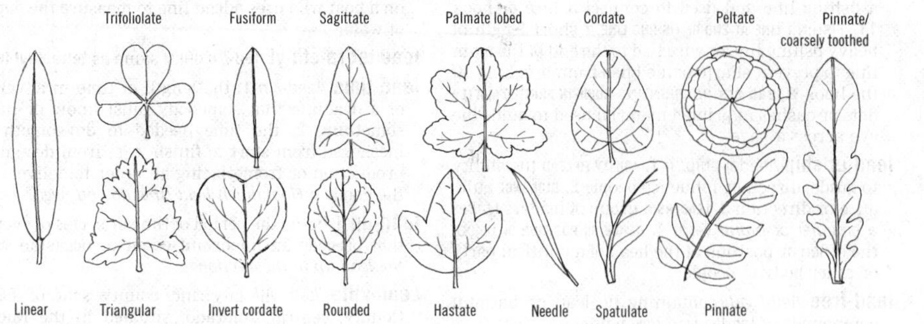

leaf

leaf mold *n* **1.** nitrogen-rich compost or soil that consists mainly of decomposed leaves **2.** a fungal growth on leaves

leaf mon·key *n* a leaf-eating monkey related to the langurs. Native to: South Asia. Genus: *Presbytis*.

leaf pri·mor·di·um *n* a group of cells that develop into a leaf

leaf roll *n* a viral disease of potatoes that is transmitted by aphids and causes the leaves to curl upward

leaf roll·er *n* a small moth whose larvae roll leaves to protect themselves while they eat them

leaf scar *n* the mark left on a stem when a leaf falls

leaf sheath *n* the part at the bottom of the leaf that surrounds the stem in grasses

leaf spot *n* a fungal or bacterial plant disease that causes discolored spots to develop on leaves

leaf spring *n* a spring made of several curved metal strips of different lengths (**leaves**) bracketed together, used in motor vehicle suspension systems

leaf·stalk /leéf stàwk/ *n* a stalk by which a leaf is attached to a stem. Technical name **petiole**

leaf trace *n* the structure that carries fluid between the main stem and the base of the leaf in plants

leaf ty·er *n* INSECTS same as **leaf roller**

leaf·y /leéfee/ (**-i·er, -i·est**) *adj* **1.** WITH MANY LEAVES covered with or having many leaves **2.** WITH MANY TREES with many trees and therefore a lot of foliage **3.** PRODUCING LEAVES producing broad leaves as distinct from blades or needles **4.** WITH EDIBLE LEAVES having edible, usually relatively large, leaves ○ *leafy vegetables* —**leaf·i·ness** *n*

~~**leag**~~, ~~**leage**~~ incorrect spelling of **league**

league[1] /leeg/ *n* **1.** GROUP WITH COMMON GOALS an association of nations, states, organizations, or businesses with common interests or goals **2.** GROUP OF SPORTS CLUBS an association of sports clubs or teams that compete with each other **3.** LEVEL OF SKILL a level of performance or skill ○ *Her painting is not in the same league as yours.* ■ *vti* (**leagued, leagu·ing, leagues**) FORM INTO LEAGUE to join with others for a common interest or goal, or bring people together for such a purpose [15C. Via French *ligue* "pact" < Italian *liga* < Latin *ligare* "bind"] ◇ **be in league (with somebody)** to collaborate with somebody, usually for a questionable purpose ◇ **be (way) out of your league** to be in a place, situation, or group where you do not belong or cannot cope (*informal*)

league[2] /leeg/ *n* a measure of distance of variable length, usually about 3 mi./5 km, no longer in general use [14C. < late Latin *leuga* < Gaulish]

League of Na·tions *n* an alliance of nations that was established in 1920 to promote world peace and cooperation and replaced by the United Nations in 1946. It was first proposed by President Woodrow Wilson after World War I, though the United States never joined, and it became increasingly ineffective in the 1930s.

lea·guer /leégər/ *n* a member of a sports league

leak /leek/ *n* **1.** HOLE OR CRACK an unintentional hole or crack that permits something such as liquid, gas, or light to escape or enter **2.** ACCIDENTAL ESCAPE OR ENTRY the accidental escape or unwanted entry of something, usually by way of an unintentional hole or crack **3.** ESCAPING LIQUID OR GAS something such as liquid or gas that escapes through an unintentional hole or crack **4.** MEANS OF ESCAPE a means of escape, or the resulting loss by means of it ○ *We need to plug the leak in our finances.* **5.** DISCLOSURE OF SECRETS an unofficial release of confidential information, usually to the media **6.** ACCIDENTAL ESCAPE OF ELECTRICITY a place through which an electric current escapes accidentally, or the resulting loss of electricity **7.** URINATION an act of urination (*slang*) ■ *vti* (**leaked, leak·ing, leaks**) **1.** LET SOMETHING IN OR OUT to let something escape or enter accidentally, or escape or enter in this way **2.** DISCLOSE SECRETS, OR BE DISCLOSED to release confidential information unofficially or covertly, usually to the media, or become publicly known in such a way ○ *She leaked the details of the deal to the press.* ○ *The news has leaked.* [15C. Origin ?] —**leak·er** *n*

SPELLCHECK Do not confuse the spelling of ***leak*** and ***leek*** (the vegetable), which sound similar. ***Leak*** is a noun meaning "accidental escape of a liquid or gas" or "a disclosure of confidential information"; it is also used in these meanings as a verb. ***Leek*** denotes a green and white vegetable with an onion flavor.

leak out *vi* to become known unintentionally, or be disclosed unofficially

leak·age /leékij/ *n* **1.** UNINTENTIONAL GRADUAL ESCAPE OR ENTRANCE a gradual escape or entrance of something such as oil, gas, or electric current by a leak **2.** SOMETHING THAT ESCAPES OR ENTERS an amount of something that escapes or enters by leaking **3.** DISCLOSURE OF SECRETS the unofficial release of confidential information, usually to the media

Lea·key /leékee/, **Louis** (1903–72) British archaeologist and paleontologist. He pioneered research into human ancestry at Olduvai Gorge in Tanzania, discovering several key hominid fossils. Full name **Leakey, Louis Seymour Bazett**

Lea·key, Mary (1913–96) British archaeologist and paleontologist. Her fieldwork in Africa yielded discoveries of early hominid fossils including *Zinjanthropus*, now reclassified as *Australopithecus boisei* (1959) and *Homo habilis* (1960). She was the wife of Louis Leakey, with whom she collaborated, and the mother of Richard Leakey. Born **Nicol, Mary Douglas**

Lea·key, Richard (*b.* 1944) Kenyan-born British archaeologist and paleontologist. The son of Louis and Mary Leakey, he continued his parents' research into human ancestry in Africa, becoming director of the Kenyan Wildlife and Conservation Management Service (1989). Full name **Leakey, Richard Erskine Frere**

leak·proof /leék proòf/ *adj* **1.** designed to prevent any of the contents of something from escaping or anything unwanted from entering **2.** not allowing breaches in secrecy or confidentiality (*informal*)

leak·y /leékee/ (**-i·er, -i·est**) *adj* **1.** letting liquid or gas in or out accidentally through holes or cracks **2.** allowing breaches in secrecy or confidentiality (*informal*) —**leak·i·ly** *adv* —**leak·i·ness** *n*

lean[1] /leen/ *v* (**leaned, lean·ing, leans**) **1.** *vi* BEND OR INCLINE to be in or move to a position that is at an angle to the vertical **2.** *vti* REST SOMETHING OR BE SUPPORTED to rest against or on something for support, or rest something against something else **3.** *vi* TEND TOWARD SOMETHING to have a preference or inclination for a particular thing or course of action ○ *leaning toward a more tolerant approach* ■ *n* TILTED POSITION a position that is at an angle to the vertical [Old English *hleonian* < Indo-European, "slope"]

lean on *vt* **1.** DEPEND ON SOMEBODY to be dependent on somebody **2.** GET SUPPORT FROM SOMEBODY to gain moral support or help from somebody ○ *You can always lean on me.* **3.** INTIMIDATE SOMEBODY to put pressure on somebody to do something (*informal*)

lean[2] /leen/ *adj* **1.** WITHOUT EXCESS FAT having no excess body fat and looking muscular and fit ○ *a tall lean physique* **2.** NOT FATTY having little or no fat ○ *lean meat* **3.** NOT PRODUCTIVE not productive or profitable ○ *a lean harvest* **4.** ECONOMICAL AND EFFICIENT not using any more resources than necessary ○ *runs a lean business* **5.** LOW IN COMBUSTIBLE MATERIAL describes a mixture of fuel and air that is low in combustible material ○ *a lean fuel mixture* **6.** MIN EXTRACT WITH FEW MINERALS low in mineral content ○ *lean ore* ■ *n* MEAT WITHOUT FAT meat with little or no fat [Old English *hlǣne* < Germanic] —**lean·ly** *adv* —**lean·ness** *n*

SYNONYMS See *thin*.

Lean /leen/, **Sir David** (1908–91) British movie director. He won Academy Awards for *The Bridge on the River Kwai* (1957) and *Lawrence of Arabia* (1962).

lean-burn *adj* designed to run on a mixture that has a high proportion of air to fuel in order to reduce air pollution ○ *a lean-burn engine*

Le·an·der /lee ándər/ *n* in Greek mythology, Hero's lover, who drowned in the Hellespont while swimming to visit her

lean·ing /leéning/ *n* an inclination or tendency toward something such as a particular set of opinions

-leaning *prefix* showing a tendency towards ○ *a left-leaning think tank*

Barnaby's
Leaning Tower of Pisa

Lean·ing To·wer of Pi·sa *n* the bell tower of Pisa Cathedral, Italy, built between 1173 and 1350 and well known for its tilt. It is 180 ft./55 m high and after extensive corrective work between 1990 and 2001 leans more than 14.5 ft./4.5 m from the perpendicular.

lean-to (*plural* **lean-tos**) *n* **1.** an outbuilding with a slanted roof that rests against the wall of a larger building **2.** a shelter or small building with a roof that slopes in one direction, often reaching the ground

leap /leep/ *v* (**leaped** or **leapt** /lept/, **leap·ing, leaps**) **1.** *vi* JUMP FORCEFULLY to make a jump with a long or high arc ○ *leaped over the stream with ease* **2.** *vi* MOVE AS IF BY JUMPING to move abruptly, as if by jumping up or across something ○ *The dog leaped into her arms.* **3.** *vi* ABRUPTLY SWITCH TO SOMETHING to move abruptly to a new thought or action ○ *immediately leaped to the wrong conclusion* **4.** *vi* GO UP SUBSTANTIALLY to increase suddenly and sizably ○ *Stock prices leaped to new highs.* **5.** *vt* JUMP OVER SOMETHING to jump over an obstacle ○ *didn't think he could leap the fence* **6.** *vt* MAKE ANIMAL JUMP to cause an animal to jump over something ■ *n* **1.** FORCEFUL JUMP a long and high jump **2.** DISTANCE OF JUMP the distance covered by a leap ○ *a leap of almost eight feet* **3.** PLACE TO JUMP a place over or from which to leap **4.** LARGE INCREASE a sudden and sizable increase ○ *a leap in profits* **5.** MUSIC MUSICAL INTERVAL a large interval in music [Old English *hlēapan* < Germanic, "run"] —**leap·er** *n* ◇ **a leap in the dark** an action taken without knowing what the outcome or consequences will be ◇ **in** *or* **by leaps and bounds** extremely rapidly

leap at *vt* to be quick to accept or take advantage of something ○ *leaped at the chance to come with us*

leap out at *vt* to be suddenly or immediately obvious to somebody ○ *The answer just leaps out at you.*

leap·frog /leép fràwg, -fròg/ *n* **VAULTING GAME** a game in which players take turns bending over so that another player can vault over them with the legs wide apart and the hands placed on their backs ■ *v* **(-frogged, -frog·ging, -frogs) 1.** *vt* **VAULT OVER SOMEBODY OR SOMETHING** to vault over somebody in leapfrog, or over something in a manner similar to that used in leapfrog **2.** *vti* **PASS EACH OTHER ALTERNATELY** to take turns passing each other ○ *The two drivers were leapfrogging down the racetrack.* **3.** *vi* **ADVANCE QUICKLY** to advance quickly in status or position, usually bypassing competitors or colleagues ○ *leapfrogged over more senior senators* **4.** *vt* **CIRCUMVENT SOMETHING** to evade something by passing around it **5.** *vt* **ADVANCE MILITARY UNITS BY TURN** to advance military units by having one engage the enemy while the other passes around the battle

leap sec·ond *n* a second added at the end of June or December to a timekeeping system in order to keep measured time synchronized with the movement of Earth around the Sun [After LEAP YEAR]

leapt past participle, past tense of **leap**

leap year *n* a year with an extra day, February 29, added to make up the difference between the 365-day calendar and the actual duration of the Earth's orbit of the Sun. Leap years occur every four years, except for years ending in 00 that are not divisible by 400. [Probably because any given date falls two days later than in the preceding year, instead of one]

Lear /leer/, **Edward** (1812–88) British writer and artist. His limericks and cartoons for children were first published in *A Book of Nonsense* (1846).

> "The Owl and the Pussy-Cat went to sea / In a beautiful pea-green boat, / They took some honey, and plenty of money, / Wrapped up in a five-pound note."
> [Edward Lear, "The Owl and the Pussy-Cat," *Nonsense Songs*; 1871]

learn /lurn/ **(learned** or **learnt** /lurnt/, **learn·ing, learns)** *v* **1.** *vti* **ACQUIRE INFORMATION OR SKILL** to acquire knowledge of a subject or skill through education or experience ○ *I'm learning to play the piano.* **2.** *vti* **FIND OUT** to gain information about somebody or something ○ *learned that they're arriving tomorrow* **3.** *vt* **MEMORIZE SOMETHING** to memorize something such as facts, a poem, a piece of music, or a dance ○ *learn the periodic table* **4.** *vt* **TEACH SOMEBODY SOMETHING** to teach a topic or skill to somebody (*nonstandard*) [Old English *leornian* < Indo-European, "track"] —**learn·a·ble** *adj*

learn·ed /lúrnəd/ *adj* **1. HIGHLY EDUCATED** well educated and very knowledgeable ○ *a learned professor* **2. SCHOLARLY** showing or requiring much education and knowledge ○ *a learned journal* **3.** LAW **HONORABLE** used in addressing or referring to a lawyer in court ○ *my learned colleague* **4.** /lúrnd/ PSYCHOL **ACQUIRED, NOT INSTINCTUAL** describes behavior or knowledge that is acquired through training or experience rather than being instinctual [14C. Past participle of LEARN "teach"] —**learn·ed·ly** *adv* —**learn·ed·ness** *n*

learned help·less·ness /lùrnd-/ *n* somebody's failure to take action to make his or her life better, arising from a sense of not being in control

learn·er /lúrnər/ *n* somebody who studies or learns to do something

learn·er's per·mit *n* a driver's license for those who have not yet passed a driving test, and subject to various restrictions

learn·ing /lúrning/ *n* **1. ACQUIRING OF KNOWLEDGE** the acquisition of knowledge or skill **2. ACQUIRED KNOWLEDGE** knowledge or skill gained through education ○ *a man of great learning* **3.** PSYCHOL **CHANGE IN KNOWLEDGE** a relatively permanent change in, or acquisition of, knowledge, understanding, or behavior

SYNONYMS See ***knowledge.***

learn·ing curve *n* **1.** the rate at which a new subject or skill is learned **2.** a graph that shows the relation between the rate at which knowledge or a skill is learned and the time spent acquiring it

learn·ing dis·a·bil·i·ty *n* a condition that either prevents or significantly hinders somebody from learning basic skills or information at the same rate as most people of the same age (*often used in the plural*)

learn·ing-dis·a·bled *adj* prevented or hindered by a learning disability from learning basic skills or information at the same rate as most people of the same age (*not hyphenated when used after a verb*) ○ *materials aimed specifically at learning-disabled children*

learn·ing the·o·ry *n* the theory that behavior can be explained in terms of how people and animals learn to respond to a stimulus, especially learning by rewards and punishments **(operant conditioning)** and learning by association **(classical conditioning)**

learnt past participle, past tense of **learn**

lear·y *adj* another spelling of **leery**

lease /leess/ *n* **1. RENTAL CONTRACT** a legal contract allowing somebody exclusive possession of another's property for a specific time in return for a payment **2. LENGTH OF LEASE** the period of time covered by a lease ■ *vt* **(leased, leas·ing, leas·es) 1. RENT PROPERTY TO SOMEBODY** to allow somebody to use property under the terms of a lease **2. RENT PROPERTY FROM SOMEBODY** to rent property from somebody under the terms of a lease ○ *We've leased a cottage from friends.* [14C. < Anglo-Norman *les* < *lesser* "to lease," variant of Old French *laissier* (see LEASH)] —**leas·a·ble** *adj* —**leas·er** *n* ◇ **a new lease on life** renewed freshness or vigor, usually resulting from a minor change

lease·back /leéss bàk/ *n* a business arrangement in which a property is sold and then leased to its former owner by its new owner

leased line /leést-/ *n* TELECOM, ONLINE same as **dedicated line**

lease·hold /leéss hōld/ *n* **1.** the holding of a property through a lease **2.** a property that is leased —**lease·hold·er** *n*

leash /leesh/ *n* **1. LINE USED TO CONTROL ANIMAL** a strap, chain, or rope used to control the animal it is attached to, especially a dog **2. RESTRAINT** something that controls or restrains somebody ○ *Our supervisor keeps us on a short leash.* **3. THREE ANIMALS TOGETHER** a set of three animals of one type, especially hounds ■ *vt* **(leashed, leash·ing, leash·es) 1. FIT WITH LEASH** to attach a leash to an animal ○ *Leash your dog!* **2. RESTRAIN FEELINGS** to restrain your emotions or impulses, or control the emotions or impulses of somebody else ○ *I tried to leash my anger.* [13C. < Old French *laisse* < *laissier* "let go" < Latin *laxare* "loosen" < *laxus* "loose"]

leash law *n* a law that requires people to keep their dogs on a leash in public places

least /leest/ CORE MEANING: the smallest or lowest quantity or degree

1. *adj, adv, pron* **SMALLEST AMOUNT POSSIBLE** a smaller amount than anything or anyone else ○ *He went up the steps without showing the least anxiety.* ○ *what I liked least of all* ○ *The least said the soonest mended.* **2.** *adv* **TO LESSER DEGREE THAN OTHERS** having less of a particular quality than most other people or things ○ *one of the least appealing movies of the year* **3.** *adj* **EXTREMELY SMALL** used to emphasize that something is so small as to be almost nonexistent ○ *She didn't have the least idea of how to begin.* **4.** *adv* **TO SMALLEST EXTENT** indicates that something happens or is true to a smaller degree than at any other time ○ *I won the award when I was least expecting it.* **5.** *pron* **MINIMUM** used to indicate the minimum that should be done in a situation ○ *The least you can do is apologize.* [Old English *lǣst*, contraction of *lǣsest* < *lǣs* "less"] ◇ **at least 1.** not less than an amount ○ *It'll take at least two days to finish.* ○ *We traveled at least 45 miles without a rest.* **2.** in any case and despite anything else ○ *At least you still have a job.* **3.** indicates a correction or change ○ *I know the answer, at least I think I do.* ◇ **least of all** emphasizes that a negative applies to one case in particular ○ *No one must know of our discovery – least of all our competitors.* ◇ **not (in) the least** emphasizes that something is not at all the case ○ *He's not in the least like his sister.* ○ *I'm not the least bit tired.* ◇ **not least** emphasizes something particularly important ○ *suffered setbacks, not least a reduction in state funding* ◇ **to say the least** without exaggerating or overstating the case ○ *We were surprised at her rudeness, to say the least.*

least com·mon de·nom·i·na·tor *n* US the lowest multiple shared by all the denominators in a set of fractions. Can term **lowest common denominator**

least com·mon mul·ti·ple *n* US the lowest whole number that is divisible without a remainder by all of the members of a set of numbers. Can term **lowest common multiple**

least squares *n* a method of finding the best curve to fit a set of statistical data points. It involves squaring the distance that each point is from a given curve, summing the squares, and choosing the curve for which the sum has the minimum value.

least·ways /leést wàyz/ *adv Southern US* same as **leastwise**

least·wise /leést wìz/ *adv* in any case and despite anything else

leat /leet/ *n UK* a trench that brings water to a mill or factory [Old English *gelǣt* "channel" < Germanic]

leath·er /lét̲h̲ər/ *n* **1. TANNED AND DRESSED HIDE** the processed hide of animals with the fur or feathers removed **2. MATERIAL LIKE LEATHER** something that is like leather in appearance or texture ○ *fruit leather* **3. SOMETHING MADE OF LEATHER** an item or part of an item that is made of leather **4. DOG'S EARFLAP** the flap of a dog's ear ■ **leath·ers** *npl* **MOTORCYCLISTS' LEATHER CLOTHING** the protective leather jacket, pants, boots, and gloves worn by motorcyclists ■ *adj* **1. MADE OF LEATHER** made of leather or a material that looks like leather **2. INVOLVING SADOMASOCHISM OR FETISHISM** wearing, or intended for people who wear, leather clothing as a symbol of interest in sadomasochism or as a fetish ■ *vt* **(-ered, -er·ing, -ers) 1. COVER SOMETHING IN LEATHER** to give something a covering of leather **2. PUNISH SOMEBODY PHYSICALLY** to beat a person or animal severely, especially by using a leather strap (*dated informal*) [Old English *leþer-* < Indo-European]

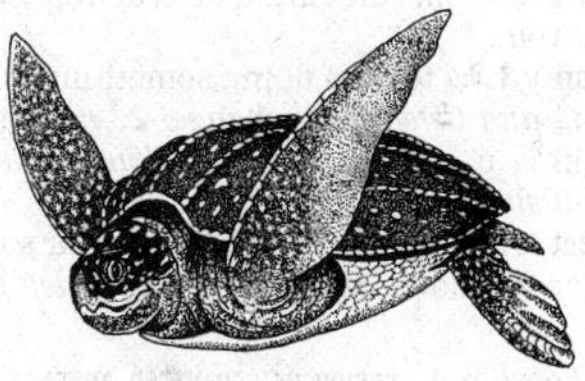

leatherback

leath·er·back /lét̲h̲ər bàk/ *n* the largest of the living sea turtles, which has a flexible shell ridged with bone and covered with leathery skin. Native to: warm seas worldwide. Latin name: *Dermochelys coriacea*.

Leath·er·ette /lèt̲h̲ə rét/ *tdmk* a trademark for a product that is colored and textured to resemble leather

leath·er·neck /lét̲h̲ər nèk/ *n US* a member of the United States Marine Corps (*slang*) [< the leather collar that was part of the uniform]

leath·er·wear /lét̲h̲ər wèr/ *n* clothing and accessories made of leather

leath·er·wood /lét̲h̲ər wòòd/ *n* **1.** a deciduous tree with pliable branches and bark. Native to: eastern North America. Latin name: *Dirca palustris*. **2.** PLANTS same as **titi**[2] (sense 2)

leath·er·work /lét̲h̲ər wùrk/ *n* **1.** the craft of sculpting, cutting, or burning designs into leather **2.** items made from leather, especially decorated leather —**leath·er·work·er** *n* —**leath·er·work·ing** *n*

leath·er·y /lét̲h̲əree/ *adj* looking or feeling like leather, especially having a grainy surface or a tough unyielding consistency —**leath·er·i·ness** *n*

leave[1] /leev/ **(left** /left/, **leav·ing, leaves)** *v* **1.** *vti* **DEPART** to go away from a person or place ○ *I leave the office at five o'clock every day.* **2.** *vt* **DESERT SOMEBODY OR SOMETHING** to abandon a person or place ○ *She has left the city to live in the country.* **3.** *vti* **GIVE UP POSITION IN SOMETHING** to end participation in a group or activity ○ *She left that job for a better one.* **4.** *vt* **CAUSE SOMETHING TO REMAIN** to give something to somebody or put something in a place before departing ○ *I left my number with Dan.* **5.** *vt* **LET SOMETHING REMAIN BEHIND ACCIDENTALLY** to forget to bring something away from a place ○ *I must have left my keys at the office.* **6.** *vt*

SET SOMETHING ASIDE to save or keep something for somebody's use ○ *I left some cake for you.* **7.** *vt* **NOT CHANGE CONDITION OF SOMETHING** to allow something or somebody to remain unchanged in a particular state ○ *I left my coat on.* ○ *Leave your sister alone.* **8.** *vt* **GIVE SOMETHING IN WILL** to bequeath something as a legacy ○ *He plans to leave all his money to charity.* **9.** *vt* **HAVE SOMEBODY AS SURVIVOR** to be survived by somebody after death ○ *He leaves a wife and two young sons.* **10.** *vt* **GIVE JOB TO ANOTHER** to transfer control of or responsibility for something to somebody ○ *Leave it to me.* **11.** *vt* **REJECT SOMETHING** to reject something offered ○ *That's the best I can offer, take it or leave it.* **12.** *vt* **HAVE SOMETHING REMAINING** to cause an amount to remain by removing some amount or part ○ *6 minus 4 leaves 2.* [Old English *lǣfan* < Indo-European, "to stick"] —**leav·er** *n* ◇ **leave go** *or* **hold of somebody** *or* **something** (*nonstandard*) **1.** to stop bothering somebody, or stop interfering in a situation **2.** to stop holding somebody or something ○ *Leave go of my arm!* ◇ **leave it at that** to do or say no more about something ◇ **leave much to be desired** to be highly unsatisfactory ◇ **leave somebody to himself** *or* **herself** to go away and allow somebody to be alone (*often passive*) ◇ **leave well enough alone** to leave a situation as it is rather than risk making it worse

USAGE leave or **let**? Either ***leave*** or ***let*** is correct if you mean "to avoid bothering somebody or to stop bothering somebody in order to allow that person to continue to do something": *Leave/let your brothers alone. Leave me to get on with my work. Let me get on with my work.* ***Let*** is the only choice if you mean "to allow or permit somebody to do something": *Let me finish this first. Let* [not *leave*] *us be.*

leave behind *vt* **1.** to travel or progress faster than somebody or something (*often passive*) **2.** to dismiss something from the mind ○ *leaving your cares behind you*

leave off *v* **1.** *vi* to stop doing something ○ *Leave off chatting and listen for a change!* **2.** *vt* to stop doing or making use of something ○ *You can leave your coats off since it's so warm.*

leave out *vt* to fail to include somebody or something, whether by choice or accident ○ *I felt left out of the party.*

leave[2] /leev/ *n* **1. PERIOD OF PERMITTED ABSENCE** time off from work or duty, with official permission ○ *He'll get a month's paternity leave.* **2. FAREWELL** the act of saying goodbye to somebody ○ *took our leave* **3. PERMISSION** permission to do something (*formal*) ○ *He was given leave to present his proposal.* [Old English *lēaf* "pleasure, approval" < Indo-European, "desire"] ◇ **take leave of your senses** to become entirely irrational or lose all sense of reality

leave[3] /leev/ (**leaved, leav·ing, leaves**) *vi* to grow foliage ○ *The oak has started to leave.* [13C. < LEAF]

leav·en /lévvən/ *n* **1.** *also* **leav·en·ing** /lévv'ning/ **RISING AGENT** a substance used to make dough rise, especially yeast or another fermenting agent **2.** *also* **leav·en·ing** /lévv'ning/ **SOMETHING ENLIVENING** something that lightens the weight or mood of something (*literary*) ○ *with a leaven of wit* ■ *vt* (**-ened, -en·ing, -ens**) **1. MIX YEAST IN SOMETHING** to add leaven to dough **2. MAKE FOOD RISE** to cause bread or cake to rise using leaven **3. ENLIVEN SOMETHING** to lighten the atmosphere or mood of something (*literary*) ○ *His story leavened the mood of the gathering.* [14C. < Old French *levain* < Latin *levare* "to raise"]

Leav·en·worth /lévvən wùrth/ city in northeastern Kansas. It is home to Fort Leavenworth, a US military post, and to Leavenworth Federal Penitentiary. Population: 35,410 (2002 estimate).

leave of ab·sence *n* **1.** permission to have time off from work or another duty for a period **2.** the time spent away from work or another duty with leave of absence

leaves plural of **leaf**

leave-tak·ing *n* a saying of goodbye before leaving somebody (*literary*) ○ *After a teary leave-taking, we set off.*

leav·ings /leévingz/ *npl* something that somebody has left behind or that is left over, usually of little value

Leb·a·non /lébbənən, -nòn/ **1.** country in Southwest Asia, on the eastern coast of the Mediterranean Sea. Language: Arabic. Currency: Lebanese pound. Capital: Beirut. Population: 3,727,703 (2003). Area: 4,036 sq. mi./10,452 sq. km. Official name **Lebanese Republic** **2.** city in Grafton County, western New Hampshire. Population: 12,788 (2002 estimate). **3.** city and county seat of Warren County, southwestern Ohio. Population: 17,896 (2002 estimate). **4.** city and county seat of Wilson County, central Tennessee. Population: 20,853 (2002 estimate). —**Leb·a·nese** /lèbbə neéz, -neéss/ *n, adj*

Lebanon

le·bens·raum /láybənz ròwm, láybənss-/ *n* **1.** additional land in Eastern Europe that the Nazi government claimed was necessary for the continued political and economic development of Germany **2.** adequate room for life or development [Early 20C. < German, "living space"]

leb·ku·chen /láyb ko͝okən, láyp ko͝okhən/ (*plural same*) *n* a rich decorated German gingerbread, traditionally baked in a wide variety of shapes and sizes for Christmas and other celebrations [Early 20C. < German, modern form of Middle High German *lebekuoche* < *lebe* "loaf" + *kuoche* "cake"]

Le·bow·a /lə bṓ ə/ former homeland in northern South Africa, now part of Northern Province

Le Car·ré /lə ka ráy/, **John** (*b.* 1931) British novelist. His popular spy novels include *Tinker, Tailor, Soldier, Spy* (1974) and *Smiley's People* (1980). Pseudonym of **Cornwell, David John Moore**

"A committee is an animal with four back legs."
[John Le Carré, *Tinker, Tailor, Soldier, Spy*; 1974]

lech /lech/, **letch** *n* (*informal*) **1.** same as **lecher** **2.** a lustful desire for somebody [Late 18C. Probably back-formation < LECHER]

Le Chate·lier's prin·ci·ple /lə shàtt'l yáyz-/ *n* the principle that a change affecting a chemical equilibrium is offset by compensatory changes in other components of the equilibrium, thus producing little overall effect [Early 20C. After Henri Louis *Le Chatelier* (1850–1936), French chemist]

le·chayim *interj, n* another spelling of **l'chaim**

lech·er /léchər/ *n* a man who behaves lewdly and lustfully in a way regarded as distasteful [12C. < Old French *lecheor* < *lechier* "to lick" < Germanic]

lech·er·ous /léchərəss/ *adj* expressing or displaying lewdness and lust in a way regarded as distasteful —**lech·er·ous·ly** *adv* —**lech·er·ous·ness** *n*

lech·er·y /léchəree/ *n* lewd and lustful behavior, especially by a man, that is regarded as distasteful

lech·we /leéchwee/ *n* **1.** an antelope with long narrow hooves and long backward-pointing horns. Native to: marshes and riverbanks in Botswana and Zambia. Latin name: *Kobus leche.* **2.** an antelope with a white shoulder patch. Native to: wetlands of the upper Nile valley. Latin name: *Kobus megaceros.* [Mid-19C. Probably < Sesotho *lets'a*]

lec·i·thin /léssəthin/ *n* a phospholipid found in cell membranes that also plays a role in fat metabolism [Mid-19C. < French *lécithine* < Greek *lekithos* "egg yolk"]

lec·i·thin·ase /léssəthi nàyss, -nàyz/ *n* BIOCHEM same as **phospholipase**

Le·clan·ché cell /lə klaán shày-/ *n* a primary cell, the common dry cell, having a carbon anode, zinc cathode, and sal ammoniac as the electrolyte [Late 19C. After Georges *Leclanché* (1839–82), French chemist]

Le Corbusier

Le Cor·bu·sier /lə kawr boo zyáy/ (1887–1965) Swiss-born French architect and designer. He pioneered functionalist architecture and his use of reinforced concrete and views on urban living influenced reconstruction after World War II. Pseudonym of **Jeanneret, Charles-Édouard**

"A house is a machine for living in."
[Le Corbusier, *Vers une architecture (Toward a New Architecture)*; 1925]

lect /lekt/ *n* a variety within a language, having its own rules [Late 20C. Back-formation < DIALECT]

lect. *abbr* EDUC **1.** lecture **2.** lecturer

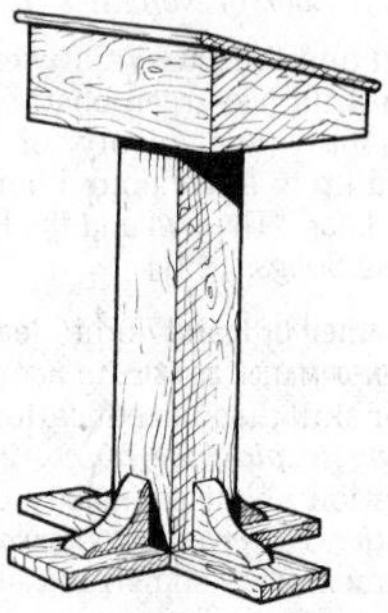
lectern

lec·tern /léktərn/ *n* **1.** a tall slender table with a slanted top on which an open book can rest, used in churches and temples for reading scriptures to the congregation **2.** a stand with a slanted top on which a book or lecture notes can rest in front of a standing speaker [14C. Via French < late Latin *lectrum* < Latin *lect-* (see LECTURE)]

lec·tin /léktin/ *n* a protein found mainly in seeds and grains and their products, belonging to a group that binds to carbohydrates and causes blood cells to clump together. Lectins may be a factor in some immune reactions and dietary intolerance. Use: testing for blood type. [Mid-20C. < Latin *lect-* (see LECTURE)]

lec·tion /lékshən/ *n* **1.** a variant reading of a text in a specific edition or translation **2.** a passage from the Bible that is set to be read on a specific day as part of the liturgy of a Christian service [Early 17C. < Latin *lection-* "reading" < *lect-* (see LECTURE)]

lec·tion·ar·y /lékshə nèrree/ (*plural* **-ies**) *n* a schedule of readings from the Bible for Christian church services during the course of the year, or a book containing such readings

lec·tor /léktər, -tàwr/ *n* **1.** a public reader of passages from the Bible to a Christian congregation or a religious community **2.** in some universities, a lecturer [14C. < Latin, "reader" < *lect-* (see LECTURE)]

lec·ture /lékchər/ *n* **1. INSTRUCTIONAL SPEECH** an educational speech on a subject made before an audience ○ *a lecture on the next generation of space probes* **2. TEACHING SESSION** a session of a class at which a lecture is given ○ *two lectures and two labs a week* **3. REPRIMAND** a lengthy reprimand or scolding concerning something ■ *v* (**-tured, -tur·ing, -tures**) **1.** *vti* **GIVE EDUCATIONAL SPEECH TO SOMEBODY** to deliver a lecture to a group of people as a method of instruction ○ *He lectures on stress management all over the country.* **2.** *vi* **BE UNIVERSITY LECTURER** to be employed as a lecturer at a university or college ○

She lectures at the university. **3.** *vt* **REPRIMAND SOMEBODY** to reprimand somebody by making a speech about how a person should behave ○ *lectured her again about her laziness* [13C. Via French < medieval Latin *lectura* "reading" < Latin *lect-*, past participle of *legere* "read"]

lec·ture hall *n* a large room with tiered or auditorium-style seating, or a building, used for holding lectures

lec·tur·er /lékchərər/ *n* **1. UNIVERSITY TEACHER IN UNITED STATES** a teacher in a college or university who neither has tenure nor is a full member of the faculty **2.** *UK* **UNIVERSITY TEACHER IN UNITED KINGDOM** a teacher at a British university or college who ranks lower than a professor **3. INFORMATIVE SPEAKER** an informative speaker on a specific topic, especially as a professional

lec·ture·ship /lékchər ship/ *n* **1. POSITION OF LECTURER IN UNITED STATES** the position of a lecturer at a college or university, especially a nontenured teaching position **2.** *UK* **ACADEMIC POSITION IN UNITED KINGDOM** a position at the rank of lecturer in a British university or college **3. FINANCE FOR LECTURES** a fund that provides financing for a series of lectures

lec·ture the·a·tre *n UK* same as **lecture hall**

led /led/ past participle, past tense of **lead**[1] (*often in combination*) ○ *The push for safety regulations is consumer-led, not industry-led.*

USAGE See *lead*[1].

LED *n* a semiconductor that emits light when a current passes through it. Use: indicator lights on electronic equipment. Full form **light-emitting diode**

Le·da /léedə/ *n* **1.** in Greek mythology, a queen of Sparta. She was the mother of Helen of Troy, Clytemnestra, and Castor and Pollux. **2.** a very small natural satellite of Jupiter. It is approximately 6 mi./10 km in diameter.

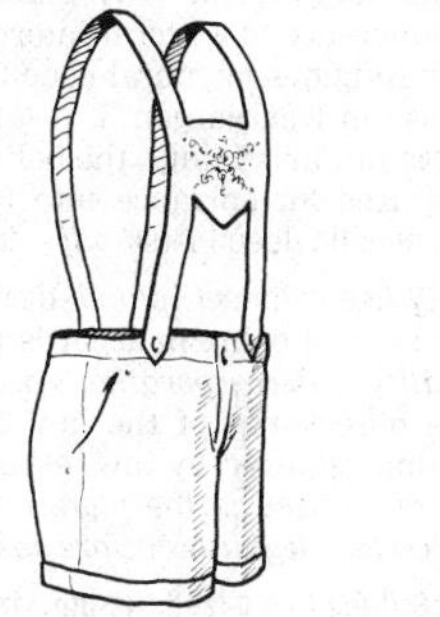

lederhosen

le·der·ho·sen /láydər hōz'n/ *npl* Bavarian leather shorts, usually with suspenders, worn by men and boys [Mid-20C. < German, "leather trousers"]

ledge /lej/ *n* **1. FLAT SURFACE PROJECTING FROM ROCK FACE** a narrow flat projecting rock shelf, e.g., on the vertical surface of a cliff **2.** OCEANOG **UNDERWATER RAISED SURFACE** a raised surface underwater, e.g., a reef or ridge, especially one found near a shore **3. NARROW SHELF AGAINST WALL** a narrow shelf or molding attached to a wall that serves a decorative or protective purpose **4.** MIN EXTRACT **ROCK LAYER** a layer of ore-bearing rock [Mid-16C. Origin ?] —**ledged** *adj* —**ledg·y** *adj*

ledg·er /léjjər/ *n* **1. FINANCIAL RECORD BOOK** a book or page with columns for debits and credits, on which to transcribe financial records **2. HORIZONTAL GRAVESTONE** a gravestone that lies flat on the ground **3.** CONSTR **SCAFFOLDING BEAM** a horizontal beam in a scaffolding that is attached to the uprights and supports the beams (**putlogs**) [Early 16C. Probably < *leggen*, earlier form of LAY[1]]

ledg·er board *n* **1.** a horizontal board, especially the top rail of a fence **2.** a narrow horizontal board attached to a row of studs to support joist ends

ledg·er line, **leg·er line** *n* a short line added above or below a musical staff to accommodate notes that are higher or lower than those on the staff

Le·duc /lə dóok/ town in Alberta, Canada, situated 20 mi./32 km south of Edmonton. Population: 15,032 (2001).

lee /lee/ *n* **1. SHIP SIDE AWAY FROM WIND** the side of a ship away from the source of the wind **2. PROTECTIVE COVER** shelter from the wind ○ *in the lee of the wall* ■ *adj* **AWAY FROM WIND** on or toward the side of a ship, natural feature, or object that is away from the wind [Old English *hlēo* "shelter" < Indo-European, "warm"]

Lee /lee/, **Ann** (1736–84) British-born American religious leader. She led the British Shakers to America (1774).

Lee, Charles (1731–82) British-born American army officer. Having left the British army to fight with the Americans in the American Revolution, his retreat at the Battle of Monmouth (1778) resulted in his court-martial and dismissal.

Lee, David M. (*b.* 1931) US physicist. With Robert C. Richardson and Douglas D. Osheroff he shared the Nobel Prize in physics (1996) for research into the superfluidity of helium-3. Full name **Lee, David Morris**

Lee, Francis Lightfoot (1734–97) American politician. A member of the Continental Congress (1775–79) from Virginia, he signed the Declaration of Independence (1776).

Lee, Gypsy Rose (1914–70) US entertainer and novelist. The musical *Gypsy* (1959) was in part based on her life as a striptease artist. Born **Hovick, Rose Louise**

> "God is love, but get it in writing."
> [Attributed to Gypsy Rose Lee]

Lee, Harper (*b.* 1926) US novelist. She was awarded the Pulitzer Prize in 1961 for her only novel, *To Kill a Mockingbird* (1960). See Cultural note at **mockingbird**

> "Folks don't like to have somebody around knowin' more than they do. It aggravates 'em. You're not gonna change any of them by talkin' right, they've got to want to learn themselves."
> [Harper Lee, *To Kill a Mockingbird*; 1960]

Lee, Henry (1756–1818) American revolutionary leader. He was governor of Virginia (1792–95) and a member of the US Congress (1799–1801). Known as **Light-Horse Harry Lee**

> "To the memory of the Man, first in war, first in peace, and first in the hearts of his countrymen."
> [Henry Lee, resolutions to the US House of Representatives on the death of George Washington; December 1799]

Lee, Richard Henry (1732–94) American politician. He made the motion in the Continental Congress that led to the writing of the Declaration of Independence (1776), of which he was a signatory.

> "That these United Colonies are, and of right ought to be, free and independent states."
> [Richard Henry Lee. This resolution, of the Continental Congress, Philadelphia (1776) gave rise to the Declaration of Independence; June 7, 1776]

Library of Congress

Robert E. Lee

Lee, Robert E. (1807–70) US Confederate general. He commanded the Confederate army during the last three years of the Civil War, and surrendered to Ulysses S. Grant at Appomattox. Full name **Lee, Robert Edward**

> "It is well that war is so terrible; else we would grow too fond of it."
> [Attributed to Robert E. Lee, remarks made after the battle of Fredericksburg; December 1862]

Lee, Spike (*b.* 1957) US movie writer and director. His movies, including *Do the Right Thing* (1989) and *Malcolm X* (1992), are concerned with racial issues. Born **Lee, Shelton Jackson**

> "I agree that agents are necessary, but they're still one of the lowest forms of life."
> [Spike Lee, *Do The Right Thing*; 1989]

lee·board /lée bàwrd/ *n* either of two movable wooden or metal shelves on the outside of a ship's hull that prevent sideways movement caused by the wind

leech[1] /leech/ *n* **1. BLOOD-SUCKING WORM** a worm that sucks blood or eats flesh. One species has been used in medical treatments to bleed patients or to eat away putrid flesh from a wound. Native to: warm shallow fresh water. Class: Hirudinea. **2. EXPLOITER OF OTHERS** somebody who clings to or exploits somebody else, e.g., for financial support **3.** same as **physician** (*archaic informal*) ■ *v* (**leeched, leech·ing, leech·es**) **1.** *vt* **DRAIN OFF SOMETHING** to draw off or deplete a supply of something **2.** *vt* MED **TREAT SOMEBODY WITH LEECHES** to bleed a patient using leeches **3.** *vi* **EXPLOIT SOMEBODY** to cling to or take advantage of somebody, e.g., for financial support (*informal*) [Old English *lǣce*] —**leech·like** *adj*

leech[2] /leech/, **leach** *n* **1.** a vertical edge of a square sail **2.** the edge of a fore-and-aft sail that is farthest from the mast or stay [15C. Origin ?]

Leeds /leedz/ university and industrial city in Yorkshire, northern England. Population: 715,402 (2001).

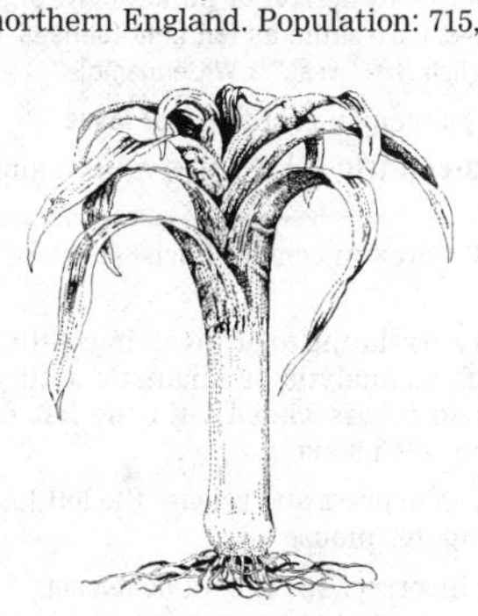

leek

leek /leek/ *n* an edible plant with dark green leaves rising from a close-set white base, related to the onion. Latin name: *Allium porrum*. [Old English *lēac* < Germanic]

SPELLCHECK See *leak*.

Lee Kuan Yew /lée kwáan yóo/ (*b.* 1923) prime minister of Singapore (1959–90). He was Singapore's first prime minister.

leer /leer/ *vi* (**leered, leer·ing, leers**) to look or smile in a way that suggests unpleasantly lustful or malicious intent ■ *n* an unpleasantly lustful or malicious look or smile [Mid-16C. Probably < obsolete *leer* "cheek" < Old English *hlēor*]

leer·y /léeree/ (**-i·er, -i·est**), **lear·y** *adj* regarding somebody or something with suspicion ○ *Many scientists are leery of the new claims.* [Early 18C. Origin ?] —**leer·i·ness** *n*

lees /leez/ *npl* sediment that settles in wine or other alcoholic beverages during fermentation [14C. Plural of obsolete *lee*, via French < medieval Latin *lia*]

lee shore *n* a shore that is in the direction away from the wind, relative to a ship

leet /leet/ *n* formerly, a court held at regular intervals by the lords of English manors [13C. < Anglo-Norman *lete*]

Leeu·war·den /láy vaàrd'n, -waàrd'n/ capital of Friesland Province, in the northern Netherlands. Population: 87,495 (1994).

Leeu·win, Cape /loo ín/ headland in southwestern Western Australia, the most southwesterly point on the continent

lee·ward /léewərd/; *nautical* /lóo ərd/ *adj* **AWAY FROM WIND** situated away from the wind, or on the side of something, especially a boat, that is away or sheltered from the wind ■ *adv* **AWAY FROM WIND** away from where the wind is coming from ■ *n* **PLACE AWAY FROM WIND** a place or direction away or sheltered from the wind

Lee·ward Is·lands /léeward-/ group of islands in the northeastern Caribbean. The principal islands include Antigua and Barbuda, Guadeloupe, Montserrat, and St. Kitts. Area: 1,273 sq. mi./3,297 sq. km.

lee·way /lée wày/ *n* **1.** the permissible margin for variation or deviation from something **2.** the sideways movement of a ship or aircraft from its course, caused by strong winds

left[1] /left/ *adj* **1. WEST WHEN FACING NORTH** on or toward the west when somebody or something is facing north ○ *Her left leg is broken.* **2.** *also* **Left** POL **ADVOCATING POLITICAL AND SOCIAL CHANGE** supporting liberal, socialist, or communist political and social changes or reform **3.** GEOG **ON LEFT WHEN LOOKING DOWNSTREAM** on the river bank to the left of somebody facing downstream **4.** THEATER **TO RIGHT OF AUDIENCE** on or relating to that part of a stage that is to the left of somebody standing on it and facing the audience ○ *Exit stage left.* ■ *adv* **ON LEFT SIDE** on or toward the left side of somebody or something ○ *Turn left at the light.* ■ *n* **1. LEFT SIDE** the left side of somebody or something ○ *The house is on your left.* **2.** *also* **Left** POL **LIBERALS, SOCIALISTS, AND COMMUNISTS** people who support liberal, socialist, or communist political and social changes or reform **3.** BOXING **LEFT-HANDED PUNCH** a blow delivered with the left hand ○ *took a hard left to the jaw* **4.** BOXING **LEFT-HANDED PUNCHING ABILITY** a boxer's left hand with respect to its ability to deliver a punch ○ *He's got a good left.* **5.** BASEBALL same as **left field** (senses 1–2) [13C. < Old English *lyft-* "weak" < W Germanic]

left[2] past participle, past tense of **leave**[1]

left a·tri·o·ven·tric·u·lar valve *n* ANAT same as **mitral valve**

Left Bank *n* area in central Paris, south of the Seine River

left-brain *adj* relating to or involving skills or knowledge such as analytic or linguistic ability that are believed to be associated with the left half of the cerebrum —**left brain** *n*

left-click *vti* to press and release the left-hand button on a computer mouse

~~**leftenant**~~ incorrect spelling of **lieutenant**

left-face *US vi* to turn 90° to the left (*usually used as a command*) ■ *n* a turn 90° to the left

left field *n* **1. SECTION OF OUTFIELD** in baseball, the part of the outfield that is to the batter's left **2. OUTFIELDER'S POSITION** in baseball, the position held by the player who is responsible for fielding balls that are hit to left field **3. VERY UNUSUAL POSITION** a position that is so different from mainstream beliefs that it is not generally taken seriously (*informal*) ◇ **out in left field** in an erroneous or very unconventional position or state (*informal*)

left field·er *n* a baseball player who is responsible for fielding balls hit to left field

left-hand *adj* **1.** on or toward the left **2.** intended for or done by the left hand

left-hand·ed *adj* **1. USING LEFT HAND** using the left hand, instead of the right, for tasks such as writing and manipulating objects **2. STARTING SWING FROM LEFT** in sports, swinging from the left to the right ○ *a left-handed batter* **3. DONE WITH LEFT HAND** intended for or done using the left hand **4. NOT SINCERE** ironic and insincere ○ *a left-handed compliment* **5. CLUMSY** lacking skill or grace **6. TURNING RIGHT TO LEFT** spiraling toward the left **7.** LAW same as **morganatic** ■ *adv* **1. WITH LEFT HAND** with the left hand, especially when it is used instead of the right for tasks such as writing **2. WITH LEFT-HANDED SWING** in sports, with a swing that moves from the left to the right

left-hand·er *n* somebody who uses chiefly the left hand for ordinary tasks

left·ie /léftee/ *n* another spelling of **lefty** (*informal*)

left·ish /léftish/, **Left·ish** *adj* tending to be relatively left-wing in politics

left·ism /léf tìzzəm/, **Left·ism** *n* the advocating of liberal, socialist, or communist political and social change or reform —**left·ist** *adj, n*

left-lug·gage of·fice *n UK* same as **baggage check**

left·most /léft mōst/ *adj* in the position farthest to the left

left·o·ver /léft ōvər/ *adj* **REMAINING UNUSED** remaining after the rest of something has been used or eaten ■ *n* **SOMETHING REMAINING** something that remains or was not used ■ **left·o·vers** *npl* **SAVED FOOD** food remaining from a previous meal or meals, saved and served again or made into a new dish ○ *I made this soup from leftovers.*

left·ward /léftwərd/ *adj* moving toward or located on the left ■ *adv also* **left·wards** /-wərdz/ toward or on the left

left wing *n* a subgroup of a larger organization that is more liberal or radical than the rest of the organization —**left-wing** *adj* —**left-wing·er** *n*

left·y /léftee/ (*informal*) *n* (*plural* **-ies**) **1. LEFT-HANDER** somebody who is left-handed ○ *How many lefties are on the team?* **2. LEFTIST** somebody with left-wing beliefs ■ *adv US* **WITH LEFT HAND** with the left hand or in a left-handed way ○ *He bats lefty.*

leg /leg/ *n* **1. LOWER LIMB** a limb that animals and people use for standing, walking, running, or jumping, either including or excluding the foot **2. SUPPORTING POLE** a part of an object that looks like a human or animal lower limb and is used for support ○ *a table leg* **3. CLOTHING FOR LEG** the portion of a piece of clothing that covers all or part of the human leg ○ *a pants leg* **4. MEAT FROM ANIMAL'S OR FOWL'S LEG** the meat, including the bone, from the back hindquarter of a four-legged mammal, or from the leg of a bird, that is cooked and eaten as food **5. BRANCH OF OBJECT** one of the extensions of a branched or jointed object **6. SECTION OF TRIP** a part of a trip that is separated from other parts by a period of rest or by a change in direction or the manner of travel **7.** SPORTS **RELAY RACE PORTION** one of the parts of a relay race that a single athlete completes **8.** SPORTS **PORTION OF SPORTS COMPETITION** one of several stages, events, or games that is part of a larger competition but is treated independently of the other parts and has its own winner **9.** SAILING **SAILING COMPLETED ON ONE TACK** the distance traveled by a sailboat on a single tack **10.** MATH **RIGHT-ANGLE SIDE OF TRIANGLE** either of the two sides of a right triangle that extends from the right angle ■ **legs** *npl* WINE **TRAILS OF WINE ON SIDE OF GLASS** the vertical trails of wine that cling to the side of a glass after wine has been swirled around in it. The length and movement of these trails are taken as an indication of the wine's body. [13C. < Old Norse *leggr*] ◇ **have legs** to be likely to enjoy a sustained period of popularity or success (*informal*) ◇ **leg it** to walk or run (*informal*) ◇ **not have a leg to stand on** to have nothing to justify or support an attitude or position (*informal*) ◇ **on your last legs** on the verge of collapse or breakdown ◇ **pull somebody's leg** to tell somebody something untrue in teasing or for fun (*informal*) ◇ **shake a leg 1.** to hurry up (*usually used as a command*) **2.** same as **dance** *v* (sense 1) (*dated informal*) ◇ **stretch your legs** to go for a walk after a period of being seated or stationary

leg. *abbr* **1.** LAW legal **2.** CHR, POL legate **3.** MUSIC legato **4.** LAW, GOV legislation **5.** LAW, GOV legislative **6.** LAW, GOV legislature

leg·a·cy /léggəssee/ *n* (*plural* **-cies**) **1. BEQUEST MADE IN WILL** money or property that is left to somebody in a will **2. SOMETHING FROM PAST** something that is handed down or remains from a previous generation or time ■ *adj* **OUTDATED OR DISCONTINUED** associated with something that is outdated or discontinued ○ *legacy software* ○ *legacy currency* [14C. Via Old French *legacie* "office of a delegate" < medieval Latin *legatia* < Latin *legatus* (see LEGATE)]

le·gal /léeg'l/ *adj* **1. LAW-RELATED** relating to the law or to courts of law ○ *took legal action* **2. OF OR FOR LAWYERS** relating to lawyers or to law as a profession **3. PERMITTED BY LAW** allowed under the law ○ *Parking on the grass isn't legal.* **4. UNDER LAW** established under the law, or by common law or legislation ○ *the legal age of consent* **5. ESTABLISHED BY LAW COURT** recognized or established by a court of law, rather than a court of equity **6. OLD ENOUGH UNDER LAW** older than a minimum age established by law for some activities such as driving (*informal*) [15C. Via French < Latin *legalis* < *leg-* "law"] —**le·gal·ly** *adv*

ORIGIN The Latin stem *leg-* "law," from which ***legal*** is derived, is also the source of English *colleague, college, delegate, legacy, legate, legislate, legitimate, loyal, privilege,* and *relegate.*

SYNONYMS ***legal, lawful, decriminalized, legalized, legitimate, licit***

CORE MEANING: describes something that is permitted, recognized, or required by law

legal established or allowed under the law ○ *It is perfectly legal to charge a reasonable interest rate on unpaid accounts.* ○ *Your spouse will still have a legal right to inherit from you.* **lawful** a less common word meaning legal ○ *The rate increases were found to be reasonable and lawful.* ○ *He believed he had lawful authority to ride the bike.* **decriminalized** no longer categorized as a criminal offense ○ *decriminalized activities* **legalized** previously categorized as illegal and now declared legal ○ *casino-style and other legalized gambling* **legitimate** complying with the law, or having official status defined by law ○ *claimed the deposit was a legitimate business transaction* ○ *legitimate travel documents* **licit** allowed by law ○ *What had been licit and reasonably commonplace practices were now forbidden.*

le·gal age *n* the age, according to the law, at which somebody is considered to be an adult

le·gal aid *n* legal advice or representation that is provided by an organization at low or no cost to people who cannot afford to pay for legal services

le·gal cap *n US* ruled white writing paper measuring 8½ in./216 mm by 14 in./350 mm to 16 in./406 mm, with the fold at the top, typically used by lawyers

le·gal ea·gle *n* a lawyer, especially a skillful or successful one (*slang*)

le·gal·ese /léeg'l éez, -éess/ *n* language that is typically used in legal documents and is generally considered by lay people to be difficult to understand

le·gal hol·i·day *n* a day established as a holiday by law, when government offices, schools, and post offices are typically closed

le·gal·ism /léeg'l ìzzəm/ *n* **1. ADHERENCE TO LETTER OF LAW** strict adherence to a literal interpretation of a law, rule, or religious or moral code **2. LAW TERM** a word or phrase in legal jargon **3.** CHR **BELIEF IN NECESSITY OF GOOD DEEDS** in Christianity, the belief that good deeds are required for entrance into Heaven —**le·gal·ist** *n* —**le·gal·is·tic** /léeg'l ístik/ *adj* —**le·gal·is·ti·cal·ly** *adv*

le·gal·i·ty /lee gállətee/ (*plural* **-ties**) *n* **1. CONFORMITY TO LAW** the state of being in accordance with the law ○ *the legality of the corporation's activities* **2. OBEYING OF LAW** the observance of the law **3. LEGAL REQUIREMENT** something required by law, especially a technical detail (*often used in the plural*) ○ *We have to take care of certain legalities before opening the business.*

le·gal·ize /léeg'l ìz/ (**-ized, -iz·ing, -iz·es**) *vt* to make an activity legal by introducing or changing a law that governs it —**le·gal·ized** *adj* —**le·gal·i·za·tion** /lèeg'li záysh'n/ *n*

SYNONYMS See ***legal.***

Le Gal·lienne /lə gal yén/, **Eva** (1899–1991) British-born US actor. She was known for her roles in plays by Ibsen and Chekhov. She also directed and taught acting.

le·gal med·i·cine *n* LAW same as **forensic medicine**

le·gal pad *n* a pad of yellow ruled paper measuring 8½ in./216 mm by 14 in./356 mm, typically used by lawyers

le·gal re·serve *n US* an amount of money that a financial organization such as a bank or insurer is required to keep as security against debts (*often used in the plural*)

le·gal sep·a·ra·tion *n* **1.** the court decree establishing the separation of a married couple **2.** separation of a married couple that is recognized by a court of law. This is often required as a first step toward divorce.

le·gal-size *adj* equal in size to a piece of legal pad paper, 8½ in./216 mm by 14 in./350 mm, or of a size that will hold such paper

le·gal ten·der *n* currency that is valid for the payment of a debt and must be accepted by a creditor

Le·gas·pi /lə gáspee/, **Le·gaz·pi** city and capital of Albay Province, the Philippines, situated at the head of Albay Gulf. Population: 160,501 (1999).

leg·ate /léggət/ *n* **1.** an emissary of the pope, especially one who represents the Vatican in another country **2.** an official representative of a government, especially a diplomat [12C. Via French < Latin *legatus* < *legat-* past participle of *legare* "send as an envoy, bequeath"]

leg·a·tee /lèggə tée/ *n* a recipient of a bequest made in a will [Late 17C. < *legate* "bequeath" < Latin *legat-* (see LEGATE)]

le·ga·tion /lə gáysh'n/ *n* **1.** DIPLOMATS ON MISSION a group of representatives sent on a mission, especially a diplomatic mission **2.** DIPLOMAT'S RESIDENCE the official local residence of a senior diplomat assigned to a country. It ranks below an embassy in importance. **3.** DIPLOMATIC STAFF the staff of a legation **4.** SENDING OF DIPLOMATIC REPRESENTATIVE the sending of a representative on a diplomatic mission **5.** DIPLOMATIC MISSION a mission performed by a diplomatic representative **6.** LEGATE'S POSITION the status or office of a papal legate [14C. Directly or via French < Latin *legation-* < *legat-* (see LEGATE)]

le·ga·to /lə gaátō/ *adv* in a smooth even manner, often indicated in a musical score by a curved line (**slur**) connecting the notes to be so played (*used as a musical direction*) ■ *n* (*plural* **-tos**) a piece of music, or a section of a piece, played legato [Mid-18C. < Italian, "tied together"] —**le·ga·to** *adj*

le·ga·tor /lə gáytər/ *n* somebody who has made a will to bequeath something [Mid-17C. < Latin < *legat-* (see LEGATE)]

Le·gaz·pi another spelling of **Legaspi**

leg·end /léjjənd/ *n* **1.** OLD STORY a story that has been passed down for generations, especially one that is presented as history but is unlikely to be true **2.** OLD STORIES a group of stories presented as history but unlikely to be true **3.** MODERN MYTH a popular myth that has arisen in modern times **4.** CELEBRITY somebody famous admired for a skill or talent **5.** INSCRIPTION an inscription, especially a title or motto, on an object **6.** PUBL CAPTION a caption for an illustration **7.** MAPS MAP KEY an explanation of the symbols used on a map [14C. Via French *légende* < medieval Latin *legenda* "things to be read" < Latin *legere* "to read"]

leg·en·dar·y /léjjən dèrree/ *adj* **1.** BELONGING TO LEGEND described or commemorated in a legend ○ *the legendary figure of Hercules* **2.** CONTAINING LEGENDS retold for generations as history but unlikely to be completely or even partially true ○ *the legendary tales of ancient warriors* **3.** LIKE SOMETHING IN LEGEND appropriate for a legend ○ *an organization of legendary size* **4.** FAMOUS very famous in contemporary society ○ *Her generosity is legendary.* —**leg·en·dar·i·ly** *adv*

leg·end·ry /léjjəndree/ (*plural* **-ries**) *n* a collection or group of legends

Lé·ger /láy zhay/, **Fernand** (1881–1955) French painter. One of the founders of the cubist movement, he developed a personal style that used rounded and cylindrical forms.

Lé·ger, Jules (1913–80) Canadian government official. He was governor-general of Canada (1974–79).

leg·er·de·main /lèjjərdə máyn/ *n* **1.** a display of skill or cleverness, especially for deceitful purposes ○ *a dazzling display of political legerdemain* **2.** ARTS same as **sleight of hand** (sense 1) [15C. < French *léger de main* "light of hand"]

leg·er line *n* MUSIC another spelling of **ledger line**

le·ges LAW plural of **lex**

-legged /léggəd/ *suffix* **1.** with a particular number of legs ○ *four-legged* **2.** with a particular type or position of legs ○ *bandy-legged* ○ *cross-legged*

leg·ging /légging/ *n* PROTECTIVE COVERING FOR LOWER LEG a protective covering made of a strong material that is wrapped around the lower leg by laborers and players in some sports ■ **leg·gings** *npl* **1.** CLOSE-FITTING PANTS women's pants or footless tights made of elastic material that fit very closely to the legs and hips **2.** PROTECTIVE OUTER PANTS waterproof or insulated outer pants that are worn for protection from snow, rain, and cold

leg·gy /léggee/ (**-gi·er, -gi·est**) *adj* **1.** WITH LONG LEGS having very long legs in relation to the rest of the body **2.** WITH SHAPELY LEGS having long good-looking legs **3.** BOT SPINDLY IN GROWTH with long thin stems that have few and widely spaced leaves

leg·horn /lég hàwrn, -gərn/ *n* **1.** BLEACHED STRAW fine bleached straw made from a type of Italian wheat **2.** STRAW FABRIC a fabric made from plaited leghorn straw **3.** STRAW HAT a hat made from leghorn straw [Mid-18C. After LEGHORN[2]]

Leg·horn[1] /lég hàwrn, -gərn/ *n* a small domestic fowl. Raised for: white eggs. [Mid-19C. After LEGHORN[2]]

Leg·horn[2] /lég hàwrn/ ➧ **Livorno**

leg·i·ble /léjjəb'l/ *adj* clear enough to be read [15C. < late Latin *legibilis* < Latin *legere* "to read"] —**leg·i·bil·i·ty** /lèjjə bíllətee/ *n* —**leg·i·bly** *adv*

ORIGIN The Latin word *legere* "to collect, choose, read," from which ***legible*** is derived, is also the source of English *coil, collect*[1], *cull, elect, elegant, intelligent, lecture, legend, legion, lesson, neglect,* and *select.*

le·gion /léejən/ *n* **1.** MULTITUDE a large number of people or things ○ *Their complicated affairs are managed by a legion of accountants.* **2.** ANCIENT HIST ROMAN ARMY DIVISION in ancient Rome, an army division of 3,000 to 6,000 soldiers, including cavalry **3.** MIL LARGE BODY OF SOLDIERS a large military unit, especially an army ○ *the French Foreign Legion* **4.** MIL ORGANIZATION OF EX-MILITARY PERSONNEL an association of former members of the armed services ○ *the American Legion* ■ *adj* MANY very numerous ○ *dissatisfied customers and their legion complaints* [12C. Via French < Latin *legion-* < *legere* "choose"]

le·gion·ar·y /léejə nèrree/ *adj* belonging to, associated with, or forming a legion ■ *n* (*plural* **-ies**) a member of a legion, especially a Roman legion

le·gion·ar·y ant *n* INSECTS same as **army ant**

le·gion·naire /lèejə nér/, **Le·gion·naire** *n* **1.** a soldier in a legion, especially the French Foreign Legion **2.** a member of the American Legion [Early 19C. < French *légionnaire* < *légion* (see LEGION)]

le·gion·naires' dis·ease *n* a virulent and sometimes fatal form of pneumonia caused by a bacterium and spread mainly by the water droplets in air conditioning systems [< its first recognized occurrence at an American Legion convention in Philadelphia in 1976]

Le·gion of Hon·or *n* a French order of merit awarded for illustrious military or civil service

Le·gion of Mer·it *n* a US military decoration awarded to military personnel from any country for exceptional and outstanding service

legis. *abbr* LAW, GOV **1.** legislation **2.** legislative **3.** legislature

leg·is·late /léjji slàyt/ (**-lat·ed, -lat·ing, -lates**) *v* **1.** *vi* to write and pass laws **2.** *vt* to make laws or rules designed to bring about an action or condition ○ *The candidates all promise to legislate change.* [Early 18C. Back-formation < LEGISLATOR, LEGISLATION]

leg·is·la·tion /lèjji sláysh'n/ *n* **1.** the process of writing and passing laws **2.** a law or laws passed by an official body, especially a governmental assembly [Mid-17C. < late Latin *legis lation-* "proposing of a law" < forms of *lex* "law" + *latus*, past participle of *ferre* "bring"]

leg·is·la·tive /léjji slàytiv/ *adj* **1.** RELATING TO LAWMAKING involved in the writing and passing of laws **2.** RELATING TO LAWMAKING BODY relating to or being part of a legislature **3.** ENACTED BY LAW created by governmental legislation ○ *There is no legislative solution to this problem.* [Mid-17C. < LEGISLATOR, LEGISLATION] —**leg·is·la·tive·ly** *adv*

leg·is·la·tive as·sem·bly *n* an official body with law- or rule-making powers

Leg·is·la·tive As·sem·bly *n* **1.** US LAWMAKING BODY the two-chamber legislature of some US states **2.** SINGLE-CHAMBER BRITISH COMMONWEALTH LEGISLATURE the single-chamber legislature of most Canadian provinces and some Australian states **3.** LOWER HOUSE OF BRITISH COMMONWEALTH LEGISLATURE the lower house of a two-chamber state legislature in some British Commonwealth countries, especially that of some Australian states

Leg·is·la·tive Coun·cil *n* **1.** *also* **leg·is·la·tive coun·cil** COMMITTEE OF STATE SENATORS AND REPRESENTATIVES a permanent committee consisting of members of both houses of a two-chamber state legislature who discuss issues of common concern and plan legislative programs **2.** UPPER HOUSE OF BRITISH COMMONWEALTH LEGISLATURE the upper house of the two-chamber legislature in some British Commonwealth countries, e.g., in most South Asian and Australian states **3.** LEGISLATURE IN FORMER BRITISH COLONY the single-chamber legislature of some former British colonies

leg·is·la·tor /léjji slàytər/ *n* a writer of or voter on laws, especially as a member of a legislature [15C. < Latin *legis lator* "proposer of a law" < forms of *lex* "law" + *latus*, past participle of *ferre* "bring"]

leg·is·la·ture /léjji slàychər/ *n* LAW, GOV an official body, usually chosen by election, with the power to make, change, and repeal laws [Late 17C. < LEGISLATOR]

le·gist /léejist/ *n* a specialist in law, especially Roman or civil law [15C. < French *légiste* < Latin *leg-* "law"]

le·git /lə jít/ *adj* (*slang*) **1.** same as **legitimate** *adj* (sense 1) **2.** telling the truth and not trying to deceive ○ *Is his story legit?* **3.** THEATER same as **legitimate** *adj* (sense 5) [Late 19C. Shortening of LEGITIMATE]

~~legitamate~~ incorrect spelling of **legitimate**

le·git·i·mate *adj* /lə jíttimət/ **1.** LEGAL complying with the law, or having official status defined by law ○ *legitimate tax deductions* ○ *a legitimate claim to the land* **2.** CONFORMING TO ACKNOWLEDGED STANDARDS complying with recognized rules, standards, or traditions **3.** WELL-FOUNDED well reasoned and sincere ○ *We have legitimate reasons for worrying about the quality of our water.* **4.** BORN IN WEDLOCK born of legally married parents **5.** THEATER RELATING TO SERIOUS PROFESSIONAL DRAMA performing or involving professionally produced dramatic works that are considered to be serious art, in contrast to such forms as burlesque, revues, and musical comedy ■ *vt* /lə jítti màyt/ (**-mat·ed, -mat·ing, -mates**) **1.** LAW LEGALIZE SOMETHING to make somebody or something lawful, by making, changing, or repealing laws or by decree **2.** PROVE SOMETHING TO BE LAWFUL to argue or prove that a claim or action is lawful or reasonable [15C. < medieval Latin *legitimatus*, past participle of *legitimare* "make legal" < Latin *legitimus* "lawful" < *lex* "law"] —**le·git·i·ma·cy** *n* —**le·git·i·mate·ly** *adv* —**le·git·i·ma·tion** /lə jìtti máysh'n/ *n*

SYNONYMS See ***legal.***

le·git·i·ma·tize /lə jíttimə tìz/ (**-tized, -tiz·ing, -tiz·es**) *vt* LAW same as **legitimate** —**le·git·i·ma·ti·za·tion** /lə jìttiməti záysh'n/ *n*

le·git·i·mist /lə jíttimist/ *n* **1.** a believer in monarchy through inheritance or in a specific person's claim to inherit a throne **2.** in the 19th century, a supporter of the Bourbon claimants to the French throne [Mid-19C. < French *légitimiste* < *légitime* "legitimate" < Latin *legitimus* (see LEGITIMATE)] —**le·git·i·mism** *n* —**le·git·i·mist** *adj*

le·git·i·mize /lə jítti mìz/ (**-mized, -miz·ing, -miz·es**) *vt* same as **legitimate** [Mid-19C. < Latin *legitimus* (see LEGITIMATE)] —**le·git·i·mi·za·tion** /lə jìttimi záysh'n/ *n* —**le·git·i·miz·er** *n*

leg·less /légglәss/ *adj* having no legs

leg·man /lég màn, légmən/ (*plural* **-men** /-mèn, -mən/) *n US* **1.** somebody employed in an office to run errands and gather information **2.** a reporter who gathers information for a story, especially from firsthand sources

Leg·o /léggō/ *tdmk* a trademark for a toy consisting of plastic building blocks and other components

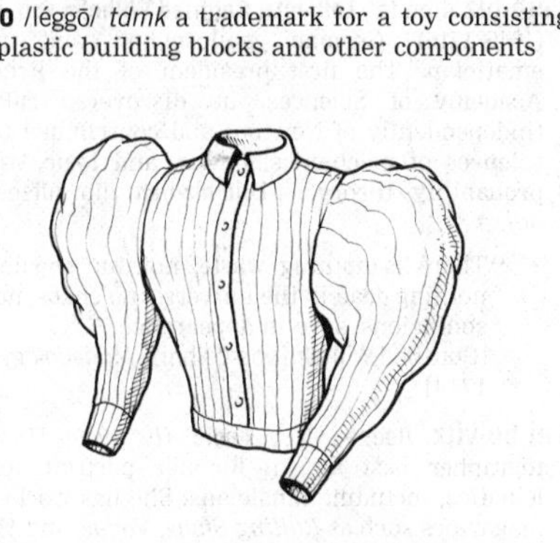

leg-of-mutton sleeve

leg-of-mut·ton, leg-o'-mut·ton *adj* shaped like a sharply tapered triangle ○ *a blouse with leg-of-mutton sleeves*

leg-pull *n UK* an amusing deception or practical joke (*informal*) [< *pull somebody's leg*] —**leg-pull·er** *n* —**leg-pull·ing** *n*

leg·room /lég ro͝om, -ro͝om/ *n* space in front of a seat for somebody's legs, especially enough space to stretch out and move the legs

Le Guin /lə gwín/, **Ursula** (*b.* 1929) US writer. Her science fiction novels include *The Left Hand of Darkness* (1969). Born **Kroeber, Ursula**

> "He had grown up in a country run by politicians who sent the pilots to man the bombers to kill the babies to make the world safe for children to grow up in."
> [Ursula Le Guin, *The Lathe of Heaven*; 1971]

leg·ume /lé gyo͝om, lə gyo͝om/ *n* **1.** a seed, pod, or other part of a plant such as a pea or bean, used as food **2.** a plant that has pods as fruits and roots that bear nodules containing nitrogen-fixing bacteria. Peas and beans are legumes. [Mid-17C. Via French *légume* < Latin *legumen* "bean"]

le·gu·mi·nous /lə gyo͝ominəss/ *adj* **1.** belonging to or typical of the family of plants that has pods as fruits and roots that bear nodules containing nitrogen-fixing bacteria **2.** resembling a legume or a leguminous plant [Mid-17C. < Latin *leguminosus* < *legumin-* stem of *legumen* "bean"]

leg up *n* (*informal*) **1. UPWARD BOOST** help for somebody to get onto something such as a horse or a wall by lifting the person's leg upward or using your linked hands as a support **2. CAREER HELP** help for somebody to move up in a hierarchy or a field of activity **3. POSITION OF SUPERIORITY** an advantage that other people do not have in an activity

leg·warm·er /lég wàwrmər/ *n* a knit tube that covers the calf of the leg and sometimes also the top of the foot, and is typically worn by a dancer during practice (*usually used in the plural*)

leg·work /lég wùrk/ *n* preparatory research for a project that is usually physically demanding or involves a lot of walking (*informal*)

Le Ha·vre /lə haávrə/ city in Seine-Maritime Department, Haute-Normandie Region, northwestern France. Population: 190,905 (1999).

le·ha·yim *n, interj* JUDAISM another spelling of **l'chaim**

Lehr·er /lérrər/, **Tom** (*b.* 1928) US teacher and songwriter. A university professor, he became a successful entertainer in the 1960s with his humorous songs, many of them political satires. Full name **Lehrer, Thomas Andrew**

> "Life is like a sewer. What you get out of it depends on what you put into it."
> [Tom Lehrer, *We Will All Go Together When We Go*; 1953]

le·hu·a /lay hoó ə/ (*plural* **-as**) *n* TREES, PLANTS a common evergreen bush. Flowers: large, red. Native to: Pacific Islands. Latin name: *Metosideros collinus*. [Late 19C. < Hawaiian]

lei[1] /lay, láy ee/ (*plural* **leis**) *n* a garland of flowers, especially one worn around the neck in Hawaii and other parts of Polynesia [Mid-19C. < Hawaiian]

lei[2] /lay/ MONEY plural of **leu**

Leib·niz /líbnits/, **Leib·nitz, Gottfried Wilhelm von, Baron** (1646–1716) German philosopher and mathematician. The first president of the Prussian Academy of Sciences, he discovered calculus (independently of Newton) and contributed to the sciences of mechanics, optics, and logic, and to probability theory. —**Leib·niz·i·an** /līb nítsee ən/ *adj, n*

> "There is nothing waste, nothing sterile, nothing dead in the universe; no chaos, no confusions, save in appearance."
> [Gottfried Wilhelm von Leibniz, *Monadology*; 1714]

Lei·bo·vitz /leébə vìtz/, **Annie** (*b.* 1949) US photographer best known for her portraits of celebrities, including musicians. She has worked for magazines such as *Rolling Stone*, *Vogue*, and *Vanity Fair*. Born **Leibovitz, Anna-Lou**

Leices·ter /léstər/ industrial city in Leicestershire, central England. Population: 279,921 (2001).

Leices·ter, Robert Dudley, 1st Earl of (1532–88) English courtier. A favorite adviser to and unsuccessful suitor of Queen Elizabeth I, he helped involve England in the Protestant struggle against Philip II of Spain.

Leices·ter·shire /léstər sheer, -shər/ county in central England. Population: 609,578 (2001). Area: 986 sq. mi./2,553 sq. km.

Lei·den /líd'n/, **Ley·den** university city in Zuid-Holland Province, western Netherlands. Population: 117,196 (2000).

Leigh /lee/, **Mike** (*b.* 1943) British playwright and movie director. His plays and films, including *Abigail's Party* (1977) and *Secrets and Lies* (1996), are developed with the actors in improvisation.

Vivien Leigh

Leigh, Vivien (1913–67) British actor. She won Academy Awards for her performances in *Gone with the Wind* (1939) and *A Streetcar Named Desire* (1951).

> "In Britain, an attractive woman is somehow suspect. If there is talent as well it is overshadowed. Beauty and brains just can't be entertained; someone has been too extravagant."
> [Vivien Leigh, *Light of a Star*; 1967]

Lein·ster /lénstər/ historic province in the eastern Republic of Ireland

Leip·zig /lípsig/ city and cultural and university center in east central Germany, known for its international trade fairs. Population: 481,526 (1997).

leish·man·i·a·sis /leeshmə nī əssiss/ *n* an infection such as kala-azar and some other skin diseases caused by a protozoan that is a parasite in the tissue of vertebrates [Early 20C. < modern Latin *Leishmania*, after Sir William Boog *Leishman* (1865–1926), Scottish pathologist]

leis·ter /leéstər/ *n* a stick with three prongs, used for spearing fish ■ *vt* (**-tered, -ter·ing, -ters**) to catch fish using a three-pronged spear [Mid-16C. < Old Norse *ljóstr* < *ljósta* "to strike"]

lei·sure /leézhər, lézhər/ *n* time during which somebody has no obligations or work responsibilities, and therefore is free to engage in enjoyable activities [13C. < Anglo-Norman *leisour* < Old French *leisir* "be permitted" < Latin *licere*] ◇ **at your leisure** at the time and pace that suits you ◇ **gentleman** *or* **lady** *or* **man** *or* **woman of leisure** a man or woman who does not have to work for a living (*humorous*)

lei·sured /leézhərd, lézhərd/ *adj* **1.** having a lot of free time, especially as a result of not having to work for a living **2.** same as **leisurely**

lei·sure·ly /leézhərlee, lézh-/ *adj* relaxed, unhurried, and enjoyable, e.g., because done during free time ○ *a leisurely stroll in the park* ■ *adv* in a slow and relaxed manner —**lei·sure·li·ness** *n*

lei·sure so·ci·e·ty *n* a society in which a greater proportion of people's time is spent in leisure than in work

lei·sure suit *n* a man's casual outfit, usually made of synthetic double-knit fabric, consisting of a jacket styled like a shirt and matching pants, first popular in the 1970s

lei·sure vi·si·tor *n* same as **tourist**

lei·sure·wear /leézhər wèr, lézhər-/ *n* comfortable informal clothing such as a sweat suit, appropriate for relaxation or play

Leith /leeth/ seaport of Edinburgh, Scotland, situated on the Firth of Forth

leit·mo·tif /līt mō teéf, līt mō teéf/, **leit·mo·tiv** *n* **1.** a musical theme that recurs in the course of a work to evoke a particular character or situation. Leitmotifs are typical of the operas of Richard Wagner. **2.** a recurring theme, e.g., in literature or history [Late 19C. < German < *leiten* "to lead" + *Motiv* "motif"]

Lei·trim /leétrim/ county in Connacht Province, northern Republic of Ireland. The county town is Carrick-on-Shannon. Population: 25,000 (1996). Area: 589 sq. mi./1,525 sq. km.

~~**leiu**~~ incorrect spelling of **lieu**

Leix /layks/ ➧ **Laois**

Lei·zhou Pen·in·su·la /lày jō-/ peninsula in Guangdong Province, southeastern China, stretching from Guangdong Bay in the east to the Gulf of Tonkin in the west

lek[1] /lek/ *n* the basic currency unit of Albania. See table at **currency** [Early 20C. < Albanian, after *Lek* Dukagjin, Albanian lawyer]

lek[2] /lek/ *n* an area used for the performance of communal breeding displays and courtship during the mating season by birds such as the black grouse or other animals [Late 19C. Origin ?]

lek·var /lék vaar/ *n* a sweet spread made of prunes or apricots, often used as pastry filling [Mid-20C. Via Hungarian *lekvár* < late Latin *electuarium* "electuary"]

LEM /lem/ *abbr* AEROSP lunar excursion module

Le·maî·tre /lə méttrə/, **Georges-Henri** (1894–1966) Belgian astrophysicist and priest. He was a proponent of the big bang theory of the universe.

lem·an /lémmən, leémən/ (*plural* **-ans**) *n* somebody loved, e.g., a sweetheart or lover (*archaic*) [12C. Contracted < LIEF + MAN]

Le Mans /lə maán, lə maáN/ capital of Sarthe Department, Pays de la Loire Region, northern France. Population: 146,105 (1999).

Le·May /lə máy/, **Léon-Pamphile** (1837–1918) Canadian writer. Some of his French-language poetry was collected in *Les Vengeances* (1875). His novels include *L'Affaire Sougraine* (1884).

lem·ma[1] /lémmə/ (*plural* **-mas** or **-ma·ta** /-mətə/) *n* **1.** LOGIC **ASSUMPTION FOR SAKE OF ARGUMENT** a proposition that is assumed to be true in order to test the validity of another proposition **2.** PUBL **SUBJECT HEADING** a heading that indicates the topic of a work or passage **3.** LING **GLOSSARY WORD** a term that is defined in a glossary [Late 16C. Via Latin < Greek *lēmma* "something taken (for granted)"]

lem·ma[2] /lémmə/ *n* the lower of two dry membranous leaves (**bracts**) protecting a single flower in a flower head of a plant of the grass family [Mid-18C. < Greek, "husk" < past participle of *lepein* "peel"]

lem·ma·ta LOGIC, PUBL, LING plural of **lemma**[1]

lem·me /lémmee/ *contr* let me (*nonstandard*)

lemming

lem·ming /lémming/ *n* **1.** a rodent with a small thick furry body and furry feet that lives in subarctic regions. Lemmings are noted for their mass migrations in search of food during population explosions, which has given rise to the myth that they flock to the sea to drown themselves. Native to: Arctic and northern regions. Genus: *Lemmus* or *Dicrostonyx*. **2.** a member of a large group of people who blindly follow one another on a course of action that will lead to destruction for all of them [Early 18C. < Norwegian]

Lem·mon /lémmən/, **Jack** (1925–2001) US actor. His many movies include the Academy Award-winning *Mister Roberts* (1955) and *Some Like It Hot* (1959). Full name **Lemmon, John Uhler III**

lem·nis·cus /lem nískəss/ (*plural* **-ci** /lem ní sī, -kī, -kee/) *n* a bundle of fibers, especially a bundle of nerve fibers [Mid-19C. Via Latin < Greek *lēmniskos* "ribbon"]

Lem·nos /lém noss/ island in eastern Greece, in the Aegean Sea, near the Dardanelles. Population: 15,721 (1981).

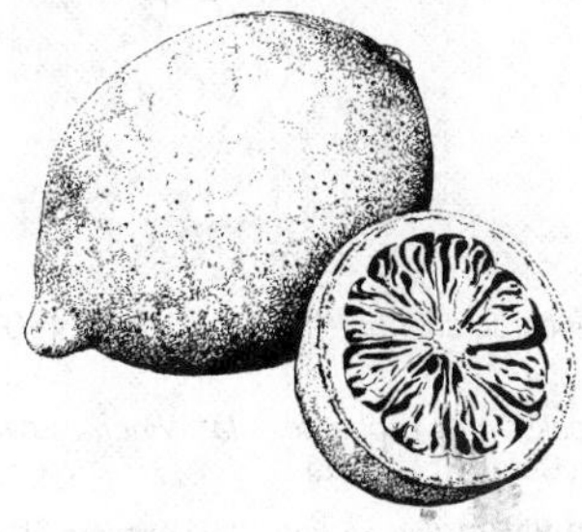

lemon

lem·on /lémmən/ *n* **1. YELLOW OR GREEN CITRUS FRUIT** a yellow or, in some climates, green oval citrus fruit with a thick fragrant rind and sour juicy flesh **2. TREE THAT BEARS LEMONS** a tree with glossy leaves and spiky branches that is widely cultivated to produce lemons. Native to: southeastern Asia. Latin name: *Citrus limon.* **3. PALE YELLOW COLOR** a pale yellow color typical of the rind of a lemon **4. DEFECTIVE PRODUCT** something that is defective or disappointing, especially a car that does not run properly (*informal*) [14C. Via French < Arabic *līmūn*] —**lem·on** *adj* —**lem·on·y** *adj*

lem·on·ade /lémmə nàyd/ *n* **1.** an uncarbonated soft drink made from fresh lemons, sugar, and water **2.** a drink of lemonade ○ *ordered a lemonade and two coffees*

lem·on·ade ber·ry *n* an evergreen bush with leathery leaves, clusters of small pink flowers, and acidic dark red fruits that are used in flavoring drinks. Native to: California. Latin name: *Rhus integrifolia.*

lem·on balm *n* a widely cultivated plant of the mint family that has lemon-scented leaves. Flowers: small, white or pinkish. Native to: southern Europe.

lem·on-bel·ly, lem·on crab *n regional* a Chesapeake Bay female blue crab with a yellow underside

REGIONAL NOTE The term ***lemon-belly*** is used in coastal areas of Maryland and Virginia.

lem·on curd *n* a thick sweet creamy yellow spread made from lemons, sugar, eggs, and butter and usually eaten on bread

lem·on drop *n* a lemon-flavored piece of hard candy

lem·on·grass /lémmən gràss/ *n* a tropical grass cultivated for a lemon-scented oil distilled from its leaves, and for use as a flavoring in cooking. Native to: southern India. Latin name: *Cymbopogon citratus.*

lem·on law *n* a law that requires a seller or manufacturer of a faulty motor vehicle either to replace or repair it or to refund the buyer's money (*informal*)

lem·on sole *n* **1.** a common flatfish, prized as a food fish. Native to: northeastern Atlantic, North Sea. Latin name: *Microstomus kitt.* **2.** the flesh of a lemon sole used as food

lem·on-squeez·er *n UK* same as **reamer** (sense 2)

lem·on ver·be·na, lem·on ver·vain *n* a widely cultivated bush with leaves that produce a fragrance resembling lemons when crushed. Flowers: small, lavender. Native to: South America. Latin name: *Lippia triphylla.*

lem·on yel·low *n* COLORS same as **lemon** (sense 3) —**lem·on-yel·low** *adj*

le Moyne /lə mwáN/, **Charles, Sieur de Longueuil and de Châteauguay** (1626–85) French-born Canadian colonist. The father of General Charles le Moyne, he settled in Canada in 1641 and worked among the Native North Americans.

le Moyne, Charles, Baron de Longueuil (1656–1729) Canadian soldier and colonial official. The son of the colonist Charles le Moyne, he was commandant-general of Canada (1711) and governor of Montreal (1724–29).

lem·pi·ra /lem péerə/ *n* the main unit of Honduran currency. See table at **currency** [Mid-20C. After *Lempira*, 16C chieftain who fought against the Spanish conquerors of Honduras]

lemur

le·mur /léemər/ *n* a primate with a long snout, large ears, and a long tail. Native to: Madagascar and nearby islands. Family: Lemuridae. [Late 18C. Via modern Latin < Latin *lemures* "the spirits of the dead"; because it is nocturnal]

lem·u·res /lémmyə rèez, lémmə ràyss/ *npl* in ancient Rome, the spirits of the dead (*literary*) [Mid-16C. < Latin]

Le·na /léenə/ river in Siberian Russia that rises in southern Siberia and flows northward before emptying into the Laptev Sea, an arm of the Arctic Ocean. Length: 2,700 mi./4,400 km.

Len·a·pe /lénnəpee/ *n* PEOPLES same as **Delaware** [1] [Early 18C. < Algonquian, "people"] —**Len·a·pe** *adj*

lend /lend/ (**lent** /lent/, **lend·ing, lends**) *v* **1.** *vt* **LET SOMEBODY BORROW SOMETHING** to allow somebody to take or use something on the understanding that it will be returned later **2.** *vti* **GIVE SOMEBODY MONEY FOR LIMITED TIME** to allow a person or business to use a sum of money for a particular period of time, usually on condition that a charge (**interest**) is paid in return **3.** *vt* **ADD SOMETHING** to give a particular quality or character to something ○ *The candles lend an air of intimacy to the room.* [Old English *lǣnan* < Germanic] —**lend·able** *adj* —**lend·er** *n* ◇ **lend itself to something** to be suitable for a particular purpose or occasion

USAGE See ***borrow.***

lend·ing li·brar·y /lénding-/ *n* a library or department of a library where the public can borrow books and often audio tapes, videotapes, CDs, and DVDs

Len·dl /lénd'l/, **Ivan** (*b.* 1960) Czechoslovakian-born US tennis player. Between 1981 and 1987 he won many international tournaments, including the French Open, the US Open and the Grand Prix Masters.

le·nes PHON plural of **lenis**

L'En·gle /léng'l/, **Madeleine** (*b.* 1918) US author. *A Wrinkle in Time* (1962), her novel for young readers, won the Newbery Medal (1963). Born **Camp, Madeleine L'Engle**

Popperfoto

Suzanne Lenglen: photographed playing at Wimbledon (1922)

Len·glen /léng glən, laaN glaán/, **Suzanne** (1899–1938) French tennis player. The women's champion of France for several years (1920–23, 1925–26) and Olympic champion (1920), she also won six Wimbledon singles titles.

length /length/ *n* **1. DISTANCE FROM END TO END** the distance along something from end to end, or a measurement taken of this distance ○ *The length of the garden is 25 yards.* **2. QUALITY OF BEING LONG** the condition or state of being long ○ *The garden is designed to give a sense of length and openness.* **3. HOW LONG SOMETHING TAKES** the time something lasts or takes from beginning to end ○ *The length of the second act is about 75 minutes.* **4. SIZE FROM BEGINNING TO END** the extent of something from beginning to end ○ *The second volume is a massive 400 pages in length.* **5. LONG PIECE OF SOMETHING** a piece of something long and narrow ○ *a length of copper piping* **6. UNIT OF MEASUREMENT** a piece of something such as cloth that is measured or bought in units of a standard size ○ *bought three lengths of fabric* **7.** SWIMMING **END TO END IN SWIMMING POOL** the distance from one end of a swimming pool to the other **8.** FASHION **HOW LONG GARMENT IS** how high the hem of a coat, skirt, or dress is above the ground or below the wearer's waist, or how much of the wearer's legs it shows **9.** SPORTS **WINNING DISTANCE** in something such as a boat race or horse race, the distance between two competitors, measured according to how long a single boat or horse is ○ *two lengths ahead with only 100 yards to go* **10.** PHON **HOW LONG SOUND TAKES TO MAKE** the amount of time required to articulate a vowel or syllable [Old English *lengþ* < Germanic] ◇ **at length 1.** in great detail and for a long time **2.** after some time or following a delay

-length *suffix* extending all the way to a particular part of something ○ *shoulder-length hair*

length·en /léngthən/ (**-ened, -en·ing, -ens**) *vti* to make something longer, or become longer ○ *The weeks lengthened into months and still no news came.* —**length·en·er** *n*

length·wise /léngth wìz/, **length·ways** /-wàyz/ *adv, adj* in relation to something's length from end to end ○ *attempting to force the suitcase into the trunk lengthwise*

length·y /léngthee/ (**-i·er, -i·est**) *adj* lasting for a long time, especially for an excessively long time —**length·i·ly** *adv* —**length·i·ness** *n*

le·ni·ent /léenee ənt/ *adj* showing tolerance or mercy in dealing with crime or misbehavior [Mid-17C. < Latin *lenient-*, present participle of *lenire* "soothe" < *lenis* "smooth"] —**le·ni·en·cy** *n* —**le·ni·ent·ly** *adv*

AKG London

Vladimir Ilyich Lenin

Le·nin /lénnin/, **Vladimir Ilyich** (1870–1924) Russian revolutionary leader. Founder of the Soviet Union, he led the Bolshevik revolution in 1917. He was the first leader of the Soviet Communist regime, but became less active after suffering a stroke in 1922. Born **Ulyanov, Vladimir Ilyich**

> "Under capitalism we have a state in the proper sense of the word, that is, a special machine for the suppression of one class by another."
> [Vladimir Ilyich Lenin, *The State and Revolution*; 1919]

Le·nin·a·khan /lènninə kaán/ former name for **Gyumri** (1924–90)

Len·in·grad /lénnin gràd/ former name for **St. Petersburg** (1924–90)

Len·in·ism /lénnə nìzzəm/ *n* the political, social, and economic theories of Lenin, which he developed from Marxist theory —**Len·in·ist** *n, adj* —**Len·in·ite** *n, adj*

Len·in Peak /lénnin-/ mountain in the Trans-Alai Range of the Pamirs, situated in Tajikistan. Height: 23,406 ft./7,134 m. Former name **Kaufman, Mount**

le·nis /leénəss, láy-/ *adj* describes a consonant produced using little breath and muscle power ■ *n* (*plural* **-nes** /-neez/) a consonant that is produced using little breath and muscle power [Early 20C. < Latin, "smooth"]

le·ni·tion /lə nísh'n/ *n* the use of little breath and muscle power when articulating consonants [Early 20C. < Latin *lenit-*, stem of *lenis* "smooth"]

Len·non /lénnən/, **John** (1940–80) British singer, songwriter, and musician. A member of the Beatles, he had a songwriting partnership with Paul McCartney that revolutionized popular music. His most distinctive solo recording was "Imagine" (1971). He was murdered in 1980. Full name **Lennon, John Winston**

> "Imagine there's no heaven / It's easy if you try / No hell below us / Above us only sky / Imagine all the people / Living for today."
> [John Lennon, "Imagine"; 1971]

le·no /leénō/ *n* **1.** an open weave created in textiles by twisting together pairs of warp threads to lock the weft threads in place **2.** a fabric made using a leno weave [Late 18C. < French *linon* < *lin* "flax" < Latin *linum*]

Le·no /lénnō/, **Jay** (*b.* 1950) US comedian and television host. Host of the television show *The Tonight Show* since Johnny Carson retired in 1992, he is known for his low-key, personable style. Full name **Leno, James Douglas Muir**

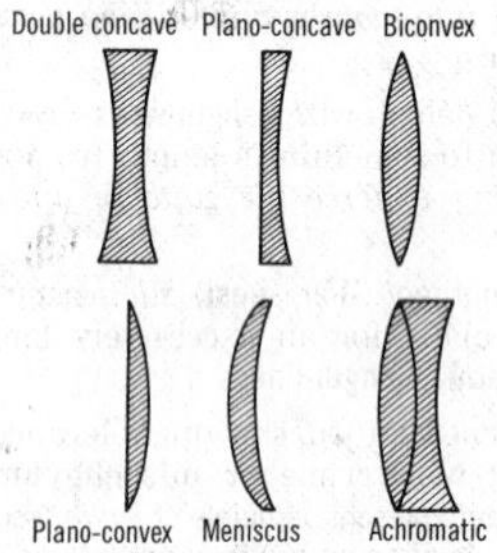

lens: cross sections of different lenses

lens /lenz/ *n* **1.** OPTICS **TRANSPARENT PIECE OF GLASS FOR FOCUSING** a piece of curved and polished glass or other transparent material that forms an image by refracting and focusing light passing through it **2.** OPTICS **SYSTEM OF LENSES** a system of two or more lenses that is used in an optical instrument such as a telescope or camera **3.** OPHTHALMOL same as **contact lens 4.** ANAT **LIGHT-FOCUSING PART OF EYE** the part of the eye that focuses light to produce an image on the light-sensitive cells of the retina. It is nearly spherical and convex on both sides, and sits behind the pupil. **5.** PHYS **BEAM-FOCUSING DEVICE** a device that focuses a beam of electrons or radiation other than light ■ *vt* (**lensed, lens·ing, lens·es**) MOVIES **FILM SOMETHING** to record a motion picture on film [Late 17C. < Latin, "lentil"; from its shape]

lens·ing /lénzīng/ *n* the bending of light as it passes through the gravitational field of a large astronomical object such as a galaxy

lent past participle, past tense of **lend**

Lent /lent/ *n* the period of 40 weekdays before Easter observed in some Christian churches as a period of prayer, penance, fasting, and self-denial. This period, starting on Ash Wednesday in Western churches, commemorates the 40 days that Jesus Christ spent fasting in the wilderness. [13C. Shortening of LENTEN]

Lent·en /léntən/, **lent·en** *adj* happening in or suitable for Lent, especially in being meager [Old English *lencten* "spring" < Germanic]

~~**lenth**~~ incorrect spelling of **length**

len·tic /léntik/ *adj* relating to or inhabiting still or slow-moving water [Mid-20C. < Latin *lentus* "slow"]

len·ti·cel /lénti sèl/ *n* a pore in the outer layer of a woody plant stem, through which gases pass from inside the stem to the atmosphere, or vice versa [Mid-19C. < modern Latin *lenticella*, literally "little lentil" < Latin *lens* "lentil"] —**len·ti·cel·late** /lènti séllət/ *adj*

len·tic·u·lar /len tíkyələr/ *adj* **1.** relating to a lens or lenses **2.** shaped like a biconvex lens in having two convex faces [15C. < Latin *lenticularis* < *lenticula* (see LENTIL)]

len·til /lént'l/ *n* **1.** an edible seed that is lens-shaped, brown, gray, green, or black on the outside and yellow or orange inside, and rich in protein **2.** a plant of the pea family grown to produce lentils. Native to: Mediterranean, western Asia. Latin name: *Lens culinaris*. [14C. Via French *lentille* < Latin *lenticula* "little lentil" < *lens* "lentil"]

len·tisk /lén tìsk/ *n* TREES same as **mastic tree** [14C. < Latin *lentiscus*]

len·tis·si·mo /len tíssə mō, -teéssə-/ *adv* very slowly (*used as a musical direction*) [Early 20C. < Italian, superlative of *lento* "slow"] —**len·tis·si·mo** *adj*

len·ti·vi·rus /léntə vìrəss/ *n* a retrovirus causing illness that characteristically does not produce symptoms until some time after infection [Late 20C. < Latin *lentus* "slow"]

len·to /léntō/ *adv* at a slow tempo (*used as a musical direction*) ■ *n* (*plural* **-tos**) a piece of music, or a section of a piece, to be played lento [Early 18C. Via Italian < Latin *lentus* "slow"] —**len·to** *adj*

Len·ya /lénnyə/, **Lotte** (1898–1981) Austrian actor and cabaret singer. She played a leading role in several works by her husband Kurt Weill, including *The Threepenny Opera* (1928). Born **Blamauer, Karoline Wilhelmine Charlotte**

Le·o /leé ō/ (*plural* **-os**) *n* **1.** **CONSTELLATION IN N HEMISPHERE** a zodiacal constellation of the northern hemisphere between Cancer and Virgo. See illustration at **constellation 2.** **5TH SIGN OF ZODIAC** the fifth sign of the zodiac, represented by the lion and lasting from approximately July 23 to August 22. Leo is classified as a fire sign and is ruled by the sun. **3.** **SOMEBODY BORN UNDER LEO** somebody whose birthday falls between July 23 and August 22 [Pre-12C. < Latin, "lion"] —**Le·o** *adj* —**Le·on·i·an** /lee ṓnee ən/ *n*

Le·o I /leé ō/, **St.** (400?–461) pope. He summoned the Council of Chalcedon in 451 and was proclaimed a doctor of the church in 1574. Known as **Leo the Great**

Le·o III, Emperor (680?–741) Byzantine monarch. He revitalized the Byzantine Empire, founded the Isaurian dynasty, and issued a legal code, the *Ecloga*.

Le·o IX, St. (1002–54) pope. During his reforming reign (1049–54), papal authority was strengthened, and this led to the Great Schism of 1054. Born **Bruno of Egisheim**

Le·o X, Pope (1475–1521) An important patron of the arts, as pope (1513–21) he initiated the rebuilding of St. Peter's Basilica, Rome. Born **de' Medici, Giovanni**

Le·o XIII, Pope (1810–1903) During his papacy (1878–1903), he upheld the authority of the church and promoted learning. His encyclical of 1896 declared Episcopalian orders invalid. Born **Pecci, Vincenzo Gioacchino**

Le·o Mi·nor *n* a small inconspicuous constellation of the northern hemisphere between Ursa Major and Leo. See illustration at **constellation**

Leom·in·ster /lémminstər/ city in central Massachusetts, southeast of Fitchburg and north of Worcester. Population: 41,895 (2002 estimate).

Le·ón /lay ṓn/ **1.** city and capital of León Province, in the Castile-León autonomous region of northwestern Spain. Population: 128,576 (2002). **2.** industrial city in central Mexico, founded in 1576. Population: 109,872 (2000).

Le·o·nard /lénnərd/, **Sugar Ray** (*b.* 1956) US boxer. He won various boxing titles in five different weight categories, mainly in the 1980s. Born **Leonard, Ray Charles**

Le·o·nar·do da Vin·ci /leé ə naárdō də vínchee/ (1452–1519) Italian painter, sculptor, architect, engineer, and scientist. One of the great masters of the High Renaissance, he painted the *Mona Lisa* (1503–06) and *The Last Supper* (1495–97). Many of his scientific observations and inventions, particularly in anatomy, optics, and hydraulics, were centuries ahead of their time.

> "A bird is an instrument working according to a mathematical law, which instrument it is within the capacity of man to reproduce, with all its movements."
> [Leonardo da Vinci. Quoted in *The Notebooks of Leonardo da Vinci*, Edward McCurdy (tr.); 1928]

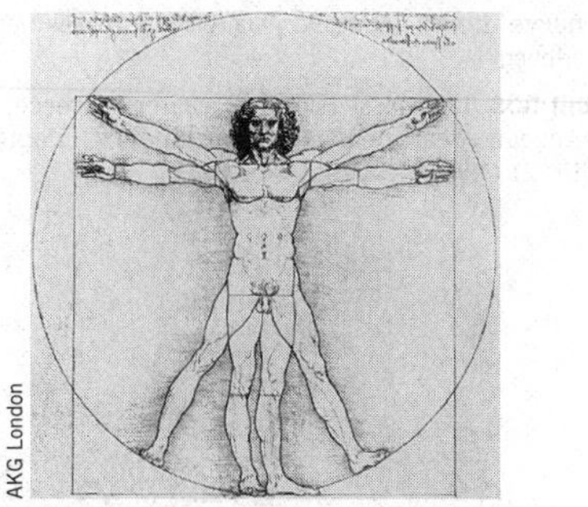

AKG London

Leonardo da Vinci: Vitruvian Man (1490?)

Le·on·ca·val·lo /lày on kə vállō/, **Ruggero** (1858–1919) Italian composer. An exponent of the verismo style in opera, he composed *I Pagliacci* (1892).

le·one /lee ṓn/ *n* the main unit of Sierra Leonean currency. See table at **currency** [Mid-20C. < Sierra *Leone*]

Le·on·i·das /lee ónnədəss/ (*d.* 480 B.C.) king of Sparta. He withstood the Persian army of Xerxes I at the battle of Thermopylae in 480 B.C.

le·o·nine /leé ə nīn/ *adj* relating to or characteristic of a lion, e.g., in strength or appearance [14C. Directly or via French < Latin *leoninus* < *leo* "lion"]

Le·on·ti·ef /lee ón tee èf/, **Wassily** (1906–99) Russian-born US economist. He received the Nobel Prize in economics (1973) for his development of the input-output economic theory.

leopard

leop·ard /léppərd/ *n* **1.** a large slender member of the cat family with a yellowish brown to orange red coat spotted with black rosettes. Native to: Africa, Asia. Latin name: *Panthera pardus*. **2.** in heraldry, an image of a lion viewed from the side facing left, with its head turned toward the viewer and one front leg raised [13C. Via French < late Greek *leopardos* < Greek *leōn* "lion" + *pardos* "big cat" (see PARD[1])]

CULTURAL NOTE ***The Leopard***, a novel (1958) by Italian writer Giuseppe Tomasi di Lampedusa. Set in late 19th-century Sicily, it describes the social and political changes resulting from the unification of Italy from the point of view of a local nobleman, Prince Salina. In addition to its political and historical insights, the novel is admired for its evocative descriptions of the Sicilian landscape and its moving and poetic meditations on mortality.

leop·ard·ess /léppərdəss/ *n* a female leopard, usually an adult one

leop·ard lil·y *n* an ornamental flowering plant. Flowers: orange red with black-speckled petals. Native to: southwestern United States. Latin name: *Lilium pardalinum*.

leop·ard moth *n* a large white moth with black spots whose caterpillars bore into trees, causing damage, and may be considered a pest. Native to: Europe, Asia, North Africa, North America. Latin name: *Zeuzera pyrina*.

leop·ard's bane *n* a plant with clusters of yellow flowers resembling daisies on long stalks. Native to: Europe, Asia. Genus: *Doronicum*.

leop·ard seal *n* a seal with a spotted dark gray back

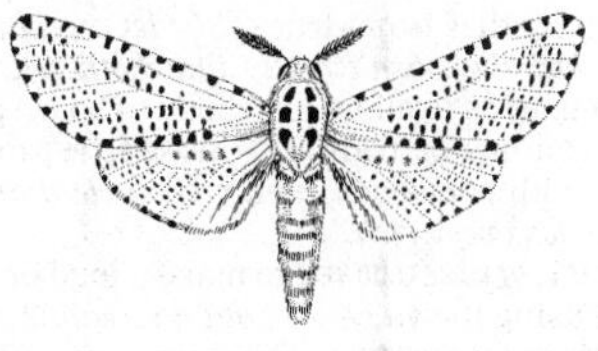

leopard moth

and paler belly that lives as a solitary hunter, feeding mainly on penguins. Native to: Antarctic waters. Latin name: *Hydrurga leptonyx*.

Le·o·pold I /lée ə pōld/, **Holy Roman Emperor, king of Bohemia, and king of Hungary** (1640–1705) As Holy Roman Emperor (1658–1705), king of Bohemia (1656–1705), and king of Hungary (1655–87) he led wars against France and the Ottoman Turks, and made efforts to extend Hapsburg territory

Le·o·pold II, Grand Duke of Tuscany and Holy Roman Emperor (1747–92) While Holy Roman Emperor (1790–92) he formed an alliance with Prussia against France to aid Marie Antoinette, his sister, during the French Revolution

Le·o·pold II (1835–1909) king of Belgium. During his reign (1865–1909), Belgium annexed the Congo Free State, which later became the Belgian Congo and is now the Democratic Republic of the Congo.

Le·o·pold III (1901–83) king of Belgium. He became king in 1934, but went into exile after the invasion by Germany during World War II. He abdicated in 1951.

Lé·o·pold·ville /lée ə pōld vìl/ former name for **Kinshasa**

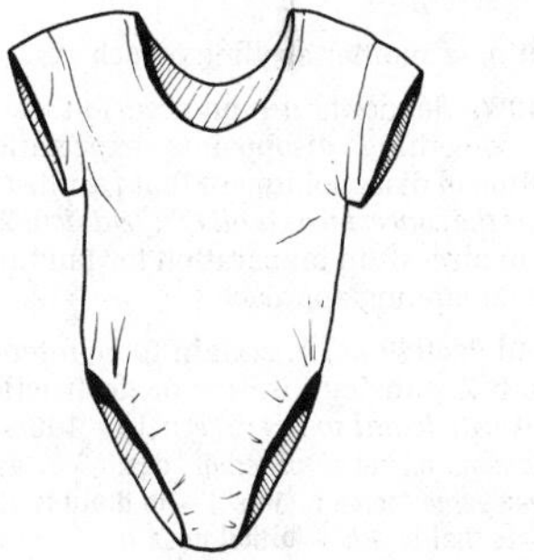

leotard

le·o·tard /lée ə taàrd/ *n* a tight-fitting one-piece elastic garment that covers the torso and is worn especially by dancers, gymnasts, and acrobats ■ **le·o·tards** *npl* a one-piece, close-fitting garment, covering the body from the neck or waist to the feet, worn by male and female dancers [Late 19C. After Jules *Léotard* (1830–70), French trapeze artist]

Le·pau·tre /lə pṓtrə/, **Pierre** (1648–1716) French interior designer. His decoration of the French royal house at Marly for Louis XV featured the arabesques and elegant curved designs that became the hallmarks of the rococo style.

Lep·cha /lépchə/ (*plural* **-chas** or *same*) *n* **1.** a member of a people who live in the northeastern Indian state of Sikkim **2.** a Tibeto-Burman language spoken in the northeastern Indian state of Sikkim. Native speakers: 65,000. [Early 19C. < Nepali *lāpche*] —**Lep·cha** *adj*

lep·er /léppər/ *n* **1.** somebody affected with leprosy **2.** somebody who is shunned by the rest of society [14C. < obsolete *leper* "leprosy," via French < late Latin *lepra* < Greek *lepros* (see LEPROUS)]

lepido- *prefix* flake, scale ○ *lepidolite* [< Greek *lepid-*]

le·pid·o·lite /lə pídd'l ìt/ *n* a mica ranging in color from pinkish purple to gray. Use: an ore of lithium.

lep·i·dop·ter·an /lèppi dóptərən/ *n* a butterfly or moth. Lepidopterans have four wings covered in tiny overlapping scales, and sucking mouthparts. Their larvae are caterpillars. Order: Lepidoptera. [Mid-19C. < modern Latin *Lepidoptera* < Greek *lepid-* "scale" + *pteron* "wing"]

lep·i·dop·ter·ist /lèppi dóptərist/ *n* an expert in or student of butterflies and moths

lep·i·do·si·ren /lèppidō sírən/ *n* an eel-shaped freshwater fish that can breathe air using a pair of lungs that it has in addition to its gills. It spends the dry season lying dormant in a burrow. Native to: South America. Latin name: *Lepidosiren paradoxa*.

lep·i·dote /léppi dōt/ *adj* covered in small scaly leaves [Mid-19C. Via modern Latin < Greek *lepidōtos* < *lepid-* "scale"]

lep·re·chaun /lépprə kàwn/ *n* in Irish folklore, a small man with magical powers, often dressed in green, who works as a shoemaker and is believed to know where treasure is hidden [Early 17C. < Irish *leipreachán* "small body"] —**lep·re·chau·nish** *adj*

lep·ro·sar·i·um /lèpprə sérree əm/ (*plural* **-i·ums** or **-i·a** /-ee ə/) *n* a hospital for the treatment of patients with leprosy [Mid-19C. < late Latin *leprosus* (see LEPROUS)]

lep·rose /lép rōss/ *adj* MED same as **leprous** (sense 2) [Mid-19C. < late Latin *leprosus* or its source *lepra* (see LEPER)]

lep·ro·sy /lépprəssee/ *n* a tropical disease mainly affecting the skin and nerves that can cause tissue change and, in severe cases, loss of sensation and disfigurement. Leprosy is transmitted following close personal contact and has an incubation period of 1–30 years. It can now be cured if treated with a combination of drugs. [Mid-16C. < LEPROUS] —**lep·rot·ic** /lə próttik/ *adj*

lep·rous /lépprəss/ *adj* **1.** having or relating to leprosy **2.** resembling the physical symptoms of leprosy, especially in being pale or scaly ○ *a leprous white deposit spreading across the cellar walls* [12C. Via French < late Latin *leprosus* < Greek *lepros* "scaly" < *lepos* "scale"; from the white scales that form on the skin]

-lepsy *suffix* seizure ○ *narcolepsy* [Via modern Latin *-lepsia* < Greek *lēpsis* < *lēp-*, stem of *lambanein* "seize"]

lept- *prefix* same as **lepto-** (*used before vowels*)

lep·tin /léptin/ *n* a hormone produced by fat cells that indicates the degree of hunger to the hypothalamus of the brain

lepto- *prefix* thin, slender ○ *leptosome* [< Greek *leptos*, past participle of *lepein* "peel"]

lep·to·ceph·a·lus /lèptō séffələss/ (*plural* **-li** /-lì/) *n* the larva of some bony fishes such as the eel, the appearance of which is markedly different from that of the adult fish [Mid-18C. < modern Latin < Greek *leptos* "small" + *kephalē* "head"]

lep·ton /lép tòn/ *n* a fundamental subatomic particle that interacts only weakly with other particles, e.g., the electron, muon, neutrino, and their antiparticles [Mid-20C. < Greek *leptos* "small"] —**lep·ton·ic** /lep tónnik/ *adj*

lep·to·spi·ro·sis /lèptə spī rṓssiss/ *n* an infectious disease occurring in human beings and domestic animals and affecting the kidneys and liver, caused by spiral-shaped bacteria **(spirochetes)** of the genus *Leptospira*. In human beings a significant form of the disease is Weil's disease. [Early 20C. < modern Latin *Leptospira*, literally "small coil"]

Le·pus /léepəss/ *n* a small constellation of the southern hemisphere located directly south of Orion. See illustration at **constellation**

Lé·ri·da /láyridə/ capital of Lérida Province in the autonomous region of Catalonia, northeastern Spain. Population: 112,199 (2001).

Ler·mon·tov /lúrmən tàwf/, **Mikhail Yuryevich** (1814–41) Russian poet and novelist. His works include *A Hero of our Time* (1840) and *The Circassian Boy* (1840).

Ler·ner /lúrnər/, **Alan Jay** (1918–86) US playwright and lyricist. He collaborated with Frederick Loewe on several musicals, including *My Fair Lady* (1956) and *Camelot* (1960).

> "You write a hit the same way you write a flop."
> [Attributed to Alan Jay Lerner]

Ler·wick /lúrwik/ seaport and largest town of the Shetland Islands, northeastern Scotland, on Mainland Island. Population: 7,336 (1991).

Le·sage /lə saázh/, **Jean** (1912–80) Canadian lawyer and politician. He was prime minister of the province of Quebec (1960–66).

les·bi·an /lézbee ən/ *n* a woman who is sexually attracted to other women ■ *adj* involving or relating to lesbians [Late 19C. LESBIAN, because the woman poet Sappho of Lesbos wrote poems to women]

Les·bi·an /lézbee ən/ *n* somebody who comes from the Greek island of Lesbos ■ *adj* relating to the Greek island of Lesbos [Mid-16C. < Latin *Lesbius*, Greek *Lesbios* < *Lesbos* "Lesbos"]

les·bi·an·ism /lézbee ə nìzzəm/ *n* sexual attraction and sexual relations between women

Les·bos /léz boss/ island in eastern Greece, in the Aegean Sea, situated 6 mi./10 km off the coast of Turkey. Population: 103,700 (1991). Area: 632 sq. mi./1,637 sq. km.

Les Cayes /lay káy/ town and seaport in southwestern Haiti, west of Port-au-Prince. Population: 45,904 (1995).

lese maj·es·ty /léez májjəstee/, **lèse ma·jes·té** *n* **1.** disrespect toward the authority or dignity of somebody or something **2.** a criminal offense against a ruler or head of state [15C. Via French < Latin *laesa majestas* "violated majesty"]

le·sion /léezh'n/ *n* **1.** a wound, especially an area of skin that is broken or infected **2.** a physical change in a body part that is the result of illness or injury [15C. Via French < Latin *laesion-* < past participle of *laedere* "injure"]

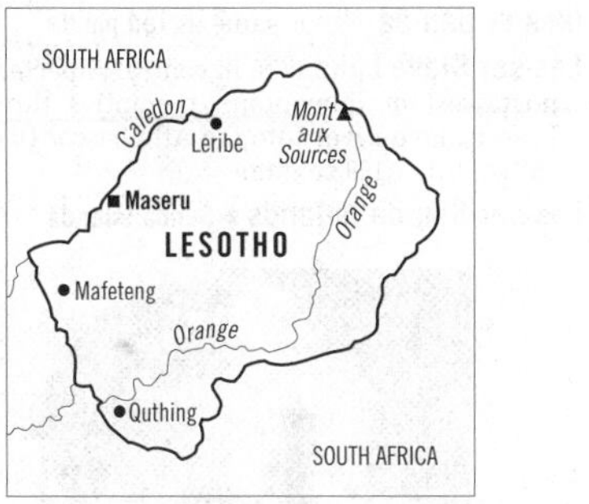

Lesotho

Le·so·tho /lə sṓtō, -sóotoo/ country in southern Africa, bordered on all sides by South Africa. It became an independent member of the British Commonwealth in 1966. Language: Sesotho (Southern Sotho) and English. Currency: loti. Capital: Maseru. Population: 1,861,959 (2003). Area: 11,720 sq. mi./30,355 sq. km. Official name **Kingdom of Lesotho**

les·pe·de·za /lèspə déezə/ (*plural* **-zas** or *same*) *n* a plant of the pea family with leaves that have three leaflets, grown for forage and to control erosion. Genus: *Lespedeza*. [Late 19C. < modern Latin, (erroneously) after Vincente Manuel de *Céspedes*, 18C Spanish governor of E Florida]

less /less/ CORE MEANING: a grammatical word used to indicate a smaller amount of something

1. *adj, pron* SMALLER AMOUNT a smaller amount or proportion of something ○ *New cars tend to emit less air pollution.* ○ *Last month less of her salary was taken up with household expenses.* **2.** *adv* TO SMALLER DEGREE to a smaller extent or degree ○ *Demanding? I've never known a less demanding patient!* ○ *I see her much less than I used to.* **3.** *prep* MINUS indicating that a number or amount is subtracted from a previously mentioned number or amount ○ *Total: $500, less $50 expenses.* ○ *I earned $45,000 last year, less tax and insurance.* [Old English *lǣssa* < Germanic] ◇ **much** *or* **still** *or* **even less** emphasizing that something is done or happens to a smaller extent than something mentioned in the previous statement (*used after a negative statement*) ○ *She could not fix her attention on any object or feel sensations, much less have conscious thoughts.* ◇ **less than** not having a particular quality ○ *Her whole attitude toward me has been less than pleasant.* ◇ **no less** used to express surprise or admiration (*often used ironically*) ○ *He* *had borrowed money at Homburg from no less a person than Lord Montbarry.*

USAGE See ***few.***

-less *suffix* **1.** without, lacking ○ *headless* ○ *restless* **2.** unable to be ○ *fathomless* [Old English *-lēas* < *lēas* "without" < Germanic]

les·see /le seé/ *n* a person or organization that leases a property from another [15C. < Anglo-Norman, past participle of *lesser* (see LEASE)]

less·en /léss'n/ **(-ened, -en·ing, -ens)** *vti* to make something less, or become less

Les·seps /léssəps/, **Ferdinand Marie, Vicomte de** (1805–94) French diplomat and engineer. While holding diplomatic posts he planned the cutting of the Suez Canal, and started work on the Panama Canal, which was eventually abandoned.

less·er /léssər/ *adj, adv* less significant or smaller in size or amount

Less·er An·til·les /lèsser an tílleez/ island group in the Caribbean comprising the Virgin Islands, Leeward Islands, and Windward Islands and stretching from Puerto Rico southeastward to the coast of Venezuela

Less·er Bai·ram *n* an Islamic festival held each year. Date: at the end of Ramadan.

less·er cel·an·dine *n* a plant of the buttercup family with heart-shaped leaves. Flowers: yellow, growing on individual stems. Native to: woodland and damp locations in Europe and Asia. Latin name: *Ranunculus ficaria.*

less·er o·men·tum *n* the fold of the peritoneum that connects to the liver

less·er pan·da *n* ZOOL same as **red panda**

Les·ser Slave Lake lake in central Alberta, Canada, northwest of Edmonton. It empties through the Lesser Slave River into the Athabasca River. Area: 451 sq. mi./1,168 sq. km.

Les·ser Sun·da Is·lands ♦ **Sunda Islands**

Doris Lessing

Les·sing /léssing/, **Doris** (*b.* 1919) British novelist. Her works such as *The Grass is Singing* (1950), *Children of Violence* (1952–69), and *The Golden Notebook* (1962) explore political and social themes. Born **Tayler, Doris May**

> "When old settlers say 'One has to understand the country,' what they mean is, 'You have to get used to our ideas about the native.' They are saying, in effect, 'Learn our ideas, or otherwise get out; we don't want you.'"
> [Doris Lessing, *The Grass is Singing*; 1950]

Les·sing, Gotthold (1729–81) German dramatist and critic. His plays and essays were highly influential in the development of the Enlightenment. Full name **Lessing, Gotthold Ephraim**

> "What we find beautiful in a work of art is not found beautiful by the eye, but by our imagination through the eye."
> [Gotthold Lessing, *Laokoon*; 1766]

Les Six /lay seéss/ *n* a group of six French composers, Louis Durey, Arthur Honegger, Darius Milhaud, Germaine Tailleferre, Francis Poulenc, and Georges Auric, who promoted an anti-Romantic aesthetic influenced by Erik Satie and the writer Jean Cocteau in the early 20th century [Early 20C. French, "the six"]

les·son /léss'n/ *n* **1.** INSTRUCTION PERIOD a period of time spent teaching or learning a subject **2.** MATERIAL TAUGHT material to be taught or studied **3.** NEW OR BETTER KNOWLEDGE some useful knowledge or sense that results from direct experience ○ *I think there's a lesson there for all of us – think ahead.* **4.** USEFUL EXPERIENCE something that acts as an example, punishment, or warning by teaching something not previously understood or accepted **5.** REBUKE a strong criticism or reproof, usually instructing or reminding somebody how to behave correctly ○ *I need to give him a lesson in how to behave properly.* **6.** *also* **Les·son** BIBLE PASSAGE a passage from the Bible that is read out to the congregation during a church service ○ *Today's lesson is from the book of Matthew.* ■ *vt* **(-soned, -son·ing, -sons) 1.** INSTRUCT SOMEBODY to teach somebody **2.** SCOLD SOMEBODY to scold somebody for doing something wrong [12C. Via French *leçon* < Latin *lection-* "reading" < *legere* "to read"]

les·sor /lé sàwr/ *n* a person or organization that leases a property to another [14C. < Anglo-Norman *lessour* < *lesser* (see LEASE)]

lest /lest/ *conj* in order to prevent something happening, especially something causing fear (*formal*) ○ *must stay out of sight lest we be discovered* [Old English *þӯ lǣs þe* "by which less that"]

let[1] /let/ **(let, let·ting, lets)** *vt* **1.** NOT PREVENT SOMETHING to allow something to happen or somebody to do something ○ *You should let him explain what happened.* ○ *I won't let anything get in the way of us living a happy life together.* ○ *I never let myself worry about the future.* **2.** GIVE SOMEBODY PERMISSION to give somebody permission to do something ○ *I want to go to the disco but Dad won't let me.* **3.** EXPRESSING SUGGESTION used to express a suggestion, an offer, or an order ○ *Let's eat – I'm starving.* ○ *Let me take that bag for you – you must be exhausted.* ○ *Let the show go on!* **4.** MAKE SOMETHING PASS SOMEWHERE to allow or cause something to pass from one place to another ○ *You need to let some air out of those tires.* ○ *Open the window and let some fresh air in.* **5.** EXPRESSING RESIGNATION used to indicate indifference to what happens or what somebody does, even though it may be unpleasant ○ *Let them do their worst.* ○ *If he wants to leave then let him – see if I care!* **6.** ENVIRON RELEASE WATER FROM POND to release or cause something to release water from a lagoon or pond by breaching a sandbar or other obstacle so that the water drains into a larger body, e.g., the sea **7.** RENT OUT PROPERTY to allow people to use land, rooms, or a building in return for rent **8.** *Ireland* UTTER SOMETHING to utter something (*informal*) **9.** MATH, LOGIC MAKE MATHEMATICAL ASSUMPTION used to introduce an assumption or hypothesis ○ *Let the point P be on a line L.* [Old English *lǣtan* "leave behind, allow" < Indo-European, "let go"] ◇ **let alone** used to introduce something that is even less likely or probable than what has just been mentioned ◇ **let go (of something)** to stop holding something ◇ **let somebody have it** to deliver a physical or verbal attack on somebody ◇ **let yourself go 1.** to start acting in a much more relaxed or less inhibited way than usual **2.** to stop caring about your appearance

USAGE See ***leave***[1].

let down *vt* **1.** LOWER SOMETHING to move something, or allow something to move, to a lower position ○ *It was getting dark, so she let down the blinds.* **2.** DISAPPOINT SOMEBODY to disappoint somebody by not meeting expectations ○ *Sorry to let you down, but I won't be able to make it tonight.* **3.** LENGTHEN GARMENT to lengthen clothing or part of a piece of clothing by shortening the hem ○ *let down the sleeves of the coat* **4.** ALLOW HAIR TO HANG DOWN to undo long hair so it falls to its full length

let in *vt* **1.** to allow somebody to enter somewhere such as a building or a room ○ *They refused to let her in the house.* **2.** to allow water or air into something that is meant to be sealed ○ *Their boat had hit a rock and was letting in water.*

let in for *vt* to become involved in something that turns out to be more difficult or complicated than expected (*informal*) ○ *I didn't realize what I was letting myself in for.*

let in on *vt* to allow somebody to know about something

let into *vt* **1.** to allow somebody to enter somewhere **2.** to allow somebody to join an organization or club

let off *vt* **1.** to allow somebody to avoid something such as an unpleasant task or a punishment ○ *I'll let you off this time, but you'd better behave from now on.* **2.** to allow somebody to get off a vehicle such as a bus or train

let on *v* **1.** *vi* PRETEND to make somebody believe something that is not true ○ *She let on that she was upset, but she wasn't really that bothered.* **2.** *vt* LET PASSENGER GET ON to allow somebody to board a vehicle such as a bus or train **3.** *vi* SHARE SECRET to share a secret with somebody (*informal*) ○ *He didn't let on that he was very rich.*

let out *v* **1.** *vt* MAKE LOUD YELL to make a loud or piercing sound using the voice ○ *let out a scream* **2.** *vt* RELEASE SOMEBODY OR SOMETHING to set a person or animal free from being confined or trapped **3.** *vt* ALLOW SOMEBODY TO LEAVE to allow somebody to leave someplace such as a building or room **4.** *vt* ENLARGE GARMENT to make a piece of clothing, or a specific part of it, wider than it was before **5.** *vt* SPREAD INFORMATION to allow previously secret information to become more widely known **6.** *vt* RENT OUT PLACE to make a place available for letting ○ *They have recently let out a suite of rooms on the third floor.* **7.** *vi* END AND RELEASE STUDENTS to come to an end and release students at the end of a session or term ○ *classes let out in early June*

let through *vt* to allow somebody or something to pass through a crowd ○ *Cars were pulling over to let an ambulance through.*

let up *vi* **1.** to become slower, calmer, or quieter ○ *Once the rain lets up a bit we'll have a look outside.* **2.** to stop working hard or being angry

let up on *vt* to treat somebody or something in a more relaxed, gentle, or kind way

let[2] /let/ *n* **1.** REPLAYED SERVICE SHOT in games such as tennis and squash, a service in which the ball is obstructed and the shot has to be played again **2.** REPLAYED POINT the point that is replayed because of a let **3.** DIFFICULTY OR OBSTACLE something that prevents somebody from doing something or makes it more difficult (*formal*) ○ *without let or hindrance* [12C. < Old English *lettan* "hinder" < Germanic]

-let *suffix* **1.** small one ○ *wavelet* **2.** something worn on [< Old French *-elet* < *-el* "small one" (< Latin *-ellus*) + *-et* (see -ET)]

letch *n, vi* another spelling of **lech**

let·down /lét dòwn/ *n* **1.** an occasion when somebody or something disappoints expectations, or the feeling of disappointment that results ○ *After all the hype the concert was a bit of a letdown.* **2.** the descent of an aircraft in preparation for landing, before the actual landing approach

le·thal /leéth'l/ *adj* **1.** certain to or intended to cause death **2.** causing disaster or destruction ○ *a move that was lethal to his career* [Late 16C. < Latin *lethalis* < *lethum*, alteration of *letum* "death," by association with Greek *lēthē* "forgetfulness"] —**le·thal·i·ty** /lee thállətee/ *n* —**le·thal·ly** *adv* —**le·thal·ness** *n*

SYNONYMS See ***deadly.***

le·thal dose *n* the amount of a drug or other substance that will cause death when administered

le·thal in·jec·tion *n* **1.** a method of capital punishment that involves injecting a deadly drug into somebody's body **2.** an injection of a deadly drug administered as capital punishment

le·thar·gic /lə thaárjik/ *adj* **1.** physically slow and mentally dull as a result of tiredness, disease, or drugs **2.** causing a state of physical slowness and mental dullness —**le·thar·gi·cal·ly** *adv*

leth·ar·gy /léthərjee/ *n* **1.** a state of physical slowness and mental dullness resulting from tiredness, disease, or drugs **2.** lack of energy, activity, or enthusiasm [14C. Via French < late Latin *lethargia* < Greek *lēthargia* < *lēthargos* "forgetful" < *lēthē* "forgetfulness"]

Leth·bridge /léth brìj/ city in southern Alberta, Canada. It is the cultural and economic center of the surrounding agricultural area. Population: 67,374 (2001).

le·the /leéthee/ *n* a dreamy state of forgetfulness or unconsciousness (*literary*) —**le·the·an** *adj*

Le·the /leéthee/ *n* in Greek mythology, a river in Hades whose water made those who drank it forget their past [Mid-16C. Via Latin < Greek *lēthē* "forgetfulness"] —**Le·the·an** *adj*

Le·to /leétō/ *n* in Greek mythology, the mother of

Apollo and Artemis by Zeus. Roman equivalent **Latona**

let's /lets/ *contr* let us ○ *Let's just wait and see what happens.*

Lett /let/ *n* PEOPLES same as **Latvian** (sense 1) [Late 16C. Via German *Lette* < Latvian *Latvi*]

let·ter /léttər/ *n* **1. MESSAGE SENT BY MAIL** a piece of handwritten or printed text addressed to a recipient and typically sent by mail **2. SYMBOL USED TO SPELL WORDS** a written or printed symbol representing a sound or set of sounds in a language and used to spell words **3. BADGE OF EXCELLENCE IN SPORTS** a badge showing the initial letter of a school's name, awarded for excellence, especially in varsity sports **4.** PRINTING **PRINTING STYLE** a style of typeface ■ *v* (**-tered, -ter·ing, -ters**) **1.** *vt* **WRITE LETTERS ON SOMETHING** to write letters or words on something such as a sign **2.** *vi US* **EARN BADGE** to earn a badge of excellence at a school, especially in varsity sports [13C. Via French *lettre* < Latin *littera* "letter of the alphabet, (plural) document"]

let·ter bomb *n* **1.** an envelope with an explosive device inside it, addressed and sent through the mail and designed to blow up when it is opened **2.** an e-mail message with a destructive code attached to it

let·ter·box /léttər bòks/ *n* **1.** *also* **let·ter·box for·mat** MEDIA a film format for television that shows a wider and shorter picture than usual to accommodate the aspect ratios of movies when shown on television **2.** *UK* MAIL same as **mail slot 3.** MAIL same as **mailbox** (sense 1) **4.** *UK* a private box or other place to which mail for a specific person or organization is delivered

let·ter car·ri·er *n* somebody employed to deliver letters or other mail

let·tered /léttərd/ *adj* **1. WITH LETTERS WRITTEN ON IT** marked with letters of the alphabet **2. EDUCATED** knowledgeable and cultured, especially in literary matters **3. LITERATE** able to read and write

let·ter·form /léttər fàwrm/ *n* the shape of a letter of the alphabet

let·ter·head /léttər hèd/ *n* **1.** a printed heading for official stationery, usually containing a company's name, address, telephone and fax numbers, and often including a logo and other details **2.** a piece of writing paper with a printed letterhead

let·ter·ing /léttəring/ *n* **1.** letters of the alphabet written, printed, inscribed, or painted on something **2.** the physical process of forming letters, or the way they are formed

let·ter·man /léttər màn, -mən/ (*plural* **-men** /-men, -mèn/) *n US* a secondary or college student who has been awarded a letter for excellence in an activity, especially a varsity sport

Let·ter·man /léttərmən/, **David** (*b.* 1947) US television host. Host of the television show *The Late Show* from 1993, he is known for his offbeat style.

> "New York now leads the world's great cities in the number of people around whom you shouldn't make a sudden move."
> [David Letterman, *Late Night with David Letterman*; February 9, 1984]

let·ter of cred·it *n* a letter from a bank, usually for presentation to another branch or bank, authorizing it to issue credit or money to the person named

let·ter of in·tent *n* a signed statement outlining an intention to form an agreement or arrangement

let·ter of in·tro·duc·tion *n* a letter written by somebody to introduce one person to another

let·ter o·pen·er *n* a blunt knife for slitting open envelopes, or for slitting folded paper, especially leaves of books

let·ter-per·fect *adj* memorized, spoken, or sung with total accuracy

let·ter·press /léttər prèss/ *n* **1. PRINTING BY USE OF PRESSURE** a printing technique that transfers ink by pressing raised type onto paper **2. PRINTED MATERIAL** material that is printed using the letterpress technique **3.** *UK* **TEXT** text as opposed to illustrations

let·ter-qual·i·ty *adj* describes printer output of a quality high enough to be compared to conventional printing, or a printer capable of producing such output

let·ters /léttərz/ *n* (*takes a singular or plural verb*) **1.** literature or literary culture **2.** knowledge and education

let·ters cre·den·tial *npl* LAW same as **letters of credence**

let·ters of ad·min·is·tra·tion *npl* an official court order appointing somebody as the administrator of a deceased person's estate when no valid will exists

let·ters of cre·dence *npl* an official document presented to a government in order to authenticate the official status of a diplomatic representative of another country

let·ters of marque *npl* **1.** a formal document issued by one country authorizing one of its private citizens to take possession of goods, or sometimes citizens, belonging to another country **2.** an official document issued by one country authorizing one of its citizens to fit a ship with weapons in order to attack or seize another country's ships and cargo [*Marque* "reprisals" via French < Provençal *marca* < *marcar* "seize as a pledge"]

let·ters pat·ent *npl* an official document stating that somebody has been granted the exclusive right to make and sell a new product. Letters patent are issued by the government and specify the length of time a patent will remain valid.

let·ters tes·ta·men·tar·y *npl* an official document authorizing somebody to assume the responsibilities and duties of executor of the will of a deceased person

let·ter·win·ner /léttər wìnnər/ *n* a secondary or college student who has been awarded a letter for excellence in an activity, especially a varsity sport

Let·tish /léttish/ *n* LANG same as **Latvian** (sense 2) —**Let·tish** *adj*

let·tre de ca·chet /lèttrə də kaa sháy/ (*plural* **let·tres de ca·chet** /lèttrə-/) *n* a letter sealed with the royal seal authorizing the arrest and indefinite imprisonment of somebody who has offended the monarch [Early 18C. < French, "letter of seal"]

let·tuce /léttəss/ *n* **1.** a common plant that is widely grown for its edible leaves, which are usually eaten in salads. Genus: *Lactuca.* **2.** paper money as opposed to coins (*slang*) [13C. Via Old French *letuës* (plural) < Latin *lactuca* < *lac* "milk"; from the milky sap of its stalk]

let·tuce bird *n regional* same as **goldfinch** [Because it feeds on lettuce seeds]

REGIONAL NOTE As well as ***lettuce bird***, the goldfinch is also called *salad bird* and *thistle bird*, all three terms being related to its feeding habits. These terms have a scattered occurrence in Midland territory, especially Indiana.

---

let-up /lét ùp/ *n* a pause, especially in something unpleasant (*informal*)

le·u /lé òò/ (*plural* **lei** /lay/) *n* the main unit of currency in Romania and Moldova. See table at **currency** [Late 19C. < Romanian, "lion"]

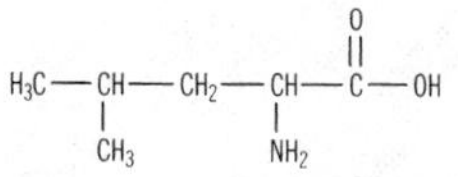

leucine

leu·cine /lóo seen/ *n* an essential amino acid. Formula: $C_6H_{13}NO_2$. [Early 19C. < Greek *leukos* "white"]

leu·cite /lóo sìt/ *n* a white or gray mineral that is a silicate of aluminum containing potassium. Source: igneous rocks. Use: source of aluminum and potash for fertilizers. [Late 18C. < Greek *leukos* "white"]

leuco- *prefix* another spelling of **leuko-**

leu·co·blast *n* ANAT another spelling of **leukoblast**

leu·co·cyte *n* MED another spelling of **leukocyte**

leu·co·cy·to·sis *n* MED another spelling of **leukocytosis**

leu·co·der·ma *n* MED another spelling of **leukoderma**

leu·co·dys·tro·phy *n* MED another spelling of **leukodystrophy**

leu·co·ma *n* MED another spelling of **leukoma**

leu·co·pe·ni·a *n* MED another spelling of **leukopenia**

leu·co·plak·i·a *n* MED another spelling of **leukoplakia**

leu·co·plast /lóokə plàst/, **leu·co·plas·tid** /lóokə plástid/ *n* a common minute colorless body (**plastid**) found inside plant cells and used for storing food

leu·co·sis *n* VET another spelling of **leukosis**

leu·cot·o·my *n* SURG another spelling of **leukotomy**

leu·co·tri·ene *n* BIOCHEM another spelling of **leukotriene**

leu·kae·mi·a *n* MED UK spelling of **leukemia**

leu·ke·mi·a /loo keémee ə/ *n* an often fatal cancer in which white blood cells displace normal blood, leading to infection, shortage of red blood cells (**anemia**), bleeding, and other disorders. Certain types of childhood leukemias respond well to treatment, which includes drugs (**chemotherapy**) and radiotherapy. —**leu·ke·mic** *adj, n*

leuko-, **leuco-** *prefix* **1.** white, pale, colorless ○ *leukoplakia* **2.** leukocyte ○ *leukopenia* **3.** white matter of the brain ○ *leukodystrophy* [< Greek *leukos* "white, clear" < Indo-European]

leu·ko·blast /lóokə blàst/, **leu·co·blast** *n* an immature white blood cell (**leukocyte**)

leu·ko·cyte /lóokə sìt/, **leu·co·cyte** *n* a white blood cell (*technical*) —**leu·ko·cyt·ic** /lóokə síttik/ *adj* —**leu·ko·cy·toid** /-sí tòyd/ *adj*

leu·ko·cy·to·sis /lóokə sī tóssiss/, **leu·co·cy·to·sis** *n* a marked increase in the number of white blood cells (**leukocytes**), usually because of infection or disease —**leu·ko·cy·tot·ic** /-tóttik/ *adj*

leu·ko·der·ma /lóokə dúrmə/, **leu·co·der·ma** *n* MED same as **vitiligo** [Late 19C. < LEUKO- + Greek *derma* "skin"]

leu·ko·dys·tro·phy /lóokō dístrəfee/, **leu·co·dys·tro·phy** *n* a degenerative disease of nerve fibers or white matter that impairs brain function, sight, and motion, leading to death, often at an early age. It involves progressive loss of the fatty myelin layer surrounding the nerve fibers.

leu·ko·ma /loo kṓmə/, **leu·co·ma** *n* a dense white scar on the cornea of the eye, caused by disease or injury [Early 18C. Via modern Latin < Greek *leukōma* "white tumor" < *leukos* "white"]

leu·ko·pe·ni·a /lóokə peénee ə/, **leu·co·pe·ni·a** *n* an excessive reduction in the number of white blood cells (**leukocytes**) —**leu·ko·pe·nic** *adj*

leu·ko·plak·i·a /lóokə pláykee ə, -plák-/, **leu·co·plak·i·a** *n* a precancerous condition that is seen as small thickened white patches, usually inside the mouth or vulva. Oral leukoplakia may be caused by smoking or by alcohol abuse. [Late 19C. < LEUKO- + Greek *plak-* "flat surface"]

leu·kor·rhe·a /lóokə reé ə/, **leu·cor·rhe·a** *n* thick whitish or yellowish discharge from the vagina —**leu·kor·rhe·al** *adj*

leu·ko·sis /loo kṓssiss/, **leu·co·sis** *n* any animal disease in which the blood contains an unusually high number of white blood cells (**leukocytes**) [Early 18C. < Greek *leukōsis* < *leukon* "make white" < *leukos* "white"]

leu·kot·o·my /loo kóttəmee/ (*plural* **-mies**), **leu·cot·o·my** *n* a surgical operation that involves cutting nerve fibers, especially in the frontal lobes of the brain. It is now rarely performed, and only as a treatment for severe psychiatric disorders.

leu·ko·tri·ene /lóokə trí een/, **leu·co·tri·ene** *n* a short-range chemical messenger in various tissues that plays a role in inflammation. Leukotrienes help regulate the state of blood vessels and airways, and influence the activities of some white blood cells. [Late 20C. < LEUKO- + *triene* "chemical compound containing three double bonds"]

~~**leutenant**~~ incorrect spelling of **lieutenant**

lev /lev/ (*plural* **lev·a** /lévvə/) *n* the main unit of Bulgarian currency. See table at **currency** [Late 19C. < Bulgarian, variant of *lăv* "lion," probably < Greek *leōn*]

LEV *abbr* AUTOMOT low emission vehicle

Lev. *abbr* BIBLE Leviticus

lev- *prefix* another spelling of **levo-** (*used before vowels*)

Le·vant /lə vánt/ *n* the region in the eastern Mediterranean comprising modern-day Lebanon, Israel, and parts of Syria and Turkey (*archaic*) [15C. < French, literally "rising"; because the sun appears to rise there] —**Le·van·tine** /lévv'n tīn, -teen, lə ván-/ *n, adj*

le·vant·er /lə vántər/ *n* a strong easterly wind that blows in the western Mediterranean area, especially in the late summer [Late 18C. < LEVANT]

le·va·tor /lə váytər/ *n* **1.** a muscle that helps to lift the body part to which it is attached **2.** a surgical instrument used to lift up a body part, especially a bone or a tooth [Early 17C. < Latin, "lifter" < *levare* (see LEVER)]

lev·ee[1] /lévvee/ *n* **1.** NATURAL EMBANKMENT BESIDE RIVER a natural embankment alongside a river, formed by sediment during times of flooding **2.** ARTIFICIAL EMBANKMENT BESIDE RIVER an artificial embankment alongside a river, built to prevent flooding of the surrounding land ■ *vt* (**-eed, -ee·ing, -ees**) BUILD LEVEE ON RIVER to provide a river with an embankment to prevent flooding [Early 18C. < French *levée*, form of past participle of *lever* (see LEVER)]

lev·ee[2] /lévvee, lə váy/ *n* **1.** in former times, an occasion when a noble or royal person received visitors informally soon after getting up in the morning **2.** in former times, a court reception at which a prince or sovereign received visitors. It is usually held in the early afternoon. [Late 17C. < French *levé*, variant of *lever* "rising" < *lever* (see LEVER)]

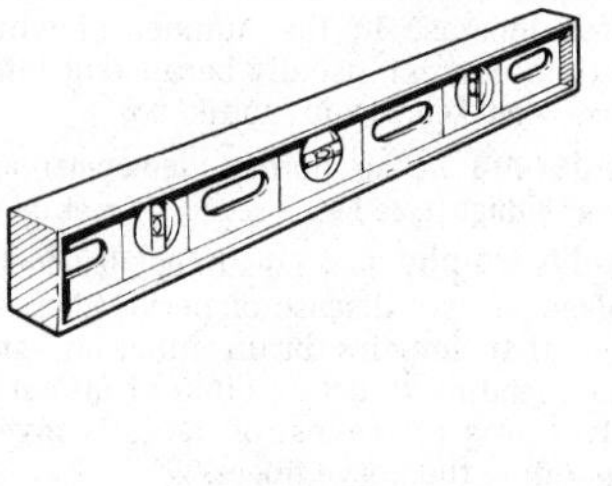

level (sense 12)

lev·el /lévv'l/ *n* **1.** AMOUNT the amount or concentration of something ○ *My job has a low stress level but few prospects.* **2.** ASPECT a quality or aspect of something ○ *It's a movie that works well on a number of different levels.* **3.** RANK OR SCALE a particular position in a range of relative scales or values ○ *playing tennis at the professional level* **4.** COMPUT GAMES SECTION OF COMPUTER GAME a part of a computer game that must be completed before moving to the next, often more difficult, stage **5.** POSITION OF PARTICULAR FLOOR the relative position of a particular floor or other plane in a structure such as a building or bridge ○ *The storeroom is down on the second level.* **6.** HEIGHT FOR MEASUREMENT a position, line, or flat surface according to which height is measured ○ *10,000 feet above sea level* **7.** HEIGHT OF SURFACE FROM BOTTOM the height of a surface from the ground or from the bottom of its container ○ *The level of the river had fallen alarmingly during the summer.* **8.** STATED HEIGHT a particular height ○ *flying below the level of the tree tops* **9.** GEOG HORIZONTAL SURFACE a horizontal surface or area of land **10.** CIV ENG SURVEYING INSTRUMENT in surveying, an instrument used to measure the relative heights of different points in the landscape **11.** CIV ENG MEASUREMENT OF HEIGHT in surveying, a measurement taken of the relative heights of different points in a landscape **12.** CONSTR TOOL FOR DETERMINING LEVELNESS a calibrated glass tube containing liquid with an air bubble in it, mounted in a frame and used for measuring whether surfaces are horizontal **13.** MIN EXTRACT HORIZONTAL MINE TUNNEL a horizontal tunnel in a mine ■ *adj* **1.** NOT SLOPING flat and horizontal, with an even surface or top **2.** EQUAL equal to or even with another individual or group in rank, ability, or condition ○ *The two teams have drawn level after six games.* **3.** ALONGSIDE next to or alongside somebody or something else ○ *His car drew level as we approached the bend.* **4.** STEADY steady, consistent, or unchanging ○ *maintaining a level pressure* **5.** CALM showing calmness and self-control ○ *keep a level head* **6.** UNWAVERING not blinking or looking away, and showing penetrating or determined calm ○ *a level gaze* **7.** OF PARTICULAR LEVEL relating to or characteristic of a particular rank or condition (*usually used in combination*) ○ *an entry-level job* ■ *v* (**-eled** or **-elled, -el·ing** or **-el·ling, -els**) **1.** *vt* FLATTEN SOMETHING EVENLY to make something even, flat, and horizontal ○ *We spent days leveling the ground before we could start building.* **2.** *vti* MAKE OR BECOME EQUAL to make two things or people equal in position or of the same standard or value, or become equal in position, standard, or value ○ *Another goal in the final few minutes leveled the scores again.* **3.** *vt* DEMOLISH AND FLATTEN SOMETHING to completely destroy a building, place, or area and leave it flattened ○ *The village had been leveled by the hurricane.* **4.** *vti* AIM GUN to aim or point a weapon ○ *He leveled his pistol at the target.* **5.** *vt* DIRECT ATTENTION AT SOMEBODY to direct criticism or an attack toward somebody in a purposeful way ○ *Criticism has been leveled at a number of prominent politicians.* **6.** *vti* MEASURE ELEVATION OF LAND in surveying, to measure the elevation of an area of land **7.** *vt* KNOCK SOMEBODY DOWN to knock somebody to the ground, especially with a punch or blow (*informal*) ○ *leveled him with one punch* **8.** *vi* BE HONEST WITH SOMEBODY to speak frankly and honestly to somebody (*informal*) ○ *I'd better level with you right now – I'm leaving the company and going it alone.* [14C. < Old French *livel* "tool for determining levelness" < Latin *libra* "balance, scales"] —**lev·el·ly** *adv* —**lev·el·ness** *n* ◇ **on the level** honest and trustworthy (*informal*)

level off *vti* **1.** *also* **level out** to fly level with the ground, especially after climbing or descending, or make an aircraft do this ○ *We passed through the clouds and eventually leveled off at about 10,000 feet.* **2.** to reach a level and become stable and unchanging, or make something do this ○ *Stock prices seem to have leveled off.*

level up *vti* **1.** same as **level** *v* (senses 1–2) **2.** to increase the capabilities of a character in a computer game

lev·el cross·ing *n UK* same as **grade crossing**

lev·el·er /lévv'lər/, **lev·el·ler** *n* **1.** a factor that makes situations or people more equal, especially by removing distinctions based on status or privilege ○ *Time is the great leveler.* **2.** somebody who advocates equality in society for everyone

lev·el-head·ed *adj* remaining rational and fully in control in difficult situations or emergencies —**lev·el-head·ed·ly** *adv* —**lev·el-head·ed·ness** *n*

lev·el·ing screw /lévelíng-/ *n* one of usually several screws on the bottom of something such as a scientific instrument or a washing machine that can be adjusted to make the piece of equipment stand level

lev·el·ler *n* SOC SCI, POL another spelling of **leveler**

Lev·el·ler *n* a member or supporter of a radical Parliamentarian movement during the English Civil War, calling for religious tolerance, legal equality, a universal male vote, and the abolition of the monarchy. The movement was later suppressed by Cromwell.

Le·ven, Loch /leevən/ lake in east central Scotland, north of the Firth of Forth. Area: 10 sq. mi./26 sq. km.

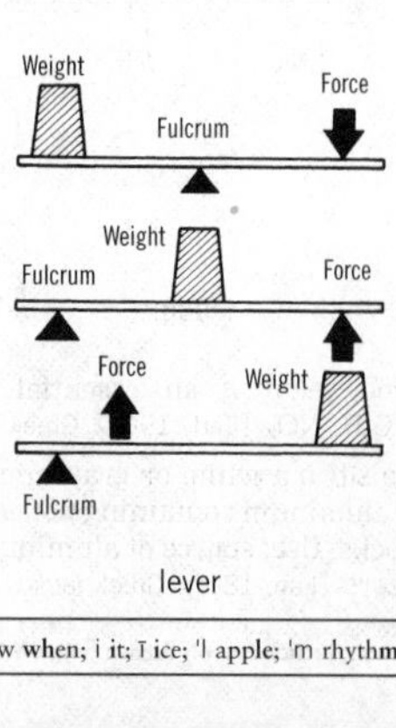

lever

lev·er /lévvər, leevər/ *n* **1.** RIGID BAR USED FOR LEVERAGE a rigid bar that pivots about a point (**fulcrum**) and is used to move or lift a load at one end by applying force to the other end **2.** DEVICE OR MACHINE a mechanical device or machine that operates using leverage **3.** WAY OF ACHIEVING SOMETHING a device, tactic, or situation that can be used to advantage ■ *vt* (**-ered, -er·ing, -ers**) MOVE SOMETHING WITH LEVER to move something using a lever [13C. < Anglo-Norman, "something that raises" < Old French, "to raise" < Latin *levare* < *levis* "light (in weight)"]

lev·er·age /lévvərij/ *n* **1.** ACTION OF LEVER the action of a lever pivoting about a point **2.** MECHANICAL ADVANTAGE the mechanical advantage gained by using a lever **3.** POWER TO GET THINGS DONE power over other people, especially something that gives an advantage but is not referred to openly ○ *He uses the leverage of seniority with the more junior employees.* **4.** FIN BORROWING OF MONEY TO PURCHASE COMPANY the borrowing of money to purchase a company, in the hope that it will make enough profit to cover the interest payable on the loan **5.** FIN PROPORTION OF CAPITAL AS DEBT the ratio of a company's debt capital to the value of its ordinary shares ■ *vti* (**-aged, -ag·ing, -ag·es**) FIN BORROW MONEY HOPING TO MAKE MORE to borrow money in order to buy a company, relying on it to make enough profit to cover the interest payable on the loan

lev·er·aged buy·out /lèvvərijd-/ *n* a takeover strategy in which a controlling proportion of a company's shares is bought using borrowed money, the collateral for which is assets belonging to the purchased company

lev·er·et /lévvərət/ *n* a young hare, especially one less than a year old [14C. < Anglo-Norman, "little hare" < *levre* "hare" < Latin *lepus*]

Le·ver·rier /lə vérree yày, -ver yáy/, **Urbain** (1811–77) French astronomer. He predicted the existence of Neptune before it was discovered and improved the astronomical tables for Mercury. Full name **Leverrier, Urbain Jean Joseph**

Le·vesque /lə vék/, **René** (1922–87) Canadian journalist and political leader. In 1968 he founded the Parti Québecois (Quebec Party), whose primary goal is Quebec's sovereignty, and became prime minister of the province (1976–85).

Le·vi /lee vī/ *n* in the Bible, the third son of Jacob and patriarch of the house of Levi (Genesis 29:34)

Le·vi /lévvee, láyvee/, **Primo** (1919–87) Italian novelist, poet, and scientist. His book *If This Is a Man* (1947) recorded his experiences in Auschwitz.

> "Our language lacks words to express this offense, the demolition of a man."
> [Primo Levi, on a year spent as a prisoner in Auschwitz, *If This is a Man*; 1947]

le·vi·a·than /lə vī əthən/ *n* **1.** *also* **Le·vi·a·than** MONSTER in the Bible, a large beast or sea monster **2.** SOMETHING HUGE something extremely large and powerful in comparison with others of its kind **3.** WHALE a whale or other large sea animal (*literary*) [14C. Via late Latin < Hebrew *liwyāṯān*]

CULTURAL NOTE ***Leviathan***, a treatise (1651) by English philosopher Thomas Hobbes. Hobbes's major work is a defense of the principle of absolute monarchy. It argues that human beings can only live in peace if they agree to subject themselves to a single, absolute ruler. Since this ruler should be answerable only to God, the Church too must be subject to civil authority.

lev·i·gate /lévvi gàyt/ (**-gat·ed, -gat·ing, -gates**) *v* **1.** *vt* GRIND MINERAL INTO POWDER to grind a mineral into a fine powder with water, forming a smooth paste or slurry **2.** *vt* SEPARATE PARTICLES BY SUSPENSION to separate fine particles from coarser ones by suspending them in a liquid **3.** *vti* FORM MIXTURE to form a smooth uniform liquid mixture such as a paste or gel, or make something do this [15C. < Latin *levigat-*, past participle of *levigare* "make smooth"] —**lev·i·ga·tion** /lèvvi gáysh'n/ *n*

Le·vi-Mont·al·ci·ni /làyvee mònt'l cheenee/, **Rita** (*b.* 1909) Italian-born US neurobiologist. She shared the Nobel Prize in physiology or medicine (1986) for research into growth factor in human development.

Le·vine /lə veen/, **James Lawrence** (*b.* 1943) US pianist and conductor. He was made principal conductor of the Metropolitan Opera in New York City (1973), and later became its artistic director (1986).

lev·i·rate /lévvərət, -ràyt, leév-/ *n* the practice by which a man may be required to marry his brother's widow. This custom was practiced in ancient Jewish society and is common in parts of Africa today. [Early 18C. < Latin *levir* "husband's brother"] —**lev·i·rat·ic** /lèvvə ráttik, leèvə-/ *adj*

Le·vi-Strauss /làyvee strówss/, **Claude** (*b.* 1908) French social anthropologist. A proponent of structuralism, he originated the thesis that all cultures have a common framework. Full name **Levi-Strauss, Claude Gustave**

Levit. *abbr* Leviticus

lev·i·tate /lévvi tàyt/ (**-tat·ed, -tat·ing, -tates**) *v* **1.** *vti* to rise and float in the air, or make something rise and float in the air, seemingly in defiance of gravity **2.** *vt* to support a patient on a cushion of air during treatment for severe burns [Late 17C. < Latin *levis* "light (in weight)," after GRAVITATE] —**lev·i·ta·tion** /lèvvi táysh'n/ *n* —**lev·i·ta·tor** *n*

Le·vite /leé vīt/ *n* a member of the Hebrew tribe of Levi, chosen to assist the priests of the Jewish Temple. The Levites were descended from Jacob's son Levi and constituted one of the twelve tribes of Israel. [14C. < ecclesiastical Latin *levita* < Greek *levitēs*, after *Levi* "Levi"]

Le·vit·i·cal /lə víttik'l/ *adj* **1.** belonging or relating to the Levites **2.** relating to the book of Leviticus, especially those portions containing laws relating to ritual or moral precepts

Le·vit·i·cus /lə víttikəss/ *n* a book of the Bible that contains the priestly tradition of the Levites, traditionally attributed to Moses. It is the third book of the Pentateuch, continuing from the end of the book of Exodus. See table at **Bible** [14C. < late Latin, "of the Levites" < Greek *levitēs* (see LEVITE)]

Lev·itt /lévvit/, **William J.** (1907–94) US housing developer. The construction company that he founded with his brother (1929) built whole towns of affordable family homes, first for the US Navy and then for armed forces families after World War II. He sold the company in 1968. Full name **Levitt, William Jaird**

Lev·it·town /lévvit tòwn/ **1.** city in Nassau County, New York, situated on Long Island. Population: 53,286 (1996). **2.** city in Bucks County, southeastern Pennsylvania. Population: 55,362 (2002 estimate).

lev·i·ty /lévvətee/ *n* remarks or behavior intended to be amusing, especially when they are out of keeping with a serious occasion [Mid-16C. < Latin *levitas* < *levis* "light (in weight)"]

le·vo /leévō/ *adj US* SCI same as **levorotatory** [Mid-20C. Shortening]

levo- *prefix* **1.** leftward, counterclockwise ○ *levorotation* **2.** levorotatory ○ *levulose* [< French *lévo-* < Latin *laevus* "left"]

le·vo·do·pa /leèvə dṓpə, lèvvə-/ *n* PHARM full form of **L-dopa**

le·vo·ro·ta·tion /leèvə rō táysh'n/ *n* a rotation to the left or counterclockwise, especially of the plane of polarized light

le·vo·ro·ta·to·ry /leèvə rṓtə tàwree/ *adj* **1.** turning or circling in a counterclockwise direction or to the left **2.** turning the plane of polarized light in a counterclockwise direction

lev·u·lose /lévvyə lōss, -lōz/ *n* BIOCHEM same as **fructose** [Late 19C. < LEVO- + -ULE]

lev·y /lévvee/ *v* (**-ied, -y·ing, -ies**) **1.** *vt* **IMPOSE TAX** to use government authority to impose or collect a tax **2.** *vt* **RAISE ARMY** to enlist troops for military service, often by force **3.** *vt* **DECLARE WAR** to declare war on somebody **4.** *vi* **SEIZE PROPERTY TO FULFILL JUDGMENT** to seize property in accordance with a legal ruling ■ *n* (*plural* **-ies**) **1. TAX** money raised under government authority **2. RAISING OF TAX** the act of collecting taxes under government authority **3. ARMY** a group of soldiers drafted under government authority **4. CONSCRIPTION** the act of drafting soldiers under government authority [15C. < French *levée* (see LEVEE[1])] —**lev·i·a·ble** *adj* —**lev·i·er** *n*

lewd /lood/ *adj* sexual in an offensive way [Old English *lǣw(e)de* "lay, not in holy orders," origin ?] —**lewd·ly** *adv* —**lewd·ness** *n*

Lew·in /loō in/, **Kurt** (1890–1947) German-born US psychologist. He pioneered research in behavior, personality, and group dynamics.

lew·is /loō iss/ *n* an iron attachment consisting of linked pieces that fit into a dovetailed opening in a stone, used to grip heavy stones before lifting them [Mid-18C. Probably < French *lous*, plural of *lou(p)* "kind of siege engine," literally "wolf" < Latin *lupus*]

Lew·is /loō iss/, **Carl** (*b.* 1961) US athlete. He won nine Olympic gold medals for 100- and 200-meter races and the long jump between 1984 and 1996.

Lew·is, C. S. (1898–1963) Irish-born British critic, scholar, and novelist. He wrote books on moral and religious issues, e.g., *The Screwtape Letters* (1942), and a children's book series known as *The Chronicles of Narnia* (1950–56). Full name **Lewis, Clive Staples**

> "Telling us to obey instinct is like telling us to obey "people." People say different things: so do instincts. Our instincts are at war…Each instinct, if you listen to it, will claim to be gratified at the expense of the rest."
> [C. S. Lewis, *The Abolition of Man*; 1943]

Lew·is, Edward B. (*b.* 1918) US geneticist. He shared the Nobel Prize in physiology or medicine (1995) with Eric Wieschaus and Christiane Nüsslein-Volhard for his research into embryonic development.

Lew·is, Gilbert Newton (1875–1946) US chemist. He was noted for his study in chemical thermodynamics and theory of chemical attraction and valence.

Lew·is, Jerry (*b.* 1926) US actor, screenwriter, movie director, and movie producer. He formed a comic duo with Dean Martin, with whom he made 16 movies, and later starred in his own movies. Born **Levitch, Joseph**

Lew·is, Meriwether (1774–1809) US explorer. With William Clark he explored territory between the Mississippi River and the Pacific Ocean (1804–06).

Lew·is, Sinclair (1885–1951) US novelist. He wrote *Babbitt* (1922) and other novels that ridicule middle-class life in the United States, and won a Nobel Prize in literature (1930). Full name **Lewis, Harry Sinclair**. See Cultural note at **Main Street**

> "In other countries, art and literature are left to a lot of shabby bums living in attics and feeding on booze and spaghetti, but in America the successful writer or picture painter is indistinguishable from any other decent business man."
> [Sinclair Lewis, *Babbitt*; 1922]

Lew·is ac·id *n* a substance that can accept a pair of electrons from a base to form a covalent bond [Mid-20C. After Gilbert Newton LEWIS]

Lew·is base *n* a substance that donates an electron pair to an acid during the formation of a covalent bond [Mid-20C. After Gilbert Newton LEWIS]

Lew·is gun *n* a gas-powered machine gun with a circular magazine, first used in World War I [Early 20C. After Colonel Isaac Newton *Lewis* (1858–1931), US soldier]

lew·is·ite /loō i sīt/ *n* a colorless or brownish oily poisonous liquid. Use: in gaseous form in chemical warfare during World War I. Formula: $C_2H_2AsCl_3$. [Early 20C. After Winford Lee *Lewis* (1878–1943), US chemist]

Lew·is rule of eight *n* the observation that chemical elements react together by losing, gaining, or sharing electrons so that they attain eight electrons in their outer shells [Mid-20C. After Gilbert Newton LEWIS]

lew·is·son /loō əss'n/ *n* CONSTR same as **lewis**

Lew·is·ton /loō istən/ **1.** city in northwestern Idaho, where the Clearwater River joins the Snake River near Washington State. Population: 30,487 (2002 estimate). **2.** city in southwestern Maine, on the eastern bank of the Androscoggin River across from Auburn. Population: 35,648 (2002 estimate).

Lew·is with Har·ris /loō iss with hárriss/ largest and northernmost island of the Outer Hebrides, western Scotland. Population: 21,737 (1991). Area: 824 sq. mi./2,134 sq. km.

Le·Witt /lə wít/, **Sol** (*b.* 1928) US artist. An important figure in minimalist and conceptual art, he is best known for his wall drawings and geometric sculptures of cubes, grids, or pyramids.

> "In Conceptual art the idea or concept is the most important aspect of the work…all planning and decisions are made beforehand and the execution is a perfunctory affair. The idea becomes the machine that makes the art."
> [Sol LeWitt, "Paragraphs on Conceptual Art," *Artforum*; Summer, 1967]

lex /leks/ *n* a named law or set of laws [Late 18C. < Latin, "law"]

lex·eme /lék seēm/ *n* a fundamental unit of the vocabulary of a language that may exist in a number of different forms, e.g., "make" existing as "makes, making, maker, made" [Mid-20C. < LEXICON]

lex·i·ca plural of **lexicon**

lex·i·cal /léksik'l/ *adj* **1.** relating to the individual words that make up the vocabulary of a language **2.** relating to a lexicon or to lexicography [Mid-19C. < Greek *lexikos* (see LEXICON)] —**lex·i·cal·i·ty** /lèksi kállətee/ *n* —**lex·i·cal·ly** *adv*

lex·i·cal·ize /léksik'l īz/ (**-ized, -iz·ing, -iz·es**) *vti* to form a single word from existing words, or be formed in this way, in order to express something previously conveyed by several words or a phrase. For example, "front-runner" was lexicalized from "runner at the front of the race." —**lex·i·cal·i·za·tion** /lèksik'li záysh'n/ *n*

lex·i·cal mean·ing *n* the meaning of the base word in the set of inflected forms (**paradigm**). In the paradigm "throw, throws, throwing, threw, thrown," the lexical meaning is "throw."

lexicog. *abbr* **1.** lexicographic **2.** lexicography

lex·i·cog·ra·phy /lèksi kóggrəfee/ *n* the writing and editing of dictionaries [Mid-17C. < Greek *lexikos* (see LEXICON)] —**lex·i·cog·ra·pher** *n* —**lex·i·co·graph·ic** /lèksikə gráffik/ *adj* —**lex·i·co·graph·i·cal·ly** *adv*

lex·i·col·o·gy /lèksi kólləjee/ *n* the branch of linguistics dealing with the use and meanings of words and the relationships between items of vocabulary [Early 19C. < Greek *lexikos* (see LEXICON)] —**lex·i·co·log·i·cal** /lèksikə lójjik'l/ *adj* —**lex·i·co·log·i·cal·ly** *adv* —**lex·i·col·o·gist** *n*

lex·i·con /léksəkən, -kòn/ (*plural* **-cons** or **-ca** /-kə/) *n* **1.** a reference book that alphabetically lists words and their meanings, e.g., of an ancient language **2.** the entire stock of words belonging to a branch of knowledge or known by somebody [Early 17C. Via modern Latin < Greek *lexikon*, form of *lexikos* "of words" < *lexis* "word" < *legein* "speak"]

lex·i·gra·phy /lek síggrəfee/ *n* a system of writing in which each character stands for a word [Early 19C. < Greek *lexis* (see LEXICON)]

Lex·ing·ton /léksingtən/ **1.** city in Fayette County, in northern central Kentucky. The surrounding area is a leading world center for horse breeding and sales. Population: 263,618 (2002 estimate). **2.** town in northeastern Massachusetts, northwest of Boston. It is the site of the first battle of the Revolution in 1775. Population: 30,663 (2002 estimate). **3.** town in the Shenandoah Valley, west central Virginia. It is home to Washington and Lee University, and Virginia Military Institute. Population: 6,910 (2002 estimate).

lex·is /léksiss/ *n* the entire stock of words in a language [Mid-20C. < Greek (see LEXICON)]

lex ta·li·o·nis /lèks tállee əniss/ *n* the legal principle that prescribes retaliating in kind for crimes committed [< Latin, "law of retaliation"]

ley /lay, lee/ (*plural* **leys**) *n* **1.** AGRIC same as **lea 2.** any ancient path in Britain that led from hilltop to hilltop and touched on water sources and places of worship [Early 20C. Variant of LEA]

Ley·den another spelling of **Leiden**

Ley·den ▸ **Lucas van Leyden**

Ley·den jar /līd'n-/ *n* an early device for condensing static electricity consisting of a glass jar coated inside and outside with metal foil and with a conducting rod passing through an insulated stopper [Mid-18C. After the city of LEIDEN (in an alternative spelling)]

ley line /láy-, lée-/ *n* in the United Kingdom, a straight line linking ancient landmarks and places of worship, believed to follow the course of former routes and popularly associated with mystical phenomena [< LEY]

Lez·ghi·an /lézgee ən/ *n* a Dagestanian language spoken in an area around the Caspian Sea. Native speakers: 300,000. [Mid-19C. < Russian *Lezgin*] —**Lez·ghi·an** *adj*

lf *abbr* **1.** PRINTING lightface **2.** PHYS, MEDIA low frequency

LF *abbr* **1.** BASEBALL left field **2.** BASEBALL left fielder **3.** PHYS, MEDIA low frequency

L-form *n* a bacterium that lacks cell walls [After the *Lister* Institute in London, England]

lg. *abbr* **1.** large **2.** *US* long

LGBT *abbr* lesbian, gay, bisexual, transgender (or transsexual)

lgth *abbr UK* length

LH *abbr* BIOCHEM luteinizing hormone

l.h. *abbr* left hand

Lha·sa /laassə, lássə/ city and capital of the autonomous region of Tibet, southwestern China. Population: 161,788 (1991).

Lhasa apso

Lha·sa ap·so /-ap sō, -aap sō, -ápsō/ (*plural* **Lha·sa ap·sos**) *n* a small dog belonging to a Tibetan breed with a long straight coat, hair that falls heavily over the eyes, and a fluffy tail that curls over the back [Early 20C. *Apso* < Tibetan, literally "sentinel"]

lhd *abbr UK* left-hand drive

LHD *abbr* Litterarum Humaniorum Doctor

lher·zo·lite /lúrzə līt/ *n* a coarse-grained rock containing minerals high in iron and magnesium that is believed to originate in the Earth's mantle [After the *Lherz* massif, French Pyrenees]

Lhot·se /lṓt sè/ fourth highest mountain in the world. It is situated in the eastern part of the Himalayan system on the border between China and Nepal. Height: 27,940 ft./8,516 m.

LHRH *abbr* BIOCHEM luteinizing hormone-releasing hormone

li[1] *abbr* **1.** ONLINE Liechtenstein (*used in Internet addresses*) See table at **domain name 2.** link

li[2] /lee/ (*plural same*) *n* a traditional Chinese unit of distance, now standardized at 547 yd./500 m [Late 16C. < Chinese *lǐ*]

Li *symbol* CHEM ELEM lithium

L.I. *abbr US* Long Island

li·a·bil·i·ty /lī ə bíllətee/ *n* (*plural* **-ties**) **1. OBLIGATION UNDER LAW** legal responsibility for something, especially costs or damages **2. DEBT** something for which somebody is responsible, especially a debt **3. DISADVANTAGE** something that holds somebody back or causes trouble **4. SOMEBODY WHO IS BURDEN** somebody who prevents a successful outcome or causes social embarrassment **5. LIKELIHOOD OF SOMETHING** likelihood or probability of something happening ■ **li·a·bil·i·ties** *npl* **MONEY OWED** all debts and other financial obligations that appear on a balance sheet

li·a·ble /lī́ əb'l/ *adj* **1.** having legal responsibility for something, especially costs or damages **2.** likely to experience or do something, often something unpleasant or hazardous [15C. Probably < French *lier* (see LIAISON)]

li·aise /lee áyz/ (**-aised, -ais·ing, -ais·es**) *vi* to establish or maintain close cooperation with somebody [Early 20C. Back-formation < LIAISON]

li·ai·son /lée ay zòn, lee áy-/ *n* **1. COORDINATION** the exchange of information or the planning of joint efforts by two or more people or groups, often of military personnel **2. COORDINATOR** somebody who coordinates communication between two or more people or groups **3. UNMARRIED LOVE AFFAIR** a romantic and sexual relationship between people who are not married to each other, especially when secret **4. PRONOUNCED CONSONANT LINKING TWO WORDS** in spoken French, the pronunciation of the usually silent final consonant of a word when it is followed by another word beginning with a vowel **5. SOMETHING USED TO THICKEN LIQUID** a thickening agent used in soups and sauces, e.g., egg yolks or flour [Mid-17C. < French < *lier* "bind" < Latin *ligare*]

li·an·a /lee áanə, -ánnə/, **li·ane** /-áan, -án/ *n* a woody climbing tropical vine [Late 18C. < French *liane*, originally "clematis"] —**li·a·noid** *adj*

Liao /lyow/ river in northeastern China. Length: 836 mi./1,345 km.

Liao·ning /lyòw níng/ province in northeastern China. Capital: Shenyang. Population: 41,160,000 (1997). Area: 58,301 sq. mi./151,000 sq. km.

Liao·yang /lyòw yáang/, **Liao-yang** city in Liaoning Province, northeastern China, situated 35 mi./56 km south of Shenyang. Population: 559,719 (1991).

Li·a·quat A·li Khan /lee ə kwáat aalee káan/ (1895–1951) prime minister of Pakistan (1947–51). Pakistan's first prime minister, he was assassinated while in office.

li·ar /lī́r/ *n* somebody who tells lies

li·ard /lee áard, -áar/ *n* a coin of small value formerly used in various European countries, including France [Mid-16C. < French]

Li·ard /lée ərd/ river of western Canada, rising in the Yukon Territory and flowing through British Columbia and the Northwest Territories, where it joins the Mackenzie River. Length: 700 mi./1,115 km.

~~**liase**~~ incorrect spelling of **liaise**

~~**liason**~~ incorrect spelling of **liaison**

Li·as·sic /lī ássik/ *adj* belonging to or dating from the oldest division of the European Jurassic period, noted for its fossils of dinosaurs [Mid-19C. < French *liassique* < *Lias* "division of the European Jurassic period" < Old French *liais* "hard limestone"] —**Li·as·sic** *n*

lib /lib/ *n* liberation of an oppressed group (*dated informal; used in combination in names of social campaigns*) ○ *gay lib* [Mid-20C. Shortening of *liberation*] —**lib·ber** *n*

lib. *abbr* LIBRARIES **1.** librarian **2.** library

Lib. *abbr* POL **1.** Liberal **2.** Liberalism

~~**libary**~~ incorrect spelling of **library**

li·ba·tion /lī báysh'n/ *n* **1. POURING OF LIQUID AS RELIGIOUS OFFERING** the pouring out of a liquid, e.g., wine or oil, as a sacrifice to a god or in honor of a dead person **2. SOMETHING POURED OUT AS SACRIFICE** a liquid, e.g., wine or oil, poured out as a religious offering **3. STRONG DRINK** an alcoholic drink (*humorous*) [14C. < Latin *libation-* < *libare* "pour out"] —**li·ba·tion·al** *adj*

Lib·by /líbbee/, **Willard Frank** (1908–80) US chemist. He discovered radiocarbon dating and received the Nobel Prize in chemistry (1960).

li·bel /lī́b'l/ *n* **1. DEFAMATION** a false and malicious published statement that damages somebody's reputation. Libel can include pictures and any other representations that have public or permanent form. **2. ATTACKING OF SOMEBODY'S REPUTATION** the making of false and damaging statements about somebody **3. WRITTEN STATEMENT** the plaintiff's written statement in a case under admiralty law or in an ecclesiastical court ■ *vt* (**-beled, -bel·ing, -bels**) **1. DEFAME SOMEBODY** to publish false and malicious statements about somebody that damage his or her reputation **2. ATTACK SOMEBODY VERBALLY** to give a false and damaging account of somebody **3. SUE SOMEBODY FOR LIBEL** to bring a suit for libel against somebody under admiralty law or in an ecclesiastical court [14C. Via French < Latin *libellus* "little book" < *liber* "book"] —**li·bel·ant** *n* —**li·bel·ee** /lībə lée/ *n* —**li·bel·er** *n* —**li·bel·ist** *n*

SYNONYMS See *malign*.

li·bel·ous /lī́b'l əss/ *adj* constituting or containing a false published statement that damages somebody's reputation —**li·bel·ous·ly** *adv*

Lib·er /lī́bər/ *n* in Roman mythology, a god of wine identified with Bacchus

Lib·er·a·ce /lìbbər aáchee/ (1919–87) US entertainer. A performer of popular piano pieces, he was noted for his flamboyant attire and lavish presentations. Born **Liberace, Wladziu Valentino**

lib·er·al /líbbərəl, líbbrəl/ *adj* **1. BROAD-MINDED** tolerant of different views and standards of behavior in others **2. PROGRESSIVE POLITICALLY OR SOCIALLY** favoring gradual reform, especially political reforms that extend democracy, distribute wealth more evenly, and protect the personal freedom of the individual **3. GENEROUS** freely giving money, time, or some other asset ○ *My great-aunt was liberal in her bequests.* **4. GENEROUS IN QUANTITY** large in size or amount ○ *a liberal helping* **5. NOT LITERAL** not limited to the literal meaning in translation or interpretation ○ *a liberal interpretation of the rules* **6. CULTURALLY ORIENTED** concerned with general cultural matters and broadening of the mind rather than professional or technical study ○ *a liberal education* **7. OF POLITICAL LIBERALISM** relating to a political ideology of liberalism ■ *n* **LIBERAL PERSON** somebody who favors tolerance or open-mindedness [14C. Via French < Latin *liberalis* < *liber* "free"]

SYNONYMS See *generous*.

Lib·er·al *adj* supporting, belonging to, or associated with the Liberal Party in Canada, the United Kingdom, or Australia ■ *n* a member or supporter of the Liberal Party, e.g., in Canada, the United Kingdom, or Australia

lib·er·al arts *npl* **1.** college and university subjects that are intended to provide students with general cultural knowledge, e.g., languages, literature, history, and philosophy **2.** the medieval studies known as the trivium and quadrivium

lib·er·al de·moc·ra·cy *n* a political system that has free elections, a multiplicity of political parties, political decisions made through an independent legislature, and an independent judiciary, with a state monopoly on law enforcement

lib·er·al·ism /líbbərə lìzzəm, líbbrə-/ *n* **1. PROGRESSIVE VIEWS** a belief in tolerance and gradual reform in moral, religious, or political matters **2.** POL **POLITICAL THEORY STRESSING INDIVIDUALISM** a political ideology with its beginnings in western Europe that rejects authoritarian government and defends freedom of speech, association, and religion, and the right to own property **3.** ECON **FREE-MARKET ECONOMICS** an economic theory in favor of free competition and minimal government regulation **4.** CHR **CHRISTIAN THEOLOGICAL MOVEMENT** a movement in Protestantism stressing intellectual freedom and the moral content of Christianity over the doctrines of traditional theology —**lib·er·al·ist** *n* —**lib·er·al·is·tic** /lìbbərə lístik, lìbbrə-/ *adj*

lib·er·al·i·ty /lìbbə rállətee/ *n* **1. GENEROSITY** generous provision of money, time, or another asset **2. LARGENESS** largeness in size or amount **3. BROAD-MINDEDNESS** tolerance of different views and standards of behavior in others

lib·er·al·ize /líbbərə līz, líbbrə-/ (**-ized, -iz·ing, -iz·es**) *vti* to reform and become less strict, or reform something and make it less strict —**lib·er·al·i·za·tion** /lìbbərəli záysh'n, lìbbrəli-/ *n* —**lib·er·al·iz·er** *n*

lib·er·al·ly /líbbərəlee, líbbrə-/ *adv* **1.** with generosity in giving money, time, or another asset **2.** in large quantities or amounts

lib·er·al·ness /líbbərəlnəss/ *n* same as **liberality**

Lib·er·al Par·ty *n* **1.** a major Canadian political party at both the national and provincial levels that first came to power nationally in 1873 **2.** one of the main British political parties, which evolved from the Whigs, merged with the Social Democratic Party in 1988, and later became known as the Liberal and Social Democratic Party

lib·er·ate /líbbə ràyt/ (**-at·ed, -at·ing, -ates**) *vt* **1. SET SOMEBODY FREE PHYSICALLY** to release a person, group, population, or country from political or military control or from severe physical constraint **2. RELEASE**

SOMEBODY FROM SOCIAL CONSTRAINTS to set somebody free from traditional socially imposed constraints such as those arising from stereotyping by gender or age **3.** STEAL SOMETHING to take unlawfully something that belongs to somebody else (*slang*) **4.** CHEM RELEASE GAS DURING CHEMICAL REACTION to free something such as a gas from combination in a chemical compound during a chemical reaction [Late 16C. < Latin *liberat-*, past participle of *liberare* < *liber* "free"] —**lib·er·at·ing** *adj* —**lib·er·at·ing·ly** *adv* —**lib·er·a·tion** /lìbbə ráysh'n/ *n* —**lib·er·a·tor** *n*

lib·er·at·ed /líbbə ràytəd/ *adj* **1.** RELEASED FROM SOCIAL CONSTRAINTS freed from traditional socially imposed constraints, e.g., those arising from sexual or ageist stereotyping **2.** RELEASED FROM ENEMY freed from enemy control ○ *People lined the streets of the newly liberated city and greeted the soldiers with flowers.* **3.** CHEM RELEASED FROM CHEMICAL COMBINATION freed from combination in a chemical compound

lib·er·a·tion the·ol·o·gy *n* a movement in Roman Catholic religious teaching that argues that the Church should work actively to combat social, political, and economic oppression. The movement is international but especially active in Latin America and bases its case on Jesus Christ's ministry to the poor and outcast in society. —**lib·er·a·tion the·o·lo·gi·an** *n*

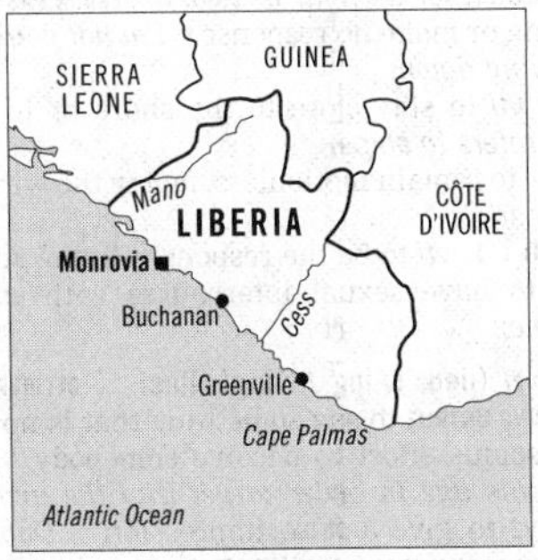

Liberia

Li·be·ri·a /lī béeree ə/ country in West Africa, on the North Atlantic Ocean. Capital: Monrovia. Population: 3,317,176 (2003). Area: 38,250 sq. mi./99,067 sq. km. Official name **Republic of Liberia** —**Li·ber·i·an** *adj, n*

li·be·ro /léebə rō, líbbə rō/ (*plural* **-ros**) *n* **1.** SOCCER same as **sweeper** (sense 3) (*informal*) **2.** in sports such as volleyball and ice hockey, a defensive player who operates freely across the whole playing area [Mid-20C. < Italian, "free" < Latin *liber*]

lib·er·tar·i·an /lìbbər térree ən/ *n* **1.** somebody who believes in the doctrine of free will **2.** somebody who believes in the principle that people should have complete freedom of thought and action [Late 18C. < LIBERTY] —**lib·er·tar·i·an·ism** *n*

Lib·er·ta·ri·an *n* a member or supporter of the Libertarian Party ■ *adj* supporting, belonging to, or associated with the Libertarian Party

Lib·er·tar·i·an Par·ty *n* a US political party founded in 1971 and advocating personal liberty, the free market, free trade, and noninterventionism

lib·er·tine /líbbər tèen/ *n* somebody, usually a man, who indulges in pleasures that are considered immoral and who has sexual relationships with many people [14C. < Latin *libertinus* < *libertus* "somebody freed from slavery" < *liber* "free"] —**lib·er·tin·age** *n* —**lib·er·tin·ism** *n*

lib·er·ty /líbbərtee/ (*plural* **-ties**) *n* **1.** RIGHT TO CHOOSE the freedom to think or act without being constrained by necessity or force **2.** FREEDOM freedom from captivity or slavery **3.** BASIC RIGHT a political, social, and economic right that belongs to the citizens of a state or to all people (*often used in the plural*) **4.** BREACH OF ETIQUETTE an action or remark that violates the polite distance usually left between people and that may strike the person at whom it is directed as insultingly familiar **5.** NAVY LEAVE FROM NAVY a short authorized leave from naval duties [14C. Via French < Latin *libertas* < *liber* "free"] ◇ **at liberty 1.** free or freed after a period of imprisonment or other constraint **2.** free or allowed to do something ◇ **take liberties with somebody** to behave inappropriately toward somebody, especially by way of excessive familiarity or sometimes sexual harassment (*disapproving*) ◇ **take liberties with something** to be deliberately inaccurate when dealing with facts (*disapproving*) ◇ **take the liberty** to be bold enough to do something, sometimes without permission

CULTURAL NOTE *On Liberty*, an essay (1859) by British philosopher John Stuart Mill. A work that has inspired civil libertarians around the world, it examines the relationship between the rights of the individual and the power of the state. Mill argues for freedom of thought and expression, asserting that the only valid restrictions on the rights of individuals are those that protect the rights of others.

CULTURAL NOTE ***Liberty Leading the People***, a painting (1830) by French artist Eugène Delacroix. Inspired by a scene witnessed by Delacroix during the antimonarchist uprisings in Paris in 1830, this mixture of allegory and realism shows a young woman leading a ragged band of rebels over razed barricades. Delacroix's declaration of solidarity with the revolutionary cause is also a powerful symbol of freedom and the struggle against oppression. The painting is sometimes called *Liberty on the Barricades*.

lib·er·ty cap *n* a soft cone-shaped cap fitting tightly on the head and falling to one side, worn as a symbol of freedom by French revolutionaries and in the United States before 1800. It was first worn in ancient Rome, when it was given to people who were set free from slavery.

Lib·er·ty Is·land /líbbərtee-/ island in New York Bay, southeastern New York. It is the site of the Statue of Liberty. Area: 12 acres/5 hectares. Former name **Bedloe's Island** (until 1956)

lib·er·ty pole *n* a tall flagpole to the top of which a liberty cap or the flag of a new republic is attached

lib·er·ty ship *n* a cargo ship mass-produced in the United States during World War II

li·bid·i·nous /li bíddənəss/ *adj* having or expressing strong sexual desires [15C. < Latin *libidinosus* < *libido* "desire"] —**li·bid·i·nous·ly** *adv* —**li·bid·i·nous·ness** *n*

li·bi·do /li béedō/ (*plural* **-dos**) *n* **1.** sexual drive **2.** in some psychoanalytical theories, the psychic and emotional energy in people's psychological makeup that is related to the basic human instincts, especially the sex drive [Early 20C. < Latin, "desire"] —**li·bid·i·nal** /lə bídd'nəl/ *adj* —**li·bid·i·nal·ly** *adv*

Li Bo /lée bṓ/, **Li Po** /lée pṓ/ (701–762) Chinese poet. His work is known for its lyrical beauty and precise imagery.

Li·bra /léebrə, lī-/ *n* **1.** CONSTELLATION IN SOUTHERN HEMISPHERE a zodiacal constellation of the southern hemisphere. See illustration at **constellation 2.** 7TH SIGN OF ZODIAC the seventh sign of the zodiac, represented by a pair of scales and lasting from approximately September 23 to October 22. Libra is classified as an air sign and its ruling planet is Venus. **3.** SOMEBODY BORN UNDER LIBRA somebody whose birthday falls between September 23 and October 22 [Pre-12C. < Latin, "balance, scales"] —**Li·bra** *adj* —**Li·bran** *n, adj*

li·brar·i·an /lī brérree ən/ *n* a worker in or manager of a library [Late 17C. < Latin *librarius* (see LIBRARY)] —**li·brar·i·an·ship** *n*

li·brar·y /lī brèrree, líbrəree, lī bèrree/ (*plural* **-ies**) *n* **1.** PLACE WHERE BOOKS ARE KEPT a room, building, or institution where a collection of books or other research materials is kept **2.** COLLECTION OF THINGS a collection of books, newspapers, records, tapes, or other materials that are valuable for research **3.** COMPUT COLLECTION OF SOFTWARE a collection of things for use on a computer, e.g., programs or diskettes, or a collection of routines or instructions used by a computer program [14C. Via French < Latin *libraria* "bookshop" < *librarius* "of books" < *liber* "book"]

PRONUNCIATION The generally preferred pronunciations of ***library*** sound both of the two *r*'s: /lī brèrree/ or /lībrəree/. A variant pronunciation, to which some people object, is /lī bèrree/, in which the first *r* is dropped. This loss of the *r* is an example of a normal process that happens when some speakers are confronted with the repeated occurrence of the same sound within a word. Finding it difficult to articulate both sounds, especially when trying to say a word fast, some speakers will simply drop one of the two sounds.

li·brar·y e·di·tion *n* a set of books, published in a series, either by a single author or on the same subject and with the same size and format

Li·brar·y of Con·gress *n* the national library of the United States, located in Washington, D.C. and founded by an Act of Congress in 1800. It contains more than 28 million books and pamphlets as well as presidential papers, music, photographs, and recordings.

li·brar·y paste *n* thick white glue made from starch that is used on paper and lightweight cardboard

li·brar·y sci·ence *n* the study of libraries and their administration, including techniques of research and principles of organization

li·bra·tion /lī bráysh'n/ *n* a real or apparent oscillation in the orbit of one astronomical object as seen from the one around which it orbits, especially as seen in the Moon from Earth [Early 17C. < Latin *libration-* < *librare* "to balance" < *libra* "balance, scales"] —**li·brate** *vi* —**li·bra·tion·al** *adj*

~~**libray**~~ incorrect spelling of **library**

lib·ret·ti MUSIC, THEATER plural of **libretto**

li·bret·tist /li bréttist/ *n* a writer of the words for a dramatic musical work such as an opera or musical

li·bret·to /li bréttō/ (*plural* **-tos** or **-ti** /-tee/) *n* the words of a dramatic musical work such as an opera, including both the spoken and the sung parts [Mid-18C. < Italian, "little book" < *libro* "book" < Latin *liber*]

Li·bre·ville /léebrə vìl/ chief port and capital of Gabon, on the Gulf of Guinea. Population: 365,650 (1993 estimate).

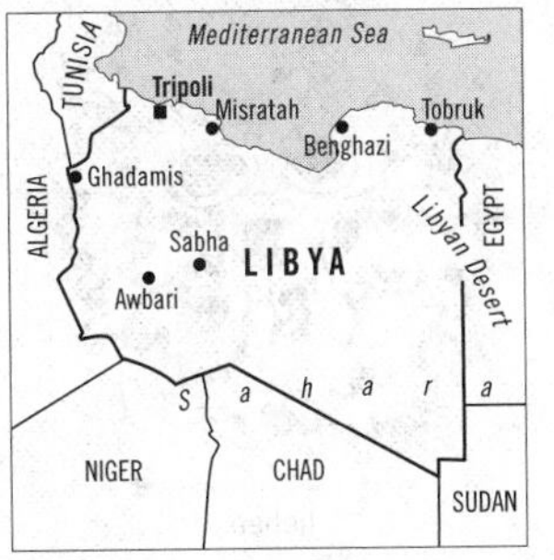

Libya

Lib·y·a /líbbee ə/ country in North Africa, south of the Mediterranean Sea. It was annexed by Italy in 1912, then became independent as a kingdom in 1951. In 1969 the monarchy was ousted in a coup led by Muammar al-Qaddafi. Language: Arabic. Currency: Libyan dinar. Capital: Tripoli. Population: 5,499,074 (2003). Area: 678,400 sq. mi./1,757,000 sq. km. Official name **Socialist People's Libyan Arab Jamahiriyah** —**Lib·y·an** *n, adj*

Lib·y·an Des·ert /líbbee ən-/ desert, the northeastern section of the Sahara, extending from eastern Libya into southwestern Egypt and the extreme northwestern part of Sudan

lice ZOOL plural of **louse**

li·cence *n* LAW, SOC SCI Can, UK spelling of **license**

li·cence plate *n Can* same as **license plate**

li·cense /līss'nss/ *n* **1.** PERMIT a printed document that gives official permission to a person or group to own something or do something **2.** *US* LAW LEGAL AUTHORIZATION official permission to do something, either from a government or under a law or regulation **3.** *US* CHANCE TO DO SOMETHING the opportunity to do something, especially when this goes beyond normal limits ○ *a license to print money* **4.** PERMISSION TO BEND TRUTH the freedom of a writer or artist to rearrange the facts of ordinary life in order to make a more striking effect ○ *artistic license* **5.** *US* LACK OF RESTRAINT freedom in behavior or speech that exceeds what is considered appropriate ■ *vt* (**-censed, -cens·ing, -cens·es**) FORMALLY ALLOW SOMEBODY TO DO SOMETHING to give official permission for somebody to do something or for an activity to take place (*often passive*) ○ *He was licensed to practice medicine in the United States.* [14C. Via French < Latin *licentia* "freedom" < *licere* "be allowed"] —**li·cens·a·ble** *adj* —**li·censed** *adj* —**li·cens·er** *n* —**li·cens·or** *n*

li·censed prac·ti·cal nurse *n* a nurse trained to

provide routine nursing care and allowed to perform more complex tasks only under the direction of a registered nurse or a doctor

li·cens·ee /lìss'n sée/ *n* a person or corporation that is officially permitted to do something

li·cense plate *n US* a thin flat piece of metal showing the registration number of a vehicle, usually attached just above the front and back bumpers. Can term **licence plate**

li·cen·sure /líss'nshər, -shòor/ *n US* the granting of a license, especially to practice a profession

li·cen·ti·ate /lī sénshee ət/ *n* **1.** SOMEBODY AUTHORIZED IN PROFESSION somebody who has been granted a license to practice or teach a profession or skill **2.** LICENSE the license granted a licentiate ○ *He has a licentiate in music.* **3.** ACADEMIC DEGREE a degree awarded by some European universities that ranks one step below that of a doctorate **4.** SOMEBODY WITH LICENTIATE DEGREE somebody holding the degree of licentiate **5.** PRESBYTERIAN PREACHER somebody licensed to preach but not perform the sacraments in a Presbyterian church, usually a trainee minister who has not yet been ordained [15C. < medieval Latin *licentiatus*, past participle of *licentiare* "permit" < Latin *licentia* (see LICENSE)]

li·cen·tious /lī sénshəss/ *adj* pursuing desires aggressively and selfishly, unchecked by morality, especially in sexual matters [15C. < Latin *licentiosus* < *licentia* (see LICENSE)] —**li·cen·tious·ly** *adv* —**li·cen·tious·ness** *n*

li·chee *n* FOOD another spelling of **lychee**

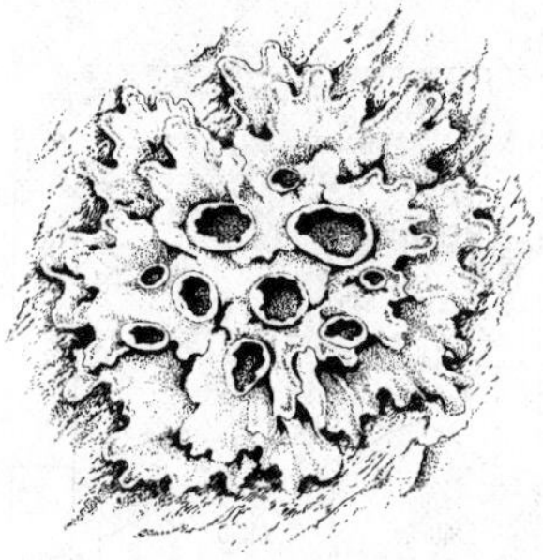

lichen

li·chen /líkən/ *n* a complex organism consisting of fungi and algae growing together in symbiosis that often appears as gray, green, or yellow patches on rocks, trees, and other surfaces [Early 17C. Via Latin < Greek *leikhēn*] —**li·chened** *adj* —**li·chen·i·form** /lī kénni fàwrm, líkəni-/ *adj* —**li·chen·oid** *adj* —**li·chen·ous** *adj*

lich-gate *n* CHR, BUILDINGS another spelling of **lychgate**

Roy Lichtenstein

Lich·ten·stein /líktən stīn/, **Roy** (1923–97) US painter, graphic artist, and sculptor. A major figure in pop art, he is noted for his paintings featuring enlarged comic-strip images.

> "Organized perception is what art is all about…It is a process. It has nothing to do with any external form the painting takes, it has to do with a way of building a unified pattern of seeing."
> [Roy Lichtenstein. Quoted in "What is Pop Art? Interviews with Eight Painters," *Art News*, G. R. Swenson; February 1964]

lic·it /líssit/ *adj* allowed by law [15C. < Latin *licitus*, past participle of *licere* "be allowed"] —**lic·it·ly** *adv* —**lic·it·ness** *n*

SYNONYMS See ***legal***.

lick /lik/ *v* (**licked, lick·ing, licks**) **1.** *vt* PASS TONGUE OVER SOMETHING to move the tongue across the surface of something, either to wet or clean it or as a way to move something into the mouth **2.** *vti* BRUSH AGAINST SOMETHING to touch or lightly move against something **3.** *vt* BEAT SOMEBODY to give somebody a physical beating (*informal*) **4.** *vt* DEFEAT COMPETITOR to defeat somebody easily or thoroughly (*informal*) ■ *n* **1.** MOVEMENT OF TONGUE OVER SOMETHING a movement of the tongue across the surface of something **2.** QUICKLY APPLIED COATING a quick coat of something, especially paint ○ *a lick of paint* **3.** *US* BIT OF SOMETHING a small amount of something (*informal*) **4.** PUNCH a punch or blow (*informal*) **5.** MUSIC BRIEF IMPROVISATION a distinctive few notes or short phrase in pop music or jazz, often improvised (*informal*) **6.** GEOG same as **salt lick** (sense 1) **7.** VET MEDICINAL BLOCK FOR ANIMALS a block of salt or chemical material to be licked by domestic animals as medicine [Old English *liccian* < Germanic] —**lick·er** *n*

lick·er·ish /líkərish/, **liq·uor·ish** *adj* (*archaic*) **1.** taking an excessive or unfair amount, without concern for the needs of others **2.** continually thinking about sex or trying to make sexual contact with others [15C. Alteration of obsolete *lickerous* < Anglo-Norman variant of Old French *lecheros* "lecherous" < *lecheor* (see LECHER)]

lick·e·ty-split /líkətee splít/ *adv* very quickly (*informal*) [*Lickety* < LICK]

lick·ing /líking/ *n* (*informal*) **1.** a beating or spanking **2.** a severe defeat or setback

lick·spit·tle /lík spìtt'l/ *n* somebody who shows undue deference toward social superiors or powerful people (*literary*)

lic·o·rice /líkərish/ (*plural same*) *n* **1.** DRIED BLACK PLANT ROOT the dried black root of a perennial plant or an extract made from it. Use: laxative, confectionery, brewing. **2.** KIND OF CANDY a dense rubbery candy that is usually made in black or red strips and flavored with licorice **3.** PLANT WITH SWEET ROOT a perennial plant with spiked blue feathery leaves and a root with a sweet flavor. Native to: Mediterranean. Latin name: *Glycyrrhiza glabra*. [12C. Via Anglo-Norman < late Latin *liquiritia* < Greek *glukurrhiza* < *glukus* "sweet" + *rhiza* "root"]

lic·tor /líktər/ *n* any of a group of minor officials in ancient Rome who carried the fasces as a symbol of authority and clearing the way for the chief magistrates [14C. < Latin]

lid /lid/ *n* **1.** TOP FOR CONTAINER a cover of a container that can be removed or raised on a hinge to open the container **2.** ANAT same as **eyelid** **3.** RESTRAINT a restraint or control on something that keeps it within acceptable bounds (*informal*) ○ *He promised to keep a lid on manufacturing costs.* **4.** BIOL same as **operculum** (sense 3) **5.** *US* AMOUNT OF MARIJUANA a quantity of marijuana, usually an ounce (*slang*) [Old English *hlid* < Indo-European, "cover, something that bends over"] —**lid·ded** *adj* —**lid·less** *adj* ◇ **flip your lid** to react to something or somebody in the strongest, most emotionally uncontrolled manner possible (*slang*)

li·dar /lī daar/ *n* a device, similar in operation to radar, that uses pulses of laser light to analyze atmospheric phenomena [Mid-20C. Acronym < *light detection and ranging*, after RADAR]

Li·di·ce /líddə sày, léedət-/ village in western Czechoslovakia, in what is now the Czech Republic. It was the scene of a retaliatory massacre of villagers by Nazi German forces during World War II.

Li·do /lée dō/ island reef in northeastern Italy, separating the Venice Lagoon from the Adriatic Sea. It is a beach resort. Population: 20,950 (1980).

li·do·caine /lídə kàyn/ *n* a local anesthetic drug given topically or by injection. It can also be given intravenously to control heart irregularities. [Mid-20C. < ACETANILIDE + *-caine*, INN stem]

lie[1] /lī/ *vi* (**lay** /lay/, **lain** /layn/, **ly·ing** /lī ing/, **lies**) **1.** RECLINE to stretch out on a surface that is slanted or horizontal ○ *She was lying on the sofa.* **2.** BE PLACED FLAT ON SURFACE to be positioned on and supported by a horizontal surface ○ *A book lay open on his bedside table.* **3.** BE LOCATED SOMEWHERE to be located in a particular place ○ *Mexico lies south of the United States.* **4.** BE BURIED to be buried in a particular place ○ *Here lies Martha, beloved daughter of John and Mary.* **5.** BE IN PARTICULAR STATE to be or continue to be in a particular condition or state ○ *It lay hidden for years.* **6.** BE IN PARTICULAR DIRECTION to extend or be in a particular direction ○ *The city lies beneath us, glittering with a thousand lights.* **7.** BE IN STORE to be still to come ○ *A great deal of hard work lies ahead of us.* **8.** STAY UNDISTURBED to remain undiscussed or undisturbed ○ *Let sleeping dogs lie.* **9.** BE ACCEPTABLE IN LAW to be acceptable as an assertion or as evidence in court ■ *n* **1.** ANIMAL'S RESTING PLACE a place where an animal returns to rest or hide **2.** POSITION OF GOLF BALL the position of a golf ball after it comes to rest, as regards the ease with which the next shot can be taken ○ *The ball has quite a good lie, in spite of being in the rough.* [Old English *licgan* < Indo-European]

USAGE See ***lay***[1].

lie around, lie a·bout *vti* to sit around doing nothing in particular (*informal*)
lie back *vi* to relax by stretching out flat on the back or reclining in a chair, especially one that tilts backward
lie down *vi* **1.** LIE ON SURFACE to stretch out flat **2.** REST to rest with the body flat, especially in bed ○ *I need to lie down for an hour or two.* **3.** REMAIN PASSIVE to do nothing or make no response ○ *I'm not going to take this lying down.*
lie off *vti* to stay close to the shore or to another ship (*refers to ships*)
lie to *vi* to remain motionless, facing the wind (*refers to ships*)
lie with *v* **1.** *vti* to be the responsibility of somebody **2.** *vi* to have sexual intercourse with somebody (*archaic*)

lie[2] /lī/ *vi* (**lied, ly·ing** /lī ing/, **lies**) **1.** DELIBERATELY SAY SOMETHING UNTRUE to say something that is not true in a conscious effort to deceive somebody ○ *He lied about his age in order to get into the army.* **2.** BE DECEPTIVE to give a false impression ○ *Don't forget that appearances can lie.* ■ *n* **1.** FALSEHOOD a false statement made deliberately ○ *She told me she wasn't seeing anyone else, but that was a lie.* **2.** FALSE APPEARANCE a situation based on deception or a false impression ○ *beginning to feel that my whole life is a lie* [Old English *lēogan* (verb), *lyge* (noun) < Germanic]

SYNONYMS ***lie, untruth, falsehood, fabrication, fib, white lie***

CORE MEANING: something that is not true

lie a false statement made deliberately ○ *He described the evidence of his accusers as "a pack of lies."* ○ *A police spokesperson declared that the allegation was "a blatant lie."* **untruth** something that is presented as being true but is actually false ○ *This young woman was clearly quite able to tell untruths when it suited her.* **falsehood** an intentionally untrue statement ○ *The account was full of inaccuracies, even falsehoods.* **fabrication** an invented statement, story, or account devised with intent to deceive ○ *She claims that the infamous Richard III of Shakespeare and history books is a Tudor fabrication.* **fib** (*informal*) an insignificant or harmless lie ○ *That's a fib! I know you haven't been sick.* **white lie** a lie not intended to harm, but told in order to avoid distress or embarrassment ○ *telling little white lies in order to avoid conflict* ○ *Why hadn't she told a white lie and said the color was flattering?*

Lieb·frau·milch /léeb frow mìlk/ *n* a slightly sweet white wine from southwestern Germany [Mid-19C. < German *lieb* "dear" + *Frau* "lady" (after Mary, mother of Jesus Christ, patron of the convent where it was produced) + *Milch* "milk"]

Lie·big /léebig/, **Justus, Baron von** (1803–73) German chemist. Noted for his contribution to organic analysis and biochemistry, he established the first chemical research laboratory for students at Giessen, Germany.

> "We are too much accustomed to attribute to a single cause that which is the product of several, and the majority of our controversies come from that."
> [Attributed to Justus Liebig]

Liech·ten·stein /líkt'n stīn/ small independent principality in central Europe, lying between Switzerland, with which it has close ties, and Austria.

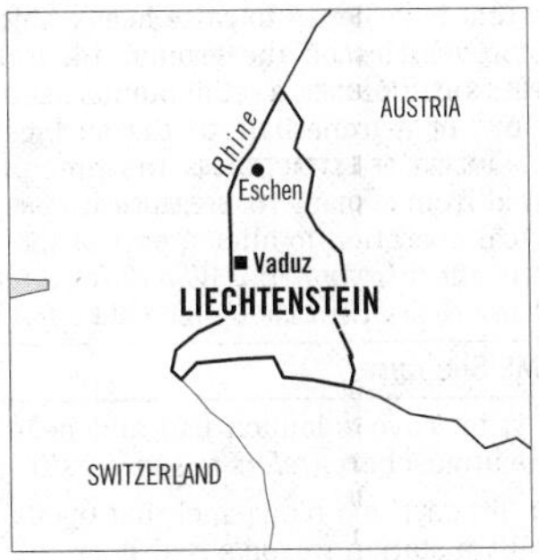

Liechtenstein

Language: German. Currency: Swiss franc. Capital: Vaduz. Population: 33,145 (2003). Area: 62 sq. mi./160 sq. km. Official name **Principality of Liechtenstein**

lied /leet/ (*plural* **lie·der** /leédər/) *n* a German folk or art song, especially an art song of the 19th century with a solo voice part and interwoven piano accompaniment of equal importance. Schubert, Brahms, and Schumann were major composers of lieder. (*usually used in the plural*) [Mid-19C. < German, "song"]

lie de·tec·tor *n* a device for finding out whether somebody is telling the truth during questioning. It has sensors that measure changes in blood pressure and pulse, which are supposed to reflect the uneasiness caused by lying.

lief /leef, leev/ (*archaic*) *adv* WILLINGLY readily or without reluctance ■ *adj* **1.** WILLING ready or desirous **2.** BELOVED dear or treasured [Old English *lēof* < Germanic]

liege /leej, leezh/ *n* **1.** a lord or sovereign who deserves loyalty and service under feudal law **2.** a vassal or subject who owes loyalty and service to a lord or sovereign under feudal law [13C. Via French *lige* < medieval Latin *leticus* < *letus* "colonist with limited freedom," probably < Germanic, "free"] —**liege·dom** *n*

Li·ège /lee áyzh, lyezh/ city and capital of Liège Province, eastern Belgium. Population: 187,538 (1999).

liege·man /leéjmən, leézh-/ (*plural* **-men** /-mən/) *n* **1.** HIST same as **liege** (sense 2) **2.** a faithful or loyal follower

lien /leen, leé ən/ *n* the legal right to keep or sell somebody else's property as security for a debt [Mid-16C. Via French < Latin *ligamen* "bond" < *ligare* "bind"]

lie of the land *n UK* same as **lay of the land** (*informal*)

lierne

li·erne /lee úrn/ *n* a reinforcing rib in the vaulting of a Gothic cathedral or other roofed structure [Mid-19C. < French < *lier* "bind" < Latin *ligare*]

~~**liesure**~~ incorrect spelling of **leisure**

lieu /loo/ *n* place or stead (*archaic*) [Mid-16C. Via French < Latin *locus* "place"] ◇ **in lieu** instead of something else already mentioned or that is usual in the current situation

Lieut. *abbr* MIL Lieutenant

lieu·ten·ant /loo ténnənt/ *n* **1.** DEPUTY an assistant to or substitute for somebody else **2.** NAVY OFFICER an officer in the US Navy or Coast Guard of a rank above lieutenant junior grade, or an officer in the British or Canadian navies of a rank above sublieutenant **3.** POLICE OFFICER OR FIREFIGHTER a US police or fire department officer of a rank above sergeant **4.** ARMY OFFICER a first or second lieutenant in the US Army, Air Force, or Marine Corps of a rank above second lieutenant [14C. < French, "somebody who holds a place" < *lieu* (see LIEU) + *tenant* (see TENANT)] —**lieu·ten·an·cy** *n*

lieu·ten·ant colo·nel *n* an officer in the US, British, or Canadian armies, the US and Canadian air forces, and the US Marine Corps of a rank above major

lieu·ten·ant com·man·der *n* an officer in the US, Canadian, or British navies or the US Coast Guard of a rank above lieutenant

lieu·ten·ant gen·er·al *n* an officer in the US, Canadian, or British armies and the US Marine Corps of a rank above major general

lieu·ten·ant gov·er·nor *n* **1.** an elected official in a state government of a rank below governor **2.** an official appointed by the Canadian federal government who acts for the Crown as the representative of the British monarch in a province —**lieu·ten·ant gov·er·nor·ship** *n*

lieu·ten·ant jun·ior grade (*plural* **lieu·ten·ants jun·ior grade**) *n* an officer in the US Navy or Coast Guard of a rank above ensign

Li·far /lee faár/, **Serge** (1905–86) Russian-born French dancer and choreographer. Director of the Paris Opéra Ballet, he created over 50 ballets, including *Promethée* (1929) and *Icare* (1935).

life /līf/ (*plural* **lives** /līvz/) *n* **1.** EXISTENCE IN PHYSICAL WORLD the quality that makes living animals and plants different from dead organisms and inorganic matter. Its functions include the ability to take in food, adapt to the environment, grow, and reproduce. **2.** LIVING INDIVIDUAL a living being, especially a person, often used when referring to the number of people killed in an accident or a war (*usually used in the plural*) ○ *Two hundred lives were lost in the crash.* **3.** LIVING THINGS CONSIDERED TOGETHER a group of living things, usually of a particular kind ○ *She was an expert on plant life in the Amazon.* **4.** WHOLE TIME SOMEBODY IS ALIVE the entire period during which somebody is, has been, or will yet be alive ○ *All my life I've wanted to learn to fly.* **5.** TIME WHEN SOMETHING FUNCTIONS the period during which something continues to function ○ *Cheap batteries usually have short lives.* **6.** PART OF SOMEBODY'S LIFE a particular aspect of somebody's life ○ *social life* **7.** HUMAN ACTIVITY human existence or activity in general ○ *real life* **8.** WAY IN WHICH SOMEBODY LIVES the character or conditions of somebody's existence ○ *Most people in this city lead hard lives.* **9.** CHARACTERISTIC WAY OF LIVING a way of living that is characteristic of a particular place or group ○ *country life* **10.** VITALITY animation and vitality, or something that produces animation or vitality ○ *We liked him because he was so full of life.* **11.** CHANCE IN GAME PLAYING in various games, a chance to be unsuccessful without being put out of a game (*usually plural*) **12.** LIFE IMPRISONMENT a sentence of life imprisonment (*informal*) **13.** BIOGRAPHY an account of somebody's life, usually in writing, but sometimes in other media such as film, video, or radio ○ *He was the author of "The Life of Aristotle."* **14.** ARTIST'S SUBJECT something real used as a subject by an artist, especially human models, who are often nude ○ *She always insisted on painting from life.* [Old English *līf* < Germanic] ◇ **get a life** to do something to improve your situation or change your lifestyle for the better (*slang*) ◇ **take somebody's** *or* **your life** to kill somebody or yourself. see Synonyms at **kill**[1]

CULTURAL NOTE ***The Life of Samuel Johnson***, a biography (1791) by Scottish writer James Boswell. Generally considered the finest biography in the English language, it is a rounded, revealing, and respectful portrait of one of the great scholars of the day. But its greatness also derives from its vivid descriptions of contemporary society and the candid revelations of its author.

life-and-death *adj* extremely important or serious, especially when somebody's life is at stake ○ *a life-and-death struggle*

life as·sur·ance *n UK* same as **life insurance**

life belt *n* a belt made of material that floats, worn by people taking part in water sports such as sailing to keep them from sinking or drowning

life·blood /līf blùd/ *n* **1.** something that is vitally important to the welfare of a larger entity ○ *Donations are the lifeblood of this organization.* **2.** blood when considered as necessary in maintaining life (*literary*)

life·boat /līf bōt/ *n* **1.** a small boat kept on the deck or railings of a larger ship, for use if the ship has to be abandoned **2.** a boat used for rescuing people from ships in trouble at sea

life buoy *n* a ring-shaped float used in an emergency to keep somebody's head and shoulders above water until help arrives

life coach *n* somebody who provides advice and support to people who wish to improve their lives, helping them to make decisions, solve problems, and achieve goals

life cri·sis *n* a major disruptive event that happens in somebody's lifetime, e.g., bereavement or divorce

life cy·cle *n* **1.** the series of changes of form and activity that a living organism undergoes from its beginning through its development to sexual maturity ○ *the life cycle of the snail* **2.** the complete process of change and development during somebody's lifetime or during the useful life of something such as an organization, institution, or manufactured product

life ex·pec·tan·cy *n* the number of years that somebody can be expected to live, according to statistics

life force *n* PHILOSOPHY same as **élan vital**

life form *n* **1.** a living organism ○ *They scanned the surface of the planet for life forms.* **2.** the characteristic form of an organism at maturity

life·guard /līf gaàrd/ *n* somebody trained in rescue techniques whose job is to watch over swimmers at a beach or swimming pool and save those in danger of drowning

life his·to·ry *n* **1.** ENTIRE STAGES OF LIFE all the changes experienced by a living organism, from its conception to its death **2.** SOMEBODY'S LIFE STORY the story of somebody's life **3.** SOMEBODY'S LIFE STORY USED FOR RESEARCH an account of somebody's life derived from oral or documentary evidence and used in social research. It may shed light on issues of social concern or add to the sum of knowledge about society and social institutions.

life im·pris·on·ment *n* a punishment in which somebody convicted of a crime must remain in prison for the rest of his or her life, or for a very lengthy period. The period of imprisonment may be shortened for good behavior.

life in·sur·ance *n* a plan under which regular payments are made to a company during somebody's lifetime, and in return the company pays a specific sum to the person's beneficiaries after the person's death

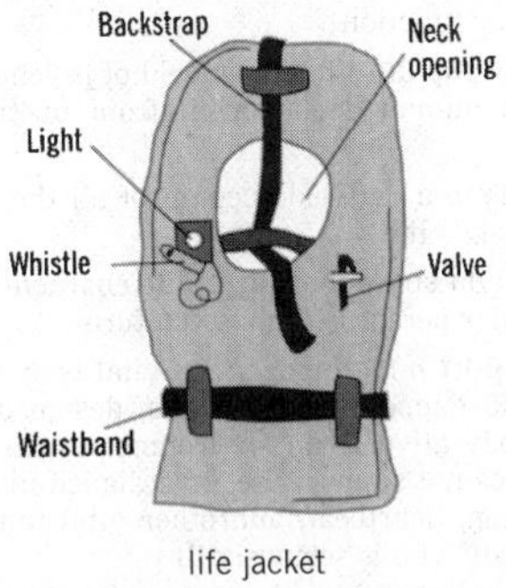

life jacket

life jack·et *n* a sleeveless jacket made of light material or filled with air, used to keep somebody afloat in water

life·less /līfləss/ *adj* **1.** DULL lacking excitement or animation **2.** DEAD dead, or seeming to be dead **3.** WITHOUT LIFE not capable of supporting life —**life·less·ly** *adv* —**life·less·ness** *n*

SYNONYMS See *dead.*

life·like /līf līk/ *adj* looking alive or representing real life accurately

life·line /līf līn/ *n* **1.** a rope or cable used for safety in dangerous maneuvers, especially at sea, e.g., attached to a diver's helmet or stretched along the deck of a boat **2.** a means of communication or support that is extremely important to the survival of an isolated person or group

life list *n* a birdwatcher's record of all the species of birds sighted in a lifetime

life·long /lîf làwng/ *adj* lasting the whole of a lifetime

life mask *n* a cast made of a living person's face, using plaster or another soft substance that hardens when it dries

life mem·ber *n* a member of an organization whose membership is valid for the rest of his or her life and does not require periodic renewal —**life mem·ber·ship** *n*

life-or-death *adj* same as **life-and-death**

life part·ner *n* the person with whom somebody has decided to spend the rest of his or her life in a sexual and romantic relationship ○*"... makes people believe that somewhere there really is the life partner who will provide the ecstatic happiness depicted in opera..."* (*The New York Times*; April 1999)

life peer *n* somebody who is granted a title and seat in the British House of Lords that cannot be inherited —**life peer·age** *n*

life pre·serv·er *n* a ring, belt, or jacket made of material that floats in water, designed to prevent drowning by keeping the wearer's head and shoulders above water

lif·er /lîfər/ *n* (*informal*) **1.** somebody sentenced to life imprisonment **2.** *US* somebody who spends an entire career in one of the armed forces

life raft *n* a raft usually made of inflatable plastic designed for use during an emergency at sea

life·sav·er /lîf sàyvər/ *n* a provider or source of greatly needed help (*informal*)

life·sav·ing /lîf sàyving/ *adj* RESCUING OR REVIVING used to rescue people or keep them alive ■ *n* **1.** RESCUING OF PEOPLE techniques or efforts to rescue people from danger, especially from drowning **2.** MULTIACTIVITY WATER-BASED SPORT in Australia, the activities of a lifeguard or a team of lifeguards formalized as a multiactivity sport. This forms the basis of the Iron Man and Iron Woman contests.

life sci·ence *n* a branch of science that is concerned with plants, animals, and other living organisms, e.g., biology, botany, and zoology (*often used in the plural*)

life sen·tence *n* a court verdict that condemns a convicted felon to spend the rest of his or her life, or a very lengthy period, in prison. It may be shortened for good behavior.

life-size *adj* being the size of the original in life

life span *n* **1.** the length of time that a member of a particular species can be expected to remain alive **2.** the length of time that something can be expected to last or function

life span psy·chol·o·gy *n* a field of psychology that studies human development from birth through death

life sto·ry *n* a detailed account of all the events of somebody's life

life·style /lîf stîl/ *n* the way of life characteristic of a particular person, group, or culture

life-sup·port *n* maintenance of vital body functions by a life-support system ■ *adj* designed to keep somebody alive in an environment such as space that does not support life, or designed to maintain breathing, heartbeat, and other vital functions in somebody who is seriously ill

life-sup·port sys·tem *n* **1.** a piece of technical equipment that temporarily performs a vital body function such as respiration when somebody's own organ cannot because of injury or disease **2.** a piece of technical equipment that is designed to provide normal living conditions when these are not available, especially in space

life's work *n Can, UK* same as **lifework**

life ta·ble *n* INSUR same as **mortality table**

life-threat·en·ing *adj* very dangerous or serious with the possibility of death as an outcome

life·time /lîf tîm/ *n* **1.** TIME REMAINING ALIVE the length of time that somebody or something remains alive **2.** TIME REMAINING USEFUL the length of time that something remains useful or in working order **3.** LONG TIME an extremely long time (*informal*) ◇ **chance** *or* **opportunity of a lifetime** a highly favorable situation that is unlikely to recur

life vest *n* SAFETY same as **life jacket**

life·work /lîf wùrk/ *n* something that is the product, result, or culmination of somebody's working life

life zone *n US* an area with a characteristic or identifiable set of animal or plant life forms

Lif·fey /liffee/ river in the eastern part of the Republic of Ireland. It rises in the Wicklow Mountains southwest of Dublin and empties into Dublin Bay. Length: 50 mi./80 km.

LIFO /lîfō/ *abbr* ACCT last in, first out

lift /lift/ *v* (**lift·ed, lift·ing, lifts**) **1.** *vt* RAISE SOMETHING to move something from one position to another, higher position **2.** *vi* MOVE HIGHER to move to a higher level than before **3.** *vt* MOVE SOMETHING UPWARD to direct something upward ○ *lifting her eyes from the book* **4.** *vi* GO UPWARD to move, especially mechanically, in an upward direction ○ *Just press the button, and the car trunk will lift automatically.* **5.** *vt* TAKE SOMETHING FROM PLACE to grasp something and move it somewhere else ○ *She lifted the CD from the rack.* **6.** *vt* AVIAT CARRY SOMEBODY OR SOMETHING IN AIRCRAFT to transport somebody or something in an aircraft ○ *The rescue helicopter lifted the stranded climbers to safety.* **7.** *vt* MAKE SOMETHING INVALID to revoke something or make something no longer apply ○ *The government has decided to lift the trade restrictions.* **8.** *vt* REMOVE WRINKLES SURGICALLY to perform cosmetic surgery on a face to tighten the skin and so reduce wrinkling, or on a woman's breasts to reduce or eliminate sagging **9.** *vti* CHEER SOMEBODY OR BECOME CHEERED to make somebody happier or more cheerful, or become happier or more cheerful ○ *A cup of hot tea will lift your spirits.* ○ *His low spirits lifted after a few songs.* **10.** *vi* DIMINISH to clear, disappear, or become less severe ○ *I think we should wait until this fog lifts.* **11.** *vt* STEAL SOMETHING to steal something or take something away without the owner's permission or knowledge (*informal*) ○ *A pickpocket lifted my wallet.* **12.** *vt* PLAGIARIZE SOMEBODY'S WORK to take and use somebody else's work without attributing it to its creator (*informal*) ○ *She was accused of lifting her first two paragraphs from a report on a webpage.* **13.** *vt* SPORTS HIT BALL HIGH INTO AIR to hit a baseball or golf ball high into the air ○ *lifting one straight down the fairway* **14.** *vt* MAKE SOMETHING BE HEARD to increase the sound from something such as the voice to make it be heard or be heard more easily or clearly ○ *The choir lifted their voices in song.* **15.** *vt* IMPROVE SOMETHING to raise the level of a performance or enhance a skill ○ *She managed to lift her grades last semester.* **16.** *vt* FIN PAY BACK MONEY to pay something back, especially a debt, mortgage, or another obligation **17.** *vt* RAISE STATUS OF SOMEBODY OR SOMETHING to have the effect of raising somebody or something in terms of status, respect, or public or official estimation ○ *Her latest novel has lifted her into the league of best-selling authors.* **18.** *vt* MIL STOP MILITARY ASSAULT to cease the firing of artillery or naval guns during a combat operation or assault so as to allow ground personnel to move forward **19.** *vt* AGRIC HARVEST UNDERGROUND VEGETABLE to dig up a plant for its edible underground tubers ○ *lift potatoes* **20.** *vt* GARDENING DIG UP PLANT FOR TRANSPLANTING to dig up a plant in order to transplant it ■ *n* **1.** RISE IN SPIRITS a rise in spirits, mood, or emotions that can often be attributed to a specific cause ○ *audiences turning to feel-good movies to give themselves a lift* **2.** TRANSP RIDE IN VEHICLE a free ride as a passenger in somebody else's motor vehicle (*informal*) ○ *Do you want a lift to the airport?* **3.** SOMETHING ADDED TO SHOE a layer of material that is put inside a shoe or added to the heel of a shoe to make the wearer appear taller **4.** AVIAT UPWARD FORCE ACTING ON AIRCRAFT the combination of forces that act to cause an aircraft to leave the ground and stay in the air **5.** RAISING OF PARTNER IN AIR an act of raising a partner in pairs skating or ice dancing as part of a choreographed sequence **6.** RAISING OF SOMEBODY OR SOMETHING a placing of somebody or something in a higher position **7.** DEGREE OF RISE the degree or distance by which something rises ○ *a moderate lift in temperature* **8.** FORCE NEEDED TO RAISE SOMETHING the power or force available, necessary, or used for raising something **9.** WEIGHT RAISED a weight or an amount of something that is or can be raised **10.** *UK* same as **elevator** (sense 1) **11.** PHYS FORCE MAKING HOT-AIR BALLOON RISE the force, usually provided by heated air, that makes a hot-air balloon or airship rise into the sky **12.** CLOTHING same as **heeltap** (sense 2) **13.** AUTOMOT MECHANICAL RAISING DEVICE a typically hydraulic-powered device that is designed to raise heavy objects such as motor vehicles off the ground **14.** MIN EXTRACT WATER PUMPS USED IN MINING a set of pumps used to pump water out of a mineshaft to the surface **15.** MIN EXTRACT AMOUNT OF EXTRACTED ORE the amount of ore extracted from a seam **16.** OPERATION ALTERING BODY PART a surgical operation to alter a part of the body for cosmetic effect (*informal*) ○ *Who did your lift?* [12C. < Old Norse *lypta* < Germanic] —**lift·a·ble** *adj* —**lift·er** *n*

SYNONYMS See ***raise***.

lift off *vi* to leave a launch pad and head upward into the atmosphere (*refers to spacecraft*)

lift·gate /lift gàyt/ *n* a rear panel that opens upward, especially a station wagon's rear door

lift·off /lift àwf, -ôf/ *n* **1.** the time when a rocket or spacecraft leaves the launch pad **2.** the initial thrust that sends a rocket or spacecraft upward from the launch pad into the atmosphere

lig·a·ment /liggəmənt/ *n* **1.** a sheet or band of tough fibrous tissue that connects bones or cartilage at a joint or supports an organ, muscle, or other body part **2.** something that forms a connection or bond [14C. < Latin *ligamentum* < *ligare* "bind"] —**lig·a·ment·al** /liggə mént'l/ *adj* —**lig·a·men·ta·ry** /-méntəree/ *adj* —**lig·a·men·tous** /-méntəss/ *adj*

ORIGIN The Latin word *ligare* "to bind," from which ***ligament*** is derived, is also the source of English *ally, liaison, lien, ligature, oblige,* and *rely,* and probably also of *liable* and *religion*.

li·gan *n* NAUT same as **lagan**

li·gand /lîgənd, liggənd/ *n* an atom, molecule, group, or ion that is bound to a central atom of a molecule, forming a complex [Mid-20C. < Latin *ligandus* < *ligare* "bind"]

li·gase /lî gàyss, -gàyz/ *n* an enzyme that joins two molecules, especially in living organisms [Mid-20C. < Latin *ligare* "bind"]

li·gate /lî gàyt/ (**-gat·ed, -gat·ing, -gates**) *vt* to bind something or tie something up (*technical*) [Late 16C. < Latin *ligat-* (see LIGATURE)] —**lig·a·tive** /liggətiv/ *adj*

li·ga·tion /lî gáysh'n/ *n* **1.** the tying of something with a surgical ligature **2.** something that is used for binding things or tying things up (*formal*)

lig·a·ture /liggəchər, liggə chòor/ *n* **1.** SOMETHING USED FOR TYING something that is used for binding things or tying things up **2.** TYING PROCESS the process of binding something or tying something up **3.** BOND a unifying link or bond (*formal*) **4.** SURG SURGICAL THREAD FOR TYING OFF DUCT a piece of surgical thread used to tie off a duct or blood vessel in order to cut off the supply of body fluid normally running through it **5.** PRINTING CHARACTER CONSISTING OF JOINED LETTERS a character or piece of type that consists of two or more letters joined together, e.g., "æ" **6.** MUSIC same as **tie** *n* (sense 8) **7.** MUSIC SYMBOL IN MEDIEVAL MUSIC in the notation of medieval music, a symbol indicating a group of notes to be sung to one syllable **8.** MUSIC REED-HOLDER ON WOODWIND INSTRUMENT on a woodwind instrument, a band, usually made of metal, that holds the reed to the mouthpiece [14C. Directly or via French < late Latin *ligatura* < Latin *ligat-*, past participle of *ligare* "bind"]

li·ger /lîgər/ *n* the offspring that results from breeding a male lion with a female tiger [Mid-20C. Blend of LION + TIGER]

Li·ge·ti /li géttee/, **György** (*b.* 1923) Hungarian composer. His choral and orchestral works explore slowly moving colors and textures.

light[1] /lît/ *n* **1.** ENERGY PRODUCING BRIGHTNESS the energy producing a sensation of brightness that makes seeing possible **2.** QUALITY OF LIGHT a particular kind or quality of brightness ○ *We won't get good photographs in this fading light.* **3.** ARTIFICIAL SOURCE OF LIGHT an artificial source of illumination, e.g., an electric lamp or a candle ○ *turn the light on* **4.** PATH TAKEN BY LIGHT the path that light takes or somebody's share or access to light ○ *asked her to move out of my light* **5.** DAYLIGHT the condition of brightness created by the rays of the sun during the day ○ *keep filming while there's still some light left* **6.** DAWN the arrival of the sun's brightness at the beginning of the day ○ *get up before light to go running* **7.** TRAFFIC SIGNAL a signal that controls the movement of traffic ○ *Turn right at the first set of lights.* **8.** GENERAL NOTICE general or public notice, attention, or knowledge ○ *facts that only recently came to light* **9.** WAY SOMETHING IS VIEWED the manner in which somebody or something is regarded, especially by the public ○ *Those actions have shown the commission in an exceptionally bad light.* **10.** SOMETHING THAT IGNITES SOMETHING a source of fire, especially a match **11.** GLEAM IN SOMEBODY'S EYE a glint in somebody's eye that is taken to indicate a particular mood or expression ○ *had a mischievous light in her eye* **12.** ARTS REPRESENTATION OF LIGHT IN ART the representation of light or the effect it has in a work of art **13.** ENTRY IN CROSSWORD GRID an entry in the grid of a cryptic crossword **14.** BUILDINGS WINDOW a window or other opening in a building, designed to let sunlight in **15.** PHYS VISIBLE ELECTROMAGNETIC RADIATION electromagnetic radiation in the range visible to the human eye, between approximately 4,000 and 7,700 angstroms **16.** PHYS ELECTROMAGNETIC RADIATION electromagnetic radiation that has wavelengths of any length ■ *adj* **1.** FULL OF BRIGHTNESS full of illumination, or relatively well lit ○ *a light airy room* **2.** PALE of a relatively pale shade ○ *decorated in light green* **3.** *US* WITH MILK served with milk or cream added ○ *Do you want your coffee light or black?* ■ *v* (**lit** /lit/ or **light·ed, light·ing, lights**) **1.** *vti* START BURNING to begin to burn, or cause something to begin to burn ○ *Still trying to light the grill?* **2.** *vt* ILLUMINATE SOMETHING to illuminate, brighten, or shine on something ○ *A full moon lit the night sky.* **3.** *vt* GIVE SOMETHING ANIMATED LOOK to give somebody's eyes or face a happy or animated look ○ *A playful smile lit his face.* **4.** *vt* LEAD SOMEBODY WITH LIGHT to lead or direct somebody with a source of illumination such as a flashlight ○ *The usher lit the way to our seats.* [Old English *lēoht* < Indo-European] ◇ **bring something to light** to reveal something, especially after an investigation ◇ **cast light on something** same as **shed** *or* **throw light on something** ◇ **come to light** to be revealed or made evident ◇ **go out like a light** to fall asleep very quickly and deeply (*informal*) ◇ **in the cold light of day, in the hard light of morning** when things are seen for what they really are rather than being seen in an unrealistically favorable light ◇ **in (the) light of something** taking into consideration what is known or what has just been said or found out ◇ **the light of day** the early hours of daylight, especially at dawn ◇ **the light of somebody's life** the person somebody cherishes the most ◇ **punch** *or* **put somebody's lights out** to give somebody a severe beating (*informal*) ◇ **see the light 1.** to have a sudden understanding or appreciation of something **2.** to be converted to a faith, belief, or point of view ◇ **see the light of day** to be published or made publicly known ◇ **shed** *or* **throw light on something** to make it possible or easier to understand something

light into *vt* to attack somebody or something, either verbally or physically (*informal*)

light out *vi US* to leave a place in a hurry (*informal*)

light up *v* **1.** *vti* LIGHT CIGARETTE OR PIPE to light something such as a cigarette, cigar, or pipe and begin smoking it **2.** *vt* ILLUMINATE SOMETHING to direct light on somebody or something **3.** *vti* MAKE OR BECOME CHEERFUL to become animated or cheerful, or cause something or somebody to become animated or cheerful **4.** *vi* BEGIN SHINING to start to shine

light[2] /līt/ *adj* **1.** NOT HEAVY weighing comparatively little **2.** LIGHTWEIGHT made of thin fabric ○ *light summer apparel* **3.** LESS SEVERE THAN POSSIBLE considered less severe or harsh than might have been the case ○ *a light sentence* **4.** NOT FORCEFUL performed with little physical force ○ *She felt a light tap on her shoulder.* **5.** EASY TO DO involving relatively little effort or exertion ○ *a little light weeding* **6.** EASILY DIGESTED easily digested, or not very filling ○ *a light snack* **7.** FOOD LOW IN CALORIES low in calories, especially containing less than the usual amount of sugar or fat **8.** CONSUMING LITTLE OF SOMETHING consuming something in small quantities only ○ *a light eater* **9.** NOT DENSE low in density or intensity ○ *only a light shower* **10.** EASILY AWAKENED easily awakened or disturbed when asleep ○ *a light sleeper* **11.** NOT INTELLECTUALLY DEMANDING not meant for serious study or contemplation ○ *some light vacation reading* **12.** BEVERAGES LOW IN ALCOHOL having a very low alcohol content **13.** UNIMPORTANT of relatively little importance or seriousness ○ *a light throwaway remark* **14.** WEIGHING TOO LITTLE weighing less than is correct or less than would be expected ○ *This sack is a couple of ounces light.* **15.** NIMBLE moving with grace and agility ○ *She's very light on her feet.* **16.** FOOD FLUFFY AND WELL RISEN of a light, flaky, fluffy, and well-risen consistency ○ *a very light pastry* **17.** SHORT OF SOMETHING lacking the usual or expected quantity of something ○ *a nice guy, if a little light on brains* **18.** UNWORRIED not burdened by worries ○ *a light heart* **19.** DIZZY slightly dizzy or not quite thinking clearly, e.g., because of fatigue, alcohol, or drugs ○ *a light head* **20.** MANUFACTURING SMALL PRODUCTS involved in the manufacture of comparatively small products, especially consumer goods made without the use of heavy machinery **21.** WINE DELICATELY FLAVORED having a fresh delicate flavor ○ *a light rosé wine* **22.** CARRYING SMALL WEIGHTS designed to carry something that is relatively low in weight or relatively small in bulk ○ *a light delivery van* **23.** MIL NOT HEAVILY ARMED carrying only hand-held weapons ○ *a light infantry brigade* **24.** NOT LOADED not containing or carrying a full load **25.** CHEM WITH LOW BOILING POINT having a relatively low boiling point **26.** AGRIC, GARDENING EASILY WORKED loose, well aerated, and therefore easily worked ○ *light soil* **27.** PHON UNSTRESSED describes a syllable that is not stressed or accented **28.** CARDS OF LOW VALUE describes a bid in bridge that is made on a fewer than normal number of points **29.** CARDS WITH TOO FEW TRICKS describes a bridge player who has taken too few tricks to make a contract **30.** IMMORAL with low moral standards, especially relating to sexual behavior (*archaic*) ■ *adv* **1.** WITH LITTLE LUGGAGE with only a small amount of luggage ○ *traveling light* **2.** LENIENTLY in a casual or lenient way ○ *Go light on him – he didn't mean to break the window.* ■ *vi* (**light·ed** or **lit** /lit/, **light·ing, lights**) **1.** COME TO REST to come to rest on a branch after flight (*refers to birds*) **2.** GET DOWN FROM VEHICLE to get down from a horse, vehicle, or other form of transportation (*dated*) [Old English *lēocht, līht* < Indo-European] ◇ **make light of something** to treat something as unimportant

Light *n* **1.** God as a source of spiritual illumination and strength **2.** CHR same as **Inner Light**

light ad·ap·ta·tion, light ad·ap·tion *n* the rapid changes that occur in the eye to permit vision when moving from darkness to light. The pupil constricts and the retina is bleached of visual pigment, making it less sensitive to light. [< LIGHT[1]] —**light-a·dapt·ed** *adj*

light air *n* a wind of between 1 and 3 mi./1.6 and 4.8 km per hour, classified as force one on the Beaufort scale [< LIGHT[2]]

light air·craft *n Can, UK* an aircraft that has a takeoff weight that does not exceed 12,500 lbs./5,670 kg. US term **light plane** [< LIGHT[2]]

light bread *n Southern US* same as **white bread** [< LIGHT[2]]

REGIONAL NOTE The term ***light bread*** is used in the southern United States from the Atlantic coast to Texas, with scattered usage in the Rocky Mountain and Pacific states.

light breeze *n* a wind of between 4 and 7 mi./6.4 and 11 km per hour, classified as force two on the Beaufort scale [< LIGHT[2]]

light bulb *n* a near-spherical glass case containing a filament that emits light when an electric current is passed through it. The filament is usually made of tungsten and is surrounded by argon or neon. [< LIGHT[1]]

light chain *n* the shorter of the two main polypeptides that make up an antibody molecule [< LIGHT[2]]

light-col·ored *adj* of a pale shade or hue [< LIGHT[1]]

light-e·mit·ting di·ode *n* ELEC ENG full form of **LED** [< LIGHT[1]]

light·en[1] /līt'n/ (**-ened, -en·ing, -ens**) *vti* **1.** REDUCE IN WEIGHT to become less heavy, or make something less heavy **2.** REDUCE IN UNPLEASANTNESS to become less of a burden or chore, or cause something to become less of a burden or chore **3.** INCREASE IN CHEERFULNESS to become more relaxed or lively, or make somebody or something become more relaxed or lively ○ *The mood of the gathering lightened a little.* [14C. < LIGHT[2]]

SPELLCHECK See ***lightening***.

lighten up *vi* to become less gloomy, serious, or angry (*informal*)

light·en[2] /līt'n/ (**-ened, -en·ing, -ens**) *v* **1.** *vti* INCREASE IN PALENESS to become pale or paler in color, or cause something to become pale or paler in color **2.** *vi* GLOW to give off shining or glowing illumination **3.** *vi* FLASH to flash across the sky (*refers to lightning*) [13C. < LIGHT[1]]

SPELLCHECK See ***lightening***.

light·en·ing /līt'ning/ *n* the process or time during late pregnancy when the fetal head begins to descend into the mother's pelvis, resulting in a lessening of pressure on the diaphragm [< LIGHTEN[1]]

SPELLCHECK lightening or **lightning**? Do not confuse the spelling of ***lightening*** and ***lightning***, which sound similar. ***Lightening*** is the present participle of either of the verbs *lighten* (as in *lightening the load, lightening his hair*), and as a verbal noun is also used with specific reference to a stage of pregnancy. The noun meaning "a flash of light in the sky during a storm" is spelled ***lightning*** (as in *thunder and lightning*), as is the corresponding adjective meaning "very fast or sudden" (as in *with lightning speed*).

light en·ter·tain·ment *n* entertainment that is not serious or highbrow in content, usually involving comedy, singing, dancing, or popular music

light·er[1] /lītər/ *n* **1.** a small typically gas-filled container with a flint or other spark-producer that produces a flame used for lighting something that is smoked, e.g., a cigarette, cigar, or pipe **2.** a person or device that lights, illuminates, or ignites something (*usually used in combination*) ○ *a lamplighter* [Mid-16C. < LIGHT[1] (verb)]

light·er[2] /lītər/ *n* a flat-bottomed open cargo boat or barge, used especially for taking goods to or from a larger vessel when it is being loaded or unloaded ■ *vt* (**-ered, -er·ing, -ers**) to transport cargo using a lighter [14C. Origin ?]

light·erd /lītərd/, **light·ered** *n Southern US* resinous pine used for kindling [Alteration of LIGHTWOOD]

light·erd knot float·er, light·ered knot float·er, light·er knot float·er *n regional* a storm whose violent winds or heavy rains spread debris

REGIONAL NOTE See ***trashmover***.

light·er-than-air *adj* describes aircraft such as hot-air balloons and dirigibles that weigh less than the air they displace [< *lighter* comparative of LIGHT[2] adj] —**light·er-than-air** *n*

light·face /līt fàyss/ *adj also* **light-faced** describes printed type with characters formed from relatively narrow lines ■ *n* printed type that is lightface [< LIGHT[2]]

light·fast /līt fàst/ *adj* describes a dye or dyed fabric whose shade or color is unchanged by exposure to light, especially sunlight [Early 20C. < LIGHT[1], after COLORFAST] —**light·fast·ness** *n*

light-fin·gered *adj* **1.** skilled at and likely to try shoplifting, pickpocketing, or petty stealing **2.** able to move the fingers quickly and nimbly, and therefore good at doing intricate jobs [< LIGHT[2]] —**light-fin·gered·ness** *n*

light fly·weight *n* **1.** in amateur boxing, a weight category for competitors whose weight does not exceed 106 lb./48 kg **2.** an amateur boxer who competes at light flyweight level [< LIGHT[2]]

light·foot /līt fòot/ *adj* same as **light-footed**

Light·foot /līt fòot/, **Gordon** (*b.* 1938) Canadian-born US folk-pop singer and writer. His songs include "If You Could Read My Mind" (1971).

light-foot·ed *adj* able to walk or run with light agile easy-flowing steps [< LIGHT[2]] —**light-foot·ed·ly** *adv* —**light-foot·ed·ness** *n*

light-hand·ed *adj US* having a steady, delicate touch [< LIGHT[2]] —**light-hand·ed·ly** *adv* —**light-hand·ed·ness** *n*

light·head·ed /līt héddəd/ *adj* **1.** slightly dizzy or euphoric, experienced as an effect of caffeine, alcohol, or fatigue **2.** having a tendency to behave in a frivolous or immature way [15C. < LIGHT[2]] —**light·head·ed·ly** *adv* —**light·head·ed·ness** *n*

light·heart·ed /līt haártəd/ *adj* **1.** not weighed down with worries or troubles **2.** entertaining in an amusing carefree way [15C. < LIGHT[2]] —**light·heart·ed·ly** *adv* —**light·heart·ed·ness** *n*

light heav·y·weight *n* **1.** WEIGHT CATEGORY IN PROFESSIONAL BOXING in professional boxing, a weight category for competitors who weigh between 160 and 175 lb./72.5 and 79.5 kg **2.** WEIGHT CATEGORY IN AMATEUR BOXING in amateur boxing, a weight category for competitors who weigh between 165 and 178 lb./75 and 81 kg **3.** BOXER COMPETING AT LIGHT HEAVYWEIGHT a professional or amateur boxer who competes at light heavyweight level **4.** WEIGHT CATEGORY IN WRESTLING in wrestling, a weight category for competitors who weigh between 192 and 214 lb./87 and 97 kg **5.** WRESTLER COMPETING AT LIGHT HEAVYWEIGHT a wrestler who competes at light heavyweight level [< LIGHT[2]]

lighthouse

light·house /lĭt hòwss/ (*plural* **-houses** /-hòwzəz/) *n* a strategically placed coastal building, often a tall round tower, with a powerful flashing light, designed to guide sailors or warn them of dangers such as rocks [Early 17C. < LIGHT[1]]

CULTURAL NOTE ***To the Lighthouse***, a novel (1927) by British writer Virginia Woolf. Typical of Woolf's more experimental novels in its unusual structure and use of stream-of-consciousness narrative, it is set at the vacation home of the Ramsay family on a Scottish island. Through the relationship between Mrs. Ramsay and a young painter, Lily Briscoe, Woolf explores the changing roles and attitudes of contemporary women.

light-in·de·pend·ent re·ac·tion *n* BOT same as **dark reaction** [< LIGHT[1]]

light·ing /lĭting/ *n* **1.** TYPE OF LIGHT light of a particular quality or type, or the equipment that produces it ○ *subdued lighting* ○ *lighting fixtures* **2.** EQUIPMENT FOR PROVIDING ARTIFICIAL LIGHT the equipment used for providing artificial light and light effects on a theater stage or a television or movie set **3.** EFFECT PRODUCED BY LIGHTS the overall effect produced by the lights used on a theater stage or a television or movie set **4.** QUALITY OF LIGHT IN ARTWORK the amount or type of light in a photograph, painting, or other artwork [Pre-12C. < LIGHT[1]]

light·ly /lĭtlee/ *adv* **1.** WITH LITTLE FORCE without exerting much pressure, force, or weight **2.** SPARINGLY in small or sparing amounts **3.** WITH LEVITY without seriousness **4.** GRACEFULLY in an easy graceful way [Pre-12C. < LIGHT[2]]

light me·ter *n* PHOTOGRAPHY same as **exposure meter** [< LIGHT[1]]

light mid·dle·weight *n* **1.** in amateur boxing, a weight category for competitors who weigh between 148 and 156 lb./67 and 71 kg **2.** an amateur boxer who competes at light middleweight level [< LIGHT[2]]

light-mind·ed *adj* not capable of thinking seriously, or not likely to think about serious issues [< LIGHT[2]] —**light-mind·ed·ly** *adv* —**light-mind·ed·ness** *n*

light·ness[1] /lĭtnəss/ *n* **1.** the illumination of something relative to its surroundings **2.** OPTICS the attribute of an object or a color that enables an observer to quantify the amount of light it appears to reflect [Pre-12C. < LIGHT[1]]

light·ness[2] /lĭtnəss/ *n* **1.** RELATIVE SLIGHTNESS OF WEIGHT the condition of something that weighs relatively little **2.** RELATIVE SLIGHTNESS OF FORCE the condition of something that has relatively little force ○ *lightness of touch* **3.** EASE OR DELICACY the ease or delicacy with which something is done **4.** NIMBLENESS ease and rapidity of movement **5.** UNTROUBLED STATE total freedom from worry and trouble **6.** LEVITY lack of the seriousness that is required or expected [12C. < LIGHT[2]]

light·ning /lĭtning/ *n* flashes of light seen in the sky when there is a discharge of atmospheric electricity in the clouds or between clouds and the ground, usually occurring during a thunderstorm ■ *adj* very fast and often very sudden [14C. < LIGHTEN[2]]

SPELLCHECK See ***lightening***.

light·ning ar·rest·er *n* a device, often an antenna, that protects a piece of electrical equipment from damage by lightning or some other electrical surge by diverting the electricity to the ground

light·ning bug *n* INSECTS same as **firefly**

light·ning chess *n* a fast form of chess in which players either have a limited time to make each move or have to complete all their moves within a set time

light·ning con·duc·tor *n UK* same as **lightning rod** (sense 1)

light·ning rod *n* **1.** a metal rod attached to the highest point of a building or other structure to protect it from lightning by conducting the lightning to the ground **2.** somebody who attracts public disapproval or criticism, diverting attention from other issues

light·ning strike *n* a military attack carried out suddenly and without warning

light op·er·a *n* MUSIC same as **operetta** [< LIGHT[2]]

light or·gan *n* ZOOL same as **photophore** [< LIGHT[1]]

light pen *n* a pen-shaped light-sensitive device used to manipulate information on a computer screen by touching the screen directly [< LIGHT[1]]

light pipe *n* **1.** a refracting tube lined with reflective material, used to transmit natural light into an otherwise dark interior space **2.** a fiber-optic cable capable of transmitting light [Early 21C.]

light plane *n US* an aircraft with a takeoff weight that does not exceed 12,500 lb./5,670 kg, especially a privately operated one. Can term **light aircraft** [< LIGHT[2]]

light pol·lu·tion *n* excessive artificial light, especially street lighting in towns and cities that prevents people from seeing the night sky clearly [< LIGHT[1]]

light·proof /lĭt pro͝of/ *adj* designed so as not to be penetrated or affected by light [< LIGHT[1]]

light re·ac·tion *n* the first stage of photosynthesis, when light energy is absorbed by chlorophyll and converted into chemical energy that is stored as ATP. It also generates NADPH, a substance that, like ATP, is essential for subsequent stages of photosynthesis. [< LIGHT[1]]

light re·flex *n* the normal contracting of the pupil of the eye in response to increased light [< LIGHT[1]]

lights /lĭts/ *npl* the lungs of domestic animals, especially those of hogs, sheep, or cattle when they are used in making pet food or, occasionally, food for people [Pre-12C. < LIGHT[2]; because the lungs are full of air]

light sa·ber *n* an imaginary weapon that is used as a sword but has a blade of visible light, or a toy imitating this

light-sen·si·tive *adj* affected in some way by the presence of light, as are some materials such as photographic film or silicon sheets [< LIGHT[1]]

light·shade /lĭt shàyd/ *n* HOUSEHOLD same as **lampshade** [< LIGHT[1]]

light shelf *n* a device fitted to the inside of a window, used to reflect sunlight toward the ceiling of a room and then farther into the building [20C.]

light·ship /lĭt shìp/ *n* a ship with a bright flashing light that functions as a lighthouse, especially one that is anchored in a place where a permanent structure would be impracticable [Mid-19C. < LIGHT[1]]

light show *n* **1.** a spectacle in the form of a display of colorful moving lights, often a feature of a live pop or rock concert **2.** a form of entertainment in which moving colored lights are synchronized with recorded music, usually synthesized instrumental music [< LIGHT[1]]

light·some /lĭtsəm/ *adj* (*archaic or literary*) **1.** feeling and displaying happiness and freedom from worry **2.** with a graceful lightness of movement [15C. < LIGHT[2]] —**light·some·ly** *adv* —**light·some·ness** *n*

lights out *n* **1.** TIME WHEN PEOPLE MUST SLEEP the time at night when people, especially those in the armed forces, prison, boarding schools, and other institutions, are supposed to go to sleep **2.** SIGNAL SOUNDED AT LIGHTS OUT a bugle call, gong, or other signal sounded at lights out ■ *adj* AUTOMATED automated, or controlled from a remote location ○ *lights-out system administration*

light·stick /lĭt stìk/ *n* a plastic tube containing two chemicals that mix when the tube is bent to create a glow, used as an emergency light source or for amusement

light-struck *adj US* describes photographic material that has become fogged through being accidentally exposed [< LIGHT[1]]

light sty·lus *n* COMPUT same as **light pen** [< LIGHT[1]]

light wa·ter *n* ordinary water, as opposed to heavy water [< LIGHT[2]]

light·weight /lĭt wàyt/ *adj* **1.** NOT HEAVY IN WEIGHT OR TEXTURE relatively light in weight and in texture **2.** LACKING INTELLECTUAL DEPTH fairly frivolous or trivial and requiring little or no intellectual effort ■ *n* **1.** INSIGNIFICANT PERSON OR THING somebody or something regarded as insignificant or without influence, often in a particular area ○ *a political lightweight* **2.** WEIGHT CATEGORY IN PROFESSIONAL BOXING in professional boxing, a weight category for competitors who weigh between 130 and 135 lb./59 and 61 kg **3.** WEIGHT CATEGORY IN AMATEUR BOXING in amateur boxing, a weight category for competitors who weigh between 126 and 132 lb./57 and 60 kg **4.** BOXER COMPETING AT LIGHTWEIGHT a professional or amateur boxer who competes at lightweight level **5.** WEIGHT CATEGORY IN WRESTLING in wrestling, a weight category for competitors who weigh between 115 and 126 lb./52 and 57 kg **6.** WRESTLER WHO COMPETES AT LIGHTWEIGHT a wrestler who competes at lightweight level [Late 18C. < LIGHT[2]]

light wel·ter·weight *n* **1.** in amateur boxing, a weight category for competitors who weigh between 132 and 139 lb./60 and 63.5 kg **2.** an amateur boxer who competes at light welterweight level [< LIGHT[2]]

light·wood /lĭt wo͝od/ *n regional* resinous pine used for kindling [Late 17C. < LIGHT[1]]

REGIONAL NOTE ***Lightwood***, meaning "kindling," is also called *fat lightwood* and *lighterd*, the latter reflecting a common South Midland pronunciation.

light-year, **light year** *n* a unit of distance in astronomy equal to the distance that light travels in a vacuum in one mean solar year, approximately 5.88 trillion mi./9.46 trillion km ■ **light-years** *npl* a very long way in time, distance, or other quantity or quality (*informal*) [< LIGHT[1]]

lign- *prefix* same as **ligni-** (*used before vowels*)

lig·nan /lígnən/ *n* a phenolic compound of a group found mainly in plants that are believed to protect human beings from tumors and viruses

lig·ne·ous /lígnee əss/ *adj* consisting of or with the appearance or texture of wood [Early 17C. < Latin *ligneus* < *lignum* (see LIGNI-)]

ligni- *prefix* wood ○ *lignicole* [< Latin *lignum* "wood, firewood" < Indo-European, "to collect"]

lig·ni·cole /lígnə kōl/, **lig·ni·co·lous** /lig níkələss/ *adj* living or growing in or on wood [Mid-19C. < LIGNI- + Latin *colere* "inhabit"]

lig·ni·fy /lígnə fī/ (**-fied, -fy·ing, -fies**) *vti* to become woody and relatively rigid as lignin is deposited in cell walls, or make plant parts woody in this way [Early 19C. < Latin *lignum* (see LIGNI-)] —**lig·ni·fi·ca·tion** /lìgnəfi káysh'n/ *n*

lig·nin /lígnin/ *n* the complex polymer in plant cell walls that gives the plant rigidity and strength, and is the major component of wood [Early 19C. < Latin *lignum* (see LIGNI-)]

lig·nite /líg nīt/ *n* GEOL same as **brown coal** —**lig·nit·ic** /lig níttik/ *adj*

ligno- *prefix* wood ○ *lignocellulose* [< Latin *lignum* (see LIGNI-)]

lig·no·caine /lígnə kàyn/ *n UK* PHARM same as **lidocaine**

lig·no·cel·lu·lose /lìgnō séllyə lōss, -lōz/ *n* a strengthening substance composed of lignin and cellulose, found in woody tissues of plants

lig·num vi·tae /lígnəm vítee/ *n* TREES same as **guaiacum** [Late 16C. < Latin, "wood of life"; from the medicinal uses of the wood and its resin]

lig·ro·in /líggrō in/ *n* a solvent in the form of a flammable liquid mixture of hydrocarbons. Source: distillation of petroleum. [Late 19C. Origin ?]

lig·u·la /líggyələ/ (*plural* **-lae** /-lèe/ or **-las**) *n* **1.** the tip of the lower lip **(labium)** of an insect, which typically has four lobes **2.** BOT same as **ligule** (sense 1) [Mid-18C. < Latin, "strap," variant of *lingula* "little tongue" < *lingua* "tongue"] —**lig·u·lar** *adj*

lig·ule /líggyool/ *n* **1.** an outgrowth at the junction of the leaf sheath and leaf blade in a grass, typically a membranous or scaly flap but in some grasses a ring of hairs **2.** the strap-shaped extension of florets found in the flower heads of some members of the daisy family and in some grasses [Early 19C. < Latin *ligula* (see LIGULA)] —**lig·u·late** *adj*

Li·gu·ri·an Sea /li gŏoree ən-/ part of the Mediterranean Sea, lying between the northwestern coast of Italy and the islands of Corsica and Elba

lik·a·ble /líkəb'l/, **like·a·ble** *adj* pleasant and friendly and therefore easy to like —**lik·a·bil·i·ty** /līkə bíllətee/ *n* —**lik·a·ble·ness** *n* —**lik·a·bly** *adv*

Li·ka·si /li kaassee/ mining and industrial city in the southeastern part of the Democratic Republic of the Congo. Population: 299,118 (1994).

like[1] /līk/ CORE MEANING: a grammatical word indicating that two things or people are similar or share some of the same features, qualities, or characteristics; it also introduces an example of the set of things or people that have just been mentioned ○ *Vivid red phone booths, looking like London imports, stood nearby.*

1. *prep* **RESEMBLING** having a resemblance to somebody or something, or so as to have a resemblance to somebody or something ○ *She wrapped the towel like a turban on her head.* ○ *He looks like the hero type to me!* **2.** *prep* **SUCH AS** introduces a typical instance or an example of a particular category or type ○ *She won't go to loud places like bars.* ○ *I bought things like fishing tackle and waders.* **3.** *prep* **INDICATES CHARACTERISTICS** indicates qualities, characteristics, or features (*often used in questions*) ○ *What's it like, being a mother?* ○ *When you go on like this, do you know what you sound like?* **4.** *prep* **TYPICAL OF** characteristic of somebody or something (*often negative*) ○ *It's not like him to be this late coming home.* **5.** *prep* **INCLINED TOWARD** having a tendency or desire to do something ○ *I felt like screaming when I found the kitchen floor flooded.* **6.** *prep* **WITH SUGGESTION OF** as though something might happen ○ *It looks like rain this morning.* **7.** ⚠ *conj* **AS** in the same way or manner that (*informal*) ○ *To ski like she does requires great athletic ability.* **8.** ⚠ *conj* **AS IF** as though or as if (*nonstandard*) ○ *Butch hops out of the car like it was on fire.* ○ *Like I'd tell you a secret!* **9.** ⚠ *adv* **USED AS FILLER OR FOR EMPHASIS** used especially in conversation as a filler, for emphasis, to indicate possible exaggeration, or to convey uncertainty or approximation (*informal*) ○ *You're, like, feeling stressed today, aren't you?* ○ *There were, like, hundreds of people there.* ○ *She has, like, six brothers and sisters.* **10.** ⚠ *adv* **INTRODUCES DIRECT SPEECH** used especially in conversation to introduce a quotation of what somebody said (*nonstandard*) ○ *Susan is like "It's not for me" and Brandon is like, "You had me worried" and Susan is like, "Don't worry, I'm not going anywhere."* **11.** *n* **SOMETHING SIMILAR** a thing or set of things similar to another ○ *window boxes, planters, flower pots, and the like* **12.** *n* **COUNTERPART** one person or thing that is regarded as similar or almost identical to another ○ *Have you ever tasted the like of this cheesecake?* ○ *We won't see his like again in this decade.* **13.** *adj* **ALIKE** having exactly the same or almost identical qualities or characteristics ○ *These two cats are as like as though they were of the same litter.* ○ *The new laws affect hospitals, nursing homes, clinics, and other like institutions.* [12C. < Old Norse *líkr*, shortening of *glíkr*, equivalent to Old English *gelīc* (see ALIKE)] ◇ **like as not** to a probable or likely extent (*informal*) ○ *Like as not he'll show up very late.* ◇ **like new** in pristine condition (*informal*) ○ *looked like new* ◇ **like so** in the manner demonstrated ○ *Spread the fabric out like so.* ◇ **the likes of** people or things of the particular sort ○ *Such luxuries aren't for the likes of us.*

USAGE like as a conjunction and a filler: In writing and formal contexts, it is best to avoid using ***like*** as a conjunction meaning "as" or "as if" or "as though" when introducing a fully developed clause (i.e., one with a subject and a verb). Avoid constructions like these: *It sounds like she may resign. This pizza smells and tastes like a good pizza should.* Recast the sentences: *It sounds as if she may resign. This pizza smells and tastes good, just the way it should.* It is acceptable to use ***like*** in a comparison as long as you do not include a verb in the matter following ***like***: *She ran the company just like a tyrant.* Avoid using ***like*** as a meaningless filler: *"What were the main characters doing in Chapter One?" "They were, like, trying to understand the reasons why people go to war,"* or to introduce speech: *She was like, "Don't worry, I'll do it."* Such usage is nonstandard in oral and written communications on any level except in fictional dialogue.

like[2] /līk/ *v* (**liked, lik·ing, likes**) **1.** *vt* **ENJOY SOMETHING** to regard something as enjoyable ○ *I like cross-country skiing.* ○ *Do you like prunes?* **2.** *vt* **CONSIDER SOMEBODY PLEASANT** to regard somebody as pleasant and enjoy that person's company ○ *I like a man with a sense of humor.* ○ *Do you like your new teacher?* ○ *I really like her.* **3.** *vt* **WANT SOMETHING** to want to have or do something ○ *Would you like some coffee?* ○ *I'd like to meet your brother.* **4.** *vt* **REGARD SOMEBODY OR SOMETHING POSITIVELY** to have a positive opinion about something or somebody ○ *How do you like her prose style?* **5.** *vi* **HAVE PREFERENCE** to have a preference or inclination ○ *We can leave later than seven if you like.* ■ *n* **PREFERENCE** something that is preferred over others ○ *a full litany of her likes and dislikes* [Old English *līcian* "to please" < Germanic, "body"]

CULTURAL NOTE ***As You Like It***, a play (1599?) by English dramatist William Shakespeare. Based on Thomas Lodge's romance *Rosalynde* (1590), it is one of Shakespeare's most charming romantic comedies. Its complex plot revolves around Rosalind, daughter of Duke Ferdinand, and her love for a young knight, Orlando, which results in her being banished to the forest, where she is eventually reunited with her lover. The observation "All the world's a stage" comes from this play.

like[3] /līk/, **liked** /līkt/ *vi Southern US* to have been on the verge or point of doing or almost doing a particular thing (*informal; only in the past tense*) ○ *I like to have died when I saw her in that getup.* [15C. < LIKE[1]]

-like *suffix* resembling or characteristic of ○ *workmanlike* [< LIKE[1]]

like·a·ble *adj* another spelling of **likable**

liked *vi Southern US* same as **like**[3] (*informal*)

like·li·hood /líklee hŏŏd/ *n* **1.** the chance of something happening **2.** something that is likely to happen ◇ **in all likelihood** very probably

like·ly /líklee/ *adj* (**-li·er, -li·est**) **1.** **PROBABLE** probably going to happen **2.** **PLAUSIBLE** fit to be believed (*often used ironically*) **3.** **SUITABLE** appropriate for a particular activity or purpose **4.** **PROMISING** with a good chance of success or victory **5.** **PLEASING** pleasant or good-looking ○ *a likely young woman* ■ *adv* **PROBABLY** to a probable degree or extent ○ *It will very likely snow tomorrow.* [14C. < Old Norse *(g)líkligr* < *líkr* (see LIKE[1])] ◇ **(as) likely as not** very probably

~~**likelyhood**~~ incorrect spelling of **likelihood**

like-mind·ed *adj* sharing the same or similar views, opinions, tastes, values, or outlook —**like-mind·ed·ness** *n*

lik·en /líkən/ (**-ened, -en·ing, -ens**) *vt* to compare something or somebody with another, especially in order to point out the similarities [14C. < LIKE[1]]

like·ness /líknəss/ *n* **1.** a representation of somebody or something, e.g., a painting or statue, often considered in terms of how accurately it represents the person or thing **2.** similarity of appearance among or between people or things [Old English *(ge)līcnes* < *gelīc* (see ALIKE)]

Li·kert scale /líkərt-/ *n* a scale measuring the degree to which people agree or disagree with a statement, usually on a 3–, 5–, or 7-point scale [Mid-20C. After Rensis *Likert* (1903–81), US psychologist]

like·wise /līk wīz/ *adv* **1.** in the same or a similar way **2.** used to state that the same applies in a second or subsequent case ○ *She works as a teacher; her brother likewise.* [15C. Contraction of *in like wise* "in similar manner"]

lik·ing /líking/ *n* **1.** a feeling of enjoying something or finding something pleasant **2.** personal taste or choice [14C. < LIKE[2]]

SYNONYMS See *love.*

~~**likly**~~ incorrect spelling of **likely**

li·ku·ta /lee kŏŏtə/ (*plural* **ma·ku·ta** /maa kŏŏtə/) *n* a former subunit of currency of the Democratic Republic of Congo, 100 of which were worth one new zaïre [Mid-20C. < Kikongo, "the cloth"; because a piece of cloth was a unit of currency]

li·lac /līlək/ (*plural* **-lacs** or *same*) *n* **1.** an ornamental bush or small tree. Flowers: fragrant, white, mauve, or purple, in sprays. Native to: Europe, Asia. Genus: *Syringa*. **2.** a pale pinkish purple color tinged with blue [Early 17C. Via French < Persian *līlak* "bluish"] —**li·lac** *adj*

li·lan·ge·ni /li laang gènnee/ (*plural* **em·a·lan·ge·ni** /émmə laang génnee/) *n* the main unit of currency of Swaziland. See table at **currency** [Late 20C. < Bantu]

lil·i·a·ceous /lìllee áyshəss/ *adj* belonging to the lily family of plants [Mid-18C. < late Latin *liliaceus* < Latin *lilium* "lily"]

Lil·ith /líllith/ *n* **1.** in Hebrew Scripture, the first woman, believed to have been created before Eve **2.** in Jewish folklore, an evil spirit of a woman, believed to lurk in deserted places and attack children

Li·li·u·o·ka·la·ni /lə lèe ō kə laanee/, **queen of the Hawaiian Islands** (1838–1917) She was the last Polynesian sovereign to govern the Hawaiian Islands before its annexation by the United States, which she strongly opposed

Lille /leel/ industrial city and capital of Nord Department, Nord-Pas-de-Calais Region, northern France. Population: 184,657 (1999).

Lil·li·pu·tian /lìllə pyóosh'n/, **lil·li·pu·tian** *n* **SMALL PERSON OR THING** a person or thing that is unusually small in height ■ *adj* **1.** **TINY** unusually small **2.** **TRIVIAL OR PETTY** of little or no importance or significance [Mid-18C. After *Lilliput*, country in *Gulliver's Travels* (1726) by Jonathan Swift whose people were only 6 in./15 cm tall]

LILO /līlō/ *n* a data storage method in which data stored last is retrieved last. Full form **last in, last out**

Li·long·we /li lóng way/ capital and second largest city of Malawi. Population: 1,000,000 (1998).

lilt /lilt/ *n* **1.** **VARIATION IN VOICE PITCH** a pleasant rising and falling variation in the pitch of a person's voice **2.** **BOUNCY STEP** a light bouncy way of walking, often taken as an indication of a cheerful disposition **3.** **CHEERFUL PIECE OF MUSIC** a cheerful song or piece of music, especially one that is easy to sing along with ■ *v* (**lilt·ed, lilt·ing, lilts**) **1.** *vti* **SAY OR SING SOMETHING CHEERFULLY** to say, sing, or play something in a cheerful way, often with pleasant variations in pitch **2.** *vi* **WALK BOUNCILY** to walk or move in a bouncy cheerful way [14C. Origin ?] —**lilt·ing** *adj*

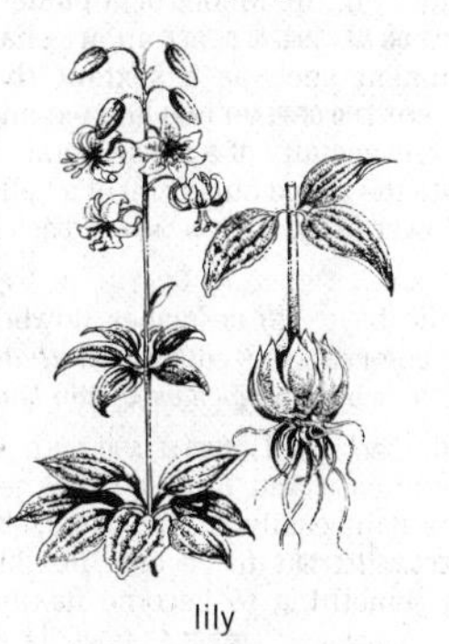

lily

lil·y /líllee/ *n* (*plural* **-ies**) **1.** **PERENNIAL PLANT** a perennial plant that grows from a bulb. Flowers: single, large, sometimes trumpet-shaped. Genus: *Lilium*. **2.** PLANTS **PLANT LIKE LILY** a plant that resembles a true lily **3.** **WHITE OR PURE THING** somebody or something that is particularly white or pure (*dated*) **4.** HERALDRY same as **fleur-de-lis** (sense 1) ■ *adj* **PALE** unusually pale in color or shade [Pre-12C. < Latin *lilium*] ◇ **gild the lily** to try to improve something that is already good or beautiful enough

lil·y-liv·ered /-lìvərd/ *adj* lacking courage (*dated*) [< the idea that a cowardly person's liver is pale through lack of bile, thought to engender courage]

lil·y of the Nile (*plural* **lil·ies of the Nile** or *same*) *n US* PLANTS same as **African lily**

lil·y of the val·ley (*plural* **lil·ies of the val·ley** or *same*) *n* a small poisonous ornamental plant with two long oval dark green leaves. Flowers: small, white or pale pink, sweet-scented, bell-shaped, drooping, growing from a single spike. Native to: North America, Europe, Asia. Genus: *Convallaria.* [Translation of Latin *lilium convallium*, unidentified plant]

lil·y pad *n* a floating leaf of a water lily

lil·y trot·ter *n* BIRDS same as **jacana** [Because its elongated toes let it walk on floating vegetation]

lil·y-white *adj* **1.** PALE AND UNBLEMISHED unusually pale in tone and unblemished **2.** *US* PREJUDICED AGAINST BLACK PEOPLE discriminating against or excluding people of African American origin (*disapproving; sometimes considered offensive*) **3.** UNMIXED without any admixture

Li·ma[1] /léemə/ *n* a code word for the letter "L," used in international radio communications

Li·ma[2] /léemə/ capital city of Peru, situated in the west central part of the country, on the Pacific Ocean and adjacent to the Rímac River in a dry coastal region. Population: 7,443,000 (2000).

li·ma bean /límə-, léemə-/ *n* **1.** a pale green flattish edible seed produced by a cultivated plant of the bean family **2.** the plant that produces lima beans. Native to: Central America. Latin name: *Phaseolus limensis* or *Phaseolus lunatus.* [Mid-18C. After LIMA[2]]

lim·a·cine /límmə sèen, límə-/ *adj* **1.** belonging or relating to the slug family of invertebrate terrestrial mollusks **2.** resembling a slug in appearance or movement [Late 19C. < Latin *limac-* "slug, snail"]

lim·a·çon /léemə sáwN, límmə sòn/ *n* a heart-shaped mathematical curve that is generated by a point on a line that intersects with a circle and rotates about a point on the circle [Late 19C. < French, "snail shell" < Latin *limac-* "slug, snail"]

Li·mas·sol /límmə sàwl/ city and port in southern Cyprus. It is the capital of Limassol District. Population: 152,900 (1997).

limb[1] /lim/ *n* **1.** BODY PART an arm, leg, or similar appendage to the body such as a wing or flipper **2.** LARGE BRANCH a major branch of a tree **3.** ASSOCIATED PERSON OR ORGANIZATION somebody or something affiliated with a larger group or organization **4.** PART STICKING OUT a part that sticks out, e.g., on a building or a mountain range **5.** ARCHERY PART OF BOW either of the two halves of a bow used in archery [Old English *lim*] —**limbed** *adj* —**limb·less** *adj* ◇ **be out on a limb** to be in an isolated position, without support ◇ **go out on a limb** to express a viewpoint that risks being controversial

limb[2] /lim/ *n* **1.** ASTRON RIM OF PLANET the illuminated edge of the Sun, the Moon, or a planet **2.** MATH ARC-SHAPED SCALE ON MEASURING DEVICE an arc-shaped scale on an instrument such as a sextant that measures angles **3.** BOT END OF PLANT PART the expanded end of a plant part, especially of a sepal, petal, or leaf **4.** BOT RIM OF FLOWER the flared outer rim of a bell- or trumpet-shaped flower [14C. Directly or via French < Latin *limbus* "edge"]

lim·bate /lím bàyt/ *adj* describes flowers that are a different color at the edges ○ *limbate carnations* [Early 19C. < late Latin *limbatus* < Latin *limbus* "edge"]

lim·ber[1] /límbər/ *adj* **1.** SUPPLE AND AGILE able to move with elastic ease and nimble quickness **2.** FLEXIBLE able to be bent easily ■ *vti* (**-bered, -ber·ing, -bers**) MAKE OR BECOME FLEXIBLE to become flexible or supple, or cause something to become flexible or supple [Mid-16C. Probably < LIMBER[2], from its ease of movement] —**lim·ber·ness** *n*

limber up *vi* to do gentle physical exercises to loosen and warm the muscles prior to taking part in more strenuous physical activity

lim·ber[2] /límbər/ *n* a two-wheeled vehicle that forms the detachable front part of a gun carriage. It was also used for transporting ammunition and other supplies on the battlefield. ■ *vt* (**-bered, -ber·ing, -bers**) to attach a gun or other piece of field equipment to a limber [Early 17C. Origin ?]

lim·bi ANAT plural of **limbus**

lim·bic /límbik/ *adj* **1.** belonging to a limbus, or situated in or near a limbus **2.** belonging to or situated in the limbic system [Late 19C. < French *limbique* < Latin *limbus* "edge"]

lim·bic sys·tem *n* an interconnected system of brain nuclei associated with basic needs and emotions such as hunger, pain, pleasure, satisfaction, sex, and instinctive motivation. The most primitive part of the brain, it is situated close to the inner wall of each cerebral hemisphere and includes the brain system concerned with the sense of smell.

lim·bo[1] /límbō/ *n* **1.** a state in which somebody or something is neglected or is simply left in oblivion **2.** *also* **Lim·bo** in Roman Catholic theology, the place that is believed to be home to the souls of children who died before baptism, and the souls of the righteous who died before Jesus Christ. Although they are barred from entry to heaven, they are not condemned to the eternal suffering of hell. [14C. < Latin, "on the border (of hell)," form of *limbus* "border, edge"] ◇ **in limbo** in a state of uncertainty or of being kept waiting

lim·bo[2] /límbō/ (*plural* **-bos**) *n* a Caribbean dance in which the body is bent backward from the knees and moved under a horizontal boundary that is placed progressively lower. An expert at this dance needs very little clearance between the bar or rope and the floor. (*often used before a noun*) ○ *a limbo dancer* [Mid-20C. Alteration of LIMBER[1]] —**lim·bo** *vi*

Lim·bourg broth·ers /lím bùrg-/, **Pol**, **Herman**, and **Jehanequin** (*fl* 1400–16) Flemish illuminators. They are credited with the brightly-colored and highly detailed illustrations in the famous prayer book *Les très riches heures de duc du Berry* (1413?–16), considered one of the finest examples of the French International Gothic style.

Lim·burg·er /lím bùrgər/, **Lim·burg·er cheese**, **Lim·burg cheese** /lim burg-/ *n* a soft white Belgian cheese with a strong smell and taste [Mid-19C. < Dutch or German, after *Limburg*, province of NW Belgium]

lim·bus /límbəss/ (*plural* **-bi** /-bì/) *n* the edge of various organs or body parts, e.g., the area in the eyeball where the cornea and sclera meet [15C. < Latin, "edge"]

lime[1] /līm/ *n* **1.** CHEM same as **calcium oxide** **2.** CALCIUM USED FOR IMPROVING SOIL a form of calcium that is added to soil with a low calcium content **3.** HUNTING same as **birdlime** ■ *vt* (**limed, lim·ing, limes**) **1.** SPREAD CALCIUM ON SOIL to treat soil with calcium, often in the form of ground limestone, in order to reduce its acidity **2.** PAINT WITH WHITEWASH to cover a surface with whitewash **3.** HUNTING SMEAR WITH BIRDLIME to smear twigs or branches with birdlime in order to catch small birds **4.** HUNTING CATCH BIRDS OR ANIMALS USING BIRDLIME to catch small birds or animals using birdlime or some other sticky substance [Old English *līm* < Germanic]

lime[2] /līm/ *n* **1.** SMALL GREEN FRUIT a small acid-tasting citrus fruit with a thin green rind and green flesh (*often used before a noun*) ○ *lime juice* **2.** EVERGREEN TREE a small evergreen citrus tree that bears limes. Native to: Asia. Latin name: *Citrus aurantifolia.* **3.** LIME GREEN the color lime green [Mid-17C. Via French and Spanish < Arabic *līma* "citrus fruit"] —**lime** *adj*

lime[3] /līm/ *n* **1.** *also* **lime tree** *Can, UK* a deciduous hardwood tree with heart-shaped leaves and clusters of white, yellowish, or green flowers, often planted for shade or ornament, or grown for timber. Native to: northern hemisphere. Genus: *Tilia.* US term **linden** **2.** the wood of the lime tree [Early 17C. Alteration of obsolete *line* < Old English *lind* (see LINDEN)]

lime[4] /līm/ (**limed, lim·ing, limes**) *vi Carib* to spend time lazily (*slang*) [Late 20C. Back-formation < *limey* "low-class Caucasian person"]

lime·ade /lī máyd/ *n* a nonalcoholic drink made from or tasting of lime juice [Late 19C. < LIME[2]]

lime-green *adj* of a pale green color [< LIME[2]] —**lime green** *n*

lime·kiln /līm kìln/ *n* an oven that is used for heating limestone to produce quicklime [13C. < LIME[1]]

lime·light /līm līt/ *n* **1.** FOCUS OF ATTENTION the focus of attention or public interest **2.** LAMP IN WHICH QUICKLIME IS HEATED a lamp used as an early form of stage lighting in which quicklime is heated to produce a brilliant light **3.** LIGHT FROM LIMELIGHT the light that a limelight lamp produces [Early 19C. < LIME[1]]

lime·light·er /līm lītər/ *n US* somebody who desires and enjoys celebrity

lim·er·ick /límmərik/ *n* a five-line humorous poem with a characteristic rhythm, often dealing with a risqué subject and typically opening with a line such as "There was a young lady called Jenny." Lines one, two, and five rhyme with each other and have three metrical feet, and lines three and four rhyme with each other and have two metrical feet. [Late 19C. After LIMERICK, probably from nonsense songs with this rhyme scheme and the refrain "will you come up to Limerick"]

Lim·er·ick /límmərik/ **1.** port and chief city of Limerick County, southwestern Republic of Ireland. Population: 52,039 (2002). **2.** county in the southwestern Republic of Ireland, in Munster Province. Population: 165,042 (2002). Area: 1,039 sq. mi./2,686 sq. km.

lime·stone /līm stòn/ *n* sedimentary rock formed from the skeletons and shells of marine organisms that consists chiefly of calcium carbonate. Use: in construction, in making lime and cement. [15C. < LIME[1]]

lime tree *n* TREES same as **linden**

lime tree loop·er *n US* a North American moth whose inchworm larvae are destructive to citrus trees. Latin name: *Erannis tiliaria.*

lime·wa·ter /līm wàwtər/ *n* **1.** a clear alkaline solution of calcium hydroxide in water. Use: in skin lotions, as an antacid. **2.** water that is naturally high in dissolved calcium carbonate or calcium sulfate [Late 17C. < LIME[1]]

lim·ey /līmee/ *n* **1.** OFFENSIVE TERM an offensive term for a British person (*slang*) **2.** BRITISH SHIP a British commercial or naval vessel (*slang disapproving*) ■ *adj* OFFENSIVE TERM an offensive term meaning coming from or relating to the United Kingdom (*slang*) [Late 19C. Shortening and alteration of *lime-juicer*, because sailors in the British Navy drank lime juice to prevent scurvy]

lim·i·nal /límmin'l/ *adj* belonging to the point of conscious awareness below which something cannot be experienced or felt [Late 19C. < Latin *limin-* "threshold"]

lim·it /límmit/ *n* **1.** FARTHEST POINT, DEGREE, OR AMOUNT the farthest point, degree, amount, or boundary, especially one that cannot or should not be passed or exceeded ○ *The car was tested to its limits on the test track.* **2.** MAXIMUM OR MINIMUM AMOUNT ALLOWED the maximum or minimum amount, or the largest or lowest quantity, that is available or allowed ○ *an upper age limit of 12 years* **3.** BOUNDARY OF AREA the boundary or edge of an area, or something that marks a boundary or edge (*often used in the plural*) ○ *the city limits* **4.** RESTRICTION a feature or circumstance that restricts what can be done ○ *a time limit* **5.** GAMBLING MAXIMUM MONEY ALLOWED IN BETTING the maximum amount of money that can be staked at any one time in various games of chance **6.** MATH MAXIMUM OF MATHEMATICAL FUNCTION a numerical value approached by a mathematical function as the independent variable of the function approaches infinity or a specific value **7.** MATH VALUE SPECIFYING INTEGRAL'S RANGE one of the two given values specifying the range over which a definite integral is evaluated ■ *vt* (**-it·ed, -i·ting, -its**) **1.** RESTRICT SOMETHING to restrict something or somebody in number or quantity, or restrict something to a particular group ○ *had to limit the number of guests because of space problems* **2.** BE BOUNDARY TO AREA to be or act as a boundary to an area [14C. < Latin *limit-* "boundary"] —**lim·it·a·ble** *adj* ◇ **be the limit** to be so bad as to be almost beyond what somebody is able or prepared to tolerate

lim·i·tar·y /límmi tèrree/ *adj* (*archaic*) **1.** on which limits are imposed **2.** imposing limits

lim·i·ta·tion /lìmmi táysh'n/ *n* **1.** RESTRICTION an imposed restriction that cannot be exceeded or sidestepped ○ *limitations on the height of vehicles* **2.** RESTRICTING FLAW a disadvantage or weakness in somebody or something (*often used in the plural*) ○ *One of the limitations of the program is the amount of memory it requires.* **3.** SETTING OF LIMIT the act of limiting something ○ *damage limitation* **4.** LAW MAXIMUM DELAY ALLOWED a particular period of time within which a legal action must start **5.** LAW LEGAL RESTRICTION a legal restriction on the powers that somebody has

lim·it down *n* under futures exchange rules, the point reached by a commodity price that has fallen by the maximum amount allowed in a single day's trading

lim·it·ed /límmitəd/ *adj* **1.** WITH LIMIT IMPOSED on which some form of limit or restriction is imposed ○ *We* *have limited space available.* **2.** LACKING FULL SCOPE existing at or below the full degree or extent, usually far below ○ *limited powers* **3.** OF RELATIVELY LITTLE TALENT with talents or skills that fall short of what is expected or required **4.** POL LACKING FULL AUTHORITY lacking a full range of powers, especially because of constitutional or legal limitations **5.** COMM WITH RESTRICTED STOCKHOLDER LIABILITY describes a British-registered business enterprise whose stockholders' liability for any debts or losses is restricted —**lim·i·ted·ly** *adv* —**lim·i·ted·ness** *n*

lim·it·ed-ac·cess high·way *n US* ROADS same as **expressway**

lim·it·ed com·pa·ny *n* a British-registered company in which the stockholders' liability for any debts or losses is restricted

lim·it·ed e·di·tion *n* an edition, especially of a book or an art print, of which only a specific number of copies have been made. This has the effect of increasing the item's value. (*hyphenated when used before a noun*) ○ *limited-edition prints*

lim·it·ed li·a·bil·i·ty *n* an investor's liability for no greater a proportion of a company's debt than is represented by the value of his or her financial stake in the business

lim·it·ed part·ner *n* a business partner who has no management responsibility and whose liability for company debts is limited to his or her financial stake —**lim·it·ed part·ner·ship** *n*

lim·it·ed war *n* a war in which it is not the objective of the participants to defeat or destroy the enemy totally, especially a war in which nuclear weapons are available but are not used

lim·it·er /límmitər/ *n* **1.** an electronic circuit that limits the amplitude of an output wave to a specific value **2.** somebody or something that has a restricting effect

lim·it·ing /límmiting/ *adj* **1.** imposing limits, especially limits on the scope for development, progress, or improvement ○ *a limiting factor* **2.** describes an adjective that identifies rather than describes the referent of a noun, as the possessive "your" does in "your house"

lim·it·less /límmitləss/ *adj* very great in amount, extent, or degree ○ *limitless resources* —**lim·it·less·ly** *adv* —**lim·it·less·ness** *n*

lim·it or·der *n* an order instructing an investment broker to buy or sell something at a specific price or one better than it within a limited period of time

lim·it point *n* a point in a set of mathematical points, such that for every neighborhood around the point at least one other point in the set is contained in the neighborhood

lim·it up *n* under futures exchange rules, the point reached by a commodity price that has risen by the maximum amount allowed in a single day's trading

limn /lim/ (**limned, limn·ing, limns**) *vt* (*literary*) **1.** to draw or paint a picture of somebody or something, especially in outline **2.** to describe something in words [15C. Alteration of obsolete *lumine* "illustrate a manuscript," via French < Latin *luminare* "illumine" < *lumin-* "light"] —**limn·er** *n*

lim·net·ic /lim néttik/ *adj* relating to or living in the deep open water of a freshwater pond or lake [Late 19C. < Greek *limnētēs* "living in marshes" < *limnē* "marshy lake"]

lim·nol·o·gy /lim nólləjee/ *n* the scientific study of lakes and other bodies of fresh water, including their physical and biological features [Late 19C. < Greek *limnē* "marshy lake"] —**lim·no·log·i·cal** /lìmnə lójjik'l/ *adj* —**lim·no·log·i·cal·ly** *adv* —**lim·nol·o·gist** *n*

lim·o /límmō/ (*plural* **-os**) *n* same as **limousine** (*informal*) [Mid-20C. Shortening]

Li·moges[1] /lee mṓzh/ *n* a fine porcelain made in the town of Limoges, France, since the 19th century

Li·moges[2] /lee mṓzh/ capital of Haute-Vienne Department and Limousin Region, central France. Famous for its enamel work and porcelain, it is situated on the Vienne River, about 110 mi./177 km northeast of Bordeaux. Population: 133,968 (1999).

Li·món /li mṓn/, **José** (1908–72) Mexican-born US dancer and choreographer. In 1946 he founded the José Limon American Dance Company.

lim·o·nene /límmə neen/ *n* a liquid unsaturated hydrocarbon that smells like lemon and is found in the essential oils of citrus fruits and peppermint. Use: a wetting agent and in making resins. Formula: $C_{10}H_{16}$. [Mid-19C. < German *Limonen* < *Limone* "lemon"]

li·mo·nite /límə nīt/ *n* a hydrated iron oxide ore that varies in color from dark brown to yellow [Early 19C. < German *Limonit* < Greek *leimōn* "meadow"] —**li·mo·nit·ic** /lìmmə níttik/ *adj*

Li·mou·sin /límmə zeen, lìmmoo záN/ *n* a large hardy beef cow, belonging to a breed that originated in Limousin, a region of central France

lim·ou·sine /límmə zeen, lìmmə zeen/ *n* **1.** a large luxurious automobile, usually chauffeur-driven, with a partition between the chauffeur and passengers **2.** a vehicle used to transport passengers to and from an airport, usually between a hotel and airport [Early 20C. < French, form of *limousin* "cloak with a cape," after *Limousin*, France]

limp[1] /limp/ *vi* (**limped, limp·ing, limps**) **1.** WALK UNEVENLY to walk with an uneven step because of an injury or disability **2.** PROCEED WITH DIFFICULTY to move or continue with great difficulty ○ *The business limped through the recession.* ■ *n* IMPAIRED GAIT a way of walking or running that involves a degree of motion impairment (*sometimes offensive*) [Late 16C. Probably back-formation < obsolete *limphalt* "walking unevenly" < Old English *lempheal*t < *lemp-* (< Indo-European) + HALT[2]] —**limp·er** *n*

limp[2] /limp/ *adj* **1.** FLEXIBLE without stiffness or rigidity **2.** WEAK without strength, power, or firmness ○ *a limp handshake* **3.** LACKING FORCE without energy, vitality, or enthusiasm **4.** LACKING VOLUME OR SUBSTANCE without a firm or substantial feel or texture **5.** NOT STIFFENED BY BOARDS describes a book cover that is not stiffened by boards but is made of more durable material than a paperback **6.** UNCONVINCING not very convincing [Early 18C. Origin ?] —**limp·ly** *adv* —**limp·ness** *n*

lim·pet /límpət/ (*plural* **-pets** or *same*) *n* a small invertebrate ocean animal that has a low rough conical shell and clings to rocks. Native to: cool Atlantic and Pacific waters. Order: Archeogastropoda. [Pre-12C. Via medieval Latin *lampreda* < late Latin *lampetra*]

lim·pet mine *n* an explosive device that can be attached to the hull of a ship

lim·pid /límpid/ *adj* **1.** CLEAR clear and transparent **2.** LUCID expressing something in a way that is clear and easy to understand ○ *limpid prose* **3.** UNWORRIED emotionally calm and composed [Early 17C. Directly or via French < Latin *limpidus* "clear"] —**lim·pid·i·ty** /lim píddətee/ *n* —**lim·pid·ly** *adv* —**lim·pid·ness** *n*

limp·kin /límpkin/ (*plural* **-kins** or *same*) *n* a wading bird with a long neck, a long curved beak, long legs, and short rounded wings. Native to: South America, southeastern North America. Latin name: *Aramus guarauna*. [Late 19C. < LIMP[1]; from its limping walk]

Lim·po·po /lim pṓpō/ river in southeastern Africa. Length: 1,100 mi./1,800 km.

Lim·po·po Prov·ince province in South Africa, in the northernmost part of the country. Capital: Polokwane. Population: 5,273,647 (2001). Area: 47,830 sq. mi./123,910 sq. km. Former name **Northern Province**

limp-wrist·ed *adj* an offensive term meaning effeminate (*insult*) [< a posture of the wrists and hands offensively associated with effeminate men]

lim·u·lus /límmyələss/ (*plural* **-li** /-lee/ or *same*) *n* a member of a group of arthropods that includes the horseshoe crab. Genus: *Limulus*. [Mid-19C. Via modern Latin < Latin, "somewhat sidelong" < *limus* "oblique"; from the crab's motion]

lim·y /līmee/ (**-i·er, -i·est**) *adj* **1.** smeared with birdlime **2.** consisting of, containing, or similar to lime

lin. *abbr* **1.** lineal **2.** linear

lin·ac /línn ak/ *n* PHYS same as **linear accelerator** [Mid-20C. Contraction]

lin·age /līnij/, **line·age** *n* **1.** the number of lines in a printed text **2.** a fixed payment per line of printed text made to the author

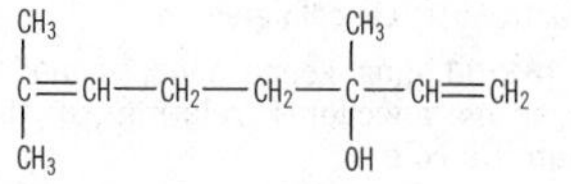

linalool

lin·al·o·ol /li nállō àwl, línnə lōol/, **lin·al·ol** /línnə làwl/ *n* a colorless liquid with a pleasant smell. Source: essential plant oils. Use: manufacture of perfumes. Formula: $C_{10}H_{18}O$. [Late 19C. < Mexican Spanish *linaloë*, via Spanish < late Latin *lignum aloes* "wood of the aloe"]

Lin Biao /lìn byów/ (1907?–71) Chinese military and political leader. He successfully commanded Communist forces during the Chinese Civil War, and died in an air crash after a failed coup attempt.

linch·pin /línch pin/, **lynch·pin** *n* **1.** somebody or something that is an essential element in the success of something such as a team or a plan **2.** a pin placed crosswise through an axle to prevent a wheel from coming off [14C. < obsolete *linch* "linchpin" < Old English *lynis*]

Lin·coln[1] /língkən/ *n* a heavy-fleeced sheep belonging to a breed originally developed in Lincolnshire, England. Raised for: mainly meat. [Mid-19C. After LINCOLNSHIRE]

Lin·coln[2] /língkən/ **1.** historic cathedral city in eastern England. Population: 85,616 (2002). **2.** city and seat of Logan County, central Illinois. Abraham Lincoln practiced law there between 1847 and 1859. Population: 15,070 (2002 estimate). **3.** state capital of Nebraska and seat of Lancaster County, situated in the southeastern part of the state. It is home to the University of Nebraska, Union College, and Nebraska Wesleyan University. Population: 232,362 (2002 estimate).

Library of Congress

Abraham Lincoln

Lin·coln, Abraham (1809–65) 16th president of the United States. A Republican, he took office in 1861, led the Union to victory in the Civil War, and announced the emancipation of slaves in the southern Confederate states (1863). His Gettysburg Address, delivered on November 19, 1863, became one of the great texts of US history. Lincoln was assassinated by John Wilkes Booth while attending a performance at Ford's Theatre in Washington, D.C. See table at **president** —**Lin·coln·esque** /lìngkə nésk/ *adj*

> "The world will little note, nor long remember, what we say here, but it can never forget what they did here. It is for us, the living, rather to be dedicated here to the unfinished work which they who fought here have thus far so nobly advanced. It is rather for us...that government of the people, by the people, and for the people, shall not perish from the earth."
> [Abraham Lincoln, *Address, Gettysburg*; November 19, 1863]

Lin·coln, Mary Todd (1818–82) US first lady (1861–65). A native of the South, she was alleged to have been a secret southern sympathizer during the Civil War.

Lin·coln green *adj* of a bright green color [After LINCOLN[2] (sense 1) where cloth of this color was first manufactured] —**Lin·coln green** *n*

Lin·col·ni·a·na /ling kōnee áanə, -ánnə/ *n* objects, writings, or anecdotes relating to the life of Abraham Lincoln

Lin·coln·shire /língkən shèer, -shər/ county in eastern England, bordering the North Sea and its inlet the Wash. Population: 646,646 (2001). Area: 2,272 sq. mi./5,885 sq. km.

linc·tus /língktəss/ *n* a medicinal syrup given to relieve coughs and soothe sore throats [Late 17C. < medieval Latin, "(medicine) for licking" < Latin *lingere* "to lick"]

Lind /lind/, **Jenny** (1820–87) Swedish soprano. The best-known singer of her day, she established the Mendelssohn Scholarships and various charities. Born **Johanna Maria Lind Goldschmidt**. Known as **the Swedish Nightingale**

lin·dane /lín dàyn/ *n* a white poisonous crystalline powder that biodegrades very slowly. Use: insecticide, weedkiller. Formula: $C_6H_6Cl_6$. [Mid-20C. After Teunis van der *Linden*, 20C Dutch chemist]

Lind·bergh /lind bùrg/, **Anne** (1906–2001) US aviator and writer. The wife of Charles Lindbergh, she accompanied him on many of his flights and wrote a number of books including *North to the Orient* (1935) and *A Gift from the Sea* (1955). Full name **Lindergh, Anne Spencer Morrow**

Charles Augustus Lindbergh and Anne Lindbergh

Lind·bergh, Charles (1902–74) US aviator and engineer. In 1927 he became the first person to fly solo across the Atlantic, which he described in *The Spirit of St Louis* (1953). Full name **Lindbergh, Charles Augustus**. Known as **Lucky Lindy**

lin·den /líndən/ (*plural* **-dens** or *same*) *n US* a deciduous hardwood tree with heart-shaped leaves and clusters of white, yellowish or green flowers, often planted for shade or ornament, or grown for timber. Native to: northern hemisphere. Genus: *Tilia*. Can term **lime**[3] [Late 16C. < *linden* "made of linden wood" < Old English *lind* "linden" < Germanic]

Lin·dis·farne /líndiss faarn/ island off the northeastern coast of England, separated from the shore by tidal waters. It is the site of a seventh-century monastery founded by St. Aidan. Area: 1.93 sq. mi./5 sq. km.

Lind·say /línzee/, **Vachel** (1879–1931) US poet. He wrote *General Booth Enters into Heaven* (1913) and *The Congo and Other Poems* (1914). Full name **Lindsay, Nicholas Vachel**

> "A nation of one hundred fine, mob-hearted, lynching, relenting, repenting millions."
> [Vachel Lindsay, "Bryan, Bryan, Bryan, Bryan," *Collected Poems*; 1923]

lin·dy /líndee/ (*plural* **-dies**), **lin·dy hop** *n* a lively dance for couples that is similar to the jitterbug [Early 20C. After *Lindy*, nickname of Charles LINDBERGH]

line[1] /līn/ *n* **1. LONG NARROW MARK** a long narrow mark or stroke made on or in a surface **2. ROW** a row of people or things **3. PEOPLE WAITING** a row of people or things waiting for a turn at something or for admittance to a place ○ *He's too impatient to wait in line.* **4. DIRECTION** a path or direction of movement ○ *The object was moving in a straight line toward us.* **5. SHAPE** the characteristic shape or contour of something (*often used in the plural*) ○ *the car's sleek lines* **6. BORDER** a boundary or division between two properties, jurisdictions, or political units ○ *The driver was heading for the county line.* **7.** SPORTS **CONFINING BOUNDARY** a long narrow mark that shows the boundary of any of the divisions of a playing area or race track **8. LIMIT** any limit or division ○ *a thin line between happiness and misery* **9. SERIES OF PEOPLE** a series of people, usually in the same family, who follow one another in the same job or role ○ *the last in a long line of musicians* **10. SERIES OF EVENTS** a series of related events or situations ○ *the latest in a long line of disasters for the company* **11. FACIAL MARK** a wrinkle or crease in the skin of the face (*often used in the plural*) **12. APPROACH** a course or approach followed in doing something ○ *his line of reasoning* ○ *We have to decide what line to take before the meeting.* **13. POLICY** a policy, a way of thinking, or a version of something ○ *What's the government line on this?* **14. DECEIVING TALK** something said to deceive, impress, or attract somebody (*informal*) ○ *gave me that old line about the dog eating his homework* **15. BRIEF MESSAGE** a short written message ○ *Why not drop me a line?* **16. CONNECTION** a telephone connection **17. TYPE OF MERCHANDISE** a particular type of product or merchandise ○ *our new line of children's wear* **18. THIN ROPE** a length of rope or wire **19. SPECIALIZED FIELD** a particular area of interest, work, activity, or expertise ○ *in my line of work* **20.** INSUR **KIND OR AMOUNT OF INSURANCE** a type of insurance, or the amount of insurance an underwriter will sell to cover a specific risk **21. USEFUL INFORMATION** useful information or an insight into something **22. ELECTRIC CABLE** a cable used for transmitting electric power or electronic messages **23. ROW OF PRINT** a row of words or numbers on a page or other surface ○ *a few lines of doggerel* **24.** MEDIA **PART OF TELEVISION PICTURE** a horizontal scan that with many others forms the picture on a television screen **25.** RAIL **TRACK** the track on which a railroad train runs **26.** RAIL **FIXED RAILROAD ROUTE** a particular part of a railroad network **27.** TRANSP **TRANSPORT COMPANY** a company that runs a regular service of buses, ships, or aircraft on a route **28.** TRANSP **ROUTE** a rail, sea, or air route served by a transport organization **29.** FOOTBALL **FOOTBALL PLAYERS** in football, either of the two rows of opposing players facing each other on either side of the line of scrimmage **30.** FOOTBALL same as **line of scrimmage** **31.** MUSIC **MELODY** the notes that make up a melody **32.** MUSIC **PART OF STAFF** a horizontal mark that is one of five that make up a staff **33.** MIL **POSITIONED FORMATION** a formation of troops, ships, weapons, or fortifications positioned in a place (*often used in the plural*) ○ *behind enemy lines* **34.** MIL **FIGHTING FORCE** the military or naval units of a country that actually go into battle **35.** MATH **ONE-DIMENSIONAL ELEMENT** in mathematics, a straight geometric element that has length but not width or thickness and whose identity is determined by two points **36.** MATH **TRACED PATH OF POINT** in mathematics, an imaginary path that has length but not width, traced by a moving point **37.** ELECTRONICS **NARROW BAND OF FREQUENCIES** a narrow band of frequencies in an electromagnetic spectrum **38.** SPORTS **ODDS** odds for wagering **39.** DRUGS **AMOUNT OF DRUG** a portion of a drug such as cocaine scraped into a long thin row to be inhaled (*slang*) **40.** GEOG **EQUATOR** the equator (*dated*) ■ **lines** *npl* **ACTOR'S WORDS** the spoken words that make up an actor's part ■ *v* (**lined, lin·ing, lines**) **1.** *vt* **MARK LINE ON SOMETHING** to mark something with lines **2.** *vt* **ARRANGE SOMETHING ALONG EDGE** to arrange or be arranged along the edge or length of something ○ *shrubs lining the driveway* **3.** *vti* BASEBALL **HIT LINE DRIVE** to hit a line drive in baseball [Pre-12C. Directly or via French *ligne* < Latin *linea* "linen string, line" < *linum* "flax, linen"; partly < Old English *līne*, probably via Germanic < Latin *linea*] —**lin·a·ble** *adj* ◇ **all along the line** throughout or at every stage in something ◇ **down** *or* **along the line 1.** at some time in the future ○ *looking for improvements down the line* **2.** at every stage ○ *poor communications all down the line* ◇ **draw the line** to restrict or set limits at a particular point ◇ **hold the line 1.** to keep a telephone connection open while waiting to speak to somebody **2.** to resist a military attack without giving ground or allowing a formation to be broken **3.** to be firm under pressure in maintaining an existing condition or situation (*informal*) ◇ **in line 1.** arranged in an orderly row **2.** in keeping with a policy or obedient to a set of rules ◇ **in line for** likely to receive something such as a promotion or position ◇ **in line with** in agreement or conformity with something ◇ **lay it on the line** to speak about something frankly (*informal*) ◇ **lay** *or* **put something on the line** to risk by some action the loss of something valuable (*informal*) ◇ **out of line** (*informal*) **1.** rude and disrespectful **2.** unruly or out of control ◇ **read between the lines** to deduce something that is not made explicit (*informal*) ◇ **shoot a line** to exaggerate abilities or attributes in order to impress somebody (*informal*) ◇ **toe the line** to comply with what is expected

line out *vi* to be put out when at bat by hitting a line drive that is caught by a fielder

line up *v* **1.** *vti* **FORM ROW** to form a row, or form people or things into a row **2.** *vi* **FORM LINE** to form a line to wait for a turn **3.** *vt* **PROVIDE SOMETHING** to organize, provide, or make something available to somebody ○ *had lined up a program of entertainments for us* **4.** *vti* **ALIGN THINGS** to align two or more things, or be in alignment

line[2] /līn/ (**lined, lin·ing, lines**) *vt* **1. REINFORCE SOMETHING** to cover or reinforce the inside or unexposed surface of something ○ *a jacket lined with silk* **2. COVER SOMETHING** to completely cover something with something else ○ *The walls were lined with books.* **3. FILL SOMETHING** to fill or supply something with something else ○ *a good hot meal to line your stomach* [14C. < obsolete *line* "spun flax" < Old English *līn*, probably via Germanic < Latin *linum* "flax"; from the use of linen to line garments]

lin·e·age[1] /línnee ij/ *n* **1.** the line of descent from an ancestor to a person or family **2.** a group of people related by descent from a common ancestor [14C. < French *lignage* < *ligne* (see LINE[1])]

lin·e·age[2] /línij/ *n* MEDIA another spelling of **linage**

lin·e·al /línnee əl/ *adj* **1.** in a direct line from an ancestor ○ *a lineal descendant of Charlemagne* **2.** relating to or derived from direct descent ○ *a lineal claim to the throne* **3.** MATH, ART, ELECTRONICS, BOT same as **linear** —**lin·e·al·ly** *adv*

lin·e·a·ment /línnee əmənt/ *n* **1. FACIAL FEATURE** a feature or contour of a face (*literary*) **2. CHARACTERISTIC FEATURE** a characteristic feature, especially of something immaterial (*literary*) **3. FEATURE OF LAND** a major topographical feature such as a long fault plane that reveals something about its subsurface [15C. < Latin *lineamentum* "line" < *lineare* "make straight" < *linea* "line"]

lin·e·ar /línnee ər/ *adj* **1. RELATING TO LINES** relating to, consisting of, or using lines **2. RELATING TO STRAIGHT LINE** relating to a straight line or capable of being represented by a straight line **3. CHANGING PROPORTIONALLY** describes variables that change proportionally and are representable on a graph as a straight line ○ *There's no linear relation between mortality and size.* **4. UNIMAGINATIVE** developed sequentially from the obvious without in-depth understanding ○ *takes a somewhat linear approach to the problem* **5.** ART **WITH CLEARLY DEFINED LINES** relying for its visual effect on clearly defined lines rather than on color **6.** MATH **OF FIRST DEGREE** about or in the first degree relative to a mathematical variable **7.** ELECTRONICS **WITH OUTPUT VARYING AS INPUT DOES** with an output that varies directly with the input **8.** BOT **LONG AND NARROW** describes a leaf that is long and narrow —**lin·e·ar·i·ty** /linnee árrətee/ *n* —**lin·e·ar·ly** *adv*

Lin·e·ar A *n* an undeciphered writing system, dating from about 1500 B.C. and found on clay remains in Crete

lin·e·ar ac·cel·er·a·tor *n* a device that propels charged particles in straight paths by using alternating high-frequency voltages

lin·e·ar al·ge·bra *n* a branch of algebra dealing with linear transformations, vector spaces, matrices, and determinants

Lin·e·ar B *n* an early form of Greek that dates from about 1400 B.C., found on clay remains in Crete and the Greek mainland, and deciphered around 1952

lin·e·ar e·qua·tion *n* an equation with no variable raised to a power

lin·e·ar func·tion *n* MATH same as **linear transformation**

lin·e·ar in·duc·tion mo·tor *n* ENG same as **linear motor**

lin·e·ar·ize /línnee ə rīz/ (**-ized, -iz·ing, -iz·es**) *vt* to form or project something into a line (*technical*) —**lin·e·ar·i·za·tion** /línnee əri záysh'n/ *n*

lin·e·ar meas·ure *n* any system or unit used to measure length

lin·e·ar mo·men·tum *n* PHYS same as **momentum** (sense 3)

lin·e·ar mo·tor *n* an electric motor in which the motion between the rotor and stator is linear so that thrust is produced along a straight line

lin·e·ar per·spec·tive *n* a form of perspective in which drawings or paintings are given apparent depth by showing parallel lines as converging on the horizon

lin·e·ar pro·gram·ming *n* in mathematics, a method of finding the maximum and minimum values of a linear transformation using variables that are subject to constraints

lin·e·ar trans·for·ma·tion *n* a mathematical transformation in which the resulting variables are neither multiplied together nor raised to any power

lin·e·a·tion /lìnnee áysh'n/ *n* **1.** division into or arrangement of lines **2.** the outline of an image

line·back·er /lī́n bàkər/ *n* in football, a player who takes a position near and behind the defensive line —**line·back·ing** *n*

line breed·ing *n* the deliberate mating of closely related individuals in order to retain characteristics of a common ancestor

line cut *n* a photoengraving made from a line drawing

lined /līnd/ *adj* **1.** WITH LINES with marked horizontal lines ○ *Use lined paper.* **2.** WRINKLED with wrinkles and signs of age ○ *a lined face* **3.** WITH LINING having a lining

line danc·ing *n* a style of dancing to country and western music in which dancers perform in rows —**line dance** *n, vi* —**line danc·er** *n*

line draw·ing *n* a drawing done entirely in lines, with tones shown by the thickness or closeness of the lines

line drive *n* in baseball or softball, a ball batted so that it moves fast, straight, and low

line en·grav·ing *n* an engraving in which lines are cut by hand into a metal plate from which the print is made

line i·tem *n* an item of financial or other data presented on a separate line, e.g., in a ledger or an annual report

line judge *n* in sports such as tennis, an official who assists the umpire by signaling that the ball is out of play

line·man /lī́nmən/ (*plural* **-men** /-mən/) *n* **1.** somebody, especially a man, who installs or repairs telephone or power lines **2.** in football, a player on the forward line, especially a center, guard, tackle, or tight end

line man·age·ment *n UK* the managers in a company who are involved in production or the central part of the business, as opposed to managers of service sectors

lin·en /línnən/ (*plural same* or **-ens**) *n* **1.** a thread or durable fabric made from the spun fibers of flax **2.** clothes, table coverings, underwear, or bedclothes made from linen or cotton (*often used in the plural*) [Old English *līnen* "made of flax" < *līn* (see LINE[2])]

lin·en pa·per *n* fine paper that is made from flax fibers or given a finish to resemble linen

line of cred·it *n* the amount of credit that a customer is allowed to draw on

line of·fi·cer *n* an officer who serves in combat

line of fire *n* **1.** a position in which somebody is exposed to a threat, attack, or criticism **2.** the path taken by a bullet or missile fired from a weapon

line of force *n* an imaginary curve whose tangent at any point is that of the electric or magnetic field that is operating there

line of scrim·mage *n* in football, an imaginary line across the field at which the ball rests and where the players of the opposing teams line up facing each other for a play

line of sight *n* **1.** an imaginary line from an observer to a distant object **2.** a straight path, unobstructed by the horizon, between a transmitting and receiving antenna

line·per·son /lī́n pùrss'n/ (*plural* **-per·sons** or **-peo·ple** /-peep'l/) *n* somebody who installs or repairs telephone or power lines

line print·er *n* a printing device that prints a line at a time rather than one character at a time

lin·er[1] /lī́nər/ *n* **1.** a passenger ship or airplane run by a shipping line or airline **2.** COSMETICS same as **eyeliner 3.** BASEBALL same as **line drive** [< LINE[1]]

lin·er[2] /lī́nər/ *n* **1.** something used as a lining or padding **2.** RECORDING same as **jacket** *n* (sense 4) **3.** a protective sleeve, usually made of metal, fitted inside or outside a cylindrical component [< LINE[2]]

lin·er·board /lī́nər bàwrd/ *n* a thick stiff cardboard used for containers, especially corrugated boxes

lin·er notes *npl* printed information about a recording that appears on the cover or as part of the packaging

line score *n* the score of a baseball game giving the runs scored by both teams in each inning as well as the total number of runs, hits, and errors

lines·man /lī́nzmən/ (*plural* **-men** /-mən/) *n* **1.** UMPIRE'S ASSISTANT in sports such as tennis an official, especially a man, who assists the umpire by signaling that the ball is out of play **2.** FOOTBALL OFFICIAL in football, an official who watches for fouls, marks the downs, and places the ball in position **3.** REFEREE'S ASSISTANT in soccer, an assistant referee positioned along a touchline (*dated*) **4.** *UK* same as **lineman** (sense 1)

line spec·trum *n* a spectrum produced by a gas emitting light or a gas selectively absorbing light emitted by another source that consists of a series of distinct parallel lines

lines·per·son /lī́nz pùrss'n/ (*plural* **-sons**) *n* in sports such as tennis, soccer, and football, an official who assists the referee or umpire, e.g., by signaling that a ball is out of play

line squall *n* a strong storm advancing along a weather front

line storm *n* an equinoctial storm

lines·wom·an /lī́nz wŏŏmmən/ (*plural* **-wom·en** /-wìmmin/) *n* in sports such as tennis, soccer, ice hockey, and football, a woman official who assists the referee or umpire, e.g., by signaling that a ball is out of play

line-up /lī́n ùp/, **line-up** *n* **1.** LIST OF PLAYERS a list of players in a team together with the positions they play **2.** TELEVISION SCHEDULE a programming schedule of a television network **3.** CRIME PEOPLE ASSEMBLED BY POLICE a group of people, including a crime suspect, assembled by the police so that a witness or victim of the crime can identify the person responsible for the crime **4.** GROUP UNITED IN PURPOSE a group of people or organizations recruited for a cause or common purpose such as raising funds for a charity **5.** SOMETHING FORMING A LINE a line of people or things

ling[1] /ling/ (*plural same* or **lings**) *n* **1.** a fish related to cod. Native to: coastal waters of Greenland and northern Europe. Genus: *Molva.* **2.** the flesh of a ling used as food [13C. Probably < Dutch or Low German]

ling[2] /ling/ *n* PLANTS same as **heather** (sense 1) [14C. < Old Norse *lyng*]

-ling[1] *suffix* **1.** one connected with or resembling ○ *hatchling* **2.** small one ○ *princeling* ○ *spiderling* [Old English, < Germanic]

-ling[2] *suffix* in a particular manner or condition ○ *darkling* [Old English, < Germanic]

Lin·ga·la /ling gáalə/ *n* a Bantu language used as a lingua franca in the Democratic Republic of Congo. Native speakers: 10 million. [Early 20C. < Bantu]

lin·gam /líng gəm/ *n* in Hinduism, a stylized phallus, used to represent the god Shiva [Early 18C. < Sanskrit *liṅga* "mark, phallus"]

ling·cod /líng kòd/ (*plural same* or **-cods**) *n* a spiny-finned large-mouthed game fish whose flesh is used as food. Native to: North Pacific Ocean. Latin name: *Ophidion elongatus.* [Mid-20C. < LING[1] + COD[1]]

lin·ger /líng gər/ (**-gered, -ger·ing, -gers**) *v* **1.** *vi* PUT OFF LEAVING to delay leaving somewhere because of reluctance to go **2.** *vi* WAIT AROUND to wait around or move around a place slowly and idly **3.** *vi* BE BARELY ALIVE to remain alive, although very weak, while gradually dying **4.** *vi* TAKE TIME TO DO SOMETHING to take longer than is usual to do something, e.g., to complete a task or look at somebody or something, usually because you are enjoying yourself ○ *Her eyes lingered on the letter.* **5.** *vi* PERSIST to remain fixed in the mind or noticed by the senses for a long time **6.** *vt* PASS TIME to pass time in a relaxed or uneventful way [13C. < obsolete *ling* "delay, linger" < Old English *lengan* "lengthen"] —**lin·ger·er** *n*

lin·ge·rie /laánzhə ráy, laánzharee, laáNzh ə rée/ *n* women's underwear and nightgowns [Early 19C. < French, "things made of linen" < *linge* "linen" < Latin *lineus* "made of flax" < *linum* "flax"]

lin·ger·ing /líng gəring/ *adj* **1.** DRAWN-OUT long and drawn-out, especially with pain **2.** SLOW done slowly in order to prolong something as long as possible **3.** PERSISTING IN MIND remaining for some time in the thoughts or mind —**lin·ger·ing·ly** *adv*

lin·go /líng gō/ (*plural* **-goes**) *n* (*informal*) **1.** a language that is not the speaker's native language **2.** a specialized set of terms requiring to be learned like a language ○ *the complicated lingo of lawyers* [Mid-17C. Origin ?]

SYNONYMS See *jargon*[1].

lin·gon·ber·ry /líng gən bèrree/ (*plural same* or **-ries**) *n* BOT same as **cowberry** [Mid-20C. < Swedish *lingon* "cowberry"]

lin·gua /líng gwə/ (*plural* **-guae** /-gwee/) *n* the tongue or a part resembling one [Late 17C. < Latin, "tongue"]

lin·gua fran·ca /lìng gwə frángkə/ (*plural* **lin·gua fran·cas** or **lin·guae fran·cae** /-gwee frángkee/) *n* **1.** a language or mixture of languages used for communication by people who speak different first languages **2.** the mixed language used chiefly by merchants throughout Mediterranean ports until the 18th century, consisting mainly of Italian with features of French, Spanish, Greek, Arabic, and Turkish [Late 17C. < Italian, "Frankish tongue"]

lin·gual /líng gwəl/ *adj* **1.** OF TONGUE relating to, using, or similar to the tongue **2.** FORMED WITH TONGUE describes speech sounds formed with the tongue **3.** OF LANGUAGE relating to language or languages [Mid-17C. < medieval Latin *lingualis* < Latin *lingua* "tongue"] —**lin·gual·ly** *adv*

lin·gui·ne /ling gweénee/, **lin·gui·ni** *n* pasta made in long narrow flat strips [Mid-20C. < Italian, plural of *linguina* "little tongue" < *lingua* "tongue" < Latin]

lin·guist /líng gwist/ *n* **1.** a speaker or adept learner of several languages **2.** an expert in or student of linguistics [Late 16C. < Latin *lingua* "tongue"]

lin·guis·tic /ling gwístik/ *adj* **1.** relating to language or languages **2.** relating to linguistics —**lin·guis·ti·cal·ly** *adv*

lin·guis·tic at·las *n* a collection of maps showing the distribution of varying language features in a region

lin·guis·tic form *n* an identifiable unit of speech, e.g., a word, prefix, phrase, or sentence

lin·guis·tic ge·og·ra·phy *n* the study of regional variation in speech —**lin·guis·tic ge·og·ra·pher** *n*

lin·guis·tics /ling gwístiks/ *n* the systematic study of language (*takes a singular verb*)

lin·gu·late /líng gyə làyt/ *adj* shaped like a tongue [Mid-19C. < Latin *lingulatus* < *lingula* "little tongue" < *lingua* "tongue"]

lin·i·ment /línnəmənt/ *n* a liquid rubbed into the skin to relieve aches or pain, e.g., one containing alcohol and camphor [15C. < late Latin *linimentum* < Latin *linire* "to smear"]

li·nin /lī́nin/ *n* a connective material in a cell nucleus [Mid-19C. < Greek *linon* "thread"]

lin·ing /lī́ning/ *n* a layer or a material used to cover, protect, or insulate the inner or unexposed surface of something [14C. < LINE[2]]

link[1] /lingk/ *n* **1.** PART OF CHAIN a ring that connects with others to make up a chain, or something resembling a ring in a chain **2.** CONNECTION something that ties, connects, or relates two or more things **3.** JEWELRY same as **cuff link 4.** TRANSP ROUTE any part of a transportation system, especially a connection between major routes **5.** BROADCAST UNIT FOR COMMUNICATING BROADCASTS a broadcasting unit or system used to relay radio or television signals, e.g., a transmitter, receiver, or relay station **6.** MEASURE SURVEYOR'S UNIT OF LENGTH a unit of length used in surveying, equal to 7.92 in./20.12 cm and one hundredth of a chain ■ *vti* (**linked, link·ing, links**) CONNECT THINGS, OR BE CONNECTED to connect, join, or associate somebody or something with another, or become joined with another ○ *There was no evidence to link him to the crime.* [14C. < Old Norse *hlekkr* < Germanic, "bending"] —**link·er** *n*

link up *v* **1.** *vti* to join, connect, or unite somebody or something with another, or become joined with another **2.** *vi* to meet and join with somebody or something else

link[2] /lingk/ *n* a burning torch used in the past to give light [Mid-16C. Origin ?]

link·age /língkij/ *n* **1.** LINK a link or connection, or the fact of being connected **2.** POL DIPLOMATIC PROCEDURE a procedure in diplomacy that requires progress toward an overall objective to depend on concessions made by the various parties on other related issues **3.** MECH ENG SYSTEM OF INTERCONNECTED PARTS a system of interconnected rods, springs, or levers that transmit motion in a mechanism **4.** GENETICS ASSOCIATED GENES the proximity of two or more genes on a chromosome, which tends to cause them to be inherited together

link·age group *n* two or more genes on a chromosome that tend to be inherited as a group

linked list *n* a chain of data items, each associated with a pointer to the next, and sometimes also to the previous one

Lin·kö·ping /lìn chŏping/ industrial city and capital of Östergötland County, southeastern Sweden. Population: 131,948 (1998).

links /lingks/ *n* (*takes a singular or plural verb*) **1.** a golf course **2.** *Scotland* an area of gently undulating sandy ground near a seashore [Old English *hlincas*, plural of *hlinc* "ridge"]

link·up /língk up/ *n* a connection or association between two or more things or people

Lin·nae·us /li neé əss/, **Carolus** (1707–78) Swedish naturalist. A pioneer of taxonomy, he devised the standard system of binomial nomenclature for plants and animals. Born **Carl von Linné** —**Lin·nae·an** /li neé ən/ *adj*

> "Nature does not proceed by leaps."
> [Carolus Linnaeus, *Philosophia Botanica*; 1750]

lin·net /línnət/ (*plural* **-nets** or *same*) *n* a small brownish songbird of the finch family, the male of which has a red breast and forehead. Native to: Europe, Africa, Asia. Latin name: *Carduelis cannabina.* [Early 16C. < Old French *linette* < *lin* "flax" < Latin *linum*; from its diet of flax seed]

li·no·cut /lĭnō kùt/ *n* a print made from a design that has been cut in relief into a piece of linoleum and mounted on a block of wood, or the design itself

li·no·le·ate /li nṓlee àyt/ *n* a salt or ester of linoleic acid [Mid-19C. < *linoleic* (see LINOLEIC ACID)]

li·no·le·ic ac·id /lìnnə leé ik-/ *n* an essential fatty acid, found in grains and seeds. Formula: $C_{18}H_{32}O_2$. [< Latin *linum* "flax" + OLEIC]

lin·o·len·ic ac·id /lìnnə lènnik-/ *n* a colorless liquid, essential to human nutrition. Source: linseed and other natural oils. Use: manufacture of paints and synthetic resins. Formula: $C_{18}H_{30}O_2$. [Translation of German *Linolensäure* < *Linolsäure* "linoleic acid," with insertion of *-en* "-ene"]

li·no·le·um /li nṓlee əm/ *n* a tough washable floor covering, made from canvas or other material coated under heat and pressure with powdered cork, rosin, and linseed oil [Late 19C. < Latin *linum* "flax" + *oleum* "oil"]

lin·sang /lín sàng/ (*plural* **-sangs** or *same*) *n* **1.** a carnivorous mammal related to and resembling the civet and genet that has spotted or banded fur and a long tail. Native to: forests of South Asia. Genus: *Prionodon.* **2.** an animal similar to the Asian linsang. Native to: forests of West Africa. Genus: *Poiana.* [Early 19C. < Javanese *lingsang*]

lin·seed /lín seèd/ *n* the seed of the flax plant, especially when used as the source of linseed oil [Old English *līnsǣd* "flax seed" < *līn* (see LINE[2])]

lin·seed oil *n* oil obtained from the seeds of flax plants. Use: as a binder in linoleum, paints, inks.

lin·sey-wool·sey /lìnzee wŏolzee/ *n* a coarse cloth made from linen interwoven with wool or cotton [15C. < *linsey* (probably after *Lindsey*, S England) + WOOL + *-sey* for rhyme]

lin·stock /lín stòk/ *n* a long staff with a forked end designed to hold a lighted match, used in the past to fire cannons [Mid-16C. < Dutch *lontstok* < *lont* "match" + *stok* "stick"]

lint /lint/ *n* **1.** THREAD OR FLUFF little pieces of thread or fluff **2.** COTTON FIBERS the fibers that surround unprocessed cotton seeds **3.** MATERIAL FOR MEDICAL DRESSINGS a soft absorbent material made from cotton or linen. Use: wound dressing. [14C. Origin ?] —**lint·y** *adj*

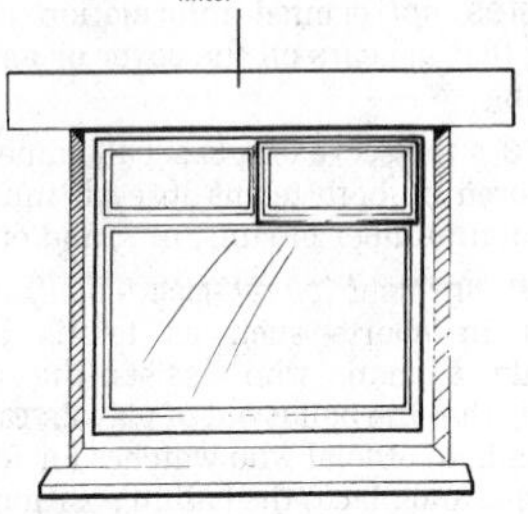

lintel

lin·tel /línt'l/ *n* a horizontal beam that supports the weight of the wall above a window or door [14C. < Old French < Latin *limit-* "boundary"; influenced by Latin *limin-* "threshold"]

lint·er /líntər/ *n* a machine for removing fibers sticking to cottonseeds ■ **lint·ers** *npl* fibers that stick to cottonseeds

LINUX /línnəks, lĭnəks/ *tdmk* a trademark for a computer operating system that is a free implementation of the UNIX operating system

Lin Yu·tang /lìn yŏo taáng/ (1895–1976) Chinese-born US philologist and novelist. He brought together Chinese and Western culture in his novels, and worked on the standard system of romanizing Chinese script.

Linz /lints/ capital of Upper Austria Province, northern Austria. Population: 189,073 (1999).

lion

li·on /lĭ ən/ *n* **1.** BIG WILD PREDATORY CAT a large wild member of the cat family that lives in extended family groups and hunts cooperatively for prey. It has a tawny yellow coat and the males have a shaggy mane. Native to: Africa, South Asia. Latin name: *Panthera leo.* **2.** SOMEBODY BRAVE AND STRONG a brave, strong, or fierce person **3.** CELEBRITY an admired and celebrated person [13C. Via Anglo-Norman *liun* < Latin *leon* < Greek *leōn*]

Li·on *n* **1.** ZODIAC same as **Leo** (sense 2) **2.** a member of a Lions Club

Li·on, Gulf of /lee ón/ gulf in the Mediterranean Sea. It extends eastward from the border between Spain and France to the French islands, les d'Hyères.

li·on dance *n* a traditional Chinese ritual performed to bring good luck, especially at Chinese New Year, in which two men dance costumed in a large ornamental lion head and body

li·on·ess /lĭ ənəss/ *n* a female lion

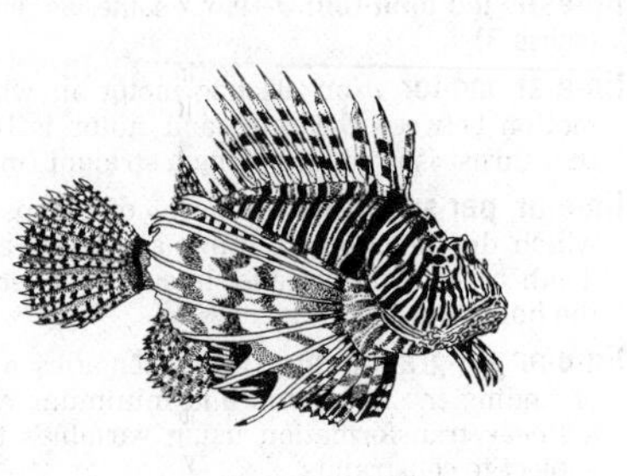

lionfish

li·on·fish /lĭ ən fish/ (*plural same* or **-fish·es**) *n* a scorpion fish with a striped body, long spiny fins, and venomous dorsal spines. Native to: tropical Pacific Ocean. Genus: *Pterois.*

li·on·heart·ed /lĭ ən haártəd/ *adj* very brave —**li·on·heart·ed·ness** *n*

li·on·ize /lĭ ə nīz/ (**-ized, -iz·ing, -iz·es**) *vt* to make somebody into a celebrity, or treat somebody like a celebrity —**li·on·i·za·tion** /lĭ əni záysh'n/ *n* —**li·on·iz·er** *n*

Li·ons Club *n* a club belonging to the International Association of Lions Clubs, an organization founded in the United States in 1917 to promote fellowship and service in local communities

li·on's share *n* the largest part or share of something [< Aesop's story in which a lion manages to get the whole kill in a hunt for himself]

lip /lip/ *n* **1.** PART OF MOUTH either of two fleshy folds around the mouth that help control eating, drinking, and the production of sounds by the mouth **2.** SOMETHING LIKE LIP something like a lip, especially an edge or rim of something hollow **3.** ANAT same as **labium** (sense 1) **4.** IMPERTINENCE impudent or disrespectful talk (*slang*) ■ *vt* (**lipped, lip·ping, lips**) **1.** STRIKE RIM WITH GOLF BALL to putt a golf ball so that it strikes the lip of a cup, but does not go in **2.** TOUCH SOMETHING WITH LIPS to bring the lips into contact with something **3.** FORM LIP OF SOMETHING to form or be a lip of something [Old English *lippa* < Indo-European, "lip"] ◇ **a stiff upper lip** *UK* a brave and composed bearing, with no giving way to emotion (*informal*) ◇ **bite your lip** (*informal*) **1.** to stop yourself from saying something you want to say **2.** to show that you are angry ◇ **button your lip** to stop speaking, not begin speaking, or keep a secret (*slang*) ◇ **give somebody a fat lip** to punch somebody hard in the mouth (*slang*)

lip- *prefix* same as **lipo-** (*used before vowels*)

li·pa /leépə/ (*plural same* or **-pas**) *n* a subunit of Croatian currency. See table at **currency** [< Croatian]

Li·pan /li paán/ (*plural same*) *n* a member of a Native North American people who lived in Texas and now live mainly in New Mexico

Lip·a·ri Is·lands /líppəree-/ group of volcanic islands off the northern coast of Sicily in the Tyrrhenian Sea. Area: 44 sq. mi./114 sq. km.

lip·ase /lĭ pàyss, -pàyz/ *n* a pancreatic enzyme that breaks down fats

lip balm *n* an ointment used on the lips, often in stick form, especially to relieve chapping or dryness

Lip·chitz /lípshits/, **Jacques** (1891–1973) Lithuanian-born French sculptor. The Cubist style of his early work was replaced by more sensual sculpture, much of it innovative and experimental. Born **Lipchitz, Chaim Jacob**

lip·ec·to·my /li péktəmee, lĭ-/ (*plural* **-mies**) *n* the surgical removal of fatty tissue from beneath the skin

li·pe·mi·a /li peémee ə, lĭ-/ *n* the presence of excessive fat in the blood

Li Peng /leè péng/ (*b.* 1928) prime minister of China (1987–98). Having become premier in 1987, he crushed the pro-democracy movement whose members had occupied Tiananmen Square (1989).

lip gloss *n* a cosmetic used on the lips to make them look shiny

lip·id /líppid, lĭpid/, **lip·ide** /lí pīd, lĭ-/ *n* a biological compound that is not soluble in water, e.g., a fat.

The group also includes waxes, oils, sterols, triglycerides, phosphatides, and phospholipids. [Early 20C. < French *lipide* < Greek *lipos* (see LIPO-) + French *-ide* "-id"] —**lip·id·ic** /li píddik, lī-/ *adj*

Li·pin·ski /lə pínskee/, **Tara** (*b.* 1982) US figure skater who, at the age of 15, became the youngest gold medalist in the history of the Winter Olympic Games (1998)

Lip·iz·zan·er /lìppit sáanər/, **Lip·piz·an·er** *n* a compact, usually white or gray horse belonging to a breed often used in equestrian displays [Early 20C. < German, after *Lipizza,* near Trieste, Italy]

lip lin·er *n* a cosmetic, usually in soft pencil form, used to outline the lips before lipstick is applied

Lip·mann /lípmən/, **Fritz Albert** (1899–1986) German-born US biochemist. He discovered the coenzyme that helps living cells derive energy from food, for which he shared the Nobel Prize in physiology or medicine (1953) with Sir Hans Krebs.

Li Po /lée pṓ/ ♦ **Li Bo**

lipo- *prefix* fat, fatty tissue ○ *lipolysis* [< Greek *lipos* "fat" < Indo-European, "to stick"]

li·po·gen·e·sis /lìppə jénnəssiss/ *n* the formation of fatty acids and other lipids in the body

lip·o·ic ac·id /li pṑ ik-/ *n* a sulfur-containing fatty acid that plays a role in carbohydrate metabolism

lip·oid /lí pòyd, lī́-/ *adj* containing or resembling fat ■ *n* a substance resembling fat —**li·poi·dal** /li póyd'l, lī-/ *adj*

li·pol·y·sis /li pólləssiss, lī-/ *n* the breakdown of fats into fatty acids and glycerol —**lip·o·lyt·ic** /lìppə líttik, lìpə-/ *adj*

li·po·ma /li pṓmə, lī-/ (*plural* **-mas** or **-ma·ta** /-mətə/) *n* a benign tumor made up of fatty tissue —**li·pom·a·tous** /li pómmətəss, lī-/ *adj*

lip·o·phil·ic /lìppə fíllik, lìpə-/ *adj* having a chemical affinity for lipids

lip·o·pol·y·sac·cha·ride /lìppō poli sákə rīd, lìpō-/ *n* a complex of lipid and polysaccharide that forms the outer layer of some bacteria

lip·o·pro·tein /lìppō prṓ teen, lìpō-/ *n* a complex of lipids and proteins that carries lipids around the body

lip·o·some /lìppə sōm, lìpə-/ *n* a microscopic artificial sac whose walls are a double layer of phospholipids, used to carry substances such as drugs, vaccines, and enzymes to specific cells or organs of the body

lip·o·suc·tion /líppə sùksh'n, lípə-/ *n* cosmetic surgery in which fat is removed from under the skin by vacuum suction

lip·o·trop·ic /lìppō tróppik, lìpō-/ *adj* preventing or reducing the accumulation of fat in the liver

lip·o·tro·pin /lìppō trṓpin, lìpō-/ *n* either of two pituitary hormones that trigger the breakdown of fats in the body

-lipped *suffix* having a particular kind of lip or lips

Lip·pi /líppee/, **Fra Filippo** (1406?–69) Italian painter. The imposing formality of his early works gave way to a more decorative and informal style in his later works, e.g., *Madonna and Child* (1455).

Lip·piz·an·er *n* SHOW JUMPING another spelling of **Lipizzaner**

Lipp·mann /lípmən/, **Walter** (1889–1974) US journalist. He was joint founder of *The New Republic* magazine (1914) and won two Pulitzer Prizes.

> "The tendency of the casual mind is to pick out or stumble upon a sample which supports or defines its prejudices, and then to make it representative of a whole class."
> [Walter Lippmann, *Public Opinion*; 1922]

lip·py /líppee/ (**-pi·er, -pi·est**) *adj* tending to say impudent things (*informal*)

lip-read /líp reed/ *vti* to understand what is said by watching how somebody's lips move rather than by listening —**lip-read·er** *n*

lip-read·ing *n* understanding spoken words by watching lip movements, rather than by listening

lip salve *n UK* same as **lip balm**

Lip·scomb /lípskəm/, **William** (*b.* 1919) US chemist. He conducted pioneering research on the molecular structure and chemical bonding of boron compounds and was awarded the Nobel Prize in chemistry (1976). Full name **Lipscomb, William Nunn, Jr.**

lip ser·vice *n* support or agreement that does not appear to be sincere because the words spoken are not followed up by appropriate action or behavior

lip·stick /líp stìk/ *n* an oily cosmetic in stick form, in a plastic or metal tube, used to color the lips

lip·stick cam·era *n* a cylindrical digital device smaller than a pack of cigarettes, typically mounted on a military helmet, motor vehicle, or combat aircraft and used to make visual records of operations or potential targets

lip·stick les·bi·an *n* a lesbian whose clothing and makeup are conventionally feminine and glamorous (*slang; sometimes considered offensive*)

lip-synch, **lip-sync** *vti* to pretend to sing or speak by moving the lips in synchronization with a recorded song or speech, or perform a song or speech in this way

Lip·ton /líptən/, **Seymour** (1903–86) US sculptor. His innovative works are constructed of sheet metal hammered into shape.

lip·u·ri·a /li pyóoree ə/ *n* the unusual presence of fat in the urine [Late 19C. < modern Latin < Greek *lipos* "fat" + *ouron* "urine"]

liq. *abbr* **1.** SCI, PHON liquid **2.** BEVERAGES, COOK, PHARM liquor

li·quate /lī́ kwàyt/ (**-quat·ed, -quat·ing, -quates**) *vt* to heat an alloy or ore to a temperature high enough to separate the constituents with the lowest melting point from the rest [Mid-17C. < Latin *liquat-*, past participle of *liquare* "liquefy"] —**li·qua·tion** /lī kwáysh'n/ *n*

liq·ue·fa·cient /lìkwə fáysh'nt/ *n* something that liquefies or helps to liquefy something else ■ *adj* capable of liquefying or helping to liquefy something [Mid-19C. < Latin *liquefacient-*, present participle of *liquefacere* (see LIQUEFY)]

liq·ue·fac·tion /lìkwə fáksh'n/ *n* the process of liquefying something, or the state of having been liquefied [14C. < late Latin *liquefaction-* < Latin *liquefacere* (see LIQUEFY)]

liq·ue·fied pe·tro·le·um gas *n* a mixture of petroleum gases liquefied under pressure. Use: as heating or engine fuel.

liq·ue·fy /líkwə fī/ (**-fied, -fy·ing, -fies**), **liq·ui·fy** *vti* to become liquid, or cause something to become liquid [14C. Via French *liquéfier* < Latin *liquefacere* < *liquere* "be liquid" + *facere* "make"] —**liq·ue·fi·a·ble** *adj* —**liq·ue·fi·er** *n*

~~**liquer**~~ incorrect spelling of **liqueur**

li·ques·cent /li kwéssənt/ *adj* becoming or tending to become liquid [Early 18C. < Latin *liquescent-*, present participle of *liquescere* "become liquid" < *liquere* "be liquid"] —**li·quesce** *vi* —**li·ques·cence** *n* —**li·ques·cen·cy** *n*

li·queur /li kúr, -kyóor/ *n* a sweet flavored alcoholic drink usually considered an after-meal beverage [Mid-18C. Via French < Latin *liquor* "fluid"]

liq·uid /líkwid/ *n* **1.** FLOWING SUBSTANCE a substance in a condition in which it flows, that is a fluid at room temperature and atmospheric pressure, and whose shape but not volume can be changed **2.** PHON CONSONANT PRONOUNCED WITHOUT FRICTION a consonant that is pronounced without friction and is capable of being prolonged like a vowel. In modern English, "l" and "r" are liquids. ■ *adj* **1.** CONSISTING OF LIQUID relating to, characteristic of, or consisting of a liquid or liquids **2.** SMOOTH AND FLUENT moving or produced in a smooth and fluent way **3.** FIN CONVERTIBLE TO CASH easily converted into cash **4.** CLEAR clear and shining **5.** PHON ARTICULATED WITHOUT FRICTION describes a consonant that is articulated without friction and is capable of being prolonged like a vowel [14C. Via French < Latin *liquidus* "fluid" < *liquere* "be fluid"] —**liq·uid·ly** *adv* —**liq·uid·ness** *n*

liq·uid air *n* a pale blue mixture of gases, mainly oxygen and nitrogen, that has been cooled and liquefied to be used in manufacturing pure gases and as a refrigerant

liq·uid·am·bar /lìkwid ámbər/ (*plural* **-bars** or *same*) *n* a tree that exudes a yellowish aromatic balsam. Native to: North and Central America, Asia. Genus: *Liquidambar*. [Late 16C. < modern Latin < Latin *liquidus* (see LIQUID) + medieval Latin *ambar* "amber"]

liq·uid as·sets *npl* assets that can easily be converted into cash

liq·ui·date /líkwi dàyt/ (**-dat·ed, -dat·ing, -dates**) *v* **1.** *vti* PAY DEBT to pay a debt or other financial obligation **2.** *vti* SHUT DOWN BUSINESS to shut down a business, paying off its liabilities from its assets, or cease trading as a business in this way **3.** *vt* CASH ASSETS to turn assets into cash **4.** *vt* KILL SOMEBODY to kill or dispose of somebody [Mid-16C. < late Latin *liquidat-*, past participle of *liquidare* "melt" < Latin *liquere* "be liquid"] —**liq·ui·da·tion** /lìkwi dáysh'n/ *n*

liq·ui·da·tor /líkwi dàytər/ *n* somebody appointed to oversee the liquidation of a business

li·quid ban·dage *n* a sterile liquid covering that is spread over a wound and then dries, used to treat minor cuts and scrapes

liq·uid crys·tal *n* a liquid that changes between being clear and cloudy depending on variations in temperature or applied voltage. Use: visual display units.

liq·uid-crys·tal dis·play *n* a display of numbers or letters in a calculator, watch, or other electronic device, created by applying electricity to cells made of liquid crystal to make some of them look darker

li·quid·i·ty /li kwíddətee/ *n* **1.** the state or quality of being liquid **2.** assets that can easily be converted into cash

liq·uid·ize /líkwi dīz/ (**-ized, -iz·ing, -iz·es**) *v* **1.** *vti* to become liquid, or cause something to become liquid **2.** *vt* to make something solid into a liquid using a blender

liq·uid·iz·er /líkwə dīzər/ *n UK* HOUSEHOLD same as **blender** (sense 1)

liq·uid lunch *n* alcoholic drinks consumed with little or no food in place of a midday meal (*humorous*)

liq·uid meas·ure *n* a unit or system of units for measuring liquid volume or capacity

liq·uid par·af·fin *n UK* same as **mineral oil**

liq·uid re·fresh·ment *n* a drink or drinks, especially alcohol (*humorous*)

liq·ui·fy *vti* CHEM another spelling of **liquefy**

liq·uor /líkər/ *n* **1.** ALCOHOLIC BEVERAGE an alcoholic drink, especially of the type produced by distillation, e.g., whiskey, rather than of the type produced by fermentation, e.g., wine or beer **2.** COOKING LIQUID a reduced liquid or juice left after cooking food, used as a sauce or as a basis for sauces **3.** SOLUTION OF DRUG a concentrated solution of a drug in a liquid, usually water **4.** WATER IN WHICH MALT IS STEEPED warm water added to malt in order to produce wort in the brewing process ■ *vti* (**-uored, -uor·ing, -uors**) STEEP MALT IN WATER to steep malt in warm water in order to form wort in the brewing of beer [13C. Via French < Latin]

liq·uor cab·i·net *n* a cabinet or cupboard in which alcoholic and other drinks are kept

liq·uored up /lìkərd úp/ *adj* having drunk too much alcohol (*informal*)

liq·uor store *n* a store that sells alcoholic beverages for consumption off the premises

li·ra /léerə/ (*plural* **-re** /léer ay, -rə/) *n* **1.** the main unit of currency of Turkey and Malta. See table at **currency 2.** the former unit of Italian currency [Early 17C. Via Italian < Latin *libra,* measure of weight]

Lis·bon /lízbən/ capital and largest city of Portugal. Population: 564,657 (2001).

li·sin·o·pril /lee sínnōpril/ *n* an oral drug that acts as an ace inhibitor. Use: treatment of high blood pressure and heart failure.

lisle /līl/ *n* a strong smooth fine cotton thread or fabric. Use: gloves, stockings. [Mid-16C. After LILLE (in former spelling)]

lisp /lisp/ *n* **1.** SPEECH DIFFICULTY a minor speech difficulty in which the sounds "s" and "z" are pronounced like the "th" sound. Small children whose front teeth have not come in yet often have a temporary lisp. **2.** SPEECH SOUND the sound produced when "s" and "z" are pronounced like the soft "th" sound in "third" or "thick" ■ *vti* (**lisped, lisp·ing, lisps**) **1.** PRONOUNCE "S" LIKE "TH" to pronounce something or speak so that "s" and "z" are pronounced like the soft "th" sound in "third" or "thick" **2.** **SPEAK LIKE CHILD** to speak in a childish or halting way [Old English *wlyspian* < Germanic, an imitation of the sound] —**lisp·er** *n* —**lisp·ing** *adj, n* —**lisp·ing·ly** *adv*

LISP /lisp/ *n* a high-level computer programming language, used in artificial intelligence, that converts data into lists [Mid-20C. Acronym < *list processing*]

Lis·sit·zky /lə síttskee/, **El** (1890–1941) Russian artist, architect, typographer, and designer. His series of abstract geometric compositions, *Prouns* (1919–23), established him as a pioneer of the constructivist movement. Full name **Lissitzky, Eliezer Markovich**

lis·some /líssəm/, **lis·som** *adj* **1.** slender and able to bend easily and gracefully **2.** quick, light, and graceful in movement [Late 18C. Alteration of *lithesome*] —**lis·some·ly** *adv* —**lis·some·ness** *n*

list[1] /list/ *n* **1.** **ORDERED SERIES** a series of related words, names, numbers, or other items that are arranged in order, one after the other ○ *a list of people to call* **2.** COMPUT **SET OF DATA** an ordered set of data ■ *v* (**list·ed, list·ing, lists**) **1.** *vt* **ARRANGE ITEMS AS ORDERED SERIES** to arrange a series of related words, names, numbers, or other items one after the other ○ *She listed the things she needed to do.* **2.** *vt* **PUT SOMEBODY OR SOMETHING IN LIST** to include somebody or something in a series of words, numbers, or other items arranged one after the other ○ *He's listed among the founding members.* **3.** *vt* **CATEGORIZE SOMEBODY** to place somebody in a category or classification ○ *She lists herself as a club member but never attends meetings.* **4.** *vt* FIN **ADMIT SECURITY TO EXCHANGE** to admit a security for trading on an exchange ○ *is listed on the New York Stock Exchange* **5.** *vti* COMM **SET OFFICIAL PRICE** to set an official retail price, e.g., in a catalog or advertisement ○ *lists at $40* **6.** *vti* MIL same as **enlist** (sense 1) (*archaic*) [Late 16C. < French *liste* < Germanic]

list[2] /list/ *vti* (**list·ed, list·ing, lists**) to lean to one side, or make a ship lean to one side ■ *n* an inclination to one side, especially one developed by a ship [Mid-17C. Origin ?]

list[3] /list/ *n* **1.** AGRIC **FURROWS FORMING RIDGE** a ridge of earth formed by two furrows plowed side by side **2.** ARCHIT same as **fillet** *n* (sense 3) ■ **lists** *npl* HIST, MIL **FENCED AREA IN TOURNAMENT** an area of combat in a medieval tournament enclosed by a fence of high stakes ■ *vt* (**list·ed, list·ing, lists**) AGRIC **FORM RIDGE FROM FURROWS** to plow together two furrows of earth to form a ridge [Old English *līste* < Germanic, "band, strip"] ◇ **enter the lists** to begin to take part in a fight or argument (*formal*)

list[4] /list/ (**list·ed, list·ing, lists**) *vti* to listen, or listen to something (*archaic*) [Old English *hlystan* < Germanic]

list[5] /list/ (**list·ed, list·ing, lists**) *vt* to choose, wish, or like something (*archaic*) [Old English *lystan* < Indo-European, "be eager"] —**list** *n*

list·ed com·pa·ny *n* a business whose stock may be traded on an exchange

lis·tel /líst'l/ *n* ARCHIT same as **fillet** *n* (sense 3) [Late 16C. < Italian *listello* "small border" < *lista* "border" < Germanic]

lis·ten /líss'n/ *vi* (**-tened, -ten·ing, -tens**) **1.** **MAKE CONSCIOUS EFFORT TO HEAR** to concentrate on hearing somebody or something ○ *We listened for the sound of the geese overhead.* **2.** **PAY ATTENTION** to pay attention to something and take it into account ○ *She wouldn't listen to my advice.* ■ *n* **ACT OF HEARING** an act of making an effort to hear something (*informal*) [Old English *hlysnan* (influenced by LIST[4]) < Indo-European, "hear"]
listen in *vi* **1.** **EAVESDROP** to listen to other people, sometimes without their knowing it **2.** **LISTEN TO RADIO** to listen to a radio broadcast **3.** **MONITOR TELECOMMUNICATIONS** to monitor radio or telephone communications
listen up *vi* to pay attention, or listen carefully (*slang*)

lis·ten·a·ble /líss'nəb'l/ *adj* pleasant to listen to, or suitable for listening to —**lis·ten·a·bil·i·ty** /lìss'nə bíllətee/ *n*

lis·ten·er /líss'nər/ *n* somebody who listens, especially to a radio broadcast

lis·ten·er·ship /líss'nər shìp/ *n* the number or kind of people who listen to a radio broadcast, program, or station

lis·ten·ing de·vice *n* a device that enables somebody to listen secretly to other people's conversations, e.g., in a room or on the telephone

lis·ten·ing post *n* **1.** **FORWARD POSITION** an advanced position near enemy lines from which troops can detect the enemy's movements **2.** **MONITORING PLACE** a post or area where information or intelligence is gathered **3.** MUSIC **POINT FOR LISTENING TO MUSIC** a module equipped with headphones and control buttons in record stores, where customers can listen to music before purchasing it

lis·ter /líster/ *n* a plow that heaps earth on both sides of a furrow [Late 17C. < LIST[3]]

Lis·ter /líster/, **Joseph, 1st Baron** (1827–1912) British surgeon. His discoveries in antisepsis greatly reduced surgical mortality.

> "There are people who do not...object to shooting a pheasant with the considerable chance that it may be only wounded and may have to die after lingering in pain...and yet who consider it something monstrous to introduce under the skin of a guinea pig a little inoculation of some microbe to ascertain its action."
> [Joseph Lister, *British Medical Journal*; 1897]

lis·te·ri·a /lə steéree ə/ *n* a rod-shaped aerobic parasitic bacterium that causes disease, especially listeriosis. Genus: *Listeria*. [Mid-20C. < modern Latin, after Joseph LISTER]

lis·te·ri·o·sis /lə steèree óssiss/ *n* a disease of the nervous system of mammals, birds, and occasionally humans that can cause fever, meningitis, miscarriage, or premature birth and is spread by eating food contaminated with listeria [Mid-20C. < LISTERIA]

list·ing /lísting/ *n* **1.** **SOMETHING ENTERED IN LIST** an entry in a list, catalog, or directory **2.** **LIST** a list, catalog, or directory **3.** COMPUT **PRINTOUT** a printout of a computer file or program **4.** FIN **PLACE ON OFFICIAL LIST OF SECURITIES** a place on an official list of securities that can be traded on an exchange ■ **list·ings** *npl* ARTS, COMMUNICATION **LISTS OF EVENTS** published lists of movies, plays, or other cultural events, containing information such as times, locations, and ticket prices [Mid-17C. < LIST[1]]

list·less /lístləss/ *adj* lacking energy, interest, or the willingness to make an effort [15C. < LIST[5] "pleasure"] —**list·less·ly** *adv* —**list·less·ness** *n*

Lis·ton /lístən/, **Sonny** (1932–70) US boxer. As world heavyweight champion (1962–64), he was noted for his power and physical stature. Born **Liston, Charles**

list price *n* a published or advertised retail price of something that can often be discounted by the seller

List·serv /líst sùrv/ *tdmk* a trademark for a mailing list management system that allows subscribers to take part in e-mail discussions

LISW *abbr* SOC WELFARE Licensed Independent Social Worker

Franz Liszt

Liszt /list/, **Franz** (1811–86) Hungarian pianist, composer, and conductor. His compositions, including *A Faust Symphony* (1857), arrangements, and transcriptions for piano, influenced other composers. He was a brilliant virtuoso pianist.

lit[1] /lit/ past participle, past tense of **light**[1] ■ *adj* having drunk too much alcohol (*slang*)

lit[2] /lit/ past participle, past tense of **light**[2]

lit. *abbr* **1.** MEASURE liter **2.** literal **3.** literally **4.** LITERAT literary **5.** LITERAT literature

lit·a·ny /lítt'nee/ (*plural* **-nies**) *n* **1.** a long and repetitious list of things such as complaints or problems ○ *recited a litany of grievances against the administration* **2.** in a Christian service, a series of sung or spoken liturgical prayers or requests for the blessing of God, including invocations from a priest or minister and responses from a congregation [13C. Via French < ecclesiastical Latin *litania* < Greek *litaneia* "prayer" < *litanos* "entreating" < *litē* "supplication"]

li·tas /leé taàss/ (*plural same*) *n* the main unit of Lithuanian currency. See table at **currency** [Late 20C. < Lithuanian]

Lit.B. *abbr* EDUC **1.** Bachelor of Letters **2.** Bachelor of Literature [Latin *Litterarum Baccalaureus*]

li·tchi *n* FOOD same as **lychee**

lit crit /lìt krít/ *n* LITERAT same as **literary criticism** (*informal*) [Mid-20C. Shortening]

Lit.D. *abbr* EDUC **1.** Doctor of Letters **2.** Doctor of Literature [Latin *Litterarum Doctor*]

lite /līt/ *adj* low in alcohol, calories, sugar, or fat (*used especially in labeling or advertising foods and beverages*) [Mid-20C. Respelling of LIGHT[2]]

-lite *suffix* mineral, rock, fossil ○ *halite* ○ *coprolite* [Via French < Greek *lithos* "stone"]

li·ter /leétər/ *n* a unit of volume equal to 1 cubic decimeter or 1.056 liquid quarts [Late 18C. Via French *litre* < medieval Latin *litra* < Greek, unit of measure]

lit·er·a·cy /líttərəssee, líttrəssee/ *n* **1.** the ability to read and write to a competent level **2.** knowledge of or competence in a subject or area of activity ○ *computer literacy* ○ *emotional literacy*

lit·er·al /líttərəl/ *adj* **1.** **FOLLOWING BASIC MEANING** adhering strictly and concisely to the basic meaning of a word or text ○ *a literal interpretation* **2.** **WORD FOR WORD** exactly following the order or meaning of a word or text ○ *a literal transcript* **3.** **USED TO EMPHASIZE TRUTH OF STATEMENT** used to emphasize that something is true ○ *It's the literal truth.* **4.** **FACTUAL AND UNIMAGINATIVE** simple in an unimaginative way that sticks solely to the facts ○ *a literal account of the incident* **5.** **USING ALPHABETICAL LETTERS** involving or expressed by letters of the alphabet [14C. Via French < Latin *literalis* < *littera* "letter"] —**lit·er·al·ness** *n*

lit·er·al·ism /líttərə lìzzəm/ *n* **1.** strict adherence to the basic meaning of a word or text **2.** the realistic representation of something in art or literature —**lit·er·al·ist** *n* —**lit·er·al·is·tic** /líttərə lístik/ *adj*

lit·er·al·ly /líttərəlee/ *adv* **1.** **STRICTLY ADHERING TO BASIC MEANING** in a way based on the basic or explicit meaning of a word or text ○ *You shouldn't interpret these lyrics literally.* **2.** **WITHOUT EXAGGERATION** used to show that a statement is actually true and not exaggerated ○ *He had literally thousands of books in his home.* **3.** ⚠ **USED FOR EMPHASIS** used with figurative expressions to add emphasis (*informal*) ○ *I was literally freezing.*

USAGE literally used for emphasis: In formal contexts, avoid using ***literally*** in a consciously exaggerated way to add emphasis, especially in combination with a colorful figure of speech: *We were literally swamped with offers.* Say instead *We had a huge number of offers*, or *We had more offers than we could deal with.*

lit·er·ar·y /líttə rèrree/ *adj* **1.** **RELATING TO LITERATURE** relating to literature, writing, or the study of literature **2.** **FORMALLY EXPRESSED** typical of literature rather than everyday speech **3.** **PROFESSIONALLY INVOLVED WITH LITERATURE** involved with literature or writing as a profession **4.** **KNOWLEDGEABLE ABOUT LITERATURE** well-read or knowledgeable about literature [Mid-17C. < Latin *literarius* < *littera* "letter"] —**lit·er·ar·i·ly** *adv* —**lit·er·ar·i·ness** *n*

lit·er·ar·y a·gent *n* somebody whose job is to negotiate business contracts on behalf of an author

lit·er·ar·y crit·i·cism *n* the process or art of analyzing, commenting on, and judging the contents, qualities, and techniques of literary texts —**lit·er·ar·y crit·ic** *n*

lit·er·ar·y ex·ec·u·tor *n* a manager of literary property on behalf of an author's estate

lit·er·ar·y for·en·sics *n* the scientific examination of documents of disputed authenticity (*takes a singular verb*)

lit·er·ate /líttərət/ *adj* **1.** **ABLE TO READ AND WRITE** having the ability to read and write **2.** **KNOWLEDGEABLE** having a good understanding of a particular subject ○ *Chil-*

a at; aa father; aw all; ay day; ə about, item, edible, common, circus; e egg; ee eel; er hair; hw when; i it; ī ice; 'l apple; 'm rhythm; 'n fashion; o odd; ō open; ŏŏ good; oo pool; ow owl; oy oil; th thin; t͟h this; u up; ur urge;

dren have to become computer-literate.* **3.** WELL-EDUCATED AND WELL-READ well-educated and cultured, especially with respect to literature or writing **4.** SKILLFULLY WRITTEN showing skill in the techniques of writing ○ *a literate account of the voyage* ■ *n* **1.** SOMEBODY CAPABLE OF READING AND WRITING somebody who is able to read and write **2.** SOMEBODY WITH EXTENSIVE EDUCATION a well-educated, learned, or cultured person [15C. < Latin *litteratus* < *littera* "letter"] —**lit·er·ate·ly** *adv*

lit·er·a·ti /lìttə raatee/ *npl* (*formal*) **1.** intellectuals or the educated class **2.** authors and other people closely or professionally involved with literature and the arts [Early 17C. Directly or via Italian < Latin *litterati* "lettered people" < *littera* "letter"]

lit·er·a·tion /lìttə ráysh'n/ *n* the representation of sounds or words by means of alphabetical letters [Early 20C. < Latin *littera* "letter"]

lit·er·a·ture /líttərəchər, líttrəchər, -choor/ *n* **1.** WRITTEN WORKS WITH ARTISTIC VALUE written works, e.g., fiction, poetry, drama, and criticism, that are recognized as having important or permanent artistic value **2.** BODY OF WRITTEN WORKS the body of written works of a culture, language, people, or period of time ○ *Russian literature* **3.** WRITINGS ON SUBJECT the body of published work concerned with a particular subject ○ *scientific literature* **4.** BODY OF MUSIC the body of musical compositions for a particular instrument or group of instruments ○ *literature for the piano* **5.** PRINTED INFORMATION printed matter such as brochures or flyers that give information ○ *the company's promotional literature* **6.** PRODUCTION OF LITERARY WORKS the creation of literary work, especially as an art or occupation [14C. Via French < Latin *litteratura* < *litteratus* (see LITERATE)]

lith. *abbr* PRINTING **1.** lithograph **2.** lithography

Lith. *abbr* **1.** Lithuania **2.** Lithuanian

lith- *prefix* same as **litho-** (*used before vowels*)

-lith *suffix* **1.** mineral, rock, stone ○ *batholith* **2.** stone structure or implement ○ *megalith* ○ *microlith* **3.** calculus, concretion ○ *otolith* [Via modern Latin *-lithus* < Greek *lithos* "stone"]

lith·arge /líth aarj, li thaarj/ *n* CHEM same as **lead monoxide** [14C. Via French < Latin *lithargyrus* < Greek *litharguros* < *lithos* "stone" + *arguros* "silver"]

lithe /līth/ (**lith·er, lith·est**), **lithe·some** /líthsəm/ *adj* able to move or bend the body lightly and gracefully ○ *a lithe gymnast* [Old English *līþe* "gentle" < Indo-European, "flexible"] —**lithe·ly** *adv* —**lithe·ness** *n*

lith·i·a /líthee ə/ *n* CHEM same as **lithium oxide** [Early 19C. < Greek *lithos* "stone"]

li·thi·a·sis /li thī əssiss/ *n* the formation or presence of stones formed by mineral concretions in the body, e.g., in the kidney, gallbladder, pancreas, or salivary glands [Mid-17C. Via modern Latin < Greek < *lithos* "stone"]

lith·ic[1] /líthik/ *adj* **1.** consisting of stone **2.** relating to undesirable mineral concretions in the body, e.g., kidney stones [Late 18C. < Greek *lithikos* < *lithos* "stone"]

lith·ic[2] /líthik/ *adj* relating to lithium [Early 19C. < LITHIUM]

-lithic *suffix* of a particular stage in human beings' use of stone implements ○ *Neolithic* [< Greek *lithos* "stone"]

lith·i·fy /líthə fī/ (**-fied, -fy·ing, -fies**) *vti* to change from loose sediments into solid rock, or change something in this way [Late 19C. < Greek *lithos* "stone"] —**lith·i·fi·ca·tion** /lìthəfi káysh'n/ *n*

lith·i·um /líthee əm/ *n* a soft silver-white element that is the lightest metal known. Source: spodumene, lepidolite. Use: alloys, ceramics, batteries, in compounds as a medical treatment for bipolar disorder. Symbol **Li**. See table at **element** [Early 19C. < LITHIA]

lith·i·um car·bon·ate *n* a white crystalline salt. Use: in ceramics and glass, treatment of bipolar disorder. Formula: Li_2CO_3.

lith·i·um fluo·ride *n* a white, slightly water-soluble powder. Use: manufacture of ceramics. Formula: LiF.

lith·i·um hy·dride *n* a white translucent powder or crystal. Use: organic synthesis, production of hydrogen. Formula: LiH.

lith·i·um-ion bat·ter·y *n* a lightweight battery charged with lithium atoms that provides more energy for a longer time than a standard battery

lith·i·um ox·ide *n* a white alkaline solid that absorbs carbon dioxide and water vapor. Use: manufacture of ceramics and glass. Formula: Li_2O.

litho. *abbr* PRINTING **1.** lithograph **2.** lithography

litho- *prefix* **1.** stone ○ *lithosphere* **2.** calculus, concretion ○ *lithotomy* [< Greek *lithos* "stone"]

lithog. *abbr* PRINTING **1.** lithograph **2.** lithography

lith·o·gen·ous /li thójjənəss/ *adj* describes organisms such as coral that secrete stony deposits

li·thog·ra·phy /li thógrəfee/ *n* a printing process using a plate on which only the image to be printed takes up ink. The area that is not to be printed is treated to repel ink. [Early 19C. < German *Lithographie* < Greek *lithos* "stone" + *graphein* "write"; because the plate was originally a porous stone] —**lith·o·graph** /líthə gràf/ *n, vti* —**li·thog·raph·er** *n* —**lith·o·graph·ic** /lìthə gráffik/ *adj* —**lith·o·graph·i·cal·ly** *adv*

lith·oid /lí thòyd/, **lith·oid·al** /li thóyd'l/ *adj* consisting of or resembling stone [Mid-19C. < Greek *lithoeidēs* < *lithos* "stone"]

li·thol·o·gy /li thólləjee/ *n* **1.** the scientific study of rocks **2.** the physical characteristics of a rock or a rock formation —**lith·o·log·i·cal** /lìthə lójjik'l/ *adj* —**lith·o·log·i·cal·ly** *adv* —**li·thol·o·gist** *n*

lith·o·phane /líthə fàyn/ *n* a piece of thin translucent porcelain or china with an intaglio design

lith·o·phyte /líthə fīt/ *n* **1.** a plant that grows on rock and absorbs nutrients from the atmosphere **2.** an organism that is composed in part of stony material, e.g., a coral —**lith·o·phyt·ic** /lìthə fíttik/ *adj*

lith·o·pone /líthə pōn/ *n* a white pigment that is a mixture of barium sulfate and zinc sulfide. Use: making paints and linoleum. [Late 19C. < LITHO- + Greek *ponos* "product"]

lith·o·sol /líthə sàwl/ *n* a soil with poorly defined layers (**horizons**) that consists mainly of partially weathered rock fragments [Early 20C. < LITHO- + Latin *solum* "soil"]

lith·o·sphere /líthə sfeer/ *n* the solid outer layer of the Earth above the asthenosphere, consisting of the crust and upper mantle —**lith·o·sphe·ric** /lìthə sféerik, -sférrik/ *adj*

li·thot·o·my /li thóttəmee/ (*plural* **-mies**) *n* the surgical removal of a stone from an organ or duct of the body, especially the urinary tract or bladder

lith·o·trip·sy /líthō trìpsee/ *n* the fragmentation of a stone in the urinary system or gallbladder, e.g., with ultrasound shock waves, so that the gravel can be passed naturally [Mid-19C. < LITHO- + Greek *tripsis* "rubbing"]

lith·o·trip·ter /líthō trìptər/, **lith·o·trip·tor** *n* a device that breaks up kidney stones using ultrasound shock waves [Early 19C. Alteration of *litho(n)triptor* < Greek *lithōn thruptika* "capable of pulverizing stones" < *lithos* "stone" + *thruptein* "to crush"]

Lithuania

Lith·u·a·ni·a /lìthoo áynee ə/ country bordering the Baltic Sea in northeastern Europe. Language: Lithuanian. Currency: litas. Capital: Vilnius. Population: 3,592,961 (2003). Area: 25,200 sq. mi./65,300 sq. km. Official name **Republic of Lithuania**

Lith·u·a·ni·an /lìthoo áynee ən/ *n* **1.** somebody who comes from Lithuania **2.** the official Balto-Slavic language of Lithuania, also spoken in western European Russia. Native speakers: 4 million. —**Lith·u·a·ni·an** *adj*

lit·i·gant /líttigənt/ *n* somebody engaged in a lawsuit [Mid-17C. Via French < Latin *litigant-*, present participle of *litigare* (see LITIGATE)] —**lit·i·gant** *adj*

lit·i·gate /lítti gàyt/ (**-gat·ed, -gat·ing, -gates**) *vti* to contest or be involved in a lawsuit [Early 17C. < Latin *litigat-*, past participle of *litigare* < *lit-* "lawsuit" + *agere* "to drive"] —**lit·i·ga·ble** /líttigəb'l/ *adj* —**lit·i·ga·tor** *n*

lit·i·ga·tion /lìtti gáysh'n/ *n* **1.** the act or process of bringing about or contesting a lawsuit or all lawsuits collectively ○ *The matter is in litigation.* **2.** same as **lawsuit** (*technical*)

li·ti·gious /li tíjjəss/ *adj* **1.** INCLINED TO GO TO LAW tending or wanting to take legal action ○ *a litigious person* **2.** OF LEGAL ACTION relating to litigation **3.** QUARRELSOME inclined to quarrel or argue (*formal*) [14C. < French *litigieux* < Latin *litigium* "litigation" < *litigare* (see LITIGATE)] —**li·ti·gious·ness** *n*

lit·mus /lítməss/ *n* a powdery substance obtained from lichens, which turns red in acids and blue in bases. Use: indicator for acids or bases. [14C. < Old Norse *litmosi* < *litr* "dye" + *mosi* "moss"]

lit·mus pa·per *n* a strip of paper treated with litmus. Use: to find out if something is an acid or a base.

lit·mus test *n* **1.** a test in which a single factor determines the outcome **2.** a test in which litmus is used to find out if something is an acid or a base

li·to·tes /lítə teez, líttə-, lī tṓ-/ (*plural same*) *n* a deliberate understatement, often expressed negatively, as in "I am not unmindful of your devotion" [Late 16C. Via late Latin < Greek *litotēs* < *litos* "simple"]

~~litrature~~ incorrect spelling of **literature**

li·tre *n* MEASURE Can, UK spelling of **liter**

Litt.B. *abbr* EDUC **1.** Bachelor of Letters **2.** Bachelor of Literature [Latin *Litterarum Baccalaureus*]

Litt.D. *abbr* EDUC **1.** Doctor of Letters **2.** Doctor of Literature

lit·ter /líttər/ *n* **1.** SCATTERED TRASH pieces of trash that have been carelessly left on the ground, especially in a public place or outdoors **2.** MESSY STATE OR PLACE a large number of objects that have been scattered around untidily, or a place that is in a messy state ○ *working away amid the litter of her study* **3.** ANIMAL OFFSPRING a group of young animals born at the same time from the same mother **4.** BEDDING FOR ANIMALS material, e.g., hay or straw, that is used as bedding for animals **5.** MATERIAL FOR PET'S TOILET BOX a dry absorbent substance, often in the form of granules, that is spread in a shallow container where a pet, especially a cat, can urinate or defecate when indoors **6.** GROUND SURFACE OF FOREST the surface layer of a forest floor, consisting of partly decomposed leaves and twigs **7.** COUCH FOR CARRYING PASSENGER a couch with poles on either side, used to transport a single passenger on people's shoulders or on animals **8.** STRETCHER WITH LONG SHAFTS a piece of cloth stretched between two long poles on either side that is used to carry a sick person or a dead body (*dated*) ■ *v* (**-tered, -ter·ing, -ters**) **1.** *vti* DROP TRASH to make a place, especially a public place or the outdoors, messy by leaving pieces of trash behind **2.** *vt* BE SCATTERED OVER PLACE to lie or be scattered over a place, making it messy, or put a place in disorder by leaving scattered objects in it ○ *Toys littered the playroom floor.* **3.** *vt* FILL SOMETHING WITH THINGS to fill something with many examples of something undesirable ○ *littered with mistakes* **4.** *vti* HAVE YOUNG to give birth to young (*refers to animals*) **5.** *vt* SUPPLY ANIMAL WITH BEDDING to provide an animal with hay or straw for bedding [14C. Via Anglo-Norman *litere* < medieval Latin *lectaria* < Latin *lectus* "bed"] —**lit·ter·er** *n*

~~litterature~~ incorrect spelling of **literature**

lit·ter·bug /líttər bùg/ *n* somebody who leaves litter, especially in public places or outdoors (*informal disapproving*)

lit·ter lout *n UK* same as **litterbug** (*informal disapproving*)

lit·ter·mate /líttər màyt/ *n* each of several animal young born or reared in the same litter

lit·tle /lítt'l/ (**-tler, -tlest**) CORE MEANING: an adjective meaning "small" or "young," or a grammatical word indicating that something exists in small quantities ○ (adj) *It was only a very little mistake!* ○ (adj) *He was helping the little boy put on his boots.* ○ (adj) *I'll bring my little sister with me.* ○ (adj) *There*

was a little food left. ○ (adj) *There was little chance of winning.*
1. *adj* **SMALL** small, or of less than average size ○ *He gave her a little Christmas tree ornament.* **2.** *adj* **YOUNG** not yet grown up ○ *I met her when she was just a little girl.* **3.** *adj* **YOUNGER** refers to a younger sister or brother ○ *my little sister* **4.** *adj* **SMALL AND PLEASANT** small in a pleasant or good-looking way ○ *his cute little habits* **5.** *adj* **SHORT** short in duration, or executed quickly ○ *gave a little smile* **6.** *adj* **TRIVIAL** of no importance ○ *the little things he does that bother me* **7.** *pron* **a little SMALL QUANTITY** a small amount of something ○ *I only ate a little.* **8.** *adj, pron* **NOT MUCH** only a very small amount ○ *had little or no effect* **9.** *adv* **HARDLY** hardly or not at all ○ *little did they know* **10.** *adv* **NOT OFTEN** on rare occasions ○ *visiting them little* [Old English *lȳtel* < Germanic, "small"] —**lit·tle·ness** *n* ◇ **little by little** gradually or by small degrees ○ *growing drowsy little by little* ◇ **no little** considerable ○ *ate with no little appetite* ◇ **not a little** a lot ○ *not a little embarrassed*

lit·tle auk *n UK* BIRDS same as **dovekie**

Lit·tle Bear *n* ASTRON same as **Ursa Minor**

Lit·tle Big·horn /-bíg hawrn/ river in southern Montana. General George Custer and his army were defeated by Native Americans on its banks in 1876. Length: 90 mi./145 km.

lit·tle-bit·ty *adj* extremely small (*informal*)

lit·tle black dress *n* a short black dress in any fashionable style for evening or party wear

Lit·tle Di·o·mede /lìtt'l dí̄ ə mēēd/ smaller of two islands in the Bering Strait between Alaska and Russia. It belongs to the United States. Area: 2 sq. mi./6 sq. km.

Lit·tle Dip·per *n* ASTRON same as **Ursa Minor**

Lit·tle Falls city and administrative seat of Morrison County, central Minnesota, situated 25 mi./40 km south of Brainerd. Population: 7,848 (2002 estimate).

lit·tle fin·ger *n* the smallest finger of the human hand, located farthest from the thumb

lit·tle folk *npl* same as **little people** (sense 2)

lit·tle grebe *n* BIRDS same as **dabchick**

lit·tle green man *n* an imaginary person from outer space (*humorous*)

lit·tle guy *n* an average person, as opposed to an important or wealthy one (*informal*)

lit·tle hours *npl* the hours of prime, terce, sext, and nones in the divine office to be recited every day by members of Roman Catholic orders

Lit·tle Ice Age *n* a period of colder weather marked by growth in alpine glaciers that began 5,000 years ago and lasted until the 19th century in some parts of the world

Lit·tle I·vies *npl* three colleges in the northeastern US, Amherst, Williams, and Wesleyan, that have high academic standards and long traditions but are smaller than those in the Ivy League

Lit·tle League *n* a baseball league for boys and girls from 8 to 12 years old, divided into administrative bodies for the United States, Canada, South America, East Asia, and Europe —**Lit·tle Leag·uer** *n*

lit·tle mag·a·zine *n* a literary magazine primarily made up of work by writers who have yet to become established, usually having a limited circulation and a small format

lit·tle man *n* an average person, as opposed to an important or wealthy one

Lit·tle Mis·sou·ri river in the northwestern United States, rising in Wyoming, and flowing eastward into the Missouri River. Length: 560 mi./900 km.

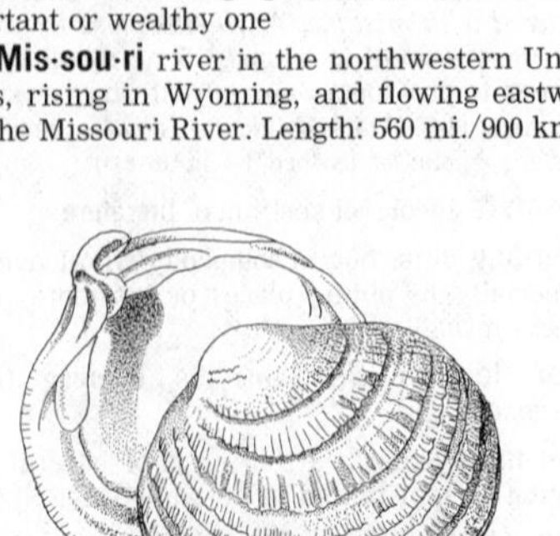

littleneck

lit·tle·neck /lítt'l nèk/, **lit·tle·neck clam** *n* a small young quahog clam, often eaten raw [Mid-19C. After *Little Neck* Bay, Long Island, New York]

lit·tle of·fice *n* a Roman Catholic office similar to but shorter than a divine office, especially a liturgical service of psalms and prayers to the Virgin Mary

lit·tle peo·ple *npl* **1. PEOPLE LACKING MONEY AND POWER** people who are typical in having a small or average income and minimal power and influence **2. SMALL SUPERNATURAL BEINGS** tiny imaginary or mythological beings, e.g., fairies, elves, and leprechauns **3. CHILDREN** small children (*informal*)

Lit·tle Rhod·y /-rṓdee/ *n* a nickname for Rhode Island

Lit·tle Rich·ard (*b.* 1935) US pianist and singer. A pioneer of rock and roll, his performance of songs such as "Tutti Frutti" (1955) and "Good Golly Miss Molly" (1958) made them classics of the genre. Born **Penniman, Richard Wayne**

Lit·tle Rock capital of Arkansas, in the central part of the state, on the Arkansas River. Population: 184,055 (2002 estimate).

lit·tle slam *n* in the game of bridge, the winning of 12 out of the 13 tricks in a deal

lit·tle the·a·ter *n* **1. SMALL EXPERIMENTAL THEATER** a small, usually noncommercial theater that produces experimental drama **2. EXPERIMENTAL NONCOMMERCIAL DRAMA** a form of noncommercial drama emphasizing experimental work **3. THEATER GROUP IN SMALL TOWN** an amateur theatrical group that puts on plays in small cities and towns

lit·tle toe *n* the fifth and smallest toe of the human foot, located farthest from the big toe

Lit·tle·ton /lítt'ltən/ city and county seat of Arapahoe County, central Colorado, situated 8 mi./13 km south of Denver. In April 1999, 15 people were killed and 23 wounded during a shooting massacre at Columbine High School. Population: 40,376 (2002 estimate).

lit·to·ral /líttərəl/ *adj* **1. ON OR NEAR SHORE** on or near a shore, especially the zone between the high and low tide marks **2. SHORE-LIVING** living on or near a shore ■ *n* **SHORE** a shore or coastal region, especially the zone between the high and low tide marks [Mid-17C. < Latin *littoralis* < *litor-* "shore"]

lit up *adj* having drunk too much alcohol (*slang*)

li·tur·gi·cal /li túrjik'l/, **li·tur·gic** /li túrjik/ *adj* **1.** relating to liturgy **2.** relating to religious worship or to a service of worship, especially the celebration of Communion in a Christian service —**li·tur·gi·cal·ly** *adv*

li·tur·gics /li túrjiks/ *n* the study of public worship or liturgies (*takes a singular verb*)

li·tur·gi·ol·o·gy /lə tùrjee óllәjee/ *n* CHR same as **liturgics** —**li·tur·gi·ol·o·gist** *n*

lit·ur·gist /líttərjist/ *n* **1. SOMEBODY WHO STUDIES LITURGIES** somebody who studies or compiles liturgies **2. PRACTITIONER OF LITURGY** somebody who performs the liturgy **3. SUPPORTER OF LITURGIES** somebody who favors using liturgies —**lit·ur·gism** *n* —**lit·ur·gis·tic** /lìttər jístik/ *adj*

lit·ur·gy /líttərjee/ (*plural* **-gies**) *n* **1.** a form and arrangement of public worship laid down by a church or religion **2.** CHR another spelling of **Liturgy** [Mid-16C. Directly or via French < late Latin *liturgia* < Greek *leitourgia* "service, worship" < *leitourgos* "public servant" < *leitos* "public"]

Lit·ur·gy *n* the form of service used to celebrate Communion in a Christian denomination, especially in Eastern churches

Liu Shao·qi /lyṓō shòw chée/, **Liu Shao-ch'i** (1898–1969) Chinese political leader. He became vice chairman of the Communist Party in 1959, but was forced from office during the Cultural Revolution (1966–69).

liv·a·ble /lívvəb'l/, **live·a·ble** *adj* **1.** comfortable or suitable for living in ○ *a very livable apartment* **2.** endurable and worth continuing ○ *It's very tense at home, but still livable.* —**liv·a·bil·i·ty** /lìvvə bílləteel/ *n*

live[1] /liv/ (**lived, liv·ing, lives**) *v* **1.** *vi* **HAVE LIFE** to be alive **2.** *vi* **STAY ALIVE** to remain alive ○ *lived through a serious illness* **3.** *vi* **RESIDE** to make your home in a particular place or condition or with a particular person ○ *lives alone* **4.** *vti* **LEAD PARTICULAR TYPE OF EXISTENCE** to spend your life in a particular way or under particular circumstances ○ *live comfortably* **5.** *vi* **MAKE LIVING** to earn or make a living ○ *lives by waiting on tables* **6.** *vti* **FULLY ENJOY LIFE** to enjoy life to the fullest ○ *really knew how to live* **7.** *vi* **CONTINUE** to persist or continue in existence ○ *Her fame lives on.* **8.** *vt* **EXPERIENCE SOMETHING** to experience or go through something ○ *living a dream* **9.** *vti* **MAKE LIFE CONFORM** to make your life conform to something such as a philosophy or religion ○ *lived her faith* ○ *lived by strict rules* **10.** *vi* **BE KEPT SOMEWHERE** to be found or kept in a particular place (*informal*) ○ *The spare car keys live in this drawer.* [Old English *libban, lifian* < Indo-European, "to stick"] ◇ **live and learn** to constantly gain new knowledge or learn from mistakes (*informal*) ○ *I thought it was safe to eat the berries, but you live and learn!* ◇ **live and let live** to be tolerant of others ◇ **live it up** to live or celebrate in an extravagant way (*slang*)

live down *vt* to live in a blameless or commendable way long enough for something shameful to be forgotten

live in *vi* to live at your place of work

live off *vt* to depend on somebody or something as a source of financial support or for a livelihood ○ *He lived off his parents.*

live on *vt* **1.** to eat a particular type of food in order to survive or thrive ○ *The koala lives on eucalyptus leaves.* **2.** same as **live off**

live out *v* **1.** *vt* **DO SOMETHING PREVIOUSLY IMAGINED** to do in reality what had previously only been imagined or fantasized about ○ *live out a fantasy* **2.** *vt* **LIVE UNTIL END OF PERIOD** to spend the rest of your life or a period of time in a particular manner or place **3.** *vi* **LIVE SOMEWHERE OTHER THAN WORKPLACE** to live away from the place where you work

live through *vt* to experience and survive something difficult or dangerous

live together *vi* to share the same home and have a sexual relationship without being married

live up to *vt* to meet somebody's expectations or desires or match somebody's good example

live with *vt* **1.** to accept or tolerate something difficult or unpleasant ○ *The house is tiny, but we'll just have to live with it.* **2.** to share a home and have a sexual relationship with somebody without being married

live[2] /līv/ *adj* **1. LIVING** alive rather than dead or inanimate **2. BROADCAST AS IT HAPPENS** broadcast while an event is happening ○ *Tonight's show is live from Los Angeles.* **3. IN PERSON** appearing, performing, or performed in front of an audience or in person, rather than recorded or filmed ○ *I'd rather dance to live music.* **4. RECORDED DURING PERFORMANCE** recorded while a performance is happening ○ *live footage of the concert* **5.** ELEC **CONNECTED TO POWER SOURCE** connected to an electrical power source ○ *a live cable* **6. CHARGED WITH EXPLOSIVE** containing an explosive and able to be used ○ *live ammunition* **7. CURRENTLY RELEVANT** relevant to current interests or concerns ○ *a live issue* **8. BURNING** burning or glowing ○ *live coals* **9. WITH LIVING BACTERIA** made using living bacteria ○ *live yogurt cultures* **10. HIGHLY RESONANT** with highly resonant or reverberant acoustics **11.** GEOL **ACTIVE** describes a volcano that is still active **12.** GEOL **FOUND AS ORIGINAL ROCK** describes a rock or mineral that is found free and not mined or quarried **13.** SPORTS **IN PLAY** in sports such as baseball or football, used to describe a ball that remains in play because officials have not halted action (*informal*) ■ *adv* **1. IN PERSON** in front of an audience or in person ○ *performing live here tomorrow night* **2. WHILE EVENT HAPPENS** so as to be broadcast at exactly the same time as a performance or event happens [Mid-16C. Shortening of ALIVE]

live·a·ble *adj* another spelling of **livable**

live·bear·er /līv bèrrər/ *n* a fish that gives birth to living young, rather than producing eggs —**live·bear·ing** *adj*

live birth /līv-/ *n* the birth of a living infant —**live-born** *adj*

lived-in *adj* **1.** with a comfortable but slightly worn or untidy look that it is consistent with actual or current occupation **2.** showing the effects of life's experiences

li·ve·do /li vēēdō, lī-/ (*plural* **-dos**) *n* a bluish black patch of discolored skin caused by the settling of blood, especially after death [< modern Latin < Latin *livere* "be bluish in color"]

live-fire /līv-/ *adj* using live ammunition and loaded weapons, usually for military tests or training

live-for·ev·er /lĭv-/ *n* PLANTS **1.** same as **houseleek 2.** same as **orpine** [Because it lives for a long time]

live-in /lĭv-/ *adj* **1.** living in your place of employment ○ *a live-in nanny* **2.** sharing a home with a sexual partner —**live-in** *n*

live·li·hood /lívlee hòod/ *n* something that provides income to live on, especially paid work [13C. Alteration of Old English *līflād* "way of living" < *līf* "life"]

live load /lĭv-/ *n* the variable load or weight borne by a structure such as a bridge, in addition to its own weight

live·long[1] /lív làwng/ *adj* used to emphasize how long a period of time seems to last or how tedious it feels (*literary*) ○ *worked all the livelong day* [14C. < LIEF; influenced by LIVE[1]]

live·long[2] /lív làwng/ *n* PLANTS same as **orpine** [Late 16C. < LIVE[1] + LONG[1]; because it lives for a long time]

live·ly /lívlee/ (**-li·er, -li·est**) *adj* **1.** FULL OF ENERGY full of life and energy ○ *two lively children* **2.** ANIMATED animated, exciting, or intellectually stimulating ○ *a lively discussion* **3.** ENTHUSIASTIC active and enthusiastic ○ *takes a lively interest in everything* **4.** FULL OF MOVEMENT full of activity or movement ○ *a lively dance* **5.** REFRESHING stimulating or refreshing ○ *a lively little breeze* **6.** SPRINGY bouncy or springy ○ *a lively rubber ball* **7.** NAUT RESPONSIVE TO STEERING describes a boat that is responsive to the helm [Old English *līflīc* "lifelike"] —**live·li·ness** *n* ◇ **look** *or* **step lively** to hurry up and get going

~~**livelyhood**~~ incorrect spelling of **livelihood**

li·ven /lívən/ (**-vened, -ven·ing, -vens**) *v* **1.** *vti* to become lively or cheerful, or make somebody or something lively or cheerful ○ *What can we do to liven up the party?* **2.** *vt* to make something more attractive or interesting, e.g., by brightening its color or intensifying its flavor ○ *livened up the sauce with some lemon juice* [Early 18C. < LIFE]

live oak /lĭv-/ *n* a very large evergreen oak with a short broad trunk, leathery leaves, and hard timber, often grown for shade. Native to: Texas, east through the southeastern United States. Latin name: *Quercus virginianus.* [< LIVE[2]; from its being evergreen]

live one /lĭv-/ *n* (*informal*) **1.** same as **live wire** (sense 2) **2.** somebody who is easily cheated or duped

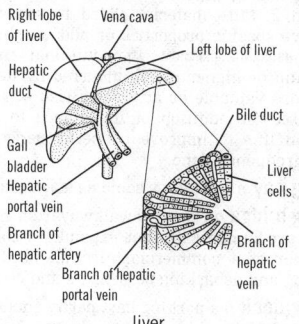

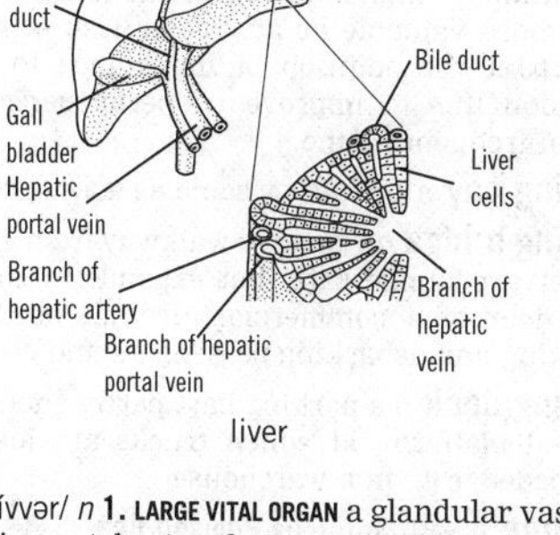

liver

liv·er[1] /lívvər/ *n* **1.** LARGE VITAL ORGAN a glandular vascular organ in vertebrates that secretes bile, stores and filters blood, and takes part in many metabolic functions such as the conversion of sugars into glycogen. The liver is reddish brown, multilobed, and in humans is located in the upper right part of the abdominal cavity. **2.** INVERTEBRATE ORGAN a glandular organ of invertebrates involved with digestion and metabolism **3.** LIVER AS FOOD the liver of a mammal, bird, or fish eaten as food **4.** COLORS DARK BROWN COLOR a dark brown color tinged with red or gray [Old English *lifer* < Germanic] —**liv·er** *adj*

liv·er[2] /lívvər/ *n* somebody who lives in a particular way ○ *a fast liver* [14C. < LIVE[1]]

liv·er fluke *n* a parasitic worm that infests the liver of mammals, including humans. Latin name: *Fasciola hepatica.*

liv·er·ish /lívvərish/ *adj* **1.** IRRITABLE bad-tempered or irritable **2.** WITH LIVER DISORDER affected by a liver disorder **3.** LIKE LIVER resembling liver, especially in color (*informal*)

Liv·er·more /lívvər màwr/ city in Alameda County, western California, situated 23 mi./37 km east of San Francisco Bay. The Lawrence Livermore National Laboratory, which pioneers nuclear research, is there.

Liv·er·pool /lívvər pòol/ port and university city in northwestern England, on the Mersey River. Population: 439,473 (2001).

liv·er sau·sage *n UK* same as **liverwurst**

liv·er spot *n* a brown patch of pigmentation on the skin, usually occurring later in life [< its color]

liv·er·wort /lívvər wùrt, -wàwrt/ *n* a small dense green plant that grows on moist surfaces and resembles moss. Class: Hepaticae. [Old English *liferwyrt*, translation of medieval Latin *hepatica*; from its lobed shape]

liv·er·wurst /lívvər wùrst/ *n* a sausage containing cooked ground liver, usually eaten cold as a spread [Mid-19C. Partial translation of German *Leberwurst* "liver sausage"]

liv·er·y[1] /lívvəree/ (*plural* **-ies**) *n* **1.** UNIFORM an identifying uniform worn by members of a group or trade, especially men and boys who are servants of a household or feudal retainers **2.** CHARACTERISTIC APPEARANCE a distinctive coloring, marking, dress, or outward appearance (*literary*) **3.** PROFESSIONAL CARE OF HORSES the care, feeding, and stabling of horses for money **4.** RENTING OF HORSES the business of renting out horses **5.** COMM same as **livery stable 6.** BUSINESS THAT RENTS VEHICLES a company that rents vehicles such as cars, bicycles, or boats [14C. < Old French *livree* "delivery" < Latin *liberare* "liberate" < *liber* "free"] —**liv·er·ied** *adj*

liv·er·y[2] /lívvəree/ *adj* same as **liverish** (*informal*) [Mid-18C. < LIVER[1]]

liv·er·y·man /lívvəreemən, lívvreemən/ (*plural* **-men** /-mən/) *n* somebody who owns or works in a livery stable

liv·er·y sta·ble *n* **1.** a stable where horses and carriages are kept for rent **2.** a stable that accommodates and takes care of horses for their owners

live·stock /lív stòk/ *n* animals raised for food or other products, or kept for use, especially farm animals such as meat and dairy cattle, pigs, and poultry

live trap /lív-/ *n* a trap designed to catch a wild animal without injuring it

live wire /lív-/ *n* **1.** a wire connected to a source of voltage **2.** an enthusiastic and energetic person (*informal*)

live·yere /lív yér/ *n Can* a permanent resident of Newfoundland [Mid-19C. Variant of *livier* "lifelong tenant" < LIFE + -IER]

liv·id /lívvid/ *adj* **1.** FURIOUS very angry **2.** WITH BLUISH BRUISED COLOR bluish or discolored as a result of bruising **3.** ASHEN very pale, especially unnaturally so **4.** GRAYISH tinged with gray [15C. Directly or via French < Latin *lividus* < *livere* "be bluish in color"] —**li·vid·i·ty** /li víddətee/ *n* —**liv·id·ly** *adv*

liv·ing /lívving/ *adj* **1.** ALIVE having life, not dead or nonexistent ○ *every living thing* **2.** LIKE REAL THING realistic or true to life ○ *the living image of her grandmother* **3.** SUITABLE FOR DOMESTIC LIFE designed for living in, especially for social and recreational activities ○ *lots of living space* **4.** STILL USED still used or in existence ○ *a living language* **5.** INTERESTING AND RELEVANT interesting in a way that is relevant and useful ○ *make a dry academic discipline into a living subject* **6.** ABSOLUTE used to emphasize how real, intense, or thorough something is ○ *went through living torment* **7.** NATURAL in a natural condition or place ○ *living water* ■ *n* **1.** MONEY OR MEANS OF EARNING a means of earning money to live on, or the money somebody earns to live on ○ *What do you do for a living?* **2.** MAINTENANCE OF WAY OF LIFE the process of sustaining or maintaining a way of life ○ *the cost of living* **3.** MANNER OF LIFE quality of life, or a particular way of life ○ *healthy living* ■ *npl* THOSE WHO ARE ALIVE people who are alive

liv·ing death *n* a life or period of time that is full of misery or pain

liv·ing do·nor *n* somebody who, while still alive, donates all or part of one or more organs for transplantation

liv·ing fos·sil *n* an organism that is almost unchanged from early geologic time and belongs to a group whose other members are extinct. Gingko trees and coelacanths are living fossils.

liv·ing hell *n* an extremely unpleasant situation that somebody is forced to endure, often for a considerable length of time (*informal*) ○ *The weeks of waiting were a living hell.*

liv·ing leg·end *n* somebody who becomes very famous during his or her own lifetime

liv·ing pic·ture *n* THEATER same as **tableau vivant**

liv·ing quar·ters *npl* the parts of a building, ship, or spacecraft where people eat, sleep, and spend their leisure time, as opposed to the parts where work is done

liv·ing room *n* a room in a house where people usually relax or entertain guests

liv·ing stan·dards *npl* the conditions in which people live, especially in terms of their level of material comfort and disposable income

Liv·ing·ston /lívvingstən/, **Henry Brockholst** (1757–1823) US Supreme Court associate justice (1806–23). A former officer in the American Revolution, he was appointed by Thomas Jefferson to the US Supreme Court.

Liv·ing·ston, Philip (1716–78) American patriot, merchant, and philanthropist. He was one of the signatories of the Declaration of Independence (1776).

Liv·ing·ston, Robert (1654–1728) Scottish-born American patriot and politician. He was a major figure in New York colonial politics after 1695.

Liv·ing·ston, Robert R. (1746–1813) American patriot, lawyer, diplomat. After independence, he administered the presidential oath to George Washington in New York. He became the first US secretary of foreign affairs (1781–83), and negotiated the Louisiana Purchase.

Liv·ing·ston, William (1723–90) American patriot, lawyer, and politician. He opposed British policies in colonial New York, and was one of the signatories of the Declaration of Independence (1776).

Liv·ing·stone /lívvingstən/ city and tourist center in southern Zambia, north of the Victoria Falls. Population: 82,218 (1990).

Liv·ing·stone, David (1813–73) British physician, missionary, and explorer. One of the most important explorers of the African interior, he was the first European to visit many areas of the continent.

liv·ing wage *n* a wage that will allow a worker to support a family in reasonable comfort

liv·ing will *n* a document, typically signed in advance while in good health, that specifies the decisions somebody wishes to be taken about his or her medical treatment in the event of becoming incapable of making or communicating them

Li·vo·ni·a /li vónee ə/ ancient Baltic region, comprising most of present-day Estonia and Latvia. Russia annexed it in 1721. —**Li·vo·ni·an** *adj, n*

Li·vor·no /lee váwrnō/ port and industrial city in northwestern Italy, on the Ligurian Sea. Population: 156,274 (2001).

li·vre /léevrə/ *n* an old unit of French currency, equivalent to a pound of silver [Mid-16C. Via French < Latin *libra* "pound"]

Liv·y /lívvee/ (59 B.C.–A.D. 17) Roman historian. His *History of Rome*, ranging from the foundation of the city in 753 B.C. to 9 B.C., was the basis for the Western tradition of historical writing, and remained the primary source of information about Rome until the 18th century. Full name **Livius, Titus**

lix·iv·i·um /lik sívvee əm/ (*plural* **-i·ums** *or* **-i·a** /-ee ə/) *n* a solution obtained by leaching, e.g., lye [Mid-17C. < late Latin < Latin *lixivius* "made into ashes or lye" < *lix* "lye"]

lizard

liz·ard /lízzərd/ *n* **1.** FOUR-LEGGED REPTILE a reptile with a long scaly body, movable eyelids, a long tapering tail, and four legs, typically living in hot dry regions. Lizards include the gecko, iguana, chameleon, and horned toad. Suborder: Sauria. **2.** LARGE REPTILE LIKE LIZARD a large reptile such as an alligator or crocodile that resembles a true lizard **3.** LEATHER FROM LIZARD SKIN leather made from the skin of a lizard. See illustration on previous page [14C. Via Old French *lesard* < Latin *lacertus*]

Liz·ard /lízzərd/ peninsula in southwestern England. Its tip, Lizard Head or Lizard Point, is the southernmost point in England.

liz·ard·fish /lízzərd fish/ *n* a slender, large-mouthed, predatory sea fish with a head shaped like that of a lizard. Family: Synodontidae.

Lju·blja·na /lóoblee aàna, lyóo blyaà naa/ capital of Slovenia, in the central part of the country, near Trieste. Population: 330,000 (1997).

lk *abbr* Sri Lanka (*used in Internet addresses*) See table at **domain name**

ll, ll. *abbr* lines

'll *after a vowel* /l/; *after a consonant* /'l/ *contr* **1.** shall **2.** will

LL *abbr* late Latin

llama

lla·ma /laáamə/ *n* **1.** a domesticated longhaired South American animal related to camels. Raised for: load-carrying, wool. Latin name: *Llama glama*. **2.** wool or cloth made from llama hair [Early 17C. Via Spanish < Quechua]

Lla·nel·li /hla néthlee/ market town and port in Carmarthenshire, Wales, on the Burry Inlet of Carmarthen Bay. Population: 44,953 (1991).

lla·no /laánō/ (*plural* **-nos**) *n* especially in Latin America and the southwestern United States, a large open grassy plain [Early 17C. Via Spanish < Latin *planus* "flat"]

Lla·no Es·ta·ca·do /laánō èstə kaádō/ extensive semiarid plateau in western Texas, southeastern New Mexico, and northwestern Oklahoma, forming the southernmost region of the Great Plains

LL.B. *abbr* LAW, EDUC Bachelor of Laws [Latin *Legum Baccalaureus*]

LL.D. *abbr* LAW, EDUC Doctor of Laws [Latin *Legum Doctor*]

LL.M. *abbr* LAW, EDUC Master of Laws [Latin *Legum Magister*]

Lloyd /loyd/, **Harold** (1893–1971) US comedian. He made almost 500 silent movies and talking pictures, including *Safety Last* (1923), many of which featured stunts and chase sequences. Full name **Lloyd, Harold Clayton**

> "I am just turning 40 and taking my time about it."
> [Harold Lloyd, *Times (London)*; September 23, 1970]

Lloyd George /lòyd jáwrj/, **David, 1st Earl of Dwyfor** (1863–1945) British prime minister (1916–22). As the last Liberal prime minister of the United Kingdom, he was a strong wartime leader during World War I. See table at **prime minister**

Lloyd Web·ber /-wébbər/, **Andrew, Lord Lloyd Webber of Sydmonton** (*b.* 1948) British composer. His popular stage musicals include *Jesus Christ Superstar* (1971), *Cats* (1981), *Phantom of the Opera* (1986), and *Sunset Boulevard* (1993).

David Lloyd George

Llyw·el·yn ap Gruf·fudd /lə wèllin ap griffith/, **Llew·el·yn ap Gruf·fudd, prince of Gwynedd** (*d.* 1282) prince of Gwynedd (1258–82). Grandson of Llywelyn ap Iorwerth, in 1258 he won recognition as Prince of Wales, and rebelled unsuccessfully against the English.

Llyw·el·yn ap Ior·werth /-ap yáwrwərth/, **Llew·el·yn ap Ior·werth, prince of Gwynedd** (1173–1240) prince of Gwynedd. He extended his sovereignty over almost all of Wales and successfully fought against the English. Known as **Llewelyn the Great**

lm *symbol* PHYS lumen

LM *abbr* **1.** MIL Legion of Merit **2.** AEROSP lunar module

LMDS *abbr* TELECOM, ONLINE Local Multipoint Distribution Service

LMK *abbr* ONLINE let me know (*used in e-mails*)

LMT *abbr* local mean time

ln *symbol* MATH natural logarithm

LNG *abbr* liquefied natural gas

lo /lō/ *interj* used to draw attention to something (*archaic or literary*) [Old English *lā*, natural exclamation]

loach[1] /lōch/ *n* a freshwater fish related to carp, with a long slender body and barbels around its mouth. Native to: Europe, Asia. Family: Cobitidae. [14C. < Old French *loche*]

loach[2] /lōch/ *n* a US army light helicopter (*informal*) [Mid-20C. Origin ?]

load /lōd/ *n* **1.** SOMETHING CARRIED OR TRANSPORTED something that is carried by an animal, person, or vehicle, especially something heavy or bulky **2.** AMOUNT CARRIED IN ONE TRIP the amount of material, goods, or people that are carried in one trip (*often used in combination*) ○ *delivered a boatload of passengers to the island* **3.** WORK DEMANDED OF SOMEBODY the amount of work that a person is required to do ○ *unhappy about his teaching load this term* **4.** MENTAL BURDEN something that makes somebody feel mentally weighed down, e.g., responsibility, worry, or guilt ○ *a heavy load to bear* **5.** QUANTITY THAT MACHINE CAN COPE WITH the amount that can be handled by a machine at one time, especially the amount of clothes that can be handled by a washing machine ○ *six loads of wash* **6.** SINGLE CHARGE FOR GUN a single charge of ammunition for a firearm **7.** ELEC AMOUNT OF DRAWN ELECTRICAL POWER the amount of electrical power that is drawn from a line or source **8.** ELEC ENG DEVICE DRAWING ELECTRICAL POWER any device to which electrical power is delivered **9.** MECH ENG FORCE AND WEIGHT ON STRUCTURE the total force and weight that a structure such as a bridge is designed to withstand. For a bridge, this includes the dynamic loads of traffic, wind, snow, and ice and the static load of the bridge's own weight. **10.** MECH ENG WORK REQUIRED OF MECHANICAL DEVICE the work required of or placed on an engine or machine, measured in kilowatts or horsepower **11.** FIN CHARGE ADDED TO MUTUAL SHARE PRICE a charge that is added to the price of some mutual fund shares as a commission or marketing cost ■ **loads** *npl* LARGE AMOUNT OR NUMBER a large amount or a lot of (*informal*) ○ *We had loads of guests at the party.* ■ *adv* **loads** *UK* VERY MUCH very much or a great deal (*informal*) ○ *feeling loads better* ■ *v* (**load·ed, load·ing, loads**) **1.** *vti* PUT SOMETHING ON VEHICLE to put cargo or passengers on a vehicle, ship, or aircraft or to have cargo or passengers put on ○ *The aircraft is now loading.* **2.** *vt* PUT SOMETHING ON PERSON OR ANIMAL to put a load on an animor or give a load to a person so that it can be carried **3.** *vt* PUT SOMETHING IN MACHINE to put into a machine the items that it will work on, e.g., clothes for washing **4.** *vti* PUT SOMETHING IN CAMERA to put a film, plate, or tape in a camera, or take in a film, plate, or tape **5.** *vt* PUT DISK IN DRIVE ON COMPUTER to put a disk or tape in a drive on a computer **6.** *vt* PUT PROGRAM IN COMPUTER to transfer data or a program to the main memory of a computer **7.** *vti* PUT ROUNDS IN GUN to put ammunition into a firearm ○ *loaded the rifle* **8.** *vt* BASEBALL PUT RUNNERS ON ALL BASES to cause runners to occupy first, second, and third bases (*often passive*) ○ *hit a home run with the bases loaded* **9.** *vt* GAMBLING WEIGHT ONE SIDE OF DIE to weight one side of each die in a pair or one side of a roulette wheel to prevent it from operating randomly ○ *He must have loaded the dice.* **10.** *vt* FIN ADD EXTRA CHARGE TO INSURANCE PREMIUM to add an extra charge to an insurance premium, e.g., because of an increased risk **11.** *vt* ELEC INCREASE ELECTRIC OUTPUT OF GENERATOR to increase the output produced by or drawn from a circuit or generator **12.** *vt* MECH ENG INCREASE WORK REQUIRED OF ENGINE to increase the work required from an engine or motor [Old English *lād* "course, way" < Indo-European, "go ahead"] ◇ **a load of** used to say emphatically that something is ridiculous or nonsensical (*informal*) ○ *a load of nonsense* ◇ **a load off your mind** a relief from anxiety or worry ◇ **get a load of something** to look at or listen to something or somebody (*slang*)

load·bear·ing /lōd bèrring/ *adj* supporting the gravitational force exerted on a structure or part of one ○ *a loadbearing wall*

load·ed /lṓdəd/ *adj* **1.** WITH FULL LOAD carrying a full load **2.** CONTAINING AMMUNITION containing bullets or other ammunition and ready to fire **3.** WITH HIDDEN IMPLICATION having a hidden or secondary implication designed to trick somebody into making an admission or commitment ○ *That is a loaded question.* **4.** WEIGHTED UNFAIRLY with one side weighted to prevent dice or a roulette wheel from operating randomly **5.** WITH MANY EXTRAS supplied with many luxurious extras ○ *a top-of-the-line car that's really loaded* **6.** RICH extremely rich (*slang*) ○ *Her parents are loaded.* **7.** DRUNK very drunk (*slang*) **8.** INTOXICATED BY DRUGS under the influence of drugs (*slang*)

load fac·tor *n* **1.** the payload of an aircraft for a particular flight, expressed as a percentage of the maximum allowable payload **2.** an external load divided by the weight of an aircraft

load·ing /lṓding/ *n* **1.** WEIGHT CARRIED a load or weight carried **2.** FILLER material added to something to improve specific properties or add weight **3.** ADDITIONAL INSURANCE PREMIUM an additional insurance premium or higher rating incurred by items that are more valuable or at greater risk **4.** ADDITION OF INDUCTANCE the addition of inductance to a transmission line to improve its performance over a given frequency band

load·ing bay *n UK* TRANSP same as **loading dock**

load·ing bridge *n* a covered walkway from an airport departure-lounge gate that expands to connect to the door of a commercial aircraft, used by embarking and debarking passengers and crew

load·ing dock *n* a parking bay, partly enclosed by a raised platform, at which trucks are loaded and unloaded, e.g., in a warehouse

load line *n* NAUT same as **Plimsoll line**

load·mas·ter /lōd màstər/ *n* somebody who oversees the loading of cargo on a military or commercial transport aircraft

load shed·ding *n* a temporary reduction in a supply of electricity as a method of reducing the demand on the generator

load·star *n* ASTRON another spelling of **lodestar**

load·stone *n* GEOL another spelling of **lodestone**

loaf[1] /lōf/ (*plural* **loaves** /lōvz/) *n* **1.** a quantity of bread, shaped and baked as a whole **2.** a quantity of food baked in a loaf pan or shaped to form a rectangular block and baked (*used in combination*) ○ *meat loaf* [Old English *hlāf* < Germanic]

loaf[2] /lōf/ (**loafed, loaf·ing, loafs**) *vi* to do very little and spend time in a lazy, wasteful way [Mid-19C. Probably back-formation < LOAFER]

loaf·er /lṓfər/ *n* a lazy person who avoids work and wastes time [Mid-19C. Origin ?]

Loaf·er /lṓfər/ *tdmk* a trademark for a casual leather shoe that is like a moccasin but has a wide flat heel

loam /lōm/ *n* 1. FERTILE WORKABLE SOIL an easily-worked fertile soil consisting of a mixture of clay, sand, and silt and sometimes also organic matter 2. CLAY AND SAND MIXED FOR BUILDING a mixture of moist clay and sand used for making bricks and in plastering ■ *vt* (**loamed, loam·ing, loams**) PUT LOAM IN OR ON SOMETHING to use loam in the process of covering, filling, or coating something [Old English *lām* "clay, earth" < Indo-European, "slippery"] —**loam·y** *adj*

loan /lōn/ *n* 1. MONEY LENT an amount of money given to somebody on the condition that it will be paid back later 2. LENDING the act of letting somebody use something temporarily 3. LING same as **loanword** ■ *vt* (**loaned, loan·ing, loans**) ⚠ LEND SOMETHING to allow somebody to borrow something on the condition that it is returned ○ *Loan me five bucks, will you?* [12C. < Old Norse *lán*] ◇ **on loan** 1. being lent or borrowed 2. working at a temporary location because additional help or expertise is needed there

USAGE loan or **lend**? If you are letting somebody else temporarily use physical property or money of yours, it is quite acceptable, especially in less formal contexts, to use the verb ***loan***, as in *I loaned him some lunch money.* In more formal settings ***lend*** is by far the safer choice: *According to the terms of this agreement, we will lend you the stipulated amount of cash.* The verb ***loan*** can be used only with reference to the temporary lending of physical property or assets. If the context is not literal or physical, ***lend*** is the only choice: *The evidence lends* [not *loans*] *credence to the witness's previous testimony. The subtle use of strings lends* [not *loans*] *fluidity to the composition.*

USAGE See ***borrow***.

loan shark *n* somebody who lends money at excessively high rates of interest (*informal; disapproving*)

loan·shark·ing /lón shaàrking/ *n* the activity or business of lending money at excessively high rates of interest (*informal disapproving*)

loan trans·la·tion *n* a word or expression that enters a language as a direct translation from another

loan·word /lón wùrd/, **loan word** *n* a word from one language that has become part of everyday usage in another, often with slight modification

loath /lōth, lō*th*/, **loth** *adj* unwilling or reluctant to do something [Old English *lāþ* "loathsome" < Germanic]

SPELLCHECK loath, loth, or **loathe**? Do not confuse the spelling of ***loath*** (or its variant ***loth***) and ***loathe***. ***Loath*** (or ***loth***) is an adjective meaning "unwilling or reluctant" and is usually followed by *to*, as in *I was loath* [or *loth*] *to admit it.* It is also occasionally encountered in the fixed phrase *nothing loath* (or *nothing loth*). ***Loathe*** is a verb meaning "dislike intensely": *I loathe this kind of music.*

SYNONYMS See ***unwilling***.

loathe /lō*th*/ (**loathed, loath·ing, loathes**) *vti* to dislike somebody or something intensely [Old English *lāþian* < Indo-European, "despise"] —**loath·er** *n* —**loath·ing·ly** *adv*

SPELLCHECK See ***loath***.

~~**loathesome**~~ incorrect spelling of **loathsome**

loath·ing /lō*th*ing/ *n* intense dislike of somebody or something

SYNONYMS See ***dislike***.

loath·some /lṓthssəm/ *adj* arousing intense dislike and disgust —**loath·some·ly** *adv* —**loath·some·ness** *n*

loaves plural of **loaf**[1]

lob /lob/ *v* (**lobbed, lob·bing, lobs**) 1. *vti* HIT BALL IN HIGH ARC to hit or throw a ball in a high curving trajectory 2. *vt* THROW SOMETHING CASUALLY to throw something in a casual careless way ■ *n* 1. HIGH ARCHING SHOT a ball hit or thrown in a high curving path 2. BALL OVER TENNIS PLAYER'S HEAD a ball that travels over the head of a tennis player [Late 16C. Probably < Low German] —**lob·ber** *n*

Lo·ba·chev·sky /lòbə chéfskee/, **Nikolay Ivanovich** (1793–1856) Russian mathematician. His system of non-Euclidian geometry undermined various previously held theories.

lo·bar /lṓbər, -baàr/ *adj* relating to or affecting a lobe, e.g., in the lungs

lo·bate /lṓ bàyt/ *adj* having or resembling a lobe or lobes —**lo·bate·ly** *adv*

lob·ber /lóbbər/, **lob·ber milk, lop·per milk** /lóppər-/ *n* milk that has curdled (*dated or regional*) [Probably < an obsolete verb < Old Norse *hlaup* "coagulation"]

REGIONAL NOTE ***Lobber*** is also called *lopper milk* and *labberd milk*. In the East, the term is old-fashioned and restricted mainly to New York State, Connecticut, and New Jersey, with a striking concentration of usage in the Great Lakes state of Michigan.

lob·by /lóbbee/ *n* (*plural* **-bies**) 1. ENTRANCE AREA IN PUBLIC BUILDING a large entrance hall or foyer immediately inside the door of a hotel, theater, or other public building 2. PUBLIC AREA IN LEGISLATIVE BUILDING a public area in or near a legislative building where people can meet and petition their political representatives 3. GROUP TRYING TO INFLUENCE POLICY a group of supporters and representatives of particular interests who try to influence political policy on a particular issue ○ *the welfare lobby* ○ *a lobby group* 4. *UK* BRITISH VOTING CORRIDOR either of the two rooms in the British Parliament where members of both houses of Parliament vote for or against bills and proposals ■ *vti* (**-bied, -by·ing, -bies**) POL PETITION POLITICIANS OR INFLUENTIAL PEOPLE to attempt to persuade a political representative or influential person to support or oppose a particular cause [Mid-16C. < medieval Latin *lobia* "cloister, covered walk" < Germanic] —**lob·by·er** *n*

lob·by·gow /lóbbee gòw/ *n* a messenger or errand boy, especially in the Chinese area of a city (*slang*) [Early 20C. Origin ?]

lob·by·ist /lóbbee ist/ *n* somebody who is paid to lobby political representatives on an issue —**lob·by·ism** *n*

lobe /lōb/ *n* 1. ANAT same as **earlobe** 2. ROUNDED BODY PART a rounded division or projection of an organ or part in the body, especially in the lungs, brain, or liver 3. ROUNDED PROJECTING PART a rounded part that projects from the main body of something 4. ROUNDED PLANT PART a rounded segment on a leaf that is not divided all the way to the midrib [15C. Via late Latin < Greek *lobos*]

lo·bec·to·my /lō béktəmee/ (*plural* **-mies**) *n* the surgical removal of a lobe, e.g., of the lungs, liver, or thyroid

lobed /lōbd/ *adj* 1. having lobes or shapes like lobes ○ *feather-lobed leaves* 2. describes birds' toes that have a rounded flap on either side

lobe·fin /lōb fìn/ *n* FISH same as **crossopterygian** —**lobe·finned** *adj*

lo·be·li·a /lō beélee ə, -beélyə/ *n* a low-growing or trailing summer-flowering plant. Flowers: white to purple. Genus: *Lobelia.* [Mid-18C. After Matthias de *Lobel* (1538–1616), Flemish botanist]

Lo·bi·to /lō beétō/ city and port in western Angola. Population: 150,000 (1983).

Lo·bi·to Bay arm of the Atlantic Ocean forming the harbor of the city of Lobito in western Angola

lob·lol·ly pine /lób lòllee-/, **lob·lol·ly** *n* a pine with flaky bark, long needles grouped in threes, and oblong cones. Native to: southeastern United States. Genus: *Pinus taeda.* [< *loblolly* "thick gruel"]

lo·bo /lṓbō/ (*plural* **-bos**) *n* ZOOL same as **gray wolf** [Mid-19C. Via Spanish < Latin *lupus* "wolf"]

lo·bo·la /lób ələ/, **lo·bo·lo** /lə bṓlō/ *n* payment, often in cattle, made by a groom's family to his bride's family before their wedding in some parts of southern and eastern Africa [Mid-19C. < Bantu]

lo·bot·o·mize /lə bóttə mìz/ (**-mized, -miz·ing, -miz·es**) *vt* 1. to carry out a surgical operation in which nerves to the prefrontal lobe of the brain are severed 2. to make somebody feel sluggish, mentally numb, or lacking in energy or vitality (*informal*)

lo·bot·o·my /lə bóttəmee/ (*plural* **-mies**) *n* same as **prefrontal lobotomy** [Mid-20C. < LOBE]

lob·scouse /lób skòwss/ *n* a stew of meat and vegetables thickened with hardtack, traditionally eaten by sailors [Early 18C. Origin ?]

lob·ster /lóbstər/ *n* 1. HARD-SHELLED SEA CRUSTACEAN a hard-shelled sea crustacean with a pair of large pincers, five pairs of limbs, eyes on stalks, and long antennae. Native to: Atlantic coasts of North America, Europe. Family: Homaridae. 2. CRUSTACEAN LIKE LOBSTER a crustacean similar in appearance to the true lobster but without the two large pincers, especially the spiny lobster. Native to: subtropical, tropical coastal waters. Family: Palinuridae. 3. LOBSTER AS FOOD the flesh of a lobster used as food. The tail meat and meat extracted from the claws is particularly valued for its fine, slightly sweet flavor. ■ *vi* (**-stered, -ster·ing, -sters**) CATCH LOBSTERS to catch lobsters using a boat and pot [Old English *loppestre*, origin ?]

lob·ster·man /lóbstərmən/ (*plural* **-men** /-mən/) *n* 1. somebody whose profession is fishing for lobsters 2. a boat designed for catching lobsters

lob·ster New·burg /-noō bùrg/ *n* lobster meat cooked in a rich sherry sauce with butter and cream and usually served on small pieces of toast or croutons or in a pastry shell [Early 20C. Origin ?]

lob·ster pot *n* a trap in the form of a basket, used for catching lobsters

lob·ster shift *n* the night shift of a factory, newspaper, or other workplace (*informal*)

lob·ster ther·mi·dor /-thúrmə dàwr/ *n* cooked lobster with a wine and cream sauce served in the shell with a topping of melted cheese [Late 19C. After *Thermidor* (1891), play by Victorien Sardou (1831–1908), French dramatist]

lob·ule /lób yoōl/ *n* 1. a small lobe 2. a section or division of a lobe [Late 17C. < LOBE] —**lob·u·lar** *adj* —**lob·u·lar·ly** *adv* —**lob·u·late** *adj* —**lob·u·lose** *adj*

lob·worm /lób wùrm/ *n* ZOOL same as **lugworm** [Mid-17C. < LOB "something hanging"]

lo·cal /lṓk'l/ *adj* 1. IN NEARBY AREA relating to, situated in, or providing a service for a particular area, especially the area near home or work ○ *the local school* 2. CHARACTERISTIC OF PARTICULAR AREA characteristic of, or only found in, a particular area ○ *the local dialect* 3. NOT WIDESPREAD confined to a fairly small area ○ *There have been local outbreaks of the disease.* 4. RELATING TO GOVERNMENTAL REGION relating to a comparatively small region that controls some aspects of practical government such as housing or education ○ *local elections* 5. AFFECTING SMALL PART affecting only a specific part of a human's or animal's body ○ *local infection* 6. STOPPING EVERYWHERE stopping at all the stations or bus stops on a route ○ *local trains and buses* 7. TO PHONE NUMBER NEARBY made to a phone number within a fairly small radius and therefore not itemized on a phone bill ○ *a phone for local calls only* 8. COMPUT PROCESSED WITHIN SAME COMPUTER OR NETWORK performed, processed, or transmitted within the same computer or one in a readily accessible network ■ *n* 1. SOMEBODY WHO COMES FROM PARTICULAR AREA a native or long-term resident of a place 2. STOPPING TRAIN OR BUS a train or bus that stops at all the stations or stops on the route 3. same as **local anesthetic** (*informal*) 4. BRANCH OF ORGANIZATION a branch or office, especially of a labor union, situated in and serving members or clients only in one locale [14C. Via French < late Latin *localis* < Latin *locus* "place"] —**lo·cal·ly** *adv* —**lo·cal·ness** *n*

lo·cal an·es·thet·ic *n* a drug, usually given by injection, that eliminates pain, though not necessarily all sensation, in a particular area of the body without affecting consciousness

lo·cal ar·e·a net·work *n* a network of personal computers and peripheral devices linked by cable and able to share resources

lo·cal au·thor·i·ty *n UK* same as **local government** (sense 2)

lo·cal col·or *n* unusual or traditional features of a particular place that make it interesting

lo·cale /lō kál/ *n* the place in which something happens or in which the action in a book or movie takes place [Late 18C. Alteration of French *local* (see LOCAL), after MORALE]

lo·cal gov·ern·ment *n* 1. the government of a town, city, county, or region at a local level by locally elected politicians ○ *worked in local government all his life* 2. an organization of people, most of whom are elected, that governs an area smaller than a state, usually a county, district, or town

lo·cal·ism /lṓk'l ìzzəm/ *n* 1. a phrase, expression, or custom peculiar to the people in a particular area 2. interest in local matters and customs rather than in national or global issues, sometimes resulting in a limited perspective —**lo·cal·ist** *n*

lo·cal·i·ty /lō kállətee/ (*plural* **-ties**) *n* 1. a particular place, district, or neighborhood **2.** the fact of being situated at a particular point in space or time

lo·cal·ize /lṓk'l ìz/ (**-ized, -iz·ing, -iz·es**) *v* **1.** *vti* **CONFINE OR BE CONFINED TO PLACE** to become confined to, or restrict something to, a particular area **2.** *vt* **FIND LOCATION OF SOMETHING** to find the source or location of something **3.** *vt* **DECENTRALIZE CONTROL OF SOMETHING** to transfer power or control from a central authority to local bodies —**lo·cal·iz·a·ble** *adj* —**lo·cal·i·za·tion** /lṑk'li záysh'n/ *n*

lo·cal·ized /lṓk'l ìzd/ *adj* restricted to a specific place or area ○ *a localized infection*

lo·cal op·tion *n* the power granted to a local government to decide whether to implement a particular policy, especially with regard to the sale of alcohol

lo·cal time *n* the time in a particular region, calculated according to the time zone in which the place is situated

Lo·car·no /lo kaárnō/ town and resort in Ticino Canton, southern Switzerland. Population: 14,312 (1998).

lo·cate /lṓ kàyt, lō káyt/ (**-cat·ed, -cat·ing, -cates**) *v* **1.** *vt* **FIND SOMETHING** to discover where something is **2.** *vi* **ESTABLISH BUSINESS IN PLACE** to establish a residence or business in a particular place **3.** *vt* **POSITION SOMETHING** to put something in a particular place [Early 16C. < Latin *locat-*, past participle of *locare* < *locus* "place"] —**lo·cat·a·ble** *adj* —**lo·cat·er** *n*

lo·ca·tion /lō káysh'n/ *n* **1.** **POSITION** the site or position of something **2.** **MOVIE SETTING** a place away from a studio where scenes for a movie are shot ○ *The movie was shot on location in Scotland.* **3.** **DISCOVERY** the discovery of something ○ *A metal detector is an essential aid in the location of buried treasure.* **4.** **POSITIONING OF SOMETHING** the positioning or siting of something or somebody in a particular place —**lo·ca·tion·al** *adj*

loc·a·tive /lókətiv/ *n* **1.** **GRAMMATICAL CASE** a grammatical case in some languages that indicates place or direction **2.** **FORM IN LOCATIVE** a word or phrase in the locative ■ *adj* **INDICATING PLACE OR DIRECTION** in or relating to the locative [Early 19C. < LOCATE]

lo·ca·tor /lṓ kàytər, lō káytər/ *n* **1.** somebody who establishes the boundaries of a piece of land or a mining claim **2.** a device that helps somebody locate something such as a table or index

loc. cit. *adv* in the place cited. Full form **loco citato**

loch /lok, law<u>kh</u>/ *n Scotland* **1.** same as **lake**[1] (sense 1) **2.** a narrow arm of the sea stretching inland [14C. < Scottish Gaelic]

loch·an /lókən, láw<u>kh</u>ən/ *n Scotland* a small lake or pool [Late 17C. < Scottish Gaelic, "small loch"]

lo·chi·a /lṓkee ə, ló-/ *n* the normal vaginal discharge of cell debris and blood after childbirth [Late 17C. < Greek *lokhia* < *lokhos* "childbirth"] —**lo·chi·al** *adj*

lo·ci LAW, MATH, GENETICS plural of **locus**

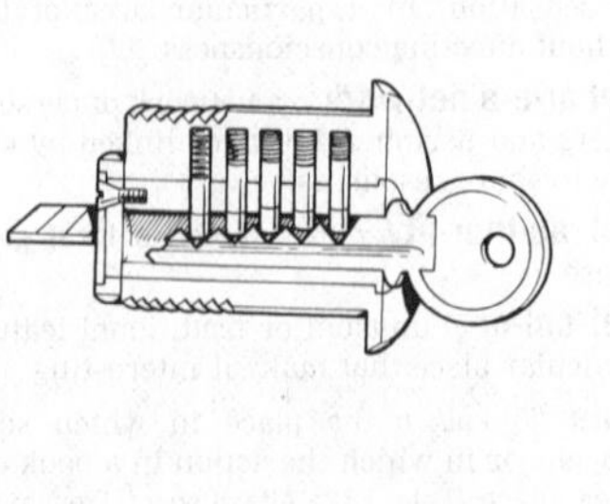

lock: cross section of a key-operated lock

lock[1] /lok/ *n* **1.** **FASTENING MECHANISM** a mechanism used to fasten or secure a door, window, or lid, especially one operated by a key **2.** **GATED SECTION OF CANAL** a short section of a canal or river in which the water level can be altered to enable boats to pass to a higher or lower part of the waterway. The lock has gates at each end with a mechanism for letting water in or out. **3.** **WRESTLING HOLD** a wrestling hold in which a wrestler twists or puts pressure on part of the other wrestler's body **4.** **GUN PART** the part of a gun that makes the charge explode **5.** **BLOCKING DEVICE** a device that prevents an unauthorized person from using something, e.g., one operated by a password **6.** **FIRM POSSESSION** firm possession or control of something ○ *a manufacturer with a lock on the market for luxury trucks* **7.** RUGBY **PLAYER IN RUGBY SCRUM** either of the two players in the second row in a rugby scrum **8.** ENG same as **airlock** ■ *v* (**locked, lock·ing, locks**) **1.** *vti* **FASTEN WITH LOCK** to fasten something or become fastened using a lock **2.** *vt* **PUT SOMETHING IN SECURE PLACE** to put something into a safe place or container that can be locked ○ *Her diamonds are locked in a safe deposit box.* **3.** *vt* **SECURE PLACE** to make a building or vehicle secure by locking the doors and windows **4.** *vt* **PREVENT UNAUTHORIZED USE** to prevent something from being used by an unauthorized person, e.g., via software **5.** *vti* **FIX OR BE FIXED IN PLACE** to become fixed in one position, or fix something in one position, so that it cannot move normally **6.** *vt* **HOLD SOMEBODY FIRMLY** to hold somebody tightly ○ *locked in a passionate embrace* **7.** *vt* **TRAP SOMEBODY IN DIFFICULT SITUATION** to put somebody in a situation or conflict from which it is difficult to escape ○ *locked in a lengthy argument* **8.** *vt* BOATING **PUT LOCKS ON WATERWAY** to put locks on a stretch of canal or river **9.** *vi* BOATING **GO THROUGH CANAL LOCKS** to go through a series of locks on a boat, or take a boat through a series of locks **10.** *vt* PRINTING **FIX TYPE IN PRINTING PRESS** to secure metal type in a printing press **11.** *vt* FIN same as **lock up** (sense 4) [Old English *loc* < Germanic] —**lock·able** *adj* ◇ **lock, stock, and barrel** completely

lock away *vt* CRIME, SAFETY same as **lock up** (senses 1–2)

lock in *vt* **1.** to prevent somebody from leaving a room or building by locking the door **2.** to fix something at a particular level for a long period ○ *locked in a good rate on their mortgage*

lock on *vti* to find a target and track it automatically, or make a radar or missile find and track a target

lock out *vt* **1.** to prevent somebody from entering a place by locking the door **2.** to prevent workers from entering their workplace, usually as a strategy in an industrial dispute

lock up *v* **1.** *vt* **IMPRISON SOMEBODY** to put somebody into prison, a secure hospital, or other institution that deprives him or her of freedom **2.** *vt* **STORE SOMETHING IN SECURE PLACE** to put valuables in a secure locked place **3.** *vti* **SECURE BUILDING** to make a building secure by locking all the doors and windows **4.** *vt* **INVEST IN LONG-TERM PLAN** to put money into a form of savings or investment that does not allow easy access to the funds

lock[2] /lok/ *n* **1.** **PIECE OF HAIR** a group of hairs that hang together, on somebody's head or cut off **2.** **WISP OF FIBER** a small bunch of wool, cotton, or other fiber ■ **locks** *npl* **1.** **HAIR** somebody's hair (*literary*) **2.** HAIR same as **dreadlocks** (*slang; used in Black English*) [Old English *locc* < Germanic]

CULTURAL NOTE ***The Rape of the Lock*** a poem (1712) by English poet Alexander Pope. Written in mock-heroic style, it satirizes a major quarrel between families that arose when a young gentleman snipped off a lock of a young lady's hair. The poem's message is summarized in the opening lines: "What dire offence from am'rous causes springs/ What mighty contests rise from trivial things.".

lock·age /lókij/ *n* **1.** **PASSAGE THROUGH LOCK** the passage of a boat through a canal or river lock **2.** **FEE** a fee paid by a boat to pass through a lock **3.** **LOCKS** a number of locks on a canal or river

lock·box /lók bòks/ *n* a strong lockable box for keeping items secure, e.g., a strongbox, safe-deposit box, or post office box

lock·down /lók dòwn/ *n* **1.** **CONFINEMENT FOR SAFETY** an emergency safety procedure in which people remain in a locked indoor space ○ *When an unknown intruder entered the building, the principal ordered the school into lockdown.* **2.** **COMPUTER LOCKING DEVICE** a locking device that prevents a computer from being moved or stolen **3.** **COMPUTER SECURITY PROCEDURE** the prevention of access by users of a computer network or intruders from the Internet to files essential to the integrity of a computer system **4.** **CONFINEMENT TO PRISON CELL** the state of being confined to a prison cell for all or most of the day (*slang*)

Locke /lok/, **Alain** (1886–1954) US writer. A leader of the Harlem Renaissance, his works include *Four Negro Poets* (1927). Full name **Alain LeRoy Locke**

Locke, John (1632–1704) English philosopher. He developed the doctrine of empiricism according to which knowledge was acquired by experience, not by intuition.

> "What can be more silly arrogant and misbecoming, than for a Man to think that he has a Mind and Understanding in him, but yet in all the Universe beside, there is no such thing?"
> [John Locke, *An Essay Concerning Human Understanding*; 1690]

locked-in syn·drome /lokt-/ *n* a condition resulting from massive brain stem damage that leaves the higher mental functions intact but prevents any movement except for that of the eyes and eyelids

lock·er /lókər/ *n* **1.** **LOCKABLE COMPARTMENT** a small lockable cupboard or compartment where personal belongings can be left, e.g., at a swimming pool, gym, school, or workplace **2.** **FREEZER** a walk-in food freezer **3.** **TRUNK** a trunk or low chest used for storage **4.** **SOMEBODY OR SOMETHING THAT LOCKS** somebody who or device that locks something

Lock·er·bie /lókərbee/ town in Dumfries and Galloway, southwestern Scotland. In 1988, an airliner was destroyed over the town by a terrorist bomb, killing all the passengers and crew and 11 of the town's residents. Population: 3,982 (1991).

lock·er room *n* a room containing lockers, where people change their clothes for sports or swimming

lock·er-room *adj* characteristic of or appropriate only for a men's locker room ○ *telling locker-room jokes*

lock·et /lókət/ *n* a small decorative metal case with a hinged cover containing a picture or memento, worn on a neck chain or bracelet [14C. < Old French *locquet* "small latch" < *loc* "latch" < Germanic]

lock for·ward *n* RUGBY same as **lock**[1] *n* (sense 7)

lock-in *n* FIN **1.** a written commitment fixing something at a particular level or rate ○ *got a lock-in on his mortgage rate* **2.** a fixing of a rate of payment for a long period, or a fixed rate ○ *a mortgage lock-in*

lock·jaw /lók jàw/ *n* MED **1.** same as **trismus** **2.** same as **tetanus** (sense 1)

lock·keep·er /lók keèpər/, **lock·mas·ter** /lók màstər/ *n* somebody employed to look after or control a lock on a waterway and collect any fees payable

lock·nut /lók nùt/ *n* **1.** a second nut tightened on a first to prevent it from loosening **2.** a nut designed to lock itself in place once tightened

lock-on *n* the point at which a radar or missile locates and starts to track a target

lock·out /lók òwt/ *n* an occasion when workers are prevented from entering their workplace, a tactic sometimes used by management in an industrial dispute

Lock·port /lók pàwrt/ city in western New York, northeast of Niagara Falls and west of Rochester. Population: 21,775 (2002 estimate).

lock·ram /lókrəm/ *n* a coarse linen fabric [15C. < French *locrenan*, alteration of *Locronan*, village in Brittany]

lock·smith /lók smìth/ *n* somebody who makes, sells, installs, and repairs locks and keys. A locksmith can also open a lock when the owner has lost the key or has become locked out.

lock·step /lók stèp/ *n* **1.** a form of military marching with soldiers close together and all moving forward with the same foot at the same time **2.** a process or routine that is standardized and inflexible ○*"It's a lockstep process, and if at any point the virus makes a mistake, the host will almost certainly kill it."* (Virginia Morell, "The Killer Cat Virus that Doesn't Kill Cats," *Discover Magazine*; July 1995)

lock stitch *n* the usual stitch made by a sewing machine, formed by the thread above the fabric interlocking with the bobbin thread

lock·up /lók ùp/ *n* **1.** **PLACE WITH PRISON CELLS** a small prison, a block of cells at a police station, or a similar place where prisoners are kept for a short time **2.** **SECURING OF BUILDING** the securing of a building by locking it **3.** **TIME FOR LOCKING BUILDING** the time at which a building is locked **4.** FIN **LONG INVESTMENT** a long-term investment (*informal*)

Lock·wood /lók wòòd/, **Belva Ann** (1830–1917) US lawyer, reformer, and women's rights activist. She secured equal pay for women employees of federal government (1872) and was the first woman to practice before the US Supreme Court (1879). Born **Bennett, Belva Ann**

lo·co[1] /lṓkō/ *adj* WILDLY IRRATIONAL wildly irrational (*informal*) ■ *n* (*plural* **-cos**) **1.** BOT same as **locoweed 2.** VET same as **loco disease** ■ *vt* (**-coed, -co·ing, -cos**) **1.** POISON ANIMAL to poison an animal with locoweed **2.** MAKE SOMEBODY WILDLY IRRATIONAL to make somebody wildly irrational (*informal*) [Late 19C. < Spanish, "irrational"]

lo·co[2] /lṓ kō/ *adj* indicating that the performer should return to playing notes in the original register, negating a previous direction that they should be played an octave higher [Early 19C. < Italian, "at the place"] —**lo·co** *adv*

lo·co ci·ta·to /lṑkō sī táy tō, -si taátō/ *adv* full form of **loc. cit.** [< Latin, "in the place cited"]

lo·co dis·ease *n* a disease of cattle, sheep, and horses in the western United States and Canada, caused by eating locoweed. It affects the animals' nervous systems, with symptoms of weakness, trembling, and inability to move.

Lo·co·fo·co /lṓkō fṓkō/ (*plural* **-cos**) *n* a member of a group of New York Democrats organized in 1835 to oppose the existing, more conservative members of the party [Mid-19C. Also originally "self-igniting match"]

lo·co·mote /lṑkə mṓt/ (**-mot·ed, -mot·ing, -motes**) *vi* to move under your own power [Mid-19C. Back-formation < LOCOMOTION]

lo·co·mo·tion /lṑkə mṓsh'n/ *n* movement or the power to move from one place to another [Mid-17C. < Latin *loco* "from a place"]

locomotive

lo·co·mo·tive /lṑkə mṓtiv/ *n* RAIL ENGINE a railroad engine ■ *adj* **1.** MOVABLE able to move about freely **2.** RELATING TO LOCOMOTION relating to, allowing, or aiding in the ability to move ○ *locomotive organs* [Early 17C. < modern Latin *locomotivus* < Latin *loco* "from a place" + late Latin *motivus* "moving" (see MOTIVE)]

lo·co·mo·tor /lṑkə mṓtər/ *adj* relating to or aiding in locomotion ○ *locomotor hyperactivity* [Late 19C. < Latin *loco* "from a place"]

lo·co·mo·tor a·tax·i·a *n* MED same as **tabes dorsalis**

lo·co·mo·to·ry /lṑkə mṓtəree/ *adj* able to move independently

lo·co·weed /lṓkō weed/ (*plural* **-weeds** or *same*), **lo·co** *n* **1.** a perennial plant of the pea family. Animals that eat it can contract loco disease. Native to: western North America. Genera: *Oxytropis* or *Astragalus*. **2.** DRUGS same as **cannabis** (*slang*) [Late 19C. < LOCO[1]]

Loc·ri·an mode /lókree ən-/ *n* a medieval scale of notes that consists of the eight notes of the diatonic scale rising from B to B [Late 19C. < Greek *Locris*, region of ancient Greece]

loc·ule /ló kyool/, **loc·u·lus** /lókyələss/ (*plural* **-li** /-lī/) *n* a small cavity, chamber, or cell in a plant or animal [Late 19C. Via French < Latin *loculus* "small place" < *locus* "place"] —**loc·u·lar** *adj*

lo·cum /lṓkəm/, **lo·cum te·nens** /-ténnənz/ (*plural* **lo·cum te·nen·tes** /-tə nén teez/) *n* somebody, especially a member of the clergy, who stands in to do the job of another who is away or unwell [Mid-17C. < medieval Latin *locum tenens* "somebody holding the place" < Latin *locus* "place" + *tenere* "to hold"]

lo·cus /lṓkəss/ (*plural* **-ci** /lṓ sī, lṓssee, lṓkee/) *n* **1.** PLACE a place where something happens **2.** SET OF POINTS in mathematics, a set of points, the positions of which satisfy a set of algebraic conditions **3.** GENE POSITION the position of a gene on a chromosome [Early 18C. < Latin, "place"]

lo·cus clas·si·cus /-klássikəss/ (*plural* **lo·ci clas·si·ci** /-klássi sī/) *n* a much-quoted passage from an authoritative or standard text [< Latin, "classical place"]

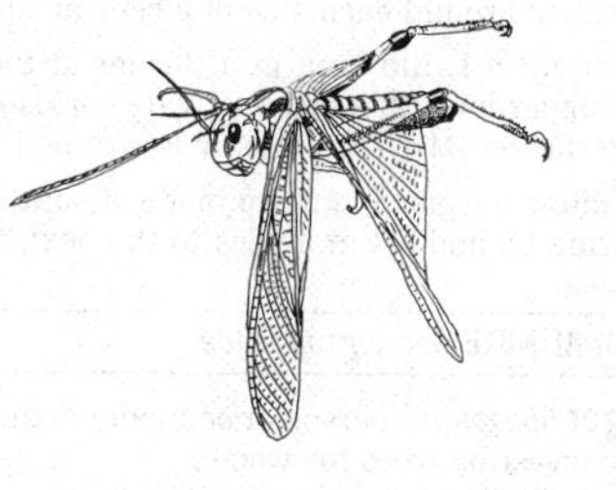

locust

lo·cust /lṓkəst/ *n* **1.** SWARMING GRASSHOPPER a migratory grasshopper that often swarms and devours crops and vegetation. Native to: southern Europe, Asia, Africa, North America. Family: Acrididae. **2.** INSECTS same as **seventeen-year locust 3.** TREES DECIDUOUS N AMERICAN TREE a thorny deciduous tree with hanging clusters of fragrant flowers, compound leaves, and long seed pods. Native to: North America. Genus: *Robinia*. **4.** POD-BEARING TREE a pod-bearing tree of the family that includes the honey locust, swamp locust, and carob. Family: Leguminosae. **5.** HARD WOOD the hard yellowish wood of a locust tree [14C. Via French < Latin *locusta*]

lo·cu·tion /lō kyoosh'n, lə-/ *n* **1.** a phrase or expression typically used by a group of people **2.** the way in which somebody speaks [15C. Directly or via French < Latin *locution-* < *locut-*, past participle of *loqui* "speak"]

Lod /lod/ city in Israel, situated 23 mi./37 km northwest of Jerusalem. Population: 61,100 (1999).

lode /lōd/ *n* **1.** a deposit or vein of ore **2.** an abundant supply of something [Old English *lād* (see LOAD)]

lo·den /lṓd'n/ *n* **1.** a thick waterproof woolen cloth. Use: coats, jackets. **2.** the dark-green color of loden cloth [Early 20C. < German] —**lo·den** *adj*

lode·star /lṓd staar/, **load·star** *n* **1.** the North Star (**Polaris**), used for navigation or as a reference position in astronomy **2.** something that somebody uses as a model or principle to guide behavior (*literary*) [14C. < LODE "course"]

lode·stone /lṓd stṑn/, **load·stone** *n* **1.** magnetite or a piece of magnetite with magnetic properties **2.** somebody or something that attracts others like a magnet [Early 16C. < LODE "leading"]

lodge /loj/ *n* **1.** COUNTRY BUILDING a cabin or other building in the country providing temporary accommodations, e.g., as a vacation home or a temporary shelter for campers, walkers, skiers, or hunters **2.** TRAVEL BUILDING IN VACATION COMPLEX the main building or all the buildings in a vacation complex, usually providing meals, overnight accommodations and other guest services. Lodges, including park lodges, hunting lodges, and ski lodges are usually located in or near mountains or tourist attractions. **3.** INN OR HOTEL a large house or hotel **4.** BRANCH OF UNION OR ORGANIZATION a local branch or chapter of a fraternal organization or union **5.** MEETING HALL a hall or other meeting place used by a branch of a society **6.** NATIVE NORTH AMERICAN DWELLING a dwelling traditionally used by Native North American people, e.g., a wigwam, hogan, or longhouse **7.** SMALL GATEKEEPER'S HOUSE in Britain, a small house in the grounds of a large country house or park, usually near the main gate, traditionally occupied by a gatekeeper, gardener, or estate worker **8.** BEAVER'S DEN a dome-shaped structure with an underwater entrance built by a beaver ■ *v* (**lodged, lodg·ing, lodg·es**) **1.** *vt* REGISTER COMPLAINT OR APPEAL to make a formal complaint, accusation, or appeal by handing the documents to the appropriate authority **2.** *vt* DEPOSIT SOMETHING IN SAFE PLACE to put something somewhere or give it to somebody for safekeeping **3.** *vti* STICK OR GET STUCK to become jammed or embedded somewhere, or jam or embed something somewhere ○ *His head was lodged between the railings.* **4.** *vi* LIVE IN SOMEBODY'S HOUSE to live in somebody's house, free or as a paying guest (*dated*) **5.** *vt* PUT SOMEBODY IN ACCOMMODATIONS to place somebody in temporary accommodations ○ *They were evacuated and lodged in a nearby school overnight.* **6.** *vt* GIVE SOMEBODY POWER TO ACT to invest somebody with the power or authority to do something ○ *powers that are lodged with the cabinet* **7.** *vti* BEAT CROPS FLAT to flatten crops, or be flattened by the wind and rain [13C. < Old French *loge* "hut" < Germanic, "roof made of bark"]

Lodge /loj/, **Henry Cabot** (1850–1924) US politician. As Republican leader in the Senate, he promoted US entry into World War I but opposed the League of Nations (1919).

Lodge, Henry Cabot, Jr. (1902–85) US politician and diplomat. Richard Nixon's running mate in their unsuccessful bid for the presidency (1960), he later became ambassador to South Vietnam (1963–67).

lodge·ment *n* another spelling of **lodgment**

lodge·pole pine /lój pōl-/ *n* a pine with two types of cones, one of which releases seeds only after a forest fire. Native to: western North America. Genus: *Pinus contorta*. [< Native North Americans' use of the trunks as supports for lodges]

lodg·er /lójjər/ *n* **1.** somebody who rents a room in somebody else's house (*dated*) ○"*...the small kitchen in which she cooked the food for her lodgers*" (Jack London, *The People of the Abyss*; 1905) **2.** somebody who lodges something such as a complaint

lodg·ing /lójjing/ *n* somewhere to stay temporarily ○ *We asked where we could find lodging for the night.* ■ **lodg·ings** *npl* a room or rooms in a boarding house or private home available for rent (*dated*)

lodg·ment /lójmənt/, **lodge·ment** *n* **1.** ACCUMULATION OR BLOCKAGE a build-up of something, especially when this causes a blockage **2.** FOOTHOLD IN ENEMY TERRITORY a small area of land that has been captured and held on the edge of enemy territory **3.** LODGING the lodging of somebody or something

Lo·di /lṓdee/ **1.** city in San Joaquin County, central California, situated 12 mi./19 km north of Stockton. Population: 60,656 (2002 estimate). **2.** borough in Bergen County, northeastern New Jersey, situated 5 mi./8 km southeast of Paterson. Population: 24,141 (2002 estimate).

lod·i·cule /lóddi kyool/ *n* a tiny scale at the base of the ovary in a grass flower [Mid-19C. < Latin *lodicula* "small coverlet" < *lodix* "blanket"]

Lodz /looj, lodz/, **Łódź** /wooj/ industrial city in central Poland, situated about 75 mi./121 km southwest of Warsaw. Population: 812,300 (1997).

Loeb /lōb/, **Jacques** (1859–1924) German-born US physiologist. He produced pioneering work in artificial parthenogenesis, and conducted important research in physiology and psychology.

lo·ess /lṓ əss, less, luss/ *n* a fine-grained yellowish brown deposit of soil left by the wind. The loess deposited by winds from Central Asia provided the basis for productive farming in early China. [Mid-19C. < German *Löss* < Swiss German *lösch* "loose"]

Loewe /lō/, **Frederick** (1904–88) US composer. His musical comedies, produced in collaboration with Alan Jay Lerner, include *My Fair Lady* (1956) and *Camelot* (1960).

Loe·wi /lṓ ee/, **Otto** (1873–1961) German pharmacologist and physiologist. He shared a Nobel Prize in physiology or medicine (1936) for his work on the chemical transmission of nerve impulses.

lo-fi /lṓ fī/ *adj* (*informal*) **1.** ELECTRONICS relating to the production or reproduction of audio in which the sound is deliberately unpolished and rough **2.** of a quality and design that is neither advanced nor sophisticated [Shortening]

Lo·fo·ten Is·lands /lṓfōt'n-/ chain of two groups of rock islands, northwestern Norway, in the Norwegian Sea. The southernmost group is in the north. Lofoten, and the Vesterålen are to the north. Population: 26,241 (1970). Area: 1,600 sq. mi./4,044 sq. km.

loft /loft/ *n* **1.** UPPER FLOOR OF BARN the upper floor of a barn or stable, used for storing hay ○ *a hay loft* **2.** GALLERY a gallery or balcony, especially the gallery where the organ is situated in a church ○ *the organ loft* **3.** UPPER FLOOR OF WAREHOUSE OR FACTORY an upper floor of a commercial building such as a factory or warehouse, typically converted to residential or studio use **4.** **BUILDINGS ELEVATED ROOM IN HOUSE** a platform, reachable by a ladder or stairs, that serves as an extra room in a high-ceilinged house **5.** *UK* **ROOF SPACE** the area between the ceiling of the top floor of a building and the roof (*often used before a noun*) **6.** **SLANTING ANGLE ON GOLF CLUB** the angle of the face of a golf club designed to drive the ball high into the air **7.** **THICKNESS OF FABRIC** the thickness and fluffiness of fabric, especially as an indication of its warmth ■ *vt* (**loft·ed, loft·ing, lofts**) **1.** **HIT BALL HIGH** to hit a ball in a high arching path **2.** **KEEP SOMETHING IN LOFT** to store something in a loft [Pre-12C. < Old Norse *lopt* "air, upstairs room"]

loft·y /lóftee/ (**-i·er, -i·est**) *adj* **1.** **VERY HIGH** very high or tall ○ *lofty peaks* **2.** **EXALTED** exalted and refined **3.** **HIGH-RANKING** of the highest rank or status **4.** **HAUGHTY** behaving in a falsely superior or haughty manner

log[1] /log/ *n* **1.** **PIECE CUT FROM TREE** a section of the trunk or a thick branch of a tree that has been cut for fuel or building material **2.** **RECORD OF JOURNEY** a record of a journey made by a ship or aircraft, detailing all events, or the book in which it is kept **3.** **RECORD OF EVENTS** any detailed record of events **4.** **DEVICE FOR MEASURING SHIP'S SPEED** a float attached to a ship by a line, formerly used for measuring the ship's speed ■ *v* (**logged, log·ging, logs**) **1.** *vt* **INCLUDE EVENT IN LOG** to record information or an event in a log ○ *The computer will log all these transactions automatically.* **2.** *vt* **TRAVEL PARTICULAR DISTANCE OR SPEED** to travel a particular distance, time, or speed that is then recorded in a log ○ *These checks are made routinely once the aircraft has logged 100,000 miles.* **3.** *vt* **HAVE WORK TIME IN CREDIT** to spend time or accumulate a particular number of hours, especially for a job, that are usually recorded somewhere **4.** *vti* **FELL TREES** to cut down the trees growing on a particular area of land **5.** *vti* **CUT UP TREE FOR LOGS** to cut up a tree to produce logs for fuel or building [14C. Origin ?] ◇ **sleep like a log** to sleep very soundly

log in *vti* COMPUT same as **log on**

log off *vi* to end a session on a computer by typing in the appropriate command

log on *vti* to gain access to a computer system by entering a name and password or other appropriate commands

log out *vi* COMPUT same as **log off**

log[2] /log/ *n* MATH same as **logarithm** (*informal*) [Mid-17C. Shortening]

lo·gan /lṓgən/ *n Can* GEOG same as **bogan** [Probably < Algonquian]

Lo·gan, Mount /lṓgən/ the highest peak in Canada, located in the St. Elias Range in southwestern Yukon Territory. Height: 19,551 ft./5,959 m.

Lo·gan, Sir William Edmond (1798–1875) Canadian geologist. He was a founder and the first director of the Geological Survey of Canada (1842–69).

loganberry

lo·gan·ber·ry /lṓgən bèrree/ (*plural* **-ries**) *n* **1.** a purplish red fruit similar to a large raspberry **2.** a prickly trailing hybrid plant that bears loganberries. Native to: western United States, northwestern Mexico. Latin name: *Rubus ursinus loganobaccus.* [Late 19C. After James H. *Logan* (1841–1928), US horticulturist]

lo·ga·oed·ic /lòggə éedik/ *adj* describes a poem or line of verse in which different metrical feet are mixed to give an effect like speech or prose [Mid-19C. Via late Latin < Greek *logaoidikos* < *logos* "speech" + *aoidē* "song"]

log·a·rithm /lóggə ri̱thəm/ *n* the power to which a base must be raised to equal a given number. For example, the logarithm of 8 to the base 2 is 3, since $2^3 = 8$. [Early 17C. < modern Latin *logarithmus* < Greek *logos* "word, relation, ratio" + *arithmos* "number"] —**log·a·rith·mic** /lòggə rítḫmik/ *adj* —**log·a·rith·mi·cal·ly** *adv*

log·book /lóg bo͝ok/ *n* a book containing a record of a journey made by a ship or aircraft [Late 17C. < LOG[1]]

log cab·in *n* **1.** a simple house made with logs **2.** a patchwork design formed from strips of fabric attached around each side of a central square

loge /lōzh/ *n* **1.** the area in a theater at the front of the upper level **2.** a small private enclosure or box in a theater [Mid-18C. < French (see LODGE)]

log fence *n regional* a fence made of split rails each resting on and set at angles to the next, forming a zigzag

REGIONAL NOTE See ***zigzag fence.***

log·ger /lóggər/ *n* a person or company in the business of harvesting trees for wood

log·ger·head /lóggər hèd/ *n* **1.** ZOOL same as **loggerhead turtle** **2.** BIRDS same as **loggerhead shrike** **3.** a tool consisting of a ball or bulb on a long handle that can be heated and used to melt pitch [Late 16C. Probably < *logger* "block for hobbling a horse" < LOG[1]] ◇ **at loggerheads** involved in a quarrel or feud

log·ger·head shrike *n* a bird with gray feathers, black and white wings and tail, and a black facial mask. Native to: North America. Latin name: *Lanius ludovicianus.*

log·ger·head tur·tle *n* a large flesh-eating sea turtle that lives in warm waters and has a large head and rounded shell. Latin name: *Caretta caretta.*

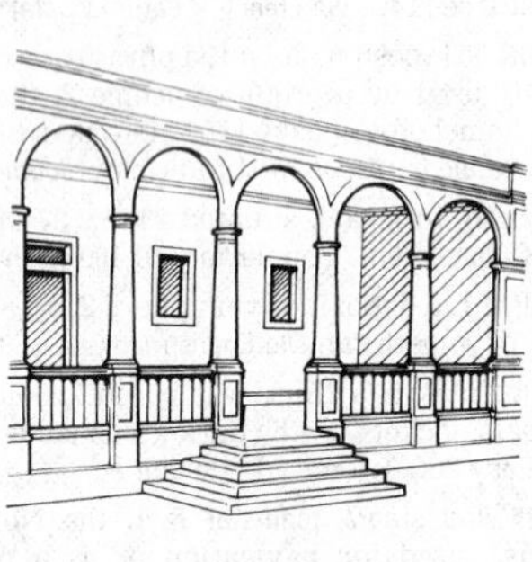

loggia

log·gi·a /láwjee ə/ (*plural* **-gi·as** or **-gie** /-jày/) *n* **1.** a covered open-sided walkway, often with arches, along one side of a building **2.** a balcony in a theater [Mid-18C. Via Italian < Old French *loge* (see LODGE)]

log·ging /lógging/ *n* the job of felling, trimming, and transporting trees

lo·gi·a CHR plural of **logion**

log·ic /lójjik/ *n* **1.** PHILOSOPHY **THEORY OF REASONING** the branch of philosophy that deals with the theory of deductive and inductive arguments and aims to distinguish good from bad reasoning **2.** **SYSTEM OR INSTANCE OF REASONING** any system of, or an instance of, reasoning and inference **3.** **SENSIBLE ARGUMENT AND THOUGHT** sensible rational thought and argument rather than ideas that are influenced by emotion or whim **4.** **REASONING OF PARTICULAR FIELD** the principles of reasoning relevant to a particular field **5.** **RELATIONSHIP AND PATTERN OF EVENTS** the relationship between specific events, situations, or objects, and the inevitable consequences of their interaction **6.** COMPUT **CIRCUIT DESIGN IN COMPUTER** the circuit design and principles used by a computer in its operation [14C. Via French *logique* < Greek *logikē (tekhnē)* "(art) of reason" < *logos* "word, reasoning"]

log·i·cal /lójjik'l/ *adj* **1.** **SENSIBLE AND BASED ON FACTS** based on facts, clear rational thought, and sensible reasoning **2.** **ABLE TO THINK RATIONALLY** able to think sensibly and come to a rational conclusion based on facts rather than emotion **3.** **OF PHILOSOPHICAL LOGIC** relating to philosophical logic —**log·i·cal·i·ty** /lòjji kállətee/ *n* —**log·i·cal·ly** *adv* —**log·i·cal·ness** *n*

log·i·cal at·om·ism *n* the philosophical theories of Bertrand Russell and Ludwig Wittgenstein's early period, which analyze a proposition in terms of its relation to some philosophically basic propositions

log·i·cal con·se·quence *n* a proposition that is implied by valid reasoning from true propositions

log·i·cal con·stant *n* a connective expression that is used in formal logic, e.g., "not," "or," "if ... then" or "if and only if"

log·i·cal pos·i·tiv·ism *n* a theory in linguistic philosophy that holds that in order for a sentence to be cognitively meaningful, it has to be verifiable

log·i·cal truth *n* a proposition that is necessarily true

log·ic bomb *n* a piece of software that interferes with the proper working of the computer's operating system

log·ic cir·cuit *n* a computer switching circuit that performs operations on input signals

lo·gi·cian /lō jísh'n/ *n* somebody whose special training is in philosophical logic

log·i·cism /lójji sìzzəm/ *n* the theory at the base of mathematics that mathematics is reducible to logic broadly construed to include set theory

log·in /lóggin/ *n* COMPUT same as **logon**

lo·gi·on /lṓjee òn, -gee-/ (*plural* **-gi·a** /-ə/) *n* a saying attributed to Jesus Christ that is not in the Bible [Late 19C. < Greek, "oracle" < *logos* "word"]

lo·gis·tic[1] /lə jístik, lō-/ *adj* relating to an uninterpreted calculus or system of symbolic logic [Early 17C. < medieval Latin *logisticus* < Greek *logos* "word, reckoning"] —**lo·gis·ti·cian** /lōji stísh'n/ *n*

lo·gis·tic[2] /lə jístik, lō-/, **lo·gis·ti·cal** /-ik'l/ *adj* **1.** involving the planning and management of how things are moved, especially military forces or industrial goods **2.** involving the planning and management of any complex task [Mid-20C. < French *logistique* (see LOGISTICS)] —**lo·gis·ti·cal·ly** *adv*

lo·gis·ti·cal /lō jístik'l, lə jístik'l/ *adj* same as **logistic**[2]

lo·gis·tics /lə jístiks, lō-/ *n* (*takes a singular or plural verb*) **1.** **ORGANIZATION OF COMPLEX TASK** the planning and implementation of a complex task **2.** **MOVEMENT MANAGEMENT** the planning and control of the flow of goods and materials through an organization or manufacturing process **3.** **ORGANIZATION OF TROOP MOVEMENTS** the planning and organization of the movement of troops, their equipment, and supplies [Late 19C. < French *logistique* < *loger* "to lodge" < Old French *loge* (see LODGE)]

log·jam /lóg jàm/ *n* **1.** a situation where something is blocked or at a standstill and is unable to progress **2.** a blockage caused by floating logs in a river

log line *n* a line from a ship trailing a floating log to determine the ship's speed

lo·go /lṓgō/ (*plural* **-gos**) *n* a design used by an organization on its letterhead, advertising material, and signs as an emblem by which the organization can easily be recognized [Mid-20C. Shortening of LOGOGRAM, LOGOTYPE]

logo- *prefix* word, thought, speech ○ *logotype* [< Greek *logos* "word"]

log·o·gram /lóggə gràm/, **log·o·graph** /-gràf/ *n* a symbol that represents the meaning of a whole word or phrase, e.g., the symbols used in shorthand, or the symbol "&" used instead of the word "and" —**log·o·gram·mat·ic** /lòggəgrə máttik/ *adj* —**log·o·gram·mat·i·cal·ly** *adv*

log·o·griph /lóggə grìf/ *n* a word puzzle, especially an anagram [Late 16C. < French *logogriphe* < Greek *logos* "word" + *griphos* "fishing-basket"]

lo·gom·a·chy /lō gómməkee/ (*plural* **-chies**) *n* an argument about the use or meaning of words [Mid-16C. < Greek *logomakhia* < *logomakhein* "to fight with words" < *logos* "word"]

log·on /lóggon/ *n* **1.** the act of logging on to a computer **2.** a name and password or other appropriate commands used for logging on to a computer

log·or·rhe·a /lòggə rée ə/ *n* excessive talkativeness, especially when the words are uncontrolled or incoherent, as in some psychiatric conditions —**log·or·rhe·ic** *adj*

log·or·rhoe·a *n* UK spelling of **logorrhea**

Lo·gos /lṓ gòss, ló-/ *n* **1.** Jesus Christ, so named in St. John's Gospel, as the word of God, and divine wisdom as the means for human salvation. **2.** in

Judaism, the divine wisdom of the word of God [Late 16C. < Greek, "word, reason"]

log·o·type /lóggə tìp/ *n* **1.** a single piece of type that has different unconnected characters on it **2.** same as **logo**

log·roll /lóg ròl/ (**-rolled, -roll·ing, -rolls**) *vti* to trade votes with political colleagues to support one another's interests [Mid-19C. Back-formation < LOGROLLING]

log·roll·ing /lóg ròling/ *n* **1. EXCHANGE OF POLITICAL SUPPORT** the striking of a deal between colleagues in a legislature whereby support is given to a piece of legislation on the understanding that the favor will be returned at a later date ○ *"The national interest will lose out to the logrolling tradeoffs of Congressional business."* (*Bush speeches in campaign '92*; 1992) **2. MUTUAL SUPPORT** mutual praise, support, or favors **3. BALANCING GAME** a game played by lumberjacks in which players have to balance on spinning floating logs [Early 19C. < the custom of neighbors helping each other to clear land by rolling logs to burn them]

-logue *suffix* speech ○ *monologue* [Via French < Greek *-logos* "speaking" < *logos* "word"]

log·wood /lóg wòòd/ *n* **1.** a spiny leguminous tree. Native to: Caribbean, Central America. Latin name: *Haematoxylon campechianum*. **2.** the wood of the logwood, which yields a purplish red dye [Late 16C. Because the tree's wood was imported in log form]

lo·gy /lṓgee/ (**-gi·er, -gi·est**) *adj* with no energy or enthusiasm [Mid-19C. Origin ?]

-logy *suffix* **1.** speech, expression ○ *haplology* **2.** science, study ○ *musicology* [Directly or via French < Greek *-logia* < *logos* "word, reason" and < *-logos* "speaking"]

loin /loyn/ *n* **1.** ANAT **BACK BETWEEN RIBS AND HIPS** the area on each side of the backbone of a human or animal between the ribs and hips **2.** FOOD **MEAT CUT FROM LOIN OF ANIMAL** a prime cut of tender meat taken from the backbone and rib area of a pig, lamb, or calf ■ **loins** *npl* **AREA BELOW WAIST** the hips and the front of the body below the waist, considered as the part of the body that should be covered and as the site of the sexual organs (*literary*) [14C. Via Old French *loigne* < Latin *lumbus*] ◇ **gird (up) your loins** to prepare yourself to do something difficult and challenging

loin·cloth /lóyn klàwth, -klòth/ *n* a cloth covering the hips and the genital area typically worn by men in hot countries

Loire /lwaar/ longest river in France, rising in the Cévennes mountains, southeastern France. Length: 634 mi./1,020 km.

loi·ter /lóytər/ (**-tered, -ter·ing, -ters**) *vi* **1.** to stand around without any obvious purpose **2.** to do something in a slow lazy way, stopping often to rest [15C. Origin ?] —**loi·ter·er** *n*

loi·ter·ing /lóytəring/, **loi·ter·ing with in·tent** *n* formerly in English law, the offense of standing around in a public place with the apparent intention of committing a crime, especially soliciting ○ *No loitering*

Lo·ki /lṓkee/ *n* in Norse mythology, a handsome giant god who was the embodiment of mischief or evil

Lok Sab·ha /lòk súbbə, -sáabə/ *n* the lower chamber of the Indian Parliament [< Hindi, "people's assembly"]

Lo·li·ta /lō léetə/ *n* a young teenage girl regarded or depicted as the object of sexual desire [Mid-20C. After the main character in *Lolita* (1958), novel by Vladimir Nabokov]

loll /lol/ (**lolled, loll·ing, lolls**) *vi* **1.** to relax in a reclining or leaning position **2.** to droop or hang down in a loose floppy way [14C. Origin ?]

Lol·land /lólland/ island of southeastern Denmark, situated in the Baltic Sea. Population: 72,026 (1994). Area: 479 sq. mi./1,241 sq. km.

lol·la·pa·loo·za /lòlləpə lóozə/, **lal·a·pa·loo·za** /làlləpə-/, **lal·la·pa·loo·za** *n* something that or somebody who is particularly wonderful and impressive or an outstanding example of something (*informal*) [Early 20C. Origin ?]

lol·li·pop /lóllee pòp/, **lol·ly·pop** *n* a piece of hard candy, usually spherical or disk-shaped, attached to a stick [Late 18C. Origin ?]

lol·lop /lólləp/ (**-loped, -lop·ing, -lops**) *vi* **1.** to move in a bouncy clumsy way **2.** *UK* to loll or lounge about [Mid-18C. < LOLL, influenced by GALLOP] —**lol·lop·y** *adj*

lol·ly /lóllee/ (*plural* **-lies**) *n UK* (*informal*) **1.** same as **lollipop 2.** same as **money** (sense 1) [Mid-19C. Shortening of LOLLIPOP]

lol·ly·gag /lóllee gàg/ (**-gagged, -gag·ging, -gags**), **lal·ly·gag** *vi* to waste time in a pleasant idle way (*dated*) [Mid-19C. Origin ?] —**lol·ly·gag·ger** *n*

lol·ly·pop /lóllee pòp/ *n* FOOD another spelling of **lollipop**

lo·ma /lṓmə/ *n* a rounded hill or ridge [Mid-19C. < Spanish, form of *lomo* "back, ridge" < Latin *lumbus* "loin"]

Lo·max /lṓ màks/, **Alan** (1915–2002) US ethnomusicologist. He was noted for his work in the collection of American folk songs, in collaboration with his father John Lomax.

Lo·max, John (1867–1948) US ethnomusicologist. He was noted for his work in the collection of American folk songs, in collaboration with his son Alan Lomax.

Lom·bard /lóm baard, lúm-/ *n* **1.** somebody who comes from Lombardy in Italy **2.** a member of an ancient Germanic people who settled in northern Italy during the 6th century A.D. and soon became the dominant group there

Lom·bar·di /lom báardee/, **Vince** (1913–70) US football coach. As head coach and then general manager, he led the Green Bay Packers to two Super Bowl victories (1967, 1968). Full name **Lombardi, Vincent Thomas**

> "Winning isn't everything, but wanting to win is."
> [Vince Lombardi, *Interview*; 1962]

Lom·bar·dy /lómbərdee, lúm-/ region in northern central Italy, a major commercial and industrial center. Area: 9,213 sq. mi./23,861 sq. km. Population: 9,065,440 (2000). —**Lom·bar·dic** /lom báardik, lum-/ *adj*

Lom·bar·dy pop·lar *n* a variety of poplar that has upright branches and a tall narrow shape. Latin name: *Populus nigra italica*.

Lom·bok /lóm bók/ island of the Lesser Sunda Islands, West Nusa Tenggara Province, southern Indonesia, situated east of Bali. Population: 2,403,399 (1990). Area: 2,000 sq. mi./5,180 sq. km.

Lo·mé /lṓ mày/ capital and largest city of Togo, situated on the Bight of Benin, close to the Ghana border. Population: 700,000 (1997).

lo·ment /lṓ mènt/ *n* a pod or fruit that splits and separates at maturity into one-seeded segments [Mid-19C. < Latin *lomentum* "cosmetic made of bean-meal" < *lavare* "to wash"]

lo·mo /lṓmō/ (*plural* **-mos**) *n Hispanic* a cured tenderloin sausage [Via American Spanish < Spanish, "loin"]

Lo·mond, Loch /lṓmənd/ largest lake in Scotland, located north of Glasgow. Area: 27 sq. mi./71 sq. km.

Lom·poc /lóm pòk/ city in Santa Barbara County, southwestern California, situated near the Pacific Ocean 45 mi./72 km northwest of the city of Santa Barbara. Population: 41,389 (2002 estimate).

Lon·don /lúndən/ **1.** capital city of the United Kingdom of Great Britain and Northern Ireland. It is one of the world's leading financial, industrial, and cultural centers. Population: 7,172,091 (2001). Area: 610 sq. mi./1,580 sq. km. **2.** city in Middlesex County, southwestern Ontario, Canada, on the Thames River. Population: 337,318 (2001). —**Lon·don·er** *n*

Lon·don, Jack (1876–1916) US writer. He wrote realist and humanitarian novels, including *The Call of the Wild* (1903), which was inspired by his experiences in the Klondike. Born **Chaney, John Griffith**. See Cultural note at **call**

> "He must master or be mastered; while to show mercy was a weakness. Mercy did not exist in the primordial life. It was misunderstood for fear, and such misunderstandings made for death."
> [Jack London, *The Call of the Wild*; 1903]

Lon·don·der·ry /lúndən dèrree/ **1.** city in northwestern Northern Ireland, officially called "Derry" until it was fortified by people from London, England, in 1613. Population: 72,334 (1991). **2.** former county of Northern Ireland

lone /lōn/ *adj* **1. SOLITARY** having no one else around **2. ONLY** only or sole ○ *a lone survivor* **3. ISOLATED** situated in an isolated position **4. SINGLE** without a husband, wife, or partner **5. LONELY** lonely and having no companions (*literary*) [14C. Shortening of ALONE]

lone hand *n* **1.** in some card games, a hand played without help from a partner, or a player without a partner **2.** somebody who lives or works alone

lone·ly /lṓnlee/ (**-li·er, -li·est**) *adj* **1. FEELING ALONE** feeling sad through being without friends or company ○ *I felt so lonely after he'd gone.* **2. ISOLATED** isolated and rarely visited ○ *a lonely farmhouse in the middle of the moor* **3. WITHOUT COMPANIONSHIP OR SUPPORT** done or lived through without companionship or support from other people ○ *a lonely existence* **4.** same as **lone** (sense 2) (*informal*) ○ *one lonely pea left on the plate* —**lone·li·ly** *adv* —**lone·li·ness** *n*

lone·ly-hearts *adj* relating to people who are looking for a partner for a romantic relationship

~~**lonelyness**~~ incorrect spelling of **loneliness**

lon·er /lṓnər/ *n* somebody who prefers to work or be alone

lone·some /lṓnssəm/ *adj* **1. SAD FROM BEING ALONE** feeling sad, or causing a feeling of sadness, because of being alone **2. DESOLATE** isolated from human habitation **3. ALONE** having no one or nothing else around —**lone·some·ly** *adv* —**lone·some·ness** *n*

Lone Star State *n* a nickname for Texas

lone wolf *n* same as **loner**

long[1] /lawng, long/ *adj* **1. EXTENDING CONSIDERABLE DISTANCE** extending a relatively great length or height **2. GOING ON FOR LENGTHY PERIOD** lasting for an extended period of time **3. HAVING MANY ITEMS** containing a relatively large number of parts or individual items ○ *a long list* **4. OF PARTICULAR LENGTH** of a particular length, height, total, number, or duration ○ *a book 300 pages long* **5. LONGER THAN IT IS WIDE** with a greater length than width ○ *Look in the long box, not the square one.* **6. BEYOND WHAT IS WANTED** extending in time or space beyond what is considered normal, reasonable, or desirable ○ *The speech was rather long, don't you think?* **7. MORE DISTANT OR LENGTHY** the more or most distant or lengthy of two or more things ○ *the long way home* **8. ABLE TO REACH CONSIDERABLE DISTANCE** capable of reaching or traveling far ○ *a long fly ball* **9. SEEMING TO LAST FOREVER** appearing to be or take more time than is really the case ○ *a long hour waiting* **10. GOING FAR BACK IN TIME** extending back in time ○ *a long memory* **11. EXTENSIVE** exhaustive and critical ○ *Take a good long look at yourself.* **12. RISKY** with an uncertain outcome ○ *long odds* **13. HAVING PLENTY OF SOMETHING** possessing enough or more than enough of something (*informal*) ○ *a politician who is long on rhetoric* **14.** FIN **HOLDING STOCK IN ANTICIPATION OF RISE** describes shares and other securities or commodities that are held with the expectation that prices will rise **15.** PHON **DRAWN OUT IN PRONUNCIATION** describes a speech sound that is relatively drawn out **16.** PHON **DESCENDED FROM LONG VOWEL** describes an English vowel sound that is historically descended from vowels that were drawn out in pronunciation, e.g., the ones in English "beet" and "bite" **17.** LITERAT **ACCENTED** describes a syllable in accentual verse that is stressed **18.** LITERAT **OF GREATER METRICAL DURATION** describes a syllable in quantitative verse that is the one of the two types that is of greater duration ■ *adv* **1. FOR LONG TIME** for or during a lengthy period of time ○ *Have you been here long?* **2. FAR** at or over a great distance ○ *hit the ball long* **3. FOR CERTAIN TIME** for or during a particular length of time ○ *work all day long* **4. AT ANOTHER TIME** at a time much later or earlier than the time specified ○ *long after he left* **5. AFTER PARTICULAR TIME** beyond a particular time ○ *Don't stay longer than two hours.* **6.** FIN **IN LONG STOCK POSITION** in a long position in securities or commodities ○ *selling long* ■ *n* **1. A LONG TIME** a lengthy period of time ○ *Will you be visiting for long?* **2.** PHON **LONG SOUND** a long syllable or sound **3.** CLOTHING **SIZE FOR TALL PEOPLE** a garment or garment size designed for somebody tall [Old English, < Germanic] —**long·ness** *n* ◇ **as** *or* **so long as 1.** for the whole of the time that **2.** provided that or on condition that **3.** because of the fact that ◇ **before long** before much time passes ◇ **long·er term** insofar as a longer period of future time is concerned ◇ **long since** a long time ago ◇ **no longer**

until the present but not for any further time ◇ **not long for** with little time remaining for ◇ **so long** good-bye (*informal*) ◇ **the long and the short of it** the basic idea or facts

long[2] /lawng, long/ (**longed, long·ing, longs**) *vi* to have a strong desire for a person, place, or thing, especially somebody or something unattainable or not within immediate reach ○ *She longed for a bit of excitement in her life.* [Old English *langian* < Germanic]

SYNONYMS See *want.*

Long /lawng, long/, **Huey P.** (1893–1935) US politician. As governor of Louisiana (1928–32) and member of the US Senate (1932–35), he was noted for his oratory and populist views. Full name **Long, Huey Pierce.** Known as **the Kingfish**

Long, Richard (*b.* 1945) British artist. His works often feature natural landscapes, either in photographs, *A Hundred Mile Walk* (1971–72), or materials, *Red Slate Circle* (1980). He was awarded the Turner Prize in 1989.

long. *abbr* GEOG longitude

long-a·go *adj* relating to or existing in the distant past ○ *long-ago civilizations*

lon·gan /láwng gən/, **lun·gan** /lúng-/ *n* **1.** a small juicy fruit with a yellowish brown exterior, white juicy flesh, and a large black seed **2.** an evergreen tree that produces longans. Native to: tropical and subtropical Asia. Latin name: *Euphoria longan.* [Mid-18C. < Chinese *lóngyan* "dragon's eye"]

long-a·wait·ed *adj* hoped for and expected for a considerable time

Long Beach 1. city in Los Angeles County, southwestern California, situated on San Pedro Bay. Population: 472,412 (2002 estimate). **2.** city in Nassau County, southeastern New York, situated off the southern shore of Long Island 21 mi./34 km southeast of New York City. Population: 35,593 (2002 estimate).

long·boat /láwng bōt, lóng-/ *n* the longest boat, usually a seaworthy rowing boat, carried on board a sailing ship, especially a merchant ship

long bone *n* any long cylindrical limb bone in vertebrates that contains marrow and ends in an enlarged head that unites to form a joint with another bone

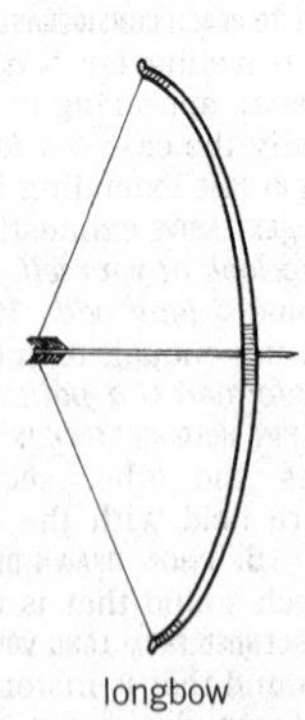

longbow

long·bow /láwng bō, lóng-/ *n* a large powerful hand-drawn bow made from a long piece of slightly curved wood and a bowstring, used, especially in medieval England, for hunting and in warfare —**long·bow·man** *n*

Long Branch city in Monmouth County, eastern New Jersey, situated on the Atlantic Ocean, 21 mi./34 km southeast of Perth Amboy. Population: 31,573 (202 estimate).

long·case clock /làwng kayss-, lòng-/ *n* FURNITURE same as **grandfather clock**

long-chain *adj* describes a molecule or substance that has a relatively long chain of atoms, especially carbon atoms

long-day *adj* requiring long periods of daylight, usually more than 12 hours, followed by short nights in order to mature and flower

long-dis·tance *adj* **1.** FOR LONG WAY traveling or extending a relatively long way **2.** BETWEEN DISTANT PHONES relating to or providing a telephone service between places that are far apart **3.** BETWEEN DISTANT PLACES occurring between places that are far apart ○ *a long-distance romance* ■ *n* TELECOM **PROVISION OF LONG-DISTANCE TELEPHONE SERVICES** the business of providing long-distance telephone services ■ *adv* USING LONG-DISTANCE CONNECTION using a long-distance telephone line

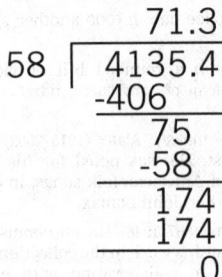

```
        71.3
 58 ) 4135.4
     -406
        75
       -58
       174
       174
         0
```

long division

long di·vi·sion *n* a method or instance of dividing one number by another in which each step is written out in full

long doz·en *n* a set of 13 items

long-drawn-out *adj* going on for an undesirably long period of time

long drink *n* a large cold refreshing drink, usually containing little or no alcohol

lon·ge·ron /lónjə ròn/ *n* a main structural component of an airplane's fuselage that runs from one end of the airplane to the other [Early 20C. < French]

long-es·tab·lished *adj* having existed for a long time in a position of general respect or widespread success

lon·gev·i·ty /lon jévvətee/ (*plural* **-ties**) *n* **1.** LONG LIFE long duration of life **2.** DURATION OF LIFE the length of a person's or animal's life **3.** CAREER SPAN the length of somebody's employment or career [Early 17C. < late Latin *longaevitas* < Latin *longaevus* "of a long age" < *longus* "long" (< Germanic) + *aevum* "age"] —**lon·ge·vous** /lon jeévəss/ *adj*

long face *n* a facial expression showing unhappiness, disappointment, or seriousness —**long-faced** *adj*

Long·fel·low /láwng fèl ō, lóng-/, **Henry Wadsworth** (1807–82) US poet. He wrote many romantic verse narratives, including *The Song of Hiawatha* (1855) and *Paul Revere's Ride* (1863).

> "Under a spreading chestnut tree / The village smithy stands; / The smith, a mighty man is he, / With large and sinewy hands; / And the muscles of his brawny arms / Are strong as iron bands."
> [Henry Wadsworth Longfellow, "The Village Blacksmith"; 1839]

long green *n* money, especially paper money (*slang*)

long·hair /láwng hèr, lóng-/ *n* **1.** SOMEBODY DEDICATED TO ARTS AND MUSIC somebody dedicated to the arts and especially to classical music (*informal*) **2.** IMPRACTICAL INTELLECTUAL an intellectual who is unconcerned with practical matters (*informal*) **3.** LONG-HAIRED MAN somebody with long hair, especially a hippie man (*dated informal disapproving*) **4.** CAT WITH LONG FUR a domestic cat with long fur —**long·haired** *adj*

long·hand /láwng hànd, lóng-/ *n* **1.** words and letters written by hand in full, rather than in shorthand **2.** cursive writing

long haul *n* (*informal*) **1.** LENGTHY PERIOD a long period of time **2.** LOT OF WORK a long-lasting job or ordeal **3.** LONG DISTANCE a long journey or distance ◇ **for** *or* **over the long haul** for a long period of time

long-haul *adj* relating to travel or transportation over long distances

long·head·ed /láwng héddəd, lòng-/ *adj* perceptive and wise (*archaic or literary*) [< the belief that a long head indicated wisdom]

long·horn /láwng hàwrn, lóng-/ (*plural* **-horns** or *same*) *n* **1.** REDDISH COW WITH LONG HORNS a red or variegated cow with long horns, belonging to a breed of beef cattle of Spanish origin that was once very common in the SW United States **2.** COW WITH LONG HORNS a cow belonging to a breed that has long horns **3.** US CYLINDRICAL CHEESE a mild cylinder-shaped Cheddar cheese made in the United States

long-horned bee·tle *n* a beetle with long antennae, long legs and a narrow, often brightly colored body. The larvae of many species are wood borers. Family: Cerambycidae.

long-horned grass·hop·per *n* a large, usually green grasshopper with long antennae and often a characteristic song. Family: Tettigoniidae.

long horse *n* GYMNASTICS same as **vaulting horse**

long·house /láwng hòwss, lóng-/ (*plural* **-hous·es** /-hòwzəz/) *n* **1.** a long bark-covered communal dwelling place built by some Native North American peoples, especially the Iroquois. It had compartments for families around central meeting areas. **2.** a communal dwelling housing accommodating entire extended families and found especially in Borneo or Sarawak

long hun·dred·weight *n* MEASURE same as **hundredweight** (sense 2)

lon·gi·corn /lónji kàwrn/ *n UK* INSECTS same as **long-horned beetle** ■ *adj* having long antennae [Mid-19C. < modern Latin *Longicornia* "long-horned ones" < Latin *longus* "long" (< Germanic) + *cornu* "horn"]

long·ing /láwnging, lónging/ *n* a persistent and strong desire, usually for somebody or something unattainable or not within immediate reach ■ *adj* expressing yearning or desire —**long·ing·ly** *adv*

Long Is·land largest island in the continental United States, in southeastern New York. Queens and Brooklyn, two boroughs of New York City, are situated at the western end of the island. The Hamptons, a series of resort towns, are located on the island's eastern stretch. Population: 6,882,362 (2002 estimate). Area: 1,723 sq. mi./4,463 sq. km.

Long Is·land Sound body of salt water situated between the southern shore of Connecticut and the north shore of Long Island, New York. Area: 1,299 sq. mi./3,364 sq. km.

lon·gi·tude /lónji to͞od/ *n* **1.** the angular distance east or west of the prime meridian that stretches from the North Pole to the South Pole and passes through Greenwich, England. Longitude is measured in degrees, minutes, and seconds. **2.** a region near a particular longitude [14C. < Latin *longitudo* "length" < *longus* "long" < Germanic]

lon·gi·tu·di·nal /lònji to͞od'nəl/ *adj* **1.** RUNNING LENGTHWAYS extending or placed along the length of something, as opposed to across it **2.** OVER TIME relating to development over a period of time **3.** OF LONGITUDE relating to longitude or length —**lon·gi·tu·di·nal·ly** *adv*

lon·gi·tu·di·nal stud·y (*plural* **lon·gi·tu·di·nal stud·ies**), **lon·gi·tu·di·nal sur·vey** *n* a study repeated over time, e.g., following the health of 20,000 people over the age of 50 over a period of 20 years

lon·gi·tu·di·nal wave *n* a wave, e.g., a sound wave, that is propagated in the same direction in which the particles of the medium vibrate

long johns *npl* underpants with full-length legs, or one-piece underwear covering the torso, arms, and legs [< the name *John*]

long jump *n* a track-and-field event in which the contestants jump for distance, usually from a running start into a sand pit —**long jumper** *n*

long-last·ing *adj* continuing for a long time

long·leaf pine /láwng leēf-, lóng-/ *n* **1.** a pine tree with long needles, orange-brown bark, and dense resinous wood. Native to: southeastern United States. Latin name: *Pinus palustris.* **2.** the wood of the longleaf pine, used for lumber

long-life *adj UK* specially treated to last for a long time ○ *long-life milk*

long list *n* a selection from a large number of items or people that will be used to form a short list

long-list *vt* to draw up a long list (*often passive*) ○ *was long-listed for the Booker prize*

long-lived /-lĭvd, -lívd/ *adj* living, lasting, or enduring for a long time

long-lost *adj* not seen for a long period of time

Long·mea·dow /láwng mèddō, lóng-/ town in southern Massachusetts, on the Connecticut River, directly north of the Massachusetts-Connecticut border, and south of Springfield. Population: 15,652 (2002 estimate).

long meas·ure *n* 1. MEASURE same as **linear measure** 2. LITERAT same as **long meter**

long me·ter *n* a four-line stanza in which the second and fourth lines always rhyme and the first and third sometimes rhyme. It is often used for hymns.

Long·mont /láwng mònt, lóng-/ city in Boulder County, northern Colorado, situated 30 mi./48 km north of Denver. Population: 78,654 (2002 estimate).

long pig *n* human flesh as eaten by cannibals [Translation of a Polynesian name]

long-play·ing rec·ord *n* RECORDING full form of **LP**

long-range *adj* 1. EXTENDING WELL INTO FUTURE extending a long time into the future 2. TRAVELING LONG DISTANCES able to travel long distances 3. ARMS ABLE TO HIT DISTANT TARGET relating to weapons that are capable of hitting a target a considerable distance away

long-run·ning *adj* 1. continuing for a long time ○ *a long-running war of words* 2. having been performed or broadcast for many weeks, months, or years in succession ○ *a long-running Broadway musical*

long·ship /láwng shìp, lóng-/ *n* a narrow wooden ship with oars and a large square sail used by the Vikings

long·shore /láwng shàwr, lóng-/ *adj* living, working, or situated on the coast [Early 19C. Shortening of ALONGSHORE]

long·shore·man /láwng shàwrmən, lóng-/ (*plural* **-men** /-mən/) *n* somebody whose job is to load and unload cargo vessels in a port

long shot *n* 1. SOMEBODY OR SOMETHING UNLIKELY TO WIN somebody or something that is unlikely to win a race or competition 2. GAMBLING BET UNLIKELY TO WIN a bet on somebody or something that is unlikely to win a race or competition 3. VENTURE UNLIKELY TO SUCCEED a venture that has little chance of success, although, if successful, an excellent chance of profit or reward 4. PHOTOGRAPHY CAMERA SHOT OF DISTANT OBJECT a camera shot taken some distance from the object or scene ◇ **(not) by a long shot** (not) in any way at all (*informal*)

long-sight·ed *adj UK* OPHTHALMOL same as **farsighted** (sense 1) —**long-sight·ed·ly** *adv* —**long-sight·ed·ness** *n*

long·some /láwngssəm, lóng-/ *adj* very long and boring (*archaic*)

Longs Peak /làwngz-, lòngz-/ mountain in northern Colorado, the highest peak in Rocky Mountain National Park. Height: 14,255 ft./4,345 m.

long·spur /láwng spùr, lóng-/ (*plural* **-spurs** or *same*) *n* a bird with brownish feathers and long-clawed hind toes. Native to: northern United States, Canada, the Arctic. Genus: *Calcarius*.

long-stand·ing *adj* having existed or been going on for a long period of time

Long·street /láwng strēet, lóng-/, **James** (1821–1904) US Confederate general. A Mexican War veteran, he was one of Robert E. Lee's most senior Confederate commanders during the Civil War. His indecisiveness at the Battle of Gettysburg (1863) was widely but unfairly blamed for the Confederate loss there.

long-suf·fer·ing *adj* patient and enduring in the face of suffering or difficulty ■ *n* patience and endurance in the face of suffering or difficulty —**long-suf·fer·ing·ly** *adv*

long suit *n* 1. the suit to which the majority of cards in a player's hand belongs 2. somebody's strongest quality or talent (*informal*)

long-tailed duck *n UK* BIRDS same as **oldsquaw**

long term *n* the period of time extending from the present far into the future

long-term *adj* 1. IN FUTURE relating to or affecting a time long into the future 2. ACCT WITH LONGER ACCOUNTING PERIOD with or relating to an accounting period of longer than one year 3. FIN MATURING IN NUMBER OF YEARS maturing only after a long time, usually a number of years 4. LONG-LASTING continuing for a long period of time

long-term mem·o·ry *n* the part of the mind that retains information permanently or nearly so

long·time /láwng tìm, lóng-/ *adj* having continued in existence for a long period of time

Long Tom *n* 1. a swiveling cannon with a long barrel, used in the past by the navy 2. a long-range cannon used by the army. In the United States, the term has usually designated some 155 mm howitzers.

long ton *n* MEASURE same as **ton**[1] (sense 2)

Lon·gueuil /làwng gáyl/ city in southern Quebec Province, Canada, situated on the St. Lawrence River. Population: 128,016 (2001).

lon·gueur /làwng gúr, lòng-/ *n* a boring section, stretch, or period within something, e.g., a dull passage in a book or tedious scene in a play [Late 18C. < French, "length" < *long* "long" < Latin *longus* < Germanic]

long va·ca·tion, **long vac** *n UK* a period of roughly three months in the summer when law courts and universities are closed

long view *n* the consideration of how events or circumstances are likely to develop in the long term

Long·view /láwng vyo͞o, lóng-/ city in Cowlitz County, southwestern Washington State. Population: 35,464 (2002 estimate).

long wave *n* 1. a radio wave with a wavelength of 1,000 m or more 2. the broadcasting or receiving of radio waves of 1,000 m or more in length (*hyphenated before a noun*)

long·ways /láwng wàyz, lóng-/ *adj, adv* same as **lengthwise**

long week·end *n* a weekend with a holiday or vacation day either on the Friday before, or the Monday after, or both

long-wind·ed *adj* 1. tediously wordy in speech or writing 2. capable of doing physical exercise for a relatively long period of time without getting short of breath —**long-wind·ed·ly** *adv* —**long-wind·ed·ness** *n*

SYNONYMS See ***wordy***.

long·wise /láwng wìz, lóng-/ *adj, adv* same as **lengthwise**

loo[1] /loo/ (*plural* **loos**) *n UK* same as **toilet** (senses 1–2) (*informal*) [Mid-20C. Origin ?]

ORIGIN The most widely claimed source of ***loo*** is *gardy loo* (based on pseudo-French *gare de l'eau* "mind the water"), used in 18th-century Edinburgh to warn passers-by when a chamber pot was about to be emptied into the street below. However, this is chronologically unlikely, as there is no evidence of ***loo*** being used for "toilet" before the 1930s. Other possible candidates include *Waterloo* (the link with "water" gives this some plausibility) and *louver*, from the use of slatted screens for a makeshift lavatory. The likeliest source is perhaps French *lieux d'aisances*, literally "places of ease," hence "toilet," possibly picked up by British service personnel in France during World War I.

loo[2] /loo/ (*plural* **loos**) *n* 1. a gambling card game in which players place the money they are betting in a pool 2. a bet placed in the pool in a game of loo [Late 17C. < French *lantur(e)lu*, refrain of a song]

loo·fa /lo͞ofə/, **loo·fah**, **luf·fa** /lo͞ofə, lúffə/ *n* 1. a sponge made from the dried fibrous interior of an oblong fruit of a tropical gourd 2. a vine of the gourd family that produces the large oblong fruits from which loofa sponges are made. Native to: tropical regions of the eastern hemisphere. Genus: *Luffa*. [Late 19C. < Arabic *lūfa*]

look /lo͝ok/ *v* (**looked, look·ing, looks**) 1. *vti* DIRECT EYES AT SOMETHING to turn the eyes toward or on something ○ *What are you looking at?* ○ *Look me in the eye.* 2. *vi* USE EYES TO SEARCH to use the eyes to examine, watch, or find somebody or something ○ *We looked everywhere.* 3. *vi* SEEM AS SPECIFIED to have the appearance of being or seem to be as specified ○ *He looks tired.* 4. ⚠ *vi* CONSIDER SOMETHING to direct the attention toward something in order to consider it ○ *Let's look at the possible options.* 5. *vt* APPEAR FITTING FOR SOMETHING to have an appearance that is in accordance with something ○ *He looks his age.* 6. *vi* USE EYES IN SPECIFIED WAY to use the eyes in a particular way ○ *He looked intently at the ball.* 7. *vi* FACE PARTICULAR WAY to face a particular direction or have a particular view ○ *The room looks over the lake.* 8. *vi* TEND TOWARD SOMETHING to show a tendency or inclination ○ *The outcome looks good.* 9. *vt* EXPRESS SOMETHING to communicate something by an expression ○ *She looked her anger at all of us.* 10. *vi* PAY ATTENTION used to tell somebody to pay attention or see something ○ *Look, why don't we split the difference?* ○ *Look! There he goes!* ■ *n* 1. ACT OR INSTANCE OF LOOKING an act or instance of looking, e.g., to examine, watch, or find something ○ *Take a look at this.* 2. WAY SOMEBODY OR SOMETHING APPEARS an impression conveyed by a manner or quality ○ *He has the look of someone enjoying himself.* 3. EXPRESSION a facial expression that communicates something ○ *a meaningful look* 4. FASHION an appearance, style, or fashion, especially of dress or hairstyle ■ **looks** *npl* OUTWARD APPEARANCE somebody's outward physical appearance, especially if it is pleasing ○ *good looks* [Old English *lōcian* < Germanic]

USAGE look at meaning "consider": Though ***look at*** is often used orally and in informal writing to mean *give attention to*, as in *Informed sources tell us that the court is going to look at the case*, some people object to this wording as vague and unacceptably casual when used in formal settings. For such contexts, choose a more precise word such as *examine, study, investigate, analyze*, or *scrutinize*, depending on your intended meaning.

look after *vt* to care for or be responsible for somebody or something

look ahead *vi* to think about or plan for the future

look back *vi* to think about the past or past experiences

look down on, **look down up·on** *vt* to regard or treat somebody or something as inferior or with contempt

look for *vt* 1. SEARCH FOR SOMEBODY OR SOMETHING to try to find somebody or something 2. EXPECT SOMETHING to hope for or anticipate something ○ *We're looking for a successful year.* 3. EXPECT SOMEBODY'S ARRIVAL to expect somebody to arrive at a particular time (*informal*) ○ *We're looking for the grandchildren at noon next Friday.*

look forward to *vt* to anticipate a future event with excitement or pleasure

look in *vi* to pay a short visit (*informal*)

look into *vt* to carry out a careful investigation of something such as a possibility, problem, or crime

look on *v* 1. *vi* to be a spectator or witness 2. *also* **look upon** *vt* to regard somebody or something in a particular way

look out *vi* to be careful to avoid danger

look out for *vt* 1. to watch for somebody or something to appear (*informal*) 2. to take particular care of somebody or something

look over *vt* to inspect or examine somebody or something either quickly or carefully

look through *vt* to fail to acknowledge somebody's presence, either intentionally or unintentionally ○ *I smiled at her, but she looked right through me.*

look to *vt* 1. to hope or expect that somebody or something will do or provide something ○ *We always look to you for new ideas.* 2. to want or hope to do something (*informal*) ○ *if you're looking to upgrade your computer*

look up *v* 1. *vt* SEARCH FOR INFORMATION to search for information, e.g., by consulting a reference book 2. *vi* IMPROVE to become better 3. *vt* VISIT SOMEBODY to locate somebody, especially for a visit

look upon *vt* same as **look on** (sense 2)

look up to *vt* to have respect and admiration for somebody

look-a·like *n* somebody or something that looks like somebody or something else (*informal*)

look·down /lo͝ok dòwn/ (*plural* **-downs** or *same*) *n* a silvery ocean fish in the jack family with a compressed body, a steeply sloping face, and eyes high on the head. Native to: Atlantic Ocean. Latin name: *Selene vomer*.

look·er /lo͝okər/ *n* 1. a watcher, observer, or spectator 2. a good-looking person, especially a girl or woman (*informal; sometimes considered offensive*)

look·er-on (*plural* **look·ers-on**) *n* same as **onlooker**

look-in *n* a visit of short duration (*informal*)

look·ing glass /lo͝oking-/ *n* a mirror for people to look at themselves in (*archaic*)

CULTURAL NOTE ***Through the Looking-Glass and What Alice Found There***, a children's story (1871) by British writer Lewis Carroll. In this inspired sequel to *Alice's Adventures in Wonderland*, Alice climbs through a mirror into a magical world where chesspieces come alive, and flowers, insects, and animals all talk. The story features bizarre characters such as Tweedledum and Tweedledee and Humpty Dumpty, and the well-known poems "Jabberwocky" and "The Walrus and the Carpenter."

look·ing-glass *adj* characterized by the complete reversal of everything normal (*dated*) [< *Through the Looking-Glass* (1871) by Lewis Carroll]

look·ist /lóokist/ *adj* involving judgments based on physical appearance, especially showing discrimination against people on this basis ■ *n* somebody who judges people on the basis of their physical appearance, especially somebody who discriminates against people in this way —**look·ism** *n*

look·out /lóok òwt/ *n* **1. CAREFUL WATCH** an act of watching carefully for somebody or something **2. SOMEBODY WATCHING FOR DANGER** somebody who watches carefully for signs of attack or danger **3. PLACE GIVING GOOD VIEW** a place or structure that affords a good view for observation **4. PROBLEM** a problem or concern (*informal*) ○ *That's your lookout.*

look-see *n* a brief look or inspection (*informal*)

look-up *n* a computer procedure in which a term or value is matched against a table of stored information

loom[1] /loom/ *vi* (**loomed, loom·ing, looms**) **1. BE ABOUT TO HAPPEN** to be imminent, often in a threatening way **2. BE SEEN AS LARGE SHAPE** to appear as a large or indistinct, and sometimes menacing, shape ■ *n* **APPEARANCE OF SOMETHING LARGE** an appearance of something, usually something large and threatening (*literary*) [Mid-16C. Origin ?]

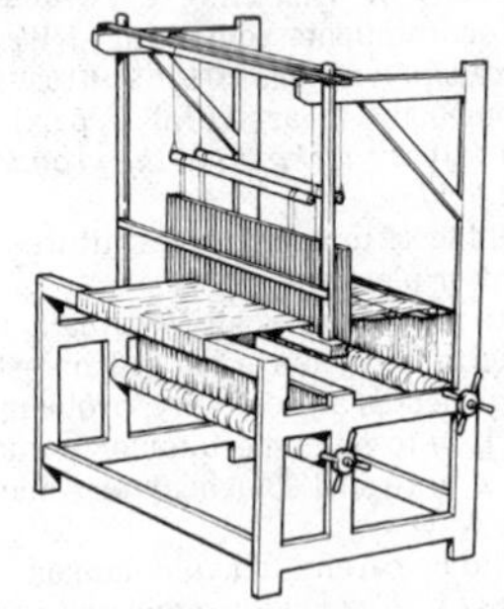

loom

loom[2] /loom/ *n* **1.** a hand-operated or machine-operated device for weaving thread or yarn into cloth **2.** the middle part of an oar between the blade and the handle [Old English *gelōma* "tool"]

loon[1] /loon/ *n* **1.** a fish-eating diving bird with a short tail, webbed feet, smooth black-and-white plumage, and a distinctive laughing call. Native to: northern hemisphere. Genus: *Gavia*. **2.** *Can* MONEY same as **loonie** (*informal*) [Mid-17C. Origin ?]

loon[2] /loon/ *n* **1.** an offensive term that deliberately insults somebody's mental condition or intelligence (*slang insult*) **2.** *Scotland* a boy or young man [15C. Origin ?]

loon·ey *adj, n* another spelling of **loony**

loon·ie /loonee/ *n Can* a Canadian one-dollar coin with an image of a loon on the back (*informal*) [Late 20C. < LOON[1]]

loons /loonz/ *npl* pants made of cotton fabric with a low waist and widely flared legs that were fashionable in the late 1960s and early 1970s

loon·y /loonee/, **loon·ey** *adj* (**-i·er, -i·est**) **1. OFFENSIVE TERM** an offensive term meaning irrational **2. SILLY** considered silly, thoughtless, or strange (*informal*) ○ *loony ideas* ■ *n* (*plural* **-ies**; *plural* **-eys**) **1. OFFENSIVE TERM** an offensive term that deliberately insults somebody's intelligence and ability to act rationally (*slang insult*) **2. SOMEBODY SILLY** somebody who behaves eccentrically or thoughtlessly (*informal*; *often offensive*) [Mid-19C. Shortening and alteration of LUNATIC] —**loon·i·ly** *adv* —**loon·i·ness** *n*

loon·y bin *n* an offensive term for a hospital for people who have psychiatric disorders (*informal*)

loon·y tune *n* an offensive term for somebody who is regarded as highly eccentric or irrational (*informal insult*)

loop[1] /loop/ *n* **1. CIRCLE OR OVAL** a circular or oval shape formed by a line or something such as a piece of string that curves back over itself **2. CIRCULAR OR OVAL FASTENER OR HANDLE** something that has a closed or nearly closed circular or oval shape and is often used to carry or fasten something **3. CONTRACEPTIVE DEVICE** a contraceptive device in the shape of a loop of plastic or metal that is placed in a woman's womb **4.** ELEC **CLOSED CIRCUIT** a closed electric circuit **5.** COMPUT **SET OF COMMANDS IN COMPUTER PROGRAM** a set of instructions in a computer program that is repeated a particular number of times or until a specific objective has been achieved **6.** AVIAT **FLIGHT MANEUVER** a flight maneuver in which a plane flies up, over, and down again describing a circle vertically **7.** *UK* RAIL **RAILROAD BRANCH LINE** a railroad branch line that leaves the main line and then joins it again later on **8.** MOVIES **PIECE OF FILM OR TAPE** a piece of film or tape joined at both ends to allow repeated use of images or sound, especially in dubbing procedures **9.** ANAT **COMMON FINGERPRINT PATTERN** the most common pattern of a human fingerprint formed by U-shaped ridges **10.** ICE SKATING **SKATING JUMP AND TURN** a jump in which a skater takes off from the outer back edge of a blade, turns in the air, and lands again on the same blade's outer back edge ■ *v* (**looped, loop·ing, loops**) **1.** *vti* **MAKE LOOP** to form the shape of a loop, or make something form the shape of a loop **2.** *vt* **FIX SOMETHING WITH LOOP** to fasten, join, or arrange something using a loop **3.** *vi* **CURVE** to move in a curved path [14C. Origin ?] ◇ **in** *or* **out of the loop** being *or* not being among the people who are decision-makers or are fully informed (*informal*) ◇ **knock** *or* **throw somebody for a loop** to surprise, shock, or upset somebody (*informal*)

loop[2] /loop/ *n* a loophole in a wall (*archaic*) [14C. Origin ?]

looped /loopt/ *adj* **1.** formed into a circular or oval shape **2.** same as **drunk** (*dated slang*)

loop·er /loopər/ *n* **1.** a maker of loops **2.** INSECTS same as **inchworm**

loop·hole /loop hōl/ *n* **1. GAP IN LAW** a small mistake or omission in a rule or law that allows it to be circumvented **2.** MIL **SLIT IN WALL** a small slit or hole in a wall, especially one in a fortified wall through which guns or other weapons are fired ■ *vt* (**-holed, -hol·ing, -holes**) **MAKE LOOPHOLES IN WALL** to provide a wall with loopholes [< LOOP[2]]

loop knot *n* a square knot that leaves a single loop hanging free

loop line *n UK* RAIL same as **loop**[1] *n* (sense 7)

loop of Hen·le /-hénnlee, -hénnlə/ *n* the part of the kidney tubule in birds and mammals that forms a loop between the cortex and medulla [Mid-19C. After Friedrich Gustav *Henle* (1801–85), German anatomist and pathologist]

loop·y /loopee/ (**-i·er, -i·est**) *adj* **1.** an offensive term meaning considered to be irrational **2.** having or consisting of loops

Loos /looss/, **Adolf** (1870–1933) Austrian architect. He was a pioneer of functionalism in architecture, and his Steiner House in Vienna, Austria (1910) was a landmark of modernism and the use of concrete.

loose /looss/ *adj* (**loos·er, loos·est**) **1. NOT FIRMLY ATTACHED** not firmly fastened or fixed in place ○ *a loose floorboard* **2. SLACK** not fastened or pulled tight ○ *a loose knot* **3. NOT TIGHT-FITTING** not fitting closely and thus baggy **4. FREE** allowed to move around freely without any restraint ○ *broke loose* **5. NOT PACKAGED** not enclosed in a container or bound together ○ *loose tea* **6. NOT FIRMLY PACKED** not compact or dense in texture or arrangement ○ *loose soil* **7. IMPRECISE** not exact, literal, or precise ○ *a loose translation* **8. FLEXIBLE** not strictly controlled or organized ○ *a loose arrangement* **9. AVAILABLE** not earmarked for a particular purpose ○ *loose funds* **10. IRRESPONSIBLE** lacking restraint or a sense of propriety ○ *loose talk* **11. TOO FLUID** too fluid in consistency ○ *characterized by stomach cramps and loose stools* **12. ACCOMPANIED BY PHLEGM** accompanied by the production of phlegm or mucus ○ *a loose cough* **13. RELAXED** relaxed or free from tension (*informal*) **14. PROMISCUOUS** having many sexual partners (*dated; disapproving*) ■ *adv* (**loos·er, loos·est**) **FREELY** freely or without restraint ■ *v* (**loosed, loos·ing, loos·es**) **1.** *vt* **SET SOMEBODY OR SOMETHING FREE** to release a person or animal from restraint or confinement **2.** *vt* **UNTIE KNOT** to undo, untie, or unfasten something **3.** *vti* **MAKE SOMETHING LESS TIGHT** to make something less tight, or be made less tight **4.** *vt* **RELEASE SOMEBODY FROM OBLIGATION** to release somebody from an obligation or pressure **5.** *vti* **FIRE MISSILE** to fire an arrow, bullet, or other missile [12C. < Old Norse *lauss* < Germanic] —**loose·ly** *adv* —**loose·ness** *n* ◇ **be on the loose 1.** to be free from confinement, e.g., a prison **2.** to be free from responsibilities and having a good time (*informal*) ◇ **let loose** to obtain relief from tension or worry (*informal*)

USAGE loose or **lose**? ***Lose*** is a verb only, meaning variously "to mislay," "to fail to win," etc., as in *Don't lose* [not *loose*] *possession of the ball, or you'll lose the game.* ***Loose*** is an adjective, adverb, and verb. As an adjective it means variously "not firmly fixed," "not restrained," etc., as in *loose* [not *lose*] *floorboards; loose* [not *lose*] *dogs running through the alley.* As an adverb it means "freely," as in *dogs running loose* [not *lose*]. As a verb it means variously "to untie," "to make less tight," and "to fire a projectile," as in *loosed her grip; loosed the taut anchor line; loosed a volley of arrows.*

loose·box /looss bòks/ *n UK* RIDING same as **box stall**

loose can·non *n* an unpredictable or indiscreet person, often causing trouble for colleagues or associates (*slang*)

loose change *n* a small amount of money in the form of coins

loose cov·er *n UK* FURNITURE same as **slipcover**

loose end *n* a small part of something such as a project or a story that has not been completed or fully explained (*informal*; *often used in the plural*) [Referring to the end of a string left hanging] ◇ **at loose ends** not knowing what to do, either because of restlessness or boredom or unfamiliarity with a situation

loose-fill *n* lightweight, often peanut-shaped, foam packing material

loose-fit·ting /looss fitting/ *adj* large, baggy, and not fitting closely to the body ○ *loosefitting pants*

loose-joint·ed *adj* **1.** agile and supple in movement **2.** having joints that move freely —**loose-joint·ed·ness** *n*

loose-leaf *adj* with pages that can be removed and replaced easily

loose-limbed *adj* having supple legs and arms

loose-meat sand·wich *n regional* a sandwich made with a bun filled with shredded meats

REGIONAL NOTE The term ***loose-meat sandwich*** is most common in the Upper Midwest, especially Iowa.

loos·en /looss'n/ (**-ened, -en·ing, -ens**) *v* **1.** *vti* **BECOME, OR MAKE SOMETHING, LESS TIGHT** to become less tight or less firmly fixed, or make something become less tight or less firmly fixed **2.** *vt* **UNTIE HAIR OR KNOT** to untie something such as hair or a knot **3.** *vt* **RELAX CONTROL** to lessen control, pressure, or strictness **4.** *vt* **MAKE BOWELS MORE REGULAR** to make somebody's bowel movements more fluid or regular

loosen up *v* **1.** *vti* to do exercises, or exercise muscles or joints, in order to become more limber, e.g., prior to strenuous activity **2.** *vi* to become less tense, strict, or serious

loose smut *n* a disease of cereal grasses in which powdery spore masses replace the grain head

loose·strife /looss strīf/ (*plural* **-strifes** or *same*) *n* **1.** a plant of the primrose family with clusters of yellow flowers. Native to: northern temperate regions. Genus: *Lysimachia*. **2.** a plant with spikes of purple flowers that has become an invasive species in North American wetlands. Native to: Europe. Latin name: *Lythrum salicaria*. [Mid-16C. Translation (wrongly, as if < Greek *lusimakhos* "loosening strife") of Latin *lysimachia*, after *Lysimachus*, Greek physician]

loose-tongued *adj* liable to gossip or reveal information that should be kept secret (*informal*)

loot /loot/ *n* **1.** MIL **SPOILS OF WAR OR RIOT** money or goods that have been pillaged during wartime or a riot **2.** CRIME **STOLEN GOODS** money or goods that have been stolen or obtained illegally **3.** same as **money** (sense 1) (*informal*) **4. LOT OF PRESENTS OR PURCHASES** a large amount of goods that have been bought or given on one occasion (*informal*) ■ *vti* (**loot·ed, loot·ing, loots**) **STEAL LOOT FROM PLACE** to steal valuables from a place during a time of disorder or confusion, e.g., during wartime or a riot [Mid-19C. < Hindi *lūṭ*] —**loot·er** *n*

lop[1] /lop/ *vt* (**lopped, lop·ping, lops**) **1. CUT BRANCH OFF TREE** to cut a branch off a tree cleanly **2. CUT OFF SOMETHING**

to cut off something such as hair or a limb with one stroke **3.** GET RID OF SOMEBODY OR SOMETHING to eliminate somebody or something as superfluous **4.** TAKE AMOUNT OFF PRICE to deduct an amount from a price ■ *n* CUT-OFF BRANCH a branch that has been cut off [Early 16C. Origin ?] —**lop·per** *n*

lop[2] /lop/ (**lopped, lop·ping, lops**) *v* **1.** *vti* to hang, or allow something to hang, loosely **2.** *vi* to move with an awkward slouching posture [Late 16C. Probably suggesting the action of flopping about]

lope /lōp/ *v* (**loped, lop·ing, lopes**) **1.** *vi* RUN IN LONG EASY STRIDES to run in a relaxed and easy way, taking long strides **2.** *vti* CANTER to canter with a long easy stride, or make a horse canter with a long easy stride ■ *n* LONG-STRIDING GAIT a relaxed and easy gait with long strides [13C. < Old Norse *hlaupa* "to leap"] —**lop·er** *n*

lop-eared *adj* describes domestic rabbits, dogs, and goats that have loosely hanging ears

Lo·pe de Ve·ga /lōpay de váygə/ (1562–1635) Spanish playwright and poet. He is considered the founder of Spanish national drama. More than 400 of his 2,000 plays survive. Full name **Vega Carpio, Lope Félix de**

lo·per·a·mide /lō pérrə mīd/ *n* an opiate drug that slows down the movements of the intestines. Use: treatment of acute and chronic diarrhea. [Late 20C. Contraction of *chloroprophenyl piperidine butyramide*]

Ló·pez Por·til·lo /lò pez pawr tée ō/, **José** (*b.* 1920) president of Mexico (1976–82). He attempted to make the country more financially independent of the United States.

lo·pho·phore /lóffə fàwr, lṓfə-/ *n* a circular or horseshoe-shaped structure of tentacles around the mouth of a bryozoan or brachiopod that is used for capturing food [Mid-19C. < Greek *lophos* "crest"]

lop·o·lith /lóppə lìth/ *n* a basin-shaped body of igneous rock formed by the penetration of magma between existing layers of rock [Early 20C. < Greek *lopas* "basin"]

lop·per /lóppər/, **lop·per milk** *n* milk that has curdled (*dated or regional*) [< dialect *lopper* "curdle," probably < Old Norse *hlaup* "coagulation"]

lop·sid·ed /lóp sīdəd, lop sīdəd/ *adj* **1.** leaning or drooping to one side **2.** unevenly balanced because one side is larger, stronger, or heavier than the other [Early 18C. < LOP[2]]

lo·qua·cious /lō kwáyshəss/ *adj* tending to talk a great deal [Mid-17C. < Latin *loquaci-* < *loqui* "speak"] —**lo·qua·cious·ly** *adv* —**lo·qua·cious·ness** *n* —**lo·qua·ci·ty** /lō kwássətee/ *n*

SYNONYMS See *talkative*.

lo·quat /lṓ kwàat, -kwàt/ (*plural* **-quats** or *same*) *n* **1.** a small pear-shaped orange-yellow sweet but slightly tangy fruit, eaten raw or cooked **2.** an evergreen tree that produces loquats. Native to: China, Japan. Latin name: *Eriobotrya japonica*. [Early 19C. < Chinese *luh kwat* "rush orange"]

lo·ran /láw ràn/ *n* a long-distance radio navigation system by which a ship or aircraft determines its position using radio signals sent out by two ground stations [Mid-20C. Acronym < *long-range navigation*]

lo·raz·e·pam /lō rázzə pàm/ *n* a mild tranquilizer. Use: relief of anxiety, often before surgery. [Late 20C. Contraction of *chlorodiazepam*]

AKG London

Federico García Lorca

Lor·ca /láwrkə/, **Federico García** (1898–1936) Spanish poet and playwright. A popular poet and powerful dramatist, he was assassinated by Nationalists during the Spanish Civil War. His works include *Blood Wedding* (1933) and *The House of Bernarda Alba* (1936).

lord /lawrd/ *n* **1.** ARISTOCRAT a man who is a member of the nobility, especially in Great Britain **2.** FEUDAL SUPERIOR in medieval Europe, a powerful land- or property-owner, with authority over an area, castle, or community, e.g., the lord of a manor **3.** POWERFUL MAN a man who has considerable power, authority, or influence over others, e.g., a business tycoon **4.** MASTER a master, ruler, or head of a household, or a woman's husband regarded as her master (*archaic*) [Old English *hlāford*, contraction of *hlāfweard* "loaf-guardian" < *hlāf*, earlier form of LOAF[1]] ◇ **lord it (over somebody)** to act in a superior, masterful, or bullying way toward somebody (*disapproving*)

Lord *n* **1.** CHRISTIAN GOD in Christianity, God or Jesus Christ **2.** JEWISH GOD in Judaism, God **3.** TITLE FOR GOD used as a title for a deity in Hinduism and some other religions ○ *Lord Krishna* **4.** TITLE FOR NOBLE used as an alternate title for a British marquess, earl, viscount, or baron **5.** TITLE FOR NOBLE'S SON used as a courtesy title for the younger son or sons of a British marquess or duke **6.** FORM OF ADDRESS FOR NOBLE used as a form of address for a British earl, viscount, or baron, and for the younger son of a duke or marquess **7.** TITLE OF HIGH-RANKING OFFICIAL a title given to some high-ranking British officials ■ *interj* EXPRESSING SURPRISE used to express surprise, concern, or annoyance about something (*informal*) ■ **Lords** *npl* GOV same as **House of Lords**

Lord Chan·cel·lor *n* the cabinet minister in the British government who is responsible for the administration of justice in England and Wales and is also the Speaker in the House of Lords. The post is to be abolished and the role will be undertaken by the Secretary of State for Constitutional Affairs.

lord·ling /láwrdling/ *n* a young, minor, or insignificant lord (*disapproving*)

lord·ly /láwrdlee/ (**-li·er, -li·est**) *adj* **1.** arrogant, aloof, and behaving in a superior way **2.** very grand, magnificent, and suitable for a lord —**lord·li·ness** *n*

Lord of Hosts *n* in Christianity, God

Lord of the Flies *n* JUD-CHR same as **Beelzebub**

lor·do·sis /lawr dṓsiss/ (*plural* **-dos·es** /-dṓ seez/) *n* **1.** an unusual inward curving of the spine in the lower part of the back, which may be medically significant **2.** an inward arching of the back of female mammals during sexual stimulation [Early 18C. Via modern Latin < Greek *lordōsis* < *lordos* "bent backward"] —**lor·dot·ic** /-dóttik/ *adj*

Lord Pro·tec·tor *n* HIST, POL same as **Protector**

Lord's Day *n* in Christianity, Sunday, the Christian Sabbath

lord·ship /láwrd shìp/ *n* **1.** the position held by a lord, or the period of tenure of a lord **2.** the land owned by a lord

Lord·ship *n* in the United Kingdom, used as a respectful way to refer to or address a judge, a bishop, or some nobles

Lord's Prayer *n* the most important prayer in Christianity, which Jesus Christ taught to his disciples according to the Gospels of Luke and Matthew

Lord's Sup·per *n* CHR same as **Communion** (sense 1)

Lord's Ta·ble *n* the altar or Communion table in a Protestant church

lord·y /láwrdee/ *interj* used to express surprise, shock, or disappointment (*dated informal*)

lore[1] /lawr/ *n* **1.** acquired knowledge or wisdom on a subject such as local traditions, handed down by word of mouth and usually in the form of stories or historical anecdotes **2.** knowledge that has been acquired through teaching or experience (*archaic*) [Old English *lār* "teaching, learning" < Germanic]

lore[2] /lawr/ *n* **1.** the part on either side of a bird's head between its eyes and the base of the beak **2.** the area on a snake's or a fish's face between its eyes and its mouth [Early 17C. < Latin *lorum* "strap, thong"]

Lo·re·lei[1] /láwrə lī/ *n* in German legend, a beautiful woman said to live on a rock near the Rhine River and lure sailors onto the rocks with enchanting songs

Lo·re·lei[2] /láwrə lī/ cliff overlooking the Rhine River between Mainz and Koblenz, west central Germany. Height: 390 ft./120 m.

Lo·ren /lər én/, **Sophia** (*b.* 1934) Italian actor. Her movie career includes both Italian comedies, often with Marcello Mastroianni, and work in Hollywood. Born **Scicolone, Sofia**

Lo·rentz /láwrənts/, **Hendrik Antoon** (1853–1928) Dutch theoretical physicist. He shared the Nobel Prize in physics with Pieter Zeeman (1902) for his work on electromagnetic radiation.

Lo·rentz-Fitz·ger·ald con·trac·tion /làwrənts fits jérrəld-/ *n* the consequence of relativity that causes a reduction in length of an object traveling at a speed approaching that of light [Early 20C. After Hendrik Antoon LORENTZ and G.F. FITZGERALD]

Lo·renz /lṓ rents, láw-/, **Konrad** (1903–89) Austrian zoologist and ethologist. He founded the science of ethology, and his research on animal behavior included work on imprinting in birds and on human and animal aggression. He shared the Nobel Prize in physiology or medicine (1973). Full name **Lorenz, Konrad Zacharias**

> "Just as the transmitting apparatus of animals is considerably more efficient than that of man, so also is their receiving apparatus."
> [Konrad Lorenz, *King Solomon's Ring*; 1949]

lo·res /lṓ rèz/, **low-res** *adj* COMPUT same as **low-resolution** (*informal*) [Shortening and alteration]

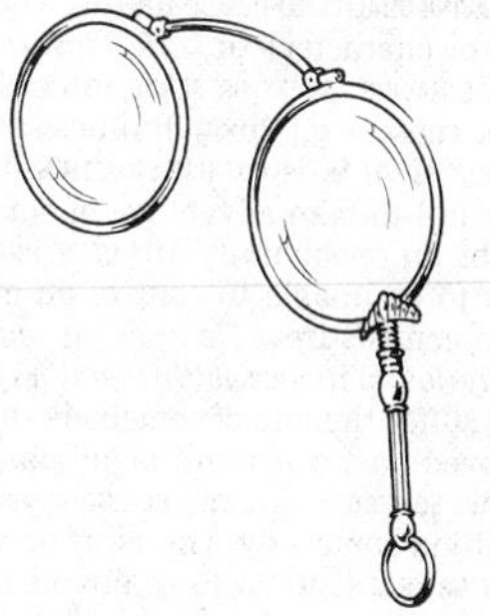

lorgnette

lor·gnette /lawrn yét/ *n* a pair of glasses or opera glasses held to the eyes by a short handle at one side [Early 19C. < French < *lorgner* "squint, peer at" < Germanic]

lo·ri·ca /law rīkə, lə-/ (*plural* **-cae** /-seē/) *n* **1.** a light loose external shell that protects ciliated or flagellated protozoans **2.** a protective metal or leather garment covering the chest and back worn by ancient Romans [Early 18C. < Latin, "breastplate" < *lorum* "strap"]

lor·i·keet /láwri keet/ (*plural* **-keets** or *same*) *n* a small brightly colored parrot with a bristle-tipped tongue for extracting nectar and pollen from flowers. It is smaller than a lory. Native to: Australia, Pacific Islands. Subfamily: Loriinae. [Late 18C. < LORY, after PARAKEET]

lo·ris /láwriss/ (*plural same*) *n* a small slow-moving tree-dwelling nocturnal primate with large eyes, dense wooly fur, a vestigial index finger, and no tail. Native to: tropical South Asia. Genera: *Loris* or *Nycticebus*. [Late 18C. < French]

lorn /lawrn/ *adj* forsaken or forlorn (*literary or archaic*) [13C. Past participle of obsolete *lese* "lose" < Old English *-lēosan*]

Lor·raine /lə ráyn/ region in eastern France. Capital: Metz. Population: 2,310,376 (1999). Area: 9,100 sq. mi./23,540 sq. km.

lor·ry /láwree/ (*plural* **-ries**) *n UK* a large vehicle for transporting goods by road [Mid-19C. Origin ?]

lo·ry /láwree/ (*plural* **-ries** or *same*) *n* a small brightly colored parrot with a bristle-tipped tongue for extracting nectar and pollen from flowers. Native to: Australia, New Guinea, Indonesia. Subfamily: Loriinae. [Late 17C. < Malay *lori*]

LOS *abbr* **1.** TRAVEL length of stay **2.** FOOTBALL line of scrimmage **3.** BROADCAST line of sight

Los Al·a·mi·tos /loss àllə meétōss/ city in Orange County, southwestern California, situated east of Long Beach. Population: 11,710 (2002 estimate).

Los Al·a·mos /loss állə mōss/ city in Los Alamos County, central New Mexico, situated approximately 35 mi./55 km northwest of Santa Fe. Home to the Los Alamos National Laboratory, it was the site chosen in 1942 for research and development of nuclear weapons. Population: 18,305 (2002).

Los Al·tos /loss áltōss/ city in Santa Clara County, western California, situated southeast of Palo Alto. Population: 27,314 (2002 estimate).

Los An·ge·les /los ánjələss, -lèez/ city and county seat of Los Angeles County, southwestern California. Located on the Pacific Ocean, it is the second most populous city in the United States and home to UCLA. Population: 3,798,981 (2002 estimate).

lose /looz/ (**lost** /lawst, lost/, **los·ing**, **los·es**) *v* **1.** *vt* HAVE SOMETHING TAKEN AWAY to cease to possess or have something such as a job or home **2.** *vt* MAKE SOMEBODY FORFEIT SOMETHING to be the cause of somebody's failure to obtain, win, or maintain something ○ *a mistake that lost us the game* **3.** *vt* MISLAY SOMETHING to be unable to find something, often only temporarily **4.** *vti* FAIL TO WIN to fail to win a victory at something, e.g., in a contest, argument, war, game, or in court **5.** *vti* EARN LESS MONEY THAN YOU SPEND to be worse off, or worse off by a particular amount of money, as the result of a financial transaction or through expenditure exceeding income ○ *lost millions when the stock markets crashed* ○ *will lose on the deal* **6.** *vt* EXPERIENCE REDUCTION IN SOMETHING to experience a reduction in something such as weight or heat **7.** *vt* CEASE HAVING QUALITY to cease having a quality, belief, attitude, or characteristic ○ *He's lost the will to live.* **8.** *vt* CEASE HAVING ABILITY OR SENSE to cease having an ability or sense, e.g., through illness or an accident ○ *lose your sight* **9.** *vt* NOT USE SOMETHING TO ADVANTAGE to waste or fail to take advantage of something such as time or an opportunity **10.** *vt* BE UNABLE TO CONTROL SOMETHING to be unable to control an emotion or to maintain composure ○ *He loses his temper easily.* ○ *He finally lost patience with them.* **11.** *vt* HAVE LOVED ONE DIE to suffer the loss of somebody through death, e.g., a loved one, a patient, or a baby before term **12.** *vt* LEAVE SOMEBODY FOLLOWING BEHIND to escape from or leave behind somebody who is in pursuit **13.** *vt* NO LONGER SEE OR HEAR SOMEBODY to be unable to see or hear somebody or something any longer **14.** *vt* CONFUSE SOMEBODY to fail to make somebody understand something ○ *You've lost me there.* **15.** *vt* DISPOSE OF SOMETHING to get rid of something or somebody that is unwanted or undesirable ○ *Lose that extra space on the left.* **16.** *vti* RUN SLOW to be or become slow by an amount of time (*refers to timepieces*) [Old English *losian* "perish, destroy, lose" < *los* (see LOSS)] —**los·a·ble** *adj* ◇ **lose it** (*informal*) **1.** to become removed from reality **2.** to be unable to maintain emotional control or composure

USAGE See *loose.*

lose out *vi* to fail to win or obtain something in a competition or rivalry (*informal*)

~~**loseing**~~ incorrect spelling of **losing**

los·er /loozər/ *n* **1.** SOMEBODY WHO HAS NOT WON a person or team that has failed to win a specific contest **2.** SOMEBODY PUT AT DISADVANTAGE a person or thing adversely affected by a situation or course of action ○ *If this measure goes through, the real losers will be college-leavers.* **3.** SOMEBODY UNSUCCESSFUL OR UNLUCKY an unsuccessful or unlucky person who seems destined to fail repeatedly (*informal insult*) **4.** SOCIAL MISFIT a socially maladjusted person (*informal insult*)

los·er cruis·er *n* a public transportation vehicle such as a bus or minivan, used by, e.g., college students or service members without personal vehicles (*humorous*)

Los·ey /lōzee/, **Joseph** (1909–84) US movie director. Influential for its camerawork, his work encompassed political and social commentaries, thrillers, and psychological drama, and included *The Servant* (1963), *Accident* (1967), and *The Go-Between* (1971). Full name **Losey, Joseph Walton**

Los Ga·tos /loss gáttəss/ town in Santa Clara County, western California, situated 8 mi./13 km southwest of San Jose. Population: 28,209 (2002 estimate).

los·ings /loozingz/ *npl* money or possessions that are lost, especially through gambling

Los Pinos /los pée nōs/ *n* the presidential mansion and its grounds in Mexico City, Mexico [< Spanish, "the pine trees"]

loss /lawss, loss/ *n* **1.** FACT OF NO LONGER HAVING SOMETHING the fact of no longer having something or of having less of something **2.** SOMEBODY OR SOMETHING LOST somebody or something that has been lost **3.** DEATH the death of somebody **4.** MONEY SPENT IN EXCESS OF INCOME the amount of money by which a company's or person's expenses exceed income or profit (*often used in the plural*) **5.** INSTANCE OF LOSING CONTEST an instance of losing a competition, race, or contest **6.** REDUCTION a reduction in the level of something, especially in the body ○ *weight loss* **7.** SAD FEELING a feeling of sadness, loneliness, or emptiness at the absence of somebody or something **8.** INSUR INSTANCE OR AMOUNT OF CLAIM an instance or the amount of a claim made by an insurance policyholder [Old English *los* "ruin, destruction" < Germanic] ◇ **at a loss** uncertain what to say or do ◇ **cut your losses** to withdraw from a situation in which there is no possibility of winning

loss ad·just·er *n UK* same as **adjuster**

loss lead·er *n* an item sold at a price below its cost in the hope that customers who buy it will also buy other things

loss-mak·ing /láwss màyking/ *adj* describes a business, organization, or industry that does not make a profit

loss ra·tio *n* the ratio of the losses paid out in a year by an insurance company against the income from premiums

lost /lawst, lost/ *v* past participle, past tense of **lose** ■ *adj* **1.** UNABLE TO FIND WAY unable to find the way to a place **2.** MISLAID unable to be found temporarily **3.** GONE no longer in existence or use **4.** NOT USED PROPERLY wasted or not taken advantage of ○ *a lost opportunity* **5.** CONFUSED BY SOMETHING COMPLICATED confused or bewildered by something complicated or poorly explained **6.** DESTROYED destroyed or killed ○ *The ship was lost in a storm.* **7.** PREOCCUPIED completely absorbed or involved in something ○ *lost in thought* **8.** LACKING CONFIDENCE unable to cope with a job or situation, usually because of inexperience or lack of confidence ○ *feels lost in front of an audience* **9.** UNAPPRECIATED not understood or appreciated by somebody ○ *His jokes were lost on me.* **10.** LACKING MORALS morally or spiritually past hoping for (*formal*) ◇ **get lost** used to tell somebody in a blunt and rude way to go away (*slang*)

lost and found *n* an area or container in a public building where personal possessions that have accidentally been left behind are kept for reclaiming by their owners

lost cause *n* somebody who cannot be made to change, or something that cannot succeed

Lost Gen·er·a·tion *n* the group of US authors, including Ernest Hemingway and F. Scott Fitzgerald, who rejected American values and lived in Paris in the 1920s

lost prop·er·ty *n UK* same as **lost and found**

lost tribes *npl* the ten Hebrew tribes that separated from the other two to create a kingdom in northern Israel after Solomon's death. They were defeated by the Assyrians in 721 B.C. and may have become assimilated, but legend predicts their return.

lost wax *n* a method of casting metal in which a wax model is coated with a material with a high melting point. The wax is melted and replaced by the molten metal.

lot /lot/ *pron* **a lot**, **lots** /lots/ MUCH OR MANY a large amount, or a large number of people or things (*takes a singular or plural verb*) ○ *I learned a lot.* ○ *A lot of people came.* ○ *Lots of exercise is what you need.* ○ *You have lots of choices.* ■ *adv* (*informal*) **1. a lot, lots** MUCH to a great extent or degree ○ *laughed a lot* ○ *I'm feeling lots better, thanks.* **2. a lot, lots** OFTEN often or much of the time ○ *went out to restaurants a lot* ■ *n* **1.** PIECE OF LAND a small area of land that has fixed boundaries ○ *a vacant lot* **2.** MOVIES FILM STUDIO a film studio together with the land that belongs to it **3.** ITEMS IN AUCTION an item or group of items on sale at an auction ○ *I bought the silver as one lot.* **4.** SET a set or group of things or people ○ *One lot of tourists has left the hotel already.* ○ *That lot go over there.* **5.** TYPE OF GROUP a group of people or things of a particular kind (*informal; takes a singular or plural verb*) ○ *They're a cheerful lot.* **6.** DESTINY the things somebody has or experiences in life ○ *our lot in life* **7.** RANDOM CHOICE the process of choosing something at random, especially by taking from a set of pieces of paper or straws, one of which has a concealed mark or is shorter than the others ○ *chosen by lot* [Old English *hlot* "object used to make decisions by chance, portion, destiny" < Germanic] ◇ **a bad lot** an unpleasant or disreputable person (*informal*) ○ *Don't have anything to do with him: he's a bad lot.* ◇ **all over the lot** (*informal*) **1.** everywhere **2.** in a state of disorder or confusion ◇ **a whole lot** very much or a great deal (*informal*) ◇ **draw** *or* **cast lots** to choose something at random, e.g., a straw or piece of paper, to determine an outcome ○ *We cast lots to decide who should go first.* ◇ **the lot** everything, or everything considered as one (*informal*)

USAGE a lot or alot? The superficial similarity of ***a lot*** to adjectives and adverbs like *alone* and *aloud* gives rise to a temptation to treat the expression as one word, but this is nonstandard usage. In formal writing *much, many, a great deal of,* and the like can be substituted for ***a lot.***

Lot[1] /lot/ *n* in the Bible, the son of Haran, brother of Abraham. He is mentioned as Lut in the Koran.

Lot[2] /lot/ **1.** river in southwestern France. Length: 300 mi./483 km. **2.** department in Midi-Pyrénées Region, southwestern France, known for its scenic beauty. Population: 160,197 (1999). Area: 2,014 sq. mi./5,217 sq. km.

lo·ta /lṓtə/, **lo·tah** *n* a small round water container, usually made of brass or copper, used in South Asia [Early 19C. < Hindi *lotā*]

loth *adj* another spelling of **loath**

Lo·thair II /lō thér/, **king of Germany and Holy Roman Emperor** (1075–1137) His election as king of Germany (1125) led to a war between two rival families, the Guelphs and the Ghibellines

Lo·thar·i·o /lō thérree ō/ (*plural* **-os**), **lo·thar·i·o** *n* a man who attempts to persuade women to enter sexual affairs with him [Mid-18C. After a character in *The Fair Penitent* (1703), tragedy by Nicholas Rowe]

lo·ti /lṓtee/ (*plural* **ma·lo·ti** /maa lṓtee/) *n* the main unit of currency in Lesotho. See table at **currency** [Late 20C. < Sesotho, after the *Maloti* Mountains in Lesotho]

lo·tic /lṓtik/ *adj* describes ecological communities that live in swift-flowing water [Early 20C. < Latin *lot-* (see LOTION)]

lo·tion /lṓsh'n/ *n* a thick liquid preparation that is applied to the skin for cosmetic or medical reasons [14C. Directly or via French < Latin *lotion-* < *lot-*, past participle of *lavare* "wash"]

lot·ter·y /lóttəree/ (*plural* **-ies**) *n* **1.** a large-scale gambling game, usually organized to raise money for a public cause, in which numbered tickets are sold and a draw is held to select the winning numbers **2.** an activity, situation, or enterprise with an outcome dependent on chance [Mid-16C. Probably < Dutch *loterij* < *lot* "lot" < Germanic]

lot·to /lóttō/ *n* **1.** a game resembling bingo, in which numbers are called at random and players try to be the first to cover all the corresponding numbers on their cards **2.** *also* **Lot·to** a state-run lottery in some US states and some other countries, in which players buy tickets bearing combinations of numbers. Periodically a combination of numbers is selected at random and people with matching tickets win cash prizes. [Late 18C. Directly or via French < Italian < assumed Frankish *lot* "lot" < Germanic]

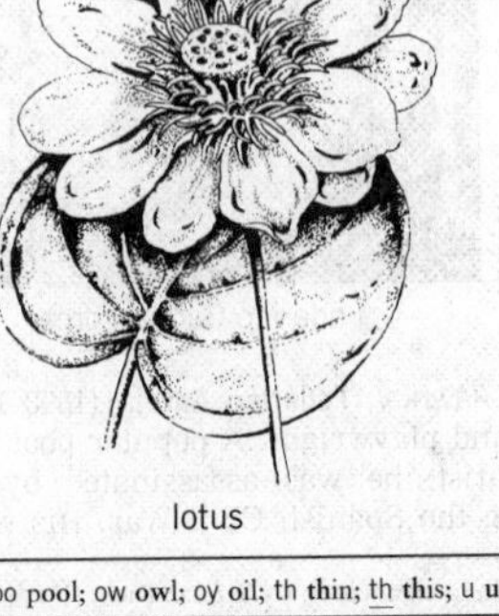

lotus

lo·tus /lṓtəss/ (*plural* **-tus·es** or *same*) *n* **1.** SACRED PINK WATER LILY a water lily with large leaves, regarded as sacred in South Asia, China, and Tibet. Flowers: fragrant, pink. Native to: South Asia, Australia. Latin name: *Nelumbo nucifera*. **2.** SACRED WHITE WATER LILY a water lily sacred to the ancient Egyptians. Flowers: white. Native to: tropical Africa and South Asia. Latin name: *Nymphaea lotus*. **3.** MYTHOLOGICAL FRUIT CAUSING DROWSINESS in Greek mythology, a fruit that made people who ate it feel a pleasant drowsiness. See illustration on previous page [15C. Via Latin < Greek *lōtos*, applied to a variety of plants]

lo·tus-eat·er *n* **1.** a lazy, self-indulgent person **2.** in Greek mythology, somebody who lived in a state of idle stupor after eating the lotus fruit

lotus position: seated Buddha, Uttar Pradesh, northern India

lo·tus po·si·tion *n* a sitting position, used especially in yoga and meditation, in which the legs are crossed in such a way that each foot rests on top of the other leg's thigh [< its supposed resemblance to a lotus blossom]

Lou·ang·phra·bang /loo àng prə báng/ city in northern Laos, on the Mekong River. Population: 68,000 (1995).

louche /loosh/ *adj* disreputable or of doubtful morality [Early 19C. Via French, "cross-eyed, shady" < Latin *luscus* "one-eyed"]

loud /lowd/ *adj* **1.** HIGH IN VOLUME high in volume of sound **2.** EXPRESSING SOMETHING NOISILY expressing something forcefully and frequently ○ *loud protests* **3.** VISUALLY SHOCKING shockingly bright in color or bold in design ○ *a loud shirt* **4.** OFFENSIVE noisy, coarse, and offensive [Old English *hlūd* < Indo-European, "hear"] —**loud·ly** *adv*

loud·en /lówd'n/ (**-ened, -en·ing, -ens**) *vti* to become louder, or make a sound louder

loud·hail·er /lòwd háylər/ *n UK* same as **bullhorn**

loud·mouth /lówd mòwth/ (*plural* **-mouths** /-mòwthz/) *n* a loud and talkative person, especially a gossip or braggart (*informal*) —**loud·mouthed** /lówd mòwthd, -mòwtht/ *adj*

loud·ness /lówdnəss/ *n* **1.** DEGREE OF SOUND VOLUME the degree of volume of sound **2.** PHYS VOLUME PERCEIVED BY EAR the magnitude of the physiological effect produced when a sound stimulates the ear **3.** MUSIC RELATIVE LEVEL OF BASS TO TREBLE the relative level of bass to treble in high-fidelity equipment that is adjusted depending on the overall volume level

Lou·don·ville /lówd'n vìl/ town in Albany County, eastern New York, situated directly north of Albany. Population: 10,822 (1996).

loud ped·al *n* MUSIC same as **sustaining pedal**

loud·speak·er /lòwd spéekər/ *n* an electronic or electromagnetic device used to convert electrical energy into sound energy, providing the audible sound in equipment such as televisions, radios, CD players, and public-address systems

loud·speak·er van *n UK* same as **sound truck**

Lou Geh·rig's dis·ease /lòo gérrigz-/ *n* MED same as **amyotrophic lateral sclerosis** [Mid-20C. After Henry Louis ("Lou") Gehrig (1903–41), US baseball player who died from it]

lough /lok, lawkh/ *n Ireland* **1.** same as **lake**[1] (sense 1) **2.** a long inlet of the sea [Pre-12C. Probably < Old Irish *loch* "lake"]

lou·ie /lóo ee/ *n* a left turn (*slang*)

lou·is /lóo ee/ (*plural same*) *n* MONEY same as **louis d'or** [Late 17C. Shortening]

Lou·is XIV /lóo ee/ (1638–1715) king of France. He was a strong military leader and patron of the arts whose long reign (1643–1715) saw a great strengthening of the monarchy. Known as **the Sun King**

"The function of kings consists primarily of using good sense, which always comes naturally and easily. Our work is sometimes less difficult than our amusements."
[Louis XIV, *Memoir for the Instruction of the Dauphin*; 1661]

Lou·is XV (1710–74) king of France. His weak leadership and despotic rule (1715–74) contributed to the crisis that led to the French Revolution.

Lou·is XVI (1754–93) king of France. Coming to the throne (1774) when France was impoverished, he was deposed during the French Revolution and executed.

Lou·is /lóo iss/, **Joe** (1914–81) US boxer. He was the world heavyweight champion from 1937 to 1949. Born **Barrow, Joseph Louis**, Known as **the Brown Bomber**

"Once that bell rings you're on your own. It's just you and the other guy."
[Joe Louis. Quoted in *A Hard Road to Glory*, Arthur Ashe; 1988]

Lou·is·bourg /lóo iss bùrg/ town on Cape Breton Island, eastern Nova Scotia, Canada. It is Canada's largest national historic site. Population: 1,265

lou·is d'or /lòo ee dáwr/ (*plural same*) *n* **1.** a former gold coin of France used from the 17th century to the Revolution **2.** a former gold coin worth 20 francs used in France after the Revolution [Mid-17C. < French, "louis of gold," after *Louis* XIII of France]

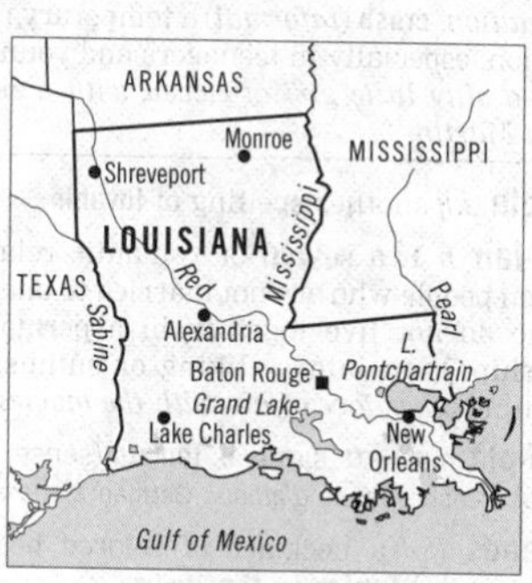

Louisiana

Lou·i·si·an·a /loo èezee ánnə/ state in the southern United States bordered by the Gulf of Mexico, Texas, Arkansas, and Mississippi. Capital: Baton Rouge. Population: 4,482,646 (2002 estimate). Area: 49,651 sq. mi./128,595 sq. km. —**Lou·i·si·an·an** *n, adj*

Lou·i·si·an·a French *n* the dialect spoken by the French-speaking descendants of the early French settlers of Louisiana —**Lou·i·si·an·a French** *adj*

Lou·i·si·an·a Pur·chase *n* territory of the western United States purchased from France in 1803. The largest single territorial addition ever made to the United States, it comprised 800,000 sq. mi./2,100,000 sq. km, extending from the Gulf of Mexico northward to the Canadian border and from the Mississippi River westward to the Rocky Mountains.

Lou·is Phi·lippe /lòo ee fə léep/ (1773–1850) king of France. Proclaimed king after the July Revolution (1830), he ruled as a constitutional monarch until the Revolution of 1848. Known as **the Citizen King**

Lou·is·ville /lóo i vìl, -ee vìl/ city in northern Kentucky, on the Ohio River at Kentucky's border with Indiana. The largest city in the state, it is the site of Churchill Downs, home of the Kentucky Derby. Population: 251,399 (2002 estimate).

lounge /lownj/ *n* **1.** PUBLIC ROOM FOR RELAXING a room in which people may relax or wait, e.g., in a public building such as a hotel or airport, or in a vehicle such as a ship **2.** LEISURE same as **cocktail lounge 3.** *UK* LIVING ROOM IN HOUSE a sitting or living room in a house **4.** BACKLESS COUCH WITH HEADREST a couch without a back but with a headrest at one end ■ *v* (**lounged, loung·ing, loung·es**) **1.** *vi* LIE OR SIT LAZILY to sit or act in a casual, relaxed way **2.** *vti* PASS TIME LAZILY to pass time in a relaxed or lazy way ○ *lounged the afternoon away* [Early 16C. Origin ?]

lounge bar *n UK* an area in a bar or hotel with more comfortable or elegant furnishings than the public area, and sometimes selling more expensive drinks

lounge car *n* RAIL same as **club car**

lounge liz·ard *n* **1.** a man who goes to places or events attended by the rich and famous, especially in order to approach wealthy women (*slang insult*) **2.** a frequent patron of cocktail lounges (*slang*) [Probably < the negative associations of reptiles]

loung·er /lównjər/ *n* **1.** an extendable chair or a lightweight, usually adjustable, couch designed to be comfortable for the user **2.** somebody who sits or walks in a casual relaxed way

lounge·wear /lównj wèr/ *n* clothing designed to be worn when relaxing, usually at home

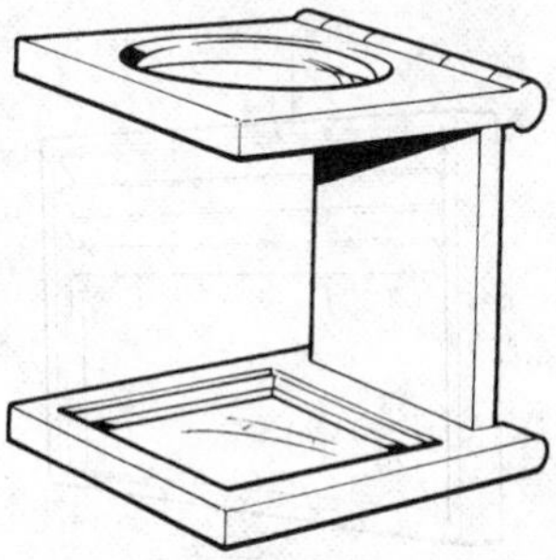

loupe

loupe /loop/ *n* a magnifying glass used especially by jewelers and watchmakers [Late 19C. < French, "flawed gem"]

loup-ga·rou /lòo gə róo, -gaa róo/ (*plural* **loups-ga·rous** /*pronunc. same*/) *n* same as **werewolf** (*dated*) [Late 16C. < French < Old French *leu* "wolf" (< Latin *lupus*) + *garoul* "werewolf" (< Germanic, "man-wolf")]

lour *vi, n* another spelling of **lower**[2]

Lourdes /loord, loordz/ town in southwestern France, famous for its Roman Catholic shrine. Population: 15,203 (1999).

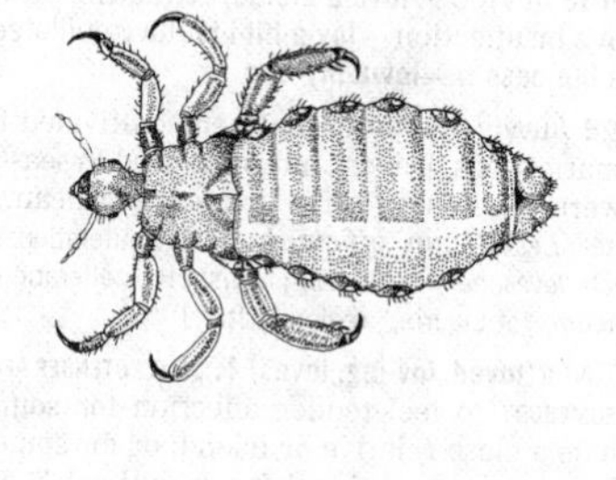

louse

louse /lowss/ (*plural* **lice** /līss/) *n* **1.** PARASITIC INSECT a small wingless insect that lives as a parasite on humans and other animals. There are sucking lice, e.g., head and body lice, and biting lice, e.g., bird lice. **2.** SMALL INVERTEBRATE ANIMAL a small invertebrate animal, e.g., a wood louse (*often used in combination*) **3.** (*plural* **lous·es**) OFFENSIVE TERM an offensive term that deliberately insults somebody's behavior and attitude toward others (*insult*) [Old English *lūs* < Indo-European]
louse up *vti* to mishandle a situation or task so that it is ruined (*informal*)

louse fly *n* a parasitic fly that clings to birds and mammals with its strong bristly legs and that is typically wingless. Family: Hippoboscidae.

louse·wort /lówss wùrt, -wàwrt/ *n* a plant of the snapdragon family with feathery leaves. Flowers: white, yellow, or pinkish purple, in spikes. Native to: northern regions. Genus: *Pedicularis*. [< the belief that sheep feeding on it became infested with lice]

lous·y /lówzee/ (**-i·er, -i·est**) *adj* **1.** LOUSE-INFESTED infested with lice **2.** INFERIOR inferior or second-rate (*informal*)

○ *lousy food* **3. UNPLEASANT** unpleasant or unacceptable (*informal*) ○ *a lousy way to treat somebody* **4. ILL** painful or in bad health (*informal*) ○ *I feel lousy today.* **5. HAVING LOT OF SOMETHING** having a large amount of something (*informal*) ○ *lousy with money* —**lous·i·ly** *adv* —**lous·i·ness** *n*

lout /lowt/ *n* an offensive term that deliberately insults the behavior and attitude of somebody, especially a young man (*insult*) [Mid-16C. Origin ?]

Louth /low*th*/ county in Leinster Province, the eastern Republic of Ireland. Population: 92,166 (2002). Area: 318 sq. mi./823 sq. km.

lout·ish /lówtish/ *adj* marked by crude and unpleasant behavior —**lout·ish·ly** *adv* —**lout·ish·ness** *n*

Lou·vain /loo váN/ city in central Belgium, near Brussels, famous for its old buildings and churches. Population: 88,245 (1999).

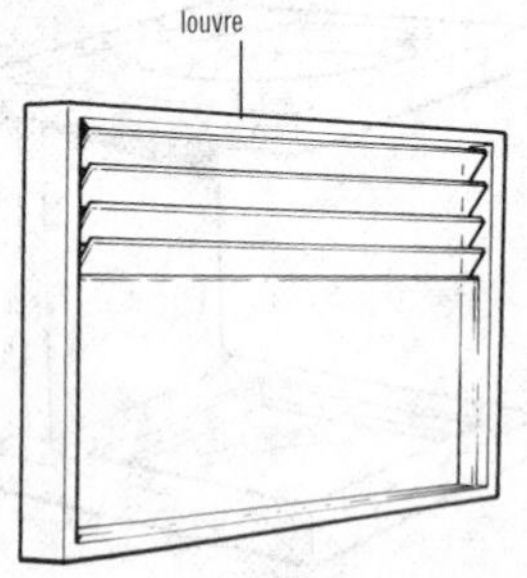

louver

lou·ver /loóvər/, **lou·vre** *n* **1. FRAME WITH HORIZONTAL SLATS** a frame on a door or window supporting spaced horizontal slats angled to admit air and light but not rain **2. SLAT IN FRAME** an individual slat in a louver **3. SLATTED OPENING** a slatted opening, generally for ventilation or cooling **4. ROOF STRUCTURE RELEASING SMOKE** a structure such as a lantern or turret on the roof of a building, especially a medieval building, that allows smoke to escape [14C. < Old French *lover* "skylight" < Germanic] —**lou·vered** *adj*

Louv·re /loóvrə, loóvər/ *n* a museum in Paris, France, that contains the national art collection, including such famous works as the *Mona Lisa* and *Venus de Milo*

lov·a·ble /lúvvəb'l/, **love·a·ble** *adj* attracting or worthy of love or affection —**lov·a·bil·i·ty** /lùvvə bíllətee/ *n* —**lov·a·ble·ness** *n* —**lov·a·bly** *adv*

lov·age /lúvvij/ *n* a perennial herb cultivated for its aromatic seeds, leaves, and roots used in seasoning. Flowers: greenish. Native to: Mediterranean. Latin name: *Levisticum officinale*. [14C. Alteration of Old French *levesche* < late Latin *levisticum*, alteration of *ligusticum*, "of Liguria," region in Italy]

love /luv/ *v* (**loved, lov·ing, loves**) **1.** *vti* **FEEL TENDER AFFECTION FOR SOMEBODY** to feel tender affection for somebody such as a close relative or friend, or for something such as a place, an ideal, or an animal **2.** *vti* **FEEL DESIRE FOR SOMEBODY** to feel romantic and sexual desire and longing for somebody **3.** *vt* **LIKE SOMETHING VERY MUCH** to like something, or like doing, something very much ○ *I love watching old movies on TV.* **4.** *vt* **SHOW KINDNESS TO SOMEBODY** to feel and show kindness and charity to somebody ○ *love your enemies* **5.** *vt* **HAVE SEX WITH SOMEBODY** to have sexual intercourse with somebody (*dated*) ■ *n* **1. PASSIONATE ATTRACTION AND DESIRE** a passionate feeling of romantic desire and sexual attraction **2. VERY STRONG AFFECTION** an intense feeling of tender affection and compassion ○ *Young children need unconditional love.* **3. ROMANTIC AFFAIR** a romantic affair, possibly sexual **4. SOMEBODY MUCH LOVED** somebody who is loved romantically or sexually ○ *He was her first real love.* **5. STRONG LIKING** a strong liking for or pleasure gained from something ○ *his love of music* **6. SOMETHING ELICITING ENTHUSIASM** something that elicits deep interest and enthusiasm in somebody ○ *Music was his greatest love but he also liked ballet.* **7. BELOVED** used as an affectionate word to somebody loved (*informal*) **8.** *UK* **TERM OF FRIENDLY ADDRESS** used as a friendly term of address, usually to a woman (*informal*) **9.** CHR **GOD'S LOVE FOR HUMANITY** in Christian belief, the mercy, grace, and charity shown by God to humanity **10.** CHR **WORSHIP OF GOD** in Christian belief, the worship and adoration of God **11.** SPORTS, LEISURE **SCORE OF ZERO** a score of zero in some sports and games, e.g., tennis, squash, and whist [Old English *lufian* (verb) < *lufu* (noun) < Indo-European, "to love"] ◇ **for love nor money** *or* **for love or money** used with a negative to indicate that something is quite impossible ○ *You can't get a cab after midnight for love nor money.*

SYNONYMS ***love, liking, affection, fondness, passion, infatuation, crush***

CORE MEANING: a strong positive feeling toward somebody or something

love an intense feeling of positive emotion toward, or enjoyment of, a person or thing, especially strong romantic or sexual feelings between people. ○ *When Lynn met Derek it was love at first sight.* ○ *He was mortally ill, but his strength of will and love of life were indomitable.* **liking** a feeling of enjoying something or or finding somebody or something pleasant ○ *He sipped his coffee, which was just to his liking.* ○ *She'd begun to develop a liking for Maurice.* **affection** fond or tender feelings toward somebody or something ○ *a man with a deep affection for the countryside* ○ *Fifteen-year-old boys don't usually welcome displays of affection.* **fondness** a feeling of affection or preference ○ *gazing with fondness at the two blond-headed little boys* ○ *He developed a fondness for music as a child.* **passion** intense or overpowering emotion, either love for somebody, usually of a strong sexual nature, or strong liking or enthusiasm for something ○ *Begun from sheer sexual passion, her marriage had quickly gone sour.* ○ *His great passion was mountaineering.* **infatuation** an intense but short-lived, often unrealistic love for somebody, usually of a romantic or sexual nature ○ *her infatuation with a young English poet* ○ *She had thought herself in love, but it had only been an infatuation.* **crush** (*informal*) a temporary romantic infatuation, especially in teenagers and young people ○ *I was a silly little girl of eleven with a schoolgirl crush on Martin.*

love·a·ble *adj* another spelling of **lovable**

love af·fair *n* **1.** a sexual or romantic relationship between people who are not married to one another or who do not live together in a permanent relationship **2.** an intense liking or enthusiasm for something ○ *her love affair with the movies*

love ap·ple *n* PLANTS same as **tomato** (sense 1) [Translation of French *pomme d'amour*, German *Liebesapfel*]

love beads *npl* a necklace of colored beads, first popular with hippies in the 1960s

love·bird /lúv bùrd/ *n* **1.** a lover, especially one who is publicly affectionate (*usually used in the plural*) **2.** a small greenish short-tailed parrot often kept as a cagebird, noted for close bonding and mutual preening between mates. Native to: Africa. Genus: *Agapornis*.

love·bite /lúv bìt/ *n UK* a small patch of bruised skin, often on the neck, caused by a partner's sucking kiss

Love Ca·nal /lúv-/ section of the city of Niagara Falls, western New York. It was evacuated in the 1970s because of toxic waste pollution.

love child *n* the child of parents who are not married to each other

Love·craft /lúv kràft/, **H. P.** (1890–1937) US writer. His horror and fantasy novels and short stories such as *The White Ship* (1919) and *The Rats in the Wall* (1923) became popular only after his death. Full name **Lovecraft, Howard Phillips**

> "The most merciful thing in the world, I think, is the inability of the human mind to correlate all its contents."
> [H. P. Lovecraft, *The Call of Cthulhu*; 1928]

loved one /lúvd-/ *n* a spouse, partner, or close family member (*often used in the plural*)

loved up *adj* feeling pleasurably empathic with and affectionate toward those around you (*informal*; *hyphenated when used before a noun*)

love feast *n* **1.** a meal held with the intention of stimulating goodwill **2.** a symbolic meal shared among Christians as a symbol of love and charity

love han·dles *npl* two regions of fat located at either side of the back just above the pelvis (*informal humorous*)

love-in *n* a relatively large gathering in which participants experience feelings of love and mutual support (*dated*)

love-in-a-mist *n* an annual flowering plant. Flowers: white or pale blue, surrounded by very fine bracts. Native to: Mediterranean. Latin name: *Nigella damascena*. [*Mist* < the mass of fine bracts that surrounds the flower]

~~**loveing**~~ incorrect spelling of **loving**

Love·joy /lúv jòy/, **Elijah Parish** (1802–37) US abolitionist and editor. He promoted the antislavery movement through the *Observer* newspaper, from 1833 until his murder in 1837.

love knot *n* a knot or bow of ribbon used to symbolize love

Love·lace /lúv làyss/, **Ada** (1815–52) British writer and mathematician. Her *Sketch of the Analytical Engine* (1843) was the best account until recent times of Babbage's computing machine and included the pioneering use of "programs." Full name **Lovelace, Augusta Ada, Countess of.** Born **Byron, Ada**

Love·land /lúvlənd/ city in Larimer County, northern Colorado, situated 12 mi./19 km south of Fort Collins. Population: 55,273 (2002 estimate).

love·less /lúvləss/ *adj* **1. EMPTY OF LOVE** devoid of feelings of love ○ *a loveless marriage* **2. NOT SHOWING LOVE** not exhibiting or giving love ○ *a loveless glance* **3. UNLOVED** not receiving love ○ *a loveless child* —**love·less·ness** *n*

love-lies-bleed·ing *n* **1.** a tropical plant. Flowers: small, red, in drooping clusters. Native to: South Asia, Africa, South America. Latin name: *Amaranthus candatus*. **2.** PLANTS same as **bleeding heart** (sense 1) [< the resemblance of the flowers to a flow of blood]

love life *n* the romantic or sexual relationships in somebody's life

love·lock /lúv lòk/ *n* a long lock of hair separated from the rest by a ribbon, worn forward over the shoulder in the 16th century, or worn on the forehead in later periods

love·lorn /lúv làwrn/ *adj* exceedingly unhappy because of unrequited love or difficulties with love

love·ly /lúvvlee/ *adj* (**-li·er, -li·est**) **1. BEAUTIFUL AND PLEASING** beautiful and pleasing, especially in a harmonious way ○ *a lovely view* **2. DELIGHTFUL** very enjoyable or pleasant ○ *We had a lovely time.* **3. CARING** loving or friendly and caring ○ *She's a lovely person.* **4. ATTRACTING LOVE** attracting or inspiring love in others ■ *n* (*plural* **-lies**) **SOMEBODY OR SOMETHING GOOD-LOOKING** an attractive or good-looking person or thing, especially a woman (*often used in the plural; sometimes considered offensive*) —**love·li·ness** *n*

SYNONYMS See ***good-looking***.

love·mak·ing /lúv màyking/ *n* **1.** sexual activity between lovers, especially sexual intercourse **2.** courtship or wooing (*dated*)

love match *n* a marriage based on love between the couple rather than economic or social considerations

love nest *n* a place where lovers can be together, e.g., a small apartment or secluded house (*informal*)

love po·tion *n* a drink that supposedly causes the person who consumes it to feel sexual desire for the person who gives it

lov·er /lúvvər/ *n* **1. SEXUAL PARTNER** somebody's sexual partner, especially if the two are not married to each other **2. SOMEBODY HAVING LOVE AFFAIR** either of two people involved in a love affair (*often used in the plural*) **3. SOMEBODY DEVOTED TO SOMETHING** somebody who is devoted to or adores a particular thing (*often used in combination*) ○ *opera-lovers* —**lov·er·ly** *adj, adv*

CULTURAL NOTE ***Lady Chatterley's Lover***, a novel (1928) by British writer D. H. Lawrence. Lawrence's last novel, it describes an aristocratic woman's search for love and sexual satisfaction after her husband is injured in war. The novel's notoriety, and the fact that the publishers of the first unexpurgated British edition were prosecuted for obscenity in 1960, has obscured its many qualities, including its insightful analysis of contemporary social and political values.

lov·er boy *n* an attractive young man, especially somebody's boyfriend or lover (*humorous*)

lov·er's knot *n* same as **love knot**

love·seat /lúv seet/ *n* a small sofa that seats two people

love·sick /lúv sìk/ *adj* listless or distracted because of love —**love·sick·ness** *n*

love tri·an·gle *n* same as **eternal triangle**

lov·ey /lúvvee/ (*plural* **-eys**) *n UK* used as an affectionate form of address, especially to a woman (*informal*)

lov·ey-dov·ey /-dúvvee/ *adj* showing affection in an excessive or excessively sentimental way (*informal*) [< pet forms of LOVE, DOVE[1]]

lov·ing /lúvving/ *adj* **1.** showing or feeling affection **2.** done with enjoyment and careful attention —**lov·ing·ly** *adv* —**lov·ing·ness** *n*

loving cup

lov·ing cup *n* **1.** an ornamental vessel with two handles awarded to the winner of a sports contest **2.** a large drinking vessel with two or more handles, sometimes passed between people at a banquet

lov·ing-kind·ness *n* tender compassion for other people

~~**lovly**~~ incorrect spelling of **lovely**

low[1] /lō/ *adj* **1.** CLOSE TO GROUND located close or closer than usual to the ground or the base of something ○ *The sinking sun was low in the sky.* **2.** WITHOUT GREAT HEIGHT relatively little in height between the top and bottom ○ *a low fence* **3.** BELOW AVERAGE below the average or expected degree, amount, or intensity ○ *The lowest rainfall in fourteen years.* **4.** CONTAINING SMALL AMOUNT having or containing a relatively small amount ○ *low in calories* **5.** WITH LITTLE MONETARY VALUE small in monetary value ○ *low prices* **6.** OF LITTLE IMPORTANCE having little importance or urgency ○ *low priority* **7.** NEAR DEPLETION approaching or near depletion ○ *We're low on supplies.* **8.** TURNED DOWN OR DIMMED adjusted so that there is less of something ○ *low lighting* **9.** QUIET at a quiet, soft, or hushed level ○ *a low murmur* **10.** DEEP IN PITCH with a relative pitch that is closer to bass than soprano sounds ○ *Her voice was gentle and low.* **11.** SMALL small or relatively small in degree ○ *a low risk* **12.** NEAR BOTTOM OF SCALE near the beginning or bottom of something measured on a scale ○ *The temperature was in the low 80s.* **13.** DISPIRITED melancholy, hopeless, or dispirited ○ *felt sad and low after the parting* **14.** LACKING PHYSICAL STRENGTH lacking in physical strength or vitality ○ *feeling low after her operation* **15.** SHOWING NECK AND CHEST cut to show more than usual of the wearer's neck and bosom ○ *a low neckline* **16.** LACKING STATUS lacking status or rank, or closer to the bottom of a class system **17.** UNPRINCIPLED without principles or morals **18.** VULGAR full of vulgarity or coarseness **19.** GEOG NEAR EQUATOR situated near to the equator **20.** BIOL NOT COMPLEX simple in organic structure **21.** PHON PRONOUNCED LOW IN MOUTH pronounced with the tongue lying low on the bottom of the mouth ○ *a low vowel* ■ *adv* **1.** IN LOW POSITION in or to a low position, state, degree, or level ○ *Turn the gas down low.* **2.** NEAR GROUND near or nearer to the ground ○ *flew low over the trees* **3.** WITH DEEP PITCH with a low or deep pitch ○ *Play it a half-step lower.* **4.** QUIETLY in a soft or quiet way **5.** AT SMALL PRICE at a low or small price ■ *n* **1.** SOMETHING LOW something, e.g., a position or degree, that is low ○ *Sales dropped to an all-time low.* **2.** UNHAPPY PERIOD an unhappy or unfortunate experience or period of somebody's life **3.** METEOROL BAD WEATHER REGION a region of low barometric pressure that results in bad weather [12C. < Old Norse *lágr*] —**low·ness** *n* ◇ **lay somebody low** to cause somebody to feel overcome or helpless, e.g., with illness or exhaustion (*usually passive*) ○ *laid low with flu*

SYNONYMS See *mean*[2].

low[2] /lō/ *vti* (**lowed, low·ing, lows**) to make a mooing sound ■ *n* a characteristic mooing sound made by a cow or similar animal [Old English *hlōwan* "bellow" < Indo-European, "shout"]

Low /low/, **Juliette** (1860–1927) US youth leader. She started the first United States troop of Girl Scouts in Savannah, Georgia (1912). Full name **Low, Juliette Magill Kinzie Gordon**

low·ball /lṓ bàwl/ (**-balled, -bal·ling, -balls**) *vti* to deliberately quote a price or estimate that is lower than the eventual cost [< *lowball*, game of draw poker in which the player with the lowest-ranking hand wins the pot]

low beam *n* the headlight beam of a road vehicle that illuminates the road near the vehicle

low blow *n* an unfair comment or blow (*informal*) [< an illegal blow in boxing]

low·born /lṓ bàwrn/ *adj* being of common rather than aristocratic parentage

low·boy /lṓ bòy/ *n* a low chest of drawers, often with cabriole legs, that is similar to the lower part of a highboy [Late 19C. After TALLBOY]

low·bred /lṓ brèd/ *adj* with a rude and vulgar manner (*insult*)

low·brow /lṓ bròw/ *adj* unsophisticated or trivial and not requiring intellectual effort to be understood or appreciated ■ *n* somebody considered to have unsophisticated or unintellectual tastes [Early 20C. After HIGHBROW]

low-cal /-kàl/, **low-cal·o·rie** *adj* with few calories or fewer calories than usual

Low Church *n* a branch of the Anglican Church that favors less ritual and ceremony and prefers an evangelical approach to services

low com·e·dy *n* comedy based on slapstick and coarse actions rather than more sophisticated forms of humor

Low Coun·tries /lṓ-/ region in Northwestern Europe, made up of Belgium, the Netherlands, and Luxembourg. Population: 26,016,000 (1995). Area: 28,550 sq. mi./73,943 sq. km.

low-cut *adj* describes a woman's garment with a low neckline that shows the top part of the chest and cleavage

low-den·si·ty *adj* having a low concentration of something in an area

low-den·si·ty lip·o·pro·tein *n* the lipoprotein that carries cholesterol to cells and tissue

low·down /lṓ dòwn/ *n* significant information about somebody or something, especially information that is not widely known (*informal*) ○ *gave me the lowdown on buying a used car* [Early 20C. < *low down* "very low" or *low-down* "contemptible"]

low-down *adj* (*informal*) **1.** mean and contemptible ○ *a low-down trick* **2.** very disheartened

low earth or·bit *n* an orbit that is nearer to Earth than a geostationary orbit

Low·ell /lṓ əl/ city in northeastern Massachusetts, at the junction of the Concord and Merrimack rivers. Population: 104,901 (2002 estimate).

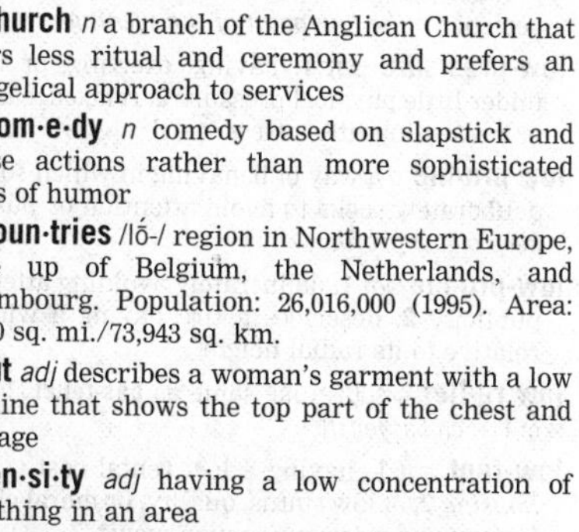

US Office of War Information

Amy Lawrence Lowell

Low·ell, Amy (1874–1925) US poet and critic. A leader of the imagist school, she wrote poems that exhibit a terseness of style and a use of free verse. Full name **Lowell, Amy Lawrence**

> "All books are either dreams or swords, / You can cut, you can drug, with words."
> [Amy Lowell, "Sword Blades and Poppy Seed"; 1914]

Low·ell, James Russell (1819–91) US magazine editor and diplomat. He edited the *Atlantic Monthly* (1857–61) and *North American Review* (1864–72) and campaigned against slavery.

> "Democracy gives every man a right to be his own oppressor."
> [James Russell Lowell, *The Bigelow Papers*; 1867]

Low·ell, Percival (1855–1916) US astronomer. He perceived what he thought were canals on Mars and claimed them as evidence of life there.

Low·ell, Robert (1917–77) US poet. A lyric poet with a concern for social issues, he won the Pulitzer Prize for *Lord Weary's Castle* (1946). Full name **Lowell, Robert Traill Spence, Jr.**

> "When the whale's viscera go and the roll / Of its corruption shall overrun this world, / Beyond tree-swept Nantucket and Wood's Hole / And Martha's Vineyard, Sailor, will your sword / Whistle and fall and sink into the fat?"
> [Robert Lowell, "The Quaker Graveyard in Nantucket," *Poems 1938–49*; 1950]

> "If we see light at the end of the tunnel, / It's the light of the oncoming train."
> [Robert Lowell, "Since 1939"; 1977]

low-end *adj* inexpensive compared to a group of similar products

low·er[1] /lṓ ər/ *adj* **1.** BELOW SOMETHING physically below another thing, especially one of the same type ○ *the lower lip* **2.** REDUCED OR LESS reduced or less in amount ○ *lower wages* **3.** CLOSER TO BOTTOM closer to the bottom or base of something ○ *the lower slopes* **4.** OF LESS IMPORTANCE of less importance or inferior status ○ *lower rank* **5.** GEOL EARLIER IN GEOLOGIC PERIOD relating to the earlier part of a geologic period or system **6.** ZOOL LESS ADVANCED DEVELOPMENTALLY describes organisms that are less advanced in terms of development or complexity ○ *a lower life form* **7.** FARTHER FROM SOURCE indicating that part of a river that is farthest away from the source ○ *the lower river* ■ *adv* SO AS TO BE BELOW to or at a lower position ■ *v* (**-ered, -er·ing, -ers**) **1.** *vt* BRING SOMETHING TO LOWER POSITION to move something down to a lower level or to move something downward ○ *lower the flag* **2.** *vti* REDUCE OR FALL to reduce something in quantity, quality, or value, or fall in quantity, quality, or value ○ *Interest rates have been lowered by the Federal Reserve Bank.* **3.** *vt* REDUCE SOMETHING IN DEGREE to reduce something in degree **4.** *vt* MOVE HEAD DOWNWARD to move the head or eyes downward **5.** **low·er your·self** *vr* HUMILIATE YOURSELF to reduce your dignity or the respect in which you are held ○ *I wouldn't lower myself to discuss it.* **6.** *vt* REDUCE VOLUME OF SOUND to reduce the volume of sound that something produces ○ *lower your voice* **7.** *vt* MUSIC REDUCE SOUND PITCH to bring a sound to a lower pitch **8.** *vt* PHON MODIFY VOWEL SOUND to change the sound of a vowel by pushing the tongue to the bottom of the mouth ■ *n* SOMETHING LOWER something that is the lower of two or more things [12C. Comparative of LOW[1]]

low·er[2] /lów ər, lowr/, **lour** *vi* (**-ered, -er·ing, -ers; loured, lour·ing, lours**) **1.** BE OVERCAST to be overcast and threatening storms or heavy rain **2.** LOOK ANGRY to look angry or sullen ■ *n* SCOWL a scowl or miserable look [13C. Origin ?] —**low·er·ing** *adj*

low·er bound *n* a number that is less than or equal to all the members of a set

Low·er Cal·i·for·ni·a /lṑ ər-/ ♦ **Baja California**

Low·er Can·a·da southern portion of present-day Quebec. It was a British province separate from Upper Canada from 1791 to 1840.

Low·er Car·bon·if·er·ous *n* GEOL same as **Mississippian** (sense 2)

low·er·case /lṑ ər káyss/ *n* SMALL LETTERS NOT CAPITALS the small rather than capital form of letters ○ *a striking ad printed entirely in lowercase* ■ *adj* NOT CAPITAL written or printed in small rather than capital form ○ *written with a lowercase "p"* ■ *vt* (**-cased, -cas·ing, -cas·es**) PUT SOMETHING IN SMALL LETTERS to put typescript or written material in lowercase form [Late 17C. Because types for small letters were kept in the lower of two type cases]

low·er cham·ber *n* GOV same as **lower house**

low·er class *n* the social group considered to occupy the lowest position in a hierarchical society, typically composed of manual workers and their families (*often used in the plural*) —**low·er-class** *adj*

low·er·class·man /lṓ ər klássmən/ (*plural* **-men** /-mən/) *n* EDUC same as **underclassman**

low·er ground floor *n UK* same as **basement**

low·er house *n* one of two legislative houses, generally more directly representative and larger than the other house

low·er·most /lṓər mṓst/ *adj* very lowest

low·er or·ders *npl UK* (*dated*) **1.** the lower classes of society **2.** people who belong to the lower orders

Low·er Pen·in·su·la southern part of Michigan, a peninsula between Lake Michigan and Lake Huron, separated from the Upper Peninsula of Michigan by the Straits of Mackinac

low·er world *n* in mythology, the dwelling place of the dead, often considered to be beneath the ground

low·est com·mon de·nom·i·na·tor /lṓ əst-/ *n* **1.** the mass of ordinary people, particularly when considered to have low critical standards and to lack taste **2.** *Can, UK* MATH same as **least common denominator**

low·est com·mon mul·ti·ple /lṓ əst-/ *n Can, UK* MATH same as **least common multiple**

low-fat *adj* prepared with a reduced amount of fat

low-fi *n* another spelling of **lo-fi** (*informal*) [Shortening]

low fre·quen·cy *n* a radio frequency ranging from 30 to 300 kilohertz

low gear *n* **1.** a gear such that the driven end of the drive shaft turns more slowly than the driving end, thus providing a relatively slow speed **2.** a state or period of little energy or activity

Low Ger·man *n* the German dialects that are spoken in northern Germany [Because spoken in the low-lying part of Germany]

low-grade *adj* **1.** bad or inferior in quality or grade **2.** describes a medical condition, especially a fever, that is mild and not serious

low-hang·ing fruit *n* a target that is easy to achieve, or a problem that is easy to solve ○ *Pick the low-hanging fruit first by identifying the most obvious opportunities.*

low-im·pact *adj* **1.** NOT STRENUOUS not requiring much energy or effort **2.** EASY ON ENVIRONMENT causing little or no damage to the surrounding environment **3.** EASY ON JOINTS describes exercise that involves little compression of the joints ○ *low-impact aerobics*

low-in·come *adj* having a relatively small income, or used by people on a relatively small income ○ *low-income families* ○ *low-income housing*

low-key, low-keyed *adj* **1.** restrained and understated in character ○ *a relatively low-key campaign* **2.** describes a photograph or painting made up of dark tones and containing few highlights

low·land /lṓlənd/ *n* land that is relatively flatter or lower than adjacent land —**low·land** *adj*

Low·land·er /lṓləndər/ *n* **1.** somebody who comes from the Scottish Lowlands **2.** somebody who comes from a lowland area

Low·lands /lṓləndz/ region of Scotland lying south of the Highlands —**Low·land** *adj*

low-lev·el *adj* **1.** situated or done at a low or lower than usual level ○ *low-level aircraft* **2.** relatively low in terms of importance, status, expertise, or intensity ○ *low-level talks*

low-lev·el lan·guage *n* a computer-oriented programming language, e.g., assembly language, in which instructions are in a code closer to machine code than to human language

low·life /lṓ līf/ (*plural* **-lifes** or **-lives** /-līvz/) *n* **1.** CRIMINAL a criminal, or somebody who associates with criminals (*informal*) **2.** SOMEBODY IMMORAL a disreputable and immoral person (*informal insult*) **3.** CRIMINAL OR IMMORAL PEOPLE people who are thought to have criminal tendencies or extremely low morals, regarded as a group (*informal insult*) —**low·life** *adj*

low·lights /lṓ līts/ *npl* strands of hair that are deliberately made darker than the rest of the hair —**low·light** *vt*

low·ly /lṓlee/ *adj* (**-li·er, -li·est**) **1.** LOW IN STATUS low in rank, status, or importance **2.** MEEK with a meek and humble way of behaving **3.** SIMPLE AND MODEST simple, plain, and modest in character ■ *adv* (**-li·er, -li·est**) **1.** IN MEEK WAY in a humble or meek way **2.** AT LOW VOLUME at a subdued pitch or volume —**low·li·ness** *n*

low-ly·ing *adj* at a lower level or closer to sea level than neighboring ground

low-main·te·nance *adj* requiring only a little attention or effort to maintain (*informal*) ○ *As clients go, they're pretty low-maintenance.*

Low Mass *n* a plain Mass celebrated in a Roman Catholic or Anglican church that is recited, not sung

low-mind·ed *adj* thinking or behaving in a coarse vulgar way —**low-mind·ed·ly** *adv* —**low-mind·ed·ness** *n*

low-necked *adj* cut to have a low neckline

low-paid *adj* receiving or offering relatively low wages, salary, or other remuneration

low-pass fil·ter *n* an electronic filter that blocks signals above a specific cutoff frequency but allows those below it to pass through unchanged

low-pitched *adj* **1.** low in pitch or tonal range ○ *a low-pitched hum* **2.** with a shallow slope ○ *a low-pitched roof*

low point *n* the least successful, enjoyable, or important part of a period of time, activity, or experience ○ *the low point of the evening*

low-pres·sure *adj* **1.** having, exerting, or working under little physical pressure **2.** relaxed, easygoing, or presenting little stress

low pro·file *n* a way of behaving in which somebody deliberately seeks to avoid attention or publicity ○ *keep a low profile*

low-pro·file *adj* **1.** deliberately avoiding attention or publicity **2.** describes a tire having a wide tread relative to its radial height

low re·lief *n* SCULPTURE same as **bas-relief** [Translation of French *bas-relief*]

low-rent *adj* **1.** having a low rental cost ○ *low-rent housing* **2.** of low status, quality, or moral character (*informal*) ○ *a low-rent action movie*

low-res *adj* COMPUT another spelling of **lo-res** (*informal*)

low-res·o·lu·tion *adj* relating to a device such as a computer screen or printer in which the text or pictures are not sharply defined

low rid·er *n* (*slang*) **1.** a car on which the springs have been shortened, so that the body of the car is closer to the ground than usual **2.** a driver of a low rider

low rise *n* a building consisting of only a few stories ■ *adj* describes pants, especially jeans, that sit low on the hips, usually revealing the navel [After HIGH-RISE] —**low-rise** *adj*

low road *n* activities that are immoral or contemptible

Low·ry /lówree/, **Malcolm** (1909–57) British writer and poet. He traveled extensively, and his most important work, *Under the Volcano* (1947), was inspired by his experience of living in Mexico. Full name **Lowry, Clarence Malcolm**. See Cultural note at **volcano**

low sea·son *n* the period of the year when resorts or travel operators are the least busy

low-slung *adj* closer to the ground or the floor than usual

low spir·its *npl* a state of unhappiness, hopelessness, or despondency ○ *The search party was in low spirits after three days.* —**low-spir·it·ed** *adj*

Low Sun·day *n* in the Christian calendar, the Sunday after Easter [Probably in contrast to the "high" feast of Easter Sunday]

low tech *n* same as **low technology** [Shortening] —**low-tech** *adj*

low tech·nol·o·gy *n* simple technology, especially that used to make basic items or perform basic tasks

low-ten·sion *adj* capable of carrying low voltage or operating under low-voltage conditions

low-test *adj* describes something that has low volatility and a high boiling point ○ *low-test gasoline*

low-tick·et *adj* moderately inexpensive (*informal*)

low tide *n* **1.** LOWEST TIDE LEVEL a tide at its lowest level **2.** TIME OF LOWEST TIDE the time of day when low tide occurs **3.** WORST POINT a lowest or worst point

low wa·ter *n* low tide, or the lowest level of water in a lake or river

low-wa·ter mark *n* **1.** a natural or artificial line marking a low-water mark **2.** a lowest or most difficult point

lox[1] /loks/ *n* smoked salmon [Mid-20C. Via Yiddish < German *Lachs* "salmon"]

lox[2] /loks/ *n* liquid oxygen, especially when used as an oxidizer for rocket fuel [Early 20C. < *l(iquid) o(xygen) (e)x(plosive)*; later interpreted as < *l(iquid) ox(ygen)*]

lox·o·ce·mus py·thon /lòksə seemәss-/ *n* a stout burrowing snake that is considered by many to be the only member of the python family in the Americas. Native to: Pacific coast of Mexico. Latin name: *Loxocemus bicolor*.

lox·o·drome /lóksə drōm/ *n* MAPS same as **rhumb line** (sense 1) [Late 19C. Back-formation < LOXODROMIC]

lox·o·drom·ic /lòksə drómmik/, **lox·o·drom·i·cal** /-drómmik'l/ *adj* relating to a map in which the rhumb lines appear straight, or to the rhumb lines on such a map [Late 17C. < French *loxodromique* < Greek *loxos* "oblique" + *dromos* "course"] —**lox·o·drom·i·cal·ly** *adv*

lox·o·drom·ic curve *n* MAPS same as **rhumb line** (sense 1)

loy·al /lóy əl/ *adj* **1.** remaining faithful to a country, person, ruler, government, or ideal **2.** expressing or relating to loyalty [Mid-16C. < French, modern form of Old French *loial*, variant of *leial* < Latin *legalis* (see LEGAL)] —**loy·al·ly** *adv* —**loy·al·ness** *n*

loy·al·ist /lóy əlist/ *n* a firm supporter of a country, ruler, or government —**loy·al·ism** *n*

Loy·al·ist *n* **1.** AMERICAN WHO SUPPORTED BRITISH an American who supported the British during the American Revolution **2.** SPANISH CIVIL WAR SUPPORTER OF GOVERNMENT a supporter of the republican government during the Spanish Civil War **3.** *UK* SUPPORTER OF ULSTER UNION WITH BRITAIN a Northern Ireland Protestant who wishes to continue Northern Ireland's political union with Britain —**Loy·al·ism** *n*

loy·al·ty /lóy əltee/ (*plural* **-ties**) *n* **1.** the quality or state of being loyal **2.** a feeling of devotion, duty, or attachment to somebody or something (*often used in the plural*) [14C. < Old French *loialté* < *loial* (see LOYAL)]

loy·al·ty card *n Can, UK* a card issued to customers by a supermarket or chain store allowing them to qualify for rewards or discounts if they continue to shop there. US term **fidelity card**

loz·enge /lózzənj/ *n* **1.** MEDICATED TABLET a medicated tablet that soothes the throat **2.** DIAMOND SHAPE a diamond-shaped figure **3.** DIAMOND-SHAPED IMAGE a diamond-shaped design or device on heraldic arms [14C. < Old French *losenge* "windowpane, small square cake"] —**loz·enged** *adj*

Lo·zi /lṓzee/ *n* a language of western Zambia, related to Sotho. Native speakers: 450,000. [Mid-20C. < Bantu] —**Lo·zi** *adj*

LP[1] *n* a long-playing phonograph record that turns at $33\frac{1}{3}$ revolutions per minute

LP[2] *abbr* low pressure

LPG *abbr* liquefied petroleum gas

LPGA *abbr* GOLF Ladies Professional Golf Association

L-plate *n* in the United Kingdom, a small white square sign bearing a red letter "L" displayed on vehicles driven by people who have not yet passed their driver's test. By law, such a sign must be displayed on the front and rear of any vehicle driven by a beginner. [*L* abbreviation of *learner*]

LPM, lpm *abbr* COMPUT lines per minute (*refers to computer printers*)

LPN, L.P.N. *abbr* MED licensed practical nurse

LPS *abbr* MICROBIOL lipopolysaccharide

lr *abbr* ONLINE Liberia (*used in Internet addresses*) See table at **domain name**

Lr *symbol* CHEM ELEM lawrencium

LR *abbr* BUILDINGS living room (*in advertisements*)

LRV *abbr* RAIL light rail vehicle

ls *abbr* ONLINE Lesotho (*used in Internet addresses*) See table at **domain name**

LSAT /él sàt/ *abbr* LAW, EDUC Law School Admissions Test

LSD *n* a hallucinogenic drug made from lysergic acid that was used experimentally as a medicine and is taken as an illegal drug [< German *L(yserg)s(äure)-D(iäthylamid)* "lysergic acid diethyl amide"]

LSI *abbr* ELECTRONICS large-scale integration

lt *abbr* ONLINE Lithuania (*used in Internet addresses*) See table at **domain name**

lt. *abbr* light

Lt., LT *abbr* MIL Lieutenant

l.t. *abbr* TIME local time

LTC *abbr* MIL Lieutenant Colonel

Lt. Col. *abbr* MIL Lieutenant Colonel

Lt. Comdr. *abbr* NAVY Lieutenant Commander

Ltd., ltd. *abbr* LAW limited (liability) (*used after the name of a British company*)

Lt. Gen. *abbr* MIL Lieutenant General

Lt. Gov. *abbr* POL Lieutenant Governor

LTJG *abbr* NAVY lieutenant junior grade

LTR *abbr* ONLINE long-term relationship

lu *abbr* ONLINE Luxembourg (*used in Internet addresses*) See table at **domain name**

Lu *symbol* CHEM ELEM lutetium

Lu·a·la·ba /lo͝o aa la͡a baa/ headstream of the Congo River in southeastern Democratic Republic of the Congo. Length: 1,100 mi./1,800 km.

Lu·an·da /loo ánda/ seaport and capital of Angola, situated in the northwestern part of the country, on the Atlantic Ocean. Population: 2,080,000 (1995).

lu·au /lo͞o ów/ *n* a Hawaiian feast, usually with music and entertainment [Mid-19C. < Hawaiian *lū'au*]

Lu·ba /lo͞obə/, **Lu·ba-Lu·lua** /-loo wa͡a/ *n* a group of Bantu languages or dialects of the southern Congo, around Kinshasa. Native speakers: 8 million. [Late 19C. < Bantu] —**Lu·ba** *adj*

lub·ber /lúbbər/ *n* **1.** a big person who is regarded as clumsy or unintelligent (*insult*) **2.** same as **landlubber** [14C. Origin ?] —**lub·ber·ly** *adj, adv*

lub·ber line *n* a mark on a ship's compass that indicates the vessel's heading

lub·ber's hole *n* a space in a platform around a mast, allowing a sailor to climb through the space and stand on the platform

lub·ber's line *n* NAUT same as **lubber line**

Lub·bock /lúbbək/ city and county seat of Lubbock County in north central Texas, situated in the eastern part of the Llano Estacado region, south of Amarillo. It is a manufacturing and commercial center. Population: 203,715 (2002 estimate).

lube /loob/ (*informal*) *n* same as **lubricant** (sense 1) ■ *vt* (**lubed, lub·ing, lubes**) to apply lubricant to something

Lü·beck /lo͞o bek/ port and city in Schleswig-Holstein State, north central Germany. Population: 216,854 (1997).

Lu·bitsch /lo͞obich/, **Ernst** (1892–1947) German-born US actor and movie director. He started making movies in Germany, then moved to Hollywood as a director of comedies and costume epics.

Lu·blin /lo͞oblin/ city in southeastern Poland, situated about 95 mi./153 km southeast of Warsaw. Population: 356,000 (1997).

lu·bri·cant /lo͞obrikənt/ *n* **1.** a substance, typically oil or grease, applied to a surface to reduce friction between moving parts **2.** somebody or something that eases or facilitates a solution to a potentially difficult or awkward situation —**lu·bri·cant** *adj*

lu·bri·cate /lo͞obri kàyt/ (**-cat·ed, -cat·ing, -cates**) *v* **1.** *vti* APPLY LUBRICANT to apply an oily or greasy substance to something in order to reduce friction to moving parts **2.** *vt* MAKE SOMETHING SLIPPERY to make something slippery **3.** *vt* MAKE SOMETHING RUN SMOOTHLY to make something run smoothly and without problems [Early 17C. < Latin *lubricat-*, past participle of *lubricare* < *lubricus* "slippery"] —**lu·bri·ca·tion** /lo͞obri káysh'n/ *n* —**lu·bri·ca·tion·al** *adj* —**lu·bri·ca·tive** *adj* —**lu·bri·ca·tor** *n*

lu·bri·cious /loo bríshəss/, **lu·bri·cous** /lo͞obrikəss/ *adj* (*literary*) **1.** lewd, obscene, or intended to be sexually exciting **2.** slippery or oily [Late 16C. < Latin *lubricus* "slippery"] —**lu·bri·cious·ly** *adv*

lu·bric·i·ty /loo bríssətee/ *n* behavior that is obscene or unchaste (*formal*) [15C. Directly or via French < late Latin *lubricitas* < Latin *lubricus* "slippery"]

lu·bri·cous *adj* same as **lubricious** (*literary*)

Lu·bum·ba·shi /lo͞obo͞om ba͡ashee/ industrial city and mining center in Shaba Administrative Region, southeastern Democratic Republic of the Congo. Population: 851,381 (1994). Former name **Elizabethville**

Lu·ca·ni·a, Mount /loo káynee ə/ mountain in the St. Elias Range, southwestern Yukon Territory, Canada, near the Alaskan border. Height: 17,146 ft./5,226 m.

lu·carne /loo ka͡arn/ *n* a dormer window [Mid-16C. Via French < Provençal *lucana*]

Lu·cas /lo͞okəss/, **George** (*b.* 1944) US movie director and producer. After making such successful movies as *American Graffiti* (1973) and *Star Wars* (1977), he built up a pioneering special effects company.

Lu·cas van Ley·den /-van líd'n/ (1494–1533) Dutch painter and engraver. One of the earliest painters of genre scenes, he also produced engravings of religious and allegorical subjects.

Luc·ca /lo͞okə/ historic city and capital of Lucca Province, Tuscany Region, north central Italy. Population: 81,862 (2001).

Luce /looss/, **Clare Boothe** (1903–87) US playwright, politician, and diplomat. Her three plays *The Women* (1936), *Kiss the Boys Goodbye* (1938), and *Margin for Error* (1939) were all noted for their dry wit and later filmed. She was ambassador to Italy (1953–56).

> "A great man is one sentence...and it is a sentence that has an active verb."
> [Clare Boothe Luce, recalled on her death, *Time*; October 19, 1987]

Luce, Henry Robinson (1898–1967) US editor and publisher. Among the magazines he founded were *Time* (1923), *Life* (1936), and *Sports Illustrated* (1954). He edited *Time* for more than 40 years.

> "The businessman makes money in America, typically by serving his fellow man in ways his fellow man wants to be served."
> [Henry Robinson Luce. Quoted in *The American Idea of Success*, Richard M. Huber; 1971]

Luce, Maximilien (1858–1941) French artist. A supporter of the anarchist movement and founder of the neoimpressionist school, he is best known for his industrial landscapes and paintings of Parisian street life.

lu·cent /lo͞oss'nt/ *adj* **1.** shining with a glowing light **2.** translucent or clear [15C. < Latin *lucent-*, present participle of *lucere* (see LUCID)] —**lu·cen·cy** *n* —**lu·cent·ly** *adv*

lu·cerne /loo súrn/ *n UK* PLANTS same as **alfalfa** [Mid-17C. Via French < modern Provençal *luzerno*, originally "glowworm" < Latin *lucerna* "lamp" < *lucere* (see LUCID)]

Lu·cerne /loo súrn/ city and capital of Lucerne Canton, central Switzerland. It is a tourist center. Population: 57,193 (1998).

Lu·cerne, Lake of lake and popular tourist region in central Switzerland. Area: 44 sq. mi./114 sq. km.

lu·cid /lo͞ossid/ *adj* **1.** RATIONAL rational, and mentally clear, especially only for a period between episodes of delirium or psychosis **2.** EASILY UNDERSTOOD clear and easily understood ○ *a lucid explanation* **3.** SHINING emitting light [Late 16C. < Latin *lucidus* < *lucere* "to shine" < *luc-* "light"] —**lu·cid·i·ty** /loo síddətee/ *n* —**lu·cid·ly** *adv* —**lu·cid·ness** *n*

Lu·cid /lo͞ossid/, **Shannon Wells** (*b.* 1943) US astronaut and biochemist. One of the first women astronauts from the United States, she flew on several space missions and spent 188 days on the Russian space station Mir.

lu·ci·fer /lo͞ossəfər/ *n* a friction match (*archaic*) [Mid-19C. < *lucifer match*, originally a brand name]

Lu·ci·fer /lo͞ossəfər/ *n* **1.** in Christianity, a rebellious archangel who is usually held to be the same as Satan **2.** the planet Venus appearing before sunrise as the morning star [Pre-12C. < Latin, "the planet Venus," literally "light-bearing" < *luc-* "light"]

lu·cif·er·ase /loo síffə ràyss, -ràyz/ *n* an enzyme that stimulates the oxidation of luciferin

lu·cif·er·in /loo síffərin/ *n* a substance in the cells of bioluminescent organisms that emits light on enzymatic oxidation

lu·cif·er·ous /loo síffərəss/ *adj* bringing or emitting light (*literary*)

Lu·ci·na /loo sínə/ *n* in Roman mythology, Juno in her capacity as goddess of childbirth

~~**lucious**~~ incorrect spelling of **luscious**

luck /luk/ *n* **1.** GOOD FORTUNE success that seems to happen by chance ○ *a stroke of luck* **2.** CHANCE the arbitrary distribution of events or outcomes ○ *a game of luck* **3.** EVENT DETERMINED BY CHANCE something that seems to happen by chance rather than as a logical consequence ○ *bad luck* **4.** FORTUNATE OR UNFORTUNATE EVENT something fortunate or unfortunate that happens to somebody, or a series of such events ○ *Just my luck!* **5.** SOMETHING BEARING LUCK an event, action, or object regarded as bringing good or bad luck ○ *It's said to be bad luck to walk under ladders.* [15C. Probably < Low German *luk*] ◇ **push your luck** to test how far you can go before running out of good fortune

luck into *vt* to obtain something desirable or experience something pleasurable by chance

luck out *vi* to be lucky enough to succeed by chance (*informal*)

luck·i·ly /lúkəlee/ *adv* as a result of or the occasion for good luck

luck·less /lúkləss/ *adj* without success or fortune —**luck·less·ly** *adv* —**luck·less·ness** *n*

Luck·now /lúk nòw/ capital of Uttar Pradesh state, northern India, situated in the Ganges valley, about 40 mi./64 km northeast of Kanpur. Population: 2,266,933 (2001).

luck·y /lúkee/ (**-i·er, -i·est**) *adj* **1.** FORTUNATE having success or advantage, especially when it is unexpected ○ *You were lucky not to be seriously injured.* **2.** BRINGING GOOD FORTUNE producing or bringing good fortune ○ *lucky charm* **3.** RESULTING FROM GOOD LUCK as a result of good luck ○ *lucky escape* —**luck·i·ness** *n*

SYNONYMS ***lucky, fortunate, happy, providential, serendipitous***

CORE MEANING: relating to advantage or good fortune

lucky having or producing success and advantage, especially when it is unexpected ○ *We were lucky to be born in prosperous times.* ○ *The ancient coins were a lucky find for the archaeologists.* **fortunate** happening as a result of good luck ○ *She was fortunate enough to win the prize.* **happy** resulting unexpectedly in something pleasant or welcome ○ *By happy coincidence my brother was there too.* **providential** so favorable that it seems determined by providence ○ *The firefighters' arrival was providential.* **serendipitous** favorable and happening entirely by chance ○ *Reading through the letters he made the serendipitous discovery of a small sketch of his great-great-grandmother.*

---

luck·y-bone *n* same as **wishbone** (*regional*)

REGIONAL NOTE See ***pulley bone.***

luck·y dip *n UK* a game in which somebody takes a prize out of a container which is filled with soft material such as sawdust or shredded paper and within which prizes are hidden

lu·cra·tive /lóokrətiv/ *adj* producing profit or wealth [15C. < Latin *lucrativus* < *lucrari* "to gain" < *lucrum* "gain"] —**lu·cra·tive·ly** *adv* —**lu·cra·tive·ness** *n*

lu·cre /lóokər/ *n* money, wealth, or profit (*dated or humorous*) ○ *filthy lucre* [14C. Directly or via French < Latin *lucrum* "gain"]

Lu·cre·tius /loo kreéshəss/ (94?–55 B.C.) Roman poet and philosopher. His *De Rerum Natura*, based on the theories of Democritus and Epicurus, expounds his materialist philosophy. Full name **Carus, Titus Lucretius**

"Nothing can be created out of nothing."
[Lucretius, *De Rerum Natura (On the Nature of Things)*; 1st century B.C.]

lu·cu·bra·tion /lóokyə bráysh'n/ *n* **1.** a written work resulting from prolonged study, often having a scholarly or pedantic style (*usually used in the plural*) **2.** long hard study, especially at night [Late 16C. < Latin *lucubration-* < *lucubrare* "compose at night" < *luc-* "light"] —**lu·cu·brate** /lóokyə bràyt/ *vi*

lu·cu·lent /lóokyələnt/ *adj* **1.** easy to understand **2.** shining or glowing [15C. < Latin *luculentus* < *luc-* "light"]

Lu·cul·lan /loo kúllən/ *adj* lavish or overindulgent, especially with regard to food [Mid-19C. < Latin *Lucullanus*, after Lucius Licinius LUCULLUS]

Lu·cul·lus /loo kúlləss/, **Lucius Licinius** (110?–56 B.C.) Roman general. A distinguished public career brought him great wealth. He was also a patron of artists and writers.

Lud·dite /lú dìt/ *n* **1.** an opponent of technological or industrial change **2.** a worker who was involved in protests in the United Kingdom in the 1810s against new factory methods of production and who favored traditional methods of work [Early 19C. Perhaps after Ned *Ludd*, 18C farm worker in Leicestershire, England, who destroyed machinery] —**Lud·dism** /lú dìzzəm/ *n* —**Lud·dite** *adj*

lu·dic /lóodik/ *adj* playful in a way that is spontaneous and without any particular purpose (*literary*) [Mid-20C. < French *ludique* < Latin *ludere* "to play" < *ludus* "game"]

lu·di·crous /lóodikrəss/ *adj* utterly ridiculous because of being absurd, incongruous, impractical, or unsuitable [Early 17C. < Latin *ludicrus* < *ludus* "play"] —**lu·di·crous·ly** *adv* —**lu·di·crous·ness** *n*

ORIGIN The Latin word *ludus* "play," from which ***ludicrous*** is derived, is also the source of English *allude, collude, delude, elude*, and *illusion*.

Lud·low /lúdlō/ town in southwestern Massachusetts, on the Chicopee River, directly northeast of Springfield and southwest of Worcester. Population: 21,678 (2002 estimate).

Lud·wigs·ha·fen /lóodvigs haàfən/ port in Rhineland-Palatinate State, southwestern Germany, situated on the western bank of the Rhine River, opposite Mannheim. Population: 167,883 (1997).

lu·es /lóo eez/ *n* MED same as **syphilis** [Mid-17C. < Latin, "plague"]

luff /luf/ *v* (**luffed, luff·ing, luffs**) **1.** *vt* **SAIL TOO CLOSE TO WIND** to bring a boat closer in to the wind, or sail too close to the wind, so that the sails flap **2.** *vi* **FLAP** to flap when a boat is in a position too close to the wind (*refers to a sail*) ■ *n* **SAIL'S FRONT EDGE** the front edge of a sail [12C. < Old French *lof*]

luf·fa *n* PLANTS another spelling of **loofa**

Luft·waf·fe /lóoft vaàfə/ *n* the German Air Force [Mid-20C. < German, "air weapon"]

lug[1] /lug/ *vt* (**lugged, lug·ging, lugs**) **1.** **PULL SOMETHING WITH EFFORT** to carry or pull something that is heavy or bulky, using great effort **2.** **INTRODUCE SOMETHING IRRELEVANTLY INTO DISCUSSION** to introduce irrelevant material into a discussion or conversation ■ *n* **ACT OF PULLING LOAD** the effort or action of pulling something very heavy [15C. Probably < N Germanic]

lug[2] /lug/ *n* **1.** **PROJECTING PART** a projecting part, especially one by which something can be moved, rotated, or supported **2.** **PROJECTION FOR ELECTRICAL CONTACT** a small metal projection to which an electrical conductor or wire may be attached, usually by soldering or using mechanical pressure **3.** **SMALL PROJECTION IMPROVING TRACTION** a small projection on a tire or shoe that helps provide traction **4.** **FRUIT OR VEGETABLE BOX** a box for vegetables or fruit **5.** **CLUMSY MAN** a man who is regarded as unintelligent or clumsy (*informal insult*) [14C. Probably < N Germanic]

lug[3] /lug/ *n* SAILING same as **lugsail** [Mid-19C. Shortening]

lug[4] /lug/ *n* ZOOL same as **lugworm** [Early 17C. Origin ?]

Lu·gan·da /loo gándə, -gaàndə/ *n* LANG same as **Ganda** [Late 19C. < Bantu] —**Lu·gan·da** *adj*

Lu·ga·no /loo gaànō/ town and tourist center in Ticino Canton, southern Switzerland. Population: 25,771 (1998).

Lu·ga·no, Lake lake in southern Switzerland and northern Italy. Area: 19 sq. mi./49 sq. km.

luge /loozh/ *n* a racing toboggan on which the riders lie on their backs with their feet pointing forward ■ *vi* (**luged, lug·ing, luges**) to race on a luge [Late 19C. Via Swiss French < medieval Latin *sludia*] —**lug·er** *n*

lug·gage /lúggij/ *n* suitcases, bags, and other items for carrying personal belongings during a journey (*often used before a noun*) ○ *the luggage compartment* [Late 16C. < LUG[1]]

lug·gage rack *n* **1.** *US* a frame attached to the top of a motor vehicle, used for carrying things, especially luggage ○ *The tent can go on the luggage rack.* Can term **roof rack 2.** an overhead frame in a train or bus for passengers to keep small items of luggage on

lug·gage van *n UK* RAIL same as **baggage car**

lug·ger /lúggər/ *n* a small boat for fishing or pleasure sailing that is rigged with a lugsail [Mid-18C. Origin ?]

lug nut *n* a large nut that screws onto a heavy bolt, especially one used to attach a wheel to a motor vehicle

Lu·go·si /loo gōssee/, **Bela** (1882–1956) Hungarian-born US actor. He starred in numerous horror movies, and was especially closely identified with the title role in *Dracula* (1931). Born **Blasko, Bela Ferenc Dezso**

lug·sail /lúgs'l, lúg sàyl/ *n* an irregularly shaped four-sided sail fixed to a beam that crosses the mast at an angle [Late 17C. Probably < LUG[3]]

lu·gu·bri·ous /loo góobree əss, lə-/ *adj* extremely mournful, sad, or gloomy [Early 17C. < Latin *lugubris* < *lugere* "mourn"] —**lu·gu·bri·ous·ly** *adv* —**lu·gu·bri·ous·ness** *n*

lug·worm /lúg wùrm/ *n* a segmented sea worm that burrows in sandy shores, has rows of tufted gills, and is often used as fishing bait. Genus: *Arenicola*. [Early 19C. < LUG[4]]

Lu·hansk /loo haánsk/, **Lu·hans'k** industrial city in eastern Ukraine. Population: 475,000 (1998).

Lu·kács /lóo kaàch/, **György** (1885–1971) Hungarian philosopher, critic, and politician. Marxist in thought, his work *History and Class Consciousness* (1923) attempts to combine socialism and humanism.

Luke /look/ *n* a book of the Bible, the third of the gospels in which the life and teachings of Jesus Christ are described, traditionally attributed to St. Luke. See table at **Bible**

Luke /look/, **St.** (*fl* A.D. 1st century) evangelist companion to St. Paul. Perhaps a physician, he was by tradition author of the biblical Acts of the Apostles and the third Gospel.

luke·warm /look wàwrm/ *adj* **1.** just slightly warm, especially when expected to be hot **2.** showing or having little enthusiasm, interest, support, or conviction [14C. < obsolete *luke* "lukewarm," origin ?] —**luke·warm·ly** *adv* —**luke·warm·ness** *n*

Luks /luks/, **George Benjamin** (1867–1933) US artist. A member of the artistic group called the Eight, he produced realistic paintings of urban deprivation.

Lu·la ♦ **Silva, Luis Inacio Lula da**

Lu·le·å /lóo lay ō/ seaport at the head of the Gulf of Bothnia, northern Sweden. Population: 71,238 (1997).

lull /lul/ *v* (**lulled, lull·ing, lulls**) **1.** *vt* **SOOTHE OR CALM SOMEBODY** to soothe or calm a person or animal, especially by using gentle sounds or motions **2.** *vt* **MAKE SOMEBODY FEEL SAFE** to give somebody a false sense of security so that an unpleasant situation takes the person by surprise ○ *They lulled us into thinking we still had time.* **3.** *vi* **BECOME CALM** to become calm or calmer ■ *n* **PERIOD OF CALM** a brief interval of calm or decreased activity [14C. Probably representing a sound made to soothe a child]

lull·a·by /lúllə bì/ *n* (*plural* **-bies**) **1.** **GENTLE SONG** a gentle song for soothing a child, especially into sleep **2.** **MUSIC FOR LULLABY** instrumental music in the style of a lullaby ■ *vt* (**-bied, -by·ing, -bies**) **SING LULLABY TO CHILD** to soothe a child with a lullaby [Mid-16C. < obsolete *lulla* "lullaby" < a sound made to soothe a child + *-by* as in BYE-BYE[2]]

Lul·ly /loo leé/, **Jean-Baptiste** (1633–87) Italian-born French composer. He wrote ballets and other musical entertainments for the court of Louis XIV of France.

lu·lu /lóo loo/ *n* a remarkable or outstanding person, object, or idea (*slang*) [Late 19C. Alteration of *looly* in *looliest looly of the loolies*, said in admiration, origin ?]

Lu·lu·a·bourg /lóo loo ə boorg/ former name for **Kananga**

lum·ba·go /lum báygō/ *n* pain in the lower or lumbar region of the back [Late 17C. < Latin < *lumbus* "loin"]

lum·bar /lúmbər, -baàr/ *adj* relating to or situated in the loins or the small of the back [Mid-17C. < medieval Latin *lumbaris* < Latin *lumbus* "loin"]

SPELLCHECK lumbar or **lumber**? Do not confuse the spelling of ***lumbar*** and ***lumber***, which sound similar. The adjective ***lumbar*** is used in medical expressions referring to the lower part of the back, as in *the lumbar vertebrae, a lumbar puncture*. ***Lumber*** is a noun meaning "logs sawed for use" or a verb meaning "to turn trees into lumber."

lum·bar punc·ture *n* the insertion of a needle between two lumbar vertebrae into the spinal cord in order to obtain a sample of cerebrospinal fluid for diagnosis or to introduce medication

Lum·bee /lúm bee/ *npl* a Native American people who lived in North Carolina but left 60 or 70 years ago, and whose descendants have now returned. There are currently 40,000 Lumbee.

lum·ber[1] /lúmbər/ *n* **1.** **LOGS SAWED FOR USE** trees that have been sawed and prepared for use in building, woodworking, or cabinetmaking **2.** *UK* **UNWANTED OBJECTS** large objects that are not being used and are stored out of sight ■ *v* (**-bered, -ber·ing, -bers**) **1.** *vti* **TURN TREES INTO LUMBER** to cut down the trees in a region and convert them into salable lumber **2.** *vt UK* **BURDEN SOMEBODY WITH SOMETHING** to burden somebody with something unpleasant or unwanted, especially a responsibility or a task (*informal*) **3.** *vt UK* **PILE THINGS TOGETHER** to pile things together haphazardly [Mid-16C. Origin ?] —**lum·ber·er** *n*

SPELLCHECK See ***lumbar***.

lum·ber[2] /lúmbər/ (**-bered, -ber·ing, -bers**) *vi* to move clumsily or heavily [14C. Origin ?]

lum·ber·jack /lúmbər jàk/ *n* **1.** a cutter and transporter of trees for lumber **2.** CLOTHING same as **lumberjacket** [Mid-19C. < JACK[1]]

lum·ber·jack·et /lúmbər jàkət/ (*plural* **-jack·ets** or **-jacks**) *n* a work jacket made from thick, warm material, usually brightly colored with a checked pattern [Mid-20C. < its being of a type worn by lumberjacks]

lum·ber·man /lúmbərmən/ (*plural* **-men** /-mən/) *n* **1.** a dealer in lumber **2.** FORESTRY same as **lumberjack** (sense 1)

lum·ber·yard /lúmbər yaàrd/ *n* a business that sells or stores lumber and sometimes other building materials

lu·men /lóomən/ (*plural* **-mens** or **-mi·na** /lóomənə/) *n* **1.** **UNIT OF LUMINOUS FLUX** the SI unit of luminous flux, equal to the amount of light crossing a unit area at a unit distance from a light source of luminous intensity of one candela. Symbol **lm 2.** **SPACE WITHIN TUBE** the space inside any tubular structure in the body such as an intestine, artery, or vein **3.** **CAVITY IN PLANT** the cavity within a plant cell wall [Late 19C. < Latin, "light, opening"]

Lu·met /loo mét/, **Sidney** (*b.* 1924) US actor, director, and screenwriter. Among his greatest successes are *Murder on the Orient Express* (1974), *Dog Day Afternoon* (1975), and *Network* (1976).

Lu·mière /lōō myér/, **Auguste** (1862–1954) and his brother **Louis** (1864–1948), French inventors. They invented the cinema camera and projector, and made the first film, *Workers Leaving the Lumière Factory* (1895).

lu·mi·nance /lóomənənss/ *n* **1.** the condition or quality of emitting or reflecting light. Symbol L **2.** a measure of the brightness of a surface, equal to the amount of luminous flux arriving at, passing through, or leaving a unit area of surface. It is measured in candelas per square meter. [Late 19C. < *luminant* "luminous" < Latin *luminant-*, present participle of *luminare* "illuminate" < *lumin-* "light"]

lu·mi·nar·i·a /lòomə nérree ə/ *n Southwest US* a small candle set inside a paper bag that has been weighted with sand, usually placed outdoors with others as a Christmas decoration [Mid-20C. Via Mexican Spanish < Spanish, "decorative light" < late Latin, "lamp," plural of *luminarium* (see LUMINARY)]

lu·mi·nar·y /lóomə nèrree/ *n* (*plural* **-ies**) **1.** EMINENT PERSON an eminent or famous person **2.** SUN, MOON, OR STAR an object, especially an astronomical one, that emits light (*literary*) ■ *adj* CHARACTERIZED BY LIGHT relating to or characterized by light [15C. Directly or via Old French *luminarie* < late Latin *luminarium* < Latin *lumin-* "light"]

lu·mi·nesce /lòomə néss/ (**-nesced, -nesc·ing, -nesc·es**) *vi* to emit light by phosphorescence, fluorescence, or bioluminescence [Late 19C. Back-formation < *luminescent* (see LUMINESCENCE)]

lu·mi·nes·cence /lòomə néss'nss/ *n* **1.** the emission of light produced by means other than heat (**incandescence**), e.g., by phosphorescence, fluorescence, or bioluminescence **2.** the light emitted by luminescence [Late 19C. < *luminescent* < Latin *lumin-* "light"] —**lu·mi·nes·cent** *adj*

lu·mi·nif·er·ous /lòomə nífərəss/ *adj* generating or giving off light [Early 19C. < Latin *lumin-* "light"]

lu·mi·nol /lóomi nàwl/ *n* a white crystalline compound. Use: chemical testing. Formula: $C_8H_7N_3O_2$. [Mid-20C. < Latin *lumin-* "light"]

lu·mi·nos·i·ty /lòomə nóssətee/ (*plural* **-ties**) *n* **1.** STATE OF BEING LUMINOUS the state or quality of being luminous **2.** ENERGY RADIATED BY ASTRONOMICAL OBJECT the energy radiated per second by an astronomical body. Symbol L **3.** STRENGTH OF LIGHT EMITTED the visual perception of the extent to which an object emits light **4.** SOMETHING LUMINOUS something that emits light

lu·mi·nous /lóomənəss/ *adj* **1.** LIGHT-EMITTING emitting or reflecting light **2.** BRIGHT startlingly bright ○ *luminous orange* **3.** ILLUMINATED brightly illuminated **4.** UNDERSTANDABLE clear and easy to understand **5.** INSPIRING enlightened and inspiring **6.** PHYS RELATING TO LIGHT evaluated on the basis of the visual sensation produced in an observer rather than energy measurements [15C. Directly or via French < Latin *luminosus* < *lumin-* "light, opening"] —**lu·mi·nous·ly** *adv* —**lu·mi·nous·ness** *n*

lu·mi·nous en·er·gy *n* the total amount of light emitted by a source. Symbol Q_v

lu·mi·nous flux *n* the rate of emission of light evaluated by the visual sensation it produces. Symbol Φ_v

lu·mi·nous in·ten·si·ty *n* the amount of light emitted by a source in a particular direction. Symbol I_v

lum·mox /lúmməks/ *n* somebody considered clumsy or unintelligent (*informal insult*) [Early 19C. Origin ?]

lump[1] /lump/ *n* **1.** SOLID CHUNK a small irregularly shaped solid mass or piece **2.** TUMOR a tumor or other swelling in the body **3.** SUGAR CUBE a small cube of solid sugar **4.** LARGE AND CLUMSY PERSON somebody regarded as large and unintelligent or clumsy (*informal insult*) ■ **lumps** *npl* HARDSHIP harsh, often undeserved, criticism, punishment, or hardship (*informal*) ○ *You have to take your lumps like everyone else.* ■ *v* (**lumped, lump·ing, lumps**) **1.** *vt* GROUP THINGS TOGETHER CARELESSLY to consider people, ideas, or objects as a single group, often without good reason ○ *All the students were lumped together as lazy.* **2.** *vi* MOVE HEAVILY to move in a heavy and clumsy manner ○ *He lumped along.* ■ *adj* IN LUMPS in small cubes or lumps ○ *lump sugar* [14C. Origin ?] ◇ **take** *or* **get your lumps** to get or endure difficult experiences, often undeserved, such as hardship, punishment, and physical blows (*informal*)

lump[2] /lump/ (**lumped, lump·ing, lumps**) *vt* to endure something unpleasant that cannot be changed (*informal*) ○ *like it or lump it* [Late 16C. Origin ?]

lump·ec·to·my /lum péktəmee/ (*plural* **-mies**) *n* a surgical operation for breast cancer in which the surgery is limited to the removal of the visible and palpable tumor only [Late 20C. < LUMP[1]]

lum·pen /lúmpən, lóom-/ (*disapproving*) *adj* **1.** MARGINALIZED living, or regarded as living, on the margins of society **2.** NOT EDUCATED OR ENLIGHTENED stupidly content with a life regarded as intellectually empty and socially inferior ■ *npl* LUMPEN PEOPLE people regarded by others as lumpen (*takes a plural verb*) [Mid-20C. Back-formation < LUMPENPROLETARIAT]

lum·pen·pro·le·tar·i·at /lùmpən prōlə térree ət, lòom-/ *n* (*takes a singular or plural verb*) **1.** in Marxist analysis, people regarded as living on the margins of society, particularly criminals, homeless people, and the long-term unemployed **2.** people from the lowest social class who are regarded as too content with a life that is supposedly intellectually empty and socially inferior (*disapproving*) [Early 20C. < German < *Lumpen*, plural of *Lump* "ragamuffin" + French *prolétariat* (see PROLETARIAT)]

lump·fish /lúmp fìsh/ (*plural* **-fish·es** or *same*) *n* a northern ocean fish with a short scaleless body covered with rows of thorny lumps. Family: Cyclopteridae. [Early 17C. < Middle Dutch *lumpe* "cod"]

lump·ish /lúmpish/ *adj* **1.** tending to move awkwardly or slowly and heavily **2.** regarded as having no intelligence, energy, or enthusiasm (*insult*) —**lump·ish·ly** *adv* —**lump·ish·ness** *n*

lump·suck·er /lúmp sùkər/ *n* FISH same as **lumpfish** [Mid-18C. < obsolete *lump* "lumpfish" < Middle Low German *lumpen*, Middle Dutch *lumpe*]

lump sum *n* an amount of money that is given in a single payment, rather than being divided into smaller periodic payments

lump·y /lúmpee/ (**-i·er, -i·est**) *adj* **1.** WITH LUMPS having or filled with lumps, especially when lumps are unwanted, e.g., in the upholstery of a chair or the mattress of a bed **2.** LACKING SMOOTHNESS OF TEXTURE describes semiliquid foods such as sauces and soups that lack the normal appetizing smoothness of texture **3.** CUMBERSOME with a cumbersome quality or appearance **4.** CHOPPY having or exhibiting short choppy waves —**lump·i·ly** *adv* —**lump·i·ness** *n*

Lu·mum·ba /lōō móombə/, **Patrice** (1925–61) prime minister of the Republic of the Congo (now the Democratic Republic of the Congo). He was the first prime minister of the newly independent country (1960), but was overthrown in a military coup and assassinated the following year.

"Without dignity there is no liberty, without justice there is no dignity, and without independence there are no free men."
[Patrice Lumumba, *Letter to his wife, Congo, My Country*; 1962]

Lu·na /lóonə/ *n* In Roman mythology, the goddess of the Moon. Greek equivalent **Selene** [14C. < Latin, "moon"]

lu·na·cy /lóonəssee/ (*plural* **-cies**) *n* **1.** behavior that is regarded as unintelligent, inconsiderate, or misguided, or an example of it **2.** an offensive term for any psychiatric disorder that rendered patients legally incompetent and required them to be taken into care. This term has never been used by physicians in medical or psychiatric contexts. (*archaic*) [Mid-16C. < LUNATIC]

lu·na moth /lóonə-/ *n* a large moth that has spotted light-green wings with long thin extensions at the back that look like tails. Native to: North America. Latin name: *Actias luna.* [< Latin, "moon"; from the crescent-shaped spots on its wings]

lu·nar /lóonər/ *adj* **1.** RELATING TO MOON relating to a moon or its movement around a planet, especially the Moon in relation to Earth **2.** USED FOR TRAVEL TO MOON for use in space travel to or on the Moon **3.** CRESCENT-SHAPED in the shape of a crescent moon **4.** PALE pale and cold-looking, as the Moon is compared to the Sun [15C. < Latin *lunaris* < *luna* "moon"]

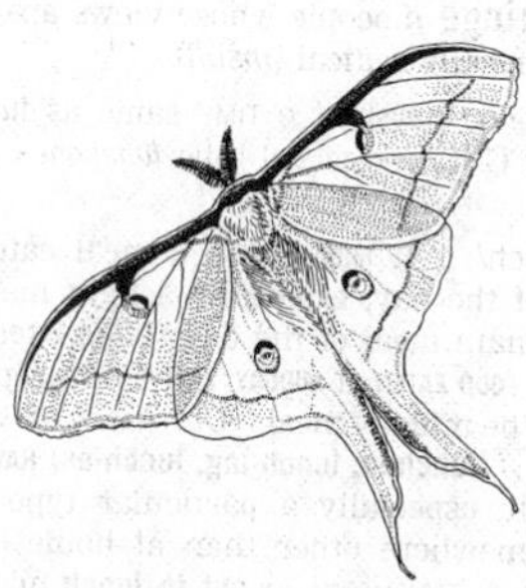

luna moth

UPI/Corbis-Bettmann

lunar: a lunar rover used by astronaut James Irwin on the moon (1971)

lu·nar caus·tic *n* silver nitrate, especially when formed into small sticks (*archaic*)

lu·nar cy·cle *n* a means of establishing a calendar that is based on the cycles of the moon. The Muslim calendar is based on the lunar cycle. It requires constant revision or intercalation, which the solar calendar does not.

lu·nar e·clipse *n* an eclipse of the Moon caused by Earth passing between the Sun and the Moon and casting its shadow on the Moon

lu·nar ex·cur·sion mod·ule *n* AEROSP same as **lunar module**

lu·nar·i·an /loo nérree ən/ *n* in mythology and science fiction, an inhabitant of the Moon [Early 18C. < Latin *lunaris* (see LUNAR)]

lu·nar mod·ule *n* a small spacecraft used to travel from an orbiting command module to the surface of the Moon and back

lu·nar month *n* **1.** the time between one new moon and the next, a period of about 29.5 days. It is the time the Moon takes to make one complete orbit of Earth. **2.** a period of four weeks

Lu·nar New Year *n* the Chinese New Year, which usually occurs at a point between late January and mid-February

lu·nar·scape /lóonər skàyp/ *n* a rugged barren landscape of strange rock formations, similar to the surface of the Moon

lu·nar year *n* a period of 12 lunar months

lu·nate /lóo nàyt/ *adj also* **lu·nat·ed** /lóo nàytəd/ shaped like a crescent moon ■ *n* ANAT same as **lunate bone** [Late 18C. < Latin *lunatus* < *luna* "moon"]

lu·nate bone *n* a bone of the wrist that articulates with the bones of the forearm [< its shape]

lu·nat·ed /lóo nàytəd/ *adj* same as **lunate**

lu·na·tic /lóonətik/ *adj* **1.** THOUGHTLESS considered thoughtless, ridiculous, or reckless **2.** OFFENSIVE TERM an offensive term meaning affected by a psychiatric disorder (*archaic*) ■ *n* **1.** IRRESPONSIBLE PERSON somebody considered wildly reckless (*informal insult*) **2.** OFFENSIVE TERM an offensive term for somebody who has a psychiatric disorder (*archaic*) [13C. Via French < late Latin *lunaticus* "moonstruck" < Latin *luna* "moon"]

lu·na·tic a·sy·lum *n* same as **asylum** (sense 3) (*offensive*)

lu·na·tic fringe *n* people whose views are regarded as eccentrically radical (*insult*)

lu·na·tion /loo náysh'n/ *n* TIME same as **lunar month** (sense 1) [14C. < medieval Latin *lunation-* < Latin *luna* "moon"]

lunch /lunch/ *n* **1. MIDDAY MEAL** a meal eaten in the middle of the day, especially a light meal that is not the main meal of the day (*often used before a noun*) **2. FOOD EATEN AT MIDDAY** the food prepared and eaten at the midday meal ○ *Our lunch was soup and salad.* ■ *vi* (**lunched, lunch·ing, lunch·es**) **HAVE LUNCH** to eat lunch, especially a particular type of lunch eaten somewhere other than at home [Early 19C. Shortening of LUNCHEON] ◇ **out to lunch** an offensive term that means displaying thoughtlessness or unusual behavior in a way that suggests a loss of touch with reality (*insult*)

CULTURAL NOTE ***The Naked Lunch***, a novel (1959) by William S. Burroughs. This controversial portrayal of drug abuse, written by Burroughs in Tunisia as he attempted to free himself of his own addiction, consists of a series of surreal episodes linked by themes and characters and described in language that is by turns clinical, hallucinatory, poetic, and scatological.

lunch·box /lúnch bòks/ *n* a container for sandwiches or other foods carried somewhere, e.g., to work, to eat for lunch

lunch count·er *n* a long counter where sandwiches and snacks are served and sold, especially at lunchtime

lunch·eon /lúnchən/ *n* **1.** FOOD same as **lunch** *n* (sense 1) (*formal*) **2.** an organized gathering in the middle of the day, with invited guests being served a meal and often offered some form of entertainment, e.g., a guest speaker [Mid-17C. Probably alteration of archaic *nuncheon* "snack" < NOON + obsolete *shench* "drink" < Old English *scenc* < Germanic]

lunch·eon·ette /lùnchə nét/ *n* a small fairly simple restaurant serving full lunch menus and snacks, and often breakfast

lunch·eon meat, **lunch·meat** /lúnch meet/ *n* processed meat, e.g., ham, sold in a loaf or sliced, and usually eaten cold

lunch·pail /lúnch pàyl/ *n* same as **lunchbox**

lunch·room /lúnch ròom, -ròom/ *n* **1.** a room in a school or office where people can buy lunch or eat a packed lunch **2.** same as **luncheonette**

lunch·time /lúnch tìm/ *n* the time, around the middle of the day, when lunch is usually eaten (*often used before a noun*)

Lund /lund/ historic city in southern Sweden, situated about 11 mi./18 km northeast of Malmö. Population: 97,638 (1998).

Lun·da /lóondə, lóon-/ *n* a Bantu language spoken in western central Africa, especially in Zaïre. Native speakers: 82,000. [Late 19C. < Bantu] —**Lun·da** *adj*

Lun·dy /lúndee/ island in southwestern England, lying in the Bristol Channel off the Devon coast. Area: 1.64 sq. mi./4.24 sq. km.

lune /loon/ *n* **1.** in geometry, a crescent-shaped area on the surface of a plane or sphere defined by two semicircles whose common end points are diametrically opposed **2.** CHR same as **lunette** (sense 6) [Early 18C. Via French < Latin *luna* "moon"]

Lü·ne·burg /lóonə bùrg/ city in Lower Saxony State, north central Germany. Population: 64,030 (1997).

Lu·nen·berg bump /lóonən burg-/ *n Can* in Nova Scotia, a jutting window on an upper floor of a multistory house [Named for *Lunenberg*, a city in Nova Scotia.]

lu·nette /loo nét/ *n* **1. CRESCENT-SHAPED OBJECT** any object that has a crescent shape **2. WINDOW IN DOMED CEILING** an arch-shaped window at the height of a domed ceiling **3. SEMICIRCULAR PANEL** a semicircular panel on a wall, containing a window, painting, or frieze **4. VEHICLE'S TOWING RING** a metal ring on a vehicle to which a rope can be attached for towing **5.** GEOG **CRESCENT-SHAPED MOUND OF SILT** a crescent-shaped mound of fine silt or clay similar in form to a sand dune, found especially near the edge of a temporary lake **6.** CHR **CONTAINER USED IN ROMAN CATHOLIC MASS** in the Roman Catholic Church, a crescent-shaped container in which the consecrated bread is placed during a Mass [Late 16C. < French, literally "little moon" < *lune* (see LUNE)]

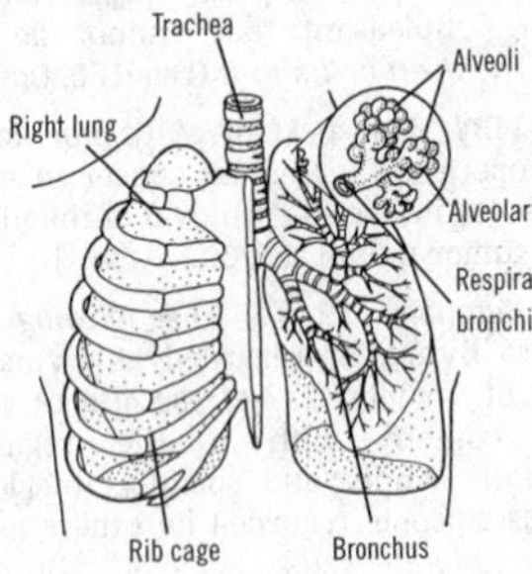

lung

lung /lung/ *n* **1.** in air-breathing vertebrate animals, either of the paired spongy respiratory organs, situated inside the rib cage, that transfer oxygen into the blood and remove carbon dioxide from it (*often used before a noun*) **2.** a respiratory organ found in invertebrate animals, especially the highly vascular region of the mantle cavity in some terrestrial snails [Old English, < Indo-European, "light"] —**lung·ful** *n* ◇ **at the top of your lungs** extremely loudly (*informal*)

lun·gan *n* BOT, FOOD same as **longan**

lunge /lunj/ *n* **1. SUDDEN FORWARD MOVEMENT** a sudden strong attacking movement forward **2. QUICK THRUST IN FENCING** in fencing, a sudden thrust made at an opponent ■ *vi* (**lunged, lung·ing, lung·es**) **1. MOVE SUDDENLY FORWARD THREATENINGLY** to make a sudden attacking movement, thrusting forward **2. MAKE QUICK THRUST IN FENCING** in fencing, to execute a sudden thrust at an opponent, especially with the sword or épée extended parallel to the floor [Mid-18C. Alteration of French *allonger* < Old French *alongier* "lengthen" < Latin *longus* "long"]

lung·fish /lúng fish/ (*plural* **-fish·es** or *same*) *n* a bony freshwater fish with one or two lungs for breathing air, as well as gills, that often becomes inactive during the dry season. Native to: swamps and pools in Australia, Africa, and South America. Order: Dipneusti.

lun·gi /lóong gee, lóonjee/, **lun·gyi** *n* a long piece of cloth, often brightly colored, traditionally worn like a skirt by men and women in Myanmar and as a loincloth by men in parts of South Asia [Early 17C. < Hindi *lungī*]

lung·worm /lúng wùrm/ *n* a parasitic nematode worm that inhabits the lungs of mammals and birds, sometimes causing coughs or respiratory distress

lung·wort /lúng wùrt, -wàwrt/ *n* **1. WOODLAND PLANT** a perennial woodland plant. Flowers: tubular, purple or blue, often pink as buds. Native to: Europe, Asia. Genus: *Pulmonaria*. **2. PLANT OF BORAGE FAMILY** a plant of the borage family. Flowers: blue, in dangling clusters. Native to: northern temperate regions. Genus: *Mertensia*. **3. LICHEN RESEMBLING LUNG TISSUE** a lichen that has a superficial resemblance to lung tissue and is dark green when wet and pale greenish brown when dry. It was used in the past to treat lung diseases. Latin name: *Lobaria pulmonaria*. [< the belief that such plants cured lung disorders]

lun·gyi *n* CLOTHING another spelling of **lungi**

lu·ni·so·lar /lòonee sólər/ *adj* relating to both the Sun and the Moon, especially to the gravitational pull of both the Sun and the Moon

lu·ni·ti·dal in·ter·val /lòoni tíd'l-/ *n* the time between the Moon's passing a given point and the next high tide at that point

lunk·er /lúngkər/ *n* something, especially a game fish, that is very big compared with others of the same type (*informal*) [Early 20C. Origin ?]

lunk·head /lúngk hèd/ *n* somebody considered to be unintelligent (*informal insult*) [Mid-19C. Probably alteration of LUMP[1]]

Lunt /lunt/, **Alfred** (1893–1977) US actor and director. Appearing in plays with his wife Lynn Fontanne, he enjoyed a successful career as a comedy actor. Full name **Lunt, Alfred David**

lu·nu·la /lóonyələ/ (*plural* **-lae** /-lee/), **lu·nule** /lóon yool/ *n* a semicircular mark, especially the white crescent-shaped area at the base of the fingernail (*technical*) [Late 16C. < Latin, "small moon" < *luna* "moon"] —**lu·nu·lar** *adj* —**lu·nu·late** /-làyt/ *adj*

Lu·o /lóo ò/ (*plural same* or **-os**) *n* **1.** a member of an African people who migrated from the Upper Nile Valley, founding a dynasty among Bantu-speaking people in the lake region of eastern Africa **2.** a Nilotic language spoken in parts of Kenya and Tanzania. Native speakers: 6 million. [Early 20C. < Luo] —**Lu·o** *adj*

Luo·yang /lwò yaáng/ city in Henan Province, northern China, situated on the Luo River. It alternated with Xi'an as the capital of ancient China, and after 1948 became a major industrial center. Population: 1,370,000 (1995).

lu·pine[1] /lóopən/, **lu·pin** *n* an annual or perennial plant with seeds in pods. Flowers: various colors, in tall spikes. Native to: northern hemisphere. Genus: *Lupinus*. [14C. < Latin *lupinus* (see LUPINE[2])]

lu·pine[2] /lóo pìn/ *adj* **1.** relating to a wolf or wolves **2.** wildly hungry or greedy in behavior or character [Mid-17C. < Latin *lupinus* < *lupus* "wolf"]

lu·pu·lin /lóopyəlin/ *n* a sticky yellow powder found in hop cones and containing the resins and essential oils that give beer its bitter taste. It was formerly used as a sedative. [Early 19C. < modern Latin *lupulus* < Latin, "hop plant," literally "little wolf" < *lupus* "wolf"]

lu·pus /lóopəss/ *n* MED **1.** same as **lupus erythematosus** **2.** same as **lupus vulgaris** [Late 16C. < Latin, "wolf"]

Lu·pus /lóopəss/ *n* a constellation of the southern hemisphere lying in the Milky Way, located between Scorpius and Centaurus. See illustration at **constellation**

lu·pus er·y·the·ma·to·sus /-èrrə theemə tóssəss, -themmə-/ *n* either of two inflammatory diseases affecting connective tissue, one largely confined to the skin, the other affecting the joints and internal organs [*Erythematosus* < modern Latin < Greek *eruthēma* (see ERYTHEMA)]

lu·pus vul·gar·is /-vul gérriss/ *n* tuberculosis of the skin in which reddish brown patches develop on the face, leading to tissue destruction and scarring [< modern Latin, "common lupus"]

lurch[1] /lurch/ *vi* (**lurched, lurch·ing, lurch·es**) **1. MOVE VIOLENTLY** to lean or pitch suddenly to one side **2. MOVE UNSTEADILY** to move along unsteadily, swaying from side to side ■ *n* **SUDDEN SIDEWAYS MOVEMENT** a sudden unbalanced movement to the side [Late 17C. Origin ?] —**lurch·ing·ly** *adv*

lurch[2] /lurch/ *n* in the card game cribbage, the state of being left with less than 30 points or half the winner's score at the end of a game [14C. Origin ?] ◇ **leave somebody in the lurch** to leave somebody in a difficult or embarrassing situation and offer no help

lurch·er /lúrchər/ *n* **1.** *UK* a long-limbed crossbred dog that has predominant greyhound features, especially one used by poachers for catching rabbits **2.** a petty thief or poacher (*archaic*) [Early 16C. < obsolete *lurch* "lurk," probably variant of LURK]

lure /loor/ *vt* (**lured, lur·ing, lures**) **1. ENTICE SOMEBODY** to persuade somebody to go somewhere or do something by offering something tempting **2. RECALL FALCON** to persuade a falcon to return by swinging a device in the air to attract its attention ■ *n* **1. SOMETHING THAT ENTICES** something that attracts or entices somebody to do something or go somewhere **2. ATTRACTION** the attractive or tempting quality that something has **3. DEVICE ATTRACTING FISH** a device attached to a fishing line to attract fish **4. DEVICE FOR RECALLING FALCON** a device swung through the air to attract or recall a falcon, usually a leather bag attached to the end of a line [13C. < Old French *luere* < Germanic] —**lur·er** *n*

Lur·ex /lóor èks/ *tdmk* a trademark for a plastic-coated metallic thread or fabric made from this

lur·gy /lúrgee/ *n UK* any illness or infection (*informal*) [Mid-20C. Origin ?]

Lu·ri·a /lóoree ə/, **Isaac ben Solomon** (1534–72) Palestinian mystic and scholar. He founded a school of Kabbalistic thought. Known as **The Lion**

Lu·ri·a /lóoree ə/, **Salvador** (1912–91) Italian-born US microbiologist. He shared the Nobel Prize in physiology or medicine (1969) for his research into virus reproduction. Full name **Luria, Salvador Edward**

lu·rid /lŏŏrid/ *adj* **1. HORRIFYING OR SHOCKING** sensational and shocking, with graphic details of horror, devastation, or violence **2. UNATTRACTIVELY BRIGHT** of a sickeningly intense brightness or boldness of color ○ *a lurid green* **3. GLOWING UNNATURALLY** glowing with an unnaturally vivid brightness **4. PALLID** with a pale sickly complexion [Mid-17C. < Latin *luridus* "pale yellow, ghastly"] —**lu·rid·ly** *adv* —**lu·rid·ness** *n*

Lu·rie /lŏŏree/, **Alison** (*b.* 1926) US novelist and scholar. Her best-known novel is *The War Between the Tates* (1974), which was made into a movie (1977). She won the Pulitzer Prize for fiction for the novel *Foreign Affairs* (1985).

lurk /lurk/ (**lurked, lurk·ing, lurks**) *vi* **1. MOVE OR WAIT FURTIVELY** to move about furtively, or wait in a concealed position or a shadowy corner, especially with the intention of doing something wrong ○ *a figure lurking in the bushes* **2. EXIST UNSUSPECTED** to exist as an unsuspected threat or danger **3.** ONLINE **READ BUT NOT SEND ONLINE MESSAGES** to read messages sent to an online discussion forum without contributing (*slang*) [13C. Probably < Low German or N Germanic] —**lurk·er** *n* —**lurk·ing** *adj*

Lu·sa·ka /loo saáka/ capital city of Zambia, situated in the south central part of the country, about 90 mi./145 km northeast of Kariba Dam, on the Zimbabwe border. Population: 1,640,000 (2000).

lus·cious /lúshəss/ *adj* **1. SWEET AND JUICY** with a rich, sweet, and juicy taste **2. ROMANTIC AND EMOTIONAL** written in a dramatic and romantic style with a strong appeal to the emotions and senses **3. DESIRABLE** very desirable physically, especially with a strong and direct sexual presence (*informal*) [14C. Alteration of obsolete *licious,* probably shortening of DELICIOUS] —**lus·cious·ly** *adv* —**lus·cious·ness** *n*

lush[1] /lush/ *adj* **1. GROWING VIGOROUSLY** producing a lot of vigorous rich young growth **2. WITH RICH TASTE** tasting rich, sweet, and juicy **3. LUXURIOUS** with luxurious decoration and furnishings **4. IN DRAMATIC STYLE** written in a dramatic style that is intended to produce an emotional response **5. SEXY** voluptuously sensual in appearance or behavior (*informal*) [15C. Probably alteration of obsolete *lash* "loose, weak," via Old French, "soft" < Latin *laxus* "loose"] —**lush·ly** *adv* —**lush·ness** *n*

lush[2] /lush/ (*slang*) *n* **1. HEAVY DRINKER** a drunkard **2. ALCOHOL** alcoholic drink ■ *vi* (**lushed, lush·ing, lush·es**) **DRINK HEAVILY** to drink too much alcohol regularly [Late 18C. Origin ?]

Lu·shun /lŏŏ shŏŏn/, **Lü·shun** town and seaport in Liaoning Province, northeastern China, situated opposite the northern coast of Shandong. Former name **Port Arthur**

Lu·si·ta·ni·a /lŏŏssi táynee ə/ ancient region and Roman province, corresponding approximately to present-day Portugal and the Spanish provinces of Salamanca and Cáceres —**Lu·si·ta·ni·an** *adj, n*

lust /lust/ *n* **1. SEXUAL DESIRE** the strong physical desire to have sex with somebody, usually without associated feelings of love or affection **2. EAGERNESS** great eagerness or enthusiasm for something ○ *a lust for power* ■ *vi* (**lust·ed, lust·ing, lusts**) **1. DESIRE SEXUALLY** to feel a strong desire to have sex with somebody **2. BE EAGER FOR SOMETHING** to have a very strong desire to obtain something [Old English, "pleasure, desire" < Indo-European, "be eager"] —**lust·ful** *adj* —**lust·ful·ly** *adv* —**lust·ful·ness** *n*

lus·ter /lústər/ *n* **1. SOFT SHEEN** a soft sheen of reflected light, especially from metal that has been polished gently **2. SHININESS** a bright and shiny condition or tone **3. SPLENDOR** the glory and magnificence of a great achievement **4. POLISH** polish or wax used to give something a shiny finish **5. CHANDELIER** a chandelier or candelabrum made of cut glass, designed to reflect the light **6. GLASS PENDANT ON CHANDELIER** any decorative piece of cut glass hanging from a chandelier **7. GLAZE ON POTTERY** an opalescent metallic glaze on pottery, especially porcelain **8.** MINERALS **LIGHT REFLECTED BY MINERAL** the quality and amount of light reflected from the surface of a mineral. This is one of the ways in which a mineral is defined, the highest degree of luster being splendent. **9.** TEXTILES **GLOSSY FABRIC** fabric with a sheen or glossy surface **10.** TIME same as **lustrum** (sense 1) (*formal*) ■ *vt* (**-tered, -ter·ing, -ters**) **1. IMPART GLOSSY FINISH TO SOMETHING** to impart a glossy finish or coating to something **2. GLORIFY SOMETHING** to give something a glorious or magnificent quality [Early 16C. < French *lustre* < Latin *lustrare* "brighten, purify by lustral rights" < *lustrum* "purification"]

lus·tra TIME, ANCIENT HIST plural of **lustrum** (*formal*)

lus·tral /lústrəl/ *adj* **1.** serving to purify the spirit, or relating to ceremonies of religious purification **2.** taking place once every five years [Mid-16C. < Latin *lustralis* < *lustrum* "purification"]

lus·trate /lú strayt/ (**-trat·ed, -trat·ing, -trates**) *vt* to make somebody or something spiritually pure by means of a special religious ceremony [Early 17C. < Latin *lustrat-,* past participle of *lustrare* (see LUSTER)] —**lus·tra·tion** /lu stráysh'n/ *n* —**lus·tra·tive** /lústrətiv/ *adj*

lus·tre *n, vt* Can, UK spelling of **luster**

lus·trous /lústrəss/ *adj* with a soft shine or gloss —**lus·trous·ly** *adv* —**lus·trous·ness** *n*

lus·trum /lústrəm/ (*plural* **-trums** or **-tra** /-trə/) *n* (*formal*) **1.** a period of five years **2.** purification of the entire ancient Roman people, which took place every five years after the census [Late 16C. < Latin, "purification"]

lust·y /lústee/ (**-i·er, -i·est**) *adj* **1. STRONG AND HEALTHY** in extremely good physical health, especially possessing great stamina and strength **2. ENERGETIC** full of energy, vitality, and enthusiasm **3. LUSTFUL** strongly desiring sex —**lust·i·ly** *adv* —**lust·i·ness** *n*

lu·sus na·tu·rae /lŏŏssəss nə tŏŏree/ (*plural same* or **lu·sus·es na·tu·rae**) *n* something that has developed in a typical way (*formal*) [< Latin, "sport of nature"]

lute

lute[1] /loot/ *n* a plucked musical instrument of the 14th to the 17th centuries resembling the guitar but with a flat, pear-shaped body [13C. Via Old French *lut* < Arabic *al-'ūd* "wood"]

lute[2] /loot/ *n* a substance, e.g., clay or cement, used in the construction industry for sealing apertures, joints, or porous surfaces ■ *vt* (**lut·ed, lut·ing, lutes**) to seal, pack, or coat something using lute [14C. Directly or via French < medieval Latin *lutum* < Latin, "mud, potter's clay"]

lu·te·al /lŏŏtee əl/ *adj* relating to the stage of the menstrual cycle between the formation of a yellow mass of tissue (**corpus luteum**) after the release of an ovum and the start of the next period [Early 20C. < Latin *luteus* "yellow"]

lu·te·fisk /lŏŏtə fisk/, **lut·fisk** /lŏŏt fisk/ *n* a Scandinavian dish of dried cod, preserved in potash lye, then skinned, boned, and boiled [Early 20C. < Norwegian < *lut* "lye" + *fisk* "fish"]

lu·te·in /lŏŏtee in, -teen/ *n* **1.** a yellow carotenoid pigment found in many plants and egg yolks **2.** a powdered preparation of the tissue (**corpus luteum**) formed after the release of an ovum [Mid-19C. < Latin *luteus* "yellow"]

lu·te·in·iz·ing hor·mone /lŏŏtee i nīzing-, lŏŏti-/ *n* a hormone released by the pituitary gland that causes the ovary to produce one or more eggs, secrete progesterone, and form the corpus luteum, and causes the testes to secrete male sex hormones

lu·te·in·iz·ing hor·mone-re·leas·ing hor·mone, lu·te·in·iz·ing hor·mone-re·leas·ing fac·tor *n* BIOCHEM same as **gonadotropic-releasing hormone**

lu·te·nist /lŏŏt'nist/ *n* somebody who plays a lute [Early 17C. < medieval Latin *lutanista* < *lutana* "lute"]

lu·te·o·lin /lŏŏtee ə lin/ *n* a yellow pigment found in some plants [Mid-19C. < French < modern Latin *luteola* < Latin *luteolus* "yellowish" < *luteus* "yellow"]

lu·te·ti·um /loo teéshee əm/ *n* a silvery white metallic element that belongs to the rare-earth group. Source: monazite. Use: catalyst in the nuclear industries. Symbol **Lu**. See table at **element** [Early 20C. < Latin *Lutetia* "Paris," native city of its discoverer, chemist Georges Urbain]

lut·fisk *n* FOOD another spelling of **lutefisk**

Lu·ther /lŏŏthər/, **Martin** (1483–1546) German theologian and religious reformer. His 95 theses against papal indulgences (1517) launched the Protestant Reformation.

> "I shall never be a heretic, I may err in dispute; but I do not wish to decide anything finally; on the other hand, I am not bound by the opinions of men."
> [Martin Luther, *Letter,* August 28, 1518]

Lu·ther·an /lŏŏthərən/ *n* a Christian who is a member of the Protestant church established by Martin Luther (**Lutheran Church**) ■ *adj* relating or belonging to Lutheranism

Lu·ther·an·ism /lŏŏthərə nìzzəm/ *n* the first form of Protestantism, founded by Martin Luther in 16th-century Germany. It focuses on the teachings of Jesus Christ and stresses individual faith over collective church authority. Spreading first through northern Europe, particularly Scandinavia, it now has adherents worldwide.

lu·thi·er /lŏŏtee ər/ *n* a maker and repairer of violins and other stringed instruments [Late 19C. < French < *luth* "lute" < Old French *lut* (see LUTE [1])]

lu·tist /lŏŏtist/ *n* MUSIC same as **lutenist**

Lu·ton /lŏŏt'n/ city in Bedfordshire, central England. Population: 184,371 (2001).

Lu·to·sław·ski /lŏŏtō slávskee/, **Witold** (1913–94) Polish composer and conductor. His use of the 12-tone system and of chance elements in his compositions produced works of considerable variety.

Lut·yens /lúttyənz/, **Sir Edwin** (1869–1944) British architect. He designed houses, gardens, and furniture, but his most monumental work is the layout and design of new public buildings for the new national capital at New Delhi, India (1912–31). Full name **Lutyens, Sir Edwin Landseer**

lutz /luts/ *n* a figure-skating jump from the back edge of one skate, landing on the back edge of the other, with one or more full rotations [Mid-20C. Probably after Gustave *Lussi* (1898–1993), Swiss figure skater and skating coach]

luv /luv/ *n* used as a written representation of "love," especially at the end of a message, in chat groups, or in e-mail or text messaging (*informal*)

Lu·wi·an /lŏŏ ee ən/ *n* an extinct Anatolian language belonging to Indo-European [Early 20C. Alteration of German *Luwisch* < *Luwia* "Luvia," region in Asia Minor] —**Lu·wi·an** *adj*

lux /luks/ (*plural* **lu·ces** /lŏŏ seez/) *n* the SI unit of illumination, equal to one lumen per square meter. Symbol **lx** [Late 19C. < Latin, "light"]

Lux. *abbr* Luxembourg

lux·ate /lúk sàyt/ (**-at·ed, -at·ing, -ates**) *vt* to displace the bones of a joint (*technical*) [Early 17C. < Latin *luxat-,* past participle of *luxare* < *luxus* "dislocated"] —**lux·a·tion** /luk sáysh'n/ *n*

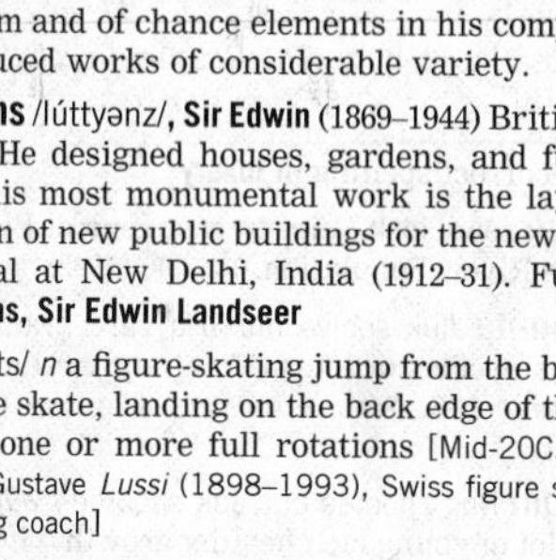

Luxembourg

Lux·em·bourg /lúksəm bùrg/ **1.** country in western Europe bordered by Belgium, Germany, and France. Language: French, German, Luxembourgish. Currency: Luxembourg franc. Capital: Luxembourg (City). Population: 454,157 (2003). Area: 998 sq. mi./2,586 sq. km. Official name **Grand Duchy of Luxembourg** 2. *also* **Lux·em·bourg City** capital of Luxembourg, in the south central part of the country. Population: 76,687 (2001). 3. largest and southernmost province of Belgium. Capital: Arlon. Population: 246,820 (2000). Area: 1,714 sq. mi./4,440 sq. km. —**Lux·em·bourg·er** *n*

Lux·em·bourg·ish /lúksəm bùrgish/ *n* the official language of Luxembourg, a form of German with many French features —**Lux·em·bourg·ish** *adj*

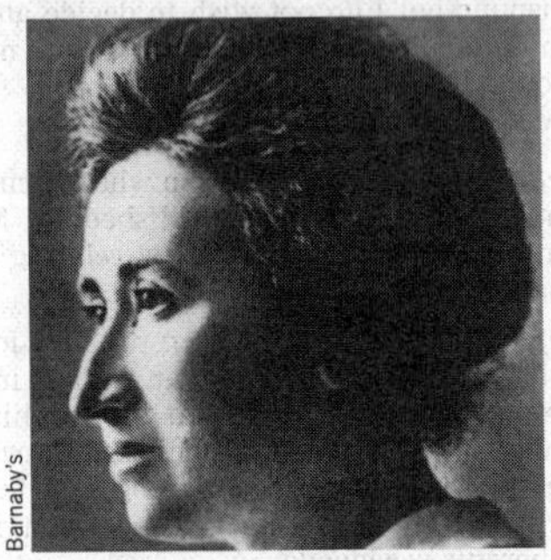

Rosa Luxemburg

Lux·em·burg /lúksəm bùrg/, **Rosa** (1871–1919) Polish-born German political activist. She cofounded the Spartacus League (1916), which became the German Communist Party. She was murdered by German soldiers.

"Freedom is always and exclusively the freedom for the one who thinks differently."
[Rosa Luxemburg, *The Russian Revolution*; 1918]

~~**luxery**~~ incorrect spelling of **luxury**

Lux·or /lúk sàwr, lóok-/ city in east central Egypt, on the Nile River. Population: 146,000 (1992).

lux·ul·yan·ite /luk sóolyə nìt/ *n* a rare granite that contains needles of tourmaline in quartz and feldspar [Late 19C. After *Luxullian*, village in Cornwall, England]

lux·u·ri·ant /lug zhóoree ənt, luk shóoree-/ *adj* 1. LUSH with a lot of young rich healthy growth ○ *luxuriant ground cover* 2. GROWING PROFUSELY growing thickly and profusely ○ *a luxuriant mane of dark curly hair* 3. ELABORATELY WRITTEN written in an elaborate, showy, and dramatic style 4. PRODUCTIVE producing vast quantities of something 5. LUXURIOUS of a luxurious rich character [Mid-16C. < Latin *luxuriant-*, present participle of *luxuriare* (see LUXURIATE)] —**lux·u·ri·ance** *n* —**lux·u·ri·ant·ly** *adv*

USAGE luxuriant or **luxurious**? Both these adjectives are related to the noun ***luxury***, but their meanings do not overlap. ***Luxuriant*** is used to describe something that grows in rich profusion, for example, hair or vegetation. ***Luxurious*** means "characterized by or suggestive of luxury," as in *a luxurious bedroom* or *a luxurious lifestyle*.

lux·u·ri·ate /lug zhóoree àyt, luk shóoree-/ (**-at·ed, -at·ing, -ates**) *vi* 1. to enjoy something in a self-indulgent way, taking great pleasure from the luxury and comfort that it offers 2. to grow vigorously and successfully [Early 17C. < Latin *luxuriat-*, past participle of *luxuriare* < *luxuria* (see LUXURY)]

lux·u·ri·ous /lug zhóoree əss, luk shóoree-/ *adj* 1. very comfortable, with high-quality expensive furnishings or fabrics 2. with a liking for luxury, or used to living in luxury —**lux·u·ri·ous·ly** *adv* —**lux·u·ri·ous·ness** *n*

USAGE See ***luxuriant***.

lux·u·ry /lúgzhəree, lúkshəree/ *n* (*plural* **-ries**) 1. GREAT COMFORT expensive high-quality surroundings, and the great comfort that they provide 2. NONESSENTIAL ITEM an item that is desirable but not essential, and often expensive or hard to get (*often used before a noun*) 3. PLEASURABLE SELF-INDULGENT ACTIVITY an activity that gives great pleasure, especially one only rarely indulged in ■ *adj* LUXURIOUS luxurious, or of the character of a luxury [14C. Via French < Latin *luxuria* "profusion, excess" < *luxus* "dislocated"]

Lu·zon /loo zón/ largest island in the Philippines, in the northern part of the country. Population: 30,759,000 (1990). Area: 40,421 sq. mi./104,690 sq. km.

lv *abbr* ONLINE Latvia (*used in Internet addresses*) See table at **domain name**

lv. *abbr* MIL leave

Lv. *abbr* BIBLE Leviticus

Lviv /lə víf/, **L'viv, Lvov** /lə vóf/ industrial city in western Ukraine, capital of L'viv Oblast. Population: 794,000 (1998).

LVN, L.V.N. *abbr* MED licensed vocational nurse

Lvov ♦ **Lviv**

lwei /lway/ (*plural* **lweis** or *same*) *n* a subunit of Angolan currency. See table at **currency** [Late 20C. < Bantu]

lx *symbol* PHYS lux

ly *abbr* ONLINE Libya (*used in Internet addresses*) See table at **domain name**

-ly *suffix* 1. like, having the characteristics of ○ *brotherly* ○ *kindly* 2. in a particular manner ○ *briefly* 3. recurring at a particular interval of time ○ *monthly* [< Old English *-līc* (adjective), *-līce* (adverb) < Indo-European, "body"]

USAGE See ***adverb***.

ly·ase /lī àyss, -àyz/ *n* an enzyme that catalyzes either the formation of a double bond, or the addition of a chemical group at a double bond [Mid-20C. < Greek *luein* "loosen"]

ly·can·thrope /líkən thròp, lī kán-/ *n* same as **werewolf** (*literary*) [Early 17C. Via modern Latin < Greek *lukanthrōpos* < *lukos* "wolf" + *anthrōpos* "human being"]

ly·can·thro·py /lī kánthrəpee/ *n* in horror stories and legends, the transformation of a person into a wolf

ly·ce·um /lī sée əm/ *n* 1. a building where concerts, lectures, and other public events take place (*usually used in names of buildings*) 2. an organization that arranges or sponsors public events and entertainment [Late 16C. Via Latin < Greek *Lukeion (gymnasion)*, school near Athens < *Lukeios*, epithet of Apollo]

ly·chee /léechee/, **li·tchi, li·chee** *n* 1. a small round fruit with a reddish skin, sweet whitish translucent pulp eaten fresh or dried, and a smooth hard seed 2. a tree of the soapberry family that produces lychees. Native to: southern China. Latin name: *Litchi chinensis*. [Late 16C. < Chinese *lìzhī*]

lych-gate /lích-/, **lich-gate** *n* a covered gateway into a churchyard. Traditionally, pallbearers would rest the coffin there before carrying it into the church. [15C. < Old English *līc* "body, corpse" < Germanic]

Ly·ci·a /líshee ə, líshə/ ancient region on the coast of southwestern Asia Minor —**Ly·ci·an** *n, adj*

ly·co·pene /líkə peen/ *n* a powerful antioxidant of the carotenoid group, found in tomatoes and used in many antioxidant dietary supplements [Mid-20C. < modern Latin *Lycopersicon* < Greek *lukos* "wolf" + *persikos* "peach"]

ly·co·po·di·um /lìkə pódee əm/ *n* 1. a plant that is a kind of club moss, with long branching stems covered in small leaves. It has small spore-carrying cones. Genus: *Lycopodium*. 2. a flammable powder, composed of spores of lycopodium and other club mosses. Use: formerly for coating for pills and suppositories, in fireworks, in foundry work. [Early 18C. < modern Latin < Greek *lukos* "wolf" + *pod-* "foot"; from its claw-shaped root]

Ly·cra /líkrə/ *tdmk* a trademark for a lightweight elastic polyurethane fiber, or a fabric made from this

lyd·dite /lí dìt/ *n* a powerful explosive consisting mainly of picric acid mixed with 10 percent nitrobenzene and 3 percent petroleum jelly. Use: in shells. [Late 19C. After *Lydd*, Kent, England, where first tested]

Lyd·i·a /líddee ə/ ancient country in present-day northwestern Turkey, on the Aegean Sea. It reached its peak of wealth in the 7th and 6th centuries B.C. before being conquered by Cyrus the Great of Persia about 546 B.C. —**Lyd·i·an** *adj, n*

Lyd·i·an mode *n* a scale of notes originating in ancient Greek music and consisting of the eight notes of the diatonic scale rising from F to F

lye /lī/ *n* a strong solution of sodium hydroxide or potassium hydroxide in water. Use: industrial drain and oven cleaners. [Old English *lēag* < Indo-European, "to wash"]

Lye·le /lyé lày/ *n* a language spoken in parts of Burkina Faso, belonging to the Gur branch of Niger-Congo. Native speakers: 60,000. —**Lye·le** *adj*

Ly·ell /lī əl/, **Sir Charles** (1797–1875) British geologist. His theories and research influenced the development of modern geology.

"Amidst the vicissitudes of the earth's surface, species cannot be immortal, but must perish, one after another, like the individuals which compose them. There is no possibility of escaping from this conclusion."
[Sir Charles Lyell, *Principles of Geology*; 1830–33]

ly·gus bug /lígəss-/ *n* a plant-eating insect that is especially common in North America, where it is a pest of cotton and other crops. Genus: *Lygus*. [Via modern Latin < Greek *lugos* "chaste tree, withy"]

ly·ing[1] present participle of **lie**[1]

ly·ing[2] present participle of **lie**[2]

ly·ing-in (*plural* **ly·ings-in**) *n* the period of time leading up to and immediately following childbirth, during which women used to be confined to bed (*archaic; often used before a noun*) [< LIE[1]]

Lyme dis·ease /līm-/ *n* an infectious bacterial disease transmitted by ticks, in which skin rash, fever, and headache precede arthritis and nervous disorder [Late 20C. After *Lyme*, Connecticut]

lyme grass *n* a perennial grass with broad bluish green leaves that is found on sand dunes. Native to: northern temperate regions. Latin name: *Elymus arenarius*. [Origin ?]

lymph /limf/ *n* a fluid containing white cells, chiefly lymphocytes, that is drained from tissue spaces by the vessels of the lymphatic system. It can transport bacteria, viruses, and cancer cells. [Late 17C. Directly or via French < Latin *lympha* "water"]

lymph- *prefix* same as **lympho-** (*used before vowels*)

lym·phad·e·nop·a·thy /lim fàdd'n óppəthee, lìmfəd'n-/ (*plural* **-thies**) *n* a disease, disorder, or enlargement of the lymph nodes

lym·phat·ic /lim fáttik/ *adj* 1. PHYSIOL RELATING TO LYMPH SYSTEM relating to lymph or the lymphatic system 2. SLUGGISH without any energy or enthusiasm (*archaic*) ■ *n* ANAT VESSEL TRANSPORTING LYMPH a vessel that transports or contains lymph

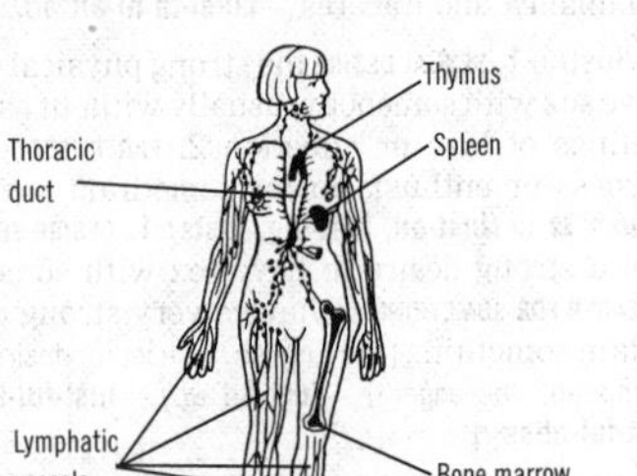

lymphatic system

lym·phat·ic sys·tem *n* a network of vessels that transport fluid, fats, proteins, and lymphocytes to the bloodstream as lymph, and remove microorganisms and other debris from tissues

lymph gland *n* ANAT same as **lymph node** (*not in technical use*)

lymph node *n* an oval body in the lymphatic system that produces and houses lymphocytes and filters microorganisms and other particles from lymph, thus reducing the risk of infection

lympho- *prefix* lymph, lymphocyte, lymphatic system ○ *lymphocytosis* [< LYMPH]

lym·pho·blast /límfə blàst/ *n* an immature cell that develops into a lymphocyte

lym·pho·blas·tic /lìmfə blástik/ *adj* relating to the production of lymphocytes

lym·pho·blas·tic leu·ke·mi·a *n* a disease in which there is great overproduction of immature lymphocytes

lym·pho·cyte /límfə sīt/ *n* an important cell class in the immune system that produces antibodies to attack infected and cancerous cells, and is responsible for rejecting foreign tissue —**lym·pho·cyt·ic** /lìmfə síttik/ *adj*

lym·pho·cy·to·sis /lìmfō sī tṓssiss/ *n* an increase in the number of lymphocytes in the bloodstream, occurring, e.g., in some persistent infections and forms of leukemia

lym·pho·gran·u·lo·ma ve·ne·re·um /lìmfō granyə lṓmə və neéree əm/ *n* a sexually transmitted disease caused by a bacterial infection, in which there is swelling of the genital lymph nodes and, especially in men, a genital ulcer [< modern Latin, "venereal granuloma of the lymph nodes"]

lym·phoid /lím fòyd/ *adj* relating to lymph, lymphatic tissue, or the lymphatic system

lym·pho·kine /límfə kīn/ *n* a soluble substance released by lymphocytes that influences other immune cells [Mid-20C. < LYMPHO- + Greek *kinein* "to move"]

lym·pho·ma /lim fṓmə/ (*plural* **-mas** or **-ma·ta** /-mətə/) *n* a malignant tumor originating in a lymph node, e.g., Hodgkin's disease or any of the range of cancers known as non-Hodgkin's lymphomas

lym·pho·poi·e·sis /lìmfō poy eéssiss/ *n* the production of lymphocytes, which occurs mainly in the bone marrow, thymus, lymph nodes, spleen, and tonsils —**lym·pho·poi·et·ic** /-éttik/ *adj*

lym·pho·trop·ic /lìmfō tróppik, -trṓpik/, **lym·pho·troph·ic** /lìmfō trṓfik/ *adj* stimulating or acting on the lymphatic system

lynch /linch/ (**lynched, lynch·ing, lynch·es**) *vt* to seize somebody believed to have committed a crime and put him or her to death immediately and without trial, usually by hanging [Early 19C. < LYNCH LAW] —**lynch·er** *n* —**lynch·ing** *n*

Lynch /linch/, **David** (*b.* 1946) US movie director. His distinctively bizarre and surreal work includes the movies *Eraserhead* (1977) and *Blue Velvet* (1986) and the cult television series *Twin Peaks* (1989–90).

Lynch, Thomas, Jr. (1749–79) American patriot. He signed the Declaration of Independence (1776), and was a member of the Continental Congress (1776–77).

Lynch·burg /línch bùrg/ city in central Virginia, on the James River. It is home to Randolph-Macon Woman's College and Lynchburg College. Population: 64,616 (2002 estimate).

lynch law *n* the condemnation and punishment of somebody by a mob or self-appointed group without a legal trial [Early 19C. After Capt. William *Lynch* (1724–1820), Virginian planter and justice of the peace]

lynch mob *n* a group of people who capture and hang somebody without legal arrest and trial, because they think the person has committed a crime

lynch·pin *n* ENG another spelling of **linchpin**

Lynn /lin/ industrial city in northeastern Massachusetts, on Massachusetts Bay. Population: 89,590 (2002 estimate).

Lynn·wood /lín wòōd/ city in Snohomish County, central Washington, on Puget Sound, 15 mi./24 km north of Seattle

Lyn·wood /lín wòōd/ city in Los Angeles County, southwestern California, on the Los Angeles River. Population: 71,387 (2002 estimate).

lynx

lynx /lingks/ (*plural same* or **lynx·es**) *n* a short-tailed cat with a lightly mottled yellowish to reddish brown coat and tufted ears. Native to: northern coniferous forests. Genus: *Lynx*. [14C. Via Latin < Greek *lugx*]

Lynx *n* a faint constellation of the northern hemisphere. See illustration at **constellation**

lynx-eyed *adj* with very good eyesight

lyo- *prefix* dissolution, dispersion ○ *lyophobic* [< Greek *luein* "loosen, dissolve"]

ly·ol·y·sis /lī óllәssiss/ *n* the reaction of a salt with a solvent to form an acid and a base

Ly·on /lī́ ən/ another spelling of **Lyons**

Ly·on, Mary Mason (1797–1849) US educator. She pioneered higher education for women, founding the Mount Holyoke Female Seminary (1837), which became Mount Holyoke College (1893).

Ly·on·nais /lee ənáy/ historic region of France, comprising the present-day Loire and Rhône departments

ly·on·naise /lī́ ə náyz, leè ə néz/ *adj* cooked with onions, or containing fried onions [Early 19C. < French (*à la*) *lyonnaise* "in the manner of Lyons"]

Ly·ons /lee óN/, **Ly·on** city in east central France, capital of the Rhône Department and the Rhône-Alpes Region. Population: 445,452 (1999).

ly·o·phil·ic /lī̀ ə fíllik/ *adj* describes a finely dispersed solid (**colloid**) that forms a stable dispersion

ly·oph·i·lize /lī óffə līz/ (**-lized, -liz·ing, -liz·es**) *vt* same as **freeze-dry** (*technical*) —**ly·oph·i·li·za·tion** /lī òffəli záysh'n/ *n* —**ly·oph·i·liz·er** *n*

ly·o·pho·bic /lī̀ ə fṓbik/ *adj* describes a finely dispersed solid (**colloid**) that forms an unstable dispersion

Ly·ra /lī́rə/ *n* a small prominent constellation of the northern hemisphere between Cygnus and Hercules. It contains a very bright star (**Vega**) and a planetary nebula (**Ring Nebula**). See illustration at **constellation**

ly·rate /lī́ ràyt, lī́rət/ *adj* **1.** in the shape of a lyre **2.** describes a leaf that has a broad rounded apex and small lateral lobes at the base [Mid-18C. < Latin *lyra* (see LYRE)]

lyre

lyre /līr/ *n* a plucked string instrument associated with ancient Greece and consisting of a U-shaped frame with a crossbar from which the strings stretch down to the soundbox [12C. Via French < Latin *lyra* < Greek *lura*]

lyre·bird /līr bùrd/ *n* a ground-dwelling bird, the male of which has long tail feathers that form into the shape of a lyre during courtship. Native to: mountain forests of southeastern Australia. Family: Menuridae.

lyr·ic /lírrik/ *adj* **1.** EXPRESSING PERSONAL FEELINGS relating to poetry that often has a musical quality and expresses personal emotions or thoughts ○ *a lyric poet* **2.** WITH LIGHTNESS OF VOICE singing with a voice that has a light quality and a vocally undramatic delivery ○ *a lyric tenor* **3.** WITH LIGHTNESS OF MUSICAL QUALITY having or played with a light smooth nondramatic quality that suggests singing **4.** RELATING TO LYRE relating to or written for the lyre, or for accompaniment by the lyre ■ *n* **1.** SONG WORDS the words of a song, especially a popular song (*often used in the plural*) **2.** SHORT PERSONAL POEM a short poem expressing personal feelings or thoughts [Late 16C. Via French < Greek *lurikos* "singing to the lyre" < *lura* "lyre"]

lyr·i·cal /lírrik'l/ *adj* **1.** wildly enthusiastic and emotional about something ○ *critics waxing lyrical about the new exhibition* **2.** LITERAT, MUSIC same as **lyric** *adj* (senses 1–3) —**lyr·i·cal·ly** *adv*

lyr·i·cism /lírrə sìzzəm/ *n* **1.** a lyric style in poetry or music **2.** emotional and enthusiastic expression of feelings or opinions

lyr·i·cist /lírrəsist/ *n* **1.** a writer of words for songs, especially popular songs **2.** a writer of lyric poems

lyr·ist /lírrist/ *n* **1.** somebody who plays a lyre **2.** MUSIC same as **lyricist** (sense 1) [Mid-17C. Via Latin *lyrista* < Greek *luristēs* < *lura* "lyre"]

lys- *prefix* same as **lyso-** (*used before vowels*)

lyse /līss, līz/ (**lysed, lys·ing, lys·es**) *vti* to undergo destruction by disruption of the bounding membrane (**lysis**), or cause cells to undergo this process [Early 20C. Back-formation < LYSIS]

Ly·sen·ko /li séngkō/, **Trofim Denisovich** (1898–1976) Russian geneticist and agronomist. As director of the Institute of Genetics of the Soviet Academy of Sciences (1940–65), he propounded the erroneous belief that acquired characteristics can be inherited.

Ly·sen·ko·ism /lī séngkō ìzzəm/ *n* a biological doctrine, presented by Trofim Denisovich Lysenko in the 1930s, maintaining that environmental characteristics acquired by an organism during its lifetime can be inherited by its offspring

ly·ser·gic ac·id /li sùrjik-, lī-/ *n* a crystalline acid, soluble in most organic solvents. Source: ergot fungus. Formula: $C_{16}H_{16}N_2O_2$. [< LYSO- + ERGOT]

ly·ser·gic ac·id di·eth·yl·am·ide *n* DRUGS full form of **LSD**

ly·sin /lī́ssin/ *n* an agent, e.g., an enzyme or antibody, that is able to destroy cells by disruption of the bounding membrane (**lysis**) [Early 20C. < LYSIS]

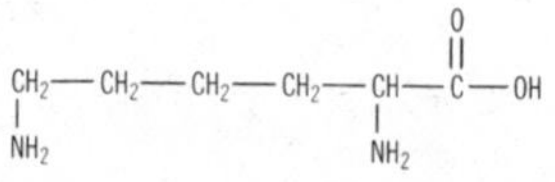

lysine

ly·sine /lī́ seèn, lī́ssin/ *n* an essential amino acid that is a constituent of most proteins. Formula: $C_6H_{14}N_2O_2$. [Late 19C. < German *Lysin* < Greek *lusis* "loosening" (see LYSIS)]

ly·sis /lī́ssiss/ *n* **1.** the destruction of cells by disruption of the bounding membrane, allowing the cell contents to escape **2.** a gradual reduction in severity of a patient's signs and symptoms during the course of a disease [Mid-16C. Via Latin, "loosening" < Greek *lusis* < *luein* "loosen"]

-lysis *suffix* **1.** dissolution, decomposition,

disintegration ○ *thermolysis* **2.** hydrolysis ○ *proteolysis* [Via Latin < Greek *lusis* (see LYSIS)]

Ly·sith·e·a /lī síthee ə/ *n* a very small natural satellite of Jupiter. It is approximately 22 mi./35 km in diameter and occupies an intermediate orbit.

lyso- *prefix* lysis ○ *lysosome* [< LYSIS]

ly·so·gen /lī́ssəjən/ *n* **1.** a bacterium that is capable of releasing a bacterium-destroying virus **(bacteriophage) 2.** an agent, particularly an antigen, that provokes the production of cell-destroying agents **(lysins)** by cells of the immune system

ly·so·gen·ic /lī̀ssə jénnik/ *adj* describes a bacterium that is capable of producing and releasing a bacterium-destroying virus **(bacteriophage)** in response to specific stimuli

ly·sog·e·nize /lī sójjə nīz/ (**-nized, -niz·ing, -niz·es**) *vt* to convert a bacterium to a lysogenic state by infection with a bacterium-destroying virus **(bacteriophage)**

ly·sog·e·ny /lī sójjənee/ *n* the ability of a bacterial cell to produce and release a bacterium-destroying virus **(bacteriophage)** in response to specific stimuli

ly·so·some /lī́ssə sōm/ *n* a membrane-bound cavity in living cells that contains enzymes that are responsible for degrading and recycling molecules — **ly·so·so·mal** /lī́ssə sṓm'l/ *adj*

ly·so·zyme /lī́ssə zīm/ *n* an enzyme in body secretions that can help destroy bacteria [Early 20C. < LYSO- + ENZYME]

-lyte *suffix* a substance that can be decomposed by a particular process ○ *electrolyte* [< Greek *lutos* "soluble" < past participle of *luein* "loosen"] —**-lytic** *suffix*

lyt·ic /líttik/ *adj* relating to, resulting from, or causing the destruction of cells by disruption **(lysis)** of the bounding membrane [Late 19C. < Greek *lutikos* "able to loosen" < *luein* (see LYSIS)]

-lyze *suffix* to cause or undergo lysis ○ *plasmolyze* [Back-formation < -LYSIS]

LZ *abbr* MIL landing zone

Mm

m[1] /em/ (*plural* **m's**), **M** (*plural* **M's** or **Ms**) *n* **1. 13TH LETTER OF ENGLISH ALPHABET** the 13th letter of the English alphabet, representing a consonant sound **2. LETTER "M" WRITTEN** a written representation of the letter "m" **3. 1,000** the Roman numeral for 1,000

m[2] *abbr* PHYS modulus

m[3] *symbol* **1.** PRINTING em dash **2.** PHYS magnetic moment **3.** PHYS mass **4.** MEASURE meter^2 **5.** MATH milli- **6.** MEASURE million

M[1] /em/ (*plural* **M's** or **Ms**) *n* something shaped like a letter "M"

M[2] *abbr* **1.** male **2.** CHEM mass **3.** EDUC Master (*used in degree titles*) **4.** CLOTHING medium (*used of clothes size*) **5.** mega- **6.** Member **7.** LOGIC middle term **8.** million **9.** CHEM molar

M[3] *symbol* **1.** PRINTING em dash **2.** PHYS mutual inductance

m. *abbr* **1.** male **2.** manual **3.** married **4.** GRAM masculine **5.** medium **6.** mile **7.** TIME minute *or* minutes **8.** CALENDAR month

M. *abbr* **1.** Majesty **2.** male **3.** Manitoba **4.** CALENDAR March **5.** CALENDAR May **6.** medieval **7.** LANGUAGE middle **8.** MONEY mill **9.** CALENDAR Monday **10.** Monsieur **11.** mountain

M'- *prefix* same as **Mac-**

M0 /èm zeérō/ *n* an assessment of the amount of money in public circulation, the money represented by banks' balances, and the money held in banks' tills **(narrow money)**

M1 /èm wún/ *n* an assessment of the amount of money in coins, bills, and checking accounts

M-1 ri·fle *n* a .30 caliber semiautomatic rifle invented by John C. Garand and adopted by the US Army in 1936.

M2 /èm tóo/ *n* an assessment of the amount of money in coins, bills, checking accounts, savings accounts, and deposits

M3 /èm threé/ *n* an assessment of the amount of money in M1, M2, and also large denomination repurchase agreements, institutional money market accounts, and some Eurodollar time deposits

M8 *abbr* ONLINE mate (*used in e-mails or text messages*)

ma /maa/ (*plural* **mas**) *n* **1.** same as **mother**[1] *n* (sense 1) (*informal*) **2.** a way of addressing or referring to a woman past middle age (*often offensive*) [Early 19C. Shortening of MAMA]

mA *symbol* MEASURE milliampere

MA *abbr* **1.** Maritime Administration **2.** Massachusetts **3.** EDUC Master of Arts **4.** PSYCHOL mental age

M.A. *abbr* EDUC Master of Arts

maa·ga *adj Carib* same as **mawger**

ma'am /mam/, **marm** /maarm/ *n* **1.** used when addressing a woman in a polite and respectful way (*dated informal*) **2.** used when addressing royal women or other women of high status (*formal*) [Mid-17C. Contraction of MADAM]

ma-and-pa *adj* same as **mom-and-pop**

maar /maar/ (*plural* **maars** or **maa·re** /maáree/) *n* a broad flat volcanic crater formed by a single explosive eruption and often filled with water [Early 19C. Via German dialect, "crater lake" < Latin *mare* "sea"]

Ma'a·riv /maáriv/, **Maa·riv** *n* in Judaism, the evening service of prayer [Late 20C. < Hebrew *ma'ărībh* "evening prayer"]

Maa·sai *n, adj* LANG, PEOPLES another spelling of **Masai**

Maas·tricht /maásstrìkt, maass tríkt/, **Maes·tricht** city in the southeastern Netherlands, the capital of Limburg Province. Population: 122,087 (2000).

Maat /maat/ *n* in Egyptian mythology, the goddess of the underworld who tested the value of a person's soul after death by weighing the heart on an ostrich feather

maat·jes her·ring *n* FISH another spelling of **matjes herring**

Mab /mab/ *n* in Celtic mythology, the god of light, who mediated between humankind and the divine

M.A.B.E. *abbr* EDUC Master of Agricultural Business and Economics

mabe pearl /máyb-/ *n* a cultured pearl with a flat base and a rounded top [Origin ?]

mac /mak/, **mack** *n UK* same as **mackintosh** (sense 1) (*informal*) [Early 20C. Shortening]

Mac /mak/ *n N Am, Scotland* used as an informal way of addressing a man whose name is not known (*informal*) [Mid-20C. < MAC-]

MAC /mak/ *n* a system for transmitting pictures to color televisions using satellites. Full form **multiplexed analog component**

Mac. *abbr* BIBLE Maccabees

M.A.C. *abbr* Municipal Assistance Corporation

Mac-, Mc-, M'- *prefix* surname meaning "son of" ○ *MacArthur* ○ *Macmillan* ○ *McCoy* [Via Scottish Gaelic and Irish < Old Irish *macc* "son"]

ma·ca·bre /mə kaábrə, -kaábr/ *adj* including gruesome and horrific details of death and decay [15C. < French *(danse) macabre* "dance of death," probably alteration of *danse Macabé* "dance of the Maccabees"]

ma·ca·co /mə kaákō/ (*plural* **-cos**) *n* a lemur, especially one belonging to a species in which the male is black and the female brown. Native to: Madagascar. Latin name: *Eulemur macaco macaco* or *Eulemur macaco flavifrons*. [Mid-18C. < French *mococo*]

mac·ad·am /mə káddəm/ *n* a smooth hard road surface made from small pieces of stone, usually mixed with tar or asphalt, in compressed layers [Early 19C. After John Loudon *McAdam* (1756–1836), Scottish civil engineer]

mac·a·da·mi·a /màkə dáymee ə/ *n* **1.** same as **macadamia nut 2.** an evergreen tree cultivated for its macadamia nuts. Native to: Australia, Southeast Asia. Genus: *Macadamia*. [Early 20C. < modern Latin, after John *Macadam* (1827–65), Scottish-born Australian chemist]

mac·a·da·mi·a nut *n* an edible, round, hard-shelled, waxy nut with a mild creamy flavor, produced by the macadamia tree

mac·ad·am·ize /mə káddə mīz/ (**-ized, -iz·ing, -iz·es**) *vt* to build or surface a road with macadam —**mac·ad·am·i·za·tion** /mə kàddəmi záysh'n/ *n* —**mac·ad·am·iz·er** *n*

Ma·cao another spelling of **Macau**

macaque

ma·caque /mə kák, -kaák/ (*plural* **-caques** or *same*) *n* a short-tailed sturdily built monkey. Native to: Asia, North Africa. Genus: *Macaca*. [Late 17C. Via French < Bantu *makaku* "some monkeys"]

ma·ca·re·na /màkə ráynə/ *n* a simple solo dance of Spanish origin mainly involving placing the hands on different parts of the body in sequence and swinging the hips [Late 20C. < *Macarena*, song to which it was performed]

mac·a·ro·ni /màkə rṓnee/ *n* **1.** hollow tubular pasta, usually produced in short lengths **2.** (*plural* **mac·a·ro·nis** or **mac·a·ro·nies**) in 18th-century Britain, an affected, foppish young man who adopted the fashions, manners, and customs of the other countries he had visited [Late 16C. < Italian dialect *maccarone* "macaroni, dumpling"]

mac·a·ron·ic /màkə rónnik/ *adj* **1. MIXING LANGUAGES IN VERSE** describes verse containing words and phrases from everyday language mixed with Latin, other foreign words and phrases, or vernacular terms with Latinate endings, usually for comic effect **2. RELATING TO MIXTURE OF LANGUAGES** relating to or involving a combination of two or more languages ■ *n* **MACARONIC VERSE** a macaronic poem, or macaronic poetry in general [Early 17C. Via modern Latin < obsolete Italian *macaronico* < dialect *maccarone* "macaroni, dumpling"]

mac·a·roon /màkə róon/ *n* a cookie made from sugar and egg whites, with ground almonds or pieces of dried coconut folded in [Late 16C. Via French *macaron* < Italian dialect *maccarone* "macaroni, dumpling"]

Mac·Ar·thur /mik aárthər/, **Douglas** (1880–1964) US general. He was the commander of Allied armed forces in the South Pacific during World War II. He lost the Philippines to the Japanese (1942), recaptured the islands (1944–45), and ultimately accepted the Japanese surrender in 1945. During the early stages of the Korean War, he was the UN commander in Korea (1950–51).

> "There is no security on this earth; there is only opportunity."
> [Douglas MacArthur. Quoted in *MacArthur: His Rendezvous with History*, Courtney Weaver; 1955]

> "It is fatal to enter any war without the will to win it."
> [Douglas MacArthur, *Speech to the Republican National Convention*; July 7, 1952]

Ma·cau /mə ków/, **Ma·cao** Special Administrative Region in southeastern China, on the South China Sea, west of Hong Kong. Population: 453,733 (2001). Area: 8.3 sq. mi./21 sq. km.

ma·caw /mə káw/ (*plural* **-caws** or *same*) *n* a large parrot with a huge beak, a long tail and brilliant plumage. Native to: Central and South America. Genera: *Anodorhynchus* or *Ara*. [Early 17C. < Portuguese *macao*]

Mac·beth /mək béth/, **king of Scotland** (c. 1005–57) After murdering Duncan I in 1040, he held the throne until he was killed by Duncan's son, Malcolm III

Macc. *abbr* BIBLE Maccabees

Mac·ca·bees /mákə bēez/ *npl* **1.** the followers of Judas Maccabeus, who led the revolt of the Jews against Syria in 168 B.C. **2.** four books of Jewish history, the first two of which are included in the Roman Catholic Bible and Protestant Apocrypha. See table at **Bible** [14C. Via Latin *Maccabaeus* < Greek *Makkabaios*, epithet of Judas] —**Mac·ca·be·an** /màkə bēe ən/ *adj*

mac·chi·a·to /maàkee aàtō/ *n* a drink of espresso coffee with a small amount of steamed milk on top [Late 20C. < Italian, "stained"]

Mac·Diar·mid /mək dúrmid/, **Hugh** (1892–1978) Scottish poet, editor, and critic. A pioneer in the Scottish literary renaissance and active in reviving literary Scots, he was a founder of the Scottish National Party. Pseudonym of **Grieve, Christopher Murray**

Mac·don·ald /mək dónn'ld/, **Flora** (1722–90) Scottish Jacobite. She helped Charles Edward Stuart, pretender to the British throne, escape to Skye after the uprising of 1745.

Mac·don·ald, Sir John Alexander (1815–91) Scottish-born lawyer, business executive, and prime minister of Canada (1867–73 and 1878–91). He was the first prime minister of the Dominion of Canada (1867–73).

Mac·don·ald, John Sandfield (1812–72) Canadian lawyer and political leader. He served as the premier of Ontario (1867–71).

Mac·Don·ald /mək dónn'ld/, **Ramsay** (1866–1937) British prime minister (1924, 1929–35). He was a founding member of the British Labor Party and the United Kingdom's first Labour prime minister. Full name **MacDonald, James Ramsay**. See table at **prime minister**

> "We hear war called murder. It is not: it is suicide."
> [Ramsay MacDonald, *Observer (London)*; May 4, 1930]

Mac·Don·nell Rang·es /mək dónn'l-/ group of mountain ranges in the Northern Territory, central Australia. The highest peak is Mount Zeil, 4,953 ft./1,510 m.

Mac·Dow·ell /mək dów əl/, **Edward Alexander** (1861–1908) US composer. He produced romantic piano music such as *Woodland Sketches* (1896).

mace

mace[1] /mayss/ *n* **1.** a stick or rod, usually with an ornamental head, carried by officials on ceremonial occasions as a symbol of authority **2.** a medieval weapon in the form of a heavy club with a round spiked metal head [13C. < Old French < Latin *mateola* "mallet"]

mace[2] /mayss/ *n* a spice made from the covering of the nutmeg seed, used in the form of dried pieces or as a yellow-orange powder [13C. Via Anglo-Norman *macis* < Latin *macir*, an Asian spice]

mace·bear·er /máyss bèrrər/ *n* an official who carries a mace on ceremonial occasions

mac·é·doine /màssə dwaán/, **mac·e·doine** *n* **1. MIXED CHOPPED FRUITS** a salad of small diced pieces of fruit, often in syrup or gelatin **2. MIXED CHOPPED VEGETABLES** a mixture of diced vegetables served hot or cold as a garnish, appetizer, or side dish **3. MEDLEY** a mixed-up jumble or medley (*literary*) [Early 19C. < French *Macédoine* "Macedonia"; because ALEXANDER THE GREAT ruled over many different peoples]

F. Y. R. O. Macedonia

Mac·e·do·ni·a /màssə dṓnee ə/ **1.** country in southeastern Europe. Formerly a constituent republic of Yugoslavia, it became independent in 1991. Language: Macedonian. Currency: dinar. Capital: Skopje. Population: 2,063,122 (2003). Area: 9,928 sq. mi./25,713 sq. km. Official name **Republic of Macedonia**. Former name **Former Yugoslav Republic of Macedonia** **2.** mountainous region of northeastern Greece. Capital: Thessaloniki. Area: 13,200 sq. mi./34,177 sq. km. Population: 1,710,513 (1991). **3.** district in southwestern Bulgaria. Area: 2,496 sq. mi./6,465 sq. km. **4.** *also* **Mac·e·don** /mássədən, -dòn/ ancient kingdom in northern Greece, centralized under Philip II, who, with his son, Alexander the Great, created a vast empire in the 4th century B.C. —**Mac·e·do·ni·an** *n, adj*

mac·er·ate /mássə ràyt/ *vti* (**-at·ed, -at·ing, -ates**) **1. SOFTEN BY SOAKING** to soften something by soaking it in liquid, or become soft by soaking in liquid **2. SEPARATE BY SOAKING** to make something break up into pieces or into its various parts by soaking it in liquid, or break up in this way **3. REDUCE OR WASTE AWAY** to make somebody or something thin or lean, or become thin or lean, especially by starvation or fasting ■ *n* **SOMETHING PRODUCED BY SOAKING** something prepared by soaking in a liquid [Mid-16C. < Latin *macerat-*, past participle of *macere* "soften"] —**mac·er·a·tion** /màssə ráysh'n/ *n*

Mac·gil·li·cud·dy's Reeks /mə gìllee kudeez rēeks/ mountain range in the southwestern Republic of Ireland. Highest peak: Carrantuohill 3,415 ft./1,041 m.

Mac·Guf·fin /mə gúffin/ *n* in a movie, play, or book, something that starts or drives the action of the plot but later turns out to be unimportant [Mid-20C. Said to come from a story in which a man pretends to have a "macgruffin," a Scottish mountain lion, but admits it does not exist]

Mach /maak/ *n* PHYS same as **Mach number**

Mach /maakh/, **Ernst** (1838–1916) Austrian physicist and philosopher. He was noted for his pioneering work in ballistics. The Mach number is named for him.

> "Physics is experience, arranged in economical order."
> [Ernst Mach, *The Economical Nature of Physical Inquiry*; 1882]

ma·cha /maáchə/ *adj* describes a woman with characteristics conventionally regarded as typically male, especially physical strength, courage, and aggressiveness (*slang; sometimes considered offensive*) [Form of MACHO]

mache /maash/, **mâche** *n* PLANTS same as **corn salad** [Late 17C. < French]

ma·chet·e /mə shéttee, -chéttee/ *n* a large heavy knife with a broad blade used as a weapon or as a tool for cutting through vegetation, especially in Central and South America and the Caribbean [Late 16C. < Spanish, "little sledgehammer" < *macho* "sledgehammer" < Latin *mateola* "mallet"]

Mach·i·a·vel·li /màkee ə véllee, mà kya-/, **Niccolò** (1469–1527) Italian historian, politician, and philosopher. He wrote several works on statecraft, of which *The Prince* (1532) had a profound and lasting influence.

machete

> "Cunning and deceit will every time serve a man better than force."
> [Niccolò Machiavelli, *The Prince*; 1532]

Mach·i·a·vel·li·an /màkee ə véllee ən, mà kya-/ *adj* **1.** using clever trickery, amoral methods, and expediency to achieve a desired goal, especially in politics **2.** relating to or characteristic of Niccolò Machiavelli or his political philosophy —**Mach·i·a·vel·li·an** *n* —**Mach·i·a·vel·li·an·ism** *n*

Mach·i·a·vel·li·an in·tel·li·gence *n* in psychology, social intelligence, especially the intelligence that involves deception and the formation of coalitions

ma·chic·o·late /mə chíkə làyt/ (**-lat·ed, -lat·ing, -lates**) *vt* to provide a castle wall with projecting galleries along its top [Late 18C. < Anglo-Latin *machicolare* < Provençal *machacol* "neck-crusher"]

machicolation

ma·chic·o·la·tion /mə chìkə láysh'n/ *n* **1. GALLERY ON TOP OF CASTLE WALL** a projecting gallery on top of a castle wall, supported by a row of arches and containing openings through which rocks and boiling oil could be dropped on attackers **2. OPENING IN MACHICOLATION** an opening in the floor of a machicolation **3. ROW OF PROJECTING ARCHES** an ornamental row of supported arches that project from a building

mach·i·nate /mákə nàyt, máshə-/ (**-nat·ed, -nat·ing, -nates**) *vti* to devise secret, cunning, or complicated plans and schemes to achieve a goal or to cause harm to others [Late 16C. < Latin *machinat-*, past participle of *machinari* < *machina* (see MACHINE)] —**mach·i·na·tor** *n*

mach·i·na·tion /màkə náysh'n, màshə-/ *n* **1.** the devising of secret, cunning, or complicated plans and schemes **2.** a secret, cunning, or complicated plan or scheme (*usually plural*)

ma·chine /mə shēen/ *n* **1. MECHANICAL DEVICE** a device with moving parts, often powered by electricity, used to perform a task, especially one that would otherwise be done by hand ○ *a washing machine* **2. SIMPLE UNPOWERED DEVICE** a simple device used to overcome resistance at one point by applying force at another point, e.g., a lever, pulley, or an inclined plane **3. POWERED FORM OF TRANSPORTATION** an engine-driven means of transportation, e.g., an aircraft, car, or motorcycle **4. GROUP OF PEOPLE IN CONTROL** an organized group of people that controls or directs something, especially a political group ○ *the party machine* **5. COMPLEX SYSTEM** a complex system structured so as to accomplish a particular goal ○ *the war machine* **6. SOMEBODY WHO BEHAVES MECHANICALLY**

somebody who is regarded as behaving like a mechanical device, e.g., somebody who is efficient but uncreative ○ *men trained as deadly machines* **7.** THEATER **DEVICE TO PRODUCE STAGE EFFECTS** a mechanical device used in the theater, especially in classical drama, to create special effects such as the entrance of a supernatural being **8.** LITERAT **LITERARY DEVICE** a character or factor introduced into a work of literature to produce an effect or to resolve the plot ■ *v* (**-chined, -chin·ing, -chines**) **1.** *vti* **WORK WITH POWER-DRIVEN TOOL** to cut, shape, or finish a piece of work using a power-driven tool such as a lathe or drilling device, or be cut, shaped, or finished in this way **2.** *vt* **USE MACHINE ON SOMETHING** to make or do something using a machine [Mid-16C. Via French < Latin *machina* "device" < Greek *mēkhanē* < *mēkhos* "means"] —**ma·chin·a·ble** *adj*

ma·chine bolt *n* a bolt with a square or hexagonal head, usually of heavy duty construction for use in aircraft and automobiles

ma·chine code *n* COMPUT same as **machine language**

ma·chine fin·ish *n* PAPER same as **mill finish**

ma·chine gun *n* an automatic weapon that fires rapidly and repeatedly without requiring separate squeezes on the trigger each time

ma·chine-gun *vt* **1. SHOOT SOMEBODY WITH MACHINE GUN** to shoot or kill somebody with a machine gun, or fire a machine gun at somebody or something **2. ADDRESS SOMEBODY RAPIDLY** to speak rapidly to somebody (*informal*) ■ *adj* **STACCATO** rapid, abrupt, and staccato in delivery —**ma·chine-gun·ner** *n*

ma·chine lan·guage *n* instructions, usually written in binary code, telling a computer how to process data

ma·chine pis·tol *n* a light automatic or semi-automatic submachine gun that can be discharged using only one hand

ma·chine-read·a·ble *adj* in a form that is able to be used directly by a computer

ma·chin·er·y /mə sheenəree/ *n* **1. MACHINES** machines collectively or in general **2. MECHANICAL PARTS** the aggregate parts that make up a machine or group of machines **3. SYSTEM OF MACHINES** a system of machines working together ○ *our office machinery* **4. SET OF PROCEDURES** an interconnected series of parts or processes that works like a mechanical system to produce a result ○ *the machinery of government* **5.** LITERAT **LITERARY DEVICES** literary devices used for effect, especially in poetry, or to resolve the plot of a play or book

ma·chine screw *n* a slotted or hexagonal-headed screw with a standardized thread. Use: to connect machine parts together.

ma·chine shop *n* a workshop where various materials, especially metals, are cut, shaped and worked, often to tight specifications using machine tools

ma·chine tool *n* a machine used for shaping and finishing metals and other solid materials, e.g., a lathe or grinder —**ma·chine-tooled** *adj*

ma·chine trans·la·tion *n* the translation of text from one language to another by computer

ma·chine-wash *vt* to wash something in a washing machine

ma·chine-wash·a·ble *adj* able to be washed in a washing machine without being damaged

ma·chin·ist /mə sheenist/ *n* **1. SOMEBODY WHO MACHINES SOMETHING** somebody whose job involves machining something or operating a machine or machine tool, especially in a factory **2. MACHINE MAKER OR REPAIRER** somebody who makes or repairs machines **3.** US NAVY **POSITION** a naval petty officer who is assigned to a ship's engine room

ma·chis·mo /mə kízmō, -chízmō/ *n* an exaggerated sense or display of masculinity, emphasizing characteristics that are conventionally regarded as male, usually physical strength and courage, aggressiveness, and lack of emotional response [Mid-20C. < Mexican Spanish < *macho* (see MACHO)]

Mach·me·ter /maák meetər/ *n* an instrument for measuring the Mach number of an aircraft

Mach num·ber /maák-/ *n* the speed of an object relative to the speed of sound. An aircraft traveling at twice the speed of sound has a Mach number of 2. [Early 20C. After Ernst MACH]

ma·cho /maáchō/ *adj* having or showing characteristics conventionally regarded as male, especially physical strength and courage, aggressiveness, and lack of emotional response ■ *n* (*plural* **-chos**) a male who displays conventional masculine characteristics [Early 20C. Via Mexican Spanish, "masculine" < Spanish < Latin *masculus*] —**ma·cho·ism** *n*

Barnaby's

Machu Picchu

Ma·chu Pic·chu /maáchoo peékchoo, -peéchoo/ ruined ancient Inca city in the Andes in southern Peru. It is well known for its architecture and system of terraces.

Mac·i·as Ngue·ma /maa seé əss əng gwáymə/ former name for **Bioko** (1973–79)

mac·in·tosh *n* CLOTHING another spelling of **mackintosh**

Mack /mak/, **Connie** (1862–1956) US baseball player and manager. He guided the Philadelphia Athletics to five world championships (1910–30). Born **McGillcuddy, Cornelius**

Mac·ken·zie /mə kénzee/ river in the Northwest Territories, Canada. It originates in Great Slave Lake. Length: 1,120 mi./1,800 km.

Mac·ken·zie, Sir Alexander (1764–1820) Scottish-born Canadian explorer. He explored western Canada from the Arctic to the Pacific and was the first European to cross North America overland.

Mac·ken·zie, Alexander (1822–92) Canadian prime minister (1873–78). He was the first Liberal prime minister of the Dominion of Canada.

Mac·Ken·zie /mə kénzee/, **William Lyon** (1795–1861) Canadian insurgent and politician. He was leader of the Rebellion of 1837, advocating independent government for Toronto. He became a member of the Canadian Assembly (1851–58).

Mac·ken·zie Moun·tains mountain range in western Canada that spans the border between the Northwest Territories and the Yukon Territory. Highest peak: Keele Peak 9,750 ft./2,972 m.

~~mackeral~~ incorrect spelling of **mackerel**

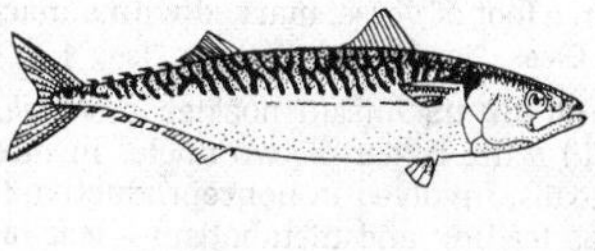

mackerel

mack·er·el /mákrəl/ (*plural* **-els** or *same*) *n* **1. OILY FISH OF N ATLANTIC** a bony oily fish with a greenish blue body, dark blue bars, and a forked tail. Native to: North Atlantic coastal waters. Latin name: *Scomber scombrus*. **2.** FOOD **MACKEREL AS FOOD** the flesh of a mackerel used as food **3. FISH LIKE MACKEREL** a fish that is similar to the true mackerel, e.g., the Spanish mackerel. Family: Scombridae. [13C. < Anglo-Norman]

mack·er·el shark *n* a large fierce shark with a pointed snout, related to the great white shark, mako shark, and porbeagle. Family: Lamnidae.

mack·er·el sky *n* a sky covered with cirrocumulus or altocumulus clouds in a pattern that resembles the markings on a mackerel (*regional*)

Mack·i·nac, Straits of /máki nàw/ channel in Michigan connecting Lake Huron and Lake Michigan. Length: 30 mi./48 km.

Mack·i·nac Is·land island in northern Michigan, in the Straits of Mackinac, between Michigan's northern and southern peninsulas. Area: 6.2 sq. mi./16 sq. km.

mack·i·naw /máki nàw/ *n* **1. HEAVY WOOLEN FABRIC** a thick heavy woolen cloth, usually with a plaid design **2. SHORT HEAVY COAT** a short double-breasted coat made from mackinaw or a similar fabric **3.** HOUSEHOLD same as **Mackinaw blanket** **4. FLAT-BOTTOMED BOAT** a boat with a pointed bow, a square stern, and a flat bottom, formerly used on the Great Lakes [Early 19C. After a former trading post on MACKINAC ISLAND near *Mackinaw* City, Michigan]

Mack·i·naw blan·ket *n* a thick blanket made of heavy woolen cloth, sometimes striped, formerly used by Native North Americans, trappers, and traders in northern and western North America

mack·i·naw trout *n* FISH same as **lake trout** (sense 1)

Mac·kin·non /mə kínnən/, **Catherine** (*b.* 1946) US legal scholar. A pioneer in changing the legal attitude toward sex discrimination, she wrote the influential *Sexual Harassment of Working Women* (1979).

mack·in·tosh /mákin tòsh/, **mac·in·tosh** *n UK* **1.** a waterproof coat worn for protection against the rain (*dated*) **2.** a waterproof fabric, especially rubberized cotton [Mid-19C. After Charles *Macintosh* (1766–1843), Scottish inventor]

AKG London

Charles Rennie Mackintosh

Mack·in·tosh /mákin tòsh/, **Charles Rennie** (1868–1928) British architect and interior designer. Noted for his art nouveau designs, he worked primarily on buildings and interiors in and around Glasgow, Scotland.

mack·le /mák'l/ *n* a blurred or double impression caused by the movement of paper or type during the printing process ■ *vti* to cause a printed impression to blur, or appear blurred [Late 16C. Directly or via French < Latin *macula* "spot, stain"]

Mac·Laine /mə kláyn/, **Shirley** (*b.* 1934) US movie actor. She won an Academy Award for her role in *Terms of Endearment* (1983). Born **MacLean Beaty, Shirley**

> "We are not victims of the world we see. We are victims of the way we see the world."
> [Shirley MacLaine, *Dancing in the Light*; 1985]

mac·le /mák'l/ *n* **1.** MINERALS same as **chiastolite** **2.** a crystal that is composed of two mirror-image crystals sharing a common plane (**twinned**) **3.** a discolored spot within a crystal [Early 19C. Via French < Latin *macula* "spot, mesh"]

Mac·Leish /mə kleésh/, **Archibald** (1892–1982) US poet, playwright, and public official. He won three Pulitzer prizes, for his volumes of poetry *Conquistador* (1932) and *Collected Poems, 1917–52* (1953), and for his verse drama *J.B.* (1958).

> "A poem should be wordless / As the flight of birds."
> [Archibald MacLeish, "Ars Poetica" "(The Art of Poetry)"; 1926]

Mac·Len·nan /mə klénnən/, **Hugh** (1907–90) Canadian writer, known for his novels and critiques of Canadian life, including *Barometer Rising* (1941). Full name **MacLennan, John Hugh**

Mac·leod /mə klówd/, **John** (1876–1935) British physiologist. He discovered insulin with Sir Frederick Grant Banting and Charles Best, for which he shared the Nobel Prize in physiology or medicine (1923). Full name **Macleod, John James Rickard**

Harold Macmillan

Mac·mil·lan /mək míllən/, **Harold, 1st Earl of Stockton** (1894–1986) prime minister of the United Kingdom (1957–63). Full name **Macmillan, Maurice Harold**. See table at **prime minister**

"When you're abroad you're a statesman: when you're at home you're just a politician."
[Harold Macmillan, *Speech*; 1958]

ma·co /mákō/, **ma·ko** *Carib n* (*plural* **-coes**; *plural* **-koes**) a gossip or busybody ■ *vi* (**-coed, -co·ing, -coes; -koed, -ko·ing, -koes**) to gossip or be overly curious about other people's affairs [Late 20C. Shortening of French Creole *makomè* < French *macommère* "my child's godmother, my intimate woman friend," hence "gossip"]

Ma·comb /mə kṓm/ city in western Illinois. Population: 18,588 (2002 estimate).

Ma·con /máykən/ city in central Georgia. It is the seat of Bibb county. Population: 95,862 (2002 estimate).

Mâ·con[1] /maa kóN/, **Ma·con** *n* a red or white wine from Burgundy, east central France [Mid-19C. < MÂCON[2]]

Mâ·con[2] /maa kóN/ city in east central France, the capital of Saône-et-Loire Department. Population: 34,469 (1999).

Mac·Phail /mək fáyl/, **Agnes Campbell** (1890–1954) Canadian politician. She was a member of parliament (1921–40) and of the Ontario legislature (1943–45 and 1948–51).

Mac·quar·ie, Lake /mə kwáwree/ coastal lake in New South Wales, Australia. Area: 43 sq. mi./110 sq. km.

Mac·quar·ie Har·bor large natural harbor in western Tasmania, Australia. Area: 110 sq. mi./285 sq. km.

Mac·quar·ie Is·land uninhabited Australian island located in the Southern Ocean, southeast of Tasmania. Area: 47 sq. mi./123 sq. km.

macr- *prefix* same as **macro-** (*used before vowels*)

mac·ra·mé /mákrə mày/ *n* pieces of string or cord knotted together to form a coarse ornamental lacy pattern, or something made using this method [Mid-19C. Via Turkish *makrama* "towel" < Arabic *miḳrama* "bed cover"]

mac·ro /mákrō/ (*plural* **-ros**) *n* a computer instruction that initiates a series of additional instructions [Mid-20C. < MACRO-]

macro- *prefix* **1.** large, inclusive ○ *macroeconomics* **2.** long ○ *macrobiotics* [< Greek *makros* < Indo-European, "long, thin"]

mac·ro·bi·ot·ics /màkrō bī óttiks/ *n* a vegan diet of seeds, grains, and organically grown fruit and vegetables, said to prolong life and balance the body's systems (*takes a singular verb*) [Late 18C. < Greek *makrobiotos* "long life"] —**mac·ro·bi·ot·ic** *adj*

mac·ro·ceph·a·ly /màkrō séffəlee/, **mac·ro·ce·pha·li·a** /-sə fáylee ə/ *n* the condition of having a head that is excessively large —**mac·ro·ce·phal·ic** /-sə fállik/ *adj*—**mac·ro·ceph·a·lous** *adj*

mac·ro·cli·mate /mákrō klīmət/ *n* the general climate of a large region such as a continent —**mac·ro·cli·mat·ic** /màkrō klī máttik/ *adj*

mac·ro·cosm /mákrə kòzzəm/ *n* a complex structure, e.g., the world or the universe, considered as a single entity that contains numerous similar smaller-scale structures [Early 17C. < medieval Latin *macrocosmus* < Greek *makro-* (see MACRO-) + *kosmos* "world"] —**mac·ro·cos·mic** /màkrə kózmik/ *adj*

mac·ro·cyte /mákrō sīt/ *n* an unusually large red blood cell that commonly occurs in cases of anemia —**mac·ro·cyt·ic** /màkrō síttik/ *adj*

mac·ro·cy·to·sis /màkrō sī tṓssiss/ *n* the presence of unusually large red cells in the blood

mac·ro·ec·o·nom·ics /màkrō ekə nómmiks, -eekə-/ *n* a branch of economics that focuses on the general features and processes that make up a national economy and the ways in which different segments of the economy are connected (*takes a singular verb*) —**mac·ro·ec·o·nom·ic** *adj*—**mac·ro·e·con·o·mist** /-i kónnəmist/ *n*

mac·ro·e·con·o·my /màkrō i kónnəmee/ *n* the economy viewed as a whole and in terms of all those factors that control its overall performance ○ *Employment rates did not respond to the macroeconomy as expected.*

mac·ro·ev·o·lu·tion /màkrō evə lo͞osh'n, -eevə-/ *n* evolution theorized to occur over a long period of time, producing major changes in species and other taxonomic groups —**mac·ro·ev·o·lu·tion·ar·y** *adj*

mac·ro·fos·sil /mákrō fòss'l/ *n* a fossil that is large enough to be observed or examined without the aid of a microscope

mac·ro·gam·ete /màkrō gá meet, -gə meet/ *n* the larger, usually female, sex cell (**gamete**) in a pair of conjugating cells of a heterogamous species

mac·ro·glob·u·lin /màkrō glóbbyəlin/ *n* a soluble protein in the blood with a high molecular weight

mac·ro·glob·u·lin·e·mi·a /màkrō glòbbyələ neemee ə/ *n* a medical condition marked by an increase in the blood of soluble proteins with high molecular weight

mac·ro·graph /mákrō gràf/ *n* a drawing, photograph, or other representation in which something appears at its actual size or larger

mac·ro·in·struc·tion /màkrō in strúksh'n/ *n* COMPUT same as **macro**

mac·ro lens *n* a lens used for close-up photography that produces a life-size or larger image on film, with a minimum of 1:1 object-to-image ratio

mac·ro·mere /mákrō meer/ *n* a large yolk-filled cell (**blastomere**) formed from the unequal splitting of a fertilized egg [Late 19C. < MACRO- + BLASTOMERE]

mac·ro·mol·e·cule /màkrō móllə kyo͞ol/ *n* a large molecule such as that of a protein or polymer, made up of smaller components connected to one another —**mac·ro·mo·lec·u·lar** /màkrō mə lékyələr/ *adj*

ma·cron /máy kròn, máykrən, má kròn/ *n* **1.** a short horizontal line placed over a vowel sound to indicate that it is long or stressed. Macrons are used in the spelling system of some languages, in some phonetic transcription systems, and in the study or analysis of poetic meter. **2.** a stressed or long syllable in a foot of verse, marked with a macron [Mid-19C. < Greek, "long thing" < *makros* "long"]

mac·ro·nu·cle·us /màkrō no͞oklee əss/ (*plural* **-cle·i** /-klee ī/) *n* the larger of two nuclei in most ciliate protozoans, involved in nonreproductive functions such as feeding and metabolism —**mac·ro·nu·cle·ar** *adj*

mac·ro·nu·tri·ent /màkrō no͞otree ənt/ *n* a chemical element needed in large amounts by plants for normal growth and development, e.g., nitrogen, carbon, or potassium

mac·ro·phage /mákrō fàyj/ *n* a large cell that is present in blood, lymph, and connective tissues, removing waste products, harmful microorganisms, and foreign material from the bloodstream —**mac·ro·phag·ic** /màkrō fájjik/ *adj*

mac·ro·pho·tog·ra·phy /màkrō fə tóggrəfee/ *n* close-up photography that produces images on the film that are life-size or larger than life

mac·ro·phys·ics /màkrō fízziks/ *n* a branch of physics that studies systems and objects large enough to be easily observed (*takes a singular verb*)

mac·ro·phyte /mákrō fīt/ *n* a plant large enough to be studied and observed using the unaided eye, especially a water plant —**mac·ro·phyt·ic** /màkrō fíttik/ *adj*

ma·crop·sia /mə krópsee ə/ *n* a medical condition in which everything perceived by the eye appears to be larger than it really is, often as a result of a retinal disease or a brain disorder [Late 19C. < MACRO- + Greek *opsia* "seeing"]

mac·ro·scop·ic /màkrō skóppik/, **mac·ro·scop·i·cal** /-skóppik'l/ *adj* **1.** large enough to be seen and examined without the aid of magnifying equipment **2.** relating to or concerned with large units [Late 19C. < MACRO-, after MICROSCOPIC] —**mac·ro·scop·i·cal·ly** *adv*

mac·ro·scop·ic a·nat·o·my *n* ANAT same as **gross anatomy**

mac·ro·so·ci·ol·o·gy /màkrō sōssee óllәjee, -shee-/ *n* the branch of sociology concerned with the study and analysis of societies in their entirety —**mac·ro·so·ci·o·log·i·cal** /màkrō sōssee ə lójjik'l, -shee ə-/ *adj*

mac·ro·spore /mákrō spàwr/ *n* BIOL same as **megaspore**

mac·ro·struc·ture /mákrō strùkchər/ *n* a structure such as that of a metal that is large enough to be seen or examined with little or no magnification —**mac·ro·struc·tu·ral** /màkrō strúkchərəl/ *adj*

mac·u·la /mákyələ/ (*plural* **-lae** /-lee/ or **-las**) *n* **1.** PHYSIOL a small pigmented spot on the skin that is neither raised nor depressed **2.** OPHTHALMOL a small yellowish spot in the middle of the retina that provides the greatest visual acuity and color perception **3.** ASTRON same as **sunspot** (*technical*) [14C. < Latin, "spot, stain"] —**mac·u·lar** *adj*

mac·u·la lu·te·a /-lo͞otee ə/ (*plural* **mac·u·lae lu·te·ae** /-lee lo͞otee ee/) *n* OPHTHALMOL same as **macula** (sense 2) [< Latin *luteus* "yellow"]

mac·u·late /mákyə làyt/ (*literary*) *vt* (**-lat·ed, -lat·ing, -lates**) to mark somebody or something with a spot, blotch, or blemish ■ *adj also* **mac·u·lat·ed** /mákyə làytəd/ marked with spots, blotches, or blemishes [15C. < Latin *maculat-*, past participle of *maculare* < *macula* "spot"]

mac·u·la·tion /màkyə láysh'n/ *n* **1.** the pattern of spots on some animals and plants **2.** the act of marking something with a spot, blotch, or blemish, or the state of being marked in this way (*archaic or literary*)

mac·ule[1] /mákyool/ *n* PHYSIOL same as **macula** (sense 1) [Mid-19C. Directly or via French < Latin *macula* "spot, stain"]

mac·ule[2] /mákyool/ *n* PRINTING same as **mackle** [15C. Directly or via French < Latin *macula* "spot, stain"]

Ma·cu·si /mə ko͞ossee/, **Ma·cu·shi** /-ko͞oshee/ *n* a Cariban language spoken in the border region between Brazil, Guyana, and Venezuela. Native speakers: over 10,000. [Early 20C. < Macusi] —**Ma·cu·si** *adj*

mad /mad/ (**mad·der, mad·dest**) *adj* **1.** ANGRY affected by great displeasure or anger ○ *She'll get mad when she finds out.* **2.** FRANTIC done with great haste, excitement, or confusion (*offensive in some contexts*) ○ *There was a mad stampede to the fire exits.* **3.** MARKEDLY AGGRESSIVE unusually aggressive or ferocious (*refers to animals; offensive in some contexts*) ○ *a mad bull* **4.** RABID describes an animal that has rabies **5.** OFFENSIVE TERM an offensive term meaning affected with a psychiatric disorder **6.** VERY UNWISE OR RASH lacking common sense and not reasoning logically (*insult; offensive in some contexts*) **7.** WILDLY EXCITED completely unrestrained and out of control (*offensive in some contexts*) ○ *When the band finally appeared, the audience went mad.* ○ *went mad after the last-minute victory* **8.** RAMBUNCTIOUS very exciting or boisterous (*sometimes offensive*) **9.** SEIZED BY UNCONTROLLABLE EMOTION overcome with a violent emotion (*sometimes offensive*) ○ *She was mad with jealousy.* **10.** PASSIONATE ABOUT SOMETHING very fond of, enthusiastic about, or interested in something, often to the exclusion of everything else (*often used in combination, offensive in some contexts*) ○ *I'm not mad about the color.* [Old English *gemǣd* "deprived of reason" < *gemād* "irrational" < Indo-European, "change"] ◇ **like mad** *UK* with great speed or energy (*offensive in some contexts*)

MAD *abbr* 1. PSYCHIAT major affective disorder 2. MIL mutual assured destruction

Mad. *abbr* Madagascar

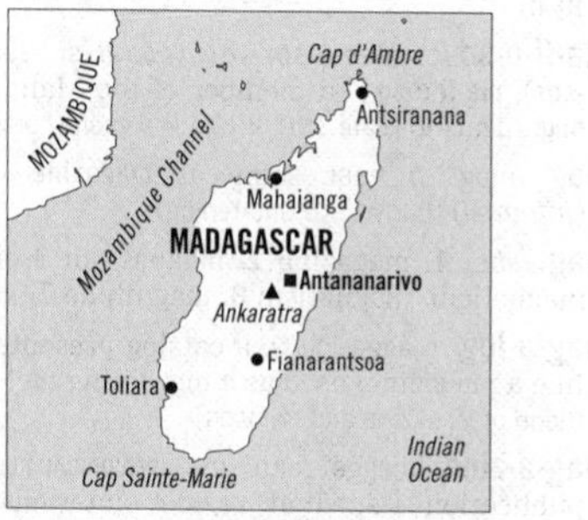

Madagascar

Mad·a·gas·car /màddə gáskər/ island country in the Indian Ocean, separated from southeastern mainland Africa by the Mozambique Channel. Language: Malagasy, French. Currency: Malagasy franc. Capital: Antananarivo. Population: 15,982,563 (2001). Area: 226,658 sq. mi./587,041 sq. km. Official name **Democratic Republic of Madagascar**. Former name **Malagasy Republic** (1958–75) —**Mad·a·gas·can** *adj, n*

Mad·a·gas·car aq·ua·ma·rine *n* a blue beryl found in Madagascar. Use: gems.

Mad·a·gas·car per·i·win·kle *n* a perennial plant that is poisonous to domestic animals. Flowers: white, pink. Native to: India, Madagascar. Use: production of substances used to treat cancer. Latin name: *Catharanthus roseus.*

mad·am /máddəm/ *n* 1. a polite term of address for a woman, especially a customer in a store, restaurant, or hotel (*formal*) 2. a woman who manages a brothel [13C. < Old French *ma dame* "my lady" < Latin *mea domina*]

Mad·am (*plural* **Mes·dames** /may dám, -daám/ or **Mad·ams**) *n* 1. used at the beginning of a formal letter to a woman, especially one whose name is not known (*formal*) 2. used before the name of a woman's official position as a term of address ○ *Madam President*

Ma·dame /máddəm, mə daám/ (*plural* **Mes·dames** /may dám, -daám/), **ma·dame** (*plural* **mes·dames**) *n* the title of a Frenchwoman or French-speaking woman, especially if married, used before her name or as a polite term of address [Mid-16C. < French < Old French *ma dame* (see MADAM)]

CULTURAL NOTE ***Madame Bovary***, a novel (1857) by French writer Gustave Flaubert. It tells the story of Emma Bovary, a young married woman who seeks refuge from the mundaneness of her provincial life in a series of reckless and ultimately disastrous affairs. The novel's frank depiction of middle-class society and its almost scientific analysis of human behavior made it a pioneering work of modern realism.

Ma·dang /mə dáng/ port on the northeastern coast of New Guinea in Papua New Guinea. Population: 27,057 (1990).

mad·cap /mád kàp/ *adj* acting or behaving without caring or stopping to think about possible consequences [Late 16C. *Cap* represents the head] —**mad·cap** *n*

mad cow dis·ease *n* VET same as **BSE** (*informal*)

MADD /mad/ *abbr* Mothers Against Drunk Driving

mad·den /mádd'n/ (**-dened, -den·ing, -dens**) *vti* 1. to make a person or animal extremely angry, or become extremely angry (*usually passive*) 2. to make somebody irrational or cause somebody to have psychiatric problems, or become irrational or have psychiatric problems

mad·den·ing /mádd'ning/ *adj* causing anger, annoyance, impatience, or frustration —**mad·den·ing·ly** *adv*

mad·der[1] /máddər/ comparative of **mad**

mad·der[2] /máddər/ *n* 1. PLANT a perennial plant with a fleshy red root. Native to: Europe, Asia. Latin name: *Rubia tinctorum.* 2. ROOT YIELDING DYE the root of a madder plant. Use: formerly, red dye. 3. RED DYE a red dye formerly obtained from madder roots 4. RED PIGMENT a red pigment obtained from the dye alizarin. Use: dyes, inks, paints. 5. REDDISH PURPLE a deep reddish purple color [Old English *mædere* < Germanic] —**mad·der** *adj*

mad·dest /máddəst/ superlative of **mad**

mad·ding /mádding/ *adj* acting in a way that suggests or reveals the presence of a psychiatric disorder (*literary*)

CULTURAL NOTE ***Far from the Madding Crowd***, a novel (1874) by British writer Thomas Hardy. The first of Thomas Hardy's Wessex novels, it is the story of a capricious, forceful young woman, Bathsheba Everdene, and the three men who want to marry her. It was made into a movie by John Schlesinger in 1967.

mad-dog skull·cap *n* a perennial plant that is 2–4 ft./1–1.25 m tall with many branches. Flowers: two-lipped, blue, in clusters. Native to: North America. Use: antispasmodic drug. Latin name: *Scutellaria lateriflora.* [< its former use to treat rabies and the appearance of its flowers, resembling caps]

made /mayd/ past participle, past tense of **make** ■ *adj* 1. ARTIFICIALLY PRODUCED produced by artificial means 2. SUCCESSFUL certain of achieving success 3. ACCEPTED INTO CRIMINAL GROUP accepted as a member of an underworld crime syndicate (*slang*) 4. CONTRIVED fictitious, invented, or contrived (*dated*)

Ma·dei·ra[1] /mə deérə/ *n* a sweet or dry wine fortified with brandy, made in the Madeira islands and usually served as a dessert wine or after a meal

Ma·dei·ra[2] /mə deérə/ river in western Brazil. It is the main tributary of the Amazon, flowing northeast from the Bolivian border and into the Amazon near Manaus. Length: 2,000 mi./3,220 km.

Ma·dei·ra Is·lands group of islands with many resorts in the eastern North Atlantic Ocean. Population: 256,000 (1992). Area: 307 sq. mi./794 sq. km.

Ma·dei·ra vine *n* a tropical ornamental vine with small fragrant flowers. Native to: South America. Latin name: *Anredera cordifolia.*

mad·e·leine /mádd'lən, máddə làyn/ *n* 1. a small light whisked sponge cake baked in the form of a shell 2. a sponge cake that is cooked in a small cup-shaped mold, coated in raspberry jam, rolled in desiccated coconut, and topped with a glacé cherry [Mid-19C. Probably after *Madeleine* Paulmier, 19th-century French pastry chef]

mad·e·moi·selle /màddəmwə zél, màdmə-/ (*plural* **mes·de·moi·selles** /màydəmwə zél/ or **mad·e·moi·selles**) *n* 1. a young Frenchwoman or French-speaking woman 2. *UK* a female French teacher or French governess (*dated*) 3. FISH same as **silver perch** (sense 2) [Mid-18C. Use of MADEMOISELLE]

Mad·e·moi·selle /màdmwə zél/ (*plural* **Mes·de·moi·selles** /màydəmwə zél/) *n* the title of a French woman or French-speaking young or unmarried woman, used before her name or as a polite term of address (*sometimes considered offensive*) [15C. < Old French *ma demoiselle* "my damsel"]

made-to-or·der *adj* 1. made in accordance with a customer's specifications or requirements 2. perfectly suitable or exactly as required

made-up *adj* 1. UNTRUE lacking any basis in fact or reality 2. WEARING COSMETICS having applied cosmetics to the face 3. ASSEMBLED completely put together and prepared

mad·house /mád hòwss/ (*plural* **-hous·es** /-howzəz/) *n* 1. a place where there is much noise and activity and little order or control (*informal; sometimes considered offensive*) 2. an offensive term for a hospital or residential facility for people who have psychiatric disorders (*dated*)

Ma·dhya Pra·desh /mùddyə prə désh/ state in north central India. Capital: Bhopal. Population: 60,385,118 (2001). Area: 118,985 sq. mi./308,250 sq. km.

mad·i·son /máddiss'n/ *n* a cycling event in which competitors ride as teams, each rider relieving the other in turn

Mad·i·son /máddiss'n/ 1. river in southwestern Montana. Rising in Yellowstone National Park, it joins the Gallatin and Jefferson rivers to form the Missouri River. Length: 180 mi./241 km. 2. capital city of Wisconsin, in the south central part of the state. It is home to the University of Wisconsin-Madison. Population: 215,211 (2002 estimate). 3. town in southern Connecticut. Population: 18,546 (2002 estimate). 4. city in northern New Jersey. Population: 15,356 (2002 estimate).

Mad·i·son, Dolley (1768–1849) US first lady. The wife of James Madison, she was popular in Washington society during his terms as secretary of state (1801–9) and president (1809–17). She saved state papers during the British invasion of the capital in 1814. Full name **Madison, Dolley Payne Todd**

James Madison

Mad·i·son, James (1751–1836) 4th president of the United States. He played a leading role in the Constitutional Convention (1787) and served two terms as president (1809–17). See table at **president**

"Democracies...have in general been as short in their lives as they have been violent in their deaths."
[James Madison, *Independent Journal*; November 23, 1787]

Mad·i·son Av·e·nue *n* the center of the US advertising and public-relations industries, or the US advertising industry itself [After the street in New York]

mad·ly /máddlee/ *adv* 1. INTENSELY with an extraordinary degree of intensity or devotion ○ *madly in love* 2. TO NO PURPOSE with great haste or activity but without accomplishing much ○ *She ran madly through the house looking for her keys.* 3. WILDLY in a wild and uncontrolled way ○ *He struck out madly in all directions.* 4. RASHLY in a rash or thoughtless way ○ *I madly agreed to go with her.* 5. OFFENSIVE TERM an offensive term meaning in the manner of somebody who is affected by a psychiatric disorder

mad·man /mád màn, -mən/ (*plural* **-men** /-mèn, -mən/) *n* an offensive term for a man with a psychiatric disorder

mad mon·ey *n* a small amount of money set aside for emergency use or for frivolous self-indulgence (*informal*)

mad·ness /mádnəss/ *n* 1. OFFENSIVE TERM an offensive term for a psychiatric disorder 2. RASHNESS rash or thoughtless behavior 3. ANGER great anger or fury 4. EXCITEMENT great enthusiasm or excitement

Madonna: Byzantine mosaic, Athens, Greece

Ma·don·na /mə dónnə/ *n* 1. VIRGIN MARY Mary, the mother of Jesus Christ 2. *also* **ma·don·na** IMAGE OF VIRGIN MARY a picture, statue, or other artistic representation of Mary, the mother of Jesus Christ 3. SPIRITUAL SAINTLY WOMAN a woman portrayed as exhibiting characteristics such as saintliness, patience, or spirituality (*informal*) [Late 16C. < obsolete Italian *ma donna* "my lady" < Latin *mea domina*]

Madonna

Ma·don·na /mə dónnə/ (*b.* 1958) US pop singer and actor. Her career, which started in the early 1980s, shows an ability to change her style and image ahead of current trends. She has also written storybooks for children. Born **Ciccone, Madonna Louise Veronica**

Ma·don·na lil·y *n* a tall lily. Flowers: white, trumpet-shaped. Native to: eastern Mediterranean. Latin name: *Lilium candidum*. [Traditional symbol of purity, often included in pictures of the Madonna, the mother of Jesus Christ]

mad·ras /máddrəss, mə dráss/ *n* **1. STRONG FINE CLOTH** a strong fine cotton or silk fabric, often with a woven striped or checked design **2. LIGHT CLOTH** a light cotton or rayon fabric. Use: curtains. **3. BRIGHTLY COLORED SCARF** a scarf or handkerchief made from brightly colored cotton or silk [Early 19C. After MADRAS]

Mad·ras /mə draáss/ former name for **Chennai**

ma·dra·sa /mə draássə/, **ma·dras·sa** *n* a school for the study of Islamic religion and thought, especially the Koran [Mid-17C. < Arabic, "place to study"]

mad·re·pore /máddrə pàwr/ *n* a reef-building coral that lives in tropical waters. Genus: *Madreporaria*. [Mid-18C. Via French or modern Latin < Italian *madrepora* < *madre* "mother" + either *poro* "pore" or Latin *porus* "calciferous stone" < Greek *poros*] —**mad·re·po·ral** /màddrə páwrəl/ *adj* —**mad·re·po·ri·an** /-páwree ən/ *adj* —**mad·re·por·ic** /-páwrik/ *adj* —**mad·re·por·it·ic** /-pə ríttik/ *adj*

mad·re·por·ite /màddrə páw rīt/ *n* a porous plate in an echinoderm that takes in water to the vascular system [Early 19C. < MADREPORE]

Ma·drid /mə dríd/ capital and largest city of Spain, in the center of the country. Noted for its museums, historic monuments, and active street life, it is the country's financial and administrative center. Population: 3,016,788 (2002).

mad·ri·gal /máddrig'l/ *n* **1. ENGLISH PART SONG** a song with parts for several usually unaccompanied voices that was popular in England in the 16th and 17th centuries **2. MEDIEVAL ITALIAN SONG** a secular Italian song of the 13th and 14th centuries, written for two or three unaccompanied voices singing in harmony **3. LYRIC POEM** a short pastoral or love poem suitable for singing as a madrigal [Late 16C. < *Italian* < Latin *matricalis* "of the mother" < *matrix* (see MATRIX)] —**mad·ri·gal·ist** *n*

ma·dri·lène /màddri lén, máddri làyn, màddri láyn/, **ma·dri·lene** *n* a clear soup flavored with tomato, usually served cold [Early 20C. Via French < Spanish *madrileño* "of Madrid"]

ma·dri·na /mə dreénə/ (*plural* **-nas**) *n Hispanic* a godmother of a young girl who is having a rite of passage party (**quinceañera**) welcoming her into adulthood, and who pays for flowers, invitations, and other things [< Spanish, "godmother" < *madre* "mother"]

ma·dro·ña /mə drṓnə/, **ma·dro·ño** /mə drṓnō/ (*plural* **-ños**) *n* an evergreen tree with smooth crimson peeling bark, glossy leaves, and orange-yellow berries. Flowers: cream. Native to: North America. Latin name: *Arbutus menziesii*. [Mid-19C. < Spanish]

mad tom *n* a small common freshwater catfish with poisonous pectoral spines, a long adipose fin, and a rounded dorsal fin. Native to: central United States. Genus: *Noturus*. [Short for "mad tom cat," since the fish inflicts nasty wounds with its poisonous spines]

Ma·du·ra /mə dóorə/ island in southwestern Indonesia, off the northeastern coast of Java. Population: 3,015,972 (1990). Area: 2,157 sq. mi./5,587 sq. km.

Ma·du·rai /maàdə rī/ historic city and pilgrimage center in southern India. Population: 1,194,665 (2001).

ma·du·ro /mə dóorō/ (*plural* **-ros**) *n* a dark strong cigar [Late 19C. < Spanish, "ripe, mature"]

mad·wom·an /mád wòommən/ (*plural* **-wom·en** /-wìmmin/) *n* an offensive term for a woman with a psychiatric disorder

mad·wort /mád wùrt, -wàwrt/ (*plural* **-worts** or *same*) *n* a low-growing plant of the borage family. Flowers: small, blue. Native to: Europe, Asia. Latin name: *Asperugo procumbens*. [Late 16C. Translation of modern Latin *alyssum* "removing rabies"; because it was believed to cure the bites of rabid dogs]

Mae·ce·nas /mī seénəss/ (*plural same*) *n* a rich patron of the arts (*literary*)

Mae·ce·nas /mī seénəss, mee-/, **Gaius** (74?–8 B.C.) Roman politician. He was an adviser to Augustus and a generous patron of artists and writers, notably Horace and Virgil.

mael·strom /máylstrəm/ *n* **1.** an exceptionally large or violent whirlpool **2.** a situation marked by confusion, turbulence, strong feelings, violence, or destruction [Late 17C. < early modern Dutch, < *maalen* "whirl round" + *stroom* "stream"]

Mael·strom /máyl strəm/ marine whirlpool in northwestern Norway between two islands of the Lofoten Islands

mae·nad /meé nàd/ *n* **1.** in ancient Greece, a woman who belonged to the cult of Dionysus and took part in orgiastic rites **2.** a woman affected by wild, uncontrollable emotion (*literary*) [Late 16C. Via Latin < Greek *Mainad-*, stem of *Mainas* < *mainesthai* "rave"] —**mae·nad·ic** /mee náddik/ *adj*

maes·to·so /mī stṓsō/ *adv* in a dignified or majestic manner (*used as a musical direction*) ■ *n* (*plural* **-sos**) a section of a piece of music played maestoso [Early 18C. < Italian, "majestic" < Latin *majestas* (see MAJESTY)] —**ma·es·to·so** *adj*

Maes·tricht /maa strítkt, maástrikt/ ♦ **Maastricht**

maes·tro /místrō/ (*plural* **-tros** or **-tri** /-tree/) *n* an expert in an art or skill, especially an accomplished musician, conductor, or composer [Early 18C. Via Italian, "master" < Latin *magister*]

maes·tro di cap·pel·la /-dee kə péllə/ (*plural* **maes·tri di cap·pel·la**) *n* formerly, especially in 17th-century Italy, the director of a group of musicians, especially a chapel choir or the private orchestra of a royal court or noble household [*Di capella* < Italian, "of the chapel"]

Mae·ter·linck /máytər lìngk, méttər-/, **Maurice, Comte** (1862–1949) Belgian poet and playwright. He was an exponent of symbolism, exemplified by his play *Pelléas et Mélisande* (1892) and a volume of poetry, *Hothouses* (1889). Full name **Maeterlinck, Maurice Polydore Marie Bernard**

"The living are just the dead on vacation."
[Attributed to Maurice Maeterlinck]

Mae West /mày wést/, **mae west** *n* (*informal*) **1.** an inflatable life jacket, especially one issued to US pilots during World War II **2.** a parachute malfunction in which a suspension line goes over the top of the canopy, creating what appears to be a huge bra [Mid-20C. Because the shape reminded airmen of Mae WEST's large bosom]

Maf·e·king /maáfi kìng/ former name for **Mafikeng**

ma·fi·a /maáfee ə/, **Ma·fi·a** *n* a close-knit or influential group of people who work together and protect one another's interests or the interests of a particular person

Ma·fi·a /maáfee ə/ *n* a secret criminal organization originating in Sicily that spread to mainland Italy and the United States and is involved in international drug-dealing, racketeering, gambling, and prostitution [Mid-19C. < Italian dialect (Sicilian), "bragging"]

maf·ic /máffik/ *adj* relating to dark-colored minerals or rocks that are high in magnesium and iron [Early 20C. < MAGNESIUM + FERRIC]

Maf·i·keng /maáfi kèng/ capital of North West Province, South Africa. Its garrison, commanded by Lord Robert Baden-Powell, was besieged by Boer troops between October 1899 and May 1900. Population: 6,900 (1994). Former name **Mafeking** (until 1980)

Ma·fi·o·so /maàfee ṓssō, -ṓzō/ (*plural* **-si** /-see, -zee/ or **-sos**), **ma·fi·o·so** *n* a member of the Mafia criminal organization [Late 19C. < Italian < *mafia* "bragging"]

mag /mag/ *n* PUBL same as **magazine** (sense 1) (*informal*) [Early 19C. Shortening]

mag. *abbr* **1.** magazine **2.** magnesium **3.** magnet **4.** magnetic **5.** magnetism **6.** magnitude **7.** magnum

mag·a·log /mággə lòg/ *n* a catalog presented to look like a magazine, used as a marketing tool [Late 20C. Blend of MAGAZINE and CATALOG]

mag·a·zine /mággə zeén/ *n* **1. PERIODICAL PUBLICATION** a publication issued at regular intervals, usually weekly or monthly, containing articles, stories, photographs, advertisements, and other features, with a page size that is usually smaller than that of a newspaper but larger than that of a book **2. BULLET OR CARTRIDGE HOLDER** a detachable container for cartridges or bullets that can be quickly inserted or removed from a gun **3. STOREHOUSE FOR MILITARY SUPPLIES** a structure on land or a part of a ship where weapons, ammunition, explosives, and other military equipment or supplies are stored **4. STOCK OF AMMUNITION** a stock of ammunition or other supplies kept in a storehouse **5. SLIDE HOLDER** a container designed to hold a number of photographic slides and feed them automatically through a projector **6. FILM CONTAINER** a space or compartment in a camera from which film is loaded without exposing it to light **7. SUPPLY DEVICE** a device or container attached to a machine that holds or supplies necessary material **8. PROGRAM CONTAINING ASSORTED ITEMS** a television or radio program made up of an assortment of short factual items, often of interest to a particular group of people [Late 16C. Via French *magazin* < Italian *magazzino* < Arabic *makzan* "storehouse"]

Mag·da·le·na /màgdə láynə/ major river of Colombia. It flows north from the Andes into the Caribbean Sea. Length: 957 mi./1,540 km.

Mag·da·lene /mágdələn, -leén/ *n* BIBLE same as **Mary Magdalene**

Mag·de·burg /mágdə bùrg/ capital of Saxony-Anhalt State, north central Germany. Population: 265,379 (1997).

Ma·gel·lan, Strait of /mə géllən/ channel separating mainland South America and Tierra del Fuego, between the Atlantic and Pacific oceans. Length: 350 mi./560 km.

Ma·gel·lan /mə géllən/, **Ferdinand** (1480?–1521) Portuguese explorer. He sailed around South America through the Strait of Magellan and across the Pacific Ocean (1519–21). Although he died in the Philippines, his ship returned to Spain, completing the first circumnavigation of the Earth.

Mag·el·lan·ic Cloud /màjjə lánnik-/ *n* either of two small galaxies near the south celestial pole that are irregularly shaped and closest to the Milky Way [Early 17C. After Ferdinand MAGELLAN]

Ma·gen Da·vid /maágən dáyvid/ *n* JUDAISM same as **Star of David** [< Hebrew, "shield of David"]

ma·gen·ta /mə jéntə/ *n* **1.** a brilliant purplish pink color that is one of the three subtractive colors **2.** CHEM same as **fuchsin** ■ *adj* brilliant purplish pink in color [Mid-19C. After *Magenta*, N Italy]

mag·gid /maágid/ (*plural* **-ma·gid·im** /maa geédim/) *n* a popular teacher traveling among the Ashkenazi Jewish communities of Eastern Europe [Late 19C. < Hebrew *maggīd* "narrator"]

mag·gio·re /mə jáw ràyl/ *n* in music, a section of a fugue or set of variations in the major mode that occurs especially after a section in a minor mode [Late 19C. < Italian, "major"]

Mag·gio·re, Lake /mə jáw ràyl/ lake that lies partly in the Ticino Canton, Switzerland, and partly in the Lombardy Region of northern Italy. Area: 82 sq. mi./212 sq. km.

mag·got /mággət/ *n* **1. INSECT LARVA** the worm-shaped larva of various members of the fly family, found in decaying matter **2. SOMEBODY DESPICABLE** somebody who is despised (*insult slang*) **3. FANCY** a fanciful notion or idea (*archaic*) [14C. < *maddock* "worm, maggot" < Germanic]

mag·got·y /mággətee/ (**-i·er, -i·est**) *adj* full of or containing maggots

Mag·ha /múggə/ *n* in the Hindu calendar, the 11th month of the year, lasting 30 days and falling about the same time as January to February. See table at **calendar** [Late 20C. < Hindi]

Ma·ghreb /múgrəb/, **Ma·ghrib** loosely defined region in northwestern Africa, centered on Algeria, Morocco, and Tunisia

ma·gi RELIG plural of **magus**

Ma·gi /máy jì/ *npl* in the Bible, the group of three men who came to Bethlehem from the East to celebrate the birth of Jesus Christ. (Matthew 2: 1–12). They are sometimes known individually as Caspar, Melchior, and Balthazar, and jointly as the Three Wise Men or the Three Kings. [Plural of MAGUS] —**Ma·gi·an** /máyjee ən, -jən/ *adj, n* —**Ma·gi·an·ism** *n*

mag·ic /májjik/ *n* **1.** CONJURING TRICKS conjuring tricks and illusions that make apparently impossible things seem to happen, usually performed as entertainment **2.** INEXPLICABLE THINGS a special, mysterious, or inexplicable quality, talent, or skill ○ *watched the dancer's feet work their magic* **3.** SUPPOSED SUPERNATURAL POWER a supposed supernatural power that makes impossible things happen or gives somebody control over the forces of nature. Magic is used in many cultures for healing, keeping away evil, seeking the truth, and for vengeful purposes. **4.** PRACTICE OF MAGIC the use of supposed supernatural power to make impossible things happen ■ *adj* **1.** OF OR FOR MAGIC relating to magic or used in the working of magic ○ *a magic potion* **2.** PARTICULARLY IMPORTANT particularly important or desirable ○ *reach the magic number of 100 points* ■ *vt* (**-icked, -ick·ing, -ics**) SUBJECT SOMETHING TO MAGIC to make somebody or something seem to appear, disappear, change, or move by using magic [14C. Via Old French *magique* < Greek *magikē* < *magos* (see MAGUS)] ◇ **like magic 1.** inexplicably, as though by magic **2.** rapidly **3.** without obstacles or difficulties

CULTURAL NOTE ***The Magic Mountain***, a novel (1924) by German writer Thomas Mann. It describes young engineer Hans Castorp's lengthy stay in a Swiss TB clinic. The clinic is a microcosm of European society at the time of World War I, with a cosmopolitan group of patients reflecting a range of contemporary political, philosophical, and scientific viewpoints.

mag·i·cal /májjik'l/ *adj* **1.** created by or as if by magic **2.** so beautiful or pleasing as to seem supernaturally created —**mag·i·cal·ly** *adv*

mag·i·cal re·al·ism *n* ART same as **magic realism**

mag·ic bul·let *n* **1.** a drug that treats a serious disease with no undesirable side effects on the patient **2.** a quick and easy solution for a difficult problem, or a means of accomplishing the impossible

mag·ic car·pet *n* in fairy stories, a carpet that flies through the air and is used as a form of transportation

ma·gi·cian /mə jísh'n/ *n* **1.** CONJURER OR ILLUSIONIST an entertainer who performs conjuring tricks and illusions **2.** SOMEBODY WHO PRACTICES SORCERY somebody who uses supposed supernatural powers **3.** SOMEBODY WITH EXCEPTIONAL ABILITY an extraordinarily skilled or powerful person

Mag·ic Mark·er *tdmk* a trademark for a felt-tip pen that comes in various colors of ink

mag·ic mush·room *n* a fungus that contains a hallucinogenic substance (*informal*)

mag·ic num·ber *n* any of the numbers 2, 8, 20, 28, 50, 82, and 126 that represent the number of protons or neutrons in very stable atomic nuclei

mag·ic re·al·ism, **mag·i·cal re·al·ism** *n* a style of art or literature that depicts fantastic or mythological subjects in a realistic manner —**mag·ic re·al·ist** *n*

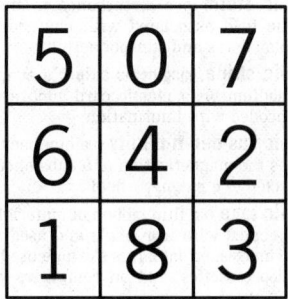

5	0	7
6	4	2
1	8	3

magic square

mag·ic square *n* a square containing rows and columns of numbers arranged in such a way that each horizontal, vertical, and diagonal line has the same sum

mag·ic wand *n* **1.** a small thin stick used by a sorcerer or conjurer while performing magic **2.** something fanciful or imaginary that would, if it existed, be able to solve a difficult or impossible problem immediately

ma·gilp *n* ART another spelling of **megilp**

Ma·gi·not line /mázhənō-, maazhə nṓ-/ *n* **1.** a line of fortifications constructed by the French along the border between France and Germany before World War II that failed to stop the German army from invading **2.** an ineffective defensive strategy that is relied on with unthinking confidence [Mid-20C. After André *Maginot* (1877–1932), French war minister]

mag·is·te·ri·al /màjjə steéree əl/ *adj* **1.** DIGNIFIED showing great dignity and authority **2.** DOMINEERING behaving in an overbearing or dictatorial way **3.** MASTERLY AND AUTHORITATIVE produced by or characteristic of a teacher, scholar, or expert **4.** OF MAGISTRATE relating to or characteristic of a magistrate —**mag·is·te·ri·al·ly** *adv* —**mag·is·te·ri·al·ness** *n*

mag·is·te·ri·um /màjji steéree əm/ *n* in the Roman Catholic tradition, the authority of the church to teach religious doctrine [Late 16C. < Latin < *magister* "master"]

mag·is·tra·cy /májjistrəssee/ (*plural* **-cies**) *n* **1.** OFFICE OF MAGISTRATE the position or function of a magistrate **2.** MAGISTRATE'S TERM OF OFFICE the term of office of a magistrate **3.** AREA OF MAGISTRATE'S JURISDICTION the district over which a magistrate has the power and authority to administer justice **4.** MAGISTRATES COLLECTIVELY magistrates considered as a group

mag·is·tral /májjistrəl/ *adj* **1.** OF MAGISTRATE relating to or characteristic of a magistrate **2.** OF EXPERT relating to or characteristic of an expert or scholar (*formal or archaic*) **3.** DETERMINING POSITION OF OTHER FORTIFICATIONS describes a line of fortifications that determines the position of other lines ■ *n* MAGISTRAL LINE OF FORTIFICATIONS a line of fortifications that determines the position of other lines —**mag·is·tral·i·ty** /màjji strállətee/ *n* —**mag·is·tral·ly** *adv*

mag·is·trate /májji stràyt, -strət/ *n* **1.** a judge in a lower court whose jurisdiction is limited to the trial of misdemeanors and the conduct of preliminary hearings on more serious charges **2.** a minor law officer or member of a local judiciary with extremely limited powers, e.g., a justice of the peace who deals with traffic violations [14C. < Latin *magistratus* < *magister* "master"] —**mag·is·trate·ship** *n*

mag·lev /mág lèv/, **Mag·lev** *n* an electrically operated high-speed train that glides above a track by means of a magnetic field. ◊ **magnetic levitation** [Late 20C. Blend of MAGNETIC + *levitation*]

mag·ma /mágmə/ (*plural* **-mas** or **-ma·ta** /-maatə/) *n* **1.** molten rock deep within the Earth from which igneous rock is formed by solidification at or near the Earth's surface **2.** a soft paste or thick suspension made from fine solid particles mixed with liquid [15C. Via Latin < Greek < *massein* "knead"] —**mag·mat·ic** /mag máttik/ *adj*

mag·ma cham·ber *n* an underground cavity that contains magma, often located below a volcano

Mag·na Car·ta /màgnə kaartə/, **Mag·na Char·ta** /-chaartə/ *n* **1.** a charter establishing the rights of English barons and free citizens, granted by King John at Runnymede in 1215 and regarded as the basis of civil and political liberty in England **2.** a document that recognizes or guarantees rights, privileges, or liberties [< Latin, "great charter"]

mag·na cum lau·de /màgnə kum lówdə, -lówdee/ *adv, adj* with the second-highest level of academic honors at graduation [< Latin, "with great praise"] —**mag·na cum lau·de** *adj*

Mag·na Grae·cia /màgnə greéshə/ *n* in ancient times, the parts of southern Italy and Sicily that contained numerous Greek colonies [< Latin, "great Greece"]

mag·na·nim·i·ty /màgnə nímmətee/ (*plural* **-ties**) *n* **1.** great generosity or noble-spiritedness **2.** a generous or noble-spirited act [14C. Via French *magnanimité* < Latin *magnanimitas* < *magnanimus* (see MAGNANIMOUS)]

mag·nan·i·mous /mag nánnəməss/ *adj* very generous, kind, or forgiving [Late 16C. < Latin *magnanimus* < *magnus* "great" + *animus* "mind"] —**mag·nan·i·mous·ly** *adv* —**mag·nan·i·mous·ness** *n*

SYNONYMS See ***generous***.

mag·nate /mág nàyt, -nət/ *n* somebody who has a lot of wealth and power, especially somebody in business or industry [15C. < late Latin *magnat-* < Latin *magnus* "great"] —**mag·nate·ship** *n*

mag·ne·sia /mag neézhə, -neéshə/ *n* CHEM same as **magnesium oxide** [14C. Via medieval Latin < Greek *magnēsia* "mineral from *Magnesia*," Asia Minor] —**mag·ne·sial** *adj* —**mag·ne·sian** *adj* —**mag·ne·sic** /-neéssik/ *adj*

mag·ne·site /mágnə sìt/ *n* a white or colorless magnesium carbonate mineral. Use: source of magnesium oxide, insulation, refractory lining of furnaces. [Early 19C. < MAGNESIA]

mag·ne·si·um /mag neézee əm/ *n* a light silver-white metallic element. Source: magnesite, dolomite, seawater. Use: alloys, metallurgy, photography, fireworks. Symbol **Mg**. See table at **element** [Early 19C. < MAGNESIA]

mag·ne·si·um car·bon·ate *n* a white crystalline salt. Source: dolomite, magnesite. Use: in antacids, glass, refractories. Formula: $MgCO_3$.

mag·ne·si·um chlo·ride *n* a colorless or white crystalline compound. Use: source of magnesium, in fireproofing, paper making, ceramics, fire extinguishers. Formula: $MgCl_2 6H_2O$.

mag·ne·si·um hy·drox·ide *n* a white crystalline powder. Use: antacid, laxative. Formula: $Mg(OH)_2$.

mag·ne·si·um ox·ide *n* a white powder. Source: periclase. Use: antacid, laxative, refractories, cements, electrical insulation, fertilizers. Formula: MgO.

mag·ne·si·um sul·fate *n* a colorless crystalline salt. Use: in medicine, fertilizers, manufacturing. Formula: $MgSO_4$.

mag·net /mágnət/ *n* **1.** a piece of metal that has the power to draw iron or steel objects toward it and to hold or move them **2.** same as **electromagnet 3.** somebody or something that has a great power of attraction over people [15C. Directly or via French < Latin *magneta* form of *magnes* < Greek *Magnēs lithos* "stone from Magnesia," Asia Minor]

mag·ne·tar /mágnə taar/ *n* a neutron star with an extremely strong magnetic field that emits gamma rays and X-rays. A magnetar's magnetic field can be a thousand trillion times stronger than that of the Earth. [Late 20C. Blend of MAGNETIC and QUASAR]

mag·net·ic /mag néttik/ *adj* **1.** HAVING POWER OF MAGNET able to attract iron or steel objects **2.** ABLE TO BE MAGNETIZED able to be magnetized, or attracted by a magnet **3.** RELATING TO MAGNETISM relating to, involving, or produced by magnetism **4.** USING MAGNET OR MAGNETISM containing or using a magnet or magnetism **5.** POWERFULLY CHARMING having a great power of attraction over people ○ *a magnetic personality* **6.** OF EARTH'S MAGNETISM relating to the Earth's magnetism ○ *magnetic North Pole* —**mag·net·i·cal·ly** *adv*

mag·net·ic bot·tle *n* a strong magnetic field. Use: to confine plasma in nuclear fusion experiments.

mag·net·ic bub·ble *n* a small movable magnetic region in a thin film of magnetic material. Use: to store data in computer memory.

mag·net·ic com·pass *n* an instrument used to indicate magnetic north and other directions, containing a magnetic needle that swings horizontally around a circle marked in degrees or with the points of the compass

mag·net·ic dec·li·na·tion *n* the angle between magnetic north and true north at a particular point on the Earth's surface

mag·net·ic disk *n* a computer disk consisting of one or more thin magnetically etched plates

mag·net·ic ep·och *n* a long period of geologic time between reversals of the Earth's magnetic field

mag·net·ic e·qua·tor *n* an imaginary line that lies near the geographic equator and passes through all points where a magnetic needle has no dip

mag·net·ic field *n* a region of space surrounding a magnetized body or current-carrying circuit in which the resulting magnetic force can be detected

mag·net·ic flux *n* the strength of a magnetic field represented by lines of force. Symbol ϕ

mag·net·ic flux den·si·ty *n* the strength of a magnetic field multiplied by the porosity of a medium, measured in teslas or gauss. Symbol *B*

mag·net·ic head *n* an electromagnetic device that reads, writes, or erases data on a magnetic medium

mag·net·ic in·duc·tion *n* PHYS same as **magnetic flux density**

mag·net·ic lev·i·ta·tion *n* a system of high-speed rail travel using magnetism both to suspend and to propel trains above and along the track

mag·net·ic me·rid·i·an *n* an imaginary line around the Earth's surface that passes through both magnetic poles

mag·net·ic mine *n* an underwater mine equipped with magnetic sensors that cause it to detonate when a large metal object, usually a ship, passes into its magnetic field

mag·net·ic mir·ror *n* PHYS same as **magnetic bottle**

mag·net·ic mo·ment *n* a vector quantity representing the torque experienced by a magnetic system in a magnetic field. Symbol *m*

mag·net·ic nee·dle *n* a thin bar of magnetized metal used in navigational instruments, mounted or suspended so that it swings freely in a horizontal circle and indicates the direction of the Earth's magnetic poles

mag·net·ic north *n* the direction of the north magnetic pole, indicated by the needle of a magnetic compass

mag·net·ic pole *n* **1.** either of the two points at the end of a magnet where the magnet's field is most intense **2.** either of the two regions on the Earth's surface near the geographic poles where the Earth's magnetic field is most intense

mag·net·ic re·cord·ing *n* **1.** the storage of analog or digital data on a magnetized medium such as audio, video, or computer data on tape, disk, or cards **2.** a surface on which information has been magnetically recorded

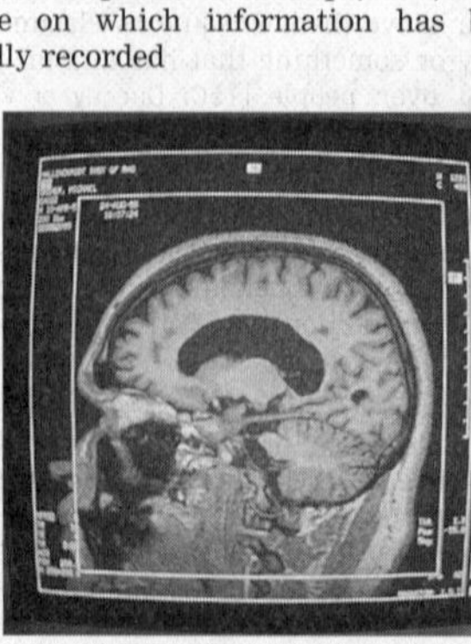

Roger Ressmeyer/Corbis

magnetic resonance imaging

mag·net·ic res·o·nance im·ag·ing *n* an imaging technique that uses electromagnetic radiation to obtain images of the body's soft tissues, e.g., the brain and spinal cord. The body is subjected to a powerful magnetic field, allowing tiny signals from atomic nuclei to be detected and then processed and converted into images by a computer.

mag·net·ic re·vers·al *n* the reversal of the Earth's magnetic poles that has occurred at irregular intervals averaging approximately one million years

mag·net·ic sense *n* BIOL same as **compass sense**

mag·net·ic storm *n* a disturbance in the Earth's magnetic field associated with charged particles from solar flares and sunspot activity

mag·net·ic stripe, mag·net·ic strip *n* a strip of magnetic medium on a plastic card such as a credit card, encoded with information

mag·net·ic sus·cep·ti·bil·i·ty *n* a number that characterizes the magnetization of a substance when it is subjected to a magnetic field

mag·net·ic tape *n* a thin ribbon of material, usually plastic, coated with iron oxide and used to record sounds, images, or data. It is the tape used in audio and video cassettes, and on computers with tape drives.

mag·net·ic tran·si·tion tem·per·a·ture *n* PHYS same as **Curie point**

mag·net·ic var·i·a·tion *n* PHYS same as **magnetic declination**

mag·net·ism /mágnə tìzzəm/ *n* **1.** ATTRACTION OF MAGNETS FOR IRON the phenomenon of physical attraction for iron, inherent in magnets or induced by a moving electric charge or current **2.** FORCE OF MAGNETIC FIELD the force exerted by a magnetic field **3.** PERSONAL ATTRACTION the strong attractiveness of something, especially the power of somebody's personality to influence others ○ *"He was a born boon companion, with a magnetism which drew good humor from all around him."* (Arthur Conan Doyle, *The Valley of Fear*; 1915)

mag·net·ite /mágnə tìt/ *n* a common black magnetic mineral consisting of iron oxide. Use: source of iron.

mag·net·ize /mágnə tìz/ (**-ized, -iz·ing, -iz·es**) *v* **1.** *vti* to become magnetic, or make an object or material magnetic **2.** *vt* to hold a strong attraction for somebody ○ *prospectors magnetized by the possibility of finding gold in the hills* —**mag·net·iz·a·ble** *adj* —**mag·net·i·za·tion** /màgnəti záysh'n/ *n* —**mag·net·iz·er** *n*

mag·ne·to /mag neétō/ (*plural* **-tos**) *n* a small alternator that uses permanent magnets to generate a spark in an internal-combustion engine, especially in marine and aircraft engines [Late 19C. Shortening of *magnetoelectric machine*]

magneto- *prefix* magnetic field ○ *magnetograph* [< MAGNET]

mag·ne·to·e·las·tic /mag neétō i lástik/ *adj* describes a ferromagnetic material in which the elastic strain imposed on it determines its magnetization —**mag·ne·to·e·las·ti·ci·ty** /-i lass tíssətee, -ee lass-/ *n*

mag·ne·to·e·lec·tron·ics /mag neétō i lek trónniks, -ee lek-/ *n* PHYS same as **spintronics** —**mag·ne·to·e·lec·tron·ic** *adj*

mag·ne·to·graph /mag neétō gràf/ *n* an instrument used to record variations in a magnetic field, usually that of the Earth

mag·ne·to·hy·dro·dy·nam·ics /mag neétō hìdrō dī námmiks/ *n* the study of magnetic and electric fields in relation to the movement of electrically conducting fluids such as plasmas and molten metal (*takes a singular verb*) —**mag·ne·to·hy·dro·dy·nam·ic** *adj*

mag·ne·tom·e·ter /màgnə tómmətər/ *n* a device for measuring the direction and intensity of a magnetic field

mag·ne·to·mo·tive /mag neétō mṓtiv/ *adj* relating to or producing a magnetic flux [Late 19C. After ELECTROMOTIVE]

mag·ne·to·mo·tive force *n* a force that produces magnetic flux. Symbol F_m

mag·ne·ton /mágnə tòn/ *n* a unit that expresses the combined force and direction of a magnetic field (**magnetic moment**) such as that of an atom or elementary particle [Early 20C. < MAGNETIC]

mag·ne·to·pause /mag neétə pàwz/ *n* the region between the magnetosphere and outer space

mag·ne·to·sphere /mag neétō sfeer/ *n* the region surrounding an astronomical object such as the Earth, in which charged particles are trapped and affected by the object's magnetic field —**mag·ne·to·spher·ic** /mag neétō sférrik, -sfeérik/ *adj*

mag·ne·to·tac·tic /mag neétō táktik/ *adj* describes a cell or microorganism that is able to orient itself in relation to a magnetic field ○ *magnetotactic bacteria*

mag·ne·to·tail /mag neétō tàyl/ *n* the long tapering region of plasma that is driven away from an astronomical object's magnetosphere by the solar wind

mag·ne·to·tax·is /mag neétō táksiss/ (*plural* **-tax·es** /-ták seez/) *n* a movement of a cell or microorganism in response to a magnetic field

mag·ne·to·the·ra·py /mag neétō thérrəpee/ *n* the use or wearing of magnets to prevent, alleviate, or remedy medical conditions

mag·ne·tron /mágnə tròn/ *n* a vacuum tube in which the flow of electrons is manipulated by electric and magnetic fields to generate microwaves. The microwave radiation produced is either pulsed, for use in radar applications, or continuous, as required for microwave cooking.

mag·net school *n* a public school that specializes in particular subjects, in addition to providing general education, and draws students from inside and outside the local area

~~magnificant~~ incorrect spelling of **magnificent**

Mag·nif·i·cat /mag níffi kàt/ *n* **1.** in the Bible, Mary's hymn of praise to God when she learns she is to be the mother of Jesus Christ, sometimes sung or chanted in church (Luke 1: 46–55) **2.** any hymn of praise sung or chanted in church [12C. < Latin, "(my soul) magnifies," a form of *magnificare* (see MAGNIFY), from the opening word of the Latin version]

mag·ni·fi·ca·tion /màgnəfi káysh'n/ *n* **1.** INCREASE IN APPARENT SIZE the process of causing an object or image to appear larger than it really is, especially by using a lens or microscope **2.** DEGREE OF ENLARGEMENT the amount by which an image is made bigger **3.** RATIO INDICATING SIZE the size of the image of an object, expressed as a ratio of its actual size **4.** INCREASING OF ACTUAL SIZE the process of increasing the actual size or magnitude of something **5.** GROWTH IN IMPORTANCE the increasing of the importance attributed to somebody or something **6.** ENLARGED COPY OF SOMETHING a copy of a map, photograph, or other image that has been made larger than the original

mag·nif·i·cence /mag níffiss'nss/ *n* **1.** the impressive beauty or grandeur of somebody or something **2.** the great richness and splendor of somebody or something, usually indicating great wealth [14C. Directly or via Old French < Latin *magnificentia* < *magnificent-* (see MAGNIFICENT)]

mag·nif·i·cent /mag níffiss'nt/ *adj* **1.** beautiful and impressive ○ *a magnificent view of Rome from our balcony* **2.** exceptionally good of its kind [15C. Directly or via Old French < Latin *magnificent-* "performing great actions" < *magnus* "great"] —**mag·nif·i·cent·ly** *adv*

CULTURAL NOTE ***The Magnificent Ambersons***, a movie (1942) by director Orson Welles. Based on a novel by Booth Tarkington, it is set in the US Midwest during the Industrial Revolution and contrasts the declining fortunes of the upper-class Amberson family with the rise of a young entrepreneur. Despite suffering savage cuts at the hands of the studio, it is regarded as one of Welles's masterpieces.

mag·nif·i·co /mag níffikō/ (*plural* **-coes** or **-cos**) *n* **1.** a rich or powerful person **2.** a nobleman of the Venetian Republic [Late 16C. < Italian, "magnificent"]

mag·ni·fy /mágnə fì/ (**-fied, -fy·ing, -fies**) *v* **1.** *vt* INCREASE APPARENT SIZE OF SOMETHING to cause something to appear larger than it is, especially by using a microscope or lens ○ *a virus magnified 50,000 times* **2.** *vt* INCREASE ACTUAL SIZE OF SOMETHING to increase the actual size or magnitude of something **3.** *vt* INCREASE IMPORTANCE OF SOMETHING to increase the importance attributed to somebody or something ○ *The complexities of today's medicine only magnify the need for better hospital management.* **4.** *vt* OVERSTATE IMPORTANCE to cause somebody or something to appear more important than is in fact the case ○ *The report was highly inaccurate, magnifying the dangers posed by the new vaccine.* **5.** *vi* HAVE ENLARGING ABILITY to have the ability to increase the size or magnitude of something **6.** *vt* PRAISE GOD to give praise or thanks to God (*formal*) ○ *"my heart doth magnify his holy name"* (*The Book of Mormon [part 1]*) [14C. Directly or via Old French *magnifier* < Latin *magnificare* "make greater" < *magnus* "great"] —**mag·ni·fi·a·ble** *adj* —**mag·ni·fi·er** *n*

mag·ni·fy·ing glass /mágnə fì ing-/ *n* a convex lens in a frame with a handle, used to make objects viewed through it appear larger

mag·nil·o·quent /mag níllәkwənt/ *adj* employing impressive words and an exaggeratedly solemn and dignified style (*formal*) [Mid-17C. < Latin *magniloquus* < *magnus* "great" + *-loquus* "speaking"] —**mag·nil·o·quence** *n* —**mag·nil·o·quent·ly** *adv*

Mag·ni·to·gorsk /mag neetə gáwrsk/ city in southwestern Siberian Russia, on the Ural River. Population: 462,766 (1995).

mag·ni·tude /mágnə to͞od/ *n* **1. GREATNESS OF SIZE** greatness of size, volume, or extent ○ *computing the magnitude of heavenly bodies* **2. IMPORTANCE** the importance or significance of something ○ *the magnitude of the discovery* **3. STATUS** great personal importance or status ○ *a baseball star of unrivaled magnitude* **4.** GEOL **MEASURE OF EARTHQUAKE SIZE** a measure of the energy of an earthquake, specified on the Richter scale **5.** MATH **NUMBER ASSIGNED TO MATHEMATICAL QUANTITY** a numerical value that describes the amount of something, usually expressed in terms of a multiple of standard units, or the item measured in this way **6.** ASTRON **BRIGHTNESS OF ASTRONOMICAL OBJECT** a numerical measure of the apparent brightness of an astronomical object, on a scale in which a lower number represents greater brightness [14C. < Latin *magnitudo* < *magnus* "great"] —**mag·ni·tu·di·nous** /màgnə to͞od'nəss/ *adj*

mag·no·lia /mag nṓlyə/ (*plural same* or **-lias**) *n* **1.** an evergreen or deciduous tree or bush with typically large simple leaves, widely cultivated as an ornamental. Flowers: yellow, white, pink, or green. Native to: North America, Asia. Genus: *Magnolia.* **2.** a creamy white color [Mid-18C. After Pierre *Magnol* (1638–1715), French botanist] —**mag·no·lia** *adj*

Mag·no·lia State *n* a nickname for Mississippi

mag·num /mágnəm/ *n* **1.** a wine bottle that holds approximately 1.5 liters, the equivalent of two normal bottles **2.** the volume of liquid contained in a magnum [Late 18C. < Latin, a form of *magnus* "large"]

ORIGIN The Latin word *magnus* "great," from which ***magnum*** is derived, is also the source of English *magnanimous, magnate, magnificent, magnify, magnitude, major, maximum,* and *mayor.*

Mag·num /mágnəm/ *tdmk* a trademark for cartridges that have a larger charge and casing than other gun cartridges of the same caliber, or firearms capable of shooting these

mag·num o·pus *n* a great work of art or literature, especially the finest work produced by one artist or author [< Latin, "great work"]

Ma·gog *n* BIBLE ➧ **Gog and Magog**

ma·got /ma gṓ, mággət/ *n* **1.** ZOOL same as **Barbary ape** **2.** a crouching, often grotesque figurine in the Japanese or Chinese style [Early 17C. < Old French *magos,* a kind of monkey < *Magog* "Magog" (see GOG AND MAGOG, used as emblems of ugliness in medieval romance)]

magpie

mag·pie /mág pī/ *n* **1. BLACK AND WHITE BIRD** a bird of the crow family with black and white feathers, a long wedge-shaped tail, and a chattering call. Genus: *Pica.* **2. ASIAN BIRD** a brightly colored long-tailed bird of the crow family. Native to: mainly Southeast Asia. Genera: *Cissa* or *Urocissa* or *Cyanopica.* **3. TALKATIVE PERSON** an incurable chatterer (*informal*) **4. AVID COLLECTOR** an enthusiastic or compulsive collector, especially of small objects (*informal*) [Late 16C. < *Mag,* shortening of the name *Margaret* + PIE[4]]

Ma·gritte /maa greet/, **René** (1898–1967) Belgian painter. A leading member of the Belgian surrealists, his work consists of strange juxtapositions of ordinary objects and parodies of famous paintings. Full name **Magritte, René François Ghislain**

Mag·say·say /maag sī sī/, **Ramón** (1907–57) Philippine president (1953–57). As defense secretary (1950–53), he crushed the communist Huk guerilla movement. He left the Liberal party in 1953 and successfully ran for president as the Nationalist candidate.

mag tape *n* same as **magnetic tape** (*informal*)

ma·guey /ma gáy, mág wày/ *n* **1.** fiber made from the stalk of a tropical plant, or a rope made of this fiber **2.** a tropical plant that forms a cluster of 20–50 stiff upright leaves edged with prickles. Use: source of fiber, pulque production. Native to: Mexico. Genus: *Agave.* [Mid-16C. Via Spanish < Taino]

ma·gus /máygəss/ (*plural* **-gi** /-jī/) *n* **1.** in the ancient Persian religion of Zoroastrianism, a priest **2.** especially in ancient times, a man with supernatural or magical powers [Early 17C. Via Latin < Greek *magos* < Old Persian *maguš*] —**ma·gi·an** /máyjee ən/ *adj* —**ma·gi·an·ism** /-jee ə nìzzəm/ *n*

CULTURAL NOTE ***The Magus,*** a novel (1966) by British writer John Fowles. The plot concerns a young teacher, Nicholas Urfe, who takes a job on a Greek island and finds himself lured into an elaborate fiction staged by a wealthy resident, Maurice Conchis. Fowles uses this enigmatic story to explore the nature of individual identity and freedom of choice.

Ma·gus *n* BIBLE ➧ **Magi** (*literary*)

Mag·yar /mág yaar, maag-/ (*plural* **-yars** or *same*) *n* **1.** a member of the Hungarian people that forms the largest population group of Hungary **2.** LANG same as **Hungarian** (sense 2) [Late 18C. < Hungarian] —**Mag·yar** *adj*

Ma·ha·bha·ra·ta /mə haa baarətə/ *n* one of India's two great national epic poems, with nearly 100,000 verses, written in Sanskrit from about 300 B.C. It tells of the great war in northern India between the Pandava and Kaurava families. The "Bhagavad-Gita" is the most celebrated section of the Mahabharata. [Late 18C. < Sanskrit, "the great history of the Bharata dynasty"]

Ma·ha·jang·a /maa haazhángə/ port on the northwestern coast of Madagascar. Population: 100,807 (1993).

ma·ha·leb /maahə lèb/ *n* a tree whose seeds are used in southwestern Asian and southeastern European cookery. It is used as a grafting stock in the United States. Latin name: *Prunus mahaleb.* [Mid-16C. Via French < Arabic *maḥaleb*]

Ma·han /mə hán/, **Alfred Thayer** (1840–1914) US naval officer. He devised theories about naval power, published in *The Influence of Sea Power upon History 1660–1783* (1870).

ma·ha·ra·jah /maahə raajə, -raazhə/, **ma·ha·ra·ja** *n* **1.** an Indian prince of a rank above a rajah, especially the ruler of one of the former Native States of India **2.** *S Asia* a person of aristocratic tastes and behavior [Late 17C. < Sanskrit < *mahā* "great" + *rājan* "raja"]

ma·ha·ra·ni /maahə raanee/ *n* **1.** the wife or widow of a maharajah **2.** an Indian princess of a rank above a rani, especially the ruler of one of the former Native States of India [Mid-19C. < Hindi < Sanskrit *mahā* "great" + *rājñī*]

Ma·ha·rash·tra /maahə raashtrə/ state in western India, situated in the northwestern part of the Deccan plateau. Capital: Mumbai. Population: 96,752,247 (2001). Area: 118,800 sq. mi./307,690 sq. km. Language: mainly Marathi.

ma·ha·ri·shi /maahə reeshee/ *n* a Hindu religious teacher [Late 18C. < Sanskrit *maharṣi* < *mahā* "great" + *ṛṣi* "inspired sage"]

ma·hat·ma /mə haatmə, -hát-/ *n* *S Asia* a title given to somebody who is deeply revered for wisdom and virtue [Late 19C. < Sanskrit *mahātman* < *mahā* "great" + *ātman* "soul"]

Ma·ha·ya·na /maahə yaanə/ *n* the branch of Buddhism that includes Tibetan, Chinese, and Zen Buddhism, developed around A.D. 1. It stresses compassion for all sentient beings and universal salvation. [Mid-19C. < Sanskrit < *mahā* "great" + *yanā* "vehicle"]

Mah·di /maadee/ *n* in Islamic belief, a prophet or messiah who is expected to appear in the world sometime before it ends [Early 19C. < Arabic *al-mahdī* "he who is rightly guided" < *hadā* "lead in the right way"] —**Mah·dism** *n* —**Mah·dist** *n*

Ma·hé /maa háy/ largest island in the Seychelles, in the western Indian Ocean. Population: 59,500 (1987). Area: 57 sq. mi./148 sq. km.

Mah·fouz /maa fo͞oz/, **Naguib** (*b.* 1911) Egyptian novelist and screenwriter. He is author of *The Cairo Trilogy* (1956–57) and other works that explore Egyptian society and culture. He won the Nobel Prize in literature (1988).

Ma·hi·can /mə heekən/ *n* **1.** a member of a Native North American confederacy of peoples who lived in the upper Hudson River Valley of New York. Their descendants live in Wisconsin and Oklahoma. **2.** the Algonquian language of the Mahican people [Early 17C. < Mahican *muhheakunneuw* "people of the tidal water"] —**Ma·hi·can** *adj*

ma·hi·ma·hi /maahee maahee/ *n* a tropical sea fish with a bright blue body and long dorsal fin. Latin name: *Coryphaena hippurus.* [< Hawaiian]

mah·jongg /maa zhóng, -jóng/, **mah·jong** *n* a game of Chinese origin using 144 small tiles bearing various designs, played by four people around a square table. The winning player is the first one who completes a particular pattern using 13 tiles. [Early 20C. < Chinese *má jiàng*]

Bettmann/Corbis

Gustav Mahler

Mah·ler /maalər/, **Gustav** (1860–1911) Czech-born Austrian composer and conductor. He is best known for his songs and large-scale orchestral works, many of them involving voices, as in *Das Lied von der Erde* (*The Song of the Earth*) (1908).

Mah·mud II /maa mo͞od/ (1785–1839) Turkish national leader. He was the sultan of the Ottoman Empire (1808–39).

Mah·mud of Ghaz·na /-gaaznə/ (971–1030) Afghan sultan. He developed Ghazni, formerly Ghazna, into a center of power and culture, through conquest.

ma·hog·a·ny /mə hóggənee/ (*plural* **-nies**) *n* **1. REDDISH BROWN HARDWOOD** a hard reddish brown wood. Use: construction, furniture-making. **2. TROPICAL HARDWOOD TREE** an evergreen hardwood tree cultivated for its timber. Native to: tropical America. Genus: *Swietenia.* **3. REDDISH BROWN** a dark reddish brown color [Mid-17C. < obsolete Spanish *mahogani*] —**ma·hog·a·ny** *adj*

ma·ho·ni·a /mə hṓnee ə/ *n* an evergreen bush typically with spiny leaflets, widely cultivated as an ornamental. Flowers: small, yellow, in clusters. Native to: America, Asia. Genus: *Mahonia.* [Early 19C. After Bernard *McMahon* (1775–1816), US botanist]

Ma·ho·ning /mə hṓning/ river rising in northeastern Ohio and flowing westward through northwestern Pennsylvania. Length: 90 mi./140 km.

ma·hout /mə hówt/ *n* in South and Southeast Asia, somebody who trains, drives, and takes care of elephants [Mid-17C. Via Hindi *mahāut* < Sanskrit *mahāmātra* "high official" < *mahā* "great" + *mātra* "measure"]

Mah·rat·ta *n* PEOPLES another spelling of **Maratha**

Mah·rat·ti *n, adj* LANG, PEOPLES another spelling of **Marathi**

mah·zor /maakh zàwr, maakh záwr/ (*plural* **-zor·im** /maakh záwrim, maakh zaw reem/ or **-zors**), **mach·zor** *n* a Jewish prayer book that details the rituals prescribed for festivals and holidays [Mid-19C. < Hebrew *maḥzōr*]

maid /mayd/ *n* **1. WOMAN DOMESTIC WORKER** a female domestic employee such as one working in a hotel or tourist accommodations **2. YOUNG UNMARRIED WOMAN** a young unmarried woman (*archaic or literary; sometimes offensive*) **3.** UNMARRIED WOMAN an unmarried woman past middle age (*archaic or literary; often offensive*) **4.** VIRGIN a woman who has never had sexual intercourse (*archaic or literary*) **5.** WOMAN SERVANT a female servant, especially one working in a large private house (*dated*) [12C. Shortening of MAIDEN]

maid·en /máyd'n/ *n* **1.** YOUNG UNMARRIED WOMAN a young unmarried woman (*archaic or literary; sometimes offensive*) **2.** VIRGIN a woman who has never had sexual intercourse (*archaic or literary*) **3.** HORSE YET TO WIN a horse that has never won a race **4.** GUILLOTINE in 16th- and 17th-century Scotland, a guillotine used to execute criminals ■ *adj* **1.** FIRST done for the very first time (*sometimes offensive*) ○ *a maiden voyage* **2.** UNTOUCHED still in its original, unused, untouched, or unexplored condition (*literary; sometimes offensive*) ○ *maiden territory* **3.** FOR HORSES YET TO WIN for horses that have never won a race [Old English *mægden* < Germanic, "young woman"]

maid·en·hair fern /máyd'n her-/ *n* an ornamental fern with slender dark stems and delicate fronds of numerous leaflets. Native to: warm moist regions worldwide. Genus: *Adiantum.*

maid·en·hair tree *n* TREES same as **ginkgo**

maid·en·head /máyd'n hèd/ *n* (*literary*) **1.** same as **hymen 2.** a woman's virginity [13C. < MAIDEN + *-head,* a variant of HOOD[1]]

maid·en·hood /máyd'n hòod/ *n* the period of a woman's life before she marries or becomes sexually active (*archaic; sometimes considered offensive*)

maid·en·ly /máyd'nlee/ *adj* of, like, or thought suitable for a maiden —**maid·en·li·ness** *n*

maid·en name *n* the former family name of a married woman who has assumed her husband's family name

maid-in-wait·ing (*plural* **maids-in-wait·ing**) *n* a young, usually unmarried, lady-in-waiting

Maid Mar·i·an /mayd mérree ən/ *n* in English legend, the beautiful young noblewoman loved by Robin Hood

maid of hon·or *n* **1.** a young unmarried woman who is the bride's chief attendant at a wedding **2.** an unmarried woman of noble birth who attends a queen or princess

maid·ser·vant /máyd sùrvənt/ *n* same as **maid** (sense 5) (*dated*)

Maid·stone /máydstən/ city in Kent, southeastern England, on the Medway River. Population: 138,948 (2001).

Maid·u·gu·ri /mī dóogəree/ city in Borno State, northeastern Nigeria. Population: 312,100 (1995).

ma·ieu·tic /may yóotik, mī-/, **ma·ieu·ti·cal** /may yóotik'l, mī-/ *adj* PHILOSOPHY same as **Socratic** [Mid-17C. < Greek *maieutikos* "acting as midwife" < *maia* "midwife"]

mai·gre /máygər, méggrə/ *adj* **1.** containing no meat and therefore suitable for eating on days when abstinence from meat is prescribed by the Roman Catholic Church **2.** describes a day when abstinence from meat is prescribed by the Roman Catholic Church [Late 17C. < French, "lean"]

mail[1] /mayl/ *n* **1.** ITEMS SENT the letters, cards, periodicals, and packages that are handled and distributed in a postal system ○ *Is there any mail for me?* **2.** *also* **mails** POSTAL SYSTEM the system that handles the collection and delivery of mail (*often used before a noun*) ○ *send it by mail* **3.** SPECIFIC MAIL COLLECTION OR DELIVERY a particular collection or delivery of letters, cards, periodicals, and packages ○ *It came in yesterday's mail.* **4.** VEHICLE DELIVERING MAIL a car, train, ship, aircraft, or other vehicle used to collect and deliver mail **5.** same as **e-mail** (*informal*) ■ *vt* (**mailed, mail·ing, mails**) **1.** SEND SOMETHING BY MAIL to send a letter, card, periodical, or package by mail **2.** E-MAIL SOMEBODY to send somebody a message by e-mail [13C. < Old French *male* "bag, trunk" < Germanic, "bag, wallet"] —**mail·a·ble** *adj*

mail[2] /mayl/ *n* **1.** ARMOR flexible armor made of interlocking metal rings or overlapping metal plates **2.** ANIMAL'S BODY COVERING the hard protective body covering of some animals such as turtles and crabs ■ *vt* (**mailed, mail·ing, mails**) PROTECT WITH ARMOR to cover or protect the body with mail armor [13C. < French *maille* "mesh" < Latin *macula* "spot, holes in a net"]

mail·bag /máyl bàg/ *n* **1.** BAG FOR TRANSPORTING MAIL a bag used for transporting mail, typically a sack made of coarse material **2.** MAIL CARRIER'S BAG a large bag, usually with a shoulder strap, used by mail carriers **3.** MAIL RECEIVED mail received by a person or organization ○ *This week's mailbag is bursting with complaints about the schedule change.* [Early 19C. < MAIL[1]]

mail bomb *n* **1.** an explosive device sent by mail in a package or letter and set to explode when the package or letter is opened **2.** a form of electronic harassment in which massive amounts of e-mail are sent to a single system and crash it by filling up the available disk space —**mail-bomb** *vt*

mail·box /máyl bòks/ *n* **1.** PUBLIC COLLECTION BOX FOR MAILING LETTERS a box in a public place where letters can be left for later collection by a mail carrier **2.** BOX FOR RECEIVING MAIL a container into which mail is delivered **3.** MESSAGE STORAGE FILE a storage area on a computer for e-mail or voice-mail messages [Early 19C. < MAIL[1]]

mail car·ri·er *n* a post office employee who delivers mail to homes and businesses

mail·drop /máyl dròp/ *n* **1.** a container into which delivered mail is placed **2.** a place where mail or messages can be left for later pickup by somebody else, often secretly

mailed fist *n* the threat of military force (*literary*) [< MAIL[2]]

mail·er /máylər/ *n* **1.** MAIL CONTAINER a carton or tube for sending objects of a particular kind through the mail **2.** MAIL SENDER a person or organization that uses the postal system ○ *Mailers of valuables are advised to insure them.* **3.** SOMEBODY WHO PREPARES MAIL somebody whose job it is to address, stamp, weigh, and sort items for mailing **4.** MACHINE THAT PREPARES MAIL a machine that seals, stamps, and sorts letters **5.** ADVERTISEMENT an advertising leaflet sent with a letter [Late 19C. < MAIL[1]]

Mail·er /máylər/, **Norman** (*b.* 1923) US writer. Famed for his World War II novel *The Naked and the Dead* (1948), he founded New Journalism with his coverage of 1960s political events, and shared a Pulitzer Prize for *Armies of the Night* (1968). See Cultural note at **naked**

> "Once a newspaper touches a story, the facts are lost forever, even to the protagonists."
> [Norman Mailer, *The Presidential Papers;* 1963]

mail form *n* a webpage designed to be used as an online order form

mail·ing /máyling/ *n* **1.** ACT OF SENDING BY MAIL the act of sending items for delivery by mail **2.** SOMETHING SENT BY MAIL a letter, card, or package sent by mail ○ *send out a mailing advertising the service* **3.** BATCH OF LETTERS mail sent by one sender at one time ○ *a big mailing to her constituents* ■ *adj* RELATING TO MAIL suitable for or associated with mail ○ *a mailing label* ○ *mailing costs* [Late 19C. < MAIL[1]]

mail·ing ad·dress *n* an address to which mail can be delivered

mail·ing list *n* a list, typically computerized, of names and addresses to which advertising material or information can be mailed

mail·lot /maa yṓ/ *n* **1.** STRETCHY FABRIC a soft stretchable jersey fabric **2.** LEOTARD OR TIGHTS a leotard or a pair of tights made of maillot, worn for dancing or gymnastics **3.** SWIMSUIT a woman's one-piece bathing suit made of stretchy fabric, especially one with a high-cut leg **4.** CLOSE-FITTING TOP a tight-fitting knitted top or jersey [Late 19C. < French, "swaddling clothes" < *maille* (see MAIL[2])]

mail·man /máyl màn, -mən/ (*plural* **-men** /-mèn, -mən/) *n* a man who delivers mail [Late 19C. < MAIL[1]]

mail merge *n* the process of producing a personalized letter for each person on a mailing list by combining a database of names and addresses with a form letter created in a word processing program

mail or·der *n* **1.** a method of buying and selling goods, in which customers usually select what they want to buy from a catalog, then send and receive their orders by mail (*hyphenated when used before a noun*) ○ *a mail-order catalog* **2.** an order for goods to be sent by mail

mail·per·son /máyl pùrss'n/ (*plural* **-per·sons** or **-peo·ple** /-peep'l/) *n* somebody who delivers mail

mail·room /máyl ròom, -ròom/ *n* a room in an organization where mail is sorted, sent out, received, and distributed [Late 19C. < MAIL[1]]

mail serv·er *n* a remote computer controlling the sending and receiving of e-mail

mail slot *n* a narrow opening in a door through which a mail carrier can push envelopes, cards, and periodicals [Mid-20C. < MAIL[1]]

mail·wom·an /máyl wòommən/ (*plural* **-wom·en** /-wìmmin/) *n* a woman who delivers mail

maim /maym/ (**maimed, maim·ing, maims**) *vt* to inflict a severe and permanent injury on a person or animal, especially one that renders a limb useless ○ *maimed by a land mine* [14C. < Old French *mahaignier*]

main /mayn/ *adj* **1.** PRINCIPAL greatest in size or importance ○ *the main reason we're here* **2.** UTMOST exerted to the full or the utmost ○ *main force* **3.** NAUT OF MAINMAST on or relating to a sailing ship's mainmast ■ *n* **1.** LARGE PIPE OR CABLE a large and important pipe or line for the distribution of water, gas, or electricity ○ *a ruptured water main* **2.** SEA the open sea (*archaic or literary*) [Old English *mægen,* influenced by Old Norse *magn* < Germanic, "have power"] ◇ **in the main** largely or in general

Main /mīn, mayn/ river in south central Germany. Length: 325 mi./523 km.

main chance *n* somebody's chief opportunity ○ *our main chance for victory*

main course *n* the most substantial dish eaten at a meal with several courses

main drag *n* the principal street of a town or city (*informal*)

Maine

Maine /mayn/ state in the northeastern United States, bordered by New Hampshire, Canada, and the Atlantic Ocean. Capital: Augusta. Population: 1,294,464 (2002 estimate). Area: 33,741 sq. mi./87,389 sq. km.

Maine coon, Maine coon cat *n* a large domestic cat with a longhaired coat that is usually brown with bold black stripes, belonging to a breed that developed in North America

main·frame /máyn fràym/ *n* a fast powerful computer with a large storage capacity that can accommodate several users simultaneously

main·land /máynlənd, -lànd/ *n* the principal landmass of a continent or country as distinct from its islands, and sometimes also excluding its peninsulas (*often used before a noun*) ○ *a ferry from the mainland* —**main·land·er** *n*

Main·land /máynlənd/ **1.** largest of the Orkney Islands, northeastern Scotland. Population: 15,123 (1991). Area: 195 sq. mi./500 sq. km. **2.** largest of the Shetland Islands, northeastern Scotland. Population: 17,562 (1991). Area: 406 sq. mi./1,053 sq. km.

main line *n* **1.** MAIN RAIL ROUTE a major rail route between two cities, from which branch lines often lead off **2.** ROADS MAIN ROAD a major road route **3.** PRINCIPAL VEIN a major vein in the arm or leg into which drugs may be injected (*slang*)

main·line /máyn līn/ *vti* (**-lined, -lin·ing, -lines**) (*slang*) **1.** TAKE DRUGS INTRAVENOUSLY to inject an illicit drug, especially heroin or cocaine, intravenously **2.** CONSUME EXCESSIVELY to consume or do something excessively, or be affected by something excessively ■ *adj* **1.** ESTABLISHED well established, accepted, or mainstream ○ *mainline charitable organizations* **2.** **OF MAIN RAIL LINE** situated on or relating to a main rail line ○ *a mainline station* —**main·lin·er** *n* —**main·lin·ing** *n*

main·ly /máynlee/ *adv* to a large extent or in most cases ○ *bacteria that live mainly in the small intestine*

main man *n* somebody's best, most trusted and respected male mentor or friend (*slang*)

main·mast /máyn màst, -məst/ *n* the principal mast on a sailing ship or sailboat with more than one mast, usually either the foremost mast or the second from the bow

main mem·o·ry *n* the random access memory of a computer, which executes instructions in real time

main·sail /máynsəl, -sàyl/ *n* the largest and most important sail on a sailing ship or sailboat

main se·quence *n* a grouping of stars that consists of most of the known stars in the universe, represented on a graph of luminosity (**Hertzsprung-Russell diagram**) as a diagonal band

main·sheet /máynsheet/ *n* the rope that controls the angle of the mainsail on a sailboat

main·spring /máyn spring/ *n* **1.** the largest and most important spring in the mechanism of a watch or clock **2.** the driving or motivating force behind something ○ *It is the small companies that are the mainspring of this economy.*

main squeeze *n* somebody's boyfriend or girlfriend (*slang*)

main·stay /máyn stày/ *n* **1.** somebody or something that plays the most important role in a particular group, place, or situation ○ *Tourism is the mainstay of the country's economy.* **2.** the strong rope or cable that secures the mainmast on a sailing ship

main stem *n* the principal waterway of a river, excluding its tributaries

main·stream /máyn strèem/ *n* **MAIN CURRENT OF THOUGHT OR BEHAVIOR** the ideas, actions, and values that are most widely accepted by a group or society, e.g., in politics, fashion, or music ○ *views well outside those of the mainstream* ■ *adj* **REFLECTING NORM** reflecting the most widely accepted views or tastes of a nation or culture and therefore not exceptional, extreme, or avant-garde ○ *The scandal, previously ignored by the mainstream media, is now on the front pages.* ■ *vti* **(-streamed, -stream·ing, -streams) ENROLL SPECIAL STUDENTS IN GENERAL CLASSES** to enroll students with physical disabilities or learning difficulties in general school classes —**main·stream·er** *n* —**main·stream·ing** /máyn strèeming/ *n*

main·stream·ing /máyn strèeming/ *n* the practice of educating students with special needs in regular classes during specific time periods based on their skills

main street *n* the most important street in a small town

Main Street *n* people living in small towns, considered as a group and often described as conservative and unsophisticated ○ *Main Street will never accept those fashions.*

CULTURAL NOTE ***Main Street***, a novel (1920) by Sinclair Lewis. This indictment of the narrow-minded complacency of small-town America is a satirical account of the stifling grip of Gopher Prairie, Minnesota, on Carol Milford, an intelligent young woman who marries a plodding local doctor. Her efforts to inject the townspeople with some of her own vitality are thwarted, and she runs away with a lover, only to be drawn back into the soul-destroying community she tried to leave behind.

main·street·ing /máyn strèeting/ *n Can* the practice of walking around a town or city to meet and talk with its inhabitants as a way of soliciting votes during an election campaign —**main·street** *vi*

main·tain /màyn táyn/ **(-tained, -tain·ing, -tains)** *v* **1.** *vt* **MAKE SOMETHING CONTINUE** to continue, or keep in existence, a situation, course of action, or condition without changing or impairing it ○ *They maintained production even with half the staff out sick.* ○ *The government maintained its confidence in the economy despite discouraging news from Wall Street.* **2.** *vt* **KEEP SOMETHING IN WORKING ORDER** to ensure that something continues to work properly by checking it regularly and making repairs and adjustments if required ○ *The machine will give years of service if maintained properly.* **3.** *vt* **PROVIDE SOMEBODY WITH FINANCIAL SUPPORT** to provide somebody with the money required for a reasonable standard of living ○ *She maintains a big family on a tight budget.* **4.** *vt* **ENABLE LIFE TO CONTINUE** to sustain life in a person or animal ○ *nutrients essential to maintain life* **5.** *vt* **DECLARE SOMETHING TO BE TRUE** to insist on the truth of something in the face of challenge or disbelief ○ *He maintains that she knew all along.* **6.** *vt* **DEFEND SOMETHING AGAINST CRITICISM** to defend an opinion, idea, or argument against criticism ○ *The governor continues to maintain his position on cleaning up the environment.* **7.** *vi* **KEEP GOING** to continue in the present state or situation without losing control (*informal*) ○ *Until the reorganization is complete, we're maintaining, and that's about it.* **8.** *vt* MIL **DEFEND PLACE** to continue to hold and defend a position when physically attacked ○ *The unit maintained its position in spite of heavy enemy shelling.* **9.** *vt* COMPUT **UPDATE WEBSITE OR SOFTWARE** to ensure that a website, a piece of software, or something similar is kept up-to-date and in good order for the benefit of users [13C. < Old French *maintener*, literally "hold in the hand" < Latin *manus* "hand"] —**main·tain·a·bil·i·ty** /mayn tàynə bíllətee/ *n* —**main·tain·a·ble** *adj* —**main·tain·er** *n*

main·te·nance /máyntənənss/ *n* **1. CONTINUING REPAIR WORK** work that is done regularly to keep a machine, building, or piece of equipment in good condition and working order (*often used before a noun*) ○ *We take the car in for maintenance every six months.* **2. UPKEEP** the general condition of something with respect to repairs ○ *a car in a poor state of maintenance* **3. CONTINUATION OF SOMETHING** the continuation or preservation of something unchanged or unimpaired ○ *The maintenance of our security depends on constant vigilance.* **4. PROVISION OF FINANCIAL SUPPORT** the provision of enough money to ensure a reasonable standard of living ○ *responsible for the maintenance of two retired parents* **5. MEANS OF SUPPORT** the money that somebody has to pay to ensure a reasonable standard of living ○ *couldn't get by without the maintenance provided by their daughter* **6.** LAW **INTERFERENCE IN LEGAL ACTION** unlawful interference in a lawsuit by an outsider who provides one party with the means to carry on the action

~~maintenence~~ incorrect spelling of **maintenance**

Mainz /mīnts/ historic city and river port in southwestern Germany, on the Rhine River. Population: 184,627 (1997).

ma·iol·i·ca *n* CERAMICS another spelling of **majolica**

Mai·son·neuve /mày zon nőv, mè zoN-/, **Paul de Chomedey, Sieur de** (1612–76) French colonial administrator. He was the founder of Montreal (1642) and the governor of Montreal Island (1642–65).

Mait·land /máytlənd/ city in eastern New South Wales, Australia, a center of coal mining, light industry, and agriculture. Population: 57,782 (2002 estimate).

maî·tre d' /màytrə dée/ *n* OCCUPATIONS same as **maître d'hôtel** (sense 1) (*informal*)

maî·tre d'hô·tel /màytrə dō tél/ (*plural* **maî·tres d'hô·tel** /*pronunc. same*/) *n* **1.** a headwaiter in a restaurant or a hotel dining room **2.** same as **major-domo** (sense 1) [Mid-16C. < French, literally "master of house"]

maize /mayz/ *n UK* same as **corn**[1] *n* (senses 1–2) (*often used before a noun*) [Mid-16C. Directly or via French *maïs* < Spanish *maíz* < Taino *mahis*]

Maj., **MAJ** *abbr* MIL Major

ma·jes·tic /mə jéstik/ *adj* **1.** greatly impressive in appearance ○ *the majestic plains* **2.** showing great dignity and grandeur ○ *her majestic bearing* —**ma·jes·ti·cal·ly** *adv*

maj·es·ty /májjəstee/ *n* **1. SPLENDOR** awesomely large size or great splendor ○ *the majesty of the Rocky Mountain peaks* **2. DIGNITY** a deeply impressive dignified quality ○ *a duchess whose majesty was clearly present in her every move* **3. POWER** supreme authority and power [13C. Via Old French *majesté* < Latin *majestas* < *major* (see MAJOR)]

Maj·es·ty (*plural* **-ties**) *n* the title used to address or refer to a king or queen

Maj. Gen. *abbr* MIL Major General

maj·lis /maj líss/ *n* in various countries in North Africa and Southwest Asia an assembly or parliament [Early 19C. < Arabic, "place of session" < *jalasa* "be seated"]

ma·jol·i·ca /mə jóllikə, -yólli-/, **ma·iol·i·ca** /mə yóllikə/ *n* Italian earthenware that is coated with a tin oxide glaze and highly decorated [Mid-16C. < Italian, old form of MAJORCA]

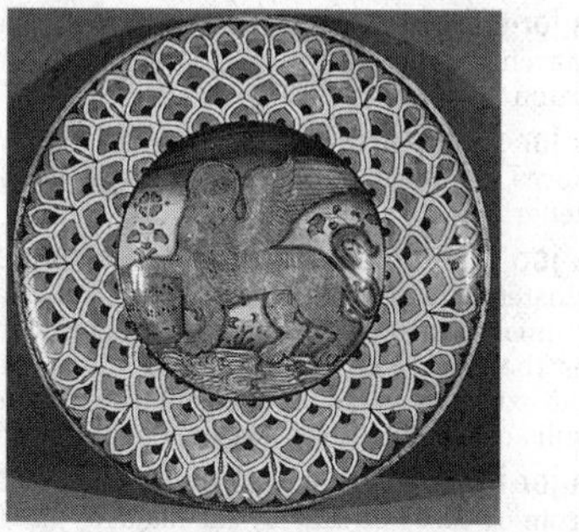

Corbis

majolica

ma·jor /máyjər/ *n* **1.** MIL **MILITARY RANK** an officer in the US, Canadian, or British armies, the US or Canadian air forces, and the US Marine Corps of a rank above captain **2.** LAW **SOMEBODY OF LEGAL AGE** somebody who has reached the age at which a person is deemed fully responsible for his or her actions **3.** EDUC **COURSE CONCENTRATION** the field of study in which a college or university student chooses to specialize ○ *a major in philosophy* **4.** EDUC **STUDENT IN SPECIALTY** a student studying a particular academic specialty ○ *a math major* **5.** MUSIC **MUSICAL KEY** a key or harmony based on a musical scale that has intervals of a semitone between the third and fourth and the seventh and eighth notes (**major scale**) ■ **ma·jors** *npl* SPORTS **MAJOR LEAGUES** the major leagues, e.g., in football or baseball ■ *adj* **1. OF HIGH STANDING** greater in importance than most others ○ *a major recording artist* **2. SIGNIFICANT** of considerable size, extent, degree, or significance ○ *major bridge repairs* **3. SERIOUS** of great severity ○ *a major illness* **4. LARGE** great in number or proportion ○ *A major part of the meeting was devoted to agreeing on our report.* **5.** LAW **OF LEGAL AGE** of the age at which a person is deemed fully responsible for his or her actions **6.** EDUC **OF PRINCIPAL SUBJECT** relating to a subject studied as a specialty in a college or university **7.** MUSIC **DESCRIBES MUSICAL SCALE** describes a musical scale that has intervals of a semitone between the third and fourth and the seventh and eighth notes ○ *in a major key* ○ *a major sixth* **8.** MUSIC **DESCRIBES MUSICAL INTERVAL** describes the interval between the keynote of a major scale and any other note in it, excluding the perfect intervals ○ *a major sixth* **9.** MUSIC **DESCRIBES MUSICAL KEY** describes a key that is based on a major scale ○ *in B major* ■ *vi* **(-jored, -jor·ing, -jors)** EDUC **STUDY AS COURSE CONCENTRATION** to make a particular subject the main field of study in a college or university ○ *She majored in economics.* [13C. < Latin, "greater" < *magnus* "great"]

Ma·jor /máyjər/, **John** (*b.* 1943) British prime minister (1990–97). During his premiership he worked to set up peace talks in Northern Ireland, but in some areas of policy he was hampered by splits within the Conservative party on the issue of closer European integration. See table at **prime minister**

> "It is time to get back to basics: to self-discipline and respect for the law, to consideration for others, to accepting responsibility for yourself and your family, and not shuffling it off on the state."
> [John Major, *Speech, Conservative party conference*; October 8, 1993]

Ma·jor·ca /mə yáwrkə, -jáwr-/, **Mal·lor·ca** /mə yáwrkə/ largest of the Balearic Islands, an autonomous region of Spain, in the western Mediterranean Sea. Population: 676,516 (2001). Area: 1,399 sq. mi./3,624 sq. km. Spanish name **Mallorca** —**Ma·jor·can** *n, adj*

ma·jor·do·mo /mī awr dőmō/ *Southwest US* somebody whose job is to maintain an irrigation canal (**acequia**), make sure all users get water according to agreed schedules, and maintain good relations among the users [See MAJOR-DOMO]

ma·jor-do·mo /màyjər dőmō/ (*plural* **ma·jor-do·mos**), **ma·yor·do·mo** (*plural* **-mos**) *n* **1.** the chief manservant in a large household, especially a royal or noble household, responsible for managing domestic affairs **2.** somebody responsible for managing affairs and making arrangements for somebody else (*humorous*) [Late 16C. Via French, Italian, Spanish < medieval Latin *major domus* "chief of the house" < Latin *magnus* "great" + *domus* "house"]

ma·jor·ette /màyjə rét/ *n* a girl or young woman who marches in front of a marching band, twirling a baton

ma·jor gen·er·al *n* an officer in the US Army, Air Force, or Marine Corps of a rank above brigadier general

ma·jor his·to·com·pat·i·bil·i·ty com·plex *n* a cluster of genes occurring in humans and other animals that determines the recognizable pattern on the surface of the body's cells. This determines the extent to which an individual's immune system will accept or reject tissue from another individual.

ma·jor·i·tar·i·an /mə jàwri térree ən/ *adj* resulting from or based on rule by the majority in any given group ■ *n* somebody who believes that a group should be ruled in the way chosen by the majority of its members —**ma·jor·i·tar·i·an·ism** *n*

ma·jor·i·ty /mə jáwrətee/ (*plural* **-ties**) *n* **1. GREATER NUMBER OF PEOPLE OR THINGS** most of the people or things in a large group (*takes a singular or plural verb*) ○ *The majority of women now work.* **2. DIFFERENCE IN NUMBER OF VOTES** the number of votes by which the winning party or group beats the opposition ○ *swept to power with an overwhelming majority* **3.** POL **GROUP IN POWER** the most powerful party or group voting together in a legislature ○ *The Democrats were the majority in Congress for many years.* **4.** LAW **AGE OF LEGAL RESPONSIBILITY** the age, generally either 18 or 21, at which somebody is legally responsible and can assume civil duties and rights such as serving on a jury or voting ○ *Until you've reached the age of majority you can't buy a car without a co-signer.* **5.** MIL **RANK OF MAJOR** the rank and tenure of a major

USAGE majority as a singular or plural? When you use ***majority*** to refer to a group of people or things as a unit or whole, use a singular verb: *A majority of the Senate intends to vote "Nay."* When you use ***majority*** to refer to people within a group, use a plural verb: *The majority of our students live on campus, with a minority living in the surrounding neighborhoods.* In that sentence, each student is under consideration; hence, the plural verb. Ensure that any pronouns referring to ***majority*** are in the same number denoted by ***majority.*** Thus, it is incorrect to say *A majority of the Senate has cast their votes.* Say instead *A majority of the Senate has cast its vote*, or, if you are speaking of the senators as individuals, say *A majority of the senators have cast their votes.*

ma·jor·i·ty lead·er *n* the head of the majority party in a legislature

ma·jor·i·ty mi·nor·i·ty *n* a majority of people in an area who belong to a minority group overall ○ *a majority minority district*

ma·jor·i·ty rule *n* control of an organization or institution according to the wishes or votes of the majority of its members

ma·jor league *n* **1. MAIN BASEBALL LEAGUE** either of the two main professional baseball leagues **2. TOP SPORTS LEAGUE** a top league of professional football, hockey, or basketball teams ■ **ma·jor leagues** *npl* **HIGH PLACES** the highest spheres of influence (*informal*) ○ *a politician operating in the major leagues*—**ma·jor-league** *adj*

ma·jor·ly /máyjərlee/ *adv* in a large degree or to a great extent (*informal*)

ma·jor med·i·cal *n* health insurance that covers most if not all of the costs incurred during a serious illness, including a hospital stay

ma·jor or·der *n* in the Roman Catholic Church, one of the higher holy orders of bishop, priest, deacon, or subdeacon

ma·jor pen·al·ty *n* in sports such as hockey and lacrosse, a player's removal from the game for five minutes for a serious violation of the rules

ma·jor scale *n* a musical scale with intervals of a semitone between the third and fourth notes and the seventh and eighth notes and whole tones between all other consecutive notes. Major scales potentially have a bright and joyful quality.

ma·jor suit *n* in bridge and some other card games, spades or hearts, owing to their greater scoring potential

Ma·ju·ro /mə jŏŏrō/ atoll and capital island of the Marshall Islands, in Micronesia, lying in the central North Pacific Ocean. Population: 19,664 (1988). Area: 4 sq. mi./10 sq. km.

ma·jus·cule /mə jú skyōōl, májjə-/ *n* a large letter used in writing or printing, e.g., a capital letter or any of the large rounded letters (**uncials**) used in ancient manuscripts [Early 18C. Via French < Latin *majuscula (littera)* "somewhat larger (letters)" < *major* (see MAJOR)] —**ma·jus·cu·lar** *adj*

Mak·a·lu /múkə lōō/ mountain in the Himalaya range, on the Nepal-China border, estimated to be the fifth highest in the world. Height: 27,824 ft./8,481 m.

ma·kan /mə kán/ *n Malaysia, Singapore* food (*informal*) [Early 20C. < Malay]

Ma·ka·ri·os III /mə kárree òss/ (1913–77) Cypriot archbishop (1950–74) and first president of Cyprus (1959–77). He was noted for his efforts to unify Greek and Turkish Cypriots. Born **Mouskos, Mihail Christodolou**

Ma·ka·ro·va /mə kaárəvə/, **Natalia** (*b.* 1940) Russian-born US dancer. A member of the American Ballet Theater, she excelled in classical roles, and later played a ballet dancer on Broadway in *On Your Toes* (1983).

Ma·kas·sar /mə kássər/, **Ma·cas·sar** former name for **Udjung Pandang**

Ma·kas·sa·rese /mə kàssə reéz/ (*plural same*), **Ma·kas·a·rese** *n* **1.** somebody who was born or raised in Makassar (now Udjung Pandang) in Sulawesi, Indonesia **2.** the Austronesian language of the Makassarese people. Native speakers: 1,600,000.

make /mayk/ *v* (**made** /mayd/, made, **mak·ing, makes**) **1.** *vt* **DO SOMETHING** used with a range of nouns to describe an action, where "make" is used rather than a more specific verb ○ *She made no effort whatsoever to pass her exams.* **2.** *vt* **CONSTRUCT SOMETHING** to assemble something from constituent parts ○ *The exhibit contains items made out of recyclable materials.* **3.** *vt* **MANUFACTURE SOMETHING** to manufacture something as a business ○ *The company makes surgical instruments.* **4.** *vt* **PREPARE SOMETHING TO EAT OR DRINK** to prepare food or drink by mixing and usually cooking a number of ingredients ○ *Let's make soup.* **5.** *vt* **SHOW SOMETHING BY GESTURE** to perform movements or gestures that show the form of something or signal something ○ *She made the signs for "I'll see you later."* ○ *He made a circular motion with his hands.* **6.** *vt* **SAY SOMETHING** to say or deliver a statement or speech ○ *He made an emotional speech about his parents' struggle to get ahead in a new country.* **7.** *vt* **FORMULATE SOMETHING** to form something in the mind ○ *These politicians have made a commitment to try to solve the problem.* **8.** *vt* **UNDERSTAND SOMETHING** to comprehend the meaning or truth of something ○ *I couldn't make anything of her last remark.* **9.** *vt* **RECKON SOMETHING** to reckon or estimate something ○ *What time do you make it?* **10.** *vt* **BRING SOMETHING ABOUT** to cause a condition or situation to arise or exist ○ *The state made it illegal to sell fireworks.* ○ *Some people here have made this a personal issue.* **11.** *vt* **CHANGE SOMEBODY OR SOMETHING** to transform somebody or something into something else ○ *They made old clothes into patchwork quilts.* **12.** *vt* **APPOINT SOMEBODY** to appoint somebody to a particular role or position ○ *She's made me her deputy.* **13.** *vt* **PROVIDE SOMETHING** to provide something out of what already exists ○ *Make room for one more.* ○ *Can you make change for a dollar?* **14.** *vt* **CAUSE SOMEBODY TO ACT** to cause somebody to do something or act in a particular way ○ *I made him realize how wrong he'd been.* ○ *You made me lose my place.* **15.** *vt* **FORCE SOMEBODY TO ACT** to force somebody or something to do something or act in a particular way ○ *You can't make me wear that dress.* **16.** *vt* **BE MEANT TO BE SOMETHING** to cause somebody or something to exist for a particular reason (*usually passive*) ○ *She was made to be a star.* **17.** *vt* **EARN MONEY** to earn or be paid a sum of money ○ *He makes $50,000 from rental properties.* **18.** *vt* **CAUSE SOUND TO BE HEARD** to produce or give rise to a sound ○ *She made a choking noise in her throat.* **19.** *vt* **PREPARE SOMETHING FOR USE** to arrange something properly for later use ○ *He made the bed carefully.* **20.** *vt* **SCHEDULE MEETING** to fix a meeting or time ○ *Let's make a date for Friday.* **21.** *vt* SPORTS **SCORE POINTS** to score a goal or points in a game ○ *made a touchdown* **22.** *vt* **REPRESENT SOMETHING** to count as one in a series ○ *That makes the third time he's lied to me.* **23.** *vt* **TOTAL PARTICULAR AMOUNT** to amount to a total ○ *Five and three make eight.* **24.** *vt* **HAVE NECESSARY QUALITIES FOR SOMETHING** to have the qualities required to be something ○ *She'll make a very good doctor.* **25.** *vt* **DEVELOP RELATIONSHIP** to acquire a friend, enemy, or acquaintance ○ *They made friends right away.* **26.** *vt* **CAUSE SOMEBODY TO SUCCEED** to cause somebody to be successful, or cause something to seem successful ○ *the novel that made her career* **27.** *vt* **REACH PLACE** to reach or arrive at a place ○ *I'm not sure we can make the island in this boat.* **28.** *vt* **BE IN TIME FOR SOMETHING** to be in time to do something or for something to happen ○ *We can make the 10:05 train if we hurry.* **29.** *vt* **COVER DISTANCE** to travel a particular distance ○ *They made only five miles a day on the ascent.* **30.** *vt* **BE INCLUDED IN SOMETHING** to succeed in being included or mentioned in something ○ *He made captain just last Saturday.* ○ *stories that never make the national news* **31.** *vi* **SIGNAL INTENTIONS** to act so as to indicate what is coming ○ *They made as if to leave.* **32.** *vt* **HAVE SEX WITH SOMEBODY** to succeed in having sex with somebody (*dated slang*) **33.** *vt* CARDS **FULFILL BRIDGE CONTRACT** to fulfill a contract in a game of bridge by winning the required number of tricks **34.** *vt* CARDS **WIN TRICK IN CARDS** to win a trick in a card game **35.** *vt* ELECTRONICS **CLOSE CIRCUIT** to close an electric circuit **36.** *vi* AGRIC **MATURE** to dry and mature (*refers to hay*) ■ *n* **1. BRAND** a brand of something such as an appliance, car, or machine ○ *Specify the make and model of the car.* **2. PROCESS AND OUTPUT** the process of making something, or the amount or number made **3. IDENTIFICATION** the identification of somebody or something, usually made with the help of police records or information (*slang*) ○ *The police got a make on him from their records.* **4. BUILD OR APPEARANCE** the way that something has been made, or the size or shape it naturally has (*literary*) ○ *a woodland cabin of rustic make* [Old English *macian* < Indo-European, "kneading"] —**mak·a·ble** *adj* ◇ **have it made, have got it made** to be in a position to succeed at something without obstacles or serious problems (*informal*) ◇ **made for somebody** *or* **something** ideally suited to somebody or something ◇ **make do (with something)** to use something that is an unsatisfactory substitute or temporary alternative for the real thing ◇ **make it 1.** to be successful (*informal*) ○ *You'll never make it as an actor.* **2.** to succeed in getting somewhere ○ *We finally made it to the top of the hill.* **3.** to be able to attend ○ *I can't make it to the party tonight.* ◇ **make like** to pretend or pretend to be (*informal*) ○ *She made like she was doing the breaststroke.* ○ *They played a game where they made like statues.* ◇ **on the make 1.** trying hard to gain a profit or advantage, especially using underhand or dishonest means (*informal*) **2.** looking for or making efforts to persuade somebody to be a sexual partner (*slang*) ◇ **make nice (to** *or* **with somebody)** to be conciliatory and often ingratiatingly friendly toward somebody (*informal*)

SYNONYMS ***make, produce, create, fashion, manufacture***
CORE MEANING: to bring something into existence
make to bring something into existence ○ *It is possible to make artificial snow.* ○ *Both bottles are made from the same recyclable plastic.* **produce** to make something in large quantities or in a commercial setting ○ *There is little demand for goods produced at inefficient state factories.* **create** to make something using imagination and artistic skill, or to cause something such as a job or opportunity to exist ○ *computer systems to design and create artwork ready for printing* ○ *a building project designed to create employment and training opportunities* **fashion** to make something by shaping and working raw materials, especially when using only the hands or handheld tools ○ *an exquisite rose fashioned from mother-of-pearl and spun gold* **manufacture** to make something in large numbers, usually in a factory using machinery ○ *a plant manufacturing synthetic rubber*

make after *vt* to chase after somebody or something

make away *vi* same as **make off**

make away with *vt* **1. STEAL SOMETHING** to steal something and abscond with it ○ *They made away with the week's receipts.* **2. ABDUCT SOMEBODY** to carry somebody off by force **3. DESTROY SOMETHING INCRIMINATING** to destroy or get rid of something incriminating ○ *We think someone's made away with the evidence.* **4. KILL SOMEBODY** to kill somebody (*dated*)

make for *vt* **1.** to move in the direction of somebody or something ○ *The reporters made for the courtroom.* **2.** to result in a particular situation ○ *This plan will make for a successful product launch.*
make off *vi* to leave a place quickly, usually with good reason
make off with *vt* same as **make away with**
make out *v* **1.** *vt* **SEE OR HEAR SOMETHING INDISTINCTLY** to see or hear somebody or something, but usually with difficulty or not clearly ○ *I could just make out her profile in the darkness.* **2.** *vt* **COMPREHEND SOMETHING** to identify or understand something ○ *I can't make out the suspect's motive.* **3.** *vt* **COMPLETE SOMETHING IN WRITING** to write necessary information such as the date and the recipient's name on a bill or similar document ○ *The deed is made out in my spouse's name.* **4.** *vt* **INTIMATE SOMETHING** to suggest or imply something that may not be true ○ *The kids make him out to be a real tyrant.* **5.** *vt* **ARGUE IN SUPPORT OF SOMETHING** to try to prove something is true or valid by giving good reasons ○ *made out a case for keeping the work in-house* **6.** *vi* **MANAGE** to perform in a situation ○ *How did you make out on the test?* **7.** *vi* **ENGAGE IN SEXUAL ACTIVITIES WITHOUT INTERCOURSE** to kiss and caress somebody as an expression of sexual desire (*slang*) **8.** *vi* **HAVE SEX** to have sexual intercourse (*slang*)
make over *vt* **1.** **MAKE SOMEBODY ELSE OWNER OF SOMETHING** to transfer the ownership of money or property to somebody, usually by means of a legal document ○ *half of her estate was made over to her cousin* **2.** **CHANGE APPEARANCE OF SOMEBODY OR SOMETHING** to make major changes to the way somebody or something looks **3.** **REFASHION GARMENT** to alter or remodel a garment
make up *v* **1.** *vt* **PREPARE SOMETHING** to get something ready, especially by putting a number of items together ○ *I've made up a box lunch.* **2.** *vt* **FORM WHOLE** to be the constituent members or parts that together form a whole ○ *a group made up of four men and six women* **3.** *vt* **CONSTITUTE SOMETHING** to be a particular part or proportion of something ○ *Women make up more than half the country's work force.* **4.** *vt* **PROVIDE SUPPLEMENTARY QUANTITY** to provide something, e.g., an additional sum of money, to raise an existing amount to the required amount ○ *You three pay $10 each and I'll make up the rest.* **5.** *vi* **COMPENSATE** to compensate for a failing such as a disappointment, deficiency, or shortcoming ○ *I'll buy lunch to make up for being late.* **6.** *vt* **FABRICATE STORY** to invent an excuse, fact, or story ○ *made the whole story up to shock her parents* **7.** *vt* **PUT ON FACIAL COSMETICS** to apply cosmetics to your own face or somebody else's face **8.** *vti* **PREPARE APPEARANCE FOR PERFORMANCE** to prepare somebody or yourself for an acting performance by applying cosmetics and fitting costumes necessary for assuming a given role ○ *It takes her two hours to make up for the role.* **9.** *vti* **RESOLVE QUARREL** to become friends again after a quarrel ○ *Haven't you two made up yet?* **10.** *vt* EDUC **TAKE EXAM OR COURSE AGAIN** to take an examination or course of study again because of absence or failure ○ *make up a French exam* **11.** *vt* PRINTING **ARRANGE LAYOUT OF PAGE** to arrange columns of print and illustrations on a page
make up to *vt* **1.** to try to gain somebody's favor by behaving in a flattering and attentive way ○ *making up to the general manager's assistant* **2.** to flirt with somebody
make with *vt* to start doing, using, or producing something (*dated slang*) ○ *Hey, let's make with the party, huh?*

Ma·ke·ba /mə káybə/, **Miriam** (*b.* 1932) South African-born US jazz and folk singer. She introduced African song to international audiences. Born **Makeba, Zensile**

> "Age is other things too. It is wisdom, if one has lived one's life properly. It is experience and knowledge. And it is getting to know all the ways the world turns, so that if you cannot turn the world the way you want, you can at least get out of the way so you won't get run over."
> [Miriam Makeba, *My Story*; 1988]

make-be·lieve *n* imaginary situations or events that somebody, especially a child playing, pretends are true (*often used before a noun*) ○ *watching them in their make-believe world*

make-do *n* (*plural* **make-dos**) a substitute, often an inferior one ■ *adj* temporarily substituting for something else ○ *used a lid as a make-do plate*

make·fast /máyk fàst/ *n* a strong ring, post, or buoy to which a boat or ship is moored

make-nice *adj* smoothly, often ingratiatingly friendly and conciliatory (*informal*)

make-or-break *adj* likely to result in either complete success or complete failure

make·o·ver /máyk ṑvər/ *n* **1.** an alteration of the way somebody looks, usually including changes of hairstyle, makeup, and clothing **2.** a remodeling of something that completely changes the way it looks

mak·er /máykər/ *n* **1.** **CREATOR OR CAUSE** a creator, source, or cause of something (*often used in combination*) ○ *a mischief-maker* **2.** **PRODUCER OF GOODS** a person or organization that produces goods (*often used in combination*) ○ *a maker of mid-priced textiles* **3.** LAW **SIGNATORY OF DOCUMENT** somebody who signs a promissory note

Mak·er *n* in the Christian religion, God, regarded as the creator of everything

make·shift /máyk shìft/ *adj* providing a temporary and usually inferior substitute ■ *n* a temporary and usually inferior substitute [Mid-16C. < *to make shift* "try all means"]

make·up /máyk ùp/, **make-up** *n* **1.** **COSMETICS** cosmetic products, especially for the face, e.g., lipstick and mascara **2.** **THEATRICAL COSMETICS** the cosmetics and costumes that actors wear to alter their appearance on stage **3.** **APPEARANCE WHEN MADE UP** the appearance or effect produced by applying cosmetics, especially theatrical cosmetics, to the face ○ *He changed his makeup to reappear as an old man in the second act.* **4.** **APPLYING ACTORS' COSMETICS** the work of applying actors' cosmetics and other appearance-altering accessories such as false hair ○ *working in makeup* **5.** **COMBINATION OF PARTS OR QUALITIES** the way parts or qualities combine or are arranged, especially in somebody's personality ○ *Self-deprecation is an intrinsic part of her makeup.* **6.** PRINTING **ARRANGEMENT OF TYPE** the arrangement of typographical elements on a page **7.** EDUC **SPECIAL EXAM** a special examination arranged for students who failed or missed the previous one

make·weight /máyk wàyt/ *n* **1.** something placed on a scale to bring a weight up to a required level **2.** a counterbalancing object, or one that fills in a required number of objects

make-work *n* unimportant or needless work assigned merely to keep workers busy

ma·ki·mo·no /maàki mṓnō/ (*plural* **-nos**) *n* a horizontal Japanese scroll decorated with paintings or calligraphy [Late 19C. < Japanese, "a scroll, something rolled up"]

mak·ing /máyking/ *n* **1.** **CREATIVE ACTIVITY** the activity of somebody who makes something ○ *during the making of the movie* **2.** **CAUSE OF SUCCESS** something that causes somebody's success or progress ○ *a book that was the making of her career* ■ *npl* **1.** **POTENTIAL** the qualities required to become a particular thing ○ *He has the makings of a great musician.* **2.** **NECESSARY INGREDIENTS** the things required to make something, especially a dish of food ◇ **in the making** in the process of being made, formed, or developed ○ *a success story in the making*

ma·ko *n, vi Carib* another spelling of **maco**

ma·ko shark /maákō-/ *n* a large slender blue-gray shark with a sharp nose and ferocious teeth that is prized as a game fish. Native to: southern oceans. Genus: *Isurus.* [Early 18C. < Maori]

mak·tak *n Can* FOOD same as **muktuk**

Ma·kur·di /mə kúrdee/ city in northern Benue State, eastern central Nigeria. Population: 120,110 (1995).

ma·ku·ta MONEY plural of **likuta**

Mal. *abbr* **1.** BIBLE Malachi **2.** Malay **3.** Malayan **4.** Malaysia **5.** Malaysian

mal- *prefix* **1.** bad, badly ○ *malpractice* **2.** improper or inadequate ○ *malnutrition* ○ *malfunction* [Via Old French < Latin *malus* "bad," *male* "badly"]

Mal·a·bar Coast /mállə baar-/ region on the southwestern coast of India, that stretches from Goa southward and includes most of Kerala State

Mal·a·bo /mállə bṑ/ capital, port, and largest city of Equatorial Guinea, on the northern coast of Bioko Island. Population: 30,000 (1995).

mal·ab·sorp·tion /màl əb sáwrpsh'n, -záwrp-/ *n* the inadequate absorption of nutrients from digested food in the alimentary canal, especially by the small intestine in celiac disease

malac- *prefix* same as **malaco-** (*used before vowels*)

ma·lac·ca /mə lákə/, **Ma·lac·ca** *n* **1.** a walking stick made from the stem of the rattan palm **2.** the stem of the rattan palm, used to make walking sticks [Mid-19C. After MALACCA]

Ma·lac·ca /mə lákə/ former name for **Melaka**

Ma·lac·ca, Strait of strait in Southeast Asia connecting the Andaman Sea with the South China Sea. Length: 500 mi./800 km.

ma·lac·ca cane, Ma·lac·ca cane *n* same as **malacca** (sense 1)

Mal·a·chi /mállə kī/ *n* **1.** in the Bible, a Hebrew prophet who wrote in the 5th century B.C. **2.** a book of the Bible that contains writings traditionally attributed to Malachi. See table at **Bible**

mal·a·chite /mállə kìt/ *n* a green copper carbonate mineral. Use: decorative stones, source of copper. [14C. < Old French *melochite* < Greek *molokhitis*, a stone similar in color to the mallow leaf < *malakhē* "mallow"]

malaco- *prefix* soft ○ *malacology* [< Greek *malakos* < Indo-European]

mal·a·col·o·gy /màllə kólləjee/ *n* the branch of zoology that involves the study of mollusks [Mid-19C. < French < modern Latin *Malacozoa* "soft-bodied creatures" < Greek *malakos* (see MALACO-)] —**mal·a·co·log·i·cal** /màlləkə lójjik'l/ *adj* —**mal·a·col·o·gist** *n*

mal·a·cos·tra·can /màllə kóstrəkən/ *n* a member of a common group of crustaceans that usually have stalked eyes, a carapace, and a tail fan formed from the rear limbs, e.g., a lobster. Subclass: Malacostraca. [Mid-19C. < modern Latin *Malacostraca* < Greek *malakos* "soft" + *ostrakon* "shell"] —**mal·a·cos·tra·can** *adj*

mal·a·dap·ted /màllə dáptəd/ *adj* unsuitable for or poorly adapted to a particular situation, function, or purpose —**mal·ad·ap·ta·tion** /màl a dap táysh'n, -addəp-/ *n*

mal·a·dap·tive /màllə dáptiv/ *adj* **1.** poorly adapted, or unable to adapt well, to a particular situation, function, or purpose **2.** not facilitating or encouraging adaptation —**mal·a·dap·tive·ly** *adv*

mal·ad·just·ed /màllə jústəd/ *adj* unable to cope with everyday social situations and personal relationships —**mal·ad·just·ment** *n*

mal·ad·min·is·tra·tion /màlləd mìnni stráysh'n/ *n* incompetent or dishonest management or administration, especially in public affairs —**mal·ad·min·is·ter** /màlləd mínnistər/ *vt*

mal·a·droit /màllə dróyt/ *adj* clumsy or insensitive in speech or behavior [Late 17C. < French, "not adept" < *adroit* (see ADROIT)] —**mal·a·droit·ly** *adv* —**mal·a·droit·ness** *n*

mal·a·dy /mállədee/ (*plural* **-dies**) *n* **1.** a physical or psychological disorder or disease **2.** a condition or situation that is problematic and requires a remedy [13C. < French *maladie* < Latin *male habitus* "in bad condition"]

Ma·la·ga /mállәgə/, **Má·la·ga** city, seaport, and holiday resort in southern Spain, on the Mediterranean Sea. It is the center of the Costa del Sol, a major tourist region. Population: 535,686 (2002).

Mal·a·gas·y /màllə gássee/ (*plural same or* **-ies**) *n* **1.** somebody who comes from Madagascar **2.** an Austronesian language, one of the official languages of Madagascar. Native speakers: 12 million. [Mid-19C. Variant of MADAGASCAR] —**Mal·a·gas·y** *adj*

Mal·a·gas·y Re·pub·lic /màllə gàssee-/ former name for **Madagascar** (1958–75)

ma·la·gue·ña /màllə gáynyə, maàlə-/, **ma·la·gue·na** *n* **1.** a Spanish dance that is similar to a fandango **2.** a Spanish folk melody that is the music for a malagueña [Late 19C. < Spanish, "from Málaga"]

mal·aise /mə láyz, ma-, -léz/ *n* **1.** a general feeling of illness or sickness of no diagnostic significance **2.** a general feeling of worry, discontent, or dissatisfaction, often resulting in lethargy [Mid-18C. < French, "ill ease" < *aise* "comfort"]

Mal·a·mud /mállәməd/, **Bernard** (1914–86) US novelist and short-story writer. Known for his parables of

Jewish life, he won a Pulitzer Prize for *The Fixer* (1966).

"I work with language. I love the flowers of afterthought."
[Bernard Malamud, *Writers at Work*, George Plimpton (ed.); 1984]

"If your train's on the wrong track, every station you come to is the wrong station."
[Bernard Malamud. Quoted in *Natural Born Winners*, Robin Sieger; 1999]

mal·a·mute /málla myoòt/, **mal·e·mute** *n* a dog with a thick gray, black, or white coat, belonging to a breed developed in Alaska for pulling sleds [Late 19C. < Inupiaq *Malimiut*, an Alaskan people]

Ma·lang /mə laáng/ city in southwestern Indonesia, on the island of Java. Population: 720,534 (1997).

mal·a·pert /málla pùrt/ *adj* impudent or bold in speech or behavior (*archaic or literary*) [15C. < Old French, "not experienced" < Latin *expertus* (see EXPERT)] —**mal·a·pert** *n* —**mal·a·pert·ly** *adv* —**mal·a·pert·ness** *n*

mal·ap·por·tioned /màllə páwrsh'nd/ *adj* describes a distribution of representatives within a legislative body that is unequal or unfair —**mal·ap·por·tion·ment** *n*

mal·a·prop·ism /málla pro pìzzəm/ *n* **1.** the misuse of a word through confusion with another word that sounds similar, especially when the effect is ridiculous **2.** an instance of using malapropism [Early 19C. After Mrs. *Malaprop* (< MALAPROPOS), character in Richard Sheridan's play *The Rivals*] —**mal·a·prop·ist** /-pròppist/ *n*

mal·a·pro·pos /màl aprə pṓ, ma lápprə pṓ/ (*formal*) *adj* not appropriate to the situation in which something is done or said ■ *adv* in an inappropriate way or at an inopportune moment [Mid-17C. < French *mal à propos* "ill-suited to the purpose"]

ma·lar /máylər/ *adj* relating to the cheek, the cheekbone, or the side of the head ■ *n* ANAT same as **cheekbone** [Late 18C. < modern Latin *malaris* < Latin *mala* "jaw, cheekbone"]

ma·lar bone *n* ANAT same as **cheekbone**

Mä·lar·en /máy laàrən/ lake in southeastern Sweden. Stockholm lies on its eastern shore. Area: 440 sq. mi./1,140 sq. km.

ma·lar·i·a /mə lérree ə/ *n* an infectious disease caused by a parasite that is transmitted by the bite of infected mosquitoes. Common in tropical countries, the disease is characterized by recurring chills and fever. [Mid-18C. < Italian *malaria* "bad air," once thought to be its cause] —**ma·lar·i·al** *adj* —**ma·lar·i·an** *adj* —**ma·lar·i·ous** *adj*

ma·lar·i·ol·o·gy /mə lèree óllәjee/ *n* the scientific study of malaria —**ma·lar·i·ol·o·gist** *n*

ma·lar·key /mə laárkee/, **ma·lar·ky** *n* nonsense or rubbish, especially insincere talk (*informal*) [Early 20C. Origin ?]

mal·ate /má làyt, máy-/ *n* a chemical compound that is a salt or ester of malic acid

Malawi

Ma·la·wi /mə laáwee/ country in southeastern Africa. It became an independent member of the British Commonwealth in 1964 and a republic in 1966. Language: English. Currency: kwacha. Capital: Lilongwe. Population: 11,651,239 (2003). Area: 45,747 sq. mi./118,484 sq. km. Official name **Republic of Malawi**. Former name **Nyasaland** —**Ma·la·wi·an** *n, adj*

Ma·la·wi, Lake same as **Nyasa, Lake**

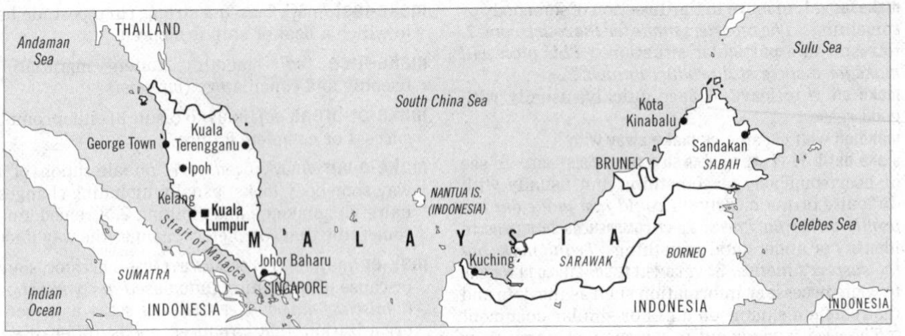

Malaysia

WORLD ENGLISH ***Malaysian English*** is the variety of English used in Malaysia since the formation of the nation-state in 1963. Prior to independence from Britain the term *Anglo-Malay* was used, indicating the influence of the Malay language. From the earlier period come such general English words of Malay origin as *amok, durian, kampong, mango, orang-utan, sago,* and *sarong.* Malaysian English pronounces *r* in such words as *art, door,* and *worker.* There is a tendency toward full vowels in all syllables (e.g. *seven* pronounced "seh-ven," not "sevn"), and a reduction in consonant clusters at the ends of words ("muss" for *must,* "bes" for *best,* "liv" *lived,* "relac" *relax*). In grammar, reflexive pronouns are used for emphasis, often without the verb *to be,* as in "Himself sick," and certain general-purpose particles are used, such as *lah,* indicating informality and intimacy, as in "Can do it lah?" ("Can you do it?"). There is considerable hybridization between Malay and English, as in: "She wanted to beli some barang-barang" ("She wanted to buy some things").

Ma·lay /mə láy, máy lày/ *n* **1.** a member of a people who inhabit the Malay Peninsula, Indonesia, and other islands of the Malay Archipelago and the Philippines **2.** an Austronesian language spoken in Malaysia and in parts of Singapore, Borneo, Sumatra, Java, and surrounding areas. Native speakers: 22 million. Other speakers: 100 million. [Late 16C. < Malay *malayu*] —**Ma·lay** *adj*

Ma·la·ya, Fed·er·a·tion of /mə láy ə/ former state in the Malay Peninsula. It was incorporated into the Federation of Malaysia in 1963. —**Ma·lay·an** *adj, n*

Mal·a·ya·lam /màllə yaálәm/ *n* a Dravidian language that is the official language of the Indian state of Kerala. Native speakers: 30 million. [Early 19C. < Malayalam *Malayālam* "mountain man"] —**Mal·a·ya·lam** *adj*

LANGUAGE HERITAGE See ***Dravidian***.

Ma·lay Ar·chi·pel·a·go world's largest system of island groups, comprising over 20,000 islands, mainly in Indonesia and the Philippines. Area: 1,100,000 sq. mi./2,800,000 sq. km.

Ma·lay·o-Pol·y·ne·sian /mə lày ō pòllə neézh'n/ *n* LANG same as **Austronesian** —**Ma·lay·o-Pol·y·ne·sian** *adj*

Ma·lay Pen·in·su·la peninsula in Southeast Asia that includes parts of Myanmar, Thailand, and Malaysia. Length: 750 mi./1,210 km.

Ma·lay·sia /mə láyzhə, -láyshə/ country in Southeast Asia, on the South China Sea, comprising the southern portion of the Malay Peninsula and parts of the Island of Borneo. It became an independent member of the British Commonwealth in 1957. Language: Bahasa Malaysia. Currency: ringgit. Capital: Kuala Lumpur. Population: 23,092,940 (2003). Area: 127,320 sq. mi./329,758 sq. km. Official name **Federation of Malaysia** —**Ma·lay·sian** *n, adj*

Ma·lay·sian Eng·lish *n* a variety of English spoken in Malaysia

Mal·bec /mál bek/ *n* a red grape variety from Argentina and Chile. Use: to make red wine.

Mal·colm III /málkəm/, **king of Scotland** (1031?–93) He became king after killing Macbeth in 1057 and ruled until his death. He made peace with the King of England, William I (the Conqueror), in 1072.

Mal·colm X /màlkəm éks/ (1925–65) US political activist. He was a prominent member of the Black Muslims and founder of the Organization of Afro-American Unity (1964). Over time he moderated his views on Black separatism, and was later assassinated. Born **Little, Malcolm**

mal·con·tent /málkən tènt/ *n* **1.** somebody who is discontented or dissatisfied, especially somebody who seems continually or chronically discontented **2.** somebody who opposes the established social or political system [Late 16C. < French, "ill contented" < *content* "content" < Latin *contentus* (see CONTENT[1])] —

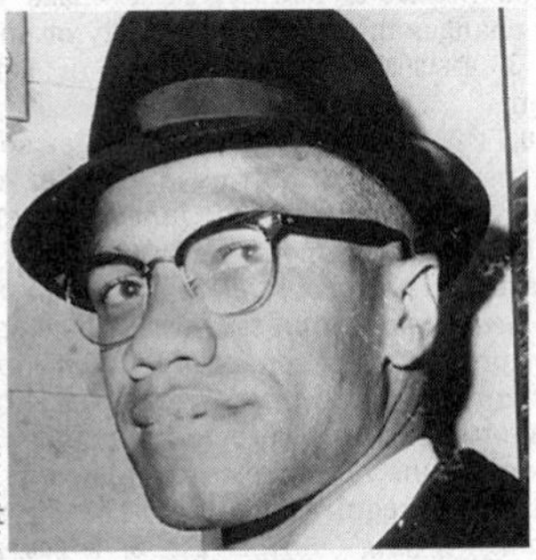

Malcolm X

mal·con·tent *adj* —**mal·con·tent·ed** /màlkən téntəd/ *adj* —**mal·con·tent·ed·ly** *adv* —**mal·con·tent·ed·ness** *n*

mal de mer /màl də mér/ *n* seasickness [Late 18C. < French, "sea sickness"]

Mal·den /máwldən/ city in northeastern Massachusetts, a northern suburb of Boston. Population: 56,155 (2002 estimate).

mal·dis·tri·bu·tion /màl distri byoōsh'n/ *n* unequal and unfair distribution of something, especially resources or wealth

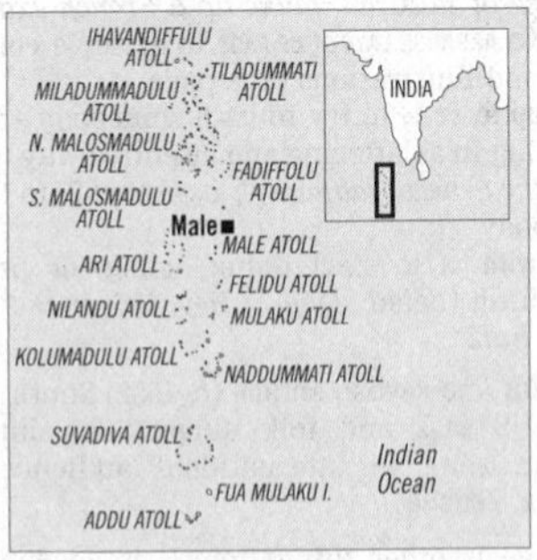

Maldives

Mal·dives /máwl deèvz, mál dìvz/ island country in South Asia, located southwest of the southern tip of India and consisting of a chain of almost 2000 small coral islands. It became an independent member of the British Commonwealth in 1982. Language: Maldivian. Currency: rufiyaa. Capital: Male. Population: 329,684 (2003). Area: 115 sq. mi./298 sq. km. Official name **Republic of the Maldives**

Mal·di·vi·an /mawl dívvee ən, mal-/ *n* **1.** somebody who was born or raised on the Maldives off the coast of southwestern India **2.** the Indic language of the Maldives, also spoken in Minicoy Island, India. Native speakers: 200,000. —**Mal·di·vi·an** *adj*

male /mayl/ *adj* **1.** **PRODUCING SPERM** relating or belonging to the sex that produces sperm to fertilize female eggs **2.** **RELATING TO MEN OR BOYS** relating to, involving, or traditionally characteristic of men or boys **3.** BIOL **FERTILIZING FEMALE SEX CELL** capable of fertilizing a female reproductive cell (**gamete**) during sexual reproduction **4.** BOT **BEARING ONLY STAMENS** describes a flower or plant that bears stamens but not pistils and does not produce fruit or seeds **5.** ENG **MACHINE PART OR FITTING** describes a projecting part such as a bolt or plug that is designed to fit into a hollow part or socket that is the female counterpart ■ *n* **1.** BIOL **MALE PERSON OR ANIMAL** a person or animal belonging to the sex that produces sperm **2.** BOT **PLANT WITH MALE FLOWERS ONLY** a plant that has only male flowers [14C. < Old French < Latin *masculus* < *mas* "male person"] —**male·ness** *n*

Ma·le /máalee/ capital city of the Maldives, on the Male atoll. Population: 62,973 (1995).

male al·to *n* MUSIC same as **countertenor**

ma·le·ate /máylee àyt, -ət/ *n* any salt or ester of maleic acid

Ma·le·bo Pool /mə làybō-/ broad section of the Congo River. Area: 170 sq. mi./450 sq. km. Former name **Stanley Pool**

male chau·vin·ist *n* a man who believes in the innate superiority of men over women (*disapproving*) —**male chau·vin·ism** *n*

male chau·vin·ist pig *n* an offensive term for a man who believes that men are innately superior to women, especially one who expresses his opinions in an aggressive or offensive way (*dated insult*)

Mal·e·cite /málə sìt/ (*plural* **-cites** or *same*), **Mal·i·seet** /-sèet/ (*plural* **-seets** or *same*) *n* **1.** a member of a Native North American people who live in New Brunswick, Quebec, and Maine. The Malecites joined the Abenaki confederacy and fought against both the Iroquois confederacy and the British. **2.** the Algonquian language of the Malecite people [Mid-19C. < Mi'kmaq *malisiit* "somebody who speaks an incomprehensible language"] —**Mal·e·cite** *adj*

mal·e·dic·tion /mállə díkshən/ *n* (*formal*) **1.** a curse **2.** slander or evil talk about somebody [14C. < Latin *malediction-* < *maledicere* "speak ill of" < *dicere* "speak"] —**mal·e·dic·tive** *adj*

mal·e·fac·tor /mállə fàktər/ *n* a wrongdoer, especially a criminal [15C. < Latin < *male facere* "do evil"] —**mal·e·fac·tion** /màllə fáksh'n/ *n*

male fern *n* a fern that has creeping rhizomes and erect, spreading fronds with scaly stalks. The rhizomes produce an oil that is used to expel tapeworms. Native to: Europe, Asia, North America. Latin name: *Dryopteris filix-mas*.

ma·lef·ic /mə léffik/ *adj* having a harmful or evil effect or influence (*literary*) [Mid-17C. < Latin *maleficus* "evil-doing" < *male* "badly"]

ma·lef·i·cent /mə léffiss'nt/ *adj* causing harm or doing evil intentionally, or capable of such acts [Mid-17C. Back-formation < *maleficence* < Latin *maleficentia* "evil doing" < *male* "badly"] —**ma·lef·i·cence** *n* —**ma·lef·i·cent·ly** *adv*

ma·le·ic ac·id /mə lée ik-/ *n* a colorless crystalline solid. Use: manufacture of polymers. Formula: $C_4H_4O_4$. [< French *maléique*, alteration of *malique* (see MALIC)]

male men·o·pause *n* a period in middle age when some men experience feelings of insecurity and anxiety about physical decline, sometimes compared to the effects of menopause in women

mal·e·mute *n* ZOOL another spelling of **malamute**

Ma·ler /máalər/ (*plural same* or **-lers**) *n* **1.** a member of a Dravidian people of northern India **2.** LANG same as **Malto** [Early 19C. < Dravidian, "hill men" < *mala* "mountain"]

Ma·le·vich /mállivich/, **Kasimir** (1878–1935) Russian painter. He formulated an approach he called suprematism and contributed to the development of geometric abstraction.

ma·lev·o·lent /mə lévvələnt/ *adj* **1.** having or showing a desire to harm others **2.** having a harmful or evil effect or influence [Early 16C. Directly or via Old French < Latin *malevolent-* < *male* "badly" + *volent-*, present participle of *velle* "wish"] —**ma·lev·o·lence** *n* —**ma·lev·o·lent·ly** *adv*

mal·fea·sance /mal féez'nss/ *n* **1.** conduct by a public official that cannot be legally justified or that conflicts with the law **2.** an act carried out by a public official that cannot be legally justified or that conflicts with the law [Late 17C. < Anglo-Norman *malfaisance* < Old French *malfaire* "do ill" < Latin *malefacere*] —**mal·fea·sant** *adj, n*

mal·for·ma·tion /màl fawr máysh'n/ *n* variation from the usual structure or form of something, or an instance of this —**mal·formed** /màl fáwrmd/ *adj*

mal·func·tion /mal fúngkshən/ *vi* (**-tioned, -tion·ing, -tions**) to fail to function properly or normally, or stop functioning altogether, usually because of a fault or bad design ■ *n* a breakdown or failure to function properly or normally, usually because of a fault or bad design

Mali

Ma·li /máalee/ landlocked country in West Africa. A former French colony, it gained independence in 1960. Language: French. Currency: C.F.A. franc. Capital: Bamako. Population: 11,626,219 (2002). Area: 478,841 sq. mi./1,240,192 sq. km. Official name **Republic of Mali**

mal·ic /mállik, máylik/ *adj* relating to or derived from malic acid [Late 18C. < French *malique* < Latin *malum* "apple"]

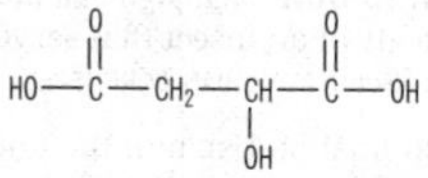

malic acid

mal·ic ac·id *n* a colorless crystalline solid. Source: fruits such as apples. Formula: $C_4H_6O_5$.

mal·ice /málliss/ *n* **1.** the intention or desire to cause harm or pain to somebody **2.** LAW the intention to commit an unlawful and unjustifiable act that will result in harm to another [13C. Via French < Latin *malitia* < *malus* "bad"]

ma·li·cious /mə líshəss/ *adj* motivated by or resulting from a desire to cause harm or pain to another —**ma·li·cious·ly** *adv* —**ma·li·cious·ness** *n*

ma·li·cious mis·chief *n* deliberate destruction of or damage to somebody's property

ma·lign /mə lín/ *vt* (**-ligned, -lign·ing, -ligns**) **CRITICIZE SOMEBODY SPITEFULLY** to criticize somebody or something in a spiteful and false or misleading way ■ *adj* **1.** **HARMFUL OR EVIL** harmful or evil in nature, effect, or intention **2.** **WISHING TO HARM OTHERS** having or showing a desire to cause harm or pain to others [15C. Via French < Latin *malignus* "of evil kind"] —**ma·lign·er** *n* —**ma·lign·ly** *adv*

SYNONYMS ***malign, defame, slander, libel, vilify***

CORE MEANING: to say or write something damaging about somebody

malign to criticize somebody in a spiteful and false or misleading way ○ *It was an old-fashioned firm and, as such, was much maligned by younger people.* ○ *You're maligning a man who was once your partner and a friend.* **defame** to attack somebody or somebody's reputation, character, or good name by making slanderous or libelous statements ○ *The lawyer claims his client defamed him in a television news program.* ○ *The company spokesperson explained, "Our rivals have defamed our character and called us pirates."* **slander** to make a false and malicious oral statement about somebody ○ *Tensions remain high between the two families, with each side slandering the other.* ○ *The general sued, claiming she had slandered him by saying he helped cover up military atrocities.* **libel** to publish false and malicious statements about somebody ○ *The detective claimed that he was libeled in a television documentary.* **vilify** to make malicious and abusive statements about somebody ○ *There is nothing to be gained by vilifying these vulnerable homeless people.* ○ *The leader of the party has been vilified as a racist.*

ma·lig·nan·cy /mə lígnənssee/ (*plural* **-cies**) *n* **1.** *also* **ma·lig·nance** the condition or quality of being malignant **2.** a tumor that invades surrounding tissue and may spread to distant parts of the body by way of the lymphatic or circulatory system

ma·lig·nant /mə lígnənt/ *adj* **1.** **WANTING TO DO EVIL** full of hate and showing a desire to harm others **2.** **HARMFUL** likely to cause harm **3.** MED **LIKELY TO SPREAD** describes a tumor that invades the tissue around it and may spread to other parts of the body **4.** MED **LIKELY TO CAUSE DEATH** used to describe a disease or condition that is liable to cause death or serious disablement unless effectively treated [Mid-16C. < late Latin, "plotting against" < Latin *malignus* "of evil kind"] —**ma·lig·nant·ly** *adv*

ma·lig·ni·ty /mə lígnətee/ (*plural* **-ties**) *n* **1.** **DESIRE TO DO EVIL** intense hatred and a strong desire to do harm **2.** **INTENTIONALLY HARMFUL ACT** an intentionally harmful or evil act **3.** **HARMFUL POTENTIAL** potential to cause harm or death

ma·lines /mə léen/, **ma·line** *n* **1.** thin stiff net with hexagonal holes. Use: dressmaking. **2.** TEXTILES same as **Mechlin** [Mid-19C. < French, after MALINES]

Ma·lines /mə léen/ ➧ **Mechelen**

ma·lin·ger /mə líng gər/ (**-gered, -ger·ing, -gers**) *vi* to pretend to be ill, especially in order to avoid work [Late 18C. < French *malingre* "sickly"] —**ma·lin·ger·er** *n*

Ma·lin·ke /mə língkee/ (*plural same* or **-kes**) *n* **1.** a member of a people who live in parts of West Africa, especially in Côte d'Ivoire, Mali, Senegal, and Gambia. They have traditionally used cowrie shells as a medium of exchange. **2.** the Mande language of the Malinke people. Native speakers: 4 million. [Late 19C. < Malinke] —**Ma·lin·ke** *adj*

Ma·li·now·ski /màlli nófskee/, **Bronislaw** (1884–1942) Polish-born British social anthropologist. He is regarded as the founder of the functional school of anthropology and was noted for his research into the formation of human culture. Full name **Malinowski, Bronislaw Kasper**

Mal·i·seet *n, adj* PEOPLES, LANG another spelling of **Malecite**

mal·i·son /málliss'n, -z'n/ *n* same as **curse** (*archaic*) [13C. Via Old French *maleiçon* < Latin *malediction-* (see MALEDICTION)]

mal·jo /máljō/ *n Carib* **1.** the belief that a conscious or unconscious look of envy or ill will can harm somebody **2.** a disease attributed to ill will, characterized by fever, changed color, inability to urinate, a greenish stool, and loss of appetite and weight [Mid-20C. Probably < French *mal* "evil" + *d'yeux* "of the eyes" or Spanish *mal de ojo* "evil of the eye"]

mall /mawl/ *n* **1.** **LARGE INDOOR SHOPPING COMPLEX** a large enclosed building complex containing stores, restaurants, and other businesses and facilities serving the general public **2.** **SHADY AVENUE** a sheltered and shady avenue or promenade **3.** URBAN PLAN **PEDESTRIAN SHOPPING AREA** an urban shopping area along a street that is closed to traffic **4.** *Northeast US* ROADS **STRIP OF LAND BETWEEN ROADWAYS** a paved or grassy strip of land between two roadways **5.** **PALL-MALL ALLEY** in former times, an alley used for playing the game of pall-mall [Mid-17C. Shortening of PALL-MALL]

mal·lard /mállərd/ (*plural* **-lards** or *same*) *n* a wild duck, the male of which has a dark green head with a white ring around the neck. Native to: northern

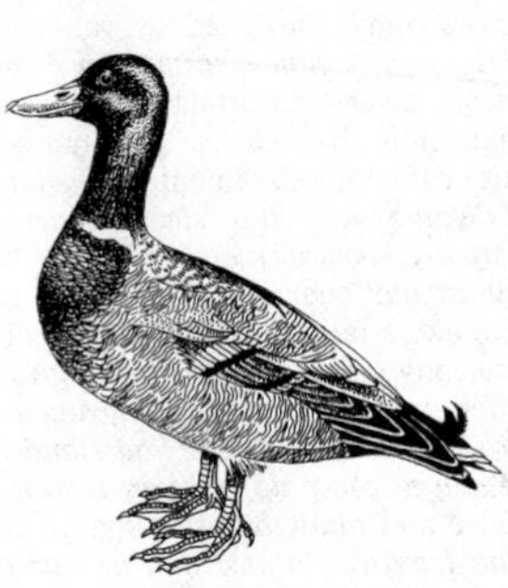

mallard

hemisphere. Latin name: *Anas platyrhynchos*. [14C. < Old French]

Mal·lar·mé /màl aar máy/, **Stéphane** (1842–98) French poet. The author of "The Afternoon of a Faun" (1876) and an originator of the symbolist movement, his work is characterized by obscurity and allusion.

mall crawl *n* the act of going to a large number of different stores in a shopping mall (*informal*)

mal·le·a·ble /mállee əb'l/ *adj* **1.** describes a metal or other substance that can be shaped or bent without breaking **2.** easily persuaded or influenced by others [14C. < Old French < Latin *malleus* "hammer"] —**mal·le·a·bil·i·ty** /màllee ə bíllətee, màllə-/ *n* —**mal·le·a·ble·ness** *n* —**mal·le·a·bly** *adv*

SYNONYMS See ***pliable***.

mal·lee /mállee/ *n* **1.** a low-growing eucalyptus tree. Native to: Australian deserts. Genus: *Eucalyptus*. **2.** a thicket of mallee trees [Mid-19C. < Australian Aboriginal]

mal·le·muck /málla mùk/ *n* a seabird, e.g., a fulmar, petrel, or albatross [Late 17C. < *mal* "foolish" + *mok* "gull"]

mal·le·o·lus /mə lée ələss/ (*plural* **-li** /-lī/) *n* either of the hammer-shaped bony protuberances at the sides of the ankle joint that project from the lower end of the tibia and fibula [Early 17C. < Latin, "little hammer" < *malleus* "hammer"] —**mal·le·o·lar** *adj*

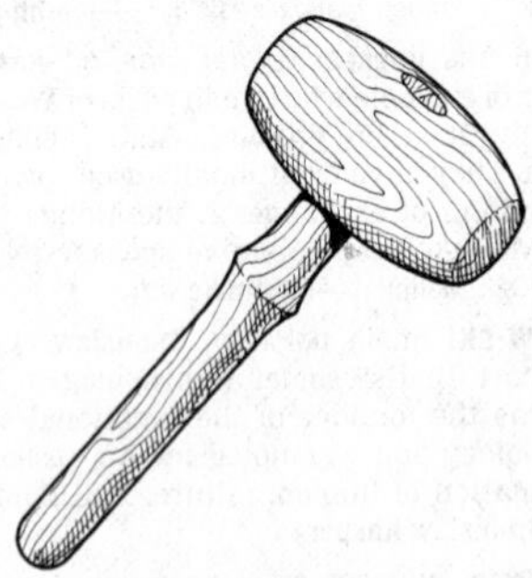

mallet

mal·let /mállət/ *n* **1.** TOOL RESEMBLING HAMMER a tool with a large usually wooden or metal head that is used for driving another tool such as a chisel or for striking or molding a material. The head of a mallet is larger than that of a hammer and usually cylindrical in shape. **2.** STICK USED IN CROQUET OR POLO a long stick with a cylindrical head, used to hit the ball in the games of croquet and polo **3.** HAMMER USED TO PLAY PERCUSSION INSTRUMENT a small hammer often with a padded head used for playing musical instruments such as the marimba and xylophone [15C. < French *maillet* "small hammer" < *mail* (see MAUL)]

mal·le·us /mállee əss/ (*plural* **-i** /-lee ī/) *n* a hammer-shaped bone, the outermost of three small bones in the middle ear that transmit sound waves from the eardrum to the inner ear. ◊ **incus** (sense 1), **stapes** [Mid-17C. < Latin, "hammer"]

Mal·lor·ca another spelling of **Majorca**

mal·low /mállō/ (*plural* **-lows** or *same*) *n* **1.** a wild or cultivated plant with fine hairs on its stem and leaves, and disk-shaped fruit. Flowers: pink, purple, white. Genus: *Malva*. **2.** a plant such as lavatera that resembles or is related to mallow [Pre-12C. < Latin *malva*]

malm /maam/ *n* **1.** TYPE OF LIMESTONE a limestone that is grayish in color and crumbles easily **2.** CHALKY SOIL a chalky soil produced by the crumbling of malm **3.** MIXTURE OF CLAY AND CHALK a mixture of clay and chalk used to make bricks [Old English *mealm* < Indo-European, "pound, grind"]

Mal·mö /málmō/ industrial city and port in southwestern Sweden, opposite Copenhagen on the Danish side of the Øresund. Population: 254,904 (1998).

malm·sey /maámzee/ *n* a dark fortified wine produced in Madeira, the sweetest type of Madeira wine [14C. Via Middle Dutch < medieval Latin *malmasia*, after *Monemvasia*, S Greece]

mal·nour·ished /mal núr risht/ *adj* having a poor or inadequate diet —**mal·nour·ish·ment** *n*

mal·nu·tri·tion /màl noo trísh'n/ *n* a lack of healthy foods in the diet, or an excessive intake of unhealthy foods, leading to physical harm

mal·oc·clu·sion /màllə kloózh'n/ *n* an undesirable relative positioning of the upper and lower teeth when the jaw is closed —**mal·oc·clud·ed** *adj*

mal·o·dor·ous /mal ṓdərəss/ *adj* smelling unpleasant or offensive —**mal·o·dor·ous·ly** *adv* —**mal·o·dor·ous·ness** *n*

ma·lo·nic ac·id /mə lōnik-, -lònnik-/ *n* a colorless crystalline solid. Source: sugar beet. Use: manufacture of pharmaceuticals. Formula: $C_3H_4O_4$. [< French *malonique*, alteration of *malique* (see MALIC)]

ma·lo·ti MONEY plural of **loti**

Ma·louf /mállоof, mə lóof/, **David** (*b.* 1934) Australian writer. His works include the novel *The Great World* (1990). Full name **Malouf, David George Joseph**

Mal·pigh·i·an cor·pus·cle /mal píggee ən-/, **Mal·pigh·i·an bod·y** *n* a cluster of small blood vessels enclosed in a capsule (**Bowman's capsule**) at the end of each of the tiny urine-secreting tubules (**nephrons**) of the kidney [Mid-19C. After Marcello *Malpighi* (1628–94), Italian physician and anatomist]

Mal·pigh·i·an lay·er *n* the deepest layer of the outermost part of the skin (**epidermis**), now called the basal cell layer [See MALPIGHIAN CORPUSCLE]

Mal·pigh·i·an tu·bule, **Mal·pigh·i·an tube** *n* a narrow tube in the body of an insect that serves as an organ of excretion [See MALPIGHIAN CORPUSCLE]

mal·po·si·tion /màl pə zísh'n/ *n* the undesirable position of something, especially a part of the body or a fetus in the womb —**mal·posed** /mal pṓzd/ *adj*

mal·prac·tice /mal práktiss/ *n* **1.** illegal, unethical, negligent, or immoral behavior by somebody in a professional or official position, resulting in a failure to fulfill the duties or responsibilities associated with that position **2.** an act or instance of malpractice —**mal·prac·ti·tion·er** /màl prak tísh'nər/ *n*

Mal·raux /mal rṓ/, **André** (1901–76) French novelist, art theorist, archaeologist, and public servant. Although known chiefly for his novels, his writings reflect the many fields in which he worked.

> "Man knows that the world is not made on a human scale; and he wishes that it were."
> [André Malraux, *Les Noyers de l'Altenburg (The Walnut Trees of Altenburg)*; 1945]

> "Art is a revolt against fate."
> [André Malraux, *Les Voix du silence (Voices of Silence)*; 1951]

malt /mawlt/ *n* **1.** GRAIN USED TO MAKE ALCOHOLIC DRINKS cereal grain, especially barley, that has begun germination by being soaked in water. Use: brewing beer, distilling whiskey. **2.** BEVERAGES same as **malt liquor** **3.** BEVERAGES same as **malted milk** (sense 2) **4.** *UK* BEVERAGES same as **malt whiskey** ■ *v* (**malt·ed, malt·ing, malts**) **1.** *vti* CHANGE GRAIN INTO MALT to make cereal grain into malt by soaking it in water to start germination and then drying it in a kiln, or to undergo this process **2.** *vt* MAKE OR MIX SOMETHING WITH MALT to make something with malt, or add malt to something [Old English *mealt* < Germanic]

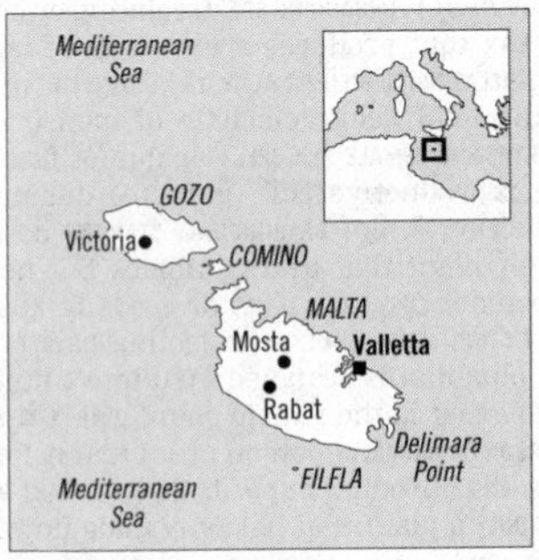

Malta

Mal·ta /máwltə/ country consisting of two main islands and nearby islets in the central Mediterranean Sea. It became an independent member of the British Commonwealth in 1964 and a member of the European Union in 2004. Language: Maltese, English. Currency: Maltese lira. Capital: Valletta. Population: 400,420 (2003). Area: 122 sq. mi./316 sq. km. Official name **Republic of Malta**

Mal·ta fe·ver *n* MED same as **brucellosis**

mal·tase /máwl tàyss, -tàyz/ *n* an enzyme that breaks down maltose into glucose

malt·ed /máwltəd/ *n* BEVERAGES same as **malted milk**

malt·ed milk *n* **1.** a soluble powder made from dried milk and malted grain **2.** a drink made from malted milk, whole milk, ice cream, and flavoring

malt·er·na·tive /mawl túrnətiv/ *n* a bottled alcoholic malt beverage, brewed like light beer but with added flavoring such as vodka, tequila, or citrus

Mal·tese /mawl téez, -téess/ (*plural same*) *n* **1.** somebody who comes from Malta **2.** an official language of Malta, belonging to the Semitic branch of Afro-Asiatic and featuring many words adopted from Italian. Native speakers: 300,000. **3.** (*plural* **Mal·tes·es**) BREED same as **Maltese cat** —**Mal·tese** *adj*

Mal·tese cat *n* a shorthaired domestic cat belonging to a breed that has silky bluish gray hair

Mal·tese cross *n* a cross with four arms resembling arrowheads that taper toward the center

mal·tha /málthə, máwl-/ *n* a black viscous bitumen that is a naturally occurring mixture of hydrocarbons [Early 17C. Via Latin < Greek, a mixture of pitch and wax]

Mal·thus /málthəss/, **Thomas Robert** (1766–1834) British economist. His theory of population growth led to fears that the rising number of living people would produce widespread famine. He advocated birth control as a means of combating poverty. —**Mal·thu·sian** /mal thóozh'n, -thóozee ən/ *adj*, *n* —**Mal·thu·sian·ism** *n*

> "Population, when unchecked, increases in a geometrical ratio. Subsistence only increases in an arithmetical ratio."
> [Thomas Robert Malthus, *Essay on the Principle of Population*; 1798]

malt liq·uor *n* an alcoholic drink that is brewed from malt, especially one having a higher alcohol content than most beer or ale

Mal·to /máltō/ *n* the Dravidian language of the Maler people. Native speakers: 100,000. [Late 19C. < Malto, "language of the Maler"] —**Mal·to** *adj*

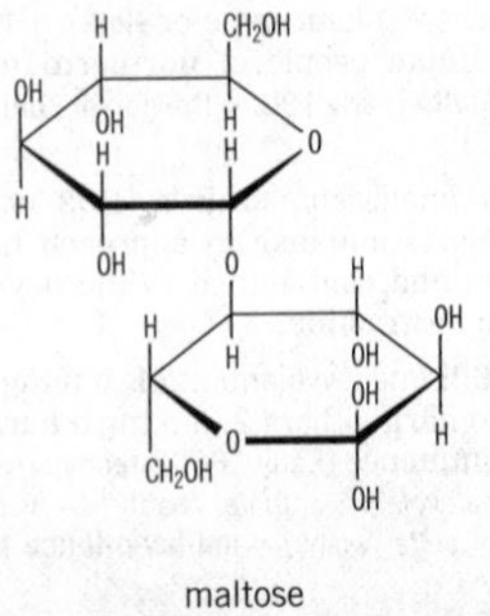

maltose

mal·tose /máwl tṑss, -tṑz/ *n* a sugar composed of two units of glucose. Formula: $C_{12}H_{22}O_{11}$. See illustration on previous page [Mid-19C. < MALT]

mal·treat /mal trée̅t/ (**-treat·ed, -treat·ing, -treats**) *vt* to behave cruelly or unkindly toward a person or animal, especially by neglecting their welfare [Early 18C. < French *maltraiter* "treat badly" < Old French *traitier* (see TREAT)] —**mal·treat·er** *n* —**mal·treat·ment** *n*

SYNONYMS See *mistreat.*

malt·ster /máwltstər/ *n* somebody whose job involves producing or selling malt

malt sug·ar *n* BIOCHEM same as **maltose**

malt whis·key *n* **1.** a whiskey distilled from malted barley, often one that is not a blend **2.** a drink or measure of malt whiskey

mal·va·si·a /màlvə zée ə/ *n* the variety of grape that is used to make malmsey wine [Mid-19C. Via Italian < medieval Latin, variant of *malmasia* (see MALMSEY)] —**mal·va·si·an** *adj*

Mal·vern Hills /màwlvərn-/ range of hills in west central England. Its highest peak is the Worcestershire Beacon, 1,395 ft./425 m.

mal·ver·sa·tion /màlvər sáysh'n/ *n* dishonest or unethical conduct by somebody in a professional position or public office, often involving bribery, extortion, or embezzlement (*formal*) [Mid-16C. < French < Latin *male versari* "behave badly"]

mal·ware /mál wèr/ *n* software such as viruses or Trojans designed to cause damage or disruption to a computer system [Early 21C. Blend of MALICIOUS + SOFTWARE]

ma·ma /maámə, mámmə/, **mam·ma** *n* **1.** same as **mother**[1] *n* (sense 1) (*informal; usually used by or to children*) **2.** a woman, especially somebody's girlfriend or wife (*slang; sometimes considered offensive*) [Late 16C. < children's first attempts at speech]

ma·ma·guile /maámə gìl/ *n, v* (**-guiled, -guil·ing, -guiles**) *Carib* same as **mamaguy** [Late 20C. Alteration of MAMAGUY, after GUILE]

ma·ma·guy /maámə gì/ *Carib vt* (**-guyed, -guy·ing, -guys**) to try to get something by flattery, especially by making exaggerated comments or compliments ■ *n* flattery or teasing [Late 20C. Alteration of Venezuelan Spanish *mamar gallo* "feed the rooster," used to describe the behavior of a rooster that only pretends to fight]

Ma·mar·o·neck /mə márrə nèk/ village in southeastern New York, on Long Island Sound. It is a suburb of New York City. Population: 29,090 (2002 estimate).

ma·ma's boy *n* an offensive term that deliberately insults a man's strength of character, courage, or independence (*insult*)

mam·ba /maámbə/ *n* a large venomous snake, especially a green or black snake that lives in trees. Native to: tropical Africa. Genus: *Dendroaspis*. [Mid-19C. < Zulu *imamba*]

mam·bo /maámbō/ *n* (*plural* **-bos**) **1.** DANCE RESEMBLING RUMBA a modern Latin American dance in 4/4 time that is similar to the rumba. It originated in Cuba. **2.** MUSIC the music for a mambo ■ *vi* (**-boed, -bo·ing, -bos**) DANCE MAMBO to dance the mambo [Mid-20C. < American Spanish]

Mam·e·luke /mámmə lo͝ok/, **Mam·luk** /mám lo͝ok/ *n* a member of a former military caste, originally comprising enslaved Turks, that ruled Egypt between the 13th and the 16th centuries, remaining powerful until the early 19th century [Early 16C. Via French < Arabic *mamlūk* "enslaved person" < *malaka* "possess"]

Mam·et /mámmit/, **David** (*b.* 1947) US playwright and movie director. His work, e.g., the play *Glengarry Glen Ross* (1992), is noted for its stylized dialog and its focus on the alienation of lower middle-class life.

> "We live in oppressive times. We have, as a nation, become our own thought police; but instead of calling the process by which we limit our expression of dissent and wonder 'censorship,' we call it 'concern for commercial viability.'"
> [David Mamet, "Radio Drama," *Writing in Restaurants*; 1986]

ma·mey /maa mée/ (*plural* **-meys**) *n* **1.** a fruit with red skin, yellow flesh, and poisonous seeds **2.** the tree that produces mameys. Native to: Caribbean. Latin name: *Mammea americana*. [Late 16C. Via American Spanish *mamei* < Taino]

ma·mil·la /mə míllə, ma-/ *n* Can spelling of **mammilla**

Mam·luk *n* HIST same as **Mameluke**

mamm- *prefix* same as **mammo-** (*used before vowels*)

mam·ma[1] /mámmə/ (*plural* **-mae** /-mee/) *n* the milk-secreting organ of female mammals, e.g., a woman's breast or a cow's udder. It includes the mammary gland and associated exterior structures such as the nipple or teat. (*technical*) [Pre-12C. < Latin] —**mam·mate** /mámàyt/ *adj* —**mam·mi·form** /mámmi fàwrm/ *adj*

mam·ma[2] /maámə, mámmə/ *n* another spelling of **mama**

mam·mae ANAT plural of **mamma**[1]

mam·mal /mámm'l/ *n* a class of warm-blooded vertebrate animals that have, in the female, milk-secreting organs for feeding the young. The class includes human beings, apes, many four-legged animals, whales, dolphins, and bats. [Early 19C. < modern Latin *mammalia* < Latin *mamma* "breast"] —**mam·ma·li·an** /mə máylee ən/ *adj*

mam·mal·o·gy /mə mállәjee, ma-/ *n* the branch of zoology that deals with the study of mammals —**mam·ma·log·i·cal** /màmmə lójjik'l/ *adj*—**mam·mal·o·gist** *n*

mam·ma·plas·ty *n* SURG another spelling of **mammoplasty**

mam·ma·ry /mámməree/ *adj* relating or belonging to the milk-secreting organ of a female mammal, e.g., the breast or udder [Late 17C. < MAMMA[1]]

mam·ma·ry gland *n* a large milk-producing gland in female mammals that consists of a network of ducts and cavities leading to a nipple or teat. Mammary glands usually occur in pairs.

mam·mee /maa mée/ *n* TREES same as **mamey** (sense 2) [Variant]

mam·mee ap·ple *n* PLANTS same as **mamey** (sense 1)

mam·mie *n* another spelling of **mammy** (*informal*)

mam·mif·er·ous /mə míffərəss, ma-/ *adj* having mammary glands

mam·mil·la /mə míllə, ma-/ (*plural* **-lae** /-lee/) *n* **1.** a nipple or teat **2.** a protuberance or organ that resembles a nipple or teat [Late 17C. < Latin, "little breast" < *mamma* "breast"] —**mam·mil·lar·y** /mámmə lèrree/ *adj*—**mam·mil·late** /-làyt/ *adj*

mammo- *prefix* breast ○ *mammogram* [< MAMMA[1]]

mam·mo·gram /mámmə gràm/ *n* the procedure of taking an X-ray of all or part of the breast [Mid-20C. < MAMMA[1]]

mam·mog·ra·phy /ma móggrəfee/ *n* X-ray examination of the breast, used for the early detection of developing tumors, especially cancerous ones —**mam·mo·graph·ic** /màmmə gráffik/ *adj*

mam·mon /mámmən/ *n* wealth and riches considered as an evil and corrupt influence [14C. Via late Latin < Aramaic *māmōnā* "riches"] —**mam·mon·ism** *n* —**mam·mon·ist** *n*

Mam·mon *n* in the Bible, the personification of wealth portrayed as a false god

mam·mo·plas·ty /mámmə plàstee/ (*plural* **-ties**), **mam·ma·plas·ty** *n* plastic surgery performed on a woman's breast to alter the shape or size, e.g., as reconstruction following a mastectomy or as cosmetic surgery

mam·moth /mámməth/ *n* (*plural* **-moths** or *same*) **1.** EXTINCT ELEPHANT a large extinct elephant that had long curved tusks and was covered with hair. It existed mainly in the northern hemisphere and died out more than 10,000 years ago. Genus: *Mammuthus*. **2.** SOMETHING ENORMOUS something that is a particularly large example of its kind ■ *adj* VERY LARGE of very great size or extent [Early 18C. < obsolete Russian *mámot*]

ORIGIN In its original Siberian language (possibly Ostyak) ***mammoth*** meant literally "earth, soil": the first remains of ***mammoths*** to be found were dug out of the frozen soil of Siberia, and it came to be believed that the animals burrowed in the earth. The adjectival use of ***mammoth*** for "huge" dates from the early 19th century.

Mam·moth Cave Na·tion·al Park /màmməth kàyv-/ national park in southwestern Kentucky, established in 1941. Its multilevel cave system is the longest in the world. Area: 83 sq. mi./214 sq. km.

mam·my /mámmee/ (*plural* **-mies**), **mam·mie** *n* same as **mother**[1] *n* (sense 1) (*informal; usually used by children*) [Early 16C. Variant of MAMMA[2]]

Ma·mo·ré /maa mō ráy/ river in northern Bolivia, flowing northward into the Madeira River on the Brazilian border. Length: 1,200 mi./1,900 km.

ma·mou *n* ➧ **big mamou** (*informal*)

Mam·pru·li /mam pro͞olee/ *n* a Niger-Congo language spoken in Ghana and Togo. Native speakers: 200,000. [Mid-20C. < Mampruli] —**Mam·pru·li** *adj*

mam·zer /maámzər/ (*plural* **-zers** or **-zer·im** /maámzə rím/), **mom·ser** /mómzər/ **mom·zer** *n* **1.** in Jewish religious law, a child born of an adulterous or incestuous relationship **2.** an offensive term for somebody regarded as untrustworthy or contemptible (*slang insult*) [Mid-16C. Via late Latin < Hebrew *mamzēr*]

man /man/ *n* (*plural* **men** /men/) **1.** ADULT MALE HUMAN an adult male human being **2.** PARTICULAR TYPE OF MAN an adult male human being with a particular occupation, responsibility, background, or nationality (*usually used in combination*) ○ *the TV repairman* **3.** PERSON a person, regardless of sex or age (*often offensive*) ○ *a six-man crew* **4.** HUMAN RACE the human race in general (*often offensive*) **5.** MODERN OR EARLIER HUMAN BEING a member of the group that comprises modern humans and their ancestors. Genus: *Homo*. (*sometimes considered offensive*) **6.** EMPLOYEE OR WORKER an employee or worker of either gender (*often offensive*) **7.** MALE MEMBER OF ARMED FORCES a male member of the armed forces, especially one who is not an officer (*usually used in the plural*) **8.** SERVANT a man who is a servant (*dated*) **9.** VIRILE PERSON the personification of qualities traditionally associated with the male sex, including courage, strength, and aggression, or somebody with such qualities **10.** HUSBAND OR MALE COMPANION a husband, or a man who is another person's companion or lover (*slang*) **11.** TERM OF ADDRESS a term of address to a person of either sex (*slang; sometimes considered offensive*) ○ *Cool it, man!* **12.** *also* **Man** AUTHORITY FIGURE somebody in a position of authority, or a group that is seen as having an unfair advantage or undue power over others (*dated slang; sometimes considered offensive*) ○ *in trouble with the Man* **13.** PIECE USED IN BOARD GAMES a piece used in playing board games such as checkers **14.** MEDIEVAL VASSAL in feudal societies of the early Middle Ages, an adult male human who swore allegiance to a lord in return for help and protection **15.** SHIP a ship, especially one of a particular kind (*used in combination*) ○ *man-of-war* ■ *vt* (**manned, man·ning, mans**) (*often offensive*) **1.** SUPPLY SOMETHING WITH WORKERS to provide something with workers, operators, or military personnel **2.** BE READY TO USE SOMETHING to be ready to operate or defend something ■ *interj* USED FOR EMPHASIS used to add emphasis (*slang*) ○ *Man, that was exciting!* [Old English *man(n)* < Indo-European, "person, man"] —**man·like** *adj* ◇ **a poor man's...** a cheaper or inferior version of something, especially one that is more widely available than the original ◇ **as one man** unanimously or without exception (*often offensive if used of women*) ◇ **be your own man** to have the resources or confidence to be responsible for yourself or your actions (*often offensive if used of women*) ◇ **to a man** everyone, without any exceptions (*often offensive if used of women*)

USAGE See *person.*

ORIGIN The etymologically primary sense of ***man*** is "human being, person," and that is what it generally meant in Old English: the sexes were usually distinguished by *wer* "man" (which survives probably in *werewolf*) and *wīf* (source of modern English *wife*) or *cwene* "woman." But during the Middle English and early modern English periods "male person" gradually became the primary meaning, and today ***man***, meaning "person," is decidedly on the decline (helped on its way by those who feel that the usage discriminates against women).

Man ➧ **de Man, Paul**

Man, Isle of ➧ **Isle of Man**

MAN /man/ *abbr* COMPUT metropolitan area network

man. *abbr* manual

Man. *abbr* **1.** PAPER Manila paper **2.** Manitoba

man a·bout town (*plural* **men a·bout town**), **man-a·bout-town** (*plural* **men-a·bout-town**) *n* a sophisticated and cultured man who socializes in fashionable circles (*dated*)

man·a·cle /mánnək'l/ *n* either of a pair of metal rings joined by a chain and fastened around the wrists of a prisoner to be restrained (*usually used in the plural*) ■ *vt* (**-cled, -cling, -cles**) to restrain somebody using manacles [14C. Via French *manicle* "handcuff" < Latin *manicula* < *manus* "hand"]

man·age /mánnij/ (**-aged, -ag·ing, -ag·es**) *v* **1.** *vti* ADMINISTER OR RUN SOMETHING to be in charge of something such as a store, department, or project and be responsible for its smooth running and for any personnel employed ○ *manages a department of 25 people* **2.** *vti* ACHIEVE SOMETHING WITH DIFFICULTY to succeed in doing something, especially something that seems difficult or impossible ○ *I finally managed to open the door.* **3.** *vi* COPE IN DIFFICULT SITUATION to survive or continue despite difficulties, especially a lack of resources ○ *He manages with very little money.* **4.** *vt* HANDLE AND CONTROL SOMETHING to handle and keep control of something such as a weapon or tool ○ *could manage a computer without difficulty* **5.** *vt* DEAL WITH SOMETHING SUCCESSFULLY to deal with a situation or process that requires skillful control or handling ○ *managing patient care* **6.** *vt* DISCIPLINE OR CONTROL PERSON OR ANIMAL to keep control of a person or animal, or a number of people or animals, especially when they are wild or unruly **7.** *vt* BE SOMEBODY'S MANAGER to guide the career and control the business affairs of somebody such as a professional entertainer or athlete **8.** *vti* BASEBALL DIRECT TEAM ON PLAYING FIELD to direct the day-to-day operations, especially play on the field, of a team and its members (*used in professional baseball*) [Mid-16C. < Italian *maneggiare* "train a horse" < Latin *manus* "hand"]

man·age·a·ble /mánnijəb'l/ *adj* able to be handled or controlled without much difficulty —**man·age·a·bil·i·ty** /mànnijə bíllətee/ *n* —**man·age·a·ble·ness** *n* —**man·age·a·bly** *adv*

man·aged care *n* a system of managing medical care in which nonmedical administrators such as insurance companies control and limit the provision of such things as procedures and medicines

man·aged fund /mánnijd-/ *n* a mutual fund that makes considered investments rather than just following the performance of specific companies' shares

man·age·ment /mánnijmənt/ *n* **1.** ADMINISTRATION OF BUSINESS the organizing and controlling of the affairs of a business or a sector of a business **2.** MANAGERS AS GROUP managers and employers considered collectively, especially the directors and executives of a business or organization **3.** HANDLING OF SOMETHING SUCCESSFULLY the act of handling or controlling something successfully ○ *crisis management* **4.** SKILL IN HANDLING OR USING SOMETHING the skillful handling or use of something such as resources

man·age·ment game *n* a computer game that simulates managing something such as a sports team or a business

man·age·ment in·for·ma·tion sys·tem *n* a system for gathering the financial, production, and other information that managers need to operate a business, especially a system that is computerized

man·age·ment sim *n* COMPUT GAMES same as **management game**

man·ag·er /mánnijər/ *n* **1.** ORGANIZER OF BUSINESS somebody who is responsible for directing and controlling the work and staff of a business, or of a department within it **2.** ORGANIZER OF SOMEBODY'S BUSINESS AFFAIRS somebody who organizes and controls the business affairs of somebody such as a professional entertainer **3.** ORGANIZER OF AFFAIRS OF ATHLETE somebody who organizes and controls the training of an athlete or a sports team **4.** COMPETENT HANDLER somebody who handles or controls something, especially somebody who works skillfully **5.** COMPUT PROGRAM FOR BASIC COMPUTER OPERATIONS a computer program designed to carry out the basic functions of a computer's operations **6.** STUDENT IN CHARGE OF TEAM'S EQUIPMENT a student who takes care of the equipment and records of a high school or college sports team under the supervision of a coach —**man·ag·er·ship** *n*

man·a·ge·ri·al /mànni jéeree əl/ *adj* involving or characteristic of a manager or management, especially in business —**man·a·ge·ri·al·ly** *adv*

man·ag·ing di·rec·tor /mánnijing-/ *n* a member of a board of directors who is responsible for the day-to-day operations of a company

man·ag·ing ed·i·tor *n* an editor of books, newspapers, or other publications who oversees editorial process, budget, and schedules

managment incorrect spelling of **management**

Ma·na·gua /mə náagwə/ capital city of Nicaragua, located in the west of the country, near the Pacific Ocean. Population: 1,200,000 (1995).

Ma·na·gua, Lake lake in western Nicaragua, the country's second largest. It is drained by the Tipitapa River. Area: 405 sq. mi./1,050 sq. km.

man·a·kin /mánnəkin/ *n* a small bird with a short beak and bright colorful feathers. Native to: South and Central America. Family: Pipridae. [Early 17C. Variant of MANIKIN]

Ma·na·ma /mə náamə/ capital city of Bahrain, situated in the northeastern part of the country. Population: 148,000 (1995).

ma·ña·na /maa nyáanə/ *adv* **1.** *Hispanic* on the day following the present day **2.** at some unspecified time in the future [Mid-19C. < Spanish, "morning, tomorrow" < Latin *mane* "in the morning"]

Man·a·pou·ri, Lake /màanə póoree/ lake in the southwestern part of the South Island, New Zealand. At 1,455 ft./444 m deep, it is the deepest lake in New Zealand. Area: 55 sq. mi./142 sq. km.

Ma·na·slu /múnnə sloo/ eighth highest mountain in the world. It is situated in the eastern part of the Himalayan system in the Ghurka massif of Nepal. Height: 26,781 ft./8,163 m.

Ma·nas·sas /mə nássəss/ independent city in northeastern Virginia. It was the site of two Confederate victories at the Civil War battles of Bull Run in 1861 and 1862. Population: 37,288 (2002 estimate).

man·at /mánnət/ *n* the main unit of currency in Azerbaijan and Turkmenistan. See table at **currency** [Late 20C. < Azeri]

man-at-arms (*plural* **men-at-arms**) *n* a soldier, especially a medieval mounted soldier who was heavily armed

man·a·tee /mánnə tee/ *n* a large plant-eating sea mammal with front flippers and a broad flattened tail. Native to: warm Atlantic coastal waters. Genus: *Trichechus*. [Mid-16C. Via Spanish *manatí* < Carib *manáti* "breast"]

Ma·naus /mə nówss/ city and river port in northwestern Brazil. It is the capital of Amazonas State. Population: 1,157,357 (1996).

Man·a·wa·tu-Wang·a·nu·i /mànnə waatoo wóng gə nóo ee/ administrative region of New Zealand, situated in the southwestern part of the North Island. Population: 220,089 (2001). Area: 9,775 sq. mi./25,317 sq. km.

man bag *n* a bag in which a man carries small personal belongings

Mance /maNss, maanss/, **Jeanne** (1606–73) French-born Canadian missionary. She was the founder of the first hospital in Canada, the Hôtel-Dieu, Montreal (1644).

Man·che·go *n* a firm Spanish cheese that has a relatively high fat content and is made with ewes' milk [< Spanish, "of La Mancha"]

Man·ches·ter /mán chèstər/ **1.** historic town in central Connecticut. Population: 55,084 (2002 estimate). **2.** largest city in New Hampshire, located in the south of the state. Population: 108,398 (2002 estimate). **3.** city in northwestern England. Population: 392,819 (2001).

Man·ches·ter ter·ri·er *n* a small terrier with a short-haired coat that is mainly black with tan patches

man-child (*plural* **men-chil·dren**) *n* a male child (*literary*)

man·chi·neel /mànchə néel/ (*plural* **-neels** or *same*) *n* a tree with poisonous apple-shaped fruit and milky sap that causes blistering. Native to: tropical America. Latin name: *Hippomane mancinella*. [Mid-17C. Via French *mancenille* < Spanish *manzanilla* "little apple" < *manzana* "apple" < Latin *matiana*, kind of apple, after *Matia*, a Roman gens]

Man·chu /man chóo/ (*plural same* or **-chus**) *n* **1.** a member of a people who invaded China from Manchuria in the 17th century, establishing a dynasty that lasted until the start of the 20th century **2.** a Tungusic language spoken in northeastern People's Republic of China. Native speakers: 20,000. [Late 17C. < Manchu, "pure"] —**Man·chu** *adj*

Man·chu·ri·a /man chóoree ə/ historical name for the mountainous region of northeastern China comprising the modern-day provinces of Heilongjiang, Jilin, and Liaoning —**Man·chu·ri·an** *n, adj*

Man·chu-Tun·gus *n* LANG same as **Tungusic** —**Man·chu-Tun·gus** *adj*

Man·cu·ni·an /man kyóonee ən/ *n* somebody who comes from Manchester, England [Early 20C. < Latin *Mancunium* "Manchester"] —**Man·cu·ni·an** *adj*

-mancy *suffix* divination ○ *geomancy* [< Old French *-mancie* < Greek *mantis* (see MANTIC)]

M & A *abbr* BUSINESS mergers and acquisitions

Man·dae·an /man dée ən/, **Man·de·an** *n* **1.** a member of a Gnostic religious group who believe themselves to be descendants of John the Baptist. The group originated in Jordan and still exists in Iraq and Iran. **2.** a form of Aramaic used in the sacred writings of the Mandaeans [Late 18C. < Mandaean *mandaia* "having knowledge" < *manda* "knowledge"] —**Man·dae·an** *adj* —**Man·dae·an·ism** *n*

mandala

man·da·la /mándələ/ *n* **1.** in Buddhism and Hinduism, a geometric or pictorial design usually enclosed in a circle, representing the entire universe and used in meditation and ritual **2.** in Jungian psychology, a symbol representing the self and inner harmony [Mid-19C. < Sanskrit *maṇḍalam* "circle"] —**man·dal·ic** /man dállik/ *adj*

Man·da·lay /màndə láy/ city and transportation center on the Irrawaddy River in central Myanmar. Population: 532,949 (1983).

man·da·mus /man dáyməss/ (*plural* **-mus·es**) *n* an order from a high court to a lower court, or to an authority, instructing it to perform an action or duty [Mid-16C. < Latin, "we command"]

Man·dan /mán dàn/ (*plural same* or **-dans**) *n* **1.** a member of a Native American people of North Dakota who lived along the Missouri River and now mainly live near Lake Sakakawea **2.** the language of the Mandan people, belonging to the Siouan branch of Hokan-Siouan languages. Native speakers: 1,200. [Late 18C. < N American French *Mandane*] —**Man·dan** *adj*

man·da·rin[1] /mándərin/ *n* **1.** FORMER CHINESE OFFICIAL in the Chinese Empire, a member of any of the nine highest ranks of public officials, attained by examinations **2.** CIVIL SERVANT a high-ranking civil servant or bureaucrat with wide-ranging powers **3.** MEMBER OF ELITE GROUP an influential member of an elite group, especially a literary or intellectual group [Late 16C. < Spanish *mandarín*, Portuguese *mandarim* < Sanskrit *mantrin-* "counselor" < *mantraḥ* "counsel"] —**man·da·ri·nate** *n* —**man·da·ri·nic** /màndə rínnik/ *adj* —**man·da·ri·nism** *n*

man·da·rin[2] /mándərin/ *n* **1.** a small citrus fruit, similar to a tangerine but with easily peelable yellow-orange skin. The segments are commonly sold as canned fruit. **2.** a small citrus tree that produces mandarins. Native to: China. Latin name: *Citrus reticulata*. [Late 18C. Via French *mandarine*

< Spanish *mandarín* (see MANDARIN[1]), because its color is similar to that of mandarins' yellow robes]

Man·da·rin *n, adj* LANG same as **Modern Standard Chinese**

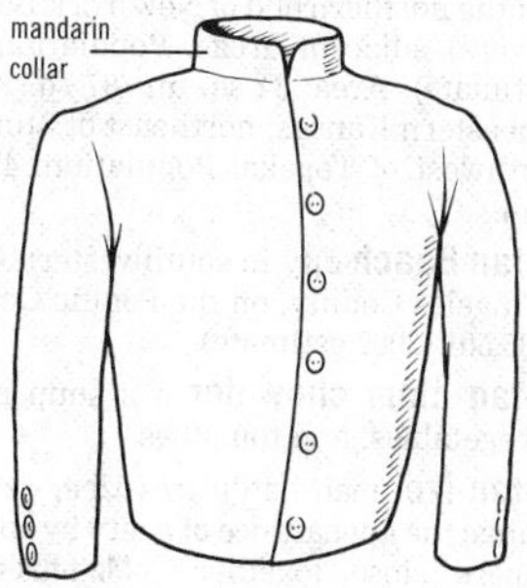

mandarin collar

man·da·rin col·lar *n* a narrow collar that stands up from a close-fitting neckline and has an opening at the front

mandarin duck

man·da·rin duck *n* a duck with a crested head and colorful feathers, the male of which has one enlarged orange feather on each wing for use in displays. Native to: Asia. Latin name: *Aix galericulata*.

man·da·rin or·ange *n* FOOD same as **mandarin**[2] (sense 1)

Man·da·rin Chi·nese *n, adj* LANG same as **Modern Standard Chinese**

man·da·tar·y /mándə tèrree/ (*plural* **-ies**), **man·da·tor·y** *n* a person or state that has been given a mandate

man·date /mán dàyt/ *n* **1.** AUTHORITATIVE ORDER an official command or instruction from an authority **2.** SUPPORT FROM ELECTORATE the authority bestowed on a government or other organization by an electoral victory, effectively authorizing it to carry out the policies for which it campaigned ○ *The party in power has a clear mandate for reform.* **3.** AGREEMENT FOR FREE SERVICE a contract by which somebody agrees to perform a service without payment **4.** INSTRUCTION FROM SUPERIOR COURT an order from a superior court or official to a lower one **5.** REGION RULED BY OUTSIDE POWER any territory that was placed by the League of Nations under the administration of one of its European member states after World War I **6.** COMMISSION TO ADMINISTER STATE the power conferred by the League of Nations on a member state to administer a region ■ *vt* (**-dat·ed, -dat·ing, -dates**) **1.** ASSIGN TERRITORY to assign a territory or region to a state under a mandate **2.** ORDER SOMETHING OFFICIALLY to require or order something officially or formally ○ *The law mandates systematic tracking and reporting of hazardous wastes.* [Early 16C. < Latin *mandat-*, past participle of *mandare* "give into somebody's hand" < Indo-European, "hand"] —**man·da·tor** *n*

man·dat·ed ter·ri·tory /mán daytəd-/ *n* HIST same as **mandate** *n* (sense 5)

man·da·to·ry /mándə tàwree/ *adj* **1.** COMPULSORY needing to be done, followed, or complied with, usually because of an official requirement **2.** WITH POWER OF MANDATE resembling or having the power of a mandate **3.** AUTHORIZED TO ADMINISTER TERRITORY having a mandate to administer a region or territory ■ *n* (*plural* **-ries**) POL another spelling of **mandatary** —**man·da·to·ri·ly** *adv*

man·da·to·ry min·i·mum *n* a minimum sentence that must be imposed for a particular crime, without consideration of mitigating circumstances

man-day *n* the work done by one person in one day (*sometimes offensive*)

Man·de /maan dày/ (*plural same* or **-des**) *n* **1.** a group of around 20 languages spoken in West Africa, especially in Sierra Leone, Mali, Guinea, and the Ivory Coast. It is a branch of the Niger-Congo family of languages. Native speakers: 9 million. **2.** a member of a West African group of people who speak a Mande language [Late 19C. < Mande, "little mother"] —**Man·de** *adj*

Man·de·an *n, adj* RELIG, LANG another spelling of **Mandaean**

Nelson Mandela

Man·de·la /man déllə, -dáylə/, **Nelson** (*b.* 1918) president of South Africa (1994–99). After a long incarceration as a political prisoner (1964–90), he became the first Black president of the Republic of South Africa (1994–99). He was awarded the Nobel Peace Prize with F. W. de Klerk (1993). Full name **Mandela, Nelson Rolihlahla**

> "Years of imprisonment could not stamp out our determination to be free. Years of intimidation and violence could not stop us. And we will not be stopped now."
> [Nelson Mandela, *Press conference*; April 26, 1994]

> "People…learn to hate, and if they can learn to hate, they can be taught to love, for love comes more naturally to the human heart than its opposite."
> [Nelson Mandela, *Long Walk to Freedom*; 1994]

Man·de·la, Winnie (*b.* 1934) South African political activist. She married Nelson Mandela in 1958 (divorced 1996), and continued his work after his imprisonment. She is an African National Congress (ANC) member of parliament and president of the ANC Women's League. Born **Madikizela, Nkosikazi Nomzamo**

Man·del·stam /mánd'l stàm/, **Osip Yemilyevich** (1891?–1938?) Russian poet. A critic of Joseph Stalin, he was arrested in 1934 and is believed to have died in a Soviet labor camp.

man·di·ble /mándib'l/ *n* **1.** LOWER JAW OF VERTEBRATE the lower jaw of a person or animal, usually containing a single bone (*technical*) **2.** INSECT'S MOUTHPART either of a pair of parts in insects and similar animals used for biting and cutting food **3.** BIRD'S BEAK the upper or lower part of a bird's beak [Mid-16C. Directly or via Old French < late Latin *mandibula* < Latin *mandere* "chew"] —**man·dib·u·lar** /man díbbyələr/ *adj* —**man·dib·u·late** /-lət, -làyt/ *adj, n*

Man·din·go /man díng gō/ (*plural* **-gos** or **-goes** or *same*) *n* **1.** a member of any of several peoples who live in parts of West Africa, especially along the Niger River valley **2.** a group of Mande languages spoken in parts of West Africa, especially along the Niger River valley. Native speakers: 6 million. [Early 17C. < Mande] —**Man·din·go** *adj*

Man·din·ka /man díngkə/ (*plural same* or **-kas**) *n* **1.** a member of a West African people living in parts of the Gambia, Senegal, and Sierra Leone **2.** the Niger-Congo language of the Mandinka people. Native speakers: 700,000. [Mid-20C. < Mande]

man·dir /mún deer/ *n S Asia* a Hindu temple [Via Hindi < Sanskrit *mandiram* "dwelling, mansion"]

man·do·lin /màndə lín, mánd'lin/ *n* **1.** a stringed instrument of the lute family with a pear-shaped body and four or more pairs of strings, usually played with a plectrum **2.** a kitchen tool for slicing vegetables, consisting of adjustable blades in a frame [Early 18C. Via French < Italian *mandolino* "small lute" < *mandola* "mandola" an early form of lute] —**man·do·lin·ist** /-línnist/ *n*

man·drag·o·ra /màndrə gáwrə, man drággərə/ *n* PLANTS same as **mandrake** (sense 1) [Pre-12C. Directly or via French *mandragore* < medieval Latin *mandragora* < Greek *mandragoras*]

man·drake /mán dràyk/ *n* **1.** a plant with a forked root resembling a human body that was formerly believed to have magical powers and was made into a drug. Flowers: yellow, purplish. Native to: Europe, Asia. Latin name: *Mandragora officinarum*. **2.** FOOD same as **May apple** (sense 1) [14C. Alteration of medieval Latin *mandragora*, influenced by MAN, DRAKE "dragon" (from its emetic and narcotic properties)]

man·drel /mándrəl/, **man·dril** *n* **1.** TAPERED SHAFT FOR SECURING WORK TO a tapered shaft or arbor to which work is secured during machining or turning, e.g., on a lathe **2.** CORE ROD a rod around which materials such as metal or glass are molded, forged, or shaped **3.** SHAFT FOR MOUNTING TOOL a shaft on which a tool such as a dentist's drill or machining tool is mounted [Early 16C. Origin ?]

man·drill /mándril/ *n* a large baboon with a beard, mane, and crest. The male also has a brilliant ribbed blue, white, and scarlet muzzle. Native to: West Africa. Latin name: *Mandrillus sphinx*. [Mid-18C. Said to be < MAN + DRILL[4]]

Man·du·rah /mán dóorə/ coastal town in southwestern Western Australia, on the Peel Inlet south of Perth. Population: 50,845 (2002 estimate).

mane /mayn/ *n* **1.** long hair on the head and neck of an animal such as a lion or horse **2.** a large amount of thick long hair on somebody's head (*literary or informal*) [Old English *manu* < Germanic] —**maned** *adj*

man-eat·er *n* **1.** an animal that eats or is thought to eat human flesh, e.g., a tiger or a great white shark **2.** same as **cannibal** **3.** an offensive term for a woman who is thought to pursue men in order to make them her lovers and then discard them —**man-eat·ing** *adj*

ma·nège /ma nézh/, **ma·nege** *n* **1.** ART OF RIDING the art of riding or training horses **2.** HORSE MOVEMENTS the movements that a horse has been trained to make **3.** RIDING SCHOOL a school where people are taught to ride and horses are trained [Mid-17C. < French < Italian *maneggio* < *maneggiare* (see MANAGE)]

ma·nes /maa nàyz, máy neez/, **Ma·nes** *n* the revered spirit of a dead person (*literary; takes a singular verb*) ■ *npl* in ancient Roman religion, the divine spirits of the dead (*takes a plural verb*) [14C. < Latin, "good ones" < *manus* "good"]

Édouard Manet: portrait drawing by Edgar Degas

Ma·net /man áy/, **Édouard** (1832–83) French painter. His innovative work such as *The Bar at the Folies-Bergère* (1882) contributed to the development of impressionism.

ma·neu·ver /mə nóovər/ *n* **1.** SKILLED MOVEMENT a movement or action that requires skill or dexterity **2.** MILITARY MOVEMENT a planned movement of one or several military or naval units **3.** DEVIOUS ACT an action, especially a devious or deceptive one, done to gain advantage ○ *a maneuver to avoid accountability* **4.** CHANGE OF COURSE a controlled change of course of a vehicle or vessel ■ **ma·neu·vers** *npl*

MILITARY EXERCISES large-scale military exercises used for training or practice ■ *v* (**-vered, -ver·ing, -vers**) **1.** *vti* MOVE SKILLFULLY to move or cause something to move skillfully ○ *maneuvered the boat into the berth* **2.** *vti* DO MILITARY EXERCISES to perform military maneuvers, or cause somebody or something to perform military maneuvers **3.** *vt* MANIPULATE SOMEBODY OR SOMETHING to manipulate somebody or something to gain advantage ○ *trying to maneuver her into agreeing* **4.** *vi* BEHAVE DEVIOUSLY to use devious means in order to gain advantage ○ *politicians maneuvering for choice committee assignments* [15C. < French *manoeuvre* "manipulation," later form of Old French *maneuvre* "manual labor" < medieval Latin *manuoperare* "work with the hands" < Latin *manus* "hand"] —**ma·neu·ver·a·bil·i·ty** /mə no͞ovərə bíllətee/ *n* —**ma·neu·ver·a·ble** *adj*

man Fri·day (*plural* **man Fri·days** or **men Fri·day**) *n* a man acting as an assistant or servant who is loyal and able to do many things [After the servant in *Robinson Crusoe* (1719) by Daniel Defoe]

man·ful /mánfəl/ *adj* brave, strong, and resolute, as a man is conventionally supposed to be —**man·ful·ly** *adv* —**man·ful·ness** *n*

man·ga /máng gə/ *n* a Japanese style of comic books or animated cartoons, often very violent or erotic [Late 20C < Japanese < *man* "indiscriminate" + *ga* "picture"]

man·ga·bey /máng gə bày, -bee/ (*plural* **-beys** or *same*) *n* a large agile monkey with a long tail, slender body, and white eyelids. Native to: Africa. Genus: *Cercocebus*. [Late 18C. After *Mangabey*, Madagascar]

Man·ga·lore /màng gə láwr/ city and seaport in Karnataka state in southwestern India, on the Arabian Sea. Population: 238,560 (2001).

mangan- *prefix* manganese ○ *manganous* [< MANGANESE]

man·ga·nate /máng gə nàyt/ *n* any mixed-metal salt containing manganese and oxygen in the form of an anion

man·ga·nese /máng gə neez, -neess/ *n* a brittle grayish white metallic element. Source: pyrolusite, rhodonite. Use: alloys, strengthening steel. Symbol **Mn**. See table at **element** [Late 17C. Via French < Italian < medieval Latin *magnesia* "magnesia"]

man·ga·nese nod·ule *n* a stony nodule rich in manganese, found on the ocean floor

man·ga·nese steel *n* steel containing 11 to 14 percent manganese. Use: manufacture of drills, blades, tools.

man·gan·ic /man gánnik/ *adj* containing or derived from manganese, especially with a valence of three or six

man·ga·nite /máng gə nìt/ *n* a grayish crystalline mineral consisting of manganese hydroxide

man·ga·nous /máng gənəss/ *adj* containing or derived from manganese, especially with a valence of two

mange /maynj/ *n* an infectious skin disease of animals and sometimes humans that is caused by mites and results in hair loss, scabs, and itching [15C. < French *manjue* "itch" < Old French *mangier* "eat" < Latin *manducare* "chew" < (see MANGER)]

man·gel /máng g'l/, **man·gel-wur·zel** /-wùrz'l/, **man·gold** /máng g'ld, -gōld/, **man·gold-wur·zel** *n* a large yellow or reddish variety of beet that is grown as food for livestock [Late 18C. < German *Mangoldwurzel* "beet root"]

man·ger /máynjər/ *n* a trough from which livestock eat [14C. < Old French *mangeoire* < *mangier* "eat" < Latin *manducare* "chew" < *mandere*]

Popperfoto
Lata Mangeshkar

Man·gesh·kar /man gésh kaar/, **Lata** (*b.* 1929) Indian singer. She provided playback singing voices in Hindi films for more than 30 years, making over 30,000 recordings. Full name **Mangeshkar, Lata Dinanath**

mange·tout /màwNzh to͞o/, **mange·tout pea** *n UK* same as **snow pea** [Early 19C. < French, "eat-all"]

man·gle[1] /máng g'l/ (**-gled, -gling, -gles**) *vt* **1.** to mutilate or disfigure somebody or something by violent tearing, cutting, or crushing **2.** to spoil or ruin something through carelessness or ineptitude ○ *a reading that mangled the rhythm of the poem* [14C. < Anglo-Norman *mahangler*] —**man·gler** *n*

man·gle[2] /máng g'l/ *n* **1.** a large machine for pressing sheets of fabric by passing it between two heated rollers **2.** *UK* HOUSEHOLD same as **wringer** [Late 17C. < Dutch *mangelstok* "mangling roller"] —**man·gle** *vt*

mango

man·go /máng gō/ (*plural* **-goes** or **-gos**) *n* **1.** a red or green fruit with juicy, sweet, orange-yellow pulp and a large pit **2.** an evergreen tree that produces mangoes. Native to: tropical Asia. Latin name: *Mangifera indica*. [Late 16C. Via Portuguese *manga* < Malay *mangga* < Tamil *mānkāy* "mango-tree fruit"]

man·gold, man·gold-wur·zel *n* AGRIC same as **mangel**

man·go·nel /máng gə nèl/ *n* a medieval military machine used for hurling stones at an enemy [13C. Via Old French *mangonel(le)* < medieval Latin *manganellus* "little war engine" < Greek *magganon* "war engine"]

man·go·steen /máng gə steen/ *n* **1.** a fruit with a hard reddish brown rind and sweet juicy pulp **2.** an evergreen tree that has leathery leaves and produces mangosteens. Native to: Southeast Asia. Latin name: *Garcinia mangostana*. [Late 16C. < Malay *manggustan*, alteration of *manggis*]

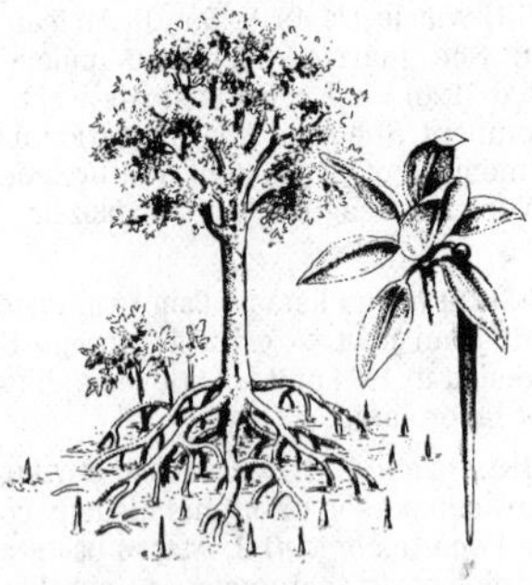
mangrove

man·grove /mán grōv, máng-/ *n* an evergreen tree or bush with straight slender stems and intertwined roots that are exposed at low tide. Native to: tropical coasts. Families: Combretaceae, Verbenaceae, Rhizophoraceae. [Early 17C. Blend of Portuguese *mangue* or Spanish *mangle* (< Taino) + GROVE]

Man·gue /maáng gày/ *n* an extinct Native Central American language of Costa Rica, belonging to the Oto-Manguean family of languages [Late 18C. Origin ?] —**Man·gue** *adj*

mang·y /máynjee/ (**-i·er, -i·est**) *adj* **1.** affected by or caused by mange **2.** having a dirty or shabby appearance (*informal*) —**mang·i·ly** *adv* —**mang·i·ness** *n*

man·han·dle /mán hànd'l/ (**-dled, -dling, -dles**) *vt* **1.** to pull or push somebody or something around roughly **2.** to move something using human strength alone rather than machinery

Man·hat·tan[1] /man hátt'n/, **man·hat·tan** *n* a cocktail made from sweet vermouth, whiskey, and a dash of bitters [Late 19C. After MANHATTAN[2] (sense 1)]

Man·hat·tan[2] /man hátt'n/ **1.** borough and main economic hub of New York City, occupying Manhattan Island at the northern end of New York Bay together with several adjacent areas. Population: 1,487,536 (2002 estimate). Area: 34 sq. mi./87 sq. km. **2.** city in northeastern Kansas, northeast of Junction City and northwest of Topeka. Population: 43,794 (2002 estimate).

Man·hat·tan Beach city in southwestern California, in Los Angeles County, on the Pacific Ocean. Population: 35,501 (2002 estimate).

Man·hat·tan clam chow·der *n* a soup made from clams, vegetables, and tomatoes

Man·hat·tan·ize /man hátt'n ìz/ (**-ized, -iz·ing, -iz·es**) *vt* to change the appearance of a city by constructing skyscrapers close together —**Man·hat·tan·i·za·tion** /man hàtt'ni záysh'n/ *n*

Man·hat·tan Proj·ect *n* the top-secret research and development in several places in the United States that led to the successful construction and detonation of the first atomic bombs [Mid-20C. < *Manhattan District*, the code name it was given]

man·haul /mán hàwl/ *vti* (**-hauled, -haul·ing, -hauls**) to pull a sled along on foot or on skis, or pull equipment or supplies in a sled in this way ■ *n* a journey made manhauling a sled —**man·haul·er** *n*

man·hole /mán hōl/ *n* an opening with a detachable cover that gives access to an enclosed area, especially a sewer, drain, or tank

man·hood /mán ho͝od/ *n* **1.** STATE OF BEING MAN the state of being an adult male human **2.** TRADITIONAL MANLINESS the qualities and attributes conventionally thought to be appropriate to a man, especially physical strength, courage, and determination **3.** MEN men considered collectively ○ *the nation's manhood* **4.** PENIS a man's penis (*literary or humorous*)

man-hour *n* the amount of work that can be done by one person in one hour, used as a means of assessing requirements, production, and performance (*sometimes offensive*) ○ *the number of man-hours lost through sickness*

man·hunt /mán hùnt/ *n* an organized search, especially by the police, for an escaped criminal or other wanted person —**man·hunt·er** *n*

ma·ni·a /máynee ə/ *n* **1.** an excessive and intense interest in or enthusiasm for something **2.** a psychiatric disorder characterized by excessive physical activity, rapidly changing ideas, and impulsive behavior [14C. Via late Latin < Greek, "loss of reason" < *mainesthai* "to rage"]

-mania *suffix* excessive enthusiasm for or attachment to ○ *pyromania* [< MANIA]

ma·ni·ac /máynee àk/ *n* **1.** OFFENSIVE TERM an offensive term for somebody who behaves in such an uncontrolled manner as to appear to be affected by mania **2.** ENTHUSIAST somebody who is obsessively interested in or enthusiastic about something **3.** OFFENSIVE TERM an offensive term for somebody affected by mania ■ *adj* PSYCHIAT same as **maniacal** (sense 2) (*offensive*) [Late 16C. Via late Latin *maniacus* < late Greek *maniakos* < *mania* (see MANIA)]

ma·ni·a·cal /mə nī ək'l/ *adj* **1.** an offensive term meaning so uncontrolled as to appear to be affected by mania **2.** an offensive term meaning characteristic of or indicative of mania —**ma·ni·a·cal·ly** *adv*

man·ic /mánnik/ *adj* **1.** RELATING TO MANIA relating to or affected by mania **2.** HECTIC extremely or excessively busy (*informal; sometimes considered offensive*) **3.** OVEREXCITED in a state of unusually high excitement, especially because of tension (*informal*) [Early 20C. < MANIA] —**man·i·cal·ly** *adv*

man·ic-de·pres·sive *n* somebody affected by bipolar disorder ■ *adj* characteristic of or affected by bipolar disorder

man·ic-de·pres·sive dis·or·der, man·ic-de·pressive ill·ness *n* MED same as **bipolar disorder**

Man·i·chae·ism /mànni kee ìzzəm/, **Man·i·che·ism** *n* **1.** a religious doctrine based on the separation of matter and spirit and of good and evil that originated in 3rd-century Persia and combined elements of Zoroastrianism, Buddhism, Christianity, and Gnosticism **2.** a heretical Christian belief in the separate nature of matter and spirit [Early 17C. < late Latin *Manichaeus* < *Mani,* (216?–276?), Persian sage] —**Man·i·chae·an** *adj* —**Man·i·chee** /mánni kee/ *n*

man·i·cot·ti /mànni kóttee/ *n* a dish of large pasta tubes that are usually stuffed with a ricotta or meat filling and then baked, and often served with a tomato sauce [Mid-20C. < Italian, "sleeves"]

man·i·cure /mánni kyoor/ *n* **HAND AND NAIL COSMETIC TREATMENT** a cosmetic treatment for the hands and nails that usually involves shaping and polishing the fingernails, pushing back the cuticles, and treating rough skin ■ *vt* (**-cured, -cur·ing, -cures**) **1. TREAT HANDS AND NAILS** to treat the hands and fingernails by cutting, shaping, and polishing the nails, and softening the hands **2. CUT AND SHAPE SOMETHING CAREFULLY** to cut and shape something with great care and precision ○ *a neatly manicured lawn* [Late 19C. < French < Latin *manus cura* "hand care"]

man·i·cur·ist /mánni kyoorist/ *n* somebody whose job is to give people manicures

man·i·fest /mánnə fèst/ *adj* **OBVIOUS** clear to see or understand ■ *v* (**-fest·ed, -fest·ing, -fests**) **1.** *vt* **SHOW SOMETHING CLEARLY** to make something evident by showing or demonstrating it very clearly **2.** *vi* **APPEAR** to appear or be revealed **3.** *vt* **INCLUDE SOMETHING IN CARGO LIST** to include something in a ship's cargo list ■ *n* **1. SHIP'S CARGO LIST** a list giving details of a ship's cargo, its destination, and other particulars for customs purposes **2. PLANE OR TRAIN CARGO LIST** a list of cargo or passengers on a plane or train [14C. Directly or via French < Latin *manifestus* "apprehensible" < *manus* "hand" + *festus* "seizable"] —**man·i·fest·a·ble** *adj* —**man·i·fest·ly** *adv*

man·i·fes·ta·tion /mànnə fe stáysh'n/ *n* **1. ACT OF SHOWING SOMETHING** an act of showing or demonstrating something **2. STATE OF BEING SHOWN** the condition of being shown or being perceptible **3. SIGN** an indication that something is present, real, or exists ○ *one of the first manifestations of the disease* **4. PUBLIC DEMONSTRATION** a public demonstration, usually over a political issue **5. MATERIALIZATION OF SPIRIT** a supposed appearance in visible form by a spiritual being **6. VISIBLE FORM OF DIVINE BEING** a visible form in which a divine being, idea, or person is believed to be revealed or expressed —**man·i·fes·ta·tion·al** *adj*

man·i·fest con·tent *n* in dream analysis, the overt meaning of a dream remembered by the dreamer on waking that requires analysis to interpret its latent content or real meaning

Man·i·fest Des·ti·ny *n* the doctrine or belief prevalent in the 19th century that the United States had the God-given right to expand into and possess the whole of the North American continent

man·i·fes·to /mànnə féstō/ (*plural* **-tos** or **-toes**) *n* a public written declaration of principles, policies, and objectives, especially one issued by a political movement or candidate [Mid-17C. < Italian < *manifestare* "make evident" < Latin *manifestus* (see MANIFEST)]

man·i·fold /mánnə fòld/ *adj* **1. MANY AND VARIOUS** of many different kinds ○ *The reasons for the crisis are manifold.* **2. HAVING MANY FORMS** having many parts, forms, or applications ○ *a manifold political system* ■ *n* **1. CHAMBER WITH PORTS** a chamber or pipe with several openings for receiving or distributing a fluid or gas, e.g., the intake or exhaust manifolds of an internal-combustion engine **2.** MATH **TOPOLOGICAL SPACE** a topological space or surface satisfying specific conditions ■ *vt* (**-fold·ed, -fold·ing, -folds**) **1. MULTIPLY SOMETHING** to make multiply something **2. MAKE COPIES OF SOMETHING** to make several copies of a book or page [Old English *manigfeald* < earlier forms of MANY + -FOLD] —**man·i·fold·er** *n* —**man·i·fold·ly** *adv* —**man·i·fold·ness** *n*

man·i·kin /mánnikin/, **man·ni·kin** *n* **1.** CLOTHING, COMM same as **mannequin** (sense 1) **2.** an anatomical model of the human body, used in teaching art or medicine **3.** an offensive term for a very short man [Mid-16C. < Dutch *manneken* "little man" < *man* "man"]

ma·nil·a /mə níllə/, **Ma·nil·a** *adj* made of Manila paper ○ *a manila envelope* ■ *n* **1.** a cigar made in Manila **2.** TEXTILES same as **Manila hemp 3.** PAPER same as **Manila paper** [Late 17C. After MANILA]

Ma·nil·a /mə níllə/ capital city of the Philippines, located on the coast of Luzon Island. Population: 1,673,000 (2000).

Ma·nil·a Bay bay of the South China Sea in the northern Philippines, on Luzon Island. Area: 770 sq. mi./2,000 sq. km. Length: 37 mi./60 km.

Ma·nil·a hemp, Ma·nil·la hemp *n* a strong fiber obtained from the Philippine abaca plant. Use: rope, paper. [Mid-19C. After MANILA]

Ma·nil·a pa·per, Ma·nil·la pa·per *n* a strong pale brown paper with a smooth surface, made from Manila hemp. Use: wrapping, envelopes. [Late 19C. After MANILA]

ma·nille /mə níl/ *n* the second-best trump in the card games ombre and quadrille [Late 17C. < French < Spanish *malilla* "little bad (card)"]

man in the moon *n* the imaginary being behind the apparent face on the moon when it is full

man in the street, man on the street *n* the average person, as opposed to an expert, celebrity, or prominent person (*sometimes considered offensive*)

man·i·oc /mánnee òk/ *n* PLANTS, FOOD same as **cassava** [Mid-16C. < Tupi *mandioca* (influenced by French *manihot*) < Guarani *mandio*]

man·i·ple /mánnəp'l/ *n* **1.** in the ancient Roman army, a subdivision of a legion, containing 60 or 120 men **2.** in the Christian church, a silk band or folded napkin formerly worn on the left arm of somebody administering Communion [Late 16C. < Latin *manipulus* "handful" < *manus* "hand"]

ma·nip·u·lar /mə níppyələr/ *adj* **1.** relating to an ancient Roman maniple **2.** relating to or constituting manipulation

ma·nip·u·late /mə níppyə làyt/ (**-lat·ed, -lat·ing, -lates**) *vt* **1. OPERATE SOMETHING** to move, operate, or handle something, especially a machine or mechanical parts ○ *manipulating the crane into position* **2. HANDLE NUMBERS** to work with data on a computer **3. CONTROL SOMEBODY OR SOMETHING** to control or influence somebody or something in an ingenious or devious way **4. FALSIFY SOMETHING** to change or present something in a way that is false but personally advantageous **5. TREAT BODY PART USING HANDS ONLY** to treat a part of the body, or to move a part such as a joint during examination, using the hands only [Early 19C. Back-formation < *manipulation* < French < *manipule* "handful" < Latin *manipulus* (see MANIPLE)] —**ma·nip·u·la·bil·i·ty** /mə nìppyələ bíllətee/ *n* —**ma·nip·u·la·ble** *adj* —**ma·nip·u·lat·a·ble** *adj* —**ma·nip·u·la·tion** /mə nìppyə láysh'n/ *n* —**ma·nip·u·la·tor** *n* —**ma·nip·u·la·to·ry** /mə níppyələ tàwree/ *adj*

ma·nip·u·la·tive /mə níppyələtiv, -làytiv/ *adj* **1.** using clever, devious ways to control or influence somebody or something ○ *a manipulative personality* **2.** relating to or involved in manipulation ○ *a manipulative technique* —**ma·nip·u·la·tive·ly** *adv* —**ma·nip·u·la·tive·ness** *n*

Man·i·pur /mùnnə poor/ state in northeastern India. Capital: Imphal. Population: 2,388,634 (2001). Area: 8,620 sq. mi./22,327 sq. km.

man·i·to *n* RELIG another spelling of **manitou**

Manitoba

Man·i·to·ba /mànni tṓbə/ province in south central Canada, the easternmost of Canada's three Prairie provinces. Capital: Winnipeg. Population: 1,150,800 (2002). Area: 250,116 sq. mi./647,797 sq. km. —**Man·i·to·ban** *adj, n*

Man·i·to·ba, Lake lake in southern Manitoba, Canada. It discharges through the Dauphin River to Lake Winnipeg. Area: 1,799 sq. mi./4,659 sq. km.

man·i·tou /mánni too/, **man·i·tu, man·i·to** /-tō/ (*plural* **-tos**) *n* a supernatural force or spirit believed by Algonquian peoples to exist within various living things and inanimate objects [Late 16C. < Narraganset *manittówock*]

Man·i·tou·lin Is·land /mànni toolin-/ world's largest freshwater island, in the Manitoulin Islands, an archipelago in northern Lake Huron on the border between the United States and Canada. Area: 1,068 sq. mi./2,766 sq. km.

man·i·tu *n* RELIG another spelling of **manitou**

Ma·ni·za·les /mànni zaáləss/ city in western Colombia. It is the capital of Caldas Department, in the Andes mountains. Population: 362,000 (1999).

Man·kie·wicz /máng kye vìch/, **Joseph L.** (1909–93) US movie director and screenwriter. He won Academy Awards for *A Letter to Three Wives* (1949) and *All About Eve* (1950). Full name **Mankiewicz, Joseph Lee**

Man·kil·ler /mán killər/, **Wilma** (*b.* 1945) Cherokee leader. She was the first woman chief of the Cherokee Nation (1985–95).

man·kind /mán kínd/ *n* **1.** human beings considered collectively (*often considered offensive*) **2.** men considered collectively, as distinct from women (*dated*)

man·ky /mángkee/ (**-ki·er, -ki·est**) *adj UK* dirty, greasy, or otherwise unpleasant (*informal*) [Mid-20C. < Scots dialect *mank* "mutilated, defective," via Old French *manc* "maimed" < Latin *mancus*]

Man·ley /mánnlee/, **Michael** (1923–97) Jamaican politician. He served twice as prime minister of Jamaica (1972–80 and 1989–92). Full name **Manley, Michael Norman**

> "Where poverty is shared it may be endured. Where poverty is mocked by extravagance it becomes the condition within which resentment smolders."
> [Michael Manley, *Jamaica: Struggle in the Periphery*; 1982]

man·ly /mánnlee/ (**-li·er, -li·est**) *adj* **1.** having or showing qualities conventionally thought to be characteristic of or appropriate to a man, especially physical strength or courage **2.** considered suitable or appropriate for a man —**man·li·ness** *n*

man-made, man·made /mán màyd/ *adj* made by human beings and not occurring naturally (*often considered offensive*)

Mann /man/, **Horace** (1796–1859) US lawyer and public official. A Massachusetts state legislator, he became the first secretary of the Massachusetts Board of Education (1837–48) and instituted reforms that transformed US public education. He later served in the US House of Representatives and as president of Antioch College in Ohio.

Mann /man, maan/, **Thomas** (1875–1955) German-born US novelist and critic. His work often explores the relationship between society and the creative artist, and includes *The Magic Mountain* (1924). He won the Nobel Prize in literature (1929). See Cultural note at **magic**

> "Speech is civilization itself. The word, even the most contradictory word, preserves contact-it is silence that isolates."
> [Thomas Mann, *The Magic Mountain*; 1924]

man·na /mánnə/ *n* **1. DIVINELY PROVIDED SUSTENANCE** in the Bible, food provided miraculously to feed the Israelites in the wilderness **2. UNEXPECTED BENEFIT** something very welcome or of great benefit that comes unexpectedly **3. SWEET SUBSTANCE FROM ASH TREE** a pale yellow sugary gum exuded by the European ash tree. Use: formerly, as a laxative. **4. SWEET SUBSTANCE FROM TAMARISK TREE** a sweet substance exuded by a tamarisk tree when its bark is punctured by a scale insect [Pre-12C. Via late Latin and Greek < Hebrew *mān*]

Mann Act /mán-/ *n* a 1910 US federal law that criminalized the interstate transportation of women for immoral purposes

man·nan /má nàn, mánnən/ *n* a polysaccharide composed of mannose [Late 19C. < MANNOSE]

Man·nar, Gulf of /mə naár/ inlet of the Indian Ocean between the southern tip of India and western Sri Lanka

manned /mand/ *adj* (*often offensive*) **1.** having a human crew **2.** operated or attended by staff

man·ne·quin /mánnikin/ *n* **1.** a usually life-size model of the human body used to display or fit clothes **2.**

a fashion model (*dated*) **3.** ARTS same as **lay figure** (sense 1) [Mid-18C. Via French < Dutch *manneken* (see MANIKIN)]

man·ner /mánnər/ *n* **1.** WAY SOMETHING IS DONE the way in which something is done or happens ○ *His manner of doing things is often a little unconventional.* **2.** WAY OF BEING the characteristic way in which somebody behaves ○ *had a capricious manner about him* **3.** TYPE a type or kind (*literary*) ○ *What manner of insect makes this hole?* **4.** ARTS STYLE OF WORK OF ART the style in which a work of art is executed ○ *painted in the manner of Vermeer* ■ **man·ners** *npl* **1.** SOCIAL BEHAVIOR social behavior, especially in terms of what is considered correct or unacceptable **2.** CUSTOMS AND PRACTICES the customs and practices of a particular society or period in time [12C. < Anglo-Norman *manere* "way of handling" < Latin *manuarius* "of the hand" < *manus* "hand"] ◇ **all manner of something** many different kinds of something ◇ **in a manner of speaking** in some ways, though not exactly or not in all ways ◇ **to the manner born** naturally adapted to something as though accustomed to it from birth

man·nered /mánnərd/ *adj* **1.** affected or artificial ○ *spoke in mannered tones* **2.** behaving in a particular way or having manners of a particular kind (*usually used in combination*) ○ *an ill-mannered child*

man·ner·ism /mánnər ìzzəm/ *n* **1.** IDIOSYNCRASY a distinctive gesture, habit, or way of doing something ○ *one of his odd little mannerisms* **2.** AFFECTED BEHAVIOR affected or exaggerated speech, behavior, or writing **3. Man·ner·ism** STYLE OF ART AND ARCHITECTURE a style of art and architecture, predominant in Italy in the late 16th century, characterized by stylized and elongated forms and vivid colors —**man·ner·ist** *adj, n* —**man·ner·is·tic** /mànnə rístik/ *adj* —**man·ner·is·ti·cal·ly** *adv*

man·ner·less /mánnərləss/ *adj* having or showing bad manners —**man·ner·less·ness** *n*

man·ner·ly /mánnərlee/ *adj* well-mannered or polite —**man·ner·li·ness** *n*

Mann·heim /mán hìm/ city and river port in southwestern Germany, on the Rhine River. Population: 316,223 (1997).

Mann·heim school *n* a style of orchestral and string playing associated with the rise of the Classical period, developed at the court of Mannheim in the 18th century

man·ni·kin *n* another spelling of **manikin**

Man·ning /mánning/ river in eastern New South Wales, Australia. Length: 140 mi./225 km.

Man·ning, Patrick (*b.* 1946) prime minister of Trinidad and Tobago (1991–95, 2001–). A member of the People's National Movement since the early 1970s, he held a variety of ministerial posts before winning the 1991 election. He was asked to form a government by the country's president in 2001 after the two parties contesting the election won the same number of seats. Full name **Manning, Patrick Augustus Mervyn**

man·nish /mánnish/ *adj* **1.** resembling or suitable for a man rather than a woman (*often considered offensive*) ○ *a mannish haircut* **2.** considered characteristic of a man —**man·nish·ly** *adv* —**man·nish·ness** *n*

man·ni·tol /mánni tàwl/, **man·nite** /má nìt/ *n* a sweet white alcohol found in many plants. Source: mannose. Use: sweetener. [Late 19C < MANNA]

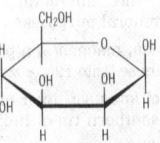

man·nose /má nōss/ *n* a six-carbon sugar found in many plant cell walls. Formula: $C_6H_{12}O_6$. [Late 19C. < *manna*]

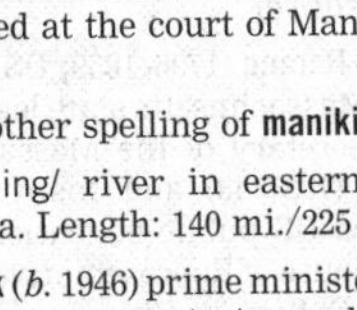

mannose

man·ny /mánnee/ (*plural* **-nies**) *n* a young man employed to look after children (*informal*) [Blend of MAN + NANNY]

ma·no /maánō/ (*plural* **-nos**) *n* the stone held in the hand when grinding grain on a stone block [Early 20C. Via Spanish < Latin *manus* "hand"]

ma·no a ma·no /maánō aa maánō/ *n* (*plural* **ma·nos a ma·nos**) **1.** FACE-TO-FACE CONFRONTATION a face-to-face confrontation between opposing people or sides **2.** BULLFIGHT IN WHICH MATADORS TAKE TURNS a bullfight during which two competing matadors take turns fighting several bulls each ■ *adj, adv* COMPETING DIRECTLY competing directly with somebody or something [Late 20C. < Spanish, "hand to hand"]

ma·noeu·vre *vti, n* Can, UK spelling of **maneuver**

man of God *n* **1.** a man who is a member of the clergy **2.** a saint or godly man

man of let·ters *n* a man who is a writer or scholar (*formal*)

man of straw *n UK* same as **straw man** (senses 1–2)

man of the cloth *n* a man who is a member of the clergy

man of the hour (*plural* **men of the hour**) *n* a man, often a public figure, who is currently publicly admired because of his accomplishments or actions

man-of-war /mànnə wáwr/ (*plural* **men-of-war**), **man o'war** (*plural* **men o'war** /mènnə-/) *n* **1.** same as **warship** **2.** MARINE BIOL same as **Portuguese man-of-war**

man-of-war bird, **man-o'-war bird** *n* BIRDS same as **frigatebird**

ma·nom·e·ter /mə nómmətər/ *n* an instrument used to measure the pressure of a gas [Mid-18C. < Greek *manos* "thin, rare"] —**man·o·met·ric** /mànnə méttrik/ *adj* —**man·o·met·ri·cal·ly** *adv* —**ma·nom·e·try** *n*

man on horse·back *n* **1.** a powerful man, usually a member of a nation's armed forces, who uses his popularity and influence to become the head of state, often in a dictatorship **2.** a military dictator

man on the street *n* same as **man in the street**

man·or /mánnər/ *n* **1.** a house and the land surrounding it, owned by a medieval noble **2.** in North America before 1776, an area of land in some colonies with hereditary rights granted by royal charter to the proprietor **3.** BUILDINGS same as **manor house** [13C. Via Anglo-Norman *maner* < Old French *maneir* "dwelling place" < Latin *manere* "remain, stay"] —**ma·no·ri·al** /mə náwree əl/ *adj*

ORIGIN The Latin word *manere* "to remain, to stay," from which ***manor*** is derived, is also the source of English *manse, mansion, permanent,* and *remain.*

man·or house *n* the residence of the lord or lady of a manor

~~manouver~~ incorrect spelling of **maneuver**

~~manouvre~~ incorrect spelling of **maneuver**

man·pow·er /mán pòwr/ *n* (*sometimes offensive*) **1.** power in terms of the number of people available or needed to do something **2.** power supplied by the physical work of people rather than machines ○ *canals dug entirely by manpower*

man·qué /maaN káy/ *adj* having wanted but failed to be or do something ○ *an artist manqué* [Late 18C. < French, past participle of *manquer* "fail, lack"]

man·sard /mán saàrd/ *n* the part of a building enclosed by a mansard roof [Mid-18C. < French, after the architect François *Mansard* (1598–1666)]

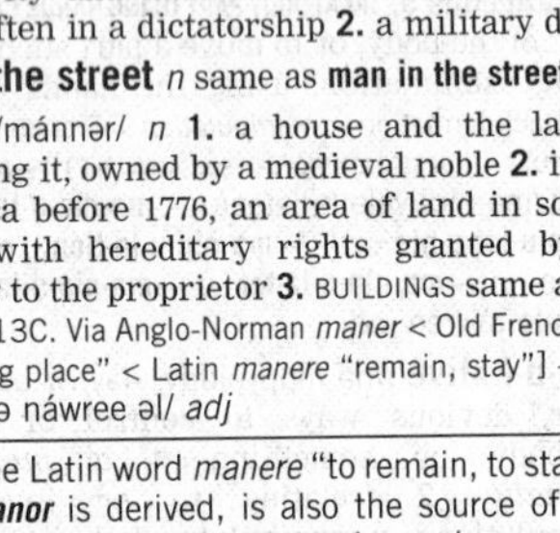

mansard roof

man·sard roof *n* a roof that slopes on all four sides, with each side divided into a gentle upper slope and a steeper lower slope

manse /manss/ *n* **1.** a house provided for a church minister by some Christian denominations, especially in the Presbyterian Church **2.** a large, stately house [Late 15C. < medieval Latin *mansus* "unit of land" < Latin *manere* "remain"]

man·ser·vant /mán sùrvənt/ (*plural* **men·ser·vants** /mén sùrvənts/) *n* a man who is a servant, especially somebody's valet

Mans·field /mánz feèld, mánss-/ city in Nottinghamshire, east central England. Population: 98,181 (2001).

Mans·field, Mount /mánz feèld/ highest peak in the Green Mountains, in north central Vermont. Height: 4,393 ft./1,339 m.

Mans·field, Jayne (1933–67) US movie actor. She played leading roles in the comic films *The Girl Can't Help It* (1956) and *Will Success Spoil Rock Hunter?* (1957). Born **Palmer, Vera Jayne**

Mans·field, Katherine (1888–1923) New Zealand-born British writer. She was a major figure in the development of the short-story form. Pseudonym of **Beauchamp, Katherine Mansfield**

"How idiotic civilization is! Why be given a body if you have to keep it shut up in a case like a rare, rare fiddle?"
[Katherine Mansfield, "Bliss," *Bliss and Other Stories*; 1920]

man·sion /mánshən/ *n* **1.** a large and stately house **2.** one of the 28 divisions of the zodiac through which the Moon passes successively each month [14C. < French, "dwelling place" < Latin *manere* "remain"]

man-sized, **man-size** *adj* **1.** larger than the ordinary size ○ *a man-sized appetite* **2.** the same size as or big enough for a man ○ *a man-sized hole in the fence*

man·slaugh·ter /mán slàwtər/ *n* the unlawful killing of one person by another without advance planning

man's man (*plural* **men's men**) *n* a man who prefers the company of other men to that of women (*informal*)

Man·son /mánssən/, **Charles** (*b.* 1934) US cult leader and murderer. Founder of the "Manson Family," he was sentenced to death for ritual murders carried out in California in 1969, but his sentence was later commuted to life imprisonment by a Supreme Court ruling.

man·sue·tude /mánsswə tood/ *n* a meek or gentle attitude or behavior (*archaic*) [14C. Via French or directly < Latin *mansuetudo* < *mansuetus* "tame," literally "accustomed to the hand" < *suescere* "accustom"]

Man·su·ra /man sóorə/ city in northeastern Egypt, in the Nile delta. Population: 371,000 (1992).

man·ta /mántə/ *n* **1.** a large warm-water ray with wide pectoral fins, a long tail, and two fins resembling horns that project from the head. Family: Mobulidae. **2.** *Southwest US* a square piece of rough cloth. Use: cape, shawl, horse blanket. [Late 17C. < Spanish, "blanket" (from its shape)]

man-tai·lored *adj* cut and styled like a man's suit

man·ta ray *n UK* FISH same as **manta** (sense 1)

Man·te·gna /man ténnyə/, **Andrea** (1431–1506) Italian painter. He was a master of illusionistic perspective and foreshortening.

man·tel /mánt'l/, **man·tle** *n* an ornamental frame around a fireplace, usually made of stone or wood [15C. < Old French *mantel* (see MANTEL)]

man·tel·board /mánt'l bàwrd/ *n Southern US* a mantel over a fireplace [Late 19C. < MANTEL + FIREBOARD]

man·tel·et /mánt'lət, mántlət/, **mant·let** /mántlət/ *n* a short cape worn by women in the 19th century

man·tel·piece /mánt'l peèss/, **man·tle·piece** *n Can, Northeast US, Southern US, UK* the mantel of a fireplace, especially its projecting top

REGIONAL NOTE See ***fireboard.***

man·tel·shelf /mánt'l shèlf/ (*plural* **-shelves** /-shèlvz/), **man·tle·shelf** (*plural* **-shelves**) *n* the projecting top of the mantel of a fireplace, used as a shelf

man·tel·tree /mánt'l treè/, **man·tle·tree** *n* a stone or beam that acts as a support for the masonry above a fireplace

man·tic /mántik/ *adj* relating to or having powers of divination or prophecy [Mid-19C. < Greek *mantikos* < *mantis* "prophet" < *mainesthai* "to rage"]

man·tid /mántid/ *n* INSECTS same as **mantis**

man·til·la /man téeyə, -tíllə/ *n* **1.** a lace scarf that covers the head and shoulders, often worn by women in church, in countries such as Spain and Latin America **2.** a short light cape [Early 18C. < Spanish, "little mantle"]

man·tis /mántiss/ (*plural* **man·tis·es** or **man·tes** /mán teez/) *n* a large, usually green insect that feeds on other insects and has a long body, large eyes, and strong grasping front legs that it holds up at rest. Family: Mantidae. [Mid-17C. Via modern Latin < Greek (see MANTIC)]

man·tis crab *n* MARINE BIOL same as **squilla**

man·tis·sa /man tíssə/ *n* the fractional part of a logarithm, to the right of the decimal point [Mid-17C. < Latin, "makeweight"]

man·tis shrimp *n* MARINE BIOL same as **squilla**

man·tle /mánt'l/ *n* **1.** SLEEVELESS CLOAK a loose sleeveless cloak **2.** WIRE MESH FOR LIGHT a small circle of wire mesh in a gas or oil lamp that gives out incandescent light when heated by the flame it surrounds **3.** TRANSFERRED POSITION a role or position, especially one that can be passed from one person to another (*formal*) ○ *assumed the mantle of the presidency* **4.** COVERING something that envelops or covers something else (*literary*) ○ *a mantle of snow* **5.** ZOOL SHELL-PRODUCING GLAND a layer of epidermis in a mollusk or brachiopod with glands that secrete a shell-producing substance **6.** GEOL CENTRAL PART OF EARTH the part of Earth or another planet that lies between the crust and core **7.** BIRD'S BACK AND SHOULDER the upper back of a bird, lying between the scapulars **8.** ARCHIT another spelling of **mantel** ■ *v* (**-tled, -tling, -tles**) **1.** *vt* COVER SOMETHING to cover something with a mantle or something resembling a mantle ○ *hilltops mantled with snow* **2.** *vi* TO BECOME FLUSHED to be filled or suffused with something (*refers to the face*) ○ *a stern brow mantled with care* [Pre-12C. Via Old French *mantel* < Latin *mantellum* "cloak"]

Man·tle /mánt'l/, **Mickey** (1931–95) US baseball player. He played center field for the New York Yankees (1951–69), where his many achievements included a Triple Crown in batting, home runs, and runs batted in.

man·tle·piece, etc. *n* FURNITURE another spelling of **mantelpiece, etc.**

mant·let *n* CLOTHING another spelling of **mantelet**

mant·ling /mántling/ *n* ornamental drapery around a shield on a coat of arms

man-to-man *adj* **1.** honest, intimate, and treating somebody as an equal ○ *a man-to-man talk* **2.** in sports such as soccer, hockey, or basketball, having each defensive player of one team guard a corresponding offensive player of the other team ○ *a man-to-man defense* —**man-to-man** *adv*

Man·toux test /man tóo-/ *n* a test to determine whether somebody has ever had a tuberculosis infection and so has a measure of immunity to the disease [Mid-20C. After Charles *Mantoux* (1877–1947), French physician]

man·tra /mántrə/ *n* **1.** in Hindu and Buddhist religious practice, a sacred word, chant, or sound that is repeated during meditation to facilitate spiritual power and transformation of consciousness **2.** an expression or idea that is repeated, often without thinking about it, and closely associated with something [Late 18C. < Sanskrit, "thought" < *man* "think"]

man·trap /mán tràp/ *n* an illegal trap set to catch poachers or trespassers on private land, usually in the form of a metal device that snaps shut onto somebody's leg

man·tu·a /mánchoo ə, -too ə/ *n* a woman's gown, fitted above the waist, with an open front and draped skirt to show the underskirt, worn in Europe in the late 17th and 18th centuries [Late 17C. Alteration of *manteau* (< French, later form of *mantel*: see MANTLE), after MANTUA]

Man·tu·a /mánchoo ə/ historic city in central northern Italy, a tourist and agricultural center. Population: 47,790 (2001). Italian name **Mantova**

man·u·al /mánnyoo əl/ *adj* **1.** USING HANDS relating to, done with, or involving the hands ○ *manual dexterity* **2.** PHYSICAL involving physical rather than mental exertion ○ *manual tasks* **3.** OPERATED BY HUMAN BEING operated by a person rather than a machine or computer, or by human effort rather than electricity or another type of power ○ *switching to manual control* ■ *n* **1.** HANDBOOK a book that contains information and instructions about the operation of a machine or how to do something **2.** MUSIC KEYBOARD PLAYED WITH HANDS an organ or harpsichord keyboard that is played with the hands alone **3.** ARMS RIFLE DRILL a drill or exercise in the use of a handheld weapon ○ *cadets practicing the manual of arms* [15C. Directly or via French *manuel* < Latin *manualis* "of the hand" < *manus* "hand"] —**man·u·al·ly** *adv*

ORIGIN The Latin word *manus* "hand," from which ***manual*** derives, is also the source of English *amanuensis, command, demand, manacle, manage, mandate, maneuver, manifest, manipulate, manner, manufacture, manure, mastiff, maundy,* and *remand.*

man·u·al al·pha·bet *n* an alphabet in which finger movements and positions stand for letters, used with other hand signs by hearing-impaired people

man·u·al trans·mis·sion *n* a vehicle transmission that requires the driver to shift gears using a clutch

ma·nu·bri·um /mə nóobree əm/ (*plural* **-bri·a** /-bree ə/ or **-bri·ums**) *n* a handle-shaped anatomical part, e.g., the upper part of the sternum or part of the inner ear [Mid-17C. < Latin, "handle" < *manus* "hand"]

Man·uel I Com·ne·nus /man wèl kom néenəss/ (1122–80) Byzantine emperor. He reigned from 1143 to 1180 and expanded his empire to the west.

Ma·nuel·i·to /màn we léetō/ (1818–93) Navajo leader. He opposed and fought against white settlement of Navajo land. In 1872 he became head of the first Navajo police force.

manuf., manufac. *abbr* **1.** manufacture **2.** manufactured **3.** manufacturer

man·u·fac·to·ry /mànnyə fáktəree/ (*plural* **-ries**) *n* MANUF same as **factory** (*archaic*) [Early 17C. < MANUFACTURE]

man·u·fac·ture /mànnyə fákchər/ *v* (**-tured, -tur·ing, -tures**) **1.** *vti* PRODUCE SOMETHING INDUSTRIALLY to make something into a finished product using raw materials, especially on a large industrial scale ○ *a business manufacturing lightweight metal goods* **2.** *vt* PRODUCE SOMETHING MECHANICALLY to produce something in the manner of a machine, without creativity **3.** *vt* INVENT SOMETHING to invent or make something up ○ *manufactured an excuse* **4.** *vt* BIOCHEM MAKE BODY CHEMICAL to produce a substance needed by the body ○ *Bile is manufactured in the liver.* ■ *n* **1.** PRODUCTION OF GOODS the production of finished goods from raw materials, especially on a large industrial scale ○ *engaged in the manufacture of arms for the military* **2.** PRODUCT something that has been produced from raw materials, especially on a large industrial scale (*often used in the plural*) **3.** BIOCHEM MAKING OF BODY CHEMICAL the production of a substance needed by the body [Mid-16C. Via French < Italian *manifattura* "something made by hand" < Latin *manu factum* "made by hand" < *manus* "hand"] —**man·u·fac·tur·a·ble** *adj*

SYNONYMS See ***make.***

man·u·fac·tured home *n* **1.** a dwelling produced in prefabricated sections that are quickly erected onsite **2.** BUILDINGS same as **mobile home**

man·u·fac·tured hous·ing *n* prefabricated dwellings considered collectively

man·u·fac·tur·er /mànnyə fákchərər/ *n* a factory, person, or organization that produces finished goods from raw materials, especially on a large industrial scale

Man·u·kau Cit·y /mànnə kow-/ city in the northwest of the North Island, New Zealand, near Auckland. Population: 283,197 (2001).

man·u·mit /mànnyə mít/ (**-mit·ted, -mit·ting, -mits**) *vt* to free somebody from slavery (*formal*) [14C. < Latin *manumittere* < *manu emittere* "send out from your hand"] —**man·u·mis·sion** *n* —**man·u·mit·ter** *n*

ma·nure /mə nóor/ *n* animal excrement, often mixed with straw, used as fertilizer for soil ■ *vt* (**-nured, -nur·ing, -nures**) to spread manure on land or soil to fertilize it [14C. < Anglo-Norman < Old French *manouvrer* "work with the hands" < medieval Latin *manuoperare* (see MANEUVER)] —**ma·nur·er** *n*

ORIGIN When English originally took the word ***manure*** over from Anglo-Norman, its connotations of manual labor had been channeled into the management of land, and in particular the cultivation of land. It was not until the middle of the 16th century that the noun ***manure*** came to denote "fertilizer made from dung." The related *maneuver,* reborrowed from French in the 18th century, has remained in more refined use. See also ***manual.***

ma·nus /máynəss, máanəss/ (*plural same*) *n* the wrist and hand of humans or the carpus and forefoot of other vertebrates (*technical*) [Early 16C. < Latin, "hand"]

man·u·script /mánnyə skrìpt/ *n* **1.** HANDWRITTEN BOOK a book or other text written by hand, especially one written before the invention of printing ○ *rare medieval manuscripts* **2.** AUTHOR'S ORIGINAL TEXT an author's text for a book, article, or other piece of written work as it is submitted for publication **3.** HANDWRITING handwriting as opposed to the printed word ○ *a manuscript of the text* [Late 16C. < medieval Latin *manuscriptus* "written by hand" < *scribere* "write"]

Manx /mangks/ *adj* OF ISLE OF MAN relating to the Isle of Man or its former Celtic language ■ *n* LANGUAGE a language formerly spoken on the Isle of Man, belonging to the Goidelic group of Celtic languages ■ *npl* MANX PEOPLE the people of the Isle of Man [Early 16C. Alteration of assumed Old Norse *manskr* < Old Irish *Manu* "Isle of Man"] —**Manx·man** *n* —**Manx·wom·an** *n*

Manx cat, manx cat *n* a shorthaired tailless domestic cat [< the origin of the breed in the Isle of Man]

man·y /ménnee/ CORE MEANING: a grammatical word referring to a considerable number of people or things ○ (adj) *Many people own their homes.* ○ (pron) *Many believe that the matter will never come to trial.* ○ (pron) *Many of you may have heard this.* ○ (adj) *He was among the many visitors to this town.*

1. *adj, pron* CONSIDERABLE NUMBER a considerable number of people or things ○ (adj) *Many children are in the park today.* ○ (pron) *He is a friend to many.* ○ (pron) *Many of us agree with you.* ○ (adj) *Among his many faults is self-importance.* **2.** *adj, pron* LARGE NUMBER a large number of people or things (*used after "so," "too," "not," "as," "the," "that," and possessives*) ○ (adj) *She has so many clocks, she can't be sure exactly what time it is.* ○ (adj) *I've just seen too many government studies get bogged down in politics.* ○ (adj) *There aren't that many people who would agree with you.* ○ (adj) *Among his many interests is mountaineering.* ○ (pron) *Help yourself – you can have as many as you like.* **3.** *adj* EACH OF CONSIDERABLE NUMBER each of a considerable number (*used before "a," "an," or "another"*) ○ *The situation has caused them many a sleepless night.* ○ *We did better than many another regiment.* **4.** *pron* MAJORITY the majority of people ○ *All these advantages should be available to the many – not just the few.* [Old English *manig* < Indo-European, "many, often"]

man·y·fold /ménnee fòld/ *adv* many times over

man·y·plies /ménni plìz/ (*plural same*) *n* ZOOL same as **omasum** [Late 18C. < MANY + PLY[2]; from its many folds]

man·y-sid·ed *adj* having a large number of sides, aspects, or abilities —**man·y-sid·ed·ness** *n*

man·y-val·ued log·ic *n* a system of logic in which propositions may have values in addition to true or false

man·za·nil·la /mànzə néeyə, -níllə/ *n* a pale dry Spanish sherry [Mid-19C. < Spanish, "chamomile," because its smell resembles chamomile]

man·za·ni·ta /mànzə néetə/ *n* an evergreen bush or tree with drooping clusters of pink or white flowers. Native to: western North America. Genus: *Arctostaphylos.* [Mid-19C. < Spanish, "little apple"]

Mao ♦ **Mao Zedong**

MAOI *abbr* MED monoamine oxidase inhibitor

Mao·ism /mów ìzzəm/ *n* the Marxist-Leninist doctrines, teachings, and policies of the former Chinese leader Mao Zedong —**Mao·ist** *n, adj*

Mao jack·et /mów-/ *n* a plain tunic-style jacket with a stand-up collar often worn by Chairman Mao Zedong and the Chinese people under his regime

Mao·ri /mówree/ (*plural same* or **-ris**) *n* **1.** a member of a Polynesian people living in New Zealand and on the Cook Islands **2.** the Austronesian language of the Maori people. Native speakers: 300,000. [Mid-19C. < Maori] —**Mao·ri** *adj*

Mao suit *n* a style of suit consisting of plain loose-fitting trousers and a tunic-style jacket with a stand-up collar often worn by Chairman Mao Zedong and the Chinese people under his regime

AKG London

Mao Zedong

Mao Ze·dong /mòw dzə dóong/, **Mao Tse-tung** /-tsay tóong/ (1893–1976) chairman of the People's Republic of China (1949–76). The leader of the Long March in the Chinese Civil War (1934), he became head of the Chinese Communist Party in the same year. He defeated Chiang's Nationalists after World War II and declared the People's Republic of China in 1949. Known as **Chairman Mao**

> "We are advocates of the abolition of war, we do not want war; but war can only be abolished through war, and in order to get rid of the gun it is necessary to take up the gun."
> [Mao Zedong, "Problems of War and Strategy"; November 6, 1938]

map /map/ *n* **1. GEOGRAPHIC DIAGRAM** a visual representation that shows all or part of the Earth's surface with geographic features, urban areas, roads, and other details **2. DIAGRAM OF STARS** a representation of the stars or the surface of a planet, usually in the form of a diagrammatic drawing **3. DRAWING SHOWING ROUTE OR LOCATION** a diagrammatic drawing of something such as a route or area made to show the location of a place or how to get there **4.** MATH same as **function** *n* (sense 6) ■ *vt* **(mapped, map·ping, maps) 1. CREATE MAP OF SOMETHING** to represent a geographic or other defined area on a map ○ *mapping the heavens* **2. DISCOVER AND SHOW SOMETHING** to discover something and create a visual representation of it **3.** GENETICS **NOTE GENE SEQUENCE** to determine and record the sequence of encoded information on a gene or chromosome **4.** MATH **MATCH SET ELEMENTS** to assign an element in one set to an element in another through a mathematical correspondence [Early 16C. < medieval Latin *mappa (mundi)* "sheet (of the world)" < Latin *mappa* "towel"] —**map·pa·ble** *adj* —**map·per** *n* ◇ **off the map** so as to be no longer famous or important (*slang*) ◇ **on the map** so as to be famous or important (*slang*)

map out *vt* to arrange or devise something such as a plan in detail

MAP *abbr* modified American plan

maple

ma·ple /máyp'l/ *n* **1. TREE** a deciduous tree with winged seeds and lobed leaves producing attractive fall colors. Native to: northern temperate regions. Genus: *Acer*. **2. WOOD** the hard wood of the maple tree. Use: furniture, flooring. **3. FLAVOR** the flavor of the processed sap of the sugar maple [Old English *mapul-* < W Germanic]

Ma·ple Leaf *n* the Canadian flag, showing a stylized red maple leaf on a white background between vertical red bars

ma·ple sug·ar *n* a sugar made by boiling down the sap of the sugar maple

ma·ple syr·up *n* a sweet syrup made from the sap of the sugar maple, or from various other sugars and artificial flavoring

map·mak·er /máp màykər/ *n* somebody who makes maps —**map·mak·ing** *n*

map·ping /mápping/ *n* **1.** the act or process of making maps **2.** MATH same as **function** *n* (sense 6)

Map·ple·thorpe /máyp'l thàwrp/, **Robert** (1946–89) US photographer. Acclaimed for his elegant photographic technique and experimentation with printing, light, and color, he was controversial for the sexually explicit content of his work.

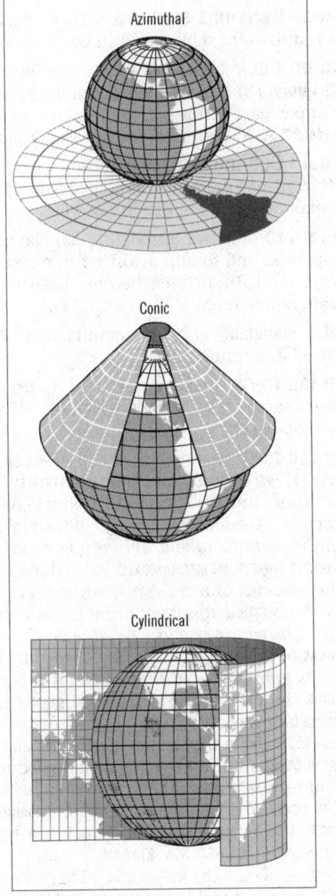

map projection

map pro·jec·tion *n* a representation of or way of representing a three-dimensional object, especially part of the Earth's surface, on a two-dimensional surface

Ma·pu·che /mə póochee/ (*plural same* or **-ches**) *n* **1.** a member of a subgroup of the Araucanian people of central Chile and areas of western Argentina **2.** the Araucanian language of the Mapuche people. Native speakers: 400,000. [Early 20C. < Mapuche, "country people"] —**Ma·pu·che** *adj*

Ma·pu·to /mə póotō/ capital of Mozambique, in the southeast of the country on the Indian Ocean. Population: 1,098,000 (1991 estimate).

ma·quette /ma két/ *n* a small model of a planned sculpture or architectural work [Early 20C. Via French < Italian *macchietta* "little spot" < Latin *maculare* "to spot"]

ma·qui·la·do·ra /maa keelaa dáw raa, mə keelə-/, **ma·qui·la** /mə keelə, maa kee laa/ *n Hispanic* an assembly plant in Mexico run by US or other foreign interests. Parts are shipped to Mexico, products are assembled, and finished goods are returned for sale in the markets of origin. [Late 20C. < Mexican Spanish < *maquilar* "assemble"]

ma·quil·lage /màakee àazh/ *n* **1.** makeup **2.** the art of applying makeup [Late 19C. < French < *maquiller* "make up the face" < Old French *masquiller* "to stain"]

ma·quis /ma kée, maa-/ (*plural same*) *n* **1. DENSE COASTAL VEGETATION** dense shrubby vegetation of Mediterranean coastal regions **2.** *also* **Ma·quis FRENCH RESISTANCE** the underground French Resistance movement that fought against the German occupying forces during World War II **3.** *also* **Ma·quis FRENCH RESISTANCE FIGHTER** a member of the World War II French Resistance movement [Mid-19C. Via French < Italian *macchia* "spot" < Latin *macula* (from the vegetation's resemblance to spots)]

Ma·qui·sard /màkee zaárd, -zaár/ *n* HIST same as **maquis** (sense 3) [Mid-20C. < French < *maquis* (see MAQUIS)]

mar /maar/ **(marred, mar·ring, mars)** *vt* to spoil or detract from something [Old English *merran* "waste, spoil" < Germanic]

mar. *abbr* **1.** maritime **2.** married

Mar. *abbr* March

ma·ra /mə raá/ (*plural* **-ras** or *same*) *n* a large long-legged member of the cavy family that resembles a hare. Native to: Argentine pampas. Latin name: *Dolichotis patagonum.* [Mid-19C. < American Spanish *mará*]

Ma·ra /maá raa/ *n* in Buddhism, a force of evil, sometimes conceived of as a being [Late 19C. < Sanskrit *Māra* "death" < *mṛ-* "die"]

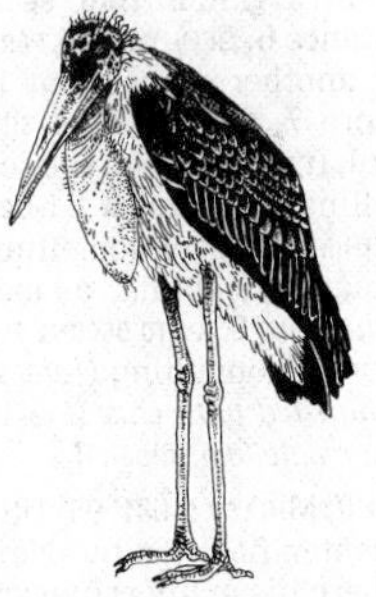

marabou

mar·a·bou /márrə bòo/, **mar·a·bout** *n* **1. LARGE AFRICAN STORK** a large stork that has dark gray feathers and a short naked neck with a pink pouch at the front. Marabous are closely related to adjutants. Native to: Africa. Latin name: *Leptoptilos crumeniferus.* **2. MARABOU FEATHERS** down taken from the tail of the marabou. Use: trimming for clothes. **3. RAW SILK** a fine white raw silk [Early 19C. Via French < Arabic *murābiṭ* "holy man"]

mar·a·bout[1] /márrə bòo/ *n* **1.** a Muslim hermit, monk, or holy man, especially in North Africa **2.** the tomb or a shrine of a marabout, often a destination for pilgrims [Early 17C. Via French < Portuguese *marabuto* < Arabic *murābiṭ* < *ribāṭ* "frontier post," because hermits would go to such places to gain merit]

mar·a·bout[2] /márrə bòo/ *n* BIRDS another spelling of **marabou**

mar·a·bun·ta /márrə bùntə/ *n Carib* a red-brown wasp that nests in trees and house eaves. Family: Vespidae. [Late 19C. < a Guyanan name]

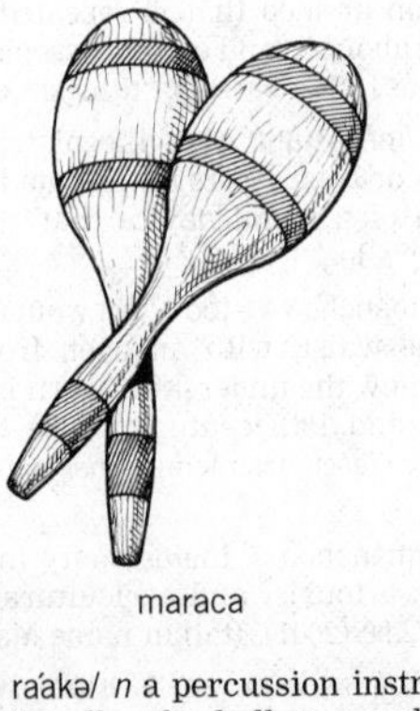

maraca

ma·ra·ca /mə raákə/ *n* a percussion instrument consisting traditionally of a hollow gourd filled with small pebbles or beans. Maracas are usually shaken in pairs as an accompaniment to Latin American music. [Early 17C. Via Portuguese *maracá* < Tupi *maráka*]

Ma·ra·cai·bo, Lake /màrrə kī́bō/ largest lake in South America, in northwestern Venezuela, connected by a channel with the Gulf of Venezuela. Area: 5,140 sq. mi./13,300 sq. km.

Ma·ra·cay /màrra káy/ city in northern Venezuela, near Lake Valencia. Population: 354,196 (1990).

ma·ra·ging steel /maá ràyjing-/ *n* a strong low-carbon steel formed by aging and heating and containing up to 25 percent nickel with lesser amounts of titanium, aluminum, and niobium [< blend of MARTENSITE + AGE]

Mar·a·jó /màrrə zhṓ/ island in northeastern Brazil, in the delta of the Amazon River. Area: 15,500 sq. mi./40,100 sq. km.

Ma·ra·ñón /màrrə nyṓn/ river in northern South America, flowing northward from the Andes into the Amazon River. Length: 990 mi./1,600 km.

ma·ran·ta /mə rántə/ *n* a plant with variegated thin leaves. Native to: tropical America. Genus: *Maranta.* [Early 19C. < modern Latin, after Bartolomeo *Maranta* (1500–71), Italian herbalist]

ma·ras·ca /mə ráskə/ *n* a cultivated variety of sour cherry tree whose fruit is used to make maraschino. Latin name: *Prunus cerasus.* [Mid-19C. < Italian, alteration of *amarasca* < *amaro* "bitter"]

mar·a·schi·no /màrrə skeénō, -sheénō/ *n* a cordial distilled from marasca cherries [Late 18C. < Italian < *marasca* (see MARASCA)]

mar·a·schi·no cher·ry *n* a bright red cherry preserved in a sweet syrup flavored with maraschino or an imitation of this. Use: in cocktails, cake decoration.

ma·ras·mus /mə rázməss/ *n* a gradual wasting away of the body, generally associated with severe malnutrition or inadequate absorption of food and occurring mainly in young children [Mid-17C. < modern Latin < Greek *marasmos* "decay" < *marainein* "waste away"] —**ma·ras·mic** *adj*

Ma·rat /mə raá/, **Jean-Paul** (1743–93) French journalist and politician. He was a radical leader of the French Revolution. He was murdered in his bath by Charlotte Corday.

Ma·ra·tha /mə raátə, -rúttə/, **Ma·rat·ta, Mah·rat·ta** *n* a member of a people living mainly in the Deccan plateau in the Indian state of Maharashtra [Mid-18C. < Marathi *marāṭhā*, or Hindi *marhaṭṭā* < Sanskrit *Mahārāṣṭra* "great kingdom"]

Ma·ra·thi /mə raátee, -rúttee/, **Mah·rat·ti** *n* an official language of the Indian state of Maharashtra, belonging to the Indo-Iranian branch of Indo-European. Native speakers: 70 million. ■ *adj* relating to the Indian state of Maharashtra, or its people, language, or culture [Late 17C. < Marathi *marāṭhī* < Sanskrit *Mahārāṣṭrī* < *Mahārāṣṭra* "great kingdom"]

mar·a·thon /márrə thòn/ *n* **1. LONG-DISTANCE RACE** a long-distance footrace run over a distance of 26 mi. 385 yds./42.195 km **2. DIFFICULT UNDERTAKING** a lengthy and difficult task, event, or activity **3. ENDURANCE TEST** a test of endurance, especially in a competition ○ *a dance marathon* [Late 19C. After MARATHON] —**mar·a·thon·er** *n*

ORIGIN According to tradition, when the Greek army defeated the Persians at Marathon in 490 B.C., the runner Pheidippides was dispatched to bring the good news to Athens (in fact there is no contemporary evidence for the story, which is not recorded until 700 years after the event). When the modern Olympic Games were first held, in Athens in 1896, a long-distance race was introduced to commemorate the ancient feat, run over a course supposedly equal in distance to the journey from Marathon to Athens (about 22 mi./35 km). The present distance was established at the 1948 Olympics in London, England.

Mar·a·thon /márrə thòn/ plain in southeastern Greece that was the site of an important Athenian military victory over the Persians in 490 B.C.

Ma·rat·ta *n* PEOPLES another spelling of **Maratha**

ma·raud /mə ráwd/ (**-raud·ed, -raud·ing, -rauds**) *vti* to rove around carrying out violent attacks or looking for plunder, or raid a place in search of plunder [Late 17C. < French *marauder* < *maraud* "rogue, vagabond"] —**ma·raud·er** *n* —**ma·raud·ing** *adj*

mar·ble /maárb'l/ *n* **1. DENSE CRYSTALLIZED ROCK** a form of limestone transformed through the heat and pressure of metamorphism into a dense, variously colored, crystallized rock. Use: building, sculpture, monuments. **2. MARBLE SCULPTURE** a sculpture made from marble **3. SMALL GLASS BALL** a small hard ball, usually made of glass, used in the game of marbles **4. SOMETHING RESEMBLING MARBLE** something that resembles marble in being cold, hard, smooth, or white (*literary*) ■ *vt* (**-bled, -bling, -bles**) **COLOR SOMETHING WITH MOTTLED STREAKS** to color something, usually paper, with mottled streaks to give the appearance of marble [12C. Via French *marbre* < Latin *marmor* < Greek *marmaros* "hard, shiny stone" (influenced by *marmairein* "to shine")] —**mar·bly** *adj*

mar·ble cake *n* a cake made with two different flavors of sponge, often chocolate and plain, dropped into the same cake pan and very lightly mixed before baking

mar·bled /maárb'ld/ *adj* **1. OF OR PATTERNED LIKE MARBLE** made of marble or resembling marble in coloring or mottling ○ *a marbled pediment* **2. COLORED WITH MOTTLED STREAKS** describes paper or other material colored with mottled streaks to create the appearance of marble ○ *an 18th-century volume with marbled endpapers* **3. STREAKED WITH FAT** describes lean meat that contains streaks of fat ○ *marbled steak*

Mar·ble·head /maárb'l hèd/ resort town in northeastern Massachusetts, on Massachusetts Bay. Population: 20,482 (2002 estimate).

mar·bles /maárb'lz/ *n* **1.** a game, played mainly by children, in which small hard balls are rolled on the ground with the aim of hitting the opponent's ball (*takes a singular verb*) **2.** mental abilities or sense of reality (*slang; takes a plural verb*)

mar·ble·wood /maárb'l wòod/ *n* **1.** a mottled black-banded wood. Use: cabinetmaking. **2.** a tree of the ebony family that produces marblewood. Native to: Malaysia. Latin name: *Diospyros marmorata.*

mar·bling /maárbling/ *n* **1. COLORING LIKE MARBLE** coloring or mottling that looks like marble **2. CREATION OF MARBLED EFFECT** the process of applying mottled streaks of color to paper or other material to create the appearance of marble **3. STREAKS OF FAT** streaks of fat in lean meat

Mar·burg dis·ease /maár bùrg-/ *n* a severe viral infection causing high fever, hemorrhaging, rashes, vomiting, and often death [Mid-20C. After *Marburg*, city in west central Germany]

marc /maark/ *n* **1.** brandy made from the skins and pulp that remain when grapes and other fruit have had their juice pressed out **2.** the skins and pulp remaining after grapes, apples, or other fruit have had their juice pressed out, e.g., for wine making [Early 17C. < French < *marcher* "trample" (see MARCH[1])]

Marc /maark/, **Franz** (1880–1916) German painter. He was a founder of the expressionist group Der Blaue Reiter (The Blue Rider). Semiabstract paintings of horses and deer are characteristic of his work.

mar·ca·site /maárkə sīt, -zīt/ *n* **1.** a yellowish iron sulfide mineral. Use: jewelry. **2.** polished steel or other white metal cut with facets and used in jewelry, or something made from this [15C. Via medieval Latin *marcasita* < Arabic *marḳašīṭa* < Persian or Aramaic]

mar·ca·to /maar kaátō/ *adv* with a heavy accentuation of individual notes that are often also played in a detached style (*used as a musical direction*) [Mid-19C. < Italian, "marked, accented"] —**mar·ca·to** *adj*

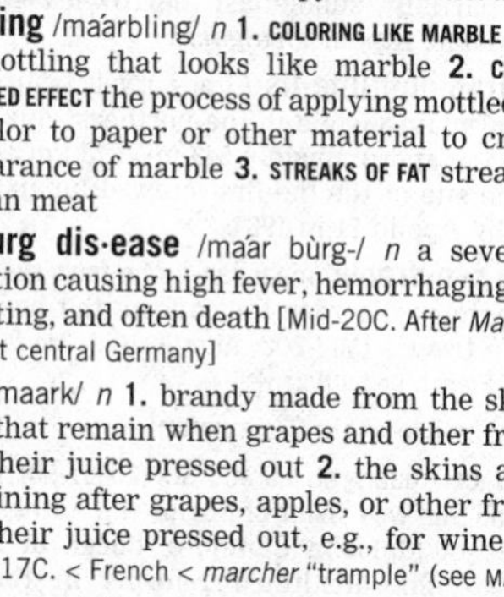

AKG London

Marcel Marceau

Mar·ceau /maar sṓ/, **Marcel** (*b.* 1923) French mime artist. His white-faced character, Bip, became for a time synonymous with mime.

"Words can be deceitful, but pantomime necessarily is simple, clear and direct."
[Marcel Marceau, *Theater Arts*; March 1958]

mar·cel /maar sél/ *n also* **mar·cel wave** a women's hairstyle, popular in the 1920s, consisting of regular deep waves created with curling irons ■ *vt* (**-celled, -cell·ing, -cels**) to style somebody's hair in a marcel [Late 19C. After François *Marcel* Grateau (1852–1936), French hairdresser]

mar·ces·cent /maar séss'nt/ *adj* remaining attached to a plant when withered ○ *marcescent blossom* [Early 18C. < Latin *marcescent-*, present participle of *marcescere* "begin to wither" < *marcere* "wither, decay"]

march[1] /maarch/ *v* (**marched, march·ing, march·es**) **1.** *vi* **WALK IN MILITARY FASHION** to walk with regular formalized movements of the arms and legs at a steady rhythmic pace, often in formation **2.** *vti* **MOVE IN MILITARY-STYLE FORMATION** to proceed somewhere, or direct a body of people or troops to proceed somewhere, on foot, in a disciplined military or military-style formation ○ *marched the troops off to battle* **3.** *vi* **SET OFF** to set off, usually on foot, on a military campaign or expedition ○ *Our orders are to march at daybreak.* **4.** *vi* **WALK WITH DETERMINATION** to walk quickly and with an air of determination ○ *marched in and demanded to see the manager* **5.** *vt* **FORCE SOMEBODY TO GO SOMEWHERE** to force somebody to accompany you, usually by physically taking hold of the person ○ *grabbed the boys and marched them into the house* **6.** *vi* **WALK TO PROTEST OR PUBLICIZE SOMETHING** to take part in a political demonstration or protest in the form of an organized walk in procession by a group of people to a place in support of a cause ○ *remembered crowds marching against the war* **7.** *vi* **PASS STEADILY** to pass steadily or inexorably ○ *Time marches on.* ■ *n* **1. ACT OR EXTENT OF MARCHING** a journey on foot, especially under military discipline or in a military formation ○ *a four-hour march back to the camp* **2. WALK FOR PROTEST OR PUBLICITY** a political demonstration or protest in the form of an organized walk in procession by a group of people to a place in support of a cause ○ *a protest march* **3. MARCHING SPEED** a particular speed or style of marching ○ *advanced at a slow march* **4. MOVEMENT FORWARD** a steady forward movement or progression ○ *the march of time* **5. MUSIC IN MARCHING RHYTHM** a piece of music especially written or suitable to accompany marching, usually with a regular emphatic beat and in a military style [14C. < French *marcher* < Germanic, "measure off"] —**march·er** *n* ◇ **on the march 1.** proceeding somewhere on foot, especially purposefully and in a military or military-style formation **2.** advancing or making progress ◇ **steal a march on somebody** to do or achieve something before somebody else, thereby gaining an advantage over that person

march[2] /maarch/ *n* an area along the border between two countries, especially an outlying area that is subject to territorial disputes and hostile incursions ■ *vi* (**marched, march·ing, march·es**) to share a border with a country or territory (*formal*) [13C. < Old French *marche* < Germanic]

March /maarch/ *n* in the Gregorian calendar, the third month of the year, lasting 31 days. See table at **calendar** [< Anglo-Norman < Latin *Martius (mensis)* "(month) of Mars"]

March /maarch/, **Fredric** (1897–1975) US stage and movie actor. He won Academy Awards for *Dr. Jekyll and Mr. Hyde* (1931) and *The Best Years of Our Lives* (1946). Born **Bickell, Fredric Ernest McIntyre**

March. *abbr* Marchioness

M.Arch. *abbr* Master of Architecture

mar·che·sa /maar káyzə/ (*plural* **-se** /-zày/) *n* an Italian marchioness, holding the title either in her own right or as the wife or widow of a marchese [Late 18C. < Italian, form of *marchese* (see MARCHESE)]

mar·che·se /maar káy zày/ (*plural* **-si** /-zee/) *n* an Italian marquis, a nobleman of a rank above count [Early 16C. < Italian < medieval Latin *(comes) marcensis* "count of the border" < *marca* "border" < Germanic]

march·ing band /maárching-/ *n* a band that plays while marching and performing maneuvers

march·ing or·ders *npl* **1.** a summary dismissal or request to leave (*informal*) ○ *The manager was given* *his marching orders when the mistake came to light.* **2.** orders to soldiers to set off on a military campaign or expedition

mar·chio·ness /maárshənəss, maárshə néss/ *n* in the United Kingdom, a noblewoman of a rank above countess, or the wife or widow of a marquess [Late 16C. < medieval Latin *marchionissa* < *marca* "borderland" < Germanic]

march·land /maárch lànd, -lənd/ *n* an area along the border between two countries [Mid-16C. < MARCH²]

march·pane /maárch pàyn/ *n* same as **marzipan** (*archaic*) [15C. Origin ?]

march-past *n* a formal parade by troops or other people who march in formation past somebody who reviews them from a stand or other vantage point

Mar·ci·a·no /maárssee aánō, -ánnō/, **Rocky** (1923–69) US boxer. At the end of his four years holding the heavyweight title (1952–56), he was the only heavyweight champion to retire undefeated. Born **Marchegiano, Rocco Francis**

Mar·co·ni /maar kōnee/, **Guglielmo, Marchese** (1874–1937) Italian electrical engineer. He pioneered the practical development of radio signaling. He shared the Nobel Prize in physics (1909) for his work in wireless telegraphy.

Mar·co·ni rig *n* SAILING same as **Bermuda rig** [After Guglielmo MARCONI] —**Mar·co·ni-rigged** *adj*

Mar·co Po·lo ♦ **Polo, Marco**

Mar·cos /maár kōss/, **Ferdinand** (1917–89) Philippine national leader and president of the Philippines (1965–86). For most of his presidency, he ruled the Philippines under martial law, amassing a large personal fortune. Ousted after allegations of corruption and irregularities in the national elections of 1986, he died in exile. Full name **Marcos, Ferdinand Edralin**

Mar·cus Au·re·li·us ♦ **Aurelius, Marcus**

Mar·cy, Mount /maárssee/ highest peak in the Adirondack Mountains, in northeastern New York 5,344 ft./1,629 m

Mar·dal Wa·ter·fall /maár daal-/ waterfall in western Norway, one of the highest in the world. Height: 1,696 ft./517 m.

Mar del Pla·ta /maár del plaá taa/ resort city and fishing port in eastern Argentina. Population: 512,880 (1991).

Mar·di Gras /maárdee graá/ (*plural* **Mar·dis Gras** /*pronunc. same*/) *n* **1.** in some countries, Shrove Tuesday, the last day before the beginning of Lent in the Christian calendar **2.** in some places, a carnival held or ending on Mardi Gras, often celebrated with costumes, parades, balls, and other festivities [< French, literally "fat Tuesday" (the day rich foods were used up before Lent)]

Mar·duk /maár dŏŏk, -dùk/ *n* in Babylonian mythology, the god who defeated the great goddess Tiamat and created humankind

mare¹ /mer/ *n* an adult female horse, or an adult female of a species closely related to the horse such as the zebra [Old English *mearh* < Indo-European, "horse"]

ma·re² /maá rày, maáree/ (*plural* **-ri·a** /-ree ə/ or **-res**) *n* a large dark plain on the surface of the Moon or Mars [Mid-19C. < Latin, "sea"]

Mare ♦ **de la Mare, Walter**

ma·re clau·sum /maá ray kláwssəm, -klów sŏŏm/ *n* a sea or other area of water that is under the jurisdiction of one country and closed to all others [< Latin, "closed sea," title of a work (1635) by John Selden defending the right of a single nation to control parts of the sea]

Ma·re Cris·i·um /maá ray kríssee əm/ lunar lowland plain visible in the northeast quadrant of the Moon, approximately 260 mi./418 km across

Ma·re Fe·cun·di·ta·tis /-fe kùndi taátiss/ lunar lowland plain visible in the southeast quadrant of the Moon, approximately 909 mi./1,463 km across

Ma·re Fri·gor·is /-fri gáwriss/ lunar lowland plain visible near the Moon's north pole, approximately 1,596 mi./2,569 km across

Ma·re Hu·mor·um /-hyoo máwrəm/ lunar lowland plain visible in the southwest quadrant of the Moon, approximately 389 mi./626 km across

Ma·re Im·bri·um /-ímbree əm/ lunar lowland plain visible in the northwest quadrant of the Moon, approximately 1,123 mi./1,807 km across

ma·re li·be·rum /-leébə rŏŏm/ *n* an area of sea that is open to the ships of all countries [Mid-17C. < Latin, "free sea," title of a treatise (1609) by Dutch jurist Hugo Grotius, defending free access to the ocean by all nations]

mar·em·ma /mə rémmə/ (*plural* **-me** /-mee/) *n* an area of marshy ground near the sea, especially in Italy [Mid-19C. Via Italian < Latin *maritimus* < *mare* "sea"]

Ma·re Nec·tar·is /-nek taáriss/ lunar lowland plain visible in the southeast quadrant of the Moon, approximately 333 mi./536 km across

Ma·ren·go /mə réng gō/ *adj* browned in oil and cooked in a sauce of tomatoes, mushrooms, garlic, onion, and white wine ○ *chicken Marengo* [Mid-19C. After *Marengo*, N Italy, where such a dish is said to have been served to Napoleon in 1800]

ma·re nos·trum /maá ray nóstrəm, -ŏŏm/ *n* an area of sea that is under the jurisdiction of one country or shared by two or more countries [< Latin, "our sea" (name for the Mediterranean)]

Ma·re Nu·bi·um /-nyŏŏbee əm/ lunar lowland plain visible in the southwest quadrant of the Moon, approximately 715 mi./1,151 km across

Ma·re O·ri·en·ta·le /-àwree en taálee/ lunar lowland plain on the side of the Moon that is furthest from the Earth, approximately 327 mi./526 km across

Ma·re Se·ren·i·ta·tis /-sə rènni taátiss/ lunar lowland plain, visible in the northeast quadrant of the Moon, approximately 707 mi./1,138 km across. It is where Apollo 17 landed.

mare's nest /mèrz-/ *n* **1.** a complicated or confused situation **2.** a discovery at first thought to be important or valuable but subsequently found to be an illusion, a hoax, or valueless

mare's-tail /mèrz-/ *n* **1.** a long wispy strand of cloud (*usually used in the plural*) **2.** a water plant with erect, partially submerged, narrow-leaved stems. Latin name: *Hippuris vulgaris*.

Ma·re Tran·quil·li·ta·tis /-trang kwìlli taátiss/ lunar lowland plain visible in the northeast quadrant of the Moon, approximately 543 mi./873 km across. It was the site of the the first crewed lunar landing, made by Apollo 11 in 1969.

Mar·fan syn·drome /maár fan-/, **Mar·fan's syn·drome** *n* a hereditary disorder that affects the body's connective tissues [Mid-20C. After A. B. J. *Marfan* (1858–1942), French pediatrician]

marg. *abbr* **1.** margin **2.** marginal

Mar·gar·et /maárgrət, -ərət/, **St.** (1046?–93) **queen of Scotland** She was sister of Edgar (the Aetheling) and as wife of Malcolm Canmore, queen of Scotland (1070–93). She instituted reforms in the Celtic Church.

Mar·gar·et II, Mar·gre·the II (*b.* 1940) **queen of Denmark** The Danish constitution was revised (1953) to allow her to become the first queen to rule the country in her own right. She acceded to the throne in 1972.

Mar·gar·et (of An·jou) /maárgrət, -gərət/ (1430?–82) queen of England. She was the wife of Henry VI of England, and led the Lancastrians in the Wars of the Roses from 1455 until her final defeat in 1471.

Mar·gar·et, Princess, Countess of Snowdon (1930–2002) She was the younger sister of Elizabeth II, queen of the United Kingdom. Born **Princess Margaret Rose**

mar·ga·rine /maárjərin/ *n* a yellow fat that usually consists of a blend of vegetable oils or animal fats mixed with water, flavoring, and other ingredients [Late 19C. < French]

mar·ga·ri·ta /maàrgə reétə/ *n* a cocktail made with tequila, lemon or lime juice, and an orange-flavored liqueur, typically served in a chilled glass whose rim has been dipped into salt [Early 20C. < Spanish < the name *Margarita*]

Mar·ga·ri·ta /maár gə reétə/ island in Nueva Esparta State, northern Venezuela, in the Caribbean Sea. Population: 117,700 (1979). Area: 414 sq. mi./1,072 sq. km.

Mar·gas·ir·sa /maàrgə seérssə/ *n* in the Hindu calendar, the ninth month of the year, lasting 30 days and falling about the same time as November to December. See table at **calendar**

Mar·gate /maár gàyt/ city in southeastern Florida, a suburb of Fort Lauderdale. Population: 54,786 (2002 estimate).

mar·gay /maár gày/ *n* a wild cat slightly larger than a domestic cat, with coloring and markings similar to those of a leopard. Native to: rain forests of Central and South America. Latin name: *Felis wiedi*. [Late 18C. < French < Portuguese *maracaj'a* < Tupi *marakaya*]

mar·gin /maárjin/ *n* **1.** BLANK SPACE AT SIDE OF PAGE a blank space on the left or right edge, or at the top or bottom, of a written or printed page ○ *comments scribbled in the margin* **2.** LINE DOWN SIDE OF PAGE a straight line drawn down the left- or right-hand side of a page to separate a narrow section from the main part ○ *Draw a margin an inch in from the edge.* **3.** OUTER EDGE the edge of something, especially the outer edge, or the area close to it ○ *dark-green leaves with reddish margins* **4.** PART FARTHEST FROM CENTER a part of something such as a society or organization that is least integrated with its center, least often considered, least typical, or most vulnerable (*often used in the plural*) ○ *on the margins of society* **5.** LIMIT a boundary indicating the limit beyond which something should not go or below which something should not fall (*often used in the plural*) ○ *beyond the margins of good taste* **6.** DIFFERENCE BETWEEN ONE AMOUNT AND ANOTHER the difference between two amounts or scores ○ *won by a small margin* **7.** ADDITIONAL AMOUNT an amount over and above what is strictly necessary, included for safety reasons or to allow for mistakes or delays ○ *no margin for error* **8.** COMM PROFIT the profit on a transaction, or the amount by which the price of something exceeds its cost ○ *We've cut our margins to the minimum.* **9.** FIN BROKER'S LOSS COVER the amount or percentage deposited with a stockbroker by a client to cover possible losses on transactions made on account **10.** FIN DIFFERENCE BETWEEN LOAN AND COLLATERAL VALUES the difference between the face value of a loan and the value of the collateral given to secure the loan **11.** ECON LOWEST ACCEPTABLE PROFIT the minimum profit that a business must make in order to remain viable ■ *vt* (**-gined, -gin·ing, -gins**) **1.** CREATE MARGIN AROUND SOMETHING to create a margin around something **2.** FIN PLACE SOMETHING AS DEPOSIT WITH BROKER to place something such as collateral with a broker as a deposit [14C. < Latin *margin-* < *margo* < Indo-European, "boundary, border"]

mar·gin ac·count *n* an account with a brokerage that allows the investor to borrow money to buy securities, up to a permitted maximum

mar·gin·al /maárjin'l/ *adj* **1.** IN MARGIN written in a margin **2.** SMALL IN SCALE very small in scale or importance ○ *Progress has been marginal so far.* **3.** IRRELEVANT not of central importance or relevance ○ *ignored everything marginal to his main thesis* **4.** ON FRINGE operating or existing on the fringes of a group or movement ○ *a marginal artist* **5.** VERY LOW at or close to the lowest acceptable or viable limit ○ *a marginal standard of living* **6.** ECON BARELY COVERING COSTS barely able to cover the costs of production when sold or when producing goods for sale **7.** AGRIC DIFFICULT TO CULTIVATE difficult to cultivate and therefore only brought into use if profits are high enough to make it worth the effort ○ *marginal land* —**mar·gin·al·i·ty** /maàrji nállətee/ *n*

mar·gin·al cost *n* the additional cost of producing one more item for sale

mar·gi·na·li·a /maàrji náylee ə, -náylyə/ *npl* notes written in a margin

mar·gin·al·ize /maárjin'l ìz/ (**-ized, -iz·ing, -iz·es**) *vt* to take or keep somebody or something away from the center of attention, influence, or power —**mar·gin·al·i·za·tion** /maàrjin'li zàysh'n/ *n*

mar·gin·al·ly /maárjin'lee/ *adv* **1.** very slightly **2.** only just or barely

mar·gin·al u·til·i·ty *n* the increase in utility prompted by one extra unit of a given service or product

mar·gin·ate /maárji nàyt/ *vt* (**-at·ed, -at·ing, -ates**) to add a margin to something, or provide something with a margin ■ *adj also* **mar·gin·at·ed** /maárjə nàytəd/ with a border or edge of a different color or pattern ○ *a marginate leaf* —**mar·gin·a·tion** /maàrji náysh'n/ *n*

mar·gin call *n* a demand by a broker to an investor

to provide cash or other assets to supplement a margin account

mar·gra·vate /maárgrə vàyt/, **mar·gra·vi·ate** /maar gráyvee ət, -gráyvee àyt/ *n* **1.** the territory ruled by a margrave or margravine **2.** the rank or position of a margrave or margravine

mar·grave /maár gràyv/ *n* formerly, a German nobleman of a rank equivalent to a British marquess [Mid-16C. < Middle Dutch *markgrave* "count of the border"]

mar·gra·vi·ate *n* HIST same as **margravate**

mar·gra·vine /maárgrə veén/ *n* formerly, a German noblewoman who was the wife or widow of a margrave or who held the rank in her own right [Late 17C. < Dutch *markgravin*, form of *markgraaf* "margrave"]

Mar·gre·the II /maar gráytə/ ♦ **Margaret II**

mar·gue·rite /maárgə reét, -gyə reét/ *n* a widely cultivated garden plant. Flowers: white or pale yellow petals, yellow center. Native to: Canary Islands. Latin name: *Chrysanthemum frutescens*. [Early 17C. < French < the name *Marguerite*]

Ma·ri /maáree/ (*plural same* or **-ris**) *n* **1.** a member of a people living around western and central stretches of the Volga River in Russia, and in Kazakhstan **2.** the Finno-Ugric language of the Mari people. Native speakers: 700,000. [Early 20C. < Mari] —**Ma·ri** *adj*

ma·ri·a ASTRON plural of **mare**[2]

ma·ri·a·chi /maaree aáchee, màrree-/ (*plural* **-chis**) *n* *Hispanic* **1.** MEXICAN MUSIC traditional Mexican folk music as played by a small group of musicians **2.** MEXICAN STREET BAND a Mexican street band that plays traditional folk music, traditionally consisting of stringed instruments, especially violins and guitars, brass instruments and singers **3.** MEXICAN BAND PLAYER a member of a mariachi band [Mid-20C. < Mexican Spanish]

~~mariage~~ incorrect spelling of **marriage**

Mar·i·an /mérree ən/ *adj* **1.** OF VIRGIN MARY relating to, characteristic of, or devoted to Mary, the mother of Jesus Christ **2.** OF QUEEN MARY relating to any Mary other than the Virgin Mary, especially Mary, Queen of Scots or Queen Mary I of England ■ *n* DEVOTEE OF VIRGIN MARY a Christian who is especially devoted to Mary, the mother of Jesus Christ

Ma·ri·an·a Is·lands /màrree aánə-/ island group in the western North Pacific Ocean, east of the Philippines, comprising Guam and the Commonwealth of the Northern Mariana Islands. Population: 226,500 (2000). Area: 370 sq. mi./958 sq. km.

Ma·ri·a·na·o /maaree aa naá ō/ city in western Cuba, on the northern coast. Population: 133,016 (1989).

Mar·i·an·a Trench deepest ocean trench in the world, in the western Pacific Ocean, east of the Mariana Islands. Length: 1,580 mi./2,550 km. Depth: 36,200 ft./11,000 m.

Mar·i·anne /màrree án/ *n* an image of a woman personifying the French republic, e.g., on French coins, usually depicted in a light flowing robe and wearing the Phrygian cap of liberty [Late 19C. < French]

Ma·ri·a The·re·sa /mə reé ə tə ráyzə/ (1717–80) archduchess of Austria and queen of Hungary and Bohemia (1740–80). Her succession as ruler of the Hapsburg dominions led to the War of the Austrian Succession (1740–48) and the Seven Years' War (1756–63).

Ma·ri·co·pa /màrri kṓpə/ (*plural same* or **-pas**) *n* **1.** a member of a Native North American people who live in Arizona **2.** the language of the Maricopa people —**Ma·ri·co·pa** *adj*

mar·i·cul·ture /márrə kùlchər/ *n* the cultivation of sea animals and plants in their usual habitats, generally for commercial purposes [Early 20C. < Latin *mari-* (stem of *mare* "sea")]

Ma·rie An·toi·nette /mə reé àntwə nét/ (1755–93) Austrian-born queen of France. The wife of Louis XVI, she was unpopular for promoting the interests of her native Austria and for her extravagance. After attempting to escape the French Revolution, she was captured, imprisoned, and guillotined.

Ma·rie Byrd Land /maáree búrd-/ region of western Antarctica, on the Amundsen Sea, east of the Ross Ice Shelf

Ma·rie de Mé·di·cis /mə reé də méddichee/ (1573–1642) queen of France. As widow of Henry IV of France, she became regent during Louis XIII's minority. Political intrigue resulted in her exile in 1630.

Ma·rie-Ga·lante /maa reé gaa laáNt/ island in the eastern Caribbean, a dependency of Guadeloupe. Population: 13,757 (1982). Area: 61 sq. mi./158 sq. km.

Ma·rie-Lou·ise (of Aus·tri·a) /mə reé loo eéz-/ (1791–1847) empress of France. She was Napoleon Bonaparte's second wife.

Mar·i·et·ta /màrree éttə/ city in northwestern Georgia, 20 mi./32 km northwest of Atlanta. Population: 62,020 (2002 estimate).

marigold

mar·i·gold /márrə gṑld/ *n* a common garden plant with a strong smell sometimes thought unpleasant. Flowers: yellow, orange. Native to: tropical America. Genus: *Tagetes*. [14C. < the name *Mary* (referring to the Virgin Mary) + Old English *golde* "marigold, corn marigold"]

mar·i·gram /márrə gràm/ *n* a printed record of tide levels at a particular place [Late 19C. < Latin *mari-*, stem of *mare* "sea"]

mar·i·graph /márrə gràf/ *n* an instrument for recording tide levels [Mid-19C. < Latin *mari-*, stem of *mare* "sea"]

mar·i·jua·na /màrrə waánə, -hwaánə/, **mar·i·hua·na** *n* **1.** same as **cannabis** (sense 1) **2.** the Indian hemp plant that is the source of the drugs marijuana and cannabis. Latin name: *Cannabis sativa*. [Late 19C. < Mexican Spanish *mariguana*]

ma·rim·ba /mə rímbə/ *n* a large musical instrument like a xylophone, with resonators made from metal or hollow gourds beneath the bars, used especially in African and Latin American music [Early 18C. Via Portuguese < Bantu] —**ma·rim·bist** *n*

Ma·rin /márrin/, **John** (1870–1953) US painter. He is famous for his watercolor paintings of New York City and Maine landscapes, e.g., *Downtown, New York* (1912) and *Maine Islands* (1922).

ma·ri·na /mə reénə/ *n* a harbor specially designed to cater to the needs of pleasure boats and their owners [Early 19C. < Italian or Spanish, "seashore" < Latin *marinus* < *mare* "sea"]

Ma·ri·na /mə reénə/ city in Monterey County, western California. Population: 21,146 (2002 estimate).

mar·i·nade *n* /màrrə náyd/ a liquid or paste made with ingredients such as vinegar, wine, oil, spices, and herbs, in which food is soaked or allowed to stand to give extra flavor and tenderness before cooking ■ *vti* /márrə nàyd/ (**-nad·ed, -nad·ing, -nades**) COOK same as **marinate** [Early 18C. < French < Italian *marinare* or Spanish *marinar* (see MARINATE)]

ma·ri·na·ra /màrrə nérrə, maàrə naárə/ *adj* **1.** made with tomatoes and garlic, often with other ingredients such as onions, parsley, capers, or olives, to serve on pasta or as a pizza topping ○ *marinara sauce* **2.** served with marinara sauce ○ *spaghetti marinara* [Mid-20C. < Italian *alla marinara* "in sailor style" < *marinaro* "sailor" < *marino* "marine" < Latin *marinus* < *mare* "sea"] —**ma·ri·na·ra** *n*

mar·i·nate /márrə nàyt/ (**-nat·ed, -nat·ing, -nates**) *vti* **1.** to be placed or soaked in a marinade, or place or soak food in a marinade **2.** to be exposed to something for a long time, or cause somebody or something to be thoroughly immersed in something ○ *marinated in history* [Mid-17C. < Italian *marinare* or Spanish *marinar* "pickle in brine" < Latin *(aqua) marina* "sea (water)," form of *marinus* < *mare* "sea"] —**mar·i·na·tion** /màrrə náysh'n/ *n*

Ma·rin·du·que /màrrən do͝ok ay/ island in the northwestern Philippines, south of Luzon and east of Mindoro. Population: 173,715 (1980). Area: 370 sq. mi./960 sq. km.

ma·rine /mə reén/ *adj* **1.** OF SEA relating to, found in, or living in the sea **2.** NAUT OF SHIPS relating to ships or sailing **3.** MIL OF SEAGOING SOLDIERS relating to soldiers who serve at sea as well as on land ■ *n* **1.** *also* **Marine** MIL SEAGOING SOLDIER a soldier who serves at sea as well as in the air and on land, e.g., a member of the US Marine Corps **2.** ART SEA SCENE a painting or photograph of a seascape, ship, or scene at sea **3.** SHIPPING NATION'S COMMERCIAL FLEET a fleet of merchant or naval ships and their crews (*formal*) [14C. Via French < Latin *marinus* < *mare* "sea"] ◇ **tell that to the marines** used to express disbelief (*slang*)

ma·rine ar·chi·tect *n* somebody specially trained to design ships —**ma·rine ar·chi·tec·ture** *n*

ma·rine bi·ol·o·gy *n* the branch of biology that deals with the plants and animals of the oceans —**ma·rine bi·ol·o·gist** *n*

Ma·rine Corps *n* a branch of the US armed forces, trained to operate on land, at sea, and in the air, especially in amphibious assaults

ma·rine en·gi·neer *n* somebody who attends to the engines and other heavy machinery of a ship or other offshore structure

mar·i·ner /márrənər/ *n* a sailor or navigator of vessels at sea [13C. Via Anglo-Norman or French *marinier* < Latin *marinarius* < *marinus* (see MARINE)]

CULTURAL NOTE ***The Rime of the Ancient Mariner***, a poem (1798) by the British writer Samuel Taylor Coleridge. A cautionary tale of sin and redemption, it describes a curse placed on a sailor after he kills an albatross that has led his ship out of danger. The vessel is becalmed and the rest of the crew die of thirst. After his rescue, the sailor is compelled to recount his story for the remainder of his days. The expression "Water, water, every where/ Nor any drop to drink" comes from this poem.

mar·i·ner's com·pass *n* a navigational ship's compass set within a binnacle

ma·rine snow *n* small particles of organic and inorganic debris that drift down from the upper layers of the ocean to the bottom

ma·rin·ière /màrrə nyér/ *adj* cooked with a little wine, herbs, and chopped onion or shallot in a closed pan, so that the main ingredient, which is usually mussels, is partly poached and partly steamed [< French, "sailor-style"]

Mar·i·ol·a·try /màrree óllətree/ *n* in Christian doctrine, extreme devotion to Mary, the mother of Jesus Christ [Early 17C. < Latin *Maria* "Mary"]

Mar·i·ol·o·gy /màrree óllǝjee/ *n* in Christianity, the study of the doctrines and beliefs concerning Mary, the mother of Jesus Christ [Mid-19C. < Latin *Maria* "Mary"] —**Mar·i·o·log·i·cal** /màrree ə lójjik'l/ *adj*

Mar·i·on /márree ən/ city in southern Illinois. Population: 16,168 (2002 estimate).

Mar·i·on, Francis (1732–95) American military officer. He engaged in successful anti-British guerrilla tactics in South Carolina during the American Revolution (1775–83). Known as **the Swamp Fox**

mar·i·o·nette /màrree ə nét/ *n* a puppet operated by means of strings attached to its hands, legs, head, and body [Early 17C. < French, "little Mary" < *Marion*]

mar·i·po·sa /màrrə pṓssə, -pṓzə/ *n* a bulbous plant of the lily family. Flowers: brightly colored, tulip-shaped. Native to: western North America. Genus: *Calochortus*. [Mid-19C. < Spanish, "butterfly" (from its brightly colored flowers)]

Mar·is /márriss/, **Roger** (1934–85) US baseball player. He played for the New York Yankees (1960–66) and in 1961 broke Babe Ruth's single-season record by hitting 61 home runs. Full name **Maris, Roger Eugene**

Mar·ist /mérrist/ *n* **1.** a member of the Society of Mary (**Marist Fathers**), a Roman Catholic order **2.** a member of the Little Brothers of Mary or (**Marist Brothers**), a Roman Catholic order [Late 19C. < French *mariste* < *Marie* "Mary"] —**Mar·ist** *adj*

mar·i·tal /márrət'l/ *adj* **1.** relating to marriage or the marriage of a particular couple **2.** relating to a husband or husbands (*formal*) [15C. < Latin *maritalis* < *maritus* "married"] —**mar·i·tal·ly** *adv*

ma·ri·tal sta·tus *n* the fact of somebody's being unmarried, married, or formerly married

mar·i·time /márrə tīm/ *adj* **1.** OF SEA relating to the sea, shipping, sailing in ships, or living and working at sea **2.** CLOSE TO SEA situated or living close to the sea ○ *the maritime region* **3.** METEOROL INFLUENCED BY SEA describes a climate influenced by the sea, and therefore generally temperate and with relatively small variations in seasonal temperatures [Mid-16C. Directly or via French < Latin *maritimus* < *mare* "sea"]

Mar·i·time Prov·inc·es /màrrə tīm-/, **Mar·i·times** /márrə tīmz/ collective name for the eastern Canadian provinces of New Brunswick, Nova Scotia, and Prince Edward Island —**Mar·i·tim·er** *n*

Ma·ri·tsa /mə réétsə/ river in southeastern Europe, in the Balkan Peninsula. Length: 300 mi./480 km.

Ma·ri·u·pol /màrree óò pol/ city in southeastern Ukraine, on the Sea of Azov. Population: 500,000 (1998).

Ma·ri·vaux /márri vō, maree vṓ/, **Pierre Carlet de Chamblain de** (1688–1763) French playwright and novelist. His romantic comedies and novels portray 18th-century French middle-class life.

mar·jo·ram /máarjərəm/ *n* an herb with aromatic leaves and small purple or white flowers. Use: seasoning in cooking and salads. Native to: Mediterranean. Latin name: *Origanum majorana.* [14C. Via Old French *marjorane* < medieval Latin *majorana*]

mark[1] /maark/ *n* **1.** SPOT, SCRATCH, OR DENT a spot, scratch, or dent on the surface of something ○ *The hot plate left a mark on the table.* **2.** SYMBOL a recognizable sign or symbol used to indicate, e.g., ownership or the quality or origin of goods, or punctuation in a piece of writing (*often used in combination*) ○ *a question mark* **3.** SUBSTITUTE FOR SIGNATURE a cross or other symbol used in place of a signature by somebody who cannot write **4.** INDICATION OF FEELING an action, gesture, or other outward sign of somebody's feeling or attitude ○ *a mark of respect* **5.** SIGN OF INFLUENCE OR INVOLVEMENT evidence of the influence or involvement of somebody or something ○ *He left his mark on the firm.* **6.** IDENTIFYING FEATURE OR CHARACTERISTIC a distinctive and identifying feature or characteristic ○ *That perfect finish is the mark of the true professional.* **7.** INDICATION OF CORRECTNESS OR QUALITY a number, letter, or percentage indicating somebody's assessment of the correctness or quality of something such as answers to examination questions or somebody's performance in a contest ○ *She always gets top marks in English.* **8.** INDICATOR OF POSITION OR EXTENT an object, sign, or line that indicates the position, extent, or amount of something ○ *the high-water mark* **9.** AMOUNT the amount, distance, or level reached by something ○ *The temperature is way above the 90 degree mark.* **10.** STANDARD the desired or required standard for something ○ *Your work is simply not up to the mark these days.* **11.** TYPE a model or variety, e.g., of a car, aircraft, or weapon, usually distinguished from earlier or later models by a number **12.** TARGET a target or something that somebody aims at with a weapon ○ *He missed the mark.* **13.** GOAL a goal or standard that somebody wishes to achieve **14.** CRIME VICTIM OF CRIME the victim or intended victim of a theft or swindle (*slang*) ○ *an easy mark* **15.** TRACK AND FIELD STARTING LINE the starting line for a race **16.** RUNNER'S STARTING POSITION an individual runner's starting position for a race **17.** BOXING MIDDLE OF STOMACH in boxing, the middle of an opponent's stomach **18.** same as **jack**[1] *n* (sense 5) **19.** NAUT INDICATOR OF WATER DEPTH a knot or other marker used to indicate intervals of fathoms on a sounding line **20.** NAVIG GUIDE TO POSITION OR DIRECTION a conspicuous object or another point of reference that serves as a visual guide **21.** HIST COMMON LAND in medieval Germany and England, land held in common by the members of a community ■ *v* (**marked, mark·ing, marks**) **1.** *vti* MAKE UNSIGHTLY MARK ON SOMETHING to make a dent, scratch, or other mark on something, or become damaged in this way ○ *The mugs have marked the table.* **2.** *vt* PUT SIGN OR SYMBOL ON SOMETHING to put writing or a recognizable sign or symbol on something, e.g., to show ownership, to indicate price, or to give a warning or instruction ○ *All items of clothing must be clearly marked with the student's name.* **3.** *vt* SHOW SOMETHING CLEARLY to make something clearly visible, recognizable, or traceable by indicating it with a mark ○ *I've marked on the map where our house is.* **4.** *vt* INDICATE LOCATION to be an indicator showing where something is situated, how far it extends, or where an event took place ○ *This monument marks their last resting place.* **5.** *vt* INDICATE POINT OF CHANGE to indicate something, especially a significant point in time or in a process, has been reached ○ *It marks the end of an era in American theater.* **6.** *vt* COMMEMORATE EVENT to give prominence to a particular event or anniversary, usually by holding a celebration ○ *a party to mark their 50th anniversary* **7.** *vt* SELECT SOMEBODY FOR SPECIAL ATTENTION to select or destine somebody or something for particular attention or treatment ○ *He was always marked for success.* **8.** *vt* MAKE SOMEBODY WORTHY OF NOTICE to characterize, distinguish, or set somebody or something apart in some way ○ *The originality of her approach marks her as a candidate of real distinction.* **9.** *vti* ASSESS QUALITY OR CORRECTNESS OF SOMETHING to assess the quality or correctness of something and indicate the assessment by means of a mark such as a check or cross, a letter, number, or percentage ○ *marking exam papers* **10.** *vt* ASSESS WORK OF SOMEBODY to assess somebody on the basis of the quality or correctness of his or her work or performance ○ *marked him high on the test* **11.** *vt* TAKE NOTICE OF to pay attention to something or somebody (*often used as a command*) ○ *Mark my words: this'll make them sit up and take notice.* **12.** *vt* SEE SOMETHING to see or notice something (*archaic*) **13.** *vt* STAY CLOSE TO PLAYER in games such as soccer and field hockey, to stay close to an attacking player in the opposing team to prevent the player from receiving the ball or scoring **14.** *vti* KEEP SCORE to keep a note of the score [Old English *mearc* "boundary, marker" < Indo-European, "boundary"] ◇ **make your mark** to achieve recognition or success, usually in a particular field ◇ **mark you** *UK* used to call somebody's attention to a point or remark that you are making ◇ **on your mark** used as a command to runners to take up their starting positions for the start of a race ◇ **quick** *or* **slow off the mark** quick *or* slow to begin, react to, or understand something ◇ **up to the mark** of an acceptable standard or quality, or at an acceptable level ◇ **wide of the mark, off the mark** inaccurate or incorrect

SPELLCHECK Do not confuse the spelling of ***mark*** and ***marque*** ("a commercial brand"), which sound similar. The confusion may arise because of the sense of the noun ***mark*** meaning "a model or variety of a car, weapon, etc., usually distinguished from an earlier or later one." ***Marque*** denotes a make rather than a specific model of car, and is restricted to prestigious cars.

mark down *vt* **1.** LOWER PRICE to lower the price of something **2.** MAKE WRITTEN NOTE OF SOMETHING to make a written note of something somewhere **3.** GIVE SOMEBODY OR SOMETHING LOWER MARK to reduce the mark given to something or somebody in a test, examination, or contest ○ *You get marked down for bad spelling.* **4.** FORM OPINION OF SOMEBODY to make a judgment as to the character or likely behavior of somebody

mark off *vt* **1.** to separate one area from another by means of a boundary line or barrier **2.** to put a mark such as a check, cross, or line beside, through, or around something, to show that it has been dealt with or to highlight it

mark out *vt* to draw lines, or use some similar method, to indicate the boundaries and divisions of something, especially the playing area for a game or a racecourse

mark up *vt* **1.** BUSINESS INCREASE PRICE OF SOMETHING to increase the price of something, especially in order to provide the seller with a profit **2.** PUBL CORRECT TEXT FOR PRINTING to prepare a piece of written work for printing or rekeying by making corrections to it or adding instructions to the typesetters or keyboarders **3.** EDUC INCREASE GRADES OR SCORES FOR SOMETHING to increase the grades awarded to somebody or something on a test, examination, or contest

mark[2] /maark/ *n* **1.** MONEY same as **deutsche mark 2.** a former unit of currency in England and Scotland that was worth 13 shillings and 4 pence, or two thirds of a pound **3.** a former unit of weight for gold and silver [Old English *marc*, a unit of weight < Germanic]

Mark /maark/ *n* a book of the Bible, the second of the gospels in which the life and teachings of Jesus Christ are described, traditionally attributed to St. Mark. See table at **Bible**

Mark /maark/, **St.** (*fl* 1st century) evangelist. A disciple of St. Peter and one of the apostles of Jesus Christ, he is credited with writing the second Gospel in the Bible.

mar·ka /múrkə/ *n* the main unit of currency in Bosnia and Herzegovina. See table at **currency** [< Serbo-Croatian < German *Mark* "mark" (currency)]

Mark An·to·ny ➧ **Antony, Mark**

mark·down /máark dòwn/ *n* a reduction in price

marked /maarkt/ *adj* **1.** NOTICEABLE very noticeable ○ *a marked contrast* **2.** SINGLED OUT singled out for surveillance, suspicion, hostility, or an unpleasant fate ○ *a marked man* **3.** WITH CONCEALED SYMBOL having a concealed identifying mark that enables somebody to cheat in card games or perform conjuring tricks ○ *marked cards* **4.** LING WITH DISTINCTIVE LINGUISTIC FEATURE having an extra or less usual distinctive linguistic feature —**mark·ed·ness** /máarkədnəss/ *n*

mark·ed·ly /máarkədlee/ *adv* to a significant extent or degree

mark·er /máarkər/ *n* **1.** INDICATOR an object or sign that indicates the position or presence of something or the direction in which somebody is to go **2.** SOMETHING THAT MAKES MARKS something used to make marks, especially a felt-tip pen **3.** IOU a debt to be paid off (*slang*) **4.** SCOREKEEPER in games such as pool and billiards, somebody who records the score, or a record of the score **5.** GRADER somebody who grades examination papers or student exercises **6.** PLAYER GUARDING ANOTHER in games such as soccer and field hockey, a player who guards a player on the opposing team

mar·ket /máarkət/ *n* **1.** GATHERING FOR BUYING AND SELLING a gathering in a public place for buying and selling merchandise or farm products, especially one held regularly ○ *a cattle market* **2.** MARKET BUILDING OR PLACE a building or open space where a market is regularly held **3.** COLLECTION OF SHOPS OR STALLS a number of small independently operated shops or stalls, housed in the same building and sometimes all selling the same type of goods **4.** ECON, POL SUPPLY AND DEMAND the whole area of economic activity in which the laws of supply and demand operate, often thought of as a regulatory force affecting both economic and political affairs ○ *market forces* **5.** SHOP a shop, especially one that sells goods or food of a particular type **6.** COMM REGION OR GROUP AS CUSTOMERS a geographic area or a section of the population, considered from the point of view of the amount of goods that can be sold to it ○ *the teenage market* **7.** COMM DEMAND the demand for goods or services being offered for sale ○ *You've got to go out and create a market if you want to succeed.* **8.** FIN BUYING AND SELLING the trade in a particular commodity ○ *the futures market* **9.** FIN same as **stock market** ○ *Prices rose on the New York and Chicago markets this morning.* **10.** FIN TRADING IN STOCKS trading in stocks and commodities ○ *The market was very slow this morning but picked up later.* **11.** FIN PRICES OR EXCHANGE RATES the prices or rates of exchange offered for stocks or commodities ○ *The market fell this morning but rallied later.* ■ *v* (**-ket·ed, -ket·ing, -kets**) **1.** *vt* PROMOTE PRODUCT to use advertising and other promotional techniques to attract buyers for something when it is put on sale ○ *If this is marketed in the right way, it'll sell very well.* **2.** *vt* OFFER SOMETHING FOR SALE to offer something for sale, or sell something, in a market ○ *We market a wide range of products.* **3.** *vi Malaysia, S Asia, Singapore* SHOP AT MARKET to go shopping at a market [Pre-12C. Via Old French dialect < Latin *mercat-*, past participle of *mercari* "buy" < *merx* "goods"] —**mar·ket·er** *n* ◇ **come onto the market** to become available for customers to buy ◇ **in the market (for something)** interested in buying or ready to buy something ◇ **on the market** available for customers to buy ◇ **on the open market** freely available and priced according to the law of supply and demand ◇ **price something out of the market** to charge so high a price for something as to make its sale unlikely ◇ **put something on the market** to offer something for sale

mar·ket·a·ble /máarkətəb'l/ *adj* **1.** SUITABLE FOR SELLING fit to be sold ○ *a highly marketable property* **2.** IN DEMAND in demand and therefore relatively easy to sell ○ *skills that are readily marketable* **3.** FIN CONVERTIBLE INTO CASH able to be converted into cash quickly, but at a price that is determined by the market in that commodity ○ *marketable value* —**mar·ket·a·bil·i·ty** /maárkətə bílləteel/ *n*

mar·ket bas·ket *n* **1.** a supermarket or grocery store cart **2.** a selection of foods representing the theoretical requirements of a household of 3.2 people or a family of four, the cost of which is a factor in cost-of-living statistics

mar·ket ca·pi·ta·li·za·tion *n* a method of assessing the value of a company by multiplying the number of shares by the stock market price

mar·ket e·con·o·my *n* an economy in which prices and wages are determined mainly by supply and demand, rather than being regulated by a government

mar·ket·eer /maárkə teér/ *n* **1.** a buyer or seller in a market **2.** an advocate or supporter of a specific type of market (*usually used in combination*) ○ *a free marketeer*

mar·ket gar·den *n* a plot of ground or small farm where fruit, vegetables, and sometimes flowers are grown for sale rather than for the grower's own use —**mar·ket gar·den·er** *n* —**mar·ket gar·den·ing** *n*

mar·ket·ing /maárkəting/ *n* **1.** the business activity of presenting products or services in such a way as to make them desirable **2.** the buying of household supplies, especially food ○ *did our marketing for the week*

mar·ket·ing board *n Can, UK* an organization set up by a government to promote and regulate the sale of a particular agricultural product

mar·ket·ing mix *n* a mixture of marketing techniques such as pricing, packaging, and advertising used to promote the sale of a product

mar·ket lead·er *n* a company or brand that has a very large, or the largest, share of the market for a particular product

mar·ket mak·er *n* a dealer in securities who offers to buy and sell at a guaranteed price

mar·ket or·der *n* an order instructing a broker to buy or sell an asset immediately at the best prevailing price

mar·ket·place /maárkət pláyss/ *n* **1. OPEN SPACE FOR MARKET** an open space where a market is held **2. SPHERE OF TRADING** the commercial sphere where buying and selling takes place and the laws of supply and demand operate **3. SETUP WHERE IDEAS CAN BE DISCUSSED** a forum in which ideas are exchanged, discussed, and compete for recognition

mar·ket price *n* the price at which something is currently being bought by the majority of customers

mar·ket re·search *n* the gathering and analysis of information about what people want or like or what they actually buy —**mar·ket re·search·er** *n*

mar·ket share *n* the proportion of the total sales of a product secured by one particular company or brand

mar·ket town *n* a town in which a market is held regularly, usually the chief town of a farming area

mar·ket val·ue *n* the amount that a seller could expect to obtain for property or goods sold on the open market

Mark·ham /maárkəm/, **Edwin Ansan** (1852–1940) US poet. His social protest poem "The Man with the Hoe" (1899) made him nationally famous. Full name **Markham, Charles Edwin Ansan**

> "O masters, lords and rulers in all lands, /
> Is this the handiwork you give to God?"
> [Edwin Ansan Markham, "The Man with the Hoe," *The Man with the Hoe and Other Poems*; 1899]

mar·khor /maár kàwr/ (*plural* **-khors** or *same*) *n* the largest wild goat, which has a reddish brown coat, spiral horns, and a shaggy beard on the male. Native to: Himalayan range. Latin name: *Capra falconeri*. [Mid-19C. < Persian *mār-kwār* "serpent-eater"]

mark·ing /maárking/ *n* **1. NATURAL PATTERN** a mark or pattern of marks that occurs naturally, e.g., on an animal's coat (*often used in the plural*) **2.** AVIAT **AIRCRAFT IDENTIFYING MARK** an identifying mark, usually a colored symbol, on an aircraft (*often used in the plural*) **3.** EDUC **ASSESSMENT AND GRADING OF WRITTEN WORK** a teacher's correction and assessment of students' written work

mark·ing ink *n* an ink used for writing on such things as clothes and bed linen because it does not wash out

mark·ka /maár kaà, -kə/ (*plural* **-kaa** or **-kas**) *n* the main unit of the former Finnish currency [Early 20C. Via Finnish < Swedish *marka*]

Dame Alicia Markova: in *Mr. Puppet* with Anton Dolin

Mar·ko·va /maar kṓvə/, **Dame Alicia** (*b.* 1910) British ballerina. She was a cofounder of the London Festival Ballet (1950) and director of the Metropolitan Opera Ballet (1963–69). Born **Marks, Lillian Alicia**

Mar·kov chain /maár kàwv-/ *n* a random process in which events are discrete rather than continuous, and the future development of each event is independent of all historical events, or dependent only on the immediately preceding event [See MARKOV PROCESS]

Mar·kov proc·ess *n* a continuous random process in which the probability of occurrence of each random event in a series is independent of all historical events, or dependent only on the immediately preceding event [After A. A. *Markov* (1856–1922), Russian mathematician]

marks·man /maárksmən/ (*plural* **-men** /-mən/) *n* **1. SOMEBODY SKILLED IN SHOOTING** somebody, especially a man, who is an accurate shooter, especially with a rifle **2. SOMEBODY CONSIDERED GOOD OR BAD SHOT** somebody, especially a man, considered from the point of view of his or her ability to shoot accurately **3. RATING FOR SKILL USING RIFLE** in the US Army or Marine Corps, the lowest of three ratings of proficiency in the use of a rifle, or a person holding this rating —**marks·man·ship** *n*

marks·wom·an /maárks wòommən/ (*plural* **-wom·en** /-wìmmin/) *n* **1.** a woman who is an accurate shooter, especially with a rifle **2.** a woman considered from the point of view of her ability to shoot accurately

mark·up /maárk up/ *n* **1.** the difference between the manufacturing cost or wholesale price of an item and its retail price **2.** the addition to a text that is to be printed of coding or instructions for layout and style

mark·up lan·guage *n* a computer coding system specifying the layout and style of a document

marl[1] /maarl/ *n* a naturally occurring fine crumbly mixture of clay and limestone, often containing shell fragments and sometimes other minerals. Use: fertilizer, water softener. ■ *vt* (**marled, marl·ing, marls**) to add marl to soil as a fertilizer [14C. Via Old French *marle* < medieval Latin *margila* < Latin *marga*, after *argilla* "white clay"] —**marl·y** *adj*

marl[2] /maarl/ (**marled, marl·ing, marls**) *vt* to bind something with a marline [Early 18C. < Dutch *marlen* "keep binding" < Middle Dutch *marren* "to bind"]

Marl·bor·ough /maárlbərə/, **John Churchill, 1st Duke of** (1650–1722) English general. He won a string of brilliant victories as commander in chief of English forces during the War of the Spanish Succession (1701–14).

> "I have not time to say more, but to beg you will give my duty to the Queen, and let her know her army has had a glorious victory. Monsieur Tallard and two other generals are in my coach, and I am following the rest."
> [John Churchill Marlborough, *Message written on a tavern bill*; August 13, 1704]

Mar·ley /maárlee/, **Bob** (1945–81) Jamaican musician. His music, much of which he wrote himself, established reggae internationally as an important part of pop music. Full name **Marley, Robert Nesta**

> "Reggae is a music that has plenty fight. But only the music should fight, not the people."
> [Bob Marley. Quoted in *Bob Marley in His Own Words*, Ian McCann; 1993]

mar·lin /maárlin/ (*plural* **-lins** or *same*) *n* a large game fish with a very long thin upper jaw, like a spear. Native to: warm regions of the Atlantic and Pacific oceans. Family: Istiophoridae. [Early 20C. Shortening of *marlinspike*; from the shape of its upper jaw]

mar·line /maárlin/, **mar·lin** *n* a light two-stranded rope, used especially for binding the ends of larger ropes to prevent them from fraying [15C. < Dutch *marlijn* "binding line," *marling* "binding" < Middle Dutch *marren* "to bind"]

mar·line·spike /maárlin spìk/, **mar·lin·spike** *n* a pointed metal tool used to separate strands of rope that are being spliced [Early 17C. Alteration (influenced by MARLINE) of *marlingspike* < MARL[2] + SPIKE[1]]

mar·lite /maár lìt/ *n* a rock with the same composition as marl but with a harder, more resistant texture [Late 18C. < MARL[1]] —**mar·lit·ic** /maar líttik/ *adj*

Mar·lowe /maárlō/, **Christopher** (1564–93) English playwright. Often considered the first great English playwright, he wrote tragedies including *The Tragical History of Doctor Faustus* (1604?) and *Edward II* (1594).

> "Was this the face that launch'd a thousand ships /And burnt the topless towers of Ilium? /Sweet Helen, make me immortal with a kiss."
> [Christopher Marlowe, *Doctor Faustus*; 1592?]

marl·stone /maárl stōn/ *n* GEOL same as **marlite**

marm *n* same as **ma'am**

mar·ma·lade /maármə làyd/ *n* a clear thick preserve made with citrus fruits, usually containing the shredded rind of the fruit ■ *adj UK* describes cats with orange fur or orange fur streaked with yellow or brown [15C. Via French *marmelade* "quince jam" < Portuguese *marmelada* < *marmelo* "quince" < Greek *melimēlon* "honey-apple," a kind of apple grafted onto the quince]

mar·ma·lade box *n* the reddish brown edible fruit of the genipap tree

mar·ma·lade plum *n* FOOD same as **sapote** (sense 1)

mar·ma·lade tree *n* TREES same as **sapote** (sense 2)

Mar·ma·ra, Sea of /maármərə/, **Mar·mo·ra, Sea of** inland sea in northwestern Turkey, separating the Asian and European regions of the country. It is connected with the Black Sea by the Bosporus and with the Aegean Sea by the Dardanelles. Area: 4,382 sq. mi./11,350 sq. km.

mar·mite /maár mìt, maar meét/ *n* a deep earthenware or metal cooking pot with a close-fitting lid, used for making soups, stews, or stock [Early 19C. Via French < Old French, "hypocritical" < *marmouser* "to murmur" + *mite* "cat," imitations of sounds]

Mar·mo·la·da /maármə laádə, maàrmō-/ highest mountain in the Dolomites, located in northeastern Italy. Height: 10,965 ft./3,342 m.

Mar·mo·ra, Sea of another spelling of **Marmara, Sea of**

mar·mo·re·al /maar máwree əl/ *adj* made of marble, or like marble, especially in being white, cold, or aloof and impressive (*literary*) [Late 18C. < Latin *marmoreus* < *marmor* (see MARBLE)] —**mar·mo·re·al·ly** *adv*

mar·mo·set /maármə sèt, -zèt/ (*plural* **-sets** or *same*) *n* a small monkey that has soft thick fur, tufts of fur around its head and ears, a long tail, and clawed digits. Native to: Central and South America. Family: Callithricidae. [14C. < French *marmouset* "grotesque figure"]

mar·mot /maármət/ (*plural* **-mots** or *same*) *n* a large brownish rodent of the squirrel family that lives on the ground and in burrows. Native to: North America, Europe, northern Asia. Genus: *Marmota*. [Early 17C. < French *marmotte*]

Marne /maarn/ river in northern France. Length: 326 mi./525 km.

mar·o·cain /márrə kàyn, màrrə káyn/ *n* a ribbed crepe fabric [Early 20C. < French, "Moroccan"]

Mar·o·nite /márrə nìt/ *adj* belonging or relating to the Christian Uniat Church of Lebanon, an Eastern Catholic church [Early 16C. < medieval Latin *Maronita*, after *Maro*, 4C Syrian hermit] —**Mar·o·nite** *n*

Ma·roo·chy·dore /ma ro͝ochee dàwr/ coastal town in southeastern Queensland, Australia, located at the mouth of the Maroochy River. Population: 36,406 (1996).

ma·roon[1] /mə ro͞on/ *n* a deep purplish red color tinged with brown [Late 18C. < French *marron* "large sweet chestnut" < medieval Greek *maraon*] —**ma·roon** *adj*

ma·roon[2] /mə ro͞on/ *vt* (**-rooned, -roon·ing, -roons**) **1. LEAVE SOMEBODY ISOLATED** to leave somebody or something somewhere with no means of getting away **2. ABANDON SOMEBODY ON ISLAND** to put somebody ashore on a lonely island or coast and leave him or her there with no means of escape ■ *n* **1.** *also* **Ma·roon DESCENDANT OF ESCAPED SLAVES** a descendant of people escaped from slavery in Guyana and the remoter parts of the Caribbean **2. MAROONED PERSON** somebody who has been marooned, especially on a desert island [Mid-17C < French *marron* "fugitive from slavery," shortening of American Spanish *cimarrón* "wild, untamed," probably < *cima* "peak"]

mar·o·quin /márrəkin/ *n* INDUST same as **morocco** [Early 16C. < French < *Maroc* "Morocco"]

Marq. *abbr* **1.** Marquess **2.** Marquis

marque /maark/ *n* a brand or make of product, especially a make of a luxury or high-performance car [Early 20C. < French < *marquer* "to mark" < Germanic]

SPELLCHECK See *mark*[1].

mar·quee /maar kée/ *n* **1. COVERING LIKE ROOF** a permanent canopy, often of metal and glass, projecting out over the entrance to a large building such as a hotel or theater **2.** *UK* **LARGE TENT** a very large tent with straight sides that can be rolled up or removed, used for large gatherings such as parties, meetings, sales, and exhibitions **3.** ONLINE **SCROLLING SCREEN MESSAGE** a piece of text that scrolls across a screen horizontally or vertically in a highlighted band ■ *adj* **HAVING PUBLIC APPEAL** having public appeal or considered in connection with public appeal ○ *a team with no marquee names* ○ *a star with great marquee value* [Late 17C. Alteration of French *marquise* "canopy over a nobleman's tent" (see MARQUISE)]

Mar·que·sas Is·lands /maar káyssəss-/ group of volcanic islands in French Polynesia, 740 mi./1,200 km north of Tahiti, in the South Pacific Ocean. Population: 7,538 (1988). Area: 492 sq. mi./1,274 sq. km.

mar·quess /máarkwəss/ *n* in the United Kingdom, a nobleman ranking between a duke and an earl [15C. < Old French *marchis* < *marche* (see MARCH[2])] —**mar·ques·sate** /máarkwə sàyt, -zàyt/ *n*

Michael Boys/Corbis

marquetry

mar·que·try /máarkətree/, **mar·que·terie** *n* **1.** designs or pictures made of thin pieces of wood, metal, shell, or other materials, inlaid in a wood veneer and often applied as decoration to pieces of furniture **2.** the craft of making marquetry designs or pictures [Mid-16C. < French *marqueterie* < *marqueter* "variegate" < *marquer* "to mark"]

Mar·quette /maar két/, **Jacques** (1637–75) French Jesuit missionary and explorer. He explored the upper reaches of the Mississippi River (1673–74) with Louis Jolliet. Known as **Père Marquette**

Már·quez ➧ **García Márquez, Gabriel**

mar·quis /máarkwiss, maar kée/ (*plural* **-quis·es** /-kwissəz/ or **-quis** /-kéez/) *n* in various European countries, a nobleman ranking above a count [14C. < Old French, alteration of *marchis* (see MARQUESS)] —**mar·quis·ate** /máarkwəzət, -wəssət/ *n*

Mar·quis /máarkwiss/, **Don** (1878–1937) US writer. He is best known for his humorous poems supposedly written by a cockroach called "archy." Full name **Marquis, Donald Robert Perry**

> "...now and then / there is a person born / who is so unlucky /that he runs into accidents / which started out to happen /to somebody else."
> [Don Marquis, "archy says," *archy's life of mehitabel*; 1933]

mar·quise /maar kéez/ *n* **1. NOBLEWOMAN** in various European countries, a noblewoman ranking above a countess, or the wife or widow of a marquis **2.** BUILDINGS same as **marquee** *n* (sense 1) **3. POINTED OVAL GEM** a gem cut into the shape of a pointed oval and usually faceted **4. RING WITH POINTED OVAL** a ring set with a pointed oval gem or a cluster of stones arranged in a pointed oval shape **5. COLD CREAMY FRENCH DESSERT** a cold French dessert consisting of whipped cream folded into fruit-flavored ice **6. FRENCH CHOCOLATE DESSERT** a French dessert consisting of either a rich chocolate mousse or a spongy chocolate cake, or a combination of chocolate mousse and cake [Early 17C. < French, form of MARQUIS]

mar·qui·sette /màarkə zét, màarkwə zét/ *n* a fine woven fabric, often cotton or silk. Use: curtains, mosquito nets. [Early 20C. < French, "little marquise"]

Mar·quis wheat *n Can* a variety of hard, early-ripening wheat, developed for the Canadian prairies in the early 20th century

~~marrage~~ incorrect spelling of **marriage**

Mar·ra·kesh /màrrə késh/, **Mar·ra·kech** city in western Morocco. Population: 745,541 (1994).

Mar·ra·no /mə ráanō/ (*plural* **-nos**) *n* in the Middle Ages, a Jew from Spain or Portugal who converted to Christianity under duress and without conviction, and who continued to practice Judaism in secret [Late 16C. < Spanish, "pig" (from the Jewish prohibition against pork)]

mar·riage /márrij/ *n* **1. LEGAL RELATIONSHIP BETWEEN SPOUSES** a legally recognized relationship, established by a civil or religious ceremony, between two people who intend to live together as sexual and domestic partners **2. SPECIFIC MARRIAGE RELATIONSHIP** a married relationship between two people, or a somebody's relationship with his or her spouse ○ *They have a happy marriage.* **3. JOINING IN WEDLOCK** the joining together in wedlock of two people **4. MARRIAGE CEREMONY** the ceremony in which two people are joined together formally in wedlock **5. UNION OF TWO THINGS** a close union, blend, or mixture of two things ○ *Civilization is based on the marriage of tradition and innovation.* **6.** CARDS **KING AND QUEEN OF SAME SUIT** in card games such as pinochle and bezique, a combination of the king and queen of the same suit [13C. < French *mariage* < *marier* (see MARRY)]

mar·riage·a·ble /márrijəb'l/ *adj* suitable or ready for marriage, or old enough to be married ○ *of marriageable age* —**mar·riage·a·bil·i·ty** /màrrijə bíllətee/ *n* —**mar·riage·a·ble·ness** *n*

mar·riage com·mis·sion·er *n* in Canada, a public official empowered by law to perform civil marriages and civil unions

mar·riage coun·sel·ing *n* advice given by professionals to help married couples resolve problems in their relationship

mar·riage of con·ven·ience *n* a marriage between two people that is intended to serve a practical, financial, or political purpose and is not based on their love for each other [Translation of French *mariage de convenance*]

mar·ried /márreed/ *adj* **1. HAVING SPOUSE** having a wife or husband ○ *married people* **2. JOINED IN MARRIAGE** joined together in marriage ○ *get married* ○ *married couples* **3. RELATING TO MARRIAGE** arising from or relating to marriage ○ *her married name* **4. COMPLETELY DEDICATED TO SOMETHING** completely dedicated to something and devoting a lot of time and effort to it ○ *married to her job* ■ **mar·rieds** *npl* **MARRIED PEOPLE** people who are married ○ *young marrieds*

mar·ron gla·cé /ma ràwN glə sáy/ (*plural* **mar·rons gla·cés** /ma ròN glə sáy, mə ròN-/) *n* a chestnut cooked and preserved in sugar syrup, drained and then coated with a sugar glaze finish [< French, "frosted chestnut"]

mar·row /márrō/ *n* **1.** soft red or yellow fatty tissue that fills the central cavities of bones. Red marrow is the site of blood cell production. **2.** the essence, core, or key part of something (*literary*) **3.** *UK* same as **marrow squash** [Old English *mærh* < Indo-European] ◇ **to the marrow (of your bones)** used to emphasize how intensely or deeply somebody is affected by something, especially the cold or an unpleasant experience ○ *I was chilled to the marrow.*

mar·row·bone /márrō bòn/ *n* a hollow bone that contains edible marrow, traditionally considered to be a culinary delicacy

mar·row·fat /márrō fàt/, **mar·row·fat pea** *n* **1.** a particularly large type of pea **2.** a plant that produces marrowfats as its seed [Mid-18C. < MARROW "substance like tallow, obtained by boiling down marrow," which the pea's texture resembles]

mar·row pea *n* PLANTS, FOOD same as **marrowfat**

mar·row squash *n* **1.** a large long cylindrical vegetable with a tough green or green and yellow rind, creamy white flesh, and a core of seeds that is usually scraped out before it is cooked and eaten **2.** a plant in the cucumber family that produces marrow squash as fruit. Latin name: *Cucurbita pepo.*

mar·ry /márree/ (**-ried, -ry·ing, -ries**) *v* **1.** *vti* **TAKE SOMEBODY IN MARRIAGE** to commit yourself to somebody, or yourselves to each other, formally in marriage **2.** *vt* **JOIN TWO PEOPLE IN MARRIAGE** to officiate at somebody's marriage ceremony and give legal sanction or a religious blessing to the marriage **3.** *vt* **GIVE SOMEBODY IN MARRIAGE** to give somebody, usually a child or ward, to somebody in marriage, or bring about his or her marriage to somebody **4.** *vt* **ACQUIRE SOMETHING BY MARRIAGE** to acquire something, especially money, by marrying somebody who has it ○ *wanted to marry wealth and power, and got both* **5.** *vti* **COMBINE THINGS SUCCESSFULLY** to brings things together, or to come together, to form a close and successful combination ○ *The meat and the spices marry well.* **6.** *vti* **FIT TOGETHER** to fit and join together, or make things fit and join together **7.** *vt* NAUT **MATCH TWO PIECES OF ROPE TOGETHER** to equalize the strands of two pieces of rope, especially before splicing them [13C. Via French *marier* < Latin *maritare* < *maritus* "married person, husband"]

marry into *vt* to become part of something, or gain something, through marriage ○ *married into a wealthy family*

marry off *vt* to find a husband or wife for a daughter or son

marry up *vti* same as **marry** (sense 5)

mar·ry·ing /márree ing/ *adj* likely or inclined to get married ○ *Neither of them was the marrying kind.*

Popperfoto

Mars: View of the surface of Mars from the Sojourner rover (1997)

Mars /maarz/ *n* **1.** in Roman mythology, the god of war and the father of Romulus, the founder of Rome. Greek equivalent **Ares 2.** the third smallest planet in the solar system and the fourth planet from the Sun. Mars has two small satellites and its surface is reddish orange in color.

Mar·sa·la /maar sáalə/ *n* a sweet or dry dark red fortified wine from Sicily [Early 19C. After a port in Sicily]

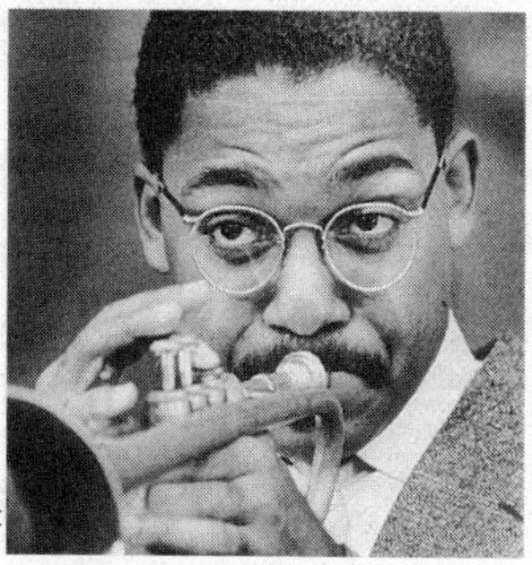
Popperfoto
Wynton Marsalis

Mar·sal·is /maar sáaliss/, **Wynton** (*b.* 1961) US musician and bandleader. His virtuosity on the trumpet has won him renown as both a jazz and a classical performer.

> "Jazz is music that really deals with what it means to be American…Louis Armstrong, the grandson of a slave, is the one more than anybody else who could translate into music that feeling of what it is to be an American."
> [Wynton Marsalis, "We Must Preserve Our Jazz Heritage," *Ebony (Chicago)*; February 1986]

Mar·seil·laise /màarssə yéz, -ə láyz/ *n* the French national anthem, written in Strasbourg in 1792 by Claude-Joseph Rouget de Lisle, a captain in the French revolutionary army. Originally called "War Song of the Army of the Rhine," its present name derives from its popularity with army units from Marseilles, the first to sing it in Paris.

mar·seille /maar sáy, -sáyl/, **mar·seilles** *n* a heavy cotton fabric with a raised pattern. Use: bedspreads. [Mid-18C. After MARSEILLES]

Mar·seilles /maar sáy/, **Mar·seille** chief port and capital of Bouches-du-Rhône Department, Provence-Alpes-Côtes d'Azur Region, southeastern France. Population: 798,430 (1999). [Late 18C. < French, "of Marseilles"]

marsh /maarsh/ *n* an area of low-lying waterlogged land, often beside water, that is poorly drained and liable to flood, difficult to cross on foot, and unfit for agriculture or building [Old English *merisc* < Germanic] —**marsh·y** *adj*

Marsh /maarsh/, **Dame Ngaio** (1899–1982) New Zealand writer and theater director. She wrote more than 30 crime novels, and played an important part in the development of live theater in New Zealand. Full name **Marsh, Dame Edith Ngaio**

Marsh, Othniel Charles (1831–99) US paleontologist. He discovered many dinosaur fossils in North America. He strongly supported Darwin's theory of evolution.

Marsh, Reginald (1898–1954) US painter. He depicted scenes of New York City life in works such as *The Bowery* (1930).

mar·shal /máarsh'l/ *n* **1.** LAW **FEDERAL LAW OFFICER** a federal law enforcement officer who carries out court orders in a federal judicial district and has duties resembling those of a local sheriff **2. SENIOR FIRE OR POLICE OFFICER** the head of the fire or police departments in some US cities **3. CITY LAW OFFICER** a municipal law enforcement officer in some US cities **4. SOMEBODY IN CHARGE OF EVENT** somebody in charge of or controlling an event or gathering such as a parade, ceremony, or sports event **5. PARADE HONOREE** somebody who is honored in a parade and usually rides in a vehicle in front of the marchers and floats **6. HIGH-RANKING OFFICER** the highest-ranking officer in some nations' armed forces ■ *v* (**-shaled** or **-shalled, -shal·ing** or **-shal·ling, -shals**) **1.** *vt* **ORGANIZE THINGS** to arrange things in an appropriate order so that they can be used effectively ○ *marshal your thoughts* **2.** *vti* **GATHER AND ORGANIZE TROOPS** to gather troops together and organize them, or gather together and organize, before embarking on a military campaign or expedition **3.** *vt* **GATHER PEOPLE TOGETHER** to gather people together and organize them into an effective body ○ *marshal your supporters* **4.** *vt* **GUIDE OR LEAD SOMEBODY** to guide or lead somebody carefully or in an officious or ceremonious way **5.** *vti* **ACT AS MARSHAL** to act as a marshal at something such as a ceremony, parade, or sports event [13C. < Old French *mareschal* "royal court official" < Germanic, "groom," literally "horse-servant"] —**mar·shal·cy** *n* —**mar·shal·ship** *n*

mar·shal·ing yard /máarsh'ling-/ *n* an area occupied by many parallel railroad tracks, where railroad cars are made up into trains

Mar·shall /máarsh'l/, **George** (1880–1959) US army general and secretary of state (1947–49). He initiated the Marshall Plan (1947) to coordinate European economic recovery after World War II. He won the Nobel Peace Prize (1953) for this initiative. Full name **Marshall, George Catlett**

> "If man does find the solution for world peace it will be the most revolutionary reversal of his record we have ever known."
> [George Marshall, *Biennial Report of the Chief of Staff, United States Army*; September 1, 1945]

Mar·shall, John (1755–1835) chief justice of the US Supreme Court (1801–35). He established the principle of judicial review and is considered responsible for developing the power of the Supreme Court and formulating constitutional law in the nation.

> "The people made the Constitution, and the people can unmake it. It is the creature of their own will, and lives only by their will."
> [John Marshall, *Decision, Cohens v. Virginia*; 1821]

Mar·shall, Sir John Ross (1912–88) prime minister of New Zealand (1972). A National Party politician, he held several ministerial posts from 1951 until he succeeded Keith Holyoake as prime minister. See table at **prime minister**

Mar·shall, Thurgood (1908–93) US civil rights lawyer and associate justice of the US Supreme Court. As chief counsel of the NAACP Legal Defense Fund (1940–61), he won the landmark *Brown v. Board of Education* case (1954) that ended racial segregation in public schools. He was the first African American member of the US Supreme Court (1967–91).

> "The United States has been called the melting pot of the world. But it seems to me that the colored man either missed getting into the pot or he got melted down."
> [Thurgood Marshall, *The Encyclopaedia of Black Folklore and Humor*, Henry D. Spalding; 1972]

> "If the 1st Amendment means anything, it means that a State has no business telling a man, sitting alone in his own house, what books he may read or what films he may watch."
> [Thurgood Marshall, unanimous opinion in an obscenity case; April 7, 1969]

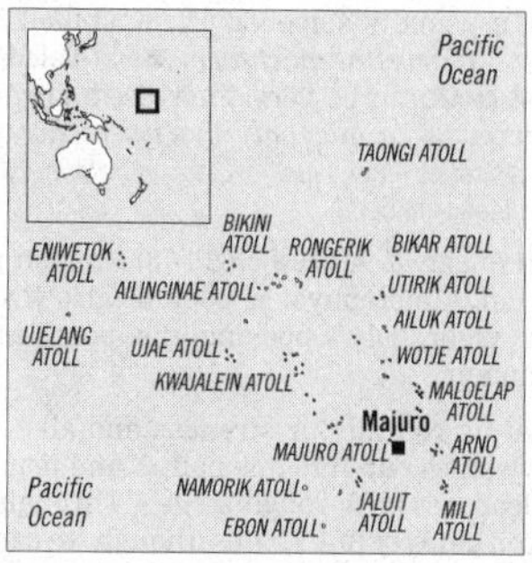

Marshall Islands

Mar·shall Is·lands country consisting of 34 islands in the central North Pacific Ocean. Capital: Majuro. Population: 56,429 (2003). Area: 70 sq. mi./181 sq. km. Official name **Republic of the Marshall Islands**

Mar·shall Plan *n* a program of loans and other economic assistance provided by the US government between 1947 and 1952 to help western European nations rebuild after World War II [Mid-20C. After George C. MARSHALL]

Mar·shall·town /máarsh'l tòwn/ city in central Iowa, on the Iowa River, northeast of Des Moines and west of Cedar Rapids. Population: 26,102 (2002 estimate).

marsh el·der *n* a bush with unisexual flowers and greenish flower heads. Native to: marshes of central and eastern North America. Genus: *Iva*.

marsh fe·ver *n* MED same as **malaria**

marsh gas *n* a mixture of gases, mostly methane, produced by decomposing plant matter in the absence of air. Spontaneous combustion of marsh gas is usually supposed to be the cause of the phenomenon known as a will-o'-the-wisp or ignis fatuus.

marsh hawk *n* BIRDS same as **northern harrier**

marsh·land /máarsh lànd, -lənd/ *n* marshy ground, or an area or expanse of it

marsh mal·low *n* a perennial shrubby plant that grows in marshes and has sticky roots that were used in the past to make marshmallow and are still used in some medicines. Flowers: pink. Native to: Europe. Latin name: *Althacea officinalis*.

marsh·mal·low /máarsh mèllō/ *n* a soft spongy candy made from sugar syrup, egg whites, and flavoring [Because formerly made from the root of the marsh mallow plant] —**marsh·mal·low·y** *adj*

marsh mar·i·gold *n* a plant of the buttercup family that has round or kidney-shaped leaves and grows in swampy areas. Flowers: bright yellow. Native to: Europe, North America. Latin name: *Caltha palustris*.

marsh tread·er *n* a slender insect with an elongated head that crawls on floating vegetation and the surface of water, preying on mosquito larvae and tiny crustaceans. Family: Hydrometridae.

mar·su·pi·al /maar sóopee əl/ *n* a mammal, e.g., a kangaroo, wombat, opossum, or koala, having no placenta and bearing immature young that are developed in a pouch on the mother's abdomen. Order: Marsupialia. [Late 17C. < modern Latin *marsupialis* < Latin *marsupium* (see MARSUPIUM)]

mar·su·pi·al frog *n* a tree frog of which the female carries the eggs in a pouch on her back

mar·su·pi·um /maar sóopee əm/ (*plural* **-pi·a** /-pee ə/) *n* a pouch on the abdomen of most marsupials that encloses the mammary glands and in which the animal's newly born offspring complete their development [Mid-17C. Via Latin *marsupium* < Greek *marsupion* "pouch," literally "little purse" < *marsippos* "purse"]

mart /maart/ *n* a market, salesroom, or large store [15C. < obsolete Dutch, variant of *markt* < Latin *mercat-* (see MARKET)]

Mart. *abbr* Martinique

Mar·ta·ban, Gulf of /màartə báan/ inlet of the Andaman Sea, east of the Irrawaddy delta, southern Myanmar

mar·ta·gon /máartəgən/, **mar·ta·gon lil·y** *n* an ornamental lily. Flowers: mottled, pinkish purple, resembling turbans. Native to: Europe, Asia. Latin name: *Lilium martagon*. [15C. Via French < Turkish *marṭağān*, kind of turban, which the flower is thought to resemble]

mar·te·lé /màart'l áy/, **mar·tel·la·to** /-aátō/ *adv* with the strings played in a strongly accented way (*used as a musical direction*) [Late 19C. < French, "hammered"]

Mar·tel·lo /maar téllō/ (*plural* **-los**), **Mar·tel·lo tow·er** *n* a fort in the form of a small circular tower, especially one built on the coast for defense against invasion during the Napoleonic Wars [Early 19C. Alteration, influenced by Italian *martello* "hammer," of Cape *Mortella* in Corsica, where such a tower was captured by the British fleet in 1794]

mar·ten /máart'n/ (*plural same* or **-tens**) *n* a short-legged bushy-tailed animal with a long slender body that lives in trees. Native to: northern forests. Genus: *Martes*. [13C. Via Middle Dutch *martren* < Old French *martre* < Germanic]

mar·ten·site /máart'n zìt/ *n* the hard solid solution of iron and carbon used in making hardened steel tools [Late 19C. After Adolf *Martens* (1850–1914), German metallurgist] —**mar·ten·sit·ic** /màart'n zíttik/ *adj*

Mar·tha /máarthə/ *n* in the Bible, the sister of Mary

and Lazarus, and friend of Jesus Christ (Luke 10: 38–42)

Mar·tha's Vine·yard /maárthəz-/ island in southeastern Massachusetts, in the Atlantic Ocean, near Cape Cod. It is a popular summer resort. Area: 100 sq. mi./280 sq. km.

Mar·tí /maartée/, **José** (1853–95) Cuban revolutionary leader and poet. He fought for Cuban independence from Spain and wrote many poems and essays on the theme of political freedom. Full name **Martí, José Julian**

> "The dagger plunged in the name of Freedom is plunged into the breast of Freedom."
> [Attributed to José Martí]

mar·tial /maársh'l/ *adj* **1.** characteristic of or suitable for soldiers, the military life, or war **2.** warlike and fierce [14C. Directly or via French < Latin *martialis* < *Mars*, the god of war] —**mar·tial·ism** *n* —**mar·tial·ist** *n* —**mar·tial·ly** *adv* —**mar·tial·ness** *n*

mar·tial art *n* a system of combat and self-defense, e.g., judo or karate, developed especially in Japan and Korea and now usually practiced as a sport

mar·tial law *n* the control and policing of a civilian population by military forces and according to military rules, imposed, e.g., in wartime or when the civilian government no longer functions

Mar·tian /maársh'n/ *adj* found on, typical of, or originating from the planet Mars ■ *n* a supposed inhabitant of the planet Mars [14C. Directly or via Old French *martien* < Latin *Martianus* < *Mart-* "Mars"]

mar·tin /maárt'n/ *n* a bird of the swallow family with a notched or square tail, which builds its nest on cliffs or houses [15C. Origin ?]

Mar·tin /maárt'n/, **St.** (316?–397?) Roman monk. The bishop of Tours, he spread Christianity throughout Gaul, establishing monasticism in the country, and became the patron saint of France.

Mar·tin V /maártin thə fífth/, **Pope** (1368–1431) His election in 1417, at the Council of Constance, ended the Great Schism. He reunified the Western Church and the Papal States.

Mar·tin /maárt'n/, **Archer** (1910–2002) British biochemist. He shared the Nobel Prize in chemistry (1952) for his study of protein structure and later developed chromatography for protein analysis. Full name **Martin, Archer John Porter**

Mar·tin, Dean (1917–95) US singer and actor. He appeared in a number of films opposite Jerry Lewis, including *My Friend Irma* (1949). His television shows included *The Dean Martin Show* (1964–75). Born **Crocetti, Dino**

Mar·tin, Glenn Luther (1886–1955) US airplane manufacturer. He designed the China Clipper and the Hawaiian Clipper, as well as World War II bombers.

Mar·tin, Paul (*b.* 1938) Canadian politician. A member of the Liberal Party, he was Minister of Finance (1993–2002) and became leader of the party and prime minister (2003). See table at **prime minister**

Mar·tin, Steve (*b.* 1945) US comedian and actor. He became known for his appearances on television's *Saturday Night Live* during the 1970s and has since acted in numerous movie comedies.

> "Talking about music is like dancing about architecture."
> [Attributed to Steve Martin]

mar·ti·net /maárt'n ét/ *n* **1.** a military officer who demands absolute adherence to military rules and behavior **2.** somebody who imposes strict discipline on others [Late 17C. After Jean *Martinet* (died 1672), French drillmaster] —**mar·ti·net·tish** *adj*

Mar·ti·nez /maar téenəss/ city in western California. It is the administrative seat of Contra Costa County. Population: 36,707 (2002 estimate).

mar·tin·gale /maárt'n gàyl/ *n* **1.** PART OF HORSE HARNESS a strap of a horse's harness connecting the girth to the reins to keep the horse from throwing its head back **2.** *also* **mar·tin·gale shroud** PART OF SHIP'S RIGGING a rope or cable that supports the forward-projecting spar (**bowsprit**) on some sailing ships **3.** GAMBLING SYSTEM gambling in which the stakes are doubled after each loss [Late 16C. < French]

mar·ti·ni /maar téenee/ *n* a cocktail made of gin or vodka with vermouth [Late 19C. < Italian *Martini*, surname of a winemaker]

Mar·ti·ni /maar téenee/, **Simone** (1280?–1344?) Italian painter. One of the most influential artists of the 14th century, he painted mainly frescoes and altar panels, and introduced refinements of line, expression, and color in works such as *The Annunciation* (1333).

Mar·ti·nique /maártə néek, maárt'n éek/ island in the eastern Caribbean Sea, an overseas department of France. Population: 418,454 (2001). Area: 425 sq. mi./1,100 sq. km.

Mar·tin Lu·ther King Day *n* a legal holiday in the United States marking the life of Martin Luther King, Jr. Date: 3rd Monday in January.

Mar·tin·mas /maárt'nməss/ *n* one of the Scottish quarter days. Date: November 11. [13C. < St. MARTIN + MASS]

Mar·tins /maártinz/, **Peter** (*b.* 1946) Danish-born US dancer and choreographer. He became director of the New York City Ballet in the 1980s.

Mar·tins·burg /maárt'nz bùrg/ city in northeastern West Virginia, in the Shenandoah Valley, southwest of Hagerstown, Maryland. Population: 15,119 (2002 estimate).

Mar·ti·nů /maártinoo/, **Bohuslav** (1890–1959) Czech composer. His music, ranging from operas to piano pieces, often combines a vibrant dissonance with elements of Czech folk music. Full name **Martinů, Bohuslav Jan**

mart·let /maártlət/ *n* on coats of arms, a footless bird used to represent a fourth son [Early 16C. < French *martelet*, alteration of *martinet*, form of the name *Martin*]

mar·tyr /maártər/ *n* **1.** SOMEBODY PUT TO DEATH somebody who chooses to die rather than deny a strongly held belief, especially a religious belief **2.** SOMEBODY WHO MAKES SACRIFICES somebody who makes sacrifices or suffers greatly in order to advance a cause or principle **3.** SOMEBODY IN PAIN somebody who experiences frequent or constant pain from something **4.** SOMEBODY SEEKING ATTENTION a frequent complainer who hopes to elicit sympathy from others ■ *v* (**-tyred, -tyring, -tyrs**) **1.** *vt* KILL SOMEBODY FOR HOLDING BELIEFS to kill somebody for refusing to deny a strongly held belief, especially a religious belief **2. mar·tyr your·self** *vr* MAKE SACRIFICES FOR SOMETHING to bring difficulties, suffering, or hardship on yourself for something [Pre-12C. Via ecclesiastical Latin < Greek *martur* "witness"] —**mar·tyr·dom** *n*

mar·tyr·ol·o·gy /maártə róllәjee/ (*plural* **-gies**) *n* **1.** the study of the lives and history of religious martyrs **2.** a catalog or list of religious martyrs, or a collection of stories about martyrs

Ma·ru·ya·ma Ok·yo /màrroo yaámə ókì ō/ (1733–95) Japanese artist. He was founder of the Maruyama school of painting. Born **Maruyama Mondo**

~~**marvalous**~~ incorrect spelling of **marvelous**

mar·vel /maárv'l/ *n* **1.** WONDERFUL THING something that inspires awe, amazement, or admiration ○ *one of the marvels of the ancient world* **2.** SKILLFUL PERSON somebody who does wonderful or astonishing things, especially somebody very skilled in something ○ *a marvel at machinery* ■ *vi* (**-veled, -vel·ing, -vels**) BE AMAZED to be very impressed, surprised, or bewildered ○ *I could only marvel at her stamina.* [13C. < French *merveille* < Latin *mirabilis* "wonderful" < *mirari* (see MIRACLE)]

Mar·vell /maárv'l/, **Andrew** (1621–78) English poet and politician. A metaphysical poet, he also wrote verse satires vigorously opposing the post-Restoration government.

> "Let us roll all our strength and all / Our sweetness up into one ball, / And tear our pleasures with rough strife / Through the iron gates of life: / Thus, though we cannot make our sun / Stand still, yet we will make him run."
> [Andrew Marvell, "To His Coy Mistress"; 1650?]

mar·vel·ous /maárvələss/, **mar·vel·lous** *adj* **1.** extraordinarily wonderful ○ *a marvelous example of Baroque architecture* **2.** very good or pleasing ○ *It was marvelous to see them all again.* —**mar·vel·ous·ly** *adv* —**mar·vel·ous·ness** *n*

Karl Marx

Marx /maarks/, **Karl** (1818–83) German philosopher. His books, especially the *Communist Manifesto* (1848) and *Das Kapital* (1867, 1885, 1894), were the basis of Communism. Full name **Marx, Karl Heinrich** —**Marx·i·an** *adj*

> "The workers have nothing to lose but their chains. They have a world to gain. WORKERS OF THE WORLD, UNITE."
> [Karl Marx, *The Communist Manifesto*; 1848]

Marx Broth·ers US comedians. Chico (born Leonard, 1891–1961), Groucho (born Julius Henry, 1895–1977), and Harpo (born Adolph, 1888–1964), the three most prominent of the brothers, appeared in comedy films such as *A Night at the Opera* (1935) and were known for their anarchic verbal and visual humor. Groucho later hosted the television game show *You Bet Your Life* (1950–61). Two other brothers, Gummo (born Milton, 1893–1977) and Zeppo (born Herbert, 1901–79), appeared in some of the Marx Brothers' early work.

Marx·ism /maárk sìzzəm/ *n* **1.** the political and economic theories of Karl Marx and Friedrich Engels, in which class struggle is a central element in the analysis of social change in Western societies **2.** political ideology based on the theories of Karl Marx and Friedrich Engels —**Marx·ist** *n, adj*

Marx·ism-Len·in·ism *n* Marxism with the inclusion of Lenin's idea that imperialism is the final stage of capitalism, and Lenin's shifting of the focus of class struggle from industrialized to nonindustrialized societies —**Marx·ist-Len·in·ist** *n, adj*

Mar·y /mérree/ *n* in the Bible, the mother of Jesus Christ. Christian tradition holds that she conceived Jesus Christ without human contact, through the direct intervention of God. In Islam she is venerated as Maryan.

Mar·y /mérree/ (1867–1953) queen of the United Kingdom. A great-granddaughter of George III, she was the queen consort of George V and the mother of Edward VIII and George VI. She is remembered especially for her charitable and relief work during World War II. Known as **Mary of Teck**

Mar·y I (1516–58) queen of England and Ireland. She was the daughter of Henry VIII and Catherine of Aragon. As queen (1553–58) she tried to restore Roman Catholicism in England, and to cement union with Spain by marrying Philip II (1554). Known as **Bloody Mary**

Mar·y II (1662–94) queen of England, Scotland, and Ireland. She was the daughter of James II. After the Glorious Revolution (1688) she was made coregent with her husband William III (Prince of Orange), during whose absences she governed as regent.

Mary (Queen of Scots): anonymous 16th-century portrait

Mar·y, Queen of Scots (1542–87) queen of Scotland. Daughter of James V of Scotland, she was married successively to King Francis II of France, Lord Darnley, and the Earl of Bothwell. Her reign (1542–67) was marked by conflict between Catholics and Protestant reformers in Scotland. The Protestant lords forced her to abdicate in 1567 in favor of her son James VI, and she fled to England. Through her grandmother, she had a claim to the English throne, and became a focus for Catholic discontent. Elizabeth I imprisoned her after 1568 and signed the warrant under which she was executed for treason in 1587. Born **Stuart, Mary**. See illustration on previous page

"In my end is my beginning."
[Mary, Queen of Scots. Motto embroidered on her canopy of state, quoted by William Drummond of Hawthornden in a letter to Ben Jonson; 1619]

Mar·y Jane /mérree jáyn/ *n* same as **marijuana** (*slang*) [Early 20C. Origin ?]

Mar·y Janes *tdmk* a trademark for shoes and boots, especially low-cut patent-leather shoes for girls with a strap fastening near the ankle at the side

Mar·y·knol·ler /mérree nōlər/ *n* a member of the Catholic Foreign Mission Society of America [Mid-20C. After *Maryknoll*, New York]

Maryland

Mar·y·land /mérrilənd/ state in the eastern United States, bordered by Delaware, the District of Columbia, Virginia, West Virginia, Pennsylvania, and the Atlantic Ocean. Capital: Annapolis. Population: 5,458,137 (2002 estimate). Area: 12,297 sq. mi./31,849 sq. km. —**Mar·y·land·er** *n*

Mar·y Mag·da·lene /-mágdə léen/ *n* in the Bible, a follower of Jesus Christ, who cured her of evil spirits (Luke 8:2)

mar·zi·pan /máarzə pàn, máartsə-/ *n* a sweet paste made of ground almonds and sugar, often with egg whites or yolks, used as a layer in cakes or molded into ornamental shapes [15C. Via German < Italian *marzapane* "type of box," originally for candy or coins]

ORIGIN Arabic *mawtabān* meant literally "enthroned king." It was used by the Saracens as the name of a medieval Venetian coin that had a figure of the seated Jesus Christ on it. In the Italian dialect of Venice the word became *matapan*, and eventually, in general Italian, *marzapane*; and its meaning supposedly progressed from the "coin" via "measure of weight or capacity," "box of such capacity," and "such a box containing confectionery" to "the contents of such a box." After English originally acquired the word (possibly via French) it became Anglicized to *marchpane*, and that remained the standard form until the 19th century. Around this time ***marzipan*** was borrowed from German. This was an alteration of Italian *marzapane*, based on the misconception that it came from Latin *marci panis* "St. Mark's bread."

ma·sa /mássə/ *n Hispanic* dough made from corn flour, sometimes also dried and ground into a powder used as a thickening agent [< Spanish, "dough"]

Ma·sac·ci·o /mə sáachee ō, maa sáachō/ (1401?–27) Italian painter. He is considered the first great painter of the Italian Renaissance, whose innovations in the use of scientific perspective inaugurated the modern era in painting. Born **Tommaso Cassai**

Ma·sa·da /mə sáadə/ ancient ruined fortress in Israel, on a mountaintop 30 mi./48.3 km southeast of Jerusalem, southwest of the Dead Sea. It was used as a stronghold by the Jewish Zealots in the final two years of their rebellion against Roman rule (A.D. 66–73). After a siege lasting nearly two years, almost all the occupants of the fortress killed themselves rather than surrender to the Romans.

Ma·sai /maa sí, máa sì/ (*plural same* or **-sais**), **Maa·sai** *n* **1.** a member of a pastoral people with strong warrior traditions who live in East Africa, mainly in Kenya and Tanzania. They are characteristically tall and slender in build. **2.** the Nilotic language of the Masai people. Native speakers: 700,000. [Mid-19C. < Masai] —**Ma·sai** *adj*

ma·sa·la /mə sáalə/ *n S Asia* gossipy embellishments in repeating a story (*informal*) [Late 18C. < Urdu *maṣālah*]

Mas·ba·te /maa báatee/ island in the central Philippines, in Masbate Province. Area: 1,600 sq. mi./4,000 sq. km. Population: 599,900 (1990).

masc. *abbr* GRAM masculine

mas·car·a /ma skárrə, mə-/ *n* thick colored paste applied to the eyelashes with a fine brush to darken them and give the appearance of greater length and thickness ■ *vt* (**-aed, -a·ing, -as**) to apply mascara to eyelashes [Late 19C. Probably < Italian *maschera* "mask"]

Mas·ca·rene Is·lands /màskə réen-/ group of islands east of Madagascar in the Indian Ocean, including Réunion, Mauritius, and Rodrigues. Population: 1,798,000 (1996). Area: 1,700 sq. mi./4,500 sq. km.

mas·car·po·ne /maàss kaar pṓnee, -pṓn/ *n* a rich fatty unsalted Italian cream cheese with a spreadable texture [Mid-20C. < Italian, "rich whey cheese"]

mas·cle /másk'l/ *n* a design on coats of arms in the form of a lozenge with a lozenge-shaped hole in the middle [13C. < Anglo-Norman < Latin *macula* "mesh"]

mas·con /máss kòn/ *n* an area of higher-than-normal gravity on the surface of the Moon [Mid-20C. Contraction of *mass concentration*]

mas·cot /máss kòt, máskət/ *n* a person, animal, or thing that is believed to bring good luck, usually one that becomes the symbol of a particular group, especially a team [Late 19C. Via French *mascotte* < modern Provençal *mascotto* "little witch"]

mas·cu·line /máskyəlin/ *adj* **1.** OF MEN AND BOYS relating or belonging to men and boys rather than women and girls **2.** OF TRADITIONAL MANLY CHARACTER having traits or qualities traditionally associated with men or boys rather than women or girls **3.** GRAM OF CERTAIN GRAMMATICAL GENDER relating to one of the classes that words and grammatical forms are divided into in some languages **4.** MUSIC CONCLUDING ON ACCENTED BEAT ending on a beat that is accented ■ *n* GRAM MASCULINE GENDER the masculine gender, or a word or form in the masculine gender [14C. Via French < Latin *masculinus* < *masculus*] —**mas·cu·line·ly** *adv* —**mas·cu·line·ness** *n*

mas·cu·line ca·dence *n* a closing section of music (**cadence**) that ends on a strong beat

mas·cu·line end·ing *n* **1.** a stressed syllable that ends a line of poetry **2.** an ending that marks a word as belonging to the masculine gender in some languages

mas·cu·line rhyme *n* a rhyme between two monosyllabic words, e.g., "gab" and "blab," or between the final stressed syllables of polysyllabic words, e.g., "connive" and "survive"

mas·cu·lin·i·ty /màskyə línnətee/ *n* **1.** the state of being a man or boy **2.** those qualities conventionally supposed to belong to a man such as physical strength and courage

mas·cu·lin·ize /máskyələ nīz/ (**-ized, -iz·ing, -iz·es**) *vt* **1.** to give something or somebody features conventionally associated with maleness **2.** to cause a female animal or a plant to acquire male sexual characteristics, e.g., as a result of administering steroids —**mas·cu·lin·i·za·tion** /màskyələni záysh'n/ *n*

Mase·field /máyss feéld/, **John** (1878–1967) British poet. The author of vigorous narrative verse, collected in *Salt Water Ballads* (1902) and other volumes, he was named poet laureate in 1930.

"I must down to the seas again, to the lonely sea and the sky, / And all I ask is a tall ship and a star to steer her by, / And the wheel's kick and the wind's song and the white sail's shaking, / And a gray mist on the sea's face and a gray dawn breaking."
[John Masefield, "Sea Fever," *Salt Water Ballads*; 1902]

ma·ser /máyzər/ *n* **1.** a device used in radar and radio astronomy to boost the strength of microwaves **2.** a galactic source of polarized microwave radiation [Mid-20C. Acronym < *microwave amplification by stimulated emission of radiation*]

Mas·er·u /mázzə ròo/ capital of Lesotho, situated on the Caledon River, near the border with South Africa. Population: 297,000 (1995).

mash /mash/ *n* **1.** GRAIN AND WATER MIX a fermentable mixture of hot water and grain, usually barley or wheat, from which alcohol is brewed or distilled **2.** ANIMAL FOOD a mixture of ground feeds for livestock or poultry **3.** PULPY MASS the consistency of a soft pulp ■ *vt* (**mashed, mash·ing, mash·es**) **1.** SOAK GRAIN to soak grain in hot water to make a mash for brewing or for feeding to animals **2.** MAKE SOMETHING INTO PULP to squash something into a pulpy mass **3.** CRUSH SOMETHING to crush or grind something (*informal*) **4.** MAKE ADVANCES to make sexual advances toward somebody, especially a man to a woman (*slang*) **5.** *Carib* STEP ON to step on something ○ *The driver had to mash brakes suddenly.* [Old English *masc* "mash for brewing" < Indo-European]

MASH /mash/, **M.A.S.H.** *abbr* ARMY mobile army surgical hospital

CULTURAL NOTE ***M*A*S*H***, a movie (1970) by director Robert Altman. Set in a mobile army surgical hospital during the Korean War, this dark satire focuses on a group of eccentric medics who combat the horrors of war with cynicism, ribald humor, and practical jokes. The movie, which was based on a novel, gave rise to a long-running television series.

mash·er /máshər/ *n* **1.** a utensil used for mashing food **2.** a man who inflicts his attentions on a woman (*dated slang*)

mash·gi·ah /maash gée áakh/ (*plural* **-gi·him** /-gée khim, maash gee khéem/), **mash·gi·ach** (*plural* **-gi·chim**) *n* an Orthodox rabbi, or a man appointed or approved by such a rabbi, who inspects slaughterhouses, meat markets, and restaurants to check that kosher food has been properly prepared and served [Mid-20C. < Hebrew *mašgīaḥ* "supervisor"]

mash·ie /máshee/ *n* an obsolete golf club similar to the modern five-iron [Late 19C. Origin ?]

mash·ie nib·lick *n* an obsolete golf club similar to the modern six-iron

Ma·sho·na /mə shṓnə/ *n* PEOPLES same as **Shona** (sense 1) —**Ma·sho·na** *adj*

mash up *adj* (*slang; used in Black English*) **1.** broken or no longer operating properly **2.** not in good health

mash·up /másh ùp/ *n* a song in digital format created by combining parts of different songs, e.g., the music track of one song and the vocal track of another

mash-up, mashed-up *adj Carib* broken or damaged

mas·int /mássint/, **MASINT** *n* intelligence data acquired, typically electronically, about possible attacks using weapons of mass destruction. Full form **materials intelligence**

Ma·si·rah /ma zéerə/ island in the Arabian Sea off the southeastern coast of Oman

mas·jid /máss jid/ *S Asia* RELIG same as **mosque** [Mid-19C. < Arabic, "place of prostration"]

mask /mask/ *n* **1.** FACE COVERING TO HIDE IDENTITY a covering for the face, worn by somebody to conceal his or her identity ○ *a Halloween mask* ○ *two gunmen wearing masks* **2.** PROTECTIVE FACE COVERING a covering for the eyes, mouth, or face, worn for protection or for medical reasons ○ *an oxygen mask* **3.** CONCEALING THING something that conceals or disguises something else such as true motives or feelings **4.** ORNAMENT RESEMBLING FACE a representation of a face used as an ornament or decoration **5.** ZOOL ANIMAL'S FACE MARKINGS the face or facial markings of some animals such as foxes and raccoons **6.** MIL CONCEALMENT FOR

TROOPS a natural or artificial feature that hides military troops and installations from an enemy **7.** ELECTRONICS TEMPLATE FOR ELECTRONIC CHIPS a template used to control the pattern of conducting material deposited or etched onto a semiconductor chip **8.** COSMETICS BEAUTY TREATMENT a facial preparation used to tighten the skin and remove impurities, applied to the skin as a paste and allowed to dry before being removed **9.** PHOTOGRAPHY PHOTOGRAPHIC GUARD a guard, often a sheet of paper, placed over areas of unexposed photographic film to stop light from hitting it ■ *vt* (**masked, mask·ing, masks**) **1.** PUT MASK ON SOMETHING to cover something with a mask ○ *masked their faces* **2.** CONCEAL SOMETHING to conceal something in order to protect or disguise it ○ *alleged that the company masked its true corporate identity* **3.** HIDE SOMETHING FROM VIEW to prevent something from being seen by covering it ○ *Thick vines masked the cave entrance.* **4.** SHIELD PART OF SOMETHING to cover part of a surface using masking tape before painting or spraying **5.** PHOTOGRAPHY SHIELD PHOTOGRAPHIC FILM FROM LIGHT to prevent stray or unwanted light from reaching areas of unexposed photographic film, either using hands or a special shield **6.** CHEM STOP CHEMICAL FROM REACTING to prevent a chemical substance from reacting by the addition of another chemical [Early 16C. Via French *masque* < late Latin *masca* "ghost, mask"] —**mask·a·ble** *adj*

masked /maskt/ *adj* **1.** WEARING MASK with the face covered in order to prevent recognition **2.** MED NOT DETECTABLE describes diseases and symptoms that are present but not yet perceptible **3.** BOT same as **personate**[2] **4.** ZOOL WITH MARKINGS LIKE MASK with markings on the head or around the eyes that resemble a mask

masked ball *n* a ball at which people wear masks

mask·er /máskər/ *n* somebody who wears a mask at a masked ball

mask·ing /másking/ *n* **1.** the hiding or screening of one sensory process such as hearing by another such as sight **2.** scenery that is used to hide a part of the stage from the audience

mask·ing tape *n* easy-to-remove adhesive tape used to cover parts of a surface that are not meant to be painted

Mas·low /mázzlō, másslō/, **Abraham Harold** (1908–70) US psychologist. He developed the principles of humanistic psychology, most notably in *Toward a Psychology of Being* (1962).

> "A musician must make music, an artist must paint, a poet must write, if he is to be ultimately at peace with himself. What one can be, one must be."
> [Abraham Harold Maslow, *Motivation and Personality*, 1954]

mas·och·ism /mássə kìzzəm/ *n* **1.** SEXUAL PLEASURE THROUGH HUMILIATION sexual gratification achieved through humiliation and physical and verbal abuse **2.** PSYCHOLOGICAL DISORDER the psychological disorder in which somebody needs to be emotionally or physically abused in order to be sexually satisfied **3.** SEARCH FOR ABUSIVE SEXUAL PARTNERS the active seeking out of sexual partners who will dominate, humiliate, and physically and verbally abuse **4.** ENJOYMENT OF HARDSHIP the tendency to invite and enjoy misery of any kind, especially in order to be pitied by others or admired for forbearance [Late 19C. After Leopold von *Sacher-Masoch* (1836–95), Austrian novelist] —**mas·o·chist** *n*

mas·och·is·tic /màssə kístik/ *adj* **1.** relating to or experiencing the desire to be humiliated and abused by others in order to feel sexually fulfilled **2.** tending to invite and enjoy misery —**mas·och·is·ti·cal·ly** *adv*

ma·son /máyss'n/ *n* somebody who works with stone or brick, especially in the building trades ■ *vt* (**-soned, -son·ing, -sons**) to build or strengthen something using stone or brick [12C. < Old N French *machun* or Old French *masson*]

Ma·son *n* same as **Freemason**

Ma·son /máyss'n/, **George** (1725–92) American patriot. He wrote the constitution of Virginia, which became the model for the Declaration of Independence (1776) and the Bill of Rights (1791).

> "The freedom of the press is one of the greatest bulwarks of liberty, and can never be restrained but by despotic governments."
> [George Mason, *Virginia Bill of Rights*, June 12, 1776]

ma·son bee *n* a solitary bee that builds nests of sand or clay held together with saliva

Ma·son Ci·ty /màyss'n-/ city in northern Iowa, north of Iowa Falls and northwest of Cedar Falls. Population: 28,464 (2002 estimate).

Ma·son-Dix·on Line /màyss'n díks'n-/ *n* the boundary that separates Pennsylvania from Maryland and West Virginia, regarded as the dividing line between free and slave states before the Civil War [After Charles *Mason* and Jeremiah *Dixon*, 18C surveyors]

ma·son·ic /mə sónnik/ *adj* relating to stonemasons or brick masons or their work —**ma·son·i·cal·ly** *adv*

Ma·son·ic *adj* relating to Freemasons or Freemasonry

Ma·son·ite /máyss'n ìt/ *tdmk* a trademark for fiberboard products. Used for insulation, paneling, and building partitions.

Ma·son jar *n* a wide-mouthed glass jar with a lid that screws or clips on and forms a vacuum seal, used for preserving food, especially fruits and vegetables [Late 19C. After John *Mason* (1832–1902), US metalworker]

ma·son·ry /máyss'nree/ *n* **1.** MASON'S TRADE the trade of a mason **2.** MASON'S WORK the work done by a mason **3.** STONEWORK the stone or brick parts of a building or other structure

Ma·son·ry /máyss'nree/ *n* same as **Freemasonry** (sense 1)

ma·son wasp *n* a solitary wasp that builds mud nests or digs out nests in old mortar. Genus: *Odynerus*.

Ma·sor·ete /mássə reet/, **Ma·sor·ite** /-rìt/ *n* any of the scholars who produced the Masoretic text [Late 16C. Via French or modern Latin *Massoreta* < a misuse of Hebrew *māsōret*] —**Mas·o·ret·ic** /màssə réttik/ *adj*

Mas·o·ret·ic text *n* the traditional text of the Hebrew Bible, revised and annotated by Jewish scholars between the 6th and 10th centuries A.D.

Ma·sor·ite *n* JUDAISM, BIBLE same as **Masorete**

Mas·qat ♦ **Muscat**

masque /mask/ *n* **1.** a dramatic entertainment similar to opera, popular in England in the 16th and 17th centuries, in which masked performers represented mythological or allegorical characters **2.** the music and words written for a masque **3.** LEISURE same as **masquerade** *n* (sense 1) [Early 16C. < French (see MASK)]

mas·quer /máskər/ *n* same as **masker**

mas·quer·ade /màskə ráyd/ *n* **1.** PARTY WITH MASKS a party at which masks and costumes are worn, whether an informal gathering of friends or a formal ball **2.** DISGUISING COSTUME a costume worn to a masquerade **3.** DISGUISING PRETENSE a pretense or disguise ■ *vi* (**-ad·ed, -ad·ing, -ades**) **1.** PRETEND to pretend to be somebody or something else **2.** WEAR COSTUME to wear a particular costume to a party [Late 16C. Via French *mascarade* < Italian *mascherata* < *maschera* "mask"] —**mas·quer·ad·er** *n*

mass /mass/ *n* **1.** LUMP a body of matter that forms a whole but has no definable shape **2.** COLLECTION a collection of many individual parts ○ *The garden is a mass of weeds.* **3.** GREAT UNSPECIFIED QUANTITY a large but unspecified number or quantity ○ *decaying into a mass of rust* **4.** MAJOR PART the greater part or majority ○ *The mass of respondents oppose the legislation.* **5.** PHYS PHYSICAL QUANTITY the property of an object that is a measure of its inertia, the amount of matter it contains, and its influence in a gravitational field. Symbol *m* ■ **mass·es** *npl* ORDINARY PEOPLE ordinary people in society, as distinct from people who are rich or powerful ■ *vti* (**massed, mass·ing, mass·es**) COLLECT to gather things in a mass, or be gathered in a mass ○ *Troops are massing on the border.* ■ *adj* **1.** OF LARGE NUMBER made up of or containing a large number ○ *a mass demonstration* **2.** GENERAL broadly general, in scope or effect ○ *The mass effect is rather disappointing.* [14C. Via French *masse* < Latin *massa* < Greek *maza* "barley cake"]

Mass /mass/, **mass** *n* **1.** in the Roman Catholic Church and some Protestant churches, the religious ceremony of Communion **2.** a part of the text of a Roman Catholic Mass set to music, to be sung by a choir [Pre-12C. < ecclesiastical Latin *missa* < Latin *mittere* "send away"]

Mass. *abbr* Massachusetts

Mas·sa·chu·sett /màssə chóossət/ (*plural same* or **-setts**), **Mas·sa·chu·set** (*plural same* or **-sets**) *n* **1.** a member of a Native North American people who lived in the Massachusetts Bay area **2.** an extinct Algonquian language formerly spoken in eastern Massachusetts —**Mas·sa·chu·sett** *adj*

Massachusetts

Mas·sa·chu·setts /màssə chóossəts/ state in the northeastern United States, bordered by Vermont, New Hampshire, the Atlantic Ocean, Rhode Island, Connecticut, and New York. Capital: Boston. Population: 6,427,801 (2002 estimate). Area: 9,241 sq. mi./23,934 sq. km. Official name **Commonwealth of Massachusetts**

Mas·sa·chu·setts Bay inlet of the Atlantic Ocean, in eastern Massachusetts

mas·sa·cre /mássəkər/ *n* **1.** KILLING OF MANY PEOPLE the vicious killing of large numbers of people or animals **2.** BAD DEFEAT a contest in which one side is badly beaten (*informal*) ■ *vt* (**-cred, -cring, -cres**) **1.** KILL PEOPLE IN LARGE NUMBERS to kill large numbers of people or animals **2.** DEFEAT SOMEBODY COMPLETELY to defeat somebody completely, especially in a sports contest (*informal*) [Late 16C. < French, "butchery"]

mas·sage /mə saázh, -saáj/ *n* RUBBING OF BODY a treatment that involves rubbing or kneading the muscles, either for medical or therapeutic purposes or simply as an aid to relaxation ■ *vt* (**-saged, -sag·ing, -sag·es**) **1.** RUB SOMEBODY'S MUSCLES to rub or knead somebody's muscles **2.** MANIPULATE INFORMATION DECEPTIVELY to manipulate statistics or other information in order to create a more suitable or falsely impressive result ○ *massaged their sales figures* **3.** ENHANCE SOMETHING to give something a boost with kind or uplifting treatment, especially somebody's ego with flattery [Late 19C. < French < *masser* "apply massage to"] —**mas·sag·er** *n*

mas·sage par·lor *n* **1.** a place that provides massages to paying customers **2.** a place that offers sex services for money, including sexual massages

Mas·sa·pe·qua /màssə péekwə/ town in southeastern New York, in Nassau County. Population: 17,555 (2002 estimate).

mas·sa·sau·ga /màssə sáwgə/ *n* a small rattlesnake that has variable coloring. Native to: North America. Latin name: *Sistrurus catenatus*. [Mid-19C. Alteration of *Mississagi*, river in SE Ontario, Canada]

Mas·sa·soit /mássə sòyt/ (1580?–1661) Wampanoag leader. He negotiated peace with the pilgrims of Plymouth Colony, and shared the first Thanksgiving feast (1621).

mass bal·ance *n* a mathematical equation, table, or quantitative chart showing the mass inputs and outputs of a process, plant, or machine, the principle being that what goes in must come out

mass com·mu·ni·ca·tion *n* communication by means of broadcasting and newspapers, which reaches all or most people in society

mass·cult /máss kùlt/ *n* culture as it is presented and interpreted by the mass media (*informal*) [Shortening of *mass culture*]

mass de·fect *n* the difference between the mass of an isotope and the element's mass number

mas·sé /ma sáy/ *n* in a cue game, a shot in which the cue is held almost vertically to strike the cue ball off center, making it curve around one ball to hit another [Late 19C. < French < *masse* "large hammer"]

Mas·se·na /mə séenə/ village in northeastern New York, near the St. Lawrence River. Population: 12,931 (2002 estimate).

mass-en·er·gy e·quiv·a·lence *n* the principle in the theory of relativity that mass and energy are equivalent and interchangeable according to the equation E = mc^2

Mas·se·net /màssə náy/, **Jules** (1842–1912) French composer. Famous for his opera *Manon* (1884), he also wrote oratorios, cantatas, and orchestral pieces. Full name **Massenet, Jules Émile Frédéric**

mas·se·ter /mə séetər, ma-/ *n* a muscle in the cheek that moves the jaws during chewing [Late 16C. < Greek *masētēr* < *masasthai* "chew"]

mas·seur /ma súr, mə-, ma sóor/ *n* a man who gives massages professionally [Late 19C. < French < *masser* "apply massage to"]

mas·seuse /ma sóoss, -sóoz, -sőz/ *n* a woman who gives massages professionally [Late 19C. < French, form of *masseur* (see MASSEUR)]

mass ex·tinc·tion *n* the destruction of a whole species by a force of nature such as climate change, volcanic eruption, or asteroid collision, thought by many scientists to have wiped out the dinosaurs

Mas·sey /mássee/, **Charles Vincent** (1887–1967) Canadian politician and diplomat. He was Canada's first native-born governor-general (1952–59).

Mas·sey, William (1856–1925) Irish-born prime minister of New Zealand (1912–25). A Reform Party politician, he is the second longest-serving New Zealand prime minister after Richard Seddon. See table at **prime minister**. Full name **Massey, William Ferguson**

mas·si·cot /mássi kòt, -kō/ *n* a yellow mineral consisting of lead oxide, or a powdered form of it used as a pigment [15C. < French]

mas·sif /ma séef/ *n* **1.** a large mountain mass, or a group of connected mountains that form a mountain range **2.** a part of the Earth's crust that is surrounded by faults and may be shifted or displaced by tectonic movements [Early 16C. < French (see MASSIVE)]

Mas·sif Cen·tral /ma séef sen tráal/ highland region in south central France. Area: 36,000 sq. mi./93,000 sq. km.

mas·sive /mássiv/ *adj* **1. BULKY** large, solid, and heavy **2. COMPARATIVELY LARGE** large in comparison with what is typical or usual ○ *a massive increase in funding* **3. LARGE-SCALE** extremely large in amount, degree, or scope ○ *massive internal bleeding* **4. EXCELLENT** of the highest quality (*slang*) [15C. Via French *massif* < Old French *massiz* < Latin *massa* (see MASS)] —**mas·sive·ly** *adv* —**mas·sive·ness** *n*

Mas·sive, Mount /mássiv/ mountain in central Colorado in the Sawatch Range of the Rocky Mountains. Height: 14,421 ft./4,396 m.

mass·less /mássləss/ *adj* with a mass of zero

mass-mar·ket *adj* designed for sale to as wide a range of people as possible, rather than to a particular group in society ■ *vt* to sell something to as many people as possible by advertising and promoting it widely

mass me·di·a *n* all of the communications media that reach a large audience, especially television, radio, and newspapers (*takes a singular or plural verb*)

mass noun *n* a noun representing something that cannot be counted, e.g., "water," or something that can only be counted if the meaning is a single type or serving, e.g., "coffee"

mass num·ber *n* the number of protons and neutrons in the nucleus of an atom of a particular substance. Symbol **A**

mass-pro·duce *vt* to manufacture a product in very large quantities in factories, especially using mechanization and assembly-line methods —**mass-pro·duc·er** *n*

mass pro·duc·tion *n* the manufacturing of products in very large quantities in factories, especially using mechanization and assembly-line methods

mass so·ci·e·ty *n* a society in which the national or global nature of the influences on life, e.g., mass production and the mass media, has stripped the population of its diversity

mass so·ci·o·gen·ic ill·ness /-sōsee ō jènnik-/ *n* PSYCHIAT a situation in which large numbers of people who, as a group, develop symptoms of physical illness as a result of intense perceived danger [Early 21C]

mass spec·trom·e·ter *n* an instrument that separates atoms and molecules according to their mass and that records the resulting mass spectrum —**mass spec·tro·met·ry** *n*

mass spec·trum *n* a record of the chemical constituents of a substance separated according to their mass and presented as a spectrum

mass tran·sit *n* TRANSP same as **public transportation**

mass wast·ing *n* the downward movement of loose rock and soil along a slope

mast[1] /mast/ *n* **1. VERTICAL SUPPORT FOR SAILS** a vertical spar that supports sails, rigging, or flags on a ship **2. UPRIGHT POLE** a vertical pole, especially one that supports a flag **3. BROADCAST TOWER** a tall broadcasting antenna **4.** NAVY same as **captain's mast** ■ *vti* (**mast·ed, mast·ing, masts**) NAVY **DISCIPLINE SAILOR, OR BE DISCIPLINED** to subject somebody charged with a usually shipboard or on-base crime or infringement to a disciplinary hearing (**captain's mast**), or undergo such a hearing [Old English *mæst* < Indo-European] ◇ **at half mast 1.** partway down a flagpole, usually as a sign of respect following a death ○ *flags flying at half mast* **2.** partway up or down from the usual position at which something is worn (*informal humorous*) ○ *jeans at half mast* ◇ **before the mast** serving as an ordinary sailor or apprentice seaman

mast[2] /mast/ *n* the nuts of some trees, e.g., beech, oak, and chestnut, especially when used as food for hogs [Old English *mæst* "fodder" < Germanic, "meat"]

mast- *prefix* breast, nipple, mammary gland ○ *mastitis* [< Greek *mastos*]

mas·ta·ba /mástəbə/, **mas·ta·bah** *n* in ancient Egypt, a brick tomb built with a flat base, sloping sides, and a flat roof. Its design inspired the pyramids. [Early 17C. < Arabic *maṣṭaba*]

mas·tal·gia /ma stáljə, -stáljee ə/ *n* pain in the breast

mast cell *n* a large cell in connective tissue consisting of granules that release histamine and heparin during allergic reactions [< German *Mast* "fattening, feeding"]

mas·tec·to·my /ma stéktəmee/ (*plural* **-mies**) *n* the surgical removal of a breast, usually as a treatment for breast cancer [Early 20C. < Greek *mastos* "breast"]

mas·ter /mástər/ *n* **1. BOSS** especially formerly, a man in a position of authority, e.g., over a business or servants (*sometimes considered offensive*) **2. SOMEBODY IN CONTROL** somebody or something controlling or influencing events or other things (*sometimes considered offensive*) **3. ABSTRACT CONTROL** an abstract idea or force that is thought of as having control or influence (*sometimes considered offensive*) ○ *She believes strongly that fate is the master of our lives.* **4. OWNER OF ANIMAL** a man who owns or has control of a horse, dog, or other domesticated animal **5. SOMEBODY HIGHLY SKILLED** somebody highly skilled at something **6. SKILLED WORKER** somebody who is highly skilled in a trade or craft and is qualified to teach apprentices (*usually used in combination*) ○ *master craftsman* **7. PLAYER AT HIGH LEVEL** in some games, a player who has reached a high level of achievement, especially in chess or bridge **8. ORIGINAL COPY** an original copy of something, e.g., a recording tape or a stencil, from which other copies can be made **9. LEADER** somebody whose philosophy or religious belief has attracted followers (*sometimes considered offensive*) **10. SHIP'S CAPTAIN** the captain of a merchant ship **11.** LAW **SPECIALIST ASSISTING JUDGE** a specialist, sometimes a retired judge, who assists a court by making a report to the judge presiding over a case, often a highly complex case **12.** COMPUT **CONTROLLING MACHINE** a device or computer that controls the operation of one or more other connected devices or computers (*sometimes considered offensive*) ■ *adj* (*sometimes considered offensive*) **1. MAIN** devised to operate on the broadest level ○ *a master plan* **2. CONTROLLING** controlling the operation of everything or of all others ○ *the master switch* **3. PRINCIPAL** biggest or primary among several ○ *the master bedroom* ■ *vt* (**-tered, -ter·ing, -ters**) **1. BECOME SKILLED IN SOMETHING** to become highly skilled in something or acquire a complete understanding of it **2. CONTROL SOMETHING** to learn to control feelings or behavior (*sometimes considered offensive*) **3. MAKE SOMEBODY OR SOMETHING SUBMIT** to break the will of a person or animal (*sometimes considered offensive*) **4. MAKE MASTER RECORDING** to produce a master recording of something [Pre-12C. < Old French *maistre* < Latin *magister* "chief" < *magis* "more"] —**mas·ter·less** *adj*

Mas·ter *n* **1.** a title sometimes prefixed to a boy's surname in formal circumstances **2.** a title used to address a man who is a religious leader or teacher (*sometimes considered offensive*)

mas·ter-at-arms (*plural* **mas·ters-at-arms**) *n* a noncommissioned officer aboard a naval vessel who is responsible for maintaining order and enforcing discipline in the ship's company

mas·ter build·er *n* an especially accomplished builder, especially one licensed to employ others as labor (*sometimes considered offensive*)

CULTURAL NOTE ***The Master Builder***, a play (1845) by Norwegian dramatist Henrik Ibsen. Typical of Ibsen's more symbolic later works, it is the story of a successful architect, Halvard Solness, who is disturbed by his continued good fortune and fearful that he will eventually have to pay a price for it. His search for redemption eventually leads to his own death.

mas·ter chief pet·ty of·fi·cer *n* a noncommissioned officer in the US Navy or Coast Guard of a rank above senior chief petty officer

mas·ter class *n* a class for advanced students given by an acknowledged expert in a field (*sometimes considered offensive*)

mas·ter cor·po·ral *n* a noncommissioned officer in the Canadian Army, of a rank above corporal and below sergeant

mas·ter·ful /mástərf'l/ *adj* (*sometimes considered offensive*) **1.** demonstrating exceptional skill or ability **2.** showing the ability or tendency to lead others —**mas·ter·ful·ly** *adv* —**mas·ter·ful·ness** *n*

USAGE **masterful** or **masterly**? These two adjectives are interchangeable in the sense of "exceptionally skillful." Some people prefer to use ***masterly*** for this purpose, to prevent confusion with the other meaning of ***masterful***, "showing the ability or tendency to lead others," which has derogatory overtones. Others avoid both adjectives, in view of the masculine associations of the word *master*.

mas·ter gun·ner·y ser·geant *n* a noncommissioned officer in the US Marine Corps of a rank above master sergeant or first sergeant

mas·ter key *n* a key that will open all the locks in a set or place

mas·ter·ly /mástərlee/ *adj* demonstrating outstanding skill (*sometimes considered offensive*) —**mas·ter·li·ness** *n*

USAGE See ***masterful***.

mas·ter mar·i·ner *n* NAUT same as **master** *n* (sense 10)

mas·ter·mind /mástər mīnd/ (*sometimes considered offensive*) *n* somebody who plans, organizes, and oversees a complex operation ■ *vt* (**-mind·ed, -mind·ing, -minds**) to plan, organize, and oversee a complex operation

Mas·ter of Arts *n* an academic degree in a nonscience subject, usually awarded after one or two years of postgraduate study

mas·ter of cer·e·mo·nies *n* (*sometimes considered offensive*) **1.** somebody who makes the opening speech and introduces speakers or performers at a formal event **2.** a performer who acts as the host of a variety show performed in front of an audience

Mas·ter of Sci·ence *n* an academic degree in a science subject, usually awarded after one or two years of postgraduate study

Mas·ter of Sur·ger·y *n* a postgraduate degree awarded for research in some area of medicine [Translation of Latin *Chirurgiae Magister*]

mas·ter·piece /mástər peess/ *n* **1. GREAT ARTISTIC WORK** an exceptionally good piece of creative work, e.g., a book, movie, or performance (*sometimes considered offensive*) **2. ARTIST'S BEST WORK** the best piece of work by a particular artist or craftsperson (*sometimes* *considered offensive*) **3. WORK EARNING RECOGNITION BY GUILD** the piece of work presented to a medieval guild to show that its maker was worthy of the rank of master craftsman [Early 17C. After Dutch *meesterstuk* or German *Meisterstück*]

mas·ter race *n* a group of people who consider themselves a race superior to all others, especially the Aryans in the ideology of Nazi Germany (*sometimes considered offensive*)

Mas·ters /maástərz/, **Edgar Lee** (1869–1950) US poet. He is best known for his free-verse small-town epic *Spoon River Anthology* (1915).

> "What is this I hear of sorrow and weariness, / Anger, discontent and drooping hopes? / Degenerate sons and daughters, / Life is too strong for you— / It takes life to love life."
> [Edgar Lee Masters, "Lucinda Matlock," *Spoon River Anthology*; 1915]

Mas·ter's de·gree *n* an academic degree, usually awarded after one or two years of postgraduate study

mas·ter sea·man *n* a noncommissioned officer in the Canadian Navy of a rank below petty officer

mas·ter ser·geant *n* a noncommissioned officer in the US Army of a rank above sergeant first class, in the Marine Corps, of a rank above gunnery sergeant, and in the Air Force, of a rank above technical sergeant

mas·ter·sing·er /mástər sìngər/ *n* MUSIC same as **Meistersinger** [Early 19C. Anglicization]

Mas·ter·son /maástərssən/, **Bat** (1853–1921) Canadian-born US sheriff. He was a notorious gambler and lawman in the American West between 1877 and 1902, when he became a sportswriter on the *New York Morning Telegraph*. Born **Masterson, Bartholomew**. Full name **Masterson, William Barclay**

mas·ter·stroke /mástər stròk/ *n* a brilliant idea or very clever tactic (*sometimes considered offensive*)

mas·ter switch *n* a switch that controls the supply of electricity to a place or to a set of equipment

mas·ter·work /mástər wùrk/ *n* ARTS same as **masterpiece** (senses 1–2) (*sometimes considered offensive*)

mas·ter·y /mástəree/ *n* (*sometimes considered offensive*) **1.** expert knowledge or outstanding ability **2.** total control over somebody or something

mast·head /mást hèd/ *n* **1.** MEDIA **TITLE OF NEWSPAPER** the name of a newspaper or magazine as it appears in large letters on the front page or cover **2.** MEDIA **NEWSPAPER INFORMATION** the list in a newspaper or magazine that provides information about staff, owners, and circulation in a newspaper or magazine **3. TOP OF MAST** the top of a ship's mast

mas·tic /mástik/ *n* **1.** a flexible cement. Use: filler, adhesive, sealant in woodwork, plaster, brickwork. **2.** an aromatic resin produced by a Mediterranean tree. Use: manufacture of lacquer, varnish, adhesives, condiments. [14C. < French < Greek *mastikhan* "grind the teeth"]

mas·ti·cate /másti kàyt/ (**-cat·ed, -cat·ing, -cates**) *v* **1.** *vti* to grind and pulverize food inside the mouth, using the teeth and jaws **2.** *vt* to grind or crush something until it turns to pulp [Mid-17C. < Latin *masticat-*, past participle of *masticare* < Greek *mastikhan* "grind the teeth"] —**mas·ti·ca·tion** /màsti káysh'n/ *n* —**mas·ti·ca·tor** *n*

mas·ti·ca·to·ry /mástikə tàwree/ *adj* relating to chewing ■ *n* (*plural* **-ries**) a medicine made to be chewed in order to increase the production of saliva

mas·tic tree *n* a small evergreen bush of the cashew family, grown for its resin. Native to: Mediterranean. Latin name: *Pistachia lentiscus*.

mas·tiff /mástif/ *n* a large powerful dog belonging to a breed with smooth-haired, often tan or grayish coats, and dark faces [14C. < Old French *mastin* < Latin *mansuetus* "used to the hand, tame" < *manus* "hand"]

mas·tiff bat *n* a snub-nosed bat. Native to: warm regions. Family: Molossidae.

mas·ti·gure /másti gyòor/ *n* a lizard that blocks its burrow with its very spiny tail. Native to: North Africa, Southwest Asia. Genus: *Uromastix*. [Mid-19C. < modern Latin *mastigura* < Greek *mastig-* "whip" + *oura* "tail"]

mastiff

mas·ti·tis /ma stítiss/ *n* inflammation of a woman's breast or an animal's udder, usually as a result of bacterial infection [Mid-19C. < Greek *mastos* "breast"] —**mas·tit·ic** /ma stíttik/ *adj*

mas·to·don /mástə dòn/ *n* a large extinct mammal that resembled an elephant, with shaggy hair and two sets of tusks. Genus: *Mastodon*. [Early 19C. < Greek *mastos* "breast" + *odōn* "tooth"]

mas·toid /máss tòyd/ *adj* **1.** shaped like a nipple or breast **2.** relating to the mastoid process ■ *n* ANAT same as **mastoid process** [Mid-18C. Via French *mastoïde* or modern Latin *mastoides* < Greek *mastoeidēs* < *mastos* "breast"]

mas·toid bone *n* ANAT same as **mastoid process**

mas·toid cell *n* an air-filled space in the mastoid process

mas·toid·ec·to·my /màss toy déktəmee/ (*plural* **-mies**) *n* a surgical operation to remove part of an infected mastoid process

mas·toid·i·tis /màss toy dítəss/ *n* inflammation of the mastoid process and mastoid cells

mas·toid proc·ess *n* a bony protuberance on the skull, found behind the ear in many vertebrates, including humans

Mas·troi·an·ni /maástroy aánee/, **Marcello** (1924–96) Italian movie actor. Specializing in romantic or bittersweet comedy, he worked with many of the great Italian directors, including Federico Fellini in *La Dolce Vita* (1960).

> "The less you do, the better you do it."
> [Marcello Mastroianni, *Interview, Il Corriere della Sera*; August 3, 1985]

mas·tur·bate /mástər bàyt/ (**-bat·ed, -bat·ing, -bates**) *vti* to give yourself or somebody else sexual pleasure by stroking the genitals, usually to orgasm [Mid-19C. < Latin *masturbat-*, past participle of *masturbari*] —**mas·tur·ba·tion** /màstər báysh'n/ *n* —**mas·tur·ba·tor** *n* —**mas·tur·ba·to·ry** /-bə tàwree/ *adj*

ma·sur·i·um /mə sóoree əm/ *n* CHEM ELEM same as **technetium** [Early 20C. < German, after *Masuria*, region of NE Poland]

mat[1] /mat/ *n* **1. PIECE OF CARPET** a flat piece of material placed on a floor for decoration or protection or for wiping the feet **2. PIECE OF PADDED MATERIAL** a piece of padded material placed on the floor for use in some sports and activities, e.g., to absorb the impact of falling in judo **3. PROTECTIVE COVER** a piece of fabric or board used to protect surfaces from damage by heat or scratching **4. THICK MASS** a thick or interwoven mass, e.g., a tangle of hair ■ *vti* (**mat·ted, mat·ting, mats**) **FORM TANGLED MASS** to make something into a thick tangled mass, or become a thick tangled mass [Pre-12C. < Latin *matta*]

mat[2] /mat/ *n* **1.** ARTS **PICTURE BORDER** a border of stiff material placed around a picture to act as a simple frame or as a decorative edge within a frame **2.** *also* **matte** *US* **NONGLOSS FINISH** a dull or nonglossy finish, e.g., on paintwork or photographic prints. Can term **matt** ■ *vt* (**mat·ted, mat·ting, mats**) **FRAME SOMETHING WITH MAT** to put a mat around a picture ■ *adj also* **matte** *US* **HAVING MAT FINISH** with a mat finish. Can term **matt** [Mid-17th C. < French *mat* "dull"]

mat., **mat** *abbr* matinée

M.A.T. *abbr* Master of Arts in Teaching

Mat·a·be·le·land /màttə beélə lànd/ region in southern Zimbabwe, between the Limpopo and Zambezi rivers. The region's main city is Bulawayo. Area: 70,118 sq. mi./181,605 sq. km.

Ma·ta·di /mə taádee/ city in the western Democratic Republic of the Congo, on the Congo River. Population: 172,730 (1994).

mat·a·dor /máttə dàwr/ *n* the main bullfighter in a bullfight, whose job is to kill the bull [Late 17C. < Spanish < *matar* "kill"]

Ma·ta Ha·ri /maátə haáree/ (1876–1917) Dutch dancer and spy. An intelligence agent for the Germans during World War I, she was executed by the French. Born **Zelle, Margaretha Geertruida**

> "I am a woman who enjoys herself very much; sometimes I lose, sometimes I win."
> [Mata Hari. Quoted in *Mata Hari, the True Story*, Russell Howe; 1986]

Ma·ta·mo·ros /màttə máwrəss/ city and port in northeastern Mexico, near the mouth of the Rio Grande opposite Brownsville, Texas. Population: 418,141 (2000).

match[1] /mach/ *n* **1. COUNTERPART** somebody who or something that is identical to another person or thing or is one half of a pair **2. EQUAL** somebody or something capable of competing equally with another person or thing **3. SOMETHING SIMILAR** a close likeness of somebody or something **4. GOOD COMPLEMENT** something that combines well with something else **5. CONTEST** a contest between opponents, especially a sports contest **6. MARRIAGE** a relationship of marriage **7. POTENTIAL PARTNER** an appropriate marriage partner ■ *v* (**matched, match·ing, match·es**) **1.** *vt* **BE LIKE SOMEBODY OR SOMETHING** to be similar or identical to somebody or something **2.** *vt* **COMPETE EQUALLY WITH SOMEBODY OR SOMETHING** to be as good, or sometimes as bad, as somebody or something else ○ *She knows she can match him for speed any day.* **3.** *vti* **COMBINE WELL** to make a suitable or pleasing combination, or put things together to make such a combination **4.** *vt* **BE IN HARMONY WITH SOMETHING** to correspond with something or reflect particular features **5.** *vt* **FIND SOMETHING THAT COMBINES WITH SOMETHING** to find something that makes a suitable accompaniment **6.** *vti* **JOIN CLEANLY** to fit or join something smoothly, or fit or join together smoothly **7.** *vt* **PLACE SOMEBODY OR SOMETHING IN OPPOSITION** to provide somebody or something with an opponent **8.** *vti* **TOSS COINS** to toss coins to see which sides land face up in order to determine a choice or decision [Old English *gemæcca* "spouse, lover" < Germanic] —**match·a·ble** *adj* —**match·er** *n*

match[2] /mach/ *n* **1.** a thin stick of wood whose tip is coated with a combustible material that ignites when scraped against a rough surface **2.** a slow-burning fuse used in cannons and explosives [14C. < Old French *meiche* < Greek *muxa* "wick for a lamp"]

match·board /mách bàwrd/ *n* a board that has a tongue along one edge and a groove along the other so that it can be fitted together with other boards [< MATCH[1]]

match·book /mách bòok/ *n* a small cardboard folder with safety matches inside and a striking surface usually on the outside [Mid-20C. < MATCH[2]]

match·box /mách bòks/ *n* a small cardboard box for matches, with a striking surface along one or both sides [Late 18C. < MATCH[2]]

match·less /máchləss/ *adj* so outstandingly great as to have no rival [Mid-16C. < MATCH[1]]

match·lock /mách lòk/ *n* **1.** formerly, a trigger mechanism in guns that ignited the powder with a slow-burning fuse **2.** a gun equipped with a matchlock [Mid-17C. < MATCH[2]]

match·mak·er /mách màykər/ *n* somebody who arranges romantic partnerships or marriages [Mid-17C. < MATCH[1]] —**match·mak·ing** *n*

match play *n* in golf, a method of scoring in which the number of holes won is counted rather than the number of strokes [< MATCH[1]] —**match play·er** *n*

match point *n* **1.** the final point needed to win a match, especially in tennis and other racket games **2.** a unit used for scoring in bridge tournaments [< MATCH[1]]

match·stick /mách stìk/ *n* **STEM OF MATCH** the wooden part of a match ■ *adj* **1. MADE FROM MATCHES** built of matchsticks **2. THIN OR IN STRIPS** as thin as matchsticks, or in the form of thin strips or simple lines [Late 18C. < MATCH[2]]

match·up /mách ùp/ *n* a competition or contest between two people or two teams, e.g., in a competitive sport [< MATCH[1]]

match·wood /mách wŏŏd/ *n* fragments or splinters, especially resulting from the destruction of something [Late 16C. < MATCH[2]]

mate[1] /mayt/ *n* 1. PARTNER IN SEX OR WEDLOCK a sexual or marriage partner (*informal*) 2. BREEDING PARTNER either of a pair of animals that breed together 3. OFFICER IN MERCHANT MARINE a deck officer of a rank below the master on a merchant ship 4. PETTY OFFICER a petty officer in the US Navy who assists a warrant officer 5. SKILLED WORKER'S HELPER an assistant to a skilled worker ○ *a plumber's mate* 6. SOMETHING THAT MATCHES either of a pair of things that belong together 7. *UK* FRIEND a friend, also used as a friendly, or sometimes hostile, form of address to a man 8. *UK* USED TO ADDRESS SOMEBODY used as a friendly, or sometimes hostile, form of address to a man (*informal; usually used in combination*) ■ *v* (**mat·ed, mat·ing, mates**) 1. *vti* BREED to come together or bring animals together to breed 2. *vi* HAVE SEX to engage in sex 3. *vt* CONNECT TWO OBJECTS to combine or connect two things 4. *vti* MARRY to join two people in marriage, or become joined in marriage (*informal or humorous*) [14C. < Middle Low German *gemate*] —**mate·less** *adj*

mate[2] /mayt/ *n, vt* (**mat·ed, mat·ing, mates**), *interj* CHESS same as **checkmate** *n* (senses 1–2), *v* (sense 1), *interj* [14C. See CHECKMATE]

ma·té /maá tày, maa táy/ *n* 1. a milky drink popular South America that contains caffeine and is made from dried leaves 2. an evergreen tree grown for its leaves, which are used to make maté. Native to: South America. Latin name: *Ilex paraguariensis.* [Early 18C. Via Spanish < Quechua *mati*]

mat·e·lote /mátt'l ŏt, maátə lŏt/ *n* a chunky fish stew made with wine [Early 18C. Via French, "sailor" < Middle Dutch *mattenoot* "bed companion"]

ma·ter /máytər/ *n UK* same as **mother**[1] *n* (sense 1) (*dated informal or humorous*) [Late 16C. < Latin]

ORIGIN The Latin word *mater* "mother," from which *mater* is derived, is also the source of English *madrigal, material, maternal, matriculate, matrimony, matrix, matron,* and *matter.* Its Indo-European ancestor in turn gave rise to English *mammal, metropolis,* and *mother*[1].

ma·ter·fa·mil·i·as /màytər fə míllee ass/ *n* a woman described in her role as head of a household or as the mother of her children (*formal*) [Mid-18C. < Latin, "mother of the family"]

ma·te·ri·al /mə teéree əl/ *n* 1. FABRIC woven flat cloth or fabric 2. SOMETHING USED IN MAKING ITEMS the substance used to make things 3. INFORMATION information such as facts, notes, and research used in the making of a book, movie, or other work 4. SOMEBODY SUITABLE somebody regarded in terms of his or her suitability to perform a particular job or task ○ *She's certainly executive material.* ■ **ma·te·ri·als** *npl* EQUIPMENT the tools and other things needed to perform a particular task ■ *adj* 1. PHYSICAL relating to or consisting of solid physical matter ○ *the material universe* 2. WORLDLY relating to physical well-being rather than emotional or spiritual well-being ○ *material comforts* 3. PERTINENT relevant or important 4. LAW IMPORTANT IN COURT crucial to the outcome of a court case or to the validity of a legal document ○ *a material witness* 5. PHILOSOPHY OF CONTENT NOT FORM relating to the substance of reasoning rather than the form it takes [14C. Via French *matériel* < late Latin *materialis* < Latin *materia* (see MATTER)] —**ma·te·ri·al·i·ty** /mə teéree állətee/ *n*

ma·te·ri·al·ism /mə teéree ə lìzzəm/ *n* 1. devotion to material wealth and possessions at the expense of spiritual or intellectual values 2. the philosophical theory that physical matter is the only reality and that psychological states such as emotions, reason, thought, and desire will eventually be explained as physical functions

ma·te·ri·al·ist /mə teéree əlist/ *n* 1. somebody who values material wealth and possessions rather than spiritual or intellectual things 2. a supporter of the philosophical theory that physical matter is the only reality and that psychological states can be explained as physical functions ■ *adj* same as **materialistic**

ma·te·ri·al·is·tic /mə teéree ə lístik/ *adj* concerned with material wealth and possessions at the expense of spiritual or intellectual values —**ma·te·ri·al·is·ti·cal·ly** *adv*

ma·te·ri·al·ize /mə teéree ə lìz/ (**-ized, -iz·ing, -iz·es**) *v* 1. *vi* BECOME REAL to become real or become fact 2. *vi* APPEAR to appear suddenly, as if out of nowhere 3. *vti* ASSUME PHYSICAL FORM to assume a physical form, or cause a supposed ghost or spirit to assume a physical form —**ma·te·ri·al·i·za·tion** /mə teéree əli záysh'n/ *n*

ma·te·ri·al·ly /mə teéree əlee/ *adv* 1. in a real sense or to a significant degree 2. in terms of material wealth and possessions

ma·te·ri·als sci·ence *n* the study of the features and applications of materials such as metals, plastics, and ceramics as used in science and technology

ma·té·ri·el /mə teéree él/, **ma·te·ri·el** *n* the supplies, weapons, and equipment associated with a military force [Early 19C. < French (see MATERIAL)]

ma·ter·nal /mə túrn'l/ *adj* 1. OF OR LIKE MOTHER belonging or relating to motherhood, a mother, or mothers in general ○ *maternal pride* 2. CARING kind, caring, and protective in a motherly way ○ *a very maternal person* 3. ON OR FROM MOTHER'S SIDE relating to or inherited from the mother or the mother's side of a family ○ *my maternal grandfather* [15C. < French *maternel* < Latin *maternus* < *mater* "mother"] —**ma·ter·nal·ism** *n* —**ma·ter·nal·is·tic** /mə tùrn'l ístik/ *adj* —**ma·ter·nal·ly** *adv*

ma·ter·ni·ty /mə túrnətee/ *n* 1. TIME DURING OR AFTER PREGNANCY the period during pregnancy or around the time of childbirth (*usually used in combination*) ○ *maternity clothes* 2. MOTHERHOOD the condition of being a mother (*usually used in combination*) 3. MOTHERLY CHARACTERISTICS the characteristics and emotions traditionally associated with being a mother, e.g., loving kindness and protectiveness 4. HOSPITAL SECTION CARING FOR NEWBORNS a ward, floor, or other section of a hospital where mothers and newborn babies are cared for [Early 17C. < French *maternité* < Latin *maternus* (see MATERNAL)]

ma·ter·ni·ty leave *n* paid or unpaid leave from work that a woman is entitled to take before, at, and after the time that she gives birth to or adopts a child

mat·ey /máytee/ *adj* (**-i·er, -i·est**) *UK* friendly, especially in a way that is familiar or seems insincere ■ *n* used by a man to address another man he does not know and, usually, feels hostile toward (*informal*) —**mat·i·ness** *n*

math /math/ *n* mathematics (*informal*) [Late 19C. Shortening]

math. *abbr* 1. mathematical 2. mathematically 3. mathematician 4. mathematics

math·e·mat·ic /màthə máttik/ *adj* same as **mathematical** (*archaic or literary*) ■ *n* same as **mathematics** (*archaic*) [14C. Directly or via French *mathématique* < Latin *mathematicus* < Greek *mathēmat-* "something learned," related to *manthanein* "learn"]

math·e·mat·i·cal /màthə máttik'l/ *adj* 1. OF MATHEMATICS belonging to, relating to, or used in mathematics 2. ACCURATE as accurate as if calculated by mathematics ○ *crafted the strategy with mathematical precision* 3. WORKED OUT BY MATHEMATICS calculated or proved by mathematics ○ *It's a mathematical certainty that two numbers in the set will be the same.* —**math·e·mat·i·cal·ly** *adv*

math·e·mat·i·cal ex·pec·ta·tion *n* STATS same as **expected value**

math·e·mat·i·cal in·duc·tion *n* MATH same as **induction** (sense 9)

math·e·ma·ti·cian /màthəmə tísh'n/ *n* a student or expert in mathematics, or somebody whose job involves mathematics

math·e·mat·ics /màthə máttiks/ *n* the study of the relationships among numbers, shapes, and quantities. It uses signs, symbols, and proofs and includes arithmetic, algebra, calculus, geometry, and trigonometry. (*takes a singular verb*) ■ *npl* the calculations involved in a process, estimate, or plan (*takes a plural verb*) ○ *It's a simple idea, though the mathematics of it are very complex.*

math·e·ma·tize /máthəmə tìz/ (**-tized, -tiz·ing, -tiz·es**) *vt* to consider something in, or reduce it to, purely mathematical terms —**math·e·ma·ti·za·tion** /màthə məti záysh'n/ *n*

Ma·ther /má<u>th</u>ər/, **Cotton** (1663–1728) American puritan minister and theologian. He published works on witchcraft, ethics, religion, natural history, medicine, and science, and championed inoculations against smallpox. Increase Mather was his father.

> "I write the wonders of the Christian religion, flying from the depravations of Europe, to the American strand: and, assisted by the Holy Author of that religion…I report the wonderful displays of His infinite power, wisdom, goodness, and faithfulness, wherewith his Divine Providence hath irradiated an Indian wilderness."
>
> [Cotton Mather, *Magnalia Christi Americana*; 1702]

Ma·ther, Increase (1639–1723) American Puritan minister. The father of Cotton Mather, he was president of Harvard College (1685–1701). He campaigned against the prevailing witchcraft hysteria of the day.

Math·ew·son /máthyooss'n/, **Christy** (1880–1925) US baseball player. He was the dominant pitcher in baseball throughout his career with the New York Giants (1901–16). Full name **Mathewson, Christopher.** Known as **Big Six**

math·lete /máth leèt/ *n* a student who competes in the International Mathematical Olympiad [Blend of MATH + ATHLETE]

~~mathmatics~~ incorrect spelling of **mathematics**

maths /maths/ (*informal*) *n, npl UK* same as **mathematics** [Early 20C. Contraction]

Ma·thu·ra /mŭttərə/ city in north central India, on the Yamuna River. Population: 319,235 (2001).

Ma·til·da /mə tíldə/ (1102–67) English princess. Though she was the daughter and acknowledged heir of Henry I of England, the throne was seized by her cousin Stephen, and she was never crowned queen.

ma·til·i·ja pop·py /mə tíllee haà-/ *n* a perennial plant of the poppy family. Flowers: single, large, white. Native to: California, Mexico. Latin name: *Romneya coulteri.* [After *Matilija* Canyon in California]

mat·in /mátt'n/, **mat·in·al** /mátt'nəl/ *adj* belonging or relating to matins, or taking place during matins [13C. < French *matines* (see MATINS)]

mat·i·née /màtt'n áy/, **mat·i·nee** *n* a performance of a play, concert, or motion picture that is given during the day, especially in the afternoon, often with cheaper seats than the evening performance [Mid-19C. < French, "morning" < *matin*, singular of *matines* (see MATINS)]

mat·i·née i·dol *n* an actor who is particularly attractive to women, especially a good-looking leading man in movies of the 1930s and 1940s (*dated*)

mat·ins /mátt'nz/ *n* 1. *also* **Mat·ins** MORNING LITURGY in the Roman Catholic Church, the morning hours of the divine office 2. MORNING PRAYER in the Church of England, the ceremony of morning prayer 3. HOURS BEFORE VIGIL in some Roman Catholic monastic communities, the hours before a vigil 4. DAWN CHORUS a morning song, especially one sung by birds (*literary*) [13C. < French *matines* < Latin *matutinus* "of the morning" < *Matuta* "goddess of dawn"]

Henri Matisse: photographed in 1948 working on his paper cutouts

Ma·tisse /mə teéss/, **Henri** (1869–1954) French artist. A leader of the fauve group from 1905, and an influential 20th-century artist, he used bold color to create rhythmic forms and a flat perspective, later working with brightly colored paper cutouts on canvas. Full name **Matisse, Henri Émile Benoît**

> "An old brush has vitality, it's a brush that has lived, that has had a life of its own."
> [Henri Matisse. Quoted in *Matisse, Picasso, Miro*, Rosamond Bernier; 1992]

mat·jes her·ring /máatyəss-/, **maat·jes her·ring** *n* a fillet or fillets of herring, especially of a young herring that has not spawned, that is lightly salted, usually sweetened and flavored, and eaten raw [Partial translation of Dutch *maatjesharing* "maiden's herring" < *maatjes* "maiden's" (from its use for young herring) + *haring* "herring"]

Mat·o Gros·so /màttō gróssō/ state in southwestern Brazil. Capital: Cuiabá. Population: 2,235,832 (1996). Area: 350,120 sq. mi./906,806 sq. km.

Ma·to·po Hills /mə tṓpō-/ region of granite hills in southwestern Zimbabwe. Area: 1,250 sq. mi./3,240 sq. km.

~~matress~~ incorrect spelling of **mattress**

matri- *prefix* mother, maternal ○ *matriarchy* ○ *matrilineal* [< Latin *matr-*, stem of *mater* "mother"]

ma·tri·arch /máytree àark/ *n* **1. WOMAN HEAD OF FAMILY** a woman who is recognized as being the head of a family, community, or people **2. STRONG SENIOR WOMAN** a woman, usually a grandmother, who is highly respected by her family and to whom the family turns for advice and help **3. WOMAN IN POWERFUL POSITION** a woman who holds a position of dominance, authority, or respect [Early 17C. < Latin *matr-* "mother," after *patriarch*] —**ma·tri·ar·chal** /màytree àark'l/ *adj*

ma·tri·ar·chy /máytree àarkee/ (*plural* **-chies**) *n* **1. SOCIAL ORDER WHERE WOMEN HAVE POWER** a form of social order where women are in charge and are recognized as the heads of families, with power, lineage, and inheritance passing, where possible, from mothers to daughters **2.** *also* **ma·tri·ar·chate** /-àarkət/ **COMMUNITY WHERE WOMEN HAVE POWER** a community, society, or social group that is based on matriarchy **3. ORGANIZATION WHERE WOMEN HAVE POWER** an organization or government where women have power [Late 19C. After PATRIARCHY]

ma·tri·ces SCI plural of **matrix**

mat·ri·cide /máttrə sìd/ *n* **1.** the act of murdering your own mother **2.** somebody who kills his or her own mother [Late 16C. Directly or via French < Latin *matricidium* < *matr-* "mother"] —**mat·ri·ci·dal** /màttrə sìd'l/ *adj*

mat·ri·cli·nous /màttrə klīnəss/ *adj* having obvious characteristics that are inherited predominantly from the woman parent

ma·tric·u·la con·su·lar /matrì kŏolə kon sŏo láar/, **ma·tric·u·la** *n* an identity card with information about, and a photograph of the bearer, issued by Mexican consulates to Mexican nationals without drivers' licenses and Social Security numbers who work in the United States [< Spanish *matrícula* "register, roll" + *consular* "consular"]

ma·tric·u·lant /mə tríkyələnt/ *n* EDUC same as **matriculate** [Mid-19C. < medieval Latin *matriculant-*, present participle of *matriculare* (see MATRICULATE)]

ma·tric·u·late *v* /mə tríkyə làyt/ (**-lat·ed, -lat·ing, -lates**) **1.** *vt* **ADMIT SOMEBODY AS STUDENT** to admit a student to membership of a college or university **2.** *vi* **BE ENROLLED AS STUDENT** to be enrolled at a college or university, after meeting the academic standard required to be accepted for a course of further education ■ *n* /mə tríkyələt, -làyt/ **SOMEBODY ENROLLED** somebody who has matriculated [Late 16C. < medieval Latin *matriculat-*, past participle of *matriculare* < *matricula* "little list" < *matrix* (see MATRIX)] —**ma·tric·u·la·tion** /mə trìkyə láysh'n/ *n*

mat·ri·lin·e·age /màttrə línnee ij/ *n* **1.** the line of genealogical relationship or descent that follows the women's side of a family **2.** a group of people related by descent through mothers

mat·ri·lin·e·al /màttrə línnee əl/ *adj* **1. FEMALE** describes the line of genealogical relationship or descent that follows the female side of a family **2. RELATED THROUGH MOTHERS** describes a group that is related by descent through mothers **3. COMING THROUGH WOMEN'S LINE** inherited or traced through the women's line of descent —**mat·ri·lin·e·al·ly** *adv*

mat·ri·lo·cal /màttrə lṓk'l/ *adj* **1.** describes a form of marriage in which, after the wedding, the bridegroom moves to his new wife's family home **2.** describes a culture in which young men live with their brides' families after marriage —**mat·ri·lo·cal·ly** *adv*

mat·ri·mo·ni·al /màttrə mṓnee əl/ *adj* belonging or relating to marriage or to a particular marriage [15C. Directly or via French < Latin *matrimonialis* < *matrimonium* (see MATRIMONY)] —**mat·ri·mo·ni·al·ly** *adv*

mat·ri·mo·ny /máttrə mṑnee/ *n* **1.** the state or condition of being married **2.** the religious ceremony of marriage [13C. Directly or via Anglo-Norman *matrimonie* < Latin *matrimonium* "state of motherhood" (because of the association of marriage with parenthood) < *matr-* "mother"]

mat·ri·mo·ny vine *n* a sometimes thorny bush, some species of which are cultivated for their orange or red berries. Native to: Europe, Asia. Genus: *Lycium.*

ma·trix /máytriks/ (*plural* **-tri·ces** /-tri seez/ or **-trix·es**) *n* **1. ARRANGEMENT OF CONNECTED THINGS** an arrangement of parts that shows how they are interconnected **2. SUBSTANCE CONTAINING SOMETHING** a substance in which something is embedded or enclosed **3. SITUATION IN WHICH SOMETHING DEVELOPS** a situation or set of circumstances that allows or encourages the origin, development, or growth of something ○ *The matrix of video and computers is producing new forms of art.* **4. TISSUE-FORMING SUBSTANCE** the substance that exists between cells and from which tissue such as cartilage and bone develops **5. SOIL OR ROCK CONTAINING SOMETHING** the soil or rock in which something such as a fossil, crystal, or mineral is embedded **6. MAIN PART OF ALLOY** the main metal component in an alloy **7. ARRANGEMENT OF MATHEMATICAL ELEMENTS** a rectangular array of mathematical elements, e.g., the coefficients of linear equations, whose rows and columns can be combined with those of other arrays to solve problems **8. NETWORK OF CIRCUIT PARTS** in computing, a network of circuit parts such as transistors and resistors **9. SURROUNDING MASS OF MATERIAL** a bed or surround of material that gives protection or absorbs a force [14C. Directly or via French *matrice* < Latin *matrix* "womb," later "list" < *matr-* "mother"]

ma·trix sen·tence *n* the main clause in a complex sentence

matro- *prefix* ANTHROP same as **matri-**

ma·tro·cli·nous /màttrə klīnəss/ **ma·tro·cli·nal** /-klīnəl/ *adj* GENETICS same as **matriclinous**

ma·tron /máytrən/ *n* **1. MATURE WOMAN** a woman, especially a married woman of middle age or later, who has had children and is thought of as being mature, sensible, and of good social standing **2.** *UK* **SUPERVISOR** a woman in charge of the medical and housekeeping arrangements in an institution such as a boarding school **3. WOMAN WARDEN** a woman who is a warden in a women's correctional institution **4.** *UK* **HEAD NURSE** a woman who is head of the nursing staff in a hospital, nursing home, or other medical institution, equivalent to a nursing director (*not in technical use*) [14C. Directly or via French *matrone* < Latin *matrona* < *matr-* "mother"]

ma·tron·ly /máytrənlee/ *adj* **1. LIKE MATRON** having qualities associated with a matron, especially dignity and placidity **2. MATURE AND FULL-FIGURED** mature and plump, especially with a large bosom **3. OF MATRON** relating to or characteristic of a matron ○ *matronly duties*

ma·tron of hon·or *n* a married woman who is the bride's chief attendant at a wedding

mat·ro·nym·ic /màttrə nímmik/, **met·ro·nym·ic** /mèttrə-, meetrə-/ *n* a name derived from a mother or a matrilineal ancestor [Late 18C. < Latin *matr-* "mother"]

mat sal·leh /màt sa láy/ *n Malaysia* a white foreigner [Early 20C. < Malay, alteration of English *mad sailor*, because drunken sailors were the Westerners that most Malayans had contact with]

mat·su·ri /mat sŏoree/ (*plural same* or **-ris**) *n* in Okinawa, a summer fair or festival [Early 18C. < Japanese]

ma·tsu·ta·ke /maatsoo taakee/, **ma·tsu·ta·ke mush·room** *n* an edible dark brown mushroom with a cinnamon fragrance. Native to: Japan. Latin name: *Tricholoma matsutake.* [< Japanese, "pine mushroom"]

Ma·tsu·ya·ma /maatsŏo yaamə/ industrial city in southwestern Japan, on the island of Shikoku. Population: 473,039 (2002).

matt /mat/ *Can, UK* PHOTOGRAPHY *n* same as **mat**[2] *n* (sense 2) ■ *adj* same as **mat**[2]

Matt. BIBLE Matthew

mat·tar /múttər/ *n S Asia* green peas [< Hindi]

matte[1] /mat/ *adj* ARTS another spelling of **mat**[2] *n* (sense 2), *adj*

matte[2] /mat/ *n* **1.** a mixture of metal sulfides formed during the smelting of sulfide ores such as ores of copper or nickel **2.** a mask used for obscuring part of an image so that another image can be put on top of the original [Mid-19C. < French, form of *mat* "dull"]

mat·ted /máttəd/ *adj* **1.** forming a thick tangled mass **2.** covered with mats or matting

mat·ter /máttər/ *n* **1. SOMETHING UNDER CONSIDERATION** something that is being considered or needs to be dealt with ○ *This is a matter for serious thought.* **2. CAUSE OF PROBLEM** the reason why something is wrong or not working properly, or why somebody is annoyed, upset, or not feeling well ○ *What's the matter?* ○ *There's something the matter with the alarm.* **3. SUBSTANCE** a substance or material of a particular kind ○ *reading matter* **4. SUBSTANCE CONSTITUTING UNIVERSE** the material substance of the universe that has mass, occupies space, and is convertible to energy **5. PRINTED TEXT** text or other material that is printed ○ *cheaper rates for printed matter* **6. SUBJECT OF SPEECH OR WRITING** the subject that is dealt with in speech or writing, as opposed to its presentation **7. WHAT IS PERCEIVED BY MIND** in Cartesian philosophy, something that is extended in space and persists through time, and is contrasted with mind **8. SOMETHING TO BE PROVED** a case to be proved or resolved in a court of law ○ *Who is the defendant in this matter?* **9. BODILY DISCHARGE** something that is discharged from the body, e.g., pus ■ **mat·ters** *npl* **CIRCUMSTANCES** the current situation or circumstances ○ *Getting angry will make matters worse.* ■ *vi* (**-tered, -ter·ing, -ters**) **1. HAVE IMPORTANCE** to be important ○ *The only thing that matters is for you to get better.* **2. MAKE DIFFERENCE** to make a difference ○ *It doesn't matter how you tell her, just make sure she knows.* [12C. Directly or via Anglo-Norman *mater(i)e*, French *matière* < Latin *materia* "timber, stuff" < *mater* "mother"] ◇ **a matter of opinion** a subject about which there are varying views ◇ **as a matter of course** in accordance with normal procedure or expected events ◇ **for that matter** as far as that is concerned ◇ **no mat·ter 1.** regardless of ○ *No matter how many we distribute, there are never enough.* **2.** it is not important ◇ **no matter what** used to express determination in the face of uncertain circumstances or consequences

SYNONYMS See *subject.*

Popperfoto

Matterhorn

Mat·ter·horn /máttər hàwrn/ mountain in the Pennine Alps, on the Italian-Swiss border. Height: 14,692 ft./4,478 m.

mat·ter of fact *n* **1.** something that is true and that cannot be denied ○ *It's a matter of fact that our scores improved.* **2.** a question to be decided by a court of law that involves deciding on the truth of a statement, rather than interpreting a point of law or forming an opinion ◇ **as a matter of fact 1.** used to add a statement that completes what you are saying or emphasizes its truth **2.** used to contradict what somebody else has said or to express disagreement

mat·ter-of-fact *adj* **1.** straightforward and not fanciful or emotional ○ *She told us the bad news in a chillingly matter-of-fact way.* **2.** dealing with facts and not emotions or opinions ○ *a matter-of-fact account of the incident* —**mat·ter-of-fact·ly** *adv* —**mat·ter-of-fact·ness** *n*

mat·ter of law *n* a question to be decided by a court of law that involves the interpretation of a point of law

mat·ter·y /máttəree/ *adj* secreting or discharging pus

matte shot *n* in filmmaking, a visual effect that is achieved by masking out part of an image using a matte and superimposing another image so that it combines with the rest of the original

Mat·thau /mát ow/, **Walter** (1920–2000) US actor. He is best known for his part in both stage and movie versions of *The Odd Couple* (1965, 1968). He won an Academy Award for *The Fortune Cookie* (1966). Born **Matuschanskayasky, Walter**

Mat·thew /máthyoo/ *n* a book of the Bible, the first of the Gospels in which the life and teachings of Jesus Christ are described, traditionally attributed to St. Matthew. See table at **Bible**

Mat·thew /máthyoo/, **St.** (*fl* A.D. 1st century) one of the 12 apostles of Jesus Christ. By tradition he is considered to be the author of the first Gospel in the Bible.

Mat·thi·as /mə thī́ əss/ disciple chosen to replace Judas as one of the 12 apostles of Jesus Christ (Acts 1:15–26)

Mat·thi·as Cor·vin·us /-kawr vī́nəss/ (1443–90) king of Hungary. His acquisition of Austria and various provinces made him a powerful ruler.

mat·ti·fy /máttə fī/ (**-fied, -fy·ing, -fies**) *vt* to remove or remedy oiliness or shininess of the complexion [< MAT²]

mat·ting[1] /mátting/ *n* **1.** MATERIAL WOVEN FROM NATURAL FIBERS a coarse material woven from natural fibers. Use: mats, coverings. ○ *coconut matting* **2.** MATS mats, taken collectively ○ *Matting is integral to Japanese interior design.* **3.** LAYER OF NATURAL MATERIALS a bed or layer formed by natural materials, e.g., by fallen leaves in a forest ○ *We walked through the pines on a matting of needles.* **4.** MAKING MATS the process of making a mat or mats [Early 17C. < MAT¹]

mat·ting[2] /mátting/ *n* **1.** a surface that is dull or without sheen **2.** the process of giving a surface, especially a metallic one, a dull finish [Late 17C. < MAT²]

mat·tock /máttək/ *n* a tool like a pickax with one end of its blade flattened at right angles to its handle, used for loosening soil and cutting through roots [Pre-12C. Origin ?]

mat·tress /máttrəss/ *n* **1.** PAD FOR SLEEPING ON a large pad on which to sleep, usually containing springs or a soft springy filling. Some modern mattresses have electronic controls that allow them to tilt into different positions. **2.** INFLATABLE PAD a large pad that can be filled with air or water and used as a bed or for floating on, e.g., in a pool **3.** FOUNDATION FOR BUILDING a slab or platform used as a foundation for a building [13C. < Old French *materas* < Arabic *al-matraḥ* "cushion"; from the practice of sleeping on cushions]

mat·u·rate /máchə ràyt/ (**-rat·ed, -rat·ing, -rates**) *vti* to mature, ripen, or develop, or develop or ripen something [Mid-16C. Either < Latin *maturat-*, past participle of *maturare* < *maturus* "ripe" or back-formation < MATURATION] —**mat·u·ra·tive** *adj*

mat·u·ra·tion /màchə ráysh'n/ *n* **1.** PROGRESS TO MATURITY the process of becoming mature, ripe, or more developed **2.** PROCESS OF MAKING SOMETHING MORE MATURE the process of ripening or developing something or of making it more mature **3.** PROCESS OF CELL DEVELOPMENT the process in which immature cells in the ovary and testes develop into ova and spermatozoa [14C. Directly or via French < medieval Latin *maturation-* < *maturare* < *maturus* "ripe"] —**mat·u·ra·tion·al** *adj*

mat·u·ra·tion di·vi·sion *n* the process of cell division by which the ova and spermatozoa are developed

ma·ture /mə chóor/ *adj* **1.** ACTING OR SEEMING LIKE ADULT showing the mental, emotional, or physical characteristics associated with a fully developed adult person ○ *Philip is only 12 but he's very tall and already quite mature.* **2.** EXPERIENCED showing qualities gained by development and experience ○ *in the author's mature writings* **3.** ADULT adult or fully grown ○ *a mature animal capable of breeding* **4.** FULLY DEVELOPED describes an organism that is fully developed to a complete or final stage **5.** OLD AND OF GOOD FLAVOR old enough to have acquired the maximum flavor ○ *mature cheddar* **6.** IN LATER LIFE no longer young ○ *the wisdom shown by the mature dramatist* ○ *The role is that of a mature woman with a successful career behind her.* **7.** FOR ADULTS made up of or suitable only for adults ○ *Because of the subject, this movie is recommended for mature audiences only.* **8.** INVOLVING SERIOUS THOUGHT involving or reached by a period of serious thought ○ *On mature reflection, I feel it would be wiser to sell.* **9.** DUE FOR PAYMENT describes a financial arrangement that has reached a previously set or mutually agreed-on time limit and is therefore due for payment or repayment ○ *mature bonds* **10.** NOT SUBJECT TO MAJOR CHANGE no longer subject to the instability of early development or expansion ○ *Hydroelectric power is a mature industry in the region.* **11.** IN MIDDLE OF EROSION CYCLE describes a natural feature or landform that is in the middle stages of an erosion cycle ■ *v* (**-tured, -tur·ing, -tures**) **1.** *vti* DEVELOP to go through a developmental process, or make something or somebody go through a developmental process ○ *Children begin to mature at different ages.* **2.** *vi* FALL DUE FOR PAYMENT to reach a previously set or mutually agreed-on time limit and therefore fall due for payment or repayment (*refers to financial arrangements*) ○ *When will those Treasury bonds mature?* **3.** *vti* DEVELOP INTO SOMETHING FINISHED to become fully worked out, or work something out fully, especially through long consideration ○ *The plan had matured over the intervening months.* [14C. Directly or via French < Latin *maturus* "ripe"] —**ma·ture·ly** *adv* —**ma·ture·ness** *n*

ma·ture-on·set di·a·be·tes *n* MED same as **non-insulin-dependent diabetes**

ma·ture stu·dent *n* a student aged 25 or over who has gone into higher education later than is usual, especially after working or raising a family

ma·tur·i·ty /mə chóorətee/ *n* **1.** FULL GROWTH OR DEVELOPMENT the state of being fully grown or developed ○ *Girls tend to reach maturity earlier than boys.* **2.** MATURE STATE the condition of being ripe, fully aged, or fully grown, especially mentally or emotionally ○ *I'm amazed at the maturity shown by these young people.* **3.** TIME FOR REPAYMENT the time when a financial arrangement falls due for payment or repayment **4.** READINESS FOR REPAYMENT the state of a financial arrangement when it falls due for payment or repayment **5.** MATURE STATE OF LANDFORM the stage in the development of a landform at which there is maximum relief and drainage is well developed [15C. Directly or via French *maturité* < Latin *maturitas* < *maturus* "ripe"]

ma·tu·ti·nal /mə tóot'nəl, màchə tī́n'l/ *adj* relating to or happening in the morning or the early part of the day (*formal*) [Mid-16C. < late Latin *matutinalis* < *Matuta*, goddess of the dawn] —**ma·tu·ti·nal·ly** *adv*

MATV *abbr* master antenna television

mat·zo /maátsə/, **mat·zoh** *n* (*plural* **-zos** or **-zoth** /maáts òt/; *plural* **-zohs** or **-zoth**) unleavened bread traditionally eaten during Passover in commemoration of the unleavened bread eaten by the ancient Hebrews escaping from slavery in Egypt ■ *adj* made from or like matzo, or used to make matzo ○ *matzo meal* ○ *matzo balls* [Mid-19C. Via Yiddish *matse* < Hebrew *maṣṣāh*]

mat·zo ball *n* a dumpling made from matzo meal

mau·by /máwbee/ *n Carib* a drink made from the bark of a tree of the buckthorn family [Late 18C. < Carib *mabi* "sweet potato (drink)"]

maud·lin /máwdlin/ *adj* overly or tearfully sentimental, especially because affected by alcohol [Early 16C. Via French *Madeleine* "Madeleine" < Greek *Mariaē Magdalēnē* "Mary Magdalene," because she was commonly represented in medieval art weeping in repentance] —**maud·lin·ly** *adv* —**maud·lin·ness** *n*

Maugham /mawm/, **W. Somerset** (1874–1965) British author best known for his short stories and novels such as *Of Human Bondage* (1915). Full name **Maugham, William Somerset**

> "Impropriety is the soul of wit."
> [W. Somerset Maugham, *The Moon and Sixpence*; 1919]

> "I [Death] was astonished to see him in Baghdad. I had an appointment with him tonight in Samarra."
> [W. Somerset Maugham, *Sheppey*, Act 3; 1933]

Mau·i /mów ee/ second largest island of Hawaii, consisting of two oval peninsulas connected by an isthmus. Population: 134,007 (2002 estimate). Area: 727 sq. mi./1,884 sq. km.

maul /mawl/ *vt* (**mauled, maul·ing, mauls**) **1.** ASSAULT SOMEBODY to beat, batter, or tear at a person or animal ○ *He got mauled in the ring by a better boxer.* **2.** HANDLE SOMEBODY OR SOMETHING ROUGHLY to handle somebody or something too roughly or clumsily ○ *Children may need to be taught not to maul their pets.* **3.** CRITICIZE SOMEBODY OR SOMETHING FIERCELY to criticize somebody or something severely or mercilessly ○ *Despite being a box-office success, her new movie was mauled by the critics.* **4.** SPLIT WOOD to split wood using a large heavy hammer and a wedge ■ *n* **1.** PILE-DRIVING HAMMER a large heavy hammer, usually with a wooden head, used for driving in piles, stakes, or wedges **2.** LOG-SPLITTING HAMMER a heavy hammer that has one side of the head shaped like a wedge, making it suitable for splitting logs or wood [13C. < French *mail* "hammer" < Latin *malleus*] —**maul·er** *n*

Maul·din /máwldin/, **Bill** (1921–2003) US cartoonist. He is known for his cartoons of World War II seen from the combat soldier's point of view, particularly via his two characters Willie and Joe. Full name **Mauldin, William Henry**

> "I feel like a fugitive from th' law of averages."
> [Bill Mauldin, *Up Front*; 1944]

maul·vi /mówl wee/ (*plural* **-vis**), **moul·vi** *n* a respected Muslim teacher or highly educated man, especially somebody with special knowledge of Islamic law [Early 17C. Via Urdu < Arabic *mawlawī* < *mawlā* "mullah, master"]

Mau Mau /mów mòw/ *npl* a secret Kenyan organization set up in 1952 with the objective of forcing European settlers from the land and ending British rule in Kenya [Mid-20C. < Kikuyu]

mau-mau /mow mów/ (**mau-maued, mau-mau·ing, mau-maus**) *vt* to confront somebody such as a public official or bureaucrat with the intent of gaining concessions, benefits, or advantage through intimidation (*slang*) [Late 20C. < MAU MAU]

Mau·na Ke·a /mòwnə káy ə, mawnə-/ dormant volcano in Hawaii, on northern Hawaii Island. It is the highest peak in the state. Height: 13,796 ft./4,205 m.

Mau·na Lo·a /-lṓ ə/ active volcano on Hawaii Island. It is one of the world's largest volcanoes. Height: 13,680 ft./4,170 m.

maund /mawnd/ *n* a unit of weight formerly used in South Asia, with a value that varies from place to place but is often equal to 82 lb./37 kg [Late 16C. < Arabic *mann*]

maun·der /máwndər/ (**-dered, -der·ing, -ders**) *v* **1.** *vti* to talk or say something in a vague, rambling, or incoherent way **2.** *vi* to move or act in a vague or aimless way [Early 17C. Origin ?]

maun·dy /máwndee/ *n* a ceremony held in some Christian churches on Maundy Thursday that involves an actual or symbolic washing of people's feet in commemoration of Jesus Christ's washing of his disciples' feet (John 13:3–34) [13C. < Old French *mandé* < Latin *mandatum (novum)* "(new) commandment," first words of an antiphon sung in the ceremony]

Maun·dy Thurs·day *n* a Christian holy day marking the Last Supper. Date: Thursday before Easter Day.

Mau·pas·sant /mṓ pass aa, mṑ pass aáN/, **Guy de** (1850–93) French novelist and short-story writer. His short stories have been particularly influential and are written with a direct realism, portraying ordinary people in extraordinary situations. Full name **Maupassant, Henri René Albert Guy de**. See illustration on next page

> "The least thing contains something unknown. Let us find it."
> [Guy de Maupassant, *Pierre et Jean*; 1887]

Mau·riac /màwree yák/, **François** (1885–1970) French poet, novelist, and playwright. Much of his work,

Guy de Maupassant

colored by his Roman Catholicism, centers on moral conflict and psychological analysis.

Mau·ri·er ➧ **du Maurier, Dame Daphne**

Mauritania

Mau·ri·ta·ni·a /màwrə táynee ə/ country in northwestern Africa, on the Atlantic Ocean. It became independent from France in 1960. Language: Arabic, French. Currency: ouguiya. Capital: Nouakchott. Population: 2,912,584 (2003). Area: 398,000 sq. mi./1,031,000 sq. km. Official name **Islamic Republic of Mauritania** —**Mau·ri·ta·ni·an** *n, adj*

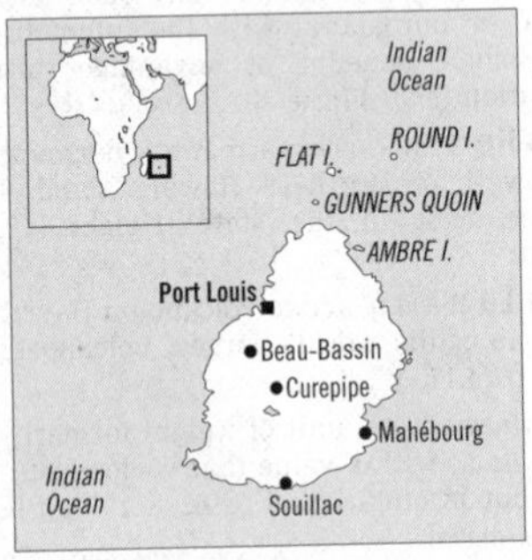

Mauritius

Mau·ri·tius /mə ríshəss/ island country in the southwestern Indian Ocean, east of Madagascar, consisting of the islands of Mauritius and Rodrigues and some islets. It became an independent member of the British Commonwealth in 1968 and a republic in 1992. Language: English. Currency: Mauritian rupee. Capital: Port Louis. Population: 1,189,825 (2001). Area: 788 sq. mi./2,040 sq. km. Official name **Republic of Mauritius** —**Mau·ri·tian** /mə rísh'n/ *n, adj*

mau·so·le·um /màwzə lée əm, màwssə-/ (*plural* **-le·ums** or **-le·a** /-lée ə/) *n* **1. TOMB** a large tomb, especially one that is ornately decorated or made from expensive stone **2. BUILDING CONTAINING TOMBS** a building, often a highly decorated or elaborate one, that houses a tomb or several tombs **3. GLOOMY INTERIOR** a large gloomy oppressive room or building ○ *a huge mausoleum of a library* [15C. Via Latin < Greek *Mausōleion* "tomb of Mausolus" (4C B.C. king of Caria in Asia Minor), built in 353 B.C. at Halicarnassus] —**mau·so·le·an** *adj*

mauve /mōv/ *n* a pale color between purple and blue or pink [Mid-19C. Via French < Latin *malva* "mallow plant"; from the color of its flowers] —**mauve** *adj*

mav /mav/, **MAV** *interj* especially in Internet communication, used to indicate an apology after inadvertently causing a problem as the result of an error [Probably < a personal name]

ma·ven /máyvən/, **ma·vin** *n* an expert or knowledgeable enthusiast [Mid-20C. Via Yiddish *meyvn* < Hebrew *mēḇīn* "somebody who understands"]

mav·er·ick /mávvərik, mávvrik/ *n* **1.** an independent thinker who refuses to conform to the accepted views on a subject **2.** an unbranded animal, especially a calf that has become separated from its mother and herd. By convention, it can become the property of whoever finds it and brands it. [Mid-19C. Probably after Samuel Augustus *Maverick* (1803–70), Texas cattle-owner]

ma·vin *n* another spelling of **maven**

mav·ing /mávving/ *n* especially in Internet communication, inadvertently creating confusion as the result of an error [< MAV]

ma·vis /máyviss/ *n* same as **song thrush** (*literary*) [14C. < French *mauvis*]

maw /maw/ *n* **1. ANIMAL'S MOUTH** the mouth, jaws, throat, or stomach of an animal, especially a carnivorous animal that devours food greedily **2. GREEDY PERSON'S MOUTH** the mouth, throat, or stomach of a greedy person (*informal*) **3. GAPING HOLE** anything that seems like a gaping hole that devours things or people ○ *the ravenous maw of readers' expectations* [Old English *maga* "stomach" < Germanic]

maw·ger /máwgər/, **maw·ga, maa·ga** /máagə/ *adj Carib* slim or lean [Late 20C. < Dutch *mager*]

mawk·ish /máwkish/ *adj* **1.** sentimental, especially in a contrived or off-putting way **2.** bland or unappetizing in taste or smell [Mid-17C. < *mawk* "maggot" < Old Norse *maðkr*] —**mawk·ish·ly** *adv* —**mawk·ish·ness** *n*

Maw·lid al-Na·bi /máwlid al náabee/ *n* in Islam, the celebrations marking the prophet Muhammad's birthday. Date: 12th day of Rabi I. [< Arabic, "birthday of the prophet"]

max /maks/ *adv* **AT MOST** as a maximum (*slang*) ○ *We were offered $200 max.* ■ *adj* **MOST** most or highest (*slang*) ○ *Turn up the volume to get the max effect.* ■ *n* **MAXIMUM** the maximum limit or amount of something (*informal*) ○ *I could lend you $100, but that's my max.* ■ *vi* (**maxed, max·ing, max·es**) **REACH HIGHEST LIMIT** to come to the point that it is impossible to exceed (*slang*) ○ *The car maxes at 120 mph.* [Mid-19C. Shortening of MAXIMUM]

max out *vti* to reach a limit in a personal attribute or ability, or reach the limit of a resource (*slang*) ○ *I maxed out my credit card last week.*

max. *abbr* maximum

max·i /máksee/ *n* **1. ANKLE-LENGTH PIECE OF CLOTHING** an ankle-length coat, skirt, or dress **2. MAXIMUM SECURITY PRISON** a maximum security prison (*informal*) ■ *adj* **ANKLE-LENGTH** used to describe an article of clothing that is ankle-length [Mid-20C. < MAXIMUM]

max·il·la /mak síllə/ (*plural* **-lae** /-lee/ or **-las**) *n* **1.** either of a pair of bones that are fused at the midline and together form the upper jawbone in vertebrates **2.** a mouthpart that is one of one or two pairs behind the mandibles of arthropods [Late 17C. Directly and via Old French *maxille* < Latin *maxilla* "little jaw" < *mala* "jaw"] —**max·il·lar·y** *adj*

max·il·li·ped /mak síllə pèd/ *n* one of the six specialized feeding appendages arranged in pairs and located just behind the maxillae on the heads of crustaceans [Mid-19C. < MAXILLA] —**max·il·li·ped·ar·y** /mak sìllə péddəree, -pedəree/ *adj*

max·il·lo·fa·cial /mak sìllō fáysh'l/ *adj* relating to, located in, or affecting the face in the region of the upper jaw [Early 20C. < MAXILLA]

max·im /máksim/ *n* **1.** a succinct or pithy saying that has some proven truth to it **2.** a general rule, principle, or truth [15C. Via French < medieval Latin *maxima (propositio)* "largest (proposition)," form of *maximus* (see MAXIMUM)]

Max·im /máksim/ *n* ARMS same as **Maxim gun**

Max·im /máksim/, **Sir Hiram** (1840–1916) US-born British engineer and inventor. He is best known for inventing the Maxim gun, an automatic machine gun.

max·i·ma plural of **maximum**

max·i·mal /máksim'l/ *adj* **1.** relating to or constituting a maximum **2.** the best or greatest possible —**max·i·mal·ly** *adv*

max·i·mal·ist /máksiməlist/ *n* an uncompromising person who is determined to achieve a political aim, directly if necessary [Early 20C. < MAXIMAL after Russian *maksimalist*] —**max·i·ma·list** *adj*

Max·i·mal·ist *n* a member of a Russian group that, in the early 20th century, advocated terrorist action to get rid of the tsar and the setting up of a temporary proletarian dictatorship

Max·im gun *n* an early single-barreled machine gun that was cooled by an outer casing containing water [Late 19C. After Sir Hiram MAXIM]

Max·i·mil·ian /màksi míllyən/ (1832–67) archduke of Austria. He was made emperor of Mexico by Napoleon III of France in 1863, but was executed by Mexican republicans.

Max·i·mil·ian I (1459–1519) Holy Roman Emperor. He made the Hapsburg dynasty a major power through diplomacy and marriage policy.

max·i·min /máksimin/ *n* **1.** in mathematics, the largest of a set of minimum values **2.** in game theory, a strategy of attempting to maximize the smallest possible advantage [Mid-20C. Blend of MAXIMUM + MINIMUM; modeled on MINIMAX]

max·i·mize /máksi mìz/ (**-mized, -miz·ing, -miz·es**) *vt* **1. INCREASE SOMETHING TO MAXIMUM** to make something as great as possible ○ *maximize the chances of success* **2. EMPHASIZE IMPORTANCE OF SOMETHING** to attach the greatest importance to something ○ *Historians maximize the treaty's benefits to trade and tend not to mention its political costs.* **3.** COMPUT **MAKE IMAGE LARGER** to increase the size of a computer image **4.** MATH **FIND LARGEST VALUE OF FUNCTION** in mathematics, to find or work out the largest value of a function —**max·i·mi·za·tion** /màksimi záysh'n/ *n* —**max·i·miz·er** *n*

max·i·mum /máksiməm/ *n* (*plural* **-ma** /-mə/ or **-mums**) **1. GREATEST POSSIBLE AMOUNT** the largest amount, number, extent, or degree possible or allowed ○ *The stadium seats a maximum of 60,000.* **2. LARGEST AMOUNT OR HIGHEST LEVEL REACHED** the largest amount or value or highest level that something variable can reach or reaches during a period ○ *Even at its maximum, the noise did not exceed legal levels.* **3. LARGEST NUMBER** the largest number in a mathematical set **4. GREATEST VALUE OF FUNCTION** in mathematics, the greatest value that a continuous function can attain over a specific interval **5. TIME OF GREATEST BRIGHTNESS OF STAR** the interval during which a variable star is most luminous **6. GREATEST MAGNITUDE OF STAR** the magnitude of a variable star at its greatest ■ *adj* **GREATEST POSSIBLE** of the greatest possible or permitted amount or value ○ *visual effects with maximum impact* ○ *Maximum occupancy in this building is 235.* ■ *adv* **AT MAXIMUM** at the greatest extent ○ *The hall seats 400 maximum.* [Mid-16C. Directly or via French < modern Latin, form of Latin *maximus* "greatest" < *magnus* "great"]

max·i·mum-se·cu·ri·ty *adj* protected or made secure by tight and elaborate security arrangements ○ *a maximum-security prison*

ma·xixe /mə shéesh, -shéeshə/ *n* **1.** a Brazilian dance performed in duple time **2.** the music for a maxixe [Early 20C. < Brazilian Portuguese]

max·well /máks wèl, mákswəl/ *n* the centimeter-gram-second unit of magnetic flux, equal to the flux over one square centimeter perpendicular to a magnetic field of one gauss. Symbol **Mx** [Late 19C. After James Clerk *Maxwell* (1831–79), Scottish physicist]

may[1] /may/ (**might** /mìt/, **may**) CORE MEANING: a modal verb indicating that something could be true, or could have happened, or will possibly happen in the future ○ *I may not be able to meet you.* ○ *He may have been working too hard.* ○ *A verdict may be announced today.*

modal v **1. INDICATES POSSIBILITY** indicates that something is possibly true ○ *That may be the best way to do it.* **2.** ⚠ **INDICATES THAT SOMETHING COULD HAPPEN** indicates that something could have happened, or could happen in the future ○ *The crash may well have been caused by faulty brakes.* ○ *The comet may be remembered best for its nonscientific impact.* **3. INDICATES PERMISSION** indicates that somebody is asking somebody for permission or giving somebody permission to do something (*formal*) ○ *"May I leave the table?" "No, you may not."* **4. INDICATES RIGHT** indicates that somebody has a legal or moral right to do something ○ *You may withdraw money from this* *account at any time.* **5. INDICATES REQUESTS OR SUGGESTIONS** indicates polite requests, suggestions, or offers ○ *May I remind you of our earlier agreement?* ○ *May I help you with that bag?* **6. INDICATES WISH** indicates that somebody wishes for something very strongly (*formal*) ○ *May God bless us, every one.* [Old English *mæg*, form of *magan* "be able" < Indo-European] ◇ **be that as it may** indicates that somebody wants to go on to a new topic after conceding the possible truth of a previous statement ○ *"He doesn't earn much money." "Be that as it may, he's been successful in what he set out to do."*

USAGE See *can*[1].

may[2] /may/ *n UK* PLANTS same as **may blossom** [< MAY; from the time it comes into flower]

May /may/ *n* in the Gregorian calendar, the fifth month of the year, lasting 31 days. See table at **calendar** [12C. Via French *mai* < Latin *Maius*, a form of *Maia* "Maia" (a fertility goddess)]

May, Cape /may/ cape at the southern tip of New Jersey, at the entrance to Delaware Bay

ma·ya /maá yə/ *n* **1.** in Hinduism, the material world, considered in reality to be an illusion **2.** in Hinduism, the ability to create illusion through supernatural, magical, or sacred power [Late 18C. < Sanskrit *māyā*] —**ma·yan** *adj*

Ma·ya[1] /maá yə/ (*plural same* or **-yas**) *n* **1.** a member of a Native American people of Central America and southern Mexico whose classical culture flourished between the 4th and the 8th centuries A.D. **2.** a Mayan language spoken in Mexico, Guatemala, and Belize. Native speakers: 500,000. [Early 19C. Via Spanish < Maya] —**Ma·ya** *adj*

Ma·ya[2] /maá yə/ *n* the mother of the Buddha, in Buddhist belief by a miraculous virgin birth

Ma·ya·güez /mī ə gwéz/ city and seaport in western Puerto Rico. Population: 100,371 (1990).

AKG London

Vladimir Mayakovsky

Ma·ya·kov·sky /maàyə káwfskee/, **Vladimir** (1893–1930) Russian poet and propagandist. He wrote propaganda for the Bolsheviks after the Russian Revolution, but later fell from favor and committed suicide. Full name **Mayakovsky, Vladimir Vladimirovich**

> "Today's poetry—is the poetry of strife. / Each word must, like a soldier in the army, be made of meat that is healthy, meat that is red! / Those who have it—join us!"
> [Vladimir Mayakovsky, "We Also Want Meat!"; 1914]

Ma·yan /maá yən/ *n* **1.** a member of the Maya people **2.** a group of Penutian languages spoken in Mexico, Guatemala, and Belize. Native speakers: 3 million. —**Ma·yan** *adj*

Ma·ya·pán /maá yaa paán/ ruined ancient Maya city in southeastern Mexico, in Yucatán State

May ap·ple *n* **1.** an oval yellowish fruit with edible pulp **2.** a poisonous plant of the barberry family that produces May apples. Flowers: single, white. Native to: eastern North America. Latin name: *Podophyllum peltatum*. [Because the fruit is produced in May]

may·be /máybee/ *adv* **1. PERHAPS** expresses uncertainty ○ *Maybe I'm being too optimistic, but I really think we can get the best players.* ○ *"Can I have a new bike?" "Maybe."* **2. NEITHER YES NOR NO** used to give a response that is neither yes nor no ○ *"So do you want to come with us or not?" "Well, maybe."* **3. INTRODUCES SUGGESTIONS** used to introduce advice or suggestions ○ *Maybe you should ask her what she means before you jump to conclusions.* **4. APPROXIMATELY** indicates an approximate estimation, e.g., of frequency or a number ○ *The coastal glacier gives off large icebergs maybe every three or four years.* ○ *The forests in this region are no more than 60, maybe 70, years old.* [14C. < *(it) may be*]

May bee·tle *n* INSECTS **1.** same as **June bug 2.** *UK* same as **cockchafer** [Because they appear around May]

may blos·som *n UK* the flower of the hawthorn

May bug *n* INSECTS **1.** same as **June bug 2.** *UK* same as **cockchafer** [See MAY BEETLE]

may·day /máy dày/ *n* the internationally recognized communications distress call, used especially by ships and aircraft [Early 20C. Representing the pronunciation of French *m'aider* in *venez m'aider* "come and help me!"]

May Day *n* **1.** traditionally, a day for celebrating the coming of spring. Date: May 1. **2.** a national holiday in some countries that marks the importance of working people. Date: May 1.

May·er /máy ər/, **Louis B.** (1885–1957) Russian-born US movie producer. He created and ran the Metro-Goldwyn-Mayer movie studio (1924–51). Born **Meir, Eliezer**

may·flow·er /máy flòwr/ (*plural* **-ers** or *same*) *n* **1.** a plant that flowers in May **2.** PLANTS same as **trailing arbutus**

may·fly /máy flī/ (*plural* **-flies**) *n* **1.** an insect that lives as an adult for only a few days, typically having two or four pairs of flimsy wings and two or three long slender tail appendages. The female lays her eggs in fresh water, where the larvae develop without a chrysalis stage. Order: Ephemeroptera. **2.** a fishing fly that looks like a mayfly [Mid-17C. < the mistaken belief that they appear only in May]

may·hap /máy hàp/ *adv* same as **perhaps** (*archaic*) [Mid-16C. < *it may hap* "it may happen"]

may·hem /máy hèm/ *n* **1.** absolute chaos or severe disruption ○ *Whenever the teacher left the room, it was mayhem.* **2.** LAW malicious injury that disfigures or disables a person [15C. Via Anglo-Norman *mahem*, Old French *mahaing* "mutilating injury" < assumed Vulgar Latin *mahagnare* "injure"]

may·ing /máy ing/, **May·ing** *n* May Day celebrations, or participation in them

may·n't /maynt/ *contr* may not

may·o /máy ō/ *n* same as **mayonnaise** (*informal*) [Mid-20C. Shortening]

May·o /máy ō/ county in Connacht Province, northwestern Republic of Ireland. Castlebar is the county town. Population: 111,524 (2002). Area: 2,084 sq. mi./5,398 sq. km.

Ma·yo /máy ō/, **William Worral** (1819–1911) US physician and surgeon. He ran St. Mary's Hospital in Minnesota, which later became the Mayo Clinic.

~~mayonaise~~ incorrect spelling of **mayonnaise**

may·on·naise /máy ə nàyz, mày ə náyz/ *n* a rich creamy sauce or dressing made from egg yolks, vegetable oil, and flavorings [Early 19C. Probably < French]

ORIGIN There are several conflicting theories about the origin of *mayonnaise*, among them that it is an alteration of *bayonnaise*, as if the sauce originated in Bayonne, in southwestern France; that it was derived from the French verb *manier* "to stir"; and that it goes back to Old French *mayou* "egg yolk." But the early variant spelling *mahonnaise* suggests that it originally meant literally "of Mahon," and that the sauce was so named to commemorate the taking of Port Mahon, the capital of the island of Minorca, by the duc de Richelieu in 1756.

Ma·yon Vol·ca·no /ma yŏn-/ active volcano in the northeastern Philippines, on Luzon Island, beside the city of Legaspi. Height: 8,284 ft./2,525 m.

may·or /máy ər/ *n* somebody elected to be head of government in a city, town, or borough in many countries including the United States, and the United Kingdom except for Scotland [13C. Via French *maire* < Latin *major* "more great" < *magnus* "great"] —**may·or·al** *adj* —**may·or·ship** *n*

CULTURAL NOTE ***The Mayor of Casterbridge***, a novel (1886) by British writer Thomas Hardy. It is the tragic story of Michael Henchard, a laborer whose success in business raises him to the position of mayor of his town, but who then loses his fortune as a result of a petty dispute with his assistant. A rich character study, it is also a revealing portrait of contemporary rural mores.

may·or·al·ty /máy əraltee/ (*plural* **-ties**) *n* **1.** the official position held by a mayor ○ *The mayoralty was fiercely contested.* **2.** the length of time that a mayor holds office ○ *a five-year mayoralty* ○ *one of the longest mayoralties in New York history*

ma·yor·do·mo *n Southwest US* same as **major-domo** (sense 3)

Ma·yotte /ma yáwt/ island in the western Indian Ocean near Madagascar, an overseas dependency of France. One of the Comoros Islands, it stayed under French control when the remaining islands declared independence in 1975. Language: French. Currency: French franc. Capital: Mamoudzou. Population: 163,366 (2001). Area: 144 sq. mi./374 sq. km.

may·pole /máy pōl/ *n* a tall pole that is traditionally erected for May Day celebrations, usually decorated with flowers and with long colored ribbons attached at the top. Dancers each take hold of the end of a ribbon and dance around the pole so that the ribbons become interlaced in colored patterns around the pole.

may·pop /máy pòp/ *n* **1.** a climbing plant with three-lobed leaves and edible but somewhat tasteless fruit. Flowers: purple, white. Native to: southeastern United States. Latin name: *Passiflora incarnata*. **2.** the yellow fruit of the maypop plant [Mid-19C. Alteration of *maycock*, kind of melon < obsolete *maracock* "maypop"]

May queen *n* a young woman chosen to preside over a May Day celebration

Mays /mayz/, **Willie** (*b.* 1931) US baseball player. Considered one of the greatest players of all time, he was the first player to hit 300 home runs and steal 300 bases. Full name **Mays, Willie Howard, Jr.** Known as **the Say Hey Kid**

> "I remember the last season I played. I went home after a ballgame one day, lay down on my bed, and tears came to my eyes...It's like crying for your mother after she's gone. You cry because you love her. I cried I guess, because I knew I had to leave it."
> [Attributed to Willie Mays]

mayst /mayst/, **may·est** /máyəst/ *modal v* 2nd person singular present of **may**[1] (*archaic*)

may've /mayv/ *contr* may have (*informal*)

may·weed /máy weèd/ *n* a straggly weed of the daisy family that has foul-smelling leaves. Flowers: white. Latin name: *Anthemis cotula*. [Mid-16C. *May*, alteration of *maythe* "mayweed, camomile" < Old English *magoþe*]

May wine *n* **1.** a white wine flavored with woodruff **2.** a punch of champagne, claret, and other wines flavored with woodruff [Translation of German *Maiwein*]

ma·zal·tov, **ma·zal tov** *interj* JUDAISM another spelling of **mazeltov**

Maz·a·rin /mázzər ìn, ma za ráN/, **Jules, Cardinal** (1602–61) Italian-born French cardinal. He controlled France during the minority of Louis XIV, when his absolutist policies resulted in the antiroyalist rebellions known as the Fronde (1648–53). He negotiated the Peace of Westphalia (1648) and the Treaty of the Pyrenees (1659), ending major European wars. Born **Mazzarino, Giulio Raimondo**

Ma·za·tlán /maà zat laán/ city, seaport, and tourist resort in western Mexico. Population: 380,509 (2000).

Maz·da·ism /mázdə ìzzəm/, **Maz·de·ism** *n* RELIG same as **Zoroastrianism** [Late 19C. < Avestan *mazdā* < *Ahura Mazda*, supreme god of ancient Persian religion]

maze /mayz/ *n* **1. PUZZLE MADE OF CONNECTING PATHS** an area of interconnected weaving paths that it is difficult to find a way through, especially one in a garden with hedges between the paths or one designed for laboratory animals **2. ROUTE TRACING PUZZLE** a diagrammatic version of a maze, where the object is to arrive at a finish point by tracing a route with a pen or pencil **3. CONFUSING NETWORK OF PATHS** a network of paths, streets, or passageways that a walker or driver might easily become lost in ○ *a maze of narrow passageways* **4.** CONFUSING MUDDLE any confusing tangle or muddle, e.g., of regulations or procedures, that is difficult to negotiate ○ *a maze of official rules* ■ *vt* (**mazed, maz·ing, maz·es**) *Southern US, UK regional* ASTONISH SOMEBODY to astonish, stun, or stupefy somebody [13C. Shortening of AMAZE]

ma·zel·tov /maáz'l tàwv, -tàwf/, **ma·zel tov, ma·zal·tov, ma·zal tov** *interj* used to express good wishes or congratulations [Mid-19C. < modern Hebrew *mazzāl ṭōḇ* "good star"]

Ma·zen /maáz'n/, **Abu** Prime Minister of the Palestine Territory (2003–)

mazer

ma·zer /máyzər/ *n* a large drinking cup or bowl, usually made from hardwood or metal [13C. < Old French *masere* "kind of hardwood, maple" < Germanic]

ma·zour·ka *n* DANCE, MUSIC another spelling of **mazurka**

ma·zu·ma /mə zóomə/ *n* money, especially cash or loose change (*informal*) [Early 20C. < Yiddish]

ma·zur·ka /mə zúrkə, -zóorkə/, **ma·zour·ka** *n* **1.** a Polish national dance, similar to the polka **2.** the music for a mazurka [Early 19C. Probably via Russian < Polish *mazurek* "dance of an inhabitant of Mazovia (ancient part of Poland)" < *mazur* "inhabitant of Mazovia"]

maz·y /máyzee/ (**-i·er, -i·est**) *adj* **1.** tangled and interwoven like a maze **2.** confusing or complicated —**maz·i·ly** *adv* —**maz·i·ness** *n*

maz·zard /mázzərd/ *n* a wild sweet cherry tree often used as grafting stock for cultivated cherries. Latin name: *Prunus avium*. [Late 16C. Origin ?]

Mb *abbr* millibar

MB *abbr* **1.** EDUC Bachelor of Medicine **2.** Manitoba **3.** MIL Medal of Bravery **4.** COMPUT megabyte **5.** message board

M.B.A., MBA *abbr* Master of Business Administration

Mba·bane /əm baa baánee/ capital of Swaziland, located in the western part of the country near the border with South Africa. Population: 73,000 (2000).

mbal·ax /əm bálaa/ *n* a blend of Senegal's traditional percussion music and praise-singing with modern Afro-Cuban arrangements [Late 20C. < Wolof, "rhythm"]

mba·qan·ga /əm baa káng gə/ *n S Africa* a rhythmic form of South African popular music [Mid-20C. < Zulu *umbaqanga*, literally "steamed maize bread"]

Mbe·ki /əm békee/, **Thabo** (*b.* 1942) South African president. He was the first Black deputy president of the Republic of South Africa in 1994 and became leader of the African National Congress in 1997, before being elected president in 1999. Full name **Mbeki, Thabo Mvuyelwa**

mbi·ra /əm beérə/ *n* an African musical instrument with a resonating box, often a hollow gourd, with tuned attached strips of wood or metal that are plucked [Late 19C. < Shona]

MBO *abbr* **1.** management buyout **2.** management by objectives

Mbps *abbr* megabytes per second

Mbu·ji-Ma·yi /əm boójə mí ee/ city in south central Democratic Republic of the Congo, the capital of Kasai-Oriental Region. Population: 806,475 (1994).

Mbyte *abbr* COMPUT megabyte

mc *abbr* **1.** PHYS millicurie **2.** Monaco (*used in Internet addresses*) See table at **domain name**

MC[1] *abbr* **1.** MIL Marine Corps **2.** MIL Medical Corps **3.** ASTRON Midheaven **4.** MIL Military Cross

MC[2] /em seé/ *n* **1.** RAP MUSICIAN a rapper whose role is to excite a crowd at a party or in a club and involve them in the music **2.** MASTER OR MISTRESS OF CEREMONIES a person in charge of the proceedings at an event or entertainment ■ *vi* (**MCed, MC·ing, MCs**) RAP TO MUSIC to speak rhythmically and often in rhyme over music [Abbreviation of MASTER OF CEREMONIES] —**MC·ing** *n*

M.C. *abbr* Member of Congress

Mc- *prefix* same as **Mac-**

MCA *abbr* E-COMMERCE merchant certificate authority

Mc·Ad·oo /mə káddoo/, **William Gibbs** (1863–1941) US businessman and politician. He twice unsuccessfully sought a Democratic US presidential nomination (1920 and 1924).

MCAT /ém kàt/ *tdmk* a trademark for a standardized test taken by applicants to medical schools. Full form **Medical College Admissions Test**

Mc·Cain /mə káyn/, **John** (*b.* 1936) US politician. After military service and a long imprisonment as a POW in North Vietnam, he became a US senator (1986) and unsuccessfully ran for the Republican presidential nomination in 2000.

Mc·Car·thy /mə kaárthee/, **Joseph R.** (1908–57) US politician. While serving as a Republican US senator (1947–57), he instigated highly publicized Senate hearings in the early 1950s into alleged Communist subversion of the US government. His often unsubstantiated charges and extreme methods led to a Senate censure, and the period is often referred to as "the McCarthy era." Full name **McCarthy, Joseph Raymond**

Mc·Car·thy, Mary (1912–89) US writer and critic. She is best known for her novel *The Group* (1963). Full name **McCarthy, Mary Therese**

> "...a rebel demands a strong authority, a worthy opponent, God to his Lucifer."
> [Mary McCarthy, *How I Grew*; 1986]

> "There are no new truths, but only truths that have not been recognized by those who have perceived them without noticing."
> [Mary McCarthy, "Vita Activa," *On the Contrary*; 1961]

Mc·Car·thy·ism /mə kaárthee ìzzəm/ *n* **1.** the practice of publicly accusing somebody, especially somebody in government or the media, of subversive or Communist activities or sympathies, especially without real evidence to substantiate this **2.** the practice of using unsubstantiated accusations or unfair methods of investigation to discredit people [Mid-20C. After Joseph R. MCCARTHY] —**Mc·Car·thy·ist** *n, adj* —**Mc·Car·thy·ite** *n, adj*

Mc·Cart·ney /mə kaártnee/, **Sir Paul** (*b.* 1942) British singer, songwriter, and musician. He was a founding member, singer, and bass guitarist of the Beatles (1959–70), cowriting most of their songs with John Lennon. He later formed the band Wings (1971–81) with his wife, Linda McCartney. Full name **McCartney, Sir James Paul**

> "The issues are the same. We wanted peace on earth, love, and understanding between everyone around the world. We have learned that change comes slowly."
> [Sir Paul McCartney, *Observer (London)*; June 7, 1987]

Mc·Clel·lan /mə kléllən/, **George Brinton** (1826–85) US Union army commander. He lost his bid for the US presidency to Abraham Lincoln (1864).

> "All quiet along the Potomac."
> [Attributed to George Brinton McClellan at the time of the Civil War]

Mc·Clin·tock /mə klíntək, -òk/, **Barbara** (1902–92) US botanist and geneticist. Her research into "jumping genes" (**transposons**) won her the Nobel Prize in Physiology or Medicine (1983).

> "I never thought of stopping, and I just hated sleeping. I can't imagine having a better life."
> [Barbara McClintock, *Time*; October 24, 1983]

Mc·Cor·mack /mə káwrmək, -àk/, **John** (1884–1945) Irish-born US tenor. He was noted for his solo performances of Irish folk songs, and also enjoyed a successful career as an opera singer.

Mc·Cor·mick /mə káwrmik/, **Cyrus Hall** (1809–84) US inventor. He patented a mechanical reaping machine (1834) which had a major impact on agriculture.

Mc·Coy /mə kóy/ [Early 20C. Origin ?] ◇ **the real McCoy** somebody or something that is genuine (*informal*)

ORIGIN Among the suggested origins of the phrase ***the real McCoy*** are that it may be an alteration of *the Reay Mackay*, a title applied to Lord Reay, the name of the chief of the northern branch of the Scots Mackay clan, the leadership of which was disputed by various branch factions; that it may be from *Mackay*, a whiskey named for its makers A. and M. Mackay of Glasgow (once referred to as *the clear McCoy*); and that it may be from the professional name of the US welterweight boxing champion Kid McCoy (1873–1940), called "Kid" to distinguish him from another boxer of the same name.

Mc·Crae /mə kráy/, **John** (1872–1918) Canadian poet. He is best known for his war poem "In Flanders Fields" (1915).

> "In Flanders fields the poppies blow / Between the crosses, row on row, / That mark our place."
> [John McCrae, "In Flanders Fields"; 1915]

Mc·Cul·lers /mə kúllərz/, **Carson** (1917–67) US writer. Her novels include Southern Gothic tales such as *Ballad of the Sad Café* (1951). Born **Smith, Lula Carson**. See Cultural note at **hunter**

> "I suppose my central theme is the theme of spiritual isolation. Certainly I have always felt alone."
> [Carson McCullers. Quoted in *The World We Imagine*, Mark Schorer; 1968]

> "He was a man watching a clock without hands."
> [Carson McCullers, on someone terminally ill, *Clock Without Hands*; 1953]

Mc·Cul·lough /mə kúllək, -əkh/, **Colleen** (*b.* 1937) Australian novelist. Her novel *The Thorn Birds* (1977) was an international bestseller. Full name **McCullough, Colleen Margaretta**

Mc·Dan·iel /mək dánnyəl/, **Hattie** (1895–1952) US actor. She was the first African American to win an Academy Award, for best actress in a supporting role in *Gone with the Wind* (1940).

Mc·En·roe /mákən rō/, **John** (*b.* 1959) US tennis player. He was four times the winner of the US Open (1979, 1980, 1981, and 1984) and won the Wimbledon men's singles title three times (1981, 1983, and 1984). Full name **McEnroe, John Patrick, Jr.**

Mc·Gil·li·vray /mə gíllə vrày/, **Alexander** (1759–93) Creek leader. His Treaty of New York (1790) helped to maintain the independence of his people.

Mc·Gil·li·vray, William (1764–1825) Scottish-born Canadian fur trader. He was chief director of the North West Company, and fought in the War of 1812 at the capture of Detroit.

Mc·Gov·ern /mə gúvvərn/, **George** (*b.* 1922) US political leader. A Democratic US representative (1957–61) and senator (1963–81) from South Dakota, he was a leading opponent of the Vietnam War. He lost a populist run for the presidency to Richard Nixon's landslide victory in 1972. Full name **McGovern, George Stanley**

Mc·Guf·fey /mə gúffee/, **William Holmes** (1800–73) US educator and writer. He wrote a series of influential reading texts called the *Eclectic Readers* (1836–57).

Mc·Gwire /mə gwír/, **Mark David** (*b.* 1963) US baseball player. He played for the Oakland Athletics (1984–97) and the St. Louis Cardinals (1997–2001). In 1998 he hit a record-breaking 70 home runs.

mCi *symbol* MEASURE millicurie

Mc·Kay /mə káy/, **Claude** (1890–1948) Jamaican-born US writer. He depicted the experience of African Americans and Jamaicans in his poems and fiction. His *Harlem Shadows* (1922) was a seminal work of the Harlem Renaissance. Full name **McKay, Festus Claudius**

Mc·Kean /mə kéen/, **Thomas** (1734–1817) US political leader. He was a signatory of the Declaration of Independence (1776) and governor of Pennsylvania (1799–1808).

Mc·Kim /mə kím/, **Charles Follen** (1847–1909) US architect. His designs include the Boston Public Library (1887–95).

Barnaby's

Mount McKinley

Mc·Kin·ley, Mount /mə kínnlee/ highest mountain in North America, in Denali National Park and Preserve, south central Alaska. Height: 20,320 ft./6,194 m.

Library of Congress

William McKinley

Mc·Kin·ley /mə kínnlee/, **William** (1843–1901) 25th president of the United States (1897–1901). During many years in the US House of Representatives (1877–83 and 1885–91), he was instrumental in enacting protective tariffs. A Republican president, he presided over the Spanish-American War (1898), which made the United States a world power. He was assassinated by the anarchist Leon Czolgosz shortly after his election to a second term. See table at **president**

> "There was nothing left for us to do but to take them all, and to educate the Filipinos, and uplift and civilize and Christianize them, and by God's grace do the very best we could for them, as our fellowmen for whom Christ also died."
> [Attributed to William McKinley]

Mc·Leish /mə kléesh/, **Henry** (*b.* 1948) Scottish Labor politician. Appointed Minister of State and Scottish Office Minister for Devolution, Home Affairs and Local Government in 1997, he was elected First Minister of Scotland in October 2000.

Mc·Lu·han /mə klóo ən/, **Marshall** (1911–80) Canadian-born US critic and theorist. His writings dealt with the effects of media technology on the public. Full name **McLuhan, Herbert Marshall**

> "The new electronic independence re-creates the world in the image of a global village."
> [Marshall McLuhan, *The Gutenberg Galaxy*; 1962]

> "The medium is the message."
> [Marshall McLuhan, on the pervasive influence of television, *Understanding Media*; 1964]

> "Vietnam was lost in the living rooms of America and not on the battlefield."
> [Marshall McLuhan, *Montreal Gazette*; May 16, 1975]

Mc·Ma·hon /mək maá ən/, **Sir William** (1908–88) Australian prime minister. A Liberal Party politician, he served as foreign minister (1969–71) before serving as prime minister of a coalition government (1971–72). See table at **prime minister**

Mc·Mur·do Sound /mək múrdō-/ bay in eastern Antarctica, in the southern Ross Sea. It is in the south of the Pacific Ocean.

Mc·Na·ma·ra /màknə márrə/, **Robert** (*b.* 1916) US business executive and public official. He left the presidency of Ford Motor Company to serve as secretary of defense (1961–68) during the Vietnam War, which he championed while in office. He was later president of the World Bank (1968–81). Full name **McNamara, Robert Strange**

> "Although we sought to do the right thing—and believed we were doing the right thing—in my judgment, hindsight proves us wrong."
> [Robert McNamara, *In Retrospect: The Tragedy and Lessons of Vietnam*; 1995]

> "Military force—especially when wielded by an outside power—cannot bring order in a country that cannot govern itself."
> [Robert McNamara, *Daily Telegraph (London)*; April 10, 1995]

M.Com. *abbr* Master of Commerce

m-com·merce /ém kòmmərss/ *n* business transactions conducted over the Internet using cell phone technology [< abbreviation of MOBILE]

MCP *abbr* male chauvinist pig (*dated informal insult*)

Mc·Pher·son /mək fúrss'n/ city in central Kansas, south of Salina and northwest of Wichita. Population: 13,774 (2002 estimate).

Mc·Pher·son, Aimee Semple (1890–1944) Canadian-born US preacher. She founded the Church of the Four Square Gospel (1927) and was one of the first evangelists to use the radio. Born **Kennedy, Aimee Elizabeth**

> "We are all making a crown for Jesus out of these daily lives of ours, either a crown of golden, divine love, studded with gems of sacrifice and adoration, or a thorny crown, filled with the cruel briars of unbelief, or selfishness, and sin, and placing it upon His brow."
> [Aimee Semple McPherson, *This is That*; 1923]

MCPO *abbr* master chief petty officer

Mc·Queen /mə kwéen/, **Steve** (1930–80) US actor. He achieved his greatest success in tough-guy and loner roles in movies such as *The Magnificent Seven* (1960) and *Bullitt* (1968). Full name **McQueen, Terence Steven**

md *abbr* Moldova (*used in Internet addresses*) See table at **domain name**

Md *symbol* CHEM ELEM mendelevium

MD *abbr* **1.** MED Doctor of Medicine **2.** mailed (*used in e-mails or text messages*) **3.** Maryland **4.** medical department **5.** BANKING memorandum of deposit **6.** HOUSEHOLD minidisc **7.** MED muscular dystrophy **8.** MUSIC musical director

Md. *abbr* Maryland

M.D. *abbr* Doctor of Medicine

m/d *abbr* COMM months after date

M-day *abbr* mobilization day

M.Div. *abbr* Master of Divinity

MDMA *n* the drug Ecstasy. Full form **methylenedioxymethamphetamine**

M.D.S. *abbr* Master of Dental Surgery

mdse. *abbr* COMM merchandise

MDT *abbr* Mountain Daylight Time

me[1] /mee/ *pron* **1.** used to refer to the speaker or writer (*used as the object or complement of a verb or preposition*) ○ *asked her to do me a big favor* ○ *Listen to me!* ○ *Was it me?* **2.** used to refer to the personality of the speaker or writer, or something that may express it (*informal*) ○ *I don't think I like this hat; it isn't really me.* **3.** same as **myself** (*informal*) ○ *I'll get me a new boyfriend, see if I don't.* [Old English *mē, me* < Indo-European]

me[2] *n* MUSIC another spelling of **mi**

Me *symbol* CHEM methyl

ME[1] *abbr* **1.** Maine **2.** mechanical engineer **3.** CHR Methodist Episcopal **4.** *also* **M.E.** LANG Middle English **5.** ENG mining engineer **6.** Most Excellent

ME[2] *n UK* chronic fatigue syndrome (*informal*) Full form **myalgic encephalomyelitis**

Me. *abbr* Maine

me·a cul·pa /mày ə kóol paà/ *interj* used to express an admission of your own guilt (*formal or humorous*) ■ *n* a formal apology or acknowledgment of responsibility or guilt ○ *His grudging mea culpa failed to soothe feelings.* [< Latin, "(through) my fault," from the prayer of confession in the Roman Catholic Church's Latin liturgy]

mead[1] /meed/ *n* an alcoholic drink made by fermenting honey with water, often with added spices [Old English *me(o)du* < Indo-European, "honey, sweet drink"]

mead[2] /meed/ *n* same as **meadow** (sense 1) (*archaic or literary*) [Old English *mǣd* (see MEADOW)]

Mead, Lake /meed/ artificial lake in Arizona and Nevada formed by the Hoover Dam, which was built across the Colorado River. Area: 233 sq. mi./603 sq. km.

Mead /meed/, **George Herbert** (1863–1931) US philosopher and social psychologist. He developed theories of self and self-consciousness.

Popperfoto

Margaret Mead

Mead, Margaret (1901–78) US anthropologist. In such influential books as *Coming of Age in Samoa* (1928), she formalized her fieldwork research on child care, adolescence, and sexual behavior in North American society and nonindustrial societies.

> "The best way to learn is to learn from the best."
> [Margaret Mead, *Blackberry Winter*; 1972]

> "Never doubt that a small group of thoughtful committed citizens can change the world. Indeed, it's the only thing that ever has."
> [Margaret Mead. Quoted in *Utne Reader*; March/April 1991]

Meade /meed/, **George** (1815–72) US Union general. He commanded the Army of the Potomac (1863–65) in the Civil War. Full name **Meade, George Gordon**

mead·ow /méddō/ *n* **1.** a grassy field used for producing hay or for grazing domestic livestock **2.** an area of low-lying grassland, especially a marshy one near a river [Old English *mǣdwe*, form of *mǣd* < Indo-European, "cut grass with a scythe"] —**mead·ow·y** *adj*

mead·ow beau·ty (*plural* **mead·ow beau·ties** *or same*) *n* a low-growing perennial plant that grows in marshy ground. Flowers: purple. Native to: North America. Genus: *Rhexia*.

mead·ow fern *n* PLANTS same as **sweet gale**

mead·ow fes·cue *n* a perennial grass that has shiny leaves and stem bases that are surrounded by brown sheaths. Native to: Europe, Asia. Latin name: *Festuca pratensis*.

mead·ow·land /méddō lànd/ *n* a large area of land that is made up of meadows

mead·ow·lark /méddō laàrk/ (*plural* **-larks** *or same*) *n* a songbird with brown speckled feathers and a yellow breast with a black crescent-shaped mark across it. Native to: North America. Genus: *Sturnella*.

mead·ow mouse *n* a field mouse or vole

mead·ow mush·room *n US* an edible white-capped mushroom that grows in grassland. Native to: Europe. Latin name: *Agaricus campestris*. Can term **field mushroom**

mead·ow nem·a·tode *n* a parasitic nematode worm that infests and destroys the roots of plants. Genus: *Pratylenchus*.

mead·ow rue *n* a plant related to the buttercup with small yellow flowers. Native to: northern temperate zones. Genus: *Thalictrum*.

mead·ow saf·fron *n* PLANTS same as **autumn crocus**

mead·ow·sweet /méddō swēet/ (*plural* **-sweets** or *same*) *n* **1.** an ornamental bush. Flowers: small, white, in clusters. Native to: North America. Genus: *Spiraea*. **2.** a tall perennial plant that grows in damp and marshy places. Flowers: tiny, creamy-white, sweet-smelling, in clusters. Native to: Europe. Latin name: *Filipendula ulmaria*.

mea·ger /méegər/, **mea·gre** *adj* **1.** UNSATISFACTORILY SMALL unsatisfactory in quantity, substance, or size ○ *a company that is notorious for paying meager salaries* **2.** OF BAD QUALITY bad and unsatisfying in quality, strength, or effectiveness ○ *The street outside my window furnished meager entertainment.* **3.** THIN very thin, especially through malnutrition or illness [14C. Via Anglo-Norman *megre*, French *maigre* "lean, thin" < Latin *macr-*] —**mea·ger·ly** *adv* —**mea·ger·ness** *n*

meal[1] /meel/ *n* **1.** a substantial amount of food, often more than one course, that is provided and eaten at one time **2.** any occasion, e.g., breakfast or lunch, when a substantial amount of food is provided and eaten [Old English *mǣl* "measure, mealtime" < Germanic] ◇ **make a meal of something** (*informal*) **1.** to put more time or effort into something than is usual or necessary **2.** to exaggerate the importance, intensity, or severity of something

meal[2] /meel/ *n* **1.** the edible part of a cereal crop that has been ground to a powder **2.** any substance ground to a fine or coarse powder ○ *fish meal* [Old English *melu* < Indo-European, "crush, grind"]

meal·ie /méelee/ *n S Africa* an ear or cob of corn, or the plant on which it grows (*often plural*) [Early 19C. < Afrikaans *mielie* < Portuguese *milho* < Latin *milium* "millet"]

meals on wheels *n* a service, usually provided by a social work department or charity, whereby hot meals are brought to seniors, physically challenged people, or homebound people (*takes a singular verb*)

meal tick·et *n* **1.** somebody or something that can be counted on or exploited for money (*informal*) **2.** a ticket that entitles the holder to a meal

meal·time /méel tīm/ *n* the time when a meal is usually or regularly served

meal·worm /méel wùrm/ (*plural* **-worms** or *same*) *n* a larva that feeds on stored grain or flour and can cause severe damage and loss. Genus: *Tenebrio*.

meal·y /méelee/ (**-i·er, -i·est**) *adj* **1.** LIKE MEAL powdery or granular, like meal or grain ○ *mealy potatoes* **2.** MADE OF MEAL containing, made of, or covered with meal **3.** DAPPLED having a spotted or dappled hide or coat **4.** PALE exceptionally pale, especially through malnutrition or illness —**meal·i·ness** *n*

meal·y bug *n* a scale insect that is covered with a white powdery secretion and feeds on plants, often causing significant damage to citrus crops and greenhouse plants. Family: Pseudococcidae.

meal·y-mouthed *adj* overly wary of speaking plainly or openly, especially of admitting unpleasant truths

mean[1] /meen/ (**meant** /ment/, **mean·ing, means**) *vt* **1.** HAVE PARTICULAR SENSE to indicate or represent a particular sense ○ *I don't know what half these words mean.* ○ *When he raises his hand, it means he's making a bid.* **2.** INTEND TO EXPRESS SOMETHING to intend or be intended to express a particular idea in speech or writing ○ *That's not quite what I meant.* ○ *Just what's that supposed to mean?* **3.** INTEND TO DO SOMETHING to have an intention to do something ○ *I didn't mean to upset you.* ○ *I've been meaning to call you for weeks.* **4.** EXPRESS OPINION OR INTENTION to be serious in expressing a definite opinion or intention ○ *She says she's resigning, and I think this time she means it.* **5.** BE CAUSE OR SIGN OF SOMETHING to be a cause or indication of something ○ *The strike will mean a hard winter for many families.* ○ *A red sunset means fine weather.* **6.** GO WITH SOMETHING to accompany or be associated with something ○ *For Sam, summer meant golf.* [Old English *mǣnan* < Indo-European]

mean[2] /meen/ *adj* **1.** UNKIND unkind or malicious ○ *You hurt her feelings – that was a mean thing to do.* **2.** BAD-TEMPERED behaving in an angry, often violent way ○ *He can be pretty mean at times.* **3.** SHABBY shabby and poor-looking ○ *streets full of small mean houses* **4.** EXCELLENT excellent or skillful (*informal*) ○ *He plays a mean sax.* **5.** BASE base or unworthy **6.** HUMBLE of low social position (*archaic*) ○ *living among the poor and mean* **7.** UNCOMFORTABLE uncomfortable or disagreeable ○ *This is the meanest climate I've ever lived in.* **8.** NOT GENEROUS unwilling to spend money on other people ○ *the meanest person I know* [Old English *mǣne* < *gemǣne* "shared by everyone" < Germanic] —**mean·ly** *adv* —**mean·ness** *n*

SYNONYMS *mean, nasty, vile, low, base, ignoble*

CORE MEANING: below normal standards of decency

mean unkind or malicious ○ *All he does is give me a hard time. He's got to be the meanest man I've ever had the misfortune to work for.* **nasty** showing spitefulness or malice ○ *She's got a nasty streak.* ○ *a nasty snide way of putting things* **vile** despicable or shameful. ○ *vile manners* ○ *a vile unspeakable act* **low** without principles or morals ○ *How could he be so low as to make political mileage out of last week's tragedy?* **base** lacking proper social values or moral principles ○ *baser instincts* **ignoble** dishonorable and contrary to the high standards of conduct expected of somebody ○ *Can you assure us that these confidential communications were not ultimately put to any ignoble use?*

---

mean[3] /meen/ *n* **1.** INTERMEDIATE VALUE in mathematics, a value that is intermediate between other values, e.g., an average or expected value **2.** MEDIUM TERM OF PROPORTION in mathematics, either the second or third term of a proportion **3.** MIDDLE WAY a medium or moderate alternative or course of action, in the middle of a range of possibilities ○ *We need to find the mean between these extremes.* ■ *adj* **1.** MEDIUM medium or intermediate in size, strength, or quality **2.** IN INTERMEDIATE POSITION occupying an intermediate position in a range ○ *Speech was achieved in 74.3% of patients within a mean time interval of 63 days.* [14C. < Old French *meien* < Latin *medianus* (see MEDIAN)]

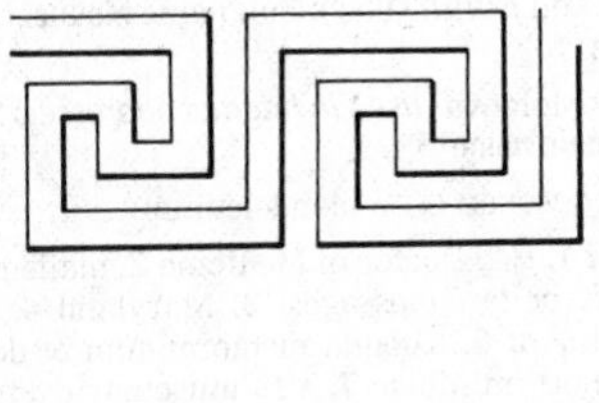

meander *n.* (sense 4)

me·an·der /mee ándər/ *vi* (**-dered, -der·ing, -ders**) **1.** FOLLOW TWISTING ROUTE to follow an indirect route or course, especially one with a series of twists and turns ○ *The river meanders to the sea.* **2.** WANDER SLOWLY AND AIMLESSLY to move in a leisurely way, especially for pleasure or because of a lack of motivation ○ *meandering through the park* ■ *n* **1.** RELAXED WALK a slow leisurely walk or journey ○ *We went for a meander in the woods.* **2.** TWIST OR BEND a twist or bend in something, especially a river, path, or street **3.** TWISTING ROUTE an indirect course or route, especially one with a series of twists and turns ○ *We followed the meanders of the path.* **4.** ORNAMENTAL DESIGN an ornamental design, popular in ancient Greek art and architecture, made by a continuous line that forms square shapes by doubling back on itself [Late 16C. Directly or via French < Latin, "winding course" < Greek *maiandros*, after a river (now the Büyük Menderes) in Turkey] —**me·an·der·er** *n* —**me·an·der·ing·ly** *adv* —**me·an·drous** /mee ándrəss/ *adj*

mean de·vi·a·tion *n* in statistics, the mean of the absolute values of the differences between individual values and the mean or median, used as a measure of dispersion

mean dis·tance *n* the average distance between an orbiting astronomical object and the object it is orbiting

mean free path *n* the average distance that a gas molecule travels before it collides with another molecule or with the containing vessel. Symbol λ

mean·ie /méenee/, **mean·y** (*plural* **-ies**) *n* a mean, bad-tempered, small-minded person (*informal*)

mean·ing /méening/ *n* **1.** WHAT SOMETHING MEANS what a word, sign, or symbol means ○ *Do you know the meaning of this word?* **2.** WHAT SOMEBODY WANTS TO EXPRESS what somebody intends to express, either in words or action ○ *I want to make my meaning very clear.* **3.** WHAT SOMETHING SIGNIFIES what something signifies or indicates ○ *I could not fathom the meaning of their glances.* **4.** INNER IMPORTANCE psychological or moral sense, purpose, or significance ○ *an empty life without meaning* ■ *adj* SIGNIFICANT conveying a significance that is not directly expressed ○ *A meaning silence followed these words.* —**mean·ing·ly** *adv*

mean·ing·ful /méeningfəl/ *adj* **1.** WITH MEANING having a discernible meaning ○ *To me, that is not a meaningful expression.* **2.** SIGNIFICANT conveying a meaning or significance that is not directly expressed ○ *She gave me a meaningful glance.* **3.** ADDING VALUE TO LIFE adding significance, meaning, or purpose to somebody's life ○ *I'm not claiming that we have a deep and meaningful relationship, but we do have fun.* —**mean·ing·ful·ly** *adv* —**mean·ing·ful·ness** *n*

mean·ing·less /méeningləss/ *adj* **1.** having no discernible meaning ○ *meaningless scrawl* **2.** lacking purpose or significance ○ *Offering to help now would be a meaningless gesture.* —**mean·ing·less·ly** *adv* —**mean·ing·less·ness** *n*

mean le·thal dose *n* SCI same as **median lethal dose**

mean-mind·ed *adj* ungenerous or malicious toward others —**mean-mind·ed·ly** *adv* —**mean-mind·ed·ness** *n*

means /meenz/ *n* something that is available and makes it possible for somebody to do something (*takes a singular or plural verb*) ○ *You can't live out there alone with no means of transportation.* ■ *npl* the money and other resources that somebody has to live on (*takes a plural verb*) ○ *It'll be impossible to find a house in this area that's within their means.* [< MEAN[3]] ◇ **by all means** used as a polite way to give permission ◇ **by no means** used to emphasize a negative ○ *You were by no means the worst player.*

means of pro·duc·tion *npl* in Marxism, the raw materials, tools, machinery, and other necessities required in the manufacturing process

mean so·lar day *n* the constant interval between two successive transits of the mean sun across the meridian. Symbol **d**

mean-spir·it·ed *adj* malicious or bad-tempered —**mean-spir·it·ed·ly** *adv* —**mean-spir·it·ed·ness** *n*

mean square *n* the mean of the squares of a set of values

means test *n* an examination of somebody's income and savings, carried out in order to determine whether the criteria for a type of assistance or financial aid are met —**means-test·ed** *adj* —**means test·ing** *n*

mean sun *n* in timekeeping, an imaginary sun that moves uniformly in the celestial equator and takes the same time to complete a circuit as the real Sun takes in the ecliptic

meant past participle, past tense of **mean**[1]

mean time *n* time measured with reference to the mean sun crossing a given meridian

mean·time /méen tīm/ *n* the intervening period of time between two events, or from now until something else happens ○ *I'll start dinner now and in the meantime you can have an apple.* ○ *I'll come as soon as I can; just wait there for the meantime.* ○ *Repairs will be done tomorrow and meantime please don't use the sink.*

mean val·ue *n* MATH, STATS same as **expected value**

mean·while /méen wīl, -hwīl/ *adv* **1.** during the period of time between two events ○ *I'll meet you later;*

meanwhile I'll leave you to your food. 2. at the same time as something is happening ○ *I tried to keep everybody calm, meanwhile struggling to open the car door.*

mean·y *n* another spelling of **meanie** (*informal*)

Mean·y /méenee/, **George** (1894–1980) US labor leader. A former plumber, he became the first president of the AFL-CIO (1955–79).

meas. *abbr* 1. measure 2. measurement

mea·sles /méez'lz/ *n* a contagious acute viral disease with symptoms that include a bright red rash of small spots that spread to cover the whole body. Small white spots, known as Koplik's spots, appear in the mouth on the inside of the cheeks a few days before the rash appears and can be used in diagnosis. (*takes a singular or plural verb*) ■ *npl* the spots that are characteristic of measles (*takes a plural verb*) [14C. Probably < Middle Low German *masele* or Middle Dutch *masel* "spot, blemish," and by folk etymology < *mesel* "leper"]

mea·sly /méezlee/ (**-sli·er, -sli·est**) *adj* 1. ridiculously or disappointingly small or inadequate (*informal*) ○ *He tipped me a measly dime.* 2. infected with measles

meas·ur·a·ble /mézhərəb'l/ *adj* capable of being measured or perceived [13C. Via French *mesurable* < late Latin *mensurabilis* < Latin *mensura* (see MEASURE)] —**meas·ur·a·bil·i·ty** /mèzhərə bílləteel/ *n* —**meas·ur·a·bly** *adv*

meas·ure /mézhər/ *n* 1. **SIZE** the size or extent of something, especially in comparison with a known standard 2. **STANDARD USED FOR FIGURING SIZE** a standard used for determining the dimensions, area, volume, or weight of something 3. **SYSTEM FOR DETERMINING SIZE** a particular system used to determine the dimensions, area, volume, or weight of something 4. **UNIT IN SYSTEM** a unit in a system that is used to determine the dimensions, area, volume, or weight of something 5. **SOMETHING USED TO FIGURE QUANTITY** something used to determine a quantity, e.g., a ruler, or a small container that holds a known volume 6. **WAY OF EVALUATING** a way of evaluating something, or a standard against which something can be compared 7. **ACTION TAKEN** an action taken to make something happen or prevent something (*often used in the plural*) ○ *to take precautionary measures* 8. **STANDARD AMOUNT OF SOMETHING** a standard amount of something, e.g., of an alcoholic beverage poured into a glass for drinking 9. **DEGREE OF SOMETHING** an extent or amount that is limited, appropriate, or has its size specified ○ *Their help contributed in no small measure to our success.* 10. **LIMITS** a limit or limits, especially one that is reasonable or appropriate ○ *His rage had no measure.* 11. MUSIC same as **bar**[1] *n* (sense 14) 12. **LAW** a bill to be enacted into law, or a law that has been enacted 13. **POETIC METER** the rhythm of a piece of poetry 14. **METRICAL FOOT** a unit of meter in poetry 15. same as **dance** *v* (sense 1) (*archaic*) ■ **meas·ures** *npl* MIN EXTRACT, GEOL **ROCK LAYERS** strata of rock, especially when they contain a particular material ■ *v* (**-ured, -ur·ing, -ures**) 1. *vt* **FIND SIZE OR QUANTITY OF SOMETHING** to find out the size, length, quantity, or rate of something using a suitable instrument or device 2. *vt* **BE PARTICULAR SIZE, LENGTH, QUANTITY** to be a particular size, length, quantity, or rate 3. *vt* **ASSESS SOMETHING** to assess the effect or quality of something, often against a standard ○ *You can't measure a hospital just by its facilities.* 4. *vt* **DETERMINE SOMEBODY'S SIZE FOR CLOTHES** to determine somebody's size in order to make a garment or garments that will fit ○ *She was being measured for her wedding dress.* 5. *vt* **COMPARE SOMETHING** to compare the size, effect, or quality of something with another thing ○ *The champion needs to measure his skill against a worthy challenger.* 6. *vt* **ADJUST SOMETHING FOR EFFECT** to adjust something so that it is suitable or effective ○ *He measured his punch exactly to catch his opponent on the jaw.* 7. *vi* **JOURNEY** to travel a particular distance (*archaic*) [12C. Via French *mesure* < Latin *mensura* < *mens-*, past participle of *metiri* "measure"] —**meas·ur·er** *n* ◇ **beyond measure** very greatly or to an enormous extent ◇ **for good measure** as something extra to the amount required, especially to make sure of something ◇ **get** *or* **have** *or* **take somebody's measure** to arrive at an accurate assessment of somebody's qualities or abilities

CULTURAL NOTE ***Measure for Measure***, a play (1604) by English dramatist William Shakespeare. Set in the court of the Duke of Vienna, this tragicomedy tells of a sister's attempts to win clemency for her brother, who has been condemned to death for the relatively minor crime of permissive behavior. It deals broadly with morality and the nature of justice.

ORIGIN The Latin stem *mens-*, from which ***measure*** derives, is also the source of English *commensurate, dimension,* and *immense.*

measure off *vt* 1. to determine a particular length of something so that this amount may be cut off 2. to find or mark the limits of an area

measure out *vt* 1. to take a particular amount from a larger amount of something for use 2. to find or mark the limits of an area

measure up *vi* to be good enough to meet a standard ○ *Her new play didn't measure up to expectations.*

meas·ured /mézhərd/ *adj* 1. **UNHURRIED OR REASONABLE** slow, deliberate, or carefully considered ○ *spoke in measured tones* 2. **ADJUSTED FOR EFFECT** adjusted to be suitable or effective ○ *a measured response to the criticism* 3. **BY MEASUREMENT** determined as a result of measuring ○ *a measured mile* —**meas·ured·ly** *adv*

meas·ure·less /mézhərləss/ *adj* too great to be measured ○ *"Through caverns measureless to man"* (Samuel Taylor Coleridge, *Kubla Khan*; 1816) —**meas·ure·less·ly** *adv* —**mea·sure·less·ness** *n*

meas·ure·ment /mézhərmənt/ *n* 1. **SIZE OF SOMETHING MEASURED** the size, length, quantity, or rate of something that has been measured. See table on next page 2. **BODY DIMENSION MEASURED FOR CLOTHING** the size of a part of somebody's body, especially used to fit or make clothing (*often used in the plural*) 3. **MEASURING OF SOMETHING** an act of measuring something

meas·ur·ing worm /mézhəring-/ *n UK* same as **inchworm**

meat /meet/ *n* 1. **EDIBLE ANIMAL FLESH** the flesh of an animal that is considered edible, especially that of a mammal or bird 2. **EDIBLE FRUIT OR NUT PART** the edible part of a fruit or nut, inside a shell or rind 3. **IMPORTANT PART** the essence or important part of something ○ *the meat of the argument* 4. **MATERIAL FOR THOUGHT** material that is interesting or stimulates thought ○ *There is plenty of meat in the book.* [Old English *mete* "food" < Indo-European, "measure"] —**meat·less** *adj* ◇ **meat and drink** something that somebody particularly enjoys ◇ **meat and potatoes** the most basic or important idea or aspect of something

SPELLCHECK **meat, meet** or **mete?** Do not confuse the spelling of ***meat*** and ***meet***, which sound similar. ***Meat*** is chiefly used as a noun denoting edible flesh, as in *roast meat.* ***Meet*** is chiefly used as a verb meaning "to encounter" or "to come together": *I'll meet you outside the theater. The lines meet at this point.* ***Meet*** is occasionally used as a noun, denoting a gathering of people for a sporting event or a hunt, and there is also an archaic adjective with this spelling, meaning "appropriate": *It is meet to do so.* ***Mete*** appears mainly in ***mete out*** meaning "to give out something such as punishment": *appalled at the mistreatment meted out to them.*

ORIGIN The sense of ***meat*** as "animal flesh (eaten as food)" developed in the 13th century, but the original English sense "food" still survives in phrases such as "meat and drink" and "one man's meat is another man's poison" (and is also seen in the word's relatives Danish *mad,* Icelandic *matur,* and Swedish *mat*).

meat-and-po·ta·toes *adj* fundamental or most important

meat·ball /méet bàwl/ *n* 1. a small round ball made from ground meat, usually with seasonings and a binding ingredient such as breadcrumbs or egg, that is then cooked 2. an offensive term that deliberately insults somebody's intelligence or energy level (*slang insult*)

meat·bot /méet bòt/ *n* ONLINE same as **human being** (*slang*) [Late 20C. Blend of MEAT + ROBOT]

Meath /meeth, meeth/ county in Leinster Province, northeast of Dublin in the eastern part of the Republic of Ireland. The county town is Navan. Population: 109,732 (2002). Area: 902 sq. mi./2,336 sq. km.

meat·head /méet hèd/ *n* an offensive term that deliberately insults somebody's intelligence or perceptiveness (*slang insult*)

meat hook *n* a large hook used for hanging carcasses of meat ■ **meat hooks** *npl* the hands or fists (*slang*)

meat loaf *n* a mixture of ground meat and other ingredients, usually cooked in a loaf pan and served hot or cold

meat lock·er *n* a large refrigerated store or storeroom for meat

meat mar·ket *n* a place such as a bar or nightclub where people go to find sexual partners (*slang*)

meat·pack·ing /méet pàking/ *n* the industry that deals with the slaughtering and butchering of meat —**meat·pack·er** *n*

me·a·tus /mee áytəss/ (*plural* **-tus·es** or *same*) *n* a body opening, e.g., the passage in the ear that leads to the eardrum [15C. < Latin, "passage," past participle of *meare* "go, pass"]

meat·y /méetee/ (**-i·er, -i·est**) *adj* 1. **CONTAINING OR TASTING OF MEAT** containing a high proportion of meat or tasting strongly of meat 2. **INTERESTING AND THOUGHT-PROVOKING** full of interesting and thought-provoking material ○ *a meaty role* 3. **FLESHY OR MUSCLED** big and fleshy or muscular —**meat·i·ness** *n*

mec·ca /mékə/ *n* a place that is an important center for a particular activity or that is visited by a great many people [Mid-19C. < MECCA]

Mec·ca /mékə/ city in western Saudi Arabia, the birthplace of Muhammad. It is considered by Muslims the most sacred of the holy cities of Islam. Population: 770,000 (1995).

mech. *abbr* 1. mechanical 2. mechanics 3. mechanism

mechan- *prefix* same as **mechano-** (*used before vowels*)

me·chan·ic /mə kánnik/ *n* a skilled worker who is employed to repair or operate machinery or engines [Mid-16C. Directly or via French < Latin *mechanicus* < Greek *mēkhanē* (see MACHINE)]

me·chan·i·cal /mə kánnik'l/ *adj* 1. **MACHINE-OPERATED** operated by or using a machine or mechanism 2. **INVOLVING MACHINE OR ENGINE** involving or located in or on a machine or engine ○ *mechanical failure* 3. **LACKING HUMAN QUALITIES** done automatically or as if by a machine instead of a thinking and feeling human being ○ *His playing was mechanical.* 4. **UNDERSTANDING MACHINES** having an aptitude for using or understanding machines ○ *I'm not very mechanical.* 5. **INVOLVING PHYSICAL FORCES** relating to, involving, or done by physical forces such as wind and rain ○ *mechanical erosion* 6. PHYS **OF MECHANICS** relating to, involving, or typical of the science of mechanics ○ *mechanical energy* 7. PHILOSOPHY same as **mechanistic** (sense 2) ■ *n* PRINTING **MATERIAL READY FOR PRINTING** copy consisting of type proofs and artwork that is laid out and ready to be photographed or electronically scanned for the purpose of preparing printing plates —**me·chan·i·cal·ly** *adv* —**me·chan·i·cal·ness** *n*

me·chan·i·cal draw·ing *n* 1. a drawing done to scale using specialized instruments and showing, e.g., machinery or an architectural plan 2. the process of making mechanical drawings

me·chan·i·cal en·gi·neer·ing *n* the branch of engineering that deals with the design, production, and use of machinery and tools, as well as the generation and transmission of heat and mechanical power —**me·chan·i·cal en·gi·neer** *n*

me·chan·i·cal pen·cil *n* a pencil with replaceable lead that may be advanced as needed

me·chan·i·cal weath·er·ing *n* the breakdown of rocks and minerals by physical agents such as frost, wind, and tree roots, with no chemical alteration

me·chan·ics /mə kánniks/ *n* 1. **STUDY OF ENERGY AND FORCES** the branch of physics and mathematics that deals with the effect of energy and forces on systems (*takes a singular verb*) 2. **MAKING AND RUNNING OF MACHINES** the application of the science of mechanics to the design, making, and operating of machines (*takes a singular or plural verb*) ■ *npl* **HOW SOMETHING WORKS** the details of how something works or the way it is done (*takes a plural verb*) ○ *She's a strategic player who really understands the mechanics of the game.*

mech·a·nism /mékə nìzzəm/ *n* 1. **MACHINE PART** a machine or part of a machine that performs a

MEASUREMENTS

SI Metric System

The SI (Système Internationale d'Unités) is founded on seven base units that can be multiplied or divided by each other to yield derived units. Values of the base and derived units can be increased or decreased by using SI prefixes indicating decimal multiplication factors. Units and prefixes are assigned internationally accepted symbols.

Base Units

Name	Physical Quantity	Symbol
meter	length	m
kilogram	mass	kg
second	time	s
ampere	electric current	A
kelvin	thermodynamic temperature	K
mole	amount of substance	mol
candela	luminous intensity	cd

Derived Units With Special Names and Symbols

Name	Physical Quantity	Symbol
becquerel	radioactivity	Bq
coulomb	electric charge	C
degree Celsius	temperature	°C
farad	electric capacitance	F
gray	absorbed radiation dose	Gy
henry	inductance	H
hertz	frequency	Hz
joule	energy, work	J
lumen	luminous flux	lm
lux	illumination	lx
newton	force	N
ohm	electric resistance	Ω
pascal	pressure, stress	Pa
radian	plane angle	rad
siemens	electric conductance	S
sievert	radiation dose equivalent	Sv
steradian	solid angle	sr
tesla	magnetic flux density	T
volt	electric potential difference	V
watt	power	W
weber	magnetic flux	Wb

Some Derived Units Without Special Names and Symbols

Name	Physical Quantity	Symbol
ampere per meter	magnetic field strength	A/m
cubic meter	volume	m^3
henry per meter	permeability	H/m
joule per kelvin	heat capacity, entropy	J/K
kilogram per cubic meter	mass density	kg/m^3
meter per second	linear speed	m/s
meter per second squared	linear acceleration	m/s^2
mole per cubic meter	concentration of substance	mol/m^3
newton meter	moment of force, torque	N·m
radian per second	angular speed	rad/s
square meter	area	m^2
volt per meter	electric field strength	V/m
watt per meter kelvin	thermal conductivity	W/(m·K)
watt per steradian	radiant intensity	W/sr

Prefixes

Multiplication Factor			Name	Symbol
1 000 000 000 000 000 000 000 000	or	10^{24}	*yotta-*	Y
1 000 000 000 000 000 000 000	or	10^{21}	*zetta-*	Z
1 000 000 000 000 000 000	or	10^{18}	*exa-*	E
1 000 000 000 000 000	or	10^{15}	*peta-*	P
1 000 000 000 000	or	10^{12}	*tera-*	T
1 000 000 000	or	10^{9}	*giga-*	G
1 000 000	or	10^{6}	*mega-*	M
1 000	or	10^{3}	*kilo-*	k
100	or	10^{2}	*hecto-*	h
10	or	10^{1}	*deca-* or *deka-*	da
0.1	or	10^{-1}	*deci-*	d
0.01	or	10^{-2}	*centi-*	c
0.001	or	10^{-3}	*milli-*	m
0.000 001	or	10^{-6}	*micro-*	μ
0.000 000 001	or	10^{-9}	*nano-*	n
0.000 000 000 001	or	10^{-12}	*pico-*	p
0.000 000 000 000 001	or	10^{-15}	*femto-*	f
0.000 000 000 000 000 001	or	10^{-18}	*atto-*	a
0.000 000 000 000 000 000 001	or	10^{-21}	*zepto-*	z
0.000 000 000 000 000 000 000 001	or	10^{-24}	*yocto-*	y

Other Units Used With the SI

Some units technically outside of the SI are nevertheless employed with it owing to their practical or special significance or because they are already in wide use. Excepting the electronvolt, liter, tex, and tonne, prefixes are not used with these units. The tonne does not take prefixes indicating a multiplication factor of less than ten.

Name	Symbol	Quantity	SI Equivalent
astronomical unit	–	length	≈ 149.598 Gm
barn	b	area	= 100 fm^2
day, mean solar	d	time	= 86,400 s
degree	°	plane angle	= (Π/180) rad
electronvolt	eV	energy	≈ 0.1602177 aJ
hectare	ha	area	= 10,000 m^2 or 1 hm^2
hour, mean solar	h	time	= 3,600 s
knot	kn	linear speed	= 1,852 m/h
liter	L or l	volume	≈ 1 dm^3 or 1,000 cm^3
millibar	mbar	pressure	= 0.1 kPa
minute, mean solar	min	time	= 60 s
minute	'	plane angle	= (Π/10,800) rad
nautical mile	M	length	= 1,852 m
parsec	pc	length	≈ 30.857 Pm
revolution	r	plane angle	= 2Π rad
second	"	plane angle	= (Π/648,000) rad
tex	tex	linear density	= 1 mg/m
tonne	t	mass	= 1,000 kg or 1 Mg
unified atomic mass unit	u	mass	≈ 1.6605402 yg
year	a	time	= 31.536 Ms (calendar) = 31.556926 Ms (solar) = 31.558150 Ms (sidereal)

Conversion of Common SI Units

Conversions for some common SI units or those used with the SI to imperial or US customary units are given below.

SI Unit	Conversion
length	
micrometer	= 0.00003937 inches
millimeter	= 0.03937 inches
centimeter	= 0.3937 inches
meter	= 39.37 inches or ≈ 1.094 yards
kilometer	≈ 0.621 miles
area	
square millimeter	≈ 0.00155 square inches
square centimeter	≈ 0.155 square inches
square meter	≈ 1.196 square yards or 10.76 square feet
hectare	≈ 2.471 acres
square kilometer	≈ 0.386 square miles
volume or capacity	
cubic millimeter	≈ 0.000061 cubic inches
cubic centimeter or milliliter	≈ 0.0610 cubic inches, 0.0352 Imp. fluid ounces, or 0.0338 US fluid ounces
cubic decimeter or liter	≈ 61.0 cubic inches, 0.880 Imp. quarts, 1.057 US liquid quarts, or 0.908 US dry quarts
cubic meter	≈ 1.308 cubic yards
mass	
gram	≈ 0.0353 oz avoirdupois or 0.0322 oz troy
kilogram	≈ 2.205 pounds avoirdupois
tonne	≈ 2,205 pounds avoirdupois
temperature	
degree Celsius	(°C × 1.8) + 32 = degrees Fahrenheit

Foot-Pound-Second and Troy Systems

The imperial and US customary systems are the last foot-pound-second systems still used nationally in everyday trade and commerce, while the troy system of weights continues to find use in the precious metals market, chiefly in North America. All have been supplanted by the SI in scientific and technical work and in nearly all international trade.

Imperial and US Customary System Units

Units of the imperial and US customary systems are equal except for some units of volume and capacity.

Unit	Relation	Conversion
length		
inch	–	= 25.4 mm
foot	12 inches	= 0.3048 m
yard	3 feet, 36 inches	= 0.9144 m
rod	$5\frac{1}{2}$ yards, $16\frac{1}{2}$ feet	= 5.0292 m
furlong	220 yards, $\frac{1}{8}$ mile	≈ 0.201 km
mile (statute)	1,760 yards, 5,280 feet	≈ 1.609 km
area		
square inch	–	= 645.16 mm^2
square foot	144 sq. inches	= 929.0304 cm^2
square yard	9 sq. feet	≈ 0.836 m^2
acre	4,840 sq. yards	≈ 0.405 ha
volume or capacity		
cubic inch	–	≈ 16.387 cm^3
cubic foot	1,728 cubic inches	≈ 28.316 dm^3
cubic yard	27 cubic feet	≈ 0.765 m^3
(Imperial)		
fluid ounce	–	≈ 28.413 cm^3
pint	20 Imp fl. oz	≈ 0.568 dm^3
quart	2 Imp. pints	≈ 1.136 dm^3
gallon	4 Imp. quarts	≈ 4.546 dm^3
peck	8 Imp. quarts	≈ 9.092 dm^3
bushel	4 Imp. pecks	≈ 36.369 dm^3
barrel	36 Imp. gallons	≈ 163.7 dm^3
(US, liquid)		
fluid ounce	–	≈ 29.573 cm^3
pint	16 US fl. oz	≈ 0.473 dm^3
quart	2 US fl. pints	≈ 0.946 dm^3
gallon	4 US fl. quarts	≈ 3.785 dm^3
barrel, wine	$31\frac{1}{2}$ US gallons	≈ 119.2 dm^3
barrel, oil	42 US gallons	≈ 0.159 m^3
(US, dry)		
pint	–	≈ 0.551 dm^3
quart	2 US dry pints	≈ 1.101 dm^3
peck	8 US dry quarts	≈ 8.810 dm^3
bushel	4 pecks	≈ 35.239 dm^3
weight or mass		
ounce	–	≈ 28.349 g
pound	16 ounces	≈ 0.454 kg
(avoirdupois)		
stone (UK)	14 pounds	≈ 6.350 kg
hundredweight (UK)	112 pounds	≈ 50.80 kg
(long) ton (UK)	2,240 pounds	≈ 1.016 Mg
(short) ton (US)	2,000 pounds	≈ 0.907 Mg
(troy)		
ounce	–	≈ 31.103 g
pound	12 oz troy	≈ 373.242 g
temperature		
degree Fahrenheit	(°F – 32) ÷1.8 = degrees Celsius	

Some Volumetric Measurement Comparisons

Imperial Units	In US Units	In SI Units
1 UK fluid ounce	≈ 0.961 US fluid ounce	≈ 28.413 cm^3
1 UK pint	≈ 1.201 US liquid pint	≈ 0.568 dm^3
1 UK pint	≈ 1.032 US dry pint	≈ 0.568 dm^3
1 UK gallon	≈ 1.201 US gallon	≈ 4.546 dm^3

US Units	In Imperial Units	In SI Units
1 US fluid ounce	≈ 1.041 UK fluid ounce	≈ 29.573 cm^3
1 US liquid pint	≈ 0.833 UK pint	≈ 0.473 dm^3
1 US gallon	≈ 0.833 UK gallon	≈ 3.785 dm^3
1 US dry pint	≈ 0.969 UK pint	≈ 0.551 dm^3

specific task **2. SOMETHING LIKE MACHINE** something that resembles a machine in having a structure of interrelated parts that function together ○ *the fragile mechanism of the planet's ecology* **3. METHOD OR MEANS** a method or means of doing something ○ *Interest rates are only one mechanism for controlling inflation.* **4. WAY THAT SOMETHING WORKS** the methods, procedures, or processes involved in the way something works or is done ○ *the mechanism of international diplomacy* **5.** PSYCHOL **INSTINCTIVE BEHAVIORAL REACTION** a natural unconscious reaction or type of behavior that comes into action when somebody is faced with a particular situation ○ *defense mechanisms* **6.** PHILOSOPHY **PHILOSOPHICAL THEORY** the philosophical theory that all natural phenomena, including human behavior, can be explained by physical causes and processes [Mid-17C. < modern Latin *mechanismus* < Greek *mēkhanē* (see MACHINE)]

mech·a·nist /mékənist/ *n* somebody who believes that all natural phenomena, including human behavior, can be explained by physical causes and processes [Early 17C. < MECHANIC]

mech·a·nis·tic /mèkə nístik/ *adj* **1. LIKE MACHINE** typical of a machine rather than a thinking and feeling human being **2.** PHILOSOPHY **EXPLAINING BEHAVIOR MECHANICALLY** explaining all natural phenomena, including human behavior, in terms of physical causes and processes **3.** PHYS **OF SCIENCE OF MECHANICS** relating to, involving, or typical of the science of mechanics —**mech·a·nis·ti·cal·ly** *adv*

mech·a·nize /mékə nīz/ (**-nized, -niz·ing, -niz·es**) *vt* **1. USE MACHINERY TO DO SOMETHING** to change a process so that it is performed by machinery instead of human or animal labor **2. EQUIP SOMEBODY OR SOMETHING WITH MACHINERY** to equip a place of work or a work force with machines to do work previously done by human or animal labor **3.** MIL **EQUIP ARMY WITH VEHICLES** to equip an armed force with trucks and armored vehicles [Late 17C. < MECHANIC] —**mech·a·ni·za·tion** /mèkəni záysh'n/ *n* —**mech·a·nized** *adj* —**mech·a·niz·er** *n*

mechano- *prefix* mechanical ○ *mechanoreceptor* [< Greek *mēkhanē* (see MACHINE)]

mech·a·no·chem·is·try /mèkənō kémmistree/ *n* the branch of chemistry concerned with the conversion of chemical energy into mechanical work —**mech·a·no·chem·i·cal** *adj*

mech·a·no·re·cep·tor /mèkənō ri séptər/ *n* a sensory receptor of a nerve that responds to pressure, vibration, or another mechanical stimulus —**mech·a·no·re·cep·tion** *n* —**mech·a·no·re·cep·tive** *adj*

mech·a·no·ther·a·py /mèkənō thérrəpee/ *n* the treatment of injuries through mechanical means such as massage and exercise machines —**mech·a·no·ther·a·pist** *n*

Mech·e·len /mékələn, mékh-/ city in northern Belgium, famous for the lace produced there since the 15th century. Population: 75,689 (1991).. French name **Malines**

Mech·lin /méklin/, **Mech·lin lace** *n* a bobbin lace made at Mechelen, Belgium [15C. After *Mechlin*, former English name for MECHELEN]

me·co·ni·um /mi kṓnee əm/ *n* the dark greenish feces that have collected in the intestines of an unborn baby and are released shortly after birth [Early 17C. Via Latin, "poppy juice" < Greek *mēkōnion* < *mēkōn* "poppy"]

me·cop·ter·an /mə kóptərən/ *n* an insect with long legs and wings and a structure resembling a beak at the front of the head, e.g., the scorpion fly. Order: Mecoptera. [< modern Latin *Mecoptera* < Greek *mēkos* "length" + *ptera* "wings"] —**me·cop·ter·ous** *adj*

Med /med/ *n* the Mediterranean Sea (*informal*) [Mid-20C. Shortening]

med. *abbr* **1.** medical **2.** medicine **3.** medieval **4.** medium

M.Ed. *abbr* Master of Education

mé·dail·lon /mày da yáwN/ *n UK* COOK same as **medallion** (sense 3) [Early 20C. < French (see MEDALLION)]

me·da·ka /mə daákə/ *n* a small freshwater fish of the killifish family that is often kept in aquariums. Native to: Japan. Latin name: *Oryzias latipes*. [Mid-20C. < Japanese, "eye-high"]

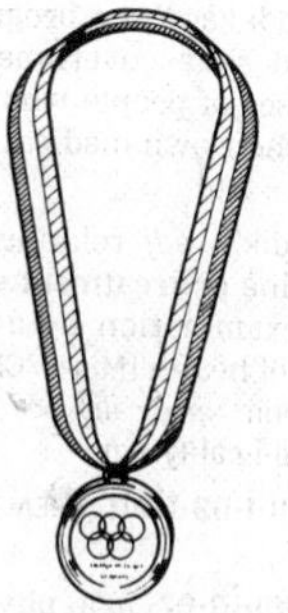

medal

med·al /médd'l/ *n* **1. PIECE OF METAL GIVEN AS AWARD** a small flat piece of metal, usually shaped like a coin and stamped with an inscription or design, awarded to somebody for outstanding achievement or bravery or to commemorate something **2. RELIGIOUS IMAGE WORN AS ACCESSORY** a cut and shaped piece of metal on which a religious image is often stamped, worn as a pin or on a chain ■ *vi* (**-aled** or **-alled, -al·ing** or **-al·ling, -als**) **WIN MEDAL** to win a medal in a competition ○ *She medaled in the javelin throw.* [Late 16C. < French *médaille* < assumed Vulgar Latin *medalia* "coins worth half the value of a denarius" < late Latin *medialis* "medial"] —**me·dal·lic** /mə dállik/ *adj*

Med·al for Mer·it *n* a medal awarded by the US government to civilians for outstanding service

med·al·ist /médd'list/ *n* **1. SOMEBODY AWARDED MEDAL** somebody who has been awarded a medal, especially in a competition **2. SOMEBODY INVOLVED WITH MEDALS** somebody who designs, makes, collects, or is an expert on medals **3.** GOLF **WINNER OF MEDAL PLAY TOURNAMENT** a golfer who wins a medal play tournament

me·dal·lion /mə dállyən/ *n* **1. MEDAL** a large medal **2. LARGE DECORATIVE METAL DISK** a large decorative metal disk worn on a chain around the neck **3. ROUND DECORATION** a round or oval decoration on something such as a building, vase, or piece of material **4.** COOK **ROUND THIN FOOD SLICE** a round thin slice or portion of meat or another food **5.** E-COMMERCE **MICROCHIP** the microchip inside a smart card [Mid-17C. Via French *médaillon* < Italian *medaglione* "large medal" < *medaglia* "medal"]

med·al·list *n* Can, UK spelling of **medalist**

Med·al of Free·dom *n* an award given to US civilians for outstanding achievement

Med·al of Hon·or *n* MIL same as **Congressional Medal of Honor**

med·al play *n US* a way of scoring in golf in which the total number of strokes taken for the round is counted rather than the number of holes won. Can term **stroke play**

Me·dan /may daán/ industrial city in western Indonesia on the island of northern Sumatra. Population: 1,974,300 (1997).

Med·a·war /méddəwər/, **Sir Peter** (1915–87) Brazilian-born British zoologist and immunologist. He shared a Nobel Prize in physiology or medicine (1960) for his work on immunology in organ transplants and skin grafts. Full name **Medawar, Sir Peter Brian**

> "The human mind treats a new idea in the same way the body treats a strange protein; it rejects it."
> [Attributed to Sir Peter Medawar]

med·dle /médd'l/ (**-dled, -dling, -dles**) *vi* to become involved in somebody else's concerns or with somebody else's property in an intrusive or unwanted way ○ *I don't mean to meddle, just to offer advice.* [13C. < Old French *me(s)dler*, variant of *mesler* < assumed Vulgar Latin *misculare* "mix thoroughly"] —**med·dler** *n*

med·dle·some /médd'lsəm/ *adj* tending to interfere in other people's concerns —**med·dle·some·ly** *adv* —**med·dle·some·ness** *n*

Mede /meed/ *n* a member of an Indo-European people who ruled an empire northwest of Persia in ancient times [< Latin *Medi*, plural of *Medus*]

Me·de·a /mə deé ə/ *n* in Greek mythology, a woman with magical powers who was the daughter of the king of Colchis. She helped Jason to steal the Golden Fleece and, when he deserted her, killed their children in revenge.

~~**medecine**~~ incorrect spelling of **medicine**

~~**medeival**~~ incorrect spelling of **medieval**

Me·del·lín /màydə yeén/ major city and capital of Antioquia Department in west central Colombia. Population: 1,958,000 (1999).

med·e·vac /méddə vàk/ *n* **1. MEDICAL EVACUATION OF INJURED** the removal of injured people from the scene of their injury to the nearest hospital or place of treatment by helicopter or airplane **2. HELICOPTER USED TO EVACUATE INJURED** an aircraft, especially a helicopter, used to take injured people from the scene of their injury to the nearest hospital or place of treatment ■ *vt* (**-vaced, -vac·ing, -vacs**) **EVACUATE INJURED PERSON** to remove somebody who is injured from the scene of his or her injury to the nearest hospital or place of treatment [Mid-20C. Blend of MEDICAL + EVACUATION]

med·fly /méd flī/ (*plural* **-flies**) *n* same as **Mediterranean fruit fly** (*informal*)

Med·ford /médfərd/ **1.** city in northeastern Massachusetts, a northwestern suburb of Boston. Population: 55,137 (2002 estimate). **2.** city in Oregon. It is the administrative seat of Jackson County. Population: 64,653 (2002 estimate).

Med. Gr. *abbr* medieval Greek

me·di·a[1] /meédee ə/ *n* the various means of mass communication considered as a whole, including television, radio, magazines, and newspapers, together with the people involved in their production (*takes a singular or plural verb*) ■ plural of **medium** [Early 20C. Plural of MEDIUM]

USAGE media – singular or plural? Even though ***media*** is historically a plural of the Latin word *medium*, in some instances you can safely use ***media*** with a singular verb, depending on what is meant by ***media***. When ***media*** means the broadcast and print press in general, including all its personnel, equipment, and policies, a singular verb is acceptable. The word is also invariably preceded by *the* in such usages: *The media has covered the story ad nauseam.* If the writer's idea is to indicate, using ***media***, various separate journalistic outlets and their activities, a plural verb goes with ***media***: *The media have differed markedly in their approaches to coverage of the scandal.* Avoid using the plural ***media*** to refer to a single system or method of communication; use the singular *medium* instead: *Cable television is a relatively inexpensive advertising medium* [not *media*]. Never use the false plural "medias" as in *new medias*. The correct form is ***media***, as in *new media*.

me·di·a[2] /meédee ə/ (*plural* **-di·ae** /-dee eé/) *n* **1.** the middle, muscular layer of the wall of a blood or lymph vessel **2.** a primary vein in an insect's wing [Mid-19C. < Latin, "middle," a form of *medius*]

Me·di·a /meédee ə/ ancient country corresponding to modern-day northwestern Iran —**Me·di·an** *adj, n*

me·di·a cir·cus *n* a situation in which there is so much frantic activity by the news media around an event that the coverage overshadows the event and distorts its significance (*informal*)

me·di·a·cy /meédee əssee/ *n* the condition of being intermediate or of having an intermediate effect [Mid-19C. < MEDIATE]

me·di·ae ANAT plural of **media**[2]

me·di·ae·val, etc. *adj* HIST another spelling of **medieval, etc.**

me·di·a e·vent *n* an event that attracts great attention from the news media, often arranged specifically for that purpose

me·di·a·gen·ic /meédee ə jénnik/ *adj* appealing or attractive when covered by the media and thus highly suitable for media exposure

me·di·al /meédee əl/ *adj* **1. IN MIDDLE** situated in or toward the middle **2. ORDINARY** not extreme or exceptional **3.** STATS same as **median** *adj* (sense 2) **4.** ZOOL **NEAR MEDIAN PLANE** near the median plane of an organism or body part **5.** LING **IN MIDDLE OF LANGUAGE UNIT** occurring between the first and last positions in a word or linguistic unit (**morpheme**) **6.** PHON **CENTRAL** pronounced in the middle of the mouth ■ *n* PHON **SOUND BETWEEN STRONG AND SOFT SOUND** a speech sound midway between a strong sound (**fortis**) and a soft sound (**lenis**) [Late 16C. < late Latin *medialis* < Latin *medius* "middle"] —**me·di·al·ly** *adv*

me·di·a mes·sag·ing *n* the sending of images, sound, and text from one cell phone to another —**me·di·a mes·sage** *n*

me·di·an /meédee ən/ *n* 1. MIDDLE POINT a point, line, part, or plane that is in the middle 2. ROADS same as **median strip** 3. STATS MIDDLE IN SET OF ORDERED VALUES the middle value in a set of statistical values that are arranged in ascending or descending order 4. STATS MIDPOINT IN FREQUENCY DISTRIBUTION the value in a frequency distribution above and below which values with equal total frequencies appear 5. MATH LINE DIVIDING TRIANGLE a line connecting a vertex of a triangle and the midpoint of the opposite side 6. MATH LINE DIVIDING TRAPEZOID a line connecting the midpoints of the nonparallel sides of a trapezoid ■ *adj* 1. IN, TO, OR THROUGH MIDDLE located in, going toward, or passing through the middle 2. STATS OF OR AS STATISTICAL MEDIAN relating to, involving, or constituting a statistical median 3. ZOOL IN MIDDLE OF ANIMAL lying in the plane that divides a bilaterally symmetrical animal into right and left halves [14C. Directly or via French (*veine*) *médiane* "median (vein)" < Latin *medianus* "median" < *medius* "middle"] —**me·di·an·ly** *adv*

me·di·an le·thal dose *n* the dose of a substance such as a drug or ionizing radiation that in a specific time period will kill half the experimental animals to whom it is given. Symbol LD_{50}

me·di·an plane *n* a vertical plane that divides a bilaterally symmetrical animal or human body into right and left halves

me·di·an strip *n* a strip of land down the center of a road that separates lanes of traffic traveling in opposite directions

me·di·ant /meédee ənt/ *n* the third note of a major or minor musical scale, or the harmony built upon this note [Mid-18C. < French *médiante* < late Latin *mediare* "be in the middle" < Latin *medius* "middle"]

me·di·as·ti·num /meédee ə stínəm/ (*plural* **-na** /-nə/) *n* in mammals, the region of the chest between the lungs that contains the heart, trachea, and other organs [15C. < medieval Latin, form of *mediastinus* "medial" < Latin, "common servant" < *medius* "middle"] —**me·di·as·ti·nal** *adj*

me·di·a stud·ies *n* an academic subject in which the role and operation of the mass media are studied (*takes a singular or plural verb*)

me·di·ate /meédee àyt/ *v* (**-at·ed, -at·ing, -ates**) 1. *vi* INTERVENE TO RESOLVE CONFLICT to work with both sides in a dispute in an attempt to help them to reach an agreement ○ *mediating between the government and the rebels* 2. *vt* OVERSEE AGREEMENT to oversee an attempt to solve a dispute by working with both sides to help them to reach an agreement ○ *appointed to mediate the talks* 3. *vt* ACHIEVE AGREEMENT to achieve a solution, settlement, or agreement by working with both sides in a dispute ○ *Negotiators have mediated a ceasefire.* 4. *vt* PHYSIOL TRANSFER SOMETHING to act as a medium that transfers something from one place to another in the body 5. *vi* BE BETWEEN to be between two stages, ideas, times, or things ■ *adj* DEPENDING ON INTERMEDIATE ACTION involving or depending on an intermediary or an intermediate action [15C. < late Latin *mediat-*, past participle of *mediare* "halve" < Latin *medius* "middle"] —**me·di·ate·ly** *adv* —**me·di·a·tion** /meédee áysh'n/ *n* —**me·di·a·tive** /-ətiv/ *adj*

me·di·a·tize /meédee ə tìz/ (**-tized, -tiz·ing, -tiz·es**) *vt* to take control of another country but allow its ruler to retain his or her title and have some role in governing the country [Early 19C. < French *médiatiser* < late Latin *mediare* (see MEDIATE)] —**me·di·a·ti·za·tion** /meédee əti záysh'n/ *n*

me·di·a·tor /meédee àytər/ *n* 1. somebody who works with both sides in a dispute in an attempt to help them to reach an agreement 2. a substance that acts as a medium in transferring something from one place to another in the body [14C. Directly or via French < ecclesiastical Latin < late Latin *mediare* (see MEDIATE)]

med·ic[1] /méddik/ *n* 1. an enlisted person or non-commissioned officer in a military medical corps 2. a doctor or medical student (*informal*) [Mid-17C. < Latin *medicus* (see MEDICINE)]

med·ic[2] /méddik/ *n* PLANTS another spelling of **medick**

Med·i·caid /méddi kàyd/ *n* a program funded by the US federal and state governments that pays the medical expenses of people who are unable to pay some or all of their own medical expenses [Mid-20C. Blend of MEDICAL + AID]

med·i·cal /méddik'l/ *adj* relating to, involving, or used in medicine or treatment given by doctors ■ *n* a physical examination by a doctor to check a patient's state of health [Mid-17C. Directly or via French < medieval Latin *medicalis* < Latin *medicus* (see MEDICINE)] —**med·i·cal·ly** *adv*

med·i·cal ex·am·i·na·tion *n* HEALTH SERVICES same as **medical**

med·i·cal ex·am·in·er *n* a physician who is appointed by a state or local government to establish the cause of somebody's death, especially in cases where death is not the result of natural causes

med·i·cal food *n* food specially processed or formulated to be given, under medical supervision, to patients who require a special diet

med·i·cal ju·ris·pru·dence *n* MED same as **forensic medicine**

med·i·cal mall *n* a complex of facilities under one roof offering diagnostics, primary and outpatient care, a pharmacy, and therapy along with banks, dry cleaners, and restaurants for patients and their families

med·i·cal te·le·mat·ics *n* the development and use of computer networks for the international exchange and retrieval of medical data (*takes a singular verb*)

me·dic·a·ment /mə díkəmənt, méddikə-/ *n* a substance used to treat an illness [15C. Directly or via French < Latin *medicamentum* < *medicari* (see MEDICATE)]

med·i·care /méddi kèr/ *n* in Canada, a government health insurance scheme funded by a tax levy in each province [Mid-20C. Blend of MEDICAL + CARE]

Med·i·care /méddi kèr/ *n* 1. in the United States, a health insurance program under which medical care and hospital treatment for people over 65 is partly paid for by the government 2. in Australia, a national health insurance scheme funded by a tax levy [Mid-20C. Blend of MEDICAL + CARE]

med·i·cate /méddi kàyt/ (**-cat·ed, -cat·ing, -cates**) *vt* 1. to treat a patient with a drug (*often passive*) 2. to add a drug to something, e.g., an antibacterial agent to a soap, or an anesthetic to a throat lozenge [Early 17C. Either < Latin *medicari* "heal" < *medicus* (see MEDICINE); or back-formation < MEDICATION] —**med·i·cat·ed** *adj* —**med·i·ca·tive** *adj*

med·i·ca·tion /mèddi káysh'n/ *n* 1. a drug used to treat an illness 2. the treatment of an illness using drugs [15C. Directly or via French < Latin *medication-* < *medicari* (see MEDICATE)]

Med·i·ce·an /mèddee seé ən/ *adj* relating to the Medici family and the period of their rule over Florence and Tuscany between the 15th and 17th centuries

Med·i·ci /méddə cheè/, **Cosimo de'** (1389–1464) Italian banker and political leader. He established the Medici as virtual rulers of Florence without holding public office himself and was a patron of the arts and learning. Known as **Cosimo the Elder**

Med·i·ci, Cosimo I de', 1st Grand Duke of Tuscany (1519–74) He became the sovereign ruler of Florence (1570) and established firm autocratic control over Florence and Tuscany.

Med·i·ci, Lorenzo de' (1449–92) Italian banker and politician. He was the virtual ruler of the Florentine Republic, a poet, and a patron of the arts. Known as **Lorenzo the Magnificent**

> "How beautiful is youth, that is always slipping away! Whoever wants to be happy, let him be so: about tomorrow there's no knowing."
> [Lorenzo de' Medici, "The Triumph of Bacchus and Ariadne"; 15th century]

med·i·cide /méddi sìd/ *n* suicide assisted by a physician (*informal*) [Late 20C. Blend of MEDICAL + SUICIDE]

me·dic·i·nal /mə díssən'l, -díssnəl/ *adj* 1. CAPABLE OF TREATING ILLNESS having properties that can be used to treat illness ○ *a medicinal plant* 2. INTENDED TO IMPROVE SOMEBODY'S WELL-BEING intended to improve somebody's physical or emotional well-being in the way that a medicine does ○ *a drink taken for medicinal purposes* 3. LIKE MEDICINE like medicine, especially in having a bitter taste [14C. Directly or via French < Latin *medicinalis* < *medicina* (see MEDICINE)] —**me·dic·i·nal·ly** *adv*

me·dic·i·nal leech *n* a large freshwater leech that lives on blood, formerly used in bloodletting and still occasionally used to prevent coagulation. Native to: Europe. Latin name: *Hirudo medicinalis.*

med·i·cine /méddəssin/ *n* 1. DRUG FOR TREATING ILLNESS a drug or remedy used for treating illness ○ *cough medicine* 2. TREATMENT OF ILLNESS the diagnosis and treatment of illnesses, wounds, and injuries 3. TREATMENT USING DRUGS the treatment of illness or injury using drugs rather than surgery 4. MEDICAL PROFESSION the profession of treating illness as a doctor 5. CULTL ANTHROP RITUAL PRACTICE OR SACRED OBJECT a ritual practice or sacred object believed, especially by Native North Americans, to control supernatural powers or to work as a preventive or remedy of illness [12C. Directly or via French < Latin *medicina* "practice of medicine" < *medicus* "doctor" < *mederi* "heal"] ◇ **a dose** *or* **taste of your own medicine** unpleasant treatment of the same kind that you have given others (*informal*)

med·i·cine ball *n* a large heavy ball that people throw to each other as a strength-building exercise

med·i·cine chest *n* a small cupboard or chest where medicines, bandages, and other things used in treating illness or injury are stored

med·i·cine dance *n* a ceremonial religious dance performed by one or more Native North Americans to obtain supernatural assistance for something, e.g., to cure illness

Med·i·cine Hat /mèddəssin hát/ city in southeastern Alberta, Canada, on the South Saskatchewan River. Population: 55,724 (2001).

med·i·cine line *n Can* among Native North Americans, the border between Canada and the United States west of Ontario (*archaic*) [Probably referring to the power this line had, for example, when the Sioux fled over it after defeating George Armstrong Custer]

med·i·cine lodge *n* a wooden building used by some Native North American peoples for rituals such as ceremonial curing

med·i·cine man *n* a man believed to be able to heal others by making use of supernatural powers, especially among Native North American peoples

med·i·cine person (*plural* **med·i·cine peo·ple**) *n* somebody believed to heal others by making use of supernatural powers, especially among Native North American peoples

med·i·cine show *n* especially in the United States in the 19th century, a traveling show in which medicines were sold to the people who came to see the entertainments

med·i·cine wo·man *n* a woman believed to heal others by making use of supernatural powers, especially among Native North American peoples

med·ick /méddik/, **med·ic** *n* a plant of the pea family with three-lobed leaves. Use: fodder. Genus: *Medicago.* [14C. Via Latin *medica* < Greek *Mēdikē* (*poa*) "(poppy) of Media"]

med·i·co /méddi kō/ (*plural* **-cos**) *n* a doctor or medical student (*informal*) [Late 17C. Via Italian < Latin *medicus* (see MEDICINE)]

me·di·e·val /meèdee eév'l, mèddee-/, **me·di·ae·val** *adj* 1. relating to, involving, belonging to, or typical of the Middle Ages in Europe 2. old-fashioned, especially because lacking modern enlightened attitudes ○ *Some of the attitudes in the industry were positively medieval.* [Early 19C. < modern Latin *medium aevum* "middle age"] —**me·di·e·val·ly** *adv*

me·di·e·val Greek *n* the form of Greek used between the 7th and 13th centuries —**me·di·e·val Greek** *adj*

me·di·e·val·ism /meèdee eév'l ìzzəm, mèddee-/, **me·di·ae·val·ism** *n* 1. CUSTOMS AND BELIEFS OF MIDDLE AGES the customs, practices, or beliefs during the Middle Ages in Europe 2. DEVOTION TO MIDDLE AGES devotion to the spirit or beliefs of the Middle Ages in Europe 3. SOMETHING FROM MIDDLE AGES a belief, custom, or style from or like one from the Middle Ages

me·di·e·val·ist /meèdee eév'list, mèddee-/, **me·di·ae·**

val·ist *n* somebody who studies, teaches the history of, or is an expert in the Middle Ages in Europe

me·di·e·val Lat·in *n* the form of Latin used in Europe during the Middle Ages —**me·di·e·val Lat·in** *adj*

me·di·na /mə déenə/, **Me·di·na** *n* the oldest part of many North African cities [Early 20C. < Arabic, "town"]

Me·di·na /mə déenə/ city in western Saudi Arabia, the site of the Mosque of the Prophet that houses the tomb of Muhammad. Population: 608,300 (1992).

me·di·o·cre /mèe dee ṓkər, mée dee òkər/ *adj* adequate or acceptable, but not very good [Late 16C. Directly or via French < Latin *mediocris* "of middle height" < *ocris* "rugged mountain"] —**me·di·o·cre·ly** *adv*

me·di·oc·ri·ty /mèedee ókratee/ (*plural* **-ties**) *n* **1.** a quality that is adequate or acceptable, but not very good ○ *His poetry seldom rises above the level of mediocrity.* **2.** somebody who lacks any special skill or flair [15C. Directly or via French *médiocrité* < Latin *mediocritas* < *mediocris* (see MEDIOCRE)]

Medit. *abbr* Mediterranean

med·i·tate /méddi tàyt/ (**-tat·ed, -tat·ing, -tates**) *v* **1.** *vi* **EMPTY OR CONCENTRATE MIND** to empty the mind of thoughts, or concentrate the mind on one thing, in order to aid mental or spiritual development, contemplation, or relaxation **2.** *vi* **THINK CAREFULLY ABOUT SOMETHING** to think about something carefully, calmly, seriously, and for some time **3.** *vt* **PLAN SOMETHING** to plan or consider doing something [Mid-16C. Either < Latin *meditat-*, past participle of *meditare* "keep on measuring," related to *mederi* "to cure"; or back-formation < MEDITATION] —**med·i·ta·tive** *adj* —**med·i·ta·tive·ly** *adv* —**med·i·ta·tive·ness** *n* —**med·i·ta·tor** *n*

med·i·ta·tion /mèddi táysh'n/ *n* **1. EMPTYING OR CONCENTRATION OF MIND** the emptying of the mind of thoughts, or the concentration of the mind on one thing, in order to aid mental or spiritual development, contemplation, or relaxation **2. PONDERING OF SOMETHING** the act of thinking about something carefully, calmly, seriously, and for some time, or an instance of such thinking **3. SERIOUS STUDY OF TOPIC** an extended and serious study of a topic [15C. Directly or via French < Latin *meditation-* < *meditari* (see MEDITATE)] —**med·i·ta·tion·al** *adj*

Med·i·ter·ra·ne·an /mèdditə ráynee ən/ *n* **1. MEDITERRANEAN SEA OR SURROUNDING AREA** the Mediterranean Sea, or the lands bordering it ○ *vacationing in the Mediterranean* **2. SOMEBODY FROM AROUND MEDITERRANEAN** somebody who comes from a region bordering the Mediterranean Sea ■ *adj* **1. IN OR NEAR MEDITERRANEAN** located in the Mediterranean Sea, or in a region that borders it **2. RELATING TO MEDITERRANEAN PEOPLE** relating to or associated with the people living in a region that borders the Mediterranean Sea **3.** METEOROL **WITH HOT SUMMERS AND WARM WINTERS** having hot summers and warm winters, with most of the rainfall occurring in the winter **4.** ANTHROP **WITH DARK HAIR AND OLIVE SKIN** resembling people from countries around the Mediterranean Sea, who often have dark hair and olive complexions [Mid-16C. < Latin *mediterraneus* "inland" < *medius* "middle" + *terra* "earth"]

Med·i·ter·ra·ne·an fe·ver *n* MED same as **brucellosis** [Because it is common in that region]

Med·i·ter·ra·ne·an flour moth *n* a small gray moth, common worldwide, whose larvae feed on grain and grain products. Latin name: *Anagasta kuehniella.*

Med·i·ter·ra·ne·an fruit fly *n* a black-and-white two-winged fly that lays its eggs in citrus and other types of fruit, which the maggots then destroy. Native to: Mediterranean, but spread elsewhere. Latin name: *Ceratitis capitata.*

Med·i·ter·ra·ne·an Sea /mèddi tə ràynee ən-/ inland sea of Europe, Asia, and Africa, linked to the Atlantic Ocean at its western end by the Strait of Gibraltar. Area: 968,700 sq. mi./2,509,000 sq. km.

~~Mediterranean~~ incorrect spelling of **Mediterranean**

me·di·um /méedee əm/ *adj* **1. NEITHER LARGE NOR SMALL** of middling size or dimensions, neither large nor small ○ *a man of medium build* **2.** COOK **BETWEEN RARE AND WELL DONE** cooked so that the meat is brown on the outside but slightly pink and moist inside ■ *n* (*plural* **-di·a** /-dee ə/ or **-di·ums**) **1. STATE BETWEEN EXTREMES** an intermediate state or condition halfway between two extremes **2. MEANS OF MASS COMMUNICATION** a means of mass communication, e.g., television, radio, or newspapers **3. VEHICLE FOR IDEAS** a means of conveying ideas or information ○ *French is the medium of instruction in all subjects.* **4. SUBSTANCE CARRIER** a substance through which something is carried or transmitted **5.** PARANORMAL **SOMEBODY SUPPOSEDLY COMMUNICATING WITH DEAD** somebody believed to transmit messages between living people and the spirits of the dead **6. MEANS TO END** the means by which something is carried out or achieved **7. MEDIUM-SIZED PIECE OF CLOTHING** a piece of clothing that is medium in size **8.** COMPUT **MATERIAL HOLDING DATA** a material on which data is stored or printed, e.g., paper, tape, or disk **9.** BIOL **PRESERVING SUBSTANCE** a substance in which specimens of animals and plants are preserved or mounted **10.** BIOL **NATURAL ENVIRONMENT** a substance or environment in which an organism naturally lives or grows **11.** ARTS **TYPE OF ART** a method that an artist uses or a category such as sculpture in which an artist works **12.** ARTS **ARTIST'S MATERIALS** the materials that an artist uses in creating a work **13.** INDUST **SOLVENT** a solvent mixed with a pigment or paint to make it thinner **14.** PAPER **PAPER SIZE** a size of paper, especially 18.5 in. by 23 in./47 cm by 58.5 cm [Late 16C. < Latin, neuter of *medius* "middle"]

ORIGIN The Latin word *medius* "middle," from which ***medium*** is derived, is also the source of English *immediate, intermezzo, mean*[3], *media*[1], *mediate, medieval, mediocre, meridian, mezzanine, mitten,* and *moiety.*

me·di·um fre·quen·cy *n* a radio frequency lying between 300 and 3,000 kilohertz

me·di·um of ex·change *n* something commonly recognized in a country or community as a standard of value and used in the same way as money, e.g., gold

me·di·um shot *n* a filmed view, midway between long shot and close-up, that shows a standing person from the waist up or the full body of a sitting person ○ *a medium shot of the two characters in conversation*

me·di·um wave *n* a radio wave with a wavelength that lies between 100 and 1,000 m (*hyphenated when used before a noun*)

med·lar /méddlər/ *n* **1.** a small apple-shaped fruit that is not edible until it is overripe. Use: preserves. **2.** a small fruit tree that produces medlars. Native to: Europe, Asia. Latin name: *Mespilus germanica.* [14C. < Old French *medler* < *medle* "medlar fruit" (a variant of *mesle*) < Greek *mespilē*]

Med. Lat. *abbr* medieval Latin

med·ley /méddlee/ (*plural* **-leys**) *n* **1. MIXTURE OF THINGS** a mixture or assortment of various things **2.** MUSIC **MUSICAL SEQUENCE OF DIFFERENT SONGS** a continuous piece of music consisting of two or more different tunes or songs played one after the other **3.** SWIMMING **RACE USING DIFFERENT STROKES** a swimming race between individual swimmers or relay teams in which sections are swum using different strokes **4. RELAY RACE WITH DIFFERENT LENGTHS** a relay race in which each member of a team runs a different length [14C. < Old French *medlee*, variant of *meslee* "melee" < medieval Latin *misculare* "mix thoroughly" < *miscere* "mix"]

med·ley re·lay *n* **1.** a relay swimming race between teams of four swimmers, each of whom uses a different stroke **2.** TRACK AND FIELD same as **medley** (sense 4)

me·dul·la /mə dúllə/ (*plural* **-las** or **-lae** /-lee/) *n* **1.** BIOL the innermost area of a part or organ of an animal or plant ○ *the adrenal medulla* **2.** ANAT same as **medulla oblongata 3.** BOT same as **pith** *n* (sense 2) [14C. < Latin, "pith"] —**me·dul·lar** *adj*

me·dul·la ob·lon·ga·ta /mə dùllə ob long gaátə/ (*plural* **me·dul·la ob·lon·ga·tas** or **me·dul·lae ob·lon·ga·tae** /-lée ob long gaá tee/) *n* the lowermost part of the brain in vertebrates. It is continuous with the spinal cord and controls involuntary vital functions such as those involved with the heart and lungs. [< Latin, literally "prolonged marrow"]

med·ul·lar·y ray /mə dùllaree-/ *n* any of the bands or sheets of connective tissue that radiate between the pith and bark in the stems of some higher woody plants

med·ul·lar·y sheath *n* ANAT same as **myelin sheath**

med·ul·lat·ed /médd'l àytəd, méjjə làytəd/ *adj* **1.** ANAT same as **myelinated 2.** having a medulla ○ *medullated fibers*

med·ul·lo·blas·to·ma /mə dùllō bla stṓmə/ (*plural* **-mas** or **-ma·ta** /-mətə/) *n* a rapidly growing malignant tumor of the central nervous system arising in the brain, especially in children [Early 20C. < MEDULLA + BLASTO-]

me·du·sa /mə dóossə, -zə/ (*plural* **-sas** or **-sae** /-ssee, -zee/) *n* **1.** the free-swimming reproductive stage of an animal such as a jellyfish, during which it has a transparent umbrella-shaped body with tentacles **2.** ZOOL same as **jellyfish** (sense 1) [Mid-18C. < modern Latin < Greek *Medousa* "Medusa"; from the resemblance of the tentacles to the snakes on Medusa's head] —**me·du·san** *adj* —**me·du·soid** *adj, n*

Barnaby's

Medusa: Roman mosaic, Sousse, France

Me·du·sa /mə dóossə, -zə/ *n* in Greek mythology, a Gorgon who could turn anyone who looked at her to stone. She was killed by Perseus. —**Me·du·san** *adj*

meed /meed/ *n* something given as a reward or compensation (*archaic or literary*) [Old English *mēd* "price, compensation" < Germanic]

meek /meek/ *adj* **1.** showing mildness or quietness of nature **2.** showing submissiveness and lack of initiative or will [12C. < Old Norse *mjúkr* "soft, pliant"] —**meek·ly** *adv* —**meek·ness** *n*

meerkat

meer·kat /méer kàt/ *n* a burrowing mongoose with four-toed feet and a grayish coat with faint black markings. Native to: southern Africa. Latin name: *Suricata suricatta.* [Early 19C. Via Afrikaans < Middle Low German *meerkatte* < *meer* "sea" + *katte* "cat"]

meer·schaum /méershəm, méer shàwm/ *n* **1.** a fine whitish mineral like clay, consisting of hydrous magnesium silicate **2.** *also* **meer·schaum pipe** a tobacco pipe with a bowl made of meerschaum [Late 18C. < German < *Meer* "sea" + *Schaum* "foam," translation of Persian *kef-i-daryā*; from its frothy appearance]

meet[1] /meet/ *v* (**met** /met/, **meet·ing, meets**) **1.** *vti* **COME ACROSS SOMEBODY** to encounter somebody without having arranged to do so beforehand ○ *Guess who I met in the supermarket?* **2.** *vti* **GET TOGETHER** to get together with somebody by arrangement ○ *We could meet for lunch tomorrow.* **3.** *vti* **ENCOUNTER SOMEBODY FOR FIRST TIME** to encounter somebody or each other for the first time ○ *They met exactly a year ago.* **4.** *vt* **GREET SOMEBODY** to go somewhere to greet or pick up somebody who is arriving there ○ *I'll come and meet you at the airport.* **5.** *vi* **GATHER FOR DISCUSSION** to gather in a place to discuss something ○ *The committee meets monthly.* **6.** *vti* **JOIN SOMETHING** to join, cross, or be adjacent to something or each other ○ *where the two roads meet* **7.** *vti* **TOUCH SOMETHING** to bring something into contact with something else, or be brought into contact ○ *I can't get the two ropes to meet.* **8.** *vti* **EXPERIENCE SOMETHING** to experience something such as a difficulty, challenge, or success ○ *All our attempts met with failure.* **9.** *vt* SATISFY SOMETHING to cope with, satisfy, or fulfill what is required ○ *The new system meets all our computing requirements.* **10.** *vt* AGREE WITH SOMEBODY to come to an agreement with somebody on something ○ *I think we can meet you on that price.* **11.** *vti* LOOK AT SOMETHING to look at or confront something, or look at or confront each other ○ *Their glances met.* **12.** *vti* COMPETE OR FIGHT WITH SOMEBODY to come together to compete or fight with somebody or each other ○ *The two teams have already met this year.* **13.** *vt* RESPOND IN PARTICULAR WAY to respond to a situation with a particular type of behavior ○ *He met success and failure with equal indifference.* **14.** *vi* OCCUR TOGETHER to happen or come together in the same place or person ○ *The extremes of creativity and irresponsibility meet in this genius.* ■ *n* **1.** SPORTS OCCASION an occasion at which numbers of competitors and spectators come together **2.** *UK* HUNTING GATHERING BEFORE HUNT the period before a hunt when the riders and hounds gather together [Old English *mētan* "come upon" < Germanic, "meeting"]

SPELLCHECK See *meat.*

meet up *vi* to get together with somebody
meet with *vt* **1.** GET TOGETHER WITH to have a meeting with other people **2.** RECEIVE to get a particular reaction or result ○ *The suggestion met with his approval.* **3.** EXPERIENCE to experience something unpleasant (*formal*) ○ *He met with an accident.*

meet[2] /meet/ *adj* suitable or fitting (*archaic*) [Old English *gemǣte* < Germanic, "measure"] —**meet·ly** *adv*

meet·ing /meeting/ *n* **1.** GATHERING OF PEOPLE FOR DISCUSSION an occasion when people gather together to discuss something **2.** GROUP AT MEETING the people attending a meeting ○ *The speaker stood up to address the meeting.* **3.** OCCASION WHEN PEOPLE MEET an occasion when somebody encounters somebody else, either accidentally or by arrangement **4.** OCCASION FOR WORSHIP a regular occasion when a group of people, especially Quakers, gather for worship

meet·ing·house /meeting hòwss/ *n* a room or building where some religious groups, especially Quakers, meet to worship

mef·e·nam·ic ac·id /mèffə nàmmik-/ *n* a drug that reduces inflammation. Use: pain relief from rheumatoid arthritis, menstruation. [< METHYL + *-fen-* (alteration and shortening of PHENYL) + *am-* (shortening of *amino-*) + *-ic* (shortening of *benzoic*)]

meg /meg/ *n* COMPUT same as **megabyte** (*informal*)

meg- *prefix* same as **mega-** (*used before vowels*)

me·ga /méggə/ *adj UK* extremely enjoyable, impressive, excellent, or large (*informal*) [Late 20C. < MEGA-]

mega- *prefix* **1.** one million (10^6) ○ *megavolt* Symbol **M** **2.** COMPUT in the binary system, a million (2^{20}) ○ *megabyte* **3.** very large ○ *megadose* **4.** very great or excellent ○ *megastar* **5.** to a great extent (*slang*) ○ *megarich* [< Greek *megas* "great" < Indo-European, "large"]

meg·a·bar /méggə baar/ *n* a unit of pressure equal to one million bars

meg·a·bit /méggə bìt/ *n* COMPUT **1.** 1,048,576 bits **2.** one million bits

meg·a·buck /méggə bùk/ (*slang*) *n* a million dollars ■ **meg·a·bucks** *npl* a large unspecified amount of money ○ *an actor earning megabucks in Hollywood*

meg·a·byte /méggə bīt/ *n* **1.** a unit of computer data or storage space equivalent to 1,024 kilobytes **2.** one million bytes

meg·a·ceph·a·ly /mèggə séffəlee/ *n* MED same as **macrocephaly** —**meg·a·ce·phal·ic** /mèggə sə fállik/ *adj* —**meg·a·ceph·a·lous** *adj*

meg·a·church /méggə chùrch/ *n* a church with a very large membership, usually in the thousands, and often nondenominational and evangelical or charismatic in character

meg·a·cy·cle /méggə sīk'l/ *n* PHYS same as **megahertz**

meg·a·death /méggə dèth/ *n* one million deaths, used as a unit for recording deaths in a nuclear war

meg·a·dose /méggə dōss/ *n* a very large dose of a medical drug or food supplement

Me·gae·ra /mə jeérə/ *n* in Greek mythology, one of the three Furies. The others were Alecto and Tisiphone.

meg·a·faun·a /mèggə fáwnə/ *n* the animal life in a particular place that is larger than microscopic in size —**meg·a·faun·al** *adj*

meg·a·gam·ete /méggə gà meet/ *n* BIOL same as **macrogamete**

meg·a·hertz /méggə hùrts/ (*plural same*) *n* one million hertz. Symbol **MHz**

meg·a·kar·y·o·cyte /mèggə kárree ə sīt/ *n* a large cell in bone marrow that fragments to produce blood platelets

megal- *prefix* same as **megalo-** (*used before vowels*)

meg·a·lith /méggə lìth/ *n* an enormous stone, usually standing upright or forming part of a prehistoric structure —**meg·a·lith·ic** /mèggə líthik/ *adj*

megalo- *prefix* exceptionally large ○ *megalocardia* [< Greek *megal-*, stem of *megas* (see MEGA-)]

meg·a·lo·blast /méggəlō blàst/ *n* an unusually large red blood cell that has failed to mature properly, found especially in people affected by anemia

meg·a·lo·blas·tic a·ne·mi·a /meggəlō blàstik-/ *n* a form of anemia in which the red blood cells are unusually large because they have failed to mature properly. It includes the type formerly known as pernicious anemia.

meg·a·lo·car·di·a /mèggəlō kárdee ə/ *n* MED same as **cardiomegaly**

meg·a·lo·ceph·a·ly /mèggəlō séffəlee/ *n* MED same as **macrocephaly** (*not in technical use*) —**meg·a·lo·ce·phal·ic** /-sə fállik/ *adj* —**meg·a·lo·ceph·a·lous** *adj*

meg·a·lo·ma·ni·a /mèggəlō máynee ə, mèggələ-/ *n* **1.** an excessive enjoyment in having power over other people and a craving for more of it **2.** a psychiatric disorder in which the patient experiences delusions of great power and importance —**meg·a·lo·ma·ni·ac** *n, adj* —**meg·a·lo·ma·ni·a·cal** /-mə nī ək'l/ *adj* —**meg·a·lo·ma·ni·a·cal·ly** *adv*

meg·a·lop·o·lis /mèggə lóppəliss/ *n* **1.** an area in which there are several large cities whose suburbs meet or nearly meet **2.** an extremely large and populous city [Mid-19C. < MEGALO- + Greek *polis* "city"] —**meg·a·lop·o·lis·tic** /-lopə lístik/ *adj* —**meg·a·lo·pol·i·tan** /-lə póllit'n/ *adj*

meg·a·lo·saur /méggələ sàwr/ *n* a very large carnivorous dinosaur of the Jurassic and early Cretaceous periods. Genus: *Megalosaurus*. [Mid-19C. Anglicization of modern Latin *megalosaurus* < MEGALO- + Greek *sauros* "lizard"] —**meg·a·lo·sau·ri·an** /mèggələ sáwree ən/ *adj*

-megaly *suffix* unusual enlargement ○ *hepatomegaly* [< modern Latin *-megalia* < Greek *megal-* (see MEGALO-)]

meg·a·ma·ser /méggə màyzər/ *n* an intense source of galactic maser radiation

Meg·an's Law /méggənz-/ *n* an amendment to the Violent Crime Control and Law Enforcement Act of 1994, requiring community notification when a paroled or released sex offender moves into a neighborhood [Late 20C. After *Megan* Kanka, seven-year-old girl killed by a convicted child molester]

meg·a·phone /méggə fōn/ *n* a device shaped like a funnel, used to channel the voice in one direction and increase its volume ■ *vti* (**-phoned, -phon·ing, -phones**) to speak using a megaphone, or say something through one —**meg·a·phon·ic** /mèggə fónnik/ *adj* —**meg·a·phon·i·cal·ly** *adv*

meg·a·pix·el /méggə pìks'l, -pìk sel/ *n* a unit of graphics data transfer speed or image resolution equal to 1,048,576 pixels

meg·a·plex /méggə plèks/ *n* **1.** a large movie theater complex housing at least fifteen screens, often with the same movie playing simultaneously in three or four of the theaters **2.** a very large complex of buildings

meg·a·pode /méggə pōd/ *n* a large ground-dwelling bird that builds a large mound of earth in which to incubate its eggs. Native to: Australasia. Family: Megapodiidae. [Mid-19C. < modern Latin *Megapodius* "with big feet"]

me·gap·o·lis /mə gáppəliss/ *n* GEOG same as **megalopolis** (sense 1) [Mid-17C. < MEGA- + Greek *polis* "city"]

Meg·a·ra /méggərə/ historic town in southern Greece. It once rivaled ancient Athens in power. Population: 25,061 (1991).

meg·a·rich /méggə rìch/ *adj* extremely rich (*informal*) ○ *You need 500 million dollars to be considered megarich these days.*

meg·a·ron /méggə ròn/ (*plural* **-ra** /-rə/) *n* the largest room in a house built during the Mycenaean period of ancient Greek civilization [Late 19C. < Greek, "large room"]

meg·a·scop·ic /mèggə skóppik/ *adj* PHYS same as **macroscopic** —**meg·a·scop·i·cal·ly** *adv*

meg·a·spore /méggə spàwr/ *n* the larger of two kinds of spore produced by seed plants and some ferns, which develops into a female gametophyte

meg·a·spo·ro·gen·e·sis /mèggə spàwrə jénnəssiss/ *n* the formation and maturing of megaspores

me·ga·sprawl /méggə spràwl/ *n* a very large area of uncontrolled urbanization [20C.]

meg·a·star /méggə staar/ *n* an extremely famous person, especially an entertainer

me·ga·store /méggə stàwr/ *n* an extremely large store that sells a range of goods

meg·a·there /méggə theer/ *n* a large extinct American ground sloth that lived in the Miocene and Pleistocene epochs. Family: Megatheriidae. [Mid-19C. Anglicization of modern Latin *Megatherium* < Greek *mega-* "large" + *thērion* "animal"] —**meg·a·the·ri·an** /mèggə theeree ən/ *adj*

meg·a·ton /méggə tùn/ *n* **1.** a unit of explosive power, e.g., in a nuclear weapon, that is equivalent to one million tons of TNT **2.** one million tons —**meg·a·ton·ic** /mèggə túnnik/ *adj* —**meg·a·ton·nage** *n*

meg·a·vi·ta·min /mèggə vītəmin/ *n* a dose of a vitamin or vitamins that is much higher than the usual dose —**meg·a·vi·ta·min** *adj*

meg·a·volt /méggə vōlt/ *n* one million volts —**meg·a·volt·age** *n*

meg·a·watt /méggə wòt/ *n* one million watts —**meg·a·watt·age** /méggə wòttij/ *n*

Me·gha·la·ya /màygə láy ə/ state in northeastern India. Capital: Shillong. Population: 2,306,069 (2001). Area: 8,660 sq. mi./22,429 sq. km.

Me·gid·do /mə geédō/ ruined ancient city in northern Israel, thought to be the site of the predicted battle of Armageddon described in the Bible

meg·il·lah /mə gíllə/ (*plural* **-lahs** or **-loth** /-lōt/) *n* **1.** a scroll containing part of the Hebrew Bible, especially the scroll containing the Book of Esther **2.** an overly elaborate and unnecessarily lengthy account of something (*slang*) [Mid-17C. < Hebrew, "roll, scroll" < *gālal* "roll"]

me·gilp /mə gílp/, **ma·gilp** *n* a mixture of linseed oil and mastic varnish or turpentine. Use: solvent for oil paints. [Mid-18C. Origin ?]

me·grim /meegrim/ (*archaic*) *n* **1.** MED same as **migraine** **2.** a sudden change of mind, or something about which somebody is briefly enthusiastic (*often pl*) ■ **me·grims** *npl* a period of melancholy or low spirits [15C. Variant of MIGRAINE]

mei·bo·mi·an cyst /mī bōmee ən-/ *n* a painless pea-shaped swelling in the eyelid, caused by the blockage of the outlet duct of a meibomian gland and the resulting accumulation of fatty secretion [See MEIBOMIAN GLAND]

mei·bo·mi·an gland *n* a sebaceous gland in the eyelid [Early 19C. After Heinrich *Meibom* (1638–1700), German anatomist]

Meigh·en /máygən/, **Arthur** (1874–1960) Canadian prime minister (1920–21 and 1926). A member of the Liberal-Conservative Party, he held a series of cabinet posts from 1915 until his election as prime minister in 1920. See table at **prime minister**

Mei·ji /máy jee/ *n* the reign of the Japanese emperor Meiji Tenno (1867–1912), a period of extensive reform, including the abolition of feudalism [Late 19C. < Japanese, "enlightened government"]

Mei·ji Ten·no /mày jee ténnō/, **emperor of Japan** (1852–1912) During a long reign (1867–1912), he modernized Japanese industry and introduced a new constitution that abolished feudalism (1889). Born **Mutsuhito**

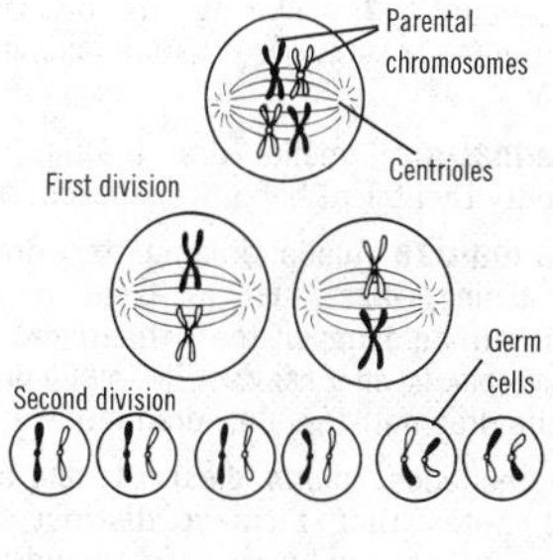

meiosis

mei·o·sis /mī ṓssiss/ *n* **1.** in organisms that reproduce sexually, a process of cell division during which the nucleus divides into four nuclei, each of which contains half the usual number of chromosomes **2.** LITERAT same as **litotes** [Mid-16C. < modern Latin < Greek *meiōn* "less"] —**mei·o·tic** /mī óttik/ *adj*

Golda Meir

Me·ir /mī ər, may éer/, **Golda** (1898–1978) Ukrainian-born Israeli politician. She served in the Labor government of Israel from 1949 and as prime minister from 1969 until 1974, when she resigned after the Yom Kippur War (1973). Born **Goldie Mabovich**

> "We intend to remain alive. Our neighbors want to see us dead. This is not a question that leaves much room for compromise."
> [Golda Meir, "The Indestructible Golda Meir," *Reader's Digest*; July 1971]

> "We who have such an intimate knowledge of boxcars and deportation...cannot be silent."
> [Golda Meir, *Speech to the UN General Assembly on bellicose Soviet actions in Hungary*; November 21, 1956]

mei·shi *n* a business card carried by a Japanese businessperson

Meis·sen[1] /míss'n/ *n US* fine and delicate porcelain as made in Meissen since the early 18th century. Can term **Dresden china** [Mid-19C. < MEISSEN[2]]

Meis·sen[2] /míss'n/ town in east central Germany, famous for its porcelain manufacture. Population: 32,900 (1997).

Meiss·ner's cor·pus·cle /míssnərz-/ *n* ANAT same as **tactile corpuscle** [Late 19C. After Georg *Meissner* (1829–1905), German anatomist]

-meister /místər/ *suffix* a highly skilled or prominent person (*humorous*) ○ *webmeister* ○ *spinmeister*

Meis·ter·sing·er /místər sìngər/ (*plural* **-ers** or *same*) *n* a member of a German guild for poets and musicians in the 14th to 16th centuries who had completed an apprenticeship and composed original work [Mid-19C. < German, "master-singer"]

Meit·ner /mítnər/, **Lise** (1878–1968) Austrian physicist. She was the first scientist to identify nuclear fission, and discovered the element protactinium in association with Otto Hahn.

meit·ner·i·um /mīt néeree əm/ *n* a highly unstable radioactive chemical element. Source: produced artificially by nuclear fusion. Symbol **Mt.** See table at **element** [Late 20C. After Lise MEITNER]

Me·jí·a /me hée a/, **Hipólito** (*b.* 1941) president of the Dominican Republic (2000–). A member of the left-wing Dominican Revolutionary Party, he has stated that fighting poverty and corruption are his primary objectives.

Mek·nès /mèk néss/ city and former capital of Morocco, located in the north of the country. Population: 530,171 (1994).

Me·kong /mee kóng/ major river in Southeast Asia, flowing through a number of countries before emptying into the South China Sea. Length: 2,610 mi./4,200 km.

me·la /máy laà/ *n S Asia* a large gathering [Early 19C. Via Hindi < Sanskrit *melā*]

mel·ae·na *n* MED UK spelling of **melena**

Me·la·ka /mə lákə/ city and seaport in Malaysia, on the southern coast of the Malay Peninsula. Population: 75,909 (1996). Former name **Malacca**

mel·a·leu·ca /mèllə lóokə/ *n* a tree or bush of the myrtle family that flourishes in wetlands and has become a pest in parts of North America. Native to: Australia. Genus: *Melaleuca.* [Early 19C. < modern Latin < Greek *melas* "black" + *leukos* "white"]

mel·a·mine /méllə meen/ *n* **1.** a plastic made from copolymerizing a white crystalline solid with formaldehyde **2.** a white crystalline solid. Use: manufacture of synthetic resins, in leather tanning. Formula: $C_3H_6N_6$. [Mid-19C. Probably < German *Melamin*, substance obtained from the distillation of ammonium thiocyanate]

melan- *prefix* same as **melano-** (*used before vowels*)

mel·an·cho·li·a /mèllən kólee ə/ *n* depression as a form of psychiatric disorder (*dated*) [Early 17C. < late Latin (see MELANCHOLY)] —**mel·an·cho·li·ac** /mèllən kólee àk/ *n, adj*

mel·an·chol·ic /mèllən kóllik/ *adj* feeling or tending to feel a thoughtful or gentle sadness [14C. Either < MELANCHOLY or < French *mélancolique* < Greek *melankholia* (see MELANCHOLY)] —**mel·an·chol·i·cal·ly** *adv*

mel·an·chol·y /méllən kòllee/ *adj* **FEELING OR CAUSING SADNESS** feeling or making somebody feel a thoughtful or gentle sadness ■ *n* **1. PENSIVE SADNESS** a thoughtful or gentle sadness **2. GLOOMY CHARACTER** the gloomy character of somebody said to have an excess of black bile, one of the four bodily humors that were once thought to determine people's health and emotional state **3.** MED same as **black bile** (*archaic*) [14C. Directly or via French *mélancholie* < late Latin *melancholia* < Greek *melankholia* < *melan-* "black" + *kholē* "bile"] —**mel·an·chol·i·ly** *adv* —**mel·an·chol·i·ness** *n*

Me·lanch·thon /mə lángkthən, me laánkh ton/, **Philipp** (1497–1560) German religious reformer. Working in association with Martin Luther, he produced some of the most important theological works of the Protestant Reformation, including *Commonplaces of Theology* (1521) and the Augsburg Confession (1530). Born **Schwartzert, Philipp**

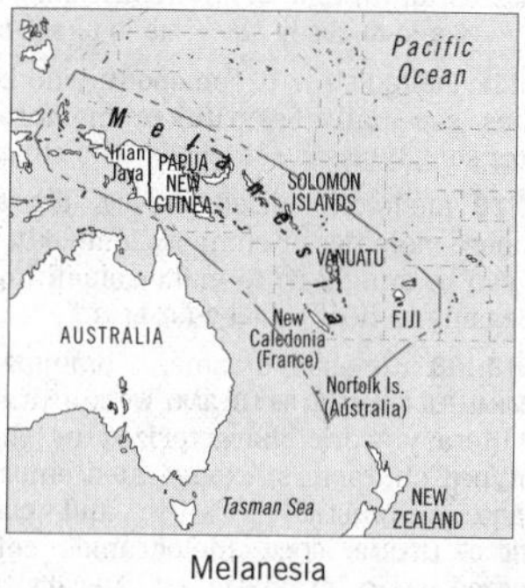

Melanesia

Mel·a·ne·sia /mèllə néezhə, -néeshə/ ethnographic grouping of Pacific islands, encompassing the islands of the western Pacific Ocean south of the equator, including New Guinea, the Solomon Islands, New Caledonia, Vanuatu, and Fiji

Mel·a·ne·sian /mèllə néezh'n/ *n* **1.** a group of Austronesian languages, including Fijian, spoken in Melanesia. Native speakers: 300,000. **2.** a member of any people living on the islands of Melanesia —**Mel·a·ne·sian** *adj*

mé·lange /may laáNzh, -laánzh/, **me·lange** *n* **1.** a collection of things of different kinds (*literary or formal*) **2.** a region of rock that consists of a mixture of dissimilar rocky materials [Mid-17C. < French *mélange* < *mêler* "to mix" < Latin *miscere*]

mel·a·nin /méllənin/ *n* a dark brown or black pigment that is naturally present to varying degrees in the skin, hair, eyes, fur, or feathers of people and animals as well as in plants —**me·lan·ic** /mə lánnik/ *adj* —**mel·a·noid** *adj*

mel·a·nism /méllə nìzzəm/ *n* **1.** dark pigmentation of the skin, hair, fur, or feathers in a human being, animal, or plant, resulting from the presence of melanin **2.** MED same as **melanosis** —**mel·a·nis·tic** /mèllə nístik/ *adj*

mel·a·nite /méllə nìt/ *n* a black andradite garnet containing titanium —**mel·a·nit·ic** /mèllə níttik/ *adj*

melano- *prefix* black, dark ○ *melanocyte* [< Greek *melan-* "black"]

mel·a·no·blast /mèllənō blàst, mə lánnə-/ *n* a cell that gives rise to either a melanocyte or melanophore, which produce the dark brown or black pigment melanin —**mel·a·no·blas·tic** /mèllənō blástik, mə lànnə-/ *adj*

mel·a·no·cyte /méllənō sìt, mə lánnə-/ *n* a cell in the epidermal layer of the skin that produces the dark brown or black pigment melanin

mel·a·no·cyte-stim·u·lat·ing hor·mone *n* either of two hormones in vertebrates produced in the pituitary gland that darken the skin by regulating melanin dispersal

mel·a·noid /méllə nòyd/ *adj* **1.** similar to melanin **2.** similar to melanosis

mel·a·no·ma /mèllə nṓmə/ (*plural* **-mas** or **-ma·ta** /-mətə/) *n* a malignant tumor, most often on the skin, that contains dark pigment and develops from a melanin-producing cell (**melanocyte**)

mel·a·no·phore /méllənō fàwr, mə lánnə-/ *n* a cell in fishes, amphibians, and reptiles that contains the dark brown or black pigment melanin

mel·a·no·sis /mèllə nṓssis/ *n* an unexpected presence of dark pigmentation in the tissues [Early 19C. < modern Latin < Greek *melan-* "black"] —**mel·a·not·ic** /-nóttik/ *adj*

me·la·no·some /méllənə sṑm, mə lánnə-/ *n* a small sac within an epidermal cell (**melanocyte**) in which the dark brown or black pigment melanin is synthesized

mel·a·nous /méllənəss/ *adj* having a dark complexion and dark hair [Mid-19C. < Greek *melan-* "black"] —**mel·a·nos·i·ty** /mèllə nóssətee/ *n*

mel·a·to·nin /mèllə tṓnin/ *n* a hormone derived from serotonin and secreted by the pineal gland that produces changes in the skin color of vertebrates, reptiles, and amphibians and is important in regulating biorhythms [Mid-20C. Blend of MELANO- + SEROTONIN]

Dame Nellie Melba

Mel·ba /mélbə/, **Dame Nellie** (1859–1931) Australian opera singer. She was a soprano who won international acclaim for her performances in roles such as Mimì in *La Bohème.* Born **Mitchell, Helen Porter**

> "Music is not written in red, white and blue. It is written in the heart's blood of the composer."
> [Dame Nellie Melba, *Melodies and Memories*; 1925]

Mel·ba sauce *n* a sauce consisting of puréed sweetened raspberries, served especially with poached peaches and ice cream in peach Melba [Early 20C. After Dame Nellie MELBA]

Mel·ba toast *n* very thin slices of bread toasted on both sides, sliced horizontally to expose two untoasted sides of bread that are then toasted too, so that the bread curls [Early 20C. After Dame Nellie MELBA]

Mel·bourne /mélbərn/ **1.** city in southeastern Australia, the capital of the state of Victoria. Population: 3,371,300 (1998). **2.** coastal city in eastern Florida. Population: 73,804 (2002 estimate).

Mel·chi·or /mélkee àwr/, **Lauritz** (1890–1973) Danish-born US opera singer. As a tenor he is known for his Wagnerian roles, especially at the Metropolitan Opera House (1926–50). Full name **Melchior, Lauritz Lebrecht Hommel**

Mel·chite *n* CHR another spelling of **Melkite**

Mel·chiz·e·dek /mel kízzə dèk/ *n* **1.** in the Bible, a priest and king of Salem who blessed Abraham **2.** the senior order of priests in the Church of Jesus Christ of Latter-Day Saints

meld[1] /meld/ *vti* (**meld·ed, meld·ing, melds**) to cause things to combine or blend and become one thing or substance, or be combined or blended in this way ■ *n* a combination or blend of various things [Mid-20C. Origin ?]

meld[2] /meld/ *vti* (**meld·ed, meld·ing, melds**) in games such as canasta or pinochle, to show or declare some or all of a hand of cards in order to score points ■ *n* in games such as canasta or pinochle, a hand of cards that are shown or declared in order to score points, or an act of showing or declaring these cards [Late 19C. < German *melden* "announce"]

me·lee /máy lày, may láy/, **mê·lée** /me láy/ *n* **1.** a noisy confused fight **2.** a confused, often noisy mixing of people or things, usually in a public place [Mid-17C. < French *mêlée*, later form of Old French *meslee* (see MEDLEY)]

me·le·na /mə leénə/ *n* a condition characterized by the production of black stools that are caused by bleeding into the bowel and the subsequent chemical changes in the blood effected by the bowel fluids [Early 19C. Via modern Latin < Greek *melaina*, feminine of *melas* "black"]

mel·ic /méllik/ *adj* describes an ancient Greek lyric poem that is meant to be sung rather than recited [Late 17C. Via Latin < Greek *melikos* < *melos* "song"]

Mé·liès /máyl yèss/, **Georges** (1861–1938) French movie director. A pioneer of cinematography, he built the first movie studio, devised trick effects, and created his own production company.

Me·lil·la /mə leélə/ Spanish enclave and port on the Mediterranean coast of Morocco. Population: 60,108 (1998). Area: 4,63 sq. mi./12 sq. km.

mel·i·lot /méllə lòt/ *n* a plant with compound leaves consisting of three oval leaflets, sometimes grown as forage. Flowers: small, yellow, fragrant on tall flower heads. Genus: *Melilotus.* [14C. Via French < Greek *melilōtos* < *meli* "honey" + *lōtos* "lotus, clover"]

mel·i·nite /méllə nìt/ *n* an explosive made from picric acid [Late 19C. < French < Greek *mēlinos* "quince-colored" < *mēlon* "quince, apple"; from its yellow color]

mel·io·rate /meélee ə ràyt/ (**-rat·ed, -rat·ing, -rates**) *vti* to become better, or make something better [Mid-16C. < late Latin *meliorare* < Latin *melior* "better"] —**mel·io·ra·ble** *adj* —**mel·io·ra·tion** /meélee ə ráysh'n/ *n* —**mel·io·ra·tive** *adj* —**mel·io·ra·tor** *n*

mel·io·rism /meélee ə rìzzəm/ *n* the belief that human society has a natural tendency to improve and that people can consciously assist this process [Mid-19C. < Latin *melior* "better"] —**mel·io·rist** *n* —**mel·io·ris·tic** /meélee ə rístik/ *adj*

me·lis·ma /mə lízmə/ (*plural* **-ma·ta** /-mətə/ or **-mas**) *n* **1.** a decorative phrase or passage in vocal music, especially one in which one syllable of a plainsong text is sung to a melodic sequence of several notes **2.** an embellishment or decoration of a melody **3.** MUSIC same as **cadenza** [Late 19C. Via modern Latin < Greek, "tune" < *melizein* "sing" < *melos* "song"] —**mel·is·mat·ic** /mèlliz máttik/ *adj*

Mel·kite /mél kìt/, **Mel·chite** *n* a member of any of several Christian churches in North Africa and Southwest Asia that use the Greek Orthodox liturgy but acknowledge the authority of the Roman Catholic Pope [Early 17C. Via ecclesiastical Latin < Byzantine Greek *Melkhitai* "Melkites" < Syriac *malkāyē* "royalists" < *malkā* "king"]

melli- *prefix* honey ○ *melliphagous* [< Latin *mel* < Indo-European]

mel·lif·er·ous /mə líffərəss/, **mel·lif·ic** /mə líffik/ *adj* producing or bearing large quantities of honey [Mid-17C < Latin *mellifer* "honey-bearing" < *mel* "honey"]

mel·lif·lu·ous /mə líffloo əss/, **mel·lif·lu·ent** /-ənt/ *adj* pleasant and soothing to listen to, and sweet or rich in tone [15C. < late Latin *mellifluus* "flowing like honey" < Latin *mel* "honey"] —**mel·lif·lu·ous·ly** *adv* —**mel·lif·lu·ous·ness** *n*

Mel·lon /méllən/, **Andrew** (1855–1937) US industrialist, financier, and philanthropist. He endowed the Washington National Gallery of Art. Full name **Mellon, Andrew William**

mel·lo·phone /méllə fōn/ *n* a portable brass musical instrument similar in tone to a French horn, used mainly in brass bands and marching bands [Early 20C. < MELLOW]

mel·low /méllō/ *adj* **1.** SOFT IN COLOR OR TONE comfortingly soft, warm, and rich in color or tone **2.** SMOOTH AND RICH IN TASTE matured to a long-lasting smooth rich taste **3.** FULLY RIPE soft, juicy, fully ripened, and sweet **4.** EASYGOING good-humored, tolerant, and approachable, especially as a result of maturity or a feeling of security **5.** MILDLY INTOXICATED mildly intoxicated by drink or drugs **6.** MOIST AND RICH IN TEXTURE describes soil that has a moist rich loamy texture ■ *vti* (**-lowed, -low·ing, -lows**) **1.** BECOME OR MAKE SOMEBODY MORE EASYGOING to become more good-humored, tolerant, and approachable, or make somebody become so **2.** INCREASE IN OR GIVE SOMETHING RICHNESS to become richer, smoother, or softer in taste, color, tone, or atmosphere, or make something become so [15C. Origin ?] —**mel·low·ly** *adv* —**mel·low·ness** *n*

mellow out *vti* (*slang*) **1.** to become more relaxed and friendly, or make somebody more relaxed and friendly **2.** to become calm, or make somebody calm

me·lo·de·on /mə lōdee ən/ *n* **1.** a small reed organ, similar to a harmonium, that uses suction bellows to draw air through its reeds **2.** a small accordion, used especially by German folk musicians [Mid-19C. Probably alteration of *melodium* "small reed organ" < MELODY after HARMONIUM]

me·lod·ic /mə lóddik/ *adj* **1.** consisting of the melody of a piece of music ○ *the melodic line* **2.** relating to or characteristic of melody or the composition of melodies **3.** MUSIC same as **melodious** —**me·lod·i·cal·ly** *adv*

me·lod·ic mi·nor scale *n* a scale with the sixth and seventh notes raised a half step when played in ascending order but in the natural minor pitch when played in descending order

me·lo·di·ous /mə lōdee əss/ *adj* **1.** tuneful or varied and interesting in tone **2.** having the character of a melody —**me·lo·di·ous·ly** *adv* —**me·lo·di·ous·ness** *n*

mel·o·dist /mélladist/ *n* **1.** somebody who composes melodies, especially beautiful or memorable melodies for song lyrics **2.** somebody who sings sweetly

mel·o·dize /méllə dìz/ (**-dized, -diz·ing, -diz·es**) *v* **1.** *vti* to compose melodies or compose a melody to which lyrics can be sung **2.** *vt* to make something tuneful and pleasing to hear —**mel·o·diz·er** *n*

mel·o·dra·ma /méllə draàmə, -dràmmə/ *n* **1.** SENSATIONALIZED DRAMATIC OR LITERARY WORK a dramatic or other literary work characterized by the use of stereotyped characters, exaggerated emotions and language, simplistic morality, and conflict **2.** DRAMATIC OR LITERARY GENRE melodramas collectively considered as a dramatic or literary genre **3.** HISTRIONIC BEHAVIOR exaggerated behavior or emotional displays, like those characteristic of a melodrama **4.** DRAMA INTERSPERSED WITH MUSIC formerly, a play with a sensational or romantic plot that is interspersed with musical numbers and often has music accompanying the action **5.** SPOKEN WORDS WITH MUSICAL ACCOMPANIMENT a piece of poetry or a scene in a dramatic or operatic work in which the text is recited to a musical accompaniment [Early 19C. < French *mélodrame* "drama with songs" < Greek *melos* "song"]

mel·o·dra·mat·ic /mèllə drə máttik/ *adj* **1.** behaving, speaking, done, or said in a way that is more dramatic, shocking, or highly emotional than the situation demands **2.** relating to or typical of melodrama [Early 19C. < MELODRAMA] —**mel·o·dra·mat·i·cal·ly** *adv*

mel·o·dra·mat·ics /mèllə drə máttiks/ *npl* exaggeratedly theatrical behavior, speech, or writing

mel·o·dra·ma·tize /mèllə draàmə tìz, -drámmə tìz/ (**-tized, -tiz·ing, -tizes**) *vti* to treat or react to something in an exaggeratedly theatrical way [Early 19C. < MELODRAMA, after DRAMATIZE] —**mel·o·dra·ma·ti·za·tion** /mèllə draàməti záysh'n, -dràmməti-/ *n*

mel·o·dy /mélladee/ (*plural* **-dies**) *n* **1.** TUNE a series of musical notes that form a distinct unit, are recognizable as a phrase, and usually have a distinctive rhythm **2.** LINEAR MUSICAL STRUCTURE the linear structure of a piece of music in which single notes follow one another **3.** MAIN TUNE the primary and most recognizable part in a harmonic piece of music **4.** MUSICALLY EXPRESSIVE QUALITY the musically expressive quality of something, especially poetry **5.** MUSICAL LYRIC a poem that lends itself easily to being set to music or sung [12C. < French *mélodie* < Greek *melōidia* "choral song" < *melos* "tune" + *ōidē* "song"]

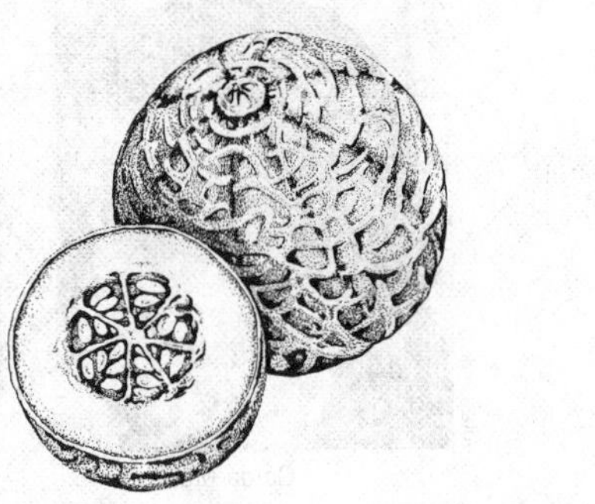

melon

mel·on /méllən/ *n* **1.** ROUND JUICY GOURD FRUIT the round edible fruit of vines belonging to the gourd family, with a tough rind and sweet juicy flesh ranging in color from pale yellow to deep orange **2.** PLANT THAT PRODUCES MELONS a vine of the gourd family widely grown to produce melons. Latin name: *Cucumis melo* or *Citrullus lanatus.* **3.** SOUND ORGAN IN DOLPHIN'S HEAD a rounded waxy mass found in the head of some dolphins and toothed whales that is thought to play a part in the focusing of sound signals **4.** FIN SURPLUS PROFIT a surplus of profit that can be distributed to stockholders (*informal*) **5.** FIN FINANCIAL WINDFALL an unexpected financial gain (*informal*) ■ **mel·ons** *npl* OFFENSIVE TERM an offensive term for a woman's breasts, especially when large (*slang*) [14C. < late Latin *melon-* < Greek *mēlopepōn*, a kind of gourd < *mēlon* "apple" + *pepōn* "gourd"]

Me·los /meé làwss/, **Mí·los** island in southeastern Greece, one of the Cyclades. Population: 4,554 (1981). Area: 61 sq. mi./158 sq. km.

Mel·pom·e·ne /mel pómmənee/ *n* in Greek mythology, the Muse of tragedy, one of the nine Muses believed to inspire and nurture the arts

Mel·rose /mél rōz/ city in northeastern Massachusetts, north of Malden, a northern suburb of Boston. Population: 26,963 (2002 estimate).

Mel·rose Park village in northeastern Illinois, west of Oak Park. It is a western suburb of Chicago. Population: 23,029 (2002 estimate).

melt[1] /melt/ *v* (**melted, melt·ing, melts**) **1.** *vti* CHANGE FROM SOLID TO LIQUID STATE to change a substance from a solid to a liquid state by heating it, or be changed in this way **2.** *vti* DISSOLVE to dissolve something such as sugar in a liquid, or be dissolved in a liquid **3.** *vi* DISAPPEAR to disappear gradually and inconspicuously **4.** *vi* BECOME MERGED to change into, or blend with, something in such a way that the actual point of change or blending is almost imperceptible **5.** *vti* BE MOVED EMOTIONALLY to cause somebody to be moved emotionally so as to become gentler and more sympathetic, or be moved in this way **6.** *vi* FEEL HOT to feel uncomfortably hot (*informal*) ■ *n* **1.** MASS OF MELTED MATERIAL a mass or an amount of melted material, especially metal, produced in a single operation or during a specific period of time **2.**

MOLTEN MATERIAL a material, e.g., metal or glass, in a molten state **3.** MELTING OF SOMETHING the process of melting something **4.** LIQUEFACTION the state or condition of being liquefied **5.** METEOROL PERIOD OF THAW the period of time during which snow and ice thaw **6.** FOOD GRILLED SANDWICH an open-faced hot sandwich with melted cheese on top [Old English *m(i)eltan* < Indo-European] —**melt·a·bil·i·ty** /mèltə bíllətee/ *n* —**melt·a·ble** *adj* —**melt·er** *n*

melt down *vti* to liquefy metal or glass by heating in order to reuse it, or be liquefied in this way

melt[2] /melt/ *n* the spleen of a slaughtered animal, used mainly for animal food (*often used in the plural*) [Late 16C. Variant of MILT]

melt·age /méltij/ *n* **1.** the process of melting something **2.** a liquefied substance produced by a heating process, or an amount of such a substance

melt·down /mélt dòwn/ *n* **1.** MELTING OF NUCLEAR REACTOR FUEL RODS the melting of fuel rods in a nuclear reactor because of overheating that results in the escape of radioactive materials or radiation **2.** OVERLOAD OF COMPUTER NETWORK the shutdown of a computer network as a result of a deluge of illegal or wrongly routed packets that saturate the network and force multiple hosts to respond simultaneously **3.** COMPLETE COLLAPSE OF ORGANIZATION a situation of complete collapse of an organization or institution (*informal*) **4.** EXTREMELY ANGRY STATE a loss of composure, especially an extremely angry response to something (*informal*)

melt·ing /mélting/ *adj* full of or causing sweet and tender or sentimental emotion —**melt·ing·ly** *adv*

melt·ing point *n* the temperature at which a substance changes from a solid to a liquid form

melt·ing pot *n* **1.** CONTAINER FOR MELTING AND MIXING a container in which substances, especially metals, are placed to be liquefied and mixed together **2.** SOCIETY COMPOSED OF MANY DIFFERENT CULTURES a place where people of different ethnic groups are brought together and can assimilate, especially a country that takes immigrants from many different ethnic backgrounds **3.** PROCESS THAT CREATES SOMETHING NEW a situation or process in which distinct elements can be brought together to produce something new

mel·ton /méltən/ *n* smooth heavy wool cloth. Use: overcoats. [Mid-19C. After the town of *Melton* Mowbray in Leicestershire, England]

melt·wa·ter /mélt wàwtər/ *n* water formed by the melting of ice or snow, especially from a glacier

Mel·ville /mélvil/, **Herman** (1819–91) US writer. His allegorical sea novel *Moby Dick* (1851) is sometimes held to be the greatest work of American fiction.

> "I always go to sea a sailor, because they make a point of paying me for my trouble, whereas they never pay passengers a single penny."
> [Herman Melville, *Moby Dick*; 1851]

Mel·ville Is·land uninhabited island in northwestern Canada, divided between Nunavut and Northwest Territories, in the Arctic Ocean. Area: 2,239 sq. mi./5,800 sq. km.

Mel·ville Pen·in·su·la peninsula in Nunavut, northern Canada. Foxe Basin lies to its west, and Committee Bay to its east. Area: 25,100 sq. mi./65,000 sq. km.

mem /mem/ *n* the 13th letter of the Hebrew alphabet, represented in the English alphabet as "m." See table at **alphabet** [Early 19C. < Hebrew *mēm* "water"]

mem. *abbr* **1.** member **2.** memoir **3.** memorandum **4.** memorial

mem·ber /mémbər/ *n* **1.** ADHERENT OF PARTICULAR GROUP somebody who belongs to and participates in a particular group by birth or choice **2.** *also* **Mem·ber** POLITICAL REPRESENTATIVE somebody elected to a legislative body such as the US Congress or UK Parliament **3.** LIMB a part or organ of a plant or animal body, especially a limb **4.** same as **penis** (*formal or humorous*) **5.** INDIVIDUAL PART a separate and distinct part of a whole, e.g., an object belonging to a mathematical set, a clause in a sentence, or a proposition in a syllogism **6.** STRUCTURAL UNIT a beam, wall, or similar structural unit in a building or other construction **7.** ELEMENT IN MATHEMATICAL EQUATION either of the expressions in a mathematical equation linked by an equal sign [14C. Via French *membre* < Latin *membrum* "limb, part"] —**mem·bered** *adj*

mem·ber firm *n* a company that trades in securities and belongs to an organized exchange

Mem·ber of Con·gress *n* somebody elected to the US Congress, especially to the House of Representatives

Mem·ber of Par·lia·ment *n* somebody who has been elected to a parliament

mem·ber·ship /mémbər shìp/ *n* **1.** the state or condition of belonging to a group such as a species, social class, team, club, or political party **2.** the members of a group such as a species, social class, organization, or mathematical set considered collectively

mem·brane /mém bràyn/ *n* **1.** THIN LAYER OF TISSUE a thin flexible sheet of tissue connecting, covering, lining, or separating various parts or organs in animal and plant bodies, or forming the external wall of a cell **2.** THIN POROUS SHEET a thin, pliable, and often porous sheet of any natural or artificial material **3.** PIECE OF PARCHMENT a piece of parchment forming part of a roll [15C. Directly or via French < Latin *membrana* "skin" < *membrum* "limb, part"] —**mem·bra·nal** /mémbrən'l/ *adj*

mem·brane bone *n* a bone that develops directly out of membranous connective tissue rather than from cartilage, e.g., the clavicle and some cranial bones

mem·brane trans·port *n* the process by which substances in solution pass through a biological membrane

mem·bra·no·phone /mem bráynə fòn/ *n* a musical instrument that uses a stretched membrane to produce sound, e.g., a drum or kazoo

mem·bra·nous /mémbrənəss/ *adj* **1.** relating to or similar to a membrane, especially in being thin, pliable, and often translucent **2.** resulting in the formation of a membrane or of a thin layer similar to a membrane

mem·bra·nous lab·y·rinth *n* the structure of fluid-filled sacs in the inner ear that are vital to hearing and balance

meme /meem/ *n* any characteristic of a culture, e.g., its language, that can be transmitted from one generation to the next in a way analogous to the transmission of genetic information [Late 20C. < Greek *mimēma* "something imitated," after GENE]

me·men·to /mə méntō/ (*plural* **-tos** or **-toes**) *n* an object given or kept as a reminder or in memory of somebody or something [Mid-18C. < Latin, "remember!" (originally the first word in prayers for the dead) < *meminisse* "remember"]

me·men·to mo·ri /-máwree/ (*plural same*) *n* **1.** an object, especially a skull, intended as a reminder of the fact that humans die **2.** a reminder of the fact that humans fail and make mistakes (*literary*) [< Latin, "remember (that you have) to die"]

Mem·non /mém nòn/ *n* in Greek mythology, the Ethiopian king who fought for the Trojans in the siege of Troy and was killed by Achilles

mem·o /mémmō/ (*plural* **-os**) *n* **1.** a written communication similar to a letter but without the formal address blocks at the beginning, especially one that is circulated to people within an office or organization **2.** a note intended to serve as a reminder of something [Early 18C. Shortening of MEMORANDUM]

mem·oir /mém waar/ *n* **1.** BIOGRAPHY OR HISTORICAL ACCOUNT a biography or an account of historical events, especially one written from personal knowledge **2.** ESSAY ON SCHOLARLY SUBJECT a short essay, article, or report on a scholarly subject, usually one in which the writer is a recognized specialist ■ **mem·oirs** *npl* **1.** AUTOBIOGRAPHY somebody's written account of his or her own life or of events in which he or she took part **2.** PROCEEDINGS the records of the business and discussions of a learned society [Mid-17C. < French *mémoire* "memory" < Old French *memorie* (see MEMORY)] —**mem·oir·ist** *n*

mem·o·ra·bil·i·a /mèmmərə bíllee ə/ *npl* **1.** objects associated with a famous person or event, especially considered as collectors' items **2.** objects collected as souvenirs of important personal events or experiences [Late 18C. < Latin, "memorable things" < *memorabilis* (see MEMORABLE)]

mem·o·ra·ble /mémmərəb'l/ *adj* **1.** sufficiently interesting, exciting, or unusual to be worth remembering or likely to be remembered **2.** easy to remember [15C. Via French < Latin *memorabilis* < *memorare* "bring to mind" < *memor* "mindful"] —**mem·o·ra·bil·i·ty** /mèmmərə bíllətee/ *n* —**mem·o·ra·ble·ness** *n* —**mem·o·ra·bly** *adv*

mem·o·ran·dum /mèmmə rándəm/ (*plural* **-dums** or **-da** /-də/) *n* **1.** BRIEF DIPLOMATIC COMMUNICATION a brief, often unsigned communication circulated among diplomats, especially one that summarizes a country's position on an issue **2.** same as **memo** (sense 2) (*formal*) **3.** COMM same as **memo** (sense 1) **4.** SUMMARY OF LEGAL AGREEMENT a written statement summarizing the terms of a contract or a similar legal transaction **5.** CONSIGNOR'S STATEMENT a consignor's brief statement about a shipment of returnable goods [15C. < Latin, "thing to be remembered" < *memorare* (see MEMORABLE)]

me·mo·ri·al /mə máwree əl/ *n* **1.** COMMEMORATIVE OBJECT OR EVENT something that is intended to remind people of somebody who has died or an event in which people died, e.g., a statue, speech, or ceremony **2.** STATEMENT OF FACTS ACCOMPANYING PETITION a written statement of facts accompanying a petition presented to a person or group in authority ■ *adj* COMMEMORATIVE intended as a reminder of a person or event or as a celebration of somebody's life and work [14C. < French < Latin *memoria* (see MEMORY)] —**me·mo·ri·al·ly** *adv*

Me·mo·ri·al Day *n* a public holiday to commemorate soldiers who died in war. Date: last Monday in May, formerly May 30.

me·mo·ri·al·ist /mə máwree əlist/ *n* **1.** a writer of memoirs **2.** a writer, signer, or presenter of a memorial accompanying a petition

me·mo·ri·al·ize /mə máwree ə lìz/ (**-ized, -iz·ing, -iz·es**) *vt* **1.** to serve as a memorial to somebody or something, or provide somebody or something with a memorial **2.** to present a written memorial accompanying a petition to a person or group in power —**me·mo·ri·al·i·za·tion** /mə màwree əli záysh'n/ *n* —**me·mo·ri·al·iz·er** *n*

me·mo·ri·al park *n* same as **cemetery**

mem·o·rize /mémmə rìz/ (**-rized, -riz·ing, -riz·es**) *vt* to commit something to memory —**mem·o·riz·a·ble** *adj* —**mem·o·ri·za·tion** /mèmməri záysh'n/ *n* —**mem·o·riz·er** *n*

mem·o·ry /mémməree/ (*plural* **-ries**) *n* **1.** ABILITY TO RETAIN KNOWLEDGE the ability of the mind or of a person or organism to retain learned information and knowledge of past events and experiences and to retrieve that information and knowledge ○ *have a good memory for faces* **2.** SOMEBODY'S STOCK OF RETAINED KNOWLEDGE somebody's stock of retained knowledge and experience ○ *recite the poem from memory* **3.** RETAINED IMPRESSION OF EVENT the knowledge or impression that somebody retains of a person, event, period, or subject ○ *memories of a happy childhood* **4.** RECOLLECTION the act or an instance of remembering **5.** PRESERVATION OF KNOWLEDGE the preservation of knowledge of and, usually, celebration of a deceased person or past event ○ *a poem in memory of her father* **6.** POSTHUMOUS IMPRESSION the knowledge or impression of somebody retained by other people after that person's death **7.** TEMPORAL EXTENT OF RECOLLECTION the period of past time that a person or group is able to remember **8.** STORAGE AREA IN COMPUTER the area of storage in a computer that maintains information for instant retrieval and processing, as distinct from disk storage **9.** COMPUTER STORAGE CAPACITY the storage capacity of a computer that determines how much information can be maintained for instant retrieval and processing **10.** ABILITY TO RETURN TO ORIGINAL SHAPE the ability of some materials such as plastics and metals to return to their original shape after being subject to deformation [13C. Via French < Latin *memoria* < *memor* "mindful"] ◇ **within living memory** in the time experienced and remembered by people now alive

mem·o·ry bank *n* COMPUT same as **memory** (sense 8)

mem·o·ry en·gram *n* PSYCHOL same as **engram**

mem·o·ry lane *n* the past, especially the past shared and remembered by a group of people, thought of as a path that can be traveled along to revisit former times

mem·o·ry span *n* a measure of somebody's memory, often for units of information such as nonsense syllables or sequences of random numbers, over a short period of time

mem·o·ry trace *n* PSYCHOL same as **engram**

Mem·phis /mémfiss/ **1.** ruined city and capital of ancient Egypt, located at the head of the Nile delta in the north of the country **2.** largest city in Tennessee, located in the southwestern corner of the state. Population: 648,882 (2002 estimate). —**Mem·phi·an** *n, adj*

Mem·phre·ma·gog, Lake /mèmfrə máy gòg/ lake in Quebec, Canada, and Vermont. It is the second largest lake in Vermont. Length: 27 mi./43 km. Area: 39.4 sq. mi./102 sq. km.

MEMS *n* a computer chip that has integrated miniaturized mechanical devices for sensing, processing, or carrying out various functions. Full form **micro-electromechanical system**

mem·sa·hib /mem saab/ *n S Asia* a respectful form of address to a woman, formerly used by Indians to European married women [Mid-19C. < MA'AM + SAHIB]

men plural of **man**

men- *prefix* same as **meno-** (*used before vowels*)

men·ace /ménnəss/ *n* **1. POSSIBLE SOURCE OF DANGER** a possible source of danger or harm **2. NUISANCE** a constant source of trouble and annoyance (*informal*) **3. THREATENING QUALITY** a threatening quality, feeling, or tone **4. THREATENING ACT** a threatening act, gesture, or speech ○ *demanding money with menaces* ■ *v* (**-aced, -ac·ing, -ac·es**) **1.** *vt* **BE THREAT TO SOMEBODY OR SOMETHING** to be a possible or actual source of danger or harm to somebody or something **2.** *vti* **MAKE THREAT AGAINST SOMEBODY** to behave toward or speak to somebody in a way that threatens injury or harm (*often passive*) [14C. < French < Latin *minac-* "threatening" < *minari* "threaten" < *minae* "threats," literally "projecting points"] —**men·ac·er** *n* —**men·ac·ing** *adj* —**men·ac·ing·ly** *adv*

men·a·di·one /mènnə dī ōn/ *n* a yellow crystalline solid. Use: fungicide, vitamin K supplement in medicines and animal feedstuffs. Formula: $C_{11}H_8O_2$. [Mid-20C. Contraction of METHYL + NAPHTHALENE + DI-[1]]

mén·age /may naazh/ *n* (*formal*) **1.** a group of people living together as a household **2.** the running of a household [Late 17C. < French; < Latin *manere* "dwell, stay"]

mén·age à trois /mày naazh aa trwaa/ (*plural* **mén·ages à trois** /*pronunc. same*/) *n* a sexual relationship involving three people [< French, literally "household for three"]

me·nag·er·ie /mə nájjəree/ *n* **1. WILD ANIMAL EXHIBIT** a collection of wild animals kept in captivity for the curiosity and entertainment of the public, sometimes as part of a traveling show **2. WILD ANIMAL ENCLOSURE** an enclosure in which wild animals are kept for public exhibition **3. DIVERSE OR EXOTIC GROUP** a diverse, exotic, or unusual group of people or things [Late 17C. < French < *ménage* (see MÉNAGE)]

Men·ai Strait /mèn ī-/ narrow arm of the Irish Sea in northwestern Wales, separating the island of Anglesey from the mainland. Length: 14 mi./23 km.

me·nar·che /mə naarkee/ *n* the first time that a girl or young woman menstruates [Early 20C. < MENO- + Greek *arkhē* "beginning"] —**me·nar·che·al** *adj*

Me·nash·a /mə náshə/ city in Wisconsin, in Winnebago County. Population: 16,412 (2002 estimate).

men·a·zon /ménnə zòn/ *n* a colorless crystalline solid. Use: killing aphids. Formula: $C_6H_8N_5O_2PS_2$. [Mid-20C. Contraction of METHYL + AMINO- + AZO- + *thionate*]

Men·ci·us /ménshee əss/ (371?–289 B.C.) Chinese philosopher. The successor of Confucius, he argued that humans are born good and are made better or worse by their environment. Born **Meng-tzu**

Menck·en /méngkən/, **H. L.** (1880–1956) US journalist and critic. An authority on the American language, he was also an effective satirist. Full name **Mencken, Henry Louis**

> "The public...demands certainties.... But there *are* no certainties."
> [H. L. Mencken, *Prejudices, First Series*; 1919]

> "Conscience is the inner voice which warns us that someone may be looking."
> [H. L. Mencken, *A Little Book in C Major*; 1916]

mend /mend/ *v* (**mend·ed, mend·ing, mends**) **1.** *vti* **RESTORE SOMETHING TO SATISFACTORY CONDITION** to restore something that is damaged or faulty to its original condition or a satisfactory condition **2.** *vt* **REMOVE DAMAGE** to fill, cover, or otherwise remove damage such as a hole or break **3.** *vti* **IMPROVE SOMETHING** to improve something or make it more acceptable, or be improved or made more acceptable ○ *You'd better mend your ways.* **4.** *vi* **RECOVER OR HEAL** to return to a healthy state after illness or injury ■ *n* **REPAIR WORK** an instance of repair work or a repaired place on a damaged object, especially a darn on a piece of clothing [12C. Partly shortening of AMEND, and partly < Anglo-Norman *mender*, shortening of *amender*; (see AMEND)] —**mend·a·ble** *adj* —**mend·er** *n* ◇ **on the mend** recovering or healing after illness or injury

men·da·cious /men dáyshəss/ *adj* **1.** having lied in the past, or prone to lying at any time **2.** deliberately untrue [Early 17C. < Latin *mendac-* "lying"] —**men·da·cious·ly** *adv* —**men·da·cious·ness** *n*

men·dac·i·ty /men dássətee/ (*plural* **-ties**) *n* **1.** deliberate untruthfulness **2.** a lie or falsehood [Mid-17C. < French *mendacité* < Latin *mendax* "lying"]

Men·de /méndee/ (*plural same* or **-des**) *n* **1.** a member of a people living in Sierra Leone **2.** the Niger-Congo language of the Mende people. Native speakers: 1 million. [Mid-18C. < Mende] —**Men·de** *adj*

Men·del /ménd'l/, **Gregor** (1822–84) Austrian monk and scientist. Through his experiments he developed the principles of heredity, and so laid the basis of modern genetics. Full name **Mendel, Gregor Johann** —**Men·de·li·an** /mèn deelyən/ *adj*

men·de·le·vi·um /mèndə leevee əm/ *n* a synthetic short-lived radioactive element. Source: bombardment of einsteinium atoms with helium particles. Symbol **Md**. See table at **element** [Mid-20C. After Dmitry Ivanovich MENDELEYEV]

Men·de·le·yev /mèndə láyəv/, **Dmitry Ivanovich** (1834–1907) Russian chemist. He formulated the periodic law of elements and devised the periodic table (1869), using it to predict the existence of several then-unknown elements. He wrote a classic text, *Principles of Chemistry* (1868–70).

Men·del·ism /ménd'l ìzzəm/, **Men·de·li·an·ism** /men déllee ə nìzzəm/ *n* the theory of heredity formulated by Mendel, which explains how some characteristics are passed on from one generation to the next through genes

Men·del's Laws *npl* the laws of heredity formulated by Mendel to explain the transmission of characteristics from one generation to the next. There are two laws, the Law of Segregation and the Law of Independent Assortment.

Men·dels·sohn /ménd'lssən/, **Felix** (1809–47) German composer. His orchestral, choral, and keyboard works are key pieces of the romantic tradition. Full name **Mendelssohn-Bartholdy, Jakob Ludwig Felix**

> "Anything but national music! May ten thousand devils take all folklore. Here I am in Wales...a harpist sits in the lobby of every inn of repute playing so-called folk melodies at you—i.e. dreadful, vulgar, fake stuff, and *simultaneously* a hurdy-gurdy is tootling out melodies...it's even given me a toothache."
> [Felix Mendelssohn. Quoted in *A Life in Letters*, Rudolf Elvers (ed.), Craig Tomlinson (tr.); 1986]

Men·de·res /men dérrəss/ river in southwestern Turkey, flowing west from the Anatolian Plateau into the Aegean Sea. Length: 363 mi./584 km.

men·di·cant /méndikənt/ *adj* **LIVING ON CHARITY** begging for and living on money given by strangers ■ *n* **1. BEGGAR** a beggar, especially somebody who begs in the street (*formal*) **2. FRIAR WHO LIVES BY BEGGING** a member of a religious order such as the Franciscans, Dominicans, Carmelites, or Augustinians that forbids the ownership of property and encourages working or begging for a living [14C. < Latin *mendicant-*, present participle of *mendicare* "beg" < *mendicus* "beggar" < *mendum* "a defect"]

mend·ing /ménding/ *n* articles, especially clothes, to be mended

Men·do·za /men dṓzə/ city in western Argentina, the capital of Mendoza Province. Population: 121,620 (1991).

men·eer /mə neer/ *n S Africa* in Afrikaans, v equivalent to "Mr.", or a respectful form of address equivalent to "sir." [Mid-17C. Via Afrikaans < Dutch *mijnheer* "my lord"]

Men·e·la·us /mènnə láy əss/ *n* in Greek mythology, the king of Sparta and husband of Helen of Troy

Men·e·lik II /ménnilik/, **emperor of Ethiopia** (1844–1913) He formed a united Ethiopian empire, resisting incursions by Italy and embarking on a program of colonial expansion

Men·em /mén em/, **Carlos** (*b.* 1930) president of Argentina (1989–99). A Peronist politician, he was first elected president in 1989 and then allowed to stand for a second term in 1995 after a constitutional amendment in 1994. He ran for president again in 2003, but withdrew on the ee of the election. Full name **Menem, Carlos Saúl**

men·folk /mén fōk/, **men·folks** /-fōks/ *npl* **1.** the male members of a family or group **2.** men in general or considered collectively

M.Eng. *abbr* Master of Engineering

Men·gis·tu Hai·le Mar·i·am /meng gìstoo hīlee maaree əm/ (*b.* 1937) Ethiopian politician. He served on the executive committee of the military government that succeeded Haile Selassie in 1974 and emerged as its leader in 1977. He made Ethiopia a Communist state and served as president from 1987 until he was forced to flee the country in 1991.

men·ha·den /men háyd'n/ (*plural* **-dens** or *same*) *n* a sea fish of the herring family. Use: mainly as a source of oil, fertilizer, bait. Native to: North America. Latin name: *Brevoortia tyrannus*. [Mid-17C. Origin ?]

menhir: le grand menhir, Dol, Brittany, France

men·hir /mén heer/ *n* a large single upright stone, erected by prehistoric people and thought to have been used for astronomical observations, found in the British Isles and northern France [Mid-19C. Directly or via French < Breton *maen-hir* < *men* "stone" + *hir* "long"]

me·ni·al /meenee əl/ *adj* **1. UNSKILLED** relating to or involving work that requires little skill or training, is not interesting, and confers low social status on somebody doing it **2. RELATING TO SERVANTS** suitable for, done by, or relating to a servant or servants ■ *n* **1. DOMESTIC SERVANT** a domestic servant, especially one of low status **2. SOMEBODY WHO DOES MENIAL WORK** somebody employed to do work that requires no skill or training (*formal*) [14C. < Anglo-Norman, "of a household" < Latin *mansion-* < *manere* "remain"] —**me·ni·al·ly** *adv*

Mén·i·ère's dis·ease /mayn yérz-/, **Mén·i·ère's syn·drome** *n* a disorder caused by an accumulation of fluid in the labyrinths of the inner ear. Symptoms include vertigo, persistent ringing in the ears, and some loss of hearing. [Late 19C. After Prosper *Ménière* (1799–1862), French physician]

mening- *prefix* same as **meningo-** (*used before vowels*)

me·nin·ges /mə nínjeez/ *npl* the three membranes that surround and protect the brain and the spinal cord, called the dura mater, the arachnoid mater, and the pia mater [Early 17C. Via modern Latin < Greek *mēnigg-* "membrane"] —**me·nin·ge·al** *adj*

meningi- *prefix* same as **meningo-**

me·nin·gi·o·ma /mə nìnjee ṓmə/ (*plural* **-mas** or **-ma·ta** /-mətə/) *n* a slow-growing benign tumor that affects the meninges of the brain or spinal cord and may cause serious damage by compression [Early 20C.

Shortening of *meningothelioma* < MENINGO- + ENDOTHELIOMA]

men·in·gi·tis /mènnin jítiss/ *n* a serious, sometimes fatal illness in which a viral or bacterial infection inflames the meninges, causing symptoms such as severe headaches, vomiting, stiff neck, and high fever —**men·in·git·ic** /-jíttik/ *adj*

meningo- *prefix* meninges ○ *meningocele* [< Greek *mēnigg-*, stem of *mēninx* "membrane"]

men·in·go·cele /mə níng gə seel/ *n* the protrusion of the meninges through the skull or backbone to form a cyst

me·nin·go·coc·cus /mə nìng gə kókəss/ (*plural* **-coc·ci** /-kók sī, -kó kī/) *n* a bacterium that causes cerebrospinal meningitis. Latin name: *Neisseria meningitidis*. —**me·nin·go·coc·cal** *adj* —**me·nin·go·coc·cic** /-kóksik/ *adj*

me·nin·go·en·ceph·a·li·tis /mə nìng gō en sèffə lítiss/ *n* an inflammation of the brain and the meninges —**me·nin·go·en·ceph·a·lit·ic** /-líttik/ *adj*

me·ninx /mén ingks/ *n* ANAT singular of **meninges**

me·nis·cus /mə nískəss/ (*plural* **-ci** /-kī/ or **-cus·es**) *n* **1. UPPER SURFACE OF LIQUID** the curved upper surface of a still liquid in a tube, concave if the liquid wets the walls of the container, convex if it does not, caused by surface tension **2. CARTILAGE DISK** a crescent-shaped cartilage disk cushioning the end of a bone where it meets another bone in a joint, especially in the knee **3. CONCAVO-CONVEX LENS** a lens that is convex on one side and concave on the other **4. CRESCENT SHAPE** a crescent-shaped body or figure [Late 17C. Via modern Latin < Greek *mēniskos* "little moon" < *mēnē* "moon"] —**me·nis·cal** *adj* —**me·nis·cate** *adj* —**me·nis·coid** *adj* —**men·is·coi·dal** /mènniss kóyd'l/ *adj*

Men·lo Park /mènlō-/ **1.** city in western California, in San Mateo County. Population: 30,277 (2002 estimate). **2.** village in central New Jersey. It was home to the laboratory of inventor Thomas Edison.

Men·non·ite /ménnə nīt/ *n* a member of a Protestant denomination emphasizing adult baptism and pacifism and rejecting church organization and, in many cases, the holding of public office and the taking of oaths. There are many different bodies of Mennonites throughout the world, with especially large communities in the United States and Canada. [Mid-16C < German *Mennonit*, after *Menno* Simons (1496–1561), early Frisian leader of the group] —**Men·non·it·ism** *n*

me·no /máynō, ménnō/ *adv* less quickly or softly (*used as a musical direction*) [Late 19C. < Italian, "less"]

meno- *prefix* menstruation ○ *menopause* [< Greek *mēn(ē)* "month" < Indo-European]

me·nol·o·gy /mə nólləjee/ (*plural* **-gies**) *n* a church calendar of the months, especially in the Eastern Orthodox Church, that shows saints' days and gives biographies of the saints [Early 17C. Via modern Latin < ecclesiastical Greek *mēnologion* "month-reckoning" < *mēn* "month"]

Me·nom·i·nee[1] /mə nómmə nee/ (*plural same* or **-nees**), **Me·nom·i·ni** (*plural same* or **-nis**) *n* **1.** a member of a Native North American people of northeastern Wisconsin **2.** the extinct Algonquian language of the Menominee people [Mid-18C. < Ojibwa *manōmīnī* "wild-rice person"] —**Me·nom·i·nee** *adj*

Me·nom·i·nee[2] /mə nómmə nee/ river in Wisconsin, formed by the Brule and Michigamme rivers, and flowing into Lake Michigan. Length: 125 mi./201 km.

Me·nom·o·nee Falls /mə nòmmənee-/ village in Wisconsin, in southeastern Waukesha County. Population: 33,309 (2002 estimate).

me·no mos·so /-máwssō/ *adv* at a slower speed (*used as a musical direction*) [< Italian, "less agitated"]

men·o·pause /ménnə pàwz/ *n* the time in a woman's life when menstruation diminishes and ceases, usually between the ages of 45 and 50 [Late 19C. < MENO- + Greek *pausis* "pause" < *pausein* "to stop"] —**men·o·paus·al** /mènnə páwz'l/ *adj* —**men·o·paus·ic** /-páwzik/ *adj*

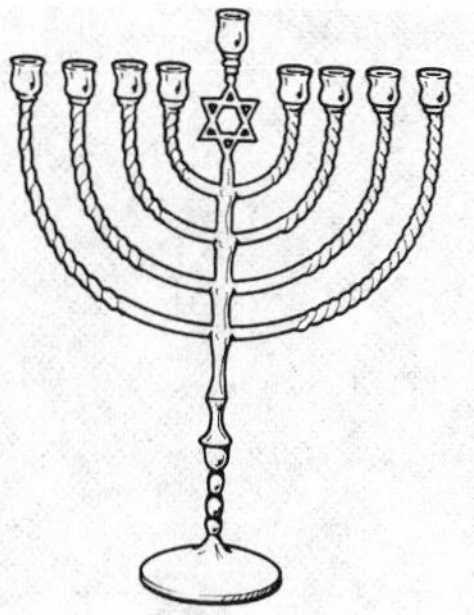

menorah

me·no·rah /mə náwrə/ *n* **1.** a ceremonial candleholder consisting of a central stem surrounded by six curved branches, used in the Jewish Temple and as an emblem of Judaism and the state of Israel **2.** an eight-branched candleholder, lit during the Jewish festival of Hanukkah [Late 19C. < Hebrew *mĕnōrāh* "candlestick"]

Me·nor·ca /mə náwrkə/, **Mi·nor·ca** /mi-/ Spanish island in the western Mediterranean Sea, the second largest of the Balearic Islands. Population: 66,900 (1989). Area: 268 sq. mi./695 sq. km. Spanish name **Menorca** —**Me·nor·can** *adj, n*

men·or·rha·gi·a /mènnə ráyjee ə/ *n* unusually heavy or prolonged bleeding during menstruation —**men·or·rha·gic** *adj*

men·or·rhea /mènnə rée ə/ *n* normal bleeding during menstruation [Mid-19C. Back-formation < AMENORRHEA]

men·or·rhoea *n* MED UK spelling of **menorrhea**

Me·not·ti /mə nóttee/, **Gian-Carlo** (*b.* 1911) Italian-born US composer. He is known for his operas, including *The Consul* (1950) and *The Saint of Bleecker Street* (1954).

Men·sa /ménssə/ *n* **1.** a faint constellation of the southern hemisphere that forms part of the larger Magellanic Cloud **2.** an international organization for people with a very high IQ. Members are admitted after passing an IQ test. [Mid-20C. < Latin, "table"]

men·sal[1] /ménssəl/ *adj* occurring monthly [Mid-19C. < Latin *mensis* "month"]

men·sal[2] /ménssəl/ *adj* used or done at the meal table, or connected with eating meals [15C. < late Latin *mensalis* < Latin *mensa* "table"]

mensch /mensh/ (*plural* **mensch·en** /-shən/ or **mensch·es**), **mensh** (*plural* **mensh·en** or **mensh·es**) *n* somebody good, kind, decent, and honorable (*informal*) [Mid-20C. Via Yiddish < Old High German *mennisco* "person, human"]

men·ses /mén seez/ *n* (*technical; takes a singular or plural verb*) **1.** menstruation, or the period of time that it lasts **2.** the blood and other matter discharged from the womb during menstruation [Late 16C. < Latin, plural of *mensis* "month"]

mensh *n* another spelling of **mensch** (*informal*)

Men·she·vik /ménshə vìk/ (*plural* **-viks** or **-vi·ki** /mènshə veekee/) *n* a member of the moderate minority faction of the Marxist Social Democratic Party in prerevolutionary Russia that advocated a gradual approach to social reform, in contrast to the Bolsheviks [Early 20C. < Russian *men'shevik* < *men'she* "less"; because the Socialist reform they favored was less extreme than that favored by the Bolsheviks] —**Men·she·vism** *n* —**Men·she·vist** *n*

mens re·a /mènz rée ə, -ráy ə/ *n* prior intention to commit a criminal act, with the knowledge that the act is a crime. For all but some minor statutory offenses, mens rea is basic to establishing the actual guilt of somebody alleged to have committed a crime. [< modern Latin, "guilty mind"]

men's room *n* a public toilet for men

mens sa·na in cor·po·re sa·no /menz saanə in kawrpə ray saanō/ *n* a healthy mind in a healthy body, as an ideal in living [< Latin]

men·stru·al /ménstroo əl/ *adj* occurring during, or connected with, menstruation

men·stru·al cy·cle *n* the monthly process of ovulation and menstruation that occurs between puberty and menopause in women and female primates who are not pregnant

men·stru·ate /ménstroo àyt/ (**-at·ed, -at·ing, -ates**) *vi* to discharge blood and other matter from the womb as part of the menstrual cycle [Early 19C. < late Latin *menstruat-*, past participle of *menstruare* < Latin *menstruus* "monthly, menstrual" < *mensis* "month"]

men·stru·a·tion /mènstroo áysh'n/ *n* the monthly process of discharging blood and other matter from the womb that occurs between puberty and menopause in women and female primates who are not pregnant

men·stru·ous /ménstroo əss/ *adj* PHYSIOL same as **menstrual**

men·su·ra·ble /ménssərəb'l, ménshə-/ *adj* **1.** capable of being measured **2.** MUSIC same as **mensural** (sense 2) [Late 16C. < late Latin *mensurabilis* < Latin *mensura* (see MEASURE)] —**men·su·ra·bil·i·ty** /mènssərə bíllətee, mènshə-/ *n* —**men·su·ra·ble·ness** *n*

men·su·ral /ménssərəl, ménshə-/ *adj* **1.** relating to or involving measurement or measurable values **2.** describes notes, particularly in medieval music, that have a fixed length or time value relative to one another [Late 16C. < Latin *mensuralis* < *mensura* (see MEASURE)]

men·su·ra·tion /mènssə ráysh'n, mènshə-/ *n* **1.** the calculation of geometric quantities such as length, area, and volume from dimensions and angles that are already known **2.** the act, process, or skill of measuring something (*formal*) [Late 16C. < late Latin *mensuration-* < Latin *mensura* (see MEASURE)] —**men·su·ra·tive** /ménsə ràytiv, ménshə-/ *adj*

mens·wear /ménz wèr/, **men's wear** *n* **1.** clothing designed to be worn by men **2.** the department in a store that sells menswear

-ment *suffix* **1.** action, process ○ *arraignment* ○ *betterment* **2.** result of an action, or condition resulting from an action ○ *bewilderment* **3.** instrument or agent of an action ○ *refreshment* **4.** place ○ *emplacement* ○ *escarpment* [Directly or via French < Latin *-mentum*]

men·tal /mént'l/ *adj* **1. RELATING TO MIND** relating to, found in, or occurring in the mind ○ *mental stimulation* **2. CARRIED OUT IN MIND** carried out in the mind without any physical action or the use of any physical aid ○ *mental arithmetic* **3. PRODUCED BY MIND** produced by the mind and visible only in the mind ○ *mental imagery* **4. OFFENSIVE TERM** an offensive term meaning having a psychiatric disorder **5. OFFENSIVE TERM** an offensive term meaning extremely unintelligent or silly (*insult*) [15C. < French < Latin *ment-* "mind"] —**men·tal·ly** *adv*

men·tal age *n* a measure of intellectual development using norms against which children can be compared with other children of the same chronological age ○ *a four-year-old with a mental age of seven*

men·tal block *n* an inability to carry out a mental task such as remembering something, especially when caused by subconscious emotional factors

men·tal chal·lenge *n* a condition that limits the ability to learn and to function independently, as a result of congenital causes, brain injury, or disease

men·tal cru·el·ty *n* the infliction of psychological pain on somebody

men·tal hand·i·cap *n* an offensive term for a mental challenge

men·tal ill·ness *n* any psychiatric disorder that causes untypical behavior

men·tal·ism /mént'l ìzzəm/ *n* the belief that all objects of knowledge, including the physical universe, ultimately have no existence except as creations of the mind —**men·tal·ist** *n* —**men·tal·is·tic** /mènt'l ístik/ *adj*

men·tal·i·ty /men tállətee/ (*plural* **-ties**) *n* **1.** a habitual way of thinking or interpreting events peculiar to a person or type of person, especially with reference to the behaviors that it produces **2.** somebody's intellectual ability

men·tal lex·i·con *n* the words of a language that somebody knows the meanings of, can use, or uses habitually

men·tal·ly chal·lenged *adj* affected by a mental challenge

men·tal re·tar·da·tion *n* an offensive term for difficulty in learning or functioning independently (*dated*)

men·ta·tion /men táysh'n/ *n* (*formal*) **1.** mental activity, especially thinking **2.** somebody's state of mind or general attitude [Mid-19C. < Latin *ment-* "mind"]

ment·ee /men tée/ *n* somebody who is mentored [Late 20C. < MENTOR]

men·thol /mén thàwl/ *n* an organic compound that has a cool minty taste. Source: peppermint oil. Use: flavorings, perfumes, mild anesthetic. Formula: $CH_3C_6H_9(C_3H_7)OH$. [Late 19C. < German, "mint-oil" < Latin *mentha* (see MINT [1])]

men·tho·lat·ed /ménthə làytəd/ *adj* flavored with or containing menthol

men·tion /ménshən/ *v* (**-tioned, -tion·ing, -tions**) **1.** *vti* **SAY OR WRITE SOMETHING** to refer to something when speaking or writing, often in a brief or casual way ○ *I happened to mention your name to her.* ○ *He mentioned that the word was spelled wrongly.* **2.** *vt* **CITE SOMEBODY FOR BRAVERY** to refer to somebody by name in an official report as a way of acknowledging exceptional conduct, especially during a military action ■ *n* **1. CASUAL REFERENCE** a reference to a particular person or thing, often made in a brief or casual way **2. ACKNOWLEDGMENT OF SOMEBODY'S EXCEPTIONAL CONDUCT** an acknowledgment, especially in an official report, of somebody's exceptional conduct **3.** same as **honorable mention** [14C. Via French < Latin *mention-* "calling to mind"] —**men·tion·a·ble** *adj* ◇ **don't mention it** used in reply to an expression of thanks as a polite way of saying that none is necessary ◇ **not to mention** used to emphasize a point by introducing somebody or something that needs to be taken into consideration and is even more significant than what has been spoken of before

men·to /méntō/ (*plural* **-tos**) *n Carib* **1.** Jamaican music similar Calypso that is based on a folk dance rhythm **2.** a composition or dance in mento style [Early 20C. Origin ?]

men·tor /mén tàwr, méntər/ *n* **1. EXPERIENCED ADVISER AND SUPPORTER** somebody, usually older and more experienced, who advises and guides a younger, less experienced person **2. TRAINER** a senior or experienced person in a company or organization who gives guidance and training to a junior colleague ■ *vt* (**-tored, -tor·ing, -tors**) **BE MENTOR TO SOMEBODY** to act as a mentor to somebody, especially a junior colleague [Mid-18C. Via French < Latin < Greek *Mentōr* "Mentor"]

Men·tor /mén tàwr, méntər/ *n* in Greek mythology, the friend whom Odysseus left in charge of the household while he was at Troy and who was the teacher and protector of Telemachus, Odysseus's son

men·tor·ing /méntəring/ *n* the task of acting as a mentor to somebody, especially a junior colleague, or the system of appointing mentors

men·u /ménnyoo/ *n* **1. LIST OF DISHES AVAILABLE** a list of the dishes that can be ordered in a restaurant or that are to be served at a formal meal **2. LIST OF PROGRAM OPTIONS** a list on a computer screen of the options available to the user **3. LIST OR COLLECTION** a list of things available, or a collection of things from which a selection can be made [Mid-19C. < French, "minute, detailed" < Latin *minutus* (see MINUTE [1])]

men·u-driv·en *adj* describes computer software that is operated by selecting options from a menu

Men·u·hin /ménnyoo in, ménnoo̅ in/, **Yehudi, Baron Menuhin of Stoke d'Abernon** (1916–99) US-born British violinist. He was known as much for mentoring younger players as for his own virtuoso performances.

> "Music creates order out of chaos; for rhythm imposes unanimity upon the divergent, melody imposes continuity upon the disjointed, and harmony imposes compatibility upon the incongruous."
> [Yehudi Menuhin, *Sunday Times (London)*; October 10, 1976]

Hulton-Deutsch Collection/Corbis

Sir Robert Menzies

Men·zies /ménzeez/, **Sir Robert** (1894–1978) Australian prime minister (1939–41, 1949–66). During his premierships, he pursued close political ties with the United Kingdom and firmly aligned Australia economically and militarily with the United States. Full name **Menzies, Sir Robert Gordon**. See table at **prime minister**

me·ow /mee ów/ *n* **CHARACTERISTIC CRY OF CAT** the characteristic cry made by a domestic cat ■ *vi* (**-owed, -ow·ing, -ows**) **UTTER MEOW** to utter a meow ■ *interj* **DESIGNATING SPITEFUL OR MEAN COMMENT** used to indicate that you think somebody's comment is spiteful or malicious (*informal*) [Late 16C. An imitation of the sound]

MEP *abbr* EDUC Master of Engineering Physics

mep·a·crine /méppə krin/ *n UK* a synthetic drug. Use: formerly, treatment of malaria and worm infections. [Mid-20C. Blend of *methoxy* + *pentane* + *acridine*]

me·per·i·dine /mə pérrə deen/ *n* a white crystalline compound. Use: painkiller, sedative. Formula: $C_{15}H_{21}NO_2$. [Mid-20C. Blend of METHYL + PIPERIDINE]

Meph·i·stoph·e·les /mèffi stóffə leez/, **Me·phis·to** /mə fístō/ *n* in medieval legend, a subordinate to the devil, one of the seven archangels cast out of heaven, to whom Faust sold his soul —**Me·phis·to·phe·le·an** /mə fìstō féelyən, -féelee ən/ *adj*

me·phit·ic /mə fíttik/, **me·phit·i·cal** /-ik'l/ *adj* relating to or resembling a poisonous or foul smell (*formal*) [Early 17C. < late Latin *mephiticus* "pestilential" < Latin *mephitis* "foul smell"] —**me·phit·i·cal·ly** *adv*

me·phi·tis /mə fítiss/ *n* **1.** a foul-smelling or poisonous vapor coming out of the ground **2.** a foul smell (*literary*) [Early 18C. < Latin]

mep·ro·bam·ate /mèpprō bá màyt, mə prṓbə-/ *n* a bitter white powder. Use: tranquilizer, muscle relaxant. Formula: $C_9H_{18}N_2O_4$. [Mid-20C. Blend of METHYL + PROPYL + CARBAMATE]

mer. *abbr* GEOG meridian

mer- *prefix* same as **mero-** (*used before vowels*)

-mer *suffix* polymer ○ *oligomer* [Back-formation < -MERISM]

Mer·a·no /me ráanō/ city and health resort in Bolzano Province, Trentino-Alto Adige Region, northeastern Italy. Population: 33,504 (1996).

mer·bro·min /mər brṓmin/ *n* a green crystalline solid that forms a red solution when dissolved in water. Use: antiseptic. Formula: $C_{20}H_8Br_2HgNa_2O_6$. [Mid-20C. < MERCURIC + BROM-]

Mer·cal·li scale /mer kállee-/ *n* a scale for measuring the intensity of earthquakes, ranging from 1 to 12, in which 1 denotes a weak earthquake and 12 one that causes complete destruction [Early 20C. After Giuseppe *Mercalli* (1850–1914), Italian geologist]

mer·can·tile /múrkən tìl, -teel/ *adj* **1.** used for trade or by merchants, or characteristic of merchants or trading **2.** relating to or characteristic of mercantilism [Mid-17C. < French < Italian *mercante* "merchant" < Latin *mercari* (see MERCHANT)]

mer·can·til·ism /múrkənti lìzzəm/ *n* **1.** an early modern European economic theory and system that actively supported the establishment of colonies that would supply materials and markets and relieve home nations of dependence on other nations **2.** the principles and methods of commerce —**mer·can·til·ist** *n, adj* —**mer·can·til·is·tic** /mùrkənti lístik/ *adj*

mer·cap·tan /mər káp tàn/ *n* CHEM same as **thiol** [Mid-19C. < modern Latin *(corpus) mercurium captans* "(substance) that seizes mercury"]

mer·cap·to·pu·rine /mər kàptō pyóorin/ *n* a drug that interferes with the synthesis of purines. Use: treatment of leukemia. Formula: $C_5H_4N_4S$. [Mid-20C. < MERCAPTAN + PURINE]

Mer·ca·tor /mər káytər/, **Gerardus** (1512–94) Flemish geographer, cartographer, and mathematician. His map projection allowed compass courses to be plotted as straight lines, and is widely used in navigation. Born **Kremer, Gerhard**

Mer·ca·tor Pro·jec·tion *n* a method of making a map of the globe on a flat surface in which the meridians and latitudes are shown as straight lines that cross at right angles [Mid-17C. After Gerardus MERCATOR]

Mer·ced /mər séd/ city in central California, the administrative seat of Merced County. Population: 68,225 (2002 estimate).

mer·ce·nar·y /múrss'n èrree/ *n* (*plural* **-ies**) **1. SOLDIER FIGHTING FOR MONEY** a professional soldier paid to fight for an army other than that of his or her country **2. SOMEBODY INTERESTED ONLY IN PROFIT** an employee who works only for personal gain ■ *adj* **1. MOTIVATED ONLY BY MONEY** motivated solely by a desire for money **2. RELATING TO MERCENARIES** paid to serve in a foreign army, or consisting of mercenaries [14C. Directly or via French *mercenaire* < Latin *mercen(n)arius* "hireling" < *merces* "wages"] —**mer·ce·nar·i·ly** *adv* —**mer·ce·nar·i·ness** *n*

mer·cer·ize /múrssə rìz/ (**-ized, -iz·ing, -iz·es**) *vt* to treat cotton fabric or thread with an alkali to strengthen it and make it more lustrous and more receptive to dyes [Mid-19C. After John *Mercer* (1791–1866), British calico printer] —**mer·cer·i·za·tion** /mùrssəri záysh'n/ *n*

mer·chan·dise *n* /múrchən dìz, -dìss/ **GOODS** goods bought and sold for profit ■ *v* /múrchən dìz/ **1. mer·chan·dise** (*past and past participle* **-dised,** *present participle* **-dis·ing,** *3rd person present singular* **-dis·es**), **mer·chan·dize** (*past and past participle* **-dized,** *present participle* **-diz·ing,** *3rd person present singular* **-dizes**) *vti* **TRADE COMMERCIALLY** to trade in or buy and sell products for profit **2.** (*past and past participle* **-dised,** *present participle* **-dis·ing,** *3rd person present singular* **-dis·es**) **mer·chan·dize** (*past and past participle* **-dized,** *present participle* **-diz·ing,** *3rd person present singular* **-dizes**) *vt* **MARKET PRODUCTS** to promote a product by developing strategies for packaging, display, and publicity [13C. < French *marchandise* "goods" < Old French *marchant* (see MERCHANT)] —**mer·chan·dis·able** *adj* —**mer·chan·dis·er** *n*

mer·chan·dis·ing /múrchən dìzing/, **mer·chan·diz·ing** *n* **1.** the promotion of a product by developing strategies for packaging, displaying, and publicizing it **2.** commercial products that are developed as spin-offs from the success of a movie, TV program, sports team, or event

mer·chan·dize *vti* COMM another spelling of **merchandise** *v*

mer·chant /múrchənt/ *n* **1. COMMERCIAL DEALER** somebody who buys and sells goods, especially as a wholesaler or internationally **2. SOMEBODY NOTED FOR PARTICULAR ACTIVITY** somebody who is noted for a particular activity or quality (*informal; usually used in combination*) ○ *a speed merchant in a souped-up car* ■ *adj* **1. RELATING TO TRADE** used for or relating to commerce, wholesalers, or retailers **2. OF MERCHANT MARINE** relating to, belonging to, or involving a merchant marine ■ *vt* **DEAL IN SOMETHING** to trade or deal in products [12C. < Old French *marchant* < Latin *mercari* "to trade" < *merc-* "merchandise"]

CULTURAL NOTE ***The Merchant of Venice***, a play (1596–97) by English dramatist William Shakespeare. The story revolves around a loan made by usurer Shylock to Venetian merchant Antonio, and Shylock's subsequent attempts to claim the pound of flesh he has stipulated as security. Among the more serious issues raised in this blend of comedy, romance, and realism are the correct administration of justice and the power conferred by wealth. The well-known saying "It is a wise father that knows his own child" comes from this play.

Mer·chant /múrchənt/, **Ismail** (*b.* 1936) Indian movie producer and director. In partnership with James Ivory, he produced films set in South Asia and created adaptations of Western literary classics.

mer·chant·a·ble /múrchəntəb'l/ *adj* suitable or of a sufficiently high quality for buying and selling

mer·chant ac·count *n* **1.** a bank account that enables a merchant to receive the proceeds of credit card purchases **2.** a bank account that enables the holder to deposit payments made by credit card, used especially in connection with trading on the Internet

mer·chant bank *n UK* a bank that provides financial services mainly for companies and large-scale investors —**mer·chant bank·er** *n* —**mer·chant bank·ing** *n*

mer·chant cer·tif·i·cate au·thor·i·ty *n* in e-commerce, a certificate authority that provides certificates to merchants

mer·chant·man /múrchəntmən/ (*plural* **-men** /-mən/) *n* SHIPPING same as **merchant ship**

mer·chant ma·rine *n* a country's fleet of merchant ships, or the sailors who serve in them

mer·chant na·vy *n UK* same as **merchant marine**

mer·chant prince *n* an extremely wealthy, powerful, and prestigious merchant, especially in Renaissance Italy

mer·chant ship *n* a seagoing ship designed to carry goods, especially for international trade

Mer·ci·a /múrshee ə, múrshə/ ancient Anglo-Saxon kingdom of central England —**Mer·ci·an** *adj, n*

mer·ci·ful /múrssif'l/ *adj* **1.** showing mercy or compassion to somebody **2.** welcome because of putting an end to something unpleasant or distressing —**mer·ci·ful·ness** *n*

mer·ci·ful·ly /múrssif'lee/ *adv* **1.** so as to show mercy or compassion **2.** in a way or at a time that prevents or ends something unpleasant

USAGE See ***sentence adverb***.

mer·ci·less /múrsiləss/ *adj* **1.** LACKING MERCY showing no mercy or compassion toward somebody or something **2.** SEVERE very harsh in the judgment and treatment of others **3.** RELENTLESS continuing at a high level of violence or unpleasantness without pause or relief —**mer·ci·less·ly** *adv* —**mer·ci·less·ness** *n*

mercur- *prefix* mercury ○ *mercurous* [< MERCURY]

mer·cu·rate /múrkyə ràyt/ (**-rat·ed, -rat·ing, -rates**) *vt* to treat or combine something with mercury —**mer·cu·ra·tion** /mùrkyə ráysh'n/ *n*

mer·cu·ri·al /mər kyŏŏree əl/ *adj* **1.** LIVELY AND UNPREDICTABLE lively, witty, fast-talking, and likely to do the unexpected **2.** CONTAINING MERCURY containing or caused by mercury ■ *n* MEDICINE CONTAINING MERCURY formerly, a drug or chemical preparation containing mercury [Late 16C. < MERCURIAL] —**mer·cu·ri·al·i·ty** /mər kyŏŏree álləte/ *n* —**mer·cu·ri·al·ly** *adv* —**mer·cu·ri·al·ness** *n*

Mer·cu·ri·al /mər kyŏŏree əl/ *adj* **1.** relating to the Roman god Mercury **2.** relating to the planet Mercury [14C. Directly or via French *mercuriel* < Latin *mercurialis* < *Mercurius* (see MERCURY)]

mer·cu·ri·al·ism /mər kyŏŏree ə lìzzəm/ *n* poisoning caused by ingesting mercury

mer·cu·ri·al·ize /mər kyŏŏree ə lìz/ (**-ized, -iz·ing, -izes**) *vt* to treat somebody or something with mercury or with a compound containing mercury —**mer·cu·ri·al·i·za·tion** /mər kyŏŏree əli záysh'n/ *n*

mer·cu·ric /mər kyŏŏrik/ *adj* relating to or containing mercury with a valence of two

mer·cu·ric chlo·ride *n* a white crystalline solid that is poisonous and soluble. Use: insecticide, fungicide, wood preservative, in photography. Formula: $HgCl_2$.

mer·cu·ric ox·ide *n* a poisonous orange-yellow solid. Use: pigment. Formula: HgO.

mer·cu·ric sul·fide *n* a poisonous compound existing as a red or black solid. Use: pigment. Formula: HgS.

mer·cu·rous /múrkyərəss/ *adj* relating to or containing mercury with a valence of one

mer·cu·ry /múrkyəree/ (*plural* **same** or **-ries**) *n* **1.** LIQUID METALLIC ELEMENT a poisonous heavy silver-white metallic element that is liquid at room temperature. Source: cinnabar. Use: thermometers, barometers, pharmaceuticals, dental fillings, lamps. Symbol **Hg**. See table at **element 2.** TEMPERATURE OR PRESSURE the mercury in a weather thermometer or barometer, or the air temperature or pressure it indicates ○ *The mercury rose steadily throughout the early part of the day.* **3.** WEEDY PLANT a weedy plant of either of two genera, especially one belonging to the spurge family. Genera: *Mercurialis* or *Acalypha*. [14C. < Latin *Mercurius* (see MERCURY)]

Mer·cu·ry /múrkyəree/ *n* **1.** in Roman mythology, the god of commerce and rhetoric, who also acted as a messenger between humans and gods. His symbol is the caduceus, a staff with two snakes entwined around it. Greek equivalent **Hermes 2.** the smallest planet in the solar system and the one nearest the Sun [12C. < Latin *Mercurius* < *merc-* "merchandise"]

mer·cu·ry chlo·ride *n* CHEM same as **mercuric chloride**

mer·cu·ry-va·por lamp *n* an electric lamp whose bluish green light is generated when electricity is passed through a vapor of low-pressure mercury. Its light has a strong ultraviolet component, and these rays are used for cosmetic and therapeutic treatment.

mer·cy /múrssee/ (*plural* **-cies**) *n* **1.** COMPASSION kindness or forgiveness shown especially to somebody a person has power over ○ *The judge showed mercy and imposed the shortest sentence he could.* **2.** COMPASSIONATE DISPOSITION a disposition to be compassionate or forgiving of others ○ *a killer completely without mercy* **3.** SOMETHING TO BE THANKFUL FOR a welcome event or situation that provides relief or prevents something unpleasant from happening ○ *It was a mercy that no one was hurt in the accident.* **4.** EASING OF DISTRESS the easing of distress or pain ○ *The supply convoy was on a mission of mercy.* [12C. Via French *merci* "thank you" < Latin *merces* "reward, wages"] ◇ **at the mercy of somebody** *or* **something** completely unprotected against whatever somebody *or* something does

Mer·cy Corps *n* a group of trained American Red Cross volunteers, ready to assist during sudden disasters

mer·cy kill·ing *n* **1.** euthanasia regarded as motivated by compassion **2.** an act of killing somebody out of compassion, often at that person's request, in order to end his or her pain or distress

mer·cy seat *n* **1.** in Judaism, the gold covering on the Ark of the Covenant, regarded as God's resting place **2.** in Christianity, the throne of God in heaven

mere[1] /meer/ (*superlative* **mer·est**) *adj* **1.** just what is specified and nothing more, usually emphasizing the smallness, humbleness, or unimportance of the thing or person designated ○ *She was no mere journalist.* ○ *The merest hint of danger sent them all running for cover.* **2.** by itself and without anything more ○ *The mere mention of Arthur's name would make him upset.* [14C. Directly or via Anglo-Norman *meer*, Old French *mier* < Latin *merus* "pure, unmixed"]

mere[2] /meer/ *n* a body of standing fresh water, especially a lake (*archaic or literary; often used in place names*) [Old English, "sea" < Indo-European]

-mere *suffix* part, segment ○ *centromere* [< Greek *meros* "part"]

Mer·e·dith /mérrə dith/, **George** (1828–1909) British novelist and poet. His novels are noted for their psychological analysis and distinctive style. They include *The Egoist* (1879) and *Diana of the Crossways* (1885).

> "A kiss is but a kiss now! and no wave / Of a great flood that whirls me to the sea / But, as you will! we'll sit contentedly, / And eat our pot of honey on the grave."
> [George Meredith, "Modern Love"; 1862]

> "Speech is the small change of silence."
> [George Meredith, *The Ordeal of Richard Feverel*; 1859]

mere·ly /méerlee/ *adv* no more than as described, or doing no more than what is described ○ *I was merely pointing out where you had gone wrong.* ○ *merely a temporary setback*

me·ren·gue /mə réng gày/ *n* **1.** a ballroom dance, originally from the Dominican republic, characterized by hip and shoulder movements **2.** the music for a merengue [Mid-20C. Via American Spanish < Haitian creole *méringue* "meringue" < French]

mer·e·tri·cious /mèrrə tríshəss/ *adj* **1.** SUPERFICIALLY ATTRACTIVE attractive in a superficial or vulgar manner but without real value (*formal*) ○ *meretricious extras that don't really add to the car's value* **2.** MISLEADINGLY PLAUSIBLE seemingly plausible or significant, but actually insincere or false (*formal*) ○ *Don't be swayed by this meretricious argument in the project's favor.* **3.** OF PROSTITUTES relating to or like a prostitute (*archaic*) [Early 17C. < Latin *meretricius* < *meretric-* "prostitute" < *mereri* "serve for hire"] —**mer·e·tri·cious·ly** *adv* —**mer·e·tri·cious·ness** *n*

merganser

mer·gan·ser /mər gánssər/ *n* a fish-eating diving duck with a crested head and a long beak notched like a saw blade. Genus: *Mergus*. [Mid-17C. < modern Latin < Latin *mergus* "diver" + *anser* "goose"]

merge /murj/ (**merged, merg·ing, merg·es**) *vti* **1.** to combine or unite with something to form a single entity, or make two or more things do this ○ *Two of the country's largest banks have decided to merge.* **2.** to blend, or make two or more things blend, gradually ○ *The sky and sea seem to merge at the horizon.* [Mid-17C. < Latin *mergere* "to plunge, dip"] —**mer·gence** *n* —**merg·ing** *n*

merg·er /múrjər/ *n* **1.** the joining together of two or more companies or organizations **2.** a blending, combining, or joining of something with something else, or the state of being blended, combined, or joined together [Early 18C. < Anglo-Norman < Latin *mergere* "to plunge"]

mer·guez /mər géz/ (*plural* **same**) *n* a highly spiced North African sausage, usually made with lamb or mutton

Mé·ri·da /mérree daa/ **1.** city in southeastern Mexico, the capital of Yucatán State. It was founded by the Spanish on a Maya site in 1542. Population: 705,055 (2000). **2.** city in western Spain, in Badajoz Province. Population: 50,790 (2002).

Mer·i·den /mérridən/ city in southern Connecticut, on the Quinnipiac River. Population: 58,675 (2002 estimate).

me·rid·i·an /mə ríddee ən/ *n* **1.** GEOG LINE OF LONGITUDE an imaginary line between the North and South poles that crosses the equator at right angles. A meridian is designated by the degrees of longitude that it is west or east of the prime meridian. **2.** GEOG HALF OF CIRCLE BETWEEN POLES either half of the circle of the meridian, from pole to pole **3.** ASTRON CELESTIAL GREAT CIRCLE a great circle of the celestial sphere that passes through the celestial poles and the zenith of the observer **4.** *Midwest* ROADS same as **median strip 5.** ALTERN MED LINE OF ACUPUNCTURE POINTS in acupuncture, one of the pathways in the body along which the body's energy is believed to flow and along which acupuncture points are located **6.** HIGHEST POINT the peak or a high point, e.g., of development or success (*literary*) ○ *the decade when the empire's power reached its meridian* [14C. Directly or via French < Latin *meridianum* < *meridies* "midday," alteration of *medidies* < *medius* "middle" + *dies* "day"]

Me·rid·i·an /mə ríddee ən/ city in eastern Mississippi. Population: 39,518 (2002 estimate).

me·rid·i·o·nal /mə ríddee ən'l/ *adj* **1.** OF MERIDIAN along, belonging to, relating to, or like a meridian **2.** OF SOUTHERN REGIONS characteristic of or located in the south, especially southern Europe **3.** OF SOUTHERN PEOPLES relating to or characteristic of people who live in the south, especially southern Europe ■ *n* SOUTHERN PERSON somebody who comes from the south, especially southern France [14C. Via French < late Latin *meridionalis* < Latin *meridies* (see MERIDIAN)] —**me·rid·i·on·al·ly** *adv*

Mé·ri·mée /mèrri máy/, **Prosper** (1803–70) French writer. His works include the novella *Carmen*

(1846), the basis of Bizet's opera. He was also a historian.

"Like most men he was much more eloquent in asking than in thanking."
[Prosper Mérimée, *La Double Méprise (A Slight Misunderstanding)*; 1833]

me·ringue /mə ráng/ *n* **1.** a mixture of egg whites and sugar beaten until stiff, cooked, and used as a topping for pies or to make cookies and shells **2.** a cake, cookie, or shell made of meringue, often with a cream filling [Early 18C. < French]

me·ri·no /mə réenō/ *n* (*plural* **-nos**) **1.** *also* **me·ri·no sheep** SHEEP BRED FOR WOOL a sheep belonging to a breed originally developed in Spain that is raised for its wool in many parts of the world, especially Australia **2.** WOOL the long fine white wool of the merino sheep **3.** YARN OR FABRIC a fine yarn or fabric made from the wool of the merino sheep, often mixed with cotton ■ *adj* OF MERINO WOOL made of merino wool ○ *a merino shawl* [Late 18C. Via Spanish < Arabic (*banū*) *marīn*, a Berber people]

-merism *suffix* denoting a relationship between chemical constituents ○ *isomerism* [< Greek *meros* "part"]

mer·i·stem /mérri stèm/ *n* embryonic plant tissue that is actively dividing, as found at the tip of stems and roots [Late 19C. < Greek *meristos* "divided" < *merizein* "to divide" < *meros* "part"] —**mer·i·ste·mat·ic** /mèrristə máttik/ *adj* —**mer·is·te·mat·i·cal·ly** *adv*

me·ris·tic /mə rístik/ *adj* **1.** divided into or having segments **2.** involving a change in the number or arrangement of body parts or segments [Late 19C. < Greek *meris, meros* "part"] —**me·ris·ti·cal·ly** *adv*

mer·it /mérrit/ *n* **1.** VALUE value that deserves respect and acknowledgment ○ *a work of considerable technical and artistic merit* **2.** GOOD QUALITY a good or praiseworthy characteristic that somebody or something has (*often used in the plural*) **3.** ABILITY proven ability or accomplishment ○ *She got her promotion based on merit.* **4.** RELIG SPIRITUAL CREDIT spiritual worthiness achieved by doing good works ■ **mer·its** *npl* FACTS OF CASE the facts of a matter considered without regard for emotional, procedural, or other issues ○ *to consider a proposal on its merits* ■ *vt* (**-it·ed, -it·ing, -its**) DESERVE SOMETHING to be worthy of or earn something ○ *Some people feel the award wasn't merited.* ○ *This merits closer inspection.* [12C. Via French *mérite* < Latin *meritum* "price," form of the past participle of *merere* "earn"]

mer·i·toc·ra·cy /mèrri tókrəssee/ (*plural* **-cies**) *n* **1.** SYSTEM BASED ON ABILITY a social system that gives opportunities and advantages to people on the basis of their ability rather than, e.g., their wealth or seniority **2.** ELITE GROUP an elite group of people who achieved their positions on the basis of ability and achievement **3.** LEADERSHIP BY ELITE leadership by an elite group of people who are chosen on the basis of their abilities and achievements —**mer·it·o·crat·ic** /mèrritə kráttik/ *adj*

mer·i·to·ri·ous /mèrri táwree əss/ *adj* deserving honor and recognition ○ *She was awarded a medal for meritorious service.* [15C. < Latin *meritorius* < *merere* "earn"] —**mer·i·to·ri·ous·ly** *adv* —**mer·i·to·ri·ous·ness** *n*

mer·it sys·tem *n* a system of appointing and promoting civil servants on the basis of their ability rather than their political connections

merle /murl/, **merl** *n* same as **blackbird** (sense 2) (*archaic or literary*) [15C. < French < Latin *merula*]

Mer·leau-Pon·ty /mur lō pawN tée/, **Maurice** (1908–61) French philosopher. An existentialist, he was noted for his critical writings on behaviorism and the phenomenology of perception.

"We should not ask ourselves if we perceive the world truly; on the contrary: the world is that which we perceive."
[Maurice Merleau-Ponty, *Phenomenology of Perception*; 1945]

mer·lin /múrlin/ *n* a small dark falcon with a broad black band on the end of its tail. Native to: northern hemisphere. Latin name: *Falco columbarius*. [14C. < Anglo-Norman *merilun*, alteration of Old French *esmirillon* "large merlin" < *esmiril* "merlin"]

merlin

Mer·lin /múrlin/ *n* in Arthurian legend, a magician and adviser to King Arthur

mer·lon /múrlən/ *n* a solid part between two openings (**crenels**) in a battlement, e.g., on a castle [Early 18C. Via French < Italian *merlone* "large battlement" < *merlo* "battlement"]

mer·lot /mər lṓ, mer lṓ/, **Mer·lot** *n* **1.** a red wine made from a variety of black grape originally grown in France **2.** a black grape that is used to make merlot wine [Early 19C. < French, "small blackbird" < *merle* "blackbird," probably from the color of the grape]

mer·maid /múr màyd/ *n* a mythical sea creature with the head and upper body of a woman and the tail of a fish instead of legs [14C. < MERE[2]]

mer·maid's purse *n* MARINE BIOL same as **sea purse**

mer·man /múr màn, -mən/ *n* a mythical sea creature with the head and upper body of a man and the tail of a fish instead of legs [Early 17C. < MERE[2]]

mero- *prefix* part, partial ○ *merozoite* ○ *meroplankton* [< Greek *meros* "part"]

mer·o·blas·tic /mèrrə blástik/ *adj* used to describe an egg undergoing only partial division after being fertilized, with the undivided cells becoming the yolk —**mer·o·blas·ti·cal·ly** *adv*

mer·o·crine /mérrəkrin, -krīn/ *adj* relating to or produced by glands that make secretions without cell damage or disintegration [Early 20C. < MERO- + Greek *krinein* "to separate"]

Mer·o·ë /mérrō èe/ **1.** ruined city in northern Sudan, on the Nile River **2.** ancient kingdom of Nubia, in present-day northern Sudan

mer·o·plank·ton /mèrrə plángktən/ (*plural* **-tons** or *same*) *n* organisms that are plankton only for part of their life cycle, usually during the larval stage —**mer·o·plank·ton·ic** /-plangk tónnik/ *adj*

-merous *suffix* having a particular number or kind of parts ○ *tetramerous* ○ *heteromerous* [< Greek *meros* "part"]

Mer·o·vin·gi·an /mèrrə vínjee ən, -vínjən/ *adj* belonging or relating to a dynasty of Frankish kings that was founded by Clovis I and reigned in Gaul and Germany from about A.D. 500 to 751 ■ *n* a member of the Merovingian dynasty [Late 17C. < French *mérovingien* < Latin *Meroveus* "Merowig" (d. 458), grandfather of Clovis]

mer·o·zo·ite /mèrrə zṓ īt/ *n* any protozoan cell produced by the fission of a schizont, e.g., that of the malaria protozoan

mer·per·son /múr pùrss'n/ (*plural* **-peo·ple** /-pèep'l/ or **-per·sons**) *n* in legends and fairy tales, a mermaid or merman [After MERMAID]

Mer·ri·am /mérree əm/ city in northeastern Kansas, a southwestern suburb of Kansas City. Population: 10,844 (2002).

Mer·ri·mack /mérri màk/, **Mer·ri·mac** river in the northeastern United States, flowing south through New Hampshire and Massachusetts. Length: 110 mi./177 km.

mer·ri·ment /mérrimənt/ *n* fun and enjoyment marked by noise and laughter

Mer·ritt Is·land /mèrrit-/ island off the eastern coast of central Florida, lying between Cape Canaveral and the mainland. Area: 93 sq. mi./179 sq. km.

mer·ry /mérree/ (**-ri·er, -ri·est**) *adj* **1.** LIVELY AND CHEERFUL full of or showing lively cheerfulness or enjoyment ○ *a merry laugh* **2.** DELIGHTFUL tending to produce cheerfulness or happiness in people (*archaic*) ○ *the merry month of May* **3.** QUICK IN MOVEMENT quick in movement or manner ○ *The train moved at a merry clip.* [Old English *myrige* "pleasant" < Germanic, "short"] —**mer·ri·ly** *adv* —**mer·ri·ness** *n* ◇ **make merry** to enjoy yourself, especially by taking part in a celebration or festivity ◇ **the more the merrier** extra people are welcome to come along or join in

CULTURAL NOTE ***The Merry Wives of Windsor***, a play (1600–01) by English dramatist William Shakespeare. Shakespeare's only play wholly in prose was written to exploit the popularity of Falstaff, a comic character in *Henry IV*. It tells of Falstaff's attempts to seduce two married women in order to gain access to their wealth, the wives' discovery of his plan, and their imaginative revenge.

mer·ry-bells (*plural same*) *n* BOT same as **bellwort**

mer·ry-go-round *n* **1.** AMUSEMENT PARK RIDE an amusement park or fairground ride with a rotating circular platform fitted with seats that are usually shaped like animals such as horses and move up and down to music **2.** REVOLVING RIDE IN PLAYGROUND a piece of playground equipment in the form of a revolving structure for children to sit on and push, or be pushed, around and around **3.** WHIRL OF ACTIVITY a busy or continuous cycle of fast-paced activities or events ○ *a merry-go-round of press interviews and promotional events*

mer·ry·mak·ing /mérree màyking/ *n* lively celebration, fun, or enjoyment —**mer·ry·mak·er** *n*

mer·ry men *npl* somebody's followers (*humorous*)

Mer·sey /múrzee/ river of northwestern England. Liverpool is situated on its estuary. Length: 70 mi./110 km.

Mer·thyr Tyd·fil /mùrthər tídvil/ town in southern Wales, formerly an important center of coalmining and iron smelting. Population: 55,981 (2001).

Mer·ton /múrt'n/, **Robert K.** (1910–2003) US sociologist. He published important work on social deviance and mass persuasion, and helped to establish sociology as an academic discipline. Full name **Merton, Robert King**

"It would be a curious reading of the history of thought to suggest that the absence of disagreement testifies to a developing discipline."
[Robert K. Merton, "Now the Case *for* Sociology," *New York Times*; July 16, 1961]

mer·wom·an /múr wòomman/ (*plural* **-wom·en** /-wimmin/) *n* in legends and fairy tales, an older or mature mermaid [Early 19C. After MERMAID]

mes- *prefix* same as **meso-** (*used before vowels*)

Library of Congress/Corbis

mesa: Devil's Tower, Wyoming

me·sa /máyssə/ *n Southwest US* a relatively flat elevated area with steep sides that is less extensive than a plateau [Mid-18C. < Spanish, "table" < Latin *mensa*]

REGIONAL NOTE ***Mesa*** is most common in the Southwestern states, including Colorado. The term contrasts with *butte*, which is used more frequently in the Northwest: compare the place names *Mesa County*, Colorado, and *Mesa*, Arizona, with *Butte County*, South Dakota, and *Butte*, Montana.

Me·sa /máyssə/ city and resort in south central Arizona, a southeastern suburb of Phoenix. Population: 426,841 (2002 estimate).

Me·sa, Carlos (*b.* 1953) president of Bolivia (2003–). He was vice president (2002–3) when conflict over the country's natural gas reserves forced his predecessor to resign. Full name **Gisbert, Carlos Diego Mesa**

Me·sa·bi Range /mə saábee-/ narrow range of hills in northeastern Minnesota, parallel to Lake Superior. They are rich in iron ore. Length: 130 mi./210 km.

mé·sal·li·ance /may zállee ənss, may zàl yaáNs/ *n* a marriage with somebody of a lower social position, regarded as a bad match [Late 18C. < French, "bad alliance" < *alliance* "alliance" < Old French *aliance*]

me·sarch /mé zaárk, meé-/ *adj* describes a succession of plant or animal communities (**sere**) that originates in a moist habitat [Late 19C. < MESO- + Greek *arkhē* "beginning, origin"]

Me·sa Verde Na·tion·al Park /màyssə vúrd-/ national park in southwestern Colorado, established in 1906. It is noted for its well-preserved ancient cliff dwellings. Area: 81 sq. mi./211 sq. km.

mes·cal /mess kál/ (*plural* **-cals** or *same*) *n* **1.** *Hispanic* a colorless Mexican liquor distilled from the fermented sap of some species of agave plant **2.** *Southwest US* DRUGS, PLANTS same as **peyote** [Early 18C. Via Spanish *mezcal* < Nahuatl *mexcalli* "mescal liquor"]

Mes·ca·le·ro /mèsskə lérrō/ (*plural same* or **-ros**) *n* a member of a Native North American people who lived in Mexico, New Mexico, and Texas, and now live mainly in southern New Mexico [Mid-19C. < Spanish < *mezcal* (see MESCAL)]

mes·ca·line /méskə leén, -lin/ *n* a hallucinogenic drug that is extracted from the button-shaped nodules on the stem of the peyote [Late 19C. < German *Mezcalin* < Spanish *mezcal* (see MESCAL)]

mes·cla /mésklə/ *n Hispanic* a drug made from the residue of processing cocaine, which is mixed with marijuana and smoked [< American Spanish, "mixture"]

mes·clun /méssklən/ *n* a green salad made from several types of young leaves, typically including arugula, dandelion, radicchio, and endive [Late 20C. < Provençal *mesclar* "to mix" < Old French *mescler* < Latin *miscere*]

Mes·dames 1. plural of **Madame 2.** plural of **Madam**

mes·de·moi·selles plural of **mademoiselle**

mes·en·ceph·a·lon /mèz en séffə lòn, -lən/ *n* same as **midbrain** (*technical*) —**mes·en·ce·phal·ic** /mèz enssə fállik/ *adj*

mes·en·chyme /mézz'n kīm/ *n* the cells within the embryo that develop into connective tissue, bone, cartilage, blood, and the lymphatic system [Late 19C. < Greek *mesos* "middle" + *egkhuma* "infusion"] —**mes·en·chy·mal** /mə zéngkim'l/ *adj* —**mes·en·chym·a·tous** /mèzz'n kímmətəss/ *adj*

mes·en·ter·a ANAT plural of **mesenteron**

mes·en·ter·i·tis /mez èntə rītiss, mess-/ *n* inflammation of the mesentery of the peritoneum

mes·en·ter·on /mez éntə ròn, mess-/ (*plural* **-ter·a** /-tərə/) *n* the middle section of the embryonic intestine, which develops into the stomach, small intestine, and most of the large intestine —**mes·en·ter·on·ic** /mez èntə rónnik, mess-/ *adj*

mes·en·ter·y /mézz'n tèrree, méss'n-/ (*plural* **-ies**) *n* **1.** a membrane that supports an organ or body part, especially the double-layered membrane of the peritoneum attached to the back wall of the abdominal cavity that supports the small intestine **2.** a supportive membrane surrounding and giving structure to the inner organs of invertebrates [15C. Via modern Latin *mesenterium* < Greek *mesenterion* "middle intestine" < *enteron* "intestine"] —**mes·en·ter·ic** /mèzz'n térrik, mèss'n-/ *adj*

mesh /mesh/ *n* **1.** MATERIAL LIKE NET material, or a piece of material, made of plastic, thread, or wire woven together like a net ○ *wire mesh* **2.** OPENING IN NET the open space between the threads or wires of a net **3.** STRANDS OF NET the threads or wires that make up a net **4.** TRAP something that holds or entangles like a net or a trap (*often used in the plural*) ○ *caught in the meshes of the criminal underworld* **5.** SOMETHING INTERWOVEN an interwoven or interlinked arrangement or construction ○ *the mesh of the girders against the sky* **6.** INTERLOCKING METAL LINKS a material consisting of interlocking metal links, used in jewelry **7.** MECH ENG ENGAGEMENT OF GEARS engagement of the teeth on gearwheels **8.** INDUST OPENING IN SCREEN a measure of the number of openings in a screen for sorting things into different sizes, usually per inch. A 20-mesh screen has 20 openings per inch. ■ *vti* (**meshed, mesh·ing, mesh·es**) **1.** FIT TOGETHER to fit or work closely or well together, or make things work closely or well together ○ *Her vision of the company's future meshes perfectly with ours.* **2.** CATCH OR ENTANGLE to catch or entangle somebody or something, or become caught or entangled, in a mesh **3.** MECH ENG ENGAGE GEARWHEELS to engage together, or make the teeth on gearwheels engage together [14C. Probably < Middle Dutch *maesche* < Indo-European, "knot"] —**mesh·y** *adj*

me·shu·ga /mə shoóggə/, **me·shu·gah** *adj* totally unreasonable or thoughtless (*slang insult*) [Late 19C. Via Yiddish *meshuge* < Hebrew *mĕshuggā*]

me·shug·gen·er /mə shoógənər/, **me·shu·ga·na** /-nə/ *n* somebody considered to be entirely unreasonable or thoughtless (*slang insult*) [Early 20C. Variant of MESHUGA]

mesh·work /mésh wùrk/ *n* material consisting of meshes

me·si·al /meézee əl/ *adj* relating to or occurring along the dental arch near the middle of the front of the jaw [Early 19C. < Greek *mesos* "middle"] —**me·si·al·ly** *adv*

mes·ic[1] /mézzik/ *adj* growing in or characterized by moderate moisture [Early 20C. < Greek *mesos* "middle"] —**mes·i·cal·ly** *adv*

mes·ic[2] /mézzik/ *adj* relating to a meson [Mid-20C. < MESON]

Me·sic /máysich/, **Stjepan** (*b.* 1934) president of Croatia (2000–). The last president of the former Yugoslavia before its breakup (1991), he joined the centrist Croatian People's Party (1997) but left after being elected, in order to be "president of all Croats."

mes·mer·ic /mez mérrik/ *adj* completely absorbing somebody's attention [Early 19C. < *Mesmer* (see MESMERIZE)] —**mes·mer·i·cal·ly** *adv*

mes·mer·ism /mézmə rìzzəm/ *n* **1.** the power to fascinate somebody in a way that is almost hypnotic **2.** hypnotism, formerly believed to involve animal magnetism [Late 18C. < *Mesmer* (see MESMERIZE)] —**mes·mer·ist** *n*

mes·mer·ize /mézmə rīz/ (**-ized, -iz·ing, -iz·es**) *vt* **1.** to fascinate somebody or absorb all of somebody's attention ○ *The speaker mesmerized the audience with his dramatic tale.* **2.** to hypnotize somebody, especially by a method formerly believed to involve animal magnetism [Early 19C. After F. A. *Mesmer* (1734–1815), Austrian physician] —**mes·mer·i·za·tion** /mèzmərì záysh'n/ *n* —**mes·mer·iz·er** *n* —**mes·mer·iz·ing·ly** *adv*

mesne /meen/ *adj* in law, happening or appearing between two other things, especially assignments of property [Mid-16C. < legal French, a variant of Anglo-Norman *meen* "middle"]

meso- *prefix* middle, intermediate ○ *mesopelagic* [< Greek *mesos* < Indo-European]

Mes·o·a·mer·i·ca /mèzzō ə mérrikə, mèssō-/ region of Central America and southern North America that was occupied by several civilizations, especially the Maya, in pre-Columbian times —**Mes·o·a·mer·i·can** *adj, n*

mes·o·blast /mézzə blàst, méssə-/ *n* BIOL same as **mesoderm**

mes·o·carp /mézzə kaárp, méssə-/ *n* the middle layer of a fruit wall (**pericarp**), e.g., the fleshy part of some fruits

mes·o·crat·ic /mèzzə kráttik, mèssə-/ *adj* describes igneous rock containing as much as 60 percent heavy dark ferromagnesian minerals in its composition

mes·o·derm /mézzə dùrm, méssə-/ *n* the middle of the three cell layers in an embryo, from which connective tissue, muscle, blood, dermis, and bone develop —**mes·o·der·mal** /mèzzə dúrm'l, mèssə-/ *adj* —**mes·o·der·mic** /mèzzə dúrmik, mèssə-/ *adj*

mes·o·gle·a /mèzzə gleé ə, mèssə-/, **mes·o·gloe·a** *n* a layer of gelatinous substance separating the inner and outer walls of a coelenterate such as a jellyfish [Late 19C. < modern Latin, "middle glue" < Greek *glia* "glue"] —**mes·o·gle·al** *adj*

Mes·o·lith·ic /mèzzə líthik, mèssə-/, **mes·o·lith·ic** *n* the middle period of the Stone Age, between the Paleolithic and Neolithic —**Mes·o·lith·ic** *adj*

mes·o·morph /mézzə màwrf, méssə-/ *n* a husky muscular body, or somebody who has such a body

mes·on /mé zòn, meé-/ *n* an elementary particle such as a pion or kaon that has a rest mass between that of an electron and a proton and participates in the strong interaction. Mesons consist of a quark and an antiquark, and have a spin that is zero or an integer. —**me·son·ic** /me zónnik, meé-/ *adj*

mes·o·pause /mézzə pàwz, méssə-/ *n* the upper boundary of the mesosphere, approximately 50 mi./80 km above the Earth's surface

mes·o·pe·lag·ic /mèzzə pə lájjik, mèssə-/ *adj* found in or relating to the intermediate oceanic depths between approximately 300 and 3,300 ft./100 and 1,000 m

mes·o·phyll /mézzə fil, méssə-/ *n* the soft tissue (**parenchyma**) containing chlorophyll between the epidermal layers of a plant leaf —**mes·o·phyl·lic** /mèzzə fíllik, mèssə-/ *adj* —**mes·o·phyl·lous** /-fílləss/ *adj*

mes·o·phyte /mézzə fīt, méssə-/ *n* a land plant that needs moderate amounts of moisture for growth —**mes·o·phyt·ic** /mèzzə fíttik, mèssə-/ *adj*

mes·o·pore /mézzə pàwr, méssə-/ *n* a tiny pore, between 2 and 50 nanometers in diameter, in a material such as carbon used to filter objects —**mes·o·por·os·i·ty** /mèzzə paw róssətee, mèssə-/ *n* —**mes·o·por·ous** *adj*

Mes·o·po·ta·mi·a /mèssəpə táymee ə/ ancient region located between the Tigris and Euphrates rivers in modern Iraq and Syria. It was the site of several early urban civilizations, including Babylonia. —**Mes·o·po·ta·mi·an** *n, adj*

mes·o·some /mézzə sōm, méssə-/ *n* an indentation in the cell membrane of some bacteria

mes·o·sphere /mézzə sfeér, méssə-/ *n* the layer of the Earth's atmosphere in which temperature decreases rapidly, located between the stratosphere and thermosphere —**mes·o·spher·ic** /mèzzə sférrik, mèssə-, -sfeérik/ *adj*

mes·o·the·li·o·ma /mèssə theelee ṓmə/ (*plural* **-mas** or **-ma·ta** /-ṓmətə/) *n* a benign or malignant tumor of the lining of the lungs, heart, or abdomen. The malignant form is often the result of exposure to asbestos and may take more than 30 years to develop.

mes·o·the·li·um /mèzzə theélee əm, mèssə-/ (*plural* **-li·a** /-lee ə/) *n* a cell layer derived from mesoderm that lines the body cavity of a vertebrate embryo and develops into epithelia and muscle tissue —**mes·o·the·li·al** *adj*

mes·o·tho·rax /mèzzə tháw ràks, mèssə-/ (*plural* **-rax·es** or **-ra·ces** /-rə seéz/) *n* the middle of the three segments of an insect's thorax, from which the middle pair of legs and first pair of wings grow —**mes·o·tho·rac·ic** /mèzzəthə rássik, mèssə-/ *adj*

Mes·o·zo·ic /mèzzə zṓ ik, mèssə-/ *n* the era of geologic time, 248 million to 65 million years ago, during which dinosaurs, birds, and flowering plants first appeared. See table at **geologic time** —**Mes·o·zo·ic** *adj*

mes·quite /me skeét/ (*plural same* or **-quites**) *n Southwest US* **1.** a hard wood often burned in a barbecue to flavor food **2.** a small spiny leguminous tree or bush with hard wood, the pods of which are sometimes used as fodder. Native to: southwestern United States, Mexico. Genus: *Prosopis.* [Mid-18C. Via Mexican Spanish *mezquite* < Nahuatl *mizquitl*]

REGIONAL NOTE ***Mesquite*** is common in Upper Mexico and the lower Southwestern states, especially in Texas, where such growth is also called *chaparral, mesquite flat(s), mesquite thicket,* and *mesquital.*

mess /mess/ *n* **1.** UNTIDY CONDITION a dirty or untidy state ○ *The apartment was left in a terrible mess after the party.* **2.** CHAOTIC STATE a chaotic, confused, or troublesome state or situation ○ *Their business affairs were in a complete mess.* ○ *The workmen have made a complete mess of the repairs.* **3.** UNTIDY PERSON OR THING somebody or something in a confused, dirty, or untidy state (*informal*) **4.** PLACE FOR COMMUNAL MEALS a place where a group of people, especially members of the armed forces, have meals together **5.** PEOPLE WHO EAT TOGETHER a group of people, especially members of the armed forces, who have meals together **6.** COMMUNAL MEAL a meal eaten together by a group of people, especially members of the armed forces **7.** QUANTITY OF FOOD a serving or quantity of food, especially of soft or soggy food ■ *v* (**messed, mess·ing, mess·es**) **1.** *vi* MEDDLE to interfere in something ○ *Don't mess in their business.* **2.** *vti* MAKE SOMETHING DIRTY to make something dirty, muddled, or disordered ○ *She messed her jacket while checking the oil.* **3.** *vi* USE SOMETHING CARELESSLY to use something carelessly, causing a problem or damage as a result ○ *Who's been messing with my computer?* **4.** *vi* EAT TOGETHER to take meals along with a particular group of people, especially members of the armed forces ○ *I used to mess with the three of them.* ○ *We messed together in the army.* [13C. < Old French, "portion of food" < Latin *mittere* "send, put"]

mess around *v* **1.** *vi* WASTE TIME to waste time in an unproductive or aimless manner (*informal*) **2.** *vi* RELAX to spend time in a leisurely and pleasant manner (*informal*) **3.** *vt* INTERFERE to interfere or meddle in something (*informal*) ○ *Don't mess in their business.* **4.** *vi* BEHAVE IN UNSERIOUS WAY to joke or behave playfully (*informal*) ○ *I thought he was just messing around.* **5.** *vi* ASSOCIATE WITH SOMEBODY to associate with somebody, especially somebody who is seen as undesirable (*informal*) ○ *She started messing around with that crowd last summer.* **6.** *vi* BE SEXUALLY UNFAITHFUL to have sexual activity with somebody other than a spouse or regular sexual partner (*slang*)

mess up *v* (*informal*) **1.** *vti* RUIN SOMETHING to spoil or bungle something, or make a mistake ○ *The rain messed up our plans for a picnic.* **2.** *vt* MAKE SOMETHING MESSY to make something dirty or disordered **3.** *vt* UPSET SOMEBODY to confuse or upset somebody

mess with *vt* (*informal*) **1.** to interfere or meddle in something in a way that may have bad consequences **2.** to try to thwart or deceive somebody

mes·sage /méssij/ *n* **1.** COMMUNICATION a communication in speech, writing, or signals, usually a brief one, and often one left for a recipient who cannot be directly contacted at the time **2.** MEANING a lesson, moral, or important idea communicated, e.g., in a work of art **3.** ERRAND the mission or errand of a messenger (*dated*) ○ *sent on a message to her grandmother's* **4.** COMMERCIAL a commercial, especially one on television, paid for by the sponsors of a program or event ○ *and now a message from our sponsor* ■ *vt* (**-saged, -sag·ing, -sages**) **1.** COMMUNICATE WITH SOMEBODY to send a message to somebody ○ *Can you message me about that?* **2.** COMMUNICATE SOMETHING TO SOMEBODY to send something as a message ○ *to message the news to your boss* [13C. < French < Latin *missus*, past participle of *mittere* "send"] ◇ **get the message** to take something in and understand it (*informal*)

mes·sage board *n* ONLINE same as **bulletin board** (sense 2)

mes·sage code au·then·ti·ca·tion *n* the cryptographic verification of the author and integrity of an e-mail message

mes·sag·ing /méssijing/ *n* **1.** a system for sending messages to people, e.g., by computer, telephone, or pager **2.** the process of sending a message using a messaging system

mes·sa·line /mèssə leén/ *n* a soft shiny lightweight silk fabric. Use: clothing. [Early 20C. < French, after Valeria *Messalina*, wife of the Roman emperor Claudius]

~~messanger~~ incorrect spelling of **messenger**

Mes·sei·gneurs plural of **Monseigneur**

mes·sen·ger /méss'njər/ *n* **1.** SOMEBODY CARRYING MESSAGE somebody who carries messages between people **2.** PAID COURIER an employee who carries and delivers messages, especially a courier **3.** SOMEBODY RUNNING ERRAND somebody who runs an errand **4.** *also* **mes·sen·ger line** NAUT LIGHT ROPE a lightweight rope used to haul a heavier one, e.g., from one ship to another ■ *vt* (**-gered, -ger·ing, -gers**) SEND SOMETHING BY MESSENGER to send something by messenger [12C. < French *messager* < *message* (see MESSAGE)]

me·ssen·ger bag *n* a satchel-shaped bag, usually made of synthetic material, used for carrying documents or small items

mes·sen·ger line *n* NAUT same as **messenger** *n* (sense 4)

mes·sen·ger RNA *n* a form of RNA that is transcribed from a strand of DNA and translated into a protein sequence at a cell ribosome

Mes·ser·schmitt /méssər shmìt/ *n* a fighter airplane, especially the Me-109 or the Me-262, used by the German Air Force in World War II

Mes·ser·schmitt /méssər shmit/, **Willy** (1898–1978) German aircraft designer. His Messerschmitt Me-109 set a world speed record (1939), and his Messerschmitt Me-262, used by the German Air Force in World War II, was the first jet fighter plane. Born **Messerschmitt, Wilhelm**

mess hall *n* a building or room where a group of people, especially members of the armed forces, eat their meals together

Mes·siaen /mèss yaáN, -yaán/, **Olivier** (1908–92) French composer and organist. His works for organ, piano, voice, chamber ensemble, and orchestra have a mystic quality and a unique harmonic language. Full name **Messiaen, Olivier Eugène Prosper Charles**

mes·si·ah /mə sí ə/ *n* somebody regarded as or claiming to be a savior or liberator of a country, people, or the world [Mid-17C. < MESSIAH]

Mes·si·ah /mə sí ə/ *n* **1.** in Christianity, Jesus Christ regarded as the Messiah prophesied in the Hebrew Bible **2.** in the Hebrew Bible, an anointed king who will lead the Jews back to the land of Israel and establish justice in the world [12C. < French *Messie* < Greek *Messias* < Aramaic *mĕšīḥā* and Hebrew *māšīaḥ* "anointed" < *māšaḥ* "anoint"] —**Mes·si·ah·ship** *n*

mes·si·an·ic /mèssee ánnik/ *adj* **1.** *also* **Mes·si·an·ic** JUD-CHR RELATING TO MESSIAH belonging or relating to the Messiah **2.** JUDAISM OF JUDAIC GOLDEN AGE relating to, belonging to, or constituting a Judaic golden age of peace, truth, and happiness **3.** OF LIBERATOR relating or belonging to an inspirational leader, especially one claiming to be or regarded as a savior or liberator **4.** INVOLVING GREAT ENTHUSIASM done with or showing great enthusiasm or devotion ○ *preaching with messianic fervor* —**mes·si·an·i·cal·ly** *adv*

mes·si·a·nism /mə sí ə nizzəm, méssee-/, **Mes·si·a·nism** *n* belief in the coming of the Messiah or a messiah or messianic age

Mes·sieurs plural of **Monsieur**

Mes·si·na /me seénə/ historic Italian city and seaport in northeastern Sicily. Population: 261,134 (1999).

Mes·si·na, Strait of strait between Sicily and the Italian mainland, linking the Ionian and Tyrrhenian seas. Length: 20 mi./32 km.

mess jacket *n* a waist-length jacket worn as part of a military uniform, especially on formal occasions

mess kit *n* a compact set of cooking and eating utensils, usually made of metal, used especially by soldiers or campers

mess·mate /méss màyt/ *n* somebody with whom somebody regularly eats, especially in a military mess

Messrs. /méssərz/ *npl* the customary title used before the name of more than one man or in names of companies named for a person ○ *Messrs Smith and Jones* ○ *bought from Messrs Wright* [Late 18C. Abbreviation of MESSIEURS]

mes·suage /mésswij/ *n* a dwelling with its outbuildings and the surrounding land that is used by the dwelling's occupants [14C. < Anglo-Norman]

mess-up *n* a complete mistake or totally unsuccessful attempt at something (*informal*)

mess·y /méssee/ (**-i·er, -i·est**) *adj* **1.** DIRTY OR DISORDERED involving, producing, or marked by dirt or disorder ○ *Repairing a car can be a messy business.* **2.** DIFFICULT TO SORT OUT complicated and unpleasant to resolve or deal with ○ *a messy divorce* **3.** CARELESS showing a lack of carefulness or precision ○ *an erroneous conclusion resulting from messy reasoning* —**mess·i·ly** *adv* —**mess·i·ness** *n*

mes·ti·za /mess teézə/ *n* *Hispanic* a woman with mixed ancestry, especially a woman in Latin America of both Native American and European ancestry [Late 16C. < Spanish, form of MESTIZO]

mes·ti·zo /mess teézō/ (*plural* **-zos** or **-zoes**) *n* *Hispanic* somebody with mixed ancestry, especially somebody in Latin America of both Native American and European ancestry. Mestizos form the largest population group in many Latin American countries. [Late 16C. Via Spanish < Latin *mixtus*, past participle of *miscere* "mix"]

mes·tra·nol /méstrə nàwl/ *n* a synthetic estrogen. Use: oral contraceptives. [Mid-20C. < METHYL + ESTRANE]

Mes·tro·vic /méshtrō vìch/, **Ivan** (1883–1962) Croatian-born US sculptor. His works have religious and folkloric subjects. He also sculpted portrait busts.

met past participle, past tense of **meet**[1]

Met /met/ *abbr* **1.** Metropolitan Museum of Art (in New York) **2.** Metropolitan Opera House (in New York)

met. *abbr* **1.** METALL metallurgy **2.** LITERAT metaphor **3.** PHILOSOPHY metaphysics **4.** METEOROL meteorological **5.** METEOROL meteorology **6.** metropolitan

met- *prefix* same as **meta-** (*used before vowels*)

meta- *prefix* **1.** later, behind ○ *metaphase* ○ *metathorax* **2.** beyond, transcending, encompassing ○ *metagalaxy* ○ *metalanguage* **3.** change, transformation ○ *metaplasia* **4.** higher, more developed ○ *metaxylem* **5.** used in chemical names ○ *metaphosphate* [< Greek *meta* "beside, after" < Indo-European, "between"]

met·a·bol·ic /mèttə bóllik/ *adj* relating to or typical of metabolism [Mid-19C. < Greek *metabolikos* "changeable" < *metabolē* (see METABOLISM)] —**met·a·bol·i·cal·ly** *adv*

met·a·bol·ic path·way *n* a sequence of energy-producing, biochemical reactions catalyzed by enzymes

met·a·bol·ic rate *n* the speed at which the biochemical reactions of metabolism in living cells take place

me·tab·o·lism /mə tábbə lìzzəm/ *n* **1.** the series of processes by which food is converted into the energy and products needed to sustain life **2.** the biochemical activity of a particular substance in a living organism [Late 19C. < Greek *metabolē* "change" < *metaballein* "throw differently" < *ballein* "to throw"]

me·tab·o·lite /mə tábbə lìt/ *n* a byproduct of metabolism [Late 19C. < METABOLISM]

me·tab·o·lize /mə tábbə lìz/ (**-lized, -liz·ing, -liz·es**) *vti* to subject something to metabolism, or undergo metabolism [Late 19C. < Greek *metabolē* (see METABOLISM)] —**me·tab·o·liz·a·ble** *adj*

me·tab·o·lome /mə tábbə lōm/ *n* the full complement of molecules of low molecular weight present in cells in a particular physiological or developmental state [Late 20C. Blend of METABOLITE + GENOME] —**me·tab·o·lom·ic** /mə tàbbə lómmik/ *adj*

me·tab·o·lom·ics /mə tàbbə lómmiks/ *n* the measurement of the metabolites of low molecular weight in an organism's cells at a specific time under specific environmental conditions (*takes a singular verb*)

met·a·car·pal /mèttə kaárp'l/ *n* any bone in the human hand between the wrist and digits, or a corresponding bone in a vertebrate animal's forefoot ■ *adj* relating or belonging to the metacarpals —**met·a·car·pal·ly** *adv*

met·a·car·pus /mèttə kaárpəss/ (*plural* **-pi** /-pì/) *n* **1.** the set of five long bones (**metacarpals**) in the human hand between the wrist and fingers **2.** the region between the wrist and digits of the forefoot or hand of a vertebrate animal

met·a·cen·ter /méttə sèntər/ *n* the intersection of the vertical line through the center of buoyancy of an object at equilibrium with the vertical line through the center of buoyancy when the object is tilted

met·a·cen·tric /mèttə séntrik/ *adj* **1.** relating or belonging to a metacenter **2.** describes a chromosome whose centromere is located at or near the middle

met·a·chro·mat·ic /mèttə krō máttik/ *adj* **1.** taking on a color atypical of the staining solution **2.** able to produce a color in different shades in tissue or cells [Late 19C. < META- + Greek *khrōmat-* "color"]

met·a·chro·ma·tism /mèttə krómə tìzzəm/ *n* a change in color caused by a change in physical conditions such as temperature

met·a·cog·ni·tion /mèttə kog nísh'n/ *n* knowledge of your own thoughts and the factors that influence your thinking —**met·a·cog·ni·tive** /mèttə kógnitiv/ *adj*

Met·a·com·et /méttə kòmmət/, **Met·a·com** /méttə kòm/ ➧ **Philip**

met·a·da·ta /méttə dàytə, -dàttə/ *n* descriptive statistical information about the elements of a set of data (*takes a singular or plural verb*)

met·a·eth·ics /mèttə éthiks/ *n* the branch of linguistic philosophy that analyzes and seeks to clarify the meaning and use of ethical expressions such as "good" and "ought" (*takes a singular verb*) —**met·a·eth·i·cal** *adj*

met·a·fe·male /mèttə fée màyl/ *n* a female organism with an extra female chromosome

met·a·fic·tion /méttə fiksh'n/ *n* **1.** fiction writing that deals, often playfully and parodically, with the nature of fiction, the techniques and conventions used in it, and the role of the author **2.** a work of metafiction —**met·a·fic·tion·al** *adj* —**met·a·fic·tion·ist** /mèttə fíksh'nist/ *n*

met·a·gal·ax·y /méttə gálləksee/ *n* the total of all galaxies making up the universe —**met·a·ga·lac·tic** /mèttə gə láktik/ *adj*

met·age /méetij/ *n* **1.** the official measurement of the contents or weight of a load, e.g., of coal or grain **2.** a charge for making an official measurement of the contents or weight of a load [Early 16C. < METE]

me·tag·na·thous /mə tágnəthəss/ *adj* describes the condition in which a bird has the tips of its beak crossed —**me·tag·na·thism** *n*

Met·ai·rie /méttə rèe/ city in Louisiana, west of New Orleans. Population: 149,428 (1996).

met·al /mét't'l/ *n* **1.** TYPE OF CHEMICAL ELEMENT a chemical element that is malleable and ductile, usually solid, has a characteristic luster, and is a good conductor of heat and electricity, e.g., copper or iron **2.** MIXTURE OF METALS a mixture (**alloy**) of one or more metals **3.** MUSIC same as **heavy metal** (sense 1) (*slang*) **4.** PRINTING TYPE printer's type made of metal **5.** MOLTEN GLASS molten glass for use in glassmaking **6.** HERALDRY GOLD OR SILVER in heraldry, gold or silver **7.** NAVY WEIGHT FIRED IN BROADSIDE the collective weight of the projectiles a warship can fire in a broadside **8.** *UK* ROADS same as **road metal** ■ *vt* (**-aled** or **-alled, -al·ing** or **-al·ling, -als**) **1.** FIT SOMETHING WITH METAL to cover, fit, or provide something with metal **2.** *UK* MAKE OR MEND ROAD to make or repair a road with broken stones (**road metal**) [13C. Directly or via French < Latin *metallum* "mine, metal" < Greek *metallon*]

SPELLCHECK metal or **mettle**? Do not confuse the spelling of ***metal*** and ***mettle***, which sound similar. ***Metal*** is chiefly used as a noun denoting a type of chemical element, but also sometimes as a verb, meaning "to provide something with metal" or "to put broken stones on a road." ***Mettle*** is only a noun, meaning "spirit" or "mental character"

metal. *abbr* **1.** metallurgic **2.** metallurgy

met·a·lan·guage /méttə làng gwij/ *n* a language or system of symbols used to describe or analyze another language or system of symbols

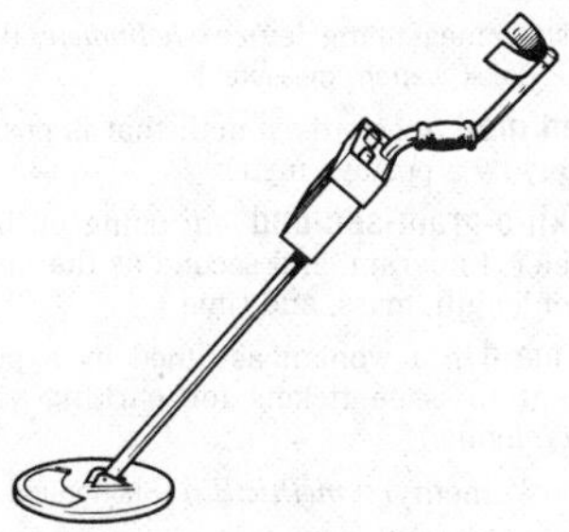

metal detector

met·al de·tec·tor *n* **1.** DEVICE FOR DETECTING BURIED METAL a portable electronic device with a search head that is swept over the ground and used to detect buried metal objects such as coins **2.** DEVICE FOR DETECTING WEAPONS an electronic device that registers the presence of metal, used, e.g., to detect metal weapons or to screen passengers at an airport **3.** DEVICE FOR DETECTING METAL IN FOOD an electronic device used in the food industry to check for the presence of pieces of metal that might have accidentally gotten into food during processing

met·a·lin·guis·tic /mèttə ling gwístik/ *adj* relating to a metalanguage or to metalinguistics

met·a·lin·guis·tics /mèttə ling gwístiks/ *n* (*takes a singular verb*) **1.** the branch of linguistics that deals with the study of metalanguages **2.** the branch of linguistics that deals with the relation between language and other aspects of culture

metall. *abbr* METALL **1.** metallurgic **2.** metallurgical **3.** metallurgy

metall- *prefix* same as **metallo-** (*used before vowels*)

me·tal·lic /mə tállik/ *adj* **1.** CONTAINING OR BEING METAL made of, containing, or constituting metal or a metal **2.** OF METAL typical of a metal **3.** SHINY shiny and highly reflective ○ *a sports car with a metallic finish* **4.** TASTING OF METAL sharp and bitter to the taste ○ *This water has a slightly metallic taste.* **5.** SOUNDING LIKE STRUCK METAL like the sound of two metal objects knocking against each other **6.** HARSH-SOUNDING harsh and unpleasant in tone ○ *speaking with a metallic edge to her voice* —**me·tal·li·cal·ly** *adv*

me·tal·lic bond *n* a chemical bond characteristic of metals, in which electrons are shared between atoms and move about in the crystal

met·al·lic·i·ty /mèttə líssətee/ *n* the amount of a specific metal contained in something such as a star, galaxy, or composite material. The ratio of iron to hydrogen in a star is used as a measure of its age.

me·tal·lic lens *n* a device consisting of louvers or slats, used to focus electromagnetic or sound waves

met·al·lif·er·ous /mètt'l íffərəss/ *adj* containing or yielding metal

met·al·line /mét't'lin, -īn/ *adj* **1.** resembling a metal **2.** containing metal ions

met·al·lize /mét't'l īz/ (**-lized, -liz·ing, -lizes**), **met·al·ize** *vt* to coat or cover something with metal

metallo- *prefix* metal ○ *metallophone* [< Latin *metallum* (see METAL)]

me·tal·lo·en·zyme /mə tàllō én zīm/ *n* an enzyme containing a bound metal ion incorporated into a protein

me·tal·lo·ful·ler·ene /mə tàllō fóollə rèen/ *n* a fullerene compound containing a metal atom or a metal oxide molecule

met·al·log·ra·phy /mètt'l óggrəfee/ *n* the study of the composition and microscopic structure of metals —**met·al·log·ra·pher** *n* —**me·tal·lo·graph·ic** /mə tàllə gráffik/ *adj* —**me·tal·lo·graph·i·cal·ly** *adv* —**met·al·lo·graph·ist** *n*

met·al·loid /mét't'l òyd/ *n* NONMETALLIC ELEMENT WITH METAL PROPERTIES a nonmetallic element such as silicon that has properties between those of a metal and nonmetal ■ *adj* **1.** *also* **met·al·loi·dal** /mètt'l óyd'l/ OF METALLOID relating to or having the characteristics of a metalloid **2.** *also* **met·al·loi·dal** LIKE METAL resembling a metal

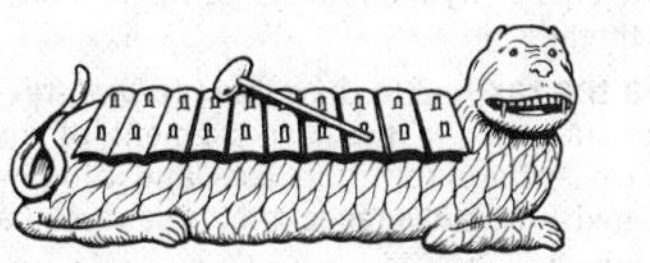

metallophone

me·tal·lo·phone /mə tállə fōn/ *n* a musical instrument resembling a xylophone, with tuned metal bars that are struck with mallets

met·al·lor·gan·ic /mètt'l awr gánnik/ *adj* relating to or composed of an organic chemical compound with a metallic component

met·al·lur·gy /mét't'l ùrjee/ *n* the study of the structure and properties of metals, their extraction from the ground, and the procedures for refining, alloying, and making things from them —**met·al·lur·gic** /mètt'l úrjik/ *adj* —**met·al·lur·gi·cal** *adj* —**met·al·lur·gi·cal·ly** *adv* —**met·al·lur·gist** /mét't'l ùrjist/ *n*

met·al·smith /mét't'l smìth/ *n* somebody who is skilled at making and repairing metal objects

met·al·ware /mét't'l wèr/ *n* objects that have been crafted from metal

met·al·work /mét't'l wùrk/ *n* **1.** MAKING OF METAL OBJECTS the craft of making objects out of metal **2.** METAL THINGS objects made of metal **3.** METAL PART OF SOMETHING the metal part of an object —**met·al·work·er** *n* —**met·al·work·ing** *n*

met·a·male /méttə màyl/ *n* a male organism with an extra male chromosome

met·a·mere /méttə mèer/ *n* a segment into which the bodies of animals such as worms or lobsters are divided

met·a·mer·ic /mèttə mérrik/ *adj* **1.** with a body divided into a series of similar segments (**metameres**) **2.** relating to or typical of metamerism —**met·a·mer·i·cal·ly** *adv*

me·tam·er·ism /mə támmə rìzzəm/ *n* the condition of having the body divided into a series of similar segments (**metameres**), or an embryonic stage in which the body is divided in this way

met·a·mor·phic /mèttə máwrfik/, **met·a·mor·phous** /-fəss/ *adj* **1.** relating to or involving a change in physical form, appearance, or character **2.** relating to or having undergone metamorphism —**met·a·mor·phi·cal·ly** *adv*

met·a·mor·phism /mèttə máwr fìzzəm/ *n* a process of change in the physical structure of rock as a result of long-term heat and pressure, especially a change that increases the rock's hardness and crystalline structure

met·a·mor·phose /mèttə máwr fōz, -fōss/ (**-phosed, -phos·ing, -phos·es**) *v* **1.** *vti* CHANGE PHYSICAL FORM to undergo a complete or marked change of physical form, structure, or substance, or make somebody or something undergo this ○ *The water had metamorphosed into ice.* **2.** *vti* CHANGE APPEARANCE OR CHARACTER to undergo a complete or marked change in appearance, character, or condition, or make somebody or something undergo this **3.** *vti* CHANGE SUPPOSEDLY BY MAGIC to undergo a transformation supposedly by magic, or make somebody or something undergo this **4.** *vi* ZOOL UNDERGO BODILY CHANGES DURING GROWTH to undergo a complete or marked change of bodily form while developing into an adult animal ○ *The tadpole has metamorphosed into a frog.* **5.** *vti* GEOL CHANGE ROCK STRUCTURE to undergo metamorphism, or make a rock undergo metamorphism [Late 16C. < French *métamorphoser* < *métamorphose* "metamorphosis" < Latin *metamorphosis* (see METAMORPHOSIS)]

met·a·mor·pho·sis /mèttə máwrfəssiss/ (*plural* **-pho·ses** /-fə sèez/) *n* **1.** CHANGE OF PHYSICAL FORM a complete or marked change of physical form, structure, or substance ○ *the overnight metamorphosis of the pond water into ice* **2.** CHANGE OF APPEARANCE OR CHARACTER a complete or marked change in appearance, character, or condition **3.** SUPPOSED SUPERNATURAL TRANSFORMATION a transformation caused by supposed supernatural powers **4.** TRANSFORMED PERSON OR THING somebody or something that has gone through a complete or marked change **5.** ZOOL CHANGE IN ANIMAL FORM a complete or marked change in the form of an animal as it develops into an adult, e.g., the change from tadpole to frog or from caterpillar to butterfly [Mid-16C. Via Latin < Greek *metamorphōsis* < *metamorphoun* "transform" < *morphē* "form"]

CULTURAL NOTE ***The Metamorphosis***, a short novel (1915) by Austrian (Czech) writer Franz Kafka. The protagonist of this bizarre tale, Gregor Samsa, awakens to find himself transformed into an insect, then dies as a result of his family's neglect and his own failure to act. Gregor's metamorphosis can be read as both a portrayal of the author's troubled family life and a metaphor for the artist's power to transform life into art.

CULTURAL NOTE ***Metamorphoses***, a poem (A.D. 8) by the Roman poet Ovid. This long narrative work consists of a series of tales in which characters undergo some kind of transformation. The stories were based on Greek myths and legends and are presented in chronological order, but much of their liveliness derives from events, characters, and details invented by the poet.

met·a·mor·phous *adj* GEOL same as **metamorphic**

met·a·neph·ros /mèttə né fròss/ (*plural* **-roi** /-fròy/) *n* an embryonic organ of excretion in reptiles, birds, and mammals that develops into the kidney [Late 19C. < META- + Greek *nephros* "kidney"]

met·a·phase /méttə fàyz/ *n* the second stage of cell division, during which chromosomes line up in preparation for separation

met·a·phase plate *n* the equatorial plane along which chromosomes line up during the second stage of cell division in preparation for separation

met·a·phor /méttə fàwr/ *n* **1. IMPLICIT COMPARISON** the use to describe somebody or something of a word or phrase that is not meant literally but by means of a vivid comparison expresses something about him, her, or it, e.g., saying that somebody is a snake **2. FIGURATIVE LANGUAGE** all language that involves figures of speech or symbolism and does not literally represent real things **3. SYMBOL** one thing used or considered to represent another [15C. Via French or Latin < Greek *metaphora* < *metapherein* "to transfer" < *pherein* "to carry"] —**met·a·phor·ic** /mèttə fáwrik/ *adj*—**met·a·phor·i·cal** /mèttə fáwrik'l/ *adj* —**met·a·phor·i·cal·ly** *adv*

met·a·phos·phate /mèttə fóss fàyt/ *n* any salt or ester of metaphosphoric acid

met·a·phos·phor·ic ac·id /mèttə foss fàwrik-/ *n* a glassy solid containing linked phosphate groups. Use: drying agent, in dental cements. Formula: HPO_3.

met·a·phrase /méttə fràyz/ *n* **LITERAL TRANSLATION** a word-for-word translation of something ■ *vt* (**-phrased, -phras·ing, -phras·es**) **1. TRANSLATE SOMETHING LITERALLY** to translate something, especially word for word **2. CHANGE WORDING OF SOMETHING** to change the wording of a text [Mid-16C. < Greek *metaphrasis* < *metaphrazein* "tell differently, translate" < *phrazein* "tell"]

met·a·phrast /méttə fràst/ *n* somebody who changes the form of a text, e.g., from prose into verse [Early 17C. < Greek *metaphrastēs* < *metaphrazein* (see METAPHRASE)] —**met·a·phras·tic** /mèttə frástik/ *adj*—**met·a·phras·ti·cal** *adj*—**met·a·phras·ti·cal·ly** *adv*

met·a·phys·ic /mèttə fízzik/ *n* PHILOSOPHY same as **metaphysics**

met·a·phys·i·cal /mèttə fízzik'l/ *adj* **1. RELATING TO METAPHYSICS** relating to the philosophical study of the nature of being and beings or a philosophical system resulting from such study **2. SPECULATIVE** based on speculative reasoning and unexamined assumptions that have not been logically examined or confirmed by observation **3. ABSTRACT** extremely abstract or theoretical ○ *metaphysical subjects removed from everyday life* **4. INCORPOREAL** without material form or substance ○ *the metaphysical realm of pure thought* **5. SUPERNATURAL** originating not in the physical world but somewhere outside it ○ *a metaphysical explanation of beauty and goodness* **6.** ARTS another spelling of **Metaphysical** —**met·a·phys·i·cal·ly** *adv*

Met·a·phys·i·cal *adj* relating to the poetic style of John Donne, George Herbert, and other early 17th-century English poets who used consciously intellectual language and elaborate metaphors that compared dissimilar things ■ *n* a poet of the Metaphysical group

met·a·phys·ics /mèttə fízziks/ *n* **1. PHILOSOPHY OF BEING** the branch of philosophy concerned with the study of the nature of being and beings, existence, time and space, and causality (*takes a singular verb*) **2. UNDERLYING PRINCIPLES** the ultimate underlying principles or theories that form the basis of a particular field of knowledge (*takes a plural verb*) ○ *Symmetry is part of the metaphysics of quantum mechanics.* **3. ABSTRACT THINKING** abstract discussion or thinking (*takes a singular verb*) [Mid-16C. < medieval Latin *metaphysica* (plural) < medieval Greek *(ta) metaphusika* "(the) metaphysics" < *ta meta ta phusika* "the (works of Aristotle) after the 'Physics'"]

met·a·pla·sia /mèttə pláyzhə, -zhee ə/ *n* the transformation of one kind of tissue into another undesirable type, as happens in tumor formation [Late 19C. < Greek *metaplassein* "mold into a new form" < *plassein* "mold"] —**met·a·plas·tic** /mèttə plástik/ *adj*

met·a·pneu·mo·vi·rus /mèttə pyóomō vīrəss/ *n* MICROBIOL same as **human metapneumovirus**

met·a·psy·chol·o·gy /mèttə sī kólləjee/ *n* the philosophical study of those aspects of psychology that cannot be examined experimentally —**met·a·psy·cho·log·i·cal** /-sīkə lójjik'l/ *adj*

met·a·se·quo·ia /mèttə si kwóyə/ (*plural* **-ias** or *same*) *n* TREES same as **dawn redwood**

met·a·so·ma·tism /mèttə sṓmə tìzzəm/, **met·a·so·ma·to·sis** /-sōmə tṓssiss/ *n* the gradual change in rock structure caused by the natural replacement of chemicals through interaction with liquids or gases [Late 19C. < META- + Greek *sōmat-* "body"] —**met·a·so·mat·ic** /mèttə sō máttik/ *adj*—**met·a·so·mat·i·cal·ly** *adv*

met·a·sta·ble /mèttə stáyb'l/ *adj* **1.** describes atoms and atomic nuclei in an apparent state of equilibrium, but likely to change to a more truly stable state if conditions change **2.** describes atoms and atomic nuclei that remain in an excited state for a relatively long time —**met·a·sta·bil·i·ty** /-stə bíllətee/ *n*

me·tas·ta·sis /mə tástəssiss/ (*plural* **-ta·ses** /-tə seez/) *n* **1.** the spread of a cancer from the original tumor to other parts of the body by means of tiny clumps of cells transported by the blood or lymph **2.** a malignant tumor that has developed in the body as a result of the spread of cancer cells from the original tumor [Late 16C. Via late Latin < Greek, "removal, change" < *methistanai* "remove" < *histanai* "to place"] —**met·a·stat·ic** /mèttə státtik/ *adj*—**met·a·stat·i·cal·ly** *adv*

me·tas·ta·size /mə tástə sīz/ (**-sized, -siz·ing, -siz·es**) *vi* to spread in the body from the site of the original tumor by means of tiny cells transported by the blood or lymph (*refers to a cancer*)

met·a·tar·sal /mèttə taárss'l/ *adj* belonging or relating to the bones between the toes and ankle ■ *n* any bone between the toes and ankle —**met·a·tar·sal·ly** *adv*

met·a·tar·sus /mèttə taársəss/ (*plural* **-tar·si** /-sī, -see/) *n* **1.** the set of five long bones (**metatarsals**) in the human foot between the toes and ankle **2.** the region between the ankle and toes of the hind foot of a vertebrate animal

met·a·tar·sus ad·duc·tus /-ə dúktəss/ *n* a condition found in newborn babies or young infants in which the front half of the foot is twisted inward at an angle to the heel

met·a·the·ri·an /mèttə theeree ən/ *adj* relating or belonging to marsupials ■ *n* same as **marsupial** [Late 19C. < modern Latin *Metatheria* "wild animals between" < Greek *thēria*, plural of *thērion* "wild animal"]

me·tath·e·sis /me táthəssiss/ (*plural* **-e·ses** /-ə seez/) *n* **1.** a reversal of the order of two sounds or letters in a word, either as a mispronunciation or as a historical development **2.** CHEM same as **double decomposition** [Late 16C. Via late Latin < Greek < *metatithenai* "transpose" < *tithenai* "to place"] —**met·a·thet·ic** /mèttə théttik/ *adj* —**met·a·thet·i·cal** *adj* —**met·a·thet·i·cal·ly** *adv*

me·tath·e·size /mə táthə sīz/ (**-sized, -siz·ing, -siz·es**) *vti* to change by metathesis, or make a word change by metathesis

met·a·tho·rax /mèttə tháw raks/ (*plural* **-rax·es** or **-ra·ces** /-rə seez/) *n* the last segment of an insect's thorax, where the hind legs and hind wings are located —**me·ta·tho·rac·ic** /mèttəthə rássik/ *adj*

met·a·xy·lem /mèttə zīləm/ *n* the rigid thick-walled tissue of plant parts that have matured

met·a·zo·an /mèttə zṓ ən/ *n* an animal whose body consists of cells that are separated into different parts such as tissues and organs. All animals except for sponges and protozoans are classified as metazoans. Group: *Metazoa*. [Late 19C. < modern Latin *Metazoa* < Greek *meta-* "beside, after" + *zoion* "animal"] —**met·a·zo·an** *adj*

mete /meet/ (**met·ed, met·ing, metes**) *vt* same as **mete out** (*literary*) [Old English *metan* "measure" < Indo-European]

USAGE See *meat*.

mete out *vt* to give out something such as punishment or justice, especially in a way that seems harsh or unfair

me·tem·psy·cho·sis /mə tèm sə kṓssiss, mèttəm sī-/ *n* the supposed passage of somebody's soul after death into the body of another person or an animal [Late 16C. Via late Latin < Greek *metempsukhōsis* < *meta* "after" + *empsukhos* "having a soul within"]

met·en·ceph·a·lon /mèt en séffə lòn/ (*plural* **-lons** or **-la** /-lə/) *n* the part of an embryo's brain that develops into the cerebellum and the pons —**met·en·ce·phal·ic** /-en sə fállik/ *adj*

me·te·or /meetee ər, -àwr/ *n* **1.** a mass of rock from space that burns up after entering the Earth's atmosphere **2.** the brief streak of light that a meteor creates, visible in the night sky [Late 16C. Via modern Latin *meteorum* "atmospheric phenomenon" < Greek *meteōron*, form of *meteōros* "raised up" < *meta* "up" + *-aoros* "lifted"]

meteor. *abbr* METEOROL meteorology

me·te·or·ic /meetee áwrik/ *adj* **1.** characterized by great speed or brilliance **2.** relating to or resembling meteors —**me·te·or·i·cal·ly** *adv*

me·te·or·ic wa·ter *n* water in the ground that has come from the atmosphere as rain or condensation, rather than forming chemically underground

me·te·or·ite /meetee ə rīt/ *n* a piece of rock that has reached Earth from outer space

me·te·or·it·ics /meetee ə ríttiks/ *n* the scientific study of meteors and meteorites (*takes a singular verb*) —**me·te·or·it·i·cist** /-ríttəssist/ *n*

me·te·or·oid /meetee ə ròyd/ *n* a mass of rock in space, often a remnant of a comet, that becomes a meteor when it enters the Earth's atmosphere and a meteorite when it falls to Earth —**me·te·or·oid·al** *adj*

meteorol. *abbr* METEOROL meteorology

me·te·or·ol·o·gy /meetee ə rólləjee/ *n* the scientific study of the Earth's atmosphere, especially its patterns of climate and weather [Early 17C. < Greek *meteōrologia* < *meteōron* (see METEOR)] —**me·te·or·o·log·i·cal** /meetee ərə lójjik'l/ *adj* —**me·te·or·o·log·i·cal·ly** *adv* —**me·te·or·ol·o·gist** *n*

me·te·or show·er *n* a number of meteors seen at regular intervals in the same area of the sky when a large group of meteors passes through the Earth's atmosphere

me·ter[1] /meetər/ *n* **1.** an arranged pattern of rhythm in a line of verse **2.** the pattern of beats that combines to form musical rhythm [Pre-12C. Directly or via French *metre* < Latin *metrum* < Greek *metron* "measure"]

me·ter[2] /meetər/ *n* the basic SI unit of length, equivalent to approximately 1.094 yd. or 39.37 in. Symbol **m** [Late 18C. Via French *metre* < Greek *metron*]

me·ter[3] /meetər/ *n* **1.** a device that measures and records the quantity or flow of something such as electricity, gas, water, distance, or time **2.** same as **parking meter** ■ *vt* (**-ter·ed, -ter·ing, -ters**) to measure the amount or flow of something such as electricity or water, using a meter [Early 19C. Origin ?] —**me·tered** *adj*

-meter *suffix* measuring device ○ *heliometer* [Via French *-mètre* < Greek *metron* "measure"]

me·tered mail /meetərd-/ *n* mail that is postmarked privately by a postage meter

me·ter-kil·o·gram-sec·ond *adj* using or based on the meter, kilogram, and second as the measuring units of length, mass, and time

me·ter maid *n* a woman assigned by a police department to issue tickets for parking violations (*dated informal*)

meth- *prefix* methyl ○ *methicillin* [Shortening]

meth·ac·ry·late /meth ákrə làyt/ *n* an ester derived from methacrylic acid

meth·a·cryl·ic ac·id /mèthə krìllik-/ *n* a synthetic colorless liquid. Use: manufacture of plastic. Formula: $C_4H_6O_2$.

meth·a·done /méthə dṓn/, **meth·a·don** /-dòn/ *n* a synthetic narcotic drug similar in its painkilling effect to morphine. Use: substitute for heroin in the treatment of addiction. [Mid-20C. < METH- + AMINO + DI-[1]]

met·haem·o·glo·bin /met heemə glṓbin/ *n* BIOCHEM UK spelling of **methemoglobin**

meth·am·phet·a·mine /mèth am féttə meen, -min/ *n* a derivative of amphetamine, used illegally as a drug. Formula: $C_{10}H_{15}N$.

meth·an·al /méthə nàl/ *n* CHEM same as **formaldehyde** [Late 19C. < METHANE]

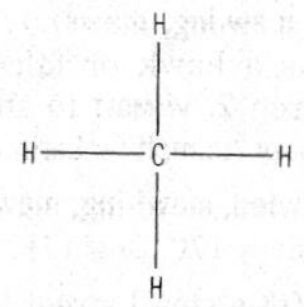

methane

meth·ane /mé thàyn/ *n* a colorless odorless flammable gas that is the main constituent of natural gas. Use: as fuel. Formula: CH_4. [Mid-19C. < METHYL]

meth·a·no·ic ac·id /mèthə nō ik-/ *n* CHEM same as **formic acid** [< METHANE]

meth·a·nol /méthə nàwl/ *n* a colorless volatile poisonous water-soluble liquid. Use: as solvent, fuel, in antifreeze for motor vehicles. Formula: CH_3OH. [Late 19C. < METHANE]

meth·a·qua·lone /mèthə kwáy lṑn/ *n* a hypnotic drug that may become habit-forming. Use: treatment of anxiety, sleep disorders. Formula: $C_{16}H_{14}N_2O$. [Mid-20C. < METH- + contraction of *quinazolinon*, a derivative of quinoline]

met·he·mo·glo·bin /met hēēmə glṑbin/ *n* an altered form of hemoglobin that cannot bind oxygen, produced by some poisons or by a genetic disorder

met·he·mo·glo·bi·ne·mi·a /met hēēmə glōbi nēēmee ə/ *n* the presence in the blood of methemoglobin

meth·i·cil·lin /mèthə síllin/ *n* a synthetic antibiotic. Use: treatment of penicillin-resistant infections. [Mid-20C. < METH- + *-cillin*, INN stem]

meth·i·cil·lin-re·sis·tant Staph·y·lo·coc·cus au·re·us *n* MED, MICROBIOL full form of **MRSA**

me·thinks /mi thíngks/ (**-thought** /-tháwt/) *vi* it seems to me (*humorous or archaic*) [Old English *mē þyncþ* "it seems to me" < *þyncan* "seem" < Indo-European]

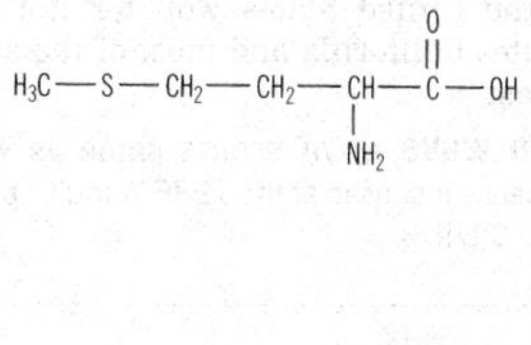

methionine

me·thi·o·nine /mə thī́ ə nēēn/ *n* an essential amino acid that contains sulfur [Early 20C. < METH- + THIO-]

meth·od /méthəd/ *n* **1. WAY OF DOING SOMETHING** a way of doing something or carrying something out, especially according to a plan ○ *a successful method of teaching reading* **2. ORDERLINESS** orderly thought, action, or technique ○ *There is no method at all in his filing system.* **3. BODY OF TECHNIQUES** the body of systematic techniques used by a particular discipline, especially a scientific one [15C. Via Latin < Greek *methodos* "pursuit, way" < *meta-* "after" + *hodos* "journey"] ◇ **there's method to** *or* **in somebody's madness** there is a good reason for somebody's apparently foolish, strange, or illogical action

Meth·od *n* a theory and system of acting that involves the actor identifying strongly with the internal motivation of the character being portrayed. It is based on the teachings of Konstantin Stanislavsky.

me·thod·i·cal /mə thóddik'l/, **me·thod·ic** /-ik/ *adj* systematic or painstaking —**me·thod·i·cal·ly** *adv* —**me·thod·i·cal·ness** *n*

Meth·od·ism /méthə dìzzəm/ *n* the doctrines, principles, or organization of the Methodist Church

Meth·od·ist /méthədist/ *n* a member of the Methodist Church ■ *adj* relating to Methodism or membership of the Methodist Church [Mid-18C. Originally applied to members of a society founded at Oxford, from the methodical habits of life and worship it promoted] —**Meth·od·is·tic** /mèthə dístik/ *adj*

Meth·od·ist Church *n* a group of evangelical Protestant denominations founded in 18th-century England by John Wesley and his followers

meth·od·ize /méthə dī̀z/ (**-ized, -iz·ing, -iz·es**) *vt* to reduce or arrange something according to a method

meth·od·ol·o·gy /mèthə dóllәjee/ (*plural* **-gies**) *n* **1. ORGANIZING SYSTEM** the methods or organizing principles underlying a particular art, science, or other area of study **2. STUDY OF ORGANIZING PRINCIPLES** in philosophy, the study of organizing principles and underlying rules **3. STUDY OF RESEARCH METHODS** the study of methods of research —**meth·od·o·log·i·cal** /mèthədə lójjik'l/ *adj* —**meth·od·o·log·i·cal·ly** *adv* —**meth·od·ol·o·gist** *n*

meth·o·trex·ate /mèthə trék sàyt/ *n* a drug that inhibits cellular reproduction. Use: cancer treatment. Formula: $C_{20}H_{22}N_8O_5$. [Mid-20C. < METH- + *-trex-*, origin ?]

me·thought past tense of **methinks** (*humorous or archaic*)

meth·ox·ide /meth ók sī̀d/ *n* a chemical derivative of methanol that has some features of a salt, e.g., sodium methoxide. Formula: $NaOCH_3$. [Late 19C. < METH- + OXY-]

me·thox·y·chlor /mə thóksee klàwr/ *n* a white crystalline compound used as an insecticide. Formula: $C_{16}H_{15}Cl_3O_2$. [Mid-20C. < METH- + OXY- + CHLORINE]

Me·thu·se·lah /mə thóózələ/ *n* **1.** in the Bible, a man who was an ancestor of Noah and lived 969 years (Genesis 5: 21–27) **2.** *also* **me·thu·se·lah** a wine bottle that holds the equivalent of eight normal bottles, approximately 208 fl. oz/6 liters

meth·yl /méth'l/ *adj* relating to the group of atoms derived from methane after the loss of a hydrogen atom. Formula: CH_3. [Mid-19C. < French *méthyl*, a back-formation < *méthylène* (see METHYLENE)] —**me·thyl·ic** /mə thíllik/ *adj*

meth·yl ac·e·tate *n* a fragrant colorless liquid. Use: solvent in paint removers. Formula: $C_3H_6O_2$.

meth·yl·al /méthə làl/ *n* a colorless flammable liquid. Use: solvent, manufacture of perfumes and adhesives. Formula: $C_3H_8O_2$.

meth·yl al·co·hol *n* CHEM same as **methanol**

meth·yl·a·mine /mèthələ mēēn, -lá mēēn/ *n* a colorless flammable derivative of ammonia. Use: as a gas, in dyes, drugs, and herbicides. Formula: CH_5N.

meth·yl·ate /méthə làyt/ *n* CHEM same as **methoxide** ■ *vt* (**-at·ed, -at·ing, -ates**) **1.** to replace one or more hydrogen atoms in a molecule with the methyl group **2.** to mix something with methanol —**meth·yl·a·tion** /mèthə láysh'n/ *n* —**meth·yl·a·tor** *n*

meth·yl·at·ed spir·it /méthə laytəd-/, **meth·yl·at·ed spir·its** *n* ethanol with methanol added, to make it undrinkable, and colored with a violet dye. Use: fuel, in solvents.

meth·yl·ben·zene /mèthèl bén zēēn, -ben zēēn/ *n* CHEM same as **toluene**

meth·yl bro·mide *n* a poisonous colorless gas or liquid. Use: solvent, fumigant, refrigerant. Formula: CH_3Br.

meth·yl·cel·lu·lose /mèth'l séllyə lṑss, -lṑz/ *n* a grayish white powder derived from cellulose that swells up in water. Use: food additive, manufacture of paints and cosmetics.

meth·yl chlo·ride *n* a colorless poisonous gas. Use: refrigerant, local anesthetic. Formula: CH_3Cl.

meth·yl·do·pa /mèth'l dṓpə/ *n* a white powdered drug. Use: treatment of hypertension. Formula: $C_{10}H_{13}NO_4$.

meth·yl·ene /méthə lēēn/ *n* a bivalent group of atoms derived from methane. Formula: CH_2. ■ *adj* relating to the group of atoms derived from methane containing one carbon atom and two hydrogen atoms [Mid-19C. < French *méthylène* < Greek *methu* "wine" + *hulē* "wood, substance"]

meth·yl·ene blue *n* a crystalline compound that turns blue when dissolved in water. Use: dye, antiseptic, antidote for cyanide poisoning, stain in laboratories. Formula: $C_{16}H_{18}ClN_3S$.

meth·yl i·so·cy·a·nate *n* a flammable, colorless, extremely toxic liquid. Use: manufacture of herbicides. Formula: CH_3NCO.

meth·yl·mer·cu·ry /mèth'l múrkyəree/ *n* an extremely toxic compound, derived from the action of microorganisms on metallic mercury. Use: seed disinfectant.

meth·yl meth·ac·ry·late *n* a colorless flammable liquid that can be converted into clear plastic resins

meth·yl·naph·tha·lene /mèth'l náfthə lēēn, -náptha-/ *n* either of two forms of naphthalene, a liquid used in making diesel fuels or a solid used in making insecticides. Formula: $C_{11}H_{10}$.

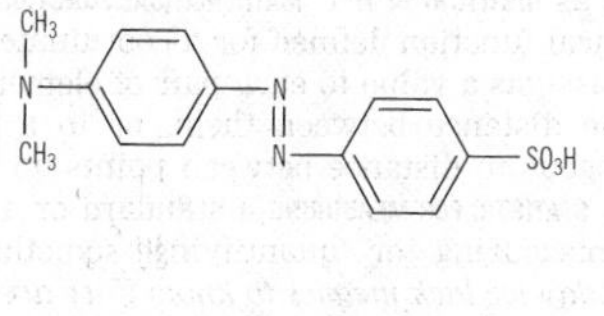

methyl orange

meth·yl or·ange *n* an alkaline dye that turns yellow when neutral and pink when acid. Use: chemical indicator.

meth·yl·phen·i·date /mèth'l fénni dàyt, -fēēni-/ *n* a drug that stimulates the central nervous system. Use: treatment of narcolepsy, attention deficit disorder. Formula: $C_{14}H_{19}NO_2$. [Mid-20C. Contraction of METHYL + PHENYL + PIPERIDINE + ACETATE]

meth·yl·pred·nis·o·lone /mèth'l pred níssə lṑn/ *n* a corticosteroid drug that reduces inflammation. Use: treatment of arthritis, allergies, and asthma.

met·i·cal /mètti kaal/ (*plural* **-cais** /-kī́sh/ or **-cals**) *n* the main unit of Mozambican currency. See table at **currency** [Late 20C. Via Portuguese *matical* < Arabic *miṯkāl*, a unit of weight < *taḳala* "weigh"]

me·tic·u·lous /mə tíkyələss/ *adj* extremely careful and precise [Early 19C. < Latin *meticulosus* "fearful, timid" < *metus* "fear"] —**me·tic·u·lous·ly** *adv* —**me·tic·u·lous·ness** *n*

SYNONYMS See *careful.*

mé·tier /me tyáy, may-/, **me·tier** *n* **1.** somebody's occupation or trade **2.** an activity that somebody is particularly good at [Late 18C. < French < Latin *ministerium* (see MINISTRY)]

Me·tis[1] /may tēē, -tēēss/ (*plural* **-tis** /-tēēz/) *n* in Canada, somebody of mixed aboriginal and European, especially French-Canadian, descent who is now defined by the Canadian Constitution Act of 1982 as an aboriginal person [Early 19C. < Canadian French *métis* < Latin *mixtus* (see MESTIZO)]

Me·tis[2] /mēētiss/ *n* the innermost known natural satellite of Jupiter. It is irregularly shaped and approximately 25 mi./40 km in diameter.

me·tol /mēē tàwl/ *n* a colorless soluble salt. Use: photographic developer. Formula: $C_{14}H_{20}N_2O_6S$. [Late 19C. Arbitrary]

Me·ton·ic cy·cle /mə tònnik-/ *n* a cycle of 235 lunar months, after which the phases of the Moon occur on the same days of the month as they did at the start of the cycle [Late 17C. After *Metōn*, 5C B.C. Athenian astronomer]

met·o·nym /méttə nìm/ *n* a word or phrase used in a figure of speech in which an attribute of something is used to stand for the thing itself, e.g., "laurels" when it is used to stand for "glory" [Late 16C. Back-formation < METONYMY] —**met·o·nym·ic** /mèttə nímmik/ *adj* —**met·o·nym·i·cal·ly** *adv*

me·ton·y·my /mə tónnəmee/ *n* a figure of speech in which an attribute of something is used to stand for the thing itself, e.g., "laurels" when it stands for "glory" or "brass" when it stands for "military officers" [Mid-16C. Via late Latin < Greek *metōnumia* "change of name" < *meta-* "beside, different" + *onuma* "name"]

me-too *adj* using products, methods, or policies copied from another person or a successful business competitor (*informal*) —**me-too·ism** *n*

met·o·pe /méttəpee/ *n* in a Doric frieze, a square space between two sets of three vertical grooves (**triglyphs**) [Mid-16C. < Greek *metopē* < *meta-* "between" + *opē* "hole"]

me·top·ic /mə tóppik/ *adj* relating to the forehead [Late 19C. < Greek *metōpon* "forehead" < *meta-* "between" + *ōps* "eye"]

metr- *suffix* same as **metro-** (*used before vowels*)

me·tral·gi·a /mə tráljee ə/ *n* pain in the womb

me·tre *n* MEASURE Can, UK spelling of **meter**[2]. Can, UK spelling of **meter**[1]

met·ric /méttrik/ *adj* **1.** RELATING TO METRIC SYSTEM relating to or using the metric system of measurement **2.** same as **metrical** ■ *n* **1.** MATHEMATICAL FUNCTION a mathematical function defined for a coordinates system that assigns a value to each pair of elements equal to the distance between them, or to a property analogous to distance between points on a line **2.** STATS STATISTIC FOR MEASURING a standard or a statistic for measuring or quantifying something else ○ *"Today we lack metrics to know if we are winning or losing the global war on terror,' Mr. [Donald] Rumsfeld wrote."* (Greg Jaffe *Wall Street Journal*; October 23, 2003)

met·ri·cal /méttrik'l/ *adj* relating to or using poetic meter —**met·ri·cal·ly** *adv*

met·ri·cate /méttri kàyt/ (**-cat·ed, -cat·ing, -cates**) *vt* to convert something from nonmetric to metric units of measurement —**met·ri·ca·tion** /mèttri káysh'n/ *n*

met·ri·cize /méttri sīz/ (**-cized, -ciz·ing, -ciz·es**) *vt* to express a measurement in metric units or change it into metric units

met·rics /méttriks/ *n* the art or study of using meter in poetry (*takes a singular verb*)

met·ric sys·tem *n* a decimal system of weights and measures based on units such as the kilogram and meter

met·ric ton *n* a unit of weight equal to 1,000 kg. Symbol **t**

met·ri·fy /méttri fī/ (**-fied, -fy·ing, -fies**) *vt* to put prose into verse or meter

met·rist /méttrist, meétrist/ *n* somebody who is skilled in using poetic meter

me·tri·tis /mi trítiss/ *n* inflammation of the womb

met·ro /méttrō/ *adj* same as **metropolitan** *adj* (senses 1–2) (*informal*) ○ *metro Atlanta* ■ *n* (*plural* **-ros**) **1.** *also* **Met·ro** a subway system in a town or city **2.** same as **metropolis** (*informal*) **3.** *Can* the government of a large city [Mid-20C. Shortening of METROPOLITAN]

metro- *prefix* womb ○ *metrorrhagia* [< Greek *mētra*, related to *mētēr* "mother" < Indo-European]

me·trol·o·gy /mə tróllǝjee/ (*plural* **-gies**) *n* **1.** the scientific study of units of measurement **2.** a system of measurement [Early 19C. < Greek *metron* "measure"] —**met·ro·log·ic** /mèttrə lójjik/ *adj* —**me·trol·o·gist** *n*

me·tro·ni·da·zole /mèttrə nídə zòl/ *n* a yellow crystalline compound. Use: treatment of vaginal infections. Formula: $C_6H_9N_3O_3$. [Mid-20C. Contraction of METHYL + NITRO- + IMIDAZOLE]

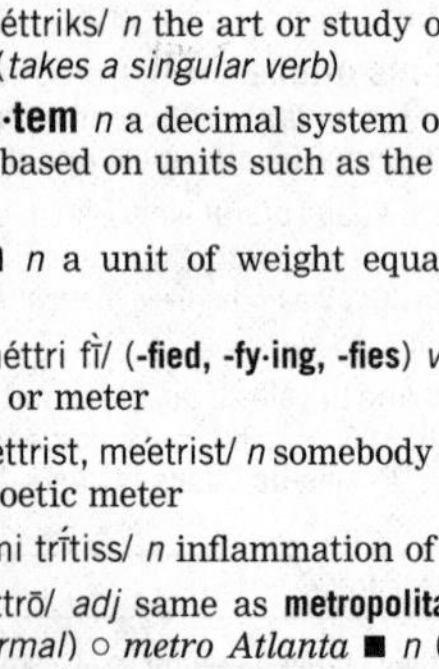

metronome

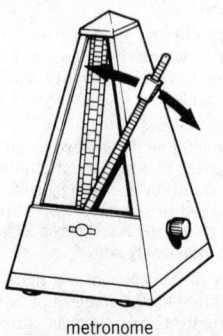

met·ro·nome /méttrə nòm/ *n* a device used to indicate a given tempo by means of a regularly recurring aural or visual signal [Early 19C. < Greek *metron* "measure, meter" + *nomos* "rule, division"] —**met·ro·nom·ic** /mèttrə nómmik/ *adj*

me·tro·nym·ic *n* LANGUAGE same as **matronymic**

me·trop·o·lis /mə tróppəliss/ *n* **1.** LARGE CITY a very large city, often the capital or chief urban center of a country, state, or region **2.** CENTER OF ACTIVITY the center or principal place for a particular activity **3.** MAIN DIOCESE in some Christian denominations, the principal diocese or see in an ecclesiastical province [Mid-16C. Via late Latin < Greek *mētropolis* "mother city" < *mētēr* "mother" + *polis* "city"]

ORIGIN *Metropolis* goes back to a Greek word meaning literally "mother city." It entered English via Latin in the mid-16th century.

met·ro·pol·i·tan /mèttrə póllit'n/ *adj* **1.** FORMING LARGE CITY constituting a large urban area, usually one that includes a city and its suburbs and outlying areas **2.** CHARACTERISTIC OF METROPOLIS characteristic of a metropolis in scale, variety, or sophistication **3.** DOMESTIC AND INTERNAL relating to the home territory of a country rather than to its territories elsewhere **4.** RELATING TO ECCLESIASTICAL METROPOLIS relating to or constituting an ecclesiastical metropolis ■ *n* **1.** CITY-DWELLER an inhabitant of a metropolis **2.** HIGH-RANKING CHURCH OFFICIAL in some Christian denominations, a high-ranking church dignitary, e.g., an archbishop or head of an ecclesiastical province **3.** HEAD OF RUSSIAN ORTHODOX CHURCH the head of the Russian Orthodox Church, based in Moscow

Met·ro·pol·i·tan France *n* the mainland departments of France along with Corsica, excluding French overseas territories

me·tror·rha·gi·a /meètrə ráyjee ə, -ráyjə, mèttrə-/ *n* excessive discharge of blood from the womb —**me·tror·rha·gic** /-ráyjik, -/ *adj*

me·tro·sex·ual /mèttrō sékshoo əl/ *n* a young, straight, sensitive urban man who is unashamed to enjoy good clothes, stylish living, the art of decorating, and improving his personal appearance (*informal*) [mid-20C.] —**me·tro·sex·u·al** *adj*

-metry *suffix* measuring ○ *cephalometry* [< Greek *-metria* < *metron* "measure"]

Met·ter·nich /méttər nìkh/, **Klemens von** (1773–1859) German-born Austrian chancellor of the Hapsburg Empire (1821–48). As an Austrian diplomat from 1814 and during his chancellorship, he was one of the most powerful political figures in Europe. He was driven from office in the Revolution of 1848. Full name **Metternich, Klemens Wenzel Nepomuk Lothar von, prince of Metternich-Winneburg-Beilstein**

met·tle /mét'l/ *n* **1.** spirited determination **2.** the mental and emotional character unique to an individual person [Mid-16C. Variant of METAL] ◇ **on your mettle** ready or determined to do your best

SPELLCHECK See *metal.*

SYNONYMS See *courage.*

met·tle·some /mét'lsəm/ *adj* spirited and courageous

Me·tuch·en /mi túchən/ town in northeastern New Jersey, in Middlesex County. Population: 13,242 (2002 estimate).

Metz /mets/ city in eastern France, the capital of Moselle Department. Population: 123,776 (1999).

meu·nière /mən yér/ *adj* dredged in flour, fried in butter, and sprinkled with lemon juice and chopped parsley ○ *sole meunière* [Mid-19C. < French *à la meunière* "in the way of a miller's wife"]

Meur·sault /mər sṓ/ *n* a dry white wine from east central France [Mid-19C. < French, a village near BEAUNE, France]

Meuse /möz/ river that flows through northeastern France, Belgium, and the Netherlands. Length: 575 mi./925 km.

MeV, **Mev**, **mev** *symbol* MEASURE million electron volts

mew[1] /myoo/ *vi* (**mewed, mew·ing, mews**) to give out a high-pitched cry (*refers to cats and kittens*) ■ *n* the high-pitched sound a cat or kitten makes [14C. An imitation of the sound]

mew[2] /myoo/ *n* a gull (*archaic*) [Old English *mǣw* < Germanic]

mew[3] /myoo/ *n* CAGE FOR HAWKS a cage for keeping hawks in ■ *v* (**mewed, mew·ing, mews**) **1.** *vt* CONFINE HAWK OR FALCON to confine a hawk or falcon, especially by tying it to a perch **2.** *vi* MOLT to shed feathers [14C. < French *mue* < *muer* "to molt" < Latin *mutare* "to change"]

mewl /myool/ (**mewled, mewl·ing, mewls**) *vi* to whimper or cry weakly [Early 17C. Origin ?]

mews /myooz/ *n UK* a small street lined with former stables that have been converted into housing (*takes a singular or plural verb*) [Early 19C. < MEW[3]]

ORIGIN In the latter part of the 14th century, the Royal Mews were built in London on the site of what is now Trafalgar Square, to house the royal hawks. By Henry VII's time, they were being used as stables, and from at least the early 17th century the term ***mews*** was used for "stabling around an open yard." The modern application to a "street of former stables converted to housing" dates from the early 19th century.

Mex. *abbr* **1.** Mexican **2.** Mexico

Mex·i·cal·i /mèksə kállee/ capital of Baja California State in northwestern Mexico, on the border with the United States. Population: 764,902 (2000).

me·xi·ca·na /méksi kaánə/ *n Hispanic* a Mexican-born woman or girl [< Spanish, form of MEXICANO]

Mex·i·can A·mer·i·can *n* an American of Mexican descent —**Mex·i·can A·mer·i·can** *adj*

Mex·i·can bean *n US* FOOD same as **frijole**

Mex·i·can bean bee·tle *n* a ladybug that feeds on the leaves of bean plants. Native to: North America. Latin name: *Epilachna varivestis.*

Mex·i·can hair·less *n* a tiny, mainly hairless dog belonging to a breed that originated in Mexico

Mex·i·can i·vy vine *n* PLANTS same as **cup-and-saucer plant**

Mex·i·can jump·ing bean *n* PLANTS same as **jumping bean**

me·xi·ca·no /méksi kaá nō/ (*plural* **-nos**) *n Hispanic* a Mexican-born man or boy [< Spanish, "Mexican"]

Mex·i·can Span·ish *n* the form of the Spanish language used in Mexico —**Mex·i·can Span·ish** *adj*

Mex·i·can stand·off *n* a dispute or argument that cannot be won (*informal*)

Mex·i·can War *n* a war between Mexico and the United States that lasted from 1846 to 1848, during which the United States won territory that now constitutes California and most of the states of the Southwest

Mex·i·can wave *n UK* SPORTS same as **wave** (sense 11) [Because first used at the 1986 World Cup soccer finals in Mexico City]

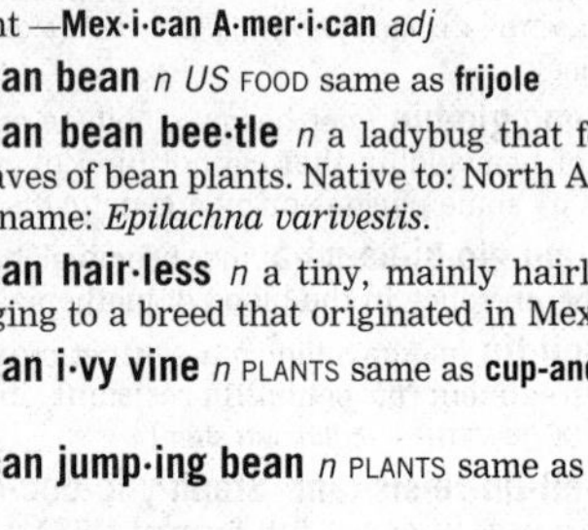

Mexico

Mex·i·co /méksi kō/ country in North America, south of the United States. Language: Spanish. Currency: peso. Capital: Mexico City. Population: 104,1907,990 (2003). Area: 758,452 sq. mi./1,964,382 sq. km. Official name **United Mexican States** —**Mex·i·can** *adj, n*

Mex·i·co, Gulf of arm of the Atlantic Ocean, bordered on the north by the United States, on the east by Cuba, and on the south and west by Mexico. Area: 579,000 sq. mi./1,500,000 sq. km.

Mex·i·co Cit·y capital city of Mexico and of the Federal District, located in the south central part of the country. With its surrounding suburbs it forms the most populous urban area in the world. Population: 8,591,309 (2000).

me·ze /mé zày, máy-/ (*plural* **-zes** or *same*), **me·zze** (*plural* **-zzes** or *same*) *n* an assortment of snacks served with drinks as an appetizer or a light meal in Greece and Southwest Asia, e.g., stuffed vine leaves, small pastries, or grilled sausages [Early 20C. < Turkish < Persian *maza* "taste, relish"]

me·ze·re·on /mə zéeree ən/ *n* a poisonous deciduous bush that flowers before the leaves emerge, and bears crimson berries. Flowers: purple, in clusters. Native to: Europe, Asia. Latin name: *Daphne mezereum*. [15C. Via medieval Latin < Arabic *māzaryūn*]

me·zu·zah /mə zŏŏzzə/ (*plural* **-zahs** or **-zot** /-zŏt/) *n* a scroll with biblical passages on one side and a name of God on the other, inserted in a small case attached by religious Jews to doorposts in the home [Mid-17C. < Hebrew *mĕzūzāh* "doorpost"]

mez·za·nine /mézz'n èen, mèzz'n éen/ *n* **1.** *also* **mez·za·nine floor** INTERMEDIATE STORY a low story, especially one between the first floor and the second floor in a building **2.** THEATER'S LOWEST BALCONY the lowest balcony in a theater ■ *adj* WITHIN INTERMEDIATE RANGE OF INVESTMENT describes an intermediate range of funding or investment that has a moderate degree of risk, such as some unsecured high-yielding loans [Early 18C. Via French < Italian *mezzanino* "small one in the middle" < *mezzano* "middle" < Latin *medianus* (see MEDIAN)]

mez·za vo·ce /mètsə vṓ chay/ *adv* with moderate volume from the voice or instrument (*used as a musical direction*) [< Italian, literally "half voice"] —**mez·za vo·ce** *adj*

mez·ze *n* FOOD another spelling of **meze**

mez·zo /métsō, médzō/ *adv* moderately (*used as a musical direction*) ■ *n* (*plural* **-zos**) MUSIC same as **mezzo-soprano** [Mid-18C. < Italian, "middle, half" < Latin *medius*]

mez·zo for·te *adv* moderately loud (*used as a musical direction*) [< Italian] —**mez·zo for·te** *adj*

mez·zo pi·a·no *adv* moderately soft (*used as a musical direction*) [< Italian] —**mez·zo pi·a·no** *adj*

mez·zo-re·lie·vo /mètsō ri léevō/ (*plural* **mez·zo-re·lie·vos**) *n* SCULPTURE same as **half relief** [< Italian, "half-relief"]

mez·zo-so·pran·o *n* a woman whose singing voice is between a soprano and a contralto in range [< Italian, literally "half soprano"]

mez·zo·tint /métsō tìnt, médzō-/ *n* **1.** ENGRAVING PROCESS an engraving process that involves scraping and burnishing the roughened surface of a copper plate **2.** MEZZOTINT PRINT a print produced by the mezzotint process ■ *vt* (**-tint·ed, -tint·ing, -tints**) ENGRAVE PLATE USING MEZZOTINT to engrave a copper plate by using the mezzotint process [Mid-18C. Anglicization of Italian *mezzotinto* "half-tint"]

mf *abbr* **1.** medium frequency **2.** MUSIC mezzo forte **3.** *also* **mF** millifarad

MF *abbr* **1.** machine finished **2.** MEDIA medium frequency

M/F, m/f *abbr* male or female (*in advertisements*)

M.F.A. *abbr* EDUC Master of Fine Arts

mfd. *abbr* manufactured

mfg. *abbr* manufacturing

mfr. *abbr* **1.** manufacture **2.** manufacturer

mg[1] *abbr* MEASURE milligram

mg[2] *abbr* Madagascar (*used in Internet addresses*) See table at **domain name**

Mg *symbol* CHEM ELEM magnesium

MG *abbr* **1.** ARMS machine gun **2.** ARMY Major General **3.** military government

mgd *abbr* million gallons per day

mgmt. *abbr* management

mgr. *abbr* manager

Mgr. *abbr* RELIG **1.** Monseigneur **2.** Monsignor

mgt. *abbr* management

mh[1] *abbr* Marshall Islands (*used in Internet addresses*) See table at **domain name**

mh[2], **mH** *abbr* MEASURE millihenry

MH *abbr* **1.** MAIL Marshall Islands **2.** Medal of Honor **3.** mental health

MHA *abbr* **1.** Master of Hospital Administration **2.** Member of the House of Assembly

MHC *n* a group of genes in mammals located next or near to one another that serve to make cells separate and distinguishable from those of other organisms. Full form **major histocompatibility complex**

MHD *abbr* PHYS magnetohydrodynamics

M.H.L. *abbr* EDUC Master of Hebrew Literature

MHz *abbr* MEASURE megahertz

mi /mee/, **me** *n* a syllable that represents the third note in a scale, used for singing solfeggio. In fixed solfeggio, it represents the note E. [15C. < medieval Latin]

MI *abbr* **1.** Michigan **2.** MIL Military Intelligence **3.** MED myocardial infarction

mi. *abbr* **1.** MEASURE mile **2.** mill

MIA[1] *abbr* Master of International Affairs

MIA[2] *n* a soldier who is reported missing during a military mission. Full form **missing in action**

Mi·am·i /mī ámmee/ port, city, and tourist resort in southeastern Florida, the county seat of Dade County. Population: 374,791 (2002 estimate).

Mi·am·i Beach city and tourist resort in southeastern Florida, on an island opposite Miami. Population: 89,575 (2002 estimate).

Miao /myow/ *n* PEOPLES, LANG same as **Hmong** [Early 20C. < Chinese *Miáo* "people"] —**Miao** *adj*

Miao-Yao /myòw yów/ *n* a group of languages, including Hmong and Yao, spoken in the People's Republic of China, Vietnam, Laos, and Thailand. Native speakers: 6 million. —**Miao-Yao** *adj*

mi·as·ma /mī ázmə, mee-/ (*plural* **-mas** or **-ma·ta** /-mətə/) *n* **1.** a harmful or poisonous emanation, especially one caused by burning or decaying organic matter **2.** an unwholesome or menacing atmosphere [Mid-17C. Directly or via French *miasme* < Greek *miasma* "defilement, pollution" < *miainein* "pollute"] —**mi·as·mal** *adj* —**mi·as·mat·ic** /mī əz máttik/ *adj*

Mic. *abbr* BIBLE Micah

mi·ca /mīkə/ *n* a shiny aluminosilicate mineral belonging to a group having varying compositions. Source: igneous and metamorphic rocks. Use: electrical insulators, heating elements. [Early 18C. < Latin, "grain, crumb"]

Mi·cah /mīkə/ *n* **1.** in the Bible, a Hebrew prophet who lived during the 8th century B.C. **2.** a book of the Bible traditionally attributed to the prophet Micah. See table at **Bible**

Mic·co·su·kee, Mic·co·su·ki *n, adj* PEOPLES, LANG another spelling of **Mikasuki**

mice ZOOL, COMPUT plural of **mouse**[2]

CULTURAL NOTE ***Of Mice and Men***, a novella (1937) by author John Steinbeck. With great compassion and realism, Steinbeck recounts the tragic tale of two itinerant laborers, George Milton and Lennie Small. When Lennie, a mentally challenged giant, accidentally kills a girl, George shoots his friend rather than surrender him to a lynch mob.

mi·celle /mī sél, mi-/ *n* an electrically charged particle formed by an aggregate of ions or molecules in soaps, detergents, and other suspensions [Late 19C. < modern Latin *micella* "small crumb" < Latin *mica* "grain, crumb"] —**mi·cel·lar** *adj*

Mich. *abbr* Michigan

Mi·chael /mīk'l/, **king of Romania** (*b.* 1921) He held the throne from 1927 to 1930 and from 1940 to 1947, when he abdicated and went into exile. Born **Hohenzollern-Sigmaringen, Michael**

Mich·ael·mas /mík'lməss/ (*plural* **-mas·es**) *n* a Christian holy day marking the feast of St. Michael the Archangel. Date: September 29. [Pre-12C. Contraction of *Michael's mass*]

Mich·ael·mas dai·sy *n* a common aster that blooms in the fall. Flowers: purple, pink, or white. Native to: North America.

Michelangelo: engraving after a 16th-century portrait by Giuliano Bugiardini

Mi·chel·an·ge·lo /mīk'l ánjəlō/ (1475–1564) Italian sculptor, painter, architect, and poet. One of the great masters of the High Renaissance, his major works, which include the ceiling of the Sistine Chapel in the Vatican, were executed for patrons in Florence and Rome. Full name **Buonarroti Simoni, Michelangelo di Lodovico**

> "There is no clime or country outside the kingdom of Italy where one can paint well...We call good painting Italian, and if good painting be produced in Flanders or in Spain...it will still be Italian painting."
> [Michelangelo. Quoted in *On Ancient Painting*, Francisco de Hollanda; 1548]

Mi·chel·son /mīk'lssən/, **Albert** (1852–1931) German-born US physicist. He won a Nobel Prize in physics (1907) for his precise measurements of the velocity of light. Full name **Michelson, Albert Abraham**

> "The most important fundamental laws of physical science have all been discovered, and these are now so firmly established that the possibility of their ever being supplemented in consequence of new discoveries is exceedingly remote."
> [Albert Michelson. Quoted in *The Arrow of Time*, Peter Coveney and Roger Highfield; 1991]

Mi·chel·son-Mor·ley ex·per·i·ment /mīk'lss'n máwrlee-/ *n* an attempt to measure the difference in speed between light beams traveling in different directions by using interference effects. The negative result is explained by special relativity. [Early 20C. After Albert MICHELSON and Edward *Morley* (1838–1923), US physicist]

Mich·e·ner /míchənər/, **James Albert** (1907–97) US writer. He wrote popular novels and short stories such as the Pulitzer Prize-winning *Tales of the South Pacific* (1947), source of the musical *South Pacific* (1949).

Michigan

Mich·i·gan[1] /míshigən/ state in the northern United States, consisting of two peninsulas situated among four of the Great Lakes. It borders the Great Lakes, Ohio, Indiana, Illinois, Wisconsin, and Minnesota. Capital: Lansing. Population: 10,050,446 (2002 estimate). Area: 96,705 sq. mi./250,465 sq. km. —**Mich·i·gan·der** /mìshi gándər/ *n* —**Mich·i·gan·ite** *n, adj*

Mich·i·gan[2] /míshigən/ *n* a gambling card game in which cards in the hand are played to match a sequence on the table [Early 20C. After MICHIGAN[1]]

Mich·i·gan, Lake lake in the northern United States,

between Michigan and Wisconsin, one of the Great Lakes. Area: 22,300 sq. mi./57,800 sq. km.

Mich·i·gan Cit·y city in northern Indiana, on the southern shore of Lake Michigan. Population: 32,564 (2002 estimate).

Mick /mik/ *n* a highly offensive term that deliberately insults somebody's Irish origin (*taboo*) [Mid-19C. < *Mick*, nickname for *Michael*]

mick·ey /míkee/ (*plural* **-eys**) *n* (*informal*) **1.** BEVERAGES same as **Mickey Finn 2.** *Can* a bottle of liquor, formerly a pint, now 375 ml, shaped to fit in a pocket

Mick·ey Finn *n* an alcoholic drink to which a strong sedative has been added to make the drinker unconscious (*informal*) [Early 20C. Origin ?]

Mic·kie·wicz /mits kyévvich/, **Adam** (1798–1855) Polish poet. A major figure in Polish romanticism, he also campaigned for his country's independence from Russia.

mick·le /mík'l/ *Scotland adj* abundant or very large ■ *adv* greatly or much [Old English *micel* < Indo-European]

Mic·mac *n, adj* PEOPLES, LANG another spelling of **Mi'kmaq**

mi·co·naz·ole /mīkə ná zōl/ *n* an imidazole drug. Use: to treat fungus infections of the skin and nails.

mi·cro /mīkrō/ *adj* very small ■ *n* (*plural* **-cros**) (*informal*) **1.** same as **microprocessor 2.** same as **microwave** *n* (sense 1) **3.** same as **microcomputer** [Mid-19C. < MICRO-]

micro- *prefix* **1.** small, minute ○ *microcosm* **2.** using a microscope or requiring magnification ○ *microbiology* **3.** one-millionth (10^{-6}) ○ *microgram* ○ *microsecond* Symbol μ **4.** of a small area or on a small scale ○ *microhabitat* ○ *micromanage* **5.** involving microfilm or microphotography ○ *microform* [< Greek *mikros* "small"]

mi·cro·ae·ro·phile /mīkrō érrə fīl/ *n* a tiny organism such as a bacterium, that is capable of living in an environment where there is not much oxygen

mi·cro·al·ga /mīkrō álgə/ *n* a microscopic alga with an undifferentiated body, e.g., a diatom or dinoflagellate —**mi·cro·al·gal** *adj*

mi·cro·am·pere /mīkrō ám peer/ *n* one-millionth part of an ampere

mi·cro·a·nal·y·sis /mīkrō ə nálləsiss/ (*plural* **-y·ses** /-ə seez/) *n* **1.** the chemical analysis of tiny samples of a substance **2.** an extremely detailed analysis of something —**mi·cro·an·a·lyst** /-ánn'list/ *n* —**mi·cro·an·a·lyt·i·cal** /-ann'l íttik'l/ *adj*

mi·cro·a·nat·o·my /mīkrō ə náttəmee/ *n* ANAT same as **histology** —**mi·cro·an·a·tom·i·cal** /-anə tómmik'l/ *adj*

mi·cro·ar·ray /mīkrō ə ràY/ *n* GENETICS same as **gene chip**

mi·cro·bal·ance /mīkrō bàllənss/ *n* a balance for precisely weighing extremely small quantities up to 0.1 g

mi·cro·bar /mīkrō baar/ *n* a unit of pressure equal to one-millionth of a bar

mi·cro·bar·o·graph /mīkrō bárrə gràf/ *n* a barograph that records tiny changes in atmospheric pressure

mi·crobe /mī kròb/ *n* a microscopic organism, especially one that transmits a disease [Late 19C. < French < Greek *mikros* "small" + *bios* "life"] —**mi·cro·bi·al** /mī kròbee əl/ *adj*

mi·cro·bi·ol·o·gy /-bī ólləjee/ *n* the scientific study of microscopic organisms and their effects —**mi·cro·bi·o·log·i·cal** /mīkrō bī ə lójjik'l/ *adj* —**mi·cro·bi·ol·o·gist** *n*

mi·cro·brew /mīkrō broo/ *n* a specialist beer produced in a microbrewery

mi·cro·brew·e·ry /mīkrō broo əree/ (*plural* **-ries**) *n* a small, usually independently owned brewery that produces limited quantities of specialized beers, often selling them on the premises —**mi·cro·brew·er** *n* —**mi·cro·brew·ing** *n*

mi·cro·burst /mīkrō bùrst/ *n* a strong localized air current that hits the ground and spreads, causing wind to rapidly change direction and speed

mi·cro·bus /mīkrō bùss/ (*plural* **-bus·es** or **-bus·ses**) *n* a vehicle resembling a small bus that has a passenger compartment with two or three rows of seats

mi·cro·busi·ness /mīkrō bìznəss/ *n* a small business, typically with fewer than six employees, that does not have access to conventional sources of capital

mi·cro·cap /mīkrō kàp/ *adj* relating to companies with very little share capital

mi·cro·cap·sule /mīkrō kàpsəl, -kàp sool/ *n* a tiny capsule used to release a drug, flavor, or chemical

mi·cro·car·ri·er /mīkrō kàrree ər/ *n* a microscopic particle to which something is attached, used especially in cell cultures and drug delivery systems

mi·cro·cas·sette /mīkrō kə sét/ *n* a small audiotape cassette designed to fit into a pocket-size tape recorder or dictation machine

mi·cro·ceph·a·ly /mīkrō séffəlee/, **mi·cro·ce·pha·li·a** /-sə fáyli ə/ *n* the condition of having a small head or having reduced space for the brain in the skull, often associated with learning difficulties —**mi·cro·ce·phal·ic** /-sə fállik/ *adj*

mi·cro·chem·is·try /mīkrō kémmistree/ *n* the scientific study of extremely small quantities of substances —**mi·cro·chem·i·cal** *adj* —**mi·cro·chem·ist** *n*

mi·cro·chip /mīkrə chìp/ *n* ELECTRONICS same as **chip** *n* (sense 4)

mi·cro·cir·cuit /mīkrō sùrkit/ *n* ELECTRONICS same as **integrated circuit** —**mi·cro·cir·cuit·ry** /-sùrkitree/ *n*

mi·cro·cli·mate /mīkrō klīmət/ *n* the climate of a confined space or small geographic area —**mi·cro·cli·mat·ic** /mīkrō klī máttik/ *adj* —**mi·cro·cli·ma·tol·o·gy** /-klīmə tólləjee/ *n*

mi·cro·cline /mīkrō klīn/ *n* a mineral of the feldspar group that contains potassium. Use: making glass, porcelain. [Mid-19C. < German *Mikroklin* < Greek *mikros* "small" + *klinein* "to lean"; because its angle of cleavage differs only slightly from 90°]

mi·cro·coc·cus /mīkrō kókəss/ (*plural* **-coc·ci** /-kó kī, -kók sī/) *n* any mainly harmless spherical bacterium, e.g., the one that ferments milk. Genus: *Micrococcus*. —**mi·cro·coc·cal** *adj*

mi·cro·com·put·er /mīkrō kəm pyootər/ *n* a small computer in which the central processing unit is a single silicon chip (**microprocessor**) [Late 20C. After MINICOMPUTER]

mi·cro·con·ti·nent /mīkrō kòntinənt/ *n* a small segment of the Earth's crust that has the same overall granitic composition as a continent but is much smaller

mi·cro·cop·y /mīkrō kòppee/ (*plural* **-ies**) *n* a photographic reproduction of something on microfilm or microfiche

mi·cro·cosm /mīkrə kòzzəm/ *n* a miniature copy of something, especially when it represents or stands for a larger whole ○ *A college is a microcosm of the larger community.* [12C. < French *microcosme* < Greek *mikros kosmos* "little world"] —**mi·cro·cos·mic** /mīkrə kózmik/ *adj*

mi·cro·cos·mic salt *n* a colorless odorless salt obtained from human urine and used to test metallic salts and oxides

mi·cro·cos·mos /mīkrō kòz moss, -kòzməss/ *n* SCI same as **microcosm**

mi·cro·cred·it /mīkrō krèddit/ *n* the extension of credit to entrepreneurs and microenterprises too poor to qualify for conventional bank loans

mi·cro·crys·tal /mīkrō krìst'l/ *n* a crystal that can only be seen under a microscope —**mi·cro·crys·tal·line** /mīkrō krístəlin/ *adj*

mi·cro·cur·ie /mīkrō kyooree, -kyoo reé/ *n* a unit of radioactivity equal to one-millionth of a curie

mi·cro·cyte /mīkrə sīt/ *n* an unusually small red blood cell —**mi·cro·cyt·ic** /mīkrə síttik/ *adj*

mi·cro·dis·sec·tion /mīkrō di séksh'n, -dī-/ *n* dissection carried out using a microscope

mi·cro·dot /mīkrə dòt/ *n* **1.** a tiny photographic reproduction of something, about the size of a dot or a pinhead **2.** a dose of LSD in a tiny tablet (*informal*)

mi·cro·e·co·nom·ics /mīkrō eekə nómmiks, -ekə-/ *n* the study of particular aspects of an economy (*takes a singular verb*) —**mi·cro·e·co·nom·ic** *adj*

mi·cro·e·lec·tro·mech·an·i·cal sys·tem *n* full form of **MEMS**

mi·cro·e·lec·tron·ics /mīkrō i lek trónniks/ *n* the technology and techniques involved in the design, development, and construction of extremely small electronic circuits such as computers on a single silicon chip (*takes a singular verb*) —**mi·cro·e·lec·tron·ic** *adj*

mi·cro·el·e·ment /mīkrō èlləmənt/ *n* CHEM same as **trace element** (sense 1)

mi·cro·en·cap·su·late /mīkrō in kápsə làyt/ (**-lat·ed, -lat·ing, -lates**) *vt* to enclose a substance in microcapsules —**mi·cro·en·cap·su·la·tion** /-in kapsə láysh'n/ *n*

mi·cro·en·gi·neer·ing /mīkrō enjə neéring/ *n* the technology and techniques involved in integrating microelectronic circuity into miniaturized mechanical devices for sensing, processing, or carrying out various functions —**mi·cro·en·gi·neer** *n, vt*

mi·cro·en·ter·prise /mīkrō èntər prīz/ *n* BUSINESS same as **microbusiness**

mi·cro·ev·o·lu·tion /mīkrō evə lóosh'n, -eevə-/ *n* minor change within a species or small group of organisms, usually within a short period of time —**mi·cro·ev·o·lu·tion·ar·y** *adj*

mi·cro·fab·ri·ca·tion /mīkrō fàbbrə káysh'n/ *n* the production of electromechanical, mechanical, chemical, or optical devices on a microscopic scale —**mi·cro·fab·ri·cat·ed** /-fábbrə kàytəd/ *adj*

mi·cro·far·ad /mīkrō fà rad, -fàrrəd/ *n* one-millionth part of a farad

mi·cro·fau·na /mīkrō fáwnə/ *npl* animals so small that they can be seen only under a microscope —**mi·cro·fau·nal** *adj*

mi·cro·fi·ber /mīkrō fībər/ *n* **1.** an extremely fine synthetic thread or yarn **2.** a wrinkle-resistant washable synthetic fabric made of microfiber. Use: clothing.

mi·cro·fib·ril /mīkrō fíbbrəl/ *n* in cells, any extremely fine structure resembling a thread

mi·cro·fiche /mīkrō feésh/ (*plural same or* **-fich·es**) *n* a sheet of microfilm containing information laid out in a grid pattern [Mid-20C. < French < Greek *mikros* "small" + French *fiche* "slip of paper"]

mi·cro·fil·a·ment /mīkrō fílləmənt/ *n* a thin thread of protein found in muscle and the cytoplasm of all cells —**mi·cro·fil·a·men·tous** /-filə méntəss/ *adj*

mi·cro·fi·lar·i·a /mīkrō fi lérree ə/ (*plural* **-as** or **-ae** /-ee/) *n* the early larval stage of a parasitic nematode worm (**filaria**), a cause of heartworm in dogs and elephantiasis in humans —**mi·cro·fi·lar·i·al** *adj*

mi·cro·film /mīkrə film/ *n* a strip of photographic film on which greatly miniaturized reproductions have been recorded ■ *vti* (**-filmed, -film·ing, -films**) to photograph something on microfilm

mi·cro·flo·ra /mīkrō fláwrə/ *npl* plants that can be seen only under a microscope —**mi·cro·flo·ral** *adj*

mi·cro·form /mīkrə fàwrm/ *n* a piece of film or paper such as microfilm or microfiche that contains miniature reproductions

mi·cro·fos·sil /mīkrō fòss'l/ *n* a fossil that can be studied only with a microscope, e.g., a bacterium fossil

mi·cro·fun·gus /mīkrō fùng gəss/ (*plural* **-gi** /-jī, -gī/ or **-gus·es**) *n* a fungus that has tiny or unobservable reproductive organs

mi·cro·gram /mīkrə gràm/ *n* one-millionth part of a gram

mi·cro·graph /mīkrə gràf/ *n* **1.** a photograph or drawing of something as seen through a microscope **2.** a device that can produce engraving or writing using very fine lines —**mi·cro·graph·ic** /mīkrə gráffik/ *adj*

mi·cro·grav·i·ty /mīkrō grávvətee/ *n* a force of gravity so low that weightlessness occurs, e.g., during space travel

mi·cro·groove /mīkrō groov/ *n* the narrow spiral groove on a phonograph record

mi·cro·hab·i·tat /mīkrō hábbi tàt/ *n* an environment that has a unique set of ecological conditions within a larger habitat and supports distinct flora and fauna

mi·cro·his·to·ry /mīkrō hìstəree/ *n* the study of and focus on a very small phenomenon in an effort to explain a larger event or an overall historical process

mi·cro·inch /mīkrō inch/ *n* a unit of linear measurement equivalent to one-millionth of an inch. Symbol μ**in**

mi·cro·in·jec·tion /mīkrō in jékshən/ *n* the injection of a very small amount of liquid into individual cells, using a specialized instrument and a microscope for observation —**mi·cro·in·ject** *vti*

mi·cro·in·struc·tion /mīkrō in strúkshən/ *n* a single instruction in a low-level computer program

mi·cro·lend·ing /mīkro lènding/ *n* same as **microcredit**

mi·cro·lens·ing /mīkrō lènzing/ *n* the temporary focusing and brightening of light from a distant background star as a result of the gravitational effect of an astronomical object passing in the foreground —**mi·cro·lens** *n*

mi·cro·lep·i·dop·ter·an /mīkrō lèppi dóptərən/ *n* a small or medium-sized moth, e.g., a leaf miner, that is of little interest to a collector

mi·cro·lith /mīkrə lìth/ *n* a tiny flint tool, usually triangular, found in Mesolithic sites in Europe and dating from 12,000 to 3,000 B.C. —**mi·cro·lith·ic** /mīkrə líthik/ *adj*

mi·cro·loan /mīkro lōn/ *n* a small loan that enables a microenterprise or impoverished person to continue or start a business. Microloans are frequently made to impoverished people in developing countries as part of a program to reduce poverty.

mi·cro·ma·chin·ing /mīkrō məsheening/ *n* the techniques used in fabricating the miniaturized devices and moving parts into which microelectronic circuitry is integrated —**mi·cro·ma·chine** *vt*

mi·cro·man·age /mīkrō mánnij/ (**-aged, -ag·ing, -ag·es**) *vt* to control a person or a situation by paying extreme attention to small details —**mi·cro·man·age·ment** *n* —**mi·cro·man·ag·er** *n*

mi·cro·ma·nip·u·la·tor /mīkrō mə níppyə làytər/ *n* a device consisting of geared controls for the manipulation of extremely small dissecting tools or miniature surgical instruments under a microscope —**mi·cro·ma·nip·u·la·tion** /-mə nìppyə láysh'n/ *n*

mi·cro·mere /mīkrō meer/ *n* either of the cells (**blastomeres**) formed by the division of a fertilized egg

mi·cro·me·te·or·ite /mīkrō meetee ə rīt/ *n* a particle of cosmic dust that falls to Earth or onto the Moon's surface

mi·cro·me·te·or·oid /mīkrō meetee ə ròyd/ *n* an extremely small dust particle found in space that may land on Earth or the Moon as a micrometeorite

mi·cro·me·te·or·ol·o·gy /mīkrō meetee ə rólləjee/ *n* the study of weather conditions in the air immediately above ground level, especially in very small areas —**mi·cro·me·te·or·o·log·i·cal** /-ərə lójjik'l/ *adj*

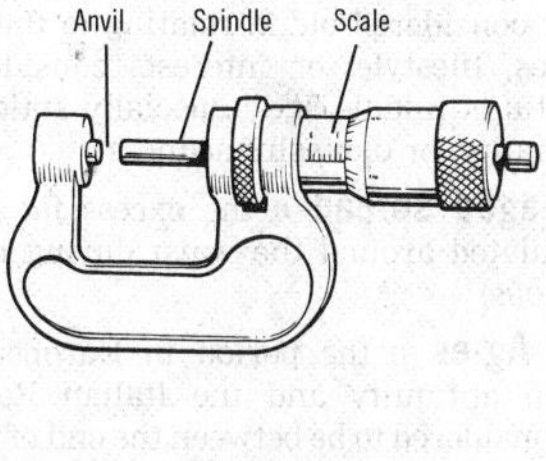

micrometer

mi·crom·e·ter[1] /mī krómmətər/ *n* a device for measuring small diameters, thicknesses, distances, or angles to a high degree of accuracy [Late 17C. < French *micromètre*] —**mi·cro·met·ric** /mīkrō méttrik/ *adj* —**mi·crom·e·try** *n*

mi·cro·me·ter[2] /mīkrō meetər/ *n* a unit of linear measurement equivalent to one-millionth of a meter. Symbol μ**m**

mi·cro·me·tre *n* MEASURE Can, UK spelling of **micrometer**[2]

mi·cro·min·i·a·tur·i·za·tion /mīkrō mìnnee əchəri záysh'n, -mìnnəchəri-/ *n* the production and use of extremely small electronic components, especially semiconductors —**mi·cro·min·i·a·tur·ize** /-mínnee əchə rīz, -mínnəchə-/ *vt* —**mi·cro·min·i·a·tur·ized** *adj*

mi·cro·mole /mīkrə mōl/ *n* a molecular weight expressed in grams that is equivalent to one-millionth of a mole. Symbol μ**mol** —**mi·cro·mo·lar** /mīkrə mōlər/ *adj*

mi·cro·mor·phol·o·gy /mīkrō mawr fólləjee/ *n* the study of the fine detail in the external form and structure of organisms, or of other objects such as metal surfaces —**mi·cro·mor·pho·log·i·cal** /-màwrfə lójjik'l/ *adj*

mi·cron /mī kròn/ *n* a unit of linear measurement equivalent to one-millionth of a meter [Late 19C. < Greek *mikros* "small" + -ON[1]]

Micronesia

Mic·ro·ne·sia /mīkrō neezhee ə, -neeshə/ **1.** ethnographic grouping of Pacific islands, encompassing the islands of the western Pacific Ocean east of the Philippines and mainly north of the equator, including Kiribati, Guam, the Mariana Islands, the Federated States of Micronesia, and Palau **2.** island nation in the western Pacific Ocean, comprising more than 600 islands, about 60 of which are inhabited. Language: English. Currency: US dollar. Capital: Palikir. Population: 136,973 (2003). Area: 271 sq. mi./702 sq. km. Official name **Federated States of Micronesia** —**Mi·cro·ne·sian** *adj, n*

mi·cron·ize /mīkrə nīz/ (**-ized, -iz·ing, -iz·es**) *vt* to reduce the particle size of a powder down to a few millionths of a meter

mi·cro·nu·cle·us /mīkrō nóoklee əss/ (*plural* **-cle·i** /-klee ī/ or **-cle·us·es**) *n* the smaller of the two nuclei in the cells of ciliate protozoans. It contains genetic material and is involved in sexual reproduction. —**mi·cro·nu·cle·ar** *adj*

mi·cro·nu·tri·ent /mīkrō nóotree ənt/ *n* a substance that an organism requires for normal growth and development but only in very small quantities, e.g., a vitamin or mineral

mi·cro·or·gan·ism /mīkrō áwrgə nìzzəm/ *n* a tiny organism such as a virus, protozoan, or bacterium that can only be seen under a microscope

mi·cro·pa·le·on·tol·o·gy /mīkrō paylee on tólləjee/ *n* a branch of paleontology that studies the microorganisms preserved as fossils in sedimentary rocks —**mi·cro·pa·le·on·to·log·ic** /-paylee ontə lójjik/ *adj* —**mi·cro·pa·le·on·tol·o·gist** *n*

mi·cro·par·a·site /mīkrō párə sīt/ *n* a microorganism that lives as a parasite on other organisms —**mi·cro·par·a·sit·ic** /-parrə síttik/ *adj*

mi·cro·phage /mīkrə fàyj/ *n* a small white blood cell, part of the immune system, that removes bacteria and other foreign bodies from blood and tissue —**mi·cro·phag·ic** /mīkrə fáyjik/ *adj*

mi·croph·a·gous /mī króffəgəss/ *adj* describes animals that live in water and feed on microscopic particles or microorganisms

mi·cro·phone /mīkrə fōn/ *n* a device that converts sounds to electrical signals by means of a vibrating diaphragm. The signals can then be amplified, transmitted for broadcasting, or used for recording the sounds. [Late 17C. Originally a device for making faint sounds louder] —**mi·cro·phon·ic** /mīkrə fónnik/ *adj*

mi·cro·phon·ics /mīkrə fónniks/ *npl* the sound heard from an electronic device, especially a loudspeaker, caused by the vibration of some mechanical part

mi·cro·pho·to·graph /mīkrō fōtə gràf/ *n* **1.** a photographic image, e.g., on microfilm, so small that it has to be magnified in order to be viewed **2.** a photograph of an object viewed through a microscope —**mi·cro·pho·to·graph·ic** /-fōtə gráffik/ *adj* —**mi·cro·pho·tog·ra·phy** /mīkrō fə tóggrəfee/ *n*

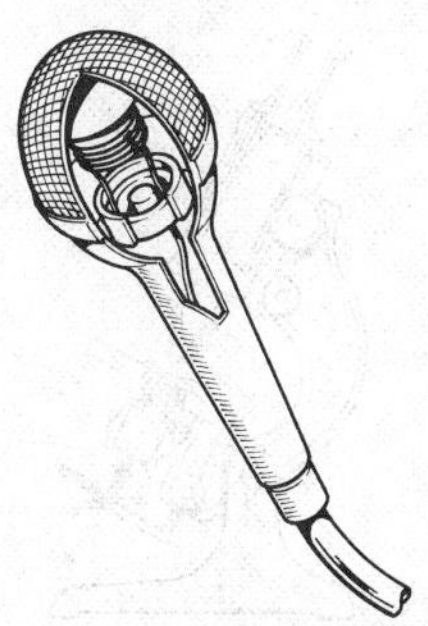
microphone: cutaway view

mi·cro·phys·ics /mīkrō fízziks/ *n* the branch of physics that studies objects and systems such as molecules, atoms, and elementary particles that are observable only microscopically or indirectly (*takes a singular verb*) —**mi·cro·phys·i·cal** *adj*

mi·cro·phyte /mīkrə fīt/ *n* a plant observable only under a microscope, especially one that is parasitic —**mi·cro·phyt·ic** /mīkrə fíttik/ *adj*

mi·cro·pi·pette /mīkrō pī pét/ *n* a very slender graduated tube that is used to measure, transfer, or remove minute amounts of something

mi·cro·pow·er /mīkrə pòwr/ *n* electrical power generated or used in relatively small quantities, usually close to the location where it is needed

mi·cro·print /mīkrə prìnt/ *n* printed text, e.g., on microfilm, so small that it has to be magnified in order to be viewed

mi·cro·prism /mīkrə prìzzəm/ *n* a small prism that is part of the focusing screen of many single-lens reflex cameras

mi·cro·proc·es·sor /mīkrō pró sèssər/ *n* the central processing unit that performs the basic operations in a microcomputer, consisting of an integrated circuit contained on a single chip

mi·cro·pro·gram /mīkrō prōgram/ *n* a built-in program within a microprocessor, consisting of a series of arithmetic and logic steps that enable basic instructions to be carried out

mi·cro·pro·gram·ming /mīkrō prōgraming/ *n* a means of programming the central processing unit of a computer by breaking down instructions into a series of small steps

mi·cro·prop·a·ga·tion /mīkrō pròppə gáysh'n/ *n* the propagation of plants by cloning a small piece of plant tissue cultured in a growth medium

mi·crop·si·a /mī krópsee ə/ *n* an eye condition in which the cones of the retina are separated by local swelling, making objects appear smaller than they really are [Mid-19C. < MICRO- + Greek *opsis* "sight" + -IA]

mi·cro·pyle /mīkrō pīl/ *n* **1.** a small opening in the covering of the ovule of a plant through which the pollen tube passes prior to fertilization **2.** a small pore in the membrane of an insect egg that allows sperm to enter and fertilize the egg [Early 19C. < French < Greek *micros* "small" + *pulē* "gate"] —**mi·cro·py·lar** /mīkrō pīlər/ *adj*

mi·cro·ra·di·og·ra·phy /mīkrō raydee óggrəfee/ *n* a technique that enlarges X-ray radiographs so that fine details can be examined

mi·cro·read·er /mīkrō reedər/ *n* a device that projects enlarged images and text from microfilm and microfiche onto a screen for easy reading

mi·cro scoot·er *n* a small, often collapsible version of a child's foot scooter, used as a quick way of getting around on the sidewalks of city streets

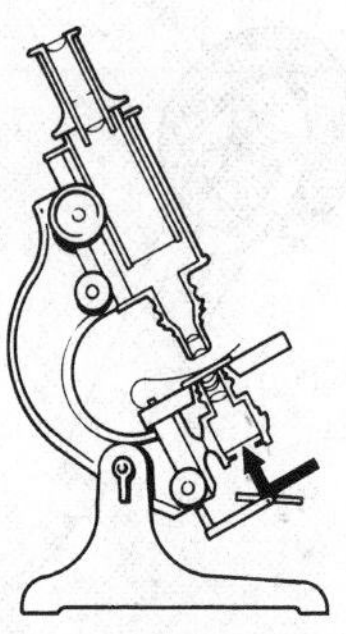

microscope

mi·cro·scope /mī́krə skōp/ *n* a device that uses a lens or system of lenses to produce a greatly magnified image of an object. An optical microscope uses transmitted or reflected light to obtain the image. An electron microscope uses a beam of electrons and a system of electron-focusing lenses to obtain images.

mi·cro·scop·ic /mī̀krə skóppik/ *adj* **1.** VERY SMALL extremely small **2.** *also* **mi·cro·scop·i·cal** /-skóppik'l/ INVISIBLE WITHOUT MICROSCOPE invisible without the use of a microscope **3.** *also* **mi·cro·scop·i·cal** INVOLVING MICROSCOPE using or involving a microscope **4.** THOROUGH very thorough and meticulous —**mi·cro·scop·i·cal·ly** *adv*

Mi·cro·sco·pi·um /mī̀krō skṓpee əm/ *n* a small inconspicuous constellation of the southern hemisphere

mi·cros·co·py /mī króskəpee/ (*plural* **-pies**) *n* **1.** the study and design of microscopes **2.** an investigation, observation, or experiment that involves the use of a microscope —**mi·cros·co·pist** *n*

mi·cro·sec·ond /mī̀krō sékənd/ *n* a measurement of time equivalent to one-millionth of a second. Symbol μ**s**

mi·cro·seism /mī́krō sī̀zəm/ *n* a recurrent low-level earth tremor caused by phenomena such as the force of crashing waves rather than by movement of rock masses —**mi·cro·seis·mic** /mī̀krō sī́zmik/ *adj*

mi·cro·some /mī́krə sōm/ *n* a small particle obtained after isolating a cell using centrifugal action, typically consisting of ribosomes associated with fragments of endoplasmic reticulum —**mi·cro·so·mal** /mī̀krə sṓm'l/ *adj*

mi·cro·spo·ran·gi·um /mī̀krō spə ránjee əm/ (*plural* **-gi·a** /-jee ə/) *n* a part of the reproductive structure of some plants, especially ferns, that produces microspores

mi·cro·spore /mī́krə spàwr/ *n* the smaller of two kinds of spores produced by seed plants and some ferns that develops into a male gametophyte

mi·cro·spo·ro·cyte /mī̀krə spáwrə sī̀t/, **mi·cro·spore moth·er cell** *n* a plant cell that divides to produce four microspores

mi·cro·spo·ro·phyll /mī̀krə spáwrə fìl/ *n* a leaf that bears a structure by which microspores are formed. In ferns, these are normal foliage leaves, the equivalent of the stamen of a flowering plant.

mi·cro·struc·ture /mī́krō strùkchər/ *n* the fine structure of a material, usually only visible through a microscope and sometimes after some form of surface preparation such as the etching of metal alloys —**mi·cro·struc·tur·al** /mī̀krō strúkchərəl/ *adj*

mi·cro·sur·ger·y /mī̀krō súrjəree/ *n* surgery performed with the aid of miniaturized precision instruments, including scalpels, needles, and a specially designed optical microscope —**mi·cro·sur·gi·cal** *adj*

mi·cro·switch /mī́krə swìch/ *n* a very small sensitive switch that acts by the movement of a small lever and is used where rapid precise movements are required, especially in keyboards and automatic control devices

mi·cro·teach·ing /mī́krə tèeching/ *n* a training exercise used in teacher training in which a student or student teacher is videotaped during part of a class for subsequent analysis and evaluation

mi·cro·tear /mī́krō tèr/ *n* a minute tear in muscle-fiber tissue, seen in competitive cyclists and other distance athletes

mi·cro·tome /mī́krə tōm/ *n* an instrument that is used to cut biological tissues into very thin transparent slices for microscopic examination

mi·crot·o·my /mī króttəmee/ *n* the process of preparing thin slices of biological tissues using a microtome, so that they can be observed under a microscope

mi·cro·tone /mī́krə tōn/ *n* a musical interval smaller than a semitone, especially a quarter tone —**mi·cro·ton·al** /mī̀krə tṓn'l/ *adj* —**mi·cro·to·nal·i·ty** /-tō nállətee/ *n*

mi·cro·tu·bule /mī̀krō tóo byoōl/ *n* a hollow tubular structure composed of the protein tubulin that helps to maintain the shape and movement of a living cell and the transportation of material within it —**mi·cro·tu·bu·lar** /-tóobyələr/ *adj*

mi·cro·vas·cu·la·ture /mī̀krō váskyələ chòor, -váskyələchər/ *n* a part of the circulatory system made up of the smallest vessels such as capillaries, arterioles, and venules —**mi·cro·vas·cu·lar** *adj*

mi·cro·vil·lus /mī̀krō vílləss/ (*plural* **-li** /-lī/) *n* a microscopic hair-shaped cell that projects from the surface of the lining of the small intestine, increasing the surface area available for the absorption of nutrients —**mi·cro·vil·lar** *adj*

mi·cro·volt /mī́krə vōlt/ *n* a unit of electric potential or electromotive force equivalent to one-millionth of a volt. Symbol μ**V**

mi·cro·watt /mī́krə wòt/ *n* a measurement of power equivalent to one-millionth of a watt. Symbol μ**W**

mi·cro·wave /mī́krə wàyv/ *n* **1.** OVEN USING ELECTROMAGNETIC RADIATION an oven that cooks or heats food or beverages relatively quickly using high-frequency electromagnetic radiation **2.** HIGH-FREQUENCY ELECTROMAGNETIC WAVE an electromagnetic wave whose wavelength ranges from 1 mm to 30 cm. Use: radar, radio transmissions, cooking or heating devices. ■ *vt* (**-waved, -wav·ing, -waves**) HEAT OR COOK SOMETHING IN MICROWAVE to heat or cook food or beverages in a microwave —**mi·cro·wav·a·ble** *adj* —**mi·cro·wave·a·ble** *adj*

mi·cro·wave ov·en *n* HOUSEHOLD same as **microwave** *n* (sense 1)

mic·tu·rate /míkchə ràyt/ (**-rat·ed, -rat·ing, -rates**) *vi* same as **urinate** (*technical*) [Mid-19C. Back-formation < *micturition* "urination" < Latin *micturire* "want to urinate" < *mict-*, past participle of *meiere* "urinate"] —**mic·tu·ra·tion** /mìkchə ráysh'n/ *n*

mid /mid/ *adj* **1.** found or occurring in or around the center of or halfway through something ○ *She cut me off in mid sentence.* **2.** describes speech sounds produced with the tongue halfway between the high and low positions, like the vowels, e.g., in the words "but" and "bet" [Old English *midd* < Indo-European]

'mid /mid/, **mid** *prep* among a group (*literary*) [15C. Shortening of AMID]

mid. *abbr* middle

Mid. *abbr* NAVY midshipman

mid- *prefix* middle ○ *midrange* ○ *midmost* [< MID]

mid·af·ter·noon /mìd aftər nóon/ *n* the part of the afternoon midway between noon and sunset —**mid·af·ter·noon** *adj*

mid·air /mid ér/ *n* a point in the air above the ground or another surface ■ *adj* occurring or located at a point in the air above the ground or another surface

Mi·das /mī́dəss/ *n* in Greek mythology, a Phrygian king who befriended Silenus, a follower of Dionysus, and was rewarded by Dionysus with the gift of making everything he touched turn into gold

Mi·das touch *n* the ability to make large amounts of money, often with very little apparent effort

mid-At·lan·tic *adj* **1.** situated or occurring in the middle of the Atlantic Ocean **2.** influenced by both North America and Britain, especially in behavior or speech

Mid-At·lan·tic Ridge submarine mountain range in the Atlantic Ocean, bisecting the ocean from north to south between Iceland and the Antarctic Circle. Its average height is 10,000 ft./3,050 m. Length: 9,300 mi./15,000 km.

Mid-At·lan·tic States *npl* same as **Middle Atlantic States**

mid·brain /míd bràyn/ *n* in vertebrates, the middle part of the three main divisions of either the embryonic or the adult brain. Technical name **mesencephalon**

mid·course /míd kàwrss/ *n* the part of a missile's flight between the end of its launch and the beginning of its re-entry ■ *adj* present or occurring partway through a course or course of action

mid·day /míd dày/ *n* noon or the period around the middle of the day

mid·den /mídd'n/ *n* **1.** a pile of dung or refuse **2.** ARCHAEOL same as **kitchen midden** [14C. < N Germanic]

mid·dle /mídd'l/ *adj* **1.** CENTRAL AND EQUIDISTANT FROM LIMITS equidistant from the sides, edges, or ends of something **2.** BEING HALFWAY BETWEEN BEGINNING AND END occurring or located halfway between the start and finish of a period of time, an event, or a series ○ *in the middle years of the 19th century* **3.** OCCUPYING INTERMEDIATE POSITION situated in an intermediate position, e.g., in age or status ○ *below middle height* **4.** BEING MIDWAY BETWEEN EXTREMES lying between two extremes or opposites and, consequently, usually moderate **5.** GRAM CONCERNING VOICE EXPRESSING REFLEXIVE ACTION relating to the voice of verbs in some languages such as ancient Greek and Sanskrit that expresses the action of a subject on or for itself ■ *n* **1.** MIDWAY PART OR POSITION the part or position farthest from the sides, edges, or ends of something ○ *the middle finger* **2.** PART BETWEEN BEGINNING AND END the part between or halfway between the beginning and end of a period of time or an event ○ *in the middle of June* ○ *arrived in the middle of a diplomatic crisis* **3.** POSITION BETWEEN HIGHEST AND LOWEST the position or rank midway between the highest and lowest **4.** INSIDE PART the interior or central part of something ○ *Remove the seeds from the middle of the melon.* **5.** CENTRAL PART OF BODY the waist, stomach, or central area of the human body (*informal*) **6.** SPORTS CENTER OF TEAM FORMATION the center of a team's formation or positioning, especially in baseball, the area around second base **7.** GRAM VOICE EXPRESSING REFLEXIVE ACTION the voice of verbs in some languages such as ancient Greek and Sanskrit that expresses the action of a subject on or for itself ■ *vti* (**-dled, -dling, -dles**) **1.** PUT SOMETHING IN MIDDLE to place something equidistant from the sides, edges, or ends of something **2.** SAILING FOLD SAIL IN HALF to fold a sail in half, or to be folded in half [Old English *middel*] ◇ **knock somebody into the middle of next week** to hit somebody very hard (*informal*)

Mid·dle *adj* relating to a language or literature between its early and later stages of development

mid·dle age *n* the period in somebody's life when that person is no longer considered young, usually between 40 and 60

mid·dle-aged *adj* **1.** no longer considered young, but not yet considered old **2.** relating to the behavior, attitudes, lifestyle, or interests considered characteristic of middle age, especially staidness, conventionality, or old-fashionedness

mid·dle-aged spread *n* the excess fat sometimes accumulated around the waist during middle age (*humorous*)

Mid·dle Ag·es *n* the period in European history between antiquity and the Italian Renaissance, often considered to be between the end of the Roman Empire in the 5th century and the early 15th century

mid·dle-age spread *n* same as **middle-aged spread** (*humorous*)

Mid·dle A·mer·i·ca *n* **1.** a section of the middle class in the United States considered by some to be politically conservative and to hold traditional social and moral values **2.** GEOG same as **Midwest 3.** *US* the area to the south of the United States and the north of South America that includes Mexico, Central America, and sometimes the Caribbean —**Mid·dle A·mer·i·can** *adj, n*

Mid·dle At·lan·tic States *npl* the states midway along the Atlantic coast of the United States, consisting of New York, New Jersey, and Pennsylvania, and usually Delaware and Maryland

mid·dle·break·er /míddʼl bràykər/ *n* AGRIC same as **lister**

mid·dle·brow /míddʼl bròw/ *n* somebody who has moderate or conventional interests in cultural and intellectual matters (*informal*) [Early 20C. After HIGHBROW and LOWBROW] —**mid·dle·brow** *adj*

mid·dle·bust·er /míddʼl bùstər/ *n* AGRIC same as **lister**

mid·dle C *n* a note roughly in the middle of a piano keyboard, written in musical notation on the first ledger line below the treble staff or above the bass staff

Mid·dle Chi·nese *n* the form of the Chinese language spoken and written during the Sui and Tang dynasties, A.D. 581–907

mid·dle class *n* the section of society between the poor and the wealthy, including business and professional people and skilled workers —**mid·dle-class** *adj*

mid·dle dis·tance *n* **1.** the portion of space that is farther away from a viewer than the foreground but nearer than the background, especially in a landscape painting or photograph **2.** a foot race between 440 yards/400 m and one mile/1500 m long

mid·dle-dis·tance *adj* relating to foot races between 440 yd./400 m and one mile/1,500 m long

Mid·dle Dutch *n* the form of the Dutch language spoken and written between the 12th and the beginning of the 16th centuries A.D.

mid·dle ear *n* the narrow air-filled space between the ear drum and the outer wall of the inner ear containing the three tiny bones that transmit sound vibrations

Mid·dle Earth *n* MYTHOL same as **Midgard**

Mid·dle East *n* **1.** the region stretching from the eastern Mediterranean to the western side of the Indian subcontinent, including Egypt, the Arabian Peninsula, Israel, Jordan, Lebanon, Syria, Turkey, Iran, and Iraq **2.** the area extending from Iran to Myanmar, including Afghanistan, South Asia, and Tibet (*dated*) —**Mid·dle East·ern** *adj* —**Mid·dle East·ern·er** *n*

Mid·dle Eng·lish *n* the form of the English language spoken and written between the 12th and the beginning of the 16th centuries. The leading dialects of this period were Kentish, West Saxon, West Midland, East Midland, and Northern.

mid·dle fin·ger *n* the longest finger of the human hand, next to the index finger

Mid·dle French *n* the form of the French language spoken and written between the 14th and the beginning of the 17th centuries A.D.

mid·dle game *n* the middle part of a game of chess, after the opening moves and before the endgame

Mid·dle Greek *n, adj* LANG same as **medieval Greek**

mid·dle ground *n* **1.** same as **middle distance** (sense 1) **2.** an intermediate position between two opposing views or factions ○ *The two parties were unable to find any middle ground.*

Mid·dle High Ger·man *n* the form of High German spoken and written between the 12th and the beginning of the 16th centuries

mid·dle-in·come *adj* earning a wage or salary that is roughly the same as the average for a population

Mid·dle I·rish *n* the form of Irish Gaelic spoken and written between the 11th and the beginning of the 15th centuries

Mid·dle King·dom *n* **1.** PERIOD OF ANCIENT EGYPTIAN HISTORY a period of Egyptian history from the late 11th dynasty, approximately 2040 B.C., to the 13th dynasty, 1670 B.C. **2.** FORMER CHINESE EMPIRE the former Chinese Empire, so called because it was supposedly at the center of the world **3.** CENTRAL TERRITORY OF CHINESE EMPIRE the central territory held by most Chinese Empires, including the Huang and Yangtze river valleys, and eventually the 18 inner provinces of China

mid·dle la·mel·la *n* a thin membrane, composed of pectin and other polysaccharides, that cements the walls of two adjacent plant cells together

Mid·dle Low Ger·man *n* the form of Low German spoken and written between the 12th and the beginning of the 16th centuries

mid·dle·man /míddʼl màn/ (*plural* **-men** /-mèn/) *n* **1.** a trader, especially a man, who buys goods from a producer and then sells them to retailers or consumers **2.** somebody, especially a man, who is a negotiator or intermediary in a transaction

mid·dle man·age·ment *n* managers who are responsible for relatively small numbers of staff and are involved in the details of running an organization rather than in making major decisions or setting policy —**mid·dle man·ag·er** *n*

mid·dle·most /míddʼl mōst/ *adj* same as **midmost**

mid·dle name *n* the name between a first name and a surname

mid·dle-of-the-road *adj* **1.** taking a course of action or adopting a point of view that is midway between two extremes **2.** intended to be musically appealing to the majority of people and avoid stylistic extremes, so often considered bland —**mid·dle-of-the-road·er** *n*

Mid·dle Pa·le·o·lith·ic *n* the period of geologic time between the Lower and Upper Paleolithic ages, from about 180,000 to 40,000 years ago

mid·dle pas·sage *n* the journey from western Africa across the Atlantic to the Caribbean or the Americas, formerly undertaken by many slave ships

mid·dle·per·son /míddʼl pùrss'n/ (*plural* **-peo·ple** /-pèep'l/ or **-per·sons**) *n* **1.** a trader who buys goods from a producer and then sells them to retailers or consumers **2.** a negotiator or intermediary in a transaction

Mid·dles·brough /míddʼlzbrə/ industrial city and port in northeastern England. Population: 134,855 (2001).

mid·dle school *n* a school for children between the ages of about 11 and 14 years, depending on the school's location

Mid·dle Scots *n* the form of the Scots language written and spoken between the late 15th and the early 17th centuries

mid·dle-sized *adj* neither very big nor very small

mid·dle term *n* in logic, a term that appears in both premises of a syllogism but not in the conclusion

Mid·dle·ton /míddʼltən/, **Arthur** (1742–87) American patriot. He was a member of the Continental Congress (1776–77) and signed the Declaration of Independence (1776).

Mid·dle·town /míddʼl tòwn/ **1.** town in central Connecticut, in Middlesex County, on the Connecticut River. Population: 44,156 (2002 estimate). **2.** town in southeastern New York, northwest of Spring Valley and southwest of Newburgh. Population: 25,775 (2002 estimate).

mid·dle·ware /míddʼl wèr/ *n* software that manages the connection between a client and a database

mid·dle watch *n* on board a vessel, the watch from midnight until 4:00 A.M.

mid·dle·weight /míddʼl wàyt/ *n* **1.** WEIGHT CATEGORY IN PROFESSIONAL BOXING in professional boxing, a weight category for competitors who weigh between 147 and 160 lb./66.5 and 72.5 kg **2.** WEIGHT CATEGORY IN AMATEUR BOXING in amateur boxing, a weight category for competitors who weigh between 157 and 165 lb./71 and 75 kg **3.** BOXER COMPETING AT MIDDLEWEIGHT a professional or amateur boxer who competes at middleweight level **4.** WRESTLER OF INTERMEDIATE WEIGHT in various sports such as wrestling, a contestant of approximately the same weight as a middleweight boxer

Mid·dle Welsh *n* the form of the Welsh language written and spoken between the 12th and the beginning of the 15th centuries

Mid·dle West *n* same as **Midwest** —**Mid·dle West·ern** *adj* —**Mid·dle West·ern·er** *n*

mid·dle·wom·an /míddʼl wòommən/ (*plural* **-wom·en** /-wìmmin/) *n* **1.** a female trader who buys goods from a producer and then sells them to retailers or consumers **2.** a female negotiator or intermediary in a transaction

mid·dling /míddling/ *adj* **1.** of average size, quantity, quality, or position **2.** neither good nor bad, especially in health or mood [Late 16C. < MID + -LING[2]] —**mid·dling·ly** *adv*

mid·dling meat *n regional* same as **salt pork**

REGIONAL NOTE See *fatback*.

mid·dlings /míddlingz/ *npl* (*takes a plural verb*) **1.** *Southern US* a cut of pork taken from between the ham and the shoulder and often cured or salted **2.** commodities or resources such as ore or petroleum that are of average quality, grade, or price

mid·dy /míddee/ (*plural* **-dies**) *n* **1.** NAVY same as **midshipman** (sense 1) (*informal*) **2.** *also* **mid·dy blouse** a loose blouse with a sailor collar worn by women and children

Mid·east /mid èest/ *n* same as **Middle East** —**Mid·east·ern** *adj* —**Mid·east·ern·er** *n*

mid·field /míd fèeld/ *n* **1.** the middle portion of a sports field, especially the area midway between the goals **2.** the group of players who contest control of the central area of the field between the two penalty areas (*takes a singular or plural verb*)

mid·field·er /míd fèeldər/ *n* a member of a soccer team active in the central area of the playing field, often both offensively and defensively

Mid·gard /míd gaàrd/, **Mid·garth** /-gaàrth/, **Mid·garthr** /-gaàrthər/ *n* in Norse mythology, the home of humankind, midway between Asgard and the underworld, encircled by a huge serpent and formed from the body of the giant Ymir

midge /mij/ *n* **1.** a small slender flying insect that occurs globally, particularly in swarms near bodies of standing water, or a related biting insect that can transmit blood-borne diseases. Family: Chironomidae or Ceratopogonidae. **2.** a person or animal of small stature [Old English *mycg* < Indo-European, probably an imitation of humming]

midg·et /míjjit/ *n* **1.** OFFENSIVE TERM an offensive term for a very short person whose skeleton and features are of standard proportions **2.** VERY SMALL VERSION OF SOMETHING a very small version of something such as a car or boat ■ *adj* MINIATURE OR SMALLER THAN USUAL miniaturized or belonging to a class smaller than the ordinary size [Mid-19C. < MIDGE, literally "little midge"]

mid·gut /míd gùt/ *n* **1.** PART OF DIGESTIVE TRACT the central section of the digestive tract of a vertebrate, in which the processes of digestion and absorption take place **2.** PART OF INVERTEBRATE ALIMENTARY CANAL the middle section of the alimentary canal of an invertebrate **3.** PART OF EMBRYO'S GUT the middle portion of the gut of an embryo that develops into most of the small intestine and part of the large intestine

Mid·heav·en /míd hèvv'n/ *n* the point on the apparent annual path of the Sun in the celestial sphere where the meridian is crossed, or the sign of the zodiac that contains it

mid·i /míddee/ (*plural* **-is**) *n* a skirt or coat that comes down to just below the knee or halfway down the calf [Mid-20C. < MID after MINI-, MAXI] —**mid·i** *adj*

Mi·di, Canal du /mee dèe/ ➧ **Canal du Midi**

MIDI /míddee/ *n* the interface between an electronic musical instrument and a computer, used in composing and editing music to allow the computer to control an instrument or one instrument to control others. Full form **musical instrument digital interface**

mid·i·ron /míd ìrn/ *n* in golf, a number 5, 6, 7, or 8 iron, used to give the ball a medium amount of lift

mid·land /míddlənd/ *n* the middle, inland, or interior part of a country ■ *adj* relating to or being in the middle or interior of a country

Mid·land *n* **1.** a variety of US English spoken in states from New Jersey south to Georgia, especially in the Appalachian and Piedmont mountains and in the Shenandoah Valley **2.** *UK* a variety of British English spoken in the Midlands of England, divided into East Midland and West Midland —**Mid·land** *adj*

Mid·lands /míddləndz/ central, largely industrialized part of England, centered on Birmingham —**Mid·land·er** *n*

mid·life /míd lìf/ *n* same as **middle age**

mid·life cri·sis *n* feelings of self-doubt and a lack of confidence experienced by some people when they become middle-aged

mid·line /míd lìn/ *n* a vertical line that divides a bilaterally symmetrical animal or human body into right and left halves

mid·morn·ing /mìd máwrning/ *n* the middle part of the morning —**mid·morn·ing** *adj*

mid·most /míd mòst/ *adj* situated at or nearest the center of something ■ *adv* in the very middle or midst of something [Old English *midmest*]

Midn. *abbr* NAVY midshipman (sense 1)

mid·night /míd nìt/ *n* **1.** 12 o'clock at night or the period around the middle of the night **2.** a period of intense darkness or gloom (*literary*) —**mid·night·ly** *adj, adv*

mid·night blue *adj* of a very dark blue color —**mid·night blue** *n*

mid·night sun *n* the Sun when it is visible from within the Arctic or Antarctic circles at midnight during their respective summer months

mid-o·cean ridge *n* a long underwater mountain range of the Atlantic, Indian, or South Pacific oceans formed from volcanic rock released during the movement of tectonic plates

mid·point /míd pòynt/ *n* **1.** the point on a line, journey, or distance that is halfway between the beginning and end **2.** the point of time halfway between the beginning and end of an event, course of action, or period

mid·range /míd ràynj/ *n* the middle of a series, array, or range ■ *adj* covering a distance midway between a short-range and long-range trajectory

Mid·rash /mí draàsh/ (*plural* **-rash·im** /mi dráwshim, mì draa shéem/) *n* a body of Rabbinic literature consisting of commentary on and clarification of biblical texts, first compiled before 500 A.D. [Early 17C. < Hebrew *midrāš* < *dāraš* "expound"]

mid·rib /míd rìb/ *n* the thick central vein that runs from the base of a leaf to its apex

mid·riff /míddrif/ *n* **1.** MIDDLE FRONT AREA OF HUMAN BODY the area of the human body between the chest and the waist **2.** CLOTHING PART OF CLOTHING OVER MIDDLE the part of clothing that covers the area of the human body from the chest to the waist **3.** ANAT same as **diaphragm** (sense 1) (*dated*) ■ *adj* **1.** NEAR MIDRIFF in the area of the midriff ○ *midriff bulge* **2.** EXPOSING MIDRIFF used to describe an article of clothing that exposes the midriff ○ *a midriff top* [Old English *midhrif* "diaphragm" < *midd* (see MID) + *hrif* "belly" (< Indo-European, "body")]

mid·rise *adj* relating to or consisting of buildings that are of moderate height, about five to ten stories ■ *n* a building of moderate height, about five to ten stories

mid·sag·it·tal /mid sájjit'l/ *adj* relating to or situated along an imaginary plane that passes through the midline of the body or an organ

mid·sec·tion /míd sèkshən/ *n* the middle part of something, especially the area of the human body between the chest and waist

mid·ship /míd shìp/ *adj* relating to or located in the middle section of a ship or vessel

mid·ship·man /míd shìpmən/ (*plural* **-men** /-mən/) *n* **1.** a student who is training to be a naval officer, especially at a naval academy **2.** a fish with rows of light-producing organs along the underside of its body that produces a buzzing sound. Native to: North America. Genus: *Porichthys*. [Late 17C. Alteration of *midshipsman*, because the sailor was originally stationed amidships]

mid·ships /míd shìps/ *adv, adj* NAUT same as **amidships** [Mid-19C. Shortening]

mid·size /míd sìz/, **mid·sized** /-sìzd/ *adj* of a size midway between large and small

midst /midst, mitst/ *n* the middle or central part of something ■ *prep* same as **amid** (*literary*) [15C. Alteration of earlier *middes* < MID] ◇ **in the midst of** in the middle of a situation, place, event, or period of time ◇ **in our midst** among us

mid·stream /mid stréem/ *n* **1.** the middle part of a river or stream where the current is often very strong **2.** a point after the beginning and before the end of something such as a speech or course of action —**mid·stream** *adv*

mid·sum·mer /míd sùmmər/ *n* the period of time in the middle of summer

CULTURAL NOTE ***A Midsummer Night's Dream***, a play (1595?) by English dramatist William Shakespeare. A comedy set in a wood outside Athens, it brings together two young aristocratic couples, a group of tradesmen who are rehearsing a play, and Oberon and Titania, king and queen of the fairies. A love potion administered by the sprite Puck has the unfortunate effect of making both the young noblemen fall in love with the same woman, and Titania with the weaver Bottom, but all is happily resolved in time for the tradesmen's performance of *Pyramus and Thisbe*. The saying "The course of true love never did run smooth" comes from this play.

Mid·sum·mer Day *n* the day of the summer solstice in the northern hemisphere marked by Christians as the feast of St. John the Baptist. Date: June 24.

mid·term /míd tùrm/ *n* **1.** MIDPOINT OF TERM the middle of an academic term or a term of office **2.** EXAM HALFWAY THROUGH ACADEMIC TERM an examination taken halfway through an academic term (*often used in the plural*) **3.** PERIOD MIDWAY THROUGH PREGNANCY the period halfway through a pregnancy ■ *adj* IN MIDDLE OF TERM OF OFFICE occurring in the middle of a term of office, especially that of a president of the United States ○ *midterm elections*

mid·town /míd tòwn/ *n* the central area of a city between the uptown and downtown areas, especially in Manhattan

mid·way /míd wày/ *adv, adj* **1.** HALF OF WAY halfway between two points, parts, or places **2.** HALFWAY THROUGH SOMETHING halfway through an event, course of action, or period of time ■ *n* AREA OF SIDESHOWS AT FAIR an area in a fair, carnival, or circus for sideshows and other amusements [Old English *midweg*]

Mid·way Is·lands /míd way-/ coral atoll consisting of two islets in the central Pacific Ocean, administered by the United States. Area: 2 sq. mi./5.2 sq. km.

mid·week /míd wéek/ *n* the period of time in the middle of a week ■ *adj, adv* on a day in the middle of the week or relating to such a day —**mid·week·ly** /mìd wéeklee/ *adj, adv*

Mid·week /míd wéek/ *n* the day of Wednesday, so called by members of the Society of Friends

Mid·west /mid wést/ *n* the northern region of the central United States east of the Rocky Mountains, generally including the states of Illinois, Indiana, Iowa, Kansas, Michigan, Minnesota, Missouri, Nebraska, Ohio, and Wisconsin —**Mid·west·ern** *adj* —**Mid·west·ern·er** *n*

mid·wife /míd wìf/ *n* (*plural* **-wives** /-wìvz/) **1.** SOMEBODY TRAINED TO DELIVER BABIES somebody trained to help deliver babies and offer support and advice to pregnant women **2.** SOMEBODY WHO HELPS TO CREATE SOMETHING somebody or something that assists in bringing something new into existence ■ *vt* (**-wifed** or **-wived** /-wìvd/, **-wif·ing** or **-wiv·ing** /-wìving/, **-wifes**) ASSIST IN BIRTH OF BABY to assist in the delivery of a baby [13C. Probably < obsolete *mid* "with" + WIFE "woman"]

mid·wife·ry /mid wíffəree, -wífəree, míd wìfəree/ *n* the technique or practice of helping to deliver babies and offering advice and support to pregnant women

mid·win·ter /mid wíntər/ *n* the period in the middle of winter

mid·year /míd yèer/ *n* **1.** the period in the middle of an academic, calendar, or fiscal year **2.** an exam taken halfway through an academic year (*informal*)

mien /meen/ *n* somebody's facial expression or general appearance, bearing, or posture, taken as an indication of his or her mood or character (*formal*) [Early 16C. Probably shortening of obsolete *demeine* "demeanor" < Old French < *demener* "lead away" < Latin *minare* "drive a herd of animals"]

Mies van der Ro·he /mèez van dər rō ə/, **Ludwig** (1886–1969) German-born US architect and designer. He was a pioneer in the design of glass-walled skyscrapers, in particular the Seagram Building, New York City (1958), on which he collaborated with Philip Johnson. His architecture and furniture are characterized by austere forms, elegant materials such as marble and chrome, and subtle proportion and detailing.

"Less is more."

AKG London

Ludwig Mies van der Rohe

[Ludwig Mies van der Rohe, *New York Herald Tribune*; 1959]

mi·fep·ri·stone /mi féppra stòn/ *n* a drug that blocks the hormone progesterone, which is essential for maintaining pregnancy. Use: fetus abortion in the first few weeks after conception. [Late 20C. Contraction of *aminophenyl* + *propyne* + *estradione* (elements of the drug's chemical name) + -ONE]

miff /mif/ *vt* (**miffed, miff·ing, miffs**) ANNOY OR OFFEND SOMEBODY to annoy or offend somebody (*informal*; *often passive*) ■ *n* **1.** ILL HUMOR an angry mood or sulk (*informal*) **2.** PETTY QUARREL a tiff or trivial quarrel [Early 17C. Origin ?]

miffed /mift/ *adj* annoyed or offended

mif·fy /míffee/ (**-fi·er, -fi·est**) *adj* **1.** oversensitive, or too easily upset or offended (*informal*) **2.** describes plants that are difficult to propagate because they require particular environmental conditions —**mif·fi·ness** *n*

MiG /mig/ *n* a high-speed high-altitude fighter aircraft built in Russia [Mid-20C. Acronym < A. I. *Mikoyan* and M. I. *Gurevich*, Soviet aircraft designers]

might[1] /mìt/ CORE MEANING: a modal verb indicating the possibility that something is true or will happen in the future ○ *She said that John might be living abroad now.* ○ *The meeting might be as early as next week.*

modal v **1.** used as a polite way of making suggestions and giving advice ○ *I thought we might go out tonight.* ○ *You might want to give him a call first.* **2.** used to indicate that somebody ought to do something, often to show annoyance that it has not been done ○ *You might at least have told me!* [Old English *mihte, meahte*, the past tense of *magan* (see MAY[1])]

SPELLCHECK might or **mite**? Do not confuse the spelling of ***might*** and ***mite***, which sound similar. ***Might*** is a verb meaning "will possibly" or "ought to": *It might rain. You might have warned me!* It is also noun meaning "power" or "strength": *the might of a multinational organization; with might and main.* ***Mite*** is a noun only, referring to a tiny eight-legged animal, a little child, or a small amount, as in *a spider mite, give the poor mite a drink*, or *feeling a mite jealous.*

might[2] /mìt/ *n* **1.** great power or influence ○ *up against the might of a huge organization* **2.** physical strength and determination ○ *We must push with all our might.* [Old English *miht* < Indo-European, "be able"]

SPELLCHECK See ***might***[1].

might-have-been *n* an event or outcome that could have occurred but did not

might·i·ly /mìtilee/ *adv* **1.** with considerable physical strength and effort ○ *struggle mightily* **2.** to a great extent or degree (*dated*) ○ *mightily relieved*

might·n't /mìt'nt/ *contr* might not (*informal*)

might've /mìtəv/ *contr* might have (*informal*)

might·y /mìtee/ *adj* (**-i·er, -i·est**) **1.** STRONG AND POWERFUL of great strength and power **2.** BIG AND IMPRESSIVE very impressive in size, scope, or extent ○ *a mighty oak tree* ■ *adv N Am, regional* VERY MUCH SO extremely or to a great degree ○ *mighty fine* [Old English *mihtig* < *miht* (see MIGHT[2])] —**might·i·ness** *n*

mig·ma·tite /mígmə tìt/ *n* a coarsely crystalline rock composed of a mixture of bands of metamorphic and igneous rocks and found in areas where high-grade metamorphic rocks are partly melted to form igneous rock [Early 20C. < Greek *migmat-*, stem of *migma* "mixture" + -ITE[1]]

mig·non *adj* /meén yòn/ very delicate and pretty (*literary*) ■ *n* /meen yáwN, meén yàwN/ a small portion of prime beef, especially filet mignon [Mid-16C. < French, alteration of Old French *mignot*]

mi·gnon·ette /mìnnyə nét/ (*plural* **-ettes** or *same*) *n* a plant with spiky leaves. Flowers: small, fragrant, greenish white flowers. Native to: Mediterranean. Genus: *Reseda*. [Early 18C. < French *mignon* "dainty" (see MIGNON)]

~~**migrain**~~ incorrect spelling of **migraine**

mi·graine /mī́ gràyn/ *n* a recurrent, throbbing, very painful headache, often affecting one side of the head and sometimes accompanied by vomiting or by distinct warning signs, including visual disturbances [14C. < French < Greek *hēmikrania* < *hēmi-* "half" + *kranion* "skull"] —**mi·grain·ous** /mī gráynəss/ *adj*

mi·grant /mī́grənt/ *n* **1.** somebody who moves from one place to another, often for employment or economic improvement **2.** an animal, especially a bird, that moves from one region to another, often at the same times each year in order to breed or avoid unsuitable weather conditions [Late 17C. < Latin *migrant-*, present participle of *migrare* "migrate"] —**mi·grant** *adj*

mi·grate /mī́ gràyt/ (**-grat·ed, -grat·ing, -grates**) *v* **1.** *vi* MOVE FROM PLACE TO PLACE to move from one region or country to another, often to seek work or other economic opportunities **2.** *vi* ZOOL MOVE BETWEEN HABITATS to move from one habitat or environment to another in response to seasonal changes and variations in food supply **3.** *vi* BIOL MOVE POSITION WITHIN ORGANISM to move from one part of an organism or substance to another, e.g., cells moving during the growth of an embryo **4.** *vt* COMPUT MOVE BETWEEN COMPUTER SYSTEMS to transfer a file from one computer system or database to another [Early 17C. < Latin *migrat-*, past participle of *migrare*] —**mi·gra·tor** *n*

mi·gra·tion /mī gráysh'n/ *n* **1.** MOVEMENT FROM ONE PLACE TO ANOTHER the act or process of moving from one region or country to another **2.** GROUP MOVING BETWEEN PLACES a group of people, birds, or other animals that are moving together from one region or country to another **3.** CHEM SHIFT OF IONS the movement of ions under the influence of an electric field **4.** CHEM MOVEMENT OF ATOMS the movement of an atom, or a group of atoms or double bonds, from one part of a molecule to another **5.** TRANSFERENCE BETWEEN COMPUTER SYSTEMS a transfer of computer data, programs, or hardware from one system to another —**mi·gra·tion·al** *adj*

mi·gra·to·ry /mī́grə tàwree/, **mi·gra·tive** /mī́grətiv/ *adj* **1.** MOVING TO ANOTHER REGION EVERY YEAR moving as part of a bird, fish, or other animal population from one region to another, usually at the same times every year, in order to breed or avoid unsuitable weather conditions **2.** RELATING TO MOVEMENT FROM PLACE TO PLACE relating to the movement of people from one place to another in order to achieve better living conditions **3.** NOT SETTLING DOWN tending to wander from one region or country to another without settling down in one place for any length of time

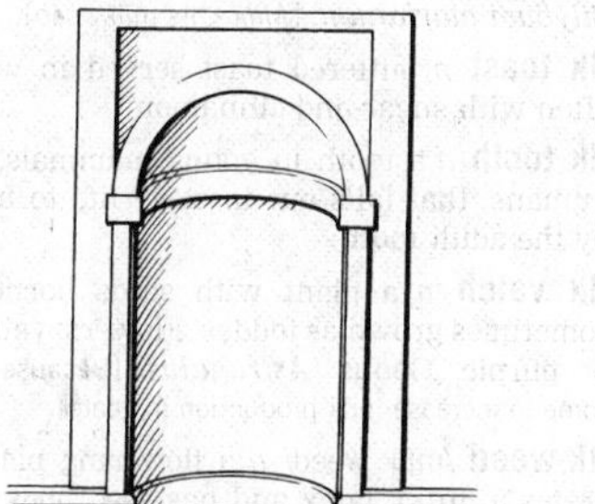

mihrab

mih·rab /meérəb/ *n* a small niche in a mosque that indicates the direction of Mecca [Early 19C. < Arabic *miḥrāb*]

mi·ka·do /mi kaá dō̆/ (*plural* **-dos**) *n* in former times, a title of a Japanese emperor [Early 18C. < Japanese, "honorable gate"]

Mi·kan /mī́kən/, **George Lawrence** (*b.* 1924) US basketball player. A player in the Minneapolis Lakers (1947–56), he was one of the first very tall players in the professional sport.

Mik·a·su·ki /mìkə soókee/ (*plural same* or **-kis**), **Mic·co·su·kee** (*plural same* or **-kees**), **Mic·co·su·ki** (*plural same* or **-kis**) *n* **1.** a member of a Native North American people who lived in northern Florida and now live mainly in southern Florida **2.** the Muskogean language of the Mikasuki people [Mid-20C. < Mikasuki, after a lake in N Florida where they first settled] —**Mik·a·su·ki** *adj*

mike /mīk/ (*informal*) *n* same as **microphone** ■ *vt* (**miked, mik·ing, mikes**) to supply somebody with, or transmit something through, a microphone [Early 20C. Shortening]

Mike /mīk/ *n* a code word for the letter "m," used in international radio communications

Mi'k·maq /mík màk/ (*plural same* or **-maqs**), **Mic·mac** (*plural same* or **-macs**) *n* **1.** a member of a group of Native North American people living in Nova Scotia, New Brunswick, Prince Edward Island, and the Gaspé Peninsula in eastern Canada **2.** an Algonquian language spoken in eastern Canada. Native speakers: 3,000. [Early 18C. Via French < Mi'kmaq *migmac* "allies"] —**Mi'k·maq** *adj*

mik·vah /míkvə, meek vaá/, **mik·veh** /míkvə/, **mik·ve** *n* among Orthodox Jews, a ritual bath for cleansing or purification, especially before the Sabbath or following menstruation, childbirth, or contact with a corpse [Mid-19C. Via Yiddish *mikve* < Hebrew *miqweh* "mass (of water)"]

mil[1] /mil/ *n* **1.** ONE THOUSANDTH OF INCH a unit of linear measurement equivalent to one thousandth of an inch/0.0254 mm, often used in measuring the diameter of wires **2.** UNIT OF ANGULAR MEASUREMENT FOR ARTILLERY a unit of measurement equivalent to the angle subtended by 1/6400th of a circumference, used in aiming artillery **3.** ONE MILLILITER a unit of volume equivalent to one milliliter or a cubic centimeter **4.** MILLION DOLLARS a million dollars (*slang*) [Early 18C. Shortening of Latin *millesimus* "thousandth" < *mille* "thousand"]

mil[2] *abbr* **1.** MIL military **2.** ONLINE military organization (*used in Internet addresses*) See table at **domain name** **3.** militia

mi·la·dy /mi láydee/ (*plural* **-dies**) *n* (*archaic or humorous*) **1.** a British gentlewoman or a woman member of the aristocracy **2.** a form of address for a gentlewoman or female member of the aristocracy [Late 18C. Via French < English *my lady*]

mil·age *n* MEASURE, TRANSP another spelling of **mileage**

Mi·lan /mi laán/ capital of Milan Province and Lombardy Region, northern Italy. Population: 1,265,211 (2001). —**Mil·a·nese** /mìllə neéz, -neéss/ *n, adj*

milch /milch/ *adj* producing milk

milch cow /mílch-, mílk-/ *n Can, UK* a source of easily gained income (*informal*) [*Milch* < Old English *-milce* "a milking" < Germanic]

mil·chig /mílkhik/, **mil·chik** *adj* under Jewish dietary laws, relating to, containing, or derived from dairy products and so not to be used with meat products [Early 20C. < Yiddish *milkhik* < *milkh* "milk" < Old High German *miluh*]

mild /mīld/ *adj* **1.** GENTLE AND AMIABLE gentle, easy-going, and slow to get angry **2.** LIGHTLY FLAVORED describes food that is lightly flavored and not strong, hot, spicy, or bitter in taste ○ *a mild sauce* **3.** PLEASANT AND TEMPERATE pleasant and temperate in climate and not excessively hot or cold ○ *one of the mildest winters on record* **4.** NOT HARSH not severe or strong ○ *a mild sedative* ○ *mild disagreement* **5.** NOT DANGEROUS not serious enough to endanger life ○ *a mild earthquake* ○ *mild to moderate hypertension* **6.** NOT CONTAINING HARMFUL CHEMICALS feeling soft and gentle and not containing any chemicals that might harm the skin or clothes ○ *mild soap* **7.** SLIGHTLY INDECENT LANGUAGE describes slightly indecent language that might offend some people [Old English *milde* < Indo-European, "soft"] —**mild·ly** *adv* —**mild·ness** *n*

mil·dew /míl doō/ *n* **1.** FUNGAL DISEASE OF PLANTS a plant disease in which the parasitic fungus is visible as white or gray powdery deposits on the leaves or fruit **2.** GRAY OR WHITE FUNGUS a gray or white fungus that grows on walls, paper, leather, and other similar materials in damp conditions ■ *vti* (**-dewed, -dew·ing, -dews**) BE AFFECTED WITH MILDEW to be affected, or affect something, with a gray or white fungus [Old English *mildēaw* "honeydew, nectar" < Indo-European "honey"] —**mil·dew·y** *adj*

mild lan·guage *n* mildly indecent language that might offend some people

mild-man·nered *adj* having a polite gentle disposition

mild steel *n* a strong steel containing a low proportion of carbon [< its being easily worked]

mile /mīl/ *n* **1.** UNIT OF DISTANCE a unit of linear measurement on land, used in English-speaking countries, equivalent to 5,280 ft. or 1,760 yd. or 1.6 km **2.** MEASURE same as **nautical mile** **3.** UNIT OF MEASUREMENT COMPARABLE TO MILE a unit of distance or length used in different historical periods or in non-English-speaking countries, e.g., the Roman mile **4.** RACE OVER ONE MILE a foot race that is a mile long ■ **miles** *npl* A LONG WAY a considerable distance ○ *We're miles from home.* ○ *We have miles to go before we sleep.* [Old English *mīl* < Latin *milia (passuum)* "a thousand (paces)" < *mille* "thousand"] ◇ **a mile a minute** very quickly ○ *talks a mile a minute* ◇ **be miles away** or **off** to be unaware of what is going on or being said through daydreaming or being preoccupied with your own thoughts (*informal*) ◇ **go the extra mile** to make an extra or special effort in order to achieve something ◇ **run a mile** *UK* used to emphasize how frightened somebody is of something, or how unwilling somebody is to do something (*informal*) ○ *He'd run a mile if he thought she was getting serious about him.* ◇ **see something a mile off** to recognize or be aware of something quickly ◇ **stick out a mile** to be extremely obvious (*informal*)

mile·age /mī́lij/, **mil·age** *n* **1.** DISTANCE IN MILES a distance or length measured in miles **2.** NUMBER OF MILES VEHICLE HAS TRAVELED the total number of miles a vehicle has traveled **3.** MILES VEHICLE TRAVELS ON FUEL the total number of miles a vehicle can travel on a particular amount of fuel, such as a gallon or a liter **4.** TRAVEL ALLOWANCE AT FIXED RATE a travel allowance, usually set and paid per mile by somebody's employer **5.** ADVANTAGE OR USEFULNESS OF SOMETHING the amount of use, advantage, profit, or service that may be obtained from something (*informal*) ○ *It's amazing how much emotional mileage she can get out of a few simple words.*

~~**milennium**~~ incorrect spelling of **millennium**

mile·om·e·ter /mīl lómmətər/, **mil·om·e·ter** *n UK* TRANSP same as **odometer**

mile·post /mī́l pōst/ *n* **1.** a post by the side of a road indicating the number of miles to a place, or placed a mile from a similar post **2.** ROADS same as **milestone** (sense 1)

mil·er /mī́lər/ *n* an athlete or horse that competes in a one-mile race

mi·les glo·ri·o·sus /meé layz glawree ṓssəss/ (*plural* **mi·li·tes glo·ri·o·si** /meélee tayz glawree ṓssee/) *n* an arrogant, bragging, and often cowardly soldier, especially one who appears as a stock character in comedies (*literary*) [< Latin, "boastful soldier," the title of a comedy by Plautus]

Mi·le·sian[1] /mī leézh'n, -leésh'n/ *n* somebody who came from the ancient Greek city of Miletus [Mid-16C. < Latin *Milesius* < Greek *Milēsios* < *Milētos* "Miletus"] —**Mi·le·sian** *adj*

Mi·le·sian[2] /mī leézh'n, -leésh'n/ *n* in Irish legend, a member of a group of people from a royal Spanish family who invaded Ireland about 1300 B.C. and became the ancestors of the modern Irish [Late 16C. After *Milesius*, the legendary head of the family]

mile·stone /mī́l stōn/ *n* **1.** a stone by the side of a road indicating the number of miles to a place **2.** a significant or important event, e.g., in the history of a country or in somebody's life

Mi·let·us /mə leétəss/ ruined ancient Greek city of western Anatolia, in modern Turkey

mil·foil /míl fòyl/ (*plural* **-foils** or *same*) *n* PLANTS **1.** same as **yarrow** **2.** same as **water milfoil** [13C. Via Old French < Latin *mil(l)efolium* "thousand-leaf," a translation of Greek *muriophullon*; from the plant's feathery leaves]

Mil·ford /mílfərd/ **1.** town in southwestern Connecticut, in New Haven County, on Long Island Sound. Population: 53,472 (2002 estimate). **2.** town in southern Massachusetts, south of Marlborough and southeast of Worcester. Population: 27,309 (2002 estimate).

Mil·ford Ha·ven seaport in Pembrokeshire, southwestern Wales. Population: 13,194 (1991).

Mil·ford Sound deep coastal inlet in the southwestern part of the South Island, New Zealand

Mil·haud /mee yō/, **Darius** (1892–1974) French composer and teacher. He was a member of the Paris-based group of composers known as "Les Six," and his work, e.g., *Le Boeuf sur le toit* (1919), was marked by polytonality and elements of jazz.

mil·i·ar·i·a /mìllee érree ə/ *n* MED same as **prickly heat** (*technical*) [Early 19C. < modern Latin < Latin *miliarius* (see MILIARY)] —**mil·i·ar·i·al** *adj*

mil·i·ar·y /míllee èrree/ *adj* **1.** resembling millet seeds **2.** describes a medical condition consisting of or characterized by small nodules or lesions resembling millet seeds [Late 17C. < Latin *miliarius* < *milium* "millet"]

mil·i·ar·y tu·ber·cu·lo·sis *n* an acute form of tuberculosis in which lesions resembling millet seeds occur in the affected organs after bacilli are spread by the blood from one point of infection

mi·lieu /mil yóō, mi lyṓ/ (*plural* **-lieus** or **-lieux** /-lyṓ/) *n* the surroundings or environment that somebody lives in and is influenced by ○ *grew up in an artistic milieu* [Mid-19C. < French < *mi* "mid" (< Latin *medius*) + *lieu* "place"]

milit. *abbr* MIL military

mil·i·tant /míllit'nt/ *adj* **1.** AGGRESSIVE extremely active in the defense or support of a cause, often to the point of extremism **2.** INVOLVED IN FIGHTING engaged in fighting or warfare ■ *n* SOMEBODY AGGRESSIVELY SUPPORTING CAUSE an aggressive defender or supporter of a cause [15C. Directly or via French < Latin *militant-*, present participle of *militare* "be a soldier" < *milit-* (see MILITARY)] —**mil·i·tan·cy** *n* —**mil·i·tant·ly** *adv*

mil·i·tar·i·a /mìlli térree ə/ *n* military objects, e.g., weapons, medals, and uniforms, that are collected as a hobby or for historical interest [Mid-20C. < MILITARY]

mil·i·ta·rism /míllitə rìzzəm/ *n* **1.** PURSUIT OF MILITARY AIMS the pursuit or celebration of military ideals **2.** STRONG INFLUENCE OF MILITARY ON GOVERNMENT a high level of influence by military personnel and ideals on the government or policies of a country or state **3.** GOVERNMENT POLICY OF INVESTING IN MILITARY a government policy of investing heavily in and strengthening the armed forces

mil·i·ta·rist /míllitərist/ *n* **1.** a zealous supporter and promoter of military ideals **2.** a student of military history and strategy —**mil·i·ta·ris·tic** /millitə rístik/ *adj* —**mil·i·ta·ris·ti·cal·ly** *adv*

mil·i·ta·rize /míllitə rìz/ (**-rized, -riz·ing, -riz·es**) *vt* **1.** EQUIP OR TRAIN FOR WAR to equip or train a person or group of people for war **2.** CONVERT FOR MILITARY USE to convert something such as a piece of land or a building for military use **3.** PERSUADE TO SUPPORT MILITARISM to persuade somebody to support a policy of aiding and promoting the military —**mil·i·ta·ri·za·tion** /mìllitəri záysh'n/ *n*

mil·i·tar·y /mílli tèrree/ *adj* **1.** OF WAR OR ARMED FORCES relating to matters of war or the armed forces **2.** OF ARMY relating to the army, especially as distinguished from the navy or air force **3.** TYPICAL OF SOLDIER characteristic of a soldier or the armed forces ■ *n* ARMED FORCES OR ITS HIGH-RANKING OFFICERS the armed forces or high-ranking members of the armed forces ○ *attempts by the military to influence government policy* ▶See table on next page [15C. Directly or via French *militaire* < Latin *militaris* < *milit-*, stem of *miles* "soldier"] —**mil·i·tar·i·ly** /mìlli térrəlee/ *adv* —**mil·i·tar·i·ness** *n*

mil·i·tar·y a·cad·e·my *n* **1.** a secondary school or college that prepares students to enter the military at officer level, and that typically emphasizes rigorous discipline **2.** a secondary school or college that follows military procedures and discipline and usually requires students to wear military uniforms but does not necessarily entitle them to become officers

mil·i·tar·y at·ta·ché *n* an officer in the armed forces who has been assigned to the official staff of an ambassador in order to gather military intelligence

mil·i·tar·y ho·tel *n S Asia* a restaurant that serves meat, fish, and poultry

mil·i·tar·y-in·dus·tri·al com·plex *n* the military and the defense industries considered as a combined influence on foreign and economic policy

mil·i·tar·y in·tel·li·gence *n* **1.** information gathered about another country's military equipment and capabilities by means of observation, exchange of information, surveillance, or spying **2.** an armed forces agency whose duties include procurement, analysis, and use of tactical and strategic data required in decision making

mil·i·tar·y law *n* the legal system, including statutes, regulations, and procedures, that applies to military personnel

mil·i·tar·y po·lice *n* a police force within the armed forces

mil·i·tar·y sci·ence *n* the academic study of the principles and procedures of warfare

mil·i·tate /mílli tàyt/ (**-tat·ed, -tat·ing, -tates**) *vi* to have an influence, especially a negative one, on something [Late 16C. < Latin *militat-*, past participle of *militare* "be a soldier, wage war" < *milit-* (see MILITARY)]

USAGE militate or **mitigate**? These two often-confused words have different, mutually exclusive meanings and they function in different ways. ***Mitigate*** needs a noun object and means "to lessen the impact or degree of seriousness of something undesirable": *A six-month suspended sentence unfairly mitigates the seriousness of a vehicular homicide. There were mitigating circumstances.* ***Militate*** does not take a noun object, but is followed by a preposition, often *against*, plus a noun. It means "to have an influence, especially a negative one, on something": *Trade sanctions militate* [not *mitigate*] *against international cooperation.*

mi·li·tia /mə líshə/ *n* **1.** SOLDIERS WHO ARE ALSO CIVILIANS an army of soldiers who are civilians but take military training and can serve full-time during emergencies **2.** RESERVE MILITARY FORCE a reserve army that is not part of the regular armed forces but can be called up in an emergency **3.** UNAUTHORIZED QUASI-MILITARY GROUP an unauthorized group of people who arm themselves and conduct quasi-military training [Late 16C. < Latin, "military service, body of soldiers" < *milit-* (see MILITARY)]

mi·li·tia·man /mə líshəmən/ (*plural* **-men** /-mən/) *n* a man who serves in a militia

mi·li·tia·wom·an /mə líshə wòommən/ (*plural* **-wom·en** /-wìmmin/) *n* a woman who serves in a militia

mil·i·um /míllee əm/ (*plural* **-i·a** /-ee ə/) *n* a whitehead on the skin (*technical*) [Mid-19C. < Latin, "millet"; so called from the nodule's size and shape]

milk /milk/ *n* **1.** NUTRITIOUS FLUID PRODUCED BY MAMMALS a nutritious white fluid, rich in protein, fats, lactose, and vitamins, that women and other female mammals produce to feed their young immediately after birth **2.** DAIRY PRODUCT an opaque white fluid produced by cows, sheep, or goats and used by human beings as a drink, in cooking, and to make products such as butter and cheese **3.** PLANT SAP a white or off-white liquid from a plant, e.g., the liquid inside a coconut or the sap of some trees **4.** COSMETIC OR PHARMACEUTICAL PRODUCT a cosmetic or pharmaceutical product that is thick and white ○ *cleansing milk* ■ *v* (**milked, milk·ing, milks**) **1.** *vti* TAKE MILK FROM COW to draw milk for use as a dairy product from the udder of a cow, goat, or sheep manually or by using a special machine **2.** *vi* PRODUCE MILK to yield or supply milk (*refers to dairy animals*) **3.** *vt* REMOVE LIQUID FROM SOMETHING to remove liquid from something, especially to drain the venom from a snake or the sap from a tree **4.** *vt* STEAL SOMETHING SLOWLY AND STEADILY to steal money from something such as a fund in small quantities over a period of time (*informal*) **5.** *vt* EXPLOIT SOMETHING UNSCRUPULOUSLY to get as much benefit from something as possible, often in a calculating or unscrupulous way (*informal*) [Old English *milc* < Indo-European, "to rub, milk"]

CULTURAL NOTE ***Under Milk Wood***, a play (1953) by the Welsh poet Dylan Thomas. This play for voices, originally written for radio but occasionally presented as a stage play, describes a day in the life of a Welsh fishing village and is noted for its poetic prose, rich humor, and vivid characterization.

Milk /milk/ river that originates in Montana and flows into Alberta, Canada, before joining the Missouri River. Length: 625 mi./1,010 km.

milk choc·o·late *n* chocolate that has been made with milk and has a sweet creamy taste

milk·er /mílkər/ *n* **1.** an animal that produces milk used for human consumption, especially a cow **2.** a milking machine, or somebody who milks animals, especially cows

milk fe·ver *n* **1.** mild fever that some new mothers have around the time that they begin to produce breast milk **2.** a disease in cows, sheep, and goats that have recently given birth, caused by mineral depletion incurred during milk production. Symptoms include temporary loss of consciousness or ability to move.

milk·fish /mílk fìsh/ (*plural* **-fish·es** or *same*) *n* a large toothless silver fish related to herring and salmon. Native to: warm waters of the Pacific and Indian oceans. Latin name: *Chanos chanos*. [Early 20C. < its color]

milk glass *n* white or translucent whitish glass used in decorative glasswork

milk house *n regional* a storage house or shed for storing milk and other perishables

REGIONAL NOTE See ***dairy***.

milk·ing /mílking/ *n* the task of drawing milk from cows, goats, or sheep for human consumption, or a time when this is done (*often used before a noun*)

milk leg *n* painful leg swelling that some women have following childbirth, caused by inflammation and clotting in the femoral vein

milk·maid /mílk màyd/ *n* a woman or girl who milks cows or does other jobs in a dairy (*dated*)

milk·man /mílk màn, -mən/ (*plural* **-men** /-mèn, -mən/) *n* a man who delivers or sells milk door to door (*dated*)

milk run *n* a routine trip, especially an airline's regular flight or an uneventful sortie made by a military aircraft (*informal*) [< the routine early morning trips of trains delivering milk]

milk shake, milk·shake /mílk shàyk/ *n* **1.** a cold drink made by whisking or blending milk, flavoring, and usually ice cream **2.** *New England* a drink made of milk and flavored syrup that is whipped until it is frothy

milk snake *n* a white or tan nonpoisonous king snake with red, yellow, brown, or black markings. Native to: North America. Genus: *Lampropeltis*. [*Milk* < its color]

milk·sop /mílk sòp/ *n* a man who is regarded as weak-willed or ineffectual (*dated insult*) [14C. The original meaning was "bread soaked in milk"]

milk sug·ar *n* BIOCHEM same as **lactose** (sense 1)

milk this·tle *n* a thistle that has dark green leaves streaked with white veins. Flowers: purple. Use: in herbal medicine, to treat the liver. Latin name: *Silybum marianum*. [*Milk* < its milky sap]

milk toast *n* buttered toast served in warm milk, often with sugar and cinnamon

milk tooth *n* a tooth in young mammals, including humans, that falls out in early life to be replaced by the adult tooth

milk vetch *n* a plant with seeds borne in pods, sometimes grown as fodder. Flowers: yellow, white, or purple. Genus: *Astragalus*. [Because thought by some to increase milk production in goats]

milk·weed /mílk wèed/ *n* a flowering plant that secretes a milky latex and has seed pods that burst open to release silky-tufted seeds. Genus: *Asclepias*. See illustration on p. 1200

milk·weed bug *n* a black crawling insect with red markings that feeds on the juice of the milkweed and is often used in scientific research. Latin name: *Oncopeltus fasciatus*.

milk·weed but·ter·fly *n* any butterfly whose larvae feed on milkweed plants, e.g., the monarch butterfly. Family: Danaidae.

MILITARY RANKS

Military ranks of the United Kingdom, Australia, and New Zealand

Navy	Marines	Army	Air Force
Admiral of the Fleet	[1]	Field Marshal	Marshal of the Royal Air Force
Admiral	General	General	Air Chief Marshal
Vice Admiral	Lieutenant General	Lieutenant General	Air Marshal
Rear Admiral	Major General	Major General	Air Vice Marshal
Commodore	Brigadier	Brigadier	Air Commodore
Captain	Colonel	Colonel	Group Captain
Commander	Lieutenant Colonel	Lieutenant Colonel	Wing Commander
Lieutenant Commander	Major	Major	Squadron Leader
Lieutenant	Captain	Captain	Flight Lieutenant
Sub Lieutenant	Lieutenant	Lieutenant	Flying Officer
	Second Lieutenant	Second Lieutenant	Pilot Officer
Midshipman			
*			
Warrant Officer	Warrant Officer (1st, 2nd Class)	Warrant Officer (1st, 2nd Class)	Warrant Officer
Chief Petty Officer	Colour Sergeant	Colour/Staff Sergeant	Flight Sergeant
			Chief Technician
Petty Officer	Sergeant	Sergeant	Sergeant
Leading Rate[2]	Corporal	Corporal	Corporal
	Lance Corporal	Lance Corporal	
Able Rate[3]	Marine 1st Class	Private	Junior Technician/ Senior Aircraftman
	Marine 2nd Class		Leading Aircraftman/ Aircraftman

Notes

NB Ranks shown are not comparative between United Kingdom, Australia, New Zealand and the United States and Canada

*** Indicates the end of officer rank**

1 Marine service not applicable for Australia and New Zealand.
2 Leading Rate: also called 'Leading Seaman' in some forces.
3 Able Rate: also called 'Able Seaman' in some forces.

Military ranks of the United States and Canada

Navy	Marine Corps	Army	Air Force
Fleet Admiral (wartime)		General of the Army (wartime)	General of the Air Force (wartime)
Admiral	General	General	General
Vice Admiral	Lieutenant General	Lieutenant General	Lieutenant General
Rear Admiral Upper Half	Major General	Major General	Major General
Rear Admiral Lower Half	Brigadier General	Brigadier General	Brigadier General
Captain	Colonel	Colonel	Colonel
Commander	Lieutenant Colonel	Lieutenant Colonel	Lieutenant Colonel
Lieutenant Commander	Major	Major	Major
Lieutenant	Captain	Captain	Captain
Lieutenant Junior Grade	First Lieutenant	First Lieutenant	First Lieutenant
Ensign	Second Lieutenant	Second Lieutenant	Second Lieutenant
*			
	Chief Warrant Officer 5	Chief Warrant Officer 5	
Chief Warrant Officer 4	Chief Warrant Officer 4	Chief Warrant Officer 4	
Chief Warrant Officer 3	Chief Warrant Officer 3	Chief Warrant Officer 3	
Chief Warrant Officer 2	Chief Warrant Officer 2	Chief Warrant Officer 2	
Warrant Officer 1 (no longer in use)	Warrant Officer 1	Warrant Officer 1	
Master Chief Petty Officer of the Navy	Sergeant Major of the Marine Corps	Sergeant Major of the Army	Chief Master Sergeant of the Air Force
Fleet/Command Master Chief Petty Officer & Master Chief Petty Officer	Sergeant Major & Master Gunnery Sergeant	Command Sergeant Major & Sergeant Major	Command Chief Master Sergeant, Chief Master Sergeant & First Sergeant
Senior Chief Petty Officer	First Sergeant & Master Sergeant	First Sergeant & Master Sergeant	Senior Master Sergeant & First Sergeant
Chief Petty Officer	Gunnery Sergeant	Sergeant First Class	Master Sergeant & First Sergeant
Petty Officer 1st Class	Staff Sergeant	Staff Sergeant	Technical Sergeant
Petty Officer 2nd Class	Sergeant	Sergeant	Staff Sergeant
Petty Officer 3rd Class	Corporal	Corporal & Specialist	Senior Airman
Seaman	Lance Corporal	Private First Class	Airman First Class
Seaman Apprentice	Private First Class	Private	Airman
Seaman Recruit	Private	Private	Airman Basic

milkweed

milk·wom·an /mílk wŏŏmmən/ (*plural* **-wom·en** /-wìmmin/) *n* a woman who delivers or sells milk door to door (*dated*)

milk·wort /mílk wùrt, -wàwrt/ *n* a plant formerly believed to increase milk production in nursing mothers. Genus: *Polygala.*

milk·y /mílkee/ (**-i·er, -i·est**) *adj* **1. MILK-COLORED** like milk in color or consistency **2. CONTAINING MILK** full of or containing milk **3. OPAQUE** cloudy or translucent, as if milk had been added —**milk·i·ly** *adv* —**milk·i·ness** *n*

milk·y dis·ease, milk·y spore dis·ease *n* a disease in the larvae of Japanese beetles and other scarabs that is caused by bacteria and turns the larvae white

Milk·y Way *n* the spiral galaxy to which Earth and its solar system belong, appearing as a faint band of light in the night sky [14C. Translation of Latin *via lactea*]

mill[1] /mil/ *n* **1. FLOUR-MAKING FACTORY** a building or group of buildings in which cereal grains are ground to make flour or meal **2. PROCESSING PLANT** a building or group of buildings used for processing raw materials and manufacturing a product such as paper, fabric, or steel **3. SMALL DEVICE FOR GRINDING GRAINS** a small device for grinding something such as coffee, pepper, or salt into granules **4. PROCESSING MACHINE** a machine that repeats a simple manufacturing procedure, e.g., one that stamps or cuts metal **5. JUICER** a machine that extracts juice from fruit or vegetables **6.** INDUST same as **milling cutter 7.** INDUST same as **milling machine 8. SOMETHING WORKING REPETITIVELY OR UNTHINKINGLY** an institution, person, or process that operates in the same automatic, repetitive, or productive manner as a factory ○ *Our family is a regular rumor mill.* **9. TEDIOUS PROCESS** a slow, unpleasant, or tedious process ○ *Getting the book through the editorial mill could take months.* **10. FIGHT** a boxing match or other fist fight (*archaic slang*) ■ *v* (**milled, mill·ing, mills**) **1.** *vt* **GRIND GRAIN BY MACHINE** to grind grain or seed by machine **2.** *vt* **MANUFACTURE BY MACHINE** to manufacture a product such as paper or fabric from raw materials by machine **3.** *vt* **PROCESS MATERIALS USING ROTARY MACHINERY** to process materials using machinery that grinds, presses, or pulverizes raw materials using a rotary motion **4.** *vt* **SHAPE METAL BY MACHINE** to use a milling cutter or milling machine to cut, shape, or finish metals **5.** *vt* **PUT RIDGES ON COIN EDGE** to cut ridges or grooves into a metal object, especially the edge of a coin **6.** *vi* **CIRCLE RESTLESSLY** to move around in a confused or restless group **7.** *vt* **PROCESS RUBBER** to pass rubber through spinning rollers as part of the manufacturing process **8.** *vt* **MAKE CREAM FROTHY** to whisk or shake something such as cream or chocolate until it is foamy **9.** *vi* **UNDERGO CRUSHING PROCESS** to undergo the process of being crushed to make flour (*refers to grain*) **10.** *vt regional* **HALT STAMPEDE** to stop a cattle stampede by turning the lead animals so that the cattle move in a circle, rather than forward [Pre-12C. < late Latin *molina* < Latin *molere* "to grind"] —**mill·a·ble** *adj* —**milled** *adj* ◇ **put somebody through the mill** to subject somebody to a difficult or unpleasant experience (*informal*)

CULTURAL NOTE ***The Mill on the Floss***, a novel (1860) by British writer George Eliot. Set in eastern England in the early 19th century, it describes the intellectual and emotional development of Maggie Tulliver, the daughter of a miller. By contrasting Maggie's independent spirit with the dreary conservatism of most of her family and acquaintances, Eliot highlights the obstacles faced by women in English society at the time.

mill about, mill around *vi* to wander about aimlessly, restlessly, or in confusion

mill[2] /mil/ *n* a monetary unit equal to one thousandth of a US dollar, used in accounts and calculations but not in everyday currency [Late 18C. Shortening of Latin *millesimum* "thousandth" (see MIL[1]), after CENT]

Mill /mil/, **James** (1773–1836) British philosopher and economist. Father of John Stuart Mill and an associate of Jeremy Bentham, he was one of the founders of utilitarianism.

Mill, John Stuart (1806–73) British philosopher and economist. The son of James Mill, he was one of the leading intellectuals of his day and a major proponent of utilitarianism. His most important works include *A System of Logic* (1843) and the essay *On Liberty* (1859).

> "If all mankind minus one were of one opinion, and only one person were of the contrary opinion, mankind would be no more justified in silencing that one person, than he, if he had the power, would be justified in silencing mankind."
> [John Stuart Mill, *On Liberty*; 1859]

mill·age /míllij/ *n* a property tax rate stated in terms of tenths of cents in tax per dollar of property value

Mil·lais /mí ay, mi láy/, **Sir John Everett** (1829–96) British painter. A leading member of the Pre-Raphaelite movement, he painted many historical scenes and worked as a portraitist.

Mil·land /mi lánd/, **Ray** (1905?–86) British-born US actor. He won an Academy Award as the alcoholic writer in *The Lost Weekend* (1945). Born **Tuscott-Jones, Reginald Alfred**

Mil·lay /mi láy/, **Edna St. Vincent** (1892–1950) US poet and playwright. She is noted for her lyrical poetry of the 1920s and the satirical play *Aria da Capo* (1919).

> "My candle burns at both ends; / It will not last the night; / But ah, my foes, and oh, my friends—/ It gives a lovely light!"
> [Edna St. Vincent Millay, "First Fig," *A Few Figs from Thistles*; 1920]

mill·board /míl bàwrd/ *n* thick paperboard used in binding books [Early 18C. Alteration of *milled board*]

mill·dam /míl dàm/ *n* a dam built near a mill in order to raise the water level of a stream so that the flow is strong enough to turn a mill wheel

Mille ♦ **De Mille, Agnes**

Mil·ledge·ville /míllij vìl/ city in central Georgia. It is the administrative seat of Baldwin County. Population: 18,762 (2002 estimate).

mille·feuille /meel fŏŏee/ (*plural* **-feuilles**) *n* a dessert or pastry consisting of several layers of puff pastry with a filling of cream and fruit preserves, topped with confectioners' sugar or frosting [Late 19C. < French, literally "a thousand leaves"]

mil·le·fi·o·ri /millə fee áwree/ *n* decorative glassware made by cutting and arranging cross sections of fused glass rods of varied color and thickness [Mid-19C. < Italian, literally "a thousand flowers"]

mille·fleurs /meel flúr, -flŏŏr, -flŏŏr/ *adj* covered with a design of small flowers or plants [Early 20C. < French, literally "a thousand flowers"]

mil·le·nar·i·an /mìllə nérree ən/ *adj* **1.** CHR **RELATING TO JESUS CHRIST'S SECOND COMING** relating to or believing in doctrines such as Jesus Christ's Second Coming, a final conflict between good and evil, or the end of the world, especially those based on the book of Revelation **2. RELATING TO FUTURE UTOPIA** relating to or believing in the coming of some future utopian age **3. RELATING TO END OF WORLD** relating to or suggesting the end of the world **4. RELATING TO 1,000** relating to units of 1,000, especially 1,000 years [Mid-17C. < Latin *millenarius* < *mille* "thousand"] —**mil·le·nar·i·an** *n*

mil·le·nar·i·an·ism /mìllə nérree ə nìzzəm/ *n* **1. BELIEF IN JESUS CHRIST'S SECOND COMING** a belief in doctrines such as Jesus Christ's Second Coming, a final conflict between good and evil, or the end of the world, especially those based on the book of Revelation **2. BELIEF IN COMING UTOPIA** a belief in the coming of a future utopian age, especially one created through revolution **3. BELIEF IN END OF WORLD** a belief that the end of the world is near

mil·le·nar·y /míllə nèrree/ *adj* CHR, CALENDAR same as **millenarian** ■ *n* (*plural* **-ies**) CALENDAR same as **millennium** (sense 1) [Mid-16C. < Latin *millenarius* (see MILLENARIAN)] —**mil·le·nar·ism** /míllənə rìzzəm/ *n*

mill end *n* either end of a roll of fabric or carpet that is finished instead of being cut

~~**millenium**~~ incorrect spelling of **millennium**

mil·len·ni·al /mi lénnee əl/ *adj* relating to a millennium ■ *n* a member of the generation of children who were born between the years 1977 and 1994

mil·len·ni·um /mi lénnee əm/ (*plural* **-ni·ums** or **-ni·a** /-nee ə/) *n* **1. 1,000 YEARS** a period of 1,000 years, especially a period that begins or ends in a year that is a multiple of 1,000 **2. PROPHESIED RULE BY JESUS CHRIST** the thousand-year period of peace that, according to one interpretation of prophecies in the book of Revelation, will follow the Second Coming of Jesus Christ **3. HOPED-FOR UTOPIAN AGE** an imagined future utopian age of joy, peace, and justice, especially one created through revolution **4. THOUSANDTH ANNIVERSARY** a thousand-year anniversary, especially the one in the year 2000 [Mid-17C. < modern Latin < Latin *mille* "thousand" + *annus* "year" (see ANNUAL)] —**mil·len·ni·al·ism** *n* —**mil·len·ni·al·ist** *n*

mil·len·ni·um bug *n* the problem posed by the year 2000 for computer software that coded dates by using only the last two digits of each year (*informal*)

Mil·len·ni·um Dome *n* a large dome-shaped structure by the Thames River in Greenwich, London, England, built to celebrate the year 2000

mil·le·pede *n* INSECTS another spelling of **millipede**

mil·le·pore /míllə pàwr/ *n* a coral that forms white or yellow reefs [Mid-18C. < modern Latin *Millepora* < Latin *mille* "thousand" + *porus* "pore" (see PORE[1])]

mill·er /míllər/ *n* **1. MILL OPERATOR** somebody who owns, manages, or operates a mill **2. MILLING MACHINE** a machine that mills materials **3. MOTH WITH POWDERY WINGS** a moth whose wings have a powdery appearance

AKG London

Arthur Miller

Mil·ler /míllər/, **Arthur** (*b.* 1915) US playwright. He won a Pulitzer Prize for his tragedy *Death of a Salesman* (1949). His play *The Crucible* (1953) was a veiled critique of the House Un-American Activities Committee of the McCarthy era. His second wife was the movie actor Marilyn Monroe. See Cultural note at **crucible, salesman**

> "For a salesman, there is no rock bottom to the life. He don't put a bolt to a nut, he don't tell you the law or give you medicine. He's a man way out there in the blue, riding on a smile and a shoeshine."
> [Arthur Miller, "Requiem," *Death of a Salesman*; 1949]

> "The structure of a play is always the story of how the birds come home to roost."
> [Arthur Miller, "Shadows of the Gods," *Harper's Magazine*; August 1958]

Mil·ler, Glenn (1904–44) US bandleader and composer. Leader of a big-band orchestra of the late 1930s and early 1940s, he was noted for swing music such as "In the Mood" (1939). Full name **Miller, Alton Glenn**

Henry Miller: photographed in 1932 by Brassaï

Mil·ler, Henry (1891–1980) US writer. His novels *Tropic of Cancer* (1934) and *Tropic of Capricorn* (1939) are sexually explicit and were banned in the United States. Full name **Miller, Henry Valentine**. See Cultural note at **tropic**[1]

> "The wallpaper with which the men of science have covered the world of reality is falling to tatters."
> [Henry Miller, *Tropic of Cancer*; 1934]

Mil·ler, Leszek (*b.* 1946) prime minister of Poland (2001–). A former textile worker and labor leader, he was elected chairman of the the Democratic Left Alliance (SLD) party when it was formed (1999).

mil·ler·ite /míllə rìt/ *n* a nickel sulfide mineral that forms long wiry crystals. Use: source of nickel. [Mid-19C. After W. H. *Miller* (1801–80), British mineralogist]

mill·er's thumb *n* a small flat spiny freshwater fish. Native to: Europe, North America. Genus: *Cottus*. [< the shape of its body, alluding to the proverbial distrust of millers' methods of measurement]

mil·les·i·mal /mə léssim'l/ *adj* **1. OF THOUSANDTHS** relating to thousandths **2. DIVIDED BY THOUSAND** divided by one thousand ■ *n* **THOUSANDTH PART** a thousandth part of something [Early 18C. < Latin *millesimus* "thousandth" < *mille* "thousand"] —**mil·les·i·mal·ly** *adv*

mil·let /míllit/ *n* **1. GRAIN** the pale shiny grain of a cereal plant. Use: flour, alcoholic drinks, birdseed, fodder. **2. CEREAL PLANT** a fast-growing cereal plant. Use: grain, fodder. Native to: warm regions. Latin name: *Panicum miliaceum*. **3. GRASS PLANT** a grass that is similar or related to millet, e.g., pearl millet. Use: grain. [15C. < Old French < Latin *milium*]

Mil·let /mi láy/, **Jean-François** (1814–75) French painter. Strong draftsmanship and mellow colors characterize his realistic scenes of rural life.

mill fin·ish *n* a particularly smooth surface on paper, made by a machine

milli- *prefix* one thousandth (10^{-3}) ○ *milligram* ○ *millisecond* Symbol **m** [< Latin < *mille* "thousand"]

mil·li·am·pere /mìllee ám peer/ *n* a unit of electric current equal to one thousandth of an ampere

mil·li·ar·y /míllee èrree/ *adj* indicating or marking a distance of one Roman mile, measured as one thousand paces [Mid-17C. < Latin *milliarius* < *mille* "thousand"]

mil·li·bar /míllə baar/ *n* a unit of atmospheric pressure equal to one thousandth of a bar

mil·li·cur·ie /mìlli kyooree/ *n* a unit of radioactivity equal to one thousandth of a curie

mil·lieme /mil yém/ *n* **1.** a former minor unit of currency in Egypt and Sudan equal to one thousandth of a pound **2.** MONEY same as **millime** [Early 20C. < French *millième* (see MILLIME)]

mil·li·far·ad /mílli fàrrad, -fàr ad/ *n* a unit of electrical capacitance equal to one thousandth of a farad

mil·li·gram /mílli gràm/ *n* a unit of mass and weight equal to one thousandth of a gram

mil·li·hen·ry /míllə hènnree/ (*plural* **-ries**) *n* a unit of electrical inductance equal to one thousandth of a henry

Mil·li·kan /míllikən/, **Robert A.** (1868–1953) US physicist. He measured the charge on the electron and coined the term "cosmic rays." He received a Nobel Prize in physics (1923). Full name **Millikan, Robert Andrews**

mil·li·lam·bert /míllə làmbərt/ *n* a unit of luminance equal to one thousandth of a lambert

mil·li·li·ter /míllə leetər/ *n* a unit of volume equal to one thousandth of a liter

mil·li·li·tre *n* MEASURE Can, UK spelling of **milliliter**

mil·lime /míllim, mí leem/ *n* a subunit of Tunisian currency. See table at **currency** [Mid-20C. Via French *millième* "thousandth" < Latin *millesimus* < *mille* "thousand"]

mil·li·me·ter /míllə meetər/ *n* a unit of length equal to one thousandth of a meter

mil·li·me·tre *n* MEASURE Can, UK spelling of **millimeter**

mil·li·met·ri·cal /míllə méttrik'l/ *adj* progressing or moving extremely slowly by degrees

mil·li·mole /míllə mōl/ *n* a unit used to measure the amount of a chemical substance, equal to one thousandth of a mole

mil·line /mí lìn, mi lín/ *n* **1.** a unit of advertising copy equal to one column line in agate type in one million copies of a newspaper or magazine **2.** COMM same as **milline rate** [Late 20C. Blend of MILLION + LINE[1]]

mil·li·ner /míllənər/ *n* somebody who designs, makes, or sells women's hats [Mid-16C. Alteration of earlier *Milaner* "importer of fancy fabrics and wares from Milan, Italy"]

mil·line rate *n* the cost per unit of advertising copy

mil·li·ner·y /míllə nèrree/ *n* **1.** hats and other accessories for women, sold by a milliner **2.** the design, manufacture, or sale of women's hats

mill·ing /mílling/ *n* the ridged edge of a coin

mill·ing cut·ter *n* a rotary tool used for cutting, shaping, or finishing metal objects

mill·ing ma·chine *n* a machine fitted with milling cutters to cut, shape, or finish metal objects

Mill·ing·ton /míllingtən/ city in New Jersey, in Marin County, on the Passaic River

mil·lion /míllyən/ *n* **1. THOUSAND THOUSAND** a thousand thousand (10^6) **2. LARGE NUMBER** an unspecified very large number of people or things (*informal*; *often used in the plural*) **3. MILLION UNITS OF CURRENCY** a million units of a currency, especially dollars or pounds **4. SEVENTH DIGIT TO LEFT OF DECIMAL** the seventh digit to the left of the decimal point in the decimal number system ○ *In the number 7,654,321, the 7 is in the millions place.* [14C. Via French < obsolete Italian *millione* "great thousand" < Latin *mille* "thousand"] —**mil·lion** *adj*

mil·lion·aire /mìllyə nér, míllyə nèr/ *n* somebody whose net worth or income is more than one million dollars, pounds, or another unit of currency (*often used before a noun*) [Early 19C. < French < *million* (see MILLION)]

mil·lion·air·ess /míllyə nérrəss/ *n* a woman whose net worth or income is more than one million dollars, pounds, or another unit of currency (*dated*)

~~millionnaire~~ incorrect spelling of **millionaire**

mil·lionth /míllyənth/ *n* one of a million equal parts of something —**mil·lionth** *adj*

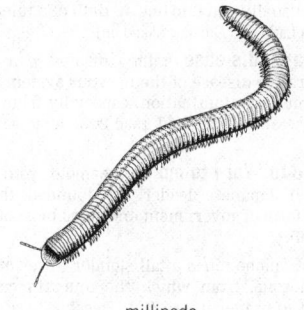

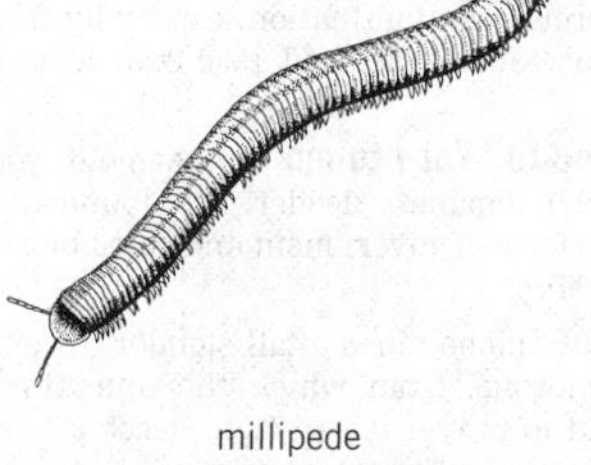
millipede

mil·li·pede /míllə peed/, **mil·le·pede** *n* a small plant-eating arthropod with a tubular body made up of segments, most of which have two pairs of legs. Class: Diplopoda. [Early 17C. < Latin *millipeda* "wood louse," literally "with a thousand feet" < *ped-* "foot"]

mil·li·sec·ond /míllə sèkənd/ *n* a unit of time equal to one thousandth of a second

mil·li·volt /míllə vòlt/ *n* a unit of electrical voltage or potential difference equal to one thousandth of a volt. Symbol **mV**

mil·li·watt /míllə wòt/ *n* a unit of electrical power equal to one thousandth of a watt. Symbol **mW**

mill·pond /míl pònd/ *n* a pond created by damming a stream in order to create a flow of water to turn a mill wheel

mill·race /míll ràyss/ *n* **1.** the stream of water that flows through a mill wheel, making it turn **2.** a channel that directs water to and from a mill wheel

mill·run /míll rùn/ *n* **1.** INDUST same as **millrace** **2. SAWMILL OUTPUT** the output of a sawmill **3. TEST OF MINERAL** a test to determine the quality of a mineral or the mineral content of an ore **4. MINERAL FROM TEST** the quantity or quality of a mineral yielded by a millrun test

mill·stone /míl stōn/ *n* **1.** either of two large circular stones used to grind grain in a mill **2.** a great burden or responsibility

mill·stream /míl streem/ *n* **1.** a stream whose water is used to turn a mill wheel **2.** INDUST same as **millrace** (sense 1)

Mill Val·ley /mìl-/ city in Marin County, California. Population: 13,557 (2002 estimate).

mill wheel *n* a wheel that powers a mill, usually turned by a flow of water

mill·work /míl wùrk/ *n* items of woodwork, e.g., doors, banisters, and moldings, made in a lumber mill

mill·wright /míl rìt/ *n* somebody who designs, builds, or maintains mills or mill machinery

Milne /miln/, **A. A.** (1882–1956) British writer. He created the character Winnie the Pooh to amuse his son Christopher Robin, and wrote four much-loved collections of children's poems and stories, including *Now We Are Six* (1927) and *The House at Pooh Corner* (1928). Full name **Milne, Alan Alexander**

> "They're changing the guard at Buckingham Palace. / Christopher Robin went down with Alice. / Alice is marrying one of the guard. / 'A soldier's life is terrible hard,' / Says Alice."
> [A. A. Milne, "Buckingham Palace," *When We Were Very Young*; 1924]

mi·lo /mílō/ *n* a type of sorghum cultivated for its grain, known for growing early and resisting drought [Late 19C. Origin ?]

REGIONAL NOTE ***Milo*** is common in the Plains states from Iowa to Texas, with scattered instances of usage to the east and west.

mi·lord /mi láwrd/ *n* **1.** a British gentleman or member of the aristocracy **2.** a form of address for a gentleman or member of the British aristocracy [Late 16C. Via French < English *my lord*]

Mí·los ♦ **Melos**

Mi·lo·se·vic /mi lóssə vìch/, **Mi·lo·še·vić, Slobodan** (*b.* 1941) Yugoslavian national leader. He served as president of Serbia (1989–97) and the Federal Republic of Yugoslavia (1997–2000). He was extradited in 2001 to stand before the International Criminal Tribunal in The Hague for war crimes in the Former Yugoslavia in the 1990s.

Mi·łosz /mee losh, mee wosh/, **Czeslaw** (*b.* 1911) Lithuanian-born US writer. He defected from Communist Poland to the West in 1951 and wrote poetry, fiction, translations, and essays, often on the relationship between culture, morality, and politics. He won the Nobel Prize in literature (1980).

mil·pa /mílpa/ (*plural* **-pas**) *n Hispanic* an agricultural field that is made by clearing forest and then farmed for only a few seasons before being abandoned, especially in Central America and Mexico [Mid-19C. Via Mexican Spanish < Nahuatl]

milque·toast /mílk tōst/, **Milque·toast** *n* somebody regarded as timid or submissive, especially a man (*dated insult*) [Mid-20C. < Caspar *Milquetoast*, cartoon character created by Harold Tucker Webster (1885–1952)]

mil·reis /mill ráyss/ (*plural* **-reis** /mill ráyz/) *n* a former Portuguese or Brazilian unit of currency and coin equal to one thousand reis [Late 16C. < Portuguese < *mil* "thousand" + *real* "real" (a unit of currency)]

Mil·stein /míl stīn, -steen/, **César** (1927–2002) Argentine-born British immunologist. He developed monoclonal antibody technology for which he shared a Nobel Prize in physiology or medicine (1984).

Mil·stein /míl stīn/, **Nathan** (1903–92) Russian-born US violinist. He studied at the St. Petersburg Conservatory and lived in the United States from 1929.

milt /milt/ *n* the semen and seminal fluid of a fish [Old English *milte* "spleen"]

milt·er /míltər/ *n* a fertile male fish during the mating season

Mil·ton /míltən/ town in eastern Massachusetts, a southern suburb of Boston. Population: 26,010 (2002 estimate).

Mil·ton, John (1608–74) English poet. His poems are considered to be among the greatest in English literature, and include the epic narrative of Adam and Eve's banishment from Paradise, *Paradise Lost* (1667). During the English Civil Wars, he wrote powerful polemics that championed religious and civil liberty. See Cultural note at **paradise** —**Mil·to·ni·an** /mil tōnee ən/ *adj* —**Mil·ton·ic** /mil tónnik/ *adj*

> "A dungeon horrible, on all sides round / As one great furnace flamed, yet from those flames / No light, but rather darkness visible / Served only to discover sights of woe, / Regions of sorrow, doleful shades, where peace / And rest can never dwell, hope never comes / That comes to all."
> [John Milton, *Paradise Lost*; 1667]

> "Who kills a man kills a reasonable creature, God's image; but he who destroys a good book, kills reason itself, kills the image of God, as it were in the eye."
> [John Milton, *Areopagitica*; 1644]

Mil·ton Keynes /-keénz/ city in Buckinghamshire, southern England. Population: 207,063 (2002).

Mil·wau·kee /mil wáwkee/ largest city in Wisconsin, located in the southeastern corner of the state. Population: 590,895 (2002 estimate). —**Mil·wau·kee·an** *adj, n*

Mi·mas /mímass, meéməss/ *n* a large natural satellite of Saturn

mim·bar *n* ISLAM same as **minbar**

Mim·bres /mímbrəss/ *n* the last period of the Native North American Mogollon culture, between the 9th and the 13th centuries, noted for its distinctive black-and-white pottery (*often used before a noun*) [< Spanish, "willows, withies" < Latin *vimen* "withy, wicker" (from the painted designs on pottery of the period)]

mime /mīm/ *n* **1. ACTING USING ONLY GESTURE AND ACTION** a style of performance in which people act out situations or portray characters using only gesture, facial expression, and action (*often used before a noun*) **2.** *also* **mime art·ist PERFORMER WHO USES MIME** a performer who does not speak, but relies solely on gesture, facial expression, and action to communicate with an audience **3. THEATRICAL PERFORMANCE IN MIME** a theatrical piece performed with gesture, facial expression, and action, and without words **4. ANCIENT FARCE** in ancient Greek and Roman theater, a lewd comedy including dialogue, dance, and gesture ■ *v* (**mimed, mim·ing, mimes**) **1.** *vti* **EXPRESS SOMETHING IN MIME** to express something or act it out without words, using only gesture, facial expression, and action **2.** *vt* same as **mimic** *v* (sense 1) [Early 17C. Via Latin *mimus* < Greek *mimos* "imitator, mimic"]

MIME /mīm/ *n* a set of Internet standards for handling multimedia and non-ASCII material. Full form **Multi-purpose Internet Mail Extensions**

mim·e·o·graph /mímmee ə gràf/, **mim·e·o** /mímmee ō/ *n* **1. COPYING MACHINE** a machine that prints copies onto paper from an inked stencil rotated on a cylinder across the pages **2. MIMEOGRAPHED COPY** a copy made on a mimeograph ■ *vt* (**-graphed, -graph·ing, -graphs; -oed, -o·ing, -os**) **MAKE COPY OF SOMETHING WITH MIMEOGRAPH** to make a copy of a document using a mimeograph [Late 19C. Originally a trademark < Greek *mimeisthai* (see MIMESIS) + -GRAPH]

mi·me·sis /mi meéssis, mī-/ *n* **1. ART'S IMITATION OF LIFE** the imitation of life or nature in the techniques and subject matter of art and literature **2.** BIOL same as mimicry (sense 2) **3.** MED **DISEASE SYMPTOMS IN HEALTHY PERSON** the occurrence of the symptoms of a disease in somebody who does not have the disease, often produced psychosomatically **4. RHETORICAL DEVICE** the rhetorical use of what somebody else might have said [Mid-16C. < Greek *mimēsis* < *mimeisthai* "imitate" < *mimos* "mime"]

mi·met·ic /mi méttik, mī-/, **mi·met·i·cal** /-méttik'l, mī méttik'l/ *adj* **1.** relating to or practicing imitation, e.g., in artistic or literary mimesis **2.** relating to mimicry in animals and plants [Mid-17C. < Greek *mimētikos* < *mimēsis* (see MIMESIS)] —**mi·met·i·cal·ly** *adv*

mim·ic /mímmik/ *vt* (**-icked, -ick·ing, -ics**) **1. MOCK SOMEBODY THROUGH IMITATION** to make fun of somebody by imitating him or her in an exaggerated way **2. IMITATE SOMEBODY** to adopt somebody else's voice, gestures, or appearance, in a deliberate and exaggerated way, especially to amuse people **3. COPY SOMETHING** to resemble something in a way that seems like a deliberate copy ○ *houses with facades that mimic the colonial style* **4.** BIOL **RESEMBLE OTHER SPECIES** to take on the appearance of another plant or animal, e.g., to discourage predators ■ *n* **IMITATOR** somebody who imitates others, especially for comic effect ■ *adj* **1. RELATING TO MIMICRY** relating to mime, mimicry, or imitation **2. SIMULATED** simulated or pretend (*literary*) **3. RESEMBLING SOMETHING** imitating or resembling something (*literary*) [Late 16C. Via Latin *mimicus* < Greek *mimikos* < *mimos* "imitator, mimic"] —**mim·ick·er** *n*

SYNONYMS See *imitate.*

mim·ic·ry /mímmikree/ *n* **1. ART OF IMITATION** the imitating of other people's voices, gestures, or appearance, often for comic effect **2.** BIOL **SIMILARITY OF APPEARANCE IN NATURE** the resemblance of a plant or animal to another species or to a feature of its natural surroundings, developed as protection from predators **3.** BIRDS **BIRD CALL IMITATION** the ability of some birds to imitate the songs of other species and use them in their own repertoire

Mi·mir /meé meér/ *n* in Norse mythology, the god of wisdom, a giant water demon who was said to reside at and drink from the well of wisdom at Yggdrasil

mi·mo·sa /mi mṓssə, -mṓzə/ *n* **1.** a tree or bush whose leaves are sensitive to touch. Flowers: white, yellow, or pink, in globular clusters. Native to: warm regions. Genus: *Mimosa.* **2.** TREES same as **silk tree 3.** a cocktail of champagne and orange juice [Mid-18C. < modern Latin < Latin *mimus* "imitator" (see MIME), because its leaves seem to flinch when touched, mimicking a recoiling animal]

mim·u·lus /mímmyələss/ (*plural same*) *n Can, UK* PLANTS a small wild or cultivated flowering plant. Flowers: shades of yellow and red, with two lips. Genus: *Mimulus.* Same as **monkey flower** [Mid-18C. < modern Latin, "little mime" < Latin *mimus* (see MIME)]

min. *abbr* **1.** SCI mineralogical **2.** SCI mineralogy **3.** MEASURE minim **4.** minimum **5.** CHR, INTERNAT REL, GOV minister **6.** EDUC minor **7.** TIME minute[1]

mi·na /mínə/ (*plural* **-nae** /mī neé/ or **-nas**) *n* a unit of weight and money used in ancient Greece and Asia Minor, usually equal to one sixtieth of a talent [Late 16C. Via Latin and Greek < Akkadian]

Min·a·ma·ta dis·ease /mìnnə maátə-/ *n* a severe degenerative disease of the nervous system caused by mercury contamination, especially from eating mercury-tainted seafood [Mid-20C. After a town in Japan]

Min·a·mo·to Yor·i·to·mo /mìnnəmṓtō yòrri tṓmō/ (1147–99) Japanese leader. He founded the shogunate form of government and ruled most of Japan (1192–99).

min·a·ret /mìnnə rét/ *n* a tall slender tower attached to a mosque, from which the muezzin calls the faithful to prayer [Late 17C. < French < Turkish *minâri* < Arabic *manāra* "lighthouse, minaret"]

Mi·nas Ba·sin /mī́nəss-/ tidal inlet on the coast of Nova Scotia, southeastern Canada. Length: 50 mi./80 km.

Mi·nas Ge·rais /meénəss zhə ríss/ inland state in eastern Brazil. Much of its terrain is mountainous. Capital: Belo Horizonte. Population: 16,672,613 (1996). Area: 227,176 sq. mi./588,383 sq. km.

minaret

min·a·to·ry /mínnə tàwree/, **min·a·to·ri·al** /mìnnə táwree əl/ *adj* menacing or threatening (*formal*) [Mid-16C. < late Latin *minatorius* < Latin *minari* "threaten" (see MENACE)] —**min·a·to·ri·al·ly** *adv* —**min·a·to·ri·ly** *adv*

min·bar /mín baar/, **mim·bar** /mím-/ *n* a pulpit in a mosque from which the sermon is delivered. It takes the form of a domed box with a door at the top of a staircase. [Mid-19C. < Arabic < *nabara* "raise"]

mince /minss/ (**minced, minc·ing, minc·es**) *v* **1.** *vt* **SHRED FOOD** to cut meat or vegetables into very small pieces **2.** *vt* **DIVIDE SOMETHING UP** to divide land or property into very small portions, especially in a way regarded as detrimental **3.** *vti* **WALK DAINTILY** to walk with small light steps in an affectedly dainty way **4.** *vti* **SPEAK DAINTILY** to speak, or say something, in an affectedly dainty way **5.** *vt* **USE TACT** to use words or deal with matters delicately in order not to offend or upset somebody (*in negatives*) ○ *She did not mince her words.* [14C. < Old French *mincier* < *minutus* (see MINUTE[1])] —**minc·er** *n*

mince·meat /mínss meet/ *n* **1.** a mixture of spiced and finely chopped fruits such as apples and raisins, usually cooked in pies **2.** finely ground meat [Mid-17C. Alteration of *minced meat*] ◇ **make mincemeat of somebody** *or* **something** to defeat somebody or something thoroughly (*informal*)

mince pie *n* an individual pie filled with mincemeat and served hot or cold

Minch /minch/, **Minch·es** /mínchəz/ sea channel in northwestern Scotland, separating the Outer Hebrides from the Inner Hebrides and the mainland. It is divided into the North Minch and the Little Minch.

Min·cha /mínkhə, min khaá/, **Min·chah** *n* a daily Jewish prayer said in the afternoon [Early 19C. < Hebrew *minḥāh* "offering"]

Minch·es ▶ **Minch**

Min·cho /mìn chṓ, mínchō/ (1352–1431) Japanese artist and Buddhist priest. He was noted for his Buddhist icons and ink paintings. Full name **Kichizan Mincho**

minc·ing /mínssing/ *adj* affectedly dainty —**minc·ing·ly** *adv*

mind /mīnd/ *n* **1. SEAT OF THOUGHT AND MEMORY** the center of consciousness that generates thoughts, feelings, ideas, and perceptions, and stores knowledge and memories **2. THINKING CAPACITY** the capacity to think, understand, and reason ○ *has a logical mind* **3. CONCENTRATION** concentration, or the ability to concentrate ○ *My mind was wandering.* **4. WAY OF THINKING** an opinion or personal way of thinking about something ○ *I've changed my mind about going with you.* ○ *Have you made up your mind about the job offer yet?* **5. STATE OF THOUGHT OR FEELING** the state of thought or feeling that is regarded as usual or desirable ○ *felt I was going out of my mind* **6. DESIRE** the desire or intention to act or behave in a particular way ○ *After such insults, I had a mind to leave right then.* **7. INTELLECTUAL PERSON** somebody considered in terms of his or her intellect or intelligence ○ *Einstein was one of the greatest minds of the modern era.* **8. THINKING CHARACTERISTIC OF PARTICULAR GROUP** a pattern of thinking or feeling characteristic of a particular group ○ *Who knows what goes through the criminal mind?* **9.** PHILOSOPHY **NONMATERIAL THINGS** in the philosophy of Descartes, all things that are not matter ■ *v* (**mind·ed, mind·ing, minds**) **1.** *vt* **PAY ATTENTION TO SOMETHING** to pay attention to something, especially so as to avoid danger or an accident ○ *Mind your step!* **2.** *vt* **CONTROL SOMETHING** to remain aware of the need to control something ○ *Mind your temper.* **3.** *vti* OBJECT TO SOMEBODY OR SOMETHING to have an objection to somebody or something ○ *Do you mind if we leave early?* **4.** *vt* TEMPORARILY WATCH OVER SOMEBODY OR SOMETHING to watch over and look after somebody or something, usually for a short time ○ *Will you mind the dog over the weekend?* **5.** *vt* OBEY SOMEBODY to listen to and obey somebody ○ *Be sure to mind your father while I'm away.* **6.** *vt* REMEMBER SOMETHING to remember or recall something ○ *Mind what I told you.* **7.** *vi* BE CAREFUL be careful or cautious ○ *If you don't mind, you'll run into bears in the forest.* **8.** *vt regional* TAKE NOTE OF SOMETHING to notice or perceive something ○ *Mind the new detour signs or you'll get lost.* **9.** *vt US regional, Scotland* REMIND SOMEBODY to remind somebody of or about something [Old English *gemynd* < Indo-European "think"] —**mind·er** *n* ◇ **bring something to mind** to remind somebody of something ○ *It brings to mind those horse-drawn carts they used to have.* ◇ **call something to mind** to remember something ○ *I can't quite call to mind the exact date they left.* ◇ **do you mind?** used to show that you object to something that somebody is doing ◇ **great minds think alike** used when two people coincidentally have the same idea ◇ **have it in mind to do something** to intend to do something ◇ **have somebody** *or* **something in mind** to be thinking of somebody or something as suitable for a specific purpose or role ◇ **keep something in mind** to remember something because it might be useful later ◇ **mind over matter** the act of making a mental effort to ignore, overcome, or control something physical ○ *They can lie on a bed of nails without feeling any pain – it's mind over matter.* ◇ **mind you** used to qualify something you have just said (*informal*) ◇ **speak your mind** to speak frankly and forthrightly

mind-al·ter·ing *adj* changing perceptions, moods, or thought patterns ○ *mild-altering drugs*

Min·da·na·o /mìndə naá ō, -nów/ island in the southern Philippines, the largest after Luzon. Population: 14,536,000 (1990). Area: 36,540 sq. mi./94,630 sq. km.

mind-bend·ing *adj* (*informal*) **1.** PSYCHOL, DRUGS same as **mind-altering 2.** very complicated or difficult for the mind to deal with —**mind-bend·er** *n* —**mind-bend·ing·ly** *adv*

mind-blow·ing *adj* (*informal*) **1.** extremely exciting, surprising, or shocking **2.** PSYCHOL, DRUGS same as **mind-altering** —**mind-blow·er** *n* —**mind-blow·ing·ly** *adv*

mind-bod·y prob·lem *n* the philosophical question of whether the mind is part of the body or separate from it, first formulated as a problem by the French philosopher René Descartes

mind-bog·gling *adj* mentally overwhelming, e.g., because of great size or complexity (*informal*) —**mind-bog·gling·ly** *adv*

mind can·dy *n* something that is entertaining but not intellectually demanding (*slang*)

mind·ed /mīndəd/ *adj* inclined to do a particular thing or act in a particular way

mind-ex·pand·ing *adj* **1.** describes drugs that heighten or intensify perceptions or moods **2.** expanding knowledge and awareness

mind·ful /mīndfəl/ *adj* actively attentive, or deliberately keeping something in mind ○ *was mindful of the difficulties that lay ahead* —**mind·ful·ly** *adv* —**mind·ful·ness** *n*

SYNONYMS See ***aware***.

mind·ful·ness train·ing *n* a program designed to reduce the psychological and physical effects of stress that involves meditation, yoga, and other relaxation methods

mind game *n* a psychologically manipulative and deceptive practice intended to deceive or confuse somebody (*informal; often used in the plural*)

mind·less /mīndləss/ *adj* **1.** BORING uninteresting as a result of requiring little mental effort **2.** PURPOSELESS having no apparent purpose or rational cause **3.** UNCONCERNED not careful or concerned —**mind·less·ly** *adv* —**mind·less·ness** *n*

mind-numb·ing *adj* inspiring no interest or thought, especially because of dullness or repetitiveness —**mind-numb·ing·ly** *adv*

Min·do·ro /min dáwrō/ island in the western Philippines, south of Luzon. Population: 282,593. Area: 3,760 sq. mi./9,738 sq. km.

mind read·er *n* somebody who claims or seems to be able to sense what others think without being told —**mind read·ing** *n*

mind·scape /mīnd skàyp/ *n* **1.** a mental scene constructed from memory or imagination **2.** an artistic representation of a mental scene constructed from memory or imagination [After LANDSCAPE]

mind·set /mīnd sèt/ *n* a set of beliefs or a way of thinking that determine somebody's behavior and outlook

mind's eye *n* the mind as a place where visual images are conjured up from memory or imagination ○ *I can see in my mind's eye how the house will look after the renovations.*

mine[1] /mīn/ *n* **1.** HOLE IN GROUND FOR EXTRACTING MINERALS an excavated area from which minerals, often in the form of ore, are extracted **2.** MINERAL-EXCAVATING BUSINESS the industrial and commercial buildings, machinery, and personnel used to work a mine **3.** MINERAL DEPOSIT an area underground or at ground level where there is a deposit of ore, minerals, or precious stones **4.** SOURCE a rich source of something, especially information ○ *a mine of information* **5.** HIDDEN EXPLOSIVE an explosive device concealed underground or underwater that detonates on contact with a person, vehicle, or ship **6.** MIL TUNNEL UNDER ENEMY TERRITORY a tunnel dug under enemy territory in order to gain entry, undermine fortifications, or lay explosives **7.** ZOOL INSECT BURROW a tunnel made by a burrowing insect or larva, especially in a plant leaf ■ *v* (**mined, min·ing, mines**) **1.** *vti* REMOVE MINERALS to extract minerals from the ground **2.** *vt* LAY MINES IN GROUND OR WATER to place explosive mines throughout an area of ground or water **3.** *vt* CONSTRUCT TUNNEL to dig a tunnel underground **4.** *vt* MAKE USE OF RESOURCE to make use of a particular resource ○ *Generations of scholars mined these archives.* [14C. Directly or via Old French < assumed Vulgar Latin *mina*] —**min·a·ble** *adj*

mine[2] /mīn/ *pron* refers to something that belongs to or relates to the speaker or writer ○ *He put on his coat, and told me to put mine on too.* ○ *She was a friend of mine.* ■ *adj* belonging to or relating to me (*archaic; used before a vowel*) ○ *By mine eyes and by mine ears I swear.* [Old English *min* < Indo-European, "me"]

mine de·tec·tor *n* an instrument used for finding explosive mines hidden under the ground or in water

mine·field /mīn feéld/ *n* **1.** an area of land or sea in which explosive mines have been placed **2.** a situation in which great care is needed to avoid the many hazards that exist in it

mine·lay·er /mīn làyər/ *n* a ship fitted with equipment for laying explosive mines under water

Min·e·o·la /minnee ólə/ village in New York, predominantly incorporated by the town of North Hempstead, in Nassau County. Population: 19,283 (2002 estimate).

min·er /mīnər/ *n* **1.** MINEWORKER somebody who works in a mine digging for minerals, especially coal **2.** MINERAL-EXTRACTING MACHINE a machine that extracts minerals, especially coal, from the ground **3.** SOMEBODY LAYING EXPLOSIVE MINES somebody whose job is to lay explosive mines underground or underwater **4.** INSECTS same as **leaf miner**

SPELLCHECK miner or **minor**? Do not confuse the spelling of ***miner*** and ***minor***, which sound similar. A ***miner*** works in a mine; a ***minor*** is somebody below the legal age of adulthood. The word ***minor*** has various other meanings and uses, principally as an adjective referring to something small or insignificant (as in *minor changes, a minor problem*) or describing a type of musical scale, key, or interval.

min·er·al /mínnərəl/ *n* **1.** INORGANIC SUBSTANCE IN NATURE a substance that occurs naturally in rocks and in the ground and has its own characteristic appearance and chemical composition **2.** MINED SUBSTANCE a naturally occurring substance that is mined or extracted from the ground **3.** MATTER NOT ANIMAL OR VEGETABLE something that is not made of animal or vegetable matter (*not in technical use*) **4.** INORGANIC NUTRITIVE SUBSTANCE an inorganic substance that must be ingested by animals or plants in order to remain healthy [15C. < medieval Latin *minerale* < Old French *miniere* "mine" < *mine* (see MINE[1])] —**min·er·al** *adj*

min·er·al·ize /mínnərə līz/ (**-ized, -iz·ing, -iz·es**) *v* **1.** *vt* to impregnate something such as water or organic matter with minerals **2.** *vti* to transform organic matter into a mineral, as happens in petrifaction, or to be transformed in this way —**min·er·al·iz·a·ble** *adj* —**min·er·al·i·za·tion** /mìnnərəli záysh'n/ *n*

min·er·al·o·cor·ti·coid /mìnnərəlō káwrti kòyd/ *n* a hormone (**corticosteroid**) such as aldosterone that controls electrolyte and fluid balance in the body and is secreted by the adrenal cortex [Mid-20C. < MINERAL + CORTICOSTEROID]

min·er·al·o·gy /mìnnə róllәjee/ (*plural* **-gies**) *n* **1.** the scientific study of minerals and how to classify, distinguish, and locate them **2.** a profile of an area's mineral deposits —**min·er·a·log·i·cal** /mìnnərə lójjik'l/ *adj* —**min·er·a·log·i·cal·ly** *adv* —**min·er·al·o·gist** *n*

min·er·al oil *n* **1.** a clear oil distilled from petroleum. Use: laxative, skin softener. **2.** an oil obtained from minerals, especially from petroleum

min·er·al spir·its *n* a liquid distilled from petroleum and used to thin paint and varnish (*takes a singular or plural verb*)

min·er·al spring *n* a spring whose water has a high mineral or gas content

min·er·al tar *n* CHEM same as **maltha**

min·er·al wa·ter *n* a drinkable water with a high mineral salt or gas content, either obtained from a mineral spring or with minerals added. It is usually sold in bottles.

min·er·al wax *n* a wax made from a mineral, especially a hydrocarbon wax (**ozocerite**) found in veins in sandstone

min·er·al wool *n* a lightweight fibrous material made from slag or glass. Use: insulation, packing material, filters.

min·er's let·tuce *n* PLANTS same as **winter purslane** [*Miner's* because it grows commonly in foothills, where gold mines were active]

Mi·ner·va /mi núrvə/ *n* in Roman mythology, the goddess of wisdom and patron of arts, trade, and the art of war, who was born fully armed from the head of Jupiter. Greek equivalent **Athena**

mine·shaft /mīn shàft/ *n* a nearly vertical passageway that provides access or ventilation to an underground mine

min·e·stro·ne /mìnnə strónee/ *n* an Italian vegetable soup [Late 19C. < Italian < Latin *ministrare* "serve" < *minister* "servant"]

mine·sweep·er /mīn sweépər/ *n* a ship fitted with equipment for detecting and clearing underwater explosive mines

mine·work·er /mīn wùrkər/ *n* somebody who works in a mine

Ming /ming/ *n* the Chinese dynasty that ruled from 1364 to 1644, under which arts, trade, and scholarship were greatly developed (*often used before a noun*) [Late 18C. < Chinese, "bright, clear"]

MING *abbr* ONLINE mailing (*used in e-mails or text messages*)

min·gle /míng g'l/ (**-gled, -gling, -gles**) *v* **1.** *vti* to mix together gently or gradually, or mix things together gently or gradually ○ *Heat gently to allow the flavors to mingle.* **2.** *vi* to circulate among a group of people such as guests at a party [15C. Alteration of obsolete *menglen* "keep mixing" < Old English *mengan* "to mix"]

Min·grel /míng grəl/, **Min·grel·i·an** /ming greélee ən/ *n* a Caucasian language closely related to Georgian that is spoken in the mountainous region to the northeast of the Black Sea. Native speakers: 500,000. [Mid-17C < Latin *Mingrelia*, region of the Caucasus] —**Min·grel** *adj* —**Min·gre·li·an** *adj*

ming tree *n* **1.** an evergreen tree used for bonsai, usually in a flat-topped asymmetric arrangement **2.** an artificial bonsai tree [*Ming*, origin ?]

Min·gus /míng gəss/, **Charlie** (1922–79) US double bassist and composer. He played in various jazz bands, establishing the double bass as a principal jazz instrument. Born **Mingus, Charles**

min·gy /mínjee/ (**-gi·er, -gi·est**) *adj* **1.** SMALL IN QUANTITY very small or tiny in quantity or degree ○ *tried to live on a mingy salary* **2. STINGY** ungenerous or stingy (*informal*) ○ *a mingy roommate who wouldn't share living expenses* **3. SHODDY IN QUALITY** creating a negative impression on others because of being shoddy (*informal*) ○*"Finally, they will have to change the mingy, defensive, consultant-driven style of recent campaigns."* (Joe Klein *Newsweek*; May 19, 2003) [Early 20C. Origin ?]

min·i /mínnee/ (*plural* **-is**) *n* something that is small in comparison with other things of its type, especially a minicomputer or a miniskirt (*informal*) [Mid-20C. < MINI-]

mini- *prefix* small, short, miniature ○ *ministroke* [Shortening of MINIATURE]

min·i·a·ture /mínnee ə chər, -ə cho͝or, mínnichər/ *n* **1. SMALLER VERSION** a smaller-than-usual version of something, e.g., a very small model or a smaller version of a particular breed of animal **2. TINY PAINTING** a very small, detailed, and well-finished painting, especially a portrait made to fit inside a locket or other piece of jewelry **3. PAINTING OF MINIATURES** the art of painting miniatures **4. ILLUMINATED MANUSCRIPT ILLUSTRATION** a small picture or decorative initial in an illuminated manuscript ■ *adj* **SMALLER THAN USUAL** smaller in size or scale than others of its type [Late 16C. Via Italian *miniatura* "illumination" < Latin *minium* "red lead"] ◇ **in miniature** on a small scale

ORIGIN Red lead was used in ancient and medieval times for making a sort of red ink with which manuscripts were decorated, and so the medieval Latin verb *miniare* was coined from *minium*, "red lead," meaning "to illuminate a manuscript." Italian took this over and derived *miniatura* "painting, illumination" from it. It referred particularly to the small paintings in manuscripts, and, after English acquired it, it was soon broadened to refer to any "small image." Association with *minute, minimum*, etc. led by the early 18th century to its adjectival use for "small."

min·i·a·ture golf *n* a novelty version of golf played with a putter on a very small course with obstacles such as tunnels and bridges for the ball to avoid or go through

min·i·a·tur·ise *vt* another spelling of **miniaturize**

min·i·a·tur·ist /mínnee ə cho͝orist, -əchərist/ *n* an artist who paints miniatures or small pictures, e.g., in illuminated manuscripts

min·i·a·tur·ize /mínnee əchə rīz, mínnichə rīz/ (**-ized, -iz·ing, -iz·es**) *vt* to make a version of something in a much smaller size or on a greatly reduced scale —**min·i·a·tur·i·za·tion** /mìnnee əchəri záysh'n, mìnnichəri-/ *n*

min·i·bar /mínnee baàr/ *n* a small refrigerator in a hotel room stocked with alcoholic beverages and often also with soft drinks and snacks

mi·ni·blind *n* a Venetian blind with narrow slits

mi·ni·break /mínnee bràyk/ *n* in a tennis match, a point won against the serve in a tie-break (*informal*)

min·i·bus /mínnee bùss/ *n* a small bus for carrying around 10 to 15 passengers, usually on short journeys

min·i·cab /mínnee kàb/ *n UK* an ordinary car used as a taxi, responding to telephone calls but not generally cruising the streets for business

Min·i·cam /mínnee kàm/ *tdmk* a trademark for a portable, shoulder-mounted television camera used in outside broadcasts

min·i·car /mínnee kaàr/ *n* an automobile that is much smaller than average

mi·ni·com·pact /mìnnee kóm pàkt/ *n* a passenger vehicle smaller than a subcompact in size

min·i·com·put·er /mínnee kəm pyo͞otər/ *n* a computer of a size, speed, and capacity intermediate between a standard personal computer and a mainframe

Min·i·con·jou /mìnni kón jo͞o/ (*plural* **-jous** or *same*), **Min·ne·con·jou** *n* a member of a Native North American people who lived in Wyoming, South Dakota, and Nebraska, and who now live mainly in South Dakota

min·i·con·ven·tion /mínnee kən vènshən/ *n* a small-scale convention, especially one that takes place before a larger political convention

min·i·course /mínnee kàwrss/ *n* a short course of study, especially an intensive introductory course lasting less than a semester

min·i·disc /mínnee dìsk/, **Min·i·Disc** *n* a small recordable compact disc housed in a rectangular plastic case. It measures 2 in./5 cm in diameter.

min·i·dress /mínnee drèss/ *n* a dress with a hemline above the knee

Min·ié ball /mínnee-, mínnee ày-/ *n* a bullet with a cone-shaped head and a hollow base that expands when fired, used in muzzle-loading rifles of the 19th century [Mid-19C. After Claude-Étienne *Minié* (1804–79), French army officer]

min·i·fy /mínnə fī/ (**-fied, -fy·ing, -fies**) *vt* to understate or reduce the size or importance of something [Late 17C. Directly or via medieval Latin < Latin *minimus* "least" after MAGNIFY] —**min·i·fi·ca·tion** /mìnnəfi káysh'n/ *n*

min·i·lab /mínnee làb/ *n* a business that does basic photographic developing and printing on site, often within an hour

min·im /mínnəm/ *n* **1.** a unit of fluid measure equal to one sixtieth of a fluid dram, 0.0616 milliliters, or approximately one drop **2.** *UK* MUSIC same as **half note 3.** a downward vertical stroke of the pen in handwriting [15C. Directly or via medieval Latin *minimus* < Latin "least"]

min·i·ma plural of **minimum**

min·i·mal /mínnəm'l/ *adj* **1. VERY SMALL** very small in amount or extent **2. SMALLEST POSSIBLE** smallest possible in amount or least possible in extent **3.** *also* **Min·i·mal RELATING TO MINIMALISM** relating to or displaying attributes associated with minimalism [Mid-17C. < Latin *minimus* "least"] —**min·i·mal·i·ty** /mìnnə mállətee/ *n* —**min·i·mal·ly** *adv*

USAGE Strictly speaking, ***minimal*** means "smallest or least possible," just as *minimize* means "to reduce something to the lowest possible amount or degree." Often, however, these words are used more generally: *a minimal amount of noise* may simply be the least amount of acceptable or possible noise, rather than none at all. If the word is to retain any sense of being a superlative, it should not be used with modifiers such as *rather, somewhat*, and *slightly. Small, limited, reduced*, and *as little as possible* are all suitable alternatives to overextending ***minimal***; and *diminish, lessen*, and *reduce* do the job that *minimize* is sometimes inappropriately asked to do.

min·i·mal art, **Min·i·mal Art** *n* **1.** ARTS same as **minimalism** (sense 1) **2.** minimalist works of art —**min·i·mal art·ist** *n*

min·i·mal·ism /mínnəm'l ìzzəm/ *n* **1.** *also* **Min·i·mal·ism ARTISTIC MOVEMENT** a movement of abstract artists who produce uncluttered paintings and sculptures that make use of basic colors and geometric shapes in impersonal arrangements. The movement originated in New York in the 1960s. **2. SIMPLICITY OF STYLE** simplicity in artwork, design, interior design, or literature, achieved by using a few very simple elements to maximum effect **3. MOVEMENT FOR SIMPLICITY IN MUSIC** a trend in music toward simplicity of rhythm and tone, including sustained or repeated rhythmic and melodic patterns resulting in a hypnotic effect

min·i·mal·ist /mínnəm'list/ *n* **1. ADVOCATE OF SMALLER ROLE FOR GOVERNMENT** somebody who advocates restricting the power and goals of something, especially somebody who wishes to limit the role of government **2. PRACTITIONER OF ARTISTIC MINIMALISM** somebody whose works of art, literature, or music display the simplicity associated with minimalism ■ *adj* **PROVIDING MINIMUM AMOUNT** providing only the least amount that is needed ■ *n* POL another spelling of **Minimalist** (sense 1)

Min·i·mal·ist /mínnəm'list/ *n* **1.** POL same as **Menshevik 2.** ARTS another spelling of **minimalist** *n* (sense 2) [Early 20C. In sense 1 translation of Russian *men'shevik*]

min·i·mal·ize /mínnəm'l īz/ (**-iz·ed** or **-is·ed**, **-iz·ing** or **-is·ing**, **-iz·es** or **-is·es**) *vt* to reduce something to the minimum —**min·i·mal·i·za·tion** /mìnnəm'li záysh'n/ *n*

min·i·mal·ly in·va·sive sur·ge·ry *n* surgery performed with lasers and other high-tech devices that involves minimal trauma to the patient's body

min·i·mal pair *n* in linguistics, a pair of words or other linguistic expressions that are the same except for one sound, e.g., "bit" and "pit"

min·i·max /mínnə màks/ *n* the lowest of a set of maximum values ■ *adj* describes options or strategies designed to minimize the risk of sustaining maximum loss in any situation that involves conflict or competition [Mid-20C. < MINIMUM + MAXIMUM]

min·i·me *n* a miniaturized clone of somebody or something [Late 20C. < the name of a clone in the films based on the Austin Powers character]

min·i·mill /mínnee mìl/ *n* a small mill, especially a steel mill that processes scrap metal

min·i·mize /mínnə mīz/ (**-mized, -miz·ing, -miz·es**) *vt* **1. REDUCE SOMETHING TO MINIMUM** to reduce something to the lowest possible amount or degree **2. UNDERRATE SOMETHING** to play down the extent or seriousness of something **3. MAKE IMAGE SMALLER** to reduce the size of a computer image —**min·i·mi·za·tion** /mìnnəmi záysh'n/ *n* —**min·i·miz·er** *n*

USAGE See ***minimal***.

min·i·mum /mínnəməm/ *n* (*plural* **-i·mums** or **-i·ma** /-əmə/) **1. LOWEST POSSIBLE DEGREE** the lowest possible amount or degree of something **2. LOWEST RECORDED DEGREE** the lowest recorded amount or degree of something **3. LOWEST PERMISSIBLE DEGREE** the lowest amount or degree of something permitted by law, e.g., the lowest speed on a highway or the youngest age at which something can be done legally **4. SUM THAT PATRON MUST SPEND** a minimum amount of money that a restaurant or nightclub requires each patron to spend **5.** MATH **LOWEST NUMBER** the lowest number in a finite set **6.** MATH **FUNCTION'S LOWEST VALUE** the smallest value of a continuous function over a particular interval ■ *adj* **LOWEST POSSIBLE** lowest possible, recorded, or permissible [Mid-17C. < Latin < *minimus* "least"]

min·i·mum-se·cu·ri·ty *adj* describes places that have security measures appropriate to inmates or patients who are not considered dangerous or who are not likely to try to escape

min·i·mum wage *n* **1.** the lowest rate of pay allowed by law or contract, either in general or for a specific type of work **2.** FIN same as **living wage**

min·i·mus /mínnəməss/ (*plural* **-i·mi** /-ə mī/) *n* a very small or insignificant person (*archaic*) [Late 16C. < Latin, "least"]

min·ing /míning/ *n* **1.** the process or business of removing minerals from the ground **2.** the process of laying explosive mines

min·ion /mínnyən/ *n* **1. ASSISTANT** a servile or slavish follower of somebody generally regarded as important **2. SERVANT** a servant or slave (*archaic* or *literary*) **3. FAVORITE** a favored person (*archaic*) [Early 16C. < French *mignon* "darling" (see MIGNON)]

min·i·park /mínnee paàrk/ *n* a small maintained grassy area or playground in an urban area

min·i·pill /mínnee pìl/ *n* an oral contraceptive that contains progesterone but not estrogen

~~**miniscule**~~ incorrect spelling of **minuscule**

min·i·se·ries /mínnee seèreez/ (*plural same*) *n* a short series of television programs, often a serialized fictional story, usually airing on consecutive nights

min·i·ski /mínnee skeè/ *n* a short snow ski for beginners or one that is attached to a vehicle used to travel over snow

min·i·skirt /mínnee skùrt/ *n* a skirt with a hemline well above the knee

min·i·state /mínnee stàyt/ *n* a country that is very small in terms both of geographic area and population

min·is·ter /mínnistər/ *n* **1. MEMBER OF CLERGY** a member of the clergy of a Christian church, especially a Protestant one **2.** CHR **HEAD OF ROMAN CATHOLIC ORDER** the superior in some orders in the Roman Catholic Church **3. SENIOR OFFICER OF STATE** a senior officer of state in a government department, especially in the parliamentary system of government **4.** INTERNAT REL **DIPLOMAT RANKED UNDER AMBASSADOR** a diplomat representing a country, especially of a rank below ambassador **5. BUSINESS REPRESENTATIVE** somebody's agent or representative (*formal or literary*) ■ *v* (**-tered, -ter·ing, -ters**) **1.** *vi* **HELP SOMEBODY** to give help to somebody in need (*formal*) **2.** *vi* CHR **DO RELIGIOUS**

MINISTER'S WORK to perform the duties of a member of the clergy **3.** *vt* **GIVE SOMETHING** to administer something such as aid, medicine, or a sacrament (*archaic*) [13C. Via French < Latin, "servant"] —**min·is·ter·ship** *n*

min·is·te·ri·al /mìnni stéeree əl/ *adj* **1. RELATING TO CLERGY** relating to a religious minister **2. RELATING TO GOVERNMENT MINISTER** relating to a government minister or the minister's department **3.** LAW **REQUIRING FOLLOWING OF INSTRUCTIONS** allowing no personal discretion, only the strict following of law **4. INSTRUMENTAL** playing an important part in achieving something (*formal*) —**min·is·te·ri·al·ly** *adv*

Min·is·ter of State *n* an assistant minister in a British government department who is usually not a member of the Cabinet

min·is·ter with·out port·fo·li·o *n* a senior officer of state who has no direct responsibility for a government department

min·is·trant /mínnistrənt/ *n* **1.** somebody serving as a religious minister (*formal*) **2.** somebody who gives aid to others (*literary*) [Mid-16C. < Latin *ministrant-*, present participle of *ministrare* "serve" < *minister* "servant"]

min·is·tra·tion /mìnni stráysh'n/ *n* **1. TREATMENT** help, treatment, or service (*formal; often used in the plural*) **2. RELIGIOUS MINISTER'S WORK** the service provided by a religious minister **3. ACT OF SUPPLYING** the supplying or administering of something (*archaic*) [14C. < Latin *ministration-* < *ministrare* (see MINISTRANT)]

min·i·stroke /mínnee strōk/ *n* a temporary blockage of blood circulation in some part of the brain, causing short-term stroke symptoms such as dizziness, inability to speak or move, or loss of senses. Technical name **transient ischemic attack**

min·is·try /mínnistree/ (*plural* **-tries**) *n* **1. WORK OF RELIGIOUS MINISTER** the profession and services of a religious minister **2. PERIOD OF SERVICE** a religious minister's career or period of service **3. MINISTERS** ministers collectively, especially religious ministers (*takes a singular or plural verb*) **4.** *also* **Min·is·try GOVERNMENT DEPARTMENT** a government department headed by a minister **5. PRIME MINISTER'S SERVICE** the period of government under a prime minister **6. GOVERNMENT BUILDING** the building in which a government department headed by a minister is housed [14C. Via Old French < Latin *ministerium* < *minister* "servant"]

~~**miniture**~~ incorrect spelling of **miniature**

min·i·um /mínnee əm/ *n* CHEM same as **red lead** [Mid-17C. < Latin]

min·i·van /mínnee vàn/ *n* a small passenger van, often with seats that can be removed or rearranged to accommodate cargo

min·i·ver /mínnivər/ *n* a white or light gray fur used as trim on ceremonial costumes [Late 16C. < Old French *menu vair* "small vair"]

mink

mink /mingk/ *n* **1.** (*plural* **minks** or *same*) **WEB-TOED MEMBER OF WEASEL FAMILY** a semiaquatic carnivorous member of the weasel family with webbed toes and a bushy tail. Raised for: fur. Native to: North America, Asia, Europe. Genus: *Mustela*. **2. MINK FUR** the thick shiny brown fur of a mink (*often used before a noun*) **3. MINK FUR GARMENT** a coat, stole, or other garment made of mink fur [15C. < Swedish]

min·ke whale /míngkee-/ *n* a small gray and white whale with a pointed snout. It is the smallest of the rorqual family, growing to only 30 ft./10 m long. Native to: oceans worldwide. Latin name: *Balaenoptera acutorostrata*. [Mid-20C. < Norwegian]

Minn. *abbr* Minnesota

Min·na /mínnə/ city in west central Nigeria, the capital of Niger State, situated about 50 mi./80 km northwest of Abuja. Population: 133,600 (1995).

Min·ne·ap·o·lis /mìnnee áppəliss/ largest city in Minnesota, in the southeastern part of the state, close to St. Paul. Population: 375,635 (2002 estimate).

Min·ne·con·jou *n* PEOPLES another spelling of **Miniconjou**

Min·ne·ha·ha Falls /mìnnə haá haa-/ waterfall on Minnehaha Creek, southern Minnesota, celebrated in Henry Wadsworth Longfellow's *The Song of Hiawatha*. Height: 50 ft./15 m.

Min·nel·li /mi néllee/, **Liza** (*b.* 1946) US stage and screen performer. Daughter of Judy Garland and Vincente Minnelli, she won an Academy Award for *Cabaret* (1972). Full name **Minnelli, Liza May**

> "Reality is something you rise above."
> [Liza Minnelli, *NY Newsday*; February 23, 1994]

min·ne·o·la /mìnnee ṓlə/ *n* an orange-colored citrus fruit that is a hybrid of a tangerine and a grapefruit [Mid-20C. After *Minneola*, town in Florida]

Min·ne·sing·er /mínnə sìngər, -zìngər/, **min·ne·sing·er** *n* in Germany between the 12th and the 14th centuries, a traveling poet-musician who wrote and performed songs of courtly love [Early 19C. Via German < Middle High German, "love singer"]

Minnesota

Min·ne·so·ta /mìnnə sṓtə/ **1.** state in the north central United States, bordered by Canada, Lake Superior, Wisconsin, Iowa, South Dakota, and North Dakota. Capital: St. Paul. Population: 5,019,720 (2002 estimate). Area: 86,943 sq. mi./225,181 sq. km. **2.** river in southern Minnesota, flowing from Big Stone Lake into the Mississippi River. Length: 332 mi./534 km. —**Min·ne·so·tan** *adj, n*

Min·ne·so·ta Mul·ti·pha·sic Per·son·al·i·ty In·ven·to·ry *n* a standardized test that uses true-false questions to assess somebody's psychological and social adjustment. It is widely used in recruitment and screening. [After the University of MINNESOTA]

min·now /mínnō/ *n* **1. BAIT FISH** a small freshwater fish of the carp family, commonly used as fishing bait. Family: Cyprinidae. **2. SMALL FISH** a small silvery freshwater fish **3. INSIGNIFICANT PERSON OR THING** a person or organization of relatively low status or little importance [15C. Probably related to Old English *myne*]

Mi·no·an /mi nṓ ən/ *adj* relating to the Bronze Age civilization on Crete that lasted from around 3000 to 1100 B.C. ■ *n* somebody who came from the island of Crete during ancient times, especially during the Minoan period [Late 19C. After *Minos*, legendary king of Crete]

mi·nor /mínər/ *adj* **1. SMALL** relatively small in quantity, size, or degree **2. LOW IN RANK** relatively low in rank or importance **3. LOW IN SEVERITY** relatively low in severity or danger **4.** MUSIC **DESCRIBES MUSICAL SCALE** describes a musical scale that has a semitone interval between the second and third, fifth and sixth, and sometimes seventh and eighth notes **5.** MUSIC **DESCRIBES MUSICAL INTERVAL** describes a musical interval that is a semitone less than a major interval **6.** MUSIC **DESCRIBES MUSICAL KEY** describes a musical key that is based on a minor scale ○ *in B minor* **7.** LAW **NOT LEGALLY ADULT** younger than the legal age of adulthood **8.** EDUC **SECONDARY** secondary to the major course of study ■ *n* **1.** LAW **SOMEBODY NOT LEGALLY ADULT** somebody who is not yet legally an adult **2.** MUSIC **MUSICAL KEY OR HARMONY** a key or harmony based on a musical scale whose third and, usually, sixth and seventh notes are lower by a semitone than those in the major scale **3.** EDUC **SECONDARY SUBJECT** a second specialization in higher education that requires fewer courses than a major **4.** EDUC **SOMEBODY FOLLOWING MINOR COURSE** a student who takes a secondary program of study ■ *vi* (**-nored, -nor·ing, -nors**) **STUDY SECONDARY SUBJECT** to have a second specialization in higher education, in addition to a major specialization ○ *She minors in Spanish.* [13C. < Latin, "lesser"]

SPELLCHECK See *miner.*

mi·nor ax·is *n* the shorter axis of an ellipse

Mi·nor·ca[1] *n* a white and black domestic chicken bred around the Mediterranean [Mid-19C. After MINORCA[2]]

Mi·nor·ca[2] ➧ **Menorca**

mi·nor el·e·ment *n* CHEM same as **trace element** (sense 2)

mi·nor·i·tar·i·an·ism /mi nàwrə térree ə nìzzəm, mī-/ *n* advocacy or political action on behalf of a minority

Mi·nor·ite /mínə rìt/ *n* a friar of the Franciscan order [Mid-16C. < *Minor Friars*, translation of medieval Latin *Fratres Minores* "lesser brethren," because the order stressed the virtue of humility]

mi·nor·i·ty /mi náwrətee, mī-/ *n* (*plural* **-ties**) **1. SMALLER GROUP** a group of people or things that is a small part of a much larger group **2. GROUP WITH INSUFFICIENT VOTES TO WIN** a group that has fewer votes in an organization than another group or groups **3. SMALLER SOCIALLY DEFINED GROUP** a group of people, within a society, whose members have different ethnic, racial, national, religious, sexual, political, linguistic, or other characteristics from the rest of society **4. OFFENSIVE TERM** an offensive term for a member of a minority group **5.** LAW **NONADULTHOOD** the state or period of being younger than the legal age of adulthood ■ *adj* **1. OF MINORITY** relating to or constituting a minority **2. OFFENSIVE TERM** an offensive term meaning belonging to, used or inhabited by, or involving a particular group of people within society who are different from the majority, especially ethnically or racially different ○ *minority schools*

mi·nor·i·ty lead·er *n* the head of a minority party in a legislature

mi·nor key *n* a musical key based on a minor scale

mi·nor league *n* a league of professional baseball, football, ice hockey, or basketball teams that do not belong to the major leagues

mi·nor-league *adj* **1.** relating to or being a team member of a minor sports league **2.** mediocre in quality or position (*informal*)

mi·nor scale *n* a scale whose third and, usually, sixth and seventh notes are lower by a semitone than those in the major scale, giving it a less bright, more emotionally suggestive quality

mi·nor suit *n* in cards, either clubs or diamonds, which in bridge and similar games are ranked below hearts and spades

Mi·nos /mínoss/ *n* in Greek mythology, the king of Crete and the son of Zeus, who kept a monster (**the Minotaur**) in a labyrinth

Mi·not /mí not/ city in northern North Dakota, west of Grand Forks and northwest of Bismarck. Population: 35,617 (2002 estimate).

Min·o·taur /mínnə tàwr, mínə-/ *n* in Greek mythology, a monster with the body of a man and head of a bull that lived in the Cretan labyrinth and was fed human sacrifices until it was killed by Theseus

mi·nox·i·dil /mi nóksəd'l/ *n* a drug that causes widening of the arteries. Use: treatment of high blood pressure and male-pattern baldness. [Late 20C. < shortening of AMINO- + OXIDE]

MINS *abbr* LAW minor in need of supervision

Minsk /minsk/ capital city of Belarus, situated in the north of the country. It is a major industrial city. Population: 1,699,000 (2001).

min·ster /mínstər/ *n* a large or important cathedral or church, usually one originally connected with a monastery [Old English *mynster* < ecclesiastical Latin *monasterium* (see MONASTERY)]

min·strel /mínstrəl/ *n* **1.** a medieval singer, musician, or reciter of poetry who traveled around from place to place giving performances **2.** any of a group of entertainers who wore black facial makeup and sang and performed in variety shows, a form of entertainment now usually considered racist and highly offensive [13C. Via Old French *menestral* "entertainer, craftsman" < late Latin *ministerialis* "official" < *ministerium* (see MINISTRY)]

min·strel·sy /mínstrəlssee/ (*plural* **-sies**) *n* **1.** MINSTREL'S ART a minstrel's art or performance, or the profession of a minstrel **2.** MINSTRELS' POEMS AND SONGS the poems and songs written and performed by minstrels or by a particular minstrel **3.** MINSTREL TROUPE a troupe of medieval minstrels [14C. < Old French *menestralsie* < *menestrel* (see MINSTREL)]

mint

mint[1] /mint/ *n* **1.** a plant with aromatic leaves. Native to: northern temperate regions. Use: food flavoring. Genus: *Mentha*. **2.** a piece of mint-flavored candy [Old English *minte*, via Germanic < Latin *mentha* < Greek *minthē*] —**mint·y** *adj*

mint[2] /mint/ *n* **1.** PLACE COINING MONEY a place where the coins used in a currency are manufactured under government control **2.** MUCH MONEY a large amount of money (*informal*) ■ *vt* (**mint·ed, mint·ing, mints**) **1.** MAKE COINS to make coins by stamping metal **2.** INVENT SOMETHING to create or invent something, especially a new word or phrase ■ *adj* IN PERFECT CONDITION in perfect condition as when first made ○ *in mint condition* [Old English *mynet*, via Germanic < Latin *moneta* (see MONEY)]

mint·age /míntij/ *n* **1.** COINS FROM MINT coins made in a mint, especially a quantity of coins minted at the same time **2.** MINTING COINS the minting of coins **3.** FEE FOR MINTING a fee paid to a mint by a government for minting its coins

mint jel·ly *n* a jelly made chiefly from mint, green in color, and served typically as a garnish for roasted lamb

mint ju·lep *n* a drink made by pouring liquor, usually bourbon, and sugar over crushed ice and flavoring or garnishing with mint

mint·mark /mínt maark/ *n* a letter or symbol stamped on a coin that identifies the mint where it was made

min·u·end /mínnyoo ènd/ *n* the number from which another number (**subtrahend**) is to be subtracted [Early 18C. < Latin *minuendus* "be made smaller" < *minuere* "diminish"]

min·u·et /mìnnyoo ét/ *n* **1.** a slow French court dance of the 17th century, performed in triple time **2.** the music for a minuet [Late 17C. < French *menuet* "small, dainty" < Latin *minutus*; from the steps taken in the dance]

Min·u·it /mínn yooit/, **Peter** (1580–1638) Dutch-born American colonial administrator. He founded the seaport of New Amsterdam on Manhattan Island, which eventually became New York City.

mi·nus /mīnəss/ *prep* **1.** LESS reduced by the subtraction of a number ○ *Seven minus four is three.* **2.** WITHOUT lacking in or deprived of something ○ *He came minus his tools, so he couldn't do much work.* ■ *adj* **1.** SHOWING SUBTRACTION relating to or showing subtraction ○ *a minus sign* **2.** LESS THAN ZERO relating to or showing a value less than zero ○ *temperatures of minus 20 degrees* **3.** HAVING DETRIMENTAL EFFECT having a negative or detrimental effect ○ *a minus factor* **4.** SLIGHTLY BELOW STANDARD LEVEL used in grading or evaluating something to show that it is slightly below the average standard indicated by a particular symbol ○ *a grade of C minus* ■ *n* **1.** MATH same as **minus sign** ○ *The minus shows that it's a subtraction.* **2.** NEGATIVE QUANTITY a quantity below zero ○ *If we take that away we're left with a minus.* **3.** DISADVANTAGE something that is detrimental or disadvantageous ○ *The power problem may prove to be a minus.* [15C. < Latin < *minor* "less"]

min·us·cule /mínnə skyool/ *adj* **1.** EXTREMELY SMALL extremely small or completely insignificant **2.** LOWERCASE in lowercase letters ■ *n* **1.** SMALL LETTER a lowercase letter **2.** MEDIEVAL WRITING STYLE a small cursive style of writing used in medieval manuscripts **3.** LETTER WRITTEN IN MINUSCULE a letter of the alphabet written in minuscule style [Early 18C. Via French < Latin *minusculus* "rather small" < *minus* "less" (see MINUS)]

mi·nus sign *n* a symbol (-) used to indicate subtraction or a negative quantity

min·ute[1] /mínnit/ *n* **1.** 60 SECONDS a period of 60 seconds or a 60th part of an hour **2.** VERY SHORT TIME a very short period of time ○ *I'll only be gone a minute.* **3.** MOMENT a particular moment ○ *The minute we got there the show began.* **4.** SHORT DISTANCE a distance that can be traveled in a minute ○ *The cottage is only a couple of minutes from the ocean.* **5.** UNIT OF ANGULAR MEASURE a unit of measurement of angles equivalent to a 60th of a degree. Symbol **'** **6.** BRIEF NOTE a brief note or memorandum ■ **min·utes** *npl* RECORD OF MEETING an official record of what is said or done during a meeting ■ *vt* (**-ut·ed, -ut·ing, -utes**) WRITE DOWN MEETING'S PROCEEDINGS to record or summarize officially what happens during a meeting, or make a note in the minutes of a particular thing that is said or done [14C. Directly or via Old French < Latin *minuta* < *minutus*, past participle of *minuere* "make small"] ◇ **up to the minute** aware of, taking account of, or reporting the very latest developments

mi·nute[2] /mī nóot/ (**-nut·er, -nut·est**) *adj* **1.** VERY SMALL extremely small in size or scope **2.** INSIGNIFICANT so very small as not to matter **3.** CONCERNED WITH EVERY DETAIL extremely or laboriously thorough and painstaking, and concerned with every detail [Early 17C. < Latin *minutus* (see MINUTE[1])] —**mi·nute·ness** *n*

min·ute gun /mínnit-/ *n* a gun fired every minute as a distress signal or sign of mourning

min·ute hand /mínnit-/ *n* the longer pointer on a watch or clock that indicates the minutes

mi·nute·ly /mī nóotlee/ *adv* **1.** IN GREAT DETAIL very thoroughly, carefully, and in great detail **2.** SLIGHTLY to a very small extent **3.** INTO SOMETHING VERY SMALL into a very small shape or very small pieces

min·ute·man /mínnit màn/ (*plural* **-men** /-mèn/) *n* an armed fighter in the Revolutionary War pledged to be ready to fight for the American cause at a minute's notice

min·ute steak /mínnit-/ *n* a piece of steak sliced so thinly that it can be cooked very quickly

mi·nu·ti·ae /mī nóoshee ee/ *npl* small or trivial details [Mid-18C. < Latin, "small things" < *minutus* (see MINUTE[1])]

minx /mingks/ *n* an offensive term that deliberately insults a woman's or girl's sense of propriety and decorous behavior [Mid-16C. Origin ?]

Min·ya, Al- /mínnyə-/ ➧ **Al-Minya**

min·yan /mínnyən, meen yaan/ (*plural* **-yan·im** /mìn yaa neem, -yə ním/ or **-yans**) *n* the minimum number, ten, of adult Jews required to be present to hold a religious service, or of Jewish men required for an orthodox religious service [Mid-18C. < Hebrew, "count, reckoning"]

Mi·o·cene /mī ə seen/ *n* the epoch of geologic time, 24 million to 5 million years ago, during which the modern ocean currents were established and Antarctica became frozen. See table at **geologic time** [Mid-19C. < Greek *meiōn* "less" + *kainos* "recent"] —**Mi·o·cene** *adj*

mi·o·ga /mee óggə/ *n* in Japanese cuisine, the shoot of a member of the ginger family that resembles a bud. It is sliced and used as a garnish. [Late 20C. < Japanese]

mi·o·sis /mī óssiss/ (*plural* **-o·ses** /-ó seez/), **my·o·sis** *n* a contraction of the pupil of the eye, e.g., a contraction caused by a reaction to a drug [Early 19C. < Greek *muein* "shut the eyes"] —**mi·ot·ic, my·ot·ic** /mī óttik/ *adj*

MIP *abbr* **1.** INSUR marine insurance policy **2.** FIN monthly investment plan

MIPS /mips/, **mips** *abbr* COMPUT million instructions per second

Mi·que·lon Is·land ➧ **St.-Pierre and Miquelon**

mir /meer/ *n* a peasant commune in tsarist Russia [Late 19C. < Russian]

Mir: photographed from the space shuttle Atlantis (1997)

Mir *n* a space station launched by the former Soviet Union in 1986, designed to be permanently crewed

Mir·a /mīrə/ *n* a variable red giant in the constellation Cetus that is only visible a few weeks a year when it becomes the brightest star in the constellation

mi·ra·bi·le dic·tu /mi raabilee dík tóo/ *interj* used to introduce the announcement of something the speaker, genuinely or ironically, considers to be amazing [< Latin, "amazing to relate"]

mir·a·cid·i·um /mìrə síddee əm/ (*plural* **-i·a** /-ee ə/) *n* the free-swimming first-stage larva of a trematode worm that hatches from an egg and then reproduces asexually [Late 19C. Via modern Latin < Greek *meirakidion* "little boy"] —**mir·a·cid·i·al** *adj*

mir·a·cle /mírrək'l/ *n* **1.** ACT OF GOD an event that appears to be contrary to the laws of nature and is regarded as an act of God **2.** AMAZING EVENT an event or action that is amazing, extraordinary, or unexpected ○ *It'll be a miracle if we get there on time.* **3.** MARVELOUS EXAMPLE something admired as a marvelous creation or example of a particular type of science or skill ○ *a miracle of modern engineering* [12C. Via French < Latin *miraculum* "object of wonder" < *mirari* "wonder at" < *mirus* "wonderful"]

mir·a·cle drug *n* a drug, usually a new one, that is extraordinarily effective and seems to represent a breakthrough in the treatment of disease

mir·a·cle play *n* a medieval play broadly depicting miracles taken from the life of a saint or a story from the Bible

mi·rac·u·lous /mi rákyələss/ *adj* **1.** REGARDED AS CAUSED BY SUPERNATURAL INTERVENTION apparently contrary to the laws of nature and caused by a supernatural power **2.** EXTRAORDINARY unexpected, extraordinary, and marvelous **3.** ABLE TO PERFORM MIRACLES believed to have the power to perform miracles [15C. < French *miraculeux* < Latin *miraculum* (see MIRACLE)] —**mi·rac·u·lous·ly** *adv* —**mi·rac·u·lous·ness** *n*

mir·a·dor /meérə dáwr/ *n* a window, balcony, or turret designed to command a wide view [Late 17C. < Spanish < *mirar* "to look" < Latin *mirare* (see MIRAGE)]

Mi·ra·flo·res, Lake /meérə fláw rayz/ lake in central Panama, through which the Panama Canal passes

mi·rage /mi raazh/ *n* **1.** an optical illusion of a sheet of water appearing in the desert or on a hot road, caused by light being distorted by alternate layers of hot and cool air **2.** something that appears to be real but is unreal or merely imagined [Early 19C. < French < *mirer* "look at" < Latin *mirare* "wonder at," variant of *mirari* (see MIRACLE)]

Mir·a·mar /mírrə maar/ city in southeastern Florida, in Broward County, near the Atlantic Ocean. Population: 90,359 (2002 estimate).

Mi·ran·da /mə rándə/ *n* a large natural satellite of Uranus

Barnaby's

Carmen Miranda

Mi·ran·da /mə rándə/, **Carmen** (1909–55) Portuguese dancer and singer. Star of Brazilian and Hollywood musicals, she is remembered particularly for her elaborate costumes and headdresses made from tropical fruit. Born **Cunha, Maria do Carmo Miranda da**

Mi·ran·da rights *npl* the rights of a person being arrested to remain silent in order to avoid self-incrimination, and to have an attorney present during questioning [Late 20C. After Ernesto A. *Miranda* (1942–76), plaintiff in the original case]

Mi·ran·dize /mə rán dìz/ (**-dized, -diz·ing, -diz·es**) *vt US* to inform somebody being arrested of his or her rights to remain silent and to have an attorney present (*informal*)

mire /mīr/ *n* **1. BOG** an area of very marshy ground or deep slushy mud **2. THICK MUD** thick slimy mud **3. DIFFICULT SITUATION** a troublesome or oppressive situation or state that is very difficult to escape from ■ *v* (**mired, mir·ing, mires**) **1.** *vti* **GET STUCK IN MUD** to sink into mud and become stuck, or make something sink into mud and become stuck **2.** *vt* **MAKE SOMETHING MUDDY** to make something muddy or dirty **3.** *vt* **ENTANGLE SOMEBODY OR SOMETHING** to involve somebody or something in difficulties (*often passive*) [13C. < Old Norse *myrr* "bog"] —**mir·y** *adj*

mire·poix /meer pwaá/, **mire·pois** *n* mixed finely diced vegetables, typically carrot, onion, and celery, lightly fried and used as a seasoning in stews, soups, and sauces, or on which to lay meat for roasting or braising [Late 19C. < French, after the Duc de Mirepoix, 1699–1757, French diplomat and general]

mi·rex /mī rèks/ *n* an insecticide used especially to kill ants. Formula: $C_{10}Cl_{12}$. [Mid-20C. Origin ?]

Mir·i·am /mírree əm/ *n* in the Bible, a Hebrew prophet, poet, and the sister of Moses

mi·rin /mírrən/ *n* a sweet liquid flavoring made from fermented sake, widely used in Japanese cooking [Mid-20C. < Japanese]

Mi·ró /mee rṓ/, **Joan** (1893–1983) Spanish painter, sculptor, and printmaker. A leading surrealist, he developed a form of abstraction that produced dreamlike, ethereal compositions.

> "I work like a gardener or a wine grower. Everything takes time. My vocabulary of forms, for example, did not come to me all at once. It formulated itself almost in spite of me."
> [Joan Miró, *Interview, XXe Siècle (Paris) (20th Century)*; February 15, 1959]

mir·ror /mírrər/ *n* **1. HIGHLY REFLECTIVE SURFACE** a surface, e.g., glass or polished metal, that reflects light without diffusing it so that it will give back a clear image of anything placed in front of it **2. SOMETHING ACCURATELY REPRESENTING SOMETHING ELSE** something that accurately reproduces, describes, or represents something else ○ *the debate whether TV shows are a mirror of our culture* **3.** ONLINE same as **mirror site** ■ *vt* (**-rored, -ror·ing, -rors**) **1. REFLECT SOMETHING IN SURFACE** to reflect something clearly in a surface (*often passive*) ○ *The mountains were mirrored in the lake.* **2. BE SIMILAR TO SOMETHING** to be very similar to or correspond closely with something else, or to reproduce it accurately ○ *The new survey mirrors several recent polls.* **3. MAINTAIN COPY OF DATA OR WEBSITE** to maintain an exact copy of a program, data, or website, usually on another file server [13C. < Old French *mirour* < Latin *mirari* (see MIRACLE)]

mir·ror im·age *n* something that, like a reflection in a mirror, is identical to something else but reversed

mir·ror site *n* a copy of a website maintained on a different file server so as to spread the distribution load or to back up data

mirth /murth/ *n* happiness or enjoyment, especially accompanied by laughter [Old English *myrgɵ* < Germanic, "pleasant, joyful"] —**mirth·ful** *adj*

mirth·less /múrthləss/ *adj* not feeling or expressing amusement, good humor, or gladness —**mirth·less·ly** *adv*

MIRV /murv/ *abbr* MIL multiple independently targeted re-entry vehicle

Mir·za /meérzə/ *n* an Iranian title of respect signifying a learned man or official when placed before a name, or, formerly, a royal prince when placed after a name [Early 17C. < Persian]

MIS *abbr* COMPUT management information system

mis- *prefix* **1.** badly, wrongly ○ *mishandle* **2.** bad, wrong ○ *misdeed* **3.** opposite, lack, failure ○ *mislike* [Partly Old English, and partly via Old French *mes-* < Germanic, "go wrong"]

mis·ad·dress *vt*
mis·ad·min·is·ter *vt*
mis·ad·min·is·tra·tion *n*
mis·ad·vise *vt*
mis·aim *vt*
mis·a·lign *vt*
mis·a·lign·ment *n*
mis·al·lo·cate *vt*
mis·al·lo·ca·tion *n*
mis·al·ly *vt*
mis·a·nal·y·sis *n*
mis·an·a·lyze *vt*
mis·ap·pli·ca·tion *n*
mis·ap·ply *vt*
mis·ap·prais·al *n*
mis·as·sem·ble *vt*
mis·as·sump·tion *n*
mis·at·trib·ute *vt*
mis·at·tri·bu·tion *n*
mis·bal·ance *vt*
mis·cat·a·log *vt*
mis·chan·nel *vt*
mis·char·ac·ter·i·za·tion *n*
mis·char·ac·ter·ize *vt*
mis·charge *vt*
mis·clas·si·fi·ca·tion *n*
mis·clas·si·fy *vt*
mis·code *vt*
mis·com·mu·ni·cate *vti*
mis·com·pute *vt*
mis·con·nect *vt*
mis·con·nec·tion *n*
mis·cre·ate *vt*
mis·cre·a·tion *n*
mis·date *vt, n*
mis·deal *vti, n*
mis·de·fine *vt*
mis·de·scribe *vt*
mis·de·scrip·tion *n*
mis·di·ag·nose *vt*
mis·di·ag·no·sis *n*
mis·di·vide *vt*
mis·di·vi·sion *n*
mis·ed·u·cate *vt*
mis·ed·u·ca·tion *n*
mis·em·ploy *vt*
mis·em·ploy·ment *n*
mis·file *vt*
mis·func·tion *n*
mis·gov·ern *vti*
mis·gov·ern·ment *n*
mis·grade *vt*
mis·hear *vti*
mis·hit *n, vt*
mis·i·den·ti·fi·ca·tion *n*
mis·i·den·ti·fy *vt*
mis·im·pres·sion *n*
mis·in·form *vt*
mis·in·for·ma·tion *n*
mis·in·form·er *n*
mis·in·ter·pret *vt*
mis·in·ter·pre·ta·tion *n*
mis·kick *vti*
mis·la·bel *vt*
mis·lo·cate *vt*
mis·num·ber *vt*
mis·or·der *vt*
mis·or·i·en·ta·tion *n*
mis·per·ceive *vt*
mis·per·cep·tion *n*
mis·play *vt, n*
mis·pro·gram *vt*
mis·pro·por·tion *n*
mis·pro·por·tioned *adj*
mis·quo·ta·tion *n*
mis·quote *vti*
mis·re·cord *vt*
mis·re·mem·ber *vti*
mis·state *vt*
mis·state·ment *n*
mis·term *vt*
mis·time *vt*
mis·trans·late *vti*
mis·trans·la·tion *n*
mis·type *vti, n*
mis·val·ue *vt*
mis·word *vt*
mis·write *vt*

mis·ad·ven·ture /mìssəd vénchər/ *n* an unfortunate event, especially something untoward, unlucky, or amusing that happens to somebody [13C. < Old French *mesaventure* < *mesavenir* "turn out badly" < *avenir* "happen" < Latin *advenire* "come to"]

mis·al·li·ance /mìssə lī́ ənss/ *n* an unsuitable alliance, especially a marriage between mismatched partners

mis·an·dry /mi sándree/ *n* hatred of men as a sexually defined group [Early 20C. < Greek *andr-* "man," after MISOGYNY] —**mis·an·drist** *n*

mis·an·thrope /míss'n thrṓp/, **mis·an·thro·pist** /mi sánthrəpist/ *n* somebody who hates humanity, or who dislikes and distrusts other people and tends to avoid them [Mid-16C. < French < Greek *misanthrōpos* < *misein* "to hate" + *anthrōpos* "man"] —**mis·an·throp·ic** /mìss'n thróppik/ *adj* —**mis·an·thro·py** /mi sánthrə pee/ *n*

mis·ap·pre·hend /miss àppri hénd/ (**-hend·ed, -hend·ing, -hends**) *vt* to fail to understand something

mis·ap·pre·hen·sion /miss àppri hénsh'n/ *n* a false impression or incorrect understanding, especially of the nature of a situation or somebody's intentions

mis·ap·pro·pri·ate /mìssə prṓpree àyt/ (**-at·ed, -at·ing, -ates**) *vt* to take something, especially money, dishonestly, or in order to use it for an improper or illegal purpose —**mis·ap·pro·pri·a·tion** /mìssə prṓpree áysh'n/ *n*

SYNONYMS See *steal*.

mis·be·got·ten /mìssbi gótt'n/ *adj* **1. ILL-CONCEIVED AND GENERALLY BAD** from a bad source, badly thought out, or generally deplorable from start to finish **2. DISHONESTLY OBTAINED** obtained by dishonest means **3. ILLEGITIMATE** born to parents who are not married to each other

mis·be·have /mìssbi háyv/ (**-haved, -hav·ing, -haves**) *vi* **1.** to be naughty and troublesome, or otherwise behave in an unacceptable way **2.** to function badly or not at all, or to cause problems (*informal*)

mis·be·hav·ior /mìssbi háyvyər/ *n* unacceptable behavior, especially naughtiness, disobedience, or troublesomeness on the part of children

mis·be·hav·iour *n UK* Can, UK spelling of **misbehavior**

mis·be·lief /mìssbi leéf/ *n* a belief that is or is considered to be false or unorthodox

mis·be·lieve /mìssbi leév/ (**-lieved, -liev·ing, -lieves**) *vi* to hold beliefs that are or are considered to be false or unorthodox, especially on religious matters (*disapproving*) —**mis·be·liev·er** *n*

mis·brand /miss bránd/ (**-brand·ed, -brand·ing, -brands**) *vt* to put a false or incorrect label on a product

misc. *abbr* **1.** miscellaneous **2.** miscellany

mis·cal·cu·late /miss kálkyə làyt/ (**-lat·ed, -lat·ing, -lates**) *vti* **1.** to calculate something incorrectly **2.** to judge or evaluate somebody or something incorrectly, or form false expectations as to the consequences of an action —**mis·cal·cu·la·tion** /miss kàlkyə láysh'n/ *n*

mis·call /miss káwl/ (**-called, -call·ing, -calls**) *vt* to use the wrong or an inappropriate name for somebody or something

mis·car·riage /miss kàrrij, miss kárrij/ *n* **1.** an involuntary ending of a pregnancy through the discharge of the fetus from the womb at too early a stage in its development for it to survive. Technical name **abortion 2.** the mishandling or failure of something such as a plan or project (*formal*)

mis·car·riage of jus·tice *n* a failure of the legal system to come to a just decision

mis·car·ry /miss kárree/ (**-ried, -ry·ing, -ries**) *vi* **1. HAVE SPONTANEOUS ABORTION** to lose a fetus, especially a human fetus, through a miscarriage **2. BE SPONTANEOUSLY ABORTED** to be expelled from the womb at too early a stage in development to be able to survive **3. FAIL** to result in failure (*formal*)

mis·cast /miss kást/ (**-cast, -cast·ing, -casts**) *vt* (*often passive*) **1.** to choose somebody to play a stage or movie part to which he or she is unsuited **2.** to give a role in a play or movie to an unsuitable actor

mis·ceg·e·na·tion /missijə náysh'n/ *n* (*offensive when used disapprovingly, as often formerly*) **1.** sexual relations between people of different races, especially of different skin colors, leading to the birth of children **2.** marriage or cohabitation between people of different races [Mid-19C. < Latin *miscere* "to mix" + *genus* "race"]

~~**miscelaneous**~~ incorrect spelling of **miscellaneous**

mis·cel·la·ne·a /mìssə láynee ə/ *npl* miscellaneous things, especially pieces of writing, brought together as a collection [Late 16C. < Latin < *miscellaneus* (see MISCELLANEOUS)]

mis·cel·la·ne·ous /mìssə láynee əss/ *adj* **1.** made up of many different things or kinds of things that have no necessary connection with each other **2.** each being different or having different abilities or qualities from the others ○ *a task force of miscellaneous specialists* [Early 17C. < Latin *miscellaneus* < *miscere* "to mix"] —**mis·cel·la·ne·ous·ly** *adv* —**mis·cel·la·ne·ous·ness** *n*

mis·cel·la·nist /míssə làynist, mi séllənist/ *n* a compiler or writer of miscellanies

mis·cel·la·ny /míssə làynee/ (*plural* **-nies**) *n* **1.** a miscellaneous collection of things **2.** a collection of miscellaneous pieces of writing in one volume, often by different authors on various subjects and in different genres [Late 16C. Via French *miscellanées* < Latin *miscellanea* (see MISCELLANEA)]

mis·chance /miss chánss/ *n* **1.** the occurrence of unfortunate events by chance **2.** something that happens through bad luck [14C. < Old French *mescheance* < late Latin *cadentia* (see CHANCE)]

~~**mischeif**~~ incorrect spelling of **mischief**

mis·chief /mísschif/ *n* **1. NAUGHTY BEHAVIOR** behavior, especially by children, that is undesirable or troublesome without being malicious **2. TENDENCY TO NAUGHTY BEHAVIOR** a tendency to mildly troublesome or undesirable behavior such as teasing or practical jokes **3. INJURY OR DAMAGE** injury or damage caused by the actions of somebody or something **4. SOURCE OF HARM OR TROUBLE** something or somebody that causes serious harm or trouble to others (*dated*) **5. HARMLESS TROUBLEMAKER** somebody who causes or enjoys causing harmless trouble (*dated*) [13C. < Old French *meschef* < *meschever* "meet with misfortune" < *chever* "come to an end" < *chef* "head"]

mis·chief-mak·er *n* a troublemaker who sets people against each other, especially by spreading malicious gossip —**mis·chief-mak·ing** *n*

~~**mischievious**~~ incorrect spelling of **mischievous**

mis·chie·vous /mísschivəss/ *adj* **1. PLAYFULLY NAUGHTY OR TROUBLESOME** behaving or likely to behave in a naughty or troublesome way, but in fun and not meaning serious harm **2. TROUBLESOME OR IRRITATING** intended to tease or cause trouble, though usually in fun or without much malice **3. FULL OF MISCHIEF** expressing somebody's intention or inclination to have fun by teasing, playing tricks, or causing trouble **4. DAMAGING** causing or meant to cause serious trouble, damage, or hurt (*formal*) —**mis·chie·vous·ly** *adv* —**mis·chie·vous·ness** *n*

misch met·al /mísh-/ *n* an alloy of cerium and rare metals used, e.g., in the flints of cigarette lighters [Early 20C. < German *Mischmetall* "mix-metal"]

mis·ci·ble /míssəb'l/ *adj* describes two or more liquids that can be mixed together [Late 16C. < medieval Latin *miscibilis* < Latin *miscere* "to mix"]

mis·com·mu·ni·ca·tion /mìsskə myo͞oni káysh'n/ *n* **1.** failure to communicate something clearly or correctly **2.** a communication that is unclear or likely to be misinterpreted

mis·com·pre·hend /mìss komprə hénd/ (**-hend·ed, -hend·ing, -hends**) *vt* to mistake the meaning or nature of something

mis·con·ceive /mìskən sée̅v/ (**-ceived, -ceiv·ing, -ceives**) *vt* to fail to understand something correctly, or form a false conception of something

mis·con·ceived /mìskən sée̅vd/ *adj* resulting from a wrong or faulty understanding or idea of something and consequently doomed to failure

mis·con·cep·tion /mìskən sépsh'n/ *n* a mistaken idea or view resulting from a misunderstanding of something

mis·con·duct *n* /miss kón dùkt/ **1. IMMORAL, UNETHICAL, OR UNPROFESSIONAL BEHAVIOR** behavior that is not in accordance with accepted moral or professional standards **2. INCOMPETENCE** incompetent or dishonest management of something, especially on behalf of others ■ *v* /mìskən dúkt/ (**-duct·ed, -duct·ing, -ducts**) **1. mis·conduct your·self** *vr* **ACT IMMORALLY** to act in an immoral or improper way **2.** *vt* **MANAGE SOMETHING BADLY** to manage something in an incompetent or dishonest way ○ *guilty of misconducting the whole affair*

mis·con·struc·tion /mìsskən strúkshən/ *n* **1.** a faulty understanding or interpretation of something **2.** a faulty grammatical construction

mis·con·strue /mìskən stro͞o/ (**-strued, -stru·ing, -strues**) *vt* to understand or interpret something incorrectly

mis·count *vti* /miss kównt/ (**-count·ed, -count·ing, -counts**) to make a mistake when counting something ■ *n* /míss kòwnt/ an incorrect count or calculation

mis·cre·ant /mískree ənt/ *n* **1.** somebody who behaves in a dishonest, malicious, or otherwise contemptible way (*literary*) **2.** somebody whose religious faith is frowned upon or loathed (*archaic insult*) [13C. < Old French, present participle of *mescroire* "disbelieve" < Latin *credere* "believe"]

mis·cue /miss kyo͞o/ *n* **1.** CUE GAMES **FAULTY SHOT IN BILLIARDS** in billiards, a shot that fails because the cue does not strike the cue ball properly **2. MISTAKE** a mistake, especially one that involves giving somebody the wrong cue to say or begin something or giving a cue at the wrong time (*informal*) ■ *v* (**-cued, -cu·ing, -cues**) **1.** *vti* CUE GAMES **MAKE FAULTY SHOT** in billiards, to fail to strike the cue ball properly, or to play a miscue **2.** *vti* **MISS CUE** to fail to respond to a cue, to give the wrong cue for something, or to give a cue at the wrong time **3.** *vi* **ERR** to make a mistake (*informal*)

mis·deed /miss dée̅d/ *n* a wicked, blameworthy, or unlawful act

mis·de·mean·ant /mìssdi mée̅nənt/ *n* somebody convicted of a misdemeanor

mis·de·mean·or /mìssdi mée̅nər/ *n* **1.** a crime less serious than a felony and resulting in a less severe punishment **2.** a relatively minor misdeed

mis·de·mean·our *n* Can, UK spelling of **misdemeanor**

mis·di·al /miss dī́ əl/ (**-aled, -al·ing, -als**) *vti* to dial a telephone number incorrectly —**mis·di·al** /míss dī̀ əl/ *n*

mis·di·rect /mìssdi rékt, -dī-/ (**-rect·ed, -rect·ing, -rects**) *vt* **1. GIVE SOMEBODY WRONG DIRECTIONS** to give somebody wrong directions or instructions **2. WRONGLY ADDRESS MAIL** to put a wrong address on an item of mail **3. AIM SOMETHING INACCURATELY** to aim something such as a punch or bullet inaccurately, or direct something such as a comment or insult at the wrong person **4. GIVE JURY WRONG INSTRUCTIONS** to give a jury incorrect information about the facts or laws pertaining to a case —**mis·di·rec·tion** *n*

mise en scène /mée̅z aaN sén/ (*plural* **mises en scène** /*pronunc. same*/) *n* **1.** MOVIES, THEATER **ARRANGEMENT OF ACTORS AND SCENERY** the positioning of actors, scenery, and properties on a stage or movie set **2. STYLE OF MOVIE DIRECTING** a style of movie directing characterized by long scenes, little camera movement, and few changes of camera position **3. SETTING FOR SOMETHING** the physical environment in which an event takes place [< French, literally "putting on stage"]

mi·ser /mī́zər/ *n* **1.** somebody who hates spending money and lives as though he or she were poor **2.** somebody regarded as ungenerous, greedy, or selfish [Mid-16C. < Latin, "unfortunate"]

mis·er·a·ble /mízzərəb'l/ *adj* **1. VERY UNHAPPY** experiencing a serious lack of contentment or happiness ○ *feeling miserable* **2. VERY UNPLEASANT** causing or accompanied by discomfort, unpleasantness, or unhappiness ○ *a miserable weekend* **3. CONTEMPTIBLE** deserving contempt or condemnation **4. INADEQUATE** inadequate, often insultingly or embarrassingly inadequate, in quantity or quality ○ *a miserable score* **5. DIRTY OR SQUALID** dirty, squalid, and lacking any comfort **6.** *Carib* **BADLY BEHAVED** troublesome and badly behaved (*especially used of children*) [15C. Via Old French < Latin *miserabilis* "pitiable" < *miser* "unfortunate"] —**mis·er·a·bly** *adv*

CULTURAL NOTE ***Les Misérables***, a novel (1862) by French writer Victor Hugo. Set in mid-19th-century France, it tells the story of Jean Valjean, whose attempts to escape his criminal past are dogged by guilt, fate, and the persistent police inspector Javert. This epic tale is noted for its gripping plot and vivid descriptions of events such as the battle of Waterloo.

mi·sère /mi zér/ *n* **1.** a call in some card games, especially solo whist, indicating that a hand is expected to win no tricks **2.** a hand that is expected to win no tricks [Early 19C < French, literally "poverty, misery"]

mis·e·re·re /mìzzə rérree, -rée̅ree/ *n* CHR same as **misericord** [Late 18C. < Latin, "have mercy!" < *misereri* "have mercy" < *miser* "unfortunate"]

Mis·e·re·re /mìzzə réree, -rée̅ree/ *n* **1.** the 50th or 51st Psalm, depending on the version of the Bible **2.** a musical setting of the Miserere [13C. < the first word of the Latin text, beginning *Miserere mei, Deus* "have mercy on me, O God" (see MISERERE)]

mis·er·i·cord /mízzəri kàwrd, mi zérri kàwrd/ *n* a projecting ledge of a seat in a church stall that, when the seat is turned up, gives a standing person something to rest against [14C < Old French < Latin *misericord* "merciful, compassionate" < *miser* "unfortunate" + *cor* "heart"]

mi·ser·ly /mī́zərlee/ *adj* **1.** greedy for money and unwilling to share or to spend it **2.** contemptibly insufficient or inadequate —**mi·ser·li·ness** *n*

mis·er·y /mízzəree/ (*plural* **-ies**) *n* **1. GREAT UNHAPPINESS** a serious lack of contentment or happiness **2. SOURCE OF GREAT UNHAPPINESS** something that causes great unhappiness **3. POVERTY** a state of extreme poverty and squalor [14C. Directly or via Anglo-Norman *miserie* < Latin *miseria* < Latin *miser* "unfortunate"] ◇ **put somebody out of his** *or* **her misery** to put an end to somebody's suspense or anxiety, especially by revealing something that he or she is desperate to know (*humorous*) ◇ **put an animal out of its misery** to kill an animal in order to prevent it from suffering further pain

mis·es·ti·mate /miss ésti màyt/ (**-mat·ed, -mat·ing, -mates**) *vt* **1.** to estimate something wrongly **2.** a wrong estimation —**mis·es·ti·ma·tion** *n*

MI-SET *abbr* E-COMMERCE merchant initiated SET™

mis·fea·sance /miss fée̅z'nss/ *n* in law, the abuse of lawful authority in order to achieve a desired result [Early 17C. < Anglo-Norman *mesfaisance* < *mesfaire* "do ill" < *mes-* "wrongly" + *faire* "to do" < Latin *facere*]

mis·fire *vi* /miss fī́r/ (**-fired, -fir·ing, -fires**) **1. FAIL TO FIRE PROPERLY** to fail to shoot a bullet or shell when fired **2. FAIL TO OPERATE PROPERLY** to fail to ignite the fuel mixture in the cylinder, or to ignite it at the wrong time (*refers to an internal-combustion engine*) **3. GO WRONG** to fail to achieve a planned result ○ *the plot misfired* ■ *n* /míss fīr, miss fī́r/ **MALFUNCTION IN FIRING** a failure to fire or function properly

mis·fit /míss fìt/ *n* **1.** somebody who does not fit comfortably into a situation or environment ○ *a social misfit* **2.** something that fits badly

mis·for·tune /miss fáwrchən/ *n* **1.** bad luck **2.** an undesirable or unhappy event or circumstance

mis·give /miss gív/ (**-gave** /-gáyv/, **-giv·en** /-gívvən/, **-giv·ing, -gives**) *vt* to feel apprehensive, or to cause a feeling of apprehension or foreboding in somebody (*literary*) [Early 16C. < GIVE in the obsolete sense "suggest"]

mis·giv·ing /miss gívving/ *n* a feeling of doubt or apprehension, especially about undertaking a course of action (*often used in the plural*) ○ *had misgivings about the plan*

mis·guide /miss gī́d/ (**-guid·ed, -guid·ing, -guides**) *vt* to lead somebody in a wrong direction or into making a mistake —**mis·guid·ance** *n*

mis·guid·ed /miss gī́dəd/ *adj* motivated by or based on ideas that are mistaken, heedless, or inappropriate —**mis·guid·ed·ly** *adv* —**mis·guid·ed·ness** *n*

mis·han·dle /miss hánd'l/ (**-dled, -dling, -dles**) *vt* **1.** to deal with something or somebody in an incompetent or ineffective way **2.** to treat something or somebody roughly

mis·hap /míss hàp/ *n* **1.** an unfortunate accident or piece of bad luck **2.** an unfortunate circumstance or set of circumstances (*formal*)

Mi·shi·ma /mi shéemə/, **Yukio** (1925–70) Japanese novelist. He celebrated Japan's nationalist and imperialist history, deploring the sterility of contemporary life, and committed ritual suicide. His novels include the tetralogy *The Sea of Fertility* (1965–70). Pseudonym of **Kimitake, Hiraoka**

mish·mash /mísh màsh/ *n* a disorderly collection or confused mixture of things [15C. < repetition of MASH]

Mish·mi /míshmee/ (*plural same* or **-mis**) *n* **1.** a member of a people living in a mountainous region of Assam in northeastern India **2.** the Tibeto-Burman language of the Mishmi people —**Mish·mi** *adj*

Mish·nah /míshnə/, **Mish·na** *n* **1. JEWISH LAW** the primary body of Jewish civil and religious law, forming the first part of the Talmud **2. JEWISH ORAL LAW** Jewish law from the oral tradition, as distinguished from law derived from the scriptures **3. JEWISH LEGAL TEACHING** the teaching of Jewish law by a rabbi or other authority on it [Early 17C. < Hebrew *mišnāh* "repetition, teaching"] —**Mish·na·ic** /mish náy ik/ *adj*

mis·join·der /miss jóyndər/ *n* an improper combining of plaintiffs, defendants, or causes of action in a single lawsuit

mis·judge /miss júj/ (**-judged, -judg·ing, -judg·es**) *v* **1.** *vti* to make a mistake when judging or evaluating something or when attempting to do something that requires accurate judgment **2.** *vt* to form an incorrect opinion about somebody or something, especially one that attributes bad qualities to somebody unjustly or mistakenly —**mis·judg·ment** *n*

Mis·ki·to /mi skéetō/ (*plural same* or **-tos**) *n* **1.** a member of a Native Central American people living along the Caribbean coasts of Nicaragua and Honduras **2.** the language of the Miskito people [Late 18C. < Miskito] —**Mis·ki·to** *adj*

Mis·kolc /mísh kōlts/ historic and industrial city in northeastern Hungary. Population: 176,629 (1999)..

mis·lay /miss láy/ (**-laid** /-láyd/, **-lay·ing, -lays**) *vt* to lose something temporarily, especially by forgetting where it was put

mis·lead /miss léed/ (**-led** /-léd/, **-lead·ing, -leads**) *vt* **1.** to cause somebody to make a mistake or form a false opinion or belief, either by employing deliberate deception or by supplying incorrect information ○ *The defendant is trying to mislead the jury.* **2.** to be responsible for making somebody, especially somebody younger, do wrong or adopt bad habits —**mis·lead·er** *n*

mis·lead·ing /miss léeding/ *adj* likely or deliberately intended to confuse people or give them a false idea of something —**mis·lead·ing·ly** *adv*

mis·led past participle, past tense of **mislead**

mis·like /miss lík/ (**-liked, -lik·ing, -likes**) *vt* (*archaic*) **1.** to dislike or disapprove of somebody or something **2.** to offend or irritate somebody

mis·man·age /miss mánnij/ (**-aged, -ag·ing, -ag·es**) *vt* to run, organize, or deal with something incompetently —**mis·man·age·ment** *n*

mis·match *n* /míss màch/ a pairing or combination of people or things that are incompatible with or apparently ill-suited to each other ■ *vt* /miss mách/ (**-matched, -match·ing, -match·es**) to fail to match or pair people or things suitably (*usually passive*) ○ *mismatching the socks as usual*

Mis·nag·ed *n* JUDAISM same as **Mitnagged**

mis·name /miss náym/ (**-named, -nam·ing, -names**) *vt* **1.** to call something by a wrong name **2.** to give somebody or something a wrong or inappropriate name

mis·no·mer /miss nómər/ *n* **1.** a wrong or unsuitable name or term for something or somebody **2.** a use of a wrong or unsuitable name or term to describe something or somebody [15C. < Old French < *mes-* "wrongly" + *nommer* "to name" < Latin *nominare*]

mi·so /méessō/ *n* Japanese fermented soybean paste used mainly in vegetarian cooking [Early 18C. < Japanese]

mi·sog·a·my /mi sóggəmee/ *n* an aversion to marriage and the married state [Mid-17C. < modern Latin *misogamia* < Greek *misein* "to hate" + *gamos* "marriage"] —**mis·og·a·mist** *n*

mi·sog·y·ny /mi sójjənee/ *n* a hatred of women, as a sexually defined group [Mid-17C. < Greek *misogunia* < *misein* "to hate" + *gunē* "woman"] —**mi·sog·y·nist** *n, adj* —**mi·sog·y·nis·tic** /mi sòjjə nístik/ *adj*

mi·sol·o·gy /mi sólləjee/ *n* a hatred of reason, logical argument, or enlightenment [Early 19C. < Greek *misologia* < *misein* "to hate" + *-logia* (see -LOGY)]

mis·o·ne·ism /missə née ìzzəm/ *n* a hatred of new things or change [Late 19C. < Italian *misoneismo* < Greek *misein* "to hate" + *neos* "new"]

~~**mispelling**~~ incorrect spelling of **misspelling**

mis·pick·el /míss pìk'l/ *n* MINERALS same as **arsenopyrite** [Late 17C. < German]

mis·place /miss pláyss/ (**-placed, -plac·ing, -plac·es**) *vt* **1.** PUT SOMETHING IN WRONG PLACE to put something in a wrong place or position **2.** MISLAY SOMETHING to lose something, especially temporarily, through forgetting where it was put **3.** TRUST SOMEBODY OR SOMETHING UNWORTHY to put confidence, faith, or trust in somebody or something unsuitable or unworthy —**mis·place·ment** *n*

misplaced mod·i·fi·er *n* a word or phrase positioned so that it is unclear what exactly it refers to, e.g., *lying in the gutter* in "Lying in the gutter, we saw a dead rat"

USAGE See ***dangling participle, kindly,*** and ***only.***

mis·plead /miss pléed/ (**-plead·ed, -pleaded** or **-pled** /-pléd/, **-plead·ing, -pleads**) *vti* to allege or claim something in a lawsuit in a manner not in accordance with procedure or the law

mis·plead·ing /miss pléeding/ *n* an error made or contained in the pleading in a lawsuit

mis·print *n* /míss prìnt/ an error in the printed copy of a text resulting from a mistake made when the text was being printed ■ *vt* /miss prínt/ (**-print·ed, -print·ing, -prints**) to print something wrongly

mis·pri·sion[1] /miss prízh'n/ *n* **1.** HIDING CRIME the failure of somebody who knows of but is not involved in a felony or treason to report it to the authorities **2.** WRONGDOING IN OFFICIAL DUTIES neglect or wrong done by a public official in the performance of the duties of his or her office **3.** SEDITION sedition against a government or court [15C. < Anglo-Norman *mesprisioun* "error" < Old French *mesprendre* "make a mistake"]

mis·pri·sion[2] /miss prízh'n/ *n* a misunderstanding of something, especially a failure to appreciate the true worth of somebody or something (*archaic*) [Late 16C. < MISPRIZE after MISPRISION [1]]

mis·prize /miss príz/ (**-prized, -priz·ing, -priz·es**) *vt* (*formal*) **1.** to fail to appreciate the true worth of something or somebody **2.** to consider somebody or something unworthy of respect or admiration [14C. < Old French *mesprisier* "misestimate value" < *prisier* "to praise"]

mis·pro·nounce /mìsprə nównss/ (**-nounced, -nounc·ing, -nounc·es**) *vti* to pronounce something incorrectly —**mis·pro·nun·ci·a·tion** /mìsprə nùnssee áysh'n/ *n*

mis·read /miss réed/ (**-read** /-réd/, **-read·ing, -reads**) *vt* **1.** to make a mistake in reading something, e.g., reading aloud inaccurately, mistaking one word for another, or misunderstanding the sense of what is written **2.** to fail to understand the true meaning or nature of something ○ *misreading the public mood*

mis·re·port /mìssri páwrt/ *vt* (**-port·ed, -port·ing, -ports**) to report something in an inaccurate or distorted way ■ *n* an inaccurate or distorted report

mis·rep·re·sent /miss rèppri zént/ (**-sent·ed, -sent·ing, -sents**) *vt* **1.** to give an inaccurate or deliberately false account of the nature of somebody or something **2.** not to be truly or typically representative of somebody or something —**mis·rep·re·sen·ta·tion** /miss rèppri zen táysh'n/ *n*

mis·rule /miss róol/ *vti* (**-ruled, -rul·ing, -rules**) RULE BADLY to govern a people or place unjustly or inefficiently ■ *n* **1.** BAD GOVERNMENT unjust or inefficient government of a people or place **2.** PUBLIC DISORDER a state of public disorder or anarchy

miss[1] /miss/ *v* (**missed, miss·ing, miss·es**) **1.** *vti* NOT HIT TARGET to fail to hit, reach, catch, or make contact with somebody or something that is being aimed at **2.** *vt* FAIL TO BE SOMEWHERE to fail to be present or on time for something **3.** *vt* NOT HEAR, SEE, OR COMPREHEND SOMETHING to fail to hear, see, or understand something, e.g., through inattention or being distracted **4.** *vt* NOT TAKE A CHANCE to fail to take an opportunity **5.** *vti* FAIL TO ACHIEVE to fail to achieve a set target or goal **6.** *vt* AVOID SOMETHING to escape or avoid a potentially harmful, dangerous, or unpleasant situation **7.** *vt* OMIT SOMETHING to leave something out **8.** *vt* REGRET ABSENCE OF SOMEBODY OR SOMETHING to feel sorry that somebody or something is absent ○ *missed her greatly while she was away* **9.** *vt* DISCOVER ABSENCE OF SOMEBODY OR SOMETHING to realize that a person or thing is not present at the expected time or in the expected place ○ *He was halfway home before he missed his wallet.* **10.** *vi* MISFIRE to fail to ignite the fuel mixture in the cylinder (*refers to an internal-combustion engine*) ■ *n* **1.** FAILURE TO MAKE CONTACT a failure to hit, reach, catch, or make contact with somebody or something aimed at **2.** A FAILURE something that does not succeed or fails to impress [Old English *missan* < Germanic, "go wrong"] —**miss·a·ble** *adj* ◇ **give something a miss** to choose not to do something or attend something (*informal*)

miss out *vi* to lose an opportunity of doing something

miss[2] /miss/ *n* **1.** WAY OF ADDRESSING YOUNG WOMAN a term of address for a girl or young woman, sometimes used in place of her name **2.** YOUNG WOMAN a girl or young woman ■ **miss·es** *npl* FASHION WOMEN'S CLOTHING SIZES a series of clothing sizes that fit women and girls of average height and build [Mid-17C. Shortening of MISTRESS]

Miss *n* **1.** a title placed before the name of a girl or unmarried woman **2.** used together with a place name or another word in the winner's title awarded in a beauty contest or similar event ○ *Miss America*

Miss. *abbr* Mississippi

mis·sal /míss'l/ *n* a book that contains all the prayers, responses, and hymns used in the Roman Catholic Mass [13C. < medieval Latin *missale* < late Latin *missa* (see MASS)]

mis·sel thrush *n* BIRDS another spelling of **mistle thrush**

mis·sense /míss sènss/ *n* a genetic mutation in which a genetic coding sequence (**codon**) for one amino acid is changed to one that codes for another

mis·shap·en /miss sháypən/, **mis·shaped** /-sháypt/ *adj* having an undesirably unusual shape —**mis·shape** *n, vt*

mis·sile /míss'l/ *n* **1.** a weapon consisting of a warhead propelled by a rocket **2.** an object thrown or launched as a weapon, e.g., a rock or bullet [Early 17C. < Latin *missilis* < *mittere* "send"]

mis·sile·ry /míss'lree/, **mis·sil·ry** *n* **1.** missiles, considered collectively **2.** the designing, building, or operating of missiles

miss·ing /míssing/ *adj* **1.** not present in an expected place ○ *There's a page missing from the book.* **2.** not yet traced and not known for certain to be alive, but not confirmed as dead ○ *missing persons*

miss·ing link *n* **1.** an animal theorized or sought as a transitional evolutionary stage between apes and humans **2.** something that is absent from a sequence or series and is needed to connect up its various parts and complete it

mis·si·ol·og·y /mìssee óllәjee/ *n* the study of Christian missionary work [Mid-20C. < MISSION]

mis·sion /mísh'n/ *n* **1.** ASSIGNED TASK a special task given to a person or group to carry out **2.** CALLING an objective or task that somebody believes it is his or her duty to carry out or to which he or she attaches special importance and devotes special care **3.** SPACE VEHICLE'S TRIP a single flight or voyage of a military aircraft or a spacecraft **4.** GROUP OF REPRESENTATIVES a group of people sent to a country to represent their government, a business, or other organization **5.** DIPLOMATIC REPRESENTATION ABROAD a permanent diplomatic delegation in another country **6.** GROUP OF CHURCH WORKERS a body of people sent by a church to another part of the country or to a foreign country to spread their faith or do medical and social work **7.** CHURCH WORK IN COMMUNITY a campaign of religious work, often including community aid at home or abroad, carried out by a church **8.** HOUSING USED BY MISSIONARIES a building or group of buildings belonging to a missionary organization **9.** PLACE THAT HELPS NEEDY a center run by a religious or charitable organization offering food, shelter, aid, and spiritual comfort to needy people ■ *adj also* **Mis·sion** IN SPANISH MISSION STYLE relating to or influenced by a style of architecture or heavy dark oak furniture used in early Spanish missions in the southwestern United States ■ *vt* (**-sioned, -sion·ing, -sions**) **1.** SEND SOMEBODY ON MISSION to send somebody on or give somebody a mission **2.** OPERATE MISSION to establish or conduct a religious mission in a place or among a people [Late 16C. Directly or via French < Latin *mission-* < *mittere* "send off"]

ORIGIN The Latin word *mittere* "to send off," from which **mission** is derived, is also the source of English *admit, commit, mess, message, missile, missive, permit, promise, remit, submit,* and *transmit.*

mis·sion·ar·y /mísh'n èrree/ *n* (*plural* **-ies**) **1.** SOMEBODY DOING CHURCH WORK ABROAD somebody sent to another country by a church to spread its faith or to do social and medical work **2.** PERSUADER somebody who tries to persuade others to accept or join something ■ *adj* OF OR LIKE MISSIONARY relating to or similar to a missionary

mis·sion·ar·y po·si·tion *n* a position for sexual intercourse in which the woman lies on her back and the man lies on top of and facing her [Because missionaries held it to be least reprehensible]

Mis·sion·ar·y Ridge /mìsh'n èrree ríj/ ridge in southeastern Tennessee and northwestern Georgia, the site of an important Union victory in the Civil War in 1863

mis·sion creep *n* a tendency of military operations in foreign countries to increase gradually in scope and demand further commitment of personnel and resources as the situation develops

mis·sion·er /mísh'nər/ *n* CHR same as **missionary** *n* (sense 1)

mis·sion state·ment *n* a formal document that states the objectives of a company or organization

Mis·sion Vi·e·jo /mìsh'n vee áyhō/ city in southwestern California, in Orange County, near the Pacific coast. Population: 96,307 (2002 estimate).

mis·sis /míssiz/, **mis·sus** /míssəz/ *n* used to refer to a man's wife or woman partner, usually either by the man himself or by another man (*informal; sometimes considered offensive*) [Late 18C. Alteration of MISTRESS]

Mis·sis·sau·ga /mìssi sáwgə/ city in southern Ontario, Canada, on the shore of Lake Ontario. Population: 612,925 (2001).

Mississippi

Mis·sis·sip·pi /mìssi síppee/ **1.** major river in the United States. It flows southward from northern Minnesota to Louisiana, emptying into the Gulf of Mexico. Length: 2,340 mi./3,770 km. **2.** state in the southeastern United States, bordered by Tennessee, Alabama, the Gulf of Mexico, Louisiana, and Arkansas. Capital: Jackson. Population: 3,871,782 (2002 estimate). Area: 48,286 sq. mi./125,060 sq. km.

Mis·sis·sip·pi·an /mìssi síppee ən/ *n* **1.** somebody who comes from Mississippi **2.** the epoch of geologic time, 360 million to 330 million years ago, during which land plants became larger and more varied, particularly in low-lying swampy areas. See table at **geologic time** —**Mis·sis·sip·pi·an** *adj*

Mis·sis·sip·pi·an cul·ture *n* the last of the Native North American mound-building cultures, which flourished from about A.D. 800 to 1300

mis·sive /míssiv/ *n* a letter or other written communication, often formal or legal communication (*formal*) [Early 16C. < medieval Latin *missivus* < Latin *mittere* "send"]

~~**missle**~~ incorrect spelling of **missile**

Mis·sou·la /mi zóolə/ city and seat of Missoula County in western Montana, on the Columbia River. Population: 59,518 (2002 estimate).

Mis·sou·ri /mi zóoree, mi zóorə/ **1.** longest river in the United States. It flows from southwestern Montana southeastward to join the Mississippi River in Missouri. Length: 2,315 mi./3,726 km. **2.** /mi zóoree, mi zóorə/ state in the central United States, bordered by Iowa, Illinois, Kentucky, Tennessee, Arkansas, Oklahoma, Kansas, and Nebraska. Capital: Jefferson City. Population: 5,672,579 (2002 estimate). Area: 69,709 sq. mi./180,545 sq. km. —**Mis·sou·ri·an** *n, adj*

Missouri

PRONUNCIATION The US state name ***Missouri***, which derives from the name of a Native American people living in the region of the Missouri River, can be pronounced two ways, the first variant being the most common: /mi zóoree, mi zóorə/.

mis·speak /miss spéek/ (**-spoke** /-spṓk/, **-spo·ken** /-spṓkən/, **-speak·ing, -speaks**) *v* **1.** *vt* PRONOUNCE INCORRECTLY to pronounce something incorrectly **2.** **mis·speak your·self** *vr* EXPRESS YOURSELF UNCLEARLY to speak or express yourself in a way that is inappropriate, inaccurate, or unclear ○ *Unfortunately the envoy misspoke himself on that particular issue.* **3.** *vi* SPEAK INCORRECTLY to speak incorrectly or imperfectly

mis·spell /miss spél/ (**-spelled, -spell·ing, -spells**) *vt* to spell a word incorrectly

mis·spell·ing /miss spélling/ *n* an incorrect spelling of a word

mis·spend /miss spénd/ (**-spent** /-spént/, **-spend·ing, -spends**) *vt* to spend money or time badly or wastefully

mis·spoke LANGUAGE past tense of **misspeak**

mis·spo·ken LANGUAGE past participle of **misspeak**

mis·step /miss stép/ *n* **1.** a bad or awkward step, or a step in a wrong direction **2.** an error in judgment or conduct

mis·sus *n* (*informal*) **1.** another spelling of **missis** (*sometimes considered offensive*) **2.** *UK* a term of address for a woman, often used in place of her name

miss·y /míssee/ *n* used as a term of address for a girl or young woman, often expressing affection or reprimand (*informal; sometimes considered offensive*)

mist /mist/ *n* **1.** THIN FOG a thin gray cloud of water droplets that condenses in the atmosphere just above the ground **2.** CONDENSED WATER VAPOR a film of water vapor that has condensed on a surface **3.** FINE SPRAY a fine spray of liquid, e.g., from an atomizer or aerosol **4.** LIQUID SUSPENSION IN GAS a suspension of liquid in a gas **5.** OBSCURING THING something that makes it difficult to see or understand something ■ *v* (**mist·ed, mist·ing, mists**) **1.** *vti* FILM OVER to cover or obscure something in a mist, or become covered in or obscured by mist ○ *misted up the windows* **2.** *vi* BECOME BLURRED BY TEARS to become blurred by tears **3.** *vt* SPRAY SOMETHING to apply a fine liquid spray to something [Old English < Indo-European, "urinate"]

mis·take /mi stáyk/ *n* **1.** INCORRECT ACT OR DECISION an incorrect, unwise, or unfortunate act or decision caused by bad judgment or a lack of information or care ○ *It's an easy mistake to make.* **2.** ERROR something in a piece of work that is incorrect, e.g., a misspelling or a misprint **3.** MISUNDERSTANDING a misunderstanding of something ○ *There must be some mistake; I didn't order this.* ■ *vt* (**-took** /-tóok/, **-tak·en** /-táykən/, **-tak·ing, -takes**) **1.** MISUNDERSTAND SOMETHING to misunderstand or misinterpret something ○ *I mistook the meaning of the phrase.* **2.** IDENTIFY SOMEBODY OR SOMETHING INCORRECTLY to identify somebody or something incorrectly, or fail to recognize somebody or something ○ *We tend to mistake infatuation for real love.* **3.** CHOOSE SOMETHING INCORRECTLY to choose something incorrectly or injudiciously [14C. < Old Norse *mistaka* "take in error"] —**mis·tak·a·ble** *adj* ◇ **by mistake** accidentally, without wishing or intending to do something

SYNONYMS ***mistake, error, inaccuracy, slip, blunder, faux pas, oversight***

CORE MEANING: something incorrect or improper

mistake an incorrect, unwise, or unfortunate act or decision caused by bad judgment or a lack of information or care ○ *He expects people to make occasional mistakes and plans accordingly.* ○ *He soon learned he'd made a big mistake in marrying Bertha.* **error** something unintentionally done wrong ○ *If not detected, this error would have had disastrous consequences.* ○ *The leadership had made a serious error of military judgment.* **inaccuracy** something that is incorrect, especially something that has been measured, calculated, copied, or conveyed incorrectly ○ *The reports were riddled with inaccuracies.* ○ *The commission's findings were criticized for containing obvious inaccuracies.* **slip** a minor mistake, especially one caused by carelessness ○ *One slip would have betrayed all I was working for.* **blunder** a serious or embarrassing mistake, usually the result of carelessness or ignorance ○ *The young Canadian scored another goal after a bad blunder by Switzerland's defense.* **faux pas** an embarrassing mistake that breaks a social convention ○ *She stopped smiling, as if I had committed a faux pas by referring to her dress.* **oversight** a mistake, especially as a result of a failure to do or notice something ○ *If the money still hasn't been transferred it's due to an oversight by my bank.*

mis·tak·en /mi stáykən/ *adj* **1.** wrong or incorrect in an assumption, belief, or understanding of something ○ *If you think that'll work, you're sadly mistaken.* **2.** based on incorrect information or values ○ *a mistaken sense of loyalty* —**mis·tak·en·ly** *adv* —**mis·tak·en·ness** *n*

Mis·tas·si·ni, Lake /mìstə séenee/ lake in central Canada, the largest in Quebec Province. Area: 840 sq. mi./2,200 sq. km.

mis·ter /místər/ *n* (*informal*) **1.** used as a term of address for a man, usually in place of his name **2.** used to refer to a woman's husband or man partner, either by the woman or by another woman (*sometimes considered offensive*) [Mid-16C. Alteration of MASTER]

Mis·ter *n* used as the full form of the courtesy title "Mr." [Mid-18C. < MISTER]

mis·throw /miss thrṓ/ (**-threw** /-thróo/, **-thrown** /-thrṓn/, **-throw·ing, -throws**) *vti* to throw something such as dice or a ball in a wrong or invalid way —**mis·throw** *n*

Mis·ti /méestee/ dormant volcano in the Andes, in southern Peru. Height: 19,101 ft./5,822 m.

mis·tle thrush /míss'l-/, **mis·sel thrush** *n* a large thrush with a spotted breast and grayish back that feeds on berries, especially those of mistletoe. Native to: Europe. Latin name: *Turdus viscivorus.* [Early 17C. < Old English *mistel* (See MISTLETOE)]

mis·tle·toe /míss'l tṑ/ *n* **1.** PARASITIC BUSH an evergreen bush that grows as a parasite on trees such as apple and oak, has leaves in horseshoe-shaped pairs, and bears white berries in winter. Native to: Europe, Asia. Latin name: *Viscum album.* **2.** PLANT RESEMBLING MISTLETOE a bush that resembles true mistletoe. Native to: North America. Latin name: *Phoradendron flavescens.* **3.** CHRISTMAS DECORATION a sprig of mistletoe traditionally used as a decoration and for kissing under at Christmas [Old English *misteltān* < *mistel* "mistletoe" + *tān* "twig" < Germanic]

mis·took past tense of **mistake**

mis·tral /místrəl, mi stráal/ *n* a powerful cold dry northeasterly wind that blows in the south of France [Early 17C. < French < Latin *magistralis* "dominant"; from its power]

mis·treat /miss tréet/ (**-treat·ed, -treat·ing, -treats**) *vt* to treat somebody or something badly or roughly —**mis·treat·ment** *n*

SYNONYMS ***mistreat, abuse, ill-treat, maltreat, ill-use***

CORE MEANING: to treat somebody or something wrongly or badly

mistreat to treat somebody or something badly or roughly ○ *It was clear that some prisoners had been mistreated.* ○ *Children should be taught that mistreating animals is not okay.* **abuse** to treat a person or animal cruelly, whether physically, psychologically, or sexually, especially on a regular or habitual basis ○ *a clinic for men who have sexually* *abused children* ○ *She has been accused of abusing the animals in her care.* **ill-treat** to behave cruelly or unkindly toward a person or animal ○ *She felt let down by the broken promises, believing that she had been ill-treated by her employers.* ○ *There was evidence that the dogs were being ill-treated.* **maltreat** to behave cruelly or unkindly toward a person or animal, especially by neglecting their welfare ○ *If one child in a family is maltreated, others in the same family are at high risk.* **ill-use** to treat somebody or something harshly or inappropriately ○ *With a feeling of being ill-used he started to clear up the remains of last night's dinner.*

mis·tress /místrəss/ *n* **1. EXTRAMARITAL LOVER OF MAN** a woman with whom a man has a usually long-term extramarital sexual relationship, often one in which he provides financial support **2. OWNER OR CONTROLLER OF SOMETHING** a woman who owns or controls something **3. PERSONIFICATION AS WOMAN** something that rules or controls, personified as a woman ○ *Venice, once mistress of the seas* **4. ABLE WOMAN** a woman who is highly skilled in a particular activity ○ *a mistress of the art of negotiation* **5. OWNER OF PET** the woman owner of a pet animal **6. LOVED WOMAN** a woman with whom a man is in love (*archaic*) [13C. < Old French *maistresse*, form of *maistre* (see MASTER)]

Mis·tress *n* used as a courtesy title to address a married woman, usually in front of the surname (*archaic*)

mis·tress of cer·e·mo·nies *n* a woman in charge of the proceedings at an event or entertainment

mis·tri·al /míss trī əl, miss trī əl, -trīl/ *n* **1.** a trial that is invalid because a mistake such as an error in procedure has been made **2.** a trial that does not come to a definitive conclusion, e.g., because the jury cannot agree on a verdict

mis·trust /miss trúst/ *n* suspicion about or lack of confidence in somebody or something ■ *vt* (**-trust·ed, -trust·ing, -trusts**) to be suspicious of and unable to trust or rely on somebody or something —**mis·trust·ful** *adj* —**mis·trust·ful·ly** *adv*

mist·y /místee/ (**-i·er, -i·est**) *adj* **1. COVERED IN MIST** with a lot of mist in the air or surrounded or covered by mist ○ *a misty mountain* ○ *a misty morning* **2. LIKE MIST** like mist, especially in being in a cloud or spray of fine drops **3. DIM AND INDISTINCT** dim and indistinct, as if veiled by mist **4. SAD AND NOSTALGIC** feeling sad or nostalgic —**mist·i·ly** *adv* —**mist·i·ness** *n*

mist·y-eyed *adj* **1.** with a film of tears in the eyes **2.** sentimental or dreamlike ○ *a misty-eyed memoir*

mis·un·der·stand /mìss undər stánd/ (**-stood** /-stŏŏd/, **-stand·ing, -stands**) *vti* to fail to realize the real or intended meaning of something, the true nature of something, or what somebody is really like

mis·un·der·stand·ing /mìss undər stánding/ *n* **1.** a failure to understand or interpret something correctly **2.** a minor disagreement or dispute

mis·un·der·stood /mìss undər stŏŏd/ past participle, past tense of **misunderstand** ■ *adj* not correctly understood, or not properly and sympathetically appreciated ○ *a misunderstood teenager*

mis·us·age /miss yoóssij/ *n* **1.** a wrong or inappropriate use of language **2.** same as **misuse** *n* (sense 1)

mis·use *n* /miss yoóss/ **1. WRONG USE** the incorrect or improper use of something **2. CRUEL TREATMENT** the cruel treatment of a person or animal ■ *vt* /miss yoóz/ (**-used, -us·ing, -us·es**) **1. USE SOMETHING WRONGLY** to use something in an incorrect or improper way, or for a dishonest purpose **2. TREAT SOMEBODY CRUELLY** to treat a person or animal cruelly —**mis·used** *adj*

SYNONYMS ***misuse, abuse, misappropriate, ill-use, misapply***

CORE MEANING: to use something for an inappropriate purpose

misuse to use something in an incorrect or improper way, or for a dishonest purpose ○ *The former president is charged with misusing money from secret government funds during his presidency.* **abuse** to use something in an improper, illegal, or harmful way ○ *A handful of cynical local officials have behaved deplorably, abusing their powers.* ○ *She admits having abused drugs and alcohol.* **misappropriate** to take something, especially money, dishonestly, or in order to use it for an improper or illegal purpose ○ *He was sentenced to 12 years in jail on charges of misappropriating foreign aid for personal gain.* **ill-use** to use something improperly ○ *He was placed under investigation to determine how much of the $35 million that had been ill-used was his responsibility.* ○ *The writing is creative, in the true sense of that ill-used word.* **misapply** to use something badly, incorrectly, or improperly ○ *He said the appeals court "disregarded the facts and misapplied the law."*

mis·us·er /miss yoózər/ *n* somebody who uses a right, privilege, or position of authority in an incorrect or improper way or for a dishonest purpose

MIT *abbr* EDUC Massachusetts Institute of Technology

Mitch·ell /míchəl/ city in southeastern South Dakota, northwest of Sioux Falls and south of Huron. Population: 14,626 (2002 estimate).

Mitch·ell, Mount mountain in western North Carolina. It is the highest point in the United States east of the Mississippi River. Height: 6,684 ft./2,037 m.

Mitch·ell /míchəl/, **Joni** (*b.* 1943) Canadian singer and songwriter. Her albums include *Clouds* (1969), *Blue* (1971), and *Wild Things Run Fast* (1982). Born **Roberta Joan Anderson**

> "To see teenagers sitting around trying to solve the problems of the world, I figured, all things considered, I'd rather be dancing."
> [Joni Mitchell. Quoted in "Joni Mitchell," *Off the Record: An Oral History of Popular Music*, Joe Smith; 1988]

Mitch·ell, Keith (*b.* 1947) prime minister of Grenada (1995–). Head of the New National Party since 1989, as premier he has called for increased political and economic integration with neighboring Caribbean states. Full name **Mitchell, Keith Claudius**

Mitch·ell, Margaret (1900–49) US writer. She wrote the enormously popular Civil War novel *Gone With the Wind* (1936), which won a Pulitzer Prize. Full name **Mitchell, Margaret Munnerlyn**

> "After all, tomorrow is another day."
> [Margaret Mitchell, closing words, *Gone with the Wind*; 1936]

Mitch·ell, Maria (1818–89) US astronomer. She discovered a comet and tracked its orbit in 1847, and also researched sunspots.

Mitch·ell, William (1879–1936) US army officer and aviation pioneer. He commanded the US Army Air Force (1917–18) during World War I, subsequently becoming an advocate of air power. Known as **Mitchell, Billy**

Mitch·um /míchəm/, **Robert** (1917–97) US movie actor. His many movies include *Night of the Hunter* (1955), *Farewell My Lovely* (1975), and *Cape Fear* (1961).

> "What's history going to say about the movies? All those rows of seats facing a blank screen? Crazy!"
> [Attributed to Robert Mitchum, *Filmgoer's Book of Quotes*, Leslie Halliwell; 1973]

mite[1] /mīt/ *n* a tiny eight-legged invertebrate animal related to spiders and ticks. Some mites live freely and some as parasites that can carry disease, attack plants, and cause human allergies. Order: Acarina. [Old English *mīte* < Germanic, "cut"]

SPELLCHECK See ***might***[1].

mite[2] /mīt/ *n* **1. SMALL CHILD** a small child or animal, especially one that inspires pity (*informal*) **2. SMALL AMOUNT** a small piece or small amount ○ *You could show just a mite of concern.* **3. SMALL COIN** a small coin of little value (*archaic*) [14C. < Middle Low German and Middle Dutch *mīte*, a small Flemish coin, also "tiny animal"]

mi·ter /mítər/ *n* **1. BISHOP'S HAT** the ceremonial headdress of a Christian bishop or abbot, consisting of a tall pointed hat creased across the top, with two ribbons hanging down the back **2.** CONSTR same as **miter joint** **3. SURFACE OF MITER JOINT** either of the surfaces that are joined together to form a miter joint **4. DIAGONAL JOIN AT CORNER BETWEEN HEMS** in sewing, a diagonal join between the edges of two hems that meet at a corner of a piece of fabric ■ *vt* (**-tered, -ter·ing, -ters**) **1. JOIN PIECES OF WOOD** to join pieces of wood using a miter joint **2. SHAPE WOOD FOR JOINT** to shape the end of a piece of wood, especially by cutting it off at an angle of 45° when making a corner or miter joint **3. DIAGONALLY JOIN HEMS AT CORNER** in sewing, to make a diagonal join at a corner between two hems **4. GIVE MITER TO SOMEBODY** to confer a miter on somebody, indicating promotion to the rank of bishop [14C. Via Old French < Latin *mitra* < Greek, "belt, turban"] —**mi·ter·er** *n*

mi·ter block *n* a block with slots cut in it to guide a handsaw at the appropriate angle when cutting a miter joint

mi·ter box *n* a box with open ends that is used to hold wood and guide a handsaw at the appropriate angle when cutting a miter joint

mi·ter joint *n* a corner joint in woodwork, usually made by cutting two ends to be joined at 45° angles and gluing or nailing them together into a right angle

mi·ter square *n* a tool used in cutting wood at an angle that has a beveled arm either fixed at an angle of 45° or adjustable to any angle

mi·ter·wort /mítər wùrt, -wàwrt/ (*plural* **-worts** or *same*) *n* a plant with seedpods that resemble a bishop's miter. Flowers: small, white, in clusters. Native to: Asia, North America. Genus: *Mitella.* [Mid-19C. < the shape of its capsule]

Mit·ford /mítfərd/, **Jessica** (1917–97) British-born US writer. Her best-known book is *The American Way of Death* (1965). *Hons and Rebels* (1960) gives an account of her unconventional family, including her sister Nancy Mitford.

> "I have nothing against undertakers personally. It's just that I wouldn't want one to bury my sister."
> [Jessica Mitford, *Saturday Review*; February 1, 1964]

Mit·ford, Nancy (1904–73) British writer. Author of *Love in a Cold Climate* (1949) and *The Blessing* (1951), she was the sister of Jessica Mitford.

> "An aristocracy in a republic is like a chicken whose head has been cut off: it may run about in a lively way, but in fact it is dead."
> [Nancy Mitford, *Noblesse Oblige*; 1956]

mi·ther /míthər/ *n Scotland* same as **mother**[1] *n* (sense 1) [Late 18C. Variant]

Mith·ra·ism /míthrə ìzzəm/ *n* a religion originating in Persia and involving worship of the god Mithras. It became popular among the Roman military in the late Roman Empire. —**Mith·ra·ic** /mi thráy ik/ *adj* —**Mith·ra·ist** *n*

Mith·ras /míthrəss/ *n* in the Zoroastrian tradition and Persian mythology, the god of light, truth, and goodness. He is often shown with a bull, which he is said to have slain before fertilizing the world with its blood. [Mid-16C. Via Latin *Mithras* < Old Persian and Avestan *Mithra*]

mith·ri·date /míthrə dàyt/ *n* a substance believed in ancient medicine and folklore to be an antidote to every poison and a cure for every disease [Early 16C. < medieval Latin *mithridatum* < late Latin *mithridatius* "relating to Mithridates," king of Pontus (132–62 B.C.), reputedly immune to poisons] —**mith·ri·dat·ic** /mìthrə dáttik/ *adj* —**mith·ri·da·tism** *n*

mi·ti·cide /míti sīd/ *n* a substance that kills mites —**mi·ti·cid·al** /mìtti sīd'l/ *adj*

mit·i·gate /mítti gàyt/ (**-gat·ed, -gat·ing, -gates**) *vt* **1.** to make an offense or crime less serious or more excusable **2.** to make something less harsh, severe, or violent [15C. < Latin *mitigat-*, past participle of *mitigare* "make mild" < *mitis* "gentle, soft" + *agere* "make"] —**mit·i·ga·ble** /míttigəb'l/ *adj* —**mit·i·ga·tion** /mìtti gáysh'n/ *n*

USAGE See ***militate.***

mit·i·gat·ing /mítti gàyting/ *adj* making an offense or a crime seem less serious or more excusable ○ *mitigating circumstances*

mit·i·ga·tion spe·cial·ist *n* a member of a criminal defense team who gathers detailed information about a defendant in order to persuade a jury not to impose the death penalty

mi·tis /mítiss, meétiss/, **mi·tis met·al** *n* a form of iron made malleable by having a small amount of aluminum added to it [Late 19C. Probably < Latin *mitis* "mild"]

Mit·nag·ged /mìt naa géd/ (*plural* **-dim** /-naagə dím/), **Mit·na·ged** (*plural* **-nag·dim**), **Mis·nag·ed** /miss naá gəd/ (*plural* **-dim** /-naágə dím/) *n* in the 18th and 19th centuries, a Jew in central and eastern Europe who believed in rationalism and opposed Hasidism [Early 20C. < Hebrew *mitnaggēd* "opponent"]

mi·to·chon·dri·a BIOL plural of **mitochondrion**

mi·to·chon·dri·al /mìtə kóndree əl/ *adj* relating to a mitochondrion or mitochondria

mi·to·chon·dri·al DNA *n* a small circular DNA molecule found in the mitochondria of a cell. Mitochondrial DNA is inherited only from the mother.

mi·to·chon·dri·on /mìtə kóndree ən/ (*plural* **-dri·a** /-dree ə/) *n* a small round or rod-shaped body that is found in the cytoplasm of most cells and produces enzymes for the metabolic conversion of food to energy [Early 20C. < Greek *mitos* "thread" + *khondrion* < *khondros* "granule, lump (of salt)"]

mi·to·gen /mítəjən/ *n* a substance or agent that induces mitosis [Mid-20C. < MITOSIS]

mi·to·my·cin /mìtə míss'n/ *n* an antibiotic produced by a soil bacterium that inhibits DNA synthesis and is used against tumors [Mid-20C. < *mito-*, origin ?]

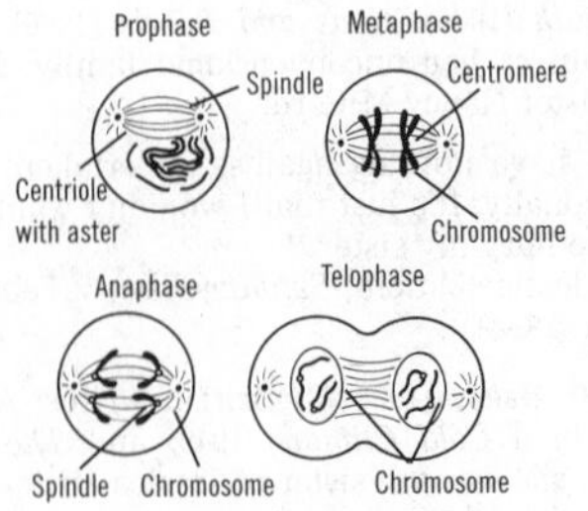

mitosis

mi·to·sis /mī tóssiss/ *n* the process by which a cell divides into two daughter cells, each of which has the same number of chromosomes as the original cell [Late 19C. < Greek *mitos* "thread"] —**mi·to·tic** /mī tóttik/ *adj*

mi·trail·leuse /meètrə yṓz/ *n* an early machine gun with 35 barrels that could be fired simultaneously or in sequence, mounted on a carriage drawn by four horses. The gun was developed in France and first used in the Franco-Prussian War of 1870. [Late 19C. < French *mitrailler* "fire mitraille" < *mitraille* "small money, pieces of metal," alteration of Old French *mitaille* < *mite*, a small coin]

mi·tral /mítrəl/ *adj* relating to a bishop's miter or like it in shape, especially in having separate front and back sections [Early 17C. < modern Latin *mitralis* < Latin *mitra* (see MITER)]

mi·tral ste·no·sis *n* the narrowing of the heart's mitral valve as the result of disease

mi·tral valve *n* the one-way valve between the upper and lower chambers, or atrium and ventricle, on the left side of the heart [< its shape]

mi·tre *n, vt* Can, UK spelling of **miter**

Mi·tro·pou·los /mi tróppoo lòss/, **Dimitri** (1896–1960) Greek-born US conductor and composer. Conductor of the New York Philharmonic Orchestra (1949–58) and the Metropolitan Opera orchestra (1954–60), he was known for championing modern music.

mit·su·ba /mit sŏŏbə/ *n* in Japanese cuisine, an herb similar to Italian parsley, having a mild flavor like that of chervil [Late 20C. < Japanese]

mitt /mit/ *n* **1.** MITTEN a mitten, especially a child's mitten (*informal*) **2.** HAND COVERING a covering for the hand and fingers, especially one shaped like a mitten ○ *an oven mitt* **3.** HAND a hand, especially when large, clumsy, or dirty (*slang*) **4.** BASEBALL PLAYER'S PADDED GLOVE in baseball, a glove, especially a large fingerless padded glove worn by the catcher **5.** GLOVE WITHOUT FINGERS a woman's glove, popular in the 19th century, that left the fingers uncovered [Mid-18C. Shortening of MITTEN]

Mit·tel·eu·ro·pe·an /mìtt'l yoorə peé ən/ *adj* relating to Central Europe, its culture, and its various inhabitants ○ *"A master of wild, at times uproarious, plots and characters whose Eastern and Mitteleuropean accents he renders with perfect pitch, the author has until now remained very much offstage."* (Elizabeth Frank, professor of literature, Bard College *New York Times Book Review*; July 20, 2003) —**Mit·tel·eu·ro·pe·an** *n*

mit·ten /mítt'n/ *n* a glove with one covering for the thumb and one covering for the four fingers [14C. < French *mitaine*]

Mit·ter·rand /meètə raàN/, **François** (1916–96) French president (1981–95). As the first socialist president of the Fifth Republic, he worked to strengthen France's position in the European Union.

> "Nothing is won forever in human affairs, but everything is always possible."
> [François Mitterrand, *Observer (London)*; June 12, 1994]

mit·ti·mus /míttəməss/ (*plural* **-mus·es**) *n* an official order to send somebody to prison [15C. < Latin, "we send," first word of this order in Latin]

mitz·vah /mítsvə, míts vaà/ (*plural* **-voth** /-vōt, -vōth/ or **-vahs**) *n* **1.** a Jewish religious duty or obligation, especially one of the commandments of Jewish religious law **2.** an act of kindness performed by or to a Jew [Mid-17C. < Hebrew *miṣwāh* "commandment"]

Mi·wok /meé wòk/ (*plural same* or **-woks**) *n* **1.** a member of a Native North American people living in central California from the Sierra Nevada foothills to the San Francisco Bay area **2.** the language of the Miwok people, in some classifications belonging to the Penutian family of Native American languages. Miwok is now spoken by very few people. [Late 19C. < Miwok, "people"] —**Mi·wok** *adj*

mix /miks/ *v* (**mixed, mix·ing, mix·es**) **1.** *vt* COMBINE INGREDIENTS to combine ingredients by putting them together or blending them to make a single new substance ○ *Mix the flour and dried fruit together.* **2.** *vi* BE COMBINED to become combined, or be capable of becoming combined ○ *Oil and water don't mix.* **3.** *vt* MAKE SOMETHING BY COMBINING to form or create something by combining separate ingredients ○ *Would you mix me a cocktail?* **4.** *vt* ADD SOMETHING EXTRA to add something as an extra or later ingredient ○ *Mix the fruit into the batter.* **5.** *vt* DO THINGS AT SAME TIME to do something at the same time as something else ○ *able to mix business with pleasure* **6.** *vt* ARRANGE THINGS BESIDE EACH OTHER to arrange things next to or alongside each other ○ *mixing browns and golds to create a sense of warmth* **7.** *vi* GO TOGETHER to go well together ○ *Reds and greens just don't mix.* **8.** *vi* MEET PEOPLE to meet other people socially, or enjoy being with other people in social situations **9.** *vi* PARTICIPATE to participate or become involved in something ○ *I heard them arguing but decided not to mix in.* **10.** *vt* CONSUME THINGS TOGETHER to consume different drinks or foods on a single occasion **11.** *vti* RECORDING BLEND MUSICAL SOUNDS to adjust and blend sounds from prerecorded tracks or live performers to create the desired combination of musical sounds. The process is done either by using a special deck (mixing deck) or a multitrack tape machine. **12.** *vt* BIOL CROSSBREED PLANTS OR ANIMALS to breed one variety of a plant or animal with another in order to create a new variety ■ *n* **1.** ACT OF MIXING SOMETHING an act of mixing something, or an occasion on which it is done ○ *Give all the ingredients a good mix.* **2.** COMBINATION a combination or blend of things ○ *There's an intriguing mix of styles on her latest CD.* **3.** SUBSTANCE USED TO PREPARE SOMETHING a substance, especially a number of dried ingredients in powder form, from which something is prepared ○ *cake mix* **4.** RECORDING MUSICAL BLEND a balanced blend of live or prerecorded musical sound ○ *He thinks the drums are too low in the mix.* **5.** RECORDING VERSION OF RECORDING a version of a musical recording that has been changed in some way to give it a different type of sound ○ *Their last hit has been rereleased in a disco mix.* **6.** CONSTR RATIO OF MORTAR INGREDIENTS the ratio of sand and cement in mortar, or of sand, cement, and gravel in concrete [15C. < MIXED] —**mix·a·ble** *adj* ◇ **mix it up** to do something unexpected to stimulate or influence a situation in a beneficial way (*informal*)

mix down *vt* to blend parts that have been recorded separately to create a final finished sound recording

mix up *vt* **1.** MISTAKE SOMEBODY OR SOMETHING FOR ANOTHER to confuse things or people and mistakenly identify one as the other ○ *People always mix her up with her sister.* **2.** CHANGE ORDER OF THINGS to change the usual or previous order of things, either deliberately or by accident ○ *The pages got mixed up on the way to the printer's.* **3.** INVOLVE SOMEBODY OR YOURSELF IN SOMETHING to involve somebody or yourself with a group of people or in an activity, especially one that is disapproved of (*usually passive*) ○ *She got herself mixed up with a bad crowd.* **4.** MAKE SOMETHING FROM INGREDIENTS to prepare or make something by mixing different ingredients

mix·down /míks dòwn/ *n* the process of converting a multitrack recording, usually a master tape recorded in a studio, into a stereo recording, usually for public release

mixed /mikst/ *adj* **1.** CONSISTING OF VARIOUS THINGS consisting of a combination of different parts or different kinds of things **2.** INVOLVING BOTH SEXES intended for, used by, or done by people of both sexes together **3.** INVOLVING DIFFERENT RACES intended for, used by, or done by people of different races together **4.** WITH INCONSISTENT ELEMENTS consisting of inconsistent or conflicting parts ○ *The play has had mixed reviews.* [15C. Via French *mixte* < Latin *mixtus*, past participle of *miscere* "to mix"]

mixed bag *n* a group of people or things of widely differing kinds

mixed bless·ing *n* something that has both advantages and disadvantages or good points and bad points

mixed dou·bles *n* in tennis, table tennis, or badminton, a match played by two pairs, each consisting of a man and a woman (*takes a singular verb*)

mixed drink *n* a drink made by mixing two or more ingredients, at least one of which is alcoholic

mixed e·con·o·my *n* an economy in which some industries and businesses are government-owned and some are privately owned

mixed farm·ing *n* farming that combines growing crops and rearing livestock on the same farm

mixed mar·riage *n* a marriage between people of different racial or religious backgrounds

mixed me·di·a *n* **1.** the use of different artistic media, e.g., painting, photography, and collage, in a single composition or work **2.** the use of different advertising media together, e.g., billboards, TV, and radio

mixed mes·sage *n* a confusing difference between the way somebody behaves and what somebody says

mixed met·a·phor *n* a combination of two or more metaphors that together evoke a strange or incongruous image, e.g., "This thorn in my side has finally bitten the dust"

mixed nerve *n* a nerve that has both motor and sensory fibers, and thus has nerve impulses passing in both directions

mixed num·ber *n* a figure that consists of a whole number and a fraction, e.g., the figure $2\frac{3}{4}$

mixed-race *adj* having or involving different racial backgrounds

mixed-up *adj* (*informal*) **1.** in a disorganized state **2.** in a state of emotional or psychological confusion

mixed-use *adj* combining commercial and residential components in a single property, e.g., an apartment building with offices or stores

mix·er /míksər/ *n* **1.** MIXING DEVICE a machine or device for mixing food, cement, or another substance **2.** NONALCOHOLIC DRINK OFTEN MIXED WITH ALCOHOL a nonalcoholic drink such as fruit juice or soda water that is often mixed with alcoholic drinks **3.** GET-TOGETHER an informal party held as a way of allowing a group of people to get to know one another **4.** SOMEBODY WITH PARTICULAR DEGREE OF SOCIABILITY somebody considered in terms of his or her ability to socialize ○ *She's a good mixer.* **5.** RECORDING ELECTRONIC DEVICE FOR MIXING SOUNDS an electronic device used to adjust and combine various inputs, e.g., performed or broadcast sounds, to create a single output **6.** BROADCAST, MOVIES SOMEBODY CREATING SOUND FOR FILM somebody who combines various sound recordings to create the final soundtrack of a motion picture

mix·ol·o·gy /mik sóllǝjee/ *n* the skill of preparing cocktails, especially cocktails containing alcohol (*informal*) —**mix·ol·o·gist** *n*

Mix·o·lyd·i·an mode /miksə líddee ən/ *n* a scale of notes originating in ancient Greek music and consisting of the eight notes of the diatonic scale rising from G to G [Late 16C. < Greek *mixoludios* "half-Lydian" < *Ludios* "Lydian"]

Mix·tec /meéss tek/ (*plural same* or **-tecs**), **Mix·tec·an** /meess tékən/ (*plural* **-ans** or *same*) *n* **1.** a member of a Native American people who originally lived in southern Mexico and are now spread throughout Mexico. They are noted for their artistic and architectural skills. **2.** an Oto-Manguean language spoken in Mexico. Native speakers: 400,000. [Late 18C. Via Spanish < Nahuatl *mixtecah* "somebody from a cloudy place"] —**Mix·tec** *adj*

mix·ture /míkschər/ *n* **1.** ACT OF MIXING the combining or mixing of different ingredients **2.** COMBINATION OF DIFFERENT PEOPLE OR THINGS a number of different components brought or existing together ○ *a mixture of old and new styles* **3.** SUBSTANCE MADE OF DIFFERENT INGREDIENTS a substance containing several ingredients mixed together ○ *cake mixture* **4.** CHEM SUBSTANCE FORMED WITHOUT CHEMICAL REACTION a substance consisting of two or more substances that have been combined without chemical bonding taking place **5.** *UK* ENG FUEL AND AIR MIX the combination of gasoline vapor and air in an internal-combustion engine [15C. Directly or via French < Latin *mixtura* < *mixt-*, past participle of *miscere*]

SYNONYMS ***mixture, blend, combination, compound, alloy, amalgam***

CORE MEANING: something formed by mixing materials

mixture a number of different components or features brought or existing together, or a substance containing several ingredients mixed together ○ *a chaotic mixture of emotions* ○ *Add the water and beat until the mixture is light and fluffy.* **blend** something formed by using together two or more things of different types, especially in a skilled way. ○ *his little-known first novel, a spirited and intricate blend of romance and mock-romance* ○ *a blend of passion fruit, peach juice, aromatic herbs, and spring water* **combination** an association of different things or factors ○ *a combination of beauty, wit, and charm* ○ *The combination of hardware and software provided a management tool that had never been available before.* **compound** a substance formed by the chemical combination of elements in fixed proportions, or anything composed of two or more separate parts ○ *volatile organic compounds* ○ *dictionaries of compounds, idioms, and common phrases* **alloy** a substance that is a mixture of two or more metals, or of a metal with a nonmetallic material ○ *Steel is basically an alloy of iron and carbon.* **amalgam** an alloy of mercury with another metal, or a combination of two or more characteristics ○ *The technique of "mercury gilding" involved using an amalgam of gold and mercury.* ○ *The culture of the United States is a complicated amalgam of various traditions.*

mix-up *n* a state of confusion, or an error resulting from confusion ○ *an administrative mix-up*

Mi·zar /mí zaàr/ *n* a multiple star in the constellation Ursa Major [< Arabic *Mi'zar* "cloak, veil"]

Mi·zo·ram /mízzō ràm/ state in northeastern India, between Bangladesh and Myanmar. Capital: Aizawl. Population: 891,058 (2001). Area: 8,139 sq. mi./21,081 sq. km.

miz·u·ma /mi zóomə/, **miz·u·na** /-nə/ *n* a Japanese salad green with a mild flavor and a delicate texture [Late 20C. < Japanese]

miz·zen /mízz'n/ *n* **1.** a sail on a mizzenmast **2.** SAILING same as **mizzenmast** ■ *adj* relating to or used on a mizzenmast or its sail [15C. < French *misaine* "foresail, foremast" < Latin *medianus* "of the middle, median"]

miz·zen·mast /mízz'n màst, -məst/ *n* **1.** on a ship with three or more masts, the third mast from the front **2.** on a boat such as a ketch or yawl, the mast nearest the back

miz·zle /mízz'l/ *regional n* a very fine rain ■ *vi* (**-zled, -zling, -zles**) to rain in very fine drops [15C. Origin ?] —**miz·zly** *adj*

mk *abbr* Macedonia (*used in Internet addresses*) See table at **domain name**

Mk *abbr* BIBLE Mark

mk. *abbr* MONEY **1.** mark **2.** markka

mks, MKS *abbr* **1.** MONEY marks **2.** MEASURE meter-kilogram-second

mksA *abbr* MEASURE meter-kilogram-second-ampere

mks u·nits *npl* the metric system of measurement, which has the meter, the kilogram, and the second as its basic units of length, mass, and time

mkt. *abbr* COMM market

mktg. *abbr* MARKETING marketing

ml[1] *abbr* MEASURE milliliter

ml[2] *abbr* ONLINE Mali (*used in Internet addresses*) See table at **domain name**

mL *abbr* MEASURE millilambert

ML *abbr* ONLINE more later (*used in e-mails or text messages*)

MLA, M.L.A. *abbr* **1.** EDUC Master of Landscape Architecture **2.** LANGUAGE Modern Language Association

Mla·dic /mláddich/, **Ratko** (*b.* 1943) Yugoslavian general. He was indicted by the International War Crimes Tribunal (1995) for genocide and crimes against humanity for actions during his time as chief of the Bosnian Serb forces in the civil war in Bosnia and Herzegovina.

MLD *abbr* MED minimum lethal dose

MLF *abbr* MIL multilateral (nuclear) force

MLG *abbr* LANG Middle Low German

Mlle. *abbr* Mademoiselle

Mlles. *abbr* Mesdemoiselles

MLR *abbr* MIL multiple-launch rockets

MLS *abbr* EDUC Master of Library Science

mm *abbr* **1.** MEASURE millimeter **2.** ONLINE Myanmar (*used in Internet addresses*) See table at **domain name**

MM. *abbr* **1.** Messieurs **2.** MIL Military Medal

Mma·bath·o /mə baàtō, əmmə-/ city in North-West Province in South Africa. Population: 13,544 (1995).

MMDS *abbr* MEDIA multipoint microwave distribution system

Mme. *abbr* Madame

Mmes. *abbr* Mesdames

mmf, m.m.f. *abbr* PHYS magnetomotive force

mmHg *n* a unit for measuring atmospheric pressure. Full form **millimeter of mercury**

MMORPG *abbr* COMPUT GAMES massively multiplayer online role-playing game

MMPI *abbr* PSYCHOL Minnesota Multiphasic Personality Inventory

MMR *n* a vaccine given to small children to protect them against measles, mumps, and rubella

MMS *n* a system that enables sounds, images, or animations to be incorporated into text messages sent, usually, from cell phones. Full form **multimedia messaging service**

M.Mus. *abbr* EDUC Master of Music

mn *abbr* ONLINE Mongolia (*used in Internet addresses*) See table at **domain name**

Mn *symbol* CHEM ELEM manganese

MN *abbr* **1.** GEOG magnetic north **2.** Minnesota

MNA *abbr* POL Member of the National Assembly (of Quebec)

MNC *abbr* COMM multinational corporation

mne·mon·ic /ni mónnik/ *n* MEMORY AID a short rhyme, phrase, or other mental technique for making information easier to memorize ■ *adj* **1.** ACTING AS MNEMONIC acting as a memory aid **2.** RELATING TO MNEMONICS relating to the practice of improving the memory, or to systems designed to improve the memory [Mid-18C. < MNEMONICS, or < Greek *mnēmonikos* "relating to memory" < *mnēmon-* "mindful"] —**mne·mon·i·cal·ly** *adv*

mne·mon·ics /ni mónniks/ *n* the practice of improving or helping the memory, or the systems used to achieve this (*takes a singular verb*) [Early 18C. < Greek *mnēmonika*, form of *mnēmonikos* (see MNEMONIC)]

Mne·mos·y·ne /ni móssənee, -mózzənee/ *n* in Greek mythology, the goddess of memory and mother of the Muses [Via Latin < Greek *Mnēmosunē*]

mngr. *abbr* MANAGEMT manager

mo /mō/ *n UK* a moment or short while (*informal*) ○ *I'll be there in half a mo.* [Late 19C. Shortening of MOMENT]

Mo *symbol* CHEM ELEM molybdenum

MO *abbr* **1.** COMPUT magneto-optical **2.** Missouri **3.** FIN money order

mo. *abbr* TIME month

Mo. *abbr* Missouri

m.o. *abbr* **1.** MAIL mail order **2.** MED Medical Officer **3.** *also* **M.O.** modus operandi **4.** FIN money order

-mo *suffix* used after numerals to indicate the number of pages made by folding a sheet of paper ○ *16mo* [< *12mo*, abbreviation of Latin *(in) duodecimo* "(in) a twelfth"; < *duodecimus* "twelfth"]

mo·a /mṓ ə/ *n* a large flightless bird similar to the ostrich that became extinct at the end of the 18th century. Native to: formerly, New Zealand. Family: Dinornithidae. [Mid-19C. < Maori]

Mo·ab[1] /mṓ ab/ *n* in the Bible, the son of Lot and his eldest daughter, whose descendants were the enemies of Israel

Mo·ab[2] /mṓ ab/ ancient kingdom situated on a plateau to the east of the Dead Sea in modern-day Jordan —**Mo·ab·ite** /mṓ ə bìt/ *n, adj*

MOAB /mṓ àb/ *n* a satellite-guided bomb weighing 21,000 lb./9,525 kg, the largest conventional bomb in the US arsenal, designed to detonate 6 ft./1.8 m from the ground. Full form **Massive Ordnance Air Blast** [Early 21C]

moan /mōn/ *v* (**moaned, moan·ing, moans**) **1.** *vi* MAKE LOW SOUND EXPRESSING PAIN to make a long low sound that expresses pain or misery **2.** *vti* COMPLAIN to complain about something, especially unreasonably or needlessly (*informal*) ○ *What's he moaning on about?* **3.** *vt* SAY SOMETHING IN PAINED VOICE to say something in a voice that expresses pain or misery ○ *"Oh no!" she moaned* **4.** *vi* MAKE SOUND LIKE SOMEBODY IN PAIN to make a long low sound similar to that made by somebody expressing pain or misery ○ *the wind moaning in the trees* ■ *n* **1.** SOUND OF PAIN a long low sound made by somebody expressing pain or misery **2.** SOUND LIKE MOAN a long, low sound that resembles an expression of pain or misery, made by something such as the wind **3.** COMPLAINT a complaint, especially one that is unreasonable or trivial (*informal*) **4.** *UK* COMPLAINING PERSON a steady complainer, especially about trivial matters (*informal*) [12C. < assumed Old English *mān* "complaint" < Germanic] —**moan·er** *n* —**moan·ful** *adj*

moat /mōt/ *n* **1.** DITCH AROUND CASTLE a wide water-filled ditch around a castle or fort, dug to give protection from attack **2.** DITCH ACTING AS BARRIER a water-filled ditch dug to prevent access or escape, e.g., to confine animals in a zoo ■ *vt* (**moat·ed, moat·ing, moats**) PUT MOAT AROUND CASTLE to surround a castle or other fortified place with a moat [14C. < Old French *mote* "mound" or medieval Latin *mota*]

mob /mob/ *n* **1.** NOISY CROWD a large and unruly crowd of people **2.** *UK* GROUP a group of people (*informal*) **3.** ORDINARY PEOPLE ordinary people, especially when thought of collectively as unintelligent or irrational (*informal*) ■ *vt* (**mobbed, mob·bing, mobs**) **1.** CROWD AROUND SOMEBODY OR SOMETHING to crowd around somebody or something noisily and excitedly **2.** CROWD INTO PLACE to crowd into and fill a place **3.** ATTACK SOMEBODY to attack somebody as a large group **4.** ZOOL ATTACK PREDATOR to surround and harass a potential predator [Late 17C. Shortening of archaic *mobile* < Latin *mobile (vulgus)* "excitable (crowd)"] —**mob·ber** *n* —**mob·bish** *adj*

Mob *n* a group of people who are involved in organized crime, or the world of organized crime (*informal*)

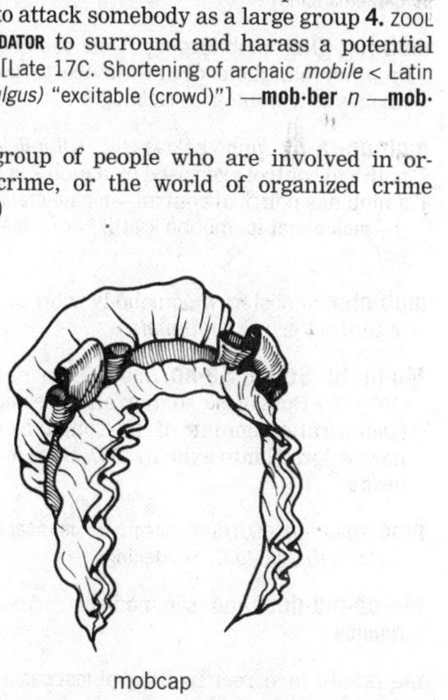

mobcap

mob·cap /mób kàp/ *n* **1.** a loose-fitting frilly cap often worn indoors by women in the 18th and early 19th centuries. See illustration on previous page **2.** a soft hat shaped like a mobcap and worn especially by small children and babies [Mid-18C. < obsolete *mob* "prostitute, negligee," variant of *mab* "promiscuous woman," origin ?]

mo·bile /mṓb'l, mṓ bèel, -bīl/ *adj* **1. MOVING EASILY** able to move freely or easily ○ *She's mobile again after her skiing accident.* **2. OPERATING FROM VEHICLE** operating from or set up in a vehicle that travels from place to place ○ *a mobile library* **3. CHANGING EXPRESSION** changing expressions quickly and easily ○ *a mobile face* **4. PREPARED FOR CHANGE** able or willing to change job, move home, or alter other arrangements at short notice if necessary **5. CHANGING SOCIALLY** moving or able to move from one social or professional class or group to another, e.g., by changing jobs or moving to a new neighborhood ■ *n* **1. HANGING DECORATION** a hanging sculpture or decoration whose parts are balanced to move in response to air currents **2.** *UK* TELECOM same as **cell phone** (*informal*) **3. OUTSIDE EMPLOYEE** an employee who works outside the company workplace, especially while using a computer link [15C. Via French < Latin *mobilis* "movable" < *movere* "to move"]

Mo·bile /mō bēel/ **1.** river in southwestern Alabama, flowing into the Gulf of Mexico. Length: 38 mi./61 km. **2.** city and port in southwestern Alabama, on the northwestern shore of Mobile Bay. Population: 194,862 (2002 estimate).

-mobile *suffix* automobile, vehicle ○ *snowmobile* [< AUTOMOBILE]

mo·bile home *n* a large trailer that can be transported on the back of a truck but is usually connected to utilities and left on a single site

mo·bile phone *n* TELECOM same as **cell phone**

Mo·bil·i·an /mō bíllee ən/ *n* a pidgin trading language containing elements of Choctaw that was used before the 20th century as a lingua franca in the Mississippi Valley and Gulf Coast [Mid-19C. < *Mobile*, town in Alabama] —**Mo·bil·i·an** *adj*

mo·bil·i·ty /mō bíllətee/ *n* **1.** the ability to move about, especially to do work or take exercise **2.** the ability of somebody to change from one social group or class to another

mo·bi·lize /mṓbə līz/ (**-lized, -liz·ing, -liz·es**) *vti* to organize people or resources in order to be ready for action or in order to take action, especially in a military or civil emergency, or to be organized for this purpose [Mid-19C. < French *mobiliser* < *mobile* "movable" (see MOBILE)] —**mo·bi·liz·a·ble** *adj* —**mo·bi·li·za·tion** /mṑbəli záysh'n/ *n*

Mö·bi·us strip /mṓbee əss-/ *n* a continuous single-sided surface formed by rotating one end of a strip through 180° and joining it to the other end [Early 20C. After August Ferdinand *Möbius* (1790–1868), German mathematician]

mob·log·ging /mób lògging/ *n* the use of a cell phone or other handheld digital device to post text and images to a weblog —**mob·log** *n*

mob·oc·ra·cy /mo bókrəssee/ (*plural* **-cies**) *n* **1.** political control exercised by a mob **2.** a place where a mob has political control —**mob·o·crat** /móbbə kràt/ *n* —**mob·o·crat·ic** /mòbbə kráttik/ *adj* —**mob·o·crat·i·cal** *adj*

mob·ster /móbstər/ *n* somebody who is involved in organized crime (*informal*)

Mo·bu·tu Se·se Se·ko /mə bōotoo say say sáykō/ (1930–97) Congolese soldier and president of Zaïre (Democratic Republic of the Congo) from 1965 until he was forced into exile in 1997. Born **Mobutu, Joseph Désiré**

moc /mok/ *n* CLOTHING same as **moccasin** (sense 2) (*informal*) [Mid-20C. Shortening]

Mo·çâ·me·des /mō sámmədish/ former name for **Namibe**

~~**mocassin**~~ incorrect spelling of **moccasin**

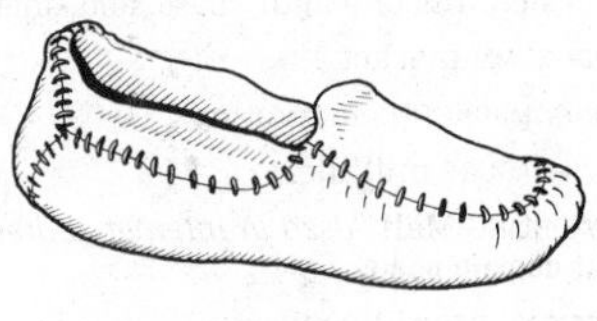

moccasin

moc·ca·sin /mókəssin/ *n* **1.** a Native North American heelless shoe made of deerskin or other soft leather wrapped around the foot and stitched on top **2.** a low-heeled leather shoe whose side panels are joined to the upper panel using prominent stitching to form a raised puckered seam **3.** REPT same as **water moccasin** (sense 1) [Early 17C. < Virginia Algonquian *mockasin*]

moc·ca·sin flow·er *n* PLANTS same as **lady's slipper** [< the shape]

moc·ca·sin tel·e·graph *n Can* the exchange of news or information through social networks, especially by casual conversation (*informal; sometimes considered offensive*) [Because such information was originally transmitted by a Native North American runner]

mo·cha /mṓkə/ *n* **1. STRONG ARABIAN COFFEE** a dark brown strong-tasting coffee from Yemen and some other countries on the Arabian peninsula **2. FLAVORING OR DRINK** a flavoring or beverage made by mixing coffee and cocoa **3. LEATHER** a soft suede leather made from sheepskin or goatskin, originally from Africa **4. DARK BROWN** a dark brown color, like mocha coffee [Late 18C. After MOCHA] —**mo·cha** *adj*

Mo·cha /mṓkə, mókə/ town and seaport in southwestern Yemen, on the Red Sea, historically a coffee-exporting center. Population: 1,163 (1977 estimate).

mo·cha·cci·no /mṑkə chéenō/ (*plural* **-nos**) *n* a cappuccino made from a mixture of coffee and chocolate

Mo·che /mṓ chày/ *adj* relating to the Mochica or their culture ■ *n* (*plural* **-ches** or *same*) PEOPLES same as **Mochica** [< archaeological site and valley in NW Peru]

Mo·chi·ca /mō chéekə/ (*plural* **-cas** or *same*) *n* a member of an ancient Native South American people who lived along the coast of northern Peru, where their civilization lasted from the 6th century B.C. to the 2nd century B.C. The Mochicas are particularly noted for their pottery, which was decorated with realistic paintings of human and animal forms. [Mid-19C. Via Spanish < a Native American language]

mock /mok/ *v* (**mocked, mock·ing, mocks**) **1.** *vti* **TREAT SOMEBODY OR SOMETHING WITH SCORN** to treat somebody or something with scorn or contempt **2.** *vt* **MIMIC SOMEBODY** to imitate somebody in a way that is intended to make that person appear silly or ridiculous **3.** *vt* **PREVENT SOMETHING** to prevent something from succeeding in a way that causes frustration or humiliation ○ *the wind mocking his efforts to light a fire* ■ *adj* **1. IMITATION** made to appear like something else, usually something older or more expensive ○ *mock leather* **2. PRETEND** done as an act, especially in order to amuse people ○ *frowned in mock disapproval* **3. PRACTICE** done as practice for the real thing ○ *mock exams* ■ *n* **1. IMITATION OBJECT** something made as an imitation **2. OBJECT OF SCORN** somebody or something ridiculed by others (*dated*) [15C. < Old French *mocquer*] —**mock·a·ble** *adj* —**mock·er** *n* —**mock·ing** *adj* —**mock·ing·ly** *adv*

SYNONYMS See ***ridicule***.

mock up /mók ùp/, **mock-up** *vt* to make a full-scale working model of something so that it can undergo testing or be used to aid research

mock·er·nut /mókər nùt/ *n* **1.** a large sweet hard-shelled nut, commonly gathered in the wild **2.** a hickory tree that produces mockernuts. Native to: North America. Latin name: *Carya tomentosa*.

mock·er·y /mókəree/ *n* **1.** words or behavior intended to make somebody or something look silly or ridiculous **2.** something that is ridiculously inadequate or wholly unsuccessful ○ *The investigation was a mockery from start to finish.*

mock-he·ro·ic *adj* describes poetry that satirizes the heroic style by using it to describe something trivial. Like heroic poetry, mock-heroic poetry traditionally used classical forms such as the iambic pentameter (**heroic couplet**) or the iambic hexameter (**alexandrine**). ■ *n* verse or a poem written in the mock-heroic style

mock·ing·bird /móking bùrd/ *n* a bird of the thrasher family, some of which incorporate the songs and calls of other birds into their own songs. Native to: North America. Family: Mimidae.

CULTURAL NOTE ***To Kill a Mockingbird***, a novel (1960) by Harper Lee. Set in the southern United States, it tells the story of a white lawyer who agrees to defend an African American man wrongly accused of the rape of a white girl. The events are narrated from the point of view of the lawyer's six-year-old daughter, Scout. It was made into a movie by Robert Mulligan in 1962.

mock moon *n* ASTRON same as **paraselene**

mock or·ange *n* **1.** an ornamental bush or tree. Flowers: fragrant, white, resembling those of an orange tree. Genus: *Philadelphus*. **2.** a bush or tree that resembles an orange tree

mock sun *n* ASTRON same as **parhelion**

mock tur·tle *n* **1.** a high tight-fitting round collar on a garment such as a sweater **2.** a sweater with a mock turtle neck

mock tur·tle soup *n* an old-fashioned soup made in imitation of turtle soup, using meat from a calf's head to replace the flesh of the green turtle

mock-up *n* **1.** a full-sized model of something, built to scale and with working parts, used especially for testing or research **2.** a preliminary layout of a newspaper, magazine, or other publication, showing the size and arrangement of material to be included

mod /mod/, **Mod** *n* in the United Kingdom in the 1960s, a member of a youth group known for their fashionable dress, motor scooters, and fights with motorcycle gangs (**rockers**) [Mid-20C. Shortening of MODERN or MODERNISM]

mod. *abbr* **1.** moderate **2.** MUSIC moderato **3.** modern

mo·dal /mṓd'l/ *adj* **1.** GRAM **EXPRESSING GRAMMATICAL MOOD** describes verbs and auxiliary verbs expressing a grammatical mood such as possibility or necessity **2.** MUSIC **RELATING TO MUSICAL MODES** relating to or using a mode, especially instead of a major or minor scale **3.** LOGIC **DESCRIBING LOGICAL MODALITIES** describes propositions involving necessity or probability, or those relating to knowledge, belief, and obligation [Mid-16C. Directly or via French < medieval Latin *modalis* < Latin *modus* "measure"] —**mo·dal·ly** *adv*

mo·dal aux·il·ia·ry *n* a verb used with other verbs to express such ideas as permission, possibility, and necessity. The modal auxiliaries in English grammar are "can," "could," "may," "might," "must," "ought to," "shall," "should," "will," and "would." Some classifications also include "dare," "need," and "used."

mo·dal·i·ty /mō dállətee/ *n* (*plural* **-ties**) **1.** GRAM **CONCEPT EXPRESSED BY MODAL VERB** the idea or concept that a modal auxiliary verb expresses **2.** PHILOSOPHY **PROPOSITIONS OF NECESSITY OR POSSIBILITY** the purely logical classification of propositions that relate to necessity or possibility **3.** MED **TREATMENT** something used in the treatment of a disorder, e.g., surgery or chemotherapy ■ **mo·dal·i·ties** *npl* POL **PROTOCOL** procedures that are followed in the course of political or diplomatic negotiations [Early 17C. Directly or via French *modalité* < medieval Latin *modalitas* < *modalis* (see MODAL)]

mo·dal log·ic *n* the branch of logic that studies the relations between modal propositions

mode /mōd/ *n* **1. MANNER OR FORM** a way, manner, or form, e.g., a way of doing something, or the form in which something exists **2. STYLE OR FASHION** a style or fashion, e.g., in art or in dress **3. MACHINE SETTING** a setting or function on a machine such as a computer **4. TYPE OF AUTOMATIC BEHAVIOR** a way of behaving, especially one that is instinctive, familiar, or habitual (*informal humorous*) ○ *in work mode* **5.** MUSIC **SET**

PATTERN OF NOTES a musical scale that is one of the seven patterns of notes that can be played over an octave using only the white notes of the piano keyboard. Some modes were widely used in European religious, folk, and art music until around 1600, after which they were largely replaced by keys, while others were used in ancient Greece. **6.** MATH, STATS **MOST FREQUENT VALUE** the value that has the highest frequency within a statistical range **7.** LOGIC **MODAL STATUS OF PROPOSITION** the modal status of a proposition, e.g., its being necessary or merely possible **8.** PHYS **RADIO FREQUENCY** one of the radio frequencies characteristic of a given resonator or oscillator **9.** PHILOSOPHY **COMBINATION OF IDEAS** a combination of ideas that cannot be worked out merely by analysis of its components [14C. < Latin *modus* "measure"]

mod·el /módd'l/ *n* **1. COPY OF OBJECT** a copy of an object, especially one made on a smaller scale than the original (*often used before a noun*) **2. SPECIFIC VERSION OF ARTICLE** a particular version of a manufactured article ○ *had traded in her car for the latest model* **3. SOMETHING COPIED** something that is copied or used as the basis for a related idea, process, or system **4. SIMPLIFIED VERSION** a simplified version of something complex used in analyzing and solving problems or making predictions ○ *a financial model* **5. PERFECT EXAMPLE** an excellent example that deserves to be imitated **6. SOMEBODY PAID TO WEAR CLOTHES** somebody who is paid to wear clothes or demonstrate merchandise, e.g., in fashion shows or in photographs **7. ARTIST'S SUBJECT** somebody who poses for a painter, sculptor, photographer, or other artist **8.** ZOOL **ANIMAL SPECIES COPIED BY ANOTHER ANIMAL** an animal species repellent to predators that another animal mimics for protection **9.** LOGIC **INTERPRETATION** an interpretation of a theory arrived at by assigning referents in such a way as to make the theory true **10.** *UK* FASHION **ORIGINAL GARMENT** the first sewn example of a couturier's or clothing manufacturer's design, from which a new line of garments is produced ■ *v* **(-eled, -el·ing, -els) 1.** *vti* **WORK AS FASHION MODEL** to work as a fashion model, or wear clothes, makeup, or other items in order to display them to others **2.** *vi* **BE ARTIST'S MODEL** to sit as a model for somebody such as a painter or photographer **3.** *vt* **BASE ONE THING ON SOMETHING ELSE** to base something, especially somebody's appearance or behavior, on that of another person ○ *She modeled herself on her older sister.* **4.** *vt* **SHAPE SOMETHING** to make something by shaping a substance or material such as clay or wood [Late 16C. Via French *modèle* < Italian *modello* "model" < Latin *modulus* "measure" < *modus*] —**mod·el·er** *n*

mo·del home *n* a house in a housing development that is decorated and furnished to show to prospective buyers

mod·el·ing *n* **1. FASHION MODEL'S WORK** the work of a fashion model **2. MAKING OF MODELS** the activity or hobby of making models **3.** PSYCHOL **DEMONSTRATION OF BEHAVIOR** the demonstration of a way of behaving to somebody, especially a child, in order for that behavior to be imitated

mod·el·ling *n* Can, UK spelling of **modeling**

mod·el the·o·ry *n* the branch of logic that deals with providing models for theories —**mod·el-the·o·ret·ic** *adj*

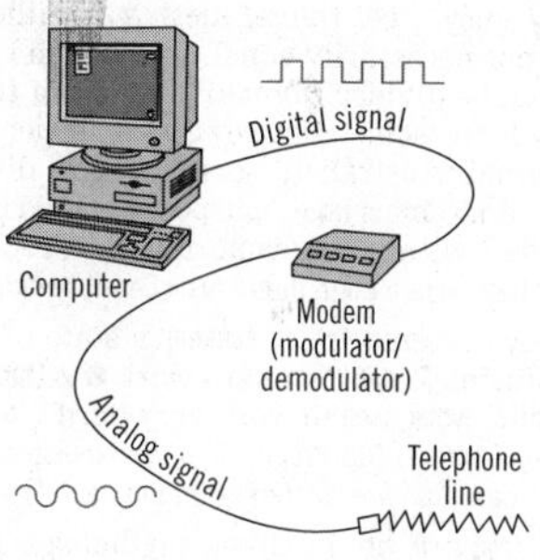

modem

mo·dem /mṓ dèm/ *n* an electronic device that connects computers via a telephone line, allowing the exchange of information. It consists of a modulator to convert computer information into a telephone signal and a demodulator to convert it back again. [Mid-20C. Blend of MODULATE + DEMODULATE]

Mo·de·na /módd'nə, mṓd'n aa/ historic city in northern Italy. It is an agricultural and industrial center. Population: 165,502 (2001).

mod·er·ate *adj* /móddərət/ **1. SMALL OR SLIGHT** not large, great, or severe ○ *a moderate portion* **2. REASONABLE** not excessive or unreasonable ○ *a moderate eater* **3. MIDDLE-OF-THE-ROAD** not extreme or radical ○ *moderate views* **4. AVERAGE** neither particularly good nor particularly bad ○ *moderate results* ■ *n* /móddərət/ **SOMEBODY WITH MODERATE VIEWS** somebody who holds views that are not extreme, especially political views ■ *vti* /móddə ràyt/ **(-at·ed, -at·ing, -ates) 1. MAKE OR BECOME LESS EXTREME** to become less great, extreme, violent, or severe, or make something become so **2. PRESIDE OVER SOMETHING** to chair or preside over something such as a meeting or discussion [14C. < Latin *moderat-*, past participle of *moderari* "regulate"] —**mod·er·ate·ly** *adv* —**mod·er·ate·ness** *n*

mod·er·ate breeze *n* a wind of between 13 and 18 mi./20.9 and 29 km per hour, classified as force four on the Beaufort scale

mod·er·ate gale *n* a wind of between 32 and 38 mi./51.5 and 61.2 km per hour, classified as force seven on the Beaufort scale

mod·er·ate-in·come *adj* having an income close to the national average

mod·er·a·tion /mòddə ráysh'n/ *n* **1. STATE OF BEING MODERATE** the state or quality of being moderate ○ *moderation in all things* **2. ACTION OF MAKING SOMETHING MODERATE** the limiting, controlling, or restricting of something so that it becomes or remains moderate **3. JOB OF MODERATOR** the position or function of moderating something ◇ **in moderation** within reasonable limits, and never to excess

mod·e·ra·to /mòddə raatō/ *adv* at a moderate tempo (*used as a musical direction*) [Early 18C. < Italian < Latin *moderat-* (see MODERATE)] —**mod·e·ra·to** *adj*

mod·er·a·tor /móddə ràytər/ *n* **1. SOMEBODY IN CHARGE OF DISCUSSION** somebody who presides over an assembly, especially a legislative assembly, or acts as a mediator in discussions or negotiations **2.** CHR **PRESIDING MINISTER** in the Presbyterian denominations of the Christian church, a minister presiding over a church court or other assembly **3.** PHYS **NEUTRON ABSORBER** a substance such as graphite or beryllium that slows neutrons in a nuclear reactor so that they can bring about the fission of uranium —**mod·er·a·tor·ship** *n*

mod·ern /móddərn/ *adj* **1. BELONGING TO PRESENT DAY** relating or belonging to the present period in history **2. OF LATEST KIND** of the latest, most advanced kind, or using the most advanced equipment and techniques available ○ *modern medicine* **3. USING LATEST STYLES** relating to or using ideas and techniques that have only recently been developed or are still considered experimental **4.** LING **OF LANGUAGE'S LATEST STAGE** relating to or belonging to the most recent stage in the development of a language ■ *n* **1. MODERN PERSON** somebody living in the present period, especially somebody whose tastes and attitudes are regarded as nontraditional or strikingly new **2.** PRINTING **TYPEFACE** a typeface with heavy vertical strokes and straight serifs [Early 16C. Directly or via French *moderne* < Latin *modernus* < *modo* "just now, in a (certain) manner" < *modus* "measure"] —**mod·ern·ly** *adv* —**mod·ern·ness** *n*

SYNONYMS See *new*.

mod·ern dance *n* a free style of theatrical dancing that developed in the early 20th century

mod·ern-day *adj* **1.** resembling a particular person or thing from the past **2.** relating to, belonging to, or existing in the present time

mo·derne /mō dérn/ *adj* describes a style of architecture and design popular in the 1920s and 1930s and characterized by streamlined and curved forms [Mid-20C. < French *moderne* (see MODERN)]

Mod·ern Eng·lish *n* the English language from about 1500, when it began to develop a more standardized form compared with the dialects of Middle English. Modern English developed mainly from the East Midland dialect, and the standardization process was accelerated by the introduction of the printing press during the 1470s. —**Mod·ern Eng·lish** *adj*

mod·ern Greek *n* the form of Greek spoken since around 1453, the year of the fall of Byzantium —**mod·ern Greek** *adj*

Mod·ern He·brew *n* the form of the Hebrew language, a revival of the ancient form, that is the official language of the state of Israel —**Mod·ern He·brew** *adj*

mod·ern his·to·ry *n* **1.** the study of the period of European history after 1789 **2.** *UK* the study of the period of history that extends from the end of the Middle Ages in Europe, around the middle of the 15th century, to the present day

mod·ern·ism /móddər nìzzəm/ *n* **1. LATEST THINGS** the latest styles, tastes, attitudes, or practices **2.** ARTS **EARLY 20C STYLES IN ART** the revolutionary ideas and styles in art, architecture, and literature that developed in the early 20th century as a reaction to traditional forms **3.** CHR **MOVEMENT WITHIN ROMAN CATHOLICISM** a movement in European Roman Catholicism in which scholars and theologians attempt to accommodate the contemporary world view within Roman Catholic theology and doctrine —**mod·ern·ist** *n, adj* —**mod·ern·is·tic** /mòddər nístik/ *adj* —**mod·ern·is·ti·cal·ly** *adv*

mo·der·ni·ty /mo dúrnətee, mō-/ (*plural* **-ties**) *n* **1.** the quality of being modern or up-to-date **2.** a modern thing

mod·ern·ize /móddər nīz/ **(-ized, -iz·ing, -iz·es)** *vti* to change something in order to make it conform to modern tastes, attitudes, or standards, or be changed in this way —**mod·ern·i·za·tion** /mòddərni záysh'n/ *n* —**mod·ern·iz·er** *n*

mod·ern jazz *n* a style of jazz that developed in the early 1940s, with rhythms and harmonies much more complex than those of traditional jazz

mod·ern pen·tath·lon *n* an athletic competition in which the contestants compete in five different events and are awarded points for each to find the best all-around athlete. The events are swimming, horseback riding, cross-country running, fencing, and pistol shooting.

Mod·ern Stan·dard Chi·nese *n* the official language of the People's Republic of China, belonging to the Chinese branch of Sino-Tibetan languages. Native speakers: 800 million. Other speakers: 100 million. —**Mod·ern Stan·dard Chi·nese** *adj*

mod·est /móddəst/ *adj* **1. HUMBLE** unwilling to draw attention to your own achievements or abilities **2. SHY** not confident or assertive, and tending to be easily embarrassed **3. REASONABLE** not large, extreme, or excessive ○ *a modest income* **4. SIMPLE** not showy, elaborate, or pretentious ○ *a modest dwelling* **5. NOT OVERTLY SEXUAL** reserved in appearance, manner, and speech, especially in relation to sexual matters [Mid-16C. Partly back-formation < MODESTY, partly via French *modeste* < Latin *modestus* "kept within due measure"] —**mod·est·ly** *adv*

Mo·des·to /mə déstō/ city in central California. It is the administrative seat of Stanislaus County. Population: 203,555 (2002 estimate).

mod·es·ty /móddəstee/ *n* **1. HUMILITY** unwillingness to draw attention to your own achievements or abilities **2. SEXUAL RESERVE** reserve in appearance, manner, and speech, especially in relation to sexual matters **3. SHYNESS** lack of confidence or assertiveness, with a tendency to embarrass easily **4. SIMPLICITY** lack of grandeur or ostentation **5. MODERATION** moderation in size, scale, or extent

mod·i·cum /móddikəm/ *n* a small amount, especially of something abstract such as a quality ○ *It only requires a modicum of common sense.* [Late 15C. < Latin, "little way, short time," form of *modicus* "moderate" < *modus* "measure"]

modif. *abbr* **1.** modification **2.** GRAM modifier

mod·i·fi·ca·tion /mòddəfi káysh'n/ *n* **1. CHANGE** a slight change or alteration made to improve something or make it more suitable ○ *made a few modifications to the original design* **2. ACT OF MODIFYING** the act or process of modifying something, or the condition of having been modified ○ *in need of modification* **3. SOMETHING MODIFIED** something that has been modified ○ *The new version is a modification and is based on existing software.* **4.** GRAM **GRAMMATICAL RELATIONSHIP WITH MODIFIER** in grammar, the relationship between a modifier and what it modifies [15C. Directly or via French < Latin *modificatio(n)-* < *modificat-*, past participle of *modificare* (see MODIFY)] —**mod·i·fi·ca·tive** /móddəfi kàytiv/ *adj* —**mod·i·fi·ca·tor** /móddəfi kàytər/ *n* —**mod·i·fi·ca·to·ry** /móddəfi kàytəree/ *adj*

mod·i·fi·er /móddə fī ər/ *n* **1.** somebody or something that makes slight changes to something, especially to improve it **2.** a word or phrase that affects the meaning of another, usually describing it or restricting its meaning. "Pink" in the phrase "the pink ribbon," "fire" in the compound "fire alarm," and "in the morning" in the sentence "She always goes jogging in the morning" are modifiers.

mod·i·fy /móddə fī/ (**-fied, -fy·ing, -fies**) *v* **1.** *vti* **MAKE SMALL CHANGES TO SOMETHING** to make a minor change or alteration to something, or change slightly, especially in order to improve **2.** *vt* **LESSEN SOMETHING** to make something less extensive, severe, or extreme **3.** *vt* GRAM **AFFECT WORD'S MEANING** to affect the meaning of a word, usually by describing or limiting it **4.** *vt* PHON **CHANGE VOWEL SOUND** to change the sound of a vowel from its usual sound, often in a way that is represented in writing by adding an umlaut [14C. Via French *modifier* < Latin *modificare* "limit" < *modus* "measure" + form of *facere* "make"] —**mod·i·fi·a·bil·i·ty** /mòddə fī ə bíllətee/ *n* —**mod·i·fi·a·ble** *adj*

SYNONYMS See *change*.

Mo·di·glia·ni /mòddil yaánee/, **Amedeo** (1884–1920) Italian painter and sculptor. His distinctive style, seen to best effect in his portraits, is characterized by graceful, elongated proportions.

mo·dil·lion /mō díllyən/ *n* a small curved ornamental bracket under the corona of a Corinthian or Composite column [Mid-16C. Via French < Italian *modiglione* < Latin *mutulus* "mutule"]

mo·di·o·lus /mō dī ələss/ (*plural* **-li** /-lī/) *n* the bony central pillar of the cochlea in the inner ear [Late 17C. < Latin, "nave of a wheel" < *modius* "measure"]

mod·ish /mṓdish/ *adj* in or conforming to the latest fashions or styles, especially those considered fads —**mod·ish·ly** *adv* —**mod·ish·ness** *n*

Mo·dred /mṓdrəd/, **Mor·dred** /máwrdrəd/ *n* in Arthurian legend, a knight of the Round Table who killed his uncle, King Arthur

mod·u·lar /mójjələr/ *adj* **1.** made up of separate modules that can be rearranged, replaced, combined, or interchanged easily ○ *modular construction techniques* ○ *a modular course structure* **2.** relating to or resembling a modulus, or made up of moduli [Late 18C. < modern Latin *modularis* < Latin *modulus* (see MODULUS)] —**mod·u·lar·i·ty** /mòjjə lárrətee/ *n* —**mod·u·lar·ly** *adv*

mod·u·lar a·rith·me·tic *n* a branch of arithmetic that deals with the remainders of whole numbers after the numbers have been divided by a modulus

mod·u·lar·ized /mójjələ rīzd/ *adj* made up of separate modules that can be rearranged, replaced, combined, or interchanged easily

mod·u·late /mójjə làyt/ (**-lat·ed, -lat·ing, -lates**) *v* **1.** *vt* **CHANGE SOUND** to change the tone, pitch, or volume of sound, e.g., of a musical instrument or the human voice **2.** *vt* **ALTER SOMETHING** to make alterations in something to make it less strong, forceful, or severe **3.** *vti* MUSIC **CHANGE KEY** in tonal music, to change from one key to another through a harmonic progression, or change one key into another **4.** *vt* PHYS **VARY WAVE CHARACTERISTICS** to vary the frequency, amplitude, or other characteristics of a radio wave or another carrier wave in order to transmit information [Mid-16C. < Latin *modulat-*, past participle of *modulari* "measure, adjust to rhythm" < *modulus* (see MODULUS)] —**mod·u·la·bil·i·ty** /mòjjələ bíllətee/ *n* —**mod·u·la·ble** *adj* —**mod·u·la·tion** /mòjjə láysh'n/ *n* —**mod·u·la·tive** *adj* —**mod·u·la·tor** *n* —**mod·u·la·to·ry** /mójjələ tàwree/ *adj*

mod·ule /mójjool/ *n* **1. SELF-CONTAINED INTERCHANGEABLE UNIT** an independent unit that can be combined with others and easily rearranged, replaced, or interchanged to form different structures or systems **2.** EDUC **SHORT COURSE OF STUDY** a short course of study that forms part of a larger academic course or training program, e.g., any of the elements that form part of a degree program **3.** AEROSP **PART OF SPACE VEHICLE** one of the self-contained units or craft that make up a space vehicle **4.** ARCHIT **UNIT OF MEASUREMENT** a unit of measurement or a standard, used especially in measuring architectural elements [Late 16C. Directly or via French < Latin *modulus* (see MODULUS)]

mod·u·lo /mójjəlō/ *prep* with respect to a particular mathematical modulus ○ *9 and 30 are congruent modulo 7 because both leave the same remainder if they are divided by 7.* [Late 19C. < Latin, form of *modulus* (see MODULUS)]

mod·u·lus /mójjələss/ (*plural* **-li** /-lī/) *n* **1.** PHYS **COEFFICIENT** a coefficient expressing the degree to which a substance exhibits a particular property **2.** MATH **DIVISION NUMBER** a number by which two other numbers can be divided so that both give the same remainder **3.** MATH **ABSOLUTE VALUE** the absolute value of a complex number **4.** MATH **LOGARITHM FACTOR** the factor by which a logarithm of one base must be multiplied to become the logarithm of another base [Mid-16C. < Latin, "small measure" < *modus* "measure"]

mo·dus op·er·an·di /mṓdəss opə rándee, -dī/ (*plural* **mo·di op·er·an·di** /mṓdee opə rándee, -dī oppə rán dī/) *n* a way of doing something [< Latin, "mode of operating"]

mo·dus vi·ven·di /mṓdəss vi véndee, -dī/ (*plural* **mo·di vi·ven·di** /mṓdee vi véndee, -dī vi vén dī/) *n* **1.** a practical arrangement that allows conflicting people, groups, or ideas to coexist **2.** the way that a person or group of people lives [< Latin, "mode of living"]

MOF *abbr* ONLINE male or female (*used in e-mails or text messages*)

mo·fette /mō fét/ *n* GEOG same as **fumarole** (*archaic*) [Early 19C. Via French < Neapolitan Italian *mofetta* < *muffa* "mold, moldy smell," probably < Germanic]

Mog·a·dish·u /mòggə díshoo/ capital city and chief port of Somalia, situated in the southeast of the country. Population: 1,162,000 (1999).

Mo·gen Da·vid /mòggən dáyvid/ *n* JUDAISM same as **Star of David**

mog·gy /móggee/ (*plural* **-gies**) *n* *UK* same as **cat** *n* (sense 1) (*informal*) [Late 17C. Variant of *Maggie* < *Mag*, shortening of *Margaret*]

Mo·ghul /mṓg'l, mō gùl/ *n* HIST same as **Mughal**

Mo·gol·lon /mògə yṓn/ (*plural* **-lons** or *same*) *n* a member of a Native North American people whose civilization in Arizona and New Mexico lasted from around the 2nd century B.C. to the 13th century A.D. The Mogollons are particularly noted for their attractive pottery, traditionally decorated with black and white designs. [After place names in Arizona and New Mexico after Juan Ignacio Flores *Mogollon*, governor of New Mexico (1712–15)]

mo·gul[1] /mṓg'l, mō gùl/ *n* an important or powerful person, especially somebody working in the media [Late 17C. < MOGUL]

mo·gul[2] /mṓg'l, mō gùl/ *n* a mound of hard compacted snow formed as an obstacle on a ski slope [Mid-20C. Origin ?]

Mo·gul *n, adj* HIST another spelling of **Mughal**

mo·hair /mṓ hèr/ *n* the soft silky wool of the Angora goat [Late 16C. Alteration of *mocayre* < Arabic *mukayyar* "cloth of goat's hair" < past participle of *kayyara* "prefer"]

Mo·ham·med ISLAM another spelling of **Muhammad**

Mo·har·ram *n* ISLAM another spelling of **Muharram**

Mo·ha·ve /mō haávee/ (*plural same* or **-ves**), **Mo·ja·ve** *n* **1.** a member of a Native North American people who lived along the Colorado River valley on the border between California and Arizona **2.** the language of the Mohave people. It belongs to the Yuman branch of Hokan-Siouan languages. [Mid-19C. < Mohave *hàmakhá:v*] —**Mo·ha·ve** *adj*

mo·hawk /mṓ hàwk/ *n* a hairstyle in which the sides of the head are shaved and the remaining hair is worn sticking up. It became associated with the punk movement and was often brightly colored. [Late 19C. < MOHAWK[1]]

Mo·hawk[1] /mṓ hàwk/ (*plural same* or **-hawks**) *n* **1.** a member of an Iroquois people who lived along the Mohawk and Hudson rivers, and who now live mainly in Ontario and New York. The Mohawk were one of the five peoples who formed the Iroquois Confederacy, which later became known as the Six Nations. **2.** an Iroquoian language spoken in Quebec, Ontario, and northern New York. Native speakers: 3,000. [Mid-17C. < Narraganset *mohowawog* "man-eaters"] —**Mo·hawk** *adj*

Mo·hawk[2] /mṓ hàwk/ river in central New York. It is the largest tributary of the Hudson River. Length: 150 mi./240 km.

Mo·he·gan /mō heégən/ (*plural same* or **-gans**) *n* **1.** a member of a Native North American people who lived in eastern Connecticut, and who now live mainly in southeastern Connecticut and Wisconsin **2.** an Algonquian language spoken in Connecticut and Wisconsin. Native speakers: 1,000. [Variant of MOHICAN] —**Mo·he·gan** *adj*

mo·hel /mṓ hèl, mṓ èl/ (*plural* **mo·he·lim** /mō he leém/) *n* somebody who is qualified under Jewish religious law to carry out circumcisions [Mid-17C. < Hebrew *mōhēl*]

Mo·hen·jo·da·ro /mō hènjō daárō/ ruined Bronze Age city in southern Pakistan. It formed part of the Indus Valley Civilization.

mo·hi·can /mō heékən, mə-/ *n* *UK* same as **mohawk** [Mid-20C. < the topknots worn in illustrations of *Last of the Mohicans* (1826), a novel by James Fenimore COOPER]

Mo·hi·can /mō heékən, mə-/ *n* (*plural same* or **-cans**), *adj* PEOPLES, LANG same as **Mahican** (*dated*) [Variant]—**Mo·hi·can** *adj*

Mo·hock /mṓ hòk/ *n* a member of a gang of hoodlums from the upper classes who terrorized people in the streets of London in the early 18th century [Mid-17C. Variant of MOHAWK[1]]

AKG London

László Moholy-Nagy

Mo·holy-Nag·y /mō hṓlee nój/, **László** (1895–1946) Hungarian-born US artist. He taught at the Bauhaus school (1923–28), founded the New Bauhaus in Chicago (1937), and was known for his artistic experiments involving modern technology.

Mohs scale /mṓz-/, **Mohs hardness scale** *n* a scale used to measure the hardness of minerals, with talc at zero and diamond at 10. Each mineral on the scale is hard enough to scratch the one below it in the scale. [Late 19C. After Friedrich *Mohs* (1773–1839), German mineralogist]

mo·hur /mṓ ər, mə hoór/ *n* a gold coin worth 15 rupees used in British India in the 19th and early 20th centuries [Late 17C. < Persian, Urdu *muhr* "seal"]

moi /mwaa/ *pron* used by a speaker or writer to refer to himself or herself (*humorous*) ○ *"I wanted to remind her that none of us would be at this juncture if it weren't for moi."* (Nelson DeMille *The Lion's Game*; 2000) [< French]

moi·dore /móy dàwr, moy dáwr/ *n* an obsolete Portuguese or Brazilian gold coin [Early 18C. < Portuguese *moeda d'ouro* "coin of gold"]

moi·e·ty /móy ətee/ (*plural* **-ties**) *n* **1.** either of two parts, not necessarily equal, into which something is or can be divided (*formal*) **2.** either of two halves into which some Native South American and Aboriginal Australian societies are divided for ritual and marriage purposes. Marriages are forbidden within the same moiety. [15C. < French *moitié* "half" < late Latin *medietas* < Latin *medius* "middle"]

moil /moyl/ *n* (*archaic*) **1. TURMOIL** a state of agitation or confusion **2. DRUDGERY** hard work ■ *vi* (**moiled, moil·ing, moils**) **WORK HARD** to work very hard ○ *toiling and moiling* [14C. < Old French *moillier* "moisten, paddle in mud" < Latin *mollire* "soften" < *mollis* "soft"] —**moil·er** *n*

Moi·rai /móy rī/ *npl* in Greek mythology, the Fates. Roman equivalent **Parcae** [< Greek]

moire /mwaar, mwaa ráy/ *n* a moiré fabric, especially silk but also, formerly, mohair [Mid-17C. < French, later form of *mouaire* "mohair"]

moi·ré /mwaa ráy/ *adj* **WITH WAVY PATTERN** describes fabric with a shiny finish and wavy pattern on the surface

■ *n* **1.** TEXTILES **WAVY PATTERN ON FABRIC** a shiny finish and wavy pattern on fabric, especially silk, created by using engraved rollers **2. WAVY PATTERN** the wavy or shimmering effect created when two similar or identical geometric patterns are superimposed slightly out of alignment with each other **3.** TEXTILES same as **moire** [Early 19C. < French *moiré,* past participle of *moirer* "water" < *moire* "moiré fabric," probably alteration of *moire* (see MOIRE)]

moi·ré ef·fect, moi·ré pat·tern *n* same as **moiré** *n* (sense 2)

moist /moyst/ *adj* **1. DAMP** slightly wet **2. FRESH** pleasantly fresh, rather than dry or stale ○ *a rich, moist fruitcake* **3. TEARFUL** full of tears ○ *moist eyes* **4. RAINY** humid or rainy, especially with light rain or drizzle [14C. < Old French *moiste* < Latin *mucidus* "moldy" < *mucus* "slime," probably influenced by *musteus* "new"] —**moist·ly** *adv* —**moist·ness** *n*

SYNONYMS See *wet.*

mois·ten /móyss'n/ (**-tened, -ten·ing, -tens**) *vti* to make something moist, or become moist ○ *Moisten the mixture with a little beaten egg.* —**mois·ten·er** *n*

mois·ture /móyschər/ *n* wetness, especially as droplets of condensed or absorbed liquid, or in a vapor [14C. < Old French *moistour* < *moiste* (see MOIST)]

mois·tur·ize /móyschə rīz/ (**-ized, -iz·ing, -iz·es**) *v* **1.** *vti* to apply a cosmetic cream or lotion to the skin, especially on the face, to keep it from drying out **2.** *vt* to make something moist or more moist

mois·tur·iz·er /móyschər īzər/ *n* a cosmetic cream or lotion used to make the skin, especially on the face, feel less dry

Mo·ja /mṓjə/ *n* an arts festival featuring African American and Caribbean theater, dance, music, arts, and crafts, especially one held annually in Charleston, South Carolina [Late 20C. < Kiswahili *moja,* literally "one"]

mo·jar·ra /mō haárə/ (*plural* **-ras** or *same*) *n* a small silvery ocean fish with mouthparts that can be thrust outward. Native to: shallow waters of tropical America. Family: Gerridae. [Mid-19C. < American Spanish]

Mo·ja·ve *n, adj* PEOPLES, LANG another spelling of **Mohave**

Mo·ja·ve Des·ert /mō haávee-/ dry region in southern California, part of the Great Basin region. Area: 20,000 sq. mi./52,000 sq. km.

mo·ji·to /mō heé tō/ (*plural* **-tos**) *n Hispanic* a rum-and-mint cocktail, especially as served in Cuba [< Cuban Spanish]

mo·jo /mṓ jō/ (*plural* **-joes** or **-jos**) *n* (*slang*) **1. MAGIC** witchcraft or magic **2. MAGNETIC QUALITY** a quality that attracts or charms others **3. MAGIC CHARM** an object believed to have magical powers, especially the power to keep away evil spirits [Early 20C. Probably of African origin]

moke /mōk/ *n UK* same as **donkey** (*slang*) [Mid-19C. Probably from a personal name]

mok·sha /mṓkshə/ *n* in Hinduism, the spiritual goal of release from reincarnation [Late 18C. < Sanskrit *mokṣa* < *muc* "set free, release"]

mol *symbol* CHEM mole⁴

mol. *abbr* CHEM **1.** molecular **2.** molecule

mo·la¹ /mṓlə/ (*plural* **-las** or *same*) *n* FISH same as **ocean sunfish** [Late 17C. < French *mole*]

mo·la² /mṓlə, mṓ laá/ *n* a square of brightly colored cloth, woven or sewn with reverse appliqué in traditional Central American style. Use: clothing, wall hanging, throw. [Mid-20C. < Cuna]

mo·lal /mṓləl/ *adj* describes a solution consisting of one mole of dissolved substance (**solute**) per 1,000 grams of solution [Early 20C. < MOLE⁴]

mo·lal·i·ty /mō lállətee/ (*plural* **-ties**) *n* the concentration of a solution, expressed as the number of moles of a dissolved substance (**solute**) that can be found in 1,000 grams of solvent

mo·lar¹ /mṓlər/ *n* a large back tooth in humans and other mammals, used for chewing and grinding. Human beings have twelve molars. [14C. < Latin *molaris* "of a mill; grindstone, molar tooth" < *mola* "mill"]

mo·lar² /mṓlər/ *adj* **1.** relating to or being a mole of a substance ○ *the molar volume of hydrogen* **2.** containing one mole of substance per liter of solution [Early 20C. < MOLE⁴] —**mo·lar·i·ty** /mə lárrətee/ *n*

mo·lar³ /mṓlər/ *adj* relating to a body of matter rather than the properties of its molecules or atoms [Mid-19C. < Latin *moles* "mass"]

mo·lar mass *n* the weight of one mole of any chemical substance [< MOLAR²]

mo·lar tooth *n* DENT same as **molar**¹ [< MOLAR¹]

mo·las·ses /mə lássəz/ *n* **1.** the thick sticky sweet syrup produced during the refining of raw sugar, which ranges in color from dark brown to gold **2.** *UK* the thick dark bitter residue produced at the end of the sugar refining process [Late 16C. < Portuguese *melaços* < late Latin *mellaceum* "new wine, must" < Latin *mel* "honey"]

mold¹ /mōld/ *n* **1. CONTAINER FOR MAKING SHAPE** a container that gives a shape to a molten or liquid substance poured into it to harden **2. FRAME** a frame on which something is formed or built **3. OBJECT MADE IN MOLD** an object formed using a mold **4. SHAPE OF MOLD** the shape or form of a mold **5. GENERAL SHAPE** the general shape or form of something **6. DISTINCTIVE TYPE** a particular type that has a distinctive character or nature ○ *a leader in the heroic mold* **7. SET OF ASSUMPTIONS** a fixed pattern or framework of assumptions, especially when regarded as restricting ○ *negotiators who break out of the traditional diplomatic mold* **8.** ARCHIT same as **molding** (sense 1) ■ *v* (**mold·ed, mold·ing, molds**) **1.** *vt* **MAKE SOMETHING IN MOLD** to shape or form something in a mold **2.** *vt* **GIVE SOMETHING SHAPE** to shape or give form to something **3.** *vt* **INFLUENCE SOMEBODY OR SOMETHING** to guide or influence the growth or development of somebody or something ○ *the childhood experience that helped mold her personality* **4.** *vti* **MAKE SOMETHING CLING** shape something, especially clothing, so that it clings to and follows the contours of the part it is fitted to, or be fitted to a part in this way **5.** *vt* METALL **MAKE MOLD FROM SOMETHING** to make a material into a mold to be used in casting metal **6.** *vt* ARCHIT **PUT MOLDING ON SOMETHING** to decorate something with a molding [12C. Via Old French *modle* < Latin *modulus* "little measure" < *modus* "measure"] —**mold·a·ble** *adj*

mold² /mōld/ *n* **1. FUNGUS** a fungus that causes organic matter to decay **2. GROWTH OF MOLD** a growth of mold on the surface of something, or the discoloration caused by the growth of mold ■ *vi* (**mold·ed, mold·ing, molds**) **BECOME COVERED WITH MOLD** to become covered with or affected by mold [15C. < obsolete *moul* "go moldy" < assumed Old Norse *mugla*]

mold³ /mōld/ *n* **1.** soil that is rich in humus and easily worked or crumbled **2.** *UK* the ground, especially surrounding a grave (*literary*) [Old English < Indo-European "to grind"]

Mold /mōld/ market town and administrative center of Flintshire, Wales. Population: 8,745 (1991).

Mol·da·vi·a /mol dáyvee ə/ former principality, located in what is now Romania and Moldova —**Mol·da·vi·an** *n, adj*

mold·board /mṓld bàwrd/ *n* **1. BLADE OF PLOW** the curved metal blade of a plow that turns over the soil **2. BLADE OF BULLDOZER OR SNOWPLOW** the large curved blade on the front of a bulldozer or snowplow that pushes the soil or snow **3.** CONSTR **SIDE OF CONCRETE MOLD** a board that forms one side or one surface of a concrete mold

mold·er¹ /mṓldər/ (**-ered, -er·ing, -ers**) *vti* to crumble or decay because of natural processes, or make something do this [Mid-16C. < *mold* "loose soil" < Germanic, "grind"]

mold·er² /mṓldər/ *n* somebody who molds things or makes molds

mold·ing /mṓlding/ *n* **1.** a strip of wood or another material used to decorate or finish a surface of a wall or a piece of furniture **2.** something produced using a mold

Mol·do·va /mol dṓvə/ country in southeastern Europe. It was a republic of the former Soviet Union until 1991. Language: Romanian. Currency: leu. Capital: Chisinau. Population: 4,439,502 (2003). Area: 13,000 sq. mi./33,700 sq. km. Official name **Republic of Moldova** —**Mol·do·van** *n, adj*

mold·y /mṓldee/ (**-i·er, -i·est**) *adj* **1. WITH MOLD** containing or covered with mold **2. STALE FROM AGE OR ROT** stale and unpleasant from old age, neglect, or fungal growth **3. OLD** old-fashioned or out-of-date (*informal*) —**mold·i·ness** *n*

Moldova

mole¹ /mōl/ *n* a small dark, sometimes raised growth on the human skin, sometimes with a hair or hairs growing from it [Old English *māl* "discolored mark" < Germanic, "spot, mark"]

mole² /mōl/ *n* **1. BURROWING ANIMAL** a small animal that usually lives underground and has large forelimbs for digging, no external ears, minute eyes, and dense velvety fur. Family: Talpidae. **2. SPY** somebody employed by a group or organization such as a government ministry who discloses sensitive information while keeping his or her own identity secret **3.** CONSTR **TUNNELING MACHINE** a machine designed for boring through hard materials such as rock [14C. Probably < Middle Dutch *mol*]

mole³ /mōl/ *n* **1.** a massive wall, usually made of stone, that extends into the sea and encloses or protects a harbor **2.** a harbor enclosed or protected by a mole [Mid-16C. Via French *môle* and medieval Greek *molos* < Latin *moles* "mass, massive structure"]

mole⁴ /mōl/ *n* the basic International System unit of amount of a substance equal to the amount containing the same number of elementary units as the number of atoms in 12 grams of carbon-12. Symbol **mol** [Early 20C. < German *Mol,* shortening of *Molekul* "molecule"]

mo·le⁵ /mṓlee/ *n Hispanic* a spicy Mexican sauce made with chocolate and a variety of chilies and spices, used especially for cooking poultry [Mid-20C. Via Mexican Spanish < Nahuatl *molli* "sauce, stew"]

Mo·lech *n* BIBLE another spelling of **Moloch**

mole crab *n* a small crustacean that has long eyestalks and hairy antennae and is often found burrowing in the sand on ocean beaches. Genus: *Emerita.* [< MOLE²]

mole crick·et *n* a cricket with a heavy body and short wings that burrows in the ground using front legs that are adapted for digging. It feeds primarily on plant roots. Family: Gryllotalpidae. [< MOLE²]

mo·lec·u·lar /mə lékyələr/ *adj* **1.** relating to or made up of molecules **2.** relating to or organized from simpler parts —**mo·lec·u·lar·i·ty** /mə lèkyə lárrətee/ *n* —**mo·lec·u·lar·ly** /mə lékyələrlee/ *adv*

mo·lec·u·lar bi·ol·o·gy *n* the branch of biology concerned with the nature and function, at the molecular level, of biological phenomena such as RNA and DNA, proteins, and other macromolecules

mo·lec·u·lar film *n* CHEM same as **monolayer** (sense 1)

mo·lec·u·lar for·mu·la *n* a chemical formula that specifies which atoms and how many of each atom there are in a molecule of a compound

mo·lec·u·lar ge·net·ics *n* the branch of genetics that studies genes, chromosomes, and the transmission of hereditary characteristics at the molecular level (*takes a singular verb*)

mo·lec·u·lar sieve *n* a crystalline compound with molecule-sized pores that can be used in separating larger molecules from smaller ones

mo·lec·u·lar vol·ume *n* the volume occupied by one mole of a substance when in the form of a gas

mo·lec·u·lar weight *n* the total of all the atomic weights of the atoms in a molecule

mol·e·cule /mólla kyoōl/ *n* **1.** the smallest physical unit of a substance that can exist independently, consisting of one or more atoms held together by chemical forces **2.** a very small amount of something [Late 18C. Via French *molécule* < modern Latin *molecula* "small mass" < Latin *moles* "mass"]

mole·hill /mṓl hìl/ *n* a small mound of earth on the surface of the ground dug up by a burrowing mole [15C. < MOLE[2]]

mole rat *n* **1.** a tailless rodent that digs burrows with its enlarged incisors and powerful head. Native to: eastern Europe, southwestern Asia. Genus: *Spalax*. **2.** a rodent that has large protruding incisors for digging burrows. Native to: sub-Saharan Africa. Family: Bathyergidae. [< MOLE[2]]

mole·skin /mṓl skìn/ *n* **1.** TEXTILES **CLOTHING FABRIC** a strong heavy cotton fabric with a brushed surface. Use: clothing. **2.** ZOOL **FUR OF MOLE** the short dense soft fur of a mole **3.** MED **PROTECTIVE PATCH** a soft fabric, usually with an adhesive backing. Use: protecting part of a foot from rubbing against a shoe. ■ **mole·skins** *npl* CLOTHING **MOLESKIN CLOTHING** clothing, especially pants, made of moleskin fabric [Mid-17C. < MOLE[2]]

mo·lest /mə lést/ (**-lest·ed, -lest·ing, -lests**) *vt* **1.** to force unwanted sexual attentions on somebody, especially a child or physically weaker adult **2.** to pester, bother, or disturb a person or animal [14C. Directly or via French < Latin *molestare* < *molestus* "troublesome"] —**mo·les·ta·tion** /mṑ le stáysh'n/ *n* —**mo·lest·er** *n*

Mo·lière /mōl yér/ (1622–73) French dramatist. He satirized contemporary society in a series of witty plays including *Tartuffe* (1664). He also wrote *Le Bourgeois gentilhomme* (*The Bourgeois Gentleman*) (1670) and *Le Malade imaginaire* (*The Imaginary Invalid*) (1673). Pseudonym of **Poquelin, Jean-Baptiste**

"Most men die of their remedies, and not of their illnesses."
[Molière, *Le Malade imaginaire*, 1673]

mo·line /mō leén, mṓlin/ *adj* describes a heraldic cross that has arms of equal length that broaden at the ends by forking and curving backward [Mid-16C. Probably < Anglo-Norman < *molin* "mill" < late Latin *molinum*]

Mo·line /mō leén/ city in northwestern Illinois, in Rock Island County, on the Mississippi River. Population: 43,221 (2002 estimate).

moll /mol/ *n* (*slang*) **1.** the woman companion of a gangster **2.** a woman prostitute [Early 17C. Shortening of *Molly*, a nickname for *Mary*]

MOLLE /móllee/, **Molle** *n* a water-repellent backpack with removable sections for carrying weapons and ammunition [Late 20C. Abbreviation of *modular lightweight load-bearing equipment*]

mol·lie *n* FISH another spelling of **molly**

mol·li·fy /móllə fī/ (**-fied, -fy·ing, -fies**) *vt* **1.** **PACIFY SOMEBODY** to calm or soothe somebody who is angry or upset **2.** **TEMPER SOMETHING** to make something less intense or severe **3.** **SOFTEN SOMETHING** to make something less hard, rigid, or stiff [15C. Directly or via French *mollifier* < Latin *mollificare* < *mollis* "soft"] —**mol·li·fi·a·ble** *adj* —**mol·li·fi·ca·tion** /mòlləfi káysh'n/ *n* —**mol·li·fi·er** *n* —**mol·li·fy·ing·ly** *adv*

mol·lusc *n* ZOOL another spelling of **mollusk**

mol·lus·ci·cide /mə lúski sīd/ *n* a chemical that kills mollusks —**mol·lus·ci·cid·al** /mə lùski sī́d'l/ *adj*

mol·lus·cum con·ta·gi·o·sum /mə lùskəm kən tayjee ṓssəm/ *n* a benign viral skin infection characterized by numerous small round dimpled pearly white nodules [Early 19C. < modern Latin, literally "contagious fungus"]

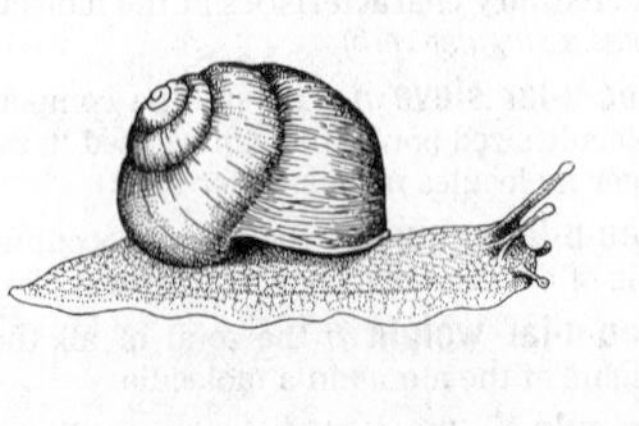
mollusk

mol·lusk /mólləsk/, **mol·lusc** *n* an invertebrate with a soft unsegmented body, usually protected by a shell in one, two, or three pieces, e.g., the snails and the octopus. Most mollusks live in or near water. Phylum: Mollusca. [Late 18C. < French *mollusque* < Latin *molluscus* "thin-shelled nut" < *mollis* "soft"] —**mol·lus·kan** /mə lúskən/ *adj, n*

mol·ly /móllee/ (*plural* **-lies**), **mol·lie** *n* a fish that bears live young and is often kept in aquariums. Native to: Central and South America. Genera: *Poecilia* or *Mollienesia*. [Mid-20C. Shortening of modern Latin *Mollienisia*, after Count F. N. *Mollien* (1758–1850), French statesman]

mol·ly·cod·dle /móllee kòdd'l/ *vt* (**-dled, -dling, -dles**) to treat somebody in an overprotective and overindulgent way ■ *n* a child, especially a boy, who is spoiled and overprotected [Mid-19C. < the name *Molly* (used for an effeminate boy or man) + CODDLE] —**mol·ly·cod·dler** *n*

Mol·ly Ma·guire /mòllee mə gwír/ *n* **1.** a member of a secret organization founded in Ireland in 1843 that used violent methods to stop evictions by the government **2.** a member of a secret Irish-American organization, active in the coalmining districts of Pennsylvania from about 1865 to 1877, that used violent methods to try to get improved working conditions [Mid-19C. < a common Irish name, and because members of the original society disguised themselves as women]

moloch

mo·loch /mṓ lòk, mólløk/ *n* a lizard with large spiny scales covering its head and back. Native to: plains and deserts of central and southern Australia. Latin name: *Moloch horridus*. [Mid-19C. Via late Latin < Greek *Molokh* < Hebrew *Mōlek*, a Canaanite idol]

Mo·loch /mṓ lèk/, **Mo·lech** *n* **1.** in the Bible, a Semitic deity to whom children were sacrificed **2.** somebody or something that requires a costly and painful sacrifice [Early 17C. Via late Latin < Greek *Molokh* < Hebrew *mōlek*, a Canaanite idol]

Mo·lo·kai /mòlō kī́, mōlə kī́/ volcanic island in central Hawaii, between the islands of Oahu and Maui. Population: 6,838 (2002 estimate). Area: 260 sq. mi./673 sq. km.

Mo·lo·tov /móllə tàwf/, **Vyacheslav Mikhailovich** (1890–1986) Soviet politician. As a close associate and adviser of Joseph Stalin, he served as premier (1930–41) and foreign minister (1939–49, 1953–56) of the Soviet Union. He negotiated the German-Soviet nonaggression pact in 1939. Born **Scriabin, Vyacheslav Mikhailovich**

Mo·lo·tov cock·tail *n* a crude bomb, usually made of a bottle filled with a flammable liquid such as gasoline and a wick that is set alight just before it is thrown

Mol·son /mṓlssən/, **John** (1763–1836) British-born Canadian entrepreneur. He made his fortune as a brewer, banker, and steamship builder.

molt /mōlt/ *vti* (**molt·ed, molt·ing, molts**) **LOSE FEATHERS, HAIR, OR SKIN** to shed feathers, hair, or skin periodically, especially seasonally, in order to allow replacement of what is lost with new growth ■ *n* **1.** **LOSS OF FEATHERS, HAIR, OR SKIN** the process or time during which a bird or other animal sheds all or part of its feathers, hair, or skin **2.** **LOST FEATHERS, HAIR, OR SKIN** the feathers, hair, or skin shed by a bird or other animal [Pre-12C. < Latin *mutare* "to change"] —**molt·er** *n*

mol·ten /mṓlt'n/ *adj* **1.** **MELTED** changed into liquid form by heat **2.** **MOLDED** produced by melting a material and then shaping it in a mold **3.** **GLOWING** glowing with great heat [13C. Originally past participle of MELT[1]]

Molt·ke /móltkə/, **Helmuth Johannes Ludwig, Count** (1848–1916) German military commander. As chief of staff of the German army, he led Germany's unsuccessful invasion of France at the beginning of World War I.

mol·to /mṓltō/ *adv* used for emphasis before or after a musical direction derived from Italian [Early 19C. < Italian < Latin *multus* "much"]

Mo·luc·cas /mə lúkəz/ group of islands in eastern Indonesia, part of the Malay Archipelago. Population: 1,741,800 (1998). Area: 28,800 sq. mi./74,500 sq. km. —**Mo·luc·can** *n, adj*

mol. wt. *abbr* CHEM molecular weight

mo·ly /mṓlee/ (*plural* **-lies**) *n* **1.** a plant of the garlic family. Flowers: yellow. Native to: southern Europe. Latin name: *Allium moly*. **2.** in Greek mythology, a magic herb with milky white flowers and black roots that Hermes gave to Odysseus to protect him from Circe's spells [Mid-16C. Via Latin < Greek *mōlu*]

mo·lyb·date /mə líb dàyt/ *n* a salt of molybdenum [Late 18C. < MOLYBDIC]

mo·lyb·de·nite /mə líbdə nīt/ *n* a grayish mineral consisting of molybdenum sulfide. Use: source of molybdenum. [Late 18C. < modern Latin *molybdenum* (see MOLYBDENUM)]

mo·lyb·de·nous /mə líbdənəss/ *adj* relating to or containing molybdenum, especially with a valence of 2 [Late 18C. < modern Latin *molybdenum* (see MOLYBDENUM)]

mo·lyb·de·num /mə líbdənəm/ *n* a very hard silvery metallic element. Use: strengthening steel alloys. Symbol **Mo**. See table at **element** [Early 19C. < modern Latin < Greek *molubdaina* "piece of lead" < *molubdos* "lead"]

mo·lyb·de·num sul·fide, **mo·lyb·de·num di·sul·fide** *n* a black crystalline powder that is insoluble in water. Use: lubricant. Formula: MoS_2.

mo·lyb·dic /mə líbdik/ *adj* relating to or containing molybdenum, especially with a valence of 6 [Late 18C. < modern Latin *molybdenum* (see MOLYBDENUM)]

mo·lyb·dous /mə líbdəss/ *adj* relating to or containing molybdenum, especially with a valence lower than 6 [Late 18C. < modern Latin *molybdenum* (see MOLYBDENUM)]

mom /mom/ *n* somebody's mother (*informal*) [Late 19C. Shortening of MOMMA] ◇ **Mom, Pop, and apple pie** the virtues, e.g., neighborliness and civic pride, that Americans believe have traditionally characterized US culture

m.o.m. *abbr* ACCT middle of month

MOMA /mṓmə/ *abbr* Museum of Modern Art (New York)

mom-and-pop *adj* **1.** describes a business that is owned and operated by a family, especially by a husband and wife ○ *a mom-and-pop store* **2.** friendly, relaxed, and pleasantly informal

Mom·ba·sa /mom bássə/ city and chief seaport of Kenya, in the southeast of the country on the Indian Ocean. It is also a tourist center. Population: 465,000 (1989).

mo·ment /mṓmənt/ *n* **1.** **SHORT TIME** a very short interval of time ○ *Wait a moment.* **2.** **PARTICULAR INSTANT** a particular instant in time ○ *At that moment she walked in the door.* **3.** **PRESENT** the present time ○ *busy at the moment* **4.** **SIGNIFICANT PERIOD** an important or significant time or occasion ○ *great moments in world history* **5.** **SHORT PERIOD OF EXCELLENCE** a brief period of excellence or interest (*often used in the plural*) ○ *It's not a great opera, but it has its moments.* **6.** **IMPORTANCE** special importance or significance (*formal*) ○ *a decision of great moment* **7.** PHILOSOPHY **SPECIFIC STAGE** a specific stage or aspect of something **8.** PHILOSOPHY same as **momentum** (sense 4) (*dated*) **9.** PHYS **TENDENCY TO PRODUCE ROTATION** a tendency to cause motion, especially rotation **10.** PHYS **PRODUCT OF FORCE TIMES DISTANCE** the product of a quantity such as a force multiplied by its perpendicular distance from a given point **11.** STATS **MEAN IN FREQUENCY DISTRIBUTION** the expected value of the deviations of a variable, compared to a fixed value, raised to a given power [14C. Via French < Latin *momentum* "movement" < *movere* "to move"]

mo·men·tar·i·ly /mṓmən térrəlee/ *adv* 1. BRIEFLY for a brief period of time 2. PROGRESSIVELY with every passing moment 3. VERY SOON within a very short period of time ○ *He'll be here momentarily.*

mo·men·tar·y /mṓmən tèrree/ *adj* 1. VERY BRIEF lasting for a very short time 2. CONSTANT present or happening at every moment 3. WITH SHORT LIFE living or continuing for only a relatively short time —**mo·men·tar·i·ness** *n*

mo·ment·ly /mṓməntlee/ *adv* 1. PROGRESSIVELY with every passing moment ○ *growing momently more uneasy* 2. VERY SOON within a very short period of time 3. FOR INSTANT for a very short period of time

~~momento~~ incorrect spelling of **memento**

mo·ment of in·er·tia *n* a measure of resistance to changes in angular speed, calculated as the sum of the products of the component masses of an object multiplied by the square of their distance from the axis. Symbol ***I***

mo·ment of truth *n* 1. a point in time when a crucial decision has to be taken or when somebody or something is put to an important test 2. in a bullfight, the point at which the bull is about to be killed with the final blow

mo·men·tous /mō méntəss/ *adj* extremely important or crucial, especially in its effect on the future course of events —**mo·men·tous·ly** *adv* —**mo·men·tous·ness** *n*

mo·men·tum /mō méntəm/ (*plural* **-ta** /-tə/ or **-tums**) *n* 1. CAPACITY FOR PROGRESSIVE DEVELOPMENT the power to increase or develop at an ever-growing pace ○ *The project was in danger of losing momentum.* 2. FORWARD MOVEMENT the speed or force of forward movement of an object ○ *the momentum gained on the downhill stretches of the course* 3. PHYS MEASURE OF MOVEMENT a quantity that expresses the motion of a body and its resistance to slowing down. It is equal to the product of the body's mass and velocity. Symbol ***p*** 4. PHILOSOPHY BASIC ELEMENT an essential part of a whole [Early 17C. < Latin *momentum* (see MOMENT)]

mom·ma /mómmə/ *n* somebody's mother (*informal*) [Early 19C. Alteration of MAMA]

mom·my /mómmee/ (*plural* **-mies**) *n* somebody's mother (*informal*) [Early 20C. Alteration of MAMMY]

mom·my track *n* a career route taken by a woman that may reduce her chances of career advancement by working flextime or fewer hours in order to look after a child or children (*informal*)

mom·ser *n* JUDAISM same as **mamzer**

Mo·mus /mṓməss/ *n* in Greek mythology, the god of fault-finding and mockery. He is a son of Night. [Late 16C. Via Latin < Greek *Mōmos*]

momz·er *n* JUDAISM same as **mamzer**

Mon /mawn/ (*plural same* or **Mons**) *n* 1. a member of a people who live in adjacent parts of Thailand and Myanmar 2. a Mon-Khmer language that is spoken in adjacent parts of Thailand and Myanmar. Native speakers: 700,000. [Late 18C. < Mon] —**Mon** *adj*

mon. *abbr* 1. monastery 2. monetary

Mon. *abbr* 1. Monday 2. CHR Monsignor

mon- *prefix* same as **mono-** (*used before vowels*)

Mo·na /mṓnə/ uninhabited island off the western coast of Puerto Rico. Area: 20 sq. mi./52 sq. km.

mon·a·chal /mónnik'l/ *adj* relating to a monastery or monks, or resembling monastic life [Late 16C. Directly or via French < ecclesiastical Latin *monachalis* < late Latin *monachus* (see MONK)] —**mon·a·chism** *n* —**mon·a·chist** *adj, n*

mon·ac·id, etc. CHEM same as **monoacid, etc.**

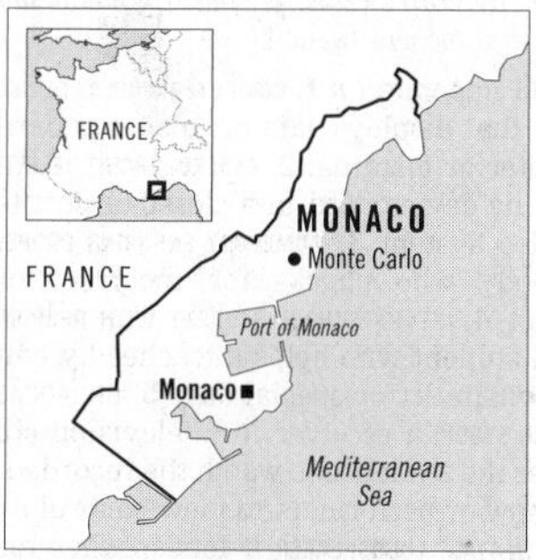

Monaco

Mon·a·co /mónnəkō/ small independent principality of Europe, bordered by France and the Mediterranean Sea. Language: French. Currency: euro. Capital: Monaco. Population: 32,130 (2003). Area: 0.75 sq. mi./2 sq. km. Official name **Principality of Monaco** —**Mon·a·can** *n, adj*

mo·nad /mṓ nàd/ *n* 1. MICROBIOL SINGLE-CELLED MICROORGANISM a microorganism consisting of just one cell, especially a flagellate protozoan. Genus: *Monas.* 2. CHEM ATOM WITH VALENCE OF ONE an atom or chemical group that has a valence of one 3. PHILOSOPHY BASIC ENTITY IN METAPHYSICS OF LEIBNITZ in the metaphysics of Leibnitz, an indivisible indestructible unit that is the basic element of reality and a microcosm of it [Mid-16C. Directly or via French *monade* < late Latin *monad-* < Greek *monos* "single"] —**mo·nad·ic** /mō náddik/ *adj* —**mo·nad·i·cal** *adj* —**mo·nad·i·cal·ly** *adv* —**mo·nad·ism** *n*

mon·a·del·phous /mònnə délfəss/ *adj* 1. describes stamens that have all the filaments united to form a single bundle in the shape of a tube 2. describes a flower that has monadelphous stamens [Early 19C. < MONO- + Greek *adelphos* "brother"]

mo·nad·nock /mə nád nòk/ *n* an isolated mountain or rock that has resisted the process of erosion and stands alone in an otherwise flat area [Late 19C. After *Monadnock*, peak in New Hampshire]

Mon·a·ghan /mónnəhən/ county in the northeastern part of the Republic of Ireland. Area: 498 sq. mi./1,291 sq. km.

mo·nan·drous /mə nándrəss/ *adj* 1. WITH ONE HUSBAND having only one husband at a time 2. WITH ONE MALE LOVER having a sexual relationship with only one man during a period of time 3. BOT WITH ONE STAMEN describes a flower that has a single stamen 4. BOT WITH MONANDROUS FLOWERS describes a plant that has monandrous flowers [Early 19C. < Greek *monandros* "having one husband" < *monos* "one, alone" + *andr-* "man"]

mo·nan·dry /mə nándree/ *n* 1. the practice of having only one husband at a time 2. the practice of having a sexual relationship with only one man during a period of time

Mo·na Pas·sage /mṓnə-/ area of sea separating the islands of Hispaniola and Puerto Rico, linking the Atlantic Ocean to the Caribbean Sea

mon·arch /mónnərk/ *n* 1. SUPREME RULER somebody, especially a king or queen, who rules a state or territory, usually for life and by hereditary right 2. EXCEPTIONALLY POWERFUL PERSON somebody who possesses exceptional power or influence in an area of activity (*literary*) 3. SOMETHING OUTSTANDING OR PREDOMINANT something that occupies a preeminent or predominant position (*literary*) 4. INSECTS same as **monarch butterfly** [15C. Directly or via French < late Latin *monarcha* < Greek *monarkhos* "rule alone" < *monos* "one, alone" + *arkhein* "to rule"] —**mo·nar·chal** /mə náark'l/ *adj* —**mo·nar·chal·ly** *adv*

mon·arch but·ter·fly *n* a large migrating orange and black butterfly whose caterpillars feed on milkweed plants. Native to: North America. Latin name: *Danaus plexippus.*

mo·nar·chic /mə náarkik/, **mo·nar·chi·cal** /-ik'l/ *adj* relating to a monarch or monarchy —**mo·nar·chi·cal·ly** *adv*

mon·ar·chism /mónnər kìzzəm/ *n* 1. the system of government in which a monarch rules 2. belief in or support for monarchy as a system of government —**mon·ar·chist** *n, adj* —**mon·ar·chis·tic** /mònnər kístik/ *adj*

mon·ar·chy /mónnərkee/ (*plural* **-chies**) *n* 1. SYSTEM OF RULE BY MONARCH a political system in which a state is ruled by a monarch 2. ROYAL FAMILY a monarch and his or her family 3. STATE RULED BY MONARCH a country ruled by a monarch

mo·nar·da /mə náardə/ *n* an aromatic plant of the mint family, e.g., bee balm and bergamot. Native to: North America. Genus: *Monarda.* [Late 18C. < modern Latin]

mon·as·ter·y /mónnə stèrree/ (*plural* **-ies**) *n* 1. a building or buildings with grounds in which a group of people observing religious vows, especially monks, live together 2. a group of people, especially monks, living together and observing religious vows [14C. Via ecclesiastical Latin *monasterium* < Greek *monazein* "live alone" < *monos* "one, alone"] —**mon·as·te·ri·al** /mònnə stéeree əl/ *adj*

mo·nas·tic /mə nástik/ *adj* 1. *also* **mo·nas·ti·cal** /-tik'l/ OF MONKS, NUNS, OR MONASTERIES relating to monks, nuns, or their way of life or the buildings in which they live ○ *monastic rule* 2. *also* **mo·nas·ti·cal** /mə nástik'l/ RECLUSIVE OR AUSTERE characteristic of the life of a monk, especially in being reclusive, self-denying, or austere ■ *n* MONK somebody, especially a monk, who lives with others in a monastery and observes religious vows [15C. Directly or via French < late Latin *monasticus* < Greek *monazein* (see MONASTERY)] —**mo·nas·ti·cal·ly** *adv*

mo·nas·ti·cism /mə násti sìzzəm/ *n* the way of life characteristic of monks or nuns, in which they withdraw entirely or in part from society to devote themselves to prayer, solitude, and contemplation

~~monastry~~ incorrect spelling of **monastery**

mon·a·tom·ic /mònnə tómmik/, **mon·o·a·tom·ic** /mònnō-/ *adj* 1. having only one atom in the molecule 2. with one atom or chemical group that can be replaced during a chemical reaction 3. CHEM same as **monovalent** (sense 1) —**mon·a·tom·ic·al·ly** *adv*

mon·au·ral /mon áwrəl/ *adj* 1. relating to or involving the hearing of sound by one ear 2. ELECTRONICS same as **monophonic** —**mon·au·ral·ly** *adv*

mon·ax·i·al /mon áksee əl/ *adj* BOT same as **uniaxial** (sense 1)

mon·a·zite /mónnə zīt/ *n* a reddish brown phosphate mineral that contains cerium, lanthanum, and some thorium [Mid-19C. < Greek *monazein* (see MONASTERY); because of its rare occurrence]

Monc·ton /múngktən/ city in southeastern New Brunswick, Canada. It is a transportation center for the country's Maritime Provinces. Population: 90,359 (2001).

Mon·dale /món dàyl/, **Walter** (*b.* 1928) US politician and diplomat. He was a US senator (1964–76), US vice president under Jimmy Carter (1977–81), and ambassador to Japan (1993–96).

> "When I hear your new ideas I'm reminded of that ad, 'Where's the beef?'"
> [Walter Mondale, televised debate with US Senator Gary Hart; March 11, 1984]

Mon·day /mún dày, múndee/ *n* the first day of the traditional working week, coming after Sunday and before Tuesday [Old English *mōnandæg* < Germanic, translation of Latin *lunae dies* "day of the moon"]

Mon·day morn·ing quar·ter·back *n* somebody who, after an event or situation has occurred, criticizes what has been done (*informal*) —**Mon·day morn·ing quar·ter·back·ing** *n*

Mon·days /mún dàyz, múndeez/ *adv* every Monday

Mon·dri·an /mòndree áan, móndree aan/, **Piet** (1872–1944) Dutch painter. A leading figure of the De Stijl art movement, he was an advocate of pure geometric abstraction, with flat planes and straight lines, and the use of primary colors along with black and white. Born **Mondriaan, Pieter Cornelis**

> "Great masters of painting have emphasized the tension characterizing the contour...What I have in mind is the most extreme transformation of the tension of the line, until it finally becomes the absolutely straight line."
> [Piet Mondrian, "Plastic Art and Pure Plastic," *Modern Artists on Art: 10 Unabridged Essays*; 1964]

mo·ne·cious *adj* BOT another spelling of **monoecious**

Mo·né·gasque /mònnə gáask/ *n* somebody who comes from Monaco ■ *adj* relating to Monaco [Late 19C. < French < *Mounegue* "Monaco"]

mon·es·trous /mon éstrəss/ *adj* used to describe mammals that have only one estrous cycle in a year or breeding season

Mo·net /mō náy/, **Claude** (1840–1926) French painter. A leading figure of the impressionist movement, he is noted for his studies of the effects of light on scenes and subjects in nature. Full name **Monet, Claude Oscar**

mon·e·tar·ism /mónnətə rìzzəm/ *n* 1. the theory that inflation and other economic variations are caused by changes in the money supply 2. the policy of controlling an economic system by increasing or decreasing the money supply, especially in a gradual manner —**mon·e·tar·ist** *n, adj*

mon·e·tar·y /mónnə tèrree/ *adj* relating to or involving money or currency [Early 19C. Directly or via French *monétaire* < late Latin *monetarius* < Latin *moneta* (see MONEY)] —**mon·e·tar·i·ly** /mònnə térrilee/ *adv*

mon·e·tar·y u·nit *n* the standard unit in a nation's currency system, e.g., the dollar in the United States or the pound in the United Kingdom

mon·e·tize /mónnə tīz/ (**-tized, -tiz·ing, -tiz·es**) *vt* **1. MAKE SOMETHING LEGAL TENDER** to make something the legal tender of a country **2. COIN METAL** to convert a metal into coins **3. CONVERT DEBT INTO AVAILABLE MONEY** to convert a government debt into available currency, especially by issuing securities [Late 19C. < Latin *moneta* (see MONEY)] —**mon·e·ti·za·tion** /mònnəti záysh'n/ *n*

mon·ey /múnnee/ *n* **1. MEDIUM OF EXCHANGE** a medium of exchange issued by a government or other public authority in the form of coins of gold, silver, or other metal, or paper bills, used as the measure of the value of goods and services **2. DENOMINATION** a form or denomination of coin or paper money **3. SOMEBODY'S COINS AND BILLS** the amount of coins and bills in somebody's possession ○ *Do you have money for lunch?* **4. SAVINGS OR CREDIT** the amount of money held in a bank account or available on credit to somebody **5. WAGES OR SALARY** the amount somebody is paid for working ○ *She earns good money.* **6. CONVERTIBLE ASSETS** assets or property that can be converted into cash **7. NATIONAL CURRENCY** the official currency of a country **8. RECOGNIZED MEDIUM OF EXCHANGE** a commodity, usually gold, that is officially recognized as a medium of exchange and a measure of value **9. RICH PEOPLE** a rich person, family, or class ○ *She married money.* ■ **mon·eys, mon·ies** *npl* **SUM OF MONEY** a sum or amount of money, especially one that has a particular origin ○ *state education monies* [13C. Via Old French *moneie* < Latin *moneta* "mint, money" < *Moneta*, epithet of the goddess Juno, in whose temple coins were minted] ◇ **for somebody's money** in somebody's opinion or judgment ○ *For my money, he's easily their best player.* ◇ **in the money** having a lot of money, especially as a change in circumstances ◇ **have mo·ney to burn** to be able to spend money extravagantly ◇ **put your money where your mouth is** to take action to show that you truly mean what you have said (*informal*) ◇ **throw good money after bad** to put more money, better used elsewhere, into a bad investment ○ *If you have the car repaired again, you'll just throw good money after bad.* ◇ **throw money about** to spend money in an extravagant, ostentatious way (*informal*)

mon·ey-back *adj* refunding money paid for something if the product or service is unsatisfactory ○ *It comes with a money-back guarantee.*

mon·ey·bags /múnnee bàgz/ (*plural same*) *n* a conspicuously rich person (*informal*)

mon·ey·chang·er /múnnee chàynjər/ *n* **1.** an exchanger of currencies, usually for a commission **2.** a machine that dispenses coins in exchange for paper money

mon·eyed /múnneed/, **mon·ied** *adj* **1.** possessing a great deal of money **2.** consisting of or resulting from money

mon·ey·grub·ber /múnnee grùbbər/ *n* somebody excessively concerned with making money at every possible opportunity —**mon·ey·grub·bing** *adj, n*

mon·ey·lend·er /múnnee lèndər/ *n* a lender of money in exchange for interest on the amount borrowed —**mon·ey·lend·ing** *n*

mon·ey·mak·er /múnnee màykər/ *n* **1.** somebody who is skilled at making money **2.** a business, product, or project that makes a lot of money —**mon·ey·mak·ing** *n, adj*

mon·ey·man /múnnee màn/ (*plural* **-men** /-mèn/) *n* (*informal*) **1.** an expert on finance and economics **2.** the financial manager or accountant of a business or organization

mon·ey mar·ket *n* **1.** the trade in low-risk securities that have a life of one year or less **2.** *also* **mon·ey mar·ket fund** a mutual fund that sells its shares to buy short-term securities and then converts the profits into additional shares for its stockholders

mon·ey of ac·count *n* a monetary unit that is used to keep accounts. It does not necessarily correspond to an actual currency unit.

mon·ey or·der *n* an order for a specific sum of money, usually purchased with cash at a bank or post office, that can be used to make payments

mon·ey plant *n* PLANTS same as **honesty** (sense 3) [Because its seedpods resemble coins]

mon·ey shell *n* the shell of the butter clam, formerly used as money by Native Americans on the coast of western North America

mon·ey sup·ply *n* the total amount of money available in a given economy. One way of measuring the money supply is the total amount of currency in circulation combined with the money available in bank deposits.

mon·ey·wort /múnnee wùrt, -wàwrt/ *n US* an evergreen creeping plant with coin-shaped leaves. Flowers: yellow. Native to: Europe, eastern North America. Latin name: *Lysimachia nummularia*. Can term **creeping Jennie**

-monger *suffix* seller, dealer, promoter ○ *fishmonger* [Old English *mangere*, via Germanic < Latin *mango* "peddler, swindler"]

mon·go /móng gō/ (*plural same* or **-gos**) *n* a subunit of Mongolian currency. See table at **currency** [Mid-20C. < Mongolian *möngö* "silver"]

mon·gol /móng g'l, móng gōl/ *n* a former term for somebody affected by Down syndrome, now considered highly offensive (*dated offensive*) [Late 19C. < MONGOL]

Mon·gol *n* **1.** a member of the originally nomadic peoples who inhabit Mongolia and established an empire in the 13th century **2.** LANG same as **Mongolian** (sense 2) ■ *adj* relating to Mongolia, its people, or their language or culture [Late 17C. < Mongol]

Mongolia

Mon·go·li·a /mong gōlee ə, mon-/ country in Central Asia, bordered on the north by Russia and on the east, south, and west by China. Language: Mongolian. Currency: tugrik. Capital: Ulaanbaatar. Population: 2,712,315 (2003). Area: 604,830 sq. mi./ 1,566,500 sq. km.

Mon·go·li·an /mong gōlee ən, mon-/ *n* **1.** somebody who comes from Mongolia **2.** a language or group of dialects of the Altaic family spoken in Mongolia and in the Chinese region of Inner Mongolia. Native speakers: 6 million. —**Mon·go·li·an** *adj*

Mon·gol·ic /mong góllik, mon-/ *n* an Altaic group of languages that includes Mongolian, Buryat, and Santa ■ *adj* **1.** relating to Mongolic **2.** ANTHROP same as **Mongoloid** (*dated*)

mon·gol·ism /móng gə lìzzəm/ *n* a former term for Down syndrome, now considered highly offensive (*dated*)

mon·gol·oid /móng gə lòyd/ *adj* a former term meaning affected by Down syndrome, now considered highly offensive (*dated*)

Mon·gol·oid *adj* in an obsolete classificatory system, relating or belonging to a racial group including the peoples of eastern Asia, the Inuit, and the Native Americans (*no longer used technically*) —**Mon·gol·oid** *n*

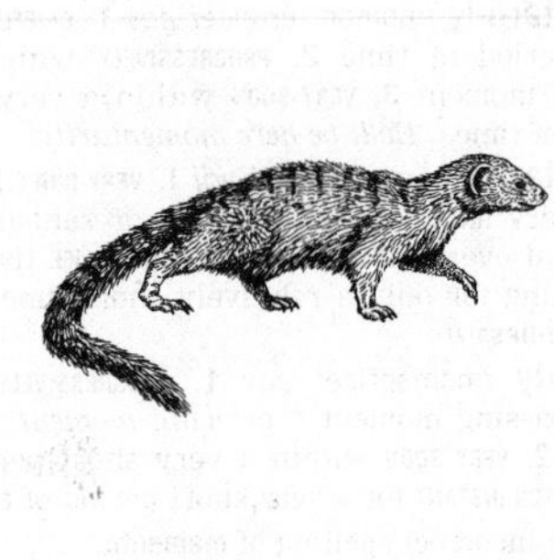

mongoose

mon·goose /món gòoss/ (*plural* **-goos·es**) *n* a small short-legged carnivorous animal that resembles a ferret and is noted for its ability to kill poisonous snakes. Native to: South Asia. Genus: *Herpestes*. [Late 17C. < Marathi *maṅgūs*]

mon·grel /móng grəl/ *n* **1. DOG OF MIXED BREED** a dog that is a mixture of different breeds **2. ANIMAL OR PLANT OF MIXED BREED** an animal or plant that is a mixture of different breeds or strains **3. OFFENSIVE TERM** an offensive term for somebody who is of mixed racial ancestry **4. STRANGE MIXTURE** a combination or mixture of different people or things, especially one that seems particularly strange ■ *adj* **MIXED IN ORIGIN OR CHARACTER** of mixed breed, descent, type, or character (*offensive in some contexts*) [15C. Probably < Germanic, "to mix"] —**mon·grel·ism** *n* —**mon·grel·ly** *adj*

mon·grel·ize /móng grə līz/ (**-ized, -iz·ing, -iz·es**) *vt* to make something or somebody become mongrel or mixed in character, type, or race (*offensive when used of people*) —**mon·grel·i·za·tion** /mòng grəli záysh'n/ *n*

'mongst /mungst/ *prep* same as **among** (*literary*) [Late 16C. Shortening of *amongst*, variant of AMONG]

Mon·i·ca·gate /mónnikə gàyt/ *n* a 1998–99 sex scandal involving US President Bill Clinton and a former White House intern, culminating in his impeachment and subsequent acquittal (*slang*) [< *Monica* S. Lewinsky, the intern]

mon·ick·er *n* another spelling of **moniker** (*slang*)

mon·ied *adj* FIN another spelling of **moneyed**

mon·ies plural of **money** (*formal*)

mon·i·ker /mónnikər/, **mon·ick·er** *n* somebody's name or nickname (*slang*) [Mid-19C. Origin ?]

mo·nil·i·form /mə níllə fàwrm, mō-/ *adj* describes a plant root or insect antenna that resembles a string of beads [Early 19C. Directly or via French < modern Latin *moniliformis* < Latin *monile* "necklace"] —**mo·nil·i·form·ly** *adv*

mo·nism /mō nìzzəm, mó-/ *n* **1.** the philosophical theory that reality is a unified whole and is grounded in a single basic substance or principle **2.** a theory or point of view that attempts to explain everything in terms of a single principle [Mid-19C. < modern Latin *monismus* < Greek *monos* "one, alone"] —**mo·nist** *n, adj* —**mo·nis·tic** /mō nístik, mo-/ *adj* —**mo·nis·ti·cal·ly** *adv*

mo·ni·tion /mə nísh'n/ *n* **1. WARNING OF DANGER** a warning, especially a warning of danger **2. URGING TO BE CAUTIOUS** a piece of advice urging caution **3.** CHR **WARNING FROM BISHOP** an official warning from a bishop to refrain from doing something **4.** LAW **SUMMONS** an order to appear in court [14C. < French < Latin *monit-*, past participle of *monere* "warn"]

mon·i·tor /mónnitər/ *n* **1. COMPUTER DISPLAY DEVICE** a video device that displays data or images generated by a computer or terminal **2. CLOSED-CIRCUIT TELEVISION SET** a receiving device used in a closed-circuit television or video system **3. SOMEBODY ENSURING PROPER CONDUCT** somebody who checks for incorrect or unfair conduct **4.** EDUC **SCHOOL STUDENT WITH RESPONSIBILITY** a school student who helps a teacher by being given a responsibility or special duty **5.** BROADCAST **VIEWING DEVICE IN STUDIO** a receiver in a television studio that enables the audience to watch the recorded portions of a show or performers to view parts of a program **6.** ARTS **STAGE LOUDSPEAKER** a loudspeaker on a stage during a concert used to let performers hear what they are playing ○ *playing a guitar solo with one foot up on the monitor* **7.** BROADCAST **SOMEBODY WHO CHECKS BROADCASTS** somebody who listens to and checks broadcasts for a client or employer, e.g., to learn foreign news or discover secret plans **8.** COMPUT **COMPUTER PROGRAM** a computer program that observes and controls other programs in a system **9.** *UK* REPT same as **monitor lizard** **10.** INDUST, EMERGENCIES **NOZZLE** a jointed device with a rotating nozzle that controls and aims a jet of water **11.** HIST **19C WARSHIP** a heavily armored warship with gun turrets used in the 19th century in coastal and inland waters ■ *vt* (**-tored, -tor·ing, -tors**) **1. CHECK SOMETHING REGULARLY** to check something at regular intervals in order to find out how it is progressing or developing **2. WATCH FOR PROPER CONDUCT** to watch over somebody or something, especially in order to ensure that good order or proper conduct is maintained **3. LISTEN TO BROADCASTS OR TELEPHONE CONVERSATIONS** to use an electronic receiver to listen in on broadcasts or telephone conversations, especially in order to discover secret or illegal plans and activities **4.** BROADCAST **CHECK QUALITY OF SIGNALS** to use an electronic receiver to check the quality of transmitted audio or visual signals [Early 16C. < Latin < *monit-* (see MONITION)] —**mon·i·to·ri·al** /mònni táwree əl/ *adj* —**mon·i·to·ri·al·ly** *adv* —**mon·i·tor·ship** *n*

ORIGIN The Latin word *monere* "to warn," from which ***monitor*** is derived, is also the source of English *admonish, monument, premonition,* and *summon.*

mon·i·tor lizard *n* a large tropical carnivorous lizard. Native to: Asia, Africa, Australia. Family: Varanidae. [< the belief that they warn of the proximity of crocodiles]

mon·i·to·ry /mónni tàwree/ *adj* communicating a warning ■ *n* (*plural* **-ries**) a letter, usually from a bishop, that warns somebody to refrain from doing something

monk /mungk/ *n* a man who withdraws entirely or in part from society and goes to live in a religious community to devote himself to prayer, solitude, and contemplation [Old English *munuc,* via Germanic < late Latin *monachus* < Greek *monos* "alone"]

AKG London

Thelonious Monk

Monk /mungk/, **Thelonious** (1920–82) US pianist and composer. An influential modern jazz musician, he was known for his compositions in the bebop style. Full name **Monk, Thelonious Sphere**

> "I hit the piano with my elbow sometimes because of a certain sound I want to hear. You can't hit that many notes with your hands."
> [Thelonious Monk. Quoted in "Round About Monk," *Jazz People*, Valerie Wilmer; 1970]

monk·er·y /múngkəree/ *n* (*disapproving*) **1.** the way of life led by monks in a monastery **2.** monks as a group

mon·key /múngkee/ *n* (*plural* **-keys**) **1. NONHUMAN PRIMATE** a medium-sized primate belonging to a group including baboons, marmosets, capuchins, macaques, guenons, and tamarins, but excluding apes, lemurs, and tarsiers. Native to: tropical regions. **2. MISCHIEVOUS CHILD** somebody, usually a child, who behaves badly, annoyingly, or high-spiritedly (*informal*) **3.** CONSTR **PILE DRIVER RAM** the ram of a pile driver **4.** DANCE **1960S DANCE** a dance of the 1960s in which partners move their hands up and down and jerk their heads back and forth ■ *vt* (**-keyed, -key·ing, -keys**) **MIMIC SOMEBODY OR SOMETHING** to copy or imitate somebody or something (*archaic*) [Mid-16C. Origin ?] ◇ **have a monkey on your back** (*slang*) **1.** to have an addiction to drugs **2.** to have a serious problem or be in serious difficulties ◇ **I'll be a monkey's uncle** used to express surprise (*dated informal*) ◇ **make a monkey (out) of somebody** to make somebody look foolish (*informal*)
monkey around, mon·key a·bout *vi* to behave in a silly, casual, or careless way
monkey with *vt* to touch or move something casually or carelessly

mon·key bars *npl* a structure, usually freestanding, consisting of metal or wooden poles and bars that children can climb on to play

mon·key bite *n regional* a mark on the skin caused by kissing, biting, or sucking and associated with physical intimacy

REGIONAL NOTE Also called *octopus bite* and *sucker bite,* **monkey bite** is primarily recorded in California, with scattered instances in the South Atlantic states.

mon·key bread *n* **1.** the gourd-shaped fruit of the baobab tree, whose pulp is eaten by monkeys **2.** *also* **mon·key bread tree** TREES same as **baobab**

mon·key busi·ness *n* (*informal*) **1.** silly or mischievous behavior **2.** illegal, dishonest, or dubious activity

mon·key-faced owl *n* BIRDS same as **barn owl**

mon·key flow·er *n US* a small wild or cultivated flowering plant. Flowers: shades of yellow and red, with two lips. Genus: *Mimulus.* Can term **mimulus** [Because spots on the flowers form a pattern reminiscent of a monkey's face]

mon·key in the mid·dle *n* a game played by children in which two people throw a ball to each other and a third person stands in the middle and tries to intercept it

mon·key jack·et *n* a tight-fitting waist-length jacket, especially one worn by a sailor or as part of a military dress uniform [Because like the kind worn by an organ grinder's monkey]

mon·key pot *n* **1.** a large bulbous woody seedpod of a tropical tree **2.** a tree that produces monkey pots. Native to: tropical America. Genus: *Lecythis.*

mon·key-puz·zle, mon·key-puz·zle tree *n* a coniferous evergreen tree with spreading branches, sharp stiff leaves, and edible seeds. Native to: Chile. Latin name: *Araucaria araucana.* [Probably because of its long intertwining limbs and leaves]

mon·key·shines /múngki shìnz/ *npl* silly or mischievous behavior (*slang*)

mon·key suit *n* (*dated informal*) **1.** a suit worn by a man as part of formal evening wear **2.** a uniform, especially a military one

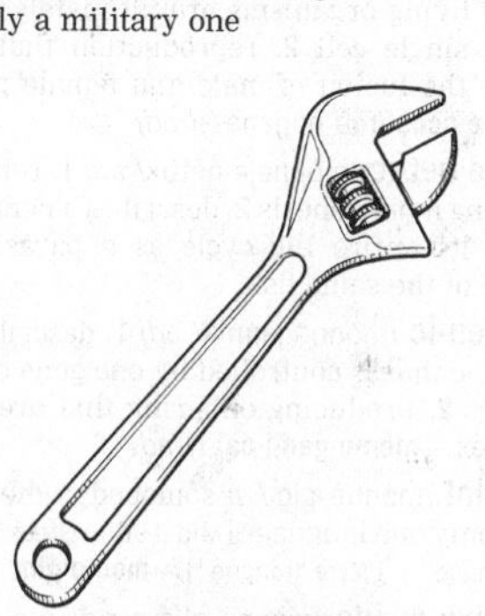

monkey wrench

mon·key wrench *n* **1.** a wrench with a jaw that can be adjusted so that it can be used to turn nuts of different sizes **2.** something that causes a problem for a plan or project (*informal*)

monk·fish /múngk fish/ (*plural same* or **-fish·es**) *n* **1.** a large bottom-dwelling anglerfish. Native to: Atlantic waters of Europe and Africa. Latin name: *Lophius piscatorius.* **2.** FISH same as **angel shark** [Early 17C. Origin ?]

Mon-Khmer /mōn kmér, -kə mér/ *n* an Austroasiatic group of languages that includes Mon and Khmer, spoken in Southeast Asia —**Mon-Khmer** *adj*

monk·ish /múngkish/ *adj* **1.** relating to monks or their way of life **2.** characteristic of the life of a monk, especially in being reclusive, self-denying, or austere —**monk·ish·ly** *adv* —**monk·ish·ness** *n*

monk's cloth *n* a heavy cotton fabric with a basket weave. Use: draperies, bedcovers.

monk seal *n* a small dark brown subtropical seal that is now endangered. Native to: the waters of the Hawaiian Islands and the Mediterranean. Genus: *Monachus.*

monks·hood /múngks hòod/ (*plural same* or **-hoods**) *n* **1.** a poisonous perennial plant. Flowers: purplish. Native to: northern Europe. Latin name: *Aconitum napellus.* **2.** PHARM same as **aconite** (sense 1) [Late 16C. < the shape of its flowers]

Mon·mouth·shire /mónməth sheer, -shər/ county in southeastern Wales. Population: 84,885 (2001). Area: 329 sq. mi./851 sq. km.

mon·o[1] /mónnō/ *n* monophonic sound reproduction [Mid-20C. Shortening]

mon·o[2] /mónnō/ *n* MED same as **infectious mononucleosis** (*informal*) [Mid-20C. Shortening]

mono- *prefix* **1.** one, single, alone ○ *monoculture* **2.** containing a single atom, radical, or group ○ *monoxide* **3.** monomolecular ○ *monolayer* [Via French and Latin < Greek *monos*]

mon·o·ac·id /mònnō ássid/, **mon·ac·id** /mən ássid/ *n* an acid that has only one replaceable hydrogen atom ■ *adj* same as **monoacidic**

mon·o·a·cid·ic /mònnō ə síddik/, **mon·a·cid·ic** /mòn ə síddik/ *adj* describes a chemical base or alcohol that has only one hydroxyl group that can react with an acid

mon·o·am·ine /mònnō á meen, -ə meen/ *n* an amine compound that contains one amino group, especially the neurotransmitters adrenaline and serotonin

mon·o·am·ine ox·i·dase *n* an enzyme that breaks down monoamine neurotransmitters

mon·o·am·ine ox·i·dase in·hib·i·tor *n* a drug that blocks the breakdown of monoamines by monoamine oxidase in the brain. Use: antidepressant.

mon·o·a·tom·ic *adj* CHEM same as **monatomic**

mon·o·ba·sic /mònnə báyssik/ *adj* describes an acid that has only one replaceable hydrogen atom in each molecule

mon·o·car·box·y·lic /mònnə kaar bok síllik/ *adj* describes an acid that has only one group. Formula: COOH.

mon·o·carp /mónnə kaarp/ *n* a plant that flowers and bears fruit only once before dying [Mid-19C. < Back-formation MONOCARPIC]

mon·o·car·pel·lar·y /mònnə káarpə lèrree/ *adj* **1.** describes a flower that has only one carpel **2.** describes a plant gynoecium that consists of only one carpel

mon·o·car·pic /mònnə káarpik/ *adj* describes a plant that flowers and bears fruit only once before dying [Mid-19C. < MONO- + Greek *karpos* "fruit"]

mon·o·car·pous /mònnə káarpəss/ *adj* BOT **1.** same as **monocarpic** **2.** same as **monocarpellary**

mon·o·ce·phal·ic /mònnō sə fállik/, **mon·o·ceph·a·lous** /mònnō séffələss/ *adj* describes a plant with a stalk that bears a single flower head, e.g., a tulip or dandelion

Mo·noc·er·os /mə nóssərəss/ *n* a constellation near the celestial equator. See illustration at **constellation** [Late 18C. Via French < Greek *monokerōs* "having one horn"]

mon·o·cha·si·um /mònnə káyzhee əm, -zhəm/ (*plural* **-si·a** /-zhee ə, -zhə/) *n* a flower cluster in which each branch bears one other branch and ends in a single flower [Late 19C. < MONO- + Greek *khasis* "separation"] —**mon·o·cha·si·al** *adj*

mon·o·chord /mónnə kàwrd/ *n* an ancient acoustic device consisting of a single string stretched over an oblong sounding box, used to determine mathematical intervals between musical tones

mon·o·chro·mat /mònnə krō màt/ *n* somebody who

cannot perceive colors and sees only shades of gray [Early 20C. Back-formation < MONOCHROMATIC]

mon·o·chro·mat·ic /mònnə krō máttik/ *adj* **1. WITH ONLY ONE COLOR** having only one color **2.** PHYS **WITH ONLY ONE WAVELENGTH** describes radiation that has only one wavelength, e.g., the light of a laser **3.** ART **PAINTED IN ONE COLOR** painted or printed in a single color **4.** MED **RELATING TO TOTAL COLORBLINDNESS** relating to or having total colorblindness (**monochromatism**) —**mon·o·chro·mat·i·cal·ly** *adv* —**mon·o·chro·ma·tic·i·ty** /mònnə krōmə tíssətee/ *n*

mon·o·chro·ma·tism /mònnə krṓmə tìzzəm/ *n* an eye condition in which the retina cannot distinguish any colors and a person sees only shades of gray

mon·o·chrome /mónnə krōm/ *adj* **1. IN SHADES OF ONE COLOR** using or displaying only shades of one color or black and white **2. DULL** dull, insipid, and lacking interest or distinctiveness **3.** ART **CONSISTING OF ONE COLOR** painted or drawn in shades of a single color ■ *n* **1.** PHOTOGRAPHY **BLACK-AND-WHITE IMAGE** a black-and-white photograph or transparency **2.** COLORS **BLACK-AND-WHITE COLORATION** the condition of being only in black and white **3.** ART **ARTWORK IN ONE COLOR** a painting, drawing, or print in shades of a single color **4.** ART **ART TECHNIQUE USING ONE COLOR** the art of painting, drawing, or printing in shades of a single color **5.** ART **CONDITION OF HAVING ONE COLOR** the condition of being painted, drawn, or printed in shades of a single color [Mid-17C. < medieval Latin *monochroma* < Greek *monokhrōmatos* "of one color" < *khrōma* "color"] —**mon·o·chro·mic** /mònnə krṓmik/ *adj* —**mon·o·chro·mist** *n*

mon·o·cle /mónnək'l/ *n* an eyeglass for correcting the vision of one eye, held in position by the muscles around the eye socket [Mid-19C. Via French < late Latin *monoculus* "single-eyed" < Greek *mono-* "single" + Latin *oculus* "eye"]

mon·o·cline /mónnə klīn/ *n* a rock structure in which all the strata slope in one direction [Late 19C. < MONO- + Greek *klinein* "to lean"] —**mon·o·cli·nal** /mònnə klī́n'l/ *adj* —**mon·o·cli·nal·ly** *adv*

mon·o·clin·ic /mònnə klínnik/ *adj* describes a crystal that has three unequal axes, with one pair not at right angles [Mid-19C. < MONO- + Greek *klinein* "to lean"]

mon·o·cli·nous /mònnə klī́nəss/ *adj* describes a flower that has both pistils and stamens [Early 19C. < French *monocline* or modern Latin *monoclinus* "in a single bed" < Greek *klinē* "bed"]

mon·o·clo·nal /mònnə klṓn'l/ *adj* describes cells or products of cells that are formed or derived from a single clone

mon·o·clo·nal an·ti·bod·y *n* an antibody with unique amino acid sequences derived from a single cell clone or cell line

mon·o·coque /mónnə kòk, -kòk/ *n* **1.** the metal outer shell of an aircraft, boat, or rocket that absorbs most of the stresses to which the craft is subjected **2.** a design of motor vehicle in which the body and frame are integrated [Early 20C. < French, "having a single shell" < *coque* "shell"]

mon·o·cot /mónnə kòt/ *n* BOT same as **monocotyledon** (*informal*) [Late 19C. Shortening]

mon·o·cot·y·le·don /mònnə kòtt'l éed'n/ *n* a flowering plant that has a single leaf in the seed and floral parts in multiples of three. Monocotyledons include grasses and lilies. Class: Monocotyledones. —**mon·o·cot·y·le·don·ous** *adj*

mo·noc·ra·cy /mo nókrəssee, mə-/ (*plural* **-cies**) *n* a form of government in which one person alone rules —**mon·o·crat** /mónnə kràt/ *n* —**mon·o·crat·ic** /mònnə kráttik/ *adj*

mo·noc·u·lar /mə nókyələr/ *n* an optical device designed for use with one eye only, e.g., a field glass or a microscope ■ *adj* relating to, affecting, or having only one eye [Mid-17C. < late Latin *monoculus* (see MONOCLE)] —**mo·noc·u·lar·ly** *adv*

mon·o·cul·ture /mónnə kùlchər/ *n* **1.** the practice of growing a single crop in a field or larger area **2.** a crop plant that is the only one grown in a field —**mon·o·cul·tur·al** /mònnə kúlchərəl/ *adj*

mon·o·cy·cle /mónnə sī̀k'l/ *n* VEHICLES same as **unicycle**

mon·o·cy·clic /mònnə sī́klik, -síklik/ *adj* **1.** CHEM **WITH SINGLE-RING MOLECULAR STRUCTURE** describes a chemical compound that has a molecular structure in which there is only one ring **2.** BOT **FORMING ONE WHORL** describes plant parts such as petals that form a single whorl **3.** BOT **LIVING DURING ONE YEAR** describes a plant that completes its life cycle within a single year

mon·o·cyte /mónnə sīt/ *n* a large circulating white blood cell, formed in the bone marrow and in the spleen, that has a single well-defined nucleus and consumes large foreign particles and cell debris —**mon·o·cyt·ic** /mònnə síttik/ *adj* —**mon·o·cy·toid** /-sī́ tòyd/ *adj*

mon·o·cy·to·sis /mònnə sī tṓssiss/ *n* an unusual increase in the numbers of monocytes

mon·o·dis·perse /mònnō diss púrss/ *adj* describes a colloid that contains particles that are all of a uniform size

mon·o·dra·ma /mónnə draàmə, -dràmmə/ *n* a dramatic piece written for one actor —**mon·o·dra·mat·ic** /mònnə drə máttik/ *adj*

mon·o·dy /mónnədee/ (*plural* **-dies**) *n* **1.** THEATER **ODE SUNG BY ONE ACTOR** in Greek tragedy, an ode for one actor to sing alone **2.** LITERAT **ELEGY** a poem that mourns somebody's death **3.** MUSIC **MUSIC WITH SINGLE MELODIC LINE** a piece of music that has a single melodic line **4.** MUSIC **17C ITALIAN VOCAL MUSIC** Italian vocal music of the 17th century for solo voice with instrumental accompaniment [Early 17C. < late Latin *monodia* < Greek *monōidos* "singing alone" < *ōidē* "song"] —**mo·nod·ic** /mə nóddik/ *adj* —**mo·nod·i·cal·ly** *adv* —**mon·o·dist** *n*

mo·noe·cious /mə néeshəss/, **mo·ne·cious**, **mo·noi·cous** /mə nóykəss/ *adj* describes a plant that has separate male and female flowers [Mid-18C. < modern Latin *Monoecia*] —**mo·noe·cious·ly** *adv*

mo·noe·strous *adj* UK spelling of **monestrous**

mon·o·eth·nic /mònnō éthnik/ *adj* relating to or belonging to the same ethnic group

mon·o·fil·a·ment /mònnō fíllәmənt/ *n* an untwisted continuous single strand of natural or artificial fiber. Use: fishing lines.

mo·nog·a·my /mə nóggəmee/ *n* **1.** CULTL ANTHROP **MARRIAGE TO ONE PERSON** the practice of being married to only one person at a time **2. PRACTICE OF HAVING ONE SEXUAL PARTNER** the practice of having a sexual relationship with only one partner during a period of time **3.** ZOOL **PRACTICE OF HAVING ONE MATE** the practice of having only one mate at a time or during a lifetime [Early 17C. < French *monogamie* < Greek *monogamos* "monogamous" < *gamos* "marriage"] —**mo·nog·a·mist** *n* —**mo·nog·a·mous** *adj* —**mo·nog·a·mous·ly** *adv*

mon·o·ge·ne·an /mònnə jéenee ən/ *n* a parasitic flatworm that spends its entire life cycle on the outside of the same fish. Order: Monogenea. [Mid-20C. < modern Latin *Monogenea* "single generation" < Greek *genea* "generation"]

mon·o·gen·e·sis /mònnə jénnəssiss/ *n* **1.** the theory that all living organisms are ultimately descended from a single cell **2.** reproduction that does not involve the fusion of male and female gametes —**mo·nog·e·nous** /mə nójjənəss/ *adj*

mon·o·ge·net·ic /mònnəjə néttik/ *adj* **1.** relating to or involving monogenesis **2.** describes a nematode that spends its entire life cycle as a parasite on the outside of the same fish

mon·o·gen·ic /mònnə jénnik/ *adj* **1.** describes a characteristic that is controlled by one gene or one pair of genes **2.** producing offspring that are all of the same sex —**mon·o·gen·i·cal·ly** *adv*

mon·o·glot /mónnə glòt/ *n* somebody who is able to speak only one language [Mid-19C. < Greek *monoglōttos* "one tongue" < *glōtta* "tongue"] —**mon·o·glot** *adj*

mon·o·glyc·er·ide /mònnə glíssə rīd/ *n* a compound derived from glycerol in which one hydroxyl group has been esterified

mon·o·gram /mónnə gràm/ *n* a design of one or more letters, usually the initials of a name, used to decorate or identify an object ■ *vt* (**-grammed** or **-gramed**, **-gram·ming** or **-gram·ing**, **-grams**) to mark or decorate something with a monogram —**mon·o·gram·mat·ic** /mònnəgrə máttik/ *adj* —**mon·o·grammed** *adj*

mon·o·graph /mónnə gràf/ *n* a scholarly article, paper, or book on a single topic —**mo·nog·ra·pher** /mə nóggrəfər/ *n* —**mon·o·graph·ic** /mònnə gráffik/ *adj* —**mon·o·graph·i·cal·ly** *adv*

mo·nog·y·ny /mə nójjənee/ *n* **1.** the practice of having only one wife at a time **2.** the practice of having a sexual relationship with only one woman during a period of time —**mo·nog·y·nist** *n* —**mo·nog·y·nous** *adj*

mon·o·hull /mónnō hùl/ *n* a boat that has a single hull

mon·o·hy·brid /mònnō hī́brid/ *n* a hybrid from parents that are different only with respect to a single gene pair

mon·o·hy·drate /mònnō hī́ dràyt/ *n* a salt that is combined with one molecule of water

mon·o·hy·dric /mònnō hī́drik/ *adj* describes an alcohol that contains one replaceable atom of hydrogen

mon·o·hy·drox·y /mònnō hī dróksee/ *adj* describes a compound that contains one hydroxyl group

mo·noi·cous *adj* BOT same as **monoecious**

mon·o·lay·er /mónnō làyr/ *n* **1.** a film or other coating of a compound that is one molecule thick **2.** a cultured layer of cells that is one cell thick

mon·o·lin·gual /mònnə líng gwəl/ *adj* **1.** able to speak only one language **2.** written, spoken, or produced in only one language —**mon·o·lin·gual·ism** *n*

mon·o·lith /mónnə lìth/ *n* **1. PILLAR OF ROCK** a tall block of solid stone standing by itself, whether a natural rock feature or a stone column shaped and erected by somebody, e.g., as a monument **2. SOMETHING LARGE AND IMMOVABLE** something massive and unchanging, especially a large and long-established organization that is slow to change, uniform in character, and difficult to deal with on a human level **3.** CONSTR **LARGE BLOCK OF BUILDING MATERIAL** a large uniform block of a single building material such as concrete pieced together with others to form a building or other structure

mon·o·lith·ic /mònnə líthik/ *adj* **1. IN FORM OF LARGE STONE BLOCK** consisting of or formed into a tall block of solid stone **2. BUILT USING LARGE BLOCKS** constructed using massive stones or large seamless blocks of material **3. LARGE AND UNCHANGING** massive, uniform in character, and slow to change —**mon·o·lith·i·cal·ly** *adv*

mon·o·lith·ic tech·nol·o·gy *n* a technology in electronic manufacturing in which all circuit components such as resistors, capacitors, and diodes are mounted on a single uniform piece of material

mon·o·logue /mónnə lòg/, **mon·o·log** *n* **1.** MOVIES **LONG SPEECH BY ONE ACTOR** a long passage in a play or motion picture spoken by one actor **2.** MOVIES **PLAY FOR ONE ACTOR** an entire play or motion picture in which only one actor appears and speaks **3. LONG UNINTERRUPTED SPEECH BY SOMEBODY** a long tedious uninterrupted speech during a conversation **4.** ARTS **PERFORMANCE BY COMEDIAN** a set of jokes or humorous stories following one another without a break, told by a solo entertainer —**mon·o·log·ic** /mònnə lójjik/ *adj* —**mo·nol·o·gist** /mə nólləjist, mónnə lòggist/ *n* —**mo·nol·o·gize** /mə nóllə jī̀z, mónnələ gī̀z/ *vti*

mon·o·ma·ni·a /mònnə máynee ə/ *n* an obsessive interest in a single thing, or a preoccupation with a single idea or thought —**mon·o·ma·ni·ac** *n* —**mon·o·ma·ni·a·cal** /mònnə mə nī́ ək'l/ *adj* —**mon·o·ma·ni·a·cal·ly** *adv*

mon·o·mer /mónnəmər/ *n* a relatively light, simple organic molecule that can join in long chains with other molecules to form a more complex molecule or polymer —**mon·o·mer·ic** /mònnə mérrik/ *adj*

mon·o·me·tal·lic /mònnō mə tállik/ *adj* **1.** describes a currency or monetary system that uses one type of metal, especially gold or silver, as a monetary standard **2.** made of one type of metal only

mon·o·met·al·lism /mònnō métt'l ìzzəm/ *n* the use of just one metal, especially gold or silver, as a basic monetary standard

mo·no·mi·al /mə nṓmee əl, mo-/ *n* **1.** an expression in algebra consisting of a single term, e.g., 3y, as distinct from one that contains two or more terms, e.g., 3x + 5y **2.** a scientific name that consists of one element only, as do the names of most families of plants and animals [Early 18C. < MONO- after *binomial*] —**mo·no·mi·al** *adj*

mon·o·mo·lec·u·lar /mònnō mə lékyələr/ *adj* **1.** relating to or involving single molecules **2.** describes a surface film that has a thickness of only one molecule. Monomolecular layers of alcohols or acids are used to retard water evaporation. —**mon·o·mo·lec·u·lar·ly** *adv*

mon·o·mor·phic /mònnō máwrfik/, **mon·o·mor·phous** /-máwrfəss/ *adj* **1.** describes an organism or species that exists in a single discrete form, as distinct from one that changes form, as a caterpillar does when it becomes a butterfly **2.** exhibiting only a single crystalline form —**mon·o·mor·phism** *n*

Mo·non·ga·he·la /mə nòng gə héelə/ river in the east central United States. It flows north through West Virginia and Pennsylvania. Length: 130 mi./210 km.

mon·o·nu·cle·ar /mònnō nóoklee ər/ *adj* **1.** describes a cell that has a single nucleus **2.** describes an organic compound with a molecular structure containing only one ring of atoms

mon·o·nu·cle·o·sis /mònnō nooklee óssiss/ *n* **1.** a significant rise in the number of atypical lymphocytes in the blood **2.** MED same as **infectious mononucleosis**

mon·o·nu·cle·o·tide /mònnō nóoklee ə tīd/ *n* a nucleotide that contains a phosphate group, a sugar, and a nitrogenous base

mo·noph·a·gous /mo nóffəgəss/ *adj* feeding on a single type of plant or animal —**mo·noph·a·gy** /-jee/ *n*

mon·o·phon·ic /mònnə fónnik/ *adj* using only one channel to carry sound from the source to the loudspeaker —**mon·o·phon·i·cal·ly** *adv*

mon·oph·thong /mónnəf thàwng, -thòng/ *n* a vowel sound that keeps the same quality for the whole syllable [Early 17C. < Greek *monophthoggos* < *phthoggos* "sound"] —**mon·oph·thon·gal** /mònnəf tháwng g'l, -thóng g'l/ *adj*

mon·o·phy·let·ic /mònnō fī léttik/ *adj* describes a group of plants or animals that are descended from a single stock or ancestral form —**mon·o·phy·let·ic·al·ly** *adv* —**mon·o·phy·let·ism** /mònnō fílə tìzzəm/ *n*

Mo·noph·y·site /mə nóffə sīt/ *n* somebody who believes that Jesus Christ has a single inseparable nature that is both human and divine [Late 17C. Via ecclesiastical Latin *Monophysita* < ecclesiastical Greek *monophusitēs* < *phusis* "nature" (see PHYSICS)] —**Mo·noph·y·sit·ic** /mə nòffə síttik/ *adj* —**Mo·noph·y·sit·ism** /mə nóffə sī tìzzəm/ *n*

monoplane

mon·o·plane /mónnə plàyn/ *n* an airplane that has just one pair of wings

mon·o·ple·gi·a /mònnə pléejee ə, -pléejə/ *n* the inability to move a single limb or a single group of muscles —**mon·o·ple·gic** *adj*

mon·o·pod /mónnə pòd/ *adj* used to describe a structure whose only support is one central pillar. Such designs are used in drilling rigs in the Arctic where the shifting ice could damage conventional supports. ■ *n* a single-legged adjustable support used to steady a camera

mon·o·pode /mónnə pōd/ *n* **1.** BOT same as **monopodium** **2.** a person or animal with a single foot, especially a member of a mythical African race of one-legged people [Early 19C. Via Latin *monopodius* < Greek *monopodios* < *pod-* "foot"] —**mon·o·po·di·al·ly** /mònnə pṓdee əlee/ *adv*

mon·o·po·di·um /mònnə pṓdee əm/ (*plural* **-di·a** /-dee ə/) *n* the main axis of some plants such as the pine tree that extends to the tip of the plant and produces lateral branches

mon·o·pole /mónnə pōl/ *n* **1.** PHYS **SINGLE MAGNETIC POLE OR ELECTRIC CHARGE** an electric charge or hypothetical magnetic pole isolated from its opposite charge or pole **2.** PHYS **HYPOTHETICAL PARTICLE** a theoretical elementary particle that has only one magnetic pole, instead of the two present in ordinary magnetic bodies **3.** MEDIA **RADIO ANTENNA** a radio antenna made of an electrically charged conducting rod with an electrical connection at one end

mo·nop·o·list /mə nóppəlist/ *n* **1.** somebody who controls a monopoly **2.** somebody who supports policies that favor monopolies —**mo·nop·o·lis·tic** /mə nòppə lístik/ *adj* —**mo·nop·o·lis·ti·cal·ly** *adv*

mo·nop·o·lize /mə nóppə līz/ (**-lized, -liz·ing, -liz·es**) *vt* **1.** to demand or take all of something such as somebody's time, attention, or affections, in a selfish way **2.** to have complete control of an industry or service and prevent other companies or people from participating or competing in it —**mo·nop·o·li·za·tion** /mə nòppəli záysh'n/ *n* —**mo·nop·o·liz·er** *n*

mo·nop·o·ly /mə nóppəlee/ (*plural* **-lies**) *n* **1.** **CONTROL OF MARKET SUPPLY** a situation in which one company controls an industry or is the only provider of a product or service **2.** **PERSONAL AND EXCLUSIVE POSSESSION** an exclusive right to have or do something ○ *He seems to think he has a monopoly on common sense.* **3.** COMM **CORPORATION WITH EXCLUSIVE CONTROL** a company with a commercial monopoly **4.** ECON **COMMODITY CONTROLLED BY ONE COMPANY** a product or service whose supply is controlled by only one company **5.** LAW **EXCLUSIVE LEGAL RIGHT** a legal right to the exclusive control of an industry or service, as granted by a government [Mid-16C. Via Latin < Greek *monopōlion* < *pōlein* "sell"] —**mo·nop·o·lism** *n*

mo·nop·so·ny /mə nópsənee/ (*plural* **-nies**) *n* a situation in which a product or service is only bought and used by one customer [Mid-20C. < MONO- + Greek *opsōnein* "purchase provisions"] —**mo·nop·so·nist** *n* —**mo·nop·so·nis·tic** /mə nòpsə nístik/ *adj*

mo·nop·ter·os /mo nóptə ròss/ (*plural* **-ter·oi** /-tə ròy/), **mo·nop·ter·on** /mo nóptə ròn/ (*plural* **-ter·a** /-tər ə/) *n* a circular classical temple surrounded by a single ring of columns [Late 17C. Via Latin < Greek, "having one wing" < *pteron* "wing"] —**mo·nop·ter·al** *adj*

mon·o·rail /mónnə ràyl/ *n* a passenger railroad transport system in which the cars straddle or are suspended from a single beam

mon·o·sac·cha·ride /mònnə sákə rīd, -rid/ *n* a simple sugar such as glucose or fructose that cannot be broken down into simpler sugars

mon·o·se·my /mo nóssəmee, mónnō séemee/ *n* the linguistic feature or fact of having only one meaning [Mid-20C. < MONO-, after POLYSEMY]

mon·o·ski /mónnō skee/ *n* a broad single ski on which a skier stands with both feet —**mon·o·ski·er** *n* —**mon·o·ski·ing** *n*

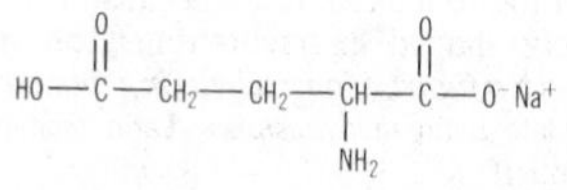

monosodium glutamate

mon·o·so·di·um glu·ta·mate /mònnə sṓdee əm-/ *n* a sodium salt of glutamic acid. Use: flavor enhancer.

mon·o·some /mónnə sōm/ *n* **1.** a single isolated chromosome, especially an unpaired X-chromosome **2.** a single protein-manufacturing particle (**ribosome**) combined with messenger RNA —**mon·o·so·mic** /mònnə sṓmik/ *adj* —**mon·o·so·my** *n*

mon·o·sper·mous /mònnə spúrməss/ *adj* describes a plant that produces only one seed

mon·o·sty·lous /mònnə stíləss/ *adj* describes a flower that has only one connecting stem (**style**) between the stigmas and the ovary

mon·o·syl·lab·ic /mònnə si lábbik/ *adj* **1.** saying very little, often in a way that gives an impression of unfriendliness or lack of intelligence **2.** consisting of one syllable only —**mon·o·syl·lab·ic·al·ly** *adv*

mon·o·syl·la·ble /mónnə sìlləb'l/ *n* a word or sentence consisting of only one syllable, e.g., "Yes" or "Me"

mon·o·the·ism /mónnə thee ìzzəm/ *n* the belief that there is only one God, as found in Judaism, Christianity, and Islam —**mon·o·the·ist** /mónnə thee ist/ *n, adj* —**mon·o·the·is·tic** /mònnə thee ístik/ *adj* —**mon·o·the·is·ti·cal·ly** *adv*

mon·o·tint /mónnə tìnt/ *n* ART same as **monochrome** *n* (sense 3)

mon·o·tone /mónnə tōn/ *n* **1.** **UNCHANGING TONE** a sound, especially a speech sound, that does not rise or fall in pitch, but stays on the same tone all the time **2.** **SERIES OF IDENTICAL SOUNDS** a sequence of sounds, e.g., a piece of speech, singing, or music, that stays at exactly the same pitch throughout **3.** **UNVARYING QUALITY** a complete lack of variety in color, expression, or style **4.** MUSIC **SINGER WITH NO SENSE OF PITCH** somebody who cannot produce or distinguish between sounds of varying pitches when singing ■ *adj* **1.** **WITH UNVARYING QUALITY** lacking variety in pitch, color, or another quality **2.** *also* **mon·o·ton·ic** /mònnə tónnik/ MATH **ASCENDING OR DESCENDING IN SEQUENCE** describes a function or a sequence of real numbers that steadily increases or decreases —**mon·o·to·nic·i·ty** /mònnə tō níssətee/ *n*

mo·not·o·nous /mə nótt'nəss/ *adj* **1.** uninteresting or boring as a result of being repetitive and unvaried **2.** uttered or performed in one unvaried tone —**mo·not·o·nous·ly** *adv* —**mo·not·o·nous·ness** *n*

SYNONYMS See ***boring***[1].

mo·not·o·ny /mə nótt'nee/ *n* **1.** boredom or dullness arising from the fact that nothing different ever happens **2.** repetitiousness or lack of variation in pitch or tone, especially in relation to music or speech

mon·o·tro·py /mónnə trōpee/ *n* a form of allotropy in which one form of an element is stable at all temperatures and pressures

mon·o·type /mónnə tīp/ *n* **1.** a plant or animal that is the only member of the taxonomic category to which it belongs **2.** an artwork created by pressing on paper laid on an inked metal plate or sheet of glass. Although similar prints can be made, each one will be unique. —**mon·o·typ·ic** /mònnə típpik/ *adj*

Mon·o·type *tdmk* a trademark for a typesetting machine run from a keyboard that activates a unit that sets type by individual characters

mon·o·un·sat·u·rat·ed /mònnō un sáchə ràytəd/ *adj* describes a fatty acid with only one carbon double bond

mon·o·va·lent /mònnə váylənt/ *adj* **1.** describes a chemical element or isotope that has a valence of one **2.** containing only one type of antibody —**mon·o·va·lence** *n* —**mon·o·va·len·cy** *n*

mon·ox·ide /mə nók sīd/ *n* a chemical compound with molecules that consist of one atom of oxygen and one or more atoms of another element

mon·o·zy·got·ic /mònnō zī góttik/ *adj* describes twins derived from a single fertilized egg (**zygote**), e.g., human identical twins

Mon·roe /mən rṓ/ city in northeastern Louisiana, on the eastern bank of the Ouachita River, northeast of Alexandria and east of Shreveport. Population: 52,360 (2002 estimate).

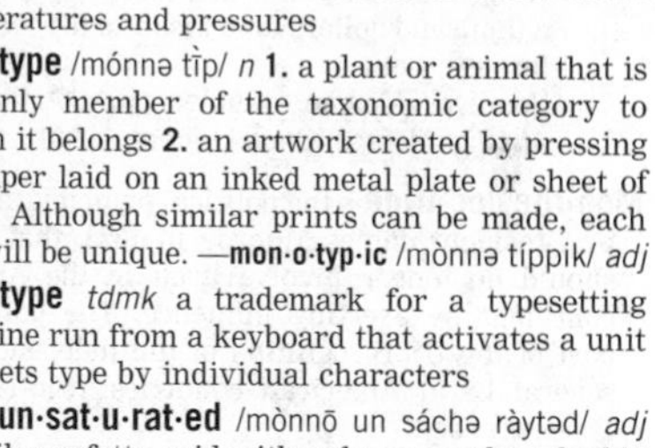

Library of Congress

James Monroe

Mon·roe, James (1758–1831) 5th president of the United States (1817–25). He held numerous state and national offices in nearly 50 years of public service, and was a popular Democratic-Republican president. He formulated the Monroe Doctrine (1823). See table at **president**. See illustration on previous page

> "The American continents, by the free and independent condition which they have assumed and maintain, are henceforth not to be considered as subjects for future colonization by any European powers...In the wars of the European powers in matters relating to themselves we have never taken any part, nor does it comport with our policy to do so."
> [James Monroe, "The Monroe Doctrine"; December 2, 1823]

Marilyn Monroe

Mon·roe, Marilyn (1926–62) US actor. She starred in movies such as *Bus Stop* (1956), *Some Like It Hot* (1959), and *The Misfits* (1961). She was married to the baseball player Joe DiMaggio and later the playwright Arthur Miller. Born **Mortenson, Norma Jean**

> "Hollywood is a place where they'll pay you a thousand dollars for a kiss and fifty cents for your soul."
> [Marilyn Monroe. Quoted in "Acting," *Marilyn Monroe*, Guus Luijters; 1990]

Mon·roe doc·trine *n* the political principle, as stated by President James Monroe in 1823, that Europe should no longer involve itself in the American continent by exerting influence. The policy was part of the US recognition of the independence of several Latin American countries. [Mid-19C. After James MONROE]

Mon·ro·vi·a /mon rṓvee ə/ **1.** capital city and chief seaport of Liberia, situated in the west of the country. Population: 479,000 (1999). **2.** city in southwestern California, in Los Angeles County, below the San Gabriel Mountains. Population: 37,848 (2002 estimate).

mons /monz/ (*plural* **mon·tes** /món teez/) *n* a fleshy body part that sticks out, especially the one formed by a pad of flesh at the juncture of the pubic bones [Mid-20C. Shortening of MONS PUBIS]

Mons /moNss/ historic city in southwestern Belgium, situated about 30 mi./48 km southwest of Brussels. Population: 91,187 (1999).

Mon·sei·gneur /mòn say nyúr, màwN-/ (*plural* **Mes·sei·gneurs** /màysay nyúr/) *n* a title given to some dignitaries, especially bishops and princes, in France and French-speaking countries [Early 17C. < French < *mon* "my" + *seigneur* "lord" < Latin *senior* "older"]

Mon·sieur /mə syúr/ (*plural* **Mes·sieurs** /may syúr, -syúrz/), **mon·sieur** (*plural* **mes·sieurs**) *n* **1.** a title for a man in France or a French-speaking country, if he has no other special title **2.** a form of address used when speaking or referring to a French or French-speaking man whose name is not known [Early 16C. < French < *mon* "my" + *sieur* "lord" < Latin *senior* "older"]

Mon·si·gnor /mon seenyər/ (*plural* **-si·gnors** or **-si·gnor·i** /-seen yáwree/) *n* a title used when speaking or referring to some clerics of the Roman Catholic Church, especially bishops or officials of the papal court [Late 16C. Via Italian < French *monseigneur* (see MONSEIGNEUR)] —**Mon·si·gnor·i·al** /mòn seen yáwree əl/ *adj*

mon·soon /mon so͞on/ *n* **1.** RAINY SEASON a period of heavy rainfall, especially during the summer over South and Southeast Asia **2.** HEAVY RAIN a very heavy fall of rain (*informal*) **3.** WINDS THAT REVERSE DIRECTION SEASONALLY a large-scale wind system that seasonally blows in opposite directions and determines the climate of large regions. The reversal of wind direction is caused by the greater annual temperature differences over large land masses than over the adjacent waters. [Late 16C. Via obsolete Dutch *monssoen* < Portuguese *monção* < Arabic *mawsim* "season"] —**mon·soon·al** *adj*

mons pu·bis (*plural* **mon·tes pu·bis**) *n* a prominence caused by the pad of fat that overlies the junction of the pubic bones in women and girls [Late 19C. < Latin, "mount of the pubes"]

mon·ster /mónstər/ *n* **1.** UGLY TERRIFYING BEING a large ugly terrifying animal or person found in mythology or created by the imagination, especially something fierce that kills people. Monsters often feature in folklore and fairy tales as evil beings resembling a mixture of different animals. **2.** EVIL PERSON somebody whose perceived inhumanity or vicious behavior terrifies and disgusts people **3.** HUGE THING something extraordinarily or unusually large (*informal*; *often used before a noun*) **4.** BIOL IMPROPERLY FORMED FETUS a fetus that is markedly improperly formed, especially one that cannot live outside the uterus (*sometimes considered offensive*) **5.** OFFENSIVE TERM an offensive term for a person, animal, or plant that is undesirably formed (*archaic*) ■ *vt* HARASS SOMEBODY to harass or pester somebody (*informal*; *often passive*) [13C. Via French *monstre* < Latin *monstrum* "monster, divine omen" < *monere* "warn, remind"]

mon·stered /mónstərd/ *adj* extremely drunk (*informal*)

monstrance

mon·strance /mónstrənss/ *n* a large gold or silver container in which the Host is placed and then shown to the congregation for adoration in a Roman Catholic Mass [13C. < medieval Latin *monstrantia* < Latin *monstrare* "to show" < *monstrum* (see MONSTER)]

mon·stros·i·ty /mon stróssətee/ (*plural* **-ties**) *n* **1.** an object, animal, or person that is very unpleasant or frightening to look at, often because it is large and strangely shaped **2.** frightening size, shape, and ugliness ○ *a figure of overwhelming monstrosity* [Mid-16C. < late Latin *monstrositas* < Latin *monstruosus* (see MONSTROUS)]

mon·strous /mónstrəss/ *adj* **1.** SHOCKING AND MORALLY UNACCEPTABLE wicked, cruel, or unpleasant to an extent that is morally unacceptable **2.** EXTREMELY LARGE extremely large, often in a way that seems ugly and frightening **3.** LIKE MONSTER resembling a monster of the type found in folklore and fairy tales [14C. Via French < Latin *monstruosus* < *monstrum* (see MONSTER)] —**mon·strous·ness** *n* —**mon·strous·ly** *adv*

mons ve·ne·ris /-vénnəriss/ (*plural* **mon·tes ve·ne·ris**) *n* ANAT same as **mons pubis** [Early 17C. < Latin, "the mount of Venus"]

Mont. *abbr* Montana

mon·ta·dale /móntə dàyl/ *n* a white-faced sheep belonging to a US breed that is raised for its wool or meat [Mid-20C. Blend of MONTANA + DALE, after names such as *Corriedale*]

mon·tage /mon tá̱azh/ *n* **1.** ARTWORK CREATED FROM SMALL PIECES a picture or other work of art composed by assembling, overlaying, and overlapping many different materials or pieces collected from different sources, e.g., photographs, magazines, and other pictures **2.** ARTS CREATION OF MONTAGE the technique of creating a montage **3.** MOVIES SEQUENCE OF OVERLAPPING FILM CLIPS a motion-picture sequence consisting of a series of dissolves, superimpositions, or cuts used to condense time or to suggest memories or hallucinations **4.** MOVIES MOVIEMAKING STYLE a style of moviemaking that makes extensive use of cuts, camera movements, and changes of camera position, particularly to set up new meanings not conveyed by the filmed action itself [Early 20C. < French < *monter* "to mount" (see MOUNT[1])]

Mon·ta·gnais /mòntən yáy/ (*plural same*) *n* **1.** a member of a Native North American people who live in parts of Quebec and Labrador **2.** the Algonquian language of the Montagnais. Native speakers: 4,000. [Early 18C. < French < *montagne* "mountain"] —**Mon·tag·nais** *adj*

Mon·ta·gnard /mòntən yáard, -yaár/ (*plural same* or **-gnards**) *n* a member of a people who live in the border region between Vietnam, Laos, and Cambodia [Mid-19C. < French, "mountaineer" < *montagne* "mountain"]

Mon·taigne /mon táyn, -ténnyə/, **Michel Eyquem de** (1533–92) French essayist. He invented the essay form in his *Essais* (*Essays*) (1572–80, 1588), original pieces on the ideas and personalities of his time.

> "To make judgments about great and lofty things, a soul of the same status is needed; otherwise we ascribe to them that vice which is our own."
> [Michel Eyquem de Montaigne, *Essais* (*Essays*); 1580]

Montana

Mon·tan·a /mon tánnə/ state in the northwestern United States, bordered by Canada, North Dakota, South Dakota, Wyoming, and Idaho. Capital: Helena. Population: 909,453 (2002 estimate). Area: 147,046 sq. mi./380,847 sq. km. —**Mon·tan·an** *n, adj*

Mon·tan·a, Joe (*b.* 1956) US football player. A quarterback, he led the San Francisco 49ers to four Super Bowl victories (1982, 1985, 1989, and 1990). Full name **Montana, Joseph**

mon·tane /mon táyn, món tàyn/ *adj* growing or living in mountainous regions [Mid-19C. < Latin *montanus* < *mont-* "mountain"]

mon·tan wax /móntən-, món tàn-/ *n* a brittle white to dark brown wax extracted from lignite and substituted in polishes and candles for carnauba and beeswax [Early 20C. < Latin *montanus* (see MONTANE), because extracted from lignite, a mountain ore]

Mon·tauk /món tàwk/ (*plural same* or **-tauks**) *n* a member of a Native North American people who lived in the eastern part of Long Island, New York [Mid-19C. < local place name]

Mont Blanc /mònt blángk, màwN blaáN/ highest mountain in western Europe, in the western Alps on the border of France and Italy. Height: 15,771 ft./4,807 m.

Mont·calm /mont kaám, màwN kálm/, **Louis-Joseph de, Marquis de Montcalm** (1712–59) French soldier. He was commander of the French forces in North America during the French and Indian War and he was mortally wounded fighting the British in the battle of the Plains of Abraham.

Mont·clair /mont klér/ **1.** city in southeastern California, in San Bernadino County. Population: 34,377 (2002 estimate). **2.** town in northeastern New Jersey, in Essex County. Population: 38,789 (2002 estimate).

mon·te /móntee/ *n* a game in which a player chooses between two cards and bets on being dealt a card of that same suit before being dealt a card of the other suit [Early 19C. Via Spanish < Latin *mont-* "mountain"; from the heap of cards on the table]

Mon·te Car·lo /mòntee ka̅a̅rlō/ tourist resort with a famous casino in Monaco, on the Mediterranean Sea. Population: 13,154 (1982).

Mon·te Cor·no /-káwrnō/ highest mountain in the Apennines, located in central Italy. Height: 9,554 ft./2,912 m.

Mon·te·go Bay /mon te̅egō-/ **1.** inlet of the Caribbean Sea in northwestern Jamaica **2.** city, seaport and tourist resort in Jamaica, located on the bay of the same name. Population: 83,446 (1991).

mon·teith /mon te̅eth/ *n* a silver or pewter basin with notches around the edge, made to hold punch or to cool punch glasses by resting their bases over the scalloped edge [Late 17C. Probably after a Scotsman *Monteith*, known for his capes with scalloped hems]

Mon·te·ne·gro /mòntə ne̅egrō, -néggrō/ smaller constituent republic of Serbia and Montenegro, in southeastern Europe. Capital: Podgorica. Population: 677,177 (2003). Area: 5,333 sq. mi./13,812 sq. km. —**Mon·te·ne·grin** *n, adj*

Mon·te·rey /mòntə ráy/ city and port in western California, on Monterey Bay. Population: 29,649 (2002 estimate).

Mon·te·rey Jack *n* a semihard cheese that is mild when young and becomes stronger and drier as it ages [Mid-20C. After *Monterey* County, California]

Mon·te·rey pine *n* a widely planted pine tree. Native to: Monterey Peninsula of California. Use: timber. Latin name: *Pinus radiata*.

Mon·te Ro·sa /mòntee rṓzə/ massif in the Pennine Alps, on the Swiss-Italian border, south of Zermatt. Height: 15,203 ft./4,634 m.

Mon·ter·rey /mòntə ráy/ industrial city in northeastern Mexico, capital of Nuevo León State. Population: 1,108,499 (2000).

Mon·tes Al·pes /mòn tayz ál pàyz/ extensive range of mountains on the Moon arching around the northeast of Mare Imbrium Height: 12,000 ft./3,658 m.

Mon·tes Ap·en·ni·nus /mòn tayz àppə nīnəss/ extensive range of mountains on the Moon surrounding the southeastern edge of Mare Imbrium

Mon·tes Ju·ra /mòn tayz jo͝orə/ range of mountains on the Moon north of Mare Imbrium. Height: 15,000 ft./4,500 m.

Mon·tes·quieu /móntə skyo͞o/, **Charles Louis de Secondat, Baron de la Brède et de** (1689–1755) French jurist and writer. His works, including his seminal comparative political study *L'Esprit des Lois* (*The Spirit of Law*) (1748), contributed to the European Enlightenment and helped to create the political climate that led to the French Revolution.

> "Liberty is the right to do everything which the laws allow."
> [Charles Louis de Secondat Montesquieu, *L'Esprit des lois* (*The Spirit of Law*); 1748]

Mon·tes·so·ri /mòntə sáwree/, **Maria** (1870–1952) Italian physician and educator. She devised a system for educating young children.

> "The task of the educator of young children lies in seeing that the child does not confound good with immobility, and evil with activity."
> [Attributed to Maria Montessori]

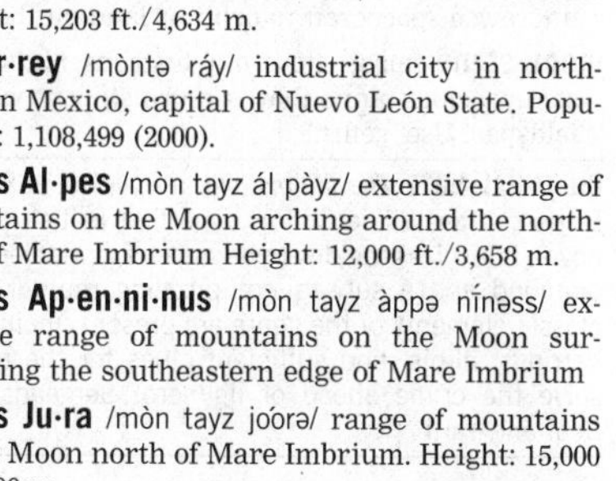
AKG London
Maria Montessori

Mon·tes·so·ri meth·od *n* a system of educating young children devised by Maria Montessori that aims to develop the child's natural interests and activities and does not use formal teaching methods

Mon·te·ver·di /mònti vérrdee/, **Claudio** (1567–1643) Italian composer. His secular and sacred choral works and his operas mark the transition from Renaissance to baroque music. Full name **Monteverdi, Claudio Giovanni Antonio**

Mon·te·vi·de·o /mòntəvi dáy ō/ capital city of Uruguay, located on the Atlantic Ocean in the south of the country. Population: 1,378,707 (1996).

Mon·te·zu·ma II /mònti zo͞omə/ (1480?–1520) Aztec emperor. His empire was brought down by Spanish invaders (1520).

Mon·te·zu·ma's re·venge *n* an offensive term for diarrhea and sickness experienced when visiting another country, originally Mexico, and eating unfamiliar food (*informal*) [Mid-20C. After MONTEZUMA II]

Mont·fort /móntfərt/, **Simon de, Earl of Leicester** (1200?–65) English aristocrat and soldier. Having captured Henry III of England in 1264, he set up a short-lived parliamentary-style assembly.

Mont·gol·fier /mont gólfee ər, màwN gòl fyáy/, **Joseph Michel** (1740–1810) and his brother **Jacques Etienne** (1745–99) French industrialists and inventors. Their development of the hot-air balloon led to the first balloon flight with human passengers, launched from Paris (1783).

Mont·gom·er·y /mont gúmmaree, -gúmree/ capital city of Alabama, in the center of the state. It is a port on the Alabama River. Population: 201,425 (2002 estimate).

Mont·gom·er·y, Bernard Law, 1st Viscount Montgomery of Alamein (1887–1976) British military commander. In World War II, he commanded the Eighth Army in North Africa, defeating Erwin Rommel, and became chief of the land forces in the Normandy invasion. After the war, he was deputy supreme commander of NATO forces (1951–58).

Mont·gom·er·y, L. M. (1874–1942) Canadian writer, known for her novel *Anne of Green Gables* (1908). Full name **Montgomery, Lucy Maud**. See Cultural note at **gable**

> "The point of good writing is knowing when to stop."
> [L. M. Montgomery, *Anne's House of Dreams*; 1917]

month /munth/ *n* **1.** MAJOR DIVISION OF YEAR a major named division of the year in various calendar systems, e.g., in the Gregorian calendar there are 12 months, varying in length from 28 to 31 days **2.** FOUR WEEKS OR 30 DAYS a period of time equivalent to about four weeks or 30 days **3.** INTERVAL BETWEEN DATES IN CONSECUTIVE MONTHS a time lasting from a date in one calendar month until the same date in the next calendar month **4.** ASTRON same as **solar month** **5.** ASTRON same as **lunar month** **6.** ASTRON same as **sidereal month** ■ **months** *npl* LONG PERIOD OF TIME a long time, often an excessively or unacceptably long time [Old English *mōnaþ* < Indo-European, "to measure"] ◇ **not** *or* **never in a month of Sundays** used to emphasize that you think that something will never happen (*informal*)

month·ly /múnthlee/ *adj* **1.** HAPPENING EACH MONTH done, held, or arranged once every month ○ *a monthly meeting* **2.** PRODUCED EVERY MONTH published or issued once a month ○ *a monthly periodical* **3.** LASTING MONTH valid for one month ○ *a monthly pass* ■ *adv* ONCE EVERY MONTH at intervals of one month ■ *n* (*plural* **-lies**) **1.** PUBL MAGAZINE ISSUED EVERY MONTH a publication or periodical that is produced once a month **2.** WOMAN'S MENSTRUAL PERIOD a woman's monthly menstruation (*informal; usually used in the plural*)

Mon·ti·cel·lo /mònti chéllō, -séllō/ estate of Thomas Jefferson in central Virginia, southeast of Charlottesville. He designed the classically inspired house and grounds, and lived there from 1770 until his death in 1826.

mon·ti·cule /mónti kyo͞ol/ *n* **1.** a subordinate volcanic cone **2.** a mound or small hill [Late 18C. Via French < late Latin *monticulus* < Latin *mont-* "mountain"]

Mont·mo·ren·cy /mòntmə rénssee/ river in southern Quebec, Canada. It flows south to join the St. Lawrence River. Length: 60 mi./97 km.

Mont·mo·ren·cy Falls highest waterfall in Quebec, Canada. They are located east of Quebec City where the Montmorency River empties into the St. Lawrence River. Height: 275 ft./84 m.

mont·mo·ril·lo·nite /mòntmə rίllə nīt/ *n* a soft clay mineral. Source: bentonite clays. [Mid-19C. After *Montmorillon*, France] —**mont·mo·ril·lo·nit·ic** /mòntmə rilə nίttik/ *adj*

Mont·pel·ier /mont pe̅elyər/ city and capital of Vermont, situated on the Winooski River in the north central part of the state. Population: 8,026 (2002 estimate).

Mont·pel·lier /màwN pə lyáy/ city in southern France, capital of the Hérault Department and administrative and commercial center of the Languedoc-Roussillon Region. Population: 225,392 (1999).

Mon·tre·al /mòntree áwl/ second largest city in Canada, situated on Montreal Island in the St. Lawrence River, Quebec. Population: 1,039,534 (2001).

Mon·treux /mon trṓ/ major resort area in western Switzerland, on the northeastern shore of Lake Geneva. Population: 21,476 (1998).

Monts /monts/, **Pierre du Guast, Sieur de** (1560?–1630?) French explorer. He colonized what are now the Maritime Provinces of Canada for France and founded Port Royal, Nova Scotia (1604).

Mont-Saint-Mi·chel /màwN saN mi shél/ steep granite hill off the Normandy coast in northern France. It becomes an island when the tides are high.

Mont·ser·rat /mòntsə rát/ island in the eastern Caribbean Sea, a dependency of the United Kingdom. It was economically devastated by volcanic eruptions in 1997. Population: 12,771 (1996). Area: 39 sq. mi./102 sq. km.

mon·u·ment /mónnyəmənt/ *n* **1.** LARGE STONE STATUE OR CARVING something designed and built as a lasting public tribute to a person, a group of people, or an event **2.** FAMOUS PLACE OR BUILDING a site or structure that is preserved because of its historical, cultural, or aesthetic importance **3.** CARVED HEADSTONE a tombstone, plaque, or ornamental stone structure placed on somebody's grave. A monument in a cemetery is usually inscribed with the name and dates of birth and death of the deceased person. **4.** WORTHY REMINDER OF SOMETHING something that remains as a reminder of something, especially something fine or distinguished **5.** MEMORIAL TRIBUTE a memorial to somebody in the form of a written or spoken tribute **6.** BOUNDARY MARKER an object that marks a boundary, e.g., a stone [13C. Via French < Latin *monumentum* < *monere* "remind"]

mon·u·men·tal /mònnyə mént'l/ *adj* **1.** LARGE great in size, importance, or intensity **2.** DESERVING SPECIAL ADMIRATION so important or enduring that people cannot fail to notice or be impressed ○ *a monumental contribution to peace* **3.** MAKING CARVED HEADSTONES related to or involved in the making of tombstones and memorial items to go in cemeteries and churches **4.** OF MONUMENTS relating to monuments or taking the form of a monument —**mon·u·men·tal·i·ty** /mònnyə men tállətee/ *n* —**mon·u·men·tal·ly** *adv*

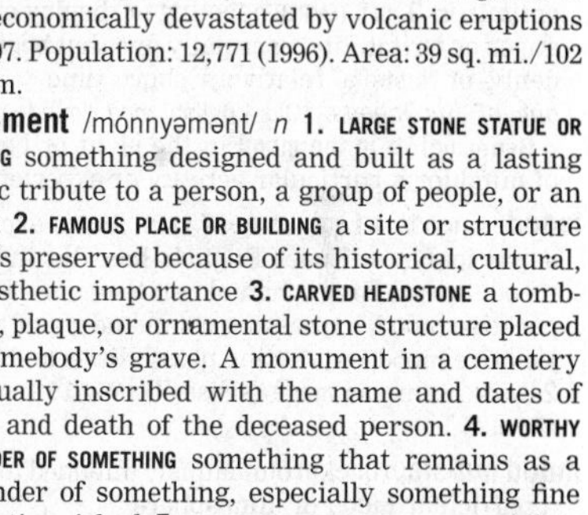
Barnaby's
Monument Valley

Mon·u·ment Val·ley /mònnyəmənt-/ region in northeastern Arizona and southeastern Utah, notable for its scenic rock formations. See illustration on previous page

mon·u·ron /mónnyə ròn/ *n* a white crystalline odorless solid. Use: herbicide. [Mid-20C. Blend of MONO- + UREA]

Mon·za /mṓntsa, mónzə/ city in northern Italy known for its motor racing course, situated about 8 mi./13 km northeast of Milan. Population: 120,204 (2001).

mon·zo·nite /mon zṓ nìt, mónzə-/ *n* a visibly crystalline, granular igneous rock composed chiefly of equal amounts of two feldspar minerals, plagioclase and orthoclase, and small amounts of a variety of colored minerals [Late 19C. After Mount *Monzoni* in the Tyrol] —**mon·zo·nit·ic** /mònzə níttik/ *adj*

moo /moo/ *vi* (**mooed, moo·ing, moos**) to produce the deep drawn-out sound that a cow makes ■ *n* (*plural* **moos**) a deep drawn-out sound made by a cow, or by somebody imitating this sound [Mid-16C. An imitation of the sound]

MOO /moo/ *n* a virtual online space in which several participants can meet at a given time to discuss a given topic. Full form **multi-user domain, object-oriented**

mooch /mooch/ (**mooched, mooch·ing, mooch·es**) *v* **1.** *vti* GET SOMETHING FOR NOTHING to get something for nothing from somebody by asking directly for it, without making any personal effort for it (*informal*) ○ *He's always mooching off friends.* **2.** *vi* WANDER AIMLESSLY to wander or linger in an aimless way (*slang*) ○ *just mooching around* **3.** *vt* STEAL to steal something (*slang*) **4.** *vi* SNEAK AROUND SUSPICIOUSLY to move around or wait somewhere quietly and secretly, trying not to be noticed (*slang*) [15C. < Old French *muchier* "to hide"] —**mooch·er** *n*

mood[1] /mood/ *n* **1.** STATE OF MIND somebody's state of mind ○ *a good mood* **2.** GENERAL FEELING OF GROUP the way a group of people think and feel about something ○ *The mood of the country after the war was generally optimistic.* **3.** BAD TEMPER a feeling or display of sullen anger or irritability, especially one that begins suddenly or lasts a relatively short time ○ *He's in one of his moods.* [Old English *mōd* "mind, courage" < Germanic] ◇ **in the mood** in the right or best state of mind for a particular activity or experience

mood[2] /mood/ *n* **1.** a group of verb forms expressing a particular attitude. English has the indicative mood, expressing factual statements, the imperative mood, expressing commands, and the subjunctive mood, expressing possibilities and wishes. **2.** LOGIC same as **mode** (sense 7) [Mid-16C. Alteration of MODE]

mood mu·sic *n* background music intended to induce a particular mood or atmosphere

mood swing *n* a sudden and extreme change in somebody's mood

mood·y /móodee/ (**-i·er, -i·est**) *adj* **1.** UNPREDICTABLY GRUMPY OR GLOOMY tending to change mood unpredictably from cheerful to bad-tempered **2.** CHANGEABLE unusually changeable or difficult to predict **3.** DISPLAYING MOOD displaying emotions, especially unhappiness or anger, clearly and intensely —**mood·i·ly** *adv* —**mood·i·ness** *n*

Mood·y /móodee/, **Dwight L.** (1837–99) US evangelist. He founded Northfield Seminary girls' school (1879) and Mount Hermon School for boys (1881). Full name **Moody, Dwight Lyman**

moo goo gai pan /moo gòo gèe pán/ *n* a spicy sautéed chicken, mushroom, and vegetable dish [< Chinese (Cantonese) *mōkhoo kai paān*, "mushroom chicken slices"]

moo·la /móolə/, **moo·lah** *n* same as **money** (*slang*) [Mid-20C. Origin ?]

moo·li /móolee/ (*plural* **-lis** or *same*) *n UK* FOOD same as **daikon** [Mid-20C. < Hindi *mūlī*]

moon /moon/ *n* **1.** ASTRON another spelling of **Moon 2.** MOON'S SHAPE AS SEEN FROM EARTH a form or view of the Moon (**phase**) at a point in the lunar cycle. Since it shines only by reflected sunlight, the phases of the Moon depend on its position in relation to the Earth and the Sun. **3.** MOONLIGHT the light given out by the Moon **4.** SYMBOLIC REPRESENTATION OF MOON a simple or stylized representation of the Moon, usually in the form of a circle or crescent **5.** ASTRON NATURAL SATELLITE OF PLANET a natural satellite revolving around a planet. Mars, Jupiter, Saturn, Uranus, and Neptune each have more than one moon. **6.** PERIOD OF TIME a month, either as a rough estimate of time or as the time it takes for the Moon to complete its cycle around Earth (*archaic or literary*) ■ *v* (**mooned, moon·ing, moons**) **1.** *vi* WANDER AIMLESSLY to wander around in a dreamy or listless state, unable to concentrate on anything **2.** *vi* YEARN FOR LOVED ONE to be stricken with longing for an absent loved one, and rendered dreamy or listless as a result (*literary or humorous*) **3.** *vti* EXPOSE BUTTOCKS TO SOMEBODY to bend over and deliberately expose the bare buttocks to somebody, either as a rude joke or as an act of defiance and disrespect (*informal*) [Old English *mōna* < Germanic] —**moon·less** *adj*

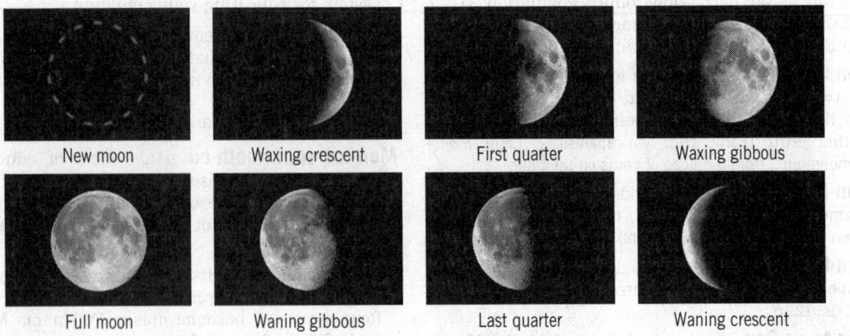

Moon: phases of the Moon

Moon *n* Earth's only natural satellite. It is the astronomical body nearest to Earth, except for some artificial satellites and occasional meteors.

moon·beam /móon bèem/ *n* a pale, milky, or iridescent beam of light reflected to the Earth by the Moon at night

moon blind·ness *n* periodic episodes of impaired vision in horses that often lead to permanent loss of sight

moon·calf /móon kàf/ (*plural* **-calves** /-kàvz/) *n* somebody regarded as unintelligent or thoughtless (*archaic insult*)

moon dog *n* ASTRON same as **paraselene**

moon·eye /móon ì/ *n* a silvery freshwater fish resembling a herring with very large eyes. Native to: North America. Latin name: *Hiodon tergisus.*

moon-faced *adj* having a large round face

moon·flow·er /móon flòwr/ *n* a plant whose flowers open at night, especially a climbing plant related to the morning glories

Moon·ie /móonee/ *n* a member of the Unification Church (*informal; often considered offensive*) [Late 20C. After Sun Myung *Moon*, the church's founder]

moon·light /móon lìt/ *n* the pale cool light that shines from the Moon on a clear night, often considered eerie or romantic. Moonlight is light from the Sun reflected from the Moon's surface. ■ *vi* (**-light·ed, -light·ing, -lights**) to have a second job in addition to a main job (*informal*) —**moon·light·ing** *n*

CULTURAL NOTE ***Moonlight Sonata***, a piano sonata (1801) by the German composer Ludwig van Beethoven. This nickname for Beethoven's somber piano sonata in C# minor, op. 27 no. 2, was coined by the poet Heinrich Renstab. In his review of the composition, he described how the first movement brought to his mind the image of moonlight on Lake Lucerne.

moon·lit /móon lìt/ *adj* brightened or illuminated by light from the Moon

moon pool *n* an open shaft in a deep-sea drilling vessel, usually located in the center of the hull, through which the drilling takes place

moon·rak·er /móon ràykər/ *n* a small sail sometimes set above the skysail on a square-rigged ship [Early 19C. Probably < its great height]

moon·rise /móon rìz/ *n* **1.** the time of day when the Moon rises over the horizon **2.** the rising of the Moon in the sky over the horizon

moon·scape /móon skàyp/ *n* **1.** the general appearance of the surface of the Moon as seen or portrayed **2.** a view or place that looks as rough, gray, and bleak as the surface of the Moon

moon·seed /móon sèed/ *n* a climbing plant that has tiny greenish flowers and red or black fruit with crescent-shaped seeds. Genera: *Menispermum* or *Cocculus.* Native to: eastern Asia, eastern North America and Mexico.

moon·set /móon sèt/ *n* **1.** the time of day when the Moon disappears below the horizon **2.** the disappearance of the Moon below the horizon [Mid-19C. < MOON after *sunset*]

moon·shee *n S Asia* another spelling of **munshi**

moon shell *n* a carnivorous sea mollusk with a smooth rounded shell. Native to: mainly tropical waters. Family: Naticidae.

moon·shine /móon shìn/ *n* **1.** whiskey or other strong liquor produced and sold illegally **2.** talk, opinions, or ideas dismissed as senseless (*informal*) **3.** same as **moonlight** —**moon·shin·er** *n*

moon·shot /móon shòt/ *n* the launch of a crewed or uncrewed spacecraft to orbit or land on the Moon

moon·stone /móon stṑn/ *n* a lustrous bluish white semiprecious stone that is a translucent variety of feldspar. Use: gems.

CULTURAL NOTE ***The Moonstone***, a novel (1868) by the British writer Wilkie Collins. The first British detective novel, it involves the disappearance of a priceless Indian diamond and a subsequent puzzling murder. All the classic elements of the genre are present, including red herrings, alibis, and sufficient clues for the reader to solve the crime ahead of its hero, Sergeant Cuff of Scotland Yard.

moon·struck /móon strùk/ *adj* **1.** acting in a rather irrational, dreamy, confused way, often out of love (*informal humorous*) **2.** behaving in a wild or confused way (*dated literary*)

moon·walk /móon wàwk/ *n* **1.** INSTANCE OF WALKING ON MOON an exploratory walk or expedition across part of the Moon's surface, carried out by an astronaut. The first person to walk on the Moon was Neil Armstrong on July 20, 1969. **2.** GLIDING DANCE MOVEMENT a dance done using gliding walking movements of the feet and legs ■ *vi* (**-walked, -walk·ing, -walks**) **1.** GO ON FOOT ACROSS MOON'S SURFACE to walk away from a spacecraft for some distance across the surface of the Moon **2.** DANCE PERFORM GLIDING DANCE to perform a dance with gliding walking movements of the feet and legs —**moon·walk·er** *n*

moon·y /móonee/ (**-i·er, -i·est**) *adj* **1.** in a distracted or dreamy state, with little energy or concentration (*informal*) **2.** relating to or resembling the Moon —**moon·i·ly** *adv* —**moon·i·ness** *n*

moor[1] /moor/ *n* a large uncultivated treeless stretch of land covered with bracken, heather, coarse grasses, or moss (*often used in the plural*) [Old English *mōr* < Germanic]

moor[2] /moor/ (**moored, moor·ing, moors**) *vti* to secure a boat, ship, or aircraft to one place with cables, chains, ropes, or an anchor, or be secured in this way [15C. Probably < Middle Low German *mōren*]

Moor /moor/ *n* a member of a nomadic people of Arab and Berber descent whose civilization flourished in

North Africa between the 8th and the 15th centuries. They also settled in Spain during this period. [14C. Via Old French *More* < Latin *Maurus* < Greek *Mauros*]

moor·age /moŏrij/ *n* **1.** NAUT, AVIAT same as **mooring** (sense 1) **2.** the fee charged for mooring somewhere

Moore /moor, mawr/, **Bobby** (1941–93) British soccer player. A skilled defensive player, he captained England to victory in the 1966 World Cup. Full name **Moore, Robert Frederick**

Moore /moŏr, mawr/, **Clement Clarke** (1779–1863) US scholar and writer. He is best known for the Christmas poem "A Visit from St. Nicholas" (1823).

> "'Twas the night before Christmas, when all through the house / Not a creature was stirring—not even a mouse; / The stockings were hung by the chimney with care, / In hopes that St. Nicholas soon would be there."
> [Clement Clarke Moore, "A Visit from St. Nicholas"; 1823]

Moore, Dudley (1935–2002) British actor, comedian, and pianist. After working in partnership with comedian Peter Cook, he appeared in Hollywood movie comedies.

Moore, Henry (1898–1986) British sculptor and printmaker. He is noted for his large-scale stylized representations of the human body, many made for outdoor locations.

> "There is a right physical size for every idea."
> [Attributed to Henry Moore]

Moore, Marianne (1887–1972) US poet. She is known for her witty ironic poetry, which covers a wide range of subjects. Her *Collected Poems* (1951) won a Pulitzer Prize. Full name **Moore, Marianne Craig**

> "They say there is a sweeter air / Where it was made, than we have here."
> [Marianne Moore, "A Carriage from Sweden"; 1944]

Moore, Mary Tyler (*b.* 1936) US actor. She is best known for her television roles, as Laura Petrie on *The Dick Van Dyke Show* (1961–66) and Mary Richards on *The Mary Tyler Moore Show* (1970–77).

Moore, Mike (*b.* 1949) New Zealand prime minister (1990). A Labour Party politician, he held a number of cabinet posts from 1984 before taking over the premiership after Geoffrey Palmer's resignation. See table at **prime minister**. Full name **Moore, Michael Kenneth**

Mòo·ré /mŏŏ ə ràyl, **Moo·ré, Mo·re** /máwree/ *n* LANG same as **Mossi** (sense 2) [< Mossi] —**Mòo·ré** *adj*

moor·hen /moŏr hèn/ *n* a medium-sized water bird with black feathers and a red beak. Native to: marshy areas. Latin name: *Gallinula chloropus.*

moor·ing /moŏring/ *n* **1.** PLACE FOR SECURING BOAT OR AIRCRAFT a place where a boat, ship, or aircraft can be moored **2.** CABLE SECURING BOAT OR AIRCRAFT a cable, chain, or rope used to stop a boat, ship, or aircraft from drifting away **3.** PHYSICAL OR EMOTIONAL TIE something that gives a feeling of emotional or physical security, e.g., a family bond (*usually used in the plural*)

moor·ing tow·er *n* a permanent structure built as a place to moor airships. The structure provides facilities for transferring passengers, crew, and freight, for refueling, and for replenishing ballast and lifting gas.

Moor·ish /moŏrish/ *adj* **1.** relating to the Moors or their culture **2.** built or designed in an architectural style popular in Spain between the 8th and the 16th centuries, noted for its use of ornate curving decoration

moor·land /moŏr lànd, -lənd/ *n* countryside, or a piece of countryside, consisting of a moor

moose /mooss/ (*plural same*) *n* a large animal of the deer family, with long legs and, in the male, large flat palmate antlers. Native to: North America, Europe, Asia. Latin name: *Alces alces.* [Early 17C. < Abenaki *mos*]

SPELLCHECK moose, mouse, or **mousse**? Do not confuse ***moose*** and ***mousse***, which have a similar sound, or ***mousse*** and ***mouse***, which have a similar spelling. A ***moose*** is a large animal with long legs and large antlers, whereas a ***mouse*** is a small animal with short legs and a long tail (or a computer input device of similar shape). ***Mousse*** is a light rich food containing whipped cream and eggs (as in *chocolate mousse, salmon mousse*) or a foamy substance used in hairdressing.

Moose (*plural same*) *n* a member of the Loyal Order of Moose, a fraternal organization

Moose Jaw /moŏss jàw/ city in southeastern Saskatchewan, Canada. It is the site of Canada's largest military jet-training base. Population: 32,631 (2001).

moose·wood /moŏss wŏŏd/ *n* TREES same as **striped maple**

moot /moot/ *adj* **1.** ARGUABLE open to argument or dispute ○ *Whether nutritional supplements are beneficial is a moot question.* **2.** NOT RELEVANT irrelevant or unimportant ○ *If they refuse to compromise, mediation is a moot issue.* **3.** LAW NOT LEGALLY RELEVANT legally insignificant because of having already been decided or settled ○ *Whether he was entitled to do business under that name was moot, because his company had ceased trading.* ■ *v* (**moot·ed, moot·ing, moots**) **1.** *vt* SUGGEST TOPIC to offer an idea for consideration or a topic for discussion (*usually passive*) **2.** *vi* LAW HAVE FORMAL ARGUMENT to take part in a debate, especially one organized as an academic exercise, e.g., a hypothetical case argued among law students ■ *n* **1.** LAW DEBATE ON HYPOTHETICAL ISSUE an academic discussion in which people such as law students argue hypothetically or plead a hypothetical legal case **2.** HIST ANGLO-SAXON LOCAL COURT in Anglo-Saxon England, a formal gathering for settling legal and administrative matters [Old English *mōt* "assembly" < Germanic, "meeting"] —**moot·ness** *n*

moot court *n* a court in which imaginary legal cases are conducted and tried by law students as part of their training

mop /mop/ *n* **1.** TOOL FOR WASHING FLOORS a long-handled tool for washing or polishing floors, with a head consisting of a large sponge or a thick mass of absorbent threads or fabric strips **2.** UNTIDY MASS a thick or scruffy-looking tangle ○ *a mop of hair* ■ *vt* (**mopped, mop·ping, mops**) **1.** WASH SOMETHING WITH MOP to use a mop to wipe a floor surface clean, usually using warm soapy water **2.** WIPE BODY TO REMOVE PERSPIRATION to wipe perspiration from a part of the body [15C. Origin ?]

mop up *v* **1.** *vti* GET RID OF LIQUID WITH CLOTH to wipe or rub a piece of material over a liquid to soak it up **2.** *vt* MIL DEAL WITH REMAINING ENEMY FORCES to capture or kill remaining enemy troops in order to secure an area after a victory **3.** *vt* CLEAR UP FINAL DETAILS to complete or carry out the final details of a task (*informal*)

MOP *n* somebody who has assets such as stocks that are nominally worth a million dollars or pounds but that may never be realizable in cash. Full form **millionaire on paper**

mop·board /móp bàwrd/ *n* CONSTR same as **baseboard** (sense 2)

mope /mōp/ *vi* (**moped, mop·ing, mopes**) **1.** BE MISERABLE to be full of self-pity or sulky unhappiness and lose interest in everything else **2.** WANDER AROUND SADLY to move in a listless or aimless way, especially one that is self-consciously sad or unhappy ■ *n* MISERABLE PERSON somebody who tends to mope and who depresses others (*informal*) ■ **mopes** *npl* GLOOMY MOOD a bout of melancholy or sulkiness (*informal*) [Mid-16C. Probably < N Germanic] —**mop·er** *n* —**mop·ey** *adj*

mo·ped /mō pèd/ *n* a lightweight pedaled motorcycle with an engine of less than 50 cc [Mid-20C. Blend of MOTOR + PEDAL [1]]

MOPP *abbr* MIL Mission Oriented Protective Posture

mop·pet /móppət/ *n* a small child (*informal*) [Early 17C. < obsolete *mop* "baby, doll," origin ?]

mo·quette /mō két/ *n* thick velvety fabric. Use: carpeting, upholstery. [Mid-19C. < French]

MOR *abbr* MUSIC middle-of-the-road (*used especially in radio programming*)

mor. *abbr* INDUST morocco

Mor. *abbr* **1.** Moroccan **2.** Morocco

mo·raine /mə ráyn/ *n* a mass of earth and rock debris carried by an advancing glacier and left at its front and side edges as it retreats [Late 18C. Via French < French dialect *morena* "mound"]

mor·al /máwrəl/ *adj* **1.** INVOLVING RIGHT AND WRONG relating to issues of right and wrong and to how individual people should behave **2.** DERIVED FROM PERSONAL CONSCIENCE based on what somebody's conscience suggests is right or wrong, rather than on what rules or the law says should be done **3.** ACCORDING TO COMMON STANDARD OF JUSTICE regarded in terms of what is known to be right or just, as opposed to what is officially or outwardly declared to be right or just ○ *a moral victory.* **4.** ENCOURAGING GOODNESS AND DECENCY giving guidance on how to behave decently and honorably **5.** GOOD BY ACCEPTED STANDARDS good or right, when judged by the standards of the average person or society at large **6.** ABLE TO TELL RIGHT FROM WRONG able to distinguish right from wrong and to make decisions based on that knowledge **7.** BASED ON PERSONAL CONVICTION based on an inner conviction, in the absence of physical proof ○ *moral certainty* ■ *n* **1.** VALUABLE LESSON IN BEHAVIOR a conclusion about how to behave or proceed drawn from a story or event **2.** FINAL SENTENCE OF STORY GIVING ADVICE a short precise rule, usually written in a rather literary style as the conclusion to a story, used to help people remember the best or most sensible way to behave ■ **mor·als** *npl* STANDARDS OF BEHAVIOR principles of right and wrong as they govern standards of general or sexual behavior [14C. < Latin *moralis* < *mor-*, stem of *mos* "custom," in plural "morals"] —**mor·al·ly** *adv*

SPELLCHECK Do not confuse the spelling of ***moral*** and ***morale*** ("level of confidence"). ***Moral*** is most often encountered as an adjective meaning "based on or involving what is right or wrong," or "generally accepted to be good or right": *moral standards; moral education.* It is also used as a noun meaning "a valuable lesson," and in the plural "principles of right and wrong": *the moral of the story; upholding society's morals.* ***Morale*** is stressed on the second rather than the first element and is used only as a noun meaning "level of enthusiasm among a group": *Morale was high as the team set off.*

mo·rale /mə rál, maw-/ *n* the general level of confidence or optimism felt by a person or group of people, especially as it affects discipline and motivation [Mid-18C. Via French *moral* < Latin *moralis* (see MORAL)]

USAGE See *moral.*

mor·al haz·ard *n* the tendency of people who are insured against a specific hazard to cease to exercise caution to avoid the hazard

mor·al im·per·a·tive *n* a thing that must be done because it is right, regardless of opposition or difficulty

mor·al·ism /máwrə lìzzəm/ *n* **1.** PIECE OF MORAL ADVICE a conventional moral maxim or saying **2.** MORAL BEHAVIOR behavior conforming to a system of moral standards that do not depend on religion **3.** MORALIZING criticism of other people's moral standards (*formal*)

mor·al·ist /máwrəlist/ *n* **1.** SOMEBODY WITH HIGH MORAL STANDARDS a follower of a strict moral code **2.** CRITIC OF MORAL STANDARDS somebody who seeks to regulate the moral standards and behavior of others **3.** SPECIALIST WHO STUDIES MORALITY a student or teacher of morals as an academic discipline —**mor·al·is·tic** /màwrə lístik/ *adj*

mo·ral·i·ty /mə rállətee, maw-/ (*plural* **-ties**) *n* **1.** ACCEPTED MORAL STANDARDS standards of conduct that are generally accepted as right or proper **2.** HOW RIGHT OR WRONG SOMETHING IS the rightness or wrongness of something as judged by accepted moral standards **3.** VIRTUOUS BEHAVIOR conduct that is in accord with accepted moral standards **4.** MORAL LESSON a lesson in moral behavior

mo·ral·i·ty play *n* a play intended to teach a moral lesson, especially a medieval play written in verse in which the characters embody human virtues and vices such as Mercy and Lust

mor·al·ize /máwrə lìz/ (**-ized, -iz·ing, -iz·es**) *v* **1.** *vi* to criticize other people's conduct or standards of behavior, or give advice on how general moral standards should be improved **2.** *vt* to consider and explain something in terms of its moral significance —**mor·al·i·za·tion** /màwrəli záysh'n/ *n* —**mor·al·iz·er** *n*

mor·al ma·jor·i·ty *n* the bulk of the population, who are thought to hold conservative religious beliefs and to approve of strict and traditional standards of sexual propriety (*takes a singular or plural verb*)

mor·al phi·los·o·phy *n* PHILOSOPHY same as **ethics**

mor·al sup·port *n* personal support and encouragement intended to bolster somebody's courage or determination

mor·al the·ol·o·gy *n* the academic study of moral and ethical questions from a Christian viewpoint

mo·rass /mə ráss, maw-/ *n* **1.** a frustrating, confusing, or unmanageable situation that impedes or prevents progress **2.** an area of low-lying ground that is soft and wet to a great depth and therefore difficult to walk on [Mid-17C. Via Dutch *moeras* < French *marais*]

mor·a·to·ri·um /màwrə táwree əm/ (*plural* **-ri·ums** or **-ri·a** /-ree ə/) *n* **1.** a formally agreed period during which an activity is halted or a planned activity is postponed **2.** a period during which a person, usually a debtor, has the right to postpone meeting an obligation [Late 19C. < modern Latin < late Latin *moratorius* "delaying" (see MORATORY)]

mor·a·to·ry /máwrə tàwree/ *adj* giving somebody the right to delay making payments on a debt [Late 19C. < late Latin *moratorius* "delaying" < Latin *morat-*, past participle of *morari* "to delay" < *mora* "delay"]

Mo·ra·va /mə ráavə/ river in the east central Federal Republic of Yugoslavia. Length: 218 mi./351 km.

Mo·ra·vi·a /mə ráyvee ə, maw-/ historic region of the eastern Czech Republic

Mo·ra·vi·an /mə ráyvee ən, maw-/ *n* **1.** PEOPLES **SOMEBODY FROM MORAVIA** somebody who comes from Moravia **2.** CHR **MORAVIAN CHURCH MEMBER** a member of the Moravian Church **3.** LANG **DIALECT OF CZECH** the dialect of the Czech language spoken in Moravia —**Mo·ra·vi·an** *adj*

Mo·ra·vi·an Church *n* a Protestant church founded in Moravia in 1722 whose members place a strong emphasis on evangelism, ecumenism, and the authority of the Bible

mo·ray /máw rày, mə ráy/ *n* a brightly colored sharp-toothed voracious eel that has no pectoral fins. Native to: rocky crevices or reefs of tropical coastal waters. Family: Muraenidae. [Early 17C. Via Portuguese *moréia* < Latin *murena* < Greek *muros* "sea eel"]

Mor·ay Firth /mùrree-/ arm of the North Sea, on the northeastern coast of Scotland

mor·bid /máwrbid/ *adj* **1. INTERESTED IN GRUESOME SUBJECTS** showing a strong interest in unpleasant or gloomy subjects such as death, murder, or accidents **2. GRISLY** inspiring disgust or horror **3.** MED **RELATING TO DISEASE** relating to or resulting in illness [Early 17C. < Latin *morbidus* "diseased" < *morbus* "sickness"] —**mor·bid·ly** *adv* —**mor·bid·ness** *n*

mor·bid·i·ty /mawr bíddətee/ *n* **1.** the presence of illness or disease **2.** the relative frequency of occurrence of a disease (*often used before a noun*)

mor·ceau /mawr số/ (*plural* **-ceaux** /-số, -sốz/) *n* **1.** a short musical or literary composition **2.** a tiny piece, e.g., a small mouthful of food [Mid-18C. < French, later form of Old French *morsel* (see MORSEL)]

mor·cil·la /mawr sée yə/ *n Hispanic* a blood sausage used in Hispanic, Mexican, and Spanish cooking [< Spanish]

mor·da·cious /mawr dáyshəss/ *adj* **1.** deliberately bitter or critical, and intended to hurt somebody's feelings (*formal or literary*) **2.** capable of biting, or tending to bite (*archaic or literary*) [Mid-17C. < Latin *mordac-* "biting" < *mordere* "to bite"]

mor·dant /máwrd'nt/ *adj* **1. SARCASTIC** sharply sarcastic or scathingly critical **2. CORROSIVE** having a corrosive effect ■ *n* **1.** INDUST **SUBSTANCE THAT FIXES DYES** a substance that fixes a dye in and on textiles or leather by combining with the dye to form a stable insoluble compound (**lake**) **2.** ART **ACID USED IN ETCHING** a corrosive substance used to etch treated areas on a metal plate ■ *vt* (**-dant·ed, -dant·ing, -dants**) INDUST **APPLY MORDANT TO SOMETHING** to apply a mordant to fabric or leather in order to fix a dye [15C. < French, present participle of *mordre* "to bite" < Latin *mordere*] —**mor·dan·cy** /máwrd'nssee/ *n* —**mor·dant·ly** *adv*

mor·dent /máwrd'nt/ *n* a musical embellishment, similar to a short trill, in which either the note above or the note below the written note is played in addition to the principal note [Early 19C. Via German < Italian *mordente* < *mordere* "to bite" < Latin]

Mor·dred *n* same as **Modred**

Mord·vin /máwrdvin/ (*plural same* or **-vins**) *n* **1.** a member of a Finnish people who live mainly in the middle of the Volga region of western Russia **2.** the Finno-Ugric language of the Mordvin. Native speakers: 1 million. [Mid-18C. < Russian] —**Mord·vin** *adj*

more /mawr/ CORE MEANING: a grammatical word, the comparative of "much" and "many," used to indicate a greater number of something, either a greater number than before, than average, or than something else ○ (adj) *a need for more adult education programs* ○ (pron) *As regards benefits, this job offers me more.*

1. *adv* **TO GREATER EXTENT** to a greater extent, or in a larger number or amount (*forming the comparative of some adjectives and adverbs*) ○ (adv) *This problem is more complex than the other one.* ○ *is more beautiful* ○ *behaved more sensibly* **2.** *adv* **FOR LONGER TIME** for a longer period of time ○ *chatted a bit more* **3.** *adv, pron* **WITH GREATER FREQUENCY OR INTENSITY** used as the comparative of "much" to mean "with greater frequency or intensity" ○ (adv) *are now going to the theater more* ○ (adv) *It inspires me more now than ever.* ○ (pron) *The more you listen, the more you hear.* **4.** *adj, pron* **ADDITIONAL** indicates something additional or further (*pronoun + singular or plural verb*) ○ (adj) *I need more light.* ○ (pron) *There aren't any more of these.* ○ (pron) *No more is expected.* [Old English *māra* < Germanic] ◇ **(all the) more so** to an even greater extent or degree ◇ **more or less 1.** approximately **2.** essentially or basically ◇ **no** *or* **neither more nor less (than something)** simply, or exactly the same as something ◇ **what is more** used to introduce an additional or reinforcing point

More /mawr/, **Sir Thomas** (1478–1535) English politician and scholar. He resigned as Henry VIII's Lord Chancellor (1529–32) in protest against the king's break with the Roman Catholic Church, and was executed after refusing to recognize Henry as the head of the English Church. His literary works include *Utopia* (1516). He was canonized as St. Thomas More in 1935.

> "For men use, if they have an evil turn, to write it in marble; and whoso doth us a good turn we write it in dust."
> [Sir Thomas, *Richard III and His Miserable End*; 1543]

mo·reen /mə réen, maw-/ *n* a thick ribbed material made of wool, cotton, or a mixture of both. Use: curtains, upholstery. [Mid-17C. Origin ?]

mo·rel /mə rél, maw-/ *n* an edible mushroom with a brown pitted spongy cap. Genus: *Morchella*. [Late 17C. < French *morille*]

mo·rel·lo /mə réllō, maw-/ (*plural* **-los**) *n* a small sour cultivated cherry with dark red skin [Mid-17C. Origin ?]

mo·ren·do /mə réndō, maw-/ *adv* growing continuously softer and sometimes slower (*used as a musical direction*) [Early 19C. < Italian, "dying," form of *morire* "die"] —**mo·ren·do** *adj*

more·o·ver /mawr ṓvər/ *adv* used to add a further piece of information that supports a previous statement

mo·res /máw ràyz, -reez/ *npl* the customs and habitual practices that a group of people accept and follow, especially as they reflect moral standards, [Late 19C. < Latin, plural of *mos* "manner, custom"]

Mo·resque /maw résk, mə-/ *adj* ARCHIT same as **Moorish** (sense 2) [Early 17C. Via French < Italian *moresco* < *Moro* "Moor" < Latin *Maurus* (see MOOR)]

MorF *abbr* ONLINE male or female (*used in e-mails or text messages*)

~~**morgage**~~ incorrect spelling of **mortgage**

mor·gan /máwrgən/ *n* a unit of chromosome length [Early 20C. After Thomas Hunt MORGAN]

Mor·gan *n* a black, bay, brown, or chestnut horse with a full mane and tail, short deep body, and slender legs, belonging to a US breed popular for hunting, jumping, and recreation [Mid-19C. After Justin *Morgan* (1747–98), owner of the stallion from which the breed descends]

Mor·gan /máwrgən/, **John Pierpont** (1837–1913) US financier. He was the founder of J. P. Morgan and Company (1895), and a noted art collector and philanthropist.

> "A man always has two reasons for doing anything—a good reason and the real reason."
> [John Pierpont Morgan. Quoted in *Roosevelt: The Story of a Friendship*, Owen Wister; 1930]

Mor·gan, Thomas Hunt (1866–1945) US geneticist and biologist. He discovered that chromosomes are the carriers of genetic information. He received the Nobel Prize in physiology or medicine (1933).

mor·ga·nat·ic /màwrgə náttik/ *adj* describes a marriage in which neither the spouse of lower social rank nor any children of the marriage may inherit the title or possessions of the higher-ranking spouse [Late 16C. Directly or via French or German < medieval Latin *(matrimonium ad) morganaticam* "(marriage for the) morning-gift" (the bridegroom's gift to the bride, which relieved him of further responsibility)] —**mor·ga·nat·i·cal·ly** *adv*

Mor·gan Cit·y city in southeastern Louisiana, on the Intracoastal Waterway. Population: 12,256 (2002 estimate).

mor·gan·ite /máwrgə nìt/ *n* a pink variety of beryl. Use: gems. [Early 20C. After John Pierpont MORGAN]

Mor·gan le Fay /màwrgən lə fáy/ *n* in Arthurian legend, an evil sorceress who was the half-sister and enemy of King Arthur

Mor·gan·ton /máwrgəntən/ city in western North Carolina. It is the seat of Burke County. Population: 17,311 (2002 estimate).

Mor·gan·town /máwrgən tòwn/ city and port in northern West Virginia, on the Monongahela River. Population: 27,342 (2002 estimate).

mor·gen /máwrgən/ *n* a unit of measurement for land area formerly used in various parts of the world and still in use in South Africa [Early 17C. < Dutch and German, "area of land that can be plowed in a morning"]

Mor·gen·thau /máwrgən thàw/, **Henry, Jr.** (1891–1967) US public official. He was US secretary of the treasury (1934–45).

morgue /mawrg/ *n* **1. PLACE FOR DEAD BODIES** a room or building usually run by a state or municipal government in which dead bodies are kept until they are autopsied or identified **2. DISMAL PLACE** a gloomy place that lacks warmth or cheer (*informal*) **3.** MEDIA **COLLECTION OF INFORMATION** a room or file in a newspaper office containing miscellaneous pieces of information kept for future reference, e.g., for writing obituaries [Mid-19C. < French *Morgue*, building in Paris]

CULTURAL NOTE ***The Murders in the Rue Morgue***, a novel (1841) by writer Edgar Allan Poe. Regarded as the world's first detective story, it begins with the brutal murder of an old woman and her daughter, a crime that perplexes the police since the women's apartment is sealed from the inside. Amateur sleuth C. Auguste Dupin comes to their aid, providing an explanation based on a brilliant analysis of scattered clues.

mor·i·bund /máwrə bùnd/ *adj* **1.** in the process of becoming obsolete **2.** nearly dead [Early 18C. < Latin *moribundus* < *mori* "die"] —**mor·i·bun·di·ty** /màwrə búndətee/ *n*

Mo·ris·co /mə rískō/ (*plural* **-cos** or **-coes**), **Mo·res·co** /-réskō/ *n* in medieval Spain, a Muslim who was forcibly converted to Christianity and often continued the secret practice of Islam, or a descendant of such a person [Mid-16C. < Spanish < *Moro* "Moor"] —**Mo·ris·co** *adj*

Mor·i·son /mórriss'n/, **Samuel Eliot** (1887–1976) US historian. He wrote the Pulitzer Prize-winning *Admiral of the Ocean Sea* (1942) and *John Paul Jones* (1959).

> "America was named after a man who discovered no part of the New World. History is like that, very chancy."
> [Samuel Eliot Morison, *The Oxford History of the American People*; 1965]

"If the American Revolution had produced nothing but the Declaration of Independence, it would have been worth while...."
[Samuel Eliot Morison, *The Oxford History of the American People*; 1965]

Berthe Morisot: portrait by Marcellin Desboutin

Mo·ri·sot /màwree zṓ/, **Berthe** (1841–95) French painter. Her paintings, in a subtle and delicate impressionistic style, often depict landscapes or women and children.

Mor·ley /máwrlee/, **Thomas** (1557–1603) English composer. He helped to establish the madrigal in England as a distinctive musical form.

Mor·mon /máwrmən/ *n* CHR same as **Latter-Day Saint** (*sometimes considered offensive*) ■ *adj* relating to the Church of Jesus Christ of Latter-Day Saints [Mid-19C. After the prophet said to be the author of the *Book of Mormon*, a sacred history of the Americas, translated by Joseph SMITH] —**Mor·mon·ism** *n*

Mor·mon crick·et *n* a large wingless grasshopper that can be a serious crop-eating pest. Native to: western United States. Latin name: *Anabrus simplex*. [< their presence in areas settled by Latter-Day Saints]

morn /mawrn/ *n* same as **morning** (*literary*) [Old English *morgen* < Germanic] ◇ **the morn** *Scotland* same as **tomorrow**

Mor·nay /mawr náy/ *adj* served in a white sauce containing grated cheese ○ *eggs Mornay* [Early 20C. Probably after Philip de *Mornay* (d. 1623), French writer]

morn·ing /máwrning/ *n* **1. EARLY PART OF DAY** the early part of the day, from dawn until noon or lunchtime **2. MIDNIGHT TO NOON** the part of the day between midnight and noon **3. DAWN** dawn or daybreak **4. EARLY PART** the beginning of something ■ *interj* same as **good morning** (*informal*) [13C. < MORN + *-ing*, after EVENING]

morn·ing-af·ter pill *n* a contraceptive pill designed to be taken after sexual intercourse

morn·ing dress *n* a man's suit worn to formal daytime events such as weddings, consisting of a black cutaway, striped black pants, usually a vest, and sometimes a top hat

morn·ing glo·ry *n* a climbing plant of the bindweed family. Flowers: trumpet-shaped, blue, purple, pink, or white, closing in the evening. Native to: tropical regions. Genus: *Ipomoea*.

morn·ing line *n* a list of entrants and their odds for a horserace, estimated by a bookmaker and posted before betting begins

Morn·ing Prayer *n* the morning service of worship in the Anglican Church

morn·ings /máwrningz/ *adv* during the morning, or every morning (*informal*)

morn·ing sick·ness *n* nausea and vomiting experienced by many pregnant women, usually in the morning and during the early months of pregnancy

morn·ing star *n* a planet, especially Venus, seen in the eastern sky around dawn

mo·roc·co /mə rókō/, **mo·roc·co leath·er** *n* a soft leather made from goatskin, or a leather made in imitation of it from sheepskin or calfskin. Use: covering books, for shoes. [Mid-17C. After MOROCCO]

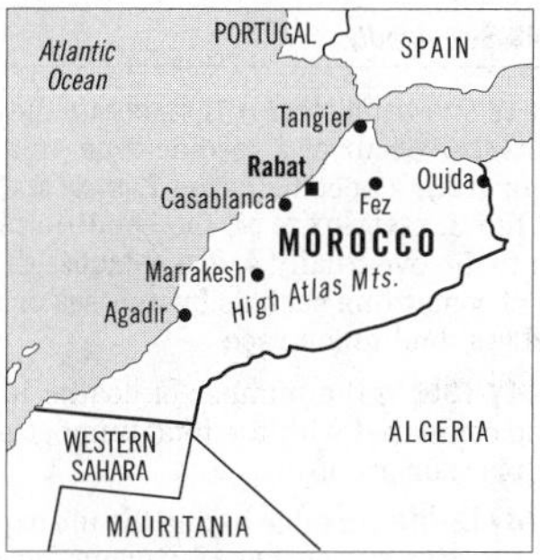

Morocco

Mo·roc·co /mə rókō/ country in northwestern Africa. Language: Arabic. Currency: dirham. Capital: Rabat. Population: 31,689,265 (2003). Area: 175,186 sq. mi./453,730 sq. km. Official name **Kingdom of Morocco** —**Mo·roc·can** *n, adj*

mo·roc·co leath·er *n* INDUST same as **morocco**

mo·ron /máw ròn/ *n* **1.** an offensive term that deliberately insults somebody's intelligence (*insult*) **2.** a former term for somebody with significant learning difficulties and impaired social skills, now considered offensive (*dated offensive*) [Early 20C. < Greek *mōron* "unintelligent, thoughtless"] —**mo·ron·ic** /mə rónnik, maw-/ *adj* —**mo·ron·i·ty** /mə rónnətee, maw-/ *n*

Mo·ro·ni /mə rṓnee/ capital of Comoros, on Grande Comore Island. Population: 49,000 (2001).

mo·rose /mə rṓss, maw-/ *adj* having a withdrawn gloomy personality [Mid-16C. < Latin *morosus* "peevish" < *mos* "manner, disposition"] —**mo·rose·ly** *adv* —**mo·rose·ness** *n*

morph[1] /mawrf/ (**morphed, morph·ing, morphs**) *vti* **1.** to transform one electronic graphic image into another or others, through the use of sophisticated computer software, or be transformed in this way **2.** to cause something to change its outward appearance completely and instantaneously, or undergo this process [Late 20C. < METAMORPHOSIS]

morph[2] /mawrf/ *n* an element of speech or writing that represents and expresses one or more morphemes [Mid-20C. Shortening of MORPHEME]

morph[3] /mawrf/ *n* one of two or more variant forms of an animal or plant [Mid-20C. < Greek *morphē* "form"]

morph. *abbr* BIOL, LING **1.** morphological **2.** morphology

-morph *suffix* something that has a particular form, shape, or structure ○ *mesomorph* [< Greek *morphē* "form"] —**-morphic** *suffix* —**-morphism** *suffix* —**-morphous** *suffix* —**-morphy** *suffix*

mor·phac·tin /mawrf áktin/ *n* a substance affecting plant growth and development [Mid-20C. Probably < Greek *morphē* "form" + ACTIVE]

mor·phal·lax·is /màwrfə láksiss/ *n* the process whereby an organism regenerates body parts by the reorganization and transformation of existing tissue, rather than by the formation of new tissue [Late 19C. < Greek *morphē* "form" + *allaxis* "exchange"]

mor·pheme /máwr fèem/ *n* the smallest meaningful element of speech or writing [Late 19C. < French < Greek *morphē* "form," after PHONEME] —**mor·phem·ic** /mawr féemik/ *adj*

mor·phem·ics /mawr féemiks/ *n* (*takes a singular verb*) **1.** the way in which morphemes combine to form words in a language **2.** the study and description of the ways in which morphemes combine in languages

Mor·phe·us /máwrfee əss, -fyòoss/ *n* in classical mythology, the god of dreams and sleep, mentioned by the Roman poet Ovid [14C. < Latin]

mor·phi·a /máwrfee ə/ *n* same as **morphine** (*dated*) [Early 19C. < MORPHEUS]

mor·phine /máwr fèen/ *n* an alkaloid drug that may become addictive with prolonged use. Source: opium. Use: relief of severe pain. [Early 19C. < French < *Morphée* "Morpheus" < Latin *Morpheus*]

mor·phin·ism /máwrfee nìzzəm, máwrfə-/ *n* addiction to morphine and the related health problems of such addiction (*dated*)

mor·pho /máwrfō/ (*plural* **-phos**) *n* a large butterfly with iridescent blue wings. Native to: tropical America. Genus: *Morpho*. [Mid-19C. Via modern Latin < Greek *Morphō*, epithet of APHRODITE]

morpho- *prefix* form, shape, structure ○ *morphogenesis* [< Greek *morphē*]

mor·pho·gen /máwrfəjən/ *n* a substance that influences the differentiation and growth of embryonic cells

mor·pho·gen·e·sis /màwrfō jénnəssiss/ *n* **1.** the origin and development of an organism or of a part of one, as it grows from embryo to adult **2.** the development of an organism or of some part of one, as it changes as a species —**mor·pho·ge·net·ic** /màwrfō jə néttik/ *adj* —**mor·pho·gen·ic** /-jénnik/ *adj*

morphol. *abbr* BIOL, LING **1.** morphological **2.** morphology

mor·phol·o·gy /mawr fólləjee/ (*plural* **-gies**) *n* **1.** BIOL **STRUCTURE OF ORGANISM** the form and structure of an organism or of a part of an organism **2.** BIOL **STUDY OF STRUCTURE OF ORGANISMS** the study of the form and structure of organisms **3.** LING **STRUCTURE OF WORDS** the structure of words in a language, including patterns of inflections and derivation **4.** LING **STUDY OF WORD FORMATION** the study of the structure of words in a language **5. STRUCTURE OF SOMETHING'S PARTS** the structure of anything made up of interconnected or interdependent parts **6. STUDY OF STRUCTURE OF SOMETHING'S PARTS** the study of the structure of anything made up of interconnected or interdependent parts —**mor·pho·log·i·cal** /màwrfə lójjik'l/ *adj* —**mor·phol·o·gist** *n*

mor·phom·e·try /mawr fómmətree/ *n* the measurement of the outside of something —**mor·pho·met·ric** /màwrfə méttrik/ *adj* —**mor·pho·met·ri·cal·ly** *adv*

mor·pho·sis /mawr fṓssiss/ (*plural* **-pho·ses** /-fō sèez/) *n* a variation in the pattern of development (**morphogenesis**) of an organism as a result of changes in the external environment [Late 17C. < Greek *morphōsis* "a shaping" < *morphē* "form"]

Mor·rill /mórril/, **Justin Smith** (1810–98) US politician. He was a Whig member of the US House of Representatives (1855–67) and US Senate (1867–98) and introduced the Tariff Act (1861) and the Land-Grant College Act (1862).

Mor·ris /máwriss, mórriss/, **Gouverneur** (1752–1816) American Federalist leader. A member of the Continental Congress, he coauthored the Constitution (1787) and served as a US senator (1800–03). He spent many years in revolutionary France.

Mor·ris, Lewis (1726–98) American patriot. He was a signatory of the Declaration of Independence (1776) and the half-brother of Gouverneur Morris.

Mor·ris, Robert (1734–1806) American patriot and financier. He was a signatory of the Declaration of Independence (1776) and helped to finance the American Revolution.

Mor·ris, William (1834–96) British artist, poet, and social activist. His decorations and furnishings drew on medieval tradition and his love of craftsmanship, and laid the foundations for the Arts and Crafts movement and art nouveau. His poetry included classical translations, some published in fine editions by Kelmscott Press, which he founded in 1890.

"Art will make our streets as beautiful as the woods, as elevating as the mountainside: it will be a pleasure and a rest, and not a weight upon the spirits to come from the open country into a town. Every man's house will be fair and decent, soothing to his mind and helpful to his work."
[William Morris. Quoted in *The Arts and Crafts Movement*, Thomas Sanderson; 1905]

Mor·ris chair *n* a light carved wooden armchair with removable cushions and a reclining back that can be set at varying angles [After William MORRIS]

mor·ris dance *n* a lively English folk dance, traditionally performed by men, usually wearing white costumes and using small bells, sticks, and handkerchiefs. [15C. < Old French *morois* "Moorish" < *More*

"Moor," because perhaps of Moorish origin] —**mor·ris danc·er** *n* —**mor·ris danc·ing** *n*

Mor·ris·on /máwriss'n, mórri-/, **Jim** (1943–71) US rock singer and songwriter. He was the lead singer of the Doors and attracted a cult following after his death. Full name **Morrison, James Douglas**

> "When you make your peace with authority, you become an authority."
> [Jim Morrison. Quoted in *In Their Own Words: The Doors*, Andrew Doe and John Tobler; 1988]

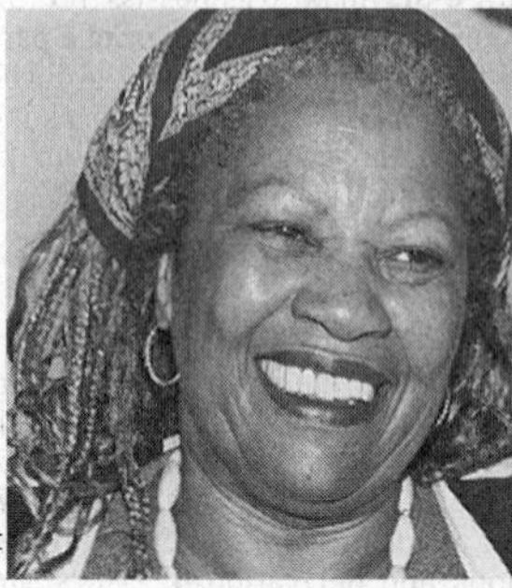

Toni Morrison

Mor·ris·on, Toni (*b.* 1931) US writer. Her novels deal with the experience of being an African American and include *Beloved* (1987), which won a Pulitzer Prize. She received the Nobel Prize in literature (1993). Born **Wofford, Chloe Anthony**. See Cultural note at **beloved**

> "If you take a life, then you own it. You responsible for it. You can't get rid of nobody by killing them. They still there, and they yours now."
> [Toni Morrison, *Song of Solomon*; 1977]

mor·ro /máwrō/ (*plural* **-ros**) *n* a hill or headland with a rounded outline [< Spanish]

mor·row /máwrō/ *n* (*literary*) **1.** the day after today or after a particular day **2.** the early part of the day [13C. < earlier form of MORN]

Mors /mawrz/ *n* in Roman mythology, the god of death. Greek equivalent **Thanatos** [< Latin, "death"]

Morse /mawrss/ *n* a system for representing letters and numbers by signs consisting of one or more short or long signals of sound or light that are printed out as dots and dashes [Mid-19C. After Samuel F. B. MORSE]

Morse /mawrss/, **Samuel F. B.** (1791–1872) US inventor and artist. He invented the electric telegraph (1837) and Morse. Full name **Morse, Samuel Finley Breese**

Morse code *n* COMMUNICATION same as **Morse**

mor·sel /máwrss'l/ *n* **1.** SMALL PIECE OF FOOD a small piece of something, especially of food **2.** SMALL AMOUNT a small amount of something **3.** SOMEBODY OR SOMETHING PLEASING somebody or something that is particularly appealing or pleasing [13C. < Old French, "little bite" < *mors* "bite" < past participle of Latin *mordere* "to bite"]

mor·ta·del·la /màwrtə déllə/ *n* a smoked, fried, or steamed Italian sausage consisting of pork and beef flavored with wine, garlic, and pepper [Early 17C. < Italian < Latin *murtatum* "(sausage) seasoned with myrtle berries"]

~~**mortagage**~~ incorrect spelling of **mortgage**

mor·tal /máwrt'l/ *adj* **1.** HUMAN relating to human beings **2.** EVENTUALLY DYING certain to die eventually **3.** FATAL causing death ○ *a mortal blow* **4.** CONTINUING UNTIL SOMEBODY DIES continuing, or intended to continue, until somebody dies ○ *mortal combat* **5.** OF DEATH relating to or accompanying death ○ *in mortal agony* **6.** EXTREMELY HATED being the object of somebody's unrelenting hatred ○ *his mortal enemy* **7.** INTENSE intensely felt ○ *mortal fear* **8.** CONCEIVABLE being within the bounds of what is imaginable or possible ○ *What mortal reason could there be for him to leave like that?* ■ *adj, adv* USED FOR EMPHASIS used for emphasis, and sometimes indicating that the speaker is frustrated or annoyed (*dated*) ■ *n* HUMAN BEING a human being, who will eventually die [14C. Directly or via French < Latin *mortalis* < *mors* "death"]

SYNONYMS See *deadly*.

mor·tal·i·ty /mawr tállətee/ *n* **1.** DEATH RATE the number of deaths that occur at a specific time, in a specific group, or from a specific cause **2.** MANY DEATHS great loss of life **3.** CERTAINTY TO DIE the condition of being certain to die eventually **4.** RATE OF FAILURE the rate of failure of something such as businesses or farms **5.** HUMAN BEINGS the human race

mor·tal·i·ty rate *n* the number of deaths in a place or group compared with the total number of people in that place or group

mor·tal·i·ty ta·ble *n* a table listing the life expectancy and death rate for people of various ages or occupations that is based on mortality statistics over a number of years

mor·tal·ly /máwrt'lee/ *adv* **1.** so badly that death follows **2.** in an extreme or intense way

mor·tal sin *n* in Roman Catholic theology, a sin considered to be so evil that it causes a complete loss of grace and leads to damnation unless it is absolved

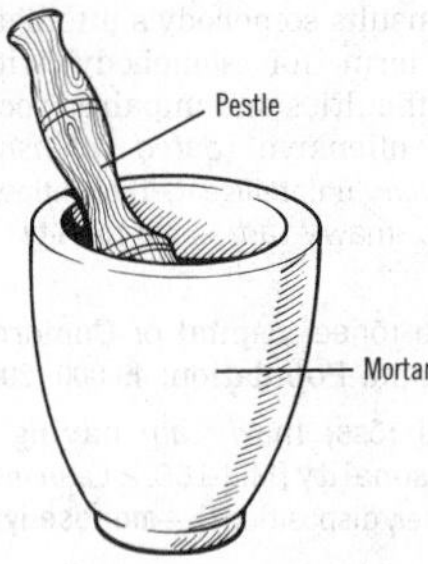

mortar (sense 4)

mor·tar /máwrtər/ *n* **1.** BONDING MATERIAL FOR BRICKS a mixture of sand, water, and cement or lime that becomes hard like stone. Use: in building to hold bricks and stones together. **2.** CANNON a cannon with a relatively short and wide barrel, used for firing shells at a high angle over a short distance **3.** GUN FIRING LIFELINE a gun for firing something other than a bullet, e.g., rope to somebody in need of rescue **4.** BOWL FOR GRINDING a hard heavy bowl designed to hold substances to be ground into small pieces or powder by means of a club-shaped tool (**pestle**) **5.** BOWL FOR CRUSHING ORE a cast-iron bowl in which ore is crushed ■ *vt* (**-tared, -tar·ing, -tars**) **1.** FIRE MORTAR AT TARGET to fire at somebody or something with a mortar **2.** SECURE MATERIALS WITH MORTAR to hold stones and bricks together with mortar [Pre-12C. Via French *mortier* "bowl for mixing" < Latin *mortarium* "bowl, substance prepared in it"]

mortarboard

mor·tar·board /máwrtər bàwrd/ *n* **1.** a hat often worn on formal academic occasions, consisting of a round cap with a hard square flat top and usually a tassel **2.** a square board with a handle in the center of the underside, used by bricklayers for carrying mortar

mort·gage /máwrgij/ *n* **1.** LOAN AGREEMENT SECURED BY PROPERTY an agreement by which somebody borrows money from a money-lending organization such as a bank or savings-and-loan association and gives that organization the right to take possession of property given as security if the loan is not repaid **2.** CONTRACT BETWEEN BORROWER AND LENDER a written contract describing the agreement between a borrower and a lending organization by which a loan is given against security **3.** TOTAL MONEY BORROWED the total amount of money lent to a borrower by a money-lending organization, with some of the borrower's property being given as security **4.** LOAN INSTALLMENT TO BE REPAID the money paid by a borrower, usually monthly, to a lending organization until the entire sum borrowed by a mortgage agreement has been repaid ■ *vt* (**-gaged, -gag·ing, -gag·es**) **1.** GRANT CLAIM TO OWNERSHIP OF PROPERTY to give a claim to legal possession of property to a money-lending organization such as a bank or savings-and-loan association as security for a loan **2.** PUT SOMETHING AT RISK to pledge something when risk is involved (*informal*) ○ *mortgaged her political future by accepting the donation* [14C. < Old French < *mort* "dead" + *gage* "pledge," because property pledged as security may be lost] —**mort·gage·a·ble** *adj*

mort·ga·gee /màwrgi jeé/ *n* an organization that lends money to a borrower by a mortgage agreement

mort·gag·er *n* FIN same as **mortgagor**

mort·gage rate *n* the interest rate charged by lenders on mortgage loans

mort·ga·gor /màwrgi jáwr, máwrgi jər/, **mort·gag·er** /-jər/ *n* a borrower of money under a mortgage agreement

mor·tice *n* CONSTR, PRINTING another spelling of **mortise**

mor·ti·cian /mawr tísh'n/ *n* same as **funeral director** [Late 19C. < Latin *mort-* "death"]

mor·ti·fi·ca·tion /màwrtəfi káysh'n/ *n* **1.** SHAME deep shame and humiliation **2.** SOMETHING CAUSING MORTIFICATION something that causes a feeling of deep shame and humiliation **3.** RELIG SELF-IMPOSED HARDSHIP the use of self-imposed discipline, hardship, abstinence from pleasure, and especially self-inflicted pain in an attempt to control or put an end to desires and passions, especially for religious purposes **4.** MED DEATH AND DECAY OF LIVING TISSUE the death and decaying of a part of a living body, e.g., because the blood supply to it has been cut off [14C. Directly or via French < late Latin *mortificatio(n-)* "destruction" < Latin *mortificat-* past participle of *mortificare* (see MORTIFY)]

mor·ti·fy /máwrtə fì/ (**-fied, -fy·ing, -fies**) *v* **1.** *vt* SHAME SOMEBODY to make somebody feel deeply ashamed and humiliated **2.** *vt* RELIG IMPOSE HARDSHIP ON SELF to attempt to subdue the body or desires and passions by self-imposed discipline, hardship, abstinence from pleasure, and especially self-inflicted pain, usually for religious purposes **3.** *vi* MED DECAY to decay and die (*refers to living tissue*) [14C. Via Old French *mortifier* < Latin *mortificare* "kill" < *mort-* "death"] —**mor·ti·fy·ing** *adj* —**mor·ti·fy·ing·ly** *adv*

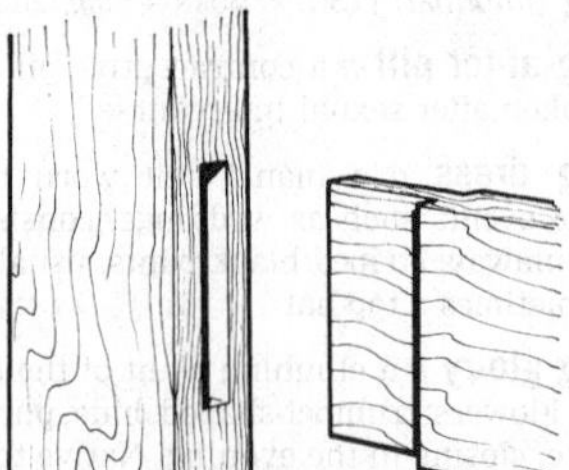
mortise

mor·tise /máwrtiss/, **mor·tice** *n* HOLE CUT TO HOLD OTHER PART a hole or slot cut into a piece of wood, stone, or other material, for a projecting part (**tenon**) to be inserted into it, in order to form a tight joint ■ *vt* (**-tised, -tis·ing, -tis·es; -ticed, -tic·ing, -tic·es**) **1.** CUT MORTISE IN SOMETHING to cut a mortise in a piece of wood, stone, or other material **2.** JOIN PARTS USING MORTISE AND TENON to join two things or parts by means of a mortise and tenon [14C. < Old French, probably < Arabic *murtaj* "locked"] —**mor·tis·er** *n*

mort·main /máwrt màyn/ *n* **1.** the perpetual, nontransferable, and nonsalable ownership of property by organizations such as churches **2.** the usually stultifying or stifling influence of the past on current events and living people [13C. Via Anglo-

Norman, Old French < medieval Latin *mortua manus* "dead hand"]

Mor·ton /máwrt'n/, **Jelly Roll** (1885–1941) US pianist and composer. He was a major figure in the development of jazz. Born **La Menthe, Ferdinand Joseph**

> "It is evidently known, beyond contradiction, that New Orleans is the cradle of *jazz*, and I, myself, happened to be the creator in the year 1902...*Jazz* music is a style, not compositions; any kind of music may be played in *jazz*, if one has the knowledge."
>
> [Jelly Roll Morton, *Downbeat*; August 1938]

Mor·ton, John (1724–77) American patriot. He was one of the signatories of the Declaration of Independence (1776).

Mor·ton, Levi Parsons (1824–1920) banker and politician. He served as vice president of the United States under Benjamin Harrison (1889–95).

Mor·ton, William Thomas Green (1819–68) US dentist. He claimed to be the first to have used ether as an anesthetic (1844).

Mor·ton Grove village in northeastern Illinois. Population: 22,502 (2002 estimate).

mor·tu·ar·y /máwrchoo èrree/ *n* (*plural* **-ies**) a room or building in which dead bodies are kept until they are buried or cremated ■ *adj* relating to death or funerals [14C. Directly or via Anglo-Norman *mortuarie* < Latin *mortuarius* "dead," past participle of *mori* "die"]

mor·tu·ar·y sci·ence *n* the study and practice of embalming bodies and administering funerals

mor·u·la /máwryələ, máwrə-/ (*plural* **-las** or **-lae** /-lee/) *n* an early stage in the development of an animal embryo, consisting of a solid ball of cells derived by cleavage of the fertilized egg (**zygote**) [Mid-19C. < modern Latin, "little mulberry" < *morum* "mulberry"]

MOS *abbr* **1.** COMPUT metal-oxide semiconductor **2.** MIL military occupational specialty

mos. *abbr* TIME months

Barnaby's

mosaic: detail of mosaic floor at the Roman settlement of Verulamium, St. Albans, England

mo·sa·ic /mō záy ik/ *n* **1.** PICTURE MADE WITH SMALL COLORED PIECES a picture or design made with small pieces of colored material such as glass or tile stuck onto a surface **2.** MAKING OF MOSAICS the art of making mosaics **3.** SOMETHING CONSISTING OF VARIETY OF COMPONENTS something consisting of a number of things of different types, forms, or colors **4.** BOT VIRAL PLANT DISEASE a plant disease, often caused by a virus, in which the foliage develops irregular patches of discoloration **5.** BOT PLANT DISCOLORATION a pattern of light green or yellowish mottling on the foliage of a plant, usually caused by a viral infection **6.** GENETICS same as **chimera** (sense 2) ■ *vt* (**-icked, -ick·ing, -ics**) DECORATE SOMETHING WITH MOSAIC to make something into, or decorate something with, a mosaic [14C. < Old French < Latin *Musa* "Muse"; from the decorations of medieval shrines dedicated to the Muses]

Mo·sa·ic /mō záy ik/, **Mo·sa·i·cal** /-ik'l/ *adj* relating to the biblical figure Moses [Mid-17C. Directly or via French < Latin *Mosaicus* < *Moses* "Moses" < Hebrew *Mōšeh*]

mo·sa·ic dis·ease *n* BOT same as **mosaic** *n* (sense 4)

mo·sa·ic gold *n* **1.** tin disulfide. Use: gilding. **2.** an alloy of copper and either zinc or tin that looks like gold. Use: to decorate such things as furniture and jewelry.

mo·sa·i·cism /mō záy ə sìzzəm/ *n* the occurrence of genetically distinct cells within tissue or an individual organism

Mo·sa·ic Law *n* the code of law of the ancient Hebrews, beginning with the Ten Commandments, believed to have been set down by Moses and contained in the Pentateuch

mo·sa·saur /mṓssə sàwr/ *n* an extinct lizard that lived in the ocean and had a long slender body with limbs resembling paddles for steering, and a long flexible tail for propulsion. Family: Mosasauridae. [Mid-19C. < modern Latin *Mosaurus* < Latin *Mosa*, the Meuse River]

mos·cha·tel /mòskə tél, móskə tèl/ (*plural* **-tels** or *same*) *n* a low-growing plant found in moist places. Flowers: small, yellowish green, in cube-shaped clusters. Native to: northern temperate regions. Latin name: *Adoxa moschatellina*. [Mid-18C. Via French < Italian *Moscatella* < *moscato* "musk," from the scent of the flowers]

Mos·cow /mós kow, -kō/ **1.** capital of Russia, located in the west central European part of the country. It was also the capital of the former Soviet Union from 1922 to 1991. Population: 8,297,900 (1999). **2.** city in northwestern Idaho. Population: 21,674 (2002 estimate).

Mo·selle[1] /mō zél/ *n* a light typically dry white wine from west central Germany [Late 17C. < MOSELLE[2]]

Mo·selle[2] /mō zél/ river in northeastern France and northwestern Germany. Length: 342 mi./550 km.

Mos·es /mṓzəz/ *n* in the Bible, a Hebrew prophet and the brother of Aaron who led the Israelites from slavery in Egypt to the Promised Land. He is believed to have written down the Ten Commandments (Exodus 20).

Popperfoto

Grandma Moses

Mos·es /mṓzəz/, **Grandma** (1860–1961) US artist. She is known for her primitivist paintings of US rural life, which she began in her late seventies. Born **Moses, Anna Mary Robertson**

Mos·es Lake city in Washington, in Grant County, on the northeastern shore of Moses Lake. Population: 15,976 (2002 estimate).

mo·sey /mṓzee/ (**-seyed, -sey·ing, -seys**) *vi* to walk somewhere at a leisurely unhurried pace (*informal*) [Early 19C. Origin ?]

mosh /mosh/ (**moshed, mosh·ing, mosh·es**) *vi* to dance to rock music in a frenzied way (*informal*) [Late 20C. Probably alteration of MASH]

mo·shav /mō shaáv/ (*plural* **-sha·vim** /-shaa véem/) *n* in Israel, a cooperative settlement consisting of independent small farms, or land farmed by the whole community with each family having its own house and garden [Mid-20C. < modern Hebrew *mōšāḇ* "dwelling, colony"]

mosh pit *n* an area in front of the stage at a rock concert where people dance wildly and energetically (*informal*)

Mos·lem /mózzləm, mósləm/ (*plural* **-lems** or *same*) *n* same as **Muslim** [Variant]

Mos·ley /mṓzlee/, **Sir Oswald** (1896–1980) British politician. He founded the British Union of Fascists in 1932. Full name **Mosley, Sir Oswald Ernald**

Barnaby's

mosque: Delhi, India

mosque /mosk/ *n* a building in which Muslims worship [15C. Via French < Arabic *masjid* "place of worship" < *sajada* "bow down"]

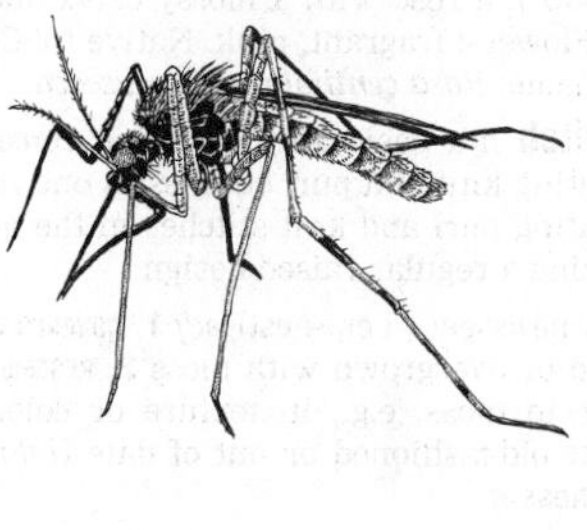

mosquito

mos·qui·to /mə skéétō/ (*plural* **-toes** or **-tos**) *n* a small slender fly that feeds on the blood of mammals, including humans, and transmits diseases such as malaria, yellow fever, and dengue. Native to: tropics. Family: Culicidae. [Late 16C. < Spanish, "little fly" < *mosca* "fly" < Latin *musca*]

mos·qui·to coil *n* a piece of coiled incense that is lit to repel mosquitoes

mos·qui·to fern *n* a small fern that has branched stems with small leaves resembling scales and floats on freshwater ponds and lakes. Genus: *Azolla*.

mos·qui·to fish *n* a small freshwater fish of the guppy family that feeds on mosquito larvae. Native to: southeastern United States. Genus: *Gambusia*.

mos·qui·to hawk *n* **1.** BIRDS same as **nighthawk** (sense 1) **2.** *regional* a dragonfly [Probably because it feeds on small flies]

REGIONAL NOTE See ***snake doctor***.

mos·qui·to net *n* a curtain of fine netting hung over a bed or across a window as a protection against mosquitoes

mos·qui·to news·pa·per *n Singapore* an ephemeral, cheaply produced newspaper, often satirical in content

moss /mawss, moss/ *n* **1.** a simple nonflowering plant (**bryophyte**) that has short stems with small leaves arranged in spirals and resembling scales, and inhabits moist shady sites. Class: Musci. **2.** a plant that resembles a true moss, e.g., a variety of seaweed known as irish moss [Old English *mos* "swamp" < Germanic]

Mos·sad /màw saád/ *n* the intelligence service of Israel, established in 1951 [Mid-20C. < Hebrew *mosad* "institution"]

moss ag·ate *n* a whitish agate containing dark green patterns resembling moss

moss an·i·mal *n* MARINE BIOL same as **bryozoan**

moss·back /máwss bàk/ *n* **1.** (*plural* **moss·backs** or *same*) an old turtle, shellfish, or fish with algae growing on its back **2.** an offensive term for somebody regarded as old-fashioned or conservative (*insult*)

moss·bunk·er /máwss bùngkər/ *n* FISH same as **menhaden** [Late 18C. < Dutch *marsbanker*]

moss cam·pi·on *n* a plant of the pink family that forms tufts of leaves resembling moss. Flowers: solitary, pink. Native to: cool alpine regions. Latin name: *Silene acaulis.*

moss green *adj* of a dull yellowish green color (*hyphenated when used before a noun*) —**moss green** *n*

moss·grown /máwss grōn/ *adj* **1.** covered with moss **2.** old-fashioned or out of date

Mos·si /máwssee/ (*plural same* or **-sis**) *n* **1.** a member of a people living in West Africa, especially in Burkina Faso **2.** the Gur language of the Mossi people. Native speakers: 6 million. [Mid-19C. < an African name] —**Mos·si** *adj*

mos·so /máwssō/ *adv* in a quick and lively way (*used as a musical direction*) [Late 19C. < Italian, past participle of *muovere* "to move"]

moss pink *n* a garden plant of the pink family with spreading mats of tiny leaves. Flowers: lavender, pink, or white. Native to: eastern North America. Latin name: *Phlox subulata.*

moss rose *n* a rose with a mossy calyx and flower stalk. Flowers: fragrant, pink. Native to: Caucasia. Latin name: *Rosa centifolia* var. *muscosa.*

moss stitch *n* a basic knitting stitch consisting of alternating knit and purl stitches in one row, then alternating purl and knit stitches in the next row, producing a regular raised design

moss·y /máwssee/ (**-i·er, -i·est**) *adj* **1.** COVERED WITH MOSS covered or overgrown with moss **2.** RESEMBLING MOSS similar to moss, e.g., in texture or color **3.** OLD-FASHIONED old-fashioned or out of date (*informal*) —**moss·i·ness** *n*

moss·y zinc *n* a form of zinc with a grainy texture. Source: pouring melted zinc into water.

most /mōst/ CORE MEANING: a grammatical word indicating nearly all or the majority of the people or things mentioned ○ *Most people enjoy watching a good movie.* ○ *We'd finished most of the work by lunchtime.*

1. *adj, pron* GREATEST indicates the greatest in number, amount, extent, or degree ○ (adj) *the candidate winning the most votes* ○ (pron) *The most I can lend you is $50.* **2.** *adv* TO GREATEST EXTENT to the greatest extent, or in the largest number or amount (*forming the superlative of some adjectives and adverbs*) ○ *It works most effectively if you heat it first.* ○ *the most expensive* **3.** *adv* SUPERLATIVE OF "MUCH" used as the superlative of "much" to mean "with the greatest frequency or intensity" ○ *He likes her most.* **4.** *adv* VERY to a great degree ○ *a most enjoyable day* **5.** *adv* ALMOST nearly but not entirely (*informal*) ○ *Most everyone was invited.* [Old English *mǣst* < Indo-European, "big"] ◇ **at (the) most** at the maximum ○ *It'll take you two hours at the most.* ◇ **make the most of something** to take full advantage of something ◇ **the most** the best of all (*dated slang*) ○ *That song is the most!*

USAGE See ***almost.***

-most *suffix* **1.** nearest to or toward ○ *endmost* **2.** most ○ *nethermost* [Old English *-mest* < Germanic, taken as < MOST]

Mos·ta·ga·nem /mə stággə nèm/ city and fishing port in northwestern Algeria. Population: 114,037 (1987).

Mos·tar /móss taàr/ city in southern Bosnia and Herzegovina, on the Neretva River. It was the scene of intense fighting during the Bosnian-Croatian-Serbian War (1991–95), when a bridge was destroyed between the Bosnian Croats and Muslims living on either side of the river. It is situated about 50 mi./80 km southwest of Sarajevo. Population: 24,606 (1991).

most-fa·vored-na·tion *adj* describes a treaty under which nations agree to allow each other their most favorable trading terms, or a nation's status under such a treaty (*often used before a noun*)

most·ly /mōstlee/ *adv* **1.** almost entirely ○ *The audience was mostly made up of younger fans.* **2.** on most occasions, or for the most part ○ *I swim mostly at weekends.*

Most Rev·er·end *adj* a title given to to cardinals and archbishops in the Roman Catholic Church and to Anglican archbishops

MOTD *abbr* ONLINE message of the day (*used in e-mails or text messages*)

mote /mōt/ *n* a tiny speck or particle [Old English *mot*, origin ?]

mo·tel /mō tél/ *n* a hotel intended to provide short-term lodging for traveling motorists, usually situated close to a highway and having rooms accessible from the parking area [Early 20C. Blend of MOTOR + HOTEL]

~~**moter**~~ incorrect spelling of **motor**

mo·tet /mō tét/ *n* a vocal composition with parts for different voices, usually based on a sacred text [14C. < Old French, "little word" < Latin *muttire* "to murmur"]

moth

moth /mawth/ *n* an insect resembling a butterfly, generally differing in having a duller color and differently shaped antennae, and in being active at night. Order: Lepidoptera. [Old English *moþþe*, origin ?]

moth·ball /máwth bàwl/ *n* MOTH-REPELLENT CHEMICAL BALL a small ball of a strong-smelling chemical such as camphor or naphthalene, used for keeping clothes moths away from clothing and other materials ■ *vt* (**-balled, -ball·ing, -balls**) **1.** PUT SOMETHING OFF INDEFINITELY to postpone work or discussion on something for an indefinite time ○ *mothballed the expansion plans* **2.** INDUST SHUT DOWN FACTORY to take a factory out of operation but protect the equipment in it so that it can be used again at some time in the future **3.** NAUT, AEROSP SEAL CRAFT FOR STORAGE to seal all the openings in a ship or aircraft in order to protect it from corrosion while it is not in use ◇ **in mothballs** put aside or stored and not in use

moth bean *n* **1.** a yellowish brown edible bean seed **2.** a plant of the pea family. Flowers: small, yellow. Use: forage, fertilizer, food. Native to: tropical regions, especially South Asia. Latin name: *Phaseolus aconitifolius.*

Mothe ♦ **Cadillac, Antoine Laumet de la Mothe**

moth-eat·en *adj* **1.** EATEN BY MOTH LARVAE damaged by clothes moth caterpillars **2.** SHABBY dilapidated and worn-out from use **3.** OUTDATED no longer usable or appropriate (*informal*)

moth·er[1] /mú*th*ər/ *n* **1.** FEMALE PARENT a woman who has a child, or a female animal that has produced young **2.** WOMAN ACTING AS PARENT a woman who acts as the parent of a child to whom she has not given birth **3.** ORIGINATOR a woman regarded as the creator, instigator, or founder of something **4.** ORIGIN OF SOMETHING the cause, source, or origin of something ○ *Necessity is the mother of invention.* **5.** PROTECTOR something that protects and nourishes like a mother **6.** GOOD OR BAD EXAMPLE OF SOMETHING something very big, good, bad, or extreme, or particularly noteworthy in some other way (*slang; sometimes considered offensive*) ○ *a real mother of a headache* **7.** TABOO TERM a highly offensive term for somebody regarded as objectionable or contemptible (*taboo*) ■ *vt* (**-ered, -er·ing, -ers**) **1.** TAKE CARE SOMEBODY WITH TENDERNESS to look after somebody with great care and affection, sometimes to an excessive degree **2.** GIVE BIRTH TO BABY to give birth to and bring up a baby **3.** BRING SOMETHING ABOUT to give rise to something [Old English *modor* < Indo-European] —**moth·er·hood** *n* ◇ **at your mother's knee** in early childhood ◇ **every mother's son** every man or boy (*dated*)

moth·er[2] /mú*th*ər/ *n* a slimy mass of bacteria and yeast cells that forms on the surface of alcohol being converted into acetic acid [Mid-16C. Probably < obsolete Dutch *moeder* < Middle Dutch *moeder* "female parent"; from its part in the production of vinegar]

Moth·er *n* **1.** used as a title or form of address for a senior nun in a religious community **2.** used as a title of respect for a woman past middle age (*archaic; sometimes considered offensive*)

moth·er·board /mú*th*ər bàwrd/ *n* a circuit board in a minicomputer or microcomputer through which all signals are directed

Moth·er Car·ey's chick·en *n* same as **storm petrel** (*dated*) [Probably < alteration of medieval Latin *mater cara* "Virgin Mary"]

moth·er cell *n* a cell that gives rise to other cells by cell division

moth·er church *n* a Christian church from which other churches derive their authority

moth·er coun·try *n* **1.** the country of origin of people who have left to found a colony or colonies elsewhere **2.** the country that somebody was born and grew up in

moth·er·ese /mù*th*ər éez/ *n* the speech patterns and restricted vocabulary used by parents and caregivers when speaking to very young children

moth·er fig·ure *n* a woman who embodies the qualities traditionally associated with a mother, especially support, advice, and affection

moth·er·fuck·er /mú*th*ər fùkər/ *n* a highly offensive term of abuse for somebody regarded as objectionable or contemptible (*taboo*) —**moth·er·fuck·ing** *adj*

Moth·er Goose *n* the supposed author of a collection of nursery rhymes first published in the 18th century

moth·er hen *n* a woman who is regarded as overprotective and fussing

moth·er·house /mú*th*ər hòwss/ *n* a Christian monastery or convent from which monks or nuns have gone out to found new monasteries and convents

Moth·er Hub·bard /mù*th*ər húbbərd/ *n* a long loose-fitting shapeless dress [Late 16C. After a nursery-rhyme character depicted wearing such a dress]

Moth·er·ing Sun·day *n* a day observed as a celebration of mothers. Date: fourth Sunday in Lent.

moth·er-in-law (*plural* **moth·ers-in-law**) *n* the mother of a person's spouse

moth·er-in-law's tongue *n* PLANTS same as **sansevieria** [< its long pointed leaves]

moth·er·land /mú*th*ər lànd/ *n* the country that somebody was born and grew up in

moth·er·less /mú*th*ərləss/ *adj* without a mother, or having lost a mother through bereavement

moth·er lode *n* **1.** the main vein of ore in a mine **2.** a plentiful supply of something

moth·er·ly /mú*th*ərlee/ *adj* having or showing qualities traditionally associated with mothers, especially kindness and protectiveness —**moth·er·li·ness** *n*

Moth·er Na·ture *n* the forces of nature personified as a willful being

Moth·er of God *n* a title given to Mary, the mother of Jesus Christ, especially by Roman Catholics

moth·er-of-pearl *n* the hard pearly internal layer of the shells of some mollusks. Use: decorative inlays. [Early 16C. Translation of obsolete French *mère perle*]

moth·er-of-thou·sands (*plural* **moth·ers-of-thous·ands** or **moth·er-of-thous·ands**) *n* a creeping or trailing plant that produces masses of small flowers, especially the ivy-leaved toadflax or the strawberry geranium

Moth·er's Day *n* **1.** a day observed as a celebration of mothers in the United States, Canada, Australia, and some other Commonwealth countries. Date: second Sunday in May. **2.** *UK* same as **Mothering Sunday**

moth·er ship *n* **1.** a ship or spaceship that provides services and supplies for a number of other, usually smaller ships **2.** an organization that oversees, or a place that acts as a base for, other activities (*informal*)

moth·er su·pe·ri·or (*plural* **moth·er su·pe·ri·ors** or **moth·ers su·pe·ri·or**) *n* the head of a Christian convent or community of Christian nuns

moth·er-to-be (*plural* **moth·ers-to-be**) *n* a woman who is expecting a baby

moth·er tongue *n* **1.** the first language somebody learns as a child at home **2.** a language from which other languages have developed

Moth·er·well /múthər wèl/, **Robert** (1915–91) US artist. He is known for his brilliantly colored or black-and-white abstract expressionist paintings. Full name **Motherwell, Robert Burns**

> "True painting is a lot more than 'picture-making.' A man is neither a decoration nor an anecdote."
> [Robert Motherwell. Quoted in *The New Decade*, Whitney Museum of American Art, New York; 1955]

moth·er wit *n* natural intelligence or good sense

moth·er·wort /múthər wùrt, -wàwrt/ (*plural* **-worts** or *same*) *n* a plant with deeply lobed leaves used in herbal medicine to treat gynecological disorders. Flowers: white or pink, purple-spotted. Native to: Europe, Asia. Latin name: *Leonurus cardiaca*. [14C. < MOTHER [1] in the obsolete sense "womb"; because formerly used as a medicinal herb during childbirth]

moth·proof /máwth proof/ *adj* treated with a substance designed to prevent damage by clothes moths —**moth·proof** *vt*

moth·y /máwthee/ (**-i·er, -i·est**) *adj* **1.** damaged by the action of clothes moths **2.** full of or infested by moths

mo·tif /mō teef/ *n* **1.** ARCHIT, DESIGN **REPEATED DESIGN** a repeated design, shape, or pattern **2.** HANDICRAFT, DESIGN **SEWN OR PRINTED DECORATION** a repetitive decorative design sewn into or printed on something such as a piece of clothing, or a single example of the pattern **3.** LITERAT **THEME IN WORK OF LITERATURE** an important and sometimes recurring theme or idea in a work of literature **4.** MUSIC **PROMINENT SEQUENCE OF NOTES** a short prominent sequence of notes forming the basis for development in a piece of music [Mid-19C. < French (see MOTIVE)]

mo·tile /mṓt'l, mṓ tìl/ *adj* capable of or demonstrating movement by independent means [Mid-19C. < Latin *motus* "motion" < past participle of *movere* "to move"] —**mo·til·i·ty** /mō tíllətee/ *n*

mo·tion /mṓsh'n/ *n* **1.** **ACT OF MOVING** the act or process of moving, or the way in which somebody or something moves ○ *walked with a swaying motion* **2.** **MOVEMENT** a movement, action, or gesture ○ *made a quick motion of the wrist* **3.** **POWER OF MOVEMENT** the power or ability to move something **4.** **PROPOSAL** a proposal put forward for discussion at a meeting **5.** LAW **APPLICATION TO JUDGE OR COURT** an application made to a court or judge for an order or ruling in a legal proceeding **6.** MUSIC **MOVEMENT FROM ONE NOTE TO ANOTHER** the movement from one note to the next by a voice or instrument **7.** *UK* PHYSIOL **PASSING OF SOLID WASTE FROM BODY** the passing of solid waste matter out of the body through the anus **8.** *UK* PHYSIOL **STOOL** a piece of evacuated fecal matter (*dated; often used in the plural*) ■ *vti* (**-tioned, -tion·ing, -tions**) **SIGNAL TO SOMEBODY** to gesture or signal something such as a request or intention to somebody ○ *motioned me over and told me to sit down* [14C. Via French < Latin *motion-* < past participle of *movere* "to move"] ◇ **go through the motions** to do something in a perfunctory or mechanical way, without enthusiasm or commitment ◇ **put** *or* **set something in motion** to cause something to start moving, functioning, or happening

mo·tion·less /mṓsh'nləss/ *adj* not moving —**mo·tion·less·ly** *adv* —**mo·tion·less·ness** *n*

mo·tion pic·ture *n* MOVIES same as **movie**

mo·tion sick·ness *n* a feeling of nausea resulting from overstimulation of the part of the ear that controls balance, caused especially by travel in a moving vehicle —**mo·tion sick** *adj*

mo·tion stud·y *n* INDUST same as **time and motion study**

mo·ti·vate /mṓtə vàyt/ (**-vat·ed, -vat·ing, -vates**) *vt* **1.** **GIVE SOMEBODY INCENTIVE** to give somebody a reason or incentive to do something **2.** **MAKE SOMEBODY WILLING** to make somebody feel enthusiastic, interested, and committed to something **3.** **CAUSE SOMEBODY'S BEHAVIOR** to be the reason for something that somebody does ○ *motivated purely by greed* [Mid-19C. < MOTIVE, after French *motiver* "motivate"] —**mo·ti·vat·ed** *adj* —**mo·ti·va·tor** *n*

mo·ti·va·tion /mṑtə váysh'n/ *n* **1.** **GIVING OF REASON TO ACT** the act of giving somebody a reason or incentive to do something **2.** **ENTHUSIASM** a feeling of enthusiasm, interest, or commitment that makes somebody want to do something, or something that causes such a feeling **3.** **REASON** a reason for doing something or behaving in a particular way **4.** PSYCHOL **FORCES DETERMINING BEHAVIOR** the biological, emotional, cognitive, or social forces that activate and direct behavior —**mo·ti·va·tion·al** *adj* —**mo·ti·va·tion·al·ly** *adv* —**mo·ti·va·tive** /mṓtə vàytiv/ *adj*

mo·ti·va·tion·al re·search, mo·ti·va·tion re·search *n* the study of the motivation of consumers in their buying practices, used to plan marketing and sales

mo·tive /mṓtiv/ *n* **1.** **REASON** the reason for doing something or behaving in a specific way **2.** ARTS same as **motif** (senses 1, 3) ■ *adj* **1.** **CAUSING MOTION** capable of causing or producing motion **2.** **CAUSING SOMEBODY TO DO SOMETHING** tending to make somebody want or be willing to do something ■ *vt* (**-tived, -tiv·ing, -tives**) **MOTIVATE SOMEBODY** to make somebody want or be willing to do something [14C. Via Old French *motif* < late Latin *motivus* < past participle of Latin *movere* "to move"]

SYNONYMS ***motive, incentive, inducement, spur, stimulus, impetus***

CORE MEANING: something that prompts action

motive the reason for doing something or behaving in a specific way ○ *a crime that appears to have no motive* ○ *He stressed the need to maintain the highest standards in this new probe, fearing there were ulterior political motives for the investigation.* **incentive** something that encourages or motivates somebody to do something ○ *The economic insecurity experienced by single mothers is another incentive for women to stay in the work force and increase their skills.* ○ *financial incentives to reduce pollution* **inducement** something that persuades somebody to do something or attracts somebody to a course of action, especially something that is offered as a reward ○ *Debt relief was promised as an inducement to the country to make peace with its neighbor.* ○ *The committee expressed the hope that "every inducement, direct or indirect, will be given to keep mothers at home."* **spur** something that encourages a person or organization to take action or to make a greater effort, for example, the hope of a reward or the fear of punishment ○ *Trade traditionally acts as a spur to economic expansion.* ○ *Storekeepers saw the outsides of their properties improved, and that provided a spur for them to improve the insides.* **stimulus** something that encourages an activity or process to begin, increase, or develop ○ *The possibility of lowering interest rates acted as a stimulus to the economy.* ○ *Although the army knew that they were defending legality, they did not have the morale stimulus of winning battles which the rebels had.* **impetus** the energy or a driving force that prompts somebody to accomplish or undertake something ○ *In the early nineteenth century almost all the impetus for setting up schools came from the churches.* ○ *concerns that give fresh impetus to a growing environmentalist movement*

---

mo·tive·less /mṓtivləss/ *adj* having no reason for doing something or behaving in a particular way ○ *a motiveless crime*

mo·tive pow·er *n* **1.** the power or energy that drives a piece of machinery, or the source of that power or energy **2.** the driving force behind an action or activity

mo·tiv·ic /mō tívvik/ *adj* relating to a musical motif or motifs

mo·ti·vi·ty /mō tívvətee/ *n* the power to move or to make something move

mot juste /mṑ zhoost/ (*plural* **mots justes** /*pronunc. same*/) *n* exactly the right word or words to express something [< French]

mot·ley /móttlee/ *adj* (**-li·er, -li·est**) **1.** **MADE UP OF DIFFERENT TYPES** consisting of people or things that are very different from one another and do not seem to belong together **2.** **OF VARIED COLORS** made up of different colors ■ *n* (*plural* **-lies**) **1.** **JESTER'S COSTUME** the multicolored clothing worn by a medieval jester **2.** **VARIED GROUP** a group of people or things that are very different from one another and do not seem to belong together [14C. Origin ?]

mot·mot /mót mòt/ *n* a bird with a broad downward-curved beak, long tail, and usually greenish feathers with a black patch on the chest. Native to: Central and South America. Family: Momotidae. [Mid-19C. < American Spanish, an imitation of its call]

mo·to·cross /mṓtō kràwss/ *n* a motorcycle race, or the sport of racing motorcycles, over a rough course with steep hills, wet or muddy areas, and turns of varying difficulty [Mid-20C. < French < *moto* "motorcycle" + English CROSS-COUNTRY]

mo·to·neu·ron /mṓtə noo ròn/ *n* ANAT same as **motor neuron** [Early 20C. < MOTOR] —**mo·to·neu·ron·al** *adj*

mo·tor /mṓtər/ *n* **1.** **MACHINE THAT CREATES MOTION** a machine that converts energy into motion and can be used as a power source, e.g., to drive another machine or to move a vehicle **2.** AUTOMOT **ENGINE** the engine of a car or other self-powered vehicle **3.** *UK* **CAR** a vehicle, especially a car, powered by a motor (*slang*) ■ *adj* **1.** **OF VEHICLES** relating to vehicles, especially cars, powered by a motor **2.** **MOTOR-DRIVEN** powered by a motor **3.** **CAUSING MOTION** causing or producing motion **4.** PHYSIOL **OF MUSCLE ACTIVITY** relating to muscle activity, especially voluntary muscle activity, and the consequent body movements ■ *vi* (**-tored, -tor·ing, -tors**) **1.** **DRIVE IN CAR** to travel by car or another form of private vehicle, especially for pleasure (*formal*) **2.** *UK* **MOVE FAST** to move or progress at a fast pace (*informal*) [15C. < Latin, "mover" < *movere* "to move"]

mo·tor·bike /mṓtər bìk/ *n* **1.** a light motorcycle **2.** a bicycle powered by a small motor

mo·tor·boat /mṓtər bṓt/ *n* a small boat powered by an engine —**mo·tor·boat·er** *n* —**mo·tor·boat·ing** *n*

mo·tor·bus /mṓtər bùss/ *n* same as **bus** *n* (sense 1) (*dated*)

mo·tor·cade /mṓtər kàyd/ *n* a procession of cars or other vehicles, especially one forming an escort for somebody important [Early 20C. < MOTOR + CAVALCADE]

mo·tor·car /mṓtər kaar/ *n* AUTOMOT same as **car** (*dated or formal*)

mo·tor car·a·van *n* *UK* same as **motor home**

mo·tor cor·tex *n* the region of the outer surface of the brain (**cortex**) where nervous impulses controlling voluntary muscle activity are initiated. The motor cortex in the right hemisphere of the brain is responsible for controlling muscles in the left side of the body, and vice versa for the left hemisphere.

mo·tor court *n* TRAVEL same as **motel**

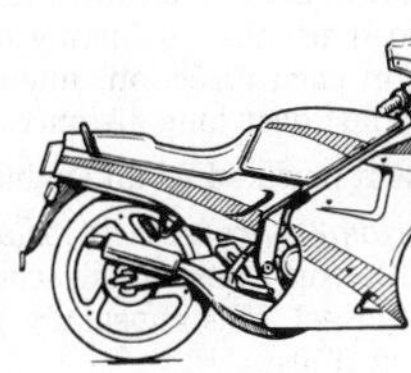

motorcycle

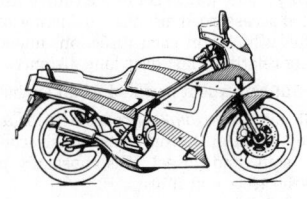

mo·tor·cy·cle /mṓtər sìk'l/ *n* a two-wheeled road vehicle powered by an engine ■ *vi* (**-cled, -cling, -cles**) to ride or travel on a motorcycle —**mo·tor·cy·clist** *n*

mo·tor drive *n* a motorized mechanism to advance film in a camera

mo·tor home *n* a motor vehicle that has facilities for cooking, living, and sleeping

mo·tor ho·tel *n* TRAVEL same as **motel**

mo·tor·ic /mō táwrik/ *adj* relating to voluntary muscle movement —**mo·tor·i·cal·ly** *adv*

mo·tor inn *n* TRAVEL same as **motel**

mo·tor·ist /mṓtərist/ *n* a driver of a motor vehicle, especially a car

mo·tor·ize /mṓtə rīz/ (**-ized, -iz·ing, -iz·es**) *vt* **1.** to fit something with a motor **2.** to provide troops with motor vehicles —**mo·tor·i·za·tion** /mṓtəri záysh'n/ *n*

mo·tor lodge *n* TRAVEL same as **motel**

mo·tor·man /mṓtərmən/ (*plural* **-men** /-mən/) *n* the driver of a streetcar, train locomotive, or subway train

mo·tor·mouth /mṓtər mòwth/ (*plural* **-mouths** /-mòwths, -mòwthz/) *n* somebody who talks too much or too fast (*informal insult*)

mo·tor neu·ron *n* a nerve cell (**neuron**) that conveys nerve impulses from the spinal cord or brainstem away from the central nervous system toward a muscle or gland

mo·tor neu·ron dis·ease *n* a progressive degenerative disease involving the motor neurons and causing weakness and wasting of the muscles

mo·tor pool *n* a number of motor vehicles kept by an organization for use as needed by its personnel

mo·tor pro·tein *n* any of a group of cell proteins that use chemical energy from ATP to create movement within cells, e.g., by separating chromosomes during cell division and transporting neurotransmitters inside nerve cells

mo·tor rac·ing *n Can, UK* the sport of racing in motor vehicles, especially in cars that are specially designed to travel at high speeds. US term **auto racing**

mo·tor rhythm *n* a rhythmic motif in a piece of music maintaining a constant pulse, usually at a fast tempo, for an extended period

mo·tor sail·er *n* a sailboat equipped with a motor

mo·tor scoot·er *n* a light motorcycle with small wheels, an enclosed engine, and a framework that includes a protective front plate and support for the rider's feet

mo·tor ship *n* a ship powered by an engine

mo·tor·sport /mṓtər spàwrt/ *n* a sport in which participants race motor vehicles, usually around a track

mo·tor tor·pe·do boat *n UK* NAVY same as **PT boat**

mo·tor u·nit *n* a motor neuron and the muscle fibers it acts on

mo·tor ve·hi·cle *n* a car, truck, or other road vehicle powered by an engine

mo·tor vo·ter *n* **1.** the National Voter Registration Act (1993), legislation that requires a state to allow citizens to register to vote when applying for or renewing a driver's license (*informal; hyphenated when used before a noun*) **2.** a citizen who registers to vote when applying for or renewing a driver's license

mo·tor·way /mṓtər wày/ *n UK* in the United Kingdom, a limited-access road usually consisting of three lanes for vehicles in each direction, intended for traveling relatively fast over long distances

mo·tor yacht *n* a yacht powered by an engine

Mo·town /mṓ tòwn/ *tdmk* a trademark for a music company based in Detroit whose music, consisting of pop, soul, and gospel, was especially popular during the 1960s and 1970s

Mott /mot/, **Lucretia** (1793–1880) US feminist and abolitionist. She ran the American Antislavery Society (1833) and the Seneca Falls women's rights convention (1848). Born **Mott, Lucretia Coffin**

> "In the marriage union, the independence of the husband and the wife will be equal, their dependence mutual, and their obligations reciprocal."
> [Lucretia Mott, "Discourse on Woman"; December 17, 1849]

motte /mot/ *n* a mound on which a castle was built [Late 19C. < French]

mot·tle /mótt'l/ *vt* (**-tled, -tling, -tles**) MARK SOMETHING WITH DIFFERENT COLORS to mark something with an irregular pattern of patches or spots of different colors ■ *n* **1.** IRREGULAR PATTERN OF COLORS an irregular pattern of patches or spots of different colors **2.** PATCH OF COLOR a patch or spot of color that forms part of an irregular pattern [Late 17C. Probably back-formation < MOTLEY]

mot·tled e·nam·el /mótt'ld-/ *n* tooth enamel that is mottled as a result of swallowing excessive amounts of fluoride at the age when teeth harden

mot·to /móttō/ (*plural* **-toes** or **-tos**) *n* **1.** RULE TO LIVE BY a short saying that expresses a rule to live by ○ *"I heartily accept the motto, 'That government is best which governs least'; and I should like to see it acted up to more rapidly and systematically."* (Henry David Thoreau, *Civil Disobedience*; 1849) **2.** HERALDRY SAYING ON COAT OF ARMS a short saying that forms part of a coat of arms and expresses something about the family or place whose coat of arms it is **3.** LITERAT QUOTATION AT BEGINNING OF WRITING a short quotation at the beginning of a piece of writing such as a book, a chapter of a book, or a poem, related in some way to its contents **4.** MUSIC same as **motif** (sense 4) [Late 16C. < Italian, probably < assumed Vulgar Latin, "word"]

Mo·tu /mṓ tòo/ (*plural same* or **-tus**) *n* **1.** a member of a Melanesian people of Papua New Guinea who live in the central province in and around Port Moresby **2.** the Austronesian language of the Motu. Native speakers: 14,000. [Late 19C. < Melanesian] —**Mo·tu** *adj*

mo·tu pro·pri·o /mṓtoo prṓpree ō/ (*plural* **mo·tu pro·pri·os**) *n* a decree issued by a pope acting independently and on his own initiative [< Latin, "on your own initiative"]

moue /moo/ *n* a look of discontent in which the lips are pressed together and forward [Mid-19C. < French]

mou·flon /mo͝o flòn/ *n* a reddish brown wild sheep with prominent curved horns. Native to: Sardinia, Corsica. Latin name: *Ovis musimon.* [Late 18C. Via French < Italian *muflone*]

mouil·lé /moo yáy/ *adj* describes a consonant pronounced with the tongue touching the palate [Mid-19C. < French, past participle of *mouiller* "wet, moisten"]

mou·lage /moo láazh/ *n* **1.** the process of making a mold or cast of something such as a footprint in the course of a criminal investigation **2.** a mold or cast made in the course of a criminal investigation [Early 20C. < French, "molding, molded copy" < Old French *mouler* "to mold"]

mould *n, vti* INDUST, FUNGI Can, UK spelling of **mold**

moul·der *vti, n* Can, UK spelling of **molder**

mould·ing *n* CONSTR Can, UK spelling of **molding**

mould·y *adj* Can, UK spelling of **moldy**

moules ma·ri·nières /mo͝ol marə nyér/ *npl* a dish of mussels cooked and served in their shells with a wine sauce [< French]

mou·lin /moo láN/ *n* an almost vertical shaft in a glacier, created by meltwater and debris boring into a crack in the surface of the ice [Mid-19C. Via French, "mill" < late Latin *molinum*]

moult *vti, n* ZOOL Can, UK spelling of **molt**

moul·vi *n* ISLAM same as **maulvi**

mound /mownd/ *n* **1.** SMALL HILL a small rounded hill **2.** CONSTRUCTED PILE OF SOMETHING a pile of earth, stones, or other material built up for some purpose, e.g., to provide shelter, defense, or concealment **3.** PILE OF OBJECTS a messy heap or pile of objects ○ *a mound of dirty laundry on the floor* **4.** LARGE AMOUNT a large amount of something ○ *a mound of mashed potato* **5.** BASEBALL BASEBALL PITCHER'S PLACE the slightly raised spot on a baseball diamond where the pitcher plays ■ *vt* (**mound·ed, mound·ing, mounds**) MAKE SOMETHING INTO MOUND to form something into a mound [Early 16C. Origin ?]

mound·bird /mównd bùrd/ *n* BIRDS same as **megapode** [Mid-19C. < its custom of depositing its eggs in a mound]

Mound Build·er *n* a member of an early Native North American people who built burial mounds and earthwork fortifications in what is now the Midwest and Southeast of the United States

mound-build·er *n* BIRDS same as **megapode** [See MOUNDBIRD]

mount[1] /mownt/ *v* (**mount·ed, mount·ing, mounts**) **1.** *vti* CLIMB SOMETHING to climb up something such as stairs or a hill **2.** *vti* GET ONTO SOMETHING FOR RIDE to get onto an animal or a form of transportation such as a bicycle **3.** *vt* PUT SOMEBODY ON FORM OF TRANSPORTATION to put somebody onto an animal or a form of transportation such as a bicycle **4.** *vt* GET ONTO SOMETHING HIGHER to get up onto a platform or other raised position **5.** *vi* GO UP INTO AIR to move upward into the air **6.** *vt* BEGIN COURSE OF ACTION to put into operation a course of action such as a campaign, rescue, or attack **7.** *vt* ORGANIZE ARTS PRODUCTION to organize something such as an exhibition or a production of a play **8.** *vi* INCREASE to become greater, stronger, or more intense ○ *Tension was mounting.* **9.** *vt* SECURE SOMETHING TO SOMETHING ELSE to attach something securely to something else, e.g., a picture into a frame, a specimen onto a slide, a stamp into an album, or an exhibit onto a stand or support **10.** *vt* PUT SOMETHING SOMEWHERE FOR USE to put something onto a support or into a position so that it is ready for use ○ *mount a camera* **11.** *vt* CLIMB ONTO ANIMAL TO COPULATE to climb onto a female animal in order to copulate (*technical; refers to male animals*) ■ *n* **1.** SOMETHING FOR FIXING SOMETHING IN PLACE something on which or with which something else can be mounted, e.g., a stand, support, frame, or backing **2.** ANIMAL FOR RIDING an animal used for riding, e.g., a horse **3.** STAMPS SOMETHING FOR MOUNTING STAMP an envelope or card on which to mount a stamp [13C. < Old French *monter* "go up" < Latin *mont-* "mountain"] —**mount·a·ble** *adj* —**mount·er** *n*

mount[2] /mownt/ *n* GEOG same as **mountain** (sense 1) (*archaic or literary; often used in place names*) [Pre-12C. Via French < Latin *mont-* "mountain"]

moun·tain /mównt'n/ *n* **1.** HIGH POINT OF LAND a high and often rocky area of a land mass with steep or sloping sides ○ *a plateau surrounded by mountains.* See table on next page **2.** LARGE PILE a large pile or heap of something ○ *a mountain of books* **3.** LARGE AMOUNT a large amount of something (*informal; often used in the plural*) ○ *a mountain of work* **4.** SURPLUS a large surplus of a particular commodity (*informal; usually used in combination*) ○ *a butter mountain* [13C. < Old French *montaigne* < Latin *mont-, mons*] ◇ **make a mountain out of a molehill** to treat something that is not important as if it were

moun·tain ash *n* a tree or bush with compound leaves and red or orange berries. Flowers: small, white, in clusters. Native to: northern hemisphere. Genus: *Sorbus.*

moun·tain av·ens *n* a small trailing plant of the rose family. Flowers: white. Native to: temperate mountainous and Arctic areas. Latin name: *Dryas octopetala.*

moun·tain bea·ver *n* a large thick-set rodent that lives in colonies made up of extensive burrows. Native to: northwestern North America. Latin name: *Aplodontia rufa.*

moun·tain bike *n* a bicycle built for rough terrain with wide fat tires, straight handlebars, a strong frame, and more gears than a standard bicycle

moun·tain blue·bird *n* a bird with a bright blue head, back, and wings and a pale blue breast. Native to: western North America. Latin name: *Sialia currocoides.*

moun·tain·board·ing *n* the sport of traveling down hillsides on a board similar to a skateboard but with bigger wheels

moun·tain cat *n regional* VERTEB same as **mountain lion**

REGIONAL NOTE See *mountain lion.*

moun·tain chain *n* a range of mountains or a string of adjacent mountain peaks

moun·tain cran·ber·ry *n* PLANTS same as **cowberry**

moun·tain dew *n* BEVERAGES same as **moonshine** (sense 1) (*informal*)

moun·tain·eer /mòwnt'n éer/ *n* **1.** MOUNTAIN CLIMBER somebody who climbs mountains for sport **2.** MOUNTAIN INHABITANT somebody who lives in a mountainous area ■ *vi* (**-eered, -eer·ing, -eers**) CLIMB MOUNTAINS to climb mountains for sport

moun·tain·eer·ing /mòwnt'n éering/ *n* the sport or pastime of climbing mountains

moun·tain goat *n* a large white wild goat with a woolly coat. Native to: North America, above the timberline in mountains from Alaska to Colorado. Latin name: *Oreamnus americanus.*

WORLD'S HIGHEST MOUNTAINS

World order (all in Asia)

1	Everest	*Himalayas*
	Height	[29,035 ft/8,850 m]
2	K2	*Himalayas*
	Height	[28,251 ft/8,611 m]
3	Kanchenjunga	*Himalayas*
	Height	[28,209 ft/8,598 m]
4	Lhotse	*Himalayas*
	Height	[27,940 ft/8,516 m]
5	Makalu	*Himalayas*
	Height	[27,824 ft/8,481 m]
6	Cho Oyu	*Himalayas*
	Height	[26,906 ft/8,201 m]
7	Dhaulagiri	*Himalayas*
	Height	[26,811 ft/8,172 m]
8	Manaslu	*Himalayas*
	Height	[26,781 ft/8,163 m]
9	Nanga Parbat	*Himalayas*
	Height	[26,657 ft/8,125 m]
10	Annapurna	*Himalayas*
	Height	[26,545 ft/8,091 m]

Highest in other continents

Europe		
1	Mont Blanc	
	Location	*Alps, France-Italy*
	Height	[15,771 ft/4,807 m]
Africa		
1	Kilimanjaro	
	Location	*Kibo Peak, Tanzania*
	Height	[19,340 ft/5,895 m]
North America		
1	McKinley (Denali)	
	Location	*Alaska Range, United States*
	Height	[20,320 ft/6,194 m]
South America		
1	Aconcagua	
	Location	*Andes, Argentina-Chile*
	Height	[22,834 ft/6,960 m]
Oceania/Australasia		
1	Puncak Jaya	
	Location	*Sudirman Range, Indonesia*
	Height	[16,502 ft/5,030 m]

moun·tain lau·rel *n* an evergreen bush with shiny poisonous leaves. Flowers: pink or white, darker stamens. Native to: eastern North America. Latin name: *Kalmia latifolia*.

moun·tain li·on *n US regional, Can* a large wild cat with a light tan coat. Native to: mountains of the western hemisphere. Latin name: *Felis concolor*.

REGIONAL NOTE The ***mountain lion*** goes by many other names, including *California cat, mountain cat,* and *mountain panther.* With scattered instances in the East, especially New York, Pennsylvania, and Georgia, ***mountain lion*** is found most frequently in the Rocky Mountain and Pacific states.

moun·tain man *n* a man who leads a solitary life in the mountains, especially an early North American pioneer

moun·tain·ous /mównt'nəss/ *adj* **1.** characterized by many mountains **2.** very large or tall ○ *The ship was battered by mountainous waves.*

moun·tain pan·ther *n regional* VERTEB same as **mountain lion**

REGIONAL NOTE See ***mountain lion.***

moun·tain range *n* a series of adjacent or interconnected mountains forming a distinct group and usually dating from the same geologic period

moun·tain res·cue *n* an organization of experienced climbers who go to the aid of people who get into difficulties in a mountainous place

moun·tain sheep *n* a wild sheep that lives in mountainous areas, e.g., the bighorn

moun·tain sick·ness *n* MED same as **altitude sickness**

moun·tain·side /mównt'n sīd/ *n* the sloping side of a mountain

Moun·tain Stan·dard Time, Moun·tain Time *n* the standard time in the time zone centered on 105° W longitude, which includes the Rocky Mountain region of North America. It is seven hours behind Universal Time.

Moun·tain State *n* a nickname for West Virginia

moun·tain·top /mównt'n tòp/ *n* the summit of a mountain

moun·tain·y /mównt'nee/ *adj* having many mountains, or forming part of a mountainous area

Mount As·pi·ring Na·tion·al Park /mòwnt ə spíring-/ national park in the southwestern part of the South Island, New Zealand. Area: 1,109 sq. mi./2,873 sq. km.

Mount·bat·ten /mownt bátt'n/, **Louis, 1st Earl Mountbatten of Burma** (1900–79) British naval commander and diplomat. After service in World War II as supreme allied commander in Southeast Asia (1943–46), he became the last viceroy of India (1947–48). He was killed by an IRA bomb.

Mount Des·ert Is·land island in the Atlantic Ocean off southeastern Maine. Approximately half of the island is occupied by Acadia National Park. Area: 110 sq. mi./285 sq. km.

moun·te·bank /mówntə bàngk/ *n* (*literary*) **1.** somebody who deceives other people **2.** formerly, somebody who sold ineffective medicines in public places [Late 16C. < Italian *montambanco* < *monta in banco* (command) "get up onto the bench"; from the quacks' practice of selling goods from a platform] —**moun·te·bank·er·y** *n*

mount·ed /mówntəd/ *adj* **1.** riding on a horse ○ *mounted police* **2.** fixed onto something for use or display

Mount Gam·bi·er /-gámbee ər/ town in southeastern South Australia, built on the slopes of an extinct volcano. Population: 21,156 (1991).

Mount·ie /mówntee/, **Mount·y** (*plural* **-ies**) *n* a member of the Royal Canadian Mounted Police (*informal*) [Early 20C. < MOUNTED]

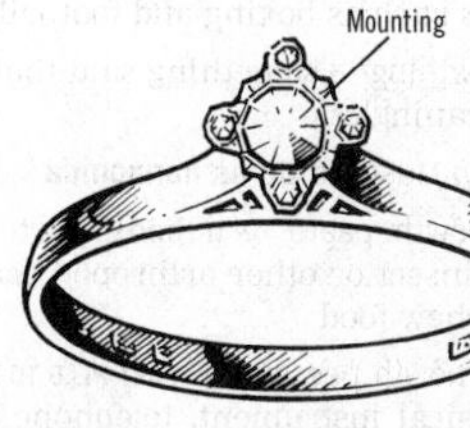

mounting

mount·ing /mównting/ *n* a support onto which something is fixed ■ *adj* becoming greater in size, number, or intensity ○ *We listened to the news with mounting alarm.*

Mount I·sa /-ízə/ city in western Queensland, Australia. Population: 20,785 (2002 estimate).

Mount Loft·y Rang·es /-lòftee-/ range of hills in South Australia, situated east of Adelaide. It forms part of the Flinders Range. Length: 200 mi./320 km.

Mount of Ol·ives /-óllivz/ ridge in central Israel, east of Jerusalem, with many biblical associations. It is separated from Jerusalem by the Valley of Kidron. Height: 2,737 ft./834 m.

Mount Rai·nier Na·tion·al Park /-rə néer-/ national park in western Washington, established in 1899 and centered around Mount Rainier and its glacier system. Area: 368 sq. mi./953 sq. km.

Mount Rush·more ♦ **Rushmore, Mount**

Mount Rush·more State *n* a nickname for South Dakota

Mount Ver·non /-vúrnən/ **1.** estate of George Washington in northeastern Virginia, situated on the Potomac River, south of Washington, D.C. He lived there from 1752 until his death in 1799 **2.** city in southeastern New York, on the Bronx River. It is a northern suburb of New York City. Population: 68,615 (2002 estimate).

Mount·y *n* POLICE another spelling of **Mountie**

mourn /mawrn/ (**mourned, mourn·ing, mourns**) *v* **1.** *vti* EXPRESS SADNESS AT SOMEBODY'S DEATH to feel and show sadness because somebody has died ○ *mourning the loss of his father* **2.** *vti* WEAR MOURNING CLOTHES to wear mourning clothes or other things that indicate grief over the death of somebody **3.** *vt* EXPRESS SADNESS AT SOMETHING LOST to feel and show sadness because something has been lost or no longer exists ○ *She mourned the loss of her independence.* [Old English *murnan* < Indo-European, "remember"] —**mourn·er** *n*

mourn·ful /máwrnfəl/ *adj* **1.** expressing or feeling deep sadness ○ *a youth with a mournful face* **2.** causing or suggesting deep sadness ○ *a mournful anniversary* —**mourn·ful·ly** *adv* —**mourn·ful·ness** *n*

mourn·ing /máwrning/ *n* **1.** SHOW OF SADNESS AT SOMEBODY'S DEATH the feeling or showing of deep sadness following somebody's death ○ *was still in mourning over the death of her mother* **2.** CLOTHING FOR SOMEBODY WHO IS MOURNING clothing worn as a sign of sorrow following somebody's death, e.g., black clothes in Christian cultures ○ *wore mourning for a year* **3.** PERIOD OF SADNESS the period during which somebody's death is mourned ○ *The family observed a period of 40 days' mourning.* —**mourn·ing·ly** *adv*

CULTURAL NOTE ***Mourning Becomes Electra***, a play (1931) by Eugene O'Neill. This drama in thirteen acts, lasting six hours, is a somewhat Freudian reworking of the *Oresteia* trilogy by the Greek author Aeschylus. Set in New England during the Civil War (O'Neill's equivalent of the Trojan Wars), it portrays Lavinia Brant's attempts to avenge her mother's infidelity by turning the rest of the family against her.

mourn·ing band *n* a band of black cloth worn on the arm as a sign of mourning

mourn·ing cloak *n* a butterfly with purplish brown wings that are spotted and rimmed with bright yellow. Native to: Europe, North America. Latin name: *Nymphalis antiopa*.

mourn·ing dove *n* a common dove with grayish brown feathers, a long pointed tail, and a mournful call. Native to: North America. Latin name: *Zenaida macroura*.

mouse[1] /mowss/ *abbr* MIL minimum orbital unmanned satellite of the Earth

mouse[2] /mowss/ *n* (*plural* **mice** /mīss/) **1.** SMALL RODENT a small rodent that has a brown or grayish brown coat and a long, mostly hairless tail. Family: Muridae or Cricetidae. **2.** (*plural* **mous·es** or **mice**) COMPUTER CONTROLLING DEVICE a handheld input device with control buttons that is moved across a pad to control the movement of a cursor on a computer screen or is clicked to transmit instructions **3.** COWARD a timid or cowardly person (*insult*) **4.** BLACK EYE a dark swelling under the eye that is caused by a blow (*dated slang*) ■ *vi* (**moused, mous·ing, mous·es**) HUNT MICE to hunt for and kill mice (*refers to cats*) [Old English *mūs* < Indo-European]

SPELLCHECK See ***moose.***

mouse over *vt* to move the cursor over text or an image on a computer screen using the mouse ○ *Simply mouse over the image and watch it change.*

mouse but·ton *n* a push button, usually one of two or three, on a computer mouse that transmits instructions to the computer

mouse-col·ored *adj* of a dull nondescript brown or gray color

mouse deer *n* ZOOL same as **chevrotain** [< the animal's small size and its similarity to a deer]

mouse-ear *n* either of two plant species with small hairy leaves supposedly resembling the ears of mice. Latin name: *Cerastium vulgatum* or *Hieracium pilosella*.

mouse·o·ver /mówss ṑvər/ *n* a feature on a webpage, e.g., a pop-up menu or graphic image, that is activated when a user moves the cursor over a contact point on the page. The feature is designed to encourage the user to select it. (*informal*)

mouse pad, mouse mat *n* a small thin piece of material that provides a surface for a computer mouse to be moved on

mouse po·ta·to *n* somebody who spends an excessive amount of time sitting at a computer (*slang*) [Late 20C. After COUCH POTATO]

mous·er /mówssər/ *n* a domestic animal that catches mice, especially a cat

mouse·tail /mówss tàyl/ *n* a plant that has long flower spikes resembling tails. Native to: temperate regions. Genus: *Myosurus*.

mouse·trap /mówss tràp/ *n* a trap for catching and often killing mice ■ *vt* (**-trapped, -trap·ping, -traps**) to trap or ensnare somebody by clever deception

mous·ey *adj* another spelling of **mousy**

mous·ing /mówssing/ *n* a cord or bar across the opening of a hook to prevent its load from slipping

mous·sa·ka /moo saákə, mo͝ossə kaá/ *n* a Greek casserole with alternating layers of eggplant and ground meat in a tomato sauce, topped with a white sauce [Mid-20C. Via Turkish *musakka* < Arabic *musakkā*]

mousse /mooss/ *n* **1.** LIGHT FOOD a light rich dish consisting mostly of whipped cream, eggs, or gelatin that is sweetened to serve as a dessert, or flavored with vegetables, meat, or fish **2.** FOAMY HAIR PRODUCT a foamy substance used to set or style hair ■ *vt* (**moussed, mouss·ing, mouss·es**) STYLE HAIR WITH MOUSSE to apply mousse to hair in order to style it [Mid-19C. < French, "moss, foam" < Germanic]

SPELLCHECK See *moose*.

---

mousse·line /mooss leén/ *n* **1.** LOOSELY WOVEN FABRIC a loosely woven fine fabric, resembling muslin and made from natural or synthetic fibers **2.** GLASS delicate blown glass **3.** ASPIC an aspic with whipped cream as one of its ingredients **4.** COOK same as **mousseline sauce** [Late 17C. Via French < Italian *mussolina*, after *Mosul*, Iraq]

mousse·line de laine /mooss leén də láyn/ *n* a thin lightweight woolen fabric, often with a printed pattern [< French, literally "muslin of wool"]

mousse·line de soie /-də swaá/ *n* a thin plain-woven rayon or silk fabric [< French, literally "muslin of silk"]

mousse·line sauce *n* a hollandaise sauce to which whisked egg white or whipped cream has been added

mous·tache *n* HAIR Can, UK spelling of **mustache**

Mous·te·ri·an /moo steéree ən/ *n* a prehistoric culture of the Paleolithic period in Europe, North Africa, and southwestern Asia associated with the Neandertals and marked by the use of flint tools [Late 19C. < French *moustérien*, after *Le Moustier*, cave in SW France]

mous·y /mówssee/ (**-i·er, -i·est**), **mous·ey** *adj* **1.** DULL BROWN dull brown in color **2.** TIMID shy or uncommunicative, especially in a boring or irritating way **3.** FULL OF MICE overrun with mice **4.** RESEMBLING MOUSE having features that resemble a mouse, e.g., big front teeth or a pointed nose —**mous·i·ly** *adv* —**mous·i·ness** *n*

mouth *n* /mowth/ (*plural* **mouths** /mowthz/) **1.** FOOD AND VOICE ORGAN in people and animals, the opening in the head and its surrounding lips, gums, tongue, and teeth, through which food is taken in and through which sounds come out **2.** PART OF FACE the part of the mouth visible to others, including the lips and the opening between them ○ *She kissed him on the mouth.* **3.** SPEECH ORGAN the mouth regarded as the organ of speech ○ *You wouldn't believe some of the things that came out of his mouth.* **4.** WAY OF SPEAKING a way of using language that other people think is inappropriate or offensive ○ *a foul mouth* **5.** WATER JUNCTION the place where a stream or river enters a sea or lake **6.** OPENING IN THE GROUND an opening to a cave, tunnel, mineshaft, or volcano **7.** OPENING IN CONTAINER the opening of a container such as a jar, tube, or bottle **8.** OPENING BETWEEN PARTS OF TOOL the opening between the two sides of a device that can be closed to hold something, e.g., in a vice or clamp **9.** MUSIC OPENING IN PIPE the slit in the pipe of a pipe organ **10.** MUSIC OPENING IN FLUTE the hole in a flute that the player blows into **11.** RUDE ANSWERS impudent challenging speech in response to a question or order (*informal*) ○ *All I got from them was a lot of mouth.* **12.** GRIMACE a facial expression that shows displeasure, distaste, or sulkiness (*dated*) ○ *She made a mouth at him and quickly turned away.* ■ *vt* /mowth/ (**mouthed, mouth·ing, mouths**) **1.** SAY SOMETHING INSINCERELY to speak or say something in a loud, affected, or insincere way ○ *How can you get up there and mouth such clichés?* **2.** FORM WORDS SILENTLY to form words with the tongue and lips without making a sound, usually in order to avoid being heard or to pretend to speak or sing something ○ *She mouthed a warning to the girl opposite as the teacher entered the room.* **3.** MUMBLE SOMETHING to say something in an indistinct way **4.** PUT SOMETHING IN MOUTH to put and hold something in the mouth as babies and young animals do **5.** CARESS SOMETHING WITH MOUTH to touch or caress something with the mouth **6.** *UK* ACCUSTOM HORSE TO BIT AND BRIDLE to train a horse to get used to a bit and bridle [Old English *mūþ* < Indo-European, "to project"] ◇ **a mouth to feed** somebody who must be provided for, especially fed ◇ **be all mouth** to boast about doing something but never actually do it (*informal*) ◇ **down in the mouth** looking sad or gloomy (*informal*) ◇ **foam at the mouth** to produce foam from the mouth as a result of exertion, illness, or anger ◇ **give mouth to something** to express something in speech or writing (*formal*)

mouth off *vi* (*informal*) **1.** to reply rudely and impudently to somebody **2.** to express views loudly and forcefully in a way that annoys others

mouth·breed·er /mówth breédər/ *n* a freshwater fish that carries its eggs and young in its mouth. Genus: *Haplochromis* or *Tilapia*.

-mouthed *suffix* **1.** having a particular kind of mouth ○ *wide-mouthed* **2.** speaking in a particular way ○ *foul-mouthed*

mouth·ful /mówth fo͝ol/ (*plural* **-fuls**) *n* **1.** QUANTITY OF FOOD OR DRINK the amount of food or drink that can comfortably be held in the mouth at one time **2.** SMALL AMOUNT OF FOOD only a very little amount to eat ○ *You can't go all day on a mouthful of food like that.* **3.** HARD-TO-PRONOUNCE WORD OR PHRASE a word or phrase that is hard to pronounce because of its unfamiliar sound combinations ○ *Her last name's a mouthful!* ◇ **say a mouthful** to say something that is very meaningful or profound

mouth guard *n* a hard plastic cover that fits inside somebody's mouth over the teeth and gums, worn as protection from injury by people involved in contact sports such as boxing and football

mouth·ing /mówthing/ *n* something said that is hypocritical or meaningless

mouth or·gan *n* MUSIC same as **harmonica**

mouth·part /mówth paàrt/ *n* a body part near the mouth of an insect or other arthropod that it uses to gather or chew food

mouth·piece /mówth peèss/ *n* **1.** PART HELD TO MOUTH the part of a musical instrument, telephone, or other device that is held to or in the mouth **2.** CONDUIT FOR VIEWS a person or publication that expresses the views of an organization (*sometimes disapproving*) ○ *He is the mouthpiece for big business in this city.* **3.** LAWYER a criminal lawyer (*slang*) **4.** SPORTS same as **mouth guard**

mouth-to-mouth, mouth-to-mouth re·sus·ci·ta·tion *n* a method of reviving somebody who is not breathing in which the rescuer places his or her mouth over the mouth of the person not breathing and inflates the lungs with air

mouth ul·cer *n* a small white ulcer that appears in groups in the mouth and on the tongue as a result of the fungal condition thrush (*usually used in the plural*) Technical name **aphtha**

mouth·wash /mówth wàwsh/ *n* a medicated liquid that is gargled and swished in the mouth to cleanse it and to freshen the breath

mouth·wa·ter·ing /mówth wàwtəring/ *adj* stimulating the appetite by having a delicious smell or appearance —**mouth·wa·ter·ing·ly** *adv*

mouth·y /mówthee, mówthee/ (**-i·er, -i·est**) *adj* tending to talk rudely, loudly, or too much (*informal*) —**mouth·i·ness** *n*

mou·ton /mo͞o tòn/ *n* sheepskin processed to resemble a fur such as seal or beaver [Mid-20C. < French]

mov /moov/ *abbr* a file extension for a movie file. Full form **movie**

mov·a·ble /mo͞ovəb'l/, **move·a·ble** *adj* **1.** EASILY MOVED able to move or be moved easily **2.** CHANGING DATE FROM YEAR TO YEAR falling on a different date each year ○ *Easter is a movable holiday.* ■ *n* LAW PROPERTY something that can be easily moved from one place to another, especially personal property such as an item of furniture (*often used in the plural*) —**mov·a·bil·i·ty** /mo͞ovə bíllətee/ *n* —**mov·a·ble·ness** *n* —**mov·a·bly** *adv*

mov·a·ble feast *n* a religious festival that is not fixed but falls on a different day from year to year, as does Easter in the Christian calendar

move /moov/ *v* (**moved, mov·ing, moves**) **1.** *vti* CHANGE POSITION to change position or location, or change the position or location of something ○ *Something moved behind that tree.* **2.** *vti* CHANGE RESIDENCE, JOB, OR SCHOOL to change your place of residence, work, or study, or make somebody do this ○ *move to the other side of town* **3.** *vti* TAKE ACTION to take action, or make somebody act ○ *It's due next week so we need to move quickly.* **4.** *vti* CHANGE VIEW to change a view or opinion, or make somebody do this ○ *She has moved to a more moderate position.* **5.** *vti* IMPROVE to make progress, or cause something to make progress ○ *Finally things have started moving.* **6.** *vi* ASSOCIATE WITH GROUP to associate with a particular group ○ *She moves among the yachting set.* **7.** *vi* PROPOSE ACTION to propose formally that something should happen or be done ○ *I move that the meeting be adjourned.* **8.** *vt* PRODUCE EMOTIONAL REACTION IN SOMEBODY to make somebody feel something, especially tender feelings ○ *Her performance moved all of us.* **9.** *vti* TAKE TURN IN GAME to change the position of one of the pieces in a board game as a turn in play ○ *Did you move yet?* **10.** *vti* SELL WELL to sell well or effectively, or sell something well or effectively ○ *The souvenir mugs aren't really moving.* **11.** *vti* EMPTY BOWELS to empty the bowels ■ *n* **1.** ACT OF MOVING an act or instance of moving ○ *One false move and we're done for.* **2.** STEP IN SERIES an action considered as one of a series ○ *Keep your rivals guessing what your next move will be.* **3.** SOMEBODY'S TURN TO PLAY somebody's turn in a board game ○ *It's your move.* **4.** CHANGE OF LOCATION a change in your place of residence, work, or study ○ *I'm considering a move across town.* **5.** MANEUVER a maneuver or way of doing something ○ *If you're interested in martial arts, I could show you a few moves.* [13C. Via Anglo-Norman *mover* < Latin *movere*] ◇ **get a move on** to start doing something immediately, or do something faster (*informal; usually used as a command*) ◇ **make a move on somebody** to proposition somebody sexually (*slang*) ◇ **move it** to hurry, or do something quickly (*informal*) ◇ **on the move 1.** going from one place to another **2.** busy doing one thing after another **3.** going forward, or making progress

---

ORIGIN The Latin word *movere* "to move," from which *move* is derived, is also the source of English *commotion, emotion, mobile, moment, motif, motion, motive, motor, mutiny, promote,* and *remote.*

---

move in *v* **1.** *vti* to begin living or doing business in a place, or set somebody up in a place **2.** *vi* to approach closer to somebody or something, especially in order to make an attack ○ *move in for the kill*

move in on *vt* **1.** TRY TO CONTROL SOMEBODY OR SOMETHING to attempt to take control of somebody or something, or take over from somebody ○ *They're trying to move in on our station's share of prime time.* **2.** APPROACH SOMEBODY OR SOMETHING to approach closer to somebody or something, especially in order to make an attack ○ *The guards are moving in on the intruders.* **3.** INTRUDE ON SOMEBODY to intrude on somebody

move into *vt* **1.** to begin living or doing business in a particular place ○ *move into a new apartment* **2.** to begin dealing with something or doing business in a particular field ○ *The company is set to move into home banking.*

move on *vi* **1.** to leave a place and go somewhere else ○ *I think I'll be moving on.* **2.** to stop doing or dealing with something and start doing something else ○ *Let's move on to the next item on the agenda.*

move out *v* **1.** *vi* to leave a place of residence or business, or help somebody do this **2.** *vti* to withdraw from a place, or make somebody do this ○ *Tell the platoon to move out, on the double.*

move over *vti* to move to one side in order to make room, or make somebody do this ○ *If you move over I'll be able to sit down.*

move·a·ble *adj, n* another spelling of **movable**

move·ment /mo͞ovmənt/ *n* **1. ACT OF MOVING** an act of changing location or position ○ *an instrument to detect subtle movements* **2. WAY OF MOVING** the way in which somebody or something moves ○ *the awkward movement of an injured arm* **3.** PHYSIOL **ACT OF EMPTYING BOWELS** an act of emptying the bowels, or the matter emptied **4.** POL **EFFORT BY MANY TO ACHIEVE SOMETHING** a collective effort by a large group of people to try to achieve something, especially a political or social reform ○ *the civil rights movement* **5.** POL **PEOPLE ORGANIZED TO EFFECT CHANGE** a large group of people who make a collective effort to achieve something, especially a political or social reform **6.** MUSIC **SECTION OF MUSICAL WORK** one of several self-contained sections that make up a large-scale musical work, usually differentiated from one another in tempo and character ○ *the concerto's third movement* **7.** MECH ENG **MOVING PARTS** the parts of a clock or watch mechanism that drive and regulate it **8.** FIN **CHANGE IN PRICE** a change in the prices of traded securities ○ *upward movement before the close of trading* **9.** LITERAT **PLOT DEVELOPMENT** the way in which a literary work develops as it progresses ○ *no movement in the plot for three chapters* **10.** LITERAT **RHYTHM** the cadence or rhythm of a piece of poetry **11.** ARTS **SUGGESTED MOTION** the illusion or suggestion of motion in a work of art such as a sculpture or painting **12.** MIL **TACTICAL CHANGE OF POSITION** a tactical change in the position or location of a military unit ■ **move·ments** *npl* **ACTIVITIES AND LOCATION** the things that somebody does and the places to which he or she goes, noted over a period of time ○ *The accused was asked to describe his movements on the day in question.*

mov·er /mo͞ovər/ *n* **1. SOMEBODY OR SOMETHING THAT CAUSES MOTION** somebody or something that causes movement or accomplishes something ○ *She's the mover behind the project.* **2. SOMEBODY IN PARTICULAR SOCIAL CIRCLE** an associate of a particular social group ○ *a mover in high places* **3. SOMEBODY PROPOSING MOTION** somebody who formally proposes something at a meeting ○ *Does the mover of the motion consent to the amendment?* **4. MOVING COMPANY** a company or person whose work is to transport the personal property of householders or businesses from one location to another

mov·ers and shak·ers *npl* people in society or in a particular sphere of activity who are powerful or influential ○ *one of the industry's movers and shakers*

mov·ie /mo͞ovee/ *n* **1. SERIES OF MOVING PICTURES** a series of real or fictional events recorded by a camera and projected onto a screen as a sequence of moving pictures, usually with an accompanying soundtrack **2.** COMPUT full form of **mov** ■ **mov·ies** *npl* **1. MOTION PICTURE INDUSTRY** the motion picture industry, considered as a whole **2. MOVIE SHOWING** the showing of a movie in a theater ○ *We went to the movies last night.* [Early 20C. Shortening of *moving picture*]

mov·ie cam·er·a *n* a camera that records live action on film

mov·ie film *n* film for use in a movie camera

mov·ie·go·er /mo͞ovee gō ər/ *n* somebody who goes to a theater to see movies

mov·ie house *n* MOVIES same as **movie theater**

mov·ie·mak·er /mo͞ovee màykər/ *n* MOVIES same as **filmmaker** —**mov·ie·mak·ing** *n*

mov·ie star *n* an extremely popular motion-picture actor

mov·ie the·a·ter, mo·vie house *n US* a theater where movies are shown. Can spelling **movie theatre**

mov·ing /mo͞oving/ *adj* **1. AROUSING EMOTION** producing a deep emotional reaction, especially sadness or compassion ○ *After such a moving speech we were all in tears.* **2. MOVABLE** able to move ○ *moving parts* **3. IN MOTION** in a state of movement (*usually used in combination*) ○ *slow-moving* **4. CAUSED BY CHANGING PLACES** involved in or caused by a change of residence or business location **5. WHILE DRIVING** happening while a vehicle is being driven ○ *a moving violation*

SYNONYMS ***moving, pathetic, pitiful, poignant, touching, heartwarming, heartrending***

CORE MEANING: arousing emotion

moving producing a deep emotional reaction, especially sadness or compassion ○ *a very moving description of life for children in these orphanages* ○ *the deeply moving funeral of a long-standing friend who had died of AIDS* **pathetic** arousing feelings of compassion and pity, often centered on somebody who is vulnerable, helpless, or unfortunate ○ *Looking at her father, she saw a pathetic and solitary figure almost like a small boy.* ○ *There was a pathetic dignity about the old animal as she stood there, patient and undemanding.* **pitiful** arousing compassion and pity ○ *a picture of a pitiful starving kid* **poignant** causing a sharp sense of sadness, pity, or regret ○ *the opera's most poignant moment* ○ *The girl died just three days after our poignant pictures were taken.* **touching** causing feelings of warmth, sympathy, and tenderness ○ *He has been a tremendous support to me and my family in many small and touching ways.* **heartwarming** inspiring warm or kindly feelings, usually by showing life and human nature in a positive and reassuring light ○ *It is heartwarming that so many voters would like to see older members of society enjoying a better standard of living.* ○ *The former president recently found a heartwarming way to repay his childhood nanny – he helped build her a new house.* **heartrending** causing intense sadness or distress, especially in arousing sympathy with somebody else's unhappiness or hardship. ○ *heartrending handmade posters depicting victims who are still missing* ○ *These refugees often have heartrending stories to tell.*

mov·ing-coil *adj* describes an electromechanical device or instrument that has a conducting coil freely suspended in a magnetic field. Current in the coil causes it to move or movement produces current.

mov·ing·ly /mo͞ovinglee/ *adv* in a way that makes people feel deep emotions, especially sadness or compassion ○ *She spoke movingly about their plight.*

mov·ing pave·ment *n UK* TRANSP same as **moving sidewalk**

mov·ing pic·ture *n* MOVIES same as **movie** (*dated*)

mov·ing side·walk *n* an endless moving belt on a long, flat, or inclined surface on which pedestrians are carried forward, typically found in airports

mov·ing spir·it *n* somebody who works hard to help to achieve something or inspires others to do this ○ *She was one of the moving spirits behind the campaign.*

mov·ing van *n* a van that is used to transport somebody's furniture and personal effects from one house to another

mow[1] /mō/ (**mowed, mown** /mōn/ or **mowed, mow·ing, mows**) *v* **1.** *vti* to cut tall grass, hay, or grain with a scythe or machine **2.** *vt* to cut the grass, hay, or grain growing in a particular place ○ *Mow the front lawn today, please.* [Old English *māwan* < Germanic]

mow down *vt* **1. KILL MANY PEOPLE QUICKLY** to kill people quickly and in large numbers **2. KNOCK SOMEBODY DOWN** to knock somebody or something down by force **3. OVERWHELM SOMEBODY** to overwhelm somebody decisively

mow[2] /mō/ *n regional* **1.** the part of a barn where hay or grain is stored when it has been harvested **2.** a pile of hay or grain, especially in a barn [Old English *mūga*, origin ?]

Mow·at /mṓ ət, mów-/, **Sir Oliver** (1820–1903) Canadian politician. He was prime minister of Ontario (1872–96).

mow·er /mṓ ər/ *n* GARDENING same as **lawn mower**

mown AGRIC past participle of **mow**[1]

MOX /moks/ *n* a reactor fuel made from plutonium that has been separated from spent nuclear fuel by chemical reprocessing and mixed with natural or depleted uranium [Blend of MIXED + OXIDE]

mox·a /móksə/ *n* in Eastern medicine, a cone or cylinder of downy or wooly material derived from various plants that is burned on the skin for its counterirritant effect [Late 17C. < Japanese *mogusa* "burning herb"]

mox·i·bus·tion /mòksi búschən/ *n* in Eastern medicine, the practice of burning a cone or cylinder of downy or woolly material derived from various plants on the skin for its counterirritant effect [Mid-19C. Blend of MOXA + COMBUSTION]

mox·ie /móksee/ *n* courage combined with inventiveness (*slang*) [Mid-20C. After a brand of soft drink originally marketed as a "nerve tonic"]

Moy·ni·han /móynə hàn/, **Daniel Patrick** (1927–2003) US academic and politician. He was ambassador to India (1973–74) and had a long and distinguished career in the US Senate (1976–2001).

> "Somehow liberals have been unable to acquire from life what conservatives seem to be endowed with at birth: namely, a healthy skepticism of the powers of government agencies to do good."
> [Daniel Patrick Moynihan, *New York Post*; May 14, 1969]

Moz. *abbr* Mozambique

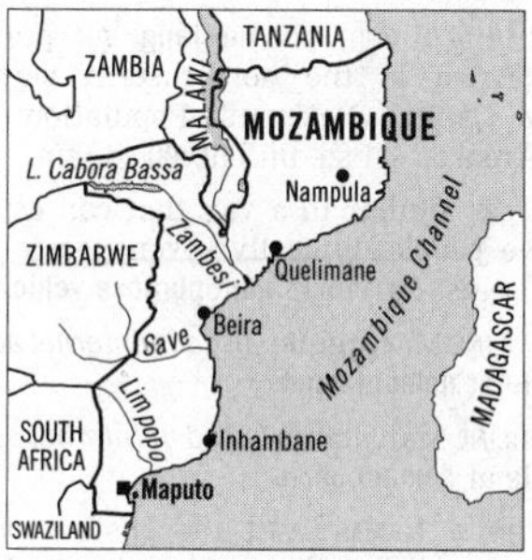

Mozambique

Mo·zam·bique /mōzəm be̅ek/ country in southeastern Africa. It became independent from Portugal in 1975 and joined the British Commonwealth in 1995. Language: Portuguese. Currency: metical. Capital: Maputo. Population: 17,479,266 (2003). Area: 308,642 sq. mi./799,380 sq. km. Official name **Republic of Mozambique** —**Mo·zam·bi·can** *n, adj*

Moz·ar·ab /mō zárrəb/ *n* in Moorish Spain, a Christian who adopted some Arab customs without converting to Islam [Early 17C. Via Spanish *mozárabe* < Arabic *musta'rib* "becoming an Arab"] —**Moz·ar·a·bic** *adj*

Mo·zart /mṓt saart/, **Wolfgang Amadeus** (1756–91) Austrian composer. A figure of key importance in Western music, his compositions, in almost every musical genre, epitomize the classical style. —**Mo·zar·ti·an** *n, adj*

> "Music must never offend the ear; it must please the hearer. In other words, it must never cease to be music."
> [Attributed to Wolfgang Amadeus Mozart]

mo·zet·ta *n* CHR another spelling of **mozzetta**

moz·za·rel·la /mòtsə réllə/ *n* a rubbery white unsalted Italian cheese used in salads, cooking, and especially on pizza [Early 20C. < Italian < *mozza*, type of cheese < *mozzare* "cut off"]

moz·zet·ta /mō zéttə, mōt séttə/, **mo·zet·ta** *n* a short hooded cape worn by the pope and other senior Roman Catholic clergymen [Late 18C. Via Italian < medieval Latin *almutia*]

mp *abbr* **1.** PHYS melting point **2.** MUSIC mezzo piano **3.** ONLINE Northern Mariana Islands (*used in Internet addresses*) See table at **domain name**

MP, M.P. *abbr* **1.** GOV Member of Parliament **2.** MIL military police **3.** LAW mounted police **4.** MAIL Northern Mariana Islands

m.p. *abbr* **1.** PHYS melting point **2.** MUSIC mezzo piano

mp3 /èm pee thrée/ *abbr* a file extension for an MP3 file. Full form **Motion Picture Experts Group, Audio Layer 3**

MP3 *n* a computer file standard for downloading compressed music from the Internet, playable on a multimedia computer with appropriate software. Full form **Motion Picture Experts Group, Audio Layer 3**

M.P.A. *abbr* EDUC **1.** Master of Professional Accounting **2.** Master of Public Accounting **3.** Master of Public Administration

MPD *abbr* PSYCHIAT multiple personality disorder

M.P.E. *abbr* EDUC Master of Public Education

mpeg /ém pèg/ *abbr* a file extension for an MPEG file. Full form **Moving Pictures Experts Group**

MPEG /ém pèg/ *n* **1.** a computer file standard for compressing, storing, and transmitting digital video and audio. Full form **Moving Pictures Experts Group 2.** a file containing digital video and audio in MPEG format

mpg[1], **m.p.g.** *abbr* MEASURE miles per gallon

mpg[2] *abbr* a file extension for an MPEG file. Full form **Moving Pictures (Experts) Group**

mph, **m.p.h.** *abbr* MEASURE miles per hour

MPH *abbr* EDUC Master of Public Health

M.Phil. /èm fíl/ *abbr* EDUC Master of Philosophy

MPP *abbr Can* GOV Member of the Provincial Parliament (of Ontario)

M·pu·ma·lang·a /əm po͝omə láng gə/ province in South Africa in the northeastern part of the country. Capital: Nelspruit. Population: 3,122,977 (2001). Area: 30,691 sq. mi./79,490 sq. km.

MPV *n* a car similar to a van that can carry more than five people, typically seven people in three rows of seats. Full form **multipurpose vehicle**

mq *abbr* ONLINE Martinique (*used in Internet addresses*) See table at **domain name**

mr *abbr* ONLINE Mauritania (*used in Internet addresses*) See table at **domain name**

Mr. /místər/ *n* **1.** MAN'S TITLE the customary title of courtesy used before the name of a man ○ *Mr. Smith* **2.** JOB OR FUNCTION TITLE a courtesy title used for a man before the name of his position or function ○ *Mr. President* **3.** DESCRIPTIVE TITLE a humorous title used for a man before a place, name, thing, or description that he is supposed to typify or represent ○ *He's not exactly Mr. Personality, is he?* **4.** JUNIOR OFFICER'S TITLE a title used to address a junior naval officer, a warrant officer, or a cadet in a service academy [15C. Contraction of MASTER]

MRAM *abbr* COMPUT magnetic random access memory

Mr. Big *n* a powerful or important man, e.g., the chief of a criminal organization (*slang*)

MRBM *abbr* MIL medium-range ballistic missile

MRCA *abbr* MIL multirole combat aircraft

Mr. Clean *n* somebody, especially a public figure, who is seen as being admirably honest and moral (*informal*) [Mid-20C. After a cleaning solution trademark]

MRE *abbr* MIL meal, ready to eat

MRI *abbr* MED magnetic resonance imaging

mri·dan·ga /mri dúng gə/, **mri·dang** /mri dúng/, **mri·dan·gam** /-gəm/ *n* a South Asian drum that is shaped like a barrel and used as an accompaniment in Karnatak music [Late 19C. < Tamil]

MRI scan·ner *n* a scanner that uses magnetic resonance imaging to obtain high-contrast detailed images in any plane of the tissues of the body

mRNA *abbr* GENETICS messenger RNA

Mr. Right *n* a man seen as being a perfect romantic or marriage partner for a specific woman (*informal*) ○ *One day Mr. Right will come along.*

Mrs. /míssiz/ *n* **1.** a customary title of courtesy for a married or widowed woman, used before her name or the name of her husband ○ *Mrs. Wright* **2.** a title used for a woman before a place name, thing, or description that she is supposed to typify or represent ○ *Mrs. Cheerful* [Early 17C. Contraction of MISTRESS]

MRSA *n* a strain of a common infection-causing bacterium that has become resistant to treatment by the antibiotic methicillin and is therefore a hazard in places such as hospitals. Full form **methicillin-resistant staphylococcus aureus**

Mrs. Grun·dy /-grúndee/ *n* an extremely conventional or rigid person, especially somebody who is prescriptive about grammatical rules [Late 18C. After a character in the play *Speed the Plough*, by Thomas Morton (1764–1838)]

ms *abbr* **1.** MEASURE millisecond **2.** ONLINE Montserrat (*used in Internet addresses*) See table at **domain name**

MS[1] *abbr* **1.** MAIL mail steamer **2.** EDUC Master of Surgery **3.** Mississippi **4.** TRANSP motor ship **5.** MED multiple sclerosis

MS[2] *abbr* sacred to the memory of (*on gravestones*) [Latin *memoriae sacrum*]

Ms. /miz/ *n* **1.** a customary title of courtesy used before the name or names of a woman without making a distinction between married and unmarried status ○ *Ms. Bennett* **2.** a title used for a woman before a place, name, thing, or description that she is supposed to typify or represent ○ *Ms. Efficiency* [Mid-20C. Blend of MISS + MRS.]

MS., **ms.** *abbr* ARTS manuscript

M.S. *abbr* EDUC Master of Science [< Latin *Magister Scientiae*]

MSB *abbr* ONLINE most significant bit (*used in e-mails or text messages*)

MSBP *abbr* MED Münchausen syndrome by proxy

M.Sc. *abbr* EDUC Master of Science [Latin *Magister Scientiae*]

MS-DOS /èm ess dáwss, -dóss/ *tdmk* a trademark for a widely used computer operating system

msec *abbr* MEASURE millisecond

Mses. plural of **Ms.**

MSG *abbr* CHEM monosodium glutamate

msg. *abbr* message

Msgr. *abbr* RELIG **1.** Monseigneur **2.** Monsignor

MSGT, **M.Sgt.** *abbr* MIL Master Sergeant

MSH *abbr* BIOCHEM melanocyte-stimulating hormone

MSI *abbr* ELECTRONICS medium scale integration

M.S.L., **m.s.l.** *abbr* GEOG mean sea level

M.S.N. *abbr* EDUC Master of Science in Nursing

Ms. Right *n* a woman seen as being the perfect romantic or marriage partner for a specific man ○ *tired of waiting for Ms. Right to come along*

MSS., **mss.** *abbr* ARTS manuscripts

MST *abbr* TIME Mountain Standard Time

MSTS *abbr* NAVY Military Sea Transportation Service

M.S.W. *abbr* EDUC Master in Social Work

mt *abbr* **1.** ONLINE Malta (*used in Internet addresses*) See table at **domain name 2.** GEOG mount **3.** GEOG mountain

Mt *symbol* CHEM ELEM meitnerium

MT *abbr* **1.** COMPUT machine translation **2.** MIL, MEASURE megaton **3.** MEASURE metric ton **4.** Montana **5.** TIME Mountain Time

mt. *abbr* **1.** MIL, MEASURE megaton **2.** GEOG mount **3.** GEOG mountain

Mt. *abbr* GEOG **1.** Mount **2.** Mountain

M·ta·ra·zi Falls /əm taa raazee-/ falls in Zimbabwe, southeastern Africa, one of the highest in the world. Height: 2,500 ft./762 m.

MTBE *n* a lead-free antiknock gasoline additive. Full form **methyl tertiary-butyl ethyl**

MTBF *abbr* COMPUT mean time between failures

M.Tech. /èm ték/ *abbr* EDUC Master of Technology

mtg. *abbr* **1.** meeting **2. mtge.** FIN mortgage

mtn., **Mtn.** *abbr* mountain

Mt. Rev. *abbr* RELIG Most Reverend

mts., **Mts.** *abbr* **1.** mountains **2.** mounts

MTTR *abbr* MANUF mean time to repair

mu[1] /myoo, moo/ *n* the 12th letter of the Greek alphabet, represented in the English alphabet as "m." See table at **alphabet** [Late 19C. < Greek]

mu[2] *abbr* ONLINE Mauritius (*used in Internet addresses*) See table at **domain name**

MU *abbr* ONLINE multiuser

muah muah *n* another spelling of **mwah mwah**

Mu'aw·i·ya /moo aávee yə/ (*d.* A.D. 680) leader of the Umayyad clan who became the first Umayyad caliph following civil war with Ali

Mu·bar·ak /mo͝o baárək, moo-/, **Hosni** (*b.* 1928) Egyptian president. He became president after the assassination of Anwar Sadat in 1981 and continued Sadat's foreign policy of peace with Israel while mending strained relations with the Arab League. Full name **Mubarak, Muhammad Hosni Said**

muc- *prefix* same as **muco-** (*used before vowels*)

much /much/ *adv* **1.** LARGELY to a great extent, intensity, or degree (*often used in combination*) ○ *She hasn't changed much over the years.* ○ *It's a much more difficult game than the other.* ○ *a much-loved figure in American political life* **2.** OFTEN often or frequently ○ *I don't get out much these days.* ○ *Do you see your children much over the holidays?* **3.** NEARLY nearly or practically ○ *One day is much like the next when you're ill.* ○ *It's much the same problem all over again.* ■ *adj, pron* LARGE AMOUNT a large amount or degree ○ (adj) *He doesn't have much free time because of the demands of work.* ○ (pron) *Much remains to be done.* ○ (pron) *She does much of her writing at home.* ■ *pron* IMPRESSIVE something impressive, important, or unusual ○ *The house isn't much to look at, but it's very comfortable.* [13C. Shortening of Old English *mycel* < Germanic] ◇ **as much** precisely that ○ *I wasn't surprised when she said she'd taken the money, as I'd suspected as much from the start.* ◇ **(as) much as** although, or even though ○ *As much as I'd like to join you, I'm afraid I can't.* ◇ **much as** to almost the same degree, or in a similar manner ○ *You cook it much as you would a potato.* ◇ **not much of a** not particularly good at something, or not a very good example of something ○ *It wasn't much of a celebration, was it?*

mu·cha·cha /moo chaa chaa/ *n* a girl (*often used as a term of address; offensive in some contexts*) [Late 19C. < Spanish, feminine of MUCHACHO]

mu·cha·cho /moo chaa chō/ (*plural* **-chos**) *n* a boy (*often used as a term of address; offensive in some contexts*) [Late 16C. < Spanish]

much·ness /múchnəss/ *n* greatness in quantity, extent, or degree (*archaic*) ◇ **much of a muchness** amounting to or being practically the same (*informal*)

muci- *prefix* same as **muco-**

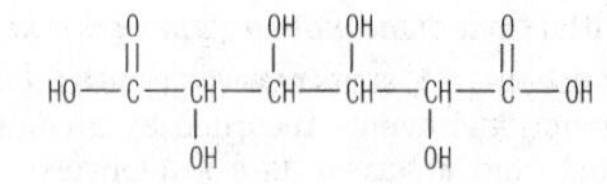

mucic acid

mu·cic ac·id /myo͞ossik-/ *n* a colorless crystalline solid. Source: lactose. Use: manufacture of chemicals. Formula: $C_4H_4(OH)_4(COOH)_2$.

mu·cif·er·ous /myoo síffərəss/ *adj* producing or containing a lot of mucus

mu·ci·gen /myo͞ossəjən/ *n* a substance in mucous cells that is converted into mucin

mu·ci·lage /myo͞ossəlij/ *n* **1.** a thick water-based solution used as an adhesive **2.** a gummy substance secreted by some plants such as seaweed that contains protein and carbohydrates [14C. Via French < late Latin *mucillago* "moldy juice" < Latin *mucus*]

mu·ci·lag·i·nous /myòossə lájjənəss/ *adj* **1.** relating to or producing mucilage **2.** moist and sticky like glue —**mu·ci·lag·i·nous·ly** *adv* —**mu·ci·lag·i·nous·ness** *n*

mu·cin /myóossin/ *n* a complex protein present in mucus —**mu·cin·ous** *adj*

muck /muk/ *n* **1.** STICKY DIRT soft moist dirt or filth (*informal*) **2.** *UK* RUBBISH something that is distasteful, disgusting, or of very poor quality (*informal*) ○ *don't know how they can publish such muck* **3.** AGRIC MANURE moist manure or compost, especially when used to fertilize land **4.** MIN EXTRACT MINE WASTE waste material from mining, e.g., earth or rubble ■ *vt* (**mucked, muck·ing, mucks**) **1.** CLEAN OUT PLACE to clean the muck out of a place such as a stable or barn **2.** MAKE SOMETHING DIRTY to pollute something or make something dirty (*informal*) **3.** AGRIC FERTILIZE LAND to fertilize land with manure or compost [13C. < N Germanic < Germanic, "soft"]

muck around *vi UK* to waste time instead of doing something useful or important (*informal*) ○ *We'd get this job finished sooner if you two stopped mucking around.*

muck up *vt* to ruin or make a mess of something (*informal*) ○ *She's really mucked up her chances now.*

muck·a·muck /múkə mùk/ *n* same as **high-muck-a-muck** (*informal*) [Early 20C. Shortening]

muck·er /múkər/ *n* somebody whose job is to remove rocky mine waste

muck·luck *n* CLOTHING another spelling of **mukluk**

muck·rake /múk ràyk/ *vi* (**-raked, -rak·ing, -rakes**) to seek out and publicize misconduct by prominent people ■ *n* a rake used to spread manure or compost —**muck·rak·er** *n* —**muck·rak·ing** *n*

muck·worm /múk wùrm/ *n* an insect larva that lives in mud or manure

muck·y /múkee/ (**-ier, -i·est**) *adj* very dirty or covered with muck (*informal*) —**muck·i·ly** *adv* —**muck·i·ness** *n*

muco- *prefix* mucus, mucous membrane ○ *mucocutaneous* [< Latin *mucus*]

mu·co·cu·ta·ne·ous /myòokō kyoo táynee əss/ *adj* involving both skin and mucous membrane

mu·co·lyt·ic /myòokə líttik/ *adj* able to break down mucus

mu·co·pep·tide /myòokō pép tīd/ *n* BIOCHEM same as **peptidoglycan**

mu·co·pol·y·sac·cha·ride /myòokō pòllee sákə rīd/ *n* a complex polysaccharide containing amino groups, found in connective tissues

mu·co·pro·tein /myòokō prṓ teen/ *n* a complex protein found in mucous secretions

mu·co·pu·ru·lent /myòokō pyóorələnt/ *adj* containing both mucus and pus

mu·co·sa /myoo kṓssə/ (*plural* **-sae** /-see/) *n* ANAT same as **mucous membrane** [Late 19C. < modern Latin *(membrana) mucosa* "mucous membrane"]

mu·cous /myóokəss/ *adj* containing, secreting, resembling, or covered with mucus [Mid-17C. < Latin *mucosus* < *mucus* "mucus"]

mu·cous mem·brane *n* a moist lining in the body passages of mammals that contains mucus-secreting cells and is open directly or indirectly to the external environment

mu·co·vis·ci·do·sis /myòokō vissi dṓssiss/ *n* MED same as **cystic fibrosis**

mu·cro /myóo krṑ/ (*plural* **-cros**) *n* a sharp point projecting from an organ or plant part [Mid-17C. < Latin, "sharp point, sword"]

mu·cro·nate /myóokrə nàyt/, **mu·cro·nat·ed** /-nàytəd/ *adj* used to describe an organ or plant part that ends in a sharp point [Late 18C. < Latin *mucronatus* < *mucron-*, stem of *mucro* "sharp point, sword"] —**mu·cro·na·tion** /myòokrə náysh'n/ *n*

mu·cus /myóokəss/ *n* the clear slimy lubricating substance consisting mostly of mucins and water that coats and protects mucous membranes [Mid-17C. < Latin] —**mu·coid** /myóo kòyd/ *adj*

mud /mud/ *n* **1.** dirt that is very wet, soft, and gummy **2.** defamatory things said or written about somebody (*informal*) [14C. Probably < Middle Low German *mudde*] ◇ **(as) clear as mud** not clear or understandable at all (*informal*) ◇ **here's mud in your eye!** used as a drinking toast (*informal*) ◇ **sling** *or* **throw mud at somebody** *or* **something** to make defamatory statements about somebody *or* something (*informal*)

MUD /mud/ *n* a virtual online space in which several participants can contribute to a communal project such as a collaboratively written story or a game for several players. Full form **multiuser domain**

mud·bath /múd bàth/ (*plural* **-baths** /-bàths, -bàthz/) *n* **1.** a bath in heated mud, thought to tone the skin and organs **2.** something, e.g., a football game, that takes place outdoors in very muddy conditions (*informal*)

mud·boat /múd bṑt/ *n Midwest* a flat-bottomed skiff propelled by means of a pole

REGIONAL NOTE The **mudboat** is also called *stone boat, mud skid, mud sled*, and *mud wagon*. Primarily an Ohio usage, the term is used less frequently to the west, in Indiana and Illinois.

mud·cat /múd kàt/ *n Southern US* a catfish

mud daub·er *n* INSECTS same as **mud wasp**

mud·dle /múdd'l/ *v* (**-dled, -dling, -dles**) **1.** *vt* MIX THINGS TOGETHER IN DISORDER to mix things together in a confused or disordered way ○ *The disks have been carefully filed, so don't muddle them.* **2.** *vt* CONFUSE THINGS to confuse things in the mind (*often passive*) ○ *They look so much alike that it's easy to muddle them up.* **3.** *vti* CONFUSE OR BE CONFUSED to be confused or bemused, or cause somebody to be so ○ *Tell me again slowly – you're muddling me.* **4.** *vt* MAKE WATER MUDDY to make water muddy and unclear by stirring it **5.** *vt* STIR ALCOHOLIC BEVERAGE GENTLY to mix or stir an alcoholic drink ■ *n* **1.** CONFUSED STATE something that is in such a confused condition that it is hard to organize or understand ○ *How did our records get into such a muddle?* **2.** MIX-UP a misunderstanding arising from or causing a confused situation or state ○ *There's been a muddle over the bookings.* [14C. Probably < Middle Dutch *moddelen* < *modden* "dabble in mud"] —**mud·dled** *adj* —**mud·dler** *n* —**mud·dly** *adj*

muddle through *vi* to succeed or manage to keep going despite being disorganized ○ *I expect we'll muddle through somehow.*

mud·dle·head·ed /mùdd'l héddəd/ *adj* **1.** unable to think clearly **2.** not clearly thought out —**mud·dle·head·ed·ly** *adv* —**mud·dle·head·ed·ness** *n*

mud·dy /múddee/ *adj* (**-di·er, -di·est**) **1.** MARKED WITH MUD full of, covered in, or dirtied with mud **2.** RESEMBLING MUD like mud in being cloudy or thick **3.** LACKING CLARITY lacking clarity, brightness, or transparency ○ *a muddy color* **4.** CONFUSED hard to understand, or lacking in logical reasoning ■ *vt* (**-died, -dy·ing, -dies**) **1.** MAKE SOMETHING MUDDY to cover or dirty something with mud **2.** MAKE SOMETHING UNCLEAR to make something confused and unclear —**mud·di·ly** *adv* —**mud·di·ness** *n*

mud eel *n* a salamander that has two short front legs, no hind legs, and external gills. Native to: southeastern United States. Latin name: *Siren lacertina*.

Mu·dé·jar /moo dé haar, -thé khaar/ *n* (*plural* **-ja·res** /-haa rayss, -khaa rayss/) a Moor who was allowed to stay in a part of Spain after it had been recaptured by the Christians ■ *adj* relating to the Mudéjares, especially their style of architecture [Mid-19C. < Spanish < Arabic *mudajjan*, past participle of *dajjana* "permit to stay"]

mud·fish /múd fish/ (*plural same* or **-fish·es**) *n* a fish that lives in muddy waters, especially the bowfin

mud flap *n Can, UK* AUTOMOT a flap attached behind the wheel of a vehicle to prevent mud and water from splashing up onto the vehicle, or onto the vehicles following. US term **splashguard**

mud·flat /múd flàt/ *n* an area of low muddy land that is underwater only at high tide, especially one near an estuary

mud·flow /múd flṑ/ *n* a fast-moving downhill flow of mud and soil loosened by rainfall or melting snow

mud·guard /múd gaard/ *n* **1.** AUTOMOT same as **splashguard 2.** *UK* CYCLING same as **fender** (sense 2)

mud hen *n* a bird that lives in marshes and low wetlands, e.g., a coot or rail

mud min·now *n* a small freshwater fish that can survive in muddy oxygen-deficient water and is often used as bait. Native to: North America. Family: Umbridae.

mud·pack /múd pàk/ *n* a beauty treatment for the face that is allowed to dry before being removed

mud pie *n* a mass of mud shaped by children as a game

mud pup·py *n* a salamander that lives on muddy banks and has dark red external gills. Native to: eastern North American. Genus: *Necturus*.

mu·dra /mə dráa/ (*plural* **-dras**) *n* a symbolic position in which the hands are held in Hindu dancing and ritual [Early 19C. < Sanskrit *mudrā* "seal, sign"]

mud·room /múd ròom, -ròom/ *n* a small room near the entrance of a house where people remove muddy or wet shoes and clothing

mud·sill /múd sìl/ *n* the lowest sill or horizontal support of a building, at or below ground level

mud skid *n Midwest* same as **mudboat**

REGIONAL NOTE See ***mudboat***.

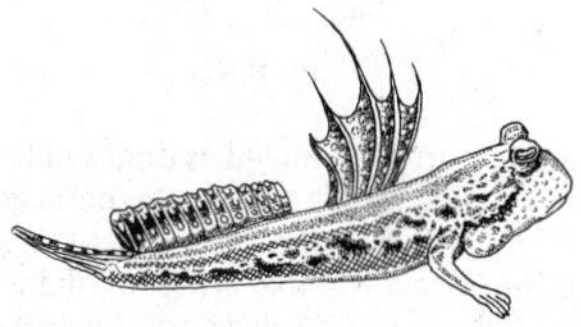

mudskipper

mud·skip·per /múd skìppər/ *n* a tropical fish of the goby family that uses its pectoral fins to leave the water to feed. Native to: Asia, Africa. Genus: *periophthalmadon*.

mud sled *n Midwest* same as **mudboat**

REGIONAL NOTE See ***mudboat***.

mud·slide /múd slīd/ *n* a slow-moving and often destructive mass of mud flowing down a slope

mud·sling·ing /múd slìnging/ *n* the making of defamatory remarks about somebody, especially a political opponent or other competitor ○ *The level of debate in this election has seldom risen above petty mudslinging.* —**mud·sling·er** *n*

mud snake *n* a nonpoisonous burrowing snake that is related to the grass snake and is dark blue and red in color. Native to: southeastern United States. Latin name: *Farancia abacura*.

mud·stone /múd stṑn/ *n* a gray sedimentary rock formed from mud, similar to shale but with less developed lamination

mud tur·tle *n* a small freshwater turtle that lives at the bottom of muddy ponds and streams. Native to: North and Central America. Genus: *Kinosternon*.

mud vol·ca·no *n* a conical mound of mud that forms around a hot spring or geyser

mud wag·on *n Midwest* same as **mudboat**

REGIONAL NOTE See ***mudboat***.

mud wasp *n* a wasp that builds multicellular nests with mud. Family: Sphecidae.

mud·wrest·ling /múd rèssling/ *n* a form of entertainment in which performers wrestle in a pit filled with mud in front of spectators —**mud·wrest·ler** /mùd résslər/ *n*

Muen·ster /múnstər, móonstər/, **Mun·ster** *n* a white to yellow semisoft mildly flavored cheese that typically has an orange edible rind [Early 20C. After *Munster*, town in NE France]

mues·li /myóozlee/ *n* a mixture of cereal flakes and rolled oats with dried fruit and nuts, eaten with milk for breakfast [Mid-20C. < Swiss German, "little purée" < German *Mus* "purée"]

mu·ez·zin /myoo ézzin, moo-/ *n* a mosque official who calls Muslims to prayer from a minaret five times a day [Late 16C. < dialect variant of Arabic *mu'addin*, form of *'addana* "call to prayer" < *'udn* "ear"]

muff[1] /muf/ *vt* (**muffed, muff·ing, muffs**) **1.** FAIL TO CATCH SOMETHING to fail to catch a ball or make a shot ○ *He got right under the ball and still muffed it.* **2.** DO SOMETHING BADLY to do something badly or awkwardly ○ *The play got off to a bad start when the actors muffed the opening lines.* ■ *n* FAILED ACTION a badly performed catch, shot, or action [Mid-19C. Origin ?]

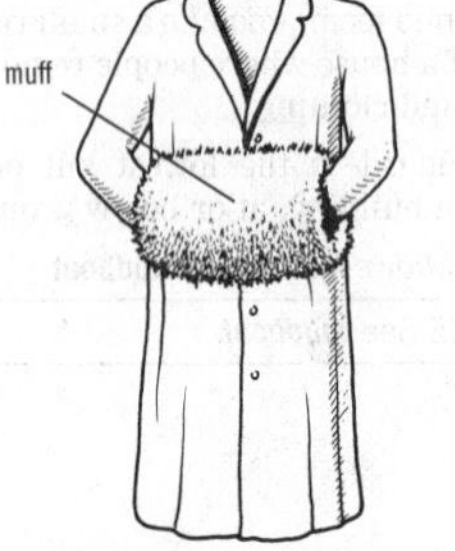

muff

muff[2] /muf/ *n* **1.** an open-ended cylinder of fur or cloth used for keeping hands warm, one hand going in at each end **2.** either of the tufts of feathers on each side of the face of some types of domestic fowl [Late 16C. < Dutch *mof*, shortening of Middle Dutch *moffel* < medieval Latin *muffula* "glove"]

muf·fin /múffin/ *n* **1.** a small round cake for one person made from a thick batter and often containing fruit or nuts, eaten at breakfast or for a snack **2.** *UK* FOOD same as **English muffin** [Early 18C. Origin ?]

muf·fle[1] /múff'l/ *vt* (**-fled, -fling, -fles**) **1.** WRAP SOMETHING TO STIFLE SOUND to wrap or pad something with material in order to deaden the sound it makes **2.** MAKE SOUND LESS LOUD to make a sound quieter or less distinct ○ *He put his hands over his ears to muffle the noise of the sirens.* **3.** PREVENT SOMETHING BEING EXPRESSED to prevent something from being said or written ○ *a government that sought to muffle all opposition* **4.** KEEP SOMEBODY WARM to wrap somebody or a part of somebody's body in a garment or cloth for warmth ○ *She muffled herself up in a thick shawl.* ■ *n* **1.** SOMETHING MUFFLING SOUND something used to muffle a sound **2.** KILN a kiln in which objects being fired are protected from direct contact with the flames [15C. Origin ?] —**muf·fled** *adj*

muf·fle[2] /múff'l/ *n* the moist fleshy hairless upper lip of some rodents and ruminants [Early 17C. < French *mufle*]

muf·fler /múfflər/ *n* **1.** a drum-shaped part of a car's exhaust pipe designed to reduce the amount of noise made by the engine **2.** a scarf worn around the neck for warmth **3.** ACOUSTICS same as **muffle**[1] *n* (sense 1)

muf·ti /múftee, mо́oftee/ *n* ordinary clothes worn by somebody who usually wears a uniform [Early 19C. Origin ?]

Muf·ti /múftee, mо́oftee/ *n* an expert on Islamic religious law [Late 16C. < Arabic *muftī*, past participle of *aftā* "decide a legal point"]

mug[1] /mug/ *n* **1.** a large round straight-sided cup typically made of earthenware and having a handle **2.** the contents of a mug, or the amount of liquid it can hold ○ *a mug of hot soup* [Early 16C. Origin ?] —**mug·ful** *n*

mug[2] /mug/ *n* **1.** SOMEBODY'S FACE somebody's face or mouth (*slang*) **2.** VIOLENT MAN a rough and violent man **3.** MUG SHOT a photograph of a suspected criminal's face (*slang*) **4.** *UK* UNINTELLIGENT PERSON somebody regarded as unintelligent or easily deceived (*slang*) ■ *v* (**mugged, mug·ging, mugs**) **1.** *vt* ROB SOMEBODY to attack and rob somebody, especially a pedestrian in a public place **2.** *vi* MAKE FACES to make exaggerated facial expressions when performing or posing for a camera ○ *The actors were playing it for laughs, mugging in every scene.* **3.** *vt* PHOTOGRAPH SUSPECTED CRIMINAL to photograph a criminal or suspect in a crime [Early 18C. Probably < MUG[1], from the representation of faces on mugs]

Robert Mugabe

Mu·ga·be /mо́o gaábee/, **Robert** (*b.* 1924) Zimbabwean politician. After leading the struggle against the white government of Rhodesia, he served as the first prime minister of Zimbabwe (1980–87) before becoming president in 1987. Full name **Mugabe, Robert Gabriel**

> "Genuine independence can only come out of the barrel of a gun."
> [Robert Mugabe. Quoted in *The Africans: Encounters from the Sudan to the Cape*, David Lamb; 1983]

mug·gar *n* REPT another spelling of **mugger**[2]

mug·ger[1] /múggər/ *n* **1.** somebody who attacks and robs somebody in a public place **2.** somebody who makes faces for comic effect, or who overacts [Mid-19C. < MUG[2]]

mug·ger[2] /múggər/, **mug·gar, mug·gur** *n* a freshwater crocodile. Native to: South Asia. Latin name: *Crocodylus palustris*. [Mid-19C. < Hindi *magar*]

mug·ging /múgging/ *n* the crime of attacking and robbing somebody in a public place

Mug·gle /múgg'l/ *n* in the Harry Potter novels by J. K. Rowling, somebody who is regarded unfavorably as a result of having no magical powers. [Late 20C. Coined by J. K. ROWLING, < ?]

mug·gur *n* REPT another spelling of **mugger**[2]

mug·gy /múggee/ (**-gi·er, -gi·est**) *adj* unpleasantly hot and humid [Mid-18C. < obsolete *mug* "rain lightly" < N Germanic] —**mug·gi·ly** *adv* —**mug·gi·ness** *n*

Mu·ghal /mо́o gù'l, mо́o gúl/, **Mo·gul** /mо́g'l, mō gúl/, **Mo·ghul** *n* **1.** a member of a Muslim dynasty of Mongol origin that ruled large parts of India from 1526 to 1857 **2.** the Mughal emperor of Delhi [Late 16C. Via Urdu *muġal* < Persian *muġul* "Mongol"] —**Mu·ghal** *adj*

mug·shot /múg shòt/ *n* a photograph of somebody's face, especially one of a suspected criminal's face or profile taken by police

mug·wort /múg wùrt, -wàwrt/ *n* an herbaceous perennial wormwood with aromatic leaves. Flowers: small, pale green. Native to: temperate regions of the northern hemisphere. Latin name: *Artemisia vulgaris*. [Old English *mucgwyrt* < earlier forms of MIDGE + WORT[1]]

mug·wump /múg wùmp/ *n* somebody who takes an independent or neutral position, especially in politics [Mid-19C. < Massachusett *mugquomp*, shortening of *muggumquomp* "war leader"] —**mug·wump·er·y** *n*

Mug·wump *n* a US Republican who refused to support the party's candidates in the 1884 presidential election

Mu·ham·mad /mо́o hámmid, mə-/, **Mo·ham·med** (A.D. 570?–632) Arabian founder of Islam. According to Islamic tradition he received his first command from Allah in 610. In 628 he made Mecca the religious capital of Islam. He recorded his visions and teachings in the Koran.

Mu·ham·mad, Elijah (1897–1975) US political activist. He was leader of the Nation of Islam (1934–75). Born **Poole, Elijah**

> "The Negro wants to be everything but himself...He wants to integrate with the white man, but he cannot integrate with himself or with his own kind. The Negro wants to lose his identity because he does not know his own identity."
> [Elijah Muhammad. Quoted in *Black Nationalism*, E. U. Essien-Udom; 1962]

Mu·ham·mad A·li ♦ **Ali, Muhammad**

Mu·har·ram /moo hárrəm/, **Mo·har·ram** *n* **1.** in the Islamic calendar, the first month of the year. See table at **calendar** **2.** an Islamic festival that marks the martyrdom of the brothers Hussein and Hassan, grandsons of the prophet Mohammed. Date: in the month of Muharram. Same as **Ashora** [Early 19C. < Arabic *muḥarram* "inviolable," past participle of *ḥarrama* "forbid"]

Muir /myoor/, **John** (1838–1914) Scottish-born US naturalist and explorer. He helped establish Yosemite, King's Canyon, and Sequoia national parks in the United States.

> "Surely all God's people, however serious or savage, great or small, like to play; whales and elephants, dancing, humming gnats, and invisibly small mischievous microbes—all are warm with divine radium and must have lots of fun in them."
> [John Muir, *The Story of my Boyhood and Youth*; 1913]

Muir Gla·cier glacier in southeastern Alaska, flowing down Mount Fairweather and into Glacier Bay. It is nearly 2 mi./3 km long and 135 to 210 ft./40 to 65 m high.

mu·ja·hi·deen /moo jaà he deén/, **mu·ja·he·din, mu·ja·hi·din, mu·ja·hed·din** *npl* Islamic guerrillas based in Iran and Pakistan who fought a holy war (**jihad**) against the Soviet forces occupying Afghanistan in the late 1970s and the 1980s [Mid-20C. < Persian or Arabic *mujāhidīn*, plural of *mujāhid* "somebody who fights a jihad"]

muk·luk /múk lùk/, **muck·luck** *n* **1.** a waterproof boot made of animal skin or canvas that is large enough to be worn over shoes or several pairs of socks **2.** a sealskin boot originally worn by the Inuit [Mid-19C. < Yupik *maklak* "bearded seal," misunderstood as "sealskin"]

muk·tuk /múk tùk/, **mak·tak** *n Can* the outer layer of skin and fat from a whale when eaten either raw or cooked [Mid-19C. < Inuit *maktak*]

mu·lat·to /mо́o láttō, -laáto/ (*plural* **-tos** or **-toes**) *n* (*dated*) **1.** an offensive term for somebody who has one Black and one white parent **2.** an offensive term for somebody who has both Black and white ancestors [Late 16C. < Spanish *mulato* "young mule" < *mulo* "mule" < Latin *mulus*]

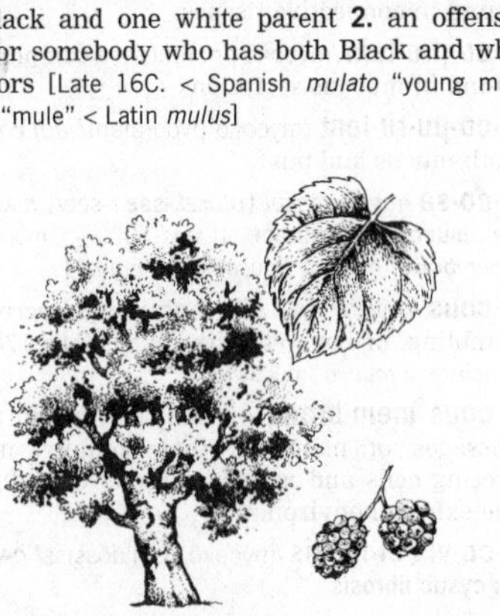

mulberry

mul·ber·ry /múl bèrree/ (*plural* **-ries**) *n* **1.** PURPLE FRUIT a small sweet fruit resembling a berry **2.** TREE WITH EDIBLE FRUIT a small deciduous tree, one species of which bears edible fruit and another species leaves that are fed to silkworms. Genus: *Morus*. **3.** PURPLE COLOR a dark purple color tinged with red or gray [Old English *mōrberie* < *mōr-* < Latin *morum* "mulberry"] —**mul·ber·ry** *adj*

mulch /mulch/ *n* a protective covering of organic material laid over the soil around plants to prevent erosion, retain moisture, and sometimes enrich the soil ■ *vti* (**mulched, mulch·ing, mulch·es**) to cover soil with mulch ○ *mulch with newspaper* [Mid-17C. Origin ?]

mulct /mulkt/ *vt* (**mulct·ed, mulct·ing, mulcts**) **1. FINE SOMEBODY** to fine somebody as a penalty **2. CHEAT SOMEBODY** to cheat somebody out of something (*archaic*) ■ *n* **PENALTY** a fine or penalty [15C. < Latin *mulctare* < *mulcta* "fine"]

mule

mule[1] /myool/ *n* **1. CROSS BETWEEN HORSE AND DONKEY** the offspring of a female horse and a male donkey **2. HYBRID ANIMAL OR PLANT** the sterile offspring of two closely related species of animal or plant **3. STUBBORN PERSON** somebody regarded as stubborn or intractable (*informal*) **4. DRUG COURIER** somebody who transports illegal drugs for a dealer (*slang*) **5. MANUF SPINNING MACHINE** a machine that draws and spins cotton fibers into yarn and winds it onto spindles [Old English *mūl*, probably via Germanic < Latin *mulus*]

mule[2] /myool/ *n* a backless slipper or shoe [Mid-16C. Via French < Latin *mulleus (calceus)* "reddish-purple (shoe)"]

mule deer *n* a large deer that has a grayish-brown coat, some white underparts, a black tail, and long ears. Native to: western North America. Latin name: *Odocoileus hemionus*. [< MULE [1]]

mule·skin·ner /myo͞ol skìnnər/ *n* OCCUPATIONS same as **muleteer** (*informal*)

mu·le·ta /moo láytə, -léttə/ (*plural* **-tas**) *n* a short red cape attached to a stick that a matador uses instead of the full cape in the final stages of a bullfight [Mid-19C. < Spanish, diminutive of *mula* "female mule" < Latin *mulus* "mule"]

mu·le·teer /myo͞olə téer/ *n* somebody whose occupation is driving mules [Mid-16C. < French *muletier* < *mulet*, diminutive of Old French *mul* "mule" < Latin *mulus*]

mu·ley /myo͞olee, mo͞ollee, moolee/ *adj* having no horns ■ *n* (*plural* **-leys**) an animal that does not have horns [Late 16C. Probably < Irish *maol* or Welsh *moel* "bald" < Indo-European, "to cut"]

mul·ga /múlgə/ *n* an acacia bush or small tree that forms dense thickets. Native to: dry regions of Australia. Genus: *Acacia*. [Mid-19C. < an Aboriginal language]

Mul·ha·cén /mool a tháyn/ highest peak on the Spanish mainland, situated in the Sierra Nevada, about 20 mi./32 km southeast of Granada. Height: 11,407 ft./3,477 m.

Mul·house /mə lo͞oz/ industrial city in Haut-Rhin Department, Alsace Region, northeastern France. Population: 110,359 (1999).

mu·li·eb·ri·ty /myo͞olee ébbrətee/ *n* (*literary*) **1.** the condition of being a woman **2.** the qualities conventionally associated with women [Late 16C. < Latin *muliebritas* < *mulier* "woman"]

mul·ish /myo͞olish/ *adj* obstinate and unwilling to cooperate or listen to suggestions [Mid-18C. < MULE [1]] —**mul·ish·ly** *adv* —**mul·ish·ness** *n*

mull[1] /mul/ *n* a period of deep thought [Mid-19C. Origin ?]

mull over *vt* to consider something thoroughly

mull[2] /mul/ (**mulled, mull·ing, mulls**) *vt* to heat, sweeten, and flavor wine, beer, or cider [Early 17C. Origin ?]

mull[3] /mul/ *n* soft cotton muslin. Use: dresses. [Late 17C. Shortening of Hindi *malmal*]

mull[4] /mul/ *n* nonacidic humus on a forest floor that eventually integrates into the soil beneath it [Early 20C. < Danish *muld* "mold"]

Mull /mul/ island in the Inner Hebrides, western Scotland. Population: 2,078 (1991). Area: 353 sq. mi./925 sq. km.

mul·lah /múllə, mo͞ollə/ *n* **1.** in Central and Southwest Asia, a Muslim cleric who specializes in the interpretation of Islamic religious law **2.** in Iran and Central and Southwest Asia, used as a term of respect for a Muslim man who is thought to be very wise [Early 17C. Via Persian or Urdu *mullā* < Arabic *mawlā*]

mul·lein /múllin/ *n* a tall plant with hairy leaves. Flowers: yellow, lavender, or white, in spikes. Native to: Europe, Asia, naturalized in the United States. Genus: *Verbascum*. [15C. < Old French *moleine*]

mul·ler /múllər/ *n* a heavy smooth object made of stone, metal, wood, or glass, used for grinding paints or drugs on a flat surface [14C. Origin ?]

Mül·ler /múllər, myo͞olər/, **Paul** (1899–1965) Swiss chemist. He demonstrated the insecticidal properties of DDT, which was widely used from the 1940s to the 1970s. Full name **Müller, Paul Hermann**

Mül·le·ri·an mim·ic·ry /myoo léeree ən-/ *n* mimicry in which two or more animals that are inedible or harmful assume one another's appearance so that predators will leave them alone [Late 19C. After J. F. T. *Müller* (1821–97), German-born Brazilian zoologist]

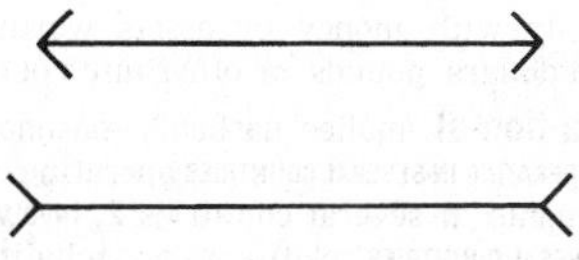

Müller-Lyer illusion

Mül·ler-Ly·er il·lu·sion /-lī ər-/ *n* an optical illusion in which a line with inward-pointing arrows is seen as longer than one of equal length with outward-pointing arrows [Late 19C. After Franz Carl *Müller-Lyer* (1857–1916), German sociologist and philosopher]

mul·let /múllət/ *n* **1.** (*plural* **mul·lets** or *same*) **FISH OF INSHORE WATERS** a fish belonging to a large family that lives in fresh or salt water. Native to: temperate and tropical coastal waters. Family: Mugilidae. **2.** (*plural* **mul·lets** or *same*) **FISH OF INSHORE WATERS** a thick-bodied fish typically found in inshore waters. Family: Mugilidae. **3. MULLET AS FOOD** the flesh of a mullet used as food [15C. < Old French *mulet* < *mul* < Latin *mullus* "red mullet" < Greek *mullos*, a sea fish]

mul·li·gan /múlligən/ *n* a shot that, against the rules, a golfer allows an opponent to take again [Mid-20C. Probably < the name *Mulligan*]

mul·li·gan bal·lot *n* a second ballot paper used if a voter records his or her vote wrongly on the first attempt (*informal*)

mul·li·gan stew *n* a stew made from whatever suitable ingredients are at hand [Origin ?]

mul·li·ga·taw·ny /mùlligə táwnee/ *n* a spicy meat and vegetable soup originally found in eastern India [Late 18C. < Tamil *miḷaku-taṇṇi* "pepper-water"]

Mul·li·ken /múllikən/, **Robert S.** (1896–1986) US chemist. He won the Nobel Prize in chemistry (1966) for his molecular studies. He helped develop the atomic bomb during World War II. Full name **Mulliken, Robert Sanderson**

mul·lion /múllyən/ *n* a vertical piece of stone, metal, or wood that divides the panes of a window or the panels of a screen [Mid-16C. Alteration of obsolete *monial* "mullion" < Anglo-Norman *moinel* "middle (part)" < *moien* "in the middle, median"] —**mul·lioned** *adj*

Mul·lis /múlliss/, **Kary B.** (*b.* 1944) US biochemist. He developed a polymerase chain reaction for which he won a Nobel Prize in chemistry (1993).

mul·lite /mú līt/ *n* a colorless mineral consisting of crystalline aluminum silicate, able to withstand corrosion and very high temperatures [Early 20C. < MULL]

Bettmann/Corbis

Brian Mulroney

Mul·ro·ney /mul ro͞onee/, **Brian** (*b.* 1939) prime minister of Canada (1984–93). He led the Progressive Conservative Party from 1983, and signed the Canadian-US Free Trade Agreement in 1988. Full name **Mulroney, Martin Brian**. See table at **prime minister**

mult- *prefix* same as **multi-** (*used before vowels*)

Mul·tan /mo͞ol taán/, **Multān** industrial city, district, and division of Punjab Province, eastern Pakistan. Population: 722,070 (1981).

multi- *prefix* many, multiple, more than one or two ○ *multilevel* ○ *multiparous* [Via French < Latin *multus* "much, many"]

mul·ti·ac·tiv·i·ty *adj*
mul·ti·armed *adj*
mul·ti·bank *adj*
mul·ti·bay *adj*
mul·ti·bil·lion *adj*
mul·ti·bil·lion·aire *n*
mul·ti·blad·ed *adj*
mul·ti·branched *adj*
mul·ti·cell *adj*
mul·ti·celled *adj*
mul·ti·cel·lu·lar *adj*
mul·ti·cel·lu·lar·i·ty *n*
mul·ti·cham·bered *adj*
mul·ti·com·mu·ni·ty *adj*
mul·ti·course *adj*
mul·ti·c·ur·ren·cy *adj*
mul·ti·dig·it *adj*
mul·ti·di·men·sion·al *adj*
mul·ti·di·men·sion·al·i·ty *n*
mul·ti·di·vi·sion·al *adj*
mul·ti·do·main *adj*
mul·ti·el·e·ment *adj*
mul·ti·em·ploy·er *adj*
mul·ti·en·gine *adj*
mul·ti·eth·nic *adj*
mul·ti·fam·i·ly *adj*
mul·ti·fil·a·ment *adj*
mul·ti·fo·cal *adj*
mul·ti·form *adj*
mul·ti·for·mi·ty *n*
mul·ti·func·tion *adj*
mul·ti·func·tion·al *adj*
mul·ti·func·tion·ing *adj*
mul·ti·gen·er·a·tion·al *adj*
mul·ti·head·ed *adj*
mul·ti·hued *adj*
mul·ti·joint·ed *adj*
mul·ti·lane *adj*
mul·ti·lay·ered *adj*
mul·ti·lobed *adj*
mul·ti·mem·ber *adj*
mul·ti·mil·lion *adj*
mul·ti·mo·dal *adj*
mul·ti·mode *adj*
mul·ti·mo·lec·u·lar *adj*
mul·ti·move·ment *adj*
mul·ti·na·tion *adj*
mul·ti·nu·cle·ar *adj*
mul·ti·page *adj*
mul·ti·part *adj*
mul·ti·par·ti·cle *adj*
mul·ti·par·ty *adj*
mul·ti·po·si·tion *adj*
mul·ti·range *adj*
mul·ti·roomed *adj*
mul·ti·screen *adj*
mul·ti·sense *adj*
mul·ti·sen·so·ry *adj*
mul·ti·sid·ed *adj*
mul·ti·site *adj*
mul·ti·span *adj*
mul·ti·speed *adj*
mul·ti·sport *adj*
mul·ti·state *adj*
mul·ti·stemmed *adj*
mul·ti·step *adj*
mul·ti·stom·ach *adj*
mul·ti·strand·ed *adj*
mul·ti·string *adj*
mul·ti·syl·lab·ic *adj*
mul·ti·tal·ent·ed *adj*
mul·ti·term *adj*
mul·ti·tiered *adj*
mul·ti·track *adj*
mul·ti·u·nit *adj*
mul·ti·use *adj*
mul·ti·us·er *adj*
mul·ti·va·lence *n*
mul·ti·va·lent *adj*
mul·ti·vol·ume *adj*
mul·ti·word *n, adj*
mul·ti·year *adj*

mul·ti·ac·cess /mùltee ák sess, mùltī-/ *adj* relating to a computer system that allows several users to access it at the same time

mul·ti·band /múltee bànd, múltī-/ *adj* enabling more than one bandwidth of a signal to be processed separately in order to achieve higher fidelity

mul·ti·cast·ing /múltee kàsting, múltī-/ *n* the process of sending data across a network to several recipients simultaneously —**mul·ti·cast** *vt*

mul·ti·cen·ter /múlti sèntər, múltī-/ *adj* having two or more centers

mul·ti·cen·ter bond *n* a chemical bond that consists of three or more atoms instead of the usual two, e.g., as found in boranes

mul·ti·chan·nel /mùlti chánn'l, múltī-/ *adj* using or providing several channels in broadcasting or communication

mul·ti·chan·nel com·mu·ni·ca·tion *n* the existence or use of two or more communication channels over the same path, e.g., in radio transmission or within a communication cable

mul·ti·col·ored /múlti kùllərd, múltī-/, **mul·ti·col·or** /-kùllər/ *adj* **1.** of many different colors **2.** able to print more than one color at once

mul·ti·cul·ti /mùltee kúltee/ *adj* SOC SCI same as **multicultural** (*slang*) [Late 20C. Alteration of MULTICULTURAL]

mul·ti·cul·tur·al /mùltee kúlchərəl, mùltī-/ *adj* **1.** relating to, consisting of, or participating in the cultures of different countries, ethnic groups, or religions **2.** advocating or encouraging the integration of people of different countries, ethnic groups, and religions into all areas of society —**mul·ti·cul·tur·al·ism** *n* —**mul·ti·cul·tur·al·ist** *n*

mul·ti·di·rec·tion·al /mùltee di rékshən'l, mùltī-/ *adj* **1.** having several objectives or covering several aspects of a situation **2.** going, operating, or pointing in several different directions

mul·ti·dis·ci·pli·nar·y /mùltee díssipli nèrree, mùltī-/, **mul·ti·dis·ci·pline** /-díssiplin/ *adj* studying or using several specialized subjects or skills

mul·ti·e·vent /múltee i vènt, múltī-/ *n* an athletic contest, e.g., the pentathlon or decathlon, that includes several different events

mul·ti·fac·et·ed /mùltee fássətəd, mùltī-/ *adj* **1.** with many different talents, qualities, or features **2.** having many facets or cut surfaces

mul·ti·fac·to·ri·al /mùlti fak táwree əl/, **mul·ti·fac·tor** /mùlti fáktər/ *adj* **1.** involving several different factors **2.** relating to inheritance depending on more than one gene. Height and weight are examples of characters determined by multifactorial inheritance. —**mul·ti·fac·to·ri·al·ly** *adv*

mul·ti·far·i·ous /mùltə férree əss/ *adj* including parts, things, or people of many different kinds [Late 16C. < Latin *multifarius* "varied, diverse" < *multi-* "many" + *-farius* "doing"] —**mul·ti·far·i·ous·ly** *adv* —**mul·ti·far·i·ous·ness** *n*

mul·ti·fid /múltə fìd/ *adj* having many lobe-shaped segments

mul·ti·flo·ra rose /mùltə fláwrə-/ *n* a wild climbing rose that is the origin of many cultivated roses. Flowers: small, fragrant. Native to: Asia. Latin name: *Rosa multiflora.*

mul·ti·flo·rous /mùltə fláwrəss/ *adj* having many flowers [Mid-18C. < late Latin *multiflorus* < Latin *multi-* "many" + *flor-* "flower"]

mul·ti·foil /múltə fòyl/ *n* in architecture, a flat shape, opening, or decorative design with many lobes or scallops at its edges

mul·ti·grade oil /mùltə grayd-/, **mul·ti·grade** *n* engine oil that has a range of viscosities and is therefore effective over a range of temperatures

mul·ti·grain /múltee gràyn/ *adj* describes bread that is made from several different types of grains

mul·ti·grav·i·da /mùlti grávvidə/ *n* a pregnant woman who has had at least one previous pregnancy

mul·ti·gym /múlti jim/ *n* an exercise apparatus with a range of weights, used for muscle toning

mul·ti·hull /múltee hùl, múltī-/ *n* a sailing vessel with two or more hulls

mul·ti·lat·er·al /mùlti láttərəl/ *adj* **1.** involving more than two parties or countries **2.** having many sides or flat surfaces [Late 17C. < medieval Latin *multilateralis* < Latin *multi-* "many" + *lateralis* (see LATERAL)] —**mul·ti·lat·er·al·ly** *adv*

mul·ti·lat·er·al·ism /mùlti láttərə lìzzəm/ *n* the principle or belief that several nations should be cooperatively involved in the process of achieving a goal, especially nuclear disarmament —**mul·ti·lat·er·al·ist** *n, adj*

mul·ti·lev·el /mùltee lévv'l, mùltī-/ *adj* **1.** WITH SEVERAL LEVELS having or operating on several layers or levels **2.** *also* **mul·ti·lev·eled** /-lévv'ld/ WITH MANY LEVELS having or operating on several or many different levels ■ *n* STRUCTURE WITH MANY LEVELS a building or structure with several or many levels

mul·ti·lin·gual /mùltee líng gwəl, mùltī-/ *adj* **1.** able to speak more than two languages fluently **2.** relating to the use of more than two languages —**mul·ti·lin·gual·ism** *n* —**mul·ti·lin·gual·ly** *adv*

mul·ti·loc·u·lar /mùlti lókyələr/ *adj* consisting of or having several different chambers or cavities [Early 19C. < LOCULE]

mul·ti·me·di·a /mùltee meédee ə, mùltī-/ *n* **1.** COMPUT SOUND AND VIDEO ON COMPUTERS programs, software, and hardware capable of using a wide variety of media such as film, video, and music as well as text and numbers **2.** ARTS USE OF VARIOUS MATERIALS AND MEDIA the use in art, especially the plastic arts, of different kinds of materials and media such as television, sound, and text **3.** MARKETING USE OF ALL COMMUNICATIONS MEDIA the use in advertising of a combination of media such as television, radio, and the press **4.** EDUC USE OF MEDIA IN TEACHING the use of film, video, and music in addition to more traditional teaching materials and methods —**mul·ti·me·di·a** *adj*

mul·ti·me·di·a mes·sag·ing ser·vice *n* TELECOM full form of **MMS**

mul·ti·me·ter /mul tímmətər/ *n* an instrument that reads and measures the values of several different electrical parameters such as current, voltage, and resistance

mul·ti·mil·lion·aire /mùltee mìllyə nér, mùltī-/ *n* somebody with money or assets worth several million dollars, pounds, or other units of currency

mul·ti·na·tion·al /mùltee náshən'l, -náshnəl, mùltī-/ *adj* **1.** OPERATING IN SEVERAL COUNTRIES operating or having investments in several countries **2.** INVOLVING PEOPLE FROM SEVERAL COUNTRIES relating to or including people from more than two countries ■ *n* LARGE COMPANY OPERATING IN SEVERAL COUNTRIES a large company that operates or has investments in several different countries —**mul·ti·na·tion·al·ism** *n*

mul·ti·no·mi·al /mùlti nṓmee əl/ *n, adj* MATH same as **polynomial**

mul·ti·pack /múlti pàk/ *n* a package that contains more than two of an item of consumer products such as batteries and is sold at a reduced price

mul·tip·a·ra /mul típpərə/ (*plural* **-rae** /-ree/ or **-ras**) *n* a woman who has borne a live child from each of two or more pregnancies [Mid-19C. < form of modern Latin *multiparus* (see MULTIPAROUS)]

mul·tip·a·rous /mul típpərəss/ *adj* **1.** describes an animal, especially a mammal, that normally gives birth to two or more offspring at one time **2.** describes a woman who has borne a child from each of two or more pregnancies, each pregnancy lasting for at least 20 weeks [Mid-17C. < modern Latin *multiparus* < Latin *multi-* "many" + *-parus* "-bearing" (see -PAROUS)] —**mul·ti·par·i·ty** /mùlti párrətee/ *n*

mul·ti·par·tite /mùlti paár tìt/, **mul·ti·par·ty** /múlti paártee/ *adj* **1.** involving more than two political parties or countries **2.** divided into many sections

mul·ti·path /múlti pàth/ *adj* relating to television or radio signals that use more than one route from the transmitter to the receiver, causing picture or sound distortion

mul·ti·plane /múlti plàyn/ *n* an aircraft with more than one pair of wings

mul·ti·play·er /mùlti pláy ər/ *adj* describes a computer game that is played with other players, typically over a local area network or the Internet —**mul·ti·play·er** *n*

mul·ti·ple /múltip'l/ *adj* INVOLVING SEVERAL THINGS involving or including several things, people, or parts ■ *n* **1.** MATH NUMBER DIVISIBLE BY ANOTHER a number that can be divided exactly by a particular smaller number **2.** TELECOM SYSTEM WITH MANY POSSIBLE ACCESS POINTS a system of wiring so arranged that a group of communication lines are accessible at a number of points [Mid-17C. Via French < late Latin *multiplus*, alteration of Latin *multiplex* (see MULTIPLEX)]

mul·ti·ple al·leles *npl* three or more different forms of a gene. Any two of these forms can be present in a normal diploid cell or organism.

mul·ti·ple-choice *adj* requiring the choice of the correct answer or answers out of several possible suggested answers ○ *a multiple-choice question*

mul·ti·ple fac·tor *n* GENETICS same as **polygene**

mul·ti·ple fis·sion *n* a form of asexual reproduction occurring in some single-celled organisms such as malaria parasites in which a single parent cell breaks up to yield numerous daughter cells

mul·ti·ple fruit *n* a fruit that is produced from the ovaries of several flowers that merge to form a single structure, e.g., a pineapple or fig

mul·ti·ple in·tel·li·genc·es *npl* the several independent forms of human intelligence that exist, according to one psychological theory, including verbal, quantitative, spatial, musical, kinesthetic, interpersonal, and intrapersonal intelligence

mul·ti·ple my·e·lo·ma *n* a form of cancer of the bone marrow characterized by swellings, malformations, and fractures of various bones and accompanied by pain, anemia, and weight loss. It affects the plasma cells that produce antibodies and can be diagnosed by the presence of unusual proteins in the blood.

mul·ti·ple neu·ri·tis *n* MED same as **polyneuritis**

mul·ti·ple per·son·al·i·ty dis·or·der *n* a psychological disorder, typically associated with childhood trauma, in which somebody appears to have two or more distinct personalities that are present at different times and dominate behavior

mul·ti·ple scle·ro·sis *n* a serious progressive disease of the central nervous system, occurring mainly in young adults and thought to be caused by a malfunction of the immune system. It leads to the loss of myelin in the brain or spinal cord and causes muscle weakness, poor eyesight, slow speech, and some inability to move.

mul·ti·ple star *n* a group of three or more stars, usually with the same gravitational center, that appears as one star to the naked eye

mul·ti·plet /múltiplət/ *n* **1.** a line in a spectrum made up of two or more component lines, caused by slight variations in atomic or molecular energy levels **2.** a group of elementary particles that have a different electric charge but have otherwise similar properties [Early 20C. < MULTIPLE, after DOUBLET, TRIPLET]

mul·ti·plex /múltə plèks/ *n* **1.** MOVIE THEATER COMPLEX a large movie theater complex that has several separate units with screens **2.** MULTIPLE TRANSMISSION the simultaneous transmission of two or more signals along one communications channel **3.** SYSTEM FOR SIMULTANEOUS TRANSMISSION a transmission system that carries two or more individual channels over a single communication path ■ *adj* COMPLEX involving or including several different things, parts, or factors ■ *vti* (**-plexed, -plex·ing, -plex·es**) SEND BY MULTIPLEX to send two or more messages or signals along one communications channel at the same time [Mid-16C. < Latin < *multi-* "many" + *-plex* "-fold"]

mul·ti·plex·er /múltə plèksər/, **mul·ti·plex·or** *n* **1.** a device for sending several data streams down a communications line and for splitting a received multiple stream into components **2.** a device for transferring projected film to video

mul·ti·plex·ing /múltə plèksing/ *n* **1.** the sending of two or more signals along one communication channel **2.** a genetic sequencing approach that uses several pooled samples simultaneously, so increasing the sequencing speed

mul·ti·plex·or *n* MEDIA, TELECOM another spelling of **multiplexer**

mul·ti·pli·cand /mùltəpli kánd/ *n* a number that is multiplied by another number (**multiplier**). The number 2 is the multiplicand in the statement $2 \times 4 = 8$. [Late 16C. < medieval Latin *multiplicandus*, form of Latin *multiplicare* (see MULTIPLY [1])]

mul·tip·li·cate /múltipli kàyt/ *adj* containing many parts [15C. < Latin *multiplicat-*, past participle of *multiplicare* (see MULTIPLY [1])]

mul·ti·pli·ca·tion /mùltipli káysh'n/ *n* **1.** ARITHMETIC OPERATION a mathematical operation, symbolized by ×, that for integers is equivalent to adding a number to itself a particular number of times **2.** MATHEMATICAL OPERATION a mathematical operation equivalent to multiplication extended to expressions such as functions or matrices that are not numbers **3.** IN-

CREASE a marked increase in number or amount ○ *a multiplication of claims* **4. REPRODUCTION** the act or process of reproduction in animals, plants, or people [14C. Directly or via French < Latin *multiplication-* < *multiplicat-*, past participle of *multiplicare* (see MULTIPLY[1])] —**mul·ti·pli·ca·tion·al** *adj* —**mul·ti·pli·ca·tive** /mùltə plíkətiv, múltəpli kàytiv/ *adj*

mul·ti·pli·ca·tion sign *n* the symbol × or •, used to indicate that one number is to be multiplied by another

mul·ti·pli·ca·tion ta·ble *n* a table giving a number from 1 to 10 or 12 multiplied by all the numbers from 1 to 10 or 12 in turn. Multiplication tables are used for teaching or remembering the basic facts of multiplication.

mul·ti·plic·i·ty /mùltə plíssətee/ (*plural* **-ties**) *n* **1. GREAT VARIETY** a considerable number or variety ○ *Her style was shaped by a multiplicity of influences.* **2. COMPLEXITY** the state of being multiple or varied **3.** PHYS **NUMBER OF MOLECULAR ENERGY LEVELS** the number of energy levels of a molecule, atom, or nucleus that result from interactions between angular momenta **4.** PHYS **PARTICLES IN MULTIPLET** the number of elementary particles that form a multiplet [15C. < late Latin *multiplicatus* < Latin *multiplic-*, stem of *multiplex* (see MULTIPLEX)]

mul·ti·pli·er /múltə plī ər/ *n* **1.** somebody or something that multiplies or increases **2.** the number by which another number (**multiplicand**) is multiplied, e.g., the number 4 is the multiplier in the statement 2 × 4 = 8 **3.** PHYS same as **photomultiplier**

mul·ti·ply[1] /múltə plī/ (**-plied, -ply·ing, -plies**) *v* **1.** *vti* **INCREASE IN AMOUNT** to increase by a considerable number, amount, or degree, or make something increase in this way **2.** *vti* MATH **PERFORM MULTIPLICATION** to perform the mathematical operation of multiplication on a number or set of numbers **3.** *vi* BIOL **BREED** to increase in number by breeding [12C. Via French *multiplier* < Latin *multiplicare* < *multiplic-* (see MULTIPLICITY)] —**mul·ti·pli·a·ble** *adj* —**mul·ti·plic·a·ble** /mùltə plíkəb'l/ *adj*

mul·ti·ply[2] /múltə plī/ *adv* many times, or in many different ways [Late 19C. < MULTIPLE]

mul·ti-ply /múltəplee/ *adj* having more than one layer ○ *multi-ply tissues*

mul·ti·point /múltee pòynt/ *n* TELECOM same as **multiple** *n* (sense 2)

mul·ti·po·lar /múlti pṓlər/ *adj* **1. WITH MORE THAN TWO MAJOR POWERS** having several countries that are centers of power or influence **2. WITH MANY CONNECTIONS** describes a nerve cell with more than two connecting fibers that carry impulses into the cell body **3. WITH MULTIPLE POLES** having several poles or extremities —**mul·ti·po·lar·i·ty** /mùltee pō lérrətee/ *n*

mul·ti·port /múlti pàwrt/ *adj* describes a computer network with more than one point of access or connection

mul·ti·po·tent /mul típpətənt/, **mul·ti·po·ten·tial** /mùltee pə ténshəl, mùltī-/ *adj* capable of developing into various types of cells, depending on the surrounding conditions

mul·ti·pro·cess·ing /mùltee pró sèssing, mùltī-/ *n* the operation of a computer in which two or more processing units work on separate parts of the same program or set of instructions to reduce processing time

mul·ti·pro·ces·sor /mùltee pró sèssər, mùltī-/ *n* a system of linked central processing units on which two or more programs can be run simultaneously by parallel processing

mul·ti·pronged /múlti prόngd/ *adj* **1.** involving several different approaches or aspects **2.** having several prongs

mul·ti·pur·pose /mùltee púrpəss, mùltī-/ *adj* designed or able to be used for several different purposes

mul·ti·ra·cial /mùltee ráysh'l, mùltī-/ *adj* relating to, made up of, or involving people from several races ○ *a multiracial society* —**mul·ti·ra·cial·ly** *adv*

mul·ti·ra·cial·ism /mùltee ráysh'l ìzzəm, mùltī-/ *n* the principle or practice of ensuring that people of various races are fully integrated into a society —**mul·ti·ra·cial·ist** *adj*

mul·ti·re·gion·al·ism /mùltee reéjən'l ìzzəm, mùltī-/ *n* a theory of evolution holding that modern human beings are descended from several separate subspecies —**mul·ti·re·gion·al·ist** *adj, n*

mul·ti·role /múlti rṑl/ *adj* having several roles or functions

mul·ti·serv·ice /múlti súrviss/ *adj* **1.** offering more than one type of service **2.** relating to or involving members of different branches of the armed forces

mul·ti·skilled /mùltee skíld, mùltī-/ *adj* trained and capable in a large variety of skills or activities

mul·ti·skill·ing /mùltee skílling, mùltī-/ *n* the training of employees to do a large variety of tasks

mul·ti·stage /múlti stàyj/ *adj* divided into or taking place in several separate stages

mul·ti·stage rock·et *n* a rocket with two or more propulsion units that are used and discarded in succession

mul·ti·sto·ry /múlti stàwree/, **mul·ti·sto·ried** /-stàwreed/ *adj* having several stories

mul·ti·task /múlti tàsk/ (**-tasked, -task·ing, -tasks**) *vi* to perform more than one task at the same time ○ *The best way to pass the time while exercising is to multitask – why just pedal when you can talk on your cell phone at the same time.*

mul·ti·task·ing /múlti tàsking/ *n* the simultaneous management of two or more tasks by a computer or a person

mul·ti·ton /múlti tùn/ *adj* weighing or capable of carrying several tons

mul·ti·tude /múlti tood/ *n* **1. CROWD** a large crowd of people **2. LARGE NUMBER** a very large number of things or people (*often used in the plural*) **3. MAJORITY** the majority of ordinary people [14C. Via French < Latin *multitudo* < *multus* "much, many"]

mul·ti·tu·di·nous /mùlti tood'nəss/ *adj* **1.** very great in number **2.** including many parts, items, or features [Early 17C. < Latin *multitudin-*, stem of *multitudo* (see MULTITUDE)] —**mul·ti·tu·di·nous·ly** *adv*—**mul·ti·tud·in·ous·ness** *n*

mul·ti·us·er do·main, ob·ject-o·ri·ent·ed /mùltee yoozər-òbjəkt áwree èntəd/ (*plural* **mul·ti·us·er do·mains, ob·ject-o·ri·ent·ed**) *n* ONLINE full form of **MOO**

mul·ti·var·i·ate /mùltee vérree ət, mùltī-/, **mul·ti·var·i·a·ble** /mùltee vérree əb'l/ *adj* relating to or used to describe a statistical distribution that involves a number of random but often related variables

mul·ti·verse /múltee vùrss, múltī-/ *n* a hypothetical cosmos that contains our universe as well as numerous other universes and space-times

mul·ti·ver·si·ty /mùlti vúrsətee/ (*plural* **-ties**) *n* a university that has many affiliated or associated institutions such as research centers and colleges [Mid-20C. < MULTI- + UNIVERSITY]

mul·ti·vi·bra·tor /mùlti vī bráytər/ *n* an oscillating electronic circuit consisting of pairs of tubes, transistors, or other components, whose oscillation is sustained by coupling the output of one to the input of the other

mul·ti·vi·ta·min /mùltə vītəmin/ *n* a tablet or capsule containing several vitamins and sometimes minerals —**mul·ti·vi·ta·min** *adj*

Mult·no·mah Falls /mult nṓmə-/ falls on Larch Mountain in northwestern Oregon, east of Portland, on a tributary of the Columbia River. Height: 620 ft./189 m.

mul·tum in par·vo /mool toom in paárvō/ *n* the quality or fact of containing, implying, or expressing much in a little space or time [< Latin, "much in little"]

mum[1] /mum/ *adj* saying nothing, especially about a sensitive piece of information (*informal*) ■ *interj* used to tell somebody to keep quiet [15C. An imitation of the sound made when the lips are closed]

mum[2] /mum/ (**mummed, mum·ming, mums**) *vi* **1.** to act in a masked folk play or mime **2.** to participate in festivities wearing a mask or disguise [Mid-16C. < French *momer* "act in a mime"]

mum[3] /mum/ *n* PLANTS same as **chrysanthemum** (*informal*) [Late 19C. Shortening]

mum[4] /mum/ *n UK* same as **mom** (*informal*)

mum[5] /mum/ *n* a strong beer of German origin [Early 17C. < German *Mumme*]

Mum·bai /moom bī/ capital of Maharashtra State and the largest city in India, situated on the Arabian Sea. Population: 11,914,398 (2001). Former name **Bombay**

mum·ble /múmb'l/ *vti* (**-bled, -bling, -bles**) **1. MUTTER** to speak or utter something quietly and indistinctly without opening the mouth very much **2. CHEW WITH DIFFICULTY** to chew food with difficulty ■ *n* **INDISTINCT SPEECH** a quiet indistinct utterance in which the mouth is not opened very much [14C. < obsolete *mum* "make an indistinct sound with closed lips"] —**mum·bler** *n* —**mum·bling·ly** *adv* —**mum·bly** *adj*

mum·ble·ty-peg /múmb'ltee-/, **mum·ble-the-peg** /múmb'l thə-/ *n* a game in which players flip a knife, trying to stick the blade into the ground, usually while standing in various prescribed positions [Because originally the unsuccessful player had to pull a peg out of the ground by biting it]

mum·bo jum·bo /mùmbō júmbō/ *n* **1. CONFUSING LANGUAGE** complicated and confusing language, especially technical jargon, that is difficult to understand (*informal*) **2. WORTHLESS BELIEFS OR RITUALS** religious beliefs, language, or rituals that appear pointless or meaningless to the speaker (*offensive in some contexts*) **3. SUPPOSEDLY SUPERNATURAL OBJECT** an object or effigy believed to hold supernatural powers [Mid-18C. Origin ?]

mu mes·on *n* PHYS same as **muon**

mum·mer /múmmər/ *n* **1.** somebody who participates in festivities wearing a mask or disguise **2.** an actor in a folk play or mime show **3.** THEATER same as **mime 4.** THEATER same as **actor** (*humorous*) [15C. < Old French *momeur* < *momer* "act in a mime"]

mum·mer·y /múmməree/ (*plural* **-ies**) *n* **1.** a performance by a group of mummers **2.** a showy or hypocritical ceremony

mum·mi·chog /múmmi chòg/ *n* a fish of the killifish family that can bury itself in mud when the tide recedes. Native to: salt marshes of the North American Atlantic coast. Latin name: *Fundulus heteroclitus.* [Late 18C. < Narraganset *moamitteaug*]

mum·mi·fy /múmmə fī/ (**-fied, -fy·ing, -fies**) *v* **1.** *vt* to preserve the corpse of a person or animal for burial by embalming it and wrapping it in cloth **2.** *vti* to dry out and shrivel, or cause something to dry out and shrivel [Early 17C. < MUMMY[2] after French *momifier*] —**mum·mi·fi·ca·tion** /mùmməfi káysh'n/ *n*

mum·my[1] /múmmee/ (*plural* **-mies**) *n UK* same as **mommy** [Late 18C. Dialectal variant of MAMMY]

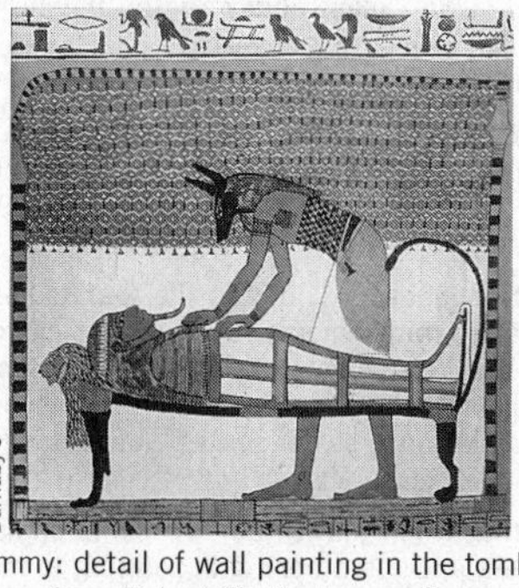

mummy: detail of wall painting in the tomb of Sennudjem, Deir-el-Medinah, near Luxor, Egypt (1295–1186 B.C.)

mum·my[2] /múmmee/ (*plural* **-mies**) *n* **1.** the body of a person or animal that has been embalmed and wrapped in cloth, especially as was the custom in ancient Egypt **2.** the body of an organism preserved by natural processes, e.g., by burial in peat or ice [Early 17C. Via Old French *momie* < Arabic *mūmiyā* "embalmed body"]

mum·my's boy *n UK* same as **mama's boy** (*insult*)

mumps /mumps/ *n* an acute contagious disease, usually affecting children, that causes a fever with swelling of the salivary glands and sometimes also affects the pancreas and ovaries or testes. It is caused by a virus and can be prevented through vaccination. It may cause sterility if contracted by a man. (*takes a singular or plural verb*) [Late 16C. Plural of obsolete *mump* "grimace," an imitation of the sounds made with a closed mouth]

mu·mu *n* CLOTHING another spelling of **muumuu**

munch /munch/ (**munched, munch·ing, munch·es**) *vti* to chew food purposefully, usually with visible movements of the jaw and sometimes with a crunching sound [14C. Origin ?] —**munch·er** *n*

AKG London

Edvard Munch

Munch /mŏŏngk/, **Edvard** (1863–1944) Norwegian painter. His work, suffused with melancholy and anguish, most famously in *The Scream* (1893), anticipates expressionism.

> "The sky was suddenly blood-red—I stopped and leaned against the fence, dead tired. I saw the flaming clouds like blood and a sword—the bluish-black fjord and town—my friends walked on—I stood there, trembling with anxiety—and I felt as though Nature were convulsed by a great unending scream."
> [Edvard Munch, *Letter*, 1892]

Mün·chau·sen syn·drome /mún chowz'n-/ *n* a psychological disorder in which somebody pretends to have a serious illness in order to undergo testing or treatment or to be admitted to a hospital

Mün·chau·sen syn·drome by prox·y *n* a diagnosis of child abuse asserting that a parent or caregiver induced symptoms of illness in a child

munch·ies /múncheez/ *npl* **1.** snack food, especially of the kind served with drinks at a party (*slang*) **2.** a craving for snack food (*informal*)

munch·kin /múnchkin/ *n* **1.** SMALL PERSON a small, sweet-natured, and harmless person **2.** CHILD a small child (*informal*) **3.** INSIGNIFICANT PERSON an insignificant person who keeps busy with trivial matters (*informal*) [Late 20C. < creatures invented by L. Frank Baum in *The Wizard of Oz* (1900)]

Mun·cie /múnssee/ city in eastern Indiana, on the White River, southwest of Fort Wayne and northeast of Indianapolis. Population: 67,195 (2002 estimate).

Mun·da /mŏŏndə/ *n* **1.** one of the four major Indian language groups spoken in eastern parts of South Asia. Native speakers: 5 million., belonging to the Austroasiatic family of languages **2.** somebody who speaks Munda as a native language [Mid-19C. < Munda *Muṇḍā*] —**Mun·da** *adj*

mun·dane /mun dáyn/ *adj* **1.** commonplace, not unusual, and often boring **2.** relating to matters of this world [15C. Via French < late Latin *mundanus* < Latin *mundus* "world"] —**mun·dane·ly** *adv* —**mun·dane·ness** *n*

Mun·de·lein /múndə līn/ village in northeastern Illinois, southwest of North Chicago. It is a northwestern suburb of Chicago. Population: 31,972 (2002 estimate).

mung bean /múng-/ *n* **1.** a small green or yellow bean that is dried and sometimes split. It is also germinated to produce bean sprouts. **2.** a plant that produces mung beans. Native to: East Asia. Latin name: *Vigna radiata*. [< Hindi *mūng*]

mun·go /múng gō/ *n* a cheap fabric made from waste wool and rags [Mid-19C. Origin ?]

Mun·go, Lake /múng gō/ dry lake in western New South Wales, Australia. It is part of Mungo National Park.

mu·ni[1] /myóonee/ (*plural* **-nis**) *n* same as **municipal bond** (*informal*) [Late 20C. Shortening]

mu·ni[2] /móonee/ (*plural* **-nis**) *n S Asia* a Hindu or Jain ascetic noted for exceptional holiness, religious inspiration, piety, or knowledge [Late 18C. < Sanskrit, literally, "silent" < *man* "think"]

Mu·nich /myóonik/ capital and largest city in the state of Bavaria, southeastern Germany. Population: 1,210,100 (2001).

Mu·nich Con·fer·ence *n* a meeting about Germany's occupation of Czechoslovakia in 1938, at which Western leaders agreed to the division of Czechoslovakia after receiving Hitler's assurances that he would take no more land

mu·nic·i·pal /myoo níssəp'l/ *adj* relating to a town, city, or region that has its own local government ■ *n* FIN same as **municipal bond** [Mid-16C. Directly or via French < Latin *municipalis* < *municip-* "holder of a civic office" < *munus* "gift, service, duty" + *capere* "take"] —**mu·nic·i·pal·ly** *adv*

mu·nic·i·pal bond *n* a bond or security issued by a city or other local government, usually to pay for public improvements

mu·nic·i·pal·i·ty /myoo nìssə pállətee/ (*plural* **-ties**) *n* **1.** a city, town, or other area that has its own local government **2.** the appointed or elected members of a local government

mu·nic·i·pal·ize /myoo níssəp'l ìz/ (**-ized, -iz·ing, -iz·es**) *vt* **1.** to bring something such as a public service or area of land under the ownership or control of a city, town, or other area with its own local government **2.** to grant a city, town, or other area powers of government in local matters —**mu·nic·i·pal·i·za·tion** /myoo nìssəp'li záysh'n/ *n*

mu·nif·i·cent /myoo níffiss'nt/ *adj* **1.** very generous in giving a lot of money **2.** characterized by generosity ○ *a munificent award* [Late 16C. < Latin *munificent-* < *munificus* "generous" < *munus* "gift, service, duty"] —**mu·nif·i·cence** *n* —**mu·nif·i·cent·ly** *adv*

SYNONYMS See ***generous***.

mu·ni·ments /myóonəmənts/ *npl* documents by which a claim to property or rights is supported, e.g., the title deeds to land [15C. < Latin *munimentum* "fortification" < *munire* (see MUNITION)]

mu·ni·tion /myoo nísh'n/ *vt* (**-tioned, -tion·ing, -tions**) to supply somebody with weapons and ammunition ■ **mu·ni·tions** *npl* military supplies, e.g., weapons and ammunition [Early 16C. Via French < Latin *munition-* < *munire* "fortify" < *moenia* "defensive walls"] —**mu·ni·tion·er** *n*

mu·ni·tion·ize /myoo nísh'n ìz/ (**-ized, -iz·ing, -iz·es**) *vt* ARMS same as **weaponize**

Mu·ñoz Ma·rín /moo nyŏz ma rín/, **Luis** (1898–1980) Puerto Rican politician. He was the first elected governor (1949–65), after Puerto Rico's status changed to that of a commonwealth (1952).

Mun·ro /mən rṓ/, **Alice** (*b.* 1931) Canadian writer, known for her short stories of rural Ontario life and sensitive portrayals of young girls. Her works include *Something I've Been Meaning to Tell You* (1974) and *Open Secrets* (1994). Pseudonym of **Laidlaw, Alice Anne**

Mun·see /múnssee/ (*plural same* or **-sees**), **Mun·si** (*plural same* or **-sis**) *n* **1.** the Algonquian language of the Delaware people. Munsee is nearly extinct. **2.** somebody who speaks Munsee as a native language [< Munsee] —**Mun·see** *adj*

mun·shi /móonshee/, **moon·shee** *n S Asia* somebody whose profession involves writing or language skills, e.g., a secretary or language teacher [Late 18C. Via Urdu and Persian < Arabic *mun šī'* "writer"]

Mun·ster[1] *n* FOOD another spelling of **Muenster**

Mun·ster[2] /múnstər/ **1.** historic province in the southwest of the Republic of Ireland **2.** town in northwestern Indiana, near the border with Illinois, southwest of Gary, part of the suburban area of Chicago. Population: 21,874 (2002 estimate).

Mün·ster /móonstər, mǘnstər/ inland port on the Dortmund-Ems Canal, North Rhine-Westphalia State, northwestern Germany. Population: 264,887 (1997).

mun·tin /múnt'n/ *n* a strip of wood or metal that separates and holds in place the panes of a window [Early 17C. Old French *montant* "upright" < present participle of *monter* (see MOUNT[1])]

munt·jac /múnt jàk/ (*plural* **-jacs** or *same*), **munt·jak** (*plural* **-jaks** or *same*) *n* a small deer with a reddish brown coat, a cry like a dog's bark, and small antlers. Native to: Southeast Asia. Genus: *Muntiacus*. [Late 18C. < Sundanese *minchek*, Malay *menjangan* "deer"]

mu·on /myóo òn/ *n* an elementary particle with a mass about 200 times that of an electron. It is a lepton with a negative charge and a half-life of two-millionths of a second. [Mid-20C. Contraction of MU MESON] —**mu·on·ic** /myoo ónnik/ *adj*

mu·on neu·tri·no *n* a lepton that exists in association with a muon. It has zero rest mass and no charge.

Mu·rad IV /myóor ad/ (1609–40) Arabian sultan. He succeeded Mustafa I as sultan of the Ottoman Empire (1623–40).

mu·ral /myóorəl/ *n* a usually large picture painted directly onto an interior or exterior wall ■ *adj* relating to or like a wall [Mid-16C. Via French < Latin *muralis* < *murus* "wall"] —**mu·ral·ist** *n*

mu·ram·ic ac·id /myoo ràmmik-/ *n* an amino sugar found in the cell walls of blue-green algae. Formula: $C_9H_{17}NO_7$. [< Latin *murus* "wall" + AMINE]

Mu·ra·sa·ki /móor aa saákee/, **Shikibu** (978?–1026?) Japanese lady-in-waiting at the imperial court and writer. She is known for *The Tale of Genji* (?1010), considered one of the world's first novels.

Mur·chi·son /múrchiss'n/ river in Western Australia that rises in the Robinson Range and flows into the Indian Ocean near the town of Kalbarri. Length: 500 mi./800 km.

Mur·cia /múrshə, múrssee ə/ capital of Murcia Province and Murcia Region, southeastern Spain. Population: 377,888 (2002).

mur·der /múrdər/ *n* **1.** CRIME OF KILLING SOMEBODY the crime of killing another person deliberately and not in self-defense or with any other extenuating circumstance recognized by law **2.** SOMETHING DIFFICULT OR UNPLEASANT something that is very difficult or unpleasant and involves great effort or hardship (*slang*) ○ *This exam is murder!* ■ *v* (**-dered, -der·ing, -ders**) **1.** *vti* KILL SOMEBODY ILLEGALLY to kill another person deliberately and not in self-defense or with any other extenuating circumstance recognized by law **2.** *vt* KILL SOMEBODY BRUTALLY to kill somebody with great violence and brutality **3.** *vt* SPOIL SOMETHING to spoil something such as a song or a piece of writing by performing it badly or changing it (*informal*) **4.** *vt* DEFEAT SOMEBODY COMPLETELY to defeat a person or team completely, especially in a sporting contest (*informal*) **5.** *vt* DESTROY SOMETHING to put an end to or destroy something (*informal*) ○ *The fire murdered their chances of selling the house.* [Old English *morþor*. < Indo-European] —**mur·der·er** *n* —**mur·der·ess** *n* ◇ **get away with murder** to escape punishment for or detection of wrongdoing

SYNONYMS See ***kill***[1].

mur·der·ous /múrdərəss/ *adj* **1.** LIKELY TO MURDER capable of, guilty of, or likely to commit murder **2.** LIKELY TO CAUSE DEATH violent and likely to result in bloodshed or murder **3.** DIFFICULT very difficult, unpleasant, or dangerous (*informal*) —**mur·der·ous·ly** *adv* —**mur·der·ous·ness** *n*

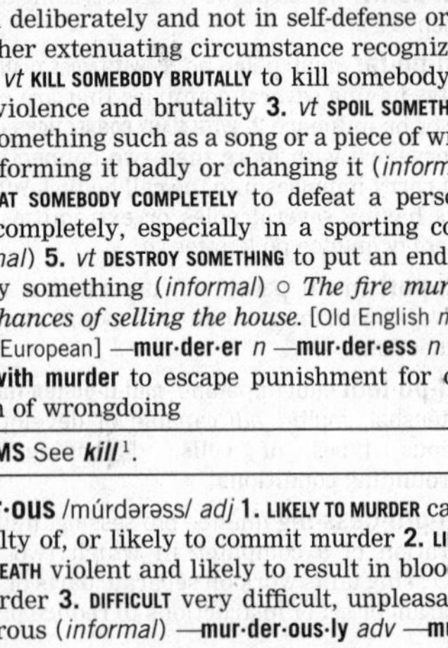

Express Newspapers

Dame Iris Murdoch

Mur·doch /múr dòk/, **Dame Iris** (1919–99) Irish-born British novelist and philosopher. Her many novels are noted for their thoughtful exploration of moral and philosophical problems. She is the author of *A Severed Head* (1961) and the Booker Prize-winning *The Sea, the Sea* (1978). Full name **Murdoch, Dame Jean Iris**. See illustration on previous page

> "We live in a fantasy world, a world of illusion. The great task in life is to find reality."
> [Dame Iris Murdoch, *Times (London)*; April 15, 1983]

Popperfoto

Rupert Murdoch

Mur·doch, Rupert (*b.* 1931) Australian-born US media proprietor, son of Sir Keith Murdoch. He turned his family's newspaper empire into a global network of media organizations. Full name **Murdoch, Keith Rupert**

> "There is no such thing as a global village. Most media are rooted in their national and local cultures."
> [Rupert Murdoch, *Business Review Weekly*; November 17, 1989]

mu·re·in /myoǒoree in, -reen/ *n* BIOCHEM same as **peptidoglycan** [Mid-20C. < Latin *murus* "wall" after PROTEIN; from its forming the walls of cells]

mu·rex /myoǒ rèks/ (*plural* **-ri·ces** /-ri seez/ or **-rex·es**) *n* an invertebrate sea animal that has a spiny shell. Native to: tropical waters. Genus: *Murex*. [Late 16C. < Latin]

mu·ri·at·ic ac·id /myoǒoree àttik-/ *n* CHEM same as **hydrochloric acid** [< Latin *muriaticus* "pickled in brine" < *muria* "brine"]

mu·ri·cate /myoǒri kàyt, -kət/, **mu·ri·cat·ed** /-kàytəd/ *adj* covered in short spines or points [Mid-17C. < Latin *muricatus* "shaped like a murex" < *murex*]

mu·ri·ces ZOOL plural of **murex**

Mu·ril·lo /myoo rílló/, **Bartolomé Esteban** (1617–82) Spanish painter. He is noted for his religious subjects and genre scenes.

mu·rine /myoǒorin, myoǒ reen/ *adj* **1. OF MOUSE AND RAT FAMILY** relating to or belonging to the family of long-tailed rodents that includes rats and mice. Family: Muridae. **2. LIKE RODENT** resembling a mouse or a rat **3. SPREAD BY RODENTS** caused or transmitted by mice or rats [Early 17C. < Latin *murinus* < *mur-* "mouse"]

mu·rine ty·phus *n* a relatively mild form of typhus that is transmitted from rats to humans by fleas or lice. Symptoms include fever, headaches, and muscular pain, and recovery is usually rapid. It is caused by the microorganism *Rickettsia typhi*.

murk /murk/ *n* **1.** gloomy darkness caused by fog, mist, smoke, or cloud **2.** *N England* a mist or thin fog (*informal*) ■ *adj* same as **murky** (*archaic or literary*) [Old English *mirce, myrce* < N Germanic]

murk·y /múrkee/ (**-i·er, -i·est**) *adj* **1. GLOOMY** dark and gloomy **2. HARD TO SEE THROUGH** thick with fog, mist, smoke, cloud, or dirt, and difficult to see through **3. OBSCURE** unclear and difficult to understand ○ *offered several murky excuses* **4. DISHONEST** involving dishonesty or illegal activities —**murk·i·ly** *adv* —**murk·i·ness** *n*

Mur·mansk /mur mánsk/ city and port in northwestern Russia, on the Kola Inlet, an arm of the Barents Sea. Population: 539,411 (1995).

~~**murmer**~~ incorrect spelling of **murmur**

mur·mur /múrmər/ *n* **1. CONTINUOUS HUM** a continuous low sound, often one that seems to be coming from some distance away **2. SOMETHING SAID QUIETLY** something said that is either very quiet or sounds indistinct **3. COMPLAINT** a complaint made in a discreet or secretive way **4.** MED **SOUND IN CHEST** a soft blowing or fluttering sound, usually heard via a stethoscope, that originates from the heart, lungs, or arteries and may indicate disease or structural concerns. It is caused by turbulent blood flow. ■ *v* (**-mured, -mur·ing, -murs**) **1.** *vti* **SAY SOMETHING SOFTLY** to say something very quietly or indistinctly **2.** *vi* **COMPLAIN DISCREETLY** to complain in a discreet or secretive way **3.** *vi* **MAKE CONTINUOUS LOW SOUND** to make a continuous low sound, often one that seems to be coming from some distance away [14C. Via French < Latin *murmurare*] —**mur·mur·er** *n* —**mur·mur·ing·ly** *adv* —**mur·mur·ous** *adj* —**mur·mur·ous·ly** *adv*

mur·mu·ra·tion /mùrmə ráysh'n/ *n* **1.** an act or sound of murmuring **2.** a flock of starlings

mur·mur·ings /múrməringz/ *npl* quiet and subdued expressions of discontent

Mur·phy /múrfee/ (*plural* **-phies**), **mur·phy** *n* CRIME same as **Murphy game** [See MURPHY GAME]

Mur·phy /múrfee/, **Audie** (1924–71) US actor and war hero. A Congressional Medal of Honor winner, he was the most decorated soldier of World War II and later starred in several movies, including *The Quiet American* (1958) and *The Unforgiven* (1960).

Mur·phy, Eddie (*b.* 1961) US actor and comedian. He came to prominence in US television's *Saturday Night Live* (1980–84) and has since appeared in numerous movies.

Mur·phy, Emily Gowan (1868–1933) Canadian writer and political and legal reformer. She was the first woman magistrate in the British Empire (1916) and an advocate of women's suffrage. Born **Ferguson, Emily Gowan**. Pseudonym **Janey Canuck**

Mur·phy, Frank (1890–1949) US Supreme Court associate justice (1940–49). In his many political and legal posts he consistently upheld civil liberties.

Mur·phy bed *n* a bed that can be folded or swung into a closet or wall recess when not in use [Early 20C. After William L. *Murphy* (1876–1959), US inventor]

Mur·phy game, **mur·phy game** *n* a confidence game in which somebody is lured into handing over money for something that is promised but never given, sometimes receiving only paper when the money is apparently returned [Mid-20C. After an imaginary prostitute, Miss *Murphy* used as a lure]

Mur·phy's Law *n* the law or principle that if anything can go wrong, it will (*informal*) [Mid-20C. After Edward A. *Murphy* (b. 1917), US engineer]

mur·rain /múrrən/ *n* **1.** an infectious disease that affects cattle, e.g., anthrax **2.** an infectious and fast-spreading disease (*archaic or humorous*) [14C. < Anglo-Norman *moryn*, Old French *morine* < *mourir* "die" < Latin *mori*]

Mur·ray /múrree/ **1.** major river in southeastern Australia. Length: 1,609 mi./2,589 km. **2.** city in southwestern Kentucky, on the Clarke River, southwest of Hopkinsville and southeast of Paducah. Population: 15,099 (1998).

Mur·ray, James (1721?–94) British military officer and colonial administrator. He was the first British governor of Quebec (1760–66).

Mur·ray, Sir James (1837–1915) British philologist and lexicographer. He laid the foundations of what became the *Oxford English Dictionary* and edited half of the first edition. Full name **Murray, James Augustus Henry**

Mur·ray, John (1741–1815) British-born American cleric. He emigrated to New England in 1770 and spent the rest of his life there preaching universal salvation and founding Universalist societies.

murre /mur/ *n* BIRDS same as **guillemot** [Late 16C. Origin ?]

murre·let /múrlət/ (*plural* **-lets** or *same*) *n* a small diving bird of the auk family. Genera: *Brachyramphus* or *Synthliboramphus*. Native to: coastal regions of north Pacific.

mur·rey /múrree/ *adj* of the color mulberry (*archaic*) [15C. Via Old French *moré* < medieval Latin *moratus* < Latin *morum* "mulberry"]

mur·rhine /múrrin, mú rīn/, **mur·rine** *n* a substance, possibly fluorite, that the ancient Romans used to make vases, cups, and other similar objects [Late 16C. < Latin *murr(h)inus* < *murra* "murrhine"]

Mur·row /múrrō/, **Edward R.** (1908–65) US journalist. His World War II radio broadcasts from wartime London helped swing US opinion behind the Allied cause. He went on to pioneer broadcast reportage in the early days of television. Full name **Murrow, Edward Roscoe**

> "This—is London."
> [Edward R. Murrow, famed sign-on, radio broadcasts from London during the Battle of Britain and World War II; 1939–45]

> "No one can terrorize a whole nation, unless we are all his accomplices."
> [Edward R. Murrow, on Joseph McCarthy and his Communist witch hunt, "See It Now," *CBS-TV*; March 7, 1954]

Mur·rum·bidg·ee /mùrrəm bíjjee/ river in southeastern Australia. Length: 980 mi./1,600 km.

mur·ther /múrthər/ (*archaic*) *n* same as **murder** *n* (sense 1) ■ *vti* (**-thered, -ther·ing, -thers**) same as **murder** *v* (sense 1) [14C. Variant]

mus. *abbr* **1.** museum **2.** music **3.** musical **4.** musician

Mu·saf /moǒssəf/ *n* in Judaism, a group of additional prayers that is included in morning services on Sabbaths, festivals, and Rosh Chodesh [< Hebrew, "addition"]

Mus.B., **Mus.Bac.** *abbr* EDUC, MUSIC Bachelor of Music [Latin *Musicae Baccalaureus*]

Mus·ca /múskə/ *n* a small constellation of the southern hemisphere. See illustration at **constellation**

mus·ca·del, **mus·ca·delle** *n* WINE same as **muscatel**

Mus·ca·det /múskə dáy/ *n* a dry white wine from western France [Early 20C. < French < *muscade* "nutmeg" < *musc* (see MUSK)]

mus·ca·dine /múskə dīn, -din/ *n* **1.** a purple grape variety with a thick skin and musky smell. Use: to make wine. **2.** a cultivated ancestor of a wild grapevine found in the southeastern United States that produces muscadine grapes. Latin name: *Vitis rotundifolia*. [Mid-16C. Probably variant of MUSCATEL]

mus·cae vol·i·tant·es /moǒ skī vōlə taán tàyz/ *npl* specks that appear to float before the eyes (*technical*) [Mid-18C. < Latin, "flies flying about"]

mus·ca·rine /múskərin, -reen/ *n* a toxic substance, found in fly agaric and some other fungi, that affects the nervous system when ingested. Among other effects it dilates the blood vessels, slows the heart rate, constricts the airways, and stimulates the gut. [Late 19C. < modern Latin *Muscaria*, species name of the fly agaric < Latin *musca* "fly"] —**mus·ca·rin·ic** /mùskə rínnik/ *adj*

mus·cat /mú skàt, múskət/ *n* a sweet white grape variety. Use: to make wine, raisins. [Mid-16C. Via French < Provençal < *musc* < Latin *muscus* (see MUSK)]

Mus·cat /mús kàt/, **Mas·qat** /máss gàt/ capital city of Oman, on the northeastern coast of the country, on the Gulf of Oman. Population: 635,000 (1995).

mus·ca·tel /mùskə tél/, **mus·ca·del** /-dél/, **mus·ca·delle** *n* **1.** a sweet white wine made from muscat grapes **2.** FOOD same as **muscat** [Mid-16C. Via Old French < Provençal, "little muscat" < *muscat* (see MUSCAT)]

Mus·ca·tine /mùskə teén/ city in southeastern Iowa, situated on the Mississippi River. Population: 22,650 (2002 estimate).

mus·ca·va·do *n* FOOD another spelling of **muscovado**

mus·cid /mússid/ *n* a fly of the family that includes the housefly and the stable fly. Family: Muscidae. [Late 19C. Back-formation < modern Latin *Muscidae* < Latin *musca* "fly"] —**mus·cid** *adj*

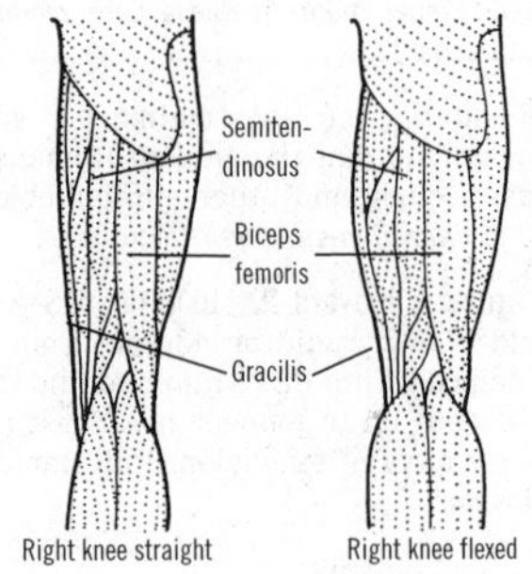

muscle: muscles of the human knee

mus·cle /múss'l/ *n* **1. BODY TISSUE PRODUCING MOVEMENT** a tissue that can undergo repeated contraction and relaxation, so that it is able to produce movement of body parts, maintain tension, or pump fluids within the body. There are three types: voluntary (**striped muscle**), involuntary (**smooth muscle**), and branched or heart muscle. **2. ORGAN COMPOSED OF MUSCLE** an organ composed of bundles or sheets of muscle tissue, bound together with connective tissue and with tendons by which the contracting part is attached to the bones that it moves **3. INFLUENCE** power and influence, especially in the political, financial, or military spheres **4. STRENGTH** physical strength (*informal*) ○ *put some muscle into it* **5. HIRED THUGS** men who are employed to intimidate, harm, or menace people (*slang*) ■ *vti* (**-cled, -cling, -cles**) **MOVE USING STRENGTH** to move using strength and force or effort, or make somebody or something move in this way (*informal*) ○ *muscled us aside to get to the head of the line* [14C. Via French < Latin *musculus* literally "small mouse" < *mus* "mouse"; from the supposed resemblance of some muscles to mice] —**mus·cly** *adj*

SPELLCHECK Do not confuse the spelling of ***muscle*** and ***mussel*** ("a shellfish"), which sound similar. ***Muscle*** is a noun meaning "a type of body organ," "influence," and "strength": *tired muscles; political muscle*; as a verb it means "to move forcefully": *muscled his way past.* ***Mussel*** meaning "a type of shellfish" is used only as a noun.

muscle in *vi* to become involved in or interfere in something by disregarding other people's wishes or by using strength, power, or influence (*informal*)

mus·cle-bound /múss'l bòwnd/, **mus·cle-bound** *adj* **1.** having muscles that are so bulky that they restrict movement **2.** too large, powerful, or overdeveloped to be capable of flexibility or a swift response

mus·cle càndy *n* a dietary supplement used by athletes to enhance bursts of high performance (*slang*)

mus·cle car *n* a flashy car with a big engine, designed to look like a sports car

mus·cle fi·ber *n* a basic contracting unit of striated muscle such as that in arms and legs, formed from several fused elongated cells (**myofibrils**) that contract when stimulated

mus·cle·man /múss'l màn/ (*plural* **-men** /-mèn/) *n* **1.** a very strong man with highly developed muscles **2.** a strong man hired by a criminal or gangster for protection and to intimidate enemies

mus·cle mar·y *n* an offensive term for a gay man with a muscular physique (*slang*)

mus·cle sense *n* PHYSIOL same as **kinesthesia**

mus·co·va·do /mùskə váydō, -vaá-/, **mus·ca·va·do** *n* a raw or unrefined sugar made by evaporating the molasses from sugar-cane juice [Early 17C. < Portuguese *mascabado* "made badly"]

mus·co·vite /múskə vìt/ *n* a common mica mineral consisting of potassium aluminum silicate. Source: igneous and sedimentary rocks. [Mid-19C. < *Muscovy glass* "mica" (from its being obtained from Russia)]

Mus·co·vite /múskə vìt/ *n* somebody who comes from Moscow, Russia ■ *adj* PEOPLES same as **Russian** (*archaic*) [Mid-16C. < modern Latin *Muscovia* < Russian *Moskva* "Moscow"]

Mus·co·vy /múskəvee/ former principality in western Russia, centered on Moscow

Mus·co·vy duck *n* a large duck with greenish black feathers, white markings, and heavy red wattles. Raised for: food. Native to: Central America. Latin name: *Cairina moschata*. [Alteration (by association with archaic *Muscovy* "of Moscow") of MUSK DUCK]

mus·cu·lar /múskyələr/ *adj* **1. OF MUSCLES** relating to, consisting of, or affecting muscles **2. STRONG** physically strong and with well-developed muscles **3. VIGOROUS** having considerable power or strength, but sometimes lacking subtlety [Late 17C. < obsolete *musculous*, directly or via French < Latin *musculosus* < *musculus* (see MUSCLE)] —**mus·cu·lar·i·ty** /mùskyə lárrətee/ *n* —**mus·cu·lar·ly** /múskyələrlee/ *adv*

mus·cu·lar dys·tro·phy *n* a medical condition in which there is gradual wasting and weakening of the skeletal muscles

mus·cu·la·ture /múskyələchər, -chòor/ *n* the way that the muscles are arranged in a body or body part [Late 19C. < French < Latin *musculus* (see MUSCLE)]

musculo- *prefix* muscle, muscular ○ *musculocutaneous* [< Latin *musculus* (see MUSCLE)]

mus·cu·lo·cu·ta·ne·ous /mùskyəlō kyoo táynee əss/ *adj* relating to or supplying the muscles and skin

mus·cu·lo·skel·e·tal /mùskyəlō skéllət'l/ *adj* relating to or involving the muscles and the skeleton

Mus.D., **Mus.Doc.** *abbr* Doctor of Music [Latin *Musicae Doctor*]

muse[1] /myooz/ *v* (**mused, mus·ing, mus·es**) **1.** *vti* **THINK ABOUT SOMETHING** to think about something in a deep and serious or dreamy and abstracted way **2.** *vti* **SAY SOMETHING THOUGHTFULLY** to say something in a thoughtful or questioning way **3.** *vi* **GAZE THOUGHTFULLY** to gaze at somebody or something thoughtfully or abstractedly ■ *n* **THOUGHTFUL STATE** a state of deep thought (*literary*) [14C. < Old French *muser* "meditate"] —**mus·er** *n* —**mus·ing·ly** *adv*

muse[2] /myooz/ *n* **1. SOMEBODY WHO INSPIRES ARTIST** somebody who is a source of inspiration for an artist, especially for a poet **2. ARTIST'S INSPIRATION** the source of inspiration that stimulates an artist, especially a poet **3. ARTIST'S PARTICULAR TALENT** the gift or talent of an artist, especially a poet ○ *"With Donne, whose muse on dromedary trots/ Wreathe iron pokers into true-love knots"* (Samuel Taylor Coleridge, *On Donne's Poetry*; 1818) [14C. Directly or via French < Latin *musa* < Greek *mousa*]

Muse *n* in Greek mythology, one of the nine daughters of Zeus and Mnemosyne, goddess of memory. The Muses inspired and presided over the creative arts. They were Calliope, Clio, Erato, Euterpe, Melpomene, Polyhymnia, Terpsichore, Thalia, and Urania, responsible for epic poetry, history, love poetry, lyric poetry, tragedy, sacred song, dance, comedy, and astronomy, respectively.

mu·se·ol·o·gy /myòozee óllәjee/ *n* the study of how museums are designed, organized, and managed [Late 19C. < MUSEUM] —**mu·se·o·log·i·cal** /myòozee ə lójjik'l/ *adj* —**mu·se·o·log·i·cal·ly** *adv* —**mu·se·ol·o·gist** *n*

mu·sette /myoo zét/ *n* **1. FRENCH BAGPIPE** French bagpipes that make a relatively soft sound. The musette was popular in the 17th, 18th, and 19th centuries. **2. PASTORAL DANCE MUSIC** a piece of pastoral dance music that imitates the sound of bagpipes or has bagpipes playing the bass line **3.** *also* **mu·sette bag** MIL **SOLDIER'S BAG** a small leather or canvas knapsack with one shoulder strap, used by soldiers [14C. < French, "little bagpipes" < *muse* "bagpipes"]

mu·se·um /myoo zée əm/ *n* **1.** a building or institution where objects of artistic, historical, or scientific importance and value are kept, studied, and put on display **2.** ONLINE the domain name for a museum (*used in Internet addresses*) See table at **domain name** [Early 17C. Via Latin, "library, academy" < Greek *mouseion* "place of the Muses" < *mousa* "muse"]

mu·se·um piece *n* **1.** an object that is so valuable, interesting, or old that it could or should be in a museum **2.** somebody or something considered very old-fashioned (*informal*)

Mus·grave Rang·es /mùss grayv-/ mountain range in central Australia, on the border between the Northern Territory and South Australia

mush[1] /mush/ *n* **1. PULP** a soft pulpy mass **2. SENTIMENTAL WORDS OR IDEAS** overly romantic and sentimental words or ideas, e.g., in a book or movie **3. FOOD COOKED CEREAL** a thick mixture made from cornmeal and milk or water ■ *vt* (**mushed, mush·ing, mush·es**) **MASH SOMETHING** to mash something into a soft pulpy mass [Late 17C. Probably variant of MASH] —**mush·y** *adj*

mush[2] /mush/ *interj* **COMMAND TO SLED DOGS** used to make sled dogs start pulling or moving faster ■ *n* **DOGSLED TRIP** a trip on a dogsled ■ *v* (**mushed, mush·ing, mush·es**) **1.** *vti* **TRAVEL BY DOGSLED** to travel on a dogsled, or drive a dogsled or team of dogs **2.** *vi Can* **TRAVEL ON SNOWSHOES** to travel on foot in difficult conditions, especially with snowshoes [Mid-19C. < *Mush on!*, probably < French *marchons* "let us march" < *marcher* "to march"] —**mush·er** *n*

Mu·shar·raf /moo shárraf/, **Pervez** (*b.* 1943) president of Pakistan. An army general, he seized power in a bloodless coup in 1999, and declared himself president and formal head of state in 2001.

mush·room /músh ròom, -ròom/ *n* **1. UMBRELLA-SHAPED FUNGUS** the usually umbrella-shaped spore-producing body of a fungus that consists of a fleshy cap on a stalk. Class: Basidiomycetes. **2. EDIBLE FUNGUS** an edible mushroom, especially the field mushroom **3. FAST-GROWING THING** something that grows very fast ■ *vi* (**-roomed, -room·ing, -rooms**) **1. GROW QUICKLY** to grow or develop very rapidly **2. BECOME MUSHROOM-SHAPED** to swell into a shape like a mushroom **3. PICK MUSHROOMS** to go mushroom picking [15C. Via French *mousseron* < late Latin *mussirion-* a type of mushroom] —**mush·room·y** *adj*

AKG London

mushroom cloud

mush·room cloud *n* the large mushroom-shaped cloud of dust and debris caused by an explosion, especially a nuclear explosion

Mu·shu·au In·nu /mə shòo aw-/ *n* a member of a Native North American people who once lived and hunted in the Canadian bush, but who now live in communities in Newfoundland and Labrador [< Montagnais] —**Mu·shu·au In·nu** *adj*

mu·sic /myòozik/ *n* **1. SOUNDS THAT PRODUCE EFFECT** sounds, usually produced by instruments or voices, that are arranged or played in order to create an effect **2. ART OF ARRANGING SOUNDS** the art of arranging or making sounds, usually those of musical instruments or voices, so as to create an effect **3. TYPE OF MUSIC** music of a particular type, place, time, instrument, or style ○ *rock-and-roll music* **4. WRITTEN MUSIC** written notation indicating the pitch, duration, rhythm, and tone of notes to be played **5. PLEASING SOUND** a sound or group of sounds that creates a desired effect ○ *the music of the wind in the trees* [13C. Via French *musique* < Greek *mousikē* "art of the Muse, music" < *mousikos* "of a Muse" < *mousa* "muse"] ◇ **be (like) music to somebody's ears** to be very pleasant, satisfying, or reassuring to hear ◇ **face the music** to deal with a pressing, difficult, or unpleasant situation arising from something you have done previously

mu·si·cal /myòozik'l/ *adj* **1. OF OR FOR MUSIC** relating to or producing music **2. PLEASANT-SOUNDING** sounding pleasant and melodious **3. GOOD AT MUSIC** having a talent for or a strong interest in music **4. WITH MUSIC** set to, consisting of, or involving music ■ *n* **PLAY OR MOVIE WITH SONGS** a lighthearted play or movie that has singing, music, and often dancing in it as important devices for developing the story and characters —**mu·si·cal·ly** *adv*

mu·si·cal box *n UK* same as **music box**

mu·si·cale /myòozi kál/ *n* a social occasion in which music is the featured entertainment [Late 19C. < French (*soirée*) *musicale* "musical evening"]

mu·si·cal·i·ty /myo͞ozi kállәtee/ *n* **1.** musical ability, especially a knowledge of or sensitivity to music **2.** the quality of being musical

mu·sic box *n* a box containing a mechanical device that plays music

mu·sic dra·ma *n* a type of opera, first composed by Richard Wagner in the late 19th century, in which the dramatic and musical content are intended to be of equal importance

mu·sic hall *n* **1.** an auditorium for musical and theatrical productions **2.** *UK* THEATER, MUSIC same as **vaudeville** (sense 1) **3.** *UK* a vaudeville theater

mu·si·cian /myoo zísh'n/ *n* somebody who plays, performs, conducts, or composes music —**mu·si·cian·ly** *adj* —**mu·si·cian·ship** *n*

mu·sic of the spheres *n* the perfect but inaudible music that Pythagoras and other later philosophers believed was created by the movement of astronomical objects

mu·si·col·o·gy /myo͞ozi kóllәjee/ *n* the academic study of music and its history —**mu·si·co·log·i·cal** /myo͞ozikә lójjik'l/ *adj* —**mu·si·co·log·i·cal·ly** *adv* —**mu·si·col·o·gist** *n*

mu·sic stand *n* a height-adjustable frame for holding printed music that is being performed

mu·sic vid·e·o *n* a short video or film made to accompany a song or piece of popular music, often as a cinematic or dramatic interpretation of it

Mu·sil /mo͞ozil/, **Robert** (1880–1942) Austrian novelist. Much of his work drew on personal experiences and often reflected Austrian culture.

mus·ings /myo͞ozingz/ *npl* thoughts, especially when aimless and unsystematic ○ *philosophical musings*

mu·sique con·crète /myoo zeék kong krét/ *n* recorded music composed by electronically combining and enhancing natural and musical sounds [Mid-20C. < French, "concrete music"]

musk /musk/ *n* **1.** GLANDULAR SECRETION OF DEER a pungent and greasy secretion from a gland in the male musk deer. Use: perfume manufacture. **2.** SUBSTANCE LIKE MUSK a secretion similar to musk from other animals such as the civet or otter, or a synthetic substance with similar properties **3.** PLANTS PLANT WITH MUSKY SCENT a plant that has a musky scent, especially the musk plant **4.** SMELL OF MUSK the smell of musk, or a similar smell **5.** ZOOL same as **musk deer** [14C. Via late Latin *muscus* < Persian *mušk*]

musk deer *n* a small mountain-dwelling deer, the male of which lacks antlers and possesses long canine teeth. Native to: central and northeastern Asia. Latin name: *Moschus moschiferus*.

musk duck *n* BIRDS same as **Muscovy duck** [< its smell]

mus·keg /mú skèg/ *n* **1.** an area of swamp or boggy land covered in sphagnum moss, leaves, and a mass of dead plant matter resembling peat **2.** the dead plant matter resembling peat that covers areas of muskeg [Late 18C. < Cree *maske:k*]

mus·kel·lunge /múskә lùnj/ (*plural* **-lun·ges** or *same*), **mas·ki·nonge** /máskә nùnj/ (*plural* **-non·ges** or *same*) *n* **1.** a large predatory freshwater fish of the pike family, caught for game. Native to: Great Lakes region. Latin name: *Esox masquinongy*. **2.** the flesh of a muskellunge used as food [Late 18C. Via Canadian French *maskinongé* < Ojibwa *maashkinoozhe* "big fish"]

mus·ket /múskәt/ *n* a shoulder gun with a long barrel and a smooth bore, used between the 16th and 18th centuries [Late 16C. Via French *mousquet* < Italian *moschetto* "crossbow bolt" < *mosca* "fly" < Latin *musca*]

ORIGIN Early *muskets* could fire crossbow bolts as well as bullets. The name was probably reinforced by Italian *moschetto* "sparrow hawk" (from its markings suggestive of flies), early guns being often named after birds of prey (e.g., *falconet*, a type of small cannon).

mus·ket·eer /múskә teér, mùskә teér/ *n* **1.** an infantryman armed with a musket **2.** a member of a company of musketeers in the French royal household's personal troops in the 17th and 18th centuries

CULTURAL NOTE ***The Three Musketeers***, a novel (1844) by French writer Alexandre Dumas. Set in France during the reign of Louis XIII, this historical romance tells the story of a young adventurer, D'Artagnan, who is taken under the wing of three musketeers, Athos, Porthos, and Aramis. The four become embroiled in a series of adventures involving love, politics, swordsmanship, and the machinations of the evil Cardinal Richelieu.

mus·ket·ry /múskәtree/ *n* **1.** a group of muskets or musketeers **2.** the technique or practice of using small arms

Mus·kho·ge·an *n, adj* LANG another spelling of **Muskogean**

mus·kie /múskee/ (*plural* **-kies** or *same*) *n* FISH same as **muskellunge** [Late 19C. Shortening]

musk mal·low *n* **1.** a plant of the mallow family with a hairy and often purple-spotted stem and a slight musky scent. Flowers: pink. Native to: Europe, North Africa. Latin name: *Malva moschata*. **2.** PLANTS same as **abelmosk**

musk·mel·on /músk mèllәn/ *n* **1.** a fruit with a ribbed or rough rind and white, yellow, or green flesh with a sweet full flavor and a pleasant, slightly musky smell **2.** a widely cultivated trailing vine that produces muskmelons. Latin name: *Cucumis melo*.

Mus·ko·ge·an /muss kṓgee әn/, **Mus·kho·ge·an** *n* a Hokan-Siouan branch of languages, including Chickasaw, Choctaw, and Creek —**Mus·ko·ge·an** *adj*

Mus·ko·gee /muss kṓgee/ (*plural same* or **-gees**) *n* a member of a Native North American people who lived in southeastern North America [Late 18C. < Creek *ma:skó:ki*]

musk ox, **musk·ox** /músk òks/ *n* a large wild ox with a black or brown shaggy coat and flat downward-curving horns. Native to: northern Canada, Greenland. Latin name: *Ovibos moschatus*.

musk plant *n* a perennial plant of the figwort family. Flowers: yellow, tubular, with a musky smell. Native to: North America. Latin name: *Mimulus moschatus*.

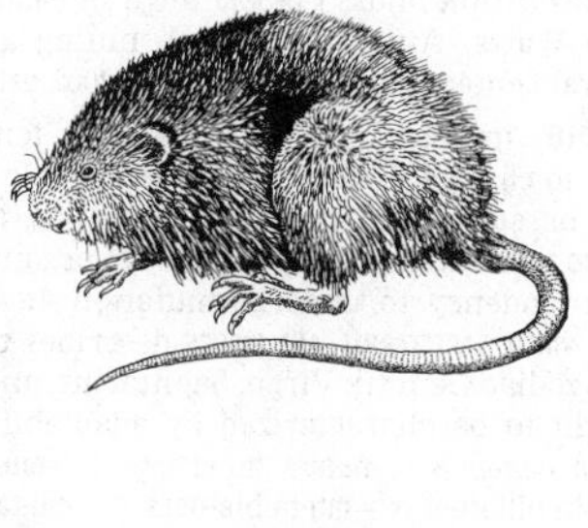

muskrat

musk·rat /mús kràt/ (*plural same* or **-rats**) *n* **1.** a large amphibious rodent, closely related to the vole and the lemming, with a thick brown coat and musk glands. Native to: North America, Europe. Latin name: *Ondatra zibethica*. **2.** the fur of the muskrat [Early 17C. < Algonquian *muscasus*, by association with MUSK and RAT]

musk·root /músk ro͝ot/ *n* PLANTS same as **moschatel**

musk rose *n* a late-flowering rose with white, musk-scented flowers. Native to: Mediterranean. Latin name: *Rosa moschata*.

musk tur·tle *n* a small freshwater turtle that gives off a pungent smell. Native to: eastern United States, Canada. Genus: *Sternotherus*.

musk·y[1] /múskee/ (**-i·er, -i·est**) *adj* having a sweet pungent smell similar to that of musk —**musk·i·ly** *adv* —**musk·i·ness** *n*

mus·ky[2] /múskee/ (*plural* **-kies** or *same*) *n* FISH same as **muskellunge**

~~**musle**~~ incorrect spelling of **muscle**

Mus·lim /múzzlәm, mo͝oz-/ *n* somebody whose religion is Islam ■ *adj* relating to the followers of Islam or to areas, cultures, or activities in which followers of Islam are especially numerous [Early 17C. < Arabic, "somebody who surrenders (to God)," active participle of *'aslama* (see ISLAM)]

Mus·lim Broth·er·hood *n* an Egyptian nationalist movement founded by Hasan al-Bannah in 1928 that is committed to the Islamic fundamentalist cause and opposes Western influence. The Muslim Brotherhood is active in several other countries throughout Southwest Asia, North Africa, South Asia, and Southeast Asia.

Mus·lim League *n* a Muslim political organization founded in India in 1906 that was instrumental in achieving the creation of Pakistan in 1947. It caused a division within the Indian nationalist movement.

mus·lin /múzzlin/ *n* a thin plain-weave cotton cloth. Use: curtains, sheets, dresses. [Early 17C. Via French *mousseline* < Italian *mussolina*, < Arabic *mawsiliy* "of Mosul," city in Iraq]

Mus.M. *abbr* Master of Music [Latin *Musicae Magister*]

mus·quash /mú skwàwsh/ *n* ZOOL same as **muskrat** [Early 17C. < Massachusett < W Abenaki *mòskwas*]

muss /muss/ (*informal*) *vt* (**mussed, muss·ing, muss·es**) to make something, especially somebody's hair or clothes, messy or ruffled ■ *n* a state of messiness or disorder [Mid-19C. Probably variant of MESS]

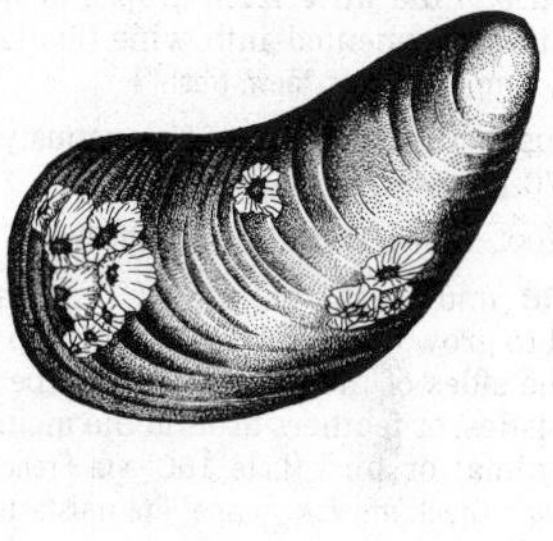

mussel

mus·sel /múss'l/ *n* **1.** an edible bivalve mollusk with a blue-black shell that lives attached to objects in the ocean. Genus: *Mytilus*. **2.** a freshwater bivalve mollusk whose shell is a source of mother-of-pearl. Genera: *Anodonta* or *Unio*. [Pre-12C. < assumed Vulgar Latin *muscula*, alteration of Latin *musculus* "small mouse" (see MUSCLE); from the mussel's supposed resemblance in shape and color to a mouse]

SPELLCHECK See ***muscle***.

Mus·so·li·ni /mo͝ossә leénee/, **Benito** (1883–1945) Italian national leader. He founded the Italian Fascist Party in 1919 and served as prime minister from 1922 and dictator (1925–43). After forming an alliance with Germany in 1939, he brought Italy into World War II (1940). He was overthrown three years later, and eventually assassinated by the Italian Resistance. Full name **Mussolini, Benito Amilcaro Andrea**. Known as **Il Duce**

Mus·sorg·sky /mә záwrgskee, -sáwrgskee/, **Modest** (1839–81) Russian composer. His works, often inspired by Russian folk music, include the opera *Boris Godunov* (1868) and the piano suite *Pictures at an Exhibition* (1874). Full name **Mussorgsky, Modest Petrovich**

> "Art is not an end in itself, but a means of addressing humanity."
> [Attributed to Modest Mussorgsky]

Mus·sul·man /múss'lmәn/ (*plural* **-men** /-mәn/ or **-mans**) *n* same as **Muslim** (*archaic*) [Late 16C. < Persian *musulmān* "Muslim" (adjective) < Arabic *muslim* (see MUSLIM)]

muss·y /mússee/ (**mus·si·er, mus·si·est**) *adj US* not neat or in an orderly state (*informal*) —**muss·i·ly** *adv* —**muss·i·ness** *n*

must[1] /must/ (**must**, *plural* **musts**) CORE MEANING: a modal verb indicating that somebody is compelled to do something because of a rule or law, or that it is necessary or advisable to do something ○ *Accidents causing injury must be reported immediately.* ○ *Employment decisions must be based on ability.* ○ *We must improve our schools.* ○ *You must give him a chance to state his case.*

1. *modal v* BE COMPELLED to be compelled to do something because of a rule or law ○ *You must stop when the light is red.* ○ *All guests must vacate their rooms by 12 noon.* **2.** *modal v* BE NECESSARY to be important or necessary for doing something ○ *Henceforth, he* *said, the central organizing principle of all governments must be the environment.* ○ *Health care insurance must be affordable.* **3.** *modal v* **BE CERTAIN** indicates that somebody is sure that something is the case ○ *This must seem strange to you.* ○ *Those must be your footprints in the garden.* **4.** *modal v* **INDICATES BELIEF** indicates that somebody concludes that something is the case on the basis of the available evidence ○ *Paleontologists know that primates must have immigrated to South America sometime before 28 million years ago.* **5.** *modal v* **USED TO MAKE SUGGESTIONS** used to make suggestions or invitations or to give advice ○ *You must see a doctor.* **6.** *modal v* **INTEND** to intend or be determined to do something (*formal*) ○ *I must call the company.* **7.** *n* **SOMETHING ESSENTIAL** something that is essential or obligatory ○ *Formal attire is a must at a state dinner.* **8.** *prefix* **ESSENTIAL** absolutely necessary or highly recommended for somebody (*informal; added to a verb to form a noun or adjective*) ○ *a must-win situation* [Old English *mōste*, past tense of assumed *mōtan* "have to, be able to" < Germanic]

must[2] /must/ *n* the juice from grapes or other fruit that is to be fermented into wine [Pre-12C. < Latin *mustum*, form of *mustus* "new, fresh"]

must[3] /must/ *n* the condition of being musty or moldy [Early 17C. Back-formation < MUSTY]

must[4] *n* ZOOL another spelling of **musth**

mus·tache /mú stàsh, mə stásh/ *n* **1.** facial hair allowed to grow on somebody's upper lip and often down the sides of the mouth or onto the cheeks **2.** hair, bristles, or feathers around the mouth or beak of an animal or bird [Late 16C. Via French < Italian *mostaccio* < Greek *mustak-* "upper lip, mustache"] —**mus·tached** *adj*

mus·ta·chi·o /mə stáshee ō/ (*plural* **-os**) *n* a mustache that is thick or trimmed into a fancy shape (*archaic or humorous; often used in the plural*) [Mid-16C. Blend of Spanish *mostacho* + Italian *mostaccio* (see MUSTACHE)] —**mus·ta·chi·oed** *adj*

mus·tang /mú stàng/ *n* a small hardy wild horse living on the plains of North America, descended from Arabian horses brought to the continent by Spanish soldiers [Early 19C. Via Mexican Spanish *mestengo* < Spanish, "ownerless" < *mesta* "ranchers who appropriated wild cattle" < Latin *mixta* "mixed"]

mus·tard /mústərd/ *n* **1.** **SPICY CONDIMENT** the powdered seeds of a brassica plant, or a hot spicy paste made from these, or sometimes whole seeds, water, and other ingredients, eaten in small quantities as a condiment **2.** PLANTS **PLANT WITH PUNGENT SEEDS** a plant with long thin seedpods containing mustard seeds. Flowers: small, yellow. Genus: *Brassica.* **3.** COLORS **DARK YELLOW COLOR** a brownish yellow color, like that of mustard **4.** **ENTHUSIASM** enthusiasm or zest (*informal*) [12C. < Old French *mo(u)starde* < Latin *mustum* "must, new wine" (originally mixed with the crushed seeds)] —**mus·tard** *adj* —**mus·tard·y** *adj* ◇ **cut the mustard** to be up to the desired standard of performance, ability, or quality (*informal*)

mus·tard gas *n* an oily liquid that evaporates into a poison gas. Used in chemical warfare, it burns the skin and causes often fatal respiratory damage. Formula: $(CH_2ClCH_2)_2S$. [Because its smell resembles mustard]

mus·tard oil *n* an oil obtained from mustard seeds. Use: making soap.

mus·tard plas·ter *n* a paste made from black mustard seeds and applied to the skin. Use: formerly, to stimulate blood flow and counter inflammation.

mus·tee /mu stée, mústee/ *n* (*dated taboo*) **1.** an offensive term for somebody with one white parent and one parent who has one Black grandparent **2.** a highly offensive term that deliberately insults somebody of mixed racial descent [Late 17C. Shortening and alteration of Spanish *mestizo* (see MESTIZO)]

mus·te·line /mústə lìn, -lin/ *adj* relating to, belonging to, or characteristic of the group of mammals that includes weasels, otters, badgers, and skunks. Family: Mustelidae. [Mid-17C. < Latin *mustelinus* < *mustel* "weasel"]

mus·ter /mústər/ *v* (**-tered, -ter·ing, -ters**) **1.** *vt* **CALL UP SOMETHING** to summon up something such as strength or courage that will help in doing something **2.** *vti* **ASSEMBLE SOLDIERS OR CREW MEMBERS** to bring together a group of soldiers or the members of a crew, e.g., for inspection, or be brought together in this way **3.** *vt* **GATHER PEOPLE OR THINGS** to gather people or things together ■ *n* **1.** **MILITARY ASSEMBLY** a gathering of soldiers or a crew, e.g., for inspection **2.** MIL, NAVY same as **muster roll** **3.** **GATHERING OR COLLECTION** a gathering of people or collection of things [14C. Via Old French *mo(u)strer* "to show," *moustre* "showing" < Latin *monstrare* < *monstrum* "(evil) omen, sign"] ◇ **pass muster** to measure up to set standards or to expectations

muster in *vti* to enroll somebody for military service, or be enrolled for military service

muster out *vti* to discharge somebody from military service, or be discharged from military service

mus·ter roll *n* a list of the members of a military or naval unit

musth /must/, **must** *n* a state of increased sexual activity accompanied by aggression in large male land mammals, especially male elephants, lasting 2 to 3 months [Late 19C. Via Urdu *mast* < Persian, "drunk, intoxicated"]

must-have *adj* absolutely necessary or highly recommended to possess ○ *a list of this year's must-have accessories* —**must-have** *n*

Mus·tique /mu stéek/ island in the eastern Caribbean Sea. It is part of St. Vincent and the Grenadines.

must·n't /múss'nt/ *contr* must not ○ *You mustn't worry.*

must-see *n* something that is considered so important, beautiful, or excellent that everyone should see it, e.g., a place, movie, or work of art (*often used before a noun*)

must·y /mústee/ (**-i·er, -i·est**) *adj* **1.** **WITH OLD DAMP SMELL** smelling old, damp, and stale because of not having been used or exposed to fresh air for a long time **2.** **WITH STALE TASTE** tasting old, stale, and moldy **3.** **OUTDATED AND UNINTERESTING** no longer relevant or interesting because of being old-fashioned [Early 16C. Origin ?] —**must·i·ly** *adv* —**must·i·ness** *n*

Mus·well·brook /múss'l bro͝ok/ town in eastern New South Wales, Australia, a coal mining and agricultural center. Population: 15,352 (2002 estimate).

mu·ta·ble /myo͞otəb'l/ *adj* **1.** **CHANGEABLE** tending or likely to change **2.** **CAPABLE OF CHANGE** capable of changing, or subject to change **3.** GENETICS **TENDING TO UNDERGO MUTATION** describes a gene or organism that has a tendency to undergo mutation **4.** ASTROL **OF GEMINI, VIRGO, SAGITTARIUS, AND PISCES** describes the signs of the zodiac Gemini, Virgo, Sagittarius, and Pisces, thought to be characterized by adaptability [14C. < Latin *mutabilis* < *mutare* "to change"] —**mu·ta·bil·i·ty** /myo͞otə bíllətee/ *n* —**mu·ta·ble·ness** *n* —**mu·ta·bly** *adv*

mu·ta·gen /myo͞otəjən/ *n* an external agent that increases the rate of mutation of cells or organisms, e.g., radiation or some chemicals or viruses [Mid-20C. < MUTATION + -GEN] —**mu·ta·gen·e·sis** /myo͞otə jénnəssiss/ *n* —**mu·ta·gen·ic** /myo͞otə jénnik/ *adj* —**mu·ta·gen·i·cal·ly** *adv* —**mu·ta·ge·nic·i·ty** /myo͞otəjə níssətee/ *n*

mu·tant /myo͞ot'nt/ *n* **1.** **SOMETHING THAT HAS MUTATED** an animal, organism, cell, or gene that has mutated **2.** **OFFENSIVE TERM** an offensive term for somebody who looks or appears strange (*slang insult*) **3.** **ODD THING** a strange-looking thing or animal (*slang*) ■ *adj* **1.** **RESULTING FROM MUTATION** undergoing or resulting from genetic mutation **2.** **APPEARING STRANGE** having an odd appearance or other qualities regarded as strange (*slang*) [Early 20C. < Latin *mutant-*, present participle of *mutare* "to change"]

Mu·tare /moo taáree/ resort city and capital of Manicaland Province in eastern Zimbabwe, close to the Mozambique border. Population: 131,367 (1992).

mu·tase /myo͞o tàyss, -tàyz/ *n* an enzyme that promotes a change in the shape of a molecule [Early 20C. < Latin *mutare* "to change"]

mu·tate /myo͞o tàyt, myoo táyt/ (**-tat·ed, -tat·ing, -tates**) *vti* to undergo mutation, or make something undergo mutation [Mid-18C. Partly back-formation < MUTATION; partly < Latin *mutat-*, past participle of *mutare* "to change"] —**mu·ta·tive** /myo͞o tàytiv, -tətiv/ *adj*

mu·ta·tion /myoo táysh'n/ *n* **1.** **CHANGE IN GENETIC MATERIAL** a random change in a gene or chromosome resulting in a new trait or characteristic that can be inherited. Mutation can be a source of beneficial genetic variation, or it can be neutral or harmful in effect. **2.** BIOL same as **mutant** *n* (sense 1) **3.** **ALTERATION** the action or process of changing something or of being changed **4.** LING same as **umlaut** *n* (sense 1) **5.** PHON **PHONETIC CHANGE** a phonetic change found in Celtic languages in which the initial consonant of a word changes according to the preceding word —**mu·ta·tion·al** *adj* —**mu·ta·tion·al·ly** *adv*

mu·ta·tion stop *n* a stop that controls a set of organ pipes that do not play the tones of the written notes, but usually a fifth or third above them

mu·ta·tis mu·tan·dis /moo taátiss moo taándiss/ *adv* with the necessary changes having been made [< Latin]

mu·ta·waa /moo taá waa/ *npl* in some Muslim countries, a police force whose duty is to ensure that the population complies with the laws of Islam [< Arabic]

Mu·taz·i·lite /moo taázə lìt/ *n* a member of an ancient Muslim religious group who subsequently became part of the Shia group [Early 18C. < Arabic, "those who keep to themselves"]

mute /myoot/ *adj* **1.** **NOT SPEAKING** unwilling or unable to speak **2.** **MAKING NO SOUND** saying nothing, or making no sound **3.** **NOT EXPRESSED IN WORDS** felt or expressed without speech **4.** LAW **NOT ANSWERING CHARGE** refusing to answer a charge brought in a court of law **5.** PHON same as **plosive** **6.** PHON **NOT PRONOUNCED** not pronounced, like the final "e" in "cheese" ■ *n* **1.** **OFFENSIVE TERM** an offensive term for somebody who is unable or unwilling to speak (*dated*) **2.** LAW **SOMEBODY REFUSING TO ANSWER CHARGE** somebody who refuses to answer a charge in a court of law **3.** MUSIC **DEVICE FOR ALTERING TONE OF INSTRUMENT** a pad, clip, or other device used to reduce or alter in some way the tone of a brass or stringed instrument **4.** PHON **SILENT LETTER** a letter that is not pronounced **5.** PHON same as **plosive** **6.** **HIRED MOURNER** somebody who was formerly paid to act as a mourner at a funeral ■ *vt* (**mut·ed, mut·ing, mutes**) **1.** **TURN DOWN SOUND** to moderate the volume of a sound **2.** **MAKE SOMETHING LESS BRIGHT** to make a color or light less bright or harsh **3.** MUSIC **ALTER TONE OF INSTRUMENT** to reduce or alter in some way the tone of a brass or stringed instrument using a pad, clip, or other device [14C. < French *muet* "slightly mute" < Old French *mu* < Latin *mutus*] —**mute·ly** *adv* —**mute·ness** *n*

mut·ed /myo͞otəd/ *adj* **1.** **NOT BRIGHT OR INTENSE** not bright, intense, or harsh in color or tone **2.** **NOT LOUD** not loud or distinct enough to be heard clearly **3.** **UNDERSTATED** subdued and understated ○ *muted criticism* **4.** MUSIC **FROM INSTRUMENT WITH MUTE** fitted with a mute, or produced by an instrument fitted with a mute —**mut·ed·ly** *adv*

mute swan *n* a large white swan with an orange bill. Native to: Europe, Asia. Latin name: *Cygnus olor*.

mu·ti·late /myo͞ot'l àyt/ (**-lat·ed, -lat·ing, -lates**) *vt* **1.** **DESTROY BODY PART** to inflict serious injury on the body or a part of the body of a person or animal by removing or destroying parts of it **2.** **RUIN SOMETHING BY REMOVING PARTS** to damage or spoil something such as a piece of writing or a movie by removing important parts of it **3.** **DAMAGE SOMETHING SERIOUSLY** to inflict serious damage on something [Mid-16C. Partly < Latin *mutilat-*, past participle of *mutilare* "cut or lop off" < *mutilus* "maimed"; partly < obsolete *mutilate* "mutilated"] —**mu·ti·la·tion** /myo͞ot'l áysh'n/ *n* —**mu·ti·la·tive** *adj* —**mu·ti·la·tor** *n*

mu·ti·neer /myo͞ot'n éer/ *n* somebody who rebels against the legal authority of others, especially a soldier or sailor [Early 17C. < French *mutinier* < Old French *mutin* "rebellious" (see MUTINY)]

mu·ti·nous /myo͞ot'nəss/ *adj* **1.** plotting, participating in, or typical of a mutiny **2.** refusing to obey or submit to control, especially military control [Late 16C. < Old French *mutineus* < *mutin* "rebellious" (see MUTINY), or < English *mutine*] —**mu·ti·nous·ly** *adv* —**mu·ti·nous·ness** *n*

mu·ti·ny /myo͞ot'nee/ *n* (*plural* **-nies**) a rebellion against legal authority, especially by soldiers or sailors refusing to obey orders and, often, attacking their officers ■ *vi* (**-nied, -ny·ing, -nies**) to take part in a rebellion against legal authority [Mid-16C. Via obsolete *mutine* "rebellion" < French *mutiner* < Old French *mutin* "rebellious" < *muete* "revolt," via assumed Vulgar Latin *movitus* < Latin *motus* "moved"]

mut·ism /myóo tìzzəm/ *n* **1.** a refusal to speak either at all times or at some times, usually as a result of trauma or stress **2.** an offensive term for the inability to speak (*dated*)

mu·ton /myóo tòn/ *n* the smallest known unit of DNA in which mutation can take place, either spontaneously or as a result of an external agent [Mid-20C. < MUTATION]

mutt /mut/ *n* **1.** a dog that is of mixed or unknown breed (*slang*) **2.** an offensive term that deliberately insults somebody's intelligence or knowledge (*slang insult*) [Late 19C. Shortening of MUTTONHEAD]

mut·ter /múttər/ *v* (**-tered, -ter·ing, -ters**) **1.** *vti* **SAY SOMETHING QUIETLY** to speak or say something quietly and indistinctly **2.** *vi* **GRUMBLE** to say something in a quiet voice, especially as a complaint or in annoyance ■ *n* **1. ACT OF UTTERING QUIETLY** an act of saying something quietly and indistinctly **2. SOMETHING SAID QUIETLY** a quiet and indistinct utterance [14C. Origin ?] —**mut·ter·er** *n*

mut·ton /mútt'n/ *n* the flesh of a fully grown sheep, eaten as food [13C. Directly or via Old French *molton* "ram, wether, sheep" < medieval Latin *multon-*] —**mut·ton·y** *adj*

mut·ton·bird *n* a seabird traditionally hunted for food, e.g., a petrel or shearwater. Native to: Australasia. Family: Procellaridae. [Because its cooked flesh is said to resemble mutton]

mut·ton·chops /mútt'n chòps/ *npl* facial hair trimmed into a narrow strip beside each ear, broadening out along the lower cheek and stopping at the side of the chin, which is kept bare [< the shape]

mut·ton·fish /mútt'n fish/ (*plural same* or **-fish·es**) *n* a bottom-dwelling sea fish with a large head and an elongated body. Native to: northeastern North America coast. Latin name: *Macrozoarces americanus*. [Because the taste of its flesh is said to resemble mutton]

mut·ton·head /mútt'n hèd/ *n* an offensive term that deliberately insults somebody's intelligence or knowledge (*informal insult*) —**mut·ton·head·ed** /mùtt'n héddəd/ *adj*

mut·ton snap·per *n* an olive-green fish of the snapper family that is caught for food and sport. Native to: tropical western Atlantic. Latin name: *Lutjanus analis*.

mu·tu·al /myóochoo əl/ *adj* **1. FELT BY EACH** done, felt, or expressed by each toward or with regard to the other ○ *mutual admiration* **2. WITH SAME FEELINGS** having or involving the same feelings toward each other ○ *mutual friendship* **3. SHARED BY PEOPLE** shared by or common to two or more people or groups **4.** INSUR **OF MUTUAL INSURANCE** relating to mutual insurance ■ *n* FIN same as **mutual fund** [15C. < French *mutuel* < Latin *mutuus* "borrowed, reciprocal, done in exchange"] —**mu·tu·al·i·ty** /myòochoo állətee/ *n* —**mu·tu·al·ly** *adv*

mu·tu·al as·sured de·struc·tion *n* the enormous reciprocal damage that the superpowers and their allies would inflict on each other in the event of a nuclear war

mu·tu·al com·pa·ny *n* a company owned by its clients, e.g., an insurance company owned by its policyholders, who receive profits in the form of bonuses instead of in share dividends

mu·tu·al fund *n* an investment company that uses members' capital to buy a diverse group of stocks from other companies

mu·tu·al in·duc·tance *n* a measure of the change in the electromotive force of a circuit caused by a change in the current flowing through an associated circuit. It is given as the ratio of the electromotive force induced to the rate of current change producing it. Symbol *M*

mu·tu·al in·duc·tion *n* the production of an electromotive force in a circuit resulting from a change in the current flowing through another circuit to which it is magnetically linked

mu·tu·al in·sur·ance *n* a method of insurance in which the customers buying policies own the company, pay premiums into a common fund to cover claims, and share in the profits

mu·tu·al·ism /myóochoo ə lìzzəm/ *n* a relationship between two organisms of different species that benefits both and harms neither. For example, lichens are a fungus and an alga living in mutualism: The fungus provides a protective structure, and the alga produces a carbohydrate as food for the fungus. —**mu·tu·al·ist** *n* —**mu·tu·al·is·tic** /myòochoo ə lístik/ *adj*

mu·tu·al·ize /myóochoo ə lìz/ (**-ized, -iz·ing, -iz·es**) *v* **1.** *vti* to become mutual, or make something mutual **2.** *vt* to alter the organization of a company so that the majority of its shares become owned by the employees and customers —**mu·tu·al·i·za·tion** /myòochoo əli záysh'n/ *n*

mu·tu·al sav·ings bank *n* a bank without shareholders in which the depositors are technically the owners

mu·tu·el /myóochoo əl/ *n* GAMBLING same as **pari-mutuel** [Early 20C. Shortening]

mu·tule /myóo chool/ *n* a projecting block that holds a conical ornament (**gutta**) under a Doric cornice [Mid-17C. Via French < Latin *mutulus*]

muu·muu /móo moo/ (*plural* **-muus**), **mu·mu** (*plural* **-mus**) *n* a loose shapeless Hawaiian dress made of brightly colored fabric [Early 20C. < Hawaiian *mu'u mu'u* "cut off" (because there was originally no yoke)]

mux /muks/ *n* COMPUT same as **multiplexer** (*informal*) [Late 20C. Contraction]

Mu·zak /myóo zàk/ *tdmk* a trademark for recorded background music played in stores, restaurants, elevators, and other public places

mu·zhik /móozhik/ *n* a Russian peasant, especially during the tsarist era [Mid-16C. < Russian, "small man" < *muzh* "man, husband"]

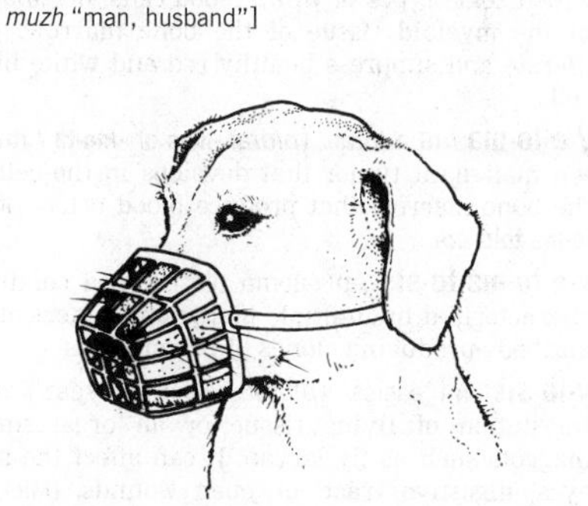

muzzle (sense 2)

muz·zle /múzz'l/ *n* **1. ANIMAL'S NOSE AND JAWS** the projecting part of an animal's face, made up of its nose and jaws **2. RESTRAINING DEVICE FOR ANIMAL** a device that is strapped over the nose and jaws of an animal to prevent it from opening its mouth, e.g., to bite, bark, or eat **3. END OF GUN BARREL** the front open end of the barrel of a firearm **4. CENSORSHIP** something that is meant to prevent free expression ■ *vt* (**-zled, -zling, -zles**) **1. PUT MUZZLE ON ANIMAL** to put a muzzle over the nose and jaws of an animal **2. CENSOR SOMEBODY** to prevent a person or group from publicly expressing their views or opinions **3.** SAILING **TAKE IN SAIL** to roll up and secure a sail [14C. < Old French *musel* "small muzzle" < *muse* "muzzle"] —**muz·zler** *n*

muz·zle·load·er /múzz'l lòdər/ *n* a firearm that is loaded through its muzzle —**muz·zle·load·ing** *adj*

muz·zle ve·loc·i·ty *n* the speed of a bullet or other projectile as it leaves the muzzle of a firearm

muz·zy /múzzee/ (**-zi·er, -zi·est**) *adj* **1.** unable to think clearly, especially as a result of illness or drinking alcohol **2.** indistinct, vague, or confused [Early 18C. Origin ?] —**muz·zi·ly** *adv* —**muz·zi·ness** *n*

mv *abbr* **1.** ONLINE Maldives (*used in Internet addresses*) See table at **domain name 2.** MUSIC mezza voce

mV *abbr* MEASURE millivolt

MV *abbr* **1.** STATS mean variation **2.** MEASURE megavolt **3.** ARMS muzzle velocity

m.v. *abbr* COMM market value

MVD *n* the Ministry for Internal Affairs of the former Soviet Union from 1946 to 1960, which acted as its secret police. Full form **Ministerstvo vnutrennikh dyel**

MVP *abbr* SPORTS most valuable player (award)

mw *abbr* ONLINE Malawi (*used in Internet addresses*) See table at **domain name**

mW *abbr* MEASURE milliwatt

MW *abbr* **1.** MEDIA medium wave **2.** MEASURE megawatt **3.** CHEM molecular weight

mwah mwah /mwàa mwàa/, **muah muah** *n* used as a humorous representation of the sound of ritual social kissing, which does not involve physical contact (*slang*)

mx *abbr* ONLINE Mexico (*used in Internet addresses*) See table at **domain name**

Mx *abbr* PHYS maxwell

MX *abbr* **1.** MIL missile experimental **2.** MOTOR SPORTS motocross

mxd. *abbr* mixed

my[1] /mī/ *adj* belonging or relating to the speaker (*first person possessive adjective*) ○ *You can borrow my car.* ○ *I always keep my promises.* ■ *interj* used to express sudden emotion such as surprise, fright, concern, or pleasure ○ *My! What a mess!* [12C. Shortening of MINE[2], originally only before consonants other than "h"]

my[2] *abbr* **1.** ONLINE Malaysia (*used in Internet addresses*) See table at **domain name 2.** million years

MY *abbr* motor yacht

my- *prefix* same as **myo-** (*used before vowels*)

my·al·gi·a /mī áljee ə, -áljə/ *n* pain or tenderness in a muscle or group of muscles —**my·al·gic** *adj*

my·al·gic en·ceph·a·lo·my·e·li·tis *n* UK MED full form of **ME**[2]

my·al·ism /mī ə lìzzəm/ *n* witchcraft practiced in the Caribbean [Mid-19C. < *myal* "myalism," origin ?] —**my·al·ist** *n*

My·all Lake /mī awl-/ coastal lake in eastern New South Wales, Australia, north of Port Stephens. Area: 120 sq. mi./310 sq. km.

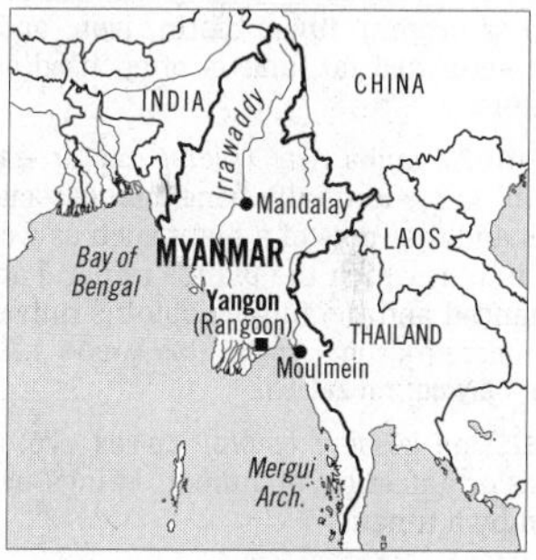

Myanmar

Myan·mar /myàan máar/ country in Southeast Asia. It became independent from Britain as the Union of Burma in 1948. Language: Burmese. Currency: kyat. Capital: Yangon. Population: 42,510,537 (2003). Area: 261,218 sq. mi./676,552 sq. km. Official name **Union of Myanmar**. Former name **Burma** (until 1989)

my·as·the·ni·a /mī əss théenee ə/, **my·as·the·ni·a gra·vis** /-gráaviss/ *n* an autoimmune disease involving extreme weakness of some muscles, caused by the blocking of the receptors for acetylcholine, the neurotransmitter that causes muscular contraction —**my·as·then·ic** /mī əss thénnik/ *adj*

my bad *interj* used to apologize for a mistake (*slang*) ○ *Whoops, my bad! You were right after all.*

my·ce·li·um /mī séelee əm/ (*plural* **-li·a** /-lee ə/) *n* a loose network of the delicate filaments (**hyphae**) that form the body of a fungus, consisting of the feeding and reproducing hyphae [Mid-19C. < modern Latin < Greek *mukēs* "fungus" after *epithelium* (see EPITHELIUM)] —**my·ce·li·al** *adj* —**my·ce·loid** /míssə lòyd/ *adj*

My·ce·nae /mī séenee/ ancient Greek city in the Peloponnese that was a center of Bronze Age culture until its destruction around 1100 B.C. —**My·ce·nae·an** /mìssə née ən/ *n, adj*

-mycete *suffix* fungus, fungi ○ *phycomycete* [Via modern Latin *-mycetes* < Greek *mukētes*, plural of *mukēs* "fungus"]

my·ce·to·ma /mìssə tṓmə/ (*plural* **-mas** or **-ma·ta**

/-mətə/) *n* a chronic inflammation of tissues, caused by a fungal or bacterial infection, that usually occurs in the feet or legs, which swell and develop pus-discharging nodules [Late 19C. < modern Latin < Greek *mukēt-*, stem of *mukēs* "fungus"] —**my·ce·to·ma·tous** *adj*

-mycin *suffix* a substance derived from a bacterium ○ *streptomycin* [< MYCO- + -IN; because the bacteria were originally thought to be fungi]

myco- *prefix* fungus, fungi ○ *mycotoxin* [< Greek *mukēs* < Indo-European, "slimy"]

my·co·bac·te·ri·um /mìkō bak te̅eree əm/ (*plural* **-ri·a** /-ree ə/) *n* a rod-shaped Gram-positive aerobic bacterium that can form branching structures resembling filaments. Some diseases in humans are caused by mycobacteria, e.g., tuberculosis and leprosy. Genus: *Mycobacterium*. —**my·co·bac·ter·i·al** *adj*

my·col·o·gy /mī kóllәjee/ *n* **1. STUDY OF FUNGI** a branch of botany that specializes in the scientific study of fungi **2. FUNGI OF PARTICULAR AREA** the fungi that live in a particular area **3. CHARACTERISTICS OF INDIVIDUAL FUNGUS** the characteristics of a particular fungus —**my·co·log·ic** /mìkə lójjik/ *adj* —**my·co·log·i·cal** *adj* —**my·co·log·i·cal·ly** *adv* —**my·col·o·gist** *n*

my·coph·a·gist /mī kóffəjist/ *n* an animal that eats fungi [Mid-19C. < *mycophagy*]

my·coph·a·gous /mī kóffəgəss/ *adj* feeding on fungi —**my·coph·a·gy** /-jee/ *n*

my·co·plas·ma /mìkō plázmə/ *n* a microorganism of a genus considered to be the smallest known living cells. Some species cause respiratory diseases in animals and human beings. Regarded by some as primitive bacteria, they need sterols such as cholesterol for growth. Genus: *Mycoplasma*. —**my·co·plas·mal** *adj*

my·co·pro·tein /mìkō prṓ te̅en/ *n* a food made by heating, draining, and texturing the fermentation product of a fungus *Fusaria graminearum*. It is a source of protein, fiber, biotin, iron, and zinc, is low in saturated fat, and is often used as a meat substitute.

my·cor·rhi·za /mìkə rī́zə/ (*plural* **-zas** or **-zae** /-zee/), **my·co·rhi·za** *n* a mutually beneficial association of a fungus and the roots of a plant such as a conifer or an orchid, in which the plant's mineral absorption is enhanced and the fungus obtains nutrients [Late 19C. < modern Latin < *myco-* (see MYCO-) + Greek *rhiza* "root"] —**my·cor·rhi·zal** *adj*

my·co·sis /mī kṓssiss/ (*plural* **-co·ses** /-kṓ se̅ez/) *n* a disease or infection of human beings or animals caused by a fungus

my·co·tox·in /mìkə tóksin/ *n* a poisonous substance produced by a fungus. Mycotoxins may affect foods such as peanuts.

my·co·troph·ic /mìkō trṓffik, -trṓfik/ *adj* describes a plant that lives in association with a fungus, as do various orchids in which the fungus lives on the roots

my·dri·a·sis /mi drī́ əssiss, mī-/ *n* excessive dilation of the pupils of the eye, usually caused by prolonged drug therapy, coma, or injury to the eye [Early 19C. Via Latin < Greek *mudriasis*]

myel- *prefix* same as **myelo-** (*used before vowels*)

my·e·len·ceph·a·lon /mì ələn séffə lòn/ *n* a part of the embryonic hindbrain formed by an extension of the spinal cord into the skull. It is the major pathway for nerve impulses leaving and entering the brain. —**my·e·len·ce·phal·ic** /mì ələn sə fállik/ *adj*

my·e·lin /mī́ əlin/ *n* a whitish material made up of protein and fats that surrounds some nerve cells in concentric sheaths, insulating adjacent nerve fibers and enabling transmission of nerve impulses

my·e·li·nat·ed /mī́ əli nàytəd/ *adj* describes nerve fibers that are surrounded by a sheath of myelin

my·e·lin sheath *n* a layer of myelin that insulates some nerve cells. In multiple sclerosis, the myelin sheath is damaged and the nerve impulse is impaired.

my·e·li·tis /mì ə lī́tiss/ *n* inflammation of the spinal cord or bone marrow

myelo- *prefix* **1.** bone marrow ○ *myelofibrosis* **2.** spinal cord, spinal column ○ *myelencephalon* [Via modern Latin < Greek *muelos* "marrow"]

my·e·lo·blast /mī́ ələ blàst/ *n* a cell that develops into a type of white blood cell (**granulocyte**) and that is normally seen only in the bone marrow where blood is formed. In some diseases such as leukemia, myeloblasts may appear in the blood. —**my·e·lo·blas·tic** /mì ələ blástik/ *adj*

my·e·lo·cyte /mī́ ələ sīt/ *n* an immature form of a type of white blood cell (**granulocyte**), usually found in the blood-forming tissue of the bone marrow —**my·e·lo·cy·tic** /mì ələ síttik/ *adj*

my·e·lo·fi·bro·sis /mì əlō fī brṓssiss/ *n* a progressive disease in which the cells of the bone marrow that produce fiber rather than blood cells proliferate, leading to anemia and enlargement of the spleen and liver —**my·e·lo·fi·brot·ic** /-fī bróttik/ *adj*

my·e·log·e·nous /mì ə lójjənəss/, **my·e·lo·gen·ic** /mì ələ jénnik/ *adj* originating in or produced by the bone marrow

my·e·log·e·nous leu·ke·mi·a *n* MED same as **myeloid leukemia**

my·el·o·gram /mī́ ələ gràm/ *n* a radiographic image created by injecting an X ray-opaque liquid into the spinal cord and used to diagnose disorders of the spine including slipped disks or tumors —**my·e·log·ra·phy** /mì ə lóggrəfee/ *n*

my·e·loid /mī́ ə lòyd/ *adj* relating to, involving, or derived from bone marrow or the spinal cord

my·e·loid leu·ke·mi·a *n* a variety of leukemia in which some types of white blood cells, originating in the myeloid tissue of the bone marrow, proliferate and suppress healthy red and white blood cells

my·e·lo·ma /mì ə lṓmə/ (*plural* **-mas** or **-ma·ta** /-mətə/) *n* a malignant tumor that develops in the cells of the bone marrow that produce blood cells —**my·e·lo·ma·toid** *adj*

my·e·lo·ma·to·sis /mì əlōmə tṓssiss/ *n* a condition characterized by multiple malignant tumors of the antibody-producing clones of plasma cells

my·i·a·sis /mī́ əssiss/ (*plural* **-i·a·ses** /-ə se̅ez/) *n* an infestation of living tissue or an organism by maggots such as fly larvae. It can affect the skin, eyes, digestive tract, or open wounds. [Mid-19C. < modern Latin < Greek *muia* "fly"]

My Lai /me̅e lī́/ village in Vietnam that was the site of a massacre of civilians by US troops during the Vietnam War (1968)

My·lar /mī́ laar/ *tdmk* a trademark for a thin strong polyester film. Use: in packaging, insulation, recording tapes, and photography.

my·lo·nite /mī́lə nīt/ *n* a fine-grained layered metamorphic rock, formed where the movement of rocks against each other causes crushing and grinding. It is found in fault zones. [Late 19C. < Greek *mulōn* "mill"]

my·nah /mī́nə/, **my·nah bird**, **my·na** *n* a bird of the starling family, some species of which are known for their ability to mimic human speech. Native to: Southeast Asia. Family: Sturnidae. [Mid-18C. < Hindi *mainā*]

Myn·heer /mə ne̅er/ *n* **1.** a title used to address a Dutch man, equivalent to "Mr." when used before a surname and to "sir" when used alone. **2.** *also* **myn·heer** same as **Dutchman** (sense 1) (*informal*) [Mid-17C. < Dutch *mijnheer* "my lord" < *heer* "lord, master"]

myo- *prefix* muscle ○ *myofibril* [Via modern Latin < Greek *mus* < Indo-European, "mouse"]

MYOB *abbr* ONLINE mind your own business

my·o·car·di·al /mì ō ka̅ardee əl/ *adj* relating to or affecting the thick muscular wall of the heart [Late 19C. < MYOCARDIUM]

my·o·car·di·al in·farc·tion *n* the death of a segment of heart muscle, caused by a blood clot in the coronary artery interrupting blood supply

my·o·car·di·tis /mì ō kaar dī́tiss/ *n* acute or chronic inflammation of the heart muscle

my·o·car·di·um /mì ō ka̅ardee əm/ (*plural* **-di·a** /-dee ə/) *n* the thick muscular wall of the heart. The myocardium is thickest around the left ventricle where the pressure generated by the heart is greatest. [Late 19C. < MYO- after PERICARDIUM]

my·oc·lo·nus /mī óklənəss/ *n* a sudden muscular contraction, or a series of these, that usually indicates a disorder of the nervous system if experienced persistently. It is normal to experience these contractions when falling asleep. —**my·o·clon·ic** /mì ə klónnik/ *adj*

my·o·cyte /mī́ ō sīt/ *n* a contractile muscle cell —**my·o·cy·tic** /mì ə síttik/ *adj*

my·o·e·lec·tric /mì ō i léktrik/, **my·o·e·lec·tri·cal** /-trik'l/ *adj* **1.** relating to or involving the electrical properties of muscle **2.** using the detection of electrical impulses in muscle to activate a bionic part such as an artificial limb

my·o·fas·cial re·lease /mì ō fáysh'l-/ *n* a form of gentle massage involving the stretching and manipulation of the tough connective tissue (**fascia**) that surrounds the body

my·o·fib·ril /mì ə fíbbril, -fībril/ *n* a structure resembling a thread running through a muscle cell that enables the muscle to contract

my·o·fil·a·ment /mì ō fílləmənt/ *n* one of the filaments that make up a myofibril, either the thicker filaments composed of the protein myosin or the thinner filaments composed of the proteins actin or troponin

my·o·gen·ic /mì ə jénnik/ *adj* originating or able to form in muscle cells, like, e.g., the contractions of heart muscle fibers, which are spontaneous and do not depend on nerve stimulation

my·o·glo·bin /mì ə glṓbin/ *n* an iron-containing protein resembling hemoglobin, found in muscle cells, that takes oxygen from the blood, releasing it to the muscles during strenuous exercise. The three-dimensional structure of myoglobin and the alpha and beta chains of hemoglobin are almost identical.

my·o·graph /mī́ ə gràf/ *n* an instrument that produces a tracing corresponding to muscle contractions —**my·o·graph·ic** /mì ə gráffik/ *adj*—**my·o·graph·i·cal·ly** *adv*

my·ol·o·gy /mī óllәjee/ *n* the study of the structure, function, and diseases of muscle [Mid-17C. Directly or via French *myologie* < modern Latin *myologia* < *myo-* (see MYO-) + *-logia* (see -LOGY)] —**my·o·log·ic** /mì ə lójjik/ *adj*—**my·ol·o·gist** /mī óllәjist/ *n*

my·o·ma /mī ṓmə/ (*plural* **-mas** or **-ma·ta** /-mətə/) *n* a benign tumor of the muscle tissue —**my·o·ma·tous** /mī ṓmətəss, -ómmə-/ *adj*

my·o·neu·ral /mì ō no͝orəl/ *adj* relating to or involving both muscles and nerves

my·op·a·thy /mī óppəthee/ (*plural* **-thies**) *n* a disease of the muscles or muscle tissues, either inherited, e.g., muscular dystrophy, or acquired, e.g., polio. All myopathies are characterized by muscle weakness and wasting, as well as pain and tenderness. —**my·o·path·ic** /mì ə páthik/ *adj*

my·ope /mī́ ōp/ *n* somebody affected by myopia [Early 18C. Via French < Latin *myop-*, stem of *myops* "short-sighted" < Greek *muōps* (see MYOPIA)]

my·o·pi·a /mī ṓpee ə/ *n* **1.** a common condition in which light entering the eye is focused in front of the retina and distant objects cannot be seen sharply. In high myopia the eyeball is unusually long, whereas in physiological myopia the eyeball length is normal but the power of the cornea is too great for the axial length. **2.** lack of foresight or long-term planning [Early 18C. Via modern Latin < late Greek *muōpia* < Greek *muōps* "short-sighted" < *muein* "blink"]

my·op·ic /mī óppik/ *adj* **1.** affected by myopia **2.** showing a lack of foresight or long-term planning —**my·op·i·cal·ly** *adv*

my·o·sin /mī́ əssin/ *n* a protein in muscles that helps them contract [Mid-19C. < MYO- + -OSE[2]]

my·o·sis *n* MED another spelling of **miosis**

my·o·si·tis /mì ō sī́tiss/ *n* muscle inflammation and soreness [Early 19C. < modern Latin < Greek *muos*, form of *mus* "mouse, muscle"]

my·o·so·tis /mì ə sṓtiss/ (*plural* **-so·tes** /-sṓ te̅ez/), **my·o·sote** /mī́ ə sōt/ *n* a plant of the borage family with hairy leaves and stems, e.g., the forget-me-not. Flowers: small, pink at first and then blue. Genus: *Myosotis.* [Early 17C. Via modern Latin < Latin, "mouse-ear (a plant)" < Greek *muōsotis* < *mus* "mouse, muscle" + *ous* "ear"]

my·o·tome /mī́ ə tōm/ *n* **1.** a cell in early embryos that gives rise to muscle in the body **2.** a muscle that is supplied by a nerve of the spine

my·o·to·ni·a /mī ə tṓnee ə/ *n* a muscle condition that results in the muscles maintaining contractions for much longer than normal and having difficulty in relaxing [Late 19C. < modern Latin < *myo-* (see MYO-) + Greek *tonos* "tone"] —**my·o·ton·ic** /mī ə tónnik/ *adj*

myr·i·ad /mérree əd/ *adj* **1.** TOO NUMEROUS TO COUNT so many that they cannot be counted **2.** VERY DIVERSE made up of many different components ■ *n* **1.** LARGE NUMBER a very large number ○ *a myriad of stars* **2.** 10,000 ten thousand (*archaic*) [Mid-16C. Directly or via French < late Latin *myriad-* < Greek *muriad-* < *murios* "countless"]

myr·i·a·pod /mérree ə pòd/ *n* an arthropod with a head, a long segmented body, and at least nine pairs of legs, e.g., a centipede or millipede. Class: Myriapoda. [Early 19C. < modern Latin *Myriapoda* "with a myriad of feet" < Greek *murias* "myriad"]

my·ris·tic ac·id /mə rístik-, mī-/ *n* a fatty acid found in plants and animals. Use: soap manufacture, flavorings, cosmetics, perfumes. [< modern Latin *Myristica* (genus name of trees) < medieval Latin *(nux) myristica* "nutmeg" < Greek *murizein* "anoint"]

myr·me·col·o·gy /mùrmə kóllәjee/ *n* the scientific study of ants [Late 19C. < Greek *murmēk-* "ant"] —**myr·me·co·log·ic** /mùrməkə lójjik/ *adj* —**myr·me·col·o·gist** *n*

myr·mi·don /múrmi dòn, -d'n/ *n* a faithful follower who obeys orders unquestioningly [Mid-17C. < MYRMIDON]

Myr·mi·don /múrmi dòn, -d'n/ *n* in Greek mythology, a member of a people who lived in Thessaly and were led by Achilles in the Trojan War [15C. Via Latin *Myrmidones* (plural) < Greek *Murmidones* < *murmèkes* "ants," (from which they were created, according to legend)]

my·rob·a·lan /mī róbbələn, mee-/ *n* **1.** the dried fruit of a tropical bush that resembles a plum. Use: dyeing, making ink. **2.** TREES same as **cherry plum** [Mid-16C. Directly or via French < Latin *myrobalanum* < Greek *murobalanon* < *muron* "balsam, ointment" + *balanos* "acorn"]

myrrh /mur/ *n* **1.** an aromatic resinous gum obtained from various trees and bushes that are native to Africa and southern Asia. Use: in perfume, incense, and medicinal preparations. **2.** PLANTS same as **sweet cicely** (sense 2) [Pre-12C. Via Latin *myrrha* < Greek *murra* < Semitic]

myrtle

myr·tle /múrt'l/ *n* **1.** a commonly cultivated evergreen bush with blue-black fruit. Flowers: fragrant, white or pink. Native to: Mediterranean region, western Asia. Latin name: *Myrtus communis.* **2.** PLANTS same as **periwinkle**[2] [14C. Directly or via French < medieval Latin *myrtilla* "small myrtle tree" < Latin *myrtus* "myrtle tree" < Greek *murtos* < Semitic]

Myr·tle Beach /múrt'l-/ town and resort in eastern South Carolina, on the Atlantic Ocean, southeast of Florence. Population: 24,525 (2002 estimate).

my·self /mī sélf/ *pron* **1.** REFERS BACK TO SPEAKER refers to the speaker or writer (*first person reflexive pronoun, used when the object of a verb or preposition refers to the same person as the subject of the verb*) ○ *I didn't enjoy myself very much.* ○ *Of all the people I am critical of, I am most critical of myself.* **2.** REFERS EMPHATICALLY TO SPEAKER refers emphatically to the speaker or writer ○ *I'm curious about that myself.* ○ *I can't expect you to be able to read my writing; I myself can't read it.* **3.** MY NORMAL SELF my normal or usual self ○ *I haven't been myself since the accident.* [Old English *mēseolf* "me self" (*self* in the obsolete sense of "same")]

USAGE The use of ***myself*** and other *-self* pronouns (reflexive pronouns) when they do not refer to the subjects of sentences is not appropriate in formal contexts. Write: *The coach chose Sarah and me* [not *myself*]. Yet another problem is the use of ***myself*** in sentences like these: *On behalf of my wife and myself, I want to thank you for your support. My wife and myself are pleased to have participated,* instead of *My wife and I want to thank you for your support.* In the second sentence ***myself***, as an object, cannot form part of a compound subject. The writer should have used *My wife and I are pleased to have served you.*

My·sore /mī sáwr/ city in the Mysore District, south central Karnataka State, southern India. Population: 785,800 (2001).

mys·ta·gogue /místə gòg/ *n* **1.** somebody who instructs candidates for initiation into sacred mysteries **2.** a believer in and disseminator of mystical doctrines [Mid-16C. Directly or via French < Latin *mystagogus* < Greek *mustagōgos* "leader of candidates for initiation" < *mustēs* "initiated person" (see MYSTERY[1])] —**mys·ta·gog·ic** /mìstə gójjik/ *adj* —**mys·ta·gog·i·cal·ly** *adv* —**mys·ta·go·gy** *n*

mys·te·ri·ous /mi stéeree əss/ *adj* **1.** UNKNOWN about whom or which little is known, but who or which excites considerable curiosity ○ *a mysterious woman in a red coat* **2.** STRANGE difficult to understand or explain ○ *the mysterious disappearance of the ship's crew* **3.** FULL OF MYSTERY full of or suggesting mystery ○ *The caves were dark and mysterious.* **4.** SECRETIVE deliberately arousing curiosity by refusing to reveal something ○ *Stop being so mysterious and tell us what you found out.* [Late 16C. < French *mystérieux* < *mystère* "mystery" < Latin *mysterium* (see MYSTERY[1])] —**mys·te·ri·ous·ly** *adv* —**mys·te·ri·ous·ness** *n*

~~mysterous~~ incorrect spelling of **mysterious**

mys·ter·y[1] /místəree/ *n* (*plural* **-ies**) **1.** PUZZLING EVENT OR SITUATION an event or situation that is difficult to understand or explain **2.** UNKNOWN ONE an unknown, secret, or hidden person or thing **3.** STRANGENESS the quality of being strange, secret, or puzzling **4.** STORY ABOUT PUZZLING EVENT a book, play, or movie about a puzzling event, especially an unsolved crime, that makes great use of suspense **5.** CHR SOMETHING KNOWN BY DIVINE REVELATION in Christian belief, a belief or truth that is considered to be beyond human understanding and can be made known only by divine revelation **6.** CHR INCIDENT FROM LIFE OF JESUS CHRIST an incident in the life of Jesus Christ that Christians believe to have special spiritual significance, especially, in Roman Catholicism, one of 15 events including the Annunciation and the Crucifixion **7.** CHR CHRISTIAN SACRAMENT one of the Christian sacraments, especially Communion **8.** RELIG RELIGIOUS RITE a secret rite or ceremony performed by a religious group, especially in one of the ancient Mediterranean religions (*often used in the plural*) **9.** RELIG GROUP OF WORSHIPERS a religious group, especially in one of the ancient Mediterranean religions, that has secret rites **10.** ARTS same as **mystery play** ■ **mys·ter·ies** *npl* **1.** SECRET KNOWLEDGE special knowledge known only to people skilled or involved in a particular activity, group, or subject **2.** CHR CONSECRATED BREAD AND WINE in Christianity, the consecrated bread and wine used in the sacrament of Communion [14C. Directly or via Anglo-Norman < Latin *mysterium* < Greek *mustērion* "secret rite" < *mustēs* "initiated person" < *muein* "close the eyes or lips, initiate"]

SYNONYMS See ***problem.***

mys·ter·y[2] /místəree/ (*plural* **-ies**) *n* a handicraft or trade (*archaic*) [13C. < medieval Latin *misterium* "service, office," contraction (influenced by Latin *mysterium* "mystery") of Latin *ministerium* < *minister* "servant"]

mys·ter·y play *n* a medieval drama staged by a craft guild and usually based on a story from the Bible, e.g., the Creation or the Flood, or an incident from the life of Jesus Christ

mys·ter·y shop·ping *n* the use of researchers posing as shoppers to determine the effectiveness of sales personnel in retail outlets —**mys·ter·y shop·per** *n*

mys·tic /místik/ *adj* RELIG, PARANORMAL same as **mystical** ■ *n* somebody who practices or believes in mysticism [14C. Directly or via French *mystique* (adjective) < Latin *mysticus* < Greek *mustikos* < *mustēs* "initiated person" (see MYSTERY[1])]

mys·ti·cal /místik'l/ *adj* **1.** WITH DIVINE MEANING having a divine meaning that is beyond human understanding **2.** OF MYSTICISM relating to, involving, or associated with mysticism or mystics **3.** WITH SUPERNATURAL SIGNIFICANCE having supernatural or spiritual significance or power **4.** MYSTERIOUS mysterious or difficult to understand —**mys·ti·cal·ly** *adv* —**mys·ti·cal·ness** *n*

mys·ti·cism /místə sìzzəm/ *n* **1.** BELIEF IN INTUITIVE SPIRITUAL REVELATION the belief that personal communication or union with the divine is achieved through intuition, faith, ecstasy, or sudden insight rather than through rational thought **2.** SPIRITUAL SYSTEM a system of religious belief or practice that people follow to achieve personal communication or union with the divine **3.** CONFUSED AND VAGUE IDEAS vague or unsubstantiated thought or speculation about something

mys·ti·fy /místə fī/ (**-fied, -fy·ing, -fies**) *vt* **1.** to make somebody unable to understand or explain something **2.** to make something mysterious or unclear [Early 19C. < French *mystifier* < *mystère* "mystery" (< Latin *mysterium*; see MYSTERY[1]) or *mystique* "mystic" (see MYSTIC)] —**mys·ti·fi·ca·tion** /mìstəfi káysh'n/ *n* —**mys·ti·fi·er** /místə fī ər/ *n* —**mys·ti·fy·ing** *adj* —**mys·ti·fy·ing·ly** *adv*

mys·tique /mi stéek/ *n* a special quality or air that makes somebody or something appear mysterious, powerful, or desirable [Late 19C. Via French < Greek *mustikos* < *mustēs* "initiated person" (see MYSTERY[1])]

myth /mith/ *n* **1.** ANCIENT STORY a traditional story about heroes or supernatural beings, often attempting to explain the origins of natural phenomena or aspects of human behavior **2.** MYTHS COLLECTIVELY myths considered as a group or as a genre **3.** IDEALIZED CONCEPTION a set of often idealized or glamorized ideas and stories surrounding a particular phenomenon, concept, or famous person ○ *the myth of the new man* **4.** FALSE BELIEF a widely held but mistaken belief ○ *exploding some of the myths about dieting* **5.** FICTITIOUS PERSON OR THING somebody who or something that is fictitious or nonexistent, but whose existence is widely believed in ○ *The loving wife turned out to be a myth.* [Mid-19C. Directly or via French *mythe* < modern Latin *mythus* < Greek *muthos* "speech, myth"]

myth. *abbr* **1.** mythological **2.** mythology

myth·i·cal /míthik'l/, **myth·ic** /míthik/ *adj* **1.** TYPICAL OF MYTH relating to, appearing in, based on, or typical of myth **2.** IMAGINARY not true or real, but existing only in somebody's imagination **3.** LEGENDARY having an extraordinary reputation ○ *a mythical figure in global politics* —**myth·i·cal·ly** *adv*

USAGE mythical or **mythological**? These two adjectives are interchangeable in the sense of "relating to or typical of myth" but ***mythical*** and its variant ***mythic*** are preferred in the senses "imaginary" (*the mythical* [or *mythic*] *quest for the Holy Grail*) and "legendary" (*the orator's mythic* [or *mythical*] *ability to excite audiences*; *a mythic* [or *mythical*] *figure in global politics*).

myth·i·cize /míthi sīz/ (**-cized, -ciz·ing, -ciz·es**) *vt* **1.** to make somebody or something into a myth **2.** to regard or explain an event or person as a myth —**myth·i·ci·za·tion** /mìthissi záysh'n/ *n* —**myth·i·ciz·er** *n*

myth·mak·er /míth màykər/ *n* a creator of myths —**myth·mak·ing** *n*

my·thog·ra·phy /mi thóggrəfee/ (*plural* **-phies**) *n* **1.** a collection of myths **2.** the representation of a mythical subject in a work of art

my·thoi plural of **mythos**

mythol. *abbr* **1.** mythological **2.** mythology

myth·o·log·i·cal /mìthə lójjik'l/, **myth·o·log·ic** /-ik/ *adj* **1.** relating to, typical of, or appearing in myth **2.**

not real, but existing only in the imagination —**myth·o·log·i·cal·ly** *adv*

USAGE See *mythical.*

my·thol·o·gize /mi thóllə jīz/ (**-gized, -giz·ing, -giz·es**) *v* **1.** *vt* **MAKE SOMETHING INTO MYTH** to make somebody or something into a myth **2.** *vti* **EXPLAIN MYTHS** to explain or relate myths **3.** *vi* **CREATE MYTHS** to create or make up myths —**my·thol·o·gi·za·tion** /mi thòlləji záysh'n/ *n* —**my·thol·o·giz·er** *n*

my·thol·o·gy /mi thóllәjee/ (*plural* **-gies**) *n* **1. BODY OF MYTHS** a group of myths that belong to a particular people or culture and tell about their ancestors, heroes, gods and other supernatural beings, and history **2. MYTHS COLLECTIVELY** myths considered as a group **3. STUDY OF MYTHS** the study of myths, or the branch of knowledge that deals with myths **4. BODY OF STORIES** a body of stories, ideas, or beliefs that are not necessarily true about a particular place or person [15C. Directly or via French < late Latin *mythologia* < Greek *muthologia* "science of myths" < *muthos* ("speech, myth")] —**myth·o·log·er** *n* —**my·thol·o·gist** *n*

myth·o·ma·ni·a /mìthō máynee ə/ *n* a very strong tendency to tell lies or exaggerate, which may be a symptom of a disorder —**myth·o·ma·ni·ac** *n*

myth·o·poe·ia /mìthō pée ə/, **myth·o·po·e·sis** /-pō éessiss/ *n* the process of creating myths [Mid-19C. Directly or via late Latin < Greek *muthopoiia* < *muthos* ("speech, myth") + *poiein* "make"] —**myth·o·poe·ist** *n*

myth·o·poe·ic /mìthō pée ik/ *adj* relating to, involving, or engaged in the production of myths [Mid-19C. < Greek *muthopoios* < *muthos* ("speech, myth") + *poiein* "make"]

my·thos /mī́ thòss, mí-/ (*plural* **-thoi** /-thoy/) *n* **1.** the interrelated set of beliefs, attitudes, and values held by a society or cultural group **2.** a myth or mythology [Mid-18C. < Greek *muthos* "speech, myth"]

myx- *prefix* same as **myxo-** (*used before vowels*)

myx·e·de·ma /mìksə déemə/ *n* **1.** a disease caused by an underactive or atrophied thyroid gland, characterized by sluggishness and weight gain. It can be treated with artificial thyroid hormone. **2.** dry swelling of the skin and subcutaneous tissues, associated with an underactive thyroid gland —**myx·e·dem·a·tous** /mìksə démmətəss, -déem-/ *adj* —**myx·e·dem·ic** /-démmik/ *adj*

myxo- *prefix* mucus ○ *myxomycete* ○ *myxedema* [Via modern Latin < Greek *muxa* "slime, mucus"]

myx·o·ma /mik sṓmə/ (*plural* **-mas** or **-ma·ta** /-mətə/) *n* a benign tumor composed of mucus and gelatinous material embedded in connective tissue, typically in the heart where it can obstruct blood flow and lead to sudden unconsciousness —**myx·o·ma·tous** /mik sómmətəss/ *adj*

myx·o·ma·to·sis /mik sòmə tṓssiss/ *n* a highly infectious disease of rabbits, caused by a virus, that leads to swelling of the mucous membranes and the formation of tumors similar to myxomas [Early 20C. < modern Latin, < *myxomat-*, stem of *myxoma* < *myxo-* (see MYXO-)]

myx·o·my·cete /mìksō mī seét/ *n* MICROBIOL same as **slime mold** [Late 19C. < modern Latin *Myxomycetes* < *myxo-* (see MYXO-) + Greek *mukētes*, plural of *mukēs* "fungus"]

myx·o·vir·us /míksə vīrəss/ *n* a group of RNA-containing viruses including those that cause influenza and other diseases of the respiratory tract, and those that cause measles and mumps (**paramyxoviruses**)

mz *abbr* ONLINE Mozambique (*used in Internet addresses*) See table at **domain name**

Nn

n[1] /en/ (*plural* **n's**), **N** (*plural* **N's** or **Ns**) *n* **1.** the 14th letter of the English alphabet, representing a consonant sound **2.** a written representation of the letter "n"

n[2] *symbol* **1.** PHYS amount of substance **2.** PRINTING en dash ■ *n* MATH an indefinite whole number ■ *symbol* **1.** PHYS, OPTICS index of refraction **2.** MEASURE nano- **3.** PHYS neutron

n' /ən/, **'n'** *conj* same as **and** (*informal*)

N[1] *abbr* **1.** CHESS knight **2.** AUTOMOT neutral (*used on gearshifts*) **3.** COMPASS north **4.** COMPASS northern **5.** CALENDAR November

N[2] /en/ (*plural* **N's** or **Ns**) *n* something shaped like a letter "N"

N[3] *symbol* **1.** PHYS Avogadro's number **2.** PRINTING en dash **3.** PHYS, MEASURE newton **4.** CHEM nitrogen

n. *abbr* **1.** COMM net **2.** GRAM neuter **3.** GRAM nominative **4.** TIME noon **5.** north **6.** northern **7.** MUSIC note **8.** GRAM noun **9.** number

N. *abbr* **1.** GEOG New (*in place names*) **2.** LANG Norse **3.** North

n- *prefix* normal

na *abbr* Namibia (*used in Internet addresses*) See table at **domain name**

Na *symbol* CHEM ELEM sodium [Shortening of modern Latin *natrium* < Greek *nitron* "niter"]

N.A. *abbr* **1.** DRUGS Narcotics Anonymous **2.** National Academy **3.** North America

n/a *abbr* **1.** not applicable **2.** not available

NAACP, **N.A.A.C.P.** *abbr* National Association for the Advancement of Colored People

naan /naan/, **naan bread** *n* FOOD another spelling of **nan**

nab /nab/ (**nabbed, nab·bing, nabs**) *vt* (*informal*) **1.** to seize, snatch, or take something suddenly **2.** to catch and arrest a criminal or fugitive [Late 17C. Probably variant of *nap* < N Germanic]

NAB *abbr* BIBLE New American Bible

Nab·a·tae·an /nàbbə tée ən/, **Nab·a·te·an** *n* **1.** a member of an Arab people who in Roman times lived in part of Jordan **2.** the extinct language of the Nabataeans, a dialect of Aramaic [Early 17C. < Latin *Nabat(h)aeus*] —**Nab·a·tae·an** *adj*

nabe /nayb/ *n* (*slang*) **1.** a neighborhood movie theater (*often used in the plural*) **2.** somebody's neighborhood [Mid-20C. < the pronunciation of *neighborhood*]

Na·bis /naábee/ *npl* a group of 19th-century French artists, including Pierre Bonnard, who embraced symbolism rather than the naturalism of the impressionist painters [Mid-20C. Plural of *nabi* "member of the Nabis" < Hebrew *nābī* "prophet"]

Na·blus ♦ **Nabulus**

na·bob /náy bòb/ *n* **1.** a rich or powerful person (*informal*) **2.** HIST same as **nawab** [Early 17C. Via Portuguese *nababo* or Spanish *nabab* < Urdu *nawwāb* "deputy governor"]

Na·bo·kov /nə báwk awf, nábbə kàwf/, **Vladimir** (1899–1977) Russian-born US writer. He is known for the stylish wordplay and intellectual subtlety of his novels, which include *Lolita* (1955) and *Pale Fire* (1962), and he was acclaimed for his translations, memoirs, and literary criticism. He lived in Switzerland after 1959. Full name **Nabokov, Vladimir Vladimirovich**. See Cultural note at **fire**

> "A novelist is, like all mortals, more fully at home on the surface of the present than in the ooze of the past."
> [Vladimir Nabokov, *Strong Opinions*; 1951]

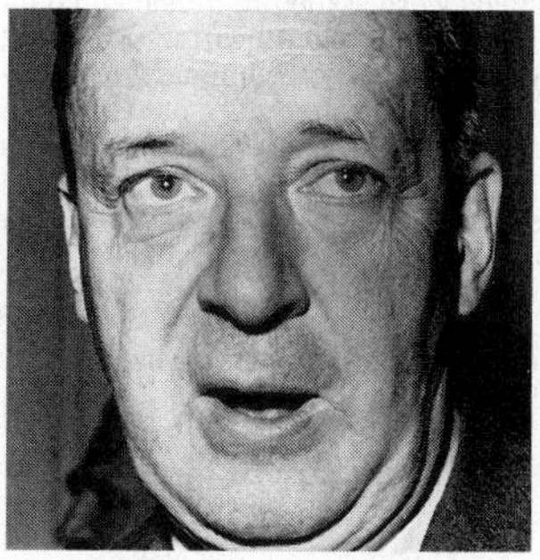

Hulton-Deutsch Collection/Corbis

Vladimir Nabokov

Nab·u·lus /nábbə lo͞oss/, **Nab·lus** /nábbləss, naábləss/, **Nāb·u·lus** city in the West Bank territory, 30 mi./48 km north of Jerusalem. Population: 100,231 (1997).

na·celle /nə sél/ *n* a separate streamlined enclosure on an aircraft for crew, cargo, or engines [Early 20C. Via French, "dinghy, gondola" < late Latin *navicella* "boat" < Latin *navis* "ship"]

na·cho /naáchō/ (*plural* **-chos**) *n* a tortilla chip, usually eaten in quantity covered with melted cheese, salsa, or sliced pickled jalapeño peppers (*often used in the plural*) [Mid-20C. < American Spanish]

Na·ci·mi·en·to Peak /nàssimee èntō-/ mountain in southern Rio Arriba County, northern New Mexico. Height: 10,045 ft./3,062 m.

na·cre /náykər/ *n* INDUST same as **mother-of-pearl** [Late 16C. Via French < Italian *naccaro* < Arabic *nāqūr* "hunting horn"]

na·cre·ous /náykree əss/ *adj* **1.** relating to, typical of, or made of mother-of-pearl **2.** with the iridescent quality of mother-of-pearl

na·cre·ous cloud *n* an iridescent cloud that looks like a cirrus and appears especially in the winter at high latitudes

NACU *abbr* National Association of Colleges and Universities

NAD *n* a coenzyme that plays a role in the electron transport chain, where it is vital in the production of energy. Formula: $C_{21}H_{27}N_7O_{14}P_2$. Full form **nicotinamide adenine dinucleotide**

Na-Den·e /naa dáynee, -dáy này/, **Na-Dén·é** *n* a group of Native North American languages spoken in parts of Alaska, Canada, and the southwestern United States. Native speakers: 200,000. [Early 20C < Athabaskan *na* + *dene* "people"] —**Na-Den·e** *adj*

Na·der /náydər/, **Ralph** (*b.* 1934) US lawyer and consumer-protection advocate. He was largely responsible for the rise of the consumer-protection movement following the publication of his book *Unsafe at Any Speed* (1965), about unsafe design and manufacture in the automobile industry. He ran unsuccessfully as a Green Party candidate for the presidency in 2000 and ran again as an Independent in 2004.

> "Trying to control corporate power and abuse by American corporate law has proven about as effective as drinking coffee with a fork."
> [Ralph Nader. Quoted in *The Times (London)*; October 23, 1976]

NADH *n* the reduced form of NAD that reverts to NAD during the generation of cellular energy [Mid-20C. < NAD + H[1] "hydrogen"]

na·dir /náydər, -deer/ *n* **1.** the lowest possible point ○ *the nadir of despair* **2.** the point on the celestial sphere directly below the observer and opposite the zenith [14C. Via French and medieval Latin < Arabic *naẓīr (as-samt)* "opposite (the zenith)"]

NADP *n* a coenzyme involved in anabolism, consisting of NAD with an extra phosphate group. It tends to participate in biochemical syntheses rather than energy-yielding reactions. Formula: $C_{21}H_{28}N_7O_{17}P_3$. Full form **nicotinamide adenine dinucleotide phosphate**

NADPH *n* the reduced form of NADP [< NADP + H[1] "hydrogen"]

nae /nay/ *adv Scotland* **1.** same as **no**[1] **2.** same as **not** [Early 18C. Variant of obsolete *na* < *ne* "not" (< Germanic) + form of AYE[2]]

nae·vus (*plural* **-vi**) *n* UK spelling of **nevus**

naff /naf/ *adj UK* lacking fashionable stylishness and appearing boring, tasteless, or unattractive (*informal*) [Mid-20C. Origin ?]

naff off (**naffed off, naffing off, naffs off**) *vi UK* used as a rude way of telling somebody to go away (*informal*)

NAFTA /náftə/ *n* a free trade agreement signed between the United States and Canada in 1989, and extended to include Mexico in 1994. Full form **North American Free Trade Agreement**

nag[1] /nag/ *v* (**nagged, nag·ging, nags**) **1.** *vti* ASK SOMEBODY REPEATEDLY to ask or urge somebody persistently and annoyingly to do something ○ *He keeps nagging me to go and see the doctor.* **2.** *vti* KEEP CRITICIZING SOMEBODY to find fault with somebody regularly and repeatedly **3.** *vi* BE PERSISTENTLY PAINFUL OR BOTHERSOME to be a persistent cause of discomfort, anxiety, or unease ○ *a nagging pain* ○ *a worry that nags into the late night hours* ■ *n* SOMEBODY WHO NAGS somebody, especially a woman, who is regarded as having a tendency to nag (*insult*) [Early 19C. Origin ?] —**nag·ger** *n* —**nag·ging** *n* —**nag·ging·ly** *adv*

SYNONYMS See ***complain***.

nag[2] /nag/ *n* **1.** OLD HORSE an old horse, especially one that is worn out **2.** RACEHORSE a horse, especially a racehorse (*slang*) **3.** SMALL HORSE a small horse for riding (*archaic*) [15C. Origin ?]

na·ga[1] /naágə/ *n S Asia* in the 19th century, a Hindu belonging to an armed group who served as mercenaries [Early 19C. < Hindi *nāgā* "naked"]

na·ga[2] *n* in Indian mythology, a creature that is part-human and part-cobra in appearance and is associated with water. It is sometimes worshipped by women who want children. [Late 18C. < Sanskrit *nāga* "snake"]

Na·ga /naágə/ (*plural same* or **-gas**) *n* **1.** a member of a South Asian people who live in Nagaland, in northeastern India and western Myanmar. They were headhunters until the 20th century and still maintain a traditional style of life. **2.** the Tibeto-Burman language of the Naga people. Native speakers: 120,000. [Mid-19C. Origin ?] —**Na·ga** *adj*

Na·ga·land /naágə lànd/ state in northeastern India, bordering Myanmar. Capital: Kohima. Area: 6,401 sq. mi./16,579 sq. km. Population: 1,988,636 (2001).

Na·ga-Mi·kir /naágə mi keér/ *n* LANG same as **Naga** (sense 2)

na·ga·na /nə gaánə/, **n'ga·na** /əng gaánə/ *n* an often fatal disease caused by trypanosome protozoan parasites that affects hoofed animals such as cattle,

> **LANGUAGE HERITAGE** ***Nahuatl*** Much of English is made up of words from other languages, and Nahuatl is a small but significant contributor in this respect, especially in the matter of cuisine. The word ***Nahuatl*** itself shows some of the distinctive structure of the language, but most loanwords have been modified in their journey through other languages (especially Spanish) to English, and less obviously indicate their Central American origins. ***Chocolate***, for example, goes back to Nahuatl *chocolatl* "bitter water," but lost its distinctive ending on its way through Spanish, and perhaps also French; ***avocado*** started out as Nahuatl *ahuacatl*, literally "testicle" (because of the shape of the fruit), but became *aguacate* in Spanish before assuming its familiar form; ***cacao*** (later also to be altered to ***cocoa***) came via a Spanish shortening of Nahuatl *cacauatl* "cacao tree"; ***tomato*** is an alteration of Spanish *tomate* from Nahuatl *tomatl*. Other culinary terms with a Nahuatl ancestry include ***chili***, ***guacamole***, ***mole***, ***pulque***, and ***tamale***. Chewing gum would be unknown without its main ingredient ***chicle*** (via American Spanish from Nahuatl *tzictli*).
> Numerous New World animals and birds that were unfamiliar to Europeans naturally acquired names from Nahuatl: ***cacomistle***, ***coyote***, ***hoatzin***, ***ocelot***, and ***quetzal***, for example. Names of indigenous peoples were also adopted from Nahuatl: ***Aztec*** (via French *Aztèque* or Spanish *Azteca* from Nahuatl *aztecatl* "somebody from Aztlan"), ***Mixtec*** (via Spanish from Nahuatl *mixtecah* "somebody from a cloudy place"), and ***Toltec*** (via Spanish from Nahuatl *toltecatl* "somebody from Tula," an ancient Toltec city).

horses, and goats in tropical Africa and is transmitted by the tsetse fly. It is related to sleeping sickness. [Late 19C. < Zulu *nakane*]

Na·ga·no /nə gáanō/ city and port in Japan, on Honshu Island. It is the commercial center and capital of Nagano Prefecture. Population: 359,045 (2002).

Na·ga·ri /náagəree/ *n* LING same as **Devanagari** [Late 18C. < Sanskrit *nagari* "script of the city"]

Na·ga·sa·ki /naàgə saákee/ city and port in southern Japan, on Kyushu Island, and capital of Nagasaki Prefecture. It was destroyed by an atomic bomb in 1945. Population: 419,901 (2002).

Na·go·ya /na góy ə/ city in Japan, on Honshu Island. It is the capital city and industrial center of Aichi Prefecture. Population: 2,109,681 (2002).

Nag·pur /nag poŏr/ city in central India, in Maharashtra State, on the Nag River. Population: 2,122,965 (2001).

Imre Nagy

Nagy /noj/, **Imre** (1896–1958) Hungarian prime minister (1953–55 and 1956). He was dismissed as prime minister in 1955 following disagreements with Stalin over policy issues. He led the Hungarian uprising (1956) and was later executed.

nah /na, naa/ *interj* same as **no**[1] *(nonstandard)* [Early 20C. Alteration]

Nah. *abbr* BIBLE Nahum

Na·han·ni Na·tion·al Park /nə haánee-/ national park and preserve in Northern Canada, in southwestern Northwest Territories, on the South Nahanni River. It is a World Heritage Site. Area: 1,840 sq. mi./4,766 sq. km.

Na·hua·tl /naá waát'l/ (*plural same* or **-tls**), **Na·hua** /naá waá/ (*plural same* or **-huas**) *n* **1.** a member of a Native Central American people who live in southern Mexico and Central America. The Nahuatl include the ancient Aztecs. **2.** *also* **Na·huat·lan** the Uto-Aztecan language of the Nahuatl people. Native speakers: 1 million. [Early 19C. Via Spanish < Nahuatl, singular of *Nahua* "the Nahuatl people"] —**Na·hua·tl** *adj*

Na·hum /náyhəm, náy əm/ *n* **1.** in the Bible, a Hebrew prophet who lived in the 7th century B.C. He was one of the minor prophets. **2.** a book of the Bible that contains the prophecies traditionally attributed to Nahum, including the prophecy foretelling the siege and sack of the Assyrian capital of Nineveh in 612 B.C. See table at **Bible**

NAIA *abbr* SPORTS National Association of Intercollegiate Athletes

nai·ad /náy əd, -àd, nī àd/ (*plural* **-ads** or **-a·des** /-ə deèz/) *n* **1.** MYTHOL **WATER NYMPH** in Greek mythology, a nymph of lakes, rivers, springs, and fountains. The naiads were skilled in music and dancing, and were supposed to have healing powers. **2.** INSECTS **WATER-DWELLING LARVA** the immature water-dwelling form **(larva)** of a dragonfly, damselfly, mayfly, or stonefly **3.** PLANTS **UNDERWATER PLANT** an underwater plant with narrow leaves. Flowers: small, white. Genus: *Najas*. [14C. Via Latin *naiad-* < Greek, "water nymph" < *naein* "to flow"]

Nai·ad *n* a small natural satellite of Neptune

na·ïf /naa eéf/, **na·if** (*plural* **-ïfs** or **-ifs**) *n* a naive person [Late 16C. < French *naïf* (see NAIVE)]

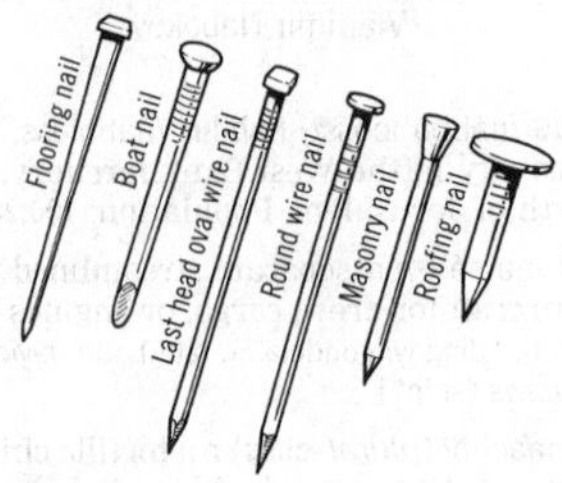

nail

nail /nayl/ *n* **1.** **SHORT POINTED METAL PIN** a strong metal pin with a flat round head and a pointed end that is hammered into wood or masonry and used to fasten objects together or hang something on **2.** **SOMETHING LIKE NAIL** something that is like a nail in its shape, in being sharp, or in the way it is used **3.** **HARD AREA ON FINGER OR TOE** in humans and other primates, the thin horny covering that grows on the upper surface of the end of each finger and toe **4.** **CLAW** the claw of a bird, mammal, or reptile **5.** **UNIT OF MEASURE** a former unit of measure for cloth that was equal to 2.25 in./5.7 cm ■ *vt* **(nailed, nail·ing, nails) 1.** **ATTACH SOMETHING WITH NAILS** to fasten, attach, or secure something using nails **2.** **FIX SOMETHING STEADILY** to keep something fixed or focused on something ○ *His gaze was nailed to the astonishing scene.* **3.** **CATCH OR CONVICT GUILTY PERSON** to catch somebody who is guilty of an offense, prove the person's guilt, or have the person convicted (*slang*) ○ *It took them five years to nail him for insider trading.* **4.** **EXPOSE UNTRUTH** to prove that something is not true or valid and so stop others from believing it (*slang*) **5.** **HIT TARGET WITH PROJECTILE** to hit or bring down somebody or something with a bullet or a projectile (*slang*) **6.** **STOP PERSON** to stop somebody and speak to him or her (*slang*) ○ *nailed me in the corridor and demanded an explanation* **7.** **DO SOMETHING PRECISELY OR WELL** to catch, hit, seize, or execute something adroitly or precisely (*slang*) ○ *nailed the high dive and won the medal* **8.** **IDENTIFY SOMEBODY OR SOMETHING** to identify somebody or establish something precisely (*slang*) ○ *I nailed him as a fraud as soon as he started talking about his wealthy background.* **9.** BASEBALL **PUT SOMEBODY OUT** in baseball, to put out a runner by tagging [Old English *nægl* < Indo-European, "fingernail, toenail"] —**nail·er** *n* ◇ **a nail in somebody's coffin** an event or action that further weakens the position of somebody or something already in decline ◇ **hit the nail on the head** to be absolutely correct or accurate ◇ **on the nail** accurate or exact

nail down *v* **1.** *vt* **PIN SOMETHING DOWN** to make somebody be definite about something **2.** *vt* **SETTLE SOMETHING FINALLY** to settle something finally or come to a final decision about something **3.** **ESTABLISH SOMETHING DEFINITIVELY** to establish something clearly and conclusively ○ *an investigation that will attempt to nail down what really happened here* **4.** **BEAT SOMEBODY CONCLUSIVELY** to defeat an opponent decisively

nail bed *n* the layer of tissue at the base of a fingernail or toenail from which new nail material develops

nail-bit·er *n* **1.** somebody who habitually bites the ends of his or her fingernails **2.** a situation or contest that is extremely tense and exciting because its outcome remains uncertain until the end (*slang*) [< the stereotype of nail-biting as a sign of anxiety]

nail-bit·ing *n* the habit of biting off the ends of the fingernails, especially out of anxiety, tension, or boredom ■ *adj* extremely tense and exciting because the outcome is uncertain [See NAIL-BITER]

nail bomb *n* a bomb packed with nails to cause widespread injuries among people who are near it when it goes off

nail·brush /náyl brùsh/ *n* a small brush used for cleaning the fingernails, with short stiff bristles on one or both sides

nail clip·pers *npl* a small pair of clippers used for trimming fingernails and toenails

nail file *n* a small file used for smoothing and shaping the ends of the fingernails

nail·head /náyl hèd/ *n* a decorative design that resembles the round head of a nail, used on furniture and leather

nail pol·ish *n* a fast-drying colored or transparent lacquer used to decorate fingernails or toenails

nail punch *n* a tool that pushes a nail level with or lower than the surrounding surface

nail scis·sors *n* small scissors, sometimes with curved blades, used for trimming fingernails or toenails (*takes singular or plural verb*)

nail set *n* CONSTR same as **nail punch**

nain·sook /náyn sŏŏk/ *n* a lightweight cotton fabric. Use: babywear, lingerie. [Late 18C. < Hindi *nainsukh* "pleasure to the eye"]

Nai·paul /nī pàwl/, **V. S.** (*b.* 1932) Trinidadian-born British novelist and cultural commentator of Indian descent. His novels include *A House for Mr. Biswas* (1961) and the Booker Prize-winning *In a Free State* (1971), while his studies of culture include *India: A Million Mutinies Now* (1990) and *Beyond Belief* (1998). His works analyze suppressed histories of peoples. He was awarded the Nobel Prize in literature (2001). Full name **Naipaul, Sir Vidiadhar Surajprasad**

> "Worse, to have lived without even attempting to lay claim to one's portion of the earth; to have lived and died as one had been born, unnecessary and unaccommodated."
> [V. S. Naipaul, *A House for Mr. Biswas*; 1961]

nai·ra /nīrə/ *n* the main unit of Nigerian currency. See table at **currency** [Late 20C. < Nigerian English, alteration of NIGERIA]

Nai·ro·bi /nī róbee/ capital city of Kenya, situated in the south central part of the country. Population: 1,810,000 (1995).

Nai·ro·bi Na·tion·al Park national park in south central Kenya, near the capital city. It was established in 1946. Area: 44 sq. mi./115 sq. km.

Nai·smith /náy smìth/, **James** (1861–1939) Canadian-born US physical education teacher. He invented basketball (1891).

nais·sance /náyss'nss/ *n* the birth or origination of something or somebody (*formal*) [15C. < French < *naissant*, present participle of *naître* "be born"]

na·ive /naa eév/ (**-iv·er, -iv·est**), **na·ïve** (**-ïv·er, -ïv·est**), **na·ïf** /-eéf/ (**-ïf·er, -ïf·est**) *adj* **1.** **EXTREMELY SIMPLE AND TRUSTING** having or showing an excessively simple and trusting view of the world and human nature, often as a result of youth and inexperience **2.** **NOT SHREWD OR SOPHISTICATED** showing a lack of sophistication and subtlety or of critical judgment and analysis ○ *a politically naive statement* **3.** **ARTLESS** admirably straightforward and uncomplicated or refreshingly innocent and unaffected **4.** ARTS **REJECTING SOPHISTICATED TECHNIQUES IN ART** not using the conventional styles and techniques of trained artists, e.g., in the treatment of perspective or light and shade **5.** SCI **NOT PREVIOUSLY EXPERIMENTED ON** not previously used in any scientific tests or experiments or not having previously used a particular drug ○ *naive laboratory* *mice* [Mid-17C. < French *naïve*, feminine of *naïf* < Latin *nativus* "born"] —**na·ive·ly** *adv* —**na·ive·ness** *n*

na·ive re·al·ism *n* the theory of perception holding that when we look at an object what we see is the actual object, not a mental representation of it

na·ive·té /naà eevə táy, naa éevə tày/, **na·ïve·té, na·ive·ty** /-tee/ *n* **1.** a naive quality or naive behavior **2.** a naive action or remark

Najd /najd, nejd/ region in central Saudi Arabia. Area: 447,100 sq. mi./1,158,000 sq. km.

NAK /nak/, **nak** *n* an ASCII control code used to indicate to the sender that a transmitted message has not been properly received. Full form **negative acknowledgment**

Na·ka·so·ne Ya·su·hi·ro /naàkə sōnee yaàssoo héérō/ (*b.* 1918) Japanese prime minister (1982–87). He was first elected to the Diet as a member of the Liberal-Democratic party in 1947 and held a series of cabinet posts before he became prime minister.

na·ked /náykəd/ *adj* **1.** WEARING NO CLOTHES not covered by clothing, especially having no clothing on any part of the body **2.** LACKING COVERING lacking the usual covering or protection ○ *a naked light bulb* **3.** NOT CONCEALED openly displayed or expressed and often threatening or disturbing ○ *naked aggression* **4.** FRANKLY UNVARNISHED direct, frank, and without embellishment ○ *the naked truth* **5.** UNARMED unarmed and defenseless ○ *"If you carry this resolution you will send Britain's Foreign Secretary naked into the conference chamber."* (Aneurin Bevan, 1957) **6.** DEVOID OF SOMETHING without or unaccompanied by a particular quality or thing ○ *naked of all pretensions to grandeur* **7.** BOT HAVING NO NATURAL COVERING having no natural covering in the form of earth, vegetation, or foliage **8.** ZOOL LACKING HAIR, FUR, OR FEATHERS having no hair, fur, scales, shell, or feathers **9.** BOT NOT ENCLOSED IN OVARY describes conifer seeds, which are not enclosed in an ovary **10.** BOT LACKING SEPALS OR PETALS describes flowers that have no sepals or petals [Old English *nacod* < Indo-European] —**na·ked·ness** *n*

CULTURAL NOTE ***The Naked and the Dead***, a novel (1948) by Norman Mailer. Set on a Pacific island during World War II, it is both a powerful account of the experience of war and, through its presentation of the conflicting political and philosophical views of the principal characters, a portrayal of some of the tensions in contemporary US society. It was made into a movie by Raoul Walsh in 1958.

SYNONYMS ***naked, bare, nude, undressed, unclothed***

CORE MEANING: without clothes or covering

naked not covered or concealed, especially having no clothing on any part of the body ○ *a ceiling decorated with frescos of naked cherubs* **bare** without the usual furnishings or decorations, or not covered by clothing ○ *The three men sat around a bare wooden table.* ○ *bare legs* **nude** not wearing any clothes at all, especially in artistic contexts ○ *the nude statue in the courtyard* **undressed** not wearing any or many clothes, or having just removed clothes ○ *The children were undressed and ready to put on their pajamas.* **unclothed** wearing little or no clothing ○ *a window full of unclothed mannequins* ○ *He felt awkwardly unclothed in just a towel.*

na·ked eye *n* human sight without the aid of a microscope, telescope, or other optical instrument

na·ked·ly /náykədlee/ *adv* without any attempt at disguise or concealment ○ *a description of the state as a nakedly repressive machine*

na·ked op·tion *n* a stock or commodity option sold by somebody who does not own the underlying asset, and who is exposed to considerable risk if the price of the underlying asset changes adversely

na·ked re·verse *n* in football, a deceptive rushing play in which the ball carrier takes a handoff from a player going in the opposite direction and goes downfield with no blockers

nak·fa /nákfə/ *n* the main unit of Eritrean currency. See table at **currency** [After *Nakfa*, town in N Eritrea]

Nakh /naak/ *n* a language family of the North Caucasian group of Caucasian languages, including Chechen and Ingush [Mid-20C. Origin ?] —**Nakh** *adj*

Na·ku·ru /nə kóoroo/ city in west central Kenya. It is the capital of Rift Valley Province. Population: 150,000 (1991).

Na·ku·ru, Lake lake in west central Kenya, noted for its flamingos and other birds. Area: 24 sq. mi./62 sq. km.

nal·bu·phine /nal byóo feèn/ *n* a drug resembling morphine. Use: relief of moderate to severe pain. [Mid-20C. Blend of NALORPHINE + BUTYL]

na·led /náy lèd/ *n* a short-lived insecticide. Use: control of mosquitoes and crop pests. Formula: $C_4H_7Br_2Cl_2O_4P$. [Mid-20C. Origin ?]

na·li·dix·ic ac·id /nàyli dìksik-/ *n* an antibacterial drug. Use: treatment of urinary infections. [< rearranged elements of NAPHTHALENE + DI-[1] + *carboxylic*]

nal·or·phine /nállər feèn/ *n* a white crystalline drug. Source: morphine. Use: in veterinary medicine as a morphine antagonist in anesthetized animals. [Mid-20C. Contraction of *N-allylnormorphine*]

nal·ox·one /nállək sòn, nə lók sòn/ *n* a drug resembling morphine. Use: diagnosis of narcotics addiction, reversal of effects of narcotics poisoning. [Mid-20C. Contraction of *N-allylnoroxymorphone*]

Nam /naam, nam/ *n* Vietnam (*informal; used particularly by veterans of the war there during the 1960s and 1970s*) [Mid-20C. Shortening]

N. Am. *abbr* **1.** North America **2.** North American

Na·ma /naámaa, -mə/ (*plural same* or **-mas**) *n* **1.** a member of a Khoikhoi people who live in southwestern Africa **2.** the San language of the Nama people. Native speakers: 25,000. [Mid-19C. < Nama] —**Na·ma** *adj*

nam·a·ble /náyməb'l/, **name·a·ble** *adj* able to be identified by name

Na·ma·qua /nə maákwə/ (*plural same* or **-quas**) *n* PEOPLES, LANG same as **Nama** (senses 1–2) [Late 17C. < Nama *nama gu a*] —**Na·ma·quan** *adj*

Na·ma·qua·land /nə maákwə lànd/ coastal region in southwestern Africa, in southern Namibia and South Africa. It is the homeland of the Nama people. Population: about 66,000. Area: 18,518 sq. mi./47,962 sq. km.

na·maste /nə mú stày/, **na·mas·kar** /nùmmə skaár/ *n* a polite bow of greeting or farewell used by Hindus, made with the hands held at chest height and both palms pressed together [Mid-20C. < Hindi, "bowing to you"]

nam·by-pam·by /nàmbee pámbee/ *adj* (*informal*) **1.** WEAK feeble and lacking strength of character **2.** SILLY silly, sentimental, or overly sensitive ■ *n* (*plural* **nam·by-pam·bies**) NAMBY-PAMBY PERSON somebody regarded as weak or silly (*informal insult*) [Mid-16C. < nickname for the English poet *Amb(rose)* Philips (1674–1749)]

name /naym/ *n* **1.** WHAT SOMEBODY OR SOMETHING IS CALLED a word, term, or phrase by which somebody or something is known and distinguished from other people or things **2.** UNCOMPLIMENTARY DESCRIPTION WORD ABOUT SOMEBODY an uncomplimentary or abusive word or phrase used to describe somebody ○ *called him names behind his back* **3.** REPUTATION the reputation or standing of somebody or something ○ *She's made quite a name for herself in the music world.* **4.** FAMOUS PERSON a famous person ○ *All the big Hollywood names were there.* ■ *adj* RESPECTED having an established and good reputation ○ *name brands* ■ *vt* (**named, nam·ing, names**) **1.** GIVE NAME TO SOMEBODY to give somebody or something a name ○ *They named the dog Sport.* **2.** IDENTIFY SOMEBODY OR SOMETHING BY NAME to identify somebody or something by giving his, her, or its name ○ *He says he can name all 50 state capitals.* **3.** SPECIFY SOMETHING to decide upon or specify something such as a date, time, or price ○ *would not name a figure* **4.** APPOINT SOMEBODY TO OFFICE to choose somebody for a particular office or honor ○ *They haven't yet named her successor.* [Old English *nama* < Indo-European] —**nam·er** *n* ◇ **in name only** supposedly or officially, but not in any real sense ◇ **in the name of 1.** by the authority of **2.** for the sake of something ◇ **name names** to mention the names of specific people in order to blame or accuse them of an error or of wrongdoing ◇ **somebody's name is mud** somebody is in trouble or is the object of disapproval ◇ **the name of the game** what something is all about, its most important element, or the kind of thing that most commonly happens in it (*informal*) ◇ **to somebody's name** credited or belonging to somebody ○ *hasn't got a penny to his name* ◇ **you name it** used to suggest that an enormous number of things are involved or an enormous number of options are possible (*informal*) ○ *They experienced cold, chills, and frostbite–you name it!*

ORIGIN The Indo-European word from which ***name*** is ultimately derived is also the ancestor of English *anonymous, nomenclature, nominate, noun, pseudonym, renown*, and *synonym*.

name·a·ble *adj* another spelling of **namable**

name-call·ing *n* verbal abuse, especially as a substitute for reasoned argument in a dispute

name·check /náym chèk/ (**-checked, -check·ing, -checks**) *vt* **1.** to mention the name of a product, brand, or performer publicly, especially in a song, a broadcast, or the press ○ *The company was delighted to be namechecked in the rap lyrics, gaining exposure to potential new consumers.* **2.** to check the name of somebody or something —**name·check** *n*

name day *n* in the Roman Catholic and Eastern Orthodox Churches, the feast day of the saint that somebody is named for

name-drop·ping *n* the practice of frequently mentioning the names of famous or influential people as friends or acquaintances in order to impress people —**name-drop** *vi* —**name-drop·per** *n*

name·less /náymləss/ *adj* **1.** LACKING NAME not having a name **2.** ANONYMOUS having a name that is unknown or not revealed **3.** INDESCRIBABLE defying accurate description ○ *a nameless fear* **4.** DISTRESSING BEYOND WORDS too unpleasant or disgusting to be described or mentioned **5.** ILLEGITIMATE illegitimate or not legally entitled to a name —**name·less·ly** *adv* —**name·less·ness** *n*

name·ly /náymlee/ *adv* used to introduce a description or explanation of something just referred to in a more general way ○ *She was given a new post, namely, that of head of department.*

name·plate /náym plàyt/ *n* a plate or plaque, e.g., on a door, bearing a name and associating the named person with the place or thing that the plate is attached to

name·sake /náym sàyk/ *n* somebody or something with the same name as somebody or something else [Mid-17C. Probably < *for your name's sake*]

name·tag /náym tàg/ *n* a small piece of metal or plastic with somebody's name on it, attached to his or her clothing for purposes of identification

name·tape /náym tàyp/ *n* a small strip of cloth with somebody's name on it, sewn onto the inside of his or her clothing as proof of ownership

Na·mib Des·ert /nə mìb-/ desert in southwestern Africa, mostly in Namibia. Length: 930 mi./1,500 km.

Na·mibe /na méeb/ city and port in southwestern Angola. It is the capital of Namibe Province. Population: 100,000 (1981). Former name **Moçâmedes** (until 1982)

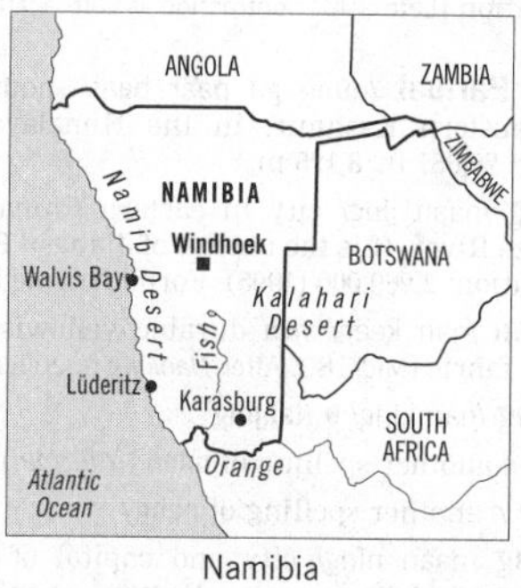

Namibia

Na·mib·i·a /nə míbbee ə/ country in southwestern Africa, with its western coast on the Atlantic Ocean, directly north of South Africa. It became an independent member of the British Commonwealth in 1990. Language: English, German, Afrikaans. Currency: Namibian dollar. Capital: Windhoek. Population: 1,927,447 (2003). Area: 318,252 sq. mi./824,269 sq. km. Official name **Republic of Namibia** —**Na·mib·i·an** *n, adj*

nam·kin /num keén/, **nam·keen** *n S Asia* any salty or spicy food eaten as a snack [< Hindi]

Nam·oi /nám oy/ river in northeastern New South Wales, southeastern Australia. Length: 525 mi./845 km.

Nam·pa /námpə/ city in southwestern Idaho, west of

Boise and east of the Oregon border. Population: 60,259 (2002 estimate).

nam pla /nám plaa/ *n* a thin sauce of fermented fish with a strong flavor and smell and a salty taste, widely used in Southeast Asian cookery [< Thai]

Na·mur /nə mo͝or-/ city in southeastern Belgium. It is the capital city of Namur Province. Population: 104,994 (1999).

nan /naan, nan/, **naan** *n S Asia* a flat round or oval bread served with South Asian food [Early 20C. < Persian, Urdu *nān*]

nan·a /nánnə, naánə/, **nan·na** *n Hispanic* **1.** same as **grandmother** (sense 1) (*informal*) **2.** MUSIC same as **lullaby** [< Spanish]

Na·nai·mo /nə nímō/ city in southwestern Canada, on Vancouver Island, on the Strait of Georgia. Population: 77,845 (2001).

Na·nai·mo bar *n* in Canada, a layered dessert consisting of a base of chocolate and coconut, a center of confectioners' sugar, and a glaze of chocolate [After NANAIMO]

Na·nak /naánək/ (1469–1539) Indian religious leader. He founded the Sikh religion, and his teachings were collected as the *Adi Granth*, the Sikh scriptures. Known as **Guru Nanak**

nance *n* same as **nancy** (*slang offensive*)

Nan·chang /naan chaáng/ city in eastern China. It is the capital of Jiangxi Province. Population: 1,410,000 (1995).

nan·cy /nánssee/ (*plural* **-cies**), **nan·cy boy, nance** /nanss/ (*plural* **nan·ces**) *n* an offensive term for an effeminate or gay man (*slang insult*) [Early 20C. < *Miss Nancy* in same sense]

Nan·cy /nawN seé/ city in northeastern France, in Lorraine Region. It is the capital of Meurthe-et-Moselle Department. Population: 103,605 (1999).

nan·cy sto·ry /nánsee-/ *n Carib* **1.** a folk tale about Anansi, a cunning spider **2.** an elaborate story that is untrue or intended to mislead people [Early 19C. < alteration of ANANSI]

NAND /nand/ (*plural* **NANDs**) *n* a logic operator used in computing that produces an output signal only if at least one of its inputs has no signal, thus being the inverse of an AND operator [Mid-20C. Blend of NOT + AND]

Nan·da De·vi /nùndə deévee/ second highest mountain in India after Kanchenjunga. It is in the extreme north of the country, in the Himalaya range, near the Tibetan border. Height: 25,646 ft./7,817 m.

NANDGATE *n* COMPUT same as **NAND**

nan·dro·lone /nándrə lōn/ *n* a muscle-building anabolic steroid that athletes are banned from using by the rules of the International Amateur Athletics Federation [Late 20C. Contraction < NOR- + ANDRO- + -*l*- + -ONE]

Nan·ga Par·bat /nùng gə paár baat/ mountain in northwestern Kashmir, in the Himalaya range. Height: 26,657 ft./8,125 m.

Nan·jing /naán jíng/ city in eastern China, on the Yangtze River. It is the capital of Jiangsu Province. Population: 2,960,000 (1995). Former name **Nanking**

nan·keen /nan keén/ *n* a durable yellowish brown cotton fabric [Mid-18C. After *Nanking* (NANJING)]

Nan·king /nan kíng/ ♦ **Nanjing**

nan·na *n* another spelling of **nana** (*informal*)

nan·nie *n* another spelling of **nanny**

Nan·ning /naán níng/ city and capital of Guangxi Zhuangzu Autonomous Region, southeastern China, situated approximately 330 mi./530 km west of Guangzhou. Population: 1,370,000 (1995).

nan·no·fos·sil *n* another spelling of **nanofossil**

nan·ny /nánnee/ (*plural* **-nies**), **nan·nie** *n* somebody who is paid to take care of one or more children in a family home, often also living there [Early 18C. Nickname for *Ann(e)*]

nan·ny goat *n* a female domestic goat

nano- *prefix* **1.** extremely small ○ *nanofossil* ○ *nanotechnology* **2.** one billionth (10^{-9}) ○ *nanosecond* Symbol **n** [< Greek *nan(n)os* "dwarf, little old man"]

nan·o·a·nal·y·sis /nànnō ə nálləssiss/ *n* the determination of the atomic structures of materials such as crystals —**nan·o·an·a·ly·tic·al** /nànnō anə líttik'l/ *adj*

nan·o·bot /nánnō bòt/ *n US* a robot of microscopic proportions built using nanotechnology (*informal*) [Blend of NANO- + ROBOT]

nan·o·cosm /nánnō kòzzəm/ *n* nanotechnology, including its developers, researchers, components, and products ○*"In the world of the nanocosm, the tiny etchings on our densest microchips are vast highways."* (Ron Bailey *Wall Street Journal*; May 23, 2003) [Early 21C.]

nan·o·crys·tal /nánnō krìst'l/ *n* a crystal with dimensions in the nanometer range —**nan·o·crys·tal·line** /nànnō krístə lìn, -krístəlin/ *adj*

nan·o·fos·sil /nánnō fòss'l/, **nan·no·fos·sil** *n* a very small fossil, especially of nanoplankton

nan·o·gram /nánnə gràm/ *n* one billionth of a gram

nan·o·me·ter /nánnə meètər/ *n* one billionth of a meter

na·no·par·tic·le /nánnō paàrtik'l/ *n* a particle of something such as a metal, polymer, or oxide, with dimensions in the nanometer range

nan·o·pho·ton·ics /nànnō fō tónniks/ *n* the study of photonic phenomena and devices with dimensions in the nanometer range (*takes a singular verb*) —**nan·o·pho·ton·ic** *adj*

nan·o·plank·ton /nánnō plàngktən/, **nan·no·plank·ton** *n* very small plankton including bacteria, algae, and protozoans. They are usually in the size range 5–60 micrometers.

nan·o·pore /nánnō pàwr/ *n* a tiny pore in a material used to filter objects such as molecules or DNA strands that are less than several nanometers in diameter —**nan·o·po·ros·i·ty** /nànnō paw róssətee/ *n* —**nan·o·po·rous** /-páwrəss/ *adj*

nan·o·sci·ence /nánnō sī ənss/ *n* the study of materials and their behavior at the level of particles measured in nanometers —**nan·o·sci·en·tif·ic** /nànnō sī ən tíffik/ *adj*

nan·o·sec·ond /nánnə sèkənd/ *n* one billionth of a second

nan·o·shell /nánnō shèl/ *n* a tiny manufactured layered sphere with dimensions in the nanometer range, used in biotechnology

nan·o·struc·ture /nánnō strùkchər/ *n* an extremely small structure such as a semiconductor or optoelectronic device with dimensions of 0.1–50 nm —**nan·o·struc·tur·ing** *n*

nan·o·tech·nol·o·gy /nànnō tek nólləjee/ (*plural* **-gies**) *n* the art of manipulating materials on a very small scale in order to build microscopic machinery

nan·o·tube /nánnō to͞ob/ *n* an extremely thin metallic or semiconducting cylinder, capped at one end, consisting of a rolled-up layer of fullerene-structured carbon atoms

nan·o·wire /nánnō wìr/ *n* a very thin strand of a material such as a polymer or metal with a diameter in the nanometer range

Nan·sen /nánss'n/, **Fridtjof** (1861–1930) Norwegian explorer. He led several expeditions to the Arctic and was also involved in humanitarian projects, for which he won the Nobel Peace Prize (1922).

Nantes /naants, naaNt/ city and major port on the Loire River in western France. In 1598, Henry IV of France issued the Edict of Nantes there, granting partial religious freedom to the Protestant Huguenots. Population: 270,251 (1999).

Nan·tong /naán to͝ong/ city and seaport in eastern China, in southeastern Jiangsu Province. Population: 323,941 (1991).

Nan·tuck·et /nan túkət/ island in southeastern Massachusetts, in the Atlantic Ocean, south of Cape Cod. Population: 10,416 (2002 estimate). Area: 57 sq. mi./148 sq. km.

Nan·u·et /nánnyo͞o ət/ town in southeastern New York, in Rockland County. Population: 14,065 (2002 estimate).

Na·o·mi /nay ómee/ *n* in the Bible, the mother-in-law of Ruth (Ruth 1:2)

na·os /náy òss/ (*plural* **-oi** /-òy/) *n* ARCHIT same as **cella** [Late 18C. < Greek, "temple"]

nap[1] /nap/ *n* **SHORT SLEEP** a period of short light sleep, especially during the day ■ *vi* (**napped, nap·ping, naps**) **1. SLEEP LIGHTLY** to have a short period of light sleep **2. BE OFF GUARD** to be inattentive or off guard ○ *caught napping* [Old English *hnappian*, origin ?]

nap[2] /nap/ *n* the small soft fibers that stick up slightly from the surface of a fabric such as velvet and that usually all lie in one direction only ■ *vt* (**napped, nap·ping, naps**) to raise the nap of a fabric by brushing it [15C. < Middle Low German, Middle Dutch *noppe* < Germanic]

nap[3] /nap/ *n* **1.** a card game similar to euchre, played with hands of five cards, in which players bid for the number of tricks they will take **2.** a bid to win all five tricks in the game of nap [Early 19C. Shortening of NAPOLEON]

NAP *n* the use of drugs by military personnel as protection against the effects of a nerve agent prior to exposure. Full form **nerve action pretreatment**

nap·a /náppə/, **nap·pa** *n* a soft leather made from sheep or kid's skin [Late 19C. After *Napa*, county, town, and valley in California]

Nap·a /náppə/ city in west central Florida. It is the administrative seat of Napa County. Population: 66,548 (1998 estimate).

na·palm /náy paàm, -paàlm/ *n* **1. JELLY USED FOR FIRE BOMBS** a highly flammable jelly produced by mixing a thickening agent with gasoline. Use: in flamethrowers and fire bombs. **2. THICKENING AGENT FOR JELLIED GASOLINE** a thickening agent, consisting of aluminum soap. Use: manufacture of jellied gasoline. ■ *vt* (**-palmed, -palm·ing, -palms**) **ATTACK SOMEBODY OR SOMETHING WITH NAPALM** to attack somebody or destroy something with napalm [Mid-20C. Blend of NAPHTHENE + PALMITATE]

Nap·a Val·ley region of west central California, Northeast of San Francisco. Extending northwestward from the city of Napa, its wineries lead the United States in grape production, and it is a major tourist destination.

nape /nayp/ *n* the back part of the neck [13C. Origin ?]

Na·per·ville /náypər vìl/ city in northeastern Illinois, southeast of Aurora, and west of Chicago. Population: 135,389 (2002 estimate).

na·per·y /náypəree/ *n* tablecloths and napkins, collectively (*archaic*) [14C. < Old French *naperie* < *nappe* (see NAPKIN)]

Naph·ta·li /náftə lì/ *n* in the Bible, the son of Jacob and Rachel's handmaid, Bilhah (Genesis 30: 7–8)

naph·tha /náfthə, nápthə/ *n* a clear colorless flammable mixture of light hydrocarbons. Source: petroleum. Use: raw material for many petrochemicals and plastics. [Late 16C. Via Latin < Greek]

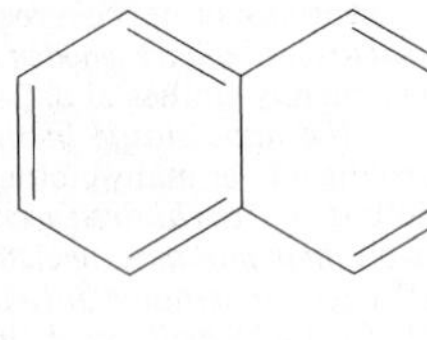

naphthalene

naph·tha·lene /náfthə leèn, nápthə-/ *n* a white crystalline hydrocarbon. Source: coal tar. Use: moth repellent, in solvents, in the manufacture of dyes, resins, plasticizers, polyesters, and explosives. Formula: $C_{10}H_8$. [Early 19C. < NAPHTHA + -AL[2]] —**naph·tha·len·ic** /nàfthə lénnik, nàpthə-/ *adj*

naph·thene /náf theèn, náp-/ *n* an alicyclic hydrocarbon. Source: petroleum. Use: formerly, in the manufacture of napalm. [Late 19C. < NAPHTHA] —**naph·then·ic** /naf theénik, nap-, -thénnik/ *adj*

naph·thol /náf thàwl, náp-/ *n* either of two derivatives of naphthalene that are isomers. Use: antiseptics, manufacturing. Formula: $C_{10}H_7OH$. [Mid-19C. < NAPHTHA]

Na·pi·er /náypee ər/ city in New Zealand, situated on the eastern coast of the North Island. Devastated by an earthquake in 1931, it was rebuilt in a distinctive art-deco style. Population: 54,537 (2001).

Na·pi·er, John (1550–1617) Scottish mathematician. He invented logarithms and a calculating device called Napier's bones.

Na·pier·i·an log·a·rithm /nay peéree ən-/ *n* MATH same as **natural logarithm** [Early 19C. After John NAPIER]

Na·pi·er's bones /này peerz-/ *npl* a set of graduated rods based on the principles of logarithms, formerly used to perform multiplication and division but now used primarily for educational purposes [Mid-17C. After John NAPIER]

na·pi·form /náypə fàwrm/ *adj* being conical at one end and spherical at the other [Mid-19C. < Latin *napus* "turnip"]

nap·kin /nápkin/ *n* a usually square piece of cloth or tissue paper used at mealtimes to protect clothes and wipe the mouth [14C. < French *nap(p)e* "tablecloth" < Latin *mappa* "napkin, cloth"]

Na·ples /náyp'lz/ **1.** city in southern Italy. It is the capital of Campania Region and of Napoli Province and an important seaport. Population: 1,004,500 (2001). Italian name **Napoli 2.** city in southwestern Florida, in Collier County, on the Gulf of Mexico. Population: 21,162 (2002 estimate).

na·po·le·on /nə pṓlee ən, -pṓlyən/ *n* **1.** a rectangular flaky pastry shape filled with custard cream **2.** a gold coin formerly used in France, equivalent to 20 francs **3.** CARDS same as **nap**[3] [Early 19C. After NAPOLEON I]

AKG London

Napoleon I, emperor of the French: portrait (1807) by Andrea Appiani

Na·po·le·on I /nə pṓlee ən, -pṓlyən/ (1769–1821) emperor of the French. He made his name as a general, was appointed first consul of France in 1799, and took the title of emperor in 1804. After conquering most of Europe, he was exiled after defeat at the battle of Waterloo (1815). Born **Bonaparte, Napoleon** —**Na·po·le·on·ic** /nə pṓlee ónnik/ *adj*

> "I want the whole of Europe to have one currency; it will make trading much easier."
> [Napoleon I, *letter to his brother Louis*; May 6, 1807]

> "It is only one step from the sublime to the ridiculous."
> [Napoleon I, *to the Polish ambassador, De Pradt, after his retreat from Moscow*; 1812]

Na·po·le·on III (1808–73) emperor of the French. A nephew of Napoleon I, he became emperor after a coup d'état in 1851, but went into exile after defeat in the Franco-Prussian War (1870–71). Full name **Bonaparte, Charles Louis Napoleon**

Na·po·le·on·ic code *n* same as **Code Napoléon**

nap·pa INDUST another spelling of **napa**

nappe /nap/ *n* **1.** SHEET OF WATER a sheet of water flowing over a dam or a spillway **2.** SHEET OF ROCK a large arch-shaped sheet of rock that has been forced over underlying rocks by internal stresses **3.** MATH PART OF CONE either of the two parts, or sheets, of a conical or pyramidal surface that are separated by a line through the vertex [Late 19C. < French (see NAPKIN)]

nap·py /náppee/ (*plural* **-pies**) *n UK* same as **diaper** *n* (sense 1) [Early 20C. Shortening and alteration of NAPKIN]

nap·py rash *n UK* same as **diaper rash**

na·prox·en /nə próksən/ *n* a drug that reduces inflammation and pain. Use: treatment of arthritis. [Late 20C. < *methoxynaphthylpropionic (acid)*]

Na·ra /naárə/ city in Japan, on southern Honshu Island. It is the capital of Nara Prefecture. Population: 364,411 (2002).

Na·ra·coorte /nárrə kàwrt/ agricultural town in southern South Australia. Population: 4,718 (1991).

~~**narative**~~ incorrect spelling of **narrative**

Na·ra·yan /nə rī́ yən/, **Jayaprakash** (1902–79) Indian politician. He was the uniting force in the Janata Party, which defeated the government of Indira Gandhi in 1977.

Na·ra·yan /nə rī́yən/, **R. K.** (1906–2001) Indian writer. Many of his gentle novels, written in English, are set in the fictional southern Indian town of Malgudi. They include *The Vendor of Sweets* (1967) and *The World of Nagaraj* (1990). Full name **Narayan, Rasipuram Krishnaswamy**

narc[1] /naark/, **nark** *n* a government agent who investigates narcotics violations (*slang*) [Mid-20C. Shortening of *narcotics agent*]

narc[2] /naark/ (**narced, narc·ing, narcs**), **nark** (**narked, nark·ing, narks**) *vi* to act as an informer, especially for the police (*slang*) UK spelling **nark** [Mid-19C. < Romany *nāk* "nose"]

nar·cis·si PLANTS plural of **narcissus**

nar·cis·sism /naárssə sìzzəm/ *n* **1.** excessive self-admiration and self-centeredness **2.** in psychiatry, a personality disorder characterized by the patient's overestimation of his or her own appearance and abilities and an excessive need for admiration. In psychoanalytic theory, emphasis is placed on the element of self-directed sexual desire in the condition. [Early 19C. After NARCISSUS] —**nar·cis·sist** *n* —**nar·cis·sis·tic** /naàrssə sístik/ *adj* —**nar·cis·sis·tic·al·ly** *adv*

nar·cis·sus /naar síssəss/ (*plural* **-si** /-sī/ or **-sus·es** or *same*) *n* a spring-blooming plant with narrow leaves that grows from a bulb. Flowers: yellow or white, with a cup-shaped center. Genus: *Narcissus*. [Mid-16C. Via Latin < Greek *narkissos* < *narkē* "numbness"; from its narcotic properties]

Nar·cis·sus /naar síssəss/ *n* in Greek mythology, a youth who was punished for repulsing Echo's love by being made to fall in love with his own reflection in a pool. He died gazing at his own image, and was turned into a flower.

nar·co /naárkō/ *n US* a drug trafficker (*informal*) [Late 20C. shortening of NARCOTIC]

narco-[1] *prefix* sleep, stupor ○ *narcolepsy* [< Greek *narkoun* "make numb" < *narkē* "numbness"]

narco-[2] *prefix* relating to illicit narcotics and the narcotics trade (*informal*) ○ *narcoterrorism* [< NARCOTIC]

nar·co·a·nal·y·sis /naàrkō ə nálləssiss/ *n* psychoanalysis using drugs to induce a state similar to sleep

nar·co·lep·sy /naárkə lèpsee/ *n* a condition characterized by frequent, brief, and uncontrollable bouts of deep sleep, sometimes accompanied by hallucinations and an inability to move —**nar·co·lep·tic** /naàrkə léptik/ *adj, n*

nar·co·sis /naar kṓssiss/ *n* a state of unconsciousness or stupor caused by a narcotic or other drug [Late 17C. < Greek *narkōsis* < *narkoun* (see NARCOTIC)]

nar·co·ter·ror·ism /naàrko tèrrər izzəm/ *n* terrorist acts carried out by groups that obtain their funds directly or indirectly from the illicit drug trade —**nar·co·ter·ror·ist** *n, adj*

nar·cot·ic /naar kóttik/ *n* **1.** DRUG a typically addictive drug, especially one derived from opium, that may produce effects ranging from pain relief and sleep to stupor, coma, and convulsions **2.** ILLEGAL DRUG a drug whose use is illegal, whether it is addictive or not **3.** SOOTHING THING something that soothes, induces sleep, relieves pain or stress, or causes a sensation of mental numbness ■ *adj* **1.** CAUSING SLEEP able to induce drowsiness, sleep, or stupor, or alter mental states through its chemical properties **2.** SOOTHING having a generally soothing, numbing, or soporific effect **3.** OF NARCOTICS relating to narcotic drugs and their use **4.** OF ADDICTS relating to people addicted to narcotics [14C. Via French and medieval Latin < Greek *narkōtikos* "numbing" < *narkoun* "make numb" < *narkē* "numbness"] —**nar·cot·i·cal·ly** *adv*

nar·co·ti·za·tion /naàrkəti záysh'n/ *n US* the process by which a society falls under the control of drugs, drug traffickers, and the illegal drug business (*informal*)

nar·co·tize /naárkə tīz/ (**-tized, -tiz·ing, -tiz·es**) *vt* **1.** to treat somebody with a narcotic **2.** to induce stupor in somebody, especially by administering a narcotic drug

nard /naard/ *n* PLANTS same as **spikenard** (senses 1–2) [14C. Via Latin *nardus* < Greek *nardos*, probably < Sanskrit *naladam* "Indian spikenard"]

nar·es /nérreez/ *npl* openings or passages leading out of the nose or nasal cavity. Most vertebrate animals have paired external nares, the nostrils, and a pair of internal nares opening into the mouth. [Late 17C. < Latin, plural of *naris* "nostril"]

nar·ghi·le /naárgəlee/, **nar·gi·leh** *n* DRUGS same as **hookah** [Mid-18C. Directly or via French and Turkish < Persian *nārgīl* "coconut, hookah" < Sanskrit *nārikela* "coconut"]

Na·ri·ta /nə reétə/ city in Japan, on southeastern Honshu Island, in Chiba Prefecture. Population: 95,850 (2002).

nark[1] /naark/ (**narked, nark·ing, narks**) *v* **1.** *vi* same as **narc**[2] (*slang*) **2.** *vt UK* to irritate, offend, or annoy somebody (*informal*) [Mid-19C. < Romany *nāk* "nose"]

nark[2] *n US* CRIME, DRUGS another spelling of **narc**[1] (*slang*)

Nar·ra·bri /nárrə brī/ town in northeastern New South Wales, southeastern Australia. Population: 14,477 (2002 estimate).

Nar·ra·gan·set /nàrrə gánssət/ (*plural* **-sets** or *same*), **Nar·ra·gan·sett** (*plural* **-setts** or *same*) *n* **1.** a member of a Native North American people who lived in Rhode Island west of Narraganset Bay. They were among the largest and strongest of the northeastern Native American peoples until large numbers of them were killed in a war against the New England colonists in the late 17th century. **2.** the extinct Iroquoian language of the Narraganset people [Early 17C. < Narraganset] —**Nar·ra·gan·set** *adj*

Nar·ra·gan·sett /nàrrə gánssət/ town and summer resort in southeastern Rhode Island, Washington County. Population: 16,809 (2002 estimate).

Nar·ra·gan·sett Bay inlet of the Atlantic Ocean in southeastern Rhode Island. Length: 26 mi./42 km.

nar·rate /ná ràyt/ (**-rat·ed, -rat·ing, -rates**) *vt* **1.** to tell a story or give an account, usually in detail **2.** to provide the narration for a film or television program [Mid-17C. < Latin *narrat-*, past participle of *narrare* < *gnarus* "knowing"] —**nar·rat·a·ble** *adj*

nar·ra·tion /na ráysh'n/ *n* **1.** ACT OF NARRATING the act of telling a story or giving an account of something **2.** SOMETHING NARRATED a narrative or story **3.** SOUNDTRACK VOICED BY ACTOR the voiced soundtrack of a broadcast or film when given by an actor or commentator who does not appear —**nar·ra·tion·al** *adj*

nar·ra·tive /nárrətiv/ *n* **1.** STORY a story or an account of a sequence of events in the order in which they happened **2.** PROCESS OF NARRATING the art or process of telling a story or giving an account of something **3.** STORY IN LITERARY WORK the part of a literary work that is concerned with telling the story ■ *adj* **1.** TELLING STORY having the objective of telling a story ○ *narrative poetry* **2.** RELATING TO NARRATION relating to or involving the art of storytelling —**nar·ra·tive·ly** *adv*

nar·ra·tor /ná ràytər/ *n* **1.** STORYTELLER somebody who tells a story or gives an account **2.** TALKING CHARACTER a character in a work of fiction who is presented as telling the story and who refers to himself or herself as "I" **3.** COMMENTATOR somebody who provides narration, e.g., for a television program

nar·row /nárrō/ *adj* **1.** SMALL IN WIDTH having a small width, especially in comparison to height or length ○ *a narrow gap* **2.** LIMITED IN SIZE limited or restricted in size or scope ○ *a narrow range of options* **3.** NARROW-MINDED limited and usually inflexible in outlook ○ *a narrow view of events* **4.** JUST ENOUGH FOR SUCCESS barely sufficient for success ○ *a narrow victory* ○ *a narrow escape* **5.** *US* NOT GENEROUS unwilling to give things or help people **6.** THOROUGH close and thorough, leaving nothing uninvestigated ○ *a narrow investigation of the scene* **7.** PHON same as **tense**[1] *adj* (sense 4) **8.** AGRIC HIGH IN PROTEIN describes animal feed that is very rich in protein ■ *n* NARROW PASSAGE a narrow place or passage ■ *vti* (**-rowed, -row·ing, -rows**) **1.** MAKE OR BECOME NARROW to make something narrow or narrower, or become narrow or narrower **2.** CONTRACT SOMETHING, OR BE CONTRACTED to restrict or limit the scope or extent of something, or become restricted or limited in scope or extent ○ *narrowed the focus of their investigation to two individuals* [Old English *nearu* < Germanic] —**nar·row·ness** *n*

nar·row·band /nárrō bànd/ *adj* functioning within a narrow band of broadcasting frequencies

nar·row·boat *n UK* a long canal barge with a width not exceeding 7 ft./2.1 m

nar·row·cast /nárrō kàst/ (**-cast** or **-cast·ed, -cast·ing, -casts**) *vt* to aim a radio or television transmission at a limited group of people such as cable subscribers or a specialized audience

nar·row gauge *n* **1.** a distance between the two rails of a railroad track that is less than the 4 ft. 8.5 in./143.5 cm distance of the standard gauge railroads **2.** a railroad line with track of a narrow gauge, or a car or locomotive designed to run on one —**nar·row-gauge** *adj*

nar·row·ly /nárrōlee/ *adv* **1.** BY SMALL MARGIN by a very small margin or distance ○ *narrowly avoided capture* **2.** INTENTLY in a very concentrated, searching, or detailed way ○ *eyed him narrowly* **3.** WITHIN NARROW LIMITS in a way that allows little freedom or scope ○ *narrowly circumscribed*

nar·row-mind·ed *adj* having or showing a limited and often prejudiced or intolerant outlook —**nar·row-mind·ed·ly** *adv* —**nar·row-mind·ed·ness** *n*

nar·row mon·ey *n* money usable as a means of exchange, especially bills and coins, but also some bank balances

nar·rows /nárrōz/ *n* a narrow section of a river, or a narrow stretch of sea usually between two larger bodies of water (*takes a singular or plural verb*)

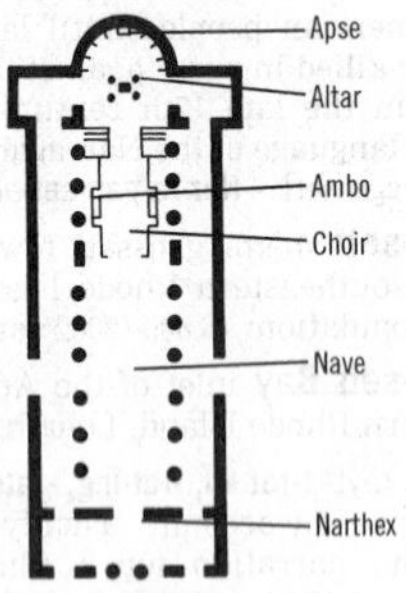

narthex

nar·thex /naar thèks/ *n* **1.** an entrance hall at the west end of a Christian church between the porch and the nave **2.** an area at the west end of the nave of an early Christian church separated off by a screen or railing behind which women, catechumens, or penitents were admitted [Late 17C. < late Greek *narthēx* "giant fennel," later "casket" (because the plant was used to make boxes)]

Nar·vá·ez /naar vī ez/, **Pánfilo de** (1470?–1528) Spanish explorer. His attempt to conquer Florida ended in disaster and his own death.

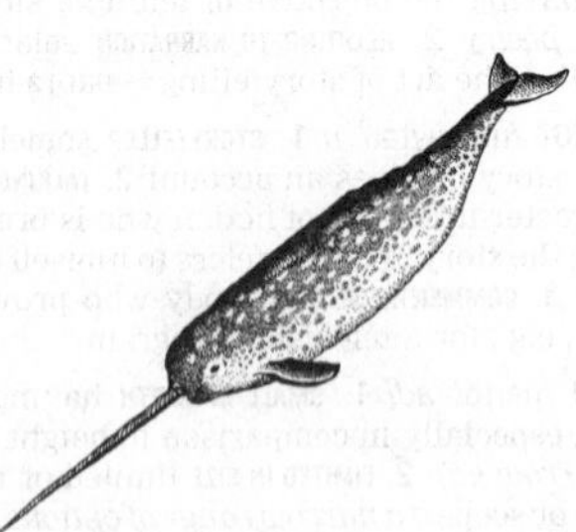
narwhal

nar·whal /naar waal, -wəl, -hwaal/ (*plural same* or **-whals**), **nar·wal** /-waal, -wəl/ (*plural same* or **-wals**), **nar·whale** /-wàyl, -hwàyl/ (*plural same* or **-whales**) *n* a small arctic whale, about 20 ft./6 m long, with a spotted body, short flippers, and, in the male, a long twisted ivory tusk. It was formerly hunted for oil and ivory. Latin name: *Monodon monoceros*. [Mid-17C. < Danish or Norwegian *narhval*]

nar·y /nérree/ *adj* not a single (*literary*) ○ *Nary a word was said.* [Mid-18C. Contraction of *ne'er a* "never a"]

NAS *abbr* **1.** SCI National Academy of Sciences **2.** NAVY naval air station

NASA /nássə/ *n* the US government agency responsible for nonmilitary programs in the exploration and scientific study of space. Full form **National Aeronautics and Space Administration**

na·sal /náyz'l/ *adj* **1.** OF NOSE forming part of or relating to the nose **2.** PRONOUNCED THROUGH NOSE describes a speech sound that is pronounced with breath escaping mainly through the nose rather than the mouth **3.** WITH NASAL SOUNDS characterized by nasal sounds ○ *a nasal accent* ■ *n* **1.** NASAL SOUND a nasal sound or a letter that represents it **2.** HELMET PART the nosepiece of a helmet [Mid-17C. Directly or via French < medieval Latin *nasalis* < Latin *nasus* "nose"] —**na·sal·i·ty** /nay zálləteel/ *n* —**na·sal·ly** *adv*

na·sal cav·i·ty *n* either of the two open spaces, located between the floor of the cranium and the roof of the mouth, that form the inner nose

na·sal con·cha *n* ANAT same as **turbinate** *n* (sense 1)

na·sal·ize /náyz'l īz/ (**-ized, -iz·ing, -iz·es**) *vti* to make a sound nasal by lowering the soft palate so that air flows through the nose —**na·sal·i·za·tion** /nàyz'li záysh'n/ *n*

NASCAR /náss kaar/ *abbr US* MOTOR SPORTS National Association of Stock Car Auto Racing

NASCAR dad *n US* a socioeconomic category characterized as a white rural blue-collar family man who is politically conservative and a fan of stock-car racing

nas·cent /náyss'nt, náss'nt/ *adj* **1.** in the process of emerging, being born, or starting to develop **2.** in the process of being created in a reaction medium, often in a highly active form [Early 17C. < Latin *nascent-*, present participle of *nasci* "be born"] —**nas·cence** *n*

NASD *abbr US* FIN National Association of Securities Dealers

NASDAQ /náz dàk/ *tdmk* a service mark for an electronic communications system in the United States that links all over-the-counter securities dealers to form a single market. Full form **National Association of Securities Dealers Automated Quotation System**

nase·ber·ry /náyz bèrree/ (*plural* **-ries**) *n* TREES same as **sapodilla** (sense 1) [Late 17C. < Spanish *níspero* or Portuguese *nespera* < Latin *mespilus* "medlar," by association with BERRY]

~~**nash**~~ incorrect spelling of **gnash**

Nash /nash/, **John** (1752–1835) British architect. His designs include the neoclassical Regent Street in London (begun 1812) and the elaborate Royal Pavilion in Brighton, England (1815–23).

Nash, Ogden (1902–71) US poet and lyricist. He is known for his comic verse and the musical *One Touch of Venus* (1943). Full name **Nash, Frederic Ogden**

> "Professional men, they have no cares; / Whatever happens, they get theirs."
> [Ogden Nash, "I Yield to My Learned Brother"; 1935]

Nash, Sir Walter (1882–1968) British-born prime minister of New Zealand (1957–60). Elected to Parliament for the Labour party in 1919, he held several ministerial posts, including finance minister (1935–40) before taking over as party leader (1949). As prime minister, he pursued a policy of social reform. See table at **prime minister**

Nash·u·a /náshoo ə/ city in southern New Hampshire. It is the administrative seat of Hillsborough County. Population: 87,705 (2002 estimate).

Nash·ville /násh vil/ capital city of Tennessee, situated in the north central part of the state. It is a major center for country-and-western music. Population: 570,785 (2002 estimate).

na·si go·reng /naassee gə réng/ *n* a Malaysian dish of fried rice with other ingredients, usually including meat or fish [< Malay, "fried rice"]

na·si·on /náyzee òn/ *n* the point where the bridge of the nose meets the forehead [Late 19C. < French < *nasal* "nasal," after INION] —**na·si·al** *adj*

naso- *prefix* nose, nasal ○ *nasogastric* [< Latin *nasus* < Indo-European, "nose"]

na·so·fron·tal /nàyzō frúnt'l/ *adj* relating to the nasal and the frontal bones jointly

na·so·gas·tric /nàyzō gástrik/ *adj* passing through the nose to the stomach

na·so·lac·ri·mal /nàyzō lákrəm'l/, **na·so·lach·ry·mal** *adj* relating to or connecting the nose and the tear-producing sacs

na·so·pha·ryn·ge·al /nàyzō fə rínjee əl, -fə rínjəl, -fàrrən jée əl/ *adj* relating to the nose and pharynx or to the nasopharynx

na·so·phar·ynx /nàyzō fárringks/ (*plural* **-pha·ryn·ges** /-fə rín jeez/ or **-phar·ynx·es**) *n* the upper part of the pharynx, behind and above the soft palate, continuous with the nasal passages

Nas·rud·din /naazroo deén/ *n* in Islamic folklore, a trickster. He first appeared in stories used by Sufis to teach their students. [Mid-20C. < Turkish]

Nas·sau /ná sàw/ capital city and principal port of the Bahamas, situated on the northeastern coast of New Providence Island. Population: 172,000 (1997).

Gamal Abdel Nasser

Nas·ser /nássər, naassər/, **Gamal Abdel** (1918–70) president of Egypt (1956–70). During his presidency, he promoted industrialization, built the Aswan High Dam, and nationalized the Suez Canal. He was the foremost Arab leader of his time.

> "Power is not merely shouting aloud. Power is to act positively with all the components of power."
> [Gamal Abdel Nasser, *The Philosophy of the Revolution*; 1952]

Nast /nast/, **Thomas** (1840–1902) German-born US satirical cartoonist. He is known for his attacks on the Tammany Ring (1869–72), and for creating the symbols of the Republican elephant and the Democratic donkey.

Na·sta·se /nə stássee/, **Ilie** (*b.* 1946) Romanian tennis player. He won the US Open (1972) and French Open (1973), and many doubles titles.

nas·tic /nástik/ *adj* describes the movement of the parts of a plant in response to external stimuli, e.g., the opening of a crocus flower in response to temperature [Early 20C. < Greek *nastos* "pressed together" < *nassein* "to press"]

nasturtium

nas·tur·tium /nə stúrshəm, na-/ *n* a plant with shield-shaped pungent edible leaves. Flowers: yellow, orange, red. Genus: *Tropaeolum*. [12C. < Latin]

nas·ty /nástee/ *adj* (**-ti·er, -ti·est**) **1.** SPITEFUL showing spitefulness or malice ○ *a nasty trick to play on someone* **2.** REPUGNANT disgusting to the senses ○ *a nasty smell* **3.** UNPLEASANT generally disagreeable, unpleasant, or causing discomfort ○ *The weather turned nasty.* **4.** SERIOUS likely to cause harm or to be painful ○ *a nasty accident* ○ *a nasty bump on the head* **5.** MORALLY OFFENSIVE morally offensive or obscene (*informal*) ○ *nasty videos* **6.** DIFFICULT difficult to solve or deal with (*informal*) ○ *a nasty problem* ■ *n* (*plural* **-ties**) UNPLEASANT PERSON OR THING somebody or something that is very disagreeable, harmful, or offensive (*informal*) ■ *vt Carib* MAKE DIRTY to make something dirty or messy [14C. Origin ?] —**nas·ti·ly** *adv* —**nas·ti·ness** *n*

SYNONYMS See *mean*[2].

-nasty *suffix* nastic response ○ *thermonasty* [< Greek *nastos* (see NASTIC)]

nat. *abbr* **1.** national **2.** native **3.** natural

na·tal[1] /náyt'l/ *adj* relating to birth or to the time and place of birth [14C. < Latin *natalis* < *nasci* "be born"]

na·tal[2] /náyt'l/ *adj* relating to the buttocks [Late 19C. < Latin *natis* "buttock"]

Na·tal /nə taál/ **1.** city and seaport in northeastern Brazil. It is the capital of Rio Grande do Norte State. Population: 656,037 (1996). **2.** British colony which became a province in the Union of South Africa in 1910. In 1994 it became the province of Kwa-Zulu Natal.

na·tal·i·ty /nə tállətee, nay-/ *n* STATS same as **birthrate**

na·tant /náyt'nt/ *adj* floating or swimming in water (*technical*) [15C. < Latin *natant-*, present participle of *natare* (see NATATORY)]

Nat·ar·a·ja /naàtə raájə/ *n* in Hinduism, the god Shiva when represented as a dancing figure with several arms and legs [Early 20C. < Hindi, "prince of dancers"]

na·ta·tion /nə táysh'n, nay-/ *n* the action or skill of swimming (*formal*) [Mid-16C. < Latin *natation-* < *natare* (see NATATORY)] —**na·ta·tion·al** *adj*

na·ta·to·ry /náytə tàwree/, **na·ta·to·ri·al** /nàytə táwree əl/ *adj* relating to or adapted for swimming (*formal*) [Late 18C. < late Latin *natatorius* < Latin *natator* "swimmer" < *natare* "keep on swimming" < *nare* "to swim"]

natch /nach/ *adv* naturally (*informal*) [Mid-20C. Shortening]

Natch·ez /náchiz/ city on the Mississippi River in southwestern Mississippi. The first state capital of Mississippi from 1817 to 1821, it was of strategic importance in the 18th and 19th centuries as the southern terminus of the Natchez Trace trade route. Population: 17,864 (2002 estimate).

Natch·ez Trace /-tráyss/ historic road between Natchez, Mississippi, and Nashville, Tennessee, that was an important commercial and military route during the settlement of the region in the late 18th and early 19th centuries

Natch·i·toches /nákə tòsh/ city in western Louisiana, just west of the Red River. Population: 17,714 (2002 estimate).

na·tes /náy teez/ *npl* the buttocks [Late 17C. < Latin, plural of *natis* "buttock, rump"]

Na·than /náythən/ *n* in the Bible, a prophet at David's court (2 Samuel 7:1–17, 12:1–15)

Na·than /náythən/, **S. R.** (*b.* 1924) president of Singapore (1999–). A former social worker, he served as ambassador to the United States (1990–96) before becoming president. Full name **Nathan, Sellapan Ramanathan**

Na·tick /náttik/ town in eastern Massachusetts, east of Framingham and southwest of Boston. Population: 32,384 (1990).

na·tion /náysh'n/ *n* **1.** PEOPLE IN LAND UNDER SINGLE GOVERNMENT a community of people or peoples living in a defined territory and organized under a single government **2.** PEOPLE OF SAME ETHNICITY a community of people who share a common ethnic origin, culture, historical tradition, and, frequently, language, whether or not they live together in one territory or have their own government **3.** NATIVE AMERICAN PEOPLE OR FEDERATION a Native American people or a federation of peoples ○ *the Apache nation* **4.** LAND OF NATIVE AMERICAN NATION a territory occupied by a Native American people or federation **5.** GROUP WITH COMMON INTEREST a group of people united by a common interest ○ *the hip-hop nation* [13C. Via French < Latin *nation-* "birth, race" < *nat-*, past participle of *nasci* "be born"] —**na·tion·hood** *n* —**na·tion·less** *adj*

Na·tion /náysh'n/, **Carry** (1846–1911) US temperance leader. Believing that she had a divine calling, she armed herself with a hatchet and carried out violent attacks on saloons in numerous US cities. Full name **Carry Amelia Moore Nation**

> "A woman is stripped of everything by them saloons. Her husband is torn from her; she is robbed of her sons, her home, her food, and her virtue."
> [Carry Nation. Quoted in *Cyclone Carry*, Carleton Beals; 1962]

na·tion·al /náshən'l, náshnəl/ *adj* **1.** OF NATION relating to, belonging to, representing, or affecting a nation, especially a nation as a whole rather than a part of it or section of its territory ○ *the national team* **2.** CHARACTERISTIC OF PEOPLE OF NATION relating to or characteristic of the people of a nation ○ *the British national character* **3.** OWNED OR CONTROLLED BY CENTRAL GOVERNMENT owned, maintained, or controlled by the central government of a nation ○ *a national film museum* ■ *n* **1.** CITIZEN OF PARTICULAR NATION a citizen of a particular nation, especially when living in another country ○ *a foreign national* **2.** SPORTS EVENT FOR CONTESTANTS FROM WHOLE COUNTRY a sports contest involving participants from every part of a country (*often used in the plural*)

na·tion·al an·them *n* a nation's official hymn or song, expressing patriotic sentiments and played or sung on public occasions

na·tion·al as·sem·bly *n* a legislative body consisting of the elected representatives of a nation or country

Na·tion·al As·sem·bly *n* **1.** the first legislative assembly set up during the French Revolution, ruling from 1789 to 1791 **2.** the legislative assembly in Quebec

Na·tion·al As·sem·bly for Wales *n* the center of devolved government for Wales, made up of elected members. It has the power to introduce secondary legislation in areas such as health and education in Wales.

na·tion·al bank *n* **1.** *US* a bank in a system of privately owned commercial banks in the United States, operating under federal charter and legally required to be a member of the Federal Reserve System **2.** a bank that acts as banker to a government and performs duties relating to national finances, especially the country's fiscal and monetary policy

Na·tion·al Cit·y /nàshən'l-/ city in southwestern California, in San Diego County, south of San Diego. Population: 55,541 (2002 estimate).

na·tion·al con·scious·ness *n* the ideas, beliefs, and attitudes regarded as characteristic of a nation

na·tion·al cos·tume *n* CLOTHING same as **national dress**

na·tion·al debt *n* the total amount of money owed by a nation's central government as a result of borrowing

na·tion·al dress *n* clothes of a distinctive design that are, or were, characteristic of the people of a particular country

na·tion·al for·est *n* *US* a forested area that is owned and maintained by the federal government

Na·tion·al Gal·ler·y *n* a museum in central London, England, that contains more than 2,000 paintings from the national collection. Founded in 1824, it opened in its present building in 1838. A new Sainsbury Wing opened in 1991.

Na·tion·al Gal·ler·y of Art *n* a museum in Washington, D.C. that contains the national collection of paintings, prints, drawings, sculptures, photographs, and other works of art. It was founded in 1937 with the gift to the nation of the art collection of the financier Andrew W. Mellon.

Na·tion·al Gal·ler·y of Aus·tra·lia *n* a museum in Canberra that contains the national collection of Aboriginal, modern Australian, and world art. The collection was begun in 1911, and is housed in a building dating from 1982. Former name **Australian National Gallery**

Na·tion·al Gal·ler·y of Can·a·da *n* a museum in Ottawa that contains the national collection of Canadian and European art. It was created by an Act of Parliament in 1913.

na·tion·al guard *n* a military organization that operates as a national defense or police force

Na·tion·al Guard *n* in the United States, the military reserve units controlled by individual states and equipped by the federal government that can be called into service by either federal or state governments

Na·tion·al Health Ser·vice *n* in the United Kingdom, the state system for providing free or subsidized medical care, established in 1948

Na·tion·al Hock·ey League *n* the major league of professional ice hockey teams in Canada and the United States

na·tion·al in·come *n* the total money earned or gained by all residents of a country over a period of time, including income from rent, profits, interest, government benefits, salaries, and wages

Na·tion·al In·sti·tutes of Health *n* an agency of the US federal government that conducts and supports medical research and programs designed to improve the health of the nation (*takes a singular verb*)

Na·tion·al In·sur·ance num·ber *n* in the United Kingdom, a unique reference number assigned to each person within the state insurance system. It remains the same throughout each person's life.

na·tion·al in·ter·est *n* actions, circumstances, and decisions regarded as benefiting a particular nation

na·tion·al·ism /náshən'l ìzzəm, náshnə-/ *n* **1.** DESIRE FOR POLITICAL INDEPENDENCE the desire to achieve political independence, especially by a country under foreign control or by a people with a separate identity and culture but no state of their own **2.** PATRIOTISM proud loyalty and devotion to a nation **3.** EXCESSIVE DEVOTION TO NATION excessive or fanatical devotion to a nation and its interests, often associated with a belief that one country is superior to all others —**na·tion·al·ist** *n, adj*

na·tion·al·is·tic /nàshən'l ístik, nàshnə-/ *adj* relating to or supporting nationalism, especially the kind that emphasizes fervent devotion to one nation and its interests above all others —**na·tion·al·is·ti·cal·ly** *adv*

na·tion·al·i·ty /nàshə nállətee/ (*plural* **-ties**) *n* **1.** CITIZENSHIP OF PARTICULAR NATION the status of belonging to a particular nation by origin, birth, or naturalization **2.** PEOPLE FORMING NATION-STATE a people with a common origin, tradition, and often language, who form or are capable of forming a nation-state **3.** ETHNIC GROUP WITHIN LARGER ENTITY an ethnic group that is part of a larger entity such as a state **4.** NATIONHOOD political independence as a separate nation **5.** NATIONAL CHARACTER the character of a nation of people

na·tion·al·ize /náshən'l ìz, náshnə-/ (**-ized, -iz·ing, -iz·es**) *vt* **1.** to transfer a business, property, or industry from private to governmental control or ownership **2.** to make something national or to give a national character to something **3.** same as **naturalize** (sense 1) —**na·tion·al·i·za·tion** /nàshən'li záysh'n, nàshnə-/ *n* —**na·tion·al·ized** *adj* —**na·tion·al·iz·er** *n*

Na·tion·al La·bor Re·la·tions Board *n* an agency of the US federal government that enforces the law regulating relations between unions and employers in the private sector

Na·tion·al Li·brar·y of Aus·tra·lia *n* the national library of Australia, in Canberra, established as an independent institution by an Act of Parliament in 1960. It was founded in 1901 as part of the Commonwealth Parliamentary Library.

Na·tion·al Li·brar·y of Can·a·da *n* the national library of Canada, founded in Ottawa in 1953

Na·tion·al Li·brar·y of New Zea·land *n* the national library of New Zealand, in Wellington, created in 1966 by combining the collections of the General Assembly Library, the Alexander Turnbull Library, and the National Library Service

na·tion·al·ly /náshən'lee, náshnəlee/ *adv* in, to, or throughout an entire nation

na·tion·al mon·u·ment *n* a structure or site of scenic, historical, or scientific significance that is protected and maintained by a national government

na·tion·al park *n* a large area of public land chosen by a government for its scenic, recreational, scientific, or historical importance and usually given special protection

Na·tion·al Par·ty *n* in South Africa until 1998, a conservative political party that developed from the Afrikaner nationalist movement, came to power in 1948, was largely responsible for instituting apartheid, and relinquished power in 1994. In 1998 it changed its name to the New National Party.

Na·tion·al Re·search Coun·cil Can·a·da *n* a Canadian government department that conducts and promotes scientific and industrial research

na·tion·al se·cu·ri·ty *n* the protection of a nation from attack or other danger by maintaining adequate armed forces and guarding state secrets

na·tion·al se·cu·ri·ty ad·vis·er *n* a member of the White House staff who advises the President on security matters

Na·tion·al Se·cu·ri·ty Coun·cil *n* a council consisting of the president, the secretary of state, the national security adviser, and top military and intelligence officers that decides on policies and measures to maintain national security

na·tion·al ser·vice *n* compulsory service in the armed forces or in a civilian role, as prescribed in some countries

na·tion·al so·cial·ism, Na·tion·al So·cial·ism *n* the ideology and practices of the Nazi Party, in Germany's Third Reich, which included national expansion, state control of the economy, the totalitarian principle of government, and anti-Semitism —**na·tion·al so·cial·ist** *n, adj*

Na·tion·al Trans·por·ta·tion Safe·ty Board *n* an agency of the US federal government that investigates civil aviation, railroad, and highway accidents and makes safety recommendations aimed at preventing future accidents

nation language *n Carib* in the Caribbean, the popularly used English language, whether considered as a dialect of English or as an English-related creole language

Na·tion of Is·lam *n* a movement of African Americans, founded in 1930, whose members follow Islamic religious practice out of a belief that Black Americans have Islamic origins. Malcolm X was a leading spokesman for the organization until he left it in 1964.

na·tion-state *n* a politically independent country, especially one in which the citizens share the same language, culture, and nationality

na·tion·wide /náysh'n wīd/ *adj* applying to, happening in, or found in all parts of a nation ○ *a nationwide advertising campaign* —**na·tion·wide** *adv*

na·tive /náytiv/ *adj* **1. INBORN** existing in or belonging to somebody by nature ○ *her native intelligence* **2. BORN OR ORIGINATING SOMEWHERE** born or originating in a particular place ○ *native to the Southwest* **3. RELATING TO SOMEBODY BECAUSE OF BIRTH** relating or belonging to somebody or something because of the place or circumstances of birth ○ *She returned to her native land.* **4. INDIGENOUS** originating, produced, growing, or living naturally in a place **5. CHARACTERISTIC OF LOCAL INHABITANTS** characteristic of, belonging to, or relating to the indigenous inhabitants of a particular place, particularly those with a traditional culture (*dated; often considered offensive*) **6. NOT EXTERNALLY AFFECTED** unaffected by artificial or outside influences ○ *the native charm of the local fishing villages* **7.** CHEM ELEM **OCCURRING NATURALLY** found in nature, especially in a pure or unadulterated form ○ *native copper* **8.** COMPUT **FOR PARTICULAR COMPUTER SYSTEM** designed exclusively for a particular computer operating system ■ *n* **1. SOMEBODY BORN IN PARTICULAR PLACE** somebody born or brought up in a particular place ○ *a native of Boston* **2. OFFENSIVE TERM** an offensive term for an original inhabitant of a place belonging to an indigenous nonwhite people with a traditional culture, as distinct from a colonial settler and immigrant (*dated*) **3. INDIGENOUS PLANT OR ANIMAL SPECIES** a plant or animal species that originates from a particular area ■ *adj* COMPUT **READABLE BY PARTICULAR APPLICATION** used to describe the format in which a software application normally saves its documents, usually readable only by that application [14C. Directly or via French *natif* < Latin *nativus* "born" < *nasci* "be born"] —**na·tive·ly** *adv* —**na·tive·ness** *n* ◇ **go native** to take up the customs and culture of the foreign place where you have settled (*humorous*)

USAGE Avoid use of the lowercase noun and adjective ***native*** to mean "an indigenous inhabitant of a place" and "relating to the indigenous people of a place," as in *the natives of Guam* and *the native people of Haiti.* Prefer *the indigenous* [or *original* or *aboriginal*] *people of Guam* or *the Haitians.* Capitalized *Native,* totally acceptable, now refers not only to Native North and South Americans but also to indigenous peoples of places such as Hawaii and Alaska, i.e., Native Alaskans, Alaska Natives, and Native Hawaiians.

ORIGIN The Latin word *nasci* "to be born," from which ***native*** is derived, and its past participle *natus* are also the source of English *cognate, impregnate, innate, naive, nascent, nation, nature, noel, pregnant, puny,* and *renaissance.*

SYNONYMS ***native, aboriginal, indigenous, autochthonous***
CORE MEANING: originating in a particular place
native born or originating in a particular place ○ *the native peoples of Siberia* ○ *Native to the region are jaguars, giant anteaters, and caymans.* **aboriginal** existing in a place from the earliest known times ○ *a tiny aboriginal island community* **indigenous** originating in and naturally living, growing, or occurring in a region or country ○ *the indigenous population of the region* **autochthonous** originating where currently found, especially used of rocks and minerals that were formed in their present position, or flora, fauna, or inhabitants descended from those present in a region from earliest times ○ *Hummingbirds are autochthonous and exclusive birds of tropical America.* ○ *autochthonous Miocene claystones*

Na·tive A·las·kan *n* PEOPLES same as **Alaska Native**

Na·tive A·mer·i·can *n* a member of any of the indigenous peoples of North, South, or Central America, belonging to the Mongoloid group of peoples ■ *adj* relating to any of the indigenous American peoples, their languages, or their cultures

USAGE See ***Indian.***

na·tive-born *adj* belonging to a place by birth

Na·tive Cen·tral A·mer·i·can *n* a member of any of the indigenous peoples of Central America ■ *adj* relating to any of the indigenous Central American peoples, their languages, or their cultures

LANGUAGE HERITAGE See ***Nahuatl.***

native frangipani

na·tive fran·gi·pan·i (*plural* **na·tive fran·gi·pan·is**) *n* an evergreen tree with fragrant cream or yellow flowers. Native to: coastal eastern Australia. Latin name: *Hymenosporum flavum.*

Na·tive Ha·wai·ian *n* a member of the indigenous people of Hawaii

na·tive land *n* the land to which somebody belongs by birth

Na·tive North A·mer·i·can *n* a member of any of the indigenous peoples of North America ■ *adj* relating to any of the indigenous North American peoples, their languages, or their cultures ▶ See panel on next page

Na·tive Peo·ple *n Can* any of the Native American peoples of Canada

na·tive son *n* somebody born in a particular place and still associated with it ○ *Illinois is expected to support its native son in the presidential primary.*

Na·tive South A·mer·i·can *n* a member of any of the indigenous peoples of South America ■ *adj* relating to any of the indigenous South American peoples, their languages, or their cultures

LANGUAGE HERITAGE See ***Tupi-Guarani.***

na·tive speak·er *n* a speaker of a language learned in infancy

na·tive tongue *n* the first language that somebody learns to speak

na·tiv·ism /náyti vìzzəm/ *n* **1. POLICY OF FAVORING INDIGENOUS INHABITANTS** a policy, especially in the United States, of favoring the interests of the indigenous inhabitants of a country over those of immigrants **2. POLICY OF REAFFIRMING INDIGENOUS CULTURE** a policy of protecting and celebrating traditional cultures **3. PHILOSOPHICAL DOCTRINE OF INNATE IDEAS** the belief that the mind possesses some ideas that are inborn and not derived from external sources **4. PSYCHOLOGICAL THEORY OF PERSONALITY** in psychology, a theory claiming that personality and behavior are determined from within, not externally —**na·tiv·ist** *n, adj* —**na·tiv·is·tic** /nàyti vístik/ *adj*

na·tiv·i·ty /nə tívvətee/ (*plural* **-ties**) *n* **1.** birth or origin, especially the place, process, or circumstances of being born **2.** a horoscope based on the time of somebody's birth [14C. Via Old French < Latin *nativitas* < *nativus* (see NATIVE)]

Na·tiv·i·ty (*plural* **-ties**) *n* **1.** the birth of Jesus Christ, which is celebrated by Christians at Christmas **2.** an artistic representation of the events surrounding the birth of Jesus Christ

natl. *abbr* national

NATO /náytō/, **Na·to** *n* an international organization established in 1949 to promote mutual defense and collective security that was the primary Western alliance during the Cold War. Full form **North Atlantic Treaty Organization**

na·tri·u·re·sis /nàytree yōō réessiss/ *n* the excretion of sodium in urine, especially in excessive amounts [Mid-20C. < *natrium* a name for sodium + Greek *ourēsis* "urination"] —**na·tri·u·ret·ic** /-yōō réttik/ *adj*

na·tro·lite /náytrə līt, náttrə-/ *n* a white sodium aluminosilicate mineral of the zeolite group [Early 19C. < NATRON]

na·tron /náy tròn, -trən/ *n* a white, yellow, or gray hydrous sodium carbonate mineral. Source: salt deposits. Use: formerly, embalming. [Late 17C. Via French, Spanish, and Arabic < Greek *nitron* "potassium or sodium nitrate"]

nat·ter /náttər/ (*informal*) *vi* (**-tered, -ter·ing, -ters**) to talk about not very serious matters, often rapidly and at length and sometimes in an irritating way ■ *n* a trivial or gossipy conversation [Early 19C. Origin ?]

nat·ty /náttee/ (**-ti·er, -ti·est**) *adj* **1.** neat and fashionable in appearance or dress **2.** describes hair worn in dreadlocks (*slang; used in Black English*) [Late 18C. Origin ?] —**nat·ti·ly** *adv* —**nat·ti·ness** *n*

nat·u·ral /náchərəl, náchrəl/ *adj* **1. OF NATURE** relating to nature ○ *natural history* **2. CONFORMING WITH NATURE** in accordance with the usual course of nature ○ *natural signs of aging* **3. PRODUCED BY NATURE** present in or produced by nature, not artificial or synthetic ○ *a natural sapphire* **4. OF PHYSICAL WORLD** relating to the physical rather than the spiritual world ○ *striking natural features* **5. LIKE HUMAN NATURE** in accordance with human nature ○ *It's only natural that they should want to be independent.* **6. INNATE** inborn, rather than acquired ○ *lots of natural charm* **7. BEING SOMETHING BY NATURE** having a particular character by nature ○ *a natural leader* **8. NOT AFFECTED** behaving in a sincere and unaffected way and not affected or adopted for a special purpose ○ *a natural manner* **9. LIKE REAL LIFE** representing something in a way that seems true to life **10. BIOLOGICAL** related by blood, rather than adoption ○ *her natural mother* **11. NOT SHARP OR FLAT** describes a note in music that is neither sharp nor flat **12. WITHOUT SHARPS OR FLATS** describes a musical key or scale containing no sharps or flats **13. WITHOUT JOKER OR WILD CARD** not made using a joker or a wild card ○ *a natural flush* **14. ILLEGITIMATE** born of unmarried parents (*archaic*) ○ *a natural child* ■ *n* **1. SOMEBODY WITH INNATE SKILLS OR ABILITIES** somebody who has seemingly innate skills or abilities ○ *a natural at bowling* **2.** MUSIC **MUSICAL SIGN CANCELING SHARP OR FLAT** a sign placed before a musical note in order to cancel a previous sharp or flat **3.** MUSIC **NOTE AFFECTED BY NATURAL SIGN** a musical note affected by a natural sign **4.** CARDS, GAMBLING **STAKE-WINNING RESULT OR COMBINATION** a result or combination in some card and dice games such as craps and blackjack that immediately wins the stake **5.** COLORS **LIGHT COLOR** a nearly white color with tints of gray, yellow, or brown, like that of undyed fibers or yarn [13C. Via French < Latin *naturalis* < *natura* (see NATURE)] —**nat·u·ral·ness** *n*

nat·u·ral child·birth *n* childbirth with little or no medication or medical intervention, in which the mother uses special techniques and exercises in order to minimize pain and assist in the delivery

nat·u·ral death *n* death caused by disease or old age rather than by an act of violence or an accident

nat·u·ral dis·as·ter *n* a disaster caused by natural forces rather than by human action, e.g., an earthquake

nat·u·ral fi·ber *n* a fiber that forms naturally, e.g., cotton, wool, or silk

nat·u·ral food *n* food that has undergone no or minimal processing and contains no additives such as preservatives or artificial coloring

LANGUAGE HERITAGE *Native North American* Much of English is made up of words from other languages, and Native North American languages, especially those in the Algonquian family, are significant contributors in this respect, particularly to US and Canadian English. To begin with, many names of states and provinces, of rivers, lakes, and other geographic features are of Native American origin. Although the early European settlers preferred European names for their political divisions, during the 19th century state names with Native North American origins were adopted with increasing frequency, from ***Ohio*** in 1803, through ***Arkansas*** in 1836 and ***Oregon*** in 1859, to ***Utah*** (named for the ***Ute*** people) in 1896. All in all 26 US states and 6 Canadian provinces or territories have such names. The older, eastern states with Native American names, ***Massachusetts*** and ***Connecticut***, share them with a bay and a river, respectively. Major rivers also give their names to the states of ***Arkansas, Mississippi, Missouri, Ohio***, and ***Tennessee***. Other landscape terms of Native American origin include four of the five Great Lakes – ***Erie, Huron, Ontario***, and ***Michigan*** – as well as others such as the ***Susquehanna River***, the ***Niagara Falls*** and ***Yosemite Falls***, and the ***Adirondack, Allegheny***, and ***Appalachian*** mountains. In Canada the name of the country itself is said to come from an Iroquoian word *kanata* meaning "village, community," and, for example, ***Quebec, Manitoba, Yukon***, and ***Saskatchewan*** are of Native North American origin; in 1991 the Inuktitut name ***Nunavut*** (literally "our land") was officially adopted for the larger part of Arctic Canada.

In identifying indigenous peoples the incoming Europeans often adopted Native North American names, either the people's own name, as ***Dakota*** (from Dakota, "allies"), ***Haida*** ("people"), or ***Tsimshian*** (from Tsimshian *čamsián* "inside the Skeena River"), or an ally's, enemy's, or stranger's name, as ***Arapaho*** (from Crow *alappahó* "many tattoo marks"), ***Menominee*** (from Ojibwa *manōminī* "wild-rice person"), or ***Mohawk*** (from Narraganset *mohowawog* "man-eaters"). Sometimes the English name is mediated through North American French, for example, ***Assiniboin*** (via French from Ojibwa), ***Cheyenne*** (via French from Dakota), and ***Sioux*** (from a shortening of French *Nadouessioux*, from Ojibwa *nātowēssiwak*), or through Spanish, as ***Comanche*** (ultimately from Southern Paiute or a related language), ***Navajo*** (via Spanish from Tewa *navahū* "fields adjoining a ravine"), and ***Yaqui*** (via Spanish from Yaqui *Hiaki*). Sometimes a word is translated, for example ***Blackfoot***, from Blackfoot *Siksika*. Occasionally a European term was adopted by Native North Americans themselves and then passed to English, as ***Seminole***, which came from Creek *simanó:li* but goes back to American Spanish *cimarrón* "wild, untamed."

Words relating to Native North American artifacts and ways of life have become familiar to English speakers, often extending far beyond their original cultural reference. The ***moccasin***, for example, (early 17th century, from Virginia Algonquian) is now a generic word for a type of shoe; ***tuxedo*** (named for a country club in Tuxedo Park, New York, but ultimately from an Algonquian word for "wolf") refers to men's evening attire; ***powwow*** (from Narraganset) has come to be used informally for any meeting or gathering to discuss something; ***sachem*** (early 17th century, from Algonquian), originally a Native North American chief, was later applied to a leader or official of ***Tammany Hall*** (itself from the name of a Delaware chief, Tamanend); the ***tomahawk*** (from Virginia Algonquian) is now any small short-handled ax; ***totem*** (from Ojibwa *nindoodem* "my totem") is used generally for something treated with the kind of respect normally reserved for religious icons. Names of food adopted into English include ***hominy*** (a contraction of Virginia Algonquian *uskatahomen* "that which is ground"), ***pone*** (from Virginia Algonquian *poan* "thing roasted or baked"), ***samp***, which has moved into South African English as well, ***squash*** (a shortening of Narraganset *asquutasquash* "green things that may be eaten raw"), and ***succotash***. Still other terms from Algonquian languages remain in their original cultural context, for example, ***manitou, sagamore, watap, wendigo*** (a demonic creature of Algonquian folklore), and ***wickiup***. From other peoples and languages come ***tepee*** (Dakota), ***muckamuck*** (Chinook Jargon), and ***kachina*** (Hopi).

Flora and fauna naturally form important categories of words of Native North American origin. Algonquian-named animals include, for example, the ***chipmunk*** (from Ojibwa *ajidamoonˀ*, literally "one that comes down trees headlong"), ***opossum, raccoon, terrapin*** (an alteration of Virginia Algonquian *torope*), and ***wapiti*** (from Shawnee). Altered by folk etymology to conform to English expectations are ***muskrat*** (from Algonquian *muscasus*) and ***woodchuck***; ***whiskey jack***, the gray jay, was originally *whiskey john*, from Cree *wiskatjan*. Showing the complexity of interaction between European and Native American languages is ***kinkajou***, from a French word *quincajou* "wolverine" that is probably a blend of one Montagnais and one Ojibwa word. Some other names of animals come from non-Algonquian languages, for example, the lizard the ***chuckwalla*** (via Mexican Spanish from Cahuilla), and the ***sewellel*** or mountain beaver (from Chinook *šwalál* "robe made of mountain beaver skin"). Algonquian is a significant source of shellfish and fish names: ***cohog*** or ***quahog, mummichog, muskellunge*** (via Canadian French *maskinongé* from Ojibwa *maashkinoozhe* "big fish"), ***scup, tautog***, and more. Representing other languages are, for example, ***abalone*** (via Spanish from Shoshonean) and ***quinnat salmon*** (first element from Chinook).

Trees and other plants, their fruits, wood, and other products have often retained or acquired Native North American names, for example, from Algonquian ***chinquapin, cohosh, hackmatack, hickory, persimmon, puccoon, saskatoon, tamarack*** (via Canadian French), ***tuckahoe***, and, combining with English, ***atamasco lily***. Names from other languages include ***catalpa*** and ***tupelo*** (from Creek), ***coontie*** (from Seminole), ***sego lily*** (first element from Southern Paiute), and ***yaupon*** (from Catawba).

nat·u·ral gas *n* a mixture of combustible hydrocarbon gases, mostly methane and ethane, found trapped in the pore spaces of some sedimentary rocks, often along with petroleum deposits

nat·u·ral his·to·ry *n* **1.** STUDY OF LIVING THINGS the study and description of living things, especially their behavior and how they relate to one another **2.** STUDY OF WHOLE NATURAL WORLD the study and description of the natural world, including minerals and fossils **3.** NATURAL PHENOMENA OF TIME OR PLACE the natural phenomena, especially plants and animals, of a particular time or place **4.** NATURAL DEVELOPMENT OF SOMETHING the natural development of something such as an organism or a disease over a period of time ○ *the natural history of the leech* **5.** WRITTEN ACCOUNT OF ASPECT OF NATURE a written account of a particular aspect of the natural world

nat·u·ral·ism /náchərə lìzzəm, náchrə-/ *n* **1.** ARTISTIC MOVEMENT ADVOCATING REALISTIC DESCRIPTION in art or literature, a movement or school advocating factual or realistic description of life, including its less pleasant aspects. In literature, it is applied especially to Zola, Maupassant, and other 19th-century French writers. In the visual arts, it refers to the practice of faithfully representing subjects. **2.** BELIEF IN RELIGIOUS TRUTH FROM NATURE a belief that all religious truth is derived from nature and natural causes, and not from revelation **3.** DOCTRINE REJECTING SPIRITUAL EXPLANATIONS OF WORLD a system of thought that rejects all spiritual and supernatural explanations of the world and holds that science is the sole basis of what can be known

nat·u·ral·ist /náchərəlist, náchrə-/ *n* **1.** SOMEBODY STUDYING NATURAL HISTORY a student of or expert in natural history, especially botany or zoology. The term is particularly used to describe a field biologist. **2.** ADVOCATE OF NATURALISM a believer in or adherent of naturalism, especially in the arts ■ *adj* RELATING TO BELIEFS OF NATURALISM relating to or in accordance with the beliefs of naturalism

nat·u·ral·is·tic /nàchərə lístik, nàchrə-/ *adj* **1.** REPRODUCING EFFECTS OF NATURE imitating or reproducing nature or perceived reality in a very exact and faithful way **2.** RELATING TO BELIEFS OF NATURALISM relating to, characteristic of, or in accordance with the tenets of naturalism, especially in art or literature **3.** OF NATURALISTS relating to naturalists or natural history —**nat·u·ral·is·ti·cal·ly** *adv*

nat·u·ral·ize /náchərə lìz, náchrə-/ (**-ized, -iz·ing, -iz·es**) *v* **1.** *vti* GRANT OR ACQUIRE CITIZENSHIP to grant citizenship to somebody of foreign birth, or to acquire citizenship in an adopted country **2.** *vt* INTRODUCE SOMETHING FOREIGN INTO GENERAL USE to introduce something foreign such as a word or custom into general use or into the language of a community **3.** *vti* ACCLIMATIZE PLANT OR ANIMAL to cause a plant or animal from another region to become established in a new environment, or adapt successfully to new environmental conditions **4.** *vt* EXPLAIN SOMETHING IN NATURAL TERMS to explain a phenomenon in terms of natural causes, rather than supernatural causes **5.** *vt* MAKE SOMETHING NATURAL to make something natural or lifelike —**nat·u·ral·i·za·tion** /nàchərəli záysh'n, nàchrə-/ *n* —**nat·u·ral·ized** *adj* —**nat·u·ral·iz·er** *n*

nat·u·ral kill·er cell *n* a white blood cell (**lymphocyte**) that can recognize microbes and tumor cells as "foreign," without requiring prior exposure to them, and destroy them

nat·u·ral lan·guage *n* **1.** a naturally evolved human language, as distinct from a created language such as a computer language **2.** naturally evolved human languages considered collectively

nat·u·ral lan·guage proc·ess·ing *n* the branch of computational linguistics concerned with the use of artificial intelligence to process natural languages, as in machine translation

nat·u·ral law *n* **1.** LAW OF MORALITY a law of morality believed to be derived from human beings' inherent sense of right and wrong, rather than from revelation or the legislation produced by society **2.** LAW OF NATURE a law that governs the behavior of natural phenomena **3.** BELIEF IN UNIVERSAL JUSTICE SYSTEM the belief that general laws of nature can be applied as a system of justice for all societies, regardless of their individual culture or customs

nat·u·ral light *n* light from a natural source, usually the sun, as distinct from artificial light

nat·u·ral log·a·rithm *n* a logarithm with the irrational number *e* as a base

nat·u·ral·ly /náchərəlee, náchrəlee/ *adv* **1.** AS EXPECTED as might be expected ○ *They naturally objected to being treated in this way.* **2.** OF COURSE without any question or doubt ○ *"You'll go then?" "Naturally."* **3.** BY NATURE as a result of a natural feature, talent, or quality that somebody possesses ○ *a naturally gifted player* ○ *Writing seems to come naturally to her.* **4.** IN NORMAL WAY in a normal and unaffected manner ○ *People seldom act naturally when being filmed.* **5.** WITHOUT ARTIFICIAL AID OR TREATMENT occurring as a natural feature or quality without artificial aid **6.** REALISTICALLY in a manner that faithfully represents nature

nat·u·ral med·i·cine *n* MED same as **naturopathy**

nat·u·ral num·ber *n* any whole number greater than zero

nat·u·ral phi·los·o·phy *n* the study of nature and natural phenomena (*archaic*)

nat·u·ral re·source *n* a naturally occurring material, e.g., coal or wood, that can be exploited by people

Nat·u·ral Re·sourc·es Can·a·da *n* the Canadian government department that oversees the use of natural resources and develops policies to regulate and protect the environment and the health and safety of Canadians

nat·u·ral sci·ence *n* any science that deals with phenomena observable in nature, e.g., biology, chemistry, and physics —**nat·u·ral sci·en·tist** *n*

nat·u·ral se·lec·tion *n* the process, according to Darwin, by which organisms best suited to survival in their environment achieve greater reproductive success, thereby passing advantageous genetic characteristics on to future generations

Nat·u·ral State *n* a nickname for Arkansas

nat·u·ral the·ol·o·gy *n* a theology that holds that knowledge of God can be derived by human reason alone, not requiring divine revelation

nat·u·ral vir·tue *n* in theology, one of the four virtues of which people are capable without direct assistance from God, specifically fortitude, justice, prudence, and temperance

nat·u·ral world *n* natural phenomena collectively, as distinct from supernatural or paranormal phenomena or those created by human activity

na·ture /náychər/ *n* **1.** PHYSICAL WORLD the physical world including all natural phenomena and living things **2.** *also* **Na·ture** FORCES CONTROLLING PHYSICAL WORLD the forces and processes collectively that control the phenomena of the physical world independently of human volition or intervention, sometimes personified as a woman called "Mother Nature" **3.** COUNTRYSIDE the countryside or the environment in a condition relatively unaffected by human activity or as the home of living things other than human beings **4.** TYPE a type or sort of thing ○ *a detective* *novel or something of that nature* **5. INTRINSIC QUALITIES OF SOMETHING OR SOMEBODY** the intrinsic or essential qualities of somebody or something ○ *the intricate nature of this kind of work* **6. TEMPERAMENT** disposition or temperament in a person ○ *It's just not part of his nature to act unkindly.* **7. REAL APPEARANCE OR ASPECT** the appearance or aspect of a person, place, or thing that is considered to reflect reality ○ *The portrait was remarkably true to nature.* **8. PRIMITIVE EXISTENCE** a basic state of existence, untouched and uninfluenced by civilization **9. NATURAL STATE OF HUMANKIND** the natural and original condition of humankind, as distinguished from a state of grace **10. UNIVERSAL HUMAN BEHAVIOR** the patterns of behavior or the moral standards that are considered to be universally found and recognized among human beings **11. GENETIC MATERIAL AFFECTING ORGANISM** the inherited characteristics of an organism, as opposed to what is learned from experience or the environment ○ *nature versus nurture* [13C. Via Old French < Latin *natura* "birth, nature" < *nasci* "be born"] ◇ **by nature** as a part of somebody's or something's essential character ○ *optimistic by nature* ◇ **in the nature of something** in the category of something ○ *Have you got anything in the nature of a computer table?*

-natured *suffix* having or showing a particular nature or disposition ○ *good-natured* —**-naturedly** *adv*

na·ture re·serve, na·ture pre·serve *n* a managed and protected area of land usually containing rare or endangered plants or animals

na·ture trail *n* a route through a natural area that is specially designed to draw attention to interesting natural features

na·tur·ism /náychə rìzzəm/ *n* **1.** the practice of going without clothes, usually in a communal setting or in designated areas, in the belief that nudity is a healthy natural state **2.** worship of nature in general, or of objects of nature such as trees and mountains

na·tur·ist /náychərist/ *n* a believer in or adherent of naturism —**na·tur·is·tic** /nàychə rístik/ *adj* —**na·tur·is·ti·cal·ly** *adv*

na·tur·op·a·thy /nàychə róppəthee/ *n* a system of medicine founded on the belief that diet, mental state, exercise, breathing, and other natural factors are central to the origin and treatment of disease —**na·tur·o·path** /náychərə pàth/ *n* —**na·tur·o·path·ic** /nàychərə páthik/ *adj* —**na·tur·o·path·i·cal·ly** *adv*

Nau·ga·hyde /náwgə hìd/ *tdmk* a trademark for an imitation leather fabric

Nau·ga·tuck /náwgə tùk/ **1.** river in southwestern Connecticut. Length: 65 mi./105 km. **2.** town in southwestern Connecticut, in New Haven County, south of Waterbury. Population: 31,429 (2002 estimate).

naught /nawt/ *n* the number zero ■ *pron* same as **nothing** *pron* (sense 1) (*archaic or literary*) ○ *Their efforts were all for naught.* [Old English *nāwiht* < *nā* NO[1] + *wiht* "thing, being" (see WIGHT)]

naugh·ty /náwtee/ (**-ti·er, -ti·est**) *adj* **1. BADLY BEHAVED** badly behaved, especially by being mischievous or disobedient **2. MILDLY INDECENT** mildly indecent or improper (*humorous*) ○ *a naughty smile* **3. SINFUL** mildly sinful (*humorous*) ○ *Would it be naughty of me to have another chocolate?* [14C. Literally "having naught, poor"] —**naugh·ti·ly** *adv* —**naugh·ti·ness** *n*

nau·pli·us /náwplee əss/ (*plural* **-pli·i** /-plee ì/) *n* a free-swimming larva that is produced by many different crustaceans, with an unsegmented body, three pairs of limbs, and a single eye [Mid-19C. Via Latin, kind of shellfish < Greek *nauplios*]

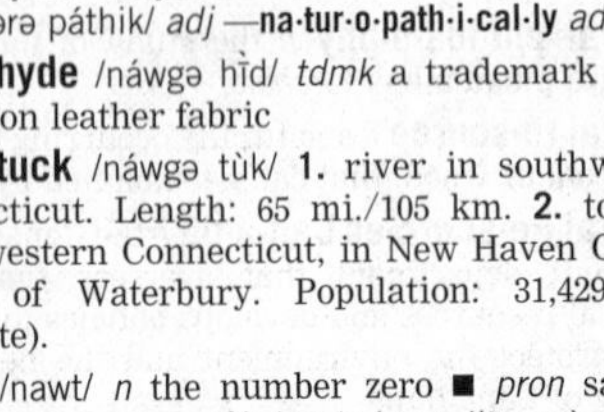

Nauru

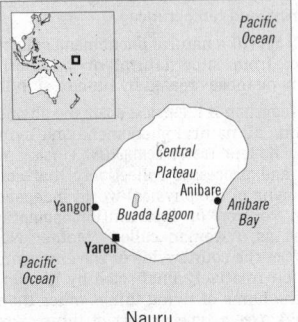

Na·u·ru /naà ŏŏ roo/ island country in the central Pacific Ocean, just south of the Equator. It became an independent member of the British Commonwealth in 1968. Language: English, Nauruan. Currency: Australian dollar. Capital: Yaren. Population: 12,570 (2003). Area: 8.2 sq. mi./21 sq. km. Official name **Republic of Nauru**

Na·u·ru·an /naà ŏŏ roo ən/ *n* **1.** somebody who comes from Nauru **2.** an Austronesian language that is one of the official languages of Nauru —**Na·u·ru·an** *adj*

nau·se·a /náwzee ə, náwshə/ *n* **1.** the unsettling feeling in the stomach that accompanies the urge to vomit **2.** deep disgust (*literary*) [15C. Via Latin < Greek *nausia* < *naus* "ship"]

nau·se·ate /náwzee àyt, náwshee-/ (**-at·ed, -at·ing, -ates**) *vti* **1.** to have the unsettling feeling in the stomach that accompanies the urge to vomit, or make somebody have this feeling **2.** to feel deep disgust, or make somebody feel deep disgust —**nau·se·a·tion** *n*

USAGE ***Nauseated, nauseating,*** or ***nauseous***? If you feel sick, you are ***nauseated***; some careful writers try to maintain the distinction between this and ***nauseous***, even though many people do commonly use ***nauseous*** in the same sense. If you experience something sickening, that thing is ***nauseous*** or ***nauseating***, as in *a nauseous/nauseating odor in the barn.*

nau·se·at·ing /náwzee àyting, náwshee-/ *adj* **1.** producing the unsettling feeling in the stomach that accompanies the urge to vomit **2.** deeply disgusting —**nau·se·at·ing·ly** *adv*

USAGE See ***nauseate.***

nau·seous /náwshəss, náwzee əss/ *adj* **1.** producing the unsettling feeling in the stomach that accompanies the urge to vomit **2.** suffering from the unsettling feeling in the stomach that accompanies the urge to vomit —**nau·seous·ly** *adv* —**nau·seous·ness** *n*

USAGE See ***nauseate.***

naut. *abbr* nautical

nautch /nawch/ *n* in North India, a professional performance of dancing by women, designed for the erotic entertainment of men [Early 19C. Via Hindi *nāc* < Sanskrit *nṛt* "dance"]

nau·ti·cal /náwtik'l/ *adj* relating to sailors, ships, or seafaring [Mid-16C. Via Latin < Greek *nautikos* < *nautēs* "sailor" < *naus* "ship"] —**nau·ti·cal·ly** *adv*

nau·ti·cal mile *n* an international unit of measurement of distance at sea equal to 1.852 km or about 6,076 ft. Symbol **M**

nau·ti·li MARINE BIOL plural of **nautilus**

nau·ti·loid /náwt'l òyd/ *n* a mollusk that belongs to the group that includes the nautiluses and many fossil species. Subclass: Nautiloidea. [Mid-19C. < NAUTILUS]

nau·ti·lus /náwt'ləss/ (*plural* **-lus·es** or **-li** /-lì/) *n* **1.** a mollusk with numerous tentacles, a horny beak, and a spiral shell with gas-filled chambers for buoyancy. Native to: South Pacific and Indian oceans. Genus: *Nautilus.* **2.** MARINE BIOL same as **paper nautilus** [Early 17C. Via Latin < Greek *nautilos* "sailor, nautilus" < *nautēs* (see NAUTICAL)]

NAV *abbr* FIN net asset value

nav. *abbr* **1.** NAUT naval **2.** NAVIG navigable **3.** NAVIG navigation

Nav·a·jo /naávə hò/ (*plural same* or **-jos**), **Nav·a·ho** (*plural same* or **-hos**) *n* **1.** a member of a Native North American people living mainly in northern New Mexico and Arizona **2.** the Athabaskan language of the Navajo people. Native speakers: 225,000. [Late 18C. Via Spanish (*Apaches de*) *Navajó* "(Apaches of) Navajó" < Tewa *navahū* "fields adjoining a ravine"] —**Nav·a·jo** *adj*

na·val /náyv'l/ *adj* relating or belonging to a navy or to warships —**na·val·ly** *adv*

SPELLCHECK naval or **navel**? Do not confuse the spelling of ***naval*** and ***navel***, which sound similar. ***Naval*** is an adjective meaning "of a navy or warships," as in *a naval officer, a naval battle.* ***Navel*** is a noun denoting the hollow on the human stomach where the umbilical cord was attached, or a similar hollow on the fruit that is called a *navel orange.*

na·val ar·chi·tect *n* a designer of ships —**na·val ar·chi·tec·ture** *n*

na·val stores *npl* products used in shipbuilding, especially, formerly, turpentine and pitch

Na·va·ra·tri /nùvvə rúttree/, **Na·va·ra·tra** /-rúttrə/ *n S Asia* a widely celebrated, major Hindu festival lasting nine days. It includes the display of dolls, the worship of female deities such as Saraswati, the goddess of learning, and Durga, the slayer of demons, and the burning of effigies. Date: autumn. [< Sanskrit, "nine nights"]

Na·varre /nə vaár/ autonomous region in northeastern Spain, between the Basque Country and Catalonia. Capital: Pamplona. Population: 555,829 (2001). Area: 4,012 sq. mi./10,391 sq. km.

nave[1] /nayv/ *n* the long central hall of a cross-shaped church, often with pillars on each side, where the congregation sits [Late 17C. Via medieval Latin < Latin *navis* "ship"]

nave[2] /nayv/ *n* the hub of a wheel [Old English *nafu* < Germanic]

na·vel /náyv'l/ *n* a small rounded hollow on the surface of the human stomach, where the end of the umbilical cord was tied after being cut. Technical name **umbilicus** [Old English *nafela* < Indo-European] ◇ **examine** *or* **contemplate your navel** to spend too much time in self-analysis to the exclusion of broader or more productive concerns (*informal*)

SPELLCHECK See ***naval.***

na·vel-gaz·ing *n* concentration on self-analysis and personal concerns in a way that excludes considering broader issues or taking practical action (*informal*)

na·vel or·ange *n* a sweet seedless orange with a small navel-shaped depression or bump at its blossom end enclosing a smaller secondary fruit. Latin name: *Citrus sinensis.*

na·vel·wort /náyv'l wùrt, -wàwrt/ *n* PLANTS same as **pennywort** (sense 1) [15C. < the navel-shaped indentation on its leaves]

na·vic·u·lar /nə víkyələr/ *n* ANAT same as **navicular bone** (sense 1) ■ *adj* **1.** shaped like a boat (*formal*) **2.** relating to a navicular bone [15C. < late Latin *navicularis* < Latin *navicula* "small ship" < *navis* "ship"]

na·vic·u·lar bone *n* **1.** a small boat-shaped bone in the human wrist or ankle **2.** a small bone in a horse's hoof. It is prone to disease (**navicular disease**), causing lameness.

nav·i·ga·ble /návvigəb'l/ *adj* **1. PASSABLE BY SHIP** passable by ship or boat, especially deep enough and wide enough to allow ships or boats to sail through **2. STEERABLE** able to be steered or otherwise controlled **3.** ONLINE **FOLLOWABLE THROUGH LINKS** describes a website that is designed to enable the user to move between or through sections by clicking on usually highlighted computer links —**nav·i·ga·bil·i·ty** /nàvvigə bíllətee/ *n*

nav·i·gate /návvi gàyt/ (**-gat·ed, -gat·ing, -gates**) *v* **1.** *vti* **FIND ROUTE** to find a way through a place, or direct the course of something, especially a ship or aircraft, using a route-finding system ○ *navigating by the stars* **2.** *vt* **PASS THROUGH PLACE** to follow a correct or satisfactory course along a route ○ *Even a champion rafter would have difficulty navigating those rapids.* **3.** *vi* **KEEP CAR ON RIGHT ROUTE** to have responsibility for keeping a car on the right route, e.g., by following a map and giving the driver instructions **4.** *vi* **PROCEED** to make your way over or through something, usually with difficulty ○ *navigated through the crowd* **5.** *vti* **WALK** to go somewhere on foot (*informal*) ○ *navigating with effort after his surgery* **6.** *vti* ONLINE **FOLLOW THROUGH LINKS** to move between the different areas of a website by using the links provided in it [Late 16C. < Latin *navigat-*, past principle of *navigare* "to sail" < *navis* "ship" + *agere* "drive"]

nav·i·ga·tion /nàvvi gáysh'n/ *n* **1. DIRECTING OF VEHICLE'S COURSE** the plotting and directing of the course of a ship, aircraft, or other vehicle **2. MOVEMENT THROUGH PLACE** the act or task of moving through a place or along a route, e.g., along a river or through a range of mountains **3. SCIENCE OF NAVIGATING** the science of plotting and following a course from one place to another and of determining the position of a moving ship, aircraft, or other vehicle —**nav·i·ga·tion·al** *adj* —**nav·i·ga·tion·al·ly** *adv*

nav·i·ga·tion light *n* a light on the outside of a ship or aircraft that alerts others to its position and direction

nav·i·ga·tion sat·el·lite *n* an artificial satellite, used as an aid to navigation, that follows a fixed orbit made known to navigators on ships and aircraft

nav·i·ga·tor /návvi gàytər/ *n* **1.** somebody who navigates something, especially a ship or aircraft **2.** a passenger of a car who gives a driver information about a route

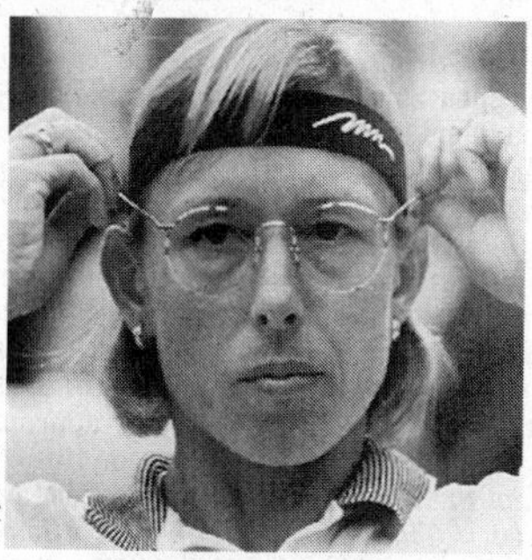

Popperfoto

Martina Navratilova

Nav·ra·ti·lo·va /nàvrəti lṓvə/, **Martina** (*b.* 1956) Czech-born US tennis player. She set the women's record of 167 singles championships (1974–94), including nine Wimbledon titles.

> "The moment of victory is much too short to live for that and nothing else."
> [Martina Navratilova, *Guardian (London)*; June 21, 1989]

NAVSAT /náv sàt/ *abbr* NAVIG navigation satellite

nav·vy /návvee/ (*plural* **-vies**) *n* *UK* an unskilled laborer, especially somebody who does the heavy digging work involved in the building of roads, railroads, and canals (*dated*) [Early 19C. Shortening of NAVIGATOR in the archaic sense "canal laborer"]

na·vy /náyvee/ (*plural* **-vies**) *n* **1.** the branch of a country's armed forces that crews, maintains, and fights on warships **2.** a fleet of ships, especially one belonging to a country **3.** COLORS same as **navy blue** [14C. < Old French *navie* "fleet" < Latin *navis* "ship"] —**na·vy** *adj*

na·vy bean *n* a small white variety of kidney bean [< its former use as a food staple in the US Navy]

na·vy blue *n* a dark blue color [< the color of the British naval uniform] —**na·vy-blue** *adj*

Na·vy Cross *n* a decoration awarded by the US Navy for outstanding heroism in armed combat

na·vy yard *n* *US* a navy-owned shipyard where warships are built and repaired

na·wab /nə wób/ *n* in India during the Mughal empire, a title for a local nobleman [Mid-18C. Via Urdu *nawāb* < Arabic *nā'ib* "deputy"]

nay /nay/ *n* **NO VOTE** a vote of no, or somebody who votes no ■ *adv* **INTRODUCING CORRECTION** used to introduce a phrase that corrects something just said, often a phrase that states the truth in stronger terms (*archaic or literary*) ○ *It was a disappointing, nay, humiliating, outcome.* ■ *interj* **NO** used to refuse, deny, or disagree with something (*archaic*) [12C. < Old Norse *nei* < *ne* "not" + *ei* "ever"]

nay·say /náy sày/ (**-say·ing, -says**) *vt* to refuse, oppose, or criticize something

nay·say·er /náy sày ər/ *n* somebody who speaks against something, especially somebody who habitually expresses contrary opinions

Naz·a·rene /nàzzə réen, názzə rèen/ *n* **1. SOMEBODY FROM NAZARETH** somebody who comes from Nazareth **2. MEMBER OF PROTESTANT CHURCH** a member of the Church of the Nazarene, a modern Protestant denomination **3. JESUS CHRIST** Jesus Christ, as connected with Nazareth (*literary*) [13C. Via late Latin < Greek *Nazarēnos* < *Nazaret* "Nazareth"] —**Naz·a·rene** *adj*

Naz·a·reth /názzərəth/ city in northern Israel. It is believed to be where Jesus Christ lived during his childhood. Population: 57,200 (1999).

Naz·a·rite /názzə rīt/, **Naz·i·rite** *n* a member of a Jewish religious group in biblical times whose members made various vows of abstinence, including a vow not to drink wine or cut their hair [Mid-16C. < late Latin *Nazaraeus* < Greek *Nazōraios* < *Nazaret* "Nazareth"]

Naz·ca Lines /názkə-/ *n* a group of long straight lines representing birds, fish, animals, or geometric figures carved into the desert near Nazca, southern Peru, believed to have been made around 200 B.C. and only visible from the air [After a place in S Peru]

Na·zi /naátsee, nát-/ (*plural* **-zis**) *n* **1. FOLLOWER OF HITLER** a member of the fascist German National Socialist Party that came to power under the leadership of Adolf Hitler in 1933 (*often used before a noun*) **2. RACIST** somebody regarded as having right-wing political views, especially on race and immigration (*insult*) **3.** *also* **na·zi BOSSY PERSON** an authoritarian or dictatorial person (*insult; sometimes offensive*) [Mid-20C. < German, shortening of *Nationalsozialist* "national socialist" or *Nationalsozialismus* "national socialism"]

Naz·i·rite *n* RELIG another spelling of **Nazarite**

Na·zism /naát sìzzəm, nát-/ *n* the philosophy of the German National Socialist Party under the leadership of Adolf Hitler

Nb *symbol* CHEM ELEM niobium

NB, N.B. *abbr* New Brunswick

N.B., NB, n.b., nb *interj* used to draw somebody's attention to something particularly important, usually an addition to or qualification of a previous statement. Full form **nota bene**

NBA, N.B.A. *abbr* **1.** BASKETBALL National Basketball Association **2.** BOXING National Boxing Association

NBC *abbr* **1.** National Broadcasting Company **2.** MIL nuclear, biological, and chemical (*refers to weapons or warfare*)

NbE *abbr* COMPASS north by east

NbW *abbr* COMPASS north by west

nc *abbr* ONLINE New Caledonia (*used in Internet addresses*) See table at **domain name**

NC *abbr* **1.** no charge **2.** noncallable **3.** *also* **N.C.** North Carolina

n/c *abbr* no charge

NC-17 /èn see sèvv'n téen/ *n* *US* a movie rating indicating that a movie cannot be seen by children under the age of 17 because of its adult content

NCAA, N.C.A.A. *abbr* *US* National Collegiate Athletic Association

NCO, N.C.O. *abbr* MIL noncommissioned officer

N'COBRA *abbr* National Coalition of Blacks for Reparations in America

NCTE *abbr* *US* National Council of Teachers of English

NCTM *abbr* *US* National Council of Teachers of Mathematics

Nd *symbol* CHEM ELEM neodymium

ND, N.D. *abbr* **1.** no date **2.** North Dakota

N. Dak. *abbr* North Dakota

NDE *abbr* near-death experience

NDEA *abbr* *US* National Defense Education Act

Nde·be·le /əndə beélee/ (*plural same* or **-les**) *n* **1.** a member of an African people who originated in northeastern South Africa, but now live mainly in southern Zimbabwe **2.** the Bantu language of the Ndebele people, which has distinct forms in Zimbabwe and South Africa. Native speakers: 1 million. [Late 19C. < Nguni] —**Nde·be·le** *adj*

N'Dja·me·na /ən jaáməna/ capital of Chad, in the southwestern part of the country. Population: 530,965 (1993).

n·dole /ən dṓlee/ *n* *W Africa* in African cuisine, a plant that must be scraped to remove bitter juice before being sliced, parboiled, and then cooked in stews and soup

NDT *abbr* Newfoundland Daylight Time

ne *abbr* Niger (*used in Internet addresses*) See table at **domain name**

né /nay/ *adj* **1.** used to introduce a man's former or original name **2.** *US* used to introduce the name that something was formerly known under ○ *Zimbabwe, né Rhodesia* [Mid-20C. < French (see NÉE)]

Ne *symbol* CHEM ELEM neon

NE *abbr* **1.** Nebraska **2.** *also* **N.E.** New England **3.** COMPASS northeast **4.** COMPASS northeastern

Ne. *abbr* BIBLE Nehemiah

NEA *abbr* **1.** EDUC National Education Association **2.** ARTS National Endowment for the Arts

Neagh, Lough /nay/ inland lake in central Northern Ireland, the largest lake in the British Isles. Area: 153 sq. mi./396 sq. km.

Ne·an·der·tal /nee ándər taal/, **Ne·an·der·thal** /-thaal/ *adj* **1. OF NEANDERTAL MAN** relating to Neandertal man **2.** *also* **ne·an·der·tal** *or* **ne·an·der·thal OFFENSIVE TERM** an offensive term meaning displaying a lack of intellect, lack of sensitivity, and boorishness (*insult*) **3.** *also* **ne·an·der·tal** *or* **ne·an·der·thal OFFENSIVE TERM** an offensive term meaning very old-fashioned or conservative (*insult*) ■ *n* *also* **ne·an·der·tal** *or* **ne·an·der·thal OFFENSIVE TERM** an offensive term that deliberately insults somebody's intelligence, manners, or sensitivity, or somebody's ability to adopt modern ideas (*insult*) [Mid-19C. After a valley in W Germany]

Ne·an·der·tal man *n* an extinct subspecies of human beings that populated Europe, North Africa, and western Asia in the early Stone Age

Ne·an·der·thal *adj, n* another spelling of **Neandertal**

neap /neep/ *n* GEOG same as **neap tide** ■ *adj* relating to or associated with a neap tide [15C. < Old English *nēp-*, origin ?]

Ne·a·pol·i·tan /neè ə póllət'n/ *adj* relating to the Italian city of Naples ■ *n* somebody who comes from Naples [15C. < Latin *Neapolitanus* < Greek *Neapolis*, literally "new town"]

Ne·a·pol·i·tan ice cream *n* ice cream made in differently colored and flavored layers

neap tide *n* a tide that shows the least range between high and low and occurs twice a month between the first and third quarters of the moon

near /neer/ (**neared, near·ing, nears, near·er, near·est**) CORE MEANING: a grammatical word that indicates that somebody or something is at or moving toward a point that is not far away in distance ○ (prep) *The art exhibit is near here.* ○ (adv) *He took a step nearer to the water.* ○ (adv) *as the car drew nearer* ○ (adj) *There must be a restaurant nearer than that.* ○ (adj) *Can you tell me where the nearest telephone is?*
1. *adv, prep, adj* **SHORT TIME AWAY** at or to a time not far away ○ (adv) *as the time for her to leave drew near* ○ (prep) *near the end of the week* ○ (adj) *the near future* **2.** *adv, adj* **CLOSE** at a point that is not far away in state, resemblance, or number ○ (adv) *a sensation near to fear* ○ (adj) *the nearest thing to a champion* **3.** *adv, adj* **ALMOST** almost in a particular state or situation ○ (adv) *near total failure* ○ (adj) *living in near poverty* **4.** *adj, n* **ON LEFT** on the left side, especially of an animal or a horse-drawn vehicle ○ *the near foreleg* **5.** *adj* **CLOSELY RELATED** closely related to somebody **6.** *adj* **MISERLY** reluctant to give or spend money (*archaic*) **7.** *v vti* **APPROACH** to approach, or approach a particular place, time, or state ○ *The project is nearing completion.* ○ *With the big event nearing, everyone was working hard.* [12C. < Old Norse *nǽr* "nearer" < *nā* "near"] —**near·ness** *n* ◇ **so near (and) yet so far** used to express frustration or regret at failure by a narrow margin

NEAR /neer/ *n* a binary operator used in searches of computer text that returns true if its operands (usually two words) occur within a specific proximity to each other, and false otherwise

near a·bout *adv regional* almost or nearly ○ *He's near about 90.*

near beer *n* *US* a malt-based drink that contains a very low amount of alcohol, specifically below 0.5%

near·by /neer bī/ *adj, adv* in, at, or to a place a short distance away ○ *a nearby grocer* ○ *His mother was waiting nearby.* ○ *The children's school is quite nearby.* ■ *adj* closest in time, especially to a stock-exchange transaction

Ne·arc·tic /nee aárktik/ *adj* relating to or located in the region of plant and animal life in the Arctic and temperate areas of Greenland and North America [Mid-19C. < NEO-]

near-death ex·pe·ri·ence *n* a sensation that people

on the brink of death have described as leaving their own bodies and observing them as though they were bystanders

near-earth ob·ject *n* an asteroid or comet that can approach, or is on course to approach, within 28 million miles of the Earth's orbit

Near East *n* same as **Middle East** (sense 1) —**Near East·ern·er** *n* —**Near East·ern** *adj*

near gale *n* METEOROL same as **moderate gale**

near let·ter qual·i·ty *adj* describes the printing quality of a computer printer that produces printed characters as clear as a typewriter's

near·ly /néerlee/ *adv* **1.** almost but not quite the case ○ *We waited for nearly an hour.* **2.** closely, in time, proximity, or relationship ○*"Brennan described to the police the man he saw in the window and then identified Oswald as the person who most nearly resembled the man he saw."* (Earl Warren et al, *The Report of the Warren Commission*; 1964) ◇ **not nearly** used to emphasize that something stated, implied, or assumed is very far from being the case ○ *not nearly enough time to answer all the questions*

near miss *n* **1. NEAR COLLISION** a situation in which two vehicles or airplanes narrowly avoid colliding with each other **2. SHOT NEAR TARGET** a shot or strike that comes very close to a target but does not quite hit it **3. BARELY AVERTED DISASTER** something, especially something undesirable, that is narrowly avoided or averted (*informal*)

near point *n* the point nearest the eye at which an object remains in focus

near·sight·ed /néer sītəd/ *adj* unable to see clearly objects that are far away —**near·sight·ed·ly** *adv* —**near·sight·ed·ness** *n*

neat[1] /neet/ *adj* **1. ORDERLY IN APPEARANCE** orderly and in a clean condition **2. ORDERLY BY NATURE** tending to keep things in an orderly and clean condition ○ *My husband's very neat in the kitchen.* **3. ELEGANT** simple, effective, and elegant ○ *a neat solution to a complex problem* **4. SKILLFULLY PERFORMED** performed with skill, ingenuity, and apparent ease ○ *a neat pirouette* **5. COMPACT** appealingly regular or compact ○ *a neat little package* **6. UNDILUTED** describes drinks that are not diluted with water, ice cubes, or a mixer **7. EXCELLENT** used as a general term of approval (*informal*) ○ *Her parents are really neat.* **8.** *US* FIN another spelling of **net**[2] *adj* (sense 1) [Mid-16C. Via French *net* < Latin *nitidus* "shiny" < *nitere* "to shine"] —**neat·ly** *adv* —**neat·ness** *n*

neat[2] /neet/ (*plural* **neats** *or same*) *n* an animal in the cattle family, e.g., a cow or ox (*archaic*) [Old English *nēat* < Germanic, "to use"]

neat·en /néet'n/ (**-ened, -en·ing, -ens**) *vt* to make something neat or orderly

neath /neeth/, **'neath** *prep* same as **beneath** (*literary*) [Late 18C. Shortening]

neat·nik /néet nik/ *n* somebody who is extremely neat and orderly (*informal*)

neat's-foot oil *n* a pale yellow oil. Source: feet and shinbones of cattle. Use: treatment of leather. [< NEAT[2]]

neb /neb/ *n N England* an animal's bill, beak, nose, or snout (*informal*) [Old English *nebb* < Germanic]

NEB *abbr* CHR New English Bible

Neb. *abbr* Nebraska

Neb·bi·o·lo /nèbbee ṓlō/ *n* a typically full-bodied red wine made from a variety of black grape grown mainly in northwestern Italy [Mid-19C. < Italian < *nebbia* "mist"; because the grapes ripen in autumn]

neb·bish /nébbish/ *n* an offensive term that deliberately insults somebody's courage, personality, and initiative (*insult*) [Late 19C. < Yiddish *nebekh* "poor thing" < assumed Slavic *ne-bogŭ* "poor"]

NEbE *abbr* COMPASS northeast by east

NEbN *abbr* COMPASS northeast by north

Nebr. *abbr* Nebraska

Nebraska

Ne·bras·ka /nə bráskə/ state in the central United States, bordered by South Dakota, Iowa, Missouri, Kansas, Colorado, and Wyoming. Capital: Lincoln. Population: 1,729,180 (2002 estimate). Area: 77,358 sq. mi./200,356 sq. km. —**Ne·bras·kan** *n, adj*

Neb·u·chad·nez·zar II /nèbbəkəd nézzər, nèbbyəkəd-/ (*fl* 6th century B.C.) Babylonian king. He conquered and destroyed Jerusalem in 586 B.C., consigning its inhabitants to captivity. He is thought to have created the Hanging Gardens of Babylon.

nebula: photographed by the Hubble Space telescope (1995)

neb·u·la /nébbyələ/ (*plural* **-lae** /-lee/ *or* **-las**) *n* a region or cloud of interstellar dust and gas appearing variously as a hazy bright or dark patch [Mid-17C. < Latin, "mist, vapor"] —**neb·u·lar** *adj*

neb·u·lar hy·poth·e·sis *n* a formerly held theory that the solar system evolved as a hot rotating flattened gaseous nebula. The theory states that as the nebula cooled, the Sun condensed at the center and planets and their moons formed from contracting concentric rings at the rim.

neb·u·lize /nébbyə līz/ (**-lized, -liz·ing, -liz·es**) *vt* to reduce a liquid to a fine spray for medical use [Late 19C. < NEBULA]

neb·u·liz·er /nébbyə līzər/ *n* a device, with a face mask attached, for administering a medicinal liquid in the form of a fine spray that is breathed in through the mouth or nose

neb·u·los·i·ty /nèbbyə lóssətee/ (*plural* **-ties**) *n* ASTRON same as **nebula**

neb·u·lous /nébbyələss/ *adj* **1.** not clear, distinct, or definite **2.** relating to or resembling a nebula —**neb·u·lous·ly** *adv* —**neb·u·lous·ness** *n*

~~**neccesary**~~ incorrect spelling of **necessary**

nec·es·sar·i·ly /nèssə sérrəlee/ *adv* **1.** inevitably, or in every case ○ *This route isn't necessarily the best one.* **2.** following as an unavoidable result or consequence ○ *Voting was a necessarily slow and complex process.*

nec·es·sar·y /néssə sèrree/ *adj* **1. REQUIRED** important in order to achieve a specific result, or desired by authority or convention ○ *Is it really necessary to contact the police?* **2. FOLLOWING INEVITABLY** inevitable given what has happened previously ○ *No doubt they will draw the necessary conclusion.* **3.** LOGIC **LOGICALLY TRUE** logically true because of being impossible to be false ■ *n* (*plural* **nec·es·sar·ies**) **SOMETHING ESSENTIAL** an essential item (*informal*) ○ *I've packed the necessaries.* [14C. Via Anglo-Norman < Latin *necessarius* < *necesse* "unyielding" < *cess-* (see CESSION)]

SYNONYMS ***necessary, essential, vital, indispensable, requisite, required, needed***

CORE MEANING: important to have

necessary important in order to achieve a specific result, or desired by authority or convention ○ *Our son says he'll get a bank loan to buy the car if necessary.* ○ *Repairs are necessary in order to ensure everyone's health and safety.* **essential** of the highest importance for achieving something ○ *Besides ability, the other essential element in political success is sheer luck.* ○ *It is essential that a social worker review the home environment before the patient's discharge.* **vital** extremely important and necessary, or indispensable to the survival or continuing effectiveness of something ○ *The president's support for the negotiations was vital to their success.* ○ *The neighborhood watch has a vital role to play in reducing crime.* **indispensable** extremely desirable or useful, or not to be done without ○ *Although not a popular leader, he created the belief that he was indispensable to political stability.* ○ *Online sources have become almost indispensable to history teachers.* **requisite** (*formal*) necessary for a specific purpose ○ *The resolution fell only four votes short of achieving the requisite two-thirds majority.* ○ *We ended up rejecting the majority of applicants because they didn't have the requisite skills.* **required** necessary or appropriate, or insisted upon or imposed as a condition ○ *They haven't got the required documents.* **needed** necessary or desired ○ *This generous donation allowed us to purchase some much-needed items.*

nec·es·sar·y con·di·tion *n* something that must happen or exist in order for something else to happen or exist

nec·es·sar·y e·vil *n* something that is unpleasant or undesirable but is needed to achieve a result

ne·ces·si·tar·i·an /nə sèssi térree ən/ *n* somebody who believes that all events are determined by previous causes —**ne·ces·si·tar·i·an·ism** *n*

ne·ces·si·tate /nə séssi tàyt/ (**-tat·ed, -tat·ing, -tates**) *vti* **1.** to make something necessary or inescapable ○ *a dry climate that necessitates water conservation* **2.** to force or oblige somebody to do something (*formal*) —**ne·ces·si·ta·tion** /nə sèssi táysh'n/ *n*

ne·ces·si·tous /nə séssitəss/ *adj* **1.** pressingly necessary **2.** in a state of poverty (*literary*) ○*"grew necessitous, pawn'd his cloaths, and wanted bread"* (Benjamin Franklin, *The Autobiography of Benjamin Franklin*; 1788)

ne·ces·si·ty /nə séssətee/ (*plural* **-ties**) *n* **1. SOMETHING ESSENTIAL** something that is essential, especially a basic requirement ○ *food, shelter, and the other necessities* **2. COMPELLING CIRCUMSTANCES** circumstances that create a need or an obligation ○ *issuing replacements as necessity dictates* **3. NEED** the condition of being needed or required ○ *We'll hire new staff when the necessity arises.* **4.** PHILOSOPHY **NECESSARY QUALITY** the quality of being necessary or of not being able to be otherwise [14C. Via French < Latin *necessitas* < *necesse* (see NECESSARY)]

neck /nek/ *n* **1. PART BETWEEN HEAD AND BODY** the part of the body that joins the head to the rest of the body **2. GARMENT PART AROUND NECK** the part of a garment that goes around or lies below the wearer's neck **3. CUT OF MEAT** a cut of meat from the neck of an animal **4. LONG OPENING** a long narrow opening ○ *the neck of a bottle* **5. STRIP OF LAND OR WATER** a long narrow strip of land or stretch of water **6. LONG NARROW FINGERBOARD** the long narrow fingerboard that projects out of the body or soundbox of a handheld string instrument such as a guitar or violin **7. WINNING MARGIN** in horseracing, a narrow winning margin equal to the distance between a horse's nose and its shoulder ○ *won the race by a neck* **8. SOMETHING IMPORTANT RISKED OR SAVED** somebody's life, job, reputation, or other important asset that has been placed at risk or saved from danger (*informal*) ○ *telling a lie to save her neck* **9.** MARINE BIOL same as **siphon** *n* (sense 3) ■ *v* (**necked, neck·ing, necks**) (*informal*) **1.** *vi* **KISS AND CUDDLE** to kiss and embrace sexually, usually sitting or lying with clothes on ○ *teenagers necking in the car* **2.** *vt* COOK **KILL POULTRY** to kill a bird to be cooked by breaking its neck or chopping its head off [Old English *hnecca* "nape" < Indo-European, "high point, ridge"] —**necked** *adj* ◇ **be breathing down somebody's neck 1.** to be close behind somebody **2.** to be putting pressure on somebody to do something more quickly ◇ **be in something up to your neck** to be very much involved in something, often something dishonest or illegal ◇ **break your neck** to try very hard to achieve something (*informal*) ◇ **get it in the neck** to be punished or scolded severely (*informal*) ◇ **neck and neck** level in a competition and with an equal chance of winning (*informal*) ◇ **neck of the woods** a particular area or part of the country (*informal*) ◇ **stick your neck out** to take a risk by saying or doing something that could bring blame or censure (*informal*)

neck·band /nék bànd/ *n* the part of a garment that fits or wraps around the neck

neck·cloth /nék klàwth/ *n UK* a cravat or scarf worn around the neck rather than around the collar, especially one worn by men between the 17th and mid-19th centuries

neck·down *n* an outward extension of the curbs at an intersection, narrowing the width of roadway and intended to slow traffic

neck·er·chief /nékər chif, -cheef/ (*plural* **-chiefs** or **-chieves** /-chìvz, -cheevz/) *n* a square of cloth worn tied around the neck as a scarf [14C. < NECK + KERCHIEF]

neck·ing /néking/ *n* kissing and embracing sexually while sitting or lying with clothes on (*informal*)

neck·lace /nékləss/ *n* a decorative chain or string of jewels worn around the neck

neck·line /nék lìn/ *n* the line formed by the edge of a garment at or under the neck, especially at the front

neck ring *n* a rigid necklace or ornamental band that fits snugly around the neck

neck·tie /nék tì/ *n* **1.** a shaped strip of cloth tied around the collar of a man's shirt, with the ends hanging down the front. Same as **tie** *n* (sense 1) **2.** a noose for hanging somebody (*slang*)

neck·wear /nék wér/ *n* garments or fashion accessories worn around the neck, e.g., ties, cravats, and scarves

necr- *prefix* same as **necro-** (*used before vowels*)

necro- *prefix* death, the dead, dead body ○ *necrophobia* [< Greek *nekros* "corpse" < Indo-European]

nec·ro·bi·o·sis /nèkrō bī óssiss/ *n* the degeneration and death of the body's cells from natural processes —**nec·ro·bi·ot·ic** /-óttik/ *adj*

ne·crol·o·gy /ne królləjee/ (*plural* **-gies**) *n* (*formal*) **1.** a list of people who have died recently or during a specific period **2.** an announcement of somebody's death [Early 18C. < medieval Latin *necrologium* < Greek *nekros* "corpse"] —**nec·ro·log·i·cal** /nèkrə lójjik'l/ *adj* —**ne·crol·o·gist** *n*

nec·ro·man·cy /nékrə mànssee/ *n* **1.** the practice of attempting to communicate with the spirits of the dead in order to predict or influence the future **2.** witchcraft or sorcery in general (*literary*) [13C. Alteration of *nigromancy*, via French < medieval Latin *nigromantia* < late Latin *necromantia* (influenced by Latin *niger* "black") < Greek *nekromanteia* < *nekros* "corpse" + *manteia* "divination"] —**nec·ro·man·cer** *n* —**nec·ro·man·tic** /nèkrə mántik/ *adj*

ne·croph·a·gous /ne króffəgəss/ *adj* describes organisms that feed on the flesh of dead animals (**carrion**)

nec·ro·phil·i·a /nèkrə fíllee ə/ *n* sexual feelings for or sexual acts with dead bodies —**nec·ro·phil·i·ac** *n* —**nec·ro·phil·ic** *adj*

nec·ro·pho·bi·a /nèkrə fṓbee ə/ *n* an irrational fear of death or of dead bodies —**nec·ro·pho·bic** *adj*

ne·crop·o·lis /ne króppəliss/ (*plural* **-lis·es** or **-leis** /-làyss/) *n* a cemetery, especially a large, elaborate, or ancient one [Early 19C. < Greek < *nekros* "corpse" + *polis* "city"]

nec·rop·sy /né kròpsee/ (*plural* **-sies**) *n* MED same as **autopsy** *n* (sense 1) [Mid-19C. < NECRO- + AUTOPSY]

ne·cro·sis /ne krṓssiss/ *n* the death of cells in a tissue or organ caused by disease or injury [Mid-17C. Via modern Latin < Greek *nekrōsis* "deadness" < *nekros* "corpse"] —**ne·crot·ic** /-króttik/ *adj*

nec·ro·tiz·ing /nékrə tìzing/ *adj* causing or undergoing the death of cells (**necrosis**) ○ *necrotizing bacteria* [Late 19C. < *necrotize* "become affected with necrosis" < *necrotic* "of necrosis" < Greek *nekroun* "to kill"]

nec·ro·tiz·ing fas·ci·it·is *n* a severe bacterial infection that causes cell tissue to decay rapidly

nec·tar /néktər/ *n* **1.** PLANT LIQUID the sweet liquid that flowering plants produce as a way of attracting the insects and small birds that assist in pollination **2.** *US* PULPY JUICE a thick drink made from puréed fruit ○ *mango nectar* **3.** DRINK OF GODS in Greek and Roman mythology, the drink of the gods that sustained their beauty and immortality **4.** ENJOYABLE DRINK an enjoyable or much appreciated drink (*informal*) [Mid-16C. Via Latin < Greek *nektar* "drink of the gods"]

nec·tar·ine /nèktə reén/ *n* **1.** a fruit similar to a peach with a smooth skin **2.** a tree that produces nectarines. Latin name: *Prunus persica.*

nec·ta·ry /néktəree/ (*plural* **-ries**) *n* the nectar-producing organ of a flowering plant

née /nay/, **nee** *adj* **1.** used to introduce a married woman's maiden name ○ *née Leppo* **2.** used to introduce the name that something was formerly known under [Mid-18C. < French form of *né*, past participle of *naître* "be born" < Latin *nasci*]

need /need/ *v* (**need·ed, need·ing, needs**) *vti* REQUIRE SOMETHING require something in order to have success or achieve a goal ○ *Do you need any money?* ○ *He told me that I didn't need to know.* ○ *This shirt needs ironing.* ■ *modal v* BE NECESSARY used to indicate that a course of action is desirable or necessary (*used in negative statements*) ○ *You don't need to thank me; I'm happy to help whenever I can.* ○ *Going to med school need not mean you can't study architecture later.* ■ *v* **1.** *vti* DESERVE SOMETHING to deserve something, especially as punishment (*informal*) ○ *That little boy needs to be given a good talking to.* ○ *Those troops need to be shown who's boss.* **2.** *vi* TO BE ESSENTIAL to be essential or necessary to something (*archaic*) ○ *"I think that we are all agreed in this matter, and therefore there needs no more words about it."* (John Bunyan, *Pilgrim's Progress*; 1678) ■ *n* REQUIREMENT something that is a requirement or is wanted ○ *an economic system that recognizes the need for financial security* ○ *His needs are few.* [Old English *nē(o)d* < Indo-European] ◇ **in need 1.** not having enough of things essential for an adequate standard of living ○ *children in need* **2.** needing something ◇ **no need to** *or* **for something** no reason or justification for something

USAGE See ***knead.***

SYNONYMS See ***necessary.***

need·ed /néed id/ *adj* necessary or desired (*usually in combination*) ○ *a much-needed rest*

SYNONYMS See ***necessary.***

need·ful /néedfəl/ *adj* necessary or required —**need·ful·ly** *adv* —**need·ful·ness** *n*

Need·ham /néedəm/ town in eastern Massachusetts. Population: 29,197 (2002 estimate).

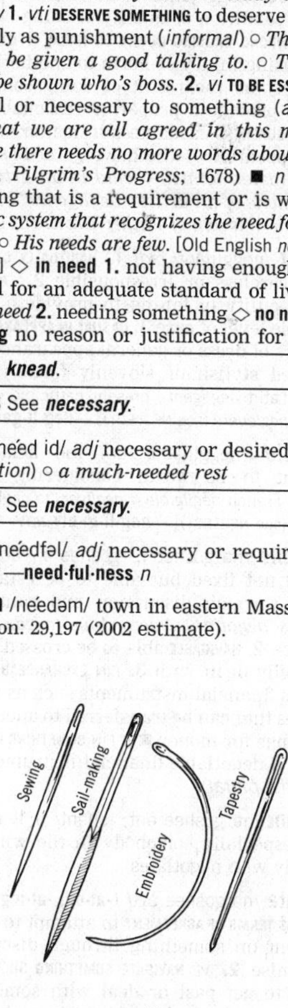

needle

nee·dle /néed'l/ *n* **1.** SEWING TOOL a small sharp metal pin used for sewing, with a hole at the blunt end for holding thread **2.** KNITTING TOOL a rod with a dull point used in knitting **3.** POINTER a pointed indicator on a dial, scale, or scientific instrument such as a compass or a car's speedometer **4.** SYRINGE a hypodermic syringe, or the hollow pointed end of one **5.** ACUPUNCTURE TOOL a small sharp metal pin used in acupuncture to stimulate points on the body **6.** STYLUS the stylus on a record player **7.** CONIFER LEAF a small pointed leaf of a conifer tree ○ *pine needles* **8.** POINTED PART a long thin pointed part of an animal's body, e.g., a porcupine quill or a sea urchin spine **9.** CRYSTALS POINTED CRYSTAL a long thin pointed crystal **10.** ARCHIT OBELISK a tall stone pillar **11.** HANDICRAFT ENGRAVING TOOL a sharp tool used in engraving **12.** PROVOCATION a remark or action intended to tease or provoke somebody (*informal*) ■ *vt* (**-dled, -dling, -dles**) **1.** PROVOKE to tease or provoke somebody, especially repeatedly in an indirect way (*informal*) **2.** HANDICRAFT USE NEEDLE ON SOMETHING to sew, prick, or pierce something with a needle [Old English *nǣdl* < Indo-European, "sew"] —**nee·dler** *n*

nee·dle·craft /néed'l kràft/ *n* sewing as a skill or craft

nee·dle ex·change *n* a public health program that allows drug addicts to exchange used hypodermic needles for new ones in an effort to stop the spread of disease and infection

nee·dle·fish /néed'l fish/ *n* a carnivorous ocean fish with a very long slender body and long jaws with sharp teeth. Native to: tropical and subtropical waters. Family: Belonidae.

nee·dle grass *n* PLANTS same as **feather grass**

nee·dle·point /néed'l pòynt/ *n* **1.** embroidery done with thick colored threads on canvas or plain cloth, usually in uniform diagonal stitches **2.** lace made with a needle worked on a paper pattern (*often used before a noun*)

need·less /néedləss/ *adj* without reason or justification —**need·less·ly** *adv* —**need·less·ness** *n*

nee·dle valve *n* a valve in which the flow of a fluid or gas is precisely controlled by a needle-shaped insert in a conical seat

nee·dle·wom·an /néed'l wŏŏmmən/ (*plural* **-wom·en** /-wìmmin/) *n* HANDICRAFT same as **seamstress**

nee·dle·work /néed'l wùrk/ *n* **1.** a craft that involves the use of a needle, e.g., sewing, needlepoint, embroidery, quilting, crochet, or knitting **2.** an example of needlework —**nee·dle·work·er** *n*

need·n't /néed'nt/ *contr* need not (*informal*)

needs /needz/ *adv* used before or after "must" to reinforce necessity, urgency, or inevitability (*archaic*) ○ *"any abstract ideas that are once true must needs be eternal"* (John Locke, *An Essay Concerning Human Understanding*; 1690)

need-to-know *adj* FOR AUTHORIZED RECIPIENTS ONLY intended for or relating to people and agencies deemed as secure recipients of classified information, so that they can use the information in fulfilling a mission ■ *n* **1.** AUTHORIZED PERSON a person regarded as a secure recipient of classified information essential in the fulfillment of a mission **2.** IMPORTANT FACT an essential fact about something ○ *a list of college need-to-knows*

need·y /néedee/ (**-i·er, -i·est**) *adj* **1.** living in poverty ○ *gifts for needy children* **2.** feeling or showing a strong need for affection, love, or other emotional support —**need·i·ly** *adv* —**need·i·ness** *n*

neem /neem/ *n* a tall evergreen tree grown for its bark, resin, and seed oil, which have medicinal and insecticidal properties. Native to: South Asia. Latin name: *Azadirachta indica.* [Early 19C. Via Hindi *nīm* < Sanskrit *nimba*]

ne'er /ner/ *adv* same as **never** (*archaic or literary*) [13C. Contraction]

ne'er-do-well *n* a lazy and irresponsible person ■ *adj* lazy and irresponsible

ne·far·i·ous /nə férree əss/ *adj* utterly immoral or wicked [Early 17C. < Latin *nefarius* < *nefas* "sin" < *ne* "not" + *fas* "divine law"] —**ne·far·i·ous·ly** *adv*

Nef·er·ti·ti /nèffər téetee/, **queen of ancient Egypt** (*fl* 14th century B.C.) As the chief wife of King Akhenaton, she supported his religious and cultural reforms. Her carved and painted image is a famous surviving Egyptian artwork.

neg. *abbr* negative

ne·gate /nə gáyt/ (**-gat·ed, -gat·ing, -gates**) *vt* **1.** to declare officially that something is invalid or ineffective, or make something invalid or ineffective (*formal*) ○ *Failure to disclose such a change of circumstances would automatically negate the policy.* ○ *a theory that negates all previous research* **2.** LOGIC to deny the truth of something, or prove something to be false [Early 17C. < Latin *negat-*, past participle of *negare* "deny"] —**ne·ga·tor** *n*

SYNONYMS See *nullify.*

ne·ga·tion /nə gáysh'n/ *n* **1.** DENIAL OR ANNULMENT the denying, disproving, or nullifying of something **2.** NEGATIVE OF SOMETHING the opposite of something regarded as positive, or the absence of such a thing ○ *The existence of happiness implies its negation.* **3.** LOGIC LOGICAL DENIAL a statement of denial or contradiction, especially an assertion that a particular proposition is false

neg·a·tive /néggətiv/ *adj* **1.** INDICATIVE OF "NO" indicating "no," or refusing or denying something ○ *a negative response* **2.** BAD unhappy, discouraging, angry, or otherwise detracting from a happy situation ○ *negative feelings* **3.** PESSIMISTIC pessimistic, or tending to have a pessimistic outlook ○ *Don't be so negative; cheer up!* **4.** MED SHOWING THAT SOMETHING IS NOT PRESENT showing the absence of a disease or condition that is being tested for ○ *The test for cancer is negative.* **5.** MATH LESS THAN ZERO indicating a quantity that is less than zero ○ *a negative number* **6.** MATH OPPOSITE TO POSITIVE describes something such as a quantity or angle of the same magnitude as, but opposite to, something considered positive **7.** PHYS HAVING SAME CHARGE AS ELECTRON with the same electric charge as that of an electron, shown by the symbol – **8.** PHYS SHOWING DIRECTION OF CURRENT indicating the direction toward which current flows in an external circuit **9.** LOGIC OPPOSING denying or contradicting a statement, proof, or argument **10.** BIOL MOVING AWAY moving or growing away from a source of stimulation such as heat or light ○ *negative tropism* ■ *n* **1.** ANSWER OF "NO" an answer meaning "no" ○ *answered in the negative* **2.** SOMETHING OR SOMEBODY UNDESIRABLE a person, thing, quality, or situation, that is bad, undesirable, discouraging, or otherwise detracts from satisfaction (*informal*) ○ *The candidate's negatives have soared since the debate.* **3.** PHOTOGRAPHIC IMAGE a photographic image, or the film containing it, that shows black and white tones reversed and colors as complementary **4.** GRAM WORD IMPLYING "NO" a word that expresses the idea "no," e.g., the words "not," "nothing," and "never" **5.** LOGIC NEGATING PROPOSITION a statement that contradicts, denies, or disproves something **6.** ELEC DESTINATION OF ELECTRONS the part of an electric circuit to which the electrons flow, e.g., a terminal or the cathode where negative ions are formed in electrolytic applications **7.** MATH QUANTITY OPPOSITE TO POSITIVE a number or quantity, e.g., speed, angle, or direction, that is less than zero or considered to be the opposite of positive ■ *interj* NO used to say "no" to something or somebody (*formal*) ■ *vt* (**-tived, -tiv·ing, -tives**) **1.** SAY "NO" TO SOMETHING to refuse, reject, deny, cancel, or forbid something (*formal*) ○*"a polite request that Elizabeth would lead the way, which the other politely and more earnestly negatived"* (Jane Austen, *Pride And Prejudice*; 1813) **2.** LOGIC DISPROVE PROPOSITION to contradict or invalidate a proposition (*informal*) —**neg·a·tive·ness** *n* —**neg·a·tiv·i·ty** /nèggə tívvətee/ *n*

neg·a·tive eq·ui·ty *n* a situation in which, as a result of falling prices, a piece of real estate is worth less than the amount of money that was borrowed to buy it

neg·a·tive feed·back *n* in an electronic or mechanical system, the redirecting of part of the output back to the input as a way of improving the quality of the output

neg·a·tive·ly /néggətivlee/ *adv* **1.** SAYING "NO" in a way that means "no" **2.** ADVERSELY in an adverse way ○ *patients reacting negatively to the medication* **3.** PESSIMISTICALLY in a pessimistic or defeatist way **4.** PHYS WITH NEGATIVE ELECTRICAL CHARGE with the same electric charge as that of one or more electrons, shown by the symbol –

neg·a·tive re·in·force·ment *n* encouragement of a desired response by giving an unpleasant stimulus when the response is absent, or discouragement of an undesired response by an unpleasant stimulus when the response is present

neg·a·tive stain·ing *n* staining of an area around a biological subject, rather than the subject itself, so that the subject can be clearly seen against it

neg·a·tive trans·fer, neg·a·tive trans·fer·ence *n* a stage in psychotherapy at which a patient relives hostile feelings toward his or her parents by experiencing hostility toward the therapist

neg·a·tiv·ism /néggəti vìzzəm/ *n* **1.** a strong tendency to be pessimistic, to assess situations in the worst light, or to be unreasonably skeptical about generally accepted beliefs **2.** persistent defiance of authority and refusal to obey instructions —**neg·a·tiv·ist** *n* —**neg·a·tiv·is·tic** /nèggəti vístik/ *adj*

Ne·gev /né gev/, **Ne·geb** /né geb/ desert region in Israel, comprising the southern half of the country. Area: 4,940 sq. mi./12,800 sq. km.

ne·glect /nə glékt/ *vt* (**-glect·ed, -glect·ing, -glects**) **1.** NOT CARE FOR SOMETHING PROPERLY to fail to give the proper or required care and attention to somebody or something **2.** FAIL TO DO SOMETHING to fail to do something, especially because of carelessness, forgetfulness, or indifference ○ *neglected to tell him* ■ *n* **1.** WITHHOLDING OF PROPER CARE the act of failing to give proper care or attention to somebody or something ○ *parents charged with criminal neglect* **2.** LACK OF CARE the effect of lack of proper care or attention ○ *The house began to suffer from neglect.* [Early 16C. < Latin *neglect-*, past participle of *neglegere* < *legere* "choose"] —**ne·glect·ful** *adj*

SYNONYMS See *overlook.*

neg·li·gee /nèggli zháy, néggli zhày/, **neg·li·gée, neg·li·gé** *n* **1.** a woman's dressing gown made of light often see-through fabric **2.** informal dress (*dated formal*) [Mid-18C. < French *négligé*, past participle of *négliger* (see NEGLIGIBLE)]

neg·li·gence /négglijənss/ *n* **1.** CONDITION OF BEING NEGLIGENT the condition or quality of being negligent **2.** LAW CIVIL WRONG CAUSING INJURY OR HARM a civil wrong (**tort**) causing injury or harm to another person or to property as the result of doing something or failing to provide a proper or reasonable level of care **3.** CASUALNESS casualness in matters of dress or general appearance, whether regarded as stylish or slovenly (*dated formal*) ○*"clad in an artist's velvet, but with none of an artist's negligence"* (G. K. Chesterton, *The Wisdom of Father Brown*; 1914)

neg·li·gent /négglijənt/ *adj* **1.** HABITUALLY CARELESS habitually careless or irresponsible **2.** LAW GUILTY OF NEGLIGENCE guilty of failing to provide a proper or reasonable level of care **3.** CASUAL IN APPEARANCE casual in matters of dress or general appearance, whether considered stylish or slovenly (*literary*) [14C. Via French < Latin *negligent-*, present participle of *negligere*, variant of *neglegere* (see NEGLECT)] —**neg·li·gent·ly** *adv*

neg·li·gi·ble /négglijəb'l/ *adj* too small or unimportant to be worth considering [Early 19C. < obsolete French *négligible* < *négliger* "to neglect" < Latin *neglegere* (see NEGLECT)] —**neg·li·gi·bly** *adv*

ne·go·tia·ble /nə góshəb'l, -góshee ə-/ *adj* **1.** OPEN TO DISCUSSION not fixed but able to be established or changed through discussion and compromise ○ *Salary is negotiable, according to education and experience.* **2.** NAVIGABLE able to be crossed, passed, or successfully dealt with **3.** FIN EXCHANGEABLE FOR MONEY describes financial instruments such as checks and securities that can be transferred to another person in exchange for money ■ *n* FIN SOMETHING EXCHANGEABLE FOR MONEY a negotiable financial instrument (*usually used in the plural*)

ne·go·ti·ant /nə góshee ənt, -shənt/ *n* **1.** a dealer or trader, especially somebody in the wine trade **2.** somebody who negotiates

ne·go·ti·ate /nə góshee àyt/ (**-at·ed, -at·ing, -ates**) *v* **1.** *vti* DISCUSS TERMS OF AGREEMENT to attempt to come to an agreement on something through discussion and compromise **2.** *vt* NAVIGATE SOMETHING SUCCESSFULLY to manage to get past or deal with something that constitutes a hazard or obstacle ○ *A canoe can negotiate these waters when the wind is calm.* **3.** *vt* FIN SELL SOMETHING to transfer ownership of a financial instrument such as a check or security to somebody else in exchange for money [Late 16C. < Latin *negotiat-*, past participle of *negotiari* "do business" < *negotium* "business" < *neg-* "not" + *otium* "leisure"] —**ne·go·ti·a·tor** *n*

ne·go·ti·a·tion /nə gòshee áysh'n/ *n* **1.** RESOLVING OF DISAGREEMENTS the reaching of agreement through discussion and compromise ○ *matters still under negotiation* **2.** NAVIGATION the tackling of a hazard or problem (*formal*) ■ **ne·go·ti·a·tions** *npl* DISCUSSION SESSIONS one or more meetings at which attempts are made to reach agreement through discussion and compromise ○ *Negotiations are already under way between the opposing factions.*

Ne·gress /néegrəss/ *n* an offensive term for a Black woman (*dated*) [Late 18C. < French *négress* < *nègre* < Latin *nigr-* "black"]

Ne·gril·lo /nə grílō/ (*plural* **-los** or **-loes**) *n* a member of a people of central and southern Africa [Mid-19C. < Spanish, "small Black person" < *negro* (see NEGRO[1])]

Ne·gri·to /nə gréetō/ (*plural* **-tos** or **-toes**) *n* a member of some of the peoples of Austronesia [Early 19C. < Spanish, "small Black person" < *negro* (see NEGRO[1])]

ne·gri·tude /néggri tòod, néegri-/ *n* identity as a Black person, especially awareness of a distinct Black history and culture as something to be proud of [Mid-20C. Via French *négritude* < Latin *nigritudo* < *nigr-* "black"]

Ne·gro[1] /néegrō/ (*plural* **-groes**) *n* an offensive term for a Black person, often considered an acceptable term in historically established phrases such as baseball's Negro Leagues [Mid-16C. < Spanish and Portuguese < Latin *nigr-* "black"]

USAGE Though ***Negro*** is still used in certain restricted formulaic expressions, it is not the preferred term for people of color such as African Americans. Use instead *African American, woman of color, man of color,* or *people of color.*

Ne·gro[2] /náygrō, néggrō/ **1.** river in northwestern South America that rises in eastern Colombia and flows southeastward to empty into the Amazon in northern Brazil. Length: 1,400 mi./2,300 km. **2.** river in central Argentina flowing eastward into the Atlantic Ocean. Length: 400 mi./640 km.

Ne·groid /née gròyd/ *adj* an offensive term meaning belonging or relating to a group, in a former classification of humankind, that originated in Africa (*dated*)

ne·gro·phile /néegrə fìl/ *n* an offensive term for a person who favors the interests of Black people

ne·gus /néegəss/ *n* a hot drink made of port or sherry with water, sugar, lemon juice, and spices [Mid-18C. After Francis *Negus* (d.1732), English colonel]

Ne·gus *n* a title formerly used for the king or emperor of Ethiopia [Late 16C. < Amharic *n'gus* "kinged, king"]

NEH *abbr* EDUC National Endowment for the Humanities

Neh. *abbr* BIBLE Nehemiah

Ne·he·mi·ah /nèehə mí ə/ *n* **1.** in the Bible, a Jewish leader and governor of Judea. He was responsible for rebuilding Jerusalem in 444 B.C. **2.** a book of the Bible that describes the rebuilding of Jerusalem in the 5th century B.C. and the reforms undertaken after its completion, traditionally attributed to Nehemiah. See table at **Bible**

Neh·ru /náy ròo/, **Jawaharlal** (1889–1964) Indian politician. He became a leading member of the Indian National Congress and the political heir of Mohandas Karamchand Gandhi, taking an active part in the civil disobedience campaigns of the 1930s and 1940s leading to Independence. He was the first prime minister of independent India (1947–64) and a leader of nonaligned nations during the Cold War. Indira Gandhi was his daughter.

> "At the stroke of the midnight hour, India will awake to life and freedom. A moment comes, which comes but rarely in history, when we step out from the old to the new, when an age ends, and when the sound of a nation, long suppressed, finds utterance."
> [Jawaharlal Nehru, *Speech to the Lok Sabha, the lower house of the Indian parliament just before independence was declared*; August 14, 1947]

Neh·ru jack·et *n* a long narrow jacket with a high standup collar. See illustration on next page [Mid-20C. After Jawaharlal NEHRU]

~~**neice**~~ incorrect spelling of **niece**

neigh /nay/ *n* the long high-pitched sound that a horse makes ■ *vi* (**neighed, neigh·ing, neighs**) to make the high-pitched sound characteristic of a horse [Old English *hnǣgan*, origin ?]

neigh·bor /náybər/ *n* **1.** SOMEBODY LIVING NEARBY somebody who lives next door or close to somebody else **2.** SOMETHING OR SOMEBODY NEARBY a person, place, or thing

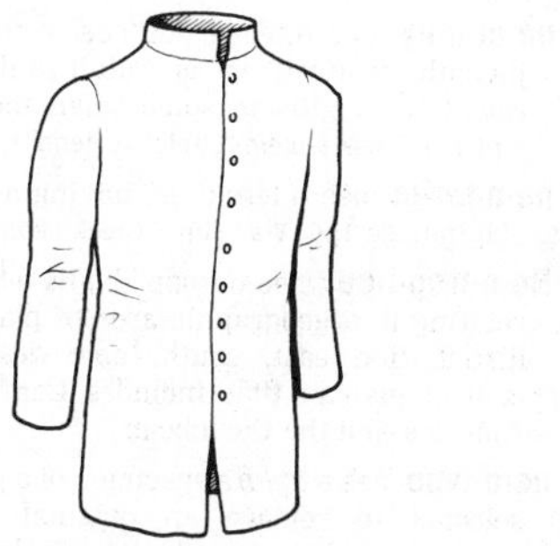
Nehru jacket

located next to another or very nearby ○ *the Spanish and their Portuguese neighbors* **3. FELLOW HUMAN** a fellow human being (*archaic or literary*) ■ *vti* (**-bored, -bor·ing, -bors**) **BE NEAR TO SOMETHING OR SOMEBODY** to be located very close to something or somebody, or be close to something in character [Old English *nēahgebūr* < *nēah* "near" + *gebūr* "dweller"]

neigh·bor·hood /náybər hòod/ *n* **1. DISTINCTIVE AREA** a district with characteristics that distinguish it from the areas around it **2. PEOPLE LIVING NEAR EACH OTHER** people who live near each other or in a specific neighborhood ○ *The whole neighborhood turned out for the picnic.* **3. VICINITY** the general vicinity or surrounding area of a place ○ *Stop by if you're in the neighborhood.* **4. APPROXIMATION OF AMOUNT** an approximate amount, size, or range (*informal*) ○ *expenses in the neighborhood of $175,000* **5.** MATH **SURROUNDING POINTS** the set of all points within a given distance from an identified point

neigh·bor·hood watch *n* a program to raise awareness of crime and crime prevention within local communities, with members taking part in various initiatives, sometimes involving the patrolling of streets

neigh·bor·ing /náybəring/ *adj* situated or located nearby

neigh·bor·ly /náybərlee/ *adj* friendly, helpful, and kind, especially to a neighbor —**neigh·bor·li·ness** *n*

neigh·bor note *n US* an auxiliary musical note a second away from its principal note

neigh·bour *n, vt* Can, UK spelling of **neighbor**

neigh·bour·hood *n* Can, UK spelling of **neighborhood**

neigh·bour·ing *adj* Can, UK spelling of **neighboring**

neigh·bour·ly *adj* Can, UK spelling of **neighborly**

Nei Mong·gol /náy-/ autonomous region of Northern China, bordered on the North by Russia and Mongolia. Capital: Hohhot. Population: 23,070,000 (1997). Area: 454,640 sq. mi./1,177,500 sq. km.

nei·ther /neéthər, nī-/ CORE MEANING: a negative grammatical word that introduces or connects two people, things, or situations, both of which are excluded ○ (adj) *Neither shirt looks good on you.* ○ (pron) *Neither of the boys wants to go.* ○ (pron) *"Would you like pork or fish?" "Neither, thank you."* ○ (conj) *Neither my father nor my mother commented.*
1. *adj, pron* **EXCLUDES BOTH** not one or the other ○ (adj) *Neither machine works.* ○ (pron) *I like neither of them.* ○ (pron) *Neither is true.* **2.** *conj* **INTRODUCES ALTERNATIVES** used preceding two alternatives joined by "nor" to indicate that both did not happen or are not true ○ *Neither my boss nor his wife can cook.* **3.** *adv, conj* **INDICATES THAT ALSO EXCLUDED** used to indicate a second person or thing, or group of people or things, that can also be included in a negative statement just made, or that the previous negative statement ought to apply in the second case also ○ *"We've never been to Paris." "Neither have I."* ○ *She doesn't want to go? Me neither!* ○ *She can't play today, and neither can her brother.* **4.** *adv* **INTRODUCES MODIFICATION OF NEGATIVE** used in a statement that indicates a modification or partial contradiction of a previous negative statement ○ *You won't find it hot, but neither will you be freezing cold.* [12C. Alteration (influenced by EITHER) of Old English *nawzzer*, contraction of *nāhwæzzer* < *nā* "not" + *hwæþer* "which of two"]

USAGE Neither meaning **none**: Do not substitute ***neither*** for the pronoun ***none*** in the sense "not one of several," as in *Neither of these (four) options has any appeal.* Say instead: *None* [or *Not one*] *of these (four) options has any appeal.* When you use ***neither*** as a conjunction, follow it with ***nor***, not *or*, and make the verb agree with the nearest noun: *Neither rain nor snow* [not *or snow*] *is* [not *are*] *going to stop mail delivery.*

nek·ton /néktən, -tòn/ *n* an organism, e.g., a fish, that lives in water and can actively swim against currents, as opposed to microorganisms that are simply carried along [Late 19C. < Greek *nēkton*, form of *nēktos* "swimming" < *nēkhein* "to swim"] —**nek·ton·ic** /nek tónnik/ *adj*

nel·lie *n* another spelling of **nelly** (*offensive*)

nel·ly /néllee/ (*plural* **-lies**), **nel·lie** *n* an offensive term for an effeminate or gay man (*insult*) [Mid-20C. < nickname for the name *Helen* or *Eleanor*]

nel·son /nélss'n/ *n* a wrestling hold in which one arm (**half nelson**) or both arms (**full nelson**) are passed through the opponent's arms from behind and pulled back, levering against the opponent's back [Late 19C. Origin ?]

Nel·son /nélss'n/ river in eastern Canada, in northern Manitoba. It rises in Lake Winnipeg and empties into Hudson Bay. Length: 400 mi./644 km.

Nel·son, Horatio, Viscount (1758–1805) British naval commander. He defeated the French and Spanish naval forces at Trafalgar (1805) but was killed during the battle. His affair with Emma, Lady Hamilton caused a considerable scandal.

> "England expects every man will do his duty."
> [Horatio Nelson, at the Battle of Trafalgar. Quoted in *Life of Nelson*, Robert Southey; 1813]

Nel·son, Thomas (1738–89) American patriot. He signed the Declaration of Independence (1776) and commanded the Virginia state forces (1777–81) during the Revolution.

Nel·son, Willie (*b.* 1933) US country-and-western singer and songwriter. His songs include "Georgia on My Mind."

> "I'm a country songwriter and we write cry-in-your-beer songs. That's what we do. Something that you can slow-dance to."
> [Willie Nelson, *Independent (London)*; May 11, 1996]

Nel·spruit /nél sprŏyt/ capital of Mpumalanga Province in northeastern South Africa. Population: 21,474 (1991).

nemat- *prefix* same as **nemato-** (*used before vowels*)

ne·mat·ic /nə máttik/ *adj* describes a phase of liquid crystals in which the axes of the molecules become parallel in response to a magnetic field [Early 20C. < Greek *nēmat-* "thread"]

nem·a·ti·cide *n* BIOCHEM same as **nematocide**

nemato- *prefix* **1.** thread, resembling a thread ○ *nematocyst* **2.** nematode ○ *nematocide* [< Greek *nēmat-* "thread" < Indo-European, "spin"]

nem·a·to·cide /némmətə sīd, nə máttə-/, **nem·a·ti·cide** *n* a substance that destroys nematodes —**nem·a·to·ci·dal** /nèmmətə sīd'l, nə màttə-/ *adj*

nem·a·to·cyst /némmətə sist, nə máttə-/ *n* a sting found in animals of the jellyfish family. It comprises a fluid-filled sac within which is a coiled hollow thread that is rapidly turned outward (**everted**) to capture food or for defense.

nem·a·tode /némmə tōd/ *n* a worm, often microscopic, with a cylindrical unsegmented body protected by a tough outer skin (**cuticle**). Phylum: Nematoda. [Mid-19C. < modern Latin *Nematoda* < Greek *nēmat-* (see NEMATO-)]

nem·a·tol·o·gy /nèmmə tóllejee/ *n* the branch of zoology that is concerned with the study of nematodes —**nem·a·to·log·i·cal** /nèmmətə lójjik'l/ *adj* —**nem·a·tol·o·gist** *n*

nem. con. /nèm kón/ *adv* without opposition ○ *The motion was carried nem. con.* [< shortening of Latin *nemine contradicente* "with no one contradicting"]

ne·mer·te·an /ni múrtee ən/ *n* same as **ribbon worm** (*technical*) [Mid-19C. < modern Latin *Nemertes* < Greek *Nēmertēs* "Nereid"] —**ne·mer·te·an** *adj* —**ne·mer·tine** /némmər tīn/ *adj*

nem·e·sis /némməssiss/ (*plural* **-e·ses** /-ə seez/) *n* (*literary*) **1. UNBEATABLE OPPONENT** a bitter enemy, especially one who seems unbeatable **2. SOURCE OF HARM** a source of harm or ruin ○ *Chocolate chip cookies are my real nemesis.* **3. DESERVED PUNISHMENT** punishment that is deserved, especially when it results in somebody's downfall **4. AVENGER** a person or force that inflicts punishment or revenge [Late 16C. < Greek, "Nemesis, righteous indignation" < *nemein* "distribute what is due"]

Nem·e·sis *n* in Greek mythology, the goddess of just punishment or vengeance [< Greek (see NEMESIS)]

Ne·mours ♦ **du Pont de Nemours, Eleuthère Irénée**

NEMS *n* a computer chip that has integrated devices on a molecular scale for sensing, processing, or carrying out various functions. Full form **nano-micro-electromechanical system**

ne·ne /náy nay/ (*plural same* or **-nes**) *n* a rare wild goose with a grayish brown body and a black face. Native to: Hawaiian Islands. Latin name: *Branta sandvicensis.* [Early 20C. < Hawaiian]

NEO *abbr* ASTRON near-earth object

neo- *prefix* new, recent ○ *neotype* ○ *neo-Darwinism* [< Greek *neos* < Indo-European]

ne·o·Con·fu·cian *adj, n*
ne·o·Con·fu·cian·ism *n*
ne·o·Freud·i·an *adj, n*
ne·o·Freud·i·an·ism *n*
ne·o·Geor·gian *adj*
ne·o·Goth·ic *adj, n*
ne·o·La·marck·i·an *adj, n*
ne·o·Mal·thu·sian *adj, n*
ne·o·Mal·thu·sian·ism *n*
ne·o·Marx·ism *n*
ne·o·Marx·ist *n, adj*
ne·o·noir *adj*
ne·o·or·tho·dox *adj*
ne·o·orth·o·dox *adj*
ne·o·or·tho·dox·y *n*
ne·o·re·al·ism *n*
ne·o·re·al·ist *n, adj*
ne·o·re·al·is·tic *adj*
ne·o·ro·man·tic *adj*
ne·o·scho·las·tic *adj*
ne·o·scho·las·ti·cism *n*
ne·o·sur·re·al·ism *n*
ne·o·sur·re·al·ist *n*
ne·o·sur·re·al·is·tic *adj*

CORBIS/G. E. Kidder Smith
neoclassical: front porch of Monticello, Charlottesville, Virginia (begun 1770)

ne·o·clas·si·cal /neè ō klássik'l/, **ne·o·clas·sic** /-sik/ *adj* **1.** ARTS, ARCHIT **OF REVIVAL OF CLASSICAL ART FORMS** relating to or belonging to a style of art and architecture prevalent in the late 18th and early 19th centuries, characterized by the simple, symmetrical forms of ancient Greek and Roman art **2.** LITERAT **OF CLASSICAL REVIVAL** relating to or characteristic of the European revival of Greek and Roman literary forms **3.** MUSIC **OF FORMAL MUSICAL STYLE** relating to a movement in the late 19th and early 20th centuries that favored the more formal style of composers before the Romantic movement **4.** ECON **OF MACROECONOMIC MONETARIST THEORY** relating to macroeconomic monetarist theories that emphasize the need for the free operation of market forces —**ne·o·clas·si·cism** *n* —**ne·o·clas·si·cist** *n, adj*

ne·o·co·lo·ni·al·ism /neè ō kə lōnee ə lìzzəm/ *n* the domination by a powerful, usually Western nation of another nation that is politically independent but has a weak economy greatly dependent on trade with the powerful nation —**ne·o·co·lo·ni·al** *adj* —**ne·o·co·lo·ni·al·ist** *n, adj*

ne·o·con /neè ō kòn/ *n US* same as **neoconservative** (*informal*) [Late 20C. Shortening]

ne·o·con·ser·va·tive /neè ō kən súrvətiv/ *n* somebody who, during the mid-1980s, began to support conservatism in society, and in politics in particular, as a reaction to the social freedoms sought throughout the 1960s and early 1970s —**ne·o·con·ser·va·tive** *adj* —**ne·o·con·ser·va·tism** *n*

ne·o·cor·tex /neè ō káwr tèks/ (*plural* **-ti·ces** /-tə seez/ or **-tex·es**) *n* the roof of the cerebral cortex that forms the part of the mammalian brain that has evolved most recently and makes possible higher brain functions such as learning —**ne·o·cor·ti·cal** /-káwrtik'l/ *adj*

ne·o·Dar·win·ism *n* a theory of evolution that combines Darwin's theory and modern genetics, especially with regard to variations in populations as a result of genetic mutations —**ne·o·Dar·win·i·an** *adj* —**ne·o·Dar·win·ist** *n, adj*

ne·o·dym·i·um /nee ō dímmee əm/ *n* a silvery-white or yellowish metallic element that is one of the lanthanide series of rare-earth elements. Source: monazite, bastnaesite. Use: lasers, glass manufacture. Symbol **Nd**. See table at **element** [Late 19C. < NEO- + DIDYMIUM]

ne·o·ex·pres·sion·ism *n* a 20th-century art movement, begun in Germany, Italy, and the United States, and based on expressionism, that focuses on the artist's inner experiences and often produces violent or erotic paintings —**ne·o·ex·pres·sion·ist** *n, adj*

ne·o·fas·cism /nee ō fá shìzzəm/ *n* **1.** the modern-day revival of Fascist beliefs of the 1930s and 1940s, which assume that a supposed Aryan race is superior to all others and attempt to justify genocide **2.** the views or actions of any modern-day white group or movement that holds racist views, especially anyone involved in the violent intimidation of people of color —**ne·o·fas·cist** *adj, n*

ne·o·fas·cist /nee ō fáshist/ *adj* **1.** OF MODERN-DAY FASCISTS relating to, or typical of, any modern-day movement inspired by the racial intolerance and militarism of the Fascists and Nazis of the 1930s and 1940s **2.** OF WHITE RACISTS relating to the members, views, or actions of any modern-day group or movement of white people with violently racist views, especially those involved in the violent intimidation of non-whites ■ *n* MODERN-DAY FASCIST OR WHITE RACIST somebody who currently holds fascist or white racist opinions

Ne·o·gene /nee ə jeen/ *n* a period of geologic time from 23.3 million to 1.64 million years ago that includes both the Miocene and Pliocene epochs [Late 19C. < NEO- + Greek *-genēs* "born"] —**Ne·o·gene** *adj*

ne·o·gen·e·sis /nee ō jénnəssiss/ *n* the regrowth of living tissue —**ne·o·ge·net·ic** /-jə néttik/ *adj* —**ne·o·ge·net·i·cal·ly** *adv*

ne·o·im·pres·sion·ism /nee ō im présh'n ìzzəm/ *n* a 19th-century movement in painting, led by the pointillist Georges Seurat, that favored stricter and more formal techniques of composition than impressionism —**ne·o·im·pres·sion·ist** *adj, n*

ne·o-La·marck·ism /nee ō lə maar kìzzəm/ *n* a theory of evolution that modifies Lamarckism by emphasizing the ways environment influences genetic variations —**ne·o-La·marck·i·an** *adj, n*

Ne·o-Lat·in *n, adj* LANG same as **New Latin** ■ *adj* relating to a language that has developed from Latin

ne·o·lib·er·al·ism /nee ō líbbərə lìzzəm, -líbbrə-/ *n* the political view, arising in the 1960s, that emphasizes the importance of economic growth and asserts that social justice is best maintained by minimal government interference and free market forces —**ne·o·lib·er·al** *adj, n*

ne·o·lith /nee ə lìth/ *n* a stone tool from the Neolithic period

Ne·o·lith·ic /nee ə líthik/ *n* the latest period of the Stone Age, between about 8000 B.C. and 5000 B.C., characterized by the development of settled agriculture and the use of polished stone tools and weapons —**Ne·o·lith·ic** *adj*

ne·ol·o·gism /nee óllə jìzzəm/, **ne·ol·o·gy** /nee óllәjee/ (*plural* **-gies**) *n* **1.** a recently coined word or phrase, or a recently extended meaning of an existing word or phrase **2.** the practice of coining new words or phrases, or of extending the meaning of existing words or phrases [Early 19C. < French *néologisme* < *néo-* "new" + Greek *logos* "word"] —**ne·ol·o·gist** *n* —**ne·ol·o·gis·tic** /nee òllə jístik/ *adj* —**ne·ol·o·gize** *vi*

ne·ol·o·gize /nee óllə jīz/ (**-gized, -giz·ing, -giz·es**) *vi* to coin new words or phrases, or extend the meaning of existing words or phrases

ne·ol·o·gy *n* LING same as **neologism**

ne·o-Mel·a·ne·sian *n* a creole language based on English with borrowings from other languages that is used in island groups of the southwestern Pacific —**ne·o-Mel·a·ne·sian** *adj*

ne·o·my·cin /nee ō míss'n/ *n* an antibiotic with a wide range of effectiveness. Source: the bacterium *Streptomyces fradiae*. Use: treatment of skin, eye, and intestinal infections.

ne·on /nee òn/ (*plural* **-ons** or *same*) *n* **1.** a colorless odorless gaseous element that occurs in very small quantities in the air and glows orange when electricity is passed through it. Symbol **Ne**. See table at **element 2.** lighting produced by neon lights or by lamps containing similar gases such as argon or krypton **3.** FISH same as **neon tetra** [Late 19C. < Greek, form of *neos* "new"]

ne·o·nate /nee ə nàyt/ *n* a newborn child, especially one less than one month old [Early 20C. < NEO- + Latin *natus*, past participle of *nasci* "be born"] —**ne·o·na·tal** /nee ō náyt'l/ *adj*

ne·o·na·tol·o·gy /nee ō nay tóllәjee/ *n* the branch of medicine that deals with the care and development of newborn babies and the treatment of their diseases —**ne·o·na·to·log·i·cal** /nee ō nàytə lójjik'l/ *adj* —**ne·o·na·tol·o·gist** *n*

ne·o-Na·zi *n* **1.** a member of a modern-day movement that promotes the idea that a supposed race of Aryans is superior to all others and that genocide is justifiable **2.** a member of any modern-day group or movement of white people who hold racist views, especially those involved in violent attacks on people of color —**ne·o-Na·zism** *n*

ne·on light, ne·on lamp *n* a light with a bulb, usually tube-shaped, containing neon gas, that glows orange when a high-voltage electric current is passed through it. Neon lights are used for display signs and television tubes.

ne·on tet·ra *n* a small iridescent blue and red fish, often kept in aquariums. Native to: Amazon River. Latin name: *Hyphessobrycon innesi*. [< its bright colors like neon glowing]

ne·o·pa·gan /nee ō páygən/ *n* a believer in a modernized version of the principles of old pre-Christian religions, especially reverence for nature and natural objects rather than worship of a transcendent supreme being

ne·o·phil·i·a /nee ō fíllee ə/ *n* a liking for new things, change for the sake of change, or novelty —**ne·o·phile** /nee ə fīl/ *n* —**ne·o·phil·i·ac** *n, adj*

ne·o·phyte /nee ə fīt/ *n* **1.** BEGINNER a beginner or novice at something **2.** RECENT CONVERT a recent convert to a religion **3.** RELIGIOUS NOVICE a new resident of a religious community who has not yet taken vows [14C. Via late Latin *neophytus* < Greek *neophutos* "newly planted" < *phuein* "plant, cause to grow"] —**ne·o·phyt·ic** /nee ə fíttik/ *adj*

ne·o·pla·sia /nee ō pláyzhə, -pláyzhee ə/ *n* the formation or existence of tumors

ne·o·plasm /nee ə plàzzəm/ *n* a tumor or tissue containing a growth [Late 19C. < NEO- + Greek *plasma* "formation" < *plassein* "to form"]

ne·o·plas·tic /nee ə plástik/ *adj* **1.** relating to neoplasms or neoplasty **2.** relating to neoplasticism

ne·o·plas·ti·cism /nee ə plástə sìzzəm/ *n* a style of abstract painting, as found in the work of Mondrian, using black, gray, white, and the primary colors, and horizontal and vertical lines and planes

ne·o·plas·ty /nee ə plàstee/ *n* the surgical construction of new tissue, or the repair of damaged tissue

ne·o-Pla·to·nism /nee ō pláyt'n ìzzəm/, **Ne·o·pla·to·nism** *n* a philosophical system combining Platonism with mysticism and Judaic and Christian ideas and positing one source for all existence, developed by Plotinus and his followers in the 3rd century A.D. —**ne·o-Pla·ton·ic** /nee ō plə tónnik/ *adj* —**ne·o-Pla·to·nist** *n*

ne·o·prene /nee ə preen/ *n* a synthetic material resembling rubber, but slower to deteriorate and more resistant to oil. Use: in the manufacture of equipment for which waterproofing is important. [Mid-20C. < NEO- + CHLOROPRENE]

Ne·o·ri·can /nee ō reekən/ *n* US a Puerto Rican who lives on the United States mainland, or who lived there for a time but has now returned to Puerto Rico [Mid-20C. Origin ?]

ne·o·stig·mine /nee ō stíg meen, -stígmin/ *n* a white crystalline compound. Use: treatment of myasthenia. [Mid-20C. < NEO- + PHYSOSTIGMINE]

ne·ot·e·ny /nee óttənee, -ótt'nee/ *n* the existence of juvenile features in an adult animal, e.g., the retention of gills in some salamanders [Late 19C. < NEO- + Greek *teinein* "stretch, extend"]

ne·o·ter·ic /nee ə térrik/ *adj* having a contemporary origin [Late 16C. Via Latin < Greek *neōterikos* "youthful"]

Ne·o·trop·i·cal /nee ō tróppik'l/, **Ne·o·trop·ic** /-pik/ *adj* relating to a geographic area of plant and animal distribution east, south, and west of Mexico's central plateau that includes Central and South America and the Caribbean

ne·o·type /nee ə tīp/ *n* a specimen of a plant or animal selected to replace an original representative example used in classification (**holotype**) that has been lost or destroyed —**ne·o·typ·i·cal** /nee ə típpik'l/ *adj*

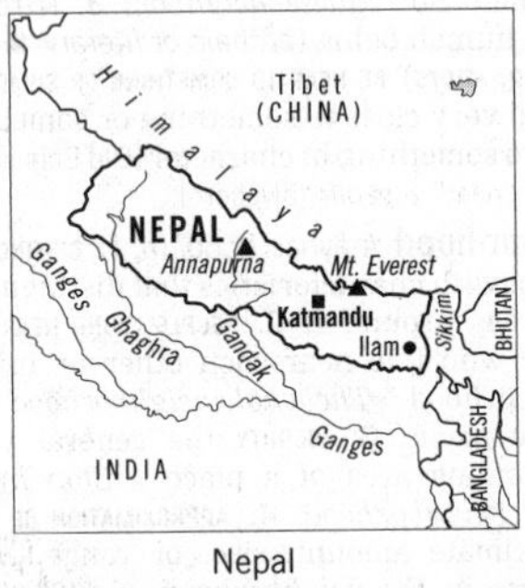

Nepal

Ne·pal /nə páwl, -paal/ country in South Asia, northeast of India, in the Himalayan range. Language: Nepali. Currency: rupee. Capital: Kathmandu. Population: 26,469,569 (2003). Area: 56,827 sq. mi./147,181 sq. km. Official name **Kingdom of Nepal** —**Nep·al·ese** /nèppə leez, -leess/ *n, adj*

Ne·pal·i /nə páwlee, -paalee/ (*plural same* or **-is**) *n* **1.** the Indic official language of Nepal, also spoken in Bhutan and northeastern India. Native speakers: 16 million. **2.** somebody who comes from Nepal —**Ne·pal·i** *adj*

ne·pen·the /nə pénthee/ *n* **1.** a supposed substance that people took in ancient times to forget their sadness or troubles, or the plant that produced the substance **2.** something that eases pain or makes people forget their troubles (*literary*) ○ *"respite and nepenthe from thy memories of Lenore"* (Edgar Allan Poe, *The Raven*; 1845) [Late 16C. < Greek *nēpenthēs* "banishing pain" < *nē* "not" + *penthos* "grief"] —**ne·pen·the·an** *adj*

ne·per /náypər, neepər/ *n* a unit for comparing two currents, voltages, or related quantities, equal to the natural logarithm of the ratio of the quantities. Symbol **Np** [Early 20C. < *neperus* Latinized name of John NAPIER]

neph·e·line /néffə leen, -lin/, **neph·e·lite** /-līt/ *n* a white aluminosilicate of potassium and sodium. Source: igneous rocks. Use: manufacture of glass and ceramics. [Early 19C. < French < Greek *nephelē* "cloud"]

neph·e·lin·ite /néffəli nīt/ *n* a fine-grained igneous rock that has nepheline and pyroxene as its main mineral ingredients

neph·e·lite *n* MINERALS same as **nepheline**

neph·e·lom·e·ter /néffə lómmətər/ *n* **1.** an instrument that uses reflected light to measure the size or density of solid particles present in a liquid **2.** an instrument used to measure the degree of cloudiness of the sky [Late 19C. < Greek *nephelē* "cloud"] —**neph·e·lo·met·ric** /nèffələ méttrik/ *adj* —**neph·e·lom·e·try** *n*

neph·ew /néffyoo/ *n* the son of somebody's brother, sister, brother-in-law, or sister-in-law [13C. Via French *neveu* < Latin *nepot-* "sister's son, grandson"]

nepho- *prefix* relating to clouds ○ *nephoscope* [< Greek *nephos* "cloud"]

neph·o·gram /néffə gràm/ *n* a photograph of a cloud formation, especially one taken from a satellite, used in predicting weather patterns

neph·o·graph /néffə gràf/ *n* a device for taking photographs of cloud formations

ne·phol·o·gy /ne fóllәjee/ *n* the branch of meteorology concerned with the study of clouds —**neph·o·log·i·cal** /nèffə lójjik'l/ *adj* —**ne·phol·o·gist** *n*

neph·o·scope /néffə skōp/ *n* an instrument for measuring the altitude, speed, and direction of movement of clouds

nephr- *prefix* same as **nephro-** (*used before vowels*)

ne·phral·gia /nə frálјə/ *n* pain in the kidneys

ne·phrec·to·my /nə fréktəmee/ (*plural* **-mies**) *n* the surgical removal of a kidney

neph·ric /néffrik/ *adj* relating to or affecting the kidneys

ne·phrid·i·um /nə fríddee əm/ (*plural* **-i·a** /-ee ə/) *n* **1.** a simple tube-shaped organ in earthworms and many other invertebrate organisms for releasing waste matter into the gut or out of the body **2.** the organ that develops into the kidney in the embryo of a vertebrate animal [Late 19C. < NEPHRO- + modern Latin *-idium* "small one" (< Greek *-idion*)] —**ne·phrid·i·al** *adj*

neph·rite /né frīt/ (*plural same* or **-rites**) *n* a variety of jade that ranges in color from white to dark green, containing calcium, magnesium, and iron

ne·phrit·ic /nə fríttik/ *adj* **1.** relating to or affected by nephritis **2.** relating to or affecting the kidneys

ne·phri·tis /ni frítiss/ *n* severe inflammation of the kidney, caused by infection, degenerative disease, or disease of the blood vessels

nephro- *prefix* kidney ○ *nephrogenous* [< Greek *nephros*]

ne·phrog·e·nous /nə frójjənəss/, **neph·ro·gen·ic** /nèffrə jénnik/ *adj* **1.** located in or moving into a kidney **2.** capable of developing into kidney tissue

ne·phrol·o·gy /nə fróllәjee/ *n* the branch of medicine concerned with the study and treatment of diseases of the kidneys —**neph·ro·log·i·cal** /nèffrə lójjik'l/ *adj* —**ne·phrol·o·gist** *n*

neph·ron /né frón/ *n* a fine tubule in the kidneys of vertebrates that filters and excretes waste materials from the blood and produces urine

ne·phrop·a·thy /nə fróppəthee/ (*plural* **-thies**) *n* a disease or medical disorder of the kidney —**neph·ro·path·ic** /nèffrə páthik/ *adj*

neph·ro·scope /néffrə skōp/ *n* a tube-shaped instrument inserted into an incision in the body wall in order to examine a patient's kidneys

ne·phro·sis /nə fróssiss/ *n* a disease that causes the kidneys to degenerate without inflaming them, especially one that affects the nephrons —**ne·phrot·ic** /nə fróttik/ *adj*

neph·ro·stome /néffrə stōm/ *n* the funnel-shaped inner opening of a nephridium that is lined with cilia and allows water and waste to enter from the body cavity [Late 19C. < NEPHRO- + Greek *stoma* "mouth"]

ne·phrot·o·my /nə fróttəmee/ (*plural* **-mies**) *n* a surgical incision into a kidney

ne plus ul·tra /này plooss óoltrə, nee pluss últrə/ *n* the highest level of excellence, or something that reaches it [Late 17C. < Latin, "not farther beyond," supposed to have been inscribed on the Pillars of Hercules]

nep·o·tism /néppə tìzzəm/ *n* favoritism shown by somebody in power to relatives and friends, especially in appointing them to good positions [Mid-17C. < French *népotisme* < Latin *nepot-* "grandson, sister's son"] —**nep·o·tist** *n* —**nep·o·tis·tic** /nèppə tístik/ *adj* —**nep·o·tis·ti·cal·ly** *adv*

Nep·tune /nép toon/ *n* **1.** the eighth planet from the Sun in our solar system **2.** in Roman mythology, the god of the sea, son of Saturn, brother of Jupiter and Pluto. Greek equivalent **Poseidon** [15C. Directly or via French < Latin *Neptunus*]

Nep·tu·ni·an /nep toonee ən/ *adj* relating or belonging to the planet Neptune

nep·tu·ni·um /nep toonee əm/ *n* a silvery radioactive metallic element. Source: uranium ores, a by-product of plutonium production in nuclear reactors. Use: neutron detection. Symbol **Np**. See table at **element** [Late 19C. After the planet NEPTUNE, discovered after uranium (named for Uranus)]

nerd /nurd/ *n* **1.** an offensive term that deliberately insults somebody's physical appearance or social skills (*slang insult*) **2.** somebody who is considered to be excessively interested in a subject or activity that is regarded as too technical or scientific (*often used in combination; offensive in some contexts*) [Mid-20C. Origin ?] —**nerd·ish** *adj* —**nerd·y** *adj*

Ne·re·id /néeree id/ *n* **1.** in Greek mythology, a sea nymph, one of the 50 daughters of Nereus, a god of the sea **2.** a large natural satellite of Neptune [Late 17C. Via Latin < Greek *Nēreid-* < *Nēreus*, a Greek god of the sea]

ne·re·is /néeree iss/ (*plural* **-i·des** /nə rée i deez/ or **-is·es**) *n* a large segmented worm usually found living in saltwater, e.g., a clamworm. Genus: *Nereis*. [Mid-18C. Via modern Latin < Latin < Greek *Nērēis* form of *nērēid-* (see NEREID)]

ne·rit·ic /nə ríttik/ *adj* relating to or found in shallow coastal waters [Late 19C. < Latin *nerita*, type of shellfish of shallow seas < Greek *Nēreus*, a Greek god of the sea]

Nernst /nernst/, **Walther** (1864–1941) German physical chemist. He developed the third law of thermodynamics and won the Nobel Prize in chemistry (1920). Full name **Nernst, Walther Hermann**

Nernst e·qua·tion /núrnst i kwàyzh'n/ *n* an equation that shows the dependence of the electromotive force in a dry cell on the activities of the reacting chemicals and the temperature [After Walther Hermann NERNST]

Ne·ro /néerō/ (A.D. 37–68) Roman emperor. He succeeded Claudius (A.D. 54), but his tyrannical and neglectful rule led to revolts against him, and he committed suicide. Born **Ahenobarbus, Lucius Domitius**. Full name **Nero, Claudius Caesar Drusus Germanicus**

ne·rol /néer àwl, né ràwl/ *n* a colorless alcohol. Source: neroli and other essential oils. Use: perfumes. [Early 20C. < NEROLI]

ner·o·li /nérrəlee/, **ner·o·li oil** *n* an oil distilled from the flowers of orange trees, especially the Seville orange. Use: aromatherapy, perfumes, food flavoring. [Late 17C. Via French < Italian, after an Italian princess who supposedly discovered the oil]

nerts /nurts/ *interj US* a word used to express contempt, disgust, or refusal (*dated slang*) [Mid-20C. Alteration of NUTS]

Ne·ru·da /ne róodə, -róothə/, **Pablo** (1904–73) Chilean poet and diplomat. He is known for his socialist poetry and won the Nobel Prize in literature (1971). Pseudonym of **Neftalí Ricardo Reyes y Basoalto**

> "Peace goes into the making of a poem as flour goes into the making of bread."
> [Pablo Neruda, *Memoirs*; 1974]

Ner·va /núrvə/ (A.D. 30–98) Roman emperor. He succeeded Domitian in 96, and introduced measures to help the poor. He was succeeded by his son Trajan. Full name **Nerva, Marcus Cocceius**

nerve /nurv/ *n* **1.** FIBER BUNDLE TRANSMITTING IMPULSES a bundle of fibers forming a network that transmits messages in the form of impulses between the brain or spinal cord and the body's organs. Motor nerves carry impulses outward to the muscles and glands, while sensory nerves carry inbound information about the body's movements and sensations. Mixed nerves perform both functions. **2.** COURAGE coolness, steadiness, and self-assurance ○ *lost his nerve* **3.** BOLDNESS boldness or impudence ○ *You've got a lot of nerve!* **4.** DENT SENSITIVE PULP IN TOOTH the sensitive tissue inside the roots of a tooth **5.** BOT LEAF VEIN a vein in a leaf **6.** INSECTS VEIN IN INSECT'S WING a thin rib visible inside an insect's wing ■ **nerves** *npl* **1.** SOMEBODY'S ABILITY TO TOLERATE STRESS somebody's ability to tolerate emotional stress or excitement ○ *My nerves are shattered.* **2.** NERVOUSNESS a state of emotional agitation (*informal*) ○ *He had a bad case of nerves before every performance.* ■ *vt* (**nerved, nerv·ing, nerves**) STEEL YOURSELF to cause somebody or yourself to muster courage or self-control in preparation for dealing with something difficult, stressful, or frightening [14C. Directly or via Old French *nerf* "sinew" < Latin *nervus* "nerve, sinew, tendon"]

SYNONYMS See *courage*.

nerve block *n* the use of a local anesthetic to numb a part of the body in order to prevent the transmission of pain messages to the brain

nerve cell *n* ANAT same as **neuron**

nerve cen·ter *n* **1.** the place from which a large organization, system, or network is controlled **2.** a cluster of interconnected nerve cells that performs a specific function in the body

nerve cord *n* a strand of nerve tissue, e.g., the spinal cord, that runs the length of the body and forms a principal part of an animal's nervous system

nerve fi·ber *n* one of the long thin extensions of a neuron such as an axon or dendrite

nerve gas *n* a poisonous gas used as a weapon of war that attacks the central nervous system and stops people from breathing

nerve im·pulse *n* a rapid and momentary change in electrical activity that passes along a nerve fiber to other neurons, muscles, or other body organs and signals instructions or information

nerve·less /núrvləss/ *adj* **1.** NUMB having no sensation or strength **2.** FEARLESS showing calmness, courage, or confidence, especially in a dangerous situation **3.** COWARDLY lacking courage or determination —**nerve·less·ly** *adv* —**nerve·less·ness** *n*

nerve net *n* a simple nervous system, found in some invertebrates such as jellyfish, consisting of interconnecting nerve cells, but lacking a control center such as a brain

nerve-rack·ing *adj* causing great anxiety or distress

nerve trunk *n* a bundle of nerve fibers surrounded by a sheath of connective tissue that forms the main stem of a nerve

nerve-wrack·ing *adj* same as **nerve-racking**

nerv·ous /núrvəss/ *adj* **1.** UNEASY having a feeling of dread or apprehension ○ *I was nervous about meeting his parents.* **2.** TIMID easily worried or frightened ○ *people of a nervous disposition* **3.** AFFECTING NERVES relating to somebody's ability to tolerate anxiety or stress ○ *a nervous illness* **4.** OF NERVES relating to or located in nerves or the nervous system ○ *nervous tissue* [14C. Originally "sinewy"] —**ner·vos·i·ty** /nur vóssətee/ *n* —**nerv·ous·ly** *adv* —**nerv·ous·ness** *n*

nerv·ous break·down *n* a psychiatric disorder, usually caused by intense stress or anxiety, in which somebody becomes incapable of coping with daily life and exhibits low self-esteem or depression

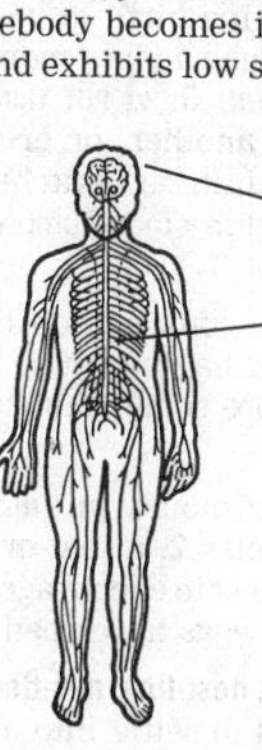

nervous system

nerv·ous sys·tem *n* the network of nerve cells and nerve fibers in most animals that conveys sensations to the brain and motor impulses to organs and muscles

nerv·ous tic *n* an involuntary twitch of a muscle, especially of the face, that is sometimes a symptom of nervousness or a nervous disease

ner·vure /núrvyər, -vyoor/ *n* **1.** a supporting structure resembling a rod that is visible inside an insect's wing **2.** BOT same as **vein** *n* (sense 4) [Early 19C. < French, "strap" < Latin *nervus* "nerve"]

nerv·y /núrvee/ (**-i·er, -i·est**) *adj* (*informal*) **1.** FEARLESS showing a lot of courage or foolhardiness **2.** AGGRESSIVE acting in ways that show lack of respect for the boundaries or feelings of other people **3.** *UK* NERVOUS feeling or easily becoming worried, upset, or frightened —**nerv·i·ly** *adv* —**nerv·i·ness** *n*

NES *abbr Can* National Employment Service

ness /ness/ *n* a section of coastline that projects into the sea (*often used in place names*) [Old English *næs(s)* < Indo-European]

Ness, Loch /ness/ long narrow lake in northern Scotland, forming part of the Caledonian Canal. It is believed by some people to be the home of an ancient monster. Length: 23 mi./37 km.

-ness *suffix* state, condition, quality ○ *callousness* [Old English *-nes* < Germanic]

nes·sel·rode /néss'l ròd/, **Nes·sel·rode** *n* a creamy frozen dessert containing puréed chestnuts, candied fruit, and usually a sweet wine or liqueur [Mid-19C. After Karl-Robert *Nesselrode* (1780–1862), Russian statesman, whose chef invented it]

nest: nest of tables

nest /nest/ *n* **1.** BIRD OR ANIMAL HOME a structure that birds and other animals such as mice build to shelter themselves and their young, using available natural materials such as grass, twigs, and mud **2.** COMMUNITY OF ANIMALS the community of animals living in a nest **3.** SOMETHING SHAPED LIKE BIRD'S NEST something shaped more or less like a bird's nest, especially something that encloses or contains things ○ *a meringue nest* **4.** COZY PLACE a cozy, protected, or secluded place **5.** BAD PLACE a place where something bad such as crime or treason flourishes ○ *a nest of vice* **6.** CRIMINALS' SECRET PLACE a hideaway for criminals, or a group of criminals hiding away there ○ *a nest of thieves* **7.** SET OF THINGS a set of things such as tables or wooden eggs that fit one inside the other **8.** GUN EMPLACEMENT a protected or camouflaged place from which a gun or other weapon is fired ■ *v* (**nest·ed, nest·ing, nests**) **1.** *vi* BUILD NEST to make or live in a nest, especially in preparation for giving birth to young **2.** *vi* MAKE PLACE MORE HOMELIKE to make a place more comfortable and homelike (*informal*) **3.** *vt* PUT THINGS TOGETHER to put one thing inside another, or group things together into a single unit, e.g., kitchen utensils of graduated size [Old English < Indo-European "place where a bird sits down"]

nest-build·ing *n* **1.** the construction of a nest by a bird in preparation for having young **2.** the process of making a place more comfortable and homelike (*informal*)

nest egg *n* **1.** a sum of money put aside for future expenses or emergencies **2.** a real or artificial egg that is put in a hen's nest to encourage it to continue laying after the other eggs have been removed

nes·tle /néss'l/ (**nes·tled, nest·ling, nes·tles**) *v* **1.** *vti* SETTLE INTO COMFORTABLE POSITION to settle into a position that feels comfortable, warm, and safe, or lay a part of the body in such a position **2.** *vi* BE SECLUDED to be in a sheltered or secluded place ○ *a village nestling in the foothills* **3.** *vt* CUSHION SOMETHING WITH SOFT MATERIAL to put something such as delicate china or glassware in a protected cushion of soft material [Old English *nestlian* < Germanic] —**nes·tler** *n*

nest·ling /néstling, néssling/ *n* a young bird that does not yet have its flight feathers, and is therefore not yet able to leave the nest [Late 14C. < NEST or NESTLE]

Nes·to·ri·an /ne stáwree ən/ *adj* relating to a Southwest Asian Christian denomination that believes that two distinct persons, one divine and the other human, existed in Jesus Christ. This doctrine was declared heresy in A.D. 431. [15C. < late Latin *Nestorianus*, after *Nestorius* (A.D. 428–31), patriarch of Constantinople] —**Nes·to·ri·an** *n* —**Nes·to·ri·an·ism** *n*

net[1] /net/ *n* **1.** MESH a material made from threads or wires knotted, twisted, or woven to form a regular pattern with spaces between the threads **2.** MESHWORK BAG a piece of meshwork fabric in a shape resembling a bag that is used for holding, carrying, trapping, or confining something ○ *a fishing net* **3.** LIGHT MESHWORK FABRIC a fine light cotton or synthetic fabric with an open weave **4.** SELECTING OR RESTRICTING SYSTEM a plan or system designed to select or restrict somebody or something ○ *those who slip through the net* **5.** BASKETBALL PART OF BASKETBALL BASKET in basketball, an open-bottomed piece of meshwork material attached to the hoop of the basket **6.** SPORTS STRIP OF MATERIAL ACROSS PLAYING AREA in some sports such as tennis and volleyball, a strip of meshwork material that divides a court into halves and over which the players must hit a ball or shuttlecock **7.** SPORTS GOAL IN SOME SPORTS in some sports such as soccer and water polo, a goal with a backing made of meshwork material **8.** BROADCAST BROADCASTING NETWORK a television or radio network **9.** COMPUT TELEPHONE OR COMPUTER NETWORK a telecommunications or computer network ■ *v* (**net·ted, net·ting, nets**) **1.** *vt* TRAP SOMEBODY OR SOMETHING to catch or snare somebody or something in a net **2.** *vt* GET SOMETHING to manage to obtain or achieve something (*informal*) ○ *We may net ourselves several new clients this way.* **3.** *vt* PROTECT SOMETHING WITH NET to cover something with a net in order to keep something else out or away ○ *Net the cherry trees to keep birds out.* **4.** *vi* MAKE NET to make a net by knotting, twisting, or weaving threads or wires together **5.** *vt* HIT BALL INTO NET TO SCORE in games such as soccer, to hit the ball into the net so as to score **6.** *vt* SERVE BALL INTO NET in games such as tennis and volleyball, to hit the ball into the net so as to lose a serve, and sometimes a point [Old English, < Indo-European, "to bind, tie"]

net[2] /net/ *adj* **1.** LEFT AFTER DEDUCTIONS remaining from an amount, especially of money, after all necessary deductions have been made ○ *net pay* **2.** RELATING TO CONTENTS relating to contents only, excluding the container or the packaging ○ *net weight* **3.** HAVING ALL THINGS CONSIDERED general or overall, after positive and negative features have been weighed against each other ○ *the net result* ■ *vt* (**net·ted, net·ting, nets**) EARN SOMETHING AS PROFIT to earn or provide a sum of money as pure profit after all necessary deductions have been made ■ *n* **1.** NET AMOUNT a net profit or weight **2.** GOLFER'S SCORE a golfer's final score after his or her handicap has been deducted [15C. Via Italian *netto* < Latin *nitidus* (see NEAT[1])]

net[3] *abbr* networking organization (*used in Internet addresses*) See table at **domain name**

Net /net/, **net** *n* ONLINE same as **Internet** (*informal*) [Late 20C. Shortening]

NET *abbr US* National Educational Television

Net·an·ya·hu /nètt'n yaáhoo/, **Binyamin** (*b.* 1949) Israeli prime minister (1996–99). As a Likud prime minister, he was criticized for failing to press for the implementation of the peace agreements with the Palestinians.

net as·set val·ue *n* the value of the securities owned by a mutual fund, calculated as the total value of assets minus the total amount of liabilities divided by the number of shares issued

net·ball /nét bàwl/ *n* an indoor or outdoor game similar to basketball, usually played by girls or women in which goals are scored by throwing a ball through a raised net. Players can hand or throw the ball to each other but not run with it.

net cord *n* **1.** a tennis shot, especially a serve, that touches the net before landing on the opponent's side. In the case of a serve, the server retakes the shot. **2.** the wire that holds up the net on a tennis court

net do·mes·tic prod·uct *n* the gross sum of domestic production minus the cost of depreciation of capital goods

Neth. *abbr* Netherlands

neth·er /né*th*ər/ *adj* located in a low or lower position or under something [Old English *neoþera* < Indo-European, "down"]

Netherlands

Neth·er·lands /né*th*ərləndz/ country in northwestern Europe, west of Germany, on the North Sea. Language: Dutch. Currency: guilder. Capital: Amsterdam. Population: 15,150,511 (2003). Area: 16,033 sq. mi./41,526 sq. km. Official name **Kingdom of the Netherlands** —**Neth·er·land·er** *n* —**Neth·er·land·ish** *adj*

Neth·er·lands An·til·les two Dutch island groups in the Caribbean Sea. One group is situated off the northern coast of Venezuela and the other lies east of Puerto Rico in the Leeward Islands. Capital: Willemstad. Population: 212,226 (2001). Area: 309 sq. mi./800 sq. km.

neth·er·most /né*th*ər mòst/ *adj* lowest or farthest down

neth·er·world /né*th*ər wùrld/ *n* **1.** HELL in the belief system of some cultures, hell or the place where evil spirits live (*formal*) **2.** ABODE OF DEAD SOULS in classical mythology, the place below the earth's surface where the souls of the dead live **3.** CRIMINAL UNDERWORLD the world of organized crime, or the people involved in it (*literary*)

net·i·quette /nétti kèt/ *n* a set of empirically derived rules for communication via the Internet (*informal*) [Late 20C. Blend of NET + ETIQUETTE]

Net·i·zen /néttiz'n/ *n* somebody who uses the Internet frequently (*informal*) [Late 20C. Blend of NET + CITIZEN]

net·lag /nét làg/ *n* a temporary loss of contact between an Internet user and a server, usually caused by network delays (*slang*) [Late 20C. After JET LAG]

net na·tion·al prod·uct *n* the amount left after subtracting a depreciation allowance for capital goods from the gross national product

net·phone /nét fòn/ *n* a phone that uses the Internet to make connections and carry voice messages

net pres·ent val·ue *n* the value of an investment project found by adding the present value of expected future cash flows and the cost of the initial investment

net prof·it *n* gross profit minus all the costs incurred by a business

net re·al·iz·a·ble val·ue *n* the value that an asset would have if sold, allowing for the costs of bringing it to a condition for sale and making the sale

net·su·ke /nét sòokee, nétskee/ (*plural same* or **-kes**) *n* a carved wooden or ivory ornamental toggle worn at the end of a cord that holds a kimono closed, originally used to fasten a purse or pouch [Late 19C. < Japanese]

Net surf·ing *n* the activity of browsing through the information and sites available on the Internet, especially casually

nett /net/ *adj Malaysia, Singapore* describes a price that cannot be changed by bartering

net·ter /néttər/ *n* somebody with an Internet address (*slang*)

net·ting /nétting/ *n* fabric made from threads or wires knotted, twisted, or woven to form a regular pattern with spaces between the threads ○ *wire netting*

net·tle /nétt'l/ *n* **1.** PLANT WITH STINGING LEAVES a wild plant with serrated-edged leaves covered with fine hairs or spines that sting when touched. Native to: found worldwide. Genus: *Urtica.* **2.** NONSTINGING PLANT RESEMBLING NETTLE a wild plant with serrated leaves like a stinging nettle, but without the stinging hairs, especially a dead nettle. Native to: north temperate regions. Genus: *Lamium.* ■ *vt* (**-tled, -tling, -tles**) **1.** IRRITATE SOMEBODY to irritate or annoy somebody (*informal*) **2.** STING SOMEBODY to sting somebody with a nettle leaf [Old English *netele* < Indo-European, "to tie"]

net·tle rash *n* MED same as **urticaria**

net ton *n* MEASURE same as **ton**[1] (sense 1) [< NET[2]]

net·war /nét wàwr/ *n* nontraditional warfare carried out by dispersed groups of activists without a central command, often communicating electronically

net weight *n* the weight of the contents only, excluding the weight of the container or packaging [< NET[2]]

net-winged *adj* describes beetles and midges that have a network of veins in their wings

net wire *n Southern US* lightweight flexible galvanized wire fencing, usually made with a hexagonal mesh

REGIONAL NOTE ***Net wire*** is sometimes called *chicken wire*, but more frequently *hog wire*. The term most frequently identifies animal fencing in the Lower Mississippi Valley states of Mississippi, Arkansas, and Louisiana, as well as Texas.

net·work /nét wùrk/ *n* **1.** SYSTEM OF LINES a pattern or system that looks like a series of branching or interconnecting lines **2.** SYSTEM OF PEOPLE OR THINGS a large and widely distributed group of people or things such as stores, colleges, or churches that communicate with one another and work together as a unit or system **3.** BROADCAST BROADCASTING AFFILIATES a group of radio or television station affiliates with a core of programs that they all broadcast at the same time, with local or regional variations at other times **4.** COMPUT SYSTEM OF COMPUTERS a system of two or more computers, terminals, and communications devices linked by wires, cables, or a telecommunications system in order to exchange data. The network may be limited to a group of users in a local area (**local area network**), or be global in scope, as the Internet is. **5.** ELEC SYSTEM OF CIRCUITS a system of interconnected electrical circuits or components **6.** NETTING net or netting ■ *v* (**-worked, -work·ing, -works**) **1.** *vt* BROADCAST BROADCAST SOMETHING SIMULTANEOUSLY to broadcast a program simultaneously on all the station affiliates that form a network **2.** *vt* COMPUT LINK COMPUTERS to link a group of computers or their users so that information can be mutually accessed or exchanged **3.** *vi* MAINTAIN RELATIONSHIPS WITH PEOPLE to build up or maintain informal relationships, especially with people whose friendship could bring advantages such as job or business opportunities

net·work-cen·tric *adj* relating to warfare that employs instantaneous electronic cooperation among air, ground, and naval forces, smart munitions, spy planes, drones, and commandos equipped with computers and laser-guided weapons, all coordinated to orchestrate highly accurate attacks ○ *"In war bad stuff happens. This is as true of network-centric warfare as the more traditional kind of an earlier day."* (Daniel Ford, *Wall Street Journal*; August 12, 2003) [Late 20C.]

net·work·ing /nét wùrking/ *n* **1.** the act of linking computers so that users can exchange information or share access to a central store of information **2.** the process or practice of building up or maintaining informal relationships, especially with people whose friendship could bring advantages such as job or business opportunities —**net·work·er** *n*

net worth *n* the difference between the assets and liabilities of a person or company ○ *services for high net worth investors*

neum *n* MUSIC another spelling of **neume**

Neu·mann ♦ **von Neumann, John**

neume /noom/, **neum** *n* in medieval Europe, an early musical notation that sometimes indicated only the approximate shape of a melody [15C. Via French < Greek *pneuma* "breath"] —**neu·mat·ic** /noo máttik/ *adj*

neur. *abbr* MED **1.** neurological **2.** neurology

neur- *prefix* same as **neuro-** (*used before vowels*)

neu·ral /nóoral/ *adj* relating to or located in a nerve or the nervous system —**neu·ral·ly** *adv*

neu·ral arch *n* a bony or cartilaginous arch enclosing the spinal cord on the outward-facing side of a vertebra

neu·ral com·put·er *n* COMPUT same as **neurocomputer**

neu·ral crest *n* a ridge of cells in the ectoderm of the vertebrate embryo that develops into cranial, spinal, and autonomic ganglia

neu·ral·gia /noo rálјə/ *n* an intermittent and often severe pain in a part of the body along the path of a nerve, especially when there is no physical change in the nerve itself —**neu·ral·gic** *adj*

neu·ral net *n* a system of electrical circuits designed to perform in a similar way to the human nervous system, especially a computer system mimicking the human brain

neu·ral net·work *n* **1.** an interconnecting system of nerve cells, e.g., the system that makes the brain function **2.** COMPUT same as **neural net**

neu·ral spine *n* a projection that points backward from the neural arch of a vertebra

neu·ral tube *n* the hollow tube of tissue in the embryo of humans and other vertebrates that develops into the spinal cord and brain

neu·ral tube de·fect *n* a disorder, e.g., spina bifida, that is present at birth and is caused by failure of the neural tube to close completely, resulting in loss of muscle function and various medical disorders

neu·ras·the·ni·a /nòorəss théenee ə/ *n* a condition marked by chronic mental and physical fatigue and depression (*dated*) —**neu·ras·then·ic** /-thénnik/ *adj* —**neu·ras·then·i·cal·ly** *adv*

neu·rec·to·my /noo réktəmee/ (*plural* **-mies**) *n* the removal of part of a nerve using surgery, e.g., as a treatment for neuralgia

neu·ri·lem·ma /nòorə lémmə/, **neu·ro·lem·ma** /nòorō-/ *n* the outermost layer of the myelin sheath that surrounds the axon of a myelinated nerve cell [Early 19C. < NEUR- + Greek *eilēma* "covering"] —**neu·ri·lem·mal** *adj* —**neu·ri·lem·mal·ly** *adv*

neu·ri·lem·mo·ma /nòorələ mṓmə/ (*plural* **-mas** or **-ma·ta** /-mətə/) *n* MED same as **neurofibroma**

neu·ri·no·ma /nòorə nṓmə/ (*plural* **-mas** or **-ma·ta** /-mətə/) *n* MED same as **neurofibroma**

neu·ri·tis /noo rítiss/ *n* inflammation of a nerve, accompanied by pain, loss of reflexes, and muscle shrinkage —**neu·rit·ic** /-ríttik/ *adj*

neuro- *prefix* nerve, neural ○ *neurosurgery* [< Greek *neuron* "nerve"]

neu·ro·ac·tive /nòorō áktiv/ *adj* having an effect on neural tissue or the nervous system

neu·ro·a·nat·o·my /nòorō ə náttəmee/ *n* **1.** the structure of the nervous system **2.** the branch of anatomy that studies the structure of the nervous system —**neu·ro·an·a·tom·i·cal** /-ànnə tómmik'l/ *adj* —**neu·ro·an·a·tom·i·cal·ly** *adv* —**neu·ro·a·nat·o·mist** *n*

neu·ro·be·hav·ior·al /nòorō bi háyvyərəl/ *adj* relating to the condition of the nervous system and its effects on behavior ○ *the neurobehavioral effects of exposure to solvents* —**neu·ro·be·hav·ior** *n* —**neu·ro·be·hav·ior·al·ly** *adv*

neu·ro·bi·ol·o·gy /nòorō bī óllәjee/ *n* BIOL same as **neuroscience** (sense 2) —**neu·ro·bi·o·log·i·cal** /nòorō bī ə lójjik'l/ *adj* —**neu·ro·bi·o·log·i·cal·ly** *adv* —**neu·ro·bi·ol·o·gist** *n*

neu·ro·blast /nòorō blàst/ *n* an embryonic cell that develops into a nerve cell

neu·ro·blas·to·ma /nòorō bla stṓmə/ (*plural* **-mas** or **-ma·ta** /-mətə/) *n* a malignant tumor of embryonic nerve cells (**neuroblasts**)

neu·ro·chem·is·try /nòorō kémmistree/ *n* the study of the chemical composition of and reactions within the nervous system —**neu·ro·chem·i·cal** /-kémmik'l/ *adj* —**neu·ro·chem·i·cal·ly** *adv* —**neu·ro·chem·ist** *n*

neu·ro·com·put·er /nòorō kəm pyootər/ *n* a computer designed to imitate the human brain's ability to identify patterns, learn by trial and error, and find relationships in information. It is used in artificial intelligence research and to perform such tasks as machine translation, process control, handwriting recognition, and weather forecasting. —**neu·ro·com·pu·ta·tion·al** /nòorō kòmpyə táyshən'l, -táyshnəl/ *adj* —**neu·ro·com·put·ing** *n*

neu·ro·en·do·crine /nòorō éndəkrin/ *adj* relating to or involving a nerve cell that releases a chemical messenger, especially a neurohormone, directly into the bloodstream

neu·ro·en·do·cri·nol·o·gy /nòorō endəkrə nóllәjee/ *n* the study of the interrelationships between the nervous system, the endocrine system, and hormones —**neu·ro·en·do·cri·no·log·i·cal** /-krinnə lójjik'l/ *adj* —**neu·ro·en·do·cri·no·log·i·cal·ly** *adv* —**neu·ro·en·do·cri·nol·o·gist** *n*

neu·ro·fi·bril /nòorə fíbrəl, -fíbbrəl/ *n* a microscopic thin strand that occurs inside the cell body, axon, and dendrites of a nerve cell —**neu·ro·fi·bril·lar·y** /-fíbbrə lèrree/ *adj*

neu·ro·fi·bro·ma /nòorō fī brṓmə/ (*plural* **-mas** or **-ma·ta** /-mətə/) *n* a usually benign tumor growing on the sheath of a nerve

neu·ro·fi·bro·ma·to·sis /nòorō fī brōmə tṓssis/ *n* an inherited disorder marked by coffee-colored patches on the skin and neurofibromas formed along nerves, causing visual and hearing impairment, other nervous disorders, and sometimes major complications

neu·ro·gen·e·sis /nòorō jénnəssiss/ *n* the formation and development of nerve cells —**neu·ro·ge·net·ic** /-jə néttik/ *adj* —**neu·ro·ge·net·i·cal·ly** *adv*

neu·ro·ge·net·ics /nòorō jə néttiks/ *n* the branch of medicine that studies the genetic influences involved in neurological disorders (*takes a singular verb*) —**neu·ro·ge·net·i·cist** *n*

neu·ro·gen·ic /nòorō jénnik/ *adj* **1.** relating to the growth of nerve tissue **2.** arising in or stimulated by nerve tissue or the nervous system —**neu·ro·gen·i·cal·ly** *adv*

neu·rog·li·a /noo rógglee ə, nòorə glée ə/ *n* US the network of supporting tissue and fibers that nourishes nerve cells within the brain and spinal cord. It comprises several layers of cells and makes up about 40% of the total volume of nerve tissue. Can term **glia** [Mid-19C. < NEURO- + Greek *glia* "glue"] —**neu·rog·li·al** *adj*

neu·ro·hor·mone /nòorō háwr mōn/ *n* a hormone secreted by specialized nerve cells —**neu·ro·hor·mo·nal** /-hawr mṓn'l/ *adj* —**neu·ro·hor·mo·nal·ly** *adv*

neu·ro·hu·mor /nòorō hyòomər/ *n* BIOL same as **neurotransmitter** —**neu·ro·hu·mor·al** /nòorō hyòomərəl/ *adj*

neu·ro·hy·poph·y·sis /nòorō hī póffəssiss/ (*plural* **-y·ses** /-ə seez/ or **-y·sis·es**) *n* the posterior lobe of the pituitary gland that secretes hormones such as vasopressin —**neu·ro·hy·po·phys·e·al** /-hīpə fízzee əl, -hī pòffə sée əl/ *adj*

neu·ro·im·ag·ing /nòorō ímmijing/ *n* the use of devices such as electroencephalographs or CAT scanners to produce a cross-sectional image of the brain —**neu·ro·im·age** *n* —**neu·ro·im·ag·er** *n*

neu·ro·lem·ma *n* MED another spelling of **neurilemma**

neu·ro·lep·tic /nòorō léptik/ *adj* reducing nerve activity and producing a tranquilizing effect ■ *n* a tranquilizing drug that works by reducing nerve activity. Use: treatment of delirium and behavioral disturbances. [Mid-20C. < NEURO- + Greek *lēptikos* "seizing" < *lambanein* "seize, take"] —**neu·ro·lep·ti·cal·ly** *adv*

neu·ro·lin·guis·tic pro·gram·ming *n* **1.** a theory and model of human behavior and communication based on linguistic insights into how people avoid change and how to assist them in changing **2.** a system of therapy in which the brain is viewed as a computer that can be reprogrammed to think and feel in a way that helps people achieve goals

neu·ro·lin·guis·tics /nòorō ling gwístiks/ *n* the branch of linguistics that explores how the brain encodes language (*takes a singular verb*) —**neu·ro·lin·guist** /nòorō líng gwist/ *n* —**neu·ro·lin·guis·tic** *adj* —**neu·ro·lin·guis·ti·cal·ly** *adv*

neu·rol·o·gy /noo róllәjee/ *n* the branch of medicine that deals with the structure and function of the nervous system and the treatment of the diseases and disorders that affect it —**neu·ro·log·ic** /nòorə lójjik/ *adj* —**neu·ro·log·i·cal** *adj* —**neu·ro·log·i·cal·ly** *adv* —**neu·rol·o·gist** *n*

neu·ro·ma /noo rṓmə/ (*plural* **-mas** or **-ma·ta** /-mətə/) *n* MED same as **neurofibroma**

neu·ro·mus·cu·lar /nòorō múskyələr/ *adj* **1.** relating to or affecting both nerve and muscle tissue **2.** having features common to both nerve and muscle tissue

neu·ro·mus·cu·lar junc·tion *n* the connection between a nerve cell and a muscle, where nerve impulses are transmitted to initiate contraction of the muscle

neu·ron /nòor òn/ *n* a cell, usually consisting of a cell body, axon, and dendrites, that transmits nerve impulses and is the basic functional unit of the nervous system. See illustration on next page [Late 19C. Via German < Greek *neuron* "sinew, cord, nerve"] —**neu·ron·al** /noo rṓn'l, nòorənəl/ *adj* —**neu·ron·al·ly** /noo rṓn'lee, nòorənəlee/ *adv*

neu·rone /nòor ōn/ *n* UK another spelling of **neuron**

neu·ro·path /nòorə pàth/ *n* somebody affected by a disorder of the nervous system

neu·ro·pa·thol·o·gy /nòorōpə thóllәjee/ *n* the branch of medicine that studies diseases and disorders of

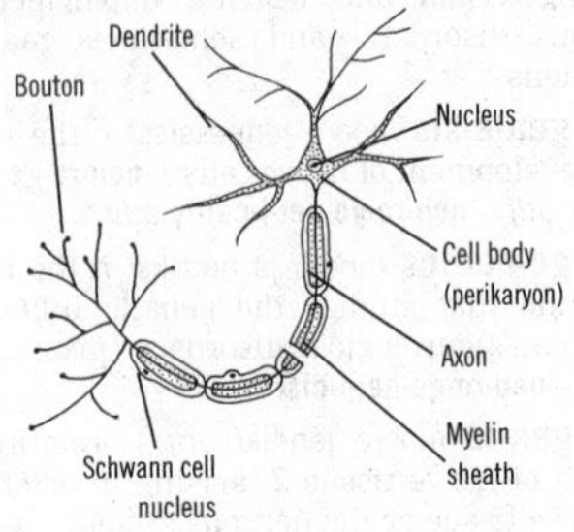

neuron

the nervous system —**neu·ro·path·o·log·i·cal** /-pàthə lójjik'l/ *adj* —**neu·ro·pa·thol·o·gist** *n*

neu·rop·a·thy /noo róppəthee/ (*plural* **-thies**) *n* a disease or disorder, especially a degenerative one, that affects the nervous system —**neu·ro·path·ic** /nòorō páthik/ *adj*

neu·ro·pep·tide /nòorō pép tīd/ *n* a peptide released by the nervous system that acts as a neurotransmitter

neu·ro·phar·ma·col·o·gy /nòorō faarmə kólləjee/ *n* the branch of medicine that studies the effects of drugs on the nervous system —**neu·ro·phar·ma·co·log·i·cal** /-kə lójjik'l/ *adj* —**neu·ro·phar·ma·col·o·gist** *n*

neu·ro·phys·i·ol·o·gy /nòorō fìzzee ólləjee/ *n* the branch of physiology that studies how the nervous system functions —**neu·ro·phys·i·o·log·i·cal** /-fìzzee ə lójjik'l/ *adj* —**neu·ro·phys·i·ol·o·gist** *n*

neu·ro·pros·thes·is /nòorō pross théessiss/ *n* a prosthetic device that uses brain waves to stimulate muscle contraction —**neur·o·pros·thet·ic** /-théttik/ *adj* —**neu·ro·pros·thet·ic·al·ly** *adv*

neu·ro·pros·thet·ics /nòorō pros théttiks/ *n* the branch of medicine that deals with prosthetic devices that are controlled by brain-wave activity (*takes a singular verb*) —**neu·ro·pros·the·tist** /nòorō prósthətist/ *n*

neu·ro·psy·chi·a·try /nòorō si kī ətree, -sī-/ *n* the study of the neurological aspects of psychiatric disorders —**neu·ro·psy·chi·at·ric** /nòorō sīkee áttrik/ *adj* —**neu·ro·psy·chi·a·trist** *n*

neu·ro·psy·chol·o·gy /nòorō sī kólləjee/ *n* the branch of neurology that studies behavior, especially in disorders such as epilepsy, memory loss, or speech impairment —**neu·ro·psy·cho·log·i·cal** /-sīkə lójjik'l/ *adj* —**neu·ro·psy·chol·o·gist** *n*

neu·rop·ter·an /noo róptərən/ *n* an insect that has two large pairs of veined wings and mouthparts adapted for chewing, e.g., the ant lion or lacewing. Order: Neuroptera. —**neu·rop·ter·ous** *adj*

neu·ro·ra·di·ol·o·gy /nòorō raydee óllәjee/ *n* the use of X-rays to diagnose and treat physiological disorders and diseases of the nervous system, or the branch of medicine that deals with their use in this way —**neu·ro·ra·di·o·log·i·cal** /-ə lójjik'l/ *adj* —**neu·ro·ra·di·ol·o·gist** *n*

neu·ro·sci·ence /nòorō sī ənss/ *n* **1.** a scientific discipline that studies nerve cells or the nervous system, e.g., neuroanatomy or neurophysiology, or all such disciplines collectively **2.** the scientific study of the molecular and cellular levels of the nervous system, of systems within the brain such as vision and hearing, and of behavior produced by the brain —**neu·ro·sci·en·tif·ic** /-sī ən tíffik/ *adj* —**neu·ro·sci·en·tist** *n*

neu·ro·sen·so·ry /nòorō sénssəree/ *adj* relating to the sensory activity of nerve cells or the nervous system —**neu·ro·sen·so·ri·ly** *adv*

neu·ro·sis /noo róssiss/ (*plural* **-ro·ses** /-rō seez/) *n* a mild psychiatric disorder characterized by anxiety, depression, or hypochondria

neu·ro·sur·ger·y /nòorō súrjəree/ *n* surgery on any part of the nervous system, including the brain —**neu·ro·sur·geon** *n* —**neu·ro·sur·gi·cal** *adj*

neu·rot·ic /noo róttik/ *adj* **1.** AFFECTED BY NEUROSIS relating to, involving, affected by, or characteristic of a mild psychiatric disorder characterized by depression, anxiety, or hypochondria **2.** PSYCHIAT OVERANXIOUS OR OBSESSIVE overanxious, oversensitive, or obsessive about everyday things (*often considered offensive*) ■ *n* **1.** SOMEBODY AFFECTED BY NEUROSIS somebody diagnosed as affected by neurosis **2.** SOMEBODY OVERANXIOUS OR OBSESSIVE somebody regarded as overanxious, oversensitive, or obsessive about everyday things (*often considered offensive*) [Mid-17C. < Greek *neuron* "nerve"] —**neu·rot·i·cal·ly** *adv*—**neu·rot·i·cism** /noo rótti sìzzəm/ *n*

neu·ro·tol·o·gy /nòorō tólləjee/ *n* the medical study of the nervous system as it affects the ear and hearing loss —**neu·ro·tol·o·gic** /nòorətə lójjik/ *adj*

neu·rot·o·my /noo róttəmee/ (*plural* **-mies**) *n* a surgical operation to cut a nerve, especially in order to relieve pain

neu·ro·tox·in /nòorō tòksin/ *n* a substance that damages, destroys, or impairs the functioning of nerve tissue —**neu·ro·tox·ic** /nòorō tóksik/ *adj* —**neu·ro·tox·ic·i·ty** /-tok síssətee/ *n*

neu·ro·trans·mit·ter /nòorō transs míttər/ *n* a chemical that carries messages between different nerve cells or between nerve cells and muscles, e.g., to trigger or prevent an impulse in the receiving cell. Excitatory neurotransmitters trigger a nerve impulse in the receiving cell, while inhibitory neurotransmitters act to prevent further transmission of an impulse.

neu·ro·troph·ic /nòorō tróffik, -trṓfik/ *adj* relating to the nutrition and maintenance of tissue of the nervous system —**neu·rot·ro·phy** /noo róttrəfee/ *n*

neu·ro·troph·in /nòorō trṓfin/ *n* a protein in the body that encourages the survival and growth of nerve cells

neu·ro·trop·ic /noo rə tróppik/ *adj* affecting or having an affinity with nerve tissue —**neu·rot·ro·pism** /noo róttrə pìzzəm/ *n*

neu·ro·ves·tib·u·lar /nòorō ve stíbbyələr/ *adj* involving the sensory systems of the inner ear and eye, and the brain's response to input from them, e.g., during space travel

neu·ro·vi·rol·o·gy /nòorō vī rólləjee/ *n* the scientific study of viruses such as HIV that occur in brain cells and of the diseases and mental illnesses caused by them —**neu·ro·vi·ro·log·i·cal** /-vīrə lójjik'l/ *adj*—**neu·ro·vi·rol·o·gist** *n*

neu·ru·la /nòorələ/ (*plural* **-lae** /-lee/ or **-las**) *n* a vertebrate embryo in an early stage, when the nervous system is beginning to develop [Late 19C. < NEURO- + Latin *-ula* "small" after BLASTULA, SCROFULA] —**neu·ru·la·tion** /nòorə láysh'n/ *n*

neus·ton /nóo stòn/ *n* a mass of minute organisms that float or swim on the surface of water [Early 20C. < German < form of Greek *neustos* "swimming" < *nein* "to swim"]

neut. *abbr* **1.** GRAM neuter **2.** neutral

neu·ter /nóotər/ *vt* (**-tered, -ter·ing, -ters**) REMOVE TESTICLES OR OVARIES OF ANIMAL to remove the testicles or ovaries of an animal ■ *adj* **1.** WITHOUT SEX ORGANS having undeveloped, nonfunctioning, or no sexual organs **2.** NOT INDICATING SEX OR OTHER CHARACTERISTICS not indicating the sex of a person, the qualities of a thing, or an attitude toward somebody or something **3.** GRAM GRAMMATICALLY NEITHER MASCULINE NOR FEMININE describes nouns and adjectives in languages such as Latin or German belonging to a separate gender that is neither masculine nor feminine **4.** GRAM INTRANSITIVE describes a verb that is neither active nor passive ■ *n* **1.** VET CASTRATED OR SPAYED ANIMAL an animal that has been castrated or spayed **2.** GRAM GRAMMATICALLY NEUTER WORD a grammatically neuter noun, adjective, or verb **3.** INSECTS INSECT WITH UNDEVELOPED SEXUAL ORGANS an insect with undeveloped sexual organs, e.g., a worker bee **4.** BOT ASEXUAL FLOWER an asexual flower without a stamen or pistil [14C. < Latin < *ne* "not" + *uter* "which of two"]

neu·tral /nóotrəl/ *adj* **1.** TAKING NO SIDES belonging to, favoring, or assisting no side in a war, dispute, contest, or controversy **2.** WITHOUT DISTINCTIVE QUALITIES possessing no distinctive quality or revealing no attitude or feeling ○ *She was careful to explain the problem in neutral terms.* **3.** WITHOUT HUE describes a color such as white, black, or gray that is not in the spectrum **4.** NOT STRONGLY COLORED not strongly or strikingly colored and thus relatively inconspicuous and able to blend easily with other colors **5.** BIOL same as **neuter** *adj* (sense 1) **6.** CHEM NOT ACID OR ALKALINE neither acidic nor alkaline **7.** PHYS WITH ZERO ELECTRIC CHARGE having zero electric charge or potential **8.** MECH ENG WITH NO MOTION TRANSMITTED describes a gear or position in which no power is transmitted from the engine to the moving parts **9.** PHON PRONOUNCED WITH TONGUE MIDWAY describes a vowel articulated with the tongue relaxed and in the mid-central position, as, e.g., in the first syllable of "away" ■ *n* **1.** AUTOMOT GEAR WITH NO MOTION TRANSMITTED a gear in which no power is transmitted from the engine to the moving parts **2.** POL NONALIGNED PERSON OR THING a person or country that remains neutral in a war, dispute, contest, or controversy [15C. < Latin *neutralis* "of neuter gender" < *neuter* (see NEUTER)] —**neu·tral·ly** *adv*

neu·tral cor·ner *n* either of the two corners of a boxing ring that are not used by boxers between rounds. If one boxer is knocked down during a round, the other must go to a neutral corner.

neu·tral ground *n Southern US* a paved or grassy strip of land between two lanes of a highway

neu·tral·ism /nóotrə lìzzəm/ *n* the policy of remaining neutral in wars and other disputes, or support for this policy —**neu·tral·ist** *n, adj* —**neu·tral·is·tic** /nòotrə lístik/ *adj*

neu·tral·i·ty /noo trállətee/ *n* the state of not taking sides, especially in a war or dispute

neu·tral·ize /nóotrə līz/ (**-ized, -iz·ing, -iz·es**) *vt* **1.** RENDER SOMETHING INEFFECTIVE to make something ineffective, especially by removing its ability to act as a threat or obstacle **2.** POL MAKE COUNTRY UNALIGNED to make or declare a country unaligned in a war or dispute **3.** CHEM MAKE SOMETHING NEITHER ACID NOR ALKALINE to render a substance neither acid nor alkaline **4.** PHYS MAKE CHARGE ZERO to make the electric charge or potential of something zero —**neu·tral·i·za·tion** /nòotrəli záysh'n/ *n* —**neu·tral·iz·er** *n*

neu·tral spir·its *n US* alcohol distilled at or above 190 proof. Use: in blending liquors. (*takes a singular or plural verb*)

neu·tral zone *n* in sports, the space between the areas of two competing teams, especially the area between the linemen of football teams or the middle area of a hockey rink between the two blue lines

neu·tri·no /noo treénō/ (*plural* **-nos**) *n* a stable neutral elementary particle of the lepton group with a zero rest mass and no charge. There are three types of neutrinos, associated respectively with the electron, muon, and tau particle, and all have a spin of 1/2. [Mid-20C. < NEUTRAL + Italian *-ino* "small"]

neu·tron /nóo tròn/ *n* a neutral elementary particle of the baryon family with a zero electrical charge and a mass approximately equal to that of a proton [Early 20C. < NEUTRAL] —**neu·tron·ic** /noo trónnik/ *adj*

neu·tron bomb *n* a nuclear bomb designed to kill all life by a heavy bombardment with neutrons, but to cause little blast damage and leave relatively low radioactive contamination

neu·tron star *n* an astronomical object consisting entirely of a very dense compact mass of neutrons, the remnant of a star that has collapsed under its own gravity

neu·tro·phil /nóotrə fil/ *adj* describes cells or tissues that are readily stainable only with chemically neutral dyes, e.g., white blood cells ■ *n also* **neu·tro·phile** /nóotrə fīl/ the most common type of white blood cell in vertebrates, responsible for protecting the body against infection and stainable with neutral dyes [Late 19C. < Latin *neutr-*, stem of *neuter* (see NEUTER)] —**neu·tro·phil·ic** /nòotrə fíllik/ *adj*

Nev. *abbr* Nevada

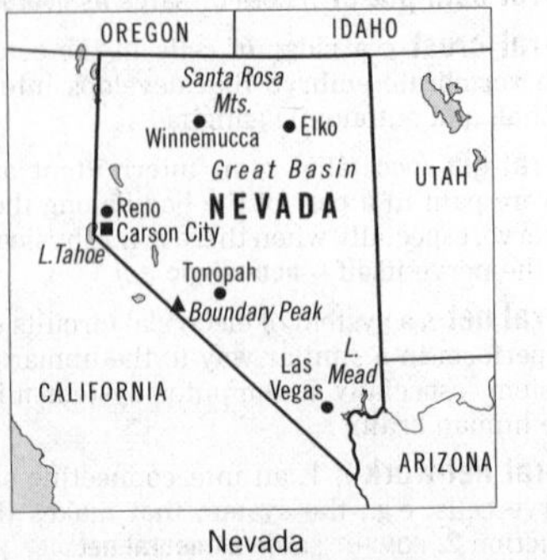

Nevada

Ne·vad·a /nə vádə/ state in the western United States, bordered by Oregon, Idaho, Utah, Arizona, and California. Capital: Carson City. Population: 2,173,491 (2002 estimate). Area: 110,567 sq. mi./286,367 sq. km. See map on previous page —**Ne·vad·an** *n, adj*

né·vé /nay váy/ (*plural* **-vés**) *n* **1.** compacted granular snow, found at the top of a glacier, that has not yet become ice **2.** a field of compacted granular snow at the top of a glacier [Mid-19C. < Swiss French < Latin *nivatus* "snow-cooled" < *niv-* "snow"]

Nev·el·son /névv'lssən/, **Louise** (1900–88) Russian-born US sculptor. She is best known for her "sculptural walls," arrangements of boxes filled with miscellaneous objects.

> "There's no denying...that Beethoven came with music in his soul, Picasso was drawing like an angel in the crib. You're born with it."
> [Louise Nevelson, *Dawns and Dusks*; 1976]

nev·er /névvər/ CORE MEANING: an adverb indicating that something will not happen at any time, or that somebody will definitely not do something ○ *The details will never be known.* ○ *I would never do anything to hurt her.*

1. *adv* **AT NO TIME** at no time in the past or the future ○ *The bird has never been seen in Iceland before. It may never appear there again.* **2.** *adv* **CERTAINLY NOT** not in any circumstances at all ○ *I would never turn my back on them.* **3.** *interj* **EXCLAMATION OF SURPRISE** an exclamation indicating surprise or shock ○ *"He won the election after all." – "Never!"* [Old English, < *ne* "not" + EVER] ◇ **never ever** used as an emphatic expression for "never" (*informal*) ◇ **something will** *or* **would never do** indicates that something is not appropriate or suitable in the circumstances (*informal*) ◇ **well I never** an exclamation of surprise or shock (*informal*) ○ *Well I never! You did it again!*

nev·er-end·ing *adj* continuing on and on and seeming unlikely ever to stop —**nev·er-end·ing·ly** *adv*

nev·er·en·dum /nèvvər éndəm/ *n* (*disapproving*) **1.** POL the holding of repeated referendums on the same subject **2.** a referendum on a subject on which there have been referendums before [< Late 20C. Blend of NEVER-ENDING + REFERENDUM]

nev·er-mar·ried *adj* describes somebody who has never been married

nev·er·more /nèvvər máwr/ *adv* never again or in the future (*literary*)

nev·er-nev·er land *n* an unreal or imaginary place, especially one where wonderful things happen ○ *My opponent's budget proposals spring from the same never-never land as his job proposals.* [< *Never Never Land* in J. M. Barrie's *Peter Pan* (1904)]

nev·er·the·less /nèvvər thə léss/ *adv* despite a situation or comment

Ne·vis /néeviss/ island in St. Kitts and Nevis, in the eastern Caribbean Sea, one of the Leeward Islands. Capital: Charlestown. Population: 10,080 (1989). Area: 36 sq. mi./93 sq. km.

Nev·is, Ben ➧ **Ben Nevis**

ne·vus /néevəss/ (*plural* **-vi** /-vī/) *n* a birthmark, mole, or any other kind of growth or mark on the skin that a person is born with [Mid-19C. < Latin *naevus*]

new /noo/ *adj* **1. RECENTLY MADE** recently made, created, or invented ○ *a new drug* **2. FIRST-HAND** not yet used by anyone else ○ *It's a totally new washing machine* **3. REPLACING EXISTING ONE** replacing or supplementing something of the same kind that already exists ○ *new rules to enhance security* ○ *I'll have a new boss from next week.* **4. RECENTLY DISCOVERED** recently discovered or noticed, though existing before ○ *The new comet will be visible at the beginning of July this year.* **5. WITH RECENTLY ACQUIRED STATUS** having recently acquired a particular status or position ○ *a new mother* ○ *the new medical school graduates* **6. PREVIOUSLY UNFAMILIAR** not seen, known, or experienced by somebody before and thus unfamiliar ○ *The city was completely new to me.* **7. UNUSED TO SOMETHING** unaccustomed to something, e.g., such as a place, job, or situation, through having only recently arrived there or experienced it for the first time ○ *He's not new to this city.* **8. CHANGED** changed, especially for the better ○ *I felt as if I had slept, and had now just awakened – a new woman, with a new mind.* **9.** *also* **New REVIVED OR DIFFERENT** constituting a revived, different, improved, or more advanced form of something, e.g., a political or artistic movement, that already exists or that existed before ○ *the New Left* ○ *the new economy* **10. EARLY** appearing early in the season ○ *new potatoes* [Old English *nēowe* < Indo-European] —**new·ness** *n*

SYNONYMS ***new, novel, innovative, fresh, newfangled, original***

CORE MEANING: never experienced before or having recently come into being

new recently made, created, or invented, or not previously known or encountered ○ *new technologies like DNA-fingerprinting* ○ *over 125,000 species of flora and fauna, many of which were entirely new to science* **novel** new and different, often in an interesting, unusual, or inventive way ○ *The company came up with a novel idea for a faster train.* ○ *The bank has introduced a novel way of detecting credit card crime.* **innovative** new and creative, especially in the way something is done ○ *a program to support flexible, innovative transportation alternatives* **fresh** excitingly or refreshingly different from what has been done or experienced previously ○ *a completely fresh approach* ○ *a fresh start in a different city* **newfangled** puzzlingly or worryingly new or different, especially because it seems gimmicky or overcomplicated ○ *one of those newfangled small cameras that do almost everything for you* ○ *A traditionalist at heart, he is instinctively suspicious of newfangled ideas.* **original** completely new and not copied or derived from something else ○ *Leonardo's highly original method of fresco working* ○ *On examination it is seen that these ideas are not so very original after all.*

NEW *abbr* ECON net economic welfare

New Age *adj* relating to a cultural movement dating from the 1980s that emphasizes spiritual consciousness, and often involves belief in reincarnation and astrology and the practice of meditation, vegetarianism, and holistic medicine ■ *n* a style of instrumental music with simple repetitive melodies, often synthesized or reproducing natural sounds, that is intended to promote mental tranquillity —**New Ag·er** *n*

New Age mu·sic *n* MUSIC same as **New Age**

New A·mer·i·can Bi·ble *n* an English translation of the Bible produced by Roman Catholic scholars in the United States and first published in 1970

New·ark /noo ərk/ **1.** city in northeastern New Jersey. It is the county seat of Essex County, situated 9 mi./14 km west of New York. Population: 277,000 (2002 estimate). **2.** city in Alameda County, western California, east of San Francisco. Population: 43,331 (2002 estimate). **3.** city in northern Delaware, in New Castle County, situated 12 mi./19 km southwest of Wilmington. Population: 29,798 (2002 estimate).

new ar·ri·val *n* **1.** a recently born baby (*informal*) ○ *I hear there's been a new arrival in the family.* **2.** somebody or something that has recently arrived somewhere ○ *She's a new arrival at the company.*

New Aus·tra·lian *n* a recent immigrant to Australia

New Bed·ford /noo-/ city and port in southeastern Massachusetts, on Buzzards Bay, southeast of Taunton. It was a major whaling center during the 1800s. Population: 94,088 (2002 estimate).

New Bern city, port, and administrative seat of Craven County, eastern North Carolina, situated 30 mi./48 km west of Pamlico Sound. Population: 23,098 (2002 estimate).

new·bie /noobee/, **New·bie** *n* somebody who is new to an activity such as using the Internet or playing a computer game

new blood *n* a person or group bringing fresh ideas and enthusiasm to a place, situation, or organization

new·born /noo bàwrn/ *adj* **1. NEWLY BORN** born very recently **2. NEWLY DISCOVERED OR RECOVERED** recently discovered, or recovered afresh ○ *newborn faith* ■ *n* **NEW BABY** a newborn child

New Brit·ain **1.** largest island in Papua New Guinea and in the Bismarck Archipelago. It is divided into the districts of East New Britain and West New Britain. Population: 311,955 (1990). Area: 14,100 sq. mi./36,500 sq. km. **2.** city in Hartford County, central Connecticut. Population: 71,589 (2002 estimate).

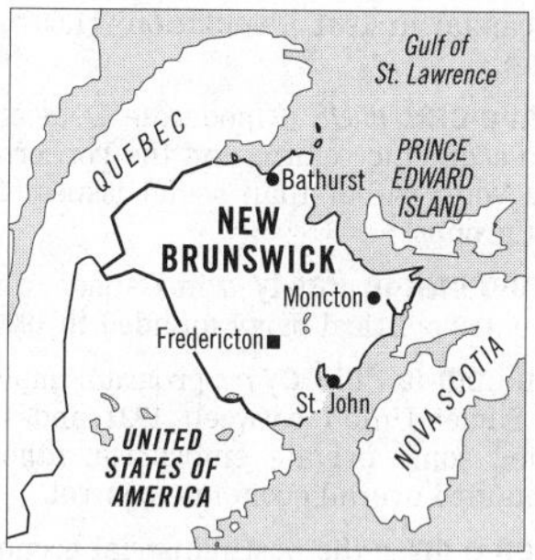

New Brunswick

New Bruns·wick **1.** province in southeastern Canada, bordering the Gulf of St. Lawrence and the Bay of Fundy. Capital: Fredericton. Population: 756,700 (2002). Area: 28,150 sq. mi./72,908 sq. km. **2.** city in central New Jersey. It is the county seat of Middlesex County, situated 9 mi./14 km west of Perth Amboy. Population: 49,397 (2002 estimate).

new build *n* newly built housing, or a newly built housing unit

New·burg /noo bùrg/ *adj* cooked and served with a rich sauce of cream, butter, sherry, and egg yolks ○ *lobster Newburg* [Early 20C. Origin ?]

New·burgh /noobərg/ city in southeastern New York, on the Hudson River, northwest of New York City. Population: 28,740 (2002 estimate).

New·bur·y·port /noobəree pàwrt/ town in northeastern Massachusetts, on the Atlantic coast, directly south of the New Hampshire border and northwest of Gloucester. Population: 17,504 (2002 estimate).

New Cal·e·do·ni·a island and overseas territory of France in the southwestern Pacific Ocean, east of Australia. Capital: Nouméa. Population: 204,863 (2001). Area: 7,376 sq. mi./19,103 sq. km.

New Ca·naan /-káynən/ town in southwestern Connecticut, in southwestern Fairfield County, situated on the New York State border. Population: 19,734 (2002 estimate).

New Car·roll·ton /-kárrəltən/ city in west central Maryland. It is a northeastern suburb of Washington, D.C. Population: 12,983 (2002 estimate).

New·cas·tle /noo kàss'l/ city in eastern New South Wales, southeastern Australia, located at the mouth of the Hunter River. Population: 143,238 (2002 estimate).

New Cas·tle city in western Pennsylvania on the Shenango River. Population: 25,708 (2002 estimate).

New·cas·tle dis·ease /noo kàss'l-/ *n* a highly infectious viral disease that affects poultry and other birds, attacking the lungs and nervous system [Early 20C. After NEWCASTLE UPON TYNE]

New·cas·tle up·on Tyne /-ə pon tīn/ city and port on the Tyne River, northeastern England. It is situated at one end of Hadrian's Wall, and the Romans built a bridge over the river there. Population: 259,536 (2001).

New Com·edy *n* a form of Greek comedy that began near the end of the 4th century and used stock characters and plots from middle-class life

new·com·er /noo kùmmər/ *n* somebody who or something that has recently arrived, appeared, or been introduced

New Coun·try *n* a form of country music, originating in the 1980s, that is influenced by pop music and is designed to appeal to an urban audience

New Crit·i·cism *n* a movement between 1930 and 1970 in the study of literature, especially poetry, that examined its structure, imagery, and ambiguities, rather than its historical setting or the author's intent

New Deal *n* **1.** the policies of social and economic reform introduced in the United States in the 1930s under the presidency of Franklin D. Roosevelt. **2.** the period during which Franklin D. Roosevelt's policies of social and economic reform were implemented. —**New Deal·er** *n*

New Del·hi capital city of India, situated in the National Capital Territory within the city of Delhi. It was built between 1912 and 1929 and inaugurated as the capital in 1931. Population: 11,680,000 (2000 estimate).

New Dem·o·crat *n US* a moderate Democrat dedicated to economic reform and the concerns of the average voter rather than social issues of special interest groups

New Dem·o·crat·ic Par·ty *n* in Canada, a national left-of-center political party founded in 1961

New Ec·o·nom·ic Pol·i·cy *n* a program implemented in the Soviet Union between 1921 and 1928 that permitted some private enterprise although the state retained overall economic control

new e·con·o·my *n* the postindustrial economy considered by some to have emerged in the late 20th century, characterized by global competition, the exploitation of information technology, and the valuing of intangible assets such as ideas and knowledge

newel

new·el /no͞o əl/ *n* **1.** *also* **new·el post** a post supporting the handrail of a staircase at the top or bottom or on a landing **2.** a vertical pillar to which the steps of a spiral staircase are attached [14C. Via French *novel* "knob" < assumed Vulgar Latin *nodellus* "little knot"]

New Eng. *abbr* New England

New Eng·land region of the northeastern United States, comprising the states of Maine, New Hampshire, Vermont, Massachusetts, Rhode Island, and Connecticut —**New Eng·land·er** *n*

New Eng·land Range mountain range in New South Wales, southeastern Australia. Its highest peak is Ben Lomond, 5,100 ft./1,550 m.

New En·glish Bi·ble *n* a version of the Bible in modern English translated by British scholars from various denominations and published in 1970

Newf *n Can* same as **Newfie** (*informal; offensive in some contexts*)

Newf. *abbr* Newfoundland

New Fair·field town in Fairfield County, southwestern Connecticut, situated 20 mi./32 km southwest of Waterbury. Population: 14,149 (2002 estimate).

new·fan·gled /noo fáng g'ld/ *adj* puzzlingly or worryingly new or different, especially because it seems gimmicky or overcomplicated [15C. < past participle of Old English *fōn* "capture"] —**new·fan·gled·ness** *n*

SYNONYMS See *new.*

new-fash·ioned *adj* up-to-date or modern (*informal*) [After OLD-FASHIONED]

New·fie /no͞ofee/, **Newf** /noof, nyoof/ *n Can* somebody who comes from Newfoundland (*informal; offensive in some contexts*) [Mid-20C. Shortening and alteration of *Newfoundland*]

New For·est region of heath, marsh, and forest in Hampshire, southern England. Area: 130 sq. mi./337 sq. km.

new·found /no͞o fòwnd/ *adj* recently discovered or met

New·found·land /no͞ofəndlənd, -lànd/ *n* a large sturdy dog with a long straight back and a dense, usually black coat, belonging to a breed formerly used in water rescues [Early 19C. After the Island of NEWFOUNDLAND]

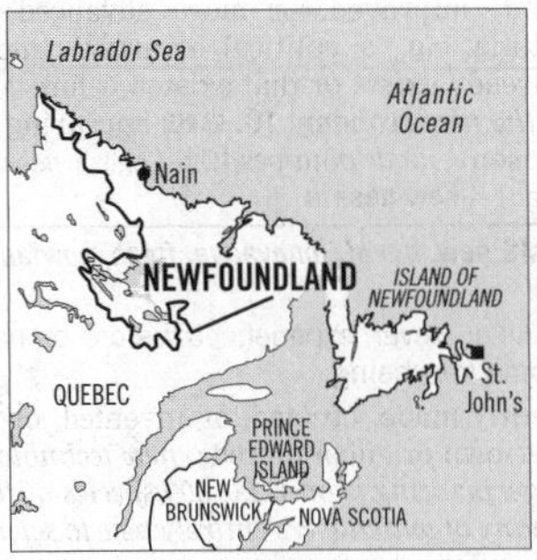

Newfoundland

New·found·land, Is·land of /no͞ofəndlənd, -lànd/ island in the Atlantic Ocean. It is part of the province of Newfoundland and Labrador. Population: 538,099 (1991). Area: 42,031 sq. mi./108,860 sq. km. —**New·found·land·er** *n*

New·found·land and Lab·ra·dor easternmost province in Canada, comprising the Island of Newfoundland and Labrador on the mainland. Capital: St. John's. Population: 531,600 (2002). Area: 156,453 sq. mi./405,212 sq. km.

New·found·land Stan·dard Time, New·found·land Time *n* the standard time in the time zone centered on 52° 30′ W longitude, which includes Newfoundland, Canada. It is three-and-a-half hours behind Universal Time.

New Fron·tier *n* a legislative program introduced during the presidency of John F. Kennedy (1961–63) that comprised economic and social legislation including housing and minimum wage laws and the creation of the Peace Corps.

new games *npl US* forms of play that attempt to minimize stress and anxiety by emphasizing participation, minimal equipment and expense, and cooperation over competition

New Geor·gia island group in the southwestern Pacific Ocean, in the central Solomon Islands, lying northwest of Guadalcanal. Area: 500 sq. mi./1,300 sq. km.

New Gra·na·da former Spanish colony in northwestern South America that included present-day Colombia, Ecuador, Venezuela, and Panama

new·ground /no͞o grównd/ *n S Atlantic US* land that has been recently cleared and prepared for the cultivation of crops

REGIONAL NOTE Also called *new land,* the term *newground* is mainly found in the Central and South Atlantic and the Gulf states, with scattered instances of usage to the north and west.

New Guin·ea second largest island in the world, in the western Pacific Ocean, off the northern coast of Australia. It is divided between the Indonesian province of Irian Jaya in the west and Papua New Guinea in the east. Population: about 5,300,000 (1995). Area: 312,170 sq. mi./808,510 sq. km. —**New Guin·e·an** *n, adj*

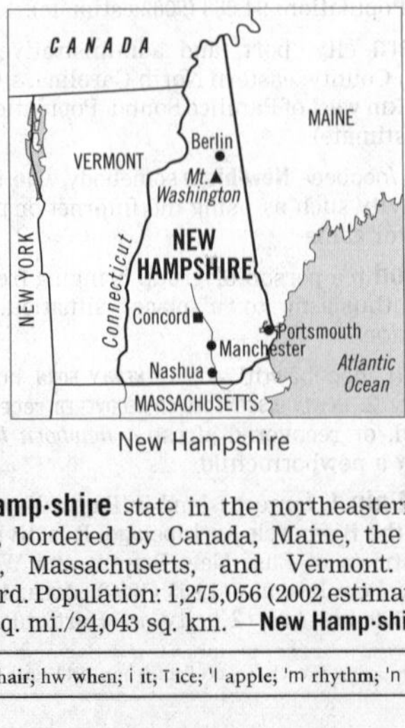

New Hampshire

New Hamp·shire state in the northeastern United States, bordered by Canada, Maine, the Atlantic Ocean, Massachusetts, and Vermont. Capital: Concord. Population: 1,275,056 (2002 estimate). Area: 9,283 sq. mi./24,043 sq. km. —**New Hamp·shir·ite** *n*

New Har·mo·ny village in Posey County, southwestern Indiana, situated 23 mi./37 km northwest of Evansville. The Harmony Society and Robert Owen both established utopian communities there in the 19th century. Population: 905 (2002 estimate).

New Ha·ven city in New Haven County, southern Connecticut, situated 36 mi./58 km southwest of Hartford. It is the home of Yale University, founded in 1701. Population: 124,176 (2002 estimate).

New Heb·ri·des former name for **Vanuatu** (until 1980)

new ho·ri·zons *npl* new and promising prospects that seem to be opening up for somebody or something

New I·be·ri·a city in southern Louisiana, southwest of Baton Rouge and southeast of Lafayette. Population: 32,506 (2002 estimate).

Ne Win /này wín/ (1911–2002) Burmese national leader. Dictator (1962–74) and president (1974–81) of Burma (now Myanmar), he nationalized the economy and suppressed dissent. Born **Maung Shu Maung**

New Ire·land island in the Bismarck Archipelago, northeastern Papua New Guinea, in the southwestern Pacific Ocean. Population: 15,743 (1990). Area: 3,340 sq. mi./8,650 sq. km.

New Jersey

New Jer·sey state on the eastern coast of the United States, bordered by New York, the Atlantic Ocean, Delaware, and Pennsylvania. Capital: Trenton. Population: 8,590,300 (2002 estimate). Area: 8,215 sq. mi./21,277 sq. km. —**New Jer·sey·an** *n, adj* —**New Jer·sey·ite** *n*

New Jour·nal·ism *n US* a style of journalism originating in the United States in the 1960s that emphasizes the subjective impressions of the reporter and uses techniques typically found in fiction writing

New King·dom *n* a period in the history of ancient Egypt, from the 18th to the 20th dynasty (approximately 1580 to 1090 B.C.)

New Lat·in *n* the form of the Latin language used since about the beginning of the 16th century, especially for scientific and taxonomic classification —**New Lat·in** *adj*

New Left *n* a political movement, chiefly among students and intellectuals in the United States and Europe during the 1960s and 1970s, that sought radical social and economic change —**New Left·ist** *n*

New Lon·don seaport in New London County, southeastern Connecticut, situated on Long Island Sound, 43 mi./69 km east of New Haven. It is home to the US Coast Guard Academy. Population: 26,068 (2002 estimate).

new look *n* a radical change in appearance, design, or style —**new-look** *adj*

New Look *n* a style in women's clothes introduced in 1947 by the designer Christian Dior that featured broad shoulders, narrow waists, and long full skirts

new·ly /no͞olee/ *adv* **1.** LATELY recently or lately **2.** AGAIN again or once more **3.** DIFFERENTLY in a different or novel way

new·ly·wed /no͞olee wèd/ *n* somebody who has recently been married —**new·ly·wed** *adj*

New·man /no͞omən/, **Barnett** (1905–70) US painter. His abstract expressionist works feature a color field broken by one or more vertical lines.

New·man, John Henry, Cardinal (1801–90) British theologian. After converting in 1845, he became the leading British Roman Catholic and was made a cardinal in 1879.

"It is as absurd to argue men, as to torture them, into believing."
[John Henry Newman, "The Usurpations of Reason (1831)," *Oxford University Sermons*; 1843]

New·man, Paul (*b.* 1925) US stage and movie actor. A popular leading man, he won an Academy Award for *The Color of Money* (1986).

"The second you step out of the confines of the personality the public has set up for you, they get incensed. Public reaction tends to keep actors as personalities instead of allowing them to act. It's a very corrupting influence."
[Paul Newman, *Photoplay*; 1977]

New Man *n* modern man characterized by emotional sensitivity, recognition of women as equals, and a desire to share in domestic chores and the work associated with child rearing

New·mar·ket[1] /nóo maárkət/ *n* **1.** a long double-breasted close-fitting jacket with a full skirt worn in the 19th century as a riding coat or overcoat **2.** *UK* same as **Michigan**[2] [Late 17C. After NEWMARKET[2]]

New·mar·ket[2] /nóo maárkət/ market town in Suffolk, England, famous for its horseracing since the early 1600s. Population: 16,498 (1991).

new math *n* a method of teaching mathematics, devised in the 1960s, in which children are introduced to elementary set theory at an early stage

New Mexico

New Mex·i·co state in the southwestern United States, bordered by Colorado, Oklahoma, Texas, Mexico, and Arizona. Capital: Santa Fe. Population: 1,855,059 (2002 estimate). Area: 121,598 sq. mi./314,937 sq. km. —**New Mex·i·can** *n, adj*

New Mil·ford town in Litchfield County, northwestern Connecticut. Population: 27,959 (2002 estimate).

new mon·ey *n* recently acquired wealth, or people who have it ○ *It's largely new money that's buying this kind of property these days.*

new moon *n* **1.** MOON AS NARROW CRESCENT the Moon at the beginning of its cycle, when it is invisible from Earth or when only a narrow crescent on the right-hand side of its surface as seen from Earth is visible **2.** PERIOD OF NEW MOON the period during which there is a new moon **3.** PHASE OF MOON one of the four phases of the Moon, during which it is directly between Earth and the Sun and invisible or seen only as a narrow crescent

New Neth·er·land /-néthərlənd/ Dutch colony in North America between 1613 and 1664, when it was conquered by the English and divided into the states of New York and New Jersey

New Nor·we·gian *n* LANG same as **Nynorsk** —**New Nor·we·gian** *adj*

New Or·leans /-áwrlee ənz, -áwrlinz/ city in southeastern Louisiana, on the eastern bank of the Mississippi River. The largest city in the state, it is known for its annual Mardi Gras festival. Population: 473,681 (2002 estimate). —**New Or·lea·ni·an** /-awr leé nee ən/ *n*

New·port /nóo pàwrt/ **1.** city on the Usk River in southeastern Wales. Population: 137,011 (2001). **2.** city in northern Kentucky, on the Ohio River, that borders Ohio, east of Covington. It is a southern suburb of Cincinnati. Population: 16,560 (2002 estimate). **3.** city in southeastern Rhode Island, on Rhode Island itself, connected to the mainland by bridges. Population: 26,312 (2002 estimate).

New·port Beach city in Orange County, southwestern California, situated on the Pacific coast, 18 mi./29 km southeast of Long Beach. Population: 78,096 (2002 estimate).

New·port News /nòo pawrt nóoz/ city at the mouth of the James River in southeastern Virginia. It is home to one of the world's largest shipyards. Population: 180,272 (2002 estimate).

New Port Rich·ey /-ríchee/ city in Pasco County, central Florida, situated 20 mi./32 km northwest of Tampa. Population: 16,465 (2002 estimate).

New Right *n* a conservative political movement that arose during the late 1960s and affirmed a commitment to established religion, patriotism, and smaller less interventionist government

New Riv·er river in the southeastern United States that flows from North Carolina into West Virginia to form the Great Kanawha River. Length: 320 mi./515 km.

New Ro·chelle /-ro shél/ city in southeastern New York, on Long Island Sound. It is a northeastern suburb of New York City. Population: 72,472 (2002 estimate).

news /nooz/ *n* **1.** RECENT INFORMATION information about recent events or developments ○ *I phoned the hospital, and the news is good.* **2.** CURRENT EVENTS information about current events printed in newspapers or broadcast by the media ○ *She has been in the news a lot lately.* **3.** PROGRAM a radio or television broadcast presenting the important events or developments that have taken place ○ *I heard about it on the news.* **4.** SOMEBODY OR SOMETHING INTERESTING somebody or something considered as being of interest to people in general **5.** SOMETHING PREVIOUSLY UNKNOWN something previously unknown to somebody that he or she is surprised to hear about ○ *Their divorce was news to me.* [15C. Plural of NEW]

news a·gen·cy *n* an organization that gathers information about current events and supplies it to the media

news·a·gent /nóoz àyjənt/ *n UK* same as **newsdealer**

news·boy /nóoz bòy/ *n* a boy who sells newspapers in the street or delivers them to houses

news·cast /nóoz kàst/ *n* a television or radio broadcast consisting of news

news·cast·er /nóoz kàstər/ *n* somebody who reads or presents the news on a television or radio broadcast

news con·fer·ence *n* MEDIA same as **press conference**

news·deal·er /nóoz deèlər/ *n US* somebody who keeps a store or stall selling mainly newspapers, magazines, and often paperback books and candy

news desk *n* an area of a newspaper office or a radio or television studio where news is prepared for publication or broadcasting

news flash *n* a brief item of urgent news, often broadcast at short notice interrupting a scheduled program

news·gath·er·ing /nóoz gàthəring/ *n* the collecting of news for possible use in a newspaper, news magazine, or broadcast —**news·gath·er·er** *n*

news·girl /nóoz gùrl/ *n* a girl who sells newspapers in the street or delivers them to houses

news·group /nóoz gròop/ *n* a discussion group maintained on a computer network such as the Internet in which people leave messages on topics of mutual interest for other participants to read

news·hound /nóoz hòwnd/ *n* a journalist, especially one who covers news in an aggressive way (*informal*)

New Si·be·ri·an Is·lands uninhabited island group in northeastern Russia, lying in the Arctic Ocean between the Laptev Sea and the East Siberian Sea. Area: 14,672 sq. mi./38,000 sq. km.

news·let·ter /nóoz lèttər/ *n* a printed report or letter that contains news of interest to a specific group, e.g., the members of a society or employees of an organization, and is circulated to them periodically

news mag·a·zine *n* **1.** a magazine, usually published weekly, containing news and news analysis from the preceding week **2.** a weekly radio or television program of interviews, investigative reportage, features, and commentary on the news

news·mak·er /nóoz màykər/ *n* somebody whose activities are considered interesting enough to qualify as news for the general public

news·man /nóozmən, -màn/ (*plural* **-men** /-mən, -mèn/) *n* a male journalist or broadcaster who reports news

news·mon·ger /nóoz mùng gər, -mòng-/ *n* somebody who gathers and spreads gossip —**news·mon·ger·ing** *n*

New South Wales state in southeastern Australia. Capital: Sydney. Population: 6,686,600 (2003). Area: 309,500 sq. mi./801,600 sq. km.

news·pa·per /nóoz pàypər, nóoss-/ *n* **1.** PRINTED ACCOUNT OF NEWS a publication containing news and comment on current events, together with features and advertisements, that usually appears daily or weekly and is printed on large sheets of paper that are folded together **2.** ORGANIZATION an organization that produces a newspaper **3.** PAPER FROM NEWSPAPER a sheet or sheets of a newspaper when used for a purpose other than reading ○ *wrapped in newspaper*

news·pa·per·man /nóoz paypər màn, nóoss-/ (*plural* **-men** /-mèn/) *n* **1.** a man who writes or edits for a newspaper **2.** a man who owns or publishes a newspaper

news·pa·per·per·son /nóoz paypər pùrss'n, nóoss-/ (*plural* **-peo·ple** /-peèp'l/ or **-per·sons**) *n* **1.** somebody who writes or edits for a newspaper **2.** somebody who owns or publishes a newspaper

news·pa·per·wom·an /nóoz paypər wòommən, nóoss-/ (*plural* **-wom·en** /-wìmmin/) *n* **1.** a woman who writes or edits for a newspaper **2.** a woman who owns or publishes a newspaper

new·speak /nóo speèk/ *n* language that is ambiguous and designed to conceal the truth, especially that sometimes used by bureaucrats and propagandists [After the language of propaganda in *Nineteen Eighty-Four*, by George ORWELL, 1949]

news·per·son /nóoz pùrss'n/ (*plural* **-per·sons** or **-peo·ple** /-peèp'l/) *n US* a journalist or broadcaster who reports news

news·print /nóoz prìnt/ *n* a relatively cheap and low-quality paper made from recycled materials or wood pulp and used for printing newspapers

news·read·er /nóoz reèdər/ *n* a computer program that allows somebody to read and post messages to Internet newsgroups

news·reel /nóoz reèl/ *n* a short film about recent news events, formerly shown before a feature film

news re·lease *n* MEDIA same as **press release**

news·room /nóoz ròom, -ròom/ *n* a room in a radio or television studio or newspaper office where news is prepared for publication or broadcasting

news ser·vice *n* MEDIA same as **news agency**

news·stand /nóoz stànd/ *n* a stall or booth where newspapers and magazines are sold

New Style *n* the reckoning of dates by the Gregorian calendar

news·ven·dor /nóoz vèndər/ *n Can, UK* a seller of newspapers

news·week·ly /nóoz weèklee/ (*plural* **-lies**) *n* a weekly newspaper or news magazine

news·wire /nóoz wìr/ *n* an Internet service providing the latest information on current events

news·wom·an /nóoz wòommən/ (*plural* **-wom·en** /-wìmmin/) *n* a female journalist or broadcaster who reports news

news·wor·thy /nóoz wùrthee/ (**-thi·er, -thi·est**) *adj* interesting or important enough to be reported in the media —**news·wor·thi·ly** *adv* —**news·wor·thi·ness** *n*

news·writ·ing /nóoz rìting/ *n* the craft of writing news stories —**news·writ·er** *n*

news·y /nóozee/ (**-i·er, -i·est**) *adj* filled with news and gossip ○ *a newsy letter* —**news·i·ness** *n*

> **WORLD ENGLISH** ***New York English*** is the variety of English used in New York City, whose idiom has been influenced by waves of immigration, especially from Central Europe (notably Jewish and Italian immigrants) and from Latin America (notably Puerto Rican immigrants). Local pronunciation on the whole does not pronounce *r* in words such as *art, door,* and *worker*. There is a distinctive "o"-sound in words such as *coffee* ("kawfee") and *ought* ("awt"). Although "broad New York" tends to have low prestige in the United States (including among its own speakers), its everyday usage has had a marked influence nationwide and abroad, notably in Yiddish-derived words like *bagel, chutzpah, klutz, maven, s(c)hmaltz,* and *s(c)hlock,* and the humorously or ironically dismissive repeated element *s(c)h-* as in "fancy-s(c)hmancy" (too fancy to be acceptable). New York English is also called New Yorkese.

newt

newt /noot/ *n* a small amphibian of the salamander family with short legs and a well-developed tail. Family: Salamandridae. [15C. < mistaken division of *an ewte, ewte* being a form of EFT]

New Ter·ri·to·ries /-térrə tàwreez/ area of Hong Kong situated mostly on the Chinese mainland north of Kowloon that was leased to Great Britain by China from 1898 to 1997. Area: 365 sq. mi./950 sq. km.

New Tes·ta·ment *n* the second section of the Christian Bible dealing with the life and teachings of Jesus Christ, containing the Gospels, the Acts of the Apostles, the Epistles, and the Book of Revelations

new·ton /nóot'n/ *n* an SI unit of force equivalent to the force that produces an acceleration of one meter per second per second on a mass of one kilogram. Symbol **N** [Early 20C. After Sir Isaac NEWTON]

New·ton /nóot'n/ city in eastern Massachusetts, composed of 14 villages, west of Boston and east of Marlborough. Population: 83,880 (2002 estimate).

New·ton, Sir Isaac (1642–1727) English scientist. He discovered gravitation, invented calculus, and formulated the laws of motion. He recognized that white light is a mixture of colored lights, and wrote *Mathematical Principles of Natural Philosophy* (1687) and *Opticks* (1704). —**New·to·ni·an** /noo tṓnee ən/ *adj*

> "If I have seen further it is by standing on the shoulders of giants."
> [Sir Isaac Newton, *Letter to Robert Hooke*; February 5, 1676]

New·to·ni·an tel·e·scope *n* a reflecting telescope in which mirrors transfer an image to an eyepiece in the side of the telescope's body

New·ton's cra·dle *n* a toy consisting of five metal balls hanging side by side in a frame. Swinging the ball at one end transmits force along the line so that the ball at the other end swings away. [After Sir Isaac NEWTON]

New·ton's rings *n* a pattern of light interference created by the contact of a convex lens with a glass plate, appearing as a series of alternating bright and dark rings [After Sir Isaac NEWTON]

new town *n* a complete self-contained town with all the usual facilities, created on an open site, usually to accommodate excess population from existing urban areas

New·town /nóo tòwn/ town in Fairfield County, Connecticut. Population: 1,849 (2002 estimate).

new var·i·ant CJD *n* MED same as **variant CJD**

new vaude·ville *n US* a form of variety entertainment performed on the street or in a theater by jugglers, magicians, acrobats, clowns, comedians, and similar artists

new wave *n* **1. POST-PUNK ROCK MUSIC** rock music made in the late 1970s after the punk rock era **2. FORM OF FRENCH MOVIEMAKING** a form of filmmaking originating in France during the 1950s that emphasized spontaneity, unconventionality, and the individual styles of directors **3. INNOVATIVE ARTS MOVEMENT** any new and innovative movement in the arts

New West·min·ster city in southwestern British Columbia, western Canada, situated on the Fraser River, 12 mi./18 km southeast of Vancouver. Population: 54,656 (2002).

New World *n* North and South America as considered by Europeans following Columbus's discovery of the Americas

new year *n* the year following the current year, especially the early part of it ○ *We hoped that things would be better in the new year.*

New Year *n* the first day or first few days of a calendar year

New Year's Day *n* the first day of the year in the Gregorian calendar, widely celebrated as a public holiday. Date: January 1.

New Year's Eve *n* the last day of the year in the Gregorian calendar, or the evening of that day. Date: December 31.

New Year's res·o·lu·tion *n* a decision to do or stop doing something, made or announced at the New Year, which is traditionally considered a time for a fresh start

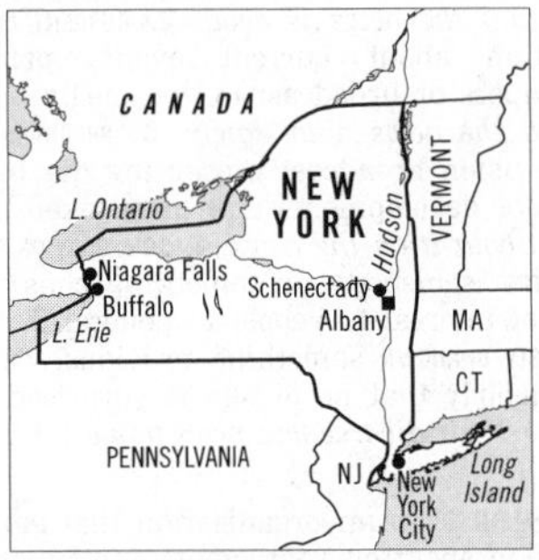

New York

New York 1. *also* **New York City** city and major port in southeastern New York State, at the mouth of the Hudson River. It is the most populous city in the United States. It comprises Manhattan, the Bronx, Brooklyn, Queens, and Staten Island boroughs. Population: 8,084,316 (2002 estimate). **2.** state in the northeastern United States, bordering Pennsylvania, the Atlantic Ocean, New Jersey, Canada, Vermont, Massachusetts, Connecticut, Lake Erie, and Lake Ontario. Capital: Albany. Population: 19,157,532 (2002 estimate). Area: 53,989 sq. mi./139,831 sq. km. —**New York·er** *n*

New York Bay inlet of the Atlantic Ocean lying at the mouth of the Hudson River at New York City

New York Eng·lish *n* a variety of English spoken in New York City

New York·ese /-yawr kéez, -kéess/ *n* same as **New York English** (*informal*)

new za·ïre *n* MONEY same as **zaïre**

New Zea·land /-zéelənd/ country in the southwestern Pacific Ocean, southeast of Australia, comprising two large islands, the North Island and the South Island, and numerous smaller islands. Its Maori name is Aotearoa, meaning "Land of the Long White Cloud." It became an independent member of the British Commonwealth in 1931. Language: English. Currency: New Zealand dollar. Capital: Wellington. Population: 3,951,307 (2003). Area: 104,454 sq. mi./270,534 sq. km. Maori name **Aotearoa** —**New Zea·land·er** *n*

New Zea·land Eng·lish *n* a variety of English spoken in New Zealand. See panel on next page

New Zild /noo zíld/ *n* same as **New Zealand English** (*informal humorous*)

NEX *abbr US* NAVY Navy exchange

next /nekst/ CORE MEANING: a grammatical word indicating that something follows something else in a series or is immediately beside it ○ (adj) *He lives next door to me.* ○ (adj) *When I returned, my next patient was waiting.* ○ (adv) *Which patient do you want to see next?*

1. *adj, adv* **IMMEDIATELY FOLLOWING** following immediately after the present or previous one ○ (adj) *Our next meeting is on April 2nd.* ○ (adv) *Are you wondering what to do next?* **2.** *adj* **FOLLOWING THIS ONE** used to describe the day, month, or year following this one ○ *The case is scheduled for trial next month.* ○ *There is no way of predicting whether this might happen next year or in 300 years.* **3.** *adj* **ADJOINING** immediately beside or nearest to something ○ *He's in the next room.* **4.** *adj* **CLOSEST IN DEGREE** closest to something in degree ○ *It's 40 times heavier than the next heaviest quark.* **5.** *adj Malaysia, Singapore* **SECOND** following the next one ○ *Take the next left turn, not the first.* [Old English *nēhsta* "most near" < Germanic, "near"] ◇ **next to 1.** adjacent to or beside something or somebody ○ *Come and sit next to me.* **2.** closest to, in comparison with something else ○ *Cleanliness, he said, was next to godliness.* **3.** almost, but not completely (*used in negative statements*) ○ *I have spent many days trying to figure out a good alternative, and it's next to impossible.* ◇ **the next best thing** the option to be preferred if a first choice is not available ○ *For healthier eating the next best thing to chocolate is carob.*

next door *adv* **1. IN NEXT HOUSE OR ROOM** in or into the house or room next to the one somebody is in ○ *Go next door and see if their phone's working.* **2. VERY CLOSE** a very short distance away ■ *adj* **IMMEDIATELY ADJACENT** situated immediately beside or very close to the one somebody is in or at, or living in the adjoining house or apartment (*hyphenated when used before a noun*) ◇ **next door to** *UK* virtually the same thing as

next friend *n* in law, somebody who acts for somebody who is not legally allowed to act independently, e.g., a child

next of kin *n* somebody's nearest relative or relatives (*takes a singular or plural verb*)

nex·us /néksəss/ (*plural same* or **-us·es**) *n* **1. CONNECTION** a connection or link associating two or more people or things **2. CONNECTED GROUP** a group or series of connected people or things **3. CENTER** the center or focus of something **4.** BIOL **SPECIALIZED PART OF CELL MEMBRANE** a specialized area of the cellular membrane that helps cells to communicate or adhere [Mid-17C. < Latin *nex-*, past participle of *nectere* "bind"]

Nez Per·cé /nèz púrss, nèss-, -pur sáy/ (*plural same* or **Nez Per·cés**), **Nez Per·ce** /nèz púrss, nèss-/ (*plural same* or **Nez Per·ces**) *n* **1.** a member of a Native North American people who lived along the Snake River, and who now live mainly in western Idaho and northeastern Washington **2.** the Sahaptin-Chinook language of the Nez Percé. Native speakers: 5,000. [Early 19C. < French, "pierced nose"] —**Nez Per·cé** *adj*

nf *abbr* Norfolk Island (*used in Internet addresses*) See table at **domain name**

NF *abbr* **1.** GEOG Newfoundland **2.** *also* **N/F** BANKING no funds **3.** LANG Norman French

n/f *abbr* BANKING no funds

NFC *abbr US* FOOTBALL National Football Conference

Nfd. *abbr* Newfoundland

NFFE *abbr US* HR National Federation of Federal Employees

NFL *abbr US* FOOTBALL National Football League

Nfld. *abbr* Newfoundland

NFS *abbr* **1.** COMPUT network file service **2.** COMPUT network file system **3.** not for sale

NFT *abbr* TIME Newfoundland Time

ng *abbr* **1.** MEASURE nanogram **2.** Nigeria (*used in Internet addresses*) See table at **domain name**

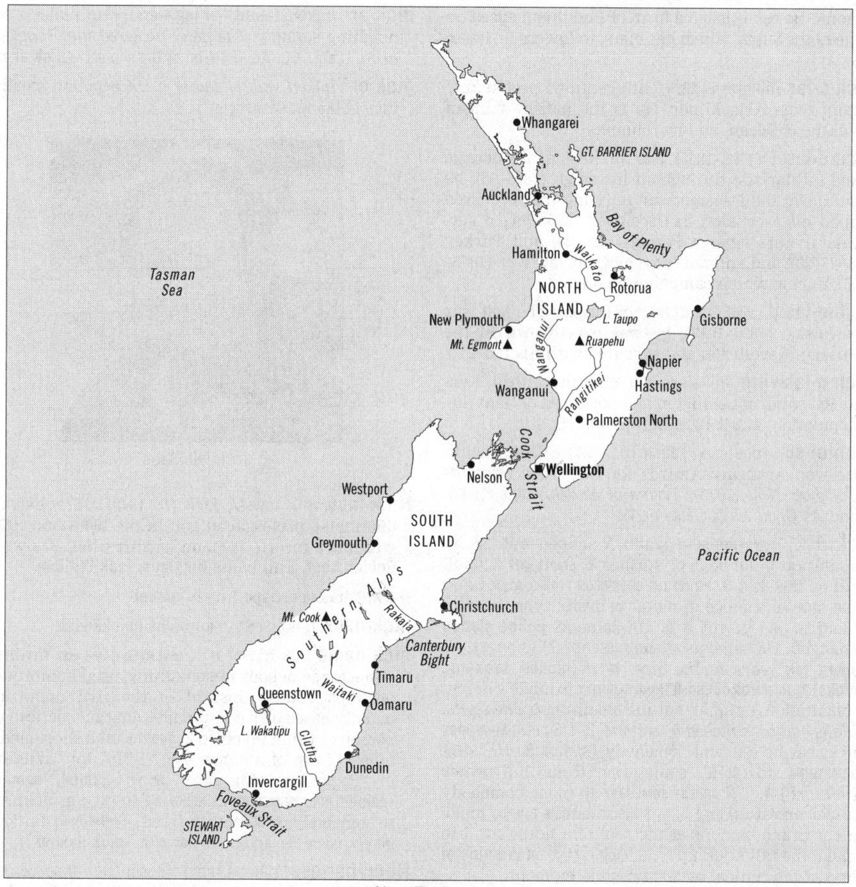

New Zealand

WORLD ENGLISH ***New Zealand English*** is the variety of English that has been used in New Zealand for over 200 years. It has much in common with Australian English, but differs from it in coexisting with, and influencing and being influenced by, Maori and other Polynesian languages. There are three varieties of pronunciation: (1) Cultivated New Zealand, similar to Received Pronunciation in the United Kingdom; (2) Broad New Zealand, with low prestige; (3) General New Zealand, occupying the social middle ground. In New Zealand English, on the whole, *r* is not pronounced in words such as *art, door,* and *worker.* Distinctive pronunciations include the vowels in words such as *ham* and *pen*, and a short *i* in "fish," these being heard by outsiders as "hem," "pin," and fush, respectively. In addition, final *y*, as in *city* and *tidy,* may be lengthened, becoming "citee" and "tidee." There is little distinctiveness in grammar, but New Zealand English vocabulary has two special features, the first being adoptions from Maori, e.g., *Pakeha* (a European, also a common name for white New Zealanders generally), *haere mai* (a term of greeting), *hongi* (to press noses, the Maori greeting), *kiwi* (a flightless bird unique to New Zealand and by extension a New Zealander), and *rahui* (a sign warning against trespassing). The second major vocabulary feature involves words shared with and borrowed from Australia, e.g., *larrikin* for *hooligan, ocker* for *boor, shanghai* for *catapult,* and *truckie* for *truck driver.* See ***Australian English.***

N.G. *abbr US* MIL National Guard

n'ga·na *n* VET another spelling of **nagana**

NGO *abbr* nongovernmental organization

Ngo Dinh Di·em /ang gō din dee ém, -dyém/ (1901–63) president of South Vietnam (1955–63). During his presidency, Communist insurgence from North Vietnam became frequent and disruptive. He was assassinated in a coup.

n·go·ma /ang gṓmə/ *n E Africa* **1.** a traditional African drum **2.** a social gathering for dancing [Early 20C. < Kiswahili, "dance, music"]

Ngo·ni /ang gṓnee/ (*plural same* or **-nis**) *n* **1.** a member of a people of eastern Africa, now mostly living in Malawi **2.** the language of the Ngoni, a dialect of Zulu or Swazi **3.** PEOPLES, LANG same as **Nguni** [Late 19C. < Bantu] —**Ngo·ni** *adj*

ngul·trum /ang go͝oltrəm, -go͝ol-/ *n* the main unit of currency in Bhutan. See table at **currency** [Late 20C. < Tibetan]

Ngu·ni /ang go͞onee/ (*plural same* or **-nis**) *n* a member of a group of Bantu-speaking peoples living in southern Africa that includes the Zulu, Swazi, Xhosa, and Ndebele [Early 20C. < Zulu] —**Ngu·ni** *adj*

ngwee /ang gwáy, -gwée/ (*plural same*) *n* a subunit of Zambian currency. See table at **currency** [Mid-20C. < Bantu]

NH *abbr* New Hampshire

NHL *abbr* HOCKEY National Hockey League

ni *abbr* Nicaragua (*used in Internet addresses*) See table at **domain name**

Ni *symbol* CHEM ELEM nickel

NI *abbr* Northern Ireland

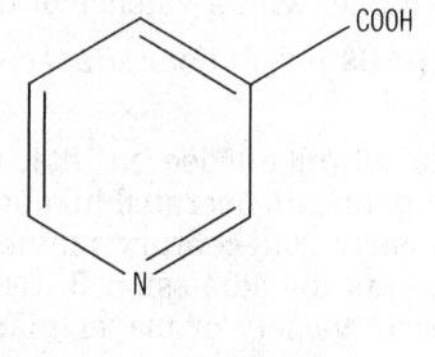

niacin

ni·a·cin /nī əssin/ *n* a B complex vitamin found in meat and dairy products. Deficiency of niacin causes pellagra. Formula: $C_6H_5NO_2$. [Mid-20C. < NICOTINE + ACID]

ni·a·cin·a·mide /nī ə sínnə mīd/ *n* a B complex vitamin that is an amide of niacin

Ni·ag·a·ra /nī ággrə, nī ággərə/ river in northeastern North America, in New York and Ontario, flowing between Lake Erie and Lake Ontario via Niagara Falls. Length: 35 mi./56 km.

Niagara Falls

Ni·ag·a·ra Falls **1.** waterfall in the Niagara River, divided by Goat Island into American Falls and Horseshoe, or Canadian, Falls. Height: 182–187 ft./ 55–57 m. **2.** city in Welland County, southeastern Ontario, Canada, situated on the Niagara River, directly below the falls. Population: 78,815 (2001). **3.** city in western New York, on Niagara Falls. Population: 54,358 (2002 estimate).

Nia·mey /nyaa máy/ capital city of Niger, situated on the Niger River in the southwestern part of the country. Population: 587,000 (1995).

Ni·ar·chos /nee áarkōss/, **Stavros** (1909–96) Greek shipowner. He was a pioneer in the construction of supertankers and the owner of a large independent fleet. Full name **Niarchos, Stavros Spyros**

~~**niave**~~ incorrect spelling of **naive**

nib /nib/ *n* **1.** a shaped detachable metal tip on the end of a pen such as a fountain pen, by means of which the ink is transferred to the paper **2.** a sharp point or tip, especially the sharpened end of a quill pen **3.** BIRDS same as **beak** (sense 1) [Late 16C. Variant of NEB]

nib·ble /nibb'l/ *v* (**-bled, -bling, -bles**) **1.** *vti* TAKE SMALL QUICK BITES to take a series of small quick bites at something, or eat something in a series of small quick bites ○ *She nibbled an apple while she read.* **2.** *vti* BITE PLAYFULLY AND CARESSINGLY to take gentle playful little bites at part of somebody's body as a form of caress ○ *The lion cubs nibbled at each other playfully.* **3.** *vi* REDUCE GRADUALLY to reduce or wear away something gradually by taking a small amount at a time ○ *These day-to-day expenses nibble away at our money.* **4.** *vi* SHOW MILD INTEREST to show a tentative interest in something ○ *Lower the price a little and the buyers will start to nibble.* ■ *n* **1.** ACT OF NIBBLING a series of small quick or gentle bites at something **2.** TINY AMOUNT OF FOOD a tiny amount of some type of food (*informal*) **3.** EXPRESSION OF MILD INTEREST an expression of tentative interest ○ *I've been trying to make a sale all day but not a nibble so far.* [Early 16C. Origin ?] —**nib·bler** *n*

Ni·be·lung /néebə lo͝ong/ (*plural* **-lungs** or **-lung·en** /-lo͝ongən/) *n* in medieval German mythology, a member of a race of dwarfs who owned a hoard of treasure that was captured by the heroic prince Siegfried [Mid-19C. < German]

nib·lick /níbblik/ *n* an obsolete golf club, similar to a modern nine-iron, having a short iron head with a steeply sloping face, used to give extra lift, e.g., when playing out of a sand trap [Mid-19C. Origin ?]

nibs /nibz/ *n* used as a mock title when referring to an important or self-important person (*informal*) ○ *His nibs will doubtless be expecting the red carpet treatment.* [Early 19C. Origin ?]

Nic. *abbr* **1.** Nicaragua **2.** COMPUT Network Interface Card

ni·cad /nī kàd/, **ni·cad bat·ter·y** *n* a dry cell battery with electrodes of nickel and cadmium in an alkaline electrolyte [Mid-20C. < NICKEL + CADMIUM]

Ni·cae·a /nī sée ə/ ancient Byzantine city of Asia Minor, on the site of present-day Iznik, northwestern Turkey. It flourished under the Romans.

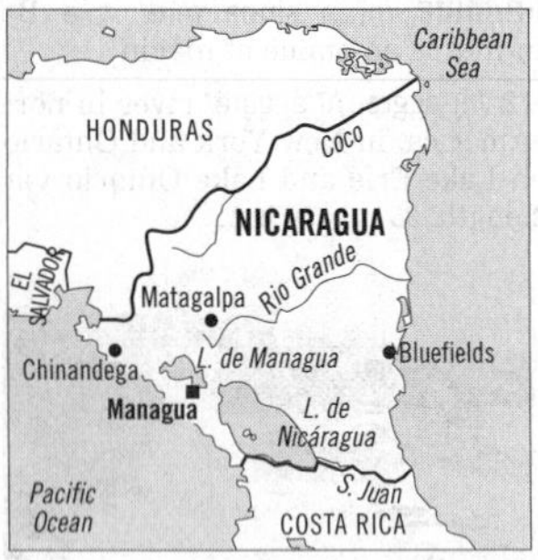

Nicaragua

Nic·a·ra·gua /nìkə raágwə/ largest country in Central America, situated between the North Pacific Ocean and the Caribbean Sea. Capital: Managua. Population: 5,128,517 (2003). Area: 49,998 sq. mi./129,494 sq. km. Official name **Republic of Nicaragua** —**Nic·a·ra·guan** *n, adj*

nic·co·lite /níkə lìt/ *n* a nickel arsenide mineral. Use: source of nickel. [Mid-19C. < modern Latin *niccolum* "nickel"]

nice /nīss/ (**nic·er, nic·est**) *adj* **1. PLEASANT** pleasant or enjoyable **2. KIND** kind, or showing courtesy, friendliness, or consideration ○ *It was a nice gesture to return the money.* **3. RESPECTABLE** respectable, or of an acceptable social or moral standard ○ *She's made some nice friends at work.* **4. GOOD-LOOKING** pleasing to look at ○ *What a nice hat you're wearing!* **5. ACCOMPLISHED** skillful and accomplished ○ *That was a nice try.* **6. SUBTLE** subtle and involving delicacy or fine discrimination ○ *You may be correct technically, but that's a nice distinction you're making.* **7. FASTIDIOUS AND FUSSY** very concerned and careful about choosing, or being seen to do, the right thing ○ *You can't be too nice about your methods if you want to get the job done.* [13C. Via Old French < Latin *nescius* "ignorant"] —**nice·ly** *adv* —**nice·ness** *n* ◇ **nice and** sufficiently or pleasingly ○ *It's nice and warm by the fire.*

Nice /neess/ city on the Mediterranean coast in southeastern France. A major tourist center, it is known for its mild climate. Population: 342,738 (1999).

Ni·cene creed /nī seen-, nī seen-/ *n* a formal statement of Christian beliefs formulated at a council held in Nicaea in A.D. 325, subsequently altered and expanded, and still in use in most Christian churches [< late Latin *Nic(a)enus* < *Nic(a)ea* "Nicaea"]

ni·ce·ty /nīssətee/ (*plural* **-ties**) *n* **1. REFINEMENT OR DETAIL** a subtle distinction or point, or a small detail, especially of proper procedure or social etiquette (*often used in the plural*) **2. REFINED FEATURE** a feature that makes something particularly refined and pleasurable (*often used in the plural*) **3. SUBTLETY** a subtle, delicate, or fastidious quality, especially in somebody's feelings or taste **4. PRECISION** the ability to be precise and accurate and make fine distinctions ○ *the nicety of his powers of judgment* ◇ **to a nicety** with great precision or exactness

niche /nich, neesh/ *n* **1. SUITABLE PLACE FOR SOMEBODY** a position or activity that particularly suits somebody's talents and personality or that somebody can make his or her own ○ *She carved out her own niche in the industry.* **2.** COMM **SPECIALIZED MARKET** an area of the market specializing in one type of product or service ○ *designed to undercut the competition in the same niche* ○ *"Thanks to the Internet, small niche companies can reach mass markets in a heartbeat."* (*Forbes Global Business and Finance*; November 1998) **3.** ECOL **PLACE IN NATURE** the role of an organism within its natural environment that determines its relations with other organisms and ensures its survival **4. WALL RECESS** a recess in a wall, especially one made to hold a statue **5. HOLLOW PLACE** any recess or hollow, e.g., in a rock formation ■ *vt* (**niched, nich·ing, nich·es**) **PUT SOMETHING IN NICHE** to place something in a niche [Early 17C. < Old French *nichier* "build a nest, nestle" < Latin *nidus* "nest"]

niche mar·ket *n* a market in which a limited and clearly defined range of products is sold to a specific group of customers

Ni·chi·ren /neéch ee rèn/ (1222–82) Japanese Buddhist monk. He established a form of Buddhism based on the Lotus Sutra, which has many followers in Japan today.

Nich·o·las /níkələss/, **St.** (*fl* 4th century) prelate and saint from Asia Minor. He is the patron saint of Russia, children, and merchants.

Nich·o·las I (1796–1855) tsar of Russia. Autocratic and militaristic throughout his reign (1825–55), he put down the Decembrists' uprising that occurred upon his ascension in December 1825, waged successful wars against Persia (1826–28) and Turkey (1827–29), and entered into the Crimean War (1853–56), during which campaign he died.

Nich·o·las II (1868–1918) tsar of Russia. The last tsar of Russia (1894–1917), he was overthrown in the Russian Revolution and executed with his family.

Nich·o·las·ville /níkələss vìl/ city in central Kentucky, south of Lexington and northeast of Danville. Population: 21,343 (2002 estimate).

Nich·ol·son /ník'lssən/, **Jack** (*b.* 1937) US film actor. He won Academy Awards for *One Flew Over the Cuckoo's Nest* (1975), *Terms of Endearment* (1983), and *As Good As It Gets* (1997).

nick /nik/ *n* **1. NOTCH** a small V-shaped cut or indentation in an edge or surface **2. SMALL CUT** a small cut on the skin **3.** PRINTING **GROOVE ON TYPE** a groove on the side of a piece of metal printing type, used to identify and orient it **4.** *UK* same as **police station** (*slang*) **5.** *UK* same as **prison** *n* (sense 1) (*slang*) ○ *He spent ten years in the nick.* ■ *vt* (**nicked, nick·ing, nicks**) **1. NOTCH OR CUT SOMETHING SLIGHTLY** to make a notch, indentation, or small cut in something ○ *The scythe blade had been nicked by a stone.* **2.** *US* **CHEAT SOMEBODY** to cheat or defraud somebody (*slang*) **3.** *UK* **STEAL SOMETHING** to steal something from its owner (*informal*) **4.** *UK* **ARREST SOMEBODY** to place somebody under arrest (*slang*) **5.** VET **INCISE HORSE'S TAIL** to make a cut in the tendons at the root of a horse's tail to make the tail stick up [15C. Origin ?] ◇ **in the nick of time** at the critical or last possible moment

SYNONYMS See *steal.*

nick·el /ník'l/ *n* **1. SILVERY WHITE METALLIC ELEMENT** a hard corrosion-resistant silvery-white metallic element. Source: sulfide and oxide ores. Use: in alloys, batteries, electroplating, catalyst. Symbol **Ni**. See table at **element 2. FIVE-CENT COIN** a coin worth five cents **3.** FOOTBALL **DEFENSE WITH FIVE BACKS** in football, a defensive formation with five backs, used when a pass is expected **4. 5-YEAR PRISON TERM** a prison sentence of five years (*slang*) ■ *vt* (**-elled, -el·ling, -els**) **COAT SOMETHING WITH NICKEL** to plate something with nickel ■ *adj US* **COSTING FIVE DOLLARS** costing or worth five dollars (*slang*) [Mid-18C. Shortening of German *Kupfernickel* "copper nickel" < *nickel* "mischievous demon," because the ore yielded no copper]

nick·el-and-dime *US adj* **1. LOW-PAID** paying or involving only a small amount of money (*slang*) ○ *a nickel-and-dime job* **2. MINOR** small-scale, or of little importance (*informal*) ■ *vt* (**nick·el-and-dimed, nick·el-and-dim·ing, nick·el-and-dimes**) **1. IMPOVERISH SOMEBODY THROUGH SMALL EXPENSES** to get somebody or something into financial trouble by accumulating many small costs and expenses (*slang*) **2. BOTHER SOMEBODY IN MANY SMALL WAYS** to hinder or harass somebody with trivialities and insignificant matters

nick·el-cad·mi·um bat·ter·y *n* ELEC ENG same as **nicad**

nick·el·ic /ni kéllik, níkəlik/ *adj* containing nickel, especially nickel with a valence of three

nick·el·if·er·ous /nìkə líffərəss/ *adj* containing or yielding nickel

nick·el·o·de·on /nìkə lódee ən/ *n* **1. EARLY JUKEBOX** an early variety of coin-operated jukebox **2. 5-CENT MOVIE THEATER** an early 20th-century movie theater, charging five cents for admission **3. COIN-OPERATED PLAYER PIANO** an early variety of player piano operated by inserting coins [Early 20C. < NICKEL + MELODEON]

nick·el·ous /níkələss/ *adj* containing nickel, especially nickel with a valence of two

nick·el plate *n* a thin coating of nickel applied to something, usually by electrolysis —**nick·el-plat·ed** *adj* —**nick·el-plat·ing** *n*

nick·el sil·ver *n* a hard durable white alloy of copper, zinc, and nickel. Use: making cutlery and wire.

nick·er[1] /níkər/ (**-ered, -er·ing, -ers**) *vi* to make a soft neighing sound ○ *The pony nickered and shook its head.* [Late 16C. An imitation of the sound] —**nick·er** *n*

nick·er[2] /níkər/ (*plural same*) *n UK* a pound sterling (*slang*) [Early 20C. Origin ?]

Jack Nicklaus

Nick·laus /ník lòwss/, **Jack** (*b.* 1940) US golfer. He dominated professional golf in the 1960s and 1970s, winning a record 20 championship titles. Known as **Golden Bear**. Full name **Nicklaus, Jack William**

~~**nickle**~~ incorrect spelling of **nickel**

nick·nack *n* HOUSEHOLD same as **knickknack**

nick·name /ník nàym/ *n* **1. INVENTED NAME** an invented name for somebody or something, used humorously or affectively instead of the real name and usually based on a conspicuous characteristic of the person or thing involved **2. SHORT NAME** a shortened or altered form of a name, e.g., "Billy" for "William" or "Peggy" for "Margaret" ■ *vt* (**-named, -nam·ing, -names**) **CALL SOMEBODY BY NICKNAME** to give a nickname to somebody or something [15C. < mistaken division of *an eke name* "an additional name"] —**nick·nam·er** *n*

Ni·co·bar·ese /nìkəbə reéz, -reéss/ (*plural same*) *n* **1.** somebody who comes from the Nicobar Islands **2.** a group of Austroasiatic languages spoken on the Nicobar Islands. Native speakers: fewer than 20,000. —**Ni·co·bar·ese** *adj*

Nic·o·bar Is·lands /níkə baár-/ island group in the Indian Ocean, east of Sri Lanka, part of the Indian union territory of the Andaman and Nicobar Islands. The Nicobar Islands consist of 19 islands. Population: 39,022 (1991). Area: 711 sq. mi./1,841 sq. km.

ni·çoise /nee swaáz/ *adj* made or garnished with tomatoes and olive oil, and often including black olives, capers, anchovies, tuna, hard-boiled eggs, and green beans (*used after the noun*) [Late 19C. < French, feminine of *niçois* "of Nice"]

Nic·o·si·a /nìkə seé ə/ capital city of Cyprus, situated on the Pedhieos River in the northern part of the island. In 1974 it was partitioned into Turkish and Greek Cypriot sectors. Population: 197,800 (2000).

ni·co·ti·an·a /ni kò shee ánnə, -áanə/ (*plural* **-as** or *same*) *n* a perennial or annual flowering plant of a genus that includes the tobacco plant. Flowers: fragrant, white, yellow, or purple. Genus: *Nicotiana*. [Early 17C. After Jacques *Nicot* (1530–1604), French ambassador to Lisbon, who introduced tobacco to France]

nic·o·tin·a·mide /nìkə tínnə mìd/ *n* BIOCHEM same as **niacinamide**

nic·o·tin·a·mide ad·e·nine di·nu·cle·o·tide *n* BIOCHEM full form of **NAD**

nic·o·tin·a·mide ad·e·nine din·u·cle·o·tide phos·phate *n* BIOCHEM full form of **NADP**

nic·o·tine /níkə teen/ *n* **1.** a toxic alkaloid. Source: tobacco. Use: insecticide. Formula: $C_{10}H_{14}N_2$. **2.** tobacco products, or the smoking of them (*informal*) [Early 19C. Shortening of NICOTIANA] —**nic·o·tin·ic** /nìkə tínnik/ *adj*

nic·o·tine gum *n* chewing gum containing nicotine, used as a substitute for tobacco by people who are trying to give up smoking

nic·o·tine patch *n* a small patch that when placed on the skin releases nicotine directly into the bloodstream, used by people who are trying to give up smoking

nic·o·tin·ic ac·id *n* BIOCHEM same as **niacin**

nic·o·tin·ism /níkə tee nìzzəm/ *n* poisoning caused by an excessive intake of nicotine through smoking

nic·ti·tate /nikti tàyt/ (**-tat·ed, -tat·ing, -tates**), **nic·tate** /nik tàyt/ *vi* to blink or wink (*technical*) [Early 19C. < medieval Latin *nictitat-*, past participle of *nictitare* "wink repeatedly" < Latin *nictare* "to wink"] —**nic·ta·tion** /nik táysh'n/ *n* —**nic·ti·ta·tion** /nìkti táysh'n/ *n*

nic·ti·tat·ing mem·brane *n* a thin transparent layer of skin underneath the eyelid that can cover the eye surface of birds, reptiles, and some mammals to moisten and protect it

ni·di BIOL, MED plural of **nidus**

ni·dic·o·lous /nī díkələss/ *adj* describes young birds that remain in the nest for some time after hatching [Early 20C. < Latin *nidus* "nest"]

nid·i·fi·cate /ni díffə kayt, nī-/ *vi* BIOL same as **nidify** [Early 19C. < Latin *nidificat-*, past participle of *nidificare* (see NIDIFY)] —**nid·i·fi·ca·tion** /nìddəfi káysh'n/ *n*

ni·dif·u·gous /nī diffyəgəss/ *adj* describes young birds that leave the nest a short time after hatching [Early 20C. < Latin *nidus* "nest" + *fugere* "flee"]

nid·i·fy /níddə fī/ (**-fied, -fy·ing, -fies**) *vi* to build a nest [Mid-17C. < Latin *nidificare* "build a nest" < *nidus* "nest"]

ni·dus /nídəss/ (*plural* **-dus·es** or **-di** /-dī/) *n* **1. SPIDER OR INSECT NEST** a nest in which spiders or insects deposit eggs **2. FOCUS OF INFECTION** a site in the body at which an infection develops **3. SPORE-DEVELOPING PLANT PART** a place in a plant where its spores develop [Early 18C. < Latin, "nest"]

Nie·buhr /neé boor/, **H. Richard** (1894–1962) US theologian who examined 20th-century Christianity and culture in works such as *Christ and Culture* (1951). Full name **Niebuhr, Helmut Richard**

> "God give us grace to accept with serenity the things that cannot be changed, courage to change the things which should be changed, and the wisdom to distinguish the one from the other."
> [H. Richard Niebuhr, "The Serenity Prayer"; 1943]

niece /neess/ *n* a daughter of somebody's brother, brother-in-law, sister, or sister-in-law [13C. Via Old French < Latin *neptis* "granddaughter, niece"]

~~**nieghbor**~~ incorrect spelling of **neighbor**

ni·el·lo /nee éllō/ *n* (*plural* **-li** /-lee/ or **-los**) **1. BLACK ALLOY USED AS INLAY** a deep black alloy of sulfur and silver, lead, or copper, used to fill lines inlaid as decoration on a metal surface **2. USE OF NIELLO** the process of using niello to decorate a metal surface **3. SOMETHING DECORATED WITH NIELLO** something decorated with niello as an inlay ■ *vt* (**-loed, -lo·ing, -los**) **DECORATE SOMETHING WITH NIELLO** to decorate something using niello as an inlay [Early 19C. Via Italian < Latin *nigellus* "blackish," diminutive of *niger* "black"] —**ni·el·list** *n*

niels·bohr·i·um /neelz báwree əm/ *n* an artificially produced radioactive element with the atomic number 105 [Late 20C. After *Niels* BOHR]

Niel·sen /neélssən/, **Carl** (1865–1931) Danish composer best known for his six symphonies. Full name **Nielsen, Carl August**

Nie·mey·er /neé mī ər/, **Oscar** (*b.* 1907) Brazilian architect. He is best known for designing the major buildings in Brasília (1956–64), the new capital of Brazil. Full name **Niemeyer Soares Filho, Oscar**

Nie·möl·ler /neé mòllər/, **Martin** (1892–1984) German pastor. A veteran of World War I, he initially supported Hitler but during the 1930s was active in the German resistance against the Nazis. Arrested for treason, he spent seven years in Dachau and Sachsenhausen concentration camps before being released by the Allies at the end of World War II. During the postwar years, he was an outspoken pacifist and advocate of reconciliation and disarmament.

~~**niether**~~ incorrect spelling of **neither**

Friedrich Wilhelm Nietzsche

Nie·tzsche /neéchə, neéchee/, **Friedrich Wilhelm** (1844–1900) German philosopher. Author of *Thus Spake Zarathustra* (1883–85) and one of the most influential thinkers of the 19th century, he founded his philosophy on the will-to-power and rejected religion. —**Nie·tzsche·an** *n, adj*

> "Species do not evolve toward perfection, but quite the contrary. The weak, in fact, always prevail over the strong, not only because they are in the majority, but also because they are the more crafty."
> [Friedrich Wilhelm Nietzsche, *The Twilight of the Idols*; 1888]

> "Truths are illusions about which one has forgotten that this is what they are; metaphors which are worn out and without sensuous power; coins which have lost their pictures and now matter only as metal, no longer as coins."
> [Friedrich Wilhelm Nietzsche, "On Truth and Lie in an Extra-Moral Sense," *The Portable Nietzsche*; 1954]

ni·fed·i·pine /nə féddə peen, nī féddəpin/ *n* a drug that stops the heart muscles from taking up calcium. Use: treatment of high blood pressure, angina pectoris. Formula: $C_{17}H_{18}N_2O_6$. [Late 20C. < NITRO- + *fe* (shortening and alteration of PHENYL) + *-dipine*, INN stem]

nif·ty /níftee/ (*informal*) *adj* (**-ti·er, -ti·est**) **1. STYLISH AND GOOD-LOOKING** fashionable and good-looking **2. AGILE** good, quick, and clever at doing something or using something **3. VERY GOOD** very good or effective ■ *n* (*plural* **-ties**) **SOMETHING CLEVER** something clever, neat, or excellent, especially a witticism [Mid-19C. Origin ?] —**nif·ti·ly** *adv* —**nif·ti·ness** *n*

Nig. *abbr* **1.** Nigeria **2.** Nigerian

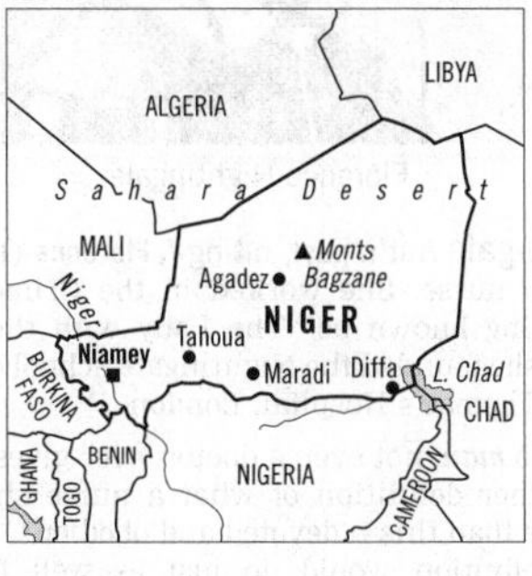

Niger

Ni·ger /níjər/ **1.** country in western Africa, north of Nigeria and south of Libya. Language: French. Currency: CFA franc. Capital: Niamey. Population: 11,058,590 (2001). Area: 489,200 sq. mi./1,267,000 sq. km. Official name **Republic of Niger 2.** river in western Africa. The third longest river in Africa, it rises in southern Guinea, and flows northward through Mali, then southeast into the Gulf of Guinea, through Niger and Nigeria. Length: 2,600 mi./4,180 km.

Ni·ger-Con·go *n* a large family of languages spoken in central and southern parts of Africa. Native speakers: 200 million. —**Ni·ger-Con·go** *adj*

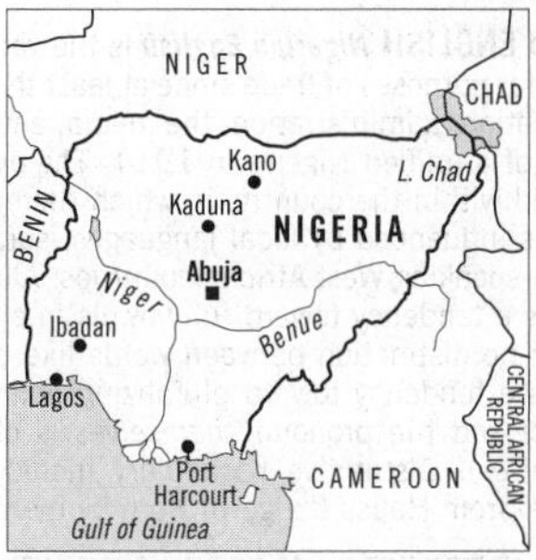

Nigeria

Ni·ge·ri·a /nī jeéree ə/ country in West Africa, on the Gulf of Guinea, south of Niger. It became an independent member of the British Commonwealth in 1960. Language: English. Currency: naira. Capital: Abuja. Population: 133,881,700 (2003). Area: 356,669 sq. mi./923,768 sq. km. Official name **Federal Republic of Nigeria** —**Ni·ge·ri·an** *n, adj*

Ni·ger·i·an Eng·lish *n* a variety of English spoken in Nigeria. See panel on next page

nig·gard /níggərd/ *n* somebody regarded as stingy or miserly [14C. Alteration of *nigon*, perhaps < *nig* "stingy" < N Germanic]

nig·gard·ly /níggərdlee/ *adj* (**-li·er, -li·est**) **1. NOT GENEROUS** very reluctant to give or spend anything **2. SMALL OR INADEQUATE** very small or inadequate in quantity ■ *adv* **IN STINGY WAY** in a miserly or stingy way —**nig·gard·li·ness** *n*

USAGE Though the etymology of ***niggardly*** and *niggard* remains subject to debate, these words probably have a Scandinavian origin not associated historically with the origin of the offensive word *Negro* and its related offensive racist slurs, which are derived ultimately from Latin. ***Niggardly***, then, is in no way a racial slur. However, the fact that the word sounds as if it might be one is reason to consider context very carefully before using it.

nig·ger /níggər/ *n* (*taboo*) **1.** a highly offensive term for a Black person **2.** a highly offensive term for a dark-skinned person [Late 17C. Alteration of NEGRO [1]]

USAGE See ***insult***.

nig·gle /nígg'l/ *v* (**-gled, -gling, -gles**) **1.** *vi* **CRITICIZE IN PETTY WAY** to criticize or find fault continually, especially about small matters **2.** *vi* **BE PREOCCUPIED WITH DETAILS** to be preoccupied with petty details **3.** *vt* **WORRY SOMEBODY** to be a source of worry and irritation to somebody, especially in a small way over a long period of time ■ *n Can, UK* **1. PETTY COMPLAINT** a small or petty complaint, criticism, or point of detail or dispute ○ *Once we have a broad agreement, we can sort out these niggles.* **2. NAGGING WORRY** a small but continuing source of annoyance or worry [Early 17C. Origin ?] —**nig·gler** *n*

nig·gling /níggling/ *adj* **1.** too preoccupied with details **2.** irritating, painful, or worrying, especially in a small but persistent way —**nig·gling** *n* —**nig·gling·ly** *adv*

nigh /nī/ *adv, adj* near in place or time ○ (adv) *Daybreak drew nigh.* ○ (adj) *Morning was nigh.* ■ *adv* nearly ○ *We talked for nigh on to two hours.* [Old English *nēah* < Germanic]

night /nīt/ *n* **1. DAILY PERIOD OF DARKNESS** the period of darkness occurring each day in most parts of the world, or the entire period between sunset and sunrise **2. TIME BETWEEN BEDTIME AND WAKING** the time between somebody's going to sleep in the evening and waking the next morning **3. PERIOD OF EVENING ACTIVITIES** the period between sunset and bedtime, especially when spent in entertainment or some other activity ○ *We had a great night at her birthday party.* **4.** *also* **Night EVENING DEVOTED TO SPECIAL ACTIVITY** any period after sunset devoted to a special activity, function, or observance ○ *Tomorrow night is Family Night at the ballpark.* **5. NIGHTFALL** the period of time just after the sun goes down, when it gets dark **6. PERIOD OF CULTURAL OR EMOTIONAL GLOOMINESS** a period marked by grief, gloom, ignorance, or obscurity ○ *Europe slipped into the long night of the Dark Ages.* **7. DARK OR DARKENED STATE** a dark or darkened state, or an absence of light, consciousness, or en-

WORLD ENGLISH ***Nigerian English*** is the variety of English that has been used in the region of the Niger, West Africa, for purposes of trade since at least the 18th century, at missions since the 19th century, and increasingly in education, administration, the media, and the 20th-century workplace, especially since the formation by the British of a unified Nigeria in 1914. The existence of a single Nigerian English continues to be debated and disputed within the country, in which there is a spectrum of usage from West African Pidgin English through varieties influenced by local languages, such as Hausa, Igbo, and Yoruba, to a general usage similar to other English-speaking West African countries. All varieties do not pronounce *r* in words such as *art, door,* and *worker.* There is a tendency toward full vowels in all syllables (e.g., *seven* pronounced "seh-ven," not "sev'n"). There is often no distinction between words like *chip* and *cheap* and ones like *caught, cot,* and *court.* In grammar, there is a tendency toward pluralizing nouns that are singular in Standard English (as in *I gave them some advices*) and the pronoun *themselves* is often used instead of *one another* (as in *That couple really love themselves*). Distinctive vocabulary includes borrowings and loan translations from local languages, e.g., *danshiki* from Hausa ("a gown worn by men") and *to throw water* ("to offer a bribe").

lightenment (*literary*) ■ *adj* **1.** OCCURRING AT NIGHT occurring, appearing, or visible at night ○ *night terrors* **2.** USED AT NIGHT used chiefly at night ○ *Use the night entrance.* **3.** WORKING AT NIGHT working at night in a job also done during the day ○ *the night porter* **4.** ACTIVE AT NIGHT awake or active at night ○ *night feeders* ■ *interj* same as **good night** (*informal*) [Old English *niht* < Indo-European] ◇ **night and day** the entire time

night blind·ness *n* an inability to see clearly in dim light while having normal vision in clear light. Technical name **nyctalopia** —**night-blind** *adj*

night-bloom·ing ce·re·us *n* a cactus whose large fragrant flowers open at night. Genera: *Hylocereus, Peniocereus, Nyctocereus, Selenicereus.*

night·cap /nīt kàp/ *n* **1.** DRINK BEFORE SLEEP a drink, often alcoholic, taken before going to bed **2.** *US* LAST EVENT the last event of a day of sports, especially the second game of a baseball double-header **3.** CAP USED AS SLEEPWEAR a soft cap worn in bed to keep the head warm, in use mainly until the late 19th century

night·clothes /nīt klōthz, -klōz/ *npl* clothes designed to be worn in bed

night·club /nīt klùb/ *n* a place of entertainment open late at night, offering live music, dancing, and drinks, and sometimes serving food and providing a floorshow

night·club·bing /nīt klùbbing/ *n* same as **clubbing** (sense 1)

night court *n* a court of law that sits at night, especially for routine matters such as the disposition of charges and the granting of bail

night crawl·er *n* a large earthworm found on the surface of the ground at night, often used as bait in fishing

REGIONAL NOTE ***Night crawler*** is a Northern term that has spread across the country to become common everywhere except in the lower Southern states.

night de·pos·i·to·ry *n* a safe in the wall of a bank that can be opened from the outside to allow people to deposit money at times when the bank is closed

night·dress /nīt drèss/ *n* **1.** *UK* same as **nightgown 2.** CLOTHING same as **sleepwear**

night·fall /nīt fàwl/ *n* the time of evening at which it becomes dark and night begins ○ *Be home by nightfall.*

night fight·er *n* a fighter aircraft designed to fly at night

night·glow /nīt glō/ *n* a dim light from the upper atmosphere seen at night

night·gown /nīt gòwn/ *n* a loose dress worn in bed by women and girls

night·hawk /nīt hàwk/ *n* **1.** a bird of the nightjar family with long pointed wings and black, white, and buff feathers, that feeds on flying insects after dark. Native to: North America. Genus: *Chordeiles.* **2.** same as **night owl** (*informal*)

night-her·on *n* a stocky heron with short legs and a thick beak that is active at night or twilight. Genus: *Nycticorax.*

night·ie /nītee/, **night·y** (*plural* **-ies**) *n* CLOTHING same as **nightgown** (*informal*) [Late 19C. Shortening and alteration]

nightingale

night·in·gale /nīt'n gàyl, nīting-/ *n* **1.** a migratory songbird of the thrush family with brownish feathers, the male of which is particularly known for its song. Latin name: *Luscinia megarhynchos.* **2.** a woman who sings sweetly (*dated*) [13C. Alteration of Old English *nihtegala* < Germanic, "night-singer"]

CULTURAL NOTE ***Ode to a Nightingale***, a poem (1819) by English writer John Keats. The poet recounts how on hearing the joyful song of the nightingale he is filled with an intense joy that provides an escape from his woes. But, as he considers the fact that the bird's song has been an inspiration throughout history, the sound fades and he is suddenly returned to reality.

AKG London

Florence Nightingale

Night·in·gale /nīt'n gàyl, nīting-/, **Florence** (1820–1910) British nurse. She worked in the Crimean War, becoming known as "The Lady with the Lamp." Later she founded the Nightingale School of Nurses at St. Thomas's Hospital, London.

> "No *man*, not even a doctor, ever gives any other definition of what a nurse should be than this—'devoted and obedient.' This definition would do just as well for a porter. It might even do for a horse. It would not do for a policeman."
> [Florence Nightingale, *Notes on Nursing*; 1860]

night·jar /nīt jaàr/ *n* a bird with a short beak, large gaping mouth, and dark feathers that is active at night and twilight and feeds on insects caught in flight. Family: Caprimulgidae. [< JAR[2] "quivering sound"]

night jas·mine *n* **1.** a bush with small fragrant orange-and-white flowers. Native to: Asia. Latin name: *Nyctanthes arbortristis.* **2.** a bush with small, greenish white flowers that release fragrance at night. Native to: Caribbean. Latin name: *Cestrum nocturnum.*

night latch *n* a door lock operated from inside by a knob and from outside by a key

night·life /nīt līf/ *n* the entertainment or social life that goes on in a place in the evenings ○ *Let's go out and check out the local nightlife.*

night·light /nīt līt/ *n* a small lamp or candle lit to give a dim light during the night, especially in a child's bedroom

night liz·ard *n* a lizard typically found in dry regions and active only at night. Native to: southwestern United States, Mexico, Central America. Family: Xantusiidae.

night·long /nīt làwng/ *adj* lasting or occurring throughout the entire night —**night·long** *adv*

night·ly /nītlee/ *adj* **1.** HAPPENING EVERY NIGHT taking place every night **2.** OCCURRING AT NIGHT typically occurring at night ■ *adv* EVERY NIGHT on or during each and every night ○ *The band is playing nightly this week.*

night·mare /nīt mèr/ *n* **1.** BAD DREAM a frightening or upsetting dream **2.** TRAUMATIC EXPERIENCE a traumatic, very upsetting, or extremely difficult and troublesome experience or situation **3.** DREADED EVENT a situation or event that somebody dreads **4.** EVIL SPIRIT a malign spirit formerly believed to suffocate or haunt people during sleep ■ *adj* EXTREMELY FRIGHTENING OR DIFFICULT extremely frightening, upsetting, or difficult to deal with [13C. < NIGHT + Old English *mære* "nightmare" < Germanic] —**night·mar·ish** *adj* —**night·mar·ish·ly** *adv*

night owl *n* somebody who stays up late at night, especially to work or socialize (*informal*)

night·rid·er /nīt rīdər/ *n* a member of a group of masked horsemen who at night terrorized or intimidated African Americans and their sympathizers in the southern United States in the period after the Civil War

nights /nīts/ *adv* during the night, or every night ○ *They work nights.*

night safe *n UK* same as **night depository**

night school *n* a school or college that holds classes in the evening, especially for people who are at work during the day

night·scope /nīt skōp/ *n* an optical device, e.g., one using infrared radiation, that gives better vision in the dark

night·shade /nīt shàyd/ *n* a wild plant, related to potatoes, tomatoes, and eggplants, with flowers that have five petals, and small berries. Some are poisonous, e.g., deadly nightshade. Family: Solanaceae.

night shift *n* **1.** a set period of work during the night **2.** a group of people who work during a set period at night ○ *The night shift finishes up at seven in the morning.*

night·shirt /nīt shùrt/ *n* a long loose garment resembling a shirt, worn in bed by men

night·side /nīt sīd/ *n* the side of a planet or moon that is not lit by the Sun

night sight *n* an infrared sight on a rifle used for taking aim in darkness

night soil *n* human excrement collected at night from toilets or cesspools, especially for use as fertilizer

night·spot /nīt spòt/ *n* same as **nightclub**

night·stand /nīt stànd/ *n* FURNITURE same as **night table**

night·stick /nīt stik/ *n* a club carried by a police officer [Because traditionally carried especially at night]

night ta·ble *n* a bedside table or stand

night ter·ror *n* a sudden awakening from sleep in a condition of extreme fear that is not associated with a dream or nightmare

night·time /nīt tīm/ *n* the period of each day when it is dark, or the time between sunset and sunrise

night vi·sion *n* somebody's ability to see in the dark ○ *They say eating carrots improves your night vision.*

night watch *n* **1.** a guard or watch kept during the night ○ *I'm on night watch this week.* **2.** same as **night watchman**

night watch·man *n* somebody who guards or watches over something at night, especially a building site or factory

night·wear /nīt wèr/ *n UK* same as **sleepwear**

night·y *n* CLOTHING another spelling of **nightie** (*informal*)

ni·gres·cence /nī gréss'nss/ *n* the process of becoming black or dark [Mid-19C. < Latin *nigrescent-*, present participle of *nigrescere* "grow black" < *niger* "black"] —**ni·gres·cent** *adj* —**ni·gres·cent·ly** *adv*

ni·gro·sine /níggrə seen, níggrəssin/, **ni·gro·sin** /níggrəssin/ *n* a black aniline pigment or dye. Use: ink, polish, textile dye. [Late 19C. < Latin *niger* "black"]

NIH *abbr* GOV National Institutes of Health

ni·hil·ism /nī ə lìzzəm, nee ə-, níhi-/ *n* **1. TOTAL REJECTION OF SOCIAL MORES** the general rejection of established social conventions and beliefs, especially of morality and religion **2. BELIEF THAT NOTHING IS WORTHWHILE** a belief that life is pointless and human values are worthless **3. DISBELIEF IN OBJECTIVE TRUTH** the belief that there is no objective basis for truth **4. BELIEF IN DESTRUCTION OF AUTHORITY** the belief that all established authority is corrupt and must be destroyed in order to rebuild a just society **5.** *also* **Ni·hil·ism RUSSIAN POLITICAL MOVEMENT** a political movement in late 19th-century Russia that sought to bring about a socially just new society by destroying the existing one through acts of terrorism and assassination [Early 19C. < German *Nihilismus* < Latin *nihil* "nothing"] —**ni·hil·ist** *n* —**ni·hil·is·tic** /nī ə lístik, nee ə-, nìhi-/ *adj* —**ni·hil·is·ti·cal·ly** *adv*

ni·hil·i·ty /nī híllətee/ *n* the condition of being nothing [Late 17C. < medieval Latin *nihilitas* < Latin *nihil* "nothing"]

ni·hil ob·stat /nī hil ób stàt/ *n* **1.** a statement by a Roman Catholic Church official that a publication is not offensive to religion or morals **2.** an official statement of nonopposition [Mid-20C. < Latin, "nothing hinders"]

Ni·i·ga·ta /nee ee gaátə/ city and port in Japan, on northern Honshu. It is the capital city of Niigata Prefecture. Population: 514,678 (2002).

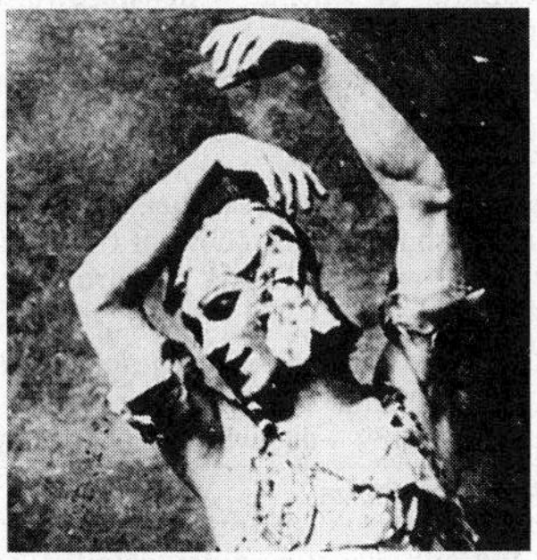

Vaslav Nijinsky: performing in *Le Spectre de la Rose* (1911)

Ni·jin·sky /ni zhínskee, -jín-/, **Vaslav** (1890–1950) Russian ballet dancer. The leading dancer of the original Ballets Russes, he choreographed several innovative ballets including *The Rite of Spring* (1913).

-nik *suffix* somebody associated with or characterized by ○ *refusenik* [Directly or via Yiddish < Russian]

Ni·ke /nīkee/ *n* in Greek mythology, the winged goddess of victory

Nik·kei In·dex /ni káy-/ *n* an index of 225 leading stocks traded on the Tokyo Stock Exchange [Late 20C. Abbreviation of Japanese *Nihon Keizai Shimbun* "Japanese Economic Journal"]

Nik·ko /neekō/ city in Japan, in Tochigi Prefecture, central Honshu, 90 mi./145 km north of Tokyo. Population: 17,527 (2002).

nil /nil/ *n* nothing or zero [Early 19C. Latin, contraction of *nihil* "nothing"]

Nile /nīl/ river in northeastern Africa. It is the longest river in the world. Rising in east central Africa near Lake Victoria, it flows 3,470 mi./5,584 km northward through Uganda, Sudan, and Egypt before emptying into the Mediterranean Sea.

Nile blue *adj* of a pale greenish blue color —**Nile blue** *n*

Nile green *adj* of a yellowish green color —**Nile green** *n*

Niles /nīlz/ city in northeastern Illinois, east of Park

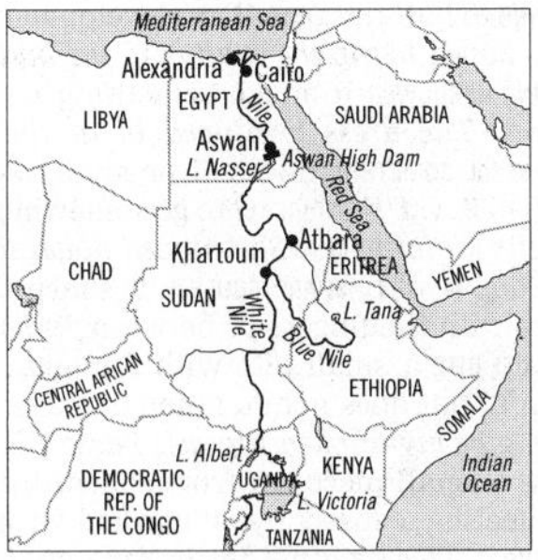

Nile

Ridge. It is a northwestern suburb of Chicago. Population: 30,076 (2002 estimate).

nil·gai /níl gī/ (*plural same* or **-gais**), **nil·gau** /-gaw/ (*plural same* or **-gaus**), **nil·ghau** (*plural same* or **-ghaus**) *n* a large antelope, the male of which is bluish gray and horned, the female brown and hornless. Native to: South Asia. Latin name: *Boselaphus tragocamelus.* [Late 18C. < Hindi *nīlgāe* < Sanskrit *nīla* "blue" + *-gāvī* "cow"]

Ni·lo-Sa·har·an /nìlo sə hárrən, -sə haárən/ *n* a large family of languages spoken in central Africa. Native speakers: 15 million. —**Ni·lo-Sa·har·an** *adj*

Ni·lot·ic /nī lóttik/ *adj* **1. RELATING TO NILE** relating to, living beside, or involving the Nile River **2. OF NILE VALLEY LANGUAGE** relating to a Nilo-Saharan group of languages spoken in parts of the Nile valley ■ *n* **NILE VALLEY LANGUAGE GROUP** a Nilo-Saharan group of languages spoken in parts of the Nile valley, mainly in Uganda and Sudan. Native speakers: 3 million. [Mid-17C. Via Latin < Greek *Neilōtikos* < *Neilos* "Nile"]

nim /nim/ *n* a game in which players remove small, differently arranged items from piles, the winner being the player who takes, or sometimes does not take, the final item [Early 20C. Origin ?]

nim·ble /nímb'l/ (**-bler, -blest**) *adj* **1.** agile, fast, and light in movement **2.** able to think quickly and cleverly [Old English *næmel, numol* "quick at grasping" < *niman* "to take"] —**nim·ble·ness** *n* —**nim·bly** *adv*

nim·bo·stra·tus /nìmbō stráytəss, -stráttəss/ (*plural* **-ti** /-tī/) *n* a low dark layer of rain-bearing cloud covering all of the sky [Late 19C. < NIMBUS]

nim·bus /nímbəss/ (*plural* **-bus·es** or **-bi** /-bī/) *n* **1.** METEOROL **DARK RAIN-BEARING CLOUD** a dense dark rain-bearing cloud **2.** RELIG **CLOUD OF LIGHT AROUND DEITY** a cloud of light surrounding a god, goddess, saint or holy person **3.** ART **IMAGE OF HALO** a bright halo or disk around the head of a deity, saint, or sovereign in a painting, icon, or medal **4. AURA OF SPLENDOR** an aura or atmosphere of splendor surrounding somebody or something [Early 17C. < Latin, "cloud, rain"]

NIMBY[1] /nímbee/ (*plural* **NIMBYs**), **Nim·by** (*plural* **-bys**) *n* **1.** somebody who objects to something unattractive or potentially dangerous being located near his or her home **2.** the attitude of a NIMBY [Late 20C. < NIMBY[2]] —**Nim·by·ism** *n*

NIMBY[2] *abbr* not in my back yard

Nim·itz /nímmits/, **Chester William** (1885–1966) US naval officer. He was commander-in-chief of the US Pacific Fleet during World War II. His strategy of relying on aircraft carriers was instrumental in defeating the Japanese fleet.

> "Uncommon valor was a common virtue."
> [Chester William Nimitz, on the US Marines' valor at Iwo Jima; May 1945]

nim·rod /ním ròd/ *n* a skillful or enthusiastic hunter (*literary*) [Mid-16C. < *Nimrod* as a "mighty hunter" (Genesis 10:9)]

Nin /nin/, **Anaïs** (1903–77) French writer. She is best known for her passionate and self-revelatory *Diaries* (1966–85).

> "Each friend represents a world in us, a world possibly not born until they arrive, and it is only by this meeting that a new world is born."
> [Anaïs Nin, *The Diary of Anaïs Nin*, volume II; 1967]

> "Life shrinks or expands in proportion to one's courage."

Anaïs Nin

> [Anaïs Nin, *The Diary of Anaïs Nin*, volume III; June 1941]

nin·com·poop /nínkəm poop, níngkəm-/ *n* an offensive term that deliberately insults somebody's intelligence or competence (*insult*) [Late 17C. Alteration of *nicompoop*, origin ?] —**nin·com·poop·er·y** *n*

nine /nīn/ *n* **1. 9** the number 9 **2. SOMETHING WITH VALUE OF 9** something in a numbered series, e.g., a playing card, with a value of 9 ○ *a nine of clubs* ○ *to play the nine* **3.** BASEBALL **BASEBALL TEAM** a team of nine baseball players **4.** GOLF **HALF OF GOLF COURSE** half of the total number of holes on a golf course, usually called the front nine or the back nine **5. GROUP OF NINE** a group of nine objects or people [Old English *nigon* < Indo-European] —**nine** *adj, pron* ◇ **dressed (up) to the nines** very elaborately or formally dressed

9/11 /nīn i lévvən/, **9–11** *n* **1.** the events of September 11, 2001, when planes hijacked by terrorists destroyed the World Trade Center in New York, damaged the Pentagon, and crashed into a field in Pennsylvania, with great loss of life **2.** any catastrophic attack, e.g., by terrorists, on a country, locale, or building, where very large numbers of innocent victims are killed or injured

nine-band·ed ar·ma·dil·lo *n* an armadillo with nine bands of hinged bony plates. Native to: Central and South America, southern United States. Latin name: *Dasypus novemcinctus.*

nine·bark /nīn baark/ *n* a bush with bark that separates into many layers. Native to: eastern North America. Genus: *Physocarpus.*

nine days' won·der, **nine day won·der** *n* something that, or somebody who, briefly arouses great interest or excitement but is soon forgotten again [Refers to Lady Jane Grey (1537–54), who was proclaimed queen of England in 1553 but was deposed after nine days and subsequently beheaded]

911 *n* in the United States and Canada, the telephone number used to call for police, fire, or ambulance emergency services ○ *The teacher sent a child to call 911 and get an ambulance.*

nine·fold *adj* /nīn fōld/ **1. BY NINE TIMES** of nine times the original figure ○ *a ninefold rise* **2. WITH NINE PARTS** made up of nine parts ○ *The problem is ninefold.* ■ *adv* /nīn fōld, nīn fōld/ **BY NINE TIMES AS MUCH** by nine times as much or as many ○ *The numbers increased ninefold.*

999 *n* in the United Kingdom, the telephone number used to call for police, fire, or ambulance emergency services ○ *When I heard the collision I dialed 999 right away.*

nine·pin /nīn pìn/ *n* a pin in the game of ninepins

nine·pins /nīn pìnz/ *n* a game in which players try to knock over nine bottle-shaped pins by bowling a ball at them (*takes a singular verb*)

nine·teen /nīn teen/ *n* **1. 19** the number 19 **2. SOMETHING WITH VALUE OF 19** something in a numbered series with a value of 19 **3. GROUP OF 19** a group of 19 objects or people [Old English *nigontȳne* < Germanic, "nine-ten"] —**nine·teen** *adj, pron*

nine·teenth /nīn teenth/ *n* one of 19 equal parts of something ○ *My share came to three-nineteenths.* —**nine·teenth** *adj, pron*

nine·teenth hole *n* a place, especially the bar of a clubhouse, where players can drink and socialize after a round of golf (*slang*) [As after the conventional 18 holes]

~~**nineth**~~ incorrect spelling of **ninth**

nine·ti·eth /nī́ntee əth/ *n* one of 90 equal parts of something ○ *a ninetieth of the whole* —**nine·ti·eth** *adj, pron*

nine-to-five *adj* requiring regular attendance, e.g., at an office job, especially between 9 a.m. and 5 p.m. (*informal*) ○ *without the self-discipline to hold down a nine-to-five job*

nine-to-fiv·er *n* somebody who works regular hours, especially from 9 a.m. to 5 p.m. (*informal*) ○ *She took the morning train with the rest of the nine-to-fivers.*

nine·ty /nī́ntee/ *n* **90** the number 90 ■ **nine·ties** *npl* **1.** NUMBERS BETWEEN 90 AND 99 the numbers between 90 and 99, particularly as a range of Fahrenheit temperatures **2.** YEARS FROM 90 TO 99 the years from 90 to 99 in a century **3.** PERIOD FROM AGE 90 TO 99 the period of somebody's life from the age of 90 to 99 [Old English *nigontig*, shortening of *hundnigontig* < *hund* "hundred" + *nigon* "nine" + *-tig* "ten"] —**nine·ty** *adj, pron*

Nin·e·veh /nínnəvə/ ancient capital of the Assyrian empire, situated on the Tigris River in northern Iraq. At the height of its importance from about 705 B.C., it was destroyed by the Babylonians and Medes in 612 B.C.

Ning·bo /níng bṓ/ city in northeastern Zhejiang Province, eastern China, situated approximately 90 mi./145 km southeast of Hangzhou. Population: 1,145,219 (1991).

Ning·xia Hui /níng shyaá hwee/ autonomous region in north central China. Capital: Yinchuan. Population: 4,655,451 (1990). Area: 25,600 sq. mi./66,400 sq. km.

Nin·i·an /nínnee ən/, **St.** (360?–432?) Scottish bishop and missionary. He was the earliest known Christian missionary in Scotland.

nin·ja /nínjə/ (*plural* **-jas** or *same*) *n* a member of a group of mercenaries in feudal Japan who were trained in stealth and the martial arts and employed as spies, saboteurs, or assassins [Mid-20C. < Japanese, "spy" < *nin* "endure" + *ja* "person" (< Middle Chinese *tšia?*)]

nin·jit·su /nin jít soō/ *n* a Japanese martial art that emphasizes stealth in movement and camouflage [Mid-20C. < Japanese, "stealth art"]

nin·ny /nínnee/ (*plural* **-nies**) *n* an offensive term that deliberately insults somebody's intelligence, common sense, or effectiveness (*insult*) [Late 16C. Origin ?] —**nin·ny·ish** *adj*

ni·non /neé nòn/ *n* a sturdy sheer silk or synthetic fabric [Early 20C. < French]

ninth /nīnth/ *n* **1.** one of 9 equal parts of something **2.** a musical tone separated from another by an interval of an octave and a second, or the interval of this tone —**ninth** *adj, pron*

ninth chord *n* a musical chord containing four thirds, including the ninth, added above the root

~~**ninty**~~ incorrect spelling of **ninety**

Ni·o·be /nī́ ə bee/ *n* in Greek mythology, the daughter of Tantalus, punished by Apollo and Artemis for claiming superiority over their mother Leto. Her children were killed and she herself was turned into stone.

ni·o·bic /nī ṓbik/ *adj* concerning or containing niobium with a valence of five [< NIOBIUM]

ni·o·bite /nī́ ə bīt/ *n* MINERALS same as **columbite** [< NIOBIUM]

ni·o·bi·um /nī ṓbee əm/ *n* a lustrous pale gray ductile metallic element that is a superconductor chemically resembling tantalum. Source: columbite. Use: steel alloys. Symbol **Nb**. See table at **element** [Mid-19C. < its association with tantalum, TANTALUS being the father of NIOBE]

ni·o·bous /nī ṓbəs/ *adj* concerning or containing niobium with a valence less than five [< NIOBIUM]

nip[1] /nip/ *v* (**nipped, nip·ping, nips**) **1.** *vt* PINCH SOMETHING to take hold of something and squeeze or compress it, often painfully, between two surfaces, e.g., to pinch skin between a forefinger and thumb **2.** *vti* TAKE BRIEF BITE AT SOMETHING to bite something briefly, often painfully, but without doing much damage **3.** *vt* SEVER SOMETHING to remove something by pinching, biting, or clipping ○ *nipped off the dead flower heads* **4.** *vt* AFFECT SOMEBODY WITH COLD to sting or chill a person or part of the body painfully with cold ○ *frost nipping his fingers and toes* **5.** *vt* STOP SOMETHING FROM DEVELOPING to halt the growth or development of something ○ *hoped to nip the conflict in the bud* **6.** *vt* MAKE SOMETHING NARROWER to make something narrower or tighter ○ *The dress is nipped in at the waist.* **7.** *vt US* STEAL SOMETHING to steal or snatch something (*informal*) **8.** *vi UK* GO QUICKLY to go somewhere quickly or briefly (*informal*) ○ *She nipped down to the shop for bread.* ■ *n* **1.** SHARP SQUEEZE a sharp or painful squeeze with the fingers or between two surfaces **2.** SMALL BRIEF BITE a small bite with the teeth that may be painful but does not do much damage ○ *The dog tried to give my ankle a nip as I passed.* **3.** SMALL CUT-OUT PIECE a small piece cut from something **4.** CHILL a chilly feeling caused by a marked drop in temperature ○ *There's a nip in the air tonight.* **5.** SHARP FLAVOR a sharp or pungent flavor [14C. < Middle Low German *nipen*] ◇ **nip and tuck** very closely and evenly contested so that the outcome remains in doubt (*informal*)

nip[2] /nip/ *n* a small portion or drink of something alcoholic ■ *vti* (**nipped, nip·ping, nips**) to drink an alcoholic beverage in small sips [Late 18C. Origin ?]

ni·pa /neépə/ *n* **1.** LEAVES OF PALM TREE the long feathery leaves of a palm tree. Use: thatching, basketry. **2.** DRINK FROM PALM SAP an alcoholic drink made from the sap of a palm tree **3.** FRUIT OF PALM TREE an edible fruit of a palm tree **4.** (*plural* **ni·pas** or *same*) ASIAN PALM TREE a palm tree that produces nipa leaves, fruit, and the sap from which the drink nipa is made. Native to: South Asia. Latin name: *Nipa fruticans.* [Late 16C. < Malay *nipah*]

Nip·i·gon, Lake /níppi gòn/ lake in west central Ontario, Canada. It empties into Lake Superior via the Nipigon River. Area: 1,870 sq. mi./4,850 sq. km. Depth: 540 ft./165 m.

Nip·is·sing, Lake /níppə sìng/ lake in southeastern Ontario, Canada. It empties into Georgian Bay via the French River. Area: 321 sq. mi./832 sq. km.

nip·per /níppər/ *n* **1.** PINCER a large claw of a crustacean, especially a lobster or crab **2.** *UK* CHILD a small child (*informal*) ■ **nip·pers** *npl* PLIERS a tool used to squeeze or clip something, e.g., pliers

nip·ping /nípping/ *adj* **1.** very cold and biting **2.** bitingly sarcastic —**nip·ping·ly** *adv*

nip·ple /nípp'l/ *n* **1.** TIP OF MAMMARY GLAND a small knob in the center of the breast that in female mammals is the outlet for the ducts that provide the young with milk **2.** RUBBER BOTTLE TOP the soft cap of a baby bottle, made of a synthetic material, through which a baby can suck milk **3.** same as **pacifier 4.** SMALL OUTLET a small knob on a device that is the outlet for fluid such as oil or grease **5.** CONSTR COUPLER FOR PIPES a short piece of pipe threaded at both ends used for coupling other pipes [Mid-16C. Origin ?]

nip·ple·wort /nípp'l wùrt, -wàwrt/ (*plural* **-worts** or *same*) *n* an annual plant with milky juice. Flowers: small, yellow. Native to: Europe, naturalized in eastern North America. Use: formerly, herbal remedy for breast tumors. Latin name: *Lapsana communis.* [Because formerly used as a herbal remedy for breast tumors]

Nip·pon /ní pon/ Japanese name for Japan —**Nip·pon·ese** /nìppə neéz/ *adj*

nip·py /níppee/ (**-pi·er, -pi·est**) *adj* **1.** CHILLY rather chilly **2.** SHARP-TASTING slightly sharp in flavor **3.** TENDING TO BITE describes a dog that is inclined to attempt to bite people or other animals —**nip·pi·ly** *adv* —**nip·pi·ness** *n*

nip-up *n* an acrobatic move in which a gymnast lying with the back flat on the floor springs to an upright position

N.Ire. *abbr* Northern Ireland

Nir·en·berg /nírən bùrg/, **Marshall Warren** (*b.* 1927) US biochemist. He shared the Nobel Prize in physiology or medicine (1968) for research into how DNA determines the structure of proteins.

Ni·ro ♦ **De Niro, Robert**

nir·va·na /neer vaánə, nur-/ *n* **1.** *also* **Nir·va·na** in Hinduism, Buddhism, and Jainism, the attainment of enlightenment and freeing of the spiritual self from attachment to worldly things, ending the cycle of birth and rebirth **2.** an ultimate experience of some pleasurable emotion such as harmony or joy [Mid-19C. < Sanskrit < *nirvā-* "be extinguished" < *nis-* "out" + *vā-* "to blow"]

Ni·san /níss'n, nee saán/ *n* in the Jewish calendar, the first month of the religious year, lasting 30 days and falling about the same time as March to April. See table at **calendar** [15C. < Hebrew *Nīsān*]

ni·sei /nee sáy/ (*plural same* or **-seis**), **Ni·sei** *n* somebody born and raised in the United States or Canada whose parents immigrated from Japan [Mid-20C. < Japanese, "second generation"]

Nis·ga'a /níssgə/ (*plural same* or **-ga'as**), **Nish·ga** /níshgə/ (*plural same* or **-gas**) *n* **1.** a member of an Aboriginal people whose traditional territory is in the Nass River Valley in northwestern British Columbia **2.** the Tsimshian language of the Nisga'a people [Late 19C. < Tsimshian]

ni·si /nī́ sī, néessee/ *adj* scheduled to take effect on a specific date unless some cause can be shown for canceling or changing the date [Mid-19C. < Latin, "unless"]

Nis·sen hut /níss'n hùt/ *n* a temporary shelter made of corrugated steel in the shape of a half cylinder that was first used by the British during World War I [Early 20C. After Lt. Col. Peter Norman *Nissen* (1871–1930)]

NIST *abbr US* TECH National Institute of Standards and Technology

nit /nit/ *n* the egg or larva of a parasitic insect, especially a louse [Old English *hnitu* < Indo-European.] —**nit·ty** *adj*

SPELLCHECK See ***knit***.

NIT *abbr US* **1.** EDUC National Intelligence Test **2.** SPORTS National Invitational Tournament

nite /nīt/ *n* a spelling of the word "night," not appropriate for use in formal writing (*informal*)

Ni·ten /neét en, nee tén/ (1584–1645) Japanese artist and soldier. He is noted for his *sumi-e,* or black ink, paintings of birds, and was renowned for developing the technique of fencing with two swords. Born **Miyamoto Musashi**

ni·ter /nī́tər/ *n* CHEM **1.** same as **potassium nitrate 2.** same as **sodium nitrate** [14C. Via Old French < Latin *nitrum* < Greek *nitron*]

Ni·te·rói /neétə róy/ city in southeastern Brazil, situated on the southeastern shore of Guanabara Bay, opposite the city of Rio de Janeiro. Population: 450,364 (1996).

nit·pick /nít pìk/ (**-picked, -pick·ing, -picks**) *vti* to find insignificant details of something unsatisfactory, often unjustifiably —**nit·pick·er** *n* —**nit·pick·y** *adj*

SYNONYMS See ***criticize***.

nit·pick·ing /nít pìking/ *n* trivial, detailed, and often unjustified faultfinding

nitr- *prefix* same as **nitro-** (*used before vowels*)

ni·trate /nī́ tràyt/ *n* **1.** CHEM CHEMICAL GROUP a salt or an ester of nitric acid **2.** AGRIC FERTILIZER a fertilizer that consists of sodium nitrate, potassium nitrate, or ammonium nitrate ■ *vt* (**-trat·ed, -trat·ing, -trates**) CHEM, INDUST USE NITRATE ON SOMETHING to treat something with a nitrate or nitric acid, usually in order to change an organic compound into a nitrate [Late 18C. < French < *nitre* "niter"] —**ni·tra·tion** /nī tráysh'n/ *n*

ni·tre /nī́tər/ *n* CHEM Can, UK spelling of **niter**

ni·tric /nī́trik/ *adj* made from or containing nitrogen, especially in a high valence state

ni·tric ac·id *n* a corrosive colorless or yellowish liquid that is a highly reactive oxidizing agent. Use: manufacture of explosives, fertilizers, rocket fuels. Formula: HNO_3.

ni·tric ox·ide *n* a colorless poisonous gas. Source: ammonia, atmospheric nitrogen. Formula: NO.

ni·tride /nī́ trīd/ *n* a compound made up of nitrogen and another more electropositive element such as phosphorus or a metal [Mid-19C. < NITROGEN]

ni·tri·fy /nī́trə fī/ (**-fied, -fy·ing, -fies**) *vt* **1.** BIOCHEM OXIDIZE AMMONIA IONS to oxidize ammonia ions into nitrite or nitrate ions, as nitrobacteria do **2.** CHEM TREAT SOMETHING WITH NITROGEN to treat or combine something with nitrogen or nitrogen compounds **3.** AGRIC FERTILIZE SOIL to introduce nitrogen or nitrogen compounds into the soil in order to increase fertility [Early 19C. < French *nitrifier* < *nitre* (see NITER)] —**ni·tri·fi·ca·tion** /nī̀trəfi káysh'n/ *n* —**ni·tri·fi·er** *n*

ni·tri·fy·ing bac·te·ri·um *n* a soil bacterium that converts ammonia to nitrites and nitrates, making nitrogen available to plants

ni·trile /nítrəl/ *n* an organic cyanide. Use: rubber, especially in latex-free gloves.

ni·trite /nī trìt/ *n* a salt or ester of nitrous acid

ni·trite bac·te·ri·um *n* a nitrifying bacterium that converts ammonia to nitrites by oxidation

ni·tro /nítrō/ *n* same as **nitroglycerin** (*informal*) [Early 20C. Shortening]

nitro- *prefix* **1.** nitrogen ○ *nitrify* **2.** niter, nitrate **3.** containing a univalent NO_2 group ○ *nitroparaffin* [< Latin *nitrum* (see NITER)]

ni·tro·bac·te·ri·um /nítrō bak tēeree əm/ (*plural* **-ri·a** /-ree ə/) *n* same as **nitrifying bacterium**

ni·tro·ben·zene /nítrō bén zēen/ *n* a poisonous organic compound that occurs either as bright yellow crystals or as an oily liquid that smells like almonds. Use: manufacture of polishes, insulating compounds. Formula: $C_6H_5NO_2$.

ni·tro·cel·lu·lose /nítrō séllyə lōss, -lōz/ *n* a chemical compound produced by the reaction of nitric and sulfuric acids on cellulose. Use: manufacture of plastics, explosives, lacquers.

ni·tro·chlo·ro·form /nítrō kláwrə fàwrm/ *n* CHEM same as **chloropicrin**

ni·tro·fu·ran /nítrō fyŏŏr àn, -fyə rán/ *n* a drug that inhibits the growth of bacteria. It has been banned from use in food-producing animals in many countries.

ni·tro·fu·ran·toin /nítrō fyoor ántō in/ *n* a drug that inhibits the growth of bacteria. Use: treatment of urinary infections.

ni·tro·gen /nítrəjən/ *n* a nonmetallic element that occurs as a colorless odorless almost inert gas and makes up four fifths of the Earth's atmosphere by volume. Use: manufacture of ammonia, explosives, fertilizers. Symbol **N**. See table at **element** [Late 18C. < French *nitrogène* < *nitre* (see NITER) + *-gène* (see -GEN)] —**ni·trog·e·nous** /nī trójjənəss/ *adj*

ni·trog·e·nase /nī trójjə nàyss, -nàyz/ *n* an enzyme found in nitrogen-fixing bacteria that catalyzes the conversion of nitrogen to ammonia. It is a key component of the nitrogen cycle, providing nitrogen compounds for plants.

ni·tro·gen bal·ance *n* **1.** the difference between the amount of nitrogen taken into the body and the amount excreted **2.** the difference between the amount of nitrogen absorbed by the soil and the amount lost

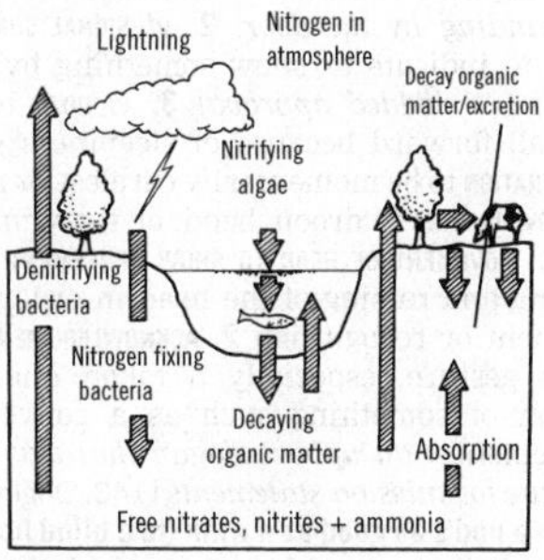

nitrogen cycle

ni·tro·gen cy·cle *n* the series of processes by which nitrogen is converted from a gas in the atmosphere to nitrogen-containing substances in soil and living organisms, then reconverted to a gas. The main chemical transformations are performed by microorganisms and include nitrogen fixation, nitrification, and denitrification.

ni·tro·gen di·ox·ide *n* a highly poisonous brown gas often present in smog and exhaust from vehicles. Use: manufacture of nitric and sulfuric acids. Formula: NO_2.

ni·tro·gen fix·a·tion *n* **1.** the natural conversion of atmospheric nitrogen by bacteria found in the nodules of legumes into compounds in the soil that plants and other organisms can use **2.** an industrial process in which nitrogen from the atmosphere is changed into compounds such as ammonia by chemical agents. Use: manufacture of fertilizers. —**ni·tro·gen-fix·er** *n* —**ni·tro·gen-fix·ing** *adj*

ni·trog·en·ize /nī trójjə nīz/ (**-ized, -iz·ing, -iz·es**) *vt* to combine or treat something with nitrogen or one of its compounds —**ni·trog·en·i·za·tion** /nī trójjəni zàysh'n/ *n*

ni·tro·gen mus·tard *n* a compound similar to mustard gas in which the sulfur is replaced by amino nitrogen. Use: treatment of some cancers.

ni·tro·gen nar·co·sis *n* light-headedness, confusion, or exhilaration caused by increased nitrogen in the blood. This occurs in deep-sea divers exposed to pressures several times that of the atmosphere.

ni·tro·glyc·er·in /nítrō glíssərin, nítrə-/, **ni·tro·glyc·er·ine** *n* a colorless thick oily flammable and explosive liquid. Use: manufacture of explosives, treatment of angina. Formula: $C_3H_5N_3O_9$.

ni·tro·hy·dro·chlo·ric ac·id /nítrō hīdrō kláwrik-/ *n* CHEM same as **aqua regia**

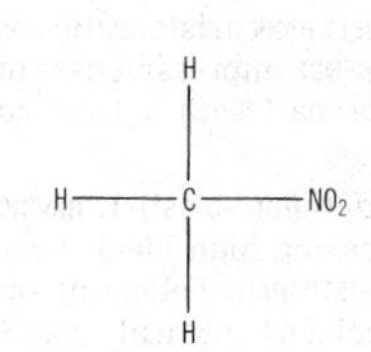

nitromethane

ni·tro·meth·ane /nítrō mé thàyn/ *n* a poisonous colorless oily slightly water-soluble liquid. Use: manufacture of dyes, resins, rocket fuels, as a solvent and gasoline additive. Formula: CH_3NO_2.

ni·tro·par·af·fin /nítrō párrəfin/ *n* a colorless simple hydrocarbon containing the chemical group NO_2

ni·tros·a·mine /nītrōssə mēen, -sá mēen/ *n* an organic carcinogenic compound found in various foods. Formula: R_2NNO. [Late 19C. < Latin *nitrosus* "nitrous"]

ni·trous /nítrəss/ *adj* made from or containing nitrogen, especially in a low valence state

ni·trous ac·id *n* a weak inorganic acid found only in solution or in the form of its salts. Formula: HNO_2.

ni·trous ox·ide *n* a colorless nonflammable sweet-smelling sweet-tasting gas. Use: anesthetic. Formula: N_2O.

nit·ty-grit·ty /nìttee gríttee/ (*informal*) *n* **BASICS** the basic and most important details of something ■ *adj* **1. BASIC AND IMPORTANT** concerning or involving the most important aspects of a subject **2. PRACTICAL** useful and direct in a practical down-to-earth way ○ *a nitty-gritty approach to teaching* [Mid-20C. Origin ?]

nit·wit /nít wìt/ *n* an offensive term that deliberately insults somebody's common sense or intelligence (*insult*) [Early 20C. Origin ?]

Ni·u·e /nee ōō ay/ island territory in free association with New Zealand, lying in the South Pacific Ocean, 350 mi./563 km southeast of Samoa. Population: 2,000 (1995). Area: 101 sq. mi./263 sq. km.

Ni·u·e·an /nee ōō ay ən/ *n* **1.** a member of a Polynesian people who inhabit the Pacific island of Niue **2.** the Polynesian language of Niue, similar to Samoan and Tongan —**Ni·u·e·an** *adj*

ni·val /nív'l/ *adj* growing in or under the snow [Mid-17C. < Latin *nivalis* < *niv-* "snow"]

niv·e·ous /nívvee əss/ *adj* resembling snow in color [Early 17C. < Latin *niveus* < *niv-* "snow"]

nix /niks/ *vt* (**nixed, nix·ing, nix·es**) to refuse, forbid, or veto something (*slang*) ■ *n* same as **nothing** (*dated slang*) ■ *interj US* used to warn somebody not to do something or stop doing something (*dated slang*) [Late 18C. < German, variant of *nichts* "nothing"] —**nixed** *adj*

nix·ie[1] /níksee/, **nix** /niks/ *n* in Germanic mythology, a female water spirit that can appear in human form or as half-human, half-fish [Early 19C. < German *Nixe*, feminine of *Nix*]

nix·ie[2] /níksee/, **nix·y** (*plural* **-ies**) *n US* an item of mail that cannot be delivered because it has the wrong address or the address is unreadable (*slang*) [Late 19C. < NIX]

Richard Nixon

Nix·on /níks'n/, **Richard** (1913–94) 37th president of the United States. A Republican president (1969–74), he was forced to resign after the Watergate scandal (1974). He was responsible for ending the US commitment in Vietnam. See table at **president**. Full name **Nixon, Richard Milhous**

> "I let down my friends, I let down my country. I let down our system of government."
> [Richard Nixon, *Observer (London)*; May 8, 1977]

> "You won't have Nixon to kick around anymore, because, gentlemen, this is my last press conference."
> [Richard Nixon, *remark to the media*; November 7, 1962]

Nix·on, Thelma Catherine Ryan (1912–93) US first lady (1969–74). She traveled extensively with her husband during his vice-presidency and presidency and was granted the title of Personal Representative of the President for her solo visits to Africa and South America. Known as **Pat**

nix·y *n US* MAIL another spelling of **nixie**[2]

Nizh·niy Nov·gor·od /nìzhnee nóvgə ròd, -náwvgə ràwd/ industrial city and major river port in western Russia where the rivers Oka and Volga meet. Population: 1,840,212 (1995).. Former name **Gorky** (1932–91)

Nizh·ny Ta·gil /nìzhnee taa gíl/ city in western Siberian Russia. Population: 579,737 (1995).

NJ, N.J. *abbr* New Jersey

n·jam·ma·n·jam·ma /ən jàmmə ən jámmə/ *n* COOK in African cuisine, large- or small-leaf cooking greens resembling arugula

Nko·mo /əng kṓmō/, **Joshua** (1917–99) Zimbabwean nationalist leader. He led the Zimbabwe African People's Union and other nationalist groups opposed to white rule in Rhodesia, and after the transition to majority rule in Zimbabwe held various government posts.

> "The hardest lesson of my life has come to me late. It is that a nation can win freedom without its people becoming free."
> [Joshua Nkomo, *The Story of My Life*; 1984]

Nkru·mah /ən krṓōmə, əng-/, **Kwame** (1909–72) first prime minister (1957–60) and president (1960–66) of Ghana. He played a prominent role in the establishment of the independent state of Ghana in 1957 and was a strong supporter of pan-Africanism.

> "Never in the history of the world has an alien ruler granted self-rule to a people on a silver platter."
> [Kwame Nkrumah, *The Autobiography of Kwame Nkrumah*; 1959]

NKVD, N.K.V.D. *n* the Soviet secret police from 1934 to 1946 [Russian, abbreviation of *Narodny Kommissariat Vnutrennikh Del* "People's Commissariat of Internal Affairs"]

nl *abbr* Netherlands (*used in Internet addresses*) See table at **domain name**

NL, N.L. *abbr* **1.** BASEBALL National League **2.** LANG New Latin

n.l. *abbr* PRINTING new line

NLF *abbr* POL National Liberation Front

NLP *abbr* **1.** COMPUT natural language processing **2.** PSYCHOL neurolinguistic programming

NLRB, N.L.R.B. *abbr US* HR, GOV National Labor Relations Board

nm *abbr* MEASURE **1.** nanometer **2.** nuclear magneton

NM *abbr* **1.** MEASURE nautical mile **2.** New Mexico

N.M. *abbr* New Mexico

NMD *abbr* POL National Missile Defense

N. Mex. *abbr* New Mexico

NMI *abbr* no middle initial

NMR *abbr* PHYS, MED nuclear magnetic resonance

NNE *abbr* north-northeast

NNP *abbr* ECON net national product

NNW *abbr* north-northwest

no[1] /nō/ *adv, interj* **1. INDICATING NEGATIVE RESPONSE** indicates a negative response, used to refuse, deny, or disagree with something ○ *"Will you be taking the car?" – "No, not today."* ○ *"Would you like coffee?" – "No, I'm fine, thanks."* **2. ACKNOWLEDGING NEGATIVE STATEMENT** used to express acceptance or understanding of a negative statement made by somebody else ○ *"Nobody seems to have the time to really listen these days." – "No, they don't."* **3. INDICATING DISBELIEF** used to indicate shock, disbelief, or disappointment at something somebody has said ○ *"The car's going to be in the shop for another week." – "Oh no!"* ■ *n* (*plural* **noes** or **nos**) **1. ANSWER OR VOTE** an answer or vote of "no" ○ *They all gave resounding noes to the proposition.* **2. SOMEBODY VOTING "NO"** somebody who answers "no" to a question or votes against something [Old English *nā* < *ne* "not" + *ā* "ever"] ◇ **not take no for an answer** not to accept a refusal ○ *I told her I couldn't do it, but she wouldn't take no for an answer.* ◇ **say no** to express disagreement or refusal ◇ **the noes have it** used to indicate that a majority has voted against something

SPELLCHECK See ***know.***

no[2] /nō/ CORE MEANING: an adjective used to indicate that there is not any or not one person or thing ○ *There is nothing in walking distance: no post office, no bank.* ○ *I had no choice in the matter.* ○ *They pay no attention to me.*

adj **1.** used to indicate that somebody or something does not have any of the characteristic or identity mentioned ○ *She's no fool.* **2.** not exceeding a particular amount or quality (*used with comparative adjectives and adverbs*) ○ *The issue was no less important to us than you.* [12C. Shortening of NONE]

no[3] *abbr* Norway (*used in Internet addresses*) See table at **domain name**

No[1] /nō/, **Noh** *n* a form of Japanese drama that presents a story in a highly stylized fashion, using music, dance, and elaborate costumes. It flourished in the 14th and 15th centuries, and its development was influenced by Zen Buddhism. [Late 19C. < Japanese *nō* "talent, ability" < Middle Chinese *nəŋ*]

No[2] *symbol* CHEM ELEM nobelium

no., No. *abbr* **1.** north **2.** northern **3.** number

NOAA *abbr US* OCEANOG, GOV National Oceanic and Atmospheric Administration

no-ac·count, no-'count *adj US* without any redeeming or useful qualities (*informal*)

No·a·chi·an /nō áykee ən/, **No·ach·ic** /-áykik/, **No·ach·i·cal** /-áykik'l/ *adj* **1.** characteristic of or relating to Noah or his time **2.** long out of date [Late 19C. < *Noach*, form of *Noah*]

No·ah /nṓ ə/ *n* in the Bible, a Hebrew patriarch who, at God's command, built a ship and saved himself, his family, and a pair of every kind of animal from the Flood (Genesis 6–9)

No·ah's ark *n* BIBLE same as **ark** (sense 1)

nob[1] /nob/ *n UK* somebody rich or socially powerful (*informal*) [Late 17C. Origin ?]

nob[2] /nob/ *n* **1.** the human head (*slang*) **2.** in cribbage, the jack of the suit that the dealer turns up, which scores one point for the player who holds it [Late 17C. Origin ?]

nob·by /nóbbee/ *adj UK* fashionable or elegant (*informal*) [Late 18C. < NOB[1]]

No·bel /nō bél/, **Alfred** (1833–96) Swedish chemist. His development of dynamite brought him great wealth, which was used after his death to set up the Nobel Prizes. Full name **Nobel, Alfred Bernhard**

No·bel·ist /nō béllist/ *n* a winner of a Nobel Prize

no·bel·i·um /nō béelee əm/ *n* a radioactive element. Source: produced artificially from curium. Symbol **No.** See table at **element** [Mid-20C. After Alfred NOBEL]

No·bel Prize /nō bèl príz/ *n* an international award made annually for outstanding achievement in chemistry, literature, physics, physiology or medicine, economics, or promoting world peace [Early 20C. After Alfred NOBEL] —**No·bel prize·win·ner** *n* —**No·bel-prize·win·ning** *adj*

no·bil·i·ar·y /nō béllee èrree, -yəree/ *adj* relating to the nobility [Mid-18C. < French *nobiliaire* < *noble* (see NOBLE)]

no·bil·i·ar·y par·ti·cle *n* a preposition used before a title or surname as a mark of rank, e.g., "de" in French or "von" in German

no·bil·i·ty /nō bíllətee/ (*plural* **-ties**) *n* **1. NOBLE CHARACTER** high ideals or excellent moral character **2. ARISTOCRATS** a noble class or people of noble rank in a country **3. NOBLE RANK** aristocratic social position or rank **4. MAGNIFICENCE** impressiveness or magnificence [14C. Directly or via French < Latin *nobilitas* < *nobilis* "noble"]

no·ble /nṓb'l/ *adj* (**-bler, -blest**) **1. HAVING EXCELLENT MORAL CHARACTER** possessing high ideals or excellent moral character **2. ARISTOCRATIC** belonging or relating to an aristocratic social or political class **3. RELATING TO HIGH MORAL PRINCIPLES** based on high ideals or revealing excellent moral character **4. MAGNIFICENT** impressive in quality or appearance **5.** CHEM **NONREACTIVE** chemically inactive or inert ■ *n* **1. ARISTOCRAT** a titled aristocrat **2. FORMER ENGLISH COIN** a gold coin worth half a mark, formerly used in England [13C. Via French < Latin *(g)nobilis*] —**no·ble·ness** *n* —**no·bly** *adv*

no·ble gas *n* a chemically inert rare gas belonging to group 18 of the periodic table. Helium, neon, argon, krypton, xenon, and radon are noble gases.

no·ble·man /nṓb'lmən/ (*plural* **-men** /-mən/) *n* a man who belongs to a titled aristocracy

no·ble met·al *n* a metal that is resistant to oxidation, e.g., gold, silver, or platinum

no·ble rot *n* a fungus that shrivels ripe grapes, increasing the proportion of sugar to liquid in them. It is desirable in the making of some wines, e.g., French Sauternes. Latin name: *Botrytis cinerea.*

no·ble sav·age *n* somebody belonging to a nontechnological culture whose life is, according to an idea popularized by Rousseau, purer because it is closer to nature (*sometimes offensive*)

no·blesse /nō bléss/ *n* **1.** aristocratic social position or rank **2.** the members of an aristocracy, especially the French aristocracy [13C. < French, "nobility" < *noble* (see NOBLE)]

no·blesse o·blige /nō blèss ə bléezh/ *n* the idea that people born into the nobility or upper social classes must behave in an honorable and generous way toward those less privileged [< French, "nobility obliges"]

no·ble·wom·an /nṓb'l wòommən/ (*plural* **-wom·en** /-wìmmin/) *n* a woman who belongs to a titled aristocracy

no·bod·y /nṓbadee, -bòddee, -bùddee/ *pron* not one single person ○ *Nobody can order the attack except the general.* ■ *n* (*plural* **-ies**) somebody regarded as unimportant or insignificant ○ *I felt like a nobody among so many important scientists.*

no-brain *adj* lacking intelligence, perception, or common sense ○ *Whose no-brain idea was that?*

no-brain·er /-bráynər/ *n* something, e.g., an idea or question, that is so easily understood or done that it requires little or no thought (*slang*)

no·cent /nṓss'nt/ *adj* causing harm, injury, or damage [15C. < Latin *nocent-*, present participle of *nocere* "to hurt"] —**no·cent·ly** *adv*

no·ci·cep·tion /nòssi sépsh'n/ *n* the perception of physical pain [Late 20C. < Latin *nocere* "to hurt" + PERCEPTION]

no·ci·cep·tive /nòssi séptiv/ *adj* **1.** describes a stimulus that causes pain **2.** caused by or reacting to pain [Early 20C. < Latin *nocere* "to hurt" + RECEPTIVE] —**no·ci·cep·tive·ly** *adv*

nock /nok/ *n* **1. GROOVE ON BOW** one of the grooves at each end of a bow that holds the bowstring **2. NOTCH ON ARROW** the notch at the end of an arrow that holds it on the bowstring ■ *vt* (**nocked, nock·ing, nocks**) **1. PREPARE TO FIRE ARROW** to place an arrow on a bowstring **2. NOTCH BOW OR ARROW** to put a notch in a bow or an arrow [14C. Probably < Middle Dutch *nocke* "projection, tip"]

no con·test *n US* LAW same as **nolo contendere**

no-'count *adj US* same as **no-account** (*informal*)

noct- *prefix* same as **nocti-** (*used before vowels*)

nocti- *prefix* night, at night ○ *noctilucent* [< Latin *noct-* "night" < Indo-European]

noc·ti·lu·ca /nòktə lóokə/ (*plural* **-cae** /-sèe/) *n* a plankton that produces light. When present in large groups they make the sea appear to glow. Genus: *Noctiluca.* [Mid-19C. < Latin, "moon, lantern"]

noc·ti·lu·cent /nòktə lóoss'nt/ *adj* describes high clouds that are visible at night [Late 19C. < NOCTI- + Latin *lucere* "to shine"]

noc·tu·id /nókchoo id/ *n* a dull-colored moth whose larvae, called army worms and cutworms, are destructive to young plants. Family: Noctuidae. [Late 19C. < Latin *noctua* "night owl"] —**noc·tu·id** *adj*

noc·tule /nók chòol/ *n* a large reddish brown bat that eats insects. Native to: Europe, Asia. Latin name: *Nyctalus noctula.* [Late 18C. Via French < Italian *nottola* "bat"]

noc·turn /nók tùrn/ *n* in the Roman Catholic Church, one of the three divisions of the service of matins, previously held at midnight but now usually at daybreak [14C. Directly or via French *nocturne* < ecclesiastical Latin *nocturnus* < Latin, "of the night" < *noct-* "night"]

noc·tur·nal /nok túrn'l/ *adj* **1. AT NIGHT** occurring at night, as opposed to during the day **2.** ZOOL **ACTIVE AT NIGHT** describes animals that are active at night rather than during the day **3.** BOT **FLOWERING AT NIGHT** describes flowers that open at night and close during the day —**noc·tur·nal·ly** *adv*

noc·turne /nók tùrn/ *n* **1.** a musical composition, especially for the piano, that suggests a tranquil dreamy mood. It evolved during the early 19th century, and Chopin was the most famous composer of nocturnes. **2.** a painting of a night scene [Mid-19C. < French (see NOCTURN)]

noc·u·ous /nókyoo əss/ *adj* likely to cause injury or damage [Mid-17C. < Latin *nocuus* < *nocere* "to hurt"] —**noc·u·ous·ly** *adv* —**noc·u·ous·ness** *n*

nod /nod/ *v* (**nod·ded, nod·ding, nods**) **1.** *vti* **MOVE HEAD IN AGREEMENT** to lower and then raise the head quickly in order to show agreement or recognition or to give a signal ○ *He nodded discreetly to a man who was standing by the door.* **2.** *vt* **SIGNAL SOMETHING BY NODDING** to indicate or show something by nodding the head ○ *nodded approval* **3.** *vi* **DOZE** to let the head fall forward because of sleepiness **4.** *vi* **LOSE CONCENTRATION** to be momentarily careless or negligent **5.** *vi* **MOVE IN WIND** to droop, bend, or sway in a breeze ■ *n* **1. MOVEMENT OF HEAD TO SHOW AGREEMENT** a quick lowering and raising of the head in order to show agreement or recognition **2. ACKNOWLEDGMENT OF SOMETHING** a gesture, especially a token one, in recognition of something such as a convention or requirement ○ *an upbeat slogan that was a nod to the vogue for mission statements* [14C. Origin ?] —**nod·der** *n* ◇ **a nod's as good as a wink (to a blind horse)** used to indicate that something expressed indirectly has been understood and that no further explanation is required ◇ **give somebody** *or* **something the nod** to select or approve somebody or something ◇ **have a nodding acquaintance with somebody** *or* **something** to have a slight knowledge of a person or subject ◇ **on the nod** *UK* agreed without formal discussion or procedures (*informal*)

nod off *vi* to fall asleep unintentionally

nod out *vi* to go into a state of drug-induced sleep or semiconsciousness (*slang*)

nod·ding don·key /nódding-/ *n* a reciprocating pump for extracting oil

nod·dle /nódd'l/ *n* the human head or brain (*dated informal*) [15C. Origin ?]

nod·dy /nóddee/ (*plural* **-dies**) *n* a dark-colored seabird of the tern family. Native to: tropical coastal waters. Genera: *Anous* or *Procelsterna.* [Early 16C. Origin ?]

nod·dy suit *n* a protective suit worn by military

personnel likely to be exposed to nuclear, biological, or chemical weapons (*slang*)

node /nōd/ *n* **1.** MATH **POINT OF INTERSECTION** a point where lines meet or intersect in a diagram or graph **2.** MATH **POINT WHERE PARTS OF CURVE INTERSECT** in geometry, a place on a curve where it crosses itself **3.** ASTRON **POINT WHERE ORBIT INTERSECTS ECLIPTIC** either of the two points where an orbit, e.g., that of a planet, crosses the ecliptic plane **4.** ANAT **LUMP OR BULGE** a lump, knob, knot, or other kind of swelling that sticks out **5.** BOT **POINT ON PLANT STEM** the place on a plant stem where a leaf is attached or has been attached **6.** COMPUT **TERMINAL OR POINT IN NETWORK** a terminal or other point in a computer network where a message can be created, received, or transmitted **7.** PHYS **POINT ON WAVE** in physics, a place in a standing wave that has little or no amplitude **8.** LING **POINT IN SENTENCE STRUCTURE** in transformational grammars, a point in a sentence diagram where a category label, indicating the part of speech, appears and from which further branches may lead off [14C. < Latin *nodus* "knot"] —**nod·al** *adj*

node of Ran·vier /-raaN vyáy/ *n* a short gap in the myelin sheath that occurs at intervals along the length of a nerve fiber [After Louis Antoine *Ranvier* (1835–1922), French histologist]

no·dose /nō dōss, -dōz/ *adj* having many points at which leaves join the stem —**no·dos·i·ty** /nō dóssətee/ *n*

nod·ule /nó joōl/ *n* **1.** **SMALL LUMP** a small protruding knob, lump, or swelling on something **2.** BOT **ROOT PROTUBERANCE** a swelling or knob on the roots of legumes that contains bacteria **3.** ANAT **CELL OR TISSUE MASS** a small mass of cells or tissue, which may be a normal part of the body or a growth such as a tumor **4.** GEOL **LARGE ROUNDED MINERAL FORM** a form of a mineral that is massive with a rounded outer surface [15C. < Latin *nodulus* "small knot" < *nodus* "knot"] —**nod·u·lar** /nójjələr/ *adj* —**nod·u·lose** /-lōss/ *adj*

no·el /nō él/, **no·ël** *n* a Christmas carol (*archaic or literary*) [Early 19C. < NOEL]

No·el /nō él/, **No·ël** *n* Christmas, especially in carols or greetings [12C. < French < Latin *(dies) natalis* "birth (day)" < *nasci* "be born"]

no·et·ic /nō éttik/ *adj* characteristic of, coming from, or understood by the human mind [Mid-17C. < Greek *noētikos* < *noein* "think" < *nous* "mind"] —**no·et·i·cal·ly** *adv*

no-fault *adj* **1.** relating to a system of motor vehicle insurance in which insurance companies compensate accident victims without determining who is responsible for the accident **2.** relating to a form of divorce in which no blame is placed on either party for the breakdown of the marriage

no-fly list *n* a computer-generated list of the names of people identified by law enforcement as being so dangerous to civil aviation that they are denied permission to fly on commercial aircraft [Early 21C.]

no-fly zone *n* **1.** an area over which aircraft, especially those of another country, are forbidden to fly, and in which they will be attacked **2.** *US* a topic of questioning or conversation that is off-limits (*slang*) ○ *The press secretary declared that issue to be a no-fly zone for reporters.*

no-frills *adj* relating to a service or establishment that does not offer extra or special treatment (*informal*)

no-fuss *adj* involving little bother or few difficulties for the user

nog[1] /nog/ *n* **1.** **WOODEN BLOCK FOR NAILING** a block of wood inserted into masonry or brickwork so that something can be nailed to it **2.** **PEG** a wooden peg or pin ■ *vt* (**nogged, nog·ging, nogs**) **FILL WITH BRICKS** to fill a wall or partition with small stones or bricks [Early 17C. Origin ?]

nog[2] /nog/ *n* BEVERAGES same as **eggnog** [Early 17C. Origin ?]

No·gal·es /nō gaáliss/ **1.** city in Sonora State in northwestern Mexico, on the United States border. Population: 159,787 (2000). **2.** city in southeastern Arizona south of Tucson, on the Mexican border opposite Nogales, Mexico. Population: 21,280 (2002 estimate).

nog·gin /nóggin/ *n* **1.** **CUP** a small cup or mug (*dated*) **2.** **ONE FOURTH OF PINT** a measure for liquor equivalent to $\frac{1}{4}$ pint/0.148 liters (*dated*) **3.** **HEAD** the human head (*dated informal*) [Mid-17C. Origin ?]

nog·ging /nógging/ *n* **1.** small stones, bricks, or bits of masonry used to fill the spaces between studs in a wall or partition **2.** one of the pieces of wood inserted between the main timbers of a half-timbered wall [Early 19C. < NOG[1]]

no-go *n* an event or situation that is prevented from occurring by adverse conditions (*informal*) ■ *adj* no longer going to happen or scheduled to occur

no-go ar·e·a *n* an area that unauthorized people are forbidden to enter

no-good (*insult*) *adj* considered as lacking merit, virtue, worth, or morals ■ *n* somebody or something considered to lack merit, virtue, worth, or morals

No·gu·chi /nō goóchee/, **Hideyo** (1876–1928) Japanese bacteriologist. He helped discover the spirochete that causes syphilis, and devised a method to diagnose the disease.

CORBIS/Nathan Benn

Isamu Noguchi

No·gu·chi, Isamu (1904–88) US sculptor. He is known for his abstract sculptures and his sculpture gardens.

Noh *n* THEATER another spelling of **No**[1]

no-hit *adj* relating to a baseball or softball game in which the opponents do not get a hit

no-hit·ter *n* a baseball or softball game in which the pitcher does not allow opponents a hit

no-holds-barred *adj* happening, or engaged in something, without restraint or control (*informal*) ○ *The debate was a no-holds-barred battle of wits.* [< a wrestling match in which any hold is permitted]

no-hop·er *n UK* an offensive term that deliberately insults somebody's achievements and likelihood of future success (*insult*)

no·how /nō hòw/ *adv* not in any way (*nonstandard*)

NOI *abbr* POL, ISLAM Nation of Islam

noil /noyl/ *n* short fibers separated during combing from the long fibers of cotton, wool, silk, or another material [Early 17C. Probably < Old French *noel* < medieval Latin *nodellus* "small knot" < Latin *nodus* "knot"]

noir /nwaar/ *adj* done or made in a style that is characteristic of film noir [< French, "black"]

noise /noyz/ *n* **1.** **UNPLEASANT SOUND** a loud, surprising, irritating, or unwanted sound **2.** **ANY SOUND** any sound or combination of sounds ○ *too much noise in the room* **3.** **OUTCRY** a loud clamor or commotion concerning something **4.** **COMPLAINT** a complaint or protest about something (*informal*) **5.** **RUMOR** idle talk, rumor, or gossip (*informal*) **6.** PHYS **ELECTRIC DISTURBANCE** a random disturbance in an electric circuit that interferes with the reception of a signal **7.** COMPUT **MEANINGLESS DATA** unwanted or meaningless data intermixed with the relevant information in the output from a computer ■ *v* (**noised, nois·ing, nois·es**) **1.** *vt* **SPREAD GOSSIP** to spread a rumor or gossip ○ *an ugly story that was being noised about in newsrooms across the nation* **2.** *vi* **TALK A LOT** to talk too much (*dated*) [13C. Via French, "uproar, brawl" < Latin *nausea* "seasickness" < Greek *naus* "ship"] ◇ **make noises** to do or say something intended to attract attention or indicate an intention ○ *He's making noises about a career change.*

noise a·bate·ment *n* the reduction of noise pollution

noise·less /nóyzləss/ *adj* not making any noise —**noise·less·ly** *adv* —**noise·less·ness** *n*

noise·mak·er /nóyz màykər/ *n* **1.** a device used to make noise at a party or a celebration, e.g., a rattle or horn **2.** *US* a maker or cause of noise —**noise·mak·ing** *n*

noise pol·lu·tion *n* irritating, distracting, or physically dangerous noise to which people are exposed in their environment and over which they usually have no control

noi·sette /nwaa zét/ *n* a piece of boned and rolled meat, especially the neck or loin of lamb [Late 19C. < French, "little nut"; from its shape]

noi·some /nóyssəm/ *adj* **1.** so offensive, especially to the senses, as to arouse feelings of disgust or repulsion **2.** extremely harmful [14C. < obsolete *noy*, shortening of ANNOY] —**noi·some·ly** *adv* —**noi·some·ness** *n*

nois·y /nóyzee/ (**-i·er, -i·est**) *adj* **1.** making a loud and annoying noise **2.** full of or characterized by loud sounds —**nois·i·ly** *adv* —**nois·i·ness** *n*

Nok /nok/ *n* a civilization located in the forests of central Nigeria that flourished between 500 B.C. and A.D. 300. It is known for its highly developed art style.

no-kill *US n* an animal shelter that does not euthanize the animals housed there, except under limited conditions ■ *adj* opposed to or not euthanizing animals housed in an animal shelter, except under limited conditions

No·land /nṓlənd/, **Kenneth** (*b.* 1924) US painter. His abstract works feature various geometric motifs, often on irregularly shaped canvases.

no·lens vo·lens /nṑlənz vṓlənz/ *adv* whether willing or not willing [< Latin, "unwilling willing"]

noli me tan·ge·re /nṑlee may táng gə rày/ *n* **1.** **PROHIBITION AGAINST TOUCHING** a warning not to touch or interfere with somebody or something **2.** **SOMEBODY OR SOMETHING NOT FOR TOUCHING** somebody or something that must not be touched or interfered with **3.** ART **PAINTING OF CHRIST WITH MARY MAGDALENE** a depiction in art of Jesus Christ appearing to Mary Magdalene after his resurrection [< Latin, "do not touch me"; from Jesus Christ's words to Mary Magdalene (John 20:17)]

nol·le pros·e·qui /nṑlee próssə kwì/ *n* an entry made in a court record when a plaintiff or a prosecutor decides not to proceed further with a case or action [< Latin, "be unwilling to pursue"]

no·lo /nṓlō/ (*plural* **-los**) *n US* same as **nolo contendere** (*informal*) [Shortening]

no-load *adj* sold directly to customers at net asset value without the addition of a sales commission or other fees ○ *a no-load mutual fund*

no·lo con·ten·de·re /nṑlō kən téndəree/ *n US* in law, a plea entered by a defendant that does not explicitly admit guilt, but subjects the defendant to punishment, while allowing denial of the alleged facts in other proceedings [< Latin, "I do not wish to contend"]

no-lose *adj* certain to result in success or be beneficial, regardless of the outcome ○ *a no-lose proposition*

nol. pros. /nòl próss/ *abbr* LAW nolle prosequi

nol-pros /nòl próss/ (**nol-prossed, nol-pros·sing, nol-pros·ses**) *vt US* to end the prosecution of a case by entering "nolle prosequi" in the court records [Shortening of Latin *nolle prosequi* "be unwilling to pursue"]

nom. *abbr* GRAM nominative

no·ma /nṓmə/ *n* a severe gangrenous inflammation of the mouth or genitals, usually occurring in children who are malnourished or otherwise debilitated [Mid-19C. < modern Latin alteration of Latin *nome* < Greek *nom-*, stem of *nemein* "to feed"]

no·mad /nṓ màd/ *n* **1.** a member of a people who move seasonally from place to place to search for food and water or pasture for their livestock **2.** somebody who wanders from place to place [Late 16C. < French *nomade* < Greek *nomas* "wandering about to find pasture" < *nemein* "to pasture"] —**no·mad·ic** /nō máddik/ *adj* —**no·mad·i·cal·ly** *adv* —**no·mad·ism** *n*

no man's land *n* **1.** **TERRITORY BETWEEN OPPOSING FORCES** the area of land that lies between two opposing armies and is held by neither side **2.** **UNCLAIMED TERRITORY** any area of land that no one has established a claim to **3.** **AMBIGUOUS AREA** any indefinite or ambiguous situation in which boundaries, rules, or authority are unclear or unfamiliar **4.** RACKET GAMES **BAD POSITION ON TENNIS COURT** in tennis and other court games, an area on a court in which a player is tactically at a disadvantage

nom·ar·chy /nómmərkee/ (*plural* **-chies**) *n* any of the administrative provinces into which modern Greece is divided [Mid-17C. < Greek *nomarkhia* < *nomos* (see NOME) + *-arkhia* "government"]

nom·bril /nómbrəl/, **nom·bril point** *n* in heraldry, the midpoint of the lower half of an escutcheon, halfway between the fess point and the base point [Mid-16C. < French, "navel"]

nom de guerre /nòm də gér/ (*plural* **noms de guerre** /*pronunc. same*/) *n* an assumed name that somebody uses, e.g., when fighting [< French, "name of war"]

nom de plume /nòm də ploóm/ (*plural* **noms de plume** /*pronunc. same*/) *n* LITERAT same as **pen name** [< French, "name of pen"]

nome /nōm/ *n* **1.** a province of ancient Egypt **2.** POL same as **nomarchy** [Early 18C. < Greek *nomos* < *nemein* "divide"]

Nome /nōm/ city in western Alaska, on the Seward Peninsula, on the northern shore of Norton Sound. Population: 3,522 (2002 estimate).

no·men /nṓmən/ (*plural* **nom·i·na** /nómmənə/) *n* in ancient Rome, a citizen's second name, which indicated the clan to which he or she belonged [Early 18C. < Latin, "name"]

no·men·cla·tor /nṓmən kláytər/ *n* an assigner of names in a scientific classification system (**taxonomy**) [Mid-16C. < Latin < *nomen* "name" + *calare* "to call"]

no·men·cla·ture /nṓmən klàychər/ *n* **1.** a system of names assigned to objects or items in a particular science or art **2.** the assigning of names to organisms in a scientific classification system (**taxonomy**) [Early 17C. Via French < Latin *nomenclatura* < *nomen* "name" + *calare* "to call"] —**no·men·cla·tur·al** *adj*

no·men·kla·tu·ra /nṓmən klə tóōrə, -klaa-/ *n* **1.** in Communist governments, the elite privileged class consisting of the people holding positions of authority in the bureaucracy (*takes a singular or plural verb*) **2.** in the former Soviet Union and other Communist countries, the system for assigning senior positions in the bureaucracy, controlled by committees in the Communist Party (*takes a singular verb*) [Mid-20C. Via Russian < Latin *nomenclatura* (see NOMENCLATURE)]

nom·i·na HIST plural of **nomen**

nom·i·nal /nómmən'l/ *adj* **1.** SO-CALLED acting or being something in name only, but not in reality **2.** VERY LOW IN COST representing very little cost when compared with the actual value received ○ *a nominal fee* **3.** BEARING SOMEBODY'S NAME assigned to a named person, and bearing that person's name **4.** OF NAMES relating to or consisting of a name or names **5.** GRAM OF NOUN relating to a noun or a group of words that functions as a noun **6.** ACCT RELATING TO CURRENT PRICES considered in terms of the stated or original value only, and ignoring changes due to inflation and other factors ■ *n* GRAM NOUN OR NOUN GROUP a word or group of words that functions as a noun [15C. Directly or via French < Latin *nominalis* < *nomen* "name"] —**nom·i·nal·ly** *adv*

nom·i·nal·ism /nómmən'l ìzzəm/ *n* the philosophical doctrine that there are no realities other than concrete individual objects —**nom·i·nal·ist** *n, adj* —**nom·i·nal·is·tic** /nòmmən'l ístik/ *adj*

nom·i·nal·ize /nómmən'l ìz/ (**-ized, -iz·ing, -iz·es**) *vt* **1.** to change a part of speech into a noun by the addition of a suffix **2.** to change an underlying clause in a sentence by a syntactic process or series of rules so that it functions like a noun —**nom·i·nal·i·za·tion** /nòmmən'li záysh'n/ *n*

nom·i·nal quote *n* an approximate price given for a security when there is no firm bid or asking price

nom·i·nal val·ue *n* FIN same as **par value**

nom·i·nal wag·es *npl* wages expressed in terms of the money actually paid, rather than in terms of the purchasing power of the wages

nom·i·nate /nómmə nàyt/ (**-nat·ed, -nat·ing, -nates**) *vt* **1.** PROPOSE SOMEBODY to suggest somebody for appointment or election to a position or for an honor or award **2.** APPOINT SOMEBODY to appoint somebody to a position, or make somebody responsible for a duty **3.** HORSERACING ENTER HORSE to enter a horse in a race [Mid-16C. < Latin *nominat-*, past participle of *nominare* "to name" < *nomin-* "name"] —**nom·i·na·tor** *n*

nom·i·na·tion /nòmmə náysh'n/ *n* **1.** PROPOSAL a suggestion of somebody for appointment or election to a position or for receiving an honor or award **2.** SOMEBODY OR SOMETHING PROPOSED somebody or something suggested for appointment or election to a position or for receiving an honor or award **3.** APPOINTMENT the appointment of somebody to a position, or assignment of somebody to a duty

nom·i·na·tive /nómmə nàytiv/; *grammatical case* /nómmənətiv/ *n* GRAM **1.** GRAMMATICAL FORM a grammatical form (**case**) of nouns and pronouns that identifies the subject of a sentence or clause. Other words, e.g., adjectives, may be in the nominative in agreement with a noun. **2.** INSTANCE OF NOMINATIVE a word or phrase in the nominative ■ *adj* **1.** APPOINTED TO OR PROPOSED FOR OFFICE appointed or suggested for election to an office or position **2.** WITH OWNER'S NAME having the name of the owner on it **3.** GRAM OF NOMINATIVE in or relating to the nominative [14C. Directly or via French *nominatif* < Latin *nominativus (casus)* "nominative (case)" < *nominat-* (see NOMINATE)]

nom·i·nee /nòmmə neé/ *n* **1.** somebody who has been proposed for a position, honor, or office **2.** a person or group that holds title to a security or piece of real estate but is not the true owner [Mid-17C. < NOMINATE]

nom·o·graph /nómmə gràf, nṓ-/, **nom·o·gram** /-gràm/ *n* **1.** a graph with three lines graduated so that a straight line intersecting any two of the lines at their known values intersects the third at the value of the related variable **2.** any graph that represents numerical relationships [Mid-18C. < Greek *nomos* "law, custom"] —**nom·o·graph·ic** /nòmmə gráffik, nṓ-/ *adj* —**no·mo·graph·y** /nō móggrəfee/ *n*

nom·o·thet·ic /nòmmə théttik, nṓ-/, **nom·o·thet·i·cal** /-k'l/ *adj* **1.** relating to the enactment of laws **2.** relating to the discovery of universal laws [Early 17C. < Greek *nomothetikos* < *nomothetēs* "lawgiver" < *nomos* "law"] —**nom·o·thet·i·cal·ly** *adv*

-nomy *suffix* system of rules, laws, or knowledge about a particular field ○ *gastronomy* [< Greek *-nomia* < *nomos* "law, custom"] —**-nomic** *suffix* —**-nomical** *suffix* —**-nomically** *suffix*

non- *prefix* not, without, the opposite of ○ *nonaggression* ○ *nonassessable* [Via Old French < Latin *non* < Indo-European]

non-Ab·o·rig·i·nal *n, adj*
non·a·bra·sive *adj*
non·ab·sor·ben·cy *n*
non·ab·sor·bent *adj*
non·a·bu·sive *adj*
non·a·bu·sive·ly *adv*
non·a·bu·sive·ness *n*
non·ac·a·dem·ic *adj*
non·ac·cel·er·at·ing *adj*
non·ac·cep·tance *n*
non·ac·ci·den·tal *adj*
non·ac·cred·it·ed *adj*
non·ac·id *adj*
non·a·cid·ic *adj*
non·act·ing *adj*
non·ac·tor *n*
non·ad·dic·tive *adj*
non·ad·her·ence *n*
non·ad·he·sive *adj*
non·ad·he·sive·ness *n*
non·ad·ja·cent *adj*
non·ad·just·a·bil·i·ty *n*
non·ad·just·a·ble *adj*
non·ad·mis·sion *n*
non·ad·mit·ted *adj*
non·a·dult *adj, n*
non·a·dult·hood *n*
non·aer·i·al *adj*
non·aer·o·bic *adj*
non-Af·ri·can *adj, n*
non·ag·gres·sive *adj*
non·ag·ri·cul·tur·al *adj*
non·air *adj*
non·al·co·hol·ic *adj*
non-Al·gon·qui·an *adj*
non·al·ler·gen·ic *adj*
non·al·ler·gic *adj*
non·al·pha·bet·ic *adj*
non·al·pha·bet·i·cal *adj*
non·am·big·u·ous *adj*
non-Am·er·i·can *adj, n*
non·an·a·lyt·ic *adj*
non·an·swer *n*
non·a·pol·o·get·ic *adj*
non·a·quat·ic *adj*
non-Ar·ab *adj, n*
non·ar·a·ble *adj*
non·ar·gu·ment *n*
non·ar·o·mat·ic *adj*
non·art *n*
non-Ar·y·an *adj, n*
non-A·sian *adj*
non·as·ser·tive *adj*
non·as·so·ci·a·tive *adj*
non·as·tro·naut *n*
non·ath·lete *n*
non·a·tom·ic *adj*
non·at·ten·dance *n*
non·at·trib·ut·a·ble *adj*
non·at·trib·ut·a·bly *adv*
non·a·vail·a·bil·i·ty *n*
non·bar·y·on·ic *adj*
non·be·ing *n*
non·be·lief *n*
non·be·liev·er *n*
non·be·liev·ing *adj*
non·bel·lig·er·ence *n*
non·bel·lig·er·en·cy *n*
non·bel·lig·er·ent *adj, n*
non·bel·lig·er·ent·ly *adv*
non·bi·na·ry *adj*
non·bind·ing *adj*
non·bi·o·de·grad·a·ble *adj*
non·bi·o·graph·i·cal *adj*
non·bi·o·log·i·cal *adj*
non·bit·ing *adj*
non-Boer *adj, n*
non·brand *adj*
non·break·a·ble *adj*
non·break·ing *adj*
non·breed·ing *adj*
non-Brit·ish *adj*
non·broad·cast *adj*
non-Bud·dhist *adj, n*
non·cak·ing *adj*
non·ca·lor·ic *adj*
non·cal·o·rif·ic *adj*
non·can·cer·ous *adj*
non·ca·non·i·cal *adj*
non·car·bon *adj*
non·car·bon·at·ed *adj*
non·car·cin·o·gen *n*
non·car·cin·o·gen·ic *adj*
non·car·niv·o·rous *adj*
non·cash *adj*
non·cat·e·gor·i·cal *adj*
non-Cath·o·lic *adj, n*
non-Cau·ca·sian *adj, n*
non·caus·al *adj*
non·cel·lu·lar *adj*
non·cer·ti·fied *adj*
non·chem·i·cal *adj*
non-Chi·nese *adj, n*
non-Chris·tian *adj, n*
non·chron·o·log·i·cal *adj*
non-Cis·ter·cian *adj, n*
non·cit·i·zen *n*
non·cit·rus *adj*
non·clas·si·cal *adj*
non·cler·i·cal *adj*
non·climb·ing *adj*
non·cling *adj*
non·clin·i·cal *adj*
non·cod·ing *adj*
non·col·le·giate *adj*
non·com·bat *adj*
non·com·bat·ive *adj*
non·com·bus·ti·bil·i·ty *n*
non·com·bus·ti·ble *adj, n*
non·com·mer·cial *adj*
non·com·mun·i·ca·ble *adj*
non·com·mun·i·cat·ing *adj*
non·com·mun·i·ca·tive *adj*
non-Com·mu·nist *adj, n*
non·com·pat·i·ble *adj*
non·com·pet·i·tive *adj*
non·com·ply·ing *adj*
non·com·pul·so·ry *adj*
non·con·cen·tric *adj*
non·con·clu·sive *adj*
non·con·cur·rent *adj*
non·con·dens·ing *adj*
non·con·duct·ing *adj*
non·con·duc·tive *adj*
non·con·duc·tor *n*
non·con·fi·den·tial *adj*
non·con·fi·den·tial·ly *adv*
non·con·form·ing *adj*
non·con·ju·gat·ed *adj*
non·con·sec·u·tive *adj*
non·con·sen·su·al *adj*
non·con·struc·tive *adj*
non·con·struc·tive·ly *adv*
non·con·struc·tive·ness *n*
non·con·ta·gious *adj*
non·con·ten·tious *adj*
non·con·ten·tious·ly *adv*
non·con·tig·u·ous *adj*
non·con·tin·u·ous *adj*
non·con·trib·ut·ing *adj*
non·con·tro·ver·sial *adj*
non·con·tro·ver·sial·ly *adv*
non·con·ven·tion·al *adj*
non·con·vert·i·ble *adj*
non·cor·po·rate *adj*
non·cor·rod·ing *adj*
non·cor·ro·sive *adj*
non·cov·er·age *n*
non·crim·i·nal *adj*
non·crit·i·cal *adj*
non·crys·tal·line *adj*
non·cu·mu·la·tive *adj*
non·cur·rent *adj*
non·cut·ting *adj*
non·dair·y *adj*
non·de·duct·i·bil·i·ty *n*
non·de·duct·i·ble *adj*
non·de·fin·ing *adj*
non·de·grad·a·ble *adj*
non·de·gree *adj*
non·de·lin·quent *adj*
non·de·liv·er·y *n*
non·dem·o·crat·ic *adj*
non·dem·o·crat·i·cal·ly *adv*
non·de·nom·i·na·tion·al *adj*
non·de·part·ment·al *adj*
non·de·riv·a·tive *adj*
non·de·vel·op·ment *n*
non·di·a·bet·ic *adj, n*
non·di·gest·i·ble *adj*
non·dig·i·tal *adj*
non·dip·lo·mat·ic *adj*
non·dis·cre·tion·ar·y *adj*
non·dis·crim·i·na·tion *n*
non·dis·crim·i·na·to·ry *adj*
non·dis·pos·a·ble *adj*
non·dis·rup·tive *adj*
non·doc·tor *n*
non·doc·tor·al *adj*
non·do·mes·tic *adj*
non·dra·mat·ic *adj*
non·drink·er *n*
non·drink·ing *adj*
non·driv·er *n*
non·droop·ing *adj*
non·dry·ing *adj*
non·du·al *adj*
non·du·al·ism *n*
non·du·al·i·ty *n*
non·du·ra·ble *adj*
non·earn·ing *adj*
non·ec·cle·si·as·ti·cal *adj*
non·ec·o·nom·ic *adj*
non·ed·i·ble *adj*
non·ed·u·ca·tion·al *adj*
non·ef·fec·tive *adj*
non·e·las·tic *adj*
non·e·lect *adj, npl*
non·e·lect·ed *adj*
non·e·lec·tion *n*
non·e·lec·tive *adj, n*
non·e·lec·tric *adj*
non·el·i·gi·ble *adj*
non·e·mer·gen·cy *adj, n*
non·emp·ty *adj*
non·en·force·a·ble *adj*
non·en·force·ment *n*
non-Eng·lish-speak·ing *adj*
non·en·zyme *n*
non·e·qui·lib·ri·um *n*
non·es·tab·lished *adj*
non·eth·i·cal *adj*
non-Eu·clid·e·an *adj*
non-Eur·o·pe·an *n, adj*
non·ev·i·dence *n*
non·ex·clu·sive *adj*
non·ex·empt *adj*
non·ex·pan·sion *n*
non·ex·pen·da·ble *adj*
non·ex·per·i·men·tal *adj*
non·ex·pert *adj, n*
non·ex·plo·sive *adj*
non·ex·po·sure *n*
non·ex·tinct *adj*
non·fac·tu·al *adj*
non·fad·ing *adj*
non·farm·er *n*
non·fas·cist *adj, n*
non·fa·tal *adj*
non·fa·tal·ly *adv*
non·fat·ten·ing *adj*
non·fat·ty *adj*
non·fed·er·al *adj*
non·fed·er·at·ed *adj*
non·fer·rous *adj*
non·fight·ing *adj*
non·fi·nan·cial *adj*
non·fi·nite *adj*
non·flex·i·ble *adj*
non·flow·er·ing *adj*
non·fluc·tu·at·ing *adj*
non·for·mal *adj*
non·for·mal·ly *adv*
non·fray·ing *adj*
non·free·hold *adj*
non·ful·fill·ment *n*
non·func·tion·al *adj*
non·func·tion·ing *adj*
non·fun·gal *adj*
non·gas·e·ous *adj*
non·ge·o·graph·ic *adj*
non·gloss *adj*
non·gloss·y *adj*
non·gov·ern·ment *adj*
non·gov·ern·men·tal *adj*
non·gran·u·lar *adj*

non·graph·ic *adj*
non·grasp·ing *adj*
non·greas·y *adj*
non·green *adj*
non·haz·ard·ous *adj*
non·he·red·i·tar·y *adj*
non·hier·ar·chi·cal *adj*
non·His·pan·ic *adj, n*
non·his·tor·i·cal *adj*
non·ho·mo·ge·ne·ous *adj*
non·hy·dro·gen *adj*
non·i·den·ti·cal *adj*
non·i·de·o·logue *n*
non·im·i·ta·tive *adj*
non·im·pact *adj*
non·im·por·ta·tion *n*
non·in·clu·sive *adj*
non·in·crim·i·nat·ing *adj*
non·in·de·pen·dent *adj*
non·in·dict·a·ble *adj*
non·in·dig·e·nous *adj*
non·in·duc·tive *adj*
non·in·dus·tri·al *adj*
non·in·dus·tri·al·ized *adj*
non·in·fect·ed *adj*
non·in·fec·tious *adj*
non·in·flam·ma·ble *adj*
non·in·flam·ma·tor·y *adj*
non·in·fla·tion·ar·y *adj*
non·in·flect·ed *adj*
non·in·form·a·tive *adj*
non·in·hab·it·a·ble *adj*
non·in·her·it·a·ble *adj*
non·in·stinct·ive *adj*
non·in·sured *adj*
non·in·te·grat·ed *adj*
non·in·tel·lec·tu·al *adj*
non·in·ter·change·a·ble *adj*
non·in·ter·est·bear·ing *adj*
non·in·ter·fer·ence *n*
non·in·tox·i·cat·ing *adj*
non·in·volve·ment *n*
non·i·on·iz·ing *adj*
non·ir·ri·gat·ed *adj*
non·ir·ri·tat·ing *adj*
non-I·tal·ian *adj, n*
non-Jew *n*
non-Jew·ish *adj*
non·judg·men·tal *adj*
non·judg·men·tal·ly *adv*
non·ju·di·cial *adj*
non·ko·sher *adj*
non·law·yer *n*
non·leaf·y *adj*
non·league *adj*
non·le·gal *adj*
non·le·gal·ly *adv*
non·le·thal *adj*
non·lex·i·cal *adj*
non·lin·guis·tic *adj*
non·liq·uid *adj, n*
non·lit·er·al *adj*
non·lit·er·al·ly *adv*
non·lit·er·ar·y *adj*
non·lit·er·ate *adj*
non·li·tur·gi·cal *adj*
non·liv·ing *adj*
non·load·bear·ing *adj*
non·lo·cal *adj*
non·lo·cal·ly *adv*
non·log·i·cal *adj*
non·lu·mi·nous *adj*
non·lym·pho·cyt·ic *adj*
non·mag·net·ic *adj*
non·main·stream *adj*
non·ma·li·cious *adj*
non·ma·lig·nant *adj*
non·mam·ma·li·an *adj*
non·man·age·ment *adj, n*
non·ma·nip·u·la·tive *adj*
non·man·u·al *adj*
non·man·u·fac·tur·ing *adj*
non-Mao·ri *adj, n*
non·mar·ket *adj*
non·mar·ket·a·ble *adj*
non·mar·ried *adj*
non·match·ing *adj*
non·ma·te·ri·al *adj*
non·ma·te·ri·al·is·tic *adj*
non·math·e·mat·i·cal *adj*
non·meas·ur·a·ble *adj*
non·me·di·a *adj*
non·med·i·cal *adj*
non·me·dic·i·nal *adj*
non·met·al *n*
non·me·tal·lic *adj*
non·met·al·lif·er·ous *adj*
non·met·ric *adj*
non·met·ro·pol·i·tan *adj*
non·mi·cro·bi·al *adj*
non·mi·grant *adj, n*
non·mi·gra·to·ry *adj*
non·mil·i·tant *adj*
non·mil·i·tar·y *adj*
non·min·is·te·rial *adj*
non·mo·bile *adj*
non·mo·lec·u·lar *adj*
non·mo·nas·tic *adj*
non·mon·e·ta·ry *adj*
non·mon·o·ga·mous *adj*
non-Mor·mon *n, adj*
non·mo·tile *adj*
non·mo·tor·ized *adj*
non·mov·ing *adj*
non·mu·si·cal *adj*
non·mu·si·cian *n*
non-Mus·lim *adj, n*
non·nar·cot·ic *adj*
non·nar·ra·tive *adj*
non·na·tion·al *adj, n*
non·na·tive *n, adj*
non·nat·u·ral *adj*
non·nat·u·ral·is·tic *adj*
non·na·val *adj*
non·ner·vous *adj*
non·news *n*
non·nu·mer·ic *adj*
non·nu·tri·ent *adj, n*
non·ob·lig·a·to·ry *adj*
non·of·fi·cial *adj*
non·oil·y *adj*
non·op·er·at·ic *adj*
non·op·er·a·tion *n*
non·op·er·a·tion·al *adj*
non·op·er·a·tive *adj*
non·op·po·si·tion *n*
non·op·tion·al *adj*
non·or·dained *adj*
non·or·gan·ic *adj*
non·or·tho·dox *adj*
non·par·al·lel *adj*
non·par·a·sit·ic *adj*
non·par·lia·men·ta·ry *adj*
non·par·tic·i·pant *n*
non·par·tic·i·pat·ing *adj*
non·par·tic·i·pa·tion *n*
non·par·ty *adj*
non·pa·ter·nal *adj*
non·pay·er *n*
non·pay·ing *adj*
non·pay·ment *n*
non·per·for·mance *adj*
non·per·form·ing *adj*
non·per·ish·a·ble *adj, n*
non·per·ma·nent *adj*
non·per·me·a·ble *adj*
non·per·sis·tent *adj*
non·per·son·al *adj*
non·pe·tro·le·um *adj*
non·phil·o·soph·i·cal *adj*
non·phys·i·cal *adj*
non·phys·i·cal·ly *adv*
non·plant *adj*
non·play·er *n*
non·poi·son·ous *adj*
non·po·lar *adj*
non·po·lit·i·cal *adj*
non·pol·lut·ing *adj*
non·po·rous *adj*
non·prac·tic·ing *adj*
non·pre·cious *adj*
non·pred·a·to·ry *adj*
non·preg·nant *adj*
non·pre·scrip·tion *adj*
non·print *adj*
non·print·ed *adj*
non·print·ing *adj*
non·pro·duc·tive *adj*
non·pro·duc·tive·ly *adv*
non·pro·duc·tive·ness *n*
non·pro·duc·tiv·i·ty *n*
non·pro·fes·sion·al *n, adj*
non·pro·fes·sion·al·ly *adv*
non·prof·it·a·ble *adj*
non·pro·gram·mer *n*
non·pro·gres·sive *adj*
non·pro·pri·e·tar·y *adj*
non·pro·tec·tive *adj*
non·pro·tein *adj, n*
non·psy·cho·log·i·cal *adj*
non·psy·chot·ic *adj*
non·pub·lic *adj*
non·pu·ni·tive *adj*
non·quan·ti·fi·a·ble *adj*
non·ra·cial *adj*
non·ra·di·o·ac·tive *adj*
non·ran·dom *adj*
non·rap·id *adj*
non·ra·tion·al *adj*
non·re·ac·tive *adj*
non·read·er *n*
non·re·al·is·tic *adj*
non·re·ceipt *n*
non·re·cip·ro·cal *adj*
non·re·cip·ro·cat·ing *adj*
non·rec·og·ni·tion *n*
non·re·cov·er·able *adj*
non·re·cur·ring *adj*
non·re·cy·cla·ble *adj*
non·re·deem·a·ble *adj*
non·re·fill·a·ble *adj*
non·re·flect·ing *adj*
non·re·flec·tion *n*
non·re·flec·tive *adj*
non·re·fund·a·ble *adj*
non·reg·u·lat·ed *adj*
non·rel·a·tive *adj, n*
non·re·li·gious *adj*
non·re·new·a·ble *adj*
non·re·new·al *n*
non·re·pay·a·ble *adj*
non·re·peat·ing *adj*
non·re·pro·duc·i·ble *adj*
non·re·pro·duc·tive *adj*
non·re·pu·di·a·tion *n*
non·re·sem·blance *n*
non·res·i·dence *n*
non·res·i·den·cy *n*
non·res·i·dent *adj, n*
non·res·i·den·tial *adj*
non·re·sis·tance *n*
non·re·sis·tant *adj*
non·re·solv·a·ble *adj*
non·res·o·nant *adj*
non·re·sponse *n*
non·re·us·a·ble *adj*
non·re·ver·si·ble *adj*
non·rho·tic *adj*
non·rhyth·mic *adj*
non·rig·id *adj*
non·ro·tat·ing *adj*
non·ru·ral *adj*
non·sal·a·ble *adj*
non·sal·a·ried *adj*
non·school *adj*
non·sci·ence *n*
non·sci·en·tif·ic *adj*
non·sci·en·tif·i·cal·ly *adv*
non·sci·en·tist *n*
non·scrip·tur·al *adj*
non·sea·son·al *adj*
non·sec·tar·i·an *adj*
non·seed·ing *adj*
non·seg·re·gat·ed *adj*
non·se·lec·tive *adj*
non·self *n*
non-Se·mit·ic *adj*
non·sep·tate *adj*
non·sex·ist *adj*
non·sex·u·al *adj*
non·sex·u·al·ly *adv*
non·shrink *adj*
non·sig·nif·i·cance *n*
non·sig·nif·i·cant *adj*
non·skat·er *n*
non·skid *adj*
non·ski·er *n*
non·skilled *adj*
non-Slav *n*
non·slave *n, adj*
non-Slav·ic *adj*
non·so·cial *adj*
non-So·cial·ist *n, adj*
non·so·lar *adj*
non·sol·dier *n, adj*
non·sol·u·ble *adj*
non·speak·ing *adj*
non·spe·cial·ist *n, adj*
non·spher·i·cal *adj*
non·spir·i·tu·al *adj*
non·sport·ing *adj*
non·stain·ing *adj*
non·stan·za·ic *adj*
non·stat·u·to·ry *adj*
non·stel·lar *adj*
non·sting·ing *adj*
non·stock *adj*
non·store *adj*
non·stra·te·gic *adj*
non·struc·tur·al *adj*
non·stu·dent *adj, n*
non·sub·mis·sive *adj*
non·sub·scrib·er *n*
non·sug·ar *n*
non·sup·port *n*
non·sur·gi·cal *adj*
non·swim·mer *n*
non·syn·chro·nous *adj*
non·sys·tem·at·ic *adj*
non·talk·a·tive *adj*
non·tan·gi·ble *adj, n*
non·tar·iff *adj*
non·tar·nish·ing *adj*
non·tax·able *adj*
non·teach·ing *adj*
non·tech·ni·cal *adj*
non·tech·no·log·i·cal *adj*
non·tec·ton·ic *adj*
non·ten·ured *adj*
non·ter·mi·nal *adj*
non·ter·ri·to·ri·al *adj*
non·text *adj*
non·tex·tile *adj*
non·the·at·ri·cal *adj*
non·the·is·tic *adj*
non·the·mat·ic *adj*
non·ther·a·peu·tic *adj*
non·ther·mal *adj*
non·think·ing *adj*
non·threat·en·ing *adj*
non·threat·en·ing·ly *adv*
non·tid·al *adj*
non·tox·ic *adj*
non·trad·a·ble *adj*
non·tra·di·tion·al *adj*
non·trans·par·ent *adj*
non·trav·el·er *n*
non·triv·i·al *adj*
non·u·ni·fied *adj*
non·u·ni·form *adj*
non·u·ni·form·i·ty *n*
non·u·ni·form·ly *adv*
non·ur·ban *adj*
non·ur·gent *adj*
non·use *n*
non·us·er *n*
non·vas·cu·lar *adj*
non·veg·e·ta·ble *adj*
non·ven·om·ous *adj*
non·vir·u·lent *adj*
non·vis·cous *adj*
non·vis·i·ble *adj*
non·vi·tal *adj*
non·vo·cal *adj*
non·vol·a·tile *adj*
non·vot·er *n*
non·vot·ing *adj*
non·wage *adj*
non-West·ern *adj*
non-Westerner *n*
non·word *n*
non·work *adj*
non·work·er *n*
non·work·ing *adj*
non·writ·ten *adj*
non·ze·ro *adj*

non-A, non-B hep·a·ti·tis *n* an acute chronic viral disease of the liver, similar to hepatitis B but caused by neither the hepatitis A nor the hepatitis B virus. Among the several new hepatitis viruses discovered relatively recently, non-A, non-B hepatitis, in most cases, is thought to be due to hepatitis C virus.

nona- *prefix* nine ○ *nonagon* [< Latin *nonus* "ninth" < Indo-European, "nine"]

non·age /nónnij, nṓnij/ *n* **1.** the status of being under the requisite age for some legal entitlement (*formal*) **2.** any time of immaturity [14C. < Anglo-Norman *nounage*, variant of Old French *nonage* "not (the full) age" < *age* (see AGE)]

non·a·ge·nar·i·an /nònnəjə nérree ən, nṑnə-/ *n* somebody who is between 90 and 99 years of age [Early 19C. < Latin *nonagenarius* "consisting of ninety" < *nonaginta* "ninety" < *nonus* "ninth"] —**non·a·ge·nar·i·an** *adj*

non·ag·gres·sion /nònnə grésh'n/ *n* a policy of not attacking other countries ○ *The two countries signed a nonaggression pact.*

non·a·gon /nónnə gòn, nṓnə-/ *n* a two-dimensional geometric figure formed of nine angles and sides —**non·ag·o·nal** /nō nággən'l/ *adj*

non·a·ligned /nònnə lī́nd/ *adj* not allied with any major world power —**non·a·lign·ment** *n*

non·a·no·ic ac·id /nonnə nṑ ik-/ *n Can, UK* same as **pelargonic acid** [< *nonane* "straight chain hydrocarbon containing nine carbon atoms"]

non·ap·pear·ance /nònnə péerənss/ *n* failure to appear or attend, especially the failure of a defendant or witness to turn up for a court appearance

non·ar·riv·al /nòn ə rī́v'l/ *n* a failure to arrive or be delivered

non·as·sess·a·ble /nònnə séssəb'l/ *adj* **1.** impossible to estimate or determine ○ *nonassessable losses* **2.** *US* describes stock for which an investor cannot be assessed or held liable for any financial loss beyond the amount of his or her investment

non·bank /non bángk/ *n* a financial enterprise that is not a bank but performs a number of the functions of a bank —**non·bank·ing** *adj*

non·black /non blák/, **non-Black** *adj* relating to a person or to people with light skin tones, ultimately of European ancestry ■ *n* a light-skinned person whose ancestry can be traced ultimately to Europe

non·book /nón bo͝ok/ *n* a book meant primarily for practical use or visual enjoyment rather than literary merit ■ *adj* not in the form of a book or books, or consisting of other things than books, e.g., as videotapes ○ *the library's nonbook holdings*

non·busi·ness /non bíznəss/ *adj* personal and not relating to business ○ *details of nonbusiness expenditure*

non·call·a·ble /non káwləb'l/ *adj US* describes a bond, stock, or security that is not subject to payment on demand or redemption prior to maturity

nonce /nonss/ *n* the present time (*archaic*) [12C. < misanalysis of *for then anes* "for the one (occasion)"] ◇ **for the nonce 1.** for the present occasion **2.** for the time being

nonce word *n* a word that is coined for a single occasion

non·cha·lant /nònshə laánt, nónshə laànt/ *adj* calm and unconcerned about things [Mid-18C. < French, "not being concerned" < *chalant*, present participle of *chaloir* "be concerned" < Latin *calere* "be hot or roused"] —**non·cha·lance** *n* —**non·cha·lant·ly** *adv*

non·com /nón kòm/ *n* same as **noncommissioned officer** (*informal*) [Late 19C. Shortening]

non·com·bat·ant /nònkəm bátt'nt/ *n* **1.** somebody who is not in the military during a war **2.** a chaplain, medical officer, or other member of the armed forces who does not take part in battle

non·com·mis·sioned of·fi·cer /nònkə mish'nd-/ *n* an enlisted member of any of the armed forces who, without being given a commission, has been appointed to a position of authority over other enlisted members

non·com·mit·tal /nònkə mítt'l/ *adj* not making clear any personal opinions or feelings about something —**non·com·mit·tal·ly** *adv*

non·com·pet·i·tive bid /nònkəm petitiv-/ *n* a method of buying United States Treasury bills by which the purchaser commits to taking a fixed amount of securities at the average weekly price

non·com·pli·ance /nònkəm plī́ ənss/ *n* a refusal or failure to obey a law, rule, contractual agreement, or a physician's order for medicine-taking —**non·com·pli·ant** *adj*

non com·pos men·tis /non kòmpəss méntiss/ *adj* in law, not mentally competent to understand what is happening and to make important decisions [< Latin, "not having control of (your) mind"]

non·con·form·ist /nònkən fáwrmist/ *adj* UNCONVENTIONAL not conforming to an established pattern of behavior ■ *n* 1. UNCONVENTIONAL PERSON somebody who does not conform to an accepted pattern of behavior 2. *also* **Non·con·form·ist** CHR MEMBER OF DISSENTING PROTESTANT CHURCH a member of a Protestant church not adhering to the doctrines or usage of a national or established church, especially in Britain —**non·con·form·ism** *n*

non·con·form·i·ty /nònkən fáwrmətee/ *n* 1. the practice of not conforming to an established pattern of behavior 2. the state of being in disagreement with something

non·con·trib·u·to·ry /nònkən tríbbyə tàwree/ *adj* 1. describes a health insurance or pension plan that does not require contributions from an employee or member ○ *a noncontributory pension plan* 2. not contributing to a health insurance or pension plan

non·co·op·er·a·tion /nònkō opə ráysh'n/ *n* 1. refusal or failure to cooperate 2. the practice of refusing to pay taxes or obey other government decrees, as a means of protest —**non·co·op·er·a·tive** /-óppərətiv, -ràytiv/ *adj*

non·count noun /nón kownt-/ *n* a noun that refers to a mass of something or to a quality rather than to one thing, and that cannot usually be used with "a" or "an," with a number, or in the plural. Examples of English noncount nouns are "milk," "freight," and "unhappiness."

non·cred·it /non kréddit/ *adj US* describes an educational course that contributes no official credit toward an academic degree

non·cus·to·di·al /nònkə stṓdee əl/ *adj* 1. not involving imprisonment or detention in custody ○ *a noncustodial sentence* 2. *US* not granted legal custody of a child ○ *a noncustodial birth parent*

non·de·script /nòndi skrípt/ *adj* having no interesting or remarkable characteristics ■ *n* somebody with no interesting or remarkable characteristics [Late 17C. < NON- + Latin *descriptus*, past participle of *describere* (see DESCRIBE)]

non·de·struc·tive /nòn di strúktiv/ *adj* not causing or capable of causing destruction

non·de·struc·tive test·ing /nòndi strùktiv-/ *n* a technique used to test for flaws in materials, components, and joints without causing damage or destruction

non·di·rec·tive /nòndi réktiv/ *adj* describes a form of psychotherapy or counseling in which the patient is encouraged to speak freely with minimal input from the therapist

non·dis·junc·tion /nòndiss júngksh'n/ *n* a failure of paired chromosomes or sister chromatids to separate during cell division —**non·dis·junc·tion·al** *adj*

non·dis·tinc·tive /nòndi stíngktiv/ *adj* describes features of speech sounds that do not distinguish meanings

non dit /nòn dée/ *n US* a taboo subject or fact that remains unspoken or is not discussed ○ *His absence was a non dit.* [Late 20C. < French *le non-dit* "what is left unsaid"]

non·drip /non dríp/ *adj* describes paint or varnish that is not likely to drip while being applied

none /nun/ *pron* 1. not one person ○ *Wealth that is free for all is valued by none.* ○ *None of us wanted the situation to continue.* 2. not any of something, not any part of something, or not a single one of something ○ *None of it seemed to matter any more.* ○ *We wrote last week demanding some answers, but so far have received none.* [Old English *nān* "not one" < *ne* "not" + *ān*, form of ONE] ◇ **have none of something** to refuse to tolerate something ○ *We asked him to explain himself, but he would have none of it.* ◇ **none the** in no degree (*used with comparative adjectives*) ○ *I'm still none the wiser.* ◇ **none too** not very ○ *The room is none too pretty, painted like that.*

USAGE See *neither.*

non·e·lec·tro·lyte /nòn i léktrə lī̀t/ *n* a substance that does not ionize readily in solution or in the molten state and is therefore a bad conductor of electricity

non·en·ti·ty /non éntətee/ (*plural* **-ties**) *n* 1. INSIGNIFICANT PERSON somebody regarded as unimportant, powerless, or insignificant 2. SOMETHING NONEXISTENT something that does not exist in reality 3. CONDITION OF NONEXISTENCE the condition or state of being nonexistent

non·e·quiv·a·lence /nòn i kwívvələnss/ *n* 1. the state of not being equal or equivalent 2. a situation in which two propositions can have different truth values —**non·e·quiv·a·lent** *adj*

nones /nōnz/ *n* (*takes a singular or plural verb*) 1. in the ancient Roman calendar, the ninth day before the ides of each month counting inclusively. The nones are the seventh day of March, May, July, and October, the fifth day of any other month. 2. in the Roman Catholic Church, the fifth of the seven separate hours (**canonical hours**) that are set aside for prayer each day. This was originally held at the ninth hour after sunrise. [15C. In sense 1 via French < Latin *nonas*, plural of a form of; *nonus* "ninth." Sense 2 plural of *none* < Latin *nona*, feminine of *nonus*]

non·es·sen·tial /nòn i sénshəl/ *adj* 1. not absolutely necessary 2. manufactured by the body and therefore not essential in the diet —**non·es·sen·tial** *n* —**non·es·sen·tial·ly** *adv*

no·net /nō nét/ *n* 1. a piece of music composed for nine voices or instruments 2. a group of nine singers or instrumentalists [Mid-19C. < Italian *nonetto* "small ninth" < *nono* "ninth" < Latin *nonus*]

none·the·less /nùnthə léss/ *adv* in spite of a situation or comment

non·e·vent /nòn i vént/ *n* an occasion that is disappointingly unexciting

non·ex·change·a·ble /nòn iks cháynjəb'l/ *adj* not able to be exchanged for an identical item or for something different
non·ex·ec·u·tive *adj*

non·ex·ist·ent /nòn ig zístənt/ *adj* not in existence —**non·ex·ist·ence** *n*

non·fat /non fát/ *adj* without fat solids, or with the fat content removed

non·fea·sance /non féez'nss/ *n* in law, the omission of some act that is expected to have been performed [Early 17C. < obsolete *feasance* "doing" < Anglo-Norman *fesa(u)nce*, French *faisance* < *fais-*, present stem of *faire* "to do" < Latin *facere*]

non·fic·tion /non fíksh'n/ *n* writings that convey factual information and are not primarily works of the creative imagination ○ *her first nonfiction work* —**non·fic·tion·al** *adj*

non·fig·u·ra·tive /non fíggyərətiv/ *adj* 1. LITERAT same as **literal** (sense 1) 2. ARTS same as **nonrepresentational**

non·flam·ma·ble /non flámməb'l/ *adj* difficult to burn or ignite

USAGE See *flammable.*

non·food /non fóod/ *adj* describes something that is sold in a supermarket that is not for eating or drinking

non·gon·o·coc·cal u·re·thri·tis /nòn gonə kók'l-/ *n US* inflammation of the urethra caused by no identified infection. It is sexually transmitted but is not caused by gonorrheal organisms. Can term **nonspecific urethritis**

non·govern·men·tal or·gan·i·za·tion *n* an independent organization that is not run or controlled by a government

non·grad·ed /non gráydəd/ *adj* 1. *US* describes an elementary school that is not divided into classes 2. not sorted into different sizes ○ *nongraded rocks*

non gra·ta /non gráatə, -gráttə/ *adj* not welcome [< PERSONA NON GRATA]

non·he·ro /nòn héerō/ (*plural* **-roes**) *n* ARTS same as **antihero**

non·hu·man /non hyóomən/ *adj* relating to a thing or being that does not belong to the human race

no·nil·lion /nō níllyən/ *n* 1. *US* the number equal to 10^{30}, written as 1 followed by 30 zeros 2. *UK* the number equal to 10^{54}, written as 1 followed by 54 zeros [Late 17C. < French < Latin *nonus* "ninth" + *-illion* as in MILLION] —**no·nil·lionth** *adj, n*

non·im·mi·grant /non ímmigrənt/ *n* 1. somebody who enters a country for a temporary stay 2. somebody who returns to his or her own country after some time spent in another country

non·in·clu·sion /nòn in klóozh'n/ *n* failure to include somebody or something, or to be included

non·in·su·lin·de·pend·ent di·a·be·tes *n* diabetes mellitus that does not require insulin for its treatment

non·in·ter·ven·tion /nòn intər vénsh'n/ *n* failure or refusal to intervene in something, especially the policy on the part of a nation of abstaining from involvement in the affairs of other states —**non·in·ter·ven·tion·ism** *n* —**non·in·ter·ven·tion·ist** *n, adj*

non·in·va·sive /nòn in váyssiv/ *adj* 1. not involving cutting into the body or entry into a body cavity such as the colon or stomach 2. not spreading or likely to spread to other parts of the body

non·i·ron /non ī́rn/ *adj UK* not needing to be ironed because of being crease-resistant

non·is·sue /non íshoo/ *n* something that is so unimportant that it is not worth considering or discussing

non·join·der /non jóyndər/ *n* failure to include a party in a lawsuit who should have been included

non·ju·ror /non jóorər, -ràwr/ *n* somebody who refuses to take an oath, especially a member of the Church of England clergy who refused to take an oath of allegiance to William and Mary in 1689 —**non·ju·ring** *adj*

non·ju·ry /non jóoree/ *adj* describes a trial where the verdict is not the responsibility of a jury but of a judge

non·lin·e·ar /non línnee ər/ *adj* 1. NOT IN LINE not lying on the same straight line 2. NOT PREDICTABLE FROM PAST varying markedly as a result of individual factors or circumstances and so difficult to anticipate or likely to depart from previous patterns 3. MATH NOT IN DIRECT PROPORTION describes a relationship or function that is not strictly proportional

non·mem·ber /non mémbər/ *n* a person, group, or nation that does not belong to a specific organization —**non·mem·ber** *adj*

non·mem·ber firm *n US* a company that is not a member of a stock exchange and thus requires an intermediary to operate on its behalf there

non·mor·al /non máwrəl/ *adj* 1. neither immoral nor moral, but unrelated to moral or ethical considerations 2. not having or showing moral principles

non·neg·a·tive /non néggətiv/ *adj* in mathematics, relating to or being a real quantity that is positive or zero

non·ne·go·tia·ble /nòn nə gṓshəb'l, -gṓshee əb'l/ *adj* 1. not open to negotiation or arbitration ○ *nonnegotiable demands* 2. not legally transferable from one owner to another ○ *nonnegotiable real property*

non·nu·cle·ar /nòn nóoklee ər/ *adj* not using nuclear power or weapons

no-no (*plural* **no-nos**) *n* something that is not allowed or is disapproved of (*informal*)

non·ob·jec·tive /nònnəb jéktiv/ *adj* 1. based on somebody's opinions or feelings, rather than on facts or evidence 2. same as **nonrepresentational** —**non·ob·jec·tiv·i·ty** /nòn ob jek tívvətee/ *n*

non·ob·ser·vance /nònnəb zúrvənss/ *n* a failure to comply with something such as a law or practice, especially a religious practice —**non·ob·ser·vant** *adj*

non ob·stan·te /nòn əb stántee, nōn-/ *prep* notwithstanding (*formal*) [< medieval Latin, "not standing in the way"]

no-non·sense *adj* 1. direct and practical in dealing with things or people 2. basic and offering no extras, frills, or luxuries

non·pa·reil /nònpə rél, nónpə rèl/ *n* 1. SOMEBODY OR SOMETHING UNPARALLELED somebody or something without an equal **2.** *US* FOOD **CONFECTIONERY DECORATION** a small crisp bead of colored sugar used to decorate cookies and other confectionery **3.** *US* FOOD **SUGAR-COVERED CHOCOLATE DISK** a small disk of chocolate covered in small beads of white nonpareils **4.** PRINTING **SIX-POINT TYPE** a size of printers' type equivalent to six point (*dated*) ■ *adj* **PEERLESS** having no equal [15C. < French, "not (having) equal" < *pareil* "equal" < popular Latin *pariculus*, diminutive of Latin *par* "equal"]

non·par·ti·san /non paártiz'n/, **non·par·ti·zan** *adj* not belonging to, supporting, or biased in favor of a political party —**non·par·ti·san** *n*

non·pen·e·tra·tive /non pénnə tràytiv/ *adj* not involving penetration of the vagina or anus by the penis

non·per·son /non púrss'n/ *n* **1.** somebody who is ignored or not mentioned, usually because his or her views are disapproved of **2.** somebody regarded as of no importance or significance

non pla·cet /non pláyssət, nōn-/ *n* a negative vote in an ecclesiastical or academic assembly [< Latin, "it does not please"]

non·play·ing /non pláy ing/ *adj* not playing in a game or competition, but usually having a coaching or advisory role

non·plus /non plúss/ *vt* (**-plussed** or **-plused, -plus·sing** or **-plus·ing, -plus·ses** or **-plus·es**) to make somebody feel confused and unable to decide what to do ■ *n* a state of confusion and nervousness (*dated*) [Late 16C. < Latin *non plus* "no more"]

non·plussed /nòn plúst/ *adj* **1.** surprised, confused, and uncertain what to do or say **2.** ⚠ calm and unperturbed (*informal*)

USAGE The adjective ***nonplussed*** means "surprised, confused, and uncertain what to do or say." It is increasingly used in the almost opposite sense of "untroubled," especially in US English (*Nonplussed by the criticism, she continued to direct her films in the very same offbeat manner for which she was famed.*). This new meaning is not yet accepted as standard, and it may cause ambiguity in sentences such as *He seemed nonplussed by the news.* It possibly derives from a misunderstanding of the *non-* element, perhaps also influenced by *nonchalant* which does mean "calm and unconcerned." But ***nonplussed*** goes back to Latin *non plus* "no more," and does not have a positive or affirmative form *plussed*.

non·prof·it /nòn próffit/ *adj* not operated with the objective of making a profit ■ *n* an organization that does not operate to make a profit ○ *a nonprofit organization*

non·prof·it·mak·ing /non próffit màyking/ *adj UK* same as **nonprofit** ○ *a nonprofitmaking organization*

non·pro·lif·er·a·tion /nòn prə liffə ráysh'n/ *n* the practice of limiting the production or spread of something, especially nuclear weapons or other weapons of mass destruction (*often used before a noun*) ○ *nonproliferation agreements*

non·pros /non próss/ (**-prossed, -pros·sing, -pros·ses**) *vt* to enter a judgment against a plaintiff who fails to appear in court (*informal*) [Late 17C. < shortening of NON PROSEQUITUR]

non pro·se·qui·tur /nòn prə sékwitər/ *n* a judgment in the defendant's favor when the plaintiff fails to appear in court [< Latin, "he or she does not prosecute"]

non·re·com·bi·nant /nòn ree kómbinənt/ *adj* not produced by artificially manipulating genetic material

non·rel·a·tiv·is·tic /nòn relàti vístik/ *adj* not affected by the phenomena of relativity —**non·rel·a·tiv·is·ti·cal·ly** *adv*

non-REM sleep *n* BIOL same as **slow-wave sleep**

non·rep·re·sen·ta·tion·al /nòn repprə zen táyshən'l, -táyshnəl/ *adj* in art, not aiming to depict an object realistically and, usually, concerned more with form, pattern, or color for its own sake —**non·rep·re·sen·ta·tion·al·ism** *n* —**non·rep·re·sen·ta·tion·al·ly** *adv*

non·re·si·dent In·di·an /non rèzzidənt-/ *n S Asia* an Indian who lives outside India

non·re·stric·tive /nòn ri stríktiv/ *adj* with few or no restrictions

non·re·stric·tive clause *n* a relative clause that gives additional information about a noun or pronoun in the main clause but that is not essential to the understanding of the main clause. A nonrestrictive clause is usually separated from the rest of the sentence by commas, e.g., "My partner, who is an artist, comes from Chicago."

non·re·turn valve /nòn ri túrn-/ *n* ENG same as **check valve**

non·run /non rún/ *adj* designed not to develop runs easily ○ *nonrun pantyhose*

non·run·ner /non rúnnər/ *n* a nonstarter in a race

non·sched·uled /non ské joold/ *adj* **1.** not planned to happen as part of a schedule **2.** operating according to demand, rather than on a published schedule

non·sense /nón sènss, nónssənss/ *n* **1. MEANINGLESS LANGUAGE OR BEHAVIOR** pointless or meaningless language or behavior ○ *You're talking utter nonsense.* **2. IRRITATING BEHAVIOR** disrespectful, obnoxious, or irritating behavior ○ *the kind of judge who won't stand for any nonsense from lawyers* **3.** LITERAT same as **nonsense verse 4.** *also* **non·sense co·don** GENETICS **DNA SECTION PRODUCING NO AMINO ACID** a set of three nucleotides (**codon**) in a DNA molecule that does not code for any amino acid. Codons are believed to signal the beginning and end of the synthesis of some protein molecules. ■ *interj* **EXPRESSION OF CONTRADICTION** used to contradict what somebody has said or written

non·sense verse *n* poetry that is written in deliberately absurd language for humorous effect, mainly for children

non·sense word *n* a word with no meaning, usually created for humorous effect

non·sen·si·cal /non sénssik'l/ *adj* **1.** having no sense or meaning **2.** deserving ridicule —**non·sen·si·cal·i·ty** /-sènssi kállətee/ *n* —**non·sen·si·cal·ly** *adv* —**non·sen·si·cal·ness** *n*

non se·qui·tur /non sékwitər/ *n* **1.** a statement that appears unrelated to a statement that it follows **2.** a conclusion that does not follow from its premises [< Latin, "it does not follow"]

non·sked /non skéd/ (*plural* **-skeds** *informal*) *n US* a nonscheduled airline or plane (*informal*) [Mid-20C. Shortening and alteration of NONSCHEDULED]

non·slip /nòn slíp/ *adj* designed to prevent people from slipping

non·smok·er /non smókər/ *n* **1.** somebody who does not smoke tobacco products **2.** a car or compartment in a train in which smoking is not allowed

non·smok·ing /non smóking/ *adj* **1. RESTRICTED TO NONSMOKERS** reserved for people who do not want to smoke cigarettes, cigars, or pipes **2. NOT SMOKING** not smoking cigarettes, cigars, or a pipe ■ *n* **AREA WHERE SMOKING IS FORBIDDEN** an area of a public space such as a restaurant or aircraft cabin, where smoking is not permitted ○ *Do you want smoking or nonsmoking?*

non·spe·cif·ic /nòn spə síffik/ *adj* **1.** not particular or detailed **2.** not attributable to a specific medical cause or condition

non·spe·cif·ic u·re·thri·tis *n Can, UK* same as **nongonococcal urethritis**

non·stan·dard /non stándərd/ *adj* **1.** not conforming to an accepted standard **2.** not conforming to a standard accepted as grammatically correct by educated native speakers, or not used by educated native speakers

non·start·er /non staártər/ *n* **1. SOMETHING OR SOMEBODY UNLIKELY TO SUCCEED** something that or somebody who seems from the beginning to have no chance of success (*informal*) **2. COMPETITOR WHO WITHDRAWS BEFORE START** a competitor who does not start a race, event, or competition in which he or she has been entered **3.** *UK* **HORSE THAT DOES NOT COMPETE** a horse that does not run in a race in which it has been entered

non·state ac·tor /nòn stayt-/ *n* an individual person or body acting independently of a state or government, e.g., a terrorist group

Non-Stat·us In·di·an, **non-sta·tus In·di·an** *n* a member of an indigenous people not recognized by the federal government of Canada as having special rights and privileges, especially the right to live on a reservation

non·ster·oid /non sté ròyd, -steér òyd/ *n* a drug that does not contain steroids ■ *adj* **non·ste·roid, non·ste·roid·al** not containing or being a steroid

non·stick /non stík/ *adj* with a coating or surface that prevents food from sticking during cooking

non·stop /non stóp/ *adj, adv* **1.** continuing without a stop ○ *a nonstop flight* **2.** continuing without interruption or rest ○ *a weekend of nonstop partying*

non·suit /non soót/ *n* the dismissal of a suit by a judge when the plaintiff fails to make out a legal case or to produce adequate evidence

non·tar·get /non taárgət/ *adj* describes cells, tissues, or organisms that are not intended for treatment, e.g., by drugs or radiation, but may be affected by such treatment aimed elsewhere

non·ter·mi·nat·ing /non túrmə nàyting/ *adj* **1.** having an infinite number of digits after the decimal point in a decimal fraction **2.** not having or coming to an end (*formal*)

non·trans·fer·a·ble /nòn transs fúr əb'l/, **non·trans·fer·ra·ble** *adj* relating to a ticket, license, or voucher that cannot be transferred to, or used by, anyone other than the person to whom it is sold or assigned

non-trea·ty In·di·an *n Can* PEOPLES same as **Non-Status Indian**

non trop·po /non tróppō/ *adv, adj* not too much (*used as a musical direction*) [< Italian]

non·un·ion /non yóonyən/ *adj* **1. NOT IN UNION** not belonging to a labor union **2. NOT USING UNION MEMBERS** not employing labor union members **3. NOT MADE BY UNION MEMBERS** not produced by labor union members —**non·un·ion·ized** *adj*

non·ver·bal /non vúrb'l/ *adj* not using or involving words —**non·ver·bal·ly** *adv*

non·ver·bal com·mu·ni·ca·tion *n* communication by other means than by using words, e.g., through facial expressions, hand gestures, and tone of voice

non·vi·a·ble /non vī əb'l/ *adj* **1.** BIOL, MED incapable of growing and developing independently ○ *a nonviable fetus* ○ *nonviable seedlings* **2.** not capable of succeeding

non·vin·tage /non víntij/ *adj* not belonging to an especially good year for a wine, or not identified by year

non·vi·o·lence /non vī ələnss, -vīlənss/ *n* **1.** the principle of refraining from using violence, especially as a means of protest **2.** the absence of or freedom from violence —**non·vi·o·lent** *adj* —**non·vi·o·lent·ly** *adv*

non·white /non wīt, -hwīt/, **non-White** *n* a person whose ancestry cannot be traced ultimately to Europe (*sometimes considered offensive*) —**non·white** *adj*

non·wood·y /non wóoddee/ *adj* **1.** not made of or containing wood or a material resembling wood **2.** describes a plant that does not form a woody stem

non·wo·ven /non wóvən/ *adj* made of fibers that have been bonded or interlocked by mechanical, chemical, thermal, or solvent methods

non·ya /nónnyə/ *adj* used to describe food or cuisine combining Chinese and Malay influences, in a style that originated in Melaka ■ *n Malaysia* a girl or woman of Chinese origin, born in Melaka and speaking Malay as a first language [< Malay, literally "grandmother"]

no·nyl·phe·nol /nònnil feé nàwl, nònnīl-/ *n* a chemical compound that is a product of the breakdown of a surfactant commonly used in detergents and cleaning agents. It is reported to be an endocrine disruptor and is especially toxic to insects and aquatic organisms.

noo·dle[1] /nóod'l/ *n* a long thin strip of pasta. Noodles are a staple of Italian and Chinese cooking. (*often used in the plural*) [Late 18C. < German *Nudel*]

noo·dle[2] /nóod'l/ *n* the head or mind (*slang*) [Mid-18C. Origin ?]

noo·dle[3] /nóod'l/ (**-dled, -dling, -dles**) *vti* to improvise on a musical instrument in a random meandering fashion, often in order to warm up (*slang*) [Mid-19C. Probably from likening such playing to the disorganized appearance of a dish of noodles]

nook /nòok/ *n* **1.** a quiet private place **2.** a corner or small recess in a room [13C. Probably < Old Norse] ◇ **every nook and cranny** every tiny part of a place

nook·ie /nóokee/, **nook·y** *n* same as **sexual intercourse** (*slang*; *offensive*) [Early 20C. Origin ?]

noon /noon/ *n* **1.** 12 o'clock in the middle of the day **2.** the most important period of something (*literary*) [Pre-12C. < Latin *nona (hora)* "ninth (hour) (of the Roman day, counted from sunrise)," feminine of *nonus*]

noon·day /no͝on dày/ (*literary*) *adj* relating to or happening at midday ■ *n* same as **noontime**

no one *pron* no person at all

noon·tide /no͝on tīd/ *n* same as **noontime** (*literary*)

noon·time /no͝on tīm/ *n* the middle of the day, around 12 o'clock

noose /nooss/ *n* **1.** LOOP IN ROPE a loop at the end of a rope, tied with a knot so that it can be tightened and slackened, and used for trapping animals or hanging people **2.** ENTRAPMENT something that traps somebody in an unpleasant or unwanted situation ■ *vt* (**noosed, noos·ing, noos·es**) **1.** CATCH SOMETHING WITH NOOSE to catch somebody or something with a noose **2.** TIE ROPE IN NOOSE to make a noose at the end of a rope or cord [15C. Probably via Old French *nos* (singular), *nous* (plural) < Latin *nodus* "knot"]

Noot·ka /no͝otkə/ (*plural* **-kas** or *same*) *n* **1.** a member of a Native North American people of the coast of western Vancouver Island, British Columbia, and Cape Flattery, on the Olympic Peninsula in Washington State **2.** the Wakashan language of the Nootka people. Few people now speak Nootka. [Early 19C. After *Nootka* Sound, an inlet on the coast of Vancouver Island, British Columbia, Canada] —**Noot·ka** *adj*

n.o.p. *abbr* not otherwise provided (for)

no·pal /nṓp'l/ (*plural* **-pals** or *same*) *n* **1.** a cactus that is a host plant to the cochineal insect. Flowers: red, with long stamens. Latin name: *Nopalea cochinellifera.* **2.** the fleshy flattened stem of a nopal cactus, sliced and cooked after removal of the spines [Mid-18C. Via French < Nahuatl *nopalli* "cactus"]

no-par, no-par-val·ue *adj* describes a security without a par or face value

nope /nōp/ *adv, interj* indicates a negative response refusing, denying, or disagreeing with something (*slang*) [Late 19C. Alteration of NO[1] (probably imitating the lips' emphatic closure)]

no-ques·tions-asked *adj* given or granted unconditionally, whatever the reason or circumstances ○ *a no-questions-asked refund*

nor /nawr/ *conj* used to introduce an alternative, after a first alternative that is preceded by "neither" (*used in negative statements*) ○ *Neither he nor his wife had profited in any way from the questionable investment.* ■ *conj, adv* used to indicate that what has just been said also applies to somebody or something else, or to add extra information to what has just been said (*used after negative statements and followed by "have," "do," or "be"*) ○ *He doesn't want to move to another town, and nor do I.* ○ *No surrounding tissue was damaged, nor did the infection spread.* ■ *prep, conj* same as **than** (*nonstandard*) ■ same as **neither** (sense 2) (*literary*) [13C. Contraction of obsolete *nouther* "neither, nor"]

NOR /nawr/ *n* a logical operator with two arguments that returns true if, and only if, both arguments are false [Mid-20C. Blend of NOT + OR[1]]

Nor. *abbr* **1.** HIST Norman **2.** North **3.** Norway **4.** Norwegian

nor- *prefix* an unaltered parent compound ○ *norepinephrine* [Shortening of NORMAL]

NORAD /náwr àd/ *abbr* North American Aerospace Defense Command

nor·a·dren·a·line /nàwrə drénnəlin/, **nor·a·dren·a·lin** *n UK* same as **norepinephrine**

nor·ad·ren·er·gic /nàwr adrə núrjik/ *adj* releasing or involving norepinephrine in the transmission of nerve impulses

NOR cir·cuit *n* a computer circuit with two inputs and one output where the output is on only when both inputs are off

Nor·co /náwrkō/ town in Riverside County, southeastern California, situated 45 mi./72 km west of Palm Springs. Population: 25,838 (2002 estimate).

Nor·dic /náwrdik/ *adj* **1.** SCANDINAVIAN relating to the countries of northwestern Europe, especially the Scandinavian countries and Iceland **2.** TALL, FAIR, AND BLUE-EYED tall, blond, fair-skinned, and blue-eyed, in a way that is considered to be characteristic of people from Scandinavian countries **3.** *also* **nor·dic** INVOLVING CROSS-COUNTRY SKIING OR JUMPING describes or relating to ski events involving either cross-country racing or ski jumping or both ■ *n* SOMEBODY FROM SCANDINAVIA somebody from a Nordic country or of Nordic appearance [Late 19C. < French *nordique* < *nord* "north" < Germanic]

Nor·dic Track *tdmk* a trademark for a cross-country ski exercise machine

Nord-Ost·see Ka·nal /nàwrt àwst zay kaa naál/ ➧ **Kiel Canal**

nor'east·er /nawr éestər/ *n* METEOROL same as **northeaster** [Mid-19C. Alteration]

nor·ep·i·neph·rine /nàwr epə néffrin/ *n* a hormone, secreted by the adrenal gland and similar to epinephrine, that is the principal neurotransmitter of sympathetic nerve endings supplying the major organs and skin. It increases blood pressure and rate and depth of breathing, raises the level of blood sugar, and decreases the activity of the intestines.

nor·eth·is·ter·one /nàwr e thístə rōn/ *n* a progestogen drug. Use: oral contraceptives, hormone replacement therapy, treatment of premenstrual syndrome, menstrual disorders, endometriosis, cancer. [< NOR- + shortening and alteration of ETHYNE + *-ster,* INN stem]

Nor·folk /náwrfək/ **1.** city in southeastern Virginia, situated southeast of Richmond at the mouth of the James and Elizabeth rivers. It is a major port and houses a number of large naval installations. Population: 239,036 (2002 estimate). **2.** county in eastern England, bordering on the Wash and the North Sea. Area: 2,069 sq. mi./5,360 sq. km.

Nor·folk jack·et *n* a loose jacket with a belt and box pleats, first worn by men and later adapted to women's fashions [After *Norfolk,* county in E England]

NOR gate *n* COMPUT same as **NOR circuit**

Nor·gay another spelling of **Norkay**

nor·ges·trel /nawr jéstrəl/ *n* a progestogen drug. Use: oral contraceptives. [Late 20C. < NOR- + PROGESTOGEN]

no·ri /náwree/ *n* an edible preparation of dried pressed seaweed, often used to wrap sushi [Late 19C. < Japanese]

no·ri·a /náwree ə/ *n* a series of buckets on a water wheel, used for raising water from a stream [Late 18C. Via Spanish < Arabic *nāy'ūra*]

No·ri·e·ga /nòrree áygə/, **Manuel** (*b.* 1934) Panamanian national leader. He took power in 1983, but was seized by US forces in 1989, and was later jailed for drug trafficking and other offenses. Full name **Noriega Morena, Manuel Antonio**

nor·ite /náw rīt/ *n* a coarse-grained igneous rock containing mainly plagioclase and orthopyroxene [Late 19C. < NORWAY] —**nor·it·ic** /naw ríttik/ *adj*

Nor·kay ➧ **Tenzing Norgay**

norm /nawrm/ *n* **1.** STANDARD PATTERN OF BEHAVIOR a standard pattern of behavior that is considered normal in a society **2.** USUAL SITUATION the customary situation or circumstances **3.** ACHIEVEMENT LEVEL a required level of achievement **4.** PSYCHOL EXPECTED RANGE OF FUNCTIONING the range of functioning that can be expected of members of a population such as babies of nine months or ten-year-old children. Psychologists use it to determine whether people functioning outside the expected range may need specialist help or support. **5.** MATH REAL-VALUED FUNCTION the magnitude of a vector expressed as the square root of the sum of the squares of the absolute values of the components of the vector **6.** MATH same as **mode** (sense 6) [Early 19C. Latin *norma* "carpenter's square, rule"]

norm. *abbr* MATH normal

Norm. *abbr* HIST, LANG Norman[1]

Nor·ma /náwrmə/ *n* a small faint constellation of the southern hemisphere lying in the Milky Way, located between Ara and Lupus

nor·mal /náwrm'l/ *adj* **1.** USUAL conforming to the usual standard, type, or custom **2.** HEALTHY physically, mentally, and emotionally healthy **3.** OCCURRING NATURALLY maintained or occurring in a natural state **4.** CHEM UNBRANCHED describes aliphatic hydrocarbons with unbranched chains of carbon atoms **5.** CHEM CONTAINING ONE GRAM PER LITER describes a chemical solution containing an equivalent weight of solute in grams per liter of solution (*dated*) **6.** MATH same as **perpendicular** *adj* (sense 1) ■ *n* **1.** USUAL STANDARD the usual standard, type, or custom **2.** MATH PERPENDICULAR LINE OR PLANE a line or plane that is perpendicular to another line or plane [15C. Directly or via French < Latin *normalis* "made according to the square" < *norma* "carpenter's square"] —**nor·mal·ly** *adv*

Nor·mal /náwrm'l/ town in north central Illinois, southeast of Peoria and northeast of Bloomington. Population: 47,078 (2002 estimate).

nor·mal curve *n* the symmetrical bell-shaped curve of a normal distribution

nor·mal·cy /náwrm'lssee/ *n* same as **normality**

nor·mal dis·tri·bu·tion *n* a probability frequency distribution for a random variable that theoretically takes on a bell shape symmetrical about the mean

nor·mal fault *n* a geologic fault in which the upper wall has slipped downward relative to the lower wall

nor·mal·i·ty /nawr mállətee/ *n* the way things are under normal circumstances

nor·mal·ize /náwrm'l īz/ (**-ized, -iz·ing, -iz·es**) *v* **1.** *vti* MAKE SOMETHING NORMAL to make something normal or return something to normal, or become or return to normal **2.** *vt* MAKE SOMETHING OR SOMEBODY CONFORM to make something or somebody conform to a standard **3.** *vt* METALL HEAT STEEL to heat steel above a specific temperature and then cool it in order to reduce internal stress —**nor·mal·i·za·tion** /nàwrm'li záysh'n/ *n*

nor·mal school *n* a school or college for training teachers, especially in France and, formerly, in England, the United States, and Canada [Mid-19C. After French *école normale*; from the first French school so named being considered a model for others]

Nor·man[1] /náwrmən/ *n* **1.** MEDIEVAL INHABITANT OF NORMANDY OR ENGLAND a member of a Viking people who raided and then settled in the French province later known as Normandy, and who invaded England in 1066 **2.** SOMEBODY FROM NORMANDY somebody who comes from the French region of Normandy **3.** LANG same as **Norman French** (sense 1) **4.** STYLE OF MEDIEVAL ARCHITECTURE in Europe, a style of Romanesque architecture developed by the Normans in the Middle Ages, characterized by vaults separated by groins, heavy walls, and deeply recessed portals [13C. < Old French *Normans,* plural of *Normant* < Old Norse *Norðmaðr* (plural *Norðmenn*) < *norð* "north"] —**Nor·man** *adj*

Nor·man[2] /náwrmən/ city in central Oklahoma, south of Oklahoma City. It is home to the University of Oklahoma. Population: 97,831 (2002 estimate).

Nor·man, Greg (*b.* 1955) Australian golfer. He was the winner of the British Open (1986, 1993), and the World Match Play Championship (1980, 1983, and 1986). Known as **Great White Shark.** Full name **Norman, Gregory John**

Nor·man, Jessye (*b.* 1945) US operatic soprano. Her 1969 operatic debut in Berlin was the first of numerous international appearances in operas and concerts, where she was admired for her rich tone and dynamic range.

Nor·man Con·quest *n* the invasion and conquest of England by the Normans, led by William the Conqueror, in 1066

Nor·man·dy /náwrmandee/ region in northwestern France, on the English Channel. Toward the end of World War II, in 1944, it was the scene of the D-day landings, the Allied invasion of German-occupied France. Capital: Rouen.

Nor·man·esque /nàwrmə nésk/ *adj* resembling the Norman style of architecture

Nor·man French *n* **1.** a variety of French spoken by the Normans in the Middle Ages **2.** the French dialect spoken in modern Normandy —**Nor·man French** *adj*

nor·ma·tive /náwrmətiv/ *adj* (*formal*) **1.** relating to standards **2.** tending to create or prescribe standards [Late 19C. < French < Latin *norma* "carpenter's square"] —**nor·ma·tive·ly** *adv* —**nor·ma·tive·ness** *n*

norm·ing /náwrming/ *n US* the practice of adjusting the scores on standardized tests in order to compensate for the possible effects that ethnic and cultural differences may have on the test results

nor·mo·ten·sive /nàwrmō ténssiv/ *adj* having or indicating normal blood pressure ■ *n* somebody with normal blood pressure [Mid-20C. < NORM or NORMAL]

nor·mo·ther·mi·a /nàwrmō thúrmee ə/ *n* the state of having a normal body temperature —**nor·mo·ther·mic** *adj*

norm-ref·er·enced *adj* using a comparison of a pupil's performance in a test with the performance of other children in the same test —**norm-ref·er·enc·ing** *n*

Norns /nawrnz/, **Norn·ir** /náwr nèer/ *npl* in Scandinavian mythology, the three goddesses of destiny [Late 18C. < Old Norse]

nor·o·vi·rus /náwrō vīrəss, nórrō-/ *n* a single-stranded RNA virus that is highly contagious and causes gastroenteritis. Genus: *Norovirus*. [Late 20C. Alteration of *Norwalk virus*, after a city in Ohio where the first outbreak occurred]

Nor·ris /náwriss/, **Frank** (1870–1902) US writer. He is known for his naturalistic novels, *McTeague* (1899) and *The Octopus* (1901). Full name **Norris, Benjamin Franklin**

Norse /nawrss/ *adj* **1.** OF OLD SCANDINAVIA relating to ancient or medieval Scandinavia, or its people or culture **2.** LANG **OF N GERMANIC LANGUAGES** relating to the North Germanic languages, especially Danish, Icelandic, and Norwegian in their earlier forms ■ *npl* **1.** VIKINGS the Viking people of medieval Scandinavia **2.** SCANDINAVIANS the people of Scandinavia **3.** LANG **N GERMANIC NATIVE SPEAKERS** the people who speak one of the North Germanic languages as their native language ■ *n* LANG **N GERMANIC LANGUAGE** a North Germanic language, especially Danish, Icelandic, or Norwegian in their earlier forms [Late 16C. Via Dutch *Noorsch* < *noordsch* "northern"]

Norse·man /náwrssmən/ (*plural* **-men** /-mən/) *n* a member of a medieval Scandinavian group, especially a Viking

nor·te /náwrtay/ *n Hispanic* the north, northern Mexico, or the United States [< Spanish]

nor·tec /náwr tèk/ *n Hispanic* a type of popular Mexican music that blends electronics and traditional music from northern Mexico [Late 20C. Blend of NORTEÑO + TECHNO]

nor·te·ño /nawr táynyō/ *n Hispanic* **1.** a type of Mexican dance music characterized by rolling accordion riffs **2. nor·te·no** (*plural* **-nos**) somebody from northern Mexico [Late 20C. Via American Spanish < Spanish, "northern"]

north /nawrth/ *n* **1.** DIRECTION the direction that lies directly to the left of somebody facing the rising Sun or that is located toward the top of a conventional map of the world **2.** COMPASS POINT one of the cardinal points on a compass. North is 90 degrees counterclockwise from east. **3.** *also* **North** AREA IN NORTH the part of an area, region, or country that is situated in or toward the north **4.** LEFT-HAND SIDE OF CHURCH the left-hand side of a church as you face the altar from the central section of the building **5.** *also* **North** POSITION EQUIVALENT TO NORTH the position equivalent to north in a diagram consisting of four points at 90-degree intervals ■ *adj* **1.** IN NORTH situated in, facing, or coming from the north of a place, region, or country **2.** BLOWING FROM NORTH describes a wind that blows from the north ○ *a north wind* ■ *adv* TOWARD NORTH in or toward the north [Old English *norþ* < Germanic] ◇ **north of** *US* in excess of (*informal*) ○ *north of $64,000*

North /nawrth/, **Frederick, 8th Baron North** (1732–92) British prime minister (1770–82). During his premiership, he pursued policies favored by George III that led to the American Revolution despite his own opposition to the war. Known as **Lord North**

North Ad·ams /nàwrth áddəmz/ town in northwestern Massachusetts, on the Hoosic River, northeast of Pittsfield. Population: 14,430 (2002 estimate8).

North Af·ri·ca northern part of the African continent, comprising Morocco, Mauritania, Algeria, Tunisia, Libya, and Northern Egypt —**North Af·ri·can** *adj, n*

North A·mer·i·ca continent in the western hemisphere, extending northward from northwestern South America to the Arctic Ocean. It comprises Central America, Mexico, the United States, Canada, and Greenland. Population: 405,000,000 (2000). Area: 9,200,000 sq. mi./23,700,000 sq. km. —**North A·mer·i·can** *adj, n*

USAGE See ***America***.

North·amp·ton /nàwr thámptən/ **1.** town in west central Massachusetts, on the western bank of the Connecticut River, north of Holyoke. It is home to Smith College. Population: 28,979 (2002 estimate). **2.** county town of Northamptonshire, central England. Population: 194,458 (2001).

North·amp·ton·shire /nàwr thámptən shèer, -shər/ county in central England. The county town is Northampton. Area: 915 sq. mi./2,370 sq. km.

North An·do·ver town in northeastern Massachusetts, at the confluence of the Shawshine and Merrimack rivers, southeast of Lawrence. Population: 27,837 (2002 estimate).

North At·lan·ta town in Georgia, United States, in DeKalb County, situated north of Atlanta. Population: 27,812 (2002 estimate).

North At·lan·tic drift *n* the relatively warm current, originating as the Gulf Stream in the Gulf of Mexico, that flows across the surface of the North Atlantic Ocean from Newfoundland to northwestern Europe, influencing the latter's climate

North At·lan·tic Trea·ty Or·ga·ni·za·tion *n* INTERNAT REL full form of **NATO**

North At·tle·bor·o /-átt'l bùr ō/ town in southeastern Massachusetts, directly east of the Rhode Island border, southwest of Brockton. Population: 27,826 (2002 estimate).

North Bat·tle·ford /-bátt'lfərd/ town in western Saskatchewan, Canada, on the North Saskatchewan River. Population: 17,117 (2001).

North Bay city on Lake Nipissing in southeastern Ontario, Canada. Population: 51,895 (2001).

North Bell·more /-bél màwr/ town in Nassau County, New York, situated on Long Island, east of New York City. Population: 19,707 (2002 estimate).

North Ber·gen town in New Jersey, in Hudson County. Population: 59,033 (2002 estimate).

North Bor·ne·o former name for **Sabah** (until 1963)

north·bound /náwrth bòwnd/ *adj* leading, going, or traveling toward the north

North·brook /náwrth bròok/ town in northeastern Illinois, northwest of Wilmette. It is a northern suburb of Chicago. Population: 33,956 (2002 estimate).

north by east *n* the direction or compass point midway between north and north-northeast —**north by east** *adj, adv*

north by west *n* the direction or compass point midway between north and north-northwest —**north by west** *adj, adv*

North Cape promontory on Magerøya Island, northern Norway, on the Barents Sea

North Carolina

North Car·o·li·na state in the eastern United States, bordered by the Atlantic Ocean, South Carolina, Georgia, Tennessee, and Virginia. Capital: Raleigh. Population: 8,320,146 (2002 estimate). Area: 52,672 sq. mi./136,420 sq. km. —**North Car·o·lin·i·an** *adj, n*

North Cas·cades Na·tion·al Park /-ka skàydz-/ national park in Northwestern Washington, established in 1968 and noted for its glaciers. Area: 789 sq. mi./2,043 sq. km.

North Cau·ca·sian *n* a group of language families spoken in the region of Caucasia, including the Abkhaz-Adyghean and Nakh languages. They are unrelated to Kartvelian, or South Caucasian. —**North Cau·ca·sian** *adj*

North Chan·nel strait of the Atlantic Ocean separating northeastern Ireland and southwestern Scotland. Width: 23 mi./37 km.

North Charles·ton city in southeastern South Carolina between the Ashley and Cooper rivers, north of Charleston. Population: 80,691 (2002 estimate).

North Chi·ca·go town in northeastern Illinois, on Lake Michigan, south of Waukegan and north of Chicago. Population: 36,097 (2002 estimate).

north·coun·try·man /nàwrth kúntreemən/ (*plural* **-men** /-mən/) *n UK* somebody who was born or raised in the north of England

North Dakota

North Da·ko·ta state in the north central United States, bordered by Minnesota, South Dakota, Montana, and Canada. Capital: Bismarck. Population: 634,110 (2002 estimate). Area: 70,704 sq. mi./183,123 sq. km. —**North Da·ko·tan** *adj, n*

North Downs range of chalk hills in Surrey and Kent, southern England. Its highest peak is Leith Hill, 965 ft./294 m.

north·east /nàwrth èest/; *nautical usage* /nàwr èest/ *n* **1.** COMPASS POINT BETWEEN N AND E the direction or compass point midway between north and east **2.** *also* **North·east** AREA IN NORTHEAST the part of an area, region, or country that is situated in or toward the northeast ■ *adj* **1.** IN NORTHEAST situated in, facing, or lying toward the northeast of a region, place, or country **2.** BLOWING FROM NORTHEAST describes a wind that blows from the northeast ○ *a northeast wind* ■ *adv* TOWARD NORTHEAST in or toward the northeast

North·east *n* **1.** *US* a part of the northeastern United States, usually thought of as consisting of the New England states, sometimes together with eastern New York, Pennsylvania, and New Jersey **2.** *UK* northeastern England, especially the area from the Tees River northward

north·east by east *n* the direction or compass point midway between northeast and east-northeast —**north·east by east** *adj, adv*

north·east by north *n* the direction or compass point midway between northeast and north-northeast —**north·east by north** *adj, adv*

north·east·er /nàwrth èestər/; *nautical usage* /nawr èestər/ *n* a storm or wind that blows from the northeast

REGIONAL NOTE The term ***northeaster*** is found in the Atlantic and Great Lakes states, from Pennsylvania to Minnesota. It is gaining ground nationwide because of its use by television weathercasters.

north·east·er·ly /nawrth èestərlee/; *nautical usage* /nawr èestərlee/ *adj* **1.** situated in or toward the northeast **2.** describes a wind that blows from the northeast ○ *a northeasterly wind* —**north·east·er·ly** *adv*

north·east·ern /nawrth èestərn/; *nautical usage* /nawr èestərn/ *adj* **1.** IN NORTHEAST situated in the northeast of a region or country **2.** COMING FROM OR FACING NORTHEAST coming or blowing from, or facing toward the northeast **3.** BLOWING FROM NE blowing from the northeast **4.** *also* **North·east·ern** OF NORTHEAST relating or native to the northeast of a region or country —**north·east·ern·most** *adj*

North·east Pas·sage sea passage extending from the North Sea eastward along the northern coast of Europe and Asia to the Pacific Ocean. It was first successfully navigated by Adolf Erik Nordenskjöld in 1878–79.

north·east·ward /nawrth éestwərd/; *nautical usage* /nawr éestwərd/ *adj* **IN NORTHEAST** toward or in the northeast ■ *n* **POINT IN NORTHEAST** a direction toward or a point in the northeast ■ *adv also* **north·east·wards** /-wərdz/ **TOWARD NORTHEAST** in a northeasterly direction —**north·east·ward·ly** *adj, adv*

north·er /náwrthər/ *n US* a very cold wind or storm that suddenly appears from the north

north·er·ly /náwrthərlee/ *adj* **1. IN NORTH** situated in or toward the north **2. BLOWING FROM NORTH** describes a wind that blows from the north ○ *a northerly wind* ■ *n* (*plural* **-lies**) **WIND FROM NORTH** a wind that blows from the north —**north·er·ly** *adv*

north·ern /náwrthərn/ *adj* **1. IN NORTH** situated in the north of a region or country **2. NORTH OF EQUATOR** lying north of the equator or north of the celestial equator **3. FACING NORTH** situated on the north side of something or facing north **4. FROM NORTH** blowing from the north ○ *a northern wind* **5.** *also* **North·ern OF NORTH** relating or native to the north of a region or country

North·ern Al·li·ance *n* a loose coalition of Afghan military forces, operating mainly in the north of Afghanistan, that ended Taliban rule in Afghanistan in 2001

North·ern Cape /nàwrthərn-/ largest province in South Africa, in the northwestern part of the country. Capital: Kimberley. Population: 822,720 (2001). Area: 139,670 sq. mi./361,830 sq. km.

North·ern Cross *n* a cross formed by six stars in the constellation Cygnus

North·ern Crown *n* ASTRON same as **Corona Borealis**

north·ern·er /náwrthərnər/, **North·ern·er** *n* somebody who comes from the northern part of a country or region

north·ern har·ri·er *n US* a slim-bodied brown or grayish hawk with a conspicuous white patch on its tail. It is the only harrier native to North America. Native to: marshy areas of North America, Europe, and Asia. Latin name: *Circus cyaneus.*

north·ern hem·i·sphere *n* **1.** the half of the Earth that lies to the north of the equator **2.** the half of the celestial sphere north of the celestial equator

North·ern Ire·land province of the United Kingdom of Great Britain and Northern Ireland, situated in the northeastern part of the island of Ireland. Capital: Belfast. Population: 1,685,267 (2001). Area: 5,467 sq. mi./14,160 sq. km.

North·ern Ire·land As·sem·bly *n* the center of devolved government for Northern Ireland, made up of elected members, suspended from October 14, 2002

North·ern·ism /náwrthər nìzzəm/, **north·ern·ism** *n* a pronunciation, word, or other linguistic construction characteristic of the northern region of a country

north·ern lights *npl* ASTRON same as **aurora borealis**

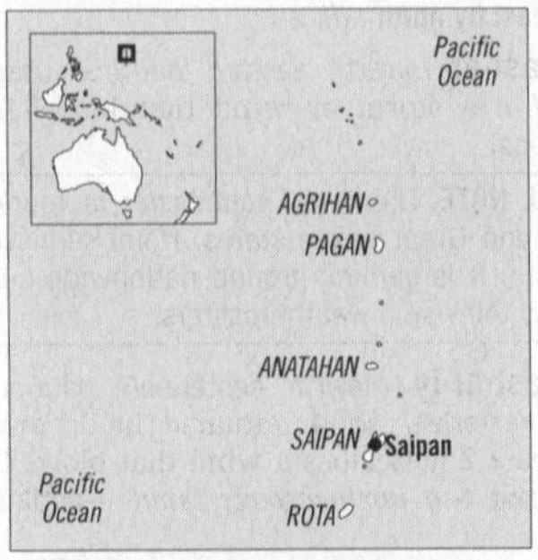

Northern Mariana Islands

North·ern Mar·i·an·a Is·lands /-màrree ánnə-/ self-governing commonwealth of the United States, situated in the western Pacific Ocean and comprising all the Mariana Islands except Guam. Population: 71,912 (2000). Area: 176 sq. mi./457 sq. km.

north·ern·most /náwrthərn mòst/ *adj* situated farthest north

north·ern o·ri·ole *n* an oriole with two subspecies, the Baltimore oriole and Bullock's oriole, the males of each having black and orange plumage. Native to: North America. Latin name: *Icterus galbula.*

North·ern Pai·ute, North·ern Pi·ute *n* **1.** a member of a Native North American people of Oregon, Nevada, and northeastern California **2.** a Uto-Aztecan language spoken in Oregon, Nevada, and northeastern California. Native speakers: 6,000. —**North·ern Pai·ute** *adj*

north·ern pike *n regional* FISH same as **pike**[1] (sense 1)

REGIONAL NOTE With scattered instances of use in the East and South, the term ***northern pike,*** denoting the fish, is common in Michigan, Wisconsin, and Minnesota.

North·ern Prov·ince former name for **Limpopo Province**

North·ern Ren·ais·sance *n* a northern European cultural and intellectual movement of the 15th century in France, England, Scotland, the Low Countries, and Germany that placed more emphasis on religion than the Italian Renaissance did

North·ern Rho·de·sia former name for **Zambia**

north·ern snake·head *n* FISH same as **snakehead** (sense 2)

North·ern So·tho *n* LANG same as **Pedi**

North·ern Ter·ri·to·ry territory in north central Australia. Capital: Darwin. Population: 198,400 (2003). Area: 519,770 sq. mi./1,346,200 sq. km. —**Nor·thern Ter·ri·tor·ian** *n, adj*

North·ern Yu·kon Na·tion·al Park national park in Northwestern Canada, in the Northwestern corner of Yukon Territory, on the Alaskan border. It is a sanctuary for arctic wildlife and Inuit archaeological sites. Area: 3,859 sq. mi./9,995 sq. km.

North Fort My·ers town in southwestern Florida, near Fort Myers, in Lee County. Population: 30,027 (1996).

North Ger·man·ic *n* **1.** a group of Germanic languages that includes Danish, Faroese, Icelandic, Norwegian, and Swedish. Native speakers: 20 million. **2.** the language that is the ancestor of modern languages belonging to North Germanic —**North Ger·man·ic** *adj*

LANGUAGE HERITAGE See ***Scandinavian.***

North Ha·ven town in southern Connecticut, in central New Haven County, northeast of New Haven. Population: 23,460 (2002 estimate).

North High·lands town in Sacramento County, north central California, northeast of Sacramento. Population: 42,105 (1996).

north·ing /náwrthing, -thing/ *n* **1.** NAUT **MOVEMENT NORTH** distance covered or movement made in a northerly direction, especially as measured by the difference in latitude between two points **2.** NAUT **PROGRESS NORTH** progress made in a northern direction **3. LATITUDINAL GRID LINE ON MAP** a grid line on a map that runs from east to west **4.** MAPS **DISTANCE NORTHWARD** the distance northward from an east-west grid line, shown in the second half of a map reference

North Is·land island in New Zealand, in the southwestern Pacific Ocean. It is the smaller and more northern of the country's two main islands. Population: 2,749,980 (1996). Area: 44,282 sq. mi./114,690 sq. km.

North Kings·town /-kíngstən/ town in south central Rhode Island, on the western shore of Narragansett Bay, southwest of Warwick. Population: 26,985 (2002 estimate).

North Ko·re·a /-kə rée ə, -kō rée ə/ country in East Asia that occupies the northern portion of the Korean Peninsula. Language: Korean. Currency: won. Capital: Pyongyang. Population: 22,466,481 (2003). Area: 46,540 sq. mi./120,538 sq. km. Official name **Democratic People's Republic of Korea** —**North Ko·re·an** *n, adj*

north·land /náwrth lànd, -lənd/ *n* the northern part of a country

North·land /náwrth lànd, -lənd/ **1.** Scandinavian peninsula containing Norway and Sweden **2.** *Can* parts of Canada in the far north

North Lau·der·dale town in southeastern Florida in Broward County, situated northwest of Fort Lauderdale. Population: 29,453 (1998).

North Lit·tle Rock city in central Arkansas, across the Arkansas River from Little Rock. Population: 60,007 (2002 estimate).

north mag·net·ic pole *n* the point on the Earth's surface to which the north-seeking pole of a compass needle is attracted

North·man /náwrthmən/ (*plural* **-men** /-mən/) *n* HIST, PEOPLES same as **Norseman**

North Mi·am·i city in southeastern Florida, in Miami-Dade County. It is a suburb of Miami. Population: 60,034 (2002 estimate).

North Mi·am·i Beach city in southeastern Florida, in Dade County, situated north of Miami Beach. Population: 40,848 (2002 estimate).

north-north·east *n* the direction or compass point midway between north and northeast ■ *adj, adv* in, from, facing, or toward the north-northeast

north-north·west *n* the direction or compass point midway between north and northwest ■ *adj, adv* in, from, facing, or toward the north-northwest

north pole *n* **1.** GEOG, NAVIG same as **north magnetic pole 2.** the north end of the axis of rotation of a planet or other astronomical object **3.** the point at infinity along the northern extension of one end of the Earth's axis of rotation **4.** another spelling of **North Pole**

North Pole *n* the northern end of the Earth's axis at a latitude of 90° N

North Prov·i·dence town in northeastern Rhode Island, southeast of Woonsocket. It is a northern suburb of Providence. Population: 33,238 (2002 estimate).

North Sas·katch·e·wan river in Canada that rises in the Canadian Rocky Mountains and flows eastward to join the South Saskatchewan River. It empties into Lake Winnipeg. Length: 760 mi./1,200 km.

North Sea arm of the Atlantic Ocean lying between the eastern coast of Great Britain and the continent of Europe. Area: 222,000 sq. mi./575,000 sq. km.

North Shore *n* **1.** *US* **CONNECTICUT SHORELINE** the Connecticut coast, which forms the northern side of Long Island Sound **2.** *US* **SHORE NORTH OF BOSTON** the area of the Atlantic coastline immediately north of Boston **3.** *Can* **NORTHERN SIDE OF BRITISH COLUMBIA INLET** in Vancouver, British Columbia, the northern side of Burrard Inlet facing the city **4.** *Can* **NORTHERN SHORE OF ST. LAWRENCE RIVER** in southeastern Quebec, the northern shore of the St. Lawrence River and the Gulf of St. Lawrence. **5.** *Can* **N NEW BRUNSWICK COASTLINE** in eastern New Brunswick, the northern coastline along the Northumberland Strait and the Gulf of St. Lawrence.

North Slope region of Northern Alaska, extending from the Arctic Ocean south to the Brooks Range. It contains the largest petroleum reserves in the United States.

North-South Di·vide *n UK* the political and economic disparities between the northern and the southern regions of England

North Star *n* ASTRON same as **Polaris** (sense 1)

North Star State *n* a nickname for Minnesota

North·um·ber·land /nawr thúmbərlənd/ northernmost county of England, and one of the largest and most sparsely populated. Area: 1,944 sq. mi./5,033 sq. km.

North·um·bri·a /nawr thúmbree ə/ ancient region in northeastern England. It was one of the most powerful of the Anglo-Saxon kingdoms of England between the 7th and 10th centuries. —**North·um·bri·an** *adj, n*

North Van·cou·ver city in southwestern Canada, in southern British Columbia, situated on Burrard Inlet across from Vancouver. Population: 44,303 (2001).

North Vi·et·nam former republic in Southeast Asia. Created by the French partition of Vietnam in 1954, it was reunited with South Vietnam in 1976 after the Vietnam War, and its capital of Hanoi became the national capital. —**North Vi·et·nam·ese** *n, adj*

north·ward /náwrthwərd/ *adj* IN NORTH toward or in the north ■ *n* POINT IN NORTH a direction toward or a point in the north ■ *adv also* **north·wards** /-wərdz/ TOWARD NORTH in a northerly direction —**north·ward·ly** *adj, adv*

north·west /nàwrth wést/; *nautical usage* /nàwr wést/ *n* **1.** COMPASS POINT BETWEEN N AND W the direction or compass point midway between north and west **2.** *also* **North·west** AREA IN NORTHWEST the part of an area, region, or country that is situated in or toward the northwest ■ *adj* **1.** *also* **North·west** IN NORTHWEST situated in, facing, or lying toward the northwest of a region, place, or country **2.** BLOWING FROM NORTHWEST describes a wind that blows from the northwest ○ *a northwest wind* ■ *adv* TOWARD NORTHWEST in or toward the northwest

North·west *n* **1.** NW UNITED STATES the northwestern area of the United States, including the states of Washington, Oregon, and Idaho **2.** FORMER AREA OF UNITED STATES formerly, a region of the United States west of the Mississippi River and north of the Missouri River **3.** *Can* CANADIAN REGION the area of Canada north and west of the Great Lakes **4.** *UK* AREA OF ENGLAND the northwestern region of England, especially Cumbria and Lancashire and including the Lake District

north·west by north *n* the direction or compass point midway between northwest and north-northwest —**north·west by north** *adj, adv*

north·west by west *n* the direction or compass point midway between northwest and west-northwest —**north·west by west** *adj, adv*

north·west·er /nawrth wéstər/; *nautical usage* /nawr wéstər/ *n* a wind that blows from the northwest

north·west·er·ly /nawrth wéstərlee/; *nautical usage* /nawr wéstərlee/ *adj* **1.** situated in or toward the northwest **2.** METEOROL describes a wind that blows from the northwest ○ *a northwesterly wind* ■ *n* (*plural* **-lies**) METEOROL same as **northwester** —**north·west·er·ly** *adv*

north·west·ern /nawrth wéstərn/; *nautical usage* /nawr wéstərn/ *adj* **1.** IN NORTHWEST situated in the northwest of a region or country **2.** FACING NORTHWEST coming or blowing from, or facing toward the northwest **3.** OF NORTHWEST relating to or native to the northwest of a region or country —**north·west·ern·most** *adj*

North·west Pas·sage /nàwrth west-/ sea passage through the Arctic regions of North America, connecting the Pacific Ocean and the Atlantic Ocean

North-West Prov·ince province in South Africa, in the north central part of the country. Capital: Mmabatho. Population: 3,669,339 (2001). Area: 44,850 sq. mi./116,190 sq. km.

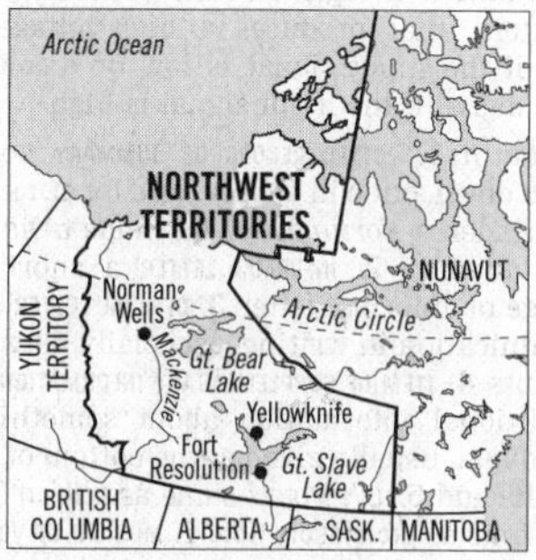

Northwest Territories

North·west Ter·ri·to·ries region in northern Canada, and its largest political subdivision, constituting a northern mainland region and numerous islands to the north. Capital: Yellowknife. Population: 441,400 (2002). Area: 519,734 sq. mi./1,346,106 sq. km.

North·west Ter·ri·to·ry territory of the north central United States ceded by England to the United States by the Treaty of Paris in 1783. The area of about 265,900 sq. mi./688,600 sq. km extended from the Ohio and Mississippi rivers northward to the Great Lakes, and included present-day Ohio, Indiana, Illinois, Michigan, Wisconsin, and eastern Minnesota.

north·west·ward /nawrth wéstwərd/; *nautical usage* /nawr wéstwərd/ *adj* IN NORTHWEST toward or in the northwest ■ *n* POINT IN NORTHWEST a direction toward or a point in the northwest ■ *adv also* **north·west·wards** /-wərdz/ TOWARD NORTHWEST in a northwesterly direction —**north·west·ward·ly** *adj, adv*

Nor·ton /náwrt'n/, **Charles Eliot** (1827–1908) US scholar and editor. He cofounded the *Nation* (1865) and pioneered the teaching of art history at Harvard (1873–97).

> "The voice of protest, of warning, of appeal is never more needed than when the clamor of fife and drum, echoed by the press and too often by the pulpit, is bidding all men fall in and keep step and obey in silence the tyrannous word of command."
> [Charles Eliot Norton, *True Patriotism*; 1898]

nor·trip·ty·line /nawr tríptə leen/ *n* a tricyclic drug. Use: antidepressant, tranquilizer, pain reliever. Formula: $C_{19}H_{21}N$. [Mid-20C. < NOR- + *triptyline*, INN stem]

Norw. *abbr* **1.** Norway **2.** Norwegian

Norway

Nor·way /náwr wày/ country in northern Europe, occupying the western and northern portions of the Scandinavian Peninsula. Language: Norwegian. Currency: krone. Capital: Oslo. Population: 4,546,123 (2003). Area: 148,896 sq. mi./385,639 sq. km. Official name **Kingdom of Norway**

Nor·way ma·ple *n* a maple with broad five-lobed green or reddish leaves, widely grown as a shade tree. Native to: central and northern Europe. Latin name: *Acer platanoides*.

Nor·way pine *n* TREES same as **red pine**

Nor·way rat *n* ZOOL same as **brown rat**

Nor·way spruce *n* a spruce tree with drooping branches and long cones, widely grown for its timber and as an ornamental. Native to: central and northern Europe. Latin name: *Picea abies*.

Nor·we·gian /nawr weéjən/ *n* **1.** somebody who comes from Norway **2.** the North Germanic language that is the official language of Norway. Native speakers: 5 million. [Early 17C. < medieval Latin *Norvegia* "Norway" < Old Norse *Norvegr*] —**Nor·we·gian** *adj*

LANGUAGE HERITAGE See *Scandinavian.*

Nor·we·gian elk·hound *n US* a sturdy medium-sized dog with pointed ears, a broad head, and a thick gray coat, belonging to a breed developed in Norway to hunt elk and other game. Can term **elkhound**

nor'west·er /nawr wéstər/ *n* **1.** METEOROL same as **northwester 2.** *UK* a strong alcoholic drink (*slang*) [Late 17C. Alteration]

Nor·wich 1. /náwr wìch/ town in southeastern Connecticut, in New London County. Population: 36,003 (2002 estimate). **2.** /nórrich/ town and administrative center of Norfolk, eastern England. Population: 121,550 (2001).

Nor·wich ter·ri·er *n* a small short-legged dog with wiry fur and erect ears, belonging to a breed that originated in East Anglia, England

nos., Nos. *abbr* numbers

n.o.s. *abbr* not otherwise specified

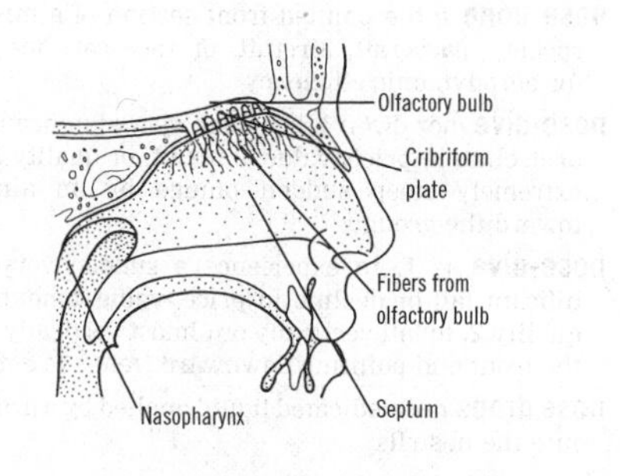

nose: cross section of the human nose

nose /nōz/ *n* **1.** ORGAN OF SMELL the part of the face or head through which a person or animal breathes and smells **2.** SENSE OF SMELL the sense of smell, especially the ability to recognize things by smell or to follow a scent **3.** TALENT FOR DISCOVERY an intuitive ability to discover, detect, or recognize something **4.** PART RESEMBLING NOSE a part that resembles the nose of a person or animal in appearance or function **5.** PROJECTING FRONT PART OF VEHICLE the pointed or rounded front end of an aircraft, spacecraft, boat, car, or other vehicle **6.** DISTINCTIVE SMELL the characteristic aroma of something such as wine or tobacco ■ *v* (**nosed, nos·ing, nos·es**) **1.** *vi* SEARCH FOR BY SCENT to try to find something by smelling or sniffing ○ *nosed out my secret hoard of chocolate* **2.** *vti* ADVANCE WITH CAUTION to move forward slowly, carefully, or cautiously, or make something move in this way ○ *nosed into the stream of traffic* **3.** *vt* TOUCH SOMETHING WITH NOSE to touch, rub, or push somebody or something with the nose (*refers to animals*) **4.** *vt* SMELL SOMETHING to smell or sniff something **5.** *vi* PRY OR SNOOP to try to make discoveries by searching or asking questions in an inquisitive, impertinent, or intrusive manner (*informal*) [Old English *nosu* < Indo-European] ◇ **as plain as the nose on your face** very obvious (*informal*) ◇ **follow your nose 1.** to go or continue straight ahead in the direction you are facing **2.** to act in accordance with your instincts or intuition ◇ **get up somebody's nose** *UK* to irritate or annoy somebody (*informal*) ◇ **keep your nose clean** to avoid getting into trouble (*informal*) ◇ **keep** *or* **put your nose to the grindstone** to keep working hard without taking a break ◇ **look down your nose at somebody** *or* **something** to regard somebody or something arrogantly or disdainfully as inferior or not worth your attention ◇ **nose to tail** so close together that the front of one vehicle almost touches the rear end of another ◇ **on the nose 1.** absolutely on target, with total accuracy, or completely correctly (*informal*) ○ *at 10 o'clock on the nose* **2.** in betting on horseraces, for a horse to win only, not to be placed second or third (*slang*) ◇ **put somebody's nose out of joint** to make somebody feel thwarted or offended because you do, obtain, or achieve something that he or she was intending or hoping for ◇ **thumb your nose at somebody** *or* **something** to express defiance or contempt of somebody or something, especially by putting a thumb to the nose and extending the fingers ◇ **turn up your nose at something** to refuse to accept something because you feel it is inferior or unworthy of you (*informal*) ◇ **under somebody's nose** in full view of or very close to somebody

nose around *vti* to look or search through a place in an inquisitive and often intrusive way (*informal*)

nose out *v* **1.** *vt* NARROWLY DEFEAT OPPONENT to defeat an opponent by a very narrow margin **2.** *vi* DRIVE CAUTIOUSLY FORWARD to move a vehicle very slowly and cautiously forward out of a place **3.** *vt* FIND SOMETHING OUT BY PRYING to discover something by thorough and often cunning or intrusive searching or questioning (*informal*) **4.** *vt* FIND SOMETHING BY SCENT to discover something by smelling or sniffing, or as if by following a scent

nose·bag /nōz bàg/ *n UK* same as **feedbag** (sense 1)

nose·band /nōz bànd/ *n* the part of a horse's bridle that goes over its nose

nose·bleed /nṓz bleèd/ *n* a flow of blood from the nose. Technical name **epistaxis** ■ *adj* extremely high or excessive, e.g., in price or profit level (*informal*)

nose can·dy *n* DRUGS same as **cocaine** (*slang*)

nose cone *n* the pointed front section of a missile, rocket, spacecraft, aircraft, or race car, designed for aerodynamic efficiency

nose·dive /nṓz dìv/ *n* **1.** a sudden very significant fall or decline in price, value, amount, or quality **2.** an extremely steep sudden plunge by an aircraft toward the ground

nose-dive *vi* **1.** to experience a sudden very significant fall or decline in price, value, amount, or quality **2.** to fall vertically or almost vertically with the front end pointing downward (*refers to aircraft*)

nose drops *npl* medicated liquid applied by a dropper into the nostrils

no-see-um /nō sée əm/ *n* INSECTS same as **punkie** [< caricatured Native American English, "you can't see them"; from its small size]

nose flute *n* a wind instrument of the South Pacific Islands, usually played by being breathed into through one nostril while the other one is plugged

nose·gay /nṓz gày/ *n* a small bouquet of flowers [< GAY "ornament"]

nose gear *n* a part of the landing gear of an airplane, consisting of a wheel and related mechanisms located forward of the plane's center and the rest of the landing gear

nose·guard /nṓz gaàrd/ *n US* in football, a defensive lineman who plays opposite the center in the offensive line

nose job *n* a surgical operation to improve the shape or size of the nose (*informal*)

nose or·na·ment *n* a decorative ring or stud worn through the nostril or septum

nose·piece /nṓz peèss/ *n* **1.** PART OF EYEGLASSES the part of a pair of eyeglasses that fits over the nose and connects the lenses **2.** PART OF MICROSCOPE the end piece of a microscope to which one or more objective lenses are attached **3.** PROTECTION FOR NOSE the part of a helmet or piece of armor that protects the nose **4.** RIDING same as **noseband**

nose ring *n* **1.** a ring put through an animal's nose to lead or control it **2.** a ring worn for adornment through a hole pierced in the nostril or septum

nose stud *n* a small stud worn for adornment in a hole pierced in the nostril or septum

nose tack·le *n US* FOOTBALL same as **noseguard**

nose wheel *n* a landing-gear wheel at the front end of an aircraft

nos·ey *adj* another spelling of **nosy** (*informal*)

nosh /nosh/ (*informal*) *n* FOOD same as **snack** *n* (sense 1) ■ *vti* (**noshed, nosh·ing, nosh·es**) to eat something, especially a snack between meals [Early 20C. Via Yiddish *nashen* "to nibble" < Middle High German *naschen*] —**nosh·er** *n*

no-show *n* somebody who fails to appear or arrive when expected, without giving notice

nos·ing /nṓzing/ *n* **1.** PROJECTING EDGE OF STAIR TREAD the rounded edge of a stair tread that projects horizontally **2.** PROTECTION FOR NOSING a shield that protects a nosing on a staircase **3.** ARCHIT PROJECTING EDGE OF MOLDING the rounded projecting edge of an architectural molding

no-smok·ing *adj* where smoking is not allowed, or that prohibits smoking ■ *n* HEALTH same as **nonsmoking**

noso- *prefix* disease ○ *nosophobia* [< Greek *nosos*]

no·so·co·mi·al /nòssō kṓmee əl/ *adj* describes a disease or infection that originates or occurs in a hospital [Mid-19C. < Greek *nosokomos* "somebody who tends the sick" < *nosos* "sickness"]

no·sog·ra·phy /nō sóggrəfee/ (*plural* **-phies**) *n* a detailed classification and description of known diseases —**no·so·graph·ic** /nòssə gráffik/ *adj*

no·sol·o·gy /nō sólləjee/ (*plural* **-gies**) *n* **1.** the branch of medicine concerned with the classification and description of known diseases **2.** a completed classification of known diseases —**no·so·log·i·cal** /nòssə lójjik'l/ *adj*—**no·sol·o·gist** /nō sólləjist/ *n*

no·so·pho·bi·a /nòssə fṓbee ə/ *n* an irrational fear of catching diseases

nos·tal·gi·a /no stáljə, nə-/ *n* **1.** SENTIMENTAL RECOLLECTION a mixed feeling of happiness, sadness, and longing when recalling a person, place, or event from the past, or the past in general **2.** THINGS THAT AROUSE NOSTALGIA something, or things, intended to arouse a feeling of nostalgia or to evoke the past in a way that arouses nostalgia **3.** HOMESICKNESS a longing for home or family when away from either (*dated*) [Late 18C. < modern Latin, "homesickness" < Greek *nostos* "homecoming" + *algos* "pain"] —**nos·tal·gic** *adj*—**nos·tal·gi·cal·ly** *adv*

nos·toc /nó stòk/ *n* a freshwater microorganism that lives in spherical colonies as coiled filaments and fixes atmospheric nitrogen. Genus: *Nostoc.* [Mid-17C. < modern Latin, invented]

nos·tol·o·gy /no stólləjee/ *n* MED same as **gerontology** [Mid-20C. < Greek *nostos* "return home" (from the former idea that later life is like a return to early years)]

Barnaby's

Nostradamus

Nos·tra·da·mus /nòstrə daáməss, -dáyməss/ (1503–66) French astrologer and physician. His prophecies, composed in rhyming quatrains and first published as *Centuries* in 1555, were consulted for hundreds of years. Born **Nostredame, Michel de**

nos·tril /nóstrəl/ *n* either of the two openings at the end of the nose of a person or animal [Old English *nosþyrl* < *nosu*, form of NOSE + *þȳrl* "hole" < *þurh*, form of THROUGH]

nos·trum /nóstrəm/ *n* **1.** a remedy for a social, political, or economic problem, especially an idea or plan that is often suggested but never proved to be successful **2.** a medicine prepared or prescribed by an unqualified person whose claims for its effectiveness have no scientific basis [Early 17C. < Latin *nostrum (remedium)* "our (remedy)"]

nos·y /nṓzee/ (**-i·er, -i·est**), **nos·ey** *adj* too curious about other people's business (*informal*) —**nos·i·ly** *adv* —**nos·i·ness** *n*

not /not/ *adv* **1.** FORMING NEGATIVES a negative adverb used to form structures indicating that something is to no degree or in no way the case or conveying the general notion "no." It is often used to express refusal, denial, or the negation of a statement just made. (*often contracted in spoken and informal written English to "n't"*) ○ *Don't you think you've done enough?* ○ *Not every household has a dishwasher.* ○ *There's nothing in my account, not one cent.* ○ *Not only was the meal expensive, the service was bad, too.* **2.** SENTENCE SUBSTITUTE used as a sentence substitute when indicating denial, refusal, or negation, in order to avoid repetition ○ *"Won't you come with us?" – "Certainly not."* ○ *I don't think I'll be late, at least I hope not.* **3.** INDICATING OPPOSITE tagged onto the end of a statement to indicate that the truth is the opposite of what has been stated (*humorous*) ○ *You're really going to enjoy this – not!* [14C. Contraction of NOUGHT] ◇ **not at all** used as a polite way of acknowledging somebody's thanks ◇ **not that** used to introduce a clause that explicitly denies something that the listener might infer from a previous or subsequent statement ○ *I'm actually seeing her tonight. Not that it's any of your business!*

USAGE See ***knot*** [1].

NOT /not/ *n* COMPUT same as **NOT circuit** [< NOT]

no·ta INSECTS plural of **notum**

no·ta be·ne /nṓtə bénnee/ *interj* full form of **N.B.** (*formal*) [< Latin < *nota*, imperative form of *notare* "mark" + *bene* "well"]

no·ta·bil·i·ty /nṓtə bíllətee/ (*plural* **-ties**) *n* **1.** same as **notable 2.** the importance of somebody or something, or the quality that makes somebody or something worth paying attention to

no·ta·ble /nṓtəb'l/ *adj* **1.** WORTHY OF NOTE significant, interesting, or unusual enough to deserve attention or to be recorded ○ *a notable contribution to our understanding of this complex phenomenon* **2.** DISTINGUISHED particularly important, distinguished, or famous ■ *n* SOMEBODY IMPORTANT somebody who is particularly important or distinguished [14C. < Old French < Latin *notare* "to note"] —**no·ta·ble·ness** *n*

no·ta·bly /nṓtəblee/ *adv* **1.** especially, or in the most significant case ○ *There has been much opposition, notably from farmers.* **2.** extremely or remarkably ○ *She seems notably unimpressed by all their arguments.*

no·tar·i·al /nō térree əl/ *adj* relating to or done by a notary public —**no·tar·i·al·ly** *adv*

no·ta·rize /nṓtə rìz/ (**-rized, -riz·ing, -riz·es**) *vt* to certify something such as a signature on a legal document as authentic or legitimate by affixing a notary's stamp and signature —**no·ta·ri·za·tion** /nṓtəri záysh'n/ *n*

no·ta·ry /nṓtəree/ (*plural* **-ries**) *n* LAW same as **notary public** [14C. Via Old French *notarie* < Latin *notarius* "shorthand writer, clerk"]

no·ta·ry pub·lic (*plural* **no·ta·ries pub·lic**) *n* somebody who is legally authorized to certify the authenticity or legitimacy of signatures and documents

no·tate /nṓ tàyt/ (**-tat·ed, -tat·ing, -tates**) *vt* to write something down using notation, especially musical notation [Early 20C. Back-formation < NOTATION]

no·ta·tion /nō táysh'n/ *n* **1.** SYMBOLIC REPRESENTATION a set of written symbols used to represent something such as the length and pitch of musical notes. See illustration on next page **2.** USE OF NOTATION the process of using a system of notation **3.** NOTE a note or annotation **4.** NOTING the act of making a note or writing something down [Late16C. Directly or via French < Latin *notation-* < *notat-*, past participle of *notare* "to note"]

notch /noch/ *n* **1.** NICK OR INDENTATION a small V-shaped cut in the edge or on the surface of something **2.** DEGREE ON SCALE a level or step on a scale, especially one measuring quality or achievement ○ *raise the tension on the wire another notch* **3.** NICK USED AS TALLY a cut made to record a score, a debt, or the number of times something has been done **4.** GEOG PASS OR GORGE a narrow valley between hills or mountains ■ *vt* (**notched, notch·ing, notch·es**) **1.** MAKE V-SHAPED CUT IN SOMETHING to make a notch in or on something **2.** RECORD SOMETHING WITH NOTCHES to record a score or debt by making a series of cuts in a surface **3.** ACHIEVE OR SCORE SOMETHING to achieve a victory or success, or score a point or goal (*slang*) ○ *notched up another win* [Mid-16C. Origin ?] —**notch·y** *adj*

notch·back /nóch bàk/ *n* a car with a sloping roof that drops sharply to the beginning of the trunk

NOT cir·cuit *n* a logic circuit, used especially in computers, that produces a high-voltage output signal if the input signal is low or a low-voltage output signal if the input signal is high

note /nōt/ *n* **1.** JOTTED RECORD OR SUMMARY something written down, often in abbreviated form, as a record or reminder ○ *Fortunately, I'd made a note of her phone number.* **2.** INFORMAL LETTER a short written message or informal letter **3.** OFFICIAL LETTER a formal communication in writing, especially between governments **4.** ITEM OF SUPPLEMENTARY INFORMATION a piece of additional information about something in a printed text, usually given at the bottom of the page or at the end **5.** *UK* MONEY same as **bill**[1] *n* (sense 7) **6.** FIN same as **promissory note 7.** MUSICAL OR VOCAL SOUND a sound of a distinct pitch, quality, or duration produced by a musical instrument or by the voice **8.** SYMBOL IN MUSIC in written or printed music, a symbol representing a specific sound **9.** KEY ON KEYBOARD a black or white key of a piano or other keyboard instrument **10.** INDICATION OF MOOD a tone in the voice or in writing, or an attitude or atmosphere, that indicates feelings or mood ○ *a note of urgency* ○ *The meeting closed on an optimistic note.* **11.** HINT a hint or suggestion of something **12.** DISTINCTION distinction or excellence ○ *a writer of note* ■ **notes** *npl* SUMMARY FOR FUTURE REFERENCE a summary of important facts or points written down by a listener, e.g., by a student during a lesson ■ *vt* (**not·ed,**

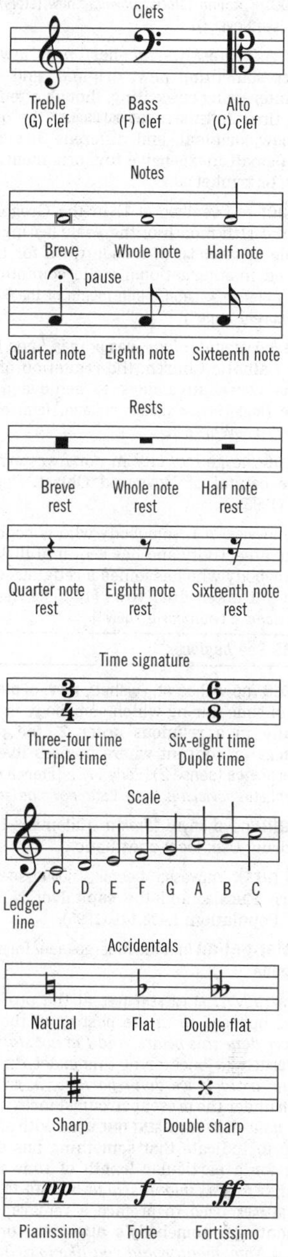

notation: musical notation

not·ing, notes) 1. OBSERVE SOMETHING to notice or remember something by paying special attention to it 2. MENTION SOMETHING to mention something important 3. WRITE SOMETHING DOWN to write down something important as a record or reminder [13C. Via Old French *note* "sign" < Latin *nota* "sign, mark"] —**not·er** *n*

noteable incorrect spelling of **notable**

note·book /nṓt bo͝ok/ *n* 1. a small book in which to write, containing blank or lined pages 2. a small thin portable personal computer

note card *n* a folded sheet of paper or thin card with a picture on the front, used for writing short informal letters

not·ed /nṓtəd/ *adj* 1. well known and especially distinguished by or admired for a particular thing or quality ○ *noted for their hospitality* 2. significant or distinctive enough to be noticeable ○ *a noted increase in applications* —**not·ed·ly** *adv*

note·let /nṓtlət/ *n UK* same as **note card**

note of hand *n* FIN same as **promissory note**

note·pad /nṓt pàd/ *n* a number of small sheets of blank or lined paper on which to write, fastened together in a way that makes it easy to detach a single page

note·pa·per /nṓt pàypər/ *n* paper for writing letters or making notes on

note row /-rṑ/ *n* MUSIC same as **tone row**

note·wor·thy /nṓt wùrthee/ (**-thi·er, -thi·est**) *adj* deserving notice or attention, usually because of significance, excellence, uniqueness, or interest —**note·wor·thi·ly** *adv* —**note·wor·thi·ness** *n*

not-for-prof·it *adj* BUSINESS same as **nonprofit**

NOT gate *n* COMPUT same as **NOT circuit**

noth·ing /núthing/ *pron* 1. NOT ANYTHING an indefinite pronoun indicating that there is not anything, not a single thing, or not a single part of a thing ○ *There is nothing more annoying than people who drop names.* 2. SOMETHING OF NO IMPORTANCE a thing or matter of no importance or significance ○ *It's nothing to me whether they win or lose.* 3. NOT HAVING QUALITY used to indicate the complete lack of the quality mentioned in somebody or something ○ *He wore an ordinary dark blue jacket, nothing special.* 4. ZERO AMOUNT a zero quantity or zero ○ *We won, three–nothing.* 5. STATE OF NONEXISTENCE a condition of nonexistence, or the absence of any perceptible qualities ○ *vanished into nothing* ■ *n* SOMEBODY OR SOMETHING UNIMPORTANT somebody or something regarded as totally unimportant ■ *adj* UNDISTINGUISHED completely lacking in distinguishing qualities, interest, or significance (*informal*) ○ *a nothing product, despite all the hype* [Old English *nāðinc* < earlier forms of NO[1] + THING] ◇ **not for nothing** for a very good reason ◇ **nothing but** only ◇ **nothing doing** used to indicate a complete refusal to do something or to cooperate (*informal*) ◇ **nothing for it** used to indicate that there is no other course of action open to somebody ○ *There was nothing for it but for us to admit our error.* ◇ **nothing if not** definitely, undoubtedly, or at the very least ○ *He's nothing if not fair.* ◇ **nothing less than, nothing short of** used to emphasize forcefully that something truly, definitely, or amazingly is as described ○ *The things they've been saying about me are nothing less than slander.* ◇ **nothing like somebody** *or* **something** having no resemblance to somebody or something else ◇ **nothing much** no item or activity of importance, significance, size, value, or interest ○ *Nothing much happened in the first hour we were there.* ◇ **there's nothing to it** used to indicate that something is very easy

USAGE nothing – singular or a plural? ***Nothing*** is a singular indefinite pronoun, and so should be treated as a singular even if followed by a phrase introduced by words like *but* and *except for* and a plural noun: *Nothing but truthful answers is* [not *are*] *acceptable on this questionnaire. Nothing except for your boxes and bags has* [not *have*] *been removed from the apartment.* Moving the subject closer to its verb, however, reduces the chance of grammatical error and more closely follows the natural flow of speech: *Except for your boxes and bags, nothing has been removed from the apartment.*

noth·ing·ness /núthingnəss/ *n* 1. ABSENCE OF EVERYTHING the absence of life, existence, and all discernible qualities 2. VACUUM space with nothing in it 3. COMPLETE WORTHLESSNESS complete worthlessness or insignificance 4. SOMEBODY OR SOMETHING COMPLETELY WORTHLESS somebody or something without any worth or significance 5. PHILOSOPHY LACK OF APPARENT MEANING the condition of lacking any apparent meaning

CULTURAL NOTE *Being and Nothingness*, an extended essay (1943) by French philosopher Jean-Paul Sartre. The fullest expression of Sartre's existential philosophy, it suggests that humans can be distinguished from the simple being or "thing-ness" of objects and other creatures by their consciousness or "no-thingness." This awareness provides humans with their freedom, but it also leaves them searching for meaning in life.

noticable incorrect spelling of **noticeable**

no·tice /nṓtiss/ *n* 1. PUBLIC SIGN a sign in a public place giving information, instructions, or a warning 2. WRITTEN ANNOUNCEMENT a written or printed announcement or statement of information, often displayed on a board or wall, or published in a newspaper or magazine 3. WARNING advance warning or notification of something ○ *turned off the electricity without notice* 4. PERIOD OF WARNING the period of time between the giving of a warning or notification and its taking effect ○ *They came at short notice, and I wasn't ready.* 5. WARNING OF END OF EMPLOYMENT official notification of the exercise of a right, especially the right to terminate employment, or the amount of time in advance that such notification is given 6. ATTENTION somebody's attention, observation, or consideration ○ *How could such a glaring error have escaped your notice?* 7. ARTS REVIEW a written or published review of a book, play, or movie ■ *v* (**-ticed, -tic·ing, -tic·es**) 1. *vti* OBSERVE SOMETHING to see or catch sight of somebody or something and register the fact in the mind ○ *Did you notice what he had in his hand?* 2. *vti* PERCEIVE SOMETHING to become aware of something or somebody and register the fact in the mind ○ *I noticed that he avoided mentioning her name.* 3. *vt* MENTION SOMETHING to mention or remark on something 4. *vt* RECOGNIZE SOMEBODY to recognize somebody, or indicate that you recognize somebody 5. *vt* TREAT SOMEBODY POLITELY to treat somebody with polite attention 6. *vt* WRITE REVIEW OF SOMETHING to write or publish a review of a book, play, or movie 7. *vt* ANNOUNCE SOMETHING TO SOMEBODY to give official notice to somebody (*formal*) [15C. Via French < Latin *notitia* "fame, knowledge" < *notus* "known"]

no·tice·a·ble /nṓtissəb'l/ *adj* 1. easy to see, hear, feel, or detect 2. important, distinctive, or worthy of comment —**no·tice·a·bil·i·ty** /nṑtissə bíllətee/ *n* —**no·tice·a·bly** *adv*

no·tice·board *n UK* same as **bulletin board** (sense 1)

no·ti·fi·a·ble /nṑtə fí əb'l/ *adj* describes an infectious disease of people or animals that must be reported to the appropriate authorities when it occurs so that control or preventive measures can be taken

no·ti·fy /nṓtə fì/ (**-fied, -fy·ing, -fies**) *vt* 1. to inform or warn somebody officially about somebody or something 2. to announce or report something officially, or make something officially known [14C. Via Old French *notifier* < Latin *notificare* "make known" < *notus* "known"] —**no·ti·fi·ca·tion** /nṑtəfi káysh'n/ *n* —**no·ti·fi·er** *n*

no-till·age *n* a method of farming in which crops are planted in narrow slit trenches, without any plowing, and weeds are controlled with chemical weedkillers

no·tion /nṓsh'n/ *n* 1. IDEA an idea, opinion, or concept 2. IMPRESSION a vague understanding or impression 3. DESIRE a sudden desire or whim ■ **no·tions** *npl* ITEMS FOR NEEDLEWORK small items used in sewing, e.g., needles, pins, thread, and buttons [14C. < Latin *notion-* "concept" < *not-*, past participle of *noscere* "know"]

no·tion·al /nṓshən'l, nṓshnəl/ *adj* 1. IMAGINARY OR HYPOTHETICAL existing only as an idea or in theory, not in reality 2. ABSTRACT OR SPECULATIVE relating to or characteristic of ideas or concepts 3. LING USED WITH DEFINITE MEANING used in a specific concrete sense as opposed to expressing a grammatical relationship. For example, "did" in "We did (= carried out) the work" is notional, whereas "did" in "Why didn't she come?" is not. —**no·tion·al·ly** *adv*

no·to·chord /nṓtə kàwrd/ *n* a long flexible rod of cells that supports the body of chordates and vertebrate embryos and is in effect a primitive backbone [Mid-19C. < Greek *nōton* "back" + CHORD[2] "line"] —**no·to·chord·al** /nṑtə káwrd'l/ *adj*

no·to·ri·e·ty /nṑtə rí ətee/ *n* the condition of being well known for some unsavory or undesirable reason [Mid-16C. Directly or via French < medieval Latin *notorietas* < *notorius* (see NOTORIOUS)]

USAGE See *fame.*

no·to·ri·ous /nō táwree əss, nə-/ *adj* 1. well known for some undesirable feature, quality, or act 2. widely known (*archaic*) [Mid-16C. < medieval Latin *notorius* < Latin *notus*, past participle of *noscere* "know"] —**no·to·ri·ous·ly** *adv*

USAGE See *fame.*

no trump *n* 1. a bid or contract to play a hand of cards without a trump suit, especially in bridge 2. a hand of cards suitable for playing without a trump suit —**no-trump** *adj*

Not·ting·ham /nóttingəm/ city and county town in Nottinghamshire, central England. Population: 266,988 (2001).

Not·ting·ham·shire /nóttingəm sheer, -shər/ county

in central England. Population: 748,510 (2001). Area: 835 sq. mi./2,165 sq. km.

no·tum /nṓtəm/ (*plural* **-ta** /-tə/) *n* a hard protective covering on an insect's thorax [Late 19C. < Greek *nōton* "back"]

not·with·stand·ing /nòt wi͟th stánding, -with-/ (*formal*) *prep* DESPITE in spite of (*often used after its object*) ○ *The lack of a catalog notwithstanding, it was a very interesting exhibit.* ■ *adv* NEVERTHELESS nevertheless or in spite of this ○ *They, notwithstanding, persisted in their inquiries.* ■ *conj* ALTHOUGH in spite of the fact that ○ *Notwithstanding they were provoked, they ought not to have reacted so violently.* [14C. After Old French *non obstante* "being of no hindrance"]

not·work /nót wùrk/ *n* a computer network that is nonfunctional (*slang humorous*) [Late 20C. Blend of NOT + NETWORK]

Nouak·chott /nwaak shót/ capital of Mauritania, in the western part of the country. Population: 707,000 (1990).

nou·gat /nóogət/ *n* a chewy candy made with egg whites, honey, and usually chopped nuts or dried fruit [Early 19C. < Provençal *nogat* < *noga* "nut" < Latin *nux*]

nought /nawt/ *n UK* same as **naught** [Old English *nōwiht* < *ne* "not" + *ōwiht* "anything," form of AUGHT]

Nought·ies /náwteez/ *npl* the years from 2000 to 2009 (*humorous*) [< NOUGHT, punning on NAUGHTY]

noughts and cross·es *n UK* same as **tick-tack-toe**

Nou·mé·a /noo máy ə/ capital of New Caledonia, on the southwestern coast of the island of New Caledonia, in the southwestern Pacific Ocean. Population: 65,110 (1989).

nou·me·non /nóomə nòn/ (*plural* **-me·na** /-nə/) *n* **1.** something beyond the tangible world that can only be known or identified by the intellect, not by the senses **2.** in Kantian philosophy, something that exists independently of intellectual or sensory perception of it, e.g., the soul in some beliefs [Late 18C. Via German < Greek < present participle of *noien* "apprehend, conceive"] —**nou·men·al** *adj*

noun /nown/ *n* a word or group of words used as the name of a class of people, places, or things, or of a specific person, place, or thing [14C. Via Anglo-Norman, "name, noun" < Old French *nom* < Latin *nōmen* "name"]

noun phrase *n* a word or group of words that functions syntactically as a noun, e.g., as the subject, object, or topic, in a clause or sentence

nour·ish /núr ish/ (**-ished, -ish·ing, -ish·es**) *vt* **1.** GIVE FOOD TO SOMEBODY OR SOMETHING to give people, animals, or plants the substances they require to live, grow, or remain fit and healthy **2.** SUPPORT OR FOSTER SOMETHING to encourage or strengthen a feeling or idea **3.** HELP SOMETHING DEVELOP to help something to grow or develop [13C. < Old French *norriss-*, a stem of *norir* < Latin *nutrire* "suckle"] —**nour·ish·er** *n*

nour·ish·ing /núr ishing/ *adj* providing people, animals, or plants with a substantial quantity of the substances they require to live, grow, or remain fit and healthy

nour·ish·ment /núr ishmənt/ *n* **1.** food, or the valuable substances in food that a person, animal, or plant requires to live, grow, or remain fit and healthy **2.** something that provides a stimulating and healthy emotional or intellectual environment for people or animals

nous /nooss, nowss/ *n* **1.** INTELLECTUAL ABILITY in ancient Greek philosophy, the capacity to reason and acquire knowledge, as distinguished from sensation **2.** INTELLECT in some philosophies, the part of the human spirit that is capable of rational thought **3.** *UK* COMMON SENSE good sense or intelligence (*informal*) [Late 17C. < Greek, "intelligence"]

nou·veau /noo vṓ/ *adj* having recently appeared or become fashionable (*humorous*) [Early 20C. < French, "new"]

nou·veau riche /nòovō réesh/ (*plural* **nou·veaux rich·es** /*pronunc. same*/) *n* somebody with recently acquired wealth who likes to display it [Early 19C. < French, "new rich"] —**nou·veau riche** *adj*

nou·veau ro·man /nòovō rō máan/ (*plural* **nou·veaux ro·mans** /nòo vō rō máan/) *n* LITERAT same as **antinovel** [Mid-20C. < French, "new novel"]

nou·velle cui·sine /noo vèl kwi zéen, -kwee-/ *n* a style of French cooking consisting of beautifully presented dishes made from fresh lightly cooked ingredients in less rich sauces than in traditional French cooking [Late 20C. < French, "new cooking"]

nou·velle vague /noo vèl váag/ *n* MOVIES same as **new wave** (sense 2) [Mid-20C. < French, "new wave"]

Nov. *abbr* November

no·va /nṓvə/ (*plural* **-vas** or **-vae** /-vee/) *n* a star that suddenly increases dramatically in brightness and then fades to its original luminosity over a short period of months or years [Late 19C. < Latin, form of *novus* "new"]

No·va /nṓvə/ *n US* FOOD same as **Nova Scotia salmon** [Shortening]

no·vac·u·lite /nō vákyə lìt/ *n* a hard dense fine-grained sedimentary rock containing quartz and feldspar. Use: whetstones. [Late 18C. < Latin *novacula* "razor"]

no·vae ASTRON plural of **nova**

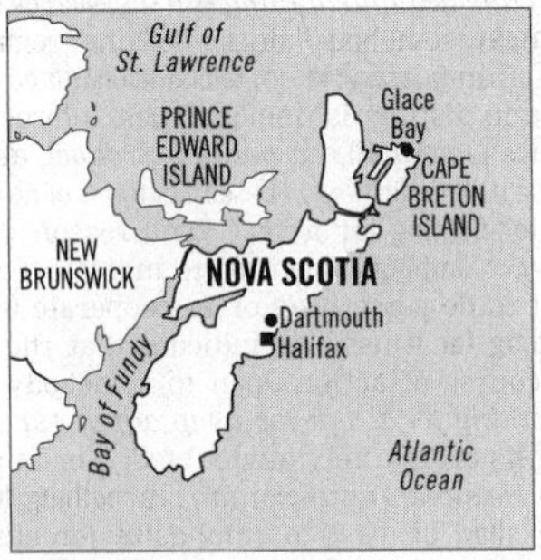

Nova Scotia

No·va Sco·tia /nṓvə skṓshə/ province in eastern Canada, bordering the Atlantic Ocean and comprising a mainland peninsula and Cape Breton Island. Capital: Halifax. Population: 944,800 (2002). Area: 21,345 sq. mi./55,284 sq. km. —**No·va Sco·tian** *n, adj*

No·va Sco·tia salm·on *n US* lox made from salmon caught near Nova Scotia

no·va·tion /nō váysh'n/ *n* the replacement of an old contract or obligation with a new one [Early 16C. < late Latin *novation-* < Latin *novare* "make new" < *novus* "new"]

No·va·to /nō vaátō/ city in western California. Population: 48,131 (2002 estimate).

nov·el[1] /nóvv'l/ *n* **1.** a fictional prose work with a relatively long and often complex plot, usually divided into chapters, in which the story traditionally develops through the thoughts and actions of its characters **2.** novels considered collectively as a literary genre [Mid-16C. < Italian *novella* (see NOVELLA)]

nov·el[2] /nóvv'l/ *adj* new and different, often in an interesting, unusual or inventive way [15C. Via Old French < Latin *novellus* "slightly new" < *novus* "new"]

SYNONYMS See ***new***.

nov·el·ese /nòvv'l éez, -éess/ *n* a style of writing or language that is typical of inferior novels

nov·el·ette /nòvv'l ét/ *n* **1.** same as **novella 2.** a light romantic novel, especially one that is considered trite or sentimental

nov·el·et·tish /nòvv'l éttish/ *adj* having the qualities of an inferior piece of writing, especially triteness or sentimentality

nov·el·ist /nóvv'list/ *n* a writer of novels

nov·el·is·tic /nòvv'l ístik/ *adj* characteristic of a novel, especially in the treatment of real people or historical events

nov·el·ize /nóvv'l ìz/ (**-ized, -iz·ing, -iz·es**) *vt* **1.** to write the story of a movie, play, or television series in the form of a novel **2.** to retell a true story in the form of a novel, sometimes adding fictional details —**nov·el·i·za·tion** /nòvv'li záysh'n/ *n*

no·vel·la /nō véllə/ *n* a fictional prose work that is longer than a short story but shorter than a novel [Early 20C. < Italian *(storia) novella* "new (story)" < Latin *novellus* (see NOVEL[2])]

nov·el·ty /nóvv'ltee/ (*plural* **-ties**) *n* **1.** NEW THING OR EXPERIENCE something new, original, and different that is interesting or exciting, though often for only a short time **2.** NEWNESS AND ORIGINALITY the quality of being new, original, and different **3.** SMALL TOY OR TRINKET a small inexpensive toy, ornament, piece of jewelry, or trinket

No·vem·ber /nō vémbər/ *n* **1.** in the Gregorian calendar, the 11th month of the year, lasting 30 days. See table at **calendar 2.** a code word for the letter "N," used in international radio communications [13C. Via French < Latin, ninth month of the Roman calendar < *novem* "nine"]

no·ve·na /nō véenə/ (*plural* **-nas** or **-nae** /-nee/) *n* in the Roman Catholic Church, the recitation of prayers for nine consecutive days to achieve a specific purpose [Mid-19C. < medieval Latin, form of *novenus* "ninefold" < *novem* "nine"]

Nov·go·rod /nóvgə ròd/ city in northwestern Russia, and the capital of Novgorod Oblast. Population: 288,910 (1995).

nov·ice /nóvviss/ *n* **1.** somebody who is beginning or learning an activity and has acquired little skill in it **2.** somebody who has joined a religious order but has not yet taken final vows [14C. Via French < late Latin *novicius* < Latin *novus* "new"]

SYNONYMS See ***beginner***.

no·vi·ti·ate /nō víshee ət, -víshət/, **no·vi·ci·ate** *n* **1.** the period of time during which somebody is a novice, especially in a religious order **2.** the part of a monastery or convent where novices live **3.** RELIG same as **novice** (sense 2) [Early 17C. < French *noviciat*, or medieval Latin *noviciatus* < late Latin *novicius* (see NOVICE)]

No·vo·cain /nṓvə kàyn/ *tdmk* a trademark for a synthetic drug. Use: local anesthetic.

No·vo·si·birsk /nṓvəssə béersk, nòvvəssə-/ city in southern Russia, and the capital of Novosibirsk Oblast. Population: 1,428,141 (1995).

Nov·yy Mar·gel·an /nòvvee maárgə laán/ former name for **Fergana**

now /now/ *adv* **1.** AT PRESENT TIME at the present time, often as opposed to in the past or in the future ○ *I've never done this before, and I'm not starting now.* **2.** IMMEDIATELY at once or at this exact time ○ *We'll miss our train if we don't go now.* **3.** GIVEN CURRENT SITUATION under the present circumstances ○ *It doesn't matter now.* **4.** UP TO PRESENT TIME used with statements of time to indicate that something has been happening for a particular length of time up to the present ○ *for six months now* **5.** USED TO PREFACE OR CLARIFY REMARK used to preface a remark, clarify a statement, get somebody's attention, or for emphasis ○ *Now, what would you like to drink?* **6.** USED IN HESITATION used in speech when hesitating and thinking of what to say next (*informal*) ○ *Now, where was I?* ■ *conj* SINCE since or in view of the fact that this is the present situation ○ *She can afford a decent car now that she's working.* ■ *n* PRESENT TIME the present time or moment ○ *Now would be a good time to tell her.* ■ *adj* FASHIONABLE in the latest fashion (*informal*) ○ *the now look in menswear* [Old English *nu* < Indo-European] ◇ **(every) now and then, (every) now and again** occasionally ◇ **for now** for the time being, as a temporary measure ◇ **just** *or* **right now 1.** a short time ago ○ *I was talking to her just now.* **2.** at the present moment ○ *Go away, I'm busy right now.* ◇ **now now** (*informal*) **1.** used as a friendly way of trying to comfort somebody **2.** used to warn or reprimand somebody gently ◇ **now then 1.** used to warn or reprimand somebody gently (*informal*) **2.** same as **now** *adv* (senses 5–6) ◇ **up to** *or* **up till** *or* **until now** up to the present time

NOW /now/ *abbr* National Organization for Women

NOW ac·count /nów-/ *n US* a savings account that pays depositors interest and against which checks can be written [Late 20C. Acronym < *negotiable order of withdrawal*]

now·a·days /nów ə dàyz/ *adv* in the present, or in the times in which we are now living, usually in contrast to the past [14C. < NOW + *adayes* "during the day" < DAY]

no·way /nṓ wày/ *adv also* **no·ways** in no way, or not at all ■ *interj also* **no way** used to express emphatic refusal or denial (*informal*)

~~nowdays~~ incorrect spelling of **nowadays**

no·where /nṓ wèr, -hwèr/ *adv* not in or to any place ○ *Nowhere does it mention any side-effects.* ■ *n* a remote or insignificant place ◇ **get** *or* **go nowhere** to fail to make any progress with something you are trying to do ◇ **nowhere near** not at all, or a long way from being a particular thing (*informal*)

no·wheres /nṓ wèrz, -hwèrz/ *adv regional* nowhere

no-win *adj* in which there is no chance of a successful outcome for a participant (*informal*) ○ *a no-win situation*

no·wise /nṓ wīz/ *adv* in no manner, or by no means at all

nox·ious /nókshəss/ *adj* **1. PHYSICALLY HARMFUL** harmful to life or health, especially by being poisonous **2. MORALLY HARMFUL** likely to cause moral, spiritual, or social harm or corruption **3. DISGUSTING** very unpleasant ○ *a noxious smell* [15C. < Latin *noxius* "hurtful, damaging"] —**nox·ious·ly** *adv* —**nox·ious·ness** *n*

noz·zle /nózz'l/ *n* **1. PROJECTING SPOUT** a narrow or tapering part at the end of a tube or pipe, used to direct or control the flow of a liquid or gas **2. SHORT TAPERED TUBE** a short tapered tube that directs or accelerates the flow of a fluid, e.g., in a jet engine **3.** *US* **NOSE** somebody's nose (*slang*) [Early 17C. < NOSE + *-le*, literally "appliance resembling a nose"]

np *abbr* Nepal (*used in Internet addresses*) See table at **domain name**

Np *symbol* **1.** TELECOM neper **2.** CHEM ELEM neptunium

NP *abbr* **1.** *US* National Park **2.** MED neuropsychiatry **3.** LING noun phrase **4.** nurse practitioner

N.P. *abbr* Notary Public

NPD *abbr* new product development

npl *abbr* GRAM plural noun

NPN *abbr* CHEM nonprotein nitrogen

NPR *abbr US* National Public Radio

NPV *abbr* **1.** net present value **2.** FIN no par value

NQA *abbr* no questions asked (*used in e-mails or text messages*)

nr *abbr* **1.** Nauru (*used in Internet addresses*) See table at **domain name 2.** near

NRA *abbr US* **1.** National Recovery Administration **2.** Naval Reserve Association **3.** National Rifle Association

NRC *abbr* **1.** National Research Council Canada **2.** Nuclear Regulatory Commission

NRCan *abbr* Natural Resources Canada

NRDS *abbr* neonatal respiratory distress syndrome

NREM *abbr* nonrapid eye movement

NREM sleep *n* BIOL same as **slow-wave sleep**

NRN *abbr* no reply necessary (*used in e-mails or text messages*)

NRV *abbr* net realizable value

ns *abbr* nanosecond

NS, **N.S.** *abbr* **1.** *UK* New Style **2.** not sufficient **3.** Nova Scotia **4.** nuclear ship

n.s. *abbr* **1.** new series **2.** not specified

n/s *abbr* **1.** nonsmoker **2.** nonsmoking **3.** BANKING not sufficient (funds)

N/S *abbr* nonsmoker

NSA *abbr US* **1.** National Security Agency **2.** National Standards Association

NSAID /én sàyd, -sèd/ *n* a nonsteroid anti-inflammatory drug taken orally or applied externally. Use: relief of headaches, muscular and joint pain, inflammation. Full form **nonsteroid anti-inflammatory drug**

NSB *abbr* **1.** National Savings Bank **2.** National Science Board

NSC *abbr US* National Security Council

NSE *abbr US* National Stock Exchange

nsec *abbr* nanosecond

NSPCA *abbr US* National Society for the Prevention of Cruelty to Animals

NST *abbr* Newfoundland Standard Time

NSU *abbr* nonspecific urethritis

NSW, **N.S.W.** *abbr* New South Wales

NT, **N.T.** *abbr* **1.** Newfoundland Time **2.** BIBLE New Testament **3.** Nome Time **4.** Northwest Territories **5.** CARDS no trump

nth /enth/ *adj* **1.** last or latest in a long and often tedious series of similar occurrences (*informal*) ○ *This is the nth revision of the text.* **2.** describes a very large, but unspecified, ordinal number, usually one that is the largest in a series of values [Mid-19C. < N^2 *n* "indefinitely large or small amount"]

NTI *abbr US* Nielsen Television Index

N.T.P., **n.t.p.** *abbr* MEASURE normal temperature and pressure

NTSB *abbr* National Transportation Safety Board

NTWS *abbr* National Threat Warning System

nt. wt. *abbr* net weight

nu[1] /noo, nyoo/ (*plural* **nus**) *n* the 13th letter of the Greek alphabet, represented in the English alphabet as "n." See table at **alphabet** [Via Greek < Semitic]

nu[2] *abbr* Niue (*used in Internet addresses*) See table at **domain name**

nu- *prefix* new, or modern (*used especially with styles of music*) ○ *nu-metal*

nu·ance /nóo aàns/ *n* **1.** a very slight difference in meaning, feeling, tone, or color **2.** the use or awareness of subtle shades of meaning or feeling, especially in artistic expression or performance [Late 18C. < French, "slight difference of tone" < *nuer* "show shading in color" < Latin *nubes* "cloud"] —**nu·anced** *adj*

nub /nub/ *n* **1. CENTRAL ISSUE** the main point or most important part of a problem or argument **2. SMALL LUMP** a small lump or chunk **3. SMALL PROJECTION** a small protuberance [Late 16C. < Middle Low German *knubbe*, variant of *knobbe* "knob"] —**nub·by** *adj*

Nu·ba /nóobə/ (*plural same or* **-bas**) *n* **1.** a member of a people inhabiting the mountains of central Sudan **2.** LANG same as **Nubian** (sense 2) [Early 19C. < Latin *Nubae* "Nubians"] —**Nu·ba** *adj*

nub·bin /núbbin/ *n* **1.** a small undeveloped part of a fruit or vegetable, e.g., an ear of corn **2.** same as **nub** (sense 1) [Late 17C. < NUB, literally "small nub"]

nub·ble /núbb'l/ *n* a small lump or knob —**nub·bly** *adj*

nu·bec·u·la /noo békyələ/ (*plural* **-lae** /-lee/) *n* ASTRON same as **Magellanic Cloud** (*technical*) [Late 17C. < Latin, "small cloud" < *nubes* "cloud"]

Nu·bi·a /nóobee ə/ region of northeastern Africa, in southern Egypt and northern Sudan, in the Nile valley

Nu·bi·an /nóobee ən, nyóo-/ *n* **1.** somebody who comes from ancient or modern Nubia **2.** a Nilo-Saharan language spoken in Sudan. Native speakers: 1 million. [15C. < medieval Latin *Nubianus* < *Nubia* "Nubia"] —**Nu·bi·an** *adj*

nu·bile /nóob'l, nóo bīl/ *adj* **1.** young and sexually desirable (*informal*) **2.** describes a young woman who is physically mature enough to have sexual intercourse and therefore suitable for marriage (*dated*) [Mid-17C. < Latin *nubilis* < *nubere* "take a husband"]

nu·cel·lus /noo séllәss/ (*plural* **-li** /-lī/) *n* the central part of a plant ovule in which the embryo develops [Late 19C. < modern Latin, probably alteration of Latin *nucleus* (see NUCLEUS)]

nucl- *prefix* same as **nucleo-** (*used before vowels*)

nu·cle·ar /nóoklee ər/ *adj* **1.** INDUST **OF NUCLEAR ENERGY** relating to, using, or producing nuclear energy through fission or fusion **2.** MIL **OF NUCLEAR WEAPONS** relating to or using weapons that produce a nuclear explosion **3.** PHYS **OF ATOM NUCLEUS** relating to the nucleus of an atom **4.** BIOL **OF CELL NUCLEUS** relating to, involving, or contained in the nucleus of a cell **5.** BIOL **FORMING NUCLEUS** forming or resembling a nucleus [Mid-19C. < NUCLEUS]

PRONUNCIATION The word ***nuclear*** is correctly pronounced /nóoklee ər/. The often-heard /nóokyələr/ is incorrect.

---

nu·cle·ar bomb *n* a bomb in which the explosive potential is controlled by nuclear fission or fusion

nu·cle·ar chem·is·try *n* the branch of chemistry in which nuclear reactions are studied

nu·cle·ar de·ter·rent *n* the nuclear weapons possessed by a country or an alliance thought of as a means of discouraging enemy attack

nu·cle·ar dis·ar·ma·ment *n* the reduction or elimination of a nation's nuclear weapons or its capacity to manufacture them

nu·cle·ar e·mul·sion *n* a photographic emulsion used to identify and show the paths of subatomic particles after development

nu·cle·ar en·er·gy *n* the energy released by nuclear fission or fusion

nu·cle·ar en·ve·lope *n* BIOL same as **nuclear membrane**

nu·cle·ar fam·i·ly *n* a social unit that consists of a mother, a father, and their children

nu·cle·ar fis·sion *n* PHYS same as **fission** (sense 1)

nu·cle·ar force *n* PHYS same as **strong interaction**

nu·cle·ar-free zone *n* an area, usually within a country, where all activities involving nuclear weapons or nuclear power are officially banned

nu·cle·ar fu·el *n* a substance that undergoes fission in a nuclear reactor and is used to provide power for electricity and submarines, e.g., an isotope of uranium

nu·cle·ar fu·sion *n* the process in which light atoms such as those of hydrogen and deuterium combine and form heavier atoms, releasing a great amount of energy, which primarily manifests itself in the form of heat

nu·cle·ar·ize /nóoklee ə rīz/ (**-ized**, **-iz·ing**, **-iz·es**) *vt* to provide or equip a military force with nuclear weapons —**nu·cle·ar·i·za·tion** /nóoklee əri záysh'n/ *n*

nu·cle·ar mag·net·ic res·o·nance *n* the energy pulse released by an atomic nucleus exposed to high-frequency radiation in a magnetic field. It is used to provide data about the atom that can be transformed into an image by computer techniques. This phenomenon is the basis of devices used in medicine, where it is called magnetic resonance imaging, to produce images of tissues, and in physics and chemistry to study molecular structure.

nu·cle·ar med·i·cine *n* the branch of medicine in which radioactive materials are used to diagnose and treat diseases

nu·cle·ar mem·brane *n* a two-layered membrane surrounding the nucleus of a living cell

nu·cle·ar phys·ics *n* the branch of physics in which the structure, forces, and behavior of the atomic nucleus are studied (*takes a singular verb*) —**nu·cle·ar phys·i·cist** *n*

nu·cle·ar pore *n* a complex opening in a nuclear membrane

nu·cle·ar pow·er *n* the power, usually electrical or motive power, produced by nuclear fission or fusion —**nu·cle·ar-pow·ered** *adj*

nu·cle·ar pow·er sta·tion, **nu·cle·ar pow·er plant** *n* a power station in which the heat for producing steam to drive electric turbogenerators is derived from a nuclear reactor

nu·cle·ar re·ac·tion *n* a process in which energy is produced by either the splitting of heavy atoms (**fission**) or the combining of light atoms (**nuclear fusion**)

nu·cle·ar re·ac·tor *n* a device in which controlled nuclear fission takes place to produce heat energy. See illustration on next page

Nu·cle·ar Reg·u·la·tory Com·mis·sion *n* an agency of the US federal government that regulates the nonmilitary use of nuclear energy

nu·cle·ar re·pro·cess·ing plant *n* a facility in which various useful isotopes are removed from used rods of nuclear reactors

nu·cle·ar sap *n* the colorless liquid in the nucleus of a living cell

nu·cle·ar sub·ma·rine *n* **1.** a submarine in which a nuclear reactor produces steam to drive turbines for propulsion **2.** a submarine that carries nuclear weapons

nu·cle·ar thresh·old *n* the point in a war being

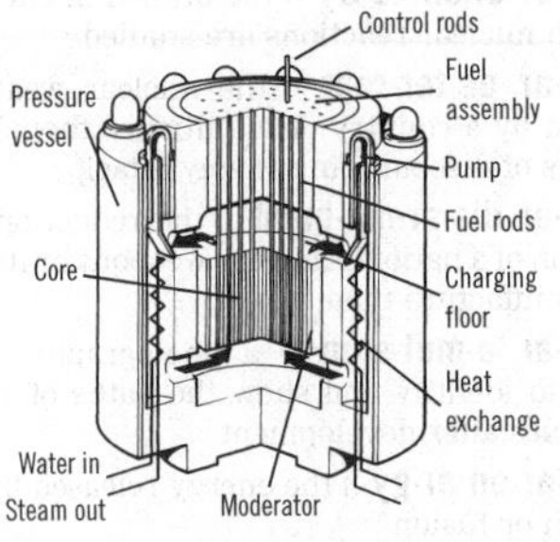

nuclear reactor

fought with conventional weapons when one of the opposing forces decides to use nuclear weapons

nu·cle·ar war·head *n* the forward part of a missile or other projectile whose explosive device derives its power from nuclear fission or fusion

nu·cle·ar waste *n* unwanted, often radioactive, material that is produced by nuclear reactors and reprocessing plants

nu·cle·ar weap·on *n* a military weapon that derives its explosive power from nuclear fission or fusion

nu·cle·ar win·ter *n* a period of continual cold and darkness believed by some scientists to be a likely consequence of a nuclear war. It would be caused by the blocking of the Sun's rays by high-altitude dust clouds, and would have disastrous environmental consequences.

nu·cle·ase /nóoklee àyss, -àyz/ *n* an enzyme that breaks down nucleic acids [Early 20C. < shortening of *nucleic*]

nu·cle·ate *adj* /nóoklee ət, -àyt/ *also* **nu·cle·at·ed** /nóoklee àytəd/ having a nucleus or nuclei ■ *vti* /nóoklee àyt/ (**-at·ed, -at·ing, -ates**) to come together as a nucleus, or bring things together to form a nucleus [Mid-19C. < shortening of NUCLEAR]

nu·cle·a·tion /nóoklee áysh'n/ *n* **1.** the process by which ice crystals and rain drops form in clouds around a solid core **2.** the formation of mineral crystals from a melt, often around a core of solid material

nu·cle·i plural of **nucleus**

nu·cle·ic ac·id /noo klée ik-, -kláy-/ *n* an acid of high molecular weight, e.g., DNA or RNA, consisting of nucleotide chains that convey genetic information and are found in all living cells

nu·cle·in /nóoklee in/ *n* BIOCHEM same as **nucleoprotein**

nucleo- *prefix* **1.** nucleus, nuclear ○ *nucleoplasm* **2.** nucleic acid ○ *nucleocapsid* [< NUCLEUS]

nu·cle·o·cap·sid /nóoklee ə kápsid/ *n* the basic viral structure consisting of a core of nucleic acid surrounded by a protein coat

nu·cle·oid /nóoklee òyd/ *n* the aggregated DNA of a bacterium, seen as a distinct region inside the cell

nu·cle·o·lar /nooklée ələr/ *adj* relating to a nucleolus or nucleoli

nu·cle·o·lar or·gan·iz·er *n* a segment of a chromosome at which a nucleolus forms

nu·cle·o·lus /noo klée ələss/ (*plural* **-li** /-lī/) *n* a small round body inside a cell nucleus, composed of protein and RNA and associated with the formation of ribosomes and ribosomal RNA [Mid-19C. < late Latin, "little nucleus" < Latin *nucleus* (see NUCLEUS)] —**nu·cle·o·late** /-ə làyt/ *adj*

nu·cle·on /nóoklee òn/ *n* a proton or neutron, especially when part of an atomic nucleus

nu·cle·on·ics /nóoklee ónniks/ *n* the branch of physics dealing with the properties of nucleons and the atomic nucleus (*takes a singular verb*)

nu·cle·on num·ber *n* PHYS same as **mass number**

nu·cle·o·phile /nóoklee ə fīl/ *n* a substance that becomes an electron donor in bonding during a chemical reaction —**nu·cle·o·phil·ic** /nóoklee ə fíllik/ *adj*

nu·cle·o·plasm /nóoklee ə plàzzəm/ *n* the matter (**protoplasm**) contained in a cell nucleus

nu·cle·o·pro·tein /nóoklee ō prō teen/ *n* a nucleic acid combined with a protein, as in a chromosome

nu·cle·o·side /nóoklee ə sīd/ *n* a compound consisting of a purine or pyrimidine base linked to a sugar, especially ribose or deoxyribose [Early 20C. < NUCLEO- + GLYCOSIDE]

nu·cle·o·some /nóoklee ə sōm/ *n* a structural unit of chromosomes, containing DNA. Nucleosomes fit together like a tightly condensed string of beads.

nu·cle·o·syn·the·sis /nóoklee ō sínthəssiss/ *n* the synthesis of heavier elements from lighter elements by fusion reactions within stars

nu·cle·o·tide /nóoklee ə tīd/ *n* a component of RNA and DNA, consisting of a nucleoside linked to a phosphate group [Early 20C. Alteration of NUCLEOSIDE]

nu·cle·us /nóoklee əss/ (*plural* **-i** /-klee ī/ or **-us·es**) *n* **1.** IMPORTANT ELEMENT a central or most important item or part that has others grouped or built around it **2.** PHYS CENTRAL REGION OF ATOM the positively charged central region of an atom, consisting of protons and neutrons and containing most of the mass **3.** BIOL CENTRAL PART OF LIVING CELL the central body, usually spherical, within a eukaryotic cell, that is a membrane-encased mass of protoplasm containing the chromosomes and other genetic information necessary to control cell growth and reproduction **4.** ASTRON CENTRAL PART OF NEBULA OR GALAXY the central brighter portion of a nebula or galaxy **5.** ASTRON CORE OF COMET HEAD the central core in the head of a comet, consisting of ice, frozen gases, and dust **6.** CHEM STABLE ATOMS IN MOLECULE a stable group of atoms in a molecule, e.g., a benzene ring, that forms the base structure of many compounds and remains unchanged in chemical reactions **7.** ANAT GROUP OF NERVE CELLS a group of nerve cells in the central nervous system or a small mass of gray matter in the brain that has a specialized function **8.** PHON MOST RESONANT PART OF SYLLABLE the most resonant part of a syllable, usually the vowel [Early 18C. < Latin, "kernel" < *nuc-* "nut"]

nu·clide /nóo klīd/ *n* one or more atomic nuclei identifiable as being of the same element by having the same number of protons and neutrons and the same energy content [Mid-20C. < NUCLEUS]

~~**nucular**~~ incorrect spelling of **nuclear**

nude /nood/ *adj* (**nud·er, nud·est**) **1.** UNCLOTHED wearing no clothes ○ *the nude figure of a man* **2.** FOR UNCLOTHED PEOPLE intended for, or done by, people wearing no clothes ○ *a nude beach* **3.** PLAIN bare or plain, with no covering or decoration **4.** *US* COLORS LIGHT-COLORED matching the skin color of a white person ○ *nude hose* **5.** LAW LACKING LEGAL REQUISITE lacking a legal requisite such as supporting evidence or a contract ■ *n* UNCLOTHED FIGURE an unclothed person, especially an unclothed figure in a painting or other artistic work [Mid-16C < Latin *nudus*] ◇ **in the nude** without clothes

SYNONYMS See *naked.*

NUDETS *abbr* nuclear detection system

nudge[1] /nuj/ *v* (**nudged, nudg·ing, nudg·es**) **1.** *vt* PUSH OR POKE SOMEBODY to push or poke somebody gently, usually with a motion of the elbow **2.** *vt* MOVE SOMETHING to move something gently, especially by pushing it slowly and carefully **3.** *vt* APPROACH LEVEL to have very nearly reached a particular level or standard ○ *Their profits are nudging the 100 million mark.* **4.** *vt* GENTLY PERSUADE SOMEBODY to persuade somebody into an action, gently and delicately **5.** *vi* MOVE SLOWLY to move slowly or little by little ■ *n* **1.** GENTLE PUSH a gentle push to get somebody's attention **2.** PERSUASIVE ACT a gentle act of persuasion [Late 17C. Origin ?]

nudge[2] /nŏoj/ (*slang*) *n* an offensive term that deliberately insults somebody for being annoying in a persistent and pestering way ■ *vt* (**nudged, nudg·ing, nudg·es**) *US* to annoy somebody in a persistent and pestering way ○ *Can you stop always nudging me about money?* [Via Yiddish *nudyen* "pester, bore" < Polish *nudzić*]

nud·ie /nóodee/ (*slang*) *adj* relating to or involving people who are unclothed ■ *n* something, e.g., a movie, or a magazine that depicts unclothed people

nud·ism /nóo dìzzəm/ *n* LEISURE same as **naturism** (sense 1)

nud·ist /nóodist/ *n* somebody who prefers not to wear clothes, especially somebody who does so in designated areas or communities —**nud·ist** *adj*

nud·ist col·o·ny *n* a place where the wearing of clothes is not allowed, intended for people who believe nudity is a healthy natural state

nu·di·ty /nóodətee/ *n* **1.** the state of having no clothes on **2.** bareness or plainness, with no covering or decoration

nud·nik /nóodnik/ *n US* an offensive term that deliberately insults somebody considered to be annoying or boring (*slang*) [Mid-20C. < Yiddish *nudne* "boring"]

nu·ée ar·dente /nóo ay aar daánt/ *n* a thick, rapidly moving, deadly, gaseous cloud produced by a volcano and consisting of steam, ash, and rock segments [< French, "burning cloud"]

Nue·vo La·re·do /nwàyvō lə ráydō/ city in northeastern Mexico. Situated on the Rio Grande opposite Laredo, Texas, it is a major crossing point by road between the United States and Mexico. Population: 310,915 (2000).

Nue·vo Le·ón /-lay ṓn/ state in northeastern Mexico where the majority of the country's iron and steel industry is located. Capital: Monterrey. Population: 3,826,240 (2000). Area: 24,792 sq. mi./64,210 sq. km.

nue·vo sol /nwàyvō sṓl/ (*plural* **nue·vos sol·es** /nwàyvōs sṓ lays/) *n* MONEY same as **sol**[2] [< Spanish, "new sol"]

nuff /nuf/ *adv, pron* same as **enough** (*slang*) [Shortening and respelling of ENOUGH]

nu·ga·to·ry /nóogə tàwree/ *adj* **1.** having no importance whatsoever **2.** having no legal force [Early 17C. < Latin *nugatorius* < *nugae* "trifling matters"] —**nu·ga·to·ri·ly** /nòo gə táwrəlee/ *adv*

nug·get /núggət/ *n* **1.** LUMP OF PRECIOUS METAL a lump of gold or other precious metal in its natural state, dug up out of the ground **2.** SMALL PRECIOUS THING a small item or piece, especially of something abstract such as knowledge or information, regarded as very precious **3.** FOOD SMALL ROUND PIECE OF FOOD a small piece of food, usually coated with breadcrumbs and fried or baked in an oven [Mid-19C. Probably < an English dialect word, "lump"]

nui·sance /nóoss'nss/ *n* **1.** an annoying or irritating person or thing **2.** something not allowed by law because it causes harm or offense, either to people in general (**public nuisance**) or to an individual person [15C. < Old French < Latin *nocere* "injure"]

nui·sance call *n* a usually anonymous telephone call made to annoy, harass, upset, or scare somebody

nui·sance grounds *n Can* a dump for garbage

nui·sance tax *n US* a tax that is collected directly from the consumer on a wide variety of goods

nui·sance val·ue *n* the relative usefulness of something based on its potential to cause problems or difficulties for somebody

nuke /nook/ *vt* (**nuked, nuk·ing, nukes**) **1.** USE NUCLEAR WEAPONS AGAINST ENEMY to attack somebody or something with nuclear weapons (*slang*) **2.** FOOD MICROWAVE SOMETHING to cook something in a microwave oven (*informal*) ■ *n* (*slang*) **1.** ARMS same as **nuclear weapon** **2.** *US* NUCLEAR POWER PLANT a nuclear power plant [Mid-20C. Shortening of NUCLEAR]

nuk·kad /nu kúd/ *n S Asia* a street corner or other place where people gather to chat [Late 20C. < Hindi]

Nu·ku'a·lo·fa /nóokoo ə lṓfə/ capital of Tonga, on Tongatapu Island in the southern Pacific Ocean. Population: 34,000 (1990).

~~**nukular**~~ incorrect spelling of **nuclear**

null /nul/ *adj* **1.** INVALID having no legal validity **2.** VALUELESS having no value or importance **3.** AMOUNTING TO NOTHING amounting to nothing in terms of context or character **4.** AT ZERO LEVEL at the level of zero or nothing **5.** MATH RELATING TO ZERO relating to or equal to zero **6.** MATH EMPTY used to describe a mathematical set containing no elements ○ *the null set* **7.** MATH ENDING IN ZERO converging to zero ○ *a null sequence* **8.** PHYS INDICATING READING OF ZERO indicating a reading of zero when a measured quantity is undetectable or equal to another in comparison ■ *n* same as **zero** (*literary*) [Mid-16C. Via Old French *nul* < Latin *nullus* "not any"] ◇ **null and void** not legally valid

nul·lah /núllə/ *n S Asia* a ditch, irrigation canal, or ravine [Late 18C. < Hindi *nālā*]

Null·ar·bor Plain /nùllər bawr-/ dry plateau in southern South Australia. Area: 115,831 sq. mi./300,000 sq. km.

nul·li·fi·ca·tion /nùlləfi káysh'n/ *n* **1.** LAW **INVALIDATION OF SOMETHING** the act of making something legally invalid **2. CANCELLATION OF SOMETHING** the act of canceling something out **3.** *US* LAW **REJECTION OF FEDERAL LAW** the refusal by a state government to allow application of a section of federal law —**nul·li·fi·ca·tion·ist** *n*

nul·li·fy /núllə fī/ (**-fied, -fy·ing, -fies**) *vt* **1.** to make something legally invalid or ineffective **2.** to have the effect of canceling something out —**nul·li·fi·er** *n*

SYNONYMS ***nullify, abrogate, annul, repeal, invalidate, negate***

CORE MEANING: to put an end to the effective existence of something

nullify to make something legally invalid or ineffective ○ *Only the courts can nullify his decision.* ○ *The country's military rulers nullified national elections after pro-democracy candidates won a landslide victory.* **abrogate** (*formal*) to declare a legal document or agreement invalid ○ *Egypt and Somalia abrogated their friendship treaties with the USSR in the 1970s.* ○ *We condemn the levity with which certain politicians speak about abrogating our international obligations.* **annul** to declare a legal document or agreement invalid ○ *A court on Wednesday annulled the decree, saying it was illegal.* ○ *Many parties have called for the election results to be annulled because of alleged fraud.* **repeal** to officially end the validity of something such as a law ○ *We intend to repeal the act when alternative regulations are in place.* **invalidate** to deprive something of its legal force or value, e.g., by failing to comply with some terms and conditions ○ *Failure to disclose all relevant changes may invalidate your policy.* ○ *Does the result of this latest poll invalidate the findings of the earlier survey?* **negate** (*formal*) to declare officially that something is invalid or ineffective, or make something invalid or ineffective ○ *This argument does not negate the point I am making.* ○ *She used her speed and experience to negate her opponent's power, winning the match in straight sets.*

nul·lip·a·ra /nə lippərə/ (*plural* **-ras** or **-rae** /-ree/) *n* a woman who has never given birth to a child [Late 19C. < Latin *nullus* "none" + English *-para* "woman who has given birth" < Latin *parere* "give birth"]

nul·li·ty /núllətee/ *n* **1.** the state of being legally invalid **2.** a lack of effectiveness or usefulness

num., **num** *abbr* **1.** number **2.** numeral

Num. *abbr* BIBLE Numbers

numb /num/ *adj* **1. WITH NO FEELING** unable to feel or have sensations, e.g., as a result of extreme cold or the application of a local anesthetic **2. EMOTIONLESS** unable to feel emotions ■ *vt* (**numbed, numb·ing, numbs**) **1. TAKE SENSATION AWAY FROM SOMETHING** to take away from a part of the body the power to feel or have sensations, or to take away the sensations themselves **2. TAKE AWAY SOMEBODY'S FEELINGS** to make somebody incapable of feeling emotion, or deaden somebody's emotions or feelings [15C. Past participle of Old English *niman* "take"] —**numb·ly** *adv* —**numb·ness** *n*

num·ber /númbər/ *n* **1. FIGURE USED IN COUNTING** a figure, symbol, or word used in calculating quantities of individual things **2. IDENTIFYING FIGURE** a figure or group of figures identifying somebody or something, e.g., a set of figures identifying somebody as a telephone subscriber, or a figure identifying a sports player or competitor ○ *Let me have your fax number.* **3. COUNTABLE QUANTITY** a total or estimated total of persons or things that can be individually counted ○ *We have received a number of complaints.* **4. SINGLE THING IN SERIES** a single one of a series of things produced in sequence, especially a single issue of a magazine **5. COUNTING** the concept of calculating quantities of individual things **6.** GRAM **GRAMMATICAL QUANTITY** quantity expressed, in some languages, by the form of a word ○ *The qualifying adjective agrees with the noun in gender and number.* **7. PIECE OF MUSIC** a self-contained piece of popular music, especially one of several that feature in a performance **8. GARMENT** an item of clothing, especially women's clothing (*informal*) ○ *a little silk number* **9. THING** a thing of any kind, especially something that gives pleasure or impresses (*informal*) **10. PERSON** somebody regarded in sexual terms (*informal; sometimes considered offensive*) ■ *v* (**-bered, -ber·ing, -bers**) **1.** *vt* **IDENTIFY SOMEBODY OR SOMETHING BY NUMBER** to give somebody or something an identifying number ○ *Don't forget to number the pages.* **2.** *vti* **ACHIEVE TOTAL** to reach a particular total amount ○ *Supporters numbered over 300, while there were only 15 dissenters.* **3.** *vt* **INCLUDE SOMEBODY OR SOMETHING** to include somebody or something as one of a group ○ *It is numbered among the world's most prestigious hotels.* [13C. < Anglo-Norman *numbre* < Latin *numerus*] —**num·ber·er** *n* ◇ **do a number on somebody** to treat somebody unfairly or harshly, e.g., by deliberate and systematic criticism or ridicule (*slang*) ◇ **have somebody's number** to understand somebody's true motives or character and so be well placed to deal with him or her ◇ **somebody's days are numbered** somebody's life or term of employment is about to come to an end

USAGE number or **quantity**? Careful writers distinguish between ***quantity*** ("an amount of something") and ***number*** ("a total or estimated total of persons or things that can be individually counted"), as in *A large number* [better than *quantity*] *of people had gathered in the square.* ***Quantity*** is best reserved for references to inanimate objects or inanimate uncountable nouns, as in *a huge quantity of wheat; a large quantity of fuel oil.*

USAGE number – singular or plural? ***Number*** is a collective noun that can take a singular or plural verb depending on how you use it. If you put the definite article *the* in front of ***number***, you are stipulating one particular number, even if *of* and a series of things comes next. Therefore, you must use a singular verb with ***number*** preceded by "*the*": *The number of lab coats available is limited.* On the other hand, if you put the indefinite article *a* before ***number***, you must use a plural verb: *A number of lab coats are available.*

USAGE See ***amount.***

num·ber crunch·er *n* (*slang*) **1.** somebody whose job consists of performing large quantities of arithmetic calculations **2.** a computer designed to perform large quantities of complex numerical calculations —**num·ber crunch·ing** *n*

num·bered ac·count /nùmbərd-/ *n* a bank account identified by a number only so that the account holder may keep his or her identity secret

num·ber·less /númbərləss/ *adj* **1.** too numerous to be counted **2.** not given a number or marked with a number

num·ber one *n* **1. FIRST PERSON OR THING** the first one in a series of people or things ○ *She's number one among the top candidates.* **2. BESTSELLING RECORD** a recording that has sold the most copies in its category in a given week **3. SELF** yourself and your own interests (*informal*) **4. MOST IMPORTANT PERSON** the leader or the most important person in a group or organization (*informal*) **5. URINATION** the act or an instance of urinating, or urine (*baby talk*) ■ *adj* **1. MOST IMPORTANT** first, best, or most important **2. EXCELLENT** of a very high standard or quality (*informal*)

Num·ber One *n* the first officer or first mate on a ship, next in rank after the captain (*informal*)

num·ber plate /númbər plàyt/ *n UK* same as **license plate**

num·bers /númbərz/ *n US* a form of gambling in which people bet on an unpredictable number to be drawn or determined later (*takes a singular or plural verb*)

Num·bers /númbərz/ *n* a book of the Bible that gives an account of the Israelites' experiences in the wilderness after they left Egypt. It is the fourth book of the Pentateuch. (*takes a singular verb*) See table at **Bible** [Probably because it records a census]

num·bers game *n* GAMBLING same as **numbers**

num·ber the·o·ry *n* the branch of mathematics that deals with the properties of integers and relationships between integers

num·ber two *n* **1.** somebody's deputy or second-in-command (*informal*) **2.** the act or an instance of defecating, or feces (*baby talk*)

numb·ing /númming/ *adj* **1.** causing numbness in a part of the body **2.** temporarily taking away somebody's ability to feel or think, e.g., as a result of shock ○ *a numbing experience* —**numb·ing·ly** *adv*

numb·nuts /núm nùts/ *npl* same as **numskull** (*slang insult*) [20C. Blend of NUMB + NUTS]

numb·skull /núm skùl/ *n* another spelling of **numskull** (*insult*)

nu·men /nóomən/ (*plural* **-mi·na** /-mənə/) *n* **1.** a god or spirit believed to inhabit a place or living object such as a tree **2.** a guiding force or influence [Early 17C. < Latin, "nod, command, divine power"]

nu·mer·a·ble /nóomərəb'l/ *adj* able to be counted

nu·mer·a·cy /nóomərəssee/ *n* a competence in the mathematical skills needed to cope with everyday life and an understanding of information presented mathematically, e.g., in graphs, charts, or tables [Mid-20C. < NUMERATE]

nu·mer·al /nóomərəl/ *n* a symbol or set of symbols used to represent a number, e.g., the Arabic numeral 5, the equivalent Roman numeral V, and the equivalent binary numeral 101 ■ *adj* relating to numbers or representing a number or numbers [14C. < late Latin *numeralis* < Latin *numerus* "number"] —**nu·mer·al·ly** *adv*

nu·mer·ar·y /nóomə rèrree/ *adj* relating to numbers [Early 18C. Via medieval Latin *numerarius* < Latin *numerus* "number"]

nu·mer·ate *adj* /nóomərət/ **1. MATHEMATICALLY COMPETENT** able to do arithmetic calculations **2.** EDUC **WITH SOME MATH KNOWLEDGE** having a basic understanding of mathematics ■ *vt* /nóomə ràyt/ (**-at·ed, -at·ing, -ates**) **ENUMERATE THINGS** to name a number of things in turn or in sequence (*archaic*) [Early 18C. < Latin *numerat-*, past participle of *numerare* "count" < *numerus* "number"]

nu·mer·a·tion /nóomə ráysh'n/ *n* **1.** the naming of numbers, e.g., by schoolchildren, or the giving of numbers to items in a set or group **2.** a system of symbols used for counting or numbering things

nu·mer·a·tor /nóomə ràytər/ *n* the part of a common fraction appearing above the line, representing the number of parts of the whole that are being considered

nu·mer·i·cal /noo mérrik'l/, **nu·mer·ic** /-mérrik/ *adj* **1.** using numbers or consisting of numbers **2.** considered in terms of the number of people or things involved ○ *numerical superiority* [Early 17C. < Latin *numerus* "number"]

nu·mer·i·cal a·nal·y·sis *n* the branch of mathematics that deals with the use of repeatedly used quantitative approximations to solve problems, and the measurement of the errors involved. Computers are usually used to perform the calculations. —**nu·mer·i·cal an·a·lyst** *n*

nu·mer·i·cal con·trol *n* a technique, often involving computerization, for controlling machine tools, where the position or action of a tool, e.g., the depth of a drill, is determined by a numerical value

nu·mer·i·cal·ly /noo mérrikəlee/ *adv* in terms of the numbers of people or things involved ○ *His forces were numerically superior to those of the enemy.*

nu·mer·i·cal or·der *n* an ordering of people or things identified by number from the lowest to the highest

nu·mer·i·cal tax·on·o·my *n* a procedure that involves comparing a large number of characteristics of one organism with the same characteristics of another

nu·mer·ic con·trol *n* ENG same as **numerical control**

nu·mer·ic key·pad *n* the section of a computer keyboard, usually to the right of the main keypad, containing numbered keys in the same layout as the numbers on a calculator. They can be used to key numbers or, in conjunction with other keys, to perform special functions.

nu·mer·ol·o·gy /nóomə róllәjee/ *n* the study of the occult use and supposed power of numbers —**nu·mer·o·log·i·cal** /nóomərə lójjik'l/ *adj* —**nu·mer·o·log·i·cal·ly** *adv* —**nu·mer·ol·o·gist** *n*

nu·me·ro u·no /nóomərō óonō/ *n* same as **number one** *n* (senses 3–4) (*informal humorous*) [Late 20C. < Spanish or Italian, "number one"]

nu·mer·ous /nóomərəss/ *adj* many in number [15C. < Latin *numerosus* < *numerus* "number"] —**nu·mer·ous·ly** *adv* —**nu·mer·ous·ness** *n*

Nu·mid·i·a /noo míddee ə/ former kingdom at the heart of the ancient Carthaginian empire in Northwestern Africa, roughly equivalent to modern-day Algeria. It became a Roman province in 46 B.C., was invaded by the Vandals in the 5th century A.D., and was conquered by the Arabs in the 8th century. —**Nu·mid·i·an** *adj, n*

Nu·mid·i·an crane *n* BIRDS same as **demoiselle** (sense 2)

nu·mi·na *n* RELIG plural of **numen**

nu·mi·nous /nóomənəss/ *adj* **1. MYSTERIOUSLY ASSOCIATED WITH DEITY** having a mysterious power that suggests the presence of a spirit or god (*formal*) **2. HOLY** filled with inextricable associations with God (*formal*) **3. OF NUMINA** relating to numina, the spirits or gods believed in some cultures to inhabit places or things [Mid-17C. < Latin *numin-* "deity"] —**nu·mi·nous·ly** *adv* —**nu·mi·nous·ness** *n*

nu·mis·mat·ic /nòomiz máttik, -miss-/ *adj* relating to the study or collecting of coins or medals [Late 18C. < French *numismatique* < Greek *nomisma* "coin, currency" < *nomizein* "have in use" < *nomos* "custom"] —**nu·mis·mat·i·cal·ly** *adv*

nu·mis·mat·ics /nòomiz máttiks, -miss-/ *n* the study and collecting of coins or medals (*takes a singular verb*) —**nu·mis·ma·tist** /noo mízmətist/ *n*

Num Lock /nùm-/ *n* a toggle feature of computer keyboards that cancels the scrolling and cursor-moving abilities of keys on the numeric keypad so that it can be used to input numbers

num·ma·ry /nùmməree/ *adj* relating to coins or banknotes [Early 17C. < Latin *nummarius* < *nummus* "coin"]

num·mu·lar /númmyələr/ *adj* shaped like a coin or disk (*formal*) [Mid-18C. < Latin *nummulus* "small coin" < *nummus* "coin"]

num·mu·lite /númmyə līt/ *n* a fossil shaped like a flat disk that is commonly found in limestone in the Mediterranean and dates from between 56.5 and 5.2 million years ago [Early 19C. < modern Latin *Nummulites* < Latin *nummulus* (see NUMMULAR); from its shape] —**num·mu·lit·ic** /nùmmyə líttik/ *adj*

num·nah /núm naá/ *n* a pad placed under a saddle [Mid-19C. Alteration of Urdu *namdā* < Persian *namad* "felt, carpet"]

num·skull /núm skùl/, **numb·skull** *n* an offensive term that deliberately insults somebody's intelligence (*insult*) [Early 18C. < NUMB]

nun[1] /nun/ *n* **1.** a member of a religious community of women who dedicate their lives to religious devotion and undertake not to marry **2.** a variety of domestic pigeon with black-and-white feathers all over and a ring of white feathers around its neck and head resembling a nun's headdress [Pre-12C. Via Old French *nonne* < ecclesiastical Latin *nonna* < *nonnus* "old man, monk"]

nun[2] /nun/ *n* the 14th letter of the Hebrew alphabet, represented in the English alphabet as "n." See table at **alphabet** [Early 19C. < Hebrew *nûn*]

nun·a·tak /núnnə tàk/ *n* a mountain peak surrounded by glacial ice, originally in Norway and Greenland [Late 19C. < Inuit *nunataq*]

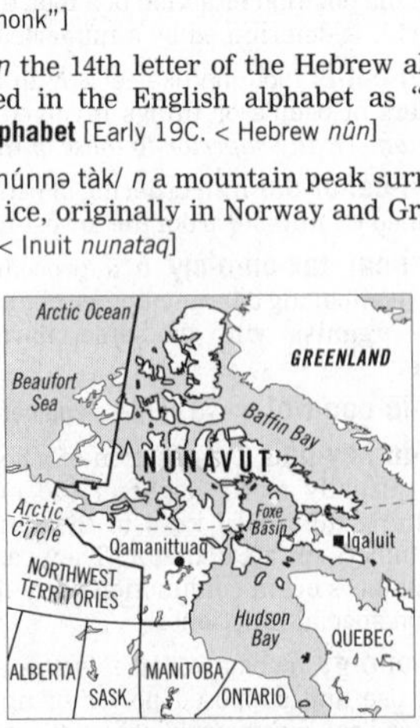

Nunavut

Nun·a·vut /nóonə vòot/ territory created in northern Canada in 1999, replacing the central and eastern part of the Northwest Territories. It is a homeland for the Inuit people (the name means "our land" in Inuit). Capital: Iqaluit. Population: 28,700 (2002). Area: 808,185 sq. mi./2,093,190 sq. km.

nun·bird /nún bùrd/ *n* a slow-moving bird with dark feathers that eats flying insects. Family: Galbulidae. [Because its white feathers resemble a nun's habit]

nun buoy *n* a buoy with a rounded middle and tapering ends, used to mark the right-hand side of a harbor channel [Early 18C. < *nun* "child's top," origin ?]

Nunc Di·mit·tis /nùngk di míttiss, nòongk-/ *n* a hymn or canticle with a text from Luke 2:29–32, starting in Latin with "Nunc dimittis servum tuum," in English meaning "Lord, now you are dismissing your servant in peace." The passage in the Bible describes Simeon being presented with the baby Jesus Christ.

nun·cha·ku /nùn chaá kòo/ *n* a martial arts weapon consisting of two thick sticks joined at their ends by a rawhide band, rope, or chain [Late 20C. < Japanese dialect]

nun·ci·a·ture /núnssee ə chòor/ *n* the rank or position of a nuncio, or the period of time somebody spends as a nuncio [Early 17C. < Italian *nunciatura* < *nuncio* (see NUNCIO)]

nun·ci·o /núnssee ō, nòon-/ (*plural* **-os**) *n* **1.** somebody with the diplomatic status of an ambassador, appointed by the pope to represent him in a country **2.** somebody sent by a person to act on his or her behalf, especially a person regarded as self-important or authoritarian (*formal or humorous*) [Early 16C. Via Italian < Latin *nuntius* "messenger"]

nun·cu·pa·tive /núngkyə pàytiv/ *adj* given or declared orally by somebody making a will, and written down later by somebody else [Mid-16C. < late Latin *nuncupativus* < Latin *nuncupare* "name, declare" < *nomen* "name" + *capere* "to take"]

Nun·ea·ton /nun eét'n/ industrial city in Warwickshire, central England. Population: 66,715 (1991).

nun·ner·y /núnnəree/ (*plural* **-ies**) *n* RELIG same as **convent**

nun·ny bag /núnnee-/ *n Can* in Newfoundland, a small knapsack made of sealskin or some other durable material [Probably < Scottish dialect *noony* "lunch"]

Nu·pe /nóo pày/ (*plural same* or **-pes**) *n* **1.** a member of a Nigerian people who live between the rivers Benue and Niger **2.** the Benue-Congo language of the Nupe people. Native speakers: 1 million. [Early 19C. After a former kingdom at the junction of the Niger and Benue] —**Nu·pe** *adj*

nup·tial /núpshəl, núpchəl/ *adj* **1. OF MARRIAGE** relating to marriage or weddings **2. OF ANIMAL BREEDING** relating to mating or breeding in animals ■ **nup·tials** *npl* **WEDDING** a wedding ceremony (*formal*) [15C. < Old French < Latin *nuptiae* "wedding" < *nubere* "take a husband"] —**nup·tial·ly** *adv*

nup·tial plum·age *n* the distinctive feathers that some birds grow during their mating season

Nu·rem·berg /nóorəm bùrg/ city in Bavaria, southern Germany. After 1933 the German Nazi Party held annual rallies in a stadium in the city, and in 1945 and 1946 it was the scene of Allied trials of German war criminals. Population: 495,845 (1997).

CORBIS/Bettmann

Rudolf Nureyev

Nu·re·yev /nòoree ef, noo ráy-/, **Rudolf** (1938–93) Russian-born dancer and choreographer. He was connected from 1962 with the British Royal Ballet, where he often partnered Dame Margot Fonteyn. Full name **Nureyev, Rudolf Hametovich**

Nu·ri·stan /nòori stán/ administrative province of eastern Afghanistan, south of the Hindu Kush. Area: 5,000 sq. mi./13,000 sq. km.

Nur·mi /núrmee/, **Paavo** (1897–1973) Finnish athlete. He won nine Olympic gold medals (1920, 1924, and 1928) in middle-distance and long-distance races. Known as **the Flying Finn**. Full name **Nurmi, Paavo Johannes**

nurse /nurss/ *n* **1. SOMEBODY CARING FOR PATIENTS** somebody trained to look after sick or injured people, especially somebody who works in a hospital or clinic, administering the care and treatment that a doctor prescribes **2.** same as **nursemaid** (*dated*) **3.** MED same as **wet nurse 4.** INSECTS **INSECT LOOKING AFTER YOUNG** an insect that looks after the young or the larvae in a colony of social insects such as ants or bees ■ *v* (**nursed, nurs·ing, nurs·es**) **1.** *vt* **CARE FOR SICK PERSON** to take care of somebody who is sick or injured **2.** *vi* **WORK AS NURSE** to do the work of a nurse, especially professionally in a hospital **3.** *vt* **TREAT HEALTH PROBLEM OR INJURY** to treat a health problem or a part of the body affected by sickness or injury in order to effect a recovery ○ *I have been nursing a bad cold for three days.* ○ *nurse a sprained ankle* **4.** *vt* **KEEP FEELING** to keep a feeling in the mind for a long time, often indulging in it and allowing it to grow or deepen ○ *nursing his resentment* **5.** *vt* **MANAGE SOMEBODY OR SOMETHING CAREFULLY** to manage, guide, or supervise somebody or something with care and devotion **6.** *vt* **CONSUME SOMETHING SLOWLY** to consume something, especially a drink, very slowly in order to make it last ○ *nursing her espresso* **7.** *vt* **HOLD SOMETHING** to hold something precious with love or care ○ *sat on the train nursing his purchase from the antique shop* **8.** *vti* **BREAST-FEED** to breast-feed a baby, or be breast-fed [13C. Via Old French *norrice* < Latin *nutricia* "wet nurse" < *nutrix*] —**nurs·er** *n*

nurse·maid /núrss màyd/ *n* a woman employed to look after somebody's child when it is young (*dated*)

nurse prac·ti·tion·er *n* a registered nurse trained in primary health care to assume some of the responsibilities once assumed only by a physician such as the diagnosis and treatment of minor illnesses

nurs·er·y /núrssəree, núrssree/ (*plural* **-ies**) *n* **1.** GARDENING **PLACE GROWING PLANTS COMMERCIALLY** a place where plants are grown commercially, either for sale direct to the public or to other retailers **2. HOSPITAL ROOM FOR NEWBORNS** a room in a hospital where newborns stay and are cared for by the nursing staff and pediatricians prior to going home **3. CHILD'S ROOM** a child's bedroom or playroom in a house **4.** EDUC same as **nursery school 5. FOSTERING PLACE** a place where talents or abilities are allowed or encouraged to develop and flourish (*literary*) [14C. < Old French *norricerie* < *norrice* (see NURSE)]

nurs·er·y·man /núrssəreemən, núrssreemən/ (*plural* **-men** /-mən/) *n* a man who works in or owns a nursery where plants are grown commercially

nurs·er·y·per·son /núrssəree pùrss'n, núrssree-/ (*plural* **-per·sons** or **-peo·ple** /-peèp'l/) *n* somebody who works in or owns a nursery where plants are grown commercially

nurs·er·y rhyme *n* a short song or poem for young children, especially one that has become traditional

nurs·er·y school *n* a prekindergarten school for children between the ages of three and five, staffed wholly or partly by qualified teachers who encourage and supervise educational play rather than simply providing childcare

nurs·er·y slopes *npl UK* same as **bunny slopes**

nurs·er·y·wom·an /núrssəree wòommən, núrssree-/ (*plural* **-wom·en** /-wimmin/) *n* a woman who works in or owns a nursery where plants are grown commercially

nurs·e's aide *n* somebody with no specialized training employed in a hospital or other healthcare facility to perform basic nursing-support tasks such as bed-making or giving patients baths

nurse shark *n* a warm-water shark that has a bristle (**barbel**) hanging from its jaw and a deep groove on either side of its mouth. Native to: subtropical to cool temperate waters of the Mediterranean Sea and Atlantic, Indian and Pacific Oceans. Family: Orectolobidae. [Because it tends its eggs until they hatch]

nurs·ing /núrssing/ *n* **1.** the profession or task of looking after people who are sick or injured **2.** breast-feeding, or the period of time that a mother spends breast-feeding her baby

nurs·ing bra *n* a bra with cups that can be removed or opened, worn by breast-feeding mothers

nurs·ing home *n* a long-term healthcare facility that provides full-time care and medical treatment for people who are unable to take care of themselves

nurs·ling /núrssling/ *n* (*literary*) **1. BREAST-FED INFANT** a baby that is being breast-fed **2. CHILD BEING CARED FOR** a baby or child that somebody is looking after or bringing up, especially somebody else's child **3. SOMETHING FOSTERED** something fostered or developed by a person, place, or set of circumstances

nur·ture /núrchər/ *vt* **(-tured, -tur·ing, -tures) 1. TAKE CARE OF YOUNG THING** to give tender care and protection to a young child, animal, or plant, helping it to grow and develop **2. ENCOURAGE SOMEBODY OR SOMETHING TO FLOURISH** to encourage somebody or something to grow, develop, thrive, and be successful ○ *an agent who nurtured several budding young playwrights* **3. KEEP FEELING** to keep a feeling in the mind for a long time, allowing it to grow or deepen ■ *n* **1. CARE GIVEN TO YOUNG THING** tender care and protection given to a young child, animal, or plant to help it to grow and develop **2. ENCOURAGEMENT TO FLOURISH** encouragement given to somebody or something to help him, her, or it grow, develop, thrive, and be successful **3. ENVIRONMENTAL INFLUENCE** the influence that an organism's environment has on the organism, especially when contrasted with what is determined genetically or by nature [14C. Via French < late Latin *nutritura* < Latin *nutrire* "suckle"] —**nur·tur·er** *n*

Nu·sa Teng·ga·ra /no͞ossə teng gaarə/ island group in southern Indonesia, lying in the Indian Ocean east of Java. Population: 7,237,600 (1995). Area: 28,241 sq. mi./73,144 sq. km.

Nuss·lein Vol·hard /nyo͞oss līn fóll haart/, **Christiane** (*b.* 1942) German geneticist. She shared the Nobel Prize in physiology or medicine (1995) with Eric Wieschaus and Edward B. Lewis for her research into embryonic development.

nut /nut/ *n* **1. HARD FRUIT** the fruit of a plant, especially a tree, with a hard outer shell containing the seed **2. EDIBLE KERNEL** the hard seed of a nut, especially when it is edible **3.** BOT **HARD FRUIT OF SOME PLANTS** the hard dry one-seeded fruit of various plants, which does not split open to scatter its seed when it is mature **4. FASTENING SCREWED ONTO BOLT** a piece of metal, usually square or hexagonal, with a hole in the middle, screwed on the end of a bolt as a fastening for it **5.** MUSIC **PART OF STRINGED INSTRUMENT** a ridge at the top end of the fingerboard of a stringed instrument that the strings pass over before reaching the tuning pegs **6.** MUSIC **PART OF INSTRUMENT'S BOW** a device like a screw at one end of a bow for a musical instrument that is turned to tighten the hairs of the bow **7. HUMAN HEAD** somebody's head (*informal*) **8. OFFENSIVE TERM** an offensive term for somebody with a psychiatric disorder **9. ENTHUSIAST** somebody with a deep interest in something (*informal*) **10.** *US* BUSINESS **COSTS OF BUSINESS** the amount of money needed to launch a business, particularly an entertainment business, or to keep it running (*slang*) ○ *The dance club's weekly nut is in the thousands.* **11.** PRINTING same as **en** ■ *vi* **(nut·ted, nut·ting, nuts) GATHER NUTS** to gather edible nuts from trees [Old English *hnutu* < Indo-European]

nu·ta·tion /noo táysh'n/ *n* **1.** ASTRON **WOBBLY ROTATION** the wobbly rotation of a spinning object, especially a planet, caused by a temporary shift in the position of its axis **2.** BOT **IRREGULAR GROWTH OF PLANT** a spiral movement of a plant part caused by varying growth rates on each side **3. NODDING** the nodding of somebody's head (*formal*) [Early 17C. < Latin *nutation-* < past participle of *nutare* "nod"] —**nu·ta·tion·al** *adj*

nut-brown *adj* dark brown or reddish brown in color —**nut-brown** *n*

nut·case /nút kàyss/ *n* an offensive term for somebody with a psychiatric disorder (*informal*)

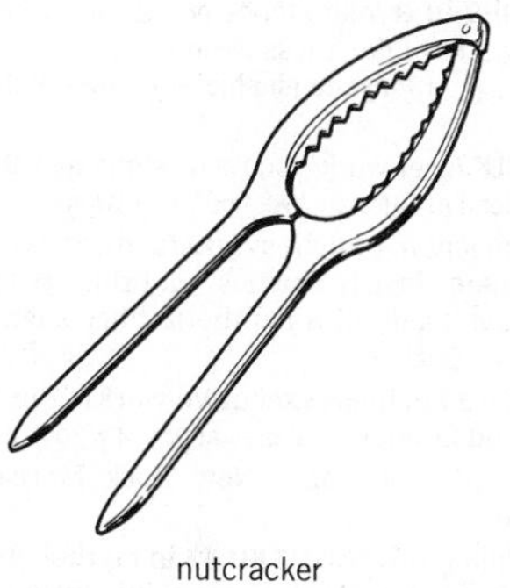

nutcracker

nut·crack·er /nút kràkər/ *n* **1.** a tool for cracking hard nutshells, usually consisting of two hinged metal arms between which the nut is squeezed **2.** a bird of the crow family that feeds mainly on nuts and the seeds of pines. Native to: Europe, Asia, western North America. Genus: *Nucifraga.*

CULTURAL NOTE ***The Nutcracker,*** a ballet (1892) by Russian composer Peter Ilyich Tchaikovsky. Based on Hoffmann's *The Nutcracker and the King of the Mice,* it depicts the dream of a young girl during which her nutcracker turns into a handsome prince who leads her to the magical realm of the Sugar Plum Fairy. Though the story is particularly popular with children, the music and choreography have universal and lasting appeal.

nut·gall /nút gàwl/ *n* a hollow nut-shaped growth on the trunks of oak and other trees caused by the gall wasp, which uses the growth as a shelter for its larvae

nut·hatch /nút hàch/ *n* a small bird with a blue-gray back that climbs on tree trunks and branches, eating insects, seeds, and nuts. Native to: North America, Europe, Asia, Australia. Family: Sittidae. [14C. < NUT + *hache* "hatchet, ax" < Old French (see HATCHET), from its habit of hacking at nuts with its beak]

nut·house /nút hòwss/ *n* (*slang*) **1.** an offensive term for a psychiatric hospital **2.** a place full of noisy, boisterous, chaotic activity

nut·let /núttlət/ *n* **1.** a small nut, especially a small hard dry one-seeded fruit of various plants **2.** the stone of fruits such as cherry and plum

nut·meat /nút meet/ *n* the edible inside part of a nut

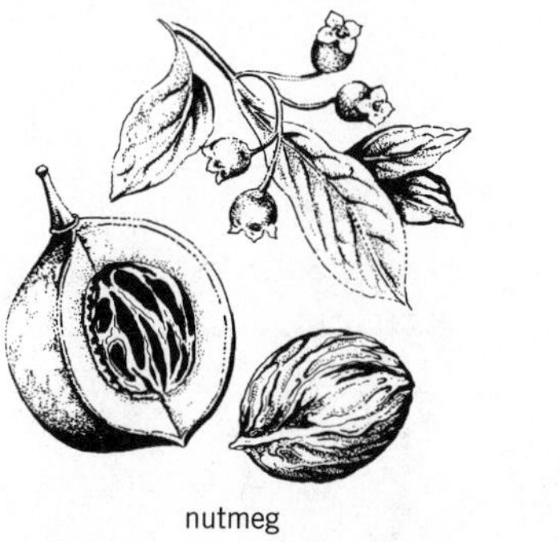

nutmeg

nut·meg /nút mèg/ *n* **1.** COOK **SPICE** an aromatic spice made by grinding or grating the large hard seed of a tropical tree **2.** TREES **TROPICAL EVERGREEN TREE** an evergreen tree widely grown in tropical regions for its seeds, which yield nutmeg and mace. Native to: eastern India. Latin name: *Myristica fragrans.* **3.** COLORS **LIGHT BROWN** a light grayish brown color [13C. Probably < medieval Latin *nux muscata* "nut smelling like musk" < *nux* "nut" + late Latin *muscus* (see MUSK)]

Nut·meg State *n* a nickname for Connecticut

nut·pick /nút pìk/, **nut pick** *n US* a sharp metal tool for digging nutmeat out of the shell

nut pine *n* TREES same as **piñon** (sense 2)

nu·tra·ceu·ti·cal /no͞otrə so͞otik'l/, **nu·tri·ceu·ti·cal** *n* PHARM same as **functional food** [Late 20C. < Latin *nutrire* "nourish" + PHARMACEUTICAL]

nu·tri·a /no͞otree ə/ *n* **1.** the light brown fur of the coypu **2.** ZOOL same as **coypu** [Early 19C. Via Spanish < Latin *lutra* "otter"]

nu·tri·ceu·ti·cal *n* PHARM another spelling of **nutraceutical**

nu·tri·ent /no͞otree ənt/ *n* a substance that provides nourishment, e.g., the minerals that a plant takes from the soil or the constituents in food that keep a human body healthy and help it to grow ■ *adj* providing nourishment [Mid-17C. < Latin *nutrient-*, present participle of *nutrire* "nourish"]

nu·tri·ment /no͞otrəmənt/ *n* nourishment or nourishing substances [Mid-16C. < Latin *nutrimentum* < *nutrire* "nourish"]

nu·tri·tion /noo trísh'n/ *n* **1. PROCESSING OF FOOD** the process of absorbing nutrients from food and processing them in the body in order to keep healthy or to grow **2. SCIENCE OF FOOD** the science that deals with foods and their effects on health **3.** FOOD **FOODS** foods, or the minerals, vitamins, and other nourishing substances that they contain [Mid-16C. Via French < Latin *nutrition-* < *nutrire* "nourish"] —**nu·tri·tion·al** *adj* —**nu·tri·tion·al·ly** *adv*

nu·tri·tion·al ther·a·py *n* the alleviation of symptoms by dietary changes, sometimes using vitamin and mineral pills

nu·tri·tion·ist /noo trísh'nist/ *n* somebody who studies or is an expert on nutrition

nu·tri·tious /noo tríshəss/ *adj* containing minerals, vitamins, and other substances that promote health —**nu·tri·tious·ly** *adv* —**nu·tri·tious·ness** *n*

nu·tri·tive /no͞otrətiv/ *adj* **1.** providing nutrients **2.** relating to nutrition [15C. Via French < medieval Latin *nutritivus* < the past participle of *nutrire* "nourish"] —**nu·tri·tive·ly** *adv*

nuts /nuts/ (*slang*) *adj* **1. OFFENSIVE TERM** an offensive term meaning having a psychiatric disorder **2. ENTHUSIASTIC** wildly enthusiastic about something, or extremely fond of somebody (*offensive in some contexts*) ■ *interj* **EXPRESSION OF ANNOYANCE** used to express annoyance, disbelief, or contempt (*sometimes offensive*) ■ *npl* **OFFENSIVE TERM** an offensive term for testicles

nuts and bolts *npl* the most basic components, elements, or constituents of something (*informal*)

nuts-and-bolts *adj* extremely basic, e.g., in attitude, approach, or strategy (*informal*) ○ *took a nuts-and-bolts approach to paring down the city's budget*

nut·shell /nút shèl/ *n* the hard outer shell of a nut that surrounds the edible inner seed ◇ **in a nutshell** in very few words, getting right to the main point

nut·sy /nútsee/ **(-si·er, -si·est)** *adj* an offensive term meaning having a psychiatric disorder (*slang*)

nut·ty /nýttee/ **(-ti·er, -ti·est)** *adj* **1. CONTAINING NUTS** containing a large amount of nuts **2. LIKE NUTS** like nuts in taste, appearance, texture, or smell **3. OFFENSIVE TERM** an offensive term meaning having or characterized by a psychiatric disorder (*slang*) —**nut·ti·ly** *adv* —**nut·ti·ness** *n*

Nuu-chah-nulth /no͞o chaa nùl/ (*plural same*) *n Can* LANG same as **Nootka** (*used by members of the Nootka people*) [< Nootka]

Nuuk /no͞ok/ capital and largest city of the Danish Island of Greenland, situated on the southwestern coast. Population: 12,483 (1994). Former name **Godthåb** (until 1979)

nux vom·i·ca /nùks vómmikə/ (*plural same*) *n* **1. MEDICINE** a medicine or homeopathic remedy made from the poisonous seeds of a South Asian tree **2. POISONOUS SEEDS** the seeds of a South Asian tree, which contain strychnine and other poisonous substances **3. SOUTH ASIAN TREE** a tree with orange-red berries and poisonous seeds. Native to: South Asia. Latin name: *Strychnos nux-vomica.* [< medieval Latin, "emetic nut"]

nuz·zle /núzz'l/ *v* **(-zled, -zling, -zles) 1.** *vti* **RUB SOMETHING WITH NOSE** to rub or push something gently with the nose, especially as a way of showing affection **2.** *vi* **RUB SOMETHING WITH FACE** to make affectionate rubbing or stroking movements with the face ■ *n* **RUBBING MOVEMENT** a rubbing or stroking movement with the nose or face [15C. Origin ?] —**nuz·zler** *n*

NV *abbr* **1.** Nevada **2.** FIN nonvoting

nvCJD *abbr* MED new variant CJD

NW *abbr* **1.** northwest **2.** northwestern

NWbN *abbr* northwest by north

NWbW *abbr* northwest by west

Nwfld. *abbr* Newfoundland

n.wt. *abbr* net weight

N.W.T. *abbr Can* Northwest Territories

NY, N.Y. *abbr* New York

nya·la /nyáalə/ (*plural same* or **-las**) *n* **1.** an antelope with vertical white stripes on its sides and, on the male, spiral horns. Native to: central Africa. Latin name: *Tragelaphus angasi.* **2.** an antelope with spiral horns on the male. Native to: mountainous regions in northeastern Africa. Latin name: *Tragelaphus buxtoni.* [Late 19C. < Zulu *i-nyala*]

Nyan·ja /nyánjə/ *n* (*plural same* or **-jas**), *adj* LANG same as **Chewa** [Mid-19C. < Bantu *nyanja* "lake"]

Ny·a·sa, Lake /nī ássə/ lake in southeastern Africa, lying between Malawi, Mozambique, and Tanzania. It is one of the world's largest lakes. Area: 8,683 sq. mi./22,490 sq. km.

Ny·as·a·land /nī ássə lànd, nee-/ former name for **Malawi** (until 1966)

nyb·ble /níbb'l/ *n* a unit of computer memory equal to half of one byte or four bits [Humorous play on the idea of a small bite]

NYC, N.Y.C. *abbr* New York City

nyc·ta·lo·pi·a /nìktə lṓpee ə/ *n* the state of being unable to see well at night (*technical*) [Late 17C. < late Latin < Greek *nuktalōps* "sightless at night" < *nukt-* "night" + *alaos* "sightless" + *ōps* "eye"] —**nyc·ta·lo·pic** /-lṓpik, -lóppik/ *adj*

nyc·tit·ro·pism /nik títtrə pìzzəm/ *n* the movement of parts of a plant in response to light and temperature differences between night and day, e.g., the opening and closing of flowers and the folding together of leaves at night [Late 19C. < Greek *nukt-* "night"] —**nyc·ti·tro·pic** /nìktə trṓpik, tróppik/ *adj*

nyc·to·pho·bi·a /nìktə fṓbee ə/ *n* an irrational fear of the night or of darkness in general [Early 20C. < Greek *nukt-* "night"] —**nyc·to·pho·bic** *adj* —**nyc·to·pho·bi·cal·ly** *adv*

nyet·work /nyét wùrk/ *n* COMPUT same as **notwork** [Late 20C. Blend of Russian *nyet* "no" + NETWORK]

ny·lon /nī́ lòn/ *n* a tough synthetic material. Use: food containers, brush bristles, clothing. ■ **ny·lons** *npl* stockings made of a synthetic fiber such as nylon [Mid-20C. Origin ?]

NY-LON *n* a business executive working in both New York and London [< abbreviations NEW YORK and LONDON]

NYMEX /nī́ mèks/ *abbr* New York Mercantile Exchange

nymph /nimf/ *n* **1.** SPIRIT OF NATURE in mythology, a minor goddess or spirit of nature inhabiting areas of natural beauty such as woods, mountains, and rivers and traditionally regarded as a beautiful young woman **2.** WOMAN a beautiful young woman (*literary*) **3.** INSECTS INSECT LARVA the larva of some insects such as mayflies, dragonflies, and grasshoppers that resembles the adult and develops into the adult insect directly, without passing through an intermediate pupa stage [14C. Via Old French < Greek *numphē* "bride, nymph"]

nym·pha /nímfə/ (*plural* **-phae** /-fee/) *n* either of the small inner folds of skin (**labia minora**) that form the opening to the vagina [Late 17C. Via Latin < Greek *numphē* "nymph"]

nym·pha·lid /nim fállid/ *adj* belonging to a family of butterflies that has brightly colored wings and includes the tortoiseshell butterfly and the red admiral. Family: Nymphalidae. [Late 19C. Via modern Latin *Nymphalidae* < Latin *nympha* (see NYMPHA)]

nym·phet /ním fèt, -fət/, **nym·phette** /nim fét/ *n* a sexually aware and sexually desirable young woman, especially a woman in her early teens

nym·pho /nímfō/ (*plural* **-phos**) *n* same as **nymphomaniac** (*slang offensive*) [Mid-20C. Shortening]

nym·pho·ma·ni·a /nìmfə máynee ə/ *n* a compulsive desire to have sex with many different men, theorized to occur in some women (*often offensive*) [Late 18C. < modern Latin < Latin *nympha* (see NYMPH) + late Latin *mania* (see MANIA)]

nym·pho·ma·ni·ac /nìmfə máynee àk/ *n* **1.** a woman supposed to have a compulsive desire to have sex with many different men **2.** an offensive term for a woman regarded as being extremely active sexually (*informal*) —**nym·pho·ma·ni·a·cal** /nìmfəmə nī́ ək'l/ *adj*

Ny·norsk /noo náwrsk/ *n* the official form of the Norwegian language, derived from the rural dialects of Norwegian spoken in the west and north of the country and standardized during the mid-19th century [Mid-20C. < Norwegian, "new Norwegian"] —**Ny·norsk** *adj*

NYP *abbr* not yet published

NYSE *abbr* New York Stock Exchange

nys·tag·mus /ni stágməss/ *n* an involuntary rhythmic movement of the eyes, usually from side to side, caused by some illnesses that affect the nerves and muscle behind the eyeball [Early 19C. Via modern Latin < Greek *nustagmos* "drowsiness" < *nustazein* "nod, be sleepy"]

nys·ta·tin /nístətin/ *n* an antibiotic drug. Use: treatment of fungal infections, especially thrush. [Mid-20C. < *N(ew) Y(ork) Stat(e)*]

Nyun·gar /nyŏŏng gaar/, **Nyun·ga** /-gə/ *n* an Aboriginal language of southwestern Australia, now extinct [Mid-19C. < Nyungar *nungar* "a man"] —**Nyun·gar** *adj*

nz *abbr* ONLINE New Zealand (*used in Internet addresses*) See table at **domain name**

N Zeal. *abbr* New Zealand

Oo

O /ō/ (*plural* **o's**), **O** (*plural* **O's** or **Os**) *n* **1.** the 15th letter of the English alphabet, representing a vowel sound **2.** a written representation of the letter "o"

o' *stressed* /ō/; *unstressed* /ə/ *contr* of

O[1] /ō/ (*plural* **O's** or **Os**) *n* **1.** **"O"-SHAPED OBJECT** something shaped like a letter "O" **2. ZERO** the number zero **3.** MED **HUMAN BLOOD TYPE** a human blood type of the ABO system containing the O antigen. Somebody with this type of blood can donate to all other types in the group but can receive only type O blood.

O[2] /ō/ *interj* **1.** used to address a person or thing, or at the start of a plea or wish **2.** used to express surprise or great wonderment (*literary*) [12C. Natural exclamation]

O[3] *symbol* CHEM ELEM oxygen

o.[1] *abbr* PHARM pint [Modern Latin *octarius*]

o.[2], **O.** *abbr* **1.** GEOG ocean **2.** PRINTING octavo **3.** old **4.** MATH order **5.** BASEBALL out

-o *suffix* **1.** used to form abbreviated words ○ *aggro* ○ *demo* ○ *hypo* **2.** somebody or something associated with or having the characteristics of something ○ *dumbo* [Origin ?]

-o- *infix* connects words and suffixes [< Greek]

OA *abbr* MED osteoarthritis

o/a *abbr* on or about

oaf /ōf/ *n* somebody regarded as unintelligent, clumsy, or uncultured (*insult*) [Early 17C. < Old Norse *álfr* "elf"]

oaf·ish /ṓfish/ *adj* unintelligent, clumsy, or uncultured (*insult*) —**oaf·ish·ly** *adv* —**oaf·ish·ness** *n*

O·a·hu /ə wáa hoo, ō áa-/ island in Hawaii, the most populous and third largest of the Hawaiian Islands. Population: 870,761 (1995).. Area: 597 sq. mi./1,546 sq. km.

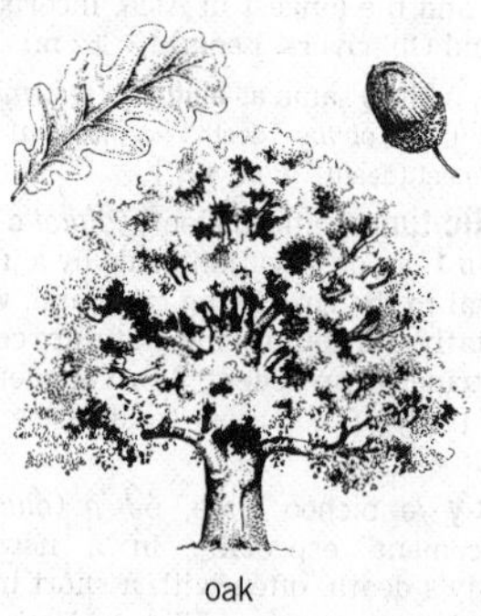

oak

oak /ōk/ *n* **1. HARD WOOD OF OAK TREE** a hard rich-colored wood. Use: furniture-making, flooring. **2. TREE** a deciduous or evergreen tree with acorns as fruit and leaves with several rounded or pointed lobes, grown for its shade and wood. Native to: northern hemisphere. Genus: *Quercus.* **3. BUSH** a bush with lobed leaves like those of an oak tree, e.g., a Jerusalem oak or poison oak **4. OAK WREATH OR GARLAND** a decoration made from the leaves of an oak tree, especially a wreath or garland ■ *adj* **OF RICH BROWN COLOR** of a rich brown color, similar to the color of oak wood [Old English *āc*]

oak ap·ple *n* a rounded hollow growth on the trunk of an oak tree caused by infestation with gall wasps, which use the growths as shelters for their larvae

oak·en /ṓkən/ *adj* made of oak wood (*literary*)

oak fern *n* a light green woodland fern. Native to: northern regions. Latin name: *Thelypteris dryopteris.*

Oak For·est /ōk-/ city in northeastern Illinois, northeast of Joliet. It is a southern suburb of Chicago. Population: 28,370 (2002 estimate).

oak gall *n* BOT same as **oak apple**

Oak·land /ṓklənd/ city and county seat of Alameda County, western California, situated on the eastern side of San Francisco Bay. Population: 402,777 (2002 estimate).

Oak·land Park city in Broward County, southeastern Florida, situated north of Fort Lauderdale. Population: 31,487 (2002 estimate).

oak leaf clus·ter *n* a small decoration shaped like a bunch of oak leaves and acorns, added to another military decoration to show that it has been awarded to the wearer more than once

Oak·ley /ṓklee/, **Annie** (1860–1926) US sharpshooter. She performed with Buffalo Bill's Wild West Show, and inspired the musical *Annie Get Your Gun* (1946). Full name **Moses, Phoebe Anne Oakley**

> "I can shoot as well as you."
> [Annie Oakley. Quoted in *Annie Oakley: Woman at Arms,* Courtney Ryley Cooper; 1927]

oak·moss /ōk mòss/ *n* a lichen that grows on oak trees and produces a resin used in the making of some perfumes. Native to: northern hemisphere. Latin name: *Evernia prunastri.*

Oak Park township in northeastern Illinois, on the western boundary of Chicago, north of Cicero. Population: 51,601 (2002 estimate).

oa·kum /ṓkəm/ *n* hemp or jute fibers, especially from old ropes unraveled and soaked in tar. Use: formerly, sealant for gaps between the planks in a wooden boat's hull. [Old English *ācumba* "broken fibers," literally "off-combing" < Indo-European, "tooth"]

Oak·ville /ōk vìl/ city in Halton Municipal Region, southeastern Ontario, Canada, situated 22 mi./35 km southwest of Toronto. Population: 144,738 (2001).

oak wilt *n* a disease of oak trees caused by a fungus that kills their leaves

O & M *abbr* organization and method

OAP *n UK* somebody who is entitled to draw a pension from the government on reaching a specific age. Full form **old-age pensioner**

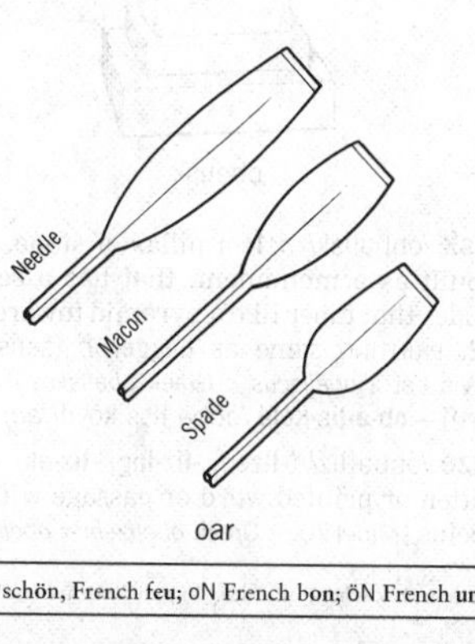

oar

oar /awr/ *n* **1.** BOATING **POLE USED TO PROPEL BOAT** a wooden pole with one broad flat end, used either singly or in pairs to propel a boat by dipping the broad end in the water **2. SOMEBODY ROWING** somebody who rows a boat, especially one of a team of rowers ■ *vti* **(oared, oar·ing, oars)** ROWING **ROW** to row a boat [Old English *ār*]

SPELLCHECK oar, or, or **ore**? Do not confuse the spelling of ***oar, or,*** and ***ore,*** which sound similar. An ***oar*** is a pole with a flat end that is used to row a boat. ***Or*** is a conjunction linking alternatives: *Would you like tea or coffee? Be quiet or leave the room!* ***Ore*** is a mineral from which metal is extracted, as in *iron ore.*

---

oar·fish /áwr fìsh/ (*plural same* or **-fish·es**) *n* a long, eel-shaped fish that grows up to 23 ft./7 m, with a red head fin and dorsal fin. Native to: tropical Atlantic waters. Latin name: *Regalecus glesne.* [Mid-19C. < the shape of its body]

oar·lock /áwr lòk/ *n* a U-shaped pivoting metal rest attached to the side of a boat, in which an oar rests [Old English *ārloc* < *ār* "oar" + *loc* "lock"]

oars·man /áwrzmən/ (*plural* **-men** /-mən/) *n* a man who rows a boat, especially as part of a team of rowers —**oars·man·ship** *n*

oars·per·son /áwrz pùrss'n/ (*plural* **-peo·ple** /-peep'l/ or **-per·sons**) *n* somebody who rows a boat, especially as part of a team of rowers

oars·wom·an /áwrz wòommən/ (*plural* **-wom·en** /-wìmmin/) *n* a woman who rows a boat, especially as part of a team of rowers

OAS *abbr* **1.** *Can* old age security **2.** Organization of American States

OASDHI *abbr US* Old Age, Survivors, Disability, and Health Insurance

o·a·sis /ō áyssiss/ (*plural* **o·a·ses** /ō áy seez/) *n* **1.** fertile ground in a desert where the level of underground water rises to or near ground level, and where plants grow and travelers can replenish water supplies **2.** a place or period that gives relief from a troubling or chaotic situation [Early 17C. Via late Latin < Greek]

oast /ōst/ *n* a kiln used for drying hops, especially hops used to flavor beer [Old English *āst* "kiln" < Indo-European, "be hot, burn"]

oast·house /ōst hòwss/ (*plural* **-hous·es** /-hòwzəz/) *n* a building constructed to contain hop-drying kilns that usually has conical or pyramid-shaped towers

oat /ōt/ *n* a plant with edible seeds that is grown as a

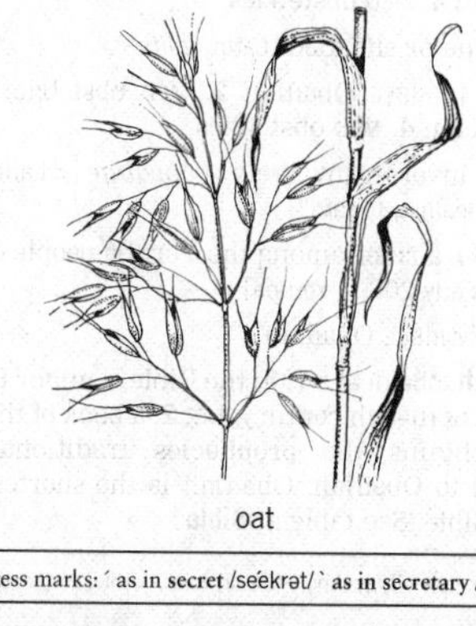

oat

cereal crop. Native to: northern regions. Latin name: *Avena sativa*. ■ **oats** *npl* the seeds of the oat grown as a cereal crop. Use: to make foods such as oatmeal, as livestock feed. [Old English *āte*]

oat·cake /ṓt kàyk/ *n US* a flat cake made of oatmeal

oat-cell *adj* describes a highly malignant form of lung cancer (**oat-cell carcinoma**) characterized by the rapid growth of undifferentiated small round cells. Oat-cell carcinoma is usually related to smoking. [Because the cells look like grains of oats]

oat·en /ṓt'n/ *adj* made from oats, oatmeal, or oat straw

oat·er /ṓtər/ *n* a movie about cowboys, Native North Americans, and settlers in the Old West (*slang humorous*) [Mid-20C. < the staple food of the horses featured]

Oates /ōts/, **Joyce Carol** (*b.* 1938) US writer. Her naturalistic novels, often depicting violence in US society, include *Them* (1969), for which she won the National Book award.

> "For what *is* passes so swiftly and irrevocably into what *was*, no human claim can be of the least significance."
> [Joyce Carol Oates, *What I Lived For*; 1994]

> "The use of language is all we have to pit against death and silence."
> [Joyce Carol Oates, *New York Times*; August 16, 1987]

Oates, Titus (1649–1705) English conspirator. He fabricated the Popish Plot (1678), a fictitious plot to assassinate Charles II and restore Roman Catholicism in England. Initially rewarded, he was later found guilty of perjury and imprisoned.

oat grass *n* a wild grass that looks like the cultivated oat. Native to: Mediterranean, USA, Australia. Genera: *Arrhenatherum* or *Danthonia* or *Themeda* or *Enneapogon*.

oath /ōth/ (*plural* **oaths** /ōthz, ōths/) *n* **1. SOLEMN PROMISE** a formal or legally binding pledge to do something such as tell the truth in a court of law, made formally and often naming God or a loved one as a witness ○ *took a solemn oath of loyalty* **2. WORDS OF PROMISE** the words said when making a formal pledge, especially when reciting a conventional formula such as that used in a court of law **3. SWEARWORD** a swearword, especially one that uses the name of God or another sacred name in a disrespectful way [Old English *āþ*]

oat·meal /ṓt mēel/ *n* **1. CRUSHED OATS** oat grains ground or crushed into flakes or powder, used to make various foods such as cereal or oatcakes ○ *oatmeal cookies* **2.** FOOD **BREAKFAST CEREAL** a breakfast cereal made from rolled oats cooked in milk or water ■ *adj* COLORS **OF LIGHT BROWN COLOR** of a light grayish brown color

Oa·xa·ca /wə haákə, waa khaá kaa/ **1.** state in southern Mexico. Capital: Oaxaca. Population: 3,438,765 (2000).. Area: 35,960 sq. mi./93,136 sq. km. **2.** historic city in southern Mexico, the capital of Oaxaca State. It was founded by the Aztecs. Population: 400,706 (2000).

Ob' /awb, ob/ river in western Siberia that rises in the Altai Mountains, joins the Irtysh River, and then empties into the Arctic Ocean. Length: 2,290 mi./3,680 km.

OB *abbr* **1.** MED obstetric **2.** MED obstetrician **3.** MED obstetrics **4.** BROADCAST outside broadcast

ob.¹ *abbr* **1.** MUSIC oboe **2.** MED obstetric **3.** MED obstetrician **4.** MED obstetrics

ob.² *abbr* he or she died [Latin *obiit*]

Ob. *abbr* **1.** BIBLE Obadiah **2.** MED obstetric **3.** MED obstetrician **4.** MED obstetrics

ob- *prefix* inverse, inversely ○ *obvolute* [< Latin *ob* "in the way, against, toward"]

o·ba /ṓbə/ *n* a ruler among the Yoruba people of West Africa [Early 20C. < Yoruba]

Obad. *abbr* BIBLE Obadiah

O·ba·di·ah /ṓbə dī́ ə/ *n* **1.** in the Bible, a minor Hebrew prophet of the 6th century B.C. **2.** a book of the Bible that contains the prophecies traditionally attributed to Obadiah. Obadiah is the shortest book of the Bible. See table at **Bible**

O·ba·san·jo /ōbə saánjō/, **Olusegun** (*b.* 1937) president of Nigeria (1999–). His election in 1999 as a representative of the People's Democratic Party ended 15 years of military rule.

obb. *abbr* MUSIC obbligato

ob·bli·ga·to /òbbli gaátō/, **ob·li·ga·to** *adj* not to be omitted from a musical piece, either as an instrumental part in the piece or as an instrumental accompaniment to a singer (*used as a musical direction*) ■ *n* (*plural* **-tos** or **-ti** /-tee/) a musical part or accompaniment that is not to be left out [Early 18C. Via Italian, "obliged" < Latin *obligare* (see OBLIGATE)]

OBC *abbr S Asia* Other Backward Classes

ob·com·pressed /òb kəm prést/ *adj* used to describe a part of a plant that is flattened from back to front, like the fruits of yellow rattle

ob·con·ic /ob kónnik/, **ob·con·i·cal** /-kónnik'l/ *adj* cone-shaped and attached to a plant by the pointed end ○ *an obconic fruit*

ob·cor·date /ob káwr dàyt/ *adj* heart-shaped and attached to a plant by the pointed end

ob·du·rate /ób doorət/ *adj* **1.** not easily persuaded or influenced **2.** not influenced by emotions, especially not inclined to feel sympathy or pity [15C. < late Latin *obduratus*, past participle of *obdurare* "be hard" < *durus* "hard"] —**ob·du·ra·cy** *n* —**ob·du·rate·ly** *adv* —**ob·du·rate·ness** *n*

O.B.E. *abbr* Officer of the (Order of the) British Empire

o·be·ah /ṓbee ə/ *n* **1.** a religion that involves witchcraft, originally practiced in Africa and surviving now in parts of the Caribbean **2.** an object believed to have magical powers, used in practicing obeah [Mid-18C. < Twi *ōbayifo*]

~~**obediance**~~ incorrect spelling of **obedience**

o·be·di·ence /ō beédee ənss, ə-/ *n* **1.** the act or practice of following instructions, complying with rules or regulations, or submitting to somebody's authority **2.** the religious authority exercised by a church, a priest, or another member of the clergy, or the people who are under this authority

o·be·di·ent /ō beédee ənt, ə-/ *adj* carrying out, or willing to carry out, instructions, or submitting to somebody's will or authority [13C. < Old French < Latin *oboediens*, present participle of *oboedire* (see OBEY)] —**o·be·di·ent·ly** *adv*

o·bei·sance /ō báyss'nss, ə-/ *n* **1.** a gesture of respect or deference, e.g., a bow of the head (*formal*) **2.** the attitude or behavior of somebody who pays respect or homage to somebody or something [14C. < Old French < *obeir* (see OBEY)]

ob·e·li PRINTING plural of **obelus**

o·be·lia /ō beélyə/ (*plural* **-lias**) *n* an ocean hydrozoan polyp that forms colonies that resemble moss on rocks, ships' hulls, and piles. Genus: *Obelia*. [Late 19C. < modern Latin < Greek *obelias* "leaf baked on a spit" < *obelos* "spit"]

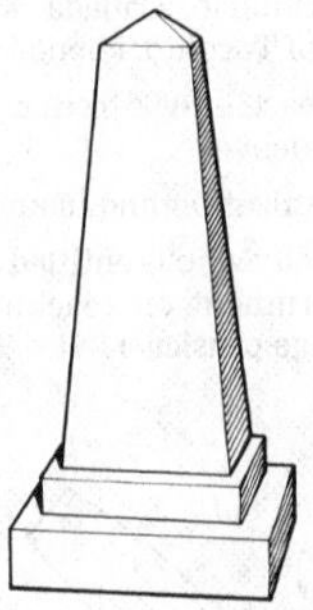

obelisk

ob·e·lisk /óbbəlisk/ *n* **1.** a pillar of stone, especially one built as a monument, that has a square base and sides that taper like a pyramid toward a pointed top **2.** PRINTING same as **dagger** *n* (sense 3) [Mid-16C. Via Latin *obeliscus* < Greek *obeliskos* < *obelos* (see OBELUS)] —**ob·e·lis·koid** /òbbə líss kòyd/ *adj*

ob·e·lize /óbbə līz/ (**-lized, -liz·ing, -liz·es**) *vt* to mark a written or printed word or passage with a dagger or obelus [Mid-17C. < Greek *obelizein* < *obelos* "spit"]

ob·e·lus /óbbələss/ (*plural* **-li** /-lī/) *n* **1.** PRINTING same as **dagger** *n* (sense 3) **2.** a printed mark (†) used in modern editions of ancient manuscripts to indicate that the passage marked is thought not to be genuine [14C. Via late Latin < Greek *obelos* "spit, obelisk"]

o·ben·to /ō béntō/ (*plural* **-tos**), **ben·to** /béntō/ *n* a Japanese meal that is packaged in a partitioned lacquer box [Late 20C. < Japanese]

O·ber·am·mer·gau /ṓbər aámər gòw/ town in Bavaria, southeastern Germany, famous for producing a Passion Play every ten years. Population: 5,225 (1997).

O·ber·on /ṓbə ròn/ *n* **1.** in medieval folklore, the king of the fairies and husband of Titania **2.** a large natural satellite of Uranus

o·bese /ō beéss/ *adj* **1.** extremely or unhealthily fat or overweight **2.** having a body weight more than 20% greater than recommended for the relevant height and thus at risk from several serious illnesses, including diabetes and heart disease [Mid-17C. < Latin *obesus*, past participle of assumed *obedere* "eat until overweight" < *edere* "eat"] —**o·bese·ly** *adv* —**o·bese·ness** *n* —**o·be·si·ty** *n*

o·bes·o·gen·ic /ōbeéssə jénnik/ *adj* tending to encourage excessive weight gain

o·bey /ō báy/ (**o·beyed, o·bey·ing, o·beys**) *vti* **1.** to follow instructions or behave in accordance with a law, rule, or order **2.** to be controlled by somebody or something [13C. Via Old French *obeir* < Latin *oboedire* "listen to" < *audire* "hear"] —**o·bey·er** *n*

ob·fus·cate /óbfə skàyt/ (**-cat·ed, -cat·ing, -cates**) *v* **1.** *vti* to make something obscure or unclear, especially by making it unnecessarily complicated **2.** *vt* to make somebody confused [Mid-16C. < late Latin *obfuscat-*, past participle of *obfuscare* "darken" < *fuscus* "dark"] —**ob·fus·ca·tion** /òbfə skáysh'n/ *n* —**ob·fus·cat·or** *n* —**ob·fus·ca·to·ry** /ob fúskə tàwree/ *adj*

ob-gyn /ō bee jeé wī én, ō bee gín/, **ob/gyn** *n* (*informal*) **1.** the branch of medicine that deals with obstetrics and gynecology **2.** a specialist in obstetrics and gynecology

o·bi¹ /ṓbee/ *n* a silk sash worn by a Japanese person in traditional dress to fasten the kimono [Late 19C. < Japanese, "belt, band, girdle"]

o·bi² *n* RELIG same as **obeah**

o·bi belt *n* a wide belt, sometimes fastened with buckles, in the style of the sash worn around a Japanese kimono

O·bie /ṓbee/ *n* an annual award for achievement in off-Broadway theater [Mid-20C. < the pronunciation of *OB* "off Broadway"]

Ob'-Ir·tysh /àwb eer tísh, òb-/ river system in western Siberia, and the longest in Asia, incorporating the Irtysh and Ob' rivers. Length: 3,362 mi./5,410 km.

o·bit /ṓbit, ō bít/ *n* same as **obituary** (*informal*) [14C. Via French < Latin *obitus* "death" < (*mortem*) *obire* "die," literally "meet (death)" < *ire* "go"]

o·bi·ter dic·tum /òbitər díktəm/ (*plural* **o·bi·ter dic·ta** /-díktə/) *n* **1.** an observation made by a judge that is incidental to the case being tried and, while being authoritative, is not binding on future courts under the doctrine of precedent **2.** a comment made in passing [Early 19C. < Latin, "said by the way, said in passing"]

o·bit·u·ar·y /ə bíchoo èrree, ō-/ *n* (*plural* **-ies**) an announcement, especially in a newspaper, of somebody's death, often with a short biography ■ *adj* relating to or recording a death [Early 18C. < medieval Latin *obituarius* < Latin *obitus* (see OBIT)]

obj. *abbr* **1.** GRAM object **2.** objection **3.** GRAM objective

ob·ject *n* /óbjəkt, ób jèkt/ **1. SOMETHING VISIBLE OR TANGIBLE** something that can be seen or touched **2. FOCUS** a focus of somebody's attention or emotion ○ *an object of public curiosity* **3. GOAL** a goal or purpose ○ *What is your object in pursuing this line of questioning?* **4.** GRAM **NOUN AFFECTED BY VERB** a noun, pronoun, or noun phrase denoting somebody or something that is acted on by a verb or affected by the action of a verb **5.** GRAM **NOUN GOVERNED BY PREPOSITION** a noun, pronoun, or noun phrase that is governed by a preposition **6.** PHILOSOPHY **SOMETHING PERCEIVED AND NAMED AS SEPARATE** something that is perceived as an entity and referred to by a name ○ *mental objects* **7.** OPTICS

SOURCE OF LIGHT RAYS the point or series of points that are or appear to be the source of light rays in an optical system **8.** COMPUT **UNIT OF INFORMATION** a block of information containing text or graphics that can be shared among applications. Changes subsequently made to the original information are reflected in all the documents in which it appears. **9.** COMPUT **UNIT OF COMPUTER PROGRAMMING** a collection of variables, data structures, and procedures stored as an entity and forming a basic building block of object-oriented programming ■ *v* /əb jékt/ (**-ject·ed, -ject·ing, -jects**) **1.** *vi* **BE OPPOSED** to be opposed to something, or express opposition to it ○ *I object to being treated like a lackey.* **2.** *vt* **PUT SOMETHING FORWARD AS OBJECTION** to state something as a reason for being opposed to something ○ *She objected that she would have insufficient time to prepare for the interview.* [14C. < medieval Latin *objectum* "thing presented (to the sight)" < Latin *obicere* "present, throw against" < *jacere* "to throw"] —**ob·ject·or** *n* ◇ **something is no object** indicates that something is not a concern or difficulty ○ *I want the best room you have – money's no object.*

SYNONYMS ***object, protest, demur, remonstrate, expostulate***

CORE MEANING: to indicate opposition to something

object to be opposed or averse to something, or express opposition to it ○ *Two companies objected strongly to the proposals.* ○ *I don't object to people smoking in the privacy of their own homes.* **protest** to express strong disapproval of or disagreement with something, or to refuse to obey or accept something, often by making a formal statement or taking action in public ○ *a noisy demonstration of several hundred workers protesting against the proposed tax* ○ *On the other side of the door, he heard Anne protesting loudly at having to meet him.* **demur** to raise objections in a hesitant or tentative way ○ *In response to Alan's offer, they at first demurred politely, but finally succumbed to his persuasion.* ○ *Janet had demurred at her aunt's room being used, especially so soon after the woman's death.* **remonstrate** to reason or argue forcefully with somebody against something ○ *"You don't mean that!" she remonstrated.* ○ *The court heard that the store owner had remonstrated with the couple for unruly behavior on his premises.* **expostulate** to express disagreement or disapproval vehemently, or to attempt to dissuade somebody from doing something ○ *"Look here, Peter, don't talk nonsense!" expostulated Dan.* ○ *Now and again someone would try to expostulate with the judge, but he never went back on a decision.*

ob·ject ball *n* in pool or billiards, the ball that a player intends to hit with the cue ball

ob·ject code *n* the binary version of a computer program that is used by the computer to run the program

ob·ject com·ple·ment *n UK* same as **objective complement**

ob·ject glass *n* OPTICS same as **objective** *n* (sense 5)

ob·jec·ti·fy /ob jéktə fī/ (**-fied, -fy·ing, -fies**) *vt* **1.** to think of or represent an idea or emotion as if it were something that actually exists **2.** to reduce somebody, or something that is complex and multifaceted, to the status of a simple object

ob·jec·tion /ob jékshən/ *n* **1.** a feeling or expression of opposition ○ *Several people raised very pertinent objections to the plan.* **2.** a reason for a feeling or expression of opposition

ob·jec·tion·a·ble /ob jékshənəb'l/ *adj* causing disapproval, offense, or opposition ○ *an objectionable habit* —**ob·jec·tion·a·bil·i·ty** /ob jèkshənə bíllətee/ *n* —**ob·jec·tion·a·ble·ness** *n* —**ob·jec·tion·a·bly** *adv*

ob·jec·tive /ob jéktiv/ *adj* **1. FREE OF BIAS** free of any bias or prejudice caused by personal feelings **2. BASED ON FACTS** based on facts rather than thoughts or opinions **3.** MED **OBSERVABLE** describes disease symptoms that can be observed by somebody other than the person who is ill **4.** PHILOSOPHY **EXISTING INDEPENDENTLY OF MIND** existing independently of the individual mind or perception **5.** GRAM **BEING OBJECT OF VERB** in or relating to the grammatical form (**case**) that identifies a noun or pronoun as the object of a verb ■ *n* **1. GOAL** a goal or purpose **2. MILITARY TARGET** the target or goal of a military operation **3.** GRAM **OBJECTIVE CASE** the objective grammatical case **4.** GRAM **NOUN IN OBJECTIVE CASE** a noun or pronoun in the objective case **5.** OPTICS **LENS NEAREST OBJECT** the lens or combination of lenses in an optical instrument nearest to and facing the object being viewed —**ob·jec·tive·ness** *n*

ob·jec·tive com·ple·ment *n* a noun, pronoun, or adjective that is a complement of a verb and qualifies its direct object, e.g., "angry" in "He makes me angry"

ob·jec·tive cor·rel·a·tive *n* something in a written or performed work that is associated with a particular emotion and used to evoke it in the reader or audience

ob·jec·tive lens *n* OPTICS same as **objective** *n* (sense 5)

ob·jec·tive·ly /ob jéktivlee/ *adv* **1.** without being influenced by personal feelings **2.** on the basis of fact, experience, or some measurable quality ○ *objectively derived measures such as test scores*

ob·jec·tiv·ism /ob jékti vìzzəm/ *n* **1.** the emphasizing of external realities rather than beliefs or feelings in literature or art **2.** a philosophical belief that moral truths or external objects exist independently of the individual mind or perception —**ob·jec·tiv·ist** *n, adj*

ob·jec·tiv·i·ty /òb jek tívvətee/ *n* **1. ABILITY TO VIEW THINGS OBJECTIVELY** the ability to perceive or describe something without being influenced by personal emotions or prejudices **2. ACCURACY** the fact or quality of being accurate, unbiased, and independent of individual perceptions **3.** PHILOSOPHY **ACTUAL EXISTENCE** the actual existence of something, without reference to people's impressions or ideas

ob·jec·ti·vize /ob jékti vīz/ (**-vized, -viz·ing, -viz·es**) *vt* same as **objectify** (sense 1)

ob·ject lan·guage *n* **1.** the language that a computer interprets in running programs **2.** COMPUT same as **target language** (sense 3)

ob·ject lens *n* OPTICS same as **objective** *n* (sense 5)

ob·ject les·son *n* an incident that provides an opportunity for learning something, especially the best way to do something ○ *an object lesson in tact*

ob·ject-o·ri·ent·ed graph·ics *npl* computer graphics images composed of individual geometric shapes such as circles and lines which, unlike bit maps, can be changed, added to, or deleted without disturbing those remaining (*takes a plural verb*)

ob·ject-o·ri·ent·ed pro·gram·ming *n* a form of computer programming based on objects arranged in a branching hierarchy

ob·ject re·la·tions *npl* a psychoanalytic theory that sees a person as motivated by a desire to form bonds with appropriate objects or people, rather than merely satisfying impulses in order to discharge tension

ob·jet d'art /àwb zhay daár/ (*plural* **ob·jets d'art** /*pronunc. same*/) *n* an object that has artistic value, especially a small piece [Mid-19C. < French, "object of art"]

ob·jet trou·vé /àwb zhay troo váy/ (*plural* **ob·jets trou·vés** /*pronunc. same*/) *n* a natural or everyday object, e.g., a pebble from a beach, treated as something of artistic value or incorporated into a work of art [Mid-20C. < French, "found object"]

ob·jur·gate /óbjər gàyt/ (**-gat·ed, -gat·ing, -gates**) *vt* to scold somebody angrily (*literary*) [Early 17C. < Latin *objurgat-*, past participle of *objurgare* "quarrel against" < *jurgium* "quarrel"] —**ob·jur·ga·tion** /òbjər gáysh'n/ *n* —**ob·jur·ga·tor** *n* —**ob·jur·ga·to·ry** /ob júrgə tàwree/ *adj*

obl. *abbr* PRINTING oblique

o·blast /ó blàst, ṓ-/ *n* a subdivision of a republic of the former Soviet Union [Late 19C. < Russian *óblast* "authority on" < *vlast* "authority, power"]

ob·late[1] /ó blàyt, o bláyt/ *adj* shaped like a sphere but with the length of the diameter at the equator greater than the length from pole to pole [Early 18C. < modern Latin *oblatus* "brought against" < Latin *latus*, past participle of *ferre* "bring"] —**ob·late·ly** *adv* —**ob·late·ness** *n*

ob·late[2] /ó blàyt/ *n* in the Roman Catholic Church, a lay person who is part of a religious community [Late 17C. Via French < medieval Latin *oblatus* "brought to" < the past participle of Latin *offerre* (see OFFER)]

ob·la·tion /ə bláysh'n, ō-/ *n* **1. OFFERING OF GIFT TO DEITY** the offering of a gift or sacrifice to a deity **2. COMMUNION OFFERING** the offering of bread and wine to God during the Christian service of Communion **3. RELIGIOUS OR CHARITABLE GIFT** something offered in a religious rite or as a charitable gift [15C. Directly or via Old French < late Latin *oblation-* < Latin *offerre* (see OFFER)] —**ob·la·tion·al** *adj*

ob·li·gate *vt* /óbbli gàyt/ (**-gat·ed, -gat·ing, -gates**) **1. COMPEL SOMEBODY LEGALLY OR MORALLY** to compel somebody to do something as a legal or moral duty **2.** *US* **COMMIT FUNDS AS SECURITY** to commit something, especially funds, to fulfill an obligation, e.g., as security ■ *adj* /-gət, -gàyt/ **ONLY EXISTING IN ONE ENVIRONMENT** describes an organism that can exist only in a particular role or under particular environmental conditions [15C. < Latin *obligatus*, past participle of *obligare* (see OBLIGE)] —**ob·li·ga·ble** /óbbligəb'l/ *adj* —**ob·li·gate·ly** *adv* —**ob·li·ga·tor** *n*

ob·li·ga·tion /òbbli gáysh'n/ *n* **1. DUTY** something that must be done because of legal or moral duty **2. STATE OF BEING OBLIGATED** the state of being under a moral or legal duty to do something **3. GRATITUDE OWED** something that somebody owes in return for something given, e.g., assistance or a favor **4.** LAW **BINDING LEGAL AGREEMENT** a legal agreement by which somebody is bound to do something, especially pay a specified amount of money **5.** LAW **LEGAL CONTRACT** a legal document such as a mortgage or bond that contains the terms of an obligation, usually including a penalty for failing to fulfill it —**ob·li·ga·tion·al** *adj*

ob·li·ga·to *adj, n* MUSIC another spelling of **obbligato**

o·blig·a·to·ry /ə blíggə tàwree/ *adj* required by law or by a moral or religious rule —**o·blig·a·to·ri·ly** *adv*

o·blige /ə blī́j/ (**o·bliged, o·blig·ing, o·blig·es**) *v* **1.** *vt* **REQUIRE SOMEBODY TO DO SOMETHING** to bind somebody morally or legally to do something **2.** *vt* **FORCE SOMEBODY TO DO SOMETHING** to make it necessary for somebody to do something **3.** *vt* **CAUSE SOMEBODY TO FEEL INDEBTED** to cause somebody to feel indebted by doing something for that person **4.** *vt* **DO FAVOR FOR SOMEBODY** to do a favor or service for somebody ○ *Would you oblige me by closing the door?* **5.** *vi* **BE HELPFUL** to do something necessary or helpful ○ *was only too happy to oblige* [13C. Via Old French *oblig(i)er* < Latin *obligare* "tie to" < *ligare* "to tie"] —**o·blig·er** *n*

ob·li·gee /òbblə jeé/ *n* somebody to whom another person is legally or morally bound, e.g., by a financial debt or obligation to do something

o·blig·ing /ə blī́jing/ *adj* willing to be helpful or do favors —**o·blig·ing·ly** *adv* —**o·blig·ing·ness** *n*

ob·li·gor /òbblə gáwr, óbblə gàwr/ *n* somebody who legally agrees to do or pay something

o·blique /ō bleék, ə-/ *adj* **1. INDIRECT** not straightforward or direct ○ *an oblique reference to the lateness of the hour* **2. SLOPING** sloping or joining something at an angle that is not a right angle **3.** MATH **NOT PARALLEL OR PERPENDICULAR** neither perpendicular nor parallel to another line or plane **4.** MATH **NOT RIGHT-ANGLED** not being or containing a right angle or a multiple of a right angle **5.** GRAM **NOT BEING SUBJECT** of or being a grammatical case of a noun or pronoun other than the nominative or vocative **6.** BOT **WITH SIDES OF DIFFERENT LENGTH** describes leaves that have sides of different length **7.** ANAT **NOT BEING ON ANATOMICAL PLANE** slanting away from any of the anatomical planes of the body such as the horizontal or perpendicular plane **8.** GEOG **BEING AT TANGENT TO EARTH'S SURFACE** relating to or from the point of view of an oblique projection ■ *adv* MIL **CHANGING DIRECTION AT 45°** changing direction to or at an angle of 45° ■ *n* **1. SOMETHING SLANTING** something that is oblique, e.g., a slanting line **2.** NAVIG **COURSE CHANGE OF LESS THAN 90°** a change of course of less than 90° ■ *vi* (**o·bliqued, o·bliqu·ing, o·bliques**) **1. TAKE OBLIQUE DIRECTION** to move or slant in an oblique direction **2.** MIL **ADVANCE IN OBLIQUE DIRECTION** to move forward at an angle of 45° in a military formation [15C. < Latin *obliquus* "slanting, sidelong"] —**o·blique·ness** *n*

o·blique·ly /ō bleéklee, ə-/ *adv* **1.** in a way that is not direct or straightforward **2.** at an angle that is not a right angle

o·blique pro·jec·tion *n* a map projection based on a plane of projection that is at a tangent to the Earth's surface at a point between the poles and the equator

o·blique-slip fault *n* a fracture in a layer of rock in which the movement is both horizontal and vertical

o·bliq·ui·ty /ə blíkwətee, ō-/ (*plural* **-ties**) *n* **1. STATE OF BEING OBLIQUE** the condition of being oblique **2. DEVIATION FROM PLANE** a deviation from the horizontal or perpendicular **3. CHARACTER FLAW** a departure from morality or reason **4. LACK OF DIRECTNESS** a lack of directness or straightforwardness in speech or conduct **5.** *also* **o·bliq·ui·ty of the e·clip·tic** ASTRON **ANGLE BETWEEN EARTH'S ORBIT AND EQUATOR** the angle between the plane of the Earth's equator and the plane of the Earth's orbit around the Sun, approximately 23.5°

o·blit·er·ate /ə blíttə ràyt, ō-/ (**-at·ed, -at·ing, -ates**) *vt* **1.** to destroy something so that nothing remains **2.** to erase or obscure something completely, leaving no trace [Late 16C. < Latin *oblitterat-*, past participle of *oblitterare* "remove letters" < *littera* "letter"] —**o·blit·er·a·tion** /ə blìttə ráysh'n, ō-/ *n* —**o·blit·er·a·tive** *adj* —**o·blit·er·a·tor** *n*

o·bliv·i·on /ə blívvee ən/ *n* **1. STATE OF BEING FORGOTTEN** a state of being completely forgotten **2. STATE OF FORGETTING** a state of complete forgetfulness or unawareness **3.** LAW **OVERLOOKING OF PAST OFFENSES** the deliberate overlooking of past offenses [14C. Via Old French < Latin *oblivion-* < *oblivisci* "forget"]

o·bliv·i·ous /ə blívvee əss/ *adj* **1.** unaware of or paying no attention to somebody or something **2.** forgetting about somebody or something —**o·bliv·i·ous·ly** *adv* —**o·bliv·i·ous·ness** *n*

ob·long /ób làwng/ *adj* having a shape that is longer than it is wide, especially a rectangular or roughly elliptical shape ■ *n* something with a length greater than its width, especially a rectangle or distorted circle [15C. < Latin *oblongus* "rather long" < *longus* "long"]

ob·lo·quy /óbbləkwee/ *n* (*formal or literary*) **1.** statements that severely criticize or defame somebody **2.** a state of disgrace brought about by being defamed [15C. < late Latin *obloquium* "talking against" < *loqui* "to talk"]

ob·nox·ious /ob nókshəss, əb-/ *adj* very offensive and unpleasant ○ *obnoxious stench* [Late 16C. < Latin *obnoxius* "vulnerable to harm" < *noxa* "harm"] —**ob·nox·ious·ly** *adv* —**ob·nox·ious·ness** *n*

o·boe /ṓbō/ *n* **1.** a woodwind instrument that produces a penetrating high sound and consists of a slim tube of conical bore with a double reed and keys operated by the fingers **2.** somebody who plays an oboe [Late 17C. Via Italian < French *hautbois* (see HAUTBOY)] —**o·bo·ist** *n*

o·boe da cac·cia /-də káachə/ *n* an early form of oboe from which the English horn was developed [Late 19C. < Italian, "hunting oboe"]

o·boe d'a·mo·re /-daa máw rày/ *n* an oboe used mainly in baroque music that has a lower pitch than the standard instrument [Late 19C. < Italian, "oboe of love"]

ob·ol /óbb'l/, **ob·o·lus** /óbbələss/ (*plural* **-li** /-lī/) *n* a coin or unit of weight used in ancient Greece, equal to one sixth of a drachma [Mid-17C. Via Latin < Greek *obolos*, variant of *obelos* "spit"]

Ob·on /ō bón/ *n* in Japan, a Buddhist festival celebrating All Souls. Date: July 13 to 31.

ob·o·vate /o bṓ vàyt/ *adj* describes leaves that are oval with the narrow end at the base

ob·o·void /o bṓ vòyd/ *adj* describes fruits that are egg-shaped, with the narrow end at the base

ob·ruk /óbb ro͝ok/ *n* in the 18th century, work obligations owed by Russian peasants to either their aristocratic landlords or the state

obs. *abbr* **1.** obscure **2.** observation **3.** ASTRON observatory **4.** obsolete **5.** MED obstetrics

Obs. *abbr* ASTRON Observatory

ob·scene /ob séen, əb-/ *adj* **1.** offensive to conventional standards of decency, especially by being sexually explicit **2.** disgusting and morally offensive, especially through an apparent total disregard for others' rights or natural justice [Late 16C. Via French < Latin *obscenus* "ill-omened"] —**ob·scene·ly** *adv*

ob·scen·i·ty /əb sénnətee, ob-/ (*plural* **-ties**) *n* **1. INDECENCY** offensiveness to conventional standards of decency, especially as a result of sexual explicitness **2. OBSCENE EXPRESSION** a word, phrase, or statement that is offensive, especially because of being sexually explicit **3. SOMETHING OBSCENE** something that is disgusting and morally offensive

ob·scur·ant·ist /əb skyo͝orəntist, ob-/ *adj* opposing or hindering the spread of new ideas and new social or political developments —**ob·scur·ant** *adj, n* —**ob·scur·ant·ism** /əb skyo͝orən tìzzəm, ob skyo͝o rán tìzzəm/ *n* —**ob·scur·ant·ist** *n*

ob·scure /əb skyo͝or, ob-/ *adj* **1. HARD TO UNDERSTAND** difficult to understand because of not being fully or clearly expressed ○ *an obscure passage in the manuscript* **2. INDISTINCT** not able to be seen or heard distinctly ○ *Its outlines are obscure, but the object seems roughly cigar-shaped.* **3. UNIMPORTANT OR UNKNOWN** not important or well-known ○ *an obscure portrait painter* **4. KNOWN TO FEW PEOPLE** unknown to most people, e.g., because of being hidden or remote **5. DIM** dark, shadowy, or clouded ○ *an obscure corner of the hall* **6.** LING **UNSTRESSED** describes a vowel that has a neutral, unstressed pronunciation (*technical*) ■ *vt* (**-scured, -scur·ing, -scures**) **1. MAKE UNCLEAR** to make something unclear, indistinct, or hidden **2. DARKEN** to make something dark or cover something with cloud [14C. Via Old French < Latin *obscurus* "covered over" < *-scurus* "covered"] —**ob·scu·ra·tion** /òbskyə ráysh'n/ *n* —**ob·scure·ness** *n*

SYNONYMS ***obscure, abstruse, recondite, arcane, cryptic, enigmatic, esoteric***

CORE MEANING: difficult to understand

obscure difficult to understand because of not being fully or clearly expressed ○ *a rather obscure branch of mathematics called graph theory* ○ *a notion which may at first seem somewhat obscure* **abstruse** not easy to understand, often because it involves specialist knowledge or is expressed in specialist language ○ *songs with abstruse titles* ○ *He is so occupied with abstruse ideas that he is incapable of coping with everyday activities.* **recondite** requiring a high degree of scholarship or specialist knowledge to be understood ○ *an excellent tutor, with an obvious knowledge of an often recondite subject* **arcane** requiring information that is secret or known only to a few people in order to be understood ○ *The current pay structure is arcane and outdated.* ○ *He had drawn several arcane symbols round the boundary of the circle.* **cryptic** deliberately mysterious or ambiguous and seeming to have a hidden meaning ○ *cryptic clues* ○ *a fax in cryptic language* **enigmatic** having a quality of mystery and ambiguity that makes it difficult to understand or interpret ○ *his enigmatic smile* ○ *the brilliant and enigmatic figure of Thomas à Becket* **esoteric** understood by or intended for only an initiated few. ○ *He was employed as a church architect and was later dismissed because of his esoteric interest in Paganism and the occult.* ○ *dictionaries for more esoteric or specialist domains*

ob·scure·ly /əb skyo͝orlee, ob-/ *adv* **1. UNCLEARLY** in a way that is not clear, definite, or easy to understand **2. DIMLY** dimly or indistinctly **3. AWAY FROM PEOPLE'S ATTENTION** in a place or position that is remote, secluded, or not prominent or well-known

ob·scu·ri·ty /əb skyo͝orətee, ob-/ (*plural* **-ties**) *n* **1. STATE OF BEING UNKNOWN** a state of being unknown or inconspicuous ○ *plucked from obscurity to star in a Broadway musical* **2. UNCLEARNESS** lack of clarity or difficulty in being understood **3. SOMEBODY OR SOMETHING OBSCURE** an obscure person or thing

~~**obsene**~~ incorrect spelling of **obscene**

ob·se·quent /óbsəkwənt/ *adj* describes a river, stream, or drainage system that flows into a subsidiary (**subsequent**) river in a direction contrary to that of the flow of the main (**consequent**) river [Late 19C. < Latin *obsequent-*, present participle of *obsequi* "comply," literally "follow towards" < *sequi* "follow"]

ob·se·quies /óbsəkweez/ *npl* rites or ceremonies carried out at a funeral [14C. Via Anglo-Norman < late Latin *obsequiae*, alteration (influenced by *obsequium* "compliance") of *exequiae* "those following out (to the grave)" < *exsequi* (see EXECUTE)]

ob·se·qui·ous /əb séekwee əss, ob-/ *adj* excessively eager to please or obey [15C. < Latin *obsequiosus* < *obsequium* "compliance"] —**ob·se·qui·ous·ly** *adv* —**ob·se·qui·ous·ness** *n*

ob·serv·a·ble /əb zúrvəb'l/ *adj* able to be seen or detected ■ *n* something that can be measured or observed directly, e.g., temperature —**ob·serv·a·bil·i·ty** /əb zùrvə bíllətee/ *n*

ob·serv·a·bly /əb zúrvəblee/ *adv* in a way or to an extent that can be seen or detected

ob·ser·vance /əb zúrvənss/ *n* **1. COMPLIANCE** the execution of or compliance with laws, instructions, or customs **2. RITUAL** a custom, ritual, or ceremony, especially a religious one **3. PERFORMANCE OF RELIGIOUS CEREMONIES** the celebration of a religious occasion, or the practice of a religious rite, ceremony, or action **4. RELIGIOUS RULE** a rule of a religious order **5. OBSERVATION** careful watching or close attention

USAGE **observance** or **observation**? These two words share the meaning "close attention," though ***observation*** is much more common: *our observation of the habits of the condor; the child's observance of the waving flags.* If you refer to "compliance," "ritual," "celebration of religious rites," or "a rule of a religious order," the only word to use is ***observance***, as in *observance* [not *observation*] *of the law; church observances* [not *observations*] *such as baptism and Communion; followed the observances* [not *observations*] *of the Jesuit order.* If you refer to "a remark or comment" or "a record of something seen or studied," ***observation*** is the correct choice: *made a few casual observations* [not *observances*] *about the foul weather; astronomical observations* [not *observances*] *in one volume.*

ob·ser·vant /əb zúrvənt/ *adj* **1.** paying such careful attention that little or nothing is unnoticed **2.** carrying out rituals or obeying laws, especially religious ones —**ob·ser·vant·ly** *adv*

ob·ser·va·tion /òbzər váysh'n/ *n* **1. PAYING ATTENTION** the attentive watching of somebody or something **2. OBSERVING OF DEVELOPMENTS IN SOMETHING** the careful watching and recording of something, e.g., a natural phenomenon, as it happens **3. RECORD OF SOMETHING SEEN OR NOTED** the result or record of observing something such as a natural phenomenon and noting developments **4. REMARK OR COMMENT** a remark or comment on something that has been noticed **5. ACT OF OBSERVING OR OBEYING** the act of observing a religious occasion or ritual or of obeying a law or rule **6.** NAVIG **SIGHTING WITH NAVIGATIONAL INSTRUMENT** a sighting with a navigational instrument to establish the observer's position in relation to an astronomical object such as the Sun **7.** NAVIG **NAVIGATIONAL INSTRUMENT READING** the reading taken from a navigational instrument that has been used to find the observer's position in relation to an astronomical object —**ob·ser·va·tion·al** *adj* —**ob·ser·va·tion·al·ly** *adv*

USAGE See ***observance.***

ob·ser·va·tion car *n* a railroad car fitted with extra or larger windows and often a partly transparent roof to allow passengers a better view of passing scenery

ob·ser·va·tion post *n* a position from which soldiers can watch enemy movements and direct artillery fire

ob·ser·va·to·ry /əb zúrvə tàwree/ (*plural* **-ries**) *n* **1.** a building, station, or artificial satellite used for scientific observation of natural phenomena such as astronomical objects, the weather, or earthquakes **2.** a place or building that commands an expansive view

ob·serve /əb zúrv/ (**-served, -serv·ing, -serves**) *v* **1.** *vt* **NOTICE SOMETHING** to see or notice something, especially while watching carefully ○ *You were observed entering the building.* **2.** *vti* **WATCH SOMETHING ATTENTIVELY** to watch somebody or something attentively, especially for scientific purposes ○ *I have been observing his movements for the last half hour.* **3.** *vti* **OFFICIALLY WITNESS SOMETHING** to be an official witness to something without taking an active part in it ○ *A UN delegation was present to observe the signing of the treaty.* **4.** *vi* **BE SPECTATOR** to watch something without taking part **5.** *vt* **COMMENT ON SOMETHING** to make a comment or remark on something seen or noticed ○ *"Your aim is definitely improving," she observed.* **6.** *vt* **COMPLY WITH SOMETHING** to carry out or comply with something such as a law or custom **7.** *vt* **CELEBRATE FESTIVAL** to celebrate or keep a religious or traditional festival [14C. Via Old French *observer* < Latin *observare* "watch toward" < *servare* "to watch"]

ob·serv·er /əb zúrvər/ *n* **1.** SOMEBODY WHO SEES OR WATCHES SOMETHING somebody who observes something that is happening **2.** NONPARTICIPATING WITNESS somebody who acts as a witness to an event, often officially and at the invitation of the participants **3.** SOMEBODY OBSERVING CEREMONY OR OBEYING LAW somebody who duly celebrates a religious ceremony or ritual, or complies with a rule or law **4.** AIR FORCE AIRCRAFT IDENTIFIER somebody trained in identifying aircraft **5.** MIL WATCHER OF ENEMY MOVEMENTS a soldier who watches enemy movements or directs artillery fire

ob·sess /əb séss, ob-/ (**-sessed, -sess·ing, -sess·es**) *v* **1.** *vt* to occupy somebody's thoughts constantly and exclusively ○ *The desire for vengeance obsesses him.* **2.** *vi* to think or worry about something constantly and compulsively ○ *You can't spend your vacation obsessing about money.* [Early 16C. < Latin *obsess-*, past participle of *obsidere* "besiege," literally "sit opposite to" < *sedere* "sit"]

ob·ses·sion /əb sésh'n, ob-/ *n* **1.** PREOCCUPATION an idea or feeling that completely occupies the mind ○ *His obsession with figures led him to make crucial economic mistakes.* **2.** STATE OF BEING OBSESSED the state of being obsessed by somebody or something ○ *Their devotion to each other borders on obsession.* **3.** PSYCHIAT UNCONTROLLABLE PERSISTENCE OF IDEA the uncontrollable persistence of an idea or emotion in the mind, sometimes associated with psychiatric disorder —**ob·ses·sion·al** *adj*—**ob·ses·sion·al·ly** *adv*—

ob·ses·sive /əb séssiv, ob-/ *adj* **1.** amounting to an obsession or as strong as an obsession **2.** worrying compulsively about something or things generally —**ob·ses·sive** *n* —**ob·ses·sive·ly** *adv* —**ob·ses·sive·ness** *n*

ob·ses·sive-com·pul·sive *adj* with or characteristic of obsessive-compulsive disorder ■ *n* somebody with obsessive-compulsive disorder

ob·ses·sive-com·pul·sive dis·or·der *n* a psychiatric disorder characterized by obsessive thoughts and compulsive behavior such as continual washing of the hands prompted by a feeling of uncleanliness

ob·sid·i·an /əb síddee ən, ob-/ *n* a jet-black volcanic glass, chemically similar to granite and formed by the rapid cooling of molten lava, that was used by early civilizations for manufacturing tools and ceremonial objects [14C. < Latin *(lapis) Obsidianus*, copyist's error for *Obsianus* "(stone) of Obsius," a Roman]

ob·so·lesce /òbssə léss/ (**-lesced, -lesc·ing, -lesc·es**) *vi* to become obsolete [Late 19C. < Latin *obsolescere* (see OBSOLESCENT)]

ob·so·les·cent /òbssə léss'nt/ *adj* in the process of becoming obsolete [Mid-18C. < Latin *obsolescent-*, present participle of *obsolescere* "wear out" < *solere* "be accustomed"] —**ob·so·les·cence** *n* —**ob·so·les·cent·ly** *adv*

ob·so·lete /òbssə léet/ *adj* **1.** NOT USED ANY MORE no longer in use **2.** OUT-OF-DATE superseded by something newer, though possibly still in use **3.** BIOL UNDEVELOPED describes a part or organ of an animal or plant that is undeveloped or no longer functional [Late 16C. < Latin *obsoletus*, past participle of *obsolescere* (see OBSOLESCENT)] —**ob·so·lete·ly** *adv*

SYNONYMS See ***old-fashioned.***

ob·sta·cle /óbstək'l/ *n* **1.** HINDRANCE somebody or something that hinders or prevents progress **2.** SOMETHING IN WAY something that blocks or impedes a road, passage, or somebody's way **3.** HURDLE a fence or hedge set up for horses to jump over in show jumping [14C. Via Old French < Latin *obstaculum* < *obstare* "stand in the way" < *stare* "to stand"]

ob·sta·cle course *n* **1.** a training area where soldiers have to get past various obstacles such as ditches or high walls as quickly as possible **2.** an area similar to a military obstacle course, used by competitors in an obstacle race

ob·sta·cle race *n* a race in which competitors have to get past a range of obstacles

obstet. *abbr* MED **1.** obstetric **2.** obstetrics

ob·stet·ric /ob stéttrik/ *adj* relating to childbirth or obstetrics [Mid-18C. < Latin *obstetricius* "of a midwife" < *obstetric-* "midwife," literally "woman who is present, stands before" < *stare* "stand"]

ob·ste·tri·cian /òbstə trísh'n/ *n* a doctor who specializes in pregnancy, delivering babies, and the care of women after childbirth

ob·stet·rics /ob stéttriks/ *n* the branch of medicine that deals with the care of women during pregnancy and childbirth, and for some six weeks following delivery (*takes a singular verb*)

~~**obsticle**~~ incorrect spelling of **obstacle**

ob·sti·nate /óbstinət/ *adj* **1.** STUBBORN determined not to agree with other people's wishes or accept their suggestions **2.** REFUSING TO CHANGE unwilling to change or give up something such as an idea or attitude **3.** DIFFICULT TO CONTROL difficult to control, get rid of, solve, or cure ○ *an obstinate blockage in the pipe* [14C. < Latin *obstinatus*, past participle of *obstinare* "be resolved," literally "stand by" < *stare* "to stand"] —**ob·sti·na·cy** *n* —**ob·sti·nate·ly** *adv*—**ob·sti·nate·ness** *n*

ob·sti·pa·tion /òbstə páysh'n/ *n* severe constipation, often caused by a blockage in the intestines [Late 16C. < late Latin *obstipation-* "pressing in the way of" < *stipare* "to press"]

ob·strep·er·ous /ob stréppərəss/ *adj* **1.** noisily and aggressively boisterous **2.** strongly objecting to something or noisily refusing to be controlled [Late 16C. < Latin *obstreperus* "clamorous," literally "rattling against" < *strepere* "to rattle"] —**ob·strep·er·ous·ly** *adv*—**ob·strep·er·ous·ness** *n*

SYNONYMS See ***unruly.***

ob·struct /əb strúkt, ob-/ (**-struct·ed, -struct·ing, -structs**) *vt* **1.** PREVENT CLEAR PASSAGE to cause a blockage in a road, course, or passage **2.** SLOW SOMEBODY OR SOMETHING DOWN to cause a serious delay in action or progress **3.** IMPEDE VIEW to be in the way and prevent a clear view of something [Early 17C. < Latin *obstructus*, past participle of *obstruere* "build up against" < *struere* "heap up, pile"] —**ob·struc·tor** *n*

SYNONYMS See ***hinder***[1].

ob·struc·tion /əb strúkshən, ob-/ *n* **1.** BLOCK OR HINDRANCE somebody or something that causes or forms a blockage or hindrance **2.** ACT OF BLOCKING an act of blocking or hindering somebody or something **3.** STATE OF BEING BLOCKED the state of being obstructed **4.** DELAYING OF SOMETHING the deliberate delaying of the business of something such as a legislative body **5.** UNFAIR IMPEDING OF OPPONENT in soccer, the unfair impeding of an opposing player

ob·struc·tion·ist /əb strúkshənist, ob-/ *adj* deliberately causing delay or impeding progress —**ob·struc·tion·ism** *n* —**ob·struc·tion·ist** *n* —**ob·struc·tion·is·tic** /əb strùkshə nístik, ob-/ *adj*

ob·struc·tion of jus·tice *n US* the criminal offense of obstructing the administration and process of the law

ob·struc·tive /əb strúktiv, ob-/ *adj* **1.** hindering or preventing the progress of something **2.** relating to or caused by the obstruction of a passage in the body —**ob·struc·tive·ly** *adv*—**ob·struc·tive·ness** *n*

ob·struc·tive sleep ap·ne·a *n* cessation or restriction of breathing during sleep that results in loud snoring

ob·stru·ent /óbstroo ənt/ *adj* **1.** MED OBSTRUCTING BODY PASSAGE obstructing or closing a passage in the body such as the intestinal tract **2.** PHON PRODUCED BY CUTOFF OF AIR describes a speech sound produced by a stoppage of air from the lungs ■ *n* **1.** MED OBSTRUCTION something that obstructs or closes a passage in the body **2.** PHON SOUND PRODUCED BY CUTOFF OF AIR a speech sound produced by a stoppage of air from the lungs [Mid-17C. < Latin *obstruent-*, present participle of *obstruere* (see OBSTRUCT)]

ob·tain /əb táyn, ob-/ (**-tained, -tain·ing, -tains**) *v* **1.** *vt* GET SOMETHING to get possession of something, especially by making an effort or having the necessary qualifications **2.** *vi* BE ESTABLISHED to be established, valid, or current ○ *under the regulations that obtained at the time* **3.** *vi* RESULT to follow as a result (*formal*) ○ *the unfortunate situation that obtains when such diverse characters are forced together* [15C. Via Old French *obtenir* < Latin *obtinere* "hold to" < *tenere* "to hold"] —**ob·tain·er** *n* —**ob·tain·ment** *n*

SYNONYMS See ***get***[1].

ob·tain·a·ble /əb táynəb'l, ob-/ *adj* able to be obtained or reached —**ob·tain·a·bil·i·ty** /əb tàynə bíllətee, ob-/ *n*

ob·trude /ob tróod/ (**-trud·ed, -trud·ing, -trudes**) *v* **1.** *vti* IMPOSE to impose something such as opinions or yourself on other people **2.** *vt* MAKE SOMETHING STICK OUT to push something out or forward **3.** *vi* APPEAR UNWELCOME to appear or be present in a way that is unwelcome but cannot be ignored ○ *"Not a leaf stirred; not a sound obtruded upon great Nature's meditation."* (Mark Twain, *The Adventures of Tom Sawyer*; 1875) [Mid-16C. < Latin *obtrudere* "thrust against" < *trudere* "to thrust"] —**ob·trud·er** *n* —**ob·tru·sion** /-tróozh'n/ *n*

ob·tru·sive /ob tróossiv/ *adj* **1.** ANNOYING tending to intrude or force opinions on other people ○ *plagued by an obtrusive photographer* **2.** HIGHLY NOTICEABLE highly noticeable, often with a bad or unwelcome effect **3.** STICKING OUT projecting or sticking out [Mid-17C. < Latin *obtrusus*, past participle of *obtrudere* (see OBTRUDE)] —**ob·tru·sive·ly** *adv* —**ob·tru·sive·ness** *n*

ob·tund /ob túnd/ (**-tund·ed, -tund·ing, -tunds**) *vt* to blunt, dull, or deaden something (*dated*) [14C. < Latin *obtundere* "strike against" < *tundere* "to strike"] —**ob·tund·ent** *adj*

ob·tuse /əb tóoss, ob-/ *adj* **1.** SLOW TO UNDERSTAND slow to understand or perceive something **2.** MATH BETWEEN 90° AND 180° describes an angle greater than 90° and less than 180° **3.** MATH WITH INTERNAL ANGLE GREATER THAN 90° describes a triangle with one internal angle greater than 90° **4.** BLUNT not sharp or pointed **5.** BOT WITH ROUNDED OR BLUNT TIP describes a leaf that has a rounded or blunt tip [Early 16C. < Latin *obtusus* "blunted," past participle of *obtundere* (see OBTUND)] —**ob·tuse·ly** *adv* —**ob·tuse·ness** *n*

OBTW *abbr* oh, by the way (*used in e-mails or text messages*)

ob·verse *n* /ób vùrss, ob vúrss, əb-/ **1.** MAIN SIDE OF COIN OR MEDAL the side of a coin or medal that has the more important design on it, especially a head **2.** COUNTERPART a counterpart, complement, or opposite **3.** LOGIC EQUIVALENT CATEGORICAL PROPOSITION a proposition derived from another proposition by denying it and then negating the predicate. The obverse of "Everything is possible" is "Nothing is impossible." ■ *adj* /ob vúrs, əb-, ób vùrs/ **1.** VISIBLE facing an observer **2.** BEING COUNTERPART forming a counterpart to something else **3.** BOT NARROWER AT BASE describes a leaf that is narrower at the base than the tip [Mid-17C. < Latin *obversus*, past participle of *obvertere* (see OBVERT)]

ob·ver·sion /ob vúrzh'n, əb-/ *n* **1.** the process of turning something so that the other side is seen **2.** LOGIC the process of forming the obverse of a proposition

ob·vert /ob vúrt/ (**-vert·ed, -vert·ing, -verts**) *vt* **1.** to turn something such as a coin or medal so that the other side is seen **2.** LOGIC to convert a proposition to its obverse [Early 17C. < Latin *obvertere* "turn toward" < *vertere* "to turn"]

ob·vi·ate /óbvee àyt/ (**-at·ed, -at·ing, -ates**) *vt* **1.** to make something unnecessary (*formal*) **2.** to anticipate and so avoid something [Late 16C. < Latin *obviat-*, past participle of *obviare* "withstand," literally "stand in the way of" < *via* "way"] —**ob·vi·a·tion** /òbvee áysh'n/ *n*

USAGE obviate the need for: Because one of the meanings of ***obviate*** is "to make unnecessary," it is sometimes argued that *obviate the need* (or *necessity*) *for* is redundant. An older but still current meaning, however, is "to avoid an anticipated difficulty." In a sentence like *Addressing these issues early can obviate any need for a joint resolution*, the need can be perceived as a difficulty — or early consideration can make the resolution unnecessary, in which case *any need for* is indeed redundant. There is little reason to prefer either interpretation to the other, except that substitution of *to make unnecessary* allows much the same thought to be expressed with fewer words.

ob·vi·ous /óbvee əss/ *adj* **1.** easy to see or understand because not concealed, difficult, or ambiguous **2.** lacking subtlety or any attempt at concealment [Late

16C. < Latin *obvius* "in the way" < *via* "way"] —**ob·vi·ous·ness** *n*

ob·vi·ous·ly /óbvee əsslee/ *adv* **1.** in a way or to an extent that is obvious **2.** used to suggest that there can be no doubt or uncertainty about something ○ *They want you to do it, obviously.*

ob·vo·lute /óbvə lo͞ot/ *adj* describes leaves or petals that are folded so as to overlap each other [Mid-18C. < Latin *obvolutus*, past participle of *obvolvere* "wrap around" < *volvere* "to roll"] —**ob·vo·lu·tion** /òbvə lo͞osh'n/ *n* —**ob·vo·lu·tive** /óbvə lo͞otiv/ *adj*

Oc., **oc.** *abbr* GEOG Ocean

o.c. *abbr* in the work cited [Latin *opere citato*]

O.C. *abbr* **1.** MIL Officer Commanding **2.** Officer of the Order of Canada **3.** STAMPS original cover

o/c *abbr* **1.** overcharge **2.** PSYCHOL obsessive-compulsive

o·ca /ṓkə/ *n* **1.** an edible tuber with firm white flesh **2.** a bushy plant whose edible tubers are oca. Native to: the Andes Mountains of South America. Latin name: *Oxalis tuberosa*. [Early 17C. Via Spanish < Quechua *ócca*]

O·cal·a /ō kállə/ city and administrative seat of Marion County, northern Florida, situated 35 mi./56 km south of Gainesville. Population: 46,931 (2002 estimate).

O Can·a·da *n* the national anthem of Canada

oc·a·ri·na /òkə reénə/ *n* a simple wind instrument related to the flute that has an oval body, finger holes, and a protruding mouthpiece [Late 19C. < Italian, "little goose" (< its shape) < *oca* "goose" < Latin *avis* "bird"]

OCAS *abbr US* POL Organization of Central American States

~~ocasionally~~ incorrect spelling of **occasionally**

occ. *abbr* **1.** GEOG occident **2.** occupation

Oc·cam's ra·zor *n* PHILOSOPHY, SCI another spelling of **Ockham's razor**

occas. *abbr* **1.** occasional **2.** occasionally

oc·ca·sion /ə káyzh'n/ *n* **1.** PARTICULAR TIME a particular time, especially a time when something happens **2.** CHANCE OR OPPORTUNITY a chance or opportunity to do something ○ *You might never have another occasion to do it.* **3.** CAUSE OR REASON a cause of or reason for something ○ *He has no occasion to criticize me.* **4.** NEED the need for something or to do something ○ *has never had occasion to use it* **5.** IMPORTANT EVENT an important or special event ■ *vt* (**-sioned, -sion·ing, -sions**) BRING SOMETHING ABOUT to cause or lead to something [14C. Via Old French < Latin *occasion-* "falling down, happening" < *cadere* "to fall"] ◇ **on occasion** from time to time

oc·ca·sion·al /ə káyzhən'l, -káyzhnəl/ *adj* **1.** INFREQUENT occurring infrequently at irregular intervals **2.** RELATING TO SPECIAL EVENT done for or connected with a special event ○ *occasional verse* **3.** DESIGNED FOR USE FROM TIME TO TIME intended for use as needed, but not essential or in constant use ○ *an occasional table* **4.** CAUSING serving as the cause of something (*formal*)

SYNONYMS See ***periodic***.

oc·ca·sion·al·ly /ə káyzhən'lee, ə káyzhnəlee/ *adv* from time to time, but not regularly or frequently

oc·ci·dent /óksidənt, -dènt/ *n* the western part of the sky, where the sun sets (*formal*) [14C. Via French < Latin *occident-*, present participle of *occidere* "fall down, set (of the sun)" < *cadere* "to fall"]

Oc·ci·dent *n* the western hemisphere, especially the countries in Europe and America (*dated formal*)

oc·ci·den·tal /òksi dént'l/ *adj* western (*formal*)

Oc·ci·den·tal (*dated formal*) *adj* relating to a country of the Occident, or its people or culture ■ *n* somebody who comes from the West

oc·ci·den·tal·ize /òksi dént'l ìz/ (**-ized, -iz·ing, -iz·es**), **Oc·ci·den·tal·ize** *vt* to make somebody or something conform to the culture of the West (*dated formal*)

oc·cip·i·ta ANAT plural of **occiput**

oc·cip·i·tal /ok síppət'l/ *adj* relating to or located at the back of the head or skull ■ *n* ANAT same as **occipital bone** [Mid-16C. < medieval Latin *occipitalis* < Latin *occiput* (see OCCIPUT)] —**oc·cip·i·tal·ly** *adv*

oc·cip·i·tal bone *n* the saucer-shaped bone at the rear of the skull that connects with the spinal column and has an opening at its base through which the spinal cord passes

oc·cip·i·tal lobe *n* the pyramid-shaped area at the back of each hemisphere of the brain that deals with the interpretation of vision

oc·ci·put /óksi pùt/ (*plural* **-ci·puts** or **-cip·i·ta** /-síppətə/) *n* the back part of the head or skull [14C. < Latin, "back of the head" < *caput* "head"]

oc·clude /ə klo͞od/ (**-clud·ed, -clud·ing, -cludes**) *v* **1.** *vt* STOP UP SOMETHING to block or stop up something such as a passage **2.** *vt* CUT OFF FLOW OF SOMETHING to cut off or prevent the flow or passage of something such as light or liquid **3.** *vti* DENT ALIGN TEETH PROPERLY to be in normal contact with another tooth when the mouth is closed, or align the upper and lower teeth for chewing or normal contact **4.** *vt* CHEM ABSORB OR ADSORB LIQUID to absorb or adsorb a liquid or gas on the surface of or within a solid **5.** *vti* METEOROL FORM OCCLUDED FRONT to form an occluded front, or undercut a mass of warm air so that it is no longer in contact with the Earth's surface [Late 16C. < Latin *occludere* "close up" < *claudere* "to close"]

oc·clud·ed front *n* a composite front formed when a cold air mass meets and undercuts a warm air mass, and forces the warm air upward and away from contact with the Earth's surface

oc·clu·sal /ə klo͞oss'l/ *adj* relating to the biting surface of a molar or premolar tooth

oc·clu·sion /ə klo͞ozh'n/ *n* **1.** ACT OF OCCLUDING an act of occluding or the condition of being occluded **2.** OBSTRUCTION something that obstructs or occludes **3.** METEOROL same as **occluded front** **4.** DENT MEETING OF UPPER AND LOWER TEETH the relation between the upper and lower teeth when the jaw is closed and their surfaces come in contact **5.** LING CLOSURE OF HOLLOW ORGAN the closure of a hollow organ such as the vocal tract in articulating a speech sound **6.** CHEM ABSORPTION OR ADSORPTION OF LIQUID the absorption or adsorption of a liquid or gas on or in a solid [Mid-17C. < Latin *occlus-*, past participle of *occludere* (see OCCLUDE)]

oc·clu·sive /ə klo͞ossiv/ *adj* relating to, involving, or producing an occlusion ■ *n* a speech sound that involves a closure of the vocal tract

oc·cult /ə kúlt/ *adj* **1.** SUPERNATURAL OR MAGIC relating to, involving, or characteristic of magic, witchcraft, or supernatural phenomena **2.** NOT UNDERSTANDABLE not capable of being understood by ordinary human beings **3.** SECRET secret or known only to the initiated **4.** MED HIDDEN describes a diseased condition that is hidden or difficult to detect **5.** MED DIFFICULT TO SEE not visible to the naked eye, and only detectable by microscope or chemical testing ■ *n* THE SUPERNATURAL the realm of magic, witchcraft, or supernatural phenomena ■ *vti* (**-cult·ed, -cult·ing, -cults**) **1.** ASTRON TEMPORARILY HIDE ASTRONOMICAL OBJECT to hide an astronomical object temporarily by moving between it and an observer, or be hidden in this way **2.** HIDE SOMETHING OR BE HIDDEN to hide something from view or be hidden from view [Early 16C. < Latin *occultus*, past participle of *occulere* "conceal"] —**oc·cul·ta·tion** /ò kul táysh'n/ *n* —**oc·cult·ly** *adv* —**oc·cult·ness** *n*

oc·cult·ism /ə kúl tìzzəm/ *n* the belief in and study of magic, witchcraft, or supernatural phenomena —**oc·cult·ist** *n*

oc·cu·pan·cy /ókyəpənsee/ (*plural* **-cies**) *n* **1.** ACT OF OCCUPYING the act or state of occupying something such as a building or an official position **2.** LEVEL OF OCCUPATION the rate or level of occupation of a place ○ *an apartment building with high occupancy* **3.** DWELLING PLACE a building or part of a building where people can live **4.** TIME OF OCCUPYING the period of time during which somebody occupies something such as a building or an official position **5.** LAW POSSESSION OF UNOWNED PROPERTY the act of taking possession of property, especially land, that has no owner, with the intention of becoming its owner **6.** LAW LEGAL PREEMPTION the presence of a higher level of government in an area of law that preempts the law of the lower level ○ *The federal government's occupancy of immigration law precludes state action.*

oc·cu·pant /ókyəpənt/ *n* **1.** a resident of a place or holder of a position **2.** somebody who takes possession of unclaimed property, especially land, with the intention of becoming its owner

oc·cu·pa·tion /òkyə páysh'n/ *n* **1.** JOB the job by which somebody earns a living **2.** ACTIVITY an activity on which time is spent **3.** ACT OF OCCUPYING an act of occupying or the state of being occupied **4.** MIL INVASION the invasion and control of a country or area by enemy forces **5.** TIME OF OCCUPYING the period of time during which something is occupied

oc·cu·pa·tion·al /òkyə páyshən'l, -páyshnəl/ *adj* relating to or caused by somebody's job —**oc·cu·pa·tion·al·ly** *adv*

oc·cu·pa·tion·al dis·ease *n* a disease that is directly caused by the conditions of somebody's work

oc·cu·pa·tion·al haz·ard *n* a risk associated with the work that somebody does

oc·cu·pa·tion·al med·i·cine *n* the branch of medicine that deals with work-related diseases and injuries incurred at work

oc·cu·pa·tion·al ther·a·py *n* the use of regular periods of suitable productive activity as part of the treatment of illness or medical condition —**oc·cu·pa·tion·al ther·a·pist** *n*

oc·cu·py /ókyə pì/ (**-pied, -py·ing, -pies**) *vt* **1.** LIVE IN PLACE to live in or be the established user of a place such as a home or office **2.** ENGAGE SOMEBODY'S ATTENTION to take up somebody's time or attention (*often passive*) ○ *something to occupy his leisure hours* **3.** FILL SPACE OR TIME to take up a space or an amount of time (*often passive*) ○ *His rambling speech occupied a good part of the hour.* **4.** MIL TAKE OVER PLACE to invade and take control of a country, area, or building **5.** HOLD POSITION to hold a position or rank [14C. Via Old French *occuper* < Latin *occupare* "take over" < *capere* "to take"] —**oc·cu·pi·er** *n*

oc·cur /ə kúr/ (**-curred, -cur·ring, -curs**) *vi* **1.** HAPPEN to happen or come about **2.** EXIST to exist or be present **3.** ENTER MIND to come into somebody's mind ○ *It didn't occur to him to lock the door.* [Early 16C. < Latin *occurrere* "run against" < *currere* "to run"]

~~occurance~~ incorrect spelling of **occurrence**

~~occured~~ incorrect spelling of **occurred**

oc·cur·rence /ə kúr rənss/ *n* **1.** something that happens **2.** the fact or act of something happening —**oc·cur·rent** *adj*

OCD *abbr* PSYCHIAT obsessive-compulsive disorder

WORLD'S LARGEST OCEANS AND SEAS

1	Pacific Ocean	Area [64 million sq. mi./165.7 million sq. km]
2	Atlantic Ocean	Area [31.8 million sq. mi./82 million sq. km]
3	Indian Ocean	Area [28.3 million sq. mi./73.4 million sq. km]
4	Arctic Ocean	Area [5.4 million sq. mi./14 million sq. km]
5	Gulf of Mexico and Caribbean Sea	Area [1.6 million sq. mi./4.2 million sq. km]
6	Mediterranean Sea	Area [0.97 million sq. mi./2.5 million sq. km]
7	Bering Sea	Area [0.87 million sq. mi./2.26 million sq. km]
8	Sea of Okhotsk	Area [0.59 million sq. mi./1.53 million sq. km]
9	Hudson Bay	Area [0.48 million sq. mi./1.2 million sq. km]
10	Sea of Japan	Area [0.39 million sq. mi./1 million sq. km]

o·cean /ṓsh'n/ *n* **1. LARGE SEA** a large expanse of salt water, especially any of the Earth's five main such areas, the Atlantic, Pacific, Indian, Arctic, and Antarctic oceans. The oceans occupy huge regions of the Earth's surface, and their boundaries are usually established by continental land masses and ridges in the ocean floor. See table on previous page **2. EARTH'S SEAS TOGETHER** the whole body of salt water on the Earth **3. LARGE AMOUNT** a vast amount or expanse of something [13C. Via French and Latin < Greek *ōkeanos*, the river surrounding the disk of the Earth]

o·cean·ar·i·um /ṑshə nérree əm/ (*plural* **-i·ums** or **-i·a** /-ee ə/) *n* a large saltwater aquarium for observing and exhibiting sea animals and plants [Mid-20C. Blend of OCEAN + AQUARIUM]

o·cea·naut /ṓshə nàwt/ *n* an underwater swimmer in an ocean who uses an underwater breathing device [Mid-20C. Blend of OCEAN + AQUANAUT]

O·cean Cit·y /ṓsh'n-/ **1.** town and resort in Worcester County, southeastern Maryland, situated on a barrier island. Population: 7,182 (2002 estimate). **2.** city in Cape May County, southern New Jersey, situated on the Atlantic Ocean 10 mi./16 km southwest of Atlantic City. Population: 15,516 (2002 estimate).

o·cean·front /ṓsh'n frùnt/ *n* **1.** land next to the ocean (*often used before a noun*) ○ *oceanfront property* **2.** the point at which two oceanic water masses of different thermal characteristics meet

o·cean·go·ing /ṓsh'n gṑ ing/ *adj* built, equipped, or used for travel on the ocean

o·cean grey·hound *n* a fast ocean liner

O·ce·an·i·a /ṑshee ánnee ə/ geographic region consisting of most of the smaller islands of the western and central Pacific Ocean, sometimes also including Australia and New Zealand —**O·ce·an·i·an** *n, adj*

o·ce·an·ic /ṑshee ánnik/ *adj* **1. IN OR FROM OCEAN** living, situated in, produced by, or taking place in an ocean, especially the depths of the open sea **2. VOLCANIC** resulting from volcanic activity in the ocean ○ *an oceanic island* **3. IMMENSE** immense, vast, or overwhelming [Mid-17C. < OCEAN]

O·ce·an·ic *n* an Austronesian group of languages spoken mainly on the Pacific islands lying to the north and east of Australia. Native speakers: 2 million. ■ *adj* relating to the countries of Oceania [Mid-19C. < OCEANIA]

o·ce·an·ic ridge *n* any section of a range of underwater mountains, found in all major oceans

o·ce·an·ic trench *n* a long narrow deep furrow in the Earth's crust at the bottom of an ocean

O·cean Is·land former name for **Banaba**

o·cean lin·er *n* an oceangoing passenger ship run by a shipping line

o·cean·og·ra·phy /ṑshə nóggrəfee/ *n* the scientific study of oceans, including their chemistry, biology, and geology —**o·cean·og·ra·pher** *n* —**o·cean·o·graph·ic** /ṑsh'nə gráffik/ *adj* —**o·cean·o·graph·i·cal·ly** *adv*

o·cean·ol·o·gy /ṑshə nólləjee/ *n* the branch of oceanography that studies how oceans may be used for economic or technological purposes —**o·cean·o·log·i·cal** /ṑsh'nə lójjik'l/ *adj* —**o·cean·o·log·i·cal·ly** *adv*

o·cean perch *n* FISH same as **rosefish** (sense 1)

o·cean rac·er *n* an oceangoing sailboat suitable for racing

O·cean·side /ṓsh'n sīd/ **1.** city in San Diego County, southwestern California, situated 45 mi./72 km north of San Diego. Population: 165,880 (2002 estimate). **2.** city in Nassau County, New York, situated on Long Island. Population: 32,423 (1996).

O·cean State *n* a nickname for Rhode Island

o·cean sun·fish *n US* a large brown and gray sunfish that frequently lies on the surface of the water. Native to: temperate or tropical waters. Family: Molidae. Can term **sunfish**

ocean tramp *n* NAUT same as **tramp steamer**

O·ce·a·nus Pro·cel·lar·um /ṑssee áanəss pròssə láarəm/ vast lunar lowland plain stretching between Mare Imbrium and Mare Humorum, visible as a dark area in the northwestern quadrant of the Moon. Area: over 775,000 sq. mi./2,000,000 sq. km.

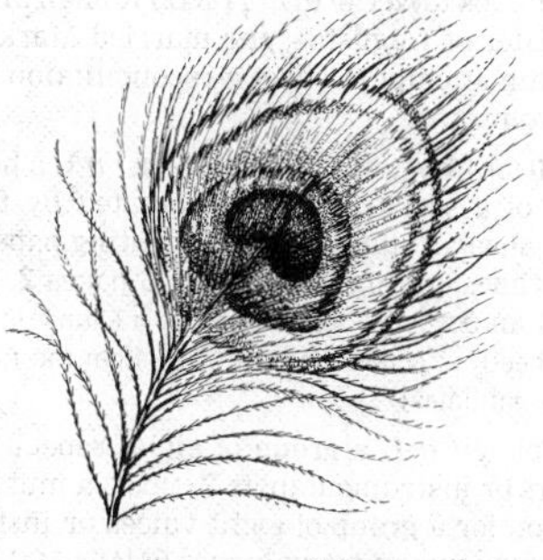

ocellus: peacock feather

o·cel·lus /ō sélləss/ (*plural* **-li** /-lī/) *n* **1.** INSECTS **SIMPLE EYE IN INVERTEBRATES** a simple eye in some insects and other invertebrates that is sensitive to light but unable to focus clearly **2.** BIRDS **EYE-SHAPED SPOT ON FEATHERS** an eye-shaped spot on the feathers of some birds such as peacocks **3.** BOT **EYE-SHAPED SPOT ON LEAF** an enlarged discolored eye-shaped spot on a leaf **4.** FISH **EYE-SHAPED SPOT ON FISH** an eye-shaped spot on a fish, usually dark-ringed with a lighter color inside, believed to deceive predators [Early 19C. < Latin, "small eye" < *oculus* "eye"]

ocelot

oc·e·lot /óssə lòt, ṓss-/ (*plural* **-lots** or *same*) *n* a small wildcat with dark spots on a light brownish coat. Native to: southern United States, Central and South America. Latin name: *Felis pardalis*. [Late 18C. Via French < Nahuatl *tlatlocelotl* "field jaguar"]

o·cher /ṓkər/, **o·chre** *n* **1.** a reddish or yellowish earthy iron oxide. Use: pigment. **2.** a brownish yellow color [14C. Via French < Latin *ochra* < Greek *ōkhros* "pale, yellow"] —**o·cher** *adj* —**o·cher·ous** *adj* —**o·cher·y** *adj*

och·loc·ra·cy /ok lókrəssee/ (*plural* **-cies**) *n* same as **mobocracy** (sense 1) [Late 16C. Via French *ochlocratie* < Greek *okhlokratia* < *okhlos* "mob"] —**och·lo·crat** /óklə kràt/ *n* —**och·lo·crat·ic** /òklə kráttik/ *adj* —**och·lo·crat·i·cal·ly** *adv*

O·cho·a /ō chṓ ə, ō kṓ ə/, **Severo** (1905–93) Spanish-born US biochemist. He shared a Nobel Prize in physiology or medicine (1959) with Arthur Kornberg for his work on synthesizing nucleic acids.

o·chre *n, adj* GEOL, COLORS another spelling of **ocher**

-ock *suffix* something small or worthless ○ *hillock* [Old English *-oc, -uc*]

Ock·ham /ókəm/, **William of** (1285?–1349) English philosopher. He revived nominalism and enunciated the principle known as Ockham's razor.

> "Entities should not be multiplied unnecessarily. / No more things should be presumed to exist than are absolutely necessary."
> [William of Ockham, *Quodlibeta Septem*; 1320?]

Ock·ham's ra·zor, **Occ·am's ra·zor** *n* the philosophical and scientific rule that simple explanations should be preferred to more complicated ones, and that the explanation of a new phenomenon should be based on what is already known

o'clock /ə klók/ *adv* **1.** in telling the time, used to indicate an exact hour of the day or night, rather than some minutes past or before the hour ○ *woke up at six o'clock in the morning* **2.** in describing a position or direction of something, comparing it to the positions of numbers on a clock face, with the observer at the center of the clock ○ *Look at the man sitting to your right, at three o'clock.* [15C. Contraction of *of the clock*]

Oc·mul·gee /ōk múl gee/ river in Georgia, United States, flowing south and joining the Oconee River to form the Altamaha River. Length: 255 mi./410 km.

AKG London

Daniel O'Connell

O'Con·nell /ō kónn'l/, **Daniel** (1775–1847) Irish politician. A Roman Catholic, he succeeded in obtaining Catholic emancipation, becoming a Member of Parliament at Westminster (1829). He agitated for repeal of the union of Ireland and Great Britain, and became Lord Mayor of Dublin (1841).

O'Con·nor /ō kónnər/, **Flannery** (1925–64) US writer. She is known for her Southern Gothic novels such as *Wise Blood* (1952). Full name **O'Connor, Mary Flannery**

> "I preach there are all kinds of truth, your truth and somebody else's. But behind all of them there is only one truth and that is that there's no truth."
> [Flannery O'Connor, *Wise Blood*; 1952]

O'Con·nor, Sandra Day (*b.* 1930) associate justice of the US Supreme Court (1981–). She was the first woman to be appointed an associate justice on the US Supreme Court.

> "The more education a woman has, the wider the gap between men's and women's earnings for the same work."
> [Sandra Day O'Connor, *Phoenix Magazine*; 1971]

o·co·til·lo /ṑkə teéyō/ (*plural* **-los** or *same*) *n* a spiny bush with red flowers at the tip of each branch. Native to: dry parts of southwestern United States, Mexico. Latin name: *Fouquieria splendens*. [Mid-19C. < American Spanish < *ocote* "Mexican pine tree" < Nahuatl *ocotl* "torch"]

OCR *abbr* COMPUT **1.** optical character reader **2.** optical character recognition

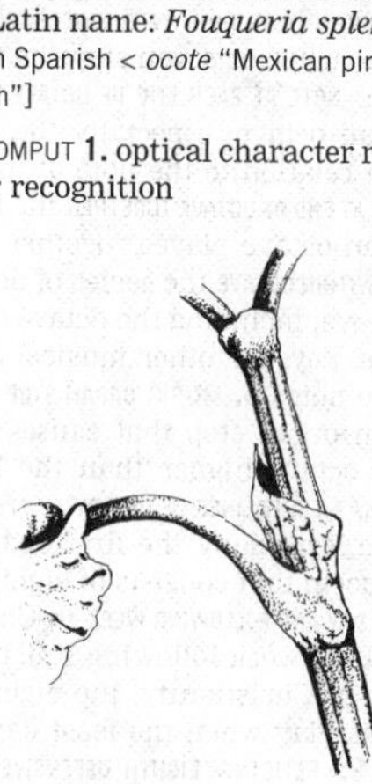

ocrea

oc·re·a /ókree ə/ (*plural* **-re·ae** /-ree ee/) *n* a cup-shaped sheath formed by appendages at the base of a leaf, as in rhubarb [Mid-19C. < Latin, "soldier's leg-armor"]

OCS *abbr* MIL Officer Candidate School

oct. *abbr* PRINTING octavo

Oct. *abbr* CALENDAR October

oct- *prefix* same as **octo-** (*used before vowels*)

octa- *prefix* same as **octo-**

oc·tad /ók tàd/ *n* a group or series of eight [Mid-19C. < Greek *oktad-* < *oktō* (see OCTO-)] —**oc·tad·ic** /ok táddik/ *adj*

oc·ta·gon /óktə gòn/ *n* a two-dimensional geometric figure formed of eight sides and eight angles [Late 16C. Via Latin < Greek *oktagōnon* < *oktagōnos* "eight-angled" < *okto* "eight" + < *gōnia* "angle"] —**oc·tag·o·nal** /ok tággən'l/ *adj*

oc·ta·he·dron /òktə heédrən/ (*plural* **-drons** or **-dra** /-drə/) *n* a three-dimensional geometric figure formed of eight faces —**oc·ta·he·dral** *adj*

oc·tal /ókt'l/ *adj* using or having a number system based on eight instead of ten ■ *n* **1.** COMPUT same as **octal notation** **2.** a number with eight as its base

oc·tal no·ta·tion *n* a number system used in writing computer programs that is based on eight and uses numerals 0 through 7, one octal unit equaling three bits

oc·tam·e·ter /ok támmətər/ *n* a line of verse consisting of eight metrical units or feet

oc·tane /ók tàyn/ *n* **1.** a liquid hydrocarbon found in petroleum that exists in 18 structurally different forms. Formula: C_8H_{18}. **2.** AUTOMOT same as **octane number** [Late 19C. < OCTO-; from the number of carbon atoms in the hydrocarbon]

oc·tane num·ber, **oc·tane rat·ing** *n* a number that measures the ability of a liquid motor fuel such as gasoline to prevent preignition or knocking. Fuels with higher numbers are less likely to cause knocking.

oc·ta·nol /óktə nàwl/ *n* a colorless oily aromatic liquid hydrocarbon. Use: solvent, in perfumes, in organic synthesis. Formula: $C_8H_{17}OH$.

Oc·tans /ók tànz/ *n* a faint constellation of the southern hemisphere incorporating the south celestial pole. See illustration at **constellation**

oc·tant /óktənt/ *n* **1.** ASTRON **EIGHTH OF ASTRONOMICAL CIRCLE** the position of one body in the sky one-eighth of a circle (45°) from another **2.** MATH **EIGHTH OF CIRCLE** one-eighth of a circle, with or without the enclosed area **3.** MATH **REGION OF SPACE IN CARTESIAN SYSTEM** any one of the eight regions into which space is divided by the three planes of the Cartesian coordinate system [Late 17C. < Latin *octant-* "half-quadrant" < *octo* (see OCTO-)] —**oc·tan·tal** /ok tánt'l/ *adj*

oc·ta·pep·tide /òktə pép tīd/ *n* a peptide consisting of eight amino acids

oc·ta·va·lent /òktə váylənt/ *adj* describes an element, atom, or group that has a valence of eight

oc·tave /óktiv, ók tàyv/ *n* **1.** MUSIC **INTERVAL ON MUSICAL SCALE** an interval between two notes consisting of eight notes inclusive or seven steps on the diatonic scale **2.** MUSIC **NOTE AT EACH END OF OCTAVE** the note at each end of an octave, especially the higher one, considered in relation to the note at the other end **3.** MUSIC **NOTES AT END OF OCTAVE TOGETHER** the two notes at each end of an octave played together **4.** MUSIC **ALL NOTES INCLUDED WITHIN OCTAVE** the series of notes that fall within an octave, including the octave on each end, or the strings, keys, or other musical devices that produce these notes **5.** MUSIC **ORGAN STOP FOR PRODUCING HIGHER NOTES** an organ stop that causes tones to be produced an octave higher than the keys played alone **6.** LITERAT **EIGHT LINES OF POETRY** a group of eight lines of verse, especially the first eight lines of a sonnet, or a poem that consists of eight lines **7.** CHR **CHRISTIAN FEAST DAY AND FOLLOWING WEEK** in Christianity, a feast day and the week following it **8.** CHR **EIGHTH DAY AFTER FEAST DAY** in Christianity, the eighth day after an octave feast day when the feast day is counted as day one **9.** FENCING **EIGHTH DEFENSIVE POSITION** the eighth of eight basic defensive positions in fencing, known as a rotating perry **10.** **EIGHTH ITEM** the eighth in a series **11.** **SET OF EIGHT** a set or series of eight [14C. Via French < Latin *octava*, form of *octavus* "eighth" < *octo* "eight"]

oc·tave cou·pler *n* a mechanism on an organ or harpsichord that allows somebody simultaneously to play one note and another one an octave higher or lower

Oc·ta·vi·a /ok táyvee ə/ (69?–11 B.C.) Roman aristocrat. The sister of Augustus, she married Mark Antony in a vain attempt to effect a reconciliation between the two men.

oc·ta·vo /ok táyvō, -taávō/ (*plural* **-vos**) *n* **1.** a book with pages of a size traditionally created by folding a single sheet of standard-sized printing paper in half three times, giving 8 leaves or 16 pages **2.** the page size of an octavo book [Late 16C. < Latin, "in an eighth (of a sheet)" < *octavus* (see OCTAVE); from the folding of a sheet eight times]

oc·tet /ok tét/ *n* **1.** a group of eight, especially eight singers or instrumentalists **2.** MUSIC a musical composition for a group of eight voices or instruments **3.** LITERAT same as **octave** (sense 6) [Mid-19C. Alteration of Italian *otteto* (< Latin *octo* "eight")]

oc·tet rule *n* CHEM same as **Lewis rule of eight**

octo- *prefix* eight ○ *octosyllable* [Directly or via Latin < Greek *oktō*]

Oc·to·ber /ok tṓbər/ *n* in the Gregorian calendar, the tenth month of the year, lasting 31 days. See table at **calendar** [Pre-12C. < Latin, "eighth month" < *octo* "eight"]

oc·to·dec·i·mo /òktō déssəmō/ (*plural* **-mos**) *n* a book size of about 4 by 4¼ in./10 by 16 cm, or a book of this size [Mid-19C. < Latin, "in an eighteenth (of a sheet)" < *octodecim* "eight and ten"; from the folding of a sheet 18 times]

oc·to·ge·nar·i·an /òktə jə nérree ən/ *n* somebody between 80 and 89 years of age [Early 19C. < Latin *octogenarius* < *octoginta* "eighty," literally "eight times ten"]

oc·to·nar·y /óktə nèrree/ *adj* **1.** **BASED ON EIGHT** based on the number eight **2.** **MADE UP OF EIGHT** consisting of eight things ■ *n* (*plural* **-ies**) **1.** **GROUP OF EIGHT** a group or set of eight things **2.** COMPUT same as **octal** *n* (sense 2) [Mid-16C. < Latin *octonarius* "containing eight" < *octo* (see OCTO-)]

oc·to·pi BIOL plural of **octopus**

oc·to·ploid /óktə plòyd/ *n* a cell nucleus or an organism, especially a plant, containing eight haploid sets of chromosomes

oc·to·pod /óktə pòd/ *n* a mollusk that has no shell and a large head and eyes and eight tentacles, e.g., the octopus. Order: Octopoda. [Early 20C. < modern Latin *Octopoda* < Greek *oktōpod-*, stem of *oktōpous* (see OCTOPUS)] —**oc·to·pod·ous** /ok tóppədəss/ *adj*

oc·to·pus /óktəpəss/ (*plural* **-pus·es** or **-pi** /-pī/ or *same*) *n* **1.** a sea animal with a big head, a soft oval body, well-developed eyes, and eight arms containing rows of suckers. It usually lives on the ocean floor. Genus: *Octopus*. **2.** something, especially an organization, that has many branches and forms of influence or control [Mid-18C. < modern Latin < Greek *oktōpous* "eight feet" < *oktō* "eight" + *pous* "foot"]

oc·to·pus bite *n regional* same as **monkey bite** [Because the marks supposedly resemble those left by the suckers of an octopus]

REGIONAL NOTE See ***monkey bite***.

oc·to·roon /òktə rōōn/ *n* an offensive term for somebody who has one Black great-grandparent and no other Black ancestors (*archaic*) [Mid-19C. < OCTO- after QUADROON]

oc·to·syl·la·ble /òktə sílləb'l/ *n* a language unit of eight syllables, usually a complete line of verse but occasionally just a word —**oc·to·syl·lab·ic** /-si lábbik/ *adj*

oc·tu·ple /ók tōōp'l, ok tōōp'l, óktəp'l/ *adj* **1.** **EIGHT TIMES AS LARGE** eight times as large or effective **2.** **WITH EIGHT PARTS** consisting of eight parts ■ *vti* (**-pled, -pling, -ples**) **MULTIPLY BY EIGHT** to multiply something by eight, or be multiplied by eight ■ *n* **QUANTITY EIGHT TIMES GREATER** an amount that is eight times more than another amount

ocul- *prefix* same as **oculo-** (*used before vowels*)

oc·u·lar /ókyələr/ *adj* relating to, perceived by, or performed by the eye ■ *n* an eyepiece in an optical instrument [Late 16C. Via French *oculaire* < late Latin *ocularis* < Latin *oculus* "eye"]

ORIGIN The Indo-European word from which ***ocular*** is derived is also the ancestor of English *atrocious, eye, ferocious, inoculate, optic,* and *window.*

oc·u·list /ókyəlist/ *n* an optometrist or ophthalmologist (*dated*)

oculo- *prefix* eye ○ *oculomotor* [< Latin *oculus*]

oc·u·lo·gy·ric /òkyəlō jírik/ *adj* relating to the movement of an eyeball in its socket

oc·u·lo·mo·tor /òkyəlō mṓtər/ *adj* relating to or causing movement of the eyeball

oc·u·lo·mo·tor nerve *n* either of the third pair of cranial nerves that carry nerve fibers from the brain to the eye muscles and eyelids

~~**ocupation**~~ incorrect spelling of **occupation**

~~**ocurr**~~ incorrect spelling of **occur**

~~**ocurred**~~ incorrect spelling of **occurred**

~~**ocurrence**~~ incorrect spelling of **occurrence**

Od /od/ *interj* used euphemistically as an oath to mean "God" (*archaic*) [Late 16C. Alteration of GOD]

OD /ō deé/ (*slang*) *vi* (**OD'ed, OD'ing, ODs**) to take a dangerous amount of a drug, often causing hospitalization or death ■ *n* (*plural* **ODs**) an overdose of a drug [Mid-20C. Shortening of OVERDOSE]

o.d.[1] *abbr* **1.** MIL olive drab **2.** on demand **3.** MEASURE outside diameter

o.d.[2] *abbr* MED right eye [Latin *oculus dexter*]

O.D. *abbr* **1.** MED Doctor of Optometry **2.** MIL Officer of the Day **3.** MIL olive drab **4.** BANKING overdraft **5.** BANKING overdrawn

O/D, **o/d** *abbr* BANKING **1.** overdraft **2.** overdrawn

o·da·lisque /ṓd'l ìsk/, **o·da·lisk** *n* **1.** an enslaved woman or concubine, especially, formerly, in a Turkish harem **2.** a representation of an odalisque in art [Late 17C. Via French < Turkish *ōdalik* "somebody who works in a chamber" < *ōda* "chamber"]

O·da No·bu·na·ga /ṓdə nòbbyoo naágə/ (1534–82) Japanese feudal lord. He began the 16th-century reunification of Japan.

odd /od/ *adj* **1.** **UNUSUAL** peculiar or out of the ordinary ○ *There's something very odd about the letter.* **2.** **NOT DIVISIBLE EXACTLY BY 2** being a number that, when divided by 2, leaves a remainder of 1, e.g., 1, 3, 5, 7, 9, or 11 **3.** **LEFTOVER** leftover, and usually few in number ○ *a few odd coins* **4.** **SEPARATED FROM PAIR OR SET** left on its own without the other member or members of its pair, set, or series ○ *wearing odd socks* **5.** **IRREGULAR** irregular or occasional ○ *We get the odd day off here and there.* **6.** **SLIGHTLY GREATER THAN PARTICULAR NUMBER** used after a number to mean a little more than that particular number ○ *50-odd dollars* **7.** **REMOTE** not usually visited or reached by many people ○ *We found the papers lying about in odd corners of the house.* **8.** MATH **HAVING CHANGING MATHEMATICAL SIGNS** used to refer to a function that changes sign but not value when the sign of each independent variable is changed at the same time ■ *n* **SOMETHING ODD IN NUMBER** something that is odd in number or numerical order [14C. < Old Norse *oddi* "third or odd number"] —**odd·ish** *adj* —**odd·ly** *adv* —**odd·ness** *n*

odd·ball /ód bàwl/ *n* somebody regarded as unusual or unconventional, but usually in a harmless way (*informal insult*)

Odd Fel·low *n* a member of the Independent Order of Odd Fellows, a secret international social and charitable fraternity founded in England in the 18th century [< ODD "remote, out-of-the-way"; from the Order's mystic practices]

odd·i·ty /óddətee/ (*plural* **-ties**) *n* somebody or something unique, unusual, or unconventional

odd job *n* an unspecialized job, e.g., a household repair, usually done casually and for low pay (*often used in the plural*) ○ *does odd jobs for a living*

odd lot *n* a quantity or number of shares that is smaller than the usual trading unit, e.g., fewer than 100 shares when traded on a stock exchange, or less than one whole share when liquidated

odd man out *n* same as **odd one out**

odd·ment /ódmənt/ *n* **1.** **SOMETHING LEFT OVER** something left over when most of something has been used or disposed of (*usually used in the plural*) ○ *By the time she arrived there were only oddments left in the sale.* **2.** **ODDITY** an odd thing (*dated*) ■ **odd·ments** *npl* **ODDS**

and ends odds and ends (*dated*) [Late 18C. < ODD after FRAGMENT]

odd one out (*plural* **odd ones out**), **odd man out** (*plural* **odd men out**) *n* somebody in a group who differs from the rest of the group or is not treated as part of the group

odd-pin·nate *adj* describes a plant leaf such as that of the rose that is pinnate with a single leaflet at the top —**odd-pin·nate·ly** *adv*

odds /odz/ *npl* **1. CHANCES OF SOMETHING HAPPENING** the likelihood or probability that something will occur, sometimes expressed as a ratio such as 10 to 1 ○ *The odds are that you'll never make it.* **2. PREDICTED CHANCES IN BETTING** a ratio of probability given to people placing a bet, usually the likelihood of something happening, or of a competitor, team, or animal winning ○ *The horse was given odds of four to one.* **3. HANDICAP OR ADVANTAGE IN COMPETITION** an advantage or handicap given to a person, animal, or team in a sporting contest, to equalize the chances of winning **4. PERCEIVED ADVANTAGE OR DISADVANTAGE** a perceived advantage or disadvantage, especially one that one person is believed to have over another in a competition [Early 16C. Plural of ODD] ◇ **at odds (with somebody)** in disagreement with somebody, especially over a period of time or about a particular issue. ◇ **at odds (with something)** in conflict with something ◇ **over the odds** more than is usual or necessary ◇ **what's the odds?** *UK* used to indicate that something is of no importance

SYNONYMS See *disagree.*

odds and ends *npl* a group of miscellaneous items

odds·mak·er /ódz màykər/ *n* an official calculator of betting odds

odds-on *adj* likeliest to win, succeed, or happen (*informal*) ○ *It was odds-on that he would succeed his father.*

ode /ōd/ *n* **1.** a lyric poem, usually expressing exalted emotion in a complex scheme of rhyme and meter **2.** an ancient Greek song written either for a chorus or for a solo singer [Late 16C. Via French < Greek *ōidē* "song"] —**od·ic** *adj* —**od·ist** *n*

-ode *suffix* **1.** electrically conducting element ○ *electrode* **2.** electrode ○ *tetrode* [< Greek *hodos* "way"]

o·de·a ARCHIT, MUSIC plural of **odeum**

O·den·se /ṓd'nssə/ city and port in south central Denmark, on the island of Fyn. Population: 144,940 (1999).

o·de·on *n* ARCHIT same as **odeum**

O·der /ṓdər/ river in north central Europe. Its northern course forms part of Poland's border with Germany. Length: 563 mi./906 km.

O·des·sa /ō déssə/, **O·des·a** city and port in south central Ukraine, on the Black Sea. Population: 1,027,000 (1998).

O·dets /ō déts/, **Clifford** (1906–63) US playwright. He is best known for his social-protest play *Waiting for Lefty* (1935) and the boxing drama *Golden Boy* (1937).

> "Go out and fight so life shouldn't be printed on dollar bills."
> [Clifford Odets, *Awake and Sing!*, 1935]

o·de·um /ōdee əm/ (*plural* **o·de·a** /ōdee ə/), **o·de·on** /ṓdee ən/ (*plural* **o·de·a**) *n* an ancient Greek or Roman building in which musical performances were held [Early 17C. Directly or via French < Latin *odeum* < Greek *ōideion* < *ōidē* "song"]

O·din /ṓdin/ *n* in Scandinavian mythology, the god of war and the king of the gods who held court in Valhalla, the final resting place of famous warriors

o·di·ous /ṓdee əss/ *adj* inspiring hatred, contempt, or disgust [14C. Via French < Latin *odiosus* < *odium* "hatred, contempt"] —**o·di·ous·ly** *adv* —**o·di·ous·ness** *n*

~~**odissey**~~ incorrect spelling of **odyssey**

o·di·um /ṓdee əm/ *n* **1. HATRED** intense dislike, repugnance, or contempt for somebody or something ○ *incurred scorn and odium for his actions* **2. STATE OF BEING ODIOUS** the state of being hateful, contemptuous, or disgusting **3. DISREPUTE OR DISGRACE** a state of being considered odious by others [Early 17C. < Latin]

o·dom·e·ter /ō dómmətər/ *n* a device built into the dashboard of a vehicle that records the distance traveled [Late 18C. < French *odomètre*, or directly < Greek *hodos* "way"]

o·do·nate /ṓd'n àyt/ *n* an insect belonging to the order of insects that includes the dragonfly and damselfly. Order: Odonata. [Early 20C. < modern Latin *Odonata* < Greek *odōn*, variant of *odous* "tooth"]

odont- *prefix* same as **odonto-** (*used before vowels*)

-odont *suffix* having a particular kind of teeth ○ *acrodont* [< Greek *odont-*, stem of *odous* (see ODONTO-)]

o·don·tal·gia /ōdon táljə/ *n* DENT same as **toothache** (*technical*)

-odontia *suffix* condition or treatment of teeth ○ *anodontia* [< Greek *odont-*, stem of *odous* (see ODONTO-)]

odonto- *prefix* tooth, teeth ○ *odontology* [< Greek *odont-* "tooth" < Indo-European]

o·don·to·blast /ō dóntə blàst/ *n* one of a layer of cells lining the pulp cavity of a tooth and taking part in the formation of dentine —**o·don·to·blas·tic** /ō dòntə blástik/ *adj*

o·don·to·glos·sum /ō dòntə glóssəm/ *n* a variety of orchid that grows on other plants and is widely cultivated for its clusters of brightly colored flowers. Native to: mountainous areas from Bolivia to Mexico. Genus: *Odontoglossum.* [Late 19C < modern Latin, "tooth tongue" < Greek *odont-* "tooth" + *glōssa* "tongue"; from the projection on the end of the flower, resembling a tooth]

o·don·toid /ō dón tòyd/ *adj* resembling a tooth, especially in shape

o·don·toid proc·ess *n* a tooth-shaped peg that projects upward from the second neck vertebra to engage with the first, acting as a pivot for side-to-side movements of the head

o·don·tol·o·gy /ō don tólləjee/ *n* the branch of science that studies the teeth and their anatomy, development, and diseases —**o·don·to·log·i·cal** /ō dòntə lójjik'l/ *adj* —**o·don·to·log·i·cal·ly** *adv* —**o·don·tol·o·gist** *n*

o·dor /ṓdər/ *n* **1.** a smell, whether pleasant or unpleasant ○ *the delicious odor of baking bread* **2.** a quality or attitude that suggests or resembles a particular thing ○ *the odor of sanctity* [13C. Via French < Latin]

SYNONYMS See *smell.*

o·dor·ant /ṓdərənt/ *n* something that gives a characteristic smell to a product

o·dor·if·er·ous /ṓdə ríffərəss/ *adj* having or diffusing a strong odor (*technical*) —**o·dor·if·er·ous·ly** *adv* —**o·dor·if·er·ous·ness** *n*

o·dor·less /ṓdərləss/ *adj* having no smell that is strong enough to be detected by the human nose —**o·dor·less·ness** *n*

o·dor·ous /ṓdərəss/ *adj* same as **odoriferous** (*literary*) —**o·dor·ous·ly** *adv* —**o·dor·ous·ness** *n*

o·dour *n* Can, UK spelling of **odor**

O·dys·seus /ō díss yòoss, ō dissee əss/ *n* in Greek mythology, the king of Ithaca who is the main character in Homer's epic poem the *Odyssey.* Roman equivalent **Ulysses**

od·ys·sey /óddəssee/ (*plural* **-seys**) *n* a long series of travels and adventures [Late 19C. < the *Odyssey* < Greek *Odusseia* < ODYSSEUS]

CULTURAL NOTE ***The Odyssey***, an epic poem (?8th century B.C.) by the Greek writer Homer. The oldest surviving source of Greek mythology along with the *Iliad*, it describes Odysseus's ten-year journey home to Ithaca after the Trojan War. It provides both an insight into a long-lost civilization and a gripping narrative rich in evocative details, complex characters, and universal themes.

Oe *symbol* MEASURE oersted

OE, **O.E.** *abbr* LANG Old English

OECD *abbr* COMM Organization for Economic Co-operation and Development

oe·de·ma *n* MED another spelling of **edema**

Oed·i·pus /éddəpəss, éed-/ *n* in Greek mythology, a son of Jocasta and Laius, king of Thebes, who unwittingly killed his father and married his mother —**Oed·i·pal** *adj*

Oed·i·pus com·plex *n* according to the psychoanalytic theory of Sigmund Freud, feelings or desires originating when a child, especially a son, unconsciously seeks sexual fulfillment with the parent of the opposite sex

Ō·e Ken·za·bu·rō /ō ay kenzə bóorō/ (*b.* 1935) Japanese writer. Perhaps the greatest Japanese novelist since World War II, he won the Nobel Prize in literature (1994).

OEM *abbr* original equipment manufacturer

oe·nol·o·gy *n* WINE Can, UK spelling of **enology**

oe·no·mel /éenə mèl/ *n* (*literary*) **1.** a drink of wine and honey made in ancient Greece **2.** words or ideas that combine strength and sweetness [Late 16C. Via late Latin *oenomeli* < Greek *oinomeli* "honey wine" < *oinos* "wine" + *meli* "honey"]

oe·no·phile /éenə fìl/ *n* a lover of or expert on wine [Mid-20C. < French < *oeno-* < Greek *oinos* "wine"]

o'er /awr/ *prep, adv* same as **over** (*literary*) ○ *The sun rose o'er the mountain.* [14C. Contraction]

oer·sted /úr stèd, -stəd/ *n* the unit measure of magnetic field strength in the centimeter-gram-second system. It is equal to the magnetic field strength experienced by a magnetic pole when undergoing a force of one dyne in a free space. Symbol **Oe** [Late19C. After Hans Christian *Oersted* (1777–1851), Danish physicist]

oe·soph·a·gus *n* ANAT another spelling of **esophagus**

oes·tri·ol *n* BIOCHEM UK spelling of **estriol**

oes·tro·gen *n* BIOCHEM another spelling of **estrogen**

oes·trone *n* BIOCHEM another spelling of **estrone**

oes·trus *n* ZOOL another spelling of **estrus**

oeu·vre /ṓvrə, óovvrə/ *n* a work of art or literature, or such works considered as a unit, especially the complete work of a single artist [Late 19C. Via French < Latin *opera*, the plural of *opus* "work"]

of *stressed* /uv, ov/; *unstressed* /əv/ CORE MEANING: a preposition introducing a noun or noun phrase that provides more information about a preceding word or phrase, usually, but not always, also a noun ○ *Most software has complex sets of commands and options.* ○ *She let out a little squeal of delight.* ○ *I'm very fond of onions.* ○ *He thought of the consequences too late.*

prep **1. AFFECTED BY ACTION** used to indicate the person or thing affected by or performing an action ○ *the promotion of junior staff* ○ *the death of her father* **2. USED IN MEASURING QUANTITIES** used after words or phrases expressing quantities to indicate the substance or thing being measured ○ *millions of dollars* ○ *a herd of cows* ○ *10 gallons of oil* **3. CONNECTED WITH** used to indicate the place that somebody or something belongs to or is connected with ○ *the president of France* **4. CONTAINING** containing a particular substance ○ *a mug of coffee* ○ *a busload of schoolchildren* **5. TAKEN FROM** used to indicate a part of something that is normally considered as a whole ○ *a slice of cake* ○ *a square of fabric* **6. MADE FROM** made from or used as a material to form something ○ *ruled with a rod of iron* ○ *a paste of flour and water* **7. INDICATING RELATIONSHIP OR ASSOCIATION** used to indicate a relationship, association, or cause ○ *I'll be thinking of you.* ○ *accused of negligence* **8. RELATING TO** used after words describing feelings and qualities to indicate the person or thing they relate to ○ *He's very sure of himself.* ○ *It's very kind of you to come.* **9. INDICATING PARTICULAR TYPE** used to describe somebody or something in terms of a particular type or kind ○ *one heck of a gymnast* **10. HAVING PARTICULAR QUALITY** used to indicate a quality that somebody or something has, or the person or thing having a particular quality ○ *announcements of a general nature* ○ *a musician of great talent* ○ *the gentleness of his manner* **11. INDICATING AMOUNT** used to indicate an amount, age, or value ○ *There is a limit of eight characters in a computer user name.* ○ *a young boy of 12* **12. ON EVERY** used to indicate a day or other period of time when an activity regularly occurs (*informal*) ○ *We usually go out for a meal of a Friday.* **13. BEFORE** before the hour of ○ *It was a quarter of ten before she returned.* [Old English < Germanic]

USAGE of and **'ve**: Note that *could've, should've,* and *would've* are contracted forms of *could have, should have,* and *would have.* The *'ve* contraction is sometimes wrongly interpreted as ***of***, because it sounds similar: *He could've* [not *could of*] *been killed. You should've* [not *should of*] *followed the instructions. It would've* [not *would of*] *been quicker to walk.*

OF *abbr* BASEBALL **1.** outfield **2.** outfielder

o·fay /ō fày/ *n US* an offensive term that deliberately insults a white person (*slang*) [Early 20C. Origin ?]

off /awf, of/ CORE MEANING: a grammatical word used to indicate separation or distance between two points, especially movement away from the speaker ○ (adv) *He ran off before I could stop him.* ○ (prep) *The bottle rolled off the ledge and fell to the floor.*
1. *prep, adv* **SO AS TO LEAVE** so as to come out of or leave a bus, train, or plane ○ *Check you have all your belongings before getting off the bus.* ○ *He got off at the next stop.* **2.** *prep, adv* **SO AS TO KEEP AWAY FROM** so as to keep away from, avoid stepping on, or be at a distance from or to the side of ○ *The sign said "Please keep off the grass."* ○ *I stepped off the curb.* **3.** *prep, adv* **AWAY FROM WORK** away from work or usual duties owing to illness, holidays, or normal nonwork time ○ *trying to get time off work to visit her in the hospital* ○ *I didn't see Jane – it must be her night off.* **4.** *prep, adv* **REDUCED BY** so as to be reduced by a particular amount ○ *10 percent off all swimwear this week* ○ *She knocked $10 off for the slight stain on the sleeve.* **5.** *prep, adv* **IN FUTURE** a particular distance away in the future ○ *My fortieth birthday is only two years off!* **6.** *prep, adv* **SO AS TO REMOVE** so as to eliminate or remove something from view ○ *The dirt should wash off easily.* ○ *He was rubbing something off the board when I came in.* **7.** *adv* **TO DISTANT PLACE** so as to be away from the present location ○ *He hopped in the car, started it up, and took off.* **8.** *adv* **AWAY** at a particular physical distance away ○ *The nearest stop's about two miles off.* **9.** *adv* **MEASURED** so as to be divided or measured ○ *Measure the gap, mark it off with a pencil, and cut the wood to size.* **10.** *adv* **TO COMPLETION** to the point of completion ○ *We're trying to get our bills paid off.* **11.** *adv* **INTO PARTICULAR STATE** into a particular state, especially an unconscious state ○ *The baby dozed off on the way over here.* **12.** *prep* **ABSTAINING FROM** no longer participating in or using ○ *I'm off caffeine for a week.* **13.** *prep* **ON DIET OF** using as a means of subsistence ○ *living off vegetables from our garden* **14.** *prep* **LEADING AWAY FROM** near or next to, and leading or branching away from ○ *He lives in an apartment block just off the main street.* **15.** *prep* **NOT LIKING** no longer inclined toward ○ *I'm really off horror movies at the moment.* **16.** *prep* **FROM** used to show the initiator or source of an action (*nonstandard*) ○ *I got these sunglasses off my sister for my birthday.* **17.** *adv, adj* **NOT IN OPERATION** not functioning or in use ○ *Shall I switch the engine off?* ○ *Make sure the lights are off before you leave.* ○ *the off switch* **18.** *adv, adj* **CANCELED** so as to be no longer taking place ○ *The deal's off.* **19.** *adj* **NO LONGER FRESH** smelling and tasting bad because of being no longer fresh ○ *We had to throw the fish away – it was going off.* **20.** *adj* **IN PARTICULAR CONDITION** in a particular condition with regard to something ○ *How are you off for cash?* **21.** *adj* **NOT CORRECT** in error or out of alignment **22.** *adj* **ON THE RIGHT OF** situated on the right side of a vehicle, farthest away from the curb **23.** *adj* **UNACCEPTABLE** not up to normal or acceptable standards (*informal*) ○ *He was off his game today.* [Old English. Originally an emphatic variant of OF] ◇ **off and on** occasionally

USAGE There are two usages of ***off*** that should be avoided in formal writing. The first involves ***off*** plus *of*: *The actors stepped off* [not *off of*] *the stage.* The second problem involves the use of ***off*** after certain verbs like *buy* or *borrow,* which mean "to obtain something from a source": *I bought the computer from* [not *off*] *my roommate.*

off. *abbr* **1.** office **2.** officer **3.** official

off-air *adj* spoken or occurring in broadcasting studios but not used during a broadcast —**off air** *adv*

of·fal /áwf'l, óff'l/ *n* **1.** the edible, mainly internal organs of an animal, e.g., the heart, liver, brains, and tongue, sometimes regarded as unpalatable **2.** something discarded as refuse [14C. < OFF + FALL]

Of·fa·ly /óffəlee/ county in Leinster Province, Republic of Ireland. The county town is Tullamore. Population: 59,117 (2002).. Area: 771 sq. mi./1,998 sq. km.

off beat *n* any unaccented beat in a bar of music

off·beat /áwf bèet, óf-/ *adj* not conforming to convention or to expectations

off-brand *adj* made and sold inexpensively under a brand name that is not well-known

off-Broad·way *n* in New York City, professional theater productions, sometimes experimental or innovative in nature, that are staged outside the principal theater district, Broadway

off-cam·er·a *adj* out of sight of the camera —**off cam·er·a** *adv*

off-cam·pus *adj* done, taking place, or existing outside the area of a university, college, or other campus —**off cam·pus** *adv*

off-cen·ter *adj* **1.** not at the center and therefore sometimes causing a lack of symmetry, balance, or evenness of movement **2.** slightly unconventional or eccentric —**off cen·ter** *adv*

off chance, off-chance *n* a slight or remote possibility ◇ **on the off chance** just in case something happens

off-col·or *adj* **1.** **SLIGHTLY SMUTTY** mildly sexually indecent or suggestive (*informal*) **2.** *UK* **ILL** ill or not very well ○ *I'm feeling a bit off-color today.* **3.** **NOT COLORED NORMALLY** not having the usual or desired color

off-course *adj UK* same as **off-track**

off·cut /áwf kùt, óf-/ *n* a remnant left after the main pieces of something such as fabric or paper have been cut

off day *n* **1.** a day of not feeling or performing very well **2.** *Malaysia* a day on which somebody does not have to work

Of·fen·bach /áwf'n baakh, -baak/ city in Hesse State, west central Germany, on the Main River. Population: 116,482 (1997).

Of·fen·bach, Jacques (1819–80) German-born French composer. He wrote witty satirical operettas, one of which includes the famous example of the cancan dance music, as well as the opera *The Tales of Hoffmann* (1880). Born **Eberst, Jacob**

of·fence *n* Can, UK spelling of **offense**

of·fend /ə fénd/ (**-fend·ed, -fend·ing, -fends**) *v* **1.** *vti* to hurt somebody's feelings, or cause resentment, irritation, anger, or displeasure ○ *The book offended too many people.* **2.** *vi* to violate a law or code of conduct ○ *He offended against the club's rules of proper dress.* [14C. Directly or via French < Latin *offendere* "to strike"] —**of·fend·er** *n* —**of·fend·ing** *adj*

of·fense /ə fénss/; *sense 3* /ó fènss/ *n* **1.** **LEGAL OR MORAL CRIME** an official crime, or a crime against moral, social, or other accepted standards ○ *mail fraud is a federal offense* **2.** **ATTACK** an attack or assault, usually in the military or in sports ○ *The army launched its great offense that spring.* **3.** **ATTACKING PLAYERS ON TEAM** the players making up the part of a team that attempts to score in a game, as distinct from the defense that tries to stop the other team from scoring ○ *We lacked a good offense last spring.* **4.** **ANGER OR RESENTMENT** anger, resentment, hurt, or displeasure ○ *"Please don't take offense."* ○ *His remarks caused great offense.* **5.** **CAUSE OF DISPLEASURE OR ANGER** something that causes displeasure, humiliation, anger, resentment, or hurt ○ *The request was an offense to their dignity.* [14C. Via French < Latin *offens-*, past participle of *offendere* "to strike"]

of·fen·sive /ə fénssiv/ *adj* **1.** **UPSETTING, INSULTING, OR IRRITATING** causing anger, resentment, or moral outrage ○ *removed the offensive material from the play* **2.** **UNPLEASANT TO SENSES** causing physical repugnance ○ *an offensive smell* **3.** **USED WHEN ATTACKING** used, or designed to be used, when attacking ○ *an offensive weapon* **4.** **AGGRESSIVE** demonstrating aggression ○ *warned that this would be seen as an offensive action* **5.** **IN POSSESSION** relating to the team that has possession of the ball or puck in a game ■ *n* MIL **ATTACK OR ASSAULT** an attack, assault, or siege ○ *The platoon braced itself for the dawn offensive.* —**of·fen·sive·ly** *adv* —**of·fen·sive·ness** *n*

of·fer /áwfər, óf-/ *vt* (**-fered, -fer·ing, -fers**) **1.** **PRESENT SOMETHING FOR ACCEPTANCE OR REJECTION** to attempt to give somebody something that may be taken or refused, usually something desirable ○ *They offered me the job.* **2.** **HAVE SOMETHING FOR USE OF OTHERS** to provide something, or make something available for those who want it ○ *The town offered many attractions.* **3.** **VOLUNTEER TO DO SOMETHING** to suggest doing something yourself as a favor for somebody else ○ *I offered to bring the salad.* **4.** **HAVE SOMETHING FOR SALE OR RENT** to present or have something for sale or rental ○ *the first gym to offer professional trainers at a low cost* **5.** **GIVE SOMETHING AS WORSHIP** to present something to God, often as part of worship ○ *We offer hymns of praise to God.* **6.** **EXHIBIT QUALITY** to exhibit or demonstrate a particular quality ○ *The city offered little resistance against the army.* ○ *a plan that offers hope to millions* **7.** **MAKE BID** to make a bid or financial proposal for something ○ *They offered 40 cents a share.* ■ *n* **1.** **PROPOSAL OF SUGGESTED GIFT OR ACTION** a suggestion from somebody to give something or do something for somebody else ○ *A home-cooked meal and a place to stay: that's the best offer I've had all day!* **2.** **FINANCIAL PROPOSAL OR BID** a sum of money suggested as payment for something ○ *They made an offer for the house but we refused it.* **3.** **REDUCED PRICE** a reduced price for something, or something for sale at a reduced price ○ *this week's special offer* **4.** LAW **PROPOSAL LEADING TO BINDING CONTRACT** a proposal that, if accepted, creates a binding contract [Old English *offrian*, via Germanic < Latin *offerre* "bring to" < *ferre* "bring"] —**of·fer·er** *n*

offer up *vt* RELIG same as **offer** *v* (sense 5)

of·fer·ing /áwfəring, óf-/ *n* **1.** **CONTRIBUTION** something that is offered, or the act of offering ○ *What are the bookstores' latest offerings?* **2.** **GIFT FOR GOD** something offered as a sacrifice to a deity **3.** **MONEY GIVEN DURING CHURCH SERVICE** a financial contribution to a church, often made during a church service

of·fer price *n* the price at which something, especially a share of a stock or mutual fund, is offered for sale

~~**offerred**~~ incorrect spelling of **offered**

of·fer·to·ry /áwfər tàwree, óffər-/ (*plural* **-ries**) *n* **1.** **OFFERING OF COMMUNION BREAD AND WINE** the offering of the bread and wine during the Christian service of Communion **2.** **CHURCH COLLECTION** the offering of money or gifts made by a church congregation **3.** **PART OF CHRISTIAN SERVICE** a part of a church service during which prayers are said or sung while offerings are received [14C. Via ecclesiastical Latin *offertorium* "offering place" < Latin *offerre* (see OFFER)]

off-glide *n* a sound produced by the vocal organs prior to their making another sound or assuming a neutral position

off-guard *adj* not anticipating a possible attack or approach (*not hyphenated when used after a verb*) ○ *caught the enemy off guard*

off·hand /awf hánd, of-, áwf hànd, óf-/ *adv* **1.** **CASUALLY** casually, thoughtlessly, or spontaneously **2.** **WITHOUT PREPARATION** without preparation or research ○ *Offhand, I'd say there must be 50 people in there.* ■ *adj also* **off·hand·ed** /awf hándəd, of-, áwf hàndəd, óf-/ **1.** **UNCONCERNED AND UNCARING** so casual, uninterested, or blunt as to appear impolite or uncaring ○ *She was pretty offhand about the whole affair.* **2.** **CASUALLY DONE** taken or made casually or without planning, usually on the spur of the moment ○ *Only through her offhand comment did I realize who she was.* —**off·hand·ed·ly** *adv* —**off·hand·ed·ness** *n*

off-hour *n US* (*informal*) **1.** a period of time that is not crowded with cars or people (*often used before a noun*) ○ *We try to visit the zoo during off-hours.* **2.** a period of time outside of normal business hours

of·fice /áwfiss, óf-/ *n* **1.** **ROOM USED FOR BUSINESS ACTIVITY** a room in which business or professional activities take place, often occupied by a single person or a single section of the business **2.** **PLACE OF BUSINESS** the quarters in which a commercial, professional, or government organization carries out its activities **3.** **OFFICIAL ORGANIZATION** a commercial or professional organization **4.** **STAFF IN OFFICE** the people who work in an office ○ *get-well cards from the office* **5.** **LARGE DEPARTMENTS IN SOME GOVERNMENTS** a major executive branch in some national governments ○ *He works for the British Home Office.* **6.** **US GOVERNMENT AGENCY OR**

DEPARTMENT a US government agency or subdivision, especially an agency or subdivision of the federal government **7.** POSITION OF RESPONSIBILITY an official post or position of duty, trust, or responsibility ○ *The mayor has been in office four years now.* **8.** PLACE FOR TICKETS OR INFORMATION a booth or other place where tickets or information may be obtained **9.** CHR SET FORM OF CHRISTIAN SERVICE the prescribed order or form of a Christian church service, or of daily prayers **10.** TASK OR ASSIGNMENT a task, assignment, or chore (*formal; usually used in the plural*) ■ **of·fic·es** *npl* **1.** SOMETHING DONE ON BEHALF OF ANOTHER something said or done by somebody to or for another person (*formal*) ○ *I got the job through her kind offices.* **2.** UK AREAS OR BUILDINGS WHERE SERVANTS WORK the outbuildings or parts of a large house in which the servants work (*dated*) [13C. Via French < Latin *officium* "doing work" < *opus* "work" + *facere* "do"]

of·fice-bear·er *n UK* same as **officeholder** (sense 2)

of·fice block *n Can, UK* same as **office building**

of·fice boy *n* a boy or man who does errands around an office (*dated*)

of·fice build·ing *n US* a large building holding offices. Can term **office block**

of·fice creep·er *n* a well-dressed, well-spoken, professionally attired thief who walks into an office, pretends to be, e.g., a sales or repair person, and steals valuable items such as laptop computers (*informal*) —**of·fice creep·ing** *n*

of·fice-free *adj US* relating to or involving a work force that is not required to work from or at an office

of·fice·hold·er *n* **1.** an official in a government position **2.** somebody who holds office in a society, club, or voluntary organization, e.g., the President or Treasurer

of·fice hours *npl* the regular times during which a business or profession, or business as a whole, is conducted

of·fi·cer /áwfissər, óf-/ *n* **1.** SOMEBODY OF RANK IN THE ARMED FORCES somebody in a military force authorized to command others **2.** ELECTED OR APPOINTED OFFICIAL an official who holds an administrative position **3.** POLICE same as **police officer** **4.** SOMEBODY IN AUTHORITY ON SHIP somebody with a position of authority on a civilian ship ■ *vt* (**-cered, -cer·ing, -cers**) MIL, NAVY SUPPLY SOMETHING WITH OFFICERS to provide something such as a military unit or a ship with officers

of·fi·cer of arms *n* a herald, especially one who devises, grants, or confirms coats of arms

of·fi·cial /ə físh'l/ *n* SOMEBODY HOLDING OFFICE a holder of office in an organization, corporation, or government department ■ *adj* **1.** OF GOVERNMENT OR AUTHORITY relating to the role of a government, public body, or authority ○ *official rules and regulations* **2.** AUTHORIZED BY AUTHORITY approved, recognized, or issued by a government, public body, or authority ○ *No official statement has been issued.* **3.** FORMAL formal or ceremonial ○ *invited to attend the official opening* —**of·fi·cial·ly** *adv*

of·fi·cial·dom /ə físh'ldəm/ *n* bureaucracy and those who work within it, especially when viewed as inefficient or pompous (*informal*) ○ *caught up in the red tape of officialdom*

of·fi·cial·ese /ə físh'l éez, -éess/ *n* unclear, pedantic, and verbose language considered characteristic of official documents

of·fi·cial·ism /ə físh'l ìzzəm/ *n* excessive respect or adherence to official routines and regulations, considered to be characteristic of officials (*informal*)

Of·fi·cial Un·i·on·ist Par·ty *n* same as **Ulster Unionist Party**

of·fi·ci·ar·y /ə físhee èrree/ *adj* derived from the holding of an office, or having a title that is derived from an office held ○ *an officiary title* ■ *n* an official, or an organized group of officials [Early 17C. < medieval Latin *officiarius* < Latin *officium* (see OFFICE)]

of·fi·ci·ate /ə físhee àyt/ (**-at·ed, -at·ing, -ates**) *v* **1.** *vti* to preside in an official capacity, especially at a religious ceremony **2.** *vt* to act as a referee at a sports event [Mid-17C. Via medieval Latin *officiat-*, past participle of *officiare* "conduct sacred service" < Latin *officium* (see OFFICE)] —**of·fi·ci·ant** *n*

of·fic·i·nal /ə físsən'l/ (*archaic*) *n* a stocked medicine rather than one specially prepared according to a prescription ■ *adj* having medicinal properties, especially those recognized by a pharmacopoeia [Late 17C. Via medieval Latin *officinalis* < *officina* "workshop" (later "storeroom for medicines") < Latin *officium* (see OFFICE)] —**of·fic·i·nal·ly** *adv*

of·fi·cious /ə físhəss/ *adj* **1.** characteristic of somebody who is eager to give unwanted help or advice ○ *whisked away our unfinished meal in an officious manner* **2.** unofficial or informal, especially in political or diplomatic dealings [Late 15C. < Latin *officiosus* < *officium* (see OFFICE)] —**of·fi·cious·ly** *adv* —**of·fi·cious·ness** *n*

off·ing /áwfing, óf-/ *n* the more distant part of the sea seen from the shore [Early 17C. Probably < OFF] ◇ **in the offing** expected or likely in the future

off·ish /áwfish, óf-/ *adj* same as **standoffish** (*informal*)

off-key *adj* (*not hyphenated when used after a verb*) **1.** OUT OF TUNE not having the correct musical pitch **2.** INAPPROPRIATE not usual, conventional, or appropriate ■ *adv* OUT OF TUNE above or below the correct musical pitch

off-la·bel *adj US* using or involving the use of a prescription drug to treat a condition for which the drug has not been approved by the US Food and Drug Administration

off-lim·its *adj* to which entry is forbidden or barred ○ *That part of town was off-limits to us.*

off-line *adj* **1.** describes a computer terminal or peripheral device that is disconnected or is functioning separately from an associated computer or computer network ○ *The printer was taken off-line for repairs.* **2.** involved in preparing but not transmitting material for broadcasting ○ *off-line editing* —**off line** *adv*

off-line news·read·er *n* a piece of software that allows a user to read newsgroup articles when the computer is not connected to the Internet

off·load /awf lṓd, of-, áwf lṑd, óf-/ (**-load·ed, -load·ing, -loads**) *v* **1.** *vti* UNLOAD GOODS to unload goods or a cargo from a vehicle or container ○ *ships waiting to offload* **2.** *vt* GET RID OF SOMETHING to get rid of something unwanted by passing it on to somebody else ○ *managed to offload some of the work onto colleagues* **3.** *vti* UNBURDEN YOURSELF to relieve yourself of a stressful emotion such as anxiety or frustration by talking to somebody (*informal*) **4.** *vti* COMPUT TRANSFER DATA to transfer data from one computer to another to create spare capacity

off-off-Broad·way *n* in New York City, theater productions that are considered to be fringe, experimental, or avant-garde

off-peak *adj* relating to the periods outside that of maximum use, frequency, or demand —**off peak** *adv*

off-piste *adj* relating to or taking place on fresh trackless snow that is away from the regular skiing runs —**off piste** *adv*

off-plan *adj* based only on the plans of a building that has not yet been built —**off plan** *adv*

off·print /áwf prìnt, óf-/ *n* a separate printing of a single article from a periodical, often given in small quantities to the contributor

off-put·ting *adj* arousing irritation, repugnance, or mild unease —**off-put·ting·ly** *adv*

off-ramp *n* a one-way road serving as an exit from a main highway

off-rhyme *n* a partial or near rhyme

off-road *adj* designed, manufactured, or used for travel off public roads, especially over rough terrain

off-road ve·hi·cle *n* a motorized vehicle designed or used for travel away from public roads or on rough terrain

off·scour·ings /áwf skòwringz, óf-/ *npl* the leftover or discarded parts of something

off-screen *adj* **1.** NOT VISIBLE ON SCREEN not visible on a television or movie screen ○ *an off-screen commentator* **2.** OCCURRING IN ORDINARY LIFE occurring in ordinary life, not as fiction on television or in a movie ○ *Her off-screen life was just as exciting.* ■ *adv* IN ORDINARY LIFE aside from television or movie performances ○ *Off-screen, he mostly played golf.*

off-sea·son *n* **1.** TIME OF LESS ACTIVITY a time of year when activity or business is at a low level (*often used before a noun*) ○ *Hotel rooms were cheaper in the off-season.* **2.** PERIOD BETWEEN SEASONS a period after the end of one annual sports season and before the beginning of the next ○ *how players spend their time in the off-season* ■ *adv* IN OFF-SEASON during the off-season ○ *He liked to travel off-season.*

off·set *n* /áwf sèt, óf-/ **1.** SOMETHING COUNTERBALANCING SOMETHING ELSE something that counterbalances or compensates, or an allowance made in order to counterbalance something (*often used before a noun*) **2.** CONSTR ABRUPT BEND IN STRAIGHT LINE an abrupt bend put into an otherwise straight bar or pipe in order to avoid an obstruction **3.** PRINTING PRINTING PROCESS USING INK TRANSFER a method of printing in which inked impressions are transferred onto paper from another surface (*often used before a noun*) **4.** PRINTING UNINTENTIONAL MARKING FROM WET INK an accidental transfer of ink, usually from one piece of paper to another (*often used before a noun*) **5.** BOT OFFSHOOT CAPABLE OF PROPAGATION an offshoot or runner from the base of a plant that can propagate the plant **6.** GENETICS OFFSHOOT OR DESCENDANT something that has developed from something else, e.g., a collateral descendant or group of descendants of a family **7.** GEOL SPUR IN MOUNTAIN RANGE a projecting spur or ridge in a mountain range (*often used before a noun*) **8.** GEOL HORIZONTAL DISPLACEMENT OF ROCK the horizontal displacement that occurs as a result of the movement of a rock mass along a fault **9.** SOMETHING SET APART something set apart from other things (*often used before a noun*) **10.** MEASURE SURVEYING LINE a short distance measured at right angles from a main survey line, used in finding the area of a piece of land **11.** BEGINNING the beginning of something (*dated*) **12.** ARCHIT same as **setback** (sense 2) ■ *v* /áwf sèt, óf-, awf sét, of-/ (**-set, -set·ting, -sets**) **1.** *vt* COUNTERACT SOMETHING to balance or make up for something (*often passive*) ○ *These improved sales were offset by last month's losses.* **2.** *vti* PRINTING PRINT SOMETHING BY TRANSFER to print something by offset printing, or to accidentally transfer ink by an offset **3.** *vti* CONSTR FORM OR BE OFFSET IN SOMETHING to make an offset in something such as a wall or pipe, or to be formed into an offset —**off·set** *adv*

off·shoot /áwf shòot, óf-/ *n* **1.** SHOOT FROM MAIN STEM OF PLANT a branch or shoot growing from the main stem of a plant **2.** SOMETHING THAT COMES FROM SOMETHING ELSE something that springs or spreads from or that is a subsidiary of a main source or origin ○ *The company was an offshoot of their leisure empire.* **3.** DESCENDANT OR BRANCH OF ANOTHER GROUP a person or group descending from an ancestral line, or branching off from a social group

off·shore /awf sháwr, of-/ *adv* **1.** FROM LAND TO WATER on or over land that is near water, especially away from the land toward the sea ○ *An icy wind blew offshore.* **2.** IN WATER SOME WAY FROM SHORE in a body of water at some distance from the shore ○ *anchored offshore* ■ *adj* **1.** BLOWING FROM LAND TO WATER blowing or moving from land toward the sea ○ *offshore breezes* **2.** AT SEA SOME WAY FROM SHORE located at sea a considerable distance from shore **3.** IN FOREIGN COUNTRY based or registered in a foreign country, usually in order to avoid taxes

off·side *adj* illegally beyond or in advance of a ball or puck during play —**off·side** *adv*

off·site /áwf sìt, óf-/ *adj* not based or occurring in an organization's principal place of activity —**off·site** *adv*

off-speed *adj US* describes a baseball pitch that is slower than is usual or expected

off·spring /áwf spring, óf-/ (*plural same or* **-springs**) *n* **1.** a person's child or an animal's young, or sometimes a descendant of a plant **2.** the product, consequence, or effect of something

off·stage /áwf stáyj, òf-/ *adv* **1.** OUTSIDE ACTING AREA away from the area of the stage used for a performance, usually out of the view of the audience **2.** IN PRIVATE LIFE in private life, especially as opposed to the character an actor plays or the personality a performer projects **3.** OUT OF PUBLIC VIEW unseen by the public and media ■ *adj* **1.** HAPPENING OFFSTAGE happening or situated outside the area of the stage visible to the audience **2.** PRIVATE occurring in or characteristic of somebody's private life **3.** **HAPPENING UNSEEN** occurring out of the gaze of the public and the media

off-street *adj* not in the street but in a parking lot, garage, driveway, or another place ○ *off-street parking*

off-the-books *adj US* **1.** not recorded in the accounts of a company **2.** not registered for the purposes of paying income tax

off-the-cuff *adj* delivered spontaneously or without preparation or notes [< the custom of scribbling extempore remarks on a starched shirt cuff] —**off the cuff** *adv*

off-the-peg *adj UK* same as **off-the-rack** —**off the peg** *adv*

off-the-rack *adj* ready-made and sold in standard sizes, not tailored for the individual customer ○ *off-the-rack evening wear* —**off the rack** *adv*

off-the-rec·ord *adj* not intended for publication or to be attributed by name to the person who said it —**off the rec·ord** *adv*

off-the-shelf *adj* readily obtainable or taken from an existing stock of merchandise or supplies —**off the shelf** *adv*

off-the-shoul·der *adj* describes a woman's dress or top with a wide neckline and short or long sleeves designed to reveal one or both shoulders

off-the-wall *adj* unusual or unconventional in a way that is particularly bizarre (*informal*) [Origin ?] —**off the wall** *adv*

off-track *adj* occurring somewhere other than a racetrack ○ *off-track betting*

off-white *adj* of a very pale color that is a shade or two away from white —**off-white** *n*

off year *n US* a year in which no major election, especially a presidential one, takes place —**off-year** *adj*

oft /awft, oft/ *adv* same as **often** (*archaic or literary; now often used in combination*) ○ *oft-repeated phrase* [Old English]

of·ten /áwf'n, óff'n, áwft'n/ *adv* at short intervals or repeatedly [13C. Alteration of OFT] ◇ **every so often** regularly but with fairly long intervals between each occurrence ◇ **more often than not, as often as not** fairly frequently, or in a majority of instances

PRONUNCIATION Pronunciation of **often**: 15th-century England saw a tendency among speakers of English to omit some consonants in an effort to pronounce some words more easily. Such was the case with the letter *t* in ***often***. To this day, the preferred pronunciations of this word are /áwf'n, óff'n/, though some speakers do pronounce the *t*. Other words, such as *listen, soften, hasten,* and *glisten*, in which the *t* is never pronounced, reflect that same 15th-century trend.

of·ten·times /áwf'n tìmz, óff'n-/, **oft·times** /áwft tìmz, óft-/ *adv* same as **often**

OG, o.g. *abbr* STAMPS original gum

og·am *n* LING another spelling of **ogham**

Og·bo·mo·sho /aágbə mṓshō/ city in Oyo state, southwestern Nigeria, situated approximately 125 mi./201 km northeast of Lagos. Population: 711,900 (1995).

Og·den /ógdən/ city and county seat of Weber County in northern Utah, situated at the confluence of the Ogden and Weber rivers, north of Salt Lake City. It is a major rail transport center. Population: 78,641 (2002 estimate).

Og·dens·burg /ógdənz bùrg/ city in St. Lawrence County, northern New York. It was the site of the Ogdensburg Declaration between Canada and the United States (1940) that marked the establishment of the Permanent Joint Board on Defense. Population: 12,040 (2002 estimate).

o·gee /ṓ jeè/ *n* **1.** a decorative double curve like an elongated and flattened S **2.** ARCHIT a decorative molding with an ogee-shaped profile **3.** ARCHIT same as **ogee arch** [Late 17C. Alteration of OGIVE]

ogee arch

o·gee arch *n* an arch whose sides curve gently inward near the top and then curve upward steeply to meet in a point

og·ham /óggəm/, **og·am** *n* **1.** **ANCIENT CELTIC WRITING SYSTEM** an ancient British and Irish Celtic alphabet consisting of twenty characters formed by inscribing lines on either side of or across a long vertical baseline **2.** **CELTIC LETTER** a character used in the ogham alphabet **3.** **CELTIC INSCRIPTION** an inscription written in ogham, or something bearing such an inscription [Early 18C. Via modern Irish < Old Irish *ogam*, after *Ogma*, the Celtic god who supposedly invented it]

o·give /ṓ jìv/ *n* **1.** ARCHIT **RIB IN GOTHIC VAULT** a diagonal rib in a Gothic vault **2.** ARCHIT **POINTED ARCH** an arch that rises to a sharp point **3.** STATS **CUMULATIVE FREQUENCY GRAPH** a graph or curve that represents the cumulative frequencies of a set of values [Origin ?]

Og·la·la /og laálə/ (*plural same or* **-las**) *n* a member of a Native North American people, a branch of the Teton, who live mainly in South Dakota [Mid-19C. < Dakota]

o·gle /ṓg'l/ *vti* (**o·gled, o·gling, o·gles**) to look at somebody for sexual enjoyment or as a way of showing sexual interest ■ *n* a prolonged flirtatious or desirous look at somebody [Late 17C. Origin ?] —**o·gler** *n*

SYNONYMS See ***gaze***.

O·gle·thorpe /ṓg'l thàwrp/, **James Edward** (1696–1785) British North American colonist. He founded Savannah, Georgia, and was the colony's governor (1733–43).

o·gon·ek /o gónnek/ *n* in some languages, a mark (˛) placed beneath vowels that signals a change in pronunciation. In Polish and in transcriptions of Native American languages it indicates nasalization. In Lithuanian it indicates a long vowel. [< Polish, literally "little tail"]

Og·o·oué /ōgə wáy/ river in Gabon, west central Africa. Length: 603 mi./970 km.

o·gre /ṓgər/ *n* **1.** in fairy tales, an evil giant or monster, especially one who eats people **2.** somebody who is particularly unpleasant and frightening —**o·gre·ish** *adj*

o·gress /ṓgrəss/ *n* in fairy tales, an evil female giant or monster, especially one who eats people

O·gun /ō gōōn/ state in southwestern Nigeria, north of Lagos State. Capital: Abeokuta. Population: 2,338,570 (1991).. Area: 6,472 sq. mi./16,762 sq. km.

oh /ō/ *interj* **1.** **USED TO EXPRESS STRONG EMOTION** used to express a strong emotional reaction such as surprise, shock, pain, or extreme pleasure ○ *Oh! That's wonderful news!* **2.** **USED TO INTRODUCE STRONG REACTION** used to introduce short phrases that express a strong emotion, such as anger, shock, delight, or triumph ○ *Oh, what a fool I've been!* **3.** **USED TO INTRODUCE RESPONSE** used to introduce a response to what somebody has just said or asked ○ *Oh, I'm fine. How are you?* **4.** **USED TO SHOW THOUGHT** used to indicate thought or hesitation about what to say next ○ *We've got, oh, fifteen minutes before the bus is due.* **5.** **USED TO ATTRACT ATTENTION** used to attract somebody's attention or call attention to something ○ *Oh, John, can you come over here?* [Mid-16C. Alteration of O²]

OH *abbr* Ohio

O'Ha·ra /ō haárə, -hárrə/, **John** (1905–70) US writer. His novels explore the themes of class conflict, status, and sexual mores. His works include the short-story collection *Pal Joey* (1940) and *Appointment in Samarra* (1934). Full name **O'Hara, John Henry**

> "An artist is his own fault."
> [John O'Hara, Introduction, *The Portable F. Scott Fitzgerald*; 1945]

OHG, O.H.G. *abbr* LANG Old High German

O'Hig·gins /ō hígginz/, **Bernardo** (1778–1842) Chilean leader. He led Chile's fight for independence from Spain (1810–17) and established himself as a virtual dictator (1817–23). Known as **the Liberator of Chile**

Ohio

O·hi·o /ō hī ō/ **1.** state in the north central United States, bordered by Michigan, Lake Erie, Pennsylvania, West Virginia, Kentucky, and Indiana. Capital: Columbus. Population: 11,421,167 (2002 estimate).. Area: 44,828 sq. mi./116,104 sq. km. **2.** major river of the eastern United States, originating from the confluence of two other rivers at Pittsburgh, Pennsylvania, and flowing southward to join the Mississippi at Cairo, Illinois. Length: 981 mi./1,580 km. —**O·hi·o·an** *adj, n*

ohm /ōm/ *n* the SI unit of electrical resistance, equal to the resistance between two points on a conductor when a potential difference of 1 volt produces a current of 1 ampere. Symbol Ω [Mid-19C. After Georg OHM]

Ohm /ōm/, **Georg** (1787–1854) German physicist. His research on electric currents led to the formulation of Ohm's law. The ohm is named for him. Full name **Ohm, Georg Simon**

ohm·age /ṓmij/ *n* electrical resistance measured in ohms

ohm·me·ter /ōm meètər/ *n* an instrument that measures electrical resistance in ohms

Ohm's law *n* the law of physics that states that electric current is directly proportional to the voltage applied to a conductor and inversely proportional to that conductor's resistance [After Georg Simon OHM]

oh·my·god /ṓmīgòd/, **oh·mi·god** (*slang*) *interj* used to express extreme dismay, shock, or surprise ■ *adj* relating to extreme dismay, shock, or surprise ○ *In an ohmygod moment, the conductor slipped and fell off the podium.* [Respelling of *Oh, my God!*]

o·ho /ō hṓ/ *interj* used to express surprise or exultation, e.g., at making a discovery [14C. < O² + HO²]

OHV *abbr* **1.** off-highway vehicle **2.** *also* **o.h.v.** MECH ENG overhead valve

OIC *abbr* oh, I see (*used in e-mails or text messages*)

-oid *suffix* like, resembling, related to ○ *toxoid* ○ *rhomboid* [< Greek *-oeidēs* < *eidos* "form, shape" (see IDOL)]

o·id·i·um /ō íddee əm/ (*plural* **-i·a** /-ee ə/) *n* a thin-walled egg-shaped fungal spore produced by the fragmentation of a hypha [Mid-19C. Via modern Latin < Greek *ōion* "egg" (see OO-)]

oil /oyl/ *n* **1.** **THICK GREASY LIQUID** a liquid fat, obtained from plant seeds, animal fats, mineral deposits, and other sources, that does not dissolve in water and will burn. Oils are used for a wide variety of purposes, most commonly as lubricants and fuels and in cooking. **2.** **PETROLEUM** petroleum, the crude product that is distilled and refined to produce industrial oils and oil-based products (*often used* *before a noun)* ○ *oil prices* **3.** PETROLEUM DERIVATIVE a liquid extracted from petroleum and used as a domestic fuel or as a machinery and engine lubricant, e.g., heating oil or motor oil (*often used before a noun*) **4.** PETROLEUM INDUSTRY the worldwide industry that is based on petroleum extraction and refining (*often used before a noun*) ○ *oil companies* **5.** THICK LIQUID CONTAINING OIL a thick liquid containing oil or with the consistency of oil, especially a cosmetic **6.** ART same as **oil paint** (*usually used in the plural*) **7.** ART same as **oil painting** (sense 1) **8.** *US* FLATTERY insincere praise or flattery ■ *v* (**oiled, oil·ing, oils**) **1.** *vt* APPLY OIL TO SOMETHING to put oil into or onto something in order to lubricate, polish, preserve, or soften it **2.** *vti* NAUT GIVE OR GET FUEL to supply a ship with oil, or be supplied with oil **3.** *vti* TURN INTO OIL to turn a solid fat such as butter or lard into an oily liquid, or be turned into an oily liquid [12C. < Old French, via Latin *oleum* "olive oil" < Greek *elaion* < *elaia* "olive"] —**oiled** *adj* ◇ **burn the midnight oil** to work or study until very late at night

oil bee·tle *n* a beetle that emits a foul-smelling oily substance from the joints of its legs to deter predators. Family: Meloidae.

oil·bird /óyl bùrd/ *n* a bird whose young have fatty flesh, formerly used as a source of oil for cooking and lighting. Native to: Central and South America. Latin name: *Steatornis caripensis.*

oil cake *n* the solid residue remaining after extraction of the oil from some seeds such as cottonseed and linseed. Use: livestock feed.

oil·can /óyl kàn/ *n* a metal container with a long thin spout, used to squirt lubricating oil into machinery

oil·cloth /óyl klàwth, -klòth/ *n* a cloth that has been treated with oil or a synthetic resin to make it waterproof. Use: table coverings.

oil-cooled *adj* fitted with a cooling system that uses oil

oil·cup /óyl kùp/ *n* a cup-shaped reservoir of oil that provides continuous lubrication for a bearing in a machine

Oil·dale /óyl dàyl/ town in Kern County, California. Population: 26,553 (1996).

oil drum *n* a large metal cylinder designed for transporting and storing oil. Empty oil drums are often used as trash cans, flotation devices, and grills and to make instruments for steel bands.

oil·er /óylər/ *n* **1.** an oil tanker, especially one that refuels ships at sea **2.** a ship that uses oil as fuel **3.** INDUST same as **oil well** (*informal*)

oil field *n* an area of land or sea under which there are substantial reserves of petroleum, especially such an area that is being exploited

oil gland *n* **1.** BOT, ZOOL a gland that secretes oil **2.** BIRDS same as **uropygial gland**

oil·man /óyl màn, -mən/ (*plural* **-men** /-mèn, -mən/) *n* **1.** an executive in the petroleum industry **2.** somebody who works in an oil field

oil of cloves *n* an essential oil extracted from clove flowers. Use: relief of dental pain, component of temporary fillings.

oil of win·ter·green *n* an aromatic oil extracted from a North American evergreen bush. Use: in liniments, as flavoring.

oil paint *n* a paint that consists of pigment mixed with a drying oil

oil paint·ing *n* **1.** a picture painted with oil paints **2.** the art of painting with oil paints

oil palm *n* a palm tree widely cultivated for its fruit and seeds, which yield palm oil. Native to: West Africa. Latin name: *Elaeis guineensis.*

oil pan *n* the lower section of the crankcase in an internal-combustion engine, which acts as a reservoir of motor oil

oil patch *n US* the region of the United States where there are substantial petroleum deposits, including the states of Oklahoma, Texas, and Louisiana (*informal*)

oil rig *n* the equipment used for drilling for oil, including the platform that supports the drilling equipment

oil·seed /óyl sèed/ *n* a seed that is rich in oil, especially one grown as a crop for oil extraction, e.g., linseed, peanut, or cottonseed

oil shale *n* a black or dark-brown shale from which petroleum can be extracted by distillation

oil·skin /óyl skìn/ *n* **1.** WATERPROOF FABRIC a cotton fabric that has been treated with oil to make it waterproof **2.** WATERPROOF GARMENT a garment, especially a coat, made of oilskin ■ **oil·skins** *npl* WATERPROOF CLOTHING waterproof outerwear consisting of a coat and pants made of oilskin

oil slick *n* a film of oil covering part of the surface of something, especially a large expanse of oil floating on the sea following a spillage of oil from an oil tanker

oil·stone /óyl stṑn/ *n* a fine-grained stone that is lubricated with oil and used to sharpen cutting tools

oil trap *n* a set of conditions within rock strata that blocks the upward movement of oil or gas, causing it to accumulate

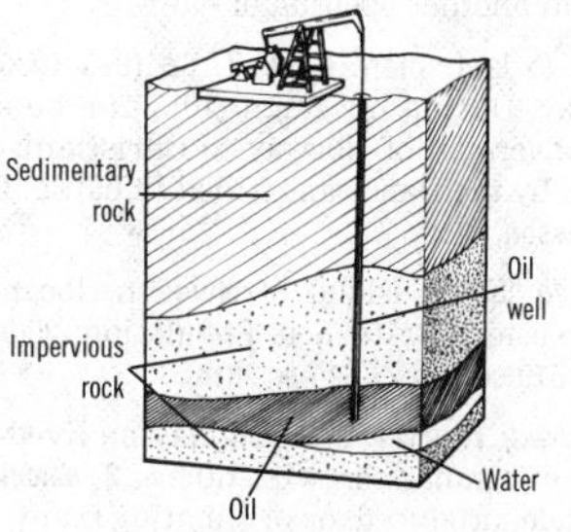

oil well

oil well *n* a shaft drilled into the ground or the bottom of the sea through which petroleum is extracted

oil·y /óylee/ (**-i·er, -i·est**) *adj* **1.** COVERED WITH OIL covered, smeared, or dirtied with oil ○ *don't want to get my hands oily* **2.** CONTAINING OIL containing or producing a lot of oil **3.** LIKE OIL resembling oil in texture, smell, or taste **4.** INGRATIATING unpleasantly eager to please or charm, or unpleasantly expert at doing this —**oil·i·ness** *n*

oink /oyngk/ *interj, n* a representation of the nasal grunting sound made by a pig ■ *vi* (**oinked, oink·ing, oinks**) to make the nasal grunting sound of a pig [Mid-20C. An imitation of the sound]

oint·ment /óyntmənt/ *n* a smooth greasy substance used on the skin to soothe soreness or itchiness, help wounds heal, or make the skin softer [13C. Via Old French *oignement* < Latin *unguentum*]

Oise /waaz/ river in western Europe, flowing from southern Belgium through France and into the Seine. Length: 188 mi./303 km.

O·i·ta /ō i taa/ city and seaport in Japan. It is the capital of Oita prefecture, on northeastern Kyushu Island. Population: 437,699 (2002).

OJ, oj *abbr* orange juice

O·jib·wa /ō jíbbwə, ō jíb wày/ (*plural* **-was** or *same*), **O·jib·way** /ō jíb wày/ (*plural* **-ways** or *same*) *n* **1.** a Native North American people who originally lived north of Lake Huron and who later moved into territories ranging from Saskatchewan across to Michigan **2.** the Algonquian language of the Ojibwa people [Early 18C. < Ojibwa *ojibwe*] —**O·jib·wa** *adj*

OJT *abbr* on-the-job training

OK[1] /ō káy/, **o·kay** (*informal*) *interj* **1.** INDICATING AGREEMENT used to indicate agreement to or approval of what somebody has said or done ○ *"Can you help?" "OK. What do you want me to do?"* **2.** USED TO CHECK FOR APPROVAL used at the end of a statement to inquire whether somebody has understood and agrees with or approves of what was said ○ *It's your job to make the arrangements, OK?* **3.** USED TO INDICATE FINISHING SOMETHING used to indicate that something is finished and that something else will now be done or discussed ○ *OK, let's move to the next item on the agenda.* ■ *adj* **1.** PASSABLE acceptable or tolerable but not exceptional ○ *It's OK for a first effort.* **2.** PHYSICALLY WELL in good health or condition ○ *I'll be OK if I can just sit down for a minute.* **3.** ALLOWABLE acceptable to somebody or permissible ○ *Is it OK for me to call home on the office phone?* **4.** FAIRLY GOOD OR PLEASANT better than just satisfactory or acceptable ○ *Her parents are OK; we get along really well.* ■ *adv* FAIRLY WELL in an acceptable, tolerable, or satisfactory manner ○ *Everything's going OK, except that we're a little bit behind schedule.* ■ *vt* (**OK'ed, OK'ing, OK's; o·kayed, o·kay·ing, o·kays**) **1.** GIVE APPROVAL FOR SOMETHING to give approval for or agreement to something ○ *I just need you to OK the agenda.* **2.** OBTAIN SOMEBODY'S CONSENT to obtain somebody's approval for or agreement to something ○ *I'll need to OK that with my boss.* ■ *n* (*plural* **OK's;** *plural* **o·kays**) APPROVAL approval for doing something or agreement to do something ○ *As soon as she gives the OK, we'll start work.* [Mid-19C. Origin ?]

ORIGIN Of the many competing theories about the origins of ***OK***, the one now most widely accepted is that the letters stand for *oll* or *orl korrect*, a facetious early-19th-century American phonetic spelling of *all correct*. This was reinforced by the fact that they were also coincidentally the initial letters of *Old Kinderhook*, the nickname of US president Martin Van Buren (who was born in Kinderhook, New York State), which were used as a slogan in the presidential election of 1840 (a year after the first record of ***OK*** in print).

OK[2] /ō káy/ *abbr* Oklahoma

O·ka·na·gan /ōkə naagən/ (*plural* **-gans** or *same*), **O·ka·nog·an** /-nóggən/ (*plural* **-ans** or *same*) *n* **1.** a member of a Native North American people who live in southern British Columbia and Washington **2.** LANG same as **Okinagan** —**O·ka·na·gan** *adj*

O·ka·na·gan, Lake /ōkə naagən/ lake in southern British Columbia, Canada. Area: 136 sq. mi./352 sq. km.

O·ka·nog·an *n, adj* PEOPLES, LANG same as **Okanagan**

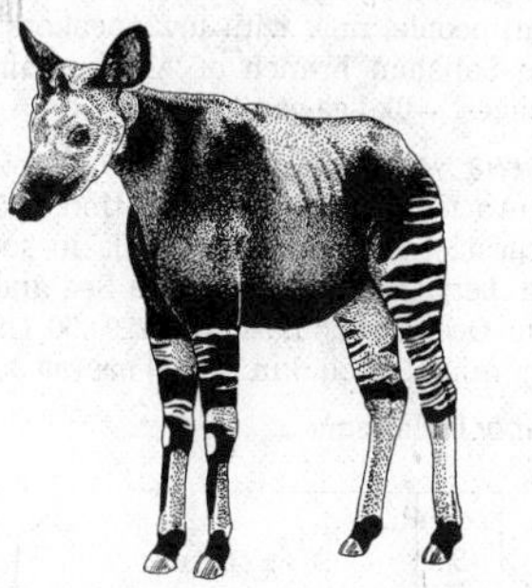

okapi

o·ka·pi /ō kaapee/ (*plural* **-pis** or *same*) *n* a plant-eating animal that resembles a small giraffe but has a short neck. It is chestnut brown with white stripes on its hindquarters. Native to: central Africa. Latin name: *Okapia johnstoni.* [Early 20C. < an African language]

O·ka·van·go /ōkə vaang gō/ river in south central Africa, rising in Angola, where it is called the Cubango, and flowing through Namibia and Botswana into the Okavango Swamp. Length: 1,120 mi./1,800 km.

O·ka·van·go Swamp marsh region in northwestern Botswana, southern Africa, occupying an inland drainage basin. Area: 5,800 sq. mi./15,000 sq. km.

o·kay *interj, adj, adv, vt, n* another spelling of **OK**[1]

O·ka·ya·ma /ōkaa yaamaa/ city and port in Japan, on western Honshu Island, on the Inland Sea. Population: 621,809 (2002).

O·kee·cho·bee, Lake /ōki chṓbee/ lake in Florida, north of the Everglades National Park, forming part of the Cross-Florida Waterway. Area: 663 sq. mi./1,720 sq. km.

O'Keeffe /ō keef/, **Georgia** (1887–1986) US artist. She is known for her stylized still lifes, especially of flowers and objects found in the desert. See illustration on next page

"You paint *from* your subject, not what you see, so you can't be bothered with changes

Georgia O'Keeffe

in light. I rarely paint anything I don't know very well."
[Georgia O'Keeffe, *The Artist's Voice: Talks with 17 Artists*, Katherine Kuh; 1962]

O·ke·fe·no·kee Swamp /ōkifə nṓkee-/ swamp in southeastern Georgia and northeastern Florida. It is noted for its rich wildlife. Area: 660 sq. mi./1,710 sq. km.

o·key·do·key /ṑkee dṓkee/, **o·key·doke** /-dṓk/ *interj* same as **OK**[1] *interj* (sense 1) (*informal*) [Mid-20C. Alteration]

Ok·hotsk, Sea of /ō kótsk, ə khótsk/ sea lying off the eastern coast of Siberia, part of the northwestern Pacific Ocean. Area: 590,000 sq. mi./1,528,000 sq. km.

Ok·ie /ṓkee/ *n US* **1.** an offensive term for a migrant farm laborer, especially one from Oklahoma or neighboring Dust Bowl states during the 1930s (*slang insult*) **2.** somebody who comes from Oklahoma (*slang*) [Mid-20C. Shortening and alteration of OKLAHOMA]

Ok·i·na·gan /ōki nóggən/ *n* the language of the Okanagan people, now with few speakers. It belongs to the Salishan branch of Algonquian-Wakashan languages. —**Ok·i·na·gan** *adj*

O·ki·na·wa /ōki naáwə/ **1.** city on south central Okinawa Island, Japan. Population: 125,762 (2002). **2.** largest of the Ryukyu Islands in southwestern Japan, between the East China Sea and the North Pacific Ocean. Population: 1,229,000 (1991).. Area: 871 sq. mi./2,255 sq. km. —**O·ki·na·wan** *adj, n*

Okla. *abbr* Oklahoma

Oklahoma

O·kla·ho·ma /ōklə hṓmə/ state in the south central United States, bordered by Colorado, Kansas, Missouri, Arkansas, Texas, and New Mexico. Capital: Oklahoma City. Population: 3,493,714 (2002 estimate).. Area: 69,903 sq. mi./181,048 sq. km. —**O·kla·ho·man** *adj, n*

O·kla·ho·ma City capital city of Oklahoma, located in the central part of the state. Population: 519,034 (2002 estimate).

O·kla·ho·ma rain·storm *n regional* same as **dust storm** (*humorous*)

o·kra /ṓkrə/ (*plural same* or **o·kras**) *n* **1.** a green finger-length seed pod, cooked and eaten as a vegetable or used to thicken soups and stews **2.** a tall tropical plant that produces okra pods. Native to: Asia. Latin name: *Abelmoschus esculentus*. **3.** FOOD same as **gumbo** (sense 1) [Early 18C. Of West African origin, related to Igbo *okuro*]

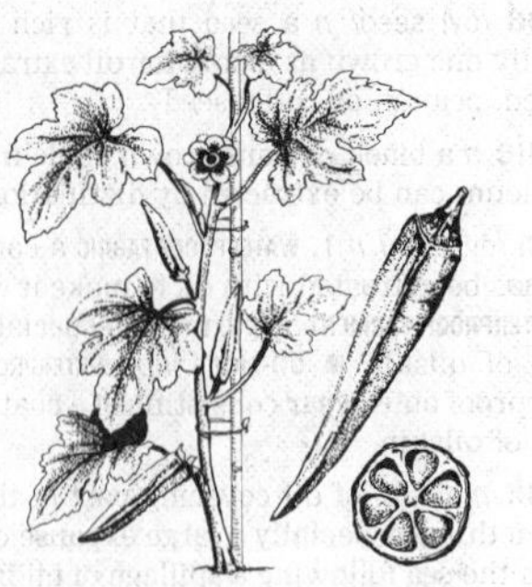
okra

ok·ta /óktə/ *n* a unit of measure used to specify the amount of cloud cover, especially over an airfield, equivalent to enough clouds to cover one eighth of the sky [Mid-20C. Alteration of OCTO-]

-ol[1] *suffix* compound containing hydroxyl, especially an alcohol or phenol ○ *glycerol* [< ALCOHOL]

-ol[2] *suffix* another spelling of **-ole**

O·laf II /ṓ laaf, ṓləf/, **O·lav II, St.** (995–1030) king of Norway. During his reign (1015–28), he completed the conversion of Norway to Christianity. He was ousted by the Danes and killed in battle. Full name **Haraldsson, Olaf**

Ö·land /ő laand/ island of Sweden, located in the southwestern Baltic Sea. Population: 25,382 (1992).. Area: 519 sq. mi./1,344 sq. km.

old /ōld/ *adj* **1.** HAVING LIVED LONG having lived for many years in comparison with others **2.** ORIGINATING YEARS AGO made, produced, or originating many years ago and still in existence **3.** SENIOR showing physical or mental characteristics sometimes associated with long life **4.** WISE showing the understanding, wisdom, or behavior that results from long experience of life ○ *She acts much older than she is.* **5.** EXISTING FOR SPECIFIC TIME having lived or existed for a particular amount of time (*usually used in combination*) ○ *The day was only a few hours old.* **6.** ANCIENT belonging to the remote past ○ *the remains of an old civilization* **7.** FORMER belonging to an earlier period of something such as somebody's life ○ *We drove past my old school.* **8.** FAMILIAR familiar from past experience ○ *She always makes the same old excuses.* **9.** EXISTING OR USED OVER TIME having existed or been used for a long time, especially if showing wear or age ○ *Change into old clothes before gardening.* **10.** *also* **Old** EARLIER existing before one or all of the other stages, forms, or instances of something, especially a particular language ○ *Old English words* **11.** USED FOR EMPHASIS used as an intensifier (*informal*) ○ *any old reason* **12.** EXPRESSING FAMILIARITY used to express affection or familiarity (*informal*) ○ *Good old Charlie!* **13.** *US* ANNOYINGLY FAMILIAR annoyingly familiar, especially as a result of repetition (*informal*) ○ *That silly joke has gotten very old.* **14.** GEOL ERODED reduced through erosion and weathering **15.** GEOL SLOWER MOVING characterized by slower moving water and broad, flat floodplains ■ *n* **1.** PERSON OF PARTICULAR AGE somebody of a particular age (*used in combination*) ○ *a two-year-old* **2.** OLD THINGS things or customs that are old ○ *to balance the old with the new* [Old English *eald*] —**old·ness** *n*

USAGE See *elder*[1].

ORIGIN *Old* is ultimately from an Indo-European word meaning "to grow, nourish," which, through Latin *alere*, is also the ancestor of English *adolescent*, *adult*, *alimony*, and *alumnus*. In Latin the meaning evolved into "high," as seen in the English derivatives *alto*, *exalt*, and *haughty*, whereas the Germanic languages preserved an old past participle meaning "grown, old," which is also the ancestor of English *elder*[1], *eldest*, and *world*.

old age *n* the latter years of somebody's life lived out to its full term

old age se·cu·ri·ty *n* in Canada, a government pension program for people over 65

Old Bailey *n* the chief criminal court in England and Wales, located in London on the site of Newgate Prison, which was demolished to make way for it in 1902

old boy *n UK* **1.** a former student of a boys' or men's school, especially a British prep school or college **2.** used as a familiar way of addressing a man or boy (*dated informal*) ○ *See here, old boy, you can't enter this club uninvited.*

old-boy net·work *n* a system of informal contacts between men who belong to the same social group, especially alumni of a school or university, and use their influence to help one another

Old Church Sla·von·ic *n* the earliest written Slavonic language, still used in religious services in some Eastern Orthodox Churches

Old Col·o·ny *n* a nickname for Massachusetts

old coun·try *n* an immigrant's country of origin

Old Do·min·ion *n* a nickname for Virginia

old·en /ṓldən/ *adj* in or from the distant past (*archaic or literary*) [14C. < OLD + -EN]

Ol·den·burg /ṓldən bùrg, -bòòrk/ city and river port in Lower Saxony State, northwestern Germany, situated approximately 25 mi./40 km west of Bremen. Population: 149,691 (1997).

Old·en·burg /ṓldən bùrg/, **Claes** (*b.* 1929) Swedish-born US sculptor. A pioneer of pop art, he is known for his sagging "soft sculptures" of everyday objects. Full name **Oldenburg, Claes Thure**

"I am for an art that tells you the time of day, or where such and such a street is. I am for an art that helps old ladies across the street."
[Claes Oldenburg, *Statement for exhibition catalogue*; 1961]

Old Eng·lish *n* **1.** the earliest form of the English language, used up to about A.D. 1150. It was first written using the runic alphabet. **2.** a form of black-letter typeface used by English printers until the 18th century —**Old Eng·lish** *adj*

Old English sheepdog

Old Eng·lish sheep·dog *n* a large dog with a long shaggy coat and dark gray and white markings [Because they were originally bred in England]

old face *n UK* same as **old style**

Old Faith·ful *n* an informal name for the best-known geyser in Yellowstone National Park, in northwestern Wyoming. It erupts on average once every 75 minutes for up to 5 minutes, shooting a column of steam and hot water up to 184 ft./56 m high. (*informal*)

old fart *n* an offensive term for somebody, usually a person in authority, who is regarded as being set in his or her ways and lacking a sense of humor or fun (*slang insult*)

old-fash·ioned *adj* **1.** OUT-OF-DATE characteristic of or belonging to a time in the past and no longer considered fashionable or suitable for the present **2.** MAINTAINING OLD-STYLE WAYS favoring or deliberately maintaining ideas, behavior, or ways of doing things from an earlier time ■ *n* BEVERAGES WHISKEY COCKTAIL a cocktail made with whiskey, bitters, sugar, and lemon peel and garnished with fruit

SYNONYMS ***old-fashioned, outdated, antiquated, archaic, obsolete, passé, antediluvian***

CORE MEANING: no longer in current use or no longer considered fashionable

old-fashioned characteristic of or belonging to a time in the past and no longer considered fashionable or suitable for the present ○ *She drove an old-fashioned car with running boards.* ○ *My uncle was old-fashioned enough to insist on silence at meals.* **outdated** superseded by something better, more fashionable, or more technologically advanced ○ *The information officers were relying on outdated sources and missed the crucial connection.* **antiquated** in need of updating or replacing ○ *The central heating was antiquated and broke down at the first sign of cold weather.* **archaic** belonging or relating to a much earlier period ○ *Much of the language of the poem is obscure or archaic.* **obsolete** superseded by something newer, though possibly still in use ○ *Spin-dry washing machines rendered the wringer obsolete.* **passé** no longer current or fashionable ○ *Coats like that are definitely passé: you need to buy a new one.* **antediluvian** (*humorous*) extremely old-fashioned or outdated ○ *condemned what he called the antediluvian attitudes of the union hierarchy*

Old French *n* the earliest form of the French language, used until about A.D. 1400 or, in some analyses, A.D. 1600 —**Old French** *adj*

old girl *n UK* **1.** a former student at a girls' or women's school, especially a British prep school or college **2.** used as a familiar way of addressing a woman or girl (*dated informal*) ○ *Sorry, old girl, didn't mean to lose my temper like that.*

old-girl net·work *n* a system of informal contacts between women who belong to the same social group, especially alumnae of a school or university, and use their influence to help one another

Old Glo·ry *n* a nickname for the flag of the United States

old gold *adj* of a dark dull yellow color, sometimes tinged with brown —**old gold** *n*

old growth *n* a long-established forest or woodland that contains some large old trees and has a relatively stable and diverse community of plants and animals (*hyphenated when used before a noun*)

old guard, **Old Guard** *n* the members of a group or organization who have been in it the longest, are the staunchest defenders of its traditions, and are the least amenable to change

Old·ham /ṓldəm/ industrial city near Manchester, northwestern England. Population: 217,273 (2001).

old hand *n* somebody who is thoroughly experienced in a field of activity

old hat *adj* boringly familiar or old-fashioned (*informal*)

Old High Ger·man *n* the form of German used in written documents up to about A.D. 1200 —**Old High Ger·man** *adj*

old·ie /ṓldee/ *n* (*informal*) **1.** something old, especially an old popular song **2.** an offensive term for somebody who has reached an advanced age

Old King·dom *n* the period of ancient Egyptian history that comprises the third to sixth dynasties, from around 2700 to 2150 B.C., when the capital was at Memphis and the great pyramids were built

old la·dy *n* (*slang*) **1.** an offensive term for somebody's mother **2.** an offensive term for a man's wife or for a woman partner in a relationship

Old Lat·in *n* the form of the Latin language used until about the middle of the first century B.C. —**Old Lat·in** *adj*

old-line *adj* **1.** conservative or traditional in principles, policy, or outlook ○ *old-line fans praising players of 40 years ago* **2.** in existence for a long time and having a high social status or good reputation that has endured ○ *an old-line publisher, still proudly independent*

Old Line State *n* a nickname for Maryland

old maid *n* **1.** OFFENSIVE TERM an offensive term for a woman in or past middle age who has never been married and seems unlikely ever to marry **2.** OFFENSIVE TERM an offensive term for a woman or man regarded as being excessively prim or fussy **3.** CARDS CARD GAME a card game played with a deck from which one card, usually a queen, has been removed. Players collect pairs of cards and the player left with the unpaired card loses. **4.** CARDS LOSER IN OLD MAID the losing player in a game of old maid —**old-maid·ish** *adj*

old maid flow·er *n Southern US* same as **zinnia**

old man *n* **1.** OFFENSIVE TERM an offensive term for somebody's father (*slang*) **2.** OFFENSIVE TERM an offensive term for a woman's husband or for a man partner in a relationship (*slang*) **3.** COMMANDING OFFICER a man in a position of authority, especially a commanding officer (*slang*) ○ *The old man is on the bridge, mad as a hornet.* **4.** *UK* FAMILIAR ADDRESS TO MAN used as a familiar way of addressing another man (*dated slang*) ○ *Look here, old man, I'm in a spot of bother and wonder if you could help me out.*

old-man's-beard *n* a plant that has trailing or hanging whitish growths, e.g., traveler's-joy, Spanish moss, or the fringe tree

old mas·ter *n* **1.** a great European painter of the period dating roughly from the late Middle Ages to the 18th century **2.** a picture painted by an old master

Old Nick *n* a nickname for the devil (*dated slang*)

Old Norse *n* the North Germanic language from which the modern Scandinavian languages are derived, in use in Scandinavia from about A.D. 700 to 1350 —**Old Norse** *adj*

LANGUAGE HERITAGE See ***Scandinavian***.

Old North State *n* a nickname for North Carolina

Old Red Sand·stone *n* a sedimentary rock, usually red in color, formed during the Devonian period and found in the United Kingdom and northwestern Europe

old rose *adj* of a deep grayish pink color —**old rose** *n*

old salt *n* a sailor who has years of experience at sea

Old Sax·on *n* LANG same as **Saxon** (sense 2) —**Old Sax·on** *adj*

old school *n* a group of people who adhere to traditional or old-fashioned values and practices ○ *As a disciplinarian of the old school, he was horrified at the laxity of the new regime.* —**old-school** *adj*

old school tie *n* **1.** *UK* NECKTIE a necktie whose colors indicate which school, especially which British prep school, the wearer attended **2.** *UK* SCHOOL LOYALTY AND TRADITION the shared attitudes, traditions, and loyalties attributed to people who attended the same school, especially the same British prep school or college **3.** CLANNISHNESS an attitude of smug self-sufficiency coupled with indifference or hostility to outsiders that is shown by members of a tight-knit group

old skool /-skool/ *adj* reminiscent of or inspired by something from a slightly earlier period of popular culture, especially in music (*slang*) [Alteration of OLD SCHOOL]

old sol·dier *n* **1.** VETERAN SOLDIER an experienced and long-serving soldier **2.** FORMER SOLDIER somebody who formerly was a soldier **3.** VETERAN somebody with a great deal of experience

old·squaw /ṓld skwàw/, **old-squaw**, **old squaw** *n* a duck with a black back and wings, a white breast, a brown-and-white head, and a long pointed tail. Native to: Arctic seas. Latin name: *Clangula hyemalis.*

USAGE See ***squaw***.

old·ster /ṓldstər/ *n* an offensive term for somebody who has reached an advanced age (*informal*) [Early 19C. After YOUNGSTER]

old style *n* a typeface that shows little difference between light and heavy strokes and has slanting serifs. It originated in the 18th century.

Old Style *n* the reckoning of dates by the Julian calendar

old-style *adj* characteristic of the past but now superseded by something else

old-talk *Carib vi* (**old-talk·ing**) to chat casually ■ *n* relaxed informal conversation [Perhaps < old people's talk]

Old Tes·ta·ment *n* the first part of the Christian Bible, corresponding to the Hebrew Bible, that recounts the creation of the world and the history of ancient Israel and contains the Psalms and the prophetic books

old-time *adj* **1.** characteristic of or dating from a time in the past ○ *old-time religion* **2.** in existence for a long time ○ *the old-time families of the town*

old-tim·er *n* **1.** a senior citizen, especially a man (*sometimes considered offensive*) **2.** somebody who has been living in a place or involved in an activity for a long time

Ol·du·vai Gorge /ṓldə vī, -vày, -wày-/ ravine in northern Tanzania, where fossil remains of early humans and hominids have been found

old·wife /ṓld wīf/ (*plural* **-wives** /-wīvz/ or *same*) *n* an edible ocean fish of several species, e.g., an alewife or a menhaden

old wives' tale *n* a traditional belief or story, passed down by word of mouth, that is now considered untrue or superstitious [< *old wife*, an old woman]

old wom·an *n* (*slang*) **1.** an offensive term for somebody's mother **2.** an offensive term for a man's wife or for a woman partner in a relationship **3.** an offensive term for a man that deliberately insults his courage and decisiveness —**old-wom·an·ish** *adj*

Old World *n* the part of the world, consisting of Europe, Asia, and Africa, that was known to Europeans before Columbus made his first voyage to the Americas

old-world *adj* considered to be characteristic of a former and more gracious age

o·lé /ō láy/ *interj* used to express triumph, excited approval, or encouragement in Spanish. It is used especially at bullfights and during flamenco dancing. ■ *n* a cry or shout of olé [Early 20C. < Spanish]

OLE /ṓlee/ *abbr* COMPUT object linking and embedding

ole- *prefix* same as **oleo-** (*used before vowels*)

-ole *suffix* **1.** a chemical compound containing a five-membered, usually heterocyclic, ring ○ *carbazole* **2.** a chemical compound, usually an ether, that does not contain hydroxyl ○ *anisole* [Via French < Latin *oleum* (see OIL)]

o·le·a CHEM plural of **oleum**

o·le·ag·i·nous /ōlee ájjənəss/ *adj* **1.** CONTAINING OIL containing or producing oil **2.** LIKE OIL similar to oil in nature or consistency **3.** INGRATIATING unpleasantly eager to please, charm, or be of service ○ *An oleaginous flunky showered me with exaggerated compliments.* [Mid-17C. Directly and via Old French *oleagineux* < Latin *oleaginus* "of an olive tree, oily" < *olea* "olive tree," alteration of *oliva* (see OLIVE)] —**o·le·ag·i·nous·ly** *adv* —**o·le·ag·i·nous·ness** *n*

O·le·an /ṓlee àn, ōlee án/ city in Cattaraugus County, southwestern New York, situated on the Allegheny River. Population: 15,024 (2002 estimate).

o·le·an·der /ṓlee ándər/ (*plural* **-ders** or *same*) *n* a poisonous evergreen bush with leathery lance-shaped leaves and long seed pods. Flowers: sweet-smelling white, pink, or purple. Native to: Mediterranean region. Latin name: *Nerium oleander.* [Mid-16C. < medieval Latin]

o·le·as·ter /ṓlee ástər/ (*plural* **-ters** or *same*) *n* **1.** an evergreen or deciduous bush with glossy leaves that are silvery underneath. Flowers: small, white, greenish yellow. Genus: *Elaeagnus.* **2.** the fruit of an oleaster, which resembles an olive [14C. Via Latin < *olea* "olive tree," alteration of *oliva* (see OLIVE)]

o·le·ate /ṓlee àyt/ *n* a salt or ester of oleic acid

o·lec·ra·non /ō lékrə nòn/ *n* the upper end of the ulna bone that extends beyond the joint of the elbow to form the elbow's hard projecting point [Early 18C. < Greek *ōlekranon* < *ōlenē* "elbow" + *kranion* "head"]

o·le·fin /ṓləfin/ *n* **1.** *also* **o·le·fin fi·ber** a synthetic fiber that is a long chain of polymers **2.** CHEM same as **alkene** [Mid-19C. < French *(gaz) oléfiant* "oil-forming (gas)" < Latin *oleum* "oil" (see OIL)]

o·le·ic /ō lée ik/ *adj* **1.** relating to or derived from oil **2.** relating to or derived from oleic acid

o·le·ic ac·id *n* a colorless oily liquid. Source: animal and vegetable fats. Use: manufacture of soap, ointments, cosmetics, and lubricating oils. Formula: $C_{18}H_{34}O_2$.

o·le·in /ṓlee in/, **o·le·ine** /ṓlee in, -een/ *n* a yellow oily liquid that occurs naturally in most fats. Use: textile lubricant.

o·le·o[1] /ólee ò/ *n* same as **margarine** (*dated*) [Shortening of OLEOMARGARINE]

o·le·o[2] /ólee ò/ (*plural* **-os**) *n* PRINTING same as **oleograph** (*informal*) [Shortening]

oleo- *prefix* **1.** oil, oily ○ *oleograph* **2.** oleic acid ○ *oleate* [Via French *oléo-* < Latin *oleum* (see OIL)]

o·le·o·graph /ólee ə gràf/ *n* a colored lithographic print made on canvas with oil colors in order to imitate an oil painting —**o·le·o·graph·ic** /ólee ə gráffik/ *adj*

o·le·o·mar·ga·rine /ólee ō maárjərin/ *n* same as **margarine** (*dated*)

o·le·o oil *n* a yellow fatty substance extracted from beef fat. Use: manufacture of margarine, soap.

o·le·o·res·in /ólee ō rézz'n/ *n* a mixture of a resin and an essential oil, either obtained naturally from plants or produced synthetically

o·le·um /ólee əm/ *n* a solution of sulfur trioxide in sulfuric acid [Early 20C. < Latin, "oil" (see OIL)]

ol·fac·tion /ol fáksh'n/ *n* **1.** the sense of smell **2.** the act of smelling something [Mid-19C. < Latin *olfacere* "to smell"]

ol·fac·tom·e·ter /òl fak tómmətər/ *n* an instrument for measuring the keenness of somebody's sense of smell [Late 19C. < OLFACTION + -METER]

ol·fac·to·ry /ol fáktəree/ *adj* used in smelling or relating to the sense of smell [Mid-17C. Via assumed Latin *olfactorius* "used for smelling" < *olfacere* "to smell" < *olere* + *facere* "do"]

ol·fac·to·ry bulb *n* the area of the brain from which the olfactory nerves extend

ol·i·ba·num /o líbbənəm/ *n* CHEM same as **frankincense** [14C. Via medieval Latin *olibanum* and Greek *libanos* < Arabic *al-lubān* "storax"]

ol·i·garch /ólli gaàrk/ *n* a ruler or leader in an oligarchy [Early 17C. < Greek *oligarkhēs* < *oligos* "few" + -ARCH]

ol·i·gar·chy /ólli gaàrkee/ (*plural* **-chies**) *n* **1.** SMALL GOVERNING GROUP a small group of people who together govern a nation or control an organization, often for their own purposes **2.** ENTITY RULED BY OLIGARCHY a nation governed or an organization controlled by an oligarchy **3.** GOVERNMENT BY SMALL GROUP government or control by a small group of people [Late 15C. Via French or medieval Latin < Greek *oligarkhia* < *oligos* "few" + *-arkhia* "-archy" (see -ARCH)] —**ol·i·gar·chic** /ólli gaárkik/ *adj*

oligo- *prefix* few ○ *oligophagous* [< Greek *oligos* "small, little, few"]

Ol·i·go·cene /ólligō seèn, ə líggə-/ *n* the epoch of geologic time, 38 million to 24 million years ago, during which primates first appeared. See table at **geologic time** —**Ol·i·go·cene** *adj*

ol·i·go·clase /ólligō klàyss, ə líggə-/ *n* a white, bluish, or reddish yellow feldspar mineral of the plagioclase series. Source: igneous and metamorphic rocks. [Mid-19C. < OLIGO- + Greek *klasis* "breaking" < *klan* "break" (see CLASTIC), from its imperfect cleavage]

o·lig·o·mer /ólligəmər, ə líggə-/ *n* a polymer consisting of fewer than five monomer units —**o·lig·o·mer·ic** /òlligə mérrik, ə lìggə-/ *adj* —**o·lig·o·mer·i·za·tion** /òlligəməri záysh'n, ə lìggəməri-/ *n*

ol·i·go·nu·cle·o·tide /òlligō nóoklee ə tìd, ə lìggə-/ *n* a polymeric chain containing ten nucleotides or fewer

ol·i·go·pep·tide /òlligō pép tìd, ə lìggə-/ *n* a peptide consisting of fewer than ten amino acids

ol·i·goph·a·gous /òlli góffəgəss/ *adj* feeding on a restricted range of foodstuffs, usually a small number of different plants

ol·i·gop·o·ly /òlli góppəlee/ (*plural* **-lies**) *n* an economic condition in which there are so few suppliers of a product that one supplier's actions can have a significant impact on prices and on its competitors [Late 19C. < OLIGO- + MONOPOLY] —**ol·i·gop·o·lis·tic** /òlli gopə lístik/ *adj*

ol·i·gop·so·ny /òlli gópsənee/ (*plural* **-nies**) *n* an economic condition in which there are so few buyers for a product that one buyer's actions can have a significant impact on prices and the market in general [Mid-20C. < OLIGO- + MONOPSONY] —**ol·i·gop·so·nis·tic** /òlli gopsə nístik/ *adj*

ol·i·go·sac·cha·ride /òlligō sákə rìd, ə lìggə-/ *n* a carbohydrate made up of a relatively small number of linked monosaccharides

ol·i·go·tro·phic /òlligō tróffik, ə lìggə-/ *adj* describes bodies of water such as lakes that contain relatively little plant life or nutrients, but are rich in dissolved oxygen

o·lin·go /ō líng gō/ (*plural* **-gos**) *n* a small tree-dwelling nocturnal mammal similar in appearance to a slim sleek raccoon. Native to: tropical South and Central America. Latin name: *Bassaricyon gabbii.* [Early 20C. < American Spanish]

o·li·o /ólee ò/ (*plural same* or **-os**) *n* **1.** ASSORTMENT a miscellaneous collection of things **2.** SPICED STEW a highly spiced stew made from a variety of meats and vegetables and usually including chickpeas **3.** ARTS MISCELLANY OR MEDLEY something made up of works of various kinds or works by different people, e.g., a literary miscellany or a musical medley [Mid-17C. Alteration of Spanish *olla* "pot, stew" (see OLLA)]

olive

ol·ive /ólliv/ *n* **1.** FOOD GREEN OR BLACK FRUIT a small oval bitter fruit with a pit, green when unripe and black when ripe, that yields olive oil **2.** TREES OLIVE TREE a widely cultivated evergreen tree that produces olives. Native to: Mediterranean region. Latin name: *Olea europaea.* (*often used before a noun*) **3.** INDUST OLIVE WOOD the wood of the olive tree. Use: decorative work. **4.** TREES TREE RESEMBLING OLIVE a tree or bush that resembles the olive tree **5.** COLORS same as **olive green** [12C. Via Latin *oliva* < Greek *elaiwa*, a variant of *elaia* "olive, olive oil"]

ol·ive branch *n* **1.** a gesture or offer intended to bring about a reconciliation **2.** a branch of an olive tree used as a symbol of peace [< Genesis 8:11]

ol·ive drab *n* **1.** GRAYISH GREEN a grayish green color **2.** *US* GREEN CLOTH a cloth dyed in an olive drab color. Use: military uniforms. **3.** GREEN MILITARY UNIFORM a military uniform made of olive drab cloth, especially one worn in the United States army —**ol·ive drab** *adj*

ol·ive green *n* a deep yellowish green color —**ol·ive green** *adj*

o·liv·e·nite /ō lívvə nìt, óllivə-/ *n* a rare olive green mineral that is a hydrated arsenate of copper. Formula: $Cu_2(AsO_4)OH$. [Early 19C. < German *Olivenit* < *Olive* "olive"; from its color]

ol·ive oil *n* a monounsaturated oil with a distinctive flavor extracted from olives. Use: salad dressings, cooking, manufacture of soap and cosmetics.

Ol·i·ver /óllivər/, **King** (1885–1938) US musician. A cornet player, he was a pioneer of early New Orleans jazz, strongly influencing Louis Armstrong. Born **Oliver, Joseph**

o·live rid·ley *n* a small endangered ocean turtle with a drab green back and a prominent beak. Native to: Pacific Ocean. Latin name: *Lepidochelys olivacea.*

Ol·ives, Mount of ➧ **Mount of Olives**

O·liv·i·er /ə lívvee ày/, **Laurence, 1st Baron Olivier of Brighton** (1907–89) British actor and director. An influential Shakespearean actor, he was a founding director of the British National Theatre (1961–73). Full name **Olivier, Laurence Kerr**

> "Shakespeare—the nearest thing in incarnation to the eye of God."

Laurence Olivier

> [Laurence Olivier. Quoted in *Kenneth Harris Talking To Sir Laurence Olivier,* Kenneth Harris; 1971]

ol·i·vine /ólli veèn/ *n* an olive-green magnesium-iron silicate mineral. Source: igneous rocks. Use: refractories, gems. —**ol·i·vin·ic** /òlli vínnik/ *adj* —**ol·i·vi·nit·ic** /òllivə níttik/ *adj*

ol·la /óllə, áwlyə, áwyə/ *n Hispanic* **1.** a large, usually unglazed pot with a spherical body and a wide mouth, used in Latin America and the southwestern United States for storing water and for cooking **2.** FOOD same as **olla podrida** (sense 1) [Early 17C. Via Spanish < Latin *aulla* "pot"]

ol·la po·dri·da /òllə pə dreédə, àwlyə-, àwyə-/ (*plural* **ol·la po·dri·das** or **ol·las po·dri·das**) *n Hispanic* **1.** a traditional Spanish and Latin American stew of meat and vegetables, usually containing sausage and chickpeas, and highly seasoned **2.** a miscellaneous mixture or assortment of things [< Spanish, "rotten pot"]

ol·lie /óllee/ *n* in skateboarding, a leap into the air on the board performed by pushing down on the rear end of the board (*slang*) [Late 20C. After the Florida skateboarder Alan "*Ollie*" Gelfand]

olm /olm, ōlm/ *n* a sightless salamander, living in caves of southeastern Europe, that has a slender white body with a narrow head, tiny limbs, and red gills. The skin-covered vestigial eyes are sensitive to light. Latin name: *Proteus anguinus.* [Early 20C. < German]

Ol·mec /ól mèk/ (*plural* **-mecs** or *same*) *n* **1.** a Central American civilization that arose around 1200 B.C., before the Maya civilization. Notable features of this civilization were irrigated agriculture, urbanism, and the beginnings of calendar and writing systems. (*often used before a noun*) **2.** a member of one of the peoples who participated in the Olmec civilization [Late 18C. < Nahuatl *olmecatl* "somebody who lives in the rubber country"]

Olm·sted /ólm stèd/, **Frederick Law** (1822–1903) US landscape architect. His naturalistic works, including New York's Central Park, greatly influenced park design throughout the United States and Canada.

> "It is one of the great purposes of the Park to supply to the hundreds of thousands of tired workers...a specimen of God's handiwork that shall be to them, inexpensively, what a month or two in the White Mountains or the Adirondacks is, at great cost, to those in easier circumstances."
>
> [Frederick Law Olmsted, *Report*; April 28, 1858]

ol·o·gy /ólləjee/ (*plural* **-gies**) *n* a science or academic field, especially one whose name ends in "-ology" (*informal*) ○ *people studying ologies you've never heard of* [Early 19C. < -LOGY]

-ology *suffix* same as **-logy**

o·lo·ro·so /òlə róssō/ *n* a golden-colored full-bodied sherry, usually medium-sweet in taste [Late 19C. Via Spanish, "fragrant" < Latin *olere* "to smell"]

O·lym·pi·a /ə límpee ə, ō-/ **1.** plain in southwestern Greece, in the western Peloponnese, near the Ionian Sea. It was an ancient religious site sacred to Zeus, and the first Olympic Games were held there in 776 B.C. **2.** city and capital of Washington, situated at the mouth of the Deschutes River on Puget Sound in the western part of the state. It has a deep-water port, and is a commercial and manufacturing center. Population: 43,519 (2002 estimate).

O·lym·pi·ad /ō límpee àd/ *n* **1.** an occasion when the modern Olympic Games take place **2.** the four-year interval between one Olympic Games and the next, used by the ancient Greeks as a way of calculating dates [14C. Via Latin < Greek *Olumpia*, where the games were held]

O·lym·pi·a Heights town in Dade County, Florida. Population: 37,792 (2002 estimate).

O·lym·pi·an /ō límpee ən/ *adj* **1.** ENORMOUS extraordinarily great or demanding **2.** LIKE GREEK DEITY characteristic of a Greek god or goddess, or resembling one in power, majesty, or beauty (*literary*) **3.** MYTHOL OF MOUNT OLYMPUS relating to Mount Olympus, the home of the gods in Greek mythology **4.** ALOOF OR SUPERIOR so superior or grand as to be above everyday events and concerns ○ *his Olympian indifference to petty squabbles* **5.** OF OLYMPIA relating to Olympia, the ancient religious site in southwestern Greece ■ *n* **1.** OLYMPIC ATHLETE a competitor in the Olympic Games **2.** SUPERIOR PERSON somebody whose status is superior to everyday events and concerns **3.** MYTHOL GREEK DEITY in Greek mythology, one of the twelve major gods or goddesses who had their home on Mount Olympus **4.** PEOPLES SOMEBODY FROM OLYMPIA somebody who lived in ancient Olympia [15C. < Latin *Olympus* < Greek *olumpios*]

O·lym·pic /ə límpik, ō-/ *adj* relating to the Olympic Games

O·lym·pic Games *npl* **1.** a large-scale international sports contest intended to promote international goodwill. It has been held every four years since 1896, except for 1940 and 1944, in different cities around the world. **2.** an ancient Greek religious festival held every four years at Olympia in honor of Zeus, with athletic, literary, and musical contests involving participants from all parts of Greece

O·lym·pic Moun·tains /ə lìmpik-, ō lìm-/ mountain range in northwestern Washington, on the Olympic Peninsula, predominantly in Jefferson and Clallam counties. The highest peak is Mount Olympus, 7,965 ft./2,428 m.

O·lym·pic Na·tion·al Park national park in northwestern Washington, in the Olympic Mountains, noted for its temperate rain forest and glaciers. It was established in 1938. Area: 1,442 sq. mi./3,734 sq. km.

O·lym·pics /ə límpiks, ō-/ *n* the modern Olympic Games (*takes a singular or plural verb*)

O·lym·pus, Mount /ə límpəss, ō-/ highest mountain in Greece, located in the north of the country. In Greek mythology it was believed to be the home of the gods. Height: 9,570 ft./2,917 m.

O·lym·pus Mons /-mónz/ large volcano in the northern hemisphere of Mars. It is three times as high as Mount Everest. Height: 16 mi./26 km.

om *abbr* Oman (*used in Internet addresses*) See table at **domain name**

Om /ōm/, **Aum** *n* a sacred syllable that is chanted in Hindu and Buddhist prayers and mantras. It is symbolic of creation, destruction, and preservation, or of the primary trinities of Hinduism or Buddhism. [Late 18C. < Sanskrit]

O.M. *abbr* Order of Merit

-oma *suffix* tumor ○ *encephaloma* [Directly and via modern Latin < Greek *-ōma*]

O·ma·ha[1] /ṓmə hàa/ (*plural* **-has** or *same*) *n* **1.** a member of a Native North American people who live in northeastern Nebraska **2.** the Siouan language of the Omaha people, now with few speakers [Early 19C. < Omaha *umonhon* "upstream people"] —**O·ma·ha** *adj*

O·ma·ha[2] /ṓmə hàa/ city in eastern Nebraska, on the Missouri River. Population: 399,357 (2002 estimate).

Oman

O·man /ō maán/ country on the southeastern Arabian Peninsula, on the Gulf of Oman. Language: Arabic. Currency: Omani rial. Capital: Muscat. Population: 2,807,125 (2001).. Area: 119,500 sq. mi./309,500 sq. km. Official name **Sultanate of Oman** —**O·man·i** /ō maánee/ *adj, n*

O·man, Gulf of arm of the Arabian Sea, situated between northern Oman and the southeastern coast of Iran

O·mar Khay·yam /ō maar kī aám/ (1050?–1122) Persian poet, mathematician, and astronomer. His *Rubáiyát* is an extensive collection of four-line stanzas, some of which were translated into English by Edward Fitzgerald (1859).

o·ma·sum /ō máyssəm/ (*plural* **-sa** /-sə/) *n* the third compartment of the stomach of a cow or other ruminant, situated between the abomasum and the reticulum. The inner surface has folds that break up food particles. [Early 18C. < Latin, "bullock's tripe"]

O·may·yad *n* HIST, ISLAM another spelling of **Umayyad**

OMB *abbr US* Office of Management and Budget

om·bre /ómbər/, **om·ber** *n* a card game, popular in the 18th century, for three players, using forty cards, in which one player competes against the other two [Mid-17C. < Spanish *hombre* "man, ombre" < Latin *homo* "man"]

om·buds·man /ómbədzmən, -bòodz-, -budz-/ (*plural* **-men** /-mən/) *n* **1.** somebody, especially a man, responsible for investigating and resolving complaints from consumers or other members of the public against a company, institution, or other organization **2.** *UK* a British government official responsible for impartially investigating citizens' complaints against a public authority or institution and trying to bring about a fair settlement [Mid-20C. Via Swedish < Old Norse *umboðsmaðr* "manager, deputy" < *umboð* "commission" + *maðr* "man"] —**om·buds·man·ship** *n*

om·buds·per·son /ómbədz pùrss'n, -bòodz-, -budz-/ (*plural* **-per·sons** or **-peo·ple** /-peèp'l/) *n* **1.** somebody responsible for investigating or resolving complaints from consumers or other members of the public against a company, institution, or other organization **2.** a government official responsible for impartially investigating citizens' complaints against a public authority or institution and trying to bring about a fair settlement [Late 20C. After OMBUDSMAN] —**om·buds·per·son·ship** *n*

om·buds·wom·an /ómbədz wòommən, -bòodz-, -budz-/ (*plural* **-wom·en** /-wimmin/) *n* **1.** a woman responsible for investigating and resolving complaints from consumers or other members of the public against a company, institution, or other organization **2.** a female government official responsible for impartially investigating citizens' complaints against a public authority or institution and trying to bring about a fair settlement [Mid-20C. After OMBUDSMAN] —**om·buds·wom·an·ship** *n*

Om·dur·man /ómdoor maán, -mán/ city in east central Sudan, on the west bank of the Nile River, opposite Khartoum. Population: 1,267,077 (1993).

-ome *suffix* mass ○ *trichome* [Via modern Latin < Greek *-ōma*]

o·me·ga /ō máygə/ *n* **1.** the 24th and final letter of the Greek alphabet, represented in the English alphabet as "o." See table at **alphabet** **2.** the end, or the last thing in a series (*literary*) [Early 16C. < Greek *ō mega* "great (i.e., long) o," as opposed to *o mikron* (see OMICRON)]

o·me·ga-3 *n* a long-chain polyunsaturated fatty acid with a double bond at the third carbon. Source: fish oils, seeds, and whole grains. Use: prevention of such conditions as high cholesterol, heart disease, and arthritis.

o·me·ga-6 oil *n* a long-chain polyunsaturated oil with a double bond at the sixth carbon, deficiency of which can cause skin problems and hormonal imbalances. Source: plants, seeds.

o·me·ga hy·per·on *n* a negatively charged elementary particle with a rest mass 3,272 times that of an electron

o·me·ga mes·on *n* an extremely short-lived neutral meson with a rest mass 1,532 times that of an electron

o·me·ga mi·nus *n* PHYS same as **omega hyperon** [< the symbol for the particle]

om·e·let /ómmlət/, **om·e·lette** *n* a dish consisting of beaten eggs cooked over high heat until set, often served folded in half over a filling such as cheese or mushrooms [Early 17C. Via French < Latin *lamella* "small thin plate" < *lamina* "thin plate"]

o·men /ṓmən/ *n* something that happens that is regarded as a sign of how somebody or something will fare in the future ■ *vti* (**o·mened, o·men·ing, o·mens**) to be a sign of how somebody or something will fare in the future [Late 16C. < Latin]

o·men·tum /ō méntəm/ (*plural* **-ta** /-tə/ or **-tums**) *n* a fold of the peritoneum, especially the fold that covers the intestines (**greater omentum**) or the fold that connects to the liver (**lesser omentum**) [Mid-16C. < Latin]

o·mep·ra·zole /o mépprə zōl/ *n* a drug that reduces the secretion of acid in the stomach. Use: treatment of ulcers and heartburn.

o·mer /ṓmər/ *n* an ancient Hebrew unit of dry measure equal to one tenth of an ephah and roughly equivalent to 3.7 quarts/3.5 liters [Early 17C. < Hebrew *ōmer*]

O·mer /ṓmər/ *n* in Judaism, a seven-week period between the second day of Passover and the first day of Shavuoth, observed as a period of mourning, except on one day. Omer is named after the custom of offering an omer or sheaf of barley as a sacrifice in the Temple on the first day of this period. [Early 17C. < Hebrew *'ōmer*]

o·mer·ta /ō mer taá, ō múrtə/, **o·mer·tà** *n* the code requirement alleged to apply to members of the Mafia, by which they must remain silent about any crimes of which they have knowledge [Late 19C. < Italian dialect < Latin *humilitas* "humility" < *humilis* "humble"]

om·i·cron /ómi kròn, ṓmi-/ *n* the 15th letter of the Greek alphabet, represented in the English alphabet as "o." See table at **alphabet** [Mid-17C. < Greek *o mikron* "small (i.e., short) o," as opposed to *ō mega* (see OMEGA)]

om·i·nous /ómminəss/ *adj* suggesting or indicating that something bad is going to happen or be revealed ○ *I think it's rather ominous that they haven't replied to your letter.* [Late 16C. < Latin *ominosus* "of an omen" < *omen* "omen"] —**om·i·nous·ly** *adv* —**om·i·nous·ness** *n*

o·mis·sion /ō mísh'n/ *n* **1.** something that has been deliberately or accidentally left out or not done ○ *errors and omissions excepted* **2.** the act of omitting something, or the state of being omitted ○ *The omission of those three words changed the sense of the whole paragraph.* [14C. Via Old French < late Latin *omission-* < *omittere* "OMIT"]

o·mit /ō mít/ (**o·mit·ted, o·mit·ting, o·mits**) *vt* **1.** to fail to include or mention somebody or something, either deliberately or accidentally **2.** to fail to do something, either deliberately or accidentally [15C. < Latin *omittere* < *ob-* "away" + *mittere* "send"] —**o·mis·si·ble** /ō míssəb'l/ *adj*

SYNONYMS See ***overlook***.

OMM *abbr Can* Officer of the Order of Military Merit

Om·mi·ad *n* HIST, ISLAM same as **Umayyad**

~~**ommission**~~ incorrect spelling of **omission**

~~**ommited**~~ incorrect spelling of **omitted**

omni- *prefix* all ○ *omnicompetent* [< Latin *omnis* < Indo-European, "abundance, to produce"]

om·ni·bus /ómni bùss, -bəss/ *n* **1.** BOOK COLLECTING SEPARATE WORKS a single book containing several works, usually by the same author, involving the same main character, or on the same subject, previously published separately **2.** *also* **om·ni·bus e·di·tion** *UK* SINGLE BROADCAST OF PROGRAMS a single continuous broadcast consisting of several radio or television programs previously broadcast separately as installments of a serial or soap opera **3.** VEHICLES same as **bus** (*archaic or formal*) ■ *adj* WITH MANY DIFFERENT THINGS bringing many different things together as a single unit ○ *an omnibus education bill* [Early 19C. Via French and directly < Latin, "for all" < *omnis* "all" (see OMNI-)]

om·ni·com·pe·tent /òmnee kómpətənt/ *adj* **1.** able to deal successfully with any task or situation **2.** competent to judge or try any kind of case

om·ni·di·rec·tion·al /òmnee di rékshən'l, -dī-/ *adj* able to transmit or receive radio or sound waves in or from any direction

om·ni·di·rec·tion·al ra·di·o range *n* MEDIA same as **omnirange**

om·nif·i·cent /om nífiss'nt/, **om·nif·ic** /om níffik/ *adj* with unlimited power to create (*literary*) [Late 17C. < Latin *omni-* (see OMNI-) + *-ficus* "-fic" (see -FIC)] —**om·nif·i·cence** *n*

om·nip·o·tent /om níppətənt/ *adj* possessing complete, unlimited, or universal power and authority [13C. Via French < Latin *omnipotent-* < *omnis* "all" + *potens*, present participle of *posse* "be able"] —**om·nip·o·tence** *n* —**om·nip·o·tent·ly** *adv*

Om·nip·o·tent *n* RELIG same as **God**

om·ni·pres·ent /òmni prézz'nt/ *adj* **1.** continuously and simultaneously present throughout the whole of creation **2.** present or seemingly present all the time or everywhere [Early 17C. < medieval Latin *omnipraesent-* < *omni-* "omni-" + *praesens* "present"] —**om·ni·pres·ence** *n*

om·ni·range /ómnee rāynj/ *n* a very-high-frequency radio navigation network that enables aircraft pilots to choose and fly any bearing relative to a transmitter on the ground

om·nis·cient /om níshənt/ *adj* knowing or seeming to know everything [Early 17C. < medieval Latin *omniscient-* < Latin *omni-* "omni-" + *scire* "know" (see SCIENCE)] —**om·nis·cience** *n* —**om·nis·cient·ly** *adv*

om·ni·um-gath·er·um /òmnee əm gáthərəm/ (*plural* **om·ni·um-gath·er·ums**) *n* a collection of many different, often unsorted ideas or items (*humorous*) [< Latin *omnium* "of all" + pseudo-Latin *gatherum*, alteration of "gathering"]

om·ni·vore /ómnə vàwr/ *n* **1.** an animal that will feed on any type or many different types of food, including both plants and animals **2.** somebody who has wide-ranging and often undiscriminating interests or tastes [Late 19C. Via modern Latin *Omnivora* "omnivores" < Latin *omnivorus* (see OMNIVOROUS)]

om·niv·o·rous /om nívvərəss/ *adj* **1.** eating any type or many different types of food, including both plants and animals **2.** wide-ranging and often undiscriminating in interests or tastes [Mid-17C. < Latin *omnivorus* < *omni-* (see OMNI-) + *-vorus* "devouring"] —**om·niv·o·rous·ly** *adv*

om·pha·los /ómfə lòss, ómfələss/ (*plural* **-los·es** or **-loi** /-loy/) *n* **1.** a conical stone with sacred significance in ancient Greek religion, especially the one at Delphi that was believed to mark the center of the world **2.** the central or focal point around which everything else revolves (*literary*) [Mid-19C. < Greek, "navel"]

Omsk /awmsk/ city and capital of Omsk Oblast, southwestern Russia, situated 480 mi./772 km east of Chelyabinsk. Population: 1,437,781 (1995).

on /on/ *prep* **1.** INDICATES POSITION used to indicate a position above and in contact with the surface of something else ○ *sitting on the bed* **2.** ATTACHED TO SOMETHING used to indicate attachment to or suspension from a surface or object ○ *a wooden wheel mounted on the wall* **3.** SUPPORTING WEIGHT used to indicate what part of the body is supporting somebody's weight ○ *They sat there leaning on their elbows.* **4.** CARRYING SOMETHING carrying something that is therefore readily accessible ○ *I didn't have any cash on me at the time.* **5.** INDICATES LOCATION OR VICINITY located in a place or situated close to or alongside a place ○ *a town on the coast of Trinidad* **6.** AT TIME used to indicate when something happens ○ *just before noon on Tuesday* **7.** RELATING TO SOMETHING concerned with or relating to a particular subject, thing, or activity ○ *a talk on international relations* **8.** WHERE SOMETHING IS AVAILABLE used to indicate that some form of information or entertainment is currently available from a machine or instrument ○ *a comedy show on the radio* **9.** AS MEANS OF FUNCTIONING used to indicate the means by which somebody or something subsists or functions ○ *animals that feed on the leaves of the trees* **10.** BY MEANS OF SOMETHING using something as a means of transport ○ *They arrived on horseback.* **11.** ENGAGED IN SOMETHING engaged in an activity ○ *My assistant is away on a course.* **12.** ACCORDING TO SOMETHING used to indicate that something is grounds for a statement, way of thinking, or action ○ *allowing them to compete on an equal basis* **13.** IN CURRENT RANK OR POSITION used to indicate somebody's current status or position in an organization or institution ○ *My sister is on the committee.* **14.** DIRECTED TOWARD SOMETHING OR SOMEBODY used to indicate that something is directed toward somebody or something ○ *I shone my flashlight on the inscription.* **15.** CHARGED TO SOMEBODY used to indicate that the cost of drinks or a meal is charged to a particular person ○ *The drinks are on me.* **16.** IN DIRECT CONTACT in direct conflict, competition, or contact with another (*informal*) ○ *spent many hours in one-on-one debate* ○ *white-on-white violence* ■ *adv* **1.** IN CONTACT WITH SOMETHING in contact with, attached to, or supported by something ○ *an envelope with a stamp on* **2.** INTO CONDITION OF ATTACHMENT OR SUSPENSION into a condition of being attached to or suspended from something ○ *sewing a button on* **3.** INTO OPERATION into the condition of operating or functioning ○ *turned the television on* **4.** WITH CLOTHING wearing clothes or placing clothing over a part of the body ○ *I pulled my tee-shirt on.* **5.** PERSISTENTLY in a continuous or persistent way ○ *decided to stay on in Cambridge* **6.** IN PROGRESS in activity or performance at the present time or at some implied time ○ *putting a play on* **7.** BASEBALL INDICATING RUNNER'S POSITION in baseball, used to indicate whether an offensive player is on the bases ○ *had left three runners on* **8.** GAMBLING WAGERED wagered as a bet ○ *put a bet on* ■ *adj* **1.** TAKING PLACE happening or being performed at the present time ○ *There's nothing good on tonight.* ○ *I've got a lot on at the moment.* **2.** ARRANGED OR PLANNED indicating that an activity is arranged and will happen ○ *Is the game still on?* **3.** FUNCTIONING indicating that a machine or device is functioning or in use ○ *There's a light on upstairs.* ■ *vt* (**onned, on·ning, ons**) *Malaysia, Singapore* SWITCH SOMETHING ON to switch on something such as a light or an electrical appliance (*usually used without inflections*) [Old English, < Indo-European] ◇ **be on** to be performing exceptionally well at something (*slang*) ◇ **be on to somebody** *or* **something** to have information on or be aware of the real nature of somebody or something (*informal*) ◇ **on and off** occasionally ◇ **on and on** in a continuous, persistent way ◇ **you're on** used to indicate that somebody is agreeing to do something proposed by somebody else (*informal*)

ON *abbr* **1.** LANG Old Norse **2.** Ontario

O.N. *abbr* LANG Old Norse

-on[1] *suffix* **1.** subatomic particle ○ *fermion* **2.** chemical substance ○ *fenuron* **3.** fundamental hereditary unit ○ *muton* **4.** unit, quantum ○ *chronon* **5.** inert gas ○ *radon* [< ION, influenced by the Greek neuter present participle *on* "being" or neuter noun ending *-on*]

-on[2] *suffix* a biological or chemical substance ○ *parathion* ○ *interferon* [Alteration of -ONE]

on·a·gain, off·a·gain, **on·a·gain-off·a·gain** *adj* happening or continuing intermittently (*informal*) ○ *an on-again, off-again romance*

on·a·ger /ónnəjər/ *n* **1.** a wild ass that is dark yellow with a stripe along its back. Native to: northern Iran and bordering areas. Genus: *Equus hemionus*. **2.** in former times, a war machine used to throw stones [14C. Via Latin < Greek *onagros* < *onos* "ass" + *agrios* "wild"]

o·nan·ism /ṓnə nìzzəm/ *n* (*literary*) **1.** the act of masturbating **2.** same as **coitus interruptus** [Early 18C. After *Onan*, a character in the Bible (Genesis 38:9), who spilled his semen onto the ground rather than impregnate his deceased brother's wife] —**o·nan·ist** *n* —**o·nan·is·tic** /ṓnə nístik/ *adj*

O·ña·te /ō nyaá tày/, **Juan de** (1550?–1630?) Spanish-American explorer. He founded New Mexico (1598) and explored territory in the southwestern part of the present-day United States.

on·board /on báwrd/, **on-board** *adj* carried or available on an aircraft, ship, or other vehicle or vessel

once /wunss/ *adv* **1.** IN PAST used to indicate that something happened or was the case at some time in the past ○ *The place must have been nice once.* ○ *a once comfortable lifestyle* **2.** ONE TIME on one occasion only **3.** BY ONE STEP distant by one place or degree ○ *a cousin once removed* **4.** MATH MULTIPLIED BY ONE indicating that a number is multiplied by one ○ *once three is three* ■ *conj* AS SOON AS happening when something else has happened ○ *Once he got started, it was clear we were dealing with an expert.* ◇ **all at once 1.** suddenly, often unexpectedly ○ *I felt really sick all at once.* **2.** all at the same time ○ *She could not read the books all at once.* ◇ **at once 1.** immediately ○ *Tell him at once.* **2.** all at the same time ○ *It's a lot to take in at once.* ◇ **for once** happening on this particular occasion, if at no other time ○ *For once my strategy worked.* ◇ **once and away 1.** conclusively **2.** occasionally ◇ **once and for all** completely and conclusively ○ *We need to clear this up once and for all.* ◇ **once or twice** *or* **once and again** on a few occasions, but not often ○ *pausing once and again to listen* ◇ **once upon a time** used at the beginning of fairy tales and children's stories to indicate that something happened a long time ago or in an imaginary world

once-o·ver *n* a rapid inspection or examination of somebody or something (*informal*) ○ *I'll give the car a quick once-over.*

on·cho·cer·ci·a·sis /òngkō sur kī́ əssiss/ *n* a disease caused by infestation with worms, especially a tropical disease of humans caused by a parasitic worm and transmitted by blackflies, causing skin nodules, lesions, and blindness [Early 20C. < modern Latin *Onchocerca*, genus of worms < Greek *ogkos* "barb" + *kerkos* "tail," from their shape]

onco- *prefix* tumor ○ *oncolysis* [< Greek *onkos* "mass"]

on·co·gene /óngkə jeen/ *n* a gene that can cause a cell to become malignant. Oncogenes are thought to be derived from normal cellular counterparts that have been taken up by viruses and altered so they malfunction when returned to the cell.

on·co·gen·e·sis /òngkō jénnəssiss/ *n* the development of a tumor or tumors

on·co·gen·ic /òngkō jénnik/ *adj* relating to or causing the formation and growth of tumors —**on·co·ge·nic·i·ty** /òngkō jə nissətee/ *n*

on·col·o·gy /ong kólləjee/ *n* the branch of medicine that deals with the study and treatment of malignant tumors —**on·co·log·i·cal** /òngkə lójjik'l/ *adj* —**on·col·o·gist** *n*

on·col·y·sis /ong kólləssiss/ *n* the destruction of tumor cells, either spontaneously or, more usually, in response to drug or radiographic treatment

on·com·ing /ón kùmming/ *adj* heading directly toward somebody or something ■ *n* the approach of something that is soon to occur

on·cor·na·vi·rus /ong kàwrnə vīrəss/ *n* a virus containing single-stranded RNA and capable of causing cancer [Late 20C. < ONCO- + RNA + VIRUS]

On·daat·je /on daátyə/, **Michael** (*b.* 1943) Sri Lankan-born Canadian writer. Among his many volumes of poetry and fiction is the Booker Prize-winning novel *The English Patient* (1992), which was made into a movie. See illustration on next page

> "We die containing a richness of lovers and tribes, tastes we have swallowed, bodies we have plunged into and swum up as if rivers of wisdom, characters we have climbed into as if trees, fears we have hidden as if in caves."
> [Michael Ondaatje, *The English Patient*; 1992]

Isolde Ohlbaum
Michael Ondaatje

on·dan·se·tron /on dánssə tròn/ *n* a drug that inhibits the production of serotonin. Use: control of nausea and vomiting caused by anticancer drug treatment and radiation therapy.

On·des Mar·te·not /àwNd maartə nṓ/ *n* an electronic musical instrument that can be played at a keyboard or with a finger slider, producing a sliding sound. The instrument was favored by the composer Olivier Messiaen. [< French *Ondes (musicales)* "(musical) waves," its original name + *(Maurice) Martenot*, 1898–1980, French inventor]

one /wun/ CORE MEANING: a grammatical word indicating a single thing or unit, and not two or more ○ (adj) *just one accident out of thousands* ○ (adj) *a one-legged man* ○ (pron) *Central Newark, once home to several bank branches, now has one.* ○ (pron) *Bill got one of his boxing gloves off.*
1. *adj, pron* **UNIQUE** used to indicate the only thing or person with a specific characteristic ○ *the one exception to this* **2.** *adj, pron* **USED TO DISTINGUISH SOMETHING** distinct from others of its kind ○ *from one thought to the next* **3.** *adj* **AT NONSPECIFIC TIME** relating to an unspecified time in the past or future ○ *one August afternoon* **4.** *adj* **USED FOR EMPHASIS** used instead of "a" and "an" to emphasize a following adjective or expression (*informal*) ○ *He's one cool customer!* **5.** *adj* **PARTICULAR** introducing the name of somebody who is not known to the speaker ○ *a letter from one Thomas Atherton of Southport* **6.** *pron* **TYPICAL INDIVIDUAL** used to refer to people in general (*formal*) ○ *One can eat well here.* **7.** *pron* **SOMEBODY OR SOMETHING UNSPECIFIED** used to indicate somebody or something not specifically identified (*dated*) ○ *the voice of one crying in the wilderness* **8.** *pron* **PREVIOUSLY MENTIONED** used instead of a preceding noun to indicate somebody or something already mentioned ○ *nothing but an old vase, and a cracked one at that* **9.** *pron* **JOKE OR STORY** used to refer to a question, joke, or remark ○ *That's a good one!* **10.** *n* 1 the number 1. It is the smallest whole number, designating a single unit, and the first cardinal number. **11.** *n* **SOMETHING WITH VALUE OF 1** something in a numbered series with a value of one ○ *to throw a one* **12.** *n US* **DOLLAR BILL** a one-dollar bill (*informal*) **13.** *n* **TIME MEASURE** used to indicate the time as one hour after twelve midday or midnight ○ *We'll stop for lunch at one.* **14.** *n* MUSIC **MUSICAL NOTATION** the numeral 1 used as the bottom figure in a time signature to indicate that the beat is measured in whole notes [Old English *ān* < Indo-European] ◇ **all one** not important enough to be of any consequence to somebody ○ *It's all one to me.* ◇ **as one** doing something at the same time or in the same way ◇ **at one** in harmony with somebody or something ◇ **be** *or* **get one up on somebody** to have or gain an advantage over somebody (*informal*) ◇ **one and all** everyone in a group ◇ **one and only 1.** unique and without comparison (*often used to introduce a performer on a show*) **2.** the person that somebody loves ◇ **one by one** happening individually in sequence ◇ **one or two** a few people or things ◇ **one time** *Carib* **1.** immediately **2.** completely **3.** used to add emphasis

USAGE one of those people who is... or **one of those people who are...?** Sense determines whether the verb in a construction of this type should be singular or plural, and in any given case one choice is right and the other wrong. To decide which verb form to choose, start with the *of.* For example, *He is one of those people who is/are always trying to impress* is not equivalent in meaning to *Of those people, he is one who is always trying to impress.* Rather, the idea is *Of those people who are always trying to impress, he is one.* Here the form of the verb *to be* is not governed by *one* but by *people*, and therefore *one of those people who are* is right. In the following example the choice of the form of "to be" is governed by "only": *He is the only one of those people who is worth talking to.* Here the idea is *Of those people, he is the only one who is worth talking to*, so in this case *one of those people who is* is right.

1 *suffix* -one in pronouns, e.g., anyone (*used in e-mails or text messages*)

-one *suffix* ketone or related compound ○ *quinone* [Origin ?]

one-act·er *n* a play that consists of only one act

O'Neal /ō neél/, **Shaquille** (*b.* 1972) US basketball player. He is considered one of the greatest players of the 1990s.

one an·oth·er *pron* each of several members of a group to the others ○ *neighbors helping one another*

USAGE See ***each other.***

one-armed ban·dit *n* a gambling machine that is operated by inserting a coin or token in a slot and pulling down a lever on one side (*informal*)

one-bag·ger *n US* BASEBALL same as **single** *n* (sense 3) (*informal*)

one-base hit *n* BASEBALL same as **single** *n* (sense 3)

one-di·men·sion·al *adj* **1.** existing in or possessing only one dimension **2.** presenting or perceiving only the most superficial aspects of something

O·ne·ga, Lake /ə nyéggə, ō neégə/ second-largest lake in Europe, in northwestern Russia, east of Lake Ladoga, to which it is linked by the Svir River. Area: 3,710 sq. mi./9,610 sq. km.

one-hand·ed tour·ni·quet *n* two concentric loops of webbing used by a person having only one hand mobile, applied by placing the bleeding extremity through the inner loop and cinching it tight by pulling on the outer loop

one-horse *adj* **1. VERY SMALL AND BORING** describes a small place where nothing of interest or importance ever happens ○ *a one-horse town* **2. HAVING ONE LIKELY WINNER** fielding only one candidate or competitor who is likely to win ○ *a one-horse race* **3. DRAWN BY SINGLE HORSE** drawn by only one horse

O·nei·da[1] /ō nídə/ (*plural same* or **-das**) *n* **1.** a member of a Native North American people who originally occupied lands in New York and whose members now live mainly in Ontario, New York, and Wisconsin. They were one of the five peoples who formed the Iroquois Confederacy, which later became known as the Six Nations. **2.** the Iroquoian language of the Oneida people [Mid-17C. < Oneida *onẽýote*, the main Oneida settlement] —**O·nei·da** *adj*

O·nei·da[2] /ō nídə/ city in Madison County, central New York, situated 13 mi./21 km southwest of Rome. Population: 10,958 (2002 estimate).

Library of Congress
Eugene O'Neill

O'Neill /ō neél/, **Eugene** (1888–1953) US playwright. His realistic psychological dramas include *Mourning Becomes Electra* (1931), *The Iceman Cometh* (1946), and *Long Day's Journey into Night* (1956). He won the Nobel Prize in literature (1936). Full name **O'Neill, Eugene Gladstone.** See Cultural note at **mourning**

"None of us can help the things life has done to us. They're done before you realize it, and once they're done they make you do other things until at last everything comes between you and what you'd like to be, and you've lost your true self forever."
[Eugene O'Neill, *Long Day's Journey into Night*; 1956]

O'Neill, Thomas Philip, Jr. (1912–94) US politician. Before becoming speaker of the US House of Representatives (1977–87), he served as a US representative from Massachusetts (1952–86) and was known for his opposition to President Lyndon B. Johnson's Vietnam War policies and for his demands for the impeachment of President Richard M. Nixon. Known as **O'Neill, Tip**

o·nei·ric /ō nírik/ *adj* relating to, in, or similar to dreams [Mid-19C. < Greek *oneiros* "dream"]

o·nei·ro·man·cy /ō nírə mànssee/ *n* the practice of divining the future through the interpretation of dreams [Mid-17C. < Greek *oneiros* "dream" + -MANCY] —**o·nei·ro·man·cer** *n*

one kind *adj Malaysia, Singapore* different from others in a way that makes somebody or something worthy of note

one-lin·er *n* a short joke or funny remark in one sentence

one-man *adj* consisting of, designed for, featuring, or performed by only one person

one-man band *n* **1.** a performer who plays several musical instruments at once **2.** a business or organization in which one person does all or most of the work

one·ness /wún nəss/ *n* **1. SINGLENESS** the quality of being one as opposed to many **2. UNIQUENESS** the quality of being unique **3. AGREEMENT** the condition of being united or agreed **4. SAMENESS** the quality of being the same or monotonous

one-night stand *n* **1.** a sexual encounter that lasts for only one night (*informal*) **2.** a single performance given at any one place for one night only

one-note *adj US* limited in ability, scope, or range (*informal*) ○ *a one-note writer*

one-off *UK adj* happening only once, not as part of a series ■ *n* a unique and unrepeatable or unrepeated thing or event

one-on-one *adj* **1. PERSONAL** involving contact or communication between only two people **2.** *US* **DIRECTLY AGAINST EACH OTHER** competing directly against only one other person ○ *a one-on-one drill* ■ *n US* **DRILL INVOLVING TWO PLAYERS** contact, communication, or competition between only two people ○ *An hour of one-on-one exhausted me.* —**one-on-one** *adv*

one-per·son *adj* consisting of, designed for, featuring, or performed by only one person

one-piece *adj* consisting of a single component, and not two or more ■ *n* a bathing suit consisting of a single piece

on·er /wúnnər/ *n* a unique or extraordinary person or thing (*informal*)

on·er·ous /ónnərəss, ṓnərəss/ *adj* **1.** representing a great burden or much trouble **2.** involving obligations that are more disadvantageous than advantageous [14C. Via Old French *onéreux* < Latin *onerosus* < *oner-*, stem of *onus* "burden"] —**on·er·ous·ly** *adv* —**on·er·ous·ness** *n*

one·self /wun sélf/ *pron* (*formal*) **1. REFERRING TO SUBJECT** the reflexive form of "one," meaning a person's own self ○ *The aim is to improve oneself and one's ability.* **2. WITHOUT HELP FROM OTHERS** used to indicate that something is done without help or interference from others ○ *One should always try and manage things oneself.* **3. NORMAL SELF** your usual or normal self ○ *In such situations one never feels oneself.* [Mid-16C. < *one's self*]

one-shot (*informal*) *adj* **1.** *US* **HAPPENING ONLY ONE TIME** happening or doing something only once **2. EFFECTIVE AT FIRST ATTEMPT** taking effect after only one application or attempt ○ *a one-shot solution to financial problems* ■ *n* **SOMETHING TRIED ONCE** something done or attempted only once ○ *It promised to be the start of a working relationship, but proved to be only a one-shot.*

one·sid·ed *adj* **1.** UNFAIRLY WEIGHTED dominated by or favoring one side more than the other in a competition **2.** BIASED presenting or considering one side of a matter while ignoring other aspects of it **3.** BIGGER ON ONE SIDE larger, more prominent, or more developed on one side than the other **4.** BEING ON ONE SIDE occurring on or having only one side —**one·sid·ed·ly** *adv* —**one·sid·ed·ness** *n*

one-size-fits-all *adj* **1.** suitable to be worn by almost everyone **2.** *US* suiting a wide variety of tastes and therefore bland and mediocre ○ *one-size-fits-all TV shows*

one-step *n* **1.** BALLROOM DANCE a ballroom dance similar to the foxtrot, in 2/4 time **2.** DANCE MUSIC the music for a one-step ■ *vi* (**one-stepped, one-step·ping, one-steps**) DANCE ONE-STEP to perform the one-step

one-stop *adj* offering a wide variety of services or goods in one location so that a customer does not have to go from place to place ○ *a one-stop home design center*

one-tailed, **one-tail** *adj* describes a statistical test in which all values of the critical region either fall below or exceed a given value, but not both

one·time /wún tīm/ *adj* **1.** having been something or played a particular role at a previous time ○ *the onetime world champion* **2.** *also* **one-time** done or occurring only once and unlikely to happen again

one-to-one *adj* **1.** with one part that corresponds to or matches another **2.** MATH describes a mathematical set in which each member can be paired with a member of another set leaving no remainder **3.** *UK* same as **one-on-one** *adj* (sense 1) —**one-to-one** *adv*

one-track *adj* focused on, obsessed with, or restricted to only one issue or subject ○ *a one-track mind*

one-two *n* **1.** *UK* BOXING same as **one-two punch** **2.** *UK* in soccer, a pass made to another player on the same team who then immediately passes to a new position taken up by the original passer

one-two punch *n* **1.** in boxing, a punch with one hand followed by a punch from the side (**cross**) with the other hand **2.** two actions or events with significant effects that happen quickly in succession ○ *the one-two punch of a hurricane and then cholera*

one-up (**one-upped, one-up·ping, one-ups**) *vt US* to gain an advantage over a rival or opponent (*informal*) ○ *Looks like I've been one-upped again.*

one-up·man·ship /wun úpmən shìp/ *n* the practice of attempting to outdo or show yourself to be superior to a rival or opponent

one-way *adj* **1.** GOING IN ONE DIRECTION moving or allowing movement in one direction only ○ *a one-way street* **2.** NOT ALLOWING RETURN allowing somebody to travel to a destination but not to return ○ *a one-way ticket* **3.** INVOLVING ONLY ONE OF TWO PEOPLE agreed on, felt by, or involving a contribution by only one of two people or parties ○ *a one-way agreement* **4.** ALLOWING VIEWING FROM ONE SIDE made in such a way that it can be looked through from one side but not from the other ○ *one-way glass*

one-way mir·ror *n* a sheet of glass that is a mirror on one side and can be seen through from the other. One use of such mirrors is to allow witnesses to identify police suspects without themselves being seen.

one-wom·an *adj* consisting of, designed for, featuring, or performed by one woman ○ *a one-woman show*

on·go·ing /ón gō ing/ *adj* **1.** having been developing or in progress for some time and continuing to do so **2.** taking place at the present time

ONI *abbr* NAVY Office of Naval Intelligence

on·i·gi·ri /ònnə gḗeree/ *npl* Japanese rice balls, bite-sized or slightly larger, sometimes filled with seaweed or other foods and wrapped in seaweed [< Japanese]

onion

on·ion /únnyən/ *n* **1.** EDIBLE BULB USED AS VEGETABLE a rounded edible bulb with hard pungent flesh in concentric layers beneath a flaky brown skin eaten raw or cooked as a vegetable **2.** PLANT WITH PUNGENT BULBS a plant of the lily family that produces onions. Native to: Asia. Latin name: *Allium cepa*. **3.** PLANT RELATED TO ONION any plant related to the onion, e.g., the Welsh onion [12C. < Latin *unio* "onion," origin ?] —**on·ion·y** *adj*

on·ion dome *n* a rounded dome resembling an onion in shape, typical of Russian and Byzantine church architecture

on·ion·skin /únnyən skìn/ *n* smooth thin translucent paper. Use: formerly, carbon copies.

O·nit·sha /ō níchə/ city in Anambra State, southeastern Nigeria, situated about 225 mi./362 km east of Lagos. Population: 362,700 (1995).

-onium *suffix* a complex positively charged ion (**cation**) ○ *diazonium* [< AMMONIUM]

on·i·um i·on /ónee əm-/ *n* a positively charged ion (**cation**) that is analogous to the ammonium ion. Formula: NH_4^+.

on-la·bel *adj US* using or involving the use of a prescription drug to treat a condition for which the drug is approved by the US Food and Drug Administration

on·lay /ón lày/ *vt* (**-laid** /-làyd/, **-lay·ing, -lays**) DECORATE SURFACE to apply something to a surface, especially for decorative purposes, so that it stands in relief ■ *n* **1.** MED SKIN GRAFT a skin graft surgically transferred to the surface of an organ or other part of the body **2.** DENT INLAY IN TOOTH an inlay fixed to the biting surface of a tooth [15C. < ON + LAY[1] (verb)]

on·line /ón līn/, **on-line** *adj* **1.** CONNECTED VIA COMPUTER attached to or available through a central computer or computer network **2.** DIRECTLY CONNECTED TO MEASURABLE PROCESS describes an instrument or sensor that is connected directly to a process being measured, thus obviating the need to take samples for analysis in a laboratory or elsewhere **3.** *US* ONGOING currently going on or being done ■ *adv* WHILE CONNECTED TO COMPUTER while connected to a central computer or computer network

on·lin·er /ón līnər/ *n* a user or a supplier of online computer services

on·load /ón lōd/ (**-load·ed, -load·ing, -loads**) *vti* to load freight onto a vehicle

on·look·er /ón lòòkər/ *n* somebody who watches an event without participating in it —**on·look·ing** *adj*

on·ly /ónlee/ *adv* **1.** SOLELY used to indicate the one thing or person that solely or exclusively happens or is involved in a situation ○ *facilities for club members only* ○ *I will act only in the best interests of our country.* ○ *The regulations apply only to new firms.* **2.** INDICATING CONDITION used to indicate the condition that exists for something to happen or be true ○ *I'll go to the party, but only if you come with me.* **3.** MERELY merely the situation, level, or amount indicated ○ *I could only stand and look.* ○ *That's only part of the picture.* **4.** NO MORE AND NO LESS just the amount specified ○ *There are only 3.3 people at work for every person retired.* **5.** AS RECENTLY AS considered as happening very recently ○ *only last March* **6.** INDICATING EVENT HAPPENING IMMEDIATELY AFTER used to introduce a surprising or unpleasant event that happens immediately after the one mentioned ○ *We rushed the cat to the vet, only to find there was nothing wrong with it.* ■ *adj* **1.** SINGLE PERSON OR THING used to indicate the single person or thing involved in a situation ○ *the only Democratic candidate* ○ *the only barrier between himself and the job* **2.** WITH NO SIBLINGS with no brothers or sisters ○ *an only child* ■ *adv Ireland* EMPHASIZING used to emphasize a statement ○ *It was only terrible.* ■ *conj* BUT but or except ○ *It's the same product, only better.* [Old English *ānlic* < *ān* "one" (see ONE)] ◇ **only too** used to emphasize the extent to which something is true ○ *Scenes like this are getting only too familiar.*

USAGE Position of **only**. Avoid ambiguity in the placement of the limiting adverb ***only***. The position of ***only*** within a sentence can determine the meaning of the entire sentence. As a general rule, put it next to the word you want it to modify: *She had only a dollar. Only she had a dollar* or *She only had a dollar.* Avoid putting ***only*** between a subject and a verb and between an auxiliary verb and a main verb: *He only does these things to get attention* where *He does these things only to get attention* is better. Similarly, *I will only stop the car once on the way there* is less desirable than *I will stop the car only once on the way there.*

Barnaby's

Yoko Ono and John Lennon

O·no /ṓnō/, **Yoko** (*b.* 1933) Japanese-born US artist. She is known for her avant-garde performance art, which after her marriage to John Lennon in 1969 included protests against the Vietnam War.

> "Keep your intentions in a clear bottle and leave it on a shelf when you rap."
> [Yoko Ono, *Chicago Tribune*; June 25, 1978]

on·o·mas·i·ol·o·gy /ònnə maysee óllәjee/ *n* **1.** the branch of linguistics that studies how meaning is expressed **2.** LING same as **onomastics** (sense 1) [Early 20C. < Greek *onomasia* "name" + -LOGY]

on·o·mas·tic /ònnə mástik/ *adj* relating to, connected with, or explaining names [Late 16C. Via French < Greek *onomastikos* < *onoma* "name"]

on·o·mas·tics /ònnə mástiks/ *n* **1.** the study of proper names, their origins, and their formation (*takes a singular verb*) **2.** the system underlying the creation and use of proper names in a specialized field (*takes a plural verb*)

on·o·mat·o·poe·ia /ònnə matə pée ə/ *n* the formation or use of words that imitate the sound associated with something, e.g., "hiss" and "buzz" [Late 16C. Via late Latin < Greek *onomatopoiia* "making of words" < *onoma* "name" + *poiein* "make" (see POEM)]

on·o·mat·o·poe·ic /ònnə matə pée ik/ *adj* imitative of the sound associated with the thing or action denoted by a word —**on·o·mat·o·poe·i·cal·ly** *adv*

On·on·da·ga /ònnən dáwgə, -daágə, -dáygə/ (*plural same* or **-gas**) *n* **1.** a member of a Native North American people who originally occupied lands in central New York and whose members mainly continue to live there, as well as in Ontario. The Onondaga were one of the five peoples who formed the Iroquois Confederacy, which later became known as the Six Nations. **2.** the Iroquoian language of the Onondaga people [Late 17C. < Onondaga *onǫ́tá?ke*, the main Onondaga settlement] —**On·on·da·ga** *adj*

On·on·da·ga, Lake /ònnən dáwgə, -daágə, -dáygə/ lake in Onondaga County, central New York. Area: 4.5 sq. mi./12 sq. km.

on·rush /ón rùsh/ *n* a forward rush or push ○ *the onrush of enemy soldiers* ○ *the onrush of events* —**on·rush·ing** *adj*

on·screen /òn skrēen/ *adj, adv* while appearing on the screen in a television program or film and therefore visible to the audience ○ *Their private life was very different from their on-screen relationship.*

on·set /ón sèt/ *n* **1.** the beginning of something, especially of something difficult or unpleasant ○ *the onset of winter* **2.** an initial attack or assault in battle [Early 16C. < SET[1] (noun)]

on·shore /on sháwr/ *adj* **1.** on land as opposed to at sea ○ *onshore drilling* **2.** toward land from the sea ○ *onshore breeze* —**on·shore** *adv*

on·side /on sīd/ *adj, adv* in sports such as soccer or hockey, in a position that is allowed within the rules of the game

on·side kick *n* in football, a kickoff used when the kicking team wants to recover the ball and keep the opposing team from getting possession of it. After the ball has traveled ten yards, either team may recover it.

on-site *adj, adv* taking place or provided at the location where work or some other activity is being carried out

on·slaught /ón slàwt/ *n* **1.** a powerful attack or force that overwhelms somebody or something **2.** a very large quantity of people or things that is difficult to deal with ○ *faced with an onslaught of junk mail* [Early 17C. Via Dutch *aanslag* < Middle Dutch *aenslach* "blow on" < *slach* "blow"]

on·stage /on stáyj/ *adj, adv* performing, happening, or existing on the stage as opposed to in the wings, backstage, or somewhere not visible to the audience

on-stream *adj, adv* in or into production or operation ○ *when the new system comes on-stream*

Ont., O.N. *abbr* Ontario

ont- *prefix* same as **onto-** (*used before vowels*)

-ont *suffix* cell, organism ○ *schizont* [< Greek *ont-* "being" (see ONTO-)]

Ontario

On·tar·i·o /on térree ō/ Canadian province situated between the Great Lakes and Hudson Bay. Capital: Toronto. Population: 11,410,046 (2001).. Area: 415,598 sq. mi./1,076,395 sq. km. Former name **Canada West** (1841–67) —**On·tar·i·an** *n, adj*

On·tar·i·o, Lake lake in North America, the easternmost and smallest of the Great Lakes, straddling the US-Canadian border and bounded by New York and Ontario Province. Its outflow is the St. Lawrence River. Area: 7,340 sq. mi./19,010 sq. km.

on-the-job *adj* provided or obtained while working at a job ○ *on-the-job training*

on·tic /óntik/ *adj* relating to real existence [Mid-20C. < the Greek stem *ont-* "being" (see ONTO-)]

on·to /ón too, óntə/ *prep* **1.** INDICATES POSITION used to indicate that somebody or something is located on something, or moves toward it so as to be on it ○ *I splashed water onto my face.* ○ *hop onto a bus* ○ *shine a flashlight onto the wall* ○ *loading the data onto a disk* ○ *come onto the market* **2.** MAKING DISCOVERY making or about to make a discovery, often about something secret or illegal ○ *I'm really onto something big here.* ○ *The police were onto them.* **3.** IN CONTACT in contact with a person or organization ○ *Get onto the suppliers.* [Early 18C. < ON + TO[1]]

USAGE on, onto, or on to? ***Onto*** is usually preferable to ***on*** where movement is involved, as in *I lifted the child onto* [not *on*] *my shoulders*, and ***onto*** is always the better choice where ***on*** would be ambiguous: *She jumped onto* [not *on*] *the platform.* Unlike ***into***, the preposition ***onto*** can be written as two separate words: *He stepped onto* [or *on to*] *the sidewalk.* Using ***onto***, however, avoids the risk of confusion with the adverb ***on*** followed by the preposition ***to***, which indicates progression and should not be joined together: *We walked on to* [not *onto*] *the end of the road. Let us move on to* [not *onto*] *the next topic.* See also ***into***.

onto- *prefix* **1.** being, existence ○ *ontology* **2.** organism ○ *ontogeny* [< Greek *ont-*, present participle of *einai* "be" < Indo-European]

on·tog·e·ny /on tójjənee/, **on·to·gen·e·sis** /òntə jénnəsiss/ *n* the development of an individual from a fertilized ovum to maturity, as contrasted with the development of a group or species (**phylogeny**) —**on·to·gen·ic** /òntə jénnik/ *adj* —**on·to·gen·i·cal·ly** *adv*

on·to·log·i·cal /òntə lójjik'l/ *adj* relating to or derived from ontology —**on·to·log·i·cal·ly** *adv*

on·to·log·i·cal ar·gu·ment *n* an argument made by St. Anselm and others to prove the existence of God by pointing to God's essence as a perfect, necessary being.

on·tol·o·gy /on tólləjee/ (*plural* **-gies**) *n* **1.** the most general branch of metaphysics, concerned with the nature of being **2.** a particular theory of being [Early 18C. < modern Latin, "study of being" < Greek *ont-* "being" (see ONTO-)] —**on·tol·o·gist** *n*

o·nus /ónəss/ *n* **1.** BURDEN a duty or responsibility ○ *The onus is on her to make the first move.* **2.** BLAME the blame for something ○ *He'll always bear the onus of having caused the accident.* **3.** LAW BURDEN OF PROOF OR PROCEEDING the burden of proof or responsibility for acting in a legal proceeding [Mid-17C. < Latin, "burden, load"]

on·ward /ónnwərd/ *adj* directed or moving forward in space, time, or development ○ *the great onward march of organization and life* ■ *adv also* **on·wards** /-wərdz/ toward a point or position ahead in space, time, or development

on·y·chol·y·sis /ònni kóllississ/ *n* the separation of all or part of a fingernail or thumbnail from its bed, associated with psoriasis or a fungal skin condition [< modern Latin < Greek *onukh-*, stem of *onux* "nail, claw"]

on·y·choph·o·ran /ònni kóffərən/ *n* a small land invertebrate that has many pairs of unjointed legs and captures insects and similar prey by spraying them with adhesive mucus. Phylum: Onychophora. [Late 19C. < modern Latin *Onychophora* < Greek *onukh-* "claw" + *-phoros* "bearing"; from the curved claws]

-onym *suffix* name, word ○ *pseudonym* [< Greek *onuma* (see ONOMASTIC)]

on·yx /ónniks/ *n* a semiprecious stone that is a fine-grained variety of chalcedony with bands of different colors. Use: gems, cameo work. [13C. Directly and via Old French and Latin < Greek *onux* "fingernail, claw"]

oo- *prefix* ovum, egg ○ *oospore* [< Greek *ōion* < Indo-European, "egg"]

ooch[1] /ooch/ *interj* same as **ouch** [Late 20C. Alteration]

ooch[2] /ooch/ (**ooched, ooch·ing, ooch·es**) *v* **1.** *vi* to try to make a sailboat go faster by moving your body forward inside the boat and then stopping abruptly, thus imparting kinetic energy to the craft. Ooching is a controversial maneuver and sometimes regarded as cheating in yacht races. **2.** *vti* to move or make something move cautiously or slowly (*slang*) ○ *told listeners the economy was just ooching along* [Perhaps < OOCH[1]]

o·o·cyst /ó ə sìst/ *n* a fertilized gamete of parasitic organisms (**sporozoans**) that is enclosed in a thick wall

o·o·cyte /ó ə sìt/ *n* a cell that develops into a female reproductive cell (**ovum**)

O.O.D. *abbr* NAVY officer of the deck

OODA Loop /óodə-/ *n* in the armed forces and other defense-related agencies, a carefully worked-out chart or guide for use in making decisions throughout varying levels of policy and command [Late 20C. Acronym of *observation, orientation, decision, accuracy*]

O'·O·dham /ó ə dàam/ (*plural same* or **-dhams**) *n* PEOPLES, LANG same as **Papago**

oo·dles /óod'lz/ *npl* a large amount or number of something (*informal*) ○ *She has oodles of friends.* [Mid-19C. Origin ?]

OOG *abbr* COMPUT object-oriented graphics

o·o·ga·mete /ò ə gá meet, -gə meet/ *n* a female reproductive cell (**ovum**)

o·o·gen·e·sis /ò ə jénnəssiss/ *n* the formation and development of a female reproductive cell (**ovum**) —**o·o·ge·net·ic** /ò əjə néttik/ *adj*

o·o·go·ni·um /ò ə gónee əm/ (*plural* **-ni·a** /-nee ə/ or **-ni·ums**) *n* **1.** a cell in the ovary that develops into an oocyte **2.** the female sex organ of some algae and fungi that contains oospheres [Mid-19C. < OO- + Greek *gonos* "generation, seed"] —**o·o·go·ni·al** *adj*

ooh /oo/ *interj* USED TO EXPRESS SURPRISE used as an exclamation of surprise, excitement, pleasure, or pain (*informal*) ■ *vi* (**oohed, ooh·ing, oohs**) EXPRESS SURPRISE OR AWE to exclaim in surprise, excitement, pleasure, or pain, especially on first encountering something ○ *When they went into the royal chambers, you could hear them oohing and aahing.* ■ *n* EXCLAMATION OF SURPRISE an exclamation of surprise, excitement, pleasure, or pain [Early 20C. Natural exclamation] ◇ **ooh la la** used to show pleasant surprise or approval, or, humorously, to suggest that something is scandalous

Ook·pik /óok pìk/ *tdmk Can* a trademark for an owl doll formerly used to identify Canadian handicrafts

o·o·lite /ó ə lìt/, **o·o·lith** /ó ə lith/ *n* **1.** a sedimentary rock, often shale, clay, or sandstone, that is made up of small spherical grains consisting of concentric layers **2.** any small spherical grain in oolite [Early 19C. Via French *oölithe* < modern Latin *oolites* < Greek *ōion* "egg" + *lithos* "stone"] —**o·o·lit·ic** /ò ə líttik/ *adj*

oo·long /óo làwng/ *n* a dark Chinese tea that is partly fermented before being dried [Mid-19C. < Chinese *wulong* < *wu* "black" + *long* "dragon"]

oom·pah /óom paa, óom-/, **oom·pah-pah** /óom paa paa, óom-/ *n* a representation of the sound made by a bass brass instrument, considered typical of some kinds of band music (*often used before a noun*) ○ *an oompah band* [Late 19C. An imitation of the sound]

oomph /óomf/ *n* **1.** energy or enthusiasm ○ *Put some oomph into it!* **2.** *US* strong or obvious sexual attractiveness (*slang*) [Mid-20C. Origin ?]

o·o·pho·rec·to·my /ò əfə réktəmee/ (*plural* **-mies**) *n* SURG same as **ovariectomy** [Late 19C. < modern Latin *oophoron* "ovary," literally "egg-bearer" < Greek *ōion* "egg"]

o·o·pho·ri·tis /ò əfə rítiss/ *n* inflammation of an ovary [Late 19C. < modern Latin *oophoron* "ovary" (see OOPHORECTOMY)]

oops /óops, oops/ *interj* used as an exclamation on dropping something, bumping into somebody, or doing something in a clumsy or awkward manner (*informal*) [Mid-20C. Natural exclamation]

Oort cloud /áwrt-/ *n* a huge, roughly spherical, orbiting collection of comets thought to exist at the edge of the solar system [Late 20C. After Jan Hendrix *Oort* (1900–92), Dutch astronomer]

o·o·sphere /ó ə sfeer/ *n* an unfertilized female reproductive cell in algae and fungi [Late 19C. < OO- + SPHERE]

o·o·spore /ó ə spàwr/ *n* a fertilized female reproductive cell in algae and fungi [Mid-19C. < OO- + SPORE] —**o·o·spor·ic** /ò ə spáwrik/ *adj* —**o·os·po·rous** /ō óspərəss, ò ə spáwrəss/ *adj*

o·o·tid /ó ə tìd/ *n* the stage in the development of an egg cell that becomes the mature ovum immediately prior to fertilization. It is a haploid cell formed by division of the secondary oocyte. [Early 20C. < OO-, modeled on SPERMATID]

ooze[1] /ooz/ *v* (**oozed, ooz·ing, ooz·es**) **1.** *vti* FLOW OR LEAK SLOWLY to exude a liquid substance slowly and in small quantities, or flow in this way ○ *Resin oozed from the trunk.* **2.** *vti* OVERFLOW WITH SOME QUALITY OR EMOTION to exude a quality or emotion in abundance, or be exuded in abundance ○ *oozing charm and self-confidence* **3.** *vi* MOVE SLOWLY BUT STEADILY to move slowly but steadily forward or outward ○ *The huge crowd oozed through the streets.* **4.** *vi* EBB to disappear or decline slowly and gradually ■ *n* **1.** VERY SLOW FLOW a slow and gradual leakage or flow **2.** TANNING SOLUTION an infusion used in tanning, made from oak bark and other plant materials [Old English *wōs* "juice, sap"]

ooze[2] /ooz/ *n* **1.** SLUDGE thick mud or slime that is found at the bottom of a river or lake **2.** SWAMP OR MARSH a soft or muddy area, e.g., a swamp or marsh **3.** MARINE BIOL SEDIMENT ON OCEAN FLOOR a layer of muddy sediment on the ocean floor consisting mainly of the remains of microscopic organisms such as plankton [Old English *wāse*]

ooze leath·er *n* a soft leather with a velvety finish [< OOZE[1] "tanning solution"]

ooz·y[1] /óozee/ (**-i·er, -i·est**) *adj* leaking moisture [Pre-12C. < OOZE[1]]

ooz·y[2] /óozee/ (**-i·er, -i·est**) *adj* wet and muddy [Pre-12C. < OOZE[2]]

op /op/ *n* a surgical operation (*informal*) [Early 20C. shortening of OPERATION]

Op /op/ *n* same as **op art** [Late 20C. Shortening]

OP *abbr* **1.** MIL observation post **2.** CHEM organophosphate **3.** PUBL out of print

op. *abbr* **1.** MUSIC opera **2.** SURG operation **3.** opposite **4.** OPTICS optical **5.** MUSIC, LITERAT opus

Op. *abbr* **1.** SURG operation **2.** MUSIC Opus

o·pac·i·fy /ō pássə fī/ (**-fied, -fy·ing, -fies**) *vti* to become opaque, or make something opaque [Early 20C. < OPACITY] —**o·pac·i·fi·er** *n*

o·pac·i·ty /ō pássətee/ *n* **1.** BEING OPAQUE the quality, condition, or degree of being opaque **2.** OBSCURITY the quality of being obscure in meaning **3.** PHOTOGRAPHY, PHYS ABILITY OF MATERIAL TO STOP LIGHT the capacity of a material such as photographic film to stop light, expressed as a comparison between light striking the material and light transmitted **4.** PHILOSOPHY PROPOSITIONS NOT ADHERING TO LEIBNIZ'S LAW propositions containing modal notions such as necessity or belief in which principles of logic such as Leibniz's law do not obtain [Mid-16C. Via French < Latin *opacus* "shaded, dark"]

o·pah /ṓpə/ *n* a brightly colored sea fish that can be up to 6 ft./1.8 m long. Latin name: *Lampris regius.* [Mid-18C. < a West African language]

o·pal /ṓp'l/ *n* a variously colored semiprecious stone that is a noncrystalline variety of silica. Use: gems. [Late 16C. Directly or via French < Latin *opalus*]

o·pal·esce /ṑpə léss/ (**-esced, -esc·ing, -esc·es**) *vi* to display shimmering milky colors [Early 19C. < OPAL + Latin *-esce* "assuming a certain state"]

o·pal·es·cent /ṑpə léss'nt/ *adj* showing or possessing shimmering milky colors —**o·pal·es·cence** *n*

o·pal·ine /ṓpə līn, -leen/ *adj* same as **opalescent** ■ *n* a semitranslucent glass made by adding fluorides

o·paque /ō páyk/ *adj* **1.** NOT TRANSPARENT OR TRANSLUCENT impervious to light, so that images cannot be seen through it **2.** NOT SHINY dull and without luster **3.** HARD TO UNDERSTAND obscure and unintelligible in meaning **4.** PHYS IMPENETRABLE BY RADIATION impenetrable by a specific form of radiation ■ *n* MATERIAL THROUGH WHICH LIGHT CANNOT PASS something opaque, especially a photographic pigment [15C. Directly or via French < Latin *opacus* "shaded, dark"] —**o·paque·ly** *adv* —**o·paque·ness** *n*

o·paque pro·jec·tor *n* an optical device that uses reflected light to project an enlarged image of an opaque object such as a photograph or printed page onto a screen

op art, Op Art *n* a 20th-century school of abstract art that uses geometric patterns and color to create the illusion of movement (*often used before a noun*) ○ *op art designs* [Shortening of OPTICAL ART, after POP ART] —**op art·ist** *n*

op. cit. /òp sít/ *abbr* in the text or texts quoted (*used in footnotes to refer to a source just mentioned*) [Latin *opus citatum* or *opere citato*]

ope /ōp/ (*archaic or literary*) *adj* open ■ *vti* (**oped, op·ing, opes**) to open, or open something [< OPEN]

OPEC /ṓ pèk/ *n* an organization of oil-producing countries that share the same policies regarding the sale of petroleum. The members are Algeria, Gabon, Indonesia, Iran, Iraq, Kuwait, Libya, Nigeria, Qatar, Saudi Arabia, the United Arab Emirates, and Venezuela. Full form **Organization of Petroleum Exporting Countries**

op-ed /op éd/ *n* **1.** a newspaper page, usually opposite the editorial page, that features signed articles expressing personal opinions (*often used before a noun*) **2.** an article expressing a personal viewpoint written for the op-ed section of a newspaper [Shortening of *opposite editorial (page)*]

Op·e·lou·sas /òppə lóossəss/ city in south central Louisiana, southeast of Alexandria and northeast of Lafayette. Population: 22,688 (2002 estimate).

o·pen /ṓpən/ *adj* **1.** NOT CLOSED OR LOCKED allowing people or things to pass through freely ○ *an open window* **2.** ALLOWING ACCESS TO INSIDE with the lid, cork, or other device removed or in a position that allows access to the inside ○ *an open box* **3.** NOT SEALED not sealed, fastened, or wrapped ○ *an open envelope* **4.** APART OR WIDE with a part of the body widened or apart ○ *The kitten's eyes were open.* **5.** UNFOLDED OR APART having been unfolded, extended, or left apart ○ *A newspaper lay open on the table.* **6.** FRANK AND HONEST not trying to hide anything or deceive anyone ○ *open hostility* **7.** PUBLIC conducted in a public manner ○ *open hearings* **8.** RECEPTIVE ready and willing to accept or listen to something such as new ideas or suggestions ○ *I'm always open to suggestions.* **9.** VULNERABLE in a position in which blame, criticism, or attack are likely ○ *That remark left him open to criticism.* **10.** NOT ENCLOSED having no boundaries or enclosures ○ *open countryside* **11.** NOT COVERED having no cover or roof ○ *an open fire* **12.** AVAILABLE TO DO BUSINESS ready for business and available for use by customers or clients ○ *The gas station is still open.* **13.** FREELY ACCESSIBLE accessible to all, with no restrictions on entry, membership, or acceptance ○ *an open meeting* **14.** POL AVAILABLE TO ALL REGISTERED VOTERS allowing all voters to participate, regardless of party affiliation ○ *an open primary* **15.** ACCESSIBLE TO PARTICULAR GROUP accessible to a particular group of interested people ○ *This competition is open to all students under the age of 18.* **16.** VACANT ready for or available to applicants ○ *The vacancy is no longer open.* **17.** US TURNED ON switched on and ready to use ○ *an open microphone* **18.** NOT PREDETERMINED OR DECIDED remaining undecided or unresolved ○ *I'm trying to keep my options open.* **19.** ALERT in a state of focused attention and alertness ○ *Keep your eyes and ears open.* **20.** WITH NO TIME RESTRICTION with no restrictions on the period of use ○ *an open ticket* **21.** US GENEROUS very free or generous, especially with money ○ *She gave to charity with an open hand.* **22.** US NOT HAVING LEGAL RESTRICTIONS not having restrictions that limit activities such as gambling or drinking ○ *an open town* **23.** MED UNPROTECTED BY SKIN unprotected and exposed, with the skin cut, torn, or missing ○ *an open wound* **24.** MED NOT BLOCKED free from blockage and therefore allowing unobstructed passage **25.** TEXTILES HAVING GAPS having small gaps or intervals between the stitches or threads ○ *an open weave* **26.** OCEANOG FREE FROM ICE OR OTHER HAZARDS not covered by ice or containing objects dangerous to shipping ○ *open water* **27.** MUSIC NOT CLOSED OR MUTED not closed off at the end, stopped by a finger, or covered with a mute ○ *an open organ pipe* **28.** METEOROL WITHOUT FROST mild and free of frost **29.** MIL KNOWN TO BE UNDEFENDED publicly declared not to be garrisoned or defended in wartime ○ *an open city* **30.** FIN AVAILABLE WITHOUT LIMITATIONS freely available without restrictions ○ *open credit* **31.** FIN CURRENTLY ACTIVE active and with transactions being made ○ *an open bank account* **32.** PRINTING HAVING UNUSUALLY WIDE SPACES having wide spacing between printed lines **33.** PHON SAID WITH LIPS APART pronounced with the tongue low in the mouth and the lips well apart ○ *an open vowel* **34.** PHON ENDING IN VOWEL describes a syllable that ends in a vowel **35.** GRAM HAVING SEPARATE ELEMENTS used to describe a compound word formed by two or more words that are spelled separately and without hyphenation **36.** CHESS WITHOUT PAWNS not having pawns as part of a file **37.** SPORTS UNGUARDED unprotected by the assigned player ○ *He left the goal wide open.* **38.** SPORTS HAVING FRONT FOOT BACK in sports, having the front foot farther from the line along which the ball is to be hit than the back foot ○ *Adopting an open stance, he began hitting the ball to the opposite field.* **39.** FOOTBALL BEYOND LINE OF SCRIMMAGE describes the part of a football field beyond the line of scrimmage, where a ball carrier encounters fewer potential tacklers **40.** MATH CONTAINING NO ENDPOINTS describes a mathematical interval that contains neither of a set's endpoints **41.** MATH REFERRING TO SET QUALITY describes a mathematical set that has at least one neighborhood of every point within the set **42.** MATH SERVING AS COMPLEMENT TO CLOSED SET describes a mathematical set that is in a complementary relation to a closed set ■ *v* (**o·pened, o·pen·ing, o·pens**) **1.** *vti* UNFASTEN FROM LOCKED OR CLOSED POSITION to change position or move so as to allow access, or change the position of or move something such as a door or window in order to allow access **2.** *vt* UNSEAL OR UNFASTEN SOMETHING to remove or unseal the lid, cork, or other device that keeps something such as a container closed **3.** *vt* UNWRAP SOMETHING to reveal the contents of something, e.g., by removing its wrapping ○ *I opened the package.* **4.** *vti* UNFOLD TO SHOW INSIDE to unfold or spread something apart so that the inner part is revealed, or become unfolded or spread in this way ○ *Open your books at page 75.* **5.** *vti* PART LIPS OR EYELIDS to move apart, or move the lips or eyelids apart **6.** *vti* START TRADING to start selling, trading, or doing business, or allow clients or customers access to premises in order to buy, trade, or do business **7.** *vti* GET UNDER WAY to start something formally, or get under way ○ *She opened the meeting with a speech about the environment.* **8.** *vt* START ACCOUNT to start an active banking or investment account **9.** *vt* DECLARE SOMETHING READY to make an official and usually public declaration that something is now ready for use or in session ○ *The sports center was officially opened by the mayor.* **10.** *vi* BEGIN PUBLIC PERFORMANCE to start being shown to or performed for the general public for the first time ○ *The show opens on Friday.* **11.** *vti* BECOME ACCESSIBLE TO PUBLIC to be visited by the public, or become accessible to the public ○ *The house opens to the public in August.* **12.** *vt* REMOVE OBSTRUCTIONS to allow people free access to something when formerly this was denied or obstructed ○ *The country had finally opened its borders to the West.* **13.** *vi* GIVE ACCESS TO PLACE to provide access directly to another place (*refers to part of a building*) ○ *The bedroom opened onto a large living room.* **14.** *vti* BE READY FOR NEW IDEAS to become ready to accept new ideas, or make somebody ready to do this ○ *Try opening your mind a bit.* **15.** *vi* BEGIN TO RAIN to produce a downpour ○ *The heavens opened.* **16.** *vi* UNCURL to become fully developed or spread out (*refers to flowers or leaves*) ○ *The daffodils will open soon.* **17.** *vi* FIN START TRADING AT PARTICULAR VALUE to have a particular value at the start of a day's trading on a stock exchange **18.** *vt* MED EMPTY BOWELS to cause the bowels to evacuate **19.** *vt Malaysia, Philippines, Singapore* SWITCH SOMETHING ON to switch on something such as a light or an electrical appliance ■ *n* **1.** COMPETITION ANYONE CAN ENTER a competition or championship in which anybody, amateur or professional, can compete **2.** OUTSIDE a large and unobstructed outdoor space ○ *in the open* **3.** UNCONCEALED STATE the state of being no longer hidden or held back ○ *It's good to get all the facts out in the open.* **4.** COMPUT PUBLICLY AVAILABLE COMPUTER SYSTEM a product or system whose internal features and interfaces can be used or modified by users or developers in any way they wish [Old English, < Indo-European, "up from under, over"] —**o·pen·ness** *n*

open out *v* **1.** *vi* WIDEN to become wider ○ *The track opened out into a clearing.* **2.** *vti* UNFOLD to unfold or spread out something, or be unfolded or spread out **3.** *vti* DEVELOP FROM BUD TO FLOWER to uncurl from a bud into a fully open flower or leaf, or cause a bud to do this **4.** *vi UK* BECOME LESS INTROVERTED to become more sociable, outgoing, and communicative

open up *v* **1.** *vi* UNFOLD to become unclosed, unfold or expand, or offer a broader and freer view to a viewer ○ *Suddenly the valley opened up before us.* **2.** *vt* MAKE OPENING IN SOMETHING to make an opening in something, especially in order to get access **3.** *vt* REMOVE COVERING OR OBSTRUCTION FROM SOMETHING to remove anything that closes or covers something, or that blocks, obstructs, or restricts it **4.** *vti* MAKE SOMETHING ACCESSIBLE to make something more accessible or available to a wider range of people, or become more accessible ○ *The Internet has opened up a whole new world of information.* **5.** *vti* same as **open**

v (sense 6) ○ *A new video store is opening up next week.* **6.** *vti* OPEN BUSINESS FOR DAY to unlock something, especially a store or business, and make it ready for the day **7.** *vi* SPEAK FREELY to speak honestly, especially about personal feelings or experiences ○ *She opens up when she gets to know you.* **8.** *vi* TELL WHAT YOU KNOW to confess to a crime or give information about a crime under coercion (*informal*) **9.** *vi* START SHOOTING WEAPON to start firing or cause a gun or other weapon to start firing **10.** *vti* BECOME OR MAKE SOMETHING MORE EXCITING to become more free-flowing and more interesting or exciting, or cause something to become so ○ *After the first goal the game opened up.* **11.** *vi* MAKE VEHICLE GO FASTER to cause a motor vehicle to accelerate, or travel at an accelerated speed (*informal*)

o·pen ad·mis·sions *n* an educational policy in which students are admitted to college regardless of their academic qualifications or record (*takes a singular or plural verb*)

o·pen a·dop·tion *n* an arrangement concerning an adopted child by which contact between the child's adoptive and biological parents is maintained

o·pen-air *adj* situated or happening outside a building

o·pen-and-shut *adj* simple and easily resolved ○ *an open-and-shut case*

o·pen bar *n* a bar at a party, wedding, or other social function where the drinks are served free of charge

o·pen book *n* somebody or something that is very easy to understand or about which everything is known

o·pen chain *adj* an arrangement of atoms in a molecule in which the atoms are not joined at the ends to form a ring

o·pen class·room *n US* a classroom in which groups of pupils work in a flexible informal way on projects and have minimal supervision

o·pen court *n* a trial or court that is open to members of the public, and whose proceedings are recorded

o·pen dat·ing *n US* the practice of providing information on food packaging that gives the date of packaging, the last day the food may be on sale, or the last day on which it should be consumed

o·pen day *n UK* EDUC same as **open house** (sense 2)

o·pen door *n* (*hyphenated when used before a noun*) **1.** a policy whereby a nation allows free and unrestricted trade with all other nations **2.** free and unrestricted access at all times ○ *open-door management*

o·pen-end *adj US* **1.** not having a limit in either time or amount ○ *an open-end contract* Can term **open-ended 2.** allowing somebody to borrow an extra amount under the terms of a loan ○ *an open-end mortgage*

o·pen-end·ed *adj* **1.** WITH NO PREARRANGED END with no planned or defined end **2.** EASILY MODIFIED not definite and easily changed ○ *We'd left everything pretty open-ended about the vacation.* **3.** NEEDING MORE THAN ONE WORD ANSWER requiring or allowing an answer that is fuller than a simple yes or no ○ *an open-ended question* **4.** *Can, UK* LAW same as **open-end** (sense 1) —**o·pen-end·ed·ly** *adv* —**o·pen-end·ed·ness** *n*

o·pen-end in·vest·ment com·pa·ny *n US* FIN same as **mutual fund**

o·pen en·roll·ment *n US* EDUC same as **open admissions**

o·pen·er /ṓpənər/ *n* **1.** OPENING DEVICE a device for opening containers such as cans or bottles **2.** INITIAL EVENT somebody or something that begins a discussion or event (*informal*) **3.** *US* FIRST ACT IN SHOW the first act in a variety show or musical concert **4.** SPORTS FIRST GAME the first game in a series or season **5.** SPORTS FIRST GOAL the first goal scored in a game **6.** CARDS OPENING PLAYER in a card game, somebody who opens the bidding, betting, or play ■ **o·pen·ers** *npl* CARDS STARTING POINT in some card games, a starting position or point, e.g., a set of cards that allow somebody to begin the betting ◇ **for openers** used to open a statement or discussion (*informal*)

o·pen-eyed *adj* **1.** WATCHFUL alert to all that is happening **2.** WITH EYES WIDE IN WONDER having the eyes wide open in wonder or surprise **3.** ASSESSING REALISTICALLY realistic in knowing and accepting all aspects of a situation

o·pen-faced *adj* with a face that suggests an honest, straightforward, and sincere character

o·pen-faced sand·wich *n* a sandwich consisting of a single slice of bread with filling on it but no second piece of bread on top, eaten with a knife and fork

o·pen-field *adj US* FOOTBALL same as **broken-field**

o·pen frac·ture *n* a bone fracture in which a broken bone pierces the skin or comes into contact with an open wound

o·pen·hand·ed /ṓpən hándəd/ *adj* generous with money or other material things —**o·pen·hand·ed·ly** *adv* —**o·pen·hand·ed·ness** *n*

o·pen·heart·ed /ṓpən ha̋artəd/ *adj* sincere and generous in spirit toward other people —**o·pen·heart·ed·ly** *adv* —**o·pen·heart·ed·ness** *n*

o·pen-hearth *adj* describes a steel-making process that uses a furnace with a shallow hearth and a low roof (**reverberatory furnace**) to produce high-quality steel

o·pen-heart sur·ger·y *n* heart surgery during which the heart is exposed and blood is circulated outside the body by mechanical means

o·pen house *n* **1.** READY HOSPITALITY a situation or occasion when visitors are welcome at any time ○ *It's open house here – come over whenever you like!* **2.** SCHOOL VISITING DAY a day on which an institution such as a school or college is open to the public for visitors to view aspects of its work and activities **3.** VIEWING PERIOD BEFORE SALE a period of time during which a house or an apartment that is for sale is open to the public for viewing **4.** HOUSE OPEN TO VIEWING a house or apartment that is open to be viewed by the public before sale

o·pen·ing /ṓpəning/ *n* **1.** GAP a gap or hole in something, especially one through which you can see or through which people or animals can pass ○ *We found an opening in the fence.* **2.** FIRST PART the first part of something ○ *The movie has a wonderful opening.* **3.** FIRST TIME OF USE the occasion on which something is formally opened or reopened for use (*often used before a noun*) ○ *the opening ceremony* **4.** CLEARING IN WOODS an area in a wood or forest in which trees do not grow **5.** FIRST PERFORMANCE FOR GENERAL PUBLIC the first public performance or showing of a play, exhibition, or other production (*often used before a noun*) **6.** OPPORTUNITY an opportunity to do something ○ *It gave her an opening to say how delighted she was.* **7.** VACANCY a job that is available ○ *We have an opening for a young person with drive and enthusiasm.* **8.** ACT OF OPENING the act of opening something **9.** BEGINNING OF GAME the first moves of a game, especially in chess and checkers

o·pen·ing night *n* ARTS same as **first night**

o·pen in·ter·val *n* in mathematics, a set of real numbers consisting of all numbers between but excluding its endpoints, usually written (a,b) or]a,b[

o·pen-jaw *adj* describes a flight or flight booking that goes to one destination and returns from another and is booked as a round-trip ticket

o·pen let·ter *n* a letter that is addressed to a person or organization but is intended for everybody to read and is published in a newspaper or magazine

o·pen·ly /ṓpənlee/ *adv* without making any attempt at concealment ○ *Many members were openly hostile to the proposed plan.*

o·pen mar·ket *n* a market with no commercial restrictions that allows free competition between buyers and sellers

o·pen mar·riage *n* a marriage in which each partner agrees to allow the other to engage in sexual relationships with other people

o·pen-mind·ed *adj* free from prejudice and receptive to new ideas —**o·pen-mind·ed·ly** *adv* —**o·pen-mind·ed·ness** *n*

o·pen mort·gage *n Can* a mortgage that allows the principal to be paid off at any time without incurring a penalty

o·pen-mouthed *adj* **1.** with the mouth wide open in surprise or wonder **2.** loudly and persistently demanding or complaining —**o·pen-mouth·ed·ly** *adv* —**o·pen-mouth·ed·ness** *n*

o·pen-necked *adj* with the top button unfastened ○ *an open-necked shirt*

o·pen peach *n Southern US* a freestone peach

REGIONAL NOTE See ***plum peach.***

o·pen-plan *adj* used to describe a large open undivided space, especially in a workplace

o·pen-pol·li·nat·ed *adj* pollinated naturally, without human intervention

o·pen punc·tu·a·tion *n* minimal punctuation, especially minimal use of commas

o·pen sand·wich *n UK* same as **open-faced sandwich**

o·pen sea·son *n* **1.** a period during the year when restrictions on the hunting and killing of game or the catching of fish are lifted **2.** a period when the usual restraints are ignored, in particular, when a particular group or category of people come under unrestrained critical attack (*informal*) ○ *It seems to be open season on lawyers at the moment.*

o·pen se·cret *n* something that is supposed to be secret but in actual fact is widely known

o·pen sen·tence *n* in logic, a formula containing a free variable, e.g., "X is human," that cannot be said to be true or false because the referent of the variable is not determined

o·pen ses·a·me /-séssəmee/ *n* a sure means of gaining access to or obtaining something [< the magical words used by Ali Baba, a character in the *Arabian Nights*, to open the door of the robbers' cave]

o·pen set *n* a mathematical set that is included within a family of sets (**topology**)

o·pen shop *n* a workplace where being a member of a union is not a condition of employment

o·pen-skies, **o·pen-sky** *adj* allowing aircraft belonging to any nation the freedom to fly over an area, and therefore placing no restrictions on aerial surveillance of military installations

o·pen so·ci·e·ty *n* a society in which there is freedom of thought, ideas, speech, and communication

o·pen stock *n* merchandise that a store keeps on hand so that customers can replenish or replace individual items in sets, e.g., dishes and glasses

o·pen sys·tem *n* a computer design system with uniform industry standards, compatible with any similar type of system or part

o·pen tick·et *n* **1.** a valid ticket for travel that does not specify a date or time, the actual date and time of travel being arranged later **2.** a request for technical assistance or customer support, especially with computer hardware or software, that has not yet been dealt with

o·pen-toe, **o·pen-toed** *adj* used to describe a shoe, especially a sandal, that is not closed at the front, allowing the toes to be seen

o·pen trad·ing pro·to·col *n* a standardized computer protocol for payment-related transactions such as purchase agreements, receipts, and payment methods (*used in e-commerce*)

o·pen wa·ter *n* an expanse of water that is not enclosed or obstructed

o·pen·work /ṓpən wùrk/ *n* **1.** decorative items that make use of patterns of holes, e.g., wrought-iron work, fretwork, or lace **2.** an embroidery technique in which holes are formed in a fabric by cutting or pulling threads and embellished with various stitches, or embroidery made by this technique

op·er·a[1] /óppərə, -prə/ *n* **1.** MUSICAL DRAMA a dramatic work where music is a dominant part of the performance, with the actors often singing rather than reciting their lines. It is usually highly stylized and typically has recurring themes intensified by musical repetitions developed as the piece progresses. **2.** OPERAS IN GENERAL operas thought of collectively or as an art form **3.** MUSIC OPERATIC SCORE the musical score or libretto of an operatic work **4.** same as **opera house** [Mid-17C. Via Italian < Latin, "works" < *opus* (see OPUS).]

o·per·a[2] /ópərə, óppərə/ ARTS plural of **opus**

op·er·a·ble /óppərəb'l, ópprəb'l/ *adj* **1.** capable of being treated by surgery **2.** capable of being done or put into practice —**op·er·a·bil·i·ty** /òppərə bíllətee, òpprə-/ *n* —**op·er·a·bly** *adv*

o·pé·ra bouffe /òppərə bóof, òpprə-/ *n* **1.** an opera with a comic or farcical theme **2.** opéra bouffes thought of collectively or as an art form [< French, "comic opera"; translation of Italian *opera buffa*]

o·pe·ra buf·fa /-bóofə/ *n* a comic opera of the kind that originated in Italy in the 18th century, using themes or characters from everyday life and usually having a happy ending. Mozart's *The Marriage of Figaro* is an example. [< Italian, "comic opera"]

o·pé·ra co·mique /òppərə kaw méek/ *n* an opera on a light-hearted theme with spoken dialogue, especially popular in 19th-century France [< French, "comic opera"]

op·er·a glass·es *npl* small decorative low-powered binoculars for use by people in the audience at theatrical, operatic, or ballet performances

op·er·a·go·er /óppərə gō ər, ópprə-/ *n* a regular attender at opera performances

op·er·a hat *n* a man's collapsible top hat that is spring-operated

op·er·a house *n* a theater that is designed for putting on operas, often grander in style than an ordinary theater

op·er·and /óppə rànd/ *n* **1.** a quantity, function, or other entity that is to have a mathematical operation performed on it **2.** the portion of a computer instruction that specifies the location in memory of the data to be manipulated [Late 19C. < Latin *operandum* "thing to be worked on" < *operari* (see OPERATE)]

op·er·ant /óppərənt/ *n* **1.** PERFORMER OF OPERATION somebody or something that operates or that carries out some kind of operation **2.** PSYCHOL VOLUNTARY ACTION in learning theory, an action or other unit of behavior that does not appear to have a stimulus ■ *adj* HAVING EFFECT producing a specific effect [Early 17C. < Latin *operant-*, present participle of *operari* (see OPERATE)] —**op·er·ant·ly** *adv*

op·er·ant con·di·tion·ing *n* a form of learning that takes place when an instance of spontaneous behavior is either reinforced by a reward or discouraged by punishment. The principles involved have had a strong influence on behavior modification as well as on other kinds of therapy.

op·er·a se·ri·a /-séeree ə/ *n* **1.** an opera that has a serious theme, often one taken from classical mythology, and usually a tragic ending. An example is Mozart's *The Clemency of Titus*. **2.** opera serias thought of collectively or as an art form [< Italian, "serious opera"]

op·er·ate /óppə ràyt/ (**-at·ed, -at·ing, -ates**) *v* **1.** *vti* FUNCTION OR MAKE SOMETHING FUNCTION to function or work, or make something function or work **2.** *vti* BUSINESS FUNCTION AS BUSINESS OR MANAGE SOMETHING to exist as a working business or organization, or oversee the running of a working business or organization **3.** *vi* MED PERFORM SURGERY to perform surgery on a person or animal **4.** *vi* EXERT EFFECT to have an effect or influence on somebody or something **5.** *vi* MIL CARRY OUT MILITARY OPERATIONS to undertake military missions or activities, usually within a particular area or from a particular base **6.** *vi* FIN TRADE IN FINANCIAL MARKET to trade or deal in securities or commodities on the stock exchange **7.** *vi* ENGAGE IN ILLEGAL ACTIVITIES to be active in some illegal or underhanded business [Early 17C. < Latin *operat-*, past participle of *operari* "work" < *oper-*, stem of *opus* "work"]

~~**operater**~~ incorrect spelling of **operator**

op·er·at·ic /òppə ráttik/ *adj* **1.** belonging or relating to opera **2.** overly or flamboyantly extravagant, especially in behavior [Mid-18C. < OPERA[1], after DRAMATIC] —**op·er·at·i·cal·ly** *adv*

op·er·at·ics /òppə ráttiks/ *n* flamboyantly exaggerated or extravagant behavior (*takes a singular or plural verb*)

op·er·at·ing room, **op·er·at·ing suite** *n* a room in a hospital where surgical operations are performed

op·er·at·ing sys·tem *n* the essential program in a computer that maintains disk files, runs applications, and handles devices such as the mouse and printer

op·er·at·ing ta·ble *n* a table on which somebody undergoing a surgical operation lies

op·er·at·ing the·a·tre *n UK* MED same as **operating room**

op·er·a·tion /òppə ráysh'n/ *n* **1.** CONTROL the act of making something carry out its function, or controlling or managing the way it works **2.** FUNCTIONING STATE the state of functioning or of being in effect ○ *The ban is to be put into operation starting next week.* **3.** SOMETHING DONE something that is carried out, especially something difficult or complex ○ *the tricky operation of removing the sting* **4.** MED SURGICAL INTERVENTION any surgical procedure, e.g., one carried out to repair damage to a body part **5.** ORGANIZED ACTION an organized campaign, maneuver, or other form of action, especially one carried out by rescue personnel, the police, or diplomatic personnel **6.** *also* **Op·er·a·tion** MIL MILITARY ACTION an action conducted by military forces that can range in scope from a reconnaissance mission to an entire campaign (*often used before a noun*) ○ *Operation Desert Storm* **7.** MATH MATHEMATICAL PROCESS a mathematical process in which entities are derived from others through the application of rules, e.g., subtraction, multiplication, or differentiation **8.** COMPUT SINGLE PART OF COMPUTER PROGRAM a series of actions performed by a computer, defined by an instruction and forming part of a computer program **9.** BUSINESS DEAL a business deal or financial transaction **10.** ILLEGAL BUSINESS an illegal, dishonest, or underhanded business ○ *He got involved in a shady gambling operation.* ■ **op·er·a·tions** *npl* CONTROLLING OF ORGANIZED ACTIVITIES the supervising, monitoring, and coordinating of the activities of a military or civilian organization or a complex machine (*often used before a noun*) ○ *the operations console of a computer*

op·er·a·tion·al /òppə ráyshən'l, -shnəl/ *adj* **1.** ABLE TO BE USED in proper working order and able to be used ○ *The new transportation link will be fully operational next month.* **2.** OF OPERATING relating to the operating of something or to the way it operates **3.** OF ORGANIZATION'S ACTIVITIES relating to the operations of an organization, especially its day-to-day activities or the basic management and control of these **4.** MIL COMBAT-READY ready for combat or maneuvers —**op·er·a·tion·al·ly** *adv*

op·er·a·tion·al am·pli·fi·er *n* an amplifier with high gain and high stability that is controlled by way of externally connected negative-feedback circuits

op·er·a·tion·al·ism /òppə ráyshən'l ìzzəm, -shnə lìzzəm/ *n* the view that terms for scientific concepts should be defined using the scientific operations such as measuring or observing performed to establish or disprove them —**op·er·a·tion·al·ist** *n, adj* —**op·er·a·tion·al·is·tic** /òppə rayshən'l ístik, -shnə lístik/ *adj*

op·er·a·tion·al·ize /òppə ráyshən'l ìz, -shnəl-/ (**-ized, -iz·ing, -iz·es**) *vt* to put something to use or into operation (*informal*)

op·er·a·tion·al re·search *n* MANAGEMT same as **operations research**

op·er·a·tion·ism /òppə ráysh'n ìzzəm/ *n* PHILOSOPHY same as **operationalism**

op·er·a·tions re·search *n* analysis of the problems that exist in complex systems such as those used to run a business or a military campaign, designed to give a scientific basis for decision-making

op·er·a·tive /óppərətiv, ópprətiv/ *adj* **1.** IN EFFECT in place and having an effect, especially the right or desired effect **2.** SIGNIFICANT carrying a special meaning or significance **3.** MED OF SURGERY relating to or resulting from a surgical procedure ■ *n* **1.** SKILLED WORKER a skilled worker, especially in a manufacturing industry **2.** WORKER somebody who performs a particular task or who works in a particular field (*formal or humorous*) ○ *a rodent operative* **3.** POL POLITICAL WORKER an employee of a political party who works in any behind-the-scenes capacity such as political troubleshooting or manipulation of media stories **4.** *US* DETECTIVE a private detective **5.** SPY a spy or secret agent —**op·er·a·tive·ly** *adv* —**op·er·a·tiv·i·ty** /òppərə tívvətee, òpprə-/ *n*

op·er·a·tor /óppə ràytər/ *n* **1.** SOMEBODY OPERATING SOMETHING somebody who operates machinery, an instrument, or other equipment **2.** BUSINESS OWNER OR MANAGER an owner or manager of a business or other commercial enterprise **3.** STOCK-EXCHANGE DEALER a dealer on the stock exchange or in a money market, especially somebody who is aggressive or speculative **4.** MANIPULATIVE PERSON somebody who behaves in a devious or manipulative way, especially in order to gain something (*informal*) ○ *a smooth operator* **5.** MATH, COMPUT SOMETHING EFFECTING MATHEMATICAL OPERATION a mathematical symbol, term, or other entity that performs or describes an operation, e.g., a multiplication or subtraction sign **6.** SOLDIER a member of the US Army Special Forces

o·per·cu·lum /ō púrkyələm/ (*plural* **-la** /-lə/ or **-lums**) *n* **1.** ANAT MUCUS PLUG IN CERVIX the plug of mucus that fills the opening of a woman's cervix while she is pregnant. It helps to prevent infection. **2.** FISH GILL-COVERING FLAP the flexible bony flap covering the gills of bony fishes **3.** BOT FLAP IN MOSSES AND FUNGI a flap covering an aperture in the spore capsules of mosses and some fungi **4.** ZOOL SEAL ON MOLLUSK'S SHELL a rounded plate that seals the mouth of the shell of some gastropod mollusks when the animal's body is inside [Early 18C. < Latin, "lid" < *operire* "to cover"] —**o·per·cu·lar** *adj* —**o·per·cu·lar·ly** *adv* —**o·per·cu·late** /-lət, -làyt/ *adj* —**o·per·cu·lat·ed** *adj*

op·e·ret·ta /òppə réttə/ *n* a theatrical production, usually with a comic theme, similar to opera but with much spoken dialogue and usually some dancing. Gilbert and Sullivan wrote many operettas. [Late 18C. < Italian, "small opera" < *opera* (see OPERA[1])] —**op·e·ret·tist** *n*

op·er·on /óppə ròn/ *n* in bacteria, a segment of a chromosome containing the genes that specify the structure of a given protein, alongside the genes that regulate its manufacture. Operons are relatively simple units of genetic control and are found only in bacteria. [Mid-20C. < French *opéron* < *opérer* "to work" < Latin *operari* (see OPERATE)]

op·er·ose /óppə ròss/ *adj* (*formal*) **1.** requiring a lot of effort **2.** busy, active, or hard working [Late 17C. < Latin *operosus* < *oper-*, stem of *opus* (see OPUS)] —**op·er·ose·ly** *adv* —**op·er·ose·ness** *n*

O·phe·li·a /ə féelee ə/ *n* a very small inner natural satellite of Uranus, discovered in 1986 by the Voyager 2 planetary probe. Its gravitational influence seems to help stabilize the outer ring of Uranus.

oph·i·cleide /óffə klìd, ṓfə-/ *n* a musical instrument resembling and superseded by the bass tuba [Mid-19C. < French *ophicléide* < Greek *ophis* "snake" + *kleid-* "key"; from its resemblance to an earlier instrument called a "serpent"]

o·phid·i·an /ō fíddee ən/ *adj* **1.** belonging or relating to snakes **2.** resembling a snake in appearance, habits, or movement [Early 19C. < modern Latin *Ophidia* < Greek *ophid-* "snake"] —**o·phid·i·an** *n*

oph·i·o·lite /óffee ə lìt, ṓfee-/ *n* any igneous and metamorphic rock that was formed from deep-sea sediment. Ophiolites are rich in iron and magnesium. [Mid-19C. < Greek *ophis* "snake" + -LITE; from its snaky texture]

oph·i·ol·o·gy /òffee óllәjee, ṑfee-/ *n* the scientific study of snakes [Early 19C. < Greek *ophis* "snake" + -LOGY] —**oph·i·o·log·i·cal** /òffee ə lójjik'l, ṑfee ə-/ *adj* —**oph·i·ol·o·gist** *n*

oph·ite /ó fìt/ *n* a mottled green rock, e.g., diabase or dolerite, that is made up of small long plagioclase crystals surrounded by larger pyroxene crystals [Mid-17C. Via Latin < Greek *ophitēs* "serpentine stone" < *ophis* "snake"; from its markings, which are like a snake's]

o·phit·ic /o fíttik, ō-/ *adj* describes rocks consisting of small elongated plagioclase crystals completely enclosed by larger pyroxene crystals

Oph·i·u·chus /òffee óokəss/ *n* a large constellation near the celestial equator. See illustration at **constellation**

ophthal. *abbr* MED **1.** ophthalmologist **2.** ophthalmology

ophthalm- *prefix* same as **ophthalmo-** (*used before vowels*)

oph·thal·mi·a /op thálmee ə, of-/ *n* inflammation of the eye, especially of the conjunctiva and surrounding area [14C. Via late Latin < Greek < *ophthalmos* "eye" (see OPHTHALMO-)]

oph·thal·mic /op thálmik, of-/ *adj* relating to the eyes, or located in the region of the eye

oph·thal·mi·tis /òpthəl mítiss, òf-/ *n* inflammation of the eye

ophthalmo- *prefix* eye, eyeball ○ *ophthalmoscope* [< Greek *ophthalmos* < Indo-European, "see"]

ophthalmol. *abbr* MED **1.** ophthalmologist **2.** ophthalmology

oph·thal·mol·o·gy /òpthəl móllәjee, òfthəl-/ *n* the branch of medicine that is concerned with the diagnosis and treatment of eye diseases and conditions —**oph·thal·mo·log·i·cal** /op thàlmə lójjik'l, of thàlmə-/ *adj* —**oph·thal·mo·log·i·cal·ly** *adv* —**oph·thal·mol·o·gist** *n*

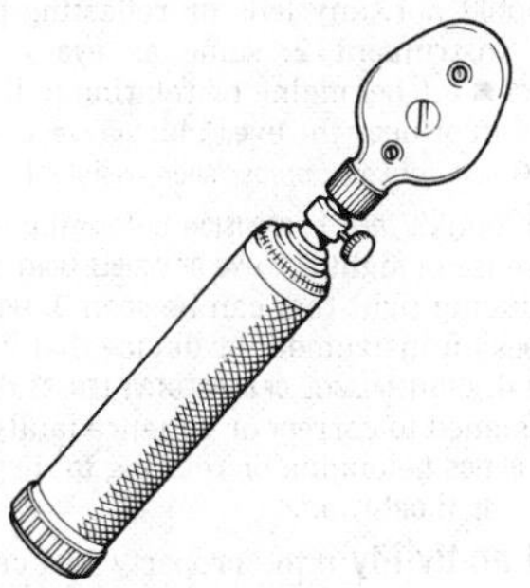

ophthalmoscope

oph·thal·mo·scope /op thálmə skōp, of-/ *n* a medical instrument used for examining the inside of the eye to detect changes to the retina such as those associated with diabetes and hypertension. A direct ophthalmoscope shines a fine beam of light into the eye and allows the examiner to see a magnified image of the spot where the beam falls. —**oph·thal·mo·scop·ic** /op thàlmə skóppik, of thàlmə-/ *adj*

oph·thal·mos·co·py /òpthəl móskəpee, òfthəl-/ (*plural* **-pies**) *n* a medical examination of the inside of the eye using an ophthalmoscope to detect changes to the retina such as those associated with diabetes and hypertension

Oph·uls /áwf'lss, óff'lz/, **Op·üls** /áwpülss/, **Max** (1902–57) German-born French movie director. His romantic, opulent movies include *La Ronde* (1950) and *Madame de...* (1953). Born **Oppenheimer, Maximilian**

-opia *suffix* condition affecting vision ○ *hyperopia* ○ *protanopia* [< Greek < *ops* "eye, face" < Indo-European, "see"]

o·pi·ate /ópee ət/ *n* **1. OPIUM-CONTAINING DRUG** a drug that contains opium or an opium derivative, e.g., morphine or heroin **2. SLEEP-INDUCING SUBSTANCE** a drug, hormone, or other substance capable of inducing drowsiness and other effects similar to those of opium or its derivatives **3. SOMETHING WITH DULLING EFFECT** something that has a relaxing, pacifying, or dulling effect ○ *TV, often described as the opiate of the masses* ■ *adj* **1. CONTAINING OPIUM** containing opium or an opium derivative **2. BORING** mind-numbingly unexciting, especially because of being simplistic, cliché-ridden, or formulaic ■ *vt* (**-at·ed, -at·ing, -ates**) **1.** PHARM **TREAT SOMEBODY WITH OPIATE** to treat somebody, or somebody's symptoms, with an opiate **2. DULL PAIN** to dull or deaden pain, anguish, or some other unwanted condition [15C. < medieval Latin *opiatus* < Latin *opium* (see OPIUM)]

o·pine /ō pín/ (**o·pined, o·pin·ing, o·pines**) *vti* to express an opinion, or express something as your opinion (*formal*) [15C. < Latin *opinari* "suppose, believe"]

o·pin·ion /ə pínnyən/ *n* **1. PERSONAL VIEW** the view somebody takes about an issue, especially when it is based solely on personal judgment ○ *In my opinion it's all a waste of time.* **2. ESTIMATION** a view regarding the worth of somebody or something ○ *They had a pretty low opinion of me.* **3. EXPERT VIEW** an expert assessment of something ○ *I told the doctor I wanted a second opinion.* **4. BODY OF GENERALLY HELD VIEWS** the view or views held by most people or by a large number of people ○ *pundits and other opinion formers* **5.** LAW **CONCLUSION OF FACT** a conclusion drawn from observation of the facts [14C. Via French < Latin *opinion-* < *opinari* "suppose"] ◇ **be a matter of opinion** to be open to dispute or debate ◇ **be of the opinion that** to think that something is the case

o·pin·ion·at·ed /ə pínnyə nàytəd/ *adj* always ready to express opinions and tending to hold to them stubbornly, unreasonably dismissing other people's views —**o·pin·ion·at·ed·ly** *adv* —**o·pin·ion·at·ed·ness** *n*

o·pin·ion·a·tive /ə pínnyə nàytiv/ *adj* (*formal*) **1.** relating to opinions or to the stating of them **2.** same as **opinionated** —**o·pin·ion·a·tive·ly** *adv*

o·pin·ion poll *n* a survey carried out to discover what the general public or some smaller group of people thinks about something

o·pi·oid /ópee òyd/ *n* any opium-containing substance that is produced naturally in the brain ■ *adj* similar in effect or properties to opium but not derived from opium [Mid-20C. < OPIUM]

o·pi·oid pep·tide *n* a naturally occurring peptide that has pain-relieving and sedative effects. The endorphins are opioid peptides.

o·pis·tho·branch /ə písthə brangk/ *n* an invertebrate ocean animal that has gills, a small or nonexistent shell, and tentacles [Mid-19C. < modern Latin *Opisthobranchiata* < Greek *opisthen* "behind" + *bragkhia* "gills," because the gills are behind the heart]

op·is·thog·na·thous /òppiss thógnəthəss/ *adj* having jaws that slope backward or mouthparts that face backward [Mid-19C. < Greek *opisthen* "behind"] —**op·is·thog·na·thism** *n*

o·pi·um /ópee əm/ *n* **1.** a brownish gummy extract from the unripe seed pods of the opium poppy that contains several highly addictive narcotic alkaloid substances such as morphine and codeine **2.** something that has a stupefying, numbing, or sleep-inducing effect ○ *Soap operas she dismissed as the opium of a bored populace.* [14C. Via Latin < Greek *opion* "poppy juice" < *opos* "vegetable juice"]

o·pi·um den *n* a place where opium is sold and smoked, especially one that has facilities where people using the drug can stay while under its influence

o·pi·um pop·py *n* a poppy with grayish green leaves, grown as a source of opium. Flowers: pink, red, or white. Native to: Europe, Asia. Latin name: *Papaver somniferum.*

OPM *abbr US* MANAGEMT Office of Personnel Management

~~**oponent**~~ incorrect spelling of **opponent**

O·por·to ➧ **Porto**

~~**oportunity**~~ incorrect spelling of **opportunity**

~~**oposite**~~ incorrect spelling of **opposite**

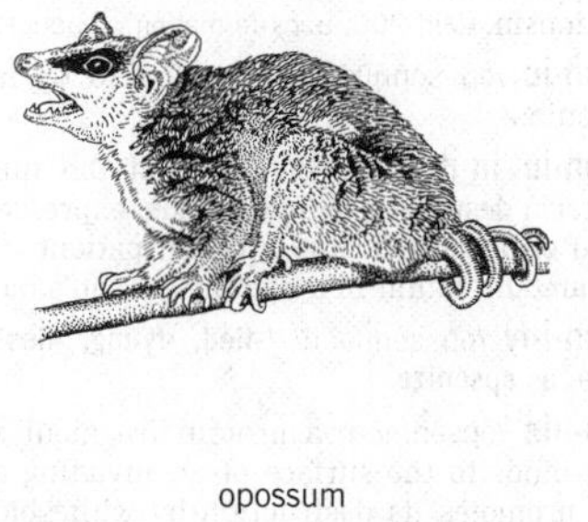

opossum

o·pos·sum /ə póssəm, póssəm/ (*plural* **-sums** or *same*) *n* **1.** a small nocturnal tree-dwelling marsupial with dense fur, a long snout, and a hairless prehensile tail. Native to: United States, Central and South America. Latin name: *Didelphis marsupialis.* **2.** any one of several similar marsupials that are mostly nocturnal plant-eating tree-dwellers. Native to: Australia, New Zealand. Family: Phalangeridae. [Early 17C. < Virginia Algonquian *aposoum* "white animal"]

o·pos·sum shrimp *n* a crustacean that resembles a shrimp, the female of which carries the eggs and newly hatched young in a pouch just below the thorax. Order: Mysidacae.

opp. *abbr* opposite

Op·pen·hei·mer /óppən hìmər/, **J. Robert** (1904–67) US nuclear physicist. He was the director of the Los Alamos atomic bomb project (1943–45) and the United States Atomic Energy Commission (1946–53). He won the Enrico Fermi Award in 1963. Full name **Oppenheimer, Julius Robert**

> "The atomic bomb...made the prospect of future war unendurable. It has led us up those last few steps to the mountain pass; and beyond there is a different country."
> [J. Robert Oppenheimer. Quoted in *The Making of the Atomic Bomb*, Richard Rhodes; 1987]

> "No man should escape our universities without knowing how little he knows."
> [J. Robert Oppenheimer, *Partisan Review*; Summer 1967]

~~**opperation**~~ incorrect spelling of **operation**

OPP film *n* plastic film used for packaging. Full form **oriented polypropylene**

op·pi·dan /óppəd'n/ (*formal*) *adj* belonging to, relating to, or found in a town, often the town in which a university is sited as distinct from the university itself ■ *n* a resident of a town [Mid-16C. < Latin *oppidanus* < *oppidum* "fort, town"]

op·pi·late /óppə làyt/ (**-lat·ed, -lat·ing, -lates**) *vt* to block up a body passage such as a duct or a body opening such as a pore [15C. < Latin *oppilat-*, past participle of *oppilare* "stop up" < *pilare* "heap up" < *pila* "heap of stones"] —**op·pi·la·tion** /òppə láysh'n/ *n*

~~**oppinion**~~ incorrect spelling of **opinion**

op·po·nent /ə pṓnənt/ *n* **1. ADVERSARY IN CONTEST** somebody who plays, fights, or competes against you in a contest **2. SOMEBODY OPPOSING SOMETHING** somebody who opposes a course of action, or a cause or belief ○ *a fierce opponent of reform of the voting system* **3.** ANAT **OPPOSING MUSCLE** any muscle that counteracts the motion of another ■ *adj* **1. CONTRARY** working or arguing against something **2. CONTRADICTORY** serving to contradict something [Late 16C. < Latin *opponent-*, present participle of *opponere* "set against" < *ponere* "to place"] —**op·po·nen·cy** *n*

op·por·tune /óppər tóon, òppər tóon/ *adj* suitable for a purpose, or occurring at just the right time [15C. Via French < Latin *opportunus* "favorable" (used of the wind) < *ob portum veniens* "coming toward port"] —**op·por·tune·ly** *adv* —**op·por·tune·ness** *n*

op·por·tun·ist /óppər tóonist, òppər tóonist/ *n* somebody who takes advantage of something, especially somebody who does so in a devious, unscrupulous, or unprincipled way ■ *adj UK* same as **opportunistic** (sense 1) —**op·por·tun·ism** *n*

op·por·tun·is·tic /òppər too nístik/ *adj* **1.** taking advantage of an opportunity, or exploiting opportunities and situations in general, especially in a devious, unscrupulous, or unprincipled way **2.** describes a microorganism or relatively minor disease that is not normally serious but that can become pathogenic or life-threatening when the host has a low level of immunity ○ *opportunistic infections* —**op·por·tun·is·ti·cal·ly** *adv*

op·por·tu·ni·ty /òppər tóonətee, óppər tóonətee/ (*plural* **-ties**) *n* **1.** a chance, especially one that offers some kind of advantage **2.** a combination of favorable circumstances or situations

op·por·tu·ni·ty cost *n* the cost of a commercial decision regarded as the value of the alternative that is forgone. For example, if the choice is between using a machine or scrapping it, the opportunity cost is the scrap value.

op·pos·a·ble /ə pṓzəb'l/ *adj* **1. RESISTIBLE** capable of being opposed or resisted **2. ABLE TO BE PLACED OPPOSITE SOMETHING** capable of being put in a position that is opposite something else **3.** ANAT **TOUCHING END OF ANOTHER DIGIT** describes a thumb or big toe that can face and touch the end of one or more of the other digits of the same hand or foot —**op·pos·a·bil·i·ty** /ə pṓzə bíllətee/ *n* —**op·pos·a·bly** *adv*

op·pose /ə pṓz/ (**-posed, -pos·ing, -pos·es**) *v* **1.** *vti* **BE**

AGAINST SOMETHING to disapprove of something and wish to, or take action to, stop it ○ *They would not state openly that they oppose violence.* **2.** *vt* COMPETE WITH OPPONENTS to be in competition, conflict, or battle with another person, team, or fighting force **3.** *vt* SET SOMETHING IN CONTRAST TO SOMETHING to set something up as a contrast to something else **4.** *vt* PUT SOMETHING OPPOSITE SOMETHING to put one thing in a position directly facing another [14C. < French *opposer*, an alteration (influenced by *poser* "place") of Latin *opponere* (see OPPONENT)] —**op·pos·er** *n* —**op·pos·ing** *adj*

op·posed /ə pṓzd/ *adj* disagreeing with or taking an active stance against somebody or something ○ *a government opposed to change of any sort* ◇ **as opposed to** used to introduce something that is a contrast to or the opposite of the first thing mentioned ○ *the acquisition of true knowledge, as opposed to mere memorizing*

op·posed-cyl·in·der en·gine *n* an engine in which cylinders or banks of cylinders are mounted on opposite sides of the crankcase in the same plane, with their connecting rods mounted on a common crankshaft. Piston strokes on each side of the camshaft work in a direction opposite to one another.

op·po·site /óppəzit/ *adj* **1.** ON FACING SIDE positioned so as to face somebody or something from the other side of an intervening space ○ *on the opposite side of the room* ○ *at the opposite end of the street* ○ *the house opposite* **2.** FACING AWAY pointing, facing, or moving away from each other ○ *went off in opposite directions* **3.** TOTALLY DIFFERENT different from or contrary to something or each other in every respect ○ *She thought the plan workable, I took the opposite view.* **4.** BOT LEVEL WITH ON OTHER SIDE describes plant parts, especially pairs of leaves or flowers, that grow at the same level on a stem but on either side of it **5.** MATH FACING ANGLE describes the side of a triangle facing an angle **6.** MATH FACING EACH OTHER GEOMETRICALLY describes sides or angles in an even-sided polygon that face each other ■ *n* **1.** SOMEBODY OR SOMETHING DIFFERENT FROM ANOTHER somebody or something that is completely different from or contrary to another or what is expected **2.** same as **opponent** *n* (sense 1) (*archaic or literary*) ■ *adv* IN OPPOSITE POSITION in or into a position that is opposite ○ *They live directly opposite.* ■ *prep* **1.** ACROSS FROM SOMETHING facing something or somebody across an intervening space ○ *They moved to a house opposite the museum.* **2.** IN COMPLEMENTING ACTING ROLE TO SOMEBODY in an acting role that is the counterpart to or complements another, especially when the two roles are played by people of different genders ○ *excited to be playing opposite the great star* [14C. Via French < Latin *oppositus*, past participle of *opponere* (see OPPONENT)] —**op·po·site·ly** *adv* —**op·po·site·ness** *n*

op·po·site num·ber *n* somebody with a similar job or post as somebody else, especially in another department or organization

op·po·site prompt *n* in a theater, the side of a stage that is to the actors' right when they face the audience

op·po·site sex *n* people of the other sex, that is, men collectively from the point of view of women, or women collectively from the point of view of men

op·po·si·tion /òppə zísh'n/ *n* **1.** HOSTILE ATTITUDE OR ACTION a disapproving attitude toward something and a wish to prevent it, or action taken to show disapproval of and prevent something ○ *Public opposition to the plan was growing.* **2.** SPORTS OPPONENT the person or team that you or another player or team have to play against ○ *He can expect stronger opposition in the semifinal.* **3.** *also* **Op·po·si·tion** POL POLITICAL GROUPS OPPOSING GOVERNMENT a political party, or political parties or groups, opposed to the government in power in a country (*often used before nouns*) **4.** *also* **Op·po·si·tion** POL PRINCIPAL PARTY OPPOSING GOVERNMENT in a British-style parliamentary system, the political party with the largest number of seats of those not in office, officially recognized as the government's main opponent (*often used before nouns*) **5.** LING LINGUISTIC CONTRAST in linguistics, the contrast between two or more similar elements in a language **6.** PHON PHONETIC CONTRAST BETWEEN SOUNDS in phonetics, the contrast between two sounds that are articulated in a similar place in the mouth, e.g., between the voiced consonant /v/ and the voiceless consonant /f/ **7.** CHESS ADVANTAGE NEAR END OF CHESS GAME a situation toward the end of a game of chess in which the two kings are in such a position that the opponent must make a king move and is therefore at a disadvantage **8.** LOGIC RELATIONS BETWEEN LOGICAL PROPOSITIONS the way in which logical propositions sharing the same subject and predicate but differing in quantity or quality relate to each other **9.** ASTRON MOON OR PLANET POSITION the position of the Moon or one of the outer planets when it is on the opposite side of the Earth as seen from the Sun **10.** ASTRON RELATIVE POSITION OF TWO ASTRONOMICAL OBJECTS the position of two astronomical objects when they are diametrically opposite on the celestial sphere **11.** ASTROLOGICALLY OPPOSING PLANETARY POSITION in astrology, a situation when two planets are 180° from each other, believed to cause friction or symbolize confrontation —**op·po·si·tion·al** *adj*

op·po·si·tion·ist /òppə zísh'nist/ *n* a member of an opposition, especially a political opposition —**op·po·si·tion·ism** *n*

op·pos·i·tion re·search *n US* research done in order to discover damaging or detrimental information about somebody

op·press /ə préss/ (**-pressed, -press·ing, -press·es**) *vt* **1.** to subject a person or a people to a harsh or cruel form of domination **2.** to be a source of worry, stress, or trouble to somebody [14C. < French *oppresser* < Latin *oppress-*, past participle of *opprimere* "press against" < *premere* "to press"] —**op·pres·sion** *n* —**op·pres·sor** *n*

op·pres·sive /ə préssiv/ *adj* **1.** DOMINATING HARSHLY imposing a harsh or cruel form of domination ○ *an oppressive regime* **2.** HIGHLY STRESSFUL exerting a worrying, troubling, or burdensome pressure on somebody **3.** STIFLING so hot and humid as to make people feel tired, irritable, or sluggish —**op·pres·sive·ly** *adv* —**op·pres·sive·ness** *n*

op·pro·bri·um /ə prṓbree əm/ (*plural* **-bri·a** /-bree ə/) *n* **1.** SCORN scorn, contempt, or severe criticism **2.** DISGRACE shame or disgrace that stems from disreputable behavior **3.** SOURCE OF SHAME something or somebody that brings shame or disgrace (*archaic*) ○*"would render him an object of scorn and an opprobrium of the religion with which he had diligently associated himself"* (George Eliot, *Middlemarch*; 1872) [Mid-17C. < Latin, "infamy, reproach" < *opprobare* "to reproach" < *probrum* "disgrace"] —**op·pro·bri·ous** *adj*

op·pugn /ə pyṓon/ (**-pugned, -pugn·ing, -pugns**) *vt* to question the validity or truthfulness of something (*formal*) [15C. < Latin *oppugnare* "fight against" < *pugnare* "to fight"] —**op·pugn·er** *n*

~~**opression**~~ incorrect spelling of **oppression**

ops /ops/ *npl* the controlling of organized military or civilian activities (*informal; often used before a noun*) ○ *Who's in the ops room tonight?* [Early 20C. Shortening of *operations*]

op·sin /ópsin/ *n* a light-sensitive pigment found in the rod cells of the eye. It is a glycoprotein, and in the vertebrate eye it combines with retinal to form rhodopsin. [Mid-20C. Back-formation < RHODOPSIN]

op·son·ic /op sónnik/ *adj* relating to or involving opsonins

op·son·ic in·dex *n* a measure of the number of bacteria destroyed by blood cells, expressed as the ratio of opsonin in the infected patient's blood to the amount found in a healthy person's blood

op·son·i·fy /op sónnə fī/ (**-fied, -fy·ing, -fies**) *vt* BIOL same as **opsonize**

op·so·nin /ópsənin/ *n* a protein fragment in blood that binds to the surface of an invading antibody and promotes its destruction by white blood cells [Early 20C. < Latin *opsonare* "cater, buy provisions" < Greek *opsōnein* "condiment"]

op·so·nize /ópsə nīz/ (**-nized, -niz·ing, -niz·es**) *vt* to make foreign bodies such as bacteria susceptible to destruction by blood cells by coating them with opsonin —**op·so·ni·za·tion** /òpsəni záysh'n/ *n*

-opsy *suffix* examination ○ *biopsy* [< Greek *-opsia* "sight" < *opsis* < Indo-European, "see"]

opt /opt/ (**opt·ed, opt·ing, opts**) *vi* to choose something or choose to do something, usually in preference to other available alternatives ○ *Offered tea or coffee, I opted for coffee.* [Late 19C. Via French *opter* < Latin *optare* "choose, desire"]

opt out *vi* to decide not to join in something or not to go along with something (*informal*)

opt. *abbr* **1.** GRAM optative **2.** OPTICS optical **3.** OPHTHALMOL optician **4.** OPTICS optics **5.** optimum **6.** optional

op·ta·tive /óptətiv/ *adj* **1.** OF CHOICE-MAKING relating to the making of choices (*formal*) **2.** GRAM OF GRAMMATICAL MOOD describes a grammatical mood in Greek and some other languages that expresses wishes or desires, or a verb in this mood **3.** GRAM CONTAINING VERB EXPRESSING WISH describes a clause or sentence containing a verb expressing a wish or desire and in the subjunctive or optative mood ■ *n* GRAM **1.** OPTATIVE MOOD the optative mood of a verb **2.** VERB IN OPTATIVE MOOD a verb in the optative mood [Mid-16C. Via French < Latin *optativus* < *optare* "choose, desire"] —**op·ta·tive·ly** *adv*

~~**opthalmology**~~ incorrect spelling of **ophthalmology**

op·tic /óptik/ *n* **1.** any lens or reflecting part in an optical instrument **2.** same as **eye** *n* (sense 1) (*archaic*) ■ *adj* belonging or relating to the eyes, or situated in or near the eye [14C. Via French or medieval Latin < Greek *optikos* < *optos* "seen, visible"]

op·ti·cal /óptik'l/ *adj* **1.** OF VISION belonging or relating to the sense of sight **2.** PHYS OF VISIBLE LIGHT relating to or producing light that can be seen **3.** LIGHT-SENSITIVE describes an instrument or device that is sensitive to light **4.** OPHTHALMOL OF CORRECTIVE LENSES describes a lens designed to correct or enhance faulty vision **5.** PHYS OF OPTICS belonging or relating to the science of optics —**op·ti·cal·ly** *adv*

op·ti·cal ac·tiv·i·ty *n* the property of a crystal or a chemical solution of rotating the plane of polarized light that passes through it. In the case of solutions, the rotation is caused by asymmetric molecules and the angle of rotation depends on the thickness of the substance.

op·ti·cal art *n* ART full form of **op art**

op·ti·cal bright·en·er *n* a chemical substance used to make the whiteness or color of fabrics brighter, e.g., in laundry detergents

op·ti·cal char·ac·ter read·er *n* a device for entering material into a computer by digitizing the image of a printed page, identifying the characters, and storing them as machine code for further processing. Initially such devices could recognize only a specially designed typeface, but modern readers can recognize a wide variety of typefaces and even handwriting.

op·ti·cal char·ac·ter rec·og·ni·tion *n* the use of light-sensing methods to identify printed and handwritten material and encode it in machine-readable form for inputting into a computer

op·ti·cal com·put·er *n* a proposed computer that uses optical switches, fibers, and laser light instead of wires, transistors, and printed circuits to achieve processing speeds far higher than those of conventional computers

op·ti·cal disk *n* a rigid computer storage disk with data stored as tiny pits in the plastic coating, readable by laser beam

op·ti·cal dou·ble star *n* a pair of stars that appear to lie close together as viewed from Earth but are actually a long way apart, lying along the same line of sight

op·ti·cal fi·ber *n* a fiber made of very pure glass or plastic that is used in modern communications systems to transmit information in the form of pulses of laser light. The core is usually of high refractive index and is enclosed in a sheath of lower refractive index, the light thus being transmitted by total internal reflection.

op·ti·cal glass *n* any high-quality glass used in lenses for its superior refractive quality

op·ti·cal il·lu·sion *n* **1.** a visual experience in which there is some kind of false perception of what is actually there **2.** something that causes an optical illusion, especially something drawn or designed deliberately to fool the eye

op·ti·cal i·som·er·ism *n* the property exhibited by a pair of molecules that differ only in being mirror images of each other and rotate plane-polarized light in opposite directions when in solution —**op·ti·cal i·so·mer** *n*

op·ti·cal mouse *n* a computer mouse that registers a change in position by detecting reflected light from a pair of light-emitting diodes and translating it into cursor movement

op·ti·cal ro·ta·tion *n* the rotation of plane-polarized light as it passes through an optically active medium

op·ti·cal scan·ner *n* COMPUT same as **scanner** (sense 2)

op·ti·cal sem·i·con·duc·tor *n* an optoelectronic semiconductor device, e.g., a laser or photodiode

op·ti·cal sound *n* a form of sound reproduction in motion pictures that employs a photographed pattern of light on the film that is read by a lamp in the projector. It has now largely been superseded by digital sound.

op·ti·cal tweez·ers *npl* a laser beam focused on a biological object of microscopic size that is used to trap it for study and manipulation. Optical tweezers are used to study molecules and by surgeons to work on a single cell.

op·tic ax·is *n* a line passing through a lens, a curved mirror, or a crystal along which light can travel without undergoing double refraction

op·tic chi·as·ma *n* the X-shaped nerve tract beneath the brain where the optic nerves from each eye meet and that enables some of their constituent nerve fibers to cross sides

op·tic cup *n* a two-walled depression in a human embryo that develops into the retina

op·tic disk *n* a small light-sensitive area of the retina marking the point where nerve fibers from the retinal cells converge to form the optic nerve

op·ti·cian /op tísh'n/ *n* **1.** a fitter and supplier of glasses and contact lenses who does not examine eyes or prescribe corrective lenses **2.** *UK* same as **optometrist**

op·tic nerve *n* either of the second pair of cranial nerves whose nerve fibers transmit visual light signals from the eye to the brain

op·tics /óptiks/ *n* the study of light or electromagnetic radiation in the visible, infrared, and ultraviolet regions (*takes a singular verb*) ■ *npl* instruments used for detecting electromagnetic radiation and for attaining highly accurate long-range vision (*takes a plural verb*)

op·tic ves·i·cle *n* a fold of the embryonic forebrain that develops into the retina and optic nerve

op·ti·ma plural of **optimum**

op·ti·mal /óptəm'l/ *adj* most desirable or favorable ○ *waited for optimal weather conditions* [Late 19C. < Latin *optimus* "best"] —**op·ti·mal·i·ty** /òptə mállətee/ *n* —**op·ti·mal·ly** *adv*

op·ti·mism /óptə mìzzəm/ *n* **1.** TENDENCY TO EXPECT BEST the tendency to believe, expect, or hope that things will turn out well **2.** CONFIDENCE the attitude of somebody who feels positive or confident **3.** PHILOSOPHY DOCTRINE THAT OUR WORLD IS BEST a philosophical doctrine, first proposed by Leibnitz, that ours is the best of all possible worlds **4.** PHILOSOPHY BELIEF IN POWER OF GOOD the belief that things are continually getting better and that good will ultimately triumph over evil [Mid-18C. < French *optimisme* < Latin *optimum* (see OPTIMUM)]

op·ti·mist /óptəmist/ *n* **1.** somebody who tends to feel hopeful and positive about future outcomes **2.** a follower of a philosophical doctrine of optimism

op·ti·mis·tic /òptə místik/ *adj* tending to take a hopeful and positive view of future outcomes —**op·ti·mis·ti·cal·ly** *adv*

op·ti·mize /óptə mìz/ (**-mized, -miz·ing, -miz·es**) *vt* **1.** to make something function at its best or most effective, or use something to its best advantage **2.** to write computer programming instructions for a task in as few lines as possible to maximize the speed and efficiency of program execution [Early 19C. < Latin *optimus* "best"] —**op·ti·mi·za·tion** /òptəmi záysh'n/ *n*

op·ti·mum /óptəməm/ *n* (*plural* **-ti·ma** /-təmə/ or **-ti·mums**) the best out of a number of possible options or outcomes ■ *adj* most desirable or favorable ○ *optimum trading conditions* [Late 19C. < Latin, "best thing" < *optimus* "best"]

USAGE Note that the word ***optimum*** refers to quality, not quantity – it means "best," not "greatest" or "most": *the optimum temperature for the storage of perishable foodstuffs*. It often happens that the best is also the greatest or most, as in *We are seeking the optimum return on our investment*, which may be the reason for the confusion about the meaning of the word.

op·tion /ópshən/ *n* **1.** CHOICE a choice that is or can be taken, especially a course of action that remains open for somebody to choose ○ *Several options were ruled out right away.* **2.** FREEDOM OF CHOICE the right, power, or freedom to make a choice ○ *I'd no option but to refuse.* **3.** BUSINESS OPPORTUNITY AVAILABLE FOR LIMITED TIME an opportunity, usually a commercial opportunity, that has been made available for a limited period only **4.** COMM OPTIONAL EXTRA an additional item or attachment, not part of the standard package, that can be purchased separately, e.g., when buying a car **5.** FIN RIGHT TO BUY OR SELL the right to buy or sell something, especially a stock-market commodity, at a fixed price during a limited time period **6.** FOOTBALL PLAY a play in football where the quarterback starts running parallel to the line of scrimmage and either keeps the ball or laterals it to another back running in the same direction **7.** POL same as **local option** ■ *vt* (**-tioned, -tion·ing, -tions**) COMM HAVE OR GIVE RIGHT TO SOMETHING to give or acquire an exclusive right to something [Mid-16C. Via French < Latin *option-* < *optare* "choose, desire"] ◇ **keep** *or* **leave your options open** to put off making a decision or selection until a later time

op·tion·al /ópshən'l, ópshnəl/ *adj* left to individual choice ○ *It comes with optional air conditioning.* —**op·tion·al·ly** *adv*

opto- *prefix* **1.** eye, vision ○ *optometry* **2.** optical ○ *optoelectronics* [< Greek *optos* "seen, visible"]

op·to·e·lec·tron·ics /òptō i lek trónniks/ *n* the branch of electronics dealing with devices that generate, modulate, transmit, and sense electromagnetic radiation in the visible-light, infrared, and ultraviolet ranges (*takes a singular verb*) [Mid-20C. < Greek *optos* "seen, visible"] —**op·to·e·lec·tron·ic** *adj*

op·tom·e·trist /op tómmətrist/ *n* somebody who is qualified to carry out eye examinations and to prescribe and supply glasses and contact lenses

op·tom·e·try /op tómmətree/ *n* the practice of examining eyes in order to determine levels of vision and then prescribing and supplying any necessary corrective lenses —**op·tom·e·ter** *n* —**op·to·met·ric** /òptə méttrik/ *adj*

~~**optomist**~~ incorrect spelling of **optimist**

~~**optomistic**~~ incorrect spelling of **optimistic**

op·to·phone /óptə fōn/ *n* a device used especially by sightless or visually impaired people that can convert written text into sounds

op·u·lent /óppyələnt/ *adj* **1.** characterized by an obvious or lavish display of wealth or affluence **2.** in richly abundant supply [Mid-16C. < Latin *opulentus* "producing much"] —**op·u·lence** *n* —**op·u·lent·ly** *adv*

Op·üls ♦ **Ophuls, Max**

o·pun·ti·a /ō púnshee ə, ō púnshə/ *n* a cactus with orange, orange-red, or yellow flowers and oval fruits, e.g., the prickly pear or cholla. Native to: North and South America. Genus: *Opuntia*. [Early 17C. < modern Latin < *Opunt-*, stem of *Opus*, city in Greece]

o·pus /ópəss/ (*plural* **o·per·a** /ópərə, óppərə/ or **o·pus·es**) *n* **1.** a musical work, especially one of a numbered series by the same composer arranged to show the order in which they were written or cataloged **2.** a creative piece of work in any field of the arts [Early 18C. < Latin, "work"]

o·pus an·gli·ca·num /-ang glə kaánəm/ *n* a form of English embroidery that was popular in the Middle Ages, usually seen on ecclesiastical robes [Mid-19C. < medieval Latin, "English work"]

o·pus·cule /ō púss kyool/, **o·pus·cu·lum** /ō púskyələm/ (*plural* **-la** /-lə/) *n* a minor or insignificant creative work, especially a musical or literary work [Mid-17C. Via French < Latin *opusculum* "little work" < *opus* "work"]

or[1] /awr/; *unstressed* /ər/ CORE MEANING: a conjunction used to link two or more alternatives. In a series of alternatives, it is usually used only before the last alternative. ○ *Which do you prefer, butter or low-fat spread?* ○ *You can accept, refuse, or ignore the offer, as you see fit.*

conj **1.** FOLLOWING "EITHER" OR "WHETHER" used to join two alternatives when the first is introduced by "either" or "whether" ○ *Either you typed the wrong name, or something is wrong with the equipment.* **2.** INDICATING APPROXIMATION used between two numbers to indicate an approximate quantity or to imply a few of something ○ *Hit the return key every three or four seconds until you get a greeting message.* **3.** REPHRASING STATEMENT used to introduce a rephrasing synonym or correction of a statement just made ○ *fetal oxygen deprivation, or hypoxia* ○ *German measles, or rubella* **4.** OTHERWISE used to give an explanation of a statement just made ○ *You'd better leave or you'll be late.* **5.** WHETHER OR EITHER a poetic word for "either" or "whether," preceding the first of two alternatives, with "or" also preceding the second alternative (*archaic or literary*) [12C. Contraction of OTHER] ◇ **or other** used to show that the preceding words you use are not exact or definite ○ *For some reason or other, the house was crowded that night.* ◇ **or so** approximately ○ *I haven't seen her for a year or so.*

SPELLCHECK See ***oar***

or[2] /awr/ *adj* describes an element of a coat of arms or other heraldic insignia that is colored gold [15C. Via French < Latin *aurum* "gold"]

OR[1] *n* a binary operator in Boolean algebra whose result is true if one or both of its operands are true and false otherwise

OR[2] *abbr* **1.** *also* **O.R.** SURG operating room **2.** BUSINESS operations research **3.** MAIL Oregon **4.** INSUR owner's risk **5.** LAW own recognizance

-or[1] *suffix* somebody or something that does or performs ○ *sailor* [Via Old French *-eor, -eur* and Anglo-Norman *-(o)ur* < Latin *-or* and *-ator*]

-or[2] *suffix* condition, state, activity ○ *horror* [Via French < Latin]

o·ra BIOL plural of **os**[1]

or·ach /áwrəch/, **or·ache** *n* a wild plant with grayish-green edible leaves resembling spinach leaves. Native to: Europe. Genus: *Atriplex*. [13C. Via Anglo-Norman *arasche* < Greek *atraphaxus*, origin ?]

or·a·cle /áwrək'l/ *n* **1.** SOURCE OF WISDOM somebody or something considered to be a source of knowledge, wisdom, or prophecy **2.** WISE SAYING a wise or prophetic statement **3.** SHRINE OF ANCIENT GOD in ancient Greece and Rome, a shrine dedicated to a particular god where people went to consult a priest or priestess in times of trouble or uncertainty. One of the most famous was the Delphic Oracle of Apollo. **4.** GREEK OR ROMAN DEITY an ancient Greek or Roman deity that a priest or priestess would consult for advice on behalf of troubled or uncertain people **5.** ADVICE FROM GREEK OR ROMAN DEITY a piece of advice, often in the form of a puzzle or an enigmatic statement, handed down by an ancient Greek or Roman deity **6.** GOD-GIVEN MESSAGE a message believed to come from God in response to a request, plea, or petition **7.** BIBLE AREA OF BIBLICAL TEMPLE the most sacred area in either of the Temples mentioned in the Bible, often referred to as the Holy of Holies ■ **or·a·cles** *npl* BIBLE SCRIPTURE the books of the Bible [14C. Via French < Latin *oraculum* < *orare* "speak" (see ORATE)]

o·rac·u·lar /aw rákyələr, ə-/ *adj* **1.** OF OR AS ORACLE relating to oracles, or in the form of an oracle **2.** WISE knowing, wise, or prophetic **3.** MYSTERIOUS puzzling, ambiguous, or enigmatic [Mid-17C. < Latin *oraculum* (see ORACLE)] —**o·rac·u·lar·i·ty** /aw ràkyə lárrətee, ə-/ *n* —**o·rac·u·lar·ly** *adv*

o·ra·cy /áwrəssee/ *n Can, UK* the ability both to convey thoughts and ideas orally in a way that others understand and to understand what others say [Mid-20C. < ORAL, after LITERACY]

o·ra et la·bo·ra /àw raa et lə báw raa, àwrə et lə báwrə/ a Latin phrase meaning "pray and work"

o·ral /áwrəl/ *adj* **1.** OF THE MOUTH relating to or belonging to the mouth ○ *oral hygiene* **2.** FOR THE MOUTH designed for use in the mouth **3.** SPOKEN existing in spoken form as distinct from written form **4.** ADMINISTERED BY

MOUTH describes medicines that are taken by mouth **5.** PHON **WITH RELEASE OF AIR THROUGH MOUTH** describes a speech sound that is produced by means of an airstream that escapes through the mouth only, with the nasal cavity sealed off by the velum **6.** PSYCHOANAL **DERIVING PLEASURE VIA MOUTH** in Freudian analysis, describes a stage in child development when erotic pleasure is derived from mouth-associated sensations, especially through feeding, thumb-sucking, and putting objects into the mouth **7.** PSYCHOANAL **DEPENDENT AND AGGRESSIVE** in Freudian analysis, describes a dependent, selfish, and aggressive personality type with a tendency to derive pleasure from mouth-related activities such as eating, drinking, or smoking **8.** BIOL **WHERE MOUTH IS SITED** describes the surface of the body of an animal on which the mouth is situated, e.g., the underside of a starfish ■ *n* **1.** EDUC **TEST REQUIRING SPOKEN ANSWERS** an examination or test that involves candidates giving spoken answers to spoken questions, as distinct from one where the questions and answers are in written form **2. ORAL SEX** oral sex, or an act of oral sex (*slang*) [Early 17C. < late Latin *oralis* < Latin *or-*, stem of *os* "mouth"] —**o·ral·ly** *adv*

USAGE See *aural*.

SYNONYMS See *verbal*.

o·ral con·tra·cep·tive *n* a pill that is taken daily to prevent conception, especially one that combines an estrogen and a progestogen

o·ral his·to·ry *n* **1. HISTORY RECORDED BY PARTICIPANTS IN EVENTS** the personal recollections of people who participated in historical events, recorded on audio or video tape or told to a younger generation **2. WRITTEN HISTORY BASED ON INTERVIEWS** a written work of history based on interviews with or recordings of participants **3. STUDY OF HISTORY RECORDED ORALLY** the branch of history that deals with personal accounts of historical events or periods recorded on audio or video tape —**o·ral his·to·ri·an** *n*

o·ral hy·giene *n* DENT same as **dental hygiene** —**o·ral hy·gien·ist** *n*

O·ral Law *n* Jewish religious law that developed out of interpretations of the Torah and was originally passed on orally by rabbis and sages before being recorded in writing, principally in the Mishnah and Talmud

o·ral re·hy·dra·tion so·lu·tion *n* a liquid specially formulated to be given as a drink to correct the water, mineral, and nutritional deficiencies in an individual, especially an infant, who is affected by dehydration

o·ral sex *n* sexual activity that involves using the mouth and tongue to stimulate a partner's genitals

o·ral so·ci·e·ty *n* a community in which people do not read or write

O·ral To·rah *n* JUDAISM same as **Oral Law**

o·ral tra·di·tion *n* a community's cultural and historical background preserved and passed on from one generation to the next in spoken stories and song, as distinct from being written down

O·ran /aw raán/ city and port in Algeria, on the northwestern coast of the country. Population: 590,000 (1987).

o·rang /áw rang/ *n* ZOOL same as **orangutan** [Late 18C. Shortening]

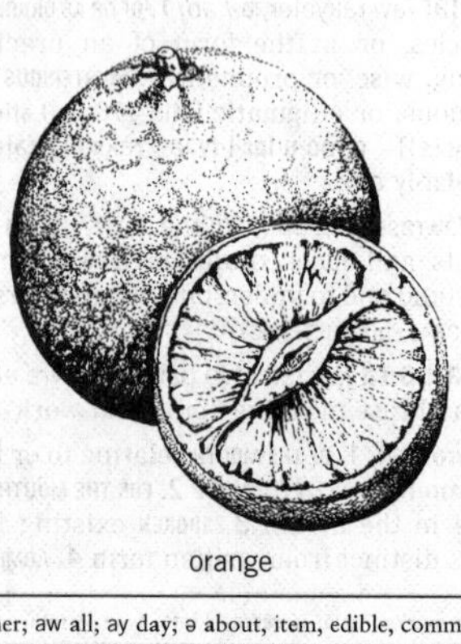

orange

or·ange /áwrənj/ *n* **1. CITRUS FRUIT** a round or oval citrus fruit with thick orange skin and juicy segmented flesh. As well as being eaten fresh, it is often squeezed for its juice. (*often used before a noun*) **2. TREE YIELDING JUICY FRUIT** an evergreen tree with glossy leaves that bears oranges. Flowers: white, fragrant. Native to: Southeast Asia. Genus: *Citrus*. **3. COLOR** the bright color of the skin of an orange, a mixture of red and yellow **4.** INDUST same as **orangewood 5. TREE WITH FRUITS SIMILAR TO ORANGE** a tree or bush that produces flowers or fruits similar to a true orange tree, e.g., mock orange or osage orange **6. BUTTERFLY THAT IS ORANGE** a butterfly that is predominantly orange, e.g., a sulphur butterfly. Family: Pieridae. **7. PIGMENT MIXING YELLOW AND RED** a pigment or dye that is a mixture of red and yellow **8. MATERIAL OF COLOR ORANGE** fabric or clothing that is orange in color **9. ORANGE-COLORED OBJECT** something that is colored orange [13C. < Old French *pomme d'orenge* < Italian *melarancia* "orange fruit," via Arabic *nāranj* and Persian *nārang* < Sanskrit *nāraṅgaḥ*] —**or·ange** *adj* —**or·ang·ey** *adj*

Or·ange[1] /áwrənj/ *n* **DUTCH ROYAL FAMILY** the royal house of the Netherlands from the accession of King William I in 1815. The family had earlier been Dutch princes and stadtholders, or magistrates. William of Orange became King William III of Great Britain and Ireland in 1689. ■ *adj* **1. OF HOUSE OF ORANGE** relating to or belonging to the house of Orange **2. OF ORANGE ORDER** relating to or belonging to the Orange Order [Mid-17C. After ORANGE[2] (sense 2) in SE France]

Or·ange[2] /áwrənj/ **1.** river in southern Africa. Its lower course forms the boundary between South Africa and Namibia. Length: 1,300 mi./2,100 km. **2.** town in Vaucluse Department, Provence-Alpes-Côte d'Azur Region, southeastern France. Population: 27,989 (1999). **3.** city in Orange County, southwestern California, situated 22 mi./35 km east of Long Beach. Population: 131,606 (2002 estimate). **4.** town in southwestern New Haven County, southern Connecticut, situated east of the Housatonic River. Population: 13,383 (2002 estimate). **5.** city in Essex County, northeastern New Jersey, situated 4 mi./6 km northwest of Newark. Population: 29,925 (2002 estimate). **6.** town in central New South Wales, Australia. It is a center for fruit and vegetable growing and light industry. Population: 37,292 (2002 estimate).

or·ange·ade /àwrən jáyd/ *n* a sometimes carbonated nonalcoholic drink flavored with orange or tasting like oranges [Early 18C. < ORANGE, after LEMONADE]

Or·ange·burg /áwrinj bùrg/ city and administrative seat of Orangeburg County, central South Carolina, situated 35 mi./56 km southeast of Columbia. Population: 91,190 (2002 estimate).

or·ange chro·mide *n* a tropical freshwater fish with distinctive orange spotty markings that is often kept in aquariums. Native to: Asia. Latin name: *Etropus maculatus*.

or·ange hawk·weed *n* a perennial variety of the hawkweed plant. Flowers: orange-red, in clusters. Native to: Europe. Latin name: *Hieracium aurantiacum*.

Or·ange·man /áwrənjmən/ (*plural* **-men** /-mən/) *n* **1.** a member of the Orange Order **2.** an Irishman of the Protestant faith [Late 18C. After the ORANGE ORDER]

or·ange milk·weed *n* PLANTS same as **butterfly weed**

Or·ange Or·der *n* a Protestant organization formed in 1795 with the objective of celebrating and defending Protestantism in Ireland, now especially in Northern Ireland, where it is prominent in Loyalist marches [Because formed out of loyalty to William of *Orange* (WILLIAM III)]

or·ange peel *n* the thick dimpled skin of an orange

or·ange-peel *adj* having a dimpled surface caused, e.g., by open pores or cellulite ○ *orange-peel skin*

or·ange pe·koe *n* a high-quality black tea grown in South Asia and made using only the small, young, tender leaves growing at the tips of the stems

or·ange·root /áwrənj root/ *n* PLANTS same as **goldenseal**

or·ange·ry /áwrənjree/ (*plural* **-ries**) *n* a building where orange trees are grown, especially a large greenhouse for use in cooler climates

or·ange stick *n* a small stick used for manicuring the fingernails and cuticles that is usually wooden or plastic, with one pointed end and one rounded end [Because it is usually made from ORANGEWOOD]

or·ange·wood /áwrənj wŏŏd/ *n* the yellowish hard fine-grained wood of the orange tree. Use: furniture, carved objects.

orangutan

o·rang·u·tan /ə ràngə tán, aw-/, **o·rang·u·tang** /ə ràngə táng/ *n* a large tailless ape with reddish brown coarse shaggy hair and long powerful arms. Native to: forests of Borneo and Sumatra. Latin name: *Pongo pygmaeus*. [Late 17C. < Malay *orang hutan* "forest person"]

o·rate /aw ráyt, áw ràyt/ (**o·rat·ed, o·rat·ing, o·rates**) *vi* **1.** to make a speech, especially a public, formal, or ceremonial speech (*formal*) **2.** to speak in a pompous or boring way or for an inappropriately long time [Early 17C. < Latin *orat-* (see ORATOR)]

o·ra·tion /aw ráysh'n/ *n* **1. FORMAL PUBLIC SPEECH** a speech, lecture, or other instance of formal or ceremonial public speaking **2. POMPOUS SPEECH** a speech that is considered pompous, boring, or inappropriately long **3. PUBLIC SPEECH SHOWING RHETORICAL SKILLS** an academic speech that is designed to show the speaker's rhetorical skills, especially a speech given as an exercise in public speaking, often in a public speaking contest [14C. < Latin *oration-* < *orat-* (see ORATOR)]

or·a·tor /áwrətər/ *n* **1.** a giver of speeches, especially somebody skilled in giving formal, ceremonial, or persuasive public addresses **2.** somebody regarded as a pompous, boring, or overlong speaker [14C. Via Anglo-Norman < Latin, "speaker, pleader" < *orat-*, past participle of *orare* "speak, pray"]

or·a·to·ri·o /àwrə táwree ō/ (*plural* **-os**) *n* **1.** a musical composition for voices and instruments that has a religious theme, often telling a sacred story but not using costumes, scenery, or dramatic staging. Handel's *Messiah* is an example of this genre. **2.** oratorios as a musical genre [Mid-17C. < Italian, after the *Oratory* of St. Philip Neri in Rome]

or·a·to·ry[1] /áwrə tàwree/ *n* **1. ART OF PUBLIC SPEAKING** the art of speaking in public with style, cogency, and grace **2. RHETORICAL SKILL AND ELOQUENCE** eloquence in public speaking, especially of the kind that shows the speaker's rhetorical skills **3. POMPOSITY IN SPEECH** pompous, boring, or inappropriately long speech [Early 16C. < Latin *(ars) oratoria* "(art) of speaking" < *orator* (see ORATOR)] —**or·a·tor·i·cal** /àwrə táwrik'l/ *adj* —**or·a·tor·i·cal·ly** *adv*

or·a·to·ry[2] /áwrə tàwree/ (*plural* **-ries**) *n* a place for private prayer or worship, e.g., a small secluded chapel, usually set aside in a church [14C. < Anglo-Norman *oratorie* < Latin *orare* "speak, pray"]

Or·a·to·ry /áwrə tàwree/ *n* a religious society that has secular priests and is a branch of the Roman Catholic Church. It was founded in 1575 by Saint Philip Neri. [Mid-17C. < ORATORY[2]]

orb /awrb/ *n* **1. SPHERE** a sphere or spherical object **2. JEWELED SPHERE OF KING OR QUEEN** a small sphere usually made from a precious metal set with jewels and with a cross set onto the top of it that forms part of a sovereign's ceremonial regalia **3. EYE** an eye or eyeball (*literary*) **4. AREA OF INTEREST** a sphere of interest, influence, or activity (*literary*) **5.** ASTRON **CONCENTRIC PLANET-HOLDING SPHERE** one of the concentric spheres that were formerly believed by astronomers to hold the planets in their orbital paths **6.** ASTRON **SPHERICAL ASTRONOMICAL OBJECT** a spherical astronomical object, especially the Sun, Moon, or Earth (*archaic or literary*) ■ *v* (**orbed, orb·ing, orbs**) **1.** *vt* **ENCIRCLE SOMETHING**

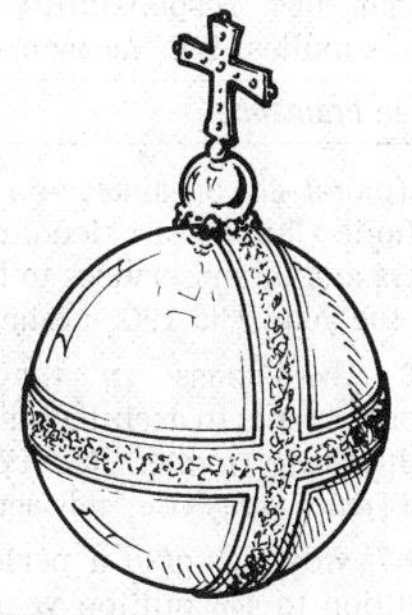

orb (sense 2)

to encircle or surround something (*literary*) **2.** *vti* **MAKE OR BECOME CIRCULAR** to become circular, or make something circular (*archaic*) [14C. < Latin *orbis* "wheel, circle"]

or·bic·u·lar /awr bíkyələr/, **or·bic·u·late** /-lət, -làyt/ *adj* **1.** having the form of a circle or sphere (*formal*) **2.** describes plant parts, especially leaves, that are flat and round or roundish [14C. < late Latin *orbicularis* < Latin *orbiculus* "small globe" < *orbis* "globe"] —**or·bic·u·lar·i·ty** /awr bìkyə lárrətee/ *n* —**or·bic·u·lar·ly** *adv* —**or·bic·u·late·ly** *adv*

or·bit /áwrbit/ *n* **1. PATH OF PLANET, SATELLITE, OR MOON** the path that an astronomical object such as a planet, moon, or satellite follows around a larger astronomical object such as the Sun **2. REVOLUTION OF ASTRONOMICAL OBJECT** a single revolution of an astronomical object around a larger astronomical object **3. AREA OF INTEREST** a sphere of interest, influence, or activity **4.** ANAT **EYE SOCKET** the round cavity in which an eye is located in the skull of a vertebrate **5.** PHYS **ELECTRON PATH AROUND ATOM NUCLEUS** the path that an electron takes as it moves around the nucleus of an atom ■ *v* (**-bit·ed, -bit·ing, -bits**) **1.** *vti* **MOVE AROUND ASTRONOMICAL OBJECT** to move around an astronomical object in a path dictated by the force of gravity exerted by that body **2.** *vt* **PUT SOMETHING INTO ASTRONOMICAL ORBIT** to send something, especially a spacecraft or an artificial satellite, into orbit **3.** *vi* **FOLLOW REGULAR PATH** to move regularly or repeatedly along the same path, especially a circular path [Mid-16C. < Latin *orbita* "wheel-track"] ◇ **go into orbit** to become suddenly extremely angry and upset (*slang*) ◇ **put somebody into orbit** *US* to make somebody suddenly extremely angry or upset (*slang*)

or·bit·al /áwrbit'l/ *adj* relating to or belonging to an orbit ■ *n* a subdivision of the available space within an atom for an electron to orbit the nucleus. An atom has many orbitals, each of which has a fixed size and shape and can hold up to two electrons. —**or·bit·al·ly** *adv*

or·bit·al space sta·tion *n* a spacecraft orbiting the Earth, designed to be occupied by a crew for extended periods and used as a base for the exploration, observation, and research of space

or·bit·al space ve·hi·cle *n* a vehicle that transports payloads to and from points in space with different orbits such as a space station, a satellite, and the Moon

or·bi·teer·ing /àwrbi teéring/ *n* the sport or practice of going up high mountains without using climbing gear and by walking in circles of ever higher altitude until reaching the top [< ORBIT, after MOUNTAINEERING or ORIENTEERING] —**or·bi·teer** *vti*

or·bit·er /áwrbitər/ *n* a spacecraft or satellite designed to orbit an astronomical object but not to land on it

orb weav·er *n* a spider that weaves a large circular web of silk to entrap its prey. Families: Araneidae or Tetragnathidae.

or·ca /áwrkə/ *n* MARINE BIOL same as **killer whale** [Mid-19C. Via modern Latin < Latin "large sea creature"]

orch. *abbr* MUSIC **1.** orchestra **2.** orchestrated by

or·chard /áwrchərd/ *n* **1.** an area of land on which fruit or nut trees are grown, especially commercially **2.** all the fruit or nut trees growing in an area, planted for commercial reasons [Old English *ortgeard* < *ort*, origin ? + YARD[2]]

CULTURAL NOTE ***The Cherry Orchard***, a play (1903–04) by the Russian dramatist Anton Chekhov. Chekhov described his last play as a comedy, but it is often played as tragedy. It depicts the decline of the Ranyevskayas, a family of upper-class landowners, who, despite being faced with bankruptcy, refuse to contemplate merchant Lopakhin's suggestion that they sell their beloved cherry orchard.

or·chard grass *n US* a tall grass grown in many countries for pasture and hay. Native to: Europe. Latin name: *Dactylis glomerata*.

or·char·dist /áwrchərdist/ *n* somebody who owns or manages an orchard

or·ches·tra /áwrkəstrə/ *n* **1. LARGE GROUP OF MUSICIANS** a large group of musicians playing classical music, consisting of sections of string, woodwind, brass, and percussion players, and directed by a conductor **2. GROUP OF MUSICIANS** a group of musicians, especially a fairly large group usually but not always playing classical music **3.** THEATER, MUSIC **PLACE FOR MUSICIANS IN THEATER** the part of a theater where the musicians sit, immediately in front of the stage or under the front part of the stage **4.** THEATER **MAIN FLOOR OF THEATER** the main floor of a theater **5.** THEATER **FRONT SEATS** the front section of seats on the lower and main floor of a theater **6.** THEATER **PLACE FOR CHORUS** the semicircular area in front of the stage in ancient Greek theaters, reserved for the chorus [Early 17C. Via Latin, "space in front of the stage where the chorus danced" < Greek *orkhēstra* < *orkheisthai* "to dance"]

or·ches·tral /awr késtrəl/ *adj* relating to orchestras, or intended for an orchestra, especially a symphony orchestra —**or·ches·tral·ly** *adv*

or·ches·tra pit *n UK* same as **orchestra** (sense 3)

or·ches·trate /áwrkə stràyt/ (**-trat·ed, -trat·ing, -trates**) *vt* **1.** to arrange or compose music to be played by an orchestra **2.** to organize a situation or event unobtrusively so that a desired effect or outcome is achieved ○ *The press conference had clearly been carefully orchestrated.* —**or·ches·tra·tion** /àwrkə stráysh'n/ *n* —**or·ches·tra·tor** *n*

or·ches·tri·on /awr késtree ən/, **or·ches·tri·na** /àwrkə streénə/ *n* a mechanical musical instrument resembling a barrel organ that can imitate the sounds of an orchestra [Mid-19C. < ORCHESTRA after *accordion*]

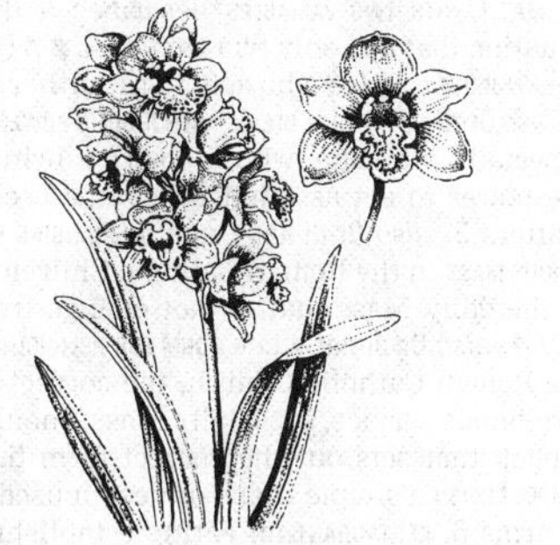

orchid

or·chid /áwrkid/ *n* a perennial plant, some varieties of which grow on other plants. Flowers: showy, delicate, fragrant, with three petals. Native to: tropical climates. Family: Orchidaceae. [Mid-19C. < modern Latin *orchid-*, mistakenly < Latin *orchis* (see ORCHIS)] —**or·chi·da·ceous** /àwrki dáyshəss/ *adj*

or·chid tree *n* either of two trees of the pea family with deeply lobed leaves. Flowers: pale to deep purple. Native to: Southeast Asia. Latin name: *Bauhinia variegata* or *Bauhinia purpurea*.

or·chi·ec·to·my /àwrkee éktəmee/ (*plural* **-mies**), **or·chi·dec·to·my** /àwrki déktəmee/ *n* the surgical removal of one or both testicles [Late 19C. < Greek *orkhis* "testicle"]

or·chil /áwrkil, -chil/ *n* **1.** a reddish dye derived from a lichen, obtained by treating the lichen with aqueous ammonia **2.** a lichen that yields orchil. Genera: *Roccella* or *Lecanora*. [15C. Via Spanish *orchilla* < Catalan *orxella* < Arabic]

or·chis /áwrkiss/ *n* an orchid with a fleshy tuber belonging to many different species. Flowers: small, with spurred lips, growing in spikes. Native to: northern temperate regions. Genus: *Orchis*. [Mid-16C. Via Latin < Greek *orkhis* "testicle" (from the tuber's shape)]

or·chi·tis /awr kítiss/ *n* inflammation of one or both testicles, usually caused by infection. It can also develop in mumps, and if both testicles are affected, it may result in sterility. [Late 18C. < modern Latin < Greek *orkhis* "testicle"] —**or·chit·ic** /awr kíttik/ *adj*

or·ci·nol /áwrssə nàwl/ *n* a colorless substance found in many lichens. Use: litmus dyes. Formula: $CH_3C_6H_3(OH)_2$. [Late 19C. < modern Latin *orcina* "orchil"]

OR cir·cuit /áwr-/ *n* a logic circuit, used especially in computers, that gives a high-voltage output if all or one of its inputs carries a high voltage, and a low-voltage output otherwise

ord. *abbr* **1.** BIOL order **2.** ordinal **3.** BIOL ordinance **4.** ordinary **5.** MIL ordnance

or·dain /awr dáyn/ (**-dained, -dain·ing, -dains**) *vt* **1.** to appoint somebody officially as a priest, minister, or rabbi **2.** to order or establish something formally, especially by law or by some other authority ○ *laws of commercial transactions that had long been ordained by the government* [13C. Via Old French *ordener* < Latin *ordinare* "set in order" < *ordo* "order"] —**or·dain·er** *n*

or·deal /awr deél/ *n* **1.** a very difficult or harrowing experience, especially one lasting a long time **2.** formerly, a trial that involved subjecting a defendant to life-threatening danger, e.g., from fire or water, with the outcome regarded as reflecting divine judgment [Old English *ordāl* "trial, judgment" < Germanic, "share out"]

or·deal bean *n* PLANTS same as **Calabar bean** [< its use in witchcraft trials]

or·der /áwrdər/ *n* **1. INSTRUCTION** an instruction to do something **2. ARRANGEMENT OF ITEMS** the way in which several items are arranged, as an indication of their relative importance or size or when each will be dealt with ○ *I will announce the winners in reverse order.* **3. NEATNESS** an organized condition, with items arranged properly, neatly, or harmoniously ○ *We all need a little order in our lives.* **4. ABSENCE OF CRIME** a peaceful condition in which laws are obeyed and misbehavior or crime is not present or is prevented ○ *maintaining order on our streets* **5. FUNCTIONING CONDITION** the condition something is in when it is functioning properly **6. INSTRUCTION TO PROVIDE SOMETHING** an instruction to bring or supply something, e.g., a spoken instruction to a waiter or waitress, or a written instruction to a manufacturer or supplier of goods ○ *Can I take your order now?* **7. SOMETHING PROVIDED** something provided in response to an instruction ○ *If you are not completely satisfied, you may return your order.* **8. SOCIAL GROUPING** the arrangement of society into groups or classes and the relationships between them ○ *a new world order* **9. SOCIAL GROUP** a group or class that is a division of society (*often used in the plural*) **10.** BIOL **SET OF RELATED FAMILIES** a taxonomic classification made up of related families of organisms ○ *the cat family, in the order Carnivora* **11. TYPE** a kind or type of something, often one judged on importance or worth ○ *Exactly what order of stupidity are we dealing with?* **12.** LAW **INSTRUCTION FROM COURT** an instruction issued by a judge or a court of law **13.** FIN **FINANCIAL INSTRUCTION** a written instruction to pay money **14.** *also* **Or·der** RELIG **RELIGIOUS COMMUNITY** a religious community in which members live according to principles that are often based on the writings of a particular saint ○ *the Order of Saint Francis* **15.** CHR **RELIGIOUS RANK** a grade or division of the ministry in some Christian denominations, e.g., that of a deacon, priest, bishop, or archbishop **16.** CHR **RELIGIOUS SERVICE** a form of Christian religious service used on particular occasions **17.** *also* **Or·der GROUP OF HONORED PEOPLE** a prestigious group consisting of people who have been awarded an honor for services to their country, or the decoration indicating such an honor ○ *the Order of the Garter* **18.** ARCHIT **ARCHITECTURAL STYLE** one of the five major styles of classical architecture, the Doric, Ionic, Corinthian, Tuscan, or Composite. They differ in the shapes and styles of columns and entablatures. **19.** MATH **NUMBER OF ROWS AND COLUMNS** the number of rows and columns in a matrix **20.** MATH **GROUP MEMBERS** the number of items in a finite group

21. MATH **NUMBER OF TIMES VARIABLE IS DIFFERENTIATED** the number of times differentiation must be applied to a mathematical expression to obtain a specific derivative **22.** MATH **NUMBER OF DIFFERENTIATIONS NEEDED IN EQUATION** in a differential equation, the number of successive differentiations required to reach the highest-order derivative **23.** CHEM **CLASSIFICATION OF CHEMICAL REACTIONS** a classification of chemical reactions based on the mathematical relationship between the rate of a given chemical reaction and the concentration of the reacting chemical compounds **24.** SCI same as **order of magnitude** ■ **or·ders** *npl* RELIG same as **holy orders** ■ *v* (**-dered, -der·ing, -ders**) **1.** *vt* **GIVE SOMEBODY INSTRUCTIONS** to command somebody to do something ○ *The colonel ordered the troops to move out.* **2.** *vti* **REQUEST SOMETHING** to give an instruction for something to be provided such as food in a restaurant or merchandise from a manufacturer or supplier **3.** *vt* **ARRANGE ITEMS** to arrange items in a particular way, especially in the sequence in which they are to be dealt with ○ *addresses ordered by zip code* **4.** *vt* **PRESCRIBE SOMETHING** to give an instruction for something to be done, e.g., for some type of medical test or treatment to be done **5.** *vt* **ARRANGE THINGS NEATLY** to put things into a neat, well organized state or into the required state ○ *ordered her business affairs prior to leaving for the summer* ■ *interj* **CALL FOR CALM** used to request calm or observance of correct procedure, e.g., by somebody chairing a debate [13C. Via French *ordre* < Latin *ordin-*, stem of *ordo*] —**or·der·er** *n* ◇ **a tall order** a request that is very difficult to fulfill (*informal*) ◇ **in order 1.** in a correct sequence or arrangement ○ *Put them in order alphabetically.* **2.** in a correct or appropriate condition ○ *The customs official was checking that the paperwork was in order.* ◇ **in order to** *or* **that** with the object or purpose of ◇ **of the order of** approximately ○ *of the order of 50,000 people in the crowd* ◇ **on order** requested, but not yet supplied or delivered ◇ **out of order 1.** not working properly or not working at all **2.** not in the correct sequence or place within a sequence **3.** *UK* not following accepted rules of procedure or conduct (*informal*) ◇ **to or·der** according to the requirements of a specific customer

order around *vt* to subject somebody to domineering or bullying treatment ○ *Don't think you can order me around.*

or·der arms *n* an act of bringing a weapon, usually a rifle, from the shoulder to a resting position on the ground alongside the right leg, performed as part of a military drill ■ *interj* used as a command in a military drill to assume the order arms position

or·der·ly /áwrdərlee/ *adj* **1. WELL-BEHAVED** well-behaved or peaceful ○ *The meeting passed off in an orderly fashion.* **2. NEATLY ARRANGED** arranged or organized in a neat, sensible, or proper way ○ *orderly bookshelves* ■ *n* (*plural* **-lies**) **1. ASSISTANT IN HOSPITAL** a hospital worker with no medical training who is employed to do various jobs such as transporting patients **2. SOLDIER WITH MINOR DUTIES** a soldier acting as a senior officer's personal assistant who carries out a variety of minor duties such as carrying messages —**or·der·li·ness** *n*

or·der of bat·tle *n* the way that military forces are organized in preparation for a battle

or·der of busi·ness *n* **1.** an issue or problem that needs to be dealt with ○ *The first order of business was a budget vote.* **2.** the order in which a number of items are to be discussed or dealt with, e.g., at a meeting

Or·der of Can·a·da *n* in Canada, an order awarded to somebody considered to have made an outstanding contribution to society. Companion, Officer, and Member are the three possible grades.

or·der of mag·ni·tude *n* the difference in size, usually expressed in powers of 10, between two quantities. For example, a quantity 100 times greater than another would be two orders of magnitude greater. ○ *The mass of the Earth is an order of magnitude greater than that of Mars.*

or·der of the day *n* **1.** a program of items to be discussed or dealt with on a particular day, e.g., by a legislative body **2.** something that is regularly done, offered, chosen, or experienced ○ *Heroism was the order of the day during the last big battle of the war.*

or·di·nal /áwrd'nəl/ *adj* **1.** MATH **SHOWING POSITION** showing the relative position in a sequence of numbers **2.** BIOL **RELATING TO BIOLOGICAL ORDERS** relating to a biological order in the classification of plants and animals ■ *n* **1. or·din·al** MATH same as **ordinal number** (sense 1) **2.** CHR **BOOKLET LISTING ORDER OF CATHOLIC SERVICES** in the Roman Catholic Church, an instruction booklet that lists the order of services in church worship **3.** CHR **BOOKLET FOR ORDINATION OF CHRISTIAN MINISTERS** an instruction booklet that outlines rules and ceremony for the ordination of Christian ministers [Late 16C. < late Latin *ordinalis* "ordered" < Latin *ordin-* (see ORDER)]

or·di·nal num·ber *n* **1.** a number used to show the relative position of somebody or something in a sequence, e.g., "first," "sixth," or "29th" **2.** a measure of the size of an ordered set

or·di·nal scale *n* a list that shows only the relative positions of items on a scale, giving no measure of the difference between them

or·di·nance /áwrd'nənss/ *n* **1.** a law or rule made by an authority such as a city government **2.** something regularly done because it is formally prescribed, especially a religious ceremony such as Communion (*formal*) [14C. < Old French *ordenance* < Latin *ordinare* (see ORDAIN)]

SPELLCHECK ordinance or **ordnance**? Do not confuse the spelling of ***ordinance*** and ***ordnance***, which sound similar. An ***ordinance*** is a law or rule, or part of a religious ceremony. ***Ordnance*** denotes military weapons, or the department responsible for them.

or·di·nand /áwrd'n ànd/ *n* somebody who is a candidate for ordination as a Christian minister [Mid-19C. < Latin *ordinandus* < *ordinare* (see ORDAIN)]

or·di·nar·i·ly /áwrd'n èrrəlee, àwrd'n érrəlee/ *adv* usually or normally

~~ordinarly~~ incorrect spelling of **ordinarily**

or·di·nar·y /áwrd'n èrree/ *adj* **1. COMMON** of a common everyday kind **2. UNREMARKABLE** not remarkable or special in any way, and therefore uninteresting and unimpressive ○ *He's just a pretty ordinary kind of guy.* **3. USUAL** usual or customary **4.** LAW **WITH IMMEDIATE JURISDICTION** having immediate jurisdiction, as opposed to jurisdiction by delegation or deputation **5.** MATH **WITH TWO VARIABLES** describes a differential equation that has only two variables ■ *n* (*plural* **-ies**) **1.** LAW **JUDGE** a judge who acts in his or her own right **2.** *also* **Or·di·nar·y** CHR **CLERIC WITH JUDGE'S POWERS** a cleric, especially a bishop, whose position brings with it the power to act as a judge in some ecclesiastical matters **3.** *also* **Or·di·nar·y** CHR **UNCHANGING PARTS OF RELIGIOUS MASS** in the Roman Catholic Church, the parts of the daily Mass that do not change from day to day **4.** *also* **Or·di·nar·y** CHR **FORM FOR RELIGIOUS SERVICE** in the Roman Catholic Church, the correct form that a religious service, especially Mass, should take, or a book that sets out the correct form **5.** HERALDRY **SIMPLE DESIGN** a simple shape or design used on a coat of arms **6. RESTAURANT** an eating establishment or a dining room in an old tavern (*archaic*) [14C. Via French < medieval Latin *ordinarius* "following the usual course" < Latin *ordin-* (see ORDER)] —**or·di·nar·i·ness** *n* ◇ **out of the ordinary** unusual or extraordinary

or·di·nar·y sea·man *n* in the British Royal Navy, a sailor of the lowest rank

or·di·nar·y shares *npl UK* same as **common stock**

or·di·nate /áwrd'nət/ *n* the vertical or y coordinate of a point on a two-dimensional graph or diagram in which pairs of numbers denote distances along fixed horizontal and vertical axes [Late 17C. < Latin *ordinare* (see ORDAIN)]

or·di·na·tion /àwrd'n áysh'n/ (*plural* **-tions** or *same*) *n* an official investiture as a Christian priest or minister, or as a rabbi, or a ceremony during which somebody is consecrated as a priest, minister, or rabbi [15C. Directly or via French < Latin *ordination-* < *ordinare* (see ORDAIN)]

ordn. *abbr* ordnance

ord·nance /áwrdnənss/ *n* **1.** military weapons, including supplies for their use and equipment for their maintenance **2.** the army or government department that has responsibility for military weapons and supplies [14C. Variant of ORDINANCE]

SPELLCHECK See ***ordinance***.

or·do /áwrdō/ (*plural* **-dos** or **-di·nes** /-də nèez/) *n* in the Roman Catholic Church, a calendar detailing the forms of Mass and other services to be followed for each day in the year [Mid-19C. < Latin, "order"]

or·don·nance /áwrd'nənss/ *n* the general arrangement of elements in architecture and in works of art and literature (*formal*) [Mid-17C. < French, alteration of Old French *ordenance* "ordinance"]

Or·do·vi·cian /àwrdə vísh'n/ *n* a period of geologic time, 495 million to 443 million years ago, during which primitive fish and other ocean organisms appeared. See table at **geologic time** [Late 19C. < Latin *Ordovices*, ancient Celtic people of N Wales] —**Or·do·vi·cian** *adj*

or·dure /áwrjər/ *n* **1.** excrement or dung (*formal*) **2.** obscene or immoral material or behavior, or an example of it (*literary*) [14C. Via Old French < Latin *horridus* "frightful" < *horrere* (see HORROR)]

ore /awr/ (*plural same* or **ores**) *n* a naturally occurring mineral from which constituents, especially metals, can be profitably extracted [Old English *ōra*, *ār* "brass, bronze"]

SPELLCHECK See ***oar***

ö·re /úr ə/ (*plural same*) *n* a subunit of Swedish currency. See table at **currency** [Early 18C. Via Swedish < Old Norse *aurar*]

ø·re /úr ə/ (*plural same*) *n* a subunit of Danish or Norwegian currency. See table at **currency** [Early 18C. Via Danish or Norwegian < Old Norse *aurar*]

Ore. *abbr* Oregon

o·re·ad /áwree àd/ *n* in Greek mythology, a mountain nymph [14C. Via Latin *Oread-* < Greek *Oreias* < *oros* "mountain"]

Ör·e·bro /úr ə bro͝o/ city and county seat of Örebro Province, central Sweden, situated 100 mi./160 km west of Stockholm. Population: 122,641 (1998).

ore dress·ing *n* the separation of the mineral content of an ore from the unwanted rock

Oreg. *abbr* Oregon

o·reg·a·no /ə réggə nō/ *n* **1.** the fresh or dried leaves of an aromatic herb, used as a flavoring **2.** a variety of wild marjoram that produces oregano. Native to: Mediterranean. Latin name: *Origanum vulgare*. [Late 18C. Via Spanish < Greek *origanon* "wild marjoram"]

Oregon

Or·e·gon /áwrəgən, órrə-/; *often by outsiders* /-gon/ state in the northwestern United States, bordered by the Pacific Ocean, Washington, Idaho, Nevada, and California. Capital: Salem. Population: 3,521,515 (2002 estimate).. Area: 97,132 sq. mi./251,571 sq. km. —**Or·e·go·ni·an** /àwrə gōnee ən, òrrə-/ *n, adj*

O·re·gon Ci·ty city in northwestern Oregon, south of Portland. It has traditionally been a trading center for the surrounding farming and forest area. Population: 27,775 (2002 estimate).

Or·e·gon grape *n* an evergreen bush of the barberry family with black berries, widely grown in gardens. Flowers: yellow. Native to: United States Pacific coast. Latin name: *Mahonia aquifolium*.

Or·e·gon myr·tle *n* TREES same as **California laurel**

Or·e·gon pine *n* TREES same as **Douglas fir**

Or·e·gon Trail *n* a 19th-century route to the western United States extending from western Missouri to northern Oregon that was used by pioneers and settlers

Or·el·la·na /ò re lá̱anə, òrrəl yáanə/, **Francisco de** (1500?–45) Spanish explorer and soldier. He was the first European to navigate the Amazon from the Andes to the Atlantic.

Ore Moun·tains /awr-/ range of mountains along the Czech-German border. Height: 4,080 ft./1,244 m.

O·ren·burg /áwrən bùrg, ərin bŏŏrk/ city in southwestern Siberian Russia, the capital of Orenburg Oblast. Population: 686,289 (1995).

O·ren·se /aw rénsse/ city in northwestern Spain and capital of Orense Province, in the autonomous region of Galicia. Population: 107,510 (2002).

O·res·tes /o rést eez/ *n* in Greek mythology, the son of Agamemnon, whose death he avenged by killing his mother, Clytemnestra, and her lover, Aegisthus

Ø·re·sund /úr ə sùn, -sŏŏnd/ channel in northern Europe, between the Kattegat and the Baltic Sea. Length: 65 mi./100 km.

O·re·ti /ō ráytee/ river in the south of the South Island, New Zealand. It rises in the Southern Alps and flows south to the Foveaux Strait. Length: 126 mi./203 km.

orf /awrf/ *n* a pox caused by a virus, affecting sheep and goats and also transmittable to humans, in which pus-filled blisters form on the animals' lips [Mid-19C. Probably < Old Norse *hrufa*]

Orff /awrf/, **Carl** (1895–1982) German composer. He is noted for his highly rhythmic oratorio *Carmina Burana* (1937).

or·fray *n* HANDICRAFT another spelling of **orphrey**

org /awrg/ *abbr* ONLINE noncommercial organization (*used in Internet addresses*) See table at **domain name**

org. *abbr* **1.** organic **2.** organization **3.** organized

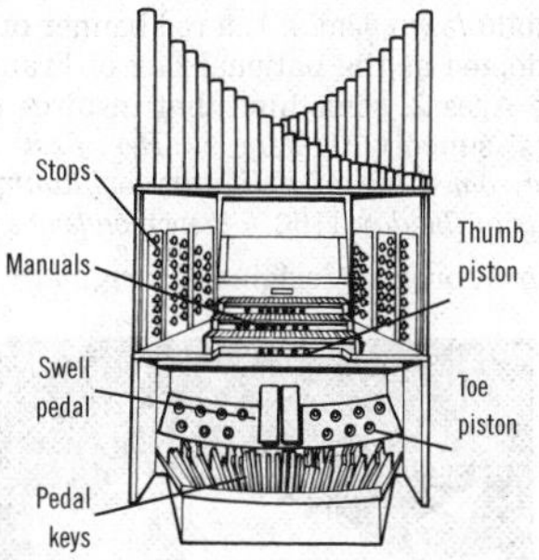

organ (sense 2)

or·gan /áwrgən/ *n* **1. BODY PART** a complete and independent part of a plant or animal that has a specific function ○ *the organs of the digestive system* **2. KEYBOARD INSTRUMENT** a large musical keyboard instrument producing sounds at different volumes using compressed air passed through pipes **3. INSTRUMENT SIMILAR TO ORGAN** a musical instrument that makes sounds resembling the organ without using pipes, e.g., electronically or with reeds **4. MEANS OF COMMUNICATION** a newspaper or magazine regarded as a means of communication, especially one communicating the views of a particular group such as a political party (*formal*) ○ *the daily organ of left-of-center politics* **5. AGENCY** an organization or body acting on behalf of a larger institution, especially a government (*formal*) ○ *There were no secrets about the institute's role as an organ of the business community.* **6.** same as **penis** (*euphemistic*) [13C. Via Old French *organe* and Latin *organum* < Greek *organon* "tool, instrument"]

or·ga·na MUSIC plural of **organon, organum**

or·gan·dy /áwrgəndee/, **or·gan·die** *n* a lightweight see-through cotton fabric, often stiffened. Use: dress-making. [Early 19C. < French *organdi*]

or·gan·elle /àwrgə nél/ *n* a specialized part of a cell that has its own function, e.g., the nucleus or the mitochondrion [Early 20C. < modern Latin *organella* "small organ" < Latin *organum* (see ORGAN)]

or·gan grind·er *n* a street musician who plays a barrel organ, traditionally accompanied by a small monkey who circulates to collect money from bystanders [< the hand-cranked barrel organ]

or·gan·ic /awr gánnik/ *adj* **1. OF LIVING THINGS** relating to, derived from, or characteristic of living things **2. DEVELOPING NATURALLY** occurring or developing gradually and naturally, without being forced or contrived **3. INTRINSIC** forming a basic and inherent part of something and largely responsible for its identity or makeup **4. NATURALLY EFFICIENTLY ORGANIZED** being made of parts that exist together in a seemingly natural relationship that makes for organized efficiency ○ *need to integrate the various functions of the department into an organic whole* **5.** AGRIC **AVOIDING SYNTHETIC CHEMICALS** relating to or employing agricultural practices that avoid the use of synthetic chemicals in favor of naturally occurring pesticides, fertilizers, and other growing aids **6.** FOOD **PRODUCED WITHOUT SYNTHETIC CHEMICALS** grown or reared without the use of synthetic chemicals ○ *a wide range of organic produce* **7.** MED **OF BODY'S ORGANS** relating to the organs of the body, specifically to basic changes in them brought about by physical disorders **8.** CHEM **BASED ON CARBON** belonging to a family of compounds that have chains or rings of carbon atoms linked to atoms of hydrogen and sometimes oxygen, nitrogen, and other elements ■ *n* **ORGANIC SUBSTANCE** an organic substance, especially a fertilizer or pesticide [15C. Directly or via French < Latin *organicus* < Greek *organikos* "of an organ, instrumental" < *organon* "tool, instrument"] —**or·gan·ic·i·ty** /àwrgə nìssətee/ *n*

or·gan·i·cal·ly /awr gánnikəlee/ *adv* **1.** in a natural or seemingly natural way ○ *paintings with key aspects organically arranged* **2.** without the use of synthetic chemicals, especially fertilizers and pesticides ○ *organically raised chickens*

or·gan·ic brain syn·drome *n* a psychiatric disorder caused by a permanent or temporary physical change in the brain

or·gan·ic chem·is·try *n* the scientific study of carbon-based compounds, originally limited to compounds that are the natural products of living things, now including the study of synthetic carbon compounds such as plastics

or·gan·ic dis·ease *n* a disorder associated with physical changes in one or more organs of the body

or·gan·i·cism /awr gánni sìzzəm/ *n* **1.** the theory that all diseases are due to structural changes in the body's organs **2.** the theory that society is analogous to, or shares characteristics with, living organisms —**or·gan·i·cist** *n* —**or·gan·i·cis·tic** /àwrgənə sístik/ *adj*

or·gan·ism /áwrgə nìzzəm/ *n* **1.** a living thing, e.g., a plant, animal, virus, or bacterium **2.** a functioning system of interdependent parts that resembles a living thing ○ *"Like any organism, public libraries and the people who run them must adapt and respond to change"* (Laurence Arnold, *Pulse of the People*; 1997) —**or·gan·is·mal** /àwrgə nízm'l/ *adj* —**or·gan·is·mic** /-nízmik/ *adj* —**or·gan·is·mi·cal·ly** *adv*

or·gan·ist /áwrgənist/ *n* a musician who plays the organ

or·gan·i·za·tion /àwrgəni záysh'n/ *n* **1. GROUP** a group of people identified by a shared interest or purpose, e.g., a business ○ *Each news organization sent its own photographer.* **2. COORDINATION OF COMPONENTS** the coordinating of separate components into a unit or structure ○ *in charge of the organization of international conferences* **3. RELATIONSHIP OF COMPONENTS** the relationships that exist between separate components in a coherent whole ○ *changes to the organization of the party* **4. EFFECTIVENESS OF ARRANGEMENT** the effectiveness of the arrangement of separate components in a coherent whole ○ *Your working method lacks organization.* —**or·gan·i·za·tion·al** *adj*

or·gan·i·za·tion·al psy·chol·o·gy *n* PSYCHOL, INDUST same as **industrial psychology**

Or·gan·i·za·tion of Af·ri·can U·ni·ty *n* an organization of African states founded in 1963 for mutual cooperation and the promotion of independence. It was superseded in 2002 by the African Union.

or·gan·i·za·tion the·o·ry *n* the branch of sociology that deals with the structure of organizations and with the systems and processes that operate within them

or·gan·ize /áwrgə nīz/ (**-ized, -iz·ing, -iz·es**) *v* **1.** *vti* **FORM SOMETHING** to form or establish something such as a club, by coming together or bringing people together into a structured group (*often passive*) **2.** *vt* **COORDINATE SOMETHING** to oversee the coordination of the various aspects of something **3.** *vt* **ARRANGE** to arrange the components of something in a way that creates a particular structure ○ *a society organized along democratic lines* ○ *candidates organized into groups of three* **4.** *vt* **MAKE SOMEBODY MORE EFFECTIVE** to apply or impose efficient working methods in order to work effectively or make somebody else work effectively ○ *Mature students are not necessarily better at organizing themselves.* **5.** *vti* **FORM LABOR UNION** to recruit the workers in a place or industry into a labor union, or come together to form a labor union [15C. Via French < medieval Latin *organizare* "provide with bodily organs" < Latin *organum* (see ORGAN)]

or·gan·ized /áwrgə nīzd/ *adj* **1.** working in a systematic and efficient way ○ *a motivated and organized self-starter* **2.** existing on a large scale and involving the systematic coordination of many different considerations ○ *organized religion*

or·gan·ized crime *n* a powerful ruthless large-scale network of professional criminals, or such networks in general

or·gan·iz·er /áwrgə nīzər/ *n* **1. SOMEBODY WHO ORGANIZES** somebody who sets up or organizes projects and motivates others to take part **2. DATEBOOK** a small portable calendar and datebook used for planning, or a handheld computerized device with a simple database for managing appointments and other information **3. CONTAINER WITH COMPARTMENTS** a container with compartments for storing items in neat groups, e.g., a desktop container with compartments for pens, pencils, and other items of stationery **4.** BIOL **EMBRYO PART** a part of an embryo that controls the differentiation of cells and contributes to the formation of organs and all the other specialized parts that make up an individual organism

organo- *prefix* **1.** organ ○ *organography* **2.** organic ○ *organophosphate* [< Greek *organon* "tool, instrument"]

or·gan·o·chlo·rine /àwrgənō kláw reen, awr gànnə-/ *n* a hydrocarbon pesticide that contains chlorine. Organochlorine pesticides such as DDT were once widely used, but their use has markedly decreased owing to problems with toxicity.

or·gan of Cor·ti /-káwrtee/ *n* a part of the cochlea of the inner ear that transforms sound energy into nerve impulses and sends those impulses to the brain [Late 19C. After Alfonso *Corti* (1822–88), Italian anatomist]

or·gan·o·gen·e·sis /àwrgənō jénnəsiss, awr gànnə-/ *n* the formation and development of animal or plant organs that takes place during the development of an embryo —**or·gan·o·ge·net·ic** /àwrgənō jə néttik, awr gànnə-/ *adj*

or·gan·og·ra·phy /àwrgə nóggrəfee/ *n* the scientific description of the organs and other main structures of plants and animals —**or·gan·o·graph·ic** /àwrgənō gráffik, awr gànnə-/ *adj* —**or·gan·o·graph·i·cal** *adj* —**or·gan·o·graph·i·cal·ly** *adv*

or·gan·o·lep·tic /àwrgənō léptik, awr gànnə-/ *adj* affecting an organ, especially a sense organ [Mid-19C. < French *organoleptique* < Greek *organon* "instrument" + *lēptikos* "receptive"] —**or·gan·o·lep·ti·cal·ly** *adv*

or·gan·ol·o·gy /àwrgə nólləjee/ *n* the study of plant and animal organs —**or·gan·o·log·ic** /àwrgənō lójjik, awr gànnə-/ *adj* —**or·gan·o·log·i·cal** *adj* —**or·gan·ol·o·gist** *n*

or·gan·o·me·tal·lic /àwrgənō mə tállik, awr gànnə-/ *adj* relating to an organic compound that contains one or more metal atoms, e.g., the gasoline additive tetraethyl lead

or·ga·non /áwrgə nòn/ (*plural* **-ga·na** /-gənə/ or **-ga·nons**) *n* a set of principles for use in philosophical or scientific investigation (*formal*) [Early 17C. < Greek (see ORGAN)]

or·gan·o·phos·phate /àwrgənō fóss fàyt, awr gànnə-/ *n* an organic compound containing phosphate groups, which may be toxic. Use: pesticides.

or·gan·o·phos·phor·us /áwrgənō fóssfərəss, awr gànnō \fóssfərəss/, **or·gan·o·phos·phor·ous** *adj* relating to organic compounds containing phosphate groups

or·gan·o·phos·phor·us com·pound /áwrgənō fóssfərəss-, awr gànnō-/ *n* an organic compound containing phosphorus

or·gan·o·ther·a·py /áwrgənō thérrəpee, awr gànnə-/ (*plural* **-pies**) *n* the treatment of diseases by administering substances derived from animal organs, e.g., bovine insulin, which is used to treat diabetes in humans —**or·gan·o·ther·a·peu·tic** /áwrgənō thèrrə pyóotik, awr gànnə-/ *adj*

or·gan-pipe cac·tus *n* a tall branched cactus. Native to: southwestern United States, northern Mexico. Latin name: *Lemaireocereus marginatus*. [< its tall pipe-shaped stems]

or·gan stop *n* **1.** a set of pipes on a musical organ, used to vary the tone and sometimes to imitate the sounds of other instruments **2.** a knob or handle that controls the flow of air to an organ stop

or·ga·num /áwrgənəm/ (*plural* **-na** /-nə/ or **-nums**) *n* **1.** a style of composition in western music of the late medieval period that combines plainsong melody with other melodies **2.** a piece of music in the organum style [Early 17C. < Latin (see ORGAN)]

or·gan·za /awr gánzə/ *n* a stiff see-through fabric, usually silk, rayon, or nylon. Use: dressmaking. [Early 19C. Origin ?]

or·gan·zine /áwrgən zeen/ *n* a yarn made from strands of silk twisted together, or a fabric made from the yarn [Late 17C. Via French *organsin* < Italian *organzino*]

or·gasm /áwr gàzzəm/ *n* the climax of sexual excitement, consisting of intense muscle tightening around the genital area experienced as a pleasurable wave of tingling sensations through parts of the body ■ *vi* (**-gasmed, -gas·ming, -gasms**) to experience sexual orgasm [Late 17C. Via French or modern Latin < Greek *orgasmos* < *organ* "swell, be excited"] —**or·gas·mic** /awr gázmik/ *adj* —**or·gas·mi·cal·ly** *adv* —**or·gas·tic** /-gástik/ *adj* —**or·gas·ti·cal·ly** *adv*

OR gate *n* COMPUT same as **OR circuit**

or·gi·as·tic /àwrjee ástik/ *adj* **1.** relating to or similar to an orgy ○ *orgiastic gatherings* **2.** characterized by excessive indulgence in an activity or emotion, especially one that is disapproved of ○ *orgiastic shopping sprees* [Late 17C. < Greek *orgiastikos* < *orgiazein* "celebrate secret rites" < *orgia* "secret Dionysian rites"] —**or·gi·as·ti·cal·ly** *adv*

or·gone /áwr gōn/ *n* a life force that is purported to exist in all living things. Some practitioners of alternative therapies claim it can be harnessed by patients sitting in specially designed booths. [Mid-20C. Probably < ORGANISM or ORGASM after HORMONE]

or·gy /áwrjee/ *n* **1.** GROUP SEX PARTY a gathering at which a group of people indulge in unrestrained sexual activity **2.** WILD PARTY a wild party or celebration characterized by excessive drinking and eating, with or without unrestrained sexual activity **3.** PERIOD OF OVERINDULGENCE a period of excessive indulgence in a particular activity or emotion, especially something that is disapproved of ○ *an orgy of self-pity* **4.** ANCIENT HIST WORSHIP OF ANCIENT GODS in ancient Greece and Rome, a secret rite in which the gods of pleasure, especially Dionysus or Bacchus, were worshiped with much dancing, drinking, and singing (*often used in the plural*) ■ *vi* (**-gied, -gy·ing, -gies**) OVERINDULGE to indulge in something without limit or restraint (*informal*) ○ *orgied on junk food* [Mid-16C. Via French < Greek *orgia* "secret Dionysian rites"]

or·i·bi /áwribee/ (*plural* **-bis** or *same*) *n* a small tan antelope with long legs and, in the male, short horns. Native to: plains of southern and eastern Africa. Latin name: *Ourebia ourebi*. [Late 18C. Via Afrikaans < Khoikhoi]

o·ri·el /áwree əl/ *n* **1.** *also* **o·ri·el win·dow** a bay window projecting from an outside wall and supported from beneath by a bracket **2.** a recess or small room formed by an oriel [15C. Via Old French *oriol* "porch" < medieval Latin *oriolum* "upper chamber"]

o·ri·ent *v* /áwree ent/ (**-ent·ed, -ent·ing, -ents**) **1.** *vt* FAMILIARIZE SOMEBODY to accustom somebody or yourself to a new situation or set of surroundings ○ *It might take you a few weeks to orient yourself.* **2.** *vt* PUT SOMEBODY OR SOMETHING IN POSITION to position somebody or something facing a particular direction ○ *old stone buildings oriented north-south* **3. o·ri·ent yourself** *vr* FIND YOUR POSITION to find out where you are and in which direction you need to travel ○ *the seaman's skill of orienting himself by the stars* **4.** *vt* DIRECT SOMETHING to direct something in a particular way, e.g., toward a particular objective or audience ○ *advertising oriented toward teenage girls* **5.** *vt* POSITION SOMETHING TOWARD EAST to position something so that it faces east, especially to build a church so that its length lies east to west, with the main altar at the eastern end ■ *n* /áwree ənt/ **1.** EASTERN SKY the eastern part of the sky, where the sun rises (*archaic or literary*) **2.** same as **dawn** (*archaic or literary*) **3.** LUSTER OF PEARL the luster of a pearl, especially a pearl of high quality (*archaic*) **4.** PEARL a pearl, especially one of high quality (*archaic*) ■ *adj* /áwree ənt/ **1.** same as **eastern** (*archaic*) **2.** RISING rising in the sky (*archaic or literary*) **3.** WITH GOOD LUSTER describes pearls with an exceptionally rich luster (*archaic*) ○ *"These pearls are orient, but they yield in whiteness to your teeth."* (Walter Scott, *Ivanhoe*; 1819) **4.** GLOWING glowing with a rich bright light (*archaic*) [14C. Via French < Latin *orient-*, present participle of *oriri* "rise"; because the Sun rises in the east]

oriel

USAGE orient or **orientate**? Since the verb ***orientate*** has never gained widespread critical acceptance, the careful writer avoids it, using ***orient***, as in *We oriented* [not *orientated*] *the telescope 50 degrees to the East. She is oriented* [not *orientated*] *toward a career in engineering.*

O·ri·ent *n* the countries of East Asia, especially China, Japan, and neighboring countries (*dated*)

O·ri·en·tal /àwree én't'l/, **o·ri·en·tal** *adj* **1.** RELATING TO EAST ASIA relating to the countries and peoples of East Asia, especially China, Japan, and neighboring countries (*dated*) **2.** HIGH IN QUALITY describes pearls and gems that are high in quality and valuable ○ *an oriental ruby* ■ *n* TABOO TERM a highly offensive term for somebody from East Asia (*dated*)

USAGE The adjective and noun ***Oriental***, with reference to people from East Asia, is now regarded as a relic of Western colonialism and should be avoided. The preferred substitute is *Asian*.

O·ri·en·tal black mush·room *n* FOOD, FUNGI same as **shiitake**

O·ri·en·tal fruit moth *n* a small moth that in the larval stage is a damaging pest to fruit trees. Native to Asia, it has been introduced to other parts of the world. Latin name: *Grapolitha molesta*.

O·ri·en·ta·li·a /àwree ən táylee ə/, **o·ri·en·ta·li·a** *n* artifacts from countries in East Asia [Early 20C. < Latin, "things from the Orient"]

o·ri·en·tal·ism /àwree ént'l ìzzəm/, **O·ri·en·tal·ism** *n* **1.** a cultural feature associated with the countries, peoples, or cultures of East Asia **2.** the study of the civilizations of East Asia —**o·ri·en·tal·ist** *n* —**o·ri·en·tal·is·tic** /àwree ent'l ístik/ *adj*

O·ri·en·tal pop·py *n* a perennial poppy, widely cultivated as a garden plant. Flowers: large, deep red. Native to: Southwest Asia. Latin name: *Papaver orientale*.

O·ri·en·tal rad·ish *n* FOOD, PLANTS same as **daikon**

or·i·en·tate /áwree ən tàyt/ (**-tat·ed, -tat·ing, -tates**) *vti* ⚠ same as **orient** [Mid-19C. Back-formation < ORIENTATION]

USAGE See ***orient***.

o·ri·en·ta·tion /àwree ən táysh'n/ *n* **1.** INTRODUCTORY SESSION a meeting or series of events at which introductory information or training is provided to somebody embarking on something new such as a course of study **2.** POSITIONING the positioning of something, or the position or direction in which something lies ○ *slopes with a southerly orientation* **3.** DIRECTION OF DEVELOPMENT the direction in which something such as a proposal is developed or focused ○ *the program's clear orientation toward the white middle class* **4.** LEANING the direction in which somebody's thoughts, interests, or tendencies lie ○ *irrespective of sexual orientation* **5.** PROCESS OF BECOMING ACCUSTOMED the process of becoming accustomed to a new situation or set of surroundings **6.** CHEM ARRANGEMENT IN CRYSTAL OR MOLECULE the arrangement of atoms, ions, radicals, or groups relative to each other in crystals or molecules **7.** BIOL REACTION TO STIMULUS movement or direction of growth in response to a stimulus, e.g., the way a plant grows in response to light —**o·ri·en·ta·tion·al** *adj*

o·ri·ent·ed /áwree èntəd/ *adj* openly supporting or favoring a particular point of view or set of beliefs (*often used in combination*) ○ *a Marxist-oriented approach to economics*

or·i·en·teer·ing /àwree ən teéring/ *n* a sport that combines map-reading and cross-country running. Competitors make their way through unfamiliar terrain using a compass and a topographical map. [Mid-20C. Anglicization of Swedish *orientering* < *orientera* "to orient" < French *orienter* < Latin *orient* (see ORIENT)] —**or·i·en·teer** *n, vi*

or·i·fice /áwrəfiss/ *n* an opening, especially the mouth, anus, vagina, or other opening into a cavity or passage in the body [Mid-16C. Via French < Latin *orificium* "making a mouth" < *or-* "mouth" + *-fic-*, stem of *facere* "make"]

or·i·flamme /áwrə flàm/ *n* **1.** a red banner or flag that was adopted as the national flag of France in the Middle Ages **2.** something that inspires people or arouses support (*literary*) ○ *Her first collection became something of a literary oriflamme for the students of the day.* [15C. < French *oriflambe*, origin ?]

orig. *abbr* **1.** origin **2.** original **3.** originally

Barnaby's

origami: an origami paper pig

o·ri·ga·mi /àwri gáamee/ *n* the Japanese art of paper folding [Mid-20C. < Japanese, "fold paper"]

or·i·gin /áwrəjin/ *n* **1.** SOURCE the thing from which something develops, or the place where it comes from (*often used in the plural*) ○ *the origins of the universe* ○ *The expression has an uncertain origin.* ○ *customs that are French in origin* **2.** ANCESTRY the ethnic group, social class, or country that somebody belongs to or that somebody's family comes from (*often used in the plural*) ○ *a great family whose origins stretch back to the Middle Ages* **3.** ANAT ROOT OF MUSCLE the place where a muscle is attached **4.** ANAT ROOT OF NERVE OR BLOOD VESSEL the root of a nerve or blood vessel **5.** MATH INTERSECTION OF AXES the point of intersection of all axes in a coordinate system. In a plane it has the coordinates (0,0), while in a three-dimensional space it has the coordinates (0,0,0). [Mid-16C. Directly or via French < Latin *origin-* < *oriri* "arise"]

CULTURAL NOTE ***On the Origin of Species by Means of Natural Selection***, a treatise (1859) by British scientist Charles Darwin. A highly controversial work, it challenged the established belief in the divine creation of life on Earth. Darwin put forward the theory that species evolved slowly in the struggle for existence: those best adapted to life in a particular environment would survive and reproduce by natural selection.

SYNONYMS ***origin, source, derivation, provenance, root***

CORE MEANING: the beginning of something

origin the thing from which something develops, or the place where something or somebody comes from ○ *Some of the concepts used now have their origins in the 19th century.* ○ *Researchers from overseas often decide not to return to their country of origin.* **source** the place, person, or thing through which something has come into being or from which it has been obtained ○ *It is important to trace the source of your error.* ○ *Inscriptions within mosaics provide a rich source of information.* **derivation** the origin or source of something such as a word or somebody's name ○ *The Latin word "regula," meaning 'straight stick,' is the derivation of the word "rule."* **provenance** the place of origin of something, especially a work of art or archaeological artifact ○ *an orange rug of Iranian provenance* ○ *Some experts have questioned the provenance and even genuineness of many of the museum's exhibits.* **root** the fundamental cause, basis, or essence of something, or the source from which something derives ○ *Various factors appear to be at the root of the inner city problem.* ○ *Lack of communication is the root of a wide range of problems.*

o·rig·i·nal /ə ríjjən'l/ *adj* **1. FIRST** existing first, from the beginning, or before other people or things ○ *The original plan was to turn the site into a shopping mall.* **2. NEW** completely new and not copied or derived from something else ○ *She doesn't have a single original idea in her head.* **3. CREATIVE** possessing or demonstrating the ability to think creatively ○ *blessed with an original mind* **4. NOT TRADITIONAL** representing a departure from traditional or previous practice ○ *a refreshingly original interpretation of the classics* **5. SOURCE FOR COPIES** relating to or being something from which a copy or alternative version has been made ○ *the original document* ■ *n* **1. FIRST VERSION** the first or unique item from which copies or alternative versions are made ○ *The meaning of the original has been lost in translation.* **2. AUTHENTIC PIECE OF ART** a genuine work of art that is not a copy or forgery ○ *verified as an original* **3. ECCENTRIC PERSON** an unusual or eccentric person **4. CREATIVE PERSON** a person of outstanding creativity or revolutionary thinking [14C. Directly or via French < Latin *originalis* < *origin-* (see ORIGIN)]

SYNONYMS See ***new***.

o·rig·i·nal·i·ty /ə rìjjə nálləteе/ *n* **1. NEWNESS** the quality of newness that exists in something not done before or not derived from anything else ○ *Improvised music lives on the tension between tradition and originality.* **2. CREATIVITY** the ability to think creatively and depart from traditional or previous forms **3.** (*plural* **o·rig·i·nal·i·ties**) **ORIGINAL THING** something original, e.g., a new idea or approach ○*"That's always the case with my originalities – they are original to nobody but myself."* (Thomas Hardy, *A Pair of Blue Eyes*; 1889)

o·rig·i·nal·ly /ə ríjjən'lee/ *adv* **1.** at first or from the beginning ○ *Originally a ballet dancer, she trained to become a circus acrobat.* **2.** in a creative or innovative way ○ *thoughtfully assembled and originally presented*

o·rig·i·nal sin *n* the sinful state, deriving from the disobedience of Adam and Eve, that Christians believe all people are born into

o·rig·i·nate /ə ríjjə nàyt/ (**-nat·ed, -nat·ing, -nates**) *v* **1.** *vi* to begin or develop somewhere or from something ○ *a custom that originated in the 19th century* **2.** *vt* to invent something, or bring something into being ○ *Einstein originated the theory of relativity.* [Mid-17C. < medieval Latin *originat-*, past participle of *originare* < Latin *origin-* (see ORIGIN)] —**o·rig·i·na·tion** /ə rìjjə náysh'n/ *n*

o·rig·i·na·tion fee *n* a charge made, e.g., by a bank, for setting up a loan

o·rig·i·na·tive /ə ríjjə nàytiv/ *adj* able to think of new ways of doing things —**o·rig·i·na·tive·ly** *adv*

o·rig·i·na·tor /ə ríjjə nàytər/ *n* **1.** a creator, inventor, or instigator of something **2.** somebody who starts a financial transaction, especially a writer of a check

o·ri·na·sal /àwri náyz'l/ *adj* describes a speech sound pronounced with both oral and nasal passages open, as the nasal vowels in French are [Mid-19C. < Latin *ori-* < *or-* "mouth" + NASAL] —**o·ri·na·sal** *n* —**o·ri·na·sal·ly** *adv*

O-ring *n* a plastic or rubber ring used in machinery as a seal against air, oil, or high pressure [Mid-20C. < its shape]

O·ri·no·co /àwri nṓkō/ long river in Venezuela. Its main channel discharges into the Atlantic Ocean, but one branch flows into the Amazon river system. Length: 1,590 mi./2,560 km.

o·ri·ole /áwree ōl/ *n* **1.** an orange and black songbird. Native to: North America. Family: Icteridae. **2.** a songbird with bold black and yellow markings. Native to: forests of Europe, Asia, Africa. Family: Oriolidae. [Late 18C. Via medieval Latin *oriolus* < Latin *aureolus* < *aurum* "gold"]

O·ri·on /ə rī́ ən, ō-/ *n* **1.** in Greek mythology, a giant and hunter, the son of the sea god Poseidon, who was killed by the goddess Artemis and transformed into a constellation **2.** a constellation near the celestial equator containing the Great Nebula and more than 200 stars visible to the naked eye. See illustration at **constellation**

O·ri·sha /ə ríshə/ *n Carib* RELIG same as **Shango**

O·ris·sa /aw ríssə/ state in eastern India bordering Bihar, Bangla, and the Bay of Bengal. Capital: Bhubaneshwar. Population: 36,706,920 (2001).. Area: 60,148 sq. mi./155,782 sq. km.

O·ri·ya /aw rée yə/ (*plural same*) *n* **1.** a member of a people who live mainly in Orissa and neighboring east Indian states **2.** an Indo-Iranian language spoken in eastern India, especially in Orissa and neighboring states on the Bay of Bengal. Native speakers: 36 million. [Early 19C. Via Oriya < Sanskrit *Odra* "Orissa"] —**O·ri·ya** *adj*

Ork·ney Is·lands /áwrknee-/ island group and council area of Scotland, lying 20 mi./32 km northeast of the Scottish mainland. Kirkwall is the administrative center. Population: 19,612 (2001).. Area: 349 sq. mi./905 sq. km.

Or·lan·do /awr lándō/ city and capital of Orange County, northern Florida, 78 mi./126 km northeast of Tampa. Population: 193,722 (2002 estimate).

orle /awrl/ *n* a border that runs inside and parallel to the edge of the shield of a coat of arms [Late 16C. < French < Latin *ora* "border, edge"]

Or·le·an·ist /awr lée ənist/ *n* a supporter of the family of the duke of Orléans and of its claim to the French throne, especially a supporter of King Louis Philippe, who reigned from 1830 to 1848 [Mid-19C. < French *Orléaniste* < *Orléans*, "Orléans"]

Or·lé·ans /awr lay a͡aN, -lée ənz/ city in north central France, the capital of Loiret Department and Centre Region. Population: 113,126 (1999).

Or·lé·ans /awr lée ənz, awr lay a͡aN/, **Louis Philippe Joseph, Duc d'** (1747–93) French nobleman. He supported the French Revolution but was executed during the Reign of Terror. He was father of the future king, Louis Philippe. Known as **Philippe Égalité**

Or·ly /awr lée, áwrlee/ southern suburb of Paris, location of an international airport. Population: 21,824 (1990).

Or·man·dy /áwrməndee/, **Eugene** (1899–1985) Hungarian-born US conductor. He worked with the Minneapolis Symphony Orchestra (1931–36) and the Philadelphia Orchestra (1936–80). Born **Blau, Eugene**

Or·mazd /áwrməzd/ *n* RELIG same as **Ahura Mazda**

or·mo·lu /áwrmə lo͞o/ *n* a gold-colored alloy of copper, zinc, and sometimes tin. Use: decorating furniture, jewelry, moldings. [Mid-18C. < French *or moulu* "ground gold"]

Or·mond Beach /àwrmənd-/ city in Volusia County, eastern Florida. Population: 37,202 (2002 estimate).

or·na·ment *n* /áwrnəmənt/ **1. SOMETHING THAT DECORATES** something that decorates or adds beauty to something else ○ *Christmas tree ornaments* **2. DECORATIVE OBJECT** a small decorative object displayed for its beauty **3. DECORATION** decoration or decorative quality ○ *manuscript pages entirely without ornament* **4.** MUSIC **EMBELLISHING NOTE** a note or set of notes added to embellish a melody or harmony **5. VALUED PERSON** somebody whose presence is a source of pride or honor (*archaic or literary*) ■ *vt* /áwrnə mènt/ (**-ment·ed, -ment·ing, -ments**) **DECORATE SOMETHING** to make something more attractive by adding decorative items to it ○ *a stone facade ornamented with gargoyles* [14C. Via Old French < Latin *ornamentum* < *ornare* "equip"] —**or·na·ment·ed** *adj*

or·na·men·tal /àwrnə mént'l/ *adj* **1. DECORATIVE** serving as a decoration and having no practical use ○ *The hitching post in the front yard was strictly ornamental.* **2. GROWN FOR SHOW** describes a plant grown for its beauty rather than for food ■ *n* **ORNAMENTAL PLANT** a plant grown for its beauty rather than for food —**or·na·men·tal·ly** *adv*

or·na·men·ta·tion /àwrnə men táysh'n, -mən-/ *n* **1. ADDITION OF DECORATION** the addition of decoration that enhances beauty or visual appeal, especially in the arts **2. DECORATION ADDED** decoration added to enhance beauty or visual appeal, especially in the arts **3.** MUSIC **ADDITION OF EMBELLISHING NOTES** the addition of a note or set of notes that embellishes a melody or harmony

or·nate /awr náyt/ *adj* **1.** having elaborate or excessive decoration **2.** using or consisting of elaborate language, especially language that is designed to impress with its complexity or literary quality ○ *expressions that are far too ornate for a TV soap opera* [Early 16C. < Latin *ornatus*, past participle of *ornare* "equip"] —**or·nate·ly** *adv* —**or·nate·ness** *n*

or·ner·y /áwrnəree/ *adj* **1. IRRITABLE** uncooperative and irritable (*informal*) ○*"The Core States crowd became as ornery as Chewbacca with a toothache"* (Keith Gave, "Game 1 Proves the Wings Have Nothing to Fear," *Detroit Free Press*; 1997) **2.** *US* **INSUFFICIENT** meager, whether out of poverty or lack of generosity (*informal*) ○*"how mean the preserves was, and how ornery and tough the fried chickens was"* (Mark Twain, *The Adventures of Huckleberry Finn*; 1884) **3.** *regional* **COMMON** ordinary ○*"It was pretty ornery preaching – all about brotherly love, and such-like tiresomeness."* (Mark Twain, *The Adventures of Huckleberry Finn*; 1884) [Early 19C. Dialectal variant of ORDINARY] —**or·ner·i·ness** *n*

ornith. *abbr* **1.** ornithological **2.** ornithology

ornith- *prefix* same as **ornitho-** (*used before vowels*)

or·ni·thine /áwrnə theen/ *n* an amino acid formed in the liver as an intermediate in the manufacture of urea [Late 19C < its presence in birds' urine]

or·nith·is·chi·an /àwrnə thískee ən/ *adj* relating to or belonging to an order of dinosaurs that had a backward-rotating pelvis similar to that of birds. The order includes the triceratops and stegosaur. Order: Ornithischia. ■ *n* an ornithischian dinosaur, e.g., an ankylosaur [Early 20C. < modern Latin *Ornithischia* < Greek *ornith-* "bird" + *iskhion* "hip joint"]

ornitho- *prefix* bird ○ *ornithology* [< Greek *ornith-*, stem of *ornis* "bird"]

or·ni·thol·o·gy /àwrnə thólləjee/ *n* the branch of zoology that deals with the scientific study of birds —**or·ni·tho·log·i·cal** /àwrnəthə lójjik'l/ *adj* —**or·ni·tho·log·i·cal·ly** *adv* —**or·ni·thol·o·gist** *n*

or·nith·o·pod /awr níthə pòd/ *n* a plant-eating dinosaur that had hind feet similar to those of a bird, e.g., the hadrosaur or the iguanodon. Suborder: Ornithopoda. [Late 19C. < modern Latin *ornithopoda* < Greek *ornith-* "bird" + *pod-* "foot"]

or·ni·thop·ter /áwrnə thóptər/ *n* an early flying machine that operated using flapping wings. Although many prototypes have been flown in the past 100 years, no ornithopter has ever been commercially successful. [Early 20C. < French *ornithoptère* < Greek *ornith-* "bird" + *pteron* "wing"]

or·ni·tho·sis /àwrnə thṓssiss/ *n* the bacterial disease psittacosis, especially when contracted by humans from birds

oro- *prefix* mountain ○ *orography* [< Greek *oros*]

or·o·gen·e·sis /àwrō jénnəssiss/ *n* GEOL same as

orogeny —**or·o·ge·net·ic** /àwrō jə néttik/ *adj* —**or·o·ge·net·i·cal·ly** *adv*

or·o·gen·ic /àwrō jénnik/ *adj* relating to or formed by the folding, faulting, and uplift of the Earth's crust —**or·o·gen·i·cal·ly** *adv*

or·o·gen·ic belt *n* a large linear feature on the Earth's surface that has undergone tectonic compression and uplift to form mountain ranges such as the Andes and the Alps

o·rog·e·ny /aw rójjənee/ *n* the folding, faulting, and uplift of the Earth's crust to form mountain ranges, often accompanied by volcanic and seismic activity

o·rog·ra·phy /aw róggrəfee/ *n* the branch of physical geography involved with the study and mapping of variations in the Earth's surface, including mountains and mountain ranges

o·ro·ide /áwrō ìd/ *n* an alloy of copper, zinc, tin, and iron that has a luster similar to gold. Use: manufacture of inexpensive jewelry. [Late 19C. < French, "like gold" < *or* "gold" (see OR²)]

o·rol·o·gy /aw róllәjee/ *n* GEOG same as **orography** —**o·ro·log·i·cal** /àwrə lójjik'l/ *adj* —**o·ro·log·i·cal·ly** *adv* —**o·rol·o·gist** *n*

OROM *abbr* COMPUT optical read-only memory

O·ro·mo /aw rṓmō/ (*plural* **-mos** or *same*) *n* **1.** a member of a people who originally occupied lands in Somalia and whose members now live in parts of eastern Africa, especially in Ethiopia and Kenya **2.** the Cushitic language of the Oromo people. Native speakers: 7 million. [Late 19C. < Oromo] —**O·ro·mo** *adj*

O·ro·no /áwrənō/ city in south central Maine, on the western bank of the Penobscot River. It is northeast of Bangor and is home to the University of Maine. Population: 9,113 (2002 estimate).

O·ron·tes /aw róntiz/ **1.** mountain in Iran, just southwest of Hamadan. Height: 11,640 ft./3,548 m. **2.** river in Southwest Asia, flowing through Lebanon, Syria, and Turkey, and into the Mediterranean Sea. Length: 355 mi./571 km.

o·ro·pen·do·la /àwrə pénd'lə/ *n* a bird with black or greenish feathers and a yellow beak that nests in colonies of long bag-shaped woven nests. Native to: Central and South America. Family: Icteridae. [Late 19C. < Spanish *oropéndola* "golden oriole" < *or* "gold" + variant of *péñola* "feather"]

o·ro·phar·ynx /àwrō fárringks/ (*plural* **-phar·ynx·es** or **-pha·ryn·ges** /-fə rínjeez/) *n* the part of the throat that is located below the soft palate and above the larynx [Late 19C. < Latin *or-* "mouth" (see ORAL) + PHARYNX] —**o·ro·pha·ryn·ge·al** /àwrō fə rínjee əl, àwrō farin jée əl/ *adj*

o·ro·tund /áwrə tùnd/ *adj* (*formal*) **1.** describes a tone or voice that is loud, clear, and strong **2.** describes language that is pompous or bombastic [Late 18C. < Latin *ore rotundo* "with a round mouth"] —**o·ro·tun·di·ty** /àwrə túndətee/ *n*

O·roz·co /o róskō/, **José Clemente** (1883–1949) Mexican artist. His murals, using fresco technique, focus on Mexican history and the suffering of humanity.

or·phan /áwrfən/ *n* **1.** CHILD WITHOUT PARENTS a child whose parents are both dead or who has been abandoned by his or her parents, especially a child not adopted by another family **2.** ANIMAL WITHOUT MOTHER a young animal whose mother is dead or has abandoned it **3.** PRINTING STRANDED FIRST LINE an opening line of a paragraph that is also the last line on a page, cut off from the rest of the paragraph by the page break ■ *vt* (**-phaned, -phan·ing, -phans**) DEPRIVE SOMEBODY OF PARENTS to make somebody an orphan ○ *a young boy orphaned by the war* ■ *adj US* **1.** MED AFFECTING VERY FEW PEOPLE describes a rare medical condition that affects only a small number of people and for which it is not commercially viable to develop drugs or therapies **2.** BUSINESS NOT COMMERCIALLY VIABLE describes a product that is not developed or marketed, often because of its perceived limited commercial potential ○ *orphan technologies* [14C. Via late Latin < Greek *orphanos* "orphaned"] —**or·phan·hood** *n*

or·phan·age /áwrfənij/ *n* a home or other institutional setting for orphans, often operated by a local government or charitable organization

or·phan as·sets *npl UK* assets held by life insurance companies and pension plans that are surplus to amounts needed to cover current or future payouts [Because deriving from policyholders who have died without making a claim or a full claim]

or·phan drug *n* an FDA category for a medication used to treat a rare condition or disease that affects only a small number of people. Orphan drug status provides financial incentives for the pharmaceutical industry to develop medications for this sector. [< the idea that the drug is of little economic interest to a manufacturer]

or·phan site *n* an area of contaminated land for which neither polluter nor owner will take responsibility. In such cases, the public sector normally assumes responsibility for decontaminating it.

or·phar·i·on /awr férree ən/ *n* a large lute, popular during the Renaissance, played by plucking or strumming the strings [Late 16C. After ORPHEUS and *Arion*, musician in Greek mythology]

Or·phe·us /áwrfee əss, áwrfyooss/ *n* in Greek mythology, a poet and musician, who descended to the underworld to seek his wife, Eurydice, after her death, but failed to bring her back —**Or·phe·an** *adj*

Or·phic /áwrfik/ *adj* **1.** relating to the poems and mystical writings associated with Orpheus **2.** mystical or magical (*literary*)

Or·phism /áwr fizzəm/ *n* an artistic movement within Cubism that flourished briefly at the beginning of the 20th century, concentrating on achieving harmony of color [Late 19C. < ORPHEUS] —**Or·phist** *n* —**Or·phis·tic** /awr fístik/ *adj*

or·phrey /áwrfree/, **or·fray** /-frày/ *n* elaborate embroidery, often done in gold [13C. Via Old French *orfreis* < medieval Latin *aurifrigium* "Phrygian gold"]

or·pi·ment /áwrpimənt/ *n* a bright yellow arsenic sulfide mineral. Use: dyeing, tanning. [14C. Via French < Latin *auripigmentum* "gold pigment"]

or·pine /áwrpin/, **or·pin** *n* a low-growing succulent plant. Flowers: pink, purple. Native to: Europe, Asia. Latin name: *Sedum telephium*. [14C. < French *orpin* < *orpiment* (see ORPIMENT)]

Orr /awr/, **Bobby** (*b.* 1948) Canadian ice-hockey player. He played for the Boston Bruins (1966–76) and Chicago Black Hawks (1976–79) and was the leading National Hockey League (NHL) scorer in 1970 and 1975. Full name **Orr, Robert Gordon**

or·re·ry /áwrəree/ (*plural* **-ries**) *n* a mechanical model of the solar system that shows the orbits of the planets around the Sun at the correct relative velocities [Early 18C. After Charles Boyle, fourth Earl of *Orrery* (1676–1731)]

or·ris /áwriss/ (*plural same* or **-ris·es** /-risseez/) *n* **1.** an iris with a fragrant root. Native to: central and southern Europe. Latin name: *Iris germanica*. **2.** same as **orrisroot** [Mid-16C. Probably alteration of IRIS]

or·ris·root /áwriss ròot/ (*plural* **-roots** or *same*) *n* the fragrant rootstock of orris. Use: perfumes, cosmetics.

ort /awrt/ *n US* a scrap or bit of food remaining after a meal is finished (*often used in the plural*) [15C. Probably < early Dutch *oorete* "leftover" < *oor* "out" + *eten* "eat"]

Or·te·ga y Gas·set /awr tàygə ee gaa sét/, **José** (1883–1955) Spanish philosopher and writer whose lectures and essays contributed to the fall of the Spanish monarchy in 1931. His best-known work, *The Revolt of the Masses* (1930), argues for the necessity of an intellectual elite.

> "He who wishes to teach us a truth should not tell it to us, but simply suggest it with a brief gesture, a gesture which starts an ideal trajectory in the air along which we glide until we find ourselves at the feet of the new truth."
> [José Ortega y Gasset, *Meditations on Quixote*; 1914]

orth. *abbr* MED **1.** orthopedic **2.** orthopedics

ortho- *prefix* **1.** correct; correction, straightening ○ *orthography* ○ *orthodontics* **2.** straight, upright, vertical ○ *orthotropous* **3.** perpendicular ○ *orthorhombic* **4.** fully hydrated or hydroxylated ○ *orthophosphate* [Via French and Latin < Greek *orthos* "straight, right"]

or·tho·cen·ter /áwrthō sèntər/ *n* the point at which the three altitudes of a triangle intersect

or·tho·chro·mat·ic /àwrthō krō máttik/ *adj* **1.** reproducing accurately the colors found naturally in a subject **2.** describes film that is sensitive to all the visible colors except red

or·tho·clase /áwrthə klàyss, -klàyz/ *n* a variously colored feldspar. Source: igneous rock.

or·tho·don·tics /àwrthə dóntiks/, **or·tho·don·tia** /-dónshə/ *n* the area of dentistry concerned with the prevention and correction of irregularities of the teeth (*takes a singular verb*) —**or·tho·don·tic** *adj* —**or·tho·don·tist** *n*

or·tho·dox /áwrthə dòks/ *adj* following the established or traditional rules of a political or religious belief, a philosophy, or a way of life ■ *n* a follower of traditional or established beliefs or rules, or a member of an Orthodox denomination [Late 16C. Via French *orthodoxe* and late Latin < Greek *orthodoxos* "having the correct opinion" < *doxa* "opinion"] —**or·tho·dox·ly** *adv*

Or·tho·dox *adj* **1.** OF ORTHODOX CHURCH relating to the Orthodox Church **2.** OF ORTHODOX JUDAISM relating to Orthodox Judaism ■ *n* MEMBER OF ORTHODOX CHURCH a member of the Eastern Orthodox Church

Or·tho·dox Church *n* **1.** a Christian church that originated in the Byzantine Empire and recognizes the Patriarch of Constantinople as primate rather than the Pope **2.** a grouping of Christian churches including the Greek Orthodox Church, the Russian Orthodox Church, and also the national churches of Bulgaria, Romania, and Serbia

Or·tho·dox Ju·da·ism *n* the branch of Judaism that accepts without reservation that the Torah was directly handed down from God to Moses

or·tho·dox·y /áwrthə dòksee/ *n* the practice of observing established social customs and definitions of appropriateness

Or·tho·dox·y *n* **1.** the beliefs and practices of the Orthodox Church **2.** the beliefs and practices of Orthodox Judaism

or·tho·e·py /awr thṓ əpee, áwrthō èppee/ *n* **1.** the study of the ways that words are pronounced **2.** the usual pronunciation of words [Mid-17C. < ORTHO- + Greek *epe-* "word, tale"] —**or·tho·ep·ic** /àwrthō éppik/ *adj* —**or·tho·ep·i·cal·ly** *adv* —**or·tho·e·pist** /awr thṓ əpist/ *n*

or·tho·gen·e·sis /àwrthō jénnəssiss/ *n* an obsolete theory that evolution can proceed in a direction determined by internal genetic factors rather than the external forces of natural selection —**or·tho·ge·net·ic** /àwrthō jə néttik/ *adj* —**or·tho·ge·net·i·cal·ly** *adv*

or·thog·o·nal /awr thóggən'l/ *adj* **1.** relating to or composed of right angles **2.** describes a set of axes all at right angles to each other in a crystal structure —**or·thog·o·nal·ly** *adv*

or·thog·o·nal mat·rix *n* a matrix in which two rows or two columns are vectors whose scalar product is zero

or·thog·o·nal pro·jec·tion *n* a way of providing a two-dimensional graphic view of an object in which the projecting lines are drawn at right angles to the plane of projection

or·tho·grade /áwrthə gràyd/ *adj* describes primates that carry the body upright [Early 20C. < ORTHO- + Latin *gradus* "walking"]

or·tho·graph·ic /àwrthə gráffik/, **or·tho·graph·i·cal** /-gráffik'l/ *adj* **1.** RELATING TO SPELLING relating to the study of spelling **2.** CORRECT IN SPELLING correctly spelled **3.** MATH MADE UP OF VERTICAL LINES composed of vertical lines —**or·tho·graph·i·cal·ly** *adv*

or·tho·graph·ic pro·jec·tion *n* ENG same as **orthogonal projection**

or·thog·ra·phy /awr thóggrəfee/ (*plural* **-phies**) *n* **1.** STUDY OF CORRECT SPELLING the study of established correct spelling **2.** STUDY OF HOW LETTERS ARE ARRANGED the study of letters of an alphabet and how they occur sequentially in words **3.** RELATIONSHIP BETWEEN SOUNDS AND LETTERS the way letters and diacritic symbols represent the sounds of a language in spelling

or·tho·mor·phic /àwrthə máwrfik/ *adj* GEOG same as **conformal** (sense 2)

or·tho·pae·dic *adj* MED another spelling of **orthopedic**

or·tho·pae·dics *n* MED another spelling of **orthopedics**

or·tho·pe·dic /àwrthə peédik/, **or·tho·pae·dic** *adj* **1.** relating to or used in orthopedics **2.** relating to or marked by disorders of the bones, joints, ligaments, or muscles [Mid-19C. < French *orthopédique* "of correct child-rearing" < Greek *paideia* "child-rearing" < *paid-* "child"] —**or·tho·pe·di·cal·ly** *adv* —**or·tho·pe·dist** *n*

or·tho·pe·dics /àwrthə peédiks/, **or·tho·pae·dics** *n* the branch of medicine concerned with the nature and correction of disorders of the bones, joints, ligaments, or muscles (*takes a singular verb*)

or·tho·phos·phate /àwrthō fóss fàyt/ *n* a salt or ester of phosphoric acid

or·tho·phos·phor·ic ac·id /àwrthə foss fàwrik-/ *n* CHEM same as **phosphoric acid** (sense 1)

or·tho·psy·chi·a·try /àwrthō si kī́ ətree, -sī-/ *n* a cross-disciplinary method of diagnosing, preventing, and treating childhood psychological problems that involves psychiatrists, child psychologists, pediatricians, and social workers —**or·tho·psy·chi·at·ric** /àwrthə sīkee áttrik/ *adj* —**or·tho·psy·chi·a·trist** *n*

or·thop·ter·an /àwr thóptərən/, **or·thop·ter·on** *n* a member of the order Orthoptera of primitive winged insects such as cockroaches, mantises, locusts, and crickets ■ *adj* INSECTS same as **orthopterous** [Late 19C. < modern Latin *Orthoptera* (plural) "those with straight wings" < Greek *pteron* "wing"]

or·thop·ter·ous /awr thóptərəss/ *adj* relating to the order Orthoptera of primitive winged insects such as cockroaches, locusts, mantises, and crickets

or·thop·tics /awr thóptiks/ *n* the study of eye disorders and their detection and correction, especially using nonsurgical treatments such as eye exercises (*takes a singular verb*) —**or·thop·tic** *adj* —**or·thop·tist** *n*

or·tho·py·rox·ene /àwrthō pī rók seen/ *n* a member of a subgroup of the pyroxene silicate minerals. Enstatite is an example.

or·tho·rhom·bic /àwrthə rómbik/ *adj* describes a crystal system that has three axes of different lengths that cross at right angles

or·tho·scop·ic /àwrthə skóppik/ *adj* **1.** able to see normally, without any visual distortion of images **2.** describes an optical instrument that gives normal vision

or·tho·stat·ic /àwrthə státtik/ *adj* associated with or caused by standing in an upright position ○ *orthostatic hypotension* ○ *orthostatic intolerance*

or·thot·ics /awr thóttiks/ *n* the branch of medical engineering concerned with the design and fitting of devices such as braces in the treatment of orthopedic disorders (*takes a singular verb*) [Mid-20C. < *orthosis* "artificial external device" < Greek *orthōsis* "making straight" < *orthos* "straight"] —**or·thot·ic** *adj* —**or·thot·ist** /àwrthətist/ *n*

or·tho·trop·ic /àwrthə tróppik, -trṓpik/ *adj* involving or characterized by vertical growth along a vertical axis —**or·tho·trop·i·cal·ly** *adv* —**or·thot·ro·pism** /awr thóttrə pìzzəm/ *n*

or·thot·ro·pous /awr thóttrəpəss/ *adj* describes an ovule that grows straight

or·to·lan /áwrtələn/ (*plural same* or **-lans**) *n* a small brownish songbird of the bunting family that has a grayish head, a yellow throat, and an orange-brown body. It was formerly sometimes eaten as a delicacy. Native to: Europe, Asia, Africa. Latin name: *Emberiza hortulana*. [Early 16C. Via French < Provençal, "gardener" < Latin *hortulanus* < *hortus* "garden"]

ORV *abbr* off-road vehicle

Or·vi·e·to /awr vyáytō/ *n* a light white blended wine from central Italy [Mid-19C. After a city]

Or·well /áwr wèl/, **George** (1903–50) British writer. A staunch critic of totalitarianism, he wrote political essays and fiction including the satirical political novels *Animal Farm* (1945) and *Nineteen Eighty-Four* (1949). Born **Blair, Eric Arthur**. See Cultural note at **farm** —**Or·well·i·an** /awr wéllee ən/ *adj*

> "If you want a picture of the future, imagine a boot stamping on a human face—for ever...And remember that it is for ever."
> [George Orwell, *Nineteen Eighty-Four*; 1949]

> "All animals are equal, but some animals are more equal than others."
> [George Orwell, *Animal Farm*; 1945]

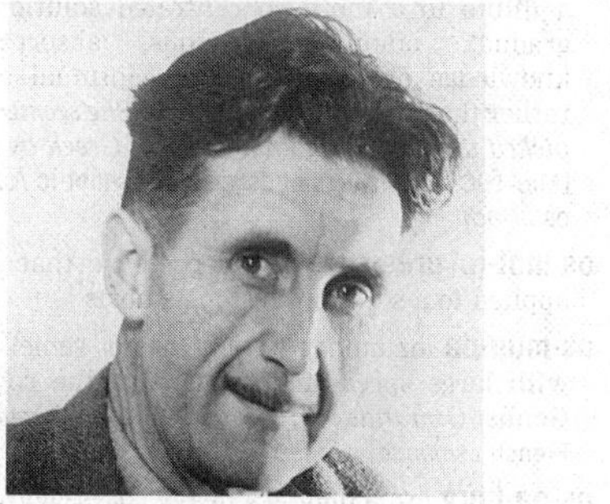
AKG London
George Orwell

-ory *suffix* **1.** of or relating to ○ *illusory* **2.** place or thing connected with or used for ○ *crematory* [Via Anglo-Norman and Old French dialect *-orie* < Latin *-orius* and *-orium*]

o·ryx /áwriks/ (*plural same* or **o·ryx·es**) *n* an antelope that has long horns, bold black and white markings on the face, and a hump above the shoulders. Native to: Africa, Arabia. Genus: *Oryx*. [14C. Via Latin < Greek *orux* "spike, pickax, oryx"]

or·zo /áwrzō/ *n* pasta that is the size and shape of rice grains, often served with lamb in Greek cooking [Early 20C. Via Italian, "barley" < Latin *hordeum*]

os[1] /oss/ (*plural* **o·ra** /áwrə/) *n* a mouth or similar opening in an organism [Mid-18C. < Latin, "mouth, face, head" (stem *or-*)]

os[2] /oss/ (*plural* **os·sa** /óssə/) *n* ANAT same as **bone** (*technical*) [Mid-16C. < Latin, "bone" (stem *oss-*)]

Os *symbol* CHEM ELEM osmium

OS *abbr* **1.** COMPUT operating system **2.** COMM out of stock

o.s. *abbr* **1.** LAW old series **2.** COMM out of stock

O.S. *abbr* **1.** MED left eye **2.** LAW old series **3.** CALENDAR Old Style **4.** ordinary seaman [in sense 1 Latin *oculus sinister*]

o/s *abbr* **1.** COMM out of stock **2.** BANKING outstanding

OSA, **O.S.A.** *abbr* Order of Saint Augustine

O·sage[1] /ṓ sàyj, ō sáyj/ (*plural same* or **O·sag·es**) *n* **1.** a member of a Native North American people who originally lived in Ohio, Missouri, and Kansas, and who now live mainly in Oklahoma **2.** the Siouan language of the Osage people. Native speakers: 1,000. [Late 17C. Alteration of Osage *Wazhazhe*, one of the three Osage bands] —**O·sage** *adj*

O·sage[2] /ṓ sàyj/ river in western Missouri, flowing northeast to join the Missouri River near Jefferson City. Length: 500 mi./800 km.

O·sage or·ange *n* **1.** a pulpy inedible fruit of a spiny tree **2.** a spiny tree that bears Osage oranges. Native to: south central United States. Latin name: *Maclura pomifera*.

O·sa·ka /ō saákə, ṓsaa kaá/ city and port in Japan, on southeastern Honshu Island. It is the capital of Osaka prefecture. Population: 2,484,326 (2002).

Os·born /óz bàwrn/, **Henry Fairfield** (1857–1935) US paleontologist. While working for the American Museum of Natural History, he assembled one of the world's major collections of vertebrate fossils.

Os·borne /óz bàwrn, ózbərn/, **John** (1929–94) British playwright and screenwriter. One of Britain's postwar generation of "angry young men," he harshly criticized the British establishment in plays including *Look Back in Anger* (1956), *The Entertainer* (1957), and *Inadmissible Evidence* (1964). Full name **Osborne, John James**

> "There aren't any good, brave causes left."
> [John Osborne, *Look Back in Anger*, Act 3; 1956]

Os·can /óskən/ *n* an extinct Italic language formerly spoken in southern Italy [Late 16C. < Latin *Oscus* "Oscan"] —**Os·can** *adj*

Os·car[1] /óskər/ *tdmk* a trademark for the golden statuette awarded annually by the Academy of Motion Picture Arts and Sciences to people in the film industry for achievement in the making of movies

Os·car[2] /óskər/ *n* a code word for the letter "O," used in international radio communications

OSCE *abbr* POL Organization for Security and Cooperation in Europe

Os·ce·o·la /óssee ṓlə/ (1800?–38) Seminole leader. He resisted government efforts to displace the Seminole people from Florida, and led them against federal troops during the Second Seminole War (1835–42).

os·cil·late /óssə làyt/ (**-lat·ed, -lat·ing, -lates**) *v* **1.** *vi* MOVE BACKWARD AND FORWARD to swing between two points with a rhythmic motion **2.** *vi* BE INDECISIVE to be unable to decide which is the better of two positions, points of view, or courses of action **3.** *vti* CAUSE SOMETHING TO CHANGE PREDICTABLY to cause something to produce rhythmic, predictable variations between two extremes, usually within a set period of time, or vary in this way [Early 18C. < Latin *oscillat-*, past participle of *oscillare* "to swing" < *oscillum* "swing, mask" (of Bacchus hung as a charm on a tree to swing) < *os* "mouth, face, head"] —**os·cil·la·tion** /óssə láysh'n/ *n* —**os·cil·la·tor** *n* —**os·cil·la·to·ry** /óssələ tàwree/ *adj*

os·cil·lo·gram /ə síllə gràm/ *n* the record produced by an oscillograph or oscilloscope [Early 20C. After OSCILLOGRAPH]

os·cil·lo·graph /ə síllə gràf/ *n* a device that produces a visual record of variations between two points or states, e.g., of electric current [Late 19C. < French *oscillographe* "that which swings while writing" < Latin *oscillare* "swing" (see OSCILLATE)] —**os·cil·lo·graph·ic** /ə sìllə gráffik/ *adj* —**os·cil·lo·graph·i·cal·ly** *adv* —**os·cil·log·ra·phy** /òssə lóggrəfee/ *n*

os·cil·lo·scope /ə síllə skṓp/ *n* a device that uses a cathode ray tube to produce a visual record of an electrical current on a fluorescent screen. Use: testing of electronic equipment, measurement of electrical impulses of the heart or the brain. [Early 20C. < *oscillation*] —**os·cil·lo·scop·ic** /ə sìllə skóppik/ *adj*

os·cine /ó sīn/ *adj* relating to, typical of, or belonging to the large subgroup of passerine birds that includes most songbirds [Late 19C. < modern Latin *Oscines* < Latin *oscen* "songbird" < *canere* "sing"]

os·ci·tan·cy /óssətənssee/ (*plural* **-cies**), **os·ci·tance** /óssətənss/ *n* (*technical*) **1.** the act of yawning **2.** a state of drowsiness or dullness [Early 17C. < Latin *oscitant-*, present participle of *oscitare* "yawn" < *os* "mouth, face, head" + *citare* "put in motion"] —**os·ci·tant** *adj*

Os·co-Um·bri·an /óskō-/ *n* a group of extinct Italic languages, including Oscan, Umbrian, and Faliscan, spoken in Italy during ancient times —**Os·co-Um·bri·an** *adj*

os·cu·lar /óskyələr/ *adj* **1.** relating to or characteristic of an osculum **2.** relating to the mouth or activities of the mouth such as kissing (*technical*) [Early 19C. < Latin *osculum* (see OSCULUM)]

os·cu·late /óskyə làyt/ (**-lat·ed, -lat·ing, -lates**) *v* **1.** *vti* KISS SOMEBODY to kiss somebody or each other (*formal or humorous*) **2.** *vi* MAKE CONTACT to make contact or come together (*technical*) **3.** *vi* MATH TOUCH AT TANGENCY POINT to touch at a point of common tangency to a line passing between two branches of a curve, each branch continuing in both directions of the line (*refers to arcs*) [Mid-17C. < Latin *osculatus*, past participle of *osculari* "kiss" < *osculum* (see OSCULUM)] —**os·cu·lant** *adj* —**os·cu·la·tion** /óskyə láysh'n/ *n* —**os·cu·la·to·ry** *adj*

os·cu·lum /óskyələm/ (*plural* **-la** /-lə/) *n* an opening like a mouth, through which a sponge expels water [Early 17C. Via modern Latin < Latin, "little mouth, kiss" < *os* "mouth"]

-ose[1] *suffix* full of, having the qualities of, resembling ○ *verbose* [< Latin *-osus*]

-ose[2] *suffix* **1.** carbohydrate, sugar ○ *maltose* **2.** product of primary hydrolysis ○ *proteose* [< GLUCOSE]

OSF, **O.S.F.** *abbr* CHR Order of Saint Francis

Osh /awsh/ city in Kyrgyzstan east-southeast of Tashkent, Uzbekistan. It is one of the most ancient settlements in Central Asia. Population: 225,600.

OSHA /óshə/ *abbr* Occupational Safety and Health Administration

Osh·a·wa /óshəwə, -waá, -wàw/ city in southeastern Ontario, Canada, on Lake Ontario, northeast of Toronto. Population: 234,779 (2001).

Osh·e·roff /óshə ràwf/, **Douglas D.** (*b.* 1945) US physicist. With David M. Lee and Robert C. Richardson he shared the Nobel Prize in physics (1996) for research into the superfluidity of helium-3.

Osh·kosh /ósh kòsh/ city and county seat of Winnebago County, eastern Wisconsin, situated on the western shore of Lake Winnebago. Population: 63,464 (2002 estimate).

O·shog·bo /ō shógbō/ capital city of Osun State, southwestern Nigeria, situated approximately 120 mi./190 km northwest of Lagos. Population: 465,000 (1995).

o·sier /ózhər, ózee ər/ *n* **1.** a willow tree with long flexible stems used in making baskets and furniture. Latin name: *Salix viminilis* or *Salix purpurea*. **2.** a branch or twig from a willow tree [14C. Via French < medieval Latin *auseria*]

O·si·ris /ō sīriss/ *n* in Egyptian mythology, the god of the underworld and the dead, husband of Isis and father of Horus

-osis *suffix* **1.** unusual or diseased condition ○ *chlorosis* **2.** condition, action, or process ○ *osmosis* **3.** formation of or increase in ○ *thrombosis* [Via Latin < Greek]

Os·lo /ózzlō, óss-/ capital city of Norway, situated in the southeast of the country, at the head of Oslo Fjord. Population: 506,923 (2001).

Os·man I /oz maán, ózmən/, **Oth·man** /óthmən, oth maán/ (1258–1324) Turkish warrior. He made himself ruler of a small state in northwestern Anatolia, from which grew the Ottoman Empire.

Os·man·li /oz mánlee, oss-/ *n* (*plural* **-lis** or *same*) **1.** SUBJECT OF OTTOMAN EMPIRE a subject of the Ottoman Empire **2.** TURKISH LANGUAGE OF OTTOMAN EMPIRE the Turkish language spoken in the Ottoman Empire, especially when written in Arabic script ■ *adj* RELATING TO OTTOMAN EMPIRE relating to the Ottoman Empire [Late 18C. < Turkish *Osmānlı* < *Osman* "Osman"]

os·mic /ózmik/ *adj* **1.** connected with or containing the element osmium, especially in a high valence state **2.** relating to odors or the sense of smell (*technical*)

os·mic ac·id *n* CHEM same as **osmium tetroxide**

os·mi·rid·i·um /ózmə ríddee əm/ *n* a very hard white or gray naturally occurring alloy of osmium and iridium, often with platinum and other metals. Use: pen nibs. [Late 19C. < German, blend of OSMIUM + IRIDIUM]

os·mi·um /ózmee əm/ *n* a hard white crystalline metallic element, the densest known. Source: osmiridium. Use: catalyst, alloyed with iridium for pen nibs. Symbol **Os**. See table at **element** [Early 19C. < modern Latin < Greek *osmē* "smell"; from the pungent smell of osmium oxides]

os·mi·um te·trox·ide *n* a colorless or yellow crystalline solid with an unpleasant-smelling poisonous vapor. Use: biological stain. Formula: OsO_4.

os·mo·con·form·er /ózmō kən fáwrmər/ *n* an ocean organism that varies the concentration of dissolved substances inside its body in accordance with that of the surrounding seawater [Mid-20C. < OSMOSIS]

os·mom·e·ter /oz mómmətər, oss-/ *n* an instrument that measures osmotic pressure [Mid-19C. < OSMOSIS] —**os·mo·met·ric** /òzzəmə méttrik, òssmə-/ *adj* —**os·mom·e·try** *n*

os·mo·reg·u·la·tion /òzmō regyə láysh'n, òss-/ *n* control of the concentration of dissolved substances in the cells and body fluids of an animal [Mid-20C. < OSMOSIS] —**os·mo·reg·u·la·to·ry** /-réggyələ tàwree/ *adj*

os·mo·reg·u·la·tor /òzmō réggyə làytər/ *n* an organism that can maintain a concentration of dissolved substances inside its body different from that of its surroundings [Mid-20C. < OSMOSIS]

os·mose /óz mòss, óss mòss/ (**-mosed, -mos·ing, -mos·es**) *vti* to cause something to diffuse by osmosis, or undergo osmosis [Mid-19C. shortening of obsolete *endosmose, exosmose*, both < French < Greek *ōsmos* "pushing"]

os·mo·sis /oz mósssiss, oss-/ *n* **1.** the diffusion of a solvent through a semipermeable membrane from a dilute to a more concentrated solution **2.** the gradual, often unconscious, absorption of knowledge or ideas through continual exposure rather than deliberate learning ○ *She seemed to have picked up a working knowledge of Greek by osmosis.* [Mid-19C. Latinization of OSMOSE] —**os·mot·ic** /oz móttik, oss-/ *adj*

os·mot·ic pres·sure *n* the pressure that must be applied to a solution to stop osmosis

os·mun·da /oz múndə/ (*plural* **-das** or *same*) *n* a fern with large spreading fronds, e.g., the royal fern. Genus: *Osmunda*. [13C. < modern Latin *Osmunda* < Old French *osmunde*]

os·na·burg /óznə bùrg/ *n* a heavy coarse cotton cloth. Use: grain sacks, upholstery, draperies. [Mid-16C. After *Osnaburg, Osnabrück*, NW Germany]

osprey

os·prey /óspree, óss prày/ (*plural* **-preys** or *same*) *n* a fish-eating hawk that has long wings and a white head with a dark strip around the eyes. Latin name: *Pandion haliaetus*. [15C. < Old French *ospres* probably < Latin *(avis) ossifraga*, a bird of prey mentioned by Pliny, identified with the lammergeier, literally "bone-breaking"]

OSS *abbr* HIST Office of Strategic Services

os·sa /óssə/ ANAT plural of **os**[2] (*technical*)

Os·sa, Mount /óssə/ mountain in northern Tasmania, Australia. It is the highest mountain in Tasmania. Height: 5,305 ft./1,617 m.

os·sa·ture /óssə chòor, -chər/ *n* the underlying structure or framework that supports a building or sculpture [Late 19C. < French < *os* "bone," after MUSCULATURE]

os·se·in /óssee in/ *n* the protein component of bone [Mid-19C. < OSSEOUS]

os·se·ous /óssee əss/ *adj* made of or resembling bone [Late 17C. < Latin *osseus* "bony" < *os* "bone"]

Os·set /óssət, ó sèt/, **Os·sete** *n* a member of a people who live in parts of southern European Russia and Georgia, especially Ossetia [Early 19C. < Russian *osetin* < Georgian *osetci* "Ossetia"]

Os·set·ic /o séttik/, **Os·se·tian** /ō seésh'n/ *n* the Iranian language of the Ossets. Native speakers: 300,000. ■ *adj* relating to the Ossets, their language, or culture

Os·sian /ósh'n, óssee ən/ *n* a legendary Gaelic hero and poet supposed to have lived in the 3rd century A.D. —**Os·sian·ic** /òshee ánnik, òssee-/ *adj*

os·si·cle /óssik'l/ *n* a small bone, especially one of three bones of the middle ear in humans [Late 16C. < Latin *ossiculum* "little bone, ossicle" < *os* "bone"] —**os·sic·u·lar** /o síkyələr/ *adj* —**os·sic·u·late** /-lət/ *adj*

os·si·fi·ca·tion /òssəfi káysh'n/ *n* **1.** PROCESS OF BONE FORMATION the natural process of forming bone **2.** HARDENING OF SOFT TISSUE the hardening of soft tissue as a result of impregnation with calcium salts **3.** BONY MASS a mass or deposit of bony material in the human body **4.** PROCESS OF BECOMING INFLEXIBLE the process of becoming set and inflexible in behavior, attitudes, and actions **5.** INFLEXIBLE CONFORMITY rigid, unthinking acceptance of social conventions

os·si·fy /óssə fī/ (**-fied, -fy·ing, -fies**) *vti* **1.** to change soft tissue such as cartilage into bone as a result of impregnation with calcium salts, or be changed in this way **2.** to become rigidly set in a conventional pattern of behavior, beliefs, and attitudes, or make somebody become so [Early 18C. < French *ossifier* "turn into bone" < Latin *os* "bone"]

Os·si·ning /óssəning/ town in southeastern New York, on the Hudson River, southeast of Peekskill. Population: 36,904 (2002 estimate).

os·so bu·co /òssō bóokō, òssō-/ (*plural* **os·so bu·cos** or **os·so bu·chi** /-bóokee/) *n* an Italian casserole of veal containing marrowbone, traditionally served with risotto [< Italian, "bone marrow"]

os·su·ar·y /óshoo əree/ (*plural* **-ies**) *n* an urn or a vault used to hold the bones of the dead (*formal*) [Mid-17C. < late Latin *ossuarium* < Latin *os* "bone"]

ost- *prefix* same as **osteo-** (*used before vowels*)

os·te·al /óstee əl/ *adj* **1.** made of, containing, or resembling bone **2.** relating to bones or the skeletons of mammals [Late 19C. < Greek *osteon* "bone"]

os·te·i·tis /òstee ítəss/ *n* inflammation of a bone or bony tissue, caused by infection or injury

Ost·end /o sténd, ós tend/ port in West Flanders Province, western Belgium. Population: 67,304 (1999). Flemish name **Oostende**

os·ten·si·ble /o sténssəb'l/ *adj* presented as being true, or appearing to be true, but usually hiding a different motive or meaning [Mid-18C. Via French < medieval Latin *ostensibilis* < Latin *ostensus*, past participle of *ostendere* "show" < *tendere* "stretch, spread"] —**os·ten·si·bly** *adv*

os·ten·sive /o sténssiv/ *adj* same as **ostensible** [Early 17C. < late Latin *ostensivus* < Latin *ostensus* (see OSTENSIBLE)] —**os·ten·sive·ly** *adv*

os·ten·so·ri·um /òss ten sáwree əm/ (*plural* **-ri·a** /-ree ə/), **os·ten·so·ry** /oss ténssəree/ (*plural* **-ries**) *n* CHR same as **monstrance** [Late 18C. < medieval Latin < past participle of Latin *ostendere* (see OSTENSIBLE)]

os·ten·ta·tion /òss ten táysh'n, òstən-/ *n* conspicuous or vulgar display of wealth and success, especially designed to impress people [15C. Via Old French < Latin *ostentation-* < *ostentare* "display, exhibit" < *ostendere* (see OSTENSIBLE)]

os·ten·ta·tious /òss ten táysh'n, òstən-/ *adj* marked by a vulgar display of wealth and success designed to impress people [Mid-17C. < OSTENTATION] —**os·ten·ta·tious·ly** *adv* —**os·ten·ta·tious·ness** *n*

osteo- *prefix* bone ○ *osteotomy* [< Greek *osteon* < Indo-European]

os·te·o·ar·thri·tis /òstee ō aar thrítəss/ *n* a form of arthritis characterized by gradual loss of cartilage of the joints, usually affecting people after middle age

os·te·o·blast /óstee ə blàst/ *n* a cell from which bone develops —**os·te·o·blas·tic** /òstee ə blástik/ *adj*

os·te·oc·la·sis /òstee ókləssiss/ (*plural* **-la·ses** /-lə seez/) *n* **1.** *also* **os·te·o·cla·sia** /òstee ō kláyzhə/ the process of disintegration and assimilation of bony tissue that occurs during normal growth of bone or as part of healing at a fracture site **2.** a surgical procedure in which a bone is broken in order to correct a natural malformation or a badly healed fracture [Early 20C. < OSTEO- + Greek *klasis* "breaking" < *klan* "to break"]

os·te·o·clast /óstee ə klàst/ *n* **1.** a large cell with many nuclei, found in growing bone. It assimilates bony tissue and is active in the formation of canals and cavities. **2.** an instrument used to break bones during surgery to correct a natural malformation or a badly healed fracture [Late 19C. < OSTEO- + Greek *klastas* "broken" < *klan* "to break"] —**os·te·o·clas·tic** /òstee ə klástik/ *adj*

os·te·o·cyte /óstee ə sīt/ *n* a branched cell within bone tissue

os·te·o·gen·e·sis /òstee ō jénnəssiss/ *n* the formation of bone in the body

os·te·o·gen·e·sis im·per·fec·ta /-ìmpər féktə/ *n* a rare hereditary disease in which poor connective tissue development causes fragile, brittle bones

os·te·o·gen·ic sar·co·ma /òstee ə jènnik-/ *n* MED same as **osteosarcoma**

os·te·oid /óstee òyd/ *adj* resembling or having the characteristics of bone ■ *n* the tissue from which bone develops, especially before it has hardened

os·te·ol·o·gy /òstee óllәjee/ (*plural* **-gies**) *n* **1.** the branch of anatomy concerned with the study of the structure and functions of bones **2.** the bone structure or skeleton of an animal —**os·te·o·log·i·cal** /óstee ə lójjik'l/ *adj* —**os·te·o·log·i·cal·ly** *adv* —**os·te·ol·o·gist** *n*

os·te·o·ma /óstee ṓmə/ (*plural* **-ma·ta** /-mətə/ or **-mas**) *n* a benign tumor made of bone, e.g., on the skull

os·te·o·ma·la·cia /óstee ō mə láyshə, -shee ə/ *n* a disease occurring mainly in women that results from a lack of vitamin D or calcium, causing softening of the bones and resulting pain and weakness

os·te·o·my·e·li·tis /óstee ō mī ə lī́təss/ *n* inflammation of bone and bone marrow, caused by infection

os·te·op·a·thy /óstee óppəthee/ *n* a system of medicine based on the theory that many diseases are caused by incorrect alignments of bones, ligaments, and muscles, and that correcting these through manipulation can cure the problems. It is often effective in treating joint and muscle disorders. —**os·te·o·path** /óstee ə pàth/ *n* —**os·te·o·path·ic** /óstee ə páthik/ *adj* —**os·te·o·path·i·cal·ly** *adv*

os·te·o·phyte /óstee ə fīt/ *n* a small outgrowth of bone that occurs within joints or at other sites where there is degeneration of cartilage as in osteoarthritis —**os·te·o·phyt·ic** /óstee ə fíttik/ *adj*

os·te·o·plas·tic /óstee ō plástik/ *adj* **1.** relating to or typical of bone surgery **2.** relating to or important in the process of bone development

os·te·o·plas·ty /óstee ō plàstee/ *n* the surgical repair or correction of distortions of bones

os·te·o·po·ro·sis /óstee ō pə rṓssiss/ *n* a disease occurring especially in women after the menopause in which the bones become very porous, break easily, and heal slowly. It may lead to curvature of the spine after the vertebrae collapse. [Mid-19C. < OSTEO- + Greek *poros* "passage"]

os·te·o·sar·co·ma /óstee ō saar kṓmə/ (*plural* **-ma·ta** /-mətə/ or **-mas**) *n* a malignant bone tumor

os·te·o·tome /óstee ə tṑm/ *n* a surgical instrument used to cut or divide bone

os·te·ot·o·my /óstee óttəmee/ (*plural* **-mies**) *n* a surgical procedure in which bone is divided or sectioned —**os·te·ot·o·mist** *n*

os·ti·a ANAT, ZOOL plural of **ostium**

Os·ti·a /áwstee ə, óstee ə/ ancient Roman port in Italy, at the mouth of the Tiber River, southwest of Rome

Os·ti·ak *n, adj* PEOPLES, LANG another spelling of **Ostyak**

os·ti·ar·y /óstee èrree/ (*plural* **-ies**) *n* a doorkeeper in a Roman Catholic church [15C. < Latin *ostiarius* "doorkeeper" < *ostium* "opening"]

os·ti·na·to /óstə naátō/ (*plural* **-tos**) *n* a short musical phrase or melody that is repeated over and over, usually at the same pitch [Late 19C. < Italian, "stubborn, obstinate"]

os·ti·ole /óstee ṑl/ *n* a small pore or opening in some algae or fungi, through which reproductive spores pass [Mid-19C. < Latin *ostiolum* "little door" < *ostium* "opening"]

os·ti·um /óstee əm/ (*plural* **-ti·a** /-tee ə/) *n* **1.** a small pore or opening in a passage or organ of the body **2.** a pore or small opening in a sponge, through which water passes [Mid-17C. < Latin, "mouth of a river, opening"]

os·tler *n* ENG, HIST another spelling of **hostler**

ost·mark /áwst maàrk/ *n* the unit of currency used in the former German Democratic Republic [Mid-20C. < German, "east mark"]

os·to·mate /óstə màyt/ *n* somebody who has had a stoma created, allowing the intestine to open at the body surface [Mid-20C. < OSTOMY]

os·to·my /óstəmee/ (*plural* **-mies**) *n* a surgical procedure in which an artificial opening for excreting waste matter is created, e.g., a colostomy or ileostomy [Mid-20C. < terms like COLOSTOMY, ILEOSTOMY]

-ostosis *suffix* formation of bone ○ *hyperostosis* [< Greek *osteon* "bone"]

os·tra·cize /óstrə sīz/ (**-cized, -ciz·ing, -ciz·es**) *vt* **1.** to banish or exclude somebody from society or from a particular group, either formally or informally ○ *She was ostracized by all her former friends.* **2.** to banish somebody by a popular vote because that person is regarded as dangerous to society, as was the practice in ancient Greece [Mid-19C. < Greek *ostrakizein* < *ostrakon* "shell, pottery fragment"] —**os·tra·cism** *n*

ORIGIN In ancient Athens, when it was proposed that somebody should be sent into exile because of becoming a danger to the state, a vote was taken on the matter. The method of voting was to inscribe the name of the prospective exile on a piece of broken pottery (*ostrakon*). If enough votes were cast against him, he was sent away for ten years.

os·tra·cod /óstrə kòd/ (*plural same* or **-cods**) *n* a tiny crustacean that lives inside a hard outer shell made of two hinged halves. Subclass: Ostracoda. [Mid-19C. < modern Latin *Ostracoda* < Greek *ostrakōdēs* "like a pottery fragment" < *ostrakon* "shell"]

Os·tra·va /áwstrəvə/ city in the northeastern Czech Republic, situated about 10 mi./16 km from the Polish border. Population: 322,111 (1999).

ostrich

os·trich /óstrich, óstrij/ (*plural* **-trich·es** or *same*) *n* **1.** a two-toed fast-running bird with a long bare neck, small head, and fluffy drooping feathers. It cannot fly, and is the largest living bird. Native to: Africa. Latin name: *Struthio camelus*. **2.** somebody who tries to avoid unpleasant situations by refusing to acknowledge that they exist (*informal*) [13C. < Old French *ostrusce* < Latin *avis* "bird" + Greek *strouthiōn-* < *strouthos* "sparrow." In sense 2 < the belief that ostriches bury their heads in sand if pursued]

Os·tro·goth /óstrə gòth/ *n* a member of the eastern branch of Gothic peoples who invaded Italy, where they ruled between the late 5th and the middle of the 6th centuries A.D. [14C. < late Latin *Ostrogothi* (plural) "Ostrogoths" < Germanic] —**Os·tro·goth·ic** /óstrə góthik/ *adj*

Os·ty·ak /óst yàk, óstee àk/ (*plural* **-aks** or *same*), **Os·ti·ak** *n* **1.** a member of a people who live in western Siberia **2.** the Finno-Ugric language of the Ostyak people. Native speakers: 15,000. [Early 18C. Via Russian < Tatar *ustyak* "one of another tribe"] —**Os·ty·ak** *adj*

Os·wald /ózzwəld/, **St.** (A.D. 604?–642) Anglo-Saxon monarch. He was king of Northumbria (634–42), where, with the help of St. Aidan, he reestablished Christianity.

Os·wald, Lee Harvey (1939–63) US alleged assassin. Accused of assassinating President John F. Kennedy (November 22, 1963), Oswald was fatally shot two days later by Jack Ruby while in police custody.

Os·we·go /oss weégō/ town and administrative seat of Oswego County, central New York, situated 33 mi./53 km northwest of Syracuse. Population: 18,027 (2002 estimate).

Os·we·go tea *n* PLANTS same as **bee balm** [Mid-18C. After the *Oswego* River, New York State]

Oś·wię·cim /áwsh vyén cheèm/ town in Poland west of Krakow. It was the location of the biggest Nazi concentration camp during World War II. Population: 43,300 (2003). Former name **Auschwitz**

OT *abbr* **1.** MED occupational therapy **2.** *also* **O.T.** BIBLE Old Testament **3.** *also* **O.T.** overtime

o.t. *abbr* overtime

ot- *prefix* same as **oto-** (*used before vowels*)

O·ta·go /ō taágō/ administrative region of New Zealand, occupying the southeastern part of the South Island. Its principal city is Dunedin. Population: 181,539 (2001).. Area: 14,918 sq. mi./38,638 sq. km.

O·ta·go Pen·in·su·la peninsula on the southeastern coast of the South Island, New Zealand. It extends 16 mi./25 km eastward from Dunedin to Cape Saunders.

O·ta·hei·te ap·ple /ōtə heetee-, -haytee-/ *n* an orange-colored, egg-shaped fruit that is eaten fresh, pickled, or preserved [< Tahitian name for Tahiti]

O·ta·hei·te or·ange *n* a popular houseplant with fragrant blossoms and small orange fruit. Latin name: *Citrus otaitense*. [< Tahitian name for Tahiti]

o·tal·gi·a /ō táljee ə, -jə/ *n* pain in the ear (*technical*) [Mid-17C. < Greek *ōtalgia* < *ōt-*, stem of *ous* "ear"]

OTB *abbr* off-track betting

OTC, O.T.C. *abbr* **1.** MIL Officers' Training Corps **2.** FIN, PHARM over-the-counter

oth·er /úthər/ CORE MEANING: a grammatical word used to show that a thing, person, or situation is additional or different ○ (adj) *He does much to help the homeless and other people in need.* ○ (adj) *They met many other children there.* ○ (adj) *I went on ahead, and the other climbers struggled on behind.* ○ (pron) *This is one problem, but there are many others.* ○ (pron) *As much as I demand of others, I am much more demanding of myself.*

1. *adj, pron* FURTHER refers to an additional or further person or thing of the type already mentioned ○ (adj) *Let me make one other suggestion.* ○ (pron) *A couple of students failed the exam, but many others passed.* **2.** *adj, pron* DIFFERENT refers to a different thing or things from that or those already mentioned ○ (adj) *Are there any other items you'd like to take home?* ○ (pron) *This problem, more than any other, has divided the critics.* **3.** *adj, pron* SECOND OF TWO THINGS refers to the second of two things when the first is known or understood ○ (adj) *He threw his other glove out of the window.* ○ (pron) *She had a cup in one hand and a glass in the other.* **4.** *adj* THE REMAINING refers to the remaining people or things in a group, apart from the one mentioned ○ (adj) *She left earlier, with the other kids.* **5.** *pron* **oth·ers** OTHER PEOPLE OR THINGS other people or things (*takes a plural verb*) ○ *Others may think differently.* ○ *Put the others in the drawer.* [Old English *ōđer* < Indo-European] ◇ **other than** indicates an exception to a statement ○ *Was anyone there other than you?* ◇ **the other day** *or* **night** a few days or nights ago ○ *A funny thing happened the other day.*

Oth·er Back·ward Class·es *npl* in India, an official categorization of people involved in tasks regarded as menial or excluded from other castes, who are considered disadvantaged and granted special treatment

oth·er-di·rect·ed *adj* more concerned with what other people think than with personal values and standards —**oth·er-di·rect·ed·ness** *n*

oth·er·ness /úthərnəss/ *n* the condition of being perceived as strange or different

oth·er·wise /úthər wīz/ *adv* **1.** OR ELSE if things had been different ○ *"I overslept," said Joe, "otherwise you would have heard from me earlier."* **2.** DIFFERENTLY different from or opposite to something stated ○ *You may take your hand luggage with you unless otherwise requested.* **3.** IN OTHER WAYS in any other ways ○ *An otherwise dull day was enlivened by her arrival.* ■ *adj* OTHER THAN SOMETHING STATED different from or other than something specified ○ *lots of information, digital and otherwise* [Old English *(on) ōđre wīsan* "(in) (an)other wise or manner"]

oth·er·world /úthər wùrld/ *n* a world or life that is beyond the conventional perception of reality

oth·er·world·ly /ùthər wúrldlee/ *adj* **1.** OF MYSTICAL WORLD relating to a world or life beyond conventional perception of reality **2.** OF INTELLECTUAL MATTERS concerned with highly intellectual or academic matters **3.** CONCERNED WITH AFTERLIFE concerned with the supposed afterlife as opposed to this life in this world —**oth·er·world·li·ness** *n*

Oth·man ◗ **Osman I**

o·tic /ṓtik, óttik/ *adj* relating to or located near the ear (*technical*) [Mid-17C. < Greek *ōtikos* < *ōt-*, stem of *ous* "ear"]

-otic *suffix* **1.** relating to a particular condition, action, or process ○ *hypnotic* **2.** having a particular disease or condition ○ *psychotic* [Via French and Latin < Greek *-ōtikos*]

o·ti·ose /óshee ōss, ṓtee-/ *adj* **1. NOT EFFECTIVE** with no useful result or practical purpose (*formal*) **2. WORTHLESS** with little or no value (*formal*) **3. LAZY** unwilling or disinclined to work or be active (*archaic*) [Late 18C. < Latin *otiosus* "at leisure, idle" < *otium* "leisure"] —**o·ti·ose·ly** *adv* —**o·ti·os·i·ty** /óshee óssətee, ōtee-/ *n*

O·tis /ṓtiss/, **Elisha** (1811–61) US inventor. He designed the first passenger elevator (1857) and founded the Otis Elevator Company (1861). Full name **Otis, Elisha Graves**

O·tis, James (1725–83) American lawyer and colonial leader. His speeches and published statements influenced American opposition to British rule.

> "Taxation without representation is tyranny."
> [Attributed to James Otis, *Slogan*; 1763]

o·ti·tis /ō tī́tiss/ *n* inflammation of the ear, caused by infection

o·ti·tis me·di·a /-meédee ə/ *n* a painful inflammation of the middle ear that can cause dizziness and temporary hearing loss

O·to /ṓtō/ (*plural* **O·tos** or *same*) *n* **1.** a member of a Native North American people who lived in the Great Lakes region and now live in Oklahoma **2.** the Siouan language of the Oto people [< Siouan *wat'ota* "lechers"] —**O·to** *adj*

oto- *prefix* ear ○ *otolith* [Via modern Latin < Greek *ōt-*, stem of *ous*]

o·to·cyst /ṓtə sìst/ *n* **1.** the structure from which the adult inner ear develops **2.** ZOOL same as **statocyst**

otol. *abbr* MED otology

o·to·lar·yn·gol·o·gy /ṓtō laring góllәjee/ *n* the branch of medicine concerned with the treatment and diagnosis of diseases of the ear, nose, and throat —**o·to·lar·yn·go·log·i·cal** /ṓtō lə ring gə lójjik'l/ *adj* —**o·to·lar·yn·gol·o·gist** *n*

o·to·lith /ṓtə lìth/ *n* **1.** a particle of calcium carbonate found in the inner ear of vertebrates and involved in sensory perception **2.** ZOOL same as **statolith** (sense 1)

o·tol·o·gy /ō tólləjee/ *n* the branch of medicine concerned with the structure and function of the ear, its diseases, and their treatment —**o·to·log·i·cal** /ṓtə lójjik'l/ *adj* —**o·tol·o·gist** *n*

O·to-Man·gue·an /ṓtə máang gee ən/, **O·to·man·gue·an** *n* a family of about 30 Native Central American languages spoken in a region extending from northern Mexico to Nicaragua [< OTOMI + MANGUE] —**O·to-Man·gue·an** *adj*

O·to·mi /ṓtə meé/ (*plural same* or **-mis**) *n* **1.** a member of a Native Central American people of central Mexico **2.** the Oto-Manguean language of the Otomi people. Native speakers: 200,000. [Late 18C. Via American Spanish < Nahuatl *otomih* "unknown"] —**O·to·mi** *adj*

O'Toole /ō tóol/, **Peter** (*b.* 1932) Irish-born British actor. Among his numerous stage and screen appearances were starring roles in *Lawrence of Arabia* (1962), *The Lion in Winter* (1968), and *The Last Emperor* (1987). Full name **O'Toole, Peter Seamus**

o·to·rhi·no·lar·yn·gol·o·gy /ṓtō rī̀nō lárring góllәjee/ *n* MED same as **otolaryngology** —**o·to·rhi·no·la·ryn·go·log·i·cal** /-lə rìng gə lójjik'l/ *adj* —**o·to·rhi·no·lar·yn·gol·o·gist** *n*

o·to·scle·ro·sis /ṓtō sklə rṓssiss/ *n* a hereditary disease of the inner ear in which spongy bone growth leads to progressive hearing impairment

o·to·scope /ṓtə skōp/ *n* an instrument incorporating a light and a magnifying lens, used to examine the external canal of the ear and the eardrum —**o·to·scop·ic** /ṓtə skóppik/ *adj*

o·to·tox·ic /ṓtə tóksik/ *adj* toxic to the ear and hence impairing hearing or balance —**o·to·tox·ic·it·y** /ṓtə tok síssətee/ *n*

OTP *abbr* E-COMMERCE open trading protocol

O·tran·to, Strait of /aw traántō, ō trántō/ sea passage between the Adriatic and Ionian seas. It separates the heel of Italy from Albania. Length: 43 mi./69 km.

OTS, O.T.S. *abbr* Officers' Training School

ot·ta·va /ō taávə/ *adj* sung or played at an octave higher or lower than the notes written on the staff, indicated by a sign placed above or below the staff [Early 19C. < Italian, "octave, eighth" < *otto* "eight" < Latin *octo*]

ot·ta·va ri·ma /-reémə/ *n* a verse form made up of eight lines in iambic pentameter with the rhyme scheme abababcc [Early 19C. < Italian, "eighth rhyme"]

Ot·ta·wa[1] /óttəwə, -waa/ (*plural same* or **-was**) *n* **1.** a member of a Native North American people who lived along Lake Huron and who now live mainly in Ontario, Michigan, Kansas, and Oklahoma **2.** the Algonquian language of the Ottawa people. Native speakers: 8,000. [Late 17C. Via Canadian French < Ojibwa *otāwā*] —**Ot·ta·wa** *adj*

Ot·ta·wa[2] /óttəwə, -waa/ **1.** river in Canada. It is the chief tributary of the St. Lawrence River, forming part of the Ontario-Quebec border. Length: 696 mi./1,120 km. **2.** capital city of Canada, located in southeastern Ontario, on the Ontario-Quebec border. Population: 774,027 (2001).

otter

ot·ter /óttər/ (*plural same* or **-ters**) *n* **1.** a fish-eating water animal with smooth dark brown fur and webbed feet that is related to weasels and minks. Native to: worldwide except Australia. Family: Mustelidae. **2.** the fur of the otter [Old English *ot(t)or* < Indo-European, "water"]

ot·ter board *n* a board or plate attached to each side of the mouth of a purse seine or other trawl net to keep it open as it passes through the water

ot·ter hound *n* a large dog belonging to an English breed developed for otter hunting

ot·to /óttō/ *n* PHARM, INDUST same as **attar** [Variant]

Ot·to I /óttō/ (A.D. 912–973) Holy Roman Emperor (962–973) and king of Germany (936–973). He consolidated the kingdom of Germany and the Holy Roman Empire through a series of military victories and alliances. Known as **Otto the Great**

Ot·to cy·cle /óttō-/ *n* a thermodynamic process for the conversion of heat into work, e.g., the sequential suction, compression, ignition, and expulsion in a four-stroke engine [Late 19C. After Nikolaus August *Otto* (1832–91), German engineer and inventor]

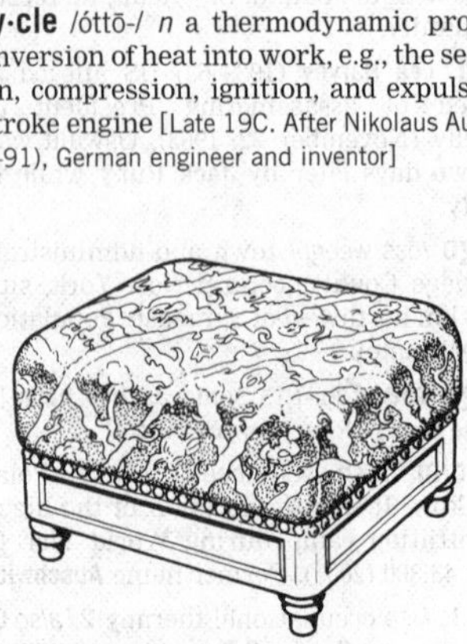

ottoman

ot·to·man /óttəmən/ *n* **1. STOOL FOR FEET** a low upholstered stool used for resting the feet or as a seat **2. LONG SEAT** an upholstered sofa that has no arms and is usually backless **3. HEAVY FABRIC** a heavy corded silk or rayon fabric. Use: coats, trimmings. [Early 19C. < French *ottomane*, feminine of adjective < *Ottoman* (see OTTOMAN)]

Ot·to·man *n* a member of a Turkish people who conquered Asia Minor in the 13th century [Late 16C. Via French or Italian < medieval Latin *ottomanus* < Arabic *'Uṯmān* "Osman"] —**Ot·to·man** *adj*

Ot·to·man Em·pire *n* a Turkish empire established in the late 13th century in Asia Minor, eventually covering much of Southwest Asia, North Africa, and southeastern Europe. It ended in 1922.

Ot·way Rang·es /ót way-/ range of hills in southern Victoria, Australia, which extends from Anglesea to Cape Otway

oua·ba·in /waa báy in, -báyn/ *n* a poisonous crystalline compound. Source: seeds of some African trees. Use: medicinally as a heart stimulant. [Late 19C. Via French *oubaïo* < Somali *wabayo* "arrow poison"]

Ouach·i·ta /wóshi taw/ river flowing from Arkansas to Louisiana, known later on its course as the Black River. Length: 605 mi./974 km.

Ouach·i·ta Moun·tains mountain range in central Arkansas and eastern Oklahoma. Highest peak: 2,950 ft./899 m.

Oua·ga·dou·gou /waágə dóogoo/ capital city of Burkina Faso, located in the center of the country. Population: 634,479 (1991).

ou·bli·ette /òoblee ét/ *n* a dungeon made so that the only way in or out is through a trapdoor at the top [Early 19C. < French < *oublier* "forget" < Latin *oblitus*, past participle of *oblivisci*]

ouch /owch/ *interj* an exclamation used to express sudden pain [Mid-19C. Origin ?]

oud /ood/ *n* a stringed instrument of southwestern Asia and North Africa that resembles a lute or a mandolin [Mid-18C. < Arabic *al-'ūd* "the wood"]

ought[1] /awt/ CORE MEANING: a modal verb indicating what somebody should do ○ *It seems to me that we ought to support their initiative.* ○ *You ought to tell her how you feel.*

modal v **1. BE MORALLY RIGHT** indicates that somebody has a duty or obligation to do something or that it is morally right to do something ○ *You ought to be ashamed of what you have done.* **2. BE IMPORTANT** indicates that something is important or a good idea ○ *You ought to see a doctor as soon as possible.* **3. BE PROBABLE** indicates probability or expectation ○ *We ought to be there by now.* **4. BE WISHED FOR** indicates a desire or wish ○ *You ought to come to dinner sometime.* **5. SHOULD BE CASE** indicates that something should be the case but may not be ○ *That ought to be easy.* [Old English *āhte*, past tense of OWE]

USAGE hadn't/shouldn't ought: Avoid in formal writing the regional constructions (called *double modal auxiliaries*) **didn't ought, hadn't ought**, or **shouldn't ought**, as in *They didn't ought to have done that.* Use instead: *They ought not to have done that.* The same holds with the regional *might could*, as in *We might could get there by three if we hurry*, which is also inappropriate in standard English.

ought[2] /awt/ *n* MATH same as **zero** [Mid-18C. < erroneous division of *a nought*]

ou·gui·ya /oo geé yə/ *n* the main unit of Mauritanian currency. See table at **currency** [Late 20C. Via French < Mauritanian Arabic *ūgiyya* < Greek *ougkia* < Latin *uncia* (see OUNCE[1])]

Oui·ja /weéjə, weéjee/ *tdmk* a trademark for a board with letters and a pointer or planchette by which answers to questions are spelled out, supposedly by spiritual forces

Ou·lu /ówloo, ṓ-/ city and port on the Gulf of Bothnia, west central Finland. Population: 117,670 (2000).

ounce[1] /ownss/ *n* **1. UNIT OF WEIGHT** a unit of weight in the avoirdupois system equal to one-sixteenth of a pound, approximately 28 g **2. FLUID OUNCE** a unit for measuring liquid, equal to 0.0284 of a litre **3. SMALL AMOUNT** a small amount of something ○ *Anyone with an ounce of common sense would take an umbrella on a day like this.* [14C. Via Old French *unce* < Latin *uncia* "twelfth part, inch, ounce" < *unus* "one"]

ounce[2] /ownss/ (*plural same or* **ounc·es**) *n* ZOOL same as **snow leopard** [14C. < Old French *once*, variant of *lonce* (the *l* being mistaken for the definite article) < Latin *lync-* "lynx"]

our /owr/ *adj* **1.** BELONGING TO US indicates that something belongs to or is associated with the speaker or writer and at least one other person (*first person plural possessive adjective*) ○ *Where are all our bags?* ○ *Today 80,000 new acres of our beautiful state are under special environmental protection.* ○ *Our house is just a few hundred yards from yours.* **2.** BELONGING TO EVERYONE indicates that something belongs to or is associated with people in general ○ *the dreams that inspire us to do our best* **3.** REFERS TO MEMBER OF FAMILY refers to a member of the speaker's family (*informal*) ○ *Our John is an electrician now.* [Old English *ūre* "of us," genitive plural of WE]

SPELLCHECK See *hour*.

Our Fa·ther *n* CHR same as **Lord's Prayer**

Our La·dy *n* a title for Mary, the mother of Jesus Christ, used mainly in Catholic churches

ours /owrz/ *pron* refers to something or somebody belonging to or associated with the speaker and at least one other person (*first person plural possessive pronoun*) ○ *It's no surprise that their team is ahead of ours.* [13C. < OUR + -'s "belonging to"]

our·selves /owr sélvz/ *pron* **1.** BELONGING TO US refers to the speaker or writer and at least one other person (*used as the object of a verb or preposition when the subject refers to the same people*) ○ *We blame ourselves for the accident.* **2.** REFERS TO PEOPLE IN GENERAL refers to people in general ○ *Many of us have secrets that we find difficult to admit even to ourselves.* **3.** REFERS EMPHATICALLY TO US refers emphatically to the speaker or writer and at least one other person ○ *We ourselves must bear the responsibility.* **4.** OUR USUAL SELVES our usual selves ○ *At home with the family, we can really be ourselves.*

-ous *suffix* **1.** full of or having the qualities of ○ *virtuous* ○ *traitorous* **2.** CHEM having a lower valence than a corresponding compound or ion the name of which ends in *-ic* ○ *chromous* [Via Old French < Latin *-osus* and *-us*]

Ouse /ooz/ **1.** river in eastern England that rises in Northamptonshire and empties into the Wash near King's Lynn, Norfolk. Length: 160 mi./257 km. **2.** river in northeastern England that rises in North Yorkshire and empties into the Humber Estuary. Length: 57 mi./92 km. **3.** river in southeastern England that rises in East Sussex and empties into the English Channel. Length: 30 mi./48 km.

oust /owst/ (**oust·ed, oust·ing, ousts**) *vt* **1.** to remove or force somebody from an office or position **2.** to use force to remove somebody from a place [15C. Via Old French *oster* < Latin *obstare* "stand in the way" < *stare* "to stand"]

oust·er /ówstər/ *n* **1.** the act of removing or forcing somebody out of a place or position **2.** the illegal removal or forceful dispossession of somebody's property

out /owt/ CORE MEANING: a grammatical word indicating that somebody or something is away from a place or removed from somewhere ○ (adv) *The child raced out and got back onto the bike.* ○ (adv) *She yanked out the weeds.* ○ (adj) *She's been out late every night.*
1. *adv* AWAY FROM PARTICULAR PLACE away from a place, especially the inside of something ○ *He reached underneath the bed and hauled out a heavy box.* ○ *The child scampered out and jumped on the bike.* **2.** *adv* OUTSIDE outside a place rather than inside ○ *It's cold out.* **3.** *adv* IN ANOTHER PLACE in another place, usually far away ○ *She's out in Australia, I think.* **4.** *adv* INDICATES END POINT indicates a goal or objective achieved in the action specified by the verb ○ *Stick it out – never give up.* **5.** *adv* EXISTING in existence ○ *It's one of the best albums out.* **6.** *adv* SO AS TO RETIRE FROM PLAY in baseball, in such a way as to retire a batter or team, or be retired from play **7.** *adj, adv* AWAY FROM HOME away from home or your place of work ○ (adj) *He's not answering the doorbell, so he must be out.* ○ (adv) *She's not answering the phone; she must have gone out.* **8.** *adj, adv* FARTHER AWAY refers to the tide when the sea moves away from the shore ○ (adj) *We can cross to the island when the tide is out.* ○ (adv) *The tide moves out at around five o'clock.* **9.** *adj, adv* NO LONGER BURNING no longer alight or no longer burning ○ (adj) *The fire is out.* ○ (adv) *The light has gone out.* **10.** *adj, adv* IN FLOWER in flower ○ (adj) *The daffodils are out at last.* **11.** *adj, adv* AVAILABLE available for people to buy ○ (adj) *Her new book is out in paperback.* **12.** *adj, adv* ON STRIKE on strike ○ (adj) *The miners have been out for a month now.* ○ (adv) *Several hundred workers came out in protest over the benefit cuts.* **13.** *adj* NO LONGER IN GAME unable to take part any longer in a game or sport **14.** *adj* CONSIDERING VERDICT describes a jury that is considering its verdict **15.** *adj* INCORRECT inaccurate or incorrect ○ *Look – the figures are way out.* **16.** *adj* UNACCEPTABLE unacceptable or not worth considering ○ *That possibility is out, I'm afraid.* **17.** *adj* UNFASHIONABLE no longer in fashion **18.** *adj* INTENT determined or intent on something ○ *He's just out for what he can get.* **19.** *adj* UNCONSCIOUS unconscious ○ *She was out cold.* **20.** *adj* USED UP used up or exhausted ○ *All our rations are out.* **21.** *adj* NOT IN GOVERNMENT no longer in power or office **22.** *adj* FINISHED completed or concluded ○ *before the year is out* **23.** *adj* NOT OPERATIONAL not in working order ○ *All the phones are out.* **24.** *adj* RETIRED FROM PLAY in baseball, retired from offensive play **25.** *adj* OPENLY GAY OR LESBIAN open about being gay or lesbian ○ *He isn't out to his parents.* **26.** *interj* AWAY FROM HERE! a command for somebody to leave a place ○ *Out! And don't come back!* **27.** *vt* (**out·ed, out·ing, outs**) EXPOSE SOMEBODY'S SEXUALITY to expose somebody as gay, lesbian, or bisexual or reveal yourself as such ○ *The action group has outed many prominent celebrities.* ○ *She outed herself to her parents last week.* **28.** *n* WAY OF AVOIDING BAD CONSEQUENCE a way of escaping from a predicament or avoiding the undesirable consequences of something (*informal*) ○ *What's my out if things go wrong?* **29.** *n* BASEBALL PLAY RETIRING PLAYER in baseball, a play that retires a batter or base runner [Old English *ūt* < Germanic] ◇ **out of 1.** indicates that somebody leaves a place ○ *Three men came out of the store.* **2.** indicates that somebody removes something from a place ○ *In her enthusiasm, she pulled the drawer right out of the desk.* **3.** toward the outside ○ *She looked longingly out of the window.* **4.** no longer available or in somebody's possession ○ *We're out of butter.* **5.** using as a source or material ○ *Plastic products are made out of petroleum.* **6.** indicates the proportion that something is true of ○ *This applies to one out of five adults.* **7.** indicates that somebody gains an advantage from something ○ *I think I got a lot out of the course.* **8.** indicates that somebody is sheltered from the weather ○ *Remember to keep out of the sun, or at least use sunblock.* **9.** beyond the range of a sound ○ *I called her, but she was out of earshot.* **10.** indicates the motivation behind an action ○ *He only did it out of spite.* **11.** indicates that somebody is not or is no longer in a situation ○ *A police officer warned them to stay out of trouble.* ◇ **out of it** very drunk, or under the influence of drugs (*informal*) ○ *You were totally out of it last night!* ◇ **out with it** a command to somebody to let something be known immediately ○ *Come on, what's going on? Out with it!*

out- *prefix* **1.** going beyond, overcoming, or outdoing ○ *outclass* **2.** positioned outside, away, or separate ○ *outback* **3.** moving or extending beyond or outward ○ *outgoing* **4.** completion or full extent ○ *outfit* [< OUT]

out·act *vt*
out·bid *vt*
out·dance *vt*
out·drink *vt*
out·eat *vt*
out·fight *vt*
out·fly *vt*
out·hit *vt*
out·learn *vt*
out·man *vt*
out·ma·neu·ver *vt*
out·ma·nip·u·late *vt*
out·match *vt*
out·matched *adj*
out·per·form *vt*
out·play *vt*
out·poll *vt*
out·price *vt*
out·pro·duce *vt*
out·punch *vt*
out·score *vt*
out·shout *vt*
out·sing *vt*
out·skate *vt*
out·spar·kle *vt*
out·sprint *vt*
out·swim *vt*
out·talk *vt*
out·think *vt*
out·vote *vt*
out·wear *vt*
out·wres·tle *vt*

out·a *prep* another spelling of **outta** (*informal*)

out·age /ówtij/ *n* **1.** a temporary loss of function or interruption of a power source, especially a loss of electric power **2.** an amount of something that is missing after delivery or storage

out-and-out *adj* being a thorough, uncompromising, or unapologetic example of something

out·back /ówt bàk/ *n* a sparsely inhabited or wilderness region of a country, especially of Australia —**out·back** *adj*

out·board /ówt bàwrd/ *adj* **1.** NAUT ON OUTSIDE OF BOAT located on the outside of the hull of a ship or boat **2.** NAUT TOWARD SIDE OF BOAT positioned away from the center of a ship or boat **3.** AVIAT AWAY FROM FUSELAGE away from the main body of an aircraft and toward the wing tips ■ *adv* NAUT, AVIAT TOWARD OUTSIDE OF CRAFT in a direction away from the center of a ship or aircraft ■ *n* **1.** BOAT WITH OUTBOARD MOTOR a boat with an engine mounted outside the stern **2.** NAUT same as **outboard motor**

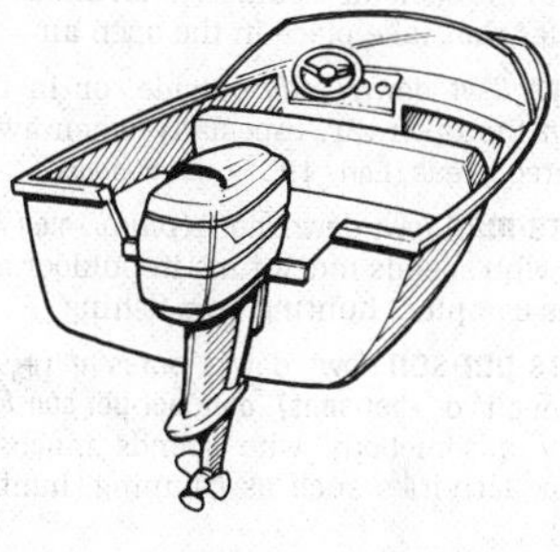

outboard motor

out·board mo·tor *n* a small or medium-sized engine with a propeller that can be mounted outside the stern of a boat

out·bound /ówt bòwnd/ *adj* traveling away from rather than toward a place ○ *an outbound journey*

out·box *n* **1.** *US* a tray or container in an office for mail ready to be sent and completed items ready to be filed **2.** a location in which outgoing e-mail messages are stored until they are sent

out·break /ówt bràyk/ *n* a sudden occurrence, usually of something unpleasant or dangerous such as illness or fighting ○ *the outbreak of war*

out·breed /owt breéd/ (**-bred** /-bréd/, **-breed·ing, -breeds**) *vti* to bring together distantly related members of a species in order to breed genetically varied offspring, or reproduce in this way [Early 20C. After INBREED]

out·build·ing /ówt bìlding/ *n* a barn, shed, or other structure that is situated away from the main building on a property

out·burst /ówt bùrst/ *n* **1.** a sudden display of strong emotion ○ *an outburst of grief* **2.** a sudden burst of energy or growth

out·call /ówt kàwl/ *n* a visit made by a doctor or other professional to the home of a client or patient

out·cast /ówt kàst/ *n* somebody who has been rejected by a group or by society ○ *a social outcast* —**out·cast** *adj*

out·caste /ówt kàst/ *n* **1.** in South Asia, somebody who has been expelled from a Hindu caste for violating its rules or customs **2.** in South Asia, somebody who does not belong to a Hindu caste

out·class /owt kláss/ (**-classed, -class·ing, -class·es**) *vt* to be so much better than others as to seem to be in a separate class altogether

out·come /ówt kùm/ *n* **1.** the way that something turns out in the end ○ *a satisfactory outcome* **2.** an expected or likely final state, achievement, or result ○ *poorer health outcomes*

out·crop /ówt kròp/ *n* the part of a rock formation that is exposed on the surface of the ground ■ *vi* (**-cropped, -crop·ping, -crops**) to stick out of the ground as an outcrop [Mid-18C. < *crop out*]

out·cross /owt kráwss/ *vt* (**-crossed, -cross·ing, -cross·es**) to mate two plants or animals not closely related but usually of the same breed in order to produce offspring ■ *n* the process of outcrossing plants or animals, or the progeny produced as a result

out·cry /ówt krī/ (*plural* **-cries**) *n* **1.** a strong, widespread public reaction against something **2.** a loud cry from a crowd of people

out·dat·ed /owt dáytəd/ *adj* superseded by something better, more fashionable, or more technologically advanced ○ *outdated notions about how to raise children*

SYNONYMS See ***old-fashioned.***

out·did *v* past tense of **outdo**

out·dis·tance /owt dístənss/ (**-tanced, -tanc·ing, -tanc·es**) *vt* **1.** to be faster than other competitors in a race and leave them behind **2.** to be considerably more successful than others

out·do /owt do͞o/ (**-did** /-díd/, **-done** /-dún/, **-do·ing, -does**) *vt* to do more or better than other people, or better than previously

out·door /òwt dáwr/ *adj* **1.** located in, belonging in, or suited to the open air ○ *outdoor activities* **2.** enjoying activities that take place in the open air

out·doors /owt dáwrz/ *adv* outside, or in the open air ■ *n* the open air, especially when away from populated areas [Early 19C. < *out of doors*]

out·doors·man /owt dáwrzmən/ (*plural* **-men** /-mən/) *n* a man who spends much time in outdoor activities such as camping, hunting, and fishing

out·doors·per·son /owt dáwrz pùrss'n/ (*plural* **-peo·ple** /-peep'l/ or **-per·sons**), **out·door·per·son** /ówt dawr pùrss'n/ *n* somebody who spends much time in outdoor activities such as camping, hunting, and fishing

out·doors·wom·an /owt dáwrz wo͝omman/ (*plural* **-wom·en** /-wìmmin/) *n* a woman who spends much time in outdoor activities such as camping, hunting, and fishing

out·door·sy /owt dáwrzee/ *adj* suited to or fond of the open air (*informal*)

out·draw /owt dráw/ (**-drew** /-dro͞o/, **-drawn** /-dráwn/, **-draw·ing, -draws**) *vt* **1.** to draw a handgun faster than another person **2.** to attract a larger audience than another performer or performance

out·er /ówtər/ *adj* **1.** ON OUTSIDE on or around the outside of something ○ *the outer surface of the spacecraft* **2.** AWAY FROM CENTER on the edge or away from the center of something ○ *the outer islands* **3.** OF BODY RATHER THAN SPIRIT concerning or belonging to external or worldly things rather than the life of the mind or spirit

Out·er Heb·ri·des island group in Scotland, comprising the westernmost islands of the Hebrides

out·er·most /ówtər mōst/ *adj* farthest away from the center [14C. < OUTER, after INNERMOST]

out·er plan·et *n* one of the five planets that have orbits lying beyond the asteroid belt, i.e. Jupiter, Saturn, Uranus, Neptune, and Pluto

out·er space *n* all space in the universe beyond Earth and its atmosphere, especially interplanetary and interstellar space, but including the region where astronauts walk and satellites orbit the Earth

out·er·wear /ówtər wèr/ *n* clothing that is designed to be worn outdoors over other clothing

out·face /owt fáyss/ (**-faced, -fac·ing, -fac·es**) *vt* **1.** to win a confrontation with somebody, especially by staring or not looking away **2.** to confront somebody boldly or confidently

out·fall /ówt fàwl/ *n* the outlet of a sewer, drain, or stream, especially where it empties into a larger body of water

out·field /ówt feeld/ *n* **1.** in baseball or softball, the part of a playing field beyond the diamond marked by the bases **2.** in baseball or softball, the players whose positions are in the outfield

out·field·er /ówt feeldər/ *n* in baseball or softball, a player who defends in the outfield

out·fit /ówt fit/ *n* **1.** SET OF CLOTHES a set of clothes worn together **2.** EQUIPMENT a set of tools or equipment for a particular task or occupation **3.** SMALL ORGANIZATION a team or group of people who work closely together, e.g., a military unit (*informal*) ■ *vt* (**-fit·ted, -fit·ting, -fits**) **1.** EQUIP SOMEBODY to provide somebody with all the equipment that is needed for a job or activity **2.** DRESS SOMEBODY to provide somebody with a set of clothes

out·fit·ter /ówt fittər/ *n* a store that sells equipment and supplies for outdoor leisure activities such as camping or hunting, and sometimes provides guides

out·flank /owt flángk/ (**-flanked, -flank·ing, -flanks**) *vt* **1.** to go around the main body of an enemy force and attack it from the side or from behind **2.** to outwit or bypass an opponent or competitor

out·flow /ówt flō/ *n* **1.** the process of flowing out or away **2.** the flow, movement, or transfer of something such as gas, water, or money away from a place

out·fox /owt fóks/ (**-foxed, -fox·ing, -fox·es**) *vt* to defeat somebody by being more cunning

out-front *adj* frank and straightforward (*informal*) ○ *wasn't very out-front about her policies*

out·gas /owt gáss/ (**-gassed, -gas·sing, -gas·es**) *vti* to remove or release trapped or absorbed gas, or be released as gas

out·gen·er·al /owt jénnərəl/ (**-aled** or **-alled, -al·ing** or **-al·ling, -als**) *vt* to defeat somebody in battle through better leadership

out·giv·ing /owt gívving/ *adj US* friendly and sociable

out·go /owt gṓ/ *vt* (**-went** /-wént/, **-gone** /-gáwn, -gón/, **-go·ing, -goes**) OUTDO SOMEBODY OR SOMETHING to go beyond or surpass somebody or something ■ *n* (*plural* **-goes**) **1.** EXPENDITURE something that goes out, especially money that is paid out **2.** SOMETHING THAT FLOWS OUT something that is flowing out **3.** GOING OUT the act of going out

out·go·ing /owt gṓing/ *adj* **1.** LEAVING OR GOING OUT in the process of departing or going out of a building or place ○ *outgoing flights* **2.** LEAVING JOB in the process of departing or being sent away after a period of office ○ *a dinner for the outgoing president* **3.** SOCIABLE confident and friendly in social situations ○ *a cheerful, outgoing child* —**out·go·ing·ness** *n*

out·gone past tense of **outgo**

out·grew past tense of **outgrow**

out-group *n* a group of people excluded from another group with higher status

out·grow /owt grṓ/ (**-grew** /-gro͞o/, **-grown** /-grṓn/, **-grow·ing, -grows**) *vt* **1.** GET TOO LARGE FOR SOMETHING to grow too large for something **2.** MOVE BEYOND PREVIOUS INTERESTS to change so that old ideas, interests, or ways of behaving are lost in favor of new ones **3.** OUTSTRIP OTHERS to grow larger or faster than other things or people

out·growth /ówt grōth/ *n* **1.** a natural development or result of something else **2.** something that is growing out from the main part

out·guess /owt géss/ (**-guessed, -guess·ing, -guess·es**) *vt* to get an advantage over somebody by anticipating what that person is thinking or planning to do

out·gun /owt gún/ (**-gunned, -gun·ning, -guns**) *vt* **1.** to have more guns or firepower than somebody else **2.** to defeat a rival or competitor by being stronger or having better resources (*informal*)

out·haul /ówt hàwl/ *n* a rope used to pull a sail taut along a boom or spar

out-Her·od (**out-Her·od·ded, out-Her·od·ding, out-Her·ods**) *vt* to behave more excessively than somebody else ○ *out-Herod Herod* [After HEROD (THE GREAT), presented in medieval mystery plays as an overdramatic character]

out·house /ówt hòwss/ (*plural* **-hous·es** /-hòwzəz/) *n* **1.** an outdoor toilet consisting of a small building that encloses a seat with a hole in it built over a pit **2.** a small building situated near the main building on a property

out·ing /ówting/ *n* **1.** EXCURSION a short pleasure trip usually lasting no more than a day **2.** PARTICIPATION IN EVENT an appearance at or participation in a public event, especially an athletic competition **3.** OUTDOOR WALK a walk or hike outdoors ○ *took the toddlers on a little outing around the block* **4.** REVELATION OF SEXUAL PREFERENCE the practice of making public the fact of being gay, lesbian, or bisexual

out·ing flan·nel *n US* a soft cotton fabric with a nap on both sides

out·jock·ey /owt jókee/ (**-eyed, -ey·ing, -eys**) *vt* to get an advantage over somebody by cleverness or trickery

out·land /ówt lànd, -lənd/ *n* **1.** the remote or outlying areas of a country (*often used in the plural*) **2.** a different country

out·land·er /ówt làndər/ *n* somebody from another country or from a different region, and thus a stranger [Late 16C. After Dutch *uitlander*, German *Ausländer*]

out·land·ish /owt lándish/ *adj* **1.** extremely unusual or bizarre **2.** alien or foreign (*archaic*) —**out·land·ish·ly** *adv* —**out·land·ish·ness** *n*

out·last /owt lást/ (**-last·ed, -last·ing, -lasts**) *vt* to last or exist longer than somebody or something else

out·law /ówt làw/ *n* **1.** FUGITIVE CRIMINAL a notorious criminal, especially one on the run **2.** SOMEBODY WITHOUT LEGAL RIGHTS somebody, often a criminal, who has been officially deprived of legal rights and so is not protected by the law **3.** REBELLIOUS PERSON somebody who is rebellious or flouts the law **4.** VICIOUS ANIMAL a savage or uncontrollable animal ■ *vt* (**-lawed, -law·ing, -laws**) **1.** BAN SOMETHING to make something illegal **2.** TAKE AWAY SOMEBODY'S LEGAL RIGHTS to deprive somebody officially of all their legal rights [12C. < Old Norse *útlagi* "person outside the law" < *útlagr* "outlawed, banished"]

out·law·ry /ówt làwree/ *n* **1.** refusal to obey the law **2.** a state in which somebody has been deprived of his or her legal rights and is no longer protected by the law, or the legal process by which this happens

out·lay *n* /ówt lày/ **1.** SPENDING the expending of resources or spending of money **2.** MONEY SPENT an amount of money spent ■ *vt* /owt láy/ (**-laid** /-láyd/, **-lay·ing, -lays**) SPEND MONEY to spend a specific amount of money

out·let /ówt lèt, -lət/ *n* **1.** STORE a store that sells the products of a particular manufacturer, often at a discount **2.** MARKET FOR GOODS a market providing goods or services **3.** RELEASE FOR EMOTIONS a way of releasing emotions or impulses ○ *an outlet for creative expression* **4.** VENT a passage or opening for letting something out, e.g., water or steam **5.** ELEC CONNECTION TO ELECTRICITY a receptacle for an electric plug to make a connection with a power supply **6.** RIVER MOUTH the mouth of a river where it flows into a lake or the sea **7.** STREAM DRAINING LAKE a stream or channel flowing from a larger body of water

out·li·er /ówt lī ər/ *n* **1.** OUTLYING PART a separate part of a system, organization, or body that is at some distance from the main part **2.** OUTSIDER somebody who chooses not to be a part of a group or community (*often used before a noun*) ○ *If we fail to ratify this treaty, we become associated with the outlier nations.* **3.** SOMEBODY LIVING AT DISTANCE FROM WORK somebody who lives far from his or her workplace **4.** STATS VALUE FAR FROM OTHERS a statistical value that is outside other values in a set of data **5.** GEOL ROCK FORMATION an outcrop of rock that is separated from a main formation

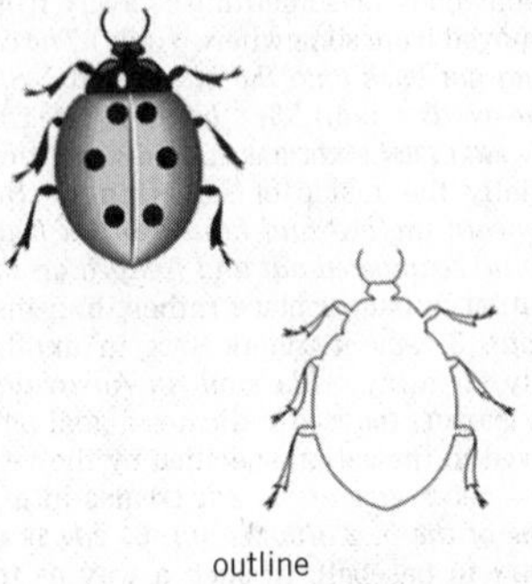

outline

out·line /ówt līn/ *n* **1.** LINE THAT SHOWS SHAPE the outer edge or edges of something thought of as a line defining its shape ○ *I could see the outline of the trees against the sky.* **2.** LINE DEPICTING SHAPE OF SOMETHING a line drawn around or depicting the outside edges of something to show its shape **3.** DRAWING WITHOUT

SHADING a style or example of drawing in which an object or figure is shown as an outline (*often used before a noun*) ○ *an outline map* **4.** ROUGH PLAN a general, preliminary, or rough plan or account of something, that concentrates on the main features and ignores detail, e.g., a list of the main points covered or to be covered in a speech (*often used before a noun*) ■ **out·lines** *npl* MAIN FEATURES the most prominent or important aspects of something ○ *The outlines of the plan have already been agreed upon.* ■ *n* BRIEF ACCOUNT a condensation of a subject or argument into its main points ○ *One of the books was an outline of European history.* ■ *vt* (**-lined, -lin·ing, -lines**) **1.** DRAW MAIN FEATURES to draw a line showing or emphasizing the shape of something **2.** GIVE ESSENTIAL POINTS to give the main points of an argument or plan

out·live /owt lív/ (**-lived, -liv·ing, -lives**) *vt* **1.** to live longer than somebody else **2.** to continue to exist beyond or last through something ○ *The policy has outlived its usefulness.*

out·look /ówt lo͝ok/ *n* **1.** ATTITUDE an attitude or point of view **2.** LIKELY FUTURE expectations for the future, especially with respect to a particular situation **3.** VIEW a view seen from a place

out loud *adv* in words that others can hear, rather than silently in the mind

out·ly·ing /ówt lī ing/ *adj* far from the central part of a place or region

out·mi·grate /ówt mī gràyt/ (**-grat·ed, -grat·ing, -grates**) *vi* to leave one region or community in order to settle in another —**out·mi·grant** /ówt mīgrənt/ *n* —**out·mi·gra·tion** *n*

out·mod·ed /owt mṓdəd /*adj* **1.** no longer fashionable or widely used **2.** having been superseded by something newer or more efficient [Early 20C. Translation of French *démodé*] —**out·mod·ed·ly** *adv* —**out·mod·ed·ness** *n*

out·most /ówt mōst/ *adj* farthest away from the center or main area [14C. Alteration of UTMOST]

out·num·ber /owt númbər/ (**-bered, -ber·ing, -bers**) *vt* to be more numerous than another group or set of things

out-of-bod·y *adj* describes an experience in which a person's consciousness appears to have an existence separate from the body, enabling the subject to see his or her own body from the outside

out-of-bounds *adj, adv* in or indicating a place that is beyond the established or official boundaries

out-of-court *adj* settled without going to court or without completing a court case

out-of-date *adj* old-fashioned or no longer current

out-of-door *adj US* same as **outdoor**

out-of-doors *adv* same as **outdoors**

out-of-pock·et *adj* **1.** describes expenses paid for with cash ○ *out-of-pocket travel expenses* **2.** out of money

out-of-state *adj US* coming from or relating to another state

out-of-stat·er *n US* a visitor to or temporary resident of one state who is a legal resident of another

out-of-the-way *adj* **1.** far from a populated area or difficult to get to **2.** uncommon or unconventional

out-of-town *adj* coming from or happening in another town or city —**out-of-town·er** *n*

out·pace /owt páyss/ (**-paced, -pac·ing, -pac·es**) *vt* to do better or go faster than something or somebody else

out·pa·tient /ówt pàysh'nt/ *n* a patient who receives treatment at a hospital without staying overnight

out·place·ment /ówt plàyssmənt/ *n* a service offered by a company to help employees who are being dismissed find new jobs

out·point /owt póynt/ (**-point·ed, -point·ing, -points**) *vt* **1.** to score more points than somebody else **2.** to sail closer to the wind than another ship

out·port /ówt pàwrt/ *n Can* a small remote fishing village, especially one on the Newfoundland coast

out·post /ówt pōst/ *n* **1.** TROOPS APART FROM MAIN FORCE a small group of troops stationed at a distance from the main body of an army and assigned to guard a place or area **2.** MILITARY BASE a small military base in a remote area or different country **3.** REMOTE SETTLEMENT a settlement in unfamiliar territory or on a frontier

out·pour *vti* /owt páwr/ (**-poured, -pour·ing, -pours**) to flow out quickly and in large quantities, or make something flow out in this way ■ *n* /ówt pàwr/ something that flows out rapidly and copiously, or the act of flowing out in this way

out·pour·ing /ówt pàwring/ *n* **1.** an extravagant, passionate, or sometimes excessive display or expression of feeling ○ *an outpouring of generosity* ○ *an outpouring of lava* **2.** same as **outpour**

out·put /ówt po͝ot/ *n* **1.** PRODUCTION the act of producing **2.** YIELD an amount of something produced or manufactured, especially during a fixed period of time **3.** PRODUCTS PRODUCED goods or services produced by an organization **4.** CREATIVE OR ARTISTIC PRODUCTION creative or intellectual work produced by somebody ○ *her literary output* **5.** ENERGY PRODUCED energy or power produced by a system **6.** ELEC ENG ELECTRICAL POWER the electrical energy, measured in watts, delivered by a generator, light bulb, amplifier, or other electric device **7.** COMPUT INFORMATION FROM COMPUTER information produced by a computer ■ *vt* (**-put** or **-put·ted, -put·ting, -puts**) COMPUT PRODUCE COMPUTER INFORMATION to display information from a computer on a monitor, or direct it to a printer or other device

out·race /owt ráyss/ (**-raced, -rac·ing, -rac·es**) *vt* to do something better or faster than others

out·rage /ówt ràyj/ *n* **1.** VIOLENT ACT an extremely violent or cruel act **2.** OFFENSIVE ACT a very offensive or insulting act **3.** FURY intense anger and indignation aroused by a violent or offensive act ■ *vt* (**-raged, -rag·ing, -rag·es**) **1.** AROUSE ANGER IN SOMEBODY to make somebody feel intense anger or indignation **2.** VIOLATE to commit a flagrant violation or infringement of something **3.** CRIME same as **rape**[1] *v* (sense 1) (*archaic*) [13C. Via French, "excess, atrocity" < Old French *outrer* "exceed" < Latin *ultra* "beyond"]

out·ra·geous /owt ráyjəss/ *adj* **1.** EXCESSIVE causing shock or indignation by exceeding the bounds of what is reasonable or expected ○ *outrageous prices* **2.** MORALLY SHOCKING violating accepted standards of decency or morality in a flagrant or shocking way ○ *It's absolutely outrageous for a judge to take bribes.* **3.** EXTRAORDINARY AND UNCONVENTIONAL extravagantly bold or unconventional, and likely to shock people ○ *She came in wearing the most outrageous hat.* **4.** VIOLENT OR CRUEL violent or unrestrained in mood or action —**out·ra·geous·ly** *adv* —**out·ra·geous·ness** *n*

~~**outragious**~~ incorrect spelling of **outrageous**

~~**outragous**~~ incorrect spelling of **outrageous**

out·range /owt ráynj/ (**-ranged, -rang·ing, -rang·es**) *vt* to have a greater range than something else of the same type

out·rank /owt rángk/ (**-ranked, -rank·ing, -ranks**) *vt* to have a higher rank or status than somebody else

ou·tré /oo tráy/ *adj* peculiarly or shockingly unusual [Early 18C. Via French < Old French, past participle of *outrer* (see OUTRAGE)]

out·reach *vt* /owt rēēch/ (**-reached, -reach·ing, -reach·es**) **1.** REACH FARTHER THAN SOMEBODY to reach or extend farther than somebody or something else **2.** EXCEED SOMETHING to exceed or go beyond a limit ■ *n* /ówt rēēch/ **1.** PROVISION OF COMMUNITY SERVICES the provision of information or services to groups in society who might otherwise be neglected ○ *an outreach program for people who cannot read* **2.** EXTENT OF REACH the length or extent of the reach of somebody or something ○ *the outreach of a communications network*

out·ride /owt rīd/ (**-rode** /-rṓd/, **-rid·den** /-rídd'n/, **-rid·ing, -rides**) *vt* **1.** to ride better, farther, or faster than somebody else **2.** to survive the violence of the wind and waves during a storm

out·rid·er /ówt rīdər/ *n* **1.** ESCORT a rider in front of or at the side of a carriage, motor vehicle, or race horse, who acts as an escort **2.** MOUNTED RANGE HAND a mounted cowboy or herdsman who rides the range watching over a herd or flock **3.** FORERUNNER somebody who precedes a group and acts as a scout

out·rig·ger /ówt rìggər/ *n* **1.** PART OF BOAT a beam or framework sticking out from the side of a boat, used to extend a rope or sail or as a brace for an oarlock **2.** FRAMEWORK ON CANOE a long float attached to a framework that projects from the side of a seagoing canoe to prevent it from capsizing **3.** KIND OF BOAT OR CANOE a boat or canoe fitted with an outrigger **4.** STRUCTURE ON AIRCRAFT a projection attached to an aircraft or other vehicle or machine to stabilize it or to support something [Mid-18C. Origin ?]

out·right *adv* /ówt rīt, òwt rīt/ **1.** CANDIDLY openly and without reservation ○ *I told him outright that he was making a big mistake.* **2.** WHOLLY completely, altogether, or as a whole in one transaction ○ *banned outright* ○ *bought the business outright* **3.** INSTANTLY immediately and finally ○ *They refused our offer outright.* ■ *adj* /ówt rīt/ **1.** TOTAL complete and utter ○ *an outright lie* **2.** CANDID open and without reservation ○ *greeted us with outright enthusiasm* **3.** WITHOUT QUALIFICATIONS without restrictions or limitations ○ *an outright gift* —**out·right·ly** *adv*

out·ri·val /owt rív'l/ (**-valed, -val·ing, -vals**) *vt* to surpass somebody or something

out·run /owt rún/ (**-ran** /-rán/, **-run, -run·ning, -runs**) *vt* **1.** RUN FASTER THAN SOMEBODY to run faster or farther than somebody else **2.** ESCAPE SOMEBODY to escape a pursuer by running or going faster than he, she, or it can ○ *outrun the bill collectors* ○ *The hare outran the wolf.* **3.** EXCEED SOMETHING to develop faster than or exceed something ○ *Demand for gasoline began to outrun supply.*

out·sell /owt sél/ (**-sold** /-sṓld/, **-sell·ing, -sells**) *vt* **1.** to be sold faster or in greater quantities than something else **2.** to sell more than another salesperson

out·set /ówt sèt/ *n* the beginning or initial stage of an activity

out·shine /owt shīn/ (**-shone** /-shṓn/ or **-shined, -shin·ing, -shines**) *v* **1.** *vt* SURPASS SOMEBODY OR SOMETHING to surpass somebody or something else, especially in terms of excellence or quality **2.** *vt* BE BRIGHTER THAN SOMETHING to shine brighter than something else **3.** *vi* PRODUCE LIGHT to give out light (*literary*)

out·shoot /owt sho͞ot/ (**-shot** /-shót/, **-shoot·ing, -shoots**) *vt* to shoot a weapon better than somebody else

out·side /owt sīd, ówt sīd/ CORE MEANING: a grammatical word indicating the outer surface or appearance of something ○ (noun) *Grill the chicken wings until the outsides are crisp.* ○ (adv) *The house still needs to be painted outside.*

1. *adv, prep, adj* BEYOND THE BOUNDARY OF SOMETHING located on or beyond the outer surface or edge of something ○ *standing outside the circle* **2.** *adv, prep, adj* OUT OF DOORS in the open air rather than inside a building ○ (adv) *We should head outside soon if we're going to start the barbecue.* ○ (prep) *I'll meet you outside the post office.* ○ (adj) *an outside toilet* **3.** *adv, prep, adj* BEYOND IMMEDIATE ENVIRONMENT happening, existing, or originating in places, people, or groups other than your own or those you are used to ○ (adj) *It was claimed that most of the substandard work had been done by outside contractors.* ○ (adv) *in the world outside* ○ (prep) *married outside her religion* **4.** *adj* SLIGHT slight or remote ○ *There's an outside chance we may still be able to get tickets.* **5.** *adj* MAXIMUM the most extreme possible or probable ○ *an outside estimate of three months to complete the job* **6.** *adj* AWAY FROM BATTER passing on the side of home plate opposite the batter in baseball or softball ○ *an outside pitch* **7.** *adj* FARTHEST FROM SIDE OF ROAD farthest from the side of a road or the center of a race track ○ *coming up fast in the outside lane* **8.** *prep* BEYOND SCOPE OF not included in the range or scope of something ○ *Such behavior is completely outside my comprehension.* **9.** *n* EXPOSED SURFACE the outer surface or appearance of something ○ *The outside of the house needs painting.* **10.** *n* EXISTENCE NOT IN INSTITUTION existence in the community and not in an institution such as prison or a psychiatric hospital ○ *We wondered what life was like on the outside.* **11.** *n* AREA FARTHEST FROM SIDE OF ROAD the part farthest from the side of a road or the center of a race track ○ *coming up fast on the outside* **12.** *n* HEAVILY POPULATED AREA OF CANADA the most populous areas of Canada and Alaska along the coasts or bordering the lower 48 states **13.** *adj* SPORTS **FARTHER FROM CENTER** in soccer, field hockey, and other sports, used to describe a position farther from the center of the field than another of the same name ○ *outside left* ◇ **at the outside** at the maximum ○ *It shouldn't last longer than three hours at the outside.* ◇ **outside of** other than the person or thing mentioned

out·side broad·cast *n UK* same as **remote** *n* (sense 3)

out·sid·er /owt sídər/ *n* **1.** somebody who is not part of a group or organization **2.** a competitor or candidate who is considered unlikely to win

out·sight /ówt sìt/ *n* the ability to take note of or judge external things [Early 17C. After INSIGHT]

out·size /owt síz, ówt sìz/ *n* an unusual size, especially one that is larger than usual ■ *adj also* **out·sized** much larger, heavier, or more extensive than is usual or expected ○ *an outsize ego*

out·skirts /ówt skùrts/ *npl* the areas at the edge of a town or city, farthest from the center

out·smart /owt smaárt/ (**-smart·ed, -smart·ing, -smarts**) *vt* to use cunning or cleverness to get an advantage over somebody

out·sold COMM past participle, past tense of **outsell**

out·sole /ówt sòl/ *n* the outer sole of a boot or shoe [Late 19C. After INSOLE]

out·source /ówt sàwrss/ (**-sourced, -sourc·ing, -sourc·es**) *vt* to buy labor or parts from a source outside a company or business rather than using the company's staff or plant —**out·sourc·er** *n* —**out·sourc·ing** *n*

out·spend /owt spénd/ (**-spent** /-spént/, **-spend·ing, -spends**) *vt* **1.** to spend more than somebody else **2.** to exceed fixed limits for something in spending ○ *outspent our budget*

out·spo·ken /owt spókən/ *adj* expressing opinions directly, frankly, and fearlessly —**out·spo·ken·ly** *adv* —**out·spo·ken·ness** *n*

out·spread /owt spréd/ *adj* **STRETCHED OUT** extended or spread out flat ■ *vt* (**-spread, -spread·ing, -spreads**) **EXTEND SOMETHING** to stretch out or extend something ■ *n* **ACT OF SPREADING OUT** the act or an example of extending outward

out·stand /owt stánd/ (**-stood** /-stood/, **-stand·ing, -stands**) *vi* to stand out or be prominent

out·stand·ing /owt stánding/ *adj* **1. CONSPICUOUSLY EXCELLENT** clearly of very high quality or clearly superior to others in the same group or category ○ *outstanding work* **2. NOT YET RESOLVED** not yet paid, resolved, or dealt with ○ *outstanding debts* **3. JUTTING OUT** jutting outward or upward **4.** FIN **PUBLICLY SOLD** publicly issued and sold as securities —**out·stand·ing·ly** *adv*

out·stare /owt stér/ (**-stared, -star·ing, -stares**) *vt* to make somebody look away or submit by staring hard

out·sta·tion /ówt stàysh'n/ *n* a post or station in a remote unsettled spot ■ *adv Malaysia* in, at, or to a place that is not where you usually live or work, often one that is in a more rural area

out·stay /owt stáy/ (**-stayed, -stay·ing, -stays**) *vt* **1.** to stay longer than other people or beyond a limit ○ *outstayed their welcome* **2.** to show greater endurance than somebody ○ *outstayed their rivals*

out·step /owt stép/ (**-stepped, -step·ping, -steps**) *vt* same as **overstep** (*literary*)

out·stood past participle, past tense of **outstand**

out·stretch /owt stréch/ (**-stretched, -stretch·ing, -stretch·es**) *vt* to hold out or extend something

out·strip /owt stríp/ (**-stripped, -strip·ping, -strips**) *vt* **1.** to achieve more or go faster than somebody, especially a competitor **2.** to be greater than something ○ *Demand for their products has already outstripped supply.*

out·ta /ówttə/, **out·a** *prep* out of (*slang*) ○ *I'm outta here.* [Mid-20C. Representing a pronunciation]

out·take /ówt tàyk/ *n* **1.** a recorded scene or sequence that is not included in the final version of a movie or television program, usually because it contains mistakes ○ *The outtakes were funnier than the movie itself.* **2.** a recording not used in the final version of an album

out-there *adj US* outgoing and positively involved with life and the world (*slang*)

out·thrust /owt thrúst/ *adj* outstretched, or extending out beyond something ○ *the dog's outthrust paw* ■ *n* something that projects or extends outward

out-tray *n UK* same as **out-box**

out·turn /ówt tùrn/ *n* the amount produced during a particular period [Late 18C. < *turn out*]

out·ward /ówtwərd/ CORE MEANING: a grammatical word indicating that something is outside or on or toward the exterior of something, or relates to the exterior of something ○ *A coconut shell is rough and hairy on the outward side.*

1. *adj* **VISIBLE** clearly observable ○ *She gave no outward indication that she was upset.* **2.** *adj* **RELATING TO PHYSICAL BODY** relating to the physical body rather than the mind or spirit ○ *His outward appearance reflected his inner turmoil.* **3.** *adj* **APPARENT** apparent or superficial ○ *can't judge by outward appearances* **4.** *adj* **OUTBOUND** heading away from a place **5.** *adv also* **out·wards** /-wərdz/ **TOWARD OUTSIDE** toward the outside and away from the inside or middle **6.** *n* **MATERIAL WORLD** the reality of the external world (*literary*) —**out·ward·ness** *n*

out·ward-bound *adj* making an outgoing journey or passage

out·ward·ly /ówtwərdlee/ *adv* **1.** in appearance rather than in reality **2.** on or toward the outside

out·wards *adv* same as **outward** (sense 5)

out·wash /ówt wòsh, -wàwsh/ *n* sand and gravel deposited by streams that are flowing away from a glacier

out·weigh /owt wáy/ (**-weighed, -weigh·ing, -weighs**) *vt* **1.** to be more important or valuable than something else **2.** to weigh more than somebody or something else

out·wit /owt wít/ (**-wit·ted, -wit·ting, -wits**) *vt* to use cunning or trickery to get an advantage over somebody

out·wore past tense of **outwear**

out·work *vt* /owt wúrk/ (**-worked, -work·ing, -works**) to work harder or faster than somebody ■ *n* /ówt wùrk/ a trench or fortification built beyond the main line of defense

out·worn /owt wáwrn/ *adj* outdated or no longer useful ■ past participle of **outwear**

ou·zel /ooz'l/ *n* a small bird of the thrush family with dark feathers and a white band across its throat. Native to: Europe. Latin name: *Turdus torquatus*. [Old English *ōsle* "blackbird" < Indo-European]

ou·zo /oozō/ *n* a colorless aniseed-flavored Greek alcoholic drink flavored with anise [Late 19C. < modern Greek]

o·va ANAT plural of **ovum**

o·val /óv'l/ *adj* **EGG-SHAPED** shaped like an egg or a flattened circle ■ *n* **1. FLATTENED CIRCLE** a two-dimensional shape like a stretched circle with slightly longer flatter sides **2. EGG SHAPE** something shaped like an egg or a flattened circle **3. TRACK** a racetrack in the shape of an oval [Late 16C. < medieval Latin *ovalis* < Latin *ovum* "egg"] —**o·val·ly** *adv* —**o·val·ness** *n*

ov·al·bu·min /òvvəl byoomən, òvəl-/ *n* the main crystalline protein or albumin found in egg whites [Mid-19C. < Latin *ovi albumen* "white of egg" < *ovum* "egg" + *albumen* (see ALBUMEN)]

O·val Of·fice *n* **1.** an oval-shaped room in the White House that is the private office used by the president of the United States **2.** the power and authority of the president of the United States

o·val win·dow *n* a membranous opening between the middle ear and the inner ear that transmits sound vibrations

O·vam·bo /ō vaámbō/ (*plural same* or **-bos**) *n* **1.** a member of a people who live in parts of southern Africa, especially in Angola and Namibia **2.** the Bantu language of the Ovambo people. Native speakers: 700,000. [Mid-19C. < Bantu, "people of leisure"] —**O·vam·bo** *adj*

o·var·i·ec·to·my /ō vèrree éktəmee/ (*plural* **-mies**) *n* the surgical removal of one or both ovaries

o·var·i·ot·o·my /ō vèrree óttəmee/ (*plural* **-mies**) *n* **1.** a surgical incision into an ovary **2.** SURG same as **ovariectomy**

o·va·ri·tis /ōvə rítiss/ *n* same as **oophoritis**

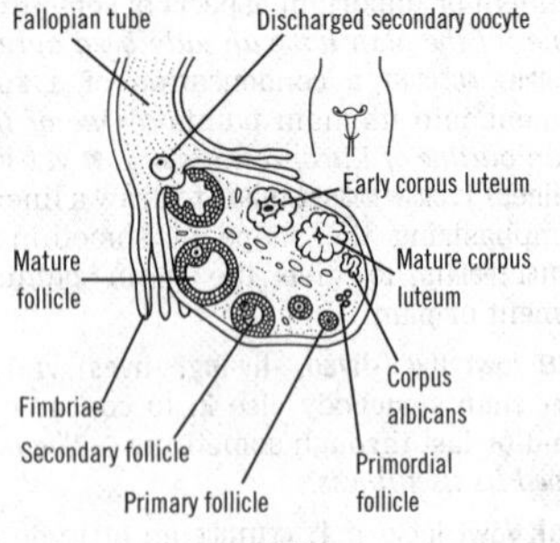

ovary

o·va·ry /óvəree/ (*plural* **-ries**) *n* **1.** either of the two female reproductive organs that produce eggs and, in vertebrates, also produce the sex hormones estrogen and progesterone **2.** the lower part of a pistil that bears ovules and ripens into a fruit [Mid-17C. < modern Latin *ovarium* < Latin *ovum* "egg"] —**o·var·i·an** /ō vérree ən/ *adj*

o·vate /ō vàyt/ *adj* **1.** shaped like an egg **2.** describes a leaf or petal that is broad and rounded at the base and tapers towards the tip [Mid-18C. < Latin *ovatus* "egg-shaped" < *ovum* "egg"] —**o·vate·ly** *adv*

o·va·tion /ō váysh'n/ *n* **1.** enthusiastic applause or cheering, especially from a crowd or large group of people **2.** an ancient Roman victory ceremony for a returning military hero [Mid-16C. Via Latin *ovation-* < *ovare* "rejoice"; from an imitation of the sound of exulting] —**o·va·tion·al** *adj*

ov·en /úvvən/ *n* a compartment warmed by a heat source and used for baking, roasting, or drying [Old English *ofen* < Indo-European, "stove"]

ov·en·bird /úvvən bùrd/ *n* **1.** a warbler with a shrill call that builds a dome-shaped nest on the ground. Native to: North America. Latin name: *Seiurus aurocapillus*. **2.** a small brown bird that builds a dome-shaped nest from clay and dried leaves. Native to: South America. Genus: *Furnarius*. [Early 19C. < the shape of the birds' nests]

ov·en mitt *n* a padded hand covering used as protection when putting hot dishes into, and taking them out of, an oven

ov·en·proof /úvvən proof/ *adj* capable of being used in an oven without being damaged by the heat

ov·en·ware /úvvən wèr/ *n* heat-resistant dishes that can be used for baking or roasting as well as for serving

o·ver /óvər/ (**o·vered, o·ver·ing, o·vers**, *plural* **o·vers**) CORE MEANING: a grammatical word used to indicate a position directly above something, either resting on the top of something, or above the upper surface of something with a space in between ○ (prep) *a framed portrait over the fireplace* ○ (prep) *He wore a red flannel shirt over a T-shirt.* ○ (prep) *Julia was bent over the sink washing glasses.* ○ (adv) *flocks of geese flying over* ○ (adv) *Heat the milk and pour it over.*

1. *prep, adv* **ON OR TO OTHER SIDE OF** positioned on or moving to the other side of something such as a barrier, obstacle, or area of land ○ (prep) *To see the cathedral you need to cross over the river.* ○ (adv) *He climbed over into the next field.* **2.** *prep, adv* **THROUGHOUT** throughout the whole extent of ○ (prep) *traveling all over Europe* ○ (prep) *In the past few years, fifties diners have sprung up all over town.* ○ (adv) *People are the same the world over.* **3.** *prep, adv* **MORE THAN** more than a particular amount, measurement, or age ○ (prep) *go over your quota* ○ (adv) *people 30 and over* **4.** *adv* **ACROSS INTERVENING SPACE** positioned at, or moving to, a point on the other side of an intervening space ○ *She reached over and turned off the TV.* ○ *Jim sent a couple of guys over to help out.* **5.** *adv* **SO AS TO FALL** so as to change position, especially so as to become horizontal after being upright ○ *knocked over a pile of books* ○ *He rolled over and turned out the light.* **6.** *adv* REMAINING remaining or surplus after what was needed has been used ○ *There was plenty of food left over from the party.* **7.** *adv* AGAIN doing something again, or again from the beginning ○ *If you make a mistake you'll just have to start over.* **8.** *prep* BY MEANS OF by means of a device for communication such as a radio or telephone ○ *talk over the phone* **9.** *prep* ABOUT indicates the cause or the subject of something ○ *grieving over the loss of her husband* **10.** *prep* AFFECTING indicates what is affected, influenced, or controlled by somebody or something ○ *exercising more control over file access* **11.** *prep* DURING during or throughout a period of time or an occasion ○ *We can discuss this over lunch.* **12.** *prep* RECOVERED FROM indicates something, e.g., an illness, that somebody has recovered from ○ *get over a virus* **13.** *prep* IN PREFERENCE TO in preference to something else ○ *I'd choose steak over fish every time.* **14.** *adj* FINISHED finished, or no longer in progress ○ *When all this is over I'm going on vacation.* **15.** *interj* MEDIA INDICATING SOMEBODY'S TURN TO SPEAK used when communicating via radio to indicate that somebody has finished talking and it is the other person's turn to speak **16.** *n* SHOT shot that hits or explodes beyond its target **17.** *n US* GAMBLING SCORE ABOVE PARTICULAR NUMBER IN WAGER in a wager, the score above a particular number of points, or an amount above a particular total ○ *bet the over in the playoff* **18.** *vt* PASS ABOVE to pass above and across something **19.** *n* CRICKET BOWLING OF SIX BALLS in cricket, a series of six correctly bowled balls, or the play during this **20.** *vt* BUSINESS CARRY AGENDA ITEM FORWARD to postpone dealing with an item on an agenda until a later meeting [Old English *ofer* < Indo-European] ◇ **over again** once more ◇ **over against** in contrast with, or in opposition to ◇ **over and above** in addition to or in excess of something ○ *benefits over and above the basic salary* ◇ **over and done with** completely finished or at an end ◇ **over and over** repeatedly, or a great deal

over- *prefix* **1.** excessively ○ *overconfident* ○ *overact* **2.** extremely ○ *overjoyed* **3.** going over something, extra ○ *overshoe* ○ *overtime* **4.** above, over, on top ○ *overcast* ○ *overlap* **5.** so as to turn over, completely ○ *overthrow* [< OVER]

o·ver·a·bun·dance *n*
o·ver·a·bun·dant *adj*
o·ver·a·bun·dant·ly *adv*
o·ver·ac·cen·tu·ate *vt*
o·ver·ag·gres·sive *adj*
o·ver·ag·gres·sive·ly *adv*
o·ver·ag·gres·sive·ness *n*
o·ver·am·bi·tion *n*
o·ver·am·bi·tious *adj*
o·ver·am·bi·tious·ly *adv*
o·ver·am·bi·tious·ness *n*
o·ver·an·al·y·sis *n*
o·ver·an·al·y·ti·cal *adj*
o·ver·an·a·lyze *vt*
o·ver·anx·i·e·ty *n*
o·ver·anx·ious *adj*
o·ver·anx·ious·ly *adv*
o·ver·anx·ious·ness *n*
o·ver·as·ser·tive *adj*
o·ver·as·ser·tive·ness *n*
o·ver·as·sess·ment *n*
o·ver·at·ten·tion *n*
o·ver·boil *vt*
o·ver·bold *adj*
o·ver·bold·ly *adv*
o·ver·bold·ness *n*
o·ver·bus·y *adj*
o·ver·buy *vti*
o·ver·cap·i·tal·i·za·tion *n*
o·ver·cap·i·tal·ize *vt*
o·ver·care·ful *adj*
o·ver·care·ful·ly *adv*
o·ver·cau·tion *n*
o·ver·cau·tious *adj*
o·ver·cau·tious·ly *adv*
o·ver·cau·tious·ness *n*
o·ver·cen·tral·i·za·tion *n*
o·ver·cen·tral·ize *vt*
o·ver·civ·il *adj*
o·ver·civ·i·lized *adj*
o·ver·clean *adj*
o·ver·com·mon *adj*
o·ver·com·pla·cen·cy *n*
o·ver·com·pla·cent *adj*
o·ver·com·plex *adj*
o·ver·com·plex·i·ty *n*
o·ver·com·pli·cate *vt*
o·ver·com·pli·cat·ed *adj*
o·ver·con·cern *n*
o·ver·con·cerned *adj*
o·ver·con·fi·dence *n*
o·ver·con·fi·dent *adj*
o·ver·con·fi·dent·ly *adv*
o·ver·con·sci·en·tious *adj*
o·ver·con·scious *adj*
o·ver·con·ser·va·tive *adj*
o·ver·con·sump·tion *n*
o·ver·cook *vt*
o·ver·crit·i·cal *adj*
o·ver·crit·i·cal·ly *adv*
o·ver·crit·i·cal·ness *n*
o·ver·cul·ti·vat·ed *adj*
o·ver·cu·ri·os·i·ty *n*
o·ver·cu·ri·ous *adj*
o·ver·dec·o·rate *vt*
o·ver·dec·o·ra·tive *adj*
o·ver·del·i·ca·cy *n*
o·ver·del·i·cate *adj*
o·ver·de·mand·ing *adj*
o·ver·de·pen·dence *n*
o·ver·de·pen·dent *adj*
o·ver·de·vel·op *vt*
o·ver·de·vel·oped *adj*
o·ver·de·vel·op·ment *n*
o·ver·dra·mat·ic *adj*
o·ver·dra·mat·i·cal·ly *adv*
o·ver·dress *vti, n*
o·ver·dressed *adj*
o·ver·drink *vi*
o·ver·drink·ing *n*
o·ver·dry *adj*
o·ver·ea·ger *adj*
o·ver·ea·ger·ly *adv*
o·ver·ea·ger·ness *n*
o·ver·ear·nest *adj*
o·ver·ed·u·cate *vt*
o·ver·ed·u·cat·ed *adj*
o·ver·ef·fu·sive *adj*
o·ver·e·lab·o·rate *adj, vti*
o·ver·e·lab·o·rate·ly *adv*
o·ver·e·lab·o·rate·ness *n*
o·ver·e·lab·o·ra·tion *n*
o·ver·em·bel·lish *vt*
o·ver·e·mo·tion·al *adj*
o·ver·e·mo·tion·al·ly *adv*
o·ver·en·large·ment *n*
o·ver·e·quipped *adj*
o·ver·ex·ag·ger·ate *vti*
o·ver·ex·ag·ger·a·tion *n*
o·ver·ex·cit·a·ble *adj*
o·ver·ex·cite *vt*
o·ver·ex·cit·ed *adj*
o·ver·ex·cite·ment *n*
o·ver·ex·er·cise *vt*
o·ver·ex·ert *vt*
o·ver·ex·er·tion *n*
o·ver·ex·pand *vti*
o·ver·ex·pan·sion *n*
o·ver·ex·pec·ta·tion *n*
o·ver·ex·plain *vt*
o·ver·ex·trav·a·gant *adj*
o·ver·far *adj, adv*
o·ver·fa·tigue *n*
o·ver·fed *adj*
o·ver·feed *vti*
o·ver·fill *vti*
o·ver·fish *vti*
o·ver·fond *adj*
o·ver·fond·ly *adv*
o·ver·fond·ness *n*
o·ver·full *adj*
o·ver·gar·ment *n*
o·ver·gen·er·ous *adj*
o·ver·graze *vt*
o·ver·hard *adj*
o·ver·har·vest *vt*
o·ver·hast·y *adj*
o·ver·hunt *vti*
o·ver·hy·drate *vt*
o·ver·hy·dra·tion *n*
o·ver·hype *vt*
o·ver·i·mag·i·na·tive *adj*
o·ver·i·mag·i·na·tive·ly *adv*
o·ver·im·press *vt*
o·ver·in·flate *vt*
o·ver·in·flat·ed *adj*
o·ver·in·gen·ious *adj*
o·ver·in·tel·lec·tu·al·ize *vi*
o·ver·in·tense *adj*
o·ver·in·ter·est *n*
o·ver·in·vest·ment *n*
o·ver·lad·en *adj*
o·ver·large *adj*
o·ver·loud *adj*
o·ver·man·y *adj*
o·ver·ma·ture *adj*
o·ver·ma·tured *adj*
o·ver·med·i·cate *vt*
o·ver·med·i·ca·tion *n*
o·ver·mod·est *adj*
o·ver·op·in·ion·at·ed *adj*
o·ver·op·ti·mism *n*
o·ver·op·ti·mis·tic *adj*
o·ver·op·ti·mis·ti·cal·ly *adv*
o·ver·or·ga·ni·za·tion *n*
o·ver·or·ga·nize *vt*
o·ver·or·ga·nized *adj*
o·ver·pay *vti*
o·ver·pay·ment *n*
o·ver·peo·pled *adj*
o·ver·pes·si·mism *n*
o·ver·pes·si·mis·tic *adj*
o·ver·pow·er·ful *adj*
o·ver·praise *vt*
o·ver·pre·scribe *vti*
o·ver·pre·scrip·tion *n*
o·ver·pres·sur·i·za·tion *n*
o·ver·pres·sur·ize *vt*
o·ver·price *vt*
o·ver·priv·i·leged *adj*
o·ver·prize *vt*
o·ver·pro·duce *vti*
o·ver·pro·duc·tion *n*
o·ver·pro·tect *vt*
o·ver·pro·tec·tion *n*
o·ver·pro·tec·tive *adj*
o·ver·pro·tec·tive·ly *adv*
o·ver·pro·tec·tive·ness *n*
o·ver·pub·li·cize *vt*
o·ver·re·fine *vti*
o·ver·re·fined *adj*
o·ver·re·fine·ment *n*
o·ver·reg·u·late *vt*
o·ver·reg·u·la·tion *n*
o·ver·re·li·ance *n*
o·ver·re·li·ant *adj*
o·ver·rep·re·sen·ta·tion *n*
o·ver·rep·re·sent·ed *adj*
o·ver·rich *adj*
o·ver·roast *vt*
o·ver·scru·pu·lous *adj*
o·ver·scru·pu·lous·ly *adv*
o·ver·scru·pu·lous·ness *n*
o·ver·se·cre·tion *n*
o·ver·sen·si·tive *adj*
o·ver·sen·si·tive·ly *adv*
o·ver·sen·si·tive·ness *n*
o·ver·sen·si·tiv·i·ty *n*
o·ver·sen·ti·men·tal *adj*
o·ver·sen·ti·men·tal·i·ty *n*
o·ver·smart *adj*
o·ver·so·phis·ti·cat·ed *adj*
o·ver·so·phis·ti·ca·tion *n*
o·ver·spe·cial·i·za·tion *n*
o·ver·spe·cial·ize *vi*
o·ver·spe·cial·ized *adj*
o·ver·stim·u·late *vt*
o·ver·stim·u·la·tion *n*
o·ver·strain *vti*
o·ver·stress *vt, n*
o·ver·strict *adj*
o·ver·stuff *vt*
o·ver·sub·tle *adj*
o·ver·sup·plied *adj*
o·ver·sup·ply *n, vti*
o·ver·sus·cep·ti·ble *adj*
o·ver·sweet *adj*
o·ver·thin *adj*
o·ver·tire *vt*
o·ver·tired *adj*
o·ver·tired·ness *n*
o·ver·top *vt*
o·ver·train *vti*
o·ver·use *n, vt*
o·ver·val·u·a·tion *n*
o·ver·val·ue *vt*
o·ver·wa·ter *vt*
o·ver·wea·ry *adj, vt*
o·ver·wind *vt*
o·ver·zeal·ous *adj*
o·ver·zea·lous·ly *adv*
o·ver·zeal·ous·ness *n*

o·ver·a·chieve /ṑvər ə chéev/ (**-chieved, -chiev·ing, -chieves**) *vi* **1.** to perform better or be more successful than expected **2.** to be excessively or unhealthily dedicated to achieving success —**o·ver·a·chieve·ment** *n* —**o·ver·a·chiev·er** *n*

o·ver·act /ṑvər ákt/ (**-act·ed, -act·ing, -acts**) *vti* to exaggerate movements or emotions, especially when acting in a performance —**o·ver·ac·tion** *n*

o·ver·ac·tive /ṑvər áktiv/ *adj* excessively or unusually active —**o·ver·ac·tiv·i·ty** /-ak tívvətee/ *n*

o·ver·age[1] /ṑvər áyj/ *adj* **1.** older than the age fixed as a standard or considered appropriate for an activity **2.** of too great an age to be useful (*offensive if used of people*) [Late 19C. < OVER prep. + AGE]

o·ver·age[2] /ṑvərij/ *n* money, goods, or something else in excess of what is proper or shown in the records [Mid-20C. < OVER adj + -AGE]

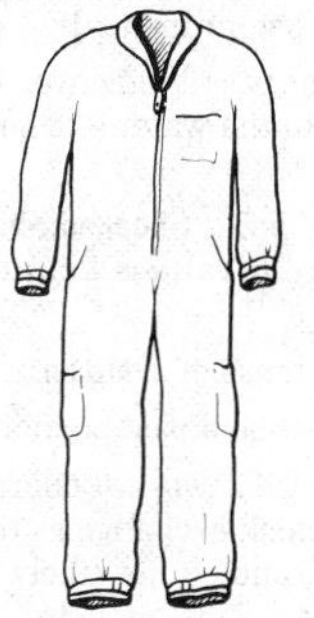
overalls (sense 1)

o·ver·all *adj* /ṑvər àwl/, *adv* /ṑvər áwl/ **1.** END TO END from one extremity to the other **2.** TOTAL including everything ■ *adj* /ṑvər àwl/ GENERAL considered as a whole ○ *an overall impression* ■ *adv* /ṑvər áwl/ **1.** GENERALLY in general ○ *Overall, we were disappointed with the results.* **2.** CONSIDERING EVERYTHING taking everything into account ○ *The frozen foods side of the business overall saw a loss.* ■ *n* /ṑvər àwl/ *UK* CLOTHING PROTECTIVE GARMENT a loose-fitting lightweight piece of clothing like a coat, worn over ordinary clothes to protect them ■ **o·ver·alls** *npl* **1.** ONE-PIECE PROTECTIVE GARMENT a one-piece garment with long sleeves and pants worn to protect a worker's clothes from dirt or wear **2.** WORK PANTS WITH BIB loose-fitting pants that have a bib and shoulder straps, originally worn over regular clothing as a protection from dirt and wear

o·ver·arch /ṑvər áarch/ (**-arched, -arch·ing, -arch·es**) *vt* to form an arch over something

o·ver·arch·ing /ṑvər áarching/ *adj* embracing or overshadowing everything —**o·ver·arch·ing·ly** *adv*

o·ver·arm /ṑvər àarm/ *adj* **1.** thrown or done with the arm raised above the shoulder and rotating forward **2.** beginning a stroke in swimming with the arm raised above the shoulder and rotating forward ■ *adv UK* same as **overhand**

o·ver·ate past tense of **overeat**

o·ver·awe /ṑvər áw/ (**-awed, -aw·ing, -awes**) *vt* to make somebody feel subdued or inhibited by inspiring respect and some fear

o·ver·bal·ance /ṑvər bálləns/ *v* (**-anced, -anc·ing, -anc·es**) **1.** *vt* EXCEED SOMETHING IN IMPORTANCE to have greater weight or importance than something else **2.** *vti* LOSE BALANCE to lose balance, or make somebody or something lose balance ■ *n* PREPONDERANCE an excess of an amount, quantity, or weight

o·ver·bear /ṑvər bér/ (**-bore** /-báwr/, **-borne** /-báwrn/ or **-born, -bear·ing, -bears**) *v* **1.** *vt* OVERPOWER SOMEBODY to defeat somebody by having superior weight or strength **2.** *vt* SURPASS SOMETHING IN IMPORTANCE to be more important than other considerations **3.** *vi* PRODUCE TOO MUCH to produce too much fruit or too many offspring

o·ver·bear·ing /ṑvər bérring/ *adj* arrogant and tending to order people around —**o·ver·bear·ing·ly** *adv* —**o·ver·bear·ing·ness** *n*

o·ver·bid /ṑvər bíd/ *v* (**-bid, -bid·den** /ṑvər bídd'n/ or **-bid, -bid·ding, -bids**) **1.** *vti* BID MORE THAN WORTH OF SOMETHING to bid more than something is worth **2.** *vi* CARDS BID FOR TOO MANY TRICKS in bridge, to bid for more tricks than can be won ■ *n* HIGHER BID a bid that is higher than somebody else's bid —**o·ver·bid·der** *n*

o·ver·bite /ṑvər bìt/ *n* a faulty alignment of the teeth in which the upper front teeth project too far over the lower teeth when the mouth is closed

o·ver·blan·ket /ṑvər blàngkət/ *n UK* same as **electric blanket**

o·ver·blouse /ṑvər blòwss, -blòwz/ *n* a blouse designed to be worn outside the waistband of a skirt or slacks

o·ver·blow /òvər bló/ (**-blew** /-blóo/, **-blown** /-blón/, **-blow·ing, -blows**) *vti* to blow a wind instrument with extra force so as to produce an overtone

o·ver·blown /òvər blón/ *adj* 1. EXAGGERATED done to excess and seeming exaggerated ○ *overblown stories that are barely credible* 2. PRETENTIOUS showing pomposity or pretentiousness ○ *His style of writing is overblown and excessively wordy.* 3. PAST BEST past full bloom and beginning to die ○ *an overblown rose*

o·ver·board /òvər bàwrd/ *adv* over the side of a ship or boat and into the water [Old English *ofer bord* "over the side"]

o·ver·book /òvər bóok/ (**-booked, -book·ing, -books**) *vti* to take more reservations than there are seats or places available

o·ver·bore past tense of **overbear**

o·ver·borne, o·ver·born past participle of **overbear**

o·ver·bought /òvər báwt/ *adj* characterized by high prices on the stock exchange as the result of recent heavy trading, and so not likely to rise further in the near future

o·ver·build /òvər bíld/ (**-built** /-bílt/, **-build·ing, -builds**) *v* 1. *vti* BUILD TOO MUCH to construct more buildings than are necessary or desirable in an area 2. *vti* BUILD OVERAMBITIOUSLY to construct something that is too large or elaborate 3. *vt* BUILD ON SOMETHING ELSE to build something on top of a particular place or thing

o·ver·bur·den *vt* /òvər búrd'n/ (**-dened, -den·ing, -dens**) OVERLOAD to place too much weight or worry on somebody or something ○ *overburdened with debt* ■ *n* /óvər bùrd'n/ 1. EXCESSIVE BURDEN an excessive or onerous burden 2. SOIL LAYERED OVER ROCK soil or other material layered over bedrock or over a geologic deposit

o·ver·call /òvər káwl/ (**-called, -call·ing, -calls**) *vti* in bridge, to bid higher than an opponent before a partner has made a positive bid —**o·ver·call** *n*

o·ver·came past tense of **overcome**

o·ver·ca·pac·i·ty /òvər kə pássətee/ *n* an ability to produce goods or provide services that exceeds demand

o·ver·cast *adj* /òvər kàst/ 1. CLOUDY very cloudy, with no sun showing 2. SEWN WITH LONG STITCHES sewn along the edge with long loose stitches that prevent a piece of fabric from raveling ■ *n* /óvər kàst/ 1. HEAVY CLOUD COVER a heavy covering of clouds in the sky 2. MIN EXTRACT MINE ARCH an arch in a mine supporting a passage above it ■ *v* /òvər kást/ (**-cast·ed, -cast·ing, -casts**) 1. *vi* BECOME CLOUDY to become cloudy or dull 2. *vt* SECURE EDGE WITH LOOSE STITCHES to sew the edge of a piece of fabric with an overcast stitch

o·ver·cast·ing /óvər kàsting/ *n* long slanting stitches sewn loosely across the edge of a piece of fabric to prevent it from raveling

o·ver·cast stitch *n* a stitch used to bind a raw edge or to form a smooth raised line, e.g., in monogramming

o·ver·charge *v* /òvər cháarj/ (**-charged, -charg·ing, -charg·es**) 1. *vti* CHARGE SOMEBODY TOO MUCH to charge somebody too much money for something 2. *vt* PUT EXCESSIVE POWER INTO BATTERY to charge a battery or circuit with more electricity than it can safely hold 3. *vt* OVERFILL OR OVERLOAD SOMETHING to fill or load something with more than it can hold or bear 4. *vt* EXAGGERATE SOMETHING to make something seem greater or more important than it actually is (*literary*) ■ *n* /óvər chàarj/ 1. EXCESSIVE CHARGE an excessively high charge for something 2. ACT OF CHARGING TOO MUCH an act of charging too much for something

o·ver·class /óvər klàss/ *n* a nation's elite governing or ruling class

o·ver·cloud /òvər klówd/ (**-cloud·ed, -cloud·ing, -clouds**) *vti* 1. to cover something with clouds, or become covered with clouds 2. to become dim and gloomy, or make something become dim and gloomy (*formal*)

o·ver·coat /óvər kòt/ *n* 1. a heavy coat worn over other outer clothes 2. *also* **o·ver·coat·ing** /-kòting/ an additional protective layer of something such as paint or varnish on top of a treated surface

o·ver·come /òvər kúm/ (**-came** /-káym/, **-come, -com·ing, -comes**) *v* 1. *vt* CONQUER PROBLEM to struggle successfully against a difficulty or disadvantage 2. *vt* MAKE SOMEBODY HELPLESS to make somebody incapacitated or helpless, or break down somebody's normal self-control (*usually passive*) 3. *vti* DEFEAT SOMEBODY to defeat somebody or something, especially in a conflict or competition 4. *vi* WIN DESPITE OBSTACLES to win or be successful, especially in spite of obstacles

SYNONYMS See *defeat.*

o·ver·com·mit /òvər kə mít/ (**-mit·ted, -mit·ting, -mits**) *vti* to undertake more than can be accomplished, or make somebody or yourself do this (*often passive*) —**o·ver·com·mit·ment** *n*

o·ver·com·pen·sate /òvər kómpən sàyt/ (**-sat·ed, -sat·ing, -sates**) *vti* 1. to try too hard to make up for a disadvantage or shortcoming and fall into a fault of another kind 2. to pay somebody too much in recompense or compensation for something done —**o·ver·com·pen·sa·tion** /òvər kòmpən sáysh'n/ *n* —**o·ver·com·pen·sa·to·ry** /òvər kəm pénssə tàwree/ *adj*

o·ver·cor·rect /òvər kə rékt/ *vti* (**-rect·ed, -rect·ing, -rects**) to do too much when trying to correct a mistake or fault, usually so that a further mistake is made ■ *adj* excessively exact or proper

o·ver·cor·rec·tion /òvər kə réksh'n/ *n* 1. LING same as **hypercorrection** 2. the fact of overcorrecting a mistake or fault

o·ver·crop /òvər króp/ (**-cropped, -crop·ping, -crops**) *vt* to make soil infertile by removing its nutrients through continuous cultivation

o·ver·crowd /òvər krówd/ (**-crowd·ed, -crowd·ing, -crowds**) *vt* to put more people or things into an area than it is comfortably able to hold —**o·ver·crowd·ed** *adj* —**o·ver·crowd·ing** *n*

o·ver·do /òvər dóo/ (**-did** /-díd/, **-done** /-dún/, **-do·ing, -does** /-dúz/) *vt* 1. DO SOMETHING TO EXCESS to do something too much, often with a harmful effect 2. SPOIL EFFECT BY EXAGGERATION to spoil the effect of something by exaggerating it ○ *You really overdid the sympathetic friend act on that occasion.* 3. OVERCOOK SOMETHING to cook food for too long —**o·ver·do·er** *n* ◇ **overdo it** 1. to work too hard and tire yourself 2. to do something to excess

o·ver·dog /óvər dàwg, -dòg/ *n US* a contestant or competitor who is favored, or somebody who is powerful or commanding (*humorous*) [Early 20C. < After UNDERDOG]

o·ver·dose *n* /óvər dòss/ DANGEROUS AMOUNT OF DRUG a dangerously large dose of a drug, especially a narcotic, causing hospitalization or death ■ *v* /òvər dóss/ (**-dosed, -dos·ing, -dos·es**) 1. *vi* TAKE OVERDOSE to take an overdose of a drug 2. *vt* GIVE SOMEBODY OVERDOSE to give somebody an overdose of a drug 3. *vi* TAKE TOO MUCH to consume or experience an excessive amount of something (*informal*) ○ *had overdosed on soap operas*

o·ver·draft /óvər dràft/ *n* 1. AMOUNT OWED TO BANK the amount that an account holder owes a bank because he or she has withdrawn or debited from the account more than has been credited to it 2. BORROWING LIMIT a limit up to which an account holder may borrow from a bank when there are no funds in his or her checking account 3. *also* **o·ver·draught** AIR CURRENT OVER FIRE a current of air passed over a fire, e.g., in a furnace or kiln

o·ver·dra·ma·tize /òvər drámmə tìz, -dráamə-/ (**-tized, -tiz·ing, -tiz·es**) *vti* to behave, or treat something, in an excessively dramatic way, e.g., by exaggerating feelings or the gravity of a situation

o·ver·draught another spelling of **overdraft** (sense 3)

o·ver·draw /òvər dráw/ (**-drew** /-dróo/, **-drawn** /-dráwn/, **-draw·ing, -draws**) *v* 1. *vti* WITHDRAW TOO MUCH FROM BANK ACCOUNT to withdraw or have debited more money from a bank account than it has credited to it, so that money is owed to the bank 2. *vt* EXAGGERATE SOMETHING to exaggerate in describing or telling about something 3. *vti* PULL BOW TOO TIGHT in archery, to pull a bow too tight

o·ver·drawn /òvər dráwn/ *adj* 1. owing money to a bank because an account has had more money withdrawn or debited from it than credited to it 2. showing exaggeration in the description of something

o·ver·drew past tense of **overdraw**

o·ver·drive *n* /óvər drìv/ 1. HIGHEST ENGINE GEAR the highest gear in the engine of a motor vehicle that is used at high speeds for fuel economy and to save engine wear 2. EXTRA HARD LEVEL OF ACTIVITY a particularly intense and productive mode of activity, usually possible only for short periods (*informal*) ○ *Production has gone into overdrive.* ■ *vt* /òvər drív/ (**-drove** /-dróv/, **-driv·en** /-drívvən/, **-driv·ing, -drives**) 1. DRIVE SOMEBODY TOO HARD to drive somebody, something, or yourself too hard 2. INCREASE ELECTRIC CURRENT TO to boost the supply of electrical current to a piece of electrical or electronic equipment beyond the recommended safe operating levels 3. AUTOMOT NOT ACCOUNT FOR DRIVING CONDITIONS to go beyond the level of safe usage recommended for a piece of equipment ○ *was overdriving his headlights when he hit the other car*

o·ver·dub /òvər dùb/ *vti* (**-dubbed, -dub·bing, -dubs**) to add supplementary sound or music to a recording ■ *n* a supplementary layer of sound or music added onto a recording

o·ver·due /òvər dóo/ *adj* late or after the scheduled time, especially in arriving, occurring, or being paid ○ *The library said the books were overdue.*

o·ver·dye /òvər dí/ (**-dyed, -dy·ing, -dyes**) *vt* 1. to use too much dye on something 2. to dye a fabric with another color over the original one

o·ver·eat /òvər éet/ (**-ate** /-áyt/, **-eat·en** /-éet'n/, **-eat·ing, -eats**) *vi* to eat too much food, especially habitually —**o·ver·eat·er** *n* —**o·ver·eat·ing** *n*

o·ver·em·pha·size /òvər émfə sìz/ (**-sized, -siz·ing, -siz·es**) *vt* to give something too much importance, attention, or force —**o·ver·em·pha·sis** *n*

o·ver·en·thu·si·asm /òvər in thóozee azzəm, -en-/ *n* more enthusiasm than is thought usual or appropriate —**o·ver·en·thu·si·as·tic** /-thoozee ástik/ *adj*

o·ver·es·ti·mate *vt* /òvər éstə màyt/ (**-mat·ed, -mat·ing, -mates**) 1. GIVE EXCESSIVE MERIT OR IMPORTANCE TO to judge somebody or something to be better, greater, or more important than he, she, or it actually is 2. CALCULATE SOMETHING TOO HIGHLY to calculate the amount, value, or quantity of something at too high a level ■ *n* /òvər éstəmət/ EXCESSIVELY HIGH ESTIMATE an estimate that is too high —**o·ver·es·ti·ma·tion** /-èstə máysh'n/ *n*

o·ver·ex·pose /òvər ik spóz/ (**-posed, -pos·ing, -pos·es**) *vt* 1. to allow somebody, or expose somebody to, too much of something, especially to allow somebody to appear in public or in the media too often 2. to expose a photographic medium such as film to too much light or for too long a time, so that the colors or tones in the resulting photograph are too light —**o·ver·ex·po·sure** /-ik spózhər/ *n*

o·ver·ex·tend /òvər ik sténd/ (**-tend·ed, -tend·ing, -tends**) *v* 1. **o·ver·ex·tend your·self** *vr* RISK FINANCIAL RUIN to risk financial ruin by borrowing excessively, spending too much, or overcommitting resources 2. *vt* MAKE TOO GREAT DEMANDS ON SOMEBODY to force somebody, something, or yourself beyond a safe or reasonable limit 3. *vt* PROLONG SOMETHING BEYOND EXPECTED DURATION to prolong something beyond its normal or expected duration

o·ver·fa·mil·i·ar /òvər fə míllee ər/ *adj* 1. more friendly, informal, or intimate than is appropriate 2. used so much or so well known as to be boring or ineffective —**o·ver·fa·mil·iar·i·ty** /-fə millee árrətee/ *n*

o·ver·flew past tense of **overfly**

o·ver·flight /óvər flìt/ *n* the flight of an aircraft or birds over an area

o·ver·flow *v* /òvər fló/ (**-flowed, -flow·ing, -flows**) 1. *vti* FLOW OR POUR OVER to pour out over the limits or edge of a container because the container is filled beyond its capacity 2. *vt* FLOOD SOMETHING to flood, cover, or flow over the surface of something 3. *vt* SPREAD BEYOND LIMITS OF SOMETHING to spread beyond the area intended to contain it ○ *The crowd overflowed the hall into the street outside.* 4. *vi* BE OVERWHELMED BY EMOTION to be so full of an emotion as to feel the need to express it ○ *overflowing with happiness* ■ *n* /óvər flò/ 1. EXCESS

CONTENTS excess contents that flow over the edge of a container **2.** EXCESS PEOPLE OR THINGS people or things that cannot be contained in the space originally set aside for them **3.** OUTLET THAT PREVENTS FLOODING an outlet that allows something, usually a liquid, to escape before it runs over the top of its container **4.** AMOUNT IN EXCESS OF LIMIT the amount by which a limit is exceeded **5.** COMPUTER'S INABILITY TO HANDLE LARGE DATA the inability of a location in computer memory to handle data of an excessively large magnitude, or an instance of this ○ *an overflow error*

o·ver·fly /ōvər flī́/ (**-flew** /-flóo/, **-flown** /-flṓn/, **-fly·ing**, **-flies**) *vti* **1.** to fly over an area **2.** to fly past a fixed point ○ *The plane has overflown the runway.*

o·ver·fold /ṓvər fōld/ *n* a geologic fold that has turned over on itself so that both sides dip in the same direction, causing the middle strata to be upside down

o·ver·gen·er·al·ize /ōvər jénnərə lī̀z/ (**-ized**, **-iz·ing**, **-iz·es**) *vti* to draw too general a conclusion about something on the basis of limited or incomplete evidence —**o·ver·gen·er·al·i·za·tion** /-jènnərəli záysh'n/ *n*

o·ver·glaze *n* /ṓvər glàyz/ **1.** EXTRA GLAZE ON POTTERY an additional coat of glaze applied to pottery or porcelain **2.** TOP LAYER OF DECORATION ON POTTERY a decoration applied to pottery or porcelain on top of the glaze ■ *vt* /ōvər gláyz, ṓvər glàyz/ (**-glazed**, **-glaz·ing**, **-glaz·es**) APPLY GLAZE OR OVERGLAZE TO POTTERY to apply a glaze or overglaze to pottery or porcelain ■ *adj* APPLIED ON TOP OF GLAZE applied on top of a ceramic glaze ○ *overglaze colors*

o·ver·grow /ōvər grṓ/ (**-grew** /-gróo/, **-grown** /-grṓn/, **-grow·ing**, **-grows**) *vti* to grow so large, dense, or extensive as to cover the area of ground or container it is planted in and hinder the growth of other plants —**o·ver·growth** /ṓvər grōth/ *n*

o·ver·grown /ōvər grṓn/ *adj* **1.** COVERED WITH VEGETATION GROWING WITHOUT CHECK covered with plants or weeds that have been allowed to grow without check **2.** GROWN TOO MUCH FOR ALLOTTED SPACE grown too dense, large, or extensive for the area of ground or container in which it is planted **3.** IMMATURE grown to a large or adult size, but remaining immature ○ *behaving like an overgrown schoolboy*

o·ver·hand /ṓvər hànd/ *adj* **1.** SPORTS MADE WITH HAND RAISED OVER SHOULDER made with the hand coming forward in a semicircular motion from behind and above the shoulder **2.** SEWN ON TOP OF SEAM sewn with small vertical stitches passing over the two edges that are being joined together to make a seam ■ *adv* WITH HAND ABOVE SHOULDER with the hand coming forward in a semicircular motion from behind and above the shoulder ■ *n* SOMETHING PERFORMED OVERHAND a stroke, throw, or delivery of something made with an overhand motion

o·ver·hand knot *n* a knot formed by passing one end of a cord or rope through a loop formed on another part of it, often used to prevent an end from fraying

o·ver·hang *v* /ōvər háng/ (**-hung** /-húng/, **-hang·ing**, **-hangs**) **1.** *vti* PROJECT OVER to project or extend over something leaving a sheltered space beneath **2.** *vt* LOOM OVER SOMEBODY to threaten or loom over somebody or something ■ *n* /ṓvər hàng/ **1.** PROJECTION something, e.g., part of a rock face or the edge of a roof, that projects out over the space beneath **2.** EXTENT OF PROJECTION the degree or amount by which something projects or extends over something **3.** AVIAT HALF DIFFERENCE IN WINGSPAN half the difference in the span of the two wings of a biplane **4.** AVIAT DISTANCE TO WING END ON MONOPLANE the distance from the last outer strut to the end of a monoplane's wing

o·ver·haul *vt* /ōvər háwl, ṓvər hàwl/ (**-hauled**, **-haul·ing**, **-hauls**) **1.** CHECK SOMETHING FOR MECHANICAL FAULTS to examine a piece of machinery thoroughly to identify faults **2.** REPAIR MACHINE EXTENSIVELY to carry out comprehensive repairs and adjustments to a piece of machinery **3.** REVISE SOMETHING THOROUGHLY to examine and revise something thoroughly **4.** GRADUALLY OVERTAKE SOMEBODY to catch up with and overtake somebody or something **5.** NAUT SLACKEN OR RELEASE SOMETHING to slacken or release something such as a rope or the blocks of a tackle ■ *n* /ṓvər hàwl/ COMPREHENSIVE REPAIR a comprehensive examination and repair of something —**o·ver·haul·er** *n*

o·ver·head *adv* /ōvər héd/ DIRECTLY ABOVE directly above somebody or something, especially in the air ■ *adj* /ṓvər hèd/ **1.** POSITIONED DIRECTLY ABOVE positioned directly above somebody or something **2.** HIT WITH RACKET ABOVE HEAD describes a stroke in racket games played hard and downward, with the racket held high above the head **3.** RELATING TO ONGOING COSTS relating to the general recurring costs of running a business such as rent, maintenance, and utilities ■ *n* /ṓvər hèd/ **1.** ONGOING BUSINESS COSTS the general recurring costs of running a business, excluding the costs of labor and materials, e.g., rent, maintenance, and utilities **2.** SHOT IN RACKET GAMES a shot in racket games played hard and downward, with the racket held above head height **3.** *also* **o·ver·head pro·jec·tion** *or* **o·ver·head trans·par·en·cy** COMM TRANSPARENCY FOR OVERHEAD PROJECTOR a transparent sheet placed on an overhead projector so that its enlarged image can be projected on a screen or other surface **4.** COMM same as **overhead projector** **5.** SOMETHING LOCATED ABOVE something that is mounted or located in an overhead position, e.g., a light **6.** EXTRA SPACE IN COMPUTER extra capacity for support, checking, or memory to run programs in a computer operating system

o·ver·head cam·shaft, **o·ver·head cam** *n* a camshaft in an internal-combustion engine that is mounted above the cylinder heads and controls the operation, opening, and closing of the cylinder's valves

o·ver·head com·part·ment *n* a luggage compartment above the passenger seats for holding carry-on luggage in an airplane

o·ver·head pro·jec·tion *n* **1.** COMM same as **overhead** *n* (sense 3) **2.** the use of or the image produced by the use of an overhead projector

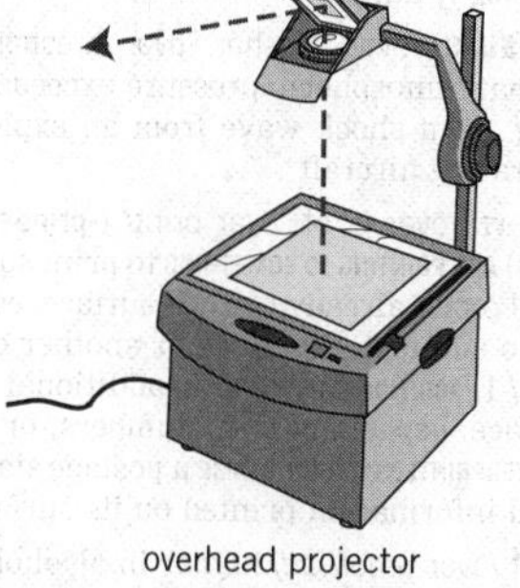

overhead projector

o·ver·head pro·jec·tor *n* a projector with a flat transparent top on which a transparent sheet carrying an image is placed for projection onto a screen or other surface

o·ver·head trans·par·en·cy *n* COMM same as **overhead** *n* (sense 3)

o·ver·head-valve en·gine *n* an internal-combustion engine with the inlet and exhaust valves located in the cylinder head above the pistons. Can term **valve-in-head engine**

o·ver·hear /ōvər héer/ (**-heard** /-húrd/, **-hear·ing**, **-hears**) *vti* to hear what somebody is saying only to others

o·ver·heat /ōvər héet/ (**-heat·ed**, **-heat·ing**, **-heats**) *vti* **1.** BECOME OR MAKE SOMETHING TOO HOT to become too hot, or make somebody or something become too hot **2.** ECON GROW TOO QUICKLY to experience too rapid growth in demand with a resultant increase in inflation, or cause too rapid growth in an economy **3.** BECOME OR MAKE SOMEBODY TOO EXCITED to become too excited, agitated, or angry, or make somebody become too excited, agitated, or angry —**o·ver·heat·ed** *adj*

o·ver·hit /ōvər hít/ (**-hit**, **-hit·ting**, **-hits**) *vti* to hit a ball too hard, or put too much force into a stroke

o·ver·hung past participle, past tense of **overhang**

~~**overide**~~ incorrect spelling of **override**

o·ver·in·dulge /ōvər in dúlj/ (**-dulged**, **-dulg·ing**, **-dulg·es**) *v* **1.** *vti* to indulge in something immoderately or too often, especially food or drink **2.** *vt* to allow somebody to do or have what he or she wants to an excessive degree —**o·ver·in·dul·gence** *n* —**o·ver·in·dul·gent** *adj* —**o·ver·in·dul·gent·ly** *adv*

o·ver·joyed /ōvər jóyd/ *adj* extremely delighted

o·ver·kill *n* /ṓvər kìl/ **1.** EXCESS action that far exceeds what is needed in order to achieve a result **2.** GREATER DESTRUCTIVE CAPACITY THAN NEEDED the capacity of weaponry, especially nuclear weapons, to cause greater damage or destruction than is necessary to accomplish a mission ■ *vti* /ōvər kíl/ (**-killed**, **-kill·ing**, **-kills**) DESTROY WITH EXCESS OF WEAPONS to use excessive force, especially far more nuclear weapons than necessary, to destroy an enemy or place

o·ver·laid past tense of **overlay**[1]

o·ver·lain past participle of **overlie**

o·ver·land /ṓvər lànd/ *adv* by or across land ■ *adj* traveling across land ○ *take the overland route* —**o·ver·land·er** /ṓvər làndər/ *n*

O·ver·land Park /ṓvər lànd-/ city in northeastern Kansas. It is a southern suburb of Kansas City. Population: 158,430 (2002 estimate).

o·ver·lap *v* /ōvər láp/ (**-lapped**, **-lap·ping**, **-laps**) **1.** *vti* PLACE OR BE PLACED OVER to position things in such a way that the edge of one thing is on top of and extending past the edge of another, or be positioned in this way ○ *The roofers overlapped the shingles.* **2.** *vt* EXTEND BEYOND SOMETHING to cover something such as a boundary or edge, and extend beyond it ○ *The tablecloth overlapped the table by several inches.* **3.** *vti* COINCIDE to coincide or correspond in part with something in time, function, or purpose, or make something coincide or correspond with something else ○ *Her area of responsibility to some extent overlaps mine.* ■ *n* /ṓvər làp/ **1.** PARTIAL OVERLAY an edge that partly covers or is covered by something else **2.** EXTENT OF OVERLAP the amount by which something overlaps something else ○ *an overlap of six inches* **3.** PARTIAL COINCIDENCE a partial coincidence or correspondence of two things in time, function, or purpose **4.** GEOL YOUNGER SEDIMENTARY ROCK OVER OLDER LAYER a younger layer of sedimentary rock that extends over an older layer and conceals it completely [Early 18C. < LAP[2]]

o·ver·lay[1] *vt* /ōvər láy/ (**-laid** /-láyd/, **-lay·ing**, **-lays**) **1.** PLACE SOMETHING AS COVERING to place a covering or covering layer of something on top of something else **2.** COVER SOMETHING to cover the surface of something with something else **3.** APPLY DECORATION TO SURFACE to apply a decorative material to a surface (*often passive*) **4.** TELECOM CREATE NEW AREA CODE to create a new area code that applies within the same geographical region as an existing area code ■ *n* /ṓvər lày/ **1.** COVERING a covering or covering layer laid on top of something else **2.** EXTRA DECORATIVE LAYER a layer of decorative material applied to a surface **3.** TRANSPARENCY LAID ON TOP a transparent sheet containing additional details that is placed on top of another graphic **4.** TELECOM NEW AREA CODE a new area code that applies to the same geographic region as an existing area code

o·ver·lay[2] past tense of **overlie**

o·ver·leaf /ṓvər lèef/ *adv* on the other side of the page

o·ver·lie /ōvər lī́/ (**-lay** /-láy/, **-lain** /-láyn/, **-ly·ing**, **-lies**) *vt* **1.** to lie on top of somebody or something **2.** to kill a newborn baby or animal by accidentally lying on and smothering it —**o·ver·ly·ing** *adj*

o·ver·load *vt* /ōvər lṓd/ (**-load·ed**, **-load·ing**, **-loads**) **1.** PUT EXCESSIVE LOAD ON SOMETHING to put too large or heavy a load on somebody or something or in something **2.** OVERBURDEN SOMEBODY to give somebody too much work, stress, or other difficulty **3.** FUSE ELECTRICAL SYSTEM to use more current than an electrical system can handle, e.g., by using too many electrical appliances simultaneously ■ *n* /ṓvər lṑd/ **1.** EXCESSIVE ELECTRICAL LOAD a greater amount of electrical current than an electrical system can handle **2.** EXCESSIVE PHYSICAL WEIGHT something that is physically too heavy or too much to carry **3.** EXCESSIVE MENTAL OR EMOTIONAL BURDEN something that is mentally or emotionally too difficult to cope with **4.** MENTAL OR EMOTIONAL EXHAUSTION the condition of having an excessive mental or emotional burden (*informal*) ○ *showed all the signs of overload and burnout*

o·ver·lock /ṓvər lòk/ *n* a sewing technique using an

invisible hem stitch made by a sewing machine or a special device

o·ver·long /ōvər láwng/ *adj* too long in extent or duration ■ *adv* for too long a time

o·ver·look *vt* /ōvər lo͝ok/ (**-looked, -look·ing, -looks**) **1. MISS SOMETHING** to fail to notice or check something as a result of inattention, preoccupation, or haste **2. IGNORE SOMETHING** to choose to disregard or ignore a shortcoming or fault **3. PROVIDE VIEW OF SOMETHING** to provide a view of something, especially from above **4. LOOK DOWN AT SOMETHING** to look at something from above **5. BE ABOVE SOMETHING** to be located high above something **6. EXAMINE SOMETHING** to look at something with care **7. SUPERVISE SOMEBODY** to observe somebody while he or she works ■ *n* /ōvər lo͝ok/ **VIEWING SPOT** a place that gives a view down over something ○ *hiked up to the scenic overlook*

SYNONYMS ***overlook, neglect, omit, forget***

CORE MEANING: to fail to do something

overlook to fail to notice or check something as a result of inattention, preoccupation, or haste ○ *You seem to have overlooked some important comments.* ○ *Despite the value of their work, caregivers' needs are often overlooked.* **neglect** to fail to do something, especially because of carelessness, forgetfulness, or indifference ○ *The survey neglected to ask how much consumers would be prepared to pay.* **omit** to fail to do something, either deliberately or accidentally ○ *The organizers somehow omitted to inform members of the time of the meeting.* **forget** to fail, or be unable, to remember something, or to do something ○ *I completely forgot to pick him up after work.*

o·ver·lord /ōvər làwrd/ *n* **1.** a ruler with overall power, usually over several subservient rulers, especially somebody who ruled over other lords in a feudal system **2.** somebody of great power or influence —**o·ver·lord·ship** *n*

o·ver·ly /ōvərlee/ *adv* to an extreme or excessive degree

o·ver·man *vt* /ōvər mán/ (**-manned, -man·ning, -mans**) HR same as **overstaff** ■ *n* /ōvər màn/ (*plural* **-men** /-mèn/) **1.** PHILOSOPHY same as **superman** (sense 2) **2.** a man who supervises other workers (*archaic*) [In sense 1 of the noun translation of German *Übermensch*] —**o·ver·man·ning** *n*

o·ver·man·tel /ōvər mànt'l/ *n* an ornamental shelf above a mantelpiece

o·ver·mas·ter /ōvər mástər/ (**-tered, -ter·ing, -ters**) *vt* to conquer somebody's resistance, or break down somebody's self-control (*formal*)

o·ver·match *vt* /ōvər mách/ (**-matched, -match·ing, -match·es**) **1. PROVIDE SOMEBODY WITH SUPERIOR OPPONENT** to provide somebody with an opponent who is likely to defeat him or her easily **2. DEFEAT SOMEBODY OR SOMETHING** to be superior enough to defeat or surpass somebody or something ■ *n* /ōvər màch/ **UNEQUAL CONTEST** a contest in which one competitor is far superior to another

o·ver·mat·ter /ōvər màttər/ *n* copy that has been typeset but is in excess of the space available and is unable to appear in the final version

o·ver·miked /ōvər mīkt/ *adj* sounding too loud or artificial because of an imperfectly positioned or adjusted microphone

o·ver·much /ōvər múch/ *adv* **TO EXCESS** to an excessive degree ■ *adj* **EXCESSIVE** too much ■ *n* **EXCESSIVE QUANTITY** an excessive quantity or amount

o·ver·night *adv* /ōvər nīt/ **1. DURING NIGHT** throughout or at some point during the night **2. VERY QUICKLY** within a very short time ○ *It became a bestseller overnight.* ■ *adj* /ōvər nīt/ **1. OCCURRING AT NIGHT** occurring during the night, or lasting throughout the night **2. EXTREMELY SUDDEN** happening in a very short time ○ *an overnight success* **3. SPENDING NIGHT** resident for the night **4. USED WHEN SPENDING NIGHT** used when staying overnight or for a short time somewhere ○ *overnight clothes* **5. INTENDED FOR NEXT-DAY DELIVERY** guaranteed to get to the intended destination by the next day ○ *sent by overnight delivery* ■ *v* /ōvər nīt/ (**-night·ed, -night·ing, -nights**) **1.** *vi* **SPEND NIGHT** to stay somewhere for the night **2.** *vt* **SEND SOMETHING FOR NEXT-DAY DELIVERY** to send something by a mail or shipping service that guarantees next-day delivery ■ *n* /ōvər nīt/ US **OVERNIGHT TRIP** an overnight stay or trip

o·ver·night bag, o·ver·night case *n* a small piece of baggage used to carry necessities for an overnight or a short trip

o·ver·night·er /ōvər nītər/ *n* **1.** somebody who takes an overnight trip or stays somewhere overnight **2.** a trip lasting one night (*informal*)

o·ver·pass /ōvər pàss/ *n* a section of a road, or a bridge or passage, that crosses over another route

o·ver·per·suade /ōvər pər swáyd/ (**-suad·ed, -suad·ing, -suades**) *vt* to persuade somebody to act contrary to his or her inclination or judgment

o·ver·play /ōvər pláy/ (**-played, -play·ing, -plays**) *v* **1.** *vt* **OVERSTATE STRENGTH OF SOMETHING** to exaggerate the importance or strength of something **2.** *vti* **OVERACT PART** to play a part or role in an exaggeratedly dramatic or theatrical way **3.** *vt* **HIT BALL TOO HARD** to hit or kick a ball too hard or too far

o·ver·plus /ōvər plùss/ *n* a larger amount than is needed or appropriate [14C. Translation of French *surplus*]

o·ver·pop·u·lat·ed /ōvər póppyə làytəd/ *adj* containing too large a population to be sustainable —**o·ver·pop·u·late** *vti* —**o·ver·pop·u·la·tion** *n*

o·ver·pow·er /ōvər pówr/ (**-ered, -er·ing, -ers**) *vt* **1. SUBDUE SOMEBODY PHYSICALLY** to use superior strength or force to defeat somebody, especially to make somebody physically helpless and unable to fight **2. OVERWHELM SOMEBODY MENTALLY** to have so strong an effect on somebody that he or she is unable to resist or control it **3. GIVE EXCESSIVE POWER TO SOMETHING** to supply something, especially a car, with more power than necessary

o·ver·pow·er·ing /ōvər pówring/ *adj* **1.** impossible to resist or control ○ *an overpowering urge to laugh* **2.** overwhelmingly superior in physical strength —**o·ver·pow·er·ing·ly** *adv*

o·ver·pres·sure /ōvər prèshər, ōvər préshər/ *n* the amount that atmospheric pressure exceeds normal levels, e.g., in a shock wave from an explosion or an accelerating aircraft

o·ver·print *vti* /ōvər prínt, ōvər prìnt/ (**-print·ed, -print·ing, -prints**) **ADD PRINTING TO SOMETHING** to print something additional on an already printed surface, especially in order to add text, numbers, or another color ■ *n* /ōvər prìnt/ **1. ADDITIONAL PRINTING** an additional printing on a surface, especially of text, numbers, or another color **2. OVERPRINTED POSTAGE STAMP** a postage stamp with additional information printed on its surface

o·ver·proof /ōvər pro͞of/ *adj* higher in alcohol content than proof spirit is

o·ver·pro·por·tion /ōvər prə páwrsh'n/ (**-tioned, -tion·ing, -tions**) *vt* to make something larger than is usual or needed and out of proportion to other things

o·ver·qual·i·fied /ōvər kwóllə fīd/ *adj* with more academic or vocational qualifications or experience than is necessary or desirable for a job

o·ver·rate /ōvər ráyt/ (**-rat·ed, -rat·ing, -rates**) *vt* to regard somebody as better or more capable, or something as greater, than is in fact the case —**o·ver·rat·ed** *adj*

o·ver·reach /ōvər re͞ech/ (**-reached, -reach·ing, -reach·es**) *v* **1.** *vr* **FAIL THROUGH OVERAMBITION** to fail through trying to do something that is too ambitious **2.** *vti* **EXTEND TOO FAR** to reach or extend too far or beyond something **3.** *vti* **DEFEAT SOMEBODY BY TRICKERY** to get the better of somebody by trickery or deception **4.** *vi* **HURT ONE FOOT WITH ANOTHER** to strike and injure the forefoot with the hind foot while moving forward (*refers to horses*) —**o·ver·reach·er** *n*

o·ver·re·act /ōvər ree ákt/ (**-act·ed, -act·ing, -acts**) *vi* to react to something with disproportionate action or excessive emotion —**o·ver·re·ac·tion** *n* —**o·ver·re·ac·tive** *adj*

o·ver·ride *vt* /ōvər rīd/ (**-rode** /-rṓd/, **-rid·den** /-rídd'n/, **-rid·ing, -rides**) **1. CANCEL SOMETHING** to cancel or change an action or decision taken by somebody else ○ *pledged to override the president's veto* **2. OUTWEIGH SOMETHING** to be more important than and take priority over something else **3. TAKE MANUAL CONTROL OF SOMETHING** to take manual control of an automatic control system **4. RIDE HORSE OVER SOMETHING** to ride a horse over or across an area **5. RIDE HORSE TOO HARD** to tire a horse by riding it too hard **6. OVERLAP SOMETHING** to extend over something, especially by overlapping it ■ *n* /ōvər rīd/ **1. ASSUMPTION OF MANUAL CONTROL** the condition, process, or action of temporarily taking manual control of an automatic system **2. SWITCH FOR MANUAL CONTROL** a switch or some other manual control that temporarily cancels or reverses the effect of an automatic system **3.** FIN **COMMISSION PAID TO EXECUTIVE** a commission that is paid to an account executive on sales made by a representative **4. REVERSAL OF DECISION** the act or process of canceling or changing an action or decision taken by somebody else

o·ver·rid·ing /ōvər rīding/ *adj* highest in priority —**o·ver·rid·ing·ly** *adv*

o·ver·ripe /ōvər rīp/ *adj* too ripe and past its best flavor and texture —**o·ver·rip·en** *vti* —**o·ver·ripe·ness** *n*

o·ver·rode past tense of **override**

o·ver·ruff /ōvər rúf, ōvər rúf/ (**-ruffed, -ruff·ing, -ruffs**) *vti* CARDS same as **overtrump**

o·ver·rule /ōvər ro͞ol/ (**-ruled, -rul·ing, -rules**) *vt* **1. RULE AGAINST SOMEBODY'S ARGUMENT** to rule authoritatively that somebody's argument is unsound, especially in the case of a judge disallowing an attorney's objection ○ *Objection overruled!* **2. DECIDE AGAINST SOMEBODY** to decide against somebody, or overturn a decision made by somebody with lesser authority **3. EXERCISE CONTROL OVER SOMEBODY** to exercise dominion or control over somebody or something (*literary*)

o·ver·run *v* /ōvər rún/ (**-ran** /-rán/, **-run, -run·ning, -runs**) **1.** *vt* **SPREAD RAPIDLY AND INFEST SOMETHING** to arrive in such large numbers or spread so rapidly in a place that it becomes infested or overcrowded (*often passive*) ○ *The cathedral square was overrun with tourists.* **2.** *vt* **CONQUER ENEMY AND TERRITORY** to attack an enemy force, defeat it conclusively, and take over the territory occupied by it ○ *The rebels overran the government forces.* **3.** *vti* **EXCEED LIMIT** to continue beyond a predetermined limit, especially a time limit or fixed budget **4.** *vt* **OVERSHOOT SOMETHING** to go on beyond an intended stopping point such as a boundary line or the end of an airport runway **5.** *vti* **OVERFLOW** to overflow or spill over something ■ *n* /ōvər rùn/ **1. AMOUNT EXCEEDING ESTIMATE** the amount by which something exceeds a preset limit, an estimated cost, or a budget **2. EXTRA QUANTITY PRODUCED** an extra quantity of something produced, e.g., manufactured items or copies of printed matter **3. ACT OF OVERRUNNING** an instance of somebody or something overrunning, especially of going on beyond the intended stopping point

o·ver·saw past tense of **oversee**

o·ver·scale /ōvər skáyl/, **o·ver·scaled** /-skàyld/ *adj* larger than usual in size or scope ○ *an overscale portrait*

o·ver·scan /ōvər skán/ *adj* describes an electronic image that extends beyond the viewing boundary of a computer screen —**o·ver·scan** *n*

o·ver·score /ōvər skáwr/ (**-scored, -scor·ing, -scores**) *vt* to draw a line over or through written text, usually so as to cancel or revise it

o·ver·seas *adv* /ōvər se͞ez, ōvər se͞ez/ **ACROSS SEA** across or beyond a sea, especially in another country ○ *They live overseas.* ■ *adj* /ōvər se͞ez, ōvər se͞ez/ **1. RELATING TO PLACE ACROSS SEA** relating to, located in, or coming from a place beyond a sea ○ *overseas visitors* **2. TRAVELING ACROSS SEA** involving travel across a sea ○ *an overseas assignment* ■ *n* /ōvər se͞ez/ **SOMEWHERE BEYOND SEA** a place or places beyond a sea (*takes a singular verb*) ○ *come from overseas*

o·ver·seas cap *n* US MIL, CLOTHING a soft wedge-shaped military cap without a visor or brim

o·ver·see /ōvər se͞e/ (**-saw** /-sáw/, **-seen** /-se͞en/, **-see·ing, -sees**) *vt* **1.** to watch over, manage, and direct somebody or a task done by somebody **2.** to observe something covertly or secretly while it is happening

o·ver·se·er /ōvər se͞e ər/ *n* somebody who supervises work done by somebody else

o·ver·sell /ōvər sél/ (**-sold** /-sṓld/, **-sell·ing, -sells**) *v* **1.** *vt* **PRAISE SOMEBODY OR SOMETHING TOO HIGHLY** to exaggerate the value or worth of somebody, something, or yourself to an implausible extent **2.** *vti* **SELL TOO AGGRESSIVELY** to use excessively aggressive sales techniques when selling a product **3.** *vti* **SELL TOO MUCH** to sell too much of a product, especially more than can be produced or supplied

o·ver·set /òvər sét/ (**-set, -set·ting, -sets**) *v* **1.** *vti* PRINTING **TYPESET TOO MUCH COPY** to set too much type or copy for the available space **2.** *vt* **TIP SOMETHING OVER** to tip or turn something over (*archaic*) **3.** *vt* **DISTURB SOMEBODY** to disturb or upset somebody (*archaic*)

o·ver·sew /ṓvər sō, òvər sṓ/ (**-sewed, -sewn** /-sṓn/, **-sew·ing, -sews**) *vt* to sew two edges together with small stitches that overlap both

o·ver·sexed /òvər sékst/ *adj* having an excessive preoccupation with or need for sex

o·ver·shad·ow /òvər sháddō/ (**-owed, -ow·ing, -ows**) *vt* **1.** to take attention away from somebody or something by appearing more important or interesting **2.** to cast a physical shadow over something, or make something become gloomy

o·ver·share /òvər shér/ *vti* (**-shared, -shar·ing, -shares**) to give inappropriately personal or detailed information to somebody else, especially a stranger ○ *a retiring person, not usually inclined to overshare* ■ *n* a set of confidences that are inappropriately personal or detailed ○ *launched into a sudden overshare about his failed plans* —**o·ver·share** *adj*

o·ver·shirt /ṓvər shùrt/ *n* a loose shirt that is worn on top of another garment such as a sweater or another shirt

o·ver·shoe /ṓvər shoo/ *n* a shoe, usually made of rubber or plastic, that is worn over an ordinary shoe to protect it from dampness or dirt

o·ver·shoot *v* /òvər shoot/ (**-shot** /-shót/, **-shoot·ing, -shoots**) **1.** *vti* **SEND OR GO FARTHER THAN INTENDED** to shoot a projectile beyond the target that was being aimed at, or be shot in this way **2.** *vti* **EXCEED LIMIT** to exceed a fixed or prearranged limit **3.** *vt* **MOVE QUICKLY OVER SOMETHING** to move at a high speed over something **4.** *vti* **RUN OFF END OF RUNWAY** to fail to complete a takeoff or landing before reaching the end of the runway and run off the end of it (*refers to aircraft*) ■ *n* /ṓvər shoot/ **1. ACT OF OVERSHOOTING** an instance of somebody or something overshooting an intended stopping point, especially the end of an airport runway **2. AMOUNT OF EXCESS** an instance of something exceeding a prearranged limit, or the amount or extent by which it exceeds it

o·ver·shot /ṓvər shòt/ *adj* **1.** describes a jaw with an upper part that is longer than and sticks out over the lower part **2.** describes a water wheel driven by water flowing onto it from above

o·ver·sight /ṓvər sīt/ *n* **1.** a mistake, especially as a result of a failure to do or notice something **2.** the responsibility of supervising something (*formal*)

SYNONYMS See *mistake*.

o·ver·sim·pli·fy /òvər símplə fī/ (**-fied, -fy·ing, -fies**) *vt* to reduce something to such a level of simplicity that it becomes distorted or falsified —**o·ver·sim·pli·fi·ca·tion** /-sìmpləfi káysh'n/ *n*

o·ver·size /òvər sīz/ *adj also* **o·ver·sized** /-sīzd/ **UNUSUALLY LARGE** larger than is usual or necessary ■ *n* **1. UNUSUALLY LARGE SIZE** a size that is larger than usual **2. EXTRA-LARGE ARTICLE** an article that comes in a larger size than usual

o·ver·skirt /ṓvər skùrt/ *n* a skirt that is worn on top of another garment, often revealing part of the lower one

o·ver·sleep /òvər sleep/ (**-slept** /-slépt/, **-sleep·ing, -sleeps**) *v* **1.** *vi* to continue sleeping for longer than desired or intended **2.** *vt* to sleep beyond the time for something

o·ver·sold /òvər sṓld/ past participle, past tense of **oversell** ■ *adj* available at or characterized by prices that are excessively low as a result of previous heavy selling on the stock market ○ *indicators pointing to an oversold market*

o·ver·spend /òvər spénd/ (**-spent** /-spént/, **-spend·ing, -spends**) *v* **1.** *vti* to spend more money than can be afforded or has been budgeted **2.** *vt* to tire somebody or something out completely

o·ver·spill *n* /ṓvər spìl/ something that spills or has spilled over from something ■ *vti* /òvər spíl/ (**-spilled** or **-spilt** /-spílt/, **-spill·ing, -spills**) to spill over, or make something spill over

o·ver·spread /òvər spréd/ (**-spread, -spread·ing, -spreads**) *vt* to spread widely over or cover the surface of something

o·ver·staff /òvər stáf/ (**-staffed, -staff·ing, -staffs**) *vt* to supply a workplace with too large a staff (*usually passive*)

o·ver·state /òvər stáyt/ (**-stat·ed, -stat·ing, -states**) *vt* to exaggerate something in talking or writing about it —**o·ver·state·ment** *n*

o·ver·stay /òvər stáy/ (**-stayed, -stay·ing, -stays**) *vti* to remain beyond the expected, planned, or desired time

o·ver·steer /òvər steer/ *vi* (**-steered, -steer·ing, -steers**) to turn more sharply than expected, especially in a motor vehicle ○ *We oversteered and landed in a ditch.* ■ *n* the tendency of a motor vehicle to turn more sharply than expected

o·ver·step /òvər stép/ (**-stepped, -step·ping, -steps**) *vt* to go beyond the limit of something ○ *overstep the bounds of your authority*

o·ver·stock *v* /òvər stók/ (**-stocked, -stock·ing, -stocks**) **1.** *vti* **STOCK IN EXCESS** to stock more of something than is necessary or desirable **2.** *vt* **KEEP TOO MANY ANIMALS ON LAND** to graze an area with more livestock than it can support ■ *n* /ṓvər stòk/ **EXCESS SUPPLY** a supply of something in excess of the amount that is needed

o·ver·stored /òvər stáwrd/ *adj* having more retail outlets than are required to meet consumer demand

o·ver·sto·ry /ṓvər stàwree/ (*plural* **-ries**) *n* the top layer of foliage in a forest, forming the canopy

o·ver·stretch /òvər stréch/ (**-stretched, -stretch·ing, -stretch·es**) *v* **1.** *vt* **STRETCH RESOURCES TOO FAR** to make too heavy demands on a person or resource, with consequent strain and, usually, poor performance (*often passive*) ○ *Absenteeism is often a sign that employees are overstretched.* **2.** *vti* **STRETCH SOMETHING TOO FAR** to stretch something such as a muscle too much, so as to cause injury or damage **3.** *vt* **STRETCH OVER SOMETHING** to extend or stretch over something

o·ver·stride /òvər strīd/ (**-strode** /-strṓd/, **-strid·den** /-strídd'n/, **-strid·ing, -strides**) *vt* **1. CROSS AREA BY STRIDING** to cross purposefully over or beyond an area **2. STAND OR SIT ASTRIDE SOMETHING** to stand or sit astride something **3. DOMINATE SOMEBODY OR SOMETHING** to have complete mastery or control of somebody or something **4. SURPASS SOMEBODY OR SOMETHING** to surpass or go beyond somebody or something

o·ver·strung /òvər strúng/ *adj* **1. TOO NERVOUS** excessively nervous and tense **2.** MUSIC **WITH DOUBLE SET OF STRINGS** describes a piano fitted with two sets of strings, one crossing the other at an angle **3.** ARCHERY **STRUNG TOO TIGHTLY** in archery, used to describe a bow with the bowstring fixed too tightly

o·ver·sub·scribe /òvər səb skrīb/ (**-scribed, -scrib·ing, -scribes**) *vt* to apply to participate in something in numbers in excess of the available number of places (*usually passive*) ○ *The course on modern poetry was heavily oversubscribed.* —**o·ver·sub·scrip·tion** /-səb skrípsh'n/ *n*

o·vert /ō vúrt, ṓ vùrt/ *adj* **1.** done openly and without any attempt at concealment **2.** done openly and intentionally, and therefore able to be taken as a sign of criminal intent [14C. < Old French, past participle of *ovrir* "open" < Latin *aperire* (see APERTURE)] —**o·vert·ly** /ō vúrtlee/ *adv* —**o·vert·ness** *n*

o·ver·take /òvər táyk/ (**-took** /-toók/, **-tak·en** /-táykən/, **-tak·ing, -takes**) *v* **1.** *vti* **GO PAST** to catch up with and pass a person or vehicle traveling in the same direction **2.** *vt* **DO BETTER THAN SOMEBODY** to reach and then surpass a level achieved by somebody or something **3.** *vt* **COME OVER SOMEBODY SUDDENLY** to come over somebody suddenly, or catch somebody by surprise ○ *Sleep overtook them.*

o·ver·tax /òvər táks/ (**-taxed, -tax·ing, -tax·es**) *vt* **1.** to impose too great a strain on somebody, something, or yourself **2.** to levy more tax on somebody or something than is justified or considered fair —**o·ver·tax·a·tion** /òvər tak sáysh'n/ *n*

o·ver-the-air *adj* transmitted by radio or television —**o·ver the air** *adv*

o·ver-the-count·er *adj* **1. BUYABLE WITHOUT PRESCRIPTION** sold directly to the customer without a doctor's prescription ○ *over-the-counter drugs* **2. BOUGHT AND SOLD ELECTRONICALLY** describes securities not quoted on an exchange, but bought and sold electronically **3. DEALING IN OVER-THE-COUNTER SECURITIES** relating to or dealing in over-the-counter securities —**o·ver the count·er** *adv*

o·ver-the-hill *adj* **1.** past the point at which talent, energy, or physical performance is at its peak **2.** an offensive term meaning middle-aged or past middle age [< the idea of being past your peak]

o·ver-the-shoul·der shot *n* a cinematographic shot taken from over the shoulder of a character whose back can be seen at the side of the frame

o·ver-the-top *adj* so exaggerated as to appear ridiculous or outrageous (*informal*)

o·ver-the-tran·som *adj* submitted to a publisher for publication without prior contact

o·ver·throw *vt* /òvər thrṓ/ (**-threw** /-throó/, **-thrown** /-thrṓn/, **-throw·ing, -throws**) **1. REMOVE SOMEBODY FROM POWER BY FORCE** to remove a person or group of people from a position of power by force **2.** BASEBALL **PITCH BASEBALL TOO HARD** to pitch a baseball so hard that the pitcher's control is adversely affected **3. THROW BALL TOO HARD** to throw a ball too far so that it goes beyond the player it was intended to reach ■ *n* /ṓvər thrṓ/ **1. REMOVAL FROM POWER BY FORCE** the removal of a person or group of people from a position of power by force **2. THROW THAT GOES TOO FAR** a throw of a ball that goes beyond the player it was intended to reach

o·ver·thrust fault /ṓvər thrust-/, **o·ver·thrust** *n* a rock fault produced by thrust action that causes older rocks to move long distances and eventually settle on top of younger rocks (**horizontal displacement**)

o·ver·time /ṓvər tīm/ *n* **1. ADDITIONAL TIME WORKED** extra time worked beyond the normal hours of employment **2. PAY FOR ADDITIONAL TIME WORKED** payment, usually at a higher rate, for time worked beyond the normal hours of employment **3.** SPORTS **EXTRA TIME IN GAME** additional time added to the normal length of a game, often in order to break a tie ■ *adv* **1. BEYOND NORMAL LENGTH OF TIME** beyond the normal or contracted length of time **2.** *UK* **VERY HARD** using a great deal of energy and effort (*informal*) ○ *had been working overtime to try and make them see sense*

o·ver·tone /ṓvər tṓn/ *n* **1.** a subtle additional meaning, nuance, or quality ○ *an overtone of malice in his manner* **2.** a musical tone whose frequency is a multiple of a fundamental tone and helps to determine the overall quality of the sound

o·ver·took past tense of **overtake**

o·ver·trade /òvər tráyd/ (**-trad·ed, -trad·ing, -trades**) *vi* to trade something such as a stock beyond the level that can be supported by the trader's financial means or the market involved

o·ver·trick /ṓvər trìk/ *n* in bridge, a trick taken in addition to the number needed to make a contract

o·ver·trump /òvər trúmp, ṓvər trùmp/ (**-trumped, -trump·ing, -trumps**) *vti* in a card game, to play a higher trump card than one already played by another player in a trick

o·ver·ture /ṓvər choor/ *n* **1. MUSICAL INTRODUCTION** a single orchestral movement that introduces an opera, play, ballet, or longer musical work, often including the work's themes **2.** MUSIC same as **concert overture** **3. INTRODUCTORY PROPOSAL OR INITIATIVE** an introductory proposal or initiative made to mark the beginning of a discussion, agreement, or relationship ○ *made overtures to me* **4. PRELUDE** something that is a first step toward something else **5. INTRODUCTION TO LITERARY WORK** an introduction to a written work such as a poem or play [15C. Via Old French, "opening" < Latin *apertura* (see APERTURE)]

o·ver·turn *v* /òvər túrn/ (**-turned, -turn·ing, -turns**) **1.** *vti* **TIP OVER** to turn somebody or something upside down, or be turned upside down **2.** *vt* **OVERTHROW SOMEBODY** to remove a person or a group of people from a position of power **3.** *vt* **REVERSE PREVIOUS DECISION** to reverse a previous decision, ruling, or law by using legal or legislative procedures ■ *n* /ṓvər tùrn/ **OVERTURNING OF**

SOMETHING an act of overturning something or somebody

~~**overun**~~ incorrect spelling of **overrun**

o·ver·view /ṓvər vyoō/ *n* **1.** a general or comprehensive outline of something **2.** a brief summary of something

o·ver·volt·age /ṓvər vṑltij, ṑvər vṓltij/ *n* a voltage that is in excess of the normal voltage for which an electrical circuit or system was designed

o·ver·wear /ṑvər wér/ (**-wore** /-wáwr/, **-worn** /-wáwrn/, **-wear·ing, -wears**) *vt* to wear somebody or something out

o·ver·ween·ing /ṑvər wéening/ *adj* **1.** intolerably arrogant or conceited **2.** excessive, especially in an arrogant and conceited way [14C. < WEEN]

o·ver·weigh /ṑvər wáy/ (**-weighed, -weigh·ing, -weighs**) *vt* **1.** same as **outweigh** (sense 2) **2.** to oppress or burden somebody heavily

o·ver·weight *adj* /ṑvər wáyt/ **1.** TOO HEAVY FOR GOOD HEALTH having more body weight than is considered healthy for the person's height, build, or age **2.** ABOVE WEIGHT LIMIT heavier than the allowed weight limit ○ *an overweight letter* ■ *vt* /ṑvər wáyt/ (**-weight·ed, -weight·ing, -weights**) **1.** OVEREMPHASIZE SOMETHING to give too much emphasis or consideration to something **2.** OVERLOAD SOMETHING to weigh something down with an excessive load ■ *npl* /ṓvər wàyt/ OVERWEIGHT PEOPLE people who weigh too much for their height, build, or age (*sometimes considered offensive*)

o·ver·whelm /ṑvər wélm, -hwélm/ (**-whelmed, -whelm·ing, -whelms**) *vt* (*often passive*) **1.** OVERPOWER SOMEBODY EMOTIONALLY to affect somebody's emotions in a complete or irresistible way **2.** PROVIDE SOMEBODY WITH HUGE AMOUNT to supply somebody with a very large or excessive amount of something **3.** OVERCOME SOMEBODY PHYSICALLY to use superior strength, force, or numbers to defeat somebody completely **4.** SURGE OVER SOMEBODY OR SOMETHING to flow over the top of and submerge or cover somebody or something

o·ver·whelm·ing /ṑvər wélming, -hwélming/ *adj* **1.** EXTREMELY LARGE extremely large in amount or proportion **2.** EMOTIONALLY OVERPOWERING having such a great effect as to be emotionally overpowering **3.** PHYSICALLY OVERPOWERING overpowering in strength, force, or numbers —**o·ver·whelm·ing·ly** *adv*

o·ver·win·ter /ṑvər wíntər/ (**-tered, -ter·ing, -ters**) *v* **1.** *vti* to keep livestock or plants alive through the winter by sheltering them, or be kept alive in this way **2.** *vi* to spend the winter by taking up residence in a particular place

o·ver·with·hold /ṑvər with hṓld, -wi<u>th</u>-/ (**-held** /-héld/, **-hold·ing, -holds**) *vti US* to deduct an amount of tax from a salary or investment that is larger than the tax to be paid, or be subjected to this

o·ver·wore past tense of **overwear**

o·ver·work *v* /ṑvər wúrk/ (**-worked, -work·ing, -works**) **1.** *vti* DO TOO MUCH WORK to work excessively, or make somebody, yourself, or an animal work excessively **2.** *vt* OVERUSE SOMETHING to use something too often, especially a word or expression **3.** *vt* WORK TOO MUCH ON SOMETHING to expend too much effort on something, especially so as to reduce its quality or effectiveness **4.** *vt* DECORATE SURFACE OF SOMETHING to apply decoration to the surface of something ■ *n* /ṓvər wùrk/ EXCESSIVE WORK too much work

o·ver·worn past participle of **overwear**

o·ver·wound past participle, past tense of **overwind**

o·ver·write /ṑvər rít/ (**-wrote** /-rṓt/, **-writ·ten** /-rítt'n/, **-writ·ing, -writes**) *v* **1.** *vti* REPLACE COMPUTER FILE to replace an electronic file containing data or a computer program in memory or on a disk with a new file of the same name **2.** *vti* WRITE TOO ELABORATELY to make a piece of writing too elaborate, polished, or decorative **3.** *vt* COVER WRITING WITH MORE WRITING to cover a piece of writing by writing on top of it

o·ver·wrought /ṑvər ráwt/ *adj* **1.** VERY UPSET extremely upset, emotional, or agitated **2.** TOO ELABORATE fashioned or decorated too elaborately **3.** ORNAMENTED ON SURFACE ornamented on the surface with decoration

ovi- *prefix* egg, ovum ○ *oviform* [< Latin *ovum* "egg"]

Ov·id /óvvid/ (43 B.C.–A.D. 17) Roman poet. His works include *Amores* and *Metamorphoses*, a collection of mythical and historical tales. See Cultural note at **metamorphosis** —**O·vid·i·an** /ō víddee ən/ *adj*

> "It is the mind that makes the man, and our vigor is in our immortal soul."
> [Ovid, *Metamorphoses*; 8? A.D.]

o·vi·duct /ṓvi dùkt/ *n* either of a pair of tubes in the body that transport eggs from the ovary to the uterus

O·vie·do /ō vyáydō, ṑv yé<u>th</u>ō/ capital of Oviedo Province, northwestern Spain. Population: 202,938 (2002).

o·vi·form /ṓvi fàwrm/ *adj* shaped like an egg

o·vine /ṓ vīn/ *adj* relating to or resembling a sheep [Early 19C. < late Latin *ovinus* < Latin *ovis* "sheep"]

o·vip·a·rous /ō víppərəss/ *adj* **1.** describes birds, fish, reptiles, and insects that reproduce by means of eggs that develop and hatch outside the mother's body **2.** relating to the production of eggs that develop and hatch outside the mother's body —**o·vip·a·rous·ly** *adv*

o·vi·pos·it /ṓvi pózzit/ (**-it·ed, -it·ing, -its**) *vi* to lay eggs (*refers usually to insects*) [Early 19C. < OVI- + Latin *posit-*, past participle of *ponere* "to place"]

o·vi·pos·i·tor /ṓvi pózzitər/ *n* a tubular organ at the end of the abdomen of some female fish or other organisms, especially insects, that is used to deposit eggs

o·vi·sac /ṓvi sàk/ *n* a sac or capsule in the ovary of a mammal that contains a mature ovum

ovo- *prefix* same as **ovi-**

o·void /ṓ vòyd/ *adj* **1.** WITH FORM OF EGG having the solid form of an egg **2.** BOT SHAPED LIKE EGG describes a fruit or similar plant part that is shaped like an egg ■ *n* SOMETHING EGG-SHAPED something with the shape or form of an egg [Early 19C. < French *ovoïde* < Latin *ovum* "egg"]

o·vo·lac·to·veg·e·tar·i·an /ṑvō laktō vèjjə térree ən/ *n* a vegetarian who eats eggs and dairy products, but no products that involve the killing of animals

o·vo·lo /ṓvə lō, óvvə-/ (*plural* **-li** /-lī/) *n* a convex architectural molding that resembles a quarter-circle or ellipse when viewed in cross section [Mid-17C. < Italian, "little egg" < Latin *ovum* "egg"]

o·von·ic /ō vónnik/ *adj* relating to, consisting of, or using glassy materials that can rapidly and reversibly become electrical conductors after a minimum voltage is applied [Mid-20C. < OVSHINSKY EFFECT + ELECTRONIC]

o·von·ics /ō vónniks/ *n* the study or use of glassy materials that can rapidly and reversibly become electrical conductors after a minimum voltage is applied (*takes a singular verb*)

o·vo·tes·tis /ṑvō téstiss/ (*plural* **-tes·tes** /-tés teez/) *n* the sexual organ of a hermaphroditic animal such as the garden snail that produces both sperm and eggs

o·vo·vi·vip·a·rous /ṑvō vī vípperəss/ *adj* describes insects, fish, and reptiles that reproduce by means of eggs that develop within the female, deriving some nutrition from her but remaining encased within an egg membrane —**o·vo·vi·vip·a·rous·ly** *adv*

OVP *abbr* GOV Office of the Vice President

Ov·shin·sky ef·fect /ov shínskee-/ *n* an effect that occurs in thin films of glass containing selenium and tellurium in which the resistance of the material drops rapidly when a specific voltage is applied across it [Mid-20C. After Stanford R. *Ovshinsky* (b. 1922), US physicist]

o·vu·late /óvvyə làyt, ṓvyə-/ (**-lat·ed, -lat·ing, -lates**) *vi* to ripen and release an egg or eggs from the ovary for possible fertilization [Late 19C. < OVULE] —**o·vu·la·tion** /òvvyə láysh'n, ṑvyə-/ *n* —**o·vu·la·to·ry** /óvvyələ tàwree, ṓvyələ-/ *adj*

o·vule /ó vyoōl, ṓ-/ *n* **1.** a small structure in a seed plant that contains the embryo sac and develops into a seed after fertilization **2.** a small or immature egg [Early 19C. Via French < modern Latin *ovulum* "little egg" < Latin *ovum* "egg"] —**o·vu·lar** /óvvyələr, ṓvyələr/ *adj*

o·vum /ṓvəm/ (*plural* **o·va** /ṓvə/) *n* a female reproductive cell [Early 18C. < Latin, "egg"]

ow /ow/ *interj* used to represent an involuntary expression of pain [Early 20C. Natural exclamation]

OW *abbr* ROADS one-way

owe /ō/ (**owed, ow·ing, owes**) *v* **1.** *vt* BE OBLIGATED TO PAY BACK MONEY to be under an obligation to pay or repay somebody an amount of money **2.** *vti* BE FINANCIALLY IN DEBT to be financially in debt to somebody or for something **3.** *vt* BE INDEBTED FOR SOMETHING to have something, usually some desirable thing, only because of something or somebody else ○ *owed his success to her* **4.** *vt* FEEL THAT RESPONSE IS DUE SOMEBODY to feel that something should be given to or done for somebody in recompense for something ○ *I owe myself a night out.* ○ *I owe you an explanation.* **5.** *vt* BEAR GRUDGE TOWARD SOMEBODY to feel a particular emotion, especially a grudge, toward somebody [Old English *āgan* < Indo-European, "to own"]

Ow·en /ṓ in/, **Robert** (1771–1858) British social reformer. A pioneer of socialist industrial communities, he wrote *Revolution in Mind and Practice* (1849).

Ow·en, Wilfred (1893–1918) British poet. Famous for his war poetry, he was killed in World War I a week before the armistice.

> "I am the enemy you killed, my friend. / I knew you in this dark: for so you frowned / Yesterday through me as you jabbed and killed. / I parried; but my hands were loath and cold. / Let us sleep now."
> [Wilfred Owen, "Strange Meeting"; 1918]

> "My subject is War, and the pity of War. The Poetry is in the pity."
> [Wilfred Owen, Preface, *Poems*; 1918]

Jesse Owens: photographed in the long jump competition at the Berlin Olympics (1936)

Ow·ens /ṓ inz/, **Jesse** (1913–80) US athlete. One of the greatest sprinters of all time, he won four gold medals at the 1936 Olympics, setting multiple Olympic and world records. Born **Owens, James Cleveland**

> "I let my feet spend as little time on the ground as possible. From the air, fast down, and from the ground, fast up."
> [Attributed to Jesse Owens]

O·wens·bor·o /ṓ ənz bùr ō/ city in northwestern Kentucky, on the Ohio River. Population: 54,176 (2002 estimate).

O·wen Sound /ō ən-/ port in southeastern Ontario, Canada. Population: 22,161 (2001).

Ow·er·ri /ō wérree/ capital city of Imo State, southern Nigeria. Population: 35,010 (1983).

ow·ing /ṓ ing/ *adj* due to be given, especially in payment or repayment of a debt ○ *amounts still owing* ◇ **owing to** as a result or consequence of something

USAGE See *due*.

owl /owl/ *n* a predatory, usually nocturnal bird with a large head, large front-facing eyes, curved and feathered talons, a small hooked beak, and a distinctive hooting call. The owl is traditionally described as wise, perhaps because of its human-looking face and fixed gaze, as if it were considering something carefully. Order: Strigiformes. See illustration on next page [Old English *ūle* < Germanic]

owl but·ter·fly *n* a butterfly that has a spot like an

owl

owl's eye on the underside of each hind wing. Native to: South America. Genus: *Caligo*.

owl·et /ówlət/ *n* a young owl

owl·et moth *n* INSECTS same as **noctuid** [Because its eyes shine in the dark when light strikes them]

owl·ish /ówlish/ *adj* **1.** physically resembling an owl or a noticeable feature of an owl, especially its large round eyes or ear tufts ○ *owlish glasses* **2.** displaying a characteristic attributed to owls, e.g., wisdom or solemnity **—owl·ish·ly** *adv* **—owl·ish·ness** *n*

owl par·rot *n* BIRDS same as **kakapo**

owl's claws *n regional* a perennial plant with large yellow flowers. Native to: western North America. Latin name: *Helenium hoopesii*.

owl's clo·ver *n* a plant of the figwort family. Flowers: variously colored, in spikes. Native to: western North America, South America. Genus: *Orthocarpus*. [Because its flowers look like owls' faces]

own /ōn/ *adj, pron* **1. EMPHASIZES POSSESSION** used to emphasize that somebody or something belongs to a particular person or thing and not to somebody or something else ○ (adj) *has her own business* ○ *Her own mother wouldn't have recognized her.* ○ (pron) *That's my paintbrush – get your own.* ○ *At last he had a house of his own.* **2. INDICATES THAT SOMEBODY DOES SOMETHING UNAIDED** used to indicate that somebody does something without help or interference ○ (adj) *makes his own clothes* ○ *I can make my own decisions.* ○ (pron) *I'd rather make my own than buy them ready-made.* ■ *adj Carib* **INDICATES SIMPLE POSSESSION** used after a possessive adjective, pronoun, or name to indicate possession or ownership ○ *That could be anybody own.* ■ *v* **(owned, own·ing, owns) 1.** *vt* **HAVE SOMETHING AS PROPERTY** to have something as your property ○ *doesn't own a car* **2.** *vt* **TAKE RESPONSIBILITY FOR SOMETHING** to acknowledge full personal responsibility for something ○ *encouraged us to own the project* **3.** *vti* **ACKNOWLEDGE** to acknowledge or admit something (*formal*) ○ *owned that the struggle was hard* [Old English *āgen* "your own," past participle of *āgan* (see OWE)] ◇ **come into your own** to start to be really effective, useful, or successful ◇ **hold your own 1.** to put up effective resistance in an argument or contest **2.** to remain in a stable condition after an illness or injury, often when it might not be expected ◇ **on your own 1.** alone **2.** without help or interference

own up *vi* to admit to having done something

own·er /ṓnər/ *n* somebody who owns something **—own·er·less** *adj*

own·er-oc·cu·pied *adj* used as a residence by the person who owns it

own·er-oc·cu·pi·er *n* somebody who owns or is buying the residence he or she is living in

own·er·ship /ṓnər ship/ *n* **1.** the legal right of possessing something **2.** the fact or condition of being an owner of something

OWTTE *abbr* ONLINE or words to that effect (*used in e-mails or text messages*)

ox /oks/ (*plural* **ox·en** /óksən/) *n* **1. BOVINE DRAFT ANIMAL** an adult castrated bull, sometimes used for pulling heavy loads and plows **2. COW OR BULL** a male or female bovine animal, especially one belonging to a domestic breed. Genus: *Bos*. **3. SOMEBODY UNINTELLIGENT AND CLUMSY** somebody who is regarded as unintelligent and clumsy, especially somebody with a large build (*insult*) [Old English *oxa* < Germanic]

ox

ox- *prefix* oxygen ○ *oxime* [< OXYGEN]

ox·a·cil·lin /òksə síllin/ *n* an antibiotic used to treat bacterial infections that are resistant to penicillin [Mid-20C. < *isoxazole* + PENICILLIN]

ox·a·late /óksə làyt/ *n* a salt or ester of oxalic acid

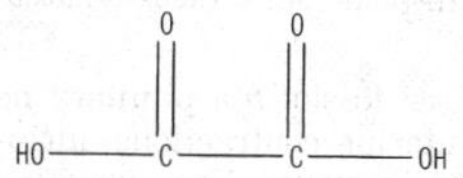

oxalic acid

ox·al·ic ac·id /ok sàllik-/ *n* a colorless poisonous acid. Source: plants, also made synthetically. Use: bleaching, dyeing, cleaning. Formula: $H_2C_2O_4$. [< Latin *oxalis* "wood sorrel" (see OXALIS), because it occurs naturally in the plant's leaves]

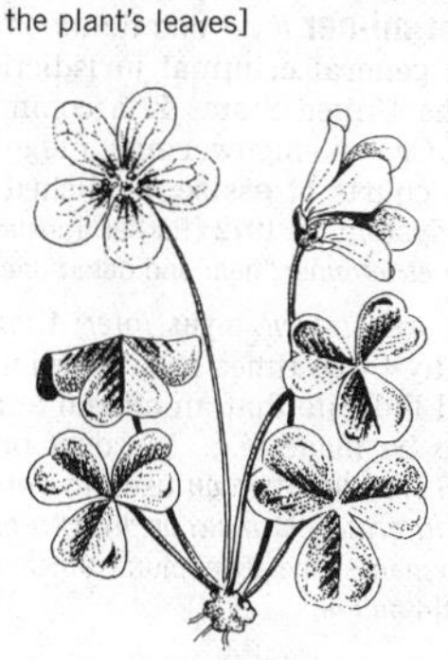

oxalis

ox·a·lis /ok sálliss, óksəliss/ *n* a plant with leaves divided into three parts similar to those of clover, e.g., wood sorrel. Genus: *Oxalis*. [Early 17C. Via Latin < Greek, "wood sorrel" < *oxus* "sour," because of the taste of its leaves]

ox·az·e·pam /ok sázzə pàm/ *n* a tranquilizer used to manage anxiety, insomnia, and alcohol withdrawal [Mid-20C. < HYDROXY + *-azepam*, INN stem]

ox·blood /óks blùd/, **ox·blood red** *adj* of a dark brownish red color **—ox·blood** *n*

ox·bow /óks bō/ *n* **1. BEND IN RIVER** a bend in a river shaped like a "U" **2. LAND IN RIVER BEND** the land that lies inside the bend of a river **3.** GEOG same as **oxbow lake 4. U-SHAPED COLLAR FOR OX** a collar for an ox used as a draft animal, consisting of a U-shaped piece of wood attached to a yoke

ox·bow lake *n* a small curved lake developed on a river floodplain by a river abandoning its original meandering course and cutting a new channel

Ox·bridge /óks brìj/ *n UK* the universities of Oxford and Cambridge, seen as forming an institution distinct from all the other more recently established universities in England [Mid-19C. Blend of OXFORD + CAMBRIDGE]

ox·cart /óks kaàrt/ *n* a cart drawn by oxen, used for transporting heavy goods

ox·en ZOOL plural of **ox**

ox·eye /óks ì/ *n* **1.** PLANTS same as **daisy** (sense 1) **2.** a plant of the daisy family. Flowers: yellow. Native to: Europe, Asia, North America. Genus: *Buphthalum* or *Heliopsis*.

ox-eyed *adj* with big round eyes like those of an ox

ox·eye dai·sy *n* PLANTS same as **daisy** (sense 1)

Ox·fam /óks fàm/ *n* an international charity dedicated to providing poverty and disaster relief [Mid-20C. Contraction of *Oxford* (*Committee for*) *Famine* (*Relief*)]

ox·ford /óksfərd/, **Ox·ford** *n* **1. STURDY LACE-UP SHOE** a sturdy leather shoe that laces over the instep **2. TAILORED COTTON SHIRT** a tailored shirt made of strong cotton fabric **3. COTTON FABRIC** a strong cotton fabric. Use: shirts. [Late 19C. After OXFORD (sense 2)]

Ox·ford /óksfərd/ **1.** city in northern Mississippi, southeast of Memphis, Tennessee. It is home to the University of Mississippi and was the home town of the author William Faulkner, who set some of his novels there. Population: 12,487 (2002 estimate). **2.** city in south central England. Population: 134,248 (2001).

Ox·ford Move·ment *n* a movement in the Church of England that began in Oxford in the 1830s and advocated a renewal of Roman Catholic doctrine and practices

Ox·ford·shire /óksfərd sheèr, -shər/ county in south central England. Oxford is the administrative center. Population: 605,488 (2001).. Area: 1,010 sq. mi./2,610 sq. km.

ox·heart /óks haàrt/ *n* a variety of cultivated cherry with large sweet heart-shaped fruits [Mid-19C. < its shape and large size]

ox·i·dant /óksidənt/ *n* **1.** a substance that oxidizes other substances **2.** a substance in a bipropellant rocket fuel that contains oxygen to support the combustion of another substance, usually liquid oxygen, hydrogen peroxide, or nitric acid [Late 19C. < French < *oxide* (see OXIDE)]

ox·i·dase /óksi dàyss, -dàyz/ *n* an enzyme that catalyzes oxidation [Late 19C. < OXIDATION]

ox·i·da·tion /òksi dáysh'n/ *n* **1.** a chemical reaction in which oxygen is added to an element or compound **2.** the process of losing electrons from a chemical element or compound [Late 18C. < French < *oxide* (see OXIDE)]

ox·i·da·tion-re·duc·tion *n* a chemical reaction in which one component loses electrons or is oxidized and another gains electrons or is reduced

ox·i·da·tion state *n* the positive or negative difference between the number of electrons associated with an atom in a chemical compound and the same atom in an element

ox·i·da·tive phos·pho·ry·la·tion /òksi dàytiv-/ *n* the production of ATP from ADP and phosphate in the final stages of aerobic respiration

ox·i·da·tive stress /òksi dàytiv-/ *n* impaired performance of cells caused by the presence of too many oxygen molecules in them

ox·ide /ók sìd/ *n* a compound containing oxygen, especially in combination with a metal [Late 18C. < French < *oxygène* "oxygen," after *acide* "acid"]

ox·i·dize /óksi dìz/ **(-dized, -diz·ing, -diz·es)** *vti* **1. REACT OR MAKE REACT WITH OXYGEN** to react with oxygen, or cause a chemical to react with oxygen, e.g., in forming an oxide **2. LOSE OR MAKE LOSE ELECTRONS** to lose electrons, or cause a chemical element or compound to lose electrons **3. COVER WITH OXIDE COATING** to form an oxide coating, or cover something with an oxide coating **—ox·i·diz·a·ble** *adj* **—ox·i·di·za·tion** /òksidi záysh'n/ *n*

ox·i·diz·er /óksi dìzər/ *n* CHEM same as **oxidant**

ox·i·diz·ing a·gent *n* a substance that oxidizes other substances and undergoes reduction in the process

ox·i·do·re·duc·tase /òksidō ri dúk tàyss, -tàyz/ *n* an enzyme that catalyzes the oxidation of one compound and reduction of another

ox·ime /ók seèm, óksim/ *n* an organic compound containing a hydroxyl group bonded to a nitrogen atom [Late 19C. < OXY- + IMIDE]

ox·im·e·ter /ok símmətər/ *n* an instrument that measures the amount of oxygen in something, especially in blood [Mid-19C. < OXY-] —**ox·im·e·try** *n*

ox·lip /óks lìp/ *n* a low-growing woodland plant. Flowers: small, yellow, in clusters on one side of a long stem. Native to: Europe, Asia. Latin name: *Primula elatior*. [Old English *oxanslyppe* "ox dung" < *oxa* "ox" + *slyppe* "slime" (see SLIP[3])]

Ox·o·ni·an /ok sṓnee ən/ *adj* **1.** relating to or characteristic of Oxford University, in England, or its students and staff **2.** relating to the city of Oxford, England, or its inhabitants [Mid-16C. < *Oxonia*, Latinized form of Old English *Ox(e)naford* "Oxford"] —**Ox·o·ni·an** *n*

ox·o·ni·um i·on /ok sṓnee əm-/ *n* a cation consisting of an oxygen atom covalently bound to three other atoms or groups of atoms [< OXY- after AMMONIUM]

ox·peck·er /óks pèkər/ *n* a bird of the starling family that climbs on the back of wild and domestic animals and eats parasites from their skin. Native to: Africa. Genus: *Buphagus*.

ox·tail /óks tàyl/ *n* the tail of a beef animal, skinned and chopped into short lengths for cooking. Oxtail is simmered for a long time to make a rich soup or stew.

oxy- *prefix* oxygen ○ *oxyacid* [Shortening]

ox·y·a·cet·y·lene /òksee ə sétt'l èen, -sétt'lin/ *n* a mixture of oxygen and acetylene. Use: cutting, welding metal.

ox·y·ac·id /òksee àssid/ *n* an acid that contains oxygen

ox·y·ceph·a·ly /òksee séffəlee/ *n* a condition in which the skull becomes slightly pointed as a result of the premature closure of some connective bones (**sutures**) [Late 19C. < Greek *oxukephalos* < *oxus* "sharp" + *kephalē* "head"]

ox·y·co·done /òksi kṓ dṑn/ *n* an opiate drug related to codeine. Use: pain relief, sedative. [< *(dihydrohydr)oxycod(ein)one*, its chemical name]

Ox·y·Con·tin /òksee kóntən/ *tdmk* a trademark for a narcotic painkiller whose active ingredient is the synthetic opiate oxycodone

ox·y·gen /óksijən/ *n* a colorless odorless gas that is the most abundant element, forms compounds with most others, is essential for plant and animal respiration, and is necessary in most cases for combustion. Symbol **O**. See table at **element** [Late 18C. < French, "acid-former" (because it was thought to be a basic component of acids) < Greek *oxus* "sharp, sour"] —**ox·y·gen·ic** /òksi jénnik/ *adj*

ox·y·gen·ase /óksijə nàyss, -nàyz/ *n* an enzyme that promotes the addition of oxygen to a compound

ox·y·gen·ate /óksijə nàyt/ *vti* (**-at·ed, -at·ing, -ates**) to combine something with oxygen, or be combined with oxygen ■ *n* a substance added to fuels, especially gasoline, to make them burn more efficiently —**ox·y·gen·a·tion** /òksijə náysh'n/ *n*

ox·y·gen bar *n* a place similar to a café where customers can pay to breathe in oxygen through a face mask for its reviving effects

ox·y·gen debt *n* the amount of oxygen needed to replenish the stores the body uses for its normal physiological processes after these have been depleted during strenuous physical exercise

ox·y·gen de·mand *n* BIOCHEM same as **biochemical oxygen demand**

ox·y·gen mask *n* a device fitting closely over the nose and mouth through which oxygen is supplied to assist breathing, e.g., at high altitudes

ox·y·gen tent *n* a structure enclosing a patient in bed and resembling a transparent plastic tent, into which oxygen can be pumped to assist breathing

ox·y·gen ther·a·py *n* the inhaling of oxygen under pressure, often inside a pressurized chamber, as a treatment for respiratory conditions

ox·y·he·mo·glo·bin /òksee hèemə glṓbən/ *n* the bright red form of hemoglobin containing bound oxygen molecules

ox·y·hy·dro·gen /òksee hī́drəjən/ *adj* using a mixture of oxygen and hydrogen gases, thus allowing hydrogen to burn in an oxygen atmosphere and giving a flame temperature of 2,400°C ○ *oxyhydrogen welding*

ox·y·me·taz·o·line /òksee mi tázzə lèen/ *n* a drug that constricts blood vessels, used as a nasal decongestant and usually administered as a spray [< HYDROXY + *-azoline*, INN stem]

ox·y·mo·ron /òksee máw ròn/ (*plural* **-ra** /-rə/ or **-rons**) *n* a phrase in which two words of contradictory meaning are used together for special effect, e.g., "wise fool" or "legal murder" [Mid-17C. < Greek *oxumōron*, form of *oxumōros* < *oxus* "sharp" + *mōros* "foolish"]

ox·yn·tic /ok síntik/ *adj* producing or secreting acid ○ *oxyntic cells* [Late 19C. < Greek *oxunteos* < *oxunein* "sharpen, make acidic" < *oxus* "sour"]

ox·y·sul·fide /òksee súl fīd/ *n* a compound in which a chemical element is combined with sulfur and oxygen

ox·y·tet·ra·cy·cline /òksee tetrə sī́ kleen/ *n* an antibiotic with a wide range of effectiveness. Source: the soil bacterium *Streptomyces rimosus*.

ox·y·to·cic /òksi tṓssik/ *adj* inducing or speeding up childbirth by causing contractions in the muscles of the uterus ■ *n* a drug that induces or speeds up childbirth [Mid-19C. < Greek *oxutokia* "sharp birth" < *tokos* "birth"]

ox·y·to·cin /òksi tṓssin/ *n* a pituitary hormone that stimulates uterine contractions during childbirth and triggers lactation. Use: sometimes given to assist labor.

ox·y·tone /óksi tṑn/ *adj* **1.** WITH STRESS ON FINAL SYLLABLE describes a word with the stress on the final syllable **2.** WITH ACUTE ACCENT ON LAST SYLLABLE describes a classical Greek word with an acute accent on the final syllable ■ *n* WORD STRESSED ON FINAL SYLLABLE an oxytone word or syllable [Mid-18C. < Greek *oxutonos* "sharp pitch" < *tonos* "pitch, force"]

ox·y·u·ri·a·sis /òksee yŏŏ rī́ əssiss/ *n* an infestation with pinworms [Early 20C. < modern Latin < *Oxyuris*, taxonomic name]

oy·er and ter·mi·ner /óyər ənd túrminər/ *n* **1.** a high court with general criminal jurisdiction in some states of the United States **2.** a commission from the British Crown empowering a judge to try cases in English courts of assize, abolished along with the assize system in 1972 [Partial translation of Anglo-Norman *oyer et terminer* "hear and determine"]

o·yez /ō yéz, -yéss, -yáy/, **o·yes** *interj* **1.** CALL FOR SILENCE used, usually three times in succession, to call for silence and indicate that an official announcement is about to be made, e.g., in court or by a town crier **2.** *US* CALL FOR ATTENTION used to get somebody's attention (*informal*) ■ *n* CRY OF "OYEZ" a cry of "oyez" [< Anglo-Norman, imperative plural ("hear ye!") of *oyer* "hear" < Latin *audire*]

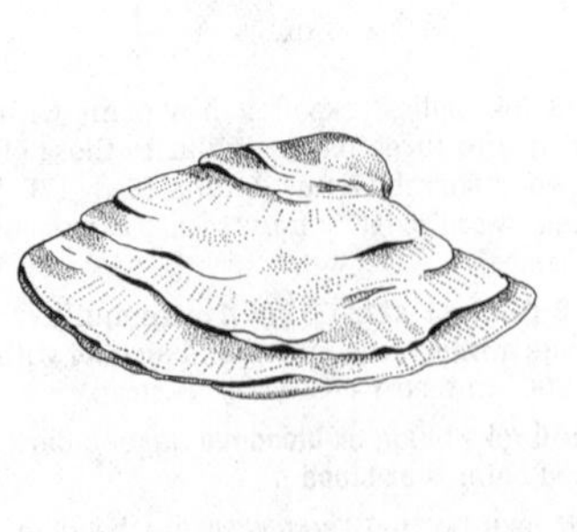

oyster

oys·ter /óystər/ *n* **1.** SHELLFISH a shellfish with a rough irregularly shaped shell in two parts. Native to: seabed of coastal waters. Genera: *Ostrea* or *Crassostrea*. **2.** SHELLFISH SIMILAR TO OYSTER any shellfish similar to an edible oyster, e.g., a pearl oyster **3.** SLIGHTLY GRAYISH OFF-WHITE a pale grayish-beige or pink color **4.** PIECE OF DARK MEAT IN FOWL a small piece of dark meat found in a hollow on either side of the pelvic bone of a fowl such as a chicken or turkey **5.** UNCOMMUNICATIVE PERSON somebody who does not say much or is secretive (*slang*) ■ *vi* (**-tered, -ter·ing, -ters**) GATHER OYSTERS to grow or gather oysters [Via Old French *oistre* < Latin *ostrea, ostreum* < Greek *ostreon*, related to *ostrakon* "shell"] —**oys·ter** *adj*

oys·ter bed *n* an area of seabed where oysters grow or are grown

oystercatcher

oys·ter·catch·er /óystər kàchər/ *n* a common large shorebird with a long flat, almost chisel-shaped red beak and black or black and white feathers that lives on shellfish and worms. Native to: found worldwide. Genus: *Haematopus*.

oys·ter crab *n* a small soft-bodied crab that lives harmlessly inside the shell of a live oyster or other mollusk. Latin name: *Pinnotheres ostreum*.

oys·ter crack·er *n* a small round salty cracker

oys·ter·man /óystərmən/ (*plural* **-men** /-mən/) *n* **1.** a grower, harvester, or seller of oysters **2.** a boat used in gathering oysters

oys·ter mush·room *n* an edible mushroom that grows on dead wood and has a soft flavorful gray cap. Latin name: *Pleurotus ostreatus*.

oys·ter plant *n* **1.** FOOD, PLANTS same as **salsify 2.** PLANTS same as **lungwort** (sense 2)

oys·ter sauce *n* a salty bottled sauce flavored with oysters, used in Chinese cooking

oys·ter shell scale *n* an insect pest of shade trees and shrubs that in its wingless and eyeless adult form lives under an impenetrable white shell and sucks the sap of its host. Latin name: *Lepidosaphes ulmi*.

oys·ters rock·e·fel·ler /-rókə fèllər/ *n* oysters topped with chopped spinach, flavored with onion, celery, parsley, and a little aniseed liqueur, and then baked [Mid-20C. Origin ?]

oz[1], **oz.** *abbr* MEASURE ounce [< Italian *ōz*, abbreviation of *onza* "ounce" < Latin *uncia* "twelfth part" (see OUNCE[1])]

oz[2] *abbr* ONLINE Australia (*used in Internet addresses*)

Oz /aaz/ *n* Australia (*informal*) [Late 20C. Shortening and alteration]

Oz /oz/, **Amos** (*b.* 1939) Israeli writer. He is best known for his novels about life in Israel and Palestine. Born **Klausner, Amos**

> "The Zionist enterprise has no other objective justification than the right of a drowning man to grasp the only plank that can save him."
> [Amos Oz, "The Meaning of Homeland," *Under This Blazing Light*, 1979]

Ö·zal /ō zaál/, **Turgut** (1927–93) prime minister (1983–89) and president (1989–93) of Turkey. The founder of the Motherland Party, he is widely credited with reforming the Turkish economy and establishing boundaries between the state and the military.

O·zark Plat·eau /ṓ zaark-/, **O·zarks** /ṓ zaarks/, **O·zark Moun·tains** mountainous region in the southern United States, predominantly in Arkansas, Missouri, and Oklahoma. Area: 50,000 sq. mi./130,000 sq. km.

AKG London

Seiji Ozawa

O·za·wa /ō záawə/, **Seiji** (*b.* 1935) Japanese conductor. He became the music director of the Boston Symphony Orchestra in 1973, and of the Vienna State Opera in 2002.

o·zo·ce·rite /ōzō séer ĭt/, **o·zo·ke·rite** /-kéer ĭt/ *n* a waxy hydrocarbon substance occurring naturally in irregular veins in sandstone rock, ranging in color from brown to jet black. Use: making candles, wax paper, and polishes. [Mid-19C. < German *Ozokerit* < Greek *ozein* "to smell" + *kēros* "beeswax"]

o·zone /ó zōn/ *n* **1.** a gaseous form of oxygen with three oxygen atoms per molecule, formed by electrical discharge in oxygen. Use: water purification. Formula: O_3. **2.** fresh pure air (*informal*) [Mid-19C. Via German *Ozon* < Greek *ozon*, neuter present participle of *ozein* "smell"; from its pungent smell]

o·zone-friend·ly *adj* causing no harm to the ozone layer

o·zone hole *n* an area of the upper atmosphere where the ozone layer is absent or has become unusually thin

o·zone lay·er *n* the layer of the upper atmosphere, from 10 to 30 mi./15 to 50 km above the Earth's surface, where most atmospheric ozone collects, absorbing harmful ultraviolet radiation from the Sun. In the 1980s it was realized that industrial pollutants such as CFCs were damaging the ozone layer and that holes had appeared in it, especially over the Antarctic.

o·zo·nide /ózō nīd/ *n* an explosive organic compound formed by the addition of ozone to any organic compound with a double or triple carbon bond

o·zo·nize /ózō nīz/ (**-nized, -niz·ing, -niz·es**) *vt* **1.** to convert oxygen into ozone **2.** to treat something with ozone, or add ozone to an organic compound with a double or triple carbon bond —**o·zon·i·za·tion** /ṑzōni záysh'n/ *n*

o·zon·iz·er /ózō nīzər/ *n* a device that produces ozone from oxygen gas

o·zo·nol·y·sis /ṑzō nóllәssis/ *n* the technique of using ozone to oxidize an organic material in the process of identifying double bonds or synthesizing chemicals

o·zo·no·sphere /ō zṓnә sfeer, ō zṓnnә-/ *n* METEOROL same as **ozone layer**

Pp

p[1] /pee/ (*plural* **p's**), **P** (*plural* **P's** or **Ps**) *n* **1.** the 16th letter of the English alphabet, representing a consonant sound **2.** a written representation of the letter "p" ◇ **mind your p's and q's, watch your p's and q's** to be careful to be polite, tactful, and well-behaved

p[2] *symbol* MUSIC piano[2] *adv* (*used as a musical direction*)

P[1] *symbol* CHEM ELEM phosphorus

P[2] *abbr* **1.** PHYS parity **2.** AUTOMOT park (*used on gearshifts*) **3.** CHESS pawn **4.** SPORTS played (*used in sports tables*) **5.** PHYS power **6.** PHYS pressure

P[3] /pee/ (*plural* **P's** or **Ps**) *n* something shaped like a letter "P"

p. *abbr* **1.** page **2.** part **3.** GRAM participle **4.** GRAM past **5.** MONEY pataca **6.** MONEY penny **7.** per **8.** MONEY peso **9.** MEASURE pint **10.** pipe **11.** population **12.** MONEY pula **13.** HANDICRAFT purl

P. *abbr* **1.** CHR Pastor **2.** POL President **3.** CHR Priest **4.** Prince

P2P /pèe tə pée/ *adj* **1.** describes payments or linkups made between two people via the Internet. Full form **person-to-person 2.** describes software enabling commercial or private users of the Internet to communicate or share resources. Full form **peer-to-peer**

pa[1] /paa/ (*plural* **pa's** or **pas**) *n* father (*informal*) [Early 19C. Shortening of PAPA[1]]

pa[2] *abbr* ONLINE Panama (*used in Internet addresses*) See table at **domain name**

Pa *symbol* **1.** PHYS pascal **2.** CHEM ELEM protactinium

PA[1] *abbr* **1.** INSUR particular average **2.** MAIL Pennsylvania **3.** BANKING personal account **4.** MIL Post Adjutant **5.** MOVIES press agent **6.** PUBL Press Association **7.** ACCT public accountant

PA[2] *n* an electronic amplification system used to increase the sound level of speech or music in a large or open space such as a stadium or auditorium. Full form **public-address system**

Pa. *abbr* Pennsylvania

p.a. *abbr* per annum

P.A. *abbr* **1.** *US* MED physician's assistant **2.** LAW power of attorney **3.** *US* LAW prosecuting attorney

P/A *abbr* LAW power of attorney

pa'an·ga /páang gə, paa áang gə/ *n* the main unit of Tongan currency. See table at **currency** [Mid-20C. < Polynesian]

PABA /pábbə, paábə/ *n* a form of aminobenzoic acid that is part of the B vitamin complex. Use: sunscreen. Full form **para-aminobenzoic acid**

pab·u·lum /pábbyələm/ *n* **1.** a source of nourishment in an easily absorbable liquid, especially the nutrient intake of plants and lower animals **2.** material whose intellectual content is thin, trite, bland, or generally unsatisfying (*literary*) [Mid-17C. < Latin < stem of *pascere* "to feed"]

PABX *abbr* TELECOM private automatic branch exchange

PAC /pak/ *abbr US* POL political action committee

paca

pa·ca /paákə, pákə/ *n* a large burrowing plant-eating rodent with a large head and brown fur with white spots. Native to: rain forests of South and Central America. Genus: *Cuniculus*. [Mid-17C. Via Spanish and Portuguese < Tupi]

Pa·ca /paákə, pákə/, **William** (1740–99) US political leader. A signatory of the Declaration of Independence (1776), he was governor of Maryland (1782–85).

pace[1] /payss/ *n* **1.** SPEED OF MOVEMENT the speed at which somebody or something moves, especially when walking or running ○ *She quickened her pace.* **2.** SPEED OF EVENTS the rate or speed at which things happen or develop ○ *the pace of modern life* **3.** STEP a step taken when walking or running **4.** DISTANCE COVERED IN STEP the distance covered in a single step or stride **5.** UNIT OF LENGTH any unit of distance, ranging from 30 to 60 in./0.76 to 1.52 m, based on the length of one or two human strides **6.** WAY OF WALKING a particular manner or style of walking ○ *an uneven pace* **7.** GAIT OF HORSE one of the distinctive ways in which a four-legged animal walks or runs at different speeds, e.g., a walk, trot, or canter, especially as executed by a trained horse **8.** 2-BEAT GAIT a two-beat gait of a four-legged animal where both legs on one side of the body move and are put down together. It is natural in camels but the product of training in horses. ■ *v* (**paced, pac·ing, pac·es**) **1.** *vti* WALK BACK AND FORTH to walk back and forth within a restricted area, especially in a state of nervous anxiety or deep thought ○ *paced up and down all night worrying* **2.** *vti* WALK ALONG SOMETHING to walk along or through something with regular strides **3.** *vti* MEASURE SOMETHING BY COUNTING STEPS to measure a distance by counting the paces taken to cover it ○ *I paced out the width of the room.* **4.** *vt* SET SPEED OF SOMETHING to set the speed at which somebody runs, moves, or does something ○ *I helped her train for the marathon by pacing her on a bicycle.* **5. pace your·self** *vr* DO SOMETHING AT CONTROLLED RATE to run or work at an even controlled speed so as not to waste energy ○ *Learn to pace yourself.* **6.** *vi* MOVE AT PACE to move at the distinctive two-beat gait known as the pace (*refers to horses*) [13C. Directly or via French *pas* "step" < Latin *passus* "stretch (of the leg)" < *pandere* "stretch, extend"] ◇ **at somebody's own pace** at the rate that is natural or comfortable for somebody ◇ **force the pace** to do something to force somebody to go faster or to make something happen more quickly ◇ **off the pace** SPORTS behind the leader, or less than the score of the leading competitor ○ *three strokes off the pace* ◇ **put something through its paces** to make something demonstrate its capabilities, as a test or in order to impress other people ◇ **set the pace** to go at a speed or establish a standard that others have to keep up with ◇ **stand** *or* **stay the pace** to be able to keep up with other people, especially when the pace is fast, the standard high, or the competition fierce

pa·ce[2] /paá chày, páyssee/ *prep* used in front of a name or title as a gesture of real or ironic respect to somebody who is mistaken and about to be corrected ○ *Pace the critic of this newspaper, the character's name is Prospero, not Prosperus.* [Late 18C. < Latin, "with peace, with permission," form of *pax* "peace"]

pace car *n* a car that leads the competitors in a car race through a pace lap before the start of a race but does not participate in the race itself

pace lap *n* a lap of the course driven by all the competitors in a motor race before the race begins, to warm up the engines

pace·mak·er /páyss màykər/ *n* **1.** DEVICE THAT REGULATES HEARTBEAT a battery-operated electrical device inserted into the body to deliver small regular shocks that stimulate the heart to beat in a normal rhythm **2.** NATURAL HEARTBEAT REGULATOR a small area of specialized heart-muscle tissue in the wall of the upper right chamber of the heart that sends out rhythmic electrical impulses to regulate the heartbeat **3.** COMPETITOR WHO SETS PACE a competitor in a race who sets the speed at which the whole or part of the race is run **4.** same as **pacesetter** (sense 1)

pac·er /páyssər/ *n* **1.** MED same as **pacemaker** (sense 3) **2.** a horse trained to move at a pace in races

pace·set·ter /páyss sèttər/ *n* **1.** a person or group regarded as being a leader in any field and one whom others may emulate **2.** SPORTS same as **pacemaker** (sense 3)

pa·chang·a /pa chángə/ *n Hispanic* same as **fiesta** (sense 2) (*slang*) [< Spanish, "party, celebration"]

pa·chin·ko /pə chíng kō/ *n* a Japanese gambling game similar to pinball played with the board vertical [Mid-20C. < Japanese]

pa·chi·si /pə chéezee/ *n* an ancient South Asian four-handed game similar to backgammon, played on a cross-shaped board with six cowrie shells used as dice [Early 19C. < Hindi *pac(c)īsī* "(throw of) 25" (the highest in the game)]

Pa·chu·ca /pə chóokə, paa chóo kaa/, **Pa·chu·ca de So·to** /-də sṓtō, -de-/ industrial city and capital of Hidalgo State, central Mexico. Population: 190,044 (2000).

pa·chu·co /pə chóo kō/ (*plural* **-cos**) *n Hispanic* a Mexican American man who wears flashy clothes, tends to be rebellious, and sometimes belongs to a local gang (*dated slang*) [Mid-20C. < Mexican Spanish]

pach·y·derm /páki dùrm/ *n* a large mammal with a thick skin, especially the elephant, rhinoceros, or hippopotamus [Mid-19C. < French *pachyderme* < Greek *pakhudermos* "thick-skinned" < *pakhus* "thick" + *derma* "skin"] —**pach·y·der·mal** /pàki dúrm'l/ *adj*

pach·y·der·ma·tous /pàki dúrmətəss/ *adj* **1.** having the thick skin or some other physical characteristic typical of a pachyderm **2.** insensitive to other people and unworried by criticism or attack (*literary or humorous*) [Early 19C. < Greek *pakhus* "thick" + *dermat-* "skin"]

pach·y·san·dra /pàki sándrə/ (*plural* **-dras** or *same*) *n* a low-growing evergreen bush with toothed leaves and tiny white flowers, often used as ground cover.

Genus: *Pachysandra.* [Early 19C. < modern Latin < Greek *pakhus* "thick" + *andr-* "man, male"; from the thick stamens]

pach·y·tene /páki teen/ *n* the third stage of cell division, during which the paired chromosomes become shorter and thicker and divide into four chromatids [Early 20C. < French *pachytène* < Greek *pakhus* "thick" + French *-tène* "ribbon" (< Greek *tainia*)]

pa·cif·ic /pə síffik/ *adj* **1.** BRINGING PEACE leading to or promoting peace and an end to conflict **2.** HAVING PEACEFUL TEMPERAMENT calm and peaceful by nature **3.** UNAGGRESSIVE avoiding the use of force [Mid-16C. Directly or via French < Latin *pacificus* < *pac-*, stem of *pax* "peace"]

Pa·cif·ic *n* the Pacific Ocean ■ *adj* relating to the Pacific Ocean, or to the territories that surround it or are surrounded by it

Pa·cif·ic Is·land·er *n* **1.** somebody who lives in or comes from one of the Pacific Islands **2.** somebody who comes from the United States and is of Melanesian, Micronesian, or Polynesian descent

Pa·cif·ic Is·lands /pə sìffik-/ more than 25,000 islands spread over the western and central Pacific Ocean, usually divided into three subregions: Melanesia, Micronesia, and Polynesia

Pa·cif·ic Is·lands, Trust Ter·ri·to·ry of the former US trust territory of over 2,000 islands in the western Pacific Ocean, consisting of the Northern Mariana Islands excluding Guam (until 1986), the Federated States of Micronesia (until 1986), the Marshall Islands (until 1986), and Palau (until 1994)

Pa·cif·ic North·west *n* a part of the northwestern United States on the Pacific coast that includes the states of Washington and Oregon and sometimes southwestern British Columbia, Canada

Pa·cif·ic O·cean largest ocean in the world, stretching from the Arctic Ocean in the north to Antarctica in the south, and from North and South America in the east to eastern Asia, the Malay Archipelago, and Australia in the west. Its deepest point is the Mariana Trench, 35,840 ft./10,924 m. Area: 63,980,000 sq. mi./165,700,000 sq. km.

Pa·cif·ic Rim *n* the countries that border the Pacific Ocean, especially the countries of East Asia, considered as a political or economic unit

Pa·cif·ic Rim Na·tion·al Park Re·serve national park in western Canada. It is divided into three sections along the western coast of Vancouver Island, British Columbia. Area: 110 sq. mi./285 sq. km.

Pa·cif·ic Stan·dard Time, Pa·cif·ic Time *n* the standard time in the time zone centered on 120° west longitude, which includes the coastal regions of western North America. It is eight hours behind Universal Time.

pac·i·fi·er /pássə fì ər/ *n* **1.** somebody or something that calms a person or situation **2.** an object made of rubber or plastic in the shape of a nipple or ring for a baby to suck on

pac·i·fism /pássə fìzzəm/ *n* **1.** BELIEF IN PEACEFUL RESOLUTION OF CONFLICTS the belief that violence, war, and the taking of lives are unacceptable ways of resolving disputes **2.** REFUSAL TO PARTICIPATE IN WAR the refusal to take up arms or participate in war because of moral or religious beliefs **3.** BELIEF IN DIPLOMACY OVER WAR the belief that international conflicts should be settled by negotiation rather than war

pac·i·fist /pássəfist/ *n* **1.** a believer in or advocate or practitioner of pacifism **2.** somebody who refuses to perform military service or take part in a war —**pac·i·fist** *adj* —**pac·i·fis·tic** /pàssə fístik/ *adj* —**pac·i·fis·ti·cal·ly** *adv*

pac·i·fy /pássə fì/ (**-fied, -fy·ing, -fies**) *vt* **1.** to calm somebody who is angry or agitated, or soothe violent or angry feelings **2.** to bring peace to an area, people, or situation, often by using military force to end conflict or unrest [15C. Directly or via French *pacifier* < Latin *pacificare* "make peace" < *pac-*, stem of *pax* "peace"] —**pac·i·fi·a·ble** /pássə fì əb'l, pàssə fì əb'l/ *adj* —**pac·i·fi·ca·tion** /pàssəfi káysh'n/ *n*

Pa·cin·i·an cor·pus·cle /pə sìnnee ən-/ *n* a pressure-sensitive nerve ending that resembles a tiny white onion and is connected to the end of nerve fibers in the skin, especially of the hands and feet, and in connective tissue [Mid-19C. After Filippo *Pacini* (1812–83), Italian anatomist]

Pa·ci·no /pə cheénō/, **Al** (*b.* 1940) US actor. He starred in *The Godfather* movies and won an Academy Award for *Scent of a Woman* (1992). Full name **Pacino, Alfredo James**

pack[1] /pak/ *n* **1.** COLLECTION OF THINGS IN PACKAGE a set of documents or other materials relating to a subject that are packaged together ○ *a free information pack* **2.** COMMERCIAL CONTAINER a container or piece of packaging holding several products or items of the same kind, or such a container and its contents ○ *a pack of matches* **3.** AMOUNT CONTAINED IN PACK the contents of a pack, or the amount of something that can be contained in a pack **4.** AMOUNT OF FOOD PRESERVED an amount of food canned or preserved in a particular year or season **5.** LARGE AMOUNT a large amount of something (*informal*) ○ *a pack of lies* **6.** ZOOL GROUP OF ANIMALS a group of animals that live and hunt together, especially wolves or dogs ○ *a pack of wolves* **7.** LARGE GROUP OF PEOPLE ACTING TOGETHER a group of people who behave in the same way, especially a group whose behavior appears to be threatening, predatory, or criminal ○ *always followed by a pack of photographers* **8.** GROUP OF CUB SCOUTS a local organized unit of Cub Scouts **9.** MAIN BODY OF COMPETITORS the main body of competitors in a race or competition **10.** SET OF CARDS a set of playing cards, comprising the four suits plus jokers ○ *a pack of cards* **11.** BAG CARRIED ON BACK a bag or bundle, especially one designed to be carried on a person's or animal's back **12.** PARACHUTE IN CONTAINER a parachute, rigged, folded, and in its container ready for use **13.** GEOG same as **pack ice 14.** MED COMPRESS USED IN SURGERY a wad of soft absorbent material applied to a wound or temporarily inserted into a body cavity to control bleeding or keep tissues dry during surgery **15.** MED HOT OR COLD PAD a compress placed on the body for medicinal purposes ○ *an ice pack* **16.** COSMETIC PASTE a quantity of moist material applied to part of the body, especially the face, for cosmetic purposes ○ *a mud pack* **17.** GROUP OF SUBMARINES OR AIRCRAFT a number of submarines, aircraft, or other military units who hunt and fight the enemy as a group ■ *v* (**packed, pack·ing, packs**) **1.** *vti* PUT BELONGINGS INTO CONTAINER to put personal belongings into a bag or other container for transportation **2.** *vti* PUT PRODUCTS IN CONTAINERS to put something into a container or fill a container with something for sale, transport, or storage **3.** *vt* MAKE SOMETHING INTO PACKAGE OR BUNDLE to make up a package or bundle, or wrap or roll something up in one **4.** *vt* FILL SOMETHING WITH LARGE QUANTITY to fill something, especially a limited space, tightly (*often passive*) ○ *The case was packed with books and letters.* **5.** *vti* CROWD INTO OR FILL PLACE to crowd into a place so that it is full or overfull, or to fill a place with people **6.** *vt* FIT SOMETHING INTO LIMITED TIME to fit many different activities or events into a limited period of time ○ *packed a lot of sightseeing into one weekend* **7.** *vt* COMPUT same as **compress** *v* (sense 3) **8.** *vti* COMPACT SOMETHING OR BECOME COMPACTED to compact a substance such as snow or soil into a dense mass, or become densely compacted **9.** *vt* PRESS SOMETHING AROUND OBJECT to wrap or press something in around an object to hold it firmly or protect it **10.** *vt* MED USE PACK ON WOUND to apply a medical pack to a wound or insert one into a body cavity **11.** *vt* MED APPLY COMPRESS TO BODY PART to apply cold compresses to part of a patient's body in order to control body temperature **12.** *vt* MECH ENG SEAL SOMETHING TO PREVENT LEAKAGE to seal a mechanical joint by inserting a layer of compressible material between the moving parts to prevent leakage of fluid **13.** *vt* MECH ENG FILL CAVITY WITH GREASE to fill a cavity containing bearings with grease **14.** *vti* CARRY GUN to carry a weapon, especially a gun (*informal*) **15.** *vt* POSSESS SOMETHING AS FORCEFUL CAPABILITY to be capable of delivering something that has a powerful or devastating effect (*informal*) ○ *new computer packs a punch* **16.** *vt* LOAD BAGGAGE ONTO ANIMAL to put goods or belongings onto a horse, donkey, or other animal in order to transport them **17.** *vti* CARRY LOAD to be carrying something loaded usually on the back [12C. < Dutch or Low German *pakken*] —**pack·a·ble** *adj*

pack in *v* **1.** *vt* to attract very large audiences ○ *The show has been running three years and is still packing them in night after night.* **2.** *vti* to stop or give up doing something (*informal*) ○ *She's packed in her job.* ◇ **pack it in** to stop doing something (*informal*)

pack off *v* **1.** *vt* to send somebody away unceremoniously to another place (*informal*) ○ *They traded him for a shortstop, and he was packed off to the minors.* **2.** *vi UK* to leave or go somewhere hastily or unceremoniously ○ *They packed off home as soon as the work was done.*

pack up *v* **1.** *vti* to stop doing something ○ *I had to pack up playing the trombone because the neighbors were always complaining.* **2.** *vi* to finish work for the day (*informal*) ○ *I'm packing up and going home.*

pack[2] /pak/ (**packed, pack·ing, packs**) *vt* to ensure that a group such as a jury or committee is made up wholly or mainly of supporters of one side [Early 16C. Probably alteration of PACT]

pack·age /pákij/ *n* **1.** PARCEL an object or set of objects wrapped, boxed, or tied in a bundle for transportation or mailing **2.** COMM PACKAGING FOR GOODS a container made of cardboard, plastic, foil, or other material in which goods are packed for sale, storage, or transportation, or a container of this type together with its contents ○ *a package of chewing gum* **3.** DIFFERENT THINGS CONSTITUTING SINGLE ITEM a number of different components intended to constitute a single item ○ *a good severance package* **4.** PIECE OF GENERAL ADAPTABLE COMPUTER SOFTWARE a piece of computer software that can be used for a range of related purposes such as word processing or financial analysis **5.** TRAVEL same as **package tour** ■ *vt* (**-aged, -ag·ing, -ages**) **1.** PUT SOMETHING INTO PACKAGE to put things into or wrap them up as a package **2.** PRODUCE ATTRACTIVE PACKAGING FOR SOMETHING to create suitable or attractive packaging in which to sell a product **3.** PROMOTE OR PRESENT SOMETHING to present somebody or something to others in a way intended to ensure appeal and acceptance ○ *It wasn't so much the policy that was wrong as the way it was packaged.* **4.** GROUP SOMETHING AS PACKAGE to group or offer several different items together in a package **5.** PRODUCE SOMETHING FOR OTHERS TO MARKET to produce a book or television program or series in finished form ready to be published or broadcast by another company —**pack·ag·er** *n*

pack·age deal *n* a proposal or agreement comprising a number of different items that must all be accepted together

pack·age hol·i·day *n UK* same as **package tour**

pack·age store *n US* BEVERAGES, COMM same as **liquor store**

pack·age tour *n* a tour organized in advance by a travel company to whom the vacationer or tourist pays a single fee covering transportation, accommodations, meals, and often entertainment

pack an·i·mal *n* **1.** an animal that is used to carry goods or equipment, e.g., a horse, donkey, or mule **2.** an animal that lives in a pack

packed /pakt/ *adj* **1.** FULL OF PEOPLE full of people and extremely crowded ○ *played to a packed house every night* **2.** CONTAINING MUCH OF SOMETHING containing or offering something in excitingly large quantities (*often used in combination*) ○ *a fun-packed adventure* **3.** COMPRESSED pressed together to form a compact mass ○ *packed snow*

packed lunch *n UK* same as **box lunch** (sense 1)

packed out *adj* crowded with or completely full of people (*informal*)

pack·er /pákər/ *n* **1.** a person or machine that packs goods in containers or in packaging **2.** a person or company involved in the processing and packing of goods, especially meat or fresh produce, for the wholesale market

pack·et /pákət/ *n* **1.** SMALL CONTAINER FOR GOODS a small box, envelope, or bag in which goods are sold or stored **2.** CONTENTS OR QUANTITY IN PACKET the contents of a packet, or the quantity of goods contained in a packet ○ *At least four packets of seeds never produced flowers.* **3.** MAIL SMALL PARCEL a small parcel or package **4.** COMPUT DATA UNIT IN COMPUTER NETWORK a message or part of a message packaged as a fixed-size segment of data for transmission through a computer network **5.** *also* **pack·et boat** BOAT ON REGULAR SHORT RUN a small ship that provides a regular service carrying passengers, freight, and mail over a fixed short route ■ *vt* (**-et·ed, -et·ing, -ets**) PUT SOMETHING IN PACKET to put something into a packet or wrap it up as a package [15C. < PACK[1]]

pack·et switch·ing *n* the transmitting and routing of data as packet segments sent rapidly and sequentially over a channel that is occupied only during the actual transmission

pack·frame /pák fràym/ *n* a lightweight frame with shoulder straps to which equipment or unwieldy loads can be strapped to be carried on a person's back

pack·horse /pák hàwrss/ *n* a horse used for carrying goods or equipment

pack ice *n* floating ice, especially in polar regions, that has formed itself into a solid mass covering a wide area

pack·ing /páking/ *n* **1.** ACT OF PUTTING THINGS INTO CONTAINERS the task of putting things into containers, usually for storage or transport **2.** MATERIAL FOR PROTECTING PACKED OBJECT material used to surround and protect something packed inside a container **3.** WATERTIGHT OR AIRTIGHT MATERIAL material used to fill or surround something such as a joint in a pipe in order to make it watertight or airtight **4.** FOOD INDUST PROCESSING AND PACKAGING OF FOOD the processing and packaging of food such as meat or produce for sale **5.** MED ABSORBENT MATERIAL FOR MEDICAL PACKS absorbent material such as gauze for insertion in body cavities or wounds **6.** MECH ENG SPACERS BETWEEN CLAMPED SURFACES shims, washers, or other pieces of metal used to adjust the distance between component surfaces before they are secured

pack·ing frac·tion *n* a measure of the stability of an atomic nucleus, arrived at by dividing the difference between its mass in atomic mass units and its mass number by that mass number

pack·ing·house /páking hòwss/ (*plural* **-hous·es** /-hòwzəz/) *n* **1.** a company that slaughters animals and processes and packages meat **2.** a company that packages food other than meat

pack·man /pák màn, pákmən/ (*plural* **-men** /-mèn, -mən/) *n* same as **peddler** (sense 1)

pack rat *n* **1.** a rat that lives in woodlands and collects and carries away objects to its nest, the best-known species of which has a long bushy tail and cheek pouches. Native to: North America. Latin name: *Neotoma cinerea*. **2.** a hoarder of objects (*informal*)

pack·sack /pák sàk/ *n* a bag with shoulder straps that can be carried on the back

pack·sad·dle /pák sàdd'l/ *n* a saddle for carrying loads on a pack animal

pack·thread /pák thrèd/ *n* strong twine used for sewing up packages wrapped in sacking or other fabric

pack train *n* a line of pack animals carrying loads

pact /pakt/ *n* an agreement made between two or more people or groups, either formally or informally, to do something together or for each other [15C. Via French < Latin *pactum* < past participle of *pacisci* "agree"]

pad[1] /pad/ *n* **1.** PIECE OF SOFT MATERIAL a piece of soft material used to protect something or give it shape, to clean or polish articles, or to absorb moisture **2.** PROTECTIVE MATERIAL WORN BY SPORTS PLAYERS a specially shaped covering of impact-absorbing material used to protect part of the body, especially when playing a sport **3.** BLOCK OF PAPER SHEETS a number of sheets of paper of the same size fastened together along one edge **4.** INK-FILLED MATERIAL a thick firm piece of material saturated with ink onto which a rubber stamp is pressed so that ink is transferred to it **5.** AREA FOR TAKING OFF AND LANDING a place where a helicopter can land and take off or from which a rocket is launched **6.** SANITARY NAPKIN a strip of absorbent material used externally during menstruation **7.** BACKING MATERIAL a firm backing or support for something that is laid on a surface **8.** FLESHY CUSHION OF ANIMAL'S PAW a small rounded fleshy cushion on the underside of an animal's paw **9.** FLESHY TIP OF FINGER OR TOE the rounded fleshy part at the end of a human finger or toe **10.** LIVING QUARTERS somebody's apartment or house (*dated slang*) **11.** BOT FLOATING LEAF OF WATER PLANT the broad leaf of a plant such as a water lily that floats on the surface of the water **12.** ELEC ENG SET OF RESISTORS a fixed configuration of resistors designed to reduce the strength of an electrical signal without distorting the signal itself **13.** COMPUT GAMES same as **joypad** (*informal*) ■ *vt* (**pad·ded, pad·ding, pads**) **1.** COVER SOMETHING WITH SOFT MATERIAL to use soft material to give something shape, to make it more comfortable, or to protect it **2.** ADD UNNECESSARY MATERIAL TO SOMETHING to add unnecessary material to something, especially a piece of writing or a speech, in order to lengthen it ○ *padded out the speech with anecdotes* **3.** INFLATE SOMETHING BY ADDING BOGUS EXPENSES to add extra charges to a bill or expense account to make it higher than it should be [Mid-16C. Probably < Low Dutch]

pad[2] /pad/ *vti* (**pad·ded, pad·ding, pads**) to walk, or to walk along or through somewhere, with soft or silent steps ○ *She padded along in her slippers.* ■ *n* the sound of soft steady footsteps [Mid-16C. Origin ?]

pad·ded cell /pàddəd-/ *n* in former times, a room in a psychiatric hospital with its walls and floor covered with padding to prevent a patient from doing himself or herself physical harm

pad·ding /pádding/ *n* **1.** THICK SOFT MATERIAL thick soft material used as a protective lining or covering or to fill and give shape to things **2.** UNNECESSARY ADDITIONS TO SPEECH OR WRITING unnecessary or irrelevant material added to a piece of writing or a speech to make it longer **3.** BOGUS ADDITIONS TO BILL extra charges added to a bill or expense account to make it higher than it should be

pad·dle[1] /pádd'l/ *n* **1.** SHORT FLAT-BLADED OAR a short oar with a flat blade at one or both ends used to propel a canoe or small boat **2.** ON PADDLE WHEEL a blade of a paddle wheel **3.** ZOOL same as **flipper** (sense 1) **4.** TABLE TENNIS RACKET a round wooden racket with a short handle used in table tennis **5.** PIECE OF WOOD FOR SPANKING a usually short piece of wood with a flattened end used for physical punishment **6.** FLAT-BLADED STIRRING TOOL a tool with a flat blade used for shaping, stirring, or beating **7.** EARLY INPUT DEVICE FOR VIDEO GAMES an input device for early video games with a dial that allowed the user to move an on-screen object either up and down or from side to side ■ *v* (**-dled, -dling, -dles**) **1.** *vti* PROPEL CANOE WITH PADDLE to propel a canoe or small boat through water using a paddle **2.** *vt* CARRY SOMETHING IN CANOE to carry somebody or something somewhere in a canoe or paddleboat **3.** *vti* ROW AT EASY PACE to row a boat at an easy pace **4.** *vt* HIT SOMEBODY to hit somebody with a paddle or with the hand **5.** *vt* STIR WITH PADDLE to stir, beat, or shape something using a paddle [15C. Origin ?] —**pad·dler** *n*

pad·dle[2] /pádd'l/ (**-dled, -dling, -dles**) *v* **1.** *vti* to move the hands or feet about gently in shallow water **2.** *vi* to walk along unsteadily like a very small child [Mid-16C. Probably < Low Dutch] —**pad·dler** *n*

pad·dle·ball /pádd'l bàwl/ *n* **1.** a game for two to four players played by hitting a ball against a wall with small paddles **2.** the ball used in paddleball

pad·dle·board /pádd'l bàwrd/ *n* a long narrow surfboard used especially in rescuing swimmers

pad·dle·boat /pádd'l bòt/ *n* a boat propelled by one or more paddle wheels

pad·dle·fish /pádd'l fish/ (*plural* **-fish·es** or *same*) *n* a large freshwater fish with a long flat snout and a cartilaginous skeleton. Native to: Mississippi River valley, Yangtze River. Family: Polyodontidae.

pad·dle steam·er *n UK* same as **paddle wheeler**

pad·dle wheel *n* a wheel with flat blades fixed all around its edge, attached to the hull of a ship and usually turned by an engine to propel the ship through water

paddle wheeler

pad·dle wheel·er *n* a steamship that is moved through the water by a paddle wheel

pad·dling pool *n UK* same as **wading pool**

pad·dock[1] /páddək/ *n* **1.** ENCLOSED FIELD FOR HORSES a small field near a house or stable with grazing for horses **2.** AREA FOR MOUNTING RACEHORSES an area on a racetrack where the racehorses are paraded before a race and the jockeys mount **3.** AREA FOR RACING CARS BEFORE RACE an area near the pits on an automobile racetrack where cars are worked on before a race ■ *vt* (**-docked, -dock·ing, -docks**) KEEP HORSES IN PADDOCK to keep animals, especially horses, in a paddock [Early 17C. Alteration of dialect *parrock* < Old English *pearroc* "fence, enclosed land" < Germanic]

pad·dock[2] /páddək/, **pud·dock** /púddək/ *n regional* a frog or toad [14C. < Old Norse *padda* "toad"]

pad·dy /páddee/ (*plural* **-dies**) *n* **1.** *also* **pad·dy field** a field, usually kept covered with shallow water, in which rice is grown **2.** rice as a crop in the field or when harvested but not yet processed [Early 17C. < Malay *padi*]

Pad·dy /páddee/ (*plural* **-dies**) *n* an offensive term for an Irish person or somebody of Irish ancestry (*slang*) [Late 18C. < nickname for Irish *Pádraig* "Patrick"]

pad·dy field *n* AGRIC same as **paddy** (sense 1)

pad·dy wag·on *n* POLICE same as **patrol wagon** (*informal*) [Late 19C. Probably < PADDY, referring to Irish policemen in New York and New England]

Pa·de·rew·ski /pàddə réfskee/, **Ignace Jan** (1860–1941) Polish pianist, composer, and prime minister (1919). An internationally renowned musician, he was prime minister of the newly independent Poland for ten months before resuming his musical career.

pad·lock /pád lòk/ *n* a detachable lock with a movable semicircular bar at the top, the free end of which is usually passed through a hasp and then locked shut ■ *vt* (**-locked, -lock·ing, -locks**) to secure something using a padlock [15C. Origin ?]

pad·pa·rad·scha /pád pə ráddshə/ *n* a rare orange-pink sapphire [Via German < Sinhalese *padmaraga* < Sanskrit *padma* "lotus flower" + *raga* "color"]

pa·dre /paá dráy, -dree/ *n* **1.** *Hispanic* used to address or refer to a Roman Catholic priest of a Spanish-speaking church in the United States, or in a country where Spanish, Italian, or Portuguese is spoken **2.** a Christian cleric who ministers to the armed forces (*informal*) [Late 16C. Via Italian, Spanish, or Portuguese < Latin *pater* "father"]

pa·dri·no /pa drée nō/ (*plural* **-nos**) *n Hispanic* **1.** a senior patron or adviser who assists non-Mexican businesspeople in starting and running commercial operations in Mexico **2.** a godfather of a young girl who is having a rite of passage party (**quinceañera**) welcoming her into adulthood, and who pays for flowers, invitations, and other things [< Spanish < *padre* "father"]

pa·dro·ne /pə drṓ này, -drṓnee/ (*plural* **-nes** /-nayz, -neez/ or **-ni** /-nee/) *n* **1.** the owner or manager of an Italian business, especially a restaurant or café **2.** a man who hires Italian immigrants to work for him, especially one who then exploits them [Late 17C. Via Italian < Latin *patronus* "protector, patron" < *pater* "father"] —**pa·dro·nism** /pə drṓ nìzzəm/ *n*

pad·saw /pád sàw/ *n UK* same as **keyhole saw** [Late 19C. < PAD[1] "handle into which different tools can be fitted"]

pad thai /pàd tī́/ *n* in Thai cooking, a dish of rice noodles stir-fried with various other ingredients, especially shrimp and chicken [< Thai]

Pad·u·a /pájjoō ə/ city in northeastern Italy, and the capital of Padua Province, Veneto Region. Population: 211,035 (1999). Italian name **Padova**

pad·u·a·soy /pájjoo ə sòy/ *n* a rich heavy silk fabric [Late 16C. Alteration (influenced by PADUA) of French *pou-de-soie*]

Pa·du·cah /pə dóokə/ city in western Kentucky, directly west of the confluence of the Tennessee and Ohio rivers. Population: 25,566 (2002 estimate).

pae·an /pée ən/, **pe·an** *n* a written, spoken, or musical expression of enthusiastic praise or rapturous joy [Late 16C. Via Latin, "religious hymn (originally in honor of Apollo)" < Greek *paian* < *Paian*, name for Apollo]

paed- *prefix* another spelling of **ped-**

pae·di·at·rics, etc. *n* MED UK spelling of **pediatrics, etc.**

paedo- another spelling of **pedo-**[1]

pa·el·la /paa éllə, paa áy yàa/ *n* a dish made of saffron-flavored rice with chicken, shellfish, and a variety of other ingredients cooked together, originally from Spain [Late 19C. Via Catalan < Latin *patella* "small dish" < *patina* "shallow dish"]

pae·on /pée ən, -òn/ *n* a metrical foot of one long and three short syllables arranged in any order [Early 17C. Via Latin < Greek *paiōn*, variant of *paian* (see PAEAN)]

Paes·tum /péstəm, péestəm/ ancient city in southern Italy, noted for its Greek ruins

Pá·ez /paá ess/, **José Antonio** (1790–1873) Venezuelan revolutionary leader and president (1831–35, 1838–43, 1846–47, and 1861–63). He fought in the South American wars of independence (1810–25) and set up an independent Venezuelan government in 1831.

pa·gan /páygən/ *n* **1. ADHERENT OF NONMAINSTREAM RELIGION** a religious adherent who does not follow one of the world's main religions, especially somebody who is not a Christian, Muslim, or Jew (*sometimes considered offensive*) **2. POLYTHEIST OR PANTHEIST** a follower of an ancient polytheistic or pantheistic religion **3. HEATHEN** somebody without a religion (*disapproving*) ■ *adj* **1. OF NONMAINSTREAM RELIGION** believing in or relating to a religion that is not one of the world's main religions and is regarded as questionable **2. FOLLOWING POLYTHEISTIC OR PANTHEISTIC RELIGION** believing in or relating to an ancient polytheistic or pantheistic religion **3. NONRELIGIOUS** having no religion (*disapproving*) [14C. < late Latin *paganus* "heathen, non-Christian," in classical Latin "villager, civilian" < *pagus* "rural district"] —**pa·gan·ish** *adj* —**pa·gan·ism** *n*

ORIGIN The Latin word *pagus*, from which ***pagan*** is derived, originally meant "something stuck in the ground as a landmark." It was extended metaphorically to "rural district, village," and the noun *paganus* was derived from it, denoting "country dweller, villager." This shifted in meaning, first to "civilian," and then (based on the early Christian notion that all members of the Church were "soldiers" of Jesus Christ) to "heathen."

Pa·ga·ni·ni /pàggə néenee/, **Niccolò** (1782–1840) Italian composer and violinist. He was renowned as a virtuoso, and his compositions include violin sonatas, caprices for solo violin, and concertos.

page[1] /payj/ *n* **1. ONE SIDE OF SHEET OF PAPER** one side of a single sheet of paper, especially one bound into a book, newspaper, or magazine, or forming part of a piece of written work **2. SINGLE SHEET IN BOOK** a single sheet of paper, especially one bound into a book, newspaper, or magazine ○ *a book with some pages missing* **3. AMOUNT OF WRITING ON PAGE** the amount of writing or printed matter that can be contained on a page **4. COMPUTER DATA PRINTING OUT AS PAGE** the amount of text or graphics in a computer document that will print out as a single page **5. SCREENFUL OF COMPUTER DISPLAY** the portion of text or graphics that can be seen on a computer screen at one time **6. NOTEWORTHY PERIOD OR EVENT** a period or event, especially a noteworthy one, in the history of something or somebody's life ○ *Antibiotics wrote an important page in the history of medical research.* ■ *v* **(paged, pag·ing, pag·es) 1.** *vi* **LOOK THROUGH PAGES** to turn and look over the pages of something **2.** *vt* LITERAT same as **paginate** [Late 16C. < French, shortening of *pagene* < Latin *pagina* "strips of papyrus fastened together"]

page[2] /payj/ *n* **1. BOY ATTENDANT** a youth acting as an attendant to somebody on a ceremonial occasion, e.g., to a bride at her wedding **2. BOY WHO RUNS ERRANDS** a youth employed to run errands or carry messages for guests in a hotel or club **3. ERRAND RUNNER IN US CONGRESS** somebody employed as a messenger, guide, and assistant in the US Congress **4. BOY SERVANT IN MEDIEVAL TIMES** a youth who acted as a personal or household servant to somebody, especially a royal or noble person, in medieval times **5. BOY APPRENTICED TO KNIGHT** a youth who acted as the personal servant to a knight in medieval times as the first stage of his training to become a knight ■ *vt* **(paged, pag·ing, pag·es) 1. SUMMON SOMEBODY BY NAME** to summon somebody by calling out his or her name, e.g., over a loudspeaker system **2. CONTACT SOMEBODY ON BEEPER** to try to contact somebody on his or her pager **3.** HIST **ACT AS PAGE TO SOMEBODY** to serve somebody in the capacity of page [13C. < French]

Page /payj/, **Sir Earle** (1880–1961) Australian politician. He was founder and leader of the Country Party (1920–39), held various ministerial posts, and was prime minister for just 19 days in 1939. See table at **prime minister**. Full name **Page, Sir Earle Christmas Grafton**

pag·eant /pájjənt/ *n* **1.** a large-scale stage production representing historical or legendary events, especially local ones, in scenes or tableaux in which dramatic interest is less important than spectacle **2.** an elaborate and colorful procession, display, or ceremonial occasion [14C. < Anglo-Latin *pagina* "scene, stage"]

pag·eant·ry /pájjəntree/ *n* highly colorful, splendid, and stately display or ceremonies, usually with a historical or traditional flavor

page·boy /páyj bòy/ *n* **1.** same as **page**[2] *n* (sense 1) **2.** a hairstyle in which the hair is cut to one length, usually jaw-length, and curls under slightly at the ends, with bangs at the front

page break *n* a code or symbol on a computer screen that shows where a printer will start a new page, e.g., in a word-processing document

~~pagent~~ incorrect spelling of **pageant**

pag·er /páyjər/ *n* a small electronic message-receiving device, often with a small screen, that beeps, flashes, or vibrates to let the user know that somebody is trying to contact him or her

Pag·et's dis·ease /pájjəts-/ *n* **1.** a disease in which the bones become enlarged and weakened and subject to fracture **2.** a cancerous inflammatory condition of the nipple and areola, associated with breast cancer [Late 19C. After Sir James *Paget* (1814–99), British surgeon]

page-turn·er *n* a book with a very gripping plot

page view *n* a count of the number of times a webpage is requested, assumed to be the number of times somebody has responded to an advertisement

pag·i·nal /pájjən'l/ *adj* **1.** exactly duplicating a previous edition or version, so that the same text appears on the same page in both **2.** consisting of, relating to, or like a page or pages [Mid-17C. < late Latin *paginalis* < Latin *pagina* "strips of papyrus fastened together"]

pag·i·nate /pájjə nàyt/ **(-nat·ed, -nat·ing, -nates)** *vt* to number the pages of a book or computer document [Late 19C. Probably back-formation < PAGINATION]

pag·i·na·tion /pàjjə náysh'n/ *n* **1.** the sequential numbers given to pages in a book or document **2.** the process or work of numbering pages [Mid-19C. < French *paginer* "paginate" < Latin *pagina* "strips of papyrus fastened together"]

pag·ing[1] /páyjing/ *n* the movement of a fixed-size block of computer data between faster main and slower auxiliary memories to optimize performance without the user being aware that the transfer has taken place [< PAGE[1]]

pag·ing[2] /páyjing/ *n* a facility that enables somebody to be contacted via a pager (*often used before a noun*) ○ *a paging service* [< PAGE[2]]

Pag·li·a /páylee ə/, **Camille** (*b.* 1947) US writer. Her books, which mainly examine art and culture, take an antifeminist position. Full name **Paglia, Camille Anna**

> "Television is actually closer to reality than anything in books. The madness of TV is the madness of human life."
> [Camille Paglia, *Harper's Magazine*; 1991]

Pa·gnol /paan yṓl/, **Marcel** (1895–1974) French playwright and movie director. Many of his movies, including *Manon des Sources* (1952), are set in southern France.

> "Honor is like a match: you can only use it once."
> [Marcel Pagnol, *Marius*; 1929]

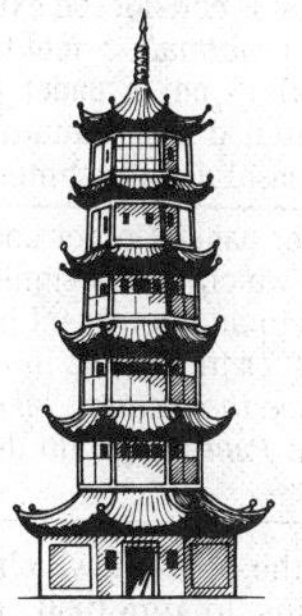

pagoda

pa·go·da /pə gṓdə/ *n* **1.** a Buddhist temple building, especially one in the form of a tower with several stories, each with an upward curving roof that tapers slightly toward the top **2.** a building that is shaped like a Buddhist pagoda but has a decorative rather than a religious purpose [Late 16C. < Portuguese *pagode*]

pah /paa/ *interj* used to show disgust, contempt, or annoyance [Late 16C. Natural exclamation]

Pah·la·vi /paálə vèe/, **Peh·le·vi** /páylə-/ *n* a literary form of classical Persian used especially in Zoroastrian and Manichaean texts [Late 18C. < Persian *pahlawī* < *pahlav* < *parthava* "Parthia" (country of ancient Asia)] —**Pah·la·vi** *adj*

Pah·la·vi /paálə vèe/, **Muhammad Reza Shah** (1919–80) shah of Iran. During his reign (1941–79) he attempted to modernize and westernize Iran, but his dictatorial rule made him unpopular. He was overthrown in the 1979 Islamic revolution.

Pah·la·vi, Reza Shah (1877–1944) shah of Iran. He seized power in a coup (1921) and became shah (1925). He initiated westernization, and abdicated in favor of his son (1941).

pa·ho·e·ho·e /pə hṓ ee hṑ ee/ *n* a form of smooth dark-colored glassy basaltic rock formed from lava flow [Mid-19C. < Hawaiian]

paid /payd/ FIN past participle, past tense of **pay**[1] ■ *adj* given money in return for work, or done for the purpose of earning money ○ *paid employment*

paid-up *adj* (*not hyphenated when used after a verb*) **1.** having paid all the money owed to an organization or individual person **2.** for which the full price or all installments have been paid ○ *a paid-up membership*

pai·gle /páyg'l/ *n UK* PLANTS same as **oxlip** [Mid-16C. Origin ?]

pail /payl/ *n* HOUSEHOLD same as **bucket** *n* (senses 1–2) [14C. < Old French *paielle* "warming pan, liquid measure"]

pail·lasse /pal yáss, pál yàss/ *n* a thin straw-filled mattress [Early 16C. Via French < Italian *pagliacchio* < Latin *palea* "straw, chaff"]

pail·lette /pī yétt/ *n* a sequin or spangle sewn onto a piece of clothing [Mid-19C. < French, literally "small straw" < *paille* "straw, chaff" < Latin *palea*]

pain /payn/ *n* **1. UNPLEASANT PHYSICAL SENSATION** the acutely unpleasant physical discomfort experienced by somebody who is violently struck, injured, or ill ○ *cried out in pain* **2. FEELING OF DISCOMFORT** a sensation of pain in a particular part of the body (*often used in the plural*) ○ *was complaining of pains in the lower abdomen* ○ *back pain* **3. EMOTIONAL DISTRESS** severe emotional or mental distress ○ *the pain of rejection* **4. SOMEBODY OR SOMETHING TROUBLESOME** somebody or something that is extremely annoying or causes many problems (*informal*) ■ **pains** *npl* **1. TROUBLE TAKEN TO DO SOMETHING** conscientious effort or trouble taken, usually in tackling a piece of work **2. LABOR PAINS** the painful spasms experienced by a woman during childbirth, caused by the contraction of the uterus ■ *v* **(pained, pain·ing, pains) 1.** *vt* **SADDEN SOMEBODY** to make somebody feel saddened or distressed ○ *It pains me to hear you speak like that.* **2.** *vti* **CAUSE OR FEEL PAIN** to cause physical pain to somebody, or experience pain [13C. Via French < Latin *poena* "penalty, punishment" < Greek *poinē* "penalty"] ◇ **a pain in the ass** *or* **butt** an offensive term for somebody or something that is considered to be extremely annoying or troublesome (*slang*) ◇ **a pain in the neck** somebody or something that is considered extremely annoying or troublesome (*informal*) ◇ **feel no pain** to be very drunk (*informal*) ◇ **on** *or* **under pain of something** risking or threatened with something such as death or instant dismissal as punishment

SPELLCHECK pain or **pane**? Do not confuse the spelling of ***pain*** and ***pane***, which sound similar. ***Pain*** is a noun and verb referring to an unpleasant physical sensation, emotional distress, or trouble, as in *a pain in my knee, if it pains you to see them suffer, taking great pains not to offend anybody.* ***Pane*** is a noun denoting a piece of glass in a window.

pain bar·rier *n* the point at which pain reaches its peak and begins to diminish, especially as experienced by an athlete

Paine /payn/, **Robert Treat** (1731–1814) US revolutionary leader. He was a delegate at the Continental Congress and a signatory of the Declaration of Independence (1776).

Library of Congress

Thomas Paine

Paine, Thomas (1737–1809) British-born American writer, political philosopher, and revolutionary. His pamphlet *Common Sense* (1776) influenced the move toward American independence. Known as **Tom Paine**

"Government, even in its best state, is but a necessary evil; in its worst state, an intolerable one."
[Thomas Paine, *Common Sense*; 1776]

"These are the times that try men's souls. The summer soldier and the sunshine patriot will, in this crisis, shrink from the service of their country; but he that stands it *now*, deserves the love and thanks of men and women."
[Thomas Paine, Introduction, *The Crisis*; December 1776]

pained /paynd/ *adj* expressing wounded feelings or a sense of being disappointed or offended by something that somebody has done ○ *a pained expression*

pain·ful /páynfəl/ *adj* **1. CAUSING PAIN** causing acute physical discomfort ○ *a painful cut* **2. HURTING** hurting as a result of an injury or disease ○ *My arm's still quite painful.* **3. CAUSING DISTRESS** causing emotional or mental distress ○ *painful memories* **4. DIFFICULT** accomplished with laborious effort ○ *making painful progress with the work* **5. VERY BAD** embarrassingly bad ○ *Her performance was painful to watch.* —**pain·ful·ly** *adv* —**pain·ful·ness** *n*

pain·kill·er /páyn kìllər/ *n* something, especially a drug, that reduces pain —**pain·kill·ing** *adj*

pain·less /páynləss/ *adj* **1.** not causing any pain **2.** involving little or no difficulty or effort ○ *a painless solution to our problem* —**pain·less·ly** *adv*—**pain·less·ness** *n*

pains·tak·ing /páynz tàyking/ *adj* involving or showing great care and attention to detail —**pains·tak·ing·ly** *adv*

SYNONYMS See ***careful***.

paint /paynt/ *n* **1. COLORED LIQUID APPLIED TO SURFACE** a colored liquid applied to a surface in order to decorate or protect it, or in order to create a painting **2. DRIED PAINT ON SURFACE** a film of dried paint on a surface (*often used before a noun*) ○ *paint remover* **3. SOLID PIGMENT** a solid block of pigment that forms liquid paint when moistened or dissolved **4. FACIAL MAKEUP** makeup for the face (*dated informal*) **5.** ZOOL, RIDING same as **pinto** ■ *adj* ZOOL, RIDING same as **pinto** ■ *v* (**paint·ed, paint·ing, paints**) **1.** *vti* **COVER SOMETHING WITH PAINT** to cover the surface of something with paint in order to decorate or protect it **2.** *vti* **CREATE PICTURE USING PAINT** to create a picture, or create a picture of something, by applying paint in different colors to paper, canvas, or some other surface **3.** *vt* **ADD SOMETHING TO SURFACE USING PAINT** to mark designs or words on a surface using paint ○ *The words "No Parking" were painted on the wall.* **4.** *vt* **APPLY LIQUID WITH BRUSH** to apply a liquid to a surface using a brush ○ *My father used to paint iodine onto our skinned knees.* **5.** *vt* **APPLY COSMETICS TO FACE OR NAILS** to apply makeup to the face or lips, or polish to the nails **6.** *vt* **DESCRIBE SOMETHING** to describe something in words, especially vividly ○ *In his autobiography, he paints his uncle's home as a palace.* [12C. < French *peint*, past participle of *peindre* "to paint" < Latin *pingere*]

paint·ball /páynt bàwl/ *n* a team game in which each player has a gun that fires gelatin capsules filled with water-soluble marking dye, the object being to shoot members of the opposing team —**paint·ball·er** *n* —**paint·ball·ing** *n*

paint·brush /páynt brùsh/ *n* a brush for putting paint onto surfaces or painting pictures

paint·ed bunt·ing *n* a brightly colored bunting. Native to: southern North America, Mexico. Latin name: *Passerina ciris.*

paint·ed cup *n* BOT same as **Indian paintbrush**

Paint·ed Des·ert /pàyntid-/ plateau region in Arizona noted for its vividly colored rocks. Parts of it lie within Native American reservations. Area: 7,500 sq. mi./19,000 sq. km.

paint·ed la·dy *n* a widely distributed migratory butterfly with reddish brown, black, and orange wings. Latin name: *Vanessa cardui.*

paint·ed tur·tle *n* a turtle found near slow-moving water that has red or yellow stripes on its legs, head, and tail and red markings on the margins of its shell. Native to: North America. Latin name: *Chrysemys picta.*

paint·er[1] /páyntər/ *n* **1.** an artist who paints pictures ○ *a portrait painter* **2.** somebody whose job is to cover surfaces with paint, especially to paint the interiors of buildings [14C. < PAINT]

pain·ter[2] /páyntər/ *n* a rope attached to the front of a boat that is used to tie it to something such as a mooring [14C. Probably < Old French *penteur* "rope running from a masthead" < *pendre* "hang" < Latin *pendere*]

pain·ter[3] /páyntər/ *n Southern US* ZOOL same as **mountain lion** [Mid-18C. Alteration of PANTHER]

paint·er·ly /páyntərlee/ *adj* **1.** characterized by the use of color rather than line to represent shapes or to structure a composition **2.** characteristic of a good painter or good painting

paint·ing /páynting/ *n* **1.** a picture made using paint **2.** the art or work of applying paint to surfaces

paint·work /páynt wùrk/ *n* the painted surfaces of something, e.g., a vehicle's bodywork or the interior of a building

pair /per/ *n* **1. TWO SIMILAR THINGS USED TOGETHER** two matching objects that are designed to be used together ○ *a pair of socks* **2. THING WITH TWO JOINED PARTS** a garment or article consisting of two matching or identical parts joined together ○ *a pair of binoculars* **3. TWO PEOPLE TOGETHER** two people who are doing something together, or who are considered together because there is some connection between them **4. COUPLE** two people in a relationship such as a marriage **5. 2 MATING ANIMALS** a male and female animal of the same species who are together for mating **6. ONE OF TWO MATCHED ARTICLES** one of two matched articles such as shoes or gloves ○ *lost the pair to his cuff link* **7. TWO HORSES HARNESSED TOGETHER** two horses harnessed together to pull a carriage ○ *a coach and pair* **8.** CARDS **TWO PLAYING CARDS** two playing cards that have the same value ○ *a pair of aces* **9.** POL **TWO OPPOSING MEMBERS MAKING VOTING AGREEMENT** two members from opposing sides in a legislative body who each agree not to vote on issues if the other is not present and able to vote. The arrangement covers occasions when members cannot vote because of illness or other commitments, the effect being to maintain the usual balance of numbers between the two opposing sides. **10.** POL **AGREEMENT TO FORM PAIR** an arrangement between two members on opposing sides in a legislative body to form a pair **11.** ROWING same as **pair-oar** **12.** MATH, LOGIC **TWO ORDERED ITEMS** a set consisting of two items in order **13.** CHEM **ELECTRON BOND** two electrons forming a bond between atoms ■ *v* (**paired, pair·ing, pairs**) **1.** *vti* **PUT INTO GROUP OF TWO** to form a pair with somebody, or partner one person with another, for a shared activity or for romance or friendship **2.** *vt* **MATCH TWO THINGS TOGETHER** to put two matching articles together **3.** *vt* POL **FORM OPPOSING MEMBERS INTO LEGISLATIVE PAIR** to arrange a pair between two members of a voting assembly, or form a pair with another member **4.** *vi* ZOOL **FORM MATING PAIR** to form a mating pair with another animal of the same species [13C. Directly or via French *paire* < Latin *paria* "equals," a plural of *par* "equal, pair"]

SPELLCHECK pair, **pare**, or **pear**? Do not confuse the spelling of ***pair***, ***pare***, and ***pear***, which sound similar. ***Pair*** is a noun or verb referring to two things, parts, or people, as in *a pair of shoes, a pair of scissors, pair a novice with a more experienced partner.* ***Pare*** is used only as a verb, meaning "to trim" or "to peel," as in *pare down the number of candidates, pare the apples.* ***Pear*** is only used as a noun, denoting a fruit or the tree on which it grows.

USAGE pair as a singular or a plural: If ***pair*** means a unit, set, or whole, it takes a singular verb: *A pair of new leather riding boots is expensive.* If the people or things constituting the ***pair*** are regarded individually and not as a set, a plural verb is used: *A pair of volunteers are walking up and down various streets and alleys, picking up trash.* Here, the two people are thought of as working not only together on one street but also separately on other streets and alleys. If ***pair*** comes after a number over *one* (as in *16 pairs of boots*), *16 pairs*, not *16 pair*, is correct.

pair bond *n* a relationship between a male and female animal, formed either during courtship and breeding or for life, that excludes others of the same species —**pair-bond** *vi* —**pair bond·ing** *n*

pair-oar *n* a racing shell in which two rowers with one oar each sit one behind the other

pair pro·duc·tion *n* the creation of a negative particle (**electron**) and a positive particle (**positron**) when a fast particle (**photon**) passes through a strong electrical field such as that surrounding an atomic nucleus

pai·sa /pī saá/ (*plural* **-se** /-sáy/ or *same*) *n* **1.** a subunit of currency in some South Asian countries. See table at **currency** **2.** *S Asia* money in general [Late 19C. < Hindi *paisā*]

pai·sa·no /pī zaánō/ (*plural* **-nos**) *n US* **1.** a friend or acquaintance (*informal; often used in direct address*) ○ *Well, paisano, how's it going today?* **2.** a countryman or ally [Mid-19C. Via Spanish, "peasant" < late Latin *pagensis* "inhabitant of a district" < Latin *pagus* "rural district"]

paisley

pais·ley /páyzlee/ (*plural* **-leys**) *n* **1.** a distinctive bold design consisting of multicolored curving shapes, stylized cones, and feathers **2.** a fabric with a paisley design, especially a type of woolen shawl popular in the 19th century [Early 19C. After PAISLEY] —**pais·ley** *adj*

Pais·ley /páyzlee/ city and administrative center of Renfrewshire, Scotland. Population: 75,526 (1991).

Pa·ís Vas·co /pī eéss baásskō/ ➧ **Basque Country**

Pai·ute /pī́ oōt/ (*plural* **-utes** or *same*), **Pi·ute** *n* **1.** a member of either of two Native North American peoples, the Northern Paiutes and the Southern Paiutes **2.** the Uto-Aztecan language of the Paiute people. Native speakers: 12,000. [Early 19C. < Spanish *payuchi*] —**Pai·ute** *adj*

pa·ja·ma par·ty *n* a party, especially for teenagers or children, at which the guests bring pajamas and spend the night

pa·ja·mas /pə jáaməz, pə jámməz/ *npl* **1.** a light loose pair of pants and a matching loose-fitting shirt or top for wearing in bed or for lounging **2.** loose-fitting pants made of silk or lightweight cotton tied at the waist, worn by both men and women in parts of Asia, particularly Turkey and South Asia [Early 19C. < Persian, Urdu *pāy-jāmah* "leg garment"]

Pak /pak, paak/ *n* (*informal*) **1.** somebody from Pakistan (*often used before a noun*) **2.** *S Asia* Pakistan ○ *Indo-Pak talks*

pak choi *n UK* same as **bok choy** [< Chinese (Cantonese) *paăk ts'oi* "white vegetable"]

Pak·i /pákee, páakee/ (*plural* **-is**) *n Can, UK* a highly offensive term for somebody from Pakistan or South Asia, or with ancestors from those areas (*taboo*) [Mid-20C. Shortening of *Pakistani*]

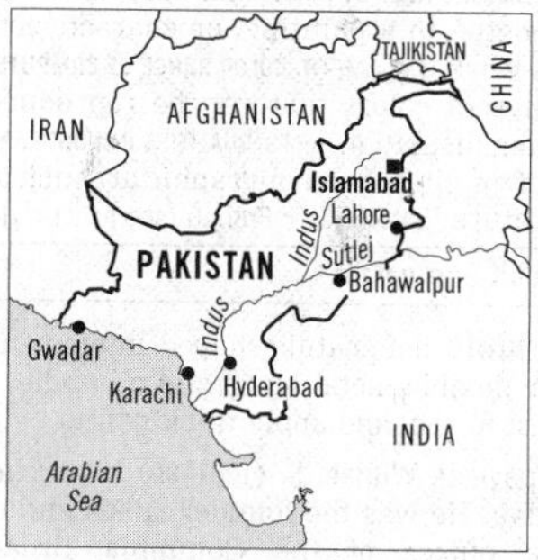

Pakistan

Pak·i·stan /páki stàn, páaki stáan/ country on the Arabian Sea in the northwestern part of South Asia. It rejoined the British Commonwealth in 1989 after withdrawing in 1972. Language: Urdu. Currency: Pakistani rupee. Capital: Islamabad. Population: 150,694,740 (2001). Area: 307,374 sq. mi./796,095 sq. km. Official name **Islamic Republic of Pakistan** —**Pak·i·stan·i** /pàki stáanee, páaki-/ *n, adj*

pal /pal/ *n* (*informal*) **1.** same as **friend** *n* (sense 1) **2.** used to address somebody, often in an unfriendly or aggressive way ○ *Listen, pal, you'd better watch out!* ■ *vi* (**palled, pal·ling, pals**) to become friends with and spend time with somebody [Late 17C. Via English Romany, "friend, brother" < Sanskrit *bhrātṛ* "brother"]

pal around *vi* to become friends with and spend time with somebody (*informal*)

pal·ace /pálləss/ *n* **1.** a grand and imposing building that is the official residence of a king or queen, a head of state such as a president, or a high-ranking aristocrat or church dignitary **2.** a large public or private building with an imposing ornate style, used for entertainment or exhibitions ○ *an old movie palace fallen into disrepair* [13C. Via Old French *palais* < Latin *palatium*, after *Palatium* "Palatine Hill," where the emperor Augustus built a house]

pal·ace rev·o·lu·tion *n* the overthrow of a ruler by those who are already in the ruling group, often carried out with little violence

pal·a·din /pálləd'n, -din/ *n* **1.** MEDIEVAL CHAMPION a champion or hero, especially in medieval legend or history **2.** CHAMPION OF CAUSE somebody known for championing a cause **3.** ONE OF CHARLEMAGNE'S COMPANIONS any one of the 12 legendary companions of Charlemagne [Late 16C. Via French < Latin *palatinus* (see PALATINE[1])]

palaeo-, etc. UK spelling of **paleo-, etc.**

pa·laes·tra *n* ANCIENT HIST, SPORTS another spelling of **palestra**

pa·la·ka /paa láa káa/ (*plural same*) *n* a Hawaiian fabric woven in a checked pattern of white and one other color, often blue [< Hawaiian]

pal·an·quin /pàllən kéen/ *n* a covered seat carried on poles held parallel to the ground on the shoulders of two or four people, used in former times to transport an important person, especially in East Asia [Late 16C. Via Portuguese *palanquim* < Sanskrit *palyaṅka* "bed, litter"]

pal·at·a·ble /pállətəb'l/ *adj* **1.** having a good enough taste to be eaten or drunk **2.** acceptable to somebody's sensibilities —**pal·at·a·bil·i·ty** /pàllətə bíllətee/ *n*

pal·a·tal /pállət'l/ *adj* **1.** ANAT FACING OR RELATING TO PALATE occurring at, facing, or relating to the palate **2.** PHON PRONOUNCED WITH TONGUE AT PALATE describes a consonant sound that is produced by raising the tongue to or near the hard palate ○ *The "sh" sound is a palatal fricative.* **3.** PHON PRONOUNCED WITH TONGUE FORWARD describes a vowel sound that is produced with the tongue moved forward in the mouth ○ *The vowel in "meet" is palatal.* ■ *n* PHON PALATAL SPEECH SOUND a speech sound pronounced with the tongue at or near the hard palate or with the tongue pushed forward, especially a palatal consonant —**pal·a·tal·ly** /pállət'lee/ *adv*

pal·a·tal·ize /pállət'l ìz/ (**-ized, -iz·ing, -iz·es**) *vt* **1.** to make a speech sound by raising the tongue to or toward the hard palate **2.** to alter a speech sound in pronunciation by placing the tongue closer to the hard palate rather than to the teeth, alveolar ridge, or velum —**pal·a·tal·i·za·tion** /pàllət'li záysh'n/ *n*

pal·ate /pállət/ *n* **1.** ROOF OF MOUTH the roof of the mouth, which separates it from the nasal cavity. It consists of a bony hard palate at the front and a muscular soft palate at the rear. **2.** SENSE OF TASTE a personal sense of taste and flavor **3.** AESTHETIC TASTE intellectual or aesthetic tastes or sensibilities **4.** BOT PART OF FLOWER the lower projection of a flower such as the snapdragon, divided into two lips [14C. < Latin *palatum*]

SPELLCHECK palate, palette, or **pallet**? Do not confuse the spelling of ***palate, palette,*** and ***pallet,*** which sound similar. A ***palate*** is the roof of the mouth, or a personal sense of taste, as in *the soft palate, dishes to please all palates*. A ***palette*** or ***pallet*** is a board for an artist's paints, or the colors available on a computer display. As well as meaning "an artist's palette," ***pallet*** also denotes a tray on which to stack loads, a board on which to dry ceramics, a tool with which to mix clay, or a straw-filled mattress.

pa·la·tial /pə láysh'l/ *adj* **1.** grand or luxurious ○ *palatial mansions* **2.** appropriate for a palace [Mid-18C. < Latin *palatium* (see PALACE)] —**pa·la·tial·ness** *n*

pa·lat·i·nate /pə látt'n àyt, pə látt'nət/ *n* the territory, office, or responsibilities of a feudal palatine

Pa·lat·i·nate *n* a part of the German Empire ruled by the Count Palatine of the Rhine, or the part of modern Germany corresponding to this

pal·a·tine[1] /pállə tìn/ *n* **1.** POWERFUL FEUDAL LORD a feudal lord in central Europe with sovereign powers within his territory **2.** IMPERIAL COURT OFFICIAL a court official in the late Roman and Byzantine empires ■ *adj* **1.** FIT FOR PALACE relating to or suitable for a palace **2.** HAVING POWER OVER TERRITORY describes an official or feudal lord who had sovereign power over a territory **3.** RULED BY LORD describes a territory ruled by a sovereign feudal lord [15C. Via French < Latin *palatinus* "of the palace, palace official" < *palatium* (see PALACE)]

pal·a·tine[2] /pállə tìn/ *adj* relating to the palate ■ *n* either of the two bones that form the hard palate [Mid-17C. < French *palatin(e)* < Latin *palatum* "palate"]

Pal·a·tine[1] /pállə tìn/ *adj* relating to the German Palatinate [Mid-17C. < PALATINE[1]]

Pal·a·tine[2] /pállə tìn/ *n* the central hill of the seven on which Rome was built, considered the oldest and the site of many of the imperial palaces [< Latin *palatinus* (see PALATINE[1])]

pal·a·to·al·ve·o·lar /pàllətō al vée ələr, -alvee ṓlər/ *adj* describes a consonant sound that is produced with the tongue touching the upper part of the mouth where the back of the ridge behind the teeth joins the front of the hard palate —**pal·a·to·al·ve·o·lar** *n*

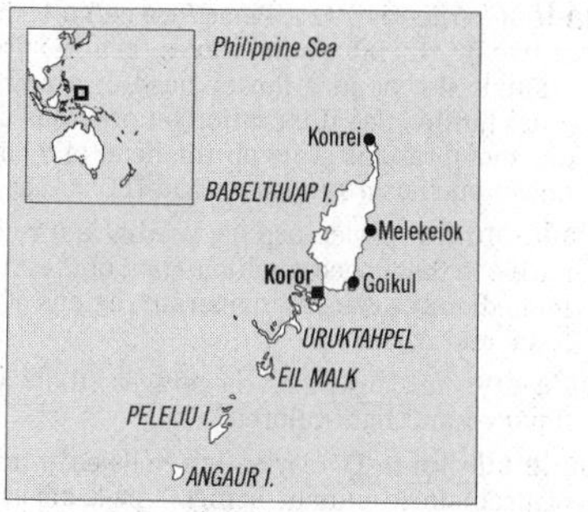

Palau

Pa·lau /paa lów/, **Be·lau** /bə-/ country in the western Pacific Ocean comprising a group of volcanic islands that are part of the Caroline Islands. Capital: Koror. Population: 19,717 (2003). Area: 188 sq. mi./488 sq. km. Official name **Republic of Palau**

pa·lav·er /pə lávvər, -láavər/ *n* **1.** CONFERENCE BETWEEN DIFFERENT PARTIES a conference or meeting between different parties (*humorous*) **2.** EMPTY TALK idle, flattering, or time-wasting talk ■ *vi* (**-ered, -er·ing, -ers**) **1.** CONFER to confer, or hold a conference (*humorous*) **2.** TALK IDLY to talk idly, emptily, or with the intention of flattering [Mid-18C. Via Portuguese *palavra* "speech" < Latin *parabola* (see PARABLE)]

Pa·la·wan /pə láawən/ island and province of the Philippines, northeast of Borneo and southwest of Luzon. Area: 4,550 sq. mi./11,790 sq. km. Population: 528,290 (1990).

pa·laz·zo /pə láatsō/ (*plural* **-zos** or **-zi** /-tsee/) *n* a large ornate building, e.g., a museum or an official residence, especially in Italy [Mid-17C. Via Italian < Latin *palatium* (see PALACE)]

pa·laz·zo pants *npl* women's loose-fitting lightweight pants with flared legs

pale[1] /payl/ *adj* (**pal·er, pal·est**) **1.** HAVING LITTLE COLOR lacking color or intensity ○ *pale blue* **2.** PALLID FROM ILLNESS unusually light in skin complexion because of illness, shock, or worry **3.** PRODUCING LITTLE LIGHT producing or reflecting little light **4.** INADEQUATE inadequate or faint ○ *a pale version of his former flamboyant self* ■ *v* (**paled, pal·ing, pales**) **1.** *vi* BECOME WHITER to become whiter or lose brilliance **2.** *vi* BECOME LESS IMPORTANT to be or become less important, remarkable, or intense, especially in comparison with something more important or serious **3.** *vt* CAUSE SOMEBODY OR SOMETHING TO FADE to cause somebody or something to lose color or brilliance [14C. Via French < Latin *pallidus* (see PALLID)] —**pale·ly** *adv* —**pale·ness** *n*

pale[2] /payl/ *n* **1.** FENCE STAKE a pointed slat of wood for a fence **2.** BOUNDARY FENCE a fence marking a boundary **3.** FENCED-IN AREA an area fenced in, or the boundary of a fenced-in area **4.** HERALDRY VERTICAL STRIPE ON SHIELD a wide vertical band down the center of a shield ■ *vt* (**paled, pal·ing, pales**) FENCE SOMETHING IN to surround an area with a fence [12C. Via French *pal* < Latin *palus* "stake"] ◇ **beyond the pale** outside the limits of what is considered to be acceptable

Pale *n* **1.** the area of Ireland, based around Dublin, that was controlled by England from the 12th century until the final conquest of the entire country in the 16th century **2.** a restricted area in Imperial Russia where Jews were allowed to settle [PALE[2]]

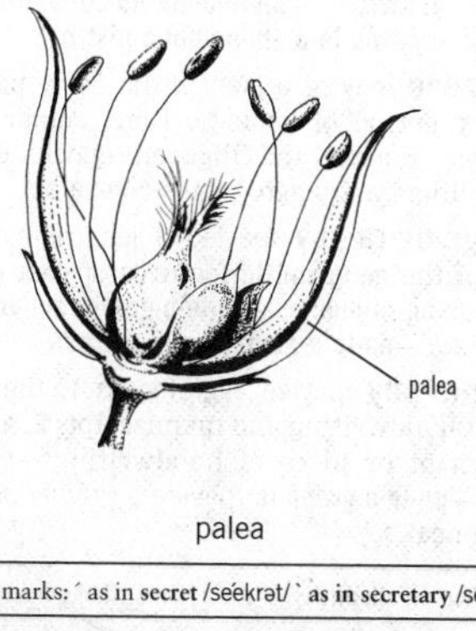

palea

pa·le·a /páylee ə/ (*plural* **-le·ae** /-lee ee/) *n* **1.** the upper of two dry membranous leaves (**bracts**) protecting a single flower in a flower head of a plant of the grass family. See illustration on previous page **2.** a dry membranous scale on the head of a composite flower such as a sunflower [Mid-18C. < Latin, "chaff"]

Pa·le·arc·tic /pàylee aárktik, -aártik/ *adj* relating or native to the biogeographic region of the Arctic and immediately adjacent temperate regions of Europe, Asia, and Africa

pale-dry *adj* describes beverages that are dry-flavored and light-colored

pa·le·eth·nol·o·gy /pàylee eth nóllәjee/ *n* the study of prehistoric human beings —**pa·le·eth·no·log·i·cal** /-ethnә lójjik'l/ *adj* —**pa·le·eth·nol·o·gist** *n*

pale·face /páyl fàyss/ *n* an offensive term for a white person (*insult*)

Pa·lem·bang /paalәm baáng, -lem-/ city in Indonesia on southeastern Sumatra. Population: 1,481,000 (2003).

Pa·len·que /paa léngke/ ancient city in southern Mexico, southeast of Villahermosa. It is the site of a temple noted for its hieroglyphics.

paleo- *prefix* **1.** ancient, prehistoric ○ *paleozoology* **2.** primitive, early ○ *Paleogene* [< Greek *palaios* < *palai* "long ago"]

pa·le·o·an·throp·ic /pàylee ō an thróppik/ *adj* relating to prehistoric human beings

pa·le·o·an·thro·pol·o·gy /pàylee ō anthrә póllәjee/ *n* the study of early human beings and related species through fossil evidence —**pa·le·o·an·thro·po·log·i·cal** /pàylee ō anthrәpә lójjik'l/ *adj* —**pa·le·o·an·thro·pol·o·gist** *n*

Pa·le·o-A·si·at·ic /pàylee ō-/ *adj* LANG same as **Paleosiberian**

pa·le·o·bi·o·ge·og·ra·phy /pàylee ō bī ō jee óggrәfee/ *n* the study of the locations of prehistoric species on the basis of fossil evidence

pa·le·o·bot·a·ny /pàylee ō bótt'nee/ *n* the study of prehistoric plants on the basis of fossil evidence —**pa·le·o·bo·tan·i·cal** /-bә tánnik'l/ *adj*—**pa·le·o·bot·a·nist** *n*

pal·e·o·cean·og·ra·phy /pàylee ōshә nóggrәfee/ *n* the study of prehistoric oceans, especially their history, conditions, and life forms —**pal·e·o·cean·og·ra·pher** *n* —**pal·e·o·cean·og·raph·ic** /-ōshәnә gráffik/ *adj*

Pa·le·o·cene /páylee ә seen/ *n* the epoch of geologic time, 65 million to 55 million years ago, during which various types of mammals flourished. See table at **geologic time** [Late 19C. < PALEO- + Greek *kainos* "new"] —**Pa·le·o·cene** *adj*

pa·le·o·cli·ma·tol·o·gy /pàylee ō klīmә tóllәjee/ *n* the study of prehistoric climates on a global or regional scale from evidence preserved in glacial deposits, sedimentary structures, and fossils —**pa·le·o·cli·ma·to·log·i·cal** /-ō klīmәtә lójjik'l/ *adj* —**pa·le·o·cli·ma·tol·o·gist** *n*

pa·le·o·cur·rent /páylee ō kùr әnt, -kùrrәnt/ *n* a prehistoric current of water or wind, revealed by the study of the sedimentary structures and textures that it deposited

pa·le·o·e·col·o·gy /pàylee ō i kóllәjee/ *n* the study of the interaction of prehistoric life forms and their environments —**pa·le·o·ec·o·log·i·cal** /-èkә lójjik'l, -eekә-/ *adj* —**pa·le·o·e·col·o·gist** *n*

pa·le·o·eth·no·bot·a·ny /pàylee ō ethnō bótt'nee/ *n* the study of fossilized seeds and grain in order to gain information about prehistoric patterns of cereal growth —**pa·le·o·eth·no·bo·tan·i·cal** /-bә tánnik'l/ *adj* —**pa·le·o·eth·no·bot·a·nist** *n*

Pa·le·o·gene /páylee ә jeen/ *n* the early part of the Tertiary period of geologic time, comprising the Paleocene, Eocene, and Oligocene epochs, 65 million to 23 million years ago —**Pa·le·o·gene** *adj*

pa·le·o·ge·og·ra·phy /pàylee ō jee óggrәfee/ *n* the study of the geographic features of past epochs —**pa·le·o·ge·og·ra·pher** *n* —**pa·le·o·ge·o·graph·ic** /-ō jee ә gráffik/ *adj* —**pa·le·o·ge·o·graph·i·cal** *adj*

pa·le·og·ra·phy /pàylee óggrәfee/ *n* **1.** the study of ancient handwriting and manuscripts **2.** an ancient manuscript or piece of handwriting —**pa·le·og·ra·pher** *n* —**pa·le·o·graph·ic** /pàylee ә gráffik/ *adj* —**pa·le·o·graph·i·cal** *adj*

Pa·le·o·In·di·an /pàylee ō-/ *adj* relating to the earliest inhabitants of the Americas, who arrived from Asia by the Bering land bridge that connected Alaska and Siberia. By 12,000 to 10,000 years ago they were hunting game and living in small groups throughout North America. —**Pa·le·o·In·di·an** *n*

pa·le·o·lib·e·ral /pàylee ō líbbәrәl, -líbbrәl/ *adj* regarded as aggressively, stubbornly, and excessively liberal in political beliefs —**pa·le·o·lib·e·ral** *n*

pa·le·o·lith /páylee ә lìth/ *n* a stone tool from the Paleolithic age

Pa·le·o·lith·ic /pàylee ә líthik/ *n* the early part of the Stone Age, when early human beings made chipped-stone tools, from 750,000 to 15,000 years ago —**Pa·le·o·lith·ic** *adj*

Pa·le·o·lith·ic man *n* a member of a people who lived in the Paleolithic period, e.g., Neandertal, Cro-Magnon, or Java man

pa·le·o·mag·net·ism /pàylee ō mágnә tìzzәm/ *n* **1.** the polarity and intensity of residual magnetism in ancient rock **2.** the study of changes in the intensity and direction of the Earth's magnetic field throughout geologic time. The recurring reversals of the Earth's magnetic field and the changing configurations of the continents have been established through such studies. —**pa·le·o·mag·net·ic** /-mag néttik/ *adj*

pa·le·on·tog·ra·phy /pàylee on tóggrәfee/ *n* the branch of paleontology concerned with describing fossils —**pa·le·on·to·graph·ic** /-ontә gráffik/ *adj* —**pa·le·on·to·graph·i·cal** *adj*

paleontol. *abbr* paleontology

pa·le·on·tol·o·gy /pàylee on tóllәjee/ *n* the study of life in prehistoric times by using fossil evidence —**pa·le·on·to·log·i·cal** /pàylee ontә lójjik'l/ *adj* —**pa·le·on·tol·o·gist** *n*

pa·le·o·path·ol·o·gy /pàylee ō pә thóllәjee/ *n* the study of the evidence of disease processes in early human and animal remains, e.g., by using DNA analysis —**pa·le·o·path·o·log·i·cal** /-pathә lójjik'l/ *adj* —**pa·le·o·path·ol·o·gist** *n*

Pa·le·o·si·be·ri·an /pàylee ō sī beeree әn/, **Pa·le·o-Si·be·ri·an** *adj* relating to a small group of languages spoken in eastern Siberia, including Chukchi, that do not belong to any of the major language families

Pa·le·o·zo·ic /pàylee ә zṓ ik/ *n* the era of geologic time, about 570 million to 248 million years ago, during which fish, insects, amphibians, reptiles, and land plants first appeared. See table at **geologic time** —**Pa·le·o·zo·ic** *adj*

pa·le·o·zo·ol·o·gy /pàylee ō zō óllәjee/ *n* the study of ancient animals and animal life using fossils and other paleontological evidence —**pa·le·o·zo·o·log·i·cal** /-zō ә lójjik'l/ *adj* —**pa·le·o·zo·ol·o·gist** *n*

Pa·ler·mo /pә lúrmō, -lér-/ city and port in Sicily, Italy. It is the largest city on the island, and is situated on the northwestern coast. Population: 686,722 (2001).

Pal·es·tine /pállә stīn/ area in Southwest Asia between the Jordan River and the eastern coast of the Mediterranean Sea. During biblical times it was the Jewish homeland, comprising the kingdoms of Israel and Judah, and was then successively occupied by the Romans, Arabs, and Ottoman Turks. In 1947 Palestine was partitioned between the new states of Israel and Jordan. Wars fought in 1948, 1967, and 1972 between Israel and the surrounding Arab states saw an increase in the land held by Israel. In 1987 a Palestinian uprising or intifada began in protest against the continued Israeli occupation. In 1993 and 1995 agreements were signed under which the Palestinian Arabs gained limited self-rule under the Palestinian National Authority in the Palestinian-Administered Territories in the Gaza Strip and on the West Bank of the Jordan River, but conflict and the Israeli presence continue. —**Pal·es·tin·i·an** /pàllә stínnee әn/ *n, adj*

pa·les·tra /pә léstrә/ (*plural* **-trae** /-tree/ or **-tras**), **pa·laes·tra** (*plural* **-trae** or **-tras**) *n* a public sports ground or gymnasium in ancient Greece [14C. Via Latin < Greek *palaistra* < *palaiein* "wrestle"]

Pa·le·stri·na /pàlli streenә/, **Giovanni Pierluigi da** (1525–94) Italian composer. A prolific composer of religious and secular choral music, he wrote 250 motets and over 100 masses.

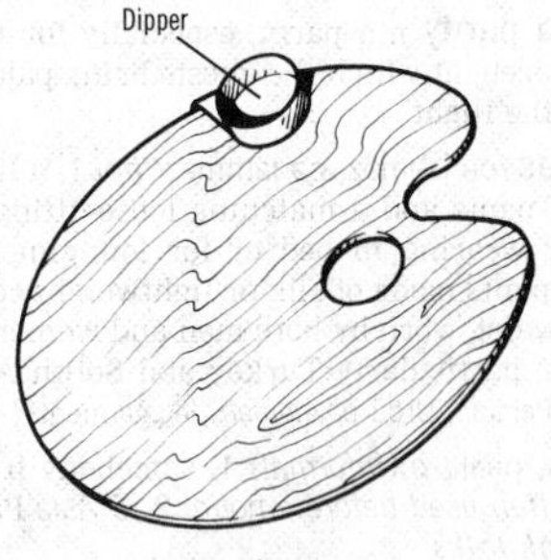

palette

pal·ette /pállәt/ *n* **1.** ART **BOARD FOR ARTIST'S PAINTS** a board or tray on which an artist arranges and mixes paints. A traditional style of palette is an oval board that curves in near a thumbhole, so that the artist can hold the board steadily from underneath. **2.** ART **RANGE OF COLORS USED BY ARTIST** the assortment of colors on a palette, in a painting, or characteristic of an artist's work **3.** COMPUT **COLOR RANGE OF COMPUTER DISPLAY** the range of colors that can be reproduced on a computer display **4.** ARTS **QUALITIES IN NONGRAPHIC ART** a range of qualities in a nongraphic art such as music or literature [Late 18C. < French (see PALLET[1])]

SPELLCHECK See *palate.*

pal·ette knife *n* a spatula-shaped implement with a slender flexible metal blade and a handle, used by an artist to mix and apply thick paints

Pa·ley /páylee/, **William S.** (1901–90) US broadcasting executive. He was the founder (1929) and chief executive officer of the Columbia Broadcasting System (CBS).

pal·frey /páwlfree/ (*plural* **-freys**) *n* a horse for everyday riding, especially one for a woman to ride (*archaic*) [12C. Via Old French *palefrei* < late Latin *paraveredus* "extra horse" < Latin *veredus* "light horse used by couriers" < Gaulish]

pa·li /paálee/ *n Hawaii* a high steep rock face [< Hawaiian]

Pa·li /paálee/ *n* an ancient Indo-European language derived from Sanskrit and formerly spoken in South Asia, surviving in Hinayana Buddhist scriptures [Late 18C. < Pali *pāli* "canonical text" (as opposed to the commentary), shortening of Sanskrit *pāli-bhāsā* "language of the line"] —**Pa·li** *adj*

pal·i·mo·ny /pállә mōnee/ (*plural* **-nies**) *n* a maintenance allowance for an ex-lover or member of an unmarried couple, when required by a court of law [Late 20C. Blend of PAL + ALIMONY]

pal·imp·sest /pállimp sèst/ *n* a manuscript written over a partly erased older manuscript in such a way that the old words can be read beneath the new ■ *adj* describes a document that has been overwritten [Mid-17C. Via Latin < Greek *palimpsestos* "something rubbed smooth again" < *palin* "again, back" + form of *psēn* "rub smooth"]

pal·in·drome /pállin drōm/ *n* **1.** a word, phrase, passage, or number that reads the same forward and backward, e.g., "Anna," "Draw, o coward," or "23832" **2.** a segment of DNA in which the nucleotide sequence in one strand read from one end is the same as the sequence in the complementary strand read from the opposite end. For example, the sequence GGTACC is a palindrome when the complementary strand is CCATGG. [Early 17C. < Greek *palindromos* "running back again" < *palin* "again, back" + form of *dramein* "to run"] —**pal·in·dro·mic** /pàllin drómmik, -drṓmik/ *adj*

pal·ing /páyling/ *n* **1.** a fence formed by a line of pointed stakes planted in the ground **2.** CONSTR same as **pale**[2] *n* (sense 1)

pal·in·gen·e·sis /pàllin jénnәssiss/ *n* **1.** BIOL same as **recapitulation** (sense 2) **2.** CHR spiritual rebirth by means of baptism **3.** RELIG the supposed transmigration of the soul of somebody who has died into the body of another person or animal [Early

19C. < Greek *palin* "again, back" + *genesis* "birth"] —**pal·in·ge·net·ic** /-jə néttik/ *adj* —**pal·in·ge·net·i·cal·ly** *adv*

pal·i·node /pállə nōd/ *n* **1.** a poem in which a poet retracts something written in a previous poem **2.** a formal retraction of a statement (*formal*) [Late 16C. Directly or via French < Latin *palinodia* < Greek *palinōdia* < *palin* "again, back" + *ōidē* "song"]

Pal·i·o /pállee ō/ *n* a traditional horserace run in Siena, Italy, twice a year, on July 2 and August 16. Of medieval origin, it is accompanied by great pageantry. The race itself comprises three circuits of the Piazza del Campo and lasts little more than one minute. [Late 17C. Via Italian < Latin *pallium* "covering"; from the cloth or banner awarded to the winner]

pal·i·sade /pàlli sáyd, pálli sàyd/ *n* **1.** FENCE a fence made of pales driven into the ground **2.** FENCE PALE a pale in a fence **3.** BOT same as **palisade cell** ■ *vt* (**-sad·ed, -sad·ing, -sades**) FENCE PLACE IN to provide a place with a fence of pales as a means of defense [Early 17C. < French *palissade* < Latin *palus* "stake"]

pal·i·sade cell *n* a soft plant tissue (**parenchyma**) cell that is long and narrow, oriented on its vertical axis, and adjacent to the upper epidermis in a leaf

pal·i·sade lay·er, pal·i·sade mes·o·phyll, pal·i·sade pa·ren·chy·ma *n* a layer of long cells under the upper epidermis of a leaf that are full of specialized chlorophyll-containing cell parts (**chloroplasts**)

pal·i·sades /pàlli sáydz, pálli sàydz/ *npl US* a row of high cliffs, usually rising sharply from the side of a river, stream, or lake

Pal·i·sades /pàlli sáydz, pálli sàydz/ row of cliffs in northeastern New Jersey, running along the western bank of the Hudson River. The cliffs are part of a park system.

Palk Strait /pàwk-, pàwlk-/ inlet of the Bay of Bengal, separating southeastern India from northwestern Sri Lanka. Length: 85 mi./137 km.

pall[1] /pawl/ *n* **1.** DARK COVERING a covering that makes a place dark and gloomy ○ *a pall of thick black smoke* **2.** GLOOMY ATMOSPHERE a prevailing gloomy mood or oppressive atmosphere ○ *Her departure cast a pall over the weekend.* **3.** CASKET COVERING a cloth covering for a casket, bier, hearse, or tomb **4.** FUNERAL CASKET a casket, especially when being carried in a funeral **5.** CHR CHALICE COVER a square cover for a Communion chalice, especially a linen-covered board **6.** CHR same as **pallium** (sense 1) (*archaic*) **7.** HERALDRY HERALDIC BEARING a heraldic bearing representing an archbishop's pallium in the form of three bands in a Y-shape, charged with crosses ■ *vt* (**palled, pall·ing, palls**) COVER SOMEBODY OR SOMETHING to cover somebody or something with a pall or with something that resembles a pall [Pre-12C. < Latin *pallium* "covering"]

pall[2] /pawl/ (**palled, pall·ing, palls**) *vi* to be or become uninteresting, unsatisfying, or insipid ○ *The music soon began to pall on us.* [14C. Shortening of APPALL]

pal·la·di·a plural of **palladium**[2]

Pal·la·di·an[1] /pə láydee ən/ *adj* typical of or similar to the classical architectural style developed by Andrea Palladio in the 16th century [Early 18C. After Andrea PALLADIO]

Pal·la·di·an[2] /pə láydee ən/ *adj* **1.** relating to the goddess Pallas Athena **2.** relating to wisdom or knowledge [Mid-16C. < Latin *palladium* (see PALLADIUM[2])]

Pal·la·di·o /pə laádee ō/, **Andrea** (1508–80) Italian architect. Working in the classical tradition of ancient Rome, he produced symmetrical designs, many for villas, and wrote his *Four Books on Architecture* (1570), which influenced several generations of architects. Born **Gondola, Andrea di Pietro della**

pal·la·di·um[1] /pə láydee əm/ *n* a malleable silvery-white metallic element resembling platinum. Source: ores of copper, gold, platinum. Use: catalyst, in electrical contacts, jewelry, dental alloys, medical instruments. Symbol **Pd**. See table at **element** [Early 19C. < Greek *Pallad-*, stem of *Pallas*, epithet of Athena and name given to an asteroid discovered shortly before the element] —**pal·la·dic** /pə láydik, -lá-/ *adj* —**pal·la·dous** /pə láydəss, pálləd əss/ *adj*

pal·la·di·um[2] /pə láydee əm/ (*plural* **-di·ums** or **-di·a** /-dee ə/) *n* **1.** a protection or safeguard, especially one protecting social and civic institutions **2.** *also* **Pal·la·di·um** an object believed to have the power to protect a city or nation, especially the statue of Pallas Athena that was believed to protect Troy [14C. Via Latin < Greek *palladion* < *Pallas*, epithet of Athena]

Pal·las /pálləss/ *n* **1.** the second largest asteroid, discovered in 1802. It has an average diameter of approximately 330 mi./530 km. **2.** *also* **Pal·las A·the·na** MYTHOL same as **Athena**

pall·bear·er /páwl bèrrər/ *n* a bearer or escort of a casket at a funeral or burial

pal·let[1] /pállət/ *n* **1.** PLATFORM FOR LOADS a standardized platform or open-ended box, usually made of wood, that allows mechanical handling of bulk goods during transport and storage **2.** CLAY-WORKING TOOL a wooden tool similar to a knife, used to mix and shape ceramic clay **3.** BOARD FOR DRYING CERAMICS a board on which ceramic pieces are dried **4.** GILDING TOOL a tool for manipulating gold leaf in gilding **5.** MECH ENG REGULATING LEVER IN TIMEPIECE a lever that regulates a ratchet wheel, especially one that regulates the movement of the balance wheel or pendulum in a timepiece by transmitting movements from the escape wheel. The pallet's function is to convert rotary to reciprocating motion, or vice versa. **6.** MUSIC VALVE ON ORGAN a valve on an organ that opens in order to let air into a pipe **7.** ART same as **palette** (sense 1) [15C. < French *palette* "small blade or spade" < Latin *pala* "spade, shovel"]

SPELLCHECK See *palate*.

pal·let[2] /pállət/ *n* **1.** a temporary and usually uncomfortable bed, made from materials at hand **2.** a straw-filled mattress [14C. < Anglo-Norman *paillete* < *paille* "straw" < Latin *palea*]

pal·let·ize /pállə tīz/ (**-ized, -iz·ing, -iz·es**) *vt* to put, transport, or store a load of something on a standardized platform

pal·li·a plural of **pallium**

pal·liasse /pal yáss, pál yàss/ *n* same as **paillasse** [Late 18C. Alteration of PAILLASSE]

pal·li·ate /pállee àyt/ (**-at·ed, -at·ing, -ates**) *vt* **1.** MITIGATE INTENSITY OF SOMETHING to reduce the intensity or severity of something **2.** PARTIALLY EXCUSE SOMETHING BAD to make or attempt to make an offense seem less serious by providing excuses or mitigating evidence **3.** ALLEVIATE SYMPTOMS to alleviate a symptom without curing the underlying medical condition [15C. < Latin *palliat-* past participle of *palliare* "cover, hide" < *pallium* "covering"] —**pal·li·a·tion** /pàllee áysh'n/ *n* —**pal·li·a·tor** *n*

pal·li·a·tive /pállee àytiv, -ətiv/ *adj* **1.** SOOTHING soothing anxieties or other intense emotions **2.** TREATING SYMPTOMS ONLY alleviating pain and symptoms without eliminating the cause ■ *n* SYMPTOM-TREATING MEDICINE something that palliates, especially a medicine that treats symptoms only —**pal·li·a·tive·ly** *adv*

pal·li·a·tive care *n* the treatment and relief of mental and physical pain without curing the causes, especially in patients suffering from a terminal illness

pal·lid /pállid/ *adj* **1.** having an unhealthily pale complexion **2.** lacking color, spirit, or intensity [Late 16C. < Latin *pallidus* < *pallere* "be pale"] —**pal·lid·i·ty** /pa líddətee, pə-/ *n* —**pal·lid·ly** *adv*

Pal·lis·er, Cape /pállissər/ southernmost point of the North Island, New Zealand, situated at the eastern end of the Cook Strait

pal·li·um /pállee əm/ (*plural* **-li·a** /-lee ə/ or **-li·ums**) *n* **1.** a white vestment that rests on the shoulders with pendants hanging at its front and back, worn by a pope, all Roman Catholic archbishops, and some bishops **2.** ZOOL, BIRDS same as **mantle** *n* (sense 7), *v* (sense 2) **3.** ANAT same as **cerebral cortex** (*technical*) **4.** ANCIENT HIST a man's rectangular cloak worn in ancient Rome [Late 16C. < Latin, "covering"] —**pal·li·al** *adj*

pall-mall /pel mél, pal mál, pawl máwl/ *n* **1.** a 17th-century game in which players used a mallet to hit a wooden ball through an iron hoop suspended at the end of a long alley **2.** an alley in which pall-mall is played [Mid-16C. Via obsolete French *palle maille* < Italian *pallamaglio* < *balla* "ball" + *maglio* "mallet"]

pal·lor /pállər/ *n* an unhealthy-looking paleness of complexion [14C. Latin *pallere* "be pale"]

pal·ly /pállee/ (**-li·er, -li·est**) *adj* having a friendly relationship (*informal*)

palm[1] /paam/ *n* **1.** INNER SURFACE OF HAND the inner surface of the hand, extending from the base of the fingers to the wrist **2.** UNDERSIDE OF MAMMAL'S FOREFOOT the part of a mammal's forefoot that is most often in contact with the ground **3.** HAND-SIZED MEASURE a unit of length, based on the length or width of a hand **4.** COVERING FOR PALM OF HAND something that covers the palm of the hand, e.g., the inner hand surface of a glove **5.** BIOL FLAT PART OF BRANCHED STRUCTURE the broad flat lobe of a branched structure such as the antler of a moose or deer or a cactus stalk **6.** ROWING OAR BLADE the blade of an oar **7.** NAUT FACE OF ANCHOR POINT the inner face of an anchor's point ■ *vt* (**palmed, palm·ing, palms**) **1.** HIDE ITEM IN HAND to hide something in the hand, especially as part of a trick **2.** TAKE SOMETHING STEALTHILY to take something secretly by hiding it in the hand **3.** TOUCH SOMETHING to touch something with the palm **4.** *US* SHAKE HANDS to shake hands with somebody (*slang*) **5.** BASKETBALL HOLD BALL BRIEFLY to let a basketball come to rest in the hands during a dribble, thereby committing a foul [12C. Via French *paume* < Latin *palma* "palm of the hand"] ◇ **have somebody** *or* **something in the palm of your hand** to have complete power or influence over somebody or something

palm off *vt* **1.** to shift something into another's possession in a deceitful way ○ *palmed off counterfeit money on unsuspecting store clerks* **2.** to give or pass on something unwanted to somebody else ○ *Don't try to palm off that old armchair on me!*

palm[2] /paam/ *n* **1.** BOT same as **palm tree** **2.** a leaf from a palm tree, used as a symbol of victory or success **3.** a small decoration shaped like a palm leaf that is added to a military decoration to show that it has been awarded to the wearer more than once [Old English, via Germanic < Latin *palma* "palm tree, palm of the hand" (because a cluster of palm leaves was thought to look like a hand and fingers)]

Pal·ma /paál maa/ port on Majorca. It is the capital city of the Spanish Balearic Islands. Population: 319,181 (1998). Full name **Palma de Mallorca**

pal·mar /paámər/ *adj* relating to the palm of the hand or to the underside of an animal's forefoot [Mid-17C. < Latin *palmaris* < *palma* "palm of the hand"]

pal·mate /pál màyt, paál-, paá-/, **pal·mat·ed** /-màytəd/ *adj* **1.** describes leaves that have five or more lobes arising from a single point, spreading like fingers from a hand **2.** describes birds' feet that have three webbed toes [Mid-18C. < Latin *palmatus* < *palma* "palm of the hand"] —**pal·mate·ly** *adv*

pal·ma·tion /pal máysh'n, paal-, paa-/ *n* **1.** a lobe of a palmate formation **2.** the state of having a palmate shape

Palm Beach /paám-/ town in southeastern Florida on the Atlantic Ocean. It is a fashionable winter resort. Population: 9,766 (2002 estimate).

palm·chat /paám chàt/ *n* a gregarious bird that is olive-brown above and yellow with dark streaks below. Native to: open woodlands and cultivated fields in the Caribbean. Latin name: *Dulus dominicus*. [< PALM[2]]

palm civ·et *n* a mammal with short legs and sharp claws that lives in trees. Native to: Africa, Asia. Family: Viverridae. [< PALM[2]]

palm·cord·er /paám kàwrdər/ *n* a small portable video camera and recorder that fits in the palm of the hand [Late 20C. < PALM[1] + RECORDER]

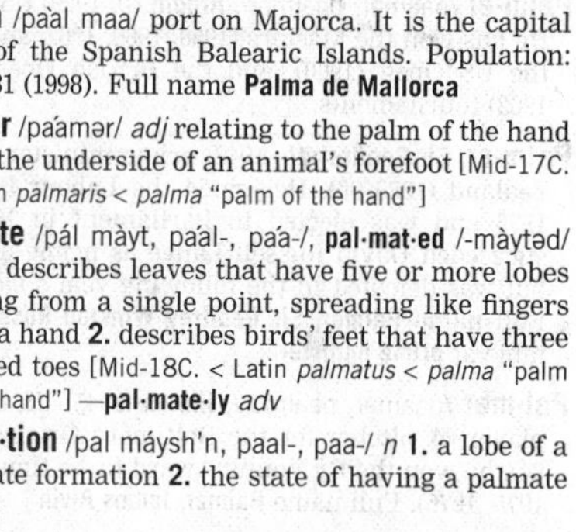

AKG London

Olof Palme

Pal·me /pálmə/, **Olof** (1927–86) prime minister of Sweden (1969–76 and 1982–86). A Social Democrat, he supported liberation movements and condemned superpower intervention in the developing world. He was killed by an unknown assassin. Full name **Palme, Sven Olof Joachim**

> "It is an illusion to believe that you can meet demands for social justice with violence and military might. It is extremely difficult to gain people's loyalty with promises to defend a freedom which, in actuality, they have never been able to experience."
> [Olof Palme, *Speech, Social Democrat conference, Gävle, Sweden*; 1965]

palm·er /paámər/ *n* **1.** a pilgrim, especially a medieval Christian pilgrim who carried or wore palm leaves as proof of a visit to the Holy Land **2.** INSECTS same as **palmer worm** [14C. Via Anglo-Norman < medieval Latin *palmarius* < Latin *palma* "palm tree" (see PALM^{2})]

Arnold Palmer

Palm·er /paámər, paálmər/, **Arnold** (*b.* 1929) US golfer. He has won the Masters (1958, 1960, 1962, and 1964), the US Open (1960), and the British Open (1961, 1962) tournaments.

Palm·er, Sir Geoffrey (*b.* 1942) prime minister of New Zealand (1989–90). He joined the Labour Party in 1975 and was elected to Parliament in 1979. He succeeded David Russell Lange as prime minister but was defeated in the following year's elections. Full name **Palmer, Sir Geoffrey Winston Russell**. See table at **prime minister**

Pal·mer /paámər, paálmər/, **Jim** (*b.* 1945) US baseball player. A pitcher for the Baltimore Orioles (1965–84), he won the Cy Young Award three times (1973, 1975, 1976). Full name **Palmer, James Alvin**

Palm·er·ston /paámərstən/, **Henry John Temple, 3rd Viscount** (1784–1865) prime minister of Great Britain (1855–58 and 1859–65). Changing from Tory to Whig (1830), he served three terms as foreign secretary and two as prime minister. Known as **Firebrand Palmerston**

> "We have no eternal allies and we have no perpetual enemies. Our interests are eternal and perpetual, and those interests it is our duty to follow."
> [Henry John Temple Palmerston, *Speech to the British Parliament*; March 1, 1848]

Pal·mer·ston North city in the south of the North Island, New Zealand, situated 87 mi./140 km north of Wellington. Population: 72,681 (2001).

palm·er worm *n* a destructive, swarming moth caterpillar

pal·mette /pal mét/ *n* a stylized palm leaf used as an ornament or in a decoration [Mid-19C. < French, literally "small palm tree" < Latin *palma* "palm tree" (see PALM^{2})]

pal·met·to /pal méttō/ (*plural* **-tos** or **-toes**) *n* **1.** a low-growing palm plant with fan-shaped leaves, especially the cabbage palmetto **2.** the blade of a palmetto leaf. Use: weaving. [Mid-16C. < Spanish *palmito* "small palm tree" < Latin *palma* "palm tree" (see PALM^{2})]

Pal·met·to State *n* a nickname for South Carolina

palm·ist /paámist/ *n* somebody who practices palmistry

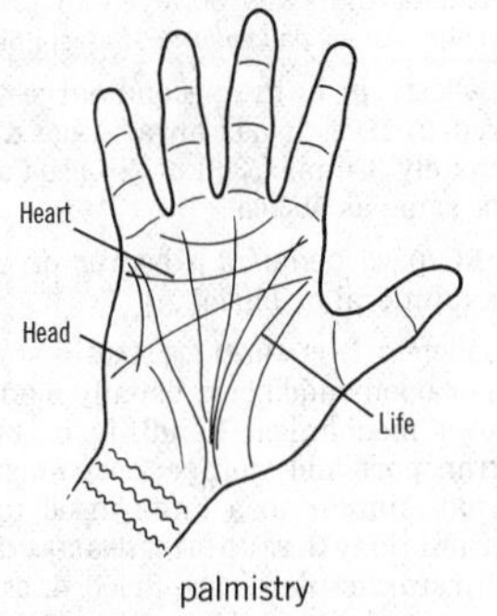

palmistry

palm·is·try /paámistree/ *n* the practice of examining the features of somebody's palms supposedly in order to predict that person's destiny [15C. < PALM^{1}]

pal·mi·tate /pálmi tàyt, paálmi-, paámi-/ *n* a salt or ester of palmitic acid

pal·mit·ic ac·id /pal mìttik-, paal mìttik-/ *n* a waxy acid. Source: plant and animal fats and oils. Use: manufacture of soap, candles, food additives. Formula: $C_{15}H_{31}COOH$. [< French *palmitique* < *palme* (see PALMITIN)]

pal·mi·tin /pálmitin, paálmi-, paámi-/ *n* an ester of palmitic acid and glycerol. Source: animal fats, palm oil. Use: soap-making. [Mid-19C. < French *palmitine* < *palme* "palm tree" < Latin *palma* (see PALM^{2})]

palm oil *n* a yellowish oil extracted from the fruit of oil palms. Use: lubricants, soap, cosmetics, foods. [< PALM^{2}]

Palm Springs town in southern California, a resort and residential center. Population: 44,526 (2002 estimate).

palm sug·ar *n* sugar made from palm tree sap [< PALM^{2}]

Palm Sun·day *n* a Christian religious day marking Jesus Christ's triumphal entry into Jerusalem through a crowd waving palm branches. Date: Sunday before Easter. [< PALM^{2}]

palm·top /paám tòp/ *n* a computer with a miniature keyboard and screen that fits into the palm of the hand [Late 20C. < PALM^{1}, after LAPTOP]

palm tree

palm tree *n* a tree, bush, or plant typically with a trunk without branches and a crown of pinnate or palmate leaves on top. Native to: tropics, subtropics. Family: Palmae. [< PALM^{2}]

palm·y /paámee/ (**-i·er, -i·est**) *adj* **1.** relating to, consisting of, or abundant in palm trees **2.** prosperous or flourishing, especially formerly (*literary*) ○ *in her palmy days* [Late 16C. < PALM^{2}]

pal·my·ra /pal mīrə/ (*plural* **-ras** or *same*) *n* a tall fan-leafed palm tree whose fronds, wood, and sap are harvested for various uses. Native to: Asia. Latin name: *Borassus flabellifer*. [Late 17C. Alteration (influenced by *Palmyra*, ancient city in Syria) of Portuguese *palmeira* "palm tree" < Latin *palma* (see PALM^{2})]

Pal·o Al·to /pàllō áltō/ city in western California on San Francisco Bay. The city developed after the establishment of nearby Stanford University, and it is a center for computer technology. Population: 57,543 (2002 estimate).

Pal·o·mar, Mount /pállə maar/ mountain in southern California, northeast of San Diego. It is the site of an astronomical observatory with one of the largest refracting telescopes in the world. Height: 6,138 ft./1,871 m.

pal·o·mi·no /pàllə meénō/ (*plural* **-nos**) *n* a golden-colored horse with a pale mane and tail, originally bred in the southwestern United States [Early 20C. Via American Spanish < Latin *palumbinus* "like a dove"]

pa·loo·ka /pə lóokə/ *n* (*slang*) **1.** an offensive term that deliberately insults somebody's physical coordination and intelligence **2.** an easily beaten athlete, especially a boxer [Early 20C. Origin ?]

Pa·louse /pə lóoss/ (*plural same* or **-lous·es**) *n* a member of a Native North American people who lived in southern Washington and northern Idaho, and who now live mainly in northern Washington —**Pa·louse** *adj*

pa·lo ver·de /pàllō vúrdee, -vúrd/ (*plural* **-des** or *same*) *n Southwest US* **1.** a spiny tree or bush with blue-green bark. Flowers: yellow. Native to: southwestern United States, Mexico. Latin name: *Cercidium floridium.* **2.** TREES same as **Jerusalem thorn** [Early 19C. < American Spanish, "green tree"]

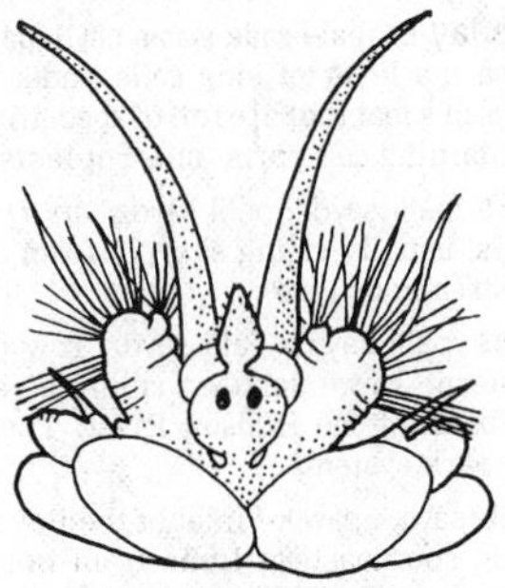
palp

palp /palp/ *n* a sensory appendage situated near the mouth of many invertebrate animals, used to assess or manipulate food before it is eaten [Mid-19C. Via French < Latin *palpus* < *palpare* "touch gently, palpate"]

pal·pa·ble /pálpəb'l/ *adj* **1.** INTENSE so intense as to be almost able to be felt physically ○ *the palpable tension in the room* **2.** OBVIOUS obvious or easily observed ○ *a palpable need for change* **3.** MED **ABLE TO BE FELT** able to be felt by the hands, especially in a medical examination ○ *a palpable lump in the abdomen* [14C. < late Latin *palpabilis* < Latin *palpare* "touch gently, palpate"] —**pal·pa·bil·i·ty** /pàlpə bíllətee/ *n* —**pal·pa·bly** *adv*

pal·pate^{1} /pál pàyt/ (**-pat·ed, -pat·ing, -pates**) *vt* to examine a part of the body by feeling with the hands and fingers, especially to distinguish between swellings that are solid and those that are filled with fluid [15C. < Latin *palpat-*, past participle of *palpare* "touch gently"]

pal·pate^{2} /pál pàyt/ *adj* describes an invertebrate organism that is equipped with one or more palps [Mid-19C. < PALP, PALPUS]

pal·pa·tion /pal páysh'n/ *n* a method of clinical examination using gentle pressure of the fingers to detect growths, changes in the size of underlying organs, and unusual tissue reactions to pressure [Late 15C. < Latin *palpation-* "stroking" < *palpat-* (see PALPATE^{1})]

pal·pe·bral /pálpəbrəl, pal peébrəl/ *adj* relating to the eyelids [Mid-19C. < Latin *palpebra* "eyelid"]

pal·pi ZOOL plural of **palpus**

pal·pi·tate /pálpi tàyt/ (**-tat·ed, -tat·ing, -tates**) *vi* to beat in an irregular or unusually rapid way, either because of a medical condition or because of exertion, fear, or anxiety (*refers to the heart*) [15C. < Latin *palpitat-*, past participle of *palpitare* < *palpare* "touch gently, palpate"] —**pal·pi·tant** *adj*

pal·pi·ta·tion /pàlpi táysh'n/ *n* an irregular or unusually rapid beating of the heart, either because of a medical condition or because of exertion, fear, or anxiety (*usually used in the plural*)

pal·pus /pálpəss/ (*plural* **-pi** /-pī/) *n* ZOOL same as **palp** [Early 19C. < Latin (see PALP)]

pals·grave /páwlz gràyv/ *n* a count palatine, especially in Germany [Mid-16C. < early Dutch *paltsgrave* < *palts* "palatinate" + *grave* "count"]

pal·sy[1] /pálzee/ *adj* same as **palsy-walsy** (*slang*) [Mid-20C. < PAL]

pal·sy[2] /páwlzee/ *n* muscular inability to move part or all of the body (*archaic*) [13C. Via Old French *paralisie* < Latin *paralysis* (see PARALYSIS)]

pal·sy-wal·sy /pàlzee wálzee/ *adj* very friendly, often in an insincere or unpleasant way (*slang*) [Mid-20C. Extension of PALSY[1]]

pal·ter /páwltər/ (**-tered, -ter·ing, -ters**) *vi* (*archaic*) **1.** to act or talk insincerely or deceitfully **2.** to haggle in bargaining [Mid-16C. Origin ?] —**pal·ter·er** *n*

Pal·trow /pál trō/, **Gwyneth** (*b.* 1972) US actor. A respected actor, she won an Academy Award for best actress for *Shakespeare in Love* (1998) and *Sliding Doors* (1998).

pal·try /páwltree/ (**-tri·er, -tri·est**) *adj* **1.** insignificant or unimportant ○ *a paltry sum of money* **2.** low and contemptible [Mid-16C. Probably < Scots, N English dialect *pelt* "coarse cloth, rubbish"] —**pal·tri·ly** *adv* —**pal·tri·ness** *n*

pa·lu·dal /pə lood'l, pállyəd'l/ *adj* relating to or living in swamps or marshes [Early 19C. < Latin *palud-* "marsh"]

pal·y /páylee/ *adj* describes a heraldic shield that is divided into equal-sized sections by vertical lines [15C. < French *palé* < *pal* (see PALE[2])]

pal·y·nol·o·gy /pàllə nólləjee/ *n* the study of spores and pollen, including fossilized spores and pollen [Mid-20C. < Greek *palunein* "to sprinkle"] —**pal·y·no·log·i·cal** /pàllənə lójjik'l/ *adj* —**pal·y·nol·o·gist** *n*

pam /pam/ *n* the jack of clubs in some card games such as loo, where it is the highest trump card [Late 17C. Shortening of French *pamphile* < Greek *Pamphilos*, personal name, literally "loved by all"]

Pa·ma-Nyun·gan /paamə nyoong gən/ *n* a large family of Aboriginal languages spoken in Australia. Native speakers: 100,000. [< two Aboriginal words for "a man" (see NYUNGAR)] —**Pa·ma-Nyun·gan** *adj*

~~**pamflet**~~ incorrect spelling of **pamphlet**

Pa·mirs /pə meérz/ mountainous region of Central Asia, located mainly in Tajikistan and extending to northeastern Afghanistan and northwestern China. The highest point is Ismail Samani Peak, 24,590 ft./7,495 m.

Pam·li·co Sound /pàm lee kō-/ inlet of the Atlantic Ocean between the eastern coast of North Carolina and some barrier islands. It is known for its commercial and recreational fishing and its waterfowl nesting sites.

pam·pa·lam /pàmpə lám/ *n Carib* confusion, fuss, or uproar [Late 20C. An imitation of the sound of noisy activity, perhaps after Twi *pam* "sound of a gun," *pam pam* "drive away"]

pam·pas /pámpəz, -pəss/ *n* treeless grassy plains in temperate South America, especially Argentina (*takes a singular or plural verb*) [Early 18C. < Spanish, plural of *pampa* < Quechua, "plain"] —**pam·pe·an** /pámpee ən, pam peé ən/ *adj*

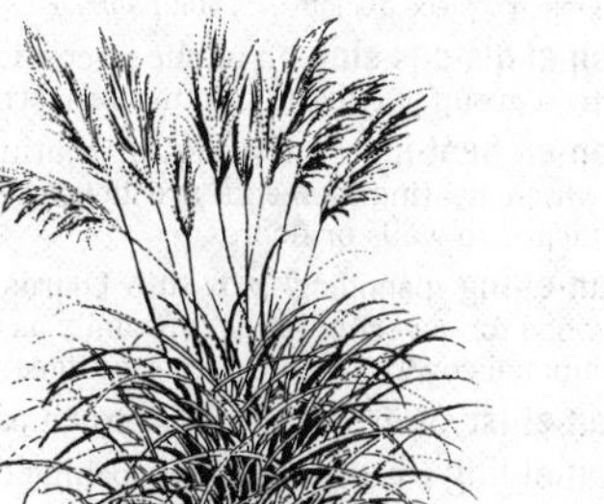

pampas grass

pam·pas grass *n* a tall grass with silky white flower plumes, often grown in parks and gardens. Native to: South America, naturalized in southern United States. Genus: *Cortaderia*.

pam·per /pámpər/ (**-pered, -per·ing, -pers**) *vt* **1.** to lavish attention on somebody, indulging his or her taste for luxury **2.** to indulge or gratify a desire or need [14C. Probably < Low German or Dutch] —**pam·per·er** *n*

pam·pe·ro /pam pérrō, paam-/ (*plural* **-ros**) *n* a strong cold dry wind that blows southwest from the Andes to the Atlantic, across the South American pampas [Late 18C. < Spanish < *pampa* (see PAMPAS)]

pam·phlet /pámflət/ *n* a small leaflet or paper booklet, usually unbound and coverless, that gives information or supports a position [14C. < *Pamphilet, Pamflet*, popular name for *Pamphilus, seu de Amore* "Pamphilus, or about Love," 12C Latin love poem]

pam·phlet·eer /pàmflə teér/ *n* a writer of opinionated pamphlets ■ *vi* (**-eered, -eer·ing, -eers**) to write material for pamphlets, especially political ones

Pam·plo·na /pam plṓnə/ city in northeastern Spain. It is the capital of the autonomous region of Navarre. Population: 198,364 (2002).

pan[1] /pan/ *n* **1.** COOKING POT a cooking pot, usually metal and with a handle, for use on the burner of a stove **2.** SHALLOW COOKING DISH a shallow metal cooking dish used for baking food in an oven **3.** SHALLOW OPEN CONTAINER a shallow open container used to store, catch, or heat liquids or other substances ○ *drained the old oil into a pan* **4.** MIN EXTRACT DISH FOR SORTING MINERALS a flat metal dish, shaped like a pie plate, used to separate precious minerals, especially gold, from loose soil, gravel, or sediment **5.** MEASURE SCALE DISH either of the dishes suspended in a balance scale **6.** GEOG HOLLOWED PLACE IN DIRT a natural shallow sink or basin in the ground, usually filled with rainwater or mud **7.** GEOG same as **hardpan 8.** MIN EXTRACT SHALLOW AREA FOR EVAPORATING BRINE a natural or artificial concavity in the earth, in which brine is evaporated, leaving behind salt **9.** OCEANOG THIN ICE FLOE a small flat thin ice floe of the type that forms near a shore or in a bay **10.** ARMS PRIMING CONTAINER IN GUN the hollow part of a flintlock gun, into which the gunpowder is loaded **11.** MUSIC STEEL DRUM a metal drum played in steel bands **12.** CRITICAL REVIEW a harshly critical review ■ *v* (**panned, pan·ning, pans**) **1.** *vt* CRITICIZE SEVERELY to criticize somebody or something severely, especially in a review (*informal*) **2.** *vi* MIN EXTRACT SORT THROUGH DIRT FOR MINERALS to use a shallow dish to separate valuable minerals from loose soil, gravel, or sediment by washing or shaking **3.** *vi* MIN EXTRACT YIELD PRECIOUS METALS to yield valuable metals when separating minerals and leavings by means of washing or shaking using a shallow dish [Old English *panne* < Germanic]

pan out *vi* (*informal*) **1.** to turn out or result ○ *After all our careful planning, it's a shame that things didn't pan out as we had hoped.* **2.** to turn out well or successfully ○ *Her new career never panned out.* [< panning for gold]

pan[2] /pan/ *vti* (**panned, pan·ning, pans**) to move a camera horizontally from a stationary point in order to capture a broad view or a moving object, or be moved in this way ■ *n* a horizontal movement of a camera from a fixed point, or the resulting filmed shot [Early 20C. Shortening of PANORAMA]

pan[3] /paan/ *n* in South and Southeast Asia, a betel leaf wrapped over a betel nut, often garnished with spices and lime, and chewed as a stimulant, especially after a meal [Early 17C. < Hindi *pān*]

Pan /pan/ *n* **1.** in Greek mythology, the god of nature, pastures, flocks, and forests, believed to have a human torso and head, and the hind legs, ears, and horns of a goat. Roman equivalent **Faunus 2.** the small innermost natural satellite of Saturn

PAN *abbr* **1.** POL Mexico National Action Party. Full form **Partido Acción Nacional 2.** E-COMMERCE primary account number

pan- *prefix* all, any, everyone ○ *panchromatic* ○ *Pan-Slavism* [< Greek]

pan·a·ce·a /pànnə seé ə/ *n* a supposed cure for all diseases or problems [Mid-16C. Via Latin < Greek *panakeia* < *panakēs* "all-healing" < *akos* "remedy"] —**pan·a·ce·an** *adj*

pa·nache /pə násh, -naásh/ *n* **1.** a sense or display of spirited style and self-confidence **2.** a plume or tuft of feathers, especially on a hat or helmet [Mid-16C. Via French < Italian *pennacchio* "plume of feathers" < Latin *pinna* "feather"]

pa·na·da /pə naádə/ *n* a very thick paste of flour or another starchy ingredient and a liquid such as milk or stock. Use: base for sauces, binding for stuffing. [Late 16C. < Spanish or Portuguese < Latin *panis* "bread"]

Pan-Af·ri·can *adj* **1.** relating to the nations of Africa, collectively or in cooperation with one another **2.** advocating freedom and independence for African people —**Pan-Af·ri·can·ism** *n*

Pan·a·ji /púnnəjee/ capital of Goa state in western India. Population: 51,872 (2001).

pan·a·ma /pánnə maa/, **Pan·a·ma** *n* CLOTHING same as **Panama hat** [Mid-19C. < PANAMA]

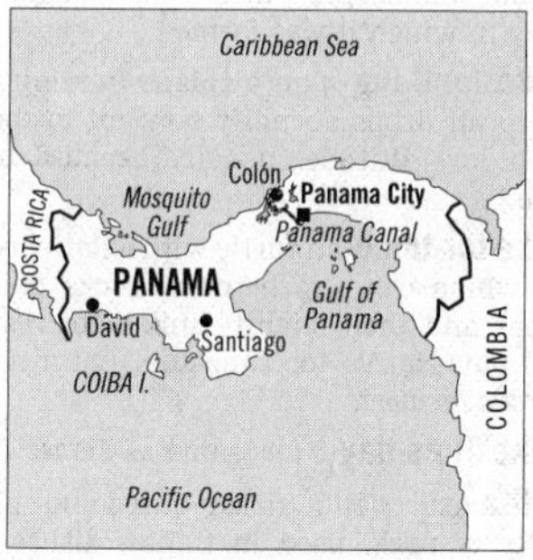

Panama

Pan·a·ma /pánnə maa/ country in Central America. It has the Caribbean Sea to its north and the Pacific Ocean to its south, connected by the Panama Canal, and is situated between Costa Rica and Colombia. Capital: Panama City. Population: 2,960,784 (2001). Area: 29,157 sq. mi./75,517 sq. km. Official name **Republic of Panama**

Pan·a·ma, Isth·mus of isthmus connecting North and South America and separating the Pacific Ocean and the Caribbean Sea

Pan·a·ma Ca·nal canal across the Isthmus of Panama, completed in 1914. Length: 40 mi./64 km.

Pan·a·ma Ca·nal Zone narrow strip of land about 10 mi./16 km wide extending across the Isthmus of Panama alongside the Panama Canal. Formerly administered by the United States, the Canal Zone was abolished in 1979 when it came under Panamanian civil control.

Pan·a·ma Cit·y 1. capital city of Panama, located in the center of the country, on the Pacific Ocean. Population: 463,093 (2000). **2.** city in northwestern Florida, on the Gulf Coast southwest of Tallahassee. It is a resort and fishing port. Population: 35,721 (2002 estimate).

Pan·a·ma hat, **pan·a·ma hat** *n* a brimmed men's hat made from the plaited leaves of the jipijapa, or an imitation of such a hat

Pan·a·ma·ni·an /pànnə máynee ən/ *n* somebody who comes from Panama ■ *adj* relating to Panama [Mid-19C. < PANAMA + *-n-* for euphony]

Pan·a·ma Red *n* a very potent reddish strain of marijuana, originally from Panama

Pan-A·mer·i·can *adj* relating to the nations of North, South, and Central America, collectively or in cooperation with one another —**Pan-A·mer·i·can·ism** *n*

Pan-A·mer·i·can High·way *n* a road system running from Alaska to Chile. It is 16,000 mi./25,744 km long, and links western hemisphere nations.

Pan-Ar·ab·ism *n* a movement for greater cooperation among and self-reliance within Arab or Islamic nations —**Pan-Ar·ab** *n, adj* —**Pan-Ar·a·bic** *adj* —**Pan-Ar·ab·ist** *n, adj*

pan·a·tel·la /pànnə téllə/, **pan·a·tel·a** *n* a long thin cigar that does not bulge in the middle [Mid-19C. Via American Spanish, "long thin biscuit" < Italian *panatello* "small loaf" < Latin *panis* "bread"]

Pan·a·the·nae·a /pàn athə neé ə/ *n* a summer festival held annually in ancient Athens but with an extra ceremony every fourth year. It involved games, sacrifices, and music and poetry contests. [Early 17C. < Greek *panathēnaia hiera* "festival of all Athenians"]

pan-broil *vt* to cook something in an ungreased pan on a direct heat source

pan·cake /pán kayk/ *n* **1.** THIN FRIED CAKE a thin flat cake made by pouring batter onto a hot greased flat pan, and cooking it on both sides **2.** AVIAT same as **pancake landing** ■ *v* (**-caked, -cak·ing, -cakes**) **1.** *vti* MAKE PANCAKE LANDING to make a pancake landing, or cause an aircraft to make a pancake landing **2.** *vt US* POSITION SOMETHING FLAT to turn something parallel to the ground, especially a tennis racket in the course of a stroke

Pan·cake Day *n* CHR same as **Shrove Tuesday** [< the practice of making pancakes to use up eggs and fat before Lent]

pan·cake ice *n* a small flat thin piece of sea ice that drifts out into deeper water from near the shore or the bay in which it was formed

pan·cake land·ing *n* an airplane landing in which the aircraft drops abruptly straight to the ground from a low altitude, usually because of engine failure

pan·cake tor·toise *n* a turtle with a flattened flexible shell, which can slip between rocks and narrow crevices and then slightly inflate to resist being pulled out. Native to: Tanzania. Latin name: *Malachersus tornieri.*

Pan·cake Tues·day *n* CHR same as **Shrove Tuesday**

pan·cet·ta /pan chéttə/ *n* a salt-cured and spiced form of belly of pork, used in Italian dishes [Mid-20C. < Italian, literally "little belly" < Latin *pantix* "bowel, intestine"]

pan·chax /pán chàks/ *n* a small freshwater fish that is olive, red, and yellow and is often kept in aquariums. Native to: Southeast Asia. Latin name: *Aplocheilus panchax.* [Mid-20C. < modern Latin]

Pan·chen La·ma /paánchən-/ *n* in Tibetan Buddhism, a lama of the second highest rank [< Tibetan, contraction of *pandi-tachen-po* "great learned one"]

pan·chro·mat·ic /pàn krō máttik/ *adj* describes photographic film that is sensitive to all visible colors and some ultraviolet light

pan·cra·ti·um /pan kráyshee əm/ (*plural* **-ti·a** /-shee ə/) *n* in ancient Greece, an athletic event involving boxing and wrestling contests [Early 17C. Via Latin < Greek *pagkration* < *kratos* "strength"] —**pan·crat·ic** /-kráttik/ *adj*

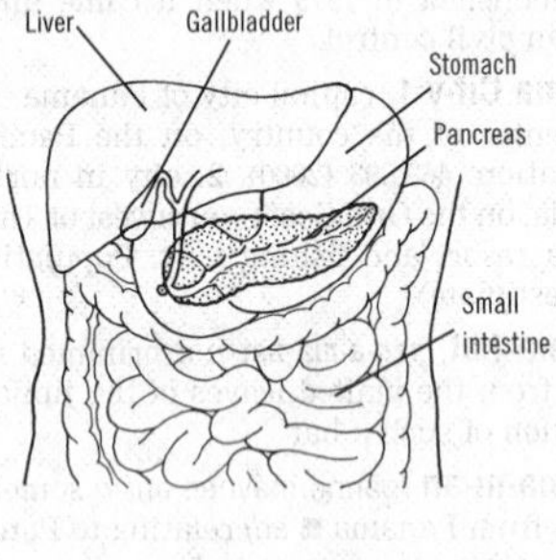

pancreas

pan·cre·as /pángkree əss, pánkree-/ *n* a large elongated glandular organ lying near the stomach. It secretes juices into the small intestine and the hormones insulin, glucagon, and somatostatin into the bloodstream. [Late 16C. Via modern Latin < Greek *pagkreas* < *kreas* "flesh"] —**pan·cre·at·ic** /pàngkree áttik, pànkree-/ *adj*

pancreat- *prefix* pancreas ○ *pancreatitis* [Via modern Latin < Greek *pagkreat-*, stem of *pagkreas* (see PANCREAS)]

pan·cre·a·tec·to·my /pàngkree ə téktəmee, pànkree-/ (*plural* **-mies**) *n* whole or partial removal of the pancreas by surgery

pan·cre·at·ic duct *n* a duct that carries pancreatic juice and, in human beings, runs from the pancreas to join the common bile duct, which empties into the small intestine

pan·cre·at·ic juice, pan·cre·at·ic flu·id *n* a watery alkaline fluid secreted by the pancreas. It contains enzymes that break down partially digested food in the small intestine.

pan·cre·a·tin /pángkree ətin, pànkree-/ *n* **1.** a digestive aid made from a mixture of pancreatic enzymes extracted from domestic animals **2.** the mixture of digestive enzymes produced by the pancreas, including amylase, lipase, and trypsin

pan·cre·a·ti·tis /pàngkree ə tītiss, pànkree-/ *n* inflammation of the pancreas

pan·cre·o·zy·min /pàngkree ō zímin, pànkree-/ *n* BIOCHEM same as **cholecystokinin** [Mid-20C. < PANCREAS + *zymin*, enzyme < Greek *zumē* "leaven"]

pan·cy·to·pe·ni·a /pàn sītə peénee ə/ *n* MED same as **aplastic anemia**

panda

pan·da /pándə/ *n* **1.** *also* **pan·da bear** a large bamboo-eating mammal with bold black-and-white markings, including black patches over the eyes. Native to: central China. Latin name: *Ailuropodia melanoleuca.* **2.** ZOOL same as **red panda** [Mid-19C. Via French < Nepalese, "red panda"]

pan·da·nus /pan dáynəss, -dánnəss/ (*plural* **-nus·es** or *same*) *n* a plant resembling a palm, with prop roots and a crown of narrow leaves. Use: mat-making. Native to: tropics. Genus: *Pandanus.* [Mid-19C. Via modern Latin < Malay *pandan*]

Pan·de·an /pan deé ən/ *adj* relating to the mythological Greek god Pan [Early 19C. Irregularly < PAN]

pan·dect /pán dèkt/ *n* **1.** a set of documents containing all the laws of a country or society **2.** a comprehensive treatise on a subject [Mid-16C. Directly or via French < Latin *pandecta* < Greek *pandektēs* "all-receiving" < *dekhesthai* "receive"]

pan·dem·ic /pan démmik/ *adj* existing in the form of a widespread epidemic that affects people in many different countries. AIDS is currently considered to be pandemic. ■ *n* a disease or condition that is found in a large part of a population [Mid-17C. < Greek *pandēmos* "of all the people" < *dēmos* "people"]

pan·de·mo·ni·um /pàndə mṓnee əm/ *n* **1.** wild uproar and chaos **2.** a place or situation that is noisy and chaotic [Late 18C. < *Pandaemonium*, capital of Hell in Milton's *Paradise Lost* < modern Latin, "home of all the demons" < Greek *daimōn* "divine power, guiding spirit"] —**pan·de·mo·ni·ac** *adj* —**pan·de·mon·ic** /-mónnik/ *adj*

Pan·de·mo·ni·um /pàndə mṓnee əm/ *n* Hell, or any place of chaos or torment [Mid-17C. Variant of *Pandaemonium* (see PANDEMONIUM)]

pan·der /pándər/ *vi* (**-dered, -der·ing, -ders**) **1.** INDULGE WEAKNESSES to indulge somebody's weaknesses or questionable wishes and tastes ○ *tired of pandering to their children's demands* **2.** PROCURE SEXUAL FAVORS to procure sexual favors for somebody ■ *n* **1.** *also* **pan·der·er** INDULGENT PERSON somebody who indulges somebody else's weaknesses or questionable wishes and tastes **2.** *also* **pan·der·er** ROMANTIC GO-BETWEEN a go-between in an illicit or secret romantic or sexual relationship **3.** same as **pimp** [14C. < *Pandare*, character in Chaucer's *Troilus & Criseyde* who procures Criseyde for Troilus]

P and H, p. and h., p&h *abbr US* MAIL postage and handling

pan·dit /pándit/ *n* a wise or learned Hindu man, especially a Brahman who is an expert in Hindu culture, law, and philosophy [Mid-19C. Variant of PUNDIT]

P & L *abbr* ACCT profit and loss

Pan·do·ra /pan dáwrə/ *n* **1.** in Greek mythology, the first woman, who was sent by the gods with a jar full of evils in order to avenge Prometheus's theft of fire. She opened the jar out of curiosity, thus releasing the evils into the world. **2.** a small inner natural satellite of Saturn, discovered in 1980 by Voyager 2. It is irregular in shape with a maximum dimension of 68 mi./110 km.

Pan·do·ra's box *n* **1.** in Greek mythology, the jar, later referred to as a box, from which Pandora allowed all the world's evils to escape **2.** the source of a great collection of ills that need not be faced unless an unwise action is taken ○ *If you criticize her work, you'll be opening a real Pandora's box.*

pan·dow·dy /pan dówdee/ (*plural* **-dies**) *n* a dish made of sliced apples and spices covered with a biscuit crust and baked in a deep pan [Mid-19C. Probably < PAN[1] + variant of DOUGH]

pan dul·ce /pàn doólsay/ *n Hispanic* Mexican-style dome-shaped sweet rolls with a sugar topping, often eaten with hot chocolate or atole [< American Spanish, "sweet bread"]

pane /payn/ *n* **1.** GLAZED SECTION OF WINDOW a glazed section of a window or door **2.** PIECE OF GLASS IN WINDOW a piece of plate glass in a window or door **3.** SECTION OF SURFACE a distinct section of a surface such as a door or wall **4.** SURFACE OF FACETED OBJECT a surface on a faceted object such as a metal nut or cut jewel **5.** SECTION OF SHEET OF STAMPS a rectangular section into which a sheet of postage stamps is divided before being sold [13C. Via French < Latin *pannus* "piece of cloth"]

SPELLCHECK See *pain.*

pa·neer /pa neér/, **pa·nir** *n S Asia* a curd cheese used especially as an ingredient in cooking [< Hindi and Persian *panir* "cheese"]

pan·e·gyr·ic /pànnə jírrik, -jīrik/ *n* extravagant praise delivered in formal speech or writing [Early 17C. Via French < Latin *panegyricus* "public eulogy" < Greek *panēguris* "public assembly" < *aguris* "assembly, marketplace"] —**pan·e·gyr·i·cal** *adj* —**pan·e·gyr·i·cal·ly** *adv* —**pan·e·gyr·ist** *n*

pan·el /pánn'l/ *n* **1.** FLAT RECTANGULAR PART a flat rectangular piece of hard material that serves as a part of something such as a door or wall, often raised above or sunk in the surface **2.** FENCE SECTION a section between two posts in a fence or gate **3.** STRIP OF FABRIC IN GARMENT a vertical section of fabric sewn onto other such sections in a flowing garment or drapery **4.** WOODEN SURFACE FOR PAINTING a thin piece of wood used as a surface for oil painting, or the painting on it **5.** COMIC STRIP FRAME a section depicting a single scene in a comic strip **6.** PART OF AIRCRAFT WING a section or surface of an airplane wing **7.** CLUSTER OF PERFORMANCE-MEASURING INSTRUMENTS a surface on which performance-measuring instruments such as gauges, dials, lights, and digital displays are clustered **8.** CONTROL AREA OF COMPUTER the collection of lights, digital displays, and switches used to monitor and control the operation of a computer **9.** DISPLAY ON COMPUTER SCREEN a display of related information on a computer screen, often a list of options **10.** GROUP OF JUDGES OR SPEAKERS a group of people who publicly discuss or judge something, usually in a situation where they sit in a row to face an audience or a competition arena **11.** LIST OF PEOPLE FOR JURY DUTY a list of people summoned as potential jurors, or the people themselves **12.** JURY a jury in a court proceeding **13.** same as **panel discussion** ■ *vt* (**-eled, -el·ing, -els**) **1.** COVER SOMETHING WITH PANELS to furnish, cover, or decorate something with panels, especially wooden paneling for walls **2.** LAW same as **impanel** [14C. < Old French, "piece of cloth" < Latin *pannus*]

pan·el dis·cus·sion *n* a public discussion of an issue by a group of experts or other concerned people

pan·el heat·ing *n* a domestic heating system in which heating elements are housed in panels attached to walls or floors

pan·el·ing /pánn'ling/ *n* **1.** thin boards or sheets of wood for covering walls, especially as decoration **2.** a panel-covered wall or other surface

pan·el·ist /pánn'list/ *n* a member of a panel

pan·el·ling *n* CONSTR Can, UK spelling of **paneling**

pan·el·list *n* LAW Can, UK spelling of **panelist**

pan·el truck *n* a small delivery truck or van that is entirely enclosed, with access to the storage area from the driver's seat

pan·et·to·ne /pànnə tṓnee/ (*plural* **-nes** or **-ni** /-tṓnee/) *n* a tall Italian yeast cake flavored with vanilla and dried and candied fruits, traditionally eaten at Christmas [Early 20C. < Italian < *pane* "bread" < Latin *panis*]

Pan-Eu·ro·pe·an *adj* relating to all the nations of Europe, collectively or in cooperation with one another

pan fish *n* any small freshwater food fish, considered too small to be classed as a game fish, that is the right size to fry whole in a frying pan

pan-fry *vt* to fry food, usually fish or meat, in a frying pan with a little fat

pang /pang/ *n* **1.** a short sharp pain **2.** a sudden, intense, and usually distressing feeling [15C. Origin ?]

pan·ga /paáng gə/ *n* an African knife with a long broad heavy blade, often used for cutting down sugar cane [Mid-20C. < Kiswahili]

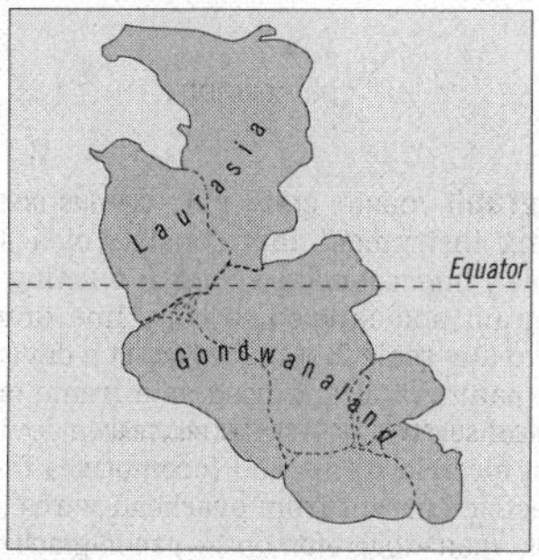

Pangaea

Pan·gae·a /pan jeé ə/, **Pan·ge·a** *n* a hypothetical ancient supercontinent incorporating all the Earth's major landmasses. It is thought to have begun splitting up about 200 million years ago.

Pan·ga·si·nan /paàn gaassee naán/ (*plural same* or **-nans**) *n* **1.** a member of a people who live in the province of Pangasinan in central Luzon in the Philippines **2.** the Austronesian language spoken by Pangasinan people [Mid-19C. < Pangasinan, "region of salty ponds"] —**Pan·ga·si·nan** *adj*

Pan·gloss·i·an /pan glóssee ən/ *adj* excessively and inappropriately optimistic (*literary*) [Mid-19C. After Dr. *Pangloss*, philosopher in Voltaire's *Candide* (1759)]

pan·go·la grass /pan gṓlə-/ *n* a fast-growing grass introduced into the southern US to provide pasture. Native to: Africa. [Mid-20C. After the *Pongola* River in South Africa]

pangolin

pan·go·lin /páng gəlin, pang gṓlin/ *n* a mammal with horny scales, a long tapering snout and tail, and a long sticky tongue for catching ants and termites. Native to: Africa and Asia. Order: Pholidota. [Late 18C. < Malay *peng-guling*, literally "roller"; because it rolls itself up when frightened]

pan·han·dle[1] /pán hànd'l/ *n* **1.** the handle of a cooking pan **2.** *also* **Pan·han·dle** a narrow section of land shaped like the handle of a cooking pan that extends away from the body of the state or territory it belongs to ○ *the Texas Panhandle* [< PAN[1]]

pan·han·dle[2] /pán hànd'l/ (**-dled, -dling, -dles**) *vti* to beg for money on the street by approaching and talking to passers-by [Late 19C. Probably < a supposed resemblance of an arm stretched out to beg to the handle of a pan] —**pan·han·dler** *n*

Pan·hel·len·ic /pàn hə lénnik/ *adj* **1.** INVOLVING ALL OF GREECE relating to all Greek peoples or all of Greece **2.** INCLUDING ALL FRATERNITIES AND SORORITIES consisting of or relating to college or university fraternities and sororities collectively ■ *n* FRATERNITY AND SORORITY COUNCIL a council or conference with representatives from all the fraternities and sororities in a college, university, or group of colleges and universities

Pan·hel·len·ism /pan héllə nìzzəm/ *n* a philosophy or movement advocating a single political system for all Greek people

pan·hu·man /pan hyṓmən/ *adj* relating to the whole of the human race

pa·ni /paánee/ *n S Asia* water [Early 19C. Via Hindi *pānī* < Sanskrit *pānīya*]

pan·ic[1] /pánnik/ *n* **1.** OVERPOWERING FEAR OR ANXIETY a sudden feeling of fear or anxiety, especially among many people, that comes on suddenly, is overwhelming, appears to be uncontrollable, and may seem to be unfounded **2.** *US* FUNNY PERSON OR THING somebody or something extremely funny (*slang*) ○ *The comedian's monologue was a panic.* ■ *adj* INVOLVING OR RESULTING FROM PANIC relating to, responding to, or resulting from panic or possible panic ○ *panic selling on the stock market* ■ *vti* (**-icked, -ick·ing, -ics**) BE OR MAKE SOMEBODY EXTREMELY AFRAID to feel panic, or make a person or animal feel panic [Early 17C. < French *panique* < modern Latin *panicus* "terrified" < Greek *panikos* < *Pan*, god of nature, thought to inspire fear] —**pan·ick·y** *adj*

pan·ic[2] /pánnik/, **pan·nick** *n* PLANTS same as **panic grass** [15C. < Latin *panicum* "foxtail"]

Pan·ic /pánnik/ *adj* same as **Pandean** [< PAN (sense 1)]

pan·ic at·tack *n* a sudden overpowering feeling of fear or anxiety that prevents somebody from functioning, often triggered by a past or present source of anxiety

pan·ic but·ton *n* an alarm to call security staff or summon help in an emergency ◇ **hit** *or* **press** *or* **push the panic button** to react to a perceived emergency or crisis by panicking and responding too hastily (*informal*)

pan·ic buy·ing *n* the buying of a product in quantity by a large number of people who fear a possible shortage

pan·ic dis·or·der *n* a condition in which somebody has recurrent panic attacks

pan·ic grass *n* a grass used for grain fodder and as a cereal, e.g., millet. Genus: *Panicum*. [< PANIC[2]]

pan·i·cle /pánnik'l/ *n* **1.** a cluster of flowers on a plant consisting of a number of individual stalks (**racemes**), each of which has a series of single flowers along its length **2.** a loose branching pyramid-shaped cluster of flowers [Late 16C. < Latin *panicula* "little ear of millet" < *panus* "swelling, ear of millet"] —**pa·nic·u·late** /pə níkyələt, -làyt/ *adj*

panic room *n* a fortified room within a house, often equipped with high-tech security devices, where people can hide to protect themselves from attack or theft

pan·ic-strick·en, **pan·ic-struck** *adj* suddenly affected by or characterized by panic

~~**panicy**~~ incorrect spelling of **panicky**

pa·ni·ni /pə neénee/ *npl* Italian white bread rolls, or sandwiches made with them [Mid-20C. < Italian, plural of *panino* "small bread" < *pane* "bread"]

Pan·is·lam·ism /pàn iz laá mìzzəm, pan ízzlə-, pàn iss laá mìzzəm, pan ísslə-/ *n* a movement that aims to unify Islamic countries and spread the Islamic religion —**Pan·is·lam·ic** /pàn iz laámik, -iss-/ *adj* —**Pan·is·lam·ist** /pàn iz laámist, pan ízzlə-, pàn iss laámist, pan ísslə-/ *n, adj*

Pan·ja·bi *n, adj* LANG another spelling of **Punjabi**

pan·jan·drum /pan jándrəm/ (*plural* **-drums** or **-dra** /-drə/) *n* somebody, especially an official, who is pompous or pretentious [Mid-18C. Invented word]

ORIGIN ***Panjandrum*** was coined in 1755 by the English actor and playwright Samuel Foote (1720–77) to test the memory of the actor Charles Macklin, who claimed to be able to memorize and repeat anything said to him (it was one of several inventions in the same vein that Foote put to him): "And there were present...the Joblillies, and the Garyulies, and the Grand Panjandrum himself, with the little round button at top." It did not spread into general use until the 19th century.

AKG London
Emmeline Pankhurst

Pank·hurst /pángk hùrst/, **Emmeline** (1858–1928) British campaigner for woman's suffrage. She founded the Women's Social and Political Union (1903) in Manchester, England. She was frequently imprisoned for destroying property, but during World War I she abandoned her campaign and encouraged women to do industrial war work.

> "We have taken this action, because as women...we realize that the condition of our sex is so deplorable that it is our duty even to break the law in order to call attention to the reasons why we do so."
> [Emmeline Pankhurst, *Speech in court*; October 21, 1908]

pan·leu·ko·pe·ni·a /pàn lookə peénee ə/, **pan·leu·co·pe·ni·a** *n* VET same as **feline distemper** (*technical*)

pan·mix·i·a /pan míksee ə/, **pan·mix·is** /-míksiss/ *n* random breeding and free interchange of genes within a population [Late 19C. Via modern Latin < German *Panmixie* "all mixing" < Greek *mixis* "mixing, mingling"] —**pan·mic·tic** *adj*

panne /pan/ *n* a lightweight silk or rayon fabric resembling velvet [Late 18C. < French]

pan·nick *n* PLANTS another spelling of **panic**[2]

pan·nier /pánnyər, pánnee ər/ *n* **1.** BASKET ON PACK ANIMAL a large basket, often one of a pair, that is placed on the back of a horse, donkey, or other pack animal **2.** *US* BASKET CARRIED ON SOMEBODY'S BACK a basket that can be carried on a person's back **3.** BAG ON BICYCLE one of a pair of bags carried on either side of the back or front wheel of a bicycle or motorcycle **4.** FRAMEWORK TO WIDEN SKIRT a framework of cane worn by women in the 18th century at each side of the hips to widen a skirt **5.** OVERSKIRT LOOPED UP AT HIPS an overskirt looped up at the hips to show the underskirt and give the impression of fullness, worn by women in the second half of the 19th century [13C. Via Old French *pannier* < Latin *panarium* "breadbasket" < *panis* "bread"]

pan·ni·kin /pánnikin/ *n UK* a small metal drinking cup [Early 19C. < PAN[1], after CANNIKIN]

Pa·no·an /pa nṓ ən/ *n* a group of languages spoken in Peru and western Brazil [Early 20C. < American Spanish *Pano*, a people of the upper Amazon basin] —**Pa·no·an** *adj*

pa·no·cha /pə nṓchə/ *n Hispanic* **1.** coarse brown sugar produced in Mexico and usually sold in hard cone-shaped pieces **2.** FOOD same as **penuche** [Mid-19C. Via Mexican Spanish < Spanish, "ear of maize" < Latin *panicula* (see PANICLE)]

pan·o·ply /pánnəplee/ (*plural* **-plies**) *n* **1.** FULL ARRAY an impressive and magnificent display or array of something **2.** FULL CEREMONIAL DRESS ceremonial dress with all the necessary accessories **3.** PROTECTIVE COVERING a covering that protects something **4.** FULL ARMOR a full suit of armor and equipment for a warrior [Late 16C. Via French < Greek *panoplia*, literally "all weapons" < *hopla* "weapons"] —**pan·o·plied** *adj*

pan·op·tic /pan óptik/, **pan·op·ti·cal** /-óptik'l/ *adj* taking in or showing everything in a single view [Early 19C. < Greek *panoptos* "seen by all," *panoptēs* "all-seeing" < *optos* "visible"] —**pan·op·ti·cal·ly** *adv*

pan·op·ti·con /pan óptikən/ *n* a prison with cell blocks situated around a central area so that the prisoners could be viewed at all times [Mid-18C. PAN- "all" + Greek *optikon*, neuter of *optikos* "optic."]

pan·o·ram·a /pànnə rámmə, -raámə/ *n* **1.** 360° VIEW an unobstructed view extending in all directions, especially of a landscape **2.** COMPREHENSIVE SURVEY an all-encompassing survey of a particular topic or issue **3.** PICTURE WITH WIDE VIEW a picture or photograph that has a wide view, especially one that is unrolled gradually in front of the spectator **4.** ARTS same as **cyclorama** (sense 1) [Late 18C. < PAN- + Greek *horama* "view" < *horan* "to see"] —**pan·o·ram·ic** /-rámmik/ *adj* —**pan·o·ram·i·cal·ly** *adv*

ORIGIN ***Panorama*** was coined in the late 1780s by an Irish artist called Robert Barker to describe a method he had invented for painting a scene on the inside of a cylinder in such a way that its perspective would seem correct to somebody viewing it from inside the cylinder. He put his invention into practice in 1793 when he opened his "Panorama," a large building in Leicester Square, London, where the public could come and gaze at such all-encompassing scenes. The modern abstract meaning was in use by the early 19th century.

pan·o·ram·ic sight *n* a sight on a military weapon that gives the user a wide-angled view of the target area

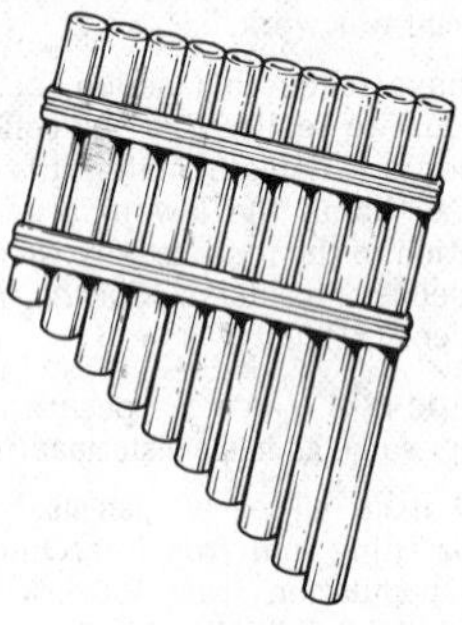

panpipes

pan·pipes /pán pīps/ *npl* a set of reeds of different lengths that are bound together in a row and played by blowing across the top of each pipe. Panpipes have been in use since ancient times and are today often associated with Peruvian music. [Early 19C. After PAN (sense 1)]

pan·sex·ual /pan sékshoo əl, -séksh'l/ *adj* relating to a sexuality that expresses itself in many different forms —**pan·sex·u·al·i·ty** /pàn sekshoo állətee/ *n*

pan·sper·mi·a /pan spúrmee ə/ *n* a theory that states that the universe is full of spores that germinate when they find a favorable environment [Mid-19C. < Greek, "belief that the elements are made of all the seeds of things" < *sperma* "seed"]

pan·sy /pánzee/ (*plural* **-sies**) *n* **1.** FLOWER WITH BRIGHT VELVETY PETALS a plant with brightly colored velvety flowers that usually have black or dark centers. Native to: Europe. Genus: *Viola* or *Achimenes.* **2.** DEEP VIOLET a deep violet color **3.** OFFENSIVE TERM an offensive term for an effeminate or gay man (*dated insult*) [15C. < French *pensée* "thought" (from its lowered head), form of past participle of *penser* "think"] —**pan·sy** *adj*

pant[1] /pant/ *v* (**pant·ed, pant·ing, pants**) **1.** *vi* TAKE SHORT FAST SHALLOW BREATHS to take short fast shallow breaths, especially when excited, hot, or after physical exertion **2.** *vt* SAY SOMETHING BREATHLESSLY to say something while trying to catch your breath **3.** *vi* YEARN to have a strong desire and yearning for somebody or something **4.** *vi* PULSATE QUICKLY to throb at a fast rhythm ■ *n* SHALLOW BREATH a short fast shallow breath [15C. Via assumed Anglo-Norman, "gasp" < Vulgar Latin *phantasiare* "gasp in horror" < Latin *phantasia* "apparition" < Greek (see FANTASY)]

pant[2] /pant/ *n* a pair of trousers [Late 19C. Back-formation < PANTS]

pant- *prefix* same as **panto-** (*used before vowels*)

pan·ta·lets /pàntə léts/, **pan·ta·lettes** *npl* **1.** long underpants extending below the skirt, usually with a frill around the bottom of each leg, worn by women in the first half of the 19th century **2.** a pair of frills, one at the bottom of each leg, on a pair of pantalets [Mid-19C. < PANTALOON]

pan·ta·loon /pàntə lóon/ *n* a character in pantomime who is the victim of the clown's jokes and tricks [Late 18C. < PANTALOON]

Pan·ta·loon /pántə lóon/ *n* a character in Italian commedia dell'arte, a very thin man of advanced years who is easily tricked and who wears pantaloons and slippers [Late 16C. Via French < Italian *Pantalone*, probably after *San Pantaleone* "St. Pantaleon," popular saint in Venice]

pan·ta·loons /pàntə lóonz/ *npl* **1.** WIDE PANTS GATHERED AT ANKLE loose-fitting pants that are gathered at the ankle **2.** 19C TIGHT-FITTING PANTS tight-fitting men's pants fastened with buttons or ribbons at the ankle and sometimes held with a strap under the instep, worn in the early 19th century **3.** 17C ENGLISH PANTS men's wide ankle-length breeches, worn especially in England in the late 17th century **4.** BAGGY PANTS pants that fit very loosely (*informal humorous*) [Mid-17C. After PANTALOON; because of a type worn by the stage character]

pan·tech·ni·con /pan téknikən, -tékni kòn/ *n UK* a large moving van (*dated*) [Late 19C. After *Pantechnicon*, a building in London, England, built as a bazaar and later used for storing furniture < PAN- + Greek *tekhnikos* "artistic"]

ORIGIN The original ***Pantechnicon*** was a huge complex of warehouses, wine vaults, and other storage facilities on Motcomb Street, in London's Belgravia. Built in 1830 and supposed to be fireproof, it was almost totally destroyed by fire in 1874. It seems originally to have been intended to be a bazaar, hence its name, literally "everything artistic," denoting that all sorts of manufactured wares were to be bought there. But it was its role as a furniture repository that brought it into the general language. Moving vans taking furniture there came to be known as "pantechnicon vans," and by the 1890s ***pantechnicon*** was a generic term for "moving van."

pan·the·ism /pánthee ìzzəm/ *n* **1.** the belief that God and the material world are one and the same thing and that God is present in everything **2.** the belief in and worship of all or many deities [Mid-18C. < PAN- + Greek *theos* "god"] —**pan·the·ist** *n* —**pan·the·is·tic** /pànthee ístik/ *adj* —**pan·the·is·ti·cal·ly** *adv*

pan·the·on /pánthee ən, -òn/ *n* **1.** TEMPLE a temple dedicated to all deities **2.** ALL DEITIES OF SPECIFIC RELIGION all the deities of a people or religion considered collectively **3.** MEMORIAL TO DEAD HEROES a monument or public building commemorating the dead heroes of a nation **4.** GROUP OF IMPORTANT PEOPLE a group of people who are the most famous or respected in their field [15C. Via Latin < Greek *pantheion* "of all the gods" < *theos* "god"]

Pan·the·on *n* a circular temple in Rome that was completed in 27 B.C. and dedicated to all the deities but which has been used as a Christian church since A.D. 609

pan·ther /pánthər/ (*plural* **-thers** or *same*) *n* **1.** a leopard, especially in its black unspotted phase **2.** VERTEB same as **mountain lion** [13C. Via French < Greek *panthēr*]

pan·tie *adj* CLOTHING another spelling of **panty**

pant·ie gir·dle, **pant·y gir·dle** *n* a woman's undergarment with a sewn-in crotch like underpants, but made of elasticized material in order to give the abdomen a flatter appearance

pant·ies /pánteez/ *npl* short light fitted underpants for women or girls (*informal*) [Mid-19C. < PANTS]

pan·ti·hose *npl* CLOTHING another spelling of **pantyhose**

pan·tile /pán tīl/ *n* a roof tile made in an "S" shape so that the downward-curving tail of the "S" overlaps the upward-curving head of the "S" of the tile next to it [Mid-17C. < PAN[1]]

pan·ti·soc·ra·cy /pàntə sókrəssee/ (*plural* **-cies**) *n* a planned utopian community in which everyone shares power and is equal [Late 18C. < PANTO- + Greek *isokratia* "equality of power"]

panto- *prefix* all ○ *pantograph* [< Greek *pant-*; form of *pan* "all"]

Pan·to·cra·tor /pan tókrətər/ *n* in Christianity, Jesus Christ as ruler of the universe, creator, and savior, represented in Byzantine church art with one hand upraised and the other holding a copy of the Gospels [Late 19C. < Greek *pantokratōr* "almighty"]

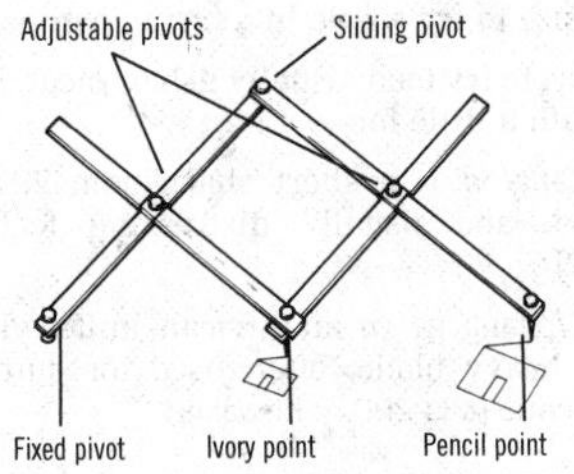

pantograph

pan·to·graph /pántə grȧf/ *n* **1.** COPYING INSTRUMENT a drawing instrument that consists of a set of adjustable interconnected bars forming a parallelogram and is used to copy line drawings or maps to any scale **2.** FRAME OR BRACKET a device shaped like a pantograph and used as a frame or bracket **3.** CURRENT-SUPPLY DEVICE FOR ELECTRIC TRAIN a device on the roof of electric trains and locomotives for picking up electric current from overhead wires —**pan·tog·ra·pher** /pan tóggrəfər/ *n* —**pan·to·graph·ic** /pàntə gráffik/ *adj* —**pan·to·graph·i·cal·ly** *adv*

pan·to·mime /pántə mīm/ *n* **1.** MIME ARTIST somebody who acts without speaking, using gesture and expression **2.** HUMOROUS BRITISH THEATRICAL ENTERTAINMENT a style of British theater, or a play in this style, traditionally performed at Christmas, in which a folktale or children's story is told with jokes, songs, and dancing **3.** ROMAN THEATRICAL PERFORMANCE in ancient Rome, a theatrical performance by one masked actor who played all the characters, using only dance, gesture, and expression, and no words, while a chorus narrated the story **4.** ROMAN ACTOR an actor in a Roman pantomime [Late 16C. Via Latin *pantomimus* "mime artist" < Greek *pantomīmos* "complete imitator" < *mīmos* "imitator"] —**pan·to·mim·ic** /pàntə mímmik/ *adj* —**pan·to·mim·ist** /pántə mīmist, -mìmmist/ *n*

pan·to·mime dame *n* the role in a British pantomime of an ill-tempered comic woman of advanced years, traditionally played by a man

~~pantomine~~ incorrect spelling of **pantomime**

pan·to·then·ate /pàntə thé nàyt, pan tóthə-/ *n* an ester of pantothenic acid [Mid-20C. < PANTOTHENIC ACID]

pan·to·then·ic ac·id /pàntə thénnik-/ *n* a B complex vitamin that is present in many foods and is essential for growth [< Greek *pantothen* "from every side"; because widely found]

pan·toum /pan tóom/ *n* a form of verse in which the second and fourth lines of each four-line verse are repeated as the first and third lines of the following verse [Late 18C. Via French < Malay *pantun*]

pan·trop·ic /pan tróppik/, **pan·trop·i·cal** /-ik'l/ *adj* found throughout the tropics

pan·try /pántree/ (*plural* **-tries**) *n* **1.** a small closed space connected to a kitchen, often with a door, in which food and utensils for food preparation can be stored **2.** a highly ventilated cold small room or walk-in cupboard with shelves and a marble surface used for storing food [13C. < Old French *paneterie* "cupboard for bread" < late Latin *panarius* "bread-seller" < Latin *panis* "bread"]

pants /pants/ *npl* **1.** an item of clothing that covers the part of the body from the waist to the ankles or, sometimes, the knees, each leg having a separate tubular piece **2.** an item of clothing worn next to the skin that covers the buttocks and genital area [Mid-19C. Shortening of PANTALOONS] ◇ **beat the pants off somebody** to defeat somebody decisively (*informal*) ◇ **bore** *or* **scare** *or* **charm the pants off somebody** to bore, scare, or charm somebody very much (*informal*) ◇ **caught with your pants down** caught in an unprepared or embarrassing position ◇ **wear the pants** to be the member of a household who makes the important decisions

pant·suit /pánt sóot/, **pants suit** *n* a woman's outfit consisting of a jacket and pants that are made of the same material

pan·ty /pántee/, **pan·tie** *adj* belonging to, concerning, suitable for, or part of women's underpants ○ *showing a panty line*

panty gir·dle *n* CLOTHING another spelling of **pantie girdle**

pant·y·hose /pántee hōz/, **pan·ti·hose** *npl* a light tight-fitting sheer covering for a woman's legs that stretches from the toes up to an elastic waistband

pant·y·lin·er /pántee līnər/ *n* a light thin sanitary napkin

pant·y·waist /pántee wàyst/ *n* **1.** an offensive term for a man that deliberately insults his courage and masculinity (*slang*) **2.** a piece of clothing for children, consisting of a shirt and pants that are buttoned together at the waist (*dated*)

pan·zer /pánzər, pántsər/ *n* a German tank used in World War II [Mid-20C. Shortening of German *Panzerdivision* "armored unit" < Old French *pancier* "armor for the belly" < *pance* "belly" (see PAUNCH)]

pap[1] /pap/ *n* **1.** SEMILIQUID FOOD soft semiliquid food, usually mashed or pulped, especially for babies or sick people **2.** TRIVIAL OR WORTHLESS MATERIAL something such as a book, movie, or television program that is regarded as lacking in depth and substance and is considered worthless **3.** *US* POLITICAL PATRONAGE political patronage in the form of money or favors (*slang*) [14C. Via French < Latin *pappa* "food," children's word] —**pap·py** /páppee/ *adj*

pap[2] /pap/ *n regional* a teat or nipple [12C. Origin ?]

pa·pa[1] /paápə, pə paá/ *n* same as **father** *n* (sense 1) (*dated*) [Late 17C. Via French and late Latin < Greek *pappas* "father"]

pa·pa[2] /paápə/ *n* a soft blue-gray clay of marine origin [Late 19C. < Maori]

Pa·pa /paápə/ *n* a code word for the letter "P," used in international radio communications [< PAPA[1]]

pa·pa·cy /páypəssee/ (*plural* **-cies**) *n* **1.** PAPAL POWER OR STATUS the power or position of the pope **2.** POPE'S PERIOD IN POWER the period of office of a pope **3.** PAPAL GOVERNMENT the system of government in the Roman Catholic Church with the pope as the head [14C. < medieval Latin *papatia* < late Latin *papa* (see POPE)]

pa·pad /páppəd/ *n S Asia* same as **poppadom** [Late 20C. Alteration of POPPADOM]

Pa·pa Doc /paápə dók/ ➧ **Duvalier, François**

pa·pa·dum *n* FOOD another spelling of **poppadom**

Pa·pa·go /páppə gō, paápə-/ (*plural same* or **-gos**) *n* **1.** a member of a Native North American people who lived in central Arizona, and now live mainly in northern Mexico and southern Arizona **2.** the Uto-Aztecan language of the Papago people, closely related to Pima. Native speakers: 9,000. [Mid-19C. Via Spanish *pápago* < Pima-Papago, "bean eaters"] —**Pa·pa·go** *adj*

pa·pa·in /pə páy in, -pī-/ *n* an enzyme found in the juice of papayas and used as a meat tenderizer and in medicine to promote digestion and healing of wounds [Late 19C. < PAPAYA]

pa·pal /páyp'l/ *adj* relating to the pope or the papacy [14C. Via French < medieval Latin *papalis* < late Latin *papa* "bishop, pope" (see POPE)] —**pa·pal·ly** *adv*

Pa·pal States /páyp'l-/ former territories in Italy over which the pope had sovereignty between A.D. 754 and 1870

Pap·an·dre·ou /pàppən dráy oo/, **Andreas** (1919–96) prime minister of Greece (1981–89 and 1993–96). The founder of the Pan-Hellenistic Socialist Movement (1974), he became the first socialist prime minister of Greece.

Pa·pa·ni·co·laou test /paápə neékə lòw tèst, pàppə níkə lòw-/, **Pa·pa·ni·co·laou smear** *n* MED same as **Pap smear** [Mid-20C. After G. N. *Papanicolaou* (1883–1962), Greek-born anatomist]

pa·pa·raz·zo /paápə raát sō/ (*plural* **-zi** /-seé/) *n* a freelance photographer who follows famous people hoping to get a newsworthy story, especially something shocking or scandalous [Mid-20C. < Italian, surname of a photographer in the film *La Dolce Vita* (1959) by Federico Fellini]

USAGE The plural form *paparazzi* is used more often than the singular, even when referring to a single photographer.

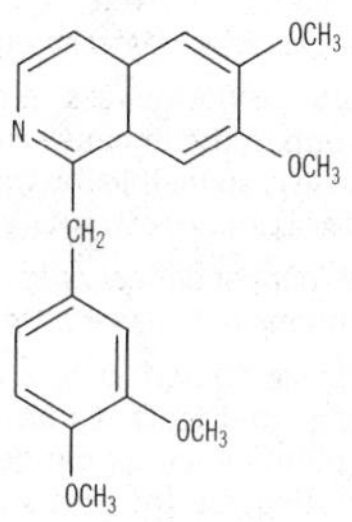

papaverine

pa·pav·er·ine /pə pávvə reèn, -rin/ *n* a toxic white crystalline nonaddictive alkaloid. Source: opium, derived synthetically. Use: antispasmodic to treat asthma and colic. Formula: $C_{20}H_{21}O_4N$. [Mid-19C. < Latin *papaver* "poppy"]

pa·paw /páw pàw/, **paw·paw** *n* **1.** a yellow medium-sized oval fruit with sweet flesh and black seeds **2.** a deciduous tree with purple flowers that bears papaws. Native to: North America. Latin name: *Asimina triloba*. **3.** TREES, FOOD same as **papaya** (sense 2) [Early 17C. Alteration of PAPAYA]

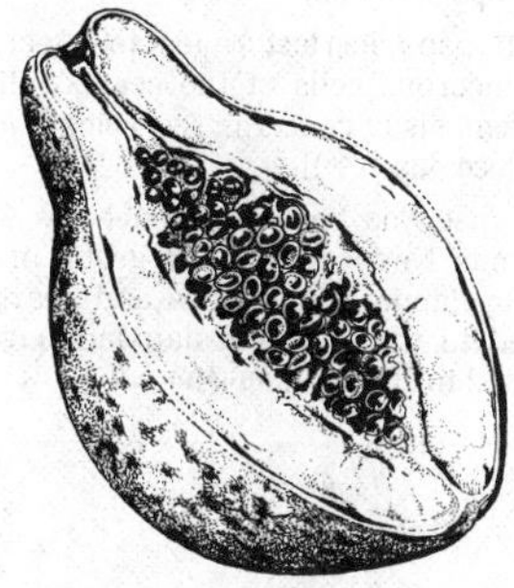
papaya

pa·pa·ya /pə pī ə/ *n* **1.** a large spherical or elongated fruit with yellow pulp and numerous seeds, eaten fresh or in salads and desserts **2.** a tropical evergreen tree with a crown of broad leaves, widely cultivated to produce papayas. Latin name: *Carica papaya*. [Late 16C. Via Spanish < Carib or Arawak]

pa·per /páypər/ *n* **1.** THIN FLAT MATERIAL FROM WOOD PULP a thin material consisting of flat sheets made from pulped wood, cloth, or fiber. Use: for writing and printing on, for wrapping things in, for covering walls. **2.** SHEET OR SHEETS OF PAPER one or more pieces or sheets of paper, for writing or drawing on **3.** MEDIA same as **newspaper** (sense 1) **4.** STUDENT'S ESSAY an essay written by a student for a class **5.** ACADEMIC ARTICLE OR TALK an essay or article, particularly an academic one, read at a conference, or submitted for publication **6.** SET OF EXAM ANSWERS a written set of answers by a student to a set of examination questions **7.** *UK* EXAMINATION a set of examination questions prepared on paper **8.** WRAPPER a piece of paper, especially one used to wrap a piece of candy or a cigarette (*often used in the plural*) **9.** COMMERCIAL NEGOTIABLE DOCUMENT a negotiable document, e.g., a bill of exchange or promissory note **10.** HOME MAINTENANCE same as **wallpaper** *n* (sense 1) (*informal*) **11.** FREE THEATER TICKET a free ticket that is given out in order to fill up a theater (*slang*) **12.** THEATERGOERS WITH FREE TICKETS members of the audience who have been given free tickets in order to fill up a theater (*slang*) ■ **pa·pers** *npl* **1.** PERSONAL IDENTITY DOCUMENTS a document or documents showing somebody's identity or status, e.g., a passport **2.** ANIMAL'S PEDIGREE OR VACCINATION RECORDS a document or documents showing an animal's pedigree or vaccination records **3.** ASSORTMENT OF DOCUMENTS a collection of documents relating to an issue or subject ○ *official papers in the archives* **4.** SOMEBODY'S PERSONAL WRITINGS somebody's diaries, letters, and other personal writings **5.** NAUT same as **ship's papers** ■ *adj* **1.** MADE OF PAPER consisting of or made of paper **2.** RESEMBLING PAPER similar to paper, e.g., in flimsiness ○ *paper walls* **3.** EXISTING IN DOCUMENTARY FORM written in a document but not necessarily effective or useful in reality ○ *mere paper guarantees of peace* **4.** IN WRITING conducted in writing ○ *a paper war* ■ *vt* (**-pered, -per·ing, -pers**) **1.** COVER WITH WALLPAPER to cover a wall or room with wallpaper **2.** COVER SOMETHING WITH PAPER to cover something with paper **3.** FILL UP THEATER to fill up a theater by giving out free tickets (*slang*) [14C. Via Anglo-Norman *papir*, Old French *papier* < Latin *papyrus* (see PAPYRUS)] —**pa·per·er** *n* ◇ **on paper 1.** in theory, but not in fact **2.** in writing ◇ **paper the walls with something** to disseminate or broadcast something (*slang*) ○ *They papered the walls with objections to the policy.*

paper over *vt* **1.** to cover something up with paper, especially to cover a wall's imperfections or old paint with wallpaper **2.** to conceal something such as a mistake or fault without resolving it

pa·per·back /páypər bàk/ *n* a book that has a thin flexible cover instead of a hard cover ■ *adj* with a thin flexible cover, instead of a hard cover

pa·per·bark /páypər baárk/ *n* a tree with pale thin papery bark that peels off in large sheets. Native to: Australia. Genus: *Melaleuca*. [< the color and texture of the bark]

pa·per birch *n* a birch tree with white peeling bark that was formerly used to cover canoes. Native to: North America. Latin name: *Betula papyrifera*. [< the white color of the bark]

pa·per·board /páypər bàwrd/ *n* thick cardboard made from compressed paper

pa·per·boy /páypər bòy/ *n* a boy who delivers newspapers to people's homes, or who sells newspapers

pa·per chase *n* an intense searching and collation of files, books, or documents

pa·per·clip /páypər klìp/, **pa·per clip** *n* a clip designed to be slipped over two or more sheets of paper to hold them together, especially a piece of wire that is bent into a long flat oval spiral

pa·per cut·ter *n* **1.** a machine or device for cutting paper, especially a flat platform with a long arm containing a blade that can be raised and lowered in order to cut straight edges **2.** HOUSEHOLD same as **letter opener**

pa·per·girl /páypər gùrl/ *n* a girl who delivers newspapers to people's homes, or who sells newspapers

pa·per·hang·er /páypər hàngər/ *n* **1.** somebody who hangs wallpaper, especially as a profession **2.** *US* somebody who regularly passes bad checks in order to obtain money (*slang*) —**pa·per·hang·ing** *n*

pa·per jam *n* a situation in which paper becomes jammed in a printer or photocopier, causing it to stop working

pa·per·knife /páypər nīf/ (*plural* **-knives** /-nīvz/) *n UK* COMM same as **letter opener**

pa·per·less /páypərləss/ *adj* using records or means of communication that are electronic rather than on paper ○ *the age of the paperless office*

pa·per mon·ey *n* currency in the form of bills, as opposed to coins

pa·per mul·ber·ry *n* a common shade tree whose inner bark was once used for making paper. Native to: Asia. Latin name: *Broussonetia papyrifera*.

pa·per nau·ti·lus *n* a cephalopod mollusk, the female of which has a thin delicate shell. Genus: *Argonauta*. [< the delicacy and whiteness of its shell]

pa·per prof·it *n* a profit that is not generated from the normal trading of a business and may or may not be realized (*often used in the plural*)

pa·per-push·er *n* somebody with a routine clerical job involving much paperwork (*informal*)

pa·per route *n* **1.** the job of delivering newspapers to people's homes **2.** the course followed from house to house by somebody delivering newspapers

pa·per-thin *adj* extremely thin, like paper —**pa·per·thin** *adv*

pa·per ti·ger *n* somebody or something, especially an organization or a nation, that appears to be very strong and powerful but is in fact weak and ineffectual

pa·per trail *n* a sequence of documents that can be used by an investigator as a record of someone's actions or decisions (*informal*)

pa·per-train (**pa·per-trained, pa·per-train·ing, pa·per-**

trains) *vt US* to train a house pet so that it urinates and defecates on paper when it is indoors

pa·per wasp *n* a large slender wasp known for its elaborate nest that is made up of individual cells built of papery material. Genus: *Polistes.*

pa·per·weight /páypər wàyt/ *n* a small heavy usually ornamental object that is used to hold down papers and keep them in place

pa·per·work /páypər wùrk/ *n* routine work that involves tasks such as filling in forms, keeping files up to date, or writing reports and letters

pa·per·y /páypəree/ *adj* similar to paper in texture or thickness —**pa·per·i·ness** *n*

Pa·phi·an /páyfee ən/ *adj* **1. RELATING TO PAPHOS** relating to the village of Paphos **2. RELATING TO APHRODITE** relating to the goddess Aphrodite, who, in Greek mythology, rose fully formed from the sea at Paphos **3. CONCERNING SEXUAL ACTIVITY** relating to sexual love (*literary*) ■ *n* **1. SOMEBODY FROM PAPHOS** somebody who comes from Paphos **2. Pa·phian, pa·phian** same as **prostitute** *n* (sense 1) (*literary*)

Pa·phos[1] /páy fòss/ town in southwestern Cyprus, on the site of the ancient city of Paphos. Population: 38,000 (1997).

Pa·phos[2] /páy fòss/, **Pa·phus** /páyfəss/ *n* in Greek mythology, a king of Cyprus who was the son of Pygmalion and Galatea

Pa·pia·men·tu /paapee ə méntoo/, **Pa·pia·men·to** /-méntō/ *n* a Spanish-based creole of the Netherlands Antilles, derived from a Portuguese pidgin and including many Dutch words. Native speakers: 200,000. [Mid-20C. < Spanish *Papiamento* < Papiamentu *papya* "talk" + *-mentu* "-ment"] —**Pa·pia·men·tu** *adj*

pa·pier col·lé /pà pyay kaw láy/ *n* scraps of paper and other objects that are glued onto a sheet as an abstract artistic composition [< French, "glued paper"]

pa·pier-mâ·ché /pàypər mə sháy, pà pyay maa sháy/ *n* sheets of paper pulp and glue stuck together in layers, usually onto a frame or mold, used to make various objects such as figures, boxes, bowls, and masks [< French, "mashed paper"] —**pa·pier-mâ·ché** *adj*

pa·pil·la /pə píllə/ (*plural* **-lae** /-lee/) *n* **1. SMALL LUMP OF TISSUE** a small nipple-shaped protuberance, e.g., on the tongue enclosing the taste buds, or at the root of a hair or feather **2. NIPPLE** a nipple or teat (*technical*) **3. SMALL PROJECTION ON PETAL OR LEAF** a small elevated pad on the surface of a stigma, petal, or leaf **4. SMALL PROJECTION RESEMBLING NIPPLE** a very small projection like a nipple on the surface of something [Late 17C. < Latin, "little swelling" < *papula* "swelling"] —**pap·il·lar·y** /páppə lèrree, pə píllaree/ *adj* —**pap·il·late** /páppə làyt, pə píllət/ *adj* —**pa·pil·lif·er·ous** /pàppə líffərəss/ *adj* —**pa·pil·li·form** /pə píllə fàwrm/ *adj*

pap·il·lo·ma /pàppə lṓmə/ (*plural* **-mas** or **-ma·ta** /-mətə/) *n* a benign tumor of the skin or mucous membrane projecting from a surface, e.g., a wart —**pap·il·lo·ma·tous** /-lómmətəss, -lṓmə-/ *adj*

pap·il·lon /páppə lòn, paapee yáwN/ *n* a small spaniel with a silky coat and heavily fringed tail and ears [Early 20C. < French, literally "butterfly"; because its pointed ears resemble the shape of a butterfly's wings]

pap·il·lote /páppə lòt, paapee yṓt/ [Mid-18C. < French < *papillon* "butterfly"] ◇ **en papillote** baked in a wrapping of waxed paper, nonstick baking parchment, or foil

Pap·i·neau /páppi nṓ/, **Louis Joseph** (1786–1871) Canadian politician. In 1837 he led the French-Canadian rebellion against British rule in Lower Canada (Quebec).

> "The most efficacious and the most immediate means which the Canadians have to protect themselves against the fury of their enemies, is to attack them in their dearest parts—their pockets—in their strongest entrenchments, the banks."
> [Louis Joseph Papineau, *Montreal Gazette*, December 11, 1834]

pa·pist /páypist/ *n* an offensive term for a member of the Roman Catholic Church [Mid-16C. < French *papiste* or modern Latin *papista* < late Latin *papa* (see POPE)] —**pa·pism** *n* —**pa·pis·tic** /pə pístik/ *adj* —**pa·pist·ry** *n*

pa·poose /pa pooss, pə-/ *n* **1.** an offensive term for a Native North American baby or young child **2.** a bag that fits over the shoulders, used for carrying a baby, especially in front of the body [Mid-17C. < Narragansett *papoòs* or Massachusett *pappouse*]

pa·po·va·vi·rus /pə pṓvə vìrəss/ *n* a DNA-containing virus of a group that can cause cancers in animals, including those responsible for warts [Mid-20C. < first two letters of PAPILLOMA + POLYOMA + *vacuolation*]

pap·par·delle /pàppər déllee/ *npl* pasta in the shape of broad flat ribbons [< Italian < *pappare* "eat ravenously"]

pap·pus /páppəss/ (*plural* **-pi** /-pì/) *n* a covering of scales, bristles, and feathery hairs that surrounds the fruit of plants such as dandelions and thistles and helps to disperse the fruits [Early 18C. Via Latin < Greek *pappos* "grandfather"] —**pap·pose** /pá pōss/ *adj*

pap·py /páppee/ (*plural* **-pies**) *n US regional, Can* same as **father** *n* (sense 1) (*dated*) [Mid-18C. < PAPA[1]]

pap·py·show /páppee shò/ *n Carib* somebody who appears ridiculous or foolish [Early 20C. Alteration of Scottish dialect *puppy show* "puppet show"] ◇ **make a pappyshow of somebody** *Carib* to ridicule somebody or make somebody appear foolish

pa·pri·ka /pa preékə, pə-, pápprikə/ *n* **1. MILD RED SPICE** a mild red spice made from various sweet red peppers, used especially in Hungarian cooking **2. SWEET RED PEPPER** a sweet red pepper or the plant on which it grows. Genus: *Capsicum.* **3. REDDISH ORANGE COLOR** a bright reddish orange color [Late 19C. < Hungarian < Serbian *pàpar* "pepper" < Latin *piper* (see PEPPER)] —**pa·pri·ka** *adj*

Pap smear /páp-/, **Pap test** *n* a test to detect cancerous or precancerous cells of the cervix, allowing for early diagnosis of cancer [< shortening of *Papanicolaou* (see PAPANICOLAOU TEST)]

Pap·u·an /páppyoo ən/ *n* **1.** somebody who comes from Papua New Guinea **2.** a group of languages spoken in Papua New Guinea and nearby islands, unrelated to the Austronesian languages. Native speakers: 2 million. —**Pap·u·an** *adj*

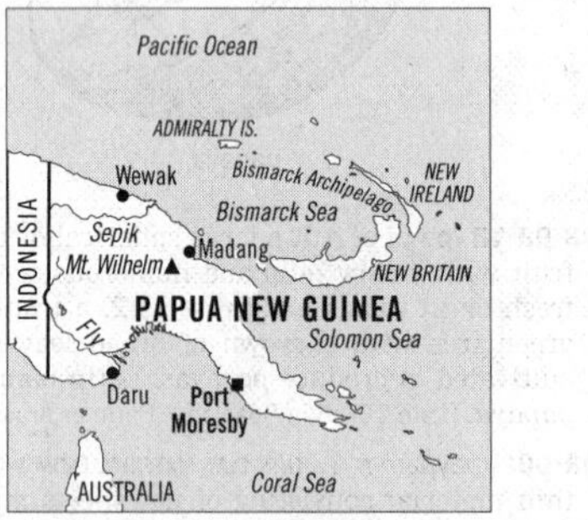

Papua New Guinea

Pap·u·a New Guin·ea /pàppyoo ə noo gínnee/ independent nation in Oceania, situated north of Australia, in the southwestern Pacific Ocean, consisting of the eastern half of the island of New Guinea together with many other islands. It became an independent member of the British Commonwealth in 1975. Language: English. Currency: kina. Capital: Port Moresby. Population: 5,295,816 (2003). Area: 178,704 sq. mi./462,840 sq. km. Official name **Independent State of Papua New Guinea** —**Pap·u·a New Guin·e·an** *n, adj*

pap·ule /páp yool/ *n* a small hard round protuberance on the skin [Early 18C. < Latin *papula*] —**pap·u·lar** /páppyələr/ *adj* —**pap·u·lif·er·ous** /pàppyə líffərəss/ *adj*

pa·py·ri plural of **papyrus**

pap·y·rol·o·gy /pàppə róllәjee/ *n* the study of ancient papyrus manuscripts —**pap·y·ro·log·i·cal** /pàppərə lójjik'l/ *adj* —**pap·y·rol·o·gist** *n*

pa·py·rus /pə pírəss/ (*plural* **-ri** /-rì/ or **-rus·es**) *n* **1. MATERIAL RESEMBLING PAPER** writing material used by the ancient Egyptians, Greeks, and Romans that was made from the pith of the stem of a water plant **2. PAPYRUS DOCUMENT** an ancient manuscript written on papyrus **3. TALL MARSH PLANT** a tall water plant. Flowers: small, like umbrellas. Use: writing material. Native to: southern Europe, Nile valley. Latin name: *Cyperus papyrus.* [14C. Via Latin < Greek *papuros* "papyrus plant"]

par /paar/ *n* **1. AVERAGE LEVEL** a level or standard considered to be average or normal **2. STANDARD SCORE IN GOLF** the standard score assigned to each hole on a golf course, or to the sum total of these holes **3. ACCEPTED VALUE OF CURRENCY** the accepted value of one country's currency in terms of the currency of another country that uses the same metal standard **4.** COMM same as **par value** ■ *adj* **AVERAGE** average or normal ■ *vt* **(parred, par·ring, pars) SCORE PAR ON HOLE OR COURSE** in golf, to score the equivalent of the par on a hole or course [Late 16C. < Latin, "equal"] ◇ **be feeling below par, be feeling under par** to feel slightly unwell or out of sorts (*informal*) ◇ **be on (a) par (with somebody** *or* **something)** to be on the same level as somebody or something, or generally have the same status or value ◇ **be par for the course** to be usual or to be expected under the circumstances (*informal*)

par. *abbr* **1.** paragraph **2.** MATH, GRAM, GEOG parallel **3.** parenthesis **4.** parish

Par. *abbr* Paraguay

par- *prefix* same as **para-**[1]

pa·ra /paarə/ (*plural* **-ras** or *same*) *n* a subunit of Yugoslav currency. See table at **currency** [Late 17C. Via Turkish < Persian *pāra* "piece, para"]

para-[1] *prefix* **1.** beside, near, along with ○ *parataxis* **2.** beyond ○ *paranormal* **3.** isomeric or related compound ○ *paraldehyde* **4.** resembling ○ *paramyxovirus* **5.** faulty, undesirable ○ *paraphasia* **6.** assistant, auxiliary ○ *paralegal* **7.** occupying the para position in the benzene ring ○ *paradichlorobenzene* [< Greek *para* "beside" < Indo-European, "next to, in front of"]

para-[2] *prefix* parachute ○ *paraskiing* [Shortening]

-para *suffix* a woman who has given birth to a particular number of children (*technical*) ○ *nullipara* [< modern Latin < Latin *parere* "give birth"]

par·a-a·mi·no·ben·zo·ic ac·id /pàrrə ə meenō ben zṓ ik-, -àmmənō-/ *n* BIOCHEM full form of **PABA**

par·a-a·mi·no·sal·i·cylic ac·id /pàrrə ə meenō sàllə síllik-, -àmmənō-/ *n* a drug similar to aspirin. Use: treatment of tuberculosis.

par·a·ben /párrə bèn/ *n* a chemical that mimics the hormone estrogen. Evidence suggests that parabens can play a role in the development of breast tumors. Use: preservative in cosmetics, deodorants, food. [Late 20C. Shortening of *parabenzene* < PARA-[1]]

par·a·bi·o·sis /pàrrə bī óssiss/ (*plural* **-o·ses** /-ṓ seez/) *n* **1.** a state in which two people are joined together and share the same circulation of blood. This is the case for conjoined twins, and it can also be induced experimentally or to establish a blood supply for some grafts. **2.** the temporary suppression of nerve conduction [Early 20C. < PARA-[1] + Greek *biōsis* "way of life" < *bios* "life"] —**par·a·bi·ot·ic** /-bī óttik/ *adj*

par·a·blast /párrə blàst/ *n* the yolk of a fertilized egg [Mid-19C. < PARA-[1] + Greek *blastos* "a bud, shoot"] —**par·a·blas·tic** /pàrrə blástik/ *adj*

par·a·ble /párrəb'l/ *n* **1.** a short simple story intended to illustrate a moral or religious lesson **2.** a parable that appears in the Bible, as told by Jesus Christ [14C. Via French < Latin *parabola* "comparison" < Greek *parabolē* < *paraballein* "put beside" < *ballein* "throw"]

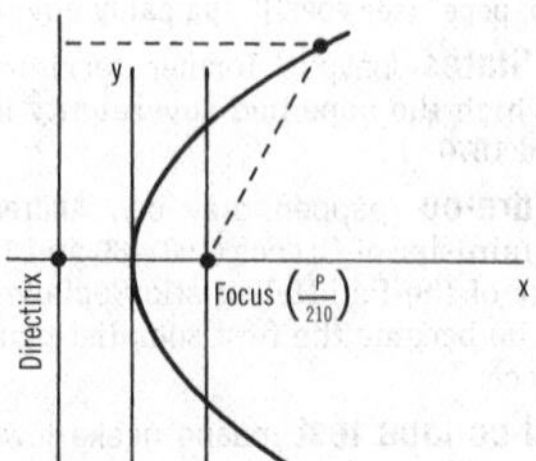

parabola

pa·rab·o·la /pə rábbələ/ *n* a curve formed by the intersection of a cone with a plane parallel to its side [Late 16C. Via modern Latin < Greek *parabolē* "application, comparison" (see PARABLE); from the relationship between the section of a cone that forms the parabola and part of the cone's surface]

par·a·bol·ic[1] /pàrrə bóllik/ *adj* **1.** relating to, resembling, or having the form of a parabola **2.** with the form of a paraboloid [Early 18C. < PARABOLA]

par·a·bol·ic[2] /pàrrə bóllik/, **par·a·bol·i·cal** /-bóllik'l/ *adj* relating to or resembling a parable [15C. Via late Latin < late Greek *parabolikos* "figurative" < Greek *parabolē* (see PARABLE)] —**pa·ra·bol·i·cal·ly** *adv*

par·a·bol·ic aer·i·al *n* COMMUNICATION same as **dish antenna**

pa·rab·o·lize /pə rábbə līz/ (**-lized, -liz·ing, -liz·es**) *vt* to explain something or tell a story by means of a parable [Early 17C. < medieval Latin *parabolizare* "speak in parables" < Latin *parabola* (see PARABLE)]

pa·rab·o·loid /pə rábbə lòyd/ *n* a mathematical surface in which intersections with planes produce parabolas, ellipses, or hyperbolas —**pa·rab·o·loi·dal** /pə ràbbə lóyd'l/ *adj*

pa·ra·bun·tal /pàrrə búnt'l/ *n* fine straw made from the leaves of a palm tree. Use: making hats.

par·a·cen·te·sis /pàrrə sen teéssiss/ *n* MED same as **thoracentesis** [Late 16C. Via Latin, "the removing of a cataract" < Greek *parakentēsis* < *parakentein* "pierce at the side" < *kentein* "prick, stab"]

par·a·cet·a·mol /pàrrə seétə màwl, -séttə-/ *n UK* PHARM same as **acetaminophen** [Mid-20C. < *par(a-)acet(yl)-am(inophen)ol*, its chemical name]

pa·rach·ron·ism /pə rákrə nìzzəm/ *n* an error in assigning a date to something, especially when the date given is later than it should be [Mid-17C. < PARA-[1] + Greek *khronos* "time," or alteration of ANACHRONISM]

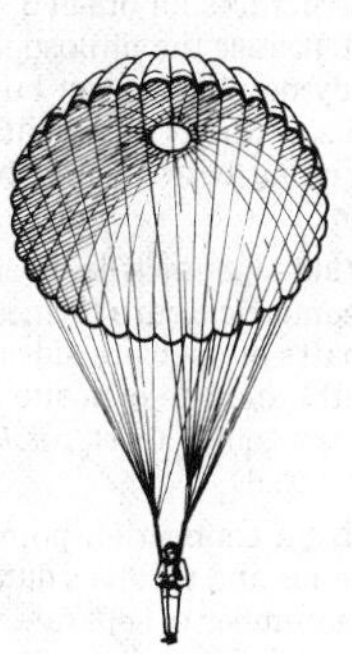

parachute

par·a·chute /párrə shoòt/ *n* **1.** a device consisting of a canopy attached to a harness that is used to slow the speed at which a person or object drops from an aircraft **2.** ZOOL same as **patagium** (sense 1) ■ *vti* (**-chut·ed, -chut·ing, -chutes**) to drop from an aircraft by parachute, or allow somebody or something to drop in this way [Late 18C. < French, "protection against a fall" < *chute* "a fall"] —**par·a·chut·ist** *n*

par·a·chute spin·na·ker *n* a very large light triangular sail used on a racing yacht

Par·a·clete /párrə kleet/ *n* in Christianity, the Holy Spirit [13C. Via French and ecclesiastical Latin < Greek *paraklētos* "advocate, intercessor" < *parakalein* "call to your side" < *kalein* "to call"]

pa·rade /pə ráyd/ *n* **1.** CELEBRATORY PROCESSION an organized procession of people celebrating a special occasion and often including decorated vehicles or floats, a marching band, people twirling batons, and people on horseback **2.** DISPLAY a long moving line of people or things intended to be publicly displayed **3.** SUCCESSION a large number of people or things in succession ○ *a parade of visitors to the palace* **4.** FLAMBOYANT DISPLAY a showy or ostentatious exhibition or display of something **5.** PROCESSION OF TROOPS a march by troops along the streets or in a large area such as a square, usually as a celebration of an important event **6.** GATHERING OF TROOPS IN FORMATION a formal gathering of a troop of soldiers in a regimented formation for a ceremonial march, inspection, or training **7.** PEOPLE IN PARADE people marching in a parade **8.** MIL same as **parade ground 9.** PARRY in fencing, a parry ■ *v* (**-rad·ed, -rad·ing, -rades**) **1.** *vti* GO ON FESTIVE PROCESSION to march in a festive public parade, or make somebody march in a parade **2.** *vti* ASSEMBLE FOR MILITARY PARADE to gather for and march in a military parade, or make troops take part in a parade **3.** *vt* SHOW SOMEBODY OR SOMETHING OFF to display somebody or something proudly and ostentatiously **4.** *vi* WALK AROUND TO BE SEEN to walk or stroll around in public, especially in order to be seen or admired **5.** *vti* CLAIM TO BE SOMETHING ELSE to present something as better than it really is, or appear falsely as better ○ *parading old ideas as new reforms* [Mid-17C. Via French < Spanish *parada* "stopping (a horse)" < Latin *parare* "prepare"] ◇ **rain on somebody's parade** to spoil things for somebody (*informal*)

pa·rade ground *n* a place where troops regularly gather in formation for inspection or training

~~paradice~~ incorrect spelling of **paradise**

par·a·di·chlo·ro·ben·zene /pàrrə dī klawrə bén zeen/ *n* a white crystalline compound. Use: moth repellent. Formula: $C_6H_4Cl_2$.

par·a·did·dle /párrə dìdd'l/ *n* a drum roll in which left and right drumsticks alternate [Early 20C. An imitation of the sound]

par·a·digm /párrə dīm/ *n* **1.** TYPICAL EXAMPLE a typical example of something **2.** MODEL THAT FORMS BASIS OF SOMETHING an example that serves as a pattern or model for something, especially one that forms the basis of a methodology or theory **3.** SET OF ALL FORMS OF WORD a set of word forms giving all of the possible inflections of a word **4.** RELATIONSHIP OF IDEAS TO ONE ANOTHER in the philosophy of science, a generally accepted model of how ideas relate to one another, forming a conceptual framework within which scientific research is carried out [15C. Via late Latin < Greek *paradeigma* "example" < *paradeiknunai*, literally "show beside" < *deiknunai* "to show"] —**par·a·dig·mat·ic** /pàrrə dig máttik/ *adj* —**par·a·dig·mat·i·cal·ly** *adv*

par·a·digm shift *n* a radical change in somebody's basic assumptions about or approach to something

par·a·dise /párrə dīss, -dīz/ *n* **1.** PLACE OR STATE OF PERFECT HAPPINESS a place, situation, or condition in which somebody finds perfect happiness **2.** *also* **Par·a·dise** HEAVEN in some religions such as Christianity, Islam, and Judaism, the place where good people are believed to go after death, or the state they are believed to attain after death **3.** *also* **Par·a·dise** GARDEN OF EDEN in the Bible, the perfect garden where Adam and Eve were placed at the Creation **4.** PLACE IDEALLY SUITED TO SOMEBODY a place where there is everything that a particular person needs for his or her interest (*informal*) ○ *a surfer's paradise* [12C. Via French and late Latin < Greek *paradeisos* "enclosed place, park" < Avestan *pairidaeza* "form around" < *diz* "to form"] —**par·a·di·sa·ic** /pàrrədi sáy ik, -záy-/ *adj* —**par·a·di·sa·i·cal·ly** *adv* —**par·a·dis·al** /párrə dīss'l, -dīz'l/ *adj* —**par·a·dis·al·ly** *adv* —**par·a·di·si·ac** /pàrrədi sī ak, -zī-/ *adj* —**par·a·di·si·a·cal·ly** *adv*

CULTURAL NOTE ***Paradise Lost***, an epic poem (1667) by the English writer John Milton. This monumental work describes Satan's rebellion against God, his corruption of Adam and Eve, and their subsequent expulsion from the Garden of Eden. The sustained brilliance of its language, structure, characterization, and imagery makes it arguably the greatest epic poem in English literature. A sequel, *Paradise Regained*, was published in 1671.

par·a·dise fly·catch·er *n* a brightly colored bird of the flycatcher family, the male of which has a very long slender tail. Native to: Asia, Africa. Genus: *Terpsiphone*.

par·a·dor /párrə dàwr/ *n* **1.** LATIN AMERICAN HOTEL in Latin America, a privately owned and operated hotel or resort **2.** CARIBBEAN HOTEL in the Caribbean, a rural hotel with few amenities **3.** SPANISH TOURIST HOTEL in Spain, a hotel operated by the national government and usually located in a castle, monastery, convent, or other historic site [Mid-19C. < Spanish < *parar* "stop, stay" < Latin *parare* "prepare"]

par·a·dos /párrə dòss/ *n* a bank built up behind a trench or other fortification that gives protection from attack from the rear [Mid-19C. < French, literally "defend the back" < *dos* "back"]

par·a·dox /párrə dòks/ *n* **1.** SOMETHING ABSURD OR CONTRADICTORY a statement, proposition, or situation that seems to be absurd or contradictory, but in fact is or may be true **2.** SELF-CONTRADICTORY STATEMENT a statement or proposition that contradicts itself **3.** PERSON OF OPPOSITES a person with seemingly self-contradictory qualities [Mid-16C. < Latin *paradoxum* < Greek *paradoxos* "contrary to opinion" < *doxa* "opinion" < *dokein* "think"] —**par·a·dox·i·cal** /pàrrə dóksik'l/ *adj* —**par·a·dox·i·cal·ly** *adv* —**par·a·dox·i·cal·ness** /-dóksik'lnəss/ *n*

par·a·dox·i·cal frog *n* a frog of which the adult is less than a third the size of the tadpole. Native to: Amazon forest, the island of Trinidad. Latin name: *Pseudis paradoxa*.

par·a·dox·i·cal sleep *n* MED same as **REM sleep** [Because its electrical brain patterns resemble those of the waking state]

par·a·drop /párrə dròp/ *n* the delivery of personnel, materials, or provisions to a place by attaching them to a parachute and dropping them from an aircraft ■ *vt* (**-dropped, -drop·ping, -drops**) to deliver somebody or something to a place by paradrop

par·aes·the·sia *n* MED UK spelling of **paresthesia**

par·af·fin /párrəfin/ *n* **1.** a mixture of liquid hydrocarbons obtained from petroleum and used as a domestic heating fuel and as fuel for aircraft. ◊ **kerosene 2.** INDUST same as **paraffin wax 3.** CHEM same as **alkane** ■ *vt* (**-fined, -fin·ing, -fins**) to treat something by saturating, impregnating, or coating it with kerosene or paraffin wax [Mid-19C. < Latin *parum* "little" + *affinis* "related"; because not closely related to any other substance] —**par·af·fin·ic** /pàrrə fínnik/ *adj*

par·af·fin wax *n* a white waxy solid mixture of hydrocarbons. Source: petroleum. Use: in making candles, pharmaceuticals, cosmetics, as a sealing agent.

~~parafin~~ incorrect spelling of **paraffin**

par·a·for·mal·de·hyde /pàrrə fawr máldə hīd/, **par·a·form** /párrə fàwrm/ *n* a white combustible polymer of formaldehyde. Use: disinfectant, fungicide, in contraceptive creams.

par·a·gen·e·sis /pàrrə jénnəssiss/, **par·a·ge·ne·sia** /-jə neézhə, -neézhee ə/ *n* the order in which the mineral constituents of a rock are formed —**par·a·ge·net·ic** /-jə néttik/ *adj* —**par·a·ge·net·i·cal·ly** *adv*

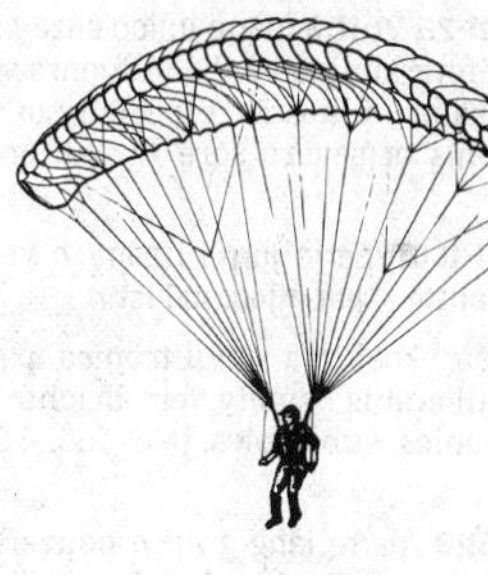

paragliding

par·a·glid·ing /párrə glīding/ *n* a sport in which somebody jumps from an aircraft or a high place wearing a rectangular parachute that allows control of direction in the descent to the ground [< PARA-[2]] —**par·a·glid·er** *n*

par·a·goge /párrə gōjee/ *n* a letter, sound, or syllable added at the end of a word as the word develops, e.g., the "s" in "towards" [Mid-16C. Via late Latin < Greek *paragōgē*, literally "carrying beyond" < *agōgē* "carrying"] —**par·a·gog·ic** /pàrrə gójjik/ *adj* —**par·a·gog·i·cal·ly** /-gójjikəlee/ *adv*

par·a·gon /párrə gòn, -gən/ *n* **1.** EXAMPLE OF EXCELLENCE somebody or something that is the very best example of something **2.** LARGE UNFLAWED DIAMOND a perfect diamond that weighs at least 100 carats **3.** LARGE PERFECTLY SPHERICAL PEARL an extremely large pearl that is a perfect sphere [Mid-16C. Via French < Italian *paragone*, originally "touchstone to test gold" < medieval Greek *parakonan* "compare," literally "sharpen against"]

par·a·graph /párrə gràf/ *n* **1.** SECTION OF WRITING a piece of writing that consists of one or more sentences, begins on a new and often indented line, and contains a distinct idea or the words of one speaker **2.** SHORT NEWS STORY a short item of news or editorial comment in a newspaper ■ *vt* (**-graphed, -graph·ing, -graphs**) **1.** SET TEXT OUT IN PARAGRAPHS to arrange text in a series of paragraphs **2.** WRITE NEWS IN PARAGRAPH to report news or a story in a short paragraph [15C. Via French or medieval Latin < Greek *paragraphos* "stroke marking a line in which there is a break in sense," literally "writing beside" < *graphein* "write"] —**par·a·graph·er** *n*

par·a·graph·i·a /pàrrə gráffee ə/ *n* the writing of words or letters different from the ones intended, as a result of a stroke or disease [Late 19C. < PARA-[1] + Greek *-graphia* "writing"]

Paraguay

Par·a·guay /párrə gwī, -gwày/ **1.** country in South America, bordered by Bolivia, Brazil, and Argentina. Language: Spanish. Currency: guaraní. Capital: Asunción. Population: 6,036,900 (2001). Area: 157,048 sq. mi./406,752 sq. km. Official name **Republic of Paraguay** **2.** river in central South America. The chief tributary of the Paraná River, it rises in western Brazil and flows south across central Paraguay to join the Paraná at the northern border of Argentina. Length: 1,580 mi./2,550 km. —**Par·a·guay·an** /párrə gwī ən, -gwáy-/ *n, adj*

Pa·ra·hy·ba /paàrə eébə/ former name for **João Pessoa**

par·a·hy·dro·gen /pàrrə hídrəjən/ *n* a form of molecular hydrogen in which the two atomic nuclei spin in opposite directions. Parahydrogen makes up about 25 percent of hydrogen molecules.

pa·ra I (*plural* **pa·ras I** or **pa·rae I**) *n* MED same as **primipara**

par·a·in·flu·en·za vi·rus /pàrrə infloo énzə-/ *n* a virus of a group of four similar to the influenza virus that causes respiratory illnesses, especially in children, with symptoms of severe sore throat, croup, and pneumonia

par·a·jour·nal·ism /pàrrə júrn'l ìzzəm/ *n* MEDIA same as **New Journalism** —**par·a·jour·nal·ist** *n*

par·a·keet /párrə keet/ *n* a small tropical parrot that has a long tail and is usually very brightly colored. Native to: tropics, subtropics. [Mid-16C. < Old French *paraquet*]

par·a·lan·guage /párrə làng gwij/ *n* nonverbal vocal nuances in communication that may add meaning to language as it is used in context, e.g., tone of voice or whispering

par·al·de·hyde /pə ráldə hīd/ *n* a colorless liquid polymer of acetaldehyde. Use: sedative, solvent. Formula: $C_6H_{12}O_3$.

par·a·le·gal /pàrrə leég'l/ *n* somebody with specialist legal training who assists a fully qualified lawyer ■ *adj* relating to a paralegal or the work of a paralegal

par·a·leip·sis *n* LITERAT same as **paralipsis**

~~paralel~~ incorrect spelling of **parallel**

par·a·lin·guis·tics /pàrrə ling gwístiks/ *n* the study of paralanguage (*takes a singular verb*) —**par·a·lin·guis·tic** *adj*

par·a·lip·o·me·na /pàrrə lī pómmənə, -li-/ *npl* material added to a literary work as a supplement [Late 17C. Via late Latin < Greek *paraleipomena* "(things) left out" < *paraleipein* (see PARALIPSIS)]

Par·a·lip·o·me·na /pàrrə lī pómmənə, -li-/ *npl* the title used for the Book of Chronicles in the Vulgate (*sometimes used in the sing*) [14C. < late Latin (see PARALIPOMENA); because it contains material omitted from the Books of Kings]

Par·a·lip·o·me·non /pàrrə lī pómmə nòn, -li-/ BIBLE singular of **Paralipomena**

par·a·lip·sis /pàrrə lípsiss/ (*plural* **-lip·ses** /-líp seez/), **par·a·leip·sis** /-lípsiss/ (*plural* **-leip·ses** /-líp seez/) *n* a rhetorical technique in which you emphasize a topic by saying in some way that you will not talk about it, e.g., by using the phrase "not to mention" [Mid-16C. Via late Latin < Greek *paraleipsis* "omission" < *paraleipein* "leave on one side" < *leipein* "leave"]

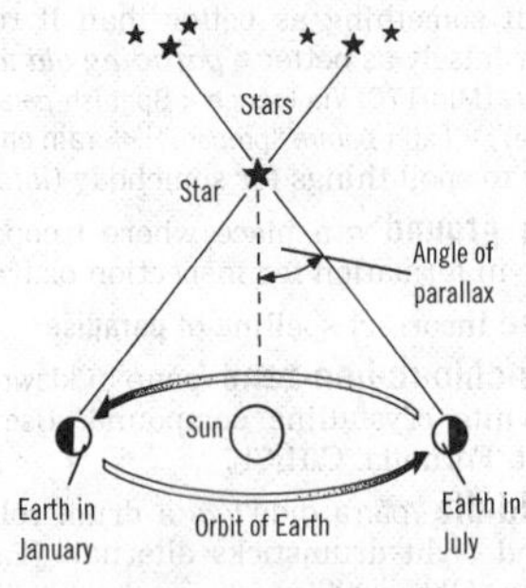

parallax (sense 2)

par·al·lax /párrə làks/ *n* **1.** an apparent change in the position of an object when the person looking at the object changes position **2.** the angle between two imaginary lines from two different observation points meeting at an astronomical object, used to measure the object's distance from Earth [Late 16C. Via French < Greek *parallaxis* "alternation, angle between two lines" < *parallassein* "alter" < *allos* "other"] —**par·al·lac·tic** /pàrrə láktik/ *adj* —**par·al·lac·ti·cal·ly** *adv*

par·al·lax view *n* a viewpoint from which you can observe and study something or somebody from a new angle, thus gaining insights unavailable before

par·al·lel /párrə lèl/ *adj* **1.** RESEMBLING EACH OTHER relating to two things that are comparable because they are similar and share many characteristics **2.** MATH ALWAYS SAME DISTANCE APART relating to or being lines, planes, or curved surfaces that are always the same distance apart and therefore never meet **3.** COMPUT USING SEVERAL ITEMS OF INFORMATION SIMULTANEOUSLY relating to a computer that processes several items of information at the same time **4.** GRAM OF IDENTICAL SYNTACTIC CONSTRUCTIONS describes two or more phrases or clauses in a single sentence that have identical syntactic constructions **5.** MUSIC KEEPING SAME MUSICAL INTERVAL THROUGHOUT describes the movement of two voices or melodies that match each other exactly in pitch, while preserving the same interval between them ■ *n* **1.** COMPARISON a comparison between two things that reveals their similarity ○ *It's easy to draw a parallel between their two careers.* **2.** SOMEBODY OR SOMETHING EQUIVALENT somebody or something that is very similar to another, sharing many characteristics **3.** MATH PARALLEL LINE OR PLANE any of a set of parallel geometric forms, especially lines or planes **4.** GEOG LINE PARALLEL TO EQUATOR an imaginary line around the Earth that lies parallel to the equator and represents a specific degree of latitude from the equator **5.** GEOG LINE ON MAP a line on a map representing a parallel of latitude **6.** ELEC ENG CONFIGURATION OF ELECTRICAL COMPONENTS the way in which electrical components or circuits are connected so that the same voltage is applied across each component or circuit ○ *connected in parallel* ■ *vt* (**-leled, -lel·ing, -lels**) **1.** CORRESPOND TO SOMETHING to be similar to something else, especially in following a similar course of events **2.** MATCH SOMEBODY OR SOMETHING to be equal to or as good as somebody or something else **3.** COMPARE SOMETHING TO SOMETHING ELSE to compare something with something else, or show something to be similar to something else **4.** BE PARALLEL to be or run parallel to something **5.** MAKE SOMETHING PARALLEL TO SOMETHING to make something be or run parallel to something else ■ *adv* ALONGSIDE in a parallel manner so as to keep the same distance away from something and never meet it [Mid-16C. Via French and Latin < Greek *parallēlos* "beside each other" < *allēlōn* "each other" < *allos* "other".] ◇ **in parallel (with somebody or something)** in conjunction with and at the same time as somebody or something else

par·al·lel bars *npl* a piece of gymnastic equipment consisting of two horizontal bars parallel to each other and supported on vertical posts (*takes a plural verb*) ■ *n* an event in a gymnastics competition that uses the parallel bars (*takes a singular verb*)

par·al·lel broad·cast *n* a broadcast that is transmitted simultaneously by radio or television and over the Internet

par·al·lel cous·in *n* a cousin who is the child of your mother's sister or your father's brother

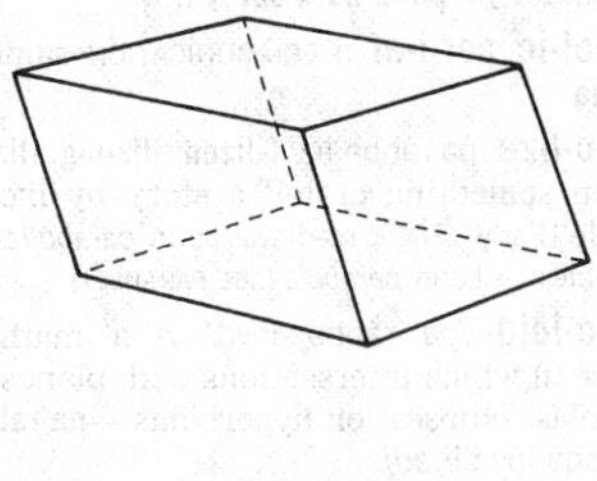
parallelepiped

par·al·lel·e·pi·ped /pàrrə lelə pípəd, -píppəd/ *n* a polyhedron consisting of six faces that are parallelograms [Late 16C. < Greek *parallēlepipedon* "parallel surface" < *epipedon* "surface" < *pedon* "ground"]

par·al·lel·ing /párrə lèlling/ *n* the exploitation of differences in commercial markets by buying an expensive product in a place where prices are relatively low and then selling it in a place where prices are higher

par·al·lel·ism /párrə le lìzzəm/ *n* **1.** PARALLEL STATE the condition of being parallel **2.** LITERAT REPETITION FOR EFFECT in writing, the deliberate repetition of words or sentence structures for effect **3.** PHILOSOPHY THEORY OF MIND-BODY RELATIONSHIP the philosophical theory that mind and body do not interact but follow separate parallel tracks, without any relationship of cause and effect existing between the two —**par·al·lel·ist** /párrə lèllist/ *n*

par·al·lel·o·gram /pàrrə léllə gràm/ *n* a two-dimensional geometric figure formed of four sides in which both pairs of opposite sides are parallel and of equal length, and the opposite angles are equal [Late 16C. Via late Latin < Greek *parallēlogrammon* < *parallēlos* (see PARALLEL)]

par·al·lel port *n* a connection point through which a computer sends and receives data simultaneously by means of a number of separate wires, commonly used for connecting a printer or external storage device. Computers transmit data through the parallel port at higher speeds and with fewer errors than through the serial port.

par·al·lel pro·cess·ing *n* the use of two or more processors to run different parts of the same computer program concurrently and merge the results, with significantly faster program execution. Parallel processing is used when many complex calculations are required, e.g., in weather modeling and digital special effects.

par·al·lel rul·er *n* a ruler designed for drawing parallel lines, constructed with two linked straight edges that remain parallel although the distance between them may be varied

par·al·lel turn *n* a skiing turn executed by shifting the body weight and keeping the skis parallel, rather than by adjusting the line of the skis

pa·ral·o·gism /pə rállə jìzzəm/ *n* in logic, an invalid argument that is unintentional or that has gone unnoticed [Mid-16C. Via late Latin < Greek *paralogismos* < *paralogos* "contrary to reason" < *logos* "reason"] —**pa·ral·o·gist** *n* —**pa·ral·o·gis·tic** /pə rállə jístik/ *adj*

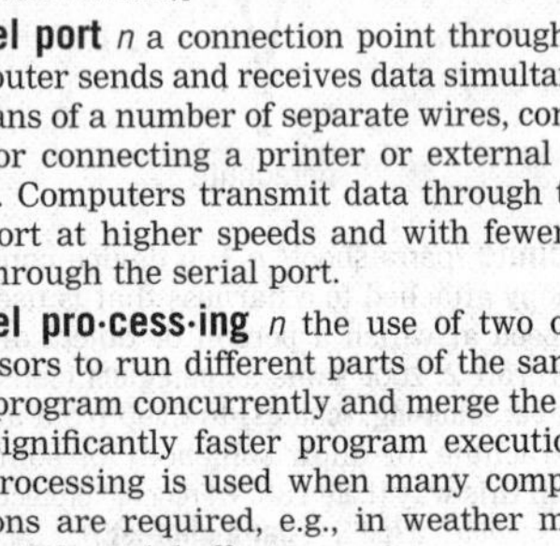
Popperfoto
Paralympic Games

Par·a·lym·pic Games /pàrrə lìmpik-/, **Par·a·lym·pics** /pàrrə límpiks/ *npl* an international sports competition for physically challenged athletes. See illustration on previous page —**Par·a·lym·pi·an** *n*

par·a·lyse *vt* UK spelling of **paralyze**

pa·ral·y·sis /pə rálləssiss/ *n* **1.** loss of voluntary movement as a result of damage to nerve or muscle function **2.** failure to take action or make progress [Pre-12C. Via Latin < Greek *paralusis* < *paraluesthai* "be unable to move" < *para-* "on one side" + *luein* "release"]

pa·ral·y·sis ag·i·tans /-ájji tànz/ *n* MED same as **Parkinson's disease** [*Agitans* < Latin, present participle of *agitare* "shake"]

par·a·lyt·ic /pàrrə líttik/ *adj* relating to loss of voluntary movement ■ *n* an offensive term for a physically challenged person [14C. Via French and Latin < Greek *paralutikos* < *paralusis* (see PARALYSIS)] —**par·a·lyt·i·cal·ly** *adv*

par·a·lyze /párrə lĩz/ (**-lyzed, -lyz·ing, -lyz·es**) *vt* **1.** DEPRIVE SOMEBODY OF VOLUNTARY MOVEMENT to cause somebody to lose the ability to move a part of the body, either by damaging nerve or muscle function, or through the use of a drug **2.** MAKE SOMEBODY TEMPORARILY UNABLE TO MOVE to make somebody temporarily unable to move, e.g., with fear **3.** BRING SYSTEM TO STANDSTILL to bring a system or network to a stop or prevent it from functioning effectively [Late 18C. < French *paralyser* < Latin *paralysis* (see PARALYSIS)]

par·a·mag·net·ic /pàrrə mag néttik/ *adj* describes a substance that is weakly magnetized so that it will lie parallel to a magnetic field. The phenomenon results from the presence of unpaired electrons in the atoms of the substance, which cause the atoms to act as tiny magnets when a magnetic field is applied.

Par·a·mar·i·bo /pàrrə márrə bō/ port and capital city of Suriname, located in the north of the country near the Atlantic Ocean. Population: 289,000 (1997).

par·a·mat·ta /pàrrə máttə/, **par·ra·mat·ta** *n* a lightweight fabric made from wool blended with silk or cotton [Early 19C. After *Parramatta*, settlement in New South Wales, Australia]

par·a·me·ci·um /pàrrə meéshee əm, -meéssee-/ (*plural* **-ci·a** /-shee ə, -ssee ə/ or **-ci·ums**) *n* a single-celled microscopic organism (**protozoan**) with fine appendages (**cilia**) around its body that it uses to move around in water and to capture bacteria. Genus: *Paramecium.* [Mid-18C. < modern Latin < Greek *paramēkēs* "oval"; from its shape]

par·a·med·ic /pàrrə méddik/ *n* somebody trained to perform emergency medical procedures in the absence of a doctor, especially a member of an ambulance crew —**par·a·med·i·cal** *adj*

pa·ram·e·ter /pə rámmətər/ *n* **1.** LIMITING FACTOR a fact or circumstance that restricts how something is done or what can be done ○ *working within the parameters of cost and manpower* **2.** VARIABLE QUANTITY DETERMINING OUTCOME a measurable quantity, e.g., temperature, that determines the result of a scientific experiment and can be altered to vary the result **3.** ⚠ NOTABLE CHARACTERISTIC a distinguishing feature or notable characteristic **4.** MATH VARIABLE MATHEMATICAL VALUE in a mathematical expression, a variable value that, when it changes, gives another different but related mathematical expression from a limited series of such expressions **5.** STATS OVERALL QUANTITY a general quantity that relates to an entire population, as distinct from an individual statistic that relates to a sample [Mid-17C. < modern Latin *parametrum* < Greek *para* "beside" + *metron* "measure"] —**par·a·met·ric** /pàrrə méttrik/ *adj*

USAGE ***Parameter***, which has special meanings in science, mathematics, and statistics, has taken on a general sense "a limiting factor," as in *had to adhere to all the parameters of tax law with regard to the establishment of family trusts and foundations.* This meaning, along with the others, is acceptable. Some people, however, object to yet another general meaning of the word, "a distinguishing feature or notable characteristic," as in *An important parameter in their culture is vegetarianism,* where *characteristic* or *feature* would be more precise and less pompous. Avoid confusing ***parameter*** with *perimeter* ("boundary"): *Guards patrolled the perimeter* [not *parameter*] *of the military installation.*

par·a·met·ric e·qua·tions *npl* mathematical equations in which coordinates of points are explicitly expressed in terms of independent parameters

par·a·mil·i·tar·y /pàrrə míllə tèrree/ *adj* **1.** MILITARY IN STYLE similar to or modeled on the military but not belonging to it **2.** ASSISTING OFFICIAL MILITARY FORCES organized and staffed by civilians to provide support for the regular military services ○ *a paramilitary unit* **3.** USING MILITARY TECHNIQUES using military weapons and tactics to fight within a country against the official ruling power ■ *n* (*plural* **-ies**) UNOFFICIAL SOLDIER a member of a paramilitary organization, especially one fighting against the official ruling power

par·am·ne·sia /pà ram neézhə/ *n* **1.** false memories of events that did not really take place **2.** an inability to recall the meanings of common words

par·a·morph /párrə màwrf/ *n* a mineral formed by the conversion of one crystalline form (**polymorph**) into another. Calcite is a paramorph of aragonite. —**par·a·mor·phism** /pàrrə máwr fìzzəm/ *n*

par·a·mount /párrə mòwnt/ *adj* greatest in importance or significance [Mid-16C. < Anglo-Norman *paramont* < *par* "by" + *amont* "above"] —**par·a·mount·cy** *n* —**par·a·mount·ly** *adv*

par·a·mour /párrə moor/ *n* a lover, especially one in a relationship with a married person (*literary*) ○*"found thee out even in the arms of thy paramour"* (Sir Walter Scott, *Ivanhoe*; 1819) [14C. < obsolete *par amour* "by way of love" < Old French]

par·a·myx·o·vi·rus /pàrrə míksə vĩrəss/ *n* a virus belonging to the group that includes the mumps and measles viruses and the parainfluenza virus

Pa·ra·ná /pàrrə naá/ **1.** river in eastern South America, flowing through Brazil, along the border with Paraguay, and through Argentina, reaching the Atlantic Ocean at the Río de la Plata. Length: 1,740 mi./2,800 km. **2.** city in northeastern Argentina, on the Paraná River. Population: 207,041 (1991).

pa·rang /paá ràng, pə raáng/ *n* a large knife with a short straight-edged blade, used in Malaysia and Indonesia as a weapon and as a tool [Mid-19C. < Malay]

par·a·noi·a /pàrrə nóy ə/ *n* **1.** extreme and unreasonable suspicion of other people and their motives **2.** a psychiatric disorder involving systematized delusion, usually of persecution [Early 19C. < Greek, "out of your mind" < *nous* "mind"]

par·a·noi·ac /pàrrə nóy àk/ *adj* characteristic of or resembling paranoia ■ *n* somebody affected by paranoia

par·a·noid /párrə nòyd/ *adj* **1.** DISTRUSTFUL obsessively anxious about something, or unreasonably suspicious of other people and their thoughts or motives **2.** SHOWING CHARACTERISTICS OF PARANOIA relating to or showing the characteristics of the psychiatric disorder paranoia ■ *n* PARANOID PERSON somebody who is paranoid (*dated*)

par·a·nor·mal /pàrrə náwrm'l/ *adj* unable to be explained or understood in terms of scientific knowledge ■ *n* paranormal events or phenomena —**par·a·nor·mal·ly** *adv*

par·a·pa·re·sis /pàrrəpə reéssiss, pàrrə párrəssiss/ *n* a medical condition in which both legs, and often the bladder, have little voluntary control —**par·a·pa·re·tic** /-réttik/ *adj*

par·a·pente /párrə pònt/ *n* a modified parachute used for paraskiing and paragliding, with a framework of inflatable tubes that give it a semirigid structure, allowing it to be steered like a hang-glider [Late 20C. < French < *parachute* + *pente* "slope"]

pa·ra·pent·ing /párrə pònting/, **pa·ra·pont·ing** *n* **1.** EXTREME SPORTS same as **paragliding 2.** the sport of taking off from a mountain top or other high place and gliding gradually to land supported by a steerable rectangular parachute [Late 20C. < *parapente* < PARACHUTE + French *pente* "slope"] —**pa·ra·pent·er** *n*

par·a·pet /párrəpət, -pèt/ *n* **1.** a low protective wall built where there is a sudden dangerous drop, e.g., along the edge of a balcony, roof, or bridge. Some parapets are battlemented, especially on castles, and many are built as ornamental features. **2.** a bank of soil, rubble, or sandbags piled up along the edge of a military trench for protection from enemy fire [Late 16C. Via French < Italian *parapetto* < *parare* "protect" + *petto* "chest" (< Latin *pectus*)]

par·aph /párrəf, pə ráf/ *n* a decorative flourish written under a signature to finish it off or, formerly, to protect against forgery [Late 16C. Via French < medieval Latin *paragraphus* (see PARAGRAPH)]

~~**paraphanalia**~~ incorrect spelling of **paraphernalia**

par·a·pha·si·a /pàrrə fáyzhə/ *n* a speech disorder of neurological origin in which the speaker's words are jumbled unintelligibly

par·a·pher·na·lia /pàrrəfər náylee ə/ *n* (*takes a singular or plural verb*) **1.** ASSORTED OBJECTS assorted objects or items, especially of equipment required for a specific activity **2.** THINGS CHARACTERISTIC OF SOMETHING things usually associated with something ○ *banks, commercial buildings, department stores, and all the paraphernalia of a sophisticated modern city* **3.** WEDDING GIFTS TO WIFE formerly, items of property given to a wife on her wedding day by her new husband and regarded by law as belonging to her [Mid-17C. < medieval Latin < Latin *parapherna* < Greek *parapherně* "beside the dowry" < *phernē* "dowry"]

par·a·phrase /párrə fràyz/ *vt* (**-phrased, -phras·ing, -phras·es**) to restate something using other words, especially in order to make it simpler or shorter ■ *n* a rephrased, simplified, and usually shorter version of written or spoken material [Mid-16C. Via French and Latin < Greek *paraphrasis* < *paraphrazein*, literally "explain alongside" < *phrazein* "explain"] —**par·a·phras·er** *n* —**par·a·phras·tic** /pàrrə frástik/ *adj*

pa·raph·y·sis /pə ráffəssiss/ (*plural* **-phy·ses** /-fə seez/) *n* an erect sterile filament that grows among the reproductive organs of fungi, algae, and mosses [Mid-19C. < modern Latin, literally "growth beside" < Greek *phusis* "growth"] —**par·a·phy·sate** /-sət, -sàyt/ *adj*

par·a·ple·gi·a /pàrrə pleéjə, -pleéjee ə/ *n* total inability to move both legs and usually the lower part of the trunk, often as a result of disease or injury of the spine [Mid-17C. Via modern Latin < Greek *paraplēgiē* "stroke on one side" < *paraplēssein* "strike on one side" < *plessein* "to strike"] —**par·a·ple·gic** *adj, n*

par·a·po·di·um /pàrrə pṓdee əm/ (*plural* **-di·a** /-dee ə/) *n* an appendage on the body of some ocean worms, occurring in pairs on each segment of the worm's body, used for swimming, crawling, or holding onto things

par·a·pont·ing *n* EXTREME SPORTS another spelling of **parapenting**

par·a·pro·fes·sion·al /pàrrəprə féshən'l, -féshnəl/ *n* a trained assistant to a professional person —**par·a·pro·fes·sion·al** *adj*

par·a·psy·chol·o·gy /pàrrə sī kóllәjee/ *n* the study of supposed mental phenomena that cannot be explained by known psychological or scientific principles, e.g., extrasensory perception and telepathy —**par·a·psy·cho·log·i·cal** /-sīkə lójjik'l/ *adj* —**par·a·psy·chol·o·gist** *n*

Pa·rá rub·ber tree /paa raá-/ *n* a tree that yields latex for making rubber. Native to: tropical South America. Latin name: ***Hevea brasiliensis.*** [After a state in N Brazil]

Par·a·Sail *tdmk* a trademark for a type of parachute

par·a·sail·ing /párrə sàyling/ *n* a sport in which somebody wearing a parachute rises high into the air from a platform at the back of a moving motorboat or from the water behind the boat and is towed along [Mid-20C. < PARA-[2]]

par·a·scend·ing /párrə sènding/ *n* a sport in which somebody wearing an open parachute is towed along by a speedboat or land vehicle, rises into the air, and descends independently using the parachute [Late 20C. < PARA-[2] + ASCEND]

par·a·sci·ence /párrə sĩ ənss/ *n* the study of phenomena that cannot be explained or tested by conventional scientific methods

par·a·se·le·ne /pàrrəssə leénee/ (*plural* **-nae** /-nee/) *n* an image of the Moon seen within a lunar halo [Mid-17C. < PARA-[1] + Greek *selēnē* "moon"] —**par·a·se·le·nic** /-sə lénnik, -leénik/ *adj*

par·a·sex·u·al /pàrrə sékshoo əl/ *adj* describes a type of reproduction, seen in some fungi, in which the recombination of parental chromosomes takes place without the usual formation of sex cells by cell division (**meiosis**) —**par·a·sex·u·al·i·ty** /-sekshoo állətee/ *n*

Pa·ra·shah /paára shaá/ (*plural* **-shoth** /paára shṓt, -shṓth/) *n* in Judaism, a passage from the Torah read during traditional weekly worship at the synagogue [Early 17C. < Hebrew *pārāšāh* "division"]

par·a·site /párrə sīt/ *n* **1.** a plant or animal that lives on or in another, usually larger, host organism in a way that harms or is of no advantage to the host **2.** somebody who exploits others without doing anything in return [Mid-16C. Via Latin < Greek *parasitos* "somebody who eats from another's table" < *sitos* "grain, food"]

par·a·sit·ic /pàrrə síttik/, **par·a·sit·ic·al** /-ik'l/ *adj* **1.** living in or on another host organism, usually causing it harm **2.** living off the generosity of others without offering anything in return —**par·a·sit·i·cal·ly** *adv*

par·a·sit·i·cide /pàrrə sítti sīd/ *n* a substance used to destroy parasites —**par·a·sit·i·ci·dal** /-sitti sīd'l/ *adj*

par·a·sit·ism /párrəssi tìzzəm, -sī-/ *n* **1.** symbiosis in which one organism lives as a parasite in or on another organism **2.** VET same as **parasitosis**

par·a·sit·ize /párrəssi tīz, -sī-/ (**-ized, -iz·ing, -iz·es**) *vt* to infest or live on an animal or plant as a parasite

par·a·sit·oid /párrəssi tòyd, -sī-/ *adj* describes an insect that lays its eggs inside the living body of another animal or insect. The hatched newborns feed off the body, eventually killing the host. ■ *n* an insect that lays its eggs within a host, eventually causing the death of the host

par·a·si·tol·o·gy /pàrrəssi tólləjee, -sī-/ *n* the scientific study of plants and animals that live as parasites —**par·a·si·to·log·i·cal** /pàrrəssitə lójjik'l, -sītə-/ *adj*

par·a·si·to·sis /pàrrəssi tṓsiss, pàrrə sī-/ (*plural* **-to·ses** /-tṓ seez/) *n* a disease that develops as a result of infestation by parasites

par·a·ski·ing /párrə skee ing/ *n* the sport of skiing off high mountains and descending through the air using a light steerable parachute (**parapente**) made of inflatable tubes of fabric [Mid-20C. < PARA-[2]]

par·a·sol /párrə sàwl/ *n* an umbrella made to provide shade from the sun [Early 17C. Via French < Italian *parasole* < *parare* "protect" + *sole* "sun"]

par·a·stat·al /pàrrə stáyt'l/ *adj* performing a function usually associated with a government and under its indirect control ■ *n* a parastatal organization, business, or industry

par·a·su·i·cide /pàrrə sóo i sīd/ *n* **1.** a suicide attempt or act of self-injury that is motivated by a desire to draw attention to personal problems rather than by a genuine wish to die **2.** somebody who carries out a parasuicide

par·a·sym·pa·thet·ic /pàrrə símpə théttik/ *adj* relating or belonging to the parasympathetic nervous system [Early 20C. < PARA-[1]; because some of the nerves run beside sympathetic nerves]

par·a·sym·pa·thet·ic nerv·ous sys·tem *n* one of the two divisions in the part of the nervous system that controls involuntary and unconscious bodily functions (**autonomic nervous system**). Its actions include slowing the heart, constricting the pupils, and relaxing the bowels.

par·a·syn·the·sis /pàrrə sínthəssiss/ *n* the formation of words by a combination of smaller words and additional elements. For example, "heavy-handed" is formed by parasynthesis, combining the adjective "heavy" with "handed," which in turn is "hand" with "-ed" added. —**par·a·syn·thet·ic** /-sin théttik/ *adj*

par·a·syn·the·ton /pàrrə sínthə tòn/ (*plural* **-ta** /-tə/) *n* a word formed by the combination of smaller words and additional elements

par·a·tax·is /pàrrə táksiss/ *n* the combination of clauses or phrases without the use of conjunctions such as "and" or "so," e.g., in "He saved my life – he deserves a medal" [Mid-19C. < Greek < *paratassein* "place side by side" < *tassein* "arrange"] —**par·a·tac·tic** /-táktik/ *adj* —**par·a·tac·ti·cal·ly** *adv*

pa·ra·tha /pə raátə/ *n* a flat unleavened bread of South Asian origin, made from flour, water, and clarified butter, often eaten with a filling [Mid-20C. < Hindi *parāṭhā*]

par·a·thi·on /pàrrə thī ón/ *n* a colorless highly toxic oil. Use: insecticide. Formula: $C_{10}H_{14}NO_5PS$. [Mid-20C. < PARA-[1] + *thiophosphate* + -ON[2]]

par·a·thy·roid /pàrrə thī ròyd/ *adj* **1.** relating to or produced by the parathyroid glands **2.** in the area around the thyroid gland ■ *n* PHYSIOL same as **parathyroid gland**

par·a·thy·roid·ec·to·my /pàrrə thī roy déktəmee/ (*plural* **-mies**) *n* the surgical removal of one or more of the parathyroid glands

par·a·thy·roid gland *n* a small gland of a group of four that lie in or near the walls of the thyroid gland and secrete a hormone that controls the depositing of calcium and phosphorus in bones

par·a·thy·roid hor·mone *n* a hormone secreted by the parathyroid glands that controls calcium and phosphorus balance in the body

par·a·troop·er /párrə tròopər/ *n* a soldier trained to go into battle by parachute, especially one who is also a member of an airborne unit —**par·a·troops** *npl*

par·a·ty·phoid fe·ver /pàrrə tī foyd-/, **par·a·ty·phoid** *n* an infectious bacterial disease similar to typhoid but with much less severe symptoms, usually limited to a pink rash, diarrhea, and some abdominal pain

Par·a·vac /párrə vàch/, **Borislav** (*b.* 1943) Serb representative of the presidency of Bosnia and Herzegovina (1998–), which rotates between a Serb, a Bosnian Muslim, and a Croat

par·a·vane /párrə vàyn/ *n* a torpedo-shaped device with sharp fins at the front, towed by a ship to cut the moorings of submerged mines [Early 20C. < *para-* "protector" (after PARASOL)]

par a·vi·on /paàr a vyáwn, -aa vyáwN/ *adv* by air mail [< French, "by airplane"]

par·a·zo·an /pàrrə zṓ ən/ (*plural* **-zo·a** /-zṓ ə/) *n* a member of the subkingdom of invertebrate animals that includes sponges. Subkingdom: *Parazoa*. [Early 20C. < modern Latin *Parazoa* < Greek *para* "beside," after *Protozoa, Metazoa*]

par·boil /paàr bòyl/ (**-boiled, -boil·ing, -boils**) *vt* **1.** to boil something until it is partly cooked, usually before frying or roasting it **2.** to make somebody uncomfortably hot [15C. Via Old French *parboillir* "boil thoroughly" < late Latin *perbullire* < Latin *bullire* "boil"]

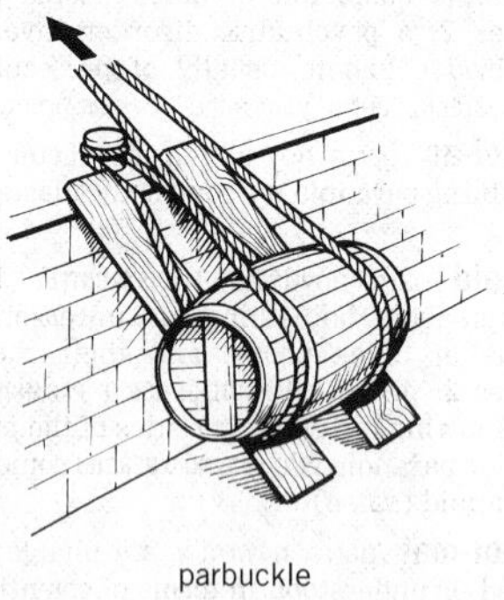

parbuckle

par·buck·le /paàr bùk'l/ *n* a rope sling for lifting or lowering barrels, logs, or similar objects [Early 17C. Origin ?]

Par·cae /paàrsee/ *npl* in Roman mythology, the Fates. Greek equivalent **Moirai** [Late 16C. < Latin]

par·cel /paàrss'l/ *n* **1.** SOMETHING WRAPPED UP one or more things wrapped up together in paper or other packaging **2.** PORTION a portion into which something is divided, especially a piece of land that was originally part of a larger area **3.** BATCH OF COMMERCIAL GOODS a quantity of wholesale merchandise treated as a unit, or a sales transaction for such a quantity of merchandise **4.** GROUP a collection of people or things (*archaic or literary*) ○ *"a parcel of rascals"* (Thomas Paine, *The Age of Reason*; 1794) ■ *vt* (**-celed, -cel·ing, -cels**) **1.** MAKE PARCEL OF SOMETHING to wrap something or a group of things into a parcel **2.** NAUT PROTECT ROPE to bind canvas tightly around rope or cable to protect it [14C. Via French < Latin *particula* "small part"]

parcel out *vt* to divide and distribute something between a number of people

par·cel-gilt *adj* partly gilded, often on the inside but not on the outside

par·cel post *n* the postal service that collects, processes, and delivers packages

parch /paarch/ (**parched, parch·ing, parch·es**) *vt* to make somebody or something extremely dry through water deprivation or exposure to heat [14C. Origin ?]

parched /paarcht/ *adj* **1.** completely lacking in moisture because of hot conditions or lack of rainfall **2.** very thirsty (*informal*)

SYNONYMS See *dry*.

parch·ment /paàrchmənt/ *n* **1.** FORMER WRITING MATERIAL a creamy or yellowish material made from dried and treated sheepskin, goatskin, or other animal hide, formerly used for books and documents **2.** DOCUMENT a manuscript or other work written, drawn, or painted on a sheet of parchment **3.** HIGH-QUALITY PAPER strong, smooth or textured, usually off-white paper used for special documents, letters, or artwork [13C. < Old French *parchemin* < alteration of Latin *pergamena*, after Greek *Pergamon* "Pergamum"]

par·ci·an·te /paàr see ántee/ *n* *Southwest US* a member of a group of people who share water rights along an irrigation canal (**acequia**) [< Mexican Spanish]

par·close /paàr klṓz/ *n* a screen or railing that separates or encloses a side chapel, private tomb, or other special area within a large church [15C. < Old French, past participle of *parclore* "close off" < Latin *claudere* "to close"]

par·course /paar kóor/ *n* *US* a training circuit in a park or other open space, where people can walk or run between stations carrying equipment and instructions as fitness exercises [Late 20C. < French *parcours* "course" < medieval Latin *percursus*, literally "running through" < *percurrere* "run through" < Latin *currere* "to run"]

pard[1] /paard/ *n* a large cat, especially a leopard or a panther (*archaic*) [13C. Via French < Greek *pardos* < Iranian]

pard[2] /paard/ *n* *US* same as **pardner** (*slang*) [Mid-19C. Shortening]

pard·ner /paárdnər/ *n* used as a term of address to a friend (*slang*) [Late 18C. Representing a pronunciation of PARTNER]

par·don /paárd'n/ *vt* (**-doned, -don·ing, -dons**) **1.** EXEMPT GUILTY PARTY FROM PUNISHMENT to officially release from any, or any further, punishment somebody who has committed a crime or wrongdoing **2.** FORGIVE GUILTY PARTY to forgive somebody who has committed a crime or wrongdoing **3.** EXCUSE SOMEBODY FOR SOMETHING IMPOLITE to excuse an impolite act or a person committing one ■ *n* **1.** RELEASE FROM PUNISHMENT the official release from any, or any further, punishment of somebody who has committed a crime or wrongdoing **2.** PAPER AUTHORIZING FREEDOM FROM PUNISHMENT an official document releasing somebody from any, or any further, punishment **3.** ACT OF EXCUSING SOMEBODY forgiveness of an impolite act or a person committing one **4.** CHR INDULGENCE in the Roman Catholic Church, a papal indulgence (*dated informal*) ■ *interj* **1.** WHAT DID YOU SAY? used as a request to somebody to repeat something that has just been said **2.** *UK* EXPRESSES APOLOGY used as an apology for doing something impolite or wrong [13C. < Old French *pardun* < *pardoner* "grant thoroughly" < medieval Latin *perdonare* < Latin *donare* "give, grant"] —**par·don·a·ble** *adj* —**par·don·a·bly** *adv* ◇ **pardon me 1.** used as a request to somebody to repeat something that has just been said **2.** used as an apology for doing something impolite or wrong

par·don·er /paárd'nər/ *n* **1.** a granter of a pardon **2.** somebody who, in medieval times, made a living by selling papal indulgences that were believed to free people from their sins

pare /per/ (**pared, par·ing, pares**) *vt* **1.** to remove the skin or outer layer of something such as a vegetable or fruit thinly and neatly **2.** to trim something such as fingernails or toenails [13C. Via French *parer* "prepare, trim" < Latin *parare*]

SPELLCHECK See *pair*.

pare down *vt* to reduce a total amount or number, usually an amount of money or a number of workers, slowly and steadily

par·e·gor·ic /pàrrə gáwrik/ *n* a camphorated tincture of opium, once a major source of opium addiction.

Use: formerly, nonprescription painkiller. ■ *adj* soothing or painkilling [Late 17C. Via late Latin < Greek *parēgorikos* "soothing" < *para* "beside" + *agoreuein* "speak"]

pa·ren·chy·ma /pə réngkəmə/ *n* **1.** BOT **PLANT TISSUE** soft plant tissue made up of thin-walled cells that forms the greater part of leaves, stem pith, roots, and fruit pulp **2.** ANAT **SPECIALIZED ORGAN TISSUE** the tissue that makes up the specialized parts of an organ, rather than the blood vessels and connective or supporting tissue **3.** ZOOL **WORM TISSUE** the loose meshwork of cells that surrounds internal organs and fills spaces inside the body of animals such as flatworms [Mid-17C. Via modern Latin < Greek *paregkhuma* "soft tissue" < *paregkhein* "pour in beside" < *khein* "pour"] —**par·en·chym·a·tous** /pèrrən kímmətəss/ *adj*

par·ent /pérrənt/ *n* **1. MOTHER OR FATHER** somebody's mother, father, or legal guardian **2. ORIGIN OF SOMETHING ELSE** something from which one or more similar and separate things have developed, or to which they are attached (*often used before a noun*) ○ *money transferred from the parent fund* **3.** CHEM **EARLIER ATOMIC FORM** an atom, molecule, or ion that undergoes change to become a new product. The starting components in a chemical reaction are the parent molecules. (*often used before a noun*) **4.** PHYS **PARTICLE'S EARLIER FORM** a radioactive particle that disintegrates to give a new particle (**nuclide**) as a subsequent member of a radioactive decay series (*often used before a noun*) ■ *vt* (**-ent·ed, -ent·ing, -ents**) **ACT AS PARENT TO SOMEBODY** to be or act as a parent to somebody or something [15C. Via French < Latin *parent-* < present participle of *parere* "give birth"] —**par·ent·hood** *n* —**par·ent·less** *adj*

par·ent·age /pérrəntij/ *n* **1.** a person's parents or ancestors, especially when regarded in terms of social characteristics or geographic origins ○ *of Irish parentage* **2.** the origins or sources that something has developed from

pa·ren·tal /pə rént'l/ *adj* **1.** relating to, belonging to, or provided by parents **2.** describes the original generation of individuals from which all subsequent generations have been bred —**pa·ren·tal·ly** *adv*

pa·ren·tal leave *n* time off from work, granted to a parent to care for a newborn or newly adopted child

par·en·ter·al /pə réntərəl/ *adj* describes drug administration other than by the mouth or the rectum, e.g., by injection, infusion, or implantation [Early 20C. < PARA-[1] + Greek *enteron* "intestine"] —**par·en·ter·al·ly** *adv*

pa·ren·the·sis /pə rénthəssiss/ (*plural* **-the·ses** /-thə seez/) *n* **1.** PRINTING **UPRIGHT CURVED MARK IN PUNCTUATION** one of a pair of shallow, curved signs, ( ), used to enclose an additional inserted word or comment and distinguish it from the sentence in which it is found **2. WORDS WITHIN PARENTHESES** a word or phrase that comments on or qualifies part of the sentence in which it is found and is isolated from it by parentheses or dashes **3. DEPARTURE FROM TOPIC** a piece of speech or writing that wanders off from the main topic **4. INTERVAL** something that acts as a pause or break in something (*formal*) [Mid-16C. Via late Latin < Greek < *parentithenai* "insert" < *tithenai* "to place"] ◇ **in parenthesis** as an additional qualifying, explanatory, or otherwise separate comment

USAGE ***Parentheses*** are used around text that adds extra information to what has gone before: *She was suffering from rubella (German measles); The noun "dessert" (with a double "s") is pronounced the same as the verb "desert"; a protest against GM (genetically modified) crops.* The information within the parentheses can usually be omitted without affecting the structure of the sentence. Note that there should be no punctuation directly before the opening parenthesis in such cases. Parentheses are also used around optional or alternative material: *Please write your forename(s) in full,* or to separate something, e.g., a number or symbol, from the surrounding text: *I disagree with the proposal, (a) because it is too expensive, and (b) because it is unlikely to be effective in the long term.* See also ***bracket***.

pa·ren·the·size /pə rénthə sīz/ (**-sized, -siz·ing, -siz·es**) *v* **1.** *vt* **PUT SOMETHING IN PARENTHESES** to enclose part of a written or printed passage in parentheses **2.** *vt* **ADD SOMETHING AS EXTRA COMMENT** to add a word, phrase, or opinion as an extra comment that is not wholly related to what is being said **3.** *vti* **INSERT EXTRA COMMENTS** to break up speech or writing with extra comments added throughout

par·en·thet·i·cal /pàrrən théttik'l/, **par·en·thet·ic** /-théttik/ *adj* **1.** added as an extra comment or parenthesis **2.** describes writing that uses or contains additional comments or notes added as parentheses —**par·en·thet·i·cal·ly** *adv*

par·ent·ing /pérrənting/ *n* the experiences, skills, qualities, and responsibilities involved in being a parent and in teaching and caring for a child (*often used before a noun*) ○ *parenting skills*

par·ent met·al *n* in welding, the metal of any of the components that are to be welded together

Par·ent-Teach·er As·so·ci·a·tion *n* a school body run by teachers and parents to organize fundraising and social events and encourage cooperation and understanding

pa·re·o *n* CLOTHING another spelling of **pareu**

pa·re·sis /pə reéssiss, párrəssiss/ *n* muscular weakness or partial inability to move caused by disease of the nervous system [Late 17C. < Greek, "letting go" < *para* "aside" + *hienai* "to throw"]

par·es·the·si·a /pàrrəs theézhə, -zhee ə/ *n* an unusual or unexplained tingling, pricking, or burning sensation on the skin [Late 19C. < PARA-[1] + Greek *aesthēsis* "feeling"]

pa·re·u /paá ray oō/, **pa·re·o** (*plural* **-os**) *n* a length of fabric worn wrapped around the hips by both men and women in Polynesian countries, or a garment resembling this for wearing [Mid-19C. < Tahitian]

pa·re·ve /paárəvə/, **par·veh** /paárvə/, **par·ve** *adj* describes a food that, under Jewish law, is neither a dairy nor a meat product and can therefore be eaten with either as part of the same meal [Mid-20C. < Yiddish]

par ex·cel·lence /paar èksə laáNss/ *adj* of the very best kind or highest quality [< French, "by virtue of preeminence"]

par·fait /paar fáy/ *n* **1.** a sweet dish composed of various layers, including ice cream, fruit, syrup, and whipped cream **2.** a rich dessert consisting of frozen whipped cream or rich ice cream flavored with fruit [Late 19C. Via French, "perfect" < Latin *perfectus* (see PERFECT)]

par·fait glass *n* a short-stemmed glass with a tall, rather narrow body designed to show off the contrasting layers of a parfait

par·fleche /paár flèsh/ *n* **1.** the hide of an animal, soaked and scraped to remove the hair, then stretched and dried, but not tanned **2.** a shield, bag, or other item made of parfleche [Early 19C. < Canadian French < French *parer* "defend" + *flèche* "arrow"]

par·get /paárjət/ *n* **1. PLASTER FOR WALLS OR CHIMNEYS** plaster, whitewash, roughcast, or any similar material used to coat walls or line chimneys **2. PLASTERWORK** ornamental plasterwork on a wall ■ *vt* (**-get·ed, -get·ing, -gets**) **COAT SOMETHING WITH PARGET** to cover walls, line chimneys, or decorate a surface with parget [14C. Alteration (influenced by Old French *parjeter* "throw about") of Old French *porgeter* "plaster a wall" < *jeter* "to throw"] —**par·get·ing** *n*

par·he·li·a ASTRON plural of **parhelion**

par·he·lic /paar heélik/, **par·he·li·a·cal** /paár hee lī ək'l/ *adj* relating to or characteristic of a parhelion

par·he·lic cir·cle *n* a luminous horizontal band in the sky that passes through the Sun and is caused by the Sun's rays reflecting off ice crystals in the atmosphere

par·he·li·on /paar heélee ən, -heélyən/ (*plural* **-li·a** /-lee ə/) *n* a bright colored spot near the Sun, often seen in pairs and caused by ice crystals in the atmosphere diffracting light [Mid-17C. Via Latin < Greek *parēlion* < *para* "beside" + *hēlios* "sun"]

pari- *prefix* equal ○ *parisyllabic* [< Latin *par* "equal"]

pa·ri·ah /pə rī ə/ *n* **1.** somebody who is despised and avoided **2.** in South Asia, somebody who has defied a social law and has therefore been rejected by a caste [Early 17C. < Tamil *paraiyan* "drummer" < *parai* "festival drum"; because hereditary drummers were outside the caste system]

Par·i·an /pérree ən/ *adj* **1. OF MARBLE FROM PAROS** describes a fine white marble that was mined on the Greek island of Paros in ancient times **2. OF PORCELAIN FROM PAROS** describes a variety of fine porcelain used mainly to make figures and originally from the Greek island of Paros **3. OF PAROS** relating to the Greek island of Paros ■ *n* **SOMEBODY FROM PAROS** somebody who comes from the Greek island of Paros [Mid-16C. < Latin *Parius* "of Paros"]

pa·ri·e·tal /pə rī ət'l/ *adj* **1.** BIOL **OF WALLS OF HOLLOW PART** relating to the walls of any hollow part of a plant or animal such as a plant's ovary or an animal's skull **2.** *US* EDUC **OF IN-COLLEGE RESIDENCE** relating to residence within a college ■ *n* BIOL **PARIETAL PART** a parietal part of a plant or animal ■ **pa·ri·e·tals** *npl* *US* EDUC **COLLEGE VISITING RULES** the rules governing who can and cannot visit a college dormitory, especially in relation to members of the opposite sex [Early 16C. Directly or via French < late Latin *parietalis* < *paries* "wall"]

pa·ri·e·tal bone *n* either of two bones, one on each side of the skull, that form a part of the sides and roof of the skull

pa·ri·e·tal cell *n* any one of the cells that make up the peptic glands of the stomach and secrete hydrochloric acid

pa·ri·e·tal lobe *n* the middle region of either of the two hemispheres of the brain, lying beneath the crown of the skull

par·i·mu·tu·el /pàrri myoōchoo əl/ (*plural* **par·i·mu·tu·els** /*pronunc. same*/ or **par·is·mu·tu·els** /*pronunc. same*/) *n US* **1.** a system of betting on horseraces using an electronic machine that totals all bets, deducts management charges and taxes, and determines the final odds and payouts **2.** a machine that records bets and calculates winnings in the pari-mutuel betting system [< French, "mutual wager"]

par·ing /pérring/ *n* something that has been pared or cut off something larger, e.g., a thin slice of fruit or vegetable peel

par·ing knife *n* a short tapered knife with a sharp blade designed for removing the outer skin of vegetables or fruit

pa·ri pas·su /pàrree pás soo, paáree paás soo/ *adv* **1.** at an equal rate or in an otherwise fair way, with no one person or group taking precedence over another **2.** together, step for step (*literary*) [< Latin, "with equal step"]

Par·is[1] /párriss/ *n* in Greek mythology, a Trojan prince whose abduction of Helen, the wife of Menelaus, started the Trojan War [Via Latin < Greek]

Par·is[2] /párriss/; *French* /pa reé/ **1.** capital city of France, situated in the north central part of the country. Population: 2,125,246 (1999). **2.** city in the Red River valley in northeastern Texas. Population: 26,212 (2002 estimate). —**Pa·ri·si·an** /pə reézh'n/ *adj, n*

Par·is green *n* a bright blue-green toxic powder. Use: pigment in paints, insecticide, wood preserver. Formula: $(CuO)_3As_2O_3.Cu(Cu_2H_3O_2)_2$. [Mid-19C. After PARIS[2]]

par·ish /párrish/ *n* **1. DISTRICT WITH OWN CHURCH** in the Episcopal, Roman Catholic, and some other churches, a division of a diocese that has its own church and member of the clergy (*often used before a noun*) ○ *the parish priest* **2.** POL **ADMINISTRATIVE AREA IN LOUISIANA** an administrative area in the state of Louisiana that corresponds to a county in other states **3. PEOPLE OF PARISH** the people who live in a parish (*takes a singular or plural verb*) [13C. Via Old French *parroche* < ecclesiastical Latin *parochia, paroechia* < Greek *paroikos* "neighbor," literally "dwelling nearby" < *oikos* "dwelling"]

pa·rish·ion·er /pə ríshənər/ *n* a resident of a religious or civil parish [15C. < obsolete *parishion* < Old French *parochien* < *parroche* (see PARISH)]

par·i·syl·lab·ic /pàrri si lábbik/ *adj* describes a noun or verb that contains the same number of syllables in all of its inflections

par·i·ty[1] /párrətee/ *n* **1. EQUALITY** equality of status or position, especially in terms of pay or rank **2. SIMILARITY BETWEEN THINGS** the quality of being similar or identical **3.** MATH **RELATIONSHIP BETWEEN NUMBERS** a relationship of oddness or evenness between two numbers (**integers**). If two numbers are both odd or both even, they are said to have the same parity. If one is odd and one is even, they have different parity. **4.** FIN **EQUALITY OF EXCHANGE RATE** equivalence in the rate of exchange between several currencies **5.** COMPUT **INTEGRITY OF TRANSMITTED DATA** equivalence between computer data transmitted, e.g., by fax or e-mail, and the data received. Errors are checked by comparing the number of 1s in the message sent with the number in the message received. [Late 16C. Directly or via French < late Latin *paritas* < Latin *par* "equal"]

par·i·ty[2] /párrətee/ *n* **1.** the condition or fact of having given birth **2.** the number of children that a woman has given birth to [Late 19C. < PAROUS]

park /paark/ *n* **1. AREA FOR PUBLIC RECREATION** a publicly owned area of land, usually with grass, trees, paths, sports fields, playgrounds, picnic areas, and other features for recreation and relaxation **2. PROTECTED AREA OF COUNTRYSIDE** an area of land reserved and managed so that it remains unspoiled, undeveloped, and as natural as possible **3. PRIVATELY OWNED RECREATION FACILITY** an area of privately owned land, developed to offer recreation or amusements to paying customers **4.** BUSINESS **BUSINESS SITE** an area of land developed for a group of related commercial enterprises ○ *a high-technology park* **5.** SPORTS **STADIUM OR SPORTS FIELD** a sports stadium or sports field **6.** URBAN PLAN **ROAD OR DISTRICT** a street or district, especially in a suburban area (*often used in place names*) **7.** MIL **AREA HOUSING MILITARY VEHICLES** a designated area where military vehicles are kept, within a military base **8.** AUTOMOT **POSITION ON AUTOMATIC TRANSMISSION** a position on the gear selector of a motor vehicle with an automatic transmission that acts as a brake when parking ■ *v* **(parked, park·ing, parks) 1.** *vti* **STOP AND LEAVE VEHICLE** to stop a motor vehicle beside or off the road and leave it there for some time **2.** *vti* **MANEUVER MOTOR VEHICLE INTO SPACE** to maneuver a motor vehicle into a space in order to park it **3.** *vt* **SETTLE SOMEWHERE** to sit down somewhere, usually with the intention of staying there for some time (*slang*) ○ *Just park yourself over there.* **4.** *vt* **LEAVE SOMETHING SOMEWHERE** to place or leave something somewhere temporarily, especially something heavy, bulky, or unwanted (*slang*) **5.** *vi* **KISS IN PARKED CAR** to kiss and cuddle in a parked car in a quiet and secluded location (*slang*) **6.** *vt* AEROSP **PLACE SPACECRAFT IN ORBIT** to place a spacecraft or satellite in orbit, usually temporarily **7.** *vt* **PUT SOMETHING ON HOLD** to stop pursuing or dealing with something temporarily [13C. Via French *parc* < medieval Latin *parricus* < Germanic, "enclosure"]

CULTURAL NOTE ***Mansfield Park***, a novel (1814) by the British writer Jane Austen. It tells the story of young Fanny Price, who is sent to live with her wealthy relatives, the Bertrams. Fanny's warmth and moral strength, which are contrasted with her uncle's stern traditionalism and the irresponsible flirtations of her neighbors Mary and Henry Crawford, eventually win her the respect of the family and the hand of her cousin Edmund.

Park /paark/, **Mungo** (1771–1806) Scottish explorer. He explored the Niger River and wrote *Travels in the Interior Districts of Africa* (1799). In a subsequent expedition his party was attacked, and he drowned.

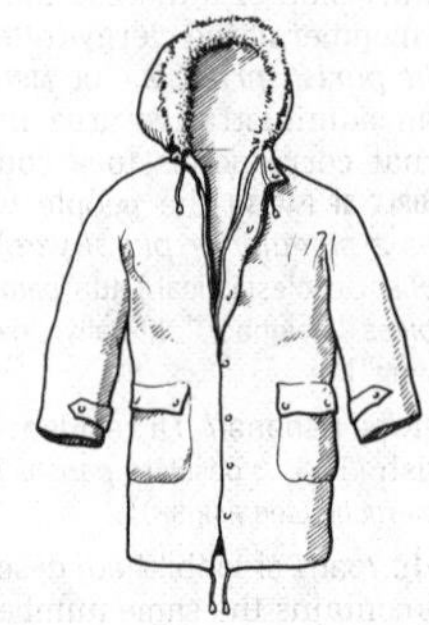

parka

par·ka /paárkə/ *n* **1.** a warm, knee- or thigh-length jacket that has a hood and is often lined with fur or imitation fur **2.** a thick, fur-lined, hooded outer garment for arctic conditions, pulled on over the head. Traditionally, parkas are made of animal hide and worn by the Inuit and Aleut people. [Late 18C. Via Aleut < Russian, "pelt, skin jacket"]

par·kade /paár kàyd/ *n Can* a multilevel parking lot [Mid-20C. < PARK, probably after ARCADE]

park day *n US* a day on which a group of people, usually parents and children, meet for communal activities in a public park

Par·ker /paárkər/, **Bonnie** (1910–34) US outlaw. With Clyde Barrow she robbed banks and killed 12 people. Both were killed in a police ambush.

Par·ker, Charlie (1920–55) US jazz musician and composer. He was an alto saxophonist and pioneer of the bebop movement. Known as **Yardbird, Bird**. Full name **Parker, Jr., Charles Christopher**

> "Music is your own experience, your thoughts, your wisdom. If you don't live it, it won't come out of your horn."
> [Charlie Parker. Quoted in *Hear Me Talkin' to Ya,* Nat Shapiro and Nat Hentoff; 1955]

Popperfoto

Dorothy Parker

Par·ker, Dorothy (1893–1967) US writer and critic. She is known for her sardonic stories, poetry, and reviews for *The New Yorker* magazine. Full name **Parker, Dorothy Rothschild**

> "Sorrow is tranquility remembered in emotion."
> [Dorothy Parker, *Here Lies*; 1939]

> "The best way to keep children at home is to make it pleasant and let the air out of the tires."
> [Dorothy Parker. Quoted in *Utne Reader*; March/April 1991]

Par·ker, Theodore (1810–60) US cleric and reformer. He supported prison reform and the abolitionist movement.

> "A democracy—that is a government of all the people, by all the people, for all the people; of course, a government of the principles of eternal justice, the unchanging law of God; for shortness' sake I will call it the idea of Freedom."
> [Theodore Parker, *Speech,* "The American Idea," *at the New England Anti-Slavery Convention, Boston*; May 29, 1850]

Par·kers·burg /paárkərz bùrg/ city and port in western West Virginia, at the confluence of the Little Kanawha and Ohio rivers. Population: 32,299 (2002 estimate).

Park For·est village in northeastern Illinois, near the Illinois-Indiana border. It is a southern suburb of Chicago. Population: 23,711 (2002 estimate).

park·ing /paárking/ *n* **1. STOPPING AND LEAVING VEHICLE** the action of driving a road vehicle into a position beside or off the road and leaving it there **2. SPACE TO LEAVE VEHICLES** spaces in which vehicles may be parked **3. KISSING IN PARKED CAR** kissing and cuddling in a parked car in a quiet and secluded location (*slang*) **4.** *Midwest* **STRIP OF GRASS** the strip of grass, often planted with trees, between a sidewalk and a street

park·ing light *n* either of the two small lights on a motor vehicle used in conditions where light is poor, but not poor enough to warrant the use of headlights

park·ing lot *n* **1.** an area in which motor vehicles can be parked temporarily **2.** same as **traffic jam** (*slang*)

park·ing me·ter *n* a coin-operated roadside meter that displays the length of time for which a vehicle may remain legally parked in a parking space

park·ing or·bit *n* a temporary orbit of a spacecraft during which preparations are made for the next step in its program. The orbit may be used while activities are being carried out aboard the craft or while waiting for the next phase of the program to begin.

park·ing ramp *n* a building or underground parking area having several levels reached by ramps, where automobiles can be parked temporarily

Par·kin·son·ism /paárkinssə nìzzəm/ *n* a nervous disorder marked by symptoms of trembling limbs and muscular rigidity, e.g., Parkinson's disease. These disorders may be caused by the frequent use of some drugs or by exposure to chemicals.

Par·kin·son's dis·ease /paárkinssənz-/ *n* a progressive nervous disorder marked by symptoms of trembling hands, lifeless face, monotone voice, and a slow shuffling walk. It is generally caused by the degeneration of dopamine-producing brain cells, and is the commonest form of Parkinsonism. [Late 19C. After James *Parkinson* (1755–1824), British physician]

Par·kin·son's law /paárkinssənz-/ *n* the observation that work always expands to fill the time set aside for it [Mid-20C. After C. Northcote *Parkinson* (1909–93), British historian]

Par·kin·son's syn·drome *n* MED same as **Parkinsonism**

park·land /paárk lànd/ *n* the land contained within a park, especially when the grassland contains shrubs and trees

Park·man /párkmən/, **Francis** (1823–93) US historian. He wrote literary studies of Native Americans and European settlers in North America.

> "France built its best colony on a principle of exclusion, and failed: England reversed the system and succeeded."
> [Francis Parkman. Introduction, *Montcalm and Wolf*; 1884]

park·out /paárk òwt/ *n regional* in Northern Virginia, a mobile drop-off point for garbage and recyclables, typically situated in a parking lot

Park Ridge city in northeastern Illinois, west of Niles. It is a northwestern suburb of Chicago. Population: 37,771 (2002 estimate).

Parks /paarks/, **Gordon** (*b.* 1912) US writer, photographer, and movie director. His movies include *The Learning Tree* (1969), which was based on his own novel, and *Shaft* (1971).

Parks, Rosa (*b.* 1913) US civil rights leader. Her arrest in Alabama for not relinquishing her bus seat to a white passenger (1955) led to Martin Luther King Jr.'s boycott campaign of the bus company and gave impetus to the campaign for civil rights. Full name **Parks, Rosa Louise**

park·way /paárk wày/ *n* a wide stretch of public highway with grassy areas on both sides, often divided by a grassy median

~~parlament~~ incorrect spelling of **parliament**

par·lance /paárlənss/ *n* **1.** the style of speech or writing used by people in a particular context or profession **2.** speech, especially in a conversation [Late 16C. < Old French < *parler* "speak" (see PARLEY)]

SYNONYMS See *jargon*[1].

par·lan·do /paar laándō/ *adv* in a style of singing that suggests speech, usually without pitch or with less clear pitch (*used as a musical direction*) [Late 19C. < Italian, "speaking"] —**par·lan·do** *adj*

par·lay /paár lày, -lee/ *vt* **(-layed, -lay·ing, -lays) 1. BET WINNINGS** to stake an original bet and its winnings on a subsequent bet **2. USE ADVANTAGE** to make good use of an asset or advantage to obtain success ○ *He parlayed his family connections into a prestigious job in the finance industry.* ■ *n* **INSTANCE OF BETTING WINNINGS** a bet in which winnings from a previous bet are gambled [Late 19C. Alteration of *paroli*, via French < Italian < *parare* "place a bet" < Latin, "prepare"]

SPELLCHECK parlay or **parley**? Do not confuse the spelling of *parlay* and *parley,* which sound similar. ***Parlay*** is a verb and noun referring to the betting of winnings on a subsequent bet. ***Parley*** is a verb and noun referring to talks or negotiations, especially with an enemy.

par·ley /paárlee/ *vi* (**-leyed, -ley·ing, -leys**) to talk or negotiate, especially with an enemy ■ *n* (*plural* **-leys**) a round of talks or negotiations, especially between opposing military forces [Late 16C. < Old French *parlee* < *parler* "speak" < late Latin *parabolare* < Latin *parabola* (see PARABLE)]

SPELLCHECK See *parlay.*

par·lia·ment /paárləmənt/ *n* **1.** a nation's legislative body, made up of elected and sometimes nonelected representatives **2.** an assembly of a parliament, created following an election and dissolved before the next election [13C. < Old French *parlement* < *parler* "speak" (see PARLEY)]

Par·lia·ment *n* the supreme legislative body in various countries. In the United Kingdom, Parliament consists of the House of Commons and the House of Lords.

par·lia·men·tar·i·an /paàrlə men térree ən, -mən-/ *n* **1.** a member of a parliament **2.** an expert in parliamentary procedures and parliamentary history

Par·lia·men·tar·i·an *n* during the English Civil War, a supporter or member of Oliver Cromwell's parliamentary army against King Charles I

par·lia·men·tar·i·an·ism /paàrlə men térree ə nìzzəm, -mən-/ *n* government of a country by a parliament, or support for this kind of government

par·lia·men·ta·ry /paàrlə méntəree, -méntree/ *adj* **1.** relating to parliaments, or in the form of a parliament ○ *parliamentary government* **2.** describes language and behavior considered to conform to the standards that apply to a parliament

Par·lia·men·ta·ry Com·mis·sion·er, Par·lia·men·ta·ry Com·mis·sion·er for Ad·min·is·tra·tion *n UK* GOV same as **ombudsman** (sense 2)

par·lia·men·ta·ry par·ty *n* the members of a political party who are members of parliament

par·lor /paárlər/ *n* **1.** a living room that is set aside for entertaining guests **2.** a room or set of rooms equipped and used to provide particular goods or services (*often used in combination*) ○ *a beauty parlor* [13C. < Old French < *parler* "to talk" (see PARLEY)]

par·lor car *n* a railroad passenger car containing individual reserved seats

par·lor·maid /paárlər màyd/ *n* a maid employed to wait on a family and guests in the living room and dining room of a large or wealthy household (*archaic*)

par·lour *n* COMM, BUILDINGS Can, UK spelling of **parlor**

par·lous /paárləss/ *adj* very unsafe, uncertain, or difficult (*archaic or humorous*) ○ *"Thou art in a parlous state, shepherd."* (William Shakespeare, *As You Like It*; 1599) ■ *adv* used to emphasize the extreme or excessive nature of something (*archaic*) [14C. Shortening and alteration of *perilous*] —**par·lous·ly** *adv* —**par·lous·ness** *n*

Par·ma /paármə/ city in northern Italy. It is the capital of Parma Province, in Emilia-Romagna Region. Population: 163,457 (2001).

Par·men·i·des /paar ménni deèz/ (*fl* 500 B.C.) Greek philosopher. He was a leader of the Eleatic school and the author of *On Nature,* which anticipates the idealism of Plato.

Par·me·san /paármə zàn, -zaàn/ *n* a pale yellow hard Italian cheese, often served grated as a garnish on pasta dishes [Mid-16C. Via French < Italian *parmigiano* "from Parma"]

par·mi·gia·na /paàrmi zhaánə, -jaánə/ *adj* describes a dish that has been prepared using Parmesan cheese ○ *veal parmigiana* [Late 19C. < Italian, form of *parmigiano* "of Parma"]

Par·mi·gia·ni·no /paàrmi jaa neénō/, **Par·mi·gia·no** /paàrmi jaánō/ (1503–40) Italian painter. His use of graceful elongated figures influenced the development of mannerism.

Par·nas·si·an[1] /paar nássee ən/ *adj* found in poetry, or associated with poetic works (*literary*) [Mid-17C. < Latin *Parnassius* < *Parnas(s)us* "Parnassus" < Greek *Parnasos*]

Par·nas·si·an[2] /paar nássee ən/ *n* a poet of a late 19th-century French school that advocated emotional detachment and purity of metrical form [< *Le Parnasse contemporain* (1866), French poetry anthology]

Par·nas·sus /paar nássəss/ mountain in central Greece, directly north of Delphi. In ancient times it was sacred to Apollo and thought to be the home of the Muses. Height: 8,061 ft./2,457 m.

Par·nell /paar nél, paárn'l/, **Charles Stewart** (1846–91) Irish politician. In 1880 he became leader of the Home Rule Party. He lost support after 1890, when he was involved in a divorce scandal.

> "No man has a right to fix the boundary of the march of a nation; no man has a right to say to his country—thus far shalt thou go and no further."
> [Charles Stewart Parnell, *Speech, Cork*; January 21, 1885]

pa·ro·chi·al /pə rṓkee əl/ *adj* **1.** concerned only with narrow local concerns without any regard for more general or wider issues **2.** relating or belonging to a parish or parishes [14C. Via French < ecclesiastical Latin *parochialis* < *parochia* (see PARISH)] —**pa·ro·chi·al·ism** *n* —**pa·ro·chi·al·ist** *n* —**pa·ro·chi·al·ly** *adv*

pa·ro·chi·al school *n* a private school that is affiliated with a church and provides children with religious instruction as well as a general education

par·o·dy /párrədee/ *n* (*plural* **-dies**) **1.** AMUSING IMITATION a piece of writing or music that deliberately copies another work in a comic or satirical way **2.** PARODIES IN GENERAL parodies as a literary or musical style or genre **3.** POOR IMITATION an attempt or imitation that is so poor that it seems ridiculous ■ *vt* (**-died, -dy·ing, -dies**) IMITATE SOMEBODY OR SOMETHING COMICALLY to write or perform a parody of somebody or something [Late 16C. Via late Latin < Greek *parōidia* < *para* "secondary, indirect" + *ōidē* "song"] —**pa·rod·ic** /pə róddik/ *adj* —**pa·rod·i·cal** *adj* —**pa·rod·i·cal·ly** *adv* —**par·o·dist** /párrədist/ *n*

pa·rol /pə rṓl, párrəl/ *adj* describes a legal contract that is oral, rather than written ■ *n* a legal contract that is made orally only [15C. < Anglo-French variant of French *parole* (see PAROLE)]

pa·role /pə rṓl/ *n* **1.** CONDITIONAL RELEASE OF PRISONER the early release of a prisoner, conditioned on good behavior and regular reporting to the authorities for a set period of time ○ *He's out on parole.* **2.** PRISONER'S PROMISE the promise to fulfill set conditions, given by a prisoner released on parole **3.** CONDITIONAL PERIOD the period of time during which a released prisoner remains on parole **4.** *US* PRISONER OF WAR'S PROMISE a promise, given by a prisoner of war as a condition of release, either not to escape or not to take up arms again **5.** LING REAL-WORLD LANGUAGE language considered as the utterances of real people, as distinct from the system of language (**langue**) that governs how those utterances are constructed ■ *vt* (**-roled, -rol·ing, -roles**) GIVE PRISONER PAROLE to release a prisoner on parole [15C. Via French < Latin *parabola* "speech, talk" (see PARABLE)] —**pa·rol·a·ble** *adj*

par·o·no·ma·sia /pàrrənō máyzhə/ *n* a play on words, especially a pun [Late 16C. < Latin < Greek *paronomazein* "name differently" < *onomazein* "to name"] —**par·o·no·mas·tic** /-mástik/ *adj* —**par·o·no·mas·ti·cal·ly** *adv*

par·o·nym /párrənim/ *n* a word derived from the same root as another word. For example, "folly" is a paronym of "fool." [Mid-19C. < Greek *parōnumon* < *para-* "beside" + *onuma* "name"] —**par·o·nym·ic** /pàrrə nímmik/ *adj* —**pa·ron·y·mous** /pə rónnəməss/ *adj* —**pa·ron·o·mous·ly** *adv*

Par·os /párross/, **Pá·ros** Greek island in the southern Aegean Sea, one of the Cyclades. Since ancient times it has been noted for its marble quarries. The chief town is Parikia. Population: 12,783 (2001). Area: 76 sq. mi./197 sq. km.

~~**parot**~~ incorrect spelling of **parrot**

pa·rot·ic /pə róttik/ *adj* ANAT same as **parotid** *adj* (sense 1) [Mid-19C. < Greek *para* "beside" + *ōt-* "ear"]

pa·rot·id /pə róttid/ *adj* **1.** situated close to or beside the ear **2.** relating to the parotid gland ■ *n* ANAT same as **parotid gland** [Late 17C. Via French and Latin < Greek *parōtid-* "beside the ear" < *ōt-* "ear"]

pa·rot·id gland *n* a salivary gland located below the ear in humans

par·o·ti·tis /pàrrə tī́tiss/, **pa·rot·i·di·tis** /pə ròtti dī́tiss/ *n* inflammation of a parotid gland or the parotid glands —**par·o·tit·ic** /pàrrə títtik/ *adj*

par·ous /párrəss/ *adj* having given birth on at least one occasion [Late 19C. < -PAROUS]

-parous *suffix* giving birth to, producing ○ *uniparous* [< Latin *-parus* < *parere* "give birth"]

Par·ou·si·a /paar oóssee ə, pə roózee ə/ *n* CHR same as **Second Coming** [Late 19C. < Greek, "presence" < present participle of *pareinai* < *einai* "be"]

pa·rox·e·tine /pə róksə teèn/ *n* a drug that allows serotonin levels in the brain to increase. Use: treatment of anxiety and depression.

par·ox·ysm /párrək sìzzəm/ *n* **1.** a sudden and uncontrollable expression of emotion ○ *paroxysms of grief* **2.** a sudden onset or intensification of a pathological symptom or symptoms, especially when recurrent [Late 16C. < medieval Latin < Greek *paroxunein* "irritate," literally "sharpen beyond" < *oxus* "sharp"] —**par·ox·ys·mal** /pàrrək sízm'l/ *adj* —**par·ox·ys·mal·ly** *adv* —**par·ox·ys·mic** /pàrrək sízmik/ *adj*

par·ox·y·tone /pə róksi tōn/ *n* **1.** WORD WITH PENULTIMATE STRESS a word in which the main stress is on the next to last syllable **2.** GREEK WORD CATEGORY in ancient Greek, a word with an acute accent on the next to last syllable ■ *adj* WITH STRESSED PENULTIMATE SYLLABLE with the main stress or accent on the next to last syllable [Mid-18C. < Greek *paroxutonos* < *para* "beside" + *oxutonos* (see OXYTONE)] —**par·ox·y·ton·ic** /pə ròksi tónnik/ *adj*

par·pen /paárpən/, **par·pend** /-pənd/ *n* same as **perpend** [15C. Via French < medieval Latin *parpannus*]

par·quet /paar káy/ *n* **1.** flooring consisting of blocks of wood laid in a decorative pattern **2.** *US* same as **orchestra** (sense 4) ■ *vt* (**-queted, -quet·ing, -quets**) to cover a floor in parquet [Early 19C. < French, literally "small enclosed space" < *parc* (see PARK)]

par·quet cir·cle *n US* the rear section of the main floor of seating in a theater, below the balcony

AKG London

parquetry: parquetry floor in an anonymous painting (1860?)

par·quet·ry /paárkətree/ *n* flooring or a decorative inlay for furniture made with blocks of wood

parr /paar/ (*plural same or* **parrs**) *n* **1.** a young salmon up to two years old that has dark transverse bands (**parr marks**) and lives in fresh water **2.** the young of some fishes other than the salmon, e.g., of the trout [Early 18C. Origin ?]

Parr /paar/, **Catherine** (1512–48) queen of England. She married Henry VIII in 1543, becoming his sixth queen. After his death in 1547 she married Thomas Seymour.

~~**parrallel**~~ incorrect spelling of **parallel**

par·rel /párrəl/, **par·ral** *n* a ring, loop, or band that secures a boom to a mast while allowing it to move up and down [15C. Shortening of APPAREL "rigging"]

par·ri·cide /párrə sīd/ *n* **1.** the murder of a parent or close relative **2.** somebody who murders his or her parent or close relative [Mid-16C. < Latin *parricidium* "kin-slaying," *parricida* "kin-slayer" < assumed *parri-* "relative"] —**par·ri·cid·al** /pàrrə sī́d'l/ *adj* —**par·ri·cid·al·ly** *adv*

Par·ring·ton /párringtən/, **Vernon L.** (1871–1929) US literary historian. He won a Pulitzer Prize for *Main Currents in American Thought* (1927–30). Full name **Vernon Louis Parrington**

Par·rish /párrish/, **Maxfield** (1870–1966) US artist. He is best known for his illustrations, posters, and murals.

parrot

par·rot /párrət/ *n* **1.** BRIGHTLY COLORED TROPICAL BIRD a bird with a strong hooked beak and variously colored, often brilliant plumage, some species of which can mimic speech. Native to: tropics, subtropics. Order: Psittaciformes. **2.** SOMEBODY WHO COPIES OTHERS a repeater of something that somebody else has said, without thought or understanding ■ *vt* (**-rot·ed, -rot·ing, -rots**) COPY OTHER PEOPLE to repeat what somebody else says or writes without having thought about it or understood it [Early 16C. Probably < French dialect *Perrot* "little Pierre"] —**par·rot·er** *n*

par·rot·bill /párrət bil/ *n* a small bird with a short strong beak for removing insects from bamboo or reed stems. Family: Psittacidae.

par·rot fe·ver *n* MED same as **psittacosis** [Because humans can contract it from pet birds such as parrots]

par·rot·fish /párrət fish/ (*plural same or* **-fish·es**) *n* a brightly colored sea fish with jaws shaped like a parrot's beak that it uses for scraping coral. Native to: tropics. Family: Scaridae.

par·rot·like /párrət līk/ *adv* mechanically and with no apparent understanding

par·ry /párree/ *v* (**-ried, -ry·ing, -ries**) **1.** *vti* TURN BLOW ASIDE to block or deflect the damaging effect of a blow or weapon **2.** *vt* AVOID ANSWERING QUESTION to evade a question by cleverly saying something that does not answer it ■ *n* (*plural* **-ries**) EVASION an act of evading a blow, criticism, or question [Late 17C. Probably < French *parez* "defend (yourself)!" < *parer* "prepare" (see PARE)]

Par·ry, Cape /párree/ headland in Canada, in the Northwest Territories, jutting into Amundsen Gulf between Franklin and Darnley bays

parse /paarss/ (**parsed, pars·ing, pars·es**) *v* **1.** *vti* DESCRIBE GRAMMATICAL ROLE OF WORD to describe the grammatical role of a word in a sentence, or undergo this process **2.** *vti* ANALYZE GRAMMATICAL STRUCTURE OF SENTENCE to analyze and describe the grammatical structure of a sentence, or undergo this process **3.** *vt* COMPUT ANALYZE COMPUTER INPUT to analyze computer input in a specific language against the formal grammar of that language, both to validate the input and to create an internal representation of it for use in subsequent processing [Mid-16C. Perhaps < obsolete *pars* "parts of speech" < Old French] —**pars·a·ble** *adj*

par·sec /paár sèk/ *n* an astronomical unit of distance equal to 3.262 light-years. A parsec is the distance from which the Earth's distance from the Sun would subtend one second of arc. Symbol **pc** [Early 20C. < PARALLAX + SECOND[2]]

Par·see /paar seé, paár seè/, **Par·si** *n* a member of a Zoroastrian group living mainly in western India, descended from Persian refugees of the 7th and 8th centuries [Early 17C. < Persian *Pārsī* < *Pārs* "Persia"] —**Par·see** *adj* —**Par·see·ism** *n*

pars·er /paárssər/ *n* **1.** a program that parses computer input. The parser determines how a sentence can be constructed from the grammar of the language, producing a tree (**parse tree**) about the statement as the output. **2.** somebody or something that analyzes something into its component parts

Par·si *n, adj* RELIG another spelling of **Parsee**

par·si·mo·ni·ous /paàrssə mṓnee əss/ *adj* very frugal or ungenerous —**par·si·mo·ni·ous·ly** *adv* —**par·si·mo·ni·ous·ness** *n*

par·si·mo·ny /paárssə mṑnee/ *n* **1.** great frugality or unwillingness to spend money **2.** economy in the use of means to achieve something, especially the principle of endorsing the simplest explanation that covers a case [15C. < Latin *parsimonia* < *pars-*, past participle of *parcere* "spare"]

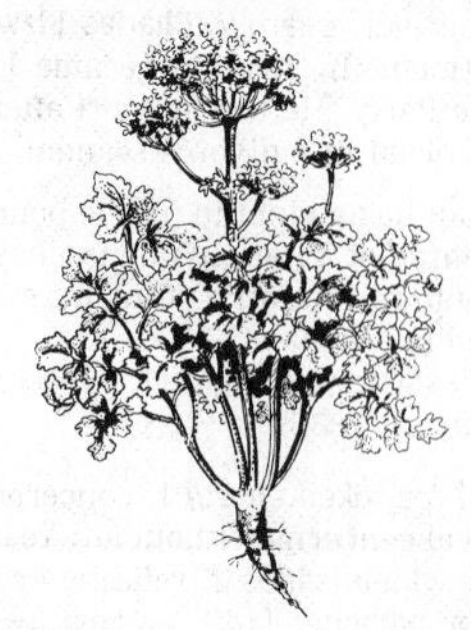

parsley

pars·ley /paársslee/ *n* a widely cultivated plant of the carrot family with small compound leaves. Use: in cooking, as a garnish. Latin name: *Petroselinum crispum*. [Pre-12C. Via late Latin *petrosilium* < Greek *petroselinon* < *petra* "rock" + *selinon* "parsley"]

pars·ley fern *n* a bright green fern with leaves that look like parsley leaves. Native to: Europe. Latin name: *Cryptogramma crispa*.

pars·ley piert /-peèrt/ *n* a small plant of the rose family with three-lobed leaves. Flowers: green, tiny. Latin name: *Aphanes arvensis*. [Late 16C. Alteration of French *perce-pierre* "stone-piercer"]

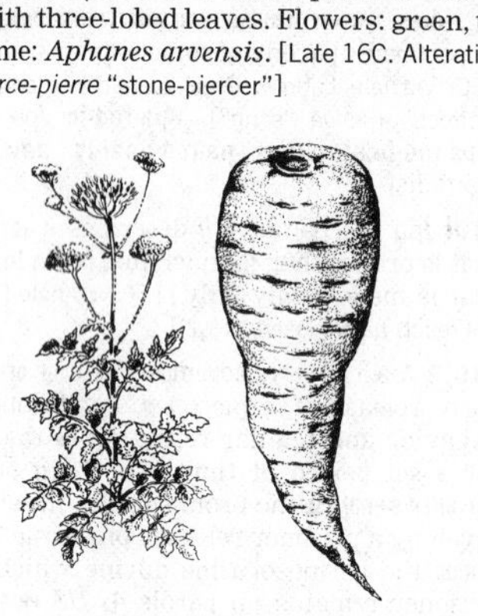

parsnip

pars·nip /paárssnip/ *n* **1.** a long tapering cream-colored root eaten cooked as a vegetable **2.** a plant of the carrot family that produces parsnips. Latin name: *Pastinaca sativa*. [14C. Alteration (influenced by Scottish and N English *neep* "turnip") of Old French *pasnaie* < Latin *pastinaca* < *pastinum* "gardening fork"; probably from its shape]

par·son /paárss'n/ *n* **1.** an Episcopal parish minister **2.** a member of the clergy, especially of the Protestant Church [13C. < variant of Old French *persone* (see PERSON)] —**par·son·ic** /paar sónnik/ *adj* —**par·son·i·cal** *adj*

par·son·age /paárss'nij/ *n* the house, usually provided by the parish or congregation, where a parson lives

Par·sons /paárss'nz/, **Talcott** (1902–79) US sociologist. He is known for functionalist theories about the mechanisms of society and the organizational principles behind societal structures.

> "Science is intimately integrated with the whole social structure and cultural tradition. They mutually support one another—only in certain types of society can science flourish, and conversely without a continuous and healthy development and application of science such a society cannot function properly."
> (Talcott Parsons, *The Social System*; 1951)

par·son's nose *n UK* same as **pope's nose**

Par·sons ta·ble *n* a square or rectangular table, the legs of which are flush with the top of the table at the four corners [After the *Parsons* School of Design in New York City]

part /paart/ *n* **1.** PORTION a portion or section of something ○ *the early part of the century* **2.** COMPONENT a separable piece or component of something such as a machine, system, or device ○ *a motor with only three moving parts* **3.** EQUAL PORTION OF WHOLE a portion of something that with other portions of the same size makes up a whole ○ *pastry that is one part butter to three parts flour* **4.** IMPORTANT ELEMENT OF SOMETHING an integral and essential feature or component of something ○ *She wants to be part of the community.* **5.** ACTOR'S ROLE a role in a dramatic performance ○ *played the part of Hamlet in the school play* **6.** INVOLVEMENT IN EVENT somebody's participation in or influence on something ○ *What part did he have to play in all this?* **7.** SIDE somebody's side or viewpoint ○ *You're always taking her part.* **8.** ORGANIC CONSTITUENT an organ, system, or other discrete element of an organism ○ *the part of the plant that carries out photosynthesis* **9.** LOGICAL DIVISION a logical division of something such as a report, book, or presentation ○ *Part three of the paper deals with environmental issues.* **10.** SEPARATE MUSICAL ROLE the score for a single voice or instrument in a symphonic, orchestral, or choral work **11.** HAIR DIVIDING LINE IN HAIR the line in a hairstyle from which the hair is combed or brushed in different directions ■ **parts** *npl* **1.** AREA a region or area (*informal*) ○ *That's unheard of in these parts.* **2.** ABILITIES intellectual abilities or talents (*literary*) ○ *a student of parts* ■ *v* (**part·ed, part·ing, parts**) **1.** *vti* SEPARATE to move apart, or move two things or people in different directions so that there is a space between them ○ *They had to part the children to keep them from fighting.* ○ *The curtains parted.* **2.** *vti* DIVIDE INTO PARTS to divide something into parts, or undergo division into parts **3.** *vti* DIVIDE HAIR to make a line in the hair by combing in opposite directions from it, or separate naturally in this way **4.** *vi* END RELATIONSHIP to finish a relationship with somebody ○ *We parted on bad terms.* **5.** *vi* GO AWAY to go away from somebody ○ *They parted at the corner.* ■ *adj* PARTIAL partial or less than the whole ○ *part owner of a beach house* ■ *adv* PARTIALLY to some extent but not completely ○ *She's part Irish, part French.* [Pre-12C. Directly or via French < Latin *part-*] ◇ **for the most part** in general, or mostly ○ *She does OK at school, for the most part.* ◇ **in good part 1.** without taking offence or becoming angry **2.** *US* largely ◇ **in part** to an extent but not completely ◇ **on the part of** as far as somebody is concerned, or with regard to somebody ◇ **part and parcel** an essential, indivisible element of something ◇ **part company** to go away in separate directions (*refers to two or more people*) ○ *They chatted for a while before parting company.* ◇ **take part (in something)** to be actively involved in something, usually as a member of a group

USAGE The idiom ***part and parcel***, meaning "an essential component of something else," is correctly worded as shown here, e.g., *Walking is part and parcel of a forest ranger's occupation. "Part and partial"* is incorrect.

part with *vt* to give something up or give something away, especially unwillingly

Part /paart/, **Arvo** (*b.* 1935) Estonian-born Austrian composer. He has written orchestral and choral works with worldwide appeal.

par·take /paar táyk/ (**-took** /-to͝ok/, **-tak·en** /-táykən/, **-tak·ing, -takes**) *vi* (*formal*) **1.** EAT OR DRINK SOMETHING to have something to eat or drink ○ *We're just about to have some tea. Would you care to partake?* **2.** HAVE OR SEEM TO HAVE to have or appear to have a quality or characteristic **3.** PARTICIPATE to share in or take part in something ○ *How many students partake in sports activities?* [Mid-16C. Back-formation < *partaker* < *part-taker, partaking* < *part-taking*, translations of Latin *particeps* "participant," *participatio* "participation"] —**par·tak·er** *n*

part·ed /paártəd/ *adj* **1.** SEPARATED separated or kept separate ○ *with parted lips* **2.** DIVIDED BY PART describes hair that has a part ○ *a hairstyle parted on the left* **3.** IN PARTS divided into parts **4.** BOT DIVIDED TO BASE describes a leaf or plant part that is separated or cleft nearly to the base

par·terre /paar tér/ *n* **1.** an ornamental garden laid out in a formal pattern that is usually marked out with low evergreen hedges and filled in with annual bedding plants **2.** THEATER same as **parquet circle** [Early 17C. < French, "ornamental garden" < *par terre* "on the ground"]

part ex·change *n UK* a payment method by which a buyer gives something he or she owns to a seller as part payment for a more expensive item —**part-ex·change** *vt*

par·the·no·car·py /paárthənō kaàrpee/ *n* the production of fruits without fertilization or seeds [Early 20C. < German *Parthenocarpie* < Greek *parthenos* "virgin" + *karpos* "fruit"] —**par·the·no·car·pic** /paàrthənō kaárpik/ *adj* —**par·the·no·car·pous** /-kaárpəss/ *adj*

par·the·no·gen·e·sis /paàrthənō jénnəssiss/ *n* a form of reproduction, especially in plants, insects, and arthropods, in which a female gamete develops into a new individual without fertilization by a male gamete [Mid-19C. < Greek *parthenos* "virgin"] —**par·the·no·ge·net·ic** /-jə néttik/ *adj* —**par·the·no·ge·net·i·cal·ly** *adv*

Parthenon, Athens, Greece

Par·the·non /paáthə nòn/ *n* a large temple on the Acropolis in Athens, Greece, built in the 5th century B.C. to the goddess Athena

Par·thi·an /paárthee ən/ *n* somebody who came from Parthia, an ancient country in Southwest Asia that ruled an empire until the 3rd century A.D. —**Par·thi·an** *adj*

Par·thi·an shot *n* a final hostile remark or gesture made while leaving [< the Parthians' legendary tactic of firing arrows over their shoulders while retreating]

par·tial /paársh'l/ *adj* **1. INCOMPLETE** not complete or total ○ *only a partial success* **2. AFFECTING PARTS** affecting a part or parts but not the whole ○ *a partial restoration of the building* **3. FOND OF SOMETHING** having a liking for something ○ *very partial to chocolate cake* **4. BIASED** showing an unfair preference for one person or thing over another ■ *n* **1.** MATH same as **partial derivative 2.** MUSIC same as **overtone** (sense 2) **3.** CARDS same as **part-score** [15C. Via French < late Latin *partialis* < Latin *part-* "part"] —**par·tial·ness** *n*

par·tial den·ture *n* an artificial tooth or row of teeth that is usually removable

par·tial de·riv·a·tive *n* the derivative of a function of two or more mathematical variables calculated with respect to one of the variables and on the assumption that the others are fixed

par·tial dif·fer·en·tial e·qua·tion *n* a differential equation that involves partial derivatives of more than one variable

par·tial e·clipse *n* an eclipse in which only part of something such as the Sun or Moon is darkened

par·tial frac·tion *n* any one of a set of simpler fractions, the sum of which composes a more complex fraction

par·ti·al·i·ty /paàrshee állətee/ *n* **1.** a liking for something **2.** an unfair preference for one person or thing over another

par·tial·ly /paársh'lee/ *adv* **1.** to a degree but not completely **2.** in a way that shows an unfair preference for one person or thing over another

USAGE See *partly.*

par·tial·ly sight·ed *adj* having a visual impairment that cannot be completely corrected by the use of glasses or contact lenses

par·tial pres·sure *n* the pressure that one gas in a mixture of gases would exert if it were the only gas present

par·tial prod·uct *n* the result when a mathematical quantity is multiplied by one digit of a number with two or more digits

par·ti·ble /paártəb'l/ *adj* able to be divided ○ *a partible inheritance* [Mid-16C. < late Latin *partibilis* < Latin *partire* "to divide" (see PARTITION)]

par·tic·i·pant /paar tíssəpənt/ *n* somebody who takes part in something ■ *adj* taking part in something [Mid-16C. < French, present participle of *participier* < Latin *participare* (see PARTICIPATE)]

par·tic·i·pate /paar tíssə pàyt/ (**-pat·ed, -pat·ing, -pates**) *vi* to take part in an event or activity [15C. < Latin *participat-*, past participle of *participare* < *particeps* "taking part" < *part-* "part"] —**par·tic·i·pa·tion** /paar tìssə páysh'n/ *n* —**par·tic·i·pa·tive** *adj* —**par·tic·i·pa·tor** *n* —**par·tic·i·pa·to·ry** /-tíssəpə tàwree/ *adj*

par·ti·cip·i·al /paàrti síppee əl/ *adj* having the form or function of a verb that can be used as both adjective and verb [Late 16C. < Latin *participialis* < *participium* (see PARTICIPLE)] —**par·ti·cip·i·al·ly** *adv*

par·ti·ci·ple /paárti sìpp'l/ *n* a form of a verb that is used to form complex tenses, as are "loving" and "loved" in English, and may also be used as an adjective [14C. < Old French < *participe* < Latin *participium* < *particeps* "sharing" (see PARTICIPATE); because it shares qualities of both adjectives and verbs]

~~particlar~~ incorrect spelling of **particular**

par·ti·cle /paártik'l/ *n* **1. TINY PIECE** a very small piece of something ○ *airborne particles* **2. TINY AMOUNT** a very small amount of something ○ *There wasn't a particle of truth in anything he said.* **3.** PHYS **OBJECT WITH FINITE MASS** a minute body that is considered to have finite mass but negligible size **4.** PHYS **BASIC UNIT OF MATTER** any one of the basic units of matter, e.g., a molecule, atom, or electron **5.** PHYS **SUBATOMIC UNIT** a unit of matter smaller than the atom or its main components **6.** GRAM **PART OF MULTIWORD VERB** an adverb or preposition that occurs as part of a multiword verb, e.g., "up" in "blow up" **7.** CHR **PIECE OF CONSECRATED BREAD OR WAFER** in the Roman Catholic Mass, a small piece of consecrated bread or wafer [14C. < Latin *particula* "small part" < *part-* "part"]

par·ti·cle ac·cel·er·a·tor *n* same as **accelerator** (sense 2)

par·ti·cle beam *n* a very narrow concentrated stream of charged particles such as electrons or protons, produced by a particle accelerator or a particle-beam weapon. Lenses are used to focus the beam and magnets change its direction.

par·ti·cle·board /paártik'l bàwrd/ *n* a board made from sawdust or wood particles bonded with a resin binder. The particles of wood used in particle board tend to be smaller than those used in chipboard.

par·ti·cle bom·bard·ment *n* a technique for inserting DNA from one organism into another by bombarding embryogenic cell cultures with DNA-coated metal particles

par·ti·cle phys·ics *n* the branch of physics that deals with the study of subatomic particles, particularly the many unstable particles produced in particle accelerators and high-energy collisions (*takes a singular verb*)

par·ti-col·ored /paárti-/, **par·ty-col·ored** *adj* having different parts in different colors [< obsolete *party* "multicolored," via French < Latin *partitus*, past participle of *partire* "to divide" (see PARTITION)]

par·tic·u·lar /pər tíkyələr/ *adj* **1. ONE OUT OF SEVERAL** relating to one person or thing out of several ○ *Which particular dress do you prefer?* **2. SPECIAL** special and worth mentioning ○ *had no particular objection to the plan* **3. EXCEPTIONAL** great or more than usual ○ *took particular care over it* **4. PERSONAL** belonging to one person and different from other people's ○ *a particular dislike* **5. FUSSY** having or demanding high standards ○ *She's very particular about standards of hygiene.* **6. CHOOSY** taking great care when making a choice ○ *They're very particular about the restaurants they go to.* **7. DETAILED** going into great detail about something (*formal*) **8.** LOGIC **NOT DEALING WITH ALL MEMBERS** in logic, used to describe a proposition that deals with some but not all members of a class ■ *n* **1. ITEM** an individual fact, item, or detail (*often used in the plural*) ○ *noted down his particulars* **2. SINGLE INSTANCE** an individual case or instance, as opposed to a more general theory **3.** PHILOSOPHY **REAL THING** in philosophy, an entity with definite spatial and temporal properties [14C. Via French < Latin *particularis* "concerned with small parts or details" < *particula* (see PARTICLE)] ◇ **in particular** specifically or especially

par·tic·u·lar·ism /pər tíkyələ rìzzəm/ *n* **1. COMMITMENT TO ONE GROUP** exclusive commitment to one group, especially when detrimental to the interests or well-being of a larger group **2. SELF-RULE PRINCIPLE** a policy of allowing political divisions within a state or federation to be self-governing, without regard to what effect this may have on the larger body **3. BELIEF THAT GOD BESTOWS GRACE INDIVIDUALLY** the belief that God chooses to bestow grace and salvation on some people, but not all —**par·tic·u·lar·ist** *n* —**par·tic·u·lar·is·tic** /pər tìkyələ rístik/ *adj*

par·tic·u·lar·i·ty /pər tìkyə lárrətee/ (*plural* **-ties**) *n* (*formal*) **1. EXACTITUDE** attention to detail and concern for accuracy **2. FASTIDIOUSNESS** the practice of taking great care when making a choice **3. USE OF DETAIL** the use of great detail in describing something **4.** same as **particular** *n* (sense 1) **5. SOMETHING CHARACTERISTIC** a peculiarity or characteristic **6. INDIVIDUALITY** the condition of being peculiar to an individual person rather than a group

par·tic·u·lar·ize /pər tíkyələ rīz/ (**-ized, -iz·ing, -iz·es**) *v* **1.** *vt* **FOCUS ON INDIVIDUAL** to make something become particular, e.g., by focusing on a particular person or thing **2.** *vt* **PROVIDE SOMETHING WITH SPECIFIC EXAMPLES** to provide something with specific examples ○ *unable to particularize her account* **3.** *vti* **GO INTO DETAIL** to go into detail about something —**par·tic·u·lar·i·za·tion** /pər tìkyələri záysh'n/ *n* —**par·tic·u·lar·iz·er** *n*

par·tic·u·lar·ly /pər tíkyələrlee/ *adv* **1. VERY MUCH** to a great degree ○ *Did you enjoy yourself? No, not particularly.* **2. MORE THAN USUALLY** more than usually or more than in other cases ○ *The trip to the museum was particularly interesting.* **3. SPECIFICALLY** as a specific example ○ *He particularly named you as one of the ringleaders.* **4. IN DETAIL** with great attention to detail

par·tic·u·late /pər tíkyələt, -làyt/ *adj* relating to or consisting of separate particles ■ *n* a substance that consists of separate particles, especially airborne pollution [Late 19C. < Latin *particula* (see PARTICLE)]

par·tic·u·late in·her·i·tance *n* a theory advanced by Gregor Mendel that parental genes do not blend in offspring but rather retain their characteristics from generation to generation

Par·ti·do Rev·o·lu·ci·o·na·ri·o In·sti·tu·ci·o·nal /paar teédō revōloossee ə naáree ō institoossee ə naál/ *n* a political body in Mexico that was in power from 1929 to 2000 [< Spanish, "Institutional Revolutionary Party"]

part·ing /paárting/ *n* **1. LEAVING** the act of leaving somebody or something, especially if the separation is sad or upsetting **2. SEPARATION** the process or action of separating or dividing **3.** *UK* HAIR same as **part** (sense 11) **4.** CRYSTALS **TENDENCY TO BREAK ALONG PLANE** the tendency of some crystals to break along a plane of weakness through deformation ■ *adj* **1. DONE WHILE LEAVING** done, made, or given when leaving ○ *a parting remark* **2. DEPARTING** leaving or coming to an end (*literary*) ○ *"The curfew tolls the knell of parting day..."* (Thomas Gray, *Elegy Written in a Country Churchyard*; 1751) **3. DIVIDING** used to divide or separate something ◇ **parting of the ways 1.** a separation of one person or group from another, e.g., after a disagreement **2.** a point at which a choice must be made between mutually exclusive courses of action

part·ing shot *n* a final, often hostile remark or gesture made by somebody who is leaving

par·ti pris /paártee preé/ (*plural* **par·tis pris** /*pronunc. same*/) *n* a preconceived opinion or bias [< French, literally "side taken"]

Par·ti Qué·béc·ois /paártee kay be kwaá/ *n* a political party of the province of Quebec that was founded in 1968 and advocates sovereignty for Quebec

par·ti·san[1] /paártiz'n, -zàn/, **par·ti·zan** *n* **1. BIASED SUPPORTER** a strong supporter of a person, group, or cause, especially one who does not listen to other people's opinions **2. RESISTANCE FIGHTER** a member of a group that has taken up armed resistance against occupying enemy forces ■ *adj* **SHOWING UNREASONING SUPPORT** showing strong and usually biased support for a cause, especially a political one [Mid-16C. Via French < Italian dialect *partisano* < Italian *parte* "part, side" < Latin *part-*] —**par·ti·san·ship** *n*

par·ti·san² /paártiz'n, ·zàn/, **par·ti·zan** *n* a weapon with a long shaft and a blade, used in the 16th and 17th centuries [Mid-16C. Via French < obsolete Italian dialect *partesana*, form (agreeing with *arma* "weapon") of *partisano* (see PARTISAN¹)]

par·ti·ta /paar teétə/ (*plural* **-te** /-tày/ or **-tas**) *n* a suite or set of musical variations, especially in baroque music [Late 19C. < Italian, "composition divided into parts" < *partire* "to divide" < Latin (see PARTITION)]

par·tite /paár tìt/ *adj* **1.** describes a plant part such as a leaf that is split almost to its base **2.** divided into or consisting of two or more parts (*usually used in combination*) [Late 16C. < Latin *partitus*, past participle of *partire* "divide" (see PARTITION)]

par·ti·tion /paar tísh'n/ *n* **1.** SOMETHING THAT DIVIDES SPACE a structure that divides a space, e.g., a wall built to make two rooms out of one **2.** DIVISION OF COUNTRY the division of a country into two or more separate states or countries ○ *the partition of India* **3.** DIVISION INTO PARTS the division of something into parts, or the state of being divided into parts (*formal*) **4.** LAW DIVISION OF PROPERTY the division of property among interested parties to settle a dispute ■ *v* (**-tioned, -tion·ing, -tions**) **1.** *vt* DIVIDE AREA WITH PARTITION to divide or separate an area such as a room by means of a partition **2.** *vti* SPLIT COUNTRY to divide a country into two or more separate states **3.** *vt* DIVIDE SOMETHING to divide something into separate parts [15C. Via French < Latin *partition-* < *partire* "to divide" < *part-* "part"] —**par·ti·tion·er** *n* —**par·ti·tion·ist** *n* —**par·ti·tion·ment** *n*

par·ti·tive /paártətiv/ *adj* **1.** SEPARATING separating or dividing something (*formal*) **2.** GRAM EXPRESSING PART OF SOMETHING describes a grammatical construction expressing a part of something, e.g., "of" in "a lump of coal" or the possessive form in "the dog's tail" ■ *n* GRAM PARTITIVE CONSTRUCTION a partitive construction [14C. Directly or via French < medieval Latin *partitivus* < Latin *partire* "to divide" (see PARTITION)] —**par·ti·tive·ly** *adv*

par·ti·zan *n* ARMS another spelling of **partisan**² ■ *n, adj* MIL another spelling of **partisan**¹

part·ly /paártlee/ *adv* to some extent, but not completely ○ *The road was partly blocked by a heavy snowfall.*

USAGE partly or **partially**? Both these adverbs mean "in part," "not completely," or "to some extent," but they are not interchangeable in all contexts: *Our first attempt was only partly* [or *partially*] *successful. He left early, partly* [not *partially*] *because he was bored. Her mother is partially* [not *partly*] *sighted.* ***Partly*** is always preferred when there is a distinct division into parts: *The houses were built partly of wood and partly of stone.* ***Partially*** should, of course, be avoided when there is any risk of confusion with its other sense of "in a biased way."

part·ner /paártnər/ *n* **1.** SOMEBODY WHO SHARES ACTIVITY somebody who is involved in an activity with somebody else ○ *his partner in crime* **2.** MEMBER OF RELATIONSHIP either member of an established couple in a relationship **3.** FELLOW PARTICIPANT IN SEXUAL ACTIVITY either of two people who have sex together **4.** ASSOCIATE IN DANCE OR GAME somebody who dances with somebody else, or plays with somebody else on the same side in a game **5.** BUSINESS BUSINESS ASSOCIATE an owner of part of a company, usually a company he or she works in, who shares both the financial risks and the profits of the business **6.** SOMETHING RELATED something that is related in some way to something else **7.** NAUT SUPPORTING TIMBER ON SHIP one of the timbers on a ship underneath the deck that is used to support the mast (*often used in the plural*) ■ *vt* (**-nered, -ner·ing, -ners**) BE SOMEBODY'S PARTNER to be somebody's partner, e.g., in a game or dance [14C. Alteration (influenced by PART) of obsolete *parcener* "sharer" < Anglo-Norman < Latin *partition-* (see PARTITION)]

part·ner·ship /paártnər shìp/ *n* **1.** RELATIONSHIP BETWEEN PARTNERS the relationship between two or more people or organizations that are involved in the same activity **2.** COOPERATION cooperation between people or groups working together ○ *scientists working in close partnership with colleagues overseas* **3.** GROUP OF PEOPLE WORKING TOGETHER an organization formed by two or more people or groups who work together for some purpose **4.** BUSINESS COMPANY OWNED BY PARTNERS a company set up by two or more people who put money into the business and share the financial risks and profits **5.** PARTNERS the people who make up a partnership, collectively

part of speech *n* a grammatical category or word group in a language to which words may be assigned on the basis of how they are used in sentences. The traditional main parts of speech in English are noun, verb, adjective, adverb, pronoun, preposition, conjunction, and interjection. Others sometimes used are article and determiner. [Translation of Latin *pars orationis*]

par·ton /paár tòn/ *n* a postulated elementary particle, proposed as a constituent of neutrons and protons [Mid-20C. < PARTICLE]

Par·ton /paárt'n/, **Dolly** (*b.* 1946) US singer, songwriter, and actor. She is known for her country-and-western songs, and for her appearances in several Hollywood movies. Full name **Parton, Dolly Rebecca**

par·took past tense of **partake**

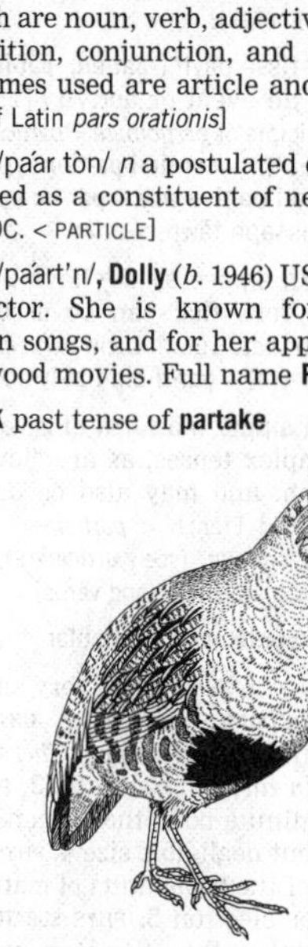

partridge

par·tridge /paártrij/ (*plural* **-tridg·es** or *same*) *n* **1.** MEDIUM-SIZED GAME BIRD a medium-sized, ground-nesting bird with variegated feathers, related to pheasants and grouse. Native to: Europe, Asia. Genera: *Alectoris* or *Perdix*. **2.** BIRD LIKE PARTRIDGE a game bird similar to the partridge, e.g., the ruffed grouse or bobwhite. Native to: North America. **3.** PARTRIDGE FLESH the flesh of the partridge as food [13C. Via Old French *perdriz* < Greek *perdix*]

par·tridge·ber·ry /paártrij bèrree/ (*plural* **-ries**) *n* **1.** the scarlet relatively tasteless berry of a trailing plant **2.** a trailing evergreen plant with rounded leaves that bears partridgeberries. Flowers: small, white, fragrant. Native to: eastern North America. Latin name: *Mitchella repens*. [Early 18C. Because partridges eat the berries]

part-score *n* a score for tricks made in bridge that is not enough to win a game

part song, **part-song** (*plural* **part songs** or **part-songs**) *n* a vocal musical composition with parts for different voices, usually performed without accompaniment

part-time *adj, adv* for less than the usual amount of time associated with a particular activity ○ *a part-time job* —**part-tim·er** *n*

par·tu·ri·ent /paar toóree ənt/ *adj* **1.** OF CHILDBIRTH relating to the process or time of childbirth **2.** GIVING BIRTH about to give birth (*technical*) **3.** ABOUT TO PRODUCE on the verge of producing something or coming forth (*literary*) [Late 16C. < Latin *parturient-*, present participle of *parturire* (see PARTURITION)] —**par·tu·ri·en·cy** *n*

par·tu·ri·fa·cient /paar toóree fáysh'nt/ *adj* inducing birth or making it easier to give birth ■ *n* a drug that induces birth or makes it easier to give birth [Mid-19C. < Latin *parturire* "be in labor" (see PARTURITION)]

par·tu·ri·tion /paártə rísh'n, paárchə-/ *n* the act of giving birth to offspring (*formal or technical*) [Mid-17C. < late Latin *parturition-* < Latin *parturire* "be in labor" < *parere* "give birth"]

part·way /paárt wày/ *adv* some but not all of the way through a process or distance

par·ty /paártee/ *n* (*plural* **-ties**) **1.** SOCIAL GATHERING FOR FUN a social gathering to which people are invited in order to enjoy themselves and often celebrate something ○ *Are you coming to my birthday party?* **2.** POLITICAL ORGANIZATION a nationally based organization of people who share the same broad political views and goals, usually one attempting to elect members to government positions **3.** GROUP ACTING TOGETHER a group of people who are doing something together ○ *a search party* **4.** PERSON an individual (*formal*) **5.** LAW ONE SIDE IN LEGAL MATTER a person or a group of people acting together and forming one side in an agreement, contract, dispute, or lawsuit **6.** MIL GROUP OF SOLDIERS a detachment of soldiers given a particular task ■ *vi* (**-tied, -ty·ing, -ties**) BE AT PARTY to socialize and have fun at a party or similar occasion (*informal*) ■ *adj* HERALDRY OF TWO COLORS divided into parts of two different colors [13C. < French *partie* "part, side in a contest" < Latin *partita*, form of past participle of *partire* "divide" (see PARTITION)] —**par·ty·er** *n* ◇ **be (a) party to something** to participate or be involved in a particular activity

par·ty an·i·mal *n* somebody who frequently goes to parties and usually drinks large amounts of alcohol (*informal*)

par·ty-col·ored *adj* another spelling of **parti-colored**

par·ty·go·er /paártee gō ər/ *n* somebody who attends a party

par·ty line *n* **1.** the official policy of a political party or other organization ○ *always toed the party line* **2.** a telephone line shared by more than one subscriber —**par·ty·lin·er** *n*

par·ty man *n* **1.** a man who is a loyal member or supporter of a political party **2.** a sociable man who enjoys going to parties

party per·son (*plural* **par·ty peo·ple**) *n* **1.** somebody who is a loyal member or supporter of a political party **2.** a sociable person who enjoys going to parties

par·ty pol·i·tics *n* political activity as carried on by political parties, especially when devoted to furthering their own interests rather than the public's (*takes a singular or plural verb*) —**par·ty-po·lit·i·cal** *adj*

par·ty poop·er *n* somebody who spoils other people's fun, often by being unenthusiastic (*informal*)

par·ty school *n* a college, university, or similar institution where students are reputed to be more interested in fun and social activities than in academic study (*informal*)

par·ty wall *n* a wall separating adjoining homes, buildings, or pieces of land

par·ty wo·man *n* **1.** a woman who is a loyal member or supporter of a political party **2.** a sociable woman who enjoys going to parties

pa·rure /pə roór/ *n* a matching set of jewelry that includes earrings, a brooch, ring, necklace, and bracelet, and sometimes other items such as buckles [Early 19C. < French < *parer* "adorn, trim" (see PARE)]

par val·ue *n* the value printed on a security such as a share certificate or bond at the time of issue. It is used to calculate interest or dividend payments.

Par·va·ti /paárvətee/ *n* in Hinduism, a mother and fertility goddess, the wife of Shiva. She is thought of as the model Hindu wife and is often depicted with a conch, mirror, and lotus.

par·ve, **par·veh** *adj* JUDAISM same as **pareve**

par·ve·nu /paárvə noò, paárvə noó/ (*plural* **-nus**) *n* somebody who has recently gained wealth or social status but who is still considered as inferior [Early 19C. < French < past participle of *parvenir* "arrive" < Latin *pervenire* < *venire* "come"]

par·vis /paárviss/, **par·vise** *n* an enclosed area or portico at the front of a building, especially a church [14C. Via French < late Latin *paradisus* "enclosed space" (see PARADISE)]

par·vo /paárvō/ *n* VET same as **parvovirus** (sense 2) [Shortening]

par·vo·vi·rus /paárvō vìrəss/ *n* **1.** any one of a group of viruses that have a single strand of DNA, especially those causing disease in mammals **2.** a contagious disease of dogs caused by a parvovirus and marked by fever, loss of appetite, and diarrhea [Mid-20C. < Latin *parvus* "small"]

pas /paa/ (*plural* **pas** /*pronunc. same*/) *n* a step in dancing, especially in ballet [Early 18C. Via French < Latin *passus* "step"]

Pas·a·de·na /pàssə deénə/ **1.** city in southwestern California, home to the California Institute of Technology. Population: 139,712 (2002 estimate). **2.** city in southeastern Texas, a center of the oil industry. Population: 145,034 (2002 estimate).

Pas·ca·gou·la /pàskə go͞olə/ city and port of entry at the mouth of the Pascagoula River on Mississippi Sound in southeastern Mississippi. It is a major shipbuilding center and resort. Population: 25,990 (2002 estimate).

pas·cal /pa skál, paa skaál/ *n* a unit of pressure or stress equal to one newton per square meter. Symbol **Pa** [Mid-20C. After Blaise PASCAL]

Pas·cal /pa skál, paa skaál/ *n* a high-level general-purpose computer language designed to encourage structured programming [Mid-20C. Acronym < French *programme appliqué à la sélection et la compilation automatique de la littérature*; also after Blaise PASCAL]

Pas·cal /pa skál, paa skaál/, **Blaise** (1623–62) French philosopher and mathematician. He is considered one of the great minds in Western intellectual history. Among his achievements are the invention of the first mechanical adding machine and the development of the modern theory of probability.

> "Had Cleopatra's nose been shorter, the whole face of the world would have changed."
> [Blaise Pascal, *Pensées*; 1670]

Pas·cal's tri·an·gle *n* a triangular arrangement of numbers with a 1 at the top and at the beginning and end of each row, with each of the other numbers being the sum of the two numbers above it [After Blaise PASCAL]

Pasch /pask/ *n* (*archaic*) **1.** the religious holiday of Passover **2.** the religious holiday of Easter [Pre-12C. < Old French *pasches* (plural) < ecclesiastical Latin *pascha*, via Greek < Aramaic *pasḥa* < Hebrew *pesaḥ* (see PESACH)]

pas·chal /pásk'l/ *adj* **1.** relating to Easter **2.** relating to Passover (*archaic*) [15C. Via French < ecclesiastical Latin *paschalis* < *pascha* "Easter," ultimately < Greek *paskha*]

pas de deux /paà də dő/ (*plural* **pas de deux** /*pronunc. same*/) *n* **1.** a dance or dance sequence for two dancers **2.** a close relationship between two people or things involved in a joint activity or venture [< French, "step for two"]

pa·se /paá sày/ *n* a movement a matador makes with a cape to attract the bull's attention and make it charge [Mid-20C. Via Spanish < Latin *passus* "step"]

~~**pasenger**~~ incorrect spelling of **passenger**

pa·se·o /paa sáy ō/ (*plural* **-os**) *n* **1.** BULLFIGHTERS' PROCESSION the procession of matadors and other bullfighters into an arena before a bullfight begins **2.** *Southwest US* LEISURELY WALK a stroll, especially in the evening **3.** *Southwest US* STREET a street or boulevard, especially used in street names [Mid-19C. < Spanish < *pasear* "take a stroll" < *paso* "step" < Latin *passus*]

pash /pash/ *n* a brief infatuation for somebody (*dated slang*) [Early 20C. Shortening of PASSION]

pa·sha /paásha, páshə/, **pa·cha** *n* formerly, in Turkey and the Ottoman Empire, an official of high rank [Mid-17C. < Turkish *paşa*]

pashm /páshəm, púshəm/ *n* the fine soft wool of some goats, especially the Kashmir goat. Use: cashmere shawls, other garments. [Late 19C. < Persian *pašm* "wool"]

pash·mi·na /pash meénə/ (*plural* **-nas**) *n* **1.** a fine woolen fabric made from the hair of goats raised in the Himalaya region **2.** a shawl made from pashmina [Late 19C. < Persian *pašmīn* "woolen" < *pašm* "wool"]

Pash·to /púshtō/ (*plural same* or **-tos**), **Push·to, Push·tu** /púsh to͞o/ (*plural same* or **-tus**) *n* **1.** an official language of Afghanistan, also spoken in northwestern Pakistan, belonging to the Indo-Iranian branch of Indo-European languages. Native speakers: 21 million. **2.** somebody who speaks Pashto as a native language [Late 18C. < Pashto *paṣ̌tō*] —**Pash·to** *adj*

Pash·tun /push to͞on/ (*plural* **-tuns** or *same*) *n* a member of a people who live in eastern and southern Afghanistan and northwestern Pakistan [Early 19C. < Pashto *paṣ̌tūn*]

Pa·siph·a·ë /pə síffə ée/ *n* **1.** in Greek mythology, the wife of Minos, King of Crete, who fell in love with a bull and gave birth to the Minotaur **2.** a small natural satellite of Jupiter, discovered in 1908 [Via Latin < Greek, literally "all-shining"]

pa·so do·ble /paásso dő blay, -dáw vle/ (*plural* **pa·so do·bles** /-blayz/) *n* **1.** a quick ballroom dance using Latin American marching movements. The movements of the man are intended to symbolize those of a bullfighter with the woman as his cape. **2.** the music for a paso doble [Early 20C. < Spanish, "double step"]

pasque·flow·er /pásk flòwr/ *n* a small spring-flowering perennial plant with hairy leaves. Flowers: blue, purple, white. Native to: prairies of North America or chalky grasslands of northern Europe and Asia. Latin name: *Anemone patens* or *Anemone pulsatilla*. [Late 16C. Alteration of French *passefleur*, after French *pasque* "Easter"; because it blooms in the spring]

pas·qui·nade /pàskwə náyd/ *n* an often anonymous lampoon or satire that was traditionally displayed in a public place (*archaic*) [Late 16C. Via French < Italian *pasquinata* < *Pasquino*, statue in Rome where lampoons were posted] —**pas·qui·nade** *vt* —**pas·qui·nad·er** *n*

pass /pass/ *v* (**passed, pass·ing, pass·es**) **1.** *vti* MOVE PAST to move past or through a place or past a person ○ *We passed several groups of refugees on our way.* ○ *dark clouds passing overhead* **2.** *vti* OVERTAKE to overtake somebody or something and move ahead **3.** *vti* GIVE BALL TO PLAYER to throw, kick, or hit a ball or other object to another player during a game **4.** *vt* HAND SOMETHING OVER to hand something to somebody ○ *Could you pass me the salt, please?* **5.** *vti* TRANSFER SOMETHING, OR BE TRANSFERRED to transfer something such as property, authority, or responsibility to somebody, or be transferred in this way ○ *The house will pass to his daughter when he dies.* **6.** *vti* MOVE INTO DIFFERENT PLACE OR CONDITION to make somebody or something move from one place or condition to another, or move from one place or condition to another **7.** *vti* MOVE IN PARTICULAR WAY to move in a particular way in relation to something else, or move something in this way ○ *He passed his hand along the banister.* **8.** *vt* GUIDE SOMETHING to guide something into a particular position ○ *Pass the wire over that hook.* **9.** *vi* EXTEND PAST SOMETHING to extend through, in front of, or along something such as a road or area ○ *The road passes by the cemetery.* **10.** *vi* CHANGE to go from one condition, stage, or state to another ○ *It sheds its skin before it passes to the pupal stage.* **11.** *vt* SPEND TIME to use up time doing something ○ *We passed the time playing cards.* **12.** *vi* ELAPSE to elapse or go by ○ *Time passes quickly.* **13.** *vi* END to come to an end ○ *The storm finally passed.* **14.** *vti* BE SUCCESSFUL, OR DECLARE SOMEBODY SUCCESSFUL to be successful in a test or examination, or officially decide that somebody has been successful in a test or examination **15.** *vti* SUCCEED IN SUBJECT to meet the requirements of a course of study **16.** *vi* BE ACCEPTABLE to be of an acceptable standard ○ *It's not the best but it will pass.* **17.** *vti* APPROVE MEASURE OR BE APPROVED to approve something such as a law, measure, or proposal, or get official approval **18.** *vi* DIE to stop living (*formal*) ○ *She passed from this life in 1967.* **19.** *vi* HAPPEN BETWEEN PEOPLE OR THINGS to happen or be exchanged between two or more people or things ○ *A look passed between them.* **20.** *vi* NOT DO SOMETHING to decide not to do something that is suggested or not to accept something that is offered **21.** *vi* NOT RAISE BID to stop raising a bid in a card game **22.** *vt* EXCRETE SOMETHING to process and excrete something from the body ○ *had been passing blood* **23.** *vt* GIVE JUDGMENT to give a judgment **24.** *vt* STATE SOMETHING to say something or give an opinion ○ *She didn't pass any comment at all.* **25.** *vt* CIRCULATE FAKE MONEY to use fake money to pay for something ○ *passing counterfeit bills* ■ *n* **1.** DOCUMENT GIVING PRIVILEGES a document that entitles the holder to do something such as enter a place ○ *a press pass* **2.** ACT OF GIVING BALL TO PLAYER an act of throwing, kicking, or hitting a ball or other object to another player in a sport **3.** SUCCESSFUL GRADE a successful outcome in a test, examination, or course of study **4.** WAY THROUGH MOUNTAINS a way through or over mountains (*often used in place names*) **5.** ATTEMPT TO KISS OR TOUCH SOMEBODY an uninvited attempt to kiss or touch somebody in a sexual way ○ *made a pass at her* **6.** ACT OF GOING BY an instance of something going past, through, over, or around a place **7.** MOVEMENT a movement of something such as the hand in conjuring tricks **8.** OPERATION a single cycle or complete operation of something such as machinery **9.** DOCUMENT EXCUSING SOMEBODY a document that excuses the holder from normal activities **10.** ACT OF NOT DOING SOMETHING an instance of not doing something that is suggested or not accepting something that is offered **11.** STATE OF AFFAIRS a state of affairs, usually of an undesirable nature ○ *How did we let things get to such a pass?* **12.** FAILURE TO BID IN CARDS an instance of not bidding or raising the bid in a card game **13.** SWORD THRUST a thrust with a sword ■ *interj* I DON'T KNOW used to indicate that you do not know the answer to a question or do not want to give an answer (*informal*) ○ *"Guess who I've just seen." – "Pass!"* ○ *"How would you rate him as a manager?" – "Pass!"* [13C. < French *passer* < Latin *passus* "step"] —**pass·er** *n* ◇ **let something pass** to make no comment or intervention ○ *It was a deliberate lie, but I let it pass.*

USAGE See *past*[1].

pass as *vt* same as **pass for**

pass away *vi* **1.** to stop living (*often used as a euphemism for "die"*) **2.** to come to an end or no longer exist

pass by *vt* to leave somebody or something unaffected or uninvolved ○ *The usual troubles of adolescence seemed to pass her by.*

pass for *vt* to be so like somebody or something as to be easily mistaken for the real person or thing

pass off *vt* to cause somebody or something to be accepted under a different, false identity ○ *She managed to pass herself off as a doctor for quite a while.*

pass on *v* **1.** *vi* to stop living (*often used as a euphemism for "die"*) **2.** *vt* to convey or transmit something that has been received to somebody else

pass out *v* **1.** *vi* to lose consciousness **2.** *vt* to distribute things among a number of people

pass over *v* **1.** *vt* IGNORE SOMEBODY to ignore somebody's right to be considered for something, especially a job or a promotion **2.** *vt* DISREGARD SOMEBODY OR SOMETHING to fail to consider or include somebody or something **3.** *vi* DIE to stop living (*dated*)

pass up *vt* to decide not to take advantage of an opportunity

pass·a·ble /pássəb'l/ *adj* **1.** ACCEPTABLE good enough but not excellent **2.** ABLE TO BE CROSSED capable of being crossed or traveled on **3.** ABLE TO BE ENACTED describes proposed legislation that is able to be passed or made law **4.** SUITABLE FOR CIRCULATION describes money that is suitable for circulation as legal and valid —**pass·a·bly** *adv*

SPELLCHECK passable or **possible**? Do not confuse the spelling of ***passable*** and ***possible***, which sound similar. ***Passable*** means "acceptable" or "able to be passed (along, around, etc.)," as in *a passable essay, roads that are not passable in winter.* ***Possible***, the more frequent of the two words, means "capable of happening or being true," as in *the only possible explanation.*

pas·sa·ca·glia /paàssə kaályə, pàssə kállyə/ *n* a baroque musical composition in slow triple time over a repeated bass line [Mid-17C. Via Italian < Spanish *pasacalle* < *pasar* "to pass" + *calle* "street"; because often played in the streets]

pas·sade /pə saád/ *n* a movement in dressage in which a horse is made to move forward and back again on the same spot [Mid-17C. Via French < Italian *passata* < Latin *passus* "step"]

pas·sa·do /pə saádō/ (*plural* **-dos** or **-does**) *n* in fencing, a thrust made while stepping forward [Late 16C. < Spanish *pasada* < Latin *passus* "step"]

pas·sage[1] *n* /pássij/ **1.** CORRIDOR OR PATHWAY a corridor in an enclosed area or a path enclosed on both sides ○ *an underground passage* **2.** WAY THROUGH a path made for somebody through an obstruction such as a crowd of people **3.** PIECE OF WRITING OR MUSIC a section of a piece of writing, speech, or music, or a section of a painting or piece of artwork **4.** CHANGE OF PLACE OR CONDITION the act of going from one place to another or changing from one condition to another (*formal*) ○ *the team responsible for easing the passage of the new President-elect into power* **5.** PROCESS OF TIME PASSING the process in which time goes by ○ *the passage of time* **6.** TRIP a journey, especially one made by sea or air **7.** FACT OF TRAVELING the fact of traveling to a place or of being allowed to enter or pass through it ○ *The guides ensured our safe passage.* **8.** APPROVAL OF NEW LAW official approval of a new law or other proposal **9. TUBE IN BODY** a tube or channel in the body **10. SEA CHANNEL** a sea channel or strait (*often used in place names*) **11. BOWEL MOVEMENT** the act or process of expelling something from the body, e.g., emptying the bowels or the bladder **12. INTERCHANGE** an exchange of words, blows, or information between people or parties (*formal*) **13.** /pa sáazh/ BIOTECH **BIOLOGICAL TECHNIQUE** the technique of introducing a microorganism or cell into a host organism or culture medium as part of the process of maintaining or modifying it ■ *vt* /pa sáazh/ (**-saged, -sag·ing, -sag·es**) BIOTECH **TRANSFER BIOLOGICAL MATERIAL** to use the biological technique of passage to introduce a microorganism or cell [13C. < French < *passer* (see PASS)]

CULTURAL NOTE ***A Passage to India***, a novel (1924) by the British writer E. M. Forster. In Forster's last and most highly regarded novel, an Englishwoman traveling in colonial India accuses a local doctor of assaulting her during a visit to the mysterious Marabar Caves. The conflicting responses of English expatriates and local Indians to the subsequent trial highlight the limitations of their belief systems and the problems of human understanding.

pas·sage[2] /pássij, pə sáazh/ *n* either of two movements in dressage, one being a sideways walk and the other a slow deliberate trot ■ *vti* (**-saged, -sag·ing, -sag·es**) to perform a passage, or make a horse do this [Late 18C. Via French < Italian *passeggiare* "to walk" < Latin *passus* "step"]

pas·sage hawk *n* a hawk or falcon captured for hawking while on migration, especially a young bird in its first year of life

pas·sage·way /pássij way/ *n* BUILDINGS same as **passage**[1] *n* (sense 1)

pas·sage·work /pássij wùrk/ *n* **1.** parts of a musical work that are thematically unrelated to the whole but enable a performer to display virtuosity **2.** the performance or execution of passagework

Pas·sa·ic Falls /pə sày ik-/ fall on the Passaic River in northeastern New Jersey. Height: 70 ft./21 m.

pass-a·long *n* something that is passed along to the consumer, e.g., a tax, usually in the form of higher prices or rents, in order to prevent a loss of profit

pas·sant /páss'nt/ *adj* in heraldry, used to describe an animal shown walking to the left or right [15C. < French, present participle of *passer* (see PASS)]

pas·sa·ta /pə sáatə/ *n* a thick tomato sauce with a rough texture, sometimes flavored with herbs

pass·back /páss bàk/ *n* the act of passing the ball or puck to another player who is closer to the home goal

pass band *n* the range of frequencies that an electronic filter will allow to pass without attenuation. A voice band filter in a telephone exchange will pass a frequency band of approximately 3,000 cycles.

pass·book /páss bòòk/ *n* **1. RECORD OF BANK TRANSACTIONS** a book in which a record is kept of the money put into and taken out of a bank account **2. BOOK RECORDING CREDIT PURCHASES** a book in which a merchant records the items a customer has bought on credit **3. IDENTITY DOCUMENT** in South Africa during the apartheid era, a mandatory identification document issued to Black people that gave details of their ancestry and spelled out restrictions on their movements

Pass·chen·daele ◆ **Passendale**

pas·sé /pa sáy/ *adj* **1.** no longer current or fashionable **2.** no longer in prime condition [Late 18C. < French, past participle of *passer* (see PASS)]

SYNONYMS See ***old-fashioned***.

passed ball /pàst-/ *n* in baseball, a ball that ought to have been caught by the catcher but is missed, thereby allowing a runner to advance

passed pawn *n* in chess, a pawn with no opposing pawn in front of it on its own or on either adjacent file that could become a queen

pas·sel /páss'l/ *n regional* a fairly large group or amount [Mid-19C. Alteration of PARCEL]

passe·men·terie /pass méntree/ *n* **1.** a decorative trimming for clothing, e.g., one made of beads, braid, or lace **2.** the craft of making fringes, tassels, and cords to embellish soft furnishings and upholstery [Early 17C. < French < *passement* "decorative lace or braid" < *passer* (see PASS)]

Pas·sen·dale /paáss'n dàyl/, **Pass·chen·daele** /paásh'n-/ village in western Belgium. It was the scene of heavy fighting during World War I in October and November 1917.

pas·sen·ger /pássʼnjər/ *n* **1.** a traveler in a motor vehicle, aircraft, train, or ship who is not a driver or crew member **2.** somebody in a team who does not do his or her fair share of the work [14C. Alteration of French *passager* "somebody who makes a passage" < *passage* (see PASSAGE[1])]

pas·sen·ger pi·geon *n* a migratory pigeon that was abundant in the early 19th century but became extinct in the early 20th century from hunting and forest clearance. Native to: North America. Latin name: *Ectopistes migratorius.* [< PASSENGER in the obsolete sense "migrating bird"]

pas·sen·ger pro·fil·ing *n* the use of profiling to identify airline passengers who, based on appearance, behavior, and personal information gathered from databases, are deemed a potential threat to the safety of the flight

pas·sen·ger seat *n* the seat in the front of a vehicle next to the driver's seat

passe-par·tout /pàss paar tóó/ (*plural* **passe-par·touts** /*pronunc. same*/) *n* **1. SOMETHING GIVING ACCESS** something that gives unrestricted access to a building or area, e.g., a master key **2. PICTURE FRAME** a decorated mat around a framed picture **3. ADHESIVE TAPE OR GUMMED PAPER** adhesive tape or gummed paper used to attach pictures to mats before framing [< French, literally "pass everywhere"]

pas·ser-by (*plural* **pas·sers-by**) *n* somebody who happens to be going past a place, especially on foot

pas·ser·ine /pássə rīn, -reen/ *adj* relating or belonging to a group of mainly perching songbirds, which forms the largest order of birds including more than half of all bird species. Order: Passeriformes. ■ *n* any bird that belongs to the passerine order [Late 18C. < late Latin *passerinus* "of sparrows" < Latin *passer* "sparrow"]

pas seul /paa sṓl/ (*plural* **pas seuls** /*pronunc. same*/) *n* a dance or passage performed by a single dancer [< French, "solo step"]

pass-fail *adj* relating to a system of grading in which a student simply passes or fails, without a grade such as A, B, or C being awarded —**pass-fail** *n*

pas·si·ble /pássəb'l/ *adj* emotionally sensitive, especially to the point of feeling pain (*formal*) [14C. Via French < Latin *passibilis* < past participle of *pati* "feel, suffer"] —**pas·si·bil·i·ty** /pàssə bíllətee/ *n* —**pas·si·bly** *adv*

pas·sim /pássim/ *adv* used especially in footnotes to indicate that what is being referred to occurs in various places in a book or other text [Early 19C. < Latin, "so as to be scattered" < *passus*, past participle of *pandere* "spread out"]

pass·ing /pássing/ *adj* **1. GOING PAST** moving past ○ *a passing car* **2. TRANSITORY** superficial and not long-lasting **3. BRIEF** done briefly and without much attention being paid ○ *a passing interest* ■ *n* **1. CEASING TO EXIST** the fact or process of something becoming obsolete or ceasing to exist **2. PROCESS OF TIME GOING BY** the elapsing of time **3. PLACE WHERE IT IS POSSIBLE TO PASS** a place where it is possible to pass or cross something **4.** same as **death** (sense 1) (*euphemistic*)

SYNONYMS See ***temporary***.

pass·ing bell *n* a bell rung to mark a death or a funeral

pass·ing lane *n* a lane designated for drivers who want to pass slower traffic

pass·ing note, pass·ing tone *n* a note played between two chords or pitches to provide a melodic transition from one to the other

pass·ing shot *n* in racket games such as tennis, a winning shot that passes beyond the reach of an opponent at the net

pass·ing tone *n* MUSIC same as **passing note**

pas·sion /pásh'n/ *n* **1. INTENSE EMOTION** intense or overpowering emotion such as love, joy, hatred, or anger ○ *Try and play it with a little more passion.* **2. STRONG SEXUAL DESIRE** strong sexual desire and excitement **3. INTENSE ENTHUSIASM** a strong liking or enthusiasm for a subject or activity ○ *a passion for music* **4. OBJECT OF ENTHUSIASM** the object of somebody's intense interest or enthusiasm ○ *Orchids are my passion.* **5. OUTBURST OF EMOTION** a sudden outburst of an emotion such as rage, hatred, or jealousy ○ *He flew into a passion.* ■ **pas·sions** *npl* **EMOTIONS** strong emotions, especially as distinct from reason or intellect ○ *a meeting at which passions were running high* [12C. Via French < ecclesiastical Latin *passion-* "suffering, affection" < Latin *pati* "feel, suffer"]

SYNONYMS See ***love***.

Pas·sion *n* **1.** in the Bible, the sufferings of Jesus Christ from the Last Supper until his crucifixion **2.** an account of the Passion in the Gospels

pas·sion·al /páshən'l, páshnəl/ *adj* relating to passion or arising from passion (*literary*) ■ *n* a book that tells of the sufferings of Christian saints and martyrs [15C. < Latin *passionalis* < *passion-* (see PASSION)]

pas·sion·ate /pásh'nət/ *adj* **1. SHOWING SEXUAL DESIRE** expressing or showing strong sexual desire ○ *a passionate kiss* **2. SHOWING INTENSE EMOTION** expressing intense feeling ○ *a passionate speech on human rights* **3. ENTHUSIASTIC** having a keen enthusiasm or intense desire for something ○ *a passionate golfer* **4. HAVING STRONG EMOTIONS** tending to have strong feelings, especially of love, desire, or enthusiasm ○ *a fiery, passionate personality* **5. QUICK-TEMPERED** easily made angry —**pas·sion·ate·ly** *adv*

passionflower

pas·sion·flow·er /pásh'n flòwr/ *n* a climbing vine with large flowers and edible fruit. Native to: Central, South America. Genus: *Passiflora.* [Mid-17C. Because parts of the flower are taken as symbols of Jesus Christ's Passion]

pas·sion fruit *n* the edible fruit of a passionflower, especially a granadilla

Pas·sion·ist /pásh'nist/ *n* a member of a Roman Catholic mendicant order devoted to commemorating the Passion of Jesus Christ by missionary work. The order was founded in Italy in 1720 by St. Paul of the Cross.

pas·sion·less /pásh'nələss/ *adj* **1.** empty of romantic or sexual love ○ *a passionless movie* **2.** feeling or expressing no emotion —**pas·sion·less·ness** *n*

Pas·sion play *n* a play that tells the story of the sufferings and crucifixion of Jesus Christ

Pas·sion Sun·day *n* **1.** the fifth Sunday in Lent, or the second Sunday before Easter, when Passiontide begins **2.** CHR same as **Palm Sunday**

Pas·sion·tide /pásh'n tīd/ *n* the last two weeks of Lent, from Passion Sunday to Easter

Pas·sion Week *n* **1.** the second week before Easter, from Passion Sunday to the Sunday before Easter **2.** Holy Week

pas·si·vate /pássə vàyt/ (**-vat·ed, -vat·ing, -vates**) *vt* to coat the surface of a metal with a substance that protects it against corrosion

pas·sive /pássiv/ *adj* **1. NOT ACTIVELY TAKING PART** tending not to participate actively, and usually letting others make decisions **2. OBEYING READILY** tending to submit or obey without arguing or resisting **3. NOT OPERATIONAL** not working or operating **4. INFLUENCED BY SOMETHING EXTERNAL** influenced, affected, or produced by something external ○ *passive solar heat gain* **5.** GRAM **EXPRESSING ACTION DONE TO SUBJECT** indicating that the apparent subject of a verb is the person or thing undergoing, not performing, the action of the verb, as in "We were given work to do" **6.** CHEM **UNREACTIVE** chemically inactive or resistant to corrosion **7.** ELECTRONICS **LACKING POWER SOURCE** describes an electronic circuit or device that does not contain a source of energy **8.** FIN **NOT MANAGED BY INVESTOR** describes a form of investment that does not involve active management by the investor ■ *n* GRAM **PASSIVE VOICE** the passive voice, or a verb in the passive voice [14C. Directly or via French < Latin *passivus* < *pati* "feel, suffer"] —**pas·sive·ly** *adv* —**pas·sive·ness** *n*

USAGE The **passive** voice: In the active voice, the subject of the verb is the one who does the action described by the verb, and the object is the one acted upon: *The waiters will collect the plates.*

In the passive voice, this situation is reversed: the subject of the verb is the one acted upon by the verb, and the one who does the action – if mentioned at all – is relegated to a separate phrase, typically beginning with *by*: *The plates will be collected by the waiters.*

The passive can be used for a variety of purposes; for example, if the identity of the doer of the action is unknown, if the writer desires to conceal the identity of the doer of the action, as in *The vase was broken*, or if the writer wants to put special emphasis on the object or the action rather than on the doer of the action, as in *The bomb was defused by experts.*

Formal writing uses the passive more frequently than informal writing, and the passive is normal style in some scientific and technical writing. However, in many contexts too much use of the passive can seem wordy or pompous, whereas the active is more direct and preferable. Compare: *Electrical appliances may be found on the fourth floor* with *You can find electrical appliances on the fourth floor*, or *Electrical appliances are on the fourth floor.*

Avoid mixing passive and active voices in sentences like this: *Our commuter railroad needs more money for major improvements, and it will probably be raised by fare increases.* Say instead: *Our commuter railroad needs more money for major improvements, and will probably raise it by fare increases.*

A less commonly encountered but awkward construction is called the *double passive*. The writer has inserted two passive constructions close together in the same sentence: *No legal remedy was sought to be obtained by the victim.* Avoid such constructions and say instead *The victim did not seek to obtain any legal remedy*, or even *The victim did not seek any legal remedy.*

USAGE See ***get***[1].

pas·sive-ag·gres·sive *adj* describes a personality type or way of behaving that seeks to manipulate others indirectly and resist their demands rather than confronting or opposing directly —**pas·sive-aggres·sion** *n*

pas·sive im·mu·ni·ty *n* immunity from disease acquired by the transfer of antibodies from one person to another, e.g., through injections or between a mother and a fetus through the placenta

pas·sive re·sis·tance *n* resistance to authority using only nonviolent methods such as peaceful demonstration or noncooperation —**pas·sive re·sist·er** *n*

pas·sive re·straint *n US* an automatic safety device in an automobile that protects a driver or passenger in the event of an accident, e.g., an air bag or a self-locking seat belt

pas·sive smok·ing *n* the involuntary breathing in of other people's tobacco smoke

pas·siv·ism /pássə vìzzəm/ *n* passive behavior or attitudes —**pas·siv·ist** *n*

pas·siv·i·ty /pa sívvətee/ *n* passive behavior, or the quality of being passive

pass·key /páss kèe/ (*plural* **-keys**) *n* **1.** same as **master key 2.** same as **skeleton key**

Pass·o·ver /páss ōvər/ *n* a Jewish festival marking the exodus of the Hebrews from captivity in Egypt. Date: seven or eight days from 14th day of Nisan. [Mid-16C. Translation of Hebrew *pesaḥ* (see PESACH)]

pass·port /páss pàwrt/ *n* **1. IDENTIFICATION DOCUMENT** an official document issued by the government of a country to a citizen that identifies the bearer and gives permission to travel to and from that country **2. ANY AUTHORIZATION TO TRAVEL** any authorization or official permission to travel in or through a country **3. MEANS OF ACCESS** something that grants somebody access to something ○ *Education can be the passport to a more fulfilling life.* [15C. < French *passeport* "pass the seaport"]

pass-through *n* **1.** an opening in a wall, often connecting a kitchen and dining area, through which food and dishes can be passed **2.** ECON same as **pass-along**

~~**passtime**~~ incorrect spelling of **pastime**

pass·word /páss wùrd/ *n* **1.** a secret word or phrase that somebody must use to gain entry to a place **2.** a sequence of characters that must be keyed in to gain access to all or part of a computer system or program ○ *Don't let anyone know your password.*

past[1] /past/ CORE MEANING: a grammatical word describing movement that involves passing or going beyond somebody or something ○ (prep) *Walk past the library and you'll arrive at the park.* ○ (adv) *She walked right past without saying a word to us.*

1. *prep* **ON FARTHER SIDE OF SOMETHING** on the farther side of or beyond something ○ *the bakery past the school* **2.** *prep, adv* **LATER** later than a particular time ○ *It's twenty past seven.* ○ *past his bedtime* **3.** *prep* **BEYOND NUMBER, AMOUNT, OR POINT** beyond a particular number, amount, or point, especially a point at which something can be done ○ *Do what you like; I'm past caring.* [13C. Past participle of PASS] ◇ **not put it past somebody** to believe that somebody is quite capable of doing something, usually something disreputable or outrageous (*informal*)

USAGE past or **passed**? Do not confuse these two words. Consider these examples: *He passed me at 80 mph; She is the past president of our sorority.* In the first example, the past tense of the verb *pass*, which is ***passed***, is required: *He passed me....* In the second sentence the adjective ***past*** ("onetime, former") is required: *She is the past president....*

past[2] /past/ *adj* **1. ELAPSED** gone by or preceding or leading up to the present ○ *in times past* ○ *during the past few days* **2. OF EARLIER TIME** having existed, occurred, been done, or been gained in a previous time ○ *my past experience* **3. ONETIME** having formerly occupied a particular position ○ *a gathering of past presidents* ○ *a past love of his* **4.** GRAM **EXPRESSING PREVIOUS ACTION** describes a verb form or tense that expresses an action that took place previously ■ *n* **1. TIME BEFORE PRESENT** the time before the present or the events that happened during that time **2. SOMEBODY'S PREVIOUS HISTORY** everything that has happened previously to somebody or something ○ *She has a mysterious past.* **3. SHAMEFUL HISTORY** a shameful or scandalous earlier period in somebody's life **4.** GRAM **PAST TENSE** the past tense of a language, or a verb form in the past tense [13C. Past participle of PASS] —**past·ness** *n*

pas·ta /paástə/ *n* **1.** a fresh or dried food of Italian origin made from a dough, usually of flour, eggs, and water, and produced in a variety of shapes and forms, e.g., in strings, ribbons, or sheets or as spaghetti, macaroni, or lasagne **2.** a dish made with cooked pasta [Late 19C. Via Italian < late Latin (see PASTE[1])]

paste[1] /payst/ *n* **1. ADHESIVE MIXTURE** a soft mixture of flour and water or starch and water used as an adhesive, especially for sticking paper to something **2. FOOD SPREAD** a soft food product that can be spread on something such as bread ○ *anchovy paste* **3. SEMISOLID MIXTURE** a soft mass or mixture with a consistency between a liquid and a solid **4. PASTRY DOUGH** pastry dough usually made with shortening and used especially to make pie crusts **5. GLASS FOR IMITATION GEMS** a hard, brilliant glass used to make imitation jewels **6. PORCELAIN CLAY** the clay mixture used to make porcelain ■ *vt* (**past·ed, past·ing, pastes**) **1. GLUE SOMETHING TO SOMETHING ELSE** to stick things together using paste **2. COVER SURFACE WITH PASTE** to cover a surface by sticking things to it with paste **3.** COMPUT **PLACE TEXT IN DOCUMENT ELECTRONICALLY** to place text, data, or an image into a document electronically [13C. Via French < late Latin *pasta* "dough, paste" < Greek *pastē* "barley porridge" < *passein* "to sprinkle"] —**past·er** *n*

paste up *vt* to take printed pages or proofs and stick them onto separate sheets of paper so that they can be read and amended

paste[2] /payst/ (**past·ed, past·ing, pastes**) *vt* to give somebody a severe beating or defeat somebody heavily (*informal*) [Mid-19C. Probably alteration of BASTE[3]]

paste·board /páyst bàwrd/ *n* **1. THICK STIFF PAPER** a stiff board made either of sheets of paper pasted together or of layers of paper pulp pressed together **2. CARD** a ticket, card, or playing card (*informal*) ■ *adj* **1. FLIMSY** not of good quality, or not very substantial ○ *pasteboard houses* **2. FAKE** intended to pass for the genuine article

pas·tel /pa stél/ *adj* **PALE IN COLOR** having a pale soft color ■ *n* **1. PALE COLOR** a pale soft color **2. PASTE USED FOR MAKING CRAYONS** a paste of powdered pigment and gum, used for making crayons **3. CRAYON** an artist's crayon made of pastel **4. DRAWING** something drawn using pastel crayons **5. ART USING PASTELS** the technique or process of drawing with pastels [Late 16C. Directly or via French < Italian *pastello* "small amount of paste" < *pasta* "paste" < late Latin (see PASTE[1])] —**pas·tel·ist** *n*

pas·tern /pástərn/ *n* **1.** the part of a horse's foot between the fetlock and the top of the hoof **2.** either of two bones in a horse's foot that connect the hoof with the fetlock [13C. < Old French *pasturon* < *pasture* "hobble for a pastured animal" < Latin *pascere* "to feed"]

Pas·ter·nak /pástər nàk/, **Boris** (1890–1960) Soviet poet and author. His novel *Doctor Zhivago* (1956) was not published in Russia until 1987 because of its critical approach to Soviet Communism. The Soviet government forced him to decline the Nobel Prize in literature (1958). Full name **Pasternak, Boris Leonidovich**

> "Man is born to live, not to prepare for life."
> [Boris Pasternak, *Doctor Zhivago*; 1956]

paste-up *n* **1. SHEETS WITH PAGES FOR CHECKING** a number of sheets of paper onto which printed pages or proofs have been pasted for checking **2. PREPARATION FOR PRINTING PLATES** cards on which pieces of typesetting or artwork have been pasted to be photographed for making printing plates **3. TECHNIQUE OF MAKING PASTE-UPS** the technique or process of making paste-ups (*often used before a noun*) ○ *a paste-up artist*

Pas·teur /pass túr, pass týúr, paass-/, **Louis** (1822–95) French scientist. He invented the process of pasteurization and developed vaccines to induce immunity against viral diseases.

> "When meditating over a disease, I never think of finding a remedy for it, but, instead, a means of preventing it."
> [Louis Pasteur, *Address to the Fraternal Association of Former Students of the École Centrale des Arts et Manufactures, Paris*; May 15, 1884]

pas·teur·ize /páschə rìz, pástə-/ (**-ized, -iz·ing, -iz·es**) *vt* to make a food product, especially milk, safer to drink or eat and improve its keeping qualities by heating it in order to destroy harmful bacteria [Late 19C. After Louis PASTEUR] —**pas·teur·i·za·tion** /pàschəri záysh'n, pàstəri-/ *n* —**pas·teur·iz·er** *n*

Pas·teur treat·ment /pass túr-/ *n* a treatment for somebody infected with rabies in which increasingly strong injections of a less infective form of the virus are given to produce antibodies against it [Late 19C. After Louis PASTEUR]

pas·tic·cio /pa stéechō, -chee ō, paa-/ (*plural* **-ci** /-chee/ or **-cios**) *n* ARTS, LITERAT same as **pastiche** [Mid-18C. < Italian, "pie, pasty" < late Latin *pasta* (see PASTE[1])]

pas·tiche /pa stéesh, paa-/ *n* **1.** a piece of creative work, e.g., in literature, drama, or art, that is a mixture of things borrowed from other works **2.** a piece of creative work, e.g., in literature, drama, or art, that imitates and often satirizes another work or style [Late 19C. Via French < Italian *pasticcio* (see PASTICCIO)]

pas·tille /pa stéel/ *n* **1.** a small flavored or medicated lozenge **2.** a substance, usually in tablet or paste form, that is burned to scent or fumigate a room [Mid-17C. Via French < Latin *pastillus* "lozenge, little loaf" < *panis* "loaf"]

pas·time /páss tīm/ *n* an interest or activity that somebody pursues in his or her spare time [15C. < PASS + TIME]

pas·ti·na /pa stéenə/ *n* tiny pieces of pasta often used in soup [Mid-20C. < Italian, literally "little pasta" < *pasta* (see PASTA)]

past·ing /páysting/ *n* a severe beating, or a complete defeat (*informal*)

pas·tis /pa stéess/ *n* a yellowish French liqueur flavored with aniseed, often drunk as an aperitif [Early 20C. Via French, "muddle, mixture" < late Latin *pasta* (see PASTE[1])]

past mas·ter *n* **1.** somebody with great experience and skill in doing something **2.** a former holder of the position of master, e.g., in the Freemasons

pas·tor /pástər/ *n* **1. CHRISTIAN MINISTER** a Christian minister or priest in charge of a congregation **2. SPIRITUAL ADVISER** somebody who is not a minister or priest but who gives spiritual advice to a group of people ■ *vti* **ACT AS PASTOR** to act as pastor for a church or congregation [14C. Via French < Latin, "herdsman, shepherd" < *past-* (see PASTURE)] —**pas·tor·ship** *n*

pas·tor·al /pástərəl/ *adj* **1. RURAL** relating to the countryside or to rural life ○ *pastoral living* **2. IDEALIZING RURAL LIFE** presenting an idealized image of rural life and nature ○ *pastoral poetry* **3. OF CLERGY** relating to Christian ministers or priests or their duties **4. GIVING ADVICE TO STUDENTS** involving the giving of personal advice and support to students on the part of a teacher as opposed to simply teaching them **5. USED FOR PASTURE** describes land that is used as pasture **6. OF SHEEP OR CATTLE** relating to or keeping sheep or cattle ■ *n* **1. DESCRIPTION OF RURAL LIFE** a literary work or painting that portrays rural life in an idealized way **2.** MUSIC same as **pastorale 3. LETTER FROM MINISTER** a letter written by a Christian minister or priest to his or her congregation **4. BISHOP'S STAFF** a staff carried by a Christian bishop as a symbol of office [15C. < Latin *pastoralis* < *pastor* (see PASTOR)] —**pas·tor·al·ly** *adv*

CULTURAL NOTE ***Pastoral Symphony,*** a composition (1808) by the German composer Ludwig van Beethoven. This is the name by which Beethoven's Symphony No. 6 in F major, op. 68, is popularly known. Beethoven described this widely performed work as a "recollection of country life." It describes a day's outing to countryside near Vienna and features peasant dances, bird songs, and a storm.

---

pas·to·rale /pàstə ráal, -rál/ (*plural* **-to·rales** or **-to·ra·li** /-ráalee/ or **-tor·als**) *n* **1.** a piece of music with a pastoral theme **2.** an opera with a rural story and setting, popular in western Europe in the 16th and 17th centuries [Early 18C. Via Italian < Latin *pastoralis* (see PASTORAL)]

Pas·tor·al E·pist·les *n* in the Bible, three epistles, the two to Timothy and the one to Titus, among those traditionally attributed to St. Paul.

pas·tor·al·ism /pástərə lìzzəm/ *n* **1.** a way of life that depends on raising livestock and living on its milk and meat **2.** a style in literary work or painting that portrays rural life, especially that of shepherds, in an idealized way

pas·tor·al·ist /pástərəlist/ *n* somebody who has a pastoral way of life

pas·tor·ate /pástərət/ *n* **1.** the office, term of office, or jurisdiction of a pastor **2.** pastors considered as a group

past par·ti·ci·ple *n* a participle that expresses past time or a completed action. It is used with auxiliaries to form perfect tenses in the active voice and all tenses in the passive voice. In the sentence "I waited until he had rung the bell," the past participle is "rung."

past per·fect *n* a verb tense formed with "had" that expresses an action completed at a more distant time in the past, that is, a time previous to the past time specified or implied elsewhere in the passage. In the sentence "She had thought seriously about the implications of what she was doing," the verb "think" is in the past perfect tense. —**past per·fect** *adj*

pas·tra·mi /pə stráamee/ *n* smoked and strongly seasoned beef, usually prepared from a shoulder cut, that is served cold or heated in thin slices [Mid-20C. Via Yiddish < Romanian *pastramă*]

pas·try /páystree/ (*plural* **-tries**) *n* **1. DOUGH FOR PIES** a dough made with flour, water, and shortening, used to make a base or covering for pies **2. FOODS MADE FROM PASTRY** sweet baked food made from pastry **3. SOMETHING MADE WITH PASTRY** a pie or small cake made with pastry [15C. < PASTE[1]]

past tense *n* a verb tense expressing something that happened or was done in the past. In the sentence "I felt very proud of them," the verb "felt" is in the past tense.

pas·tur·age /páschərij/ *n* **1.** AGRIC same as **pasture** *n* (sense 1) **2.** the grazing of livestock, or the right to graze livestock on a particular area of land

pas·ture /páschər/ *n* **1. LAND FOR GRAZING** grass-covered land used for grazing livestock **2. PLANTS FOR GRAZING** grass and other growing plants that are suitable food for livestock ■ *vti* (**-tured, -tur·ing, -tures**) **GRAZE** to graze, or put livestock somewhere to graze [13C. Via French < late Latin *pastura* < Latin *past-*, past participle of *pascere* "feed, graze"] ◇ **put somebody out to pasture** to impose early retirement on somebody (*informal*)

pas·ture·land /páschər lànd/ *n* an area of land that is used for grazing livestock

~~pasturized~~ incorrect spelling of **pasteurized**

past·y[1] /páystee/ *adj* (**-i·er, -i·est**) **1. UNHEALTHILY PALE** having a pale unhealthy appearance **2. RESEMBLING PASTE** resembling paste in consistency, color, or texture ■ *n* (*plural* **-ies**) **NIPPLE COVERING** either of a pair of small adhesive coverings for a woman's nipples, worn usually by erotic dancers [Early 17C. < PASTE[1]] —**past·i·ness** *n*

pas·ty[2] /pástee/ (*plural* **-ties**) *n UK* a turnover made from a folded-over round of pastry with a filling in the middle [13C. < Old French *pasté(e)* < late Latin *pasta* (see PASTE[1])]

PA sys·tem *n* same as **PA**[2]

pat[1] /pat/ *vt* (**pat·ted, pat·ting, pats**) **1. LAY HAND ON SOMETHING REPEATEDLY** to touch somebody or something repeatedly with the palm of the hand, e.g., to show affection or to congratulate somebody ○ *I patted the child's curly head.* **2. STRIKE LIGHTLY** to strike something lightly with the palm of the hand or something flat **3. SHAPE SOMETHING WITH HANDS** to shape or smooth something with repeated light blows with the hands or with a flat object ○ *patted the dough into shape* ■ *n* **1. LIGHT TOUCH** a light, usually repeated, touch with the hand to show affection or to congratulate somebody **2. LIGHT BLOW** a light blow with the palm of the hand or with a flat object **3. SMALL PIECE** a small piece of a soft substance, especially butter **4. SOFT SOUND** the sound made by a light blow with the hand or with a flat object, or by a light footstep [14C. An imitation of the sound made] ◇ **a pat on the back** an expression of praise or congratulation (*informal*) ◇ **pat somebody on the back** to praise or congratulate somebody (*informal*)

pat[2] /pat/ *adv* **1. EXACTLY** in an exact, accurate, or fluent way ○ *He has his part down pat.* **2. OPPORTUNELY** at the most appropriate time or place ■ *adj* **1. GLIB** so easily and readily produced as to suggest lack of proper thought ○ *pat answers* **2.** CARDS **NOT TO BE IMPROVED** describes a poker hand that is not likely to be improved by drawing additional cards [Late 16C. Probably "hitting the mark" < PAT[1]]

Pat /pat/ *n* an offensive term for an Irishman [Early 19C. Shortening of the name *Patrick*, common in Ireland]

pa·ta·ca /pə táakə/ *n* the main unit of currency of Macau. See table at **currency** [Mid-19C. Via Portuguese < Arabic *abū ṭāqah*, a coin]

pa·ta·gi·um /pə táyjee əm/ (*plural* **-gi·a** /-jee ə/) *n* **1.** a loose fold of skin between the fore and hind limbs in some mammals such as bats and flying lemurs, used as an aid to flying or gliding **2.** a thin fold of skin between a bird's wing and its shoulder [Early 19C. < Latin, "gold edging on a tunic"]

Pat·a·go·ni·a /pàttə gṓnee ə/ region of steppe and desert in southern Argentina and southeastern Chile, between the Andes Mountains and the South Atlantic Ocean. Area: 260,000 sq. mi./670,000 sq. km. —**Pat·a·go·ni·an** *n, adj*

Pat·a·go·ni·an Des·ert one of the largest deserts in the world, located in Patagonia, southern Argentina. Area: 260,000 sq. mi./670,000 sq. km.

patch /pach/ *n* **1. SOMETHING THAT COVERS OR MENDS** a piece of material used to cover, strengthen, or mend a hole in something ○ *an elbow patch* **2. SMALL AREA** a small area of something within a larger one ○ *a patch of ice* **3. SMALL GROWING AREA** a small area of land used for growing a particular crop ○ *a cabbage patch* **4. AREA OF CONTROL** an area under somebody's control or jurisdiction ○ *didn't like anyone encroaching on his patch* **5. PERIOD** a period of time in which a particular situation exists ○ *hit a bad patch* **6. EYE SHIELD** a pad worn over an injured or missing eye ○ *an eye patch* **7. COVER FOR WOUND** a piece of material used to cover a wound **8. DRUG-IMPREGNATED MATERIAL** a drug-impregnated adhesive pad worn on the skin to allow gradual absorption of the drug ○ *a nicotine patch* **9. SEWN-ON BADGE** a cloth badge sewn onto clothing as identification, a sign of rank, or to commemorate something **10. SOFTWARE BUG CORRECTOR OR UPDATE** a fragment of program code made available to fix a bug in a software application or to add a new feature before an updated version of the application is released ○ *a patch available on the Internet* **11. TEMPORARY CONNECTION** a temporary connection between parts of a communications system, especially to create a telephone hookup **12. ARTIFICIAL BEAUTY SPOT** a small piece of black silk or velvet worn on the face by men and women as an adornment in the 17th and 18th centuries ■ *vt* (**patched, patch·ing, patch·es**) **1. REPAIR SOMETHING WITH MATERIAL** to cover or mend a hole in something or to strengthen a weak place using cloth or a pasty substance **2. MAKE SOMETHING FROM CLOTH PIECES** to make something by sewing together pieces of fabric ○ *patched together a quilt* **3. AMEND COMPUTER PROGRAM USING PATCH** to fix or update software using a patch **4. CONNECT CALL** to connect one telephone or radio caller with another or transfer a call to somewhere else ○ *Patch me through to headquarters.* [14C. Origin ?] —**patch·er** *n*

patch up *vt* **1. MEND SOMETHING HURRIEDLY** to mend or assemble something hurriedly or as a temporary measure **2. BECOME FRIENDS AGAIN** to become friends with somebody again after an argument **3. GIVE TREATMENT TO SOMEBODY** to give somebody medical treatment for an injury (*informal*)

patch board *n* an electrical panel with numerous sockets into which electrical cords (**patch cords**) can be plugged to form temporary circuits

patch·ou·li /pə chóolee, páchəlee/, **pach·ou·li** *n* **1.** an aromatic oil obtained from a tropical mint. Use: perfumes, aromatherapy. **2.** a bush of the mint family whose leaves produce patchouli. Native to: tropical Asia. Latin name: *Pogostemon cablin.* [Mid-19C. < Tamil *paccuḷi*]

patch pock·et *n* a pocket made by sewing a patch of fabric onto the outside of a garment

patch test *n* a test for allergies in which small pads impregnated with allergens are applied to somebody's skin to check whether there is any negative reaction

patch·work /pách wùrk/ *n* **1.** needlework in which pieces of fabric are sewn together in a decorative way ○ *a patchwork quilt* **2.** something made up of many different parts ○ *a patchwork of fields*

patch·y /páchee/ (**-i·er, -i·est**) *adj* **1.** occurring only in patches rather than throughout an area, or consisting only of patches rather than a large expanse ○ *patchy fog* **2.** unpredictable and varying in quality depending on the place or time —**patch·i·ly** *adv* —**patch·i·ness** *n*

patd. *abbr* patented

pate /payt/ *n* the head, especially the top of the head (*archaic or humorous*) [14C. Origin ?]

pâ·té /paa táy/ *n* a paste made from meat, fish, or vegetables, often served as an appetizer [Mid-19C. < French, modern form of Old French *paste* (see PASTE[1])]

pâ·té de foie gras /paa tày də fwaa gráa/ *n* a rich pâté made from the livers of geese that are fattened specifically for this purpose [< French, "pâté of fatty liver"]

pa·tel·la /pə téllə/ (*plural* **-lae** /-lee/ or **-las**) *n* ANAT same as **kneecap** *n* (sense 1) (*technical*) [15C. < Latin, literally "small shallow dish" (from the shape) < *patina* (see PATEN)] —**pa·tel·lar** *adj*

pat·en /pátt'n/, **pat·in** *n* a shallow metal plate, often made of gold or silver, used to carry the bread at the celebration of the Christian Communion [13C. Directly or via French *patène* < Latin *patina* "shallow dish" < Greek *patanē* "plate"]

pa·ten·cy /páyt'nssee/ *n* **1.** the obvious nature of something **2.** the naturally open and unblocked state of an artery, duct, or other tube in the body

pat·ent *n* /pátt'nt/ **1. EXCLUSIVE RIGHT TO MARKET INVENTION** an exclusive right officially granted by a government to an inventor to make or sell an invention **2.** DOCUMENT GRANTING PATENT an official document setting out the terms of a patent **3.** INVENTION PROTECTED BY PATENT an invention for which a patent has been granted **4.** DOCUMENT GRANTING RIGHT an official document that grants a right to somebody **5.** GOVERNMENT GRANT a government grant that gives an individual title to public lands **6.** *US* LAND the land granted by a government in a patent ■ *adj* /páyt'nt, pátt'nt/ **1.** CLEAR OR OBVIOUS very obvious and not open to doubt ○ *his patent discomfiture* **2.** PROTECTED BY PATENT protected by a patent from being copied or sold by somebody else ○ *patent medicine* **3.** MED UNBLOCKED describes an artery, duct, or other tube in the body that is naturally open and unblocked **4.** LAW OPEN FOR INSPECTION describes a legal document that is accessible to anyone for inspection ■ *vt* /pátt'nt/ (**-ent·ed, -ent·ing, -ents**) **1.** PROTECT RIGHTS TO SOMETHING BY PATENT to obtain a patent on or for something, especially an invention **2.** GRANT PATENT TO SOMEBODY to grant a patent to somebody for something, especially for a piece of land [14C. Directly or via French < Latin *patent-*, present participle of *patere* "lie open"]

pat·ent·ee /pàtt'n tée/ *n* a person or group to whom a patent has been granted

pat·ent leath·er *n* leather that has been treated with lacquer to give it a hard, glossy surface [< the idea of protection]

pat·ent log *n* an instrument that measures a ship's speed or the distance it has traveled by means of fins that rotate as the instrument is dragged through the water behind the vessel [< PATENT "patented"]

pat·ent·ly /páyt'ntlee, pátt'ntlee/ *adv* in a way that can easily be seen or understood ○ *She was patently ill at ease.*

pat·ent med·i·cine *n* a medicine protected by a patent or trademark that can be bought without a prescription

pat·ent of·fice *n* a government office that evaluates patent claims and grants patents

pat·en·tor /pátt'ntər, pàtt'n táwr/ *n* a person or office that grants a patent

pat·ent right *n* an exclusive right to make or sell something that is granted to somebody by a patent

pa·ter /páytər/ *n UK* somebody's father (*informal dated*) [14C. < Latin, "father"]

Pa·ter /páytər/, **Walter** (1839–94) British essayist and philosopher. His *Studies in the History of the Renaissance* (1873) and phrase "art for art's sake" had an important influence on the aesthetic movement. Full name **Pater, Walter Horatio**

> "All art constantly aspires toward the condition of music."
> [Walter Pater, "The School of Giorgione," *Studies on the History of the Renaissance*; 1873]

pa·ter·fa·mil·i·as /pàytər fə míllee əss, paàtər-/ *n* a man in the role of father and head of a household [15C. < Latin, "father of a family"]

pa·ter·nal /pə túrn'l/ *adj* **1.** OF FATHERS OR FATHERHOOD relating to fathers or considered characteristic of a father **2.** RELATED THROUGH FATHER being on a father's side of a family ○ *her paternal grandfather* **3.** INHERITED FROM FATHER inherited or deriving from a father [15C. < late Latin *paternalis* < Latin *pater* "father"] —**pa·ter·nal·ly** *adv*

pa·ter·nal·ism /pə túrn'l izzəm/ *n* a style of government or management, or an approach to personal relationships, in which the desire to help, advise, and protect may neglect individual choice and personal responsibility —**pa·ter·nal·is·tic** /pə tùrn'l ístik/ *adj*

pa·ter·ni·ty /pə túrnətee/ *n* **1.** FATHERHOOD a man's role or status as a father **2.** ANCESTRY descent from a father ○ *children whose paternity has not been legally established* **3.** ORIGIN the origin or authorship of something (*literary*) [15C. Directly or via French < late Latin *paternitas* < Latin *pater* "father"]

pa·ter·ni·ty leave *n* time off work that an employer grants to a man whose partner has just given birth to a baby or who is adopting a child

pa·ter·ni·ty suit *n* a lawsuit brought by a woman against a man whom she claims is the father of her child and therefore liable for contributing to the child's financial support

pa·ter·ni·ty test *n* a medical test using DNA fingerprinting or other genetic information to determine whether or not a man is the father of a particular child

pa·ter·nos·ter /paàtər nóstər, pàytər-/ *n* **1.** *also* **Pa·ter·nos·ter** LORD'S PRAYER in Roman Catholicism, the Lord's Prayer, or a recitation of it **2.** LARGE BEAD IN ROSARY in Roman Catholicism, a large bead in a rosary, used to indicate when the Lord's Prayer is to be recited **3.** WORDS IN PRAYER OR ATTEMPTED MAGIC a set form of words used in prayer or in attempting magic **4.** NONSTOP ELEVATOR a doorless elevator in which compartments move continuously and people step on and off as they wish [Pre-12C. < Latin *pater noster* "our father," first two words of the Lord's Prayer]

path /path/ *n* **1.** TRODDEN TRACK a track that has been worn by the continual passage of feet **2.** SURFACED TRACK a surfaced track made for walking or cycling **3.** COURSE a route along which something moves ○ *the path of the Earth's orbit around the Sun* **4.** COURSE OF ACTION a course of action or a way of living ○ *her path to freedom and independence* **5.** ROUTE TO COMPUTER FILE the route that a computer operating system follows through the directories on a disk to locate a file, or the sequence of keyed characters that identifies this route [Old English *pæþ* < Indo-European, "to tread"]

-path *suffix* **1.** somebody with a particular disorder ○ *neuropath* **2.** somebody who practices a particular type of remedial treatment ○ *osteopath* **3.** somebody who possesses a particular ability ○ *telepath* [Back-formation < -PATHY]

Pa·than /pə taán/ (*plural same* or **-thans**) *n* a member of a people who live in Afghanistan, where Pathans are the largest ethnic group, and in parts of Pakistan [Mid-17C. < Hindi *Paṭhān*] —**Pa·than** *adj*

pa·thet·ic /pə théttik/ *adj* **1.** provoking or expressing feelings of compassion and pity **2.** so inadequate as to be laughable or contemptible (*informal*) [Late 16C. Via French and late Latin < Greek *pathētikos* "sensitive" < *pathos* "feeling"] —**pa·thet·i·cal·ly** *adv*

SYNONYMS See ***moving***.

pa·thet·ic fal·la·cy *n* the attribution of human characteristics to nature or to inanimate objects, as in the phrase "the angry waves"

path·find·er /páth fìndər/ *n* a discoverer of a route, especially through unmapped territories or uncharted areas of knowledge —**path·find·ing** *n*

patho- *prefix* disease ○ *pathogen* [< Greek *pathos*]

path·o·gen /páthəjən/ *n* something that can cause disease, e.g., a bacterium or a virus

path·o·gen·e·sis /pàthə jénnəssiss/, **pa·thog·e·ny** /pə thójjənee/ *n* the cause, development, and effects of a disease —**path·o·ge·net·ic** /pàthə jə néttik/ *adj*

path·o·gen·ic /pàthə jénnik/ *adj* **1.** causing disease, or able to cause disease **2.** relating to the causes and development of diseases

pa·thog·e·ny *n* BIOL same as **pathogenesis**

pa·thog·no·mon·ic /pə thògnə mónnik, pàthəgnə-/ *adj* used to describe a symptom or sign that indicates almost beyond doubt the correct diagnosis of a disease [Early 17C. < Greek *pathognōmonikos* < *pathos* "disease" + *gnōmōn* "judge"]

path·o·log·i·cal /pàthə lójjik'l/ *adj* **1.** EXTREME uncontrolled or unreasonable ○ *a pathological fear of heights* **2.** OF DISEASE relating to disease, or arising from disease **3.** OF PATHOLOGY relating to pathology, or used in pathology [Late 17C. < Greek *pathologikos* < *pathos* "disease"] —**path·o·log·i·cal·ly** *adv*

pa·thol·o·gy /pə thólləjee/ (*plural* **-gies**) *n* **1.** STUDY OF DISEASE the scientific study of the nature, origin, progress, and cause of disease ○ *plant pathology* **2.** PROCESSES OF A DISEASE the processes of a disease, observable either with the naked eye or by microscopy, or, at a molecular level, as inferred from biochemical tests ○ *the pathology of cholera* **3.** DISEASE a diseased condition ○ *a scan showing the area of suspected pathology* ○ *evidence of intestinal pathology* **4.** CONDITION THAT IS NOT NORMAL a condition that is a deviation from the normal [Late 16C. < French *pathologie* or modern Latin *pathologia* < Greek *pathos* "disease"] —**pa·thol·o·gist** *n*

path·o·phys·i·ol·o·gy /pàthō fìzzee ólləjee/ *n* the disturbance of function that a disease causes in an organ, as distinct from any changes in structure that might be caused

pa·thos /páy thòss, -thàwss/ *n* **1.** the quality in something that makes people feel pity or sadness **2.** feelings of pity, especially when they are expressed in some way [Late 16C. < Greek, "feeling, disease"]

path·way /páth wày/ *n* **1.** a path or route **2.** a sequence of biochemical reactions involved in a metabolic process

-pathy *suffix* **1.** disorder, disease ○ *retinopathy* **2.** remedial treatment ○ *hydropathy* **3.** feeling, perception ○ *telepathy* [< Greek *-patheia* < *pathos* "feeling, disease"] —**-pathic** *suffix*

pa·tience /páysh'nss/ *n* **1.** the ability to endure waiting, delay, or provocation without becoming annoyed or upset, or to persevere calmly when faced with difficulties ○ *I was beginning to run out of patience.* **2.** *UK* CARDS same as **solitaire** (sense 1) [12C. Via French < Latin *patientia* < *patient-* (see PATIENT)]

pa·tient /páysh'nt/ *adj* **1.** CAPABLE OF WAITING able to endure waiting, delay, or provocation without becoming annoyed or upset **2.** CAPABLE OF PERSEVERING able to persevere calmly, especially when faced with difficulties ■ *n* SOMEBODY GIVEN MEDICAL TREATMENT somebody who receives medical treatment [14C. Via French < Latin *patient-*, present participle of *pati* "suffer"] —**pa·tient·ly** *adv*

pat·i·na /pátt'nə, pə téenə/ (*plural* **-nas** or **-nae** /-nee/) *n* **1.** THIN GREEN LAYER ON COPPER a thin layer formed by corrosion on the surface of some metals and minerals, especially the green layer that covers copper and bronze and is valued for its color **2.** SURFACE SHEEN a pleasing surface sheen that develops on an object with age or frequent handling **3.** SUPERFICIAL LAYER a thin or superficial layer on something [Mid-18C. Via Italian < Latin (see PATEN)] —**pat·i·nat·ed** /pátt'n àytəd/ *adj*

pat·i·o /páttee ō/ (*plural* **-os**) *n* **1.** a paved area adjoining a house, used for outdoor dining and recreation **2.** a roofless inner courtyard typical of a Spanish-style house [Early 19C. < Spanish, "courtyard of a house"]

pa·tis·se·rie /pə tíssəree/ *n* **1.** a bakery that specializes in pastries and cakes **2.** sweet pastries or cakes collectively [Late 16C. < French *pâtisserie*, modern form of Old French *pastiserie* < *pasticier* "make pastry" < late Latin *pasta* (see PASTE[1])]

Pát·mos /paát moss, pátməss, -mawss/ Greek island in the southeastern Aegean Sea, one of the Dodecanese group. Population: 2,650 (1995). Area: 13 sq. mi./34 sq. km.

Pat·na /pútnə/ capital of Bihar State, northern India. Population: 1,707,429 (2001).

pat. off. *abbr* patent office

pat·ois /pát waà, pa twaà/ (*plural same*) *n* **1.** a regional form of a language, used informally and usually containing nonstandard forms **2.** the jargon used by a specific group [Mid-17C. < French, "native speech"]

Pat·ois *n* **1.** LANG same as **Creole** (sense 4) **2.** *Carib* in the Caribbean, the local popularly used vernacular, usually a French- or English-related Creole —**Pat·ois** *adj*

Pa·ton /páyt'n/, **Alan** (1903–88) South African writer and politician. His novels, in particular *Cry, the Beloved Country* (1948), deal with the racial tensions in South Africa during the apartheid era. Full name **Paton, Alan Stewart**

> "Wise men write many books, in words too hard to understand. But this, the purpose of our lives, the end of all our struggle, is beyond all human wisdom."
> [Alan Paton, *Cry, the Beloved Country*; 1948]

pat. pend. *abbr* patent pending

patr- *prefix* same as **patri-** (*used before vowels*)

Pa·tras /pə tráss, páttrəss/ port in S Greece, on the northwestern Peloponnesus. Population: 153,344 (1991).

patri- *prefix* father, paternal ○ *patrilineal* [Directly or via Latin < Greek *patr-* "father"]

~~patriachal~~ incorrect spelling of **patriarchal**

pa·tri·arch /páytree aark/ *n* **1.** HEAD OF FAMILY a man who is the head of a family or group **2.** RESPECTED SENIOR a respected and experienced senior man within a group or family **3.** BIBLICAL ANCESTOR in the Bible, a figure mentioned as the ancestor of the whole human race, e.g., Adam or Noah **4.** HEBREW LEADER in the Hebrew Scriptures, especially the book of Genesis, an ancestor or religious leader of the Hebrew people, e.g., Abraham, Isaac, or Jacob **5.** EASTERN ORTHODOX BISHOP in the Eastern Orthodox Church, a bishop of the sees of Constantinople, Alexandria, Antakya, or Jerusalem, and also of Russia, Romania, or Serbia **6.** DIGNITARY OF LATTER-DAY SAINTS a high dignitary of the Church of Latter-Day Saints with the power to invoke blessings, especially one of the Melchizedek order of priests [12C. Directly or via French < ecclesiastical Latin *patriarcha* < Greek *patriarkhēs* "head of a family" < *patria* "family"]

pa·tri·ar·chal /pàytree aárk'l/, **pa·tri·ar·chic** /-aárkik/ *adj* **1.** CHARACTERISTIC OF RULE BY MEN relating to or characteristic of a culture in which men are the most powerful members **2.** RELATING TO PATRIARCH relating to or held to be characteristic of a patriarch **3.** RULED BY BISHOP in Roman Catholicism, governed by a bishop —**pa·tri·ar·chal·ly** *adv*

pa·tri·ar·chal cross *n* a Christian cross with a second and shorter horizontal bar above the main bar

pa·tri·ar·chal·ism /pàytree aárk'l ìzzəm/ *n* institutionalized domination by men, with women being regarded as socially or constitutionally inferior

pa·tri·ar·chate /páytree aárkət, -aar kàyt/ *n* **1.** the office, term of office, area of jurisdiction, or residence of a patriarch of a Christian church **2.** SOC SCI same as **patriarchy** [Early 17C. < medieval Latin *patriarchatus* < ecclesiastical Latin *patriarcha* (see PATRIARCH)]

pa·tri·ar·chic *adj* ANTHROP, CHR same as **patriarchal**

pa·tri·ar·chy /páytree aarkee/ (*plural* **-chies**) *n* **1.** a social system in which men are regarded as the authority within the family and society, and in which power and possessions are passed on from father to son **2.** a society based on a system of patriarchy [Mid-16C. Via medieval Latin < Greek *patriarkhia* < *patriarkhēs* (see PATRIARCH)]

pat·ri·ate /páytree àyt/ *vt* to obtain control over a constitution that was formerly under the control of a colonial power (*refers to a former dependency*)

pa·tri·cian /pə trísh'n/ *n* **1.** SOMEBODY WITH UPPER-CLASS CHARACTERISTICS somebody with the qualities and manners traditionally associated with the upper class **2.** ARISTOCRAT a member of an aristocracy **3.** ARISTOCRATIC ROMAN a member of an aristocratic family of ancient Rome whose privileges included the exclusive right to hold some high offices ■ *adj* **1.** OF PATRICIANS relating to patricians, or belonging to a class of patricians **2.** ARISTOCRATIC characteristic of aristocrats or the upper class [15C. < French *patricien* < Latin *patricius* "of a noble father" < *pater* "father"]

pa·tri·ci·ate /pə tríshee ət, -àyt/ *n* **1.** the position or rank of a patrician **2.** the social class to which patricians belong [Mid-17C. < Latin *patriciatus* < *patricius* (see PATRICIAN)]

pat·ri·cide /páttri sīd/ *n* **1.** the murder of a father by his child or children **2.** somebody who murders his or her own father [Late 16C. < late Latin *patricidium* < Latin *pater* "father"] —**pat·ri·cid·al** /pàttri sīd'l/ *adj*

Pat·rick /páttrik/, **St.** (389?–461?) British-born Irish cleric. He spread Christianity throughout Ireland, and reorganized the church there. He is the patron saint of Ireland.

> "Christ beside me, Christ before me, Christ behind me, Christ within me, Christ beneath me, Christ above me."
> [St. Patrick's Breastplate]

pat·ri·cli·nous *adj* BIOL same as **patroclinous**

pa·tri·lin·e·age /pàttrə línnee ij/ *n* **1.** descent traced through the male line **2.** a group of people who are related to each other on the father's side of a family

pat·ri·lin·e·al /pàttrə línnee əl/, **pat·ri·lin·e·ar** /-ər/ *adj* describes family relationships traced through the male line, or societies in which only such relationships are recognized —**pat·ri·lin·e·al·ly** *adv*

pat·ri·lo·cal /pàttrə lṓk'l/ *adj* describes a custom in which a wife goes to live with her husband's family or people after marriage, or a society in which this custom prevails —**pat·ri·lo·cal·ly** *adv*

pat·ri·mo·ny /páttrə mōnee/ (*plural* **-nies**) *n* **1.** HERITAGE the objects, traditions, or values that one generation has inherited from its ancestors **2.** INHERITANCE FROM FATHER an inheritance from a father or male ancestor **3.** CHR ESTATE BELONGING TO CHURCH an estate or endowment that belongs to a church [14C. Via French < Latin *patrimonium* < *pater* "father"] —**pat·ri·mo·ni·al** /pàttrə mṓnee əl/ *adj*

pa·tri·ot /páytree ət, -òt/ *n* a proud supporter or defender of his or her country and its way of life [Late 16C. Via French < late Latin *patriota* "fellow countryman" < Greek *patris* "fatherland"] —**pa·tri·ot·ic** /pàytree óttik/ *adj* —**pa·tri·ot·i·cal·ly** *adv* —**pa·tri·ot·ism** *n*

Pa·tri·ot Act *n* a set of federal antiterrorism measures that lowers the standards of probable cause for obtaining intelligence warrants against suspected spies, terrorists, and other enemies of the United States

Pa·tri·ot Day *n* in the United States, a day commemorating those who were killed in the September 11, 2001, terrorist attacks on the United States. Date: September 11.

pa·tris·tic /pə trístik/, **pa·tris·ti·cal** /-tik'l/ *adj* relating to the early Christian writers such as St. Augustine or St. Ambrose whose works have helped to shape the Christian Church. [Mid-19C. < German *patristisch* < Latin *pater* "father"] —**pa·tris·ti·cal·ly** *adv*

pa·tris·tics /pə trístiks/ *n* the study of the writings and lives of the early Christian theologians (*takes a singular verb*) [Mid-19C. < German *Patristik* < Latin *pater* "father"]

patro- *prefix* same as **patri-**

pat·ro·cli·nous /pàttrə klīnəss/, **pat·ri·cli·nous** *adj* descended or inherited from the male line [Early 20C. < PATRI- + Greek *klinein* "lean"]

Pa·tro·clus /pə trṓkləss, pə trókləss/ *n* in Greek mythology, a friend of Achilles and a warrior in the Trojan War

pa·trol /pə trṓl/ *vti* (**-trolled, -trol·ling, -trols**) GUARD PLACE to guard or protect a place by moving regularly around it and watching it ○ *troops patrolling the border* ■ *n* **1.** REGULAR TOUR MADE BY GUARD a regular tour made of a place in order to guard it or to maintain order **2.** SOMEBODY CARRYING OUT PATROL a person or group that carries out a patrol **3.** MILITARY UNIT ON MISSION a military unit sent out for reconnaissance **4.** SUBDIVISION OF SCOUT TROOP a subdivision of a troop of Boy Scouts of America or Girl Scouts of America [Mid-17C. Directly or via German *Patrolle* < French *patrouille* < *patrouillier*, originally "walk through mud in a military camp" < Old French *patte* "paw"]

pa·trol car *n* same as **squad car**

pa·trol·man /pə trṓlmən/ (*plural* **-men** /-mən/) *n* a police officer who patrols a beat

pa·trol·o·gy /pə tróllәjee/ *n* the study of the writings of the Fathers of the Christian Church [Early 17C. < Greek *patēr* "father"]

pa·trol tor·pe·do boat *n US* NAVY full form of **PT boat**

pa·trol wag·on *n US* an enclosed police vehicle for transporting prisoners

pa·trol·wom·an /pə trṓl wòomən/ (*plural* **-wom·en** /-wìmmin/) *n US* a policewoman who patrols a beat

pa·tron /páytrən/ *n* **1.** REGULAR CUSTOMER a customer, especially a regular one, of a shop or business **2.** SPONSOR a giver of money or other support to somebody or something, especially in the arts **3.** ROMAN SLAVE MASTER in ancient Rome, somebody who had given a slave his or her freedom but still retained some rights over the former slave [14C. Via French < Latin *patronus* "protector" < *pater* "father"] —**pa·tron·al** *adj*

SYNONYMS See *backer*.

pa·tron·age /páytrənij, páttrə-/ *n* **1.** SUPPORT OF PATRON the encouragement, financial support, or influence of a patron **2.** POWER TO MAKE APPOINTMENTS the political power to grant privileges or appoint people to positions **3.** APPOINTMENTS ASSIGNED BY POLITICIAN the appointments or privileges that a politician can give to loyal supporters **4.** REGULAR PURCHASING FROM STORE the regular purchasing of goods from a store or business **5.** CONDESCENDING KINDNESS support or kindness offered in a condescending way [14C. < French < *patron* (see PATRON)]

pa·tron·ize /páytrə nīz, páttrə-/ (**-ized, -iz·ing, -iz·es**) *v* **1.** *vti* BE CONDESCENDING TO to treat somebody as if he or she were less intelligent or knowledgeable than yourself **2.** *vt* SUPPORT SOMEBODY to give money or other material support to somebody or something, especially in the arts **3.** *vt* BE REGULAR CUSTOMER OF BUSINESS to be a regular customer of a store or business (*formal*) —**pa·tron·iz·er** *n*

pa·tron·iz·ing /páytrə nīzing, páttrə-/ *adj* treating somebody as if he or she is less intelligent or knowledgeable than yourself —**pa·tron·iz·ing·ly** *adv*

pa·tron saint *n* a saint who is believed to be a special guardian, especially of a country, trade, or group of people

pat·ro·nym·ic /pàttrə nímmik/ *adj* describes a name derived from a male ancestor's name, especially one that adds a prefix such as "Mac-," or a suffix such as "-son," to the earlier name [Early 17C. Via late Latin < Greek *patrōnumikos* < *patrōnumos* "father's name" < *patēr* "father" + *onuma* "name"] —**pat·ro·nym·ic** *n*

pa·troon /pə tróon/ *n* the owner of a manorial estate in New York or New Jersey during the period of Dutch colonial rule [Mid-18C. Via Dutch < French *patron* (see PATRON)]

pat·sy /pátsee/ (*plural* **-sies**) *n* an easily victimized, cheated, or manipulated person (*informal insult*) [Late 19C. Origin ?]

pat·ten /pátt'n/ *n* a clog, sandal, or overshoe with a raised wooden sole to lift the wearer's feet above mud [14C. < French *patin* < *patte* "paw"]

pat·ter[1] /páttər/ *vi* (**-tered, -ter·ing, -ters**) **1.** MAKE QUICK TAPPING SOUND to make a quick light tapping sound on something ○ *The rain pattered against the window.* **2.** STEP LIGHTLY to move or run with short quick light steps ○ *She pattered across the floor in her pajamas.* ■ *n* TAPPING NOISE a quick light tapping sound [Early 17C. < PAT[1]]

pat·ter[2] /páttər/ *n* **1.** GLIB AND RAPID TALK the fast well-prepared talk of somebody such as a comedian or salesperson **2.** JARGON the language of a specific group or class of people **3.** SMALL TALK meaningless empty chatter ■ *v* (**-tered, -ter·ing, -ters**) **1.** *vi* TALK QUICKLY to speak rapidly and glibly **2.** *vt* REPEAT SOMETHING RAPIDLY to repeat something quickly in a mechanical way [14C. Shortening of PATERNOSTER]

pat·tern /páttərn/ *n* **1.** REGULAR FORM a regular or repetitive form, order, or arrangement ○ *a predictable pattern of behavior* ○ *local variations in voting patterns* **2.** DESIGN a repeated decorative design, e.g., on fabric ○ *a zigzag pattern* **3.** PLAN OR MODEL a plan or model used as a guide for making something ○ *a knitting pattern* **4.** PROTOTYPE an original design or model from which exact copies can be made **5.** GOOD EXAMPLE a model that is considered to be worthy of imitation **6.** REGULAR MANNER OF PERFORMANCE a regular or standard way of moving or behaving ○ *the flight patterns of birds* **7.** GUNSHOTS ON TARGET a series of marks made by shots from a gun on a target **8.** SPREAD OF SPENT PROJECTILES the dispersal of projectiles such as artillery shells and shrapnel on the ground around a target ■ *vt* (**-terned, -tern·ing, -terns**) **1.** MODEL SOMETHING ON SOMETHING to make something in such a way that it imitates the design, structure, or another quality of something else ○ *patterned the program after an earlier immunization campaign* **2.** PUT PATTERN ON SOMETHING to make something into, or decorate something with, a repeated decorative design [14C. Alteration of French *patron* "pattern, patron" (see PATRON)] —**pat·terned** *adj*

pat·tern bald·ness *n* hair loss that takes place gradually and in a symmetrical pattern on the head, thought to be a result of both genetic and hormonal factors

pat·tern·ing /páttərning/ *n* **1.** a design or configuration that is in accordance with a pattern **2.** a type of physical therapy in which the patient performs exercises designed to strengthen specific muscles and nerves

Pat·ter·son /páttərss'n/, **Percival** (*b.* 1935) prime minister of Jamaica (1992–). A member of the People's National Party, he was a longtime government minister before assuming the premiership. Full name **Patterson, Percival James**

USMA Archives, West Point

George S. Patton

Pat·ton /pátt'n/, **George S.** (1885–1945) US general. In World War II he commanded the Third Army in France. Full name **Patton, George Smith, Jr.**

"The quickest way to get it over with is to get the bastards."
[George S. Patton, *Speech to troops*; 1944]

pat·ty /páttee/ (*plural* **-ties**) *n* **1.** a small flat individual cake made from ground or chopped meat, vegetables, or other food **2.** a small pie or pasty **3.** *US* FOOD same as **patty shell** [Mid-17C. Anglicization of French *pâté* (see PÂTÉ), influenced by PASTY[2]]

pat·ty·pan squash /pàttee pan-/ *n* a variety of wheel-shaped summer squash with a ribbed edge. Latin name: *Cucurbita pepo.* [< PATTY + PAN[1]]

pat·ty shell *n* a decorative edible shell of baked puff pastry that is filled with other food such as meat, fish, vegetables, or fruit

pat·u·lous /páchələss/ *adj* describes branches that spread or expand from a central point [Early 17C. < Latin *patulus* "standing open" < *patere* "be open"]

Pat·wa /pát waà, pa twaà/ *n* LANG *Carib* another spelling of **Patois** [Form of PATOIS] —**Pat·wa** *adj*

pat·zer /pátsər, paàtsər/ *n* an inept player of chess (*informal insult*) [Mid-20C. Origin ?]

Pau /pō/ city in southwestern France. Population: 78,732 (1999).

PAU, P.A.U. *abbr* Pan American Union

pau·ci·ty /páwssətee/ *n* **1.** an inadequacy or lack of something **2.** a small number of something [14C. Via French < Latin *paucitas* < *paucus* "few, little"]

Paul /pawl/, **St.** (A.D. 3?–62?) early Christian missionary. He became a Christian after having a vision of Jesus Christ on the road from Jerusalem to Damascus. A major missionary of Christianity, he was also its first theologian. His life and teachings are described in the Epistles and the Acts of the Apostles in the Bible. Known as **Saul of Tarsus, Paul the Apostle** —**Paul·ine** /páw līn, -leen/ *adj*

Paul III /pàwl/, **Pope** (1468–1549) As pope (1534–49), he excommunicated King Henry VIII of England (1538) and authorized the establishment of the Jesuits. Born **Farnese, Alessandro**

Paul VI, Pope (1897–1978) As pope (1963–78), he presided over the Second Vatican Council and traveled widely to extend the Vatican's influence. Born **Montini, Giovanni Battista**

Paul, Alice (1885–1977) US feminist and social reformer. She founded the National Women's Party, campaigned for the 19th Amendment to the US Constitution, and proposed an equal rights amendment.

Paul Bun·yan /-búnnyən/ *n* in US folklore, a giant lumberjack who performs superhuman feats with his blue ox, Babe

Pauld·ing /páwlding/, **James Kirke** (1778–1860) US writer. His novels and plays draw on Native American material.

paul·dron /páwldrən/ *n* a piece of armor consisting of a metal plate worn on the shoulder [Late 16C. < Old French *espauleron* < *espaule* "shoulder" < late Latin *spatula* "shoulder blade"]

Pau·li ex·clu·sion prin·ci·ple /pòwlee-/ *n* a law of quantum physics stating that no two identical particles of a particular type **(fermions)** may occupy the same quantum state at the same time [Early 20C. After Wolfgang *Pauli* (1900–58), Austrian-born US physicist]

Pau·ling /páwling/, **Linus** (1901–94) US chemist and peace activist. He won the Nobel Prize in chemistry (1954) and the Nobel Peace Prize (1962) for his efforts to end nuclear testing. Full name **Pauling, Linus Carl**

"Science is the search for truth—it is not a game in which one tries to beat his opponent, to do harm to others."
[Linus Pauling, *No More War!*; 1958]

pau·low·ni·a /paw lṓnee ə/ (*plural* **-as** or *same*) *n* a deciduous tree with large heart-shaped leaves. Flowers: purple, white, bell-shaped, in clusters. Native to: China. Latin name: *Paulownia tomentosa.* [Mid-19C. < modern Latin, after Anna *Paulowna* (1795–1865), wife of William II of the Netherlands and daughter of Tsar Paul I of Russia]

paunch /pawnch/ *n* **1.** a large round protruding stomach **2.** ZOOL same as **rumen** [14C. Via Old French *pance, panche* < Latin *panticem* "belly, bowels"] —**paunch·y** *adj*

pau·per /páwpər/ *n* **1.** an impoverished person **2.** an impoverished person who is eligible to receive aid from public funds [15C. < Latin, "getting little" < *paucus* "little" + *parare* "get"] —**pau·per·ism** *n* —**pau·per·ize** *vt*

pau·piette /pō pyét/ *n* a piece of meat or fish that is cut or rolled out very thin, topped with a stuffing, then rolled up into a neat shape and cooked [Early 18C. Via French < Italian *polpetta* < Latin *pulpa* "pulp"]

pau·ro·pod /páwrə pòd/ *n* a small eyeless invertebrate with eleven segments and nine pairs of legs. Class: Pauropoda. [Late 19C. < modern Latin *pauropoda* "small-footed" < Greek *pauros* "small"]

Paus·a /páwzə/ *n* in the Hindu calendar, the tenth month of the year, lasting 30 days and usually falling within December and January. See table at **calendar**

pause /pawz/ *v* (**paused, paus·ing, paus·es**) **1.** *vi* STOP BRIEFLY to stop doing something briefly before continuing ○ *He paused for a moment and then went on eating.* **2.** *vi* STAY BRIEFLY to halt somewhere for a short time ○ *I paused to glance into a shop window.* **3.** *vi* HESITATE to wait intentionally for a short period before doing or saying something ○ *Selena paused. There was no easy way of saying what had to be said.* **4.** *vt* CAUSE SOMETHING TO PAUSE to cause an electronic or mechanical device to stop operating temporarily, e.g., by pressing a pause button ○ *Can you pause the video for a minute?* ■ *n* **1.** BRIEF STOP a temporary break in an activity **2.** SHORT SILENCE a brief moment of silence between words, sounds, or musical notes **3.** HESITATION a brief moment of hesitation or uncertainty before something happens or is done **4.** *also* **pause button** PAUSING MECHANISM a control on an electronic or mechanical device such as a video recorder that brings it temporarily to a halt **5.** MUSICAL SYMBOL FOR TIME EXTENSION a musical symbol indicating that a note, chord, or rest is to be held longer than the indicated time value. It is represented by a period with an upside-down "u" above it. **6.** LITERAT same as **caesura** (sense 1) [15C. Directly or via French < Latin *pausa* "stopping, cessation" < Greek *pausis* < *pauein* "stop, cease"] —**paus·al** *adj* ◇ **give somebody pause** to make somebody hesitate or reconsider

SYNONYMS See ***hesitate.***

pa·vane /pə vaàn, -ván/ *n* **1.** a slow dance that was popular in European courts in the 16th and 17th centuries **2.** the music for a pavane [Mid-16C. Via French < Italian *pavana* "Paduan" < *Pavo*, dialect name for Padua]

Pav·a·rot·ti /pàvvə róttee/, **Luciano** (*b.* 1935) Italian tenor. Known for his great vocal power and dramatic quality, he is associated with 19th-century Italian opera.

pave /payv/ (**paved, pav·ing, paves**) *vt* **1.** PROVIDE SOMETHING WITH HARD SURFACE to cover a surface with brick, concrete, or other hard materials in order to make it

AKG London

Luciano Pavarotti

suitable for walking or traveling on **2.** BE SURFACE FOR WALKING ON to serve as a hard covering for the surface of something and make it suitable for walking or traveling on ○ *Large stone slabs paved the path.* **3.** COVER to cover a surface with a flat, uniform material such as leaves or flowers [14C. Via French < Latin *pavire* "beat, tread down"] ◇ **pave the way (for something)** to prepare for and facilitate the progress of something

pa·vé /pa váy, pə váy/ *n* a jewel setting in which small stones are set very close together so as to cover the surface of the piece and obscure the metal base [Late 19C. < French, "paved"]

pave·ment /páyvmənt/ *n* **1.** PAVED SURFACE a paved surface, especially of a road **2.** CONSTR MATERIAL FOR PAVEMENTS material that is used to make a pavement, e.g., concrete or stone **3.** CIV ENG LAYERED SURFACE OF PATH the layered structure that forms the surface of a path, road, highway, or aircraft runway **4.** *UK* ROADS same as **sidewalk** [13C. Via French < Latin *pavimentum* "beaten floor" < *pavire* "beat, tread down"]

pav·er /páyvər/ *n* **1.** a stone or slab used to pave an area such as a patio **2.** somebody who installs or lays a pavement

pa·vil·ion /pə víllyən/ *n* **1.** OUTDOOR STRUCTURE a summerhouse or other often ornamental building in a park, fair, or garden, used for shelter and entertainment **2.** EXHIBITION TENT a large tent or other temporary structure used for displaying or exhibiting things **3.** BIG TENT a large and often extremely ornate tent **4.** ANNEX a detached building that forms part of a complex of a hospital or other large public building **5.** JEWELRY FACET OF GEM a facet of a brilliant-cut gem that comes below the girdle ■ *vt* (**-ioned, -ion·ing, -ions**) **1.** SET SOMETHING IN PAVILION to enclose or house something inside a pavilion **2.** ENCLOSE SOMETHING to enclose or completely surround something (*literary*) ○ *"Pavilioned in splendour, And girded with praise"* (Sir Robert Grant, *O Worship the King*; 1833) [Pre-12C. Via French *pavillon* "tent, canopy" < Latin *papilion-* "butterfly, tent"; because a tent was thought to resemble a butterfly's wings]

pavillion incorrect spelling of **pavilion**

pav·ing /páyving/ *n* **1.** MATERIAL FOR MAKING HARD SURFACE material used for making a firm hard surface, e.g., concrete or stones **2.** PAVEMENT a firm usually flat surface made of stone, brick, concrete, or other material **3.** CONSTRUCTION OF PAVED SURFACE the act of making a paved surface

Pav·lov /páv lov, -làwf/, **Ivan** (1849–1936) Russian physiologist. He became famous for his studies on conditioned reflexes with dogs. He won the Nobel Prize in physiology or medicine (1904). Full name **Pavlov, Ivan Petrovich**

Pav·lo·va /pav lṓvə, pávləvə/, **Anna** (1882–1931) Russian ballet dancer. Admired for the poetic quality of her movement, she performed many classic roles. The solo dance "The Dying Swan" was created for her. See illustration on next page

"Happiness is like a butterfly which appears and delights us for one brief moment, but soon flits away."
[Anna Pavlova. Quoted in "Pages of My Life," *Pavlova: A Biography*, A. H. Franks (ed.); 1956]

Pav·lo·vi·an /pav lṓvee ən, -láwvee-/ *adj* **1.** produced involuntarily in response to a stimulus **2.** relating to Ivan Pavlov and his work [Mid-20C. After Ivan PAVLOV]

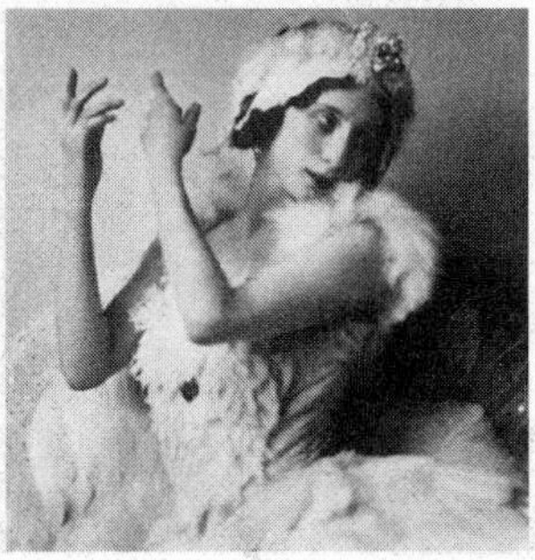

Anna Pavlova

Pav·lo·vi·an con·di·tion·ing *n* PSYCHOL same as **classical conditioning**

Pa·vo /páyvō/ *n* a constellation of the southern hemisphere containing the bright star Peacock. See illustration at **constellation**

pav·o·nine /pávvə nīn/ *adj* resembling a peacock, especially the colors and design of its tail (*literary*) [Mid-17C. < Latin *pavoninus* < *pavon-* "peacock"]

paw /paw/ *n* **1. ANIMAL'S FOOT** the foot of a four-legged mammal, usually having claws or nails **2. HUMAN HAND** a human hand, especially one that is large or clumsy (*informal*) ■ *vti* (**pawed, paw·ing, paws**) **1. STRIKE SOMETHING REPEATEDLY WITH PAW** to scrape or strike something repeatedly with a paw or hoof **2. TOUCH SOMEBODY CLUMSILY** to touch somebody or something, or caress somebody, roughly or rudely with the hands [13C. Via Old French *powe* < Frankish]

pawk·y /páwkee/ (**-i·er, -i·est**) *adj UK regional* witty or shrewd in a dry or sly manner [Mid-17C. < *pawk* "trick," origin ?] —**pawk·i·ly** *adv* —**pawk·i·ness** *n*

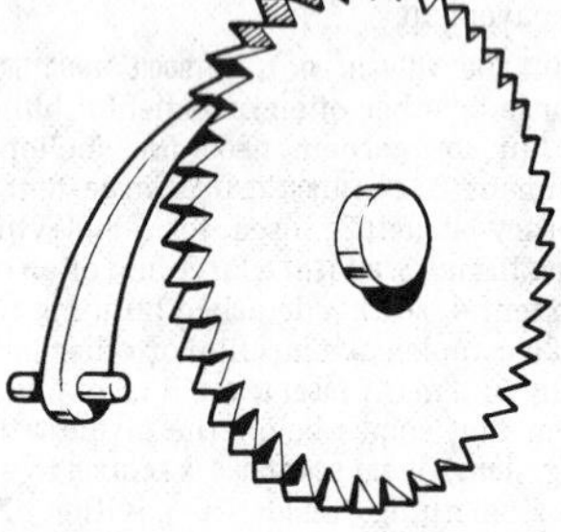

pawl

pawl /pawl/ *n* a hinged or pivoted catch, often spring-controlled, designed to engage with the teeth of a ratchet wheel to prevent reverse motion [Early 17C. Origin ?]

pawn[1] /pawn/ *vt* (**pawned, pawn·ing, pawns**) **1. DEPOSIT SOMETHING WITH PAWNBROKER** to leave something with a pawnbroker as security against money borrowed **2. PLEDGE SOMETHING** to stake or pledge your honor, life, or word on something ■ *n* **1. OBJECT DEPOSITED AS SECURITY** an object that is left as security with a pawnbroker in exchange for a loan of money **2. HOSTAGE** somebody who is held as security, usually as a hostage **3. ACT OF PAWNING** the act of pawning something [15C. < Old French *pan(d)* "pledge" < W Germanic] —**pawn·age** *n* —**pawn·er** *n*

pawn[2] /pawn/ *n* **1.** a chess piece of the lowest value that can move one square forward at a time, with an optional first move of two squares. It can take other pieces by moving diagonally and can be exchanged for any other captured piece on reaching the farthest rank of the board. **2.** somebody or something that is being used for the advantage of another person or organization [14C. Via Anglo-Norman *poun*, Old French *peon* < medieval Latin *pedon-* "foot soldier" < Latin *ped-* "foot"]

pawn·bro·ker /páwn brōkər/ *n* somebody who lends money at a fixed rate of interest in exchange for articles of personal property that are left as security

Paw·nee /páwnee/ (*plural same* or **-nees**) *n* **1.** a member of a confederation of Native North American peoples who lived in Nebraska and Kansas and who are now mainly dispersed **2.** the Caddoan language of the Pawnee people. Native speakers: 3,000. [Late 18C. Via Canadian French *Pani* < a Native N American language] —**Paw·nee** *adj*

pawn·shop /páwn shòp/ *n* a shop where articles of personal property may be left as security in exchange for a loan of money

pawn tick·et *n* a ticket that serves as a receipt for something that has been pawned

paw·paw *n* TREES, FOOD another spelling of **papaw**

Paw·tuck·et /paw túkət/ city in northeastern Rhode Island, at the confluence of the Blackstone and Seekonk rivers. Population: 74,033 (2002 estimate).

pax /paks, paaks/ *n* **1.** *also* **Pax STABLE PERIOD UNDER POWERFUL EMPIRE** a period of peace and stability under the influence of a powerful country or empire **2. KISS OF PEACE IN CHURCH** a kiss or other greeting given as a sign of peace during the Christian ceremony of Communion, especially in the Roman Catholic Mass **3. TABLET KISSED AT CHRISTIAN COMMUNION** a tablet bearing a representation of the Crucifixion that is kissed by participants in the Christian ceremony of Communion, especially during the Roman Catholic Mass [Pre-12C. < Latin, "peace"]

PAX *abbr* TELECOM private automatic exchange

Pax·il /páks'l/ *tdmk* a trademark for the antidepressant drug paroxetine

Pax Ro·ma·na /-rō maánə/ *n* the long period of peace and stability that existed under the Roman Empire, especially in the 2nd century A.D. [< Latin, "peace of the Romans"]

pax vo·bis·cum /-vō bískəm/ *interj* peace be with you [< Latin]

pay[1] /pay/ *v* (**paid** /payd/, **pay·ing, pays**) **1.** *vti* **GIVE MONEY FOR SOMETHING** to give somebody money for work done or for goods or services provided ○ *They were paid a small fortune for it.* ○ *a well-paid job* **2.** *vti* **SETTLE DEBT** to settle a debt or other obligation **3.** *vti* **BRING IN MONEY** to bring in an amount of money ○ *How much will the job pay?* **4.** *vti* **BE PUNISHED** to be punished or suffer bad consequences as the result of an action ○ *He's paid dearly for his carelessness.* **5.** *vt* **YIELD INTEREST** to yield a particular amount as a return on a sum of money invested ○ *The account pays 12% interest.* **6.** *vi* **GIVE POSITIVE RESULT** to be profitable or beneficial ○ *Crime doesn't pay.* **7.** *vt* **BESTOW ATTENTION** to give something such as attention or a compliment to somebody or something ○ *pay a compliment* **8.** *vt* **VISIT SOMEBODY** to make a visit or call to somebody **9.** *vt* same as **pay out** (sense 2) **10.** *vt* NAUT **LET VESSEL GO LEEWARD** to allow a vessel to make leeway ■ *n* **1. MONEY GIVEN IN RETURN FOR WORK** money that is given in return for work or services provided, especially in the form of a salary or wages **2. REWARD** reward, recompense, or recognition granted to somebody ■ *adj* **1. NEEDING INSERTION OF COIN TO FUNCTION** requiring the insertion of coins or a card in order to function ○ *pay TV* **2.** MIN EXTRACT **RICH IN METALS** yielding metal or minerals valuable enough to make mining them profitable [12C. Via Old French *payer* "pacify" < Latin *pacare* < *pax* "peace"] ◇ **in the pay of somebody** employed by somebody, especially for a dishonest or criminal purpose ◇ **pay the price (for something)** to suffer the unpleasant consequences of something you have done ◇ **put paid to** to put an end to or ruin something (*informal*) ◇ **pay through the nose** to pay an exorbitant sum for goods or services

SYNONYMS See *wage*.

pay back *vt* **1.** to repay money that has been loaned ○ *I'll pay you back on Friday.* **2.** to revenge yourself on somebody

pay down *vt* **1.** to pay an amount of money as a deposit or as the first installment of a larger payment **2.** to reduce the amount of a debt by repaying some of the money that has been borrowed ○*"...should have paid down its debt or invested in microchip technology..."* (*Newsweek*; November 1998)

pay in *vt* to deposit money in a bank or other account

pay off *v* **1.** *vt* **REPAY DEBT IN FULL** to repay the full amount of a bill, debt, or other financial obligation, especially one that has been paid in installments **2.** *vt* **REPAY PART OF DEBT** to repay a portion of a debt or other financial obligation **3.** *vt* **BRIBE SOMEBODY** to give somebody money as a bribe, usually to prevent that person from causing trouble (*informal*) **4.** *vt* **PAY AND LAY OFF WORKERS** to give employees or workers the money owing to them for work performed before dismissing them **5.** *vi* **BE SUCCESSFUL** to be successful or profitable ○ *All that preparation paid off in the end.* **6.** *vt UK* **TAKE REVENGE ON SOMEBODY** to take revenge on somebody for something he or she has done to you **7.** *vi* NAUT **MAKE LEEWAY** to make leeway

pay out *v* **1.** *vti* to spend or pay money **2.** *vt* to release a rope or cable gradually

pay over *vi* to transfer money to somebody officially

pay up *vi* to pay money that is due

pay[2] /pay/ (**payed, pay·ing, pays**) *vt* to make a ship's hull waterproof with pitch or tar [Early 17C. Via Old French *peier* < Latin *picare* < *pix* "pitch"]

pay·a·ble /páy əb'l/ *adj* **1. REQUIRING PAYMENT** due or needing to be paid **2. GRANTING PAYMENT TO SOMEBODY** requesting payment to be made to a particular person ○ *Shall I make the check payable to you or to Jean?* ■ **pay·a·bles** *npl* **LIABILITIES** money owed to a creditor or creditors

pay-as-you-go *n* the practice or system of paying debts or costs as they are incurred

pay·back /páy bàk/ *n* **1. RETURN ON INVESTMENT** a financial return on an investment equaling the initial capital invested **2. TIME REQUIRED TO RECOVER OUTLAY** the period of time required to recover the return on an initial investment **3. REQUITAL FOR SERVICE RENDERED** a benefit in exchange for an action or service performed (*informal*) **4. REVENGE** revenge or retaliation (*informal*)

pay ca·ble *n US* pay television that utilizes a cable system for transmission and reception

pay·check /páy chèk/ *n* **1.** a check issued to an employee as payment of salary or wages **2.** wages or salary

pay cheque *n Can* same as **paycheck**

pay·day /páy dày/ *n* the day on which employees are paid their wages or salary

pay dirt *n* **1.** a discovery or idea that is likely to be useful or profitable **2.** gravel, sand, earth, or ore that is worth mining

pay·down /páy dòwn/ *n* the repayment of part of a debt

~~**payed**~~ incorrect spelling of **paid**

pay·ee /pay eé/ *n* somebody to whom money is being paid or is due, especially the person to whom a check or money order is payable

pay en·ve·lope *n* **1.** an envelope containing an employee's wages **2.** wages received for a job or service

pay·er /páy ər/ *n* **1.** somebody who pays somebody or something **2.** the person named as responsible for the payment of a check, money order, or other financial paper when it is redeemed

pay·load /páy lòd/ *n* **1. QUANTITY OF CARGO** the quantity of cargo or number of passengers that a plane, train, or other vehicle can carry, often expressed as weight or volume, or the revenue-producing portion of its cargo or passengers **2. SPACECRAFT LOAD** the passengers, equipment, or satellites carried by a spacecraft, or the weight of these **3. EXPLOSIVE CHARGE** the explosive charge of the warhead of a rocket or missile, or the total explosive charge of the bomb load carried by an aircraft

pay·mas·ter /páy màstər/ *n* the person who is responsible for paying wages or salaries in a business or government organization

pay·ment /páymənt/ *n* **1. MONEY PAID** an amount of money that is paid or is due to be paid **2. ACT OF PAYING** the act of paying money, or fact of being paid ○ *Payment will be made at the end of the month.* **3. REWARD** a reward or punishment given in return for something [14C. < Old French *paiement* < *payer* (see PAY[1])]

pay·ment gate·way *n* a server or organization acting as an interface between the payment systems of retail seller, acquirer, and issuer with regard to Internet payments (*used in e-commerce*)

pay·ment gate·way cer·tif·i·cate au·thor·i·ty *n* a body issuing, renewing, or revoking certificates identifying an Internet payment gateway (*used in e-commerce*)

pay·mi /páymee/ *n Carib* FOOD same as **dukuna** [Late 20C. Via French Creole < French *pain de mie* "bread made from crumb" (i.e. without a crust)]

pay·nim /páynim/ *n* (*archaic*) **1.** same as **pagan** *n* (sense 1) **2.** somebody who is not a Christian, especially a Muslim [13C. Via Old French *pai(e)nime* < ecclesiastical Latin *paganismus* "paganism" < *paganus* "pagan"]

pay·off /páy àwf, -òf/ *n* **1. FULL PAYMENT** full payment of a salary, wages, or a debt **2. TIME FOR FULL PAYMENT** the time when full and final payment of a debt, salary, or wage is due **3. SETTLEMENT** a final settlement, reward, or reckoning **4. CLIMAX OF NARRATIVE** the final climax of a narrative, joke, or sequence of events **5. ADVANTAGE** an ultimate benefit or advantage **6. BRIBE** a payment made to somebody as a bribe (*informal*) **7.** PSYCHOL **HIDDEN BENEFIT OF NEGATIVE BEHAVIOR** an often unconscious or hidden benefit of a negative thought pattern or action

pay·o·la /pay ṓlə/ (*plural* **-las** *informal*) *n* a payment given in exchange for promoting a commercial product, or the system of making such payments, especially to disc jockeys [Mid-20C. < PAY[1]]

pay·out /páy òwt/ *n* the act of paying out money or the sum of money paid

pay pack·et *n UK* same as **pay envelope**

pay-per-view *n* a cable or satellite television system in which individual programs can be watched for a fee

pay·phone /páy fṓn/ *n* a public telephone that operates only when coins or a card are used to pay for calls

pay·roll /páy rṓl/ *n* **1.** a list of employees and their salaries or wages **2.** the total sum of money to be paid to employees at a given time

pay scale *n* a pay range for a particular type of work or for all types of work within a particular organization

pay·slip /páy slìp/ *n UK* same as **paystub**

pay·stub /páy stùb/ *n* a printed statement of the amount an employee is paid, showing deductions for tax, social security, and insurance

pay tel·e·vi·sion *n* a system in which television programs are transmitted in a scrambled form that can be decoded by viewers who have paid for the appropriate equipment

pay TV *n* same as **pay television**

pay·ware /páy wèr/ *n* commercial software as opposed to freeware or shareware

Octavio Paz

Paz /pass, paz/, **Octavio** (1914–98) Mexican writer. Known for his poetry and essays, he was the first Mexican to be awarded the Nobel Prize in literature (1990).

"Our democratic capitalist society has converted Eros into an employee of Mammon."
[Octavio Paz, *Observer (London)*; June 19, 1994]

Paz Es·tens·so·ro /pàss es ten sáwrō/, **Víctor** (1907–2001) president of Bolivia (1952–56, 1960–64, and 1985–89). During his presidencies, he instituted several reforms, including nationalization of foreign-owned tin companies.

Pb *symbol* CHEM ELEM lead[2] (sense 1)

PB, **P.B.** *abbr* **1.** SPORTS personal best **2.** CHR prayer book

p.b. *abbr* BASEBALL passed balls

PBA *abbr* **1.** Patrolmen's Benevolent Association **2.** Policemen's Benevolent Association

PBJ *abbr US* peanut butter and jelly (sandwich)

PBS *abbr* Public Broadcasting Service

PBX, **P.B.X.** *abbr* TELECOM private branch exchange

PC[1] *abbr* **1.** Peace Corps **2.** politically correct **3.** ELECTRONICS printed circuit **4.** BUSINESS professional corporation **5.** *UK* POL Privy Council **6.** *Can* POL Progressive Conservative

PC[2] *n* **1.** COMPUT same as **personal computer 2.** a computer compatible with IBM™ personal computers and DOS [Abbreviation of PERSONAL COMPUTER]

p.c.[1] *abbr* **1.** percent **2.** postcard

p.c.[2] *abbr* PHARM after meals (*used in prescriptions*) [Latin *post cibum* "after food"]

p.c.[3], **p/c** *abbr* **1.** BUSINESS petty cash **2.** FIN price current

P.C. *abbr* **1.** MIL Past Commander **2.** MIL Post Commander

PCB *n* a compound derived from biphenyl and containing chlorine that is a hazardous pollutant. Use: in electrical insulators, flame retardants, plasticizers. Full form **polychlorinated biphenyl**

PCI *n* a specification for extending the internal circuitry (**bus**) that transmits data from one part of a computer to another by inserting circuit boards. It allows the expansion of a computer by inserting printed circuit boards, or expansion boards, into sockets (**expansion slots**) inside the PCI bus. Full form **peripheral component interconnect**

p.c.m. *abbr* TELECOM pulse code modulation

PCMCIA *n* **1.** a specification for extending the internal circuitry (**bus**) that transmits data from one part of a computer to another, used to add memory or connect credit-card-sized peripheral devices. Full form **personal computer memory card interface adapter** **2.** an international organization that has developed a standard for adding memory to personal computers and credit-card size devices. Full form **Personal Computer Memory Card International Association**

PCO *abbr* Privy Council Office

PCOS *abbr* MED polycystic ovarian syndrome

PCP *abbr* **1.** CHEM phencyclidine **2.** MED pneumocystis carinii pneumonia **3.** *Can* POL Progressive Conservative Party

PCR *abbr* BIOCHEM polymerase chain reaction

Pd *symbol* CHEM ELEM palladium[1]

PD *abbr* public domain

pd. *abbr* paid

p.d. *abbr* **1.** PHARM per diem **2.** PHYS potential difference

P.D. *abbr* **1.** PHARM per diem **2.** POLICE police department **3.** MAIL postal district

PDA *abbr* **1.** COMPUT personal digital assistant **2.** public display of affection (*used in e-mails or text messages*)

Pd.B. *abbr US* EDUC Bachelor of Pedagogy [Latin *Pedagogiae Baccalaureus*]

Pd.D. *abbr US* EDUC Doctor of Pedagogy [Latin *Pedagogiae Doctor*]

pdf[1] *n* a format for a computer document file that enables a document to be processed and printed on any computer using any printer or word-processing program. Full form **portable document format**

pdf[2] *abbr* a file extension for a file containing information in pdf format

Pd.M. *abbr US* EDUC Master of Pedagogy [Latin *Pedagogiae Magister*]

PDN *abbr* ONLINE public data network (*used in e-mails or text messages*)

pdq *adv* at once or immediately (*informal*) Full form **pretty damn quick**

P-D ra·ti·o *abbr* FIN price-dividend ratio

PDT *abbr* TIME Pacific Daylight Time

pe[1] /pay/ *n* the 17th letter of the Hebrew alphabet, represented in the English alphabet as "p" or "f." See table at **alphabet** [Early 19C. < Hebrew *pē*]

pe[2] *abbr* **1.** ONLINE Peru (*used in Internet addresses*) See table at **domain name 2.** PRINTING printer's error

p.e. *abbr* PRINTING printer's error

P.E. *abbr* **1.** EDUC physical education **2.** PHYS potential energy **3.** CALENDAR Present Era **4.** Prince Edward Island **5.** STATS probable error **6.** ENG professional engineer **7.** CHR Protestant Episcopal

USAGE See ***A.D.***

P/E *abbr* FIN price-earnings

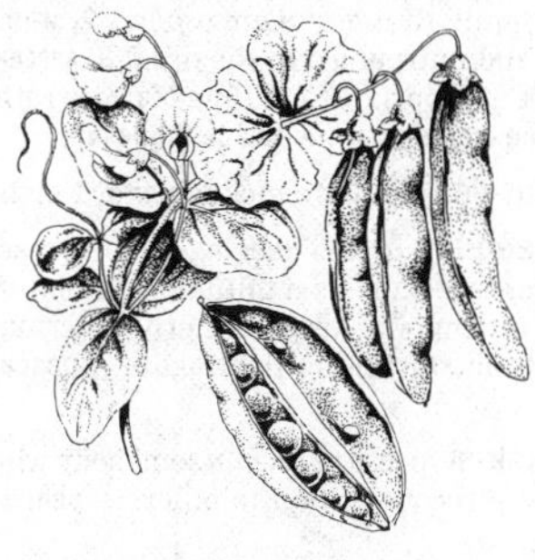

pea

pea /pee/ *n* **1. SEED AS VEGETABLE** a round green seed that grows in a pod, eaten as a vegetable **2. PLANT PRODUCING PEAS** an annual vine of the legume family with compound leaves that is widely grown for its edible seeds. Flowers: small, white. Native to: Europe, Asia. Latin name: *Pisum sativum*. **3. PLANT RELATED TO PEA** a plant related to or similar to the pea, e.g., the chickpea, sweet pea, or cowpea **4. SOMETHING RESEMBLING PEA** something resembling a pea in form or size ■ **peas** *npl US* FOOD **PEA PODS** the unopened immature pods of the pea, containing the seeds and used as a vegetable [Mid-17C. Back-formation < *pease* (singular but taken as plural) < Old English *pise*, via Latin < Greek *pison*]

pea bean *n* FOOD, PLANTS same as **navy bean**

Pea·bod·y /peé bòddee, -bədee/ city in northeastern Massachusetts, northeast of Boston and northwest of Marblehead. Population: 49,668 (2002 estimate).

Pea·bod·y /peé bòddee/, **George** (1795–1869) US businessman and philanthropist. He funded many educational institutions such as Baltimore's Peabody Institute and Yale's Peabody Museum, as well as new houses for workers in London.

~~**peacable**~~ incorrect spelling of **peaceable**

peace /peess/ *n* **1. FREEDOM FROM WAR** freedom from war, or the time when a war or conflict ends ○ *the signing of the peace agreement* **2. TRANQUILLITY** a calm and quiet state, free from disturbances or noise **3. MENTAL CALM** a state of mental calm and serenity, with no anxiety **4. HARMONY** freedom from conflict or disagreement among people or groups of people **5. PEACE TREATY** a treaty agreeing to an end of hostilities between two warring parties **6. LAW AND ORDER** the absence of violence or other disturbances within a state ○ *Peace reigned throughout the land.* ■ *interj* **BE CALM OR SILENT** used to tell somebody to be calm or silent or as a greeting or farewell [12C. Via Anglo-Norman *pes* < Latin *pax*] ◇ **at peace 1.** in a state of friendship and freedom from conflict **2.** dead (*used euphemistically*) **3.** in a state of calm and serenity ◇ **hold your peace** to refrain from speaking (*dated*) ◇ **keep the peace** to refrain from or prevent conflict or violence ◇ **make peace** to bring a disagreement or war to an end ◇ **make your peace with somebody** *or* **something** to resolve a disagreement with someone or become resigned to a situation that cannot be changed

SPELLCHECK peace or **piece**? Do not confuse the spelling of ***peace*** and ***piece***, which sound similar. ***Peace*** is a lack of noise, disturbance, disagreement, or warfare, as in *peace and quiet, a breach of the peace, make peace, not war.* A ***piece*** is a part or item, as in *fall to pieces, a piece of music.*

Peace /peess/ river in British Columbia, Canada, and an outlet of Lake Williston. It flows east into Alberta, joining the Slave River to discharge into Lake Athabasca. Length: 1,195 mi./1,923 km.

peace·a·ble /péessəb'l/ *adj* **1.** inclined toward peace and avoiding contentious situations **2.** tranquil and free from strife and disorder —**peace·a·ble·ness** *n* —**peace·a·bly** *adv*

Peace Corps *n* a US government organization that trains volunteers to work in developing countries on educational and agricultural projects

peace div·i·dend *n* savings on defense spending when a country is no longer at war or under threat of war

peace·ful /péessfəl/ *adj* **1.** QUIET AND CALM quiet, calm, and tranquil ○ *a peaceful atmosphere* **2.** MENTALLY CALM serene and untroubled in the mind **3.** APPROPRIATE FOR PEACETIME appropriate for a time of peace rather than war —**peace·ful·ly** *adv* —**peace·ful·ness** *n*

Peace Gar·den State *n* a nickname for North Dakota

peace·keep·ing /péess keeping/ *n* the preservation of peace, especially as a military mission in which troops attempt to keep formerly warring armed forces from starting to fight again —**peace·keep·er** *n*

peace·mak·er /péess màykər/ *n* somebody who brings peace and reconciliation to others —**peace·mak·ing** *n*

peace·nik /péess nìk/ *n* a pacifist, especially somebody who opposed the Vietnam War (*dated informal*)

peace of·fer·ing *n* something done for or given to an enemy or somebody you have quarreled with in the hope of bringing about a reconciliation

peace of·fi·cer *n* somebody whose main duty is to preserve public order, e.g., a police officer or sheriff

peace pipe *n* a long-stemmed ceremonial pipe used by some Native North American peoples

peace sign *n* a sign used to indicate peaceful intentions, made by holding the palm upright and outward and forming a V with the middle and index fingers

peace·time /péess tìm/ *n* a time when there is no war

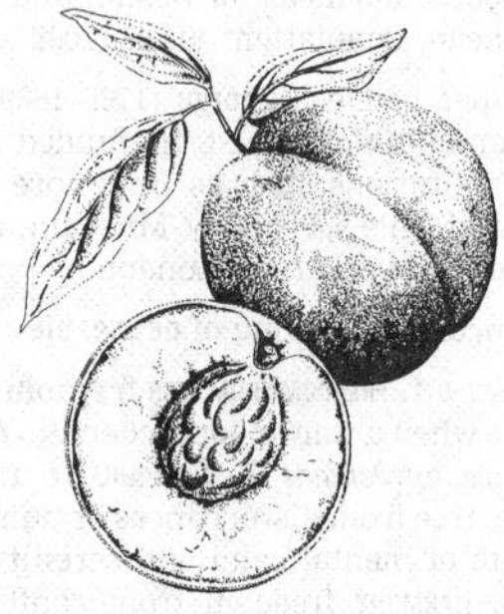
peach

peach[1] /peech/ *n* **1.** LARGE FRUIT WITH STONE a sweet round juicy fruit with yellow flesh, a single stone, and a soft downy orange-yellow skin **2.** TREE WITH EDIBLE FRUIT a tree that bears peaches, widely grown in temperate regions. Flowers: pink. Native to: China. Latin name: *Prunus persica*. **3.** SOMEBODY OR SOMETHING EXCELLENT somebody or something that is particularly good or pleasing (*informal*) ○ *That was a peach of a throw!* **4.** ORANGE-YELLOW COLOR a creamy yellowish orange color [13C. Via Old French *pe(s)che* < medieval Latin *persica* < Latin *persicum* < *malum Persicum* "Persian apple"] —**peach** *adj*

peach[2] /peech/ (**peached, peach·ing, peach·es**) *vi* to inform against somebody, especially an accomplice (*dated informal*) [15C. Shortening of obsolete *appeach*, via Anglo-Norman < late Latin *impedicare* (see IMPEACH)]

peach mel·ba *n* a dessert made with fresh or canned peaches, vanilla ice cream, and a raspberry sauce

Peach State *n* a nickname for the US state of Georgia

peach·y /péechee/ (**-i·er, -i·est**) *adj* **1.** very good or wonderful (*informal*) **2.** resembling a peach in color, taste, or texture [Late 16C. < PEACH[1]] —**peach·i·ly** *adv* —**peach·i·ness** *n*

pea coat *n* CLOTHING same as **pea jacket**

peacock

pea·cock /pée kòk/ *n* **1.** MALE PEAFOWL a male peafowl with a crested head and a large fan-shaped tail with brilliantly colored blue and green spots **2.** PEAFOWL a peafowl, either male or female **3.** VAIN PERSON a conspicuously vain person, especially as shown by his or her behavior and dress [14C. < Old English *pēa* "peacock" < Latin *pavo*] —**pea·cock·ish** *adj*

Pea·cock *n* the brightest star in the constellation Pavo

pea·cock blue *adj* of a brilliant greenish blue color, like a peacock's plumage —**pea·cock blue** *n*

pea·cock but·ter·fly *n* a butterfly with bold iridescent colors and eyespots on its wings. Native to: Europe. Latin name: *Nymphalis io*.

pea·cock ore *n* a copper ore that becomes iridescent as it tarnishes, e.g., bornite

pea·fowl /pée fòwl/ (*plural same* or **-fowls**) *n* a large pheasant, the male of which holds up its brilliant iridescent tail like a fan in courtship displays. Native to: South and Southeast Asia, Africa. Genera: *Pavo* or *Afropavo*. [Early 19C. After PEACOCK]

pea green *adj* of a medium yellowish green color —**pea green** *n*

pea·hen /pée hèn/ *n* a female peafowl, with much plainer plumage than the peacock [14C. < Old English *pēa* (see PEACOCK)]

pea jack·et *n* a heavy double-breasted jacket or short coat, made of mohair or thick wool and originally worn by sailors [Alteration of Dutch *pijjakker, pijjekker* "coarse cloth jacket" < *pij* "coarse cloth" + *jekker* "jacket"]

peak[1] /peek/ *n* **1.** MOUNTAIN TOP the pointed summit of a mountain **2.** MOUNTAIN a mountain with a pointed summit **3.** HIGHEST POINT the point of greatest success, development, or strength of a process or activity ○ *She's at the peak of her career.* **4.** POINTED PART a sharp projecting pointed part of something, e.g., the brim of a cap **5.** TOP OF CURVE the highest point in a curve, especially the curve of a wave **6.** HAIR same as **widow's peak** **7.** PHYS MAXIMUM VALUE OF QUANTITY a point at which a variable physical quantity such as temperature or voltage changes from rapidly increasing to rapidly decreasing, or the value of the quantity at such a point **8.** NAUT EXTREME END OF HULL the narrow part at the front or back end of a boat's hull **9.** SAILING CORNER OF FORE-AND-AFT SAIL the top rear corner of a fore-and-aft sail **10.** SAILING GAFF END the outermost end of a gaff sail ■ *v* (**peaked, peak·ing, peaks**) **1.** *vi* REACH HIGHEST POINT to reach the point of greatest success, development, intensity, or strength ○ *Sales peaked around July.* **2.** *vi* FORM PEAK to form a peak or peaks ○ *The waves peaked as the storm grew.* **3.** *vt* CAUSE PEAK IN SOMETHING to cause something to come to a high point ■ *adj* **1.** HIGHEST being at a maximum or highest point ○ *peak efficiency* **2.** OF GREATEST USE relating to the maximum use of something or the maximum demand on something ○ *peak viewing time* [Mid-16C. Back-formation < PEAKED[1], or variant of *pike* "long pointed object, steep summit," origin ?]

SPELLCHECK peak, peek, or **pique**? Do not confuse the spelling of ***peak***, ***peek***, and ***pique***, which sound similar. ***Peak*** is a noun, verb, or adjective referring to a high point, as in *a mountain peak, hoping that interest rates have peaked, peak viewing time.* ***Peek*** is a noun or verb referring to a quick look, as in *peek through the curtains, have a peek inside the box.* ***Pique*** is a noun or verb referring to a bad mood, as in *left in a fit of pique, piqued by their refusal.*

peak out *vi* to reach a peak or maximum level, often before beginning to decline

peak[2] /peek/ (**peaked, peak·ing, peaks**) *vi* to become thin, pale, and sickly in appearance (*archaic*) [Early 16C. Origin ?] —**peak·ish** *adj*

peaked[1] /peekt, péekəd/ *adj* having a peak or point [15C. Variant of dialect *picked* "pointed"]

peak·ed[2] /péekəd/ *adj US* thin, pale, and sickly in appearance. Can term **peaky** [Mid-19C. < archaic *peak* "be sickly," origin ?]

peak load *n* the maximum instantaneous rate of power consumption in a load circuit

peak sea·son *n* the most popular time of year for vacations, when resorts are at their busiest

peak·y /péekee/ (**-i·er, -i·est**) *adj Can, UK* same as **peaked**[2] [Early 19C. < archaic *peak* "be sickly," origin ?]

peal /peel/ *n* **1.** RINGING OF BELLS a ringing of bells, especially a change or series of changes rung on bells **2.** GROUP OF BELLS a set of tuned bells **3.** NOISY OUTBURST a loud repetitive sound, e.g., of thunder or laughter ■ *v* (**pealed, peal·ing, peals**) **1.** *vti* RING BELL to ring a bell loudly and sonorously, or be rung in this way **2.** *vt* SAY SOMETHING LOUDLY to say something loudly and sonorously [14C. Shortening of APPEAL "call, request"]

SPELLCHECK peal or **peel**? Do not confuse the spelling of ***peal*** and ***peel***, which sound similar. ***Peal*** is a noun and verb referring to the sound of bells, thunder, etc., as in *peals of laughter, when the church bells peal.* ***Peel*** is a noun denoting an outer layer or skin, as in *orange peel*, or a verb referring to the removal of such a layer, as in *paint peeling from the walls.*

Peale /peel/, **Charles Willson** (1741–1827) US artist. He was the most prominent US portraitist of his time.

pe·an *n US* ARTS another spelling of **paean**

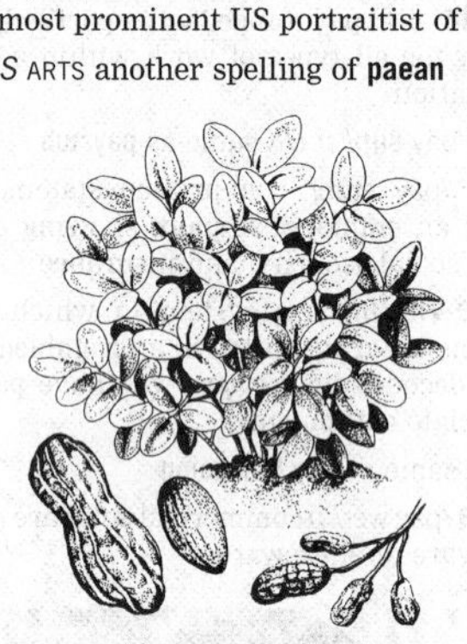
peanut

pea·nut /pée nùt/ *n* **1.** OILY EDIBLE SEED an oily edible seed with a thin shell that grows underground and is a source of vegetable oil **2.** PLANT PRODUCING PEANUTS a low-growing annual plant of the legume family whose seeds are peanuts. Latin name: *Arachis hypogaea*. **3.** *US* OFFENSIVE TERM an offensive term for a short person or somebody regarded as insignificant (*informal*) **4.** PIECE OF PACKING MATERIAL a small piece of polystyrene or similar material used in quantity to protect items during packaging and shipment ■ **pea·nuts** *npl* SMALL AMOUNT OF MONEY a very small amount of money, especially when smaller than would be expected (*informal*) ○ *They're paid peanuts!* ■ *adj US* UNIMPORTANT petty and insignificant (*informal*) [Early 19C. Because peanuts grow in a pod, as peas do]

pea·nut brit·tle *n* candy made of hard toffee and peanuts

pea·nut but·ter *n* an oily paste made from ground roasted peanuts and usually spread on bread or used in cooking

pea·nut oil *n* a combustible yellow oil extracted from peanuts. Use: cooking, medicine, soaps.

pear /per/ *n* **1.** a sweet juicy fruit with a usually green skin, firm white flesh, and roughly teardrop shape, eaten fresh or canned. See illustration on next page **2.** a tree with fine-toothed glossy leaves, widely grown to produce pears. Native to: Europe. Latin name: *Pyrus communis*. [Pre-12C. Via assumed Vulgar Latin *pira* < Latin *pirum*]

SPELLCHECK See ***pair***.

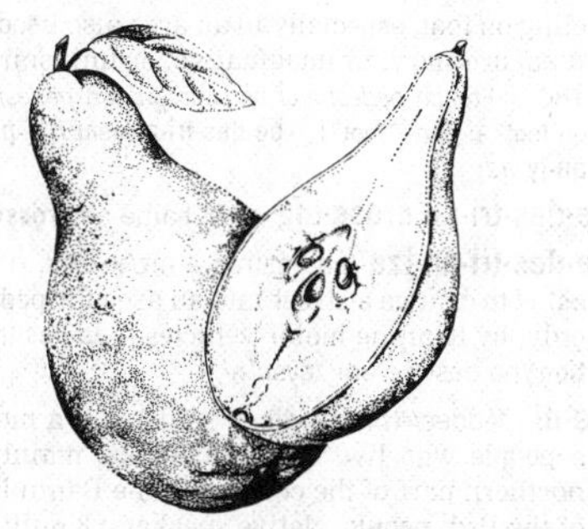

pear

pearl[1] /purl/ *n* **1. GEM FORMED IN MOLLUSK** a small lustrous sphere of calcium carbonate that forms around a grain of sand in an ocean organism such as an oyster. Use: gems. **2.** HANDICRAFT same as **mother-of-pearl 3. SOMEBODY OR SOMETHING MUCH VALUED** somebody or something highly esteemed or valued **4. PALE GRAYISH WHITE COLOR** a pale grayish white color tinged with blue ■ *v* **(pearled, pearl·ing, pearls) 1.** *vi* **HARVEST PEARLS** to fish or dive for pearls **2.** *vti* **MAKE BEADS** to form drops shaped like pearls or take on a pearlized color, or cause something to do this **3.** *vt* **DECORATE SOMETHING WITH PEARLS** to decorate something with pearls or with things that resemble pearls [14C. < Old French *perle*, probably < assumed Vulgar Latin *pernula* "little mollusk" < Latin *perna* "ham"; because of the mollusk's shape] —**pearl** *adj*

pearl[2] /purl/ *n* HANDICRAFT another spelling of **purl**[1] *n* (senses 2–3)

pearl ash *n* the commercial form of potassium carbonate

pearl bar·ley *n* grains of barley that have been polished and are used in soups and stews

pearl·er /púrlər/ *n* **1.** a diver for or dealer in natural pearls **2.** a boat used for pearl diving or for trading pearls

pearl·es·cent /pur léss'nt/ *adj* with a lustrous surface like a pearl

pearl gray *adj* of a pale blue-gray color —**pearl gray** *n*

Pearl Har·bor /pùrl-/ inlet in Hawaii, on Oahu Island. The Japanese attack on the US naval base there in 1941 prompted the United States' entry into World War II.

pearl·ite /púr lìt/ *n* a microstructure of steel or cast iron made up of bands **(lamellae)** of pure iron **(ferrite)** and iron carbide **(cementite)** [Late 19C. < PEARL[1] + -ITE[1]] —**pearl·it·ic** /pur líttik/ *adj*

pearl·ized /púr lìzd/ *adj* having a pearly iridescent luster

pearl mil·let *n* a tall cereal grass widely grown for its whitish seeds. Latin name: *Pennisetum americanum.*

pearl on·ion *n* a very small white onion that is often used for pickling

pearl oys·ter *n* a tropical ocean mollusk that is a source of pearls. Genus: *Pinctada.*

pearl·y /púrlee/ **(-i·er, -i·est)** *adj* **1. RESEMBLING PEARL** resembling pearls or mother-of-pearl, particularly in having an iridescent luster **2. DECORATED WITH PEARLS** decorated with pearls or mother-of-pearl **3. PALE GRAYISH WHITE** of a pale grayish white color tinged with blue —**pearl·i·ness** *n*

pearl·y ev·er·last·ing *n* a plant with woolly leaves and white flower heads. Native to: North America. Latin name: *Anaphalis margaritacea.*

Pearl·y Gates *npl* in Christianity, the gates of heaven (*informal*)

pearl·y nau·ti·lus *n* a mollusk that has a spiral pearl-colored multichambered shell. Genus: *Nautilus.*

pear psyl·la /-síllə/ *n* a jumping plant louse that sucks the sap from pear trees and is a serious pest in the eastern and northwestern United States. Native to: Europe, introduced to USA. Latin name: *Psylla pyricola.*

Pears /peerz/, **Sir Peter** (1910–86) British tenor. He is noted for his interpretation of music by Benjamin Britten, much of which Britten wrote for him. Full name **Pears, Sir Peter Neville Luard**

Pearse /peerss/, **Patrick** (1879–1916) Irish nationalist leader. He led the Irish Republican Brotherhood in the Easter Rising (1916), after which he was executed. Full name **Pearse, Patrick Henry**

pear-shaped *adj* **1.** having a shape similar to that of a pear with a rounded bottom part and narrower top part **2.** *US* clear and resonant, and without any unpleasant harshness of tone

Pear·son /peerss'n/, **Lester** (1897–1972) prime minister of Canada (1963–68). He had a distinguished diplomatic career playing key roles at the UN and in the creation of Israel (1948) and NATO (1949). He received the Nobel Peace Prize (1957). Full name **Pearson, Lester Bowles**

> "We prepare for war like ferocious giants, and for peace like retarded pygmies."
> [Lester Pearson, *Nobel Prize acceptance speech*; December 11, 1957]

Pea·ry /peéree/, **Robert** (1856–1920) US explorer. He is generally credited with leading the first expedition to reach the North Pole (1909). Full name **Peary, Robert Edwin**

peas·ant /pézz'nt/ *n* **1. AGRICULTURAL LABORER** an agricultural laborer or small farmer **2. RURAL PERSON** somebody who lives in the country **3. OFFENSIVE TERM** an offensive term for somebody considered to be ill-mannered or uneducated [15C. < Anglo-Norman *paisant*, Old French *païsant* < Latin *pagus* "rural district"]

peas·ant blouse, peas·ant top *n* a women's top with an elasticized low neckline, usually worn off the shoulders, and long or short sleeves

peas·ant·ry /pézz'ntree/ *n* **1.** peasants as a class in society **2.** the status or characteristic behavior of a peasant

peas·ant top *n* CLOTHING same as **peasant blouse**

pea·shoot·er /peé shootər/ *n* a toy in the form of a pipe through which dried peas or similar small pellets can be blown

pea soup *n* **1.** soup made with fresh or dried peas **2.** an extremely dense fog (*informal*)

pea·soup·er /pee sóopər/ *n* **1.** *Can* an offensive term for a French Canadian (*slang*) **2.** *UK* same as **pea soup** (sense 2) (*informal*)

peat /peet/ *n* **1.** a compacted deposit of partially decomposed organic debris, usually saturated with water **2.** a cut and dried piece of peat used as fuel [14C. < Anglo-Latin *peta*, probably < Celtic, "bit"] —**peat·y** *adj*

peat bog *n* an area of land composed primarily of peat

peat moss *n* a moss that grows in wet places, and whose partially decomposed remains form peat. Genus: *Sphagnum.*

peau de soie /pō də swaá/ *n* a silk or artificial fabric with a smooth texture and a fine grainy or ribbed surface [< French, "skin of silk"]

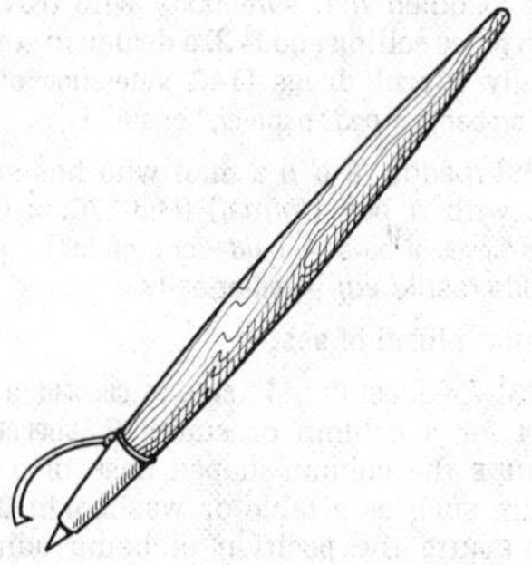

peavey

pea·vey /peévee/ (*plural* **-veys**), **pea·vy** (*plural* **-vies**) *n* a pointed lever with a hinged hook, used for handling logs [Late 19C. After Joseph *Peavey*, US inventor]

peb·ble /pébb'l/ *n* **1. SMALL ROUND STONE** a small rounded stone that has been worn smooth by erosion **2.** GEOL **ROCK FRAGMENT** a rock fragment with a diameter between 0.16 in./4 mm and 2.51 in./64 mm **3.** GEOL **QUARTZ USED FOR LENSES** a colorless form of quartz **(rock crystal)** used for making lenses **4.** OPTICS **CRYSTAL LENS** a lens made from colorless rock crystal **5.** TEXTILES **IRREGULAR SURFACE** a rough grainy surface, especially on leather ■ *adj* **THICK AND DISTORTING** being or containing lenses that make the eyes of the wearer seem very large and distorted (*informal*) ○ *wearing thick pebble glasses* ■ *vt* **(-bled, -bling, -bles) 1. COVER SOMETHING WITH PEBBLES** to cover or pave something with pebbles **2. GIVE IRREGULAR SURFACE TO SOMETHING** to give a rough grainy surface to something [Old English *papolstān*, origin ?] —**peb·bly** *adj*

pec /pek/ *n* same as **pectoral muscle** (*informal*; *often used in the plural*) ○ *exercises to strengthen the pecs* [Mid-20C. Shortening]

pe·can /pi kaán, -kán, peé kàn/ *n* **1.** an edible nut with a thin dark red shell **2.** a large hickory tree that has deeply furrowed bark and produces pecans. Native to: southern United States, Mexico. Latin name: *Carya illinoensis.* [Late 18C. Via French *pacane* < Illinois *pakani*]

pec·ca·dil·lo /pèkə díllō/ (*plural* **-loes** or **-los**) *n* a trifling offense [Late 16C. < Spanish, "little fault" < *peccado* "sin" < Latin *peccare* "to sin"]

pec·cant /pékənt/ *adj* (*formal*) **1.** guilty of a sin **2.** violating a rule or practice [Late 16C. < Latin *peccant-*, present participle of *peccare* "to sin"] —**pec·can·cy** *n* —**pec·cant·ly** *adv*

pec·ca·ry /pékəree/ (*plural* **-ries**) *n* a wild pig with a rudimentary tail and small tusks on the upper jaw that grow downward. Native to: Mexico, South America. Genus: *Tayassu.* [Early 17C. < Carib *pakira*]

pec·ca·vi /pə kaávee/ (*plural* **-vis**) *n* an admission of sin or guilt (*literary*) [Early 16C. < Latin, "I have sinned"]

Pe·cho·ra /pə káwrə/ river in northwestern European Russia, flowing northward to the Barents Sea. Length: 1,124 mi./1,809 km.

peck[1] /pek/ *v* **(pecked, peck·ing, pecks) 1.** *vt* **PICK SOMETHING UP WITH BEAK** to take small bits of food using a beak **2.** *vti* **STRIKE SOMETHING WITH BEAK** to strike somebody or something with a beak **3.** *vt* **MAKE HOLE IN SOMETHING** to make a hole in something by repeatedly striking it with a beak **4.** *vi* **NIBBLE** to eat small quantities of food with little interest ○ *She just pecked at her food.* **5.** *vt* **KISS SOMEBODY LIGHTLY** to kiss somebody lightly and briefly **6.** *vi* **NAG** to nag or carp (*informal*) ■ *n* **1. SWIFT BITE WITH BEAK** a quick light stroke, blow, or bite with a beak **2. HOLE MADE BY BEAK** a mark or hole made by a beak or pointed object **3. LIGHT KISS** a quick light kiss (*informal*) [14C. Probably variant of PICK[1]]

peck[2] /pek/ *n* **1. UNIT OF DRY MEASURE** a unit of dry measure equal to 8 quarts/7.57 liters **2. CONTAINER FOR PECK** a container that holds a peck of material **3. LARGE QUANTITY** a large amount or number of something (*informal*) [13C. Origin ?]

Peck /pek/, **Gregory** (1916–2003) US movie actor. He was an appealing presence in a wide variety of movies, including *Roman Holiday* (1953) and *To Kill a Mockingbird* (1962) for which he won an Academy Award for best actor. Born **Peck, Eldred Gregory**

peck·er /pékər/ *n* **1.** something that pecks, especially a woodpecker **2.** same as **penis** (*slang*; *sometimes considered offensive*) ◇ **keep your pecker up** *UK* used to tell somebody to keep his or her spirits up (*informal*)

peck·er·wood /pékər wòod/ *n* **1.** *Southeast US* same as **woodpecker 2.** *Can, Southeast US* an offensive term for a white person from a rural area who has a lower than average income (*slang*) [Mid-19C. Alteration of WOODPECKER]

peck·ing or·der *n* **1.** a social hierarchy in which some members of a group are established as superior to others **2.** a social hierarchy among domestic fowl in which each member maintains its place by dominance over the lower members

peck·ish /pékish/ *adj* (*informal*) **1.** *US* somewhat irritable **2.** *Can, UK* slightly hungry

Peck·sniff·i·an /pek sníffee ən/ *adj* hypocritical and making a show of having high moral principles [Mid-19C. After Mr. *Pecksniff*, character in *Martin Chuzzlewit* (1844) by Charles Dickens]

pe·co·ri·no /pèkə reénō/ (*plural* **-nos**) *n* a hard pungent Italian cheese made from ewe's milk [Mid-20C. < Italian < *pecora* "sheep"]

Pe·cos /páykəss/ river in the United States, flowing from New Mexico into Texas, where it joins the Rio Grande. Length: 926 mi./1,490 km.

Pécs /paych/ capital of Baranya County, southwestern Hungary, situated about 105 mi./170 km southwest of Budapest. Population: 159,607 (1999).

pec·tate /pék tàyt/ *n* a salt or ester of pectic acid [Mid-19C. < PECTIC ACID]

pec·tic ac·id /pèktik-/ *n* an insoluble component of pectin [< Greek *pēktikos* < *pēktos* "curdled" < *pēgnunai* "make solid"]

pec·tin /péktin/ *n* a mixture of polysaccharides found in plant cell walls. Use: gelling agent. [Mid-19C. < French *pectine* < Greek *pektos* (see PECTIC ACID)] —**pec·tic** *adj* —**pec·tin·ous** *adj*

pec·tin·es·ter·ase /pèkti néstə ràyss, -ràyz/ *n* an enzyme that catalyzes the breakdown of pectin

pec·tize /pék tīz/ (**-tized, -tiz·ing, -tiz·es**) *vt* to change something into a gel —**pec·ti·za·ble** *adj* —**pec·ti·za·tion** /pèkti záysh'n/ *n*

pec·to·ral /péktərəl/ *adj* **1.** OF CHEST relating to or located in or on the chest **2.** WORN ON CHEST worn on the chest ○ *a pectoral medal* ■ *n* **1.** CHEST MUSCLE a chest muscle or organ ○ *an exercise for the pectorals* **2.** FISH same as **pectoral fin 3.** BREASTPLATE something that is worn on the chest as a decoration or ornament **4.** CHEST MEDICINE a medicine for chest or respiratory disorders (*dated*) [15C. Via French, "something worn on the chest" < Latin *pectorale* "breastplate" < *pectus* "chest"] —**pec·tor·al·ly** *adv*

pec·to·ral fin *n* either of a pair of fins of a fish located either directly behind the gill openings or below them

pec·to·ral gir·dle *n* the part of the skeleton of a vertebrate animal that provides attachment points and support for the forelimbs

pec·to·ral mus·cle *n* any of four flat muscles, two on each side of the front of the chest, that help to move the upper arm and shoulder

pec·u·late /pékyə làyt/ (**-lat·ed, -lat·ing, -lates**) *vt* to appropriate money or property by embezzlement or theft (*formal*) [Mid-18C. < Latin *peculat-*, past participle of *peculari* < *peculium* (see PECULIAR)] —**pec·u·la·tion** /pèkyə láysh'n/ *n* —**pec·u·la·tor** *n*

pe·cu·liar /pi kyoólyər/ *adj* **1.** unusual, strange, or unconventional ○ *The situation was very peculiar.* **2.** belonging exclusively to or identified distinctly with somebody or something ○ *a form of wildlife peculiar to that region* [15C. < Latin *peculiaris* "of private property" < *peculium* "private property" < *pecus* "cattle"] —**pe·cu·liar·ly** *adv*

pe·cu·li·ar·i·ty /pi kyoòl yárrətee, -lee árrətee/ (*plural* **-ties**) *n* **1.** the quality or state of being unusual or strange **2.** a characteristic that belongs distinctively to a particular person, place, or thing

~~**peculier**~~ incorrect spelling of **peculiar**

pe·cu·li·um /pi kyoólyəm/ *n* in Roman law, property that a father allowed his child, or a master his slave, to own independently [Late 17C. < Latin (see PECULIAR)]

pe·cu·ni·ar·y /pi kyoónee èrree/ *adj* **1.** relating to or involving money **2.** involving a financial penalty such as a fine ○ *a pecuniary offense* [Early 16C. < Latin *pecuniarius* < *pecunia* "money, wealth in cattle" < *pecus* "cattle"] —**pe·cu·ni·ar·i·ly** *adv*

ped-, **paed-** *prefix* same as **pedo-**[1] (*used before vowels*)

-ped *suffix* foot ○ *biped* [< Latin *ped-*, *pes*]

ped·a·gogue /péddə gòg/ *n* **1.** a schoolteacher or educator (*formal*) **2.** a teacher who teaches in a particularly pedantic or dogmatic manner [14C. Via Latin < Greek *paidagōgos* "slave who leads a child to school" < *paid-* "child"]

ped·a·go·gy /péddə gòjjee/ *n* the science or profession of teaching [Mid-16C. Via French < Greek *paidagōgia* "duties of a slave who leads a child to school" < *paidagōgos* (see PEDAGOGUE)] —**ped·a·gog·ic** /pèddə gójjik/ *adj* —**ped·a·gog·i·cal** *adj* —**ped·a·gog·i·cal·ly** *adv*

ped·al[1] /pédd'l/ *n* **1.** FOOT-OPERATED LEVER FOR MACHINE a lever operated by the foot that powers a mechanism such as a bicycle, sewing machine, or the foot controls of a car **2.** FOOT-OPERATED LEVER FOR MUSICAL INSTRUMENT a foot-operated lever used in playing the piano, organ, and other musical instruments **3.** MUSIC same as **pedal point** ■ *vti* (**-aled, -al·ing, -als**) **1.** MAKE BICYCLE MOVE to push down on the pedals to make a bicycle or other vehicle move forward **2.** OPERATE OR PLAY INSTRUMENT USING PEDALS to operate the pedals of a piano or organ while playing it, or those of a machine in order to make it work [Early 17C. Via French < Italian *pedale (d'organo)* "(organ) pedal" < Latin *pedalis* "of the foot" < *ped-* "foot"] —**ped·al·er** *n*

SPELLCHECK pedal, peddle, or **petal**? Do not confuse the spelling of ***pedal, peddle***, and ***petal***, which sound similar. The words ***pedal*** and ***petal*** are chiefly used as nouns, ***pedal*** denoting a part pressed by the foot, for example, on a bicycle or a piano, and ***petal*** denoting one of the colored parts of a flower. ***Pedal*** can also be used as a verb, meaning "operate the pedals of," as in *pedal a bicycle*. The word ***peddle*** is only used as a verb, meaning "sell" or "promote," as in *peddling books, peddling ideas*.

---

ped·al[2] /peéd'l/ *adj* relating to the foot or feet [Early 17C. < Latin *pedalis* (see PEDAL[1])]

pe·dal·fer /pi dálfər/ *n* soil without a layer of accumulated calcium carbonate, but in which iron and aluminum have tended to accumulate [Early 20C. Blend of PEDO-[2] + ALUMINUM + Latin *ferrum* "iron"]

ped·al point *n* a note, usually in the bass, that is sustained while other musical parts and harmonies continue

ped·al push·ers *npl* calf-length pants for women, originally designed for cycling

ped·al steel, ped·al steel gui·tar *n* an electrically amplified floor-mounted guitar that is fretted with a steel bar and usually has ten strings, whose pitch can be varied by the use of pedals

ped·ant /pédd'nt/ *n* **1.** somebody who unduly emphasizes unimportant details and rules **2.** somebody who displays his or her knowledge ostentatiously [Late 16C. Via French < Italian *pedante*]

pe·dan·tic /pə dántik/ *adj* too concerned with what are thought to be correct rules and details, e.g., in language —**pe·dan·ti·cal·ly** *adv*

ped·ant·ry /pédd'ntree/ (*plural* **-ries**) *n* a pedantic attitude or an example of pedantic behavior

~~**pedastool**~~ incorrect spelling of **pedestal**

ped·dle /pédd'l/ (**-dled, -dling, -dles**) *v* **1.** *vti* SELL GOODS to sell goods, especially while traveling from place to place **2.** *vt* SELL ILLEGAL THINGS to sell something illegal, especially drugs *(dated)* **3.** *vt* PROMOTE IDEA to promote an idea or belief insistently [Mid-16C. Back-formation < PEDDLER]

SPELLCHECK See ***pedal***[1].

---

ped·dler /péddlər/ *n* **1.** somebody who travels from place to place selling goods **2.** a dealer in something, especially illegal drugs [14C. Alteration of dialectal *pedder*, probably < *ped* "pannier," origin ?]

ped·er·ast /péddə ràst/ *n* a man who has sexual relations with a boy (*formal*) [Mid-17C. < Greek *paiderastēs* "lover of boys" < *paid-* "boy, child"] —**ped·er·as·tic** /pèddə rástik/ *adj* —**ped·er·as·ty** *n*

pe·des ANAT plural of **pes**

ped·es·tal /péddəst'l/ *n* **1.** BASE OF COLUMN a base or support for a column or statue **2.** SUPPORTING BASE OF FURNITURE the column-shaped base of a piece of furniture such as a table or washbasin **3.** POSITION OF BEING EXALTED the position of being admired by somebody to the point of reverence or deification ○ *I don't want to be put on a pedestal – I just want to be treated as a normal person!* ■ *vt* (**-taled** or **-tal·led, -tal·ing** or **-tal·ling, -tals**) PUT SOMETHING ON PEDESTAL to provide somebody or something with a pedestal [Mid-16C. Via French *piédestal* < Italian *piedestallo*, literally "foot of a stall"; altered after Latin *ped-* "foot"]

pe·des·tri·an /pə déstree ən/ *n* somebody who is traveling on foot, especially in an area also used by cars ■ *adj* ordinary, unimaginative, or uninspired [Early 18C. < French *pédestre* or its source Latin *pedester* "going on foot" < *ped-* "foot"] —**pe·des·tri·an·ism** *n* —**pe·des·tri·an·ly** *adv*

pe·des·tri·an cross·ing *n UK* same as **crosswalk**

pe·des·tri·an·ize /pə déstree ə nīz/ (**-ized, -iz·ing, -iz·es**) *vt* to change a street into an area for pedestrians only, by banning motor vehicles —**pe·des·tri·an·i·za·tion** /pə dèstree əni záysh'n/ *n*

Pe·di /péddee/ (*plural* **-dis** or *same*) *n* **1.** a member of a people who live in South Africa, mainly in the northern part of the country **2.** the Bantu language of the Pedi people. Native speakers: 3 million. [Mid-20C. < Sotho *Mopedi*] —**Pe·di** *adj*

pedi- *prefix* foot, feet ○ *pedipalp* [< Latin *ped-* "foot"]

pe·di·at·rics /peèdee áttriks/ *n* the branch of medicine concerned with the care and development of children and with the prevention and treatment of children's diseases (*takes a singular verb*) —**pe·di·at·ric** *adj* —**pe·di·a·tri·cian** /peèdee ə trísh'n/ *n* —**pe·di·at·rist** /peèdee áttrist/ *n*

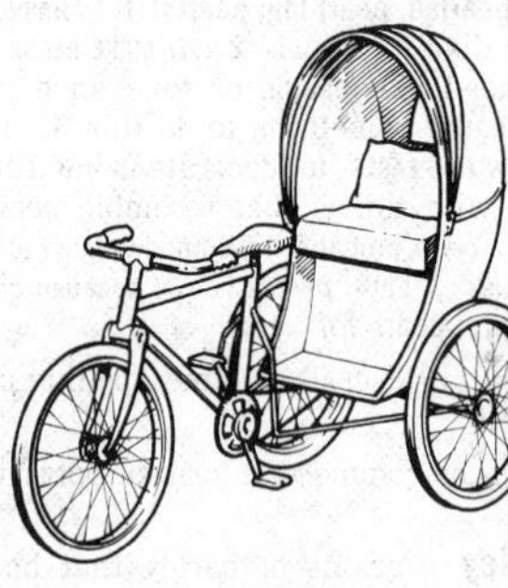

pedicab

ped·i·cab /péddi kàb/ *n* a pedal-operated tricycle with a seat in front for the driver and a passenger seat behind covered by a hood, available for hire in some Southeast Asian countries

ped·i·cel /péddiss'l, -sèl/, **ped·i·cle** /péddik'l/ *n* **1.** BOT STALK OF INDIVIDUAL FLOWER a stalk bearing a single flower or spore-producing body within a cluster **2.** ANAT STALK-SHAPED BODY PART an anatomical part that resembles a stem or stalk **3.** ZOOL NARROW SEGMENT OF BODY a narrow anatomical part, e.g., the waist between the thorax and abdomen of wasps and related insects [Late 17C. < modern Latin *pedicellus* < Latin *pediculus* "little foot" < *ped-* "foot"] —**ped·i·cel·lar** /pèddi séllər/ *adj* —**ped·i·cel·late** /-séllət, -sél àyt/ *adj*

pe·dic·u·late /pi díkyələt, -làyt/ *adj* relating to the anglerfishes, which are characterized by a modified dorsal spine with an attachment for luring prey [Mid-19C. < Latin *pediculus* (see PEDICEL)] —**pe·dic·u·late** *n*

ped·i·cu·li·cide /pèddi kyoóli sīd/ *n* a chemical substance that kills lice, used to treat infestations of humans and animals [Early 20C. < Latin *pediculus* "louse"]

pe·dic·u·lo·sis /pə dikyə lṓssiss/ *n* infestation with lice, specifically the head and body louse *Pediculus humanus*. It can cause insomnia, irritability, and depression. [Early 19C. < Latin *pediculus* "louse"] —**pe·dic·u·lous** /pə díkyələss/ *adj*

ped·i·cure /péddi kyoòr/ *n* **1.** SESSION OF TREATMENT FOR FEET a session of cosmetic or medical treatment of the feet **2.** COSMETIC TREATMENT OF FEET cosmetic treatment of the feet, e.g., the application of nail varnish **3.** MEDICAL CARE OF FEET medical treatment of the feet, e.g., the removal of corns **4.** SOMEBODY WHO TREATS FEET somebody who provides cosmetic or medical care for the feet ■ *vt* (**-cured, -cur·ing, -cures**) TREAT FEET OF SOMEBODY to give somebody a pedicure [Mid-19C. < French *pédicure* < Latin *ped-* "foot" + *cura* "care"] —**ped·i·cur·ist** *n*

ped·i·gree /péddi greè/ *n* **1.** LINE OF ANCESTORS the line of ancestors of an individual animal or person, especially a pure-bred animal **2.** LIST OF ANIMAL'S ANCESTORS a document recording the line of ancestors of an animal, especially a pure-bred animal **3.** FAMILY TREE a table showing the line of ancestors of a person, especially an aristocratic or upper class person **4.** BACKGROUND the background, history, or origin of something, especially a group [15C. < Anglo-Norman *pe de gru* "crane's foot" (likened to the branches of a family tree)] —**ped·i·greed** *adj*

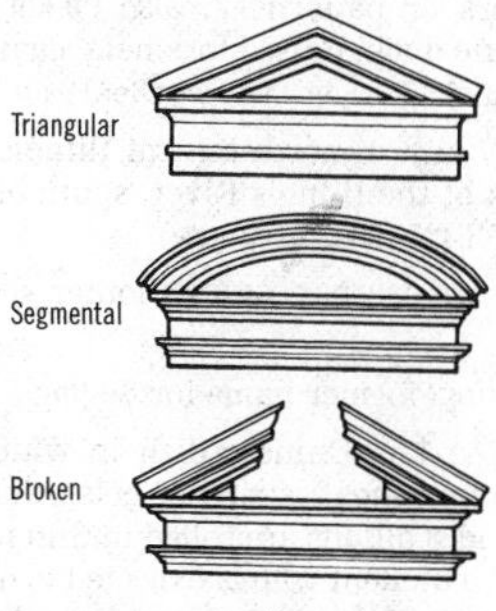

pediment

ped·i·ment /péddimənt/ *n* **1.** in classical architecture, a broad triangular or segmental gable surmounting a colonnade as the major part of a facade **2.** a broad flat rock surface of low relief adjacent to a steeper slope in a dry region, e.g., that of a mountain range, often covered with rock debris [Late 16C. Origin ?] —**ped·i·men·tal** /pèddi mént'l/ *adj*

ped·i·palp /péddi pàlp/ *n* either of a pair of appendages that are part of the mouths of spiders and other arachnids, used for various functions including manipulating food [Early 19C. < modern Latin *pedipalpi* < Latin *ped-* "foot" + *palpus* "palp"]

ped·lar /péddlər/ *n UK* same as **peddler** (sense 1) [Variant of PEDDLER]

pedo-[1], **paedo-** *prefix* child, children [< Greek *paid-* "child, boy" < Indo-European, "little"]

pedo-[2] *prefix* soil ○ *pedology* [< Greek *pedon* "ground"]

pe·do·don·tics /pe̅edə dóntiks/, **pe·do·don·tia** /-shə, -shee ə/ *n* the branch of dentistry concerned with dental care and treatment for children (*takes a singular verb*)

ped·o·gen·e·sis /pe̅edō jénnəssiss/ *n* the natural process of soil formation, including erosion and leaching —**pe·do·ge·net·ic** /-jə néttik/ *adj* —**pe·do·gen·ic** *adj*

pe·dol·o·gy[1] /pee dóllәjee/ *n* the scientific study of the physical and mental development of children —**pe·do·log·ic** /pe̅ed'l ójjik/ *adj* —**ped·o·log·i·cal** *adj* —**ped·o·log·i·cal·ly** *adv* —**pe·dol·o·gist** *n*

pe·dol·o·gy[2] /pee dóllәjee/ *n* the scientific study of soil properties and the classification of soil types —**pe·do·log·ic** /pèdd'l ójjik/ *adj* —**pe·do·log·i·cal** *adj* —**pe·do·log·i·cal·ly** *adv* —**pe·dol·o·gist** *n*

pe·dom·e·ter /pə dómmətər/ *n* an instrument that measures the distance covered by a walker by recording the number of steps taken [Early 18C. < French *pédomètre* < Latin *ped-* "foot" + French *-mètre* "-meter"]

ped·o·mor·pho·sis /pèddə máwrfəssiss, pe̅edə-/ *n* ZOOL same as **neoteny**

ped·o·phile /péddə fìl, pe̅edə-/ *n* an adult who has sexual desire for children or who has committed the crime of sex with a child —**ped·o·phil·ic** /pèddə fíllik, pe̅edə-/ *adj*

ped·o·phi·li·a /pèddə fíllee ə, pe̅edə-/ *n* sexual desire felt by an adult for children, or the crime of sex with a child

Pe·dro I /páydrō, péddrō/, **emperor of Brazil** (1798–1834) The son of the king of Portugal, he declared Brazil's independence in 1822, made himself emperor, and abdicated in 1831. He was also briefly king of Portugal (1826).

Pe·dro II, emperor of Brazil (1825–91) He was emperor from his father's abdication (1831) until his own abdication (1889). He abolished slavery in Brazil.

pe·dun·cle /pe̅e dùngk'l, pi dúngk'l/ *n* **1.** the stalk of a plant **2.** a part resembling a stalk in shape or function, e.g., the base of a fish's tail or a structure attaching an invertebrate animal to the place where it lives [Mid-18C. < modern Latin *pedunculus* "small foot" < Latin *ped-* "foot"] —**pe·dun·cled** *adj* —**pe·dun·cu·lar** /pi dúngkyələr/ *adj* —**pe·dun·cu·late** /pi dúngkyələt, -làyt/ *adj*

ped·way /péd wày/ *n* a walkway for pedestrians only

pee /pee/ (*informal; sometimes considered offensive*) *vi* (**peed, pee·ing, pees**) to pass urine ■ *n* **1.** same as **urine 2.** an act of urinating [Late 18C. < the first letter of PISS]

peek /peek/ *vi* (**peeked, peek·ing, peeks**) to take a quick look at something, especially secretively or surreptitiously ○ *I peeked at the name at the foot of the letter.* ■ *n* a quick or secret look at something [14C. Origin ?]

SPELLCHECK See *peak*[1].

peek·a·boo /pe̅ekə bo͞o/ *n* CHILDREN'S GAME a game played to amuse small children, in which the face is hidden in the hands and then suddenly uncovered as "peekaboo!" is shouted ■ *interj* WORD SAID IN GAME the word used when playing a game of peekaboo ■ *adj* CLOTHING HAVING HOLES having holes or gaps intended to reveal parts of the body [Late 16C. < PEEK + BOO]

Peeks·kill /pe̅eks kil/ city in southeastern New York, on the Hudson River, southeast of Newburgh. Population: 23,077 (2002 estimate).

peel[1] /peel/ *v* (**peeled, peel·ing, peels**) **1.** *vt* REMOVE OUTER LAYER to cut away or pull off the skin or outer layer of something, especially a fruit or vegetable **2.** *vi* HAVE REMOVABLE SKIN to have a skin that can be removed **3.** *vt* PULL SOMETHING OFF to pull or strip off something, especially something that is stuck to a surface **4.** *vi* LOSE OUTER LAYER to lose or shed an outer layer or covering, e.g., of paint or sunburned skin ○ *The skin on her nose was peeling.* **5.** *vi* COME OFF IN THIN PIECES to come off in flakes, small pieces, or thin strips **6.** *vi* UNDRESS to remove clothes (*informal*) ○ *She peeled and jumped into the pool.* **7.** *vt* PUT BALL THROUGH CROQUET HOOP in croquet, to make another player's ball go through a hoop ■ *n* **1.** FRUIT OR VEGETABLE SKIN the rind or skin of a fruit or vegetable ○ *apple peel* **2.** COSMETIC TREATMENT a beauty treatment that involves removing the top layer of skin, usually by means of abrasion or chemicals [13C. < Latin *pilare* "deprive of hair" < *pilus* "hair"] —**peel·a·ble** *adj*

SPELLCHECK See *peal*.

peel[2] /peel/ *n* a large spatula with a long handle, used by bakers to move bread in and out of an oven [14C. Via Old French *pele* < Latin *pala* "spade"]

Peel /peel/, **Sir Robert** (1788–1850) prime minister of Great Britain (1834–35 and 1841–46). As the British home secretary (1822–27 and 1828–30), he organized the London police force, later known as "bobbies" or "peelers." He founded the modern Conservative Party and led it to victory in the 1841 elections.

peel·er[1] /pe̅elər/ *n* **1.** a device for removing the skin from fruit or vegetables, usually a hand-held utensil with a blade **2.** *US* a striptease dancer (*slang*) [14C. < PEEL[1]]

peel·er[2] /pe̅elər/ *n UK* a police officer [Early 19C. After Sir Robert PEEL]

peel·ing /pe̅eling/ *n* a piece of something, especially fruit or vegetable skin, that has been peeled off (*often used in the plural*) ○ *potato peelings*

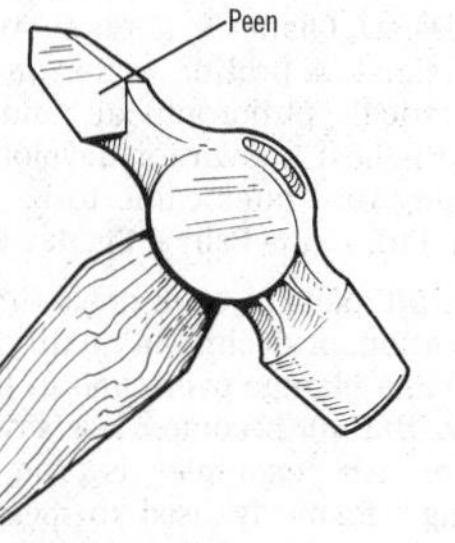

peen

peen /peen/ *n* the end of a hammerhead opposite the flat face, often rounded or wedge-shaped, and used for bending and shaping ■ *vt* (**peened, peen·ing, peens**) to bend or shape something by striking it with the peen of a hammer [Late 17C. Origin ?]

peep[1] /peep/ *v* (**peeped, peep·ing, peeps**) **1.** *vi* LOOK QUICKLY OR SECRETLY to look quickly or secretly, e.g., through a small opening or from a hiding place **2.** *vti* EMERGE, OR MAKE SOMETHING EMERGE to become partly visible or visible only for a short time, or make something become so ■ *n* **1.** QUICK LOOK a quick or secret look at something **2.** THE FIRST SIGHT OF SOMETHING the first appearance or sight of something [15C. Origin ?]

peep[2] /peep/ *vi* (**peeped, peep·ing, peeps**) **1.** MAKE SHORT, HIGH-PITCHED NOISE to make a short high-pitched noise like that made by a baby bird or a mouse **2.** SPEAK IN HIGH OR QUIET VOICE to speak in a quiet, weak, or high-pitched voice **3.** MAKE QUIET NOISE to make the quietest possible noise or remark ■ *n* **1.** SHORT HIGH-PITCHED SOUND a high-pitched sound like that of a baby bird or a mouse **2.** SMALLEST SOUND a very quiet utterance ○ *I don't want to hear another peep out of any of you!* **3.** SMALL SANDPIPER any small bird belonging to the sandpiper family of shorebirds. Genus: *Calidris*. [15C. An imitation of the sound]

peep·er[1] /pe̅epər/ *n* **1.** somebody who looks secretly at somebody or something **2.** somebody's eye (*dated slang; often used in the plural*) [Mid-17C. < PEEP[1]]

peep·er[2] /pe̅epər/ *n* AMPHIB same as **spring peeper** [Late 16C. < PEEP[2]]

peep·hole /pe̅ep hōl/ *n* **1.** a small crack or hole that somebody can look through **2.** a small hole in a door that allows somebody to see people on the other side without being observed

peep·ing Tom *n* somebody who secretly watches others, especially a man who gets sexual pleasure from watching somebody undressing or watching sexual activity between other people [Early 19C. After a tailor in English legend who was the only person to look at Lady Godiva riding naked]

peeps /peeps/ *n* ONLINE same as **people** (*slang*) [Shortening and alteration]

peep·show /pe̅ep shō/ (*plural* **peep·shows** or **peep shows**) *n* **1.** an erotic or pornographic movie or show viewed from individual booths **2.** a sequence of pictures viewed through a hole or lens in a box, regarded as a form of entertainment in former times

peep sight *n* a metal tab at the rear of a rifle barrel, containing a small circular opening through which the user looks to align the front sight with the target

pee·pul *n* TREES another spelling of **pipal**

peer[1] /peer/ (**peered, peer·ing, peers**) *vi* **1.** to look very carefully or hard, especially at somebody or something that is difficult to see, often with narrowed eyes **2.** to be partially visible or appear briefly [Late 16C. Origin ?]

SPELLCHECK peer or **pier**? Do not confuse the spelling of *peer* and *pier*, which sound similar. *Peer* is a verb meaning "to look carefully or hard" (as in *peering at the inscription on the weathered stone*) or a noun meaning "an equal" or "a member of the nobility" (as in *peer group, a peer of the realm*). *Pier* is a noun denoting a walkway jutting into the sea or a structural support.

peer[2] /peer/ *n* **1.** somebody who is the equal of somebody else, e.g., in age or social class **2.** a member of the nobility in Great Britain and Northern Ireland [13C. Via French < Latin *par* "equal"]

peer·age /pe̅erij/ *n* **1.** NOBLES AS GROUP noblemen and noblewomen considered as a class or group **2.** NOBLE RANK the rank, status, or title of a nobleman or noblewoman **3.** LIST OF NOBLES a book listing the members of the nobility and giving information about their families

peer·ess /pe̅erəss/ *n* **1.** a woman who is a peer **2.** the wife or widow of a peer

peer group *n* a social group consisting of people who are equal in such respects as age, education, or social class ○ *Teenagers usually prefer to spend time with their own peer group.*

peer·less /pe̅erləss/ *adj* so good as to have no equal —**peer·less·ly** *adv* —**peer·less·ness** *n*

peer of the realm *n* in Great Britain and Northern Ireland, a member of the nobility who has the right to sit in the House of Lords

peer pres·sure *n* social pressure on somebody to adopt a type of behavior, dress, or attitude in order to be accepted as part of a group

peer re·view *n* an assessment of an article, piece of work, or research by people who are experts on the subject —**peer-re·view** *vt* —**peer-re·viewed** *adj*

peer-to-peer *adj* ONLINE full form of **P2P**

peeve /peev/ (*informal*) *vt* (**peeved, peev·ing, peeves**) **ANNOY SOMEBODY** to make somebody feel annoyed, irritated, or resentful ■ *n* **1. SOMETHING THAT ANNOYS** something that annoys or irritates somebody **2. BAD MOOD** an irritated or resentful mood [Early 20C. Back-formation < PEEVISH]

pee·vish /peévish/ *adj* bad-tempered, irritable, or tending to complain [14C. Origin ?] —**pee·vish·ly** *adv*—**pee·vish·ness** *n*

pee·wee[1] /peé weè/ *n* **1. VERY SMALL PERSON OR THING** somebody or something that is extremely small, especially a small child **2. CHILD PLAYING SPORT** a child involved in a sport or sports league organized for children ■ *adj* **1. TINY** very small **2. FOR CHILDREN** describes a sport or sports league that is organized for children ○ *played peewee baseball* [Late 19C. Reduplication of WEE]

pee·wee[2] *n* BIRDS another spelling of **pewee**

pee·wit /peé wìt/ *n* BIRDS same as **lapwing** [Early 16C. An imitation of its cry]

~~**peform**~~ incorrect spelling of **perform**

peg /peg/ *n* **1. HOOK FOR HANGING THINGS** a hook or projecting piece of wood or metal that is attached to a surface such as a door or wall and used to hang things, especially clothes **2. PIN FOR FASTENING OR MARKING SOMETHING** a small piece of metal, plastic, or wood used to secure or mark something, or to join two parts together **3.** *UK* same as **clothespin 4. PART OF INSTRUMENT FOR TUNING** a screw or pin around which a string is wound in the head (**pegbox**) of a stringed instrument. The string can be tightened or loosened to raise or lower its pitch by turning the peg. **5. REASON FOR DOING SOMETHING** an excuse or reason for doing something, or a support for an argument **6. DEGREE OR STEP** a degree, notch, or step, especially in somebody's opinion of a person or thing **7.** BASEBALL **FAST THROW** in baseball, a fast low throw of the ball that puts a base runner out **8.** LEISURE **CROQUET PIN** in croquet, a post that must be hit with a ball in order for a player to win the game ■ *vt* (**pegged, peg·ging, pegs**) **1. SECURE SOMETHING WITH PEGS** to fasten something with one or more pegs **2. PUT PEG IN SOMETHING** to insert a peg into something **3. MARK SOMETHING WITH PEG** to mark something such as the score in a game with a peg or pegs **4. CATEGORIZE SOMEBODY** to classify somebody or something, especially as having a particular character **5.** COMM **FIX SOMETHING AT CERTAIN LEVEL** to fix the cost or value of something at a particular level **6.** BASEBALL **THROW BASEBALL** in baseball, to throw a low and fast ball (*informal*) [15C. Probably < obsolete Dutch *pegge*] ◇ **a square peg in a round hole** a person who is unsuited to the situation he or she is in ◇ **bring** *or* **take somebody down a peg (or two)** to make somebody more humble

peg out *v* **1.** *vt* **SECURE SOMETHING WITH PEGS** to fasten something such as a tent with pegs **2.** *vt* **MARK OUT LAND** to mark out a piece of land with stakes **3.** *vi* **WIN CROQUET GAME** in croquet, to hit the peg, thereby winning the game **4.** *vt* **EXCLUDE OPPONENT'S BALL IN CROQUET** to make an opponent's croquet ball hit the peg, thereby causing it to be out of the game **5.** *vi* CARDS **SCORE WINNING POINT IN CRIBBAGE** in cribbage, to score the winning point

Peg·a·sus /péggəssəss/ *n* **1.** in Greek mythology, a horse with wings, born of the shed blood of Medusa **2.** a large constellation of the northern hemisphere between Andromeda and Aquarius. See illustration at **constellation**

peg·board /pég bàwrd/ *n* **1.** a board with a pattern of holes into which pegs are placed in some games **2.** a board with a pattern of holes into which pegs are placed to keep the score in some games, especially card games such as cribbage

Peg-Board /pég bàwrd/ *tdmk* a trademark for a thin board with evenly spaced holes into which pegs or hooks can be placed for displaying, hanging, or storing things

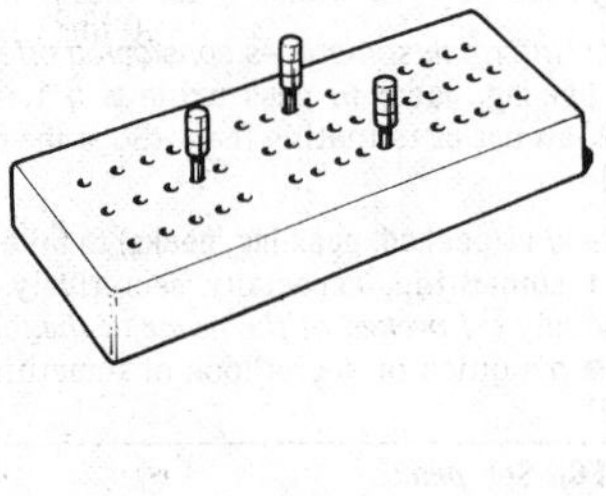

pegboard

peg·box /pég bòks/ *n* the portion of a stringed instrument that holds the tuning pegs

peg leg *n* **1.** a prosthetic leg, especially a simple wooden one fitted at the knee (*offensive*) **2.** an offensive term for somebody who has a prosthetic leg

peg·ma·tite /pégmə tìt/ *n* a coarse-grained igneous rock, usually granite, that is characterized by large well-formed crystals and often contains rare elements [Mid-19C. < Greek *pēgmat-* "something joined together"] —**peg·ma·tit·ic** /pègmə títtik/ *adj*

peg top *n* a spinning top that is thrown from the hand and is caused to spin as a string quickly unwinds from around a central metal peg ■ **peg tops** *npl* pants that are full and gathered at the hips and narrow at the ankle (*dated*)

Pe·gu /pe goó/ city in Myanmar, formerly Burma. Between 1531 and 1635 it was the country's capital. Population: 150,528 (1983).

Peh·le·vi *n, adj* LANG another spelling of **Pahlavi**

I. M. Pei

Pei /pay/, **I. M.** (*b.* 1917) Chinese-born US architect. His major urban buildings around the world combine elegance of form with functional efficiency, and include the John Hancock Tower, Boston, Massachusetts (1973) and a pyramidal glass entrance to the Louvre, Paris (1989). Full name **Pei, Ieoh Ming**

P.E.I., PEI *abbr* Prince Edward Island

~~**peice**~~ incorrect spelling of **piece**

pei·gnoir /payn waár, pen-/ *n* a woman's loose-fitting dressing gown, bathrobe, or negligee [Mid-19C. < French < *peigner* "to comb" < Latin *pecten* "comb"]

~~**peir**~~ incorrect spelling of **pier**

Peirce /peerss/, **Charles S.** (1839–1914) US philosopher and physicist. A prolific writer on a wide range of mathematical, philosophical, and scientific subjects, he is best known for developing a system of philosophy that later came to be known as pragmatism. Full name **Peirce, Charles Sanders**

pej·o·ra·tion /pèjjə ráysh'n, peéjə-/ *n* **1.** a worsening, deterioration, or decline in quality, status, or value (*formal*) **2.** a change over time in the meaning of a word so that it becomes less favorable or more negative. An example is the English word "cunning," formerly used to mean "learned" but now used to mean "cleverly deceitful." [Mid-17C. < medieval Latin *peioration-* < late Latin *peiorare* "worsen" < Latin *peior* "worse"]

pe·jor·a·tive /pə jáwrətiv, péjjə ràytiv, peéjə-/ *adj* expressing criticism or disapproval (*formal*) ■ *n* a word, expression, or affix that expresses criticism or disapproval [Late 19C. < French *péjoratif* < late Latin *peiorare* (see PEJORATION)] —**pe·jor·a·tive·ly** *adv*

peke /peek/, **Peke** *n* a Pekingese dog (*informal*) [Early 20C. Shortening]

pe·kin /peé kìn/ *n* **1.** silk fabric with broad stripes in various colors or patterns **2.** *also* **Pe·kin** a large white domestic duck. Raised for: meat, eggs. Native to: China. [Late 18C. < French *pékin*, after *Pékin* "Beijing"]

Pe·kin /peékin/ city in north central Illinois, on the eastern bank of the Illinois River, south of Peoria. Population: 33,428 (2002 estimate).

Pe·kin·ese *n, adj* BREED, PEOPLES another spelling of **Pekingese**

Pe·king /peé kíng/ former name for **Beijing**

Pe·king duck *n* **1.** a Chinese dish in which small portions of duck meat, strips of crisp duck skin, cucumber, and scallions are rolled in thin pancakes **2.** *Hong Kong* a student who is expected to deal with a large amount of school work and learn by rote

Pekingese

Pe·king·ese /peè king eéz, -eéss/, **Pe·kin·ese** /peèkə neéz, -neéss/ *n* (*plural same*) **1. SMALL CHINESE DOG** a small pet dog with a short flat nose, a long straight silky coat, and a tail that curls over its back, belonging to a breed originally developed in China **2. SOMEBODY FROM BEIJING** somebody who comes from Beijing **3.** LANG same as **Chinese** (sense 3) (*dated*) ■ *adj* **OF BEIJING** relating to Beijing, or its people or culture

Pe·king man *n* the fossilized remains of an extinct human species that lived 400,000 to 500,000 years ago, originally classified as Pithecanthropus and now regarded as a subspecies of Homo erectus [Early 20C. After PEKING, because discovered in China]

pe·koe /peékō/ *n* a high-quality black tea [Early 18C. < Chinese *pekho* "white down"]

pel·age /péllij/ *n* a mammal's coat of fur, hair, or wool (*technical*) [Early 19C. < French < Old French *pel* "hair" < Latin *pilus*]

Pe·la·gi·an·ism /pə láyjee ə nìzzəm/ *n* the belief of the heretical Christian monk Pelagius that people can earn salvation through their own efforts, without relying on the grace of God, and the rejection of the concept of original sin [Late 16C. After PELAGIUS]

pe·lag·ic /pə lájjik/ *adj* **1.** relating to, living, or occurring in the waters of the ocean or the open sea as opposed to near the shore ○ *pelagic bird populations* **2.** describes sediments deposited beneath deep ocean waters that are rich in the remains of microscopic organisms [Mid-17C. Via Latin < Greek *pelagikos* < *pelagos* "sea"]

Pe·lag·i·us /pi láyjee əss/ (360?–420?) Romano-British monk. His doctrine, known as Pelagianism, denies the existence of original sin and was condemned as heretical. —**Pe·la·gi·an** *adj, n*

pel·ar·gon·ic ac·id /pèl aar gònnik-/ *n US* a colorless to yellow oil. Source: beets, potatoes. Use: in plastics, pharmaceuticals, and synthetic flavors, additive in gasoline. Formula: $CH_3(CH_2)_7COOH$. Can term **nonanoic acid**

pel·ar·go·ni·um /pèl aar gṓnee əm/ (*plural* **-ums** *or same*) *n* a flowering plant with rounded or lobed leaves. Flowers: red, pink, white, in clusters. Native to: southern Africa. Genus: *Pelargonium.* [Early 19C. < modern Latin < Greek *pelargos* "stork"; because its capsules resemble a stork's bill]

Pe·las·gi·an /pi lázjee ən, -lázgee-/ *n* a member of an ancient people who lived in Greece and the islands of the Aegean Sea before the arrival of the Bronze Age Hellenic peoples ■ *adj also* **Pe·las·gic** /pi lázjik, -lázgik/ relating to the Pelasgian peoples or their cultures [15C. < Latin *Pelasgus* < Greek *Pelasgos*, the Pelasgians' mythical founder]

pe·lau /pi lów, pe-/ *n Carib* a spicy dish of browned meat, usually small pieces of beef or chicken, with rice, and sometimes peas [Mid-17C. Variant of PILAF]

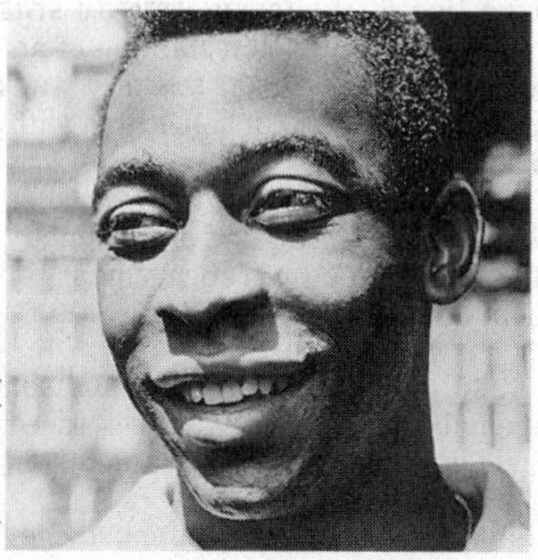
Express Newspapers
Pelé

Pe·lé /pél ay/ (*b.* 1940) Brazilian soccer player. He is considered one of the greatest players of all time. His Brazilian team won the World Cup in 1958, 1962, and 1970. He retired in 1977, having scored 1,281 goals during his career. Born **Nascimento, Edson Arantes do**

pe·lec·y·pod /pə léssə pòd/ *n* MARINE BIOL same as **bivalve** [Late 19C. < modern Latin *Pelecypoda* < Greek *pelekus* "ax" + *-podos* "footed"]

pel·er·ine /pèllə reén, -rin/ *n* a woman's short narrow cape with long pointed ends that meet at the front [Mid-18C. Via French *pèlerine*, form of *pèlerin* "pilgrim" < Latin *pelegrinus* (see PEREGRINE)]

Pe·le's hair /páy làyz-, peéliz-/ *n* fine threads of volcanic glass formed by the action of the wind on jets of lava erupting into the air [Mid-19C. Translation of Hawaiian *lauoho o Pele*, after *Pele*, goddess of volcanoes]

Pe·le·us /peélee əss, peél yòoss/ *n* in Greek mythology, the king of the Myrmidons in Thessaly. He and the sea nymph Thetis were the parents of Achilles.

pelf /pelf/ *n* money, wealth, or riches, especially if obtained dishonestly (*archaic*) [14C. < Old N French variant of Old French *pelfre* "booty"]

pel·ham /pélləm/ *n* a bit for a horse's bridle that is midway between the simple snaffle bit and the harsher curb bit [Mid-19C. After *Pelham*, surname]

pelican

pel·i·can /péllikən/ *n* a large water bird that has webbed feet and a large flat beak with a hanging pouch that can be expanded to catch and store fish. Native to: warm-water coasts and lakes worldwide. Family: Pelecanidae. [Pre-12C. Via late Latin < Greek *pelekan*]

Pel·i·can State *n* a nickname for Louisiana

pe·lisse /pə leéss/ *n* **1.** a cloak, coat, or jacket lined or trimmed with fur, often worn as part of a military uniform, e.g., by members of the Hussar regiments **2.** a woman's long fitted coat or dress that opens at the front and is often trimmed with fur [Early 18C. Via French < late Latin *pellicia* < Latin *pellis* "skin"]

pe·lite /peé lìt/, **pe·lyte** *n* aluminum-rich metamorphic rock formed by the action of temperature and pressure on clay-rich sedimentary rocks [Late 19C. < Greek *pēlos* "clay"] —**pe·lit·ic** /pə líttik/ *adj*

pel·lag·ra /pə lággrə, pə láygrə/ *n* a disease caused by a dietary deficiency of niacin and marked by dermatitis, diarrhea, and disorder of the central nervous system [Early 19C. < Italian < *pelle* "skin" + *agra* "rough" or *-agra* "seizure"] —**pel·lag·rous** *adj*

pel·let /péllət/ *n* **1.** SMALL BALL OF COMPRESSED MATERIAL a small ball or piece of material that has been pressed tightly together, e.g., for animal feed or a medicine **2.** SMALL BULLET a small bullet or ball of metal fired from a gun, especially an air gun **3.** IMITATION BULLET an imitation bullet for use in a toy gun **4.** STONE MISSILE a ball, usually made of stone, formerly used as a cannonball or as a missile fired from a catapult **5.** ZOOL ANIMAL FECES a small round piece of the feces of some animals such as sheep or rabbits **6.** BIRDS REGURGITATED MATTER an undigested mass of food, mostly bone and hair, that is regurgitated by owls and other birds of prey ■ *vt* (**-let·ed, -let·ing, -lets**) **1.** MAKE PELLETS OF SOMETHING to make or form something into pellets **2.** STRIKE SOMETHING WITH PELLETS to bombard or hit somebody or something with pellets [14C. < French *pelote* "small ball" < Latin *pila* "ball"] —**pel·let·i·za·tion** /pèlləti záysh'n/ *n* —**pel·let·ize** *vt* —**pel·let·iz·er** *n*

pel·li·cle /péllik'l/ *n* **1.** a thin film, membrane, or skin **2.** a multilayered flexible sheath that lies immediately beneath the cell membrane of many protozoans [Mid-16C. Via French < Latin *pellicula*, literally "small skin" < *pellis* "skin"] —**pel·lic·u·lar** /pə líkyələr/ *adj*

pel·li·to·ry /pélli tàwree/ (*plural* **-ri·es**) *n* a plant whose oil was formerly used for the relief of toothache. Native to: Mediterranean. Latin name: *Anacyclus pyrethrum*. [15C. < Old French *peletre*, alteration of *peretre* < Latin *pyrethrum* (see PYRETHRUM)]

pell-mell /pèl mél/ *adv* **1.** IN DISORDERLY RUSH in a disorderly frantic rush **2.** MESSILY in a confused, jumbled, or messy manner ■ *adj* DISORDERLY confused, frantic, or disorderly ■ *n* CONFUSION OR DISORDER a confused or disorderly condition or situation [Late 16C. < French *pêle-mêle*, modern form of Old French *pesle mesle* < *mesler* "to mix"]

pel·lu·cid /pə lòossid/ *adj* **1.** allowing all or most light to pass through (*literary*) **2.** easy to understand or clear in meaning (*formal*) [Early 17C. < Latin *pellucidus* < *pellucere* "shine through" < *lucere* "to shine"] —**pel·lu·cid·i·ty** /pèllyə síddətee/ *n* —**pel·lu·cid·ly** *adv* —**pel·lu·cid·ness** *n*

Pel·ly /péllee/ river in Canada. It is a tributary of the Yukon River in southeastern Yukon Territory and originates in the Mackenzie Mountains. Length: 329 mi./530 km.

pel·o·bat·id /pèllō báttid, peèlō-/ *n* a frog with the backbone development of more primitive frogs and the leg-muscle structure of more advanced ones, e.g., the European spade foot toad. Family: Pelobatidae. [Mid-20C. < Greek *pelos* "mud" + *bates* "walker"]

Pel·o·pon·ne·sus /pèlləpə neéssəss/ peninsula in southern Greece, linked to the rest of mainland Greece by the Isthmus of Corinth. Area: 8,278 sq. mi./21,440 sq. km. —**Pel·o·pon·ne·sian** /pèlləpə neézh'n, -neésh'n/ *n, adj*

Pe·lops /peé lòps/ *n* in Greek mythology, the son of Tantalus, killed by his father and served up as a meal to the gods. The gods punished Tantalus and restored Pelops to life.

pe·lo·rus /pə láwrəss/ *n* a device used to measure bearings relative to the direction in which a boat is traveling [Mid-19C. Origin ?]

Pe·lo·si /pə lóssee/, **Nancy** (*b.* 1940) US minority leader of the House of Representatives. A Democrat and congresswoman for San Francisco since 1987, she became the first woman to lead a major party in the US Congress (2002).

pe·lo·ta /pə lṓtə/ *n* **1.** a fast court game of Basque origin, in which two players use long wickerwork baskets strapped to their wrists to hurl a ball against a marked wall and catch it **2.** the ball used in pelota [Early 19C. < Spanish, "ball" < Latin *pila*]

pelt[1] /pelt/ *n* **1.** ANIMAL SKIN the skin of an animal with the fur, hair, or wool still attached **2.** ANIMAL SKIN FOR TANNING the skin of an animal with the fur, hair, or wool removed so that it is ready for tanning into leather ■ *vt* (**pelt·ed, pelt·ing, pelts**) REMOVE ANIMAL'S SKIN to remove the skin of an animal [15C. Origin ?]

pelt[2] /pelt/ *v* (**pelt·ed, pelt·ing, pelts**) **1.** *vt* THROW THINGS AT SOMEBODY OR SOMETHING to bombard somebody or something with many blows or missiles **2.** *vt* BEAT AGAINST SOMETHING to beat against something continuously **3.** *vi* RAIN HEAVILY to fall fast and hard as hail or rain **4.** *vi* MOVE QUICKLY to hurry or move quickly ■ *n* A BLOW a strong blow [15C. Origin ?] —**pelt·er** *n* ◇ **at full pelt** extremely fast

pel·tast /pél tàst/ *n* a foot soldier of ancient Greece armed with a light shield and a javelin [Early 17C. Via Latin < Greek *peltastēs* < *peltē* "small light shield"]

pel·tate /pél tàyt/ *adj* describes a leaf that has its stalk attached to the lower surface in the center rather than at the edge [Mid-18C. < Latin *peltatus*, "armed with a light shield" < *pelta* "small light shield" < Greek *peltē*] —**pel·tate·ly** *adv* —**pel·ta·tion** /pel táysh'n/ *n*

Pel·ti·er ef·fect /pélt yay-/ *n* the production or absorption of heat at the junction of two metals when an electric current is passed from one metal to another. Heat is produced or absorbed depending on the direction and amount of current flow. [Mid-19C. After J. C. A. *Peltier* (1785–1845), French scientist]

Pel·ton wheel /pélt'n-/ *n* an impulse turbine in which cup-shaped buckets on the edge of a rotor are hit with a high-pressure jet of water, causing the rotor to turn [Late 19C. After L. A. *Pelton* (1829–1908), US engineer]

pel·try /péltree/ *n* the skins of animals collectively, especially when the fur is still attached [15C. < Anglo-Norman *pelterie*, Old French *peleterie* < Old French *pel* "animal skin, pelt" < Latin *pellis* "skin, leather"]

pel·ves ANAT plural of **pelvis**

pel·vic /pélvik/ *adj* relating to, involving, or located in or near the pelvis

pel·vic fin *n* either of a pair of fins on the lower surface of a fish that have skeletal support and are analogous to the hind limbs of land animals

pel·vic in·flam·ma·to·ry dis·ease *n* an inflammation of a woman's reproductive organs in the pelvic area, which can cause infertility

pel·vim·e·try /pel vímmətree/ *n* measurement of the inlet and outlet diameters of the pelvis, usually to assess whether there will be any difficulty during childbirth

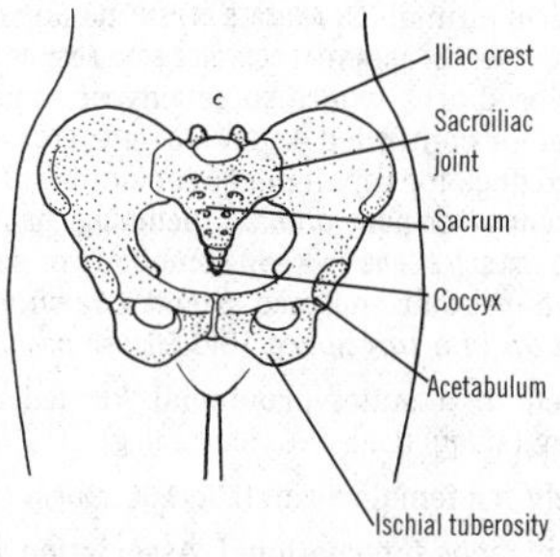

pelvis

pel·vis /pélviss/ (*plural* **pel·vis·es** *or* **pel·ves** /pél veez/) *n* **1.** the strong basin-shaped ring of bone near the bottom of the spine formed by the hip bones on the front and sides, and the triangular sacrum on the back **2.** any basin- or cup-shaped anatomical cavity, e.g., the region of the kidney into which urine is discharged before its passage into the ureter [Early 17C. < Latin, literally "basin"]

pe·ly·co·saur /péllikə sàwr/ *n* a large extinct reptile that was common in Europe and North America during the Permian period, 245 to 290 million years ago. Order: Pelycosauria. [Mid-20C. < Greek *peluk-* "bowl" + *sauros* "lizard"]

pe·lyte *n* GEOL another spelling of **pelite**

Pem·ba /pémbə/ island in northeastern Tanzania, in the Indian Ocean. Its main towns are Wete and

Chake Chake. Population: 265,039 (1988). Area: 379 sq. mi./982 sq. km.

Pem·broke /pém brŏŏk, pémbrək/ **1.** town in southeastern Massachusetts, northwest of Plymouth and southwest of Scituate. Population: 17,541 (2002 estimate). **2.** city in Canada, in southeastern Ontario, on the Ottawa River. Population: 15,019 (2001). **3.** town in southwestern Wales, in Pembrokeshire. Population: 6,773 (1991).

Pem·broke·shire /pém brŏŏk sheer, -shər/ county in southwestern Wales. Haverfordwest is its administrative center. Population: 114,131 (2001). Area: 614 sq. mi./1,591 sq. km.

Pem·broke ta·ble (*plural* **Pem·broke ta·bles** or **pem·broke ta·bles**) *n* a small four-legged table with a top that folds down on two sides and one or two drawers [Late 18C. Probably after PEMBROKE, Wales]

pem·mi·can /pémmikən/, **pem·i·can** *n* **1.** a traditional Native North American food made with strips of lean dried meat pounded into paste, mixed with melted fat and dried berries or fruits, and pressed into small cakes **2.** a nutritious food adapted from traditional Native North American pemmican and used as emergency rations, e.g., by explorers [Late 18C. < Cree *pimihkan* "he makes grease"]

pem·o·line /pémmə leen/ *n* a synthetic stimulant of the central nervous system. Use: treatment of depression, attention deficit disorder in children. Formula: $C_9H_8N_2O_2$. [Mid-20C. < parts of *phenyliminooxooxazolidine*, its chemical name]

pem·phi·gus /pémfigəss, pem fígəss/ *n* an autoimmune disease characterized by large blisters on the skin and mucous membranes, often accompanied by itching or burning sensations [Late 18C. Via modern Latin < Greek *pemphig-* "pustule"]

pen[1] /pen/ *n* **1. WRITING INSTRUMENT** a long thin instrument used for writing or drawing with ink. Early examples were made from sharpened quill feathers, but modern pens usually consist of a metal or plastic shaft with a nib, point, or revolving ball at one end. **2. WRITING** the written word considered as a means of expression ○ *They say the pen is mightier than the sword.* **3.** MARINE BIOL **SQUID'S INTERNAL SHELL** the internal feather-shaped horny shell of a squid ■ *vt* (**penned, pen·ning, pens**) **WRITE SOMETHING** to write something in letters or symbols, or compose something for others to read [13C. Via French < Latin *penna* "feather"] —**pen·ner** *n* ◇ **from the pen of somebody** composed or written by a particular author ○ *another novel from the pen of everybody's favorite thriller writer.*

pen[2] /pen/ *n* **1. ENCLOSURE FOR ANIMALS** a small fenced area of land, or an enclosure within a building, used to keep farm animals **2. ANIMALS IN PEN** the farm animals kept in a pen **3. AREA THAT CONFINES SOMEBODY OR SOMETHING** an enclosed area where somebody or something is confined or controlled **4.** NAVY **FORTIFIED DOCK** a heavily fortified dock for repairing or servicing submarines ■ *vt* (**penned** or **pent** *archaic*, **pen·ning, pens**) **CONFINE SOMEBODY OR SOMETHING** to keep somebody or something in a pen or other enclosed area ○ *The animals were penned up in a tiny space.* [Old English *penn*, origin ?]

pen[3] /pen/ *n* a state, provincial, or federal penitentiary (*slang*) [Late 19C. Shortening]

pen[4] /pen/ *n* a female swan [Mid-16C. Origin ?]

PEN /pen/ *abbr* International Association of Poets, Playwrights, Editors, Essayists, and Novelists

Pen. *abbr* **1.** Peninsula (*used in place names*) **2.** Penitentiary (*used in names of prisons*)

pe·nal /peen'l/ *adj* **1. OF PUNISHMENT** relating to, forming, or prescribing punishment, especially by law ○ *the penal system* **2. PUNISHABLE BY LAW** subject to punishment under the law **3. USED AS PLACE OF PUNISHMENT** used as a place of imprisonment and punishment ○ *a penal institution* [15C. Via French *pénal* < Latin *poenalis* < *poena* "penalty"]

pe·nal code *n* a body or system of laws concerned with the punishment of crime

pe·nal col·o·ny *n* a place of imprisonment and punishment at a remote location

pe·nal·ize /peen'l īz/ (**-ized, -iz·ing, -iz·es**) *vt* **1. SUBJECT SOMEBODY TO PENALTY** to impose a penalty on somebody or something for breaking a law or rule **2. DISADVANTAGE SOMEBODY** to put somebody or something at a disadvantage, or treat him or her unfairly ○ *The tax system heavily penalizes people with high incomes.* **3. PUNISH PLAYER FOR BREAKING RULE** to punish a team or player for breaking a rule by giving an advantage to the opposing team or player **4. MAKE SOMETHING PUNISHABLE** to make something punishable by a law or rule —**pe·nal·i·za·tion** /peen'li záysh'n/ *n*

pe·nal ser·vi·tude *n* confinement in a penal colony as a result of conviction of a crime

pen·al·ty /pénn'ltee/ (*plural* **-ties**) *n* **1. PUNISHMENT FOR CRIME** a legal or official punishment for committing a crime or other offense, e.g., a fine or imprisonment **2. PUNISHMENT FOR BREAKING CONTRACT** a punishment, e.g., a fine, for failing to fulfill the terms of a legal agreement **3. UNPLEASANT CONSEQUENCE** something unpleasant suffered as the result of an unwise action ○ *paying the penalty of being too lenient* **4. DISADVANTAGE FOR BREAKING RULE** a disadvantage imposed on a player or team for breaking a rule in a sport or game, e.g., a free shot at the goal awarded to the opposing side **5.** SOCCER same as **penalty kick** (sense 1) **6. GOAL FROM PENALTY** in soccer, a goal scored from a penalty [15C. < assumed Anglo-Norman variant of French *pénalité* < Latin *poenalis* (see PENAL)]

pen·al·ty ar·e·a *n* a rectangular area in front of a soccer goal within which the goalkeeper is allowed to handle the ball. A foul by the defending team within this area may result in a free shot at the goal awarded to the opposing side.

pen·al·ty box *n* **1.** an area with a bench beside a hockey rink where penalized players must stay during the period they have to serve as a time penalty **2.** SOCCER same as **penalty area**

pen·al·ty kick *n* **1.** in soccer, a free kick from the penalty spot at the opposing team's goal, which is defended only by its goalkeeper. It is awarded for some types of fouls within the penalty area. **2.** in rugby, a kick worth three points that can be aimed at the goal after a serious foul by a member of the opposing side

pen·al·ty shoot·out *n* SOCCER same as **shootout** (sense 2)

pen·al·ty shot *n* SPORTS same as **penalty** (sense 4)

pen·al·ty spot *n* **1.** a designated spot on a soccer field, 12 yd./11 m from the goal line, from which penalty kicks are taken **2.** in field hockey, a designated spot 23 ft./7 m from the goal line from which the shot is taken

pen·ance /pénnənss/ *n* **1. SELF-PUNISHMENT FOR SIN** self-punishment or an act of religious devotion performed to show sorrow for having committed a sin **2. DUTY IMPOSED BY PRIEST** a duty or religious devotion imposed by a priest during the sacrament of confession in some Christian churches **3. CHRISTIAN SACRAMENT OF RECONCILIATION** a sacrament in some Christian churches in which a person confesses sins to a priest and is forgiven after performing a religious devotion or duty such as praying or fasting ■ *vt* (**-anced, -anc·ing, -anc·es**) **IMPOSE PENANCE ON SOMEBODY** to make somebody do penance for a sin [13C. Via French < Latin *paenitentia* "regret" < *paenitere* "to regret"]

Pe·nang /pə náng/, **Pi·nang** state in northwestern Malaysia, comprising Penang Island and a small mainland area on the Malay Peninsula. Capital: George Town. Population: 219,603 (1996). Area: 398 sq. mi./1,031 sq. km.

pen·an·nu·lar /pen ánnyələr/ *adj* in the shape of an almost complete circle [Mid-19C. < Latin *paene* "almost"]

pe·na·tes /pə náyteez, pə naateez/ *npl* in ancient Roman religion, the gods of a household or state [Early 16C. < Latin < *penus* "provisions"]

~~**penatrate**~~ incorrect spelling of **penetrate**

pence *UK* MONEY plural of **penny**

pen·cel /pénssəl/, **pen·sil** *n* a small narrow flag (**pennon**) or streamer, especially one carried at the end of a lance [13C. < Anglo-Norman, contraction of Old French *penoncel* "small pennon" < *penon* (see PENNON)]

pen·chant /pénchənt/ *n* a strong liking, taste, or tendency for something [Late 17C. < French, present participle of *pencher* "incline" < assumed Vulgar Latin *pendicare* < Latin *pendere* "hang"]

pen·cil /pénssəl/ *n* **1. WRITING INSTRUMENT** a thin cylindrical instrument used for drawing or writing. It consists of a rod of graphite or some other erasable marking material inside a wooden or metal shaft. **2. SOMETHING RESEMBLING PENCIL** something that has a shape, structure, or function similar to a pencil, e.g., a stick for applying cosmetics ○ *an eyebrow pencil* **3.** OPTICS **CYLINDER OF LIGHT** a long narrow cylinder or cone of light with a small angle of convergence **4.** MATH **SET OF LINES THROUGH POINT** the set of all lines passing through a fixed point or of all lines parallel to a given line **5.** ART **ARTIST'S INDIVIDUAL STYLE** the individual drawing style or technique of an artist ■ *vt* (**-ciled, -cil·ing, -cils**) **WRITE SOMETHING WITH PENCIL** to draw, mark, write, or color something with a pencil [14C. Via Old French *pincel* < Latin *peniculus* "brush," literally "small tail" < *penis* "tail"]

pencil in *vt* to note something provisionally such as the time of a proposed engagement in an appointment book or on a calendar

pen·cil case *n* a small container for somebody's pens, pencils, and erasers, used especially by school, college, and university students

pen·cil mus·tache *n* a very thin mustache

pen·cil push·er *n* somebody whose work involves much paperwork, e.g., an office worker (*informal*)

pen·cil skirt *n* a narrow straight skirt

pen com·put·er *n* a computer using pattern-recognition circuitry or software to enable it to accept handwriting as data input. Many personal digital assistants are pen computers.

pend /pend/ (**pend·ed, pend·ing, pends**) *vi* **1.** to remain unsettled or wait to be judged **2.** to be suspended or drape from something (*literary*) [15C. Probably < French *pendre* (see PENDANT)]

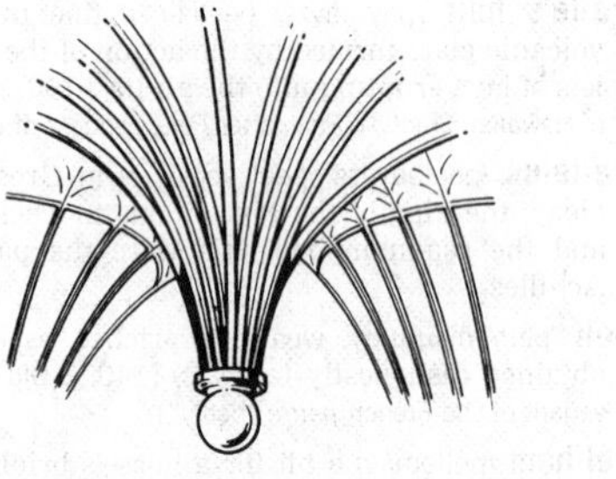

pendant (sense 4)

pen·dant /péndənt/ *n* **1. HANGING ORNAMENT OR JEWELRY** an ornament or a piece of jewelry that hangs from a necklace, bracelet, or earring **2. NECKLACE WITH ORNAMENT** a necklace with a hanging ornament attached to it **3. HANGING LIGHT** a lamp, chandelier, or other lighting fixture that hangs from the ceiling **4.** ARCHIT **ORNAMENT HANGING FROM CEILING** an architectural ornament hanging from a vaulted ceiling or roof **5.** ARTS **ONE OF MATCHING PAIR** a piece of art that matches or goes with another piece **6.** NAUT **LENGTH OF WIRE OR ROPE** a length of wire or rope attached at the upper end to a spar or similar part and at the lower end to a block and tackle ■ *adj* ARCHIT, GRAM same as **pendent** [14C. < French < present participle of *pendre* "hang" < Latin *pendere*]

pen·dent /péndənt/ *adj* **1. HANGING OR SUSPENDED** dangling, hanging, or suspended (*formal or literary*) **2. OVERHANGING** jutting, overhanging, or sticking out (*formal or literary*) **3. PENDING** not yet dealt with, decided, or settled (*formal or literary*) **4.** GRAM **GRAMMATICALLY INCOMPLETE** describes an incomplete grammatical structure ■ *n* JEWELRY, ARCHIT, ARTS, NAUT same as **pendant** [13C. Variant of PENDANT] —**pen·den·cy** *n* —**pen·dent·ly** *adv*

ORIGIN The Latin word *pendere* "to hang," from which ***pendent*** is derived, is also the source of English *append, appendix, compendium, depend, impend, penchant, pendulum, penthouse, perpendicular,* and *suspend.*

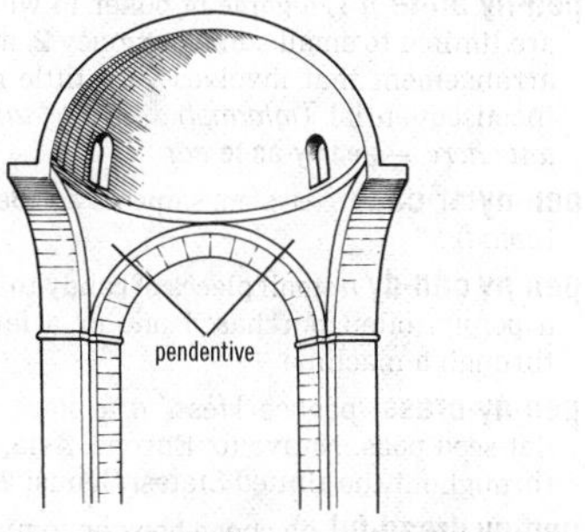

pendentive

pen·den·tive /pen déntiv/ *n* a sloping triangular piece of vaulting between the arches that support a dome and its rim [Early 18C. < French *pendentif* < Latin *pendere* "hang"]

pend·ing /pénding/ *adj* **1.** NOT YET TAKEN CARE OF not yet dealt with, decided, or settled **2.** ABOUT TO HAPPEN about to happen or come into effect ■ *prep* **1.** UNTIL until or while waiting for ○ *pending further inquiries* **2.** DURING during the course of something [Mid-17C. Anglicization of French *pendant* (see PENDANT)]

pen·drag·on /pen drággən/ (*plural* **pen·drag·ons** or **Pen·drag·ons**) *n* a supreme leader of the ancient Britons [15C. < Welsh < *pen* "head" + *dragon* "military standard" (< Latin *dracon-*)] —**pen·drag·on·ship** *n*

pen·du·lar /pénjələr, péndyələr/ *adj* swinging back and forth with the motion of a pendulum

pen·du·lous /pénjələss, péndyələss/ *adj* **1.** hanging loosely or swinging freely **2.** undecided or wavering in making a decision (*literary*) [Early 17C. < Latin *pendulus* (see PENDULUM)] —**pen·du·lous·ly** *adv* —**pen·du·lous·ness** *n*

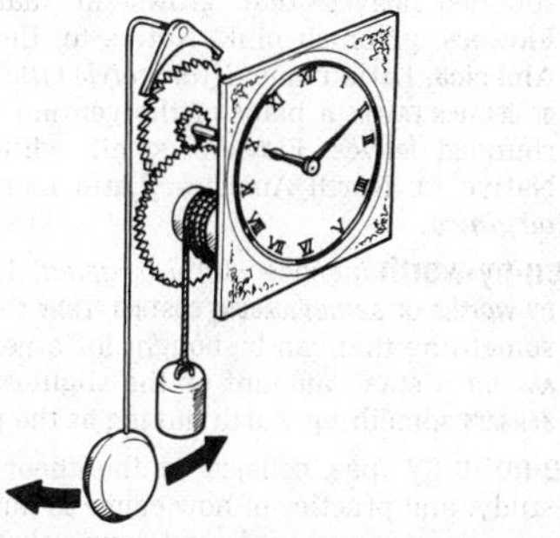
pendulum (sense 2)

pen·du·lum /pénjələm, péndyələm/ *n* **1.** HANGING WEIGHT a weight hung from a fixed point so that it can swing freely back and forth under the influence of gravity **2.** ROD CONTROLLING CLOCK a rod with a weight at its base that swings from side to side and controls the mechanism of a clock **3.** SOMETHING THAT CHANGES REGULARLY something that changes its direction or position regularly, often alternating between two extremes ○ *The pendulum has swung back to more traditional teaching methods.* [Mid-17C. < modern Latin < Latin *pendulus* "hanging" < *pendere* "hang"]

~~**penecillin**~~ incorrect spelling of **penicillin**

Pe·nel·o·pe /pə néllәpee/ *n* in Greek mythology, the wife of Odysseus, who waited for his return from the Trojan War and was the mother of his son, Telemachus

pe·ne·plain /péenə plàyn/, **pe·ne·plane** *n* an area of nearly flat featureless land that is the result of a prolonged period of erosion [Late 19C. < Latin *paene* "nearly, almost"] —**pe·ne·pla·na·tion** /pèenəplə náysh'n/ *n*

pe·nes ANAT plural of **penis**

pen·e·tra·li·a /pènnə tráylee ə/ *npl* the innermost parts of a place, especially a sanctuary within a temple (*formal*) [Mid-17C. < Latin < *penetralis* "innermost" < *penetrare* (see PENETRATE)] —**pen·e·tra·li·an** *adj*

pen·e·trance /pénnətrənss/ *n* the frequency with which a hereditary characteristic such as a genetic disease occurs among individuals carrying the gene or genes for that characteristic [Mid-20C. < German *Penetranz*]

pen·e·trant /pénnətrənt/ *n* **1.** a substance that encourages a liquid to penetrate a porous material by lowering the surface tension of the liquid **2.** somebody or something that penetrates

pen·e·trate /pénnə tràyt/ (**-trat·ed, -trat·ing, -trates**) *v* **1.** *vti* ENTER OR PASS THROUGH SOMETHING to enter or pass through something, e.g., by piercing it or forcing a way in ○ *The aim of the mission was to penetrate deep into enemy territory.* **2.** *vt* SPREAD THROUGH SOMETHING to enter and spread through something ○ *The fumes had penetrated the entire building.* **3.** *vt* GET SHARE OF MARKET to succeed in getting a share of a particular market **4.** *vt* INFILTRATE GROUP to enter something such as an organization or country, usually secretly, in order to influence or gather information from within **5.** *vt* SEE INTO SOMETHING to see into or through something that is dark or obscuring **6.** *vt* DECIPHER MEANING to understand or discover the meaning of something ○ *an enigma few were able to penetrate* **7.** *vi* BE UNDERSTOOD to be understood or taken in by the mind ○ *It took a few seconds for the news to penetrate.* **8.** *vt* INSERT PENIS INTO SOMETHING to insert the penis into a vagina or anus [Mid-16C. < Latin *penetrat-*, past participle of *penetrare* "penetrate" < *penitus* "inner, innermost"] —**pen·e·tra·bil·i·ty** /pènnətrə bíllətee/ *n* —**pen·e·tra·ble** *adj* —**pen·e·tra·tor** *n*

pen·e·trat·ing /pénnə tràyting/ *adj* **1.** ABLE OR TENDING TO PENETRATE strong enough to enter or spread through something ○ *a penetrating odor* **2.** PIERCING OR PROBING apparently able to see or understand things that are hidden ○ *a penetrating glance* **3.** LOUD loud, piercing, shrill, or unpleasant to the ears **4.** PERCEPTIVE able to understand or accurately identify something ○ *a penetrating observation* —**pen·e·trat·ing·ly** *adv*

pen·e·tra·tion /pènnə tráysh'n/ *n* **1.** ENTERING OR PASSING THROUGH the action of penetrating, entering, or passing through something ○ *Penetration of the foundations by torrential rain resulted in structural damage.* **2.** ABILITY TO PENETRATE the ability or power to penetrate, enter, or pass through something **3.** UNDERSTANDING the ability to understand or perceive something **4.** INSERTION OF PENIS the insertion of the penis into a vagina or anus **5.** DEGREE OF SUCCESS IN MARKET the extent to which a commercial product or service is recognized or bought in a particular market ○ *The launch of the new product should improve the company's market penetration.* **6.** ATTACK ENTERING ENEMY TERRITORY an attack that succeeds in penetrating an enemy's territory or defenses **7.** DEPTH PROJECTILE REACHES a measure of the depth a projectile reaches beneath the surface of its target

pen·e·tra·tive /pénnə tràytiv/ *adj* **1.** PENETRATING piercing something or able to get through something **2.** KEEN mentally perceptive or insightful **3.** INVOLVING INSERTION OF PENIS describes sexual activity that involves putting the penis into a vagina or anus

pen·e·trom·e·ter /pènnə trómmətər/, **pen·e·tram·e·ter** /-trámmətər/ *n* **1.** an instrument for measuring the penetrating power of electromagnetic radiation, e.g., gamma radiation in contaminated soils **2.** an instrument for measuring the penetrability of a solid material by measuring the depth to which it may be pierced with a standard needle [Early 20C. < PENETRATION]

pen friend *n UK* same as **pen pal**

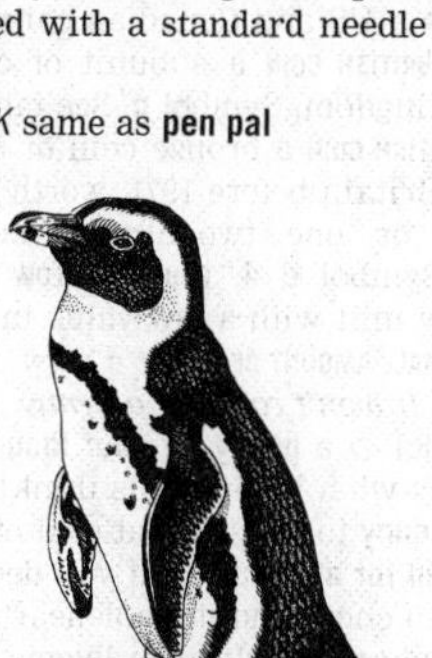
penguin

pen·guin /péng gwin/ *n* an upright web-footed seabird with contrasting black and white feathers that cannot fly but uses its flipper-shaped wings for swimming. Native to: cold regions of the southern hemisphere. Family: Spheniscidae. [Late 16C. Origin ?]

pen·hold·er /pén hòldər/ *n* **1.** a handle for a pen point or nib, consisting of a metal, plastic, or wooden rod **2.** a holder for a pen or pens in the form of, e.g., a cup, rack, or stand

-penia *suffix* deficiency ○ *thrombocytopenia* [Via modern Latin < Greek *penia* "poverty, want"]

pen·i·cil·la·mine /pènni sílla meen/ *n* a chelating agent. Source: penicillin. Use: removal of toxic metals from the body. [Mid-20C. < PENICILLIN + AMINE]

pen·i·cil·late /pènni síllət, -sí làyt/ *adj* having or resembling a tuft of hair [Early 19C. < Latin *penicillus* (see PENICILLIUM)] —**pen·i·cil·late·ly** *adv* —**pen·i·cil·la·tion** /pènnissi láysh'n/ *n*

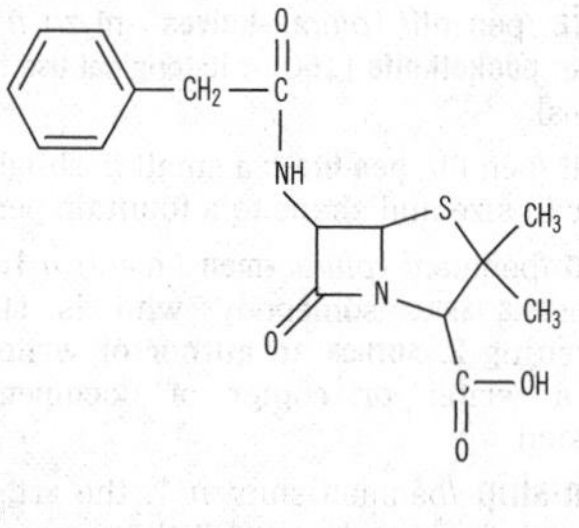
penicillin

pen·i·cil·lin /pènni síllin/ *n* an antibiotic belonging to a group originally derived from mold of the genus *Penicillium* but now produced synthetically. Formula: $C_{16}H_{18}N_2O_4S$. [Early 20C. < PENICILLIUM]

pen·i·cil·lin·ase /pènni sílli nàyss, -nàyz/ *n* an enzyme produced by some bacteria that inactivates penicillin. Use: treatment of adverse penicillin reactions.

pen·i·cil·li·um /pènni síllee əm/ *n* a bluish green fungus that grows on stale or ripening food. Use: in cheese-making, as a source of penicillin. Genus: *Penicillium.* [Mid-19C. < modern Latin < Latin *penicillus* "paintbrush" < *peniculus* (see PENCIL)]

pe·nile /pée nìl, péen'l/ *adj* relating to, affecting, or resembling the penis

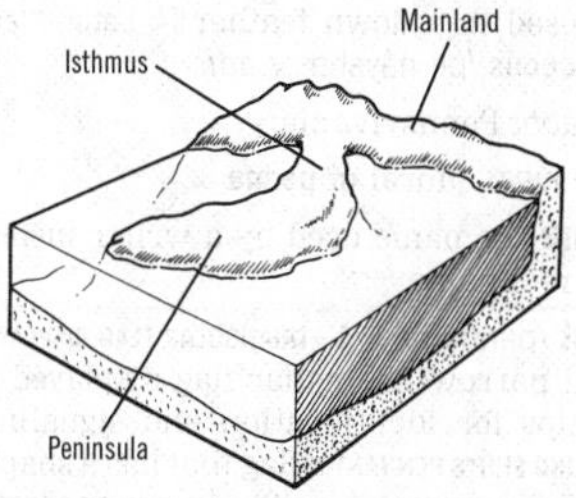

peninsula

pen·in·su·la /pə nínssyələ, pə nínssələ/ *n* a narrow piece of land that juts out from the mainland into an area of water [Mid-16C. < Latin *paeninsula* < *paene* "almost" + *insula* "island"] —**pen·in·su·lar** *adj*

pe·nis /péenəss/ (*plural* **pe·nis·es** or **pe·nes** /pée neez/) *n* the external male organ of copulation, used to transfer semen to the female. In most mammals, it is also used to expel urine from the body. [Late 17C. < Latin, "tail, penis"]

pe·nis en·vy *n* in Freudian psychoanalysis, the theory that some girls' and women's psychological problems stem from a sense of deprivation about not having a penis. Very few psychologists now accept this concept.

pen·i·tent /pénnitənt/ *adj* FEELING REGRET FOR SINS expressing or feeling regret or sorrow for having committed sins or misdeeds ■ *n* **1.** SOMEBODY WHO FEELS REGRET a sinner or wrongdoer who feels regret or sorrow for misdeeds **2.** **SOMEBODY DOING PENANCE** somebody who does a penance as directed by a priest or minister after confessing his or her sins [14C. Via French < Latin *paenitent-*, present participle of *paenitere* "regret"] —**pen·i·tence** *n* —**pen·i·tent·ly** *adv*

pen·i·ten·tial /pènni ténshəl/ *adj* constituting or expressing penance or penitence —**pen·i·ten·tial·ly** *adv*

pen·i·ten·tia·ry /pènni ténshəree/ *n* (*plural* **-ries**) **1.** **PRISON** a prison, especially for people who have been convicted of serious crimes **2.** **ROMAN CATHOLIC OFFICIAL** a high official in the Roman Catholic Church who can grant absolution in extraordinary cases **3.** **ROMAN CATHOLIC TRIBUNAL** a tribunal of the Roman Catholic Church dealing with penance ■ *adj* **1.** **OF PENANCE** relating to penance **2.** **CONCERNING PUNISHMENT OR REFORM** involving or used for the punishment or reform of offenders **3.** LAW **PUNISHABLE BY IMPRISONMENT IN PENITENTIARY** punishable by a term of imprisonment in a penitentiary [15C. < medieval Latin *paenitentiaria* < Latin *paenitentia* (see PENANCE)]

pen·knife /pén nīf/ (*plural* **-knives** /-nīvz/) *n Can, UK* same as **pocketknife** [15C. < its original use for making quill pens]

pen·light /pén līt/, **pen·lite** *n* a small flashlight that is similar in size and shape to a fountain pen

pen·man /pénmən/ (*plural* **-men** /-mən/) *n* **1.** **SOMEBODY WITH WRITING SKILL** somebody who is skilled at handwriting **2.** **AUTHOR** an author or writer **3.** HIST **SCRIBE** a writer or copier of documents as a profession

pen·man·ship /pénmən shìp/ *n* **1.** the art, skill, or technique of writing by hand **2.** the manner, quality, or style of somebody's handwriting

Penn /pen/, **John** (1741–88) US patriot. A member of the Continental Congress from North Carolina, he was a signatory of the Declaration of Independence (1776).

Penn, William (1644–1718) English-born American Quaker reformer and colonialist. After religious persecution in England, he traveled to North America in 1682, where he founded Pennsylvania.

> "They that love beyond the world cannot be separated by it. Death is but crossing the world, as friends do the seas; they live in one another still."
> [William Penn, *Some Fruits of Solitude*; 1693]

Penn. *abbr* Pennsylvania

pen·na /pénnə/ (*plural* **-nae** /-nee/) *n* a feather that helps to form the outer contour of a bird's plumage, as opposed to a down feather [< Latin, "feather"] —**pen·na·ceous** /pe náyshəss/ *adj*

Penna. *abbr* Pennsylvania

pen·nae BIRDS plural of **penna**

pen name *n* a name used by a writer instead of his or her real name

pen·nant /pénnənt/ *n* **1.** **TRIANGULAR FLAG DISPLAYED ON SHIP** a small narrow triangular flag displayed on boats and ships for identification and signaling **2.** **FLAG RESEMBLING SHIP'S PENNANT** a flag that has a shape similar to a ship's pennant **3.** NAUT same as **pendant** *n* (sense 6) **4.** **FLAG SYMBOLIZING SPORTS CHAMPIONSHIP** in some sports, especially baseball, a flag that symbolizes a championship **5.** **CHAMPIONSHIP SYMBOLIZED BY PENNANT** a championship that is symbolized by a pennant [Early 17C. Blend of PENNON + PENDANT]

pen·nate /pé nàyt/, **pen·nat·ed** /pé nàytəd/ *adj* **1.** ZOOL having feathers or wings **2.** MARINE BIOL describes diatoms which are bilaterally symmetrical. Order: Pennales. **3.** BOT same as **pinnate**

pen·ne /pé này/ *n* short tube-shaped pasta cut diagonally at the ends [Late 20C. < Italian, plural of *penna* "feather, quill pen"]

Pen·ney /pénnee/, **William George, Baron** (1909–91) British physicist. He developed the British atomic and hydrogen bombs.

pen·ni /pénnee/ (*plural* **-ni·a** /-nee ə/ or **-nis**) *n* a subunit of the former Finnish currency [Late 19C. < Finnish]

pen·ni·less /pénniləss/ *adj* very poor or without any money —**pen·ni·less·ly** *adv* —**pen·ni·less·ness** *n*

pen·nine *n* MINERALS same as **penninite**

Pen·nine Alps /pén īn-/ mountain range in southern Switzerland, along the Italian border. Its highest point is the Dufour Peak 15,200 ft./4,634 m.

Pen·nine Hills, **Pen·nines** range of hills in northern England, forming the "spine" of England

pen·ni·nite /pénni nīt/, **pen·nine** /pén īn/ *n* a green-blue mineral of the chlorite group, containing magnesium and iron. Source: metamorphic rocks. [Mid-19C. After the PENNINE ALPS]

pen·non /pénnən/ *n* **1.** a long narrow flag, usually triangular, tapering, or divided at the end, originally carried on a lance by a medieval knight **2.** NAUT same as **pennant** (sense 1) **3.** a bird's wing or the tip of a wing (*literary*) [14C. < French *penon*, literally "large feather" < Latin *penna* "feather"]

pen·non·cel /pénnən sèl/, **pen·non·celle**, **pen·on·cel**, **pen·on·celle** *n* a pennon carried at the end of a lance [14C. < Old French *penoncel* (see PENCEL)]

Pennsylvania

Penn·syl·va·nia /pènssəl váynyə/ state in the northeastern United States, bordered by New York, New Jersey, Delaware, Maryland, West Virginia, and Ohio. Capital: Harrisburg. Population: 12,335,091 (2002 estimate). Area: 46,058 sq. mi./119,290 sq. km.

Penn·syl·va·nia Dutch *npl* **GERMAN AND SWISS IMMIGRANTS IN PENNSYLVANIA** a group of people who emigrated from Germany and Switzerland to eastern Pennsylvania in the 17th and 18th centuries, or their descendants ■ *n* **1.** *also* **Penn·syl·va·nia Ger·man** **GERMAN DIALECT SPOKEN IN PENNSYLVANIA** a dialect of German mixed with some English that is spoken in eastern Pennsylvania by the Pennsylvania Dutch. Native speakers: 70,000. **2.** **FOLK ART THAT USES STYLIZED FIGURES** folk art developed by the Pennsylvania Dutch that uses stylized figures of people, plants, and animals, primarily in the decoration of household objects and in needlework [Mid-18C. Alteration of German *Deutsch* "German"] —**Penn·syl·va·nia Dutch** *adj*

Penn·syl·va·nian /pènssəl váynyən, -váynee ən/ *n* **1.** somebody who comes from Pennsylvania **2.** the period of geologic time, 330 million to 290 million years ago, during which the climate was relatively warm and damp and the major coal beds were formed. It is the second of two epochs of the Carboniferous Period used by North American geologists. See table at **geologic time** —**Penn·syl·va·nian** *adj*

pen·ny /pénnee/ (*plural* **-nies**) *n* **1.** **COIN IN UNITED STATES AND CANADA** a US and Canadian coin worth one cent **2.** **SMALL BRITISH COIN** a subunit of currency in the United Kingdom. Symbol **p.** See table at **currency** **3.** **FORMER BRITISH COIN** a bronze coin or a unit of money used in Britain before 1971, worth one twelfth of a shilling, or one two-hundred-and-fortieth of a pound. Symbol **d** **4.** **COIN WITH LOW VALUE** a coin or monetary unit with a low value in some countries **5.** **VERY SMALL AMOUNT OF MONEY** a very small amount of money ○ *It won't cost you a penny.* [Old English *penig* < Germanic] ◇ **a penny for your thoughts** used to ask somebody what he or she is thinking about ◇ **cost a pretty penny** to cost a great deal of money ◇ **in for a penny, in for a pound** *UK* if you decide to do something, you should do it wholeheartedly and boldly, and accept any resulting problems or difficulties ◇ **penny wise and pound foolish** economical with regard to small items of expenditure but extravagant with regard to large items ◇ **the penny dropped** somebody suddenly understood or realized something ◇ **turn up like a bad penny** to keep making unwelcome appearances ◇ **two** *or* **ten a penny** very numerous or common, and therefore of little value

pen·ny an·te *n* **1.** a game of poker in which the bets are limited to small sums of money **2.** any business arrangement that involves very little money or is inconsequential (*informal*) ○ *We're talking penny ante here.* —**pen·ny-an·te** *adj*

pen·ny ar·cade *n* LEISURE same as **arcade** *n* (sense 3) (*dated*)

pen·ny can·dy *n* small pieces of candy that cost about a penny, often purchased one or a few at a time through a machine

pen·ny·cress /pénnee krèss/ *n* a plant with round flat seed pods. Native to: Europe, Asia, naturalized throughout the United States. Genus: *Thlaspi*.

pen·ny dread·ful *n* a cheap book or comic containing lurid stories of adventure, crime, or passion

pen·ny pinch·er *n* somebody who is stingy or unduly careful with his or her money (*informal*)

pen·ny·roy·al /pènnee róy əl/ *n* **1.** a plant of the mint family with small purple flowers. Use: medicines, insect repellent. Native to: Europe, Asia. Latin name: *Mentha pulegium*. **2.** an aromatic plant of the mint family, especially a variety with bluish flowers. Native to: eastern North America. Latin name: *Hedeoma pulegioides*. [Mid-16C. Alteration of Anglo-Norman *puliol real* "royal thyme"]

pen·ny stock *n* a security that sells on a stock exchange, often at less than one dollar a share

pen·ny·weight /pénnee wàyt/ *n* a unit of weight in the troy system, equal to 0.05 oz/1.555 g

pen·ny whis·tle *n* a small high-pitched flute with six finger holes, similar to a recorder but made of metal

pen·ny-wise *adj* extremely careful about spending even small amounts of money

pen·ny·wort /pénnee wùrt, -wàwrt/ *n* **1.** **ROCK PLANT** a rock plant with rounded leaves. Flowers: whitish green, tubular. Native to: Europe, Asia. Latin name: *Umbilicus rupestris*. **2.** **MARSH PLANT** a plant with rounded leaves that grows in marshy areas. Flowers: greenish pink. Native to: Europe, North America. Latin name: *Hydrocotyle vulgaris*. **3.** **PLANT OF GENTIAN FAMILY** a plant of the gentian family with rounded leaves. Flowers: small, white, purplish. Native to: North America. Latin name: *Obolaria virginica*.

pen·ny·worth /pénnee wùrth/ *n* (*dated*) **1.** (*plural* **pen·ny·worths** or *same*) **AMOUNT COSTING PENNY** the amount of something that can be bought for a penny **2.** **SMALL AMOUNT** a small amount or the slightest amount **3.** **BARGAIN** something worth having at the price

pe·nol·o·gy /pee nólləjee/ *n* the theory, scientific study, and practice of how crime is punished, how prisons are managed, and how rehabilitation is handled [Mid-19C. < Latin *poena* "penalty"] —**pe·no·log·i·cal** /pēenə lójjik'l/ *adj* —**pe·no·log·i·cal·ly** *adv* —**pe·nol·o·gist** *n*

pen·on·cel, **pen·on·celle** *n* HIST another spelling of **pennoncel**

pen pal *n* either of two people, usually in different countries, who become friends through an exchange of letters but who may never meet

pen point *n* the tip, point, or nib of a pen

pen·push·er /pén pŏoshər/ *n UK* same as **pencil pusher** (*informal*) —**pen·push·ing** *adj, n*

Pen·sa·co·la /pènssə kṓlə/ city in northwestern Florida, on the Gulf of Mexico. Population: 55,240 (2002 estimate).

pen·sil *n* HIST another spelling of **pencel**

pen·sile /pén sīl/ *adj* hanging or suspended ○ *a pensile nest* [Early 17C. < Latin *pensilis* < *pens-* (see PENSION[1])]

pen·sion[1] /pénsh'n/ *n* **1.** **RETIREMENT PAY** a fixed amount of money paid regularly to somebody during retirement by the government, a former employer, or an insurance company **2.** **REGULAR SUM PAID** a sum of money paid regularly as compensation, e.g., for an injury sustained on a job, or as a reward for service, e.g., to an ex-soldier ○ *a widow's pension* ■ *vt* (**-sioned, -sion·ing, -sions**) **PAY SOMEBODY PENSION** to pay a pension to somebody [14C. Via French < Latin *pension-* "payment" < *pens-*, past participle of *pendere* "hang"] —**pen·sion·ar·y** *adj*

pension off *vt* **1.** to force somebody into retirement with a pension, e.g., as a cost-cutting measure or because of age **2.** to get rid of something because it is useless or no longer needed (*informal*)

pen·sion[2] /paàn syáwn/ *n* **1.** a boarding house or small inexpensive hotel in continental Europe, especially in France **2.** accommodations provided by a European pension **3.** TRAVEL same as **room and board** [Mid-17C. < French (see PENSION[1])]

pen·sion·a·ble /pénsh'nəb'l/ *adj* entitled to receive a pension, or relating to such entitlement —**pen·sion·a·bil·i·ty** /pènsh'nə bíllətee/ *n*

pen·sion·er /pénsh'nər/ *n* a recipient of a pension, especially somebody who has retired from work

pen·sive /pénssiv/ *adj* thinking deeply about something, especially in a sad or serious manner [14C. < French < *penser* "think" < Latin *pensare* "keep on weighing" < *pendere* "weigh"] —**pen·sive·ly** *adv* —**pen·sive·ness** *n*

pen·ste·mon /pen stéemən, pénstəmən/ *n* a plant belonging to the figwort family. Flowers: large, brightly-colored, with five stamens, one of which is sterile. Native to: North America. Genus: *Penstemon.* [Mid-18C. < modern Latin < Greek *penta-* "five" + *stēmōn* "warp, thread" (taken to mean "stamen," after Latin *stamen,* its equivalent)]

pen·stock /pén stòk/ *n* a sluice, channel, or pipe used to control or supply a flow of water to something such as a hydroelectric plant [Early 17C. < PEN[2] "enclosure"]

pent- *prefix* same as **penta-** (*used before vowels*)

penta- *prefix* five ○ *pentagon* [< Greek *pente* "five" < Indo-European]

pen·ta·chlo·ro·phe·nol /pèntə klawrə fée nàwl/ *n* a toxic white chemical compound. Use: in fungicides, disinfectants, and wood preservatives. Formula: C_6Cl_5OH.

pen·ta·cle /péntək'l/ *n* MATH same as **pentagram** [Late 16C. < medieval Latin *pentaculum,* literally "little five" < Greek *penta-* "five"]

pen·tad /pén tàd/ *n* **1.** GROUP OF FIVE any group or series of five, e.g., in mathematics **2.** CHEM ATOM WITH VALENCE OF FIVE an atom or chemical group with a valence of five **3.** METEOROL 5 DAYS in meteorology, a period of five days [Mid-17C. < Greek *pentad-* < *penta-* "five"]

pen·ta·dac·tyl /pèntə dákt'l/ *adj* having five digits on each hand or foot —**pen·ta·dac·ty·late** /pèntə dákt'lət, -àyt/ *adj* —**pen·ta·dac·tyl·ism** *n*

pen·ta·gon /péntə gòn/ *n* a two-dimensional geometric figure formed of five sides and five angles [Late 16C. Via late Latin < Greek *pentagōnon* < *pentagōnos* "five-angled" < *penta-* "five" + *gōnia* "angle"] —**pen·tag·o·nal** /pen tággən'l/ *adj* —**pen·tag·o·nal·ly** *adv*

Pen·ta·gon *n* the US Department of Defense, or the five-sided main building that houses it

Pen·ta·gon·ese /pèntəgə néez, -néess/ *n* US the euphemistic indirect jargon-ridden language considered by some to be characteristic of the US military leadership

pentagram

pen·ta·gram /péntə gràm/ *n* a two-dimensional geometric figure in the shape of a star, with five points, especially one used as a magical or occult symbol [Mid-19C. < Greek *pentagrammon,* < *pentagrammos* "of five lines"]

pen·ta·he·dron /pèntə héedrən/ (*plural* **-drons** or **-dra** /-drə/) *n* a three-dimensional geometric figure formed of five faces —**pen·ta·he·dral** *adj*

pen·tam·er·ous /pen támmərəss/ *adj* **1.** divided into or having five similar parts **2.** describes flowers that have petals or other parts such as sepals or stamens arranged in groups of five —**pen·tam·er·ism** *n*

pen·tam·e·ter /pen támmətər/ *n* a line of verse consisting of five units of rhythm such as five pairs of stressed and unstressed syllables [Early 16C. Via Latin < Greek *pentametros* "having five measures" < *penta-* "five" + *metron* "measure"]

pen·tam·i·dine /pen támmə dèen/ *n* a drug effective against protozoan infections. Use: treatment of African sleeping sickness, pneumonia in AIDS patients. Formula: $C_{19}H_{24}N_4O_2$. [Mid-20C. < PENTANE + *amidine,* type of chemical compound < AMIDE]

pen·tane /pén tàyn/ *n* an organic chemical belonging to the group containing only hydrogen and carbon (**hydrocarbons**). Use: solvent. Formula: C_5H_{12}. [Late 19C. < PENTA-]

pen·tan·gle /pén tàng g'l/ *n* MATH same as **pentagram**

pen·tan·gu·lar /pen táng gyələr/ *adj* having five angles and five sides

pen·ta·pep·tide /pèntə pép tìd/ *n* a peptide with five amino acids in its molecules

pen·ta·prism /péntə prizzəm/ *n* a prism with five faces that deviates light at a 90-degree angle, making it useful in correctly presenting an image in the viewfinder of a single-lens reflex camera

pen·ta·quine /péntə kwèen/, **pen·ta·quin** /-kwin/ *n* a synthetic drug. Use: with quinine in the treatment and prevention of malaria. Formula: $C_{18}H_{27}N_3O$. [< PENTA- + QUINOLINE]

pen·ta·stich /péntə stìk/ *n* a poem or section of a poem consisting of five lines [Mid-17C. Via modern Latin < Greek *pentastikhos* "having five rows"]

pen·ta·stome /péntə stòm/ *n* ZOOL same as **tongue worm**

Pen·ta·teuch /péntə tòok/ *n* the first five books of the Bible, traditionally attributed to Moses. See table at **Bible** [15C. Via ecclesiastical Latin < Greek *pentateukhos* "having five books"] —**Pen·ta·teuch·al** /pèntə tòok'l, pèntə tòok'l/ *adj*

pen·tath·lete /pen táthleet/ *n* an athlete who takes part in a pentathlon

pen·tath·lon /pen táthlən, -táth lòn/ *n* **1.** SPORTS same as **modern pentathlon** **2.** an athletic competition in which the contestants compete in five different track and field events and are awarded points for each to find the best all-around athlete. The events are usually sprinting, hurdling, long jumping, and discus and javelin throwing. [Early 17C. < Greek < *penta-* "five" + *athlon* "contest"]

pen·ta·tom·ic /pèntə tómmik/ *adj* having five atoms in a molecule

pen·ta·ton·ic scale /pèntə tonik-/ *n* any musical scale that has five notes to an octave, especially a major scale in which the fourth and seventh degrees are omitted

pen·ta·va·lent /pèntə váylənt/ *adj* used to describe chemical elements that have a valence of five

pen·taz·o·cine /pen tázzə sèen/ *n* a synthetic narcotic drug. Use: painkiller. [Mid-20C. < PENTA- + AZO- + OCTA- + -INE]

Pen·te·cost /péntə kòst/ *n* **1.** a Christian festival that commemorates the descent of the Holy Spirit upon the apostles, or the day on which it is celebrated. Date: 7th Sunday after Easter. **2.** JUDAISM same as **Shavuoth** [Pre-12C. Via late Latin < Greek *Pentēkostē* < *pentēkonta* "fifty"; because it falls fifty days after the second day of Passover]

Pen·te·cos·tal /pèntə kóst'l/ *adj* **1.** EMPHASIZING HOLY SPIRIT belonging or relating to any Christian denomination that emphasizes the workings of the Holy Spirit, interprets the Bible literally, and adopts an informal demonstrative approach to religious worship **2.** OF PENTECOST relating to the Christian festival of Pentecost ■ *n* MEMBER OF PENTECOSTAL DENOMINATION a member of a Pentecostal denomination —**Pen·te·cos·tal·ism** *n* —**Pen·te·cos·tal·ist** *n, adj*

pen·tene /pén tèen/ *n* a colorless flammable liquid with several isomers. Use: manufacture of organic compounds. Formula: C_5H_{10}.

pent·house /pént hòwss/ (*plural* **-houses** /-hòwzəz/) *n* **1.** ROOFTOP DWELLING an expensive and comfortable apartment on the top floor of a building or built on the roof (*often used before a noun*) ○ *a penthouse apartment* **2.** HOUSING FOR SERVICE EQUIPMENT a structure on the roof of a building to house elevator machinery, a water tank, or other service equipment **3.** ADJOINING ROOF OR SHED a sloping roof, or a shed with a sloping roof, built against the outer wall of a building **4.** ROOFED CORRIDOR in court tennis, a roofed corridor that runs along three sides of a court [14C. Alteration (influenced by HOUSE) of Anglo-Norman *pentiz* "lean-to," shortening of Old French *apentis* < Latin *appendere* "hang onto" < *pendere* "hang"]

pen·ti·men·to /pèntə méntō/ (*plural* **-ti** /-tee/) *n* **1.** the technique of removing a top layer of paint to reveal a painting or part of a painting underneath **2.** a painting or part of a painting that is revealed by pentimento [Early 20C. < Italian, "correction," literally "repentance" < Latin *paenitere* "repent"]

Pent·land Firth /pèntlənd-/ sea passage in Scotland separating the Orkney Islands from the mainland, and linking the North Sea to the Atlantic Ocean. Length: 20 mi./32 km.

pent·land·ite /péntlən dìt/ *n* a brownish yellow sulfide mineral containing iron and nickel. Use: source of nickel. [Mid-19C. After Joseph B. *Pentland* (1797–1873), Irish scientist]

pen·to·bar·bi·tal so·di·um /pèntə baàrbət'l-/ *n* a barbiturate drug used in veterinary medicine. Formula: $C_{11}H_{17}N_2O_3Na$.

pen·to·bar·bi·tone so·di·um /pèntə baàrbə tòn-/ *n* UK PHARM, VET same as **pentobarbital sodium**

pen·tode /pén tòd/ *n* **1.** a vacuum tube that has five electrodes. They are a cathode, an anode, and three grids. **2.** a point-contact transistor that has five electrodes constituting a base, three emitters, and one collector [Early 20C. < PENTA-]

pen·to·san /péntə sàn/ *n* a plant polysaccharide composed of linked pentose units

pen·tose /pén tòss/ *n* a five-carbon sugar, e.g., ribose

pen·tose phos·phate path·way *n* a series of biochemical reactions in which glucose is converted into other molecules such as those needed to synthesize nucleic acids

pent·ox·ide /pen tók sìd/ *n* a chemical element whose oxides contain five atoms of oxygen in each molecule

pent-up *adj* repressed or stifled rather than being released or freely expressed ○ *pent-up emotions*

pen·tyl /péntil/ *adj* relating to the group of atoms derived from pentane after the loss of a hydrogen atom. Formula: C_5H_{11}. [Late 19C. < PENTA-]

pen·tyl ac·e·tate *n* a colorless combustible liquid. Use: solvent for paints, in extracting penicillin, in photographic film, flavoring. Formula: $CH_3COOC_5H_{11}$.

pen·tyl·ene·tet·ra·zol /pèntəleen téttrə zàwl/ *n* a white crystalline powder. Use: stimulant for the central nervous system. Formula: $C_6H_{10}N_4$. [Mid-20C. < PENTA- + METHYLENE + *tetrazole,* acidic crystalline compound]

pe·nu·che /pə nóochee/, **pe·nu·chi** *n* Hispanic a fudge made from brown sugar, butter, milk, and nuts [Mid-20C. Variant of PANOCHA]

pe·nuch·le, **pe·nuck·le** *n* CARDS another spelling of **pinochle**

pe·nult /pée nùlt, pə núlt/ *n* the second to last item in a series of things, especially the second to last syllable of a word [15C. Shortening of Latin *penultima,* form of *paenultimus* (see PENULTIMATE)]

pe·nul·ti·mate /pə núltimət/ *adj* **1.** second to last in a series or sequence ○ *the penultimate chapter* **2.** relating to a penult [Late 17C. < Latin *paenultimus* < *paene* "almost" + *ultimus* "last" (see ULTIMATE)] —**pe·nul·ti·mate·ly** *adv*

pe·num·bra /pə númbrə/ (*plural* **-brae** /-bree/ or **-bras**) *n* **1.** PARTIAL SHADOW a partial outer shadow that is lighter than the darker inner shadow (**umbra**), e.g., the area between complete darkness and complete light in an eclipse **2.** INDETERMINATE AREA an indistinct area, especially a state in which something is unclear or uncertain **3.** PERIPHERY the outer region or periphery of something **4.** ASTRON EDGE OF SUNSPOT a grayish area surrounding the dark center of a sunspot [Mid-17C. < modern Latin < Latin *paene* "almost" + *umbra* "shadow"] —**pe·num·bral** *adj* —**pe·num·brous** *adj*

pe·nu·ri·ous /pə nŏŏree əss/ *adj* (*literary*) **1.** POOR having very little money **2.** NOT GENEROUS not generous with money **3.** BARREN barren or yielding little —**pe·nu·ri·ous·ly** *adv* —**pe·nu·ri·ous·ness** *n*

pen·u·ry /pénnyəree/ *n* extreme poverty [15C. < Latin *penuria*]

Pe·nu·ti·an /pə nóotee ən, pə nóosh'n/ *n* in some language classifications, a grouping (**phylum**) of Native American languages of California, sometimes also including some Central and South American languages, and sometimes Sahaptin-Chinook as a separate branch. Most of the Californian languages are now extinct. [Early 20C. < Yokuts *pen* "two" + Miwok *uti* "two"]

Pen·zance /pen zánss, pən-/ port and resort town in Cornwall, southwestern England, on Mounts Bay. Population: 17,500 (1994 estimate).

Pen·zi·as /péntsee əss/, **Arno** (*b.* 1933) German-born US astrophysicist. He and co-researcher Robert Wilson discovered background radiation in the Milky Way galaxy, which supported the big bang theory. They shared the Nobel Prize in physics (1978).

pe·on /pée òn, -ən/ *n* **1.** DRUDGE somebody who does boring menial tasks (*informal*) **2.** *Hispanic* LABORER in Latin America and the southern United States, especially formerly, a farm laborer who was forced to work for a creditor until a debt was paid off **3.** *S Asia* LOW-PAID WORKER formerly, in India and Sri Lanka, a low-paid office worker, soldier, or public servant [Early 17C. Via Spanish *peón*, Portuguese *peão* "foot soldier" < medieval Latin *pedon-* < Latin *ped-* "foot"]

pe·on·age /pée ənij/ *n* **1.** in Latin America and the southern United States, a former system under which a debtor was forced to work for a creditor until a debt was paid **2.** the status or condition of being a peon

pe·o·ny /pée ənee/ (*plural* **-nies**) *n* a large ornamental shrubby plant. Flowers: large, globe-shaped, red, white, pink. Native to: Europe, Asia, North America. Genus: *Paeonia*. [Pre-12C. Via medieval Latin < Greek *paiōnia*, after *Paiōn* "Paian," physician of the deities]

peo·ple /pée'p'l/ *n* NATION a nation, community, ethnic group, or nationality ○ *a proud people* ■ *npl* **1.** HUMAN BEINGS COLLECTIVELY human beings considered collectively or in general ○ *People tend not to mind if you ask them for help.* **2.** SUBORDINATES persons who are under the authority or leadership of somebody or something, e.g., employees, subjects, or followers ○ *I'll get one of my people to phone them.* **3.** ORDINARY MEN AND WOMEN the general population, as distinct from the government or higher social classes ○ *the will of the people* **4.** POLITICAL UNIT a group of persons comprising a political unit, electorate, or group **5.** FAMILY MEMBERS the members of somebody's family, especially somebody's close family (*informal*) ○ *My people were farmers.* ■ *vt* (**-pled, -pling, -ples**) POPULATE AREA to populate an area (*usually passive*) ○ *mountain regions that are sparsely peopled* [13C. Via Anglo-Norman and Old French < Latin *populus* < Etruscan]

USAGE people as singular or plural? In most cases ***people*** behaves as a plural, as in *People are funny; you never know what they will do.* When ***people*** means "a group of human beings sharing one specific nationality, culture, or language," however, it is regarded as a singular and when used in the plural, takes an *s* plural ending: *a Native American people of the Southwest, one of several such peoples noted for their peaceableness.* The possessive of ***people*** is formed by adding an apostrophe + *s* if one people is stipulated: *the people's choice of a new president.* If many peoples are stipulated, the possessive is formed by adding an apostrophe after the *s*: *various Caribbean peoples' representatives at the conference.* ***People*** is the preferred form in designating human beings in the plural generally: *Thousands of people* [not persons] *jammed the stadium. What on earth will people* [not persons] *think if you do that?* Use ***persons*** only in certain narrow, typically legalistic or otherwise official, contexts: *the Bureau of Missing Persons; the arrest of three suspicious persons loitering outside the White House gates.*

peo·ple·hood /pée'p'l hŏŏd/ *n* identity as a member of a particular people, especially a nation or ethnic group

peo·ple mov·er *n* any automated means of transporting large numbers of people over short distances

peo·ple per·son *n* a sociable and communicative person

peo·ple's re·pub·lic *n* a Socialist or Communist republic

Pe·or·i·a /pee áwree ə/ **1.** city and county seat of Peoria County in central Illinois, situated on the Illinois River, north of Springfield. It is a major inland port and manufacturing center. Population: 112,670 (2002 estimate). **2.** city in southern Arizona, a northwestern suburb of Phoenix. Population: 123,239 (2002 estimate).

pep /pep/ *n* liveliness or vigor (*informal*) [Early 20C. Shortening of PEPPER] —**pep·py** *adj*

pep up *vt* to make somebody or something more lively, energetic, or interesting (*informal*)

pep·er·o·mi·a /pèppə rṓmee ə/ *n* a plant often cultivated as a house plant for its heavily veined foliage. Native to: tropical and subtropical regions worldwide. Genus: *Peperomia*. [Late 19C. < modern Latin < Greek *peperi* (see PEPPER)]

pe·pi·no /pə péenō/ (*plural* **-nos**) *n Hispanic* **1.** OVAL FRUIT an eggplant-shaped purple-streaked fruit with a flavor resembling that of a melon **2.** SPINY PLANT a plant with spiny foliage that bears pepinos. Native to: Peru. Latin name: *Solanum muricatum*. **3.** CONE-SHAPED HILL a steep conical hill, especially in Puerto Rico [Mid-19C. Via American Spanish < Spanish, "cucumber" < Latin *pepo* (see PUMPKIN)]

Pep·in the Short /pèppin-/ (714?–768) king of the Franks (751–768). He was the founder of the Carolingian dynasty and the father of Charlemagne.

pep·la CLOTHING plural of **peplum**

pep·los /pépləss/, **pep·lus** *n* a loose-fitting garment worn by women in ancient Greece, draped in folds around the shoulders and reaching the waist [Late 18C. < Greek]

pep·lum /pépləm/ (*plural* **-lums** or **-la** /-lə/) *n* a short flared ruffle attached to the waist of a jacket or blouse [Late 17C. < Latin < Greek *peplos* "peplos"]

pep·lus *n* CLOTHING another spelling of **peplos**

pe·po /péepō/ (*plural* **-pos**) *n* a fruit of the gourd family, e.g., a melon, squash, pumpkin, or cucumber, that typically has a firm or hard rind, a large number of flat seeds, and soft watery flesh [Mid-19C. < Latin (see PUMPKIN)]

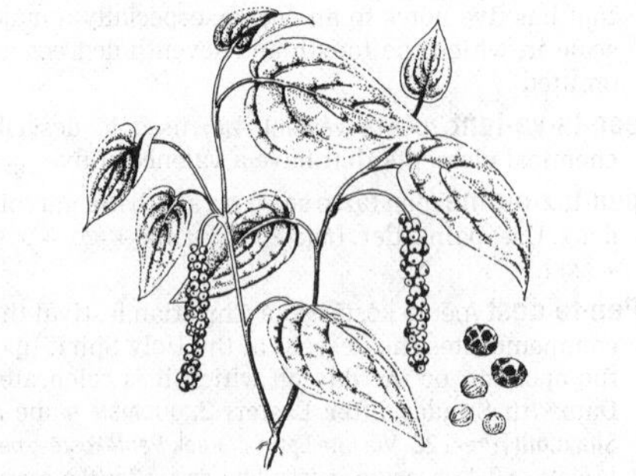

pepper (sense 2)

pep·per /péppər/ *n* **1.** SEASONING a hot condiment or seasoning made from the ground dried berries of a tropical climbing plant. Black pepper is made from berries that are dried before they ripen, and white pepper from berries that ripen before being dried. **2.** PLANT WITH BERRIES a tropical climbing plant whose berries are dried for use as pepper, e.g., betel, cubeb, or kava. Genus: *Piper*. **3.** HOLLOW VEGETABLE a green, red, purple, or yellow fruit that is hollow with firm walls containing seeds and has mild or pungent flesh that can be eaten either raw or cooked as a vegetable **4.** PLANT WITH EDIBLE PODS a tropical plant of the nightshade family that produces mild or pungent peppers. Genus: *Capsicum*. **5.** PUNGENT CONDIMENTS condiments such as chili sauce or cayenne pepper made from the more strongly pungent peppers **6.** *US* BASEBALL BASEBALL WARM-UP ROUTINE a baseball warm-up routine with fielders standing close to the batter and quickly tossing the ball to the batter, who in turn hits each toss back to the fielders ■ *v* (**-pered, -per·ing, -pers**) **1.** *vt* SPRINKLE FOOD WITH PEPPER to add or sprinkle pepper as a seasoning onto something **2.** *vt* ASSAIL SOMEBODY OR SOMETHING to bombard somebody or something with something **3.** SPRINKLE SOMETHING AROUND to scatter things liberally onto or among something (*often passive*) ○ *manuscripts peppered with typing errors* **4.** *vt* MAKE SOMETHING LIVELY to liven up something, e.g., a speech with wit [Old English *piper*, via W Germanic < Latin *piper* < Greek *peperi* < Sanskrit *pippalī* "berry, peppercorn"]

pep·per-and-salt *adj UK* same as **salt-and-pepper**

pep·per·box /péppər bòks/ *n* **1.** *US* HOUSEHOLD same as **peppershaker** **2.** a cylindrical turret or cupola **3.** a small 18th-century pistol with several short revolving barrels

pep·per·corn /péppər kàwrn/ *n* **1.** a small dried tropical berry that is ground to make pepper for use as a seasoning **2.** something that is very small or has little importance or value

pep·per·corn rent *n* a very low or nominal rent [< the custom of giving a peppercorn as a nominal rent]

pep·pered moth *n* a moth that is gray and speckled when found in rural areas and black in smoke-darkened industrial regions. Latin name: *Biston betularia*.

Pep·per·ell /péppərəl/, **Sir William** (1696–1759) colonial New England military officer. He commanded the forces that captured Louisbourg from the French in 1745.

pep·per game *n US* same as **pepper** *n* (sense 6)

pep·per·grass /péppər gràss/ *n* a plant of the mustard family whose pungent lower leaves are used in salads and to season dishes. Genus: *Lepidium*.

pep·per·idge /péppərij/ *n* TREES same as **sour gum** [Mid-16C. Origin ?]

pep·per mill *n* a kitchen utensil for storing and grinding peppercorns

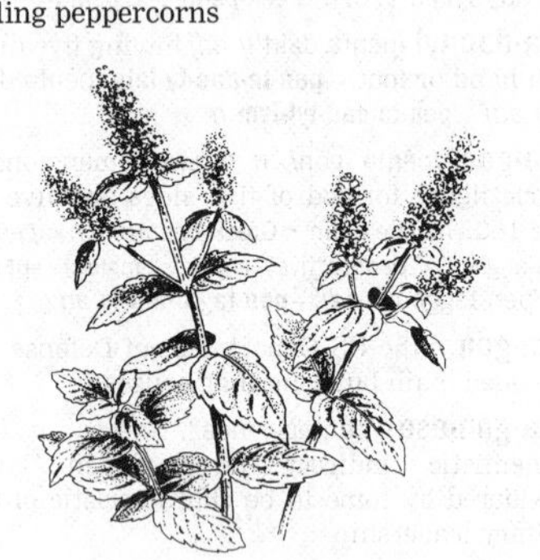

peppermint

pep·per·mint /péppər mìnt/ *n* **1.** FLAVORING a flavoring prepared from the aromatic oil of a mint plant. Use: food industry, pharmaceuticals. (*often used before a noun*) **2.** PEPPERMINT CANDY a candy flavored with peppermint **3.** AROMATIC HERB a plant of the mint family whose dark green downy leaves yield peppermint. Latin name: *Mentha piperita*.

pep·per·o·ni /pèppə rṓnee/ *n* a hard dry Italian sausage spiced with pepper, or a slice of this, often used on pizzas [Mid-20C. < Italian *peperone* "red pepper" < Latin *piper* (see PEPPER)]

pep·per pot *n* **1.** a Guyanese or Caribbean stew made with meat, rice, and vegetables and seasoned with cassava syrup **2.** a peppery Pennsylvania soup made with vegetables, tripe, or meat, and sometimes dumplings **3.** *UK* same as **peppershaker**

pep·per·shak·er /péppər shàykər/, **pep·per shak·er** *n* a small cylindrical container for ready-ground pepper with a perforated top for sprinkling

pep·per·shrike /péppər shrīk/ *n* a small stocky bird with a thick hook-tipped beak. Native to: Central and South America. Genus: *Cyclarhis*.

pep·per spray *n* an aerosol spray containing a pepper-based oleoresin, used by law enforcement officers to disable somebody who is behaving in an aggressive or violent manner

pep·per steak *n* a steak coated with crushed peppercorns before being fried or broiled

pep·per tree *n* a tree of the cashew family that is cultivated for its bright red fruits. Native to: subtropical South America. Genus: *Schinus.*

pep·per·wort /péppər wùrt, -wàwrt/ *n* **1.** a freshwater fern with floating leaves and slender tangled stems that grows in marshes and ponds. Genus: *Marsilea.* **2.** *UK* PLANTS same as **peppergrass**

pep·per·y /pépparee/ *adj* **1.** CONTAINING PEPPER strongly flavored with pepper, or tasting of pepper **2.** ANGRY angry and critical **3.** EASILY ANNOYED easily annoyed —**pep·per·i·ness** *n*

pep pill *n* any pill that contains a stimulant drug, especially an amphetamine (*slang*)

pep ral·ly *n* a gathering designed to fire enthusiasm into those attending, especially one held in a school before a sporting event

pep·sin /pépsin/ *n* an enzyme produced in the stomach that breaks down proteins into simpler compounds. It can be extracted from the stomachs of calves and hogs for use as a digestive aid and in the production of cheese. [Mid-19C. < Greek *pepsis* "digestion" < *peptein* "to digest"]

pep·sin·o·gen /pep sínnəjən/ *n* a substance produced by stomach glands that is converted into pepsin after contact with hydrochloric acid during digestion

pep talk *n* a short speech designed to give advice and generate enthusiasm, e.g., in a sports team or among a company's employees (*informal*)

pep·tic /péptik/ *adj* **1.** HELPING DIGESTION relating to or helping digestion **2.** INVOLVING PEPSIN relating to, caused by, or producing pepsin **3.** OF STOMACH relating to or involving the stomach, especially any digestive actions or their results [Mid-17C. Via Latin < Greek *peptikos* "capable of digesting" < *peptein* "to digest"]

pep·tic ul·cer *n* erosion of the mucous membrane that lines the upper digestive tract, caused by excess secretion of acid in the stomach

pep·ti·dase /pépti dàyss, -dàyz/ *n* an enzyme that splits amino acids from peptides

pep·tide /pép tìd/ *n* a linear molecule made up of two or more linked amino acids [Early 20C. < German *Peptid*, back-formation < *Polypeptid* "polypeptide" < *Pepton* (see PEPTONE)] —**pep·tid·ic** /pep tíddik/ *adj*

pep·tide bond *n* a linkage formed between the amino group of one amino acid and the carboxylic acid group of another

pep·ti·do·gly·can /pèptidō glíkən, -kàn/ *n* a large structural molecule found in the cell walls of bacteria

pep·tize /pép tìz/ (**-tized, -tiz·ing, -tiz·es**) *vt* to disperse fine particles of one substance evenly throughout another substance to create a state intermediate between a suspension and a solution (**colloid**) [Mid-19C. < PEPTONE] —**pep·tiz·a·ble** *adj*—**pep·ti·za·tion** /pèpti záysh'n/ *n* —**pep·tiz·er** *n*

pep·tone /pép tōn/ *n* a fragment of protein formed by enzyme action in the first stages of digestion [Mid-19C. Via German < Greek *pepton*, form of *peptos* "digested" < *peptein* "to digest"]

pep·to·nize /péptə nìz/ (**-nized, -niz·ing, -niz·es**) *vt* to digest protein using an enzyme —**pep·to·ni·za·tion** /pèptəni záysh'n/ *n* —**pep·to·niz·er** *n*

Pepys /peeps, péppiss/, **Samuel** (1633–1703) English diarist. His *Diary* (1660–69) includes detailed descriptions of the Plague and the Fire of London. —**Pepys·i·an** /péeps ee ən/ *adj*

> "Memoirs are true and useful stars, whilst studied histories are those stars joined in constellations, according to the fancy of the poet."
> [Samuel Pepys. Quoted in *Samuel Pepys' Naval Minutes*, J.R. Tanner (ed.); 1926 edition]

Pe·quot /pée kwòt/ (*plural same* or **-quots**) *n* **1.** a member of a Native North American people of eastern Connecticut **2.** the Algonquian language of the Pequot people. Native speakers: 7,000. [Mid-17C. < Narraganset *Pequtôog* "Pequot people"] —**Pe·quot** *adj*

per /pər/ *prep* **1.** FOR EACH for each or for every thing mentioned ○ *50 miles per hour* **2.** ACCORDING TO SOMETHING by, through, or according to something ○ *per instructions* ■ *adv* FOR EACH ONE for each one (*informal*) [14C. < Latin]

per- *prefix* **1.** through ○ *permeate* **2.** containing a large proportion of an element ○ *peroxide* **3.** containing an element in its highest oxidation state ○ *perchlorate* **4.** containing a peroxide group ○ *peracid* [< Latin *per* "through"]

per·ac·id /pə rássid/ *n* an acid in which one element is in its highest possible state of oxidation, e.g., perchloric acid or permanganic acid —**per·ac·id·i·ty** /pùrə síddətee/ *n*

per·ad·ven·ture /pùr əd vénchər/ *adv* possibly or perhaps (*archaic*) ■ *n* chance, doubt, or uncertainty (*literary*) [13C. < Old French *per aventure* "by chance"]

per·am·bu·late /pə rámbyə làyt/ (**-lat·ed, -lat·ing, -lates**) *vti* to walk about a place (*formal*) [Mid-16C. < Latin *perambulat-*, past participle of *perambulare* < *ambulare* "to walk"] —**per·am·bu·la·tion** /pə ràmbyə láysh'n/ *n* —**per·am·bu·la·to·ry** /pə rámbyələ tàwree/ *adj*

per·am·bu·la·tor /pə rámbyə làytər/ *n UK* a baby carriage (*formal*)

per an·num /pər ánnəm/ *adv* in or for every year, or by the year [< modern Latin, "by the year"]

p/e ra·tio *abbr* price-earnings ratio

per·bo·rate /pər báw ràyt/ *n* a salt compound of borate. Use: bleaching agent in washing powder.

per·cale /pər káyl/ *n* a smooth-textured closely woven cotton or polyester fabric. Use: sheets, clothing. [Early 17C. < French]

per·ca·line /pùrkə léen/ *n* a glossy lightweight cotton fabric. Use: linings, book bindings. [Mid-19C. < French < *percale* "percale"]

per cap·i·ta /pər káppitə/ *adv, adj* by or for each person ○ *earnings per capita* [< modern Latin, "per head"]

per·ceive /pər séev/ (**-ceived, -ceiv·ing, -ceives**) *vt* **1.** to notice something, especially something that escapes the notice of others **2.** to understand or interpret something in a particular way ○ *the action was perceived as a conciliatory gesture* [13C. Via variants of Old French *perçoivre* < Latin *percipere*, literally "seize completely" < *capere* "seize"] —**per·ceiv·a·ble** *adj* —**per·ceiv·a·bly** *adv* —**per·ceiv·er** *n*

per·cent /pər sént/ *adv* AS EXPRESSED IN HUNDREDTHS used to express a proportion of an amount in hundredths, sometimes represented by the symbol % ■ *n* (*plural* **-cent** /*pronunc. same*/) **1.** ONE HUNDREDTH one hundredth part of something **2.** PERCENTAGE a part or percentage [< Latin *per centum* "by a hundred"]

USAGE percent – singular or plural? If ***percent*** stands alone without a subsequent prepositional phrase, you can use a singular or a plural verb with it: *Sixty percent is accounted for; Sixty percent are accounted for.* If a prepositional phrase following ***percent*** contains a noun or pronoun object regarded as a unit or a whole, use a singular verb: *Sixty percent of the electorate is accounted for.* If the object of the preposition in such a phrase is regarded as a number of people or things, use a plural verb: *Sixty percent of the votes are accounted for.*

per·cent·age /pər séntij/ *n* **1.** PROPORTION IN ONE-HUNDREDTHS a proportion stated in terms of one-hundredths that is calculated by multiplying a fraction by 100 **2.** PROPORTION a proportion of a group or set ○ *A larger percentage of students are choosing to go on to college.* **3.** COMMISSION an amount charged that is based on the total amount involved, e.g., a commission charged on a sale, especially the commission that an agent charges a client (*informal*) **4.** ADVANTAGE advantage or benefit (*informal*) ○ *There's no percentage in accepting the proposal.*

USAGE percentage – singular or plural? If you put the definite article *the* before ***percentage***, you are stipulating just one percentage and thus you must use a singular verb: *The percentage of errors in this term paper is large.* If you put the indefinite article *a* before ***percentage***, use a plural verb when the noun or pronoun in any subsequent prepositional phrase is regarded as a countable plural, not a unit or a whole: *A large percentage of the errors are found in this text.* If the noun or pronoun object in such a phrase is singular or is regarded as a unit or a whole, use a singular verb: *A large percentage of the electorate remains undecided.*

USAGE Do not use ***a percentage of*** (or ***a proportion of***) when you mean "some," as in *A percentage of the students have laptop computers.* The words ***percentage*** and ***proportion*** are meaningless unless qualified by an adjective such as *large* or *small*, as in *a large proportion of the work*, and they are still best avoided where *many, much, a few*, or *a little* can be used instead.

per·cen·tile /pər sén tìl/ *n* in statistics, a value on a scale of one hundred that indicates whether a distribution is above or below it

per·cept /púr sèpt/ *n* something that is perceived by the senses [Mid-19C. < Latin *perceptum* "something perceived" < past participle of *percipere* (see PERCEIVE)]

per·cep·ti·ble /pər séptəb'l/ *adj* large enough, great enough, or distinct enough to be noticed ○ *a perceptible difference* —**per·cep·ti·bil·i·ty** /pər sèptə bíllətee/ *n* —**per·cep·ti·bly** *adv*

per·cep·tion /pər sépshən/ *n* **1.** PERCEIVING the process of using the senses to acquire information about the surrounding environment or situation ○ *the range of human perception* **2.** RESULT OF PERCEIVING the result of the process of perception ○ *After watching the experiment closely, he noted his perceptions in his lab notebook.* **3.** IMPRESSION an attitude or understanding based on what is observed or thought ○ *a news report that altered the public's perception of the issue* **4.** POWERS OF OBSERVATION the ability to notice or discern things that escape the notice of most people **5.** PSYCHOL NEUROLOGICAL PROCESS OF OBSERVATION AND INTERPRETATION any neurological process of acquiring and mentally interpreting information from the senses [14C. Via French < Latin *perception-* < *percipere* (see PERCEIVE)] —**per·cep·tion·al** *adj*

per·cep·tive /pər séptiv/ *adj* **1.** possessing or showing keen insight and understanding **2.** relating to perception, or capable of perceiving —**per·cep·tive·ly** *adv* —**per·cep·tive·ness** *n* —**per·cep·tiv·i·ty** /pùr sep tívvətee/ *n*

per·cep·tu·al /pər sépchoo əl/ *adj* relating to or involving sensory perception —**per·cep·tu·al·ly** *adv*

perch[1] /purch/ *n* **1.** PLACE FOR BIRD TO SIT a place for a bird to land or rest, e.g., a branch or a pole in a cage **2.** RESTING PLACE any temporary resting place for a person or thing **3.** ADVANTAGEOUS POSITION a place or position that is secure, advantageous, or prominent ○ *She now runs the organization from her new perch as director.* **4.** SOLID MEASURE FOR STONE a unit of measure for the volume of stone, equal to about 24 cu. ft./0.7 cu. m **5.** UNIT OF LENGTH a unit of length equal to $5\frac{1}{2}$ yd./5.03 m **6.** UNIT OF AREA a unit of area equal to $30\frac{1}{4}$ sq. yd./25.3 m^2 **7.** TEXTILES INSPECTION FRAME a frame that woven fabric is laid on to be inspected after weaving **8.** PEG TO HANG THINGS ON a pole, bar, or peg on which to hang things ■ *v* (**perched, perch·ing, perch·es**) **1.** *vi* SIT PRECARIOUSLY SOMEWHERE to sit or rest in a high or precarious position ○ *She perched on the edge of the desk.* **2.** *vt* PUT SOMETHING IN HIGH PLACE to place something or somebody in a high or precarious position ○ *I looked up at the old fort perched on the cliffs.* ○ *The child was perched on a high stool.* **3.** *vi* SIT ON PERCH to land or rest on a perch (*refers to birds*) ○ *A pair of doves perched on the apple tree.* **4.** *vti* TEXTILES LAY ITEM ON PERCH to place woven fabric on a perch to inspect after weaving, or be placed on a perch [13C. Via French < Latin *pertica* "pole, stick"] —**perch·er** *n* ◇ **knock somebody off his** *or* **her perch** to make somebody feel less proud or superior

perch[2] /purch/ (*plural* **perch·es** or *same*) *n* **1.** a freshwater fish with rough scales and two dorsal fins, one spiny and one soft. Native to: North America, Europe. Genus: *Perca.* See illustration on next page **2.** the flesh of a perch used as food [14C. Via French < Latin *perca* < Greek *perkē*]

per·chance /pər chánss/ *adv* (*archaic or literary*) **1.**

perch

possibly or perhaps **2.** by chance [14C. < Anglo-Norman *par chance* "by chance"]

Per·che·ron /púrchə ròn, púrshə-/ *n* a large black or gray draft horse belonging to a breed originating in France [Late 19C. < French, "of the Percheron breed," after *le Perche*, region of N France]

perch·ing bird *n* BIRDS same as **passerine**

per·chlo·rate /pər kláw ràyt/ *n* a salt or ester of perchloric acid

per·chlo·ric ac·id /pər klàwrik-/ *n* a colorless acid of chlorine that is explosive under some conditions. Use: oxidizing agent in laboratory work. Formula: $HClO_4$.

per·chlo·ride /pər kláw rīd/ *n* a chloride of an element that contains more chlorine than all other chlorides of the same element

per·chlor·o·eth·yl·ene /pər klàwrō éthə leen/ *n* a colorless toxic organic solvent. Use: in dry-cleaning fluid. Formula: C_2Cl_4.

per·cia·tel·li /pùrchə téllee/ *n* pasta in the form of long thin tubes, thicker than spaghetti [< Italian dialect, literally "little pierced thing" < *perciato*, past participle of *perciare* "pierce" < French *percer* (see PIERCE)]

Per·ci·er /pùrssi áy/, **Charles** (1764–1838) French architect. With his partner Pierre-François Fontaine, he introduced the Empire style of architecture with monumental projects such as the *Arc du Carrousel* (1806).

percieve incorrect spelling of **perceive**

per·cip·i·ent /pər síppee ənt/ *adj* showing keen understanding, observation, or discernment ■ *n* somebody or something capable of perceiving [Mid-17C. < Latin *percipient-*, present participle of *percipere* (see PERCEIVE)] —**per·cip·i·ent·ly** *adv*

per·coid /púr kòyd/ *adj* belonging or relating to a large suborder of bony spiny-finned fishes that includes the perch, sea bass, sunfishes, and red mullet. Suborder: Percoidea. [Mid-19C. < modern Latin *Percoidea* < Latin *perca* (see PERCH[2])] —**per·coid** *n*

per·co·late *v* /púrkə làyt/ (**-lat·ed, -lat·ing, -lates**) **1.** *vti* PASS THROUGH FILTER to make a liquid or gas pass through a filter or porous substance, or filter through in this way **2.** *vi* PASS THROUGH SLOWLY to pass slowly through something or spread throughout a place ○ *I let the idea percolate through my mind.* **3.** *vti* MAKE COFFEE to prepare coffee in a percolator, or undergo preparation in a percolator **4.** *vi* *US* BE LIVELY to be lively, active, or energetic (*informal*) ■ *n* /púrkə lət, púrkə làyt/ *US* SOMETHING PERCOLATED a liquid that has been percolated [Early 17C. < Latin *percolat-*, past participle of *percolare* "sieve through" < *colare* "to sieve" < *colum* "sieve"] —**per·co·la·ble** *adj* —**per·co·la·tion** /pùrkə láysh'n/ *n* —**per·co·la·tive** /púrkə làytiv/ *adj*

per·co·la·tor /púrkə làytər/ *n* a coffeepot in which boiling water rises repeatedly through a narrow stem, spills over into a sieve containing coffee grounds, mixes with them, and returns to the water below

per con·tra /pər kóntrə/ *adv* on the other hand or by way of contrast [< Italian, "by the opposite side"]

per cu·ri·am /pər kŏoree əm/ *adj* relating to a unanimous decision or opinion by a court of law, as opposed to one given by an individual justice [< Latin, "by the court"]

per·cuss /pər kúss/ (**-cussed, -cuss·ing, -cuss·es**) *vt* to gently tap a part of a patient's body in order to diagnose an illness or condition [Mid-16C. < Latin *percuss-*, past participle of *percutere* "strike hard" < *quatere* "to strike"] —**per·cus·sor** *n*

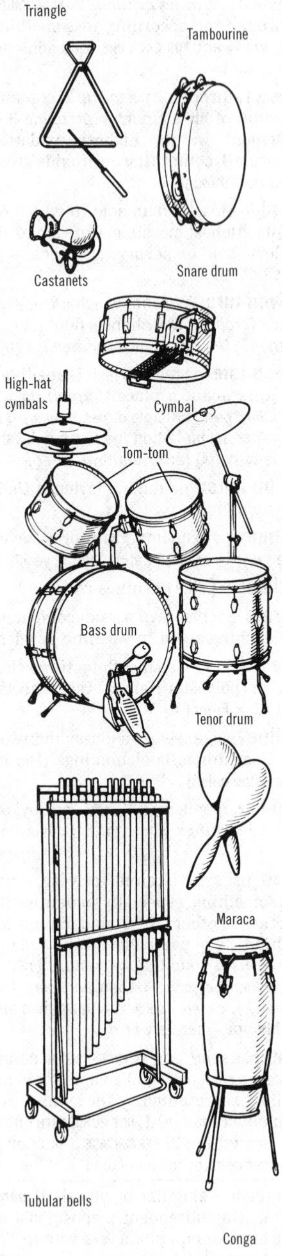

percussion

per·cus·sion /pər kúsh'n/ *n* **1.** MUSICAL INSTRUMENTS THAT ARE HIT the group of musical instruments that produce sound by being struck, including drums and cymbals, or the section of the orchestra playing such instruments **2.** ACT OF DETONATING PERCUSSION CAP the striking or detonating of a percussion cap in a firearm **3.** IMPACT the impact of one object striking another, or the noise or shock created when two objects hit each other (*formal*) **4.** MED TAPPING OF BODY examination of part of a patient's body by tapping with the fingers to assess the presence of fluid, the enlargement of organs, or the solidification of normally hollow parts [Mid-16C. < Latin *percussion-* < *percuss-* (see PERCUSS)]

per·cus·sion cap *n* a detonator consisting of a thin metal case or strip of paper containing explosive powder, formerly used to fire some pistols

per·cus·sion in·stru·ment *n* a musical instrument that is hit to produce sound, e.g., a drum, cymbal, or triangle

per·cus·sion·ist /pər kúsh'nist/ *n* a musician who plays one or more percussion instruments

per·cus·sion lock *n* a mechanism on a gun that fires by striking a percussion cap

per·cus·sion tool *n* any power tool that delivers repeated heavy blows, e.g., a jackhammer

per·cus·sive /pər kússiv/ *adj* having the effect of an impact or a blow —**per·cus·sive·ly** *adv* —**per·cus·sive·ness** *n*

per·cu·ta·ne·ous /pùrkyoo táynee əss/ *adj* describes medication that is administered or absorbed through the skin —**per·cu·ta·ne·ous·ly** *adv*

per di·em /pər dée əm/ *adv, adj* BY DAY by the day or every day ■ *n* **1.** DAILY PAYMENT a daily payment or allowance **2.** *US* WORKER PAID BY DAY somebody who is hired to work as needed and is therefore paid by the day (*informal*) [< Latin, "by the day"]

per·di·tion /pər dísh'n/ *n* **1.** in some religions, the state of everlasting punishment in hell that sinners endure after death **2.** hell itself as a location [14C. Directly or via French < late Latin *perdition-* < Latin *perdere* "put to destruction" < *dare* "put"]

per·dure /pər dŏor/ (**-dured, -dur·ing, -dures**) *vi* to last for a long time (*archaic*) [15C. Via French < Latin *perdurare* "last through" < *durare* "to last"]

père /per/ *n* **1.** the title given to Roman Catholic priests in France and French-speaking countries **2.** in France and French-speaking countries, used after a man's surname to distinguish him from his son ○ *Alexandre Dumas père* [Early 17C. Via French < Latin *pater* "father"]

Père Da·vid's deer *n* a large reddish gray deer that survives in captivity only. Native to: China. Latin name: *Elaphurus davidianus.* [Late 19C. After *Père* Armand *David* (1826–1900), French missionary and naturalist]

per·e·gri·nate /pérrəgri nàyt/ (**-nat·ed, -nat·ing, -nates**) *vti* to travel around a place or from place to place (*literary*) [Late 16C. < Latin *peregrinat-*, past participle of *peregrinari* < *peregrinus* (see PEREGRINE)] —**per·e·gri·na·tor** *n*

per·e·gri·na·tion /pèrrəgri náysh'n/ *n* a journey or voyage (*literary*) [15C. Directly or via French < Latin *peregrination-* < *peregrinari* (see PEREGRINATE)]

per·e·grine /pérrəgrin, -green/ *adj* coming from another region or country (*archaic*) ■ *n* BIRDS same as **peregrine falcon** [14C. Via French < Latin *peregrinus* "traveling" < *pereger*, literally "through fields" < *ager* "field"]

per·e·grine fal·con *n* a large falcon with a blue-gray back and whitish underparts that often catches other birds in flight. Family: Falconidae. [Because formerly captured for hawking while migrating, rather than taken from their nests]

per·emp·to·ry /pə rémptəree/ *adj* **1.** DICTATORIAL expecting to be obeyed and unwilling to tolerate disobedience, **2.** EXPRESSING URGENCY communicating urgency, command, or instruction **3.** LAW CLOSED TO FURTHER CONSIDERATION OR ACTION ending, or not open to, discussion, debate, or further action [13C. Via Anglo-Norman < Latin *peremptorius* "decisive" < Latin *perimere* "take away completely" < *emere* "buy"] —**per·emp·to·ri·ly** *adv* —**per·emp·to·ri·ness** *n*

perenial incorrect spelling of **perennial**

per·en·nate /pérrə nàyt, pə ré-/ (**-nat·ed, -nat·ing, -nates**) *vi* to survive from one growing season to the next with reduced or arrested growth between seasons [Early 17C. < Latin *perennat-*, past participle of *perennare* "last for years" < *perennis* (see PERENNIAL)] —**per·en·na·tion** /pèrrə náysh'n/ *n*

per·en·ni·al /pə rénnee əl/ *adj* **1.** LASTING OVER 2 YEARS describes a plant that lasts for more than two growing seasons, either dying back after each season, as some herbaceous plants do, or growing continuously, as some bushes do **2.** RECURRING OR ENDURING constantly recurring, or lasting for an indefinite time ○ *the perennial problem of litter* ■ *n* **1.** PERENNIAL PLANT a plant that lasts for more than two growing seasons **2.** SOMETHING HAPPENING AGAIN AND AGAIN something that recurs or appears to recur yearly or on a continuing basis [Mid-17C. < Latin *perennis* "through the year" < *annus* "year"] —**per·en·ni·al·ly** *adv*

pe·ren·tie /pə réntee/, **pe·ren·ty** (*plural* **-ties**) *n* a large burrowing lizard that has brown skin with yellow patches and can reach 8 ft./2.5 m in length. Native to: semidry and desert regions of central and northern Australia. Latin name: *Varanus giganteus.* [Early 20C. < Aboriginal, probably Diyari *pirindi*]

Per·es /pé ress/, **Shimon** (*b.* 1923) Polish-born Israeli politician. First elected to the Knesset in 1959, he has twice served as prime minister (1984–86 and 1995–96). With Yasir Arafat and Yitzhak Rabin he shared the Nobel Peace Prize (1994) for his part in negotiating the Israeli-Palestinian peace agreement (1983).

> "Peace is made with yesterday's enemies. What is the alternative?"
> [Shimon Peres, *Observer (London)*; October 16, 1994]

per·e·stroi·ka /pèrrə stróykə/ *n* **1.** the political and economic restructuring in the former Soviet Union initiated by Mikhail Gorbachev from about 1986. The stated objectives included decentralized control of industry and agriculture and some private ownership. **2.** any political, bureaucratic, or economic restructuring [Late 20C. < Russian, "rebuilding, reconstruction"]

Pé·rez de Cuél·lar /pè ress də kwáy yaar/, **Javier** (*b.* 1920) Peruvian diplomat. He was the fifth secretary-general of the United Nations (1982–91).

> "I am like a doctor…If the patient doesn't want all the pills I've recommended that's up to him. But I must warn that next time I will have to come as a surgeon with a knife."
> [Javier Pérez de Cuéllar, *Guardian (London)*; May 10, 1986]

perf. *abbr* **1.** GRAM perfect **2.** STAMPS perforated **3.** performance

per·fect *adj* /púrfikt/ **1. WITHOUT FAULTS** without errors, flaws, or faults ○ *in perfect condition* **2. COMPLETE AND WHOLE** complete and lacking nothing essential **3. EXCELLENT OR IDEAL** excellent or ideal in every way ○ *That's the perfect word to describe him.* **4. ESPECIALLY SUITABLE** having all the necessary or typical characteristics required for a given situation ○ *the perfect candidate for the job* **5. SKILLED** very proficient, skilled, or talented in a particular area ○ *a perfect host* **6. UTTER OR ABSOLUTE** used to emphasize the extent or degree of something ○ *a perfect nuisance* ○ *perfect happiness* **7. EXACT AS REPRODUCTION** exactly reproducing an original ○ *a perfect likeness* **8.** BOT **WITH STAMENS AND PISTILS TOGETHER** describes a flower that has functional stamens and pistils in the same flower **9.** MATH **EXACTLY DIVISIBLE** exactly divisible into equal roots **10.** GRAM **WITH VERB ACTION FINISHED** describes a verb or verb aspect for an action that is brought to a close **11.** MUSIC **OF MUSICAL INTERVALS** describes the differences in pitch between the fourth, the fifth, and the octave, common to both major and minor scales **12.** FUNGI **WITH SEXUAL AND ASEXUAL REPRODUCTION** describes a fungus that reproduces both sexually and asexually during its life cycle **13.** INSECTS **SEXUALLY MATURE** describes an insect that is sexually mature and completely differentiated ■ *vt* /pər fékt/ (**-fect·ed, -fect·ing, -fects**) **1. BRING SOMETHING TO COMPLETION** to make something as good as possible, or bring something to completion ○ *They perfected the process last year.* **2.** PRINTING **FINISH PAGE** to complete a printed page by printing its reverse side ■ *n* /púrfikt/ GRAM **1. PERFECT ASPECT OF VERB** the perfect aspect of a verb **2. VERB IN PERFECT ASPECT** a verb that is in the perfect aspect [13C. Directly or via French < Latin *perfectus* < *perficere* "make completely, finish" < *facere* "make"] —**per·fect·er** *n* —**per·fect·i·ble** *adj* —**per·fect·ness** *n*

per·fec·ta /pər féktə/ *n UK* same as **exacta** [Late 20C. < American Spanish *quiniela perfecta* "perfect quinella"]

per·fect bind·ing *n* a method of bookbinding in which a book's pages are cut and then bound to the spine with glue, as opposed to being stitched uncut —**per·fect bound** *adj*

per·fect com·pe·ti·tion *n* a market condition in which a product is traded freely by buyers and sellers in large numbers without any individual transaction affecting the price

per·fect game *n* **1.** a baseball game in which a pitcher plays a full game without allowing any player of the opposing team to reach a base **2.** a game of bowling in which 12 consecutive strikes occur

per·fect gas *n* PHYS, CHEM same as **ideal gas**

per·fec·tion /pər féksh'n/ *n* **1. PERFECT NATURE** the quality of something that is as good or suitable as it can possibly be ○ *to strive for perfection as a goal* **2. PROCESS OF PERFECTING** the process of becoming or making something perfect ○ *The perfection of the technique will require another two years' research.* **3. EXAMPLE OR INSTANCE OF BEING PERFECT** somebody or something that reaches the highest attainable standard, or an instance of this ○ *His cooking that evening was sheer perfection.* ◇ **to perfection** perfectly ○ *The piece showed off her talent as a pianist to perfection.*

per·fec·tion·ism /pər fékshə nìzzəm/ *n* **1.** rigorous rejection of anything less than perfect **2.** the doctrine that perfection is possible in human beings

per·fec·tion·ist /pər fékshənist/ *n* **1.** somebody who demands or seeks to achieve nothing less than perfection **2.** a believer in the philosophical doctrine of perfectionism

per·fec·tive /pər féktiv/ *adj* **1. TOWARD PERFECTION** tending toward perfection **2.** GRAM **DESCRIBING COMPLETED ACTION** describes a verb that reports a completed action as opposed to an incomplete or continuing one ■ *n* GRAM **PERFECTIVE VERB OR ASPECT** a verb in the perfective aspect, or the aspect itself —**per·fec·tive·ly** *adv* —**per·fec·tive·ness** *n* —**per·fec·tiv·i·ty** /pùr fek tívvətee/ *n*

per·fect·ly /púrfəktlee/ *adv* **1.** in exactly the way desired or required ○ *That will suit her perfectly.* **2.** used to emphasize the degree or extent of something ○ *They're perfectly capable of managing on their own.*

per·fect num·ber *n* a positive whole number that is equal to the sum of the numbers that can be multiplied to give it as a result, excluding itself

per·fec·to /pər féktō/ (*plural* **-tos**) *n* a medium-sized cigar with tapered ends and a thick center [Late 19C. < Spanish, "perfect"]

per·fect par·ti·ci·ple *n* GRAM same as **past participle**

per·fect pitch *n* MUSIC same as **absolute pitch** (sense 1)

per·fect rhyme *n* **1.** a rhyme of two words that are pronounced the same but spelled differently and have different meanings, e.g., "flew" and "flue" **2.** a rhyme in which the stressed vowel and the consonants following it are the same, e.g., "alive" and "contrive"

per·fect square *n* a rational number equal to the square of another rational number

per·fer·vid /pər fúrvid/ *adj* extremely passionate or enthusiastic (*literary*) [Mid-19C. < modern Latin *perfervidus* "extremely vehement" < Latin *fervidus* (see FERVID)] —**per·fer·vid·ly** *adv* —**per·fer·vid·ness** *n*

per·fi·dy /púrfidee/ *n* treachery or deceit (*formal*) [Late 16C. < Latin *perfidia* < *perfidus* "treacherous" < *per fidem decipere* "deceive through trustingness" < *fides* "faith, trust"] —**per·fid·i·ous** /pər fíddee əss/ *adj*

per·fin /púrfin/ *n* a postage stamp with initials perforated in it by a business or other organization to prevent misuse [Mid-20C. Blend of PERFORATED + INITIAL]

per·fo·li·ate /pər fṓlee ət/ *adj* describes a leaf that encloses a stem so that the stem seems to pass through it [Late 17C. < modern Latin *perfoliatus* "through a leaf" < Latin *folium* "leaf"] —**per·fo·li·a·tion** /pər fṑlee áysh'n/ *n*

per·fo·rate *v* /púrfə ràyt/ (**-ra·ted, -rat·ing, -rates**) **1.** *vt* **PUNCTURE SOMETHING** to make a hole or holes in something **2.** *vt* **MAKE HOLES FOR TEARING** to make a line of small holes in paper to make tearing it easier **3.** *vi* **PENETRATE SOMETHING** to penetrate or pass through something ■ *adj* /púrfərət, púrfə ràyt/ **1.** BIOL **WITH SMALL HOLES** dotted with small holes **2.** BIOL **WITH TRANSPARENT SPOTS** dotted with transparent spots **3.** STAMPS same as **perforated** (sense 1) [Mid-16C. < Latin *perforat-*, past participle of *perforare* "bore through" < *forare* "to bore"] —**per·fo·ra·ble** *adj* —**per·fo·ra·tive** /-rətiv, -ràytiv/ *adj* —**per·fo·ra·tor** *n* —**per·fo·ra·to·ry** /-rə tàwree/ *adj*

per·fo·rat·ed /púrfə ràytəd/ *adj* **1.** pierced with a hole or holes, especially with a line of small holes designed to make tearing easy **2.** in which a hole has developed ○ *a perforated eardrum*

per·fo·ra·tion /pùrfə ráysh'n/ *n* **1. HOLE** a hole made in something **2. HOLES FOR TEARING** a small hole or series of holes punched into a piece of paper to make tearing easy **3. MAKING HOLES OR HAVING THEM** the act of making a hole or holes in something or the state of being perforated **4.** MED **FORMATION OF HOLE** the formation of a hole in an organ, tissue, or tube, usually as a consequence of disease

per·force /pər fáwrss/ *adv* unavoidably or as forced by circumstances (*archaic or literary*) [14C. < Old French *par force* "by force"]

per·form /pər fáwrm/ (**-formed, -form·ing, -forms**) *v* **1.** *vt* **ACCOMPLISH SOMETHING** to carry out an action or accomplish a task, especially one requiring care or skill ○ *the surgeon who performed the operation* **2.** *vt* **FULFILL REQUIREMENT** to do what is stated or required **3.** *vti* **PRESENT ARTISTIC WORK** to present or enact an artistic work such as a piece of music or a play to an audience **4.** *vi* **FUNCTION OR BEHAVE** to function, operate, or behave in a particular way or to a particular standard ○ *athletes who perform best under pressure* **5.** *vi US* **FULFILL OBLIGATION** to fulfill a promise or obligation [14C. < Anglo-Norman *parformer*, alteration of Old French *parfornir* "accomplish completely" < *fournir* "accomplish"] —**per·form·a·ble** *adj* —**per·form·er** *n*

SYNONYMS ***perform, do, carry out, fulfill, discharge, execute***

CORE MEANING: to complete an action or task

perform to carry out an action or accomplish a task, especially one requiring care or skill ○ *Six patients had the procedure performed under local anesthesia.* ○ *Each child was asked to perform the specified task during the specified time.* **do** to take action or accomplish something ○ *I've got a load of paperwork to do tomorrow.* ○ *A robot will do anything you ask it.* **carry out** to complete a task or activity, especially something that has been ordered or planned ○ *claims of negligence in failing to carry out the duties imposed by the law* **fulfill** to do what is necessary to bring about or achieve something expected, desired, or promised ○ *Organizations are created because individuals need each other in order to fulfill goals that they consider worthwhile.* **discharge** (*formal*) to undertake a duty, responsibility, or promise successfully ○ *The people who are delegated must be competent to discharge those duties.* **execute** to put an instruction or plan into effect, or to complete an action or procedure that requires skill and expertise ○ *If a state failed to develop or execute a satisfactory plan, the agency had the authority to intervene directly.*

---

per·form·ance /pər fáwrmənss/ *n* **1. ARTISTIC PRESENTATION** a presentation of an artistic work such as a play or piece of music to an audience **2. MANNER OF FUNCTIONING** the manner in which something or somebody functions, operates, or behaves ○ *a high-performance car* **3. WORKING EFFECTIVENESS** the way in which somebody does a job, judged by its effectiveness (*often used before a noun*) ○ *performance-related pay* **4. THING ACCOMPLISHED** something that is carried out or accomplished **5. ACCOMPLISHMENT OF SOMETHING** the act of carrying out or accomplishing something such as a task or action **6. DISPLAY OF BEHAVIOR** a public display of behavior that others find distasteful, e.g., an angry outburst that causes embarrassment (*informal*) **7.** LING **LANGUAGE PRODUCED** the language that a speaker or writer actually produces, as distinct from his or her understanding of the language

per·form·ance art *n* art that combines two or more artistic media, a traditionally static medium such as sculpture or photography, and a dramatic medium such as recitation or improvisation —**per·form·ance art·ist** *n*

per·form·ance en·hanc·er *n* a dietary supplement used by athletes to enhance bursts of high performance

per·form·a·tive /pər fáwrmətiv/ *adj* describes speech that constitutes an act of some kind, e.g., the phrase "I promise I'll do my best," which constitutes a promise in itself ■ *n* a performative utterance [Mid-20C. After DECLARATIVE] —**per·form·a·tive·ly** *adv*

per·form·ing arts /pər fáwrming-/ *npl* the forms of

art that involve theatrical performance, especially drama, dance, and music

per·form·ing arts med·i·cine *n US* MED same as **arts medicine**

per·fume *n* /púr fyo͞om, pər fyo͞om/ **1. FRAGRANT LIQUID** a fragrant liquid that is sprayed or rubbed on the skin or clothes to give a pleasant smell **2. PLEASANT SCENT** a pleasant smell, especially of flowers or plants ■ *vt* /pər fyo͞om/ **(-fumed, -fum·ing, -fumes) GIVE SOMETHING PLEASANT SCENT** to give something a pleasant or sweet smell [Mid-16C. < French *parfum* < *parfumer* "fill with fumes or perfume" < obsolete Italian *parfumare*, literally "smoke through" < *fumare* "to smoke"] —**per·fumed** *adj* —**per·fum·y** *adj*

SYNONYMS See ***smell***.

per·fum·er /pər fyo͞omər/ *n* a manufacturer or seller of perfumes

per·fum·er·y /pər fyo͞omәree/ (*plural* **-ies**) *n* **1. PERFUMES** perfumes in general **2. PLACE MAKING OR SELLING PERFUMES** a place of business where perfumes are manufactured or sold **3. MAKING OF PERFUMES** the manufacture of perfumes, or the art of making perfumes

per·func·to·ry /pər fúngktəree/ *adj* **1.** done as a matter of duty or custom, without thought, attention, or genuine feeling ○ *a perfunctory kiss* **2.** done hastily or superficially ○ *a perfunctory search* [Late 16C. < late Latin *perfunctorius* < Latin *perfungi* "work through" < *fungi* "perform"] —**per·func·to·ri·ly** *adv* —**per·func·to·ri·ness** *n*

per·fuse /pər fyo͞oz/ **(-fused, -fus·ing, -fus·es)** *vt* **1.** to spread throughout something, or spread a substance or quality such as liquid, light, or color throughout something **2.** to introduce a liquid into tissue or an organ by circulating it through blood vessels or other channels within the body [Early 16C. < Latin *perfus-*, past participle of *perfundere* "pour over" < *fundere* "pour"] —**per·fused** *adj* —**per·fu·sion** *n* —**per·fu·sive** *adj*

Per·ga·mum /púrgəməm/ ancient city in northwestern Asia Minor, in present-day Turkey. It was a major cultural center in the 3rd and 2nd centuries B.C.

pergola

per·go·la /púrgələ/ *n* a frame structure consisting of colonnades or posts with a latticework roof, designed to support climbing plants [Late 17C. Via Italian < Latin *pergula*]

per·haps /pər háps, -áps/ CORE MEANING: an adverb expressing uncertainty, or indicating that something is possibly true or may possibly happen, often used to make remarks appear less definite ○ *Perhaps it will be warmer later.* ○ *He wondered if perhaps he had figured things wrong.* ○ *Perhaps his best-known ceramic work is his public mural "Voyage."*

adv used to show approximation ○ *The house is perhaps five miles from here.* [15C. < PER "by" + plural of HAP[1] "chance"]

pe·ri /péeree/ *n* **1.** in Persian mythology, a beautiful supernatural being descended from the fallen angels **2.** a graceful and beautiful girl or woman (*literary*) [Late 18C. < Persian *perī*]

peri- *prefix* **1.** around, surrounding ○ *pericarp* **2.** near ○ *perilune* ○ *perinatal* [< Greek *peri* "around, about" < Indo-European]

per·i·anth /pérree ànth/ *n* the outer structure of a flower, made up of the corolla, the calyx, or both [Early 19C. Via French < modern Latin *perianthium* < Greek *peri* "around" + *anthos* "flower"]

per·i·apt /pérree àpt/ *n* a charm worn to protect the wearer from harm [Late 16C. Via French < Greek *periapton* "something fastened around" < *peri* "around" + *haptein* "fasten"]

per·i·as·tron /pèrree ástrən, -á stròn/ *n* the points in space and time in the orbits of two stars in a binary system at which they are closest together [Mid-19C. < PERI- + Greek *astron* "star," after PERIHELION]

per·i·car·di·tis /pèrri kaar dítiss/ *n* inflammation of the pericardium —**per·i·car·dit·ic** /-díttik/ *adj*

per·i·car·di·um /pèrrə kaárdee əm/ (*plural* **-di·a** /-dee ə/) *n* a fibrous membrane that forms a sac surrounding the heart and attached portions of the main blood vessels [Late 16C. Via medieval Latin < Greek *perikardion* < *peri* "around" + *kardia* "heart"] —**per·i·car·di·ac** *adj* —**per·i·car·di·al** *adj*

per·i·carp /pérrə kaàrp/ *n* the part of a fruit that surrounds the seed or seeds, including the skin, flesh, and, in some fruits, the core —**per·i·car·pi·al** /pèrrə kaárpee əl/ *adj* —**per·i·carp·ic** /pèrrə kaárpik/ *adj*

per·i·chon·dri·um /pèrrə kóndree əm/ (*plural* **-dri·a** /-dree ə/) *n* the fibrous membrane that covers the surface of cartilage except at joints [Mid-18C. < modern Latin < Greek *peri* "around" + *khondros* "cartilage"] —**per·i·chon·dri·al** *adj*

per·i·clase /pérrə klàyss, -klàyz/ *n* a colorless, gray, green, or yellow magnesium oxide mineral. Source: limestone. [Mid-19C. Directly or via German *Periklas* < modern Latin *periclasia* < Greek *peri* "around" + *klasis* "breaking"; from its perfect cleavage] —**per·i·clas·tic** /pèrrə klástik/ *adj*

Per·i·cles /pérrə kleèz/ (495?–429? B.C.) Athenian political leader. He dominated Athens during its golden age by virtue of his oratory skills and honesty. He ordered the construction of the Parthenon and established Athens as a great center of art and literature. —**Per·i·cle·an** /pèrrə kleé ən/ *adj*

> "Our love of what is beautiful does not lead to extravagance; our love of the things of the mind does not make us soft."
> [Pericles, *Histories*, Rex Warner (tr.); 1961]

per·i·cli·nal /pèrrə klín'l/ *adj* **1.** used to describe a fold in sedimentary rocks that appears as a regular dome on the surface of the Earth **2.** describes cell walls that are parallel to the outer surface of a plant part [Late 19C. < Greek *periklinēs* "sloping all around" < *peri* "all around" + *klinein* "to slope"]

per·i·cline /pérrə klìn/ *n* **1.** a dome-shaped fold in sedimentary rock **2.** a variety of the mineral albite that forms long white crystals [Mid-19C. < Greek *periklinēs* (see PERICLINAL)]

pe·ric·o·pe /pə ríkəpee/ *n* an extract from a book, especially a passage from the Bible selected for reading during a Roman Catholic Mass [Mid-17C. Via late Latin < Greek *perikopē* "section" < *peri* "around" + *koptein* "to cut"] —**per·i·cop·ic** /pèrrə kóppik/ *adj*

per·i·cra·ni·um /pèrrə kráynee əm/ (*plural* **-ni·a** /-nee ə/) *n* the membrane of connective tissue that surrounds the skull [Early 16C. Via modern Latin < Greek *perikranion* < *peri* "round" + *kranion* "skull"] —**per·i·cra·ni·al** *adj*

per·i·cy·cle /pérrə sìk'l/ *n* the outer layer of plant tissue surrounding the inner core of the roots and stems of plants (**stele**) that conducts moisture and nutrients around the plant [Late 19C. Via French < Greek *perikuklos* "circling around" < *peri* "around" + *kuklos* "circle"] —**per·i·cy·clic** /pèrrə síklik, -síklik/ *adj*

per·i·derm /pérrə dùrm/ *n* the outer layer of plant tissue in woody roots and stems —**per·i·der·mal** /pèrrə dúrm'l/ *adj* —**per·i·der·mic** /-dúrmik/ *adj*

pe·rid·i·um /pə ríddee əm/ (*plural* **-i·a** /-ee ə/) *n* the covering of the spore-bearing organ in many kinds of fungi [Early 19C. Via modern Latin < Greek *pēridion* "small leather wallet" < *pēra* "wallet"]

per·i·dot /pérrə dòt, -dō/ *n* a pale green or yellowish green semiprecious stone that is a transparent form of olivine. Use: gems. [Early 18C. < French]

per·i·do·tite /pèrrə dṓ tìt/ *n* a coarse-grained igneous rock that is rich in iron and magnesium. It is found in meteorites and also on Earth, where it is thought to form much of the Earth's core. —**per·i·do·tit·ic** /pèrrədō títtik/ *adj*

per·i·gee /pérrəjee/ *n* the point in the orbit of a satellite, moon, or planet at which it comes nearest to the object it is orbiting [Late 16C. Via French < late Greek *perigeion* < *perigeios* "close round the earth" < Greek *peri* "around" + *gē* "earth"] —**per·i·ge·al** /pèrrə jeé əl/ *adj* —**per·i·ge·an** /-jeé ən/ *adj*

Pé·ri·gueux /pày ree gṓ/ town in southwestern France, in Dordogne Department, Aquitaine Region. Population: 30,193 (1999).

pe·rig·y·nous /pə ríjjənəss/ *adj* describes a flower that has petals, stamens, and sepals arranged around a cup-shaped receptacle that contains the ovary, as have the flowers of cherries and roses —**pe·rig·y·ny** *n*

per·i·he·li·on /pèrrə heélyən, -heélee ən/ (*plural* **-li·a** /-lee ə/) *n* the point in the orbit of a planet or other astronomical body at which it comes closest to the Sun [Mid-17C. Alteration of modern Latin *perihelium* < Greek *peri* "around" + *hēlios* "sun"] —**per·i·he·li·al** *adj*

per·i·kar·y·on /pèrrə kérree òn, -ən/ (*plural* **-y·a** /-ee ə/) *n* the part of a nerve cell that contains the nucleus —**per·i·kar·y·al** *adj*

per·il /pérrəl/ *n* **1.** exposure to risk of harm **2.** a source of possible or imagined harm [13C. Via French < Latin *periculum* "experiment, risk" < Indo-European, "try"]

pe·ril·la /pə ríllə/ *n* **1.** a pale yellow oil produced from the seeds of a mint plant. Use: varnishes, inks. **2.** an annual plant of the mint family, especially a variety with white flowers and seeds that yield perilla. Native to: Asia. Latin name: *Perilla frutescens*. [Late 18C. < modern Latin]

per·il·ous /pérrələss/ *adj* involving exposure to very great danger [13C. Via Old French *perillous* < Latin *periculosus* < *periculum* (see PERIL)] —**per·il·ous·ly** *adv* —**per·il·ous·ness** *n*

per·i·lune /pérrə lo͞on/ *n* the point at which a planet or other body orbiting the Moon comes closest to the Moon's surface [Mid-20C. < PERI- + Latin *luna* "moon"]

per·i·lymph /pérrə lìmf/ *n* the fluid that fills the space between the membranous labyrinth and the bony labyrinth in the inner ear

pe·rim·e·ter /pə rímmitər/ *n* **1. BOUNDARY ENCLOSING AREA** a boundary that encloses an area **2. OUTER EDGE OF TERRITORY** the outer edge of an area of defended territory **3.** MATH **CURVE ENCLOSING AREA** a curve enclosing an area on a plane, or the length of such a curve [Late 16C. Via Latin < Greek *perimetros* < *peri* "around" + *metron* "measure"] —**per·i·met·ric** /pèrrə méttrik/ *adj* —**per·i·met·ri·cal** *adj* —**per·i·met·ri·cal·ly** *adv*

per·i·morph /pérrə màwrf/ *n* a mineral that crystallizes around a grain of a different kind of mineral —**per·i·mor·phic** /pèrrə máwrfik/ *adj* —**per·i·mor·phism** *n* —**per·i·mor·phous** /-máwrfəss/ *adj*

per·i·my·si·um /pèrrə mízzee əm, -mízhee-/ (*plural* **-si·a** /-zee ə/) *n* the sheath of connective tissue that surrounds bundles of muscle fibers [Mid-19C. < PERI- + Greek *mus* "muscle"]

per·i·na·tal /pèrrə náyt'l/ *adj* relating to or occurring during the period around childbirth, specifically from around week 28 of pregnancy to around one month after the birth —**per·i·na·tal·ly** *adv*

per·i·na·tol·o·gy /pèrrə nay tólləjee/ *n* a medical specialty concerned with the care and treatment of mother and infant immediately prior to, during, and following childbirth —**per·i·na·tol·o·gist** *n*

per·i·neph·ri·um /pèrrə néffree əm/ (*plural* **-ri·a** /-ree ə/) *n* the fatty tissue that surrounds the kidney [Late 19C. < PERI- + Greek *nephros* "kidney"] —**per·i·neph·ric** *adj*

per·i·ne·um /pèrrə neé əm/ (*plural* **-ne·a** /-neé ə/) *n* the region of the abdomen surrounding the urogenital and anal openings [Mid-17C. Via late Latin < Greek *perinaion* < *peri* "around" + *inan* "excrete"] —**per·i·ne·al** *adj*

per·i·neu·ri·um /pèrri no͞oree əm/ (*plural* **-ri·a** /-ree ə/) *n* the sheath of connective tissue that surrounds a bundle of nerve fibers [Mid-19C. < PERI- + NEURO-] —**per·i·neu·ri·al** *adj*

pe·ri·od /péeree əd/ *n* **1. LENGTH OF TIME** an interval or portion of time **2. IDENTIFIABLE TIME** an interval of time that is identified by what happens or exists during it ○ *the early Victorian period* **3. TIMETABLE SECTION** a division of a schedule or timetable, e.g., a portion of the school day **4. DIVISION OF GAME** a division of playing time in some sports **5. PUNCTUATION MARK** the punctuation mark (.) that is used at the end of a sentence or in abbreviations **6. MENSTRUATION TIME** an occurrence of menstruation **7.** GEOL **UNIT OF GEOLOGIC TIME** a division of geologic time shorter than an era and longer than an epoch **8.** PHYS **TIME FOR SINGLE CYCLE** the time required for one complete cycle of a repetitive system, e.g., the rotation of a star or the movement of an electromagnetic wave. Symbol **T 9.** MATH **INTERVAL BETWEEN EQUAL VALUES** the interval between the points at which the values of a periodic function are equal **10.** CHEM **ROW IN PERIODIC TABLE** a horizontal row of elements in the periodic table **11.** LITERAT **UNIT OF POETIC RHYTHM** one of the longer units in the classical system of analyzing the rhythms of poetry **12.** MUSIC **MUSICAL PASSAGE** a long passage of music consisting of two or more contrasting musical phrases ■ *interj* **SHOWING FINALITY** a word added to the end of a statement to emphasize that the speaker will not discuss it further (*informal*) ○ *I'm not going, period!* ■ *adj* **RELATING TO HISTORICAL TIME** belonging to or intended to suggest a historical time ○ *actors in period costume* [14C. Via French < Greek *periodos*, literally "way around" < *hodos* "way"]

USAGE A ***period*** is used at the end of a sentence that is not a question or exclamation: *It rained last Saturday.* It is also used after some abbreviations: *at 11 a.m. on Aug. 7, 2003.* The period is increasingly omitted in abbreviations, especially after capital letters (e.g., *VCR*). Shortened forms used as words in their own right (e.g., *gym, disco, pub*) and acronyms pronounced as words (e.g., *AIDS, laser, NATO*) should not be written with periods. The same mark is used in decimal notation where it is read as "point." It is also used in Internet addresses, where it is read as "dot" (*.com*).

pe·ri·od·ic /péeree óddik/ *adj* **1. OCCASIONAL** recurring or reappearing from time to time **2. REGULAR** occurring or appearing at regular intervals or in regular cycles **3. INVOLVING PERIODS** associated with or occurring in periods [Mid-17C. Via French and Latin < Greek *periodikos* < *periodos* (see PERIOD)] —**pe·ri·od·i·cal·ly** *adv*

SYNONYMS ***periodic, intermittent, occasional, sporadic***

CORE MEANING: recurring over a period of time

periodic recurring or reappearing from time to time ○ *carry out periodic inspections* ○ *El Niño, a periodic weather pattern* **intermittent** occurring at irregular intervals ○ *The pain was usually intermittent, although in some patients it was continuous.* ○ *Thunder, lightning, and intermittent rain delayed the start of the tournament.* **occasional** occurring infrequently at irregular intervals ○ *Her family kept in contact by writing, telephoning, and occasional visits.* ○ *He sat silent, producing only an occasional suppressed grunt.* **sporadic** occurring at intervals that have no apparent pattern ○ *Despite a truce announced last month, sporadic fighting continues.* ○ *Prior to the mid-1960s, pollution issues received only limited and sporadic attention from the general public.*

pe·ri·od·ic ac·id *n* any strongly oxidizing acid of iodine [< PER- + IODIC]

pe·ri·od·i·cal /péeree óddik'l/ *n* **MAGAZINE** a magazine or journal published at regular intervals, especially weekly, monthly, or quarterly ■ *adj* **1. PUBLISHED REGULARLY** published at regular intervals **2. OCCASIONAL** recurring or reappearing from time to time

pe·ri·od·i·cal ci·ca·da *n* INSECTS same as **seventeen-year locust**

pe·ri·od·ic func·tion *n* a mathematical function whose value is the same at regular intervals

pe·ri·o·dic·i·ty /péeree ə dissétee/ *n* **1.** recurrence at regular intervals **2.** similarity between the properties of chemical elements that are close to each other in the periodic table

pe·ri·od·ic law *n* the law stating that chemical elements fall into groups sharing similar properties when they are arranged according to atomic number

pe·ri·od·ic sen·tence *n* in rhetoric, a complex sentence in which the main clause is left unfinished until the end in order to create the effect of anticipation or suspense

pe·ri·od·ic sys·tem *n* the system of arranging chemical elements in a table according to the periodic law

pe·ri·od·ic ta·ble *n* a table of the chemical elements arranged according to their atomic numbers. See table on next page

pe·ri·o·di·za·tion /péeree ədi záysh'n/ *n* the dividing of history into distinct and identifiable periods

per·i·o·don·tal /pèrree ə dónt'l/ *adj* relating to or affecting the tissues that surround the neck and root of a tooth [Mid-19C. < PERI- + Greek *odont-* "tooth"] —**per·i·o·don·tal·ly** *adv*

per·i·o·don·tics /pèrree ə dóntiks/, **per·i·o·don·tia** /-dónshə/, **per·i·o·don·tol·o·gy** /-don tólləjee/ *n* the branch of dentistry concerned with the treatment of diseases of the gums and other periodontal tissues (*takes a singular verb*) —**per·i·o·don·tic** *adj* —**per·i·o·don·ti·cal** *adj* —**per·i·o·don·ti·cal·ly** *adv* —**per·i·o·don·tist** *n*

pe·ri·od piece *n* something, especially a curio or a work of art, that dates from or evokes a historical period, often something with no other value

per·i·o·ny·chi·um /pèrree ō níkee əm/ (*plural* **-chi·a** /-kee ə/) *n* the areas of skin that surround a fingernail or toenail [Early 20C. < modern Latin < Greek *peri* "around" < *onukh-* "nail"]

per·i·os·te·um /pèrree óstee əm/ (*plural* **-te·a** /-tee ə/) *n* the sheath of connective tissue that surrounds all bones except those at joints [Late 16C. Via modern Latin < Greek *periosteon* < *peri* "around" + *osteon* "bone"] —**per·i·os·te·al** *adj*

per·i·os·ti·tis /pèrree o stítiss, -ə-/ *n* inflammation of the periosteum —**per·i·os·tit·ic** /-stíttik/ *adj*

per·i·os·tra·cum /pèrree óstrəkəm/ (*plural* **-ca** /-kə/) *n* the hard outer layer of the shell of some mollusks, especially freshwater mollusks [Mid-19C. < modern Latin < Greek *peri* "around" + *ostrakon* "shell"]

per·i·o·tic /pèrree óttik/ *adj* involving the area around the ear, especially the bones around the inner ear

per·i·pa·tet·ic /pèrrəpə téttik/ *adj* traveling from place to place, especially working in several establishments and traveling between them ■ *n* a peripatetic worker, especially a teacher who travels between schools [Early 17C. Via French or Latin < Greek *peripatētikos* < *peripatein* "walk around" < *patein* "to walk"] —**per·i·pa·tet·i·cal·ly** *adv*

Per·i·pa·tet·ic *adj* belonging or relating to the school of philosophy founded by Aristotle, who gave lectures while walking about the Lyceum in Athens ■ *n* a member of the Aristotelian school of philosophy

pe·rip·a·tus /pə ríppətəss/ *n* ZOOL same as **onychophoran** [Mid-19C. Via modern Latin < Greek *peripatos* < *peri* "around" + *patos* "way"]

pe·riph·er·al /pə ríffərəl/ *adj* **1. AT EDGE** at or relating to the edge of something, as opposed to its center **2. NOT SIGNIFICANT** minor or incidental in importance or relevance **3.** ANAT **NEAR SURFACE** near the surface of an organ or the body ■ *n* COMPUT **PERIPHERAL PIECE OF HARDWARE** a piece of computer hardware such as a printer or a disk drive that is external to but controlled by a computer's central processing unit —**pe·riph·er·al·ly** *adv*

pe·riph·er·al nerv·ous sys·tem *n* the part of the nervous system that lies outside the brain and spinal cord

pe·riph·er·y /pə ríffəree/ (*plural* **-ies**) *n* **1. BOUNDARY** the area around the edge of a place **2. SURFACE** the surface of an object **3. POSITION OF LITTLE INVOLVEMENT** the position or state of having only a minor involvement in something [Late 16C. Via late Latin < Greek *periphereia* < *peripherēs*, literally "carrying around" < *pherein* "carry"]

pe·riph·ra·sis /pə ríffrəssiss/ (*plural* **-ra·ses** /-rə seez/) *n* **1.** the use of overly long or indirect language in order to say something **2.** an expression that states something indirectly [Mid-16C. Via Latin < Greek < *periphrazein*, literally "explain around" < *phrazein* "explain"]

per·i·phras·tic /pèrrə frástik/ *adj* **1.** relating to or using periphrasis **2.** formed using two or more words rather than an inflected form, especially used to describe a verb tense formed using an auxiliary verb rather than by inflecting the main verb. "Did you have" is a periphrastic equivalent of archaic "had you." [Early 19C. < Greek *periphrastikos* < *periphrazein* (see PERIPHRASIS)] —**per·i·phras·ti·cal·ly** *adv*

pe·riph·y·ton /pə ríffə tòn/ *n* plants and animals that live in water attached to rocks and other submerged objects [Mid-20C. Probably < PERI- + Greek *phuton* "plant," after *plankton*]

per·i·plasm /pérrə plàzzəm/ *n* the area of a cell that lies immediately inside the cell wall but outside the plasma membrane

per·i·plast /pérrə plàst/ *n* a cell wall or cell membrane

per·i·proct /pérrə pròkt/ *n* the area surrounding the anus of some invertebrate animals such as sea urchins [Late 19C. < PERI- + Greek *prōktos* "anus"]

pe·rip·ter·al /pə ríptərəl/ *adj* describes a classical building that has a single row of columns on all sides [Early 19C. < Greek *peripteros* "with a wing around" < *pteron* "wing"]

pe·rique /pə réek/ *n* a strongly flavored tobacco grown in Louisiana. It is usually mixed with other tobaccos. [Late 19C. < Louisiana French]

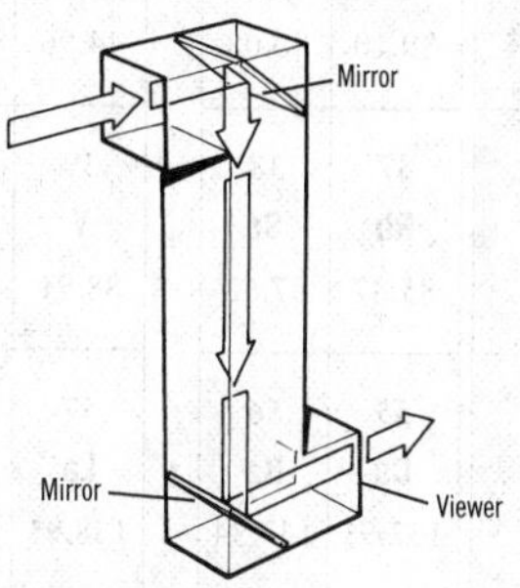

periscope

per·i·scope /pérrə skōp/ *n* a long tubular optical instrument, e.g., on a submarine, that uses lenses, prisms, and mirrors to allow a viewer to see objects not in a direct line of sight

per·i·scop·ic /pèrrə skóppik/ *adj* **1.** describes a lens that has a wide field of view **2.** relating to or using a periscope

per·ish /pérrish/ (**-ished, -ish·ing, -ish·es**) *vi* **1.** to die, e.g., because of harsh conditions or an accident **2.** to come to an end or cease to exist (*formal*) [13C. < French *périss-*, stem of *périr* < Latin *perire* "go completely" < *ire* "go"]

per·ish·a·ble /pérrishəb'l/ *adj* liable to decay, rot, or spoil ■ *n* something that is perishable, especially an item of food —**per·ish·a·bil·i·ty** /pèrrishə bíllətee/ *n* —**per·ish·a·ble·ness** *n* —**per·ish·a·bly** *adv*

per·i·sperm /pérrə spùrm/ *n* nutritive tissue from a plant nucleus that surrounds the seed embryo —**per·i·sperm·al** /pèrrə spúrm'l/ *adj*

pe·ris·so·dac·tyl /pə rìssə dákt'l/ *n* a large animal that belongs to the order of mammals with hooves and an odd number of toes, which includes horses, rhinoceroses, and tapirs. Order: Perissodactyla. [Mid-19C. < modern Latin *Perissodactyla* < Greek *perissos* "uneven" + *daktulos* "finger, toe"] —**pe·ris·so·dac·tyl** *adj* —**pe·ris·so·dac·ty·lous** *adj*

per·i·stal·sis /pèrrə stáwlsiss/ (*plural* **-stal·ses** /-stáwl seez/) *n* the waves of involuntary muscle contractions that transport food, waste matter, or other contents through a tube-shaped organ such as the intestine [Mid-19C. < modern Latin < Greek *peristaltikos* "clasping, compressing" < *peristellein* "place around" < *stellein* "to place"] —**per·i·stal·tic** *adj* —**per·i·stal·ti·cal·ly** *adv*

per·i·stome /pérrə stōm/ *n* the mouthparts of an invertebrate such as an earthworm or echinoderm —**per·i·sto·mal** /pèrrə stṓməl/ *adj*

per·i·style /pérrə stīl/ *n* **1.** a line of columns (**colonnade**) that encircles a building or a courtyard **2.** a building or courtyard that has a peristyle [Early 17C. Via French < Greek *peristulos* "having columns

PERIODIC TABLE

Period \ Group	1	2		3	4	5	6	7	8	9	10	11	12	13	14	15	16	17	18
1	1 **H** 1.01																		2 **He** 4.00
2	3 **Li** 6.94	4 **Be** 9.01												5 **B** 10.81	6 **C** 12.01	7 **N** 14.01	8 **O** 16.00	9 **F** 19.00	10 **Ne** 20.18
3	11 **Na** 22.99	12 **Mg** 24.31												13 **Al** 26.98	14 **Si** 28.09	15 **P** 30.97	16 **S** 32.06	17 **Cl** 35.45	18 **Ar** 39.95
4	19 **K** 39.10	20 **Ca** 40.08		21 **Sc** 44.96	22 **Ti** 47.90	23 **V** 50.94	24 **Cr** 52.00	25 **Mn** 54.94	26 **Fe** 55.85	27 **Co** 58.93	28 **Ni** 58.71	29 **Cu** 63.55	30 **Zn** 65.38	31 **Ga** 69.72	32 **Ge** 72.59	33 **As** 74.92	34 **Se** 78.96	35 **Br** 79.90	36 **Kr** 83.80
5	37 **Rb** 85.47	38 **Sr** 87.62		39 **Y** 88.91	40 **Zr** 91.22	41 **Nb** 92.91	42 **Mo** 95.94	43 **Tc** 98.91	44 **Ru** 101.07	45 **Rh** 102.91	46 **Pd** 106.40	47 **Ag** 107.87	48 **Cd** 112.40	49 **In** 114.82	50 **Sn** 118.69	51 **Sb** 121.75	52 **Te** 127.60	53 **I** 126.90	54 **Xe** 131.30
6	55 **Cs** 132.91	56 **Ba** 137.34	*	57 **La** 138.91	72 **Hf** 178.49	73 **Ta** 180.95	74 **W** 183.85	75 **Re** 186.2	76 **Os** 190.2	77 **Ir** 192.22	78 **Pt** 195.09	79 **Au** 196.97	80 **Hg** 200.59	81 **Tl** 204.37	82 **Pb** 207.20	83 **Bi** 208.98	84 **Po** 209	85 **At** (210)	86 **Rn** (222)
7	87 **Fr** (223)	88 **Ra** (226)	**	89 **Ac** (226)	104 **Rf** (261)	105 **Db** (262)	106 **Sg** (266)	107 **Bh** (264)	108 **Hs** (269)	109 **Mt** (268)	110 **Ds** (271)	111 **Uuu** (272)	112 **Uub** (277)	113 **Uut** (284)	114 **Uuq**	115 **Uup** (288)	116 **Uuh**	117 **Uus**	118 **Uuo**

Chemical elements are indicated by their symbols. The numbers above the elements are the atomic numbers, and those below are the atomic weights (those in parentheses are for the longest-lived isotopes, while those for Np, Pa, and Tc are for the most technologically important isotopes). The lanthanides and actinides do not fit easily into any group and are thus shown separate from the main table.

Elements 113 and 115 are reported but unconfirmed; 117 is unknown; the report of 118 has been retracted, throwing doubt on 116.

Lanthanides	*	57 **La** 138.91	58 **Ce** 140.12	59 **Pr** 140.91	60 **Nd** 144.24	61 **Pm** (145)	62 **Sm** 150.40	63 **Eu** 151.96	64 **Gd** 157.25	65 **Tb** 158.93	66 **Dy** 162.50	67 **Ho** 164.93	68 **Er** 167.26	69 **Tm** 168.93	70 **Yb** 173.04	71 **Lu** 174.97
Actinides	**	89 **Ac** (226)	90 **Th** 232.04	91 **Pa** 231.04	92 **U** 283.04	93 **Np** 237.05	94 **Pu** (244)	95 **Am** (243)	96 **Cm** (247)	97 **Bk** (247)	98 **Cf** (251)	99 **Es** (254)	100 **Fm** (257)	101 **Md** (258)	102 **No** (255)	103 **Lr** (256)

around" < *stulos* "column"] —**per·i·sty·lar** /pèrrə stī́lər/ *adj*

per·i·the·ci·um /pèrrə théessee əm, -théeshee-/ (*plural* **-ci·a** /-see ə, -shee ə/) *n* in some kinds of fungus, a flask-shaped fruiting body that contains spores [Mid-19C. < modern Latin < Greek *peri* "around" + *thēkē* "case"]

per·i·to·ne·um /pèrrət'n ée əm/ (*plural* **-ne·ums** or **-ne·a** /-n ée ə/) *n* a smooth transparent membrane that lines the abdomen and doubles back over the surfaces of the internal organs to form a continuous sac [Mid-16C. Via late Latin < Greek *peritoneion* < *peritonos* "stretched around" < *teinein* "to stretch"] —**per·i·to·ne·al** *adj* —**per·i·to·ne·al·ly** *adv*

per·i·to·ni·tis /pèrrət'n ī́tiss/ *n* inflammation of the membrane that lines the abdomen (**peritoneum**). Symptoms can include swelling of the abdomen, severe pain, and weight loss. —**per·i·ton·it·ic** /-íttik/ *adj*

per·i·track /pérrə trak/ *n* AVIAT same as **taxiway** [Late 20C. < PERIMETER]

per·i·trich /pérrə trìk/ (*plural* **per·i·tri·cha** /pə ríttrəkə/) *n* a simple microscopic invertebrate (**protozoan**) covered in tiny filaments (**cilia**) that it uses to move around [Early 20C. < modern Latin *peritricha* < Greek *peri* "around" + *trikh-* "hair"] —**pe·rit·ri·chous** /pə ríttrəkəss/ *adj*

per·i·wig /pérrə wìg/ *n* a wig, especially of the kind that men wore in the 17th and 18th centuries [Early 16C. Alteration of an earlier form of PERUKE]

per·i·win·kle[1] /pérrə wìngk'l/ *n* MARINE BIOL same as **winkle** [Mid-16C. Origin ?]

per·i·win·kle[2] /pérrə wìngk'l/ *n* a trailing evergreen plant with dark green glossy leaves. Flowers: blue, white. Native to: Europe, Asia. Genus: *Vinca*. ■ *adj* of a pale bluish purple color [Pre-12C. < late Latin *pervinca* < Latin *vincapervinca*]

perjorative incorrect spelling of **pejorative**

per·jure /púrjər/ (**-jured, -jur·ing, -jures**), **per·jure your·self** *vr* to tell a lie in a court of law and therefore be guilty of perjury [15C. Via French < Latin *perjurare* "swear falsely" < *jurare* (see JURY)] —**per·jur·er** *n*

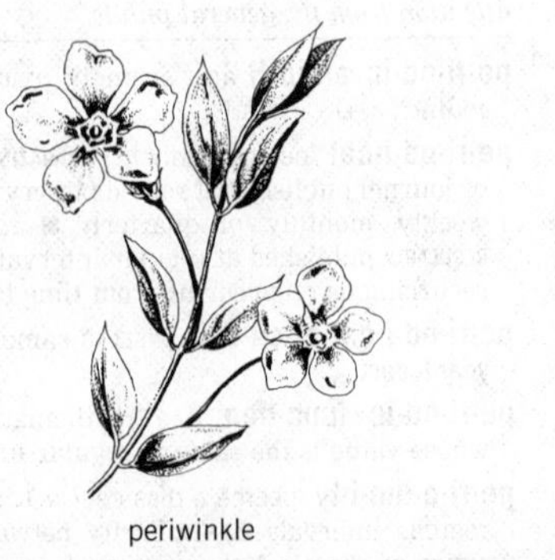

periwinkle

per·jured /púrjərd/ *adj* **1.** guilty of telling a lie in a court of law and therefore of committing perjury **2.** containing lies and therefore breaking an oath to tell the truth in a court of law

per·ju·ry /púrjəree/ (*plural* **-ries**) *n* **1.** the telling of a lie after having taken an oath to tell the truth, usually in a court of law **2.** a lie told in a court of law by somebody who has taken an oath to tell the truth [14C. Via Anglo-Norman < Latin *perjurium* < *perjurare* (see PERJURE)] —**per·ju·ri·ous** /pər jŏŏree əss/ *adj* —**per·ju·ri·ous·ly** *adv* —**per·ju·ri·ous·ness** *n*

perk[1] /purk/ *n* a benefit given to an employee in addition to a salary, e.g., the use of a car or membership in a club ○ *one of the perks of the job* [Early 19C. Shortening of PERQUISITE]

perk[2] /purk/ (**perked, perk·ing, perks**) *vti* to percolate, or percolate coffee (*informal*) [Mid-20C. Shortening]

perk[3] /purk/ (**perked, perk·ing, perks**) [14C. Probably < *perk* "perch" (now dialectical) < Old French *perche* (see PERCH[1])]

perk up *vti* **1.** to become more cheerful, positive, or active, or make somebody more cheerful, positive, or active **2.** to stick up, or make something stick up, especially quickly ○ *The dog's ears perked up.*

Per·kins /púrkinz/, **Charles** (1936–2000) Australian Aboriginal activist. He led antidiscrimination protests in the 1960s, and subsequently became head of Australia's Department of Aboriginal Affairs (1984–89). Full name **Perkins, Charles Nelson**

Per·kins, Frances (1880–1965) US secretary of labor (1933–45). She was the first woman to be appointed to a US cabinet post.

Per·kins, Maxwell (1884–1947) US book editor. He is known for his championing of writers such as F. Scott Fitzgerald and Ernest Hemingway. Full name **Perkins, Maxwell Evarts**

perk·y /púrkee/ (**-i·er, -i·est**) *adj* **1.** lively, cheerful, and energetic **2.** irritatingly self-confident —**perk·i·ly** *adv* —**perk·i·ness** *n*

Perl /purl/, **Martin L.** (*b.* 1927) US physicist. He discovered the tau lepton, a fundamental atomic particle, for which he shared the Nobel Prize in physics (1995). Full name **Perl, Martin Lewis**

per·lite /púr lìt/ *n* a grayish volcanic glass in the form of grains that resemble pearls. It is often added to potting soil as a conditioner and is also used as a heat insulator. —**per·lit·ic** /pur líttik/ *adj*

Perl·man /púrlmən/, **Itzhak** (*b.* 1945) Israeli-born US violinist. He is considered one of the finest violinists of his generation.

per·lo·cu·tion /pùrlə kyŏŏsh'n/ *n* the effect that a speaker's words have on somebody's emotions and responses

perm /purm/ *n* a hair treatment that uses chemicals to give hair long-lasting curliness or waviness [Early 20C. Shortening of PERMANENT] —**perm** *vt*

Perm /purm, perm/, **Perm'** city in eastern European Russia. Population: 1,275,482 (1995).

per·ma·frost /púrmə fràwst/ *n* underlying soil or rock that remains permanently frozen, found mainly in the polar regions [Mid-20C. < PERMANENT]

~~**permanant**~~ incorrect spelling of **permanent**

per·ma·nence /púrmənənss/, **per·ma·nen·cy** /-nənssee/ *n* existence in the same form forever or for a very long time [15C. Directly or via French < medieval Latin *permanentia* < Latin *permanent-* (see PERMANENT)]

per·ma·nent /púrmənənt/ *adj* **1.** lasting forever or for a very long time, especially without undergoing significant change **2.** never changing or not expected to change ■ *n* HAIR same as **perm** (*formal*) [15C. Directly or via French < Latin *permanent-*, present participle of *permanere* "remain through" < *manere* "remain"] —**per·ma·nent·ly** *adv* —**per·ma·nent·ness** *n*

per·ma·nent mag·net *n* a magnet that retains its properties after the magnetizing force has been removed from it. Permanent magnets are used in loudspeakers and small motors. —**per·ma·nent mag·net·ism** *n*

per·ma·nent press *n* a chemical process used to give fabric shape and make it resistant to wrinkling (*hyphenated when used before a noun*)

per·ma·nent set *n* a permanent plastic deformation of a test piece or structure once an applied load has been removed

per·ma·nent tooth *n* a tooth of the second and final set of teeth that grow to replace the milk teeth. A human adult has 32 permanent teeth.

per·ma·nent wave *n* same as **perm**

per·man·ga·nate /pur máng gə nàyt, -gənət/ *n* a chemical compound that is a salt of permanganic acid [Mid-19C. < PER- + MANGANESE]

per·man·gan·ic ac·id /pùr man gànnik-/ *n* an unstable acid that exists only in dilute solution. Formula: $HMnO_4$. [< PERMANGANATE]

per·me·a·bil·i·ty /pùrmee ə bíllətee/ (*plural* **-ties**) *n* **1.** PERMEABLE NATURE the property of being permeable **2.** RATE SUBSTANCE PASSES THROUGH POROUS MEDIUM the rate at which something such as a liquid or a magnetic field passes through a membrane or other medium **3.** MAGNETIC PROPERTY the property of a material to alter a magnetic field in which it is placed, or a measure of this property. Symbol μ

per·me·a·ble /púrmee əb'l/ *adj* allowing liquids, gases, or magnetic fields to pass through —**per·me·a·bly** *adv*

per·me·ance /púrmee ənss/ *n* **1.** the act of passing through a porous substance or membrane **2.** the ability of a magnetic component or assembly to be magnetized, measured in henries and calculated by dividing the magnetic flux by the magnetomotive force —**per·me·ant** *adj, n*

per·me·ase /púrmee àyss, -àyz/ *n* a protein in bacterial cell membranes that allows a solute to enter the cell [Mid-20C. < PERMEATE]

per·me·ate /púrmee àyt/ (**-at·ed, -at·ing, -ates**) *vti* **1.** to enter something and spread throughout it, so that every part or aspect of it is affected **2.** to pass through the minute openings in a porous substance or membrane, or make something such as a liquid pass through [Mid-17C. < Latin *permeat-*, past participle of *permeare* "pass through" < *meare* "to pass"] —**per·me·a·tion** /pùrmee áysh'n/ *n* —**per·me·a·tive** *adj*

~~**permenent**~~ incorrect spelling of **permanent**

Per·mi·an /púrmee ən/ *n* the period of geologic time, 290 million to 248 million years ago, when many marine invertebrates disappeared and reptiles flourished. See table at **geologic time** [Late 16C. After *Perm*, province in E Russia] —**Per·mi·an** *adj*

per mill /pər míl/, **per mil** *adv* in every thousand, or by the thousand [< Latin *mille* "thousand"]

~~**permissable**~~ incorrect spelling of **permissible**

per·mis·si·ble /pər míssəb'l/ *adj* allowable or permitted [15C. < French < Latin *permiss-* (see PERMISSION)] —**per·mis·si·bil·i·ty** /pər mìssə bíllətee/ *n* —**per·mis·si·bly** *adv*

per·mis·sion /pər mísh'n/ *n* agreement to allow something to happen or be done ■ *vt* (**-sioned, -sion·ing, -sions**) to give explicit permission for something, e.g., for marketing information to be sent automatically [15C. < French < Latin *permiss-*, past participle of *permittere* (see PERMIT)]

per·mis·sive /pər míssiv/ *adj* **1.** allowing or enjoying the freedom to behave in ways others might consider unacceptable, particularly in sexual matters **2.** granting permission [15C. < French, < Latin *permiss-* (see PERMISSION)] —**per·mis·sive·ly** *adv* —**per·mis·sive·ness** *n*

per·mit *v* /pər mít/ (**-mit·ted, -mit·ting, -mits**) **1.** *vti* ALLOW SOMETHING to allow something or give permission for it ○ *She will not permit talking in her class while she is speaking.* **2.** *vti* MAKE SOMETHING POSSIBLE to allow somebody the possibility of doing something ○ *New technologies will permit more people to work from home.* **3. per·mit your·self** *vr* ALLOW YOURSELF SOMETHING to allow yourself to have or do something, especially as a luxury or for a special occasion ■ *n* /púrmit, pər mít/ **1.** DOCUMENT GIVING PERMISSION an official document or certificate giving permission for something **2.** PERMISSION permission granted, especially in written form (*formal*) [15C. < Latin *permittere* "let go through" < *mittere* "let go"] —**per·mit·tee** /pùrmi tée/ *n* —**per·mit·ter** *n*

~~**permited**~~ incorrect spelling of **permitted**

per·mit·tiv·i·ty /pùrmi tívvətee/ (*plural* **-ties**) *n* the measure of the ability of a nonconducting material to retain electric energy when placed in an electric field. Symbol υ [Late 19C. < PERMIT, after *conductivity*]

per·mu·ta·tion /pùrmyə táysh'n/ *n* **1.** TRANSFORMATION a change or transformation **2.** ARRANGEMENT an arrangement of items created by moving or reordering them **3.** REARRANGING the reordering or rearranging of items in a group **4.** MATH ORDER OF MATHEMATICAL ELEMENTS an ordered arrangement of elements from a set —**per·mu·ta·tion·al** *adj*

per·mute /pər myŏŏt/ (**-mut·ed, -mut·ing, -mutes**) *vt* **1.** to change the order of items in a group, especially to rearrange them in every possible way **2.** to reorder the elements in a mathematical set [Late 19C. < Latin *permutare* "change completely" < *mutare* "to change"] —**per·mut·a·bil·i·ty** /pər myŏŏtə bíllətee/ *n* —**per·mut·a·ble** *adj* —**per·mut·a·bly** *adv*

per·ni·cious /pər níshəss/ *adj* **1.** causing great harm, destruction, or death **2.** wicked or meaning to cause harm [Early 16C. Via French < Latin *perniciosus* < *pernicies* "complete destruction" < *nec-* "destruction"] —**per·ni·cious·ly** *adv* —**per·ni·cious·ness** *n*

per·ni·cious a·ne·mi·a *n* a severe form of anemia, found mostly in older adults, that results from the body's inability to absorb vitamin B_{12}. Symptoms include weakness, breathing difficulties, and weight loss.

per·nick·e·ty /pər níkətee/ *adj* (*informal*) **1.** *UK* same as **persnickety 2.** same as **persnickety** [Early 19C. Origin ?] —**per·nick·e·ti·ness** *n*

~~**perogative**~~ incorrect spelling of **prerogative**

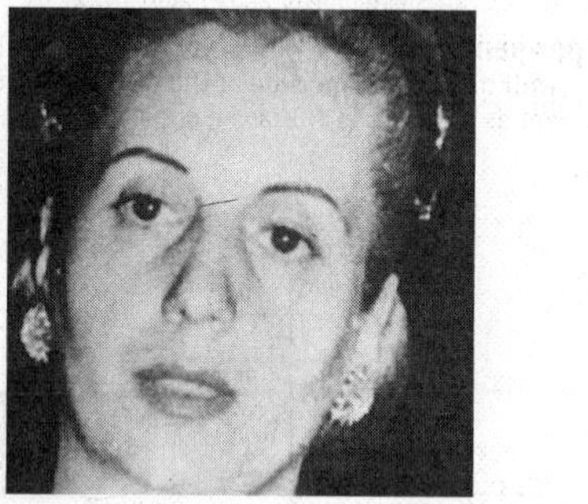

Eva Perón

Pe·rón /pə rṓn/, **Eva** (1919–52) Argentine political figure. Married to President Juan Perón, she was adored by the Argentinean people for her charitable work. Born **Duarte, María Eva**. Full name **Duarte de Perón, Maria Eva**. Known as **Evita**

> "Almsgiving tends to perpetuate poverty; aid does away with it once and for all. Almsgiving leaves a man just where he was before. Aid restores him to society as an individual worthy of all respect and not as a man with a grievance. Almsgiving is the generosity of the rich; social aid levels up social inequalities."
> [Eva Perón, *Speech to the American Congress of Industrial Medicine*; December 5, 1949]

Pe·rón, Isabel (*b.* 1931) president of Argentina (1974–76). She was the third wife of Juan Perón, and after his death succeeded him as president. Born **Martínez Cartas, María Estela**. Full name **de Perón, Isabel**

Pe·rón, Juan (1895–1974) president of Argentina (1946–55 and 1973–74). He rose to power by a military coup (1943) and enacted populist economic reforms during his presidencies. Full name **Perón, Juan Domingo** —**Per·o·nist** /pə rṓnist/ *n, adj*

per·o·ne·al /pèrrə née əl/ *adj* relating to the narrower of the two bones in the lower leg (**fibula**) [Mid-19C. < Greek *peronē* "pin of a brooch, fibula"]

per·o·ral /pər áwrəl/ *adj* occurring by way of the mouth —**per·o·ral·ly** *adv*

per·o·rate /pérrə ràyt/ (**-rat·ed, -rat·ing, -rates**) *vi* (*formal*) **1.** to finish a speech by summarizing its main points **2.** to speak at length, especially in a formal or pompous way [Early 17C. < Latin *perorat-*, past participle of *perorare* "speak all the way through" < *orare* "speak"] —**per·o·ra·tion** /pèrrə ráysh'n/ *n* —**per·o·ra·tion·al** *adj*

Pe·rot /pə rṓ/, **H. Ross** (*b.* 1930) US business executive and politician. He ran unsuccessfully as an independent candidate for president (1992), and established the political movement "United We Stand

America" (1993) and the Reform Party (1995). Full name **Perot, Henry Ross**

per·ov·skite /pə róv skīt, -ráwf-/ *n* a black, yellow, or brown calcium titanate mineral. Use: superconductive materials. [Mid-19C. After L. A. *Perovski* (1792–1856), Russian mineralogist]

per·ox·i·dase /pə róksə dàyss, pə tóksə dàyz/ *n* an enzyme in animals and plants that helps neutralize harmful peroxides

per·ox·ide /pə rók sīd/ *n* **1. CHEMICAL COMPOUND** a chemical compound that contains oxygen atoms in the group -O_2-, e.g., hydrogen peroxide **2. HAIR COLORING SUBSTANCE** a solution of hydrogen peroxide used to lighten hair color, giving a blond tint that is almost white (*often used before a noun*) ○ *a peroxide blond* ■ *vt* (**-id·ed, -id·ing, -ides**) **1. COLOR HAIR BLOND** to bleach hair using peroxide **2. TREAT SOMETHING WITH PEROXIDE** to treat something with peroxide or hydrogen peroxide

per·ox·i·some /pə róksi sōm/ *n* a tiny part within a cell containing enzymes that oxidize toxic substances such as alcohol and prevent them from doing any harm. There are many peroxisomes in the cells of the liver and kidney. [Mid-20C. < PEROXIDE + -SOME[1]]

perp /purp/ *n* somebody responsible for a crime (*slang*) [Late 20C. Shortening of *perpetrator*]

per·pend /pər pénd/ *n* a stone or brick built into a wall to go from one side of the wall to the other and act as a binder [15C. Variant of PARPEN]

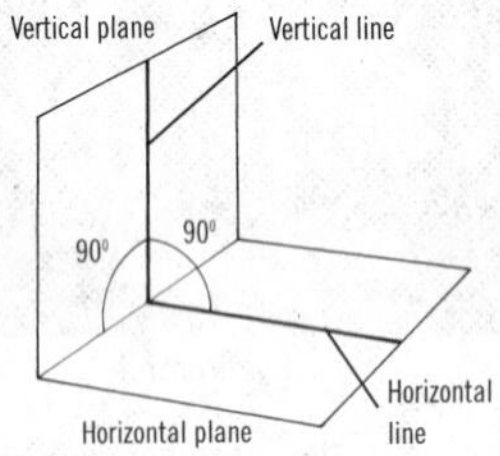

perpendicular

per·pen·dic·u·lar /pùrpən díkyələr/ *adj* **1. AT RIGHT ANGLES** at right angles to a line or plane **2. VERTICAL** perfectly vertical **3. STEEP** very steep **4.** *also* **Per·pen·dic·u·lar** ARCHIT **IN LATE GOTHIC STYLE** relating to or typical of a style of Gothic architecture in which tall narrow facades, windows, and doors, and vaulted ceilings are characteristic. It was popular in England in the 14th and 15th centuries. ■ *n* **1. PERPENDICULAR LINE** a perpendicular line or plane **2. DEVICE FINDING VERTICAL** any device used to establish a vertical line, e.g., a spirit level or a plumb line **3. SHEER ROCK** a sheer rock face [14C. Directly or via French < Latin *perpendicularis* < *perpendiculum* "plumb line" < *perpendere* "weigh thoroughly" < *pendere* "weigh"] —**per·pen·dic·u·lar·i·ty** /-dikyə lárrətee/ *n* —**per·pen·dic·u·lar·ly** *adv*

per·pe·trate /púrpə tràyt/ (**-trat·ed, -trat·ing, -trates**) *vt* to commit or be responsible for something, usually something criminal or morally wrong [Mid-16C. < Latin *perpetrat-*, past participle of *perpetrare*, literally "completely bring about" < *patrare* "bring about" < *pater* "father"] —**per·pe·tra·tion** /pùrpə tráysh'n/ *n* —**per·pe·tra·tor** *n*

per·pet·u·al /pər péchoo əl/ *adj* **1. LASTING FOREVER** lasting for all time **2. LASTING INDEFINITELY** lasting for an indefinitely long time **3. OCCURRING REPEATEDLY** occurring over and over **4.** BOT **BLOOMING THROUGHOUT SEASON** describes flowers or flowering plants that bloom throughout the season [14C. Via French < Latin *perpetualis* < *perpetuus* "continuous" < *perpes*, literally "going toward throughout" < *petere* "go toward"]

per·pet·u·al cal·en·dar *n* a calendar set out in such a way that it can be used for several years or for any year

per·pet·u·al check *n* a situation in chess in which one player's king is placed in check with every move the other player makes, resulting in a draw

per·pet·u·al·ly /pər péchoo əlee/ *adv* **1.** forever, or for a very long time **2.** repeatedly at very short intervals, and so appearing to be continuous

per·pet·u·al mo·tion *n* **1.** the hypothetical continuous operation of a mechanism without the introduction of energy from an external source, known as perpetual motion of the first kind. A device demonstrating this would violate the first law of thermodynamics, which states that energy can neither be created nor destroyed. **2.** the hypothetical operation of a mechanism that would convert heat directly into work, known as perpetual motion of the second kind. A device demonstrating this would violate the second law of thermodynamics, which states that heat cannot be converted into work without producing some other effect.

per·pet·u·ate /pər péchoo àyt/ (**-at·ed, -at·ing, -ates**) *vt* **1.** to make something continue, usually for a very long time **2.** to make something or somebody be remembered [Early 16C. < Latin *perpetuat-*, past participle of *perpetuare* < *perpetuus* (see PERPETUAL)] —**per·pet·u·a·tion** /pər pèchoo áysh'n/ *n* —**per·pet·u·a·tor** *n*

per·pe·tu·i·ty /pùrpə tóo ətee/ (*plural* **-ties**) *n* **1. PERPETUAL CONDITION** the state of continuing for a long time or indefinitely **2. ETERNITY** eternity or the rest of time ○ *a sacrifice honored in perpetuity* **3.** LAW **TRANSFER OF REAL ESTATE FOREVER** the transfer of real estate for an unlimited period of time, restricted in law by the rule against perpetuity. The maximum legal period of transferred ownership is based on the length of a life in existence at the time plus 21 years plus a nine month period of gestation. **4.** FIN **INVESTMENT** an investment designed to pay an annual return indefinitely, having no maturity date [15C. Via French < Latin *perpetuitas* < *perpetuus* (see PERPETUAL)]

per·phen·a·zine /pər fénnə zeen/ *n* an antipsychotic drug. Use: treatment of anxiety, tension and nausea. Formula: $C_{21}H_{26}ClN_3OS$. [Mid-20C. < PIPERIDINE + PHENOTHIAZINE]

Per·pi·gnan /pèr pee nyaáN/ city in southern France, near the Mediterranean Sea and the border with Spain. Population: 105,115 (1999).

per·plex /pər pléks/ (**-plexed, -plex·ing, -plex·es**) *vt* **1.** to puzzle or confuse somebody, especially causing doubt **2.** to make something overly complicated or intricate [Late 16C. Back-formation from *perplexed* < obsolete *perplex* (adj), directly or via French < Latin *perplexus* "intricate, involved" < *per-* "through" + past participle of *plectere* "plait, involve"] —**per·plexed** *adj*

per·plex·i·ty /pər pléksətee/ (*plural* **-ties**) *n* **1. BEING PERPLEXED** the state of being perplexed **2. PERPLEXING THING** something that is difficult to understand, especially because it is complex or part of a complicated whole (*often used in the plural*) **3. COMPLEX NATURE** the nature of something that is disconcertingly complex

per pro·cu·ra·ti·on·em /pər pròkə raátee ō nem, -pròkyə ràyshee-/ *prep* a fuller form of the abbreviation "p.p." that is written in formal correspondence by somebody who is signing on behalf of another person [< Latin, "by proxy"]

perp walk *n* an act of escorting a prisoner to confinement in full public view, especially in front of the media (*slang*)

per·qui·site /púrkwəzit/ *n* **1.** same as **perk**[1] (*formal*) **2.** a tip that is customary on some occasions **3.** something considered to be an exclusive right [Early 18C. < medieval Latin *perquisitum* "something searched for" < *perquirere* "seek for" < *quaerere* "seek"]

Per·rault /pe rṓ, pə-/, **Charles** (1628–1703) French writer. In *Tales of Mother Goose* (1697) he set down from oral tradition such fairy tales as *Cinderella* and *Sleeping Beauty*.

~~perrenial~~ incorrect spelling of **perennial**

per·ron /pérrən, pə rón/ *n* **1.** a raised platform at an entrance that is not at ground level **2.** an external stairway leading up to a perron [14C. < French, "large stone" < Latin *petra* "stone"]

per·ry /pérree/ *n* a drink made from fermented pear juice, similar to cider or wine [14C. < Old French *pere* < Latin *pirum* "pear"]

Per·ry /pérree/, **Fred** (1909–95) British tennis player. He was winner of the US Open (1933, 1934, 1936), Wimbledon (1934, 1935, 1936), Australian Open (1934), and French Open (1935) singles titles. Full name **Perry, Frederick John**

Per·ry, Matthew Calbraith (1794–1858) US naval officer. He negotiated the opening of Japan to United States ships and merchants (1853).

Per·ry, Oliver Hazard (1785–1819) US naval officer. He equipped and commanded the fleet of warships that defeated the British in the Battle of Lake Erie (1813).

per se /pər sáy/ *adv* in itself, by itself, or intrinsically [< Latin, "by itself"]

perse /purss/ *adj* of a dark bluish gray or purplish black color [14C. Via French < medieval Latin *persus*] —**perse** *n*

per·se·cute /púrssə kyoòt/ (**-cut·ed, -cut·ing, -cutes**) *vt* **1.** to systematically subject a race or group of people to cruel or unfair treatment, e.g., because of their ethnic origin or religious beliefs **2.** to make somebody the victim of continual pestering or harassment [15C. Via French < Latin *persecut-*, past participle of *persequi* "keep following" < *sequi* "follow"] —**per·se·cu·tee** /pùrssə kyoo teé/ *n* —**per·se·cu·tive** *adj* —**per·se·cu·tor** *n* —**per·se·cu·to·ry** /púrssəkyə tàwree/ *adj*

per·se·cu·tion /pùrssə kyóosh'n/ *n* **1.** the subjecting of a race or group of people to cruel or unfair treatment, e.g., because of their ethnic origin or religious beliefs **2.** the suffering felt by persecuted people

Per·se·id /púrssee id/ *n* a meteor in a meteor shower that appears around August 12 and seems to originate from near the constellation Perseus

Per·seph·o·ne /pər séffənee/ *n* in Greek mythology, the daughter of Demeter and Zeus who was abducted by Hades, king of the underworld. She spent half the year in the underworld and half on Earth. Her return to Earth symbolized the arrival of spring. Roman equivalent **Proserpina**

Per·sep·o·lis /pər séppəliss/ ruined city situated northeast of Shiraz in modern-day Iran. It was founded by Darius the Great in the 6th century B.C. as the Persian capital and destroyed by Alexander the Great.

Per·se·us /púrssee əss/ *n* **1.** a constellation of the northern hemisphere. See illustration at **constellation 2.** in Greek mythology, the son of Zeus and Danae. He killed the Gorgon Medusa and also rescued the princess Andromeda as she was about to be sacrificed to a sea monster.

per·se·ver·ance /pùrssə veérənss/ *n* **1. DETERMINED CONTINUATION WITH SOMETHING** steady and continued action or belief, usually over a long period and especially despite difficulties or setbacks **2. CALVINIST CONCEPT OF DIVINE GRACE** in Calvinism, the belief that God's grace brings selected people, the elect, to salvation **3. ROMAN CATHOLIC BELIEF IN GOD'S GRACE** in the Roman Catholic Church, the belief that God's grace lasts to the end of somebody's life if that person has maintained his or her good works and faith —**per·se·ver·ant** *adj*

per·sev·er·a·tion /pər sèvvə ráysh'n/ *n* a tendency to repeat the response to an experience in later situations where it is not appropriate [Early 20C. < Latin *perseverare* (see PERSEVERE)]

per·se·vere /pùrssə veér/ (**-vered, -ver·ing, -veres**) *vi* to persist steadily in an action or belief, usually over a long period and especially despite problems or difficulties [14C. Via French < Latin *perseverare* "follow strictly" < *perseverus* "very strict" < *severus* "serious"] —**per·se·ver·ing** *adj* —**per·se·ver·ing·ly** *adv*

~~perseverence~~ incorrect spelling of **perseverance**

Per·shing /púrshing/ *n* a two-stage US Army ballistic missile capable of delivering a nuclear warhead [Mid-20C. After John J. PERSHING]

Per·shing /púrshing/, **John J.** (1860–1948) US general. He led the American Expeditionary Force in Europe during World War I. Full name **Pershing, John Joseph**

> "I hope that here on the soil of France and in the school of French heroes, our American soldiers may learn to battle and vanquish for the liberty of the world."
> [John J. Pershing, *Speech, at Lafayette's tomb, Paris*; July 4, 1917]

Per·sia /púrzhə/ **1.** former name for **Iran 2.** ancient

LANGUAGE HERITAGE ***Persian*** Much of English is made up of words from other languages, and some are from Persian, the earlier form of the language now known as Farsi. Persia once had a vast empire in Southwest Asia, and Persian left a legacy to many of the languages of the region. Though relatively few purely Persian words have moved directly into English, numerous words set out from Persian and found their way by a more circuitous route. A typical much-traveled example would be Persian *lāžward* "lapis lazuli," which arrived in English in the 13th century as ***azure***, by way of Arabic *al-lāzaward* "the lapis lazuli," medieval Latin *azzurum*, and finally Old French *azur*. Even earlier was the name of the game of ***chess***, known from the 12th century and a shortening of Old French *esches*, plural of *eschec* "check in chess"; this is the word from which the English chess term ***check*** (14th century) immediately derives, though the French goes back to Persian *šāh* "king," itself imported as ***shah*** in the mid-16th century; ***checkmate*** followed ***check*** in the 15th century, from Old French *eschec mat*, from Persian *šāh māt* "the king is dead."

Travel and trade brought English speakers more directly into contact with Persian, and this is reflected by early migrants, for example, ***khan*** "inn" (14th century), and ***caravanserai*** (late 16th), from Persian *kārwānsarāī*, formed from *kārwān* "group of desert travelers" and *sarāī* "inn" (***caravan*** itself also arrived from Persian in the late 16th century, by way of French). Luxury materials such as ***taffeta*** (14th century, via medieval Latin or Old French *taffetas* from Persian *tāftah* from *tāftan* "to shine"), ***seersucker*** (early 18th, via Hindi from Persian *šīr o šakar* "milk and sugar"), and ***pashmina*** (late 19th, from Persian *pašmīn* "woolen," from *pašm* "wool") continued to come from or through Persian.

A great proportion of words of Persian origin, however, migrated through the languages of northern South Asia such as Hindi and, especially, its close relative Urdu, the official language of Pakistan and of Bangladesh, which has many loanwords from Persian. Urdu and Persian gave, for example, familiar items such as ***pajamas*** (early 19th century, from *pāy-jāmah* "leg garment"), the ***shawl*** (early 17th, from *šāl*), and ***khaki*** (mid-19th, from Urdu *kakī* "dust-colored" from Persian *kāk* "dust"). Through Persian and Urdu have migrated not only words relating to Islamic culture and religion such as ***burqa***, ***chador***, ***mullah***, ***purdah***, and ***zakat*** ("tax that goes to charity"), but also the name for those of another great faith, ***Hindu*** (mid-17th century, via Urdu from Persian *Hindū* from *Hind* "India"). South Asian terms of the military and of public administration include numerous words in *-dar*, from Persian *-dār* "holder," for example, ***havildar***, ***jamadar***, ***sardar***, ***subadar***, ***tahsildar***, and ***zamindar***.

During the 20th century, migration of people from South Asia has brought many more English speakers into contact with its cultures, and nowhere more effectively than in its food. ***Biryani*** (via Hindi from Persian *biriyān* "fried, grilled"), ***kofta*** (from Urdu and Persian *koftah* "pounded meat"), ***nan*** (from Persian and Urdu *nān*), and the ***tandoori*** (from Persian and Urdu, from Urdu *tandūr*, Persian *tanūr* "clay oven") are familiar pleasures of many non-Asian lives. See also ***Turkish***

empire in Southwest Asia that, at its height under Darius the Great in the 6th century B.C., stretched from the shores of the eastern Mediterranean to the Indus River in present-day Pakistan. It was conquered by Alexander the Great in 330 B.C.

Per·sian /púrzh'n/ *n* **1.** SOMEBODY FROM IRAN somebody who comes from Iran **2.** LANG same as **Farsi** **3.** SOMEBODY FROM ANCIENT PERSIA a member of a people who lived in ancient Persia and who founded an empire around 500 B.C. **4.** LANGUAGE OF ANCIENT PERSIANS the Iranian language spoken by the ancient Persians **5.** BREED same as **Persian cat** —**Per·sian** *adj*

Per·sian blinds *npl* outside louvered shutters for blocking sunlight while allowing ventilation

Per·sian car·pet *n* a carpet consisting of a woven backing to which wool or silk threads have been hand-knotted, made in southwestern Asia and typically having rich colors and strong designs

Persian cat

Per·sian cat *n* a longhaired domestic cat belonging to a breed originally from southwestern Asia

Per·sian Gulf /pùrzh'n-/ gulf of the Arabian Sea, with Iran to its northeast and the Arabian peninsula to its southwest. Area: 88,800 sq. mi./230,000 sq. km.

Per·sian Gulf War *n* ➧ **Gulf War** (sense 1)

Per·sian lamb *n* **1.** the soft curled usually black fur from the karakul lamb **2.** a lamb of the karakul sheep

Per·sian mel·on *n* a melon that has musky orange flesh and a rind with a netted pattern. Latin name: *Cucumis melo*.

Per·sian rug *n* TEXTILES same as **Persian carpet**

Per·sian wool *n* a loosely twisted three-strand wool yarn used in needlepoint, each strand being two-ply

per·si·ennes /pùrzee én, -énz/ *npl UK* same as **Persian blinds** [Mid-19C. < French < *persian* "Persian"]

per·si·flage /púrssi flaàzh/ *n* **1.** light or teasing good-natured talk **2.** light-heartedness or frivolity in the treatment of something [Mid-18C. < French < *persifler* "to banter" < *siffler* "to whistle" < Latin *sibilare* "to hiss"]

persimmon

per·sim·mon /pər símmən/ *n* **1.** a juicy smooth-skinned orange-red fruit that is sweet only when fully ripe **2.** a tree that has hard wood and bears persimmons. Native to: Asia, Europe, eastern North America. Genus: *Diospyros*. [Early 17C. Alteration of Virginia Algonquian *pessemmins*]

per·sist /pər síst/ (**-sist·ed, -sist·ing, -sists**) *vi* **1.** KEEP CARRYING ON to continue steadily or obstinately despite problems, difficulties, or obstacles **2.** CONTINUE TO BE BELIEVED WRONGLY to continue being widely believed or accepted despite evidence or proof to the contrary ○ *a view that persists to this day* **3.** CONTINUE to continue happening or existing [Mid-16C. < Latin *persistere*, literally "stand through" < *sistere* "make stand" < *stare* "to stand"] —**per·sis·ter** *n*

~~**persistant**~~ incorrect spelling of **persistent**

per·sist·ence /pər sístənss/, **per·sist·en·cy** /-ənssee/ *n* **1.** QUALITY OF PERSISTING the quality of continuing steadily despite problems or difficulties **2.** ACT OF PERSISTING the action of somebody who persists with something **3.** LONG CONTINUANCE OF SOMETHING continuance of an effect after its cause has ceased or been removed **4.** ZOOL RESILIENCE OF ORGANISM the ability of a living organism to resist being disturbed or altered

per·sist·ent /pər sístənt/ *adj* **1.** CONTINUING DESPITE PROBLEMS tenaciously or obstinately continuing despite problems or difficulties **2.** INCESSANT OR UNRELENTING existing or continuing for an unpleasantly long time **3.** BOT PERSISTING BEYOND MATURATION describes a plant part such as a scale on a pine cone that lasts beyond maturity without falling off **4.** ZOOL SUSTAINING CONTINUAL GROWTH describes a body part such as a tooth that grows throughout life **5.** ECOL, ENVIRON ABLE TO REMAIN IN ENVIRONMENT describes a chemical or a living organism that remains in the environment for months or years, usually because of resistance to attack by oxygen, light, and microorganisms —**per·sist·ent·ly** *adv*

per·sist·ent veg·e·ta·tive state *n* a medical condition in which a patient has severe brain damage and as a result is unable to stay alive without the aid of a life-support system, showing no response to stimuli

per·snick·e·ty /pər sníkətee/ *adj* **1.** OBSESSED WITH DETAIL overly attentive to detail and trivia (*informal*) **2.** *US* SNOBBISH snobbish in terms of choice, and thus wanting or accepting only the finest things **3.** *US* REQUIRING KEEN EYE FOR DETAIL necessitating precise, keen attention to details [Early 20C. Alteration of PERNICKETY] —**per·snick·e·ti·ness** *n*

per·son /púrss'n/ (*plural* **peo·ple** /peép'l/ or **per·sons** *formal*) *n* **1.** HUMAN BEING an individual human being **2.** HUMAN'S BODY a human being's body, often including the clothing ○ *objects found on her person* **3.** HUMAN'S APPEARANCE an individual human being's general appearance (*formal*) **4.** CHARACTER OR ROLE a character or role, e.g., in a play (*archaic*) **5.** GRAM FORM OF VERB AND PRONOUN any one of three forms of verbs and pronouns used to denote the speaker, the person addressed, or somebody else being referred to ○ *the third person singular* **6.** ETHICS OBJECT WITH SPECIAL MORAL VALUE an object with special moral value because of some spiritual status, autonomous nature, or importance for other people **7.** LAW INDIVIDUAL OR BODY OF INDIVIDUALS a living human being or a group, either or both having legal rights and responsibilities [12C. Via French *persone* < Latin *persona* "mask worn by an actor, character"] —**-person** *suffix* —**per·son·hood** *n* ◇ **in person** personally, rather than being represented by somebody or something else

USAGE Terms that are not gender-specific have increasingly grown in prominence, and ones incorporating the suffix ***-person*** are now common (*chairperson, spokesperson*). The terms that have taken hold most strongly tend to be those that do not simply replace *-man* (or *-woman*) with ***-person*** but are more subtly neutral with respect to sex: *chair* rather than *chairperson*, *representative* rather than *congressperson*. Despite the powerful trend toward inclusive terms, however, it remains true that when the members of the group at issue are predominantly male, the traditional term incorporating *-man* tends to be used more frequently (*chairman, fisherman*). Forms with *-woman* are also seen, though in most cases these are now less common than the form incorporating ***-person***. Choose gender-neutral words when they are available.

Per·son *n* in Christianity, the Father, the Son, or the Holy Spirit, together being the Trinity

per·so·na /pər sṓnə/ (*plural* **-nas** or **-nae** /-nee/) *n* **1.** ASSUMED IDENTITY OR ROLE an identity or role that somebody assumes **2.** CHARACTER IN LITERATURE a character in a literary work, especially a play (*often used in the plural*) **3.** PSYCHOL, PSYCHOANAL PERSONAL FACADE the image of character and personality that somebody wants to show the outside world. This concept originated in Jungian psychology. [Early 20C. < Latin, "mask worn by an actor, character"]

per·son·a·ble /púrss'nəb'l/ *adj* having a pleasant personality and appearance —**per·son·a·ble·ness** *n* —**per·son·a·bly** *adv*

per·son·age /púrssənij/ *n* (*formal*) **1.** a distinguished, important, or famous person **2.** a historical figure, or a character in a work of literature [15C. < Old French < *persone* (see PERSON)]

per·so·na gra·ta /pər sṓnə graátə/ (*plural* **per·so·nae gra·tae** /pər sṓnee graátee/) *n* somebody who is acceptable to others, especially as a diplomat [< late Latin, "acceptable person"] —**per·so·na gra·ta** *adj*

per·son·al /púrssən'l, púrssnəl/ *adj* **1.** RELATING TO SOMEBODY'S PRIVATE LIFE relating to the parts of somebody's life that are private ○ *personal relationships* **2.** RELATING TO ONE PERSON relating to a specific person rather than anyone else ○ *my personal opinion* **3.** DONE BY

ONE PERSON ONLY done by a specific person rather than by that person's delegate ○ *that personal touch* **4.** INTENDED FOR SOMEBODY intended for or owned by a specific person rather than anyone else **5.** REFERRING OFFENSIVELY TO SOMEBODY referring, especially in an offensive way, to somebody's beliefs, actions, or physical characteristics ○ *That personal remark was definitely uncalled-for.* **6.** UNFAIRLY REMARKING OR QUESTIONING ABOUT OTHERS making unacceptable remarks or being too probing about other people ○ *There's no need to get personal.* **7.** OF BODY relating to somebody's body ○ *personal hygiene* **8.** RELIG CONSCIOUS AND INDIVIDUAL having the character or nature of a conscious and individual entity **9.** LAW OF MOVABLE PROPERTY relating to or constituting a person's movable property ○ *personal effects* ■ *n* MEDIA AD FOR FRIENDS OR ROMANCE a usually classified newspaper or magazine advertisement in which somebody expresses interest in meeting others or sends a message of a personal nature to somebody else (*often used in the plural*) [14C. Via French < Latin *personalis* < *persona* "mask worn by an actor, character"]

per·son·al ad *n UK* same as **personal**

per·son·al ap·pear·ance *n* **1.** the visual aspect of somebody, especially with regard to personal cleanness and neatness of clothing **2.** an occasion when an important or famous person takes part in a public event

per·son·al as·sis·tant *n* somebody employed to perform secretarial and administrative tasks for somebody such as an executive who has many responsibilities

per·son·al care *n* assistance with washing, dressing, and other personal needs, often provided at home by a paid helper for somebody who is unable to manage alone

per·son·al col·umn *n* a section of a newspaper or magazine in which personals are printed

per·son·al com·put·er *n* a computer with its own operating system and a wide selection of software, intended to be used by one person

per·son·al dig·i·tal as·sis·tant *n* a small handheld computer with facilities for taking notes, storing information such as addresses, and keeping a calendar, usually operated using a stylus rather than a keyboard

per·son·al ef·fects *npl* possessions that somebody carries or wears regularly

per·son·al flo·ta·tion de·vice *n* a device, e.g., a life jacket or life buoy, for use by one person

per·son·al foul *n* a foul, especially one committed in football or basketball, involving illegal physical contact with an opponent during a game and also sometimes involving unnecessary roughness

per·so·nal i·den·ti·fi·ca·tion num·ber *n* FIN full form of **PIN**

per·son·al in·for·ma·tion man·ag·er *n* a piece of software that organizes random notes, contacts, and appointments for fast access

per·son·al in·ju·ry *n US* an actionable injury to an individual person, whether involving physical contact or not and whether fatal or not, but causing pain, discomfort, or injury

per·son·al·ism /púrssən'l izzəm, púrssnə lizzəm/ *n* a quirky or highly individualistic mode of expression or behavior —**per·son·al·ist** *n, adj* —**per·son·al·is·tic** /pùrssən'l ístik, pùrssnə lístik/ *adj*

per·son·al·i·ty /pùrss'n állətee/ (*plural* **-ties**) *n* **1.** SOMEBODY'S SET OF CHARACTERISTICS the totality of somebody's attitudes, interests, behavioral patterns, emotional responses, social roles, and other individual traits that endure over long periods of time **2.** CHARACTERISTICS MAKING SOMEBODY APPEALING the distinctive or very noticeable characteristics that make somebody socially appealing ○ *a partner with real personality* **3.** SOMEBODY REGARDED AS EPITOMIZING TRAITS somebody regarded as epitomizing particular character traits ○ *a difficult personality* **4.** FAMOUS PERSON a famous person, especially an entertainer or athlete **5.** UNUSUAL PERSON a distinctive and unusual person **6.** QUALITY OF BEING PERSON the quality of existing as a person ○ *Do you think that computers will ever achieve personality?* **7.** *US* PERSONAL COMMENT a personal comment or observation, especially one that might be considered offensive (*often used in the plural*) ○ *Let's not get into personalities.* **8.** DISTINGUISHING CHARACTERISTICS the distinguishing characteristics of a place or situation [14C. Via French < late Latin *personalitas* < Latin *personalis* (see PERSONAL)]

per·son·al·i·ty dis·or·der *n* a psychiatric disorder that makes it difficult for somebody to get along with other people or to succeed at work or in social situations but that does not involve loss of touch with reality

per·son·al·i·ty in·ven·to·ry, per·son·al·i·ty test *n* a standardized psychological test in which the subject is given questions about various aspects of personality, the answers supplying a character-trait profile unique to that person

per·son·al·i·ty type *n* a set of categories based on attitudes or behavioral tendencies into which people are grouped, e.g., introvert and extrovert

per·son·al·ize /púrssən'l īz/ (**-ized, -iz·ing, -iz·es**) *vt* **1.** PUT INITIALS OR NAME ON SOMETHING to mark something such as a wallet, pen, or item of clothing with somebody's initials or name **2.** CHANGE SOMETHING TO REFLECT PERSONALITY to change or modify something showing that it obviously originated from or belonged to you **3.** TAKE REMARK PERSONALLY to take a remark in a personal way **4.** same as **personify** (sense 3) —**per·son·al·i·za·tion** /pùrssən'li záysh'n/ *n*

per·son·al·ized med·i·cine *n* the prevention, detection, and treatment of disease taking into account a person's unique genetic profile

per·son·al·ly /púrssən'lee/ *adv* **1.** AS OWN OPINION in one's own experience or showing one's own opinion ○ *Personally, I would have given it back.* **2.** AS INDIVIDUAL in relation to a particular person ○ *I'm sure the criticisms weren't directed at you personally.* ○ *Don't take it personally.* **3.** WITHOUT OTHERS without intervention or assistance from others ○ *I'll handle it personally.* **4.** AS PERSON IN SOCIAL CONTEXT as a person, considered in a social context ○ *personally likable but professionally inept* **5.** AS SOMEBODY YOU HAVE MET by personal contact rather than by reputation ○ *I never knew your brother personally.*

per·son·al or·gan·iz·er *n* **1.** a datebook that also contains personal information and has replaceable pages so that it can be kept up to date **2.** a handheld computer with a small keyboard and display that can function as a calendar, an address book, a scheduler, and a calculator

per·son·al pro·noun *n* a pronoun that refers to the speaker, somebody being addressed, or another person, e.g., "I," "you," or "she"

per·son·al prop·er·ty *n* in law, somebody's tangible movable property, exclusive of land and including items such as automotive vehicles, boats, and money

per·son·al shop·per *n* a person, often an employee of a store, who assists others in choosing what to buy, either accompanying them or buying for them

per·son·al ster·e·o *n* a small audio cassette or CD player used with earphones, designed to be carried in a pocket or worn attached to a belt

per·son·al trans·port·er *n* a small lightweight motorized vehicle for one person, e.g., a two-wheeled vehicle similar to an upright scooter designed to be ridden while standing

per·son·al·ty /púrssən'ltee, púrssnəltee/ (*plural* **-ties**) *n* LAW same as **personal property** [Mid-16C. Via Anglo-Norman < late Latin *personalitas* (see PERSONALITY)]

per·son·al un·con·scious *n* in Jungian and related forms of psychotherapy, a section of somebody's unconscious mind that contains impulses, fears, and memories that have been repressed

per·son·al wa·ter·craft *n* a jet-propelled vehicle for one or two people, used for traveling on water. It is similar in appearance to a motorcycle.

per·so·na non gra·ta /pər sṓnə nōn graátə/ (*plural* **per·so·nae non gra·tae** /pər sṓnee nōn graátee/) *n* **1.** an unwelcome or unacceptable person **2.** a diplomat who is unacceptable to the country to which he or she is sent [< late Latin, "unacceptable person"] —**per·so·na non gra·ta** *adj*

per·son·ate[1] /púrss'n àyt/ (**-at·ed, -at·ing, -ates**) *vt* (*dated*) **1.** to play a dramatic role, especially in a play **2.** to impersonate somebody in order to deceive or defraud [Late 16C. < late Latin *personat-*, past participle of *personare* < Latin *persona* "mask worn by an actor, character"] —**per·son·a·tion** /pùrss'n áysh'n/ *n* —**per·son·a·tive** /púrss'n àytiv/ *adj* —**per·son·a·tor** *n*

per·son·ate[2] /púrss'n àyt/ *adj* describes a flower that has two lips, with one lip curling over the other to close the opening between them, e.g., a snapdragon [Late 16C. < Latin *personatus* "masked" < *persona* "mask worn by an actor, character"]

~~**personell**~~ incorrect spelling of **personnel**

per·son-hour *n* a unit that measures the amount of work that can be done by one person in one hour and the cost of that hour's work

per·son·i·fi·ca·tion /pər sònnəfi káysh'n/ *n* **1.** SOMEBODY WHO EMBODIES SOMETHING an embodiment or perfect example of something **2.** REPRESENTATION OF ABSTRACT QUALITY AS HUMAN a representation of an abstract quality or notion as a human being, especially in art or literature **3.** ATTRIBUTION OF HUMAN QUALITIES TO ABSTRACTS the attribution of human qualities to objects or abstract notions

per·son·i·fy /pər sónnə fī/ (**-fied, -fy·ing, -fies**) *vt* **1.** BE PERFECT EXAMPLE OF SOMETHING to be an embodiment or perfect example of something **2.** REPRESENT SOMETHING ABSTRACT AS HUMAN to represent an abstract quality or notion as a human being, especially in art or literature **3.** ASCRIBE HUMAN QUALITIES TO ABSTRACTS to ascribe human qualities to an object or abstract notion —**per·son·i·fi·a·ble** /pər sònnə fī əb'l/ *adj* —**per·son·i·fi·er** *n*

per·son·nel /pùrssə nél/ *n* the department of an organization or business that deals with employees' hiring, records, and problems ■ *npl* the people employed in an organization, business, or armed force [Early 19C. < French < *personne* "person" < Latin *persona* "mask worn by an actor, character"]

per·son-to-per·son *adj* **1.** FACE-TO-FACE AND DIRECT describes direct communication between two or more people **2.** *US* CHARGEABLE WHEN RECIPIENT IS REACHED used to describe a telephone call chargeable only when a specific person is reached **3.** ONLINE, COMPUT full form of **P2P** ■ *adv US* TO BE PAID IF RECIPIENT ANSWERS in such a way as to be chargeable or payable only if the person telephoned is reached

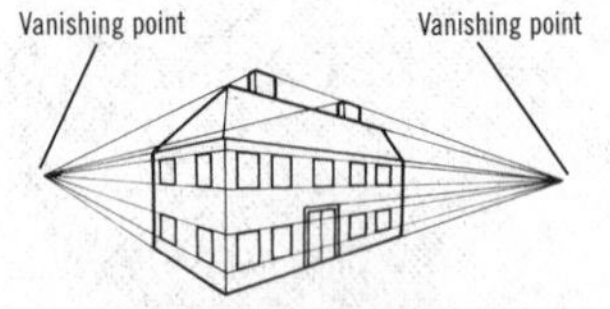

perspective (sense 3)

per·spec·tive /pər spéktiv/ *n* **1.** PARTICULAR EVALUATION OF SOMETHING a particular evaluation of a situation or facts, especially from one person's point of view ○ *a different perspective on the matter* **2.** MEASURED ASSESSMENT OF SITUATION a measured or objective assessment of a situation, giving all aspects their comparative importance ○ *He's having trouble keeping things in perspective right now.* **3.** APPEARANCE OF DISTANT OBJECTS TO OBSERVER the appearance of objects to an observer allowing for the effect of their distance from the observer **4.** ART ALLOWANCE FOR ARTISTIC PERSPECTIVE WHEN DRAWING the theory or practice of allowing for artistic perspective when drawing or painting **5.** VISTA a vista or view [14C. Via French < late Latin *perspectivus* "optical" < Latin *perspicere* "look closely" < *specere* "look at"] —**per·spec·tive·ly** *adv*

per·spi·ca·cious /pùrspi káyshəss/ *adj* penetratingly discerning or perceptive [Early 17C. < Latin *perspicac-* < *perspicere* (see PERSPECTIVE)] —**per·spi·ca·cious·ly** *adv* —**per·spi·ca·cious·ness** *n*

per·spi·cac·i·ty /pùrspi kássətee/ *n* acuteness of discernment or perception

per·spi·cu·i·ty /pùrspi kyoō ətee/ *n* **1.** the quality of being perspicuous **2.** same as **perspicacity**

per·spic·u·ous /pər spíkyoo əss/ *adj* clearly expressed and therefore easily understood [Late 16C. < Latin *perspicuus* < *perspicere* (see PERSPECTIVE)] —**per·spic·u·ous·ly** *adv* —**per·spic·u·ous·ness** *n*

per·spi·ra·tion /pùrspə ráysh'n/ *n* **1.** fluid lost from the body both in the form of sweat secreted by the sweat glands and as water that diffuses through the skin **2.** the process or act of excreting sweat —**per·spir·a·to·ry** /pər spīrə tàwree/ *adj*

per·spire /pər spīr/ (**-spired, -spir·ing, -spires**) *vti* to secrete fluid from the sweat glands through the pores of the skin [Mid-17C. Via French < Latin *perspirare*, literally "breathe through" < *spirare* "breathe"] —**per·spir·ing·ly** *adv*

Pers·son /pérss'n/, **Göran** (*b.* 1949) Swedish politician. A former minister of finance (1994–96), he became chairman of the Social Democratic Party and prime minister in 1996.

per·suad·a·ble /pər swáydəb'l/ *adj* able to be persuaded to do or accept something ■ *n* an undecided voter who is regarded as being willing to vote for a candidate, given the right motivation and rationale

per·suade /pər swáyd/ (**-suad·ed, -suad·ing, -suades**) *vt* **1.** to succeed in convincing somebody to do something, especially by reasoning, pleading, or coaxing **2.** to make somebody believe something, especially by giving good reasons for doing so [Early 16C. < Latin *persuadere* "urge strongly" < *suadere* "to urge"] —**per·suad·a·bil·i·ty** /pər swàydə bíllətee/ *n*

USAGE See *convince.*

per·suad·er /pər swáydər/ *n* **1.** somebody or something, e.g., a situation, that serves to persuade somebody to do something **2.** a weapon, e.g., a gun, used to intimidate somebody (*slang*)

per·sua·sion /pər swáyzh'n/ *n* **1.** ACT OF PERSUADING the act of persuading somebody to do something **2.** ABILITY TO PERSUADE the ability to persuade somebody **3.** SET OF BELIEFS a set of beliefs, e.g., a set of religious or political beliefs ○ *believers of all religious persuasions* **4.** GROUP WITH PARTICULAR BELIEFS a group whose members share a particular set of beliefs or views or a particular lifestyle ○ *recent recruits to the hawkish persuasion* **5.** TYPE a group of people or things with a particular characteristic in common (*informal humorous*) ○ *those of the long-legged persuasion* [14C. Via French < Latin *persuasion-* < *persuas-*, past participle of *persuadere* (see PERSUADE)]

USAGE See *conviction.*

per·sua·sive /pər swáyssiv/ *adj* having the ability to persuade people or the effect of persuading them [Late 16C. Directly or via French < medieval Latin *persuasivus* < Latin *persuas-* (see PERSUASION)] —**per·sua·sive·ly** *adv* —**per·sua·sive·ness** *n*

~~**persue**~~ incorrect spelling of **pursue**

~~**persuit**~~ incorrect spelling of **pursuit**

~~**persumably**~~ incorrect spelling of **presumably**

pert /purt/ *adj* **1.** AMUSINGLY BOLD bold and lively in a pleasant or amusing way **2.** JAUNTY jaunty and stylish in design ○ *a pert hat* **3.** SMALL AND WELL-SHAPED small, well-shaped, and pretty ○ *a pert nose* [13C. Via Old French *apert* "open, frank" < Latin *apertus* "open" < *aperire* "to open"] —**pert·ly** *adv* —**pert·ness** *n*

PERT /purt/ *n* a method of charting and scheduling a complex set of interrelated activities that identifies the most time-critical events in the process. Full form **program evaluation and review technique**

per·tain /pər táyn/ (**-tained, -tain·ing, -tains**) *vi* **1.** HAVE RELEVANCE to have relevance, reference, or a connection to something **2.** BE APPROPRIATE to be appropriate or suitable **3.** BE PART OR BELONG to be part of something or belong to something, especially as an attribute or accessory [14C. Via French < Latin *pertinere*, literally "hold to" < *tenere* "hold, keep"]

Perth /purth/ **1.** city on the Tay River in Perth and Kinross Council Area, central Scotland. Population: 41,453 (1991). **2.** capital city of Western Australia, located on the Swan River. Population: 1,341,900 (1998).

per·ti·na·cious /pùrti náyshəss/ *adj* determinedly resolute in purpose, belief, or action [Early 17C. < Latin *pertinac-* "very tenacious" < *tenac-* (see TENACIOUS)] —**per·ti·na·cious·ly** *adv* —**per·ti·na·cious·ness** *n* —**per·ti·nac·i·ty** /-nássətee/ *n*

per·ti·nent /púrt'nənt/ *adj* relevant to the matter being considered [14C. Via French < Latin *pertinent-*, present participle of *pertinere* (see PERTAIN)] —**per·ti·nence** *n* —**per·ti·nent·ly** *adv*

per·turb /pər túrb/ (**-turbed, -turb·ing, -turbs**) *vt* **1.** DISTURB SOMEBODY to disturb and trouble somebody **2.** RENDER SOMETHING INTO STATE OF DISORDER to render something into a state of confusion or disorder **3.** CAUSE SOMETHING TO UNDERGO PERTURBATION to cause a small deviation in the behavior of a physical system, e.g., in the orbit of an electron or a planet [14C. Via French < Latin *perturbare* "disturb thoroughly" < *turbare* "disturb" < *turba* "turmoil"] —**per·turb·a·ble** *adj* —**per·turb·a·bly** *adv* —**per·turb·ing** *adj* —**per·turb·ing·ly** *adv*

per·tur·ba·tion /pùrtər báysh'n/ *n* **1.** BEING PERTURBED disturbance and trouble, a disturbed and troubled state, or the act of disturbing and troubling somebody or something **2.** CAUSE OF TROUBLE something that causes disruption, trouble, or disorder **3.** PHYS DISTURBANCE CAUSED BY SECONDARY INFLUENCE a slight disturbance of a system by a secondary influence within it **4.** ASTRON DEVIATION IN ORBIT CAUSED BY GRAVITY a deviation in an astronomical object's orbit or path caused by the gravitational attraction of another astronomical object —**per·tur·ba·tion·al** *adj*

per·tus·sis /pər tússiss/ *n* MED same as **whooping cough** (*technical*) [Late 18C. < modern Latin < Latin *per-* "extreme" + *tussis* "cough"] —**per·tus·sal** *adj*

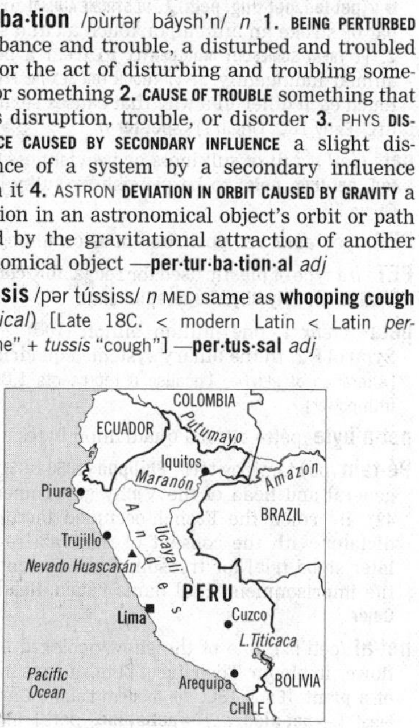

Peru

Pe·ru /pə roō/ **1.** country in western South America, bordered by Ecuador, Colombia, Brazil, Bolivia, Chile, and the Pacific Ocean. It is the third largest country in South America. Language: Spanish. Currency: nuevo sol. Capital: Lima. Population: 28,409,897 (2003). Area: 496,225 sq. mi./1,285,216 sq. km. Official name **Republic of Peru 2.** city in north central Indiana, on the Wabash River, southwest of Fort Wayne and north of Kokomo. Population: 12,915 (2002 estimate).

Pe·ru Cur·rent *n* GEOG same as **Humboldt Current**

Pe·ru·gia /pə roōjə/ city in central Italy. It is the capital of Perugia Province and Umbria Region. Population: 149,125 (2001).

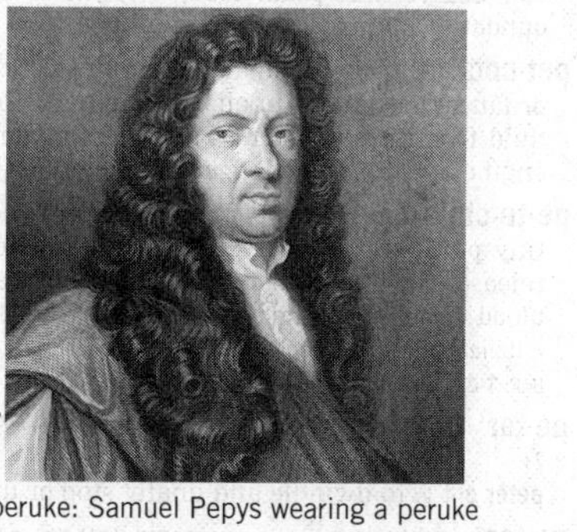

Barnaby's

peruke: Samuel Pepys wearing a peruke

pe·ruke /pə roōk/ *n* HAIR same as **periwig** (*archaic*) [Mid-16C. Via French < Italian *perrucca* "head of hair"]

pe·ruse /pə roōz/ (**-rused, -rus·ing, -rus·es**) *vt* **1.** to read or examine something, usually in a careful and thorough way or taking time to do it **2.** to read through or scan something quickly [Mid-16C. < Latin *per-* "thoroughly" + USE] —**pe·rus·a·ble** *adj* —**pe·rus·al** *n* —**pe·rus·er** *n*

Pe·rutz /pə roōts/, **Max** (1914–2002) Austrian-born British biochemist. He shared the Nobel Prize in chemistry (1962) for his work on hemoglobin, using X-ray crystallography. Full name **Perutz, Max Ferdinand**

Pe·ru·vi·an /pə roōvee ən/ *adj* relating to or originating in Peru ■ *n* somebody who comes from Peru [Early 17C. < modern Latin *Peruvia* "Peru"]

Pe·ru·vi·an bal·sam *n* PHARM same as **balsam of Peru**

Pe·ru·vi·an bark *n* the bark of a cinchona tree. Use: formerly, to make quinine. [Because the trees grew in Peru]

perv /purv/, **perve** *n* same as **pervert** (*slang insult*) [Mid-20C. Shortening of PERVERT]

per·vade /pər váyd/ (**-vad·ed, -vad·ing, -vades**) *vt* to spread through or be present throughout something [Mid-17C. < Latin *pervadere* "go throughout" < *vadere* "go"] —**per·vad·er** *n* —**per·va·sion** /pər váyzh'n/ *n*

per·va·sive /pər váyssiv/ *adj* spreading widely or present throughout something [Mid-18C. < Latin *pervas-*, past participle of *pervadere* (see PERVADE)] —**per·va·sive·ly** *adv* —**per·va·sive·ness** *n*

per·verse /pər vúrss/ *adj* **1.** INEXPLICABLY IRRATIONAL contrary to what is regarded as normal or reasonable, often for reasons that seem unaccountable or self-defeating ○ *There's a kind of perverse logic that argues that only working longer and harder can get you more free time.* **2.** STUBBORNLY UNREASONABLE deliberately and doggedly behaving in a way that seems contrary to good sense or your own best interests ○ *He knew he was being perverse, but he still refused point blank to accept the offered help.* **3.** same as **perverted** (sense 2) **4.** CRANKY cranky or peevish [14C. Via French < Latin *perversus*, past participle of *pervertere* (see PERVERT)] —**per·verse·ly** *adv* —**per·verse·ness** *n*

per·ver·sion /pər vúrzh'n/ *n* **1.** a sexual practice considered unusual or unacceptable **2.** the changing of something good, true, or correct into something bad or wrong, or a situation in which the change has occurred ○ *perversion of justice*

per·ver·si·ty /pər vúrssətee/ (*plural* **-ties**) *n* **1.** being perverse, especially willfully persisting in actions that seem contrary to good sense or your own best interests **2.** something, e.g., an action or activity, that is perverse

per·ver·sive /pər vúrssiv/ *adj* tending or able to pervert something

per·vert *vt* /pər vúrt/ (**-vert·ed, -vert·ing, -verts**) **1.** LEAD SOMEBODY AWAY FROM GOOD to lead somebody or something away from what is considered good, normal, moral, or proper **2.** MISINTERPRET OR DISTORT SOMETHING to misinterpret or distort something such as a piece of text **3.** USE SOMETHING IMPROPERLY to use something incorrectly or improperly **4.** DEBASE SOMETHING to bring something into a state regarded as morally inferior or reprehensible ■ *n* /púr vùrt/ SOMEBODY WHOSE SEXUAL BEHAVIOR IS UNACCEPTABLE somebody whose sexual behavior is considered unacceptably deviant [14C. Via French < Latin *pervertere* "turn wrong" < *vertere* "turn"] —**per·vert·er** *n* —**per·vert·i·ble** *adj*

per·vert·ed /pər vúrtəd/ *adj* **1.** DEVIATING FROM WHAT IS PROPER deviating greatly from what is accepted as right, normal, or proper **2.** RELATING TO UNUSUAL SEXUAL ACTIVITIES relating to or practicing sexual activities considered unusual or unacceptable **3.** DISTORTED misinterpreted or distorted —**per·vert·ed·ly** *adv* —**per·vert·ed·ness** *n*

per·vi·ous /púrvee əss/ *adj* **1.** susceptible to permeation **2.** open to ideas, suggestions, and change [Early 17C. < Latin *pervius* < *per-* "through" + *via* "way"] —**per·vi·ous·ly** *adv* —**per·vi·ous·ness** *n*

pes /payss/ (*plural* **pe·des** /pé dàyss/) *n* **1.** the foot, or a part resembling a foot **2.** a hind foot of a four-footed vertebrate [Mid-19C. < Latin, "foot"]

Pe·sach /páy saakh/ *n* the Passover festival [Early 17C.

< Hebrew *pesaḥ* < *pāsaḥ* "pass over"; because God passed over the Israelites' first-born (Exodus 12:11–27)]

pe·se·ta /pə sáytə/ *n* the main unit of the former Spanish currency [Early 19C. < Spanish, "small peso" < *peso* (see PESO)]

pe·se·wa /pay sáy wàa/ *n* a subunit of the Ghanaian currency. See table at **currency** [Mid-20C. < Fanti and Twi, "penny"]

Pe·sha·war /pe shaáwər/, **Pe·shā·war** city near the Khyber Pass in the North-West Frontier District, Pakistan. Population: 988,055 (1998).

Pe·shit·ta /pə sheétə/, **Pe·shit·to** /-tō/ *n* the Syriac version of the Bible, written around the 4th century [Late 18C. < Syriac *pšīṭtā* "the simple one"]

pes·ky /péskee/ (**-ki·er, -ki·est**) *adj* troublesome or irritating (*informal*) [Late 18C. Probably < alteration of PEST] —**pes·ki·ly** *adv* —**pes·ki·ness** *n*

pe·so /páyssō/ (*plural* **-sos**) *n* the main unit of currency in several South and Central American countries. See table at **currency** [Mid-16C. Via Spanish < Latin *pensum* "weight" < past participle of *pendere* "weigh"]

pes·sa·ry /péssəree/ (*plural* **-ries**) *n* **1.** a plastic device, e.g., a ring, placed in the vagina to keep the womb in position following a prolapse caused by weakened ligaments **2.** a suppository containing medication for insertion into the vagina [14C. < late Latin *pessarium* < Greek *pessos* "pessary, oval stone used in board games"]

pes·si·mism /péssə mìzzəm/ *n* **1.** a tendency to see only the negative or worst aspects of all things and to expect only bad or unpleasant things to happen **2.** a doctrine that all things become evil or that evil outweighs good in life [Late 18C. < French *pessimisme* < Latin *pessimus* "worst"]

pes·si·mist /péssəmist/ *n* somebody who always expects the worst to happen —**pes·si·mis·tic** /pèssə místik/ *adj* —**pes·si·mis·ti·cal·ly** *adv*

pest /pest/ *n* **1.** DAMAGING ORGANISM an organism that is damaging to livestock, crops, humans, or land fertility **2.** ANNOYING PERSON OR THING somebody or something that is a nuisance (*informal*) **3.** OUTBREAK OF DISEASE an epidemic of infectious or contagious disease (*archaic*) [Mid-16C. Via French, "pestilence" < Latin *pestis*]

Pes·ta·loz·zi /pèstə lótsee/, **Johann Heinrich** (1746–1827) Swiss educator. He developed teaching methods adapted to children's natural development, the basis of modern elementary education.

> "Perhaps the most fateful gift an evil genius could bestow upon our times is knowledge without skill."
> [Johann Heinrich Pestalozzi. Quoted in *The Education of Man: Aphorisms*, Heinz and Ruth Norden (trs.); 1951]

pes·ter /péstər/ (**-tered, -ter·ing, -ters**) *vt* to be a constant source of annoyance to somebody, e.g., by harassing him or her with demands [Mid-16C. < French *empestrer* "embarrass," influenced by PEST] —**pes·ter·er** *n* —**pes·ter·ing·ly** *adv*

pest·house /pést hòwss/ (*plural* **-hous·es** /-hòwzəz/) *n* a hospital where patients suffering from infectious disease were once treated [Early 17C. < PEST "contagious disease"]

pes·ti·cide /pésti sīd/ *n* a chemical substance used to kill pests, especially insects —**pes·ti·cid·al** /pèsti sīd'l/ *adj*

pes·tif·er·ous /pə stíffərəss/ *adj* **1.** ANNOYING troublesome or annoying **2.** CAUSING INFECTIOUS DISEASE breeding or spreading a virulently infectious disease **3.** CORRUPTING evil and corrupting (*formal*) [15C. < Latin *pestifer* "plague-carrying" < *pestis* "plague"] —**pes·tif·er·ous·ly** *adv* —**pes·tif·er·ous·ness** *n*

pes·ti·lence /péstilənss/ *n* (*archaic*) **1.** an epidemic of a highly contagious or infectious disease such as bubonic plague **2.** a serious infectious disease

pes·ti·lent /péstilənt/ *adj* **1.** DEADLY causing or tending to cause death **2.** ANNOYING annoying or infuriating (*literary or humorous*) **3.** DAMAGING very harmful morally or socially (*archaic*) [14C. Via French < Latin *pestilent-* < *pestis* "plague"] —**pes·ti·len·tial** /pèsti lénsh'l/ *adj* —**pes·ti·len·tial·ly** *adv* —**pes·ti·lent·ly** *adv*

pes·tle /péss'l/ *n* a rod-shaped object made from hard material with a rounded end that is used for crushing or grinding substances in a mortar ■ *vti* (**-tled, -tling, -tles**) to crush, grind, or pound a substance or object using a pestle [14C. Via French < Latin *pistillum*]

pes·to /péstō/ *n* **1.** a sauce or paste made by crushing together basil leaves, pine nuts, oil, Parmesan cheese, and garlic. It is traditionally served hot or cold with pasta or on meat. **2.** a puréed or finely minced paste of herbs and vegetables, tomatoes, or olives, used as pasta sauce, bread spread, or in cooking [Mid-20C. < Italian < past participle of *pestare* "pound, crush" < late Latin *pistare* < Latin *pinsere* "to beat"]

pet[1] /pet/ *n* **1.** ANIMAL KEPT AT HOME an animal kept for companionship, interest, or amusement **2.** FAVORITE PERSON an indulged or pampered person **3.** LOVED PERSON somebody whom others find lovable ■ *adj* **1.** KEPT AS PET kept as a pet animal **2.** SPECIAL OR FAVORITE cherished by or favorite to somebody ○ *a pet topic* ■ *v* (**pet·ted, pet·ting, pets**) **1.** *vt* STROKE ANIMAL to lovingly pat or stroke an animal, or touch a child similarly **2.** *vt* TREAT SOMEBODY INDULGENTLY to treat a person or animal indulgently **3.** *vi* TOUCH FOR SEXUAL PLEASURE to touch each other in a way that causes sexual pleasure [Early 16C. Origin ?] —**pet·ter** *n*

pet[2] /pet/ *n* a fit of sulkiness or peevishness ■ *vi* (**pet·ted, pet·ting, pets**) to be peevish or sulky [Mid-16C. Origin ?]

PET[1] /pet/ *abbr* MED positron emission tomography

PET[2] *n* a type of plastic used for recyclable containers. Full form **polyethylene terephthalate**

peta- *prefix* **1.** one million billion (10^{15}) ○ *petabyte* Symbol **P** **2.** in the binary system, a quadrillion (2^{50}) [Alteration of PENTA-; because it represents 1,000 to the fifth power]

pet·a·byte /péttə bīt/ *n* a quadrillion bytes

Pé·tain /pay tán, pay táN/, **Philippe** (1856–1951) French general and head of the Vichy government (1940–42). He ruled the French-occupied territory as a dictator with the consent of the Nazi regime. He later stood trial for treason, and was sentenced to life imprisonment. Full name **Pétain, Henri Philippe Omer**

pet·al /pétt'l/ *n* one of the showy colored parts of a flower in bloom. The ring of petals forms the corolla of a plant. [Early 18C. Via modern Latin < Greek *petalon* "leaf"] —**pet·aled** *adj* —**pet·al·ine** /pétt'l īn, pétt'lin/ *adj* —**pet·al·oid** *adj*

-petal *suffix* moving toward ○ *centripetal* [< modern Latin *-petus* < Latin *petere* "seek"]

pet·al·if·er·ous /pètt'l íffərəss/, **pet·al·ous** /pétt'ləss/ *adj* having petals

pé·tanque /pay taángk/ *n* LEISURE same as **boules** [Mid-20C. < French]

pe·tard /pə taárd/ *n* **1.** a small explosive charge or grenade used to blow a hole in a door, wall, or fortification **2.** a powerful firecracker [Mid-16C. < French *pétard* < *péter* "break wind" < Latin *pedere*] ◇ **be hoist with your own petard** to be the victim of your own attempt to harm somebody else

Pet·a·vi·us /pə táyvee əss/ crater on the Moon with a prominent crack (**rill**) across the floor and a complex central peak, located south of Mare Fecundatis, 110 mi./177 km in diameter

pet·cock /pét kòk/ *n* a small manually operated valve or faucet used to drain off waste material or excess fluid from the cylinder of an internal combustion engine [Mid-19C. < *pet*, origin ? + COCK "spout"]

pe·te·chi·a /pe teékee ə/ (*plural* **-chi·ae** /-kee ī/) *n* a tiny purplish red spot on the skin caused by the release into the skin of a very small quantity of blood from a capillary [Late 18C. Via modern Latin < Italian *petecchie* "spots on the skin" < Latin *impetigo* (see IMPETIGO)] —**pe·te·chi·al** *adj*

pe·ter[1] /peétər/ (**-tered, -ter·ing, -ters**) [Early 19C. Origin ?]

peter out *vi* to dwindle and finally stop or disappear

pe·ter[2] /peétər/ *n* same as **penis** (*slang; considered offensive by some people*) [Early 20C. < the name *Peter*]

Pe·ter /peétər/ *n* either of two books of the Bible, originally letters, traditionally attributed to St. Peter. See table at **Bible**

Pe·ter /peétər/, **St.** (*d.* A.D. 64?) one of the 12 apostles of Jesus Christ. He was a leader and missionary in the early church, and traditionally the first Bishop of Rome. Born **Simon**

Pe·ter I (1672–1725) tsar of Russia. During his reign (1682–1725), he did much to modernize and westernize his country, and his victory over Sweden established Russia as a major European power. He founded St. Petersburg as his capital in 1703. Known as **Peter the Great**

Pe·ter·bor·ough /peétər bùrō, -bərə/ **1.** city and unitary authority in eastern England. Population: 156,061 (2001). **2.** city in southeastern Ontario, Canada, approximately 25 mi./40 km north of Lake Ontario. Population: 73,303 (2001).

Pe·ter Pan *n* a man who looks very young or behaves in a boyish way (*informal*) [Early 20C. After the hero of J. M. Barrie's play *Peter Pan, or The Boy Who Wouldn't Grow Up* (1904)]

Pe·ter Pan col·lar *n* a flat collar attached to a round neck with rounded ends visible at the front

Pe·ter Prin·ci·ple *n* the theory that all members of an organization will eventually be promoted to a level at which they are no longer competent to do their job [Mid-20C. After Laurence Johnston *Peter* (1919–90), US educationalist and author]

pe·ter·sham /peétər shàm/ *n* a strong ribbed ribbon used to reinforce parts of garments such as waistbands [Early 19C. After Viscount *Petersham* (1790–1851), British army officer]

Pe·ter·son /peétərss'n/, **Oscar** (*b.* 1925) Canadian pianist. He is known for his technical brilliance in jazz. Full name **Peterson, Oscar Emmanuel**

Pe·ter's pence *n* **1.** a voluntary financial contribution made by some Roman Catholic dioceses to the Papal See **2.** a tax of one penny per household paid to the Papal See in medieval times until it was abolished by Henry VIII [After St. PETER as the first bishop of Rome]

Pe·ters' pro·jec·tion *n* a form of map projection that represents the relative size of land masses more accurately than Mercator's projection [Late 20C. After Arno *Peters* (b. 1916), German historian]

pe·thi·dine /péthi deèn/ *n UK* same as **meperidine** [Mid-20C. Blend of P(IPER)IDINE + ETH(YL)]

pé·til·lant /pàytee yaáN/ *adj* describes wine that is slightly sparkling [Late 19C. < French, present participle of *pétiller* "effervesce" < *péter* (see PETARD)]

pet·i·o·lar /pèttee ṓlər/ *adj* relating to the growth of petioles

pet·i·ole /péttee ōl/ *n* same as **leafstalk** (*technical*) [Mid-18C. < modern Latin *petiolus*, variant of Latin *peciolus* "little foot" < *pes* "foot"] —**pet·i·o·late** /-ə làyt/ *adj*

pet·i·o·lule /péttee ə lòol/ *n* the stalk of a leaflet in a compound leaf [Mid-19C. < modern Latin *petiolulus* "little petiole" < *petiolus* (see PETIOLE)]

pet·it bour·geois /pèttee boor zhwaá, pə teè-/ (*plural* **pe·tits bour·geois** /pèttee-, pə teè-/) *n* a member of the lower middle class [< French, "little citizen"]

pe·tite /pə teét/ *adj* **1.** having a small and delicate build ○ *a petite woman* **2.** designed to fit smaller women or girls [Mid-16C. < French, "little"]

pe·tite bour·geoi·sie /pəteét boor zhwaa zeé/ *n* people in the lower middle class, a group traditionally including small business operators, craftspeople, and tradespeople

pet·it four /pèttee fàwr/ (*plural* **pe·tits fours** /pèttee fàwrz/) *n* any one of a mixture of bite-size sweet cakes served at the end of a meal with coffee [< French, "little oven"]

pe·ti·tion /pə tísh'n/ *n* **1.** DEMAND FOR ACTION WITH SIGNATURES a written request signed by many people demanding a specific action from an authority or government **2.** APPEAL OR REQUEST TO HIGHER AUTHORITY an appeal or request to a higher authority or being **3.** SOMETHING REQUESTED something requested or appealed for **4.** ACT OF PETITIONING the act of making a petition **5.** *US* LAW PLEADING STATING CAUSE OF ACTION a pleading in a civil action by which the plaintiff sets down the cause of action and invokes the court's jurisdiction **6.** *Can*

LAW **APPLICATION FOR WRIT** a written application for a writ or for other legal action to be taken ■ *vti* **(-tioned, -tion·ing, -tions) 1. GIVE PETITION TO SOMEBODY** to give or address a petition to somebody, especially somebody in authority or a representative of an organization **2. MAKE DEMAND USING PETITION** to urge for or against a course of action by presenting a petition ○ *petitioning for his release* [14C. Via French < Latin *petition-* < *petere* "seek, go toward"] —**pe·ti·tion·ar·y** *adj* —**pe·ti·tion·er** *n*

ORIGIN The Latin word *petere* "to seek," from which ***petition*** is derived, is also the source of English *appetite, compete, impetus, perpetual, petulant,* and *repeat.*

pe·ti·ti·o prin·ci·pi·i /pə tìshee ō prin síppee èe/ *n* logically fallacious reasoning in which what has to be proved is already assumed [< Latin, "assuming the first thing"]

pet·it ju·ry /pèttee jóoree/ *n* a trial jury

pet·it lar·ce·ny *n* the theft of something whose value lies below a locally set level

pet·it mal /pèttee mál/ *n* a form of epilepsy marked by episodes of brief loss of consciousness without convulsions or falling. It is found most frequently in children and adolescents. [< French, "small illness"]

pet·it point /pèttee póynt/ (*plural* **pe·tits points** /*pronunc. same*/) *n* **1.** a small stitch used in needlepoint when creating details **2.** work embroidered using small stitches [< French, "small stitch"]

pe·tits pois /pèttee pwáa, pə tée-/ *npl* small sweet green peas [< French, "small peas"]

pet name *n* a special affectionate name used to address or refer to a family member or close friend

pet·nap·ping /pét nàpping/ *n* the theft of a pet animal [Late 20C. After KIDNAPPING] —**pet·nap·per** *n*

pet peeve *n* somebody's constant topic of complaint

Pe·tra /péetrə, péttrə/ ancient ruined city in southwestern Jordan, famous for its buildings and tombs that are carved out of solid rock

Pe·trarch /pée traark, pét ràark/ (1304–74) Italian lyric poet and scholar. He is best remembered for his series of love poems addressed to Laura, the *Canzoniere* (after 1327). Born **Petrarca, Francesco** —**Pe·trarch·an** /pi tràarkən/ *adj*

Pe·trarch·an son·net *n* a form of poetry that has an eight-line stanza with the rhyme scheme abbaabba followed by six lines with various rhyme schemes, usually cdcdcd or cdecde [Early 19C. After Francesco PETRARCH]

pet·rel /péttrəl/ *n* a seabird such as the storm petrel, the diving petrel, or the fulmar. Petrels are widespread in ocean environments and move awkwardly on land. Families: Hydrobatidae or Pelecanoididae or Procellariidae. [Early 17C. Probably after St. PETER, because it flies low with legs down giving the appearance of walking on water]

petri- *prefix* same as **petro-**

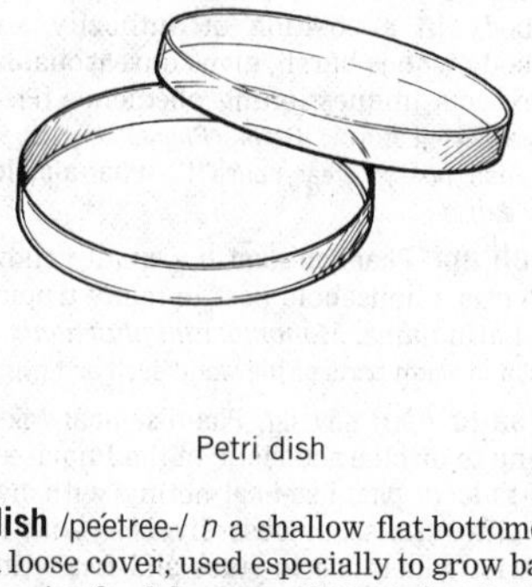

Petri dish

Pe·tri dish /péetree-/ *n* a shallow flat-bottomed dish with a loose cover, used especially to grow bacterial cultures in the laboratory [After Julius *Petri* (1852–92), German bacteriologist]

pet·ri·fac·tion /pèttrə fáksh'n/, **pet·ri·fi·ca·tion** /pèttrəfi káysh'n/ *n* **1.** the process in which the porous structure of organic material such as bone, shell, and wood is infiltrated by salt-bearing ground water, which preserves the structure when it solidifies. The Petrified Forest in Arizona contains whole tree trunks that have been turned into stone. **2.** the condition of being turned into stone

Pet·ri·fied For·est Na·tion·al Park /pèttrə fīd-/ national park in eastern Arizona, established as a national monument in 1906, and as a national park in 1962. It is noted for its petrified trees and Native American ruins. Area: 146 sq. mi./379 sq. km.

pet·ri·fy /péttrə fī/ **(-fied, -fy·ing, -fies)** *v* **1.** *vt* **IMMOBILIZE SOMEBODY WITH FEAR** to cause a person or animal to become immobile with terror **2.** *vti* **TURN SOMETHING TO STONE** to become stone, or cause something organic to turn into stone **3.** *vti* **MAKE OR BECOME DEADENED** to become dull, stiff, or deadened, or cause something to become dull, stiff, or deadened [15C. < French *pétrifier* or medieval Latin *petrificare*, both < Latin *petra* "stone, rock" < Greek, "rock"] —**pet·ri·fi·er** *n*

Pe·trine /pée trīn/ *adj* **1.** relating to or associated with St. Peter. **2.** in the Roman Catholic Church, relating to a dissolved marriage between somebody who has been baptized and somebody who has not [Mid-19C. < ecclesiastical Latin *Petrus* "Peter"]

petro- *prefix* **1.** rock, stone ○ *petrography* **2.** petroleum ○ *petrodollar* [< Greek *petros* "stone," *petra* "rock"]

pet·ro·chem·i·cal /pèttrō kémmik'l/ *n* a substance derived from petroleum or natural gas, e.g., gasoline or paraffin ■ *adj* relating to or derived from petrochemicals —**pet·ro·chem·i·cal·ly** *adv*

pet·ro·chem·is·try /pèttrō kémmistree/ *n* **1.** the branch of chemistry that is concerned with petroleum and derivatives of petroleum **2.** the chemistry of rocks, especially with reference to their composition

pet·ro·dol·lar /péttrō dòllər/ *n* any of the dollars paid to global oil producers that are deposited in US banks

pet·ro·gen·e·sis /pèttrō jénnəssiss/ *n* the origin, formation, and history of rocks —**pet·ro·gen·ic** *adj*

pet·ro·glyph /péttrə glìf/ *n* a prehistoric drawing done on rock [Late 19C. < French *pétroglyphe* < Greek *petros* "stone" + *glyphē* "carving"]

Pe·tro·grad /péttrə gràd/ former name for **St. Petersburg** (1914–24)

pe·trog·ra·phy /pi tróggrəfee/ *n* the systematic description of the texture of rocks and the minerals they contain, often using microscopy of thin slices of the rock to determine the mineral content —**pe·trog·ra·pher** *n* —**pet·ro·graph·ic** /pèttrə gráffik/ *adj* —**pet·ro·graph·i·cal·ly** *adv*

pet·rol /péttrəl/ *n UK* same as **gasoline** [Mid-16C. Via French *pétrole* < medieval Latin *petroleum* (see PETROLEUM)]

pe·tro·le·um /pə trṓlee əm/ *n* crude oil that occurs naturally in sedimentary rocks and consists mainly of hydrocarbons. A wide variety of commercially important petrochemicals, including gasoline and kerosene, are derived from it. [Early 16C. < medieval Latin < Latin *petra* "stone, rock" + *oleum* "oil"]

pe·tro·le·um jel·ly *n* a greasy gelatinous substance. Source: petroleum. Use: ointment base, lubricant, protective covering.

pe·trol·o·gy /pə tróllәjee/ *n* the study of sedimentary, igneous, and metamorphic rocks with respect to their occurrence, structure, origin, history, and mineral content —**pet·ro·log·i·cal** /pèttrə lójjik'l/ *adj* —**pet·ro·log·i·cal·ly** *adv* —**pe·trol·o·gist** *n*

pet·rol sta·tion *n UK* same as **gas station**

pet·ro·nel /péttrən'l/ *n* a short firearm with a curved butt whose length was between that of a long pistol and a short carbine, used mostly by cavalry in the 16th and 17th centuries [Late 16C. < French *petrinal*, variant of *poitrinal* < *poitrine* "chest" < Latin *pectus*; because the butt rested against the chest when the gun was fired]

pe·tro·sal /pə trṓss'l/ *adj* affecting or belonging to the hard (**petrous**) portion of the temporal bone surrounding the inner ear [Mid-18C. < Latin *petrosus* (see PETROUS)]

pet·rous /péttrəss/ *adj* **1.** relating to or resembling rock or stone **2.** describes the hard portion of the temporal bone surrounding the inner ear [Mid-16C. < Latin *petrosus* "rocky" < *petra* (see PETRIFY)]

PET scan /pét-/ *n* an image of a bodily cross section, usually of the brain, that reveals metabolic processes and that is obtained by means of positron emission tomography —**PET scan·ner** *n* —**PET scan·ning** *n*

pet·ti·coat /péttee kōt/ *n* **1. WOMAN'S UNDERGARMENT** a woman's undergarment that is sometimes decorated and consists of an underskirt with or without a bodice **2.** *US* **SOMETHING RESEMBLING SKIRT** something that resembles a petticoat, e.g., ruffles sewn on a skirt or a skirt-shaped covering for something **3. OFFENSIVE TERM** an offensive term for a woman or girl, or women in general (*dated*) ■ *adj* **OFFENSIVE TERM** an offensive term referring to women or girls (*dated*) [15C. < PETTY "small"]

pet·ti·fog·ger /péttee fòggər/ *n* **1.** somebody who quibbles or fusses about petty details **2.** a lawyer whose practice is small or insignificant [Mid-16C. Probably < PETTY + *fogger*, origin ?] —**pet·ti·fog** *vi* —**pet·ti·fog·ger·y** *n*

pet·ti·fog·ging /péttee fògging/ *adj* **1.** petty or trivial ○ *pettifogging details* **2.** quibbling or fussing over trivial matters

pet·ting /pétting/ *n* touching between people that causes sexual pleasure but does not include sexual intercourse (*informal*)

pet·ting zoo *n* a place where tame animals such as deer, goats, rabbits, and fowl are made available for small children to pet and feed

pet·tish /péttish/ *adj* peevish, irritable, or sulky [Late 16C. < PET[2]] —**pet·tish·ly** *adv* —**pet·tish·ness** *n*

pet·ty /péttee/ **(-ti·er, -ti·est)** *adj* **1. INSIGNIFICANT** of little importance **2. NARROW-MINDED** narrow-minded in nature **3. MEAN** spiteful in character **4. SUBORDINATE** subordinate in rank or importance [14C. < Old French *peti, petit* "small"] —**pet·ti·ly** *adv* —**pet·ti·ness** *n*

pet·ty cash *n* a small amount of money kept, e.g., in an office, and used to cover minor everyday expenses

pet·ty ju·ry *n* LAW another spelling of **petit jury**

pet·ty lar·ce·ny *n* CRIME another spelling of **petit larceny**

pet·ty of·fi·cer *n* NAVY **1. NONCOMMISSIONED NAVAL OFFICER** a noncommissioned officer in the US Navy or Coast Guard of a rank above seaman **2. NAVAL OFFICER** an officer in the British Navy of a rank above leading seaman **3. NAVAL OFFICER** an officer in the Canadian Navy of a rank above master seaman

pet·u·lant /péchələnt/ *adj* ill-tempered or sulky in a peevish manner [Late 16C. Via French < Latin *petulant-* "insolent" < *petere* "seek, go toward"] —**pet·u·lance** *n* —**pet·u·lant·ly** *adv*

petunia

pe·tu·nia /pə tóonee ə/ *n* a flowering plant with sticky stems. Flowers: brightly colored, funnel-shaped. Native to: tropical America. Genus: *Petunia.* ■ *adj* of a dark purple or violet color [Early 19C. < modern Latin < obsolete French *petun* "tobacco" < Tupi *pety*; because related to tobacco]

pe·tun·tze /pi tóontsə/, **pe·tun·tse** *n* a variety of feldspar that can be melted. Use: Chinese porcelain. [Early 18C. < Chinese *báidūnzi*, literally "white stone block"]

Pevs·ner /pévznər/, **Antoine** (1886–1962) Russian-born French sculptor. One of the founders of the constructivist school with his brother Naum Gabo, he emigrated to Paris (1923) and developed a highly personal style of sculpture.

pew /pyoo/ *n* a usually wooden bench with a straight back and often a kneeling bench attached to the one in front of it, used by worshipers in a church or synagogue [14C. Via Old French *puie* "balcony" < Latin *podium* (see PODIUM)]

pe·wee /pée wèe/, **pee·wee** *n* a drab medium-sized bird of the tyrant-flycatcher family with a plaintive song. Genus: *Contopus*. [Late 18C. An imitation of its call]

pe·wit /péewit, pyóo it/ *n* BIRDS same as **lapwing** [Early 16C. An imitation of its call]

pew·ter /pyóotər/ *n* **1. TIN AND LEAD ALLOY** a silver-gray alloy of tin and lead sometimes containing antimony and copper **2. PEWTER OBJECTS COLLECTIVELY** articles made from pewter **3. DARK GRAYISH COLOR** a dark dull gray color tinged with blue or purple [14C. Via Old French *peutre* < assumed Vulgar Latin *peltrum*] —**pew·ter** *adj* —**pew·ter·er** *n*

pe·yo·te /pay ṓtee/ *n Southwest US* **1.** a spineless globe-shaped cactus that has small rounded nodules containing mescaline. Native to: Mexico, southwestern United States. Latin name: *Lophophora williamsii.* **2.** *also* **pe·yo·te but·ton** a button-shaped nodule containing mescaline that forms on the stem of the peyote cactus [Mid-19C. Via American Spanish < Nahuatl *peyotl*]

pf *abbr* ONLINE French Polynesia (*used in Internet addresses*) See table at **domain name**

pF *symbol* MEASURE picofarad

pf. *abbr* **1.** GRAM perfect **2.** MONEY, HIST pfennig

PFC, Pfc *abbr US* MIL private first class

PFD *abbr* **1.** NAUT personal flotation device **2.** FIN preferred (*used of stocks*)

pfen·nig /fénnig/ (*plural* **-nigs** or **-ni·ge** /-nigə/) *n* a subunit of the former German currency [Mid-16C. < German]

pfft /ft/ *interj US* a sound indicating a sudden disappearance or failure of something (*informal*) ○ *I set out the pretzels and, pfft, they were gone!* [Early 20C. An imitation of a light burning out]

pg *abbr* ONLINE Papua New Guinea (*used in Internet addresses*) See table at **domain name**

PG[1] *tdmk* a rating indicating that a movie may be seen by anyone, but parental guidance is suggested for children

PG[2] *abbr* **1.** EDUC postgraduate **2.** pregnant (*informal*)

pg. *abbr* page

PG-13 *tdmk US* a rating indicating that a movie may be seen by anyone, but parental guidance is suggested for children under the age of 13

PGA *abbr* Professional Golfers' Association

PGCA *abbr* E-COMMERCE payment gateway certificate authority

PGP *n* a program to encrypt data for security purposes when transmitting over public networks such as the Internet. PGP uses public key encryption, a system that provides for privacy and authentication of both the sender and the receiver of the message. (*used in e-commerce*) Full form **Pretty Good Privacy**

PGx *abbr* PHARM **1.** pharmacogenetics **2.** pharmacogenomics

ph *abbr* ONLINE Philippines (*used in Internet addresses*) See table at **domain name**

pH *n* a measure of acidity or alkalinity in which the pH of pure water is 7, with lower numbers indicating acidity and higher numbers indicating alkalinity. Full form **potential of hydrogen**

Ph *symbol* CHEM phenyl group

PH, P.H. *abbr* **1.** PUBLIC ADMIN public health **2.** MIL Purple Heart

PHA *abbr US* PUBLIC ADMIN Public Housing Administration

phac·o·e·mul·si·fi·ca·tion /fákō i múlsəfi káysh'n/ *n* an ultrasonic technique using microsurgical instruments that allows a cataract-affected lens to be liquefied and removed by suction using a very small incision near the edge of the cornea. A foldable plastic lens is then inserted through the incision and unfolded. [Late 20C. < Greek *phakos* "lentil"; because of the shape of the lens]

pha·e·ton /fáy ət'n, fáyt'n/ *n* **1.** a small light four-wheeled carriage, usually with two seats and usually drawn by two horses **2.** *US* an old-fashioned touring car, now antique [Late 16C. Via French < Greek *Phaethōn*, son of Helios in Greek mythology, killed by Zeus while trying to drive his father's chariot across the sky]

phage /fayj/ *n* MICROBIOL same as **bacteriophage** [Early 20C. Shortening]

-phage *suffix* something that eats ○ *xylophage* [< Greek *-phagos* < *phagein* "eat" (see PHAGO-)]

phag·e·de·na /fàjjə déenə/, **phag·e·dae·na** *n* an ulcer that spreads rapidly [Late 16C. Via Latin < Greek *phagedaina*]

-phagia *suffix* eating ○ *aerophagia* ○ *hyperphagia* [< Greek < *phagein* "eat" (see PHAGO-)]

phago- *prefix* eating, consuming ○ *phagocyte* [< Greek *phagein* "eat" < Indo-European, "share out"]

phag·o·cyte /fággə sīt/ *n* a cell in the body's bloodstream and tissues, e.g., a white blood cell that engulfs and ingests foreign particles, cell waste material, and bacteria —**phag·o·cyt·ic** /fàggə síttik/ *adj*

phag·o·cy·to·sis /fàggə sī tṓssiss/ *n* the engulfing and ingesting of foreign particles or waste matter by phagocytes —**phag·o·cy·tot·ic** /-sī tóttik/ *adj*

-phagous *suffix* eating ○ *polyphagous* [Via Latin < Greek *-phagos* (see -PHAGE)]

Phag·wa /fágwa/ *n* HINDUISM same as **Holi** [Late 20C. < Hindi < PHALGUNA + *-wa*, masculine singular suffix]

-phagy *suffix* same as **-phagia**

Pha·lange /fáy lànj, fə lánj/ *n* a Lebanese Christian paramilitary group [Mid-20C. Variant of FALANGE] —**Pha·lang·ist** /fə lánjist, fállənjist/ *n, adj*

pha·lan·ger /fə lánjər/ *n* a small tree-dwelling marsupial with dense woolly fur and a long tail. Native to: Australia and nearby islands. Family: Phalangeridae. [Late 18C. < modern Latin < Greek *phalagg-* "toe bone"; because of the webbed or fused toes on its hind feet]

pha·lanx /fáy làngks, fá-/ (*plural* **pha·lanx·es** or **pha·lan·ges** /fə lánjeez, fay-/) *n* **1. TIGHT GROUP** a group of people, animals, or objects that are moving or standing closely together **2. ANCIENT TROOP FORMATION** especially in ancient Greece, a group of soldiers that attacked in close formation, protected by their overlapping shields and projecting spears **3.** (*plural* **pha·lan·ges**) **FINGER AND TOE BONE** a finger or toe bone of a human being or vertebrate animal [Mid-16C. Via Latin (stem *phalang-*) < Greek *phalagx* "line of battle, finger or toe bone"] —**pha·lan·ge·al** /fə lánjee əl, fay-/ *adj*

phal·a·rope /fállə rṓp/ *n* a small wading bird that is related to the sandpiper but has lobed toes adapted for swimming. Genus: *Phalaropus.* [Late 18C. Via French < modern Latin *Phalaropus* < Greek *phalaris* "coot" + *pous* "foot"]

Phal·gu·na /pál gòonə, fál-/ *n* in the Hindu calendar, the 12th month of the year, lasting 30 days and falling about the same time as February or March. See table at **calendar**

phal·li ARTS, ANAT plural of **phallus**

phal·lic /fállik/ *adj* **1. OF PHALLUS** relating to or resembling a phallus **2. OF STAGE OF PSYCHOSEXUAL DEVELOPMENT** in psychoanalytic theory, relating to a stage of psychosexual development during which a young child's sexual feelings are concentrated on the genitals **3. OF PHALLICISM** relating to phallicism [Late 18C. < Greek *phallikos* < *phallos* "phallus"]

phal·li·cism /fálli sìzzəm/ *n* the worshiping of the reproductive forces of life as symbolized by the penis —**phal·li·cist** *n*

phal·lo·cen·tric /fàllō séntrik/ *adj* centered on men or showing a preference for traditionally masculine qualities rather than traditionally feminine ones [Early 20C. < PHALLUS]

phal·lus /fálləss/ (*plural* **-lus·es** or **-li** /-lī/) *n* **1.** a picture, sculpture, or other representation of a penis, especially one regarded as a symbol of the reproductive force of life **2.** the human penis, especially when erect [Early 17C. Via late Latin < Greek *phallos*]

-phane, -phan *suffix* a substance having the appearance or qualities of ○ *cymophane* [< Greek *-phanēs* < *phainesthai* "appear" < *phainein* "bring to light"]

phan·er·o·gam /fánnərō gàm/ *n* a plant that produces seeds (*dated*) [Mid-19C. Via French < modern Latin *phanerogamus* < Greek *phaneros* "visible" (< *phainein* "bring to light") + *gamos* "sexual union"] —**phan·er·o·gam·ic** /fànnərō gámmik/ *adj*

Phan·er·o·zo·ic /fànnərə zṓ ik/ *n* the present eon of geologic time, beginning 570 million years ago, that consists of the Paleozoic, Mesozoic, and Cenozoic eras. See table at **geologic time** [Late 19C. < Greek *phaneros* "visible" + *zōē* "life"] —**Phan·er·o·zo·ic** *adj*

phan·tasm /fán tàzzəm/ *n* **1.** a supposed being, e.g., a ghost or a disembodied spirit, that can be seen but does not have physical substance **2.** an understanding or perception that is not based on reality [13C. Via French *fantasme* < Greek *phantasma* < *phantazesthai* "appear" < *phainein* "bring to light"] —**phan·tas·mal** /fan tázməl/ *adj* —**phan·tas·mal·ly** *adv* —**phan·tas·mic** /fan tázmik/ *adj* —**phan·tas·mi·cal·ly** *adv*

phan·tas·ma·go·ri·a /fan tàzmə gáwree ə/, **phan·tas·ma·go·ry** /fan tázmə gàwree/ (*plural* **-ries**) *n* **1.** a series or group of strange or bizarre images seen as if in a dream **2.** a scene or view that encompasses many things and changes constantly [Early 19C. < French *fantasmagorie* "art of making optical illusions" < *fantasme* (see PHANTASM)] —**phan·tas·ma·gor·ic** *adj* —**phan·tas·ma·gor·i·cal** *adj* —**phan·tas·ma·gor·i·cal·ly** *adv*

phan·tast *n* another spelling of **fantast**

phan·tom /fántəm/ *n* **1. UNREAL BEING OR SENSATION** something that can be seen or heard or whose presence can be felt, but that is not physically present **2. GHOST** a ghost or apparition **3. ILLUSION** somebody or something that does not exist, or whose existence is difficult to prove **4. IMAGINARY SHAPE** an imaginary embodiment in threatening form of an abstract thing or quality ○ *The phantom of disaster seemed to threaten their success.* ■ *adj* **1. LIKE PHANTOM** having the nature of a phantom, especially in being ghostly, illusory, or unreal ○ *phantom horsemen* **2. NONEXISTENT** nonexistent, but claimed to exist usually for purposes of fraud ○ *phantom voters* [13C. Via Old French *fanto(s)me* < Greek *phantasma* (see PHANTASM)]

CULTURAL NOTE ***The Phantom of the Opera***, a novel (1910) by French writer Gaston Leroux. This romantic melodrama about a disfigured musical genius who dwells in the passageways of a Paris opera house was not widely known until the appearance of Rupert Julian's movie adaptation of 1925. This in turn inspired other movie adaptations as well as Andrew Lloyd Webber's 1986 musical, one of the most successful musicals of all time.

phan·tom limb *n* the powerful sensation that an amputated limb remains attached. This sensation may persist for weeks or months after the limb has been lost.

phan·tom limb pain *n* pain that seems to come from an amputated limb

phan·tom preg·nan·cy *n UK* same as **false pregnancy**

-phany *suffix* a manifestation of something ○ *epiphany* [< Greek *phan-*, stem of *phainesthai* "appear" < *phainein* "bring to light"]

phar·aoh /férrō/ *n* **1.** a ruler of ancient Egypt **2.** somebody in a position of authority, especially somebody who is harsh, gives unreasonable orders, and expects unquestioning obedience [Pre-12C. Via ecclesiastical Latin < Greek *Pharaō* < Hebrew *par'ōh* < Egyptian *pr-' o* "great house"] —**Phar·a·on·ic** /fèr ay ónnik/ *adj*

Phar·aoh ant, Phar·aoh's ant *n* a small yellowish red ant that is a household pest in many tropical countries. Latin name: *Monomorium pharaonis.* [Because common in warm parts of the world such as Egypt]

Phar·i·sa·ic /fàrri sáy ik/, **Pha·ri·sa·i·cal** /-ik'l/ *adj* **1.** relating to or characteristic of the Pharisees **2.** *also* **phar·i·sa·ic** *or* **phar·i·sa·i·cal** acting with hypocrisy, self-righteousness, or obsessiveness with regard to the strict adherence to rules and formalities [Early 17C. Via ecclesiastical Latin < Greek *pharisaikos* < *pharisaios* (see PHARISEE)] —**Phar·i·sa·i·cal·ly** *adv* —**Phar·i·sa·i·cal·ness** *n*

Phar·i·sa·ism /fárri say ìzzəm/ *n* **1.** the beliefs and practices of the Pharisees, especially the great attention they paid to the detailed rules of everyday life **2.** *also* **phar·i·sa·ism** hypocritical, self-righteous, or obsessive behavior or attitudes toward the observing of rules and formalities [Late 16C. < French *pharisaïsme* < ecclesiastical Latin *pharisaeus* (see PHARISEE)]

Phar·i·see /fárri seè/ *n* **1.** a member of an ancient Jewish religious group who followed the Oral Law in addition to the Torah and attempted to live in a constant state of purity **2.** *also* **phar·i·see** a self-righteous, hypocritical, or sanctimonious person [Pre-12C. Via ecclesiastical Latin < Greek *pharisaios* < Aramaic *prīšayyā* "those who are separate"]

Phar·i·see·ism *n* JUDAISM, HIST same as **Pharisaism** (sense 1)

pharm /faarm/ (**pharmed, pharm·ing, pharms**) *v* **1.** *vt* to produce medicinally valuable proteins in the milk of genetically modified cows and sheep **2.** *vti* to mix and share prescription medications, especially narcotics and opiates, often with harmful effects (*slang*)

phar·ma /fáarmə/ *adj, n* same as **pharmaceutical**

pharmac- *prefix* same as **pharmaco-** (*used before vowels*)

phar·ma·ceu·ti·cal /fàarmə sóotik'l/ *adj* involved in or related to the manufacture, preparation, dispensing, or sale of drugs used in medicine ■ *n* a drug used in medicine (*usually used in the plural*) [Mid-17C. < late Latin *pharmaceuticus* < Greek *pharmakeutēs* "somebody who prepares drugs" < *pharmakon* "drug"] —**phar·ma·ceu·ti·cal·ly** *adv*

phar·ma·ceu·tics /fàarmə sóotiks/ *n* the science of the preparation and dispensing of prescribed drugs (*takes a singular verb*) ■ *npl* drugs prescribed as medicines (*takes a plural verb*)

phar·ma·cist /fáarməssist/ *n* somebody trained and licensed to dispense medicinal drugs and to advise on their use [Mid-19C. < PHARMACY]

pharmaco- *prefix* drugs, medicine ○ *pharmacodynamics* [< Greek *pharmakon* "drug, poison"]

phar·ma·co·dy·nam·ics /fàarməkō dī námmiks/ *n* the study of the effects of drugs on living organisms (*takes a singular verb*) —**phar·ma·co·dy·nam·ic** *adj*

phar·ma·co·ge·ne·tics /fàarmə kō jə néttiks/ *n* same as **pharmacogenomics** —**phar·ma·co·ge·ne·tic** *adj*

phar·ma·co·ge·nom·ics /fàarməkō jee nómmiks, -nṓmiks/ *n* the study of the relationship between a specific person's genetic makeup and his or her response to drug treatment (*takes a singular verb*) —**phar·ma·co·ge·nom·ic** *adj*

phar·ma·cog·no·sy /fàarmə kógnəssee/ *n* the branch of pharmacology that deals with active substances found in plants [Mid-19C. < PHARMACO- + Greek *gnōsis* "knowledge" (see GNOSIS)] —**phar·ma·cog·no·sist** *n* —**phar·ma·cog·nos·tic** /fàarmə kog nóstik/ *adj*

phar·ma·co·ki·net·ics /fàarməkō ki néttiks, -kī-/ *npl* the body's reaction to drugs, including their absorption, metabolism, and elimination

phar·ma·col·o·gy /fàarmə kólləjee/ (*plural* **-gies**) *n* **1.** the science or study of drugs, especially of the ways in which they react biologically at receptor sites in the body **2.** the effects that a drug has when taken by somebody, especially as a medical treatment —**phar·ma·co·log·i·cal** /fàarməkə lójjik'l/ *adj* —**phar·ma·co·log·i·cal·ly** *adv* —**phar·ma·col·o·gist** *n*

phar·ma·co·poe·ia /fàarməkə peé ə/, **phar·ma·co·pe·ia** *n* **1.** an official compendium of quality standards for pharmacologically active substances and drug products **2.** a stock or collection of drugs (*archaic*) [Early 17C. Via modern Latin < Greek *pharmakopoiia* "preparing of drugs" < *pharmakon* "drug"] —**phar·ma·co·poe·ial** *adj* —**phar·ma·co·poe·ic** *adj* —**phar·ma·co·poe·ist** *n*

phar·ma·co·ther·a·py /fàarməkō thérrəpee/ (*plural* **-pies**) *n* the use of drugs to treat conditions, especially psychiatric disorders

~~**pharmacuetical**~~ incorrect spelling of **pharmaceutical**

phar·ma·cy /fáarməssee/ (*plural* **-cies**) *n* **1.** the science or profession of dispensing medicinal drugs **2.** a place where medicinal drugs are dispensed or sold [14C. Via Old French *farmacie* < Greek *pharmakeia* "use of drugs" < *pharmakon* "drug"]

pha·ryn·ge·al /fə rínjəl, fə rínjee əl, fàrrən jeé əl/ *adj* found in, affecting, or relating to the throat [Early 19C. < modern Latin *pharyngeus* < *pharyng-* (see PHARYNX)]

phar·yng·es *n* ANAT plural of **pharynx**

phar·yn·gi·tis /fàrrən jítiss/ *n* inflammation of the pharynx, commonly known as a sore throat

pharyngo- *prefix* pharynx ○ *pharyngoscope* [< modern Latin, *pharyng-* (see PHARYNX)]

phar·yn·gol·o·gy /fàrring gólləjee/ *n* the branch of medicine concerned with the throat, its diseases, and their treatment —**phar·yn·go·log·i·cal** /fə rìng gə lójjik'l/ *adj* —**phar·yn·gol·o·gist** *n*

pha·ryn·go·scope /fə ríng gə skōp/ *n* a medical instrument for examining the throat —**phar·yn·go·scop·ic** /fə rìng gə skóppik/ *adj* —**phar·yn·gos·co·py** /fàrring góskəpee/ *n*

phar·ynx /fárringks/ (*plural* **pha·ryn·ges** /fə rínjeez/ or **phar·ynx·es**) *n* **1.** the throat, the region of the alimentary canal in humans and in vertebrate animals that lies between the mouth and esophagus **2.** a region between the mouth and the digestive system in sea anemones, worms, insects, and other invertebrate animals [Late 17C. Via modern Latin (stem *pharyng-*) < Greek *pharugx* "throat"]

phase /fayz/ *n* **1.** STAGE OF DEVELOPMENT a clearly distinguishable period or stage in a process, in the development of something, or in a sequence of events **2.** PATTERN OF BEHAVIOR a period of time when a situation or particular pattern of behavior persists and is often annoying or worrying **3.** PART OR ASPECT one of the many parts or aspects of something ○ *We needed to restructure all phases of our business.* **4.** ASTRON RECURRING SHAPE OF MOON a recurring form of the Moon or a planet seen in the sky. The four principal phases of the Moon are the first quarter, full moon, last quarter, and new moon. **5.** PHYS PART OF REPEATING CYCLE a part of a repeated uniform pattern of occurrence of a phenomenon or process, relative to a fixed starting point or time **6.** PHYS STATE OF MATTER a state in which matter can exist, depending on temperature and pressure, e.g., the solid, liquid, gaseous, and plasmatic states **7.** ZOOL VARIATION IN ANIMAL FORM an alternate stage, appearance, or coloring that distinguishes a group of animals from most of their kind, or that an animal adopts under specific conditions **8.** BIOL STAGE IN LIFE CYCLE a stage in the life cycle of an organism ■ *vt* (**phased, phas·ing, phas·es**) **1.** DO SOMETHING IN STAGES to plan or arrange something so that it is carried out in stages (*often passive*) ○ *a takeover that is being phased to minimize disruption* **2.** SYNCHRONIZE THINGS to cause two or more things to happen or operate simultaneously or in a coordinated way ○ *to phase the departure of one train with the arrival of another* [Early 19C. Partly via French < modern Latin *phasis*; partly back-formation < *phases*, plural of *phasis* "phase," via modern Latin < Greek, "appearance" < *phainein* "to show"] —**pha·sic** *adj*
◇ **in phase** in the same phase at the same time, or operating in a synchronized or coordinated way ◇ **out of phase** not in the same phase, or not synchronized or coordinated with each other

SPELLCHECK See *faze.*

phase in *vt* to introduce something in stages over a period of time

phase out *vt* to bring something to an end, or remove it, in stages over a period of time

phase-con·trast mi·cro·scope *n* a microscope sensitive to small differences in the phase of light reflected by or passing through different parts of an object. By enhancing the differences, it provides a clearly contrasted image. Phase-contrast microscopes are particularly useful for examining colorless or transparent objects.

phase di·a·gram *n* a graph on which parameters of a property such as temperature or pressure are plotted on perpendicular axes in such a way that a curve corresponds to a transition between physical states

phase·down /fáyz dòwn/ *n US* a gradual reduction in something

phase mod·u·la·tion *n* a method of transmitting a voice or other signal in which the phase of a radio carrier wave is varied in accordance with the signal

phase mu·sic *n* a musical composition, associated with minimalism, in which the different parts use the same material at the same time but only sometimes in phase with each other

phase·out /fáyz òwt/ *n* a gradual process of bringing something to an end or removing it in stages over a period of time

-phasia *suffix* speech disorder ○ *aphasia* [< Greek *phasis* "utterance" < *phanai* "to say" < Indo-European, "speak"]

phas·mid /fázmid/ *n* a tropical plant-eating insect that has a body that looks like a twig with long legs and antennae. Walking stick insects and leaf insects are phasmids. Family: Phasmidae. ■ *adj* belonging or relating to the phasmids [Late 19C. < modern Latin *Phasmida* < Greek *phasma* "apparition" < *phainein* "to show"]

phat /fat/ *adj* of a very high quality or standard (*slang*) ○ *"music...set to the phat beats of hip-hop" (The New York Times*; November 1998) [Late 20C. Origin ?]

phat·ic /fáttik/ *adj* spoken in order to share feelings, create goodwill, or set a pleasant social mood, rather than to convey information. "Have a nice day!" is a phatic phrase. [Early 20C. < Greek *phatos* "spoken" < *phanai* (see -PHASIA)]

Ph.B. *abbr* EDUC Bachelor of Philosophy [Latin *Philosophiae Baccalaureus*]

Ph.C. *abbr* Pharmaceutical Chemist

Ph.D. *abbr* EDUC Doctor of Philosophy [Latin *Philosophiae Doctor*]

pheasant

pheas·ant /fézz'nt/ (*plural* **-ants** or *same*) *n* **1.** a large bird, the male of which often has a long tail and brightly colored feathers. Pheasants are often bred for shooting. Native to: Asia, Europe, North America. Family: Phasianidae. **2.** the meat obtained from a pheasant [13C. Via Old French *fesan* < Greek *phasianos (ornis)* "(bird) from the river Phasis" in W Georgia, its supposed place of origin]

phel·lem /féllem/ *n* BOT same as **cork** *n* (sense 4) [Late 19C. < Greek *phellos* "cork," after PHLOEM, XYLEM]

phel·lo·derm /féllə dùrm/ *n* a layer of plant cells produced by the inner surface of the cork cambium in woody plants, from which cork tissue develops [Late 19C. < Greek *phellos* "cork"] —**phel·lo·der·mal** /fèllə dúrm'l/ *adj*

phel·lo·gen /félləjən/ *n* BOT same as **cork cambium** [Late 19C. < Greek *phellos* "cork"] —**phel·lo·ge·net·ic** /fèlləjə néttik/ *adj* —**phel·lo·gen·ic** /-jénnik/ *adj*

phen- *prefix* CHEM, GEOL same as **pheno-**

phe·na·caine /fénnə kàyn/ *n* a white crystalline compound. Use: local anesthetic in ophthalmology. Formula: $C_{18}H_{22}N_2O_2$. [Early 20C. < PHEN- + -CAINE]

phen·a·cite /fénnə sìt/, **phen·a·kite** /-kìt/ *n* a colorless glassy mineral that is composed of beryllium silicate. Use: gems. [Mid-19C. < Greek *phenak-* "impostor"; because mistaken for quartz]

phenanthrene

phe·nan·threne /fə nán thrēen/ *n* a colorless crystalline aromatic hydrocarbon. Use: manufacture of dyes, drugs, and explosives. Formula: $C_{14}H_{10}$. See illustration on previous page [Late 19C. < PHEN- + contraction of ANTHRACENE]

phen·cy·cli·dine /fen sī́kli dēen, -sīkli-/ *n* a drug used as an anesthetic in veterinary medicine and illegally as a hallucinogen. Formula: $C_{17}H_{25}N$. [Mid-20C. < PHEN- + CYCLO- + PIPERIDINE]

phe·net·ics /fə néttiks/ *n* a system of biological classification based on overall similarities between organisms rather than on their genetic or developmental relationships (*takes a singular verb*) [Mid-20C. < Greek *phainesthai* "appear" (see -PHANE)] —**phe·net·ic** *adj* —**phe·net·i·cal·ly** *adv* —**phe·net·i·cist** *n*

phe·nix *n US* another spelling of **phoenix**

Phe·nix Cit·y /fēeniks-/ town in Alabama, situated east of Montgomery, on the Chattahoochee River, which separates Alabama from Georgia. Population: 28,503 (2002 estimate).

pheno- *prefix* **1.** CHEM containing phenyl ○ *phenobarbital* **2.** CHEM related to or derived from benzene ○ *phenol* **3.** GEOL appearing ○ *phenocryst* [< Greek *phainein* "to show"]

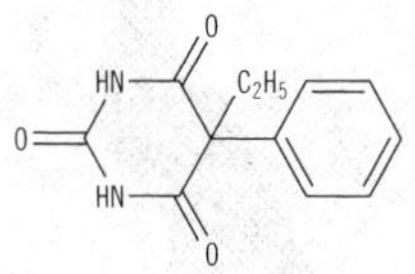

phenobarbital

phe·no·bar·bi·tal /fēenō baárbi tàwl/ *n* a crystalline barbiturate. Use: sedative, hypnotic, anticonvulsant. Formula: $C_{12}H_{12}N_2O_3$.

phe·no·bar·bi·tone /fēenō baárbi tōn/ *n UK* same as **phenobarbital**

phe·no·cop·y /fēenə kòppee/ (*plural* **-ies**) *n* a noninheritable change in an organism induced by its response to its environment but resembling a genetic mutation [Mid-20C. < PHENOTYPE]

phe·no·cryst /fēenə krìst/ *n* a large embedded crystal in a porphyritic rock [Late 19C. < French *phénocryste* < *phéno-* "appearing" (< Greek *phainein* "to show") + Greek *krustallos* "ice"] —**phe·no·crys·tic** /fēenə krístik/ *adj*

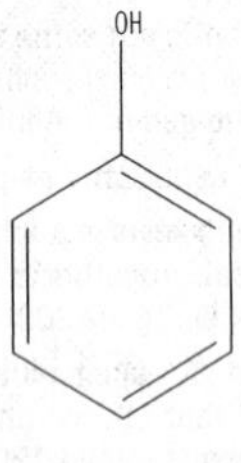

phenol

phe·nol /fēe nàwl/ *n* **1.** a poisonous caustic crystalline compound. Source: coal, wood tar, benzene. Use: manufacture of resins, dyes, and pharmaceuticals, antiseptic, disinfectant. Formula: C_6H_5OH. **2.** a chemical compound that has one or more hydroxyl groups attached to a benzene ring

phe·no·lic /fi nṓlik, -nóllik/ *n* a resin that has high temperature stability. Use: in plastics, paints, adhesives. ■ *adj* derived from or containing phenol

phe·no·lic res·in *n* CHEM same as **phenolic**

phe·nol·o·gy /fi nólləjee/ (*plural* **-gies**) *n* **1.** the study of regularly recurring biological phenomena such as animal migrations or plant budding, especially as influenced by climatic conditions **2.** the relationship between a regularly recurring biological phenomenon and climatic or environmental factors that may influence it [Late 19C. < PHENOMENON] —**phe·no·log·i·cal** /fēenə lójjik'l/ *adj* —**phe·nol·o·gist** *n*

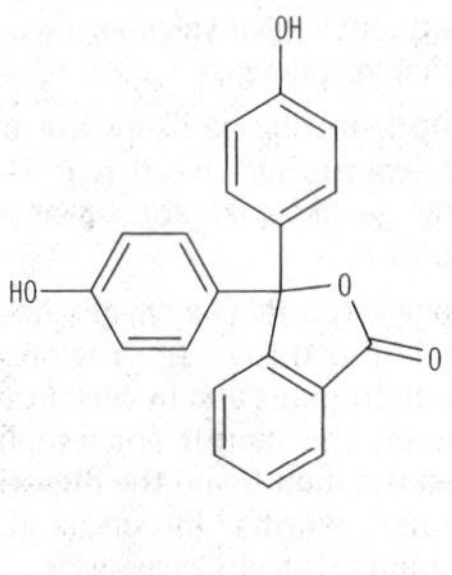

phenolphthalein

phe·nol·phthal·ein /fēe nawl tháy lēen, -nəl-/ *n* a colorless or yellowish compound. Use: chemical indicator, laxative. Formula: $C_{20}H_{14}O_4$.

phe·nol red *n* a red dye. Use: acid-base indicator, testing kidney function.

phe·nom /fə nóm/ *n* an outstanding or unusual person or thing (*slang*) [Late 19C. Shortening of PHENOMENON]

phe·nom·e·na plural of **phenomenon**

phe·nom·e·nal /fə nómmən'l/ *adj* **1.** REMARKABLE remarkably and impressively good or great ○ *a phenomenal talent* **2.** OF PHENOMENON constituting or relating to a phenomenon **3.** PHILOSOPHY PERCEIVED BY SENSES perceived by or perceptible to the senses, rather than the mind, and thus having at least an apparent external existence —**phe·nom·en·al·ly** *adv*

phe·nom·e·nal·ism /fə nómmən'l ìzzəm/ *n* a philosophical theory stating that knowledge of the external world is limited to appearances, so that we know what our senses tell us about things, not what they are. Phenomenalism is chiefly associated with the work of the 18th-century British philosopher David Hume and his followers. —**phe·nom·e·nal·ist** *n, adj* —**phe·nom·e·nal·is·tic** /fi nòmmən'l ístik/ *adj* —**phe·nom·e·nal·is·ti·cal·ly** *adv*

phe·nom·e·nol·o·gy /fə nòmmə nólləjee/ *n* **1.** in philosophy, the science or study of phenomena, things as they are perceived, as opposed to the study of being, the nature of things as they are **2.** the philosophical investigation and description of conscious experience in all its varieties without reference to the question of whether what is experienced is objectively real —**phe·nom·e·no·log·i·cal** /fə nòmmənə lójjik'l/ *adj* —**phe·nom·e·no·log·i·cal·ly** *adv* —**phe·nom·e·nol·o·gist** *n*

~~**phenomenom**~~ incorrect spelling of **phenomenon**

phe·nom·e·non /fə nómmə nòn, -nən/ (*plural* **-na** /-nə/ or **-nons**) *n* **1.** SOMETHING EXPERIENCED a fact or occurrence that can be observed **2.** SOMETHING NOTABLE something that is out of the ordinary and excites people's interest and curiosity ○ *a strange phenomenon* **3.** (*plural* **phe·nom·e·nons**) EXTRAORDINARY PERSON OR THING somebody or something that is, or is considered to be, truly extraordinary and marvelous **4.** PHILOSOPHY OBJECT OF PERCEPTION something perceived or experienced, especially an object as it is apprehended by the human senses as opposed to an object as it intrinsically is in itself [Late 16C. Via late Latin < Greek *phainomenon* "that which appears" < *phainein* "to show"]

USAGE phenomenon or **phenomena**? Usage varies for the plural ending of nouns derived from Latin and Greek words. For **phenomenon** never use the false singular *phenomena* as in *This phenomena occurs only in the southern hemisphere*; write instead *This phenomenon occurs....* Similarly, never attach an *-s* plural to the already plural ***phenomena***, as in *These physiological phenomenas are fascinating.* Write instead *These physiological phenomena are...* The variant plural *phenomenons* is appropriate only outside scientific and philosophical contexts with the meaning "extraordinary people, events, or things," as in *The dot-coms are one of the most interesting 21st-century phenomenons.* Do not overuse ***phenomenon*** in nonscientific and nonphilosophical contexts. Restrict it to people, events, and things that are extraordinary, not merely interesting or vaguely out of the ordinary.

phe·no·thi·a·zine /fēenō thī́ ə zēen, -nə-/ *n* **1.** a yellowish crystalline compound used in veterinary medicine to destroy intestinal worms and as an insecticide. Formula: $C_{12}H_9NS$. **2.** a derivative of phenothiazine used as a tranquilizer and in the treatment of schizophrenia

phe·no·type /fēenə tīp/ *n* the visible characteristics of an organism resulting from the interaction between its genetic makeup and the environment [Early 20C. < German *Phänotypus*, literally "type that shows" < Greek *phainein* "to show"] —**phe·no·typ·ic** /fēenə típpik/ *adj* —**phe·no·typ·i·cal** *adj* —**phe·no·typ·i·cal·ly** *adv*

phe·nox·ide /fi nók sīd/ *n* a chemical compound that is a salt of phenol

phen·yl /fénn'l, fēen'l/ *n* a chemical group derived from benzene by removing a hydrogen atom, thus having a valence of one. Formula: C_6H_5. [Mid-19C. < French *phényle* < Greek *phainein* "to show"; because it was used to name compounds formed from lighting gas]

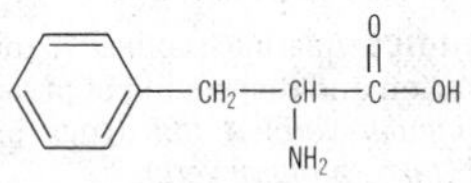

phenylalanine

phen·yl·al·a·nine /fènn'l álla nēen, fēen'l-/ *n* an essential amino acid found in many proteins and converted to a nonessential amino acid (**tyrosine**) by the body. Formula: $C_9H_{11}O_2N$.

phen·yl·bu·ta·zone /fènn'l byóotə zōn, fēen'l-/ *n* an anti-inflammatory drug. Use: treatment of arthritis, bursitis, gout. Formula: $C_{19}H_{20}N_2O_2$.

phen·yl·eph·rine /fènn'l éffrin, fēen'l-/ *n* a drug that constricts blood vessels. Use: nasal decongestant, blood pressure regulator. [Mid-20C. Contraction of PHENYL + EPINEPHRINE]

phen·yl·ke·to·nur·i·a /fènn'l keetə nóoree ə, fēen'l-/ *n* a condition, resulting from a genetic mutation, in which the body lacks the enzyme to metabolize phenylalanine. If untreated, it results in developmental deficiency, seizures, and tumors.

phen·yl·pro·pa·nol·a·mine /fènn'l prōpə nóllə mēen, fēen'l-/ *n* a drug that constricts blood vessels. Use: nasal and bronchial decongestant, appetite suppressant.

phen·yl·thi·o·car·ba·mide /fènn'l thī ō kaárbə mīd, fēen'l-/, **phen·yl·thi·o·u·rea** /fènn'l thī ō yóoree ə, fēen'l-/ *n* a crystalline compound that tastes extremely bitter to people who possess a specific dominant gene. Use: testing for that gene.

phen·y·to·in /fénni tō in, fə níttō in/ *n* a drug that controls convulsions. Use: treatment of epilepsy.

pher·o·mone /férrə mōn/ *n* a chemical compound, produced and secreted by an animal, that influences the behavior and development of other members of the same species [Mid-20C. < Greek *pherein* "carry" + HORMONE] —**pher·o·mon·al** /férrə mōn'l/ *adj*

phew /fyoo/ *interj* **1.** used to express tiredness, relief, surprise, or disgust **2.** used to express disgust at an unpleasant smell [Early 17C. An imitation of blowing through partly closed lips]

Ph.G. *abbr US* Graduate in Pharmacy

phi /fī/ (*plural* **phis**) *n* the 21st letter of the Greek alphabet, represented in the English alphabet as "ph." See table at **alphabet** [Mid-20C. < late Greek, later form of Greek *phei*]

phi·al /fí əl/ *n* same as **vial** [14C. Via French < Latin *phiala* "saucer" < Greek *phialē* "broad flat vessel"]

Phi Be·ta Kap·pa *n* **1.** an honor society of American college and university students showing high academic achievement. It was founded in 1776. **2.** a member of Phi Beta Kappa

Phid·i·as /fíddee əss/ (*fl* 490–430 B.C.) Greek sculptor considered the greatest of the classical period. His colossal statue of Zeus at Olympia was one of the Seven Wonders of the World.

phi ef·fect *n* OPTICS same as **phi phenomenon**

PHIGS /figz/ *abbr* COMPUT programmers' hierarchical interactive graphics standard

Phil. *abbr* **1.** MUSIC Philharmonic **2.** BIBLE Philippians **3.** Philippines

phil- *prefix* same as **philo-** (*used before vowels or l*)

-phil *suffix* same as **-phile**

Phila. *abbr* Philadelphia

Phil·a·del·phi·a /fíllə délfee ə/ largest city in Pennsylvania, situated on the Delaware River in the southeastern part of the state. It is known as the "Birthplace of the Nation" because both the Declaration of Independence and the Constitution of the United States were drawn up there. Population: 1,492,231 (2002 estimate).

Phil·a·del·phi·a law·yer *n* a lawyer who has a detailed knowledge of legal technicalities and exploits them for a client's benefit [After PHILADELPHIA; because of the reputed shrewdness of lawyers from eastern cities]

Phil·a·del·phi·a pep·per pot *n US* FOOD same as **pepper pot** (sense 2) [After PHILADELPHIA; because common in Pennsylvania]

Phil·a·del·phi·a scrap·ple *n regional* scrapple

phil·a·del·phus /fìllə délfəss/ *n* TREES same as **mock orange** (sense 1) [Late 18C. Via modern Latin < Greek *philadelphos* "loving your brother" < *philos* "loving" + *adelphos* "brother"]

Phi·lae /fí lee/ submerged island in southern Egypt, in the Nile River, south of Aswan. It was the site of ancient temples that were moved when the island was flooded after the building of the Aswan High Dam.

phi·lan·der /fi lándər/ (**-dered, -der·ing, -ders**) *vi* to flirt with and have casual sexual affairs with many women, especially when married to another woman [Late 17C. < Greek *philandros* "loving men" < *andr-* "man"] —**phi·lan·der·er** *n*

phil·an·throp·ic /fìllən thróppik/, **phil·an·throp·i·cal** /-ik'l/ *adj* **1.** showing kindness, charitable concern, and generosity toward other people **2.** devoted to helping other people, especially through giving charitable aid —**phil·an·throp·i·cal·ly** *adv*

phi·lan·thro·py /fi lánthrəpee/ (*plural* **-pies**) *n* **1.** DESIRE TO BENEFIT HUMANITY a desire to improve the material, social, and spiritual welfare of humanity, especially through charitable activities **2.** PHILANTHROPIC ACT OR GROUP a philanthropic action or organization **3.** LOVE FOR ALL HUMANITY general love for, or benevolence toward, the whole of humankind (*formal*) [Early 17C. Via late Latin < Greek *philanthrōpos* "humane" < *philos* "loving" + *anthrōpos* "human being"] —**phi·lan·thro·pist** *n*

phi·lat·e·ly /fi látt'lee/ *n* the collection and study of postage stamps and related items [Mid-19C. < French *philatélie* < Greek *philos* "loving" + *ateleia* "exemption from tax" < *telos* "tax"; from the freedom from charges that a stamped letter provides] —**phil·a·tel·ic** /fìllə téllik/ *adj* —**phil·a·tel·i·cal·ly** *adv* —**phi·lat·e·list** *n*

ORIGIN Monsieur Herpin, a French stamp collector, was looking for an impressive and learned-sounding term for his hobby. Because the Greeks and Romans did not have postage stamps, there was no classical term for them. So he went back a stage beyond stamps, to the days of franking with a postmark. In France, such letters were marked with the words *franc de port* "carriage-free." The nearest he could get to this in Greek was *ateleia*, and from it he created *philatélie*, the English form of which made its first recorded appearance in 1865.

Phil·by /fílbee/, **Kim** (1912–88) British intelligence agent and Soviet spy. During the 1940s and 1950s he penetrated the upper levels of British intelligence and passed vital information to the Soviet Union. Born **Philby, Harold Adrian Russell**

> "To betray, you must first belong. I never belonged."
> [Kim Philby, *Sunday Times (London)*; December 17, 1967]

-phile *suffix* **1.** somebody or something that loves or has an affinity for ○ *bibliophile* ○ *acidophil* **2.** loving or having an affinity for ○ *homophile* [Via Latin < Greek *philos* "loving"] —**-philic** *suffix* —**-philous** *suffix* —**-phily** *suffix*

Phi·le·mon /fi léemən/ *n* a book of the Bible, originally a letter, that appeals to Philemon to take pity on his slave who had escaped and converted to Christianity, traditionally attributed to St. Paul. See table at **Bible**

phil·har·mon·ic /fìl haar mónnik/, **Phil·har·mon·ic** *adj* describes an orchestra, choir, or society that promotes the study, performance, and appreciation of classical music ■ *n* a symphony orchestra, choir, or musical society that has the word "philharmonic" in its title [Mid-18C. < French *philharmonique* < Greek *philos* "loving" + *harmonika* (see HARMONIC)]

phil·hel·lene /fil hé leen/, **phil·hel·len·ist** /fil héllənist/ *n* an admirer of Greece, Greek history and culture, or the Greeks [Early 19C. < Greek *philellēn* < *philos* "loving" + *Hellēn* "a Greek"] —**phil·hel·len·ic** /fìl he lénnik/ *adj* —**phil·hel·len·ism** /fil héllə nìzzəm/ *n* —**phil·hel·len·is·tic** /fil hèllə nístik/ *adj*

-philia *suffix* **1.** intense or unusual attraction to ○ *neophilia* ○ *zoophilia* **2.** tendency toward ○ *basophilia* [Via modern Latin < Greek *philia* "fondness" < *philos* "loving"] —**-philiac** *suffix*

Phil·ip /fíllip/, **St.** (*fl* A.D. 1st century) one of the 12 apostles of Jesus Christ. He was born in Bethsaida and was present at the miracle of the loaves and fishes.

Phil·ip (*d.* 1676) Wampanoag leader. He led the uprising known as King Philip's War against New England colonists (1675–76). Born **Metacomet**

Phil·ip I, (1478–1506) duke of Burgundy and king of Castile. Father of Charles V and Ferdinand I, he founded the Hapsburg dynasty in Spain through his marriage to a Castilian princess. Known as **Philip the Handsome**

Phil·ip II[1] (382–336 B.C.) king of Macedonia. After becoming king (359) he extended Macedonian power over the whole of Greece. He was the father of Alexander the Great.

Phil·ip II[2] (1527–98) king of Spain (1556–98). He ruled over a vast empire including the Netherlands, Naples and Sicily, the Philippines, and several South American colonies. His Armada was destroyed in an attempt to invade England (1588).

> "England's chief defense depends upon the navy being always ready to defend the realm against invasion."
> [Philip II, *Submission to the Privy Council*; 1555?]

Phil·ip IV (1268–1314) king of France. He succeeded to the throne in 1285. His conflict with Pope Boniface VIII led to the residence of the popes in Avignon (1309–77). Known as **Philip the Fair**

Phil·ip V (1683–1746) king of Spain. The grandson of Louis XIV of France, he was the first of the Spanish Bourbons. His accession to the throne (1700) led to the War of the Spanish Succession.

Phil·ip, Prince, Duke of Edinburgh (*b.* 1921) The son of Prince Andrew of Greece and the great-great-grandson of Queen Victoria, he married Princess Elizabeth, later Queen Elizabeth II, in 1947

~~Philipines~~ incorrect spelling of **Philippines**

Phi·lip·pi /fi lí pī/ town in northern Greece. It was the site of a battle in 42 B.C. in which forces led by Mark Antony and Augustus defeated Marcus Brutus and Gaius Cassius Longinus.

Phi·lip·pi·ans /fi líppee ənz/ *n* a book of the Bible, originally addressed to the Christian church at Philippi and traditionally attributed to St. Paul. (*takes a singular verb*) See table at **Bible**

phi·lip·pic /fi líppik/ *n* a verbal attack on somebody or something delivered in the most savage, bitter, and insulting terms, usually as a speech [Late 16C. Via Latin < Greek *philippikos*, speech of the 4C B.C. Greek orator Demosthenes urging the citizens of Athens to rise up against Philip of Macedon (see PHILIP II, king of Macedonia)]

Phil·ip·pine /fíllə peen/ *adj* relating to the Philippines or its people or culture

Phil·ip·pine Eng·lish *n* a variety of English spoken in the Philippines. See panel on next page

Philippines

Phil·ip·pines /fíllə peenz/ country in Southeast Asia, in the western Pacific Ocean, in the Malay Archipelago. It comprises over 7,000 islands. Language: Filipino. Currency: Philippine peso. Capital: Manila. Population: 84,619,974 (2003). Area: 115,831 sq. mi./300,000 sq. km. Official name **Republic of the Philippines**

Phil·ip·pine Sea /fíllə peen-/ section of the western Pacific Ocean, south of Japan and northeast of the Philippines. Area: 2,000,000 sq. mi./5,000,000 sq. km.

phil·is·tine /fílli steen, -stīn/ (*disapproving*) *n* somebody who is regarded as being indifferent to artistic and intellectual achievements and values ■ *adj* regarded as being ignorant, uncultured, and indifferent or hostile to artistic and intellectual achievement [Early 19C. < PHILISTINE] —**phil·is·tin·ism** *n*

Phil·is·tine *n* a member of a people who settled in ancient Philistia in southern Palestine around the 12th century B.C. ■ *adj* relating to the ancient Philistines or their culture (*disapproving*)

~~Phillipines~~ incorrect spelling of **Philippines**

Phil·lips screw /fíllips-/ *tdmk* a trademark for a screw with a cross-shaped slot on its head

Phil·lips screw·driv·er *tdmk* a trademark for a screwdriver that has a cross-shaped tip so that it can be used to turn a Phillips screw

phil·lu·men·ist /fi lóomənist/ *n* a collector of matchboxes and matchbooks as a hobby [Mid-20C. < PHILO- + Latin *lumen* "light"] —**phil·lu·men·y** /fi lóomənee/ *n*

philo- *prefix* loving, having an attraction to or affinity for ○ *philoprogenitive* [< Greek *philos* "loving"]

Phi·loc·te·tes /fìllək téet eez, fi lóktə téez/ *n* in Greek mythology, a friend of Achilles and the slayer of the Trojan prince Paris

phil·o·den·dron /fìllə déndrən/ (*plural* **-drons** or **-dra** /-drə/) *n* a climbing plant of the arum family, grown as a house plant for its evergreen leaves. Native to: tropical America. Genus: *Philodendron*. [Late 19C. Via modern Latin < Greek < *philodendros* "loving trees" (because it climbs trees in its native habitat) < *dendron* "tree"]

phi·log·y·ny /fi lójjənee/ *n* a positive and admiring attitude toward women in general (*archaic*) —**phi·log·y·nist** *n* —**phi·log·y·nous** *adj*

phi·lol·o·gy /fi lólləjee/ *n* **1.** LING STUDY OF LANGUAGE IN TEXTS the scientific study of the relationship of languages to one another, and their history, especially based on the analysis of texts **2.** CULTL ANTHROP STUDY OF ANCIENT TEXTS the study and analysis of ancient texts, especially as an approach to the cultural history of a period or people **3.** LITERAT STUDY OF LITERATURE the study of literature in general (*archaic*) [14C. Via Latin < Greek *philologia* < *philologos* "fond of words" < *philos* "loving" + *logos* "word"] —**phil·o·log·i·cal** /fìllə lójjik'l/ *adj* —**phil·o·log·i·cal·ly** *adv* —**phi·lol·o·gist** *n*

WORLD ENGLISH ***Philippine English***, also Filipino English, is the variety of English used in the Philippines. It has some co-official status with Filipino. English is the second western colonial language, after Spanish; the United States took the territory in 1898 from Spain, whose colony it had been since 1521. The nation is diverse, with a Malay majority, a Chinese minority, and many people of mixed Malay, Chinese, Spanish, and US backgrounds. Because English is used in varying degrees by over half the population of about 60 million, the Philippines rightly claims to be a major English-speaking country.

Like US English, Philippine English pronounces *r* in words such as *art*, *door*, and *worker*. Also, *h* is pronounced with the tip of the tongue curled back and raised. Vowels tend to be full in all syllables (e.g., *seven* being pronounced "seh-ven," not "sev'n"). An "s" or "sh" sound may serve instead of a "z" or "zh," as in "carss" (cars), "pleshure" (pleasure). In grammar, the present progressive is commonly used for habitual behavior, rather than the simple present ("We are doing this work all the time" for "We do this work all the time"), the present perfect may be used rather than the simple past ("We have done it yesterday" for "We did it yesterday"), and the past perfect rather than the present perfect ("They had already been there" for "They have already been there").

Distinctive vocabulary includes: (1) Hispanicisms, unchanged or adapted, e.g., *asalto* (surprise party), *querida* (mistress); (2) words from Tagalog, e.g., *boondock* (mountain) – whence "the boondocks," *kundiman* (love song), *tao* (man) – as in "the common tao"; (3) local coinages, e.g., *carnap* (to steal a car), formed by analogy with *kidnap*, and *jeepney* (small bus), blending *jeep* and *jitney*, a jeep adapted for passengers.

phil·o·pro·gen·i·tive /fìllō prō jénnitiv/ *adj* **1.** producing a large number of offspring (*formal*) **2.** loving children, especially your own offspring (*literary*)

phi·lo·sophe /fíllə sòf, fèelə zóf/ *n* a leading writer or thinker of the Enlightenment in 18th-century France, who advocated a rational approach to philosophy and government and criticized the French social and political system [Late 18C. Via French < Latin *philosophus* (see PHILOSOPHER)]

phi·los·o·pher /fi lóssəfər/ *n* **1. SOMEBODY WHO STUDIES PHILOSOPHY** somebody who seeks to understand and explain the principles of existence and reality **2. SOMEBODY HOLDING PARTICULAR BELIEFS** somebody who believes in a particular philosophy and thinks and acts accordingly **3. THINKING PERSON** a thinker who deeply and seriously considers human affairs and life in general **4. CALM AND RATIONAL PERSON** somebody who calmly and rationally reacts to events, especially adversity [14C. < Anglo-Norman *philosophre*, variant of Old French *philosophe* < Latin *philosophus* < Greek *philosophos* "lover of knowledge" < *philos* "loving" + *sophia* "learning, wisdom"]

phi·los·o·pher's stone, phi·los·o·phers' stone *n* a substance that medieval alchemists believed could be used to convert other metals into gold

phil·o·soph·i·cal /fìllə sóffik'l/, **phil·o·soph·ic** /-sóffik/ *adj* **1. RELATING TO STUDY OF PHILOSOPHY** concerned with the study of the nature of life and reality, or of related areas such as ethics, logic, or metaphysics **2. CONCERNED WITH DEEP QUESTIONS OF LIFE** concerned with or given to thinking about the larger issues and deeper meanings in life and events **3. SHOWING CALMNESS AND RESIGNATION** showing calmness, restraint, or resignation, especially reacting to adversity in a restrained or resigned way —**phil·o·soph·i·cal·ly** *adv*

phi·los·o·phize /fi lóssə fìz/ (**-phized, -phiz·ing, -phiz·es**) *v* **1.** *vi* **DISCUSS NATURE OF REALITY** to comment on or attempt to explain the nature of life and reality, or a part of it such as ethics, logic, knowledge, or existence **2.** *vi* **EXPLAIN OR MORALIZE IN SUPERFICIAL WAY** to express opinions of a supposedly philosophical nature in a superficial, tedious, or moralistic way **3.** *vt* PHILOSOPHY **DEAL WITH SOMETHING FROM PHILOSOPHICAL STANDPOINT** to consider, explain, or deal with something from a philosophical standpoint —**phi·los·o·phi·za·tion** /fi lòssəfi záysh'n/ *n* —**phi·los·o·phiz·er** *n*

phi·los·o·phy /fi lóssəfee/ (*plural* **-phies**) *n* **1. EXAMINATION OF BASIC CONCEPTS** the branch of knowledge or academic study devoted to the systematic examination of basic concepts such as truth, existence, reality, causality, and freedom **2. SCHOOL OF THOUGHT** a particular system of thought or doctrine **3. GUIDING OR UNDERLYING PRINCIPLES** a set of basic principles or concepts underlying a particular sphere of knowledge **4. SET OF BELIEFS OR AIMS** a precept, or set of precepts, beliefs, principles, or aims, underlying somebody's practice or conduct **5. CALM RESIGNATION** restraint, resignation, or calmness and rationality in somebody's behavior or response to events [14C. Via French and Latin < Greek *philosophia* < *philosophos* (see PHILOSOPHER)]

phil·ter /fíltər/, **phil·tre** *n* a magical potion or charm, especially one that causes somebody to fall in love (*literary*) [Late 16C. Via French < Greek *philtron* < *philein* "to love" < *philos* "loving"]

phi·mo·sis /fī mṓssiss, fi-/ *n* a narrowing of the opening in the foreskin that prevents its being drawn back over the penis. This makes washing difficult or impossible and often leads to irritation and infection. [Late 17C. Via modern Latin < Greek *phimōsis* "muzzling"]

phi phe·nom·e·non *n* an optical illusion in which the rapid appearance and disappearance of two stationary objects such as flashing lights are perceived as the movement back and forth of a single object

phish /fish/ *vi* to trick somebody into providing bank or credit-card information by sending a fraudulent e-mail purporting to be from a bank, Internet provider, etc. asking for verification of an account number or password —**phish·ing** *n*

~~**phisical**~~ incorrect spelling of **physical**

phleb- *prefix* same as **phlebo-** (*used before vowels*)

phle·bi·tis /flə bítiss/ *n* inflammation of the wall of a vein

phlebo- *prefix* vein ○ *phlebotomy* [< Greek *phleb-* "blood vessel"]

phle·bog·ra·phy /flə bóggrəfee/ *n* MED same as **venography**

phle·bot·o·mize /flə bóttə mìz/ (**-mized, -miz·ing, -miz·es**) *vt* to make an incision into a patient's vein in order to draw blood for testing

phle·bot·o·mus fe·ver /flə bòttəməss-/ *n* MED same as **sandfly fever** [< modern Latin < Greek *phlebotomos* "opening a vein"]

phle·bot·o·my /flə bóttəmee/ (*plural* **-mies**) *n* a surgical incision made in a vein, or a puncture made by a needle to draw blood for testing —**phle·bot·o·mist** *n*

phlegm /flem/ *n* **1. THICK MUCUS** the thick mucus secreted by the walls of the respiratory passages, especially during a cold **2. UNFLAPPABILITY** calmness or composure that is not easily disturbed **3. BODILY FLUID DETERMINING HEALTH AND EMOTIONS** in medieval medicine, one of the four basic bodily fluids (**humors**). Phlegm was believed to be cold and moist in nature and to cause sluggishness and apathy. [14C. Via French < late Latin *phlegma* "clammy bodily moisture" < Greek, "inflammation, heat" < *phlegein* "to burn"] —**phlegm·y** *adj*

phleg·mat·ic /fleg máttik/, **phleg·mat·i·cal** /-máttik'l/ *adj* generally unemotional and difficult to arouse [14C. Via French and Latin < Greek *phlegmatikos* < *phlegma* (see PHLEGM)] —**phleg·mat·i·cal·ly** *adv*

SYNONYMS See ***impassive***.

~~**phlem**~~ incorrect spelling of **phlegm**

phlo·em /flṓ èm/ *n* one of the two main types of tissue in vascular plants, which conducts synthesized nutrients to all parts of the plant. It is made up of sap-conducting tubes (**sieve tubes**) and the cells that lie alongside them (**companion cells**), elongated cells of soft tissue (**parenchyma**), and fibers. [Late 19C. < German < Greek *phloos* "bark"]

phlo·gis·ton /flō jístən/ *n* a hypothetical element that some early scientists, before the discovery of oxygen, believed to be present in all combustible substances to make them burn [Mid-18C. < Greek, "inflammable thing" < *phlogizein* "set on fire" < *phlox* "flame"] —**phlo·gis·tic** *adj*

phlog·o·pite /flóggə pìt/ *n* a yellowish brown or reddish brown mineral form of mica. Source: marble, dolomite. [Mid-19C. < Greek *phlogōpos* "fiery-faced" < *phlox* "flame"; from its highly reflective flat crystals]

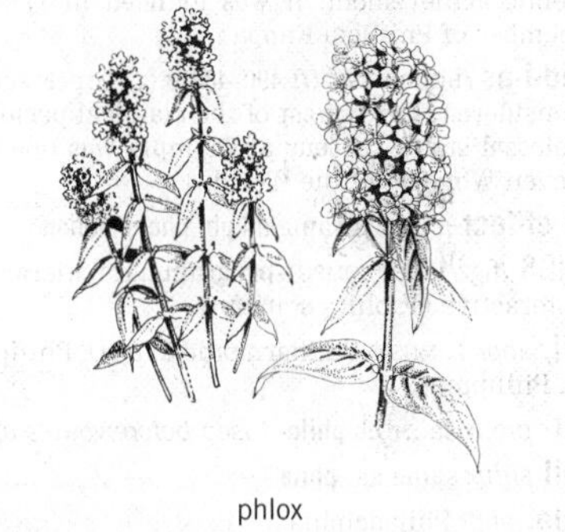

phlox

phlox /floks/ (*plural same or* **phlox·es**) *n* a common garden plant that has slim stems with oval narrow leaves. Flowers: scented, white, red, purple, in clusters. Native to: North America. Genus: *Phlox*. [Early 18C. Via modern Latin < Greek, "flame"; from its brightly colored flowers]

Phnom Penh /pə nòm pén, nòm-/ capital city of Cambodia, situated at the confluence of the Mekong and Tonle Sap rivers in the southern part of the country. Population: 999,804 (1999).

-phobe *suffix* fearing or disliking something or somebody ○ *claustrophobe* [Via French < Greek *phobos* "fear"]

pho·bi·a /fṓbee ə/ *n* an irrational or very powerful fear and dislike of something such as spiders or confined spaces ○ *a phobia about traveling in elevators* [Late 18C. < -PHOBIA]

-phobia *suffix* an exaggerated or irrational fear ○ *claustrophobia* [Via Latin < Greek *phobos* "fear"]

pho·bic /fṓbik/ *adj* **1. INTENSELY FEARFUL OF SOMETHING** having or showing an intense fear and dislike of something **2.** PSYCHIAT **RELATING TO PHOBIAS** affected with or arising out of a phobia ■ *n* PSYCHIAT **SOMEBODY WITH PHOBIA** somebody who fears or dislikes something strongly or irrationally

-phobic *suffix* with a strong or irrational fear or dislike of somebody or something ○ *claustrophobic*

Pho·bos /fṓbəss, fṓ boss/ *n* the innermost of the two natural satellites of Mars, both of which are small. It was discovered in 1877 and is ellipsoidal in shape.

pho·cine /fṓ sìn/ *adj* relating to or resembling seals [Mid-19C. < modern Latin *Phocinae* < Greek *phōkē* "seal"]

pho·co·me·li·a /fṓkə mèelee ə/ *n* a condition, present at birth, characterized by an absent or underdeveloped upper section of a limb, with a normal-sized hand or foot attached to the trunk by a short broad flat limb [Late 19C. < Greek *phōkē* "seal" + *melos* "limb"; from the short limbs of seals]

phoe·be /fèebee/ *n* a bird of the flycatcher family that has grayish brown feathers, a yellowish white breast, and is noted for the flicking of its tail. Native to: eastern North America. Genus: *Sayornis*. [Early 18C. An imitation of its song (influenced by the name PHOEBE)]

Phoe·be /fèebee/ *n* **1. TITAN GODDESS** in Greek mythology, a Titan goddess who later became identified with the goddess of the Moon, Artemis **2. MOON PERSONIFIED** a personification of the Moon (*literary*) **3.** ASTRON **SMALL OUTERMOST MOON OF SATURN** a small natural satellite of Saturn [14C. Via Latin < Greek *Phoibē*, form of *phoibos* "bright, shining"]

Phoe·bus /fèebəss/ *n* **1.** *also* **Phoe·bus A·pol·lo** in Greek mythology, the god Apollo when identified with the Sun **2.** a personification of the Sun (*literary*) [14C. Via Latin < Greek *Phoibos*, literally "bright, shining"]

Phoe·ni·cia /fə níshə, -nèeshə/ ancient region on the eastern coast of the Mediterranean Sea in modern Lebanon and Syria. It was the site of several city-kingdoms, whose people became the greatest traders and sailors of the ancient world.

Phoe·ni·cian /fə nísh'n, fə nèesh'n/ *n* **1.** a member of an ancient people who occupied Phoenicia, where they established trading ports **2.** an extinct Semitic language spoken in ancient Phoenicia —**Phoe·ni·cian** *adj*

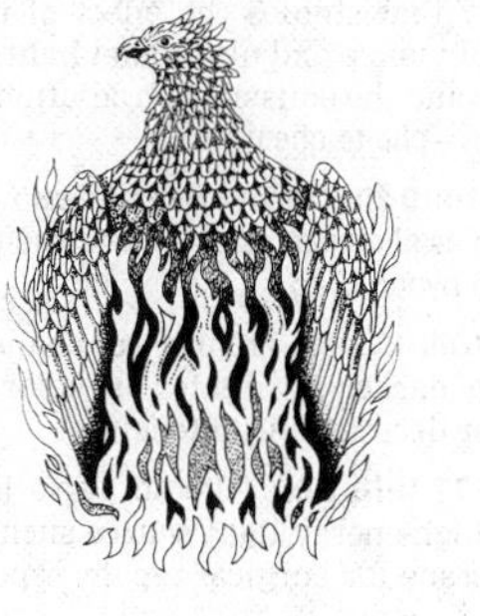

phoenix

phoe·nix /féeniks/, **phe·nix** *n* **1.** in ancient mythology, a bird resembling an eagle that lived for 500 years and then burned itself to death on a pyre from whose ashes another phoenix arose. It commonly appears in literature as a symbol of death and resurrection. **2.** a supremely beautiful, rare, or unique person or thing (*literary*) ○ *a phoenix of princes* [Pre-12C. Via French and Latin < Greek *phoinix*]

Phoe·nix[1] *n* a constellation of the southern hemisphere situated between Sculptor and Eridanus. See illustration at **constellation**

Phoe·nix[2] /féeniks/ capital of Arizona and its largest city, located in the southern part of the state. Population: 1,371,960 (2002 estimate).

phon /fon/ *n* a unit of subjective measure of loudness level. The level in phons is equal in number to the sound intensity of a 1,000-hertz reference sound, measured in decibels, judged to be the same loudness as the measured sound.

phon- *prefix* same as **phono-** (*used before vowels*)

pho·nate /fṓ nàyt/ (**-nat·ed, -nat·ing, -nates**) *vi* to produce sounds, especially speech sounds, with the voice —**pho·na·tion** /fō náysh'n/ *n* —**pho·na·to·ry** /fṓnə tàwree/ *adj*

phone[1] /fōn/ *n* same as **telephone** ■ **phones** *npl* a set of earphones or headphones (*informal*) ■ *vti* (**phoned, phon·ing, phones**) same as **telephone** *v* [Late 19C Shortening]

phone[2] /fōn/ *n* a single basic speech sound [Mid-19C. < Greek *phōnē* "sound, voice"]

-phone *suffix* **1.** a device that emits or receives sounds, e.g., a musical instrument ○ *diaphone* ○ *hydrophone* ○ *sousaphone* **2.** a telephone ○ *speakerphone* **3.** a speech sound ○ *isophone* **4.** a speaker of a particular language ○ *Francophone* [< Greek *phōnē* "sound, voice"] —**-phonic** *suffix* —**-phony** *suffix*

phone book *n* TELECOM same as **telephone book**

phone booth *n* same as **telephone booth**

phone·card /fōn kaard/ *n* a rectangular plastic card that can be used instead of money when making calls from some public telephones

phone-in *n Can, UK* a radio or television programme in which audience members can participate by telephone and ask questions or take part in discussions with the host and any guests. US term **call-in**

pho·neme /fṓ neem/ *n* a speech sound that distinguishes one word from another, e.g., the sounds "d" and "t" in the words "bid" and "bit." A phoneme is the smallest phonetic unit that can carry meaning. [Late 19C. Via French < Greek *phōnēma* "sound produced" < *phōnein* "produce a sound" < *phōnē* "sound, voice"]

pho·ne·mic /fə néemik, fō-/ *adj* **1.** OF PHONEMES relating to a phoneme **2.** OF DIFFERENT PHONEMES relating to speech sounds that belong to different phonemes rather than being different ways of pronouncing the same phoneme **3.** OF PHONEMICS relating to the branch of linguistics that studies phonemes —**pho·ne·mi·cal·ly** *adv*

pho·ne·mics /fə néemiks, fō-/ *n* the branch of linguistics involved in the classification and analysis of the phonemes of a language (*takes a singular verb*) —**pho·ne·mi·cist** *n*

phone phreak /-freek/ *n* somebody who breaks into telephone systems and other secure networks, often to make free long-distance telephone calls (*slang*)

phon·er /fṓnər/ *n* **1.** somebody who makes a telephone call **2.** an interview conducted by telephone, especially on a radio or TV program (*informal*)

phone sex *n* the act of talking in an erotic and explicit way to another person on the telephone for mutual or individual sexual pleasure

pho·net·ic /fə néttik, fō-/ *adj* **1.** OF SPEECH SOUNDS belonging to or associated with the sounds of human speech **2.** SHOWING PRONUNCIATION representing the sounds of human speech in writing, often with special symbols or unconventional spelling **3.** OF PHONETICS relating to the science of phonetics [Early 19C. Via modern Latin < Greek *phōnētikos* "spoken" < *phōnein* (see PHONEME)] —**pho·net·i·cal·ly** *adv*

pho·net·ic al·pha·bet *n* **1.** a set of letters and symbols used to represent the sounds of human speech in writing **2.** a set of words representing alphabetical letters, e.g., "Delta" for D and "Tango" for T, used in radio or telephone communications. The phonetic alphabet is used to distinguish between letters that sound similar, to spell out words, and in code names or call signs.

pho·net·ics /fə néttiks, fō-/ *n* (*takes a singular verb*) **1.** the scientific study of speech sounds and how they are produced **2.** the system or pattern of speech sounds used in a language —**pho·ne·ti·cian** /fṑnə tísh'n/ *n*

pho·net·ist /fṓnətist/ *n* a user or advocate of the use of a phonetic spelling system [Mid-19C. Shortening of *phoneticist* < PHONETIC]

pho·ney *adj, n* another spelling of **phony**

phon·ic /fónnik/ *adj* **1.** USING PHONICS using or involving phonics as a method of teaching people to read **2.** OF SOUND associated with sound or the scientific study of sound **3.** OF SPEECH SOUNDS relating to the sounds used in speech [Early 19C. < Greek *phōnē* "sound, voice"] —**phon·i·cal·ly** *adv*

phon·ics /fónniks/ *n* a method of teaching reading in which people learn to associate letters with the speech sounds they represent, rather than learning to recognize the whole word as a unit (*takes a singular verb*) [Late 17C. < Greek *phōnē* "sound, voice"]

phono- *prefix* sound, speech, voice ○ *phonogram* [< Greek *phōnē* "sound, voice" < Indo-European, "speak"]

pho·no·car·di·o·gram /fṑnə kaardee ə gràm/ *n* a visual record of heart sounds and murmurs made by a phonocardiograph

pho·no·car·di·o·graph /fṑnə kaardee ə gràf/ *n* an instrument that amplifies heart sounds and converts them into a visual display —**pho·no·car·di·o·graph·ic** /-kaardee ə gráffik/ *adj* —**pho·no·car·di·og·ra·phy** /-kaardee óggrəfee/ *n*

pho·no·chem·is·try /fṑnō kémmistree/ *n* a branch of science and technology dealing with the effect of sound and ultrasonic waves on chemical reactions

pho·no·gram /fṓnə gràm/ *n* **1.** a symbol that represents a word, part of a word, or an individual speech sound **2.** a sequence of letters that have the same pronunciation in several different words, e.g., "ear" in "earth," "heard," and "learn" —**pho·no·gram·ic** /fṑnə grámmik/ *adj* —**pho·no·gram·i·cal·ly** *adv*

pho·no·graph /fṓnə gràf/ *n* a record player

pho·nog·ra·phy /fə nóggrəfee, fō-/ *n* **1.** the use of symbols to represent speech sounds in writing **2.** a method of writing in shorthand that uses symbols to represent speech sounds —**pho·nog·ra·pher** *n* —**pho·no·graph·ic** /fṑnə gráffik/ *adj* —**pho·nog·ra·phist** *n*

pho·no·lite /fṓnə lìt/ *n* a fine-grained light-colored volcanic rock characterized by the presence of alkali feldspar and nepheline [Early 19C. < the resonance of the rock when hit with a hammer] —**pho·no·lit·ic** /fṑnə líttik/ *adj*

pho·nol·o·gy /fə nóllәjee, fō-/ (*plural* **-gies**) *n* **1.** the study of the system or pattern of speech sounds used in a particular language or in language in general **2.** the system or pattern of speech sounds used in a particular language —**pho·no·log·i·cal** /fṑnə lójjik'l/ *adj* —**pho·no·log·i·cal·ly** *adv* —**pho·nol·o·gist** *n*

pho·non /fṓ nòn/ *n* a quantum of vibrational or acoustic energy in a crystal lattice

pho·no·scope /fṓnə skṑp/ *n* a device that visually represents the vibrations of sound waves, used especially with musical instruments

pho·no·tac·tics /fṑnə táktiks/ *n* the study of the sounds it is possible to put together to form words and parts of words in a language (*takes a singular verb*)

pho·no·typ·y /fṓnə tìpee/ *n* the representation of speech sounds with phonetic symbols in writing or print —**pho·no·typ·ist** *n*

pho·ny /fṓnee/, **pho·ney** *adj* (**-ni·er, -ni·est**) **1.** NOT GENUINE not genuine and used to deceive **2.** GIVING FALSE IMPRESSION putting on a false show of something such as sincerity or expertise ■ *n* (*plural* **-nies** or **-neys**) SOMEBODY OR SOMETHING PHONY a phony person or thing ■ *vt* (**-nied** or **-neyed, -ny·ing** or **-ney·ing, -nies**) FALSIFY SOMETHING to make something appear to be genuine when it is not [Late 19C. Origin ?] —**pho·ni·ly** *adv* —**pho·ni·ness** *n*

phoo·ey /fóo ee/ *interj* used to express contempt, disbelief, disgust, or disappointment (*informal*) [Early 20C. Partly < *phoo*, natural exclamation; partly alteration of *pfui* < German]

pho·rate /fáw ràyt/ *n* an organophosphorus compound. Use: insecticide. Formula: $C_7H_{17}O_2PS_3$. [Mid-20C. Contraction of *phosphorodithioate* < PHOSPHORUS + DI-[1] + THIO- + -ATE]

-phore *suffix* something that carries ○ *sporophore* [< Greek *-phoros* "bearing" < *pherein* "carry" < Indo-European] —**-phorous** *suffix*

-phoresis *suffix* transmission ○ *diaphoresis* [< Greek *phorēsis* < *phorein* "keep carrying" < *pherein* (see -PHORE)]

pho·rid fly /fáwrid-/ *n* INSECTS a small, non-biting, two-winged fly that lives in moist, cool spots, and is a pest when it breeds in large numbers. Family: Phoridae.

phos·gene /fóss jeen, fóz-/ *n* a highly toxic colorless gas. Use: chemical weapons in World War I, manufacture of pesticides, plastics, dyes. Formula: $COCl_2$. [Early 19C. < Greek *phōs* "light"]

phos·gen·ite /fósjə nìt, fózjə-/ *n* a rare grayish fluorescent crystalline mineral consisting of a carbonate and chloride of lead. Formula: $Pb_2(Cl_2CO_3)$. [Mid-19C. Because formed from the same substances as phosgene]

phosph- *prefix* same as **phospho-** (*used before vowels*)

phos·pha·tase /fósfə tàyss, -tàyz/ *n* an enzyme that catalyzes the hydrolysis of phosphate esters and the transfer of phosphate groups [Early 20C. < PHOSPHATE]

phos·phate /fóss fàyt/ *n* a salt or ester formed by the reaction of a metal, alcohol, or other radical with phosphoric acid. A tribasic acid, phosphoric acid forms three series of phosphates by replacement of one, two, or all three of its hydrogen ions. [Late 18C. < French *phosphate* < *phosphore* "phosphorus"] —**phos·phat·ic** /foss fáttik/ *adj*

phos·phate rock *n* a sedimentary rock with a naturally high phosphate concentration. Use: fertilizer, manufacture of phosphorus compounds.

phos·pha·tide /fósfə tìd/ *n* BIOCHEM same as **phospholipid** —**phos·pha·tid·ic** /fòsfə tíddik/ *adj*

phos·pha·ti·dyl·cho·line /fòsfə tìd'l kṓ leen, foss fàttəd'l-/ *n* BIOCHEM same as **lecithin** [Mid-20C. < PHOSPHATIDE + -YL]

phos·pha·ti·dyl·eth·a·no·la·mine /fòsfə tìd'l èthə nóllə meen, foss fàttəd'l-, -nṓlə-/ *n* BIOCHEM same as **cephalin** [Mid-20C. < PHOSPHATIDE + -YL]

phos·pha·tize /fósfə tìz/ (**-tized, -tiz·ing, -tiz·es**) *v* **1.** *vt* to treat something with phosphoric acid or with a phosphate, typically to protect ferrous metal against corrosion **2.** *vti* to convert something into a phosphate or phosphates, or undergo this process —**phos·pha·ti·za·tion** /fòsfəti záysh'n/ *n*

phos·pha·tu·ri·a /fòsfə tóoree ə/ *n* the presence in the urine of a high concentration of phosphate salts, giving it a cloudy appearance. It is associated with the formation of kidney stones. [Late 19C. < PHOSPHATE] —**phos·pha·tu·ric** *adj*

phos·phene /fóss feen/ *n* a sensation of seeing light caused by pressure or electrical stimulation of the eye [Late 19C. < French *phosphène* < Greek *phōs* "light" + *phainein* "to show"]

phos·phide /fóss fīd/ *n* a compound of phosphorus with a more electropositive element, e.g., a metal

phos·phine /fóss feen/ *n* a colorless inflammable gas with a fishy smell. Use: pesticide. Formula: PH_3.

phos·phite /fóss fīt/ *n* a salt or ester of phosphorous acid

phospho- *prefix* **1.** phosphorus ○ *phosphate* **2.** phosphate ○ *phosphocreatine* [< PHOSPHORUS]

phos·pho·cre·a·tine /fòsfō kree ə teen/, **phos·pho·cre·a·tin** /-ətin/ *n* a phosphate of creatine found in muscles, providing energy for muscle contraction

phos·pho·fruc·to·ki·nase /fòsfō fruktō kī nàyss, -frooktō-, -nàyz/ *n* an enzyme that catalyzes the transfer of phosphate to a fructose compound during the metabolism of glucose

phos·pho·glu·co·mu·tase /fòsfō glookō myoo tàyss, -tàyz/ *n* an enzyme that catalyzes the breakdown and synthesis of glycogen, providing energy that can be used or stored

phos·pho·li·pase /fòsfō lí pàyss, -pàyz/ *n* an enzyme that catalyzes the hydrolysis of phospholipids in cell membranes

phos·pho·lip·id /fòsfō líppid/ *n* a phosphorus-containing lipid found in double-layered cell membranes

phos·pho·nic ac·id /foss fònnik-/ *n* CHEM same as **phosphorous acid** (sense 1)

phos·pho·ni·um /foss fōnee əm/ *n* a univalent radical derived from phosphene. Formula: PH_4. [Late 19C. < PHOSPHO- + AMMONIUM]

phos·phor /fósfər/ *n* a substance that can emit light when irradiated with particles of electromagnetic radiation [Early 17C. < Latin *phosphorus* (see PHOSPHORUS)]

phos·phor·ate /fósfə ràyt/ (**-at·ed, -at·ing, -ates**) *vt* to treat, combine, or impregnate something with phosphorus

phos·phor bronze *n* one of several alloys containing copper, tin, and phosphorus that are resistant to wear and corrosion. Use: in bearings, gears, components exposed to sea water.

phos·pho·resce /fòsfə réss/ (**-resced, -resc·ing, -resc·es**) *vi* to continue to emit light without accompanying heat after exposure to and removal of a source of stimulating radiation

phos·pho·res·cence /fòsfə réss'nss/ *n* the continued emission of light without accompanying heat after exposure to and removal of a source of stimulating radiation —**phos·pho·res·cent** *adj*

phos·phor·ic /foss fáwrik/ *adj* containing phosphorus with a valence state higher than that of the phosphorus ion or radical in an analogous phosphorous compound

phos·phor·ic ac·id *n* **1.** a water-soluble transparent solid acid. Use: fertilizer, rust-proofing, in soft drinks, pharmaceuticals, animal feeds. Formula: H_3PO_4. **2.** an acid of a group formed by the combination of phosphorus pentoxide with water, each acid having one more oxygen atom than the corresponding phosphorous acid

phos·pho·rism /fósfə rìzzəm/ *n* poisoning caused by long-term exposure to phosphorus

phos·pho·rite /fósfə rīt/ *n* **1.** a mineral deposit consisting of apatite and other phosphates **2.** GEOL same as **phosphate rock** —**phos·pho·rit·ic** /fòsfə ríttik/ *adj*

phos·pho·rol·y·sis /fòsfə róllәssiss/ *n* a process in which a phosphate group is added to a molecule, which then splits into two simpler fragments [Mid-20C. Blend of PHOSPHORUS or *phosphorylation* + HYDROLYSIS]

phos·pho·rous /fósfərəss/ *adj* relating to phosphorus with a valence state lower than that of the phosphorus ion or radical in an analogous phosphoric compound [Late 18C. < PHOSPHORUS]

phos·pho·rous ac·id *n* **1.** a white or yellowish crystalline solid that absorbs water from the atmosphere. Use: reducing agent, production of phosphite salts. Formula: H_3PO_3. **2.** an acid of a group formed by the combination of phosphorus pentoxide with water, each acid having one less oxygen atom than the corresponding phosphoric acid

phos·pho·rus /fósfərəss/ *n* **1.** a poisonous nonmetallic chemical element that ignites in air and glows in the dark. Use: matches, fireworks, incendiary devices, fertilizers. Symbol **P**. See table at **element** **2.** a phosphorescent substance or object [Early 17C. Via Latin < Greek *phōsphoros* "morning star," literally "light-bringing" < *phōs* "light"]

phos·pho·rus pent·ox·ide, phos·pho·rus ox·ide *n* a flammable white solid that absorbs moisture from the air. Source: burning phosphorus in air. Use: manufacture of phosphoric acid. Formula: P_2O_5.

phos·pho·ryl /fósfəril/ *n* a chemical group, usually with a valence of three, consisting of one phosphorus atom and one oxygen atom

phos·pho·ryl·ase /fósfərə làyss, -làyz/ *n* an enzyme that catalyzes the phosphorolysis of a molecule

phos·pho·ryl·ate /fósfərə làyt/ (**-at·ed, -at·ing, -ates**) *vt* to add a phosphate group to an organic molecule in order to produce an organic phosphate —**phos·pho·ryl·a·tion** /fòsfərə láysh'n/ *n* —**phos·pho·ryl·a·tive** /fósfərə làytiv/ *adj*

phot /fōt/ *n* the centimeter-gram-second unit of illumination equal to one lumen per square centimeter [Late 19C. Via French < Greek *phōt-* "light"]

phot- *prefix* same as **photo-** (*used before vowels*)

pho·tic /fōtik/ *adj* **1.** relating to light, especially when produced by living organisms **2.** describes the area of the ocean where light penetrates and photosynthesis occurs [Mid-19C. < Greek *phōt-* "light"]

Pho·ti·us /fōtee əss/ (820?–891?) Byzantine churchman and scholar. He was patriarch of Constantinople (858–867 and 877–886), initiating the spread of Orthodox Christianity in Eastern Europe.

pho·to /fōtō/ *n* (*plural* **-tos**) PHOTOGRAPHY same as **photograph** ■ *vt* (**-toed, -to·ing, -tos**) to take a photograph or photographs of somebody or something [Mid-19C. Shortening]

photo- *prefix* **1.** light, radiant energy ○ *photochemistry* ○ *photic* **2.** photographic ○ *photomontage* **3.** photoelectric ○ *photocurrent* [< Greek *phōt-* "light" < Indo-European, "to shine"]

pho·to·ac·tin·ic /fōtō ak tínnik/ *adj* emitting radiation similar to visible and ultraviolet light in its chemical effects on substances such as photographic emulsions

pho·to·ac·tive /fōtō áktiv/ *adj* exhibiting a reaction to electromagnetic radiation, especially visible light, either by chemical reaction or photoelectrically

pho·to·au·to·troph /fōtō áwtə tròf, -trōf/ *n* an organism that derives its energy exclusively from light and uses it to synthesize food —**pho·to·au·to·troph·ic** /-awtə tróffik, -trōfik/ *adj*

pho·to·bi·ol·o·gy /fōtō bī óllәjee/ *n* a branch of biology concerned with the interaction of living organisms with light —**pho·to·bi·o·log·i·cal** /-bī ə lójjik'l/ *adj* —**pho·to·bi·ol·o·gist** *n*

pho·to·bi·ot·ic /fōtō bī óttik/ *adj* describes organisms that need light in order to live and grow

pho·to·call /fōtō kàwl/ *n* MEDIA same as **photo opportunity**

pho·to·ca·tal·y·sis /fōtō kə tálləssiss/ *n* the acceleration or deceleration of the speed at which a chemical reaction occurs, caused by electromagnetic radiation and especially visible light

pho·to·cath·ode /fōtō ká thōd/ *n* an electrode that emits electrons when exposed to electromagnetic radiation such as light. Use: in television and digital cameras and photoelectric cells.

pho·to CD *n* a compact disk that stores images from photographs that can be displayed on a computer or television screen

pho·to·cell /fōtō sèl/ *n* PHYS same as **photoelectric cell**

pho·to·chem·i·cal /fōtō kémmik'l/ *adj* relating to photochemistry —**pho·to·chem·i·cal·ly** *adv*

pho·to·chem·i·cal smog *n* air pollution caused by the effect of strong sunlight on nitrogen dioxide and hydrocarbons emitted by motor vehicles, creating a harmful haze of minute droplets in the air

pho·to·chem·is·try /fōtō kémmistree/ *n* a branch of chemistry that studies the effect of radiation, especially of visible and ultraviolet light, on chemical reactions and the emission of radiation by chemical reactions —**pho·to·chem·ist** *n*

pho·to·che·mo·ther·a·py /fōtō keemō thérrəpee/ *n* MED same as **photopheresis** —**pho·to·che·mo·ther·a·peu·tic** /-therə pyootik/ *adj*

pho·to·chrom·ic /fōtō krómik/ *adj* changing color or becoming darker or lighter in color as light increases or decreases in intensity

pho·to·co·ag·u·la·tion /fōtō kō àggyə láysh'n/ *n* the use of a high-energy light source such as a laser to harden tissue for surgical repair, especially in eye injuries

pho·to·com·po·si·tion /fōtō kòmpə zísh'n/ *n* a typesetting process that involves projecting the characters that are to be printed onto photographic film and then making printing plates from the film —**pho·to·com·pose** /-kəm pōz/ *vt* —**pho·to·com·pos·er** *n*

pho·to·con·duc·tion /fōtō kən dúksh'n/ *n* the conduction of electricity resulting from the absorption of electromagnetic radiation, especially visible light

pho·to·con·duc·tiv·i·ty /fōtō kòn duk tívvətee/ *n* an increase in the electrical conductivity of a substance on exposure to electromagnetic radiation, especially visible light —**pho·to·con·duc·tive** /-kən dúktiv/ *adj* —**pho·to·con·duc·tor** /-dúktər/ *n*

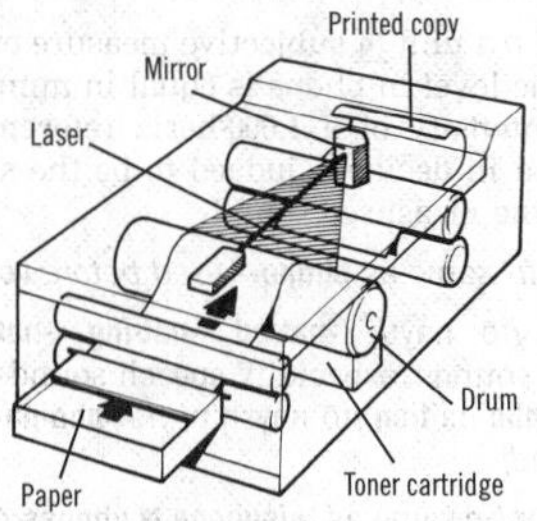

photocopier

pho·to·cop·i·er /fōtə kòppee ər/ *n* a machine that uses a photographic process to produce an almost instant copy of something printed, written, or drawn

pho·to·cop·y /fōtə kòppee/ *n* (*plural* **-ies**) a copy of something printed, written, or drawn that is produced almost instantly by a photographic process in a machine designed for this purpose ■ *vti* (**-ied, -y·ing, -ies**) to make a photocopy of something, or be photocopied

pho·to·cur·rent /fōtō kùr ənt, -kùrrənt/ *n* an electric current that is produced by and varies with the intensity of illumination. The current is a result of photoconductivity or of the photoelectric or photovoltaic effect.

pho·to·de·com·po·si·tion /fōtō dee kòmpə zísh'n/ *n* the breakdown of a chemical compound into simpler substances by means of incident electromagnetic energy, especially visible light

pho·to·de·grad·a·ble /fōtō di gráydəb'l/ *adj* able to be decomposed into simpler substances through prolonged exposure to incident electromagnetic energy, especially ultraviolet light

pho·to·der·ma·tol·o·gy /fōtō dùrmə tóllәjee/ *n* a branch of photobiology dealing with the adverse effects of sunlight on the skin and the therapeutic use of artificial light —**pho·to·der·ma·to·log·ic** /-dùrmətə lójjik/ *adj*

pho·to·di·ode /fōtō dī ōd/ *n* a semiconductor device in which the flow of current is controlled by the intensity of light and that can therefore be used to detect light

pho·to·dis·in·te·gra·tion /fōtō diss intə gráysh'n/ *n* the ejection of a proton, neutron, or other elementary particle from an atomic nucleus as a result of its absorption of a photon, usually in the form of gamma radiation —**pho·to·dis·in·te·grate** /-diss íntə gràyt/ *vti*

pho·to·driv·en /fṓtō drìvvən/ *adj* describes a physical or chemical reaction initiated by the absorption of photons

pho·to·du·pli·cate /fṓtō dóopli kàyt/ *vt* (**-cat·ed, -cat·ing, -cates**) to make a photocopy of something ■ *n* a copy of something made using a photocopier —**pho·to·du·pli·ca·tion** /-dòopli káysh'n/ *n*

pho·to·dy·nam·ic /fṓtō dī námmik/ *adj* **1.** OF PHOTODYNAMICS relating to photodynamics or to the energy of light **2.** INVOLVING ADVERSE REACTION TO LIGHT bringing about or enhancing the toxic effects of some wavelengths of light, especially ultraviolet, on living tissue **3.** OF LASER CANCER TREATMENT relating to or used to describe a cancer treatment in which the drug used is activated by a laser beam —**pho·to·dy·nam·i·cal·ly** *adv*

pho·to·dy·nam·ics /fṓtō dī námmiks/ *n* a branch of biology dealing with the effects of light on living organisms (*takes a singular verb*)

pho·to·e·lec·tric /fṓtō i léktrik/, **pho·to·e·lec·tri·cal** /-léktrik'l/ *adj* relating to electrical effects that are due to the action of electromagnetic radiation, especially visible light —**pho·to·e·lec·tri·cal·ly** *adv* —**pho·to·e·lec·tric·i·ty** /-i lek tríssətee, -ee lek-/ *n*

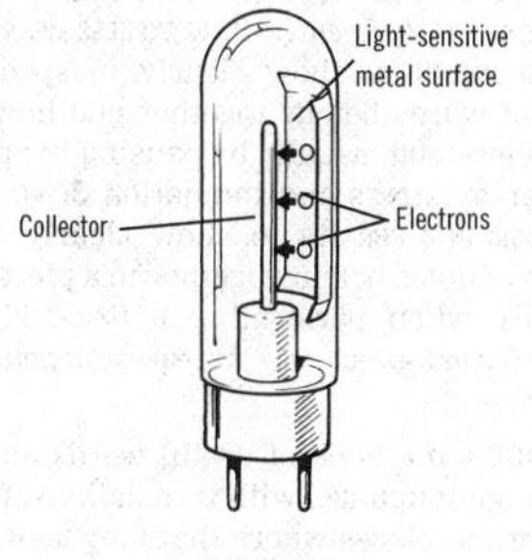

photoelectric cell

pho·to·e·lec·tric cell *n* a solid-state device sensitive to varying levels of light that is used to generate or control an electric current, e.g., in burglar alarms, smoke detectors, and exposure meters

pho·to·e·lec·tric ef·fect *n* the emission of electrons from a substance exposed to electromagnetic radiation

pho·to·e·lec·tron /fṓtō i lék tròn/ *n* an electron released from the surface of a substance that has been struck by a photon of electromagnetic radiation

pho·to·e·mis·sion /fṓtō i mísh'n/ *n* the release of electrons from a substance by incident electromagnetic radiation —**pho·to·e·mis·sive** *adj*

pho·to·en·grave /fṓtō in gráyv/ (**-graved, -grav·ing, -graves**) *vt* to make a copy of something using photoengraving —**pho·to·en·grav·er** *n*

pho·to·en·grav·ing /fṓtō in gráyving/ *n* **1.** PROCESS OF ETCHING PRINTING PLATE the process of making a printing plate by photographing an image onto a metal plate and then etching the image **2.** PRINTING PLATE MADE BY PHOTOENGRAVING a printing plate made by photographing an image onto a metal plate and then etching the image **3.** PRINT MADE BY PHOTOENGRAVING a print made by photographing an image onto a metal plate and then etching the image

~~**photoes**~~ incorrect spelling of **photos**

pho·to·es·say /fṓtō èssay/, **pho·to es·say** *n* MEDIA same as **photo story**

pho·to fin·ish *n* **1.** the end of a race in which two or more contestants are so close that the result must be determined from a photograph taken as they cross the finish line **2.** a race or competition won by a very small margin

pho·to·fis·sion /fṓtō físh'n/ *n* nuclear fission induced by gamma rays

Pho·to·fit /fṓtō fit/ *tdmk* a trademark for a way of constructing a photograph of somebody using photographs of individual facial features arranged to fit a description closely. This method is often used to try to identify criminals.

pho·to·flash /fṓtō flàsh/ *n* PHOTOGRAPHY same as **flashbulb**

pho·to·flood /fṓtō flùd/ *n* a very bright incandescent lamp used in photography and filming

pho·to·fluor·o·gram /fṓtə flóorə gràm, -fláwrə-/ *n* a photograph of an image produced using X-rays

pho·to·fluor·og·ra·phy /fṓtō floo róggrəfee, -flaw-/ *n* a technique that photographs an X-ray image onto a fluorescent screen for diagnostic purposes —**pho·to·fluor·o·graph·ic** /-floorə gráffik, -flawrə-/ *adj*

pho·tog /fə tóg/ *n* a photographer (*informal*)

pho·to·gen·ic /fṓtə jénnik/ *adj* **1.** LOOKING ATTRACTIVE IN PHOTOGRAPHS tending to look good in photographs **2.** BIOL PRODUCING LIGHT describes an organism that produces its own light, especially by phosphorescence **3.** MED CAUSED BY LIGHT describes a physical reaction such as an epileptic episode that is caused or aggravated by light —**pho·to·gen·i·cal·ly** *adv*

pho·to·ge·ol·o·gy /fṓtō jee óllәjee/ *n* the study and identification of landforms and other geologic features by means of aerial and satellite photographs —**pho·to·ge·o·log·ic** /-jee ə lójjik/ *adj* —**pho·to·ge·o·log·i·cal** *adj* —**pho·to·ge·ol·o·gist** *n*

pho·to·gram /fṓtə gràm/ *n* a photographic image produced without a camera, usually by placing an object on or near a piece of film or light-sensitive paper and exposing it to light

pho·to·gram·me·try /fṓtə grámmətree/ *n* the making of measurements or scale drawings from photographs, especially using aerial photography in the construction of maps —**pho·to·gram·met·ric** /fṓtəgrə méttrik/ *adj* —**pho·to·gram·me·trist** *n*

pho·to·graph /fṓtə gràf/ *n* PICTURE PRODUCED WITH CAMERA an image produced on light-sensitive film or array inside a camera, especially a print or slide made from the processed image, or a reproduction in a newspaper, magazine, or book ■ *v* (**-graphed, -graph·ing, -graphs**) **1.** *vti* TAKE PHOTOGRAPH OF SOMEBODY OR SOMETHING to produce an image of something or somebody using a camera **2.** *vi* BE PHOTOGRAPHED WITH PARTICULAR RESULT to be able to be photographed, or to have a particular quality or appearance in a photograph ○ *Scenes like this photograph best in bright sunlight.* —**pho·tog·ra·pher** /fə tóggrəfər/ *n*

pho·to·graph·ic /fṓtə gráffik/ *adj* **1.** relating to, used in, or produced by photography **2.** as accurate and detailed as a photograph ○ *a witness who recounted the incident in photographic detail* —**pho·to·graph·i·cal·ly** *adv*

pho·to·graph·ic mag·ni·tude *n* the magnitude of a star determined by measuring its size on a photographic plate. Depending on the color of the star, photographic magnitude and visual magnitude can differ because the eye and standard photographic plates have different color sensitivities.

pho·to·graph·ic mem·o·ry *n* the ability to recall information, especially visual images, with great accuracy and clarity

pho·tog·ra·phy /fə tóggrəfee/ *n* **1.** the art, hobby, or profession of taking photographs, and developing and printing the film or processing the digitized array image **2.** the process of recording images by exposing light-sensitive film or array to light or other forms of radiation

pho·to·gra·vure /fṓtə grə vyóor/ *n* the process of using photography to make a printing plate with an image engraved into it [Late 19C. < French < *photo-* "photo-" + *gravure* "engraving" < *graver* "engrave"]

pho·to·in·duced /fṓtō in dóost/ *adj* initiated through exposure to light —**pho·to·in·duc·tion** /-dúksh'n/ *n* —**pho·to·in·duc·tive** /-dúktiv/ *adj*

pho·to·in·ter·pre·ta·tion /fṓtō in turprə táysh'n/ *n* the science of identifying objects in photographs, especially in order to determine their potential military or topographic importance —**pho·to·in·ter·pret·er** /-in túrprətər/ *n*

pho·to·i·on·i·za·tion /fṓtō ī əni záysh'n/ *n* the removal of one or more electrons from an atom or molecule by absorption of a photon of electromagnetic radiation, especially visible or ultraviolet light. The free electrons in the ionosphere are believed to be a product of molecular absorption of ultraviolet radiation from the Sun. —**pho·to·i·on·ize** /-ī ə nīz/ *vti*

pho·to·jour·nal·ism /fṓtō júrn'l ìzzəm/ *n* a form of journalism in which photographs play a more important role than the accompanying text —**pho·to·jour·nal·ist** *n* —**pho·to·jour·nal·is·tic** /-jurn'l ístik/ *adj*

pho·to·ki·ne·sis /fṓtō ki néessiss, -kī-/ *n* the movement of an organism when stimulated by light —**pho·to·ki·net·ic** /-ki néttik, -kī-/ *adj* —**pho·to·ki·net·i·cal·ly** *adv*

pho·to·li·thog·ra·phy /fṓtō li thóggrəfee/ *n* **1.** the process of creating lithographs using photographic methods **2.** the process of producing integrated circuits and printed circuit boards by photographing the circuit pattern on a photosensitive substrate and then chemically etching away the background —**pho·to·lith·o·graph** /-líthə gràf/ *n* —**pho·to·li·thog·ra·pher** *n* —**pho·to·lith·o·graph·ic** /-lithə gráffik/ *adj* —**pho·to·lith·o·graph·i·cal·ly** *adv*

pho·to·lu·mi·nes·cence /fṓtō loomə néss'nss/ *n* the emission of light from a substance as a result of the absorption of electromagnetic radiation. The frequency of the light emitted is lower than that absorbed. —**pho·to·lu·mi·nes·cent** *adj*

pho·tol·y·sis /fō tólləsiss/ *n* the irreversible decomposition of a chemical compound as a result of the absorption of electromagnetic radiation, especially visible light —**pho·to·lyt·ic** /fṓtə líttik/ *adj* —**pho·to·lyt·i·cal·ly** *adv*

pho·to·map /fṓtə màp/ *n* a map produced by marking place names, grid lines, and other information on an aerial photograph ■ *vti* (**-mapped, -map·ping, -maps**) to make a photomap of an area

pho·to·mask /fṓtō màsk/ *n* ELECTRONICS same as **mask** *n* (sense 7)

pho·to·me·chan·i·cal /fṓtō mə kánnik'l/ *adj* describes a method of producing printed text or images that uses photography —**pho·to·me·chan·i·cal·ly** *adv*

pho·to mes·sa·ging *n* TELECOM same as **picture messaging**

pho·tom·e·try /fō tómmətree/ *n* **1.** the measurement of the luminous intensities of visible light sources. This is sometimes expanded to include near-infrared and near-ultraviolet light. **2.** the branch of physics concerned with the measurement of the intensity of light —**pho·tom·e·ter** *n* —**pho·to·met·ric** /fṓtə méttrik/ *adj* —**pho·to·met·ri·cal·ly** *adv* —**pho·tom·e·trist** *n*

pho·to·mi·cro·graph /fṓtō mīkrə gràf/ *n* a photograph made of something seen through a microscope —**pho·to·mi·cro·graph·ic** /-mīkrə gráffik/ *adj* —**pho·to·mi·crog·ra·phy** /-mī króggrəfee/ *n*

pho·to·mon·tage /fṓtō mon ta͟azh/ *n* **1.** the technique of combining a number of photographs or parts of photographs to form a composite picture, used especially in art and advertising **2.** a composite picture made up of many photographs or parts of photographs, used especially in art and advertising

pho·to·mo·sa·ic /fṓtō mō záy ik/ *n* a large picture made up of many photographs, e.g., one combining aerial photographs to produce a detailed picture of an area

pho·to·mul·ti·pli·er /fṓtō múlti plī ər/, **pho·to·mul·ti·pli·er tube** *n* an evacuated electronic device used to convert low-intensity electromagnetic radiation, especially visible light, into an electric current, and to amplify this current significantly

pho·ton /fṓ tòn/ *n* a quantum of visible light or other form of electromagnetic radiation demonstrating both particle and wave properties. A photon has neither mass nor electric charge but possesses energy and momentum. —**pho·ton·ic** /fō tónnik/ *adj*

pho·to·neg·a·tive /fṓtō néggətiv/ *adj* **1.** describes a conductive material whose electrical conductivity decreases in response to increasing illumination **2.** describes organisms that move away from a source of light

pho·ton·ics /fō tónniks/ *n* the scientific study of the properties and applications of light and other forms of radiant energy, ranging from the generation of energy to information processing (*takes a singular verb*) —**pho·ton·ic** *adj*

pho·to·nu·cle·ar /fṓtō nóoklee ər/ *adj* relating to a nuclear reaction caused by the absorption of a photon, usually in the form of gamma radiation, by an atomic nucleus

pho·to-off·set *n* a method of offset printing in which plates are created using photographic methods

pho·to op·por·tu·ni·ty, **pho·to op** *n* an opportunity for the media to photograph a politician or other public figure doing something newsworthy, especially when it is deliberately staged to produce favorable publicity

pho·to·pe·ri·od /fṓtō peéree əd/ *n* the daily cycle of light and darkness that affects the behavior and physiological functions of organisms —**pho·to·pe·ri·od·ic** /-peeree óddik/ *adj* —**pho·to·pe·ri·od·i·cal·ly** *adv*

pho·to·pe·ri·od·ism /fṓtō peéree ə dìzzəm/ *n* the influence of the daily cycle of light and darkness on the physiology and behavior of an organism

pho·to·phe·re·sis /fṓtəfə reéssiss/, **pho·to·pho·re·sis** *n* a technique used to enhance the immune system in which a photoactive drug such as psoralen is injected into the body. Blood is removed, exposed to ultraviolet light to activate the drug, then returned to the body to fight the disease.

pho·to·phil·ic /fṓtə fíllik/, **pho·toph·i·lous** /fō tóffiləss/ *adj* describes an organism such as a plant that grows well in strong light

pho·to·pho·bi·a /fṓtə fṓbee ə/ *n* **1.** very low tolerance of the eye for light, sometimes a symptom of disease or migraine **2.** an irrational fear and avoidance of light or lighted spaces

pho·to·pho·bic /fṓtə fṓbik/ *adj* **1.** AFFECTED BY PHOTOPHOBIA relating to or having a condition in which the eye has very low tolerance to light **2.** BEING AFRAID OF LIGHT having an irrational fear of light **3.** GROWING WELL IN REDUCED LIGHT describes an organism such as a plant that grows well in reduced light

pho·to·phore /fṓtə fàwr/ *n* a luminous light organ on many deep-sea and some nocturnal fish, squids, and shrimps

pho·to·pho·re·sis *n* MED same as **photopheresis**

pho·to·phos·phor·y·la·tion /fṓtō fòsfəri láysh'n/ *n* the process in photosynthesis that converts light energy to stored energy in plants and bacteria

pho·to·pi·a /fō tṓpee ə/ *n* normal vision during daylight, when the activity of the cones in the retina enables the eye to perceive color —**pho·to·pic** /fō tṓpik, -tóppik/ *adj*

pho·to·pig·ment /fṓtō pígmənt/ *n* a light-absorbing chemical that converts light into biochemical energy, e.g., in the rods and cones of the eye

pho·to·pol·y·mer /fṓtō póllәmәr/ *n* a light-sensitive plastic whose physical properties change on exposure to visible or ultraviolet light

pho·to·pos·i·tive /fṓtō pózzətiv/ *adj* **1.** describes a conductive material whose electrical conductivity increases in response to increasing illumination **2.** describes organisms that move toward a light source

pho·to·re·al·ism /fṓtō reé ə lìzzəm/ *n* an artistic style, e.g., in painting or sculpture, that produces an accurate and detailed representation of the subject without attempting to conceal any unattractive aspects —**pho·to·re·al·ist** *adj, n* —**pho·to·re·al·is·tic** /-reè ə lístik/ *adj*

pho·to·re·cep·tion /fṓtō ri sépsh'n/ *n* the perception, absorption, and use of light, e.g., for vision in animals or photosynthesis in plants —**pho·to·re·cep·tive** /-séptiv/ *adj*

pho·to·re·cep·tor /fṓtō ri séptər/ *n* a cell or organ that responds to light. Simple receptors may sense only changes in light intensity while more complex ones such as the eye may also form images of objects in the visual field.

pho·to·re·con·nais·sance /fṓtō ri kónnəss'nss/ *n* reconnaissance undertaken using cameras, usually from an aircraft

pho·to·re·sist /fṓtō ri zíst/ *n* a photosensitive material that is applied to a surface, exposed to visible or ultraviolet light, and developed prior to chemical etching during the photolithographic process

pho·to·res·pi·ra·tion /fṓtō respə ráysh'n/ *n* a pathway in photosynthesis in some plants in which oxygen is absorbed and carbon dioxide released

pho·to·sen·si·tive /fṓtō sénssətiv/ *adj* reacting to incident electromagnetic radiation, especially visible, infrared, and ultraviolet light —**pho·to·sen·si·tiv·i·ty** /-sènssə tívvətee/ *n*

pho·to·sen·si·tize /fṓtō sénssi tīz/ (**-tized, -tiz·ing, -tiz·es**) *vt* to increase the sensitivity of an organism or substance to electromagnetic radiation, especially visible light —**pho·to·sen·si·ti·za·tion** /-sènssəti záysh'n/ *n* —**pho·to·sen·si·tiz·er** *n*

pho·to·sphere /fṓtə sfeer/ *n* the intensely bright gaseous outer layer of a star, especially the Sun. Sunspots and faculae are features of the photosphere. —**pho·to·spher·ic** /fṓtə sfeérik, -sférrik/ *adj*

pho·to sto·ry *n* a collection of photographs in a magazine or book, often accompanied by a short commentary, that tells a story

pho·to·syn·the·sis /fṓtō sínthəssiss/ *n* a process by which green plants and other organisms turn carbon dioxide and water into carbohydrates and oxygen, using light energy trapped by chlorophyll —**pho·to·syn·thet·ic** /-sin théttik/ *adj* —**pho·to·syn·thet·i·cal·ly** *adv*

pho·to·syn·the·size /fṓtō sínthə sīz/ (**-sized, -siz·ing, -siz·es**) *vti* to produce carbohydrates and oxygen by photosynthesis [Early 20C. < PHOTOSYNTHESIS]

pho·to·sys·tem /fṓtə sìstəm/ *n* either of two reactions in the light phase of photosynthesis, the first (**photosystem I**) proceeding best with longer wavelengths of light, the second (**photosystem II**) with shorter wavelengths

pho·to·tax·is /fṓtō táksiss/ *n* movement of an organism either toward or away from a source of light [Late 19C] —**pho·to·tac·tic** *adj* —**pho·to·tac·ti·cal·ly** /-táktikəlee/ *adv*

pho·to·ther·a·py /fṓtō thérrəpee/ *n* the use of light, especially ultraviolet light, in the treatment of disease —**pho·to·ther·a·peu·tic** /-therə pyoótik/ *adj*

pho·to·tox·ic /fṓtō tóksik/ *adj* making the skin unusually sensitive to light and subject to damage by light, e.g., by sunburn —**pho·to·tox·ic·i·ty** /-tok síssətee/ *n*

pho·to·tran·sis·tor /fṓtō tran zístər/ *n* a light-sensitive junction transistor that amplifies the base current as the illumination increases

pho·to·tro·pic /fṓtə trṓpik, -tróppik/ *adj* describes organisms that can utilize light as a source of energy —**pho·to·troph** /fṓtə tròf, -trṓf/ *n*

pho·tot·ro·pism /fō tóttrə pìzzəm/ *n* the tendency of an organism to grow toward or away from a source of light

pho·tot·ro·py /fō tóttrəpee/ *n* a property of some solids whereby they change color in relation to the wavelength of the incident electromagnetic radiation, especially visible light

pho·to·tube /fṓtō tōōb/ *n* an electron tube that uses a cathode to convert visible light into electrical current at a rate proportional to the intensity of the illumination

pho·to·type·set /fṓtō tīp sèt/ (**-set, -set·ting, -sets**) *vt* to prepare text for printing by the use of photocomposition

pho·to·type·set·ting /fṓtō tīp sètting/ *n* PRINTING same as **photocomposition**

pho·to·vol·ta·ic /fṓtō vol táy ik, -vòl-/ *adj* able to generate a current or voltage when exposed to visible light or other electromagnetic radiation

pho·to·vol·ta·ic cell *n* a photoelectric cell that detects and measures light intensity using the potential difference that arises between unlike materials when they are exposed to electromagnetic radiation

pho·to·vol·ta·ic ef·fect *n* the production of a potential difference across the junction of unlike materials or in a nonhomogeneous semiconductor material by the absorption of visible light or other electromagnetic radiation

phrag·mi·tes /frag mī́ teez/ *n* an invasive reed of the grass family with stems that can grow as tall as 20 ft. (6 m), found around the world in marshes and wetlands. Genus: *Phragmites.* [Early 20C. Via modern Latin < Greek *phragmitēs* "growing in hedges" < *phragma* "fence"]

phras·al /fráyz'l/ *adj* consisting of or relating to a phrase

phras·al verb *n* a verb followed by an adverb, a preposition, or both, used with an idiomatic meaning that is often quite different from the literal meaning of the individual words. Examples include "put up with," meaning "tolerate," and "stand for," meaning "represent."

phrase /frayz/ *n* **1.** GRAMMATICAL UNIT a string of words that form a grammatical unit, usually within a clause or sentence **2.** FIXED EXPRESSION a string of words that are used together and have an idiomatic meaning **3.** BRIEF PITHY UTTERANCE a string of words, usually a short one, that memorably encapsulates something, e.g., a particular truth or sentiment or the character of a person or time ○ *We had certainly made progress, but this was still, in Churchill's phrase, only "the end of the beginning."* **4.** LITERAT WORDS SPOKEN AS GROUP a group of words that form a unit of meaning or rhythm in prose or poetry, often separated by punctuation in writing and by pauses in speech **5.** MUSIC MELODIC DIVISION a sequence of notes that form a unit of melody within a piece of music **6.** DANCE PART OF CHOREOGRAPHIC PATTERN a short sequence of steps within a longer pattern of dance movements ■ *v* (**phrased, phras·ing, phras·es**) **1.** *vt* EXPRESS SOMETHING IN PARTICULAR WAY to use a particular choice and order of words to express something in speech or writing ○ *She was saying more or less the same thing, but she phrased it differently.* **2.** *vt* EXPRESS MEANING THROUGH PATTERNED SPEECH to show clearly in speech which groups of words belong together and how they are to be understood, usually by pausing in appropriate places or by stress and intonation **3.** *vti* MUSIC SEPARATE MUSIC INTO PHRASES to show clearly which sequences of notes belong together in a piece of music, especially when performing it [Mid-16C. Via Latin < Greek *phrasis* "speech, way of speaking" < *phrazein* "show, explain"]

phrase book *n* a book of useful words and phrases in a foreign language, with translations, for the use of visitors to places where that language is spoken

phrase·mak·er /fráyz màykər/ *n* a maker of impressive phrases in speech or writing —**phrase·mak·ing** *n*

phrase mark·er *n* a representation of the structure of a sentence, usually in the form of a tree diagram

phra·se·o·gram /fráyzee ə gràm/ *n* a symbol used to represent a phrase in shorthand

phra·se·o·graph /fráyzee ə gràf/ *n* a phrase that is or can be represented by a symbol, usually in shorthand

phra·se·ol·o·gy /fràyzee óllәjee/ *n* **1.** the way words and phrases are chosen or used **2.** the phrases used in a particular sphere of activity [Mid-17C. < modern Latin *phraseologia* < Greek *phrasis* (see PHRASE)] —**phra·se·o·log·i·cal** /-ə lójjik'l/ *adj*

phrase-struc·ture gram·mar *n* a grammar that describes the structure and linear sequence of a sentence in terms of the phrases of which it is made up

phras·ing /fráyzing/ *n* **1.** the way words are chosen and put together to express something, or the words themselves **2.** the way sequences of notes are grouped together to form units of melody in a piece of music, especially when it is performed

phra·try /fráytree/ (*plural* **-tries**) *n* **1.** a group of clans claiming descent from a common ancestor **2.** in ancient Greece, a kinship group [Mid-19C. < Greek *phratria* < *phratēr* "clansman, brother"] —**phra·tric** *adj*

phreak /freek/ (**phreaked, phreak·ing, phreaks**) *vi* to use computer and telecommunications skills illegally to break into a telephone system to make free long-distance calls (*slang*) [Late 20C. Alteration of FREAK[1], after PHONE[1]] —**phreak·ing** *n*

phre·at·ic /free áttik/ *adj* **1.** describes soil or rock below the water level, in which all the pores and intergranular spaces are full of water **2.** describes an explosion caused by ground water coming into contact with ascending magma, e.g., in a volcano [Late 19C. < Greek *phreat-* "well, cistern"]

phre·at·o·mag·mat·ic /free àttō mag máttik/ *adj* describes a volcanic eruption caused by contact between magma and ground water in which magma, gases, and steam are expelled —**phre·at·o·mag·ma·tism** /-mágmə tìzzəm/ *n*

phren·ic /frénnik, freénik/ *adj* **1.** belonging to or supplying the diaphragm **2.** belonging to or associated with the mind [Early 18C. < French *phrénique* < Greek *phrēn* "mind, heart, diaphragm"]

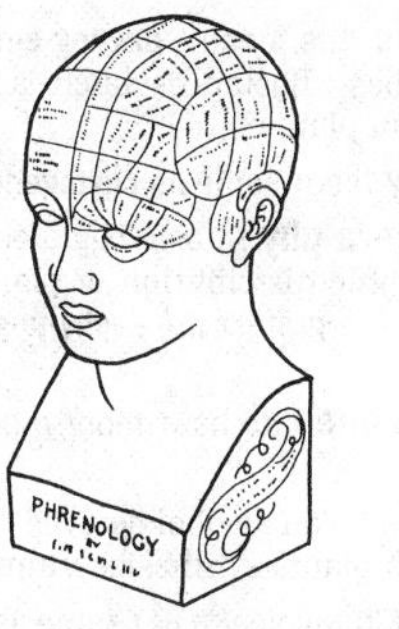

phrenology

phre·nol·o·gy /frə nóllәjee/ *n* the study of the bumps on the outside of the skull, based on the now discredited theory that these bumps reflect somebody's character [Early 19C. < Greek *phrēn* "mind, heart, diaphragm"] —**phren·o·log·i·cal** /frènnə lójjik'l, freènə-/ *adj* —**phre·nol·o·gist** *n*

Phryg·i·a /fríjjee ə/ ancient country in Asia Minor, in present-day west central Turkey. It reached the height of its importance in the 8th century B.C.

Phryg·i·an /fríjjee ən/ *n* **1.** somebody who came from ancient Phrygia **2.** an extinct Anatolian language spoken in ancient Phrygia —**Phryg·i·an** *adj*

Phryg·i·an cap *n* same as **liberty cap** [Because worn by the ancient Phrygians]

Phryg·i·an mode *n* a scale of notes originating in ancient Greek music and consisting of the eight notes of the diatonic scale rising from E to E

PHS *abbr* Public Health Service

phthal·ate /thálayt/ *n* a chemical compound used as a plastic softener and in many personal grooming products. It is reported to be a possible cause of reproductive or developmental problems because it mimics a natural hormone. [Mid-19C. < PHTHALIC ACID]

phthal·ein /thá leèn, tháy leèn/ *n* an organic dye obtained by reacting phthalic anhydride with a phenol [Late 19C. < PHTHALIC ACID]

phthal·ic ac·id /thàllik-/ *n* one of three isomers obtained by the oxidation of benzene derivatives. Use: dyes, perfumes, pharmaceuticals, synthetic fibers. Formula: $C_6H_4(CO_2H)_2$. [< shortening of NAPHTHALENE]

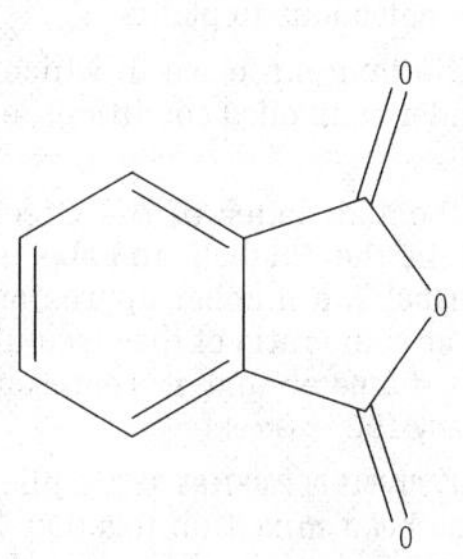

phthalic anhydride

phthal·ic an·hy·dride *n* a white crystalline organic compound. Source: naphthalene. Use: manufacture of dyes, insecticides, plastics. Formula: $C_6H_4(CO)_2O$.

phthal·o·cy·a·nine /thàllō sí̄ ə neèn/ *n* **1.** a bright greenish blue crystalline compound. Source: phthalic anhydride. Use: pigment, coating for CD-ROMs, anticancer agent. Formula: $(C_6H_4C_2N)_4N_4H_2$. **2.** a blue or green pigment developed as a metal-substituted form of phthalocyanine. Use: in enamels, plastics, printing inks, wallpaper, linoleum.

phthi·ri·a·sis /thi rí̄ əssis, thī-/ *n* an infestation of the pubic hair of human beings with lice whose bite can irritate the skin [Late 16C. Via Latin < Greek *phtheiriasis* < *phtheirian* "be infested with lice" < *phtheir* "louse"]

phthis·ic /tízzik, thízz-/ *n* MED same as **phthisis** (sense 1) ■ *adj also* **phthis·i·cal** /tízzik'l, thízz-/ relating to or having phthisis [14C. Via French and Latin < Greek *phthisikos* "consumptive" < *phthisis* (see PHTHISIS)]

phthi·sis /thī́sis, tī́ss-/ *n* **1.** a disease or condition marked by wasting of the body **2.** a disease of the respiratory system, especially asthma or tuberculosis (*archaic*) [Mid-16C. Via Latin < Greek *phthisis* "consumption" < *phthinein* "waste away"]

Phu·ket /poo két/ **1.** resort island off the western coast of Thailand. Population: 231,200 (2002). Area: 206 sq. mi./534 sq. km. **2.** resort town and port on southeastern Phuket Island. Population: 60,000 (2002).

phul·ka·ri /poòl kaàree/ *n* **1.** *S Asia* an embroidered shawl or cloth used on special occasions, especially associated with weddings **2.** a style of embroidery using long thin stitches made close together [Late 19C. < Hindi]

phyco- *prefix* relating to seaweed or algae ○ *phycology* [< Greek *phukos* "seaweed"]

phy·co·cy·a·nin /fī̀kō sí̄ ənin/ *n* a protein pigment in cyanobacteria

phy·co·er·y·thrin /fī̀kō érrithrin/ *n* a red protein pigment in red algae

phy·col·o·gy /fī kóllәjee/ *n* BOT same as **algology** —**phy·co·log·i·cal** /fī̀kə lójjik'l/ *adj* —**phy·col·o·gist** *n*

phy·co·my·cete /fī̀kō mī́ seèt, -mī́ seèt/ *n* a mold resembling algae. Class: Phycomycetes. [Mid-20C. < Greek *phukos* "seaweed" + *mukētes*, plural of *mukēs* "fungus"]

Phyfe /fī́f/, **Duncan** (1768–1854) Scottish-born US furniture designer. His neoclassical approach helped to define the federal style in the United States.

phyl- *prefix* same as **phylo-** (*used before vowels*)

phy·la BIOL, LANGUAGE plural of **phylum**

phylactery

phy·lac·ter·y /fi láktəree/ (*plural* **-ies**) *n* **1.** either of two small leather boxes containing slips of paper with scriptures written on them, traditionally worn by Jewish men during morning weekday prayers as reminders of their religious duties (*often used in the plural*) **2.** a reminder of something important [14C. Via Latin < Greek *phulaktērion* "amulet" < *phulaktēr* "guard" < *phulassein* "to guard"]

phy·le /fī́lee/ (*plural* **-lae** /-lee/) *n* any of a number of clans into which some peoples of ancient Greece were divided. The phylae formed political and administrative units within the large city-states. [Mid-19C. < Greek *phulē* "tribe"] —**phy·lic** *adj*

phy·let·ic /fī léttik/ *adj* relating to the hereditary descent of a species or its development over time [Late 19C. < Greek *phuletikos* < *phulē* "tribe"]

phyll- *prefix* same as **phyllo-** (*used before vowels*)

-phyll *suffix* leaf ○ *chlorophyll* [< Greek *phyllon* "leaf"] —**-phyllous** *suffix*

phyl·lid /fíllid/ *n* a moss or liverwort leaf

phyl·lite /fí lī́t/ *n* a fine-grained metamorphic rock with a distinctive shiny surface, containing large quantities of mica and resembling slate or schist [Early 19C. < Greek *phullon* "leaf"] —**phyl·lit·ic** /fi líttik/ *adj*

phyl·lo /feèlō/, **phyl·lo pas·try** *n* very thin sheets of pastry dough used to make papery, crisp small pastries or large dishes, especially in Greek cooking. UK spelling **filo** [Mid-20C. Via modern Greek, "leaf, sheet" < Greek *phullon* "leaf"]

phyllo- *prefix* leaf ○ *phyllotaxis* [< Greek *phullon* < Indo-European]

phyl·lo·clade /fíllə klàyd/, **phyl·lo·clad** /-klàd/ *n* BOT same as **cladophyll** [Mid-19C. < modern Latin *phyllocladium* < Greek *phullon* "leaf" + *klados* "shoot"]

phyl·lode /fí lȫd/, **phyl·lo·di·um** /fi lȫdee əm/ (*plural* **-di·a** /-dee ə/) *n* a flat leaf stalk that functions as a leaf in some plants such as the acacia [Mid-19C. < modern Latin *phyllodium* < Greek *phullōdēs* "resembling a leaf" < *phullon* "leaf"]

phyl·loid /fí lòyd/ *adj* like a leaf in shape or function [Mid-19C. < modern Latin *phylloides* < Greek *phullon* "leaf"]

phyl·lo pas·try *n* FOOD same as **phyllo**

phyl·lo·qui·none /fìllō kwi nṓn, -kwí nṑn/ *n* BIOCHEM same as **vitamin K**$_1$

phyl·lo·tax·y /fíllə tàksee/ (*plural* **-ies**), **phyl·lo·tax·is** /fìllə táksiss/ (*plural* **-tax·es** /-tákseez/) *n* **1.** the way the leaves on a plant are arranged in relation to one another **2.** the study of the factors that determine the growth patterns and arrangement of plant leaves —**phyl·lo·tac·tic** /fìllə táktik/ *adj*

phyl·lox·e·ra /fìllək seèrə, fi lóksərə/ (*plural same* or **-ras** or **-rae** /-ree/) *n* an aphid that is a major pest in wine-producing areas. Latin name: *Viteus vitifolii*. [Mid-19C. < modern Latin < Greek *phullon* "leaf" + *xēros* "dry"; from the insect's effect on leaves]

phylo- *prefix* race, kind, tribe, phylum ○ *phylogeny* [< Greek *phulon* "race"]

phy·log·e·ny /fī lójjənee/ (*plural* **-nies**), **phy·lo·gen·e·sis** /fī̀lō jénnəssiss/ (*plural* **-e·ses** /-ə seèz/) *n* the development over time of a species, genus, or group, as contrasted with the development of an individual (**ontogeny**) —**phy·lo·ge·net·ic** /fī̀lō jə néttik/ *adj* —**phy·lo·ge·net·i·cal·ly** *adv* —**phy·lo·ge·net·ics** *n* —**phy·lo·gen·ic** /-jénnik/ *adj*

phy·lum /fī́ləm/ (*plural* **-la** /-lə/) *n* **1.** a major taxonomic group into which animals are divided, made up of several classes **2.** a large group of languages or language stocks thought to be historically related, e.g., Afro-Asiatic or Indo-European [Late 19C. Via modern Latin < Greek *phulon* "race"]

phys·al·is /fī́ssəliss, físsə-, fī sálliss/ (*plural* **-al·is·es** or **-al·es** /-əleez/) *n UK* same as **Cape gooseberry** [Early 19C. Via modern Latin < Greek *phusallis* "bladder"]

physi- *prefix* same as **physio-** (*used before vowels*)

phys·i·at·rics /fìzzee áttriks/ *n US* MED (*takes a singular verb*) **1.** same as **physical medicine** **2.** same as **physical therapy** [Mid-19C. < Greek *phusis* "nature" (see PHYSICS) + *iatrikos* "medical"] —**phys·i·at·ric** *adj* —**phys·i·at·rist** /fìzzee áttrist, fi zí̄ əttrist/ *n*

phys·ic /fízzik/ *n* **1.** PICK-ME-UP something that lifts the spirits or energizes **2.** PROFESSION OF MEDICINE medicine or healing as an art or profession (*archaic*) **3.** MEDICINE a medicine, especially a purgative (*archaic*) ■ *vt* (**-icked, -ick·ing, -ics**) TREAT SOMEBODY OR SOMETHING to treat somebody or something with a medicine or cure (*archaic*) [13C. Directly or via Old French *fisique* < Latin *physica* (see PHYSICS)]

phys·i·cal /fízzik'l/ *adj* **1.** OF BODY relating to the body, rather than to the mind, the soul, or the feelings **2.** REAL AND TOUCHABLE existing in the real material world, rather than as an idea or notion, and able to be touched and seen ○ *physical evidence* **3.** NEEDING BODILY STRENGTH involving or needing a lot of bodily strength or energy ○ *hard physical work* **4.** WITH BODILY CONTACT involving a lot of bodily contact or aggression ○ *Some of the players were a little too physical.* **5.** INVOLVING TOUCHING tending to touch people or involving touching, especially in an affectionate or sexual way (*informal*) **6.** NOT SOCIAL OR BIOLOGICAL describes sciences such as physics and chemistry that deal with nonliving things such as energy and matter ■ *n* MED same as **physical examination** (*informal*) —**phys·i·cal·i·ty** /fìzzi kálləteе/ *n*

phys·i·cal an·thro·pol·o·gy *n* the branch of anthropology that studies the development over time of human physical characteristics and the differences in appearance among the peoples of the world, as distinct from cultural differences

phys·i·cal chal·lenge *n* **1.** an inability to perform some or all of the tasks of daily life **2.** a medically diagnosed condition that makes it difficult to engage in the activities of daily life

phys·i·cal chem·is·try *n* the branch of chemistry that studies the physical and thermodynamic properties of substances in relation to their structures and chemical reactions

phys·i·cal ed·u·ca·tion *n* gymnastics, athletics, team sports, and other forms of physical exercise taught to children in school

phys·i·cal ex·am·i·na·tion *n* a doctor's general examination to determine somebody's state of physical health and fitness

phys·i·cal ge·og·ra·phy *n* the branch of geography that studies the natural features of the Earth's surface as well as their formation

phys·i·cal·ism /fízzik'l ìzzəm/ *n* in philosophy, a form of materialism that explains the phenomena of reality, including perceptual and intellectual processes, in terms of the physical —**phys·i·cal·ist** *n, adj* —**phys·i·cal·is·tic** /fízzik'l ístik/ *adj*

phys·i·cal·ize /fízzik'l īz/ (**-ized, -iz·ing, -izes**) *vt* **1.** to express or exhibit something such as emotion with the body **2.** to represent something abstract in the form of a physical or concrete thing

phys·i·cal·ly /fízzik'lee/ *adv* **1.** relating to somebody's body or appearance ○ *physically unattractive* **2.** in terms of what is real or what exists in the material world, as opposed to what is theoretical or exists only in the mind ○ *physically impossible*

phys·i·cal·ly chal·lenged *adj* describes somebody with a condition that makes it difficult to perform some or all of the basic tasks of daily life

phys·i·cal med·i·cine *n* the branch of medicine concerned with the diagnosis of injuries or physical conditions and their treatment by external means, including heat, massage, or exercise, rather than by medication or surgery

phys·i·cal sci·ence *n* a science that studies nonliving things, e.g., physics and chemistry

phys·i·cal ther·a·py *n* the treatment of injuries and physical conditions by a trained person under the supervision of a specialist in physical medicine —**phys·i·cal ther·a·pist** *n*

phy·si·cian /fi zísh'n/ *n* **1.** somebody qualified to practice medicine **2.** a doctor who diagnoses and treats diseases and injuries using methods other than surgery [13C. < Old French *fisicien* < *fisique* (see PHYSIC)]

phy·si·cian as·sis·tant *n* MED same as **physician's assistant**

phy·si·cian-as·sist·ed su·i·cide *n* the suicide of somebody with an incurable disease carried out with the help of a physician. Physician-assisted suicide is illegal in most countries.

phy·si·cian's as·sis·tant, phy·si·cian as·sis·tant *n* somebody trained and authorized to carry out some medical duties under a doctor's supervision such as taking a patient's medical history

phys·i·cist /fízzissist/ *n* a scientist who specializes in physics [Mid-19C. < PHYSICS]

phys·i·co·chem·i·cal /fízzikō kémmik'l/ *adj* **1.** relating to both physical and chemical characteristics **2.** relating to physical chemistry [Mid-17C. < Greek *phusikos* (see PHYSICS)] —**phys·i·co·chem·i·cal·ly** *adv*

phys·ics /fízziks/ *n* the scientific study of matter, energy, force, and motion, and the way they relate to each other. Physics traditionally incorporates mechanics, electromagnetism, optics, and thermodynamics and now includes modern disciplines such as quantum mechanics, relativity, and nuclear physics. (*takes a singular verb*) ■ *npl* the physical processes, interactions, qualities, properties, or behavior of something (*takes a plural verb*) [15C. < PHYSIC; translation of Latin *physica* (plural) < Greek *phusika*, plural of *phusikos* "of nature" < *phusis* "nature" < *phuein* "make grow"]

phy·si·o /fízzee ō/ (*plural* **-os**) *n* UK a physical therapist (*informal*) [Mid-20C. Shortening]

physio- *prefix* physical ○ *physiopathology* [< Greek *phusis* "nature" (see PHYSICS)]

phys·i·og·no·my /fìzzee ógnəmee, -ónnəmee/ (*plural* **-mies**) *n* **1.** FACIAL FEATURES the features of somebody's face, especially when they are used as indicators of that person's character or temperament **2.** JUDGMENT OF CHARACTER FROM FACIAL FEATURES the use of facial features to judge somebody's character or temperament **3.** CHARACTER OR APPEARANCE OF SOMETHING the character or outward appearance of something, e.g., the physical features of a landscape [13C. Via French < Greek *phusiognōmonia* < *phusis* "nature" (see PHYSICS) + *gnomon* "judge" (see GNOMON)] —**phys·i·og·nom·ic** /fìzzee og nómmik, fìzzee ə-/ *adj* —**phys·i·og·nom·i·cal·ly** *adv* —**phys·i·og·no·mist** *n*

phys·i·og·ra·phy /fìzzee óggrəfee/ *n* GEOG same as **physical geography** —**phys·i·og·ra·pher** *n* —**phys·i·o·graph·ic** /-ə gráffik/ *adj* —**phys·i·o·graph·i·cal·ly** *adv*

phys·i·o·log·i·cal /fìzzee ə lójjik'l/, **phys·i·o·log·ic** /-lójjik/ *adj* **1.** relating to the way that living things function, rather than to their shape or structure **2.** relating to physiology —**phys·i·o·log·i·cal·ly** *adv*

phys·i·o·log·i·cal psy·chol·o·gy *n* a branch of psychology that studies the interactions between physical or chemical processes in the body and mental states or behavior

phys·i·o·log·i·cal sa·line *n* an aqueous salt solution used to keep cells alive and to administer medication intravenously

phys·i·ol·o·gy /fìzzee óllǝjee/ *n* **1.** the branch of biology that deals with the internal workings of living things, including functions such as metabolism, respiration, and reproduction, rather than with their shape or structure **2.** the way a particular body or organism works [Mid-16C. Directly or via French < Latin *physiologia* < Greek *phusiologia* < *phusis* "nature" (see PHYSICS)] —**phys·i·ol·o·gist** *n*

phys·i·o·pa·thol·o·gy /fìzzee ōpə thóllǝjee/ *n* the branch of medicine that studies how disease disrupts normal body functions —**phys·i·o·path·o·log·ic** /-pathə lójjik/ *adj* —**phys·i·o·path·o·log·i·cal** *adj*

phys·i·o·ther·a·py /fìzzee ō thérrəpee/ *n* Can, UK the treatment of injuries and physical disabilities by a trained person under the supervision of a specialist in physical medicine. US term **physical therapy** —**phys·i·o·ther·a·peu·tic** /fìzzee ō therrə pyóotik/ *adj* —**phys·i·o·ther·a·pist** *n*

phy·sique /fi zéek/ *n* the shape and size of somebody's body [Early 19C. < French < *physique* "physical" < Greek *phusikos* (see PHYSICS)]

phy·so·stig·mine /fìssō stíg meen/, **phy·so·stig·min** /-min/ *n* a crystalline alkaloid. Source: dried leaves of the vine that produces Calabar beans. Use: treatment of glaucoma, to counteract adverse effects of anticholinergic drugs on the central nervous system. Formula: $C_{15}H_{21}N_3O_2$. [Mid-19C. < modern Latin *Physostigma* < Greek *phusa* "bladder" + *stigma* "mark on the skin"]

phyt- *prefix* same as **phyto-** (*used before vowels*)

-phyte *suffix* **1.** plant ○ *saprophyte* **2.** pathological growth ○ *osteophyte* [< Greek *phuton* (see PHYTO-)] —**-phytic** *suffix*

phyto- *prefix* plant ○ *phytohormone* [Via modern Latin < Greek *phuton* < *phuein* "make grow" < Indo-European, "be"]

phy·to·ac·cu·mu·la·tion /fìtō ə kyoomyə láysh'n/ *n* ENVIRON same as **phytoextraction**

phy·to·a·lex·in /fìtō ə léksin/ *n* a chemical produced by a plant to protect it from infection by a pathogen or exposure to some agents of stress

phy·to·chem·i·cal /fìtō kémmik'l/ *n* a naturally occurring plant substance. Some phytochemicals have been shown in research to protect against disease.

phy·to·chem·is·try /fìtə kémmistree/ *n* the chemistry of plants and their metabolic processes —**phy·to·chem·i·cal** *adj* —**phy·to·chem·ist** *n*

phy·to·chrome /fítə krōm/ *n* a light-sensitive pigment in plants that controls flowering and germination of seeds [Late 19C. < PHYTO- + Greek *khrōma* "color"]

phy·to·es·tro·gen /fìtō éstrəjən/ *n* a sterol of a group found in plants that can have a similar effect on the body to that of a hormone

phy·to·ex·trac·tion /fìtō ik stráksh'n/ *n* the process by which plants absorb metal contaminants in soil through their roots, and store them in their upper parts, used as a means of cleaning the soil

phy·to·gen·e·sis /fìtə jénnəssiss/, **phy·tog·e·ny** /fī tójjənee/ *n* the development over time of plants —**phy·to·ge·net·ic** /fìtəjə néttik/ *adj* —**phy·to·ge·net·i·cal·ly** *adv*

phy·to·gen·ic /fìtə jénnik/, **phy·tog·e·nous** /fī tójjənəss/ *adj* describes substances such as coal that are formed from plants

phy·tog·e·ny *n* BOT same as **phytogenesis**

phy·to·ge·og·ra·phy /fìtəjee óggrəfee/ *n* the study of the geographic distribution of plants —**phy·to·ge·o·graph·ic** /-jee ə gráffik/ *adj* —**phy·to·ge·o·graph·i·cal·ly** *adv*

phy·to·hor·mone /fìtō háwr mōn/ *n* BOT same as **plant hormone**

phy·tol /fī tàwl/ *n* an alcohol derived from chlorophyll from which plants synthesize vitamins E and K

phy·tol·o·gy /fī tóllǝjee/ *n* BOT same as **botany** (*archaic*)

phy·ton /fī tòn/ *n* the smallest part of a plant, usually a leaf and its stem, that can grow when it has been cut from the parent plant [Mid-19C. < French < Greek *phuton* (see -PHYTE) + *-on* "-on"]

phy·to·path·o·gen /fìtō páthəjən/ *n* something that causes disease in plants

phy·to·pa·thol·o·gy /fìtōpə thóllǝjee/ *n* the branch of botany that studies plant diseases —**phy·to·path·o·log·i·cal** /-pathə lójjik'l/ *adj*

phy·toph·a·gous /fī tóffəgəss/ *adj* describes animals, especially insects, that feed on plants —**phy·to·pha·gy** *n*

phy·to·plank·ton /fìtō plángktən/ *n* very small free-floating plants, e.g., one-celled algae, found in plankton —**phy·to·plank·ton·ic** /-plangk tónnik/ *adj*

phy·to·pro·tect·ant /fìtō prə téktənt/ *n* a compound derived from plants that prevents the progression of diseases such as cancer

phy·to·re·me·di·a·tion /fìtō ri meedee áysh'n/ *n* the process of decontaminating soil by using plants to absorb heavy metals or other pollutants

phy·to·so·ci·ol·o·gy /fìtō sōssee óllǝjee/ *n* the branch of ecology concerned with the identification, analysis, and classification of plant communities or plant associations

phy·to·sta·bi·li·za·tion /fìtō stàyb'lī záysh'n/ *n* the use of plant roots to immobilize soil contaminants and prevent them from polluting groundwater

phy·to·tox·ic /fìtō tóksik/ *adj* poisonous to plants —**phy·to·tox·ic·i·ty** /-tok síssətee/ *n*

phy·to·tox·in /fìtō tóksin/ *n* **1.** a poisonous substance obtained from plants, e.g., the drug digitalis **2.** something that is poisonous to plants

phy·to·tron /fìtə tròn/ *n* a place in which plants can be grown under controlled conditions, e.g., a greenhouse

pi[1] /pī/ *n* **1.** the 16th letter of the Greek alphabet, represented in the English alphabet as "p." See table at **alphabet 2.** a number approximately equal to 3.14159 that is the ratio of the circumference of a circle to its diameter and is represented by the symbol π [Early 19C. < Greek]

pi[2] /pī/, **pie** *n* **1.** JUMBLE OF PRINTERS' TYPE a pile of printing type that has been mixed up together **2.** DISORDERED MIXTURE a disorganized combination of things ■ *v* (**pied, pi·ing, pies; pied, pie·ing, pies**) **1.** *vt* JUMBLE TYPE to mix printing type up together **2.** *vti* MAKE OR BECOME JUMBLED to mix things up in a confusing way, or become mixed up or confused [Mid-17C. Origin ?]

PI *abbr* **1.** US personal injury **2.** US politically incorrect **3.** private investigator

pi·a /pī ə, pée ə/ *n* ANAT same as **pia mater** [Late 19C. Shortening] —**pi·al** *adj*

PIA *abbr* COMPUT peripheral interface adaptor

Pia·cen·za /pyaa chénzə, -chént saa/ capital city of Piacenza Province, Emilia-Romagna Region, northern Italy. Population: 95,594 (2001).

pi·ac·u·lar /pī ákyələr/ *adj* **1.** done or offered in order to make up for a sin or sacrilegious action **2.** wicked or sinful and requiring the offender or sinner to atone [Early 17C. < Latin *piacularis* < *piaculum* "atonement" < *piare* "appease"]

Edith Piaf

Pi·af /pēe ăaf/, **Édith** (1915–63) French singer. Her expressive performance of songs such as "Je ne regrette rien" and "La Vie en rose" led to international fame. Born **Gassion, Édith Giovanna**

piaffe /pyaf/ *n* a dressage movement performed by a horse in which it trots in one place and raises its legs very high ■ *vi* (**piaffed, piaf·fing, piaffes**) to perform a piaffe [Mid-18C. < French < *piaffer* "to strut"]

Pia·get /pēe ə zhāy/, **Jean** (1896–1980) Swiss psychologist. His pioneering study of intellectual development in children had a major impact on psychology and education.

> "Psychoanalysis is a sort of individual history, an embryology of the personality."
> [Jean Piaget, "Psychoanalysis and its Relations with Child Psychology"; 1920]

pi·a ma·ter /pī ə máytər, pēe ə máatər/ *n* the innermost and most delicate of the three membranes (**meninges**) that surround the brain and the spinal cord [14C. < Latin, "tender mother," translated < Arabic *al-'umm ar-rakika*]

pi·a·ni MUSIC plural of **piano**[2]

pi·an·ism /pēe ə nìzzəm/ *n* piano-playing skill or technique —**pi·a·nis·tic** /pēe ə nístik/ *adj*

pi·a·nis·si·mo /pēe ə níssi mō/ *adv* very softly and quietly (*used as a musical direction*) ■ *n* (*plural* **-mos** or **-mi** /-mee/) a part of a musical composition that is played very softly [Early 18C < Italian, "very quiet" < *piano* (see PIANO[2])] —**pi·a·nis·si·mo** *adj*

pi·an·ist /pēe ənist, pee ánnist/ *n* somebody who plays the piano

pi·an·o[1] /pee ánnō/ *n* (*plural* **-os**) a large musical instrument consisting of a keyboard fixed to a wooden case containing metal wires stretched across a frame. It is played by pressing the keys, each of which is attached to a small hammer that strikes one or more of the wires to sound a note. ■ *adj* relating to or played on a piano ○ *a piano sonata* [Early 19C. < Italian, shortening of PIANOFORTE]

pi·a·no[2] /pee áanō/ *adv* softly and quietly (*used as a musical direction*) ■ *n* (*plural* **-nos** or **-ni** /-nee/) a part of a musical composition that is played softly [Late 17C. Via Italian < Latin *planus* "soft, flat"] —**pi·a·no** *adj*

pi·an·o ac·cor·di·on *n* an accordion with a keyboard on one side to play the notes of the melody on —**pi·an·o ac·cor·di·on·ist** *n*

pi·an·o bar *n* a bar, or a lounge in a hotel, where a pianist plays to entertain customers or provide background music

pi·an·o·for·te /pee ànnō fáwr tày/ *n* same as **piano**[1] (*formal*) [Mid-18C. < Italian < *gravecembalo col piano e forte* "harpsichord with soft and loud"]

pi·an·o hinge *n* a long narrow hinge that has a pin running the length of its joint

pi·an·o quar·tet *n* an ensemble consisting of a piano and three other instruments, usually a violin, viola, and cello, or a piece of music written for this combination

pi·an·o quin·tet *n* an ensemble consisting of a piano and four other instruments, usually two violins, a viola, and a cello, or a piece of music written for this combination

pi·an·o roll *n* a roll of paper with patterns of perforations whose positions determine the sequence of notes played on a player piano

pi·an·o tri·o *n* a musical ensemble consisting of a piano and two other instruments, usually a cello and a violin, or a piece of music written for this combination

pi·as·sa·va /pēe ə sáavə/, **pi·as·sa·ba** /-sáabə, -sáavə/ *n* **1.** a coarse fiber obtained from a Brazilian tree. Use: rope, brooms, brushes. **2.** a palm tree that produces piassava. Native to: Brazil. Latin name: *Attalea funifera* or *Leopoldinia piassaba*. [Mid-19C. Via Portuguese < Tupi *piaçába*]

pi·as·tre /pee ástər/, **pi·as·ter** *n* a subunit of currency in several Middle Eastern countries. See table at **currency** [Late 16C. Via French < Italian *piastra (d'argento)* "(silver) plate" < Latin *emplastrum* (see PLASTER)]

pi·az·za /pee áatsə/ (*plural* **-zas** or **-ze**) *n* **1.** (*plural* **pi·az·ze** /-áatsə, -say/ or **pi·az·zas**) ITALIAN PUBLIC SQUARE a large open square, especially one in an Italian town **2.** OPEN-SIDED PASSAGEWAY a covered passageway that has arches on one or both sides and is usually attached to a building, e.g., along the inner walls of a courtyard or quadrangle **3.** *regional* PORCH a veranda or porch, especially one attached to a house (*dated*) [Late 16C. Via Italian < Latin *platea* "open space" (see PLACE)]

REGIONAL NOTE Used to mean "porch," ***piazza*** is an old-fashioned term found in the northeastern and southeastern states, but not in the Midland territory. In the Carolinas, the use of this term, together with *earthworm* and *press peach*, marks the northern limits of Southern speech. See also ***veranda***.

---

pi bond *n* a covalent bond between two atoms and a pair of electrons having orbitals whose greatest overlap is along a plane perpendicular to a line connecting the nuclei of the atoms —**pi-bond·ing** *adj*

pi·broch /pēe bròk/ *n* a piece of music written for the Scottish Highland bagpipes, consisting of a theme and variations, often with a mournful tone [Early 18C. < Gaelic *piobaireachd* "art of piping" < English PIPE[1]]

pic /pik/ (*plural* **pics** or **pix** /piks/) *n* a picture, especially a photograph or illustration (*informal*) [Late 19C. Shortening of PICTURE]

pi·ca[1] /píkə/ *n* a unit of measurement for printing type, equal to 12 points or 0.166 in./0.422 cm [15C. < Anglo-Latin, "church almanac"; from the resemblance to the handwriting in such books]

pi·ca[2] /píkə/ *n* the indiscriminate craving for and eating of substances such as paint chips, clay, plaster, or dirt [Mid-16C. < Latin, literally "magpie," translation of Greek *kissa*]

Pi·ca·bi·a /pi káabee ə/, **Francis** (1879–1953) French avant-garde artist who painted in most major 20th-century styles. He is best known for his Dadaist and surrealist works. Born **Picabia, François Marie Martinez**

pic·a·dor /píkə dàwr, péekaa dàwr/ *n* a bullfighter on horseback, who attacks the bull with a spear early in the fight, making it easier for the main bullfighter (**matador**) to kill it with his sword [Late 18C. < Spanish < *picar* "prick, pierce"]

pi·ca em *n* PRINTING same as **pica**[1]

pic·a·nin·ny *n US* another spelling of **pickaninny** (*taboo offensive*)

pi·can·te /pi káan tày/ *adj* spicy, especially in being served with a sauce that contains tomatoes, onions, peppers, vinegar, and spices [< Italian *piccante* < present participle of *piccare* "to sting"]

Pi·card /pee káard/ *n* **1.** somebody who comes from Picardy in northern France **2.** the dialect of French spoken in Picardy [14C. < French]

Pi·car·dy /píkərdee/ region and former province of northern France, in an area between Calais and Paris and centered on the city of Amiens. There was heavy fighting there during World War I. French name **Picardie**

pic·a·resque /pìkə résk/ *adj* **1.** OF LITERATURE HAVING ROGUE AS HERO belonging to or characteristic of a type of prose fiction that features the adventures of a roguish hero and usually has a simple plot divided into separate episodes **2.** RELATING TO ROGUES relating to or characteristic of rogues or scoundrels ■ *n* PICARESQUE FICTION prose fiction featuring the adventures of a roguish hero [Early 19C. Via French < Spanish *picaresco* < *picaro* "rogue" < assumed Vulgar Latin *piccare* "to prick"]

pic·a·roon /pìkə róon/ *n* same as **rogue** *n* (sense 1) (*archaic or literary*) ■ *vi* (**-rooned, -roon·ing, -roons**) to live the adventurous life of a pirate, thief, swindler, or scoundrel (*archaic literary*) [Early 17C. < Spanish *picarón* "great rogue" < *picaro* (see PICARESQUE)]

Pablo Picasso: photographed in 1933 by Man Ray

Pi·cas·so /pi káassō, -kássō/, **Pablo** (1881–1973) Spanish painter and sculptor. An exceptionally versatile and prolific artist, he was the leading figure in the development of modern abstract art. Among his major works are the cubist masterpiece *Les Demoiselles d'Avignon* (1906–07) and *Guernica* (1937), which expresses his horror of war.

> "Painting is a blind man's profession. He paints not what he sees, but what he feels, what he tells himself about what he has seen."
> [Pablo Picasso. Quoted in "Childhood," *The Journals of Jean Cocteau*, Wallace Fowlie (tr.); 1957]

pic·a·yune /pìkə yóon/ *adj* (*informal*) **1.** TRIFLING of very little importance **2.** SMALL-MINDED tending to fuss about unimportant things and to be childishly spiteful ■ *n* **1.** TRIFLING THING something unimportant or of little value (*informal*) **2.** COINS COIN FROM SPANISH AMERICA a small silver coin formerly used in Spanish America, worth half of a real **3.** *US* COINS SMALL COIN a low-value coin, especially a five-cent piece (*archaic informal*) [Early 19C. Via French *picaillon*, Piedmontese coin < Provençal *picaioun*]

pic·ca·lil·li /pìkə líllee/ *n* a pickle relish consisting of chopped mixed vegetables with mustard, vinegar, and spices [Mid-18C. Probably < PICKLE + CHILLI]

Pic·card /pee káard, -káar/, **Auguste** (1884–1962) Swiss physicist. He is noted for his exploration of the deep sea and of the stratosphere, to which he made the first balloon ascent (1931).

pic·ca·ta /pi káatə/ *adj* describes meats sautéed in slices and served in a spicy lemon and butter sauce [< Italian < French *piqué*, past participle of *piquer* "attach ingredients, lard," literally "to prick"]

pic·co·lo /píkə lō/ (*plural* **-los**) *n* a musical instrument, the smallest member of the flute family, with a range one octave higher than the standard flute [Mid-19C. < Italian, "small"]

pice /pīss/ (*plural same*) *n* a subunit of currency formerly used in South Asia, four of which were worth an anna [Early 17C. < Hindi *paisā* "paisa"]

pich·i·ci·e·go /pìchissee áygō/ (*plural same* or **-gos**), **pich·i·ci·a·go** /-áagō/ *n* **1.** a very small armadillo with pink armor and silky hair. Native to: Argentina. Latin name: *Chlamyphorus truncatus*. **2.** a large armadillo with yellowish brown armor and coarse whitish hair. Native to: South America. Latin name: *Burmeisteria retusa*. [Early 19C. < Spanish, probably < Guarani *pichey*, type of armadillo, literally "small" + Spanish *ciego* "sightless" < Latin *caecus*]

pick[1] /pik/ *v* (**picked, pick·ing, picks**) **1.** *vt* CHOOSE SOMETHING OR SOMEBODY to take, or decide to take, one or more things or people from a larger number ○ *Pick three people for your team.* **2.** *vt* REMOVE SOMETHING FROM PLANT to remove something, especially in quantity and by hand, from a plant on which it has grown ○

picking strawberries **3.** *vt* **STRIP SOMETHING OF FRUIT OR FLOWERS** to strip a plant, or all the plants in a place, of fruit or flowers ○ *The bushes nearest the path had already been picked.* **4.** *vt* **REMOVE SOMETHING IN SMALL PIECES** to remove something part by part from the surface or middle of something using a sharp or pointed object such as a fingernail or a beak **5.** *vt* **SCRAPE BODY PART WITH FINGERNAIL** to use a fingernail to loosen and remove something, or to loosen and remove something attached to the surface of a part of the body ○ *pick a scab* **6.** *vt* MUSIC **PLUCK OR PLAY BY PLUCKING** to pluck the strings of a stringed instrument or to play a tune on such an instrument in this way **7.** *vt* **OPEN SOMETHING WITHOUT PROPER KEY** to use a special device or pointed instrument to open a lock, usually illegally ○ *pick a lock* **8.** *vt* **UNDO SOMETHING** to loosen, unfasten, or separate something into disconnected parts, especially something that was sewn together ○ *pick a seam apart* **9.** *vi* **FIND FAULT** to be petty or fault-finding **10.** *vi* **START FIGHT OR ARGUMENT** to begin a fight or argument with somebody, usually deliberately ■ *n* **1. CHOICE** the act or right of choosing somebody or something ○ *take your pick* ■ *n* **2. BEST** the very best of a wide selection of people or things ○ *the pick of the bunch* **3. CROP PORTION** the amount of a crop gathered by hand at one time [13C. Probably < assumed Old English *pīcian* "to prick," Old Icelandic *pikka*] —**pick·er** *n* ◇ **pick and choose** to select only the best of what is on offer, or make a choice in a careful or fussy manner ◇ **pick your way** to step very carefully through a dirty, messy, or dangerous area of ground

pick at *vt* **1. EAT LITTLE FOOD** to eat very little of a meal ○ *He only picked at his breakfast.* **2. SCRAPE SOMETHING WITH FINGERNAILS** to scrape away surface pieces of something with the fingernails **3. NAG SOMEBODY** to nag or criticize somebody in a petty way (*informal*)

pick off *vt* **1. SHOOT SOMETHING BY AIMING CAREFULLY** to shoot somebody or something selected as a target and deliberately aimed at, usually from a distance, or shoot a number of targets one by one **2. INTERCEPT PASS** in some sports such as football, to intercept a pass **3. PUT OUT BASE RUNNER** in baseball, to put out a base runner caught off base, often when trying to steal the next base

pick on *vt* to blame, criticize, or bully somebody repeatedly in a way that is considered unfair or unkind

pick out *vt* **1. CHOOSE SOMETHING** to choose or select something or somebody from among others ○ *She picked out her favorite chocolate.* **2. IDENTIFY SOMEBODY FROM CROWD OR BACKGROUND** to recognize or distinguish somebody or something from among others or against a background that makes this difficult ○ *I couldn't pick him out in the crowd.* **3.** MUSIC **PLAY SOMETHING NOTE BY NOTE** to play a tune slowly, note by note

pick over *vt* to go through something, selecting the best items or discarding unwanted items

pick up *v* **1.** *vt* **LIFT SOMETHING** to take hold of and raise or remove something or somebody **2.** *vt* **GATHER DROPPED THINGS** to gather up things that have been dropped or have fallen to the ground **3.** *vt* **CLEAN PLACE** to clean something, usually by gathering up things that have been carelessly left where they do not belong **4. pick your·self up** *vr* **REGAIN UPRIGHT OR STRONGER POSITION** to stand up after falling down, or recover strength, courage, or a sense of purpose after a setback ○ *She picked herself up off the floor and staggered over to the phone.* ○ *They're still picking themselves up after narrowly avoiding bankruptcy.* **5.** *vti* **TAKE ON PASSENGERS** to stop a vehicle and let a passenger or passengers in ○ *picked up a hitchhiker* **6.** *vt* **CLAIM SOMETHING** to claim something such as an item left for repair or merchandise ordered from a store ○ *pick up a library book* **7.** *vt* **PAY FOR SOMETHING** to take on the responsibility for paying something, especially a bill ○ *pick up the tab* **8.** *vt* **ACQUIRE SOMETHING CHEAPLY OR EASILY** to get or buy something cheaply or easily ○ *a book I picked up for a few dollars* **9.** *vt* **ACQUIRE SOMETHING CASUALLY** to acquire something casually, often without meaning to and without knowing it ○ *has picked up some bad habits* **10.** *vt* US **GAIN POINTS** to gain or win something such as an award, or points or yards **11.** *vt* **CATCH DISEASE** to become infected with a disease **12.** *vt* **RECEIVE SIGNAL** to receive something such as a radio or television signal or a radar image on a piece of equipment **13.** *vt* **NOTICE SOMETHING** to notice something or become aware of it **14.** *vt* **FIND SOMETHING** to find and follow something, especially a scent or trail ○ *pick up the scent* **15.** *vt* **UNDERSTAND SOMETHING** to understand something that is communicated indirectly **16.** *vt* **LEARN SOMETHING** to learn something in a casual or unsystematic way, e.g., by frequently hearing it, seeing it done, or trying to do it ○ *picked up a lot of Spanish on his trip* **17.** *vti* **ACCELERATE** to increase, or cause something to increase, in strength, speed, or intensity ○ *picking up speed* **18.** *vti* **RETURN TO SOMETHING AGAIN** to continue, or continue something, at a later time, usually after an interruption or break ○ *We can pick up our discussion after the break.* **19.** *vt* **FIND SEXUAL PARTNER** to make the acquaintance of a stranger, often in a public place, usually for sexual purposes (*informal*) ○ *picked him up in a bar* **20.** *vt* same as **arrest** (*informal*) ○ *He was picked up on a burglary charge.* **21.** *vi* **BECOME BETTER** to improve after being ill, injured, bad, or unsuccessful (*informal*) ○ *Sales picked up this quarter.* **22.** *vi* US **PACK BELONGINGS** to pack up belongings and leave without telling anyone why (*informal*)

pick up on *vt* **1.** to learn or understand something quickly **2.** to notice something, and perhaps mention or question it (*informal*)

pick up with *vt* US to become acquainted and start associating with somebody (*informal*)

pick[2] /pik/ *n* **1. TOOL FOR BREAKING UP HARD SURFACES** a tool used for breaking up hard surfaces, consisting of a long handle and a curved metal head that is pointed at one end and either pointed or like a chisel at the other **2. SMALL TOOL FOR BREAKING INTO PIECES** a small tool used to break up something into smaller pieces (*often used in combination*) **3. SHARP TOOL FOR PICKING** a sharp tool for cleaning something such as the teeth or for getting into small places, as in a lock (*often used in combination*) **4. COMB FOR CURLY HAIR** a comb having a handle and long teeth, used to comb curly hair **5.** US MUSIC **DEVICE FOR PLUCKING GUITAR STRINGS** a device used to pluck the strings of a stringed instrument such as a guitar. Can term **plectrum** ■ *vi* (**picked, pick·ing, picks**) **WORK WITH PICK** to use a pick or do work with a pick [14C. Variant of PIKE[2]]

pick·a·back /píkə bàk/ *n, adj, adv* same as **piggyback** (*dated*) [Variant]

pick·a·nin·ny /píkə nìnnee/ (*plural* **-nies**), **pic·a·nin·ny** *n* a highly offensive term for a small Black child (*taboo*) [Mid-17C. < Caribbean creole, probably < Portuguese *pequenino* "very small" < *pequeno* "small"]

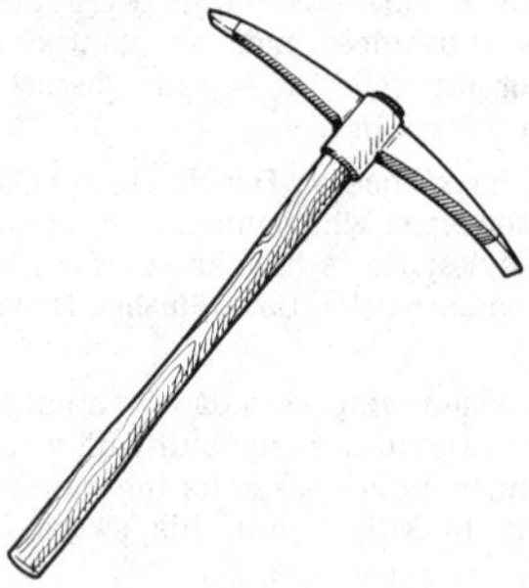

pickax

pick·ax /pík àks/ *n* same as **pick**[2] *n* (sense 1) [15C. Alteration (by association with AX) of obsolete *pikois* < Old French *picois* < Latin *picus* "woodpecker"]

pick·er·el /píkərəl/ (*plural same* or **-els**) *n* a predatory fish of the pike family, popular as a game fish. Native to: North America. Latin name: *Esox niger*. [14C. < PIKE[1]; partly after Anglo-Latin *picerellus*]

pick·er·el·weed /píkərəl wēed/ *n* a plant with heart-shaped leaves that grows in shallow water in rivers and lakes. Flowers: purple. Native to: North America. Latin name: *Pontederia cordata*.

Pick·er·ing /píkəring/, **Edward Charles** (1846–1919) US astronomer and physicist. He devised the meridian photometer with which he made more than 1,400,000 measurements of the magnitudes of stars.

pick·et /píkit/ *n* **1. POINTED POST STUCK IN GROUND** a post or plank with a pointed end that is hammered into the ground, e.g., as a marker, as a support for a fence, or to tether an animal **2. PROTESTER OR PROTESTERS OUTSIDE BUILDING** a person or group of people demonstrating or protesting outside a building **3. SOLDIER OR SOLDIERS ON GUARD** a soldier or small body of troops used to occupy ground of tactical importance ■ *v* (**-et·ed, -et·ing, -ets**) **1.** *vti* **HOLD PROTEST OUTSIDE PLACE** to hold a demonstration or protest outside a place, e.g., as part of a strike **2.** *vt* **GUARD SOMETHING** to patrol or guard a place, especially a military site or position **3.** *vt* **ENCLOSE OR MARK SOMETHING WITH STAKES** to enclose or mark something with wooden stakes driven into the ground, or enclose it with a picket fence [Late 17C. < French *piquet* "pointed stake" < *piquer* "prick, pierce" (see PIQUE[1])] —**pick·et·er** *n*

pick·et fence *n* a fence made of pointed stakes or posts driven into the ground and connected by one or more horizontal bars

pick·et line *n* a line of people such as striking workers or members of the public protesting outside a building

Pick·ett /píkit/, **George Edward** (1825–75) US Confederate general. At the Battle of Gettysburg (1863) he led his troops in an unsuccessful charge in which three-fourths of them were killed.

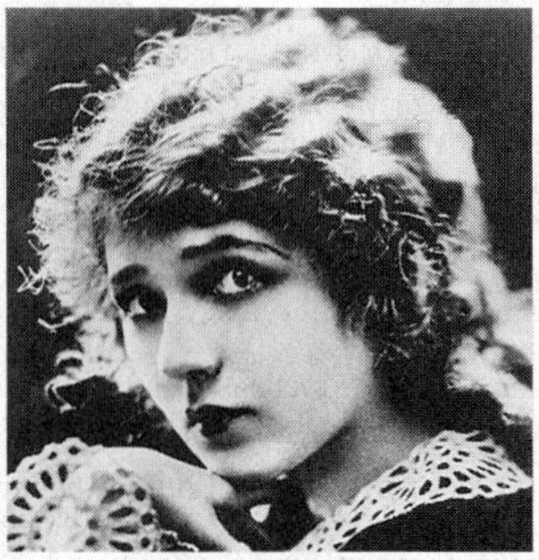

AKG London

Mary Pickford

Pick·ford /píkfərd/, **Mary** (1893–1979) Canadian-born US actor and producer. She starred in movies such as *Poor Little Rich Girl* (1917), and cofounded United Artists Studio (1919). Born **Smith, Gladys Marie**. Known as **America's Sweetheart**

pick·ings /píkingz/ *npl* things available to be earned or taken ○ *easy pickings*

pick·le /pík'l/ *n* **1. PRESERVED VEGETABLE** a small cucumber or other vegetable that has acquired a sharp taste by being preserved in vinegar or brine **2. LIQUID FOR PRESERVING FOOD** liquid, usually brine or a vinegar solution, used to preserve cold foods such as vegetables or fish **3.** *UK* **SPICY VEGETABLE PRESERVE** a lumpy mixture of chopped vegetables, typically cauliflower, onions, cucumbers, and gherkins, preserved in vinegar or brine to give it a sharp or spicy flavor and eaten with other foods **4. CLEANING OR PROCESSING SOLUTION** an industrial or commercial solution used to clean or process something **5. AWKWARD SITUATION** a difficult or problematic situation (*informal*) ■ *vt* (**-led, -ling, -les**) **1. PRESERVE FOOD** to preserve food, especially vegetables or fish, in vinegar, brine, or another solution **2. DIP OR SOAK SOMETHING IN LIQUID** to clean or process something by dipping or soaking it in a liquid [14C. < Middle Low German *pekel*] —**pick·ler** *n*

pick·led /pík'ld/ *adj* **1.** preserved in vinegar, brine, or another liquid **2.** same as **drunk** *adj* (sense 1) (*informal*)

pick·le peach *n regional* a clingstone peach

REGIONAL NOTE See ***plum peach***.

pick·le·worm /pík'l wùrm/ (*plural same* or **-worms**) *n* the larva of a moth that feeds on cucumbers, pumpkins, and other gourds. Native to: southeastern United States. Latin name: *Diaphania nitidalis*.

pick·lock /pík lòk/ *n* **1.** a tool used to open locks without using a key **2.** an opener of locks who does not use a key, especially a burglar

pick-me-up *n* something that lifts the spirits and energizes somebody, especially a stimulating drink (*informal*)

~~**picknick**~~ incorrect spelling of **picnic**

pick·off /pík àwf, -òf/ *n* **1.** in some sports such as football or basketball, an interception of a pass **2.** in baseball, a play in which a runner who is off base is thrown out

pick·pock·et /pík pòkət/ *n* a thief who steals from people's pockets and bags in public places, usually unnoticed —**pick·pock·et·ing** *n*

pick·up /pík ùp/ *n* **1.** AUTOMOT same as **pickup truck 2.** **POWER TO ACCELERATE** the ability of a vehicle to accelerate quickly (*informal*) **3.** **IMPROVEMENT** an improvement or increase (*informal*) ○ *a pickup in consumer confidence* **4.** **PROSPECTIVE SEXUAL PARTNER** somebody met casually with the idea of developing a sexual relationship (*informal*) **5.** **HITCHHIKER** somebody who hitchhikes (*informal*) **6.** **ARREST** the taking of somebody into custody by a police officer (*informal*) **7.** **SOMEBODY OR SOMETHING TAKEN SOMEWHERE** somebody or something that is moved from one place to another **8.** **FIELDING BALL** in some sports such as baseball, the act of fielding a ball after it touches the ground **9.** **LIFTING OR COLLECTING OF SOMETHING** the raising, gathering, collection, or removal of something to be taken somewhere else ○ *weekday pickups and deliveries* **10.** *also* **pick·up arm** RECORDING same as **tone arm 11.** RECORDING **PART OF TONE ARM** a device inside the tone arm of a record player that converts the stylus's vibrations into electrical signals that are converted into sound **12.** **CONVERTER OF VIBRATIONS ON MUSICAL INSTRUMENT** an electromagnetic device that converts the vibrations from the strings of an electric guitar or other amplified instrument into electrical signals that are amplified into sound **13.** **PART THAT LIFTS SOMETHING** a part of a machine or system that lifts or selects something, e.g., the rotating rake on a combine harvester that lifts and gathers straw or hay **14.** PHYS **RECEIVING OF LIGHT OR SOUND WAVES** the receiving and gathering of light or sound waves that are to be converted into electrical impulses **15.** *US* ACCT **BALANCE FORWARD** a balance carried forward in an accounting ledger **16.** MUSIC **UNSTRESSED NOTE** an unstressed note or series of notes introducing a musical phrase or composition ■ *adj* **IMPROMPTU** informally organized on the spot and made up of or involving people available at the time ○ *a pickup basketball game*

pick·up truck *n* a light truck with a low-sided open back and a tailgate that drops down for easy loading and unloading

Pick·wick·i·an /pik wíkee ən/ *adj* **1.** generous, naive, or benevolent **2.** not literal or typical in usage or meaning [Mid-19C. < Mr. *Pickwick*, character in Charles Dickens's novel *The Pickwick Papers* (1837)]

pick·y /píkee/ (**-i·er, -i·est**) *adj* having inflexible likes and dislikes and, therefore, being hard to please or satisfy [Mid-19C. < PICK[1]] —**pick·i·ly** *adv* —**pick·i·ness** *n*

pic·nic /pík nìk/ *n* **1.** **MEAL TAKEN AND EATEN OUTDOORS** an informal meal prepared for eating in the open air or the food that makes up such a meal **2.** **EASY OR PLEASANT THING** something easy to do or pleasant to experience (*informal*) ○ *Moving house was no picnic.* **3.** **CUT OF PORK** a cut of pork consisting of the shoulder with most of the butt removed ■ *vi* (**-nicked, -nick·ing, -nics**) **HAVE PICNIC** to eat an informal meal outdoors [Mid-18C. < French *pique-nique*] —**pic·nick·er** *n*

~~**picnicing**~~ incorrect spelling of **picnicking**

pico- *prefix* **1.** one trillionth (10^{-12}) ○ *picofarad* Symbol **p 2.** very small ○ *picornavirus* [Via Spanish *pico* "beak, small amount" < Latin *beccus* (see BEAK)]

Pi·co del·la Mi·ran·do·la /péekō dèllə mi rándōlə/, **Giovanni, Count** (1463–94) Italian humanist philosopher. His 900 philosophical propositions attracted accusations of heresy.

Pi·co de Tei·de /péekō day táydə, -táythə/ highest mountain in Spain, on the island of Tenerife. Height: 12,188 ft./3,715 m.

pi·co·far·ad /péekə fàrrəd, píkə-/ *n* one-trillionth of a farad

pi·co·gram /péekə gràm, píkə-/ *n* one-trillionth of a gram

pic·o·line /píkə lèen, -lin/ *n* a colorless liquid. Source: coal tar, bone oil. Use: solvent, in organic synthesis. Formula: C_6H_7N. [Mid-19C. < Latin *pic-* "pitch" + *oleum* "oil"] —**pic·o·lin·ic** /pìkə línnik/ *adj*

pi·co·mole /péekə mòl, píkə-/ *n* one-trillionth of a mole

pi·cong /pee kóng/ *n Carib* light-hearted teasing talk [Mid-20C. < Spanish *picón*]

pi·co·plank·ton /péekō plàngktən/ *n* the component of plankton in the size range 0.2–2.0 micrometers

pi·cor·na·vi·rus /pi káwrnə vìrəss/ *n* a small infectious virus, e.g., the virus that causes polio or the common cold. Family: Picornaviridae. [Mid-20C. < PICO- + RNA + VIRUS]

pi·co·sec·ond /péekə sèkənd, píkə-/ *n* one-trillionth of a second

pi·cot /péekō, pee kṓ/ *n* a loop that forms a pattern with others, e.g., in lace ■ *vt* (**-cot·ed, -cot·ing, -cots**) to embroider small loops on fabric [Early 17C. < French, "small point" < *pic* "peak, point" < *piquer* "to prick" (see PIQUE[1])]

pic·o·tee /pìkə tée/ *n* a flower, especially a carnation or tulip, that has petals edged with a different, usually darker color [Early 18C. < French *picotée*, form of past participle of *picoter* "to prick" < *picot* (see PICOT)]

pi·co·wave /péekə wàyv, píkə-/ (**-waved, -wav·ing, -waves**) *vt* to expose food to radiation in order to kill insects, worms, or bacteria

pic·quet *n* CARDS another spelling of **piquet**

picr- *prefix* same as **picro-** (*used before vowels*)

pic·rate /pík ràyt/ *n* a salt or ester of picric acid [Mid-19C. < Greek *pikros* "bitter"]

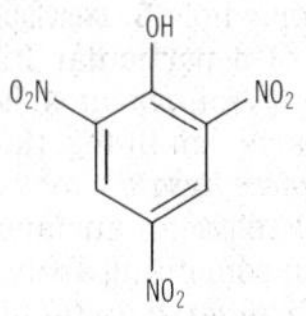

picric acid

pic·ric ac·id /píkrik-/ *n* a strong toxic yellow crystalline acid. Use: dyes, antiseptics, high explosives. Formula: $C_6H_3N_3O_7$. [< Greek *pikros* "bitter"]

pi·crite /pík rìt/ *n* a dark-colored igneous rock made up primarily of coarse grains of olivine and other ferromagnesian minerals [Early 19C. < Greek *pikros* "bitter"]

picro- *prefix* **1.** bitter ○ *picrotoxin* **2.** picric acid ○ *picrate* [< Greek *pikros* "bitter, sharp" < Indo-European, "to cut"]

pic·ro·tox·in /pìkrə tóksin/ *n* a bitter crystalline compound. Source: seeds of a South Asian vine. Use: antidote to barbiturate poisoning. Formula: $C_{30}H_{34}O_{13}$.

Pict /pikt/ *n* a member of an ancient people who occupied lands north of the Forth and Clyde rivers in Scotland between the 1st and the 4th centuries [Pre-12C. < late Latin *Picti* (plural), probably < Latin *picti* "painted or tattooed people," form of *pictus* "painted"]

Pict·ish /píktish/ *adj* relating to the Picts, their culture, or their language ■ *n* an extinct language formerly spoken in Scotland

pic·to·graph /píktə gràf/, **pic·to·gram** /-gràm/ *n* **1.** a graphic symbol or picture representing a word or idea in some writing systems, as opposed to a symbol such as a letter of the alphabet representing an individual sound **2.** a chart or diagram that uses symbols or pictures to represent values [Mid-19C. < Latin *pictus* (see PICTURE)] —**pic·to·graph·ic** /pìktə gráffik/ *adj* —**pic·tog·ra·phy** /pik tóggrəfee/ *n*

Pic·tor /píktər/ *n* an inconspicuous constellation of the southern hemisphere between Dorado and Columba. See illustration at **constellation**

pic·to·ri·al /pik táwree əl/ *adj* **1.** **OF PICTURES** relating to, composed of, or shown by pictures **2.** **ILLUSTRATED** containing illustrations or photographs, as opposed to writing or text **3.** **DESCRIPTIVE** describes language that conjures up vivid images ■ *n* **HIGHLY ILLUSTRATED PERIODICAL** a newspaper or magazine that has many pictures in it, especially one with far more pictures than text [Mid-17C. < late Latin *pictorius* < Latin *pictor* "painter" < *pictus* (see PICTURE)] —**pic·to·ri·al·ly** *adv*

pic·ture /píkchər/ *n* **1.** **SOMETHING DRAWN OR PAINTED** a shape or set of shapes and lines drawn, painted, or printed on paper, canvas, or some other flat surface, especially shapes that represent a recognizable form or object **2.** PHOTOGRAPHY same as **photograph 3.** **TV IMAGE** the image on a television screen **4.** **MOVIE** a motion picture **5.** **MENTAL IMAGE** a vivid image or impression in the mind of how somebody or something looks **6.** **ARTISTIC DESCRIPTION OR REPRESENTATION** a description or representation of something in writing, in a film, in music, or some other art form **7.** **OBSERVED SITUATION** a situation in its context ○ *get the picture* **8.** **EMBODIMENT OR EPITOME** a typical or perfect example of the way something looks, or somebody or something that embodies a quality or state perfectly ○ *She was the picture of health.* **9.** **SOMEBODY WHO CLOSELY RESEMBLES ANOTHER** somebody who closely resembles somebody else ○ *She's the absolute picture of her grandmother.* ■ **pic·tures** *npl UK* **THE MOVIES** a movie theater or movie show (*dated informal*) ○ *go to the pictures* ■ *vt* (**-tured, -tur·ing, -tures**) **1.** **IMAGINE SOMETHING** to imagine or have an image of somebody or something in mind **2.** **DESCRIBE SOMETHING** to describe somebody or something in a particular way **3.** **FEATURE PICTURE OF SOMEBODY** to feature a picture, especially a photograph, of somebody or something in a newspaper, magazine, or book (*often passive*) [15C. < Latin *pictura* < *pictus*, past participle of *pingere* "to paint"] ◇ **put somebody in the picture** to acquaint somebody with the facts of a situation

CULTURAL NOTE ***The Picture of Dorian Gray***, a novel (1890) by Irish writer Oscar Wilde. In Wilde's update of the Faust legend, the decadent young gentleman Dorian Gray trades his soul for eternal youth and beauty, but is subsequently tormented by a portrait of himself that constantly changes to reflect the ravages of time and of his debauched lifestyle. It was made into a movie by Albert Lewin in 1945.

pic·ture book *n* a highly illustrated book, especially one for children, written in a simple style

pic·ture card *n* CARDS same as **face card**

pic·ture hat *n* a woman's elaborately decorated hat with a very broad brim, of the kind often featured in informal portraits of women painted in the 18th century

pic·ture li·brar·y *n* a place where photographs and other images are stored, from which they may be borrowed for use in books, magazines, and newspapers

pic·ture mes·sa·ging *n* the sending of images and photographs from one cell phone to another

pic·ture mold·ing *n US* BUILDINGS a strip of wood or plaster molding resembling a cornice, fixed high up around the walls of a room, from which you can hang pictures. Can term **picture rail**

pic·ture-per·fect *adj* very clean, neat, ordered, and pleasing, as the subjects of paintings and photographs often are

pic·ture post·card *n* a postcard with a picture, often a photograph of a landmark or landscape, on one side (*dated*)

pic·ture puz·zle *n* HOBBIES same as **jigsaw puzzle**

pic·ture rail *n Can, UK* same as **picture molding**

pic·tur·esque /pìkchə résk/ *adj* **1.** **VISUALLY ATTRACTIVE** visually very appealing or impressive, often by virtue of quaintness or unusualness or through seeming fit for a painting or photograph **2.** **VIVID** charmingly or strikingly unusual and often very expressive ○ *a picturesque expression* ■ *n* **VISUALLY ATTRACTIVE OR DISTINCTIVE THINGS** things that are visually very pleasing or distinctive, considered collectively [Early 18C. Anglicization (after PICTURE) of French *pittoresque* < Italian *pittoresco* < *pittore* "painter" < Latin *pictor* (see PICTORIAL)] —**pic·tur·esque·ly** *adv* —**pic·tur·esque·ness** *n*

pic·ture tube *n* ELECTRONICS same as **cathode-ray tube**

WORLD ENGLISH ***Pidgin*** A *pidgin* is a simple language that arises from contacts between people with different mother tongues, in situations where relatively uncomplicated ideas are being exchanged. The speech is generally slow and supported by mime and gesture; the vocabulary is basic and taken mostly from the language of the most important group of speakers; and the grammar has much in common with that typically used by native speakers talking to non-native speakers, or by mothers talking to young children.

A simplified pidgin can develop rapidly: if it proves useful, it becomes more complex, and hence flexible. If it becomes a mother tongue, it is expanded to fulfill all its speakers' needs. Such mother tongues are known as *creoles*. Developed pidgins are most likely to be found in multilingual communities, where they are invaluable as lingua francas. They can be found in Papua New Guinea, for example, where there are over 700 languages for an estimated population of five million, and in West Africa, where as many as one-fifth of the world's languages occur.

Pidgins have probably existed for millennia. Evidence suggests that pidginized versions of Latin evolved into the Romance languages, and there was certainly a medieval lingua franca in use during the Crusades. Pidgins with vocabularies from European languages developed extensively in the wake of European expansionism from the 15th century onward.

Each pidgin, like each language, is unique but they share some characteristics: word order is fixed; there is little or no inflection; negation usually involves a "no" word in front of the verb; nouns and verbs are regular; the small vocabulary is used creatively; and speakers use local idioms, metaphors, and proverbs.

Here is an example of Kamtok, a Cameroon Pidgin English from west central Africa:

Den i bin lef dat ples, an i bin kam fo i on kontri, an i pipu bin folo i. An i bin di tich di pipu fo insai di Jew dem God haus... (Mark 6: 1–2)

(Then he left that place, and he came into his own country and his people followed him. And he was teaching the people inside the synagogue...). See also ***creole***.

pic·ture win·dow *n* a large window, usually with a single pane of glass, especially one that has a pleasant view

pic·ture writ·ing *n* **1.** a writing system that uses symbols or pictures to represent whole words or ideas rather than individual sounds, e.g., the writing system of Chinese **2.** the reporting of an event or telling of a story using pictures instead of words, e.g., in ancient cave paintings

pic·ul /pík'l/ *n* a unit of weight used in East and Southeast Asia, especially a Chinese unit equal to 133 lb./60 kg [Late 16C. < Malay, Javanese *pikul* "load"]

pic·u·let /píkyələt/ (*plural same* or **-lets**) *n* a very small woodpecker with a short tail. Native to: tropics, especially of Americas. Genus: *Picumnus*. [Mid-19C. < Latin *picus* "woodpecker"]

PID *abbr* **1.** MED pelvic inflammatory disease **2.** COMPUT personal identification device

pid·dle /píd'l/ *vi* (**-dled, -dling, -dles**) **1.** same as **urinate** (*informal; usually used by children*) **2.** to operate in a disorganized way, doing one thing and then another without a distinct purpose or method ■ *n* an act of urinating (*informal; usually used by children*) [Late 18C. Origin ?]

pid·dling /píddling/ *adj* very small, insignificant, or trivial (*informal*)

pid·dock /píddək/ *n* a saltwater mollusk that has a hinged shell with serrated edges that it uses to bore into rock and wood. Family: Pholadidae. [Mid-19C. Origin ?]

pidg·in /píjjin/ *n* a simplified language made up of parts of two or more languages, used as a communication tool between speakers whose native languages are different [Early 19C. < Chinese, alteration of BUSINESS] —**pidg·in·i·za·tion** /pìjjini záysh'n/ *n* —**pidg·in·ize** *vt*

pidg·in Eng·lish *n* a pidgin based however loosely on English, especially one formerly used between Chinese people and Europeans, or one currently spoken in West Africa and some Pacific islands

pi-dog *n* ZOOL another spelling of **pye-dog**

PIDS *abbr* MED primary immune deficiency syndrome

pie[1] /pī/ *n* **1.** a baked dish consisting of a filling such as chopped meat or fruit enclosed in pastry and usually cooked in a container **2.** something regarded as a resource to be shared or divided up ○ *Our competitors are always looking for a larger piece of the overseas pie.* [14C. Origin ?] ◇ **pie in the sky** something described very attractively that is not likely to happen or materialize

pie[2] /pī/ *n* a very small coin formerly used in India, worth one third of a pice [Mid-19C. Via Hindi *paī* < Sanskrit *pādikā* < *pāda* "quarter"]

pie[3] /pī/ *n* PRINTING another spelling of **pi**[2]

pie[4] /pī/ (*plural same* or **pies**) *n* **1.** a bird resembling a magpie, especially one with black and white feathers **2.** BIRDS same as **magpie** (*archaic*) [14C. Via French < Latin *pica* "magpie"]

pie·bald /pī bàwld/ *Can, UK* ZOOL *adj* describes a horse whose coat has patches of two or more contrasting colors, especially black and white ■ *n* (*plural same* or **-balds**) a piebald horse ► US term (all senses) **pinto** [Late 16C. < PIE[4]; from the resemblance to a magpie's plumage]

piece /peess/ *n* **1.** PART TAKEN FROM LARGER WHOLE a part that has been broken, torn, or cut from a larger whole **2.** PORTION OR SERVING a portion or serving from a larger block or whole **3.** INDIVIDUAL ITEM OR OBJECT an item or object of a particular kind or class ○ *an expensive piece of equipment* **4.** INTERCONNECTING PART one of a set of parts that fit together to form a whole or unit ○ *a 500-piece jigsaw* ○ *took the radio to pieces* **5.** EXAMPLE OF SOMETHING an instance or example of something, often something abstract such as luck ○ *a piece of good fortune* ○ *a useful piece of information* **6.** DECLARATION OF OPINION a statement of opinion on a subject, event, or situation ○ *At least I said my piece.* **7.** ARTS ARTISTIC WORK a single artistic work, e.g., a musical composition, play, or painting ○ *a piano piece* ○ *a piece of music* **8.** MEDIA PUBLISHED ARTICLE an article in a newspaper or magazine ○ *a piece of writing* **9.** COINS COIN a coin of a particular value ○ *a fifty-cent piece* **10.** BOARD GAMES OBJECT MOVED IN BOARD GAME in board games, an object that a player moves on the board **11.** FIREARM a gun, especially a handgun (*slang*) **12.** OFFENSIVE TERM an offensive term for a woman (*slang*) **13.** OFFENSIVE TERM an offensive term for sexual intercourse (*slang*) **14.** ESTIMATE OF DISTANCE an unspecified distance (*informal*) ○ *You go down the road a piece and then you come to the bridge.* ■ *vt* (**pieced, piec·ing, piec·es**) **1.** WORK SOMETHING OUT to put something together gradually, part by part ○ *We finally managed to piece together the events of that night.* **2.** MEND SOMETHING to mend something by patching it [12C. < Old French, probably < Gaulish] ◇ **fall** *or* **go to pieces 1.** to become broken into small bits **2.** to become unable to cope ◇ **give somebody a piece of your mind** to rebuke somebody severely and angrily ◇ **of a piece** alike ◇ **pull somebody** *or* **something to pieces** to reduce somebody or something to smaller parts by tugging or tearing forcefully

SPELLCHECK See ***peace***.

piece out *vt* to bring all the fragments of something such as a story together gradually

pi·èce de ré·sis·tance /pee èss də rə zeéss taánss, -ray zeéss-/ (*plural* **pi·èces de ré·sis·tance** /*pronunc. same*/) *n* **1.** the most impressive thing or something that brings the greatest pride or satisfaction **2.** the most important dish served at a meal (*formal*) [Late 18C. < French, literally "piece of resistance"]

piece-dyed *adj* dyed after being woven

piece goods *npl* fabrics made and sold in standard lengths

piece·meal /peéss meèl/ *adv* **1.** GRADUALLY little by little **2.** IN PARTS in separate parts or fragments ■ *adj* DONE PART BY PART done in a disorganized or fragmentary way ○ *His novel is a ragtag, piecemeal work.* [13C. < PIECE + obsolete *-meal* "measure" < form of MEAL[1]]

piece of cake *n* something that is very easy to do (*informal*) [< the easiness of eating cake, a soft food]

piece of eight *n* a former Spanish gold coin

piece of work *n* **1.** somebody or something remarkable or outstanding **2.** somebody or something unpleasant, troublesome, or strange

piece·work /peéss wùrk/ *n* work paid by the amount done instead of by the time spent doing it

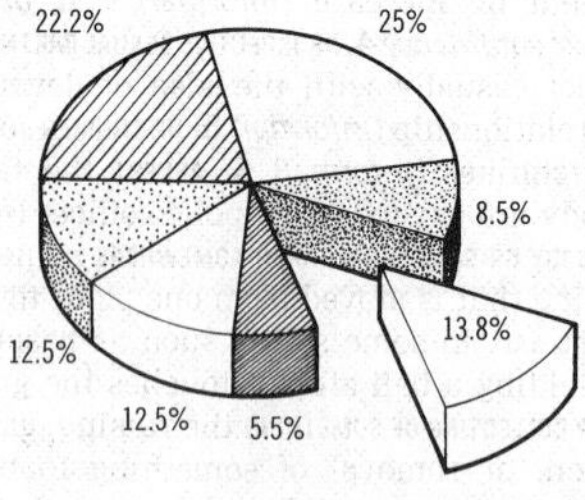

piechart

pie·chart /pī chaart/ *n* a diagrammatic representation of a group shown as a circle divided into sections by straight lines from its center with areas proportional to the relative size of the quantity represented

pied-à-terre /pee àydə tér/ (*plural* **pieds-à-terre** /*pronunc. same*/) *n* a small apartment or house used as a second home for vacations or business purposes [< French, literally "foot to earth"]

pied·mont /peéd mònt/ *n* a region at the base of a mountain range ■ *adj* lying or formed at the base of a mountain range [Mid-19C. After PIEDMONT]

Pied·mont /peéd mont/ region in northwestern Italy, a major commercial and agricultural center. Capital: Turin. Population: 4,338,262 (1991). Area: 9,807 sq. mi./25,399 sq. km. —**Pied·mon·tese** /peéd mon teéz/ *n, adj*

Pied·mont Pla·teau /peéd mont-/ upland region of the eastern United States, extending from New York to Alabama between the Appalachian Mountains and the Atlantic Coastal Plain

Pied Pip·er /pīd-/ *n* **1.** in German folklore, a visiting piper whose entrancing music rid the town of Hamelin of its rats. He later lured away its children after town officials refused to pay him for his services. **2.** *also* **pied pip·er** somebody who attracts supporters and followers, especially by making unrealistic promises

pied wag·tail *n* **1.** a small black and white bird with a long black tail. Native to: Europe. Latin name: *Motacilla alba yarrellii.* **2.** a long-tailed black-and-white bird. Native to: Africa. Latin name: *Motacilla aguimp.*

pie-eyed *adj* very drunk (*informal*)

pier /peer/ *n* **1.** WALKWAY JUTTING INTO SEA a platform built on stilts jutting out into a body of water, used as a boat dock, a place from which to fish, or as an entertainment center **2.** CONSTR BREAKWATER a barrier built out to sea to protect a harbor from heavy waves **3.** CONSTR VERTICAL STRUCTURAL SUPPORT a pillar, especially a rectangular one supporting the end of an arch, lintel, or vault **4.** CONSTR BRIDGE SUPPORT a vertical structural support between two spans of a bridge **5.** ARCHIT WALL BETWEEN ADJACENT DOORS an area of wall between two adjacent doors, windows, or other openings **6.** ARCHIT COLUMN PROJECTING FROM WALL a column of masonry projecting from a wall **7.** CONSTR WALL REINFORCEMENT a vertical structure, usually of masonry, built against a wall to support it [12C. < Anglo-Latin *pera*]

SPELLCHECK See ***peer***[1].

CULTURAL NOTE ***The Road to Wigan Pier***, a book (1937) by the British writer George Orwell. It combines a first-hand account of the appalling living conditions endured by workers in northern England with a penetrating analysis of class interests and prejudices. Its graphic and moving descriptions, compelling arguments, and restrained anger make it a classic of literary journalism.

pierce /peerss/ (**pierced, pierc·ing, pierc·es**) *v* **1.** *vti* BORE INTO SOMETHING to penetrate through or into something with a sharp pointed object **2.** *vt* PUT HOLE IN SOMETHING to make a hole through something ○ *She had her ears pierced.* **3.** *vti* PENETRATE BARRIER to break through a barrier of some kind such as a defensive line or security system **4.** *vti* GAIN SIGHT OR KNOWLEDGE to perceive something with the eyes or the mind **5.** *vti* PENETRATE SOMETHING WITH SOUND OR LIGHT to sound or shine suddenly and sharply through something such as silence or darkness ○ *A dreadful scream pierced the silence.* **6.** *vt* AFFECT SOMEBODY DEEPLY to have a sudden, intense, often painful effect on somebody ○ *A stab of fear pierced his heart.* [13C. Via French *percer* < Latin *pertundere* "bore through" < *tundere* "to bore"] —**pierc·er** *n*

Library of Congress

Franklin Pierce

Pierce /peerss/, **Franklin** (1804–69) 14th president of the United States (1853–57). A Democrat, he sided with the South on the slavery issue, yet was committed to the Union. See table at **president**

pierc·ing /peérssing/ *adj* **1.** PENETRATING having an unpleasantly intense quality ○ *a piercing cry* **2.** PERCEPTIVE capable of acute perception ○ *her piercing gaze* **3.** INTENSELY COLD having a sharp, deeply chilling coldness ○ *a piercing wind* ■ *n* **1.** MAKING OF HOLES IN BODY PARTS the practice of piercing holes in parts of the body so that rings or studs can be inserted ○ *body piercing* **2.** HOLE FOR RING IN BODY a hole pierced in a part of the body to take a ring or stud ○ *She had piercings on her eyebrow and nose.* —**pierc·ing·ly** *adv*

pier glass *n* a long narrow mirror, originally designed to fit on a wall between two windows, often above a pier table

Pi·e·ri·an Spring /pī eéree ən-/ *n* in Greek mythology, the spring at Pieria in ancient Macedonia that was sacred to the Muses, who lived there, and gave poetic inspiration to anyone who drank from it

Pie·ro del·la Fran·ce·sca /pyérrō dellə fran chéskə/ (1420?–92) Italian painter. One of the leading figures of the early Renaissance, he is noted particularly for his frescoes for the church of San Francesco in Arezzo, Italy.

Pierre /peer/ capital city of South Dakota, on the Missouri River, west of Huron and northeast of Rapid City. Population: 14,012 (2002 estimate).

Pier·rot /peé ə rō, pye rṓ/ *n* a character in traditional French pantomime. He is a white-faced clown with a white costume and pointed hat, and is often represented as sad or crying. [Mid-18C. < French, "little Peter" < *Pierre* "Peter"]

pier ta·ble *n* a small table designed to stand against a narrow section of wall between two large windows

Pie·tà /pyày taá/, **pie·tà** *n* a painting or sculpture of the Virgin Mary mourning over Jesus Christ's dead body [Mid-17C. Via Italian < Latin *pietas* (see PIETY)]

Pie·ter·mar·itz·burg /peétər márrits bùrg/ capital city of KwaZulu-Natal Province, South Africa, situated 45 mi./72 km northwest of Durban. Population: 156,473 (1991).

Pie·ters·burg /peétərz bùrg/ former name for **Polokwane**

pi·e·tism /pī́ ə tìzzəm/ *n* **1.** devotion to a deity or deities and observance of religious principles in everyday life **2.** excessive or insincere religious devotion [Early 19C. < PIETISM] —**pi·e·tist** *n* —**pi·e·tis·tic** /pī̀ ə tístik/ *adj* —**pi·e·tis·ti·cal·ly** *adv*

Pi·e·tism /pī́ ə tìzzəm/ *n* a German Protestant movement in the 17th and 18th centuries that changed the focus of Lutheranism from ritual and church government to personal piety. It was founded by Philipp Jakob Spener. [Late 17C. < German *Pietismus* < Latin *pietas* (see PIETY)]

Pie·tro da Cor·to·na /pyèttrō də kawr tṓnə/ (1596–1669) Italian architect and painter. His illusionistic frescoes, e.g., the *Allegory of Divine Providence and Baberini Power* (1633–39) and those in Roman churches, had an important influence on the development of baroque art and architecture.

pi·e·ty /pī́ ətee/ (*plural* **-ties**) *n* **1.** RELIGIOUS DEVOTION a strong respectful belief in a deity or deities and strict observance of religious principles in everyday life **2.** DEVOUT ACT an action inspired by devout religious principles **3.** INSINCERE ATTITUDE a conventional or hypocritical statement or observance of a belief **4.** FAMILY LOYALTY loyalty to parents and family (*archaic*) [14C. Via French < Latin *pietas* "dutifulness, piety, compassion" < *pius* "dutiful, devout"]

piezo- *prefix* pressure ○ *piezoelectric crystal* [< Greek *piezein* "to press" < Indo-European, "sit"]

pi·e·zo·e·lec·tric·i·ty /pee àyzō i lek tríssətee, -àytsō-/ *n* the electric current produced by some crystals and ceramic materials when they are subjected to mechanical pressure —**pi·e·zo·e·lec·tric** /-i léktrik, -àytsō-/ *adj*

pi·e·zom·e·ter /pee ə zómmətər/ *n* an instrument for measuring the compressibility of a material or fluid under pressure —**pi·e·zo·met·ric** /pee àyzō méttrik, -àytsō-/ *adj* —**pi·e·zo·met·ri·cal·ly** *adv*

pif·fle /píff'l/ *n* silly talk or ideas (*informal*) ■ *vi* (**-fled, -fling, -fles**) to behave in a silly or ineffective way (*dated informal*) [Mid-19C. Origin ?]

pif·fling /piffling/ *adj* of little use, value, or importance (*informal*)

pig /pig/ *n* **1.** FARM ANIMAL WITH BROAD SNOUT a sturdy short-legged hoofed animal with a broad snout, especially a young domesticated variety, commonly kept as a farm animal and traditionally represented as fat and pink with a curly tail. Latin name: *Sus scrofa.* **2.** PORK the meat of a pig **3.** GREEDY PERSON somebody who is regarded as slovenly, greedy, or gluttonous (*informal insult*) **4.** COARSE PERSON somebody who is thought to behave in a coarse, discourteous, or brutal manner (*informal insult*) **5.** METALL BLOCK OF METAL a casting of metal in a basic shape suitable for storage or transportation **6.** METALL METAL MOLD a basic mold for casting metal, especially iron **7.** OFFENSIVE TERM an offensive term for a member of the police force (*slang*) **8.** *US* ESTABLISHMENT FIGURE a member of the established order of society, especially somebody in authority who is regarded by youths or minorities as having outdated, racist, or sexist views (*slang insult*) **9.** *US* OFFENSIVE TERM an offensive term that deliberately insults a woman's morality (*slang*) ■ *vi* (**pigged, pig·ging, pigs**) GIVE BIRTH TO PIGS to give birth to a litter of pigs [13C. Origin ?] ◇ **a pig in a poke** something that is bought or obtained without being inspected to see whether it is worth having

pig out *vi* to eat greedily or gluttonously (*informal*)

pig·boat /píg bōt/ *n US* a submarine (*informal*)

pi·geon /píjjən/ *n* **1.** HEAVY-BODIED BIRD WITH COOING CALL a medium-sized bird with a stocky body and short legs, powerful flight and a cooing call, which eats seeds and fruit. There are more than 300 species of pigeons. Native to: found worldwide. Family: Columbidae. **2.** MEDIUM-SIZED BIRD LIVING IN CITIES a variety of rock dove, commonly seen in cities or trained for racing or carrying messages. Latin name: *Columba livia.* **3.** GULLIBLE PERSON somebody who is easily swindled or deceived (*informal*) **4.** *US* RIFLERY same as **clay pigeon** (sense 1) [14C. Via Old French *pijon* "young bird" < Vulgar Latin alteration of late Latin *pipion-*, an imitation of cheeping]

pi·geon breast *n* a condition in which the sides of the chest are flattened and the center protrudes like the keel of a boat —**pi·geon-breast·ed** *adj*

pi·geon hawk *n US* a merlin (*dated*)

pi·geon·hole /píjjən hōl/ *n* **1.** PLACE TO PUT MESSAGES a small compartment that is part of a set in a desk or wall unit into which papers or messages can be sorted or placed **2.** BROAD CATEGORY a category or label assigned to somebody or something without a great deal of thought ○ *the tendency to put writers into pigeonholes* **3.** BIRDS PIGEON'S NESTING COMPARTMENT a small nesting hole in a shelter for domestic pigeons ■ *vt* (**-holed, -hol·ing, -holes**) **1.** PUT SOMEBODY IN BROAD CATEGORY to categorize somebody or something without a great deal of thought **2.** POSTPONE SOMETHING to put something off for a while

pi·geon·ite /píjjə nīt/ *n* a yellow-green aluminosilicate mineral of the pyroxene group, containing iron, magnesium, and calcium. Source: basic igneous rocks. [Early 20C. After *Pigeon* Point, Minnesota]

pi·geon pea *n* **1.** a small nutritious seed that is popular in Caribbean cookery **2.** a woody plant of the pea family with three-lobed leaves, cultivated in tropical regions to produce pigeon peas. Flowers: yellow, orange. Native to: Africa. Latin name: *Cajanus cajan.* [< the use of its seeds as pigeon-feed]

pi·geon-toed *adj* tending to walk or stand with the toes turned inward

pig·fish /píg fish/ (*plural same* or **-fish·es**) *n* a fish of the grunt family. Native to: Atlantic coast of North America. Latin name: *Orthopristis chrysoptera.*

pig·ger·y /píggəree/ (*plural* **-ies**) *n* **1.** a farm or a building on a farm where pigs are bred and raised **2.** coarse, greedy, or otherwise distasteful behavior

pig·gish /píggish/ *adj* **1.** GLUTTONOUS eating too much too fast **2.** COARSE IN BEHAVIOR behaving in a coarse, greedy, or otherwise distasteful way **3.** OBSTINATE behaving in a stubborn, uncooperative, or obstructive way —**pig·gish·ly** *adv* —**pig·gish·ness** *n*

pig·gy /píggee/ *n* (*plural* **-gies**) (*baby talk*) **1.** a pig or piglet **2.** a toe, especially a toe of a small child ■ *adj* (**-gier, -gi·est**) same as **piggish**

pig·gy·back /píggee bàk/ *n* **1.** RIDE ON SOMEBODY'S BACK a ride on somebody's back or shoulders **2.** TRANSP HAULING OF ONE VEHICLE BY ANOTHER transportation of one vehicle by another, e.g., automobiles by truck or truck trailers by railroad car ■ *adj, adv* **1.** ON SOMEBODY'S BACK carried on the back or shoulders of another person **2.** TRANSP ON OTHER VEHICLE transported on another vehicle **3.** AS ADDITION linked with or added onto something larger or more important ■ *v* (**-backed, -back·ing, -backs**) **1.** *vt* CARRY SOMEBODY ON BACK to carry somebody on the back or shoulders **2.** *vt* TRANSP TRANSPORT VEHICLE to transport one vehicle on another **3.** *vti* ATTACH ONE THING TO ANOTHER to link or add something to a larger or more important item, or be linked or added in this way [Mid-16C. Origin ?]

pig·gy bank *n* a child's savings bank, especially one in the shape of a pig

pig·gy in the mid·dle *n UK* same as **monkey in the middle**

pig·head·ed /pig héddəd/ *adj* stubbornly adhering to a belief, decision, or course of action —**pig·head·ed·ly** *adv* —**pig·head·ed·ness** *n*

pig i·ron *n* a crude form of iron made in a blast furnace and shaped into rough blocks for storage or transportation. Pig iron is processed further to make steel, wrought iron, and other alloys.

pig Lat·in *n* a joke dialect coined and used by children, especially one in which first consonants are moved to the end of the words and extra syllables added

pig·let /pígglət/ *n* a newborn or immature pig

pig·ment *n* /pígmənt/ **1.** COLORING SUBSTANCE a substance that is added to give something such as paint or ink its color. Pigments are often available in the form of dry powders to be added to liquids. **2.** NATURAL COLORING FOR TISSUE a natural substance in plant or animal tissue that gives it its color ■ *vt* /pígmənt, pig mént/ (**-ment·ed, -ment·ing, -ments**) COLOR SOMETHING to impart color to something [Pre-12C. < Latin *pigmentum* < *pingere* "to paint"] —**pig·men·tar·y** /pígmən tèrree/ *adj*

pig·men·ta·tion /pìgmən táysh'n/ *n* **1.** the natural color of plants and animals **2.** the atypical coloring in plant or animal tissue that occurs as a result of disease

pig·my, etc. another spelling of **pygmy, etc.**

pig·nut /píg nùt/ *n US* **1.** a nut with a fleshy husk and bitter taste **2.** a hickory tree that bears pignuts. Native to: central and southern United States. Latin name: *Carya glabra* or *Carya cordiformis.*

pig·pen /píg pèn/ *n* **1.** a building or enclosure where pigs are kept **2.** a dirty or disorderly place

Pigs, Bay of ♦ **Bay of Pigs**

pig·skin /píg skìn/ *n* **1.** LEATHER FROM PIG the skin of a pig, especially when made into leather **2.** FOOTBALL a football **3.** *US* SADDLE a horse's saddle (*informal*) ■ *adj* MADE OF LEATHER FROM PIG made of leather prepared from the skin of a pig

pig·sty /píg stī/ (*plural* **-sties**) *n UK* AGRIC same as **pigpen**

pig·tail /píg tàyl/ *n* **1.** BRAID a braid or bunch of hair, often worn in pairs **2.** HAIR same as **queue** *n* (sense 4) **3.** TOBACCO STRAND a thin twisted piece of tobacco **4.** ELEC BRAIDED WIRE a short length of flexible electrical cable or wire, usually braided, connecting two terminals —**pig·tailed** *adj*

pig·weed /píg wèed/ *n* **1.** a hairy-leaved weed of the amaranth family. Flowers: green, in spikes. Native to: North America. Latin name: *Amaranthus retroflexus.* **2.** *US* a common weed whose leaves have a grainy surface and are sometimes used as a vegetable or in salads. Latin name: *Chenopodium album.* Can term **goosefoot**

pi·ka /péekə, pīkə/ (*plural* **-kas** or *same*) *n* a small short-eared burrowing animal that is related to the rabbit. Native to: rocky mountainous regions of western North America and Asia. Family: Ochotonidae. [Early 19C. < Evenki *piika*]

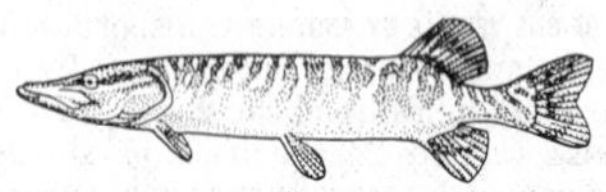

pike

pike[1] /pīk/ (*plural* **pikes** or *same*) *n* **1.** a large predatory freshwater fish with a long body, long broad snout, and sharp teeth, popular as a game fish. Native to: northern waters. Latin name: *Esox lucius.* **2.** a fish that resembles the pike or belongs to the same family, especially the muskellunge or the pickerel [14C. < Old English *pic* "long pointed object," origin ?; from its jaws]

pike[2] /pīk/ *n* a weapon, formerly used by foot soldiers, consisting of a long pole with a pointed metal head ■ *vt* (**piked, pik·ing, pikes**) to stab or kill somebody with a pike [Early 16C. < French *pique* < *piquer* (see PIQUE[1])]

pike[3] /pīk/ *n* ROADS same as **turnpike** (sense 1) [Early 19C. Shortening]

pike[4] /pīk/ *n* a diving or gymnastic position in which the body is bent at the hips with the head tucked under and the hands touching the toes or behind the knees [Early 20C. Origin ?] —**piked** *adj*

Pike /pīk/, **Zebulon Montgomery** (1779–1813) US explorer and soldier. He searched for the headwaters of the Mississippi River (1805–06) and explored Colorado and New Mexico.

pike·man /pīkmən/ (*plural* **-men** /-mən/) *n* formerly, a foot soldier armed with a pike

pike·perch /pīk pùrch/ (*plural* **-perch·es** or *same*) *n* FISH same as **walleye** (sense 1)

pik·er /pīkər/ *n US* (*informal*) **1.** STINGY PERSON somebody who is stingy with money **2.** PETTY PERSON somebody who does things in a small-minded or petty way **3.** CAUTIOUS GAMBLER somebody who gambles cautiously with little money

Pikes Peak /pīks-/ mountain in Colorado, in the Rocky Mountains, west of Colorado Springs. It was named for the explorer Zebulon Pike. Height: 14,110 ft./4,301 m.

pike·staff /pīk stàf/ *n* **1.** the wooden shaft of a pike, which forms the handle **2.** a walking stick with a pointed metal end

pi·la /péelə/ *n Hispanic* a concrete cube in which water brought in by truck is stored in Mexican desert areas [Via Mexican Spanish < Spanish, "sink, basin"]

pi·laf /pi láaf, pée laaf/, **pi·lau** /pi lów, pée lòw/ *n* a dish of spiced rice, often with chopped vegetables, fish, or meat added [Early 17C. Directly or via Turkish *pilâv* "cooked rice" < Persian *pilaw* "cooked rice and meat"]

Pi·lar /pee láar/ city and river port on the Paraguay River in southwestern Paraguay. Population: 13,135 (1982).

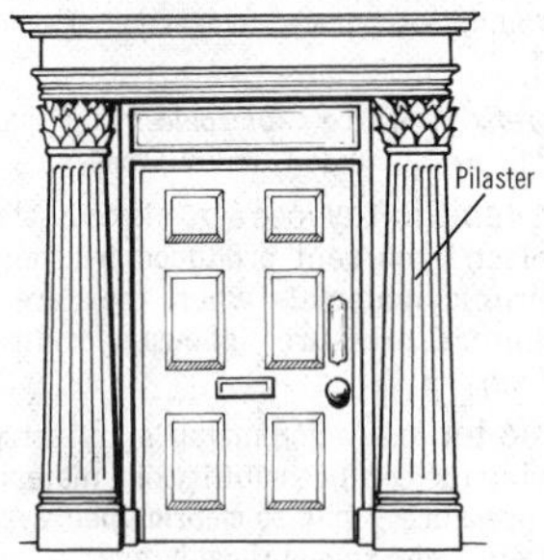

pilaster

pi·las·ter /pi lástər/ *n* a vertical structural part of a building that projects partway from a wall and is made to resemble an ornamental column by adding a base and capital [Late 16C. Via French *pilastre* < Italian *pilastro* or medieval Latin *pilastrum* < Latin *pila* "pillar"] —**pi·las·tered** *adj*

Pi·late /pīlət/, **Pontius** (*fl* A.D. 1st century) Roman administrator. As procurator of Judea (A.D. 26–36) he condemned Jesus Christ to death, albeit reluctantly, according to the Bible.

Pi·la·tes /pi láa tàyz/ *n* a holistic form of exercise and postural therapy that emphasizes the development of the deep abdominal muscles to control body movement and protect the back [Mid-20C. After Joseph H. *Pilates* (1880–1967), German fitness trainer]

pi·lau *n* another spelling of **pilaf**

Pil·ba·ra /pílbərə/ region in western Western Australia, located between the De Grey and Ashburton rivers. Area: 170,000 sq. mi./440,000 sq. km.

pil·chard /pílchərd/ (*plural* **-chards** or *same*) *n* **1.** a small ocean fish of the herring family with a rounded body and large scales. Native to: Europe. Latin name: *Sardinia pilchardus.* **2.** the flesh of a pilchard used as food [Mid-16C. Origin ?]

Pil·co·ma·yo /pìlco mīō/ river in central South America that rises in the Bolivian Andes and flows southeastward along the border between Argentina and Paraguay before joining the Paraguay River south of Asunción. Length: 700 mi./1,125 km.

pile[1] /pīl/ *n* **1.** MOUND OF THINGS a number of things heaped or stacked one on top of another **2.** LARGE QUANTITY a very large amount of something (*informal; often used in the plural*) ○ *I've got piles of work to do.* **3.** FORTUNE a very large amount of money, especially one large enough to retire on (*informal*) ○ *He'd already made his pile by the age of 30.* **4.** BUILDING a large impressive building **5.** same as **pyre** (*archaic*) **6.** ELEC same as **voltaic pile 7.** PHYS same as **nuclear reactor** (*dated*) ■ *v* (**piled, pil·ing, piles**) **1.** *vt* STACK SOMETHING INTO MOUND to heap or stack things one on top of another **2.** *vt* PLACE LARGE AMOUNT ON SOMETHING to heap a large amount of something somewhere ○ *plates piled high with ribs* **3.** *vi* GO AS CROWD to move hurriedly in a large disorganized group ○ *We all piled into the car and headed for the diner.* [15C. Via French < Latin *pila* "pillar"]

pile on ◇ **pile it on (thick)** to exaggerate something, especially its intensity or severity (*informal*)

pile up *vti* **1.** to accumulate rapidly, or accumulate something rapidly, forming a large amount **2.** to crash vehicles, or collide with other vehicles, starting a chain of collisions

pile[2] /pīl/ *n* **1.** CONSTR SUNKEN SUPPORT FOR BUILDING a vertical wood, metal, or concrete support for a building or other structure that is driven into the ground **2.** HERALDRY HERALDIC SYMBOL a heraldic figure in the shape of an arrowhead, usually displayed with the point downward **3.** ARMS ARROWHEAD the pointed head of an arrow (*technical*) **4.** ARMS ANCIENT ROMAN JAVELIN a javelin used by foot soldiers in ancient Rome ■ *vt* (**piled, pil·ing, piles**) CONSTR SUPPORT STRUCTURE WITH PILES to use piles as a support for a building or other structure [Pre-12C. < Latin *pilum* "javelin"]

pile[3] /pīl/ *n* **1.** the surface of a carpet or of a fabric such as velvet that is formed of short, sometimes cut, loops of fiber **2.** the fine soft fur or hair of an animal [Mid-16C. Probably via Anglo-Norman *peile* < Latin *pilus* "hair"]

pi·le·a BIRDS plural of **pileum**

pi·le·ate /pīlee ət, píllee-/, **pi·le·at·ed** /pīlee àytəd, píllee-/ *adj* **1.** describes the condition in which a bird has a crest of feathers on its head **2.** describes a fungus that has a cap-shaped upper part (**pileus**) [Early 18C. < Latin *pileatus* "wearing a felt cap" < *pileus* "felt cap"]

pile driv·er *n* a large mechanical hammering device that uses steam, compressed air, or gravity to drive construction piles into the ground

pi·le·i BIOL, CLOTHING plural of **pileus**

piles /pīlz/ *npl* MED same as **hemorrhoids** (*informal*) [15C. Probably < Latin *pila* "ball"; from their shape]

pi·le·um /pīlee əm, píllee-/ (*plural* **-le·a** /-lee ə/) *n* the top of a bird's head from the base of the beak to the nape of the neck [Late 19C. < modern Latin, alteration of Latin *pileus* "felt cap"]

pile-up /pīl ùp/, **pile-up** *n* (*informal*) **1.** a collision involving several vehicles **2.** an accumulated number or amount of things such as tasks

pi·le·us /pīlee əss, píllee-/ (*plural* **-le·i** /-lee ī/) *n* **1.** BOT CAP OF MUSHROOM the top cap-shaped part of a mushroom or other fungus **2.** MARINE BIOL BODY OF JELLYFISH the part of the body of a jellyfish that resembles an opened umbrella **3.** CLOTHING ROMAN SKULLCAP a close-fitting brimless cap worn by ancient Romans [Mid-18C. < Latin *pileus* "felt cap"]

pile·wort /pīl wùrt, -wàwrt/ (*plural* **-worts** or *same*) *n* a flowering plant of the buttercup family, e.g., the lesser celandine. Use: remedy for hemorrhoids. [15C. < singular of PILES]

pil·fer /pílfər/ (**-fered, -fer·ing, -fers**) *vti* to steal small items of little value, especially habitually [14C. < Anglo-Norman *pelfrer* "rob"] —**pil·fer·age** *n* —**pil·fer·er** *n* —**pil·fer·ing** *n*

SYNONYMS See ***steal***.

pil·grim /pílgrim/ *n* **1.** somebody who goes on a journey to a holy place for religious reasons **2.** somebody who makes a special journey (*literary*) [12C. Via Provençal *pelegrin* < Latin *peregrinus* (see PEREGRINE)]

CULTURAL NOTE ***The Pilgrim's Progress***, a story (1678, 1684) by the English writer John Bunyan. An allegorical account of religious conversion, it describes the journey of a man called Christian from the City of Destruction (the contemporary, corrupt world) to the Celestial City (a state of religious grace). Much of its lasting popularity can be attributed to the author's skill in rendering complex abstract issues immediate, entertaining, and accessible. It is the source of three well-known expressions in use today: *muckraker* (an investigative journalist seeking sensational stories), *slough of despond* (a state of profoundly deep depression), and *vanity fair* (a place or situation of ostentatious empty pride).

Pil·grim *n* any of the English Puritans who founded Plymouth Colony in Massachusetts in 1620

pil·grim·age /pílgrimij/ *n* **1.** a journey to a holy place, undertaken for religious reasons **2.** a journey to a place with special significance ○ *Thousands of fans make the pilgrimage to Elvis's birthplace every year.* [13C. < Provençal *pelegrinatge* < *pelegrin* (see PILGRIM)]

~~pilgrimmage~~ incorrect spelling of **pilgrimage**

pi·li BIOL plural of **pilus**

pil·ing /pī́ling/ *n* **1.** SINKING OF PILES the driving of piles into the ground for structural support **2.** PILES COLLECTIVELY piles driven into the ground, considered collectively **3.** CONSTR STRUCTURE OF PILES a structure built of piles **4.** CONSTR same as **pile**^{2} *n* (sense 1) [15C. < PILE^{2}]

Pil·i·pi·no /pìllə peénō/ *n, adj* LANG same as **Filipino**

pill /pil/ *n* **1.** ROUND TABLET OF MEDICINE a round solid tablet of medicine to be taken orally **2.** *also* **Pill** ORAL CONTRACEPTIVE a contraceptive taken orally **3.** SOMETHING ROUND something round, e.g., a baseball, bullet, or bomb (*informal*) **4.** TIRESOME PERSON an unpleasant or boring person (*slang dated*) ■ *v* (**pilled, pil·ling, pills**) **1.** *vi* FORM LITTLE BALLS WHEN RUBBED to become covered in small balls of matted fiber because of rubbing (*refers to fabrics*) **2.** *vt* EXCLUDE SOMEBODY to reject somebody either by vote or consensus (*dated slang*) [15C. < Middle Low German or Middle Dutch *pille*] ◇ **a bitter pill (to swallow)** something that is difficult or painful to accept

pil·lage /píllij/ *vti* (**-laged, -lag·ing, -lag·es**) **1.** PLUNDER PLACE to rob a place using force, especially during a war **2.** STEAL POSSESSIONS to steal goods using force, especially during a war ■ *n* **1.** STEALING OF POSSESSIONS the theft of goods from a place using force, especially during a war **2.** STOLEN POSSESSIONS goods that are stolen using force, especially during a war [14C. < French < *piller* "to plunder"] —**pil·lag·er** *n*

pil·lar /píllər/ *n* **1.** COLUMN USED FOR SUPPORT OR DECORATION a vertical column that is part of a building or other structure and can be either a support or decoration **2.** SOMETHING TALL AND NARROW something that is tall and slender like a pillar **3.** CENTRAL FIGURE a mainstay of an organization or society ○ *She was a pillar of the community.* ■ *vt* (**-lared, -lar·ing, -lars**) SUPPORT SOMETHING WITH PILLARS to support or strengthen something with pillars [13C. Via Anglo-Norman *piler* < Latin *pila*] ◇ **from pillar to post** from one place to another

Pil·lars of Her·cu·les /píllərz əv hùrkyoō leez/ two promontories, the Rock of Gibraltar and Jebel Musa, on either side of the Strait of Gibraltar at the far western end of the Mediterranean. According to legend, the two rocks were separated by Hercules.

Pil·lars of Is·lam *npl* same as **Five Pillars of Islam**

pill·box /píll bòks/ *n* **1.** PILL-CONTAINER a small container for pills **2.** *also* **pill·box hat** WOMAN'S BRIMLESS HAT a woman's shallow brimless hat with a flat top **3.** GUN SHELTER a small fortified shelter with a flat roof, in which a large gun is sited

pill bug *n* INSECTS same as **wood louse** [Because able to roll itself into a ball]

pilled-up /pìld úp/ *adj* affected by or high on drugs, especially drugs taken in tablet form (*slang*)

pil·lion /píllyən/ *n* a seat for a passenger behind the driver of a motorcycle or the rider of a horse ■ *adv* seated behind the driver of a motorcycle or the rider of a horse [15C. < Gaelic *pillean*, Irish *pillin* "little couch" < *pell* "couch" < Latin *pellis* "skin"]

pil·lo·ry /pílləree/ *n* (*plural* **-ries**) CRIME, HIST PUNISHMENT DEVICE a wooden frame with holes into which somebody's head and hands could be locked, formerly used as a means of public punishment ■ *vt* (**-ried, -ry·ing, -ries**) **1.** RIDICULE SOMEBODY to scorn or ridicule somebody or something openly **2.** CRIME PUNISH SOMEBODY IN PILLORY to put somebody into a pillory as a public punishment [13C. Via Anglo-Latin *pillorium* < Old French *pillorie*]

pil·low /píllō/ *n* **1.** CUSHION FOR HEAD IN BED a sealed fabric bag stuffed with feathers or a synthetic filling used as a soft support for the head in bed **2.** SOMETHING LIKE PILLOW something that is similar to a pillow in appearance or use **3.** HANDICRAFT same as **cushion** *n* (sense 6) ■ *vt* (**-lowed, -low·ing, -lows**) **1.** CUSHION HEAD to rest the head on a pillow or something else that is soft and comfortable **2.** ACT AS PILLOW FOR SOMETHING to provide a soft comfortable surface on which to rest something [Old English *pyle*, via W Germanic < Latin *pulvinus*]

pil·low block *n* an enclosure and support for a shaft or axle of a machine

pil·low·case /píllō kàyss/ *n* a fabric cover for a pillow

pil·low lace *n* lace made using bobbins and a firm pad or pillow as a base, as distinct from lace made with a needle and a paper pattern

pil·low la·va *n* lava that has solidified into pillow-shaped masses, formed from underwater lava flows or from lava flowing into water from land. Each pillow can be up to 6 ft./2 m across and is surrounded by a fine-grained skin.

pil·low sham *n* a decorative covering for a pillow on a bed

pil·low·slip /píllō slìp/ *n* HOUSEHOLD same as **pillowcase**

pil·low talk *n* the discussion of intimate or private matters in bed with a sexual partner

pilm /pilm/ *n Wales* same as **dust** *n* (senses 1–2) [< Welsh]

pi·lo·car·pine /pìlə kaár peen, -kaárpin/ *n* an organic compound of plant origin. Source: leaves of jaborandi trees. Use: in eye drops to treat glaucoma. [Late 19C. < modern Latin *Pilocarpus*, genus name of the jaborandi tree]

pi·lo·e·rec·tion /pìlō i réksh'n/ *n* the erection of the hairs on the surface of the skin, e.g., to conserve heat [Mid-20C. < Latin *pilus* "hair"]

pi·lose /pī́lōss/, **pi·lous** /pī́ləss/ *adj* describes plant parts that are covered with soft hair [Late 18C. < Latin *pilosus* "hairy" < *pilus* "hair"] —**pi·los·i·ty** /pī lóssətee/ *n*

pi·lot /pī́lət/ *n* **1.** SOMEBODY WHO FLIES PLANE somebody who pilots an aircraft or spacecraft **2.** SOMEBODY STEERING SHIPS THROUGH DIFFICULT AREA somebody with local knowledge whose job is to navigate ships in and out of a harbor or through a difficult stretch of water **3.** STEERER OF SHIP somebody who steers a ship or boat **4.** LEADER somebody who acts as a leader or guide **5.** BROADCAST TRIAL TELEVISION PROGRAM a television or radio program made as a prototype for a projected series **6.** TRIAL RUN a test of something such as a proposed manufacturing process to discover and solve problems before full implementation **7.** INDUST same as **pilot light** (sense 1) **8.** ENG MACHINE GUIDE a guiding part of a tool or machine ■ *vt* (**-lot·ed, -lot·ing, -lots**) **1.** AVIAT FLY AIRCRAFT to fly an aircraft or spacecraft **2.** NAUT NAVIGATE SHIP to navigate a ship **3.** BE IN CHARGE OF SOMETHING to direct the course of something such as a project or a program of research **4.** RUN TRIAL OF SOMETHING to test something such as a proposed manufacturing process to discover and solve problems before full implementation [Early 16C. Via French *pilote* < medieval Latin *pilotus*, alteration of *pedota* < Greek *pēdon* "oar"] —**pi·lot·less** *adj*

pi·lot·age /pī́lətij/ *n* **1.** PILOTING OF CRAFT the controlling of a ship, aircraft, or spacecraft **2.** FEE OF HARBOR OR RIVER PILOT the fee paid to a harbor or river pilot **3.** MANUAL NAVIGATION the manual navigation of an aircraft, using landmarks and maps

pi·lot bal·loon *n* a small balloon launched to study the speed and direction of winds at high altitudes. The balloon is visually tracked by a theodolite.

pi·lot bread, pi·lot bis·cuit *n US* FOOD same as **hardtack**

pi·lot fish *n* a small striped ocean fish, often found swimming with sharks, mantas, and other large fishes, where it finds stray scraps of food. Latin name: *Naucrates ductor.*

pi·lot·house /pī́lət hòwss/ *n* an enclosed control room on or near the bridge of a ship, containing the steering wheel and navigational and communication equipment

pi·lot lamp *n* a small light in an electric circuit to show whether the power is on or whether an electrical device is operating

pi·lot light *n* **1.** a small gas flame that remains lit in order to ignite a burner when it is turned on **2.** ELEC same as **pilot lamp**

pi·lot whale *n* a large black toothed whale with a bulbous head, found in warm seas. Genus: *Globicephala.*

pi·lous *adj* BIOL same as **pilose**

pil·sner /pílznər, pílssnər/, **pil·sener** /pílzənər, píls-/ *n* **1.** *also* **Pil·sner** *or* **Pil·sener** a lager beer with a strong hops flavor, originally and especially made in Pilsen in the Czech Republic **2.** *also* **pil·sner glass** *or* **pil·sener glass** a tall, tapering, short-stemmed glass used for drinking beer [Late 19C. < German, "of Pilsen" < *Pilsen* (Czech *Plzeň*), province in the Czech Republic]

Pił·sud·ski /pil soōtskee/, **Józef** (1867–1935) Polish nationalist leader. He fought to free Poland from Russian rule. He was Poland's head of state (1918–22) and later its virtual dictator (1926–35). Full name **Piłsudski, Józef Klemens**

Pilt·down man /pílt dòwn-/ *n* a supposed primitive form of human being represented by remains of bones found in Sussex, England in 1912, shown in 1953 to be a hoax [Early 20C. After a village in Sussex, England]

pil·ule /píl yoōl/ *n* a small pill [15C. Via French < Latin *pilula* "little ball" < *pila* "ball"]

pi·lus /pī́ləss/ (*plural* **-li** /-lī/) *n* a part of a plant or animal organism that looks like a hair [Mid-20C. < Latin, "hair"]

PIM /pim/ *abbr* COMPUT personal information manager

Pi·ma /peémə/ (*plural same or* **-mas**) *n* **1.** a member of a Native North American people who lived in southern and central Arizona and now live mainly in central Arizona **2.** the Uto-Aztecan language of the Pima people. Native speakers: 15,000. [Early 19C. < Spanish, shortening of *Pimahito* < Pima *pimahaitu* "nothing"] —**Pi·ma** *adj*

pi·ma cot·ton /peémə-/ *n* a strong cotton with medium-length fibers that was developed in the southwestern United States from selected Egyptian cottons [Mid-20C. After *Pima* County, Arizona]

Pi·ma-Pa·pa·go /peémə páppə gō/ *n* the Pima and Papago languages regarded together. They are closely related members of the Uto-Aztecan family of Native North and Central American languages. Native speakers: 24,000. —**Pi·ma-Pa·pa·go** *adj*

pi·men·to /pi méntō/ *n* **1.** FOOD same as **pimiento 2.** COOK same as **allspice** [Late 17C. Via Spanish *pimiento* < Latin *pigmentum* (see PIGMENT)]

pi mes·on *n* PHYS same as **pion**

pi·mien·to /pi méntō, -myéntō/ (*plural* **-tos**) *n* **1.** a large sweet red pepper. Use: paprika, olive stuffing, garnish. **2.** a plant that produces pimientos. Native to: Europe. Latin name: *Capsicum annuum.* [Mid-17C. < Spanish (see PIMENTO)]

pimp /pimp/ *n* somebody, usually a man, who finds customers for a prostitute in return for a portion of the prostitute's earnings [Late 16C. Origin ?] —**pimp** *vi*

pim·per·nel /pímpər nèl, -nəl/ (*plural* **-nels** *or same*) *n* a small plant with long trailing stems. Flowers: small, red, white, or purple. Genus: *Anagallis.* [15C. < Old French *pimpernelle* "burnet," alteration of *piprenelle* < Latin *piper* "pepper"; because its fruit resemble peppercorns]

pimp·ing /pímping/ *adj* **1.** of little significance (*archaic*) **2.** *regional* appearing weak and unhealthy (*regional*) [Late 17C. Origin ?]

pim·ple /pímp'l/ *n* a small inflamed or pus-filled spot on the skin [14C. Related to Old English *piplian* "break out in spots"] —**pim·pled** *adj* —**pim·ply** *adj*

pimp·mo·bile /pímp mō beél, -mə-/ *n* a very showy large automobile, typical of one that might be used by a pimp (*informal*)

pin /pin/ *n* **1.** THIN POINTED METAL STICK a small thin metal stick with a sharp point and a rounded head used for holding pieces of fabric together **2.** POINTED METAL FASTENER a fastener with a sharp metal point designed to pierce the things it is fastening **3.** CLOTHING, ARMS same as **safety pin 4.** JEWELRY SOMETHING DECORATIVE ATTACHED TO CLOTHING a badge, piece of jewelry, or other decorative item that attaches to clothing by means of a sharp metal point or a clasp **5.** HAIR same as **hairpin** (sense 1) **6.** HAIR BOBBY PIN a bobby pin **7.** MECH ENG same as **cotter pin 8.** HOUSEHOLD same as **rolling pin 9.** ELEC PART OF ELECTRICAL CONNECTOR a thin metal terminal extending from an electrical or electronic device such as a plug or a vacuum tube, used to connect the device by socket to other circuitry ○ *a three-pin plug* **10.** SURG ROD JOINING BROKEN BONE a thin metal rod used to hold the ends of a fractured bone together **11.** DENT ROD ATTACHING TOOTH CAP TO ROOT a thin metal rod used to attach a crown to the root of a tooth **12.** MECH ENG KEY PART ENTERING LOCK the part of a key that inserts into a lock **13.** MUSIC PEG HOLDING

INSTRUMENT STRING a peg on a stringed instrument such as a piano that holds the strings and can be turned to tighten or loosen them to tune the instrument **14.** BOWLING **BOWLING PIN** a club-shaped target used in various games of bowling **15.** GOLF **HOLE MARKER** a pole with a flag on it, used to mark each hole on a golf course **16.** WRESTLING **FALL BRINGING WRESTLER'S SHOULDERS ONTO FLOOR** in wrestling, a fall in which an opponent's shoulders are made to touch the mat **17.** COMPUT **GUIDE ON COMPUTER PRINTER** a peg in a set that guides the paper through a computer printer **18.** COMPUT **PART OF PRINTHEAD THAT FORMS LETTERS** a wire in a set on the printhead of a dot matrix printer that forms one dot of a letter or symbol **19.** NAUT same as **belaying pin 20.** ROWING same as **tholepin** ■ **pins** *npl* ANAT somebody's legs (*informal*) ○ *He's a bit unsteady on his pins.* ■ *vt* (**pinned, pin·ning, pins**) **1. FASTEN SOMETHING WITH PIN** to fasten, attach, or secure something with a pin **2. KEEP SOMEBODY FROM MOVING** to hold somebody or something immobile, e.g., on the ground ○ *The beam fell across his back, pinning him to the ground.* **3.** CHESS **STOP CHESS PIECE BEING MOVED** to make it impossible for a chess opponent to move a piece without exposing the king to check or a valuable piece to capture **4.** WRESTLING **HOLD WRESTLER DOWN ON FLOOR** in wrestling, to hold an opponent's shoulders to the mat **5. GIVE FRATERNITY PIN TO SOMEBODY** to give a young woman a fraternity pin as a sign of commitment to a relationship [12C. < Latin *pinna* "feather, pointed peak"]

pin down *vt* **1. IDENTIFY SOMETHING PRECISELY** to determine something with certainty ○ *Can you pin down the time of death?* **2. FORCE SOMEBODY TO DECIDE** to force somebody to keep a commitment or come to a decision ○ *I haven't managed to pin him down to a date for our meeting yet.* **3. PREVENT SOMEBODY FROM MOVING** to prevent somebody from going anywhere ○ *The platoon was pinned down by enemy fire.*

PIN /pin/ (*plural* **PINs**) *n* a multidigit number that is used by somebody to gain access to an account at an ATM, a computer, or a telephone system. Full form **personal identification number**

~~**pinacle**~~ incorrect spelling of **pinnacle**

pi·ña cloth /pe͞enyə-/ *n* a fine transparent fabric made of fiber from pineapple leaves [*Piña* via Spanish, "pineapple, pine cone" < Latin *pinea* "pine cone" < *pinus* "pine (tree)"]

pi·ña co·la·da /pe͞enyə kə la͞adə/ *n* a cocktail made from pineapple juice, rum, and coconut [< Spanish, "strained pineapple"]

pinafore

pin·a·fore /pínnə fàwr/ *n* **1.** a sleeveless collarless garment formerly worn by girls over a dress and fastened at the top of the back **2.** *also* **pin·a·fore dress** *UK* CLOTHING same as **jumper**[1] (sense 1) [Late 18C. Because originally a garment pinned to the front of a dress]

Pi·nang /pə náng/ ➧ **Penang**

pi·ña·ta /pin ya͞atə, peen-/ *n Hispanic* a decorated papier-mâché container of candy or small gifts that is hung from the ceiling and is hit and broken by blindfolded people with sticks, traditionally during Latin American festivals. It is often shaped like a donkey or a cartoon character. [Late 19C. < Spanish, "jug"]

Pi·na·tu·bo, Mount /pìnnə to͝obō/ active volcano in the Philippines, in the central part of the island of Luzon, north of Manila. It erupted in 1991 and 1992, causing heavy loss of life and widespread destruction of homes and agricultural land. Height: 5,840 ft./1,780 m.

pin·ball /pín bàwl/ *n* a game played on an electronic table fitted with obstacles, targets, and pivoted flippers. The player controls the flippers to keep a ball in play, hitting targets to score points. (*often used before a noun*)

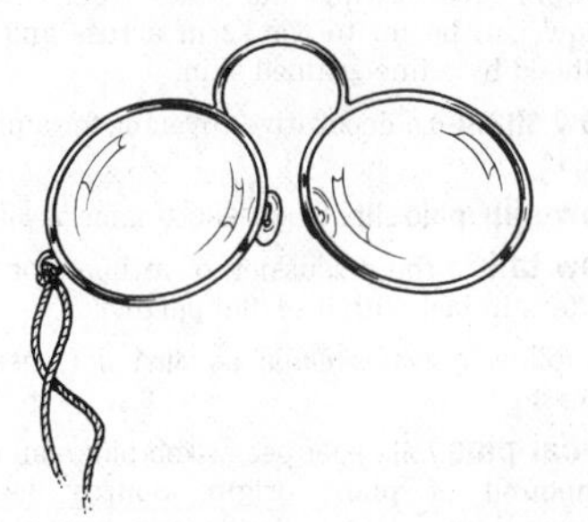
pince-nez

pince-nez /pìnss náy/ (*plural* **pince-nez** /-náyz/) *n* a pair of glasses without sidepieces, held in place by a clip that fits over the nose [< French, "pinch the nose"]

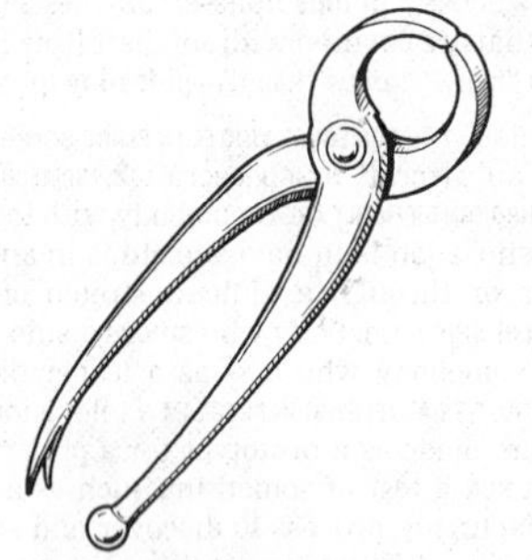
pincers

pin·cer /pínssər/ *n* a large jointed front claw of some crustaceans and arachnids such as the lobster and scorpion, used for grasping things (*usually used in the plural*) ■ **pin·cers** *npl* a tool resembling a pair of pliers or scissors that has curved pivoted jaws that are used to grip something such as a nail when they are closed [14C. < assumed Anglo-Norman *pinceour* < *pincer*, variant of Old French *pincier* (see PINCH)]

pin·cer move·ment /pínssər-/, **pin·cers move·ment** /pínssərz-/ *n* a military maneuver that attempts to surround an enemy by simultaneous attack from the front and two side columns that curve around the enemy and back toward each other

pinch /pinch/ *v* (**pinched, pinch·ing, pinch·es**) **1.** *vti* **GRIP SOMETHING BETWEEN FINGER AND THUMB** to grip or squeeze something tightly between finger and thumb or between two hard objects or edges **2.** *vti* **BE TOO TIGHT AND PAINFUL** to painfully constrict or squeeze a part of the body ○ *These shoes are pinching my feet.* **3.** *vt* **WITHER SOMETHING** to make somebody or something become shrunken or withered, especially through harsh conditions such as cold or hunger ○ *a face pinched with grief and pain* **4.** *vt* **IMPOSE FINANCIAL HARDSHIP ON SOMEBODY** to put somebody in financial difficulty ○ *Unexpected expenses have really pinched me this month.* **5.** *vti* **STEAL SOMETHING** to steal something or take something without permission (*informal*) ○ *Who's pinched my pen?* **6.** *vt* **ARREST SOMEBODY** to arrest somebody for wrongdoing (*informal*) **7.** *vt* GARDENING **REMOVE SHOOTS TO ENCOURAGE BUSHY GROWTH** to remove new shoots and buds from a plant to make it become more bushy **8.** *vt* SAILING **SAIL VESSEL INTO WIND** to sail a sailing vessel too close to the wind, so that it loses wind from its sails **9.** *vi* MIN EXTRACT **NARROW AND DISAPPEAR** to become gradually narrower, eventually disappearing entirely (*refers to a vein of ore*) ■ *n* **1. PAINFUL SQUEEZE** a painful squeeze or nip, especially with the thumb and finger ○ *a pinch on the arm* **2. VERY SMALL QUANTITY** a very small amount of a substance, especially the amount held between the thumb and first finger ○ *Add a pinch of salt.* **3.** CRIME same as **robbery** (*informal*) **4. ARREST OF SOMEBODY** an arrest made by the police (*informal*) **5. CRITICAL TIME** an emergency or critical situation [13C. Via assumed Anglo-Norman *pincher*, variant of Old French *pincier* < assumed Vulgar Latin *pinctiare* "to prick"] ◇ **feel the pinch** to have financial problems ◇ **in a pinch** if absolutely necessary, although preferably not

SYNONYMS See ***steal***.

pinch bar *n* a crowbar with a pointed end and a projection that provides a fulcrum, used as a lever, often with a notch, or claw, at the other end

pinch·beck /pínch bèk/ *n* **1. GOLD-COLORED METAL ALLOY** an alloy of copper and zinc used as imitation gold in inexpensive jewelry **2. CHEAP COPY** an inferior imitation ■ *adj* **1. MADE OF PINCHBECK** made from pinchbeck alloy **2. IMITATION** made in imitation of something and usually of inferior quality [Mid-18C. After Christopher *Pinchbeck* (d. 1732), English watchmaker]

pinch ef·fect *n* the narrowing of a beam of charged particles caused by the interaction of each particle with the magnetic field generated by the movement of the beam

pinch hit *n* in baseball, a hit made by a substitute batter —**pinch-hit** *vi* —**pinch hit·ter** *n*

pinch-hit *vi* **1.** in baseball, to replace the scheduled batter at bat, especially when a hit is needed **2.** to take somebody else's place at something —**pinch hit·ter** *n*

Pin·chot /pín shō/, **Gifford** (1865–1946) US conservationist. He advocated government protection of natural resources, and was chief of what is now the Forest Service (1898–1910).

pinch·pen·ny /pínch pènnee/ *adj* unwilling to spend or give money ■ *n* (*plural* **-nies**) somebody who is unwilling to spend or give money

pinch·point /pínch pòynt/ *n* **1.** a point in a system or process that is likely to experience or cause delays ○ *a major pinchpoint in the traffic flow* **2.** a narrow area between two surfaces that is likely to trap or catch objects and so is a potential safety hazard

pinch run·ner *n* in baseball, a runner who replaces a batter who has successfully reached base, usually because the batter is slow or injured

Pinck·ney /píngknee/, **Charles Cotesworth** (1757–1824) US patriot and political leader. He helped to draft the US Constitution, and was four times governor of South Carolina.

pin clo·ver *n* PLANTS same as **alfilaria** [< the shape of its carpels]

pin curl *n* a flat curl in hair, made by winding strands of hair into a circle and securing it with a clip or hairpin

pin·cush·ion /pín ko͝osh'n/ *n* a small stuffed pad used for sticking dressmaking pins into when they are not being used

Pin·dar /píndər/ (518–438 B.C.) Greek poet. His lyric poetry celebrated victories in the ancient Olympic Games. —**Pin·dar·ic** /pin dárrik/ *adj*

Pin·dar·ic ode /pin dàrrik-/ *n* a form of ode with three-stanza sections, the first and second stanzas having one metrical form and the third having a different form

pine

pine[1] /pīn/ *n* **1. WOOD FROM EVERGREEN TREE** the wood from an evergreen tree, varying from soft to hard. Use: furniture-making, construction, finishing material. **2. EVERGREEN TREE** an evergreen coniferous tree with needle-shaped leaves and woody cones, often grown for its wood or resin, or for ornament. Genus: *Pinus*. (*often used before a noun*) **3. TREE RESEMBLING PINE** a coniferous tree or bush that resembles a true pine, e.g., the Norfolk Island pine [Pre-12C. < Latin *pinus*] —**pine·y** /pīnee/ *adj* ◇ **ride the pine** to be removed from team play during a sports contest ○ *He's been riding the pine all season owing to injuries.*

pine[2] /pīn/ (**pined, pin·ing, pines**) *vi* **1.** to long for somebody or something, especially somebody or something unattainable **2.** to become weak and lose vitality as a result of grief or longing [Old English *pīnian* "suffer" < *pīne* "punishment" < Latin *poena* (see PAIN)]

pin·e·al /pínnee əl, pī née əl/ *adj* **1.** relating to or secreted by the pineal gland **2.** shaped like a pine cone [Late 17C. < French *pinéal* < Latin *pinea* "pine cone" (from its shape) < *pinus* "pine (tree)"]

pin·e·al gland, **pin·e·al bod·y** *n* a small cone-shaped organ of the brain that secretes the hormone melatonin into the bloodstream. It is one of the endocrine glands and is situated beneath the back part of the corpus callosum.

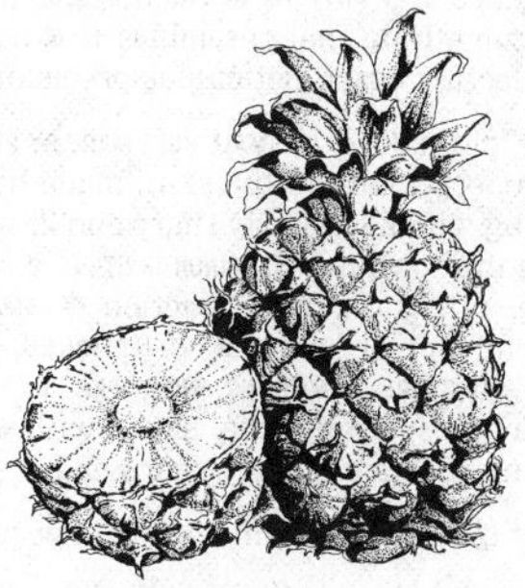

pineapple

pine·ap·ple /pīn àpp'l/ *n* **1.** JUICY YELLOW FRUIT a large fruit with juicy yellow flesh, a thick lumpy yellowish brown skin, and a tuft of tough pointed leaves at the top **2.** (*plural* **pine·ap·ples** or *same*) PLANT ON WHICH PINEAPPLES GROW a plant that produces pineapples. Native to: tropical America. Latin name: *Ananas comosus*. **3.** ARMS GRENADE WITH PATTERNED SURFACE a hand grenade with a surface of raised geometric shapes (*slang*) [14C. < the likening of the fruit to a pine cone]

pine·ap·ple weed *n* a plant with greenish yellow flower heads that smell like pineapple when crushed. Native to: Asia. Latin name: *Matricaria matri.*

Pine Bluff /pīn-/ city in southeastern Arkansas, on the Arkansas River, southeast of Little Rock. Population: 54,169 (2002 estimate).

pine cone *n* the seed case of a pine tree, usually woody, oval, and scaly

pine·drops /pīn dròps/ *n* a purplish brown leafless plant that grows under pine trees as a parasite on the roots. Flowers: drooping, reddish or white. Native to: North America. Latin name: *Pterospora andromedea*. (*takes a singular or plural verb*)

pine·land /pīn lànd/ *n* an area forested mainly with pine trees (*often used in the plural*)

pine leaf scale *n* an insect with a tough outer covering that attaches itself to pine needles and seriously inhibits their growth. Latin name: *Chionaspis pinifoliae.*

pi·nene /pī neen/ *n* either of two colorless liquid compounds. Source: turpentine, eucalyptus. Use: manufacture of plastics, solvent. Formula: $C_{10}H_{16}$. [Late 19C. < Latin *pinus* "pine (tree)"]

pine nee·dle *n* the needle-shaped leaf of a pine tree

pine nut *n* a small sweet seed of some pine trees, especially a piñon

pin·er·y /pīnəree/ (*plural* **-ies**) *n* **1.** a plantation or heated greenhouse where pineapples are grown commercially **2.** a pine forest, especially one planted for timber production

pine·sap /pīn sàp/ (*plural* **-saps** or *same*) *n* a fleshy red or yellowish plant that resembles the Indian pipe and grows as a parasite on tree roots. Native to: North America. Latin name: *Montropa hypopithys.*

pine sis·kin *n* a small finch with brown plumage and yellow markings that lives in coniferous forests and eats the seeds from pine cones. Native to: North America. Latin name: *Carduelis pinus.*

pine snake *n* a large bull snake with black-and-white markings. Native to: pine forests in the eastern United States. Latin name: *Pituophis melanoleucus.*

pine straw *n Southern US* pine needles that have fallen to the ground

pine tar *n* a thick sticky brown-to-black substance obtained by the destructive distillation of pine wood. Use: making roofing materials, paints, medicines, shampoos.

Pine Tree State *n* a nickname for Maine

pine war·bler *n* a bird of the warbler family with a yellow breast. Native to: pine forests of the eastern United States. Latin name: *Dendroica pinus.*

pine·wood /pīn wòod/ *n* **1.** the wood of a pine tree (*often used before a noun*) **2.** a small forest of pine trees (*often used in the plural*)

pin·y *adj* BOT another spelling of **piny**

Pine·y Woods /pīnee-/ large forested upland region of the southern and southeastern United States, covering parts of Texas, Oklahoma, Arkansas, Louisiana, Mississippi, Alabama, Georgia, and Florida

pin·feath·er /pín fè*th*ər/ *n* a feather only recently emerged from a bird's skin and still surrounded by a horny sheath

pin·fish /pín fish/ (*plural* **-fish·es** or *same*) *n* a small ocean fish of the porgy family with a thin dark green body and sharp dorsal spines. Native to: southern Atlantic coast of the United States. Latin name: *Lagodon rhomboides.*

pin·fold /pín fòld/ *n* **1.** an enclosure for stray animals, especially farm animals **2.** a place or situation that confines [Pre-12C. < form related to POUND[3] "enclosure" + FOLD[2]]

ping /ping/ *n* **1.** SOUND a single short ringing sound **2.** AUTOMOT same as **knock** *n* (sense 5) **3.** SONAR PULSE a brief sonic or ultrasonic pulse emitted by a sonar, the reflection or echo of which is used in detecting submarines or schools of fish **4.** RESPONSE TIME the length of time, in milliseconds, that it takes to send a message to an intranet, Internet, or web address and receive a reply ○ *super-low ping* ■ *v* (**pinged, ping·ing, pings**) **1.** *vti* RING to make a single short ringing sound, or make something such as a bell produce a ringing sound **2.** *vi* DETECT UNDERWATER OBJECTS to detect submarines or schools of fish by emitting and receiving the echo of a brief sonic or ultrasonic pulse **3.** *vti* CHECK FOR RESPONSE FROM WEB ADDRESS to send a packet of data to an intranet, Internet, or web address to check whether it is accessible or is responding **4.** *vi* AUTOMOT same as **knock** *v* (sense 8) [Mid-18C. An imitation of the sound]

ping·er /píngər/ *n* a device that produces pinging noises, especially one used as part of underwater detection equipment (*informal*)

pin·go /píng gō/ (*plural* **-gos**) *n* a large mound of soil-covered ice forced up by the pressure of water in permafrost [Mid-20C. < Inuit *pinguq*]

Ping-Pong /píng pòng/ *tdmk* a trademark for table tennis

ping-pong·ing *n* the practice of referring a customer or client from one agency or representative to another and vice versa, with no decision being made (*slang*)

pin grass *n* PLANTS same as **alfilaria**

pin·guid /píng gwid/ *adj* containing a lot of fat, oil, or grease [Mid-17C. < Latin *pinguis* "fat"] —**pin·guid·i·ty** /ping gwíddətee/ *n*

pin·head /pín hèd/ *n* **1.** BLUNT END OF PIN the rounded head of a pin **2.** SMALL THING something that is very small or trivial **3.** OFFENSIVE TERM an offensive term that deliberately insults somebody's intelligence (*informal insult*)

pin·hole /pín hòl/ *n* a tiny hole or puncture of the size made by a pin

pin·hole cam·er·a *n* a basic form of camera with a tiny hole for the aperture, and no lens. Light passes through the hole to form an inverted image on the film emulsion.

pin·ion[1] /pínnyən/ *vt* (**-ioned, -ion·ing, -ions**) **1.** RESTRAIN SOMEBODY to restrain or immobilize somebody, especially by tying his or her arms **2.** KEEP BIRD FROM FLYING to prevent a bird from flying by removing or binding its wing feathers ■ *n* BIRD'S WING a bird's wing, especially the tip of the wing where the stiff flight feathers are found, containing the carpus, metacarpus, and phalanx bones [15C. < French *pignon* < Latin *pinna* "feather"]

pin·ion[2] /pínnyən/ *n* a small gear wheel that engages with a larger gear or with a rack, e.g., in a vehicle steering system [Mid-17C. < French *pignon* < Latin *pinea* "pine cone" < *pinus* "pine (tree)"]

pin·ite /pín īt, pée nīt/ *n* a gray-green mixture of the minerals mica and chlorite. Source: alteration of cordierite. [Early 19C. < German *Pinit*, after *Pini*, mine in Saxony]

pink[1] /pingk/ *n* **1.** PALE REDDISH COLOR a pale reddish color that, as a pigment, is formed by mixing red and white **2.** PLANT WITH FRAGRANT FLOWERS a plant with narrow grayish green leaves. Flowers: fragrant, especially pink, white, or red. Genus: *Dianthus*. **3.** FRAGRANT FLOWER the fragrant pink, white, or red flower of a pink plant **4.** PLANT SIMILAR TO TRUE PINK a plant that is similar but not related to the pink, e.g., the wild pink or moss pink **5.** HIGHEST FORM the highest degree or perfect example of something ○ *the pink of perfection* **6.** RED HUNTING JACKET the scarlet riding coat traditionally worn by fox hunters **7.** POL same as **pinko** ■ **pinks** *npl* US OFFICERS' TROUSERS light colored dress trousers formerly worn by United States Army officers ■ *adj* **1.** COLORED PINK of the color pink **2.** SLIGHTLY LEFT-WING relating to or holding political views that tend toward the left (*informal disapproving*) [Late 16C. Origin ?] —**pink·ish** *adj* —**pink·ness** *n* ◇ **in the pink** in excellent physical health (*informal dated*)

ORIGIN The Dutch phrase *pinck oogen* meant literally "small eyes." It was adopted into English in the partially translated form *pink eyes*, which may have been used as the name of a plant of the genus *Dianthus*. The abbreviated form ***pink*** emerged as a plant name in the 16C. Many of these plants have pale red flowers, and by the 18C ***pink*** was being used as a color term.

pink[2] /pingk/ (**pinked, pink·ing, pinks**) *vt* **1.** CUT FABRIC WITH PINKING SHEARS to cut fabric with pinking shears to make a zigzag edge that will not easily fray **2.** STAB SOMEBODY to prick somebody's skin with a sword or other pointed weapon **3.** DECORATE SOMETHING WITH LITTLE HOLES to make a pattern on leather or other material by punching little holes in the surface [14C. Origin ?]

pink[3] /pingk/ *n* a sailing ship with a narrow overhanging stern [Late 15C. < Middle Dutch *pincke*]

pink boll·worm *n* the pinkish larva of a brown moth that is a common pest in cotton-growing areas. Latin name: *Pectinophora gossypiella.*

pink-col·lar *adj* relating to jobs, especially clerical jobs, traditionally associated with women

pink dol·lar *n* the collective spending power of gays and lesbians, especially when targeted as consumers (*sometimes offensive*)

pink el·e·phants *npl* hallucinations in any form that are sometimes experienced by somebody who has overindulged in alcohol or drugs (*informal humorous*)

Pin·ker·ton /píngkərtən/, **Allan** (1819–84) Scottish-born US detective. He founded Pinkerton's National Detective Agency (1850), which later provided strikebreakers and ran the Union's secret service in the Civil War.

pink·eye /píngk ī/ *n* **1.** a contagious form of acute conjunctivitis in human beings and some domestic animals marked by inflammation of the eyelid and eyeball **2.** a viral or bacterial eye infection of cattle that is characterized by redness of the eye, production of tears that attract flies, and sometimes blindness

pink·ie /píngkee/, **pink·y** (*plural* **-ies**) *n N Am, Scotland* the little finger (*informal*) [Late 16C. Probably < Dutch *pinkje* < *pink* "little finger"]

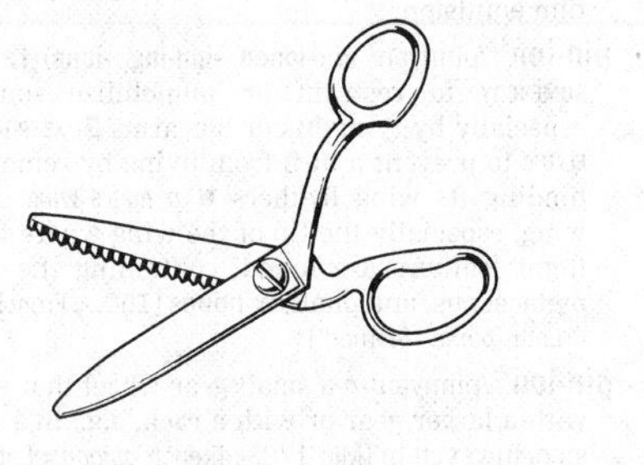
pinking shears

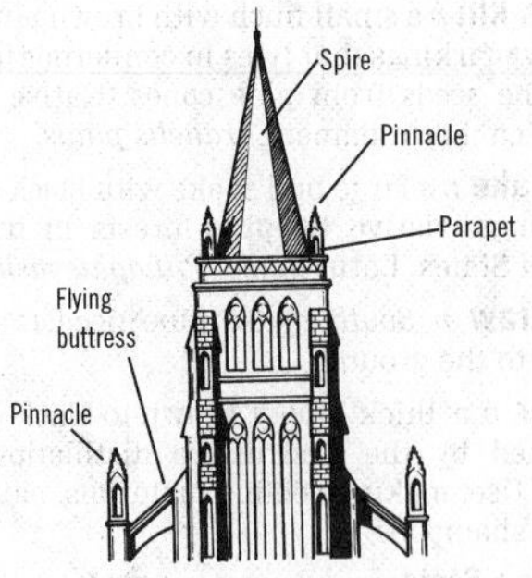

pinnacle (sense 3)

pink·ing shears, pink·ing scis·sors *npl* scissors for cutting cloth that have one blade or both blades serrated, so that whatever they cut has a zigzag edge, either for decoration or to prevent fraying [< PINK[2]]

pink la·dy *n* a cocktail that is made by mixing gin, brandy, lemon or lime juice, egg white, and grenadine

pink·o /píngkō/ (*plural* **-os** or **-oes**) *n* somebody who favors the political left (*slang disapproving*) [Early 20C. < PINK[1], alluding to RED "communist"]

pink·root /píngk ro͝ot, -ro͞ot/ (*plural* **-roots** or *same*) *n* **1.** POWDERED ROOT OF TROPICAL PLANT the powdered root of a subtropical plant. Use: formerly, to treat intestinal worms. **2.** PLANT WITH RED AND YELLOW FLOWERS a tropical or subtropical perennial plant with pinkish roots. Flowers: red, tinged with yellow on the inside. Native to: southeastern United States. Genus: *Spigella.* **3.** PLANT DISEASE a fungal plant disease that affects bulbous plants, especially onions, causing the roots to become pink and shriveled and stunting root growth

pink salm·on *n* **1.** a small salmon, the male of which has a pinkish body and a distinctive hump on its back at breeding times. Native to: northern Pacific waters. Latin name: *Oncorhynchus gorbuscha.* **2.** the pink flesh of the pink salmon used as food, often canned

pink slip *n* a termination of employment notice that an employer gives to an employee (*informal*) [< the traditional color of such notices]

Pink·ster /píngkstər/, **Pinx·ter** *n Northeast US* Whitsunday or Whitsuntide [Mid-18C. Via Dutch < Greek *Pentēkostē* (see PENTECOST)]

pink·ster flow·er *n US* PLANTS another spelling of **pinxter flower**

pink·y *n N Am, Scotland* ANAT another spelling of **pinkie**

pin mon·ey *n* **1.** MONEY FOR BUYING PERSONAL THINGS money that is earned, put aside, or used for buying personal, often nonessential things **2.** NOT MUCH MONEY a small amount of money **3.** MONEY THAT MAN GIVES TO WIFE money that a man gives to his wife, woman partner, or daughter for personal use (*dated*)

pin·na /pínnə/ (*plural* **-nae** /-nee/ or **-nas**) *n* **1.** ZOOL a feather, wing, fin, or other similarly shaped body part or appendage **2.** BOT any one of the several leaflets that make up a pinnate compound leaf **3.** ANAT same as **auricle** (sense 1) [Late 18C. < Latin, "feather"] —**pin·nal** *adj*

pin·nace /pínnəss/ *n* a small boat, e.g., a sailboat, carried by a larger vessel and used as a gig or a tender [Mid-16C. < French *pinace* < Latin *pinus* "pine (tree)"]

pin·na·cle /pínnək'l/ *n* **1.** HIGHEST POINT the highest or topmost point or level of something ○ *at the pinnacle of her career* **2.** MOUNTAIN PEAK a natural peak, especially a distinctively pointed one on a mountain or in a mountain range **3.** ARCHIT POINTED ORNAMENT a pointed ornament on top of a buttress or parapet ■ *vt* (**-cled, -cling, -cles**) **1.** ARCHIT ADD PINNACLE TO SOMETHING to provide something with a pinnacle **2.** PUT SOMETHING ON PINNACLE to put or set something on a pinnacle or on something resembling a top or peak [13C. Via French < late Latin *pinnaculum,* literally "little feather" < Latin *pinna* "feather"]

pin·nae BIOL plural of **pinna**

pin·nate /pín àyt/, **pin·nat·ed** /-àytəd/ *adj* describes a leaf that has a central axis or stem with parts branching off it [Early 18C. < Latin *pinnatus* < *pinna* "feather"] —**pin·nate·ly** *adv* —**pin·na·tion** /pi náysh'n/ *n*

pinnati- *prefix* like a feather ○ *pinnatifid* [< Latin *pinnatus* (see PINNATE)]

pin·nat·i·fid /pi náttəfid/ *adj* describes leaves that have a central axis with parts branching off it —**pin·nat·i·fid·ly** *adv*

pin·ni·ped /pínnə pèd/, **pin·ni·pe·di·an** /pìnnə péedee ən/ *n* a sea mammal that has a streamlined body and four flippers and eats fish and other meat, e.g., a walrus, sea lion, or seal. Suborder: Pinnipedia. [Mid-19C. < modern Latin *Pinnipedia* < Latin *pinna* "wing, fin" + *pes* "foot"] —**pin·ni·ped** *adj*

pin·nule /pínnyool/, **pin·nu·la** /pínnyələ/ (*plural* **-lae** /-lèe/) *n* **1.** a small fin or fin-shaped part of an organ or organism **2.** a small division or lobe of a leaf that has a central axis with parts branching off it [Late 16C. < Latin *pinnula* "little feather" < *pinna* "feather"] —**pin·nu·lar** /pínnyələr/ *adj*

PIN num·ber *n* BANKING, COMPUT same as **PIN**

pin oak *n* an oak tree that has small acorns and leaves with deep spine-tipped lobes. Native to: wet regions of eastern United States. Latin name: *Quercus palustris.* [< the pin shape of some of the tree's branches]

Pin·o·chet /péenō shày/, **Augusto** (*b.* 1915) Chilean military dictator. Under his right-wing regime (1973–90) dissidence was suppressed. Full name **Pinochet Ugarte, Augusto**

> "Don't forget that in the history of the world, there was a plebiscite, in which Christ and Barabbas were being judged, and the people chose Barabbas."
> [Augusto Pinochet, *Remark*; 1988]

pi·noch·le /pée nùk'l, -nòk'l/, **pi·noc·le, pe·nuch·le, pe·nuck·le** *n* **1.** a card game for two or four players using two decks of cards that do not include two to eight. Certain combinations of cards score points, as do tricks taken. **2.** a combination of the queen of spades and the jack of diamonds in the game of pinochle [Mid-19C. Origin ?]

pin·o·cy·to·sis /pìnnə si tṓsiss, -sī-/ *n* the ingestion of fluid into a cell by turning a portion of the cell membrane inward to form a sheath that is then pinched off to form an internal vesicle [Late 19C. < Greek *pinein* "to drink"] —**pin·o·cy·tot·ic** /pìnnə si tóttik, -sī-/ *adj* —**pin·o·cy·tot·i·cal·ly** *adv*

pi·no·le /pi nṓlee/ *n Hispanic* flour that is made by mixing parched corn with ground mesquite beans and sometimes other ingredients [Mid-19C. Via American Spanish < Nahuatl *pinolli*]

pi·ñon /pín yòn, pínnyən/ (*plural* **-ñons** or **-ño·nes** /pin yṓneez/), **pin·yon** *n* **1.** *also* **pi·ñon nut** *or* **pin·yon nut** a small sweet nut produced by a pine tree **2.** a low-growing pine tree that bears piñons. Native to: southwestern United States. Latin name: *Pinus edulis* or *Pinus monophylla.* [Mid-19C. < Spanish *piñón* < Latin *pineus* "of pines" < *pinus* "pine (tree)"]

pi·ñon jay *n* a short-tailed steel-blue bird of the jay family, often found near piñon pines and junipers. Native to: dry regions of the western United States. Latin name: *Gymnorhinus cyanocephalus.*

Pi·not Blanc /péeno blángk, -blaáN/ *n* **1.** a dry white wine made from a grape grown especially in Alsace but also in Italy and California **2.** a white grape variety. Use: to make Pinot Blanc. [< French, "white Pinot" (see PINOT NOIR)]

Pi·not Gri·gio /péenō gréejō, pee nṓ-/ *n* **1.** a crisp dry white wine made from a variety of white grape grown mainly in Italy and France **2.** a white grape variety. Use: to make Pinot Grigio. [< Italian, "gray Pinot" (see PINOT NOIR)]

Pi·not Noir /péenō nwaár, pee nṓ-/ *n* **1.** a red wine made from a variety of black grape originally grown in the Burgundy region of France **2.** a black grape variety. Use: to make Pinot Noir. [< French, "black Pinot" (grape variety) < *pin* "pine cone"; from the shape of the grape clusters]

pin·point /pín pòynt/ *vt* (**-point·ed, -point·ing, -points**) IDENTIFY SOMETHING CORRECTLY to identify or locate something accurately ■ *n* **1.** SOMETHING SMALL OR TRIVIAL something small or trivial and with no value or consequence **2.** POINTY TIP OF PIN the sharp end of a pin, or something that resembles it ■ *adj* PRECISELY EXACT reflecting exact meticulous precision

pin·prick /pín prìk/ *n* **1.** SMALL HOLE MADE BY PIN a small puncture, especially to the skin, made by a pin or something with a similarly sharp end **2.** SLIGHT WOUND a very minor wound **3.** MINOR IRRITANT a minor annoyance, nuisance, or distraction **4.** SMALL MARK a very small dot or mark ■ *vt* (**-pricked, -prick·ing, -pricks**) PUNCTURE SOMETHING WITH PIN to puncture something, especially the skin, with a pin or something with a similarly sharp end

PINS *abbr US* LAW person in need of supervision

pins and need·les *n* a tingling sensation, especially in the feet or hands, sometimes experienced when a temporarily restricted blood flow to the affected body parts returns to normal (*takes a singular or plural verb*)

pin·scher /pínshər/ *n* same as **Doberman pinscher** [Early 20C. < German]

pin·set·ter /pín sèttər/ *n* a person or machine in a bowling alley that sets up and resets the pins

Pinsk /pinsk/ city in southwestern Belarus. Population: 133,500 (1999).

Pin·sky /pínskee/, **Robert** (*b.* 1940) US poet. His collections of poetry include *The Want Bone* (1990). He was US poet laureate (1997–2000).

pin·stripe /pín strìp/ *n* **1.** NARROW LINE any one of many very narrow lines, especially in a fabric **2.** MATERIAL WITH VERY NARROW LINES material that has very narrow lines in it. Use: business suits. (*often used before a noun*) **3.** PINSTRIPE SUIT a suit made of pinstripe fabric (*often used in the plural*) —**pin·striped** *adj*

pint /pīnt/ *n* **1.** UNIT OF LIQUID MEASURE a unit of liquid measure equal to one half quart or 0.473 liter in the United States and 0.568 liter in the United Kingdom **2.** UNIT OF DRY MEASURE a unit of dry measure equal to one half a quart or 0.551 liter in the United States and 0.568 liter in the United Kingdom **3.** CONTAINER a container or measure that has the capacity of a pint **4.** *UK* PINT OF LIQUID a pint of a liquid, especially of beer or milk (*informal*) [14C. < French *pinte*]

pin·ta /píntə, péen taà/ *n* an infectious bacterial skin disease of tropical America that is marked by the formation and eruption of papules, loss of pigmentation, and thickening of the skin [Early 19C. Via Spanish, "painted spot" < assumed Vulgar Latin *pincta* < past participle of Latin *pingere* "paint"]

pin·tail /pín tàyl/ (*plural same* or **-tails**) *n* a slender duck that has a long pointed tail and brown and white feathers. Native to: northern hemisphere. Latin name: *Anas acuta.* [< the pointed tip of the male bird's tail]

Pin·ter /píntər/, **Harold** (*b.* 1930) British playwright and director. Many of his numerous plays, which include *The Caretaker* (1960) and *The Homecoming* (1964), explore the alienation and hostility beneath the surface of intimate relationships. His screenplays include *The Handmaid's Tale* (1990). See Cultural note at **birthday** —**Pin·ter·esque** /pìntə résk/ *adj*

"The earth's about five thousand million years old. Who can afford to live in the past?"
[Harold Pinter, *The Homecoming*; 1964]

pin·tle /pínt'l/ *n* a pin or bolt, especially one used as a vertical pivot or hinge, e.g., on a rudder [Old English, "peg, penis" < Germanic]

pin·to /píntō/ *US adj* describes a horse that has a coat marked with irregular patches of white and another color, usually brown, black, or gray ■ *n* (*plural* **-tos** or **-toes**) a horse with irregular patches of white and another color on its coat ▶ Can term (all senses) **piebald** [Mid-19C. Via Spanish, "painted" < past participle of Latin *pingere* "paint"]

pin·to bean *n* **1.** a mottled brown and pink kidney-shaped bean, cooked and eaten as a vegetable or used as fodder **2.** a variety of the kidney bean that produces pinto beans [< Spanish *pinto*, "painted, mottled" (see PINTO)]

pint-size, **pint-sized** *adj* very small, especially smaller than usual or than expected (*informal*)

Pin·tu·bi *n, adj* PEOPLES same as **Pintupi**

pin tuck *n* a narrow vertical fold stitched in place and used for decoration, especially on the front of clothes —**pin-tucked** *adj*

Pin·tu·pi /píntəpee/ (*plural same* or **-pis**), **Pin·tu·bi** /-bee/ (*plural same* or **-bis**) *n* a member of an Aboriginal people living in the border regions between Western Australia and Northern Territories [Mid-20C.< Aboriginal] —**Pin·tu·pi** *adj*

pin·up /pín ùp/ *n* a photograph or poster of a sexually attractive person, especially one in which the person is posing in a seductive way and scantily clothed or naked ■ *adj US* designed for hanging on, or attaching to, a wall

pin·wale /pín wàyl/ *adj* describes a fabric such as corduroy that has narrow ridges on its surface

pin·weed /pín wèed/ (*plural* **-weeds** or *same*) *n* an herb with numerous narrow leaves and small flowers. Native to: North America. Genus: *Lechea*.

pin·wheel /pín wèel, -hweel/ *n* **1.** a child's toy consisting of a stick with a set of plastic or paper blades fitted to it, which spin around when the wind blows them **2.** a firework that, when ignited, forms a multicolored wheel that spins

pin·work /pín wùrk/ *n* the delicate stitches that are raised above the main design in the embroidery of needlepoint lace

pin·worm /pín wùrm/ *n* **1.** a thread-shaped nematode worm that occurs as a parasite in the intestines of vertebrate animals, including human beings. Family: Oxyuridae. **2.** an infestation of pinworms

Pinx·ter *n Northeast US* CALENDAR, CHR another spelling of **Pinkster**

pinx·ter flow·er /píngkstər-/, **pink·ster flow·er** *n* a deciduous woodland azalea. Flowers: funnel-shaped, pink. Native to: southeastern United States. Latin name: *Rhododendron periclymenoides*. [< variant of PINKSTER; because it flowers around Whitsuntide]

pin·y /pínee/ (**-i·er, -i·est**), **pine·y** (**pin·i·er, pin·i·est**) *adj* relating to or resembling pine trees, e.g., in smell

Pin·yin /pìn yín/, **pin·yin** *n* a system for transliterating written Chinese characters into the Roman alphabet, introduced in 1959 and adopted by the People's Republic of China in 1979 [Mid-20C. < Chinese *pīnyīn*, literally "spell sound"]

pin·yon *n* TREES another spelling of **piñon**

pin·yon jay *n* BIRDS another spelling of **piñon jay**

PIO *abbr US* public information office

pi·o·let /pèe ə láy/ *n* a double-headed ice ax used by mountaineers [Mid-19C. < French dialect < *piola* "small ax" < Germanic]

pi·on /pí òn/ *n* an elementary particle of the meson group that has either single positive, negative, or zero charge, a mass approximately 270 times that of the electron, and spin zero [Mid-20C. Contraction of *pi meson*]

pi·o·neer /pì ə néer/ *n* **1.** INVENTOR OR INNOVATOR a person or group that is the first to do something or that leads in developing something new **2.** FIRST PERSON TO EXPLORE TERRITORY a person who is one of the first from another country or region to explore or settle a new area **3.** SOLDIER WHO BUILDS THINGS a foot soldier whose duties include going ahead of the main company to construct things to pave the way for them **4.** FIRST SPECIES TO GROW SOMEWHERE the first species of plant or animal life to begin living in a previously unoccupied site, e.g., a moss beginning to grow on otherwise bare rock ■ *v* (**-neered, -neer·ing, -neers**) **1.** *vt* INVENT NEW THING to experiment with or develop something new **2.** *vti* GO INTO UNEXPLORED TERRITORY to go into previously uncharted or unclaimed territory with the purpose of exploring it and possibly settling it **3.** *vi* ACT AS PIONEER to act as a pioneer in a particular field [Early 16C. < French *pionnier* < medieval Latin *pedon-* "foot soldier" < Latin *ped-* "foot"]

pi·ous /pí əss/ *adj* **1.** RELIGIOUS devoutly religious **2.** RELIGIOUSLY REVERENT characterized by religious reverence **3.** ACTING IN FALSELY MORALIZING WAY talking or acting in a falsely, hypocritically, or affectedly moralizing way **4.** HOLY OR SACRED holy or sacred, especially as distinct from worldly **5.** PRAISEWORTHY deserving to be praised **6.** VIRTUOUS AND MORAL professing or showing great virtue and morality in the strict, traditional sense of it **7.** SHOWING DUE RESPECT showing appropriate respect, especially toward parents (*archaic*) [15C. < Latin *pius* "dutiful, devout"] —**pi·ous·ly** *adv* —**pi·ous·ness** *n*

pip[1] /pip/ *n* **1.** SEED OF FRUIT a small hard seed of a fruit such as an apple that usually has several seeds **2.** SECTION OF PINEAPPLE SKIN any one of the many irregular diamond-shaped sections on the outer skin of a pineapple **3.** ROOTSTOCK OR FLOWER a rootstock or flower of some plants, especially the lily of the valley [Late 18C. Shortening of PIPPIN]

pip[2] /pip/ *n* **1.** SPOT ON DIE OR DOMINO a single spot on a die or domino **2.** MARK ON PLAYING CARD a single symbol of a club, diamond, heart, or spade on a playing card **3.** *UK* SOMETHING INDICATING RANK something that indicates rank, e.g., a diamond-shaped insignia on the shoulder of a British Army officer's uniform (*informal*) **4.** SPECK a very small mark or piece of something ■ *v* (**pipped, pip·ping, pips**) **1.** *vi* CHEEP to make a cheeping sound, especially when newly hatched (*refers to birds*) **2.** *vti* USE BEAK TO BREAK SHELL to use the beak to break through the shell during hatching (*refers to birds*) **3.** *vi* MAKE SHRILL NOISE to make or emit a short shrill noise [Late 16C. Origin ?]

pip[3] /pip/ *n* **1.** a contagious disease of birds, especially domestic poultry, characterized by the presence of a thick crust in the mouth and throat, caused by a secretion of mucus **2.** a slight ailment in humans (*slang*) [14C. Via Middle Dutch *pippe* < Latin *pituita* "phlegm"]

pip[4] /pip/ (**pipped, pip·ping, pips**) *vt UK* to wound or kill a person or animal with a bullet from a gun (*dated*) [Late 19C. Origin ?]

pi·pa[1] /péepə/ *n* a toad that lives in water, with a flat body, large webbed feet, and no eyelids or tongue. Native to: South America. Genus: *Pipa*. [Early 18C. Probably < Galibi]

pi·pa[2] /péepə, pée paa/ *n* a plucked four-stringed Chinese instrument with a fretted fingerboard like a guitar's [Mid-19C. < Chinese *píba* "loquat"; from its shape]

pi·pa[3] /péepə/ *n Hispanic* a tanker truck that delivers clean drinking water to inhabitants of Mexican desert areas [< Mexican Spanish]

pi·pal /péep'l/, **pee·pul** *n* TREES same as **bo tree** [Late 18C. Via Hindi *pīpal* < Sanskrit *pippala*]

pipe[1] /pīp/ *n* **1.** TUBE FOR TRANSPORTING LIQUID OR GAS a long cylindrical tube that water, oil, gas, or other such material passes through **2.** TUBE OF ANY KIND an object in tubular form **3.** DEVICE FOR SMOKING TOBACCO a small bowl with a hollow stem coming from it, used for smoking tobacco or other substances. Pipes are usually made of wood or clay. The tobacco is burned in the bowl and the smoke drawn into the mouth through the stem. **4.** AMOUNT IN SMOKER'S PIPE the amount of tobacco or other substance that the bowl of a smoker's pipe holds **5.** HOLLOW BODY PART a tubular part or organ in a plant or animal, especially one in an animal's respiratory system **6.** TUBULAR MUSICAL INSTRUMENT PLAYED BY BLOWING a tubular musical instrument that is played by blowing air into it **7.** TUBULAR PART OF MUSICAL ORGAN an upright tubular part of a musical organ that produces sound when air is blown into it **8.** WIND INSTRUMENT OF MIDDLE AGES a three-holed wind instrument of the Middle Ages, played with one hand while the other hand beats on a small drum **9.** SAILOR'S WHISTLE a small whistle used for signaling orders to a ship's crew, usually by a boatswain **10.** HIGH-PITCHED NOISE a high-pitched or shrill noise, e.g., a birdcall **11.** GEOL CYLINDER-SHAPED GEOLOGIC FORMATION a vertical cylinder-shaped geologic formation, e.g., a vein of ore **12.** GEOL PASSAGE THROUGH WHICH LAVA FLOWS a vertical passage through which molten lava flows **13.** METALL HOLE IN CAST METAL a conical cavity in the middle of a piece of metal, produced by gas escaping as the metal cools ■ **pipes** *npl* **1.** MUSIC BAGPIPES a pair of bagpipes **2.** VOCAL CORDS the vocal cords or voice, especially when used to sing (*slang*) **3.** HUMAN BOWEL OR RESPIRATORY PASSAGES the passages of the human respiratory or intestinal system (*slang*) ■ *v* (**piped, pip·ing, pipes**) **1.** *vt* CARRY SOMETHING BY PIPE to carry something, especially water, gas, or a semisolid, by means of a pipe, pipeline, or system of pipes ○ *The company pipes crude oil to the refinery.* **2.** *vti* INSTALL OR EQUIP WITH PIPES to equip something with pipes, or install pipes and their connections in something **3.** *vt* PLAY TUNE ON PIPE to play a tune on a musical pipe **4.** *vt* SEND PIPED MUSIC THROUGH PLACE to play prerecorded music in a public place or workplace to create a soothing atmosphere **5.** *vt* SIGNAL SOMETHING USING PIPE to signal the arrival or departure of somebody or something using a pipe **6.** *vt* ORDER CREW USING BOATSWAIN'S PIPE to give orders to a ship's crew using a boatswain's pipe **7.** *vt* DECORATE GARMENT WITH PIPING to add decorative piping to a garment **8.** *vt* DECORATE FOOD WITH PIPING to add decorative piping to food, especially by forcing it out of a bag that has a nozzle designed to create the various decorative forms **9.** *vti* MAKE HIGH-PITCHED NOISE to make a high-pitched or shrill noise, or speak or say something in a squeaky voice [Old English *pīpe*, via Germanic < assumed Vulgar Latin *pipa* < Latin *pipare* "to peep, cheep," an imitation of the sound] —**pipe·ful** *n*

pipe down *vi* to stop talking or become less noisy or boisterous (*informal; often used as a command*)

pipe up *vi* **1.** to say something, often as an interruption or a clarification **2.** to begin to sing or play a musical instrument

pipe[2] /pīp/ *n* **1.** LARGE CONTAINER FOR LIQUID a large container for wine, oil, or some other liquid **2.** UNIT OF LIQUID CAPACITY a unit of liquid measure for wine, equal to four barrels, two hogsheads, or 126 gallons **3.** CASK a cask that has the capacity of four barrels, two hogsheads, or 126 gallons [14C. Via Anglo-Norman < PIPE[1]]

pipe bomb *n* a bomb made of a length of pipe that is filled with explosives and is capped at its ends

pipe clay *n* a very fine white pure clay. Use: pottery, smokers' pipes, whitening leather and other materials.

pipe clean·er *n* a flexible wire covered with fluffy material that is used for cleaning the stems of smokers' pipes and other things that are difficult to access

piped mu·sic *n* prerecorded, usually easy-listening music played through speakers in public places and some workplaces to create a soothing atmosphere

pipe dream *n* a goal, hope, or plan so fanciful that it is very unlikely to be realized [< the dreams caused by smoking opium]

pipe·fit·ting /pīp fìtting/ *n* **1.** BRANCH OF PLUMBING INVOLVING PIPES the branch of plumbing that involves measuring, cutting, bending, and joining lengths of pipe, either in installation or repairs **2.** ACT OR PROCESS OF PIPE INSTALLATION an act or process of installing or connecting pipes **3.** SOMETHING USED IN CONNECTING PIPES something that is used in the connection or joining of pipes

pipe·line /pīp līn/ *n* **1.** LONG PIPE SYSTEM FOR TRANSPORTING SOMETHING a pipe or system of pipes designed to carry something such as oil, natural gas, or other petroleum-based products over long distances, often underground **2.** CHANNEL OF COMMUNICATIONS a channel of communications, especially a private one among several people within a single organization **3.** SYSTEM FOR SUPPLYING SOMETHING a system for the supply or transfer of something, especially goods or information ■ *vt* (**-lined, -lin·ing, -lines**) **1.** SEND SOMETHING

BY PIPE SYSTEM to send, connect, or carry something by way of a long system of pipes **2.** EQUIP SOMETHING WITH LONG PIPE SYSTEM to equip or supply something with a long system of pipes ◇ **in the pipeline** in preparation but not yet ready

pipe or·gan *n* a musical organ that uses pipes to produce the sound, as opposed to a reed organ or an electric organ. Most church organs are pipe organs.

pip·er /pīpər/ *n* **1.** somebody who plays a pipe **2.** somebody who plays the bagpipes ◇ **pay the piper** to take the consequences for something ◇ **he who pays the piper calls the tune** used to say that the person who is paying for something will control what happens

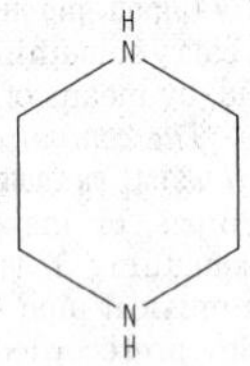

piperazine

pi·per·a·zine /pī pérrə zeen, pi-/ *n* a colorless crystalline compound. Use: parasiticide, insecticide. Formula: $C_4H_{10}N_2$. [Late 19C. < PIPERIDINE + AZINE]

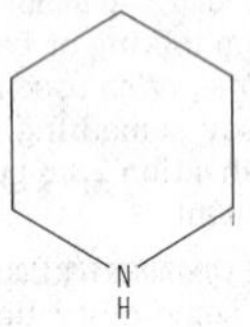

piperidine

pi·per·i·dine /pī pérrə deen, pi-/ *n* a colorless liquid compound that has a peppery odor resembling ammonia. Use: manufacture of rubber and epoxy resins. Formula: $C_5H_{11}N$. [Mid-19C. < PIPERINE + -IDINE]

pip·er·ine /píppə reen/ *n* a white crystalline alkaloid compound that is the chief active component of pepper. Formula: $C_{17}H_{19}NO_3$. [Early 19C. < Latin *piper* (see PEPPER)]

pi·per·o·nal /pī pérrə nàl, pi-/ *n* a white crystalline compound that has an odor resembling heliotrope. Use: in perfumes and flavorings. Formula: $C_{19}H_{63}$. [Mid-19C. < German < *Piperin* "piperine"]

pipe snake *n* a tropical snake with a fused inflexible skull, vestiges of hind limbs, and two unequally sized lungs. Family: Aniliidae.

pipes of Pan *npl* MUSIC same as **panpipes**

pipe·stone /pīp stṓn/ *n* a reddish or pinkish stone resembling clay in consistency that some Native North Americans harden and use for making decorative objects and long, often ornate pipes

pi·pette /pī pét/ *n* a small glass tube that liquid is drawn into so that it can be measured, often before it is delivered to another container, e.g., in experiments or in medication doses ■ *vt* (**-pet·ted, -pet·ting, -pettes**) to measure or deliver an accurate amount of liquid using a pipette [Mid-19C. < French, "little pipe" < *pipe* "pipe" < assumed Vulgar Latin *pipa* (see PIPE[1])]

pipe wrench *n* a wrench with two adjustable, usually ridged jaws, one fixed and one moveable, used to grip and turn pipes and other tubular objects

pip·ing /pīping/ *n* **1.** PIPES COLLECTIVELY pipes thought of collectively, especially when they form a connected plumbing system in a house or other building **2.** DECORATIVE TWISTED CORD a twisted cord covered with fabric inserted into a seam as a decoration. Use: clothes, upholstery. **3.** DECORATIVE EFFECT ON FOOD a decorative effect used on food, especially strands or swirls of icing in a contrasting color **4.** SKILL OF PLAYING MUSICAL PIPE the art, technique, or skill of playing the bagpipes or another kind of musical pipe **5.** SOUND OF MUSICAL PIPE the sound of bagpipes or some other musical pipe **6.** SHRILL NOISE a shrill, high-pitched, or whistling noise ■ *adj* SHRILLY PITCHED shrill and very high in pitch, as some voices are

piping hot *adj* describes food or water that is very hot

pip·i·strelle /pìppi strél, píppi strèl/, **pip·i·strel** *n* a small brown insect-eating bat found throughout the world. Genus: *Pipistrellus.* [Late 18C. Via French < Italian *pipistrello*, alteration of *vipistrello* < Latin *vespertilio* "bat" < *vesper* "evening"]

pip·it /píppit/ *n* a small songbird of the wagtail family with brown speckled feathers and a long tail. Family: Motacillidae. [Mid-18C. An imitation of its call]

pip·kin /pípkin/ *n* a small cooking pot, usually made of metal or earthenware and with a handle going across the top [Mid-16C. Origin ?]

pip·pin /píppin/ *n* **1.** VARIETY OF APPLE a variety of cultivated eating or cooking apple **2.** PIP OR SEED a pip or seed, especially an apple seed **3.** DESIRABLE OR ADMIRABLE PERSON OR THING somebody or something that is particularly desirable or admirable (*dated informal*) [14C. < French *pepin*]

pip·sis·se·wa /pip síssə wàw, -síssəwə/ (*plural* **-was** or *same*) *n* an evergreen plant with jagged astringent leaves used as a diuretic. Flowers: white or pinkish. Genus: *Chimaphila.* [Late 18C. < Abenaki *kpi-pskwàhsawe* "flower of the woods"]

pip·squeak /píp skweek/ *n* somebody or something that is small or insignificant, but nevertheless often annoying or troublesome (*informal*)

pi·quant /peekənt, -kaant, pee kaant/ *adj* **1.** SPICY OR SALTY having a flavor, taste, or smell that is spicy or salty, often with a slightly tart or bitter edge to it **2.** SHARPLY STIMULATING OR PROVOCATIVE refreshingly interesting, stimulating, or provocative **3.** SHARPLY CRITICAL AND BITING excessively severe or hurtful in tone or content [Early 16C. < French, present participle of *piquer* (see PIQUE[1])] —**pi·quan·cy** *n* —**pi·quant·ly** *adv* —**pi·quant·ness** *n*

pique[1] /peek/ *n* BAD MOOD a bad mood or feeling of resentment, especially when brought on by an insult, hurt pride, or loss of face ■ *v* (**piqued, piqu·ing, piques**) **1.** *vt* PUT SOMEBODY IN BAD MOOD to cause somebody to be in a bad mood or to feel resentful **2.** *vt* AROUSE SOMEBODY'S INTEREST to cause a feeling of interest, curiosity, or excitement in somebody ○ *piqued my curiosity* **3.** *vr* TAKE PRIDE IN SOMETHING to take pride in something, especially a personal attribute or ability [Mid-16C. Via French *piquer* "prick, irritate" < assumed Vulgar Latin *piccare*]

SPELLCHECK See ***peak***[1].

---

pique[2] /peek/ *n* in the game of piquet, a score of 30 points to an opponent's 0 from the hand as dealt ■ *vti* (**piqued, piqu·ing, piques**) in the game of piquet, to score a pique against an opponent [Mid-17C. < French *pic*]

pi·qué /pi káy, pee-, pee kày/ *n* a closely woven ribbed fabric produced from natural fibers. Use: shirts and dresses. [Mid-19C. < French, past participle of *piquer* "prick, stitch" (see PIQUE[1])]

pi·quet /pi káy/, **pic·quet** *n* a card game for two players using a deck that does not include two to six [Mid-17C. < French, origin ?]

pi·ra·cy /pīrəssee/ *n* **1.** ROBBERY ON HIGH SEAS robbery on the high seas, especially the stealing of a ship's cargo **2.** ROBBERY ON ANY FORM OF TRANSPORTATION robbery committed on board any form of transportation, especially an aircraft **3.** HIJACKING the hijacking of an aircraft or another form of transportation **4.** USE OF COPYRIGHTED MATERIAL WITHOUT PERMISSION the taking and using of copyrighted or patented material without authorization or without the legal right to do so **5.** ILLEGAL BROADCASTING the unauthorized or illegal broadcasting of TV or radio programs [Mid-16C. < medieval Latin *piratia* < Latin *pirata* (see PIRATE)]

Pi·rae·us /pī reé əss, pi ráy-/ industrial city and seaport serving Athens, Greece. Population: 182,671 (1991).

pi·ra·gua /pi raagwə/ *n* *Hispanic* CANOEING same as **pirogue** [Early 17C. Via American Spanish < Carib, "dugout"]

pi·ra·ña *n* FISH another spelling of **piranha**

Pi·ran·del·lo /pìrrən déllō/, **Luigi** (1867–1936) Italian playwright. His works, which include *Six Characters in Search of an Author* (1921), explore the human condition with grim humor. He won a Nobel Prize in literature (1934).

> "Whoever has the luck to be born a character can laugh even at death. Because a character will never die! A man will die, a writer, the instrument of creation: but what he has created will never die!"
> [Luigi Pirandello, *Six Characters in Search of an Author*; 1921]

Pi·ra·ne·si /pirrə náyzee/, **Giovanni Battista** (1720–78) Italian artist. He is noted for his *Imaginary Prisons* (1745) and other engravings and etchings of real or imaginary buildings.

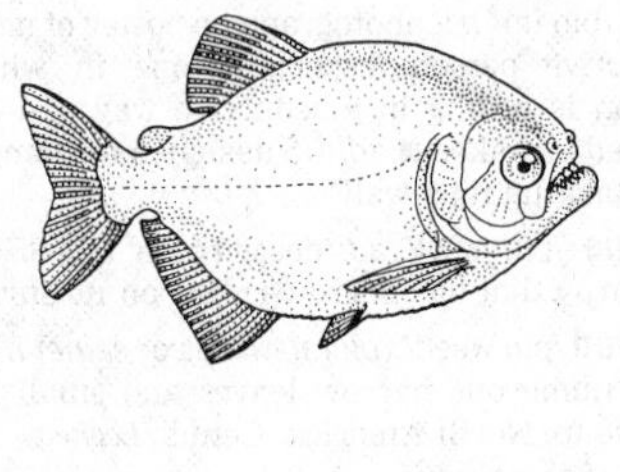

piranha

pi·ra·nha /pi raanyə, -rányə, -raanə, -rannə/ (*plural* **-nhas** or *same*), **pi·ra·ña** (*plural* **-ñas** or *same*) *n* a small freshwater fish that has sharp teeth and strong jaws and is a dangerous predator when attacking in large numbers. Native to: South America. Genus: *Serrasalmo.* [Mid-18C. Via Portuguese < Tupi *piráya*]

pi·rate /pīrət/ *n* **1.** ROBBER AT SEA a robber who operates from a ship on the ocean **2.** SHIP USED BY SEA ROBBERS a ship used by people who rob or otherwise attack shipping on the high seas **3.** SOMEBODY USING COPYRIGHTED MATERIAL WITHOUT PERMISSION somebody who duplicates or uses copyrighted or patented material illegally or without authorization **4.** SOMEBODY INVOLVED IN ILLEGAL BROADCASTING somebody who takes part in or manages the unauthorized or illegal broadcasting of TV or radio programs ■ *v* (**-rat·ed, -rat·ing, -rates**) **1.** *vti* ROB SOMETHING ON HIGH SEAS to rob a vessel or commit robbery on the high seas **2.** *vt* USE COPYRIGHTED MATERIAL WITHOUT PERMISSION to duplicate or use copyrighted or patented material without authorization or without the legal right to do so [13C. Via Latin *pirata* < Greek *peiratēs* < *peiran* "to attack"] —**pi·rat·ic** /pī ráttik/ *adj* —**pi·rat·i·cal** *adj* —**pi·rat·i·cal·ly** *adv*

pi·rog /pi rṓg/ (*plural* **-ro·gi** /-rṓgee/ or **-ro·ghi**) *n* a large rectangular pie that has a pastry crust on top and bottom, filled with chopped meat or cabbage, onions, and hard-boiled eggs [Mid-19C. < Russian]

pi·rogue /pi rṓg/ *n* a canoe made from a hollowed-out tree trunk, used especially in southern Louisiana [Early 17C. Via French < Carib *piragua* "dugout"]

REGIONAL NOTE Found in neighboring Mississippi and East Texas, the term ***pirogue***, as well as the distinctive artifact itself, is characteristic of Louisiana dialect. Although it occurs across the state, north of the Atchafalaya River, it is nearly twice as common in the southern part of the state, the Cajun bayou country, west of New Orleans.

---

pi·rosh·ki *n* FOOD another spelling of **pirozhki**

pir·ou·ette /peeroo ét/ *n* a spin of the body, especially one performed in ballet on tiptoe or on the ball of one foot [Mid-17C. < French] —**pir·ou·ette** *vi*

pi·rozh·ki /pi ráwshkee, -róshkee/, **pi·rosh·ki** *n* very small fried or baked pastries, usually filled with finely chopped meat or cabbage and onions (*takes a singular or plural verb*) [Early 20C. < Russian, "little pirog"]

Pi·sa /péezə/ capital of Pisa Province, Tuscany Region, central Italy. It is known for its leaning bell tower. Population: 89,694 (2001).

pis al·ler /péez a láy/ (*plural* **pis al·lers**) *n* something that is done as a last resort or when no other option is available [< French < *pis* "worse" + *aller* "to go"]

Pi·sa·no /pee zaánō/, **Giovanni** (1250?–1314?) Italian sculptor. The son of Nicola Pisano, he incorporated Gothic style into his sculptures for Siena Cathedral and pulpits for the cathedrals of Pistoia and Pisa, Italy.

Pi·sa·no, Nicola (1220?–84?) Italian sculptor. The father of Giovanni Pisano, his fame rests chiefly on his relief sculptures for the Pisa Baptistry, Italy.

pis·ca·ry /pískəree/ *n* the legal right to fish in a place even if it belongs to another person [15C. < medieval Latin *piscaria* < Latin *piscis* "fish"]

pis·ca·to·ri·al /pìskə táwree əl/, **pis·ca·to·ry** /pískə tàwree/ *adj* relating to fish, fishing, or fishers (*formal*) [Early 19C. < Latin *piscatorius* < *piscis* "fish"]

Pi·sces /pī́ seez/ (*plural same*) *n* **1. CONSTELLATION IN NORTHERN HEMISPHERE** a zodiacal constellation of the northern hemisphere. See illustration at **constellation 2. 12TH SIGN OF ZODIAC** the 12th sign of the zodiac, represented by two fishes and lasting from approximately February 19 to March 20. Pisces is classified as a water sign and its ruling planets are Jupiter and Neptune. **3. SOMEBODY BORN UNDER PISCES** somebody whose birthday falls between February 19 and March 20 [Pre-12C. < Latin, plural of *piscis* "fish"] —**Pi·sce·an** /pī́see ən/ *n* —**Pi·sces** *adj*

pisci- *prefix* fish ○ *piscivorous* [< Latin *piscis* < Indo-European]

pi·sci·cul·ture /pī́ssi kùlchər, píssi-/ *n* the controlled breeding, hatching, and rearing of fish, especially for scientific or commercial purposes —**pi·sci·cul·tur·al** /pìsi-, pìssi-/ *adj* —**pi·sci·cul·tur·al·ly** *adv* —**pi·sci·cul·tur·ist** *n*

pi·sci·na /pi séenə, -sī́nə, -shéenə/ (*plural* **-nas** or **-nae** /-nee/) *n* **1.** in some Christian churches, a sacred container or basin that holds holy water, used to carry it away after ablutions have been completed **2.** the place where a priest can wash his hands and the sacred containers used in Mass, located in the sacristy, especially in a Roman Catholic church [Late 16C. < medieval Latin (in classical Latin "fish pond"), < Latin *piscis* "fish"] —**pis·ci·nal** /píssən'l/ *adj*

pi·scine /pī́ seen, pí sīn/ *adj* relating to, characteristic of, or resembling fish (*formal*) [Late 18C. < medieval Latin *piscinus* < Latin *piscis* "fish"]

Pi·scis Aus·tri·nus /pī́sis o strī́nəss, pìssiss-/ *n* a small constellation of the southern hemisphere between Grus and Aquarius. See illustration at **constellation**

pi·sciv·o·rous /pi sívvərəss, pī-/ *adj* feeding habitually or mainly on fish

pish /pish/ *interj* used to express contempt, annoyance, or impatience (*dated*) [Late 16C. Natural exclamation]

pi·si·form /píssə fàwrm/ *adj* resembling a pea in shape or size ■ *n* same as **pisiform bone** [Mid-18C. < Latin *pisum* "pea"]

pi·si·form bone *n* the small knobbed bone at the place where the inner bone of the forearm (**ulna**) joins the wrist (**carpus**)

Pi·sis·tra·tus /pī sístrətəss/ (600?–527 B.C.) Athenian general and tyrant of Athens (560–527 B.C.). He extended Athenian territory, encouraged the arts, lowered taxes, and improved conditions for the poor.

pis·mire /píss mīr, píz-/ *n* same as **ant** (*archaic or informal*) [14C. < PISS (from the urinous smell of anthills) + obsolete *mire* "ant"]

pis·mo clam /pízmō-/ *n* a large edible thick-shelled ocean clam. Native to: Pacific coast of North America. Latin name: *Tivela stultorum*. [After *Pismo* Beach, California]

pi·so·lite /pīssə līt/ *n* an inorganic limestone consisting of individual spherical concretions (**pisoliths**) [Early 18C. < Greek *pisos* "pea"] —**pi·so·lit·ic** /pīsə líttik/ *adj*

pi·so·lith /pī́ssə lìth, pī́zə-, píssə-, pízzə-/ *n* a spherical concretion with concentric laminations that with others makes up an inorganic limestone. Pisoliths can be up to 4 in./10 cm in diameter. [Late 18C. < Greek *pisos* "pea"]

piss /piss/ (*slang*) *v* (**pissed, piss·ing, piss·es**) **1.** *vi* an offensive term meaning to urinate **2.** *vt* an offensive term meaning to discharge a substance such as blood when urinating **3.** *vt* an offensive term meaning to urinate on or into something ■ *n* **1.** an offensive term for urine **2.** an offensive term for an act or instance of urinating [13C. Via French *pisser* < assumed Vulgar Latin *pissiare*, an imitation of the sound] ◇ **piss and vinegar** *US* an offensive term for feisty strength of character and physical vigor (*slang*)
piss away *vt* an offensive term meaning to waste something such as money or time (*slang*)
piss off *v* (*slang*) **1.** *vt* an offensive term meaning to annoy, irritate, or upset somebody **2.** *vi* an offensive term often used as a command to tell somebody to go away and stop being annoying

piss·ant /píss ànt/, **piss ant** *US n* **1.** an offensive term for somebody who pays too much attention to small details **2.** an offensive term for somebody regarded as being of no importance, significance, or consequence ■ *adj* **1.** an offensive term meaning paying too much attention to small details **2.** an offensive term meaning regarded as being of no importance, significance, or consequence [Mid-17C. Originally "ant"; from the urinous smell of anthills]

Pis·sar·ro /pi saárō/, **Camille** (1830–1903) French painter. He was a major exponent of the impressionist style and is known for his landscapes, river scenes, and street scenes. Full name **Pissarro, Camille Jacob**

pissed /pist/ *adj* (*slang*) **1.** an offensive term meaning extremely angry or upset **2.** *UK* an offensive term meaning extremely drunk

pissed off *adj UK* same as **pissed** (sense 1) (*slang offensive*)

piss·er /píssər/ *n* (*slang*) **1.** an offensive term for somebody or something regarded as extremely annoying, upsetting, or unpleasant **2.** *US* somebody or something that is unexpectedly good or worthwhile (*offensive in some contexts*)

pis·soir /pee swaár/ *n* a public urinal, especially one on the streets of some European cities, with a circular screen around it [Early 20C. < French < *pisser* (see PISS)]

piss·pot /píss pòt/ *n US* an offensive term for somebody regarded as bad-tempered and generally mean (*slang*) [15C. Originally "chamber pot"]

pis·ta·chi·o /pi stáshee ō, -staáshee-/ (*plural* **-os**) *n* **1.** a nut with a small green kernel that is eaten fresh and also yields an edible oil **2.** (*plural* **pis·ta·chi·os** or *same*) a tree of the cashew family that produces pistachios. Native to: western Asia. Latin name: *Pistachia vera*. [15C. Directly or via Old French *pistace* < Italian *pistacchio* < Greek *pistakion* < *pistakē* "pistachio tree"]

pis·ta·chi·o green *adj* of a pale yellowish green color, like a pistachio kernel —**pis·ta·chi·o green** *n*

pis·ta·chi·o nut *n* FOOD same as **pistachio** (sense 1)

piste /peest/ *n* a downhill track or area of densely packed snow that provides good skiing conditions [Early 18C. Via French, "track" < Latin *pista* < past participle of *pinsere* "beat"]

pis·til /píst'l/ *n* a carpel or group of fused carpels forming the female reproductive part of a flower and including the ovary, style, and stigma [Early 18C. Directly or via French < Latin *pistillum* "pestle"; from its shape]

pis·til·late /píst'l àyt, -ət/ *adj* describes a flower that has one or more pistils but usually no stamens

pis·tol /píst'l/ *n* **1. SMALL GUN** a small short-barreled gun designed to be held in one hand **2. SOMEBODY OR SOMETHING EFFECTIVE** a remarkable or effective person or thing, or a forceful or energetic person (*slang*) **3. PASTRAMI SANDWICH** a hot pastrami sandwich on rye bread (*slang*) ■ *vt* (**-toled, -tol·ing, -tols**) **SHOOT SOMEBODY OR SOMETHING WITH PISTOL** to shoot somebody or something using a pistol [Mid-16C. Via French *pistole* < Czech *píšťala* "pipe" < *pištěti* "whistle," an imitation of the sound]

pis·tole /pi stṓl/ *n* a gold coin used in some European countries during the 17th and 18th centuries [Late 16C. < French]

pis·tol grip *n* a handle that resembles the butt of a pistol, especially in being shaped to fit the hand

pis·tol-whip *vt* to hit or beat somebody or something with the butt or barrel of a pistol

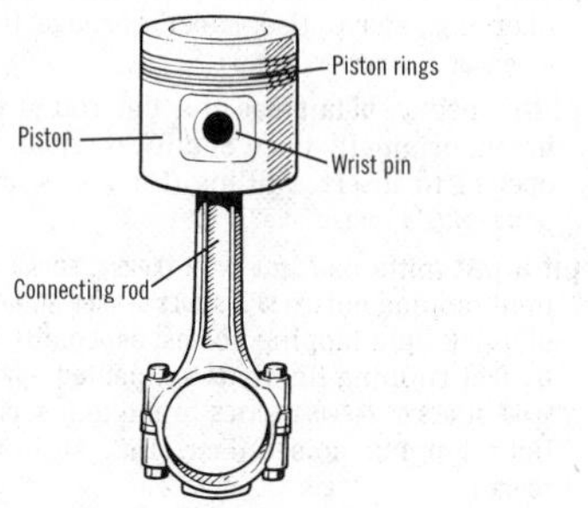

piston

pis·ton /pístən/ *n* **1.** a metal cylinder that slides up and down inside a tubular housing, receiving pressure from or exerting pressure on a fluid, especially one of several in an internal-combustion engine **2.** the valve mechanism in a brass musical instrument that is used to alter its pitch [Early 18C. Via French < Italian *pestone* "large pestle" < *pestare* (see PESTO)]

Pis·ton /pístən/, **Walter** (1894–1976) US composer and teacher. Known for his orchestral and chamber works, he won Pulitzer Prizes for two of his symphonies.

pis·ton ring *n* a metal ring or series of rings attached around a piston to ensure a tight seal with the cylinder wall and prevent gaseous leakage

pis·ton rod *n* a rod connected to a piston that transmits the motion of the piston to a pump or an engine

pis·tou /pee stoó/ *n* a sauce from Provence made of basil, garlic, and olive oil, similar to Italian pesto [Mid-20C. Via French < Provençal, past participle of *pestar* "crush" < late Latin *pistare* (see PESTO)]

pit[1] /pit/ *n* **1. BIG HOLE IN GROUND** a large hole in the ground **2. HOLE IN GROUND FOR MINING** a deep hole in the ground that gives access to a mining resource, especially coal **3. MINESHAFT** a shaft that gives access to a mine **4. BLEMISH** a blemish or indentation on a surface, especially a small circular scar left by a disease such as chickenpox **5. LOWEST PART** the very bottom of something ○ *in the pit of my stomach* **6. AREA CONTAINING PARTICULAR SUBSTANCE** an area filled with a particular material or substance ○ *a tar pit* **7.** SPORTS **ARENA FOR FIGHTING** an arena that is cordoned off for bouts of fighting, especially illegal fighting between cocks or dogs **8.** MOTOR SPORTS **SERVICING AREA FOR RACING CARS** an area, or section of an area, off the side of an auto racing track where vehicles can get fuel, fresh tires, and repairs (*often used in the plural*) **9.** AUTOMOT **SUNKEN AREA FOR EXAMINING CARS** a sunken area, especially in a garage, where the undercarriages of cars and other motor vehicles can be inspected and repaired **10.** TRACK AND FIELD **SANDY AREA WHERE JUMPERS LAND** a soft sandy area where a long jumper, triple jumper, or pole vaulter can land safely **11.** ANAT **NATURAL HOLLOW** a natural hollow, especially on the surface of a body part **12.** BOT **CONCAVE SPOT ON PLANT WALL** a tiny concavity or thin-walled area in the wall of a plant serving to help transport water and nutrients **13.** HUNTING same as **pitfall** (sense 2) **14.** GAMBLING **AREA IN CASINO** the area in a casino where the gambling takes place **15.** FIN **AREA ON FLOOR OF EXCHANGE** the area of the floor of an exchange where commodities trading takes place **16.** CHR same as **hell** *n* (sense 1) (*literary*) ■ **pits** *npl* **WORST POSSIBLE THING, PERSON, OR PLACE** the worst or most unpleasant thing, person, or place it is possible to find (*informal*) ■ *vt* (**pit·ted, pit·ting, pits**) **1.** MAKE SOMEBODY OR SOMETHING OPPONENT to set somebody or something up in opposition to somebody or something else ○ *She was pitted against the three-time world champion.* **2.** MARK SURFACE WITH SMALL HOLES to cause small holes or indentations to form in a surface **3.** BURY SOMEBODY OR SOMETHING to put somebody or something in a deep hole [Old English *pytt*, via Germanic < Latin *puteus* "pit, well"] ◇ **pit your wits against somebody** to compete with somebody in an intellectual exercise

pit[2] /pit/ *n* the hard seed of a fruit such as a peach that has only one seed ■ *vt* (**pit·ted, pit·ting, pits**) to remove the kernel or stone from a fruit [Mid-19C. Probably < Dutch]

pi·ta[1] /péetə/ *n Hispanic* a plant that yields a strong fiber, e.g., agave. Use: paper, cordage. [Late 17C. Via American Spanish < Taino]

pi·ta[2] /péetə/, **pi·ta bread** *n* a flat round unleavened bread, originally from Southwest Asia, that can be opened to insert a filling [Mid-20C. < modern Greek *pētta, pit(t)a* "bread, pie"]

pit·a·pat /pìttə pát/ *adv* WITH TAPPING SOUND with quick light tapping noises ■ *n* SERIES OF TAPPING NOISES a series of quick light tapping noises, especially those made by feet running lightly ■ *vi* (**-pat·ted, -pat·ting, -pats**) MAKE SERIES OF TAPPING NOISES to make a series of quick light tapping noises [Early 16C. An imitation of the sound]

pit boss *n* the supervisor of all gambling-table operations in a casino (*informal*)

pit bull ter·ri·er *n* a large bull terrier similar to the Staffordshire bull terrier but more muscular and powerful. The breed was first developed in the United States in dogfighting circles and remains unrecognized by the Kennel Clubs.

Pit·cairn Is·land /pít kern-/ island in the central South Pacific Ocean. It is the main island of a group forming a dependency of the United Kingdom. It was first inhabited by mutineers from HMS *Bounty* in 1790. Population: 61 (1991). Area: 14 sq. mi./36 sq. km.

pitch[1] /pich/ *v* (**pitched, pitch·ing, pitch·es**) **1.** *vti* THROW SOMETHING to throw or hurl something **2.** *vt* THROW SOMETHING AWAY to throw something out or hurl something away to get rid of it **3.** *vti* BASEBALL THROW BALL TO BATTER in baseball, to throw a ball from the mound to the batter **4.** *vti* GOLF HIT BALL HIGH in golf, to hit a high ball, usually onto the green and often with some backspin so that it does not roll too far on landing **5.** *vt* SET UP TEMPORARY STRUCTURE to set up a camp, tent, marquee, or other temporary structure **6.** *vt* SECURE SOMETHING IN GROUND to secure, embed, or implant something in the ground ○ *pitch tent stakes* **7.** *vti* FALL OR MAKE SOMEBODY FALL DOWN to fall or stumble, especially headfirst, or make somebody or something do this **8.** *vti* SLANT IN PARTICULAR WAY to slope in a particular way or to a particular degree, or make something do this ○ *a steeply pitched roof* **9.** *vi* NAUT WOBBLE UP AND DOWN to move in a rolling alternate front to rear motion, e.g., in rough water or turbulent air currents **10.** *vt* TRY TO SELL OR PROMOTE SOMETHING to try to sell or promote something, often in an aggressive way ○ *pitched his budget proposal to Congress* **11.** *vt* SET SOMETHING AT LEVEL to put, set, or have something at a particular level, e.g., of intensity or comprehension ○ *a show pitched at an audience in their 20s* **12.** *vt* MUSIC SET INSTRUMENT TO PARTICULAR KEY to set a musical instrument to a particular key **13.** *vt* CARDS LEAD CARD TO ESTABLISH TRUMPS to lead a card of a particular suit in order to establish that suit as trumps for the trick **14.** *vi* GIVE ENTHUSIASTIC SUPPORT to provide enthusiastic support for somebody or something ■ *n* **1.** PARTICULAR DEGREE OF SOMETHING a particular degree or level of something ○ *Their anticipation had been at fever pitch for days.* **2.** MUSIC PARTICULAR FREQUENCY OF SINGLE NOTE the level of a sound in a musical scale, according to its frequency **3.** *UK* FIELD FOR BALL GAME a playing area for a team ball game **4.** BASEBALL THROW OF BALL TO BATTER in baseball, the act or an instance of the pitcher throwing the ball from the mound to the batter **5.** GOLF HIGH BALL in golf, a shot, especially one from fairway to green, in which the ball lofts high in the air, often with some backspin, so that it does not roll too far on landing **6.** WAY OF THROWING SOMETHING a particular way or manner of throwing something, especially a ball **7.** METHOD OF PERSUASION an attempt to persuade somebody to accept or buy something (*informal*) ○ *unwanted telephone sales pitches at inconvenient times* **8.** CONSTR ROOF ANGLE the angle of slope of a roof expressed in degrees **9.** DEGREE OF SLOPE OF SOMETHING the degree, direction, or extent of a slope, especially of a hill, road, or other feature **10.** GEOL TILT OF GEOLOGIC FORMATION the inclination from the horizontal of a geologic formation or structure such as a vein or stratum **11.** ARCHIT VERY TOP OF SOMETHING the highest point of something such as an arch **12.** AVIAT ANGLE OF PROPELLER the angle formed between the plane of a propeller blade and the plane of rotation of the propeller **13.** TOSSING MOTION an act or instance of pitching up and down, e.g., in rough water or air turbulence **14.** MECH ENG DISTANCE BETWEEN THREADS OR GEAR TEETH the distance between corresponding points on adjacent threads on a screw or teeth on a gear **15.** CLIMBING DISTANCE SEPARATING CLIMBERS the distance between climbers making an ascent or descent using the same ropes, equal to one rope length or less [12C. Origin ?]

pitch in *vi* (*informal*) **1.** to help or cooperate, especially willingly **2.** to begin to do or participate in something, especially with great enthusiasm

pitch into *vt* to begin to attack somebody, either verbally or physically (*informal*)

pitch[2] /pich/ *n* **1.** SUBSTANCE OBTAINED FROM TAR a dark sticky substance obtained from tar and used in the building trades, especially for waterproofing roofs **2.** NATURAL TARRY SUBSTANCE a sticky dark substance such as asphalt that is found naturally **3.** RESIN a resin obtained from the sap of some pine trees ■ *vt* (**pitched, pitch·ing, pitch·es**) SPREAD PITCH ON SURFACE to coat a surface with pitch [Old English *pic*, via Germanic < Latin *pix*; partly < Anglo-Norman *piche* < Latin *pix*]

pitch-and-putt *n* **1.** a game similar to golf, but played on a much shorter course, in which players use only two clubs, an iron and a putter **2.** a course for pitch-and-putt, with holes shorter than those for golf

pitch-and-toss *n* a game of skill and luck in which each player throws a coin toward a designated mark. The player whose coin lands closest to the mark takes up then drops all the coins, and any coins that land heads up are won by that player.

pitch bend *n* an instrumental and vocal technique by which the pitch of a note is modified by raising or lowering it slightly

pitch-black *adj* so dark as to make seeing difficult or impossible

pitch·blende /pích blènd/ *n* a dark-colored form of the mineral uraninite. Use: source of uranium and radium. [Late 18C. < German *Pechblende* < *Pech* "pitch" + *Blende* (see BLENDE)]

pitch-dark *adj* same as **pitch-black**

pitched bat·tle *n* **1.** a fierce battle fought by opposing forces who take up prearranged positions in close proximity to each other **2.** a bitter conflict or confrontation ○ *a pitched battle between delegates and party leaders*

pitch·er[1] /píchər/ *n* **1.** a container for liquids with a single handle and a lip or spout for pouring **2.** a leaf of the pitcher plant [13C. Via Old French *pichier* < medieval Latin *bicarium*]

pitch·er[2] /píchər/ *n* in baseball, the player on the mound who throws the ball to the batter [Early 18C. < PITCH[1]]

Pitch·er /píchər/, **Molly** (1754–1832) US patriot. She carried pitchers of water to the soldiers at the Battle of Monmouth (1778), and may have fought in her fallen husband's place. Born **Hays, Mary**

pitch·er plant *n* a plant with leaves shaped like a pitcher for attracting, trapping, and digesting insects. Family: Sarraceniaceae.

pitch·er's mound *n* BASEBALL same as **mound** *n* (sense 5)

pitch·fork /pích fàwrk/ *n* a farming implement with a long handle and two or three widely spaced, slightly curved prongs, used for lifting and moving hay ■ *vt* (**-forked, -fork·ing, -forks**) to use a pitchfork to lift, turn, or move hay [13C. Alteration of *pickfork*, after PITCH[1]]

pitch·ing wedge *n* a golf club with a low-angled face used for hitting pitches

pitch·man /píchmən/ (*plural* **-men** /-mən/) *n* **1.** SPOKESMAN IN COMMERCIAL somebody, especially a man, who is a spokesperson in a TV or radio commercial **2.** PERSUASIVE SALESMAN somebody, especially a man, who is a very persuasive salesperson or advertiser **3.** DEALER IN CHEAP MERCHANDISE somebody, especially a man, who sells small or cheap items, especially on the streets or at carnivals

pitch·out /pích òwt/ *n* **1.** in baseball, a pitch that is high and outside the strike zone, thrown deliberately to allow the catcher to throw out a runner attempting to steal a base **2.** in football, a lateral pass after the snap made by the back, usually the quarterback, to another back behind the line of scrimmage

pitch·per·son /pích pùrss'n/ (*plural* **-per·sons** or **-peo·ple** /-peep'l/) *n* **1.** SPOKESPERSON IN COMMERCIAL a spokesperson in a TV or radio commercial **2.** PERSUASIVE SALESPERSON a very persuasive salesperson or advertiser **3.** DEALER IN CHEAP MERCHANDISE a seller of small or cheap items, especially on the streets or at carnivals

pitch pine *n* **1.** a pine tree that yields pitch or turpentine. Native to: eastern North America. Latin name: *Pinus rigida*. **2.** the hard heavy resinous wood of a pine tree

pitch·stone /pích stōn/ *n* a dark hydrated volcanic glass similar to obsidian

pitch·wom·an /pích wŏŏmmən/ (*plural* **-wom·en** /-wìmmin/) *n* **1.** SPOKESWOMAN IN COMMERCIAL a woman who is a spokesperson in a TV or radio commercial **2.** PERSUASIVE SALESWOMAN a woman who is a very persuasive salesperson or advertiser **3.** WOMAN DEALER IN CHEAP MERCHANDISE a woman who sells small or cheap items, especially on the streets or at carnivals

pitch·y /píchee/ (**-i·er, -i·est**) *adj* **1.** covered with or full of pitch **2.** resembling pitch, especially in color, smell, or consistency —**pitch·i·ness** *n*

pit·e·ous /píttee əss/ *adj* deserving pity, or causing feelings of pity [13C. < Old French *piteus* "full of pity" < Latin *pietas* (see PIETY)] —**pit·e·ous·ly** *adv* —**pit·e·ous·ness** *n*

pit·fall /pít fàwl/ *n* **1.** a potential and usually unanticipated disaster or difficulty **2.** a deep concealed hole in the ground intended as a trap

pith /pith/ *n* **1.** TISSUE UNDER RIND OF CITRUS FRUITS the soft whitish fibrous tissue that lies under the outer rind of a citrus fruit **2.** BOT TISSUE INSIDE STEM OF PLANT the central spongy tissue of the stem of a vascular plant **3.** ANAT SPONGY INTERIOR OF BODY PART the soft spongy inner tissue of a part of the body such as a hair shaft or bone **4.** CENTRAL PART OF SOMETHING the central and most important part of something such as an argument or discussion **5.** VIGOR strength or stamina ■ *vt* (**pithed, pith·ing, piths**) **1.** BIOL CUT SPINAL CORD OF LABORATORY ANIMAL to cut or destroy the spinal cord of a vertebrate as part of a laboratory experiment **2.** AGRIC KILL ANIMAL BY CUTTING SPINAL CORD to kill animals, especially cattle, by cutting through the spinal cord **3.** REMOVE PITH FROM PLANT STEM to remove the pith from the center of a plant stem [Old English *piþa* < Germanic]

Pith·e·can·thro·pus /pìthə kánthrəpəss, -kan thrṓpəss/ (*plural* **-pi** /-pī/) *n* same as **Java man** (*dated*) [Late 19C. < modern Latin < Greek *pithēkos* "ape" + *anthrōpos* "human being"] —**pith·e·can·throp·ic** /pìthəkən thróppik/ *adj* —**pith·e·can·thro·pine** /-kánthrə pīn/ *adj* —**pith·e·can·thro·poid** /-pòyd/ *adj*

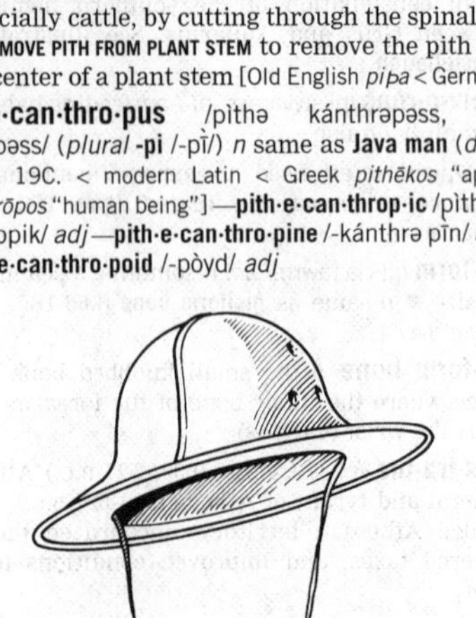

pith helmet

pith hel·met *n* a lightweight hat made from dried pith or some other material, worn in hot climates to protect the head, face, and the back of the neck from strong sunlight. See illustration on previous page

pith·os /pí thòss, pī́-/ (*plural* **-oi** /-òy/) *n* a large ceramic jar used in ancient Greece for storing oil or grain [Late 19C. < Greek]

pith·y /píthee/ (**-i·er, -i·est**) *adj* **1.** brief, yet forceful and to the point, often with an element of wit **2.** relating to, containing, or resembling pith —**pith·i·ly** *adv* —**pith·i·ness** *n*

pit·i·a·ble /píttee əb'l/ *adj* **1.** arousing or deserving pity or compassion **2.** arousing or deserving contempt or derision —**pit·i·a·ble·ness** *n* —**pit·i·a·bly** *adv*

pit·i·ful /píttif'l/ *adj* **1.** arousing or deserving pity or compassion **2.** arousing or deserving contempt or derision —**pit·i·ful·ly** *adv* —**pit·i·ful·ness** *n*

SYNONYMS See *moving*.

pit·i·less /píttiləss/ *adj* **1.** lacking in pity, mercy, or sympathy **2.** extremely severe ○ *the blazing, pitiless sun* —**pit·i·less·ly** *adv* —**pit·i·less·ness** *n*

Pit·jant·jat·ja·ra /pìchənchə chaárə/ (*plural same* or **-ras**), **Pit·jant·ja·ra** /pìchən chaárə/ *n* **1.** a member of an Australian Aboriginal people who live in the desert regions in the south of the continent **2.** the Pama-Nyungan language of the Pitjantjatjara people. Native speakers: 2,100. [< Pitjantjatjara] —**Pit·jant·jat·ja·ra** *adj*

pit·lane /pít làyn/ *n* a part of the track of an auto racing circuit that leads into the pits or from the pits back to the main track

pit·man /pítmən/ *n* (*plural* **pit·mans**) *UK* ENG same as **connecting rod**

pi·ton /peé tòn/ *n* a metal spike with an eye at one end driven into ice or a rock crevice and used for securing a rope when climbing [Late 19C. < French, "eye-bolt"]

Pi·tot-stat·ic tube /peétō-, pee tṓ-/ *n* a device consisting of a Pitot tube and a static tube, used to measure fluid velocity and especially as an air speed indicator in an aircraft [Early 20C. See PITOT TUBE]

Pi·tot tube *n* **1.** an instrument placed in a moving fluid and used along with a manometer to measure fluid velocity **2.** PHYS same as **Pitot-static tube** [Late 19C. After Henri *Pitot* (1695–1771), French physicist]

pit stop *n* **1.** MOTOR SPORTS **REFUELING STOP FOR CAR DURING RACE** a stop in the pits to allow a racecar to be refueled and serviced during a race **2. BRIEF STOP DURING ROAD JOURNEY** a brief stop during a road trip to rest, refuel, use a restroom, or buy refreshments (*informal*) **3. PLACE TO MAKE PIT STOP** a place to make a pit stop during a road trip (*informal*)

Pitt /pit/, **William, 1st Earl of Chatham** (1708–78) British politician. As secretary of state (1756–61), he was the most powerful politician in Great Britain and effectively prime minister. He headed a new government from 1766 to 1768. Known as **Pitt the Elder**

"You cannot conquer America."
[William Pitt, *Speech to the House of Lords*; November 18, 1777]

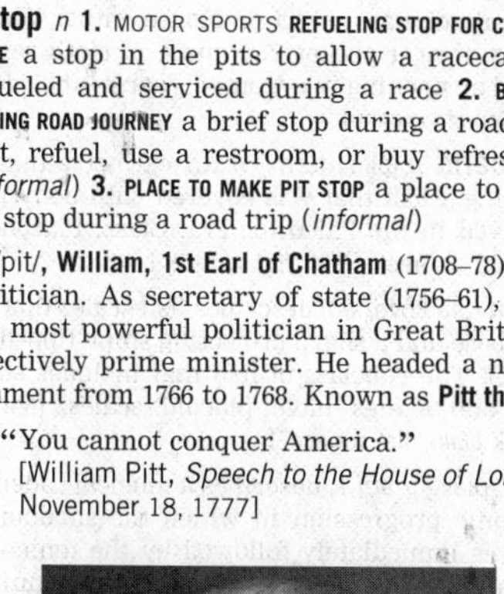

William Pitt (the Younger)

Pitt, William (1759–1806) prime minister of Great Britain (1783–1801 and 1804–06). He was Great Britain's youngest prime minister, at the age of 24. During his first premiership, the Act of Union (1800) incorporated Ireland into the United Kingdom but he resigned following George III's refusal to accept Roman Catholic emancipation. He returned to office for a second administration in 1804. Known as **Pitt the Younger**

pit·ta[1] /píttə/ *n* FOOD UK spelling of **pita**[2] [< Sanskrit]

pit·ta[2] /píttə/ *n* a brightly colored small bird. Native to: Australia, Asia, Africa. Genus: *Pitta*. [Mid-19C. Via modern Latin < Telegu *piṭṭa* "bird"]

pit·tance /pítt'nss/ *n* a very small amount of something, especially money [13C. Via Old French *pietance* < medieval Latin *pietantia* "pious or charitable gift" < Latin *pietas* (see PIETY)]

pit·ter-pat·ter /píttər-/ *n* **LIGHT CONTINUOUS TAPPING SOUND** a light, rapid, and continuous tapping sound, similar to the sound of raindrops falling on something ■ *vi* (**pit·ter-pat·tered, pit·ter-pat·ter·ing, pit·ter-pat·ters**) **MAKE LIGHT CONTINUOUS TAPPING SOUND** to make or move with a light, rapid, and continuous tapping sound ■ *adv* **WITH LIGHT CONTINUOUS TAPPING SOUND** with a light, rapid, and continuous tapping sound [15C. An imitation of the sound]

~~pittiful~~ incorrect spelling of **pitiful**

pit·tos·po·rum /pi tóspərəm, píttə spàwrəm/ *n* an evergreen bush with leathery leaves, often planted for hedges in warm regions. Flowers: white, purple, or greenish yellow. Native to: Australasia, Southeast Asia, southern Africa. Genus: *Pittosporum*. [Late 18C. < modern Latin < Greek *pitta* "pitch" + *sporos* "seed"; from the resinous pulp around the seeds]

Pitts·burgh /píts bùrg/ city in southwestern Pennsylvania. It is the second largest city in the state. Population: 327,898 (2002 estimate).

Pitts·field /píts feéld/ city in western Massachusetts, directly east of the New York border, on the eastern bank of the Housatonic River, northwest of Springfield. Population: 45,023 (2002 estimate).

pi·tu·i·tar·y /pi tóo i tèrree/ *n* (*plural* **-ies**) **1.** PHYSIOL same as **pituitary gland 2.** PHARM same as **pituitary extract** ■ *adj* PHYSIOL relating to or produced by the pituitary gland [Early 17C. < Latin *pituitarius* "of slime or mucus" < *pituita* "slime"]

pi·tu·i·tar·y ex·tract *n* a pharmaceutical preparation made from substances obtained from the pituitary gland that is rich in beneficial hormones

pi·tu·i·tar·y gland *n* a small oval gland at the base of the brain in vertebrates, producing hormones that control other glands and influence growth of the bone structure, sexual maturing, and general metabolism

pit vi·per *n* a venomous snake that has heat-sensitive pits below its eyes used to detect prey. Rattlesnakes and copperheads are pit vipers. Native to: Central, North and South America. Family: Crotalidae.

pit·y /píttee/ *n* **1. FEELING OF SYMPATHY** a feeling of sadness because of another person's trouble or suffering, or the capacity to feel this **2. REGRETTABLE THING** a sad or regrettable thing ○ *It's a pity you couldn't make it.* **3. MERCY** a willingness to help or to forgive somebody ■ *vt* (**-ied, -y·ing, -ies**) **FEEL PITY FOR SOMEBODY** to feel pity for somebody ■ *interj* **EXPRESSION OF SYMPATHY OR REGRET** used to express sympathy or regret about something (*informal*) [13C. Via Old French *pité* < Latin *pietas* "dutifulness, piety, compassion" (see PIETY)] —**pit·y·ing** *adj* —**pit·y·ing·ly** *adv* ◇ **have** *or* **take pity on somebody 1.** to feel pity for somebody **2.** to show mercy to somebody ◇ **(the) more's the pity** used to express regret, disappointment, or annoyance that something is the case (*informal*)

~~pityful~~ incorrect spelling of **pitiful**

pit·y·ri·a·sis /pìtti rī́ əssiss/ *n* a skin disease affecting humans and animals in which the skin comes off in dry flakes [Late 17C. Via modern Latin < Greek *pituriasis* < *pituron* "corn husks"]

più /pyoo/ *adv* more or increasingly (*used as a musical direction*) [Early 18C. Via Italian < Latin *plus*]

Pi·u·ra /pee óorə/ city in northwestern Peru on the Piura River. The nearby community of San Miguel de Piura, the oldest Spanish settlement in Peru, was founded in 1532 by the conquistador Francisco Pizarro. Population: 324,600 (1990).

Pi·us IX /pī́ əss/ (1792–1878) pope. His pontificate (1846–78) was marked by the loss of the Papal States, the declaration of papal infallibility, and condemnation of all forms of liberalism. Born **Mastai-Ferretti, Giovanni Maria**

Pi·us XII (1876–1958) pope (1939–58). He condemned modernism and Communism. He sought to prevent World War II, although his role in the war is the subject of controversy. Born **Pacelli, Eugenio**

Pi·us V, St. (1504–72) pope (1566–72). During his papacy, he aided French Roman Catholics in their persecution of the Huguenots, excommunicated Elizabeth I of England, and used the Inquisition to punish heretics. Born **Antonio Michele Ghisleri**

Pi·us X, St. (1835–1914) pope (1903–14). During his pontificate he opposed modernism in the Roman Catholic Church, initiated changes to canon law, and introduced a new breviary. Born **Sarto, Giuseppe Melchiorre**

Pi·ute *n, adj* LANG another spelling of **Paiute**

piv·ot /pívvət/ *n* **1.** MECH ENG **POINT ON WHICH SOMETHING TURNS** a pin, shaft, or point on which something turns **2. CRUCIAL PERSON OR THING** somebody or something that is essential to the success or effectiveness of an activity or event **3. TURNING MOVEMENT** a turning movement on a pivot or while standing in place **4.** BASKETBALL **OFFENSIVE POSITION OR PLAYER** in basketball, an offensive position in which a player faces away from the opposing basket, relays passes, and screens other team members, or a player in this position ■ *v* (**-ot·ed, -ot·ing, -ots**) **1.** *vti* **TURN ON PIVOT** to turn on a pivot, or make something do this **2.** *vti* **WHEEL OR SWING AROUND** to wheel or swing around, or make something do this **3.** *vi* **DEPEND ON SOMETHING** to be dependent on somebody or something, usually a single person, thing, or factor **4.** *vt* **PROVIDE SOMETHING WITH PIVOT** to provide something with a pivot on which it can turn [15C. < French]

piv·ot·al /pívvət'l/ *adj* **1.** vitally important, especially in determining the outcome, progress, or success of something **2.** relating to or functioning as a pivot

piv·ot bridge *n* CIV ENG same as **swing bridge**

piv·ot·man /pívvət màn/ *n* **1.** somebody on whom the success of an organization depends **2.** BASKETBALL same as **pivot** *n* (sense 4)

pix[1] /piks/ MOVIES, PHOTOGRAPHY, ARTS plural of **pic** (*informal*)

pix[2] /piks/ *n* CHR another spelling of **pyx**

pix·el /píks'l, -sèl/ *n* a tiny dot of light that is the basic unit from which images on computer or television screens are made [Mid-20C. < PIX[1] + ELEMENT]

pix·e·lat·ed /píksə làytəd/ *adj* describes an image on a computer or television screen that is made up of pixels, especially one that is unclear or distorted [Mid-20C. < PIXEL, after PIXILATED]

pix·ie /píksee/, **pix·y** (*plural* **-ies**) *n* a fairy or elf often depicted as having pointed ears, wearing a long pointed hat, and being cheerful and rather mischievous [Mid-17C. Origin ?]

pix·ie cut *n* a short tapered hairstyle for girls and women, first popular in the 1960s

pix·i·lat·ed /píksə làytəd/ *adj* **1.** *US* **BEHAVING ODDLY** behaving in a strange or whimsical way **2. BEWILDERED** feeling bewildered **3. DRUNK** intoxicated by alcohol (*slang*) [Mid-19C. < PIXIE, after words such as *elated, titillated*] —**pix·i·la·tion** /pìksə láysh'n/ *n*

pix·y *n* another spelling of **pixie**

Pi·zar·ro /pi zaárō/, **Francisco** (1476?–1541) Spanish conquistador. He conquered the Inca Empire (1532), founded the city of Lima (1535), and was governor of Peru (1532–41).

piz·azz *n* another spelling of **pizzazz** (*informal*)

piz·za /peétsə/ *n* a flat round piece of bread dough baked with a variety of toppings, often including tomato sauce and cheese [Late 19C. < Italian, "pie"]

piz·za par·lor *n* COMM, FOOD same as **pizzeria**

piz·zazz /pi záz/, **piz·azz, piz·zaz** *n* an attractive and exciting vitality, especially when combined with style and glamor (*informal*) [Mid-20C. Origin ?]

piz·ze·ri·a /peétsə reé ə/ *n* a restaurant that specializes in making and serving pizzas [Mid-20C. < Italian < *pizza* "pizza, pie"]

piz·zi·ca·to /pìtsee kaátō/ *adv* by using the fingers to pluck the strings of an instrument that is normally played with a bow, especially a violin (*used as a musical direction*) ■ *n* (*plural* **-ti** /-tee/) a piece of music, or a section of a piece, played pizzicato [Mid-19C. < Italian, past participle of *pizzicare* "pluck" < *pizzare* "to prick, sting" < *pizza* "point"] —**piz·zi·ca·to** *adj*

piz·zle /pízz'l/ *n* (*sometimes considered offensive*) **1.** the penis of an animal, especially a bull **2.** a whip made out of a bull's penis [Late 15C. < Low German *pēsel* "little penis" < Middle Low German *pēse* "penis"]

PK *abbr* PARAPSYCHOL psychokinesis

pk. *abbr* **1.** pack **2.** ONLINE Pakistan (*used in Internet addresses*) See table at **domain name** **3.** park **4.** peak **5.** MEASURE peck

PKI *abbr* E-COMMERCE public key infrastructure

pkt. *abbr* packet

PKU *abbr* MED phenylketonuria

Pky, pky, Pkwy *abbr* parkway

PL *abbr* **1.** GRAM plural **2.** LAW public law

pl. *abbr* **1.** GRAM plural **2.** Poland (*used in Internet addresses*) See table at **domain name**

Pl. *abbr* Place (*used in addresses*)

PL/1 *abbr* a high level computer programming language specially designed for both business and scientific applications. Full form **programming language 1**

plac·a·ble /plákəb'l, pláy-/ *adj* easily placated (*formal*) [14C. Directly or via French < Latin *placabilis* < *placare* "make calm"] —**plac·a·bil·i·ty** /plàkə bílləteе, plàykə-/ *n* —**plac·a·bly** *adv*

plac·ard /plá kaàrd, -kərd/ *n* **1.** NOTICE DISPLAYED IN PUBLIC a large piece of stiff paper or board with a notice on it, displayed or carried in public **2.** SMALL CARD OR METAL PLAQUE a small card or metal plaque with a name on it, e.g., a nameplate ■ *vt* (**-ard·ed, -ard·ing, -ards**) **1.** PUT PLACARDS ON SOMETHING to put placards on or in something **2.** PUBLICIZE SOMETHING WITH PLACARDS to advertise or announce something using placards [15C. < French < Old French *plaquier* "flatten, plaster" < Middle Dutch *placken* "flatten, patch"]

pla·cate /pláy kàyt, plá-/ (**-cat·ed, -cat·ing, -cates**) *vt* to make somebody less angry, upset, or hostile, usually by doing or saying things to please him or her [Late 17C. < Latin *placat-*, past participle of *placare* "make calm"] —**pla·ca·tion** /play káysh'n/ *n* —**pla·ca·to·ry** /pláykə tàwree, plákə-/ *adj*

place /playss/ *n* **1.** AREA OR PORTION OF SPACE an area, position, or portion of space that somebody or something can occupy ○ *This is a good place to plant the sapling.* **2.** LOCALITY a geographic locality, e.g., a town, country, or region ○ *People come here to work from lots of different places.* **3.** SQUARE OR STREET a public square or short street with residences on it **4.** DWELLING a house, apartment, or other living accommodations ○ *a place of our own* **5.** LOCATION WITH PARTICULAR USE a building or location with a particular purpose ○ *the firm's place of business* ○ *their regular place of worship* **6.** POINT IN SOMETHING a point or position in something such as a book, film, or story ○ *I lost my place when you interrupted me.* **7.** PROPER POSITION the usual or proper position or location for somebody or something ○ *A place for everything, and everything in its place.* **8.** OPPORTUNITY TO STUDY an opportunity to study at a school or university ○ *hoping for a place at Harvard* **9.** STATUS somebody's social position or rank in an organization ○ *know your place* **10.** RESPONSIBILITY somebody's responsibility or right, especially as it relates to the person's role or status ○ *It's not your place to tell me what to do.* **11.** JOB a job or position ○ *was offered a place on the board* **12.** SOMEWHERE TO SIT somewhere for somebody to sit, e.g., at a table or in a theater ○ *I'll keep a place for you next to me.* **13.** POSITION IN SERIES the position of somebody or something in a sequence or series **14.** HORSERACING SECOND POSITION the second position in a race, especially a horserace **15.** MATH POSITION OF DIGIT IN NUMBER the relative position of a digit in a number ■ *v* (**placed, plac·ing, plac·es**) **1.** *vt* PUT SOMETHING OR SOMEBODY SOMEWHERE to put something or somebody in a particular location or position ○ *placed the box on the table* **2.** *vt* PUT SOMEBODY IN PARTICULAR STATE to cause somebody or something to be in a particular state or condition ○ *Your actions placed all of us in danger.* **3.** *vt* SEE SOMEBODY IN PARTICULAR WAY to see or treat somebody or something as having a particular value or character ○ *He placed his family above everything else in his life.* **4.** *vt* REMEMBER SOMEBODY OR SOMETHING to recognize or remember somebody or something ○ *I can't place him.* **5.** *vt* ASSIGN SOMEBODY to assign somebody to a job, position, home, or the care of somebody else ○ *I'll see if I can place you with the sales team.* **6.** *vt* AIM SOMETHING CAREFULLY to aim or calculate something carefully in order to achieve the desired result ○ *Her observations were timely and well placed.* ○ *placed his punches well* **7.** *vt* ARRANGE FOR SOMETHING to arrange for something to be dealt with or take place ○ *placed an order for a new car* **8.** *vt* RANK SOMEBODY OR SOMETHING to put somebody in a particular position in a sequence or series ○ *The survey place her third overall.* **9.** *vi* SPORTS FINISH SECOND to finish in second position in a race, especially a horserace [Pre-12C. Via French < Latin *platea* "broad way" < Greek *plateia hodos*] ◇ **all over the place** (*informal*) **1.** everywhere **2.** in a state of disorder or confusion ◇ **a place in the sun** a position of success, happiness, or prosperity ◇ **give place (to) 1.** to be succeeded or superseded by somebody or something **2.** to make room for somebody or something ◇ **go places** to become successful (*informal*) ◇ **in place 1.** in position or ready for use **2.** in the position or location in which somebody or something belongs or ought to be ◇ **in place of** instead of or as a replacement for somebody or something ◇ **out of place 1.** not in the position or location in which somebody or something should be **2.** inappropriate or incongruous ◇ **put somebody in his** *or* **her place** to humble somebody who is behaving in an arrogant, presumptuous, or insolent way (*informal*) ◇ **take place** to happen ◇ **take the place of** to be a substitute for or replace somebody or something

pla·ce·bo /plə seébō/ (*plural* **-bos** or **-boes**) *n* **1.** PRESCRIPTION WITHOUT PHYSICAL EFFECT something prescribed for a patient that contains no medicine, but is given for the positive psychological effect it may have because the patient believes that he or she is receiving treatment **2.** PHARM INACTIVE SUBSTANCE a preparation containing no active ingredients, given to a patient participating in a clinical trial in order to assess the performance of a new drug given to other patients in the trial **3.** SOMETHING DONE TO PLACATE SOMEBODY something of no inherent benefit that is done or said simply to placate or reassure somebody **4.** /plaa cháybō/ CHR VESPERS OF OFFICE FOR DEAD in the Roman Catholic Church, the vespers of the office for the dead [13C. < Latin, "I shall please" (first word in the Vulgate text of Psalm 114:9) < *placere* "to please"]

pla·ce·bo ef·fect *n* a sense of benefit felt by a patient that arises solely from the knowledge that treatment has been given

place card *n* a small card with somebody's name on it, put on a dining table to show where that person is to sit

place·hold·er /pláyss hòldər/ *n* a symbol in a mathematical or logical expression used to show a pattern, e.g., by representing a term in an equation or a statement in an argument

place kick *n* a kick, especially in football or rugby, in which the ball is propped or held up on the ground

place·kick *vt* to kick the ball, or score a goal or points by kicking the ball, while it is propped up on the ground —**place·kick·er** *n*

place mat *n* a protective mat for a place setting at a table

place·ment /pláyssmənt/ *n* **1.** ACT OF PLACING OR BEING PLACED the act of placing or arranging something in a position or location, or the fact of being placed or arranged in this way **2.** ARRANGING OF JOB OR HOUSING the task of arranging employment or accommodations for somebody, or an instance of this **3.** ARRANGING FOR APPROPRIATE CLASS the task of helping a student to find an appropriate course or class, or an instance of this **4.** *UK* same as **practicum** **5.** SPORTS SKILLFUL PLAYING OF BALL in a sport such as tennis or soccer, a player's skill in accurately playing the ball **6.** *US* FOOTBALL PLACE KICK OR PLACING OF BALL in football, a place kick for a field goal or point after a touchdown, or the positioning of the ball for such a kick

place·ment test *n US* a test given to students entering a school, college, or university to find the most appropriate courses or classes for them

place name *n* the name of a geographic area or feature such as a town, settlement, hill, or body of water

pla·cen·ta /plə séntə/ (*plural* **-tas** or **-tae** /-tee/) *n* **1.** ANAT ORGAN IN UTERUS OF PREGNANT MAMMAL a vascular organ that develops inside the uterus of most pregnant mammals to supply food and oxygen to the fetus through the umbilical cord. It is expelled after birth. **2.** BOT PART OF OVARY OF PLANT the part of the ovary in a flowering plant that bears ovules **3.** BOT SPORE-BEARING MASS OF TISSUE the tissue in a nonflowering plant where the sporangia or spores develop [Late 17C. < Latin, "cake" < Greek *plakous* "flat cake" < *plak-* "flat surface"] —**pla·cen·tal** *adj, n* —**pla·cen·ta·ry** *adj*

plac·en·ta·tion /plàss'n táysh'n/ *n* **1.** BIOL FORMATION OR ATTACHMENT OF PLACENTA the process of forming a placenta during pregnancy, or the way in which the placenta is attached to the wall of the uterus **2.** BOT WAY OVULES ARE ATTACHED the way in which ovules are attached to the ovary of a plant **3.** BIOL PLACENTA TYPE the form, structure, or type of a placenta

plac·er /pláyssər/ *n Southwest US* a deposit of river sand or gravel containing particles of gold or another valuable mineral [Early 19C. < American Spanish, "shoal"]

place set·ting *n* a set of items such as utensils, dishes, and glasses arranged on a table to be used by one person at a meal, or the utensils or dishes alone

place val·ue *n* the value of the place that a digit occupies in a numeral

plac·id /plássid/ *adj* **1.** tending or appearing to be calm and not easily excited, upset, or disturbed **2.** *US* too easily satisfied [Early 17C. Directly or via French < Latin *placidus* "gentle" < *placere* "to please"] —**pla·cid·i·ty** /pla síddətee/ *n* —**plac·id·ly** *adv*

plac·ing /pláyssing/ *n* the issuing of securities to the public through a stockbroker or another intermediary

plack·et /plákit/ *n* **1.** an opening in a woman's garment such as a skirt or blouse, either where it fastens or at a pocket **2.** a piece of cloth sewn in behind an opening in a woman's garment [Early 17C. Alteration of PLACARD]

pla·co·derm /plákə dùrm/ *n* an extinct animal resembling a fish that was covered with bony plates and lived in the Paleozoic era. Class: Placodermi. [Mid-19C. < Greek *plak-* "flat surface"]

plac·oid /plá kòyd/ *adj* describes fish scales that have a flat base and a sharp projecting spine tipped with enamel. The subclass of fish that includes sharks, rays, and skates have placoid scales. [Mid-19C. < Greek *plak-* "flat surface"]

pla·gal /pláyg'l/ *adj* **1.** describes a musical cadence or harmonic progression in which the subdominant chord is immediately followed by the tonic chord **2.** relating to or being a musical mode beginning on the note a fourth below the keynote of its equivalent authentic mode, but ending on the same final note [Late 16C. < medieval Latin *plagalis* < medieval Greek *plagios hēkhos* "plagal mode"]

plage /plaazh/ *n* **1.** a mark on the Sun's surface often associated with sunspots **2.** a beach, especially at a fashionable seaside resort [Late 19C. Via French < Italian *plaggia* < late Latin *plagia* "plain, shore"]

pla·gia·rism /pláyjə rìzzəm/ *n* **1.** the process of copying another person's idea or written work and claiming it as original **2.** a piece of written work or an idea that somebody has copied and claimed as his or her own —**pla·gia·rist** *n* —**pla·gia·ris·tic** /plàyjə rístik/ *adj*

pla·gia·rize /pláyjə rīz/ (**-rized, -riz·ing, -riz·es**) *vti* to copy another person's idea or written work and claim it as original —**pla·gia·riz·er** *n*

plagio- *prefix* **1.** oblique, offset ○ *plagiotropism* **2.**

disturbance ○ *plagioclimax* [< Greek *plagios* "sideways" < *plagos* "side" < Indo-European, "be flat"]

pla·gi·o·clase /pláyjee ə klàyss, -klàyz/ *n* a feldspar consisting of sodium and calcium aluminum silicates [Mid-19C. < PLAGIO- + Greek *klasis* "breaking"] —**pla·gi·o·clas·tic** /plàyjee ə klástik/ *adj*

pla·gi·ot·ro·pism /plàyjee óttrə pìzzəm/ *n* the tendency of a plant's roots, stems, or branches to grow at an angle away from the vertical in response to a stimulus —**pla·gi·o·tro·pic** /plàyjee ə trṓpik, -tróppik/ *adj* —**pla·gi·o·tro·pi·cal·ly** *adv*

plague /playg/ *n* **1.** MED **EPIDEMIC DISEASE** a disease that spreads rapidly through a population, killing a great many people, or an outbreak of such a disease **2.** MED same as **bubonic plague** **3.** **APPEARANCE OF SOMETHING IN LARGE NUMBERS** a sudden appearance or outbreak of something unpleasant in very large numbers or with unusual frequency ○ *a plague of locusts* ○ *a plague of violence* **4.** **SOMEBODY OR SOMETHING TROUBLESOME** an affliction or extremely troublesome or annoying person or thing ■ *vt* (**plagued, plagu·ing, plagues**) (*often passive*) **1.** **AFFLICT SOMEBODY** to cause somebody severe and lasting distress, difficulty, or other affliction ○ *Falling prices and drought plagued the cattle industry.* **2.** **ANNOY SOMEBODY CONSTANTLY** to persistently harass or annoy somebody ○ *plagued him with requests for autographs* [14C. < Latin *plaga* "blow, stroke, wound"]

pla·guy /pláygee/, **pla·guey** (**-gui·er, -gui·est**) *adj* causing trouble or irritation —**pla·gui·ly** *adv* —**pla·guy** *adv*

plaice /playss/ (*plural same*) *n* **1.** a large flat-bodied ocean fish with brown skin and red or orange spots. Native to: European waters. Latin name: *Pleuronectes platessa.* **2.** a fish similar to and related to the European plaice. Native to: North American Atlantic. Latin name: *Hippoglossoides platessoides.* [13C. Via Old French *plaïs* < late Latin *platessa* "flatfish" < Greek *platus* "broad"]

plaid /plad/ *n* **1.** **CHECKED FABRIC** a fabric woven in a tartan or checked pattern **2.** **TARTAN PATTERN** a tartan or checked pattern **3.** **TARTAN CLOTH WORN OVER SHOULDER** a long rectangular piece of tartan material worn draped over the shoulder as part of traditional Scottish Highland dress [Early 16C. < Gaelic] —**plaid·ed** *adj*

plain /playn/ *adj* **1.** **CLEARLY VISIBLE** clearly visible and not blocked or obscured ○ *in plain view* **2.** **EASILY UNDERSTOOD** clear to the mind or senses ○ *The plain fact is that they lied to us.* **3.** **SIMPLE AND ORDINARY** simple and ordinary, without ornamentation or frills ○ *plain homely food* ○ *a plain brown envelope* **4.** **CANDID** truthful and frank ○ *a maverick general known for his plain speaking* **5.** **PURE** not combined with any other substances ○ *plain water* **6.** **UNCOLORED OR UNPATTERNED** lacking any pattern or coloration ○ *plain fabric* **7.** **NOT ATTRACTIVE** not pretty or good-looking ○ *plain looks* **8.** **ADDS EMPHASIS TO NOUN** used to emphasize a noun ○ *died of plain neglect* **9.** HANDICRAFT **IN SIMPLEST KNITTING STYLE OR STITCH** done in the simplest knitting style or stitch ■ *adv* **1.** **ADDS EMPHASIS TO ADJECTIVE OR ADVERB** used to emphasize an adjective or adverb ○ *just plain wrong* **2.** **CLEARLY** in a clear or candid way ○ *I'll tell you plain – I've had enough of this.* ■ *n* **1.** GEOG **FLAT EXPANSE OF LAND** a large expanse of fairly flat dry land, usually with few trees **2.** HANDICRAFT **KNITTING STYLE OR STITCH** the simplest knitting style or stitch ■ **plains** *npl* GEOG **TREELESS LEVEL EXPANSES** large expanses of level, almost treeless country in some central states of the United States [13C. Via French < Latin *planus* "flat"] —**plain·ly** *adv* —**plain·ness** *n*

USAGE plain or **plane**? Do not confuse ***plain*** with ***plane***, which has the same pronunciation. ***Plain*** is more frequently used as an adjective and ***plane*** as a noun. As an adjective, ***plain*** means "simple," "clear," or "not patterned, decorated, etc.", as in *a plain fabric*, whereas ***plane*** simply means "flat and level" or "two-dimensional," as in *a plane surface.* As a noun related to the adjective, ***plane*** denotes (among other things) a flat surface or a level, as in *different planes of existence*, whereas ***plain*** simply denotes a large expanse of flat land, as in *a treeless plain.* There are several other nouns ***plane***, denoting an aircraft, a tool, and a tree.

SYNONYMS See ***unattractive***.

plain·chant /pláyn chànt/ *n* MUSIC same as **plainsong**

plain clothes, plain·clothes /pláyn klṑthz, -klṑz/ *npl* ordinary civilian clothes when worn by a police officer on duty —**plain-clothes** *adj*

plain deal·ing *n* open and honest behavior or business

plain Jane *n* a woman who is regarded as not pretty or good-looking (*informal; often considered offensive*)

plain knit·ting *n* HANDICRAFT same as **garter stitch**

Plain Peo·ple *npl US* members of Christian groups such as the Amish or the Mennonites who are noted for their simple lifestyle and plain way of dressing

plain sail·ing *n* something that is straightforward and easy to do

Plains In·di·an *n* a member of any of the Native American peoples who formerly lived on the Great Plains of North America

plains·man /pláynzmən/ (*plural* **-men** /-mən/) *n* a man who lives on a plain, especially somebody who settled or lives on the Great Plains of North America

plain·song /pláyn sàwng/ *n* church music that is intended to be sung in unison without instrumental accompaniment [15C. Translation of Latin *cantus planus*]

plains·per·son /pláynz pùrss'n/ (*plural* **-peo·ple** /-peep'l/ or **-per·sons**) *n* somebody who lives on a plain, especially somebody who settled or lives on the Great Plains of North America

plain-spo·ken *adj* speaking or tending to speak truthfully and frankly —**plain-spo·ken·ness** *n*

plains·wom·an /pláynz wŏŏmmən/ (*plural* **-wom·en** /-wìmmin/) *n* a woman who lives on a plain, especially one who settled or lives on the Great Plains of North America

plaint /playnt/ *n* **1.** an expression of grief or sadness (*literary or archaic*) **2.** *US* a complaint [12C. Via French < Latin *planctus* "a beating of the breast" < *plangere* "to beat"]

plain text, plain·text /pláyn tèkst/ *n* a form of a message that is in ordinary readable language, and not in code

plain·tiff /pláyntif/ *n* somebody who begins a lawsuit against somebody else (**defendant**) in a civil court [14C. < French (see PLAINTIVE)]

plain·tive /pláyntiv/ *adj* expressing sadness or sounding sad [14C. < French *plaintive, plaintif* < *plaint* (see PLAINT)] —**plain·tive·ly** *adv* —**plain·tive·ness** *n*

plain weave *n* a weave in which the weft passes alternately under and over the warp, the threads forming a simple crisscross pattern

plait /playt, plat/ *n* **1.** same as **braid** **2.** HANDICRAFT same as **pleat** ■ *vt* (**plait·ed, plait·ing, plaits**) **1.** same as **braid** **2.** HANDICRAFT same as **pleat** [15C. < Old French *pleit* < Latin *plicit-*, past participle of *plicare* "fold"]

plan /plan/ *n* **1.** **SYSTEM FOR ACHIEVING OBJECTIVE** a method of doing something that is worked out in advance **2.** **INTENTION** something that somebody intends or has arranged to do (*often used in the plural*) ○ *What are your plans for Saturday?* **3.** **LAYOUT** a drawing or diagram on a horizontal plane of the layout or arrangement of something **4.** **LIST OR OUTLINE** a list, summary, or outline of the items to be included in something such as a piece of writing or a meeting **5.** ARCHIT **PERSPECTIVE DRAWING** a scale drawing showing the various perspectives of something, especially a building ■ *v* (**planned, plan·ning, plans**) **1.** *vti* **WORK OUT HOW TO DO SOMETHING** to work out in advance how something is to be done or organized **2.** *vt* **INTEND TO DO SOMETHING** to intend to do something, or make arrangements to do something **3.** *vt* ARCHIT **MAKE SCALE DRAWING OF SOMETHING** to make a scale drawing of something, especially a building [Late 17C. < French, "ground plan," alteration (after *plan* "flat") of *plant* < Latin *plantare* (see PLANT)]

plan ahead *vi* to make preparations or arrangements for the future

plan for *vt* to make preparations and arrangements for something on the basis of what is expected to happen

plan on *vt* to intend to do something (*informal*)

plan out *vt* to make a detailed plan for something to be done or organized

plan- *prefix* same as **plano-** (*used before vowels*)

pla·nar /pláynər, -naar/ *adj* **1.** **OF GEOMETRIC PLANE** relating to, involving, or typical of a geometric plane **2.** **FLAT** flat or lying in a single geometric plane **3.** *US* **TWO-DIMENSIONAL** having only two dimensions —**pla·nar·i·ty** /play nárrətee/ *n*

pla·nar·i·an /plə nérree ən/ *n* a small flatworm that lives mainly in freshwater, is not a parasite, and has a three-branched intestine. Order: Tricladida. [Mid-19C. Via modern Latin *Planaria* < Latin *planarius* "on level ground" < *planus* "flat" (see PLAIN)]

pla·na·tion /play náysh'n/ *n* the process of erosion and deposition by which water and wind currents produce a nearly level land surface [Late 19C. < PLANE[2]]

planch·et /plánchət/ *n* **1.** a flat disk of metal ready to be stamped as a coin or medal **2.** *US* a small metal container used to measure a radioactive substance [Early 17C. < obsolete *planch* "wooden plank, metal plate" < French *planche* (see PLANK)]

plan·chette /plan shét/ *n* a small heart-shaped or triangular wooden board on two casters and with a pencil attached that spells out messages supposed to be from the spirit world when people touch it lightly [Mid-19C. < French, "little plank" < *planche* (see PLANK)]

Planck /plangk/, **Max** (1858–1947) German physicist. He was the originator and developer of quantum theory and won the Nobel Prize in physics (1918). Full name **Planck, Max Karl Ernst Ludwig**

> "We have no right to assume that any physical laws exist, or if they have existed up to now, that they will continue to exist in a similar manner in the future."
> [Max Planck. Quoted in *The Universe in the Light of Modern Physics*, W. H. Johnston (tr.); 1931]

Planck's con·stant *n* a basic physical constant that is equal to the energy of a photon divided by its frequency, with an approximate value of 6.6261 x 10^{-34} joule-seconds. Symbol *h*

plane[1] /playn/ *n* AVIAT same as **airplane** ■ *vi* (**planed, plan·ing, planes**) to travel by airplane [Late 20C. Shortening]

USAGE See ***plain***.

plane[2] /playn/ *n* **1.** **FLAT SURFACE** a flat or level surface **2.** **LEVEL OF REALITY** a particular level of existence, mental activity, or achievement ○ *never felt he was on the same intellectual plane as the others* **3.** MATH **TWO-DIMENSIONAL SURFACE OR SPACE** a two-dimensional surface in which a straight line between any two points will lie wholly on that surface **4.** AVIAT **WING OR HYDROFOIL** a flat surface that provides lift for an aircraft or hydroplane, e.g., a wing or a hydrofoil ■ *adj* **1.** **FLAT** flat or level **2.** MATH **TWO-DIMENSIONAL** lying within a plane ■ *vi* (**planed, plan·ing, planes**) **1.** **SKIM OVER SURFACE OF WATER** to rise partly out of water and skim along the surface **2.** AVIAT, BIRDS **GLIDE** to glide through the air without propulsion [Early 17C. < Latin *planus* "flat"] —**plane·ness** *n*

USAGE See ***plain***.

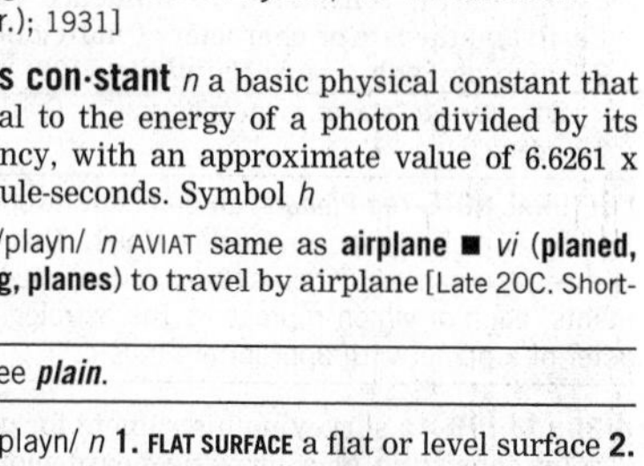

plane

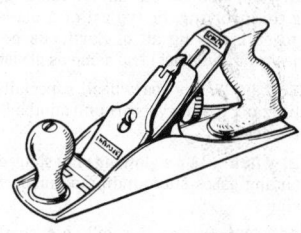

plane[3] /playn/ *n* **1.** WOODWORK **TOOL FOR SMOOTHING WOOD** a tool with an adjustable metal blade at an angle, for smoothing and leveling wood **2.** CERAMICS **SMOOTHING TROWEL** a hand tool with a flat metal blade used for smoothing clay or plaster in a mold ■ *vt* (**planed, plan·ing, planes**) WOODWORK **SMOOTH WOOD** to smooth or level wood with a plane [14C. Via French < late Latin *plana* < Latin *planare* "make level" < *planus* "flat"]

USAGE See *plain*.

plane[4] /playn/ *n* TREES same as **plane tree** [14C. Via French < Latin *platanus* < Greek *platanos* < *platus* "broad," from the shape of its leaf]

USAGE See *plain*.

plane an·gle *n* an angle formed by two straight lines meeting in the same geometric plane

plane ge·om·e·try *n* the branch of geometry that deals with two-dimensional figures

plane·load /pláyn lōd/ *n* the number of passengers or the quantity of goods that can be carried in an aircraft

plan·er /pláynər/ *n* **1.** a person or machine that planes, especially a machine used to plane wood or to cut flat surfaces into metal **2.** PRINTING a flat block of wood used to hold type level in a chase [15C. < PLANE[2]]

pla·ner tree /pláynər tree/ *n* a deciduous tree that resembles an elm and has small oval ribbed fruit. Native to: swamps of southern United States. Latin name: *Planera aquatica*. [Early 19C. After I. J. Planer (1743–89), German botanist]

plane sail·ing *n* sailing using a form of navigation that treats Earth's surface as if it were flat for the purposes of calculating a ship's position and course

plan·et /plánnət/ *n* **1.** ASTRON an astronomical object that orbits a star and does not shine with its own light, especially one of those orbiting the Sun in the solar system **2.** ASTROL in astrology, the Sun, the Moon, or any of the planets of the solar system, except Earth, considered to influence events on Earth and the fate or character of individual people **3.** same as **Earth** ○ *save the planet* [12C. Via French < Latin *planeta* "planet, wandering star" < Greek *planētēs* "wanderer"]

CULTURAL NOTE ***The Planets***, an orchestral work (1914–16) by British composer Gustav Holst. This suite for orchestra, organ, and chorus is divided into seven movements, each of which represents the astrological character of a planet with appropriate music.

plane ta·ble *n* a surveying instrument for use in the field, consisting of a drawing board mounted on adjustable legs with a sighting telescope and ruler

plan·e·tar /plánnə taar/ *n* a hypothetical young astronomical object of planetary mass that might have formed in the same way as a star

plan·e·tar·i·um /plànnə tàiree əm/ (*plural* **-i·ums** or **-i·a** /-ee ə/) *n* **1.** BUILDING WITH IMAGE OF NIGHT SKY a building with a domed ceiling onto which movable images of the stars, planets, and other objects seen in the night sky are projected for an audience **2.** PROJECTOR USED IN PLANETARIUM the special projector used to project images of the night sky for an audience in a planetarium **3.** SOLAR SYSTEM MODEL a model of the solar system, often a working model showing how the planets revolve around the Sun (*archaic*) [Mid-18C. < modern Latin < late Latin *planetarius* "astrologer" < *planeta* (see PLANET)]

plan·e·tar·y /plánnə tèrree/ *adj* **1.** relating to, belonging to, involving, or typical of a planet **2.** relating to or involving all of Earth, its people, or countries ■ *n* (*plural* **-ies**) ENG same as **planetary gear**

plan·e·tar·y gear *n* a gearwheel, especially in an epicyclic train, that travels around another, usually central gearwheel

plan·e·tar·y neb·u·la *n* a glowing ring-shaped nebula of expanding gases surrounding a small, very hot white star

plan·e·tes·i·mal /plànnə téssəm'l/ *n* a small rocky astronomical object thought to have orbited the Sun in the early stages of the solar system before coalescing with others to form the planets [Early 20C. < PLANET, after INFINITESIMAL]

plan·e·toid /plánnə tòyd/ *n* ASTRON same as **asteroid** (sense 1) —**plan·e·toi·dal** /plànnə tóyd'l/ *adj*

plan·e·tol·o·gy /plànnə tóllәjee/ *n* the branch of astronomy that studies the origin and composition of the planets and other solid bodies in the solar system such as comets and meteors —**plan·e·to·log·i·cal** /plànnətə lójjik'l/ *adj* —**plan·e·tol·o·gist** *n*

plane tree *n* a tall deciduous tree that has leaves with pointed lobes, globular fruit clusters, and flaking bark. Native to: temperate northern hemisphere. Genus: *Platanus*. [< PLANE[4]]

plan·et wheel *n* a wheel in an epicyclic gear system that rotates around the wheel with which it meshes

plan·gent /plánjənt/ *adj* **1.** making a loud and resonant or mournful sound **2.** expressing or suggesting grief or sadness (*literary*) [Early 19C. < Latin *plangent-*, present participle of *plangere* "beat"] —**plan·gen·cy** *n* —**plan·gent·ly** *adv*

plani- *prefix* same as **plano-**

pla·nim·e·ter /plə nímmətər/ *n* a mechanical instrument that measures the area of a plane figure as a pointer is moved around the figure's edge [Mid-19C. < French *planimètre* < Latin *planus* "flat"] —**pla·ni·met·ric** /plàynə méttrik/ *adj* —**pla·ni·met·ri·cal·ly** *adv*

plan·ish /plánnish/ (**-ished, -ish·ing, -ish·es**) *vt* to toughen and smooth the surface of a metal by hammering or rolling it [Late 16C. < Old French *planiss-*, stem of *planir* "to smooth" < *plain* "flat" (see PLAIN)] —**plan·ish·er** *n*

pla·ni·sphere /pláyni sfeer/ *n* a representation on a flat surface of all or part of a sphere, especially a map of the night sky as seen from one location at a point in time [< medieval Latin *planisphaerium* < Latin *planus* "flat" + *sphaera* "sphere" < Greek *sphaira*] —**pla·ni·spher·ic** /plàyni sféerik, -sférrik/ *adj*

plank /plangk/ *n* **1.** LONG FLAT PIECE OF WOOD a long flat piece of lumber sawn thicker than a board **2.** *US* WOODWORK, CONSTR same as **planking 3.** POLICY OF POLITICAL PARTY a policy that is part of a political party's platform ■ *vt* (**planked, plank·ing, planks**) PUT PLANKS OVER SOMETHING to cover something with planks [13C. Via Old N French *planke*, variant of Old French *planche* < late Latin *planca* "slab" < form of Latin *plancus* "flat"]

plank·ing /plángking/ *n* **1.** planks used as building material **2.** the work of covering something with planks or laying planks

plank·ter /plángktər/ *n* any of the tiny organisms that make up plankton [Mid-20C. Via German < Greek *plagktēr* "wanderer" < *plazein* "wander"]

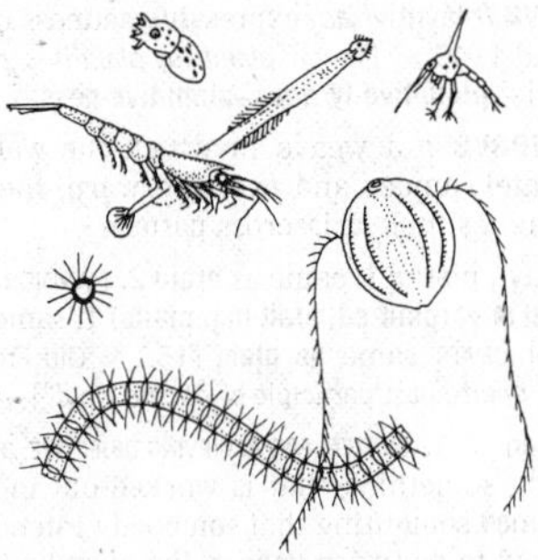

plankton

plank·ton /plángktən/ *n* a mass of tiny animals and plants floating in the sea or in lakes, usually near the surface, and eaten by fish and other water animals [Late 19C. Via German < Greek, "wandering thing" < *plazein* "wander, lead astray"] —**plank·ton·ic** /plangk tónnik/ *adj*

planned ob·so·les·cence /plànd-/ *n* a policy of designing and making products that quickly become outdated or wear out, so that they must be replaced

Planned Par·ent·hood *n US* an organization that does research and gives advice concerning family planning

plan·ner /plánnər/ *n* **1.** somebody who plans something, especially the development of an area **2.** a chart or notebook in which future events can be noted

Pla·no /pláynō/ city in northeastern Texas, an industrial suburb of Dallas. Population: 238,091 (2002 estimate).

plano- *prefix* flat ○ *planosol* ○ *plano-concave* [< Latin *planus* "flat"]

pla·no-con·cave /plàynō-/ *adj* flat on one side and concave on the other

pla·no-con·vex /plàynō-/ *adj* flat on one side and convex on the other

plan·o·gam·ete /plánnō gá meet, -gə méet/ *n* a gamete, e.g., a spermatozoon, that is capable of moving

plan·o·sol /plánnə sàwl/ *n* a soil formation found on flat uplands that have high to moderate rainfall, in which a strongly leached upper layer overlies a layer of compacted clay or silt

plant /plant/ *n* **1.** VEGETABLE ORGANISM a photosynthetic organism that has cellulose cell walls, cannot move of its own accord, grows in soil or water, and usually has green leaves. Kingdom: *Plantae*. **2.** SMALLER VEGETABLE ORGANISM a vegetable organism that does not have a permanent woody stem, e.g., a flower or herb rather than a bush or tree **3.** GARDENING CUTTING OR SEEDLING a cutting or seedling that is ready to be planted **4.** INDUST FACTORY a factory, power station, or other large industrial complex where something is manufactured or produced **5.** INDUST EQUIPMENT AND MACHINERY the equipment and machinery necessary for carrying on an industrial or engineering activity **6.** SOMETHING DISHONESTLY HIDDEN TO INCRIMINATE SOMEBODY something secretly put somewhere so that it can be discovered later, e.g., by the police, in order to incriminate somebody (*informal*) **7.** SOMEBODY SECRETLY INTRODUCED INTO GROUP somebody who has been placed secretly in an organization in order to spy on it or to influence its behavior (*informal*) ■ *v* (**plant·ed, plant·ing, plants**) **1.** *vti* PUT SOMETHING INTO GROUND TO GROW to put something such as a seed, plant, or tuber into the ground to enable it to grow ○ *plant a tree* **2.** *vti* USE AREA FOR GROWING PLANTS to place young plants or sow seeds in an area of ground ○ *wanted to plant that bed with pansies* **3.** *vt* PUT SOMETHING DOWN FIRMLY to put something down or take a position firmly or decisively ○ *planted the stakes about five feet apart* **4.** *vt* PUT IDEA IN SOMEBODY'S MIND to introduce an idea into somebody's mind ○ *She planted the notion in my head that we should move.* **5.** *vt* PLACE SOMETHING IN CONCEALED POSITION to place something such as an explosive or listening device where it will not be easily found by others **6.** *vt* HIDE SOMETHING TO INCRIMINATE SOMEBODY to put something secretly where it can be discovered later, e.g., by the police, in order to incriminate somebody (*informal*) ○ *plant evidence* **7.** *vt* INTRODUCE SPY INTO GROUP to introduce somebody into an organization in order to spy on it or to influence the behavior of its members (*informal*) ○ *planted an informer in the group* **8.** *vt* STRIKE SOMEBODY to land a blow on somebody (*informal*) **9.** *vt* FISHERIES PUT FISH IN BODY OF WATER to place spawn, young fish, or shellfish into an area of water so that they will develop there ○ *plant oysters* **10.** *vt* ESTABLISH COLONY OR COLONISTS to establish a colony or settlement in a place, or send people to a place as colonists or settlers [Pre-12C. < Latin *plantare* "plant in the ground" < *planta* "sole of the foot"] —**plant·a·ble** *adj* —**plant·like** *adj*

ORIGIN There did exist a Latin noun *planta* that meant "shoot, cutting," of uncertain origin, but the meaning of the English noun ***plant*** is not found. It is likely that this sense developed after the classical Latin period and is linked with the action of pressing on a shovel, or some other tool, with the "sole of the foot" in order to work the soil for planting. Latin *planta* "sole of the foot" is ultimately from an Indo-European word meaning "to spread," which is also the ancestor of English *flan*, *flat*[1], *flounder*[2], and *place*.

Plan·tag·e·net /plan tájjənət/ *adj* relating to or belonging to the English royal family that ruled between 1154 and 1485, or to this period of English history. The period is spanned by the reigns of Kings Henry II, Richard I, John, Henry III, Edward I, Edward II, Edward III, Richard II, Henry IV, Henry V, Henry VI, Edward IV, Edward V, and Richard III. ■ *n* a member of the Plantagenet royal family [< Latin *planta* "sprig" + *genista* "broom," from the sprig of broom used as a family emblem]

plan·tain[1] /plántən/ *n* **1.** a green fruit resembling a banana, eaten cooked as a staple food in many tropical countries **2.** a large plant of the banana family that produces plantains. Native to: tropical regions. Latin name: *Musa paradisiaca*. [16C. Via

Spanish *plátano* "plane tree" < Latin *platanus* (see PLANE[4])]

plan·tain[2] /plántən/ *n* a small wild plant with leaves that grow mainly from the plant's base. Flowers: tiny, greenish, in spikes. Native to: northern temperate regions. Family: Plantaginaceae. [14C. Via French < Latin *plantago* < *planta* "sole of the foot"]

plan·tain lil·y *n US* a perennial shade-loving plant with broad ribbed leaves. Flowers: tubular, white, blue, or lilac, in clusters. Genus: *Hosta.* Can term **hosta**

plan·tar /plántər, -taar/ *adj* relating to, affecting, or occurring on the sole of the foot [Early 18C. < Latin *plantaris* < *planta* "sole of the foot"]

plan·tar wart *n* MED same as **verruca** (sense 1)

plan·ta·tion /plan táysh'n/ *n* **1. LARGE ESTATE OR FARM** a large estate or farm, especially in a hot climate, where crops such as cotton, coffee, tea, or rubber trees are grown, usually worked by resident laborers **2. AREA OF PLANTED LAND** an area of land on which trees or crops are planted **3. GROUP OF CULTIVATED PLANTS** a large group of cultivated plants, especially trees **4. ESTATE IN S UNITED STATES** a large landed estate in the southern United States **5. COLONY** in former times, a colony or settlement

plant·cut·ter /plaánt kùttər/ *n* a bird that has a short conical beak with a serrated edge and eats fruit, leaves, and buds. Native to: South America. Family: Phytotomidae.

plant·er /plántər/ *n* **1. LARGE CONTAINER** a large decorative container for houseplants or small trees **2. HEAD OF PLANTATION** somebody who owns or manages a plantation **3. PLANTING MACHINE** a machine for planting seeds, tubers, or other plant parts **4. SETTLER** in former times, a settler or colonist

plant·er's punch *n* a drink made with rum, lime or lemon juice, sugar, water, or soda, and sometimes bitters

plant hor·mone *n* a hormone produced naturally by plants that activates or regulates their growth, or a synthetic equivalent used to promote growth in cultivated plants

plan·ti·grade /plánti gràyd/ *adj* describes an animal such as a bear or a human being that walks on the soles of the feet with the heels touching the ground ■ *n* an animal that walks on the soles of its feet [Mid-19C. Via French < modern Latin *plantigradus* < Latin *planta* "sole of the foot" + *gradus* "step"]

plant·let /plántlət/ *n* a young or very small plant

plant louse *n* INSECTS same as **aphid**

plan·toc·ra·cy /plan tókrəssee/ (*plural* **-cies**) *n* a ruling class made up of the owners and managers of large plantations, or a society ruled by them

plant sci·ence *n* the scientific study of plants

plants·man /plántsmən/ (*plural* **-men** /-mən/) *n* a man who has expert knowledge of garden plants and gardening

plants·per·son /plánts pùrss'n/ (*plural* **-peo·ple** /-peep'l/ or **-per·sons**) *n* somebody who has expert knowledge of garden plants and gardening

plants·wom·an /plánts wŏŏmmən/ (*plural* **-wom·en** /-wimmin/) *n* a woman who has expert knowledge of garden plants and gardening

plan·u·la /plánnyələ/ (*plural* **-lae** /-lee/) *n* a free-swimming larva of a coelenterate, e.g., a hydra. Planulae have cilia and usually a flattened oval body. [Late 19C. < modern Latin, "little flat one" < Latin *planus* "flat"] —**plan·u·lar** *adj*

plaque /plak/ *n* **1. INSCRIBED METAL OR STONE** a small flat piece of metal, stone, or other hard material that has an inscription or decoration on it and is fixed to a wall or other surface, often to commemorate somebody or something **2. DEPOSIT ON SURFACE OF TEETH** a film of saliva, mucus, bacteria, and food residues that builds up on the surface of teeth and can cause gum disease **3. DEPOSIT ON SKIN** a small flattened patch or deposit, e.g., on the skin in psoriasis or on the inner wall of an artery in atherosclerosis **4. CLEAR PATCH IN CULTURE** a clear patch in a bacterial or cell culture caused by a virus destroying the cells **5. SMALL PIN OR BROOCH** a small pin or brooch worn to show membership of or rank in an organization [Mid-19C. Via French < Dutch *plak* "tablet" < *plakken* "to stick" < Middle Dutch *placken* "flatten, patch"]

plash[1] /plash/ (*literary*) *n* **LIGHT SPLASH** a light splash or splashing sound ■ *v* (**plashed, plash·ing, plash·es**) **1.** *vi* **SPLASH IN OR THROUGH LIQUID** to move in or through something liquid, scattering drops and making light splashing sounds **2.** *vt* **SPLASH SOMETHING** to splash or spatter a liquid [Early 16C. An imitation of the sound]

plash[2] /plash/ (**plashed, plash·ing, plash·es**) *vt UK* same as **pleach** [15C. < Old French *pla(i)ssier* (see PLEACH)]

-plasia *suffix* growth, formation ○ *hyperplasia* [< modern Latin < Greek *plassein* "to form, mold"]

plasm /plázzəm/ *n* **1.** BIOL same as **plasma 2.** protoplasm of a particular type [Early 17C. < late Latin *plasma* "image, creation" (see PLASMA)] —**plas·mic** *adj*

plasm- *prefix* same as **plasmo-** (*used before vowels*)

-plasm *suffix* material that forms or is formed ○ *protoplasm* ○ *neoplasm* [Shortening of PROTOPLASM]

plas·ma /plázmə/ *n* **1. FLUID COMPONENT OF BLOOD** the clear yellowish fluid component of blood, lymph, or milk, excluding the suspended corpuscles and cells **2. BLOOD SUBSTITUTE** a blood substitute prepared by removing the cells and corpuscles from donated sterile blood and freezing the resulting fluid until it is needed **3. IONIZED GAS** a hot ionized gas made up of ions and electrons that is found in the Sun, stars, and fusion reactors. Plasma is a good conductor of electricity and reacts to a magnetic field, but otherwise has properties similar to those of a gas. **4. GREEN CHALCEDONY** a green variety of chalcedony. Use: gems, decorative ware. [Early 18C. Via late Latin, "image, creation" < Greek, "something molded" < *plassein* "to form, mold"] —**plas·mat·ic** /plaz máttik/ *adj*

plas·ma cell, plas·ma·cyte /plázmə sīt/ *n* a lymphocyte that produces antibodies and is derived from a B cell

plas·ma·gel /plázmə jèl/ *n* a form of cytoplasm that resembles jelly and often forms the outer layer of cells

plas·ma·gene /plázmə jeen/ *n* a particle in the cytoplasm of organisms that can replicate itself and is thought to be able to pass on hereditary characteristics in the same way as a chromosomal gene —**plas·ma·gen·ic** /plàzmə jénnik/ *adj*

plas·ma·lem·ma /plàzmə lémmə/ *n* BIOL same as **cell membrane**

plas·ma mem·brane *n* BIOL same as **cell membrane**

plas·ma·pher·e·sis /plàzmə férrə siss, -fə reessiss/ *n* a process in which blood taken from a patient is treated to extract the cells and corpuscles, which are then added to another fluid and returned to the patient's body. An example of its use is the removal of harmful antibodies or immune complexes from the blood in autoimmune diseases such as myasthenia.

plas·ma screen *n* a very thin, high-definition television or computer display consisting of many pixel-sized gas-filled cells which emit light when an electric current is channeled through them

plas·ma·sol /plázmə sàwl/ *n* a form of cytoplasm that is more fluid than plasmagel and often forms an inner layer in cells

plas·ma torch *n* a metal-cutting device in which a cutting flame is produced by the conversion of a gas into plasma

plas·mid /plázmid/ *n* a small circle of DNA that replicates itself independently of chromosomal DNA, especially in the cells of bacteria. Plasmids often contain genes for drug resistance and are used in genetic engineering, since they can be transmitted between bacteria of the same and different species.

plas·min /plázmin/ *n* a plasma enzyme that helps break down fibrin [Mid-19C. < French *plasmine* < *plasma* "plasma"]

plas·min·o·gen /plaz mínnəjən/ *n* the inactive precursor of plasmin

plasmo- *prefix* plasma ○ *plasmogamy* [< PLASMA]

plas·mo·des·ma /plàzmə dézmə/ (*plural* **-ma·ta** /-mətə/) *n* a very fine thread of cytoplasm that in some plants passes through openings in the walls of adjacent cells and forms a living bridge between them [Early 20C. < German *Plasma* "plasma" + Greek *desma* "bond"]

plas·mo·di·um /plaz mōdee əm/ (*plural* **-di·a** /-dee ə/) *n* **1.** a mass of protoplasm containing many nuclei that is a stage in the life cycle of some organisms, especially slime molds **2.** a parasitic protozoan, especially one that causes malaria. Genus: *Plasmodium.* [Late 19C. < PLASMA + modern Latin *-odium* "resembling" < Greek *-ōdēs* (see -OID)] —**plas·mo·di·al** *adj*

plas·mog·a·my /plaz móggəmee/ *n* fusion between cells in some fungi in which the cytoplasm merges but the nuclei remain distinct

plas·mol·y·sis /plaz mólləssiss/ *n* the shrinking of the protoplasm in a plant or bacterial cell away from the cell wall, caused by loss of water through osmosis —**plas·mo·lyt·ic** /plàzmə líttik/ *adj* —**plas·mo·lyt·i·cal·ly** *adv*

plas·mo·lyze /plázmə līz/ (**-lyzed, -lyz·ing, -lyz·es**) *vti* to undergo plasmolysis, or make plasmolysis happen in a cell

plas·mon /pláz mòn/ *n* the sum total of the genetic material in the cytoplasm, as opposed to the nucleus or nuclei, of a cell or an organism

-plast *suffix* living cell, small body ○ *spheroplast* [< Greek *plastos*, past participle of *plassein* "form, mold"]

plas·ter /plástər/ *n* **1. LIME MIXTURE FOR WALLS** a mixture of lime, sand, and water that is applied as a liquid paste to the ceilings and internal walls of a building and dries to a hard surface **2. PIECE OF IMPREGNATED MUSLIN** a piece of muslin spread with a curative preparation formerly used for placing over a wound or sore **3.** SCULPTURE, MED same as **plaster of Paris** (*often used before a noun*) **4.** *UK* **STICKY BANDAGE** a strip of adhesive material, usually with a dressing attached, for sticking over a cut or wound ■ *vt* (**-tered, -ter·ing, -ters**) **1. COVER WALLS WITH PLASTER** to apply plaster to the interior walls and ceilings of a building **2. APPLY SOMETHING THICKLY** to apply a thick layer of something to a surface, often in a vigorous or careless way ○ *She didn't bother with fancy brushwork, she just plastered the paint on.* **3. STICK MASS OF THINGS OVER SURFACE** to stick or spread objects in great profusion over a surface ○ *The walls were plastered with election posters.* **4. MAKE SOMETHING APPEAR IN MANY LOCATIONS** to cause a name, story, or image to appear in many conspicuous places ○ *woke up to find her name plastered on every front page* **5. MAKE SOMETHING STICK TO SOMETHING** to make something lie flat and smooth against something or stick to something, e.g., by wetting it ○ *He plastered his hair down with gel.* **6. APPLY MEDICINAL PLASTER** to apply a medicinal plaster to a wound or sore **7. BOMBARD SOMEBODY** to hit somebody or something repeatedly and effectively with blows or weapons (*informal*) **8.** *US* **DEFEAT SOMEBODY SEVERELY** to defeat an opponent severely, e.g., in a sports competition (*informal*) ○ *got plastered in the semifinals* [Pre-12C. Directly or via Old French *plastre* "wall plaster" < medieval Latin *plastrum*, alteration of Latin *emplastrum* < Greek *emplastron* < *emplassein* "plaster up" < *plassein* "form, mold"] —**plas·ter·er** *n* —**plas·ter·y** *adj*

plas·ter·board /plástər bàwrd/ *n UK* same as **drywall**

plas·ter cast *n* **1.** a rigid covering of plaster of Paris molded around a broken limb to immobilize the fracture site during healing **2.** a copy or mold of an object such as a statue or footprint in plaster of Paris

plas·tered /plástərd/ *adj* very drunk (*informal*) [Early 20C. < PLASTER "hit hard"]

plas·ter·ing /plástəring/ *n* **1. APPLICATION OF PLASTER TO WALLS** the application of a layer of plaster to walls **2. PLASTER COVERING SURFACE** the hardened plaster that covers a surface **3. SEVERE DEFEAT** a severe beating or defeat (*informal*)

plas·ter of Par·is *n* a white powder, calcium sulfate, that when mixed with water forms a quick-hardening paste. It is used in the arts for sculpting and making casts, and in medicine for molding casts around broken limbs. [Because it originated in Paris, France]

plas·ter saint *n* somebody who appears to be or makes a show of being a model of virtue, but often proves a hypocrite ○ *I mean, I'm certainly no plaster saint, but there are things even I wouldn't do.*

plas·ter·work /plástər wùrk/ *n* objects in plaster, especially the layer of plaster applied to interior wall surfaces or decorative plaster moldings on ceilings or walls

plas·tic /plástik/ *n* **1.** SYNTHETIC MATERIAL an extremely versatile synthetic material made from the polymerization of organic compounds. It can be molded into shapes or fabricated in many different forms for use in commerce and industry. **2.** CREDIT CARDS debit or credit cards as a form of payment as distinct from cash or a check (*informal*) ■ *adj* **1.** MADE OF PLASTIC made or consisting of plastic **2.** ARTIFICIAL seeming artificial and unnatural ○ *a plastic smile* **3.** ADAPTING EASILY adapting easily and readily to change **4.** ABLE TO BE MOLDED able to be shaped or modeled **5.** OF MOLDING, MODELING, OR SCULPTING relating to or involving molding, modeling, or sculpting **6.** OF PLASTIC SURGERY relating to or involving plastic surgery **7.** PHYS ABLE TO HAVE SHAPE PERMANENTLY CHANGED able to be bent, stretched, squeezed, or pulled out so that the resulting change of shape is permanent **8.** BIOL ADAPTING TO CONDITIONS capable of adapting to conditions during growth or development [Mid-17C. Directly or via French *plastique* < Latin *plasticus* < Greek *plastikos* "moldable" < *plastos*, past participle of *plassein* "form, mold"] —**plas·ti·cal·ly** *adv*

plas·tic art *n* **1.** a three-dimensional art, e.g., sculpture, modeling or bas-relief work, pottery, or ceramics **2.** an art that represents subjects for visual appreciation, e.g., painting, sculpture, or architecture

plas·tic bomb *n* a bomb that employs a plastic explosive for its destructive force

plas·tic bul·let *n* a large bullet made of PVC, sometimes used by the police for riot control in place of metal bullets

plas·tic ex·plo·sive *n* an explosive with the consistency of putty that allows it to be easily molded

plas·tic·i·ty /pla stíssətee/ *n* **1.** ABILITY TO BE MOLDED the condition of being soft and capable of being molded **2.** ABILITY TO KEEP SHAPE AFTER CHANGE the quality that will allow a substance to retain its change in shape after being bent, stretched, or squeezed **3.** THREE-DIMENSIONAL QUALITY the three-dimensional quality of an image

plas·ti·cize /plásti sìz/ (**-cized, -ciz·ing, -ciz·es**) *v* **1.** *vti* to give plastic or moldable qualities to something, or become plastic or moldable **2.** *vt* to impregnate or coat something with plastic, usually to make it waterproof —**plas·ti·ci·za·tion** /plàstəssi záysh'n/ *n*

plas·ti·ciz·er /plásti sìzər/ *n* an industrial compound that affects the physical properties of a substance to which it is added, making it more plastic

plas·tic mon·ey *n* debit and credit cards as distinct from cash or checks

plas·tic sur·geon *n* a physician who performs or specializes in plastic surgery

plas·tic sur·ger·y *n* the branch of surgery that is concerned with repairing especially external damage to the body, remedying impairments, or improving a person's appearance. Cosmetic surgery is a branch of plastic surgery.

plas·tic wrap *n* a clear plastic film that sticks to itself and to surfaces. Use: to wrap food for storage.

plas·tid /plástid/ *n* a specialized component (**organelle**) in a photosynthetic plant cell that contains pigment, ribosomes, and DNA, and serves specific physiological purposes such as food synthesis and storage [Late 19C. < Greek *plastid-* < *plastos* "molded" (see PLASTIC)]

plas·tique /pla stéek/ *n* **1.** ARMS same as **plastic explosive** **2.** graceful poses or slow movements in dance [Late 19C. < French (see PLASTIC)]

plas·ti·sol /plásti sàwl/ *n* a suspension of synthetic resin particles convertible by heat into solid plastic [Mid-20C. < PLASTIC + SOL²]

plas·to·qui·none /plàstō kwi nṓn, -kwí nōn/ *n* a compound found in plants that plays a role in photosynthesis [Mid-20C. < shortening of CHLOROPLAST + QUINONE]

plas·tron /plástrən/ *n* **1.** UNDER PART OF TORTOISE SHELL the under portion of the shell of a turtle or tortoise that is made up of several, often hinged, bony plates joined to the carapace by bridges located between the animal's legs **2.** WATER-REPELLENT GILL IN WATER INSECTS a tuft of water-repellent hairs on the bodies of some insects that live in water, having the function of trapping air bubbles and acting as an external gill **3.** STEEL BREASTPLATE a steel breastplate worn as part of medieval armor beneath a chain-mail tunic (**hauberk**) **4.** CHEST PAD FOR FENCERS a leather-covered pad for protecting the chest, worn by professional fencers [Early 16C. Via French < Italian *piastrone* "large breastplate" < *piastra* "metal plate"] —**plas·tral** *adj*

-plasty *suffix* surgical repair, plastic surgery ○ *angioplasty* ○ *rhinoplasty* [< Greek *plastos* (see PLASTIC)]

plat /plat/ *n* **1.** PLAN OR MAP a plan or map showing property boundaries and geographic features **2.** PLOT OF LAND a small plot or area of land ■ *vt* (**plat·ted, plat·ting, plats**) MAP AREA OF LAND to map an area of land to show boundaries and features [Early 16C. Probably alteration of PLOT]

Pla·ta, Rí·o de la ➧ **Río de la Plata**

plat du jour /plaa də zhŏor/ (*plural* **plats du jour** /*pronunc. same*/) *n* the featured dish of the day on the menu of a restaurant [Early 20C. < French, "dish of the day"]

plate /playt/ *n* **1.** DISH FROM WHICH FOOD IS EATEN a flat or shallow object, usually round and made of earthenware, china, glass, plastic, or metal, from which food is eaten **2.** CONTENTS OF PLATE a portion of food consisting of the amount served on a plate ○ *a plate of vegetables* **3.** SERVED FOOD a particular variety of prepared and served food ○ *a low-calorie plate* **4.** COLLECTION DISH FOR MONEY a shallow metal or wooden container passed around a church for members of the congregation to put money in **5.** DISH FOR GROWING CULTURES a small flat glass or plastic dish with a vertical rim, used in laboratories for growing cultures of microorganisms **6.** BASEBALL same as **home plate** **7.** COATING OF METAL a thin coating of metal, typically silver or gold, applied by electrolysis to copper or another base metal **8.** PRECIOUS TABLEWARE tableware and cutlery made out of gold or silver or covered with gold or silver plate **9.** THINLY BEATEN METAL metal produced in thin sheets of uniform thickness by beating, rolling, or casting **10.** PIECE OF SHEET METAL a piece, sheet, or slab of flat metal used to join or strengthen things **11.** PIECE OF ARMOR PLATE a piece or sheet of specially strengthened metal used as part of the cladding of something such as a warship or tank **12.** SECTION OF SUIT OF ARMOR a thin piece of steel or iron used in making a suit of armor, or armor made from plates **13.** THIN SHEET a thin flat rigid sheet or slice of some material, usually of uniform thickness and with a smooth surface **14.** AUTOMOT same as **license plate** **15.** SENSITIZED SHEET OF GLASS a sheet of glass or other material coated with a light-sensitive film to receive a photographic image **16.** SURFACE FROM WHICH TO PRINT a template for printing, either an engraved metal sheet or a phototypeset page **17.** PRINT TAKEN FROM ENGRAVED SURFACE a print made from a printing plate, especially one inserted into a book on paper different from that on which the text is printed **18.** ILLUSTRATION IN BOOK a full-page illustration or photograph in a book, especially on glossy or coated paper **19.** ENGRAVED PLAQUE a metal plaque that bears an engraved or printed legend, name, number, or other inscription (*often used in combination*) **20.** PRIZE OF GOLD OR SILVER CUP a prize, especially in horseracing, consisting of a silver or gold dish or similar trophy **21.** RACE WITH PLATE AS PRIZE a race, especially a horse race, in which the prize is a silver or gold dish or similar trophy **22.** ARTIFICIAL PALATE FITTED WITH FALSE TEETH a piece of plastic molded to fit the mouth and holding false teeth or an orthodontic device such as a brace **23.** SECTION OF EARTH'S CRUST any segment of the Earth's crust that moves in relation to other segments as defined by the theory of plate tectonics **24.** FLAT ANATOMICAL STRUCTURE a thin flat bony or horny anatomical part or formation **25.** ELECTRODE a thin flat piece of metal acting as an electrode in a rechargeable battery **26.** SHOE WORN BY RACEHORSE a light shoe with which racehorses are shod in preparation for racing **27.** HORIZONTAL SUPPORTING TIMBER a horizontal timber laid along the top of a wall of a building to support the ends of timbers laid at right angles to the wall **28.** *US* CUT OF BEEF a thin cut of beef from the breast or ribs ■ *vt* (**plat·ed, plat·ing, plates**) **1.** COVER SOMETHING WITH METAL to cover metal or metal objects with a thin coating or film of another metal, often a precious or shiny one **2.** COVER SOMETHING WITH METAL SHEETS to cover something, e.g., a ship or tank, with sheets of metal for protection and strength **3.** SET UP TYPE IN PAGE FORM to set up movable type into page form ready for printing **4.** STRENGTHEN BROKEN BONE WITH PLATE to hold a fractured bone in position once it has been set by screwing it, on either side of the fracture, to a metal plate **5.** PUT FOOD ON PLATE to arrange food on a plate [13C. Via French < medieval Latin *plata* "plate armor" < Greek *platus* "flat"] —**plate·ful** *n* ◇ **have something handed to you on a plate** to obtain something without having to put any effort into obtaining it (*informal*) ◇ **on your plate** requiring your attention (*informal*) ○ *I can't do it, I have too much on my plate right now.*

plate ar·mor *n* body armor made up of metal plates, as distinct from the chain mail that it superseded

pla·teau /pla tṓ/ *n* (*plural* **-teaus** or **-teaux** /-tṓz/) **1.** RAISED AREA WITH LEVEL TOP an area of high ground with a fairly level surface **2.** STABLE PHASE a period or phase in something when there is little increase or decrease **3.** PHASE OF STAGNATION a phase in mental or physical development during which little headway is made ■ *vi* (**-teaued, -teau·ing, -teaus**) LEVEL OUT to reach a stable phase after a period of movement or development [Late 18C. < French, modern form of Old French *platel* "small flat thing" < *plate* (see PLATE)]

plate bound·a·ry *n* an area on the margins of tectonic plates where seismic, volcanic, and tectonic activity takes place as a consequence of the relative motion of the plates

plat·ed /pláytəd/ *adj* **1.** OVERLAID WITH OTHER METAL covered with a thin layer of metal, especially a precious or shiny metal **2.** COVERED WITH PLATES protected and strengthened by a covering of plates **3.** KNITTED WITH TWO YARNS knitted with two kinds of yarn, one appearing on the front and one on the back of the fabric

plate glass *n* strong thick glass in large sheets used for windows and as a construction material for larger buildings (*hyphenated when used before a noun*)

plate·lay·er /pláyt làyr/ *n UK* same as **trackman** [Mid-19C < *plate rail*, early type of rail with a flange along the outer edge]

plate·let /pláytlət/ *n* a tiny colorless disk-shaped particle found in large quantities in the blood and playing an important part in the clotting process

plate·mak·er /pláyt màykər/ *n* a person or machine that prepares plates for printing

plat·en /plátt'n/ *n* **1.** METAL PLATE IN PRINTING PRESS a flat metal plate in a printing press that holds the paper against the inked type **2.** TYPEWRITER ROLLER the cylindrical roller against which the paper is held in a typewriter, and against which the type strikes **3.** WORKTABLE the movable worktable of a machine tool [Mid-16C. < Old French *platine* "metal plate" < *plat* "flat" < Greek *platus*]

plat·er /pláytər/ *n* **1.** SOMEBODY OR SOMETHING THAT PLATES a person or machine that plates things **2.** RACEHORSE IN MINOR RACES a racehorse of average quality that is entered in minor races **3.** BLACKSMITH a blacksmith who specializes in shoeing racehorses

plat·er·esque /plàttə résk/ *adj* relating to a heavily decorated architectural style fashionable in 16th-century Spain, reminiscent of elaborate silverware [Late 19C. < Spanish *plateresco* < *platero* "silversmith" < *plata* "silver"]

plate tec·ton·ics *n* a theory that ascribes continental drift, volcanic and seismic activity, and the formation of mountain belts to moving plates of the Earth's crust supported on less rigid mantle rocks (*takes a singular verb*)

~~plateu~~ incorrect spelling of **plateau**

plat·form /plát fàwrm/ *n* **1.** STAGE FOR PERFORMERS OR SPEAKERS a raised level area of flooring for speakers, performers, or participants in a ceremony, making them easily visible to the audience **2.** FLAT RAISED STRUCTURE a simple structure, especially one composed of wooden planks, serving as a base for keeping things clear of the ground **3.** RAISED AREA PROVIDING ACCESS TO TRAINS a raised structure beside the tracks at a railroad station that makes it easier to get on or off and load or unload a train **4.** PARTICULAR

POLICY OF PARTY SEEKING ELECTION the particular publicly announced policies and promises of a party seeking election, understood as the basis of its actions should it come to power **5.** OPPORTUNITY FOR DOING SOMETHING a position of authority or prominence that provides a good opportunity for doing something **6.** OFFSHORE DRILLING STRUCTURE an anchored offshore structure with living and working accommodations above water level, from which oil or gas wells can be drilled or maintained **7.** STANDARD OPERATING SYSTEM a specific configuration of hardware, a specific operating system, or other software that is a standard for the development and operation of computers and of computerized devices such as personal digital assistants and cell phones ○ *Some software will only run on a particular platform.* **8.** SHOE WITH DEEP SOLE a shoe or boot with a very thick sole **9.** RAISED AREA OF GROUND a flat raised area of ground [Mid-16C. < French *plateforme* "diagram" < *plat* "flat" + *forme* "form"]

plat·form bed *n* a bed consisting of a mattress lying on a platform raised on supports, the space under the platform being used for storage

plat·form game *n* a computer game that involves solving largely physical puzzles by finding the right sequence of moves

plat·form rock·er *n* a rocking chair with the rocker set into a stable base that lies flat on the floor

plat·form scale *n* a scale with a flat surface that supports the object to be weighed

plat·form ten·nis *n US* a game similar to tennis played with table-tennis paddles and a rubber ball on a fenced wooden platform slightly smaller than a tennis court

Sylvia Plath

Plath /plath/, **Sylvia** (1932–63) US poet. Her work is best known for its savage imagery and themes of self-destruction, anticipating her own suicide. Her works include the collected poems *The Colossus* (1960) and *Ariel* (1965) and the semiautobiographical novel *The Bell Jar* (1963). She was married to the British poet Ted Hughes.

> "I am no shadow / Though there is a shadow starting from my feet. I am a wife. / The city waits and aches. The little grasses / Crack through stone, and they are green with life."
> [Sylvia Plath, *Three Women*; 1971]

platin- *prefix* platinum ○ *platinic* [< PLATINUM]

pla·ti·na /plə téenə, plátt'nə/ *n* a naturally occurring platinum alloy [Mid-18C. < Spanish < *plata* "silver"; because of its color]

plat·ing /pláyting/ *n* **1.** THIN COVERING OF OTHER METAL a thin covering of another usually more valuable metal applied to a metal surface ○ *gold plating* **2.** COVERING OF METAL PLATES metal plates used to make an exterior covering for something, e.g., a ship's hull **3.** APPLICATION OF COVERING OF METAL the process of applying a covering of metal or metal plates to the surface of something

pla·tin·ic /plə tínnik/ *adj* relating to, containing, or consisting of platinum, especially in a valence state of four

plat·i·nize /plátt'n ìz/ (**-nized, -niz·ing, -niz·es**) *vt* to coat, combine, or treat something with platinum or a platinum compound —**plat·i·ni·za·tion** /plàtt'ni záysh'n/ *n*

plat·i·noid /plátt'n òyd/ *adj* RESEMBLING PLATINUM resembling or containing platinum ■ *n* **1.** METAL CHEMICALLY SIMILAR TO PLATINUM a metal that is chemically similar to platinum, specifically iridium, osmium, palladium, rhodium, or ruthenium **2.** ALLOY SIMILAR TO PLATINUM an alloy of copper, zinc, nickel, and tungsten that resembles platinum in not tarnishing readily and in having a strong resistance to the passage of an electric current

plat·i·nous /plátt'nəss/ *adj* relating to, containing, or consisting of platinum, especially in a valence state of two

plat·i·num /plátt'nəm/ *n* a precious silvery white metallic element, highly malleable and ductile and highly resistant to chemicals and heat. Source: copper, nickel ores. Use: jewelry, catalyst, electroplating. Symbol **Pt**. See table at **element** ■ *adj* having sold one million as a single or two million as an LP or CD [Early 19C. < PLATINA] ◇ **go platinum** to reach the level of sales designated for platinum status (*refers to musical recordings*)

plat·i·num black *n* platinum in the form of a fine black powder. Use: catalyst in organic synthesis.

plat·i·num blond, plat·i·num blonde *adj* describes hair that is pale silvery-blond in color (*hyphenated when used before a noun*)

plat·i·num met·al *n* platinum or any of the metals in its group, specifically, iridium, osmium, palladium, rhodium, or ruthenium

plat·i·tude /pláttə tòod/ *n* **1.** a pointless, unoriginal, or empty comment or statement made as though it was significant or helpful **2.** the making of platitudes [Early 19C. < French, "flatness" < *plat* "flat"] —**plat·i·tu·di·nal** /plàttə tóod'n'l/ *adj* —**plat·i·tu·di·nous** /-tóod'nəss/ *adj*

plat·i·tu·di·nize /plàttə tóod'n ìz/ (**-nized, -niz·ing, -niz·es**) *vi* to produce or talk in platitudes —**plat·i·tu·di·niz·er** *n*

Pla·to /pláytō/ distinctive dark-floored large crater on the Moon just north of Mare Imbrium, approximately 60 mi./100 km in diameter

Pla·to (428?–347 B.C.) Greek philosopher. A disciple of Socrates and teacher of Aristotle, he founded the Athenian Academy. His works, written in dialogue form, include *Phaedo*, the *Symposium*, and the *Republic*.

> "The true lover of knowledge naturally strives for truth, and is not content with common opinion, but soars with undimmed and unwearied passion till he grasps the essential nature of things."
> [Plato, *The Republic*; 370? B.C.]

pla·ton·ic /plə tónnik/ *adj* **1.** involving friendship, affection, or love without sexual relations between people who might be expected to be sexually attracted to each other **2.** perfect in form or conception but not found in reality [Mid-16C. Via Latin < Greek *Platōnikos* < *Platōn* "Plato (the philosopher)"] —**pla·ton·i·cal·ly** *adv*

Pla·ton·ic *adj* relating to Plato or his philosophy

Pla·to·nism /pláytə nìzzəm/ *n* the philosophy or teachings of Plato, especially the theory that both physical objects and instances of qualities are recognizable because of their common relationship to an abstract form or idea [Late 16C. < modern Latin *Platonismus* < Greek *Platōn* "Plato (the philosopher)"] —**Pla·to·nist** *n*

pla·toon /plə tóon/ *n* **1.** a subdivision of a company of soldiers, usually led by a lieutenant and consisting of two to three sections or squads of ten to twelve people **2.** a body of people or things with a common purpose or goal [Mid-17C. < French *peloton* "small ball" < *pelote* (see PELLET)]

pla·toon ser·geant *n* a noncommissioned officer in the US army who assists a lieutenant in leading a platoon

Platt·deutsch /plát dòych/ *n* LANG same as **Low German** [Mid-19C. Via German < Dutch *Platduitsch* "low German"; from the flat landscape of N Germany where it is spoken] —**Platt·deutsch** *adj*

Platte /plat/ river in central Nebraska, flowing from near North Platte into the Missouri River. Length: 310 mi./500 km.

plat·ter /pláttər/ *n* **1.** LARGE FLAT DISH a large flat dish for serving food **2.** SERVED FOOD a variety of prepared and served food (*often used in combination*) ○ *a seafood platter* **3.** RECORD a phonograph record (*dated informal*) **4.** COMPUT SURFACE OF HARD DISK the recording surface of a hard disk [14C. < Anglo-Norman *plater* < Old French *plat* < Greek *platus* "flat"]

plat·y[1] /pláytee/ (**-i·er, -i·est**) *adj* describes minerals that crystallize in thin sheets and tend to flake along cleavage planes [Mid-16C. < PLATE]

plat·y[2] /pláytee/ (*plural* **-ys** or **-ies** or *same*) *n* a brightly colored fish that bears live young, not eggs, often kept as an aquarium fish. Native to: Central America. Genus: *Xiphophorus*. [Early 20C. Shortening of modern Latin *Platypoecilus*, former genus name < Greek *platus* "flat" + *poikilos* "spotted"]

plat·y·hel·minth /plàttee hélminth/ *n* ZOOL same as **flatworm** (*technical*) [Late 19C. < modern Latin *Platyhelminthes* < Greek *platus* "flat" + *helminth-* "worm"] —**plat·y·hel·min·thic** /-hel mínthik/ *adj*

plat·y·pus /pláttəpəss, -pòoss/ (*plural* **-pus·es** or **-pi** /-pì/) *n* ZOOL same as **duck-billed platypus** [Late 18C. Via modern Latin *Platypus* < Greek *platupous* "flat-footed" < *platus* "flat" + *pous* "foot"]

plat·yr·rhine /pláttə rìn/ *adj* describes animals, especially New World monkeys, whose nostrils are well separated and point to either side ■ *n* a platyrrhine animal, especially a monkey [Mid-19C. Via modern Latin *Platyrrhini* < Greek *platurrhis* "broad-nosed" < *platus* "broad" + *rhis* "nose"]

plau·dit /pláwdit/ *n* an expression of praise or approval ○ *won plaudits for her skillful handling of the crisis* [Early 17C. < Latin *plaudite* "applaud!" < *plaudere* "to clap"; from the customary appeal made by Roman actors at the end of a play]

ORIGIN The Latin word *plaudere* "to clap, applaud," from which ***plaudit*** is derived, is also the source of English *applaud* and *explode*.

~~plausable~~ incorrect spelling of **plausible**

plau·si·ble /pláwzəb'l/ *adj* **1.** believable and appearing likely to be true, usually in the absence of proof **2.** having a persuasive manner in speech or writing, often combined with an intention to deceive [Mid-16C. < Latin *plausibilis* "deserving applause" < *plaus-*, past participle of *plaudere* "clap"] —**plau·si·bil·i·ty** /plàwzə bíllətee/ *n* —**plau·si·ble·ness** *n* —**plau·si·bly** *adv*

Plau·tus /pláwtəss/, **Titus Maccius** (254?–184 B.C.) Roman comic dramatist. His 21 surviving plays, modeled on Greek New Comedy, influenced both Shakespeare and Molière.

> "He whom the gods love dies young, while he has his strength and senses and wits."
> [Titus Maccius Plautus, *Bacchides*; 3rd-2nd century B.C.]

play /play/ *v* (**played, play·ing, plays**) **1.** *vi* ENGAGE IN ENJOYABLE ACTIVITIES to take part in an enjoyable activity, especially a game, simply for the sake of amusement ○ *There were some children my mother wouldn't let me play with.* **2.** *vti* TAKE PART IN GAME OR SPORT to take part in a game or a sporting activity ○ *likes to play football* **3.** *vt* COMPETE AGAINST SOMEBODY to compete against somebody in a game or sporting event ○ *They play their biggest rival tomorrow.* **4.** *vti* ASSIGN OR HAVE POSITION ON FIELD to assign a player to a particular position on the field, or be assigned such a position **5.** *vt* HIT SHOT to make a shot or stroke in a sporting event **6.** *vt* HIT BALL to hit or kick a ball, puck, or birdie in a particular direction ○ *playing the ball straight down the line* **7.** *vt* USE PIECE OR CARD IN GAME to use a card from a hand in a card game or a piece in a board game **8.** *vti* PERFORM ON MUSICAL INSTRUMENT to use a musical instrument to produce music ○ *He plays the trombone.* **9.** *vt* PERFORM MUSICAL WORK to use an instrument to perform a piece of music ○ *play a sonata* **10.** *vt* MUSIC PERFORM COMPOSER to perform the music of a particular composer ○ *Chopin is notoriously difficult to play well.* **11.** *vti* REPRODUCE RECORDED MUSIC to reproduce recorded music for listening, or be reproduced for listening ○ *played my favorite CD* **12.** *vti* ACT IN PARTICULAR MANNER to deal with a situation in a particular way to achieve a desired result ○ *We decided to play it safe.* **13.** *vti* PERFORM OR BE PERFORMED SOMEWHERE to perform a play or show a movie at a particular theater, or be performed or shown there ○ *What's playing at the Roxy?*

14. *vt* PRETEND TO HAVE PARTICULAR QUALITY to pretend to be a particular type of person ○ *Don't play the innocent with me.* **15.** *vti* ACT PART IN PLAY to portray a character in a theatrical or movie production **16.** *vi* MAKE PARTICULAR IMPRESSION ON SOMEBODY to be received in a particular way by somebody, or make a particular impression on that person ○ *a policy likely to play well with middle-class voters* ○ *How will it play in Peoria?* **17.** *vt* PERFORM IN PARTICULAR PLACES to perform in particular places or types of places ○ *plays the Catskill Mountains every summer* **18.** *vi* ACT IN FUN to do something for fun, not in earnest ○ *He's only playing, he doesn't really mean it.* **19.** *vt* PERFORM DRAMATIC WORK BY SOMEBODY to perform the work of a particular dramatist **20.** *vti* GAMBLE to gamble on a game of chance such as roulette or on horse races **21.** *vt* SPECULATE IN MARKET to speculate with securities or commodities in a market **22.** *vti* MOVE IRREGULARLY OVER SURFACE to move unsteadily or irregularly over a surface, usually in a pleasing way, or cause something to do this ○ *sunlight playing on her brown hair* **23.** *vt* LET FISH PULL ON LINE to tire an already hooked fish by letting it pull on the line as it tries to escape **24.** *vti* DIRECT LIGHT OR WATER to direct light or water over a surface or in a particular direction, or be directed in this manner ■ *n* **1.** ENJOYABLE ACTIVITIES activities bringing amusement or enjoyment, especially the spontaneous activity of young children or young animals (*often used before a noun*) ○ *young cubs at play* **2.** ACTION OR MOVE IN GAME an action or move in a game ○ *drilled the team in several new offensive plays* **3.** TURN IN GAME somebody's turn to move in a game **4.** HANDLING OF SHOT OR MOVE a player's handling of a shot or move or use of a piece or card **5.** ACTION DURING GAME the action during a game or series of games ○ *The play was skilled during the first half but then the team began to tire.* **6.** STATUS OF BALL the position or status of the ball or puck during a game, with regard to whether or not play can, according to the rules, legally continue ○ *The ball was ruled to be out of play.* **7.** EFFECTIVE OPERATION a state in which something is effective, operative, or exercises an influence ○ *The experts will come into play when the committee resumes its deliberations.* **8.** GAMBLING participation in betting or gambling **9.** PLOY a ploy or deceptive act ○ *The defendant's tears were just a play for your sympathy.* **10.** DRAMATIC COMPOSITION a dramatic work written to be performed by actors on the stage, television, or radio **11.** PUN a pun on a word **12.** FLICKERING MOVEMENT flickering or shimmering movement, especially of light through or on something **13.** ACTIVITY the free-ranging and varied activity of something, e.g., the imagination **14.** LOOSENESS the amount of looseness in something such as a rope, or the room for free movement between parts of a mechanism **15.** SCOPE the freedom to operate given to something or somebody ○ *gave free play to his inventiveness* [Old English *pleg(i)an* < Germanic, "to risk, exercise"] —**play·a·bil·i·ty** /plàyə bíllətee/ *n* —**play·a·ble** /pláyəb'l/ *adj* ◇ **make a play for somebody** *or* **something** to try openly to attract somebody or gain something ◇ **play fair** to act in an honest and reasonable way ◇ **play fast and loose** to act irresponsibly or recklessly without regard to facts or others' feelings ◇ **play hard to get** to avoid agreeing to a suggestion, invitation, or proposal, with the intention of appearing to be desirable or in demand ◇ **play it by ear** to improvise or adapt your response to a situation as it occurs rather than make plans in advance ◇ **play it safe** to exercise caution and take few risks

play along *vi* to pretend to agree with somebody or something in order to gain an advantage or avoid conflict

play around *vi* **1.** to engage in sexual activity with somebody other than a spouse or long-term partner **2.** to behave in an irresponsible or childish way

play at *v* **1.** *vt* to pretend to do or be something, usually without conviction or commitment ○ *I was tired of playing at being an entrepreneur.* **2.** *vi* to engage in a game that involves role-playing (*refers typically to children*) ○ *playing at doctors and nurses*

play back *vti* to reproduce recorded sound or video material

play down *vt* to represent something as being less important or significant than it is ○ *The spin doctors are playing down the significance of the charge.*

play off *v* **1.** *vi* TAKE PART IN DECIDING GAME to take part in a deciding game to find the winner of a tied contest **2.** *vt* BRING PEOPLE INTO CONFLICT to set one person or group against another in order to gain an advantage ○ *children playing their parents off each other* **3.** *vt* INTERACT WITH SOMETHING to interact with or react to somebody or something ○ *The women are distantly related and the subplot plays off that coincidence.*

play on *vt* **1.** to say or do things that intensify somebody's existing feelings of hope, fear, or insecurity, usually as a way of manipulating that person **2.** to make a pun on a word

play out *v* **1.** *vt* FINISH PLAYING SOMETHING to continue to play something to the finish or end ○ *We'll play out this hand, then go home.* **2.** *vt* LET SOMETHING OUT GRADUALLY to release something such as a rope bit by bit **3.** *vt* ACT OUT SOMETHING to act out a scene or situation that has been rehearsed or envisaged previously **4.** *vti US* END to bring something to an end, or come to an end ○ *The calamity has yet to play out.*

play up *vt* to emphasize or exaggerate something ○ *She played up her commercial know-how for all she was worth.*

play upon *vt* same as **play on**

play up to *vt* to attempt to please somebody by flattery and obsequiousness

play with *vt* **1.** THINK ABOUT SOMETHING to consider a plan or idea without doing very much to make it happen **2.** TREAT SOMEBODY CARELESSLY to treat somebody or somebody's feelings carelessly or irresponsibly **3.** DEAL WITH SOMETHING HALF-HEARTEDLY to deal with something unenthusiastically or haphazardly, e.g., by pushing food around a plate without eating **4.** STIMULATE SELF to stimulate your own or somebody else's genitals

pla·ya /plaáyə/ *n* the lower part of an inland desert drainage basin that is periodically filled with alkaline and briny salts washed down by rainwater from surrounding highlands [Mid-19C. Via Spanish, "beach" < late Latin *plagia* "plain, shore"]

play-act *v* **1.** *vi* BEHAVE INSINCERELY to behave in an insincere and excessively dramatic fashion, usually in order to get attention **2.** *vti* PRETEND TO BE ACTING to pretend to be acting a part, usually for fun **3.** *vi* ACT IN PLAY to take part in drama, especially as an amateur —**play-act·ing** *n* —**play-act·or** *n*

play-ac·tion pass *n* in football, a play in which the quarterback fakes a handoff to a back before passing forward to a receiver

play·back /pláy bàk/ *n* **1.** the replay of a sound or video recording after it has been made, often as a check for quality or accuracy **2.** the device or facility in a recording apparatus for replaying recordings

play·back sing·er *n S Asia* a singer who sings songs mimed to by film actors

play·bill /pláy bìl/ *n* a poster advertising a play or other theatrical performance (*dated*)

Play·bill /pláy bìl/ *tdmk* a trademark for a printed program given to theatergoers before a theatrical performance or concert

play·book /pláy bo͝ok/ *n* **1.** a book in which football plays are explained and diagrammed **2.** a book containing play scripts

play·boy /pláy bòy/ *n* a rich man who does not work and devotes himself to a life of pleasure without commitments or responsibilities

---

CULTURAL NOTE ***The Playboy of the Western World,*** a play (1907) by Irish dramatist J. M. Synge. This, Synge's best-known and most controversial work, is the story of Christy Mahon, who flees from his domineering father to a village in Mayo. There he impresses the inhabitants, particularly the women, with his exaggerated tales, claiming to have killed his father with a single blow. His period of glory is cut short, however, by the arrival in the village of his alleged victim, who suffered no more than a blow on the head from his son.

---

play-by-play *adj* consisting of a description of each event as it happens, especially in a sports contest ■ *n* a spoken description of an event as it happens, especially of a sporting event being broadcast on radio or television

play·date /pláy dàyt/ *n* an arranged time when children are brought together to play under supervision, often at one another's homes

played out /plàyd-/ *adj* (*hyphenated when used before a noun*) **1.** drained of energy or inspiration as a result of excessive or prolonged effort or of being too long in the public eye ○ *After months of intensive but not very productive research I was feeling played out and in need of a vacation.* **2.** having lost all usefulness or relevance through overuse or overexposure [Originally describing a fish caught on a line that has fought until it is exhausted]

play·er /pláy ər/ *n* **1.** SOMEBODY TAKING PART IN GAME somebody taking part in a sport or game, e.g., a member of a team (*often used in combination*) ○ *a hockey player* **2.** MUSICIAN somebody who plays a musical instrument (*usually used in combination*) ○ *a trumpet player* **3.** PARTICIPANT IN ACTIVITY a person, group, or business that has an influential role in a political or commercial activity ○ *a major player in the direct banking sector* **4.** STAGE ACTOR an actor, especially a member of a theatrical company **5.** DEVICE FOR PLAYING RECORDED SOUND a device for playing recorded sound (*usually used in combination*) ○ *a CD player*

play·er kill·er *n* in a multiplayer computer game, somebody who defeats the character of another player —**play·er kill·ing** *n*

play·er pi·an·o *n* a piano with a mechanism for playing music automatically, traditionally by means of a perforated metal disk or roll of paper

play·fel·low /pláy fèllō/ *n* a friend with whom a child plays (*archaic*)

play·ful /pláyf'l/ *adj* **1.** fond of having fun and playing games with others **2.** said or done in a teasing way or in fun ○ *a playful poke in the ribs* —**play·ful·ly** *adv* —**play·ful·ness** *n*

play·girl /pláy gùrl/ *n* a rich woman who does not work and devotes herself to a life of pleasure without commitments or responsibilities

play·go·er /pláy gō ər/ *n* a frequent attender of plays at a theater —**play·go·ing** *adj, n*

play·ground /pláy gròwnd/ *n* **1.** an outdoor recreation area for children, usually equipped with swings, slides, seesaws, and other play equipment **2.** *UK* EDUC same as **schoolyard** **3.** a resort or other place used for recreation by a particular group of people ○ *The coast has become a playground for millionaires.*

play·group /pláy gro͞op/ *n* an organized meeting for preschool children to play together under supervision

play·house /pláy hòwss/ (*plural* **-houses** /-hòwzəz/) *n* **1.** THEATER a theater, especially the main theater in a town or city **2.** LEISURE SMALL MODEL HOUSE FOR CHILDREN a model house that is large enough for small children to go inside and play in **3.** DOLLHOUSE a dollhouse

play·ing card /pláying kaàrd/ *n* a card belonging to a set printed with an identical design on the back and symbols on the face representing the numbers in different suits, used for playing various games. Playing cards, introduced to the West from Asia, were probably first used in China in the 10th century. The pack was standardized at 52 in the 15th century.

play·ing field *n* an area of level ground used for organized sporting activities ◇ **a level playing field** a situation in which all those involved have an equal chance of being successful

play·land /pláy lànd/ *n US* an area designed and equipped for children to play in

play·let /pláylət/ *n* a short play, often one with a rather slight plot

play·list /pláy lìst/ *n* a list of musical recordings that are to be played on a radio program or by a radio station —**play·list** *vt*

play·mak·er /pláy màykər/ *n* in team games, a player who initiates an offensive play designed to create a scoring opportunity

play·mate /pláy màyt/ *n* somebody, especially a child, who plays with another

play·off /pláy àwf, -òf/ *n* **1.** an additional match, game, or round to decide the winner in the case of a tie **2.** one of a series of games that decides a championship competition ○ *One more win should guarantee a spot in the playoffs.*

play on words *n* same as **pun**

play·pen /pláy pèn/ *n* a portable structure that forms a small enclosure for a baby to play in safely

~~playright~~ incorrect spelling of **playwright**

play·room /pláy ro͝om, -ro͞om/ *n* a room reserved, designed, or equipped for children to play in

play·school /pláy sko͞ol/ *n Can, UK* same as **nursery school**

play·suit /pláy so͞ot/ *n* an outfit for a child or woman to wear when relaxing, either consisting of shorts and a top or made in one piece

play·thing /pláy thìng/ *n* **1.** a toy or other object with which to play **2.** somebody or something used for amusement rather than being treated with respect or taken seriously

play·time /pláy tīm/ *n* a time set aside for play, especially as a recess for children at school

play·wear /pláy wèr/ *n US* children's clothes suitable for playing in

play·wright /pláy rīt/ *n* a writer of plays

~~playwrite~~ incorrect spelling of **playwright**

pla·za /plaázə, plázzə/ *n* **1.** WIDENED AREA IN HIGHWAY a part of a highway that has been widened as a multilane approach to a set of tollbooths **2.** PARKING AREA a parking lot adjacent to a highway **3.** SHOPPING CENTER a mall or shopping center **4.** *Hispanic* TOWN SQUARE an open square or marketplace in a Spanish-speaking country or somewhere influenced by Hispanic culture [Late 17C. Via Spanish < Latin *platea* "broad way" (see PLACE)]

PLC *abbr* **1.** MARKETING product life cycle **2.** *also* **plc** *UK* BUSINESS public limited company

plea /plee/ *n* **1.** URGENT REQUEST an urgent, often emotional, request ○ *a plea for understanding* **2.** LAW DEFENDANT'S ANSWER TO CHARGE the defendant's answer to a charge in a court of law, especially one stating that he or she is guilty or not guilty **3.** LAW STATEMENT OF DEFENDANT'S OR CLAIMANT'S CASE a statement or argument made in a court of law in support of a defendant's or claimant's case **4.** EXCUSE an excuse or pretext ○ *He managed to extricate himself on the plea of extreme pressure of work.* [13C. < Anglo-Norman *plai* "lawsuit, agreement," variant of Old French *plaid* < Latin *placitum* "decree" < past participle of *placere* "please"]

plea-bar·gain·ing *n* the practice of arranging with the prosecution, and sometimes a judge, for a defendant to plead guilty to a less serious charge rather than be tried for a more serious one —**plea bar·gain** *n* —**plea-bar·gain** *vi*

pleach /pleech/ (**pleached, pleach·ing, pleach·es**) *vt* to form or reinforce a hedge or arch by intertwining shoots or branches [14C. < Old French *plechier*, dialectal variant of *plassier* < Latin *plectere* "to plait"]

plead /pleed/ (**plead·ed** or **pled** /pled/, **plead·ed** or **pled, plead·ing, pleads**) *v* **1.** *vi* BEG EARNESTLY to make an earnest or urgent entreaty, often in emotional terms ○ *I pleaded with her to stay.* **2.** *vt* OFFER REASON AS EXCUSE to use a particular reason or circumstance to excuse or justify behavior ○ *It's no use pleading ignorance.* **3.** *vt* DECLARE GUILT OR INNOCENCE to answer "guilty" or "not guilty" in response to a charge in a court of law **4.** *vti* OFFER ARGUMENT IN SUPPORT OF SOMETHING to argue a case in support of somebody or something, especially in a court of law [13C. < Anglo-Norman *pleder* < Old French *plaid* (see PLEA)] —**plead·a·ble** *adj* —**plead·er** *n* —**plead·ing·ly** *adv*

plead·ings /pleédingz/ *npl* the formal written statements made by the plaintiff and the defendant in a lawsuit

pleas·ance /plézz'nss/ *n* a quiet tree-planted area laid out with walks and often statues and fountains [14C. < French *plaisance* < *plaisant* (see PLEASANT)]

pleas·ant /plézz'nt/ *adj* **1.** bringing feelings of pleasure, enjoyment, or satisfaction ○ *We spent a very pleasant evening together.* **2.** friendly, kind, or good-natured [14C. < French *plaisant*, present participle of Old French *plaisir* (see PLEASE)] —**pleas·ant·ly** *adv* —**pleas·ant·ness** *n*

Plea·sant Is·land /plèzz'nt-/ former name for **Nauru**

pleas·ant·ry /plézz'ntree/ (*plural* **-ries**) *n* **1.** POLITE REMARK a conventionally polite remark or inquiry **2.** WITTY REMARK a humorous or witty remark **3.** AGREEABLE CONVERSATION pleasing light conversation

please /pleez/ *adv, interj* USED IN REQUESTS used to add politeness or urgency to requests, commands, and published rules and regulations ○ *Please be quiet.* ■ *interj* USED TO EXPRESS INDIGNATION used to express astonishment or indignation, often facetiously ○ *Oh please! Do you really expect me to believe that?* ■ *v* (**pleased, pleas·ing, pleas·es**) **1.** *vti* GIVE PLEASURE to give pleasure or satisfaction to somebody **2.** *vi* LIKE to like or wish to do something ○ *He just does whatever he pleases.* **3.** *vt* BE WHAT SOMEBODY WANTS to be the wish or will of somebody (*formal or literary*) [14C. Via Old French *plaisir* < Latin *placere*] —**pleas·er** *n* ◇ **if you please 1.** used to make a polite request or command **2.** used to indicate mild annoyance, indignation, or amazement (*dated*)

pleased /pleezd/ *adj* **1.** feeling or expressing satisfaction or pleasure ○ *I'm really pleased with their progress.* ○ *Pleased to meet you.* **2.** willing to do something ○ *We would be pleased to answer any further requests you have.*

~~pleasent~~ incorrect spelling of **pleasant**

pleas·ing /pleézing/ *adj* **1.** pleasant or attractive ○ *It's not very pleasing to the eye.* **2.** welcome or satisfying ○ *She has made pleasing progress in the last few weeks.* —**pleas·ing·ly** *adv* —**pleas·ing·ness** *n*

pleas·ur·a·ble /plézhərəb'l/ *adj* giving pleasure or enjoyment —**pleas·ur·a·bil·i·ty** /plèzhərə bíllətee/ *n* —**pleas·ur·a·bly** *adv*

pleas·ure /plézhər/ *n* **1.** HAPPINESS OR SATISFACTION a feeling of happiness, delight, or satisfaction ○ *The grandchildren bring me so much pleasure.* **2.** SENSUAL GRATIFICATION gratification of the senses, especially sexual gratification **3.** RECREATION recreation, relaxation, or amusement, especially as distinct from work or everyday routine ○ *traveling for pleasure* **4.** SOMETHING SATISFYING a source of happiness, joy, or satisfaction **5.** SOMEBODY'S DESIRE somebody's desire or preference (*formal or literary*) ○ *serves at the President's pleasure* ■ *v* (**-ured, -ur·ing, -ures**) **1.** *vt* GIVE SOMEBODY PLEASURE to give somebody pleasure, especially through sensual or sexual stimulation or gratification **2.** *vi* ENJOY to derive satisfaction or happiness from something [14C. < Old French *plaisir* "please," used as a noun] —**pleas·ure·less** *adj* ◇ **my pleasure** used as a response to say that you are happy or willing to do or to have done something ○ *"Thank you for your generosity." "My pleasure."* ◇ **with pleasure** used as a response to say that something will be done willingly and happily ○ *"Join me for a walk?" "With pleasure."*

pleas·ure prin·ci·ple *n* in Freudian psychology, the principle that guides instinctive behavior, directing the subject toward gratifying immediate needs and avoiding pain

pleat /pleet/ *n* a vertical fold in cloth or other material, usually one of a number, sewn into position or pressed flat ■ *vt* (**pleat·ed, pleat·ing, pleats**) to put pleats into cloth or a piece of clothing [14C. Variant of PLAIT] —**pleat·er** *n*

pleb /pleb/ *n* **1.** ANCIENT HIST same as **plebeian** *n* (sense 1) **2.** *UK* an offensive term for an ill-educated and unrefined person, especially somebody from a lower social class (*insult*) **3.** *US* MIL same as **plebe** ■ **plebs** *npl* the ordinary citizens of ancient Rome, as distinct from the patricians [Mid-17C. Originally < plural Latin *plebs* "Roman plebs," later also shortening of PLEBEIAN] —**pleb·by** *adj*

plebe /pleeb/ *n US* a first-year student at the US Military Academy or the US Naval Academy [Mid-19C. Probably shortening of PLEBEIAN]

ple·be·ian /plə beé ən/ *n* **1.** MEMBER OF ROMAN PLEBS one of the ordinary citizens of ancient Rome as distinct from the patricians **2.** SOMEBODY REGARDED AS ILL-EDUCATED somebody thought to behave in a coarse or crude manner, and to have common or vulgar tastes, especially somebody from a lower social class (*insult*) ■ *adj* **1.** OF ROMAN PLEBS relating or belonging to the ordinary people in a society, especially the plebs of ancient Rome **2.** COMMON OR VULGAR regarded as coarse, vulgar, or tasteless (*insult*) [Mid-16C. < Latin *plebeius* < *plebs* "Roman plebs"] —**ple·be·ian·ism** *n*

~~plebian~~ incorrect spelling of **plebeian**

pleb·i·scite /plébbi sīt/ *n* **1.** VOTE OF ALL CITIZENS a vote by a whole electorate to decide a question of importance **2.** EXPRESSION OF PUBLIC WILL a public expression of the will or opinion of a whole community **3.** ANCIENT HIST COMMON PEOPLE'S LAW a law enacted by the plebs or ordinary citizens of ancient Rome gathered in assembly [Mid-16C. Via French < Latin *plebiscitum* "decree of the common people" < *plebs* "Roman plebs"] —**ple·bis·ci·tar·y** /plə bíssə tèrree/ *adj*

ple·cop·ter·an /plə kóptərən/ *n* INSECTS same as **stonefly** ■ *adj* relating or belonging to the stoneflies [Late 19C. < modern Latin *Plecoptera* < Greek *plekos* "wickerwork" + *pteron* "wing"]

plec·trum /pléktrəm/ (*plural* **-tra** /-trə/ or **-trums**) *n Can, UK* a small flat pointed piece of plastic or other material, used for plucking or strumming the strings of a guitar or similar instrument. US term **pick**[2] [Early 17C. Via Latin < Greek]

pled *N Am, Scotland* past participle, past tense of **plead**

pledge /plej/ *n* **1.** SOLEMN UNDERTAKING a solemn promise or undertaking ○ *stood by her election pledges* **2.** SOMETHING GIVEN AS SECURITY something delivered as security for the keeping of a promise or the payment of a debt or as a guarantee of good faith **3.** EDUC RECRUIT TO UNIVERSITY SOCIETY a student who has been invited, and has promised, to join a fraternity or sorority **4.** PROMISE TO GIVE MONEY a promise to donate money, e.g., to a charity or a political cause ○ *They have raised over $10,000 in donations and pledges.* **5.** *US* LAW DEPOSIT OF PROPERTY a handing over or deposit of property as security **6.** BEING HELD AS SECURITY the state of being held as security ○ *goods in pledge* **7.** TOKEN OF SOMETHING something given or received as a token of something such as love or friendship **8.** TOAST a toast drunk to somebody or something as a gesture of goodwill or support ■ *v* (**pledged, pledg·ing, pledg·es**) **1.** *vt* PROMISE SOMETHING to promise something solemnly, or promise solemnly to do something **2.** *vti* EDUC PROMISE TO JOIN UNIVERSITY SOCIETY to promise to join a society, fraternity, or sorority in a university **3.** *vt* EDUC ENROLL STUDENT IN SOCIETY to admit a student to a society as a new member **4.** *vt* BIND SOMEBODY to submit somebody to a binding pledge **5.** *vt* GIVE SOMETHING AS SECURITY to hand over something as security for the payment of a debt, repayment of a loan, or the carrying out of some obligation (*dated*) **6.** *vti* DRINK TO SOMEBODY to drink a toast to somebody (*archaic*) ○ *"Drink to me, only with thine eyes, And I will pledge with mine"* (Ben Jonson *To Celia*; 1616) [14C. Via French < late Latin *plebium* < *plebire* "to pledge," probably < Germanic] —**pledg·a·ble** *adj* ◇ **sign** *or* **take the pledge** to undertake solemnly to abstain forever from alcoholic drink (*dated*)

pledg·ee /ple jeé/ *n* **1.** *US* EDUC same as **pledge** *n* (sense 3) **2.** somebody with whom a pledge or pawned object is deposited

Pledge of Al·le·giance *n* a formula recited by citizens of the United States when saluting the US flag as a promise of loyalty to the country

pledg·er /pléjjər/, **pledg·or** *n* **1.** somebody who pledges or pawns something **2.** somebody who takes a pledge or vow

pled·get /pléjjət/ *n* a small tuft of cotton or other material used on forceps to cleanse or apply medication to a confined space such as the ear passage [Mid-16C. Origin ?]

pled·gor *n* another spelling of **pledger**

-plegia *suffix* inability to move ○ *quadriplegia* [< Greek *plēgē* "blow, stroke" < *plēg-*, stem of *plēssein* "to strike"]

Ple·ia·des /pleé ə deèz/ *npl* **1.** in Greek mythology, the seven daughters of Atlas and Pleione who were pursued by Orion and were turned into a constellation to escape him **2.** a cluster of more than 300 stars in the constellation Taurus, several of which are blue-white giants visible to the naked eye [14C. Via Latin < Greek]

plein-air /plàyn ér/ *adj* relating to or in the style of the French impressionist painters who sought to capture effects of light and atmosphere by completing their work out of doors [Late 19C. < French *(en) plein air* "(in) the open air"] —**plein-air·ist** *n*

pleio- *prefix* same as **pleo-** [< Greek *pleiōn* "more," comparative of *polus* (see POLY-)]

Plei·o·cene *adj, n* GEOL another spelling of **Pliocene**

plei·ot·ro·pism /plī óttrə pìzzəm/, **plei·ot·ro·py** /-óttrəpee/ (*plural* **-pies**) *n* the phenomenon in which a single gene determines two or more apparently unrelated characteristics of the same organism, or an instance of this —**plei·o·tro·pic** /plī ə tróppik/ *adj* —**plei·o·tro·pi·cal·ly** *adv*

Pleis·to·cene /plístə seen/ *n* the epoch of geologic time, about 1.6 million to 10,000 years ago, characterized by the disappearance of continental ice sheets and the appearance of humans. See table at **geologic time** [Mid-19C. < Greek *pleistos* "most" + *kainos* "recent"] —**Pleis·to·cene** *adj*

ple·na plural of **plenum**

ple·na·ry /pleenəree, plénnə-/ *adj* **1. ATTENDED BY EVERYONE** attended or meant to be attended by every member or delegate ○ *a plenary session* **2. FULL OR UNLIMITED** full and complete and not limited in any respect (*formal*) ■ *n* (*plural* **-ries**) **PLENARY MEETING** a plenary meeting, session, or lecture, e.g., at a conference [Early 16C. < late Latin *plenarius* < Latin *plenus* "full"] —**ple·na·ri·ly** *adv*

ple·na·ry in·dul·gence *n* in the Roman Catholic Church, a complete remission of temporal punishment

plen·i·po·ten·ti·ar·y /plènnəpə ténshee èrree/ *adj* **1. HAVING FULL POWER** invested with complete authority to act independently **2. CONFERRING FULL POWER** giving the holder complete authority to act independently ■ *n* (*plural* **-ies**) **OFFICIAL WITH FULL POWERS** an ambassador, envoy, or delegate invested with full authority to act or negotiate independently on behalf of a government or sovereign [Mid-17C. < medieval Latin *plenipotentiarius* < late Latin *plenipotent-* "having full power" < *plenus* "full" + *potent-* "powerful"] —**plen·i·po·tent** /plə níppət'nt/ *adj*

plen·i·tude /plénnə tood/ *n* (*literary*) **1.** an abundance or plentiful supply of something **2.** the state of being full or complete [15C. Via French < late Latin *plenitudo* < Latin *plenus* "full"]

plen·te·ous /pléntee əss/ *adj* (*literary*) **1.** being in plentiful supply **2.** giving an abundant yield [13C. < Old French *plentivous* < *plentet* (see PLENTY)] —**plen·te·ous·ly** *adv* —**plen·te·ous·ness** *n*

plen·ti·ful /pléntif'l/ *adj* **1.** present or existing in large quantities ○ *Water is plentiful on the island.* **2.** supplying a large quantity or number of something —**plen·ti·ful·ly** *adv* —**plen·ti·ful·ness** *n*

plen·ty /pléntee/ *pron* **LARGE AMOUNT** an adequate or more than adequate amount or quantity ○ *There's plenty for the kids to do there.* ○ *Get plenty of rest.* ■ *n* **PROSPERITY** a situation in which there is a more than adequate supply of food, money, and other necessities ○ *had grown up in a time of plenty* ■ *adj* **AMPLY SUFFICIENT** ample or more than sufficient (*informal*) ■ *adv* **SUFFICIENTLY** used to emphasize the degree to which something is the case (*informal*) ○ *It should be plenty big enough.* [13C. Via Old French *plentet* < Latin *plenitas* < *plenus* "full"]

ple·num /pleenəm, plénnəm/ (*plural* **-nums** or **-na** /-nə/) *n* **1. GENERAL ATTENDANCE AT MEETING** a full or general assembly, e.g., of all the branches of a legislature **2.** PHYS **ENCLOSURE CONTAINING GAS AT HIGHER PRESSURE** an enclosure or chamber containing gas that is at a higher pressure than the surrounding atmosphere. Plenum systems may be used in air conditioning. **3.** PHILOSOPHY **MATTER-FILLED SPACE** space entirely filled with matter [Late 17C. < Latin *plenum spatium* "full space"]

pleo- *prefix* more ○ *pleomorphism* [< Greek *pleion*, variant of *pleiōn* (see PLEIO-)]

ple·och·ro·ism /plee ókrō ìzzəm/ *n* the property in some crystals of transmitting different colors when viewed along different axes [Mid-19C. < PLEO- + Greek *khrōs* "skin, color"] —**ple·o·chro·ic** /plee ə krṓ ik/ *adj*

ple·o·mor·phism /plee ə máwr fìzzəm/, **ple·o·mor·phy** /plee ə màwrfee/ *n* the characteristic in some organisms of taking on at least two different forms during the life cycle, or the ability to do this —**ple·o·mor·phic** *adj*

ple·o·nasm /plee ə nàzzəm/ *n* **1.** the use of more words than are necessary to express a meaning **2.** an example of using more words than are necessary to express a meaning, e.g., "free gift" or "sufficient enough" [Mid-16C. Via late Latin < Greek *pleonasmos* < *pleonazein* "be in excess" < *pleōn* "more"] —**ple·o·nas·tic** /plee ə nástik/ *adj* —**ple·o·nas·ti·cal·ly** *adv*

ple·o·pod /plee ə pòd/ *n* ZOOL same as **swimmeret**

ple·o·trop·ic /plee ə tróppik/ *adj* describes a gene that affects more than one characteristic of the phenotype

~~**plesant**~~ incorrect spelling of **pleasant**

ple·si·o·saur /pleessee ə sàwr, pleezee-/ *n* an extinct ocean reptile of the Mesozoic era with limbs like paddles, a large flattened body, and a short tail. Suborder: Sauropterygia. [Mid-19C. < modern Latin *Plesiosaurus* < Greek *plēsios* "near" + *sauros* "lizard"]

pleth·o·ra /pléthərə/ *n* **1.** a very large amount of something or number of things, especially an excessive amount (*formal*) ○ *a plethora of new scholarly articles on the subject* **2.** an excess of blood in a part of the body, especially in the facial veins, causing a ruddy complexion [Mid-16C. Via late Latin < Greek *plēthorē* < *plēthein* "be full"] —**ple·thor·ic** /pléthərik, plə tháwrik/ *adj* —**ple·thor·i·cal·ly** *adv*

pleur- *prefix* same as **pleuro-** (*used before vowels*)

pleu·ra /plŏŏrə/ *n* (*plural* **-rae** /-ree/ or **-ras**) a thin transparent membrane that lines the lungs, thereby forming a continuous sac enclosing the narrow pleural cavity. The inner faces of the cavity are lubricated by fluid to ease breathing movements. ■ ZOOL plural of **pleuron** [15C. Via medieval Latin < Greek, "side, rib"] —**pleu·ral** *adj*

pleu·ral cav·i·ty *n* the cavity formed between the pleural layer surrounding the lungs and the other layer lining the chest wall

pleu·ri·sy /plŏŏrissee/ *n* inflammation of the membrane (**pleura**) surrounding the lungs, usually involving painful breathing, coughing, and the buildup of fluid in the pleural cavity [14C. Via French < late Latin *pleurisis*, alteration of Latin *pleuritis* < Greek < *pleura* "side, rib"] —**pleu·rit·ic** /plŏŏ ríttik/ *adj*

pleuro- *prefix* **1.** side, lateral ○ *pleurodont* **2.** pleura, pleural ○ *pleuropneumonia* [< Greek *pleura* "side, rib"]

pleu·ro·dont /plŏŏrə dònt/ *adj* **1.** describes teeth that are not rooted in the jawbone, but fused to its inner side, as, e.g., in some reptiles **2.** describes reptiles that have teeth not rooted in the jawbone, but fused to its inner side

pleu·ro·dyn·i·a /plŏŏrə dínnee ə/ *n* **1.** pain in the pleura, between the ribs or in the chest wall area **2.** an illness caused by a coxsackie virus (*not in technical use*) [Early 19C. < PLEURO- + Greek *odunē* "pain"]

pleu·ron /plŏŏr òn/ (*plural* **-ra** /-rə/) *n* the part of the outer layer of the skin of an arthropod that covers the side of a body segment [Early 18C. Via modern Latin < Greek, "side, rib"]

pleu·ro·pneu·mo·nia /plŏŏrə noo mṓnee ə/ *n* inflammation of the membrane (**pleura**) surrounding the lungs and of the lungs themselves at the same time

pleus·ton /plŏŏstən, plŏŏ stòn/ *n* small animals and plants such as algae that float on the surface of a pool of fresh water [Mid-20C. < Greek *pleusis* "sailing," after PLANKTON] —**pleus·ton·ic** /ploo stónnik/ *adj*

Plev·en /plévv'n/ capital city of Pleven Province, northern Bulgaria, situated about 80 mi./129 km northeast of Sofia. Population: 127,945 (1996).

plex·i·form /pléksi fàwrm/ *adj* resembling or in the form of a plexus or network [Early 19C. < PLEXUS]

Plex·i·glas /pléksi glàss/ *tdmk* a trademark for a tough transparent acrylic plastic that can be used in place of glass

plex·or /pléksər/ *n* a small rubber-headed hammer formerly used to tap the body in a medical examination by percussion and in testing reflexes, e.g., by tapping the knee [Mid-19C. < Greek *plēxis* "percussion" < *plēssein* "to strike"]

plex·us /pléksəss/ (*plural* **-us·es** or *same*) *n* **1.** a network of nerves, blood vessels, or other vessels in the body **2.** a complex network or interwoven structure [Late 17C. < Latin, past participle of *plectere* "plait"]

pli·a·ble /plī́ əb'l/ *adj* **1. FLEXIBLE** flexible and easily bent or molded **2. EASILY INFLUENCED** easily persuaded or influenced **3. ADAPTABLE** adaptable to change [15C. < French < *plier* "to fold, bend" (see PLY²)] —**pli·a·bil·i·ty** /plī ə bíllətee/ *n* —**pli·a·ble·ness** *n* —**pli·a·bly** *adv*

SYNONYMS ***pliable, ductile, malleable, elastic, pliant***

CORE MEANING: able to be bent or molded

pliable flexible and easily bent or molded ○ *a young, pliable tree branch* **ductile** used to describe metals that can be easily drawn out into a long continuous wire or hammered into thin sheets ○ *The alloy possesses a high proportion of tin to copper, giving the metal special ductile qualities.* **malleable** used to describe metals or other substances that can be shaped without breaking or cracking ○ *Iron possesses a very low carbon content, which makes it tough and malleable.* ○ *The sculptor used wet, malleable plaster to create a cast of her subject's head.* **elastic** used to describe substances or materials that can be stretched without breaking and then return to their original shape ○ *An elastic material such as rubber is easily pulled into long strings.* ○ *Add enough water to form a soft elastic dough and knead until smooth.* **pliant** supple and easily bent ○ *To execute this move, the wrist must be pliant and completely relaxed.* **plastic** easily shaped, molded, or modeled ○ *The clay is plastic and easy to use.*

pli·ant /plī́ ənt/ *adj* **1. SUPPLE** supple and bending easily ○ *a pliant tree branch* **2. ADAPTABLE** easily adapted or modified **3. EASILY INFLUENCED** easily persuaded or influenced [14C. < Old French, present participle of *plier* "to fold, bend" (see PLY²)] —**pli·an·cy** *n* —**pli·ant·ly** *adv* —**pli·ant·ness** *n*

SYNONYMS See ***pliable***.

pli·ca /plī́kə/ (*plural* **-cae** /-see, -kee/) *n* a fold or folded part, e.g., of skin [Early 18C. < medieval Latin, "fold" < Latin *plicare* "to fold, bend"] —**pli·cal** *adj*

pli·cate /plī́ kàyt/, **pli·cat·ed** /plī́ kàytəd/ *adj* **1.** arranged in folds like a fan **2.** describes rock with a folded wrinkled texture [Late 17C. < Latin *plicat-*, past participle of *plicare* "fold, bend"] —**pli·cate·ly** *adv* —**pli·cate·ness** *n*

pli·ca·tion /plī káysh'n/, **plic·a·ture** /plíkə chŏŏr, -chər/ *n* **1. PLEATING OF SIDES OF BODY ORGAN** the pleating and stitching of the walls of a body organ in order to reduce its size **2. ACT OF FOLDING** the act of folding, or the condition of being folded **3. FOLD IN SOMETHING** a fold or pleat in something

pli·é /plee áy/ *n* a ballet movement in which the knees are bent and the back is kept straight [Late 19C. < French, past participle of *plier* "fold, bend" (see PLY²)]

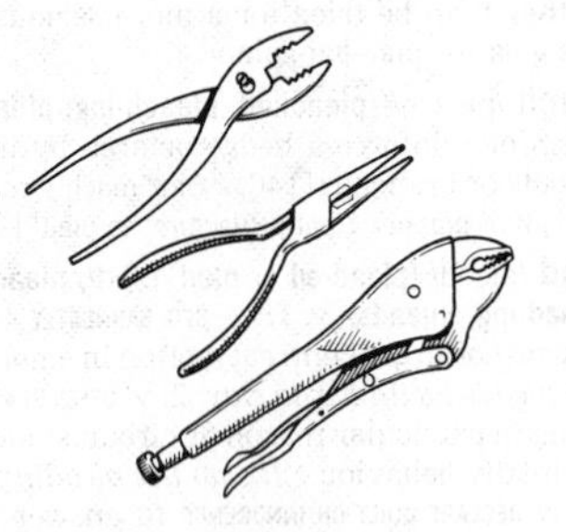

pliers

pli·ers /plī́ ərz/ *npl* a hand tool with two hinged arms ending in jaws that are closed by hand pressure to grip something [Mid-16C. < PLY¹]

plight¹ /plīt/ *n* a difficult or dangerous situation, especially a sad or desperate predicament [14C. < Anglo-Norman *plit* "wrinkle, situation" (influenced by PLIGHT²) < Latin *plicitum* < past participle of *plicare* "fold, bend"]

plight² /plīt/ *vt* (**plight·ed, plight·ed** or **plight, plight·ing, plights**) to make a formal pledge, especially when promising to marry (*dated*) ○ *plighted her word* ■ *n* a formal promise or pledge (*archaic*) [Old English *plihtan* "endanger" < *pliht* "risk, danger" < Germanic, "risk, pledge yourself"] —**plight·er** *n* ◇ **plight your troth** to promise something solemnly, especially to marry somebody (*dated*)

Plim·soll line /plímssəl-/, **Plim·soll mark** *n* a mark on the side of a merchant ship indicating the limit to which it can legally be submerged when loaded. See illustration on next page [After Samuel *Plimsoll* (1824–98), British politician and reformer]

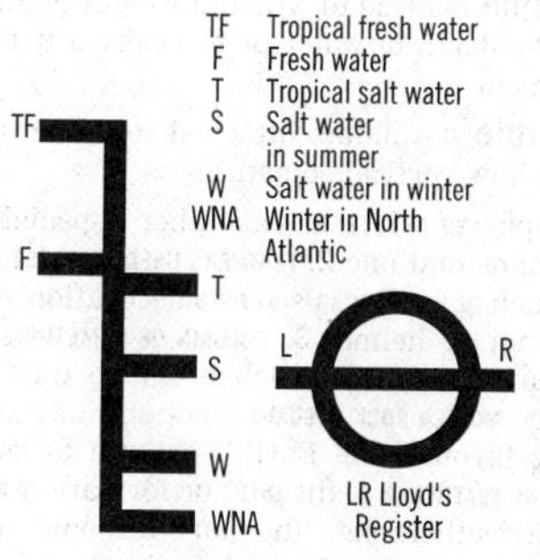

Plimsoll line

plink /plingk/ *n* **HIGH-PITCHED SOUND** a short high-pitched metallic sound ■ *vti* **(plinked, plink·ing, plinks) 1. MAKE HIGH-PITCHED SOUND** to make a short high-pitched metallic sound, or cause something to do this **2. SHOOT AT TARGET** to shoot at or hit targets for fun, especially targets that make a short high-pitched metallic sound when hit [Mid-20C. An imitation of the sound] —**plink·er** *n*

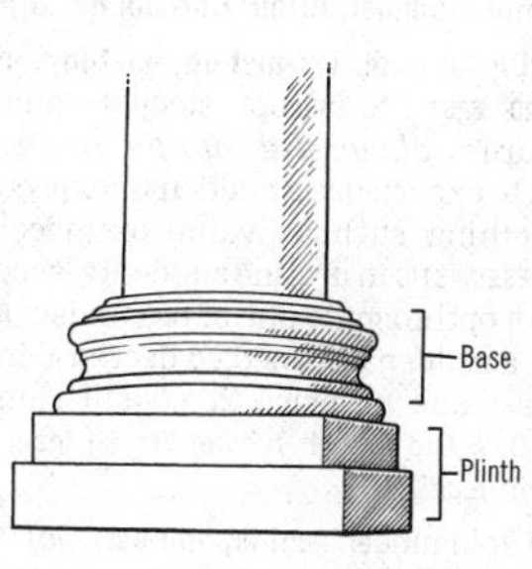

plinth

plinth /plinth/ *n* **1. SUPPORTING BLOCK** a square block beneath a column, pedestal, or statue **2. SUPPORTING PART OF WALL** the part of the wall of a building immediately above the ground, usually a course of stones or bricks **3. PART OF DOORFRAME** the square block at the base on each side of a doorframe **4. FLAT BASE** a flat block used as a base for something, e.g., underneath a heavy machine [Late 16C. Directly or via French < Latin *plinthus* < Greek *plinthos* "tile, squared building stone"]

Plin·y (the El·der) /plínnee-/ (A.D. 23–79) Roman scholar. His *Natural History* (A.D. 77) was a major source of knowledge until the 17th century.

Plin·y (the Young·er) (A.D. 62–113) Roman politician and writer. He was the nephew of Pliny the Elder and author of nine books of Letters (A.D. 100–109).

plio- *prefix* another spelling of **pleo-**

Pli·o·cene /plī̍ ə seen/, **Plei·o·cene** *n* the epoch of geologic time, 5 million to 1.6 million years ago, during which a hominid species **(Homo erectus)** first appeared. See table at **geologic time** [Mid-19C. < Greek *pleiōn* "more" + *kainos* "recent," because it is later than the Miocene] —**Pli·o·cene** *adj*

plis·sé /plee sáy/, **plis·se** *n* **1.** a permanently wrinkled finish given to a fabric by treating it chemically **2.** a fabric with a plissé finish [Late 19C. < French, past participle of *plisser* "pleat" < *pli* "fold" < *plier* (see PLY²)]

PLO *abbr* POL Palestine Liberation Organization

plod /plod/ *vi* **(plod·ded, plod·ding, plods) 1. WALK HEAVILY** to walk with a slow heavy tread **2. WORK SLOWLY BUT STEADILY** to work slowly but steadily, especially on something uninteresting or laborious ■ *n* **1. SLOW HEAVY STEPS** a walk with slow heavy steps **2. SOUND OF SOMEBODY PLODDING** the sound of slow heavy steps [Mid-16C. Probably to suggest the motion] —**plod·der** *n* —**plod·ding** *adj* —**plod·ding·ly** *adv*

-ploid *suffix* having a chromosome number in a particular relationship to the basic number of chromosomes in a group ○ *tetraploid* [< DIPLOID and HAPLOID]

ploi·dy /plóydee/ *n* the multiple of the number of chromosome sets in a cell

Ploi·eş·ti /plaw yésht, -yéshtee/ city in southeastern Romania. It is the capital of Prahova County and center of the national oil industry. Population: 253,623 (1997).

plonk¹ /plongk/ *vti, n, adv* same as **plunk**

plonk² /plongk/ *n UK* cheap inferior wine (*informal*) [Mid-20C. Shortening of *plink-plonk*, origin ?]

plop /plop/ *n* **SOUND OF SOMETHING DROPPING INTO WATER** the sound made by something dropping into water without making a large splash ■ *v* **(plopped, plop·ping, plops) 1.** *vti* **FALL OR DROP SOMETHING WITH PLOP** to fall into water without making a large splash, or make somebody or something do this **2.** *vi* **DROP DOWN QUICKLY AND HEAVILY** to drop or sit down quickly and heavily ○ *He plopped down on the nearest chair.* ■ *adv* **WITH PLOP** with a plopping sound or action ■ *interj* **IMITATES SOUND OF DROPPING INTO WATER** used to imitate the sound of somebody or something dropping into water without splashing [Early 19C. An imitation of the sound]

plo·sion /plṓzh'n/ *n* the sound made by a sudden release of breath in pronouncing some sounds, especially a stop consonant [Early 20C. Back-formation < EXPLOSION]

plo·sive /plṓziv, plóssiv/ *adj* describes a consonant such as the "p" in "pear" that is pronounced by completely closing the breath passage and then releasing air ■ *n* a consonant pronounced with a sudden release of breath [Late 19C. Back-formation < EXPLOSIVE]

plot /plot/ *n* **1. SECRET HOSTILE PLAN** a plan decided on in secret, especially to bring about an illegal or subversive act **2. STORY LINE** the story or sequence of events in something such as a novel, play, or movie **3. PIECE OF GROUND** a small piece of ground **4.** *US* ARCHIT **PLAN OF BUILDING OR ESTATE** an architectural plan of a building or estate **5. CHART** a graph, chart, or diagram of something ■ *v* **(plot·ted, plot·ting, plots) 1.** *vti* **MAKE SECRET PLAN** to make a secret plan, especially to do something illegal or subversive with others **2.** *vt* **MARK SOMETHING ON CHART** to mark something on a chart, especially the course of a ship or aircraft **3.** *vt US* ARCHIT **MAKE PLAN OF BUILDING OR ESTATE** to make a plan or map of something such as a building or estate **4.** *vti* **MARK POINTS ON GRAPH** to mark points on a graph or diagram using coordinates, or be located on a graph by coordinates **5.** *vt* **DRAW SOMETHING ON GRAPH** to draw a line or curve through points marked on a graph or diagram **6.** *vt* **PLAN EVENTS OF STORY** to devise the sequence of events in a story or script [< Old English, "area of ground," origin ?; in "plan" senses, influenced by obsolete *complot* "secret scheme" < Old French] —**plot·less** /plóttləss/ *adj* ◇ **lose the plot** to fail to make sense of something, especially a story

Plo·ti·nus /plō tī́nəss/ (A.D. 205–270) Egyptian-born philosopher, probably of Roman ancestry. He founded neo-Platonism.

plot·line /plót lī̀n/, **plot line** *n* the plot or story in a book or dramatic presentation, or the dialogue needed to develop the plot

plot·tage /plóttij/ *n US* the area of land that makes up a plot

plot·ter /plóttər/ *n* **1.** somebody who is involved in a secret plan, especially to do something illegal or subversive **2.** a computer output device that draws graphs and other pictorial images on paper, sometimes using attached pens. Large plotters are used in computer-aided design applications to produce more rapidly the engineering drawings and architectural plans once prepared by skilled draftspeople.

plough /plow/ *n, vti* UK spelling of **plow**

Plough *n UK* same as **Big Dipper**

Plov·div /pláwv dìf/ city in southern Bulgaria, the administrative center of Plovdiv Region. Population: 344,326 (1996).

plov·er /plúvvər/ (*plural* **plov·ers** or **plover**) *n* **1.** a shorebird that has a short beak and tail and long pointed wings. Family: Charadriidae. **2.** a bird that resembles a plover but is in a different family, e.g., an egyptian plover [14C. Via Anglo-Norman < assumed Vulgar Latin *pluviarius* < Latin *pluvia* "rain" (see PLUVIAL); because it lives near water]

plow /plow/ *n* **1. FARM IMPLEMENT** a heavy farming tool with a sharp blade or series of blades for breaking

plover

up soil and making furrows, usually pulled by a tractor or draft animal **2. HEAVY TOOL** a heavy tool or machine used like a plow to cut a cleared route or channel, e.g., a snowplow ■ *v* **(plowed, plow·ing, plows) 1.** *vti* **MAKE FURROWS IN EARTH** to break up soil and turn it over into furrows ○ *plowing a field* **2.** *vti* **CUT THROUGH SOMETHING** to cut or force a way through something ○ *I plowed my way through the crowd.* **3.** *vt* **MAKE CLEARING IN SOMETHING** to make a channel or cleared route in something ○ *plowed the snow-covered roads* ○ *plowed the snow from the roads* **4.** *vt* AGRIC **PUT UNDER SOIL** to put something such as fertilizer or a crop under the surface of the soil, using a plow **5.** *vti* **WORK METHODICALLY** to work at something and progress slowly and steadily ○ *We plowed through the backlog of applications.* ○ *plowing my way through pages of job ads* **6.** *vt US* **OFFENSIVE TERM** an offensive term meaning to have sexual intercourse with somebody (*slang*) [Old English *ploh* < Germanic, < N Italic] —**plow·er** *n*

plow back *vt* to invest profits from a business back into the business

plow in *vt* to contribute or devote something, especially money, to a project or place

plow into *vt* (*informal*) **1.** to crash into or hit something with a great deal of force ○ *We lost control and plowed into the car in front.* **2.** to start a job or undertaking, especially with energy and determination

plow on *vi* to persist determinedly in spite of obstacles, opposition, or warnings (*informal*)

plow under *vt* **1.** to bury something by plowing or digging ○ *Large tracts of forest had been plowed under by the bulldozers.* **2.** to overwhelm somebody with too many responsibilities or jobs, or to overwhelm something with too heavy a burden (*informal*) ○ *I was plowed under for the whole weekend trying to fix the mess in the computer files.*

plow·boy /plów bòy/ *n* a boy who leads one or more animals while they pull a plow

plow·man /plówmən/ (*plural* **-men** /-mən/) *n* **1.** somebody who operates a plow, especially a plow drawn by animals **2.** *US* a farm laborer, especially somebody not very sophisticated —**plow·man·ship** *n*

plow·share /plów shèr/ *n* the part of a plow that cuts the soil for the furrow

plow steel *n US* a strong steel used mainly in making wire rope

ploy /ploy/ *n* a tactic or maneuver, especially one calculated to deceive or frustrate an opponent [Late 17C. Origin ?]

PLS *abbr* ONLINE please

PLSS *abbr* MED portable life-support system

pluck /pluk/ *v* **(plucked, pluck·ing, plucks) 1.** *vt* **TAKE SOMETHING AWAY QUICKLY** to take something away swiftly, often by means of skill or strength **2.** *vt* **QUICKLY REMOVE FEATHERS OR HAIR** to pull out by the roots some or all of the feathers or hair from a bird or other animal **3.** *vt* **PULL SOMETHING OFF OR OUT** to pull something off or out of something else, e.g., fruit from a tree ○ *plucking flowers* **4.** *vt* **TAKE SOMETHING CASUALLY** to select something randomly or with no obvious reason **5.** *vti* **TUG AT SOMETHING** to tug quickly at something ○ *felt someone plucking at my sleeve* **6.** *vt* MUSIC **PULL AND RELEASE STRINGS** to play a stringed musical instrument by quickly pulling and releasing strings with a finger or plectrum ■ *n* **1. BRAVERY** courage and determination in meeting danger or difficulty **2. ACT OF PLUCKING** an act or instance of plucking something **3.** FOOD **ANIMAL'S HEART, LIVER, AND LUNGS** the heart, liver, and lungs of an animal, used as meat [Old English *pluccian* < Germanic] —**pluck·er** *n*

SYNONYMS See ***courage.***

pluck up *vt* to muster courage or audacity

pluck·y /plúkee/ (**-i·er, -i·est**) *adj* showing courage and determination, especially in the face of danger, difficulty, or superior odds —**pluck·i·ly** *adv* —**pluck·i·ness** *n*

plug /plug/ *n* **1. FILLER FOR HOLE** something used to fill and tightly close up a hole **2. STOPPER FOR SINK** a rubber or plastic stopper for the drainage hole in a sink or bath **3. ELECTRICAL CONNECTION** the connection at the end of the wire leading from an electrical device, with prongs or pins that allow it to fit into the socket of a power supply **4. SOCKET** an electrical socket, e.g., on a wall (*informal*) **5. PUBLICIZING MENTION** a favorable mention of something to publicize it, e.g., during a broadcast about something else (*informal*) **6. WEDGE FOR SCREW** a hollow piece of plastic pushed inside a hole to act as a holder for a screw that, when inserted, makes the plug expand and completely fill the hole **7. FIREPLUG** a fireplug **8.** AUTOMOT same as **spark plug 9. CAKE OF CHEWING TOBACCO** a cake of compressed or twisted tobacco, or a piece of it used for chewing **10.** SEISMOL same as **volcanic plug 11. SOMETHING FAULTY** something that no longer works properly, especially because it is worn out (*slang*) **12. OLD HORSE** an old and worn-out horse (*slang*) **13.** FISHING **WEIGHTED LURE** an artificial weighted lure that has hooks attached to it **14. SMALL PIECE CUT FROM SOMETHING** a small wedge cut away from something, especially as a test sample ■ *v* (**plugged, plug·ging, plugs**) **1.** *vt* **CLOSE UP SOMETHING** to close up a hole or gap **2.** *vt* **GIVE SOMETHING FAVORABLE PUBLIC MENTION** to make a favorable mention of something in order to publicize it, e.g., during a broadcast about something else (*informal*) ○ *a chance to plug her latest novel* **3.** *vt US* **SHOOT SOMEBODY** to shoot somebody with a gun (*slang*) **4.** *vt* **PUNCH SOMEBODY** to punch or hit somebody (*slang*) **5.** *vi* **WORK STEADILY** to work at something steadily and persistently (*informal*) ○ *He is still plugging away in the insurance business.* [Early 17C. < Dutch] —**plug·ger** *n* ◇ **pull the plug** to discontinue the use of life support systems attached to a terminally ill person or animal (*slang*) ◇ **pull the plug on something** to bring something abruptly to an end, especially by cutting off funds

plug in *v* **1.** *vti* to connect an electrical appliance to a power source or to another electrical appliance, or be connected in this way **2.** *vt US* to include or incorporate something (*informal*)

plug into *v* **1.** *vti* to connect something to an electric power source by means of a plug, or be connected in this way **2.** *vt* to become closely involved with or well-informed about something (*informal*)

plug and play *n* a technical standard that allows a peripheral device such as a printer or DVD drive to be connected to a computer and to function immediately without alteration of the system's configuration files

plug gage *n* a tool for checking the diameter of a hole, consisting of a plug of a known size that is put into the hole

plugged /plugd/ *adj US* made counterfeit by adding base metal

plugged-in /plùgd-/ *adj* closely involved with or well-informed about something (*informal*)

plug-in *adj* **CONNECTIBLE BY MEANS OF PLUG** capable of being connected by a plug to an electric power source ○ *a plug-in hand drill* ■ *n* **1. SOMETHING CONNECTED BY PLUG** a device or appliance that may be connected by a plug to an electric power source **2.** COMPUT **DATA FILE ALTERING APPLICATION** a data file that alters or extends the operation of an application

plug-ug·ly *adj* an offensive term meaning regarded as extremely unattractive (*informal*) ■ *n* (*plural* **plug-ug·lies**) a tough and intimidating person, especially a gangster (*slang*) [*Plug*, origin ?]

plum /plum/ *n* **1. DARK RED FRUIT** a round or oval smooth-skinned fruit, usually red or purple, containing a flattened pit **2. FRUIT TREE** a tree that bears plums. Genus: *Prunus.* **3. DARK REDDISH PURPLE COLOR** a dark reddish purple color **4. SOMETHING CHOICE** something that is highly desirable or enviable, especially a job or contract (*informal*) ■ *adj* **1. DESIRABLE** highly desirable or profitable (*informal*) ○ *a plum job* **2. DARK REDDISH PURPLE** of a dark reddish purple color [12C. Alteration of Middle Low German, Middle Dutch *prūme*, Old High German *pfrūma* < Latin *prunum* (see PRUNE[1])]

SPELLCHECK plum or **plumb**? Do not confuse the spelling of ***plum*** and ***plumb***, which sound similar. ***Plum*** denotes a fruit or, by extension, its dark reddish purple color, as in *a plum tree, a gorgeous plum velvet*, or something highly desirable, as in *a plum contract.* ***Plumb*** means "a weight attached to a line," "in a vertical position," or "exactly," as in *a plumb line, plumb in the middle.* ***Plumb*** is the only spelling of the verb: *I had plumbed the depths of despair. Do you know how to plumb in a washing machine?*

plum·age /plóomij/ *n* the feathers that cover a bird's body, considered collectively [14C. < French < *plume* (see PLUME)]

plu·mate /plóo màyt/ *adj* resembling, having, or producing feathers [Early 19C. < Latin *plumatus* "feathered" < *pluma* "down, feather"]

plumb /plum/ *n* **1. WEIGHT ATTACHED TO LINE** a weight, usually made of lead, attached to a line and used to find the depth of water or to verify a true vertical alignment **2. TRUE VERTICAL POSITION** a true vertical position or alignment ■ *adv* **1. IN TRUE VERTICAL POSITION** in perfect alignment or a true vertical position **2. EXACTLY** precisely or exactly (*informal*) ○ *plumb in the middle* **3. COMPLETELY** utterly or totally (*informal*) ○ *plumb lazy* ■ *adj* **1. VERTICAL** in a true vertical alignment ○ *Hanging the striped wallpaper he made sure the stripes were plumb.* **2. TOTAL** utter or total (*informal*) ○ *It is plumb foolishness to try that at home.* ■ *vt* (**plumbed, plumb·ing, plumbs**) **1. FULLY COMPREHEND SOMETHING** to succeed in fully understanding something, especially something mysterious **2. EXPERIENCE SOMETHING TO EXTREME DEGREE** to experience something, especially something unpleasant, to an extreme degree ○ *had plumbed the depths of despair* **3. USE PLUMB TO CHECK SOMETHING** to find the depth of water or the vertical alignment of something with a plumb **4. MAKE SOMETHING VERTICAL** to make something properly vertical **5.** CONSTR **INSTALL PLUMBING IN SOMETHING** to equip something with plumbing, seal pipes with lead, or work as a plumber [13C. Via Old French *plomb* "lead weight" < Latin *plumbum* "lead"]

SPELLCHECK See ***plum.***

plumb in *vt* to attach a device such as a washing machine to a system of inlet and drainage pipes

plum·ba·go /plum báygō/ (*plural* **-gos**) *n* **1.** an evergreen Mediterranean or tropical plant of the leadwort family. Flowers: blue, white, or red, in clusters. Genus: *Plumbago.* **2.** MINERALS same as **graphite** [Early 17C. < Latin, "lead ore, plumbago" < *plumbum* "lead"]

plum·bate /plúm bàyt/ *n* a weakly acidic compound formed by reaction of an lead oxide with an alkali [Mid-19C. < Latin *plumbum* "lead"]

plumb bob *n* the weight, usually a conical metal one, at the end of a plumb

plumb·er /plúmmər/ *n* somebody who installs and repairs water, drainage, or heating pipes and fixtures in a building [14C. Via French, "lead worker" < Latin *plumbarius* < *plumbum* "lead"]

plumb·er's help·er *n* CONSTR same as **plunger** (sense 1)

plumb·er's snake *n* CONSTR same as **snake** *n* (sense 3)

plum·bic /plúmbik/ *adj* relating to or containing lead, especially in a valence state of four [Late 18C. < Latin *plumbum* "lead"]

plumb·ing /plúmming/ *n* **1. PLUMBER'S WORK** the work that a plumber does **2. PIPES AND FIXTURES** the pipes and fixtures that carry or use water or gas in a building **3. USE OF PLUMB** the use of a plumb to test depth or show a vertical alignment **4. DIGESTIVE, URINARY, AND REPRODUCTIVE SYSTEMS** the digestive, urinary, and reproductive tracts and organs of the body (*slang humorous*)

plum·bism /plúm bìzzəm/ *n* long-term lead poisoning (*technical*) [Late 19C. < Latin *plumbum* "lead"]

plumb line *n* a line to which a weight is attached to find the depth of water or to verify a true vertical alignment

plumb rule *n* a plumb attached to a board, used to check how vertical something is

plume /ploom/ *n* **1. FEATHER** a feather, especially a large or ornamental one **2. FEATHERS USED AS CREST** a feather or bunch of feathers used as a decoration, especially on a hat or helmet **3. COLUMN OF SOMETHING** a rising column of something such as smoke, dust, or water **4.** GEOL **MOLTEN ROCK COLUMN** a column of molten rock rising through the Earth's mantle **5.** BOT **PART RESEMBLING FEATHER** a plant part or formation that looks like a feather, e.g., the part of some seeds that allows them to be blown about by the wind **6. TOKEN OF HONOR** a prize, awarded decoration, or token of honor ■ *v* (**plumed, plum·ing, plumes**) **1.** *vt* **PREEN FEATHERS** to preen, smooth, or clean the feathers **2. plume your·self** *vr* **BE PROUD OF YOURSELF** to take pride in or congratulate yourself on something **3.** *vt* **DECORATE SOMETHING WITH FEATHERS** to decorate something with a feather or feathers [14C. Via French < Latin *pluma* "down, feather"] —**plumed** *adj*

Plum·mer /plúmmər/, **Christopher** (*b.* 1927) Canadian stage and movie actor. He won Tony Awards for his roles in *Cyrano* (1974) and *Barrymore* (1997). Full name **Plummer, Arthur Christopher Orme**

plum·met /plúmmət/ *vi* (**-met·ed, -met·ing, -mets**) **1. DROP DOWNWARD FAST** to drop steeply and suddenly downward ○ *plummeted into the ravine* **2. SUDDENLY DECREASE** to experience a sudden unexpected decrease in something such as value or price **3. SUDDENLY BECOME PESSIMISTIC** to decline suddenly, especially from a state of optimism to one of pessimism ■ *n* **1. SUDDEN DECREASE** a sudden unexpected decrease in something such as value or price **2.** CONSTR same as **plumb bob** [14C. < Old French *plomet* "small lead ball" < Latin *plumbum* "lead"]

plum·my /plúmmee/ (**-mi·er, -mi·est**) *adj* **1. RESEMBLING PLUMS** resembling, full of, or tasting like plums **2. RICH AND RESONANT** having a voice or tone that is rich, resonant, and mellow **3. DESIRABLE** highly desirable or of superior quality (*informal*)

plu·mose /plóo mòss/ *adj* ZOOL same as **plumate** [Mid-18C. < Latin *plumosus* < *pluma* "down, feather"] —**plu·mose·ly** *adv* —**plu·mos·i·ty** /ploo mόssətee/ *n*

plump[1] /plump/ *adj* **1. SLIGHTLY OVERWEIGHT** rounded and somewhat overweight (*sometimes considered offensive*) **2. WELL-FLESHED** having a pleasing amount of flesh ○ *a plump chicken* **3. FILLED WITH SOMETHING** rounded and filled with something ○ *a plump cushion* ■ *vti* (**plumped, plump·ing, plumps**) **FATTEN OR ROUND** to become fatter, rounder, or softer, or make something do this ○ *plump up the pillows* [15C. < Middle Dutch or Middle Low German *plomp* "blunt, thick"] —**plump·ly** *adv* —**plump·ness** *n*

plump[2] /plump/ *vti* (**plumped, plump·ing, plumps**) **DROP ABRUPTLY OR HEAVILY** to fall or come down heavily or suddenly, or cause somebody or something to do this ○ *plumped down into an armchair* ■ *n* **ABRUPT FALL OR ITS SOUND** a heavy or sudden fall, or its sound ■ *adv* **1. HEAVILY** in a sudden or heavy way **2. DIRECTLY** directly or in a direct line **3. BLUNTLY** in a blunt and direct way ■ *adj* **FORCEFULLY DIRECT** blunt, direct, and forceful [13C. Probably < Dutch *plompen* or Low German *plumpen* "to fall into water," an imitation of the sound]

plump for *vt* to suddenly choose or support somebody or something, often after hesitating ○ *The senator has decided to plump for new energy conservation measures.*

plum peach *n Southern US* a clingstone peach

REGIONAL NOTE The clingstone peach is also called *Indian peach, pickle peach*, and *press peach.* ***Plum peach*** is a South Midland term that covers the same territory occupied by *open peach* ("freestone peach"). Usage is strongest in the Eastern Gulf states, the upper sectors of Georgia, Alabama, and Mississippi, with equally strong incidence in Tennessee and Arkansas.

plump·er /plúmpər/ *n* a pad worn by an actor between the teeth and the inside of the cheeks to make the face seem fatter

plum pud·ding *n* a rich steamed pudding made from flour, suet, dried fruit, and spices that is often flavored with brandy or rum [< PLUM "raisin"]

plum to·ma·to *n* an elongated firm-textured tomato. Use: in cooking and for canned tomatoes. [< its shape]

plu·mule /plo͞om yo͞ol/ *n* **1.** the rudimentary primary shoot of a plant embryo **2.** a soft down feather of a young bird [Early 18C. < Latin *plumula* "small feather" < *pluma* "down, feather"]

plum·y /plo͞omee/ (**-i·er, -i·est**) *adj* **1.** like a feather or plume **2.** made of, covered with, or decorated with feathers or plumes

plun·der /plúndər/ *v* (**-dered, -der·ing, -ders**) **1.** *vti* ROB PLACE OR STEAL GOODS to rob a place or the people living there, or steal goods using violence and often causing damage, especially in wartime or during civil unrest ○ *gangs of looters plundering the electronics stores* **2.** *vt* ROB PLACE BY FRAUD to rob a place or steal goods or money by fraudulent means ○ *a military government that had steadily plundered the country's wealth* **3.** *vt* GET SOMETHING BY SUPERIOR STRENGTH to gain or acquire something by superior strength or skill ○ *They plundered five goals in a one-sided game.* ■ *n* **1.** STOLEN GOODS something stolen by force, especially during wartime or civil unrest **2.** ROBBERY the theft of goods by force or fraud [Mid-17C. Via German *plündern* or Low German *plünderen* < Middle Low German *plunder* "household goods"] —**plun·der·a·ble** *adj* —**plun·der·er** *n* —**plun·der·ous** *adj*

plunge /plunj/ *v* (**plunged, plung·ing, plung·es**) **1.** *vti* MOVE SUDDENLY DOWNWARD to move suddenly downward or forward, or move something in this way ○ *plunged into the undergrowth and disappeared* **2.** *vt* PUT SOMEBODY OR SOMETHING IN DIFFICULTIES to put somebody or something suddenly into an unpleasant or undesirable situation **3.** *vt* PUT SOMETHING QUICKLY INTO SOMETHING to put something quickly or firmly into something such as a liquid or container ○ *Drain the beans and plunge them into cold water.* **4.** *vi* BECOME INVOLVED ENTHUSIASTICALLY to become involved in something with great enthusiasm ○ *She plunged into student life.* **5.** *vi* EMBARK ON RECKLESS ACTION to begin a course of action suddenly and in a reckless or impetuous way ○ *warned against plunging into hostilities without trying diplomacy first* **6.** *vi* DESCEND PRECIPITOUSLY to descend abruptly or steeply ○ *The mountains plunged to the sea.* **7.** *vi* DROP SUDDENLY IN VALUE to drop suddenly and unexpectedly in value, price, or amount ○ *Prices plunged.* **8.** *vi* GAMBLE RECKLESSLY to gamble, speculate, or take risks in a reckless way (*informal*) ■ *n* **1.** ACT OF LEAPING INTO WATER a dive or leap into water ○ *a headlong plunge into the sea* **2.** SUDDEN DROP IN VALUE a sudden unexpected drop in value, price, or amount ○ *a 38% plunge in PC sales* **3.** *US* PLACE TO SWIM a place for swimming or diving, e.g., a swimming pool **4.** SUDDEN RUSH a sudden or violent rush ○ *The dog made a plunge for the open door.* **5.** RECKLESS GAMBLE a reckless gamble or speculation (*informal*) [14C. Via Old French *plongier* < assumed Vulgar Latin *plumbicare* "heave a sounding lead" < Latin *plumbum* "lead"] ◇ **take the plunge 1.** to commit suddenly to doing something new, difficult, or irrevocable **2.** to get married or decide to get married (*informal humorous*)

plunge pool *n* a small deep swimming pool used for cooling the body

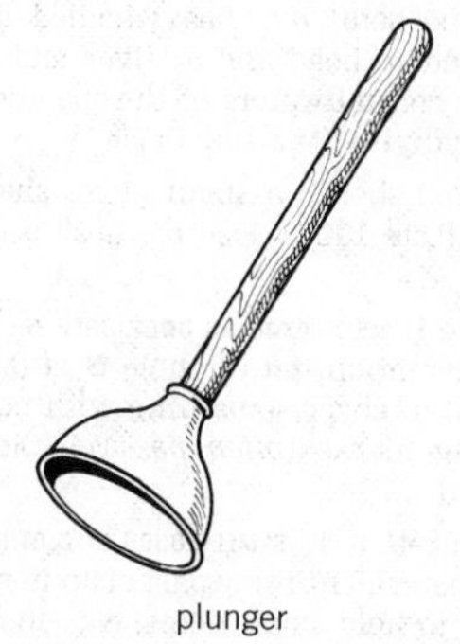

plunger

plung·er /plúnjər/ *n* **1.** TOOL FOR CLEARING DRAINS a tool for clearing clogged drains, consisting of a rubber suction cup attached to a long handle **2.** THRUSTING MACHINE PART a part of a machine that thrusts or drops downward, e.g., a piston **3.** GAMBLER somebody who gambles frequently and recklessly (*informal*)

plung·ing /plúnjing/ *adj* in a direction or at an angle that plunges downward

plunk /plungk/, **plonk** /plongk/ *vti* (**plunked, plunk·ing, plunks; plonked, plonk·ing, plonks**) **1.** PLUCK STRINGS to pluck the strings of a stringed instrument, especially in an inexpert or inexpressive way, or make the sound of a string being plucked **2.** DROP DOWN to drop, or cause something to drop, heavily or suddenly ○ *He plunked down on the nearest chair.* ■ *n* **1.** TWANGING SOUND a twanging sound, e.g., of a string on a stringed instrument being plucked, especially in an inexpert or inexpressive way **2.** SOUND OF HEAVY FALL the action or sound of a sudden heavy fall ○ *A stone hit the tin roof with a plunk.* **3.** *US* HARD BLOW a hard blow or hit (*informal*) ■ *adv US* **1.** WITH PLUNK with the action or sound of a sudden heavy fall **2.** EXACTLY precisely or exactly (*informal*) ○ *plunk in the middle* [Early 19C. An imitation of the sound]

plu·per·fect /ploo púrfikt/ *adj, n* GRAM same as **past perfect** ■ *adj* **1.** even better than perfect ○ *a pluperfect talent* **2.** extreme in degree (*informal*) ○ *a world leader who was a pluperfect tyrant* [15C. < Latin *plus quam perfectum* "more than perfect"]

plu·ral /plo͝orəl/ *adj* **1.** REFERRING TO MORE THAN ONE having a grammatical form that refers to more than one person or thing **2.** CONCERNING MORE THAN ONE concerning, involving, or made up of more than one person or thing ■ *n* **1.** PLURAL CATEGORY the plural number category **2.** GRAM PLURAL FORM OF WORD the plural form of a word ○ *What's the plural of mouse in the computer sense?* [14C. Via French < Latin *pluralis* < *plus* "more"] —**plu·ral·ly** *adv*

plu·ral·ism /plo͝orə lìzzəm/ *n* **1.** EXISTENCE OF DIFFERENT GROUPS WITHIN SOCIETY the existence of groups with different ethnic, religious, or political backgrounds within one society **2.** SOCIOL SOCIAL POLICY AND THEORY the policy or theory that minority groups within a society should maintain cultural differences, but share overall political and economic power **3.** CHR HOLDING OF MULTIPLE OFFICES the holding of more than one office or position by somebody, especially in a church **4.** PHILOSOPHY THEORY OF VARIOUS KINDS OF REALITY the philosophical theory that reality is made up of many kinds of being or substance **5.** STATE OF BEING PLURAL the state or condition of being plural —**plu·ral·ist** *n* —**plu·ral·is·tic** /plo͝orə lístik/ *adj* —**plu·ral·is·ti·cal·ly** *adv*

plu·ral·i·ty /plo͞o rállətee/ (*plural* **-ties**) *n* **1.** CONDITION OF BEING PLURAL the condition of being plural or numerous **2.** GREAT NUMBER OR PART OF SOMETHING a great number or part of something, particularly when this quantity represents more than half the whole **3.** MARGIN GAINED BY ELECTION CANDIDATE the number of votes that an election winner gets, or the number exceeding the nearest rival, when no one has more than 50 percent of the total votes cast **4.** CHR same as **pluralism** (sense 3)

plu·ral·ize /plo͝orə lìz/ (**-ized, -iz·ing, -iz·es**) *vti* to make something plural, or become plural —**plu·ral·i·za·tion** /plo͝orəli záysh'n/ *n* —**plu·ral·iz·er** *n*

plu·ral mar·riage *n* LAW same as **polygamy** (sense 1)

plus[1] /pluss/ *prep* USED FOR ADDING used to show that one number or amount is added to another ○ *The flight cost $480, plus tax.* ■ *adj* **1.** MATH RELATING TO ADDITION relating to, involving, or showing addition **2.** MATH WITH FIGURE ON POSITIVE SIDE having a figure or value on the positive side of a scale or axis (*often written as "+"*) **3.** ELEC ENG ON ELECTRICAL POSITIVE SIDE relating to, involving, or on the positive side of an electric circuit **4.** ADVANTAGEOUS favorable, desirable, or advantageous ○ *one of its plus points* **5.** SOMEWHAT MORE THAN PARTICULAR NUMBER somewhat higher than a particular number or amount ○ *earnings of $100,000 plus* **6.** SOMEWHAT MORE THAN SPECIFIC GRADE somewhat higher than a specific grade for academic work (*often written as "+"*) **7.** FUNGI REPRODUCING ONLY WITH OPPOSITE STRAIN reproducing as an alga or fungus only with an opposite strain ■ *n* (*plural* **plus·es** or **plus·ses**) **1.** MATH same as **plus sign 2.** POSITIVE QUANTITY a positive quantity or amount ○ *The figures show a plus.* **3.** ADVANTAGE something beneficial or advantageous (*informal*) ○ *Having her in the team is a real plus.* **4.** SURPLUS a surplus or excess ■ *conj* (*informal*) **1.** ⚠ AND and also ○ *Exports have been affected by cheap oil prices plus a strong dollar.* **2.** ⚠ FURTHERMORE furthermore or additionally ○ *I'm too busy, plus I'm short of cash.* [Mid-16C. < Latin, "more"]

USAGE Avoid using ***plus*** in formal contexts to introduce an independent clause: *He is the chair of the electrical engineering department, plus he has his own consulting firm.* Use instead: *As well as being the chair of the electrical engineering department, he has his own consulting firm.* ***Plus which*** should not be used to introduce any sentence or clause. Avoid: *She is the head coach of women's varsity soccer. Plus which, she is a physical education professor.* Use instead: *In addition to being the head coach of women's varsity soccer, she is a physical education professor.* In formal writing avoid using ***plus*** in place of *and* as a conjunction joining two subjects in a sentence: *Lack of practice and* [not *plus*] *a knee injury have caused her to drop out.* This use of ***plus*** as a conjunction is also contested syntactically. Some writers regard it as a preposition, in which case the verb *have caused* in the last sentence would switch from plural to the singular *has caused* with the single subject being *lack*.

plus[2] /pluss/ *suffix* and much more besides (*informal*) ○ *The show is entertainment-plus.*

plus fours *npl* baggy pants gathered and fastened just below the knee, worn mainly for sports or hunting ○ *golfers in their plus fours* [Because four inches longer in the leg than standard knickerbockers]

plush /plush/ *n* a rich smooth fabric with a long soft nap ■ *adj also* **plush·y** /plúshee/ luxurious, expensive, or lavish (*informal*) [Late 16C. < obsolete French *pluche* < Old French *peluchier* "to pluck" < Latin *pilus* "hair"] —**plush·ness** *n*

plus sign *n* the symbol "+," used to show addition or a positive quantity

plus-size *adj* of a size of clothing that is much larger than average ○ *our new range of plus-size fashions* ■ *n* an item of clothing that is much larger than average, especially an item of women's clothing

Plu·tarch /plo͞o taark/ (A.D. 46–120) Greek historian, biographer, and philosopher. His *Parallel Lives* was used by Shakespeare as a source for his history plays.

> "Caesar said to the soothsayer, 'The ides of March are come'; who answered him calmly, 'Yes, they are come, but they are not past.'"
>
> (Plutarch, "Life of Caesar," *Parallel Lives*; 1st-2nd century)

Plu·to /plo͞otō/ *n* **1.** the planet in the solar system that is the smallest in diameter and is, on average, the furthest away from the Sun **2.** in Roman mythology, the god of the underworld and husband of Proserpina. He was the god of the dead and also of riches, since precious metals and crops were believed to come from his underground realm. Greek equivalent **Hades** (sense 3) [Via Latin < Greek *Ploutōn* < *ploutos* "wealth"]

plu·toc·ra·cy /ploo tókrəssee/ (*plural* **-cies**) *n* **1.** GOVERNANCE BY WEALTHY the rule of a society by its wealthiest people **2.** SOCIETY RULED BY WEALTHY a society that is ruled by its wealthiest members **3.** WEALTHY RULING CLASS a wealthy social class that controls or greatly influences the government of a society [Mid-17C. < Greek *ploutokratia* < *ploutos* "wealth"] —**plu·to·crat** /plo͞otə kràt/ *n* —**plu·to·cra·tic** /plo͞otə kráttik/ *adj* —**plu·to·crat·i·cal·ly** *adv*

plu·ton /plo͞o tòn/ *n* a mass of intrusive igneous rock that has solidified underground by the crystallization of magma [Mid-20C. < German, back-formation < *plutonisch* "plutonic" < Greek *Ploutōn* (see PLUTO)] —**plu·ton·ic** /ploo tónnik/ *adj*

Plu·to·ni·an /ploo tṓnee ən/ *adj* **1.** relating to or characteristic of the planet Pluto **2.** relating to or characteristic of the Roman god Pluto [Mid-17C. < Greek *Ploutōn* (see PLUTO)]

plu·to·ni·um /ploo tṓnee əm/ *n* a highly toxic silvery radioactive metallic element. Source: uranium ore. Use: as plutonium-239, production of atomic energy and weapons. Symbol **Pu**. See table at **element** [Mid-20C. After the planet PLUTO, because it follows uranium and neptunium in the periodic table]

plu·vi·al /plo͞ovee əl/ *adj* **1.** RELATING TO RAIN relating to or caused by rain **2.** RAINY having or affected by much rain ■ *n* WET PERIOD a period of heavy rainfall [Mid-17C. < Latin *pluvialis* < *pluvia* "rain" < *pluere* "to rain"]

plu·vi·ous /plo͞ovee əss/, **plu·vi·ose** /plo͞ovee ōss/ *adj* relating to, involving, or typical of rain, especially heavy rainfall [15C. Via French < Latin *pluviosus* < *pluvia* "rain" (see PLUVIAL)]

ply[1] /plī/ **(plied, ply·ing, plies)** *v* **1.** *vti* WORK HARD AT SOMETHING to work at a trade or occupation, especially with diligence **2.** *vt* USE SOMETHING DILIGENTLY to use something such as a tool or weapon in a diligent or skillful way ○ *the dexterity with which she plied her needle* **3.** *vt* OFFER SOMETHING FOR SALE to offer goods or services for sale, especially regularly or as an occupation **4.** *vt* KEEP SUPPLYING SOMEBODY WITH SOMETHING to keep supplying somebody with something, especially in an insistent way ○ *kept plying us with offers of food* **5.** *vt* SUBJECT ANOTHER TO SOMETHING INSISTENTLY to keep subjecting somebody to something in an urgent and insistent way ○ *We were plied with questions.* **6.** *vti* TRAVEL ROUTE REGULARLY to travel a route regularly, especially on water **7.** *vi* SAILING ZIGZAG IN BOAT AGAINST WIND to sail a boat on a zigzag course against the wind [14C. Shortening of APPLY]

ply[2] /plī/ *n* (*plural* **plies**) (*often used in combination*) **1.** TWISTED STRAND a twisted single strand, especially of yarn or rope **2.** THIN LAYER OF SOMETHING a layer, sheet, or thickness of something such as wood or a tire ■ *vt* **(plied, ply·ing, plies)** TWIST OR FOLD SOMETHING TOGETHER to twist strands or fold layers together [14C. < Old French *pli* < *plier* "to fold, bend" < Latin *plicare*]

Plym·outh /plímməth/ **1.** port in Devon, southwestern England. Population: 240,720 (2001). **2.** town in southeastern Massachusetts, on Plymouth Bay, south of Duxbury. It was settled by the Pilgrims in 1620. Population: 53,789 (2002 estimate).

Plym·outh Breth·ren *n* a strict Protestant group founded in the United Kingdom in the late 1820s that has no organized ministry or formal creed and accepts the Bible as its sole guide [After PLYMOUTH, Devon, England]

Plym·outh Rock *n* a domestic hen with white or gray barred plumage, belonging to a US breed. After plymouth, Massachusetts. Raised for: eggs, meat.

ply·wood /plī wo͝od/ *n* board made by gluing and compressing thin layers of wood together with the grain of each layer at right angles to the layer next to it [Early 20C. < PLY[2]]

PLZ *abbr* ONLINE same as **PLS**

Pl·zeň /púl zèn/ capital city of Západoceky Region in the western part of the Czech Republic. Population: 168,422 (1999).

pm *abbr* **1.** TELECOM phase modulation **2.** MED postmortem **3.** ONLINE St.-Pierre and Miquelon (*used in Internet addresses*) See table at **domain name**

Pm *symbol* CHEM ELEM promethium

PM, **P.M.** *abbr* **1.** Past Master (*of a fraternity*) **2.** Postmaster **3.** POL Prime Minister **4.** ONLINE private message (*used in e-mails or text messages*) **5.** Provost Marshal

p.m.[1] *abbr* postmortem

p.m.[2], **P.M.** *adj, adv* between 12 noon and midnight. Full form **post meridiem**

P.M. *abbr* postmortem

P-mail /peé màyl/, **p·mail** *n* mail sent through the postal service

P.M.G. *abbr* **1.** Paymaster General **2.** Postmaster General **3.** Provost Marshal General

PMS *abbr* MED premenstrual syndrome

PMT *abbr UK* MED premenstrual tension

pn *abbr* ONLINE Pitcairn Island (*used in Internet addresses*) See table at **domain name**

PN, **P/N**, **p.n.** *abbr* FIN promissory note

PNdB *abbr* MEASURE perceived noise decibel

pneum- *prefix* same as **pneumo-** (*used before vowels*)

pneu·ma /no͞omə/ *n* in Stoicism, the vital spirit or soul [Late 19C. < Greek, "breath, spirit" < *pnein* "breathe"]

pneu·mat·ic /noo máttik/ *adj* **1.** USING COMPRESSED AIR operated by compressed air in a tool or machine **2.** FILLED WITH AIR filled with air, especially compressed air **3.** PHYS INVOLVING COMPRESSED GASES relating to, operated by, or typical of the pressure of compressed gases, especially air pressure or compressed air **4.** OF GASES OR WIND relating to or typical of air, gases, or wind **5.** RELIG OF SOUL relating to the soul or spirit **6.** BIRDS HAVING AIR-FILLED CAVITIES describes bird's bones that contain air-filled cavities **7.** FULL-BREASTED having large breasts (*informal; offensive in some contexts*) [Mid-17C. Via French and Latin < Greek *pneumatikos* < *pneuma* (see PNEUMA)] —**pneu·mat·i·cal·ly** *adv*

pneu·mat·ics /noo máttiks/ *n* the branch of physics dealing with the mechanical properties of air and other gases (*takes a singular verb*)

pneu·mat·ic tube *n* a tube through which letters and packets are propelled by compressed air

pneumato- *prefix* **1.** air, gas, vapor ○ *pneumatolysis* **2.** respiration, breathing ○ *pneumatophore* **3.** spirits, spiritual ○ *pneumatology* [< Greek *pneumat-*, stem of *pneuma* (see PNEUMA)]

pneu·ma·tol·o·gy /no͞omə tólləjee/ *n* **1.** the branch of Christian theology that deals with the Holy Spirit **2.** the study of spirits or spiritual beings —**pneu·ma·to·log·i·cal** /-tə lójjik'l/ *adj* —**pneu·ma·tol·o·gist** *n*

pneu·ma·tol·y·sis /no͞omə tólləssiss/ *n* the alteration caused in rocks by hot gases escaping from solidifying magma —**pneu·ma·to·lyt·ic** /no͞omətə líttik/ *adj*

pneu·mat·o·phore /noo máttə fàwr/ *n* **1.** a branch in swamp plants such as the mangrove or bald cypress that grows upward from the roots and carries out respiration **2.** a gas-filled sac that acts as a float in coelenterates such as the Portuguese man-of-war

pneu·mec·to·my /noo méktəmee/ (*plural* **-mies**) *n US* SURG same as **pneumonectomy**

pneumo- *prefix* **1.** air, gas **2.** lung, pulmonary ○ *pneumocystis* **3.** pneumonia ○ *pneumobacillus* **4.** respiration [< Greek *pneuma* "breath"]

pneu·mo·ba·cil·lus /no͞omōbə sílləss/ (*plural* **-li** /-lī/) *n* a Gram-negative bacterium that occurs in the respiratory tract and is one cause of pneumonia. Latin name: *Klebsiella pneumoniae.*

pneu·mo·coc·cus /no͞omə kókəss/ (*plural* **-coc·ci** /-kók sī/) *n* a Gram-positive bacterium that occurs in the respiratory tract and is one cause of pneumonia. Latin name: *Streptococcus pneumoniae.* —**pneu·mo·coc·cal** /-kók'l/ *adj*

pneu·mo·co·ni·o·sis /no͞omō kōnee ṓssiss/, **pneu·mon·o·co·ni·o·sis** /no͞omənə-/ *n* a disease of the lungs such as silicosis caused by inhaling mineral or metallic dust over a long period [Late 19C. < PNEUMO- + Greek *konis* "dust"]

pneu·mo·cys·tis /no͞omə sístiss/, **pneu·mo·cys·tis pneu·mo·nia** *n* a form of pneumonia that mainly affects people with weakened immune systems. It is caused by the microorganism *Pneumocystis carinii.*

pneu·mo·nec·to·my /no͞omə néktəmee/ (*plural* **-mies**) *n* the surgical removal of a lung [Late 19C. < Greek *pneumōn* "lung" (see PNEUMONIA)]

pneu·mo·nia /noo mṓnee ə/ *n* an inflammation of one or both lungs, usually caused by infection from a bacterium or virus or, less commonly, by a chemical or physical irritant [Early 17C. < modern Latin < Greek *pneumōn* "lung," alteration (influenced by *pneuma* "breath") of *pleumōn*]

pneu·mon·ic /noo mónnik/ *adj* **1.** relating to or affecting the lungs **2.** relating to, involving, or affected by pneumonia [Late 17C. Via French < Greek *pneumonikos* < *pneumōn* "lung" (see PNEUMONIA)]

pneu·mo·ni·tis /no͞omə nítiss/ *n* inflammation of the air sacs in the lungs, usually caused by a virus [Early 19C. < modern Latin < Greek *pneumōn* "lung" (see PNEUMONIA)]

pneu·mon·o·co·ni·o·sis *n* MED same as **pneumoconiosis**

pneu·mo·tho·rax /no͞omə tháw ràks/ *n* the presence of air or gas in the pleural cavity surrounding the lungs, causing pain and difficulty in breathing. Pneumothorax can occur spontaneously because of accidental rupture or perforation of the pleura, and in the past it was also a deliberate medical procedure in the treatment of tuberculosis.

~~pnuematic~~ incorrect spelling of **pneumatic**

~~pnuemonia~~ incorrect spelling of **pneumonia**

po *abbr* BASEBALL putout

Po[1] *symbol* CHEM ELEM polonium

Po[2] /pō/ longest river in Italy. It rises in the Alps near Italy's northwestern border and flows into the Adriatic Sea. Length: 405 mi./652 km.

PO, **P.O.** *abbr* **1.** NAVY Petty Officer **2.** AIR FORCE Pilot Officer **3.** postal order **4.** post office **5.** purchase order

p.o. *abbr* **1.** postal order **2.** BASEBALL putout

poach[1] /pōch/ **(poached, poach·ing, poach·es)** *v* **1.** *vti* CATCH GAME ILLEGALLY to catch wild animals or fish illegally on public land or while trespassing on private land **2.** *vti* ENCROACH ON SOMETHING to encroach on somebody's rights, territory, or sphere of operation in order to appropriate or remove another person or thing ○ *The rival company's sales force was poaching on our turf.* **3.** *vti* SPORTS PLAY SOMEBODY ELSE'S SHOT to play a shot that properly should be handled by a partner in badminton, tennis, squash, or handball **4.** *vti* MAKE GROUND MUDDY to become muddy, or make ground muddy by trampling it **5.** *vi* SINK INTO MUD to sink into soft earth or mud while walking across it [Early 17C. < Old French *pocher* "trample, trespass," probably < Germanic] —**poach·a·ble** *adj*

poach[2] /pōch/ **(poached, poach·ing, poach·es)** *vt* to cook something by simmering it in or over water or another liquid [15C. < Old French *pochier*, originally "enclose in a bag" < *poche* "bag"]

poach·er[1] /pṓchər/ *n* somebody who hunts or fishes illegally, usually while trespassing [Mid-17C. < POACH[1]]

poach·er[2] /pṓchər/ *n* a pan for poaching eggs that has a tightly fitting lid and small metal cups [Mid-19C. < POACH[2]]

PO Box, **P.O. Box** *abbr* Post Office Box

po'boy /pṓ bòy/ *n Southern US* a poor boy sandwich [Representing a pronunciation of POOR]

AKG London

Pocahontas: posthumous portrait (1666)

Po·ca·hon·tas /pòkə hóntəss/ (1595?–1617?) Powhatan princess. According to legend, she saved the life of colonist Captain John Smith (1608). Born **Matoaka**

Po·ca·tel·lo /pòkə téllō/ city in southeastern Idaho, east of American Falls Reservoir and southwest of Idaho Falls. Population: 51,242 (2002 estimate).

po·chard /pṓchərd/ *n* a heavy-bodied diving duck with a reddish head and a silver and black beak. Native to: coastal waters of Europe and Asia. Subfamily: Aythyini. [Mid-16C. Origin ?]

po·chette /pō shét/ *n* a small purse shaped like an envelope [Late 19C. < French, "small pouch" < *poche* "bag"]

pock /pok/ *n* **1.** MED same as **pockmark** *n* (sense 1) **2.** a small indentation, pit, or hole ■ *vt* **(pocked, pock·ing, pocks)** to cover something with pockmarks or disfiguring marks (*often passive*) [Old English *poc* < Germanic]

pock·et /pókət/ *n* **1.** SMALL POUCH IN CLOTHES a shaped piece of material forming part of an item of clothing and used to hold small items, e.g., inside pants or on the outside of a shirt **2.** SMALL FITTED POUCH a small fitted pouch, e.g., a pouch-shaped compartment on the inside of a bag ○ *The suitcase has several inside pockets.* **3.** SMALL POUCH a small pouch, bag, or purse **4.** PERSONAL MONEY somebody's personal financial resources ○ *a vacation paid for out of his own pocket* **5.** SMALL DIFFERENTIATED AREA a small area differentiated from neighboring areas by a particular feature ○ *pockets of wealth* **6.** CAVITY a type of cavity or opening **7.** ZOOL **SAC ON ANIMAL** a pouch-shaped sac on an animal's body **8.** GEOL **QUANTITY OF ORE IN CAVITY** the quantity of petroleum, natural gas, or mineral found in an underground cavity, or a cavity that contains such a substance **9.** SPORTS **BOXED-IN POSITION IN RACE** a position in a race in which a competitor is blocked by others **10.** CUE GAMES **POUCH ON PLAYING TABLE** a pouch or net at each corner and side of a billiard or pool table ○ *He sank the red in the side pocket.* **11.** FOOTBALL **AREA FOR A QUARTERBACK TO THROW** in football, a defended area behind the offensive line in which a quarterback can stand to throw the ball **12.** *US* BOWLING **SPACE SEPARATING 2 PINS** in bowling, a space between two pins, especially the head pin and one adjacent to it **13.** BASEBALL **CENTER OF BASEBALL GLOVE** the depression in the center of a baseball glove where the ball is caught **14.** AVIAT same as **air pocket** ■ *vt* (**-et·ed, -et·ing, -ets**) **1. PUT SOMETHING IN POCKET** to put something into a pocket ○ *She pocketed the change.* **2. TAKE SOMETHING DISHONESTLY** to appropriate something, often dishonestly ○ *They buy tickets cheaply, sell them for high prices, and pocket the difference.* **3.** CUE GAMES **HIT BALL INTO POCKET** to hit a ball into one of the pockets on a billiard or pool table ○ *pocket the black* **4. PUT UP WITH SOMETHING** to tolerate something unpleasant, especially an insult, without protesting or retaliating **5. SUPPRESS FEELING** to hide or suppress a feeling ○ *Pocket your pride and admit you were wrong.* **6. ENCLOSE OR SURROUND SOMEBODY OR SOMETHING** to enclose or hem in somebody or something **7.** *US* POL **RETAIN PIECE OF LEGISLATION** to retain a legislative bill without signing it, especially as a president, in order to stop it becoming approved by Congress ■ *adj* **1. SMALL ENOUGH TO CARRY IN POCKET** designed for carrying in a pocket ○ *a pocket flashlight* **2. SMALL** small, especially smaller than something larger of the same type ○ *a pocket trumpet* **3. CONTAINED** isolated and contained in small areas [15C. < Anglo-Norman *pokete* "small bag" < *poke* "bag"] —**pock·et·a·ble** *adj* ◇ **have deep pockets** to have large financial resources ○ *a price-cutting war which will be won by whoever has the deepest pockets* ◇ **in pocket** making a profit from something ◇ **in somebody's pocket 1.** fully under somebody's control **2.** almost certain to be won by somebody ○ *We thought she had the race in her pocket.* ◇ **line your pocket(s)** to profit at the expense of others ◇ **out of pocket** having lost money on something or spent money without benefit ◇ **pick somebody's pocket** to steal something from somebody's pocket without the person feeling or noticing

pock·et bat·tle·ship *n* a small but powerful and heavily armed battleship, especially one built by Germany in the 1930s to conform to limitations that were placed by treaty on size and armament

pock·et bil·liards *n* a form of billiards played with a cue ball and 15 balls on a felt-covered table with six pockets (*takes a singular or plural verb*)

pock·et·book /pókət bòòk/ *n* **1. SMALL CASE CARRIED IN POCKET** a small case or folder for money and documents, suitable for carrying in a pocket **2. PURSE** a purse or handbag **3. SOMEBODY'S FINANCES** somebody's financial resources **4. SMALL BOOK** a book small enough to be carried in a pocket

pock·et bor·ough *n* a political constituency in Great Britain before the Reform Act of 1832, whose representative in Parliament was determined by one landowner or landowning family [Because the landowner had the borough "in his pocket"]

pock·et e·di·tion *n UK* same as **pocketbook** (sense 4)

pock·et·ful /pókət fòòl/ *n* **1.** the amount of something that would fit in a pocket **2.** a large amount of something, especially money (*informal*)

pock·et go·pher *n* ZOOL same as **gopher** (sense 1)

pock·et·knife /pókət nīf/ (*plural* **-knives** /-nīvz/) *n US* a small knife with one or more blades that fold away into the handle. Can term **penknife**

pock·et mon·ey *n* **1.** a small amount of money that somebody carries for making minor purchases or to cover incidental expenses **2.** *UK* same as **allowance** *n* (sense 7)

pock·et mouse *n* a small nocturnal rodent with long hind legs, a long tail, and fur-lined cheek pouches for carrying food. Native to: deserts of western United States and Mexico. Genus: *Perognathus*.

pock·et park *n* a small park, usually located in an urban area

pock·et-sized, pock·et-size *adj* **1.** small enough or almost small enough to be carried in a pocket **2.** very small compared to other things of the same type

pock·et ve·to *n* **1.** a failure by the US president to return a bill passed by Congress during its last days in session, in order to prevent its being enacted **2.** *US* the holding of a bill by a state governor or other executive toward the end of a legislative session to prevent its enactment [< the idea of the executive's holding the bill in a coat pocket]

pock·et watch *n* a watch designed to be carried in a pocket, instead of being worn on the wrist

pock·mark /pók maark/ *n* (*often used in the plural*) **1. SMALL SCAR LEFT BY SKIN DISEASE** a small permanent circular scar on the skin, especially one left by smallpox, chickenpox, or acne **2. SMALL HOLLOW MARK** a small hollow mark disfiguring a surface ■ *vt* (**-marked, -mark·ing, -marks**) **1. COVER SKIN WITH POCKMARKS** to disfigure the skin with pockmarks **2. MAKE POCKMARKS IN SOMETHING** to make many small indentations or marks in the surface of something

po·co /pṓkō/ *adv* a little or slightly (*used in musical directions*) [Early 18C. < Italian, "little"]

po·co a po·co /-aa-/ *adv* little by little (*used in musical directions*) [< Italian, "little by little"]

po·co·cu·ran·te /pṑkō kòò rántee, -raantee/ (*literary*) *adj* uninterested, indifferent, or nonchalantly detached ■ *n* somebody who is uninterested, indifferent, or nonchalantly detached [Mid-18C. < Italian < *poco* "little" + *curare* "to care"] —**po·co·cu·ran·te·ism** *n* —**po·co·cu·ran·tism** *n*

Po·co·ma·ni·a /pṑkō máynee ə/ *n Carib* a religious group in Jamaica whose worship is characterized by singing, dancing, spirit-possession, speaking in tongues, and healing rituals [Mid-20C. Probably an alteration of an African term after Spanish *poco* "little" + MANIA]

Po·co·no Moun·tains /pṓkənō-/ range of forested mountains in northeastern Pennsylvania, reaching about 2,100 ft./640 m

po·co·sin /pə kṓssin/ *n S Atlantic US* a swamp in upland coastal regions of the southeastern United States, characterized by waterlogged soil and dense evergreen vegetation [Mid-17C. Probably < Virginia Algonquian *poquosin*]

pod[1] /pod/ *n* **1. SEED CASE** the long narrow outer case holding the seeds of a plant such as the pea, bean, or vanilla **2.** AEROSP **DETACHABLE COMPARTMENT OF SPACECRAFT** a specialized detachable compartment on a spacecraft, usually for carrying personnel or instruments **3.** AEROSP, NAVY **STREAMLINED HOUSING FOR EQUIPMENT** a streamlined housing attached to the wing or fuselage of an aircraft, or to the hull of a submarine, to carry fuel, an engine, weaponry, or other equipment **4.** ZOOL **PROTECTIVE EGG CASE** a protective case surrounding the eggs of some fishes and insects such as the grasshopper ■ *v* (**pod·ded, pod·ding, pods**) **1.** *vt* **SHELL PEAS** to strip peas out of their pod so that they can be eaten or cooked **2.** *vi* **PRODUCE PODS** to produce fruit in the form of pods **3.** *vi* **SWELL LIKE POD** to swell out, as a pod does [Late 17C. Origin ?]

pod[2] /pod/ *n* a small group of ocean animals, especially seals, whales, or dolphins [Mid-19C. Origin ?]

pod[3] /pod/ *n* **1.** a socket holding the bit in a boring tool **2.** a lengthwise channel in the barrel of a boring tool [Late 16C. Origin ?]

PO'd /pée ōd/, **p.o.'d** *adj* annoyed or irritated by somebody or something (*slang*) [Abbreviation of *pissed off*]

POD *abbr* Post Office Department

-pod *suffix* foot, part like a foot ○ *stomatopod* [< Greek *pod-* < Indo-European] —**-podous** *suffix*

po·dag·ra /pə dággrə/ *n* gout in the foot or the big toe [13C. Via Latin < Greek, "foot-trap" < *pod-* "foot" + *agra* "trap"] —**po·dag·ral** *adj* —**po·dag·ric** *adj* —**po·dag·rous** *adj*

Steve Podborski

Pod·bor·ski /pod báwrskee/, **Steve** (*b.* 1957) Canadian skier. He won eight World Cup events in downhill skiing between 1979 and 1982.

-pode *suffix* another spelling of **-pod**

po·des·ta /pō déstə, pṑde staa/ *n* in former times, a chief magistrate or governor of an Italian town, especially during the Middle Ages and Renaissance [Mid-16C. Via Italian < Latin *potestas* "power" < *potis* "powerful"]

podge /poj/ *n UK* **1.** same as **pudge** (sense 2) (*offensive insult*) **2.** same as **pudge** (sense 1) (*informal disapproving*) [Mid-19C. Probably back-formation < PODGY]

Pod·go·ri·ca /pódgo reetsə/ capital city of Montenegro, Federal Republic of Yugoslavia, situated about 12 mi./19 km north of Lake Shkoder. Population: 163,493 (1998).

podg·y /pójjee/ (**-i·er, -i·est**) *adj UK* same as **pudgy** [Mid-19C. Variant] —**podg·i·ly** *adv* —**podg·i·ness** *n*

po·di·a ARCHIT, FURNITURE plural of **podium**

po·di·a·try /pə dī ətree/ *n US* the profession concerned with the care of the feet and the treatment of foot disorders. Can term **chiropody** [Early 20C. < Greek *pod-* "foot"] —**po·di·at·ric** /pṑdee áttrik/ *adj* —**po·di·a·trist** *n*

po·di·um /pódee əm/ (*plural* **-di·ums** or **-di·a** /-dee ə/) *n* **1. SMALL RAISED PLATFORM** a small raised platform that the conductor of an orchestra, a lecturer, or somebody giving a speech can stand on **2.** ARCHIT, FURNITURE same as **lectern** (sense 2) **3. FOUNDATION WALL** a low wall forming a foundation or base, e.g., for a colonnade **4.** ARCHIT **WALL AROUND ARENA OF AMPHITHEATER** a low wall encircling the arena of an ancient amphitheater [Mid-18C. Via Latin < Greek *podion* "small foot" < *pod-* "foot"]

-podium *suffix* foot, part like a foot ○ *pseudopodium* [Via modern Latin < Greek *podion* (see PODIUM)]

pod·o·phyl·lin /pòddə fíllin/, **pod·o·phyl·lin res·in** *n* a greenish or brownish bitter resin. Source: root of the May apple. Use: removal of warts. [Mid-19C. < modern Latin *Podophyllum* < Greek *pod-* "foot" + *phullon* "leaf"]

pod·sol, etc. GEOG same as **podzol, etc.**

Po·dunk /pṓ dùngk/ *n US* a small, remote, and unimportant place (*informal*) ○ *She came from some Podunk town in the Midwest.* [Mid-19C. After a New England place name, < Algonquian]

pod·zol /pód zàwl/, **pod·sol** /pód sàwl/ *n* an infertile soil that forms in cool moist climates, usually under coniferous or mixed forests. The topsoil consists of leached clay under a layer of organic material. [Early 20C. < Russian < *pod-* "under" + *zol* "ash"] —**pod·zol·ic** /pod zóllik/ *adj*

pod·zol·i·za·tion /pòd zoli záysh'n/, **pod·sol·i·za·tion** /-soli-/ *n* the process whereby minerals are leached from the upper into the lower layers of a soil, leaving the topsoil acidic and infertile and forming a podzol —**pod·zol·ize** /pódzə līz/ *vti*

Poe /pō/, **Edgar Allan** (1809–49) US writer and critic. His poems, including "The Raven" (1845), and short stories, including "The Pit and the Pendulum" (1842), deal with the mysterious and the macabre. See Cultural note at **morgue, raven**[1]

"Once upon a midnight dreary, while I pondered, weak and weary, / Over many a quaint and curious volume of forgotten lore, / While I nodded, nearly napping, suddenly there came a tapping, / As of

American Antiquarian Society

Edgar Allan Poe

some one gently rapping, rapping at my chamber door."
[Edgar Allan Poe, "The Raven"; 1845]

POE, P.O.E. *abbr* port of entry

po·em /pṓ əm/ *n* **1. PIECE WRITTEN IN VERSE** a complete and self-contained piece of writing in verse that is set out in lines of a set length and uses rhythm, imagery, and often rhyme to achieve its effect **2. WRITING WITH POETIC EFFECT** a piece of writing that is not in verse, but that has the imaginative, rhythmic, or metaphorical qualities and the intensity usually associated with a poem **3. BEAUTIFUL OR DELIGHTFUL THING** something particularly lovely, beautiful, or delightful [15C. Directly or via French < Latin *poema* < Greek *poiēma* "making" < *poiein* "make"]

~~**poeple**~~ incorrect spelling of **people**

po·e·sy /pṓ əzee, -əssee/ (*plural* **-sies**) *n* **1.** poetry or poetic compositions in general, or a single piece of poetry (*archaic or literary*) **2.** the art or skill of writing poetry (*archaic*) [14C. Via French *poésie* and Latin *poesis* < Greek *poiēsis* "making" (see -POIESIS)]

po·et /pṓ ət/ *n* **1.** somebody who writes poems, especially as a vocation **2.** an imaginative, creative, or artistic person [13C. Via French *poète* and Latin *poeta* < Greek *poiētēs* "maker, author" < *poiein* "make"]

poet. *abbr* **1.** poetic **2.** poetical **3.** poetry

po·et·as·ter /pṓ ə tàstər/ *n* somebody who writes bad poetry (*literary*) [Late 16C. < modern Latin < Latin *poeta* (see POET)]

po·et·ic /pō éttik/, **po·et·i·cal** /-ik'l/ *adj* **1. RELATING TO POETRY** relating to, characteristic of, or in the form of poetry **2. RESEMBLING POETRY** having qualities usually associated with poetry, especially in being gracefully expressive, romantically beautiful, or elevated and uplifting **3. SENSITIVE OR INSIGHTFUL** characteristic of a poet, especially in possessing unusual sensitivity or insight, or in being able to express things in a beautiful or romantic way —**po·et·i·cal·i·ty** /pō ètti kálləteе/ *n* —**po·et·i·cal·ly** *adv* —**po·et·i·cal·ness** *n*

Po·et·ic Ed·da *n* LITERAT same as **Edda** (sense 1)

po·et·i·cize /pō étti sīz/ (**-cized, -ciz·ing, -ciz·es**) *vti* to express or describe something in a poetic style or in poetry

po·et·ic jus·tice *n* a situation in which somebody meets a fate that seems a fitting punishment or, less often, a fitting reward for his or her past actions

po·et·ic li·cense *n* deliberate misuse of or disregard for the normal rules of fact, style, or grammar by a writer or speaker in order to achieve a special effect

po·et·ics /pō éttiks/ *n* **1. BASIC PRINCIPLES OF POETRY** the literary or philosophical study of the basic principles, forms, and techniques of poetry, or of imaginative writing in general (*takes a singular verb*) **2.** (*plural same*) **TREATISE ON POETRY** a treatise on the nature or principles of poetry **3. WAY OF COMPOSING POEM** the art or technique of writing poetry (*takes a plural verb*)

po·et·ize /pṓ ə tīz/ *vti* LITERAT same as **poeticize**

po·et lau·re·ate (*plural* **po·ets lau·re·ate** or **po·et lau·re·ates**) *n* **1. BRITISH COURT POET** a poet who is appointed a member of the royal household for life by a British monarch and is expected to write poems celebrating great national or royal events **2. POETRY CONSULTANT TO THE LIBRARY OF CONGRESS** a poet appointed as a consultant to the Library of Congress for one year. The poet is required to give a poetry reading during the year. **3. EMINENT POET** a poet who is particularly honored for his or her work, or who is considered to be the most eminent poet in a particular country, state, or group

po·et·ry /pṓ ətree/ *n* **1. LITERATURE IN VERSE** literary works written in verse, in particular verse writing of high quality, great beauty, emotional sincerity or intensity, or profound insight **2. PARTICULAR POEMS CONSIDERED COLLECTIVELY** all the poems written by a particular poet, in a particular language or form, or on a particular subject ○ *a collection of love poetry* **3. WRITING OF POEMS** the art or skill of writing poems **4. PROSE LIKE POETRY** writing in prose that has a poetic quality **5. BEAUTY OR GRACE** something that resembles poetry in its beauty, rhythmic grace, or imaginative, elevated, or decorative style **6. POETIC QUALITY** a poetic or particularly beautiful or graceful quality in something [14C. < medieval Latin *poetria* < Latin *poeta* (see POET)]

po·e·try slam *n* a poetry-reading competition

po·gey /pṓgee/, **po·gy** *n Can* unemployment or any other welfare benefit provided by a government for the unemployed (*slang*) [Late 19C. Origin ?]

po·go·noph·o·ran /pṑgə nóffərən/, **po·gon·o·phore** /pə gónnə fàwr, pṓgənə-/ *n* an animal resembling a worm that has tentacles around the head area, lacks a digestive tract, and lives in vertical tubes in deep water. Phylum: Pogonophora. [Late 20C. < modern Latin *Pogonophora* < Greek *pōgōn* "beard" + *-phoros* "-bearing"] —**po·go·noph·o·ran** *adj*

po·go stick /pṓgō-/ *n* a strong metal pole with a spring at the bottom and two footrests to stand on, used to jump up and down or hop along on for play or exercise [Early 20C. Origin ?]

po·grom /pə gróm, pṓgrəm/ *n* a planned campaign of persecution or extermination sanctioned by a government and directed against an ethnic group, especially against the Jews in tsarist Russia [Early 20C. < Russian, "devastation" < *gromit* "wreak havoc" < *grom* "thunder"]

pogue /pōg/ *n* (*slang insult*) **1.** an offensive term for somebody regarded as a coward or sissy **2.** an offensive term for a member of the armed forces employed in a rear echelon support capacity

po·gy[1] /pṓgee/ (*plural* **-gies** or *same*) *n* FISH same as **menhaden** [Mid-19C. Probably < Algonquian *pauhaugen*]

po·gy[2] /pṓgi/ *n Can* SOC WELFARE another spelling of **pogey** (*slang*)

poi /poy/ *n* a Hawaiian dish made from the root of the taro, cooked, pounded to a paste, and fermented [Early 19C. < Hawaiian]

-poiesis *suffix* creation, formation, production ○ *erythropoiesis* [< Greek *poiēsis* < *poiein* "make"]

poign·ant /póynyənt/ *adj* **1. CAUSING SADNESS OR PITY** causing a sharp sense of sadness, pity, or regret **2. SHARPLY PERCEPTIVE** particularly penetrating and effective or relevant (*literary*) **3. SHARPLY PAINFUL** causing acute physical pain (*literary*) **4. STRONG SMELLING OR TASTING** having an often pleasurably strong sharp smell or taste (*archaic*) [14C. < French, present participle of *poindre* "to prick" < Latin *pungere* "to prick, sting"] —**poign·ance** *n* —**poign·an·cy** *n* —**poign·ant·ly** *adv*

SYNONYMS See *moving*.

poi·kil·o·cyte /poy kíllə sīt/ *n* an unusually shaped red blood cell [Late 19C. < Greek *poikilos* "spotted, varied, irregular"]

poi·kil·o·therm /poy kíllə thùrm/ *n* an organism such as a reptile, amphibian, insect, or fish that has a body temperature that varies according to the temperature of the local atmosphere

poi·ki·lo·ther·mic /pòykilō thúrmik/, **poi·ki·lo·ther·mal** /-thúrm'l/, **poi·ki·lo·ther·mous** /-thúrməss/ *adj* having a body temperature that varies according to the temperature of the local atmosphere. Reptiles, amphibians, insects, and fish are all poikilothermic. [Late 19C. < Greek *poikilos* "spotted, varied, irregular"] —**poi·ki·lo·ther·mism** *n* —**poi·ki·lo·therm·y** *n*

poi·lu /pwaa lóō/ *n* a soldier in the French infantry, especially during World War I [Early 20C. < French, "hairy" < *poil* "hair" < Latin *pilus*]

poin·ci·an·a /pòynssee ánnə, -áanə/ (*plural* **-as** or *same*) *n* a tree grown for its large reddish orange flowers. Native to: tropical regions. Genera: *Caesalpinia* or *Delonix*. [Mid-18C. < modern Latin, after M. de Poinci, 17C governor of the Antilles]

poinsettia

poin·set·ti·a /poyn séttee ə, -séttə/ (*plural* **-as** or *same*) *n* a bush with bright red bracts resembling petals, popular as a houseplant. Native to: Central America. Latin name: *Euphorbia pulcherrima*. [Mid-19C. After Joel R. *Poinsett* (1775–1851), US botanist]

point /poynt/ *n* **1. OPINION, IDEA, OR FACT** an opinion, idea, or fact put forward in the course of or forming a main element of a discussion or argument ○ *She made many valid points in her report.* **2. UNDERLYING ESSENTIAL IDEA** the essential idea conveyed or intended in something that is said or written ○ *He seems to have missed the point entirely.* **3. PURPOSE** the purpose or usefulness of something ○ *Is there really any point in continuing?* **4. ITEM IN LIST OR PLAN** an item or detail in something such as a plan, contract, or list ○ *a four-point plan to revive the coal industry* ○ *a point-by-point examination of the contract* **5. CONVINCING ARGUMENT OR VIEWPOINT** a cogent or persuasive argument or observation ○ *You have to admit that she has a point there.* **6. QUALITY OR FEATURE** a distinguishing quality, feature, or item in the makeup of somebody or something ○ *Generosity is one of her good points.* **7. PHYSICAL FEATURE OF LIVESTOCK ANIMAL** an external feature that is assessed when judging the overall shape of a livestock animal, e.g., the face or fetlock **8. LOCATION** a specific place or position ○ *a point six miles east of here* **9. MOMENT** an individual moment in time ○ *At that point, the door opened and the teacher walked in.* **10. PARTICULAR STAGE IN PROCESS** a particular moment or stage in a process, especially one at which a significant change or development occurs or a condition is reached ○ *We have reached the point at which a decision will have to be made.* **11. LEVEL OR DEGREE** a level or degree of a quality ○ *He was confident to the point of almost being arrogant.* **12. TIME JUST BEFORE SOMETHING HAPPENS** the moment or period of time just before something happens ○ *at the point of death* **13. SHARP END OF SOMETHING** the sharp narrowed end of something such as a needle, pencil, or weapon **14. END OR TIP** the end or tip of something such as a finger or the projecting angle of something such as the elbow or chin **15. SMALL PROJECTION** a small sharp or perceptible projection, e.g., in a piece of writing in Braille **16. ACT OF POINTING** the act of pointing, e.g., with a finger **17. DOT** a small dot or source of something such as color or light **18. UNIT ON SCALE** a single unit on a scale of measurement ○ *The earthquake measured 6 points on the Richter scale.* ○ *opened up a 10-point lead over her opponent in the polls* **19.** SPORTS, LEISURE **UNIT USED IN SCORING** a unit used in scoring a sport, game, or competition, or as a means of making a quantitative evaluation of something **20.** MUSIC **TIP OF BOW** the tip of the bow of a stringed instrument **21.** ZOOL **ANTLER PRONG** a prong on a deer's antlers **22.** GEOG **HEADLAND** a prominent headland on the coast that juts out into the sea, often the projecting tip of a peninsula (*often used in place names*) **23.** MATH **DECIMAL POINT** the dot separating the whole number and fraction in a decimal number. The term "point" is used particularly when such numbers are spoken aloud. ○ *five point nine* **24.** MATH **DIMENSIONLESS GEOMETRIC ELEMENT** a dimensionless geometric element whose location in space is defined solely by its coordinates. Geometric figures such as circles, planes, or spheres can be treated as if they are sets of points. **25.** GRAM, PRIN-

TING **PUNCTUATION MARK** in printing or writing, a punctuation mark, especially a period **26.** PHON same as **vowel point** **27.** FIN **INVESTMENT PRICE UNIT** a unit used to measure change in the value of an investment, e.g., on a stock exchange ○ *The market is up 5 points.* **28.** *US* FIN **PERCENTAGE OF LOAN** an amount equivalent to one per cent of the value of a loan, used to calculate the sum that the borrower pays to the lender as a service charge **29.** *US* LAW **PENALTY UNIT FOR MOTORIST** a penalty unit given for a driving offense recorded on somebody's driving record. Receiving a set number of points leads automatically to a penalty. **30.** *US* EDUC **UNIT OF CREDIT FOR STUDENT** a unit of academic credit for a student that is equivalent to one hour of class work per week over a period of one semester **31.** *US* EDUC **GRADING UNIT** a unit, equivalent to a letter grade, that is used to assess a student's academic performance. Four is the highest grade. **32.** CARDS **UNIT OF WINNING POTENTIAL** a unit used in assessing the strength of a hand in bridge **33.** PRINTING, MEASURE **PRINTING UNIT OF MEASUREMENT** a unit of measurement in printing equal to one twelfth of a pica or approximately 0.01384 in./0.03515 cm **34.** MEASURE **DIAMOND WEIGHT UNIT** a unit of weight for a diamond equivalent to one hundredth of a metric carat **35.** COMPASS **MARK ON COMPASS** one of the 32 direction indicators marked on a compass, e.g., west, west by north, west-northwest, or northwest **36.** COMPASS **ANGLE BETWEEN ADJACENT BEARINGS** the angle between any two adjacent bearings marked on a compass, measuring 11° 15' **37.** MIL **UNIT AHEAD OF FORMATION** a person or unit that moves ahead of a larger formation, acting as a scout and advance guard **38.** MIL **ADVANCE MILITARY POSITION** the position ahead of a larger formation taken by a person or unit acting as point **39.** BASKETBALL **OFFENSIVE POSITION** in basketball, the position in front court taken by the guard who directs the offensive **40.** HERALDRY **DIVISION OF HERALDIC SHIELD** a position on or division of a heraldic shield in which a charge can be placed ■ **points** *npl* **1.** AUTOMOT **ELECTRICAL CONTACTS IN DISTRIBUTOR** the two electrical contacts that act as circuit breakers in the distributor of an internal-combustion engine as current is passed in turn to the cylinders **2.** ZOOL **EXTREMITIES OF DOMESTIC ANIMAL** the ears, feet, and tail of a domestic animal ■ *v* (**point·ed, point·ing, points**) **1.** *vi* **INDICATE WITH EXTENDED FINGER** to extend the finger or a long thin object in the direction of something in order to draw attention to it ○ *I pointed to one of the shrubs and asked its cost.* **2.** *vt* **AIM AT SOMETHING** to hold an object so that its end is aimed at somebody or something ○ *pointed the hose at the flowers* **3.** *vi* **BE TURNED IN PARTICULAR DIRECTION** to be turned toward or aimed in a particular direction ○ *The arrow on the signpost was pointing to the right.* **4.** *vt* **DIRECT SOMEBODY TOWARD SOMETHING** to indicate the direction in which somebody should go ○ *If you can just point me in the right direction I should be able to find it.* **5.** *vti* COMPUT **AIM MOUSE OR JOYSTICK** to move a mouse, joystick, or other device so that the cursor on a computer screen is positioned over or touching something ○ *Point at the icon, then double click on it.* **6.** *vi* **SUGGEST SOMETHING IS CASE** to be strong evidence of something or lead the mind to believe or conclude something ○ *It all points to one conclusion.* **7.** *vi* **CALL ATTENTION TO SOMETHING** to call attention to a fact or situation as being important **8.** *vt* **GIVE FORCE TO REMARK** to give additional force, emphasis, or incisiveness to something said or written **9.** *vt* **SHARPEN SOMETHING** to sharpen something so that it has a point at the end **10.** *vt* **STRETCH FOOT DOWNWARD** especially in ballet, to stretch out the foot or toes so that leg and foot make one comparatively straight line **11.** *vt* CONSTR **REPAIR SOMETHING WITH MORTAR** to repair or finish a wall, chimney, or other structural component by putting mortar or cement between the bricks or stones **12.** *vti* SAILING **SAIL BOAT CLOSE TO WIND** to sail or sail a boat close to the wind **13.** *vti* HUNTING **POINT MUZZLE AT GAME** to perform the characteristic function of a hunting dog by standing still with muzzle and tail outstretched, indicating the whereabouts of game **14.** *vt* MUSIC **MARK PSALM FOR CHANTING** to mark a psalm to indicate how it is to be chanted **15.** *vt* PHON **ADD MARKS OVER LETTERS** to place diacritics or vowel points over the relevant letters in a text **16.** *vt* GRAM **PUNCTUATE TEXT** to put punctuation marks into a text **17.** *vi* MED **COME TO HEAD** to reach the stage of spontaneous rupture or surgical opening, allowing pus to drain (*refers to boils and abscesses*) [13C. Via French < Latin *punctum* "prick-mark, dot, particle" < past participle of Latin *pungere* "prick, pierce"] ◇ **a sore point** a cause of annoyance ◇ **be on the point of doing something** to be just about to do something ○ *I was just on the point of leaving.* ◇ **beside the point** irrelevant or unimportant ◇ **in point of fact** used, often when correcting something said before, to emphasize that what is now being stated represents the truth ◇ **make a point of doing something** to be careful to do something and, often, to be seen by others to do it ◇ **not to put too fine a point on it** used to indicate that somebody is being frank or blunt about something ◇ **stretch a point 1.** to make an exception to a rule **2.** to exaggerate ◇ **stretch the point** to exaggerate ◇ **to the point** relevant or worth paying attention to ◇ **(up) to a point** to some extent, but not completely

point out *vt* **1.** to point at or otherwise indicate somebody or something so that somebody will look at that person or thing ○ *Our guide pointed out the most interesting architectural features of the building.* **2.** to tell somebody about or draw somebody's attention to something ○ *She did point out some of the difficulties we might expect to face.*

point up *vt* to emphasize or draw particular attention to something

point-and-click *adj* describes an interface that allows a user to interact with a computer by using a mouse to move a cursor on the computer screen and clicking the mouse button ○ *a point-and-click adventure game*

point-and-shoot *adj* describes a camera that requires no adjustment by the user before taking a photograph, because the focus and exposure are adjusted automatically or are fixed

point bar *n* a sand or gravel ridge formed in a series by the flowing water of a meandering river

point-blank *adv* **1.** **AT CLOSE RANGE** at or from very close range when firing or shooting **2.** **OUTRIGHT** directly or bluntly and without further explanation ○ *told them point-blank what I thought of them* ■ *adj* **1.** **FIRED AT CLOSE RANGE** fired straight and from so close to the target that no adjustment to the aim is necessary for the drop in the bullet's trajectory ○ *point-blank shot* **2.** **CLOSE TO TARGET** very close to the target when shooting ○ *at point-blank range* **3.** **OUTRIGHT** direct and blunt ○ *a point-blank refusal* [Origin ?]

point con·tact *n* contact between a slender wire filament and the surface of a semiconductor so as to form a junction converting alternating current and direct current

point de·fect *n* an imperfection in the lattice structure of a crystal

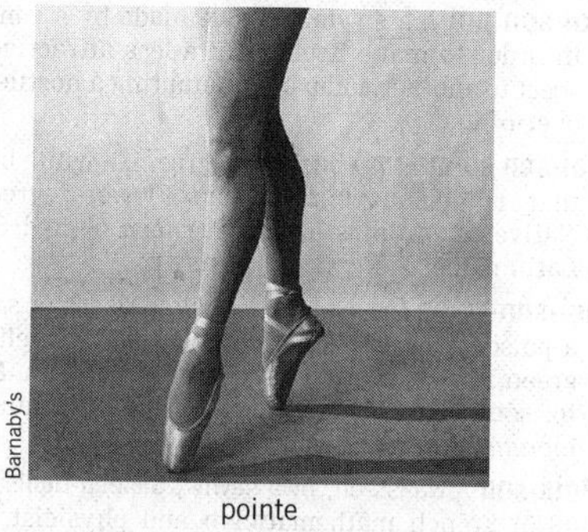

Barnaby's

pointe

pointe /pwaaNt/ *n* the ends of the toes, a position on which a ballerina wearing special shoes raises herself up for some moves and positions while performing [Mid-19C. < French, "point"]

point·ed /póyntəd/ *adj* **1.** **ENDING IN POINT** ending in a point or sharp angle **2.** **MADE WITH EMPHASIS** made with emphasis and carrying an unmistakable message, often a criticism **3.** **CONSPICUOUS** made intentionally obvious or noticeable —**point·ed·ness** *n*

point·ed arch *n* ARCHIT same as **lancet arch**

point·ed·ly /póyntədlee/ *adv* in a deliberate or emphatic way and with no attempt at tact or subtlety ○ *They pointedly ignored me.*

Pointe-Noire /pwaáNt nwaár/ city in the Republic of Congo, and the country's main port. Population: 576,206 (1995).

point·er /póyntər/ *n* **1.** **CANE USED FOR POINTING** a stick or cane used, especially by a teacher or lecturer, to point something out, e.g., on a chart or large map **2.** **INDICATOR ON MEASURING DEVICE** a needle that moves around on a measuring instrument to point to part of a dial **3.** **HELPFUL HINT** a piece of advice or information given to help somebody achieve something or do something the right way ○ *My coach gave me a few pointers on how to hold the racket.* **4.** **SIGN INDICATING SITUATION** a sign of what is happening or what might happen in the future **5.** **HUNTING DOG** a hunting dog, usually with a shorthaired white coat with colored patches, belonging to a breed trained to indicate the whereabouts of shot game by standing still with the muzzle and tail outstretched **6.** COMPUT **ARROW ON COMPUTER SCREEN** an arrow or other symbol on a computer screen that shows the current position of the mouse or other pointing device. The symbol may change shape depending on the task being performed. **7.** COMPUT **COMPUTER MEMORY ADDRESS** an address, stored as data in a computer's memory, that is the location where specific data is stored ■ **point·ers, Point·ers** *npl* **GUIDE STARS IN BIG DIPPER CONSTELLATION** the two bright stars in the Big Dipper constellation forming the side of the quadrilateral farthest from the handle and used as a guide to find Polaris

pointe shoe *n* BALLET same as **toe shoe**

point guard *n* in basketball, the guard who is mainly responsible for directing a team's offensive play

poin·til·lism /pwaántee ìzzəm, póynt'l ìzzəm/ *n* **1.** a late 19th-century style of painting in which a picture is constructed from dots of pure color that blend, at a distance, into recognizable shapes and various color tones. Pointillism developed out of impressionism and its best-known exponent is the French painter Georges Seurat. **2.** a technique of musical composition using sparse isolated notes in widely varying registers [Early 20C. < French *pointillisme*, via *pointiller* "mark with dots" < Latin *punctum* "dot"] —**poin·til·list** *n, adj* —**poin·til·lis·tic** /pwaántee ístik, pòynt'l ístik/ *adj*

point·ing de·vice *n* an input device used to manipulate a cursor or pointer on a computer display, e.g., a mouse, trackball, or joystick

point lace *n* lace made with a needle instead of bobbins [< POINT in the sense "prick, stitch"]

point·less /póyntləss/ *adj* **1.** having no purpose, use, or sense, or any positive or beneficial effect ○ *It's pointless even attempting to make sense of it.* **2.** in sports, having or scoring no points —**point·less·ly** *adv* —**point·less·ness** *n*

point man *n* **1.** the lead soldier in a military formation or patrol **2.** somebody, especially a man, who is in the forefront of an activity or endeavor

point mu·ta·tion *n* a mutation that involves a change in a single base or base pair of the nucleotides in a gene, occurring as a result of addition, deletion, or substitution

point of ac·cu·mu·la·tion *n* MATH same as **limit point**

point of de·par·ture *n* a starting point for something

point of hon·or *n* something that a sense of honor, self-respect, or pride obliges somebody to do

point of in·flec·tion *n* *UK* same as **inflection point**

point of no re·turn *n* **1.** the time or stage in a process beyond which it becomes impossible to stop or discontinue it **2.** the point in an aircraft's flight after which there will be insufficient fuel left to enable it to return to its starting point

point of or·der *n* a question raised by one of the participants in a formal debate or meeting that relates to the rules of procedure governing it, in particular as to whether those rules are being breached

point of pres·ence *n* a location where a user can connect to a network, e.g., a place where subscribers can dial in to an Internet service provider

point of ref·er·ence *n* something to which somebody can refer in order to check direction or progress, as a guide to action or conduct, or as an aid to understanding or communication

point-of-sale *adj* located, used, or occurring at the place where a product is sold ○ *a point-of-sale display* —**point of sale** *n*

point of view *n* **1. PERSPECTIVE SOMEBODY BRINGS** somebody's way of thinking about or approaching a subject, as shaped by his or her own character, experience, mindset, and history **2. OPINION** somebody's personal opinion on a subject **3. PARTICULAR PERSPECTIVE ON SUBJECT** an aspect from which a subject may be considered or judged **4.** LITERAT **ANGLE OF NARRATOR** the perspective on events of the narrator or a character in a story **5. POSITION OF OBSERVER** the position or angle from which somebody observes an event or scene

point per·son *n* somebody who is in the forefront of any activity or endeavor

point source *n* a source of something such as radiant energy or pollution that is or appears to be very small

point-to-point *n* a horse race in which horses regularly used in hunting are raced over a marked cross-country course that includes various jumps and obstacles ■ *adj* from one place to another —**point-to-point·er** *n* —**point-to-point·ing** *n*

Point-to-Point Pro·to·col *n* a protocol for dial-up access to the Internet using a modem

point wom·an *n* a woman who is in the forefront of any activity or endeavor

point·y /póyntee/ (**-i·er, -i·est**) *adj* ending in a point

point·y-head·ed *adj* regarded as intelligent or intellectual in an arrogant or impractical way (*slang*)

poise[1] /poyz/ *n* **1. COMPOSURE** calm self-assured dignity, especially in dealing with social situations **2. CONTROLLED GRACE IN MOVEMENT** a graceful controlled way of standing, moving, or performing an action **3. EQUILIBRIUM** a stable state of balance **4. SUSPENDED STATE** a state of hovering or being in suspension (*literary*) ■ *vti* (**poised, pois·ing, pois·es**) **BALANCE** to be balanced or suspended, or place or hold something in balance or suspension [14C. The noun is via Old French *pois* "weight, balance"; the verb via *peser* "weigh," both ultimately < Latin *pensare* (see PENSIVE)]

poise[2] /poyz/ *n* the centimeter-gram-second unit of viscosity equal to one dyne-second per square centimeter [Early 20C. After J. L. M. *Poiseuille* (1799–1868), French physiologist]

poised /poyzd/ *adj* **1. READY TO ACT** fully prepared or in position and about to do something ○ *We are now poised to take over the company.* **2. READY TO MOVE** motionless and balanced or suspended in the air, often just before or in the midst of an action ○ *a bird poised on a branch* **3. COMPOSED** calm, self-assured, and dignified **4. IN DANGER OF SOMETHING** teetering on the edge of a sudden change ○ *stock prices seemingly poised to rise*

~~**poisen**~~ incorrect spelling of **poison**

poi·sha /póyshə/ *n* a subunit of currency in Bangladesh. See table at **currency** [Late 20C. < Bangla, alteration of PAISA]

poi·son /póyz'n/ *n* **1. TOXIC SUBSTANCE** a substance that causes illness, injury, or death if taken into the body or produced within the body **2. NEGATIVE INFLUENCE** something that exercises a powerful destructive or corrupting force, especially in an insidious way **3.** CHEM **REACTION-INHIBITING SUBSTANCE** a substance that inhibits a chemical reaction or diminishes the activity of a catalyst **4.** PHYS **SUBSTANCE SLOWING NUCLEAR REACTION** a substance in a nuclear reactor that can absorb neutrons without undergoing fission and therefore slows down the reaction ■ *vt* (**-soned, -son·ing, -sons**) **1. GIVE POISON TO SOMEBODY** to administer poison to a person or animal, especially with malicious intention **2. HARM SOMEBODY WITH TOXIC SUBSTANCE** to cause illness, injury, or death to somebody with a poison or other harmful chemical substance **3. ADD POISON TO SOMETHING** to put poison into or onto something in order to harm or kill a person or animal ○ *poisoned bait used to kill rats* **4. POLLUTE ENVIRONMENT** to pollute water, land, or air severely with a harmful substance **5. CORRUPT OR UNDERMINE SOMEBODY OR SOMETHING** to have an evil or corrupting influence on somebody or something, especially by planting hostility or suspicion in somebody's mind against another person **6. SPOIL SITUATION** to spoil something that should be pleasant, enjoyable, or friendly **7.** CHEM **INHIBIT CHEMICAL REACTION** to inhibit a chemical reaction or activity **8.** PHYS **SLOW DOWN NUCLEAR REACTION** to slow down or stop a nuclear reaction by the addition of a substance that can absorb neutrons without undergoing fission [13C. Via Old French < Latin *potion-* < *potare* "to drink"] —**poi·son·er** *n* ◇ **what's your poison?, name your poison** used to ask what somebody would like to drink (*informal humorous*)

poi·son dog·wood *n* TREES same as **poison sumac**

poi·son el·der *n* TREES same as **poison sumac**

poi·son gas *n* a lethal or incapacitating gas used as a weapon in warfare

poi·son hem·lock *n* US a highly poisonous plant with spotted stems, delicately divided leaves, and flat-topped clusters of white flowers. Native to: Europe. Latin name: *Conium maculatum*.

poison ivy

poi·son i·vy *n* **1. VINE CAUSING ITCHING RASH** a climbing vine of the cashew family that has three-part leaves and white berries. Contact with the plant produces an itchy rash. Flowers: small, green. Native to: North America. Genus: *Rhus*. **2. PLANT RELATED TO POISON IVY** a plant related to poison ivy, e.g., poison oak **3. RASH FROM POISON IVY** a rash produced by poison ivy

poi·son oak *n* **1.** a plant similar or related to poison ivy that produces a rash on contact with the skin. Native to: North America. Genus: *Rhus*. **2.** a rash produced by poison oak

poi·son·ous /póyz'nəss/ *adj* **1.** containing, producing, or acting as a poison **2.** filled with or creating malice, distrust, or hostility —**poi·son·ous·ly** *adv* —**poi·son·ous·ness** *n*

poi·son-pen let·ter *n* a letter containing unpleasant or abusive comments that is sent anonymously to somebody

poi·son pill *n* a strategic move made by a company in order to make itself seem a less attractive prospect to another company attempting a hostile takeover of it

poi·son su·mac *n* a bush with greenish white berries that is poisonous to touch. Flowers: greenish. Native to: swamps of southeastern United States. Latin name: *Toxicodendron vernix*.

poi·son·wood /póyz'n wòod/ (*plural* **-woods** or *same*) *n* a poisonous tree with compound leaves, yellowish green flowers, and yellowish orange fruits. Native to: southern Florida, Caribbean. Latin name: *Metopium toxiferum*.

Pois·son /pwaáss on, pwa sáwN/, **Siméon-Denis** (1781–1840) French mathematician and physicist. He is noted for his work on electricity, magnetism, elasticity, and for the Poisson distribution in statistics.

> "Life is good for only two things, discovering mathematics and teaching mathematics."
> [Siméon-Denis Poisson. Quoted in *Mathematics Magazine*; February 1991]

Pois·son dis·tri·bu·tion *n* a probability distribution that represents the number of random events occurring over a fixed period of time

Poi·ti·er /pwaátee ay/, **Sidney** (*b.* 1924) US actor and director. He was the first African American Hollywood movie star. He won an Academy Award for his role in *Lilies of the Field* (1963).

Poi·tiers /pwaa tyáy/ city in west central France. It is the capital of Vienne Department in Poitou-Charente Region. Population: 83,448 (1999).

poke[1] /pōk/ *v* (**poked, pok·ing, pokes**) **1.** *vti* **PROD SOMEBODY OR SOMETHING WITH SOMETHING** to push the point of something such as an outstretched finger, elbow, or a stick against somebody or something else **2.** *vt* **MAKE HOLE IN SOMETHING** to make a hole or opening in something by pushing at it with a finger or a sharp object **3.** *vt* **PUSH SOMETHING INTO HOLE** to push a finger or a long thin object into a hole, space, or opening **4.** *vti* **PROTRUDE FROM SOMETHING** to stick out of or through an opening, surface, or covering in such a way that part of the object is visible, or make something stick out in this way ○ *One foot was poking out from under the covers.* **5.** *vi* **SEARCH HAPHAZARDLY** to search or investigate in a haphazard or aimless manner ○ *poking around in a second-hand bookstore* **6.** *vi* **MEDDLE** to pry or intrude into something, or meddle with something ○ *Stop poking around in my affairs.* **7.** *vt* **STIR FIRE** to stir a fire with a poker or similar object in order to make it burn better **8.** *vt* **PUNCH SOMEBODY** to hit somebody with a fist (*informal*) **9.** *vi* **GO SLOWLY** to move around or do things in a slow unhurried way ■ *n* **1. PROD** a push or prod with a finger, elbow, stick, or similar pointed object **2. HAPHAZARD SEARCH** a haphazard or aimless search or investigation **3. PUNCH** a blow delivered with the fist (*informal*) **4.** US same as **slowpoke** (*informal*) [13C. Origin ?]

poke[2] /pōk/ *n regional* a small bag or sack [13C. < Old N French variant of Old French *poche* "bag"]

poke[3] *n* PLANTS same as **pokeweed** [Mid-17C. < Virginia Algonquian *poughkone*]

poke·ber·ry /pók bèrree/ *n* **1.** (*plural* **poke·ber·ries**) the juicy blackish berry that grows on a pokeweed plant **2.** (*plural same* or **poke·ber·ries**) PLANTS same as **pokeweed**

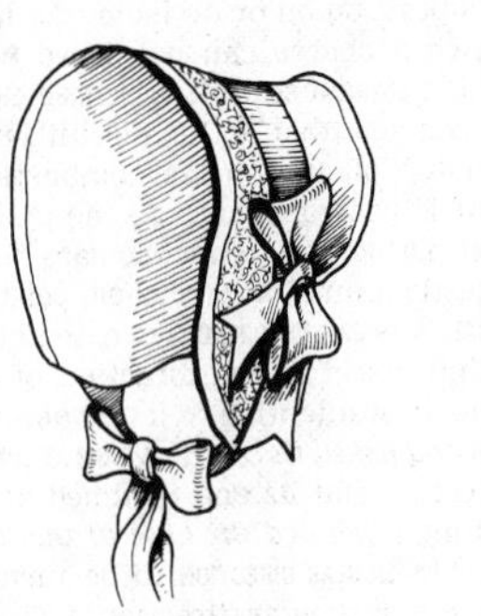

poke bonnet

poke bon·net *n* a woman's bonnet with a deep projecting rim, fashionable in the first half of the 19th century [< POKE[2]]

pok·er[1] /pókər/ *n* a card game in which players attempt to acquire a winning combination of cards and bet at every deal [Mid-19C. Origin ?]

pok·er[2] /pókər/ *n* **1.** a metal rod for stirring a fire to make it burn better **2.** somebody or something that pokes, or something used for poking [Mid-16C. < POKE[1]]

pok·er face *n* a face showing no expression and revealing nothing about what somebody is thinking or feeling [< POKER[1]] —**pok·er-faced** *adj*

poke·weed /pók weèd/ (*plural same* or **-weeds**) *n* a tall plant with blackish berries in elongated clusters, edible shoots, and a poisonous root. Flowers: white. Native to: North America. Latin name: *Phytolacca americana*. [Mid-18C. < POKE[3]]

poke·y[1] /pókee/ *adj* another spelling of **poky**[1] (*informal*)

po·key[2] /pókee/ (*plural* **-keys** or **-kies**), **po·ky** (*plural* **-kies**) *n* a jail (*slang*) [Early 20C. Origin ?]

pok·y[1] /pókee/ (**-i·er, -i·est**), **pok·ey** *adj* (*informal*) **1.** annoyingly slow **2.** US shabby and old-fashioned [Mid-19C. < POKE[1]] —**pok·i·ly** *adv* —**pok·i·ness** *n*

pok·y[2] /pókee/ *n* US CRIME another spelling of **pokey**[2] (*slang*)

pol /pol/ *n* a politician (*informal*) [Mid-20C. Shortening]

pol. *abbr* **1.** political **2.** politics

Po·lack /pṓ lăk/ *n* a highly offensive term for a Polish person or somebody of Polish descent (*taboo*) [Late 16C. Directly or via French < Polish *Polak*]

Poland

Po·land /pṓlənd/ country in eastern Europe, bordering on the Baltic Sea. It became a member of the European Union in 2004. Language: Polish. Currency: zloty. Capital: Warsaw. Population: 38,622,660 (2003). Area: 120,728 sq. mi./312,684 sq. km. Official name **Republic of Poland**

Po·land Chi·na *n* a large black hog with white markings, belonging to a breed developed in North America

po·lar /pṓlər/ *adj* **1. OF OR NEAR EARTH'S POLES** relating to, located at, or found in the regions surrounding the North or South Pole **2.** PHYS **OF POLE OR POLES** relating to a pole or poles of a rotating body, a magnet, or an electrically charged object **3.** AEROSP **PASSING OVER POLES OF PLANET** passing over, or traveling in an orbit that passes over, a planet's poles ○ *polar orbit* **4. UTTERLY UNLIKE** opposite in tendency, character, or opinions **5. PIVOTAL** of pivotal or central importance **6. GUIDING** serving as a guide or giving direction (*literary*) **7.** CHEM **HAVING DIPOLE** having a permanent dipole, or having molecules with permanent dipoles ○ *polar molecule* **8.** CRYSTALS **HAVING IONIC BOND** having an ionic bond, or having crystals with ionic bonds ○ *polar crystal* **9.** MATH **IN POLAR COORDINATE SYSTEM** relating to or measured with reference to a system of polar coordinates

po·lar ax·is *n* the fixed horizontal line in a system of polar coordinates from which the angle made by the radius vector is measured

polar bear

po·lar bear *n* a large white mainly meat-eating bear that has wide front feet for swimming. Native to: Arctic coasts and ice floes. Latin name: *Ursus maritimus.*

po·lar bod·y *n* a cell with a nucleus but little cytoplasm that is produced along with an oocyte, and later discarded, in the process of cell division that leads to an ovum

po·lar cap *n* **1.** the area around either the North Pole or South Pole that is permanently covered in ice **2.** either of the two polar regions on Mars that are permanently covered with frozen carbon dioxide and water

po·lar cir·cle *n* either of the lines of latitude that define the Arctic and Antarctic regions, 66°33' N and 66°33' S

po·lar co·or·di·nates *npl* the two coordinates that locate a point in a plane by specifying the length of a radius vector and the angle it makes with a horizontal line (**polar axis**)

po·lar front *n* a weather front separating cold polar air and warmer air

po·lar·im·e·ter /pōlə rímmətər/ *n* an instrument used to measure the rotation of the plane of polarization of light as it passes through a substance, especially a liquid or solution. It is an important tool in the analysis of sugar solutions. [Mid-19C. < modern Latin *polaris* "polar"] —**po·lar·i·met·ric** /pōləri méttrik/ *adj* —**po·lar·im·e·try** *n*

Po·lar·is /pə lárriss/ *n* **1.** the brightest star of the Little Dipper in the constellation Ursa Minor, near the celestial north pole. Because it always indicates due north from an observer anywhere on the Earth, Polaris is important for navigation. See illustration at **constellation 2.** a US intermediate-range ballistic missile that usually carries a nuclear warhead and is launched from a submarine

po·lar·i·scope /pō lárrə skōp/ *n* an instrument used to study either a substance exposed to polarized light or the effects of a substance on polarized light [Early 19C. < modern Latin *polaris* "polar"]

po·lar·i·ty /pō lárrətee/ (*plural* **-ties**) *n* **1.** a situation in which two people or groups have qualities, ideas, or principles that are diametrically opposed to each other **2.** the condition, in a system, of having opposite characteristics at different points, especially with respect to electric charge or magnetic properties

po·lar·ize /pṓlə rīz/ (**-ized, -iz·ing, -iz·es**) *vti* **1. CAUSE DIVISION OF OPINION** to make the differences between groups or ideas ever more clear-cut and extreme, hardening the opposition between them, or become ever more clear-cut and extreme in this way **2.** PHYS **ACQUIRE OR MAKE SOMETHING ACQUIRE POLARITY** to acquire polarity, or cause something to acquire polarity **3.** PHYS **RESTRICT VIBRATION OF LIGHT** to cause light to vibrate within particular planes, or vibrate in this way —**po·lar·iz·a·ble** *adj*—**po·lar·i·za·tion** /pōləri záysh'n/ *n*—**po·lar·iz·er** *n*

po·lar·iz·ing mi·cro·scope /pṓlə rīzing-/ *n* a microscope in which polarized light is used to examine specimens

po·lar nu·cle·us *n* either of the two nuclei in the center of the sac of a seed plant embryo that eventually fuse into the endosperm

po·lar·og·ra·phy /pōlə róggrəfee/ *n* an analytic technique used to study ions in a solution that compares the strength of electric currents passing through the solution during electrolysis and the voltages needed to produce them [Mid-20C. < *polarization*] —**po·lar·o·graph·ic** /pōlərə gráffik/ *adj*

Po·lar·oid /pṓlə ròyd/ *tdmk* **1.** a trademark for a camera that produces pictures that develop within seconds of being taken, or the film used in such a camera **2.** a trademark for a specially treated transparent plastic that allows polarized light through and is used to reduce glare in sunglasses

po·lar star *n* ASTRON same as **Polaris** (sense 1)

pol·der /pṓldər/ *n* an area of land reclaimed from the sea and protected by dikes, especially in the Netherlands [Early 17C. < Dutch] —**pol·der** *vt*

pole[1] /pōl/ *n* **1. NORTH OR SOUTH POLE** either of the two points on the Earth, the North and South Poles, that are the endpoints of its axis of rotation, are farthest from the equator, and are surrounded by icecaps **2. ENDPOINT OF SPHERE AXIS** either of the two endpoints of the axis of rotation of a sphere, planet, or other astronomical object **3.** ASTRON same as **celestial pole 4. EITHER OF TWO OPPOSITES** either of two completely opposed or contrasted positions, states, or views ○ *They're at opposite poles as far as their taste in music is concerned.* **5.** PHYS **END OF MAGNET** either of the two ends of a magnet or magnetized body, where the lines of force are most concentrated **6.** ELEC **POSITIVE OR NEGATIVE TERMINAL** either of two terminals in something such as a battery, generator, or motor that have opposite electric charges **7.** PHYSIOL **DISTINCT REGION IN CELL** either of two opposite regions that are physiologically or functionally distinct in an organism, cell, or structure, e.g., the opposite ends of the spindle structure formed in the nucleus of a cell during cell division **8.** MATH **ORIGIN OF POLAR COORDINATES** the origin in a polar coordinate system **9. REFERENCE POINT** a fixed point of reference (*literary*) [14C. Via Latin < Greek *polos* "axis"] ◇ **be poles apart** to be as different or as opposed as it is possible to be

SPELLCHECK pole or **poll**? Do not confuse the spelling of ***pole*** and ***poll***, which sound similar. A ***pole*** is a long straight piece of wood, metal, etc. (as in *a ski pole, the pole vault*) or either of two opposite regions of the Earth, a magnet, etc. (as in *the South Pole, be poles apart*). ***Poll*** is a noun or verb referring to an election or survey, as in *going to the polls, an opinion poll.*

pole[2] /pōl/ *n* **1. LONG STRAIGHT OBJECT** a long straight strong piece of wood, metal, or other material, usually with a round cross-section and thin enough to hold in the hands or arms **2. POLE-VAULTER'S POLE** the long flexible shaft made of wood, metal, or fiberglass used by a competitor in the pole vault **3. SHAFT ON HORSE-DRAWN VEHICLE** a single shaft projecting forward from the front of a vehicle between the animals that draw it, to which those animals are hitched **4.** *US* HORSERACING, MOTOR SPORTS **RACETRACK STARTING POSITION OR LANE** the inside lane or the inside starting position on a racetrack **5.** MOTOR SPORTS same as **pole position** (sense 2) **6.** MEASURE same as **perch[1]** *n* (senses 5–6) ■ *v* (**poled, pol·ing, poles**) **1.** *vti* **PROPEL BOAT WITH POLE** to move a boat along by pushing with a pole against a firm surface **2.** *vt* **SUPPORT PLANT WITH POLE** to use a pole to provide support for a plant **3.** *vti* **USE SKI POLES** to make forward progress on skis by pushing with ski poles [Old English *pāl*, via Germanic < Latin *palus* "stake"]

USAGE See ***pole***[1].

Pole /pōl/ *n* **1.** somebody who comes from Poland **2.** somebody who is of Polish descent [Late 16C. Via German < Old Polish *Polanie* "field-dwellers" < *pole* "field"]

pole·ax /pṓ làks/ *n* **1. BUTCHER'S AX** a specialized ax with a hammer face opposite the blade, used, especially in former times, for slaughtering animals **2. BATTLE-AX** a battle-ax with a long or short handle, especially one with a hammer or spike opposite the ax blade **3. AX FOR CUTTING RIGGING** a short-handled ax used to cut rigging or ropes on sailing ships, especially during combat ■ *vt* (**-axed, -ax·ing, -ax·es**) **1. AMAZE AND STUPEFY SOMEBODY** to leave somebody stupefied and speechless with astonishment **2. HIT SOMEBODY VERY HARD** to hit somebody hard enough to cause unconsciousness **3. HIT SOMEBODY OR SOMETHING WITH POLEAX** to hit somebody or something with a poleax [14C. Alteration of *pollax* "head-axe" < POLL]

pole·axe *n, vt* Can, UK spelling of **poleax**

pole bean *n* a climbing green bean that is grown supported on a pole

polecat

pole·cat /pṓl kàt/ *n* **1.** a woodland animal related to but larger than the weasel that has brown fur and emits a foul smell when disturbed. Native to: Europe, Asia, North Africa. Genus: *Mustela* or *Vormela.* **2.** ZOOL same as **skunk** [14C. Origin ?]

pole danc·er *n* an entertainer who dances around a pole in an erotic way in a bar or club —**pole danc·ing** *n*

po·leis ANCIENT HIST, POL plural of **polis**

pole jump *n US* TRACK AND FIELD same as **pole vault** —**pole-jump** *vti* —**pole-jump·er** *n*

po·lem·ic /pə lémmik/ *n* **1. PASSIONATE ARGUMENT** a passionate, strongly worded, and often controversial argument against or, less often, in favor of somebody or something **2. PASSIONATE CRITIC** somebody who engages in a passionate dispute about or argues passionately against somebody or something (*literary*) ■ *adj also* **po·lem·i·cal** CONTAINING PASSIONATE ARGUMENT containing or expressing passionate and strongly worded argument against or in favor of somebody or something [Mid-17C. Via medieval Latin < Greek *polemikos* < *polemos* "war"] —**po·lem·i·cal·ly** *adv*—**po·lem·i·cist** *n*

po·lem·ics /pə lémmiks/ *n* the art or practice of arguing passionately and strongly for or against something (*takes a singular verb*)

po·len·ta /pō léntə/ *n* in Italian cooking, fine yellow cornmeal cooked to a mush with water or stock, sometimes set, sliced, and served baked or fried [Mid-16C. Via Italian < Latin, "barley meal"]

pole po·si·tion *n* **1.** *US* HORSERACING, MOTOR SPORTS same as **pole**[2] *n* (sense 4) **2.** the best position on the starting grid of an automobile race, usually on the inside of the front row and taken by the driver with the fastest prerace practice time **3.** a very good or advantageous position at the beginning of something

pol·er /pṓlər/ *n* somebody who uses a pole to move a boat along [Late 17C. < POLE[2]]

pole·star /pṓl staar/ *n* something considered as a guiding light and giver of direction (*literary*)

Pole Star *n UK* ASTRON same as **Polaris** (sense 1)

Po·les'ye /pṓ lez yə/ ➧ **Pripet Marshes**

pole vault *n* **1.** a track-and-field event in which the competitors use a long flexible pole to swing themselves up and over a very high crossbar **2.** a jump in the pole vault, or any jump made with the help of a pole —**pole-vault** *vti* —**pole-vault·er** *n*

po·lice /pə léess/ *n* **1.** ORGANIZATION FOR MAINTAINING LAW AND ORDER a civil organization whose members are given special legal powers by the government and whose task is to maintain public order and to solve and prevent crimes ○ *a police car* **2.** SPECIALIZED FORCE an organized group of people whose job is maintaining order, ensuring that regulations are obeyed, and preventing crime within a particular area or sphere of activity ○ *military police* **3.** POLICE OFFICERS police officers considered as a group (*takes a plural verb*) **4.** PEOPLE ENFORCING CORRECT BEHAVIOR a group of people who seek to make others' opinions or behavior conform with their own (*informal*) ○ *fashion police* **5.** *US* MIL CLEANLINESS AND ORDER IN MILITARY the work of keeping a military base clean and orderly, or its state of cleanliness and order **6.** ENFORCEMENT OF LAW the enforcement of law and the prevention of crime in a community (*archaic*) ■ *vt* (**-liced, -lic·ing, -lic·es**) **1.** MAINTAIN LAW AND ORDER AT SOMETHING to ensure that law and order are maintained at an event or location, using the police or a military force **2.** ENSURE SOMETHING PROCEEDS ACCORDING TO RULES to ensure that rules and procedures are followed correctly in something, or that something is implemented as agreed **3.** *US* MIL CLEAN MILITARY BASE to keep a military base clean and orderly [15C. Via French and Latin < Greek *politeia* "civil organization, the state" < *politēs* "citizen" (see POLITIC)]

po·lice ac·tion *n* a relatively small-scale military action undertaken without a declaration of war, e.g., to prevent violation of an international agreement

po·lice dog *n* **1.** a dog trained to work with the police in tracking or searching for people, or in detecting illegal substances by smell **2.** BREED same as **German shepherd**

po·lice force *n* an organized body of police with jurisdiction within a geographic area or over a group of people

po·lice·man /pə léessmən/ (*plural* **-men** /-mən/) *n* a man who is a police officer

Po·lice Mo·tu /pə léess mṓtoo/ *n* LANG same as **Hiri Motu**

po·lice of·fi·cer, po·lice·per·son /pə léess pùrss'n/ (*plural* **-per·sons** or **-peo·ple** /-pèep'l/) *n* a member of a police force

po·lice pow·er *n US* the power of a government to impose what it considers reasonable restrictions on the liberties of its citizens for the maintenance of public order and safety

po·lice pro·ce·dur·al *n* a crime novel or drama in which the crime is investigated by police officers

po·lice re·port·er *n US* a journalist who is assigned to cover news about crime and police work

po·lice state *n* a country in which the government uses police, especially secret police, to exercise strict or repressive control over the population

po·lice sta·tion *n* the local headquarters of a police force

po·lice·wom·an /pə léess wòommən/ (*plural* **-wom·en** /-wìmmin/) *n* a woman who is a police officer

pol·i·cy[1] /póllәssee/ (*plural* **-cies**) *n* **1.** a program of actions adopted by a person, group, or government, or the set of principles on which they are based **2.** shrewdness or prudence, especially in the pursuit of a course of action [14C. Via Old French *policie* "government, civil organization" < Greek *politeia* (see POLICE)]

pol·i·cy[2] /póllәssee/ (*plural* **-cies**) *n* **1.** a contract that exists between an insurance company and a person or organization buying insurance services, or the document that lists the contract terms **2.** *US* a game of chance, e.g., a daily lottery, where participants bet on what the number will be [Mid-16C. Via French < Provençal *polissa*, Catalan *police*]

pol·i·cy·hol·der /póllәssee hṑldər/ *n* a named person or organization that has bought an insurance policy

pol·i·cy·mak·ing /póllәssee màyking/ *n* the drawing up of policies, especially the formulating of political policies by members of a government —**pol·i·cy·mak·er** *n* —**pol·i·cy·mak·ing** *adj*

pol·i·cy sci·ence *n* the study of how policies are made and executed in governments and bureaucracies

po·li·o /pṓlee ō/ *n* MED same as **poliomyelitis** [Mid-20C. Shortening]

po·li·o·my·e·li·tis /pṓlee ō mī ə lítiss/ *n* a severe infectious viral disease, usually affecting children or young adults, that inflames the brainstem and spinal cord, sometimes leading to loss of voluntary movement and muscular wasting [Late 19C. < modern Latin < Greek *polios* "gray"; because it affects "gray matter"] —**po·li·o·my·e·lit·ic** /-mī ə líttik/ *adj*

po·li·o·vi·rus /pṓlee ō vīrəss/ *n* one of three forms of a virus that causes poliomyelitis

po·lis /póliss/ (*plural* **po·leis** /pṓ lìss/) *n* **1.** a city-state in ancient Greece, characteristic of Greek political organization from 800 to 400 B.C. **2.** the city-state form of government [Late 19C. < Greek, "city"]

pol·ish /póllish/ *v* (**-ished, -ish·ing, -ish·es**) **1.** *vti* MAKE SMOOTH OR GLOSSY to make something smooth or shiny, or become smooth or shiny, by rubbing with something **2.** *vt* REMOVE OUTER LAYERS OF RICE to remove the outer layers of brown rice to make white rice by rotating the grain in a drum **3.** *vti* IMPROVE to make something more refined, elegant, or complete, or become more refined, elegant, or complete ○ *polish a speech* ■ *n* **1.** SUBSTANCE USED FOR POLISHING a substance used to make something smooth or shiny ○ *furniture polish* **2.** SMOOTHNESS the smoothness or glossiness of something that has been polished ○ *car paintwork with a high polish* **3.** RUB GIVEN TO SOMETHING a rubbing of something designed to make it smooth or glossy **4.** REFINEMENT refinement, especially of style, that is the mark of expertise or experience [13C. < Old French *poliss-*, stem of *polir* < Latin *polire*] —**pol·ish·er** *n*

polish off *vt* **1.** to finish something, especially food or a task, quickly and completely **2.** to kill or eliminate somebody (*informal*)

polish up *vt* **1.** to make something smooth or shiny by rubbing it **2.** to improve or refine something such as a prepared speech or knowledge of a foreign language

polish up on *vt* to improve knowledge or skill in a subject

Po·lish /pṓlish/ *npl* PEOPLE OF POLAND the people of Poland ■ *n* OFFICIAL LANGUAGE OF POLAND the official language of Poland, also spoken in North America and Europe, belonging to the Balto-Slavic branch of Indo-European. Native speakers: 44 million. See panel on next page ■ *adj* OF POLAND relating to Poland, or its people, language, or culture [Early 17C. < POLE]

Po·lish no·ta·tion *n* a notation for symbolic logic where the logical operators are placed as prefixes in front of formulas instead of between them, allowing parentheses to be dispensed with. For example, "p or (q and r)" becomes "or p and q r." [Because developed by mathematicians in Poland]

Pol·it·bu·ro /póllit byòorō/ *n* the executive and policymaking committee of a governing Communist Party, especially the committee in the former Soviet Union [Early 20C. < Russian *politbyuro* "political bureau"]

po·lite /pə lít/ (**-lit·er, -lit·est**) *adj* **1.** showing or possessing good manners or common courtesy **2.** socially superior to ordinary people and considered refined or cultivated [15C. < Latin *politus*, past participle of *polire* "polish"] —**po·lite·ly** *adv* —**po·lite·ness** *n*

pol·i·tesse /pòllee téss/ *n* politeness of a very formal or genteel kind [Early 18C. < French, "politeness"]

pol·i·tic /póllətik/ *adj* possessing or displaying shrewdness, tact, or cunning [15C. Via French and Latin < Greek *politikos* "civic, political" < *politēs* "citizen" < *polis* "city"] —**pol·i·tic·ly** *adv*

po·lit·i·cal /pə líttik'l/ *adj* **1.** CONCERNED WITH PARTY POLITICS relating to politics, especially party politics **2.** CONCERNED WITH GOVERNMENT relating to civil administration or government **3.** RESULTING FROM BELIEFS UNACCEPTABLE TO GOVERNMENT arising from somebody's opposition to a government or support for policies and principles regarded by the authorities as unacceptable, or suffering as a result of expressing such opposition or support ○ *a political trial* ○ *a political detainee* **4.** INTERESTED IN POLITICS particularly interested or active in politics ○ *I'm not usually a very political person.* **5.** CONCERNED WITH POWER relating to the balance of power in relationships, especially in a group or organization ○ *a political workplace* **6.** PRAGMATIC carried out for reasons that best serve a desired outcome rather than for other reasons such as being morally justifiable ○ *denies that this was a political decision* —**po·lit·i·cal·ly** *adv*

po·lit·i·cal ac·tion com·mit·tee *n US* a group that seeks to advance its interests by raising money to contribute to a political candidate or campaign

po·lit·i·cal e·con·o·my *n* the study of ways in which economics and government policies interact (*dated*) —**po·lit·i·cal e·con·o·mist** *n*

po·lit·i·cal·ly cor·rect *adj* relating to or supporting the use of language or conduct that deliberately avoids giving offense, e.g., on the basis of ethnic origin or sexual orientation —**po·lit·i·cal cor·rect·ness** *n*

po·lit·i·cal·ly in·cor·rect *adj* relating to or tolerant of the use of language or conduct that could give offense, e.g., on the basis of ethnic origin or sexual orientation —**po·lit·i·cal in·cor·rect·ness** *n*

po·lit·i·cal pris·on·er *n* somebody who is imprisoned because of his or her political actions or beliefs

po·lit·i·cal sci·ence *n* the study of political organizations and institutions, especially governments —**po·lit·i·cal sci·en·tist** *n*

po·lit·i·cal the·a·ter *n* dramatic performances designed to advance or promote a political cause

pol·i·ti·cian /pòllə tísh'n/ *n* **1.** SOMEBODY ACTIVE IN POLITICS somebody who actively or professionally engages in politics **2.** GOVERNMENT MEMBER a member of a branch of government **3.** *US* SOMEBODY SEEKING PERSONAL POWER somebody whose main political motive is self-advancement and whose methods are often unscrupulous (*disapproving*) **4.** SCHEMER somebody who manipulates relationships, especially in a workplace [Late 16C. < POLITIC]

po·lit·i·cize /pə lítti sīz/ (**-cized, -ciz·ing, -ciz·es**) *v* **1.** *vti* to bring something such as an issue of public interest into the political arena ○ *Educational policy has definitely become more politicized.* **2.** *vt* to make somebody politically aware or active, or introduce a political element to something —**po·lit·i·ci·za·tion** /-littissi záysh'n/ *n*

pol·i·tick·ing /póllə tiking/ *n* political activity, especially campaigning or speechmaking

po·lit·i·co /pə líttikō/ (*plural* **-cos**) *n* a politician, especially one whose words are dismissed as trite or whose motives are disapproved of as self-serving (*informal*) [Mid-17C. < Italian or Spanish, "politician"]

LANGUAGE HERITAGE ***Polish*** Much of English is made up of words from other languages, and Polish is a contributor in this respect, though less often directly than through other languages, especially Yiddish. Polish words have been transmitted through Yiddish to give us, for example, ***yarmulke*** (the small round cap worn by some Jewish men and boys), ***schmatte*** (an informal word for a rag or worthless thing), ***schav*** (a chilled soup), ***chachka*** ("inexpensive trinket or souvenir"), and the slang word ***nudge*** ("annoy somebody in a persistent or pestering way"), all these adopted into English during the course of the 20th century. Other 20th-century borrowings, this time directly from Polish, include ***kielbasa*** (a spicy smoked sausage), ***rendzina*** (a type of dark, rich soil), ***ogonek*** (a mark under vowels that usually indicates nasalization), and ***zloty*** (the unit of currency, literally in Polish "golden"). Polish *Solidarność*, the name of a federation of trade unions in Poland founded in 1980 that became famous for challenging the Soviet-backed government, was translated into English as ***Solidarity***.

19th-century borrowings from Polish include the dessert the rum ***baba***, which came through French from a Polish word meaning "married peasant woman," the dances ***mazurka*** and ***polka***, and ***britzka***, a type of horse-drawn carriage. Even earlier Polish played a part in transmitting the words ***kumiss*** ("slightly alcoholic, fermented, and sour-tasting milk from a mare or camel," ultimately from Tatar), and ***horde*** (ultimately from Turkish *ordu* "camp, army").

pol·i·tics /póllətiks/ *n* **1. ACTIVITIES ASSOCIATED WITH GOVERNMENT** the theory and practice of government, especially the activities associated with governing, with obtaining legislative or executive power, or with forming and running organizations connected with government (*takes a singular verb*) **2. POLITICAL LIFE** political activity as a profession (*takes a singular verb*) ○ *left the law to enter politics* **3. POWER RELATIONSHIPS IN SPECIFIC FIELD** the interrelationships between the people, groups, or organizations in a particular area of life especially insofar as they involve power and influence or conflict (*takes a singular or plural verb*) ○ *the politics of education* **4. CALCULATED ADVANCEMENT** the use of tactics and strategy to gain power in a group or organization (*takes a singular or plural verb*) **5.** same as **political science** (*takes a singular verb*) ■ *npl* **POLITICAL BELIEFS** political persuasions or beliefs (*takes a plural verb*)

pol·i·ty /póllətee/ (*plural* **-ties**) *n* **1. PARTICULAR FORM OF GOVERNMENT** a particular form of government that exists within a state or an institution **2. POLITICAL ENTITY** a state, society, or institution regarded as a political entity **3. POLITICS AND GOVERNMENT WITHIN SOCIETY** the aspect of society that is oriented to politics and government [Mid-16C. Via Latin < Greek *politeia* (see POLICE)]

pol·je /pōl yè/ *n* a large low-lying area in a limestone region (**karst**), often surrounded by steep walls and containing a marsh or small lake [Late 19C. < Serbo-Croatian, "field"]

Library of Congress

James Knox Polk

Polk /pōk/, **James Knox** (1795–1849) 11th president of the United States (1845–49). Under his Democratic administration, the United States expanded westward to the Pacific Ocean. See table at **president**

"The people of this continent alone have the right to decide their own destiny."
[James Knox Polk, *Speech to Congress*; December 2, 1845]

pol·ka /pólkə, pṓkə/ *n* **1. LIVELY DANCE** a lively dance for couples consisting of three quick steps and a hop and originating in Central Europe **2. MUSIC FOR POLKA** the music for a polka ■ *vi* (**-kaed, -ka·ing, -kas**) **DANCE POLKA** to dance a polka [Mid-19C. Probably via Czech < Polish, feminine form of *Polak* "Pole"]

pol·ka dot *n* a round spot repeated to form a regular pattern in a contrasting color on fabric

poll /pōl/ *n* **1. SURVEY OF PUBLIC** a questioning of the population or of a representative sample to tally opinions or gather other information ○ *a telephone poll* **2. ELECTION** a political election in its entirety, including the casting, recording, and counting of votes **3. NUMBER OF VOTES** the total number of votes cast in an election **4. HEAD** the head, or the back part of the head (*archaic*) **5. STRIKING SURFACE OF HAMMER** the broad hitting part of a hammer or ax ■ **polls** *npl* **PLACE FOR VOTING** a place where votes are recorded during an election ■ *v* (**polled, poll·ing, polls**) **1.** *vt* **SAMPLE OPINION METHODICALLY** to sample the opinions or attitudes of a group of people systematically **2.** *vt* **RECEIVE PARTICULAR NUMBER OF VOTES** to receive a particular number of votes in an election **3.** *vti* **CAST VOTE IN ELECTION** to cast a vote in an election **4.** *vt US* **RECORD JURY VOTES** to take the vote of each member of a jury in turn **5.** *vt* **CHECK AVAILABILITY OF COMPUTER COMMUNICATION LINES** to check communication lines in a computer or computer network to determine if they can receive or transmit data **6.** *vt* AGRIC, BOT **CUT OFF SOMETHING** to cut off the top of something or trim it short, especially the branches of a tree or an animal's hair or horns [13C. Probably < Middle Dutch or Middle Low German]

SPELLCHECK See *pole*[1].

pol·lack /póllək/ (*plural same*), **pol·lock** *n* **1.** an ocean fish of the cod family, with a protruding lower jaw. Native to: North Atlantic. Genus: *Pollachius*. **2.** the flesh of a pollack used as food [Early 16C. Origin ?]

pol·lard /póllərd/ *n* **1. TREE WITH BRANCHES CUT** a tree whose branches are cut back extensively to encourage denser growth **2. ANIMAL WITH HORNS REMOVED OR SHED** an animal that has shed its horns or antlers or has had its horns removed ■ *vt* (**-lard·ed, -lard·ing, -lards**) **CUT BRANCHES OR HORNS** to cut back the branches of a tree, or remove the horns of an animal [Mid-17C. < POLL]

pol·len /póllən/ *n* a powdery substance produced by flowering plants that contains male reproductive cells. It is carried by wind and insects to other plants, which it fertilizes. [Mid-18C. < Latin, "fine flour, dust"]

pol·len bas·ket *n* the hollow part of a bee's hind leg, used to transport pollen

pol·len count *n* a scientific measure of the amount of pollen in a volume of air during a 24-hour period

pol·len moth·er cell *n* a cell in a flowering plant that produces four pollen grains after cell division

pol·len sac *n* a cavity in the anther of a flower, where pollen is produced

pol·len tube *n* a hollow tube that develops from a pollen grain and conveys male reproductive cells to the egg cell

pol·lex /pó lèks/ (*plural* **-li·ces** /-lə seez/) *n* the first digit of the forelimb in birds and animals, or the thumb in humans (*technical*) [Mid-19C. < Latin]

pol·li·nate /póllə nayt/ (**-nat·ed, -nat·ing, -nates**) *vt* to transfer pollen grains from the male structure of a plant (**anther**) to the female structure of a plant (**stigma**) and fertilize it [Late 19C. < Latin *pollin-*, stem of *pollen* "fine flour, dust"] —**pol·li·na·tion** /pòllə náysh'n/ *n* —**pol·li·na·tor** *n*

poll·ing booth *n Can, UK* same as **voting booth**

poll·ing place *n* a building officially designated for casting votes during an election

pol·lin·i·a BOT plural of **pollinium**

pol·li·nif·er·ous /pòllə nífərəss/ *adj* producing or carrying pollen [Mid-19C. < Latin *pollin-* (see POLLINATE)]

pol·lin·i·um /pə línnee əm/ (*plural* **-i·a** /-ee ə/) *n* a cohering mass of pollen grains transported as a whole during pollination, typical of orchids and milkweeds [Mid-19C. < modern Latin < Latin *pollin-* (see POLLINATE)]

pol·li·no·sis /pòllə nṓssiss/ *n* MED same as **hay fever** (*technical*) [Early 20C. < Latin *pollin-* (see POLLINATE)]

pol·li·wog /póllee wòg/, **pol·ly·wog** *n* ZOOL same as **tadpole** [15C. Alteration of *pollwiggle* < POLL "head" + WIGGLE]

pol·lock *n* FISH another spelling of **pollack**

Pol·lock /póllək/, **Jackson** (1912–56) US artist. A leading abstract expressionist, he used action-painting techniques to create intricate interlaced webs of paint. Full name **Pollock, Paul Jackson**

"When I am *in* my painting, I'm not aware of what I am doing. It's only after a sort of 'get acquainted' period that I see what I have been about."
[Jackson Pollock, "Winter Possibilities I," *My Painting*; 1947–48]

poll·ster /pṓlstər/ *n* somebody who conducts public opinion polls

poll tax *n* a flat-rate tax levied on all members of a population, often as a prerequisite to voting

pol·lu·cite /pə lóo sìt, póllyə-/ *n* a rare colorless feldspathoid mineral that contains cesium [Mid-19C. Alteration of *pollux*, its earlier name, from its association with the mineral CASTOR[2] (in allusion to CASTOR AND POLLUX)]

pol·lut·ant /pə lóot'nt/ *n* a substance that pollutes something, e.g., a chemical or waste product contaminating the air, soil, or water

pol·lute /pə lóot/ (**-lut·ed, -lut·ing, -lutes**) *vt* **1. CONTAMINATE SOMETHING** to make something impure or unclean, or cause harm to an area of the natural environment, usually by introducing chemicals, waste products, or similarly damaging or poisonous substances **2. CORRUPT OR DEFILE SOMEBODY** to make somebody morally or spiritually impure **3. DESECRATE SOMETHING** to violate the sacred nature of a holy place [14C. < Latin *pollut-*, past participle of *polluere* < Indo-European, "dirt, make dirty"] —**pol·lut·er** *n*

pol·lu·tion /pə lóosh'n/ *n* **1.** the act of polluting something, especially the natural environment **2.** the state or condition of being polluted, or the presence of pollutants ○ *Pollution in the river will destroy the fish.*

Pol·lux *n* MYTHOL ➧ **Castor and Pollux**

Pol·ly·an·na /pòllee ánnə/ *n* an unrealistically optimistic person [Early 20C. After the heroine of children's stories written by Eleanor Hodgman Porter (1868–1920), US author]

pol·ly·wog *n* ZOOL another spelling of **polliwog**

po·lo /pṓlō/ *n* **1.** a game played by teams on horseback, with players using long-handled mallets to drive a wooden ball into a goal **2.** a game similar to polo, e.g., one in which the participants are mounted on bicycles rather than horses (*usually used in combination*) **3.** SPORTS same as **water polo** **4.** (*plural* **po·los**) CLOTHING same as **polo shirt** (*informal*) [Late 19C. < Tibetan *pholo* "ball game"]

Po·lo /pṓlō/, **Marco** (1254–1324) Venetian merchant and traveler. His accounts of his travels to China offered Europeans a firsthand view of Asian lands and stimulated interest in Asian trade.

po·lo coat *n* a double-breasted overcoat, usually made of camel's hair

Pol·ok·wa·ne /pòlō kwaá nay/ capital city of Limpopo Province, South Africa. Population: 39,011 (1991). Former name **Pietersburg**

pol·o·naise /pòllə náyz, pṑlə-/ *n* **1. SLOW DANCE** a stately formal dance for couples, in 3/4 time **2. MUSIC FOR POLONAISE** the music for a polonaise **3. DRESS WITH UNDERSKIRT** a dress with a tight bodice, cut away at the waist to reveal an inner skirt, worn by European women in the 18th century [Mid-18C. < French, "Polish"]

po·lo neck *n UK* same as **turtleneck** (sense 1) —**po·lo-necked** *adj*

po·lo·ni·um /pə lṓnee əm/ *n* a very rare radioactive

metallic element. Source: uranium ores. Use: removal of static electricity. Symbol **Po**. See table at **element** [Late 19C. < medieval Latin *Polonia* "Poland," the home of its discoverer, Marie CURIE]

po·lo po·ny *n* a horse ridden in the game of polo

po·lo shirt *n* a lightweight casual shirt, usually made of knitted cotton, with a small square collar and a buttoned opening at the neck [Because traditionally worn by polo players]

Pol Pot /pòl pót/ (1928–98) Cambodian national leader. He led the communist Khmer Rouge to victory, and approximately 1.7 million people died under his rule in Cambodia (1975–79). Born **Saloth Sar**

pol·ter·geist /póltər gīst/ *n* a supposed supernatural spirit that reveals its presence by creating disturbances, e.g., by knocking over objects [Mid-19C. < German, "noisy ghost"]

pol·troon /pol troōn/ *n* an offensive term for somebody regarded as a contemptible coward (*archaic*) [Early 16C. Via French < Italian *poltrone* "coward, lazy person"]

~~**polution**~~ incorrect spelling of **pollution**

pol·y /póllee/ *n* (*informal*) **1.** TEXTILES same as **polyester** (sense 2) **2.** CHEM same as **polyethylene** [Late 20C. Shortening]

poly- *prefix* **1.** more than one ○ *polyandry* **2.** more than normal ○ *polyphagia* **3.** polymer ○ *polyethylene* [< Greek *polus* "much" < Indo-European, "fill"]

pol·y·a·cryl·a·mide /pòllee ə kríllə mīd/ *n* a white solid polymer of acrylamide. Use: thickening, clouding, and absorbent agent.

pol·y·ad·e·nyl·ic ac·id /pòllee ad'n ìllik-/ *n* a segment of RNA made up of multiple units of AMP, found in messenger RNA molecules. It stabilizes RNA during protein synthesis.

pol·y·al·co·hol /pòllee álkə hàwl/ *n* CHEM same as **polyol**

pol·y·am·ide /pòllee á mīd, -ámmid/ *n* a synthetic polymer that has recurring amide groups, e.g., nylon

pol·y·a·mine /pòllee ə meēn, -á meēn/ *n* an organic compound containing more than one amino group

pol·y·an·dry /póllee àndree/ *n* **1.** SIMULTANEOUS MARRIAGE TO MULTIPLE HUSBANDS the custom of having more than one husband at a time **2.** FACT OF HAVING MULTIPLE MALE MATES animal mating in which a female mates with more than one male during any single breeding season **3.** FACT OF HAVING MANY STAMENS possession by a plant of a large number of stamens [Late 17C. < Greek *poluandria* "many husbands" < *andr-* "man, husband"] —**pol·y·an·drous** /pòllee ándrəss/ *adj*

pol·y·an·tha rose /pòllee ánthə-/ *n* a member of a class of cultivated roses. Flowers: small, mainly scentless, in dense clusters. [< modern Latin, form of *polyanthus* (see POLYANTHUS)]

pol·y·an·thus /pòllee ánthəss/ (*plural* **-thus·es** or **-thi** /-thī/) *n* **1.** a hybrid primrose with bright flowers in a variety of colors. Latin name: ***Primula polyantha***. **2.** PLANTS same as **polyanthus narcissus** [Early 18C. Via modern Latin < Greek *poluanthos* "having many flowers" < *anthos* "flower"]

pol·y·an·thus nar·cis·sus *n* a narcissus with small white or yellow flowers. Native to: Europe, Asia. Latin name: *Narcissus tazetta*.

pol·y·a·tom·ic /pòllee ə tómmik/ *adj* describes a molecule that has more than two atoms

pol·y·ba·sic /pòllee báyssik/ *adj* describes a molecule or compound that has two or more atoms of replaceable hydrogen

pol·y·ba·site /pòllee báy sīt/ *n* a rare gray to black crystalline mineral containing silver, found near silver ores [Mid-19C. < German *Polybasit* < Greek *polus* "much" + German *Basis* "base"; from its chemical composition]

pol·y·car·bon·ate /pòllee kaárbə nàyt, -kaárbənət/ *n* a strong synthetic resin. Use: molded products, unbreakable windows, optical components.

pol·y·car·box·yl·ic ac·id /pòllee kaar bok sillik-/ *n* carboxylic acid that contains more than one carboxyl group

po·ly·car·pic /pòllee kaárpik/, **pol·y·car·pous** /-kaárpəss/ *adj* describes a plant that is capable of producing flowers and fruit several times in succession —**pol·y·car·py** /póllee kaàrpee/ *n*

pol·y·chaete /pólli keēt/, **pol·y·chete** *n* an ocean worm with a segmented body and bristled fleshy appendages used in swimming. Class: Polychaeta. [Late 19C. < modern Latin *Polychaeta* < Greek *polukhaitēs* "having much hair" < *khaitē* "long hair"] —**pol·y·chae·tous** /pòlli keētəss/ *adj*

pol·y·chlo·rin·at·ed bi·phen·yl /pòllee klàwri naytəd bī fénn'l, -feēn'l/ *n* CHEM full form of **PCB**

pol·y·chro·mat·ic /pòllee krō máttik/ *adj* **1.** having, showing, or consisting of many colors, either at the same time or in sequence **2.** describes electromagnetic radiation that has multiple wavelengths

pol·y·chrome /póllee krōm/ *adj* **1.** decorated with many or varied colors **2.** PHYS same as **polychromatic** (sense 1) ■ *n* a polychrome object or artifact

pol·y·chro·my /póllee krōmee/ *n* the practice of using several different colors in painting, sculpture, or decoration

pol·y·clin·ic /pòllee klínnik/ *n* a clinic, often independent of a hospital, in which medical care is provided by a range of specialists

pol·y·clone /póllee klōn/ *n* a clone derived from groups of cells of different ancestry or genetic constitution —**pol·y·clo·nal** /pòllee klōn'l/ *adj*

pol·y·con·ic pro·jec·tion /pòllee kònnik-/ *n* a conic map projection in which all meridians, except the central, are curved and the parallels are nonconcentric arcs

pol·y·cot·y·le·don /pòllee kòtt'l eēd'n/ *n* a plant with more than two cotyledons

pol·y·crys·tal /póllee krìst'l/ *n* a crystalline structure whose crystals were formed rapidly and randomly

pol·y·crys·tal·line /pòllee krístə līn, -lin/ *adj* consisting of randomly oriented crystals

pol·y·cy·clic /pòllee sīklik, -síklik/ *adj* **1.** describes a shell that has two or more whorls **2.** describes a compound having two or more closed rings of atoms —**pol·y·cy·clic** *n*

pol·y·cys·tic /pòllee sístik/ *adj* describes an organ such as a kidney or ovary that has developed multiple cysts

pol·y·cys·tic o·var·i·an syn·drome *n* a hormonal disorder in women characterized by enlarged ovaries containing numerous small painless cysts, infertility, excessive hair growth, and acne

pol·y·cy·the·mi·a /pòllee sī theēmee ə/ *n* an increase in red blood cells, occurring on its own or in conjunction with other diseases, especially of the respiratory or circulatory systems

pol·y·dac·tyl /pòllee dákt'l/ *adj* describes vertebrates, including human beings, that have more than the normal number of fingers or toes —**pol·y·dac·tyl** *n*

pol·y·dip·si·a /pòllee dípsee ə/ *n* excessive thirst [Mid-17C. < POLY- + Greek *dipsa* "thirst"]

pol·y·e·lec·tro·lyte /pòllee i léktrə līt/ *n* an electrolyte that has a high molecular weight, e.g., a protein

pol·y·em·bry·o·ny /pòllee émbree ənee, -em brī-/ *n* the production of more than one embryo from a single egg —**pol·y·em·bry·on·ic** /pòllee èmbree ónnik/ *adj*

pol·y·ene /póllee eēn/ *n* a hydrocarbon that has many alternating single and double carbon-carbon bonds

pol·y·es·ter /póllee èstər, pòllee éstər/ *n* **1.** a synthetic polymer in which the monomers are linked together by the chemical group -COO-. Use: resins, plastics, textile fibers. **2.** a strong hard-wearing synthetic fabric with low moisture absorbency, made from a polyester

pol·y·eth·yl·ene /pòllee éthə leēn/ *n* a plastic polymer of ethylene. Use: manufacture of containers, packaging, and electrical insulation.

pol·y·eth·yl·ene gly·col *n* a polymer of ethylene compounds. Use: emulsifiers and lubricants in ointments and cosmetics.

po·lyg·a·my /pə líggəmee/ *n* **1.** the custom of having more than one spouse at the same time **2.** animal mating in which an individual mates with more than one animal during any single breeding season [Late 16C. Via French and late Latin < ecclesiastical Greek *polugamia* < *polugamos* "often married" < Greek *gamos* "marriage"] —**po·lyg·a·mist** *n* —**po·lyg·a·mous** *adj*

pol·y·gene /póllee jeēn/ *n* one of a group of genes in which the number of those genes present collectively determines the extent of a characteristic such as height —**pol·y·gen·ic** /pòllee jénnik/ *adj*

pol·y·gen·e·sis /pòllee jénnəssiss/ *n* origin from more than one species, line of ancestors, or source —**pol·y·gen·et·ic** /pòllee jə néttik/ *adj* —**pol·y·gen·et·i·cal·ly** *adv*

pol·y·glot /póllee glòt/ *adj* **1.** COMPETENT IN MANY LANGUAGES capable of reading, writing, or speaking many languages **2.** IN MANY LANGUAGES written or communicated in many languages ■ *n* **1.** MULTILINGUAL PERSON a speaker of many languages **2.** BOOK CONTAINING TEXT IN MANY LANGUAGES a book, especially a Bible, that gives the text in several languages **3.** MIX OF LANGUAGES a confused mixture of languages [Mid-17C. Via French < Greek *poluglōttos* < *glōtta* "tongue, language"]

pol·y·gon /póllee gòn/ *n* **1.** a two-dimensional geometric figure formed of three or more straight sides **2.** a building block of computer graphics ○ *The new character model sports an extremely high number of polygons, with smooth and realistic animations.* [Late 16C. Via late Latin < Greek *polugōnon*, form of *polugōnos* "many-angled" < *-gōnos* "-angled"] —**po·lyg·o·nal** /pə líggən'l/ *adj*

po·lyg·o·num /pə líggənəm/ *n* a plant with bulbous stem joints and spikes of small flowers. Genus: *Polygonum*. [Early 18C. Via modern Latin < Greek *polugonon* "knotgrass," literally "many-jointed" < *gonu* "knee, joint"]

pol·y·graph /póllee gràf/ *n* **1.** LIE DETECTOR an electrical device that registers involuntary physical processes such as pulse rate and perspiration and that is often used as a lie detector **2.** TEST USING POLYGRAPH a test using a polygraph, or a result of this test ■ *vt* (**-graphed, -graph·ing, -graphs**) GIVE SOMEBODY POLYGRAPH TEST to test somebody, usually somebody suspected of committing a crime, using a polygraph —**pol·y·graph·ic** /pòllee gráffik/ *adj*

po·lyg·y·ny /pə líjjənee/ *n* **1.** SIMULTANEOUS MARRIAGE TO MULTIPLE WIVES the custom of being married to more than one wife at the same time **2.** FACT OF HAVING MULTIPLE FEMALE MATES animal mating in which a male mates with more than one female during any single breeding season **3.** FACT OF HAVING MANY PISTILS OR STYLES the possession by a plant of many pistils or styles [Late 18C. < POLY- + Greek *gunē* "woman"] —**po·lyg·y·nous** *adj*

pol·y·he·dra MATH plural of **polyhedron**

pol·y·he·dral /pòllee heēdrəl/ *adj* relating to or in the form of a polyhedron

pol·y·he·dral an·gle *n* a geometric angle formed by the intersection of three or more planes meeting at a point such as the peak of a pyramid

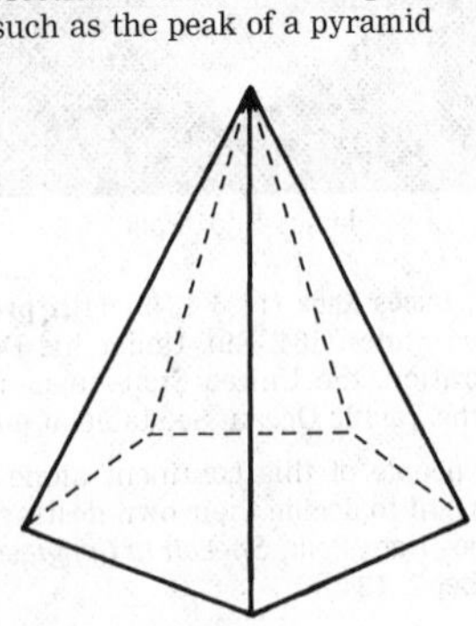

polyhedron

pol·y·he·dron /pòllee heēdrən/ (*plural* **-drons** or **-dra** /-drə/) *n* a three-dimensional geometric figure formed of many faces [Late 16C. < Greek *poluedron* "many-based figure" < *hedra* "base"]

pol·y·hy·drox·y /pòllee hī dróksee/, **pol·y·hy·dric** /-hīdrik/ *adj* describes a compound that has two or more hydroxyl groups in each molecule

Pol·y·hym·ni·a /pòllee hímnee ə/ *n* in Greek mythology, the Muse of sacred songs, one of the nine Muses believed to inspire and nurture the arts

pol·y·im·ide /pòllee í mīd, -ímmid/ *n* a tough durable polymer that contains an imide group. Use: heat-resistant coatings.

pol·y·i·so·prene /pòllee íssə prēen/ *n* a polymeric form of isoprene. Source: natural or synthetic rubber.

pol·y·math /póllee màth/ *n* somebody with knowledge of many subjects [Early 17C. < Greek *polumathēs* "somebody with much learning" < *manthanein* "learn"] —**pol·y·math·ic** /pòllee máthik/ *adj*

pol·y·mer /póllәmәr/ *n* a natural or synthetic compound that consists of large molecules made of many chemically bonded smaller identical molecules, e.g., starch and nylon [Mid-19C. < Greek *polumerēs* "having many parts" < *meros* "part"] —**pol·y·mer·ic** /pòllә mérrik/ *adj*

pol·y·mer·ase /póllimә ràyz, -ràyss/ *n* an enzyme that catalyzes the elongation of a polymer, especially in DNA or RNA

pol·y·mer·ase chain re·ac·tion *n* a technique used to replicate a fragment of DNA and produce a large amount of that sequence

po·lym·er·i·za·tion /pә lìmmәri záysh'n, pòllimәri-/ *n* the chemical reaction in which a compound is made into a polymer by the addition or condensation of smaller molecules —**pol·y·mer·ize** /póllәmә rīz, pә límmә-/ *vti*

po·lym·er·ous /pә límmәrәss/ *adj* describes an organism that consists of many parts or segments

pol·y·morph /póllee màwrf/ *n* **1. ANIMAL OR PLANT WITH DIFFERENT FORMS** an animal or plant that has several different adult forms **2. CHEMICAL COMPOUND WITH DIFFERENT FORMS** a chemical compound that has several crystalline forms **3. WHITE BLOOD CELL WITH SEGMENTED NUCLEUS** a white blood cell whose nucleus is segmented into lobes —**pol·y·mor·phic** /pòllee máwrfik/ *adj*

pol·y·mor·phism /pòllee máwr fìzzәm/ *n* **1.** the characteristic of existing in different forms **2.** a difference in DNA sequence between individuals

pol·y·mor·pho·nu·cle·ar leu·ko·cyte /pòllee màwrfō nóoklee әr-/ *n* BIOL same as **polymorph** (sense 3)

pol·y·myx·in /pòllee míksin/ *n* a peptide antibiotic. Source: a soil bacterium, *[Bacillus polymyxa]*. Use: treatment of meningitis, inner ear infections. [Mid-20C. < modern Latin *Polymyxa* < Greek *muxa* "slime"]

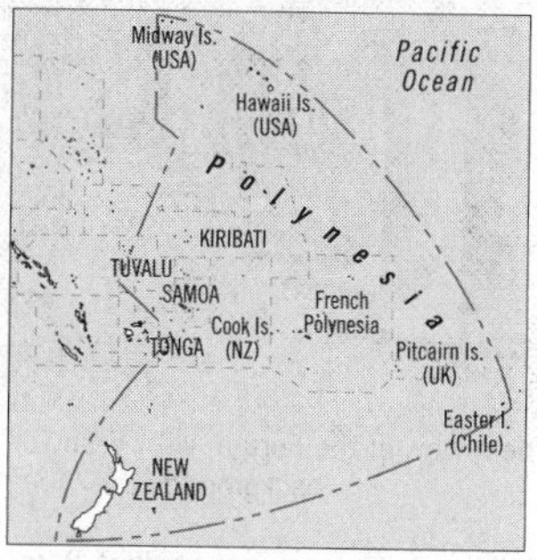

Polynesia

Pol·y·ne·sia /pòllә nēe*zh*ә/ ethnographic grouping of Pacific islands, encompassing a number of scattered islands in the central and southern Pacific Ocean, including Hawaii, Samoa, Easter Island, the Cook Islands, the Marquesas Islands, French Polynesia, Tonga, Tuvalu, and sometimes New Zealand

Pol·y·ne·sian /pòllee nēe*zh*'n/ *n* **1.** somebody who comes from an island of the central or southern Pacific **2.** a group of Austronesian languages, including Fijian, Hawaiian, and Maori, spoken on islands of the central and southern Pacific. Native speakers: 800,000. —**Pol·y·ne·sian** *adj*

pol·y·neu·ri·tis /pòllee noo rítiss/ *n* a simultaneous inflammation of several nerves

pol·y·no·mi·al /pòllә nṓmee әl/ *adj* **WITH MORE THAN TWO TERMS** describes a mathematical expression that has more than two terms, or a system of taxonomic nomenclature that uses more than two names ■ *n* **1. MULTITERM MATHEMATICAL EXPRESSION** a mathematical expression consisting of the sum of a number of terms, each of which contains a constant and variables raised to a positive integral power **2. MULTITERM TAXONOMIC NAME** a taxonomic name of a plant or animal that has more than two terms, e.g., one giving a genus, species, and subspecies [Late 17C. After BINOMIAL]

pol·y·nu·cle·o·tide /pòllee nóoklee ә tīd/ *n* a chain of chemically bonded nucleotides, as occurs in the structure of DNA and RNA

pol·y·ol /póllee àwl/ *n* an alcohol that contains more than two hydroxyl groups, e.g., glycerol

pol·y·o·ma /pòllee ṓmә/, **pol·y·o·ma vi·rus** *n* a virus in rodents that can produce tumors

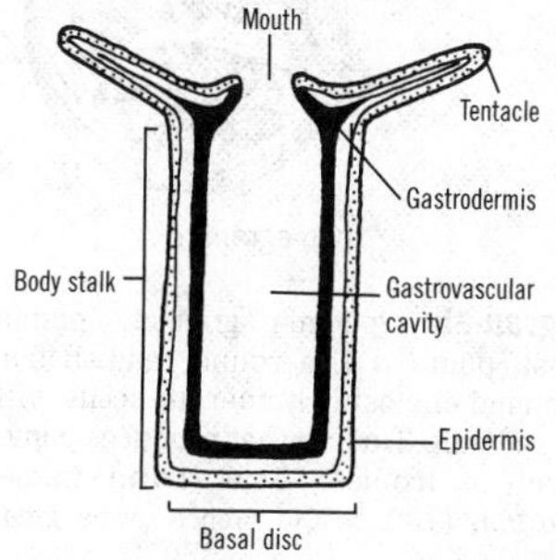

polyp: cross section of a polyp (sense 2)

pol·yp /póllip/ *n* **1.** a small stalk-shaped growth sticking out from the skin or from a mucous membrane. Polyps are usually benign, but some become malignant. **2.** a single-cavity sea invertebrate **(cnidarian)** in its sedentary stage that attaches to a rock at one end of its cylindrical body and has a tentacled mouth at the other end [14C. Via French *polipe* and Latin *polypus* < Greek *polupous* "octopus," literally "many-footed" < *pous* "foot"] —**pol·yp·oid** *adj*

pol·y·pep·tide /pòllee pép tīd/ *n* a chain of chemically bonded amino acids, as occurs in the structure of protein molecules [Early 20C. < POLY- + PEPTONE]

pol·y·pet·al·ous /pòllee pétt'lәss/ *adj* describes flowers such as roses and carnations that have many separate petals

pol·y·pha·gia /pòllee fáyjә, -jee ә/ *n* **1.** an insatiable appetite for food **2.** the habit on the part of some animals of feeding on many different types of food —**po·lyph·a·gous** /pә líffәgәss/ *adj*

pol·y·phase /póllee fàyz/ *adj* producing two or more phases of alternating current, or two or more alternating voltages of the same frequency

Pol·y·phe·mus /pòllee fēemәss/ *n* in Greek mythology, a cyclops who was blinded by Odysseus after having imprisoned him in a cave

pol·y·phone /póllee fōn/ *n* a letter or character that has more than one way of being pronounced

pol·y·phon·ic /pòllee fónnik/ *adj* **1. WITH SEVERAL MELODIES** describes music consisting of two or more largely independent melodic lines, parts, or voices that sound simultaneously **2. WITH SEVERAL POSSIBLE PRONUNCIATIONS** describes a letter or character that may be pronounced in several different ways **3. PLAYING SEVERAL NOTES TOGETHER** describes a ringtone on a cell phone that plays several notes or sounds simultaneously, making it sound more musical —**pol·y·phon·i·cal·ly** *adv*

pol·y·phon·ic prose *n* highly rhythmic prose that makes use of poetic devices such as alliteration and assonance

po·lyph·o·ny /pә líffәnee/ *n* **1.** musical composition that uses simultaneous, largely independent, melodic parts, lines, or voices **2.** the representation of different sounds by the same letter in a writing system [Early 19C. < Greek *poluphōnia* "multiplicity of sounds" < *phōnē* "voice, sound" (see PHONO-)] —**po·lyph·o·nous** *adj*

pol·y·phy·let·ic /pòllee fī léttik/ *adj* derived or descended from several groups of ancestors

pol·y·phy·o·dont /pòllee fī ō dònt/ *adj* describes a fish or other vertebrate that grows several sets of teeth in succession

Pol·y·pill /póllee pìll/ *n* a proposed drug that would contain substances to lower cholesterol and blood pressure, aspirin to interfere with blood clotting, and folic acid to help prevent atherosclerosis

pol·y·ploid /póllee plòyd/ *adj* having more than twice the basic number of chromosomes —**pol·y·ploid** *n* —**pol·y·ploi·dy** *n*

pol·y·pod /póllee pòd/ *adj* describes an insect larva such as a caterpillar with a large number of jointed legs on the thorax and unjointed legs on the abdomen, or this stage of larval development [Mid-18C. Via French < Greek *polupod-* "many-footed" < *pod-* "foot"] —**pol·y·pod** *n*

pol·y·po·dy /póllee pōdee/ (*plural* **-dies**) *n* a fern with evergreen pinnate leaves and a creeping rootstock. Genus: *Polypodium*. [15C. Via Latin < Greek *polupodion* "many-footed one" < *polupod-* (see POLYPOD)]

pol·yp·o·sis /pòllee pṓssiss/ *n* a condition in which numerous polyps develop in a hollow organ such as the bowel

pol·y·pro·pyl·ene /pòllee prṓpә lēen/, **pol·y·pro·pene** /-prō pēen/ *n* a thermoplastic substance that is a synthetic polymer of propylene. Use: pipes, industrial fibers, molded objects.

pol·yp·tych /póllip tìk/ *n* an arrangement of three or more panels with a painting or carving on each, usually hinged together and used as an altarpiece in a church [Mid-19C. After DIPTYCH]

pol·y·rhythm /póllee ri*th*әm/ *n* a technique of musical composition in which several contrasting rhythms are used simultaneously —**pol·y·rhyth·mic** /pòllee ríthmik/ *adj*

pol·y·ri·bo·some /pòllee rībә sōm/ *n* a cluster of ribosomes linked by a strand of messenger RNA and functioning as a site of protein synthesis

pol·y·sac·cha·ride /pòllee sákә rīd/, **pol·y·sac·cha·rose** /pòllee sákә rōss/ *n* a complex carbohydrate such as starch or cellulose made up of sugar molecules linked into a branched or chain structure

pol·y·sem·y /póllee sēemee, pә líssәmee/ *n* the existence of several meanings for a single word or phrase [Early 20C. < modern Latin *polysemia* < Greek *polusēmos* "having many meanings" < *sēma* "sign, mark"] —**pol·y·se·mous** /pòllee sēemәss/ *adj*

pol·y·sep·al·ous /pòllee séppәlәss/ *adj* describes flowers that have distinctly separate sepals

pol·y·some /póllee sōm/ *n* BIOCHEM same as **polyribosome** [Mid-20C. Contraction]

pol·y·so·mic /pòllee sṓmik/ *adj* describes a diploid cell or organism in which some of the chromosomes occur more than twice

pol·y·sor·bate /pòllee sáwr bàyt, -bәt/ *n* an emulsifier used in preparing some foods and drugs [Mid-20C. < POLY- + SORBITOL]

pol·y·sper·my /póllee spùrmee/ *n* the fertilization of an egg by several spermatozoa

po·lys·ti·chous /pә lístikәss/ *adj* describes parts of a plant that are arranged in two or more series of rows [Late 19C. After DISTICHOUS]

pol·y·sty·rene /pòllee stī rēen/ *n* a synthetic polymer of styrene that is stable in various physical forms. As a white rigid foam **(expanded polystyrene)** it is used for packing and insulation.

pol·y·sul·fide /pòllee súl fīd/ *n* a sulfide whose molecules have two or more atoms of sulfur

pol·y·syl·lab·ic /pòllee si lábbik/ *adj* **1.** having more than one or two syllables **2.** using or containing long words, often where shorter words would be adequate or better

pol·y·syl·la·ble /pòllee síllәb'l/ *n* a word that has more than one or two syllables

pol·y·syn·ap·tic /pòllee si náptik/ *adj* describes a reflex in the central nervous system that uses two or more synapses

pol·y·syn·de·ton /pòllee síndә tòn/ *n* the use of multiple conjunctions or coordinate clauses in close succession, as in "The bad news caused him to weep and cry and wail" [Late 16C. After ASYNDETON]

pol·y·syn·thet·ic /pòllee sin théttik/ *adj* describes a language in which the syntax is conveyed by means of multiple affixes to single words —**pol·y·syn·the·sis** /pòllee sínthəssiss/ *n*

pol·y·tech·nic /pòllee téknik/ *n* a college offering a range of courses, some of them vocational or technical, at or below the bachelor's degree level [Early 19C. < French *polytechnique* < Greek *polutekhnos* "multiskilled" < *tekhnē* "skill"]

pol·y·tene /póllee teen/ *adj* describes a giant chromosome with distinct chromosome bands in polyploid cells of some two-winged flies, comprising multiple copies of a chromosome aligned side by side

pol·y·tet·ra·fluor·o·eth·yl·ene /pòllee tetrə floorō éthə leen, -flawrō-/ *n* a durable, chemically resistant nonflammable thermoplastic substance. Use: metal coatings, especially for nonstick surfaces of cookware.

pol·y·the·ism /póllee thee ìzzəm, pòllee thee-/ *n* the worship of or belief in more than one deity, especially several deities [Early 17C. < French *polythéisme* < Greek *polutheos* "of many deities" < *theos* "deity"] —**pol·y·the·ist** *n* —**pol·y·the·is·tic** /pòllee thee ístik/ *adj*

pol·y·thene /póllə theen/ *n UK* same as **polyethylene** [Mid-20C. Contraction of POLYETHYLENE]

pol·y·to·nal·i·ty /pòllee tō nállətee/ *n* a technique of musical composition in which several keys are used at once —**pol·y·to·nal** /pòllee tṓn'l/ *adj*

pol·y·tro·phic /pòllee trṓfik, -tróffik/ *adj* describes bacteria that derive food from several different sources

pol·y·typ·ic /pòllee típpik/, **pol·y·typ·i·cal** /-ik'l/ *adj* describes a taxonomic subset, especially a species, that has many subdivisions

pol·y·un·sat·u·rat·ed /pòllee un sáchə ràytəd/ *adj* belonging to a class of fats, especially plant oils, that are less likely to be converted into cholesterol in the body. Their molecules have long carbon chains with many double bonds unsaturated by hydrogen atoms.

pol·y·ur·e·thane /pòllee yóorə thàyn/ *n* a thermoplastic polymer that contains an NHCOO chemical group. Use: resins, coatings, insulation, adhesives, foams, fibers.

pol·y·u·ri·a /pòllee yóoree ə/ *n* the passing of unusually large amounts of urine, e.g., in untreated diabetes

pol·y·va·lent /pòllee váylənt/ *adj* **1.** describes a chemical element that has more than one valence or a valence of more than two **2.** describes a vaccine that is effective against more than one strain of microorganism, toxin, antigen, or antibody

pol·y·vi·nyl /pòllee vín'l/ *adj* describes plastics and resins produced by the polymerization of vinyls

pol·y·vi·nyl ac·e·tate *n* INDUST full form of **PVA**

pol·y·vi·nyl chlo·ride *n* INDUST full form of **PVC**

pol·y·zo·an /pòllee zṓ ən/ *n* MARINE BIOL same as **bryozoan** [Mid-19C. < modern Latin *Polyzoa* < *zoon* (see -ZOON)]

POM *abbr* PHARM prescription-only medicine

pom·ace /púmməss, póm-/ *n* **1.** the pulpy mass that remains after apples or other fruits have been crushed and pressed to extract the juice, e.g., to make cider **2.** the pulpy mass that remains after nuts, fish, or other foods have been crushed and pressed to extract oil or another liquid [Mid-16C. < medieval Latin *pomacium* "cider" < Latin *pomum* "apple"]

po·ma·ceous /pō máyshəss/ *adj* describes a fruit such as an apple or pear that has a large fleshy receptacle with a central seed-bearing core (**pome**) [Early 18C. < Latin *pomum* "apple"]

po·made /pō máyd, pə-, -maad/ *n* a perfumed oil or ointment used to make hair look smooth and shiny ■ *vt* (**-mad·ed, -mad·ing, -mades**) to dress hair with pomade [Mid-16C. < French *pommade* < Latin *pomum* "apple"]

po·man·der /pṓ màndər, pō mán-/ *n* **1.** AROMATIC MIXTURE a mixture of aromatic substances enclosed in a sachet, ball, or other container, kept near stored clothes or in a room to impart a pleasant smell **2.** POMANDER CONTAINER a container for a pomander, usually a lidded pottery bowl with holes **3.** CLOVE-STUDDED ORANGE an orange or apple studded with cloves, used to scent clothes or a room [15C. < Old French *pome d'ambre* "apple of amber"]

pome /pōm/ *n* a fleshy fruit that has a central core typically containing five seeds, e.g., an apple or pear [14C. Via French < Latin *pomum* "apple"]

pomegranate

pome·gran·ate /pómmə grànnət, púmmə-, póm grànnət, púm-/ *n* **1.** a round reddish fruit with a tough rind enclosing numerous seeds within a tart juicy red pulp **2.** a tree that produces pomegranates. Native to: tropical Asia. Latin name: *Punica granatum.* [14C. < Old French *pome grenate* "seedy apple"]

~~**pomegranite**~~ incorrect spelling of **pomegranate**

pom·e·lo /pómmə lō/ (*plural* **-los**) *n* **1.** a yellowy orange citrus fruit similar to a large grapefruit **2.** a citrus tree that produces pomelos. Native to: Southeast Asia. Latin name: *Citrus maxima.* **3.** FOOD same as **grapefruit** [Mid-19C. Origin ?]

Pom·er·a·ni·a /pòmmə ráynee ə/ historic region in Northern Europe on the southern shores of the Baltic Sea in present-day northwestern Poland and northeastern Germany

Pom·er·a·ni·an /pòmmə ráynee ən/ *n* **1.** SMALL DOG a small dog belonging to a breed that has a long silky coat, pointed ears, a pointed muzzle, and a long curling tail **2.** SOMEBODY FROM POMERANIA somebody who comes from Pomerania ■ *adj* OF POMERANIA relating to Pomerania, or its people or culture

po·mi·cul·ture /pṓmi kùlchər/ *n* the cultivation of fruit [Late 19C. < Latin *pomum* "apple, fruit"]

po·mif·er·ous /pō míffərəss/ *adj* describes fruit plants that bear apples, pears, or any related fleshy fruit with five seeds (**pome**) [Mid-17C. < Latin *pomifer* < *pomum* "apple, fruit"]

pom·mel /púmm'l, póm-/ *n* **1.** FRONT OF SADDLE the front part of a saddle that curves upward **2.** PART OF SWORD HANDLE the knob at the hilt of a sword **3.** HANDLE ON POMMEL HORSE either of the two curved handles on the top of a pommel horse ■ *vt* (**pom·meled, pom·mel·ing, pom·mels**) same as **pummel** [14C. < Old French *pomel* "little fruit" < Latin *pomum* "apple, fruit"]

pom·mel horse *n* **1.** a padded oblong piece of gymnastics apparatus that is raised off the floor and has two curved handles on the top **2.** the men's gymnastics event that involves balancing and maneuvering on a pommel horse

po·mo /pṓmō/, **po-mo** *adj* relating to or characteristic of postmodernism (*informal*) ○ *"beat-generation, counterculture, and pomo literature"* (Hawkeye, *FutureCulture FAQ parts 1 & 2*; 1992) [Late 20C. Contraction and alteration of *post modern*]

Po·mo /pṓmō/ (*plural same* or **-mos**) *n* **1.** a member of a group of Native North American peoples living in northern California **2.** a Native North American language of a group of closely related languages spoken in parts of northern California and belonging to the Hokan branch of Hokan-Siouan languages [Late 19C. < N Pomo *p'ó·mo·* "at the red earth hole"] —**Po·mo** *adj*

po·mol·o·gy /pō mólləjee/ *n* the study or practice of cultivating fruit [Early 19C. < Latin *pomum* "apple, fruit"] —**po·mo·log·i·cal** /pòmə lójjik'l/ *adj* —**po·mol·o·gist** *n*

Po·mo·na /pə mṓnə/ *n* in Roman mythology, the goddess of fruit [Mid-17C. < Latin < *pomum* "apple, fruit"]

pomp /pomp/ *n* **1.** a display of great splendor and magnificence **2.** an ostentatious and vain display of importance [14C. Via French *pompe* and Latin *pompa* < Greek *pompē* "solemn procession, sendoff, escort" < *pempein* "send"]

CULTURAL NOTE ***Pomp and Circumstance***, an orchestral work (parts 1 to 4: 1901–07; part 5: 1930) by British composer Edward Elgar. The title of this series of five military marches (op. 39) derives from the reference in Shakespeare's *Othello* (Act III, scene iii) to the "pride, pomp, and circumstance of glorious war."

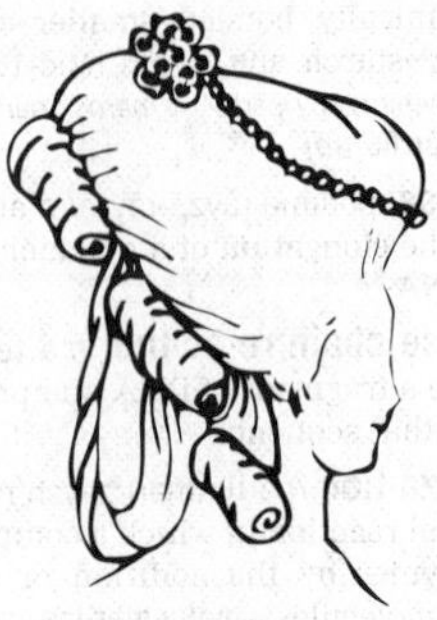

pompadour

pom·pa·dour /pómpə dàwr, -door/ *n* **1.** a woman's hairstyle, popular in Europe in the 18th century, in which the hair is swept back high off the face over a pad **2.** a man's hairstyle in which the hair is combed back off the face to form a mound above the forehead [Mid-18C. After the Marquise de POMPADOUR]

Pom·pa·dour /pómpə dàwr, -door/, **Marquise de** (1721–64) French noblewoman. She was a mistress of Louis XV and a patron of the arts. She had great influence with Louis in all important political matters. Born **Poisson, Jeanne Antoinette**

pom·pa·no /pómpə nō/ (*plural* **-nos** or *same*) *n* **1.** an ocean fish with a deep flat body and forked tail. Native to: southern Atlantic and Gulf coasts of North America. Latin name: *Trachinotus carolinus.* **2.** FISH same as **butterfish** [Late 18C. < Spanish *pámpano*]

Pompeii: view of the Forum, with Vesuvius in the background

Pom·pe·ii /pom páy, -páy ee/ ancient Roman city in southern Italy. It was buried by volcanic ash during the eruption of Mount Vesuvius in A.D. 79, and has since been partly excavated.

Pom·pey /pómpee/ (106–48 B.C.) Roman general and leader. He formed a ruling triumvirate with Caesar and Crassus, but was later defeated by Caesar at Pharsalus (48 B.C.) and escaped to Egypt, where he was assassinated. Full name **Gnaeus Pompeius Magnus.** Known as **Pompey the Great**

Pom·pi·dou /pómpi doo/, **Georges** (1911–74) French politician. He was four times prime minister (1962–68), and followed Charles de Gaulle as president (1969–74).

> "A statesman is a politician who places himself at the service of the nation. A politician is a statesman who places the nation at his service."
> [Georges Pompidou, *Observer (London)*; December 30, 1973]

pom-pom[1] /póm pòm/ *n* **1.** a cheerleader's accessory in the form of a large white or brightly colored ball-shaped mass of thin paper or plastic strips connected to a handle **2.** a small tufted ball made from wool, silk, or other material, attached as a decoration to hats, shoes, and other articles of clothing **3.** BOT same as **pompon** (sense 2) [Mid-18C. < French]

pom-pom[2] /póm pòm/ *n* a rapid-firing automatic weapon, especially a cannon used in the Boer War or a double-barreled antiaircraft gun used in World War II (*slang*) [An imitation of the sound]

pom·pon /póm pòn/ *n* **1.** CLOTHING same as **pom-pom**[1] (sense 2) **2.** a small round flower of some chrysanthemum or dahlia varieties, or a variety that has this kind of flower [Mid-18C. < French]

pom·pos·i·ty /pom póssətee/ (*plural* **-ties**) *n* **1.** an excessive sense of self-importance, usually displayed through exaggerated seriousness or stateliness in speech and manner **2.** an act, remark, or gesture that is exaggerated in its seriousness or stateliness and conveys an excessive sense of self-importance

pom·pous /pómpəss/ *adj* **1. SELF-IMPORTANT** having an excessive sense of self-importance, usually displayed through exaggerated seriousness or stateliness in speech or manner **2. REVEALING SELF-IMPORTANCE** displaying exaggerated seriousness or stateliness ○ *a pompous gesture* **3. CEREMONIALLY GRAND** full of splendor and magnificence [14C. Via French < Latin *pomposus* < *pompa* (see POMP)] —**pom·pous·ly** *adv* —**pom·pous·ness** *n*

'pon /pon/ *prep* same as **upon** (*archaic or literary*) [Mid-16C. Shortening]

Pon·ca /póngkə/ (*plural same* or **-cas**), **Pon·ka** (*plural same* or **-kas**) *n* **1.** a member of a Native North American people who formerly occupied lands around the Niobrara River in Nebraska and now live mainly in parts of Oklahoma and Nebraska **2.** a Native American language spoken in parts of Oklahoma and Nebraska. It belongs to the Siouan branch of Hokan-Siouan languages and is closely related to Omaha. [Late 18C. < Ponca *ppákka*] —**Pon·ca** *adj*

ponce /ponss/ *n UK* **1.** an offensive term for an effeminate or gay man (*insult*) **2.** same as **pimp** (*slang*) [Late 19C. Origin ?] —**pon·cy** *adj*

Pon·ce /páwn say/ city and port in southern Puerto Rico, on the Caribbean Sea. Population: 187,749 (1990).

Ponce (de Le·ón) /pònss də lee ón, pòn ssə də lée ən/, **Juan** (1460–1521) Spanish explorer. He was the first European to reach Florida (1513), but failed in his attempt to set up a colony there (1521).

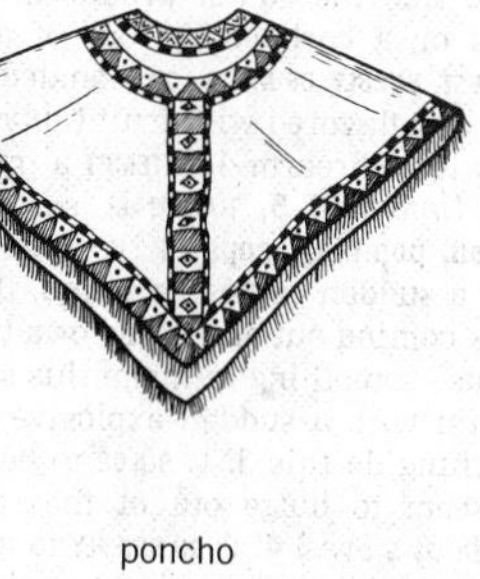

poncho

pon·cho /pónchō/ (*plural* **-chos**) *n* **1.** a simple outer garment for the upper body in the form of a single piece of heavy cloth, often wool, with a slit in it for the head **2.** *Hispanic* a waterproof outer garment with a hood, made in the style of a poncho [Early 18C. < American Spanish]

pond /pond/ *n* a small still body of water formed naturally or created artificially, e.g., as a feature in a garden ■ *vi* (**pond·ed, pond·ing, ponds**) to collect into shallow pools (*refers to water*) [13C. Alteration of POUND[3] "enclosure for fish"]

pond ap·ple *n US* an evergreen tree that has fragrant yellow flowers with red markings inside. Native to: tropical America, West Africa. Latin name: *Annona glabra*.

pon·der /póndər/ (**-dered, -der·ing, -ders**) *vti* to think about something carefully over a period of time [14C. Via French < Latin *ponderare* "weigh, consider" < *ponder-*, stem of *pondus* "weight"] —**pon·der·a·ble** *adj, n*

pon·der·o·sa pine /pòndə róssə-/ *n* a tall pine with yellowish bark and needles grouped in twos or threes, that yields valuable timber. Native to: western North America. Latin name: *Pinus ponderosa*. [< modern Latin < Latin *ponderosus* "heavy" (see PONDEROUS), because of its dense wood]

pon·der·ous /póndərəss/ *adj* **1. MOVING HEAVILY** lumbering and laborious in movement **2. DULL** without liveliness or wit **3. HEAVY-LOOKING** disproportionately thick and heavy [14C. Via French < Latin *ponderosus* < *ponder-*, stem of *pondus* "weight"] —**pon·der·ous·ly** *adv* —**pon·der·ous·ness** *n*

pond hock·ey *n Can* casual hockey played on a frozen pond

Pon·di·cher·ry /pòndi chérree/ **1.** city and port in southeastern India and capital of the Union Territory of Pondicherry. Population: 203,065 (1991). **2.** Union Territory of India, comprising Pondicherry, Karaikal, and Yanam on the east coast and the enclave of Mahé on the southwest coast. Capital: Pondicherry. Population: 973,829 (2001). Area: 190 sq. mi./492 sq. km.

pond lil·y *n* PLANTS same as **water lily**

pond scum *n* green freshwater algae that form a layer on the surface of stagnant water

pond-skat·er *n UK* same as **water strider**

pond·weed /pónd wèed/ (*plural same* or **-weeds**) *n* **1.** a plant that grows in ponds and slow streams and has jointed stems, floating or submerged leaves, and greenish flowers. Genus: *Potamogeton*. **2.** *UK* PLANTS same as **waterweed**

pone /pōn/ *n Southern US* FOOD same as **cornpone** [Early 17C. < Virginia Algonquian *poan*, "thing roasted or baked"]

pong·al /póng g'l/ *n S Asia* **1.** a Tamil festival. Date: New Year. **2.** a rice dish popular in South India, that may or may not be sweetened [Late 18C. < Tamil *ponkal* "boiling," because the festival involves the cooking of new rice]

pon·gee /pon jée, pón jèe/ *n* a soft, usually unbleached, silk fabric from China or South Asia, or a similar cotton or rayon imitation [Early 18C. < Chinese *běnjī* "own loom," or *běnzhī* "home-woven"]

pon·gid /pónjid/ *n* an ape of the family that includes the gibbon and the great apes. Family: Pongidae. [Mid-20C. < modern Latin *Pongidae* < Kongo *mpongo* "ape"]

pon·iard /pónnyərd/ (*literary*) *n* a small dagger with a slim blade that is triangular or square in its cross section ■ *vt* (**-iard·ed, -iard·ing, -iards**) to stab somebody with a poniard [Mid-16C. < French *poignard* < Latin *pugnus* "fist"]

Pon·ka *n, adj* LANG, PEOPLES another spelling of **Ponca**

pons /ponz/ (*plural* **pon·tes** /pón tèez/) *n* a whitish band of nerve fibers on the surface of the brainstem between the medulla oblongata and midbrain [Late 17C. < Latin, "bridge"]

pons as·i·no·rum /-assə náwrəm/ *n* a proposition or problem that is especially difficult for an inexperienced person to understand [< Latin, "bridge of asses"]

Pon·son·by /pónss'nbee/, **Vere Brabazon, 9th Earl of Bessborough** (1880–1956) British Canadian administrator who was governor-general of Canada (1931–35)

pons Va·ro·li·i /-və rólee ì/ *n* ANAT same as **pons** [Late 17C. < Latin, "bridge of Varolius," after C. *Varoli* (1543–75), Italian anatomist]

Pont ➧ **du Pont de Nemours, Eleuthère Irénée**

Pon·ta Del·ga·da /pòntə del gáadə/ city in Portugal, on São Miguel Island. It is the capital of the autonomous region of the Azores. Population: 21,091 (1991).

Pont·char·train, Lake /pónchər tràyn/ lake in southeastern Louisiana between the Gulf of Mexico and the Mississippi River. It is spanned by the world's longest causeway. Area: 625 sq. mi./1,620 sq. km.

Pon·te ➧ **Da Ponte, Lorenzo**

pon·tes ANAT plural of **pons**

Pon·ti·ac[1] /póntee àk/ city in southeastern Michigan, 25 mi./40 km northwest of Detroit. It is a car manufacturing center. Population: 66,137 (2002 estimate).

Pon·ti·ac[2] /póntee ak/ (1720?–69) Ottawa leader. He led the Ottawa and other Native American peoples in Pontiac's Rebellion against the British (1763–65).

pon·ti·fex /póntə fèks/ (*plural* **-tif·i·ces** /-tíffi sèez/) *n* in ancient Rome, a member of the highest council of priests [Late 16C. < Latin, "way-maker" < *pont-* "bridge, way"]

Pon·ti·fex Max·i·mus /pòntə feks máksiməss/ (*plural* **Pon·tif·i·ces Max·i·mi** /pon tíffə sèez máksə mì/) *n* in ancient Rome, the chief priest who presided over the highest council of priests

pon·tiff /póntif/ *n* **1.** the head of the Roman Catholic Church and bishop of Rome **2.** ANCIENT HIST, RELIG same as **pontifex** [Late 16C Via French < Latin *pontifex* (see PONTIFEX)]

pon·tif·i·cal /pon tíffik'l/ *adj* **1. OF PONTIFF** belonging to, befitting, or involving a pope, bishop, or pontifex **2. POMPOUS** displaying an exaggerated sense of self-importance ■ *n* **BISHOP'S BOOK** a book containing the rites that may be performed only by a bishop ■ **pon·tif·i·cals** *npl* **PONTIFF'S VESTMENTS** the vestments and insignia of a pope or bishop [15C < Latin *pontificalis* < *pontifex* (see PONTIFEX)] —**pon·tif·i·cal·ly** *adv*

Pon·tif·i·cal Mass *n* especially in the Roman Catholic Church, a High Mass that is celebrated by a bishop

pon·tif·i·cate *vi* /pon tíffi kàyt/ (**-cat·ed, -cat·ing, -cates**) **1. SPEAK POMPOUSLY** to speak about something in a knowing and self-important way, especially when not qualified to do so **2. SERVE AS BISHOP** to officiate as a bishop, especially in celebrating Mass ■ *n* /pon tíffikət, -kàyt/ **TERM OF OFFICE** the office or term of office of a pope or bishop [Early 19C. < medieval Latin *pontificat-*, past participle of *pontificare* < Latin *pontifex* (see PONTIFEX)] —**pon·tif·i·ca·tion** /pon tìffi káysh'n/ *n* —**pon·tif·i·ca·tor** *n*

pon·til /pónt'l/ *n* GLASS same as **punty** [Mid-19C. < French]

pon·tine /pón tìn, -tèen/ *adj* relating to or situated in the whitish band of nerve fibers (**pons**) on the surface of the brainstem between the medulla oblongata and midbrain [Late 19C. < Latin *pont-* "bridge, way"]

pon·toon[1] /pon tóon/ *n* **1. FLOATING SUPPORT FOR BRIDGE** a floating structure used as a support for a bridge across a river, especially one put in place temporarily **2. FLOAT ON AIRCRAFT** a float on an aircraft that provides buoyancy or stability when the aircraft is on water **3. FLOATING DOCK** a floating structure used as a dock [Late 17C. Via French < Latin *ponton-* "floating bridge" < *pont-* "bridge"]

pon·toon[2] /pon tóon/ *UK n* same as **blackjack** *n* (senses 1–2) ■ *interj* same as **blackjack** [Early 20C. Probably alteration of French *vingt-et-un* "twenty-one"]

pon·toon bridge *n* a temporary bridge built across a river, supported by floating structures

Pon·tor·mo /pon táwrmō/, **Jacopo da** (1494–1557) Italian painter. The exaggerated forms and bright colors of paintings such as *Deposition* (1526) influenced early mannerists.

Pon·ty·pool /pòntee pόol, póntee pòol/ town in Monmouthshire, Wales. Population: 35,564 (1991).

Pon·ty·pridd /pòntee préeth/ town near Cardiff, Wales. Population: 28,487 (1991).

po·ny /pónee/ *n* (*plural* **-nies**) **1. SMALL HORSE** any breed of small horse **2. POLO HORSE** a horse used in polo **3. ANY HORSE** a horse of any kind, especially a racehorse (*informal*) **4. SMALL GLASS** a small drinking glass, especially one used for liqueurs **5.** *US* **SMALL BOTTLE** a small bottle of beer or another beverage, holding seven ounces/0.2 liter **6.** *US* EDUC **CRIB SHEET** a literal translation of a text, used secretly by students during an exam or as an aid to studying a language (*informal*) **7.** *UK* **£25** the sum of £25 (*slang*) ■ *vti* (**-nied, -ny·ing, -nies**) *Northwest US, Rocky Mountains* **PAY MONEY** to pay out money that is due or owed (*informal*) ○ *They ordered some drinks, then ponied together the $8.50.* [Mid-17C. Origin ?]

pony up *vti* to pay somebody the money that is owed to him or her (*informal*)

po·ny ex·press *n* a system of carrying mail using relays of horses and riders that operated from St. Joseph, Missouri, to Sacramento, California, from 1860 to 1861.

po·ny·tail /pṓnee tàyl/ *n* a hairstyle in which long hair is pulled back and tied behind the head so that it hangs down like a pony's tail —**po·ny·tailed** *adj*

Pon·zi scheme /pónzee-/ *n US* a pyramid investment swindle in which supposed profits are paid to early investors from money actually invested by later participants [Early 20C. After Charles *Ponzi* (d. 1949)]

pooch /pooch/ *n* same as **dog** *n* (sense 1) (*informal*) [Early 20C. Origin ?]

poodle

poo·dle /pood'l/ *n* a dog with a thick curly coat, usually clipped short, belonging to either a small breed (**toy poodle**), or a large breed (**standard poodle**) originally developed in Europe for hunting [Early 19C. < German *Pudel*, shortening of *Pudelhund* < Low German *pudeln* "splash in water" + German *Hund* "dog"]

poof[1] /poof/, **pouf**, **pouffe**, **poove** *n UK* an offensive term for an effeminate or gay man (*insult*) [Mid-19C. Probably alteration (after POUF "puffed-out hairstyle") of PUFF "powder puff"] —**poof·y** *adj*

poof[2] /poof, poof/ *interj* (*informal*) **1.** used to indicate that something happens suddenly **2.** used to express disdain for or dismissal of something [Early 19C. An imitation of the sound of a rush of air or breath]

pooh /poo/ *interj* used to express disdain or dismissal (*informal*) [Late 16C. An imitation of the sound of blowing something away with the lips]

Pooh-Bah /poo baa/, **pooh-bah** *n* **1.** a pompous self-important official, especially one who holds more than one office but is ineffectual in all of them **2.** a leader, high official, or important person [Late 19C. After a character in *The Mikado*, operetta by W. S. Gilbert and Sir Arthur Sullivan]

pooh-pooh (**pooh-poohed, pooh-pooh·ing, pooh-poohs**) *vt* to dismiss or express disdain for something [Late 18C. Doubled form of POOH]

poo·ja *n Carib* another spelling of **puja**

poo·ka /pookə/ *n Ireland* in Irish folklore, a mischievous spirit, especially one that takes on the form of an animal [Early 19C. < Irish *púca*]

pool[1] /pool/ *n* **1.** SWIMMING POOL a swimming pool or wading pool **2.** PUDDLE a small amount of any liquid lying on a surface **3.** WATER a small body of still water, usually one that occurs naturally **4.** UNDERGROUND OIL OR GAS an accumulation of oil or gas in a region of porous sedimentary rock **5.** WATER BEHIND DAM a body of water collected behind a dam **6.** DEEP PART OF WATER a deep place in a river or stream where the water runs more slowly **7.** PATTERN RESEMBLING POOL a pattern or arrangement of something such as light that resembles a pool of liquid ○ *The floodlights bathed her in a pool of light.* ■ *vi* (**pooled, pool·ing, pools**) **1.** FORM POOL to collect in or form a pool **2.** ACCUMULATE IN BODY PART to collect in a body part or organ (*refers to blood*) [Old English *pōl* < Germanic]

pool[2] /pool/ *n* **1.** BALL AND CUE GAME a game played with a cue stick, cue ball and 15 balls on a felt-covered table with six pockets **2.** FORM OF GAMBLING a form of gambling in which the participants contribute an amount to a common fund that is divided among the winners **3.** TOTAL AMOUNT STAKED the collective amount that the players in a gambling game have staked **4.** COLLECTIVE RESOURCE a joint supply of vehicles, commodities, or workers that is shared and used by members of a group **5.** GROUP OF REPORTERS a selected group of reporters who cover an event and make their reports available to all participating news organizations **6.** FIN INVESTMENT FUND a collection of investments such as stocks in a mutual fund that are managed as a group for a common purpose or group of owners **7.** COMM BUSINESS TRUST an agreement between competing businesses to control production and sales in order to guarantee profits ■ *vt* (**pooled, pool·ing, pools**) SHARE RESOURCES to combine something to form a supply that can be shared by a group of people or companies [Late 17C. Via French *poule* "hen, gambling stakes" (hens were used as game prizes) < Latin *pullus* "young animal"]

Poole /pool/ port in Dorset, southern England. It is a resort and sailing center. Population: 138,288 (2001).

pool·room /pool room, -room/ *n* a room or commercial establishment where pool or billiards is played

pools /poolz/ *npl UK* in the United Kingdom, an organized form of gambling, conducted mainly by mail, that involves predicting the outcome of soccer games [Mid-20C. < POOL[2] *n* (sense 2)]

pool·side /pool sīd/ *n* the area around the sides of a swimming pool (*often used before a noun*)

pool ta·ble *n* a felt-covered rectangular table used for playing pool. It has six pockets, one at each corner and one in the middle of each of the longer sides.

poon /poon/ (*plural* **poons** or *same*) *n* a tree with leathery leaves and strong light wood. Native to: southern Asia. Genus: *Calophyllum.* [Late 17C. Via Sinhalese < Malayalam *punna* or Tamil *puṉṉai*]

Poo·na former name for **Pune**

Poons /poonz/, **Larry** (*b.* 1937) US painter. An influential figure in the op art movement in the 1960s, he later abandoned geometric patterns for more painterly compositions.

poop[1] /poop/ *n* NAUT **1.** RAISED AREA AT REAR OF SHIP the raised cabins at the stern of an old sailing ship, or the raised area at the stern of a modern ship, lying above the level of the main deck **2.** same as **poop deck** ■ *v* (**pooped, poop·ing, poops**) **1.** *vt* BREAK OVER STERN to break over a ship at the stern (*refers to waves*) **2.** *vi* HAVE WAVES BREAKING OVER STERN to have waves break over its stern, especially repeatedly (*refers to boats*) [15C. Via French < Latin *puppis*]

poop[2] /poop/ (**pooped, poop·ing, poops**) *vt* to make somebody feel exhausted (*informal; usually passive*) ○ *were pooped by the long hike* [Mid-20C. Origin ?] —**pooped** *adj*

poop out *vi* (*dated slang*) **1.** to quit doing something, usually because of exhaustion or fear **2.** to stop operating, e.g., because of mechanical failure

poop[3] /poop/ *n* candid and accurate information about something (*slang*) [Mid-20C. Origin ?]

poop[4] /poop/ (*informal; often used by or to children*) *n* excrement, a stool, or an act of defecating ■ *vi* (**pooped, poop·ing, poops**) same as **defecate** (sense 1) [Mid-16C. An imitation of a short blast of sound (part of the original meaning)]

poop[5] /poop/ *n* an offensive term that deliberately insults somebody's intelligence or competence (*slang insult*) [Early 20C. Origin ?]

poop deck *n* a raised open deck at the stern of a ship, with cabins below it

poop·er-scoop·er /poopər skoopər/ *n* a small shovel used to clean up dog excrement, used especially by a dog owner whose dog defecates in a public place (*informal*) [< POOP[4]]

poo-poo /poo poo/ (*baby talk*) *n* excrement, or an act of defecating ■ *vi* (**poo-pooed, poo-poo·ing, poo-poos**) same as **defecate** (sense 1) [Doubled form of *poo* "excrement" < variant of POOH]

poor /poor, pawr/ *adj* **1.** NOT RICH lacking money or material possessions **2.** AFFECTED BY POVERTY characterized by widespread or evident poverty ○ *a poor part of town* ○ *one of the poorest countries in the world* **3.** INFERIOR not of good quality or not in good condition ○ *We received a very poor education.* **4.** LACKING SKILL having little skill or ability ○ *I was always a poor athlete in school.* **5.** LOW OR INADEQUATE lower than expected or needed in quantity, number, or amount ○ *poor wages* ○ *Attendance at the concert was poor.* **6.** WEAK lacking strength, power, stamina, or resilience ○ *in poor health* **7.** DEFICIENT lacking or deficient in something (*often used in combination*) ○ *cash-rich but time-poor* **8.** LACKING PRODUCTIVE POTENTIAL lacking fertility or nutrients **9.** LOW IN VALUATION low in a scale of value ○ *has a poor opinion of himself* **10.** DESERVING PITY deserving pity or compassion, especially because of something that has just happened ■ *npl* PEOPLE WHO ARE POOR people who lack money or material possessions ○ *The poor are always with us.* [12C. Via Old French *povre* < Latin *pauper* (see PAUPER)] —**poor·ness** *n*

poor box *n* a box, especially one kept in a church, that is used to collect money for the poor

poor boy *n US regional, Can* a sandwich made from a long roll cut horizontally [Because originally made from discarded scraps and ends, and given to poor people]

poor farm *n* a publicly funded farm that provided employment, housing, and support for poor workers in former times

poor·house /poor hòwss, páwr-/ (*plural* **-hous·es** /-hòwzəz/) *n* a publicly funded institution that formerly existed to house people who were too poor to provide for themselves

poo·ri *n* another spelling of **puri**

poor law *n* a law or system of laws relating to the provision of support for poor people

poor·ly /poorlee, páwr-/ *adv* **1.** INADEQUATELY in an inferior or inadequate way ○ *He did poorly on the exam.* **2.** UNFAVORABLY with an unfavorable opinion or attitude ○ *They looked poorly on any suggestion of spending money.* ■ *adj* PHYSICALLY UNWELL feeling physically unwell or in poor physical health (*informal*)

poor mouth *n N Am, Ireland* complaints about being poor, regarded as made to win sympathy, sometimes when the complainer is not truly poor (*informal disapproving*)

poor-mouth *vi N Am, Ireland* to complain of a lack of money, especially when feigning or exaggerating poverty, often in order to win sympathy (*informal disapproving*)

poor re·la·tion *n* somebody or something that is inferior compared to another

poor white *n US* an offensive term for an uneducated lower-class white person who has an income considerably lower than average (*informal*)

poo·tle /poot'l/ (**-tled, -tling, -tles**) *vi UK* to move at a leisurely pace (*informal*) [Late 20C. Blend of *poodle* "move at a leisurely pace" + TOOTLE]

pop[1] /pop/ *n* **1.** SUDDEN BURSTING SOUND a sudden explosive sound, like the sound produced when a balloon bursts or a cork comes out of a bottle **2.** *Can, Midwest* BUBBLY DRINK a carbonated drink, usually sweet and flavored with fruit (*informal*) **3.** GUNSHOT a shot with a firearm **4.** ATTEMPT a try at doing something (*informal*) **5.** BASEBALL same as **pop fly** ■ *v* (**popped, pop·ping, pops**) **1.** *vti* MAKE BURSTING SOUND to make a sudden explosive sound, like the sound of a cork coming out of a bottle or a balloon bursting, or cause something to make this sound **2.** *vti* BURST to burst with a sudden explosive sound, or make something do this **3.** *vi* BULGE to become wide open and seem to bulge out of the sockets (*refers to somebody's eyes*) **4.** *vi* GO BRIEFLY to go, come, or visit for a brief time (*informal*) ○ *I might pop in later for a chat.* **5.** *vt* OPEN OR CLOSE SOMETHING to move something quickly and suddenly into an open or closed position (*informal*) ○ *He popped the lid up.* **6.** *vt* PUT QUICKLY to put or place something somewhere with a sudden rapid movement (*informal*) ○ *Before I could speak he had popped the cake into my mouth.* **7.** *vt* TAKE BY SWALLOWING to take a drug orally (*informal*) ○ *pop pills* **8.** *vti US* FIRE SHOTS to fire shots from a pistol or other firearm (*informal*) **9.** *vti* BASEBALL HIT POP FLY to hit a baseball high into the air a short distance, especially where it can be caught by an infielder ■ *adv* **1.** WITH BURSTING NOISE with a sudden bursting sound **2.** UNEXPECTEDLY suddenly or abruptly ■ *interj* INDICATING BURSTING NOISE used to indicate a sudden bursting noise [14C. An imitation of the sound] ◇ **a pop** for each one (*slang*) ○ *It'll cost you $10 a pop.*

REGIONAL NOTE See ***tonic***.

pop off *vi* (*informal*) **1.** *US* to speak out about something angrily or tactlessly **2.** to die suddenly

pop up *v* **1.** *vi* to appear suddenly and unexpectedly **2.** *vti* BASEBALL same as **pop**[1] *v* (sense 9)

pop[2] /pop/ *n* **1.** *also* **Pop** used for referring to or addressing your father (*informal*) **2.** used, either affectionately or patronizingly, to address a much older man (*dated slang*) [Mid-19C. Shortening of POPPA]

pop[3] /pop/ *n* **1.** MUSIC same as **pop music 2.** ARTS same as **pop art** ■ *adj* **1.** musically commercial, especially by being tuneful, up-tempo, and repetitive, and targeted at the general public and the youth market in particular ○ *a pop song* **2.** intended for or appreciated by a wide public, and often regarded as oversimplified for the sake of greater accessibility (*informal*) ○ *magazines full of pop psychology* [Late 19C. Shortening of POPULAR]

POP *abbr* **1.** ENVIRON persistent organic pollutant **2.** COMM point of presence **3.** METEOROL probability of precipitation **4.** COMM proof of purchase

pop. *abbr* **1.** popular **2.** population

pop art *n* an art movement in the 1950s to 1970s that incorporated modern popular culture and the mass media. It included such artists as Andy Warhol and Roy Lichtenstein.

pop·corn /póp kàwrn/ *n* **1.** the kernels of a variety of corn, heated until they become puffy, then usually flavored with butter and salt and eaten as a snack **2.** a variety of corn with hard kernels that pop open to form white puffs when heated. Latin name: *Zea mays praecox*. **3.** *US* INDUST same as **peanut** (sense 4)

pop·corn mov·ie *n* a popular and highly entertaining movie (*informal*)

pope /pōp/ *n* **1.** *also* **Pope** ROMAN CATHOLIC CHURCH HEAD the head of the Roman Catholic Church and bishop of Rome **2.** *also* **Pope** COPTIC CHURCH HEAD the head of the Coptic Church **3.** *also* **Pope** ORTHODOX PRIEST a priest in the Eastern Orthodox Church **4.** POWERFUL PERSON somebody who has great authority or status [Pre-12C. Via Latin *papa* < Greek *pappas* "father"] —**pope·dom** *n*

Pope /pōp/, **Alexander** (1688–1744) English poet. He wrote the mock-heroic poem *The Rape of the Lock* (1712) and *An Essay on Man* (1733–34).

> "To err is human; to forgive, divine."
> [Alexander Pope, *An Essay on Criticism*; 1711]

> "All nature is but art, unknown to thee; / All chance, direction, which thou canst not see; / All discord, harmony, not understood; / All partial evil, universal good; / And spite of Pride, in erring Reason's spite, / One truth is clear, 'Whatever IS, is RIGHT.'"
> [Alexander Pope, *An Essay on Man*; 1733–34]

> "Expression is the dress of thought."
> [Alexander Pope, *An Essay on Criticism*; 1711]

pop·er·y /pṓpəree/ *n* an offensive term for the Roman Catholic Church, its doctrines, or its practices

pope's nose *n* the fatty piece of flesh at the rear end of a cooked chicken, turkey, or other bird, to which the tail feathers were attached (*sometimes offensive*)

pop·eyed /póp ìd/ *adj* **1.** with the eyes bulging out **2.** with the eyes wide open in surprise or disbelief

pop fly *n* in baseball, a high fly ball that travels a relatively short distance from home plate

pop·gun /póp gùn/ *n* **1.** a toy gun that uses compressed air to shoot pellets, balls, or a cork tied to a string. It makes a popping sound. **2.** a useless or unimpressive firearm (*informal*)

pop·in·jay /póppin jày/ *n* a vain and conceited person [13C. Via Old French *papegay* "parrot" < Arabic *babbaġā*]

pop·ish /pṓpish/ *adj* an offensive term meaning associated with the Roman Catholic Church, its doctrines, or its practices —**pop·ish·ly** *adv*

pop·lar /pópplər/ *n* **1.** a slender tree of the willow family with triangular leaves, flowers in catkins, and soft wood. Native to: northern temperate regions. Genus: *Populus*. **2.** the light-colored wood of a poplar (*often used before a noun*) **3.** TREES same as **tulip tree** [14C. Via Anglo-Norman *popler* < Latin *populus*]

pop·lin /pópplin/ *n* a plain strong cotton fabric with fine ribbing. Use: clothes, upholstery. (*often used before a noun*) [Early 18C. < obsolete French *papeline* < medieval Latin *papalis* "papal" (because made at the papal town of Avignon) < Latin *papa* (see POPE)]

pop·lit·e·al /pop líttee əl, pòpplə tée əl/ *adj* relating to or located in the part of the leg behind the knee joint [Late 18C. < modern Latin *popliteus* < Latin *poples* "ham, back of the knee"]

pop mu·sic *n* modern commercial music, usually tuneful, up-tempo and repetitive, that is aimed at the general public and the youth market in particular

Po·po·ca·té·petl /pṓpə kátta pètt'l, pṓw paw kaa té pètt'l/ volcano in southern central Mexico. Height: 17,887 ft./5,452 m.

Po·po·va /po pṓvər/, **Liubov** (1889–1924) Russian painter and designer. Influenced by futurism and constructivism, she designed stage sets and textiles for Moscow's First State Textile Printing Factory.

pop·o·ver /póp ṑvər/ *n* a light hollow muffin-shaped quick bread made from eggs, flour, and milk

pop·pa /póppə/ *n* same as **father** (*informal*) [Late 19C. Alteration of PAPA[1]]

pop·pa·dom /póppədəm/, **pop·pa·dum**, **pa·pa·dum** *n* in South Asian cuisine, a fried or roasted plate-sized wafer made from bean flour, eaten as an appetizer or a side dish [Early 19C. < Tamil *pappaṭam*]

pop·per /póppər/ *n* an appliance, container, or pan for popping popcorn ■ **pop·pers** *npl* small vials of amyl nitrate or butyl nitrate for inhaling as an illicit drug (*slang*)

pop·pet /póppət/ *n* **1.** ENG same as **poppet valve 2.** a steel beam or timber that is used to support the front and back ends of a ship when it is being launched **3.** *UK* used to address a sweet and dear person, especially a child (*informal*) [14C. Origin ?]

pop·pet valve *n* a valve that is raised and lowered by a vertical guide, e.g., the intake and exhaust valves of the cylinders in an internal-combustion engine

pop·ple[1] /póppʼl/ (**-pled, -pling, -ples**) *vi* to move in an irregular tumbling or bubbling manner, like water does when it boils [14C. Probably < Middle Dutch *popelen* "to babble, murmur," an imitation of the sound]

pop·ple[2] /póppʼl/ *n* TREES same as **poplar** (sense 1) (*informal*) [14C. < Latin *populus*]

poppy

pop·py /póppee/ (*plural* **-pies**) *n* **1.** PLANT WITH RED FLOWERS an annual or perennial plant that has cup-shaped seed pods and milky sap. Flowers: large, red, orange, or white. Genus: *Papaver*. **2.** PLANT EXTRACT an extract from poppy that is used as a narcotic or medicine **3.** PLANT LIKE TRUE POPPY any flowering plant that is similar or related to a poppy, e.g., a California poppy or Welsh poppy **4.** ORANGE-RED COLOR a bright red color tinged with orange [Pre-12C. < Vulgar Latin alteration of Latin *papaver*]

pop·py·cock /póppee kòk/ *n* absurd speech or writing (*dated*) [Mid-19C. < Dutch dialect *pappekak* < *pap* "soft, pap" + *kak* "dung"]

pop·py·head /póppee hèd/ *n* an ornamental carved top on the end of a pew in a Gothic church

pop·py seed *n* the small black seed of the poppy, used in cooking and in baking

pop quiz *n* a quiz given to students without advance notice

pops /pops/ *n* a symphony orchestra that plays popular classical music and pop music (*often used before a noun*)

Pop·si·cle /pópsik'l, póp sìk'l/ *tdmk* a trademark for a colored fruit-flavored ice on one or two sticks

pop-top *n* **1.** CAN TOP the top or portion of the top of a can that can be removed by pulling an attached ring or tab **2.** CAN a can whose top is opened by pulling an attached ring or tab **3.** VAN ROOF a van roof that can be raised to create extra headroom while the van is stationary **4.** VAN a van with a pop-top

pop·u·lace /póppyələss/ *n* **1.** the inhabitants of a town, region, or other area **2.** ordinary people, as distinct from the political elite or the aristocracy [Late 16C. Via French < Italian *popolaccio* "rabble" < *popolo* "people" < Latin *populus*]

SPELLCHECK Do not confuse the spelling of ***populace*** and ***populous***, which sound similar. ***Populace*** is a noun meaning "the inhabitants or ordinary people of a place," whereas ***populous*** is an adjective meaning "densely populated."

pop·u·lar /póppyələr/ *adj* **1.** APPEALING TO GENERAL PUBLIC appealing to or appreciated by a wide range of people ○ *the most popular name for babies this year* **2.** WELL-LIKED liked by a person or group of people ○ *popular with young audiences* **3.** OF GENERAL PUBLIC relating to the general public ○ *popular appeal* **4.** AIMED AT NONSPECIALISTS designed to appeal to or be comprehensible to the nonspecialist ○ *popular science* **5.** BELIEVED BY PEOPLE IN GENERAL believed, embraced, or perpetuated by ordinary people ○ *popular myths* **6.** INEXPENSIVE designed to be affordable to people on average incomes ○ *a new popular car* [15C. Via Anglo-Norman < Latin *popularis* "of the people" < *populus* "people"]

pop·u·lar front *n* a broad-based coalition of left-wing political parties, formed to oppose fascism or institute social reforms, especially in Europe in the mid-1930s

pop·u·lar·i·ty /pòppyə lárratee/ *n* **1.** admiration, approval, or acceptance of somebody or something by people in general or by a group of people **2.** the desire or demand for something such as a manufactured product

pop·u·lar·ize /póppyələ rìz/ (**-ized, -iz·ing, -iz·es**) *vt* **1.** to make something widely liked or appreciated **2.** to make something accessible and comprehensible to a wide audience —**pop·u·lar·i·za·tion** /pòppyələri záysh'n/ *n* —**pop·u·lar·iz·er** *n*

pop·u·lar·ly /póppyələrlee/ *adv* **1.** by most people or in most situations **2.** by the general public, as distinct from specialists

pop·u·lar mu·sic *n* MUSIC same as **pop music**

pop·u·lar sov·er·eign·ty *n* **1.** the doctrine that the people are sovereign and a government is subject to the will of the people **2.** a pre-Civil War political doctrine that held that individual states should decide whether to permit slavery or not. It was espoused mainly by opponents of the abolition of slavery.

pop·u·late /póppyə làyt/ (**-lat·ed, -lat·ing, -lates**) *vt* **1.** to live in an area, region, or country (*often passive*) **2.** to supply an area with inhabitants [Late 16C. < medieval Latin *populat-*, past participle of *populare* < Latin *populus* "people"] —**pop·u·lat·ed** *adj*

pop·u·la·tion /pòppyə láysh'n/ *n* **1.** PEOPLE IN PLACE all of the people who inhabit an area, region, or country **2.** ALL PEOPLE OF GROUP all of the people of a particular nationality, ethnic group, religion, or class who live in an area **3.** NUMBER OF PEOPLE the total number of people who inhabit an area, region, or country, or the number of people in a particular group who inhabit an area **4.** ACT OF SUPPLYING INHABITANTS the populating of an area with inhabitants **5.** INDIVIDUALS OF SAME SPECIES all the plants or animals of a particular species present in a place **6.** STATS GROUP STATISTICALLY SAMPLED the entire group of individuals or items from which a sample may be selected for statistical measurement

pop·u·la·tion ex·plo·sion *n* a sudden and rapid increase in the number of individuals living in an area. In humans, this may be as a result of an increased birth rate or a decline in mortality, while in the case of animals it may be because of a lack of predators or altered environmental conditions.

pop·u·la·tion rev·o·lu·tion *n* the huge growth in population in western Europe that began about 1730. It was a prelude to the Industrial Revolution.

pop·u·lism /póppyə lìzzəm/ *n* **1.** politics or political ideology based on the perceived interests of ordinary people, as opposed to those of a privileged elite **2.** focus or emphasis on the lives of ordinary people, e.g., in the arts and in politics [Late 19C. < Latin *populus* "people"]

Pop·u·lism *n* the political philosophy and program of the Populist Party

pop·u·list /póppyəlist/ *n* an advocate of the rights and interests of ordinary people, e.g., in politics or the arts ■ *adj* emphasizing or promoting ordinary people, their lives, or their interests [Late 19C. < Latin *populus* "people"]

Pop·u·list *n* a political supporter of the Populist Party ■ *adj* belonging or relating to the Populist Party

Pop·u·list Par·ty *n US* a US political party formed in the 1890s to represent the interests of farmers and laborers. It favored free coinage of silver and other reforms and was disbanded in 1904.

pop·u·lous /póppyələss/ *adj* with a large number of inhabitants [15C. < late Latin *populosus* < Latin *populus* "people"] —**pop·u·lous·ly** *adv* —**pop·u·lous·ness** *n*

SPELLCHECK See ***populace.***

pop-up *adj* **1. UPWARD-LIFTING** having a mechanism that makes something move quickly upward ○ *pop-up headlights* **2. PRESENTED ON COMPUTER SCREEN TEMPORARILY** appearing quickly and temporarily on a computer screen when a special key is pressed or a button is clicked with a mouse ○ *a pop-up menu* **3. WITH RISING CUT-OUT FIGURES** containing cut-out figures that rise up as a page is opened ○ *a pop-up book* ■ *n* **1.** BASEBALL same as **pop fly** **2. ITEM WITH POP-UP FIGURES** a book or card that contains pop-up figures, or a pop-up figure

pop wine *n US* an inexpensive, sweet, usually fruit-flavored wine that has a low alcohol content

por·bea·gle /páwr beeg'l/ (*plural* **-gles** or *same*) *n* a large and voracious shark with a crescent-shaped tail. Native to: North Atlantic. Latin name: *Lamna nasus.* [Mid-18C. < Cornish *porbugel*]

por·ce·lain /páwrssələn, páwrsslən/ *n* **1. CERAMIC MATERIAL** a hard translucent ceramic material used for making plates, cups, and other items (*often used before a noun*) **2. ITEMS MADE OF PORCELAIN** objects made of porcelain, e.g., expensive crockery or decorative figurines **3. DECORATIVE OBJECT** a single object made from porcelain, especially a decorative object [Mid-16C. Via French < Italian *porcellana* "cowrie shell," (from its texture) "porcelain," literally "like a young sow" (because of the shell's shape) < *porca* "sow" < form of Latin *porcus* "pig"] —**por·ce·la·ne·ous** /pàwrssə láynee əss/ *adj*

por·ce·lain e·nam·el *n* a glass coating that is fused to a metal by firing

porch /pawrch/ *n* **1.** a raised platform with a roof that runs along the side of a house, partly enclosed with low walls or fully enclosed with screens or windows **2.** a covered shelter at the entrance to a building [13C. Via French < Latin *porticus* "covered entry" < *porta* "gate"]

por·cine /páwr sīn, páwrss'n/ *adj* relating to or resembling pigs [Mid-17C. Via French < Latin *porcinus* < *porcus* "pig"]

por·ci·no /pawr seénō/ (*plural* **-ni** /-nee/), **por·ci·ni mush·room** *n* FOOD same as **cep** [Late 20C. < Italian, shortening of *fungo porcino* "porcine mushroom"]

porcupine

por·cu·pine /páwrkyə pīn/ *n* a large rodent whose body is covered with long protective quills that it can erect in defense against predators. Families: Hystricidae or Erethizontidae. [14C. < Old French *porc espin* "spiny pig"]

Por·cu·pine /páwrkyə pīn/ river in North America that originates in northern Yukon Territory, Canada, joining the Yukon River in northeastern Alaska. Length: 569 mi./916 km.

por·cu·pine fish *n* a ocean fish that has strong sharp spines covering its body. Native to: tropics. Family: Diodontidae.

pore[1] /pawr/ *n* **1. TINY OPENING IN SKIN** a tiny opening in human skin, or in the skin or other outer covering of an animal, through which substances can pass. Perspiration is released through the pores. **2. TINY OPENING IN PLANT** a tiny opening in a leaf or stem of a plant used to absorb or release substances, e.g., in photosynthesis or respiration **3.** GEOL **SMALL SPACE IN ROCK** a small space that is surrounded by rock or soil. It may be filled with water, crude oil, or natural gas. [14C. Via French and Latin < Greek *poros* "passage"]

USAGE See ***pour.***

pore[2] /pawr/ (**pored, por·ing, pores**) *vi* **1.** to study something carefully and thoughtfully ○ *poring over a book* **2.** to meditate on or think carefully about something [13C. Origin ?]

USAGE See ***pour.***

pore fun·gus *n* any fungus that has spores in tiny tubules that lead to outside pores. Families: Boletaceae or Polyporaceae.

por·gy /páwrgee/ (*plural* **-gies** or *same*) *n* **1. SEA FOOD FISH** an ocean food fish that has a deep flat body with large scales. Native to: Mediterranean Sea, Atlantic Ocean. Latin name: *Pagrus pagrus.* **2. FISH RELATED TO PORGY** an ocean fish related to the porgy, with a similarly deep flat body. Family: Sparidae. **3. UNRELATED FISH LIKE PORGY** a fish that is similar to the porgy but unrelated, e.g., the menhaden [Mid-17C. Via Spanish, Portuguese *pargo* < Greek *phagros* "sea bream"]

po·rif·er·an /paw ríffərən/ *n* MARINE BIOL same as **sponge** *n* (sense 1) (*technical*) ■ *adj* belonging or relating to the sponges [Mid-19C. < modern Latin *Porifera* "passage-bearing" < Latin *porus* "pore (of the skin)"]

po·rin /páwrən/ *n* a doughnut-shaped protein that spans a membrane in living cells to create a channel for the passage of small molecules [Late 20C. < PORE[1]]

pork /pawrk/ *n* **1.** the flesh of a hog eaten as food, usually cooked fresh. Cured hog flesh is usually referred to as bacon or ham. (*often used before a noun*) **2.** *US* government money and jobs awarded by politicians to their supporters or constituents to win their favor, especially when awarded wastefully (*informal*) [13C. Via French < Latin *porcus* "pig"]

pork bar·rel *n* government-funded projects that bring jobs and other benefits to an area and give its political representative the opportunity to award favors and reap the ensuing prestige (*informal; hyphenated before a noun*)

pork bel·ly *n* a side of fresh pork, or a cut of meat from this

pork·er /páwrkər/ *n* **1.** a young fattened hog, especially one raised for its meat **2.** person or animal regarded as overweight (*informal insult*)

pork·pie hat /páwrk pī hàt/, **pork·pie** *n* **1.** a man's hat with a flat crown and small brim that can be turned up, first popular in the 1850s **2.** a woman's round hat without a brim, first popular in the 1860s [< its shape]

pork rinds *npl* small pieces of fried pork rind and fat that are eaten as a snack

pork scratch·ings *npl UK* same as **pork rinds**

por·ky[1] /páwrkee/ *adj* (**-ki·er, -ki·est**) regarded as overweight (*informal insult*) ■ *n* (*plural* **-kies**) *UK* same as **lie**[2] *n* (sense 1) (*slang; often used in the plural*) ○ *Who's been telling porkies, then?* [In noun sense < rhyming slang *pork pie*]

por·ky[2] /páwrkee/ (*plural* **-kies**) *n* a porcupine (*informal*) [Mid-20C. Shortening]

porn /pawrn/, **por·no** /páwrnō/ *n* same as **pornography** (*informal; often used before a noun*) [Mid-20C. Shortening]

por·no·graph·ic /pàwrnə gráffik/ *adj* **1.** sexually explicit and intended to cause sexual arousal **2.** producing or selling sexually explicit magazines, films, or other materials —**por·no·graph·i·cal·ly** *adv*

por·nog·ra·phy /pawr nóggrəfee/ *n* **1.** films, magazines, writings, photographs, or other materials that are sexually explicit and intended to cause sexual arousal **2.** the production or sale of sexually explicit films, magazines, or other materials [Mid-19C. Via French < Greek *pornographos* "writing about prostitutes" < *pornē* "prostitute"] —**por·nog·ra·pher** *n*

po·ros·i·ty /paw róssətee/ (*plural* **-ties**) *n* **1. POROUS QUALITY** the porous nature of something, or the extent to which something is porous **2.** GEOL **PERCENTAGE OF PORE SPACE** the ratio of the space taken up by the pores in a soil, rock, or other material to its total volume. It is expressed as a percentage. **3.** GEOL **PORE** a pore in soil, rock, or other material (*technical*) [14C. Via French < medieval Latin *porositas* < *porosus* (see POROUS)]

po·rous /páwrəss/ *adj* **1. PERMEABLE** permitting the movement of fluids or gases through it by way of pores or other passages **2. BREACHABLE** easy to cross, infiltrate, or penetrate **3. WITH PORES** having a surface that contains pores or a body that contains cavities [14C. Via French < medieval Latin *porosus* < Latin *porus* "passage, pore"] —**po·rous·ly** *adv* —**po·rous·ness** *n*

por·phyr·i·a /pawr féeree ə/ *n* a medical condition caused by the body's failure to metabolize porphyrins. Symptoms of the hereditary form include abdominal pain, sensitivity to sunlight, confusion, and excretion of porphyrins in the urine. [Early 20C. < PORPHYRIN]

por·phy·rin /páwrfərin/ *n* a metal-containing pigment in animal and plant tissue, consisting of four pyrrole rings linked by methylene groups, e.g., hemoglobin [Early 20C. < Greek *porphura* "purple," from the color of the pigments]

por·phy·rit·ic /pàwrfə ríttik/ *adj* **1.** relating to or containing porphyry **2.** containing isolated large and distinct crystals in a mainly fine-grained rock

por·phy·ry /páwrfəree/ *n* **1.** a reddish purple rock containing large distinct feldspar crystals embedded in a fine-grained groundmass **2.** any predominantly fine-grained igneous rock that contains isolated large crystals [14C. Via Old French *porfire* < Greek *porphuritēs* < *porphura* "purple," from its color]

por·poise /páwrpəss/ (*plural* **-pois·es** or *same*) *n* **1.** a toothed sea mammal, related to the whales and dolphins, that has a blunt snout and a triangular dorsal fin. Family: Phocaenidae. **2.** a popular but technically inaccurate term for a dolphin [14C. < Old French *porpeis* < Latin *porcus* "pig" + *piscis* "fish"]

por·ridge /páwrij/ *n UK* same as **oatmeal** *n* (sense 2) [Mid-16C. Alteration of POTTAGE]

por·rin·ger /páwrinjər/ *n* a small bowl, usually with a handle, used for soup, stew, or oatmeal [Early 16C. Alteration of *pottinger* < French *potager* < *potage* (see POTTAGE)]

port[1] /pawrt/ *n* **1. HARBOR** a place by the sea, or by a river or other waterway, where ships and boats can dock, load, and unload **2. TOWN WITH HARBOR** a town or city built around a port **3. WATERFRONT** the waterfront area of a port **4. COVE** a sheltered place along a coast, where boats are protected from storms and rough seas **5.** GEOG same as **port of entry** [Pre-12C. < Latin *portus*] ◇ **any port in a storm** any source of help or refuge is welcome in desperate circumstances

port[2] /pawrt/ *n* **1.** COMPUT **EXTERNAL COMPUTER CONNECTION** an external socket on a computer's main unit (**CPU**) where a peripheral device such as a printer, keyboard, or network cable is plugged in **2.** COMPUT **ADAPTATION OF SOFTWARE** the act of converting software so that it can run on a different operating system **3.** NAUT **OPENING IN BOAT** a watertight opening in the side of a boat, used for loading and unloading and as a means of general access to the holds **4.** NAUT same as **porthole** (sense 1) **5.** MIL **GUN HOLE** a small opening in an armored vehicle, military aircraft, naval vessel, or fortification through which a gun can be fired **6.** ENG **VALVE-OPERATED OPENING** an opening controlled by a valve, e.g., any of the openings in the cylinder of an internal combustion engine ■ *vt* (**port·ed, port·ing, ports**) COMPUT **CONVERT SOFTWARE FOR DIFFERENT SYSTEM** to convert software to run on a different operating system [13C. Via French, "gate" < Latin *porta*]

port[3] /pawrt/ *n* **LEFT SIDE ON SHIP OR PLANE** the left-hand side of a boat or airplane when facing forward ■ *adj, adv* **ON LEFT** on or to the left-hand side of boat or airplane when facing forward ■ *vti* (**port·ed, port·ing, ports**) **TURN TO PORT** to turn toward the port side, or make a ship do this [Mid-16C. Shortening of *port side* < PORT[1], because the side that faced the pier and over which cargo was loaded]

port[4] /pawrt/ *n* a strong sweet fortified wine usually drunk after dinner. It is usually a deep red color, but some kinds are brownish (**tawny port**) and some white. Originally from Portugal, port is now made in other countries. [Late 17C. After PORTO]

port[5] /pawrt/ *vt* (**port·ed, port·ing, ports**) to carry a weapon positioned diagonally across the body with the muzzle or blade in front of the left shoulder ■ *n* the position of a rifle or sword when ported [Mid-16C. Via French < Latin *portare* "carry"]

por·ta·bel·la *n* FUNGI another spelling of **portobello**

port·a·ble /páwrtəb'l/ *adj* **1. EASILY MOVED AROUND** designed to be light or compact enough to carry or move easily from place to place **2.** COMPUT **EASY TO CONVERT** describes software that can be easily converted to run on different computer operating systems ■ *n* **EASILY TRANSPORTED OBJECT** a device or an appliance that is designed to be easily carried or moved from place to place [14C. Via French < late Latin *portabilis* < Latin *portare* "carry"] —**port·a·bil·i·ty** /pàwrtə bílləte̊e/ *n* —**port·a·bly** *adv*

port·a·ble doc·u·ment for·mat *n* COMPUT full form of **pdf**

port·age /páwrtij, pawr ta̋azh/ *n* **1. ACT OF CARRYING** the carrying or transporting of something **2. CHARGE FOR CARRYING** a charge made for carrying or transporting something **3. CARRYING OF BOATS OVERLAND** the carrying of boats or cargo across land from one waterway to another or around an unnavigable section of a waterway **4. OVERLAND ROUTE TO WATERWAY** an overland route used when transporting a boat or its cargo from one waterway to another ■ *vti* (**-aged, -ag·ing, -ag·es**) **CARRY SOMETHING OVERLAND TO WATERWAY** to carry boats or cargo across land from one waterway to another or around an unnavigable portion of a waterway [13C. < French < Latin *portare* "carry"]

Por·tage /páwrtij/ city in northwestern Indiana, directly south of Lake Michigan, southeast of Gary and southwest of South Bend. Population: 34,498 (2002 estimate).

Por·tage la Prai·rie /-lə prérree/ city in Manitoba, Canada, situated on the Assiniboine River and the Trans-Canada Highway. Population: 13,019 (2001).

por·tal /páwrt'l/ *n* **1. LARGE GATE** a large or elaborate gate or entrance (*literary*) **2. ENTRANCE** any entrance to a place, or any means of access to something (*literary*) **3.** *also* **por·tal site** ONLINE **HOME SITE FOR WEB BROWSER** a website that provides links to information and other websites **4.** CONSTR **TUNNEL ENTRANCE** the entrance to a tunnel ■ *adj* ANAT **OF PORTAL VEIN OR SYSTEM** relating to the portal vein, portal system, or the opening in the liver through which the portal vein passes [14C. Via French < medieval Latin *portale* < Latin *porta* "gate"]

por·tal bridge *n* a bridge that is supported from beneath by an angled member at each end, often used for road bridges

por·tal site *n* ONLINE same as **portal** *n* (sense 3)

por·tal sys·tem *n* a network of blood vessels that begin in the capillaries of one organ and end in the capillaries of another, especially the portal veins connecting the liver and intestines

por·tal vein *n* a vein that carries blood from the digestive organs, gall bladder, and spleen to the liver, especially the vein from the intestines carrying nutrient-rich blood

por·ta·men·to /pàwrtə méntō/ (*plural* **-ti** /-tee/) *n* a smooth glide from one note to another when singing or playing a stringed instrument [Late 18C. < Italian, "carrying," because the finger slides from one note to the next]

Port Ar·thur /-a̋arthər/ **1.** city and deep-water port in southeastern Texas, on the Sabine Lake. Linked to the Gulf of Mexico by the Sabine-Neches Canal, it is the largest gasoline-refining center in the United States. Population: 56,885 (2002 estimate). **2.** town in Australia, in southern Tasmania. It was the site of a major penal settlement between 1830 and 1837. Population: 190 (1994). **3.** former name for **Lushun**

por·ta·tive or·gan /páwrtətiv-/ *n* a small portable organ operated by bellows, used in medieval and Renaissance music

Port Au·gus·ta city in South Australia, at the head of the Spencer Gulf. The city is a railroad junction and industrial center. Population: 13,593 (2002 estimate).

Port-au-Prince /-ō prínss/ capital city and chief port of Haiti, on Gonâve Gulf. Population: 990,558 (1999).

Port Blair port on South Andaman Island in the Bay of Bengal, and capital of the Indian Union Territory of Andaman and Nicobar Islands. Population: 49,634 (1981).

Port Ches·ter village on Long Island Sound, in southeastern New York, on the Connecticut border. Population: 27,949 (2002 estimate).

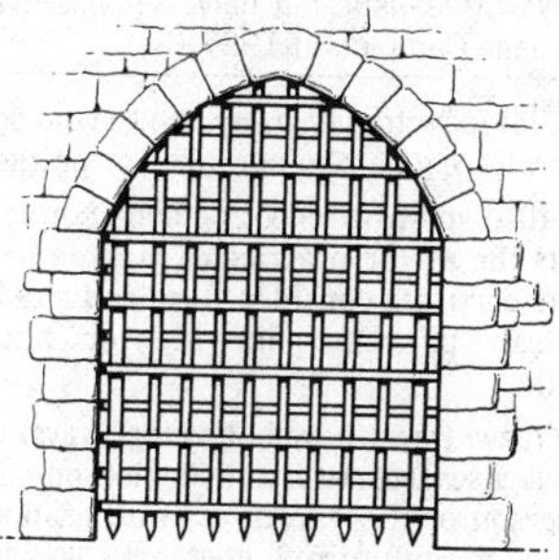

portcullis

port·cul·lis /pawrt kúlliss/ *n* a heavy iron or wooden grating that is set in vertical grooves and lowered to block the gateway to a castle or fortification [14C. < Old French *porte coleïce* "sliding door"]

port de bras /pàwr də bra̋a/ *n* the proper movement of the arms in ballet, or exercises for developing this [< French, "carriage of the arms"]

Port du Salut *n* FOOD same as **Port-Salut**

Porte /pawrt/ *n* the court or government of the Ottoman Empire. It was situated in Constantinople. [Early 17C. < French *(la Sublime) Porte* "(the exalted) Gate," translation of the Turkish title of the central office; from the palace gate where justice was administered]

porte-co·chère /pàwrt kō shér/, **porte-co·chere** *n* **1.** a large roof or awning extending from the entrance of a building to the driveway **2.** a large covered entrance for vehicles in a wall or building leading to a courtyard [Late 17C. < French *porte cochère* "door for coaches"]

Port E·liz·a·beth city in Eastern Cape Province, southeastern South Africa, situated on Algoa Bay, on the Indian Ocean. Population: 1,035,000 (1995).

por·tend /pawr ténd/ (**-tend·ed, -tend·ing, -tends**) *vt* **1.** to be an indication that something, especially something unpleasant, is going to happen **2.** to indicate or signify something [15C. < Latin *portendere* "stretch forward" < *tendere* "hold out, stretch"]

por·tent /páwr tènt/ *n* **1. OMEN** an indication that something, often something unpleasant, is going to happen **2. SIGNIFICANCE** ominous or prophetic significance **3. MARVEL** a wonderful or marvelous thing (*formal*) [Late 16C. < Latin *portentum* < *portendere* (see PORTEND)]

por·ten·tous /pawr téntəss/ *adj* **1. SIGNIFICANT** very serious and significant, especially with regard to future events **2. POMPOUS** excessively serious or pompous **3. AMAZING** inspiring wonder and amazement —**por·ten·tous·ly** *adv* —**por·ten·tous·ness** *n*

por·ter[1] /páwrtər/ *n* **1.** a worker who carries people's luggage, e.g., at an airport or railroad station, or in a hotel **2.** an attendant in a sleeping car or parlor car [14C. Via French *porteur* < medieval Latin *portator* "carrier" < Latin *portat-*, past participle of *portare* "carry"]

por·ter[2] /páwrtər/ *n UK* same as **superintendent** *n* (sense 2) [13C. Via French < late Latin *portarius* < Latin *porta* "gate"]

por·ter[3] /páwrtər/ *n* a dark sweet beer, similar to light stout, made from malt that has been browned or charred [Early 18C. Shortening of *porter's ale* < PORTER[1]]

Por·ter /páwrtər/, **Cole** (1893–1964) US composer and lyricist. He is known for his witty sophisticated songs, and for musicals such as *Kiss Me Kate* (1949). Full name **Porter, Cole Albert**

> "In olden days, a glimpse of stocking / Was looked on as something shocking, / But now, Heaven knows, / Anything goes."
> [Cole Porter, "Anything Goes," *Anything Goes*; 1934]

Por·ter, Katherine Anne (1890–1980) US writer. Regarded as one of the leading modern writers of short stories, she received the 1966 Pulitzer Prize for *Collected Short Stories* (1965).

> "Miracles are instantaneous, they cannot be summoned, but come of themselves, usually at unlikely moments and to those who least expect them."
> [Katherine Anne Porter, *Ship of Fools*; 1962]

Por·ter, Rodney (1917–85) British biochemist. He is noted for his work on the chemical structure of antibodies, for which he shared a Nobel Prize in physiology or medicine (1972). Full name **Porter, Rodney Robert**

Porter /páwrtər/, **William Sydney** ➧ **Henry, O.**

por·ter·age /páwrtərij/ *n* **1.** the work of carrying that is performed by porters **2.** a fee charged by porters for carrying things

por·ter·house /páwrtər hòwss/ (*plural* **-hous·es** /-hòwzəz/) *n* **1.** FOOD same as **porterhouse steak 2.** an establishment that sold porter and sometimes also served meals (*archaic*)

por·ter·house steak *n* a beef steak from the thick end of the sirloin

port·fo·li·o /pawrt fōlee ō/ (*plural* **-os**) *n* **1. FLAT CASE FOR DOCUMENTS** a large flat case for carrying documents such as maps, photographs, or drawings **2. PORTFOLIO CONTENTS** the contents of a portfolio, especially when they represent somebody's creative work **3. GROUP OF INVESTMENTS** all the investments held by a person or organization **4. MINISTERIAL RESPONSIBILITIES** the post or responsibilities of a cabinet minister, minister of state, or ambassador **5. RANGE OF PRODUCTS** the complete range of products or designs offered by a company (*formal*) [Early 18C. < Italian *portafoglio* < *portare* "carry" + *foglio* "sheet, page"]

port·fo·li·o work·er *n* somebody who offers skills and experience in a number of different areas, often working on a short-term or part-time basis

Port Har·court /-ha̋arkərt/ major port and capital city of Rivers State, southern Nigeria. Population: 399,700 (1995).

Porth·cawl /pàwrth káwl/ town near Bridgend in southern Wales. Population: 15,922 (1991).

Port Hed·land /-hédlənd/ town in northwestern Western Australia. Population: 12,846 (1996).

port·hole /páwrt hòl/ *n* **1.** a small round window with a metal frame in the side of a ship **2.** a small opening in a fortified wall through which weapons can be fired

Por·tia /páwrshə/ *n* a small inner natural satellite of Uranus, discovered in 1986 by the Voyager 2 planetary probe. It is approximately 68 mi./110 km in diameter.

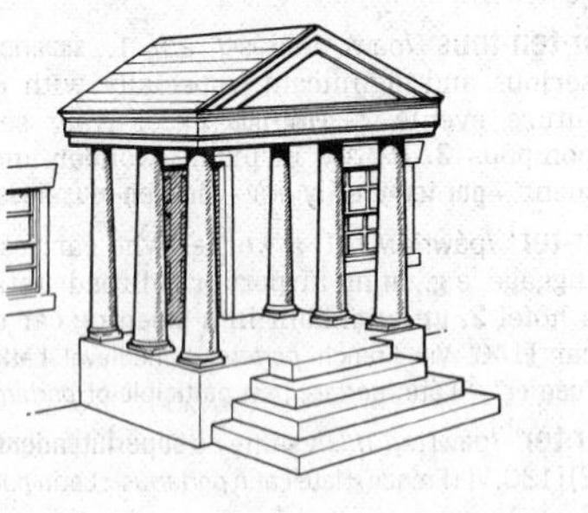

portico

por·ti·co /páwrti kō/ (*plural* **-coes** or **-cos**) *n* **1.** a covered entrance to a large building **2.** a covered walkway, often leading to the main entrance of a building, that consists of a roof supported by pillars [Early 17C. Via Italian < Latin *porticus* < *porta* "gate"]

por·tière /pàwrtee ér/, **por·tiere** *n* a heavy curtain hung across a doorway [Mid-19C. < French < *porte* "door" < Latin *porta* "gate"]

por·tion /páwrsh'n/ *n* **1. HELPING OF FOOD** an amount of food for one person **2. FRACTION** a part or section of a larger whole **3. FATE** an unavoidable event or part of somebody's life (*literary*) ○ *It was her portion in life to teach reading only.* **4. INHERITANCE** a part of an estate that has been bequeathed to an heir **5.** LAW same as **dowry** (sense 1) ■ *vt* (**-tioned, -tion·ing, -tions**) **1. DIVIDE SOMETHING** to divide something into parts for use **2. ENDOW WOMAN** to give a dowry to a woman (*archaic*) [14C. Via French < Latin *portion-*] —**por·tion·a·ble** *adj* —**por·tion·er** *n*

Port Jack·son coastal inlet in eastern New South Wales, Australia. The site of the city of Sydney, it is more commonly known as Sydney Harbour. Area: 20 sq. mi./54 sq. km.

Port·land /páwrtlənd/ **1.** city in Oregon, situated in the northwestern part of the state on the Willamette River. It is the state's largest city and its economic and cultural center. Population: 539,438 (2002 estimate). **2.** city in southwestern Maine, on the southern shore of Casco Bay, northeast of Saco. Population: 63,882 (2002 estimate).

Port·land ce·ment, port·land ce·ment *n* a cement that hardens under water, made by burning limestone and clay [Because a similar color to stone, quarried on the Isle of *Portland*, S England]

Port Lou·is /-lo͞o iss, -lo͞o ee/ capital city and chief port of Mauritius, on the northeastern coast of the island. Population: 147,131 (1998).

port·ly /páwrtlee/ (**-li·er, -li·est**) *adj* **1.** slightly overweight but dignified **2.** having an air of grandeur (*archaic*) [15C. < PORT[5] in the old sense "bearing, manner"] —**port·li·ness** *n*

port·man·teau /pawrt mántō, pàwrt man tṓ/ (*plural* **-teaus** or **-teaux** /-tōz, -tṓz/) *n* an old type of large leather suitcase, especially one that opened out into two compartments [Mid-16C. < French *portemanteau* < *porter* "carry" + *manteau* "cloak"]

port·man·teau word *n* a word that combines the sound and meaning of two words, e.g., "smog," a combination of "smoke" and "fog" [< the description (in Lewis Carroll's *Through the Looking Glass*) of the word *slithy* as a "portmanteau" because "there are two meanings packed up into one word"]

Port Mores·by /-máwrzbee/ capital city of Papua New Guinea, situated on the southern coast of the island of New Guinea. Population: 259,000 (2001).

Por·to /páwrtō/, **O·por·to** /ō páwrtō/ city and port in northwestern Portugal, situated about 170 mi./274 km north of Lisbon. Population: 285,320 (1995).

Por·to A·le·gre /-ə léggrə/ capital city of Rio Grande do Sul State, southeastern Brazil, and the country's leading river port. It lies at the junction of five rivers. Population: 1,288,879 (1996).

por·to·bel·lo /pàwrtə béllō/ (*plural* **-los**), **por·ta·bel·la** /pàwrtə béllə/ *n* a very large dark mushroom known for its meaty texture

port of call *n* **1.** any port, other than the home port, that a vessel visits on a journey **2.** a place visited during a vacation, trip, or excursion (*informal*)

port of en·try *n* a place where passengers and goods may enter a country under the supervision of customs officials, e.g., a port or an airport

Port-of-Spain /pàwrt əv spáyn/, **Port of Spain** capital city and main port of Trinidad and Tobago. It is situated in the northwestern part of the island of Trinidad. Population: 53,000 (2000).

Por·to-No·vo /pàwrto nṓvō/ capital city of Benin, and its main seaport, situated on a lagoon that extends along the Gulf of Guinea. Population: 232,756 (2000).

Port Or·ford ce·dar /-áwrfərd-/ *n* **1.** a fragrant valuable wood **2.** a tall evergreen tree that has leaves with white markings and yields Port Orford cedar. Native to: southwestern Oregon, northwestern California. Latin name: *Chamaecyparis lawsoniana*. [After a town in SW Oregon]

Port Phil·lip Bay bay in southern Victoria, Australia. The city of Melbourne lies on its southern shore. Area: 800 sq. mi./2,000 sq. km.

por·trait /páwrtrət/ *n* **1. PICTURE OF PERSON** a painting, photograph, or drawing of somebody, somebody's face, or a related group **2. DESCRIPTION** a description of something such as a person, place, or period ■ *adj* **TALLER THAN WIDE** describes a piece of paper, illustration, book, or page that is taller than it is wide [Mid-16C. < French < past participle of Old French *portraire* (see PORTRAY)]

CULTURAL NOTE ***Portrait of a Lady***, a novel (1881) by Henry James. Through the story of Isabel Archer, a young American woman who travels to Europe and is duped into marrying an urbane but materialistic fellow expatriate, the author explores the contrasting characteristics of the Old World (sophisticated but corrupt) and the New (idealistic but naive). It was made into a movie by Jane Campion in 1997.

por·trait·ist /páwrtrətist/ *n* somebody who specializes in portraits, e.g., a photographer or painter

por·trai·ture /páwrtrə cho͝or, -trəchər/ *n* **1. MAKING OF PORTRAITS** the art or practice of making portraits **2. PORTRAITS** portraits considered collectively **3. PORTRAIT** a portrait painting, drawing, or photography (*formal*)

por·tray /pawr tráy/ (**-trayed, -tray·ing, -trays**) *vt* **1. DEPICT SOMETHING OR SOMEBODY VISUALLY** to depict something such as a person or a scene in a painting, photograph, drawing, or sculpture **2. DEPICT SOMETHING OR SOMEBODY VERBALLY** to represent somebody or something in words **3. PLAY ROLE IN DRAMA** to play a character in drama [13C. < Old French *portraire* "draw out" < *traire* "draw" < Latin *trahere*] —**por·tray·a·ble** *adj* —**por·tray·al** *n* —**por·tray·er** *n*

Port Sa·id /-saa eéd/ city and port in northeastern Egypt, at the Mediterranean end of the Suez Canal. Population: 469,000 (1998).

Port-Sal·ut /pàwr sa lo͞o/, **Port du Salut** /pàwr doo sa lo͞o/ *n* a flat round mild French cheese with an orange rind, made from whole milk [Late 19C. After Notre Dame de *Port-du-Salut*, Trappist monastery in NW France]

port·side /páwrt sīd/ *US adj* situated on or near the waterfront at a port ○ *a portside café* ■ *adj, adv* NAUT same as **port**[3]

Ports·mouth /páwrtsməth/ **1.** city in southeastern New Hampshire, close to the mouth of the Piscataqua River opposite Kittery, Maine. It is an Atlantic seaport and was the colonial state capital. Population: 21,048 (2002 estimate). **2.** city in southeastern Virginia on the Elizabeth River and Hampton Roads, opposite Norfolk. It has one of the world's largest shipyards and dry dock systems. Population: 99,790 (2002 estimate). **3.** city and naval base in Hampshire, southern England. Population: 186,701 (2001).

Port Stan·ley ➧ **Stanley**

Port Su·dan city in northeastern Sudan, and the country's only seaport, situated on the Red Sea 200 mi./322 km northeast of Khartoum. Population: 305,385 (1993).

Port Tal·bot /-táwlbət, -tál-, pawr-/ town in southern Wales. It is the administrative center of Neath and Port Talbot unitary authority and was a major steel-making center. Population: 37,647 (1991).

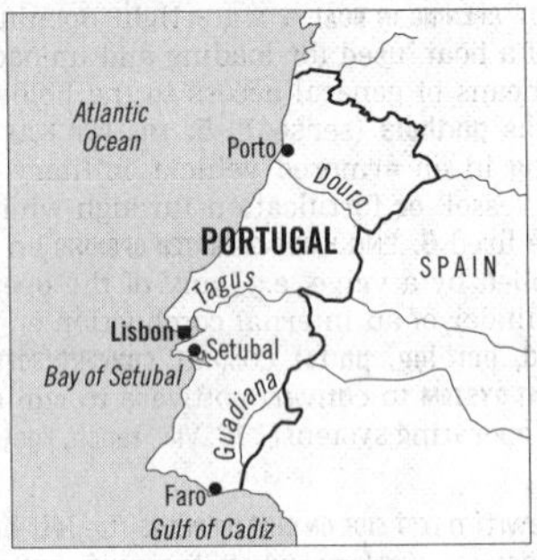

Portugal

Por·tu·gal /páwrchəgəl/ country in southwestern Europe, in the southwestern part of the Iberian peninsula. Language: Portuguese. Currency: escudo. Capital: Lisbon. Population: 10,102,022 (2003). Area: 35,655 sq. mi./92,345 sq. km. Official name **Portuguese Republic**

~~**Portugese**~~ incorrect spelling of **Portuguese**

Por·tu·guese /pàwrchə geéz, -geéss/ *n* **1.** the Romance official language of Portugal and Brazil, also an official language in some African countries. Native speakers: 150 million. Other speakers: 30 million. **2.** somebody who comes from Portugal [Late 16C. < Portuguese *português* < medieval Latin *Portus Cale*, the port of Gaya (Porto)] —**Por·tu·guese** *adj*

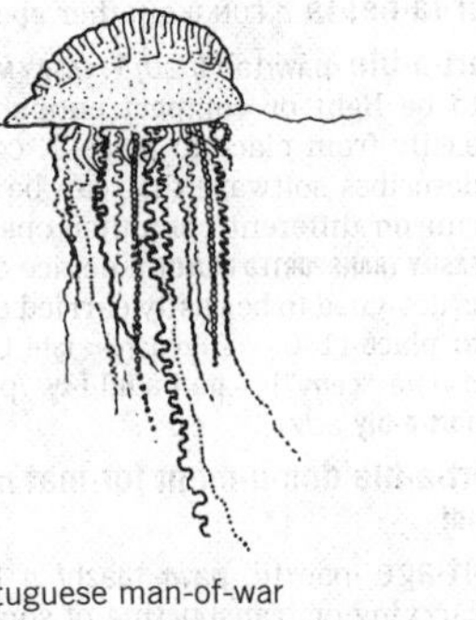

Portuguese man-of-war

Por·tu·guese man-of-war (*plural* **Por·tu·guese man-of-wars** or **Por·tu·guese men-of-war**) *n* a sea organism (**hydrozoan**) that resembles a jellyfish and lives in warm waters. It has a transparent gas-filled float and long stinging, often poisonous tentacles. Genus: *Physalia*. [< its crest, resembling a sail]

Por·tu·guese wa·ter dog *n* a dog with webbed feet and a dark coat with light markings that is an excellent swimmer, belonging to a breed originating in Portugal and trained to assist fishermen

por·tu·lac·a /pàwrchə lákə/ *n* a widely cultivated fleshy-leaved plant. Flowers: brightly colored. Native to: tropical and subtropical America. Genus: *Portulaca*. [Mid-16C. < Latin, "purslane" < *portula* "little gate" < *porta* "gate"; because the covering of the seed capsule resembles a gate]

port-wine stain *n* a conspicuous purplish birthmark, especially on the face or neck

POS *abbr* COMM point of sale

pos·a·ble *adj* another spelling of **poseable**

po·sa·da /pō saádə, pə-/ *n Hispanic* in a Spanish-speaking country, a hotel, pension, or hostel [Mid-18C. < Spanish < *posar* "stay, lodge" < late Latin *pausare* (see POSE[1])]

pose[1] /pōz/ *v* (**posed, pos·ing, pos·es**) **1.** *vti* **ADOPT POSTURE** to adopt a physical posture for a photograph or painting, or position somebody or something for this purpose **2.** *vi* **IMPERSONATE SOMEBODY OR SOMETHING** to pretend to be somebody or something else ○ *got past the security guards by posing as a reporter* **3.** *vt* **PRESENT SOMETHING** to be the cause of something such as a problem, threat, danger, or challenge ○ *a breakdown of negotiations that poses a threat to peace* **4.** *vt* **ASK QUESTION** to ask a question, often one that requires some consideration **5.** *vi* **BE PRETENTIOUS** to behave, dress, or assume a mental attitude intended to impress others (*disapproving*) ■ *n* **1. POSTURE** a physical posture, e.g., one adopted for a painting or photograph **2. PRETENSE** a way of behaving or dressing intended to impress others (*disapproving*) [14C. Via French *poser* < late Latin *pausare* "rest, cease" < Latin *pausa* (see PAUSE)]

pose[2] /pōz/ (**posed, pos·ing, pos·es**) *vt* to confuse or baffle somebody (*archaic*) [Early 16C. Partly shortening of obsolete *appose* "examine, interrogate" < Old French *aposer*, variant of *opposer* (see OPPOSE); partly < Old French *poser* "assume"]

pose·a·ble /pṓzəb'l/, **pos·a·ble** *adj* describes a doll or figure with jointed limbs and a body that can be made to pose in a variety of positions

Po·sei·don /pə sī́d'n, pō-/ *n* **1.** in Greek mythology, the god of the sea, water, earthquakes, and horses, who was the son of Cronus and brother of Zeus. Roman equivalent **Neptune 2.** a US ballistic missile capable of being launched from a submarine and carrying a nuclear warhead

pos·er[1] /pṓzər/ *n* **1.** somebody who poses for a photograph or work of art **2.** same as **poseur** (*informal*) [Late 19C. < POSE[1]]

pos·er[2] /pṓzər/ *n* a difficult question or problem [Late 16C. < POSE[2]]

~~**posess**~~ incorrect spelling of **possess**

~~**posession**~~ incorrect spelling of **possession**

po·seur /pō zúr/ *n* somebody who tries to impress others by behaving in an affected way [Late 19C. < French < *poser* (see POSE[1])]

posh /posh/ (*informal*) *adj* elegant, fashionable, and expensive ■ *adv UK* like somebody from the upper classes ○ *She talks posh to try and impress people.* [Early 20C. Origin ?] —**posh·ly** *adv* —**posh·ness** *n*

ORIGIN The legend has become widely circulated that ***posh*** is an acronym formed from the initial letters of *port out, starboard home*, an allusion to the fact that wealthy passengers could afford the more expensive cabins on the port side of the ships going out to India, and on the starboard side returning to the United Kingdom, which kept them out of the heat of the sun. Pleasant as this story is, it has never been substantiated. Another possibility is that *posh* may be the same word as the now obsolete *posh* "dandy, swell," a slang term current around the end of the 19th century. This too is of unknown origin, but it has been linked with the still earlier 19th-century slang term *posh* "halfpenny," hence broadly "money," which may have come ultimately from Romany *posh* "half."

pos·it /pózzit/ (*formal*) *vt* (**-it·ed, -it·ing, -its**) **1. PUT SOMETHING FORWARD** to put forward for consideration something such as a suggestion, assumption, or fact **2. POSITION SOMETHING** to place something firmly in position ■ *n* **SOMETHING PUT FORWARD** a suggestion, assumption, or fact put forward for consideration [Mid-17C. < Latin *posit-*, past participle of *ponere* "place"]

pos·i·tif /pózzə téef/ *n* a manual that controls the softer stops on a church organ [< Old French, "movable church organ" < Latin *positivus* (see POSITIVE)]

po·si·tion /pə zísh'n/ *n* **1. LOCATION** the place where somebody or something is, especially in relation to other things **2. POSTURE** the posture that somebody's body is in ○ *the fetal position* **3. ARRANGEMENT** the way or direction in which an object is placed or arranged ○ *the position of the hour hand* **4. SITUATION** a particular set of circumstances ○ *I wouldn't sell just yet if I were in your position.* **5. RANK** somebody's standing or level of importance in society or an organization ○ *In her position she should set an example for others.* **6. POST** a job or post in a company or organization ○ *the position of marketing manager* **7. VIEW** a policy, view, or opinion, especially an official one ○ *What's your position on the proposed highway?* **8. PLACE IN ORDER** the place that a person, team, or organization occupies in a race, contest, or list **9. CORRECT PLACE** the correct or usual place or arrangement of an object or person ○ *Once the dignitaries are in position, the ceremony can start.* **10. SEXUAL POSTURE** the posture used by a couple in sexual intercourse **11.** MIL **STRATEGIC PLACE** a strategic area or point that is occupied by military personnel or where weapons are placed **12. ROLE ON TEAM** the part of a playing area where a player is based and usually plays ○ *tried out several positions before settling on left field* **13.** BOARD GAMES **ARRANGEMENT OF PIECES** the arrangement of the pieces or counters in a board game such as chess or backgammon at a specific time **14.** FIN **DEALER'S RESPONSIBILITY** a dealer's commitment to buy or sell a specific number of stocks or commodities **15.** FIN **INVESTOR'S STATUS** an investor's status based on holdings with regard to market trends **16.** MUSIC **FINGERING ON INSTRUMENT** the placement of the fingers on a keyboard or string instrument **17.** MUSIC **EXTENSION OF TROMBONE SLIDE** the extent to which a trombone slide is pushed out **18.** MUSIC **ARRANGEMENT OF NOTES** the arrangement of individual notes within a chord. Root position is the most fundamental position. **19.** LITERAT **VOWEL LENGTH AFFECTED BY LOCATION** in classical poetry, a short vowel counting as a long vowel because it comes before two or more consonants ■ *vt* (**-tioned, -tion·ing, -tions**) **1. PUT SOMETHING IN PLACE** to put something in a particular or suitable place ○ *Position the two pieces so that they are at right angles.* **2. PLACE SOMEBODY** to place somebody or yourself in a particular or suitable area, place, or situation ○ *This strategy will position us advantageously in the market.* **3. LOCATE SOMETHING** to determine the site or location of something ○ *Air traffic controllers have positioned the unknown aircraft at 50 miles north of the airport.* [14C. Directly or via French < Latin *position-* < *posit-*, past participle of *ponere* "place"] —**po·si·tion·al** *adj* —**po·si·tion·al·ly** *adv* —**po·si·tion·er** *n*

ORIGIN The Latin word *ponere* "to place," from which ***position*** is derived, is also the source of English *component, compost, compound*[1]*, deposit, dispose, expose, impose, opponent, positive, post* ("place or position" and "letters and parcels"), *postpone, posture, repose* ("place, trust"), *suppose*, and *transpose*.

po·si·tion·al no·ta·tion *n* the method of denoting numbers by using digits in such a way that the value contributed by the digit depends on its position as well as its independent value. In the decimal system the value of the digits 37 is $(3 \times 10^1) + (7 \times 10^0)$, while in the octal system it is $(4 \times 8^1) + (5 \times 8^0)$.

po·si·tion au·dit *n* an assessment of a company's or organization's commercial standing carried out to help future planning

po·si·tion ef·fect *n* a change in a gene's expression depending on its location on the chromosome in relation to other genes

po·si·tion pa·per *n* an in-depth report on a matter that gives the official view and recommendations of a government or organization

pos·i·tive /pózzətiv/ *adj* **1. SURE** certain and not in doubt **2.** LAW **IRREFUTABLE** conclusive and beyond doubt or question ○ *positive identification of the suspect* **3. OPTIMISTIC** confident, optimistic, and focusing on good things rather than bad ○ *a positive attitude about work* **4. BENEFICIAL** producing good results because of having an innately beneficial character ○ *a very positive experience* **5. ENCOURAGING GOOD BEHAVIOR** encouraging behavior, especially in the young, that is considered morally good ○ *a positive role model* **6. AFFIRMATIVE** indicating agreement or affirmation ○ *positive feedback* **7. ADDS EMPHASIS** used to emphasize the degree to which something is true, striking, or impressive (*informal*) ○ *Hiring her is a positive triumph for the department.* **8.** SCI, MATH **QUANTIFIABLE** capable of being measured, detected, or perceived ○ *a positive correlation between investment in telecommunications and economic development* **9.** MED **INDICATING PRESENCE OF SOMETHING** indicating the presence of a particular organism or component in the results of a test or examination ○ *a positive test for diabetes* **10.** MED same as **Rh positive 11.** MATH **MORE THAN ZERO** having a value higher than zero. Symbol **+ 12. NOT NEGATIVE** measured in a direction or designated as a quantity equal in magnitude, but opposite to that regarded as negative **13.** PHYS **WITH ELECTRICAL CHARGE LIKE PROTON** having an electrical charge of an opposite polarity to that of an electron and the same polarity as that of a proton **14.** PHYS **WITH POSITIVE CHARGE** having an overall positive electrical charge, sometimes caused by the loss of one or more electrons **15.** PHYS **WITH HIGHER ELECTRICAL POTENTIAL** having a higher electrical potential than the ground or the defined neutral point ○ *a positive electrode* **16.** ELEC same as **electropositive** (sense 1) **17.** PHOTOGRAPHY **LIKE SUBJECT** describes photographic images that have colors or values of dark and light corresponding to the subject **18.** OPTICS **MAKING LIGHT CONVERGE** making a parallel beam of light converge **19.** GRAM **NOT COMPARATIVE OR SUPERLATIVE** relating to the basic form of an adjective or adverb, and not to its comparative or superlative forms **20.** PHILOSOPHY **EMPIRICAL** relating to the theory that knowledge can be acquired only through direct observation and experimentation, and not through metaphysics or theology **21.** BIOL **SHOWING RESPONSE** indicating growth, response, or movement toward a stimulus such as light **22.** ENG **WITH NO SLACK** describes a mechanical action or device having little or no play **23.** ASTROL **OF ZODIAC SIGNS** relating to the air or fire signs of the zodiac ■ *n* **1. POSITIVE THING** something that shows agreement, support, or affirmation (*informal*) ○ *Not a bad situation when we weigh all the positives.* **2.** MATH **SOMETHING GREATER THAN ZERO** a value or number higher than zero **3.** PHOTOGRAPHY **IMAGE LIKE SUBJECT** a photographic image in which the light and dark tones and colors correspond to those of the original subject **4.** ELEC **SOMETHING WITH POSITIVE CHARGE** something that carries a positive electrical charge **5.** ELEC **CELL PLATE OR TERMINAL** a positively charged plate or terminal in a cell **6.** GRAM **BASIC FORM OF MODIFIER** an adjective or adverb in its basic form, and not in the comparative or superlative **7.** MUSIC **MEDIEVAL ORGAN** a small medieval organ with just one manual and no pedals **8.** MUSIC another spelling of **positif** [14C. Via French < Latin *positivus* < *posit-* (see POSITION)] —**pos·i·tive·ness** *n* —**pos·i·tiv·i·ty** /pòzzə tívvətee/ *n*

pos·i·tive dis·crim·i·na·tion *n UK* same as **affirmative action**

pos·i·tive gloss *n* an interpretation of something unpleasant or unfavorable that is intended to make people see it in a good, rather than a bad, light ○ *sought to put a positive gloss on an increasingly difficult situation*

pos·i·tive·ly /pózzətivlee/ *adv* **1. DEFINITELY** used to emphasize that the truth of a statement or response is beyond any doubt ○ *This is positively the last chance you're going to get.* **2. ADDS EMPHASIS** used to emphasize an often already emphatic quality, characteristic, or action ○ *looking positively radiant* **3. ENCOURAGINGLY** in an encouraging, supportive, or optimistic way

pos·i·tive pre·scrip·tion *n* LAW same as **prescription** (sense 7)

pos·i·tiv·ism /pózzəti vìzzəm/ *n* **1.** the theory that knowledge can be acquired only through direct observation and experimentation, and not through metaphysics or theology **2.** the state or quality of being positive —**pos·i·tiv·ist** *n, adj* —**pos·i·tiv·is·tic** /pòzzəti vístik/ *adj* —**pos·i·ti·vis·ti·cal·ly** *adv*

pos·i·tron /pózzə tròn/ *n* an elementary particle of antimatter that has the same mass as an electron, but the opposite electrical charge [Mid-20C. Blend of POSITIVE + ELECTRON]

pos·i·tron e·mis·sion to·mog·ra·phy *n* a method of medical imaging capable of displaying the metabolic activity of organs in the body that is useful in diagnosing cancer, locating brain tumors, and investigating other brain disorders

pos·i·tro·ni·um /pòzzə trṓnee əm/ *n* a combination of a positron and an electron that rapidly decays to produce two or three photons

po·so·le /pō sṓ lày/, **po·zo·le** *n* **1.** *Hispanic* a thick Mexican soup made with hominy, chicken or pork, chilies, and cilantro **2.** a large kernel of white corn [Mid-20C. Via Mexican Spanish < Nahuatl *pozolli*]

po·sol·o·gy /pə sóllәjee/ *n* the study of the dosage of medicines [Early 19C. < French *posologie* < Greek *posos* "how much"] —**po·so·log·i·cal** /pòssə lójjik'l/ *adj*

pos·se /póssee/ *n* **1. SHERIFF'S HELPERS** especially in the western United States in the 19th-century, a group of citizens assembled by a sheriff to assist in maintaining law and order **2. ASSEMBLED GROUP** a group of people assembled for a common purpose (*informal*)

3. *US* SEARCHERS a search party [Mid-17C. Shortening of *posse comitatus* < medieval Latin, "force of the county"]

pos·sess /pə zéss/ (**-sessed, -sess·ing, -sess·es**) *vt* **1.** OWN SOMETHING to have or own something **2.** HAVE SOMETHING AS ABILITY to have something as an ability, quality, or characteristic **3.** HAVE KNOWLEDGE OF SOMETHING to have or acquire skill or knowledge of something **4.** TAKE CONTROL OF SOMEBODY to take control of somebody so that the person's behavior or thinking is affected ○ *possessed by fear and unable to speak* **5.** FILL SOMEBODY WITH AN EMOTION to cause somebody to be influenced by something, especially an emotion ○ *The news possessed us with foreboding.* **6.** CONTROL FEELING to control yourself or a feeling (*formal*) **7.** HAVE SEX WITH SOMEBODY to have sexual intercourse with somebody (*dated; sometimes considered offensive*) **8.** SEIZE SOMETHING to gain or seize something (*archaic*) [14C. Via Old French *possesser* < Latin *possess-*, past participle of *possidere* "sit on as head" < *sedere* "sit"] —**pos·ses·sor** *n*

pos·sessed /pə zést/ *adj* **1.** CONTROLLED controlled or strongly influenced, especially by a supposed evil supernatural force or a strong emotion ○ *screaming and shouting like a man possessed* **2.** HAVING QUALITY having something as a quality, characteristic, or belief (*literary*) ○ *He was possessed of a sharp wit.* **3.** OWNING having or owning something ○ *an only child possessed of a great fortune* **4.** same as **self-possessed**

pos·ses·sion /pə zésh'n/ *n* **1.** OWNERSHIP the act or state of owning or holding something ○ *You can take possession of the house on Friday.* **2.** SOMETHING OWNED something owned or held **3.** POL COLONY a country or region controlled or governed by another country (*often used in the plural*) **4.** STATE OF BEING CONTROLLED the condition of being controlled by or appearing to be controlled by a supposed supernatural force or a strong emotion **5.** CONTROL OF BALL in various sports, control of the ball or puck by a player or team **6.** CRIME ILLEGAL OWNERSHIP OF SOMETHING the crime of having or owning something illegal such as a weapon, contraband, stolen property, or illegal drugs **7.** LAW OCCUPANCY the physical occupancy of something such as a house, whether or not as its owner ■ **pos·ses·sions** *npl* PROPERTY personal property —**pos·ses·sion·al** *adj*

pos·ses·sive /pə zéssiv/ *adj* **1.** DEMANDING EXCLUSIVITY wishing to control somebody exclusively or to be the sole object of somebody's love **2.** SELFISH tending not to share possessions with others **3.** OF OWNERSHIP relating to ownership ○ *possessive pride* **4.** GRAM SHOWING OWNERSHIP IN GRAMMATICAL TERMS indicating grammatical ownership, e.g., in pronouns such as "his" or "her" ■ *n* GRAM **1.** WORD SHOWING OWNERSHIP a noun, pronoun, adjective, or form of a word that indicates ownership or association **2.** POSSESSIVE CASE the possessive or genitive case —**pos·ses·sive·ly** *adv* —**pos·ses·sive·ness** *n*

USAGE See ***apostrophe***[1].

pos·ses·so·ry /pə zéssəree/ *adj* **1.** relating to possession or a possessor (*formal*) **2.** arising from or depending on legal possession

pos·si·bil·i·ty /pòssə bíllətee/ *n* (*plural* **-ties**) **1.** SOMETHING POSSIBLE something that is possible **2.** STATE OF BEING POSSIBLE the condition or quality of being possible **3.** CONTENDER somebody who is considered a possible winner, choice, or candidate ■ **pos·si·bil·i·ties** *npl* POTENTIAL the potential for successful future development ○ *The house needs a lot of work, but it's got possibilities.*

pos·si·ble /póssəb'l/ *adj* **1.** ABLE TO HAPPEN capable of happening or likely to happen in the future **2.** MAYBE REAL OR TRUE capable of being real, present, or true **3.** CAPABLE OF HAPPENING BUT UNLIKELY theoretically capable of happening or existing, although unlikely in practice **4.** POTENTIAL having potential as a particular thing or for a particular purpose **5.** PROPER in keeping with convention, decorum, or tradition ■ *n* POSSIBILITY somebody or something that is a possibility [14C. Via French < Latin *possibilis* < *posse* "be able" (see POTENT[1])]

SPELLCHECK See ***passable***.

pos·si·bly /póssəblee/ *adv* **1.** PERHAPS likely, or maybe so, but not definitely so **2.** AS POSSIBILITY as something that is possible or may be realized ○ *a new park to include a pond and possibly a playground* **3.** SUGGESTS EFFORT used to indicate the magnitude of effort or difficulty ○ *They've done everything they possibly could.* **4.** ADDS EMPHASIS used to express shock, disbelief, or amazement ○ *What could he possibly mean?* ○ *How could you possibly have believed that?* **5.** SUGGESTS IMPOSSIBILITY used in negative sentences and phrases to emphasize that something cannot be done or cannot happen ○ *I couldn't possibly tell you.* **6.** USED AS REQUEST MODIFIER used with requests to suggest the speaker's awareness of an imposition ○ *Could you possibly mail this letter for me on your way to work?*

POSSLQ *abbr* person of the opposite sex sharing living quarters (*informal*)

pos·sum /póssəm/ *n* ZOOL same as **opossum** (*informal*) [Early 17C. Shortening] ◇ **play possum** to feign death, illness, or sleep, or pretend to be uninvolved in something, in order to protect yourself

pos·sum·haw /póssəm hàw/ *n US* PLANTS same as **dockmackie**

post[1] /pōst/ *n* **1.** UPRIGHT POLE a pole of wood or metal fixed in the ground in an upright position, serving as a support, marker, or place for attaching things **2.** CONSTR UPRIGHT FRAME PART a vertical piece in a building frame that supports a beam **3.** HORSERACING RACECOURSE INDICATOR either of two upright poles marking the starting point and finishing line on a racecourse **4.** FURNITURE SUPPORT one of the upright supports of a piece of furniture such as a chair or a four-poster bed **5.** SPORTS same as **goalpost** (*informal*) **6.** JEWELRY EARRING PART a metal stem on a pierced earring that passes through the ear and fits into a cap at the back **7.** ONLINE same as **posting**[1] (sense 1) ■ *vt* (**post·ed, post·ing, posts**) **1.** DISPLAY SOMETHING to display something such as an announcement, name, or result in a public place **2.** PUBLISH SOMETHING ELECTRONICALLY to make text appear online or at an Internet location **3.** *US* ERECT SIGNS FORBIDDING SOMETHING to put up signs around a property warning against trespassing or engaging in a forbidden activity **4.** *US* DENOUNCE PUBLICLY to denounce somebody by displaying damaging information publicly (*dated*) **5.** LEISURE SCORE POINTS to score something, e.g., points, in a game or sport ○ *posted a win in his first game of the season* **6.** GIVE NOTICE OF MARRIAGE to announce a forthcoming marriage in a church ○ *post the banns* **7.** NAUT NAME SHIP to publish the name of a ship presumed lost or sunk [Pre-12C. < Latin *postis* "something that stands in front" < Indo-European, "to stand"]

post[2] /pōst/ *n* **1.** MIL MILITARY BASE a place such as a military base, camp, or garrison where troops are stationed **2.** EMPLOYMENT POSITION a position of employment, especially one in another country **3.** WORKPLACE OR STATION a place where somebody has been assigned a duty or responsibility **4.** *Can* TROOPS the body of troops occupying a military base, camp, or garrison **5.** *US* MIL VETERANS' ORGANIZATION a local organization of military veterans ○ *a VFW post* **6.** BASKETBALL BASKETBALL POSITION in basketball, a position taken by a player near the opposing team's basket ■ *vt* (**post·ed, post·ing, posts**) *US* PAY MONEY TO SET SOMEBODY FREE to pay somebody's bond or bail ■ *n* COMM same as **trading post** (sense 1) ■ *vt* (**post·ed, post·ing, posts**) **1.** ASSIGN SOMEBODY TO DUTY to assign somebody to a particular place or station for a period of duty ○ *post a security guard at the exit* **2.** *Can, UK* SEND SOMEBODY AWAY TO WORK to send somebody somewhere, often overseas, to take up an appointment **3.** MIL TRANSFER SOLDIER to assign or transfer somebody to a military unit or command [Mid-16C. Via French *poste* < Latin *positum* < past participle of *ponere* "place"]

post[3] /pōst/ *n* **1.** *UK* MAIL LETTERS AND PARCELS letters and parcels that have been sent or are to be sent through the postal system **2.** *UK* POSTAL SERVICE the official system for collecting, conveying, and delivering letters and parcels to another place **3.** HIST STATION ON ROUTE formerly, a station along a route where mounted messengers or couriers rested and changed horses **4.** HIST MAIL DELIVERER formerly, a rider who covered the distance from one post to the next in a delivery system ■ *v* (**post·ed, post·ing, posts**) **1.** *vt UK* MAIL SEND LETTER OR PARCEL to send a letter or parcel through the postal system **2.** *vti* SEND MESSAGE ELECTRONICALLY to place or send a message on a newsgroup or bulletin board on the Internet or some other electronic network **3.** *vt* ONLINE UPDATE DATABASE to update a database record by entering or transferring information **4.** *vi* RIDING KEEP RHYTHM WITH HORSE to bob up and down in the saddle in time with a horse's trot **5.** *vi* HIST TRAVEL BY POST to travel using relays of horses **6.** *vi* TRAVEL FAST to travel at speed (*archaic*) **7.** *vt* ACCT WRITE SOMETHING IN LEDGER to enter a transaction in a ledger ■ *adv* QUICKLY quickly (*archaic*) [Early 16C. Via French, "relay station" < Latin *posita*, form of past participle of *ponere* "place"] ◇ **keep somebody posted** to keep somebody informed by supplying new information regularly

post[4] /pōst/ *n* a postmortem examination of a corpse (*informal*) [Mid-20C. Shortening]

POST *abbr* COMPUT Power On Self-Test

post- *prefix* **1.** after, later ○ *postwar* ○ *postdate* **2.** behind ○ *postorbital* [< Latin *post* < Indo-European, "off, away"]

post·a·poc·a·lyp·tic *adj*
post·ap·o·stol·ic *adj*
post·a·tom·ic *adj*
post·bap·tis·mal *adj*
post·bib·li·cal *adj*
post-Car·te·sian *adj*
post·clas·si·cal *adj*
post·co·i·tal *adj*
post·co·lo·ni·al *adj*
post-Com·mu·nist *adj*
post·con·cep·tion *adj*
post·con·cert *adj*
post·con·quest *adj*
post·con·so·nan·tal *adj*
post·coup *adj*
post·crash *adj*
post-Dar·win·i·an *adj*
post·de·pres·sion *adj*
post·di·vorce *adj*
post·e·lec·tion *adj*
post·ex·er·cise *adj*
post·flight *adj*
post-Freud·i·an *adj*
post·gla·cial *adj*
post·grad·u·a·tion *adj*
post·in·de·pend·ence *adj*
post·in·dus·tri·al *adj*
post·in·fec·tive *adj*
post·in·oc·u·la·tion *adj*
post-Keynes·i·an *adj*
post·lib·er·a·tion *adj*
post·med·i·e·val *adj*
post·men·o·paus·al *adj*
post·mid·night *adj*
post·nup·tial *adj*
post·pu·ber·ty *adj*
post·punk *adj*
post·re·ces·sion *adj*
post-Ref·or·ma·tion *adj*
post-Re·nais·sance *adj*
post·re·tire·ment *adj*
post·rev·o·lu·tion·ar·y *adj*
post·ro·man·tic *adj*
post·sea·son *n, adj*
post·show *adj*
post·strike *adj*
post·sur·gi·cal *adj*
post-Tal·mud·ic *adj*
post·the·a·ter *adj*
post·trans·fu·sion *adj*
post·trau·mat·ic *adj*
post·treat·ment *adj*
post·vac·ci·nal *adj*
post-Vic·to·ri·an *adj*

post·age /pōstij/ *n* **1.** the amount of money paid for the delivery of a piece of mail **2.** the stamps, labels, or other marks on an item of mail showing that the charge has been paid

post·age me·ter *n* an office machine that prints prepaid postage and a date stamp on items of mail

post·age stamp *n* **1.** GUMMED POSTAGE MARKER an illustrated paper stamp affixed to mail to show payment of postage **2.** PRINTED MARK a printed mark or impression on an envelope indicating that the postage charge has been paid ■ *adj* TINY extremely small (*hyphenated when used before a noun*) ○ *a postage-stamp bikini*

post·al /pōst'l/ *adj* relating to a post office or a mail delivery service —**post·al·ly** *adv* ◇ **go postal** *US* to become extremely angry, often in a way that leads to violence (*slang*)

post·al card *n US* **1.** a plain postcard with prepaid postage, sold in post offices **2.** MAIL same as **postcard** (sense 1)

post·al code *n Can* a sequence of letters and numbers assigned by the post office to addresses to facilitate mail delivery. Same as **ZIP Code**

post·al mon·ey or·der *n* a voucher for a sum of money that can be bought at a post office and that is payable to a specific person or organization

post·al vote *n UK* same as **absentee ballot**

post·bag /pōst bàg/ *n* **1.** *UK* same as **mailbag** (sense 2) **2.** *UK* same as **mailbag** (sense 3)

post-bel·lum /pōst bélləm/, **post·bel·lum** *adj* relating to or occurring in the period after a war, especially the Civil War [< Latin *post bellum* "after the war"]

post-boost phase *n* the last phase of the flight of a multistage missile, when it releases its payload

post·box /pōst bòks/ *n UK* same as **mailbox** (sense 1)

post·card /pōst kaard/ *n* **1.** a card used to carry a message, usually with a picture or a photograph on one side, that can be sent through the mail without an envelope **2.** *US* MAIL same as **postal card** (sense 1)

post chaise *n* a closed horse-drawn carriage with four wheels that was used in the 18th and 19th centuries as a fast means of transporting mail and passengers [< POST³]

post·code /pṓst kṑd/ *n UK* same as **ZIP Code**

post·date /pṑst dáyt/ (**-dat·ed, -dat·ing, -dates**) *vt* **1.** DATE CHECK LATER to put a date on a check later than the current day's date in order to delay payment **2.** HAPPEN LATER THAN SOMETHING to happen or be at a later date than something **3.** ASSIGN LATER DATE TO EVENT to assign a date to something such as an event in history that is later than the one previously assigned

post·doc /pṓst dòk/ (*slang*) *n* a postdoctoral grant, fellowship, or scholar ■ *adj* EDUC same as **postdoctoral** [Late 20C. Shortening]

post·doc·tor·al /pṑst dóktərəl/ *adj* relating to academic work or research done after a doctorate has been awarded

post·er /pṓstər/ *n* **1.** a printed picture, often a reproduction of a photograph or artwork, used for decoration or advertisement **2.** somebody who posts a message to an online or Internet address

post·er child *n* **1.** REPRESENTATIVE OF GOOD CAUSE somebody, especially a child, chosen to represent a charitable or other cause by appearing in promotional material **2.** PERFECT EXAMPLE OF SOMETHING a perfect or quintessential example of something **3.** REPRESENTATIVE EXAMPLE OF SOMETHING somebody or something appearing as a representative or illustrative example of something (*sometimes offensive*)

post·er col·or *n US* ART same as **tempera** (sense 2)

poste res·tante /pṑst re staánt/ *n UK* MAIL same as **general delivery** [< French, "mail remaining" (at the post office)]

pos·te·ri·or /po steéree ər, pō-/ *adj* **1.** BEHIND situated at the rear or behind something **2.** NEAR BACK situated near or toward the back of the body of a person or animal **3.** FOLLOWING IN SERIES coming after something in an order or series (*formal*) **4.** SUBSEQUENT following something in time (*formal*) **5.** BOT NEAREST STEM nearest the main stem or axis of a plant ○ *the posterior flower* ■ *n* BOTTOM the buttocks (*humorous*) [Early 16C. < Latin, "coming farther after" < *posterus* "coming after" < *post* "after, behind"] —**pos·te·ri·or·ly** *adv*

pos·ter·i·ty /po stérrətee/ *n* (*formal*) **1.** all future generations **2.** all of somebody's descendants [14C. Via French < Latin *posteritas* < *posterus* (see POSTERIOR)]

pos·tern /pṓstərn, póst-/ *n* a small gate or entrance at the back of a building, especially a castle or a fort [13C. Via Old French *pasterne* < late Latin *posterula* "small back door" < Latin *posterus* (see POSTERIOR)]

post·er paint *n* ART same as **tempera** (sense 2)

post ex·change *n US* MIL full form of **PX**

post·ex·il·i·an /pṑst ig zíllee ən, -ik síllee ən/, **post·ex·il·ic** /-ig zíllik, -ik síllik/ *adj* occurring or in existence after the period of Babylonian captivity of the Jewish people, 587–539 B.C.

post·fem·i·nist /pṑst fémmənist/ *adj* **1.** AFTER FEMINISM occurring or having developed after the feminist movement of the 1970s (*sometimes considered offensive*) **2.** GOING BEYOND FEMINISM differing from or showing a reevaluation of the principles of feminism **3.** REFLECTING FEMINISM developing out of or including the principles of feminism ■ *n* SUPPORTER OF POSTFEMINIST IDEAS somebody who supports or believes in postfeminist ideas —**post·fem·i·nism** *n*

post·gen·i·tive /pṑst jénnitiv/ *n* a double possessive construction in which "of" and an apostrophe + "s" are both used, e.g., a letter of Sam's

post·grad /pṑst grád/ EDUC *n* same as **postgraduate** (*informal*) ■ *adj* same as **graduate**

post·grad·u·ate /pṑst grájjoo ət/ *adj UK* EDUC same as **graduate** ■ *n* somebody who has graduated from a university or college with a bachelor's degree, especially one who is studying for a higher degree

post·haste /pṑst háyst/ *adv* as quickly as possible [Mid-16C. < *Haste, post, haste,* an instruction on letters]

post hoc /pṑst hók, -hṓk/ *n* the fallacy of arguing that since one event happened before a second, the first caused the second [Mid-19C. < Latin, "after this," referring to the fallacy *post hoc, ergo propter hoc* "after this, therefore because of this"]

post·hold·er /pṓst hṑldər/ *n* somebody who occupies a specific position of employment in a company, organization, or institution

post·hole /pṓst hṑl/ *n* a hole that has been dug in the ground for a post

post horn *n* a simple, usually valveless horn, formerly used to announce the arrival of a coach carrying mail [< POST³]

post·hu·mous /póschəməss/ *adj* **1.** AFTER SOMEBODY'S DEATH occurring after somebody's death **2.** PUBLISHED AFTER DEATH published or printed after the author's death **3.** BORN AFTER FATHER'S DEATH born after the death of the father ○ *a posthumous heir* [Early 17C. < late Latin *posthumus*, alteration (after medieval Latin *humare* "bury") of Latin *postumus* "last" < *posterus* (see POSTERIOR)] —**post·hu·mous·ly** *adv* —**post·hu·mous·ness** *n*

post·hyp·not·ic sug·ges·tion /pṑst hip nòttik-/ *n* a suggestion made to somebody under hypnosis that is to be acted upon at a later time after the period of hypnosis is over

pos·tiche /po stéesh/ *n* (*formal*) **1.** an artificial or fake version or copy of something **2.** a small hairpiece or toupee [Early 18C. Via French < Italian *posticcio*]

pos·til·ion /pə stíllyən, pō-/, **pos·til·lion** *n* somebody riding the left-hand front horse in a team of horses drawing a carriage [Early 17C. Via French *postillon* "relay rider" < Italian *postiglione* < *posta* < Latin *posita* (see POST³)]

post·im·pres·sion·ism /pṑst im présh'n ìzzəm/ *n* a school of painting in late 19th-century France that rejected the naturalism of impressionism, but adapted its use of color and form to a more subjective style —**post·im·pres·sion·ist** *n, adj* —**post·im·pres·sion·is·tic** /pṑst im presh'n ístik/ *adj*

post·ing¹ /pṓsting/ *n* **1.** ONLINE MESSAGE a message sent to and displayed on an online facility such as an Internet newsgroup or bulletin board **2.** ACCT BOOKKEEPING ACTIVITY the activity of making entries in a ledger **3.** ACCT LEDGER ENTRY an entry made in a ledger [Late 16C. < POST²]

post·ing² /pṓsting/ *n UK* an appointment to a job, position, or unit, usually overseas [Mid-19C. < POST³]

Post-it *tdmk* a trademark for self-sticking slips of paper sold in pad form

post·lude /pṓst lo͞od/ *n* **1.** a piece of organ music played at the end of a church service **2.** a final or concluding phase, chapter, or development (*literary*) [Mid-19C. After PRELUDE]

post·man /pṓstmən/ (*plural* **-men** /-mən/) *n UK* same as **mailman**

post·man's knock *n UK* same as **post office** (sense 3)

post·mark /pṓst maàrk/ *n* an official mark, usually covering a postage stamp, that indicates when and from where a piece of mail was sent ■ *vt* (**-marked, -mark·ing, -marks**) to stamp a postmark on an item of mail

post·mas·ter /pṓst màstər/ *n* **1.** POST OFFICE OFFICIAL the person in charge of a post office or postal district **2.** WEBSITE MANAGER the person responsible for the maintenance of a website and for being the contact point for information and complaints **3.** E-MAIL PROGRAM a computer program that distributes, forwards, and receives electronic mail

post·mas·ter gen·er·al (*plural* **post·mas·ters gen·er·al**) *n* the executive head of the postal service in some countries

post me·rid·i·em /-mə ríddee əm/ *adv* TIME full form of **P.M.** [< Latin, "after midday"]

post·mil·len·ni·al /pṑst mi lénnee əl/ *adj* occurring or existing after a millennium

post·mil·len·ni·al·ism /pṑst mi lénnee ə lìzzəm/, **post·mil·len·na·ri·an·ism** /-millə nérree ə nìzzəm/ *n* the belief that Jesus Christ will return after, and not at, the millennium —**post·mil·len·ni·al·ist** *n* —**post·mil·len·ni·an** *n, adj*

post·mis·tress /pṓst mìstrəss/ *n* a woman in charge of a post office (*dated*)

post·mod·ern·ism /pṑst móddər nìzzəm/ *n* a style in architecture, art, literature, and criticism developed after and often in reaction to modernism, characterized by reference to other periods or styles in a self-conscious way and a rejection of the notion of high art —**post·mod·ern** *n, adj* —**post·mod·ern·ist** *n, adj*

post·mor·tem /pṑst máwrtəm/ *adj* occurring after death ■ *n* **1.** *also* **post·mor·tem ex·am·i·na·tion** same as **autopsy** *n* (sense 1) **2.** an analysis carried out shortly after the conclusion of an event, especially an unsuccessful one ○ *the usual media postmortems the day after the election* [Mid-18C. < Latin *post mortem* "after death"]

post·na·sal drip /pṑst náyz'l-/ *n* a continual dripping of mucus from the rear of the nose into the throat, often caused by an allergy or a cold

post·na·tal /pṑst náyt'l/ *adj* **1.** occurring immediately or soon after childbirth **2.** relating to an infant immediately after birth ○ *postnatal development* —**post·na·tal·ly** *adv*

post·na·tal de·pres·sion *n UK* same as **postpartum depression**

post-o·bit *n* a bond that pays after the death of somebody from whom the issuer of the bond expects to inherit (*dated*) ■ *adj* coming into effect after somebody's death (*formal*) ○ *post-obit payments* [Mid-18C. < Latin *post obitum* "after death"]

post of·fice *n* **1.** PLACE FOR MAILING AND STAMPS an office or building where the public has access to services of the postal system **2.** NATIONAL MAIL SYSTEM the national organization or government department that is responsible for a country's mail service **3.** LEISURE PARTY GAME a children's game in which one player gives another a pretend letter and is given a kiss in return

post of·fice box *n* a private numbered box in a post office where mail is held until collected by the addressee

post·op /pṓst òp/, **post-op** *adj* MED same as **postoperative** (*informal*) [Late 20C. Shortening]

post·op·er·a·tive /pṑst ópparətiv/ *adj* occurring after a surgical operation —**post·op·er·a·tive·ly** *adv*

post·or·bi·tal /pṑst áwrbit'l/ *adj* situated behind the eye or the eye socket

post·paid /pṑst páyd/ *adj* with the postage paid in advance

post·par·tum /pṑst paártəm/ *adj* relating to or occurring in the period immediately after childbirth [Mid-19C. < Latin *post partum* "after childbirth"]

post·par·tum de·pres·sion *n* a psychiatric disorder consisting of severe depression that can affect a woman soon after giving birth to a baby

post·per·son /pṑst pùrss'n/ (*plural* **-per·sons** or **-peo·ple** /-peép'l/) *n* same as **mailperson**

post·pone /pṑst pṓn, pōss-/ (**-poned, -pon·ing, -pones**) *vt* **1.** to put something off until a later time or date **2.** to ascribe less importance to something (*formal*) [15C. < Latin *postponere* "place later" < *ponere* "place"] —**post·pon·a·ble** *adj* —**post·pone·ment** *n* —**post·pon·er** *n*

post·pose /pṑst pṓz/ (**-posed, -pos·ing, -pos·es**) *vti* to place a word or phrase after another or at the end of a sentence or construction [Late 19C. Back-formation < POSTPOSITION]

post·po·si·tion /pṑstpə zísh'n/ *n* **1.** the placement of a word or phrase after the word or phrase it qualifies, e.g., the placement of "bold and free" in the phrase "poets bold and free" **2.** GRAM same as **postpositive** [Mid-17C. After PREPOSITION] —**post·po·si·tion·al** *adj* —**post·po·si·tion·al·ly** *adv*

post·pos·i·tive /pṑst pózzətiv/ *adj* describes an adjective or modifier that is placed after the word or phrase it qualifies ■ *n* an adjective or modifier that is placed after the word or phrase it qualifies [Late 18C. < late Latin *postpositivus* < Latin *postponere* (see POSTPONE)] —**post·pos·i·tive·ly** *adv*

post·pran·di·al /pōst prándee əl/ *adj* occurring after a meal, especially an evening meal (*formal or humorous*) —**post·pran·di·al·ly** *adv*

post-print *adj* belonging to the era of electronic communication ○ *the post-print revolution*

post·pro·duc·tion /pōst prə dúksh'n/ *n* the final stage in the making of a recording, film, or television program that includes editing, sound dubbing, and adding special effects

post rid·er *n* formerly, somebody who delivered or relayed mail on horseback

post road *n* a road or route formerly used regularly by the postal delivery service

post·script /pōst skrìpt/ *n* **1.** a short message added onto the end of a letter, after the signature **2.** an addition to the end of something such as a book, story, or document [Mid-16C. < Latin *postscriptum* < past participle of *postscribere* "write after" < *scribere* "write"]

post-Sep·tem·ber 11 *adj* relating to or characteristic of the more serious values and views in the US government, military, marketplace, schools, and families after the September 11, 2001, terrorist attacks on the World Trade Center and the Pentagon

post·struc·tur·al·ism *n* an intellectual movement derived from structuralism but questioning the basis upon which the structures of society, language, and mores have been conceptualized —**post·struc·tur·al·ist** *adj, n*

post·syn·ap·tic /pōst si náptik/ *adj* describes a nerve cell, muscle cell, or region of cell membrane that receives signals transmitted across a synapse from another nerve cell

post·synch /pōst síngk/ (**-synched, -synch·ing, -synchs**) *vt* to add sound or music to a film at a later time

post·test /pōst tèst/ *n* a test administered after a lesson or instruction to see what has been assimilated

post time *n* the starting time of a horserace, after which no more bets can be accepted

post trans·ac·tion *n* submission by a retailer of a previously authorized transaction to the acquirer for payment

post·tran·scrip·tion·al /pōst tran skrípshən'l, -shnəl/ *adj* describes processes or components that become involved in carrying out the genetic instructions of a living cell only after the stage of transcription of a gene or genes

post·trans·la·tion·al /pōst transs láyshən'l, -shnəl/ *adj* describes processes or components that become involved in carrying out the genetic instructions of living cells only after translation of RNA to protein

post·trau·mat·ic stress dis·or·der *n* a psychological condition affecting people who have suffered severe emotional trauma as a result of an experience such as combat, crime, or natural disaster, and causing sleep disturbances, flashbacks, anxiety, tiredness, and depression

pos·tu·lant /póschələnt/ *n* somebody who applies to join a religious order (*formal*) [Mid-18C. Directly or via French < Latin *postulant-*, present participle of *postulare* "nominate, demand"] —**pos·tu·lan·cy** *n*

pos·tu·late *vt* /póschə làyt/ (**-lat·ed, -lat·ing, -lates**) **1.** ASSUME SOMETHING to assume or suggest that something is true or exists, especially as the basis of an argument or theory **2.** CLAIM SOMETHING to demand or claim something ■ *n* /póschələt, -làyt/ **1.** SOMETHING ASSUMED TRUE something that is assumed or believed to be true and that is used as the basis of an argument or theory **2.** PRINCIPLE a basic principle **3.** PRECONDITION an essential precondition or requirement **4.** MATH, LOGIC STATEMENT UNDERPINNING THEORY a statement that is assumed to be true but has not been proven and that is taken as the basis for a theory, line of reasoning, or hypothesis [Mid-16C. < Latin *postulat-*, past participle of *postulare* "nominate, demand"] —**pos·tu·la·tion** /pòschə láysh'n/ *n* —**pos·tu·la·tion·al** *adj*

pos·tu·la·tor /póschə làytər/ *n* **1.** in the Roman Catholic Church, an official, usually a priest, who presents a request for a deceased person to be beatified or canonized **2.** somebody who postulates something

pos·ture /póschər/ *n* **1.** PHYSICAL CARRIAGE the way in which somebody holds his or her body, especially when standing **2.** BODY POSITION a position that the body can assume, e.g., standing, sitting, kneeling, or lying down **3.** ATTITUDE a frame of mind or attitude ○ *a conciliatory posture* **4.** POSE CONVEYING ATTITUDE a physical pose that conveys a mental or emotional attitude ○ *a posture of defiance* **5.** DECEPTIVE STANCE a position, attitude, or stance that is intended to deceive **6.** CULTIVATED POSITION a practiced or cultivated arrangement of the body, e.g., a position used in yoga **7.** ARRANGEMENT OF PARTS the way that components of an object or situation are arranged in relation to one another ■ *v* (**-tured, -tur·ing, -tures**) **1.** *vi* ASSUME STANCE to assume an affected or exaggerated pose or attitude **2.** *vti* ADOPT POSTURE to adopt a particular posture, or make somebody do this [Late 16C. Via French < Latin *positura* < *posit-* (see POSITION)] —**pos·tur·al** *adj* —**pos·tur·er** *n*

post·vi·ral syn·drome /pōst vīrəl-/ *n* MED same as **chronic fatigue syndrome**

post·vo·cal·ic /pōst vō kállik/ *adj* coming after a vowel

post·war /pōst wàwr, pōst wáwr/ *adj* occurring or existing after a war, especially World War II

po·sy /pōzee/ (*plural* **-sies**) *n* a blooming flower, or a bunch of blooming flowers [Mid-16C. Alteration of POESY]

pot[1] /pot/ *n* **1.** CONTAINER FOR COOKING a container made of metal, pottery, or glass that is usually cylindrical and watertight with an open top and sometimes a lid, used especially for cooking or storage **2.** SOMETHING RESEMBLING POT something similar to a pot in shape or function, e.g., a flowerpot or teapot **3.** CONTENTS OF POT the contents of a pot, or the amount that it will hold ○ *made a pot of coffee* **4.** CLAY OBJECT a dish or container made from clay, especially one of artistic or historic interest **5.** COMMON FUND a common fund of money for an activity such as a party or trip that is contributed to by all the members of a group (*informal*) **6.** same as **potty**[2] (sense 1) **7.** LARGE AMOUNT OF MONEY a large amount of money (*informal*) ○ *made pots of money* **8.** CARDS MONEY BET IN CARD GAME all the money that is bet in a game of cards, especially poker, and that is taken by the winning player **9.** CUE GAMES HIT OF BALL INTO POCKET in billiards or pool, a hit of a ball that sends it into any of the pockets at the edge of the table **10.** FISHERIES FISH OR LOBSTER TRAP a basket or cage used for catching lobsters, eels, or fish **11.** ANAT same as **potbelly** (*informal*) **12.** SPORTS same as **potshot** (sense 2) ■ *v* (**pot·ted, pot·ting, pots**) **1.** *vt* PUT PLANT IN POT to put a plant into a pot with soil or compost **2.** *vti* SHOOT ANIMAL FOR FOOD to shoot or shoot at a bird or animal, especially for food **3.** *vti* SHOOT AT SOMETHING NEARBY to shoot or shoot at an easy target, especially casually **4.** *vt* COOK PRESERVE FOOD to preserve food in a pot **5.** *vti* CUE GAMES HIT BALL INTO POCKET in billiards or pool, to hit a ball into any of the pockets at the edge of the table **6.** *vti* CERAMICS SHAPE CLAY to shape a pot or other item from clay **7.** *vt* ELECTRONICS PROTECT ELECTRONIC COMPONENTS to encapsulate electronic components in an insulating resin in order to protect them and hold them in place. The technique is used in high technology industries such as avionics as well as in automotive, medical, and consumer electronics. [Pre-12C. Directly or (later) via French < assumed Vulgar Latin *pottus*] —**pot·ful** *n* ◇ **go to pot** to get much worse or become useless, worthless, or extremely unsatisfactory (*informal*)

pot on *vt UK* to transfer a growing plant from a smaller to a larger pot

pot[2] /pot/ *n* DRUGS same as **marijuana** (*slang*) [Mid-20C. Probably shortening of Mexican Spanish *potiguaya* "marijuana leaves"]

pot[3] /pot/ *n* PHYS same as **potentiometer** (*informal*) [Mid-20C. Shortening]

po·ta·ble /pṓtəb'l/ *adj* suitable for drinking because clean and uncontaminated ■ *n* a liquid that is suitable for drinking, especially an alcoholic drink [15C. Directly or via French < late Latin *potabilis* < Latin *potare* "to drink" (see POTION)] —**po·ta·bil·i·ty** /pōtə bíllətee/ *n* —**po·ta·ble·ness** *n*

po·tage /pō taázh/ *n* a thick soup [12C. < French "what is put in a pot" < *pot* (see POT[1])]

pot·ash /pót àsh/ *n* **1.** a potassium compound, especially potassium chloride, sulfate, or oxide. Use: in fertilizers. **2.** CHEM same as **potassium carbonate 3.** CHEM same as **potassium hydroxide** [Early 17C. < obsolete Dutch *potasschen* (plural) now *potasch*]

pot·ash al·um *n* CHEM same as **alum**[1]

po·tas·si·um /pə tássee əm/ *n* a soft silvery white highly reactive element of the alkali metal group. Source: carnallite, sylvite. Use: coolant in nuclear reactors, in fertilizers. Symbol **K**. See table at **element** [Early 19C. < modern Latin < *potassa* "potash"]

po·tas·si·um-ar·gon dat·ing *n* a technique for estimating the age of rocks older than 250,000 years, based on the time taken for the radioactive decay of the potassium-40 isotope into a stable argon isotope. The half-life of potassium-40 is about 1.28×10^9 years, and the ratio of potassium to argon in the specimen gives an indication of its age.

po·tas·si·um bi·tar·trate *n* a white powder or crystalline compound. Use: in baking powder, medicine, food preparation. Formula: $KHC_4H_4O_6$.

po·tas·si·um bro·mide *n* a white crystalline compound. Use: in lithography, medicine, photography, soap. Formula: KBr.

po·tas·si·um car·bon·ate *n* a white salt. Use: in brewing, ceramics, explosives, fertilizers, glass, soap. Formula: K_2CO_3.

po·tas·si·um chlo·rate *n* a white salt that detonates with heat. Use: fireworks, matches, explosives, textile printing, paper manufacture, as bleach and disinfectant. Formula: $KClO_3$.

po·tas·si·um chlo·ride *n* a colorless crystalline salt. Use: as fertilizer, in photography, medicine. Formula: KCl.

po·tas·si·um cy·a·nide *n* a very poisonous white crystalline chemical salt. Use: extraction of gold and silver from their ores, electroplating, photography, insecticide. Formula: KCN.

po·tas·si·um di·chro·mate *n* a yellow-red poisonous crystalline compound. Use: manufacture of explosives, safety matches, dyes. Formula: $K_2Cr_2O_7$.

po·tas·si·um fer·ri·cy·a·nide *n* a bright red poisonous crystalline compound that decomposes when heated. Use: textile printing, wool dyeing, blueprint paper, fertilizer. Formula: $K_3Fe(CN)_6$.

po·tas·si·um fer·ro·cy·a·nide *n* a yellow crystalline compound. Use: in medicine, explosives. Formula: $K_4Fe(CN)_6$.

po·tas·si·um hy·dro·gen car·bon·ate *n* a white powder or granular compound. Use: in baking powder, as antacid. Formula: $KHCO_3$.

po·tas·si·um hy·dro·gen tar·trate *n* CHEM same as **potassium bitartrate**

po·tas·si·um hy·drox·ide *n* a caustic toxic white solid. Use: manufacture of soap, detergents, liquid shampoos, matches. Formula: KOH.

po·tas·si·um i·o·dide *n* a white crystalline compound with a salty taste. Use: in medicine and photography, additive in table salt. Formula: KI.

po·tas·si·um ni·trate *n* a white crystalline salt. Use: in fireworks, explosives, matches, as fertilizer, meat preservative. Formula: KNO_3.

po·tas·si·um per·man·ga·nate *n* a dark purple toxic odorless crystalline compound. Use: bleach, disinfectant, antiseptic, in deodorizers and dyes. Formula: $KMnO_4$.

po·tas·si·um so·di·um tar·trate *n* a colorless crystalline salt. Use: mild laxative, food preservative, in electronics.

po·tas·si·um sul·fate *n* a colorless crystalline compound. Use: in aluminum, glass, cement, fertilizers, medicine. Formula: K_2SO_4.

po·ta·tion /pō táysh'n/ *n* (*literary*) **1.** the act or an instance of drinking **2.** a drink, especially an alcoholic drink [15C. Directly or via French < Latin *potation-* < *potare* "to drink" (see POTION)]

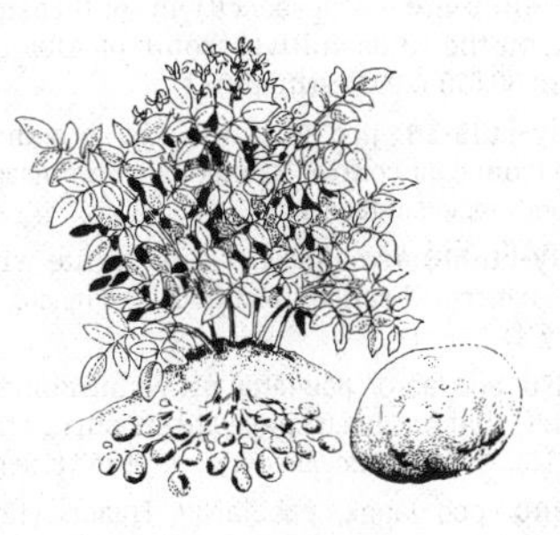

potato

po·ta·to /pə táytō/ (*plural* **-toes**) *n* **1.** a rounded white tuber cooked in a variety of ways as a vegetable. Use: industrial source of starch. **2.** a perennial plant that produces potatoes underground. Native to: South America. Latin name: *Solanum tuberosum*. **3.** FOOD, PLANTS same as **sweet potato** [Mid-16C. < Spanish *patata*, alteration of Taino *batata* "sweet potato"]

po·ta·to bee·tle *n* INSECTS same as **Colorado potato beetle**

po·ta·to blight *n* a highly destructive disease of the potato caused by the fungus *Phytophthora infestans*. It was the cause of the loss of the potato crop in Ireland in the 19th century.

po·ta·to chip *n* a very thin slice of potato that has usually been deep-fried in oil, salted, sometimes flavored, and packaged and sold to be eaten cold as a snack

~~**potatoe**~~ incorrect spelling of **potato**

po·ta·to pan·cake *n* a pancake made from a mixture of coarsely grated potato with egg, flour, and seasonings, and often eaten with applesauce

po·ta·to skin *n* a piece of skin from a hollowed-out baked potato that is then baked further, or a piece of deep-fried skin of a raw potato, served as an appetizer (*often used in the plural*)

pot-au-feu /pàwt ō fő/ (*plural same*) *n* **1.** a French stew of slowly boiled meat and vegetables, the meat usually being eaten separately from the vegetables and stock, which are served first as a soup **2.** a large earthenware pot in which pot-au-feu is traditionally cooked [< French, "pot on the fire"]

Pot·a·wat·o·mi /pòttə wóttəmee/ (*plural same* or **-mis**) *n* **1.** a member of a Native North American people who lived in the north central states, and who now live mainly in Kansas, Oklahoma, Michigan, and Ontario **2.** the Algonquian language of the Potawatomi people. Native speakers: 50. —**Pot·a·wat·o·mi** *adj*

pot·bel·lied /pót bèllid/ *adj* having a round bulging stomach or abdomen

pot·bel·lied pig *n* a small domesticated pig with a rounded shape and a dark skin with a lighter band running around its middle, sometimes kept as a pet. Native to: Vietnam.

pot·bel·lied stove *n* HOUSEHOLD same as **potbelly stove**

pot·bel·ly /pót bèllee/ (*plural* **-lies**) *n* **1.** a round bulging stomach or abdomen **2.** HOUSEHOLD same as **potbelly stove**

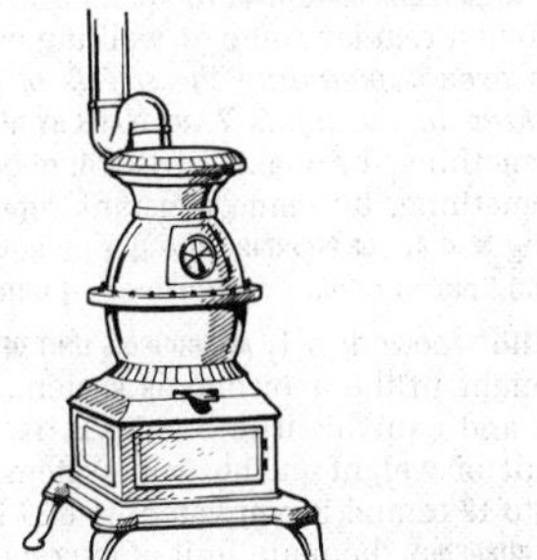

potbelly stove

pot·bel·ly stove *n* a wood- or coal-burning stove that has a rounded bulbous body

pot·boil·er /pót bòylər/ *n* a book, film, or other work that is produced quickly to make money and has little literary or artistic quality [< its purpose of "boiling the pot," providing money for food]

pot·bound /pót bòwnd/ *adj* describes a potted plant whose roots have grown very dense and have filled its pot so that its growth is restricted. Some plants thrive in this condition.

po·teen /pō téen/ *n* in Ireland, liquor that has been distilled illegally, especially from potatoes [Early 19C. < Irish *(fuisce) poitín* "small pot (whiskey)" < *pota* "pot"]

Po·tem·kin vil·lage /pə témkin-/ *n US* something that appears impressive but is ineffective and insubstantial [Mid-20C. After Grigoriĭ Aleksandrovich *Potemkin* (1739–91), who reputedly ordered villages consisting of mere facades to be built along the route of a tour by Catherine the Great]

po·ten·cy /pṓt'nssee/ (*plural* **-cies**) *n* **1.** STRENGTH OF MEDICINE the strength of something such as a drug or alcoholic drink **2.** STATE OF BEING POTENT the state or quality of being potent **3.** ABILITY TO DEVELOP a capacity for growth or development

po·tent[1] /pṓt'nt/ *adj* **1.** STRONG AND EFFECTIVE possessing great physical, political, or military strength and power ○ *a potent force* **2.** POWERFULLY PERSUASIVE exerting or capable of exerting great powers of persuasion or influence ○ *a potent symbol* **3.** WITH STRONG PHYSIOLOGICAL EFFECT producing a powerful effect on the body or mind when taken, eaten, or drunk ○ *The local brew is said to be particularly potent.* **4.** CAPABLE OF SEXUAL INTERCOURSE used to describe a man who is capable of achieving an erection or ejaculation [15C. < Latin *potent-*, present participle of *posse* "be powerful," contraction of *potis esse* < *potis* "able" + *esse* "be"] —**po·tent·ly** *adv* —**po·tent·ness** *n*

po·tent[2] /pṓt'nt/ *adj* describes a heraldic cross that has four arms with a bar across the end of each arm [14C. Alteration of obsolete *potence* "crutch," or via its French source < Latin *potentia* "power" < *potent-* (see POTENT[1])]

po·ten·tate /pṓt'n tàyt/ *n* somebody with great power or influence, especially a ruler

po·ten·tial /pə ténshəl/ *adj* **1.** POSSIBLE BUT AS YET NOT ACTUAL having a latent possibility or likelihood of occurring, or of doing or becoming something ○ *posed a potential danger* ○ *a potential investor* **2.** EXPRESSING POSSIBILITY describes a verb or verb form that expresses possibility, e.g., "may" or "might" in English ■ *n* **1.** CAPACITY FOR DEVELOPMENT a capacity to develop, succeed, or become something ○ *has the potential to be profitable* ○ *unable to use her expertise to its full potential* **2.** POTENTIAL VERB FORM a verb or verb form that expresses possibility, e.g., "may" or "might" in English **3.** PHYS same as **electric potential** [14C. Directly or via French < late Latin *potentialis* < Latin *potent-* (see POTENT[1])] —**po·ten·tial·ly** *adv*

po·ten·tial dif·fer·ence *n* the work done in moving a unit electric charge between two points in an electric field. Symbol ΔV, ΔU

po·ten·tial en·er·gy *n* the energy that a body or system has stored because of its position in an electric, magnetic, or gravitational field, or because of its configuration. Symbol V, E_p

po·ten·ti·al·i·ty /pə tènshee állətee/ (*plural* **-ties**) *n* **1.** a capacity to grow, develop, or become something **2.** somebody or something capable of growing, developing, or becoming something

po·ten·tial well *n* a region in an electric, magnetic, or gravitational field in which an object has a lower potential energy than it would have in all adjacent regions

po·ten·ti·ate /pə ténshee àyt/ (**-at·ed, -at·ing, -ates**) *vt* **1.** to improve the effectiveness of a drug or treatment, especially by adding another drug or agent **2.** to make something potent or powerful —**po·ten·ti·a·tor** *n*

po·ten·til·la /pṓt'n tíllə/ (*plural* **-las** or *same*) *n* a cultivated flowering plant or small bush. Flowers: small, yellow, white, or red, five-petaled. Genus: *Potentilla*. [Mid-16C. < medieval Latin, "powerful little (plant)" (from its use in medicine) < Latin *potent-* (see POTENT[1])]

po·ten·ti·om·e·ter /pə tènshee ómmətər/ *n* **1.** a device for measuring an unknown potential difference or electromotive force by comparing it to a known standard **2.** a three-terminal component, typically used as a volume or brightness control, that gives a variable electric potential by rotating a shaft or moving a slider [Late 19C. < POTENTIAL] —**po·ten·ti·om·e·try** *n*

po·ten·ti·o·met·ric /pə tènshee ə méttrik/ *adj* indicating the completion of a chemical reaction by a change in potential at an electrode immersed in the solution where the reaction is taking place [Early 20C. < POTENTIAL]

pot·head /pót hèd/ *n* a regular or heavy smoker of marijuana (*slang disapproving*)

poth·e·car·y /póthə kèrree/ (*plural* **-ies**) *n* COMM same as **pharmacy** (*archaic or regional*) [14C. Shortening of APOTHECARY]

poth·er /pó*th*ər/ *n* **1.** NERVOUS STATE a state of emotional agitation, especially over something trivial **2.** COMMOTION a great deal of frenzied activity or conversation, especially over something trivial **3.** CHOKING CLOUD a suffocating cloud of smoke or dust ■ *vti* (**-ered, -er·ing, -ers**) CONFUSE SOMEBODY OR BE CONFUSED to confuse or worry somebody, or become confused or worried [Late 16C. Origin ?]

pot·herb /pót hùrb/ *n* an herb or vegetable used to add flavor in cooking

pot·hold·er /pót hṓldər/ *n* a pad of fabric used to protect the hands from hot pots and cooking utensils

pot·hole /pót hṓl/ *n* **1.** HOLE IN ROAD a hole in the surface of a road **2.** VERTICAL HOLE IN LIMESTONE AREA a vertical deep hole or shaft formed naturally in limestone regions by the erosive action of running water **3.** HOLE IN RIVER BED a bowl-shaped hole in the bed of a river or stream, formed by the abrasive action of stone, gravel, or ice being churned in an eddy **4.** *Western US* PATCH OF MUD OR QUICKSAND a patch of deep mud or quicksand in which cattle might be bogged down or sink

pot·hole lake *n* a small lake formed in a limestone pothole depression

pot·hook /pót hòòk/ *n* **1.** an S-shaped hook fixed above an open fire, from which a pot or kettle is hung **2.** a handwriting mark beginning or ending in a curve

pot·hunt·er /pót hùntər/ *n* **1.** HUNTER VIOLATING RULES somebody who hunts game, often indiscriminately and disregardful of rules **2.** PRIZE-SEEKER a participant in competitions and races with more interest in the prizes than the sports (*informal disapproving*) **3.** AMATEUR ARCHAEOLOGIST somebody who digs for ancient pots and other objects but who is not a professional archaeologist

po·tion /pṓsh'n/ *n* a liquid to be drunk that is medicinal, supposedly magical, or poisonous [13C. Via French < Latin *potion-* < *potare* "to drink" < *potus* "drink"]

Pot·i·phar /póttifər/ *n* in the Bible, the Egyptian who bought Joseph as a slave and later imprisoned him when he was falsely accused of attempting to have sexual relations with his wife. (Genesis 37).

pot·latch /pót làch/ *n* among Native American peoples of the coast of northwestern North America, a ceremony of feasting in which the host gains prestige by giving gifts or, sometimes, destroying wealth [Mid-19C. < Chinook Jargon *patlă* < Nootka *p'achitl* "giving or gift"]

pot liq·uor *n US* the liquid in a pot in which meat and vegetables have been boiled

pot·luck /pót lùk/ *n* **1.** CHOICE FROM WHAT IS AVAILABLE a choice from whatever happens to be available in a particular situation ○ *take potluck* **2.** FOOD AVAILABLE FOR UNEXPECTED GUEST whatever food happens to be available to serve an unexpected guest **3.** MEAL TO WHICH EVERYONE BRINGS SOMETHING a meal to which each participant brings one dish that is shared by everyone (*often used before a noun*) ○ *a potluck dinner* [Late 16C. < POT[1]]

pot mar·i·gold *n* same as **calendula**

Po·to·mac /pə tṓmək/ river of the eastern United States, formed by the confluence of its north and south branches near Cumberland, Maryland, and emptying into Chesapeake Bay. It flows through Washington, D.C. Length: 383 mi./616 km.

po·too /pə to͞o/ (*plural same*) *n* a nocturnal bird that eats insects. Native to: Mexico, Central and South America. Genus: *Nyctibius*. [Mid-19C. Via Jamaican Creole < Twi, an imitation of the bird's call]

pot·pie /pót pī/ *n* a pie of meat and vegetables in a deep dish covered with a pastry crust

pot plant *n UK* same as **potted plant**

pot·pour·ri /pōpə rée/ (*plural* **-ris**) *n* **1.** a collection of dried flower petals, leaves, herbs, and spices that is used to scent the air **2.** a mixture of miscellaneous things [Early 17C. < French, "mixed stew," literally "rotten pot," translation of Spanish *olla podrida*]

potray incorrect spelling of **portray**

pot roast *n* a dish consisting of a piece of beef cooked slowly in the oven in a closed pot in its own juices, often on a bed of vegetables —**pot-roast** *vti*

POTS /pots/ *n US* a standard connection to a telephone system, as distinguished from a high-speed digital connection. Full form **plain old telephone system**

Pots·dam /póts dàm/ city in northeastern Germany approximately 18 mi./29 km southwest of Berlin. It was the site of the Potsdam Conference (July-August 1945), at which US, British, and Soviet leaders discussed the postwar administration of Germany. Population: 138,268 (1997).

pot·sherd /pót shùrd/, **pot·shard** /-shaard/ *n* a fragment of pottery, especially one found at an archaeological site [14C. < POT[1]]

pot·shot /pót shòt/ *n* **1.** a criticism made without careful consideration and aimed at an easy target ○ *journalists taking potshots at the government* **2.** a quick careless, and usually easy, shot taken at something such as game [Mid-19C. Because originally a shot to get food for the cooking "pot"]

pot·stick·er /pót stìkər/ *n* in Chinese cooking, a circle of dough wrapped around a filling of meat or vegetables, steamed or fried and served with a dipping sauce

pot still *n* an apparatus for distilling whiskey that applies heat directly to the container holding the mash

pot·stone /pót stōn/ *n* an impure variety of talc, used in the past to make cooking vessels

pot·tage /póttij/ *n* a thick vegetable, or meat and vegetable, soup [Mid-16C. Anglicization of POTAGE]

pot·ted /póttəd/ *adj* **1.** GROWING IN POT planted in a pot **2.** DRUNK drunk or intoxicated by a drug (*slang*) **3.** PRESERVED IN POT cooked or preserved in a vessel such as a pot or jar ○ *potted beef* **4.** *UK* SUPERFICIALLY SUMMARIZED reproduced in a brief and often superficial form (*informal*) ○ *a potted biography*

pot·ted plant *n* a plant that has been placed with soil in a flowerpot and is kept for display and decoration

pot·ter[1] /póttər/ *n* a maker of pottery [Pre-12C. < POT[1]]

pot·ter[2] /póttər/ (**-tered, -ter·ing, -ters**) *vi UK* same as **putter**[1] [Mid-16C. < obsolete *pote* "push," origin ?]

Popperfoto

Beatrix Potter

Pot·ter /póttər/, **Beatrix** (1866–1943) British children's writer and illustrator. Her illustrated animal stories, including *The Tale of Peter Rabbit* (1900) and *The Tailor of Gloucester* (1902), became children's classics. Full name **Potter, Helen Beatrix**

"Don't go into Mr. McGregor's garden: your Father had an accident there; he was put in a pie by Mrs. McGregor."
[Beatrix Potter, *The Tale of Peter Rabbit*; 1900]

Pot·ter·ies /póttəreez/ a region in Staffordshire, west central England, famous for its ceramics factories

pot·ter's clay *n* clay that does not contain any iron and is suitable for making pottery

pot·ter's field *n* **1.** in the Bible, an area of land near Jerusalem bought as a burial ground for strangers with the money that was given to Judas for betraying Jesus Christ **2.** a public burial ground for poor or unidentified people

pot·ter's wheel *n* a device for molding clay into pottery by hand, consisting of a rotating horizontal disc that holds and turns the clay between the potter's hands

pot·ter wasp *n* a small solitary wasp that constructs elaborate clay pots in which it lays its eggs and puts caterpillars to serve as food for the young. Genus: *Eumenes*.

pot·ter·y /póttəree/ (*plural* **-ies**) *n* **1.** OBJECTS MADE OF BAKED CLAY objects that are made by molding or shaping moist clay and hardening it by heating in a kiln, e.g., vases, pots, plates, or sculptured articles **2.** MAKING OF POTTERY the art, craft, or occupation of making pottery **3.** PLACE WHERE POTTERY IS MADE a workshop, factory, or other place where pottery is made

pot·ting soil *n* a mixture with a soil, peat, or fiber base and a balanced nutrient content that is used for growing plants in pots

pot·to /póttō/ (*plural* **-tos**) *n* a small primate that has small ears, large eyes, and a short bushy tail and lives in the lower branches of trees. Native to: rain forests of West and Central Africa. Latin name: *Perodicticus potto*. [Early 18C. Probably < a West African language]

Pott's dis·ease /póts-/ *n* a tubercular disease of the spine, marked by the destruction of the bone and disks and curvature of the spine [Mid-19C. After Sir Percivall *Pott* (1713–88), English surgeon]

pot·ty[1] /póttee/ (**-ti·er, -ti·est**) *adj UK* slightly irrational (*informal*) [Mid-19C. Origin ?] —**pot·ti·ness** *n*

pot·ty[2] /póttee/ (*plural* **-ties**) *n* **1.** a bowl, used especially by young children who cannot yet use a toilet, to eliminate body waste **2.** same as **toilet** (sense 1) (*informal*) [Mid-20C. < POT[1]]

pot·ty-chair *n* a small chair with a potty in the seat, used by young children who are being trained to use a toilet

pot·ty-train *vti* to train a young child to use a potty instead of a diaper (*informal*)

POTUS /pōtəss/ *n US* used as shorthand by White House staff in memos and internal documents to refer to the US president. Full form **President of the United States**

pouch /powch/ *n* **1.** SMALL SOFT BAG a small bag or container made of a soft material such as fabric or leather **2.** SOMETHING RESEMBLING POUCH something that looks like a pouch, especially a small baggy fold of skin **3.** POCKET OF SKIN IN ANIMAL a structure in an animal resembling a pouch, especially one on the abdomen of a marsupial for carrying young, or in the cheek of a rodent for carrying food **4.** BODY CAVITY RESEMBLING POCKET a pocket-shaped space or structure in the body **5.** PLANT CAVITY a cavity in a plant shaped like a pocket **6.** BAG FOR MAIL a lockable bag or sack for carrying mail, especially diplomatic correspondence **7.** *Scotland* CLOTHING same as **pocket** *n* (sense 1) ■ *v* (**pouched, pouch·ing, pouch·es**) **1.** *vt* PUT SOMETHING IN POUCH to put something into a pouch **2.** *vti* FORM POUCH to make something, or be made, into a shape resembling a pouch [13C. < Anglo-Norman *puche*, Old N French *pouche*, Old French *poche* "bag" < Germanic] —**pouch·y** *adj*

pouf /poof/, **pouffe** *n* **1.** PUFFED-OUT HAIRSTYLE a puffed-out hairstyle, similar to a bouffant, fashionable especially in the 18th century **2.** PAD IN HAIR a pad worn in the hair to help shape a pouf **3.** BUNCHED-UP PART OF DRESS a part of a dress or skirt gathered up to form a soft projecting shape **4.** *UK* same as **hassock** (sense 1) [Early 19C. < French, an imitation of the sound of a puff]

Pough·keep·sie /pə kípsee/ city in southeastern New York, on the Hudson River, south of Albany. Population: 30,073 (2002 estimate).

Pouil·ly-Fuis·sé /poo yée fwee sáy/ *n* a dry white wine from east central France [After two villages in the Burgundy region of France]

Pouil·ly-Fu·mé /-fyoo máy/ *n* a dry white wine from west central France [Mid-20C. < French, "smoked Pouilly"]

pou·lard /poo laard/, **pou·larde** *n* a young domestic hen (**pullet**) that has been spayed to encourage fattening [Mid-18C. < French *poularde* < *poule* "hen" (see PULLET)]

Pou·lenc /po͝o langk, po͝o laNk/, **Francis** (1899–1963) French composer and pianist. He was a member of the Paris-based group of composers known as "Les Six." His music, tuneful and satirical, includes ballets, operas, chamber music, and songs.

poult /pōlt/ *n* a young fowl, especially a turkey [15C. Contraction of PULLET]

poul·tice /pōltiss/ *n* a warm moist preparation placed on an aching or inflamed part of the body to ease pain, improve circulation, or hasten the expression of pus [14C. < Latin *pultes*, plural of *puls* "pottage, thick gruel"]

poul·try /pōltree/ *n* **1.** domestic fowl in general, e.g., chickens, turkeys, ducks, or geese, raised for meat or eggs (*takes a singular or plural verb*) **2.** the meat of domestic fowl [14C. < Old French *pouletrie* < *pouletier* "seller of poultry" < *poulet* (see PULLET)]

pounce[1] /pownss/ *vi* (**pounced, pounc·ing, pounc·es**) **1.** JUMP SUDDENLY ON to jump or swoop suddenly toward or onto somebody or something, especially onto prey **2.** ATTACK OR TAKE QUICKLY to move very quickly and suddenly in attacking somebody or obtaining something ○ *He pounced on the book and carried it off to his room.* **3.** REACT SWIFTLY TO SOMETHING to be quick to notice and make use of something ○ *She immediately pounced on his admission that he'd known all about it.* ■ *n* ACT OF SUDDENLY JUMPING ON an act of suddenly jumping or swooping toward or onto somebody or something, especially onto prey [14C. Either shortening of PUNCHEON[2], or < Old French *poinson* "pointed tool" < Latin *punct-* (see PUNCTURE)] —**pounc·er** *n*

pounce[2] /pownss/ *n* **1.** POWDER USED FOR PRODUCING IMAGE powdered charcoal or other fine powder sprinkled over a stencil to reproduce the main lines of a pattern or design on the surface beneath the stencil **2.** POWDER TO STOP INK FROM RUNNING a very fine powder formerly used to stop ink from spreading on unglazed paper ■ *vt* (**pounced, pounc·ing, pounc·es**) **1.** REPRODUCE SOMETHING WITH POUNCE to reproduce a pattern or design on something by sprinkling pounce over a stencil **2.** BLOT PAPER WITH POUNCE to sprinkle paper with pounce to prevent ink from running [Late 16C. < French < Latin *pumic-* "pumice"]

pound[1] /pownd/ *v* (**pound·ed, pound·ing, pounds**) **1.** *vti* STRIKE SOMETHING HARD AND REPEATEDLY to strike somebody or something with repeated heavy blows **2.** *vt* BEAT SOMETHING TO PULP OR POWDER to beat something into a pulp or powder with repeated heavy blows **3.** *vi* THROB to beat or throb heavily ○ *My heart was pounding.* **4.** *vt* BOMBARD SOMETHING to attack a place continuously with bombs or large guns ○ *pounding the city for a few weeks* **5.** *vi* RUN HEAVILY to move, especially to run, fast or energetically and with heavy, noisy steps **6.** *vt* WALK ALONG SOMETHING to spend a long time walking along a regular route or walking back and forth in an area ○ *pounding the streets of Manhattan and taking in the sights* **7.** *vt* TEACH BY REPETITION to teach something, or make sure somebody understands something, by using constant repetition and drilling ■ *n* ACT OF POUNDING the act or sound of pounding [Old English *pūnian* < Germanic] —**pound·er** *n*

pound[2] /pownd/ *n* **1.** AVOIRDUPOIS UNIT OF WEIGHT a unit of weight in the avoirdupois system, divided into 16 oz and equivalent to 0.45 kg **2.** TROY UNIT OF WEIGHT a unit of weight in the troy system that is divided into 12 oz and is equivalent to 0.37 kg **3.** COMMON UNIT OF CURRENCY the main unit of currency in the United Kingdom and several other countries. See table at **currency** **4.** FORMER IRISH CURRENCY the main unit of the former currency of the Republic of Ireland **5.** BRITISH UNIT OF FORCE a British unit of force, equal to the gravitational force experienced by a pound mass accelerating at 32.174 ft./9.80665 m per second per second [Old English *pund*, via Germanic < Latin *pondo* "weight of a pound" < *(libra) pondo* "(pound) by weight"] ◇ **get** *or* **have your pound of flesh** to get what is due to you, even if it causes difficulties or hardship to others

pound out *vt* **1.** to produce something by working in a diligent continuous way ○ *pound out an essay* **2.** to produce something with heavy blows or loud thumping noises ○ *pound out a tune on the piano*

pound[3] /pownd/ *n* **1.** ENCLOSURE FOR STRAY ANIMALS a fenced-off area or a building with cages where stray animals, especially dogs, are kept **2.** ENCLOSURE FOR VEHICLES OR OTHER GOODS a fenced-off area where vehicles or other goods that have been taken by the police or another authority are kept until a debt or fine has been paid **3.** PLACE FOR ANIMALS OR FISH an area in which animals or fish are trapped or kept **4.** PRISON AREA a place where people are held prisoner ■ *vt* (**pound·ed, pound·ing, pounds**) PUT SOMETHING IN POUND to confine an animal or person in a pound [Old English *pund-*, origin ?]

Ezra Pound

Pound /pownd/, **Ezra** (1885–1972) US writer. He was an influential poet, critic, translator, and mentor of other poets, and a founder of imagism. His major work is the *Cantos* (1915–70). Full name **Pound, Ezra Loomis**

"The apparition of these faces in the crowd; / Petals on a wet black bough."
[Ezra Pound, "In a Station of the Metro," *Dramatis Personae*; 1926]

"Great literature is simply language charged with meaning to the utmost possible degree."
[Ezra Pound, *How to Read*; 1931]

pound·age[1] /pówndij/ *n* **1.** WEIGHT IN POUNDS the weight of somebody or something expressed in pounds **2.** PAYMENT PER POUND OF WEIGHT a tax, charge, commission, or other payment for something calculated per pound of weight **3.** PAYMENT PER POUND STERLING a tax, charge, commission, or other payment for something calculated per pound sterling

pound·age[2] /pówndij/ *n* **1.** the confinement of animals in an enclosed area or pound **2.** the fee that must be paid for the return of an impounded vehicle, animal, or other goods

pound·al /pównd'l/ *n* a British unit of force, equal to the force that will impart an acceleration of one foot per second per second to a mass of one pound [Late 19C. < POUND[2]]

pound cake *n* a rich dense yellow cake that is traditionally made with a pound each of butter, sugar, flour, and eggs, or with equal weights of each of these ingredients

pound-fool·ish *adj* unwise when dealing with large amounts of money or important matters

pound sign *n* **1.** *US* the symbol (#), especially on a telephone keypad or computer keyboard. Can term **hash**[1] **2.** the symbol (£) which indicates pound sterling

pound ster·ling (*plural* **pounds ster·ling**) *n* the official name for the unit of currency used in the United Kingdom

pour /pawr/ (**poured, pour·ing, pours**) *v* **1.** *vt* MAKE SOMETHING FLOW to make a substance flow out or down in a stream ○ *poured the sugar into the bowl* **2.** *vti* SERVE DRINK to serve a drink from a container such as a pot or pitcher into a cup, mug, or glass ○ *Let me pour you some tea.* **3.** *vi* FLOW IN LARGE QUANTITIES to flow down or out, especially in large quantities ○ *Smoke poured from the burning building.* **4.** *vi* RAIN HEAVILY to rain very heavily ○ *It poured for hours.* **5.** *vi* COME IN LARGE QUANTITIES to come or go quickly and in large quantities ○ *Letters of complaint came pouring in.* **6.** *vt* EXPRESS FEELING to express a feeling at length and without restraint ○ *poured his heart out to me* **7.** *vt* GIVE SOMETHING IN LARGE AMOUNT to expend a large amount of something, e.g., time, money, or effort ○ *poured a lot of blood, sweat, and tears into that project* [13C. Probably via Old French dialect *purer* "sift, pour out" < Latin *purare* "purify" < *purus* "pure"]

USAGE pour or **pore**? "To study something carefully and thoughtfully" (***pore***) might seem to have more in common with "to make a substance flow" (***pour***) than with "a tiny opening" (***pore***). Perhaps it has, but all three words have been derived separately, despite the fact that one of the verbs has the same spelling as the noun. You ***pour*** from the pot into a teacup, ***pore*** over a text, and have ***pores*** in your skin.

pour·boire /poor bwaár/ *n* a sum of money given for services rendered or anticipated [Early 19C. < French, literally "for drinking"]

pour·down /páwr dòwn/ *n Southern US* a heavy downpour

REGIONAL NOTE See ***trashmover***.

pour point *n* the lowest temperature at which a liquid will continue to flow

pousse-ca·fé /po͝oss ka fáy/ *n* **1.** a drink consisting of different-colored liqueurs poured in one glass and forming layers because each liqueur has a different density **2.** a liqueur served after dinner, with or after coffee [< French, literally "push coffee"]

pousse-pousse /po͝oss po͝oss/ *n* in Madagascar, a small vehicle with two wheels and a seat for passengers, pulled along by somebody walking in front of it ○*"A typical scene: 'Now the road was littered with crashed taxis, broken pousse-pousses, and wandering zebu carts.'"* (Patrick Anderson, quoting book author John Robinson "The Sapphire Sea," *Washington Post Book World*; November 3, 2003) [Reduplication of French *pousse*, "to push."]

Pous·sin /poo sáN/, **Nicolas** (1594–1665) French painter. He was a master of French classicism, and was influenced by Raphael.

"The idea of beauty does not descend into matter unless this is prepared as carefully as possible."
[Nicolas Poussin. Quoted in *Lives of the Modern Painters, Sculptors and Architects*, Giovanni Pietro Bellori; 1672]

pout[1] /powt/ *v* (**pout·ed, pout·ing, pouts**) **1.** *vti* PUSH LIPS OUTWARD to push the lower lip or both lips outward in an expression of bad temper or sulkiness **2.** *vti* ADOPT SEXY EXPRESSION to push the lips outward in order to look sexually attractive **3.** *vi* SULK to show disappointment, anger, or resentment, usually in silence ○ *still pouting because he missed the game* **4.** *vt* SAY SOMETHING SULKILY to say something with a pout ○ *pouted that the whole thing wasn't fair* ■ *n* **1.** EXPRESSION WITH LIPS PUSHED OUT an expression of the face with the lower lip or both lips pushed out **2.** SULKY MOOD a period or display of sulkiness [14C. Origin ?] —**pout·y** *adj*

pout[2] /powt/ (*plural* **same** or **pouts**) *n* FISH **1.** same as **eelpout** **2.** same as **hornpout** [Old English *-pūte*, origin ?]

pout·er /pówtər/ *n* **1.** somebody who pouts **2.** *also* **pout·er pi·geon** a domesticated pigeon belonging to a breed with a pouch in its throat that can be greatly inflated

pou·tine /poo téen/ *n* a dish originating in Quebec that consists of French fries and cottage cheese, covered with tomato sauce or gravy

POV *abbr* point of view (*used in e-mails or text messages*)

pov·er·ty /póvvərtee/ *n* **1.** STATE OF BEING POOR the state of not having enough money to take care of basic needs such as food, clothing, and housing **2.** LACK a deficiency or lack of something ○ *poverty of emotion* **3.** INFERTILITY OF SOIL lack of soil fertility or nutrients [12C. Via Old French *poverte* < Latin *paupertas* < *pauper* "poor" (see PAUPER)]

pov·er·ty line, **pov·er·ty lev·el** *n* a level of income below which somebody is considered to be living in poverty. It is based on the price of basic necessities and is usually determined by a government.

pov·er·ty-strick·en *adj* in a state of extreme poverty

pow /pow/ *interj* used to imitate the sound of an explosion or gun, or of a sudden impact, e.g., of somebody being hit (*informal*) [Late 19C. An imitation of the sound]

POW *abbr* prisoner of war

pow·der /pówdər/ *n* **1.** LOOSE DRY PARTICLES a substance in the form of a mass of very small, loose dry grains **2.** PARTICULAR KIND OF POWDER powder that is produced for a particular purpose ○ *face powder* **3.** ARMS same as **gunpowder** **4.** DRY SNOW light dry snow ■ *v* (**-dered, -der·ing, -ders**) **1.** *vt* PUT POWDER ON SOMETHING to cover something with powder, or sprinkle powder on something **2.** *vti* TURN SOMETHING INTO POWDER to turn a solid into powder by crushing it, or become a powder [13C. < French *poudre*, alteration of *poldre* < Latin *pulver-* "dust"] —**pow·der·er** *n* —**pow·der·y** *adj*

Pow·der /pówdər/ **1.** river rising in the Blue Mountains in Oregon and flowing into the Snake River along the Idaho border. Length: 110 mi./177 km. **2.** river forming in central Wyoming and flowing into the Yellowstone River in Montana. Length: 375 mi./604 km.

pow·der blue *adj* of a very pale purplish blue color (*hyphenated when used before a noun*) —**pow·der blue** *n*

pow·der burn *n* a minor skin burn caused by being very close to a brief intense explosion, especially the firing of a gun, sometimes used as evidence in a court of law

pow·der flask *n* a small flask used for keeping gunpowder for loading a firearm

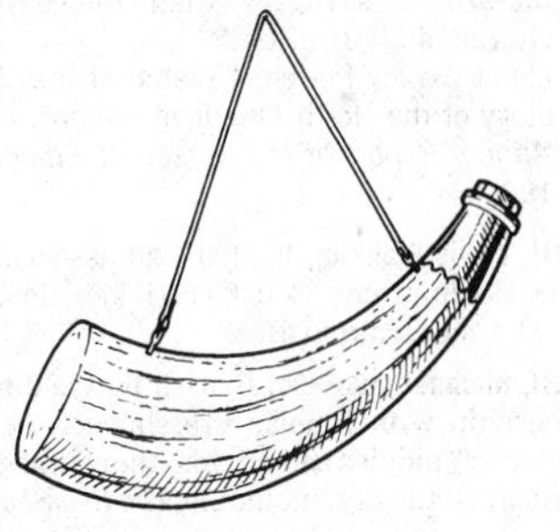
powder horn

pow·der horn *n* a small container consisting of the hollow horn of an ox or cow, used for keeping gunpowder for loading a firearm

pow·der keg *n* **1.** a small barrel used to hold gunpowder or blasting powder **2.** a tense situation that may easily erupt into violence

pow·der met·al·lur·gy *n* the technology used in producing solid objects, e.g., self-lubricating bearings, from powdered metals or carbides by compressing or heating them without melting them

pow·der mon·key *n* **1.** somebody who deals with explosives, e.g., in mining or construction (*slang*) **2.** a boy formerly employed on a warship to carry gunpowder from the store to the guns

pow·der puff *n* a soft or fluffy pad used for putting powder on the face or skin

pow·der room *n* **1.** a public restroom for women **2.** a bathroom for use by guests, situated near the main living area of a house

pow·der·y mil·dew *n* a fungal disease that produces a white powdery covering on plant leaves

Pow·ell /pów əl/, **Adam Clayton, Jr.** (1908–72) US politician and cleric. He was a Democratic congressman (1945–70), and campaigned against racial discrimination.

Pow·ell /pṓ əl/, **Sir Anthony** (1906–2000) British novelist. His major work is the series of 12 novels, *A Dance to the Music of Time* (1951–75), which examines English upper-middle-class life in the mid-20th century. Full name **Powell, Sir Anthony Dymoke**

Department of Defense, Washington, D.C.

Colin Powell

Pow·ell /pów əl/, **Colin** (*b.* 1937) US general and secretary of state (2001–). He was chairman of the Joint Chiefs of Staff during the Persian Gulf War (1991) and became secretary of state under President George W. Bush. Full name **Powell, Colin Luther**

> "One of the fondest expressions around is that we can't be the world's policeman. But guess who gets called when suddenly someone needs a cop."
> [Colin Powell, *Life*; March 1991]

> "Avoid having your ego so close to your position that when your position falls, your ego goes with it."
> [Colin Powell, "Colin Powell's Rules," *Parade*; August 1989]

Pow·ell, John Wesley (1834–1902) US ethnologist, explorer, and geologist. He classified Native American languages, and did pioneering survey work in the Rocky Mountains.

> "The scalping scene is no more the true picture of savagery than the bayonet charge of civilization."
> [John Wesley Powell, "Sketch of the Mythology of the North American Indians," *First Annual Report of the Bureau of Ethnology*; 1881]

Pow·ell, Lewis Franklin, Jr. (1907–98) associate justice of the US Supreme Court (1971–87). He was considered a moderate justice.

Pow·ell, Michael (1905–90) British movie director. In partnership with Emeric Pressburger, he made a number of movies noted for their imagery and technical virtuosity, including *The Red Shoes* (1948).

> "The real reason why *The Red Shoes* was such a success, was that we had all been told for ten years to go out and die...now that the war was over *The Red Shoes* told us to go and die for art."
> [Michael Powell, *A Life in Movies*; 1986]

pow·er /pówr/ *n* **1. CAPACITY TO DO SOMETHING** the ability, strength, and capacity to do something ○ *The pilot did everything in his power to avoid the disaster.* **2. STRENGTH** physical force or strength **3. CONTROL AND INFLUENCE** control and influence over other people and their actions ○ *She made you stay behind just to show how much power she has over you.* **4. POLITICAL CONTROL** the political control of a country, exercised by its government or leader **5. AUTHORITY TO ACT** the authority to act or do something according to a law or rule **6. SOMEBODY WITH POWER** a politically, financially, or socially powerful person **7. IMPORTANT COUNTRY** a country that has military or economic resources and is considered to have political influence over other countries **8. PERSUASIVENESS** the ability to influence people's judgment or emotions **9. SKILL** a faculty, skill, or ability ○ *musical powers* **10. MEASURE OF RATE OF DOING WORK** a measure of the rate of doing work or transferring energy, usually expressed in terms of wattage or horsepower. Symbol *P* **11. ENERGY TO DRIVE MACHINERY** energy or force used to drive machinery or produce electricity **12. ELECTRICITY** electricity made available for use **13.** MATH **NUMBER OF MULTIPLICATION OPERATIONS** the number of times a quantity is to be successively multiplied by itself, usually written as a small number to the right of and above the quantity **14.** OPTICS **MAGNIFYING ABILITY** a measure of the ability of a lens, mirror, or prism to magnify an image **15.** STATS **PROBABILITY OF REJECTING NULL HYPOTHESIS** the probability of rejecting the null hypothesis as false when an alternative hypothesis is true **16.** CHR **ANGEL OF FOURTH-HIGHEST ORDER** an angel of the fourth of the nine orders of angels in the traditional Christian hierarchy ■ *adj* **1. RUN BY ELECTRICITY OR FUEL** receiving power from a motor using electrical energy or fuel such as gasoline, instead of relying on manual labor ○ *power tools* **2. INTENDED FOR BUSINESS SUCCESS** designed or believed to improve somebody's status, influence, or effectiveness in business ○ *power dressing* ■ *v* **(-ered, -er·ing, -ers) 1.** *vt* **PROVIDE ENERGY TO OPERATE SOMETHING** to supply a machine or tool with the energy it needs to operate ○ *electrically powered* **2.** *vi* **MOVE ENERGETICALLY** to move fast and with great determination and energy ○ *He came powering down the home straight.* [13C. < Anglo-Norman *poer*, Old French *poeir* < assumed Vulgar Latin *potere* "be powerful" < Latin *potis* "able"] ◇ **the powers that be** the people in authority

power down *vti* to turn a computer off in the correct way, bringing an orderly end to system operation

power up *v* **1.** *vti* to turn on a computer, printer, or other peripheral device **2.** *vt* to give somebody or something increased energy or capability

pow·er base *n* a position, region, or group of voters providing the foundation of somebody's political power or support

pow·er·boat /pówr bṑt/ *n* SPORTS same as **motorboat** —**pow·er·boat·ing** *n*

pow·er brake *n* an automotive brake in which the pressure on a piston operates the brake cylinder

pow·er brok·er *n* a person or country that has great influence, especially in politics or commerce, and is able to use this influence to affect the policies and decisions of others

pow·er cen·tre *n Can* a shopping mall containing several large superstores or discount stores

pow·er cut *n UK* same as **power outage**

pow·er dive *n* a steep dive made by an aircraft with its engines at high power to increase the speed —**pow·er-dive** *vti*

pow·er for·ward *n* **1. TALL FORWARD WHO EXCELS UNDER BASKET** in basketball, a tall forward who plays the low-post position because his or her height provides an advantage for blocking shots and rebounding **2. POWER FORWARD'S POSITION** in basketball, the position in which a power forward plays **3. FORWARD KNOWN FOR STRENGTH AND AGGRESSIVENESS** in hockey, a forward who is valued as much for strength and aggressiveness as for playing skills

pow·er·ful /pówrf'l/ *adj* **1. INFLUENTIAL** able to exert a lot of influence and control over people and events ○ *a powerful nation* **2. STRONG** having or exerting great physical or mental strength **3. EFFECTIVE** possessing the strength or qualities to produce a fast and effective result ○ *a powerful antibiotic* **4. PERSUASIVE** able to produce a strong effect on people's ideas or emotions ○ *a powerful movie* ■ *adv Southern US* same as **extremely** ○ *He was powerful thirsty.* —**pow·er·ful·ly** *adv* —**pow·er·ful·ness** *n*

pow·er·house /pówr hòwss/ (*plural* **-hous·es** /-hòwzəz/) *n* **1.** somebody or something that is full of energy and very productive (*informal*) ○ *a publishing powerhouse* **2.** INDUST same as **power plant**

pow·er·less /pówrləss/ *adj* lacking power, strength, or effectiveness —**pow·er·less·ly** *adv* —**pow·er·less·ness** *n*

pow·er·lift·ing /pówr lìfting/ *n* weightlifting that emphasizes strength, in which the lifter competes against others in performing a bench press, a squat, and a two-handed dead lift

pow·er line *n* a cable that carries electricity from a power station to the users of the electricity or between electric utilities in a network

pow·er lunch *n* a meeting over lunch that gives somebody the opportunity to cultivate an important contact or discuss high-level business matters

pow·er mow·er *n* a lawn mower that is driven by a motor

pow·er nap *n* a short sleep taken by a businessperson in the office in order to feel revitalized

pow·er of ap·point·ment *n* the authority given to somebody to select beneficiaries and to allocate money and other property from a person's estate to those beneficiaries

pow·er of at·tor·ney *n* the legal authority to act for another person in legal and business matters

pow·er out·age *n* a temporary loss of electricity to a building or area

pow·er pack *n* a device for converting a supply of electricity to direct or alternating current at the correct voltage for a piece of electrical or electronic equipment

pow·er plant *n* **1.** an industrial complex where power, especially electricity, is generated from another source of energy such as burning coal, nuclear reactions, or flowing water **2.** a unit that supplies the power to move a self-propelled object, e.g., a diesel-electric engine in a locomotive or an internal-combustion engine in an automobile

pow·er play *n* **1. BID FOR ADVANTAGE** an attempt to gain an advantage by a display of strength or superiority, e.g., in a negotiation or relationship **2. TACTIC OF CONCENTRATING PLAYERS** a tactic used in sports consisting of concentrating players in one area, especially an attack in football that involves extra blockers preceding the person carrying the ball **3. NUMERICAL ADVANTAGE IN ICE HOCKEY** a situation or period of time in ice hockey during which one team has a numerical advantage because the other team has one or more players in the penalty box **4. TACTIC OF CONCENTRATING RESOURCES** a tactic in business, commerce, or politics that involves concentrating resources and effort in one area

pow·er point *n UK* ELEC same as **outlet** (sense 5)

pow·er pol·i·tics *n* political relations and actions based on an implied threat of the use of political, economic, or military power by a participant (*takes a singular or plural verb*)

Pow·ers /pów ərz/, **Hiram** (1805–73) US sculptor. He is known for the celebrated statue *The Greek Slave* (1843), depicting a female nude in chains.

pow·er se·ries *n* an infinite series in which the terms contain regularly increasing integral powers of a variable. A typical series would be $Sn = 1+2x+3x^2+4x^3+\ldots+nx^{n-1}$.

pow·er shov·el *n* a mobile machine for excavating and removing debris, with a movable lever arm ending in a hinged digging bucket

pow·er sta·tion *n UK* same as **power plant** (sense 1)

pow·er steer·ing *n* a system of steering for a motor vehicle in which turning the steering wheel is made easier by supplementary power from the vehicle's engine

pow·er take-off *n* a device for transferring power from a vehicle's engine to another piece of machinery

pow·er train *n* the portion of a vehicle's drive mechanism that transmits power from the engine to the wheels, tracks, or propellers. An automobile's power train includes the clutch, transmission, drive shaft, and differential.

pow·er-up *n* **1.** an act of switching on a computer system **2.** an icon in a computer game, typically appearing upon the destruction of an enemy, that gives the player a greater advantage ○ *There are plenty of rewards and power-ups that increase your maximum health and amount of ammo you can carry.*

pow·er us·er *n* a computer user who is expert in one or more software applications (*informal*)

pow·er walk·ing *n* a form of exercise involving energetic walking in which the arms are swung backward and forward, sometimes using weights, in order to increase the heart rate —**pow·er walk·er** *n*

Pow·ha·tan /pow hátt'n, pòw ə tán/ (1550?–1618) Algonquian leader. He led the Powhatan confederacy of Algonquian peoples in Virginia, and was the father of Pocahontas. Born **Wahunsonacook**

pow·wow /pów wòw/ *n* **1.** NATIVE AMERICAN CEREMONY a traditional Native American ceremony featuring dance, feasting, and a blessing by a shaman for an event such as a marriage, a major hunt, or a gathering of nations **2.** MEETING a meeting or gathering to discuss something (*informal*) ■ *vi* **(-wowed, -wow·ing, -wows)** HAVE POWWOW to hold a powwow (*informal*) [Early 19C. < Narraganset *powwaw* "shaman"]

Pow·ys /pṓ iss/ county in central Wales. Llandrindod Wells is its administrative center. Population: 126,354 (2001). Area: 2,009 sq. mi./5,205 sq. km.

pox /poks/ *n* **1.** a viral disease that causes pus-filled blisters (**pustules**) to form on the skin, and often leaves scars (**pockmarks**), e.g., smallpox or chickenpox **2.** a venereal disease, especially syphilis (*informal*) [Alteration of *pocks*, plural of POCK] ◇ **a pox on somebody** *or* **something** used to express a wish that misfortune will come to somebody or something (*archaic*)

pox·vi·rus /póks vĩrəss/ *n* an oval-shaped DNA-containing virus responsible for diseases that cause pus-filled blisters (**pustules**) to form on the skin

Poynt·ing the·o·rem /póynting-/ *n* the theorem stating that the rate of flow of electromagnetic energy per unit area equals the cross product of the electric and magnetic vectors [Late 19C. After J. H. *Poynting* (1852–1914), English physicist]

Poz·nań /pṓz nàn, -naǹn/ city in western Poland. It is the capital of Poznań Province. Population: 580,000 (1997).

po·zo·le *n* another spelling of **posole** (*Southwestern US*)

poz·zuo·la·na /pòtswə laánə/, **poz·zo·la·na** /pòtsə-/, **poz·zo·lan** /pótsələn/ *n* a porous volcanic ash that when mixed with cement hardens either in air or under water [Early 18C. < Italian *pozz(u)olana (terra)* "(earth) of Pozzuoli" (town near Naples, S Italy)]

Poz·zuo·li /pot swṓlee/ city in Campania Region, southern Italy. Population: 78,754 (2001).

PP *abbr* GRAM prepositional phrase

pp. *abbr* pages

p.p.[1] *abbr* BUSINESS by proxy (*used when signing documents on behalf of somebody else*) [Latin *per procurationem*]

p.p.[2] *abbr* **1.** MAIL parcel post **2.** CHR parish priest **3.** GRAM past participle

ppb *abbr* MEASURE parts per billion

PPO *abbr* US HEALTH SERVICES, INSUR preferred-provider organization

PPP *abbr* BUSINESS, GOV public private partnership

PPV *abbr* MEDIA pay-per-view

pr *abbr* ONLINE Puerto Rico (*used in Internet addresses*) See table at **domain name**

Pr *symbol* CHEM ELEM praseodymium

PR *abbr* **1.** Puerto Rico **2.** BUSINESS public relations

pr. *abbr* GRAM pronoun

Pr. *abbr* **1.** FIN preferred (stock) **2.** CHR Priest **3.** Prince

P.R. *abbr* **1.** Puerto Rico **2.** POL proportional representation

praam *n* NAUT another spelling of **pram**[2]

prac·ti·ca·ble /práktikəb'l/ *adj* **1.** capable of being carried out or put into effect **2.** capable of being used successfully [Mid-17C. < French < *practiquer* "put into practice" < medieval Latin *practica* < form of Greek *praktikos* "practical" (see PRACTICE)]

USAGE practicable or **practical**? These two adjectives have overlapping meanings. Both indicate that something can be done, but ***practical*** also implies that it is appropriate, sensible, or useful: *It is practicable to do the calculation in the traditional way, but far more practical to use a computer.* The difference between ***impracticable*** and ***impractical*** is rather more clear-cut: ***impracticable*** means "impossible" and ***impractical*** means "not workable when put into practice."

prac·ti·cal /práktik'l/ *adj* **1.** CONCERNED WITH MATTERS OF FACT concerned with actual facts and real life and experience, not theory ○ *the practical applications of this research* **2.** USEFUL appropriate, sensible, and likely to be effective ○ *practical advice* **3.** GOOD AT SOLVING PROBLEMS good at managing matters and dealing with problems and difficulties ○ *He's terribly clever, but not very practical.* **4.** PRACTICING involved in the actual work of a profession or activity ○ *practical physician* **5.** SUITABLE FOR EVERYDAY USE plain, functional, and suitable for everyday use **6.** VIRTUAL resembling a particular thing in almost every way (*informal*) ○ *The campaign was a practical disaster.* ■ *n* EDUC CLASS WITH HANDS-ON ACTIVITIES a class or examination that requires participation in an activity such as an experiment or a medical procedure ○ *a physics practical* [Mid-16C. < late Latin *practicus* < Greek *praktikos* (see PRACTICE)]

USAGE See ***practicable.***

prac·ti·cal·i·ty /pràkti kállətee/ (*plural* **-ties**) *n* **1.** the quality or state of being practical **2.** a practical aspect or requirement of a situation (*usually used in the plural*)

prac·ti·cal joke *n* a trick that is carried out on somebody to make him or her look silly and to amuse others —**prac·ti·cal jok·er** *n*

prac·ti·cal·ly /práktikəlee/ *adv* **1.** very nearly but not quite ○ *It was practically impossible to hear what was going on because of the noise.* **2.** in a way that is useful, sensible, or practical ○ *We've got to look at this thing practically.*

prac·ti·cal nurse *n* **1.** a nurse who has completed a level of training lower than that of a registered nurse **2.** somebody who has considerable experience in caring for people but who does not have a college degree in nursing

prac·tice /práktiss/ *v* **(-ticed, -tic·ing, -tic·es) 1.** *vti* REPEAT SOMETHING TO GET BETTER to do something repeatedly in order to improve performance in a sport, art, or hobby ○ *practices the piano daily* **2.** *vt* DO SOMETHING AS CUSTOM to do something as an established custom or habit **3.** *vti* WORK IN LAW OR MEDICINE to work in a profession, especially law or medicine ○ *She has been practicing law for 15 years now.* **4.** *vt* RELIG FOLLOW RELIGION to act according to the beliefs and customs of a particular religion ○ *We are proud to practice the religion of our ancestors.* **5.** *vt* PERPETRATE WRONG to perpetrate something morally bad such as deceit or cruelty (*archaic*) ■ *n* **1.** REPETITION IN ORDER TO IMPROVE the process of repeating something many times in order to improve performance **2.** PROCESS OF CARRYING OUT AN IDEA the process of carrying out an idea, plan, or theory ○ *It's more difficult to put these ideas into practice.* **3.** WORK OF PROFESSIONAL PERSON the business of a lawyer, doctor, dentist, or other professional **4.** USUAL PATTERN OF ACTION an established way of doing something, especially one that has developed through experience and knowledge ○ *good business practices* **5.** PERFORMANCE OF RELIGION, PROFESSION, OR CUSTOMS the performance of a religion, profession, set of customs, or established habit [14C. Directly or via French < medieval Latin *practizare*, alteration of *practicare* < Greek *praktikos* "practical" < *prattein* "do"] —**prac·tic·er** *n* ◇ **in practice 1.** in the real world and under everyday conditions, as opposed to in theory **2.** having recently practiced or exercised a skill so as to be currently proficient ◇ **out of practice** not having recently practiced or exercised a skill so as to be currently less proficient than usual

SYNONYMS See ***habit.***

prac·ticed /práktist/ *adj* expert in doing something because of long experience

prac·tice teach·ing *n* the part of a student teacher's training that consists of placement in a school where classroom teaching is undertaken by the student under the supervision of a certified teacher

prac·tic·ing /práktising/ *adj* actively involved in a particular activity such as a profession, religion, or way of life

~~**practicle**~~ incorrect spelling of **practical**

~~**practicly**~~ incorrect spelling of **practically**

prac·ti·cum /práktikəm/ *n* a period of work for practical experience as part of an academic course [Early 20C. < late Latin, form of *practicus* "active, practical" < Greek *praktikos* (see PRACTICE)]

prac·tise /práktiss/ *vti* Can, UK spelling of **practice**

prac·ti·tion·er /prak tísh'nər/ *n* **1.** somebody who practices a profession, especially medicine **2.** in Christian Science, somebody who carries out ministry and spiritual healing [Mid-16C. < obsolete *practician* < Old French *practicien* < *practiser* < medieval Latin *practizare* (see PRACTICE)]

Pra·do /praádō/ *n* a museum in Madrid that contains the Spanish national collection of paintings, sculptures, and drawings. It was founded by Fernando VII in 1810.

prae·di·al /préedee əl/, **pre·di·al** *adj* relating to land or farming [15C. < medieval Latin *praedialis* < Latin *praedium* "farm, estate"] —**prae·di·al·i·ty** /prèedee állətee/ *n*

prae·mu·ni·re /prèemyə néeree/ *n* the offense under English law of accepting the authority of some other power over that of the English crown, or an accusation to that effect [< medieval Latin *praemunire facias* "that you warn" (words in the writ)]

prae·no·men /pree nṓmən/ (*plural* **-no·mens** or **-nom·i·na** /-nómmənə, -nṓmənə/) *n* in ancient Rome, somebody's first name [Early 17C. < Latin, "forename" < *nomen* "name"] —**prae·nom·i·nal** /-nómmən'l/ *adj* —**prae·nom·i·nal·ly** *adv*

prae·tor /préetər/, **pre·tor** *n* in ancient Rome, any of several magistrates ranking immediately below the consuls and acting as the chief law officers of the state [15C. < Latin] —**prae·to·ri·al** /pree táwree əl/ *adj* —**prae·tor·ship** *n*

prae·to·ri·an /pree táwree ən/, **pre·to·ri·an** *adj* **1.** RELATING TO PRAETORS relating to praetors or to the office of praetor **2.** CORRUPT corrupt and venal (*formal*) ■ *n* ANCIENT ROMAN OF PRAETOR RANK in ancient Rome, a holder or former holder of the office of praetor

Prae·to·ri·an, Pre·to·ri·an *adj* belonging or relating to the Praetorian Guard ■ *n* a member of the Praetorian Guard

Prae·to·ri·an Guard *n* **1.** in ancient Rome, the emperor's bodyguard **2.** a soldier of the emperor's bodyguard in ancient Rome

prag·mat·ic /prag máttik/ *adj* **1.** CONCERNED WITH PRACTICAL RESULTS more concerned with practical results than with theories and principles **2.** PHILOSOPHY RELATING TO PHILOSOPHICAL PRAGMATISM relating to or characteristic of philosophical pragmatism **3.** LING RELATING TO PRAGMATICS relating or belonging to pragmatics **4.** LEARNING LESSONS FROM HISTORY relating to or analyzing the events of history with emphasis on the lessons that can be learned from them **5.** POL POLITICAL relating to affairs of state (*formal*) [Late 16C. Via late Latin < Greek *pragmatikos* < *pragma* "deed, action"] —**prag·mat·i·cal·i·ty** /prag màttə kállətee/ *n* —**prag·mat·i·cal·ly** /prag máttikəlee/ *adv*

prag·mat·ics /prag máttiks/ *n* the branch of linguistics that studies language use rather than language structure (*takes a singular verb*)

prag·mat·ic sanc·tion *n* a special decree issued by a sovereign that has the force of law

prag·ma·tism /prágmə tìzzəm/ *n* **1.** a straightforward practical way of thinking about things or dealing with problems, concerned with results rather than with theories and principles **2.** a philosophical view that a theory or concept should be evaluated in terms of how it works and its consequences as the standard for action and thought —**prag·ma·tist** *n* —**prag·ma·tis·tic** /pràgmə tístik/ *adj*

Prague /praag/ capital city of the Czech Republic, located in the west of the country. Population: 1,178,576 (2001).

pra·hu *n* same as **proa**

Prai·a /prī́ ə/ capital city of the Republic of Cape Verde, in southeastern São Tiago Island. Population: 94,757 (1999).

prai·rie /prérree/ *n* a treeless grass-covered plain in the United States and Canada, especially in the Midwest and the West ■ **prai·ries** *npl Can* the Prairie Provinces of Manitoba, Alberta, and Saskatchewan in Canada [Late 18C. Via French < assumed Vulgar Latin *prataria* < Latin *pratum* "meadow"]

prai·rie chick·en *n* a game bird of the grouse family that has mottled brownish feathers, the male of which has inflatable air sacs on its throat that it uses in courtship. Native to: grasslands of North America. Genus: *Tympanuchus.*

prai·rie dog *n* a burrowing rodent of the squirrel family with light brown fur that lives in large underground colonies. Native to: grasslands of North America. Genus: *Cynomys.*

prai·rie fal·con *n* a large falcon with a squarish head, dark brown back feathers with pale edges, and pale spotted underparts. Native to: western United States. Latin name: *Falco mexicanus.*

prai·rie oys·ter *n* **1.** a drink consisting of a raw egg, Worcestershire sauce, salt, and pepper, taken as a cure for a hangover or hiccups **2.** the fried testicle of a calf or pig, eaten as a delicacy in the Midwest (*usually used in the plural*)

prai·rie schoo·ner *n* a large covered wagon pulled by horses or oxen that was used by pioneers crossing the prairies in the 19th century

prai·rie soil *n* a rich black soil that typically forms under the grasses of a prairie

Prai·rie State *n* a nickname for the US state of Illinois

Prai·rie Vil·lage /prérree-/ city in northeastern Kansas, a southern suburb of Kansas City. Population: 21,764 (2002 estimate).

prai·rie wolf *n* VERTEB same as **coyote**

praise /prayz/ *n* **1.** EXPRESSION OF ADMIRATION words that express approval or admiration, e.g., for somebody's achievements or for something's good qualities **2.** WORSHIP worship and thanks to God or a deity (*often used in the plural*) ■ *vt* (**praised, prais·ing, prais·es**) **1.** EXPRESS ADMIRATION FOR SOMEBODY OR SOMETHING to express approval or admiration for somebody or something **2.** WORSHIP GOD to give worship and thanks to God or a deity [13C. Via French < late Latin *pretiare* "to prize" < *pretium* "price"] —**prais·er** *n* ◇ **sing somebody's** *or* **something's praises** to praise somebody or something enthusiastically ○ *She's not one to sing her own praises.*

praise·wor·thy /práyz wùrthee/ *adj* deserving praise —**praise·wor·thi·ly** *adv* —**praise·wor·thi·ness** *n*

praj·na /prúnjnə/ *n* in Buddhist teaching, direct awareness and understanding of truth not achieved by intellectual or rational means [Early 19C. < Sanskrit *prajñā* "know directly"]

Pra·krit /praá krìt/ *n* an Indic language belonging to a group spoken in northern India from approximately 400 B.C. to A.D. 1000. Prakrits are Indic languages that developed from Sanskrit, the most well-known being Pali. [Mid-18C. < Sanskrit *prākṛta* "natural, vernacular" < *pra-* "forward" + *kṛta-* "made"] —**Pra·krit** *adj*

pra·line /práy leen/ *n* **1.** a candy or dessert topping made of nuts caramelized in boiling sugar syrup **2.** a chocolate candy with a soft filling made from crushed caramelized nuts, usually almonds [Early 18C. After Marshal de Plessis-*Praslin* (1598–1675), French officer]

prall·tril·ler /praál trìllər/ *n* a musical embellishment made by the quick alternation of a note with the note immediately above it [Mid-19C. < German, "bouncing trill"]

pram[1] /pram/ *n UK* same as **baby carriage** [Late 19C. Contraction of PERAMBULATOR]

pram[2] /praam/, **praam** *n* **1.** a small fishing boat with a flat bottom and a square front **2.** a flat-bottomed barge used in Baltic ports [Mid-16C. Via Dutch < Czech *prám* "raft"]

pra·na /praánə/ *n* **1.** in yoga, the practice of inhaling, holding the breath, and exhaling according to fixed patterns **2.** in Hinduism, breath or breathing [Mid-19C. < Sanskrit *prāṇa* "breathing out"]

pra·nam /prə naám/ *n S Asia* a respectful gesture of greeting made by pressing the palms together and often followed by bending to touch the other person's feet [Mid-19C. < Hindi]

prance /pranss/ *v* (**pranced, pranc·ing, pranc·es**) **1.** *vi* MOVE IN SPRIGHTLY MANNER to walk or move in a lively, but often exaggerated way that suggests arrogance **2.** *vti* SHOW JUMPING JUMP FORWARD ON BACK LEGS to jump, or make a horse jump, forward on its hind legs with its front legs raised **3.** *vti* SHOW JUMPING WALK WITH LIVELY STEPS to walk, or make a horse walk, with lively springing steps ■ *n* PRANCING MOVEMENT a lively, springing, or carefree movement [14C. Origin ?] —**pranc·er** *n* —**pranc·ing** *adj* —**pranc·ing·ly** *adv*

pran·di·al /prándee əl/ *adj* relating to a meal, especially lunch or dinner (*formal or humorous*) [Early 19C. < Latin *prandium* "late breakfast"] —**pran·di·al·ly** *adv*

prang /prang/ (**pranged, prang·ing, prangs**) *vt UK* to crash or damage a vehicle or aircraft (*informal*) [Mid-20C. Origin ?]

prank[1] /prangk/ *n* a mischievous trick or silly stunt done for amusement [Late 16C. Origin ?] —**prank·ish** *adj*

prank[2] /prangk/ *vti* to embellish something or dress in an ostentatious manner ○ *Don't prank yourself up, it's only a family dinner.* [Mid-16C. Probably < Middle Dutch *pronken* or Middle Low German *prunken* "show off"]

prank call *n* **1.** a phone call in which the caller deceives or tricks the person called **2.** a digitized trick phone call or image that can be downloaded and sent to somebody's phone as a practical joke

prank·ster /prángkstər/ *n* somebody who enjoys playing mischievous tricks on people

~~**prarie**~~ incorrect spelling of **prairie**

Pra·sad /prə saád/, **Rajendra** (1884–1963) first president of India (1950–62). A member of the Indian National Congress, he presided over the Constituent Assembly (1946–49) before becoming president.

prase /prayz/ *n* a green form of quartz [Late 18C. Via French < Greek *prasios* "leek-colored" < *prason* "leek"]

pra·se·o·dym·i·um /pràyzee ō dímmee əm/ *n* a soft ductile silvery metallic element belonging to the rare-earth group. Use: alloys, coloring for glass. Symbol **Pr**. See table at **element** [Late 19C. < Greek *prasios* "leek-colored" (see PRASE)]

prat /prat/ *n* **1.** *UK* somebody regarded as unintelligent (*slang insult*) **2.** the buttocks (*slang*) [Mid-16C. Origin ?]

prate /prayt/ *vi* (**prat·ed, prat·ing, prates**) to talk in a silly way and at length about nothing important ■ *n* silly or idle talk [15C. < Middle Dutch *praten*] —**prat·er** *n* —**prat·ing·ly** *adv*

prat·fall /prát fàwl/ *n* (*slang*) **1.** a backward fall onto the buttocks, especially one executed deliberately for comic effect **2.** an embarrassing or humiliating mistake or failure

pra·tique /pra teék, prə-/ *n* permission granted to a ship or boat to use a port on satisfying the local quarantine regulations or on producing a clean bill of health [Early 17C. < French, "practice"]

prat·tle /prátt'l/ *vi* (**-tled, -tling, -tles**) to talk in a silly, idle, or childish way ■ *n* silly, idle, or childish talk [Mid-16C. Origin ?] —**prat·tler** *n* —**prat·tling·ly** *adv*

Pratt·ville /prát vìl/ town in central Alabama, a northwest suburb of Montgomery. Population: 25,867 (2002 estimate).

prau *n* SAILING same as **proa**

prav·as·tat·in /pràvvə státt'n/ *n* a drug used to reduce unusually high levels of blood cholesterol [Mid-20C. < *pra-* + *vastatin*, INN stem]

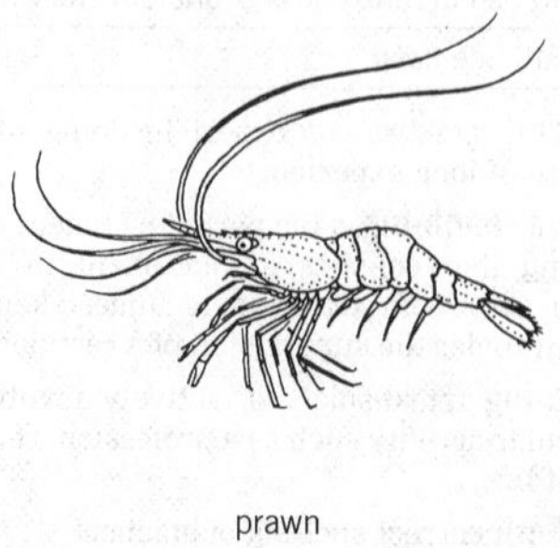

prawn

prawn /prawn/ *n* an edible sea animal resembling a shrimp, with a slender body, a long tail, five pairs of legs, and two pairs of pincers. Genera: *Palaemon* or *Penaeus.* ■ *vi* (**prawned, prawn·ing**) to fish for prawns [15C. Origin ?] —**prawn·er** *n*

prax·e·ol·o·gy /pràksee óllәjee/, **prax·i·ol·o·gy** *n* the study of human behavior and actions [Early 20C. < Greek *praxis* (see PRAXIS)] —**prax·e·o·log·i·cal** /pràksee ə lójjik'l/ *adj*

prax·is /práksiss/ *n* (*formal*) **1.** the practical side and application of something such as a professional skill, as opposed to its theory **2.** established custom or habitual practice [Late 16C. Via medieval Latin < Greek, "action, custom, behavior" < *prattein* "do"]

Prax·it·e·les /prak síttə leez/ (390?–330? B.C.) Greek sculptor. Apart from *Hermes with the Infant Dionysus*, his work is known only in the form of Roman copies.

pray /pray/ *v* (**prayed, pray·ing, prays**) **1.** *vti* RELIG SPEAK TO GOD to speak to God, a deity, or a saint, e.g., in order to give thanks, express regret, or ask for help **2.** *vti* HOPE STRONGLY to hope strongly for something ○ *I'm just praying that it won't rain on Saturday.* **3.** *vti* ADDRESS EARNEST REQUEST TO SOMEBODY to ask somebody for something, especially earnestly or with passion ○ *He prayed to be allowed to go back home to his family.* **4.** *vt* ATTEMPT TO GET SOMETHING ACHIEVED to attempt to achieve something by prayer or by wishing very hard ○ *The villagers tried to pray the drought away.* ■ *interj* EMPHASIZING QUESTION OR COMMAND used to emphasize a question or a command, either politely or sarcastically (*dated or humorous*) ○ *And what, pray, do you think you're doing?* [13C. Via Old French *preier* < Latin *precari* "entreat" < *prec-* "prayer"]

SPELLCHECK pray or **prey**? Do not confuse the spelling of ***pray*** and ***prey***, which sound similar. The verb ***pray*** means "say a prayer" or "make an earnest request," as in *pray for rain*. The verb ***prey***, always used with *on* or *upon*, means "hunt and kill," "exploit," or "cause anxiety or distress to," as in *birds that prey on small mammals, preying on the more vulnerable members of society, preying on my mind*. ***Prey*** is also a noun denoting a hunted animal or a victim, as in *lions devouring their prey, a bird of prey, be prey to panic attacks*.

prayer /prer/ *n* **1.** ADDRESS TO GOD a spoken or unspoken address to God, a deity, or a saint. It may express praise, thanksgiving, confession, or a request for something such as help or somebody's well-being. **2.** ADDRESSING OF GOD the act or practice of making spoken or unspoken addresses to God, a deity, or a saint ○ *kneeling in prayer* **3.** RELIG same as **prayers** **4.** SOMETHING WISHED FOR something that is wanted or hoped for very much ○ *My only prayer is that it doesn't last too long.* ■ **prayers** *npl* RELIGIOUS SERVICE a religious service at which prayers are said ○ *attended evening prayers at seven* [13C. Via Old French *preiere* < Latin *precarius* "obtained by entreaty" < *precari* (see PRAY)] ◇ **not have a prayer** to have not even a slight chance of achieving something ○ *I don't have a prayer of getting the manager's job.*

prayer beads *npl* a string of beads used to keep count of prayers being recited, e.g., a rosary

prayer book *n* a book containing the prayers regularly used in religious services

prayer·ful /prérf'l/ *adj* **1.** RELIG PRAYING FREQUENTLY liking to pray or praying frequently **2.** RELIG INFLUENCED BY PRAYER strongly influenced by or involving prayer **3.** EARNEST earnest or sincere —**prayer·ful·ly** *adv* —**prayer·ful·ness** *n*

prayer mat *n* ISLAM same as **prayer rug**

Prayer o·ver the Gifts *n* in the Roman Catholic Mass, a variable prayer said at the conclusion of the Preparation of the Gifts and before the Preface. Former name **the Secret**

prayer rug, **prayer mat** *n* a rug on which a Muslim kneels to pray

prayer shawl *n* JUDAISM same as **tallith**

prayer wheel *n* in Tibetan Buddhism and some other religions, a hollow cylinder containing prayers written on a scroll. It that must be turned, by hand or machinery, to make the prayers effective.

pray·ing man·tis /prày·ing-/ *n* a large greenish-brown predatory insect with long forelegs that are raised and folded at rest, as if in prayer. Native to: Europe. Latin name: *Mantis religiosis.*

PRC *abbr* People's Republic of China

Pré ➧ **du Pré, Jacqueline**

pre- *prefix* **1.** before, earlier ○ *preschool* ○ *predate* **2.** in advance, preparatory ○ *presell* ○ *prerelease* **3.** in

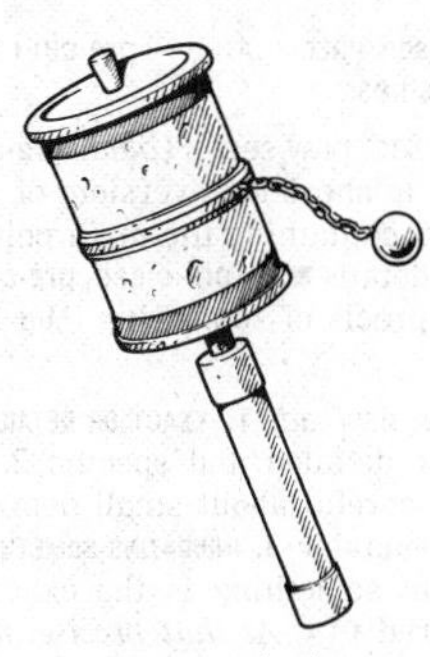

prayer wheel

front of ○ *premolar* [< Latin *prae* "in front, before" < Indo-European]

pre·ad·o·les·cence *n*
pre·ad·o·les·cent *n, adj*
pre·ag·ri·cul·tur·al *adj*
pre·an·nounce *vt*
pre·ap·prove *vt*
pre·ar·range *vt*
pre·ar·range·ment *n*
pre·as·sem·ble *vt*
pre·as·sign *vt*
pre·au·thor·ized *adj*
pre·bake *vt*
pre·bib·li·cal *adj*
pre·blend·ed *adj*
pre·break·fast *adj*
pre-Bud·dhist *adj*
pre-Cel·tic *adj*
pre-Chris·tian *adj*
pre-Christ·mas *adj*
pre-Civ·il War *adj*
pre·clas·si·cal *adj*
pre·col·lege *adj*
pre·co·lo·ni·al *adj*
pre·con·so·nan·tal *adj*
pre·con·struct·ed *adj*
pre·con·ven·tion *adj*
pre·cook *vt*
pre·cooked *adj*
pre·cool *vt*
pre·crash *adj*
pre·cre·a·tion *n*
pre·cut *adj*
pre·dawn *adj*
pre·dec·i·mal *adj*
pre·de·fine *vt*
pre·de·fined *adj*
pre·des·ig·nate *vt*
pre·des·ig·na·tion *n*
pre·din·ner *adj*
pre·dyed *adj*
pre·e·lec·tion *adj*
pre·e·rect *vt*
pre·es·tab·lish *vt*
pre·ex·ist *vti*
pre·ex·is·tence *n*
pre·fight *adj*
pre·filled *adj*
pre·flight *adj, vt, n*
pre·fo·cused *adj*
pre·fro·zen *adj*
pre·game *adj*
pre·gan·gli·on·ic *adj*
pre·gla·cial *adj*
pre·heat *vt*
pre·heat·er *n*
pre·hom·i·nid *adj, n*
pre·hu·man *adj*
pre·im·pres·sion·ism *n*
pre·im·pres·sion·ist *n*
pre-In·ca *adj*
pre-In·can *adj*
pre·in·de·pend·ence *adj, adv*
pre·in·dus·tri·al *adj*
pre·in·ter·view *adj*
pre·in·va·sion *adj*
pre·kin·der·gar·ten *adj*
pre·launch *adj*
pre·log·i·cal *adj*
pre·lunch *adj*
pre·made *adj*
pre·man·u·fac·ture *vt*
pre·match *adj*
pre·mat·ing *adj*
pre·meal *adj*
pre·mi·gra·tion *n*
pre·mix *n, vt*
pre·mod·ern *adj*
pre·no·ti·fi·ca·tion *n*
pre·no·ti·fy *vt*
pre-O·lym·pi·an *adj*
pre·or·der *vt*
pre·or·ga·ni·za·tion *n*
pre·owned *adj*
pre·packed *adj*
pre·per·for·mance *adj*
pre·pill *adj*
pre·plan *vt*
pre·pre·pared *adj*
pre·pro·fes·sion·al *adj*
pre·pu·ber·tal *adj*
pre·pu·ber·ty *n*
pre·pub·li·ca·tion *adj*
pre·pur·chase *vt*
pre·qual·i·fi·ca·tion *n*
pre·qual·i·fy *vi*
pre·race *adj*
pre·read·ing *adj*
pre-Ref·or·ma·tion *adj*
pre·reg·is·ter *vti*
pre·reg·is·tra·tion *n*
pre·re·lease *n, adj*
pre-Re·nais·sance *adj*
pre·re·tire·ment *n*
pre·rev·o·lu·tion·ar·y *adj*
pre-Ro·man *adj*

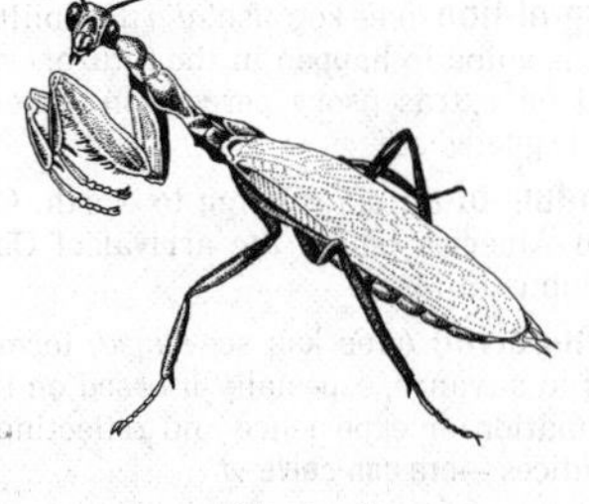

praying mantis

pre·ro·man·tic *n*
pre·sci·en·tif·ic *adj*
pre·score *vti*
pre·screen *vt*
pre·sea·son *n*
pre·se·lect *vt*
pre·se·lec·tion *n*
pre·show *adj*
pre·shrink *vt*
pre·sig·ni·fy *vt*
pre·soak *vt, n*
pre-So·crat·ic *adj*
pre·sort *vt*
pre·sur·ger·y *adj*
pre·tape *vt*
pre·tax *adj*
pre·the·a·ter *adj*
pre·tour·na·ment *adj*
pre·treat *vt*
pre·treat·ment *n*
pre·tri·al *adj*
pre·u·ni·ver·si·ty *adj*
pre·warn *vt*
pre·wrap *vt*

preach /preech/ (**preached, preach·ing, preach·es**) *v* **1.** *vti* RELIG **GIVE SERMON** to give a talk on a religious or moral subject, especially in church **2.** *vi* **GIVE ADVICE IN IRRITATING WAY** to give advice on morality or behavior in an irritatingly tedious or overbearing way **3.** *vt* **URGE PEOPLE TO ACCEPT IDEA** to make an opinion or attitude known to others and urge others to share it ○ *preached restraint in the midst of chaos* [13C. Via Old French *prechier* < Latin *praedicare* (see PREDICATE)] —**preach·a·ble** *adj*

preach·er /préechər/ *n* (*informal*) **1. MINISTER** somebody whose occupation is to give sermons, preach the gospel, or conduct religious services, especially a minister of a Protestant church **2. SOMEBODY GIVING ADVICE ON MORALS** somebody who gives advice on morality or behavior in an irritatingly tedious or overbearing way **3. SOMEBODY URGING ACCEPTANCE OF IDEA** somebody who makes an opinion or attitude known to others and urges them to share it

preach·i·fy /préechə fī/ *vi* to preach or give advice on morality or behavior in an irritatingly tedious or overbearing way (*informal*) —**preach·i·fy·ing** *n*

preach·ment /préechmənt/ *n* (*informal*) **1.** a sermon or talk on a moral or religious subject **2.** tedious or overbearing advice on morals or behavior

preach·y /préechee/ *adj* giving, or in the habit of giving, advice on morality or behavior, especially in an irritatingly tedious or overbearing way (*informal*) —**preach·i·ness** *n*

pre·ad·ap·ta·tion /prèe adəp táysh'n/ *n* an anatomical or behavioral feature of an organism that is highly suited to an adjacent habitat, thus allowing for migration and increased survival rate in response to environmental change. The lungs that developed in some fish were probably originally buoyancy aids, but became used for breathing air. —**pre·a·dapt** /-ə dápt/ *vti* —**pre·a·dapt·ed** /-ə dáptəd/ *adj* —**pre·a·dap·tive** *adj*

Preak·ness Stakes /préek ness-/ *n* a race for three-year-old horses that has been run annually since 1873 at the Pimlico Race Course in Baltimore, Maryland [After the first well-known horse to race at the course]

pre·am·ble /prée àmb'l, pree ámb'l/ *n* **1.** a section at the beginning of a speech, report, or formal document that introduces what follows **2.** something that precedes, introduces, or leads up to something else ○ *high winds as a preamble to a winter storm* [14C. < French *préambule* < late Latin *praeambulus* "going in front" < Latin *ambulare* "to walk"]

Pre·am·ble *n* the introductory section of the United States Constitution, often cited as a succinct statement of national identity

pre·am·pli·fi·er /pree ámpli fī ər/ *n* an amplifying circuit, e.g., in a radio or television, that is designed to strengthen very weak signals and then transmit them to a more powerful amplifier

pre·a·tom·ic /prèe ə tómmik/ *adj* relating or belonging to the time before atomic energy was developed or atomic weapons existed

preb·end /prébbənd/ *n* an allowance paid by a cathedral or collegiate church to a member of its clergy, or the property or tithe that is the source of this allowance [15C. Via French < late Latin *praebenda* "things to be supplied" < Latin *praebere* "offer," literally "hold in front"] —**pre·ben·dal** /pri bénd'l, prébbənd'l/ *adj*

pre·ben·dar·y /prébbən dèrree/ (*plural* **-ies**) *n* a member of the clergy of a cathedral or collegiate church —**preb·en·dar·y·ship** /prébbən deree ship/ *n*

pre·bi·o·log·i·cal /pree bī ə lójjik'l/ *adj* relating or belonging to a time in geologic history before the appearance of living organisms

pre·bi·o·tic /prèe bī óttik/ *n* a dietary supplement in the form of nondigestible carbohydrate that favors the growth of desirable microflora in the large bowel

pre·built /pree bílt/ *adj US* prefabricated or made in prefabricated sections ○ *a prebuilt structure*

pre·calc /prée kàlk/ *n* MATH, EDUC same as **precalculus** (*informal*)

pre·cal·cu·lus /pree kálkyələss/ *n US* a course in mathematics taken, especially in high school, in preparation for the study of calculus

Pre·cam·bri·an /pree kámbree ən/ *n* the period of geologic time, 4,650 to 700 million years ago, during which the Earth's crust consolidated and primitive life first appeared —**Pre·cam·bri·an** *adj*

pre·can·cel /pree kánss'l/ *vt* (**-celed, -cel·ing, -cels**) to cancel the postage stamp on an envelope before mailing it ■ *n* a stamp that has been canceled before mailing, or an item bearing such a stamp —**pre·can·cel·la·tion** /prèe kanss'l áysh'n/ *n*

pre·can·cer·ous /pree kánsərəss/ *adj* describes conditions or tissue anomalies that are capable of becoming cancerous if left untreated

pre·car·i·ous /prə kérree əss/ *adj* **1.** dangerously unstable, unsteady, uncertain, or insecure **2.** based on uncertain premises or unwarranted assumptions (*formal*) [Mid-17C. < Latin *precarius* "depending on entreaty, uncertain"] —**pre·car·i·ous·ly** *adv* —**pre·car·i·ous·ness** *n*

pre·cast /pree kást/ *adj* poured into a cast of the required shape and allowed to harden before being taken out and put into position ○ *precast concrete* —**pre·cast** *vt*

prec·a·to·ry /prékə tàwree/ *adj* expressing a wish, request, entreaty, or recommendation (*formal*) [Mid-17C. < late Latin *precatorius* < Latin *precari* "entreat" (see PRAY)]

pre·cau·tion /prə káwsh'n/ *n* **1.** an action taken to protect against possible harm or trouble or to limit the damage if something goes wrong **2.** the foresight to protect against possible harm or trouble or to limit the damage if something goes wrong [Late 16C. Via French < late Latin *precaution-* < Latin *precaut-*, past participle of *praecavere*, literally "take care before" < *cavere* "take heed"] —**pre·cau·tion·al** *adj* —**pre·cau·tion·ar·y** *adj* —**pre·cau·tious** *adj*

pre·cede /prə séed/ (**-ced·ed, -ced·ing, -cedes**) *vt* **1.** to come, go, be, or happen before somebody or something else in time, position, or importance **2.** to say or do something before something else [14C. Via French < Latin *praecedere* "go before" < *cedere* "give way"]

SPELLCHECK precede or **proceed**? Do not confuse the spelling of ***precede*** and ***proceed***, which sound similar. The verb ***precede*** has the prefix *pre-* ("before") and means "come or go before": *March precedes April.* The verb ***proceed*** has the prefix *pro-* ("forward") and means "begin or continue with an action" or "progress": *She proceeded to explain what had gone wrong.*

prec·e·dence /préssəd'nss/, **prec·e·den·cy** /-d'nssee/ *n* **1. RELATIVE IMPORTANCE** a relative importance in rank and status that determines something such as the order in which participants are placed in a formal situation **2. PRIORITY** the right or need to be dealt with before somebody or something else or to be treated as more important than somebody or something else ○ *The interests of the rest of the group take precedence over any personal wishes.* **3. GREATER IMPORTANCE** the fact of being more important than others (*formal*)

prec·e·dent /préssəd'nt/ *n* **1. EXAMPLE FOR LATER ACTION OR DECISION** an action or decision that can be used subsequently as an example for a similar decision or to justify a similar action **2. ESTABLISHED PRACTICE** an established custom or practice **3.** LAW **REQUIREMENT TO FOLLOW EARLIER COURT DECISIONS** the doctrine that requires a court to follow decisions of superior or previous courts ■ *adj* **PRECEDING** coming, going, existing, or happening before somebody or something else (*formal*) —**prec·e·dent·ly** *adv*

prec·e·den·tial /prèssə dénshəl/ *adj* (*formal*) **1.** relating to or serving as a precedent **2.** taking precedence over something or somebody else —**pre·ce·den·tial·ly** *adv*

pre·ced·ing /prə séeding/ *adj* coming, going, existing, or happening immediately before somebody or something else

~~preceed~~ incorrect spelling of **precede**

~~precence~~ incorrect spelling of **presence**

pre·cen·sor /pree sénssər/ (**-sored, -sor·ing, -sors**) *vt* to lay down rules in advance stating what will or will not be allowed in a publication, broadcast, or other item for public performance or release —**pre·cen·sor·ship** *n*

pre·cen·tor /prə séntər/ *n* **1.** a leader of the congregation or choir in a church **2.** CHR a member of the clergy of a cathedral who is in charge of the music in the cathedral [Early 17C. < Latin *praecentor* < *praecinere*, literally "sing before" < *canere* "sing"] —**pre·cen·tor·ship** *n*

pre·cept /prée sèpt/ *n* **1.** a rule, instruction, or principle that guides somebody's actions, especially one that guides moral behavior (*formal*) **2.** a warrant or writ that is issued by a legal authority [14C. < Latin *praeceptum* "something taught," < past participle of *praecipere* "teach," literally "take before" < *capere* "take"]

pre·cep·tive /prə séptiv/ *adj* giving instructions or orders, or setting out rules or principles (*formal*) —**pre·cep·tive·ly** *adv*

pre·cep·tor /prə séptər, prée sèptər/ *n* **1.** EDUC TEACHER a teacher or instructor (*formal*) **2.** MED SPECIALIZED TUTOR a specialist in a profession, especially medicine, who gives practical training to a student **3.** HIST HEAD OF PRECEPTORY the head of a community of Knights Templars —**pre·cep·tor·al** *adj* —**pre·cep·tor·ate** *n* —**pre·cep·tor·ship** *n*

pre·cep·to·ri·al /prèe sep táwree əl, prə sèp-/ *n* US in some colleges, a class consisting of a small group of students who discuss a work of literature or other subject with a professor or instructor ○ *I'm taking a preceptorial on T.S. Eliot next quarter.*

pre·cep·to·ry /prə séptəree/ (*plural* **-ries**) *n* a community of Knights Templars

pre·cess /prə séss/ (**-cessed, -cess·ing, -cess·es**) *vti* to spin with a motion in which the axis of rotation describes a cone, or make something spin in this way [Late 19C. Back-formation < PRECESSION]

pre·ces·sion /prə sésh'n/ *n* the regular motion of a spinning body such as a spinning top or a planet, in which the axis of rotation describes a cone [Late 16C. < late Latin *praecession-* < Latin *praecess-*, past participle of *praecedere* "go before" (see PRECEDE)] —**pre·ces·sion·al** *adj*

pre·ces·sion of the e·qui·nox·es *n* the slow westward movement of the equinoxes, resulting from the Earth's precessional motion, making them occur slightly earlier each year

pre·cinct /prée sìngkt/ *n* **1.** POL ELECTORAL DISTRICT a small electoral district of a city or town, forming part of a ward **2.** US PUBLIC ADMIN CITY AREA PATROLLED BY POLICE UNIT a district of a city or town under a particular unit of the police force **3.** US PUBLIC ADMIN POLICE UNIT OR STATION the police unit or police station of a city or town district **4.** BOUNDARY a boundary marking out an area **5.** UK SPECIAL PART OF TOWN a part of a town designated for a particular use, especially an area accessible only to pedestrians or a specially built area containing many stores ○ *a shopping precinct* ■ **pre·cincts** *npl* AREA AROUND SOMETHING the area surrounding a building or institution such as a cathedral or college [15C. < medieval Latin *praecinctum* "something encircled," < past participle of Latin *praecingere* "gird about" < *cingere* "gird"]

pre·ci·os·i·ty /prèshee óssətee/ (*plural* **-ties**) *n* ridiculous overrefinement in language or manners, or an example of this ○ *It might be a good poem if all the preciosities were removed.* [14C. Via French < Latin *pretiositas* < *pretiosus* "precious" (see PRECIOUS)]

pre·cious /préshəss/ *adj* **1.** VALUABLE worth a great deal of money **2.** VALUED highly valued, much loved, or considered to be of great importance ○ *Your friendship is very precious to me.* **3.** NOT TO BE WASTED rare or unique and therefore to be used wisely or sparingly or treated with care **4.** USED FOR EMPHASIS used for emphasis to express irritation, dislike, contempt, bemusement, or some other strong emotion (*informal*) ○ *I'm tempted to tell them what they can do with their precious training course!* **5.** FASTIDIOUS OR AFFECTED too carefully refined in language, dress, or manners ■ *adv* VERY very, often by way of a complaint ○ *And precious little thanks I got!* ■ *n* TERM OF ENDEARMENT used as term of affection in talking to somebody ○ *Good morning, my precious.* [13C. Via French < Latin *pretiosus* < *pretium* "price"] —**pre·cious·ly** *adv* —**pre·cious·ness** *n*

pre·cious cor·al *n* MARINE BIOL same as **red coral**

pre·cious met·al *n* gold, silver, or platinum

pre·cious stone *n* a relatively rare and valuable mineral used in jewelry, e.g., a diamond or ruby

prec·i·pice /préssəpiss/ *n* **1.** a high, vertical, or very steep rock face **2.** a very dangerous situation [Late 16C. Directly or via French < Latin *praecipitium* < *praecipit-* "headlong" (see PRECIPITATE)] —**prec·i·piced** *adj*

pre·cip·i·tant /prə síppitənt/ *n* CHEM SOMETHING CAUSING PRECIPITATION a substance that causes precipitation ■ *adj* **1.** TOO HASTY done too quickly and impulsively, often resulting in mistakes **2.** SUDDEN OR UNEXPECTED happening suddenly or unexpectedly [Early 17C. < French *précipitant*, present participle of *précipiter* < Latin *praecipitare* (see PRECIPITATE)] —**pre·cip·i·tan·cy** *n* —**pre·cip·i·tant·ly** *adv*

pre·cip·i·tate *v* /prə síppi tàyt/ (**-tat·ed, -tat·ing, -tates**) **1.** *vt* MAKE SOMETHING HAPPEN QUICKLY to make something happen suddenly and quickly **2.** *vt* SEND SOMEBODY OR SOMETHING RAPIDLY to send somebody or something suddenly and rapidly into a particular state or condition ○ *A minor border skirmish precipitated the two countries into war.* **3.** *vti* METEOROL MAKE RAIN OR SNOW FALL to cause liquid or solid forms of water, condensed in the atmosphere, to fall to the ground as rain, snow, or hail, or fall in such a form **4.** *vti* CHEM SEPARATE SOLID OUT OF SOLUTION to cause a solid to separate out from a solution as a result of a chemical reaction, or separate out in this way **5.** *vti* THROW OR FALL FROM ABOVE to throw somebody or something from a great height, or fall from a great height (*formal*) ■ *adj* /prə síppitət/ **1.** DONE OR ACTING RASHLY done or acting too quickly and without enough thought ○ *I may have been precipitate in accepting their offer.* **2.** HURRIED very hurried ○ *made a precipitate departure* **3.** SUDDEN sudden and unexpected ■ *n* /prə síppi tàyt, -tət/ CHEM SUSPENSION OF SMALL PARTICLES a suspension of small solid particles that are formed in a solution as a result of a chemical reaction and usually settle out of the solution [Early 16C. < Latin *praecipitat-*, past participle of *praecipitare* "throw down" < *praeceps* "headlong" < *caput* "head"] —**pre·cip·i·ta·ble** *adj* —**pre·cip·i·tate·ly** *adv* —**pre·cip·i·tate·ness** *n* —**pre·cip·i·ta·tive** *adj* —**pre·cip·i·ta·tor** *n*

pre·cip·i·ta·tion /prə sìppi táysh'n/ *n* **1.** RAIN, SNOW, OR HAIL rain, snow, or hail, all of which are formed by condensation of moisture in the atmosphere and fall to the ground **2.** FORMATION OF RAIN, SNOW, OR HAIL the formation of rain, snow, or hail from moisture in the air **3.** FORMATION OF SUSPENSION IN SOLUTION the formation of a suspension of an insoluble compound by mixing two solutions **4.** HASTE great or excessive haste (*formal*) ○ *He deeply regretted the precipitation of his resignation from the position.* **5.** HASTENING OF SOMETHING the act of making something happen earlier or more suddenly than expected (*formal*) ○ *circumstances that led to the precipitation of my decision to resign* **6.** THROWING DOWN OF SOMEBODY OR SOMETHING the throwing of somebody or something from a great height (*formal*)

pre·cip·i·tin /prə síppitin/ *n* an antibody that, when combined with its antigen, forms a substance that separates out of solution and can be detected visually [Early 20C. < PRECIPITATE]

pre·cip·i·tin·o·gen /prə sìppi tínnəjən/ *n* an antigen that causes the formation of a specific precipitin. This reaction can be used to identify an unknown antigen.

pre·cip·i·tous /prə síppitəss/ *adj* **1.** DONE RASHLY done or acting too quickly and without enough thought **2.** GEOG LIKE PRECIPICE very high and steep ○ *precipitous mountain slopes* **3.** GEOG WITH PRECIPICES having a number of precipices ○ *precipitous terrain* [Mid-17C. < French *précipiteux* < Latin *praecipitium* < *praecipit-* "headlong" (see PRECIPITATE)] —**pre·cip·i·tous·ly** *adv* —**pre·cip·i·tous·ness** *n*

pré·cis /práy see, pray sée/ *n* (*plural* **pré·cis** /práy seez, pray séez/) a shortened version of a speech or written text, containing the main points and omitting minor details ■ *vt* (**pré·cised, pré·cis·ing, pré·cis**) to make a précis of something [Mid-18C. < French, "abridged"]

pre·cise /prə síss/ *adj* **1.** EXACT OR DETAILED exact and accurate, or detailed and specific **2.** CAREFUL ABOUT DETAILS very careful about small details, especially of correct behavior **3.** INDICATING SOMETHING SPECIFIC indicating that something is the exact one that is being referred to ○ *At that precise moment, in he came.* **4.** HANDLING SMALL DETAILS able to assimilate details or wanting to be given details **5.** CLEAR distinct and correct ○ *a very precise speaker* [Early 16C. Via French < Latin *praecisus*, past participle of *praecidere* "cut off in front" < *caedere* "cut"] —**pre·cise·ness** *n*

pre·cise·ly /prə síslee/ *adv* **1.** EXACTLY used to indicate that something is stated exactly ○ *That is precisely what I mean.* **2.** ACCURATELY with absolute accuracy ○ *instruments that must be adjusted precisely before use* **3.** IN DETAIL in complete and accurate detail ○ *Tell me precisely what happened.* **4.** CLEARLY clearly and distinctly ○ *She speaks very precisely.* **5.** USED FOR EMPHASIS used to add emphasis when specifying something ○ *It was precisely because you didn't ask that she thought you didn't need her help.* **6.** EXPRESSING AGREEMENT used to indicate complete agreement with what has been said ○ *"But I don't think they can be relied on." "Precisely."*

pre·ci·sian /prə sízh'n/ *n* somebody who is concerned about correct rules and behavior, especially in moral and religious matters (*formal*) —**pre·ci·sian·ism** *n*

pre·ci·sion /prə sízh'n/ *n* **1.** EXACTNESS exactness or accuracy **2.** MATH ACCURACY IN CALCULATION the accuracy to which a calculation is performed, specifying the number of significant digits with which the result is expressed ■ *adj* RELATING TO EXACTNESS OR ACCURACY allowing for, made with, or requiring great exactness or accuracy ○ *precision instruments* [Late 16C. Via French < Latin *praecision-* < *praecis-*, past participle of *praecidere* (see PRECISE)]

pre·clin·i·cal /pree klínnik'l/ *adj* relating to or characteristic of a disease before the symptoms become evident —**pre·clin·i·cal·ly** *adv*

pre·clude /prə klóod/ (**-clud·ed, -clud·ing, -cludes**) *vt* **1.** to prevent something from happening or somebody from doing something ○ *That shouldn't preclude a satisfactory outcome.* **2.** to exclude somebody or something, especially in advance ○ *Having a relative in the company precludes me from entering the contest.* [Early 17C. < Latin *praecludere* "close off ahead" < *claudere* "close"] —**pre·clu·sion** /-klóozh'n/ *n* —**pre·clu·sive** /-klóossiv/ *adj* —**pre·clu·sive·ly** *adv*

pre·co·cial /prə kósh'l/ *adj* describes some animals that display independent activity at birth, especially young birds that are hatched covered with down and with open eyes [Late 19C. < modern Latin *Praecoces* "precocial birds" < plural of Latin *praecoc-* "precocious" (see PRECOCIOUS)]

pre·co·cious /prə kóshəss/ *adj* **1.** developed or mature, especially mentally, at an unusually early age, or showing such advanced development **2.** describes a plant or tree that blossoms before its leaves appear or that produces fruits only a few years after planting [Mid-17C. < Latin *praecoc-* "ripening early," literally "cooked ahead" < *coquere* "to cook"] —**pre·co·cious·ly** *adv* —**pre·co·cious·ness** *n* —**pre·coc·i·ty** /prə kóssətee/ *n*

pre·cog·ni·tion /prèe kog nísh'n/ *n* the ability to know what is going to happen in the future, especially if based on extrasensory perception —**pre·cog·ni·tive** /pree kógnətiv/ *adj*

pre-Co·lum·bi·an *adj* relating to North, Central, or South America before the arrival of Christopher Columbus in 1492

pre·con·ceived /prèe kən séevd/ *adj* formed in the mind in advance, especially if based on little or no information or experience and reflecting personal prejudices —**pre·con·ceive** *vt*

pre·con·cep·tion /prèe kən sépshən/ *n* an idea or

opinion formed in advance, especially if it is based on little or no information or experience and reflects personal prejudices

pre·con·cert /pree kónsərt/ (**-cert·ed, -cert·ing, -certs**) *vt* to agree, arrange, or organize something beforehand (*archaic*)

pre·con·di·tion /preè kən dísh'n/ *n* something that must be done or agreed before something else can happen ○ *They made a total ceasefire a precondition of the talks.* ■ *vt* (**-tioned, -tion·ing, -tions**) to prepare somebody or something for a process, or put somebody into a desired mental state

pre·con·scious /pree kónshəss/ *n* in Freudian theory, the part of the mind lying between the conscious and the unconscious. It contains information, thoughts, and feelings that are not present in conscious awareness but can readily be brought into the conscious mind. ■ *adj* relating to or contained in the preconscious —**pre·con·scious·ly** *adv* —**pre·con·scious·ness** *n*

pre·crit·i·cal /pree kríttik'l/ *adj* relating to the time or state before a crisis or before something such as a disease reaches a critical condition

pre·cur·sor /prə kúrssər, preè kùrssər/ *n* **1.** SOMEBODY OR SOMETHING THAT COMES EARLIER somebody or something that comes before, and is often considered to lead to the development of, another person or thing **2.** PREVIOUS HOLDER OF JOB somebody who held a position or job before somebody else **3.** CHEM CHEMICAL COMPOUND PRECEDING ANOTHER a chemical compound that leads to another, usually more stable, product in a series of connected reactions [Early 16C. < Latin *praecursor* < *praecurs-*, stem of *praecurrere* "run before" < *currere* "run"]

pre·cur·so·ry /prə kúrssəree, pree-/, **pre·cur·sive** /-kúrssiv/ *adj* **1.** at an initial or preparatory stage **2.** serving as an indication of something to come (*formal*)

pre·da·cious /prə dáyshəss/, **pre·da·ceous** *adj* **1.** describes animals that hunt, kill, and eat other animals (*technical*) **2.** attacking and stealing from other people (*dated*) [Early 18C. < Latin *praedari* "seize as plunder" (see PREDATORY)] —**pre·da·cious·ness** *n* —**pre·dac·i·ty** /prə dássətee/ *n*

pre·date /pree dáyt/ (**-dat·ed, -dat·ing, -dates**) *vt* **1.** to put a date on something, especially a check or a contract, that is earlier than the actual date, or say that something occurred at an earlier date than it actually did **2.** to come before somebody or something else in time

pre·da·tion /prə dáysh'n/ *n* **1.** the relationship between two groups of animals in which one species hunts, kills, and eats the other **2.** the act of plundering, stealing, or destroying [15C. < Latin *praedation-* < *praedari* "seize as plunder" (see PREDATORY)]

pred·a·tor /préddətər/ *n* **1.** CARNIVOROUS ANIMAL OR DESTRUCTIVE ORGANISM a carnivorous animal that hunts, kills, and eats other animals in order to survive, or any other organism that behaves in a similar manner **2.** SOMEBODY WHO PLUNDERS OR DESTROYS a person, group, company, or state that steals from others or destroys others for gain **3.** RUTHLESSLY AGGRESSIVE PERSON an aggressive, determined, or persistent person [Early 20C. < Latin *praedator* < *praedari* "seize as plunder" (see PREDATORY)]

pred·a·to·ry /préddə tàwree/ *adj* **1.** GREEDILY DESTRUCTIVE greedily eager to steal from or destroy others for gain **2.** RELATING TO PREDATORS relating to or characteristic of animals that survive by preying on others **3.** RUTHLESSLY AGGRESSIVE extremely aggressive, determined, or persistent [Late 16C. < Latin *praedatorius* < *praedari* "seize as plunder" < *praeda* "booty"] —**pred·a·to·ri·ly** /prèddə táwrəlee/ *adv* —**pred·a·to·ri·ness** *n*

pred·a·to·ry pric·ing *n* the act of setting prices at very low levels in order to force other companies out of the market

pre·de·cease /preè di seéss/ (**-ceased, -ceas·ing, -ceas·es**) *vt* to die before somebody else ○ *His eldest son predeceased him.* —**pre·de·cease** *n*

pred·e·ces·sor /préddə sèssər, preédə-/ *n* **1.** somebody who held a position or job before somebody else **2.** a thing previously in use or existence that has been replaced or succeeded by another **3.** same as ancestor (*archaic*) [14C. Via French < late Latin *praedecessor* "somebody who has departed before" < Latin *decedere* "depart"]

pre·de·lin·quent /preè di língkwənt/ *adj US* showing signs of becoming a delinquent ○ *a program for predelinquent youths*

pre·del·la /prə déllə/ *n* **1.** the platform for an altar, or the step on which an altar rests **2.** the decorative base of an altarpiece, embellished with small paintings or sculptures [Mid-19C. < Italian, "stool"]

pre·des·ti·nar·i·an /preè destə nérree ən/ *n* somebody who believes in predestination ■ *adj* relating to predestination or to people who believe in it —**pre·des·ti·nar·i·an·ism** *n*

pre·des·ti·nate /pree déstə nàyt/ *vt* (**-nat·ed, -nat·ing, -nates**) RELIG same as **predestine** ■ *adj* **1.** decided in advance **2.** in some religious beliefs, decided and decreed in advance by God, a deity, or fate [14C. < ecclesiastical Latin *praedestinat-*, past participle of *praedestinare* (see PREDESTINE)]

pre·des·ti·na·tion /preè destə náysh'n/ *n* **1.** ADVANCE DECISION BY GOD ABOUT EVENTS in some religious beliefs, the doctrine that God, a deity, or fate has established in advance everything that is going to happen and that nothing can change this **2.** GOD'S DECISION WHO GOES TO HEAVEN in some religious beliefs, the doctrine that God decided at the beginning of time who would go to heaven after death and who would not **3.** ACT OF FOREORDAINING the human or supposedly divine act of deciding the fate of people or things beforehand

pre·des·tine /pree déstin/ (**-tined, -tin·ing, -tines**) *vt* **1.** to decide in advance what is going to happen **2.** in some religious beliefs, to select in advance who will go to heaven after death and who will not [14C. Directly or via French < ecclesiastical Latin *praedestinare* "foreordain" < Latin *destinare* "decree"] —**pre·des·tin·able** *adj*

pre·de·ter·mine /preè də túrmən/ (**-mined, -min·ing, -mines**) *vt* **1.** to decide, agree, or arrange something in advance ○ *at a predetermined place* **2.** to ordain something in advance (*usually used in the passive*) ○ *Are our lives predetermined?* —**pre·de·ter·mi·nate** *adj* —**pre·de·ter·mi·na·tion** /preèdə tùrmə náysh'n/ *n* —**pre·de·ter·mi·na·tive** *adj*

pre·de·ter·min·er /preè də túrmənər/ *n* a word that precedes and qualifies another determiner, as "both" does in "both my hands"

pred·i·ca·ble /préddikəb'l/ (*formal*) *adj* able to be stated, or able to be said about somebody or something ■ *n* a quality or attribute by which somebody or something can be described [Mid-16C. < medieval Latin *praedicabilis* < Latin *praedicare* (see PREDICATE)] —**pred·i·ca·bil·i·ty** /prèddikə bíllətee/ *n* —**pred·i·ca·ble·ness** *n*

pre·dic·a·ment /prə díkəmənt/ *n* **1.** a difficult, unpleasant, or embarrassing situation from which there is no clear or easy way out **2.** in logic, a category or class that can be assigned to something [14C. < late Latin *praedicamentum* "class, category" (translation of Greek *katēgoria*) < Latin *praedicare* "proclaim" (see PREDICATE)]

pred·i·cate *n* /préddikət/ **1.** GRAM PART OF SENTENCE EXCLUDING SUBJECT a word or combination of words, including the verb, objects, or phrases governed by the verb that make up one of the two main parts of a sentence **2.** LOGIC EVERYTHING IN SENTENCE EXCLUDING NAMES everything in a simple sentence other than names, e.g., "runs" in "Lee runs" and "is taller than" in "Lee is taller than Glen" **3.** LOGIC SOMETHING AFFIRMED OR DENIED something that is affirmed or denied about something else ■ *vt* /préddi kàyt/ (**-cat·ed, -cat·ing, -cates**) **1.** BASE SOMETHING ON SOMETHING to base an opinion, an action, or a result on something (*formal*) ○ *predicated on reason* **2.** STATE SOMETHING to state or assert something (*formal*) **3.** IMPLY SOMETHING to imply or suggest something (*formal*) **4.** LOGIC ASSERT SOMETHING ABOUT SUBJECT OF STATEMENT to assert or affirm something about the subject of a statement **5.** LOGIC MAKE EXPRESSION PREDICATE OF STATEMENT to make an expression or term the predicate of a statement [Mid-16C. < late Latin *praedicatum* < past participle of Latin *praedicare* "declare publicly," literally "declare before" < *dicare* "declare, state"] —**pred·i·ca·tion** /prèddi káysh'n/ *n*

pred·i·cate cal·cu·lus *n* the branch of symbolic logic that uses symbols to explore relationships between and within propositions

pred·i·ca·tive /préddə kàytiv/ *adj* **1.** FORMING PREDICATE describes an adjective or noun that forms all or part of the predicate of a sentence. In "I am happy," "happy" is predicative, whereas in "a happy face" it is "attributive." **2.** GRAM STATING SOMETHING describes a use of the verb "to be" that makes a statement about the subject of the sentence **3.** LOGIC ACTING AS PREDICATE acting as a logical predicate [Mid-19C. < Latin *praeadicativus* < past participle of *praedicare* (see PREDICATE)] —**pred·i·ca·tive·ly** *adv*

pre·dict /prə díkt/ (**-dict·ed, -dict·ing, -dicts**) *vti* to say what is going to happen in the future, often on the basis of present indications or past experience [Mid-16C. < Latin *praedict-*, past participle of *praedicere* "say in advance" < *dicere* "say"] —**pre·dic·tor** *n*

pre·dict·a·ble /prə díktəb'l/ *adj* **1.** happening or turning out in the way that might have been expected or predicted **2.** rarely or never behaving or happening in an unusual or unexpected way —**pre·dict·a·bil·i·ty** /prə diktə bíllətee/ *n* —**pre·dict·a·bly** *adv*

pre·dic·tion /prə díkshən/ *n* **1.** a statement of what somebody thinks will happen in the future **2.** the making of a statement or forming of an opinion about what will happen in the future

pre·dic·tive /prə díktiv/ *adj* relating to the forecasting of a likely result or outcome ○ *a predictive medical test* —**pre·dic·tive·ly** *adv* —**pre·dic·tive·ness** *n*

pre·dic·tive text en·try *n* digital technology that anticipates the word a computer or cell phone user is in the process of keying

pre·di·gest /preè dī jést, -di-/ (**-gest·ed, -gest·ing, -gests**) *vt* **1.** to treat food with chemicals or enzymes so that it is more easily digested, especially for people with digestion problems **2.** to produce information in a simplified form so that it is easy to understand —**pre·di·ges·tion** /preè dī jésch'n, -di-/ *n*

pred·i·lec·tion /prèdd'l ékshən/ *n* a special liking or preference for something [Mid-18C. < French *prédilection* < medieval Latin *praediligere* "love above others" < Latin *diligere* "to love"]

pre·dis·pose /preèdi spṓz/ (**-posed, -pos·ing, -pos·es**) *vt* (*formal*) **1.** to make somebody feel favorably about somebody or something else in advance **2.** to make somebody liable or inclined to do something such as catch an illness or behave in a particular way ○ *Her fair skin predisposes her to sunburn.* —**pre·dis·pos·al** *n*

pre·dis·po·si·tion /preè dispə zísh'n/ *n* **1.** MED TENDENCY TO DEVELOP DISEASE a susceptibility to a disease, arising from a hereditary or other factor **2.** LIABILITY TO SOMETHING a liability or tendency to do something such as behave in a particular way **3.** FAVORABLE ATTITUDE OR INCLINATION a favorable attitude toward somebody or something, or an inclination to do something

pred·nis·o·lone /pred níssə lṑn/ *n* a synthetic steroid hormone, similar to cortisone. Use: treatment of allergies, suppression of inflammatory diseases. [Mid-20C. < PREDNISONE, by insertion of -OL[1]]

pred·ni·sone /prédnə sṑn/ *n* a synthetic steroid hormone produced from cortisone. Use: treatment of allergies and autoimmune diseases. [Mid-20C. Blend of *pregnane*, a synthetic hydrocarbon + DIENE + CORTISONE]

pre·doc·tor·al /pree dóktərəl/ *adj* **1.** relating to a degree other than a doctorate **2.** relating to or involving research or studies that will lead to a doctorate

pre·dom·i·nant /prə dómmənənt/ *adj* **1.** most common or greatest in number or amount ○ *a predominant shellfish species in the estuary* **2.** most important, powerful, or influential ○ *gave the predominant reason for instituting an embargo* —**pre·dom·i·nance** *n*

pre·dom·i·nant·ly /prə dómmənəntlee/ *adv* in the greatest number or amount

pre·dom·i·nate /prə dómmə nàyt/ (**-nat·ed, -nat·ing**) *v* **1.** *vi* BE IN MAJORITY to be the most common or greatest in number or amount **2.** *vi* BE MORE IMPORTANT to have greater importance, power, or influence than others **3.** *vt* DOMINATE SOMEBODY OR SOMETHING to dominate or control somebody or something [Late 16C. < medieval Latin *predominat-*, past participle of *predominari* "rule over" < Latin *dominari* "rule"] —**pre·dom·i·nate·ly** *adv* —**pre·dom·i·na·tion** /-dòmmə náysh'n/ *n* —**pre·dom·i·na·tor** *n*

~~**predominately**~~ incorrect spelling of **predominantly**

pre·e·clamp·si·a /prèe i klámpsee ə/ *n* a potentially dangerous condition that may develop in late pregnancy and may lead to convulsions if not treated. Symptoms are high blood pressure, fluid retention, excessive weight gain, and the presence of protein in the urine.

pre·em·bry·o /pree émbree ō/ *n* a fertilized ovum before implantation in the womb and before differentiation of embryonic tissue —**pre·em·bry·on·ic** /prèe embree ónnik/ *adj*

pree·mie /préemee/, **pre·mie** *n* a premature baby born before it is fully developed, usually before 35 weeks of gestation (*informal*) [Early 20C. < shortening of PREMATURE]

pre·em·i·nent /pree émminənt/ *adj* standing out among all others because of superiority in a field or activity [15C. < Latin *praeeminent-*, present participle of *praeeminere* "stand out in front" < *eminere* "stand out"] —**pre·em·i·nence** *n* —**pre·em·i·nent·ly** *adv*

pre·empt /pree émpt/ *v* (**-empt·ed, -empt·ing, -empts**) **1.** *vt* **ACT TO PREVENT SOMETHING** to do something that makes it pointless or impossible for somebody else to do what he or she intended **2.** *vt* **OCCUPY SOMETHING** to occupy public land in order to have the right to buy it later **3.** *vt* **REPLACE SOMETHING** to take the place of something, especially of something less important **4.** *vi* CARDS **MAKE BID THAT BLOCKS OTHERS** in bridge, to make a bid so high that it discourages further bidding ■ *n* CARDS **PREEMPTIVE BID** in bridge, a preemptive bid [Mid-19C. Back-formation < PREEMPTION] —**pre·emp·tor** *n* —**pre·emp·to·ry** *adj*

pre·emp·tion /pree émpshən/ *n* **1. ACTION PREVENTING SOMETHING** action that makes it pointless or impossible for somebody else to do what he or she intended **2. OCCUPATION OF PUBLIC LAND** the occupation of public land in order to have the right to buy it later, or the right to buy that is gained in this way **3. OPTION TO BUY PROPERTY** an option to purchase property if and when it is put up for sale **4.** MIL **STRATEGY OF FIRST ATTACK** the strategy of attacking an enemy in order to prevent that enemy from attacking first **5.** LAW **EXCLUSION OF STATE ACTION** the doctrine that prohibits a state from enacting laws in an area if the US federal government has passed laws in that area (*formal*) [Early 17C. < medieval Latin *praeemption-* < *praeempt-*, past participle of *praeemere* "buy first" < Latin *emere* "buy"]

pre·emp·tive /pree émptiv/ *adj* **1. DONE BEFORE OTHERS CAN ACT** done before somebody else has had an opportunity to act so as to make his or her planned action pointless or impossible **2.** MIL **INTENDED TO PREVENT ATTACK** intended to eliminate or lessen an enemy's capacity to attack ○ *a preemptive strike* **3.** CARDS **DISCOURAGING FURTHER BIDDING** in bridge, being so high a bid that it discourages further bidding [Late 18C. < medieval Latin *praeempt-* (see PREEMPTION)] —**pre·emp·tive·ly** *adv*

pre·emp·tive right *n* a right to be offered first refusal in selling or buying an asset

~~**preemptory**~~ incorrect spelling of **peremptory**

preen[1] /preen/ (**preened, preen·ing, preens**) *vti* **1. GROOM FEATHERS WITH BEAK** to clean, smooth, or arrange the feathers with the beak (*refers to birds*) **2. GROOM FUR WITH TONGUE** to clean and smooth the fur by licking it (*refers to a furred mammal*) **3. CARE EXCESSIVELY FOR PERSONAL APPEARANCE** to spend a long or excessive time attending to personal appearance, especially making small finishing touches to the hair, the face, or clothes ○ *busy preening in front of the mirror* **4. SHOW SELF-SATISFACTION** to feel excessively self-satisfied and display that feeling by gloating [15C. Probably < Old French *proignier* "to prune"] —**preen·er** *n*

preen[2] /preen/ *n* a decorative pin or brooch [Old English *prēon* < Germanic]

pre·en·gi·neered /prèe enji néerd/ *adj* constructed using prefabricated parts

pre·en·joyed *adj* previously owned or used (*often used euphemistically*)

pre·ex·il·i·an /prèe ig zíllee ən, prèe ik síllee ən/, **pre·ex·il·i·an** *adj* relating to or occurring in the period before the exile of the Jews to Babylon in the 6th century B.C.

pre·fab /prée fàb/ (*informal*) *n* a prefabricated house or building ■ *adj* relating to or constructed from prefabricated parts [Mid-20C. Shortening] —**pre·fabbed** *adj*

pre·fab·ri·cate /pree fábbrə kàyt/ (**-cat·ed, -cat·ing, -cates**) *vt* **1.** to manufacture sections of something, especially a building, that can be transported to a site and easily assembled there **2.** to produce something in an unoriginal or standardized way —**pre·fab·ri·ca·tion** /pree fàbbrə káysh'n/ *n* —**pre·fab·ri·ca·tor** *n*

pref·ace /préffəss/ *n* **1. INTRODUCTORY PART OF TEXT** an introductory section at the beginning of a book or speech that comments on aspects of the text such as the writer's intentions ○ *in the preface to the second edition* **2. PRELIMINARY ACTION** an action or event that precedes something more important **3.** *also* **Pref·ace** CHR **PRAYER DURING MASS** a prayer said by a priest during Mass, especially the prayer that begins "Lift up your hearts" **4.** *also* **Pref·ace** CHR **PRAYER FOR PARTICULAR PURPOSE** in the Roman Catholic Church, a prayer used for a particular purpose ■ *vt* (**-aced, -ac·ing, -ac·es**) **1. INTRODUCE SOMETHING WITH PREFACE** to introduce an action, speech, or piece of writing with something ○ *He prefaced his remarks with an apology.* **2. SERVE AS INTRODUCTION TO SOMETHING** to act as a preface to an action, speech, or piece of writing [14C. Via French < medieval Latin *praefatia* < Latin *praefat-*, past participle of *praefari* "say before" < *fari* "speak"] —**pref·ac·er** *n*

pre·fad·ed /pree fáydəd/ *adj* given an artificially faded, worn, or old appearance ○ *prefaded denim* —**pre·fade** *vt*

pref·a·to·ry /préffə tàwree/ *adj* serving to introduce something such as a main body of text or a speech ○ *prefatory remarks introducing the Vice President* [Late 17C. < Latin *praefat-* (see PREFACE)] —**pref·a·to·ri·ly** /prèffə táwrəlee/ *adv*

pre·fect /prée fèkt/ *n* **1.** EDUC **STUDENT ASSISTING WITH DISCIPLINE** a student who is given some authority over other pupils in matters of discipline in a private school **2.** CHR **SENIOR MASTER AT JESUIT SCHOOL** a senior master or administrator with special responsibilities at a Jesuit school or college **3.** POLICE **FRENCH CHIEF OF POLICE** the head of a French police force, especially in Paris **4.** PUBLIC ADMIN **HIGH-RANKING ADMINISTRATIVE OFFICIAL** the highest official in an administrative district (**department**) or former territorial possession of France or in an administrative region of Italy **5.** ANCIENT HIST **ROMAN MAGISTRATE OR COMMANDER** a senior administrative or military official in ancient Rome [14C. Via French < Latin *praefectus* "overseer" < past participle of *praeficere* "set over" < *facere* "make"] —**pre·fec·to·ri·al** /prèe fek táwree əl/ *adj*

pre·fec·ture /prée fèkchər/ *n* **1.** the district over which a prefect has jurisdiction **2.** the office or authority of a prefect —**pre·fec·tur·al** /pree fékchərəl/ *adj*

pre·fer /pri fúr/ (**-ferred, -fer·ring, -fers**) *vt* **1. LIKE SOMEBODY OR SOMETHING BETTER** to like or want somebody or something more than somebody or something else ○ *I prefer tea to coffee.* **2.** LAW **LAY CHARGE BEFORE COURT** to make a charge against somebody by submitting details of the alleged offense to a court, magistrate, or judge for examination, or prosecute such a charge ○ *preferred charges against the accused* **3.** LAW **GIVE PRIORITY TO SOMEBODY** to give priority to one person, especially a creditor, over others **4. PROMOTE SOMEBODY** to promote somebody to a higher position or rank (*archaic*) [14C. Via French *préferer* < Latin *praeferre* "put before" < *ferre* "carry, bear"] —**pre·fer·rer** *n*

pref·er·a·ble /préffərəb'l/ *adj* more likely to be enjoyable, useful, or desired than somebody or something else —**pref·er·a·bil·i·ty** /prèffərə bíllətee/ *n* —**pref·er·a·ble·ness** *n*

pref·er·a·bly /préffərəblee/ *adv* used to specify more exactly what is required or desired ○ *Plan to arrive early, preferably before the rush hour.*

~~**preferance**~~ incorrect spelling of **preference**

~~**prefered**~~ incorrect spelling of **preferred**

pref·er·ence /préffərənss/ *n* **1. SELECTION OF SOMEBODY OR SOMETHING** the view that one person, object, or course of action is more desirable than another, or a choice based on such a view ○ *The judges showed a marked preference for representational art.* **2. RIGHT TO EXPRESS CHOICE** the right or opportunity to choose a person, object, or course of action that is considered more desirable than another ○ *We exercised our preference.* **3. SOMEBODY OR SOMETHING PREFERRED** a person, object, or course of action that is more desirable than another, or the state of being that desirable choice ○ *State your preferences clearly.* **4.** LAW **PRIORITY OF ONE CREDITOR OVER OTHERS** priority given to a creditor, e.g., when a debtor goes bankrupt, or the right of one creditor to receive payment before others **5.** COMM **FAVORITISM IN INTERNATIONAL TRADE** priority given to a particular country or group of countries in international trade

pref·er·ence shares *npl UK* FIN same as **preferred stock**

pref·er·en·tial /prèffə rénsh'l/ *adj* **1.** giving advantage or priority to a person or group ○ *preferential treatment* **2.** giving advantage or priority to a country or group of countries in international trade —**pref·er·en·tial·ism** *n* —**pref·er·en·tial·ist** *adj* —**pref·er·en·ti·al·i·ty** /prèffə renshee állətee/ *n* —**pref·er·en·tial·ly** *adv*

pre·fer·ment /pri fúrmənt/ *n* (*formal*) **1.** appointment to a higher position or rank **2.** an office, appointment, or position of high rank or honor, especially one that brings social advancement or financial reward

pre·ferred pro·vid·er or·gan·i·za·tion *n US* an organization providing approved health care under contract with an insurance agency

pre·ferred stock *n* equity stock whose holders are the first to receive dividends from available profit. Preferred stock is redeemed before common stock when a company is liquidated.

pre·fig·ur·a·tion /pree figgyə ráysh'n/ *n* (*formal*) **1.** a representation, often in form or likeness, of a person, thing, or event that is to come **2.** somebody or something that represents, often in form or likeness, a person, thing, or event that is to come

pre·fig·ure /pree fíggyər/ (**-ured, -ur·ing, -ures**) *vt* **1.** to represent, often in form or likeness, a person, thing, or event that is to come ○ *designs that prefigured modern architecture* **2.** to think about or imagine a person, thing, or event in advance [15C. < ecclesiastical Latin *praefigurare* "depict beforehand" < Latin *figura* "figure"] —**pre·fig·ur·a·tive** *adj* —**pre·fig·ur·a·tive·ly** *adv* —**pre·fig·ure·ment** *n*

pre·fix[1] /prée fiks/ *n* **1. WORD ELEMENT BEGINNING VARIOUS WORDS** a linguistic element that is not an independent word, but is attached to the beginning of a word to modify its meaning. For example, "un-" is a prefix meaning "not." **2. TITLE BEFORE SOMEBODY'S NAME** a title before somebody's name, e.g., the prefix "The Honorable" before a judge's full name **3. SOMETHING PRECEDING SOMETHING ELSE** something that comes before something else, e.g., a fixed group of digits at the beginning of a telephone number ■ *vt* (**-fixed, -fix·ing, -fix·es**) **1. PUT SOMETHING BEFORE SOMETHING ELSE** to place something in front of something else ○ *You must prefix the number with the area code.* **2. INTRODUCE SOMETHING WITH SOMETHING ELSE** to say or do something by way of introduction to something else ○ *His requests for money were usually prefixed by an apology.* **3. ADD PREFIX TO WORD** to attach a prefix at the beginning of a word in order to alter its meaning [Mid-17C. Via French < Latin *praefixum* < past participle of *praefigere* "fix in front" < *figere* "fasten"] —**pre·fix·al** /pree fíks'l/ *adj* —**pre·fix·al·ly** *adv* —**pre·fix·a·tion** /prèe fik sáysh'n/ *n* —**pre·fix·ion** /pree fíksh'n/ *n*

pre·fix[2] /pree fíks/ (**-fixed, -fix·ing, -fix·es**) *vt* to decide on something such as a price, date, or meeting place beforehand ○ *They duly arrived at the prefixed hour.* [15C. < French *préfixer* < Latin *praefix-*, past participle of *praefigere* (see PREFIX[1])]

pre·form /pree fáwrm/ (**-formed, -form·ing, -forms**) *vt* **1.** to shape or form something beforehand **2.** to give something a preliminary shape —**pre·for·ma·tion** /prèe fawr máysh'n/ *n*

pre·fron·tal /pree frúnt'l/ *adj* **1.** relating to or situated in the foremost part of the brain **2.** located in front of the frontal bone

pre·fron·tal lo·bot·o·my *n* a surgical operation in which the nerves connecting the front part of the brain (**prefrontal lobe**) to the thalamus are severed. Prefrontal lobotomy was formerly a method of reducing severe emotional disturbances, but the operation had serious side effects.

preg·na·ble /prégnəb'l/ *adj* able to be captured or attacked [15C. < Old French < stem of *prendre* "take" < Latin *prehendere* "seize"] —**preg·na·bil·i·ty** /prègnə bíllətee/ *n*

preg·nan·cy /prégnənssee/ (*plural* **-cies**) *n* **1.** CONDITION OF BEING PREGNANT the physical condition of a woman or female animal carrying unborn offspring inside her body, from fertilization to birth **2.** INSTANCE OF BEING PREGNANT an individual occurrence or experience of being pregnant **3.** TIME OF CARRYING UNBORN OFFSPRING the period during which a woman or female animal carries unborn offspring inside her body, from fertilization to birth **4.** SIGNIFICANCE importance or fullness of meaning ○ *the pregnancy of his words*

preg·nant /prégnənt/ *adj* **1.** CARRYING OFFSPRING WITHIN BODY carrying unborn offspring inside the body **2.** SIGNIFICANT full of meaning or importance ○ *After a pregnant pause, the general began briefing the media on the surprise attack.* **3.** FULL OF SOMETHING pervaded by something, usually something intangible ○ *The tense, quiet operations center was pregnant with anxiety and dread.* **4.** CREATIVE full of creative power ○ *the child's pregnant imagination* **5.** PRODUCTIVE producing a lot of useful results ○ *It was a pregnant endeavor, yielding much experience, information, and help.* [15C. Directly or via French *preignant* < Latin *praegnant-*, alteration of *praegnat-*, probably < *prae-* "before" + *gnatus* "born"] —**preg·nant·ly** *adv*

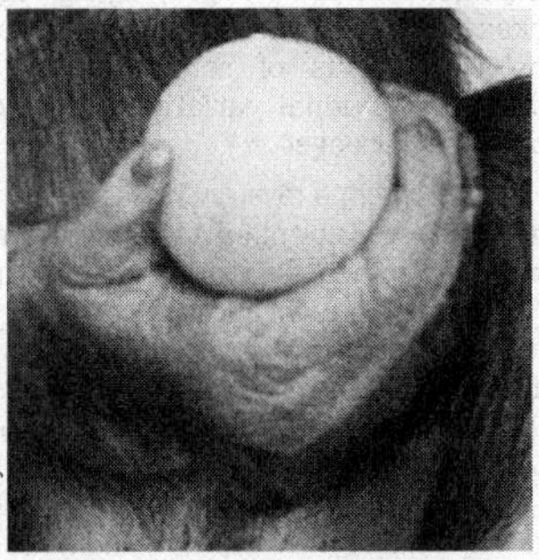

Barnaby's

prehensile: chimpanzee grasping a ball

pre·hen·sile /pree hénss'l/ *adj* **1.** ABLE TO GRASP SOMETHING able to take hold of things, especially by wrapping around them ○ *The monkey has a prehensile tail.* **2.** QUICK TO UNDERSTAND skilled at grasping ideas and concepts **3.** AGGRESSIVELY EAGER excessively eager for gain or profit [Late 18C. < French *préhensile* < Latin *prehens-*, past participle of *prehendere* "seize"] —**pre·hen·sil·i·ty** /preè hen síllətee/ *n*

ORIGIN The Latin word *prehendere* "to seize," from which ***prehensile*** is derived, is also the source of English *apprehend, apprentice, comprehend, comprise, impregnable, prey, prison, reprehend, reprieve,* and *surprise.*

pre·hen·sion /pree hénshən/ *n* (*formal*) **1.** ACT OF FIRMLY GRASPING the act of firmly taking hold of something **2.** PERCEIVING OF SOMETHING THROUGH SENSES the perception by the senses of a sight, sound, smell, taste, or texture **3.** COMPREHENSION the process of understanding [Mid-16C. < Latin *prehension-* < *prehens-* (see PREHENSILE)]

pre·his·tor·ic /preè hi stáwrik/ *adj* **1.** BEFORE RECORDED HISTORY relating to the period before history was first recorded in writing **2.** LING RELATING TO LANGUAGE BEFORE WRITING relating or belonging to a language before it was recorded in writing **3.** VERY OLD OR OLD-FASHIONED very old, old-fashioned, or out-of-date ○ *prehistoric views about nutrition* —**pre·his·tor·i·cal·ly** *adv*

pre·his·to·ry /pree hístəree/ *n* **1.** HISTORY BEFORE WRITTEN WORD the period before history was first recorded in writing **2.** STUDY OF PREHISTORIC PERIOD the study of the prehistoric period using archaeological evidence **3.** EVENTS LEADING UP TO SOMETHING the events and circumstances preceding an event or situation —**pre·his·to·ri·an** /preè hi stáwree ən/ *n*

pre·ig·ni·tion /preè ig nísh'n/ *n* ignition of fuel in an internal-combustion engine before the spark has been generated, causing inefficient operation. Preignition may be caused by a hot spot in the cylinder. —**pre·ig·nite** *vti*

pre·judge /pree júj/ (**-judged, -judg·ing, -judg·es**) *vt* to judge a person, issue, or case before sufficient evidence is available [Late 16C. Via French *préjuger* < Latin *praejudicare* < *judicare* "to judge"] —**pre·judg·er** *n* —**pre·judg·ment** *n*

prej·u·dice /préjjədiss/ *n* **1.** OPINION FORMED BEFOREHAND a preformed opinion, usually an unfavorable one, based on insufficient knowledge, irrational feelings, or inaccurate stereotypes **2.** HOLDING OF ILL-INFORMED OPINIONS the holding of preformed opinions based on insufficient knowledge, irrational feelings, or inaccurate stereotypes **3.** IRRATIONAL DISLIKE OF SOMEBODY an unfounded hatred, fear, or mistrust of a person or group, especially one of a particular religion, ethnicity, nationality, sexual preference, or social status **4.** LAW DISADVANTAGE OR HARM disadvantage or harm caused to somebody or something ■ *vt* (**-diced, -dic·ing, -dic·es**) **1.** MAKE SOMEBODY PREJUDGE SOMEBODY OR SOMETHING to make somebody form an opinion about somebody or something in advance, especially an irrational one, based on insufficient knowledge **2.** AFFECT SOMEBODY OR SOMETHING ADVERSELY to cause harm or disadvantage to somebody or something [13C. Via French < Latin *praejudicium* "judgment in advance" < *judicium* "judgment"] —**prej·u·diced** *adj* ◇ **without prejudice** without doing any harm to any legal right or claim that somebody has (*formal*)

prej·u·di·cial /prèjjə dísh'l/ *adj* **1.** causing disadvantage or harm to somebody or something **2.** leading to the formation of prejudiced ideas or opinions —**prej·u·di·cial·ly** *adv*

prel·a·cy /préllәssee/ (*plural* **-cies**) *n* **1.** the office or position of a prelate in the Christian church **2.** prelates considered as a group [14C. Via Anglo-Norman < medieval Latin *prelatia* < *praelatus* (see PRELATE)]

pre·lap·sar·i·an /preè lap sérree ən/ *adj* relating to or belonging to the biblical time before Adam and Eve lost their innocence in the Garden of Eden [Late 19C. < PRE- + Latin *lapsus* "sin, fall"]

prel·ate /préllət/ *n* a high-ranking member of the Christian clergy, e.g., an abbot, bishop, or cardinal [13C. Via French < medieval Latin *praelatus,* < past participle of Latin *praeferre* (see PREFER)] —**pre·lat·ic** /prə láttik/ *adj*

prel·a·ture /préllәchər/ *n* CHR same as **prelacy**

pre·li·ba·tion /preè lī báysh'n/ *n* same as **foretaste** (*archaic*) [Early 16C. < Latin *praelibation-* < *praelibare* "taste beforehand" < *libare* "pour out"]

pre·lim /preèlim/ (*informal*) *n* **1.** SPORTS a preliminary contest or event **2.** *US* EDUC an examination that a doctoral candidate must pass in order to be allowed to do dissertation research ■ **pre·lims** *npl UK* PUBL same as **front matter** [Late 19C. Shortening of PRELIMINARY]

pre·lim·i·nar·y /pri límmə nèrree/ *adj* COMING BEFORE SOMETHING occurring before and leading up to something, especially an event of greater size and importance ■ *n* (*plural* **-ies**) **1.** INTRODUCTORY OR PREPARATORY ACTIVITY something said or done before something else, often by way of introduction to or preparation for something of greater size and importance (*often used in the plural*) **2.** SPORTS INTRODUCTORY CONTEST a sporting contest held before the main event, especially in boxing or wrestling **3.** SPORTS ELIMINATORY CONTEST an eliminatory contest to select the finalists in a sports competition **4.** EDUC PREPARATORY EXAMINATION a test that prepares students for a subsequent examination of greater difficulty and importance [Mid-17C. Directly or via French < modern Latin *praeliminaris* < Latin *limen* "threshold"] —**pre·lim·i·nar·i·ly** /pri lìmmə nérrəlee/ *adv*

pre·lit·er·ate /pree líttərət/ *adj* describes a society that has not yet developed a written language ■ *n* a member of a society with no written language —**pre·lit·er·a·cy** *n*

prel·ude /prél yoòd, práy loòd/ *n* **1.** MUSIC INTRODUCTORY PIECE OF MUSIC a piece of music that introduces or precedes another one **2.** MUSIC FREE-STANDING PIECE OF MUSIC a short musical composition, often one for piano, and often forming part of a set of such works **3.** INTRODUCTORY EVENT OR OCCURRENCE an event or action that introduces or precedes something else, especially something longer and more important ■ *v* (**-ud·ed, -ud·ing, -udes**) **1.** *vti* ACT AS PRELUDE TO SOMETHING to act as an introduction to something else, especially something that is longer and more important **2.** *vt* INTRODUCE SOMETHING WITH PRELUDE to precede something, especially a piece of music, with a prelude [Mid-16C. Directly or via French *prélude* < medieval Latin *praeludium* < Latin *praeludere* "play before" < *ludere* "play"] —**prel·ud·er** *n* —**pre·lu·di·al** /prə loòdee əl/ *adj* —**pre·lu·sive** /-loòssiv/ *adj* —**pre·lu·sive·ly** *adv* —**pre·lu·so·ri·ly** *adv* —**pre·lu·so·ry** *adj*

CULTURAL NOTE ***The Prelude***, a poem (1805) by British writer William Wordsworth. Planned as a preface to a never-completed philosophical poem called *The Recluse*, this autobiographical account of the poet's intellectual and spiritual development was published posthumously (1850) in a revised form. Rejecting contemporary rationalist philosophies, it proclaims Wordsworth's faith in the redeeming power of poetry and the imagination.

pre·ma·lig·nant /preè mə lígnənt/ *adj* MED same as **precancerous**

pre·mar·i·tal /pree márrət'l/ *adj* occurring or existing before marriage

pre·ma·ture /preèmə choòr/ *adj* **1.** occurring, existing, or developing earlier than is expected, normal, or advisable ○ *It would be premature to suggest that there is a link between these events.* **2.** born before completing the normal gestation period, or, for a human infant, weighing less than 5 lb. 8 oz/2.5 kg at birth [Early 16C. < Latin *praematurus* "ripening too early" < *maturus* "ripe"] —**pre·ma·ture·ly** *adv* —**pre·ma·ture·ness** *n* —**pre·ma·tu·ri·ty** *n*

pre·max·il·la /preè mak síllə/ (*plural* **-lae** /-leè/) *n* either of two bones that form the front part of the upper jaw in vertebrates and that bear the incisors. In humans, it merges with the rest of the maxilla during embryonic development. —**pre·max·il·lar·y** /pree máksi lèrree/ *adj*

pre·med /pree méd/ (*informal*) *n* **1.** a student in a premedical program **2.** a premedical course of study ○ *majoring in premed* ■ *adj* same as **premedical** [Mid-20C. Shortening]

pre·med·i·cal /pree méddik'l/ *adj* relating to or engaged in the course of studies that somebody must complete before entering medical school —**pre·med·i·cal·ly** *adv*

pre·med·i·ca·tion /preè medi káysh'n/ *n* **1.** the practice of giving drugs to a patient before anesthesia to relieve anxiety, diminish body reactions to pain, or improve postoperative comfort **2.** the drugs given to a patient in premedication

pre·med·i·tate /pree méddi tàyt/ (**-tat·ed, -tat·ing, -tates**) *v* **1.** *vt* to plan or devise something, especially a crime, in advance **2.** *vti* to consider or think carefully about something beforehand [Mid-16C. < Latin *praemeditat-*, past participle of *praemeditari* "think about beforehand" < *meditare* (see MEDITATE)] —**pre·med·i·tat·ed** *adj* —**pre·med·i·ta·tive** *adj* —**pre·med·i·ta·tor** *n*

pre·med·i·ta·tion /pree mèddi táysh'n/ *n* **1.** the act of thinking about and planning a crime beforehand, rather than acting on impulse in a moment of passion or mindlessness **2.** the act of thinking about something before doing it [15C. Directly or via French < Latin *praemeditation-* < *praemeditat-* (see PREMEDITATE)]

pre·me·no·paus·al /preè mènnə páwz'l/ *adj* describes the stage in a woman's life just before the onset of menopause, or a woman at this stage. Such a woman is still menstruating, but may show some signs of menopause, e.g., irregular menstrual periods.

pre·men·stru·al /pree ménstroo əl/ *adj* relating to, or occurring in, the days immediately before the start of a woman's menstrual period

pre·men·stru·al syn·drome *n* a group of symptoms such as nervous tension, irritability, tenderness of the breasts, and headache, experienced by some women in the days preceding menstruation and caused by hormonal changes

pre·mie *n* MED another spelling of **preemie** (*informal*)

pre·mier /pri meèr/ *adj* BEST OR MOST IMPORTANT first in importance, size, or quality ■ *n* **1.** PRIME MINISTER a prime minister or head of government **2.** LEADER OF

CANADIAN PROVINCE the governmental head of a Canadian province [15C. Via French < Latin *primarius* "foremost" (see PRIMARY)]

pre·mier dan·seur /pri meer daaN súr/ (*plural* **pre·miers dan·seurs** /*pronunc. same*/) *n* the principal man dancer in a ballet company [Early 19C. < French, "first (man) dancer"]

pre·miere /pri meer/ *n* **1.** FIRST PUBLIC PERFORMANCE the first public performance or showing of something such as a play or movie **2.** LEADING WOMAN ACTOR the principal woman performer in a theatrical company ■ *v* (**-miered, -mier·ing, -mieres**) **1.** *vti* PRESENT OR BE PRESENTED AS PREMIERE to perform, show, or broadcast a play, movie, or similar piece of work publicly for the first time, or be publicly performed for the first time ○ *The play premiered in New York.* **2.** *vi* GIVE FIRST PUBLIC PERFORMANCE to appear on stage or screen for the first time, especially in a leading role ○ *Not many young performers get to premiere on Broadway.* ■ *adj* BEST OR MOST IMPORTANT first in importance, quality, or size [Mid-20C. < French, feminine form of *premier* "foremost" (see PREMIER)]

pre·mière dan·seuse /pri meer daaN sooz/ (*plural* **pre·mières dan·seuses** /*pronunc. same*/) *n* the principal woman dancer in a ballet company [Early 19C. < French, "first (woman) dancer"]

pre·mier·ship /pri meer ship/ *n* the office or position of a premier

pre·mil·len·ni·al /pree mi lénnee əl/ *adj* relating to or occurring in the period immediately before a millennium —**pre·mil·len·ni·al·ly** *adv*

pre·mil·len·ni·al·ism /pree mi lénnee ə lìzzəm/ *n* the belief that Jesus Christ will return for the Last Judgment just before the one-thousand-year reign of peace (**millennium**) mentioned in the Bible —**pre·mil·le·nar·i·an** /pree mìllə nérree ən/ *adj, n* —**pre·mil·len·ni·al·ist** *n*

Express Newspapers

Otto Preminger

Prem·in·ger /prémminjər/, **Otto** (1906–86) Austrian-born US movie director, producer, and actor. His movies include *Laura* (1944), *Carmen Jones* (1954), and *Exodus* (1960). Full name **Preminger, Otto Ludwig**

prem·ise /prémmiss/, **prem·iss** *n* BASIS OF ARGUMENT a proposition that forms the basis of an argument or from which a conclusion is drawn ○ *I question the premise on which your whole theory is based.* ■ *v* (**-ised, -is·ing, -is·es**) **1.** *vt* BASE SOMETHING ON SOMETHING to base something on the foundation of a proposition or idea, stated or assumed to be true ○ *a budget premised on growth not stability* **2.** *vti* PROPOSE AS PREMISE to put forward a proposition as a premise in an argument **3.** *vt* SAY SOMETHING BY WAY OF INTRODUCTION to state something in advance to introduce or explain what follows (*formal*) [14C. Via French < medieval Latin *praemissa (propositio)* "(the proposition) set before" < past participle of *praemittere* "set in front" < *mittere* "send"]

prem·is·es /prémmissəz/ *npl* **1.** LAND AND BUILDINGS a piece of land and the buildings on it **2.** PART OR ALL OF BUILDING a building or part of a building, especially when used for commercial purposes **3.** LAW MATTERS PREVIOUSLY MENTIONED matters previously stated or referred to in a legal document such as a deed [15C. < medieval Latin *praemissa* "things stated at the beginning" (see PREMISE)]

prem·iss *n* LOGIC another spelling of **premise**

pre·mi·um /preemee əm/ *n* **1.** COST OF INSURANCE the sum of money paid, usually at regular intervals, for an insurance policy ○ *My insurance premium went up as a result of the accident.* **2.** ADDITIONAL SUM a sum of money paid in addition to a normal wage, rate, price, or other amount **3.** PRIZE an award or prize given, e.g., to the winner of a competition **4.** INDUCEMENT TO BUY a gift or reduced price offered as an incentive to purchase another product or service ○ *The manufacturer offered premiums, in the form of free merchandise, for every purchase of a new car.* **5.** AMOUNT ABOVE PAR VALUE the amount above its nominal value at which something, especially a security, sells **6.** *US* EXTRA CHARGE FOR BORROWING MONEY an amount charged in addition to interest on a loan **7.** COST OF SECURITIES OPTION the sum or cost at which a securities option is bought or sold **8.** FEE FOR INSTRUCTION a fee paid for training or apprenticeship in a profession or trade ■ *adj* **1.** HIGH-QUALITY of very high quality **2.** UNUSUALLY HIGH higher than normal, especially in price ○ *premium gasoline prices* [Early 17C. < Latin *praemium* "reward" < *prae-* "before" + *emere* "take, buy"] ◇ **at a premium 1.** much in demand and therefore difficult to obtain **2.** selling for a high price, or for a higher price than usual, because of scarcity ◇ **put a premium on** to place a high value on somebody or something

pre·mo·lar /pree mólər/ *n* either of two teeth on each side of both jaws that lie immediately behind the canines and in front of the molars and are used for grinding and chewing ■ *adj* relating to a grinding and chewing tooth

pre·mo·ni·tion /prèmmə nísh'n, preemə-/ *n* **1.** a strong feeling, without a rational basis, that something is going to happen **2.** an advance warning about a future event [Mid-16C. Directly or via French < late Latin *praemonition-* < Latin *praemonere* "forewarn" < *monere* "warn"] —**pre·mon·i·to·ri·ly** /pree mònni táwrəlee/ *adv* —**pre·mon·i·to·ry** *adj*

pre·mum·ble /pree mùmb'l/ *n* a series of opening remarks, often gratuitous, made by a speaker prior to the beginning of his or her real presentation (*slang*) [Late 20C. After PREAMBLE]

pre·na·tal /pree náyt'l/ *adj* existing or happening during pregnancy but before childbirth —**pre·na·tal·ly** *adv*

Pren·der·gast /préndər gàst/, **Maurice Brazil** (1859–1924) US painter. He was a member of the Eight, a group of realist painters, and his subjects include landscapes with figures, painted in rich colors.

pre·nom·i·nal /pree nómmən'l/ *adj* **1.** occurring before a noun, or used only before a noun **2.** relating to an ancient Roman's first name (**praenomen**)

pre·no·tion /pree nósh'n/ *n* **1.** a preconceived idea about somebody or something **2.** a feeling that something is about to occur or may occur [Early 17C. < Latin *praenotion-* < *notion-* "concept" (see NOTION)]

pre·nup·tial /pree núpshəl/ *adj* occurring or existing before a marriage

pre·nup·tial a·gree·ment /pree núpshəl-/ *n* an agreement made between a couple before marriage relating to the arrangement of financial matters and division of property in the event of their divorce

pre·oc·cu·pa·tion /pree òkyə páysh'n/, **pre·oc·cu·pan·cy** /pree ókyəpənsee/ (*plural* **-cies**) *n* **1.** constant thought about or persistent interest in something ○ *a preoccupation with fame and fortune* **2.** a subject or activity that constantly occupies somebody's thoughts ○ *His children are his main preoccupation at the moment.* [Early 17C. Directly or via French < Latin *praeoccupation-*, literally "seizing in advance" < *praeoccupare* < *occupare* (see OCCUPY)]

pre·oc·cu·pied /pree ókyə pìd/ *adj* **1.** HAVING ATTENTION TAKEN UP WITH SOMETHING completely absorbed in thinking about something or doing something, sometimes to the extent of neglecting other things ○ *She was too preoccupied to notice what was going on.* **2.** OCCUPIED already occupied by somebody or something else ○ *a preoccupied airline seat* **3.** BIOL ALREADY IN USE describes a scientific name that has already been used to designate a species, genus, or other taxonomic group and therefore cannot be used again

pre·oc·cu·py /pree ókyə pì/ (**-pied, -py·ing, -pies**) *vt* **1.** to fill somebody's thoughts completely, sometimes in a way that blunts his or her response to other things **2.** to occupy something in advance, or before somebody else

pre·op /pree óp/ *adj* same as **preoperative** (*informal*) [Mid-20C. Shortening]

pre·op·er·a·tive /pree óppərətiv, -óppràtiv/ *adj* occurring or done before a surgical operation

pre·or·dain /pree awr dáyn/ (**-dained, -dain·ing, -dains**) *vt* **1.** to decide in advance that something will happen, or determine somebody's future, usually by fate or divine decree **2.** to decide, determine, or arrange something beforehand —**pre·or·dain·ment** *n* —**pre·or·di·na·tion** /pree àwrd'n áysh'n/ *n*

pre·o·vu·la·to·ry /pree óvyələ tàwree, pree óvvyələ tàwree/ *adj* relating to the stage of the menstrual cycle between menstruation and ovulation that lasts from 6 to 13 days

prep /prep/ *n* (*informal*) **1.** PREPARATION preparation for an activity **2.** EDUC same as **preparatory school** (sense 1) **3.** EDUC same as **preppy** *n* (sense 2) **4.** *UK* EDUC same as **preparation** (senses 5–6) ■ *v* (**prepped, prep·ping, preps**) **1.** *vi* PREPARE FOR SOMETHING to study or train for an examination, sporting event, or other activity (*informal*) **2.** *vt* MED PREPARE SOMEBODY FOR SURGERY to make a patient ready for an operation or other hospital procedure (*informal*) **3.** *vt* ART PREPARE SOMETHING FOR PAINTING to prime a surface for painting **4.** *vi* ATTEND PRIVATE SECONDARY SCHOOL to attend a preparatory school ○ *prepped at Groton* ■ *adj* PREPARATORY serving as preparation (*informal*) [Mid-19C. Shortening of PREPARATION]

prep. *abbr* **1.** preparation **2.** preparatory **3.** GRAM preposition

pre·pack·age /pree pákij/ (**-aged, -ag·ing, -ag·es**) *vt* **1.** to package a product before selling it **2.** to arrange all the components of something in advance, allowing no individual variation ○ *a prepackaged holiday* —**pre·pack·aged** *adj*

prep·a·ra·tion /prèppə ráysh'n/ *n* **1.** PREPARING SOMETHING OR SOMEBODY the work or planning involved in making something or somebody ready or in putting something together in advance (*often used before a noun*) ○ *a preparation time of about 45 minutes* **2.** READINESS a state of readiness ○ *Twenty place settings lay carefully arranged in preparation for the guests.* **3.** PREPARATORY MEASURE something done in advance in order to be ready for a future event (*often pl*) ○ *Preparations for the next Olympic Games are already under way.* **4.** MIXTURE a substance, e.g., a medicine, that is made by combining various ingredients ○ *a cough preparation* **5.** *UK* HOMEWORK at a boarding school or private school in the United Kingdom, work to be done by students outside normal school hours **6.** *UK* STUDY TIME at a boarding school in the United Kingdom, the time during which students do homework or prepare for lessons **7.** MUSIC SOFTENING APPROACH TO DISSONANCE in traditional composition, a lessening of the effect of a dissonant chord by using the discordant note harmonically in a preceding chord [14C. Via French < Latin *praeparation-* < *praeparare* (see PREPARE)]

Prep·a·ra·tion of the Gifts *n* the offertory in the Roman Catholic Mass

pre·par·a·tive /pri párrətiv/ *adj* same as **preparatory** (senses 1–2) ○ *a series of preparative lectures* ■ *n* something that prepares for or introduces a more important event or action (*formal*) ○ *Her preparative was excellent and we felt ready to perform the procedure.* [15C. Via French < medieval Latin *praeparativus* < Latin *praeparare* (see PREPARE)] —**pre·par·a·tive·ly** *adv*

pre·par·a·to·ry /pri párrə tàwree/ *adj* **1.** DONE AS PREPARATION done in preparation for something else, as a preparation for something, or to make something ready ○ *preparatory design work* **2.** INTRODUCTORY acting as an introduction to something ○ *preparatory remarks before a news conference* **3.** *US* PREPARING FOR COLLEGE relating to or engaged in a course of study that prepares students for advanced education, especially college ○ *Most of my classes this year are college preparatory.* [15C. < medieval Latin *praeparatorius* < *praeparator* "preparer" < Latin *praeparari* (see PREPARE)] —**pre·par·a·to·ri·ly** /pri pàrrə táwrəlee/ *adv* ◇ **preparatory to** before or in preparation for something

pre·par·a·to·ry school *n* **1.** *US* in the United States, a private secondary school that prepares students for college, often with academic requirements for entry **2.** in the United Kingdom, a private, usually single-sex, school that prepares students between the ages of 6 and 13 for entrance into a private boarding school

pre·pare /pri pér/ (**-pared, -par·ing, -pares**) *v* **1.** *vti* **MAKE SOMETHING READY** to take the necessary action to put something into a state where it is fit for use or action, or for a particular event or purpose ○ *preparing the aircraft for takeoff* **2.** *vti* **MAKE SOMEBODY READY** to put somebody or yourself into a suitable physical or mental state to do or experience something ○ *They prepared to go.* ○ *Prepare yourselves for a shock.* **3.** *vt* **MAKE SOMETHING BY PUTTING THINGS TOGETHER** to make something by combining various ingredients ○ *meals that can be prepared in less than half an hour* **4.** *vt* **EQUIP SOMEBODY** to provide somebody or something with the necessary equipment for an activity ○ *The expedition had not been properly prepared for arctic conditions.* **5.** *vt* MUSIC **LESSEN EFFECT OF DISSONANCE** to lessen the effect of a dissonant chord by using the discordant note harmonically in a preceding chord [15C. Directly or via French < Latin *praeparare* "make ready beforehand" < *parare* "make ready"] —**pre·par·er** *n*

pre·pared /pri pérd/ *adj* **1. WILLING** willing and able to do something ○ *Are you prepared to testify in court?* **2. READY TO DEAL WITH SOMETHING** in a suitable physical or mental state to be able to cope with something, often something hard or bad ○ *We had taken the necessary defensive measures and were prepared for the attack when it came.* **3. MADE, OR MADE READY, BEFOREHAND** made ready or put together in advance ○ *a specially prepared surface* ○ *a prepared statement* —**pre·par·ed·ly** /pri pérədlee/ *adv*

pre·par·ed·ness /pri pérədnəss/ *n* readiness for action, especially military action

pre·pared pi·an·o *n* a piano that has been modified to produce special effects, usually by placing objects on or between its strings

pre·pay /pree páy/ (**-paid** /-páyd/, **-pay·ing, -pays**) *vt* to pay in advance for goods or services —**pre·paid** *adj* —**pre·pay·a·ble** *adj* —**pre·pay·ment** *n*

pre·pense /pri pénss/ *adj* planned or contemplated in advance (*archaic*) ○ *acted with malice prepense* [Early 18C. Shortening of *prepensed*, past participle of *prepense* "premeditate," alteration of obsolete *purpense* < Anglo-Norman *purpenser* < Latin *pensare* "think"]

~~**preperation**~~ incorrect spelling of **preparation**

pre·pon·der·ance /pri póndərənss/, **pre·pon·der·an·cy** /-póndərənssee/ *n* (*formal*) **1.** a large number or the majority (*takes a singular or plural verb*) ○ *A preponderance of the settlers in this area were French.* **2.** dominance or superiority in force, importance, or influence ○ *The preponderance of the evidence is in support of this theory.*

pre·pon·der·ant /pri póndərənt/ *adj* greater in number, power, or importance than something else of the same nature or class [Mid-17C. < Latin *praeponderant-*, present participle of *praeponderare* "outweigh" < *ponderare* "weigh" (see PONDER)] —**pre·pon·der·ant·ly** *adv*

pre·pon·der·ate *vi* /pri póndə ràyt/ (**-at·ed, -at·ing, -ates**) to be greater in weight, strength, number, or importance than something else ■ *adj* /pri póndərət/ same as **preponderant** [Early 17C. < Latin *praeponderat-*, past participle of *praeponderare* (see PREPONDERANT)] —**pre·pon·der·ate·ly** *adv* —**pre·pon·der·a·tion** /-pòndə ráysh'n/ *n*

pre·pone /pree pṓn/ (**-poned, -pon·ing, -pones**) *v* *S Asia* to reschedule something for an earlier time or date [Late 20C. After POSTPONE]

prep·o·si·tion /prèppə zísh'n/ *n* a member of a set of words used in close connection with, and usually before, nouns and pronouns to show their relation to another part of a clause. An example is "off" in "He fell off his bike" and "What did he fall off?" [14C. < Latin *praeposition-* "putting before, preposition" < *praeponere* "put before" < *ponere* "put"] —**prep·o·si·tion·al** *adj*

pre·po·si·tion *vt* to put somebody or something in position beforehand, especially to deploy ships and troops to an area of possible future conflict

prep·o·si·tion·al phrase *n* a phrase made up of a preposition followed by a noun or pronoun, e.g., "over the hill." Prepositional phrases can be used adverbially or adjectivally.

pre·pos·i·tive /pree pózzətiv/ *adj* describes a word that is placed before the word it modifies ■ *n* a prepositive word or element [Late 16C. < late Latin *praepositivus* < past participle of Latin *praeponere* (see PREPOSITION)] —**pre·pos·i·tive·ly** *adv*

pre·pos·sess·ing /prèe pə zéssing/ *adj* creating a pleasing impression —**pre·pos·sess·ing·ly** *adv* —**pre·pos·sess·ing·ness** *n*

pre·pos·ses·sion /prèe pə zésh'n/ *n* **1.** prejudice or bias concerning somebody or something **2.** the occupation of the mind by thoughts or feelings

pre·pos·ter·ous /pri póstərəss/ *adj* going very much against what is thought to be sensible or reasonable [Mid-16C. < Latin *praeposterus* "inverted," literally "having the first thing last"] —**pre·pos·ter·ous·ly** *adv* —**pre·pos·ter·ous·ness** *n*

pre·po·tent /pree pṓt'nt/ *adj* **1.** greater in power, force, or influence **2.** showing great effectiveness in conferring genetic traits or in fertilization [15C. < Latin *praepotent-* "more powerful" < *potent-* (see POTENT[1])] —**pre·po·ten·cy** *n* —**pre·po·tent·ly** *adv*

prep·py /préppee/, **prep·pie** (*informal*) *adj* **RELATING TO YOUNG WELL-EDUCATED AFFLUENT PEOPLE** relating to or characteristic of well-educated, fairly affluent young people who are known for their neat, traditional, often expensive style of dress ■ *n* (*plural* **-pies**; *plural* **-pies**) **1. WELL-EDUCATED AFFLUENT YOUNG PERSON** a young person who dresses in a preppy style or behaves in a way that suggests a traditional education at a preparatory school **2. PREPARATORY SCHOOL STUDENT** a young person who is studying or has studied at a preparatory school —**prep·pi·ly** *adv* —**prep·pi·ness** *n*

pre·pran·di·al /pree prándee əl/ *adj* taking place before a meal, especially an evening meal (*formal or humorous*)

pre·proc·ess /pree pró sèss, -prṓ-/ (**-essed, -ess·ing, -ess·es**) *vt* to analyze computer data such as control statements embedded in a program, and take appropriate action before processing the data —**pre·proc·es·sor** *n*

pre·pro·duc·tion /prèe prə dúksh'n/ *n* **PRELIMINARY WORK** the plans and activities, e.g., those relating to finance, equipment, and personnel, that precede the production phase of a project, especially in the entertainment and manufacturing industries ■ *adj* **1. HAPPENING BEFORE PRODUCTION** preceding a production phase **2. PROTOTYPIC** produced as a trial or prototype

pre·pro·gram /pree prṓ gràm/ (**-grammed** or **-gramed, -gram·ming** or **-gram·ing, -grams**) *vt* **1.** to program a computer or other device in advance **2.** to prepare somebody in such a way that a later response in a desired manner is assured

prep school *n* EDUC same as **preparatory school** (*informal*)

pre·pu·bes·cent /prèe pyoo béss'nt/ *adj* at or characteristic of the stage of life just before puberty ■ *n* a child at the stage of life just before puberty —**pre·pu·bes·cence** *n*

pre·puce /prèe pyoòss/ *n* (*technical*) **1.** same as **foreskin** **2.** the loose fold of skin that covers the tip of the clitoris [14C. Via French < Latin *praeputium*] —**pre·pu·tial** /pree pyoòsh'l/ *adj*

pre·quel /prèekwəl/ *n* a movie or novel set at a time preceding the action of an existing work, especially one that has achieved commercial success [Late 20C. Blend of PRE- + SEQUEL]

Pre-Raph·a·el·ite /pree ráffee ə lìt/ *n* a member of a group of painters and writers (**the Pre-Raphaelite Brotherhood**) founded in 1848 with the objective of reviving the simpler and more direct style of Italian painting before Raphael. The group included Rossetti and Millais. ■ *adj* relating or belonging to the Pre-Raphaelites, or characteristic of their style of painting or writing —**Pre-Raph·a·el·it·ism** *n*

pre·re·cord /prèe ri káwrd/ (**-cord·ed, -cord·ing, -cords**) *vt* to record something, e.g., a message or television or radio program, for later use or broadcasting —**pre·re·cord·ed** *adj* —**pre·re·cord·ing** *n*

pre·req·ui·site /pree rékwizit/ *n* an object, quality, or condition that is required in order for something else to happen ○ *A degree is a prerequisite for entry into this profession.* ■ *adj* required in order for something else to happen ○ *A good command of Spanish is prerequisite for the Spanish literature course.*

pre·rog·a·tive /pri róggətiv/ *n* **1. PRIVILEGE RESTRICTED TO PEOPLE OF RANK** an exclusive privilege or right enjoyed by a person or group occupying a particular rank or position ○ *It was her prerogative as leader to choose a successor.* **2. INDIVIDUAL RIGHT OR PRIVILEGE** a privilege or right that allows a particular person or group to give orders or make decisions or judgments ○ *It's not his prerogative to say who can come.* **3. PRIVILEGE RESULTING FROM NATURAL ADVANTAGE** the right conferred by a natural advantage that places somebody in a position of superiority ○ *the prerogatives conferred by age* **4. SOVEREIGN POWER, PRIVILEGE, OR IMMUNITY** the power or right of a monarch or government to do something or be exempt from something **5. SUPERIORITY** superiority in rank or nature [14C. Via French < Latin *praerogativa* < *praerogare* "ask first" < *rogare* "ask"]

Pres. *abbr* President

pre·sa /práyssə/ (*plural* **-se** /práy sày/) *n* *Southwest US* a dam that diverts water from a river into an irrigation canal (**acequia**) [Early 18C. < Italian, "taking up"]

pres·age /préssij, pri sáyj/ *n* **1. PORTENT OR OMEN** a sign or warning of a future event **2. SENSE OF SOMETHING TO COME** a feeling that a particular thing, often something unpleasant, is about to happen **3. FUTURE IMPORT** significance with regard to future events ○ *a moment of great presage* ■ *v* (**pre·saged, pre·sag·ing, pre·sag·es**) **1.** *vt* **FORETELL SOMETHING** to be or give a sign or warning of a future event ○ *Clear skies that night presaged fine weather for the picnic.* **2.** *vt* **HAVE PRESENTIMENT OF SOMETHING** to know intuitively that a particular thing is going to happen **3.** *vti* **PREDICT** to predict a future event [14C. Directly or via French < Latin *praesagire* "forebode" < *sagire* "perceive"] —**pre·sag·er** *n*

pre·sale /pree sáyl/ *n* **1.** a private sale of products, objects, or works of art that takes place before a public sale **2.** the period before something is sold to somebody, or the period before a product, object, or work of art is placed on sale to the general public

pres·by·o·pi·a /prèzbee ṓpee ə/ *n* progressive reduction in the eye's ability to focus, with consequent difficulty in reading at the normal distance, associated with aging. It typically starts at middle age, and is due to age-related loss of elasticity of the lens. [Late 18C. < Greek *presbus* "man of advanced years"] —**pres·by·ope** /prézbee ṑp/ *n* —**pres·by·op·ic** /prèzbee óppik/ *adj*

pres·by·ter /prézbitər/ *n* **1. MEMBER OF EARLY CHURCH ADMINISTRATION** in early Christianity, an administrative official of a local church **2. MEMBER OF CLERGY** an ordained member of the clergy in many Christian churches **3. LAY OFFICIAL IN PRESBYTERIAN CHURCH** any layperson chosen by the congregation to govern a Presbyterian or other Reformed church **4. POWERFUL SELF-APPOINTED LEADER** a powerful, self-appointed or self-anointed person, e.g., a leader of a group or faction or a backer of a major movement (*disapproving*) [Late 16C. Via ecclesiastical Latin < Greek *presbuteros* "elder of the church" < *presbus* "man of advanced years"]

pres·byt·er·ate /prez bíttərət, -ràyt/ *n* **1.** the office or position of a presbyter **2.** an order or group of presbyters

pres·by·te·ri·al /prèzbi tèeree əl/ *adj* relating to a presbyter or presbytery

pres·by·te·ri·an /prèzbi tèeree ən/ *adj* characterized by or relating to the government of a church by democratically elected lay officials ■ *n* a supporter and advocate of church government by democratically elected lay officials

Pres·by·te·ri·an *adj* relating or belonging to the Presbyterian Church or any Protestant church governed by the presbyterian system ■ *n* a member of a presbyterian church —**Pres·by·te·ri·an·ism** *n*

pres·by·ter·y /prézbi tèrree/ (*plural* **-ies**) *n* **1. GROUP OF PRESBYTERS** a group of presbyters in the early

Christian church or in a modern Presbyterian church **2.** COURT OF PRESBYTERIAN CHURCH a court composed of ministers and lay officials in a Presbyterian Church, or the churches under the jurisdiction of such a court **3.** GOVERNMENT BY PRESBYTERS the government of a church by democratically elected lay officials **4.** PART OF CHURCH FOR CLERGY part of a church or cathedral, or a separate building, for the use of clergy only **5.** HOME OF ROMAN CATHOLIC PARISH PRIEST the home of a Roman Catholic parish priest

pre·school /preé skòol/ *adj* **1.** UNDER SCHOOL AGE below the age at which compulsory schooling begins **2.** FOR PRESCHOOL CHILDREN relating to or provided for children below the age at which compulsory schooling begins ■ *n* SCHOOL FOR YOUNG CHILDREN a school for children below the age at which they can enter kindergarten or the first grade —**pre·school·er** *n* —**pre·school·ing** *n*

pre·sci·ence /preéshee ənss, pré-, -sh'nss/ *n* knowledge of actions or events before they happen [14C. Via French < late Latin *praescientia* "foreknowledge" < Latin *praescient-* (see PRESCIENT)]

pre·sci·ent /preéshee ənt, pré-, -sh'nt/ *adj* having or showing knowledge of actions or events before they take place [Early 17C. < Latin *praescient-*, present participle of *praescire* "know beforehand" < *scire* "know"] —**pre·sci·ent·ly** *adv*

pre·scind /pri sínd/ (**-scind·ed, -scind·ing, -scinds**) *vi* to detach the mind from something, typically a concept, notion, or fixed idea (*formal*) [Mid-17C. < Latin *praescindere* "cut off in front" < *scindere* "cut off"]

Pres·cott /préskət, -kòt/ city in central Arizona, near the source of the Hassayampa River, southwest of Flagstaff. Population: 36,300 (2002 estimate).

Pres·cott, William Hickling (1796–1859) US historian. His works include *History of the Conquest of Mexico* (1843) and *History of the Conquest of Peru* (1847).

pre·scribe /pri skríb/ (**-scribed, -scrib·ing, -scribes**) *v* **1.** *vti* ORDER USE OF MEDICATION to order a course of treatment for a patient, usually the use of a particular drug at set times and dosages ○ *Most doctors are wary of prescribing antibiotics for relatively minor infections.* **2.** *vt* RECOMMEND REMEDY to recommend a particular course of action or treatment as a remedy for something ○ *I prescribe lots of tender loving care.* **3.** *vt* LAY DOWN RULE to say with authority that a course of action should be taken ○ *the penalties prescribed by law* **4.** *vi* SET DOWN REGULATIONS to lay down rules or laws **5.** *vti* LAW CLAIM PROPERTY RIGHT to claim a right to something on the grounds of possession over a long period of time [15C. < Latin *praescribere* "write before" < *scribere* "write"] —**pre·scrib·a·ble** *adj*—**pre·scrib·er** *n*

pre·script /preé skrìpt/ (*formal*) *n* a rule or regulation that has been laid down ■ *adj* laid down as a rule or regulation [Mid-16C. < Latin *praescriptum* "something prescribed" < past participle of *praescribere* (see PRESCRIBE)]

pre·scrip·tion /pri skrípshən/ *n* **1.** WRITTEN ORDER FOR MEDICINE a written order issued by a physician or other qualified practitioner that authorizes a pharmacist to supply a specific medication for a patient, with instructions on its use (*often used before a noun*) **2.** PRESCRIBED MEDICINE a drug or other medication prescribed by a physician or other qualified practitioner **3.** ORDER FOR LENS TO CORRECT EYESIGHT a written order from an optometrist or ophthalmologist for glasses or contact lenses of a particular type and strength to correct the eyesight of a particular person (*often used before a noun*) ○ *prescription sunglasses* **4.** PROVEN FORMULA FOR SOMETHING a proven formula for causing something else to happen ○ *Caring about others' feelings is a prescription for a fulfilling life.* **5.** AUTHORITATIVE RECOMMENDATION the act of ordering or recommending a particular course of action authoritatively **6.** SOMETHING ORDERED OR RECOMMENDED a practice or course of action that is authoritatively ordered or recommended **7.** LAW PRESUMPTION OF RIGHT OF POSSESSION a presumption of the right of possession of property, based on long-term exercise of property rights [14C. Via French < Latin *praescription-* < *praescribere* (see PRESCRIBE)]

pre·scrip·tion drug *n* a drug that can be dispensed only upon presentation of a legally valid prescription

pre·scrip·tive /pri skríptiv/ *adj* **1.** MAKING OR ADHERING TO REGULATIONS establishing or adhering to rules and regulations ○ *prescriptive grammarians* **2.** CUSTOMARY based on or authorized by long-standing custom (*dated*) **3.** LAW GROUNDED IN LEGAL PRESCRIPTION based on legal prescription —**pre·scrip·tive·ly** *adv* —**pre·scrip·tive·ness** *n*

pre·sell /pree sél/ (**-sold** /-sṓld/, **-sell·ing, -sells**) *vt* **1.** POPULARIZE SOMETHING BEFOREHAND to promote a product or entertainment before it is generally available to the public, by means of advertising and publicity **2.** SELL BOOK EARLY to sell a book before its official publication date **3.** ARRANGE SALE OF SOMETHING BEFOREHAND to agree to sell a house, car, or other item before it is actually available

pres·ence /préz'nss/ *n* **1.** EXISTENCE IN PLACE the physical existence or detectability of something in a place at a particular time ○ *the presence of contaminants in the water supply* **2.** ATTENDANCE somebody's attendance at an event or physical existence in a place with other people ○ *Our presence is requested at the board meeting.* **3.** AREA WITHIN SIGHT OR EARSHOT the immediate vicinity of somebody or something ○ *How dare you use that kind of language in my presence!* **4.** IMPRESSIVE QUALITY an impressive appearance or bearing ○ *has a certain presence about her that garners respect* **5.** INVISIBLE SUPPOSED SUPERNATURAL BEING a supernatural spirit that is felt to be nearby ○ *A malevolent presence filled the room.* **6.** PERSON PRESENT somebody who is notably present ○ *the venerable scholar, a dignified presence in the academic procession* **7.** GROUP OF OFFICIAL PERSONNEL a group of official personnel, especially police, military forces, or diplomats, present or stationed in a place to represent their country and maintain its interest ○ *maintained a heavy military presence in the capital* [14C. Via French < Latin *praesentia* < *praesent-* (see PRESENT[2])] ◇ **make your** *or* **its presence felt** to influence what is going on

pres·ence of mind *n* the ability to remain calm and act decisively and effectively in a crisis ○ *At least she had the presence of mind to call the fire department.*

pre·sent[1] *v* /pri zént/ (**-sent·ed, -sent·ing, -sents**) **1.** *vt* GIVE SOMETHING to give or hand something to somebody, often in a humorously formal manner ○ *Then she presented me with the bill!* **2.** *vt* AWARD SOMETHING TO SOMEBODY to give or award something to somebody in a formal or ceremonial manner or at a ceremonial occasion ○ *The mayor came in person to present the prizes.* **3.** *vt* OFFER SOMETHING FORMALLY to offer or convey something such as your compliments or apologies to somebody formally ○ *May I present my warmest congratulations?* **4.** *vt* HAND SOMETHING OVER OFFICIALLY to put something forward for inspection or consideration, typically in a formal or official manner or capacity ○ *proposals to be presented at the next meeting* **5.** *vt* MAKE SOMETHING EVIDENT to show or display something ○ *taking care to present his best side to the camera* **6.** *vt* POSE PROBLEM to pose a problem or difficulty to somebody ○ *presenting a direct threat to national security* **7.** *vt* LAW BRING CHARGE to put a charge before a court of law so that it can be considered or tried **8.** *vt* INTRODUCE SOMEBODY FORMALLY to introduce somebody formally, especially to somebody of higher rank ○ *They were presented to the Queen.* **9.** *vt* INTRODUCE WOMAN INTO SOCIETY to introduce a young woman formally into fashionable society ○ *Her family planned to present her at the Christmas debutante ball in New York.* **10.** *vt* HOST PROGRAM to introduce, or act as the host of, a television or radio program or an infomercial ○ *He used to present a game show.* **11.** *vt* OFFER PUBLIC ENTERTAINMENT to bring a movie, play, or other form of entertainment to the public **12.** *vt* PORTRAY SOMETHING ARTISTICALLY to represent something or somebody in a particular way in the arts ○ *In the film, Romeo and Juliet are presented as modern teenagers.* **13.** **pre·sent your·self** *vr* BE IN APPOINTED PLACE to appear, especially at an appointed time and place ○ *Present yourselves at the gate at eight o'clock.* **14.** *vr* ARISE to come into being or happen ○ *when an opportunity presents itself* **15.** *vi* PRODUCE SPECIFIC IMPRESSION to produce a particular impression, especially a favorable one (*formal*) ○ *She presents as a pleasant young woman.* **16.** *vi* MED HAVE PARTICULAR SYMPTOMS to exhibit a particular symptom or symptoms on examination **17.** *vi* MED EXIT BIRTH CANAL IN POSITION to appear during the process of being born (*refers to fetuses*) ■ *n* /prézzənt/ GIFT something that is given to somebody out of kindness or to celebrate an occasion such as a birthday [13C. Via French < Latin *praesentare* "make present" < *praesent-* (see PRESENT[2])] —**pres·ent·ee** /prèzz'n teé/ *n* —**pre·sent·er** *n*

SYNONYMS See *give*.

pres·ent[2] /prézz'nt/ *adj* **1.** CURRENTLY HAPPENING taking place or existing now ○ *in our present circumstances* ○ *up to the present day* **2.** IN PLACE existing, detectable, or in attendance in a place ○ *There were over a hundred people present at the reception.* **3.** NOW UNDER DISCUSSION being considered or talked about at this time **4.** GRAM RELATING TO CURRENT TIME describes a verb form or tense that expresses the current time ■ *n* **1.** THE HERE AND NOW the current time or moment ○ *The story takes place in the present.* **2.** GRAM CURRENT-TIME VERB TENSE a grammatical tense that expresses current time **3.** GRAM CURRENT-TIME VERB a form of a verb used to express the present tense, indicating that the action is happening now ■ **pres·ents** *npl* LEGAL OR FORMAL DOCUMENT this legal or formal document (*formal*) ○ *terms discussed in these presents* [13C. Via French < Latin *praesent-*, present participle of *praeesse* "be in front of" < *esse* "be"] ◇ **at present** just now ◇ **for the present** as far as the present time is concerned

pre·sent·a·ble /pri zéntəb'l/ *adj* **1.** looking or being good enough to be introduced to other people ○ *Make sure you look presentable.* **2.** good enough to be offered, shown, or given to other people ○ *still a presentable gift* —**pre·sent·a·bil·i·ty** /-zèntə bíllətee/ *n* —**pre·sent·a·bly** *adv*

pre·sent arms /pri zènt-/ *n* a drill movement in which a salute is given by bringing a rifle vertically in front of the body, or the command to give such a salute —**pre·sent arms** *vi*

pres·en·ta·tion /prèzz'n táysh'n/ *n* **1.** ACT OF PRESENTING SOMETHING an act of presenting something or the state of being presented **2.** PREPARED PERFORMANCE FOR AUDIENCE a performance, exhibition, or demonstration put on before an audience **3.** FORMAL HANDING OVER OF GIFT the action of presenting somebody with an award or a token of appreciation in front of other people, or an occasion when this is done ○ *the presentation of the trophy* **4.** PREPARED REPORT READ BEFORE AUDIENCE a formal talk made to a group of people, e.g., on somebody's recent work or some aspect of business, often with handouts, diagrams, or other visual aids ○ *He gave a presentation on modern irrigation methods.* **5.** SOMEBODY'S INTRODUCTION INTO SPECIAL SOCIAL GROUP an occasion when somebody is first presented into society or at court, or the official or recognized process of first presenting somebody in this way **6.** WAY SOMETHING APPEARS WHEN OFFERED the manner in which something is shown, expressed, or laid out for other people to see ○ *Presentation is an important part of the chef's job.* **7.** MED PART OF BABY APPEARING FIRST the part of a baby that appears first at birth, normally the crown of the head ○ *a breech presentation* **8.** PHILOSOPHY, PSYCHOL OBJECT OF PERCEPTION something that is perceived, remembered, or acquired as knowledge **9.** CHR ACT OF NOMINATING CLERGY MEMBER the act or power of nominating a member of the clergy to a paid office in a church **10.** COMM same as **presentment** (sense 3) —**pres·en·ta·tion·al** *adj*

pre·sen·ta·tion·ism /prèzz'n táysh'n ìzzəm/ *n* the theory that things in the external world are identical with people's perceptions of them —**pre·sen·ta·tion·ist** *n*

Pres·en·ta·tion of the Vir·gin Mar·y *n* a festival celebrated by the Roman Catholic and Eastern Orthodox churches marking the Virgin Mary's presentation at the temple. Date: November 21.

pre·sent·a·tive /pri zéntətiv/ *adj* able to be known directly without any reflective or cognitive process being necessary —**pre·sent·a·tive·ness** *n*

pres·ent-day /prézz'nt-/ *adj* found or existing in modern times ○ *out of touch with present-day society and the Internet culture*

pre·sent·ee·ism /prèzz'n teé ìzzəm/ *n* the practice of

spending longer hours at work than are contractually required

Pres·ent E·ra /prézz'nt-/ *n* the period after the birth of Jesus Christ (*used in dates*)

USAGE See ***A.D.***

pre·sen·tient /pree sénshənt, -shee ənt/ *adj* having a definite and usually uneasy sense that something is going to happen, or being aware of something before it occurs [Early 19C. < Latin *praesentient-*, present participle of *praesentire* "perceive beforehand" < *sentire* "feel"]

pre·sen·ti·ment /pri zéntəmənt/ *n* an awareness of some event, especially an unpleasant event, before it takes place and before there is any reason to suspect it or know about it ○ *a presentiment of doom* [Early 18C. < obsolete French *présentiment* < Latin *praesentire* (see PRESENTIENT)] —**pre·sen·ti·men·tal** /-zèntə mént'l/ *adj*

pres·ent·ly /prézz'ntlee/ *adv* **1.** not at this exact moment but in a short while ○ *I'll be there presently.* **2.** now, or during the current period, especially if not at some other time (*some people object to this usage*) ○ *Yes, he's presently engaged in a research job for the company.*

pre·sent·ment /pri zéntmənt/ *n* **1.** PRESENTATION the act of presenting something, or the way in which something is presented **2.** STATEMENT BY JURY formerly, a formal statement made on oath by a grand jury to a court concerning facts and matters within their own knowledge **3.** COMM PRESENTING OF NEGOTIABLE DOCUMENT the presenting of a negotiable document for payment

pres·ent par·ti·ci·ple /prèzz'nt-/ *n* the form of a verb that suggests a progressive or active sense and that ends in "-ing" in English, e.g., "flying"

pres·ent per·fect /prèzz'nt-/ *n* the form of a verb that suggests that an action has been completed, formed in English by preceding the verb with "have" or "has" and usually ending the verb with "-ed," e.g., "have departed" —**pres·ent per·fect** *adj*

pres·ent tense *n* the tense of a verb that suggests actions or the situation at the time of speaking or writing

pres·ent val·ue /prèzz'nt-/ *n* the value now of a sum of money expected to be received in the future, calculated by subtracting the interest and other value that will accrue in the intervening period ○ *The judge reduced the jury's award of damages to present value, as required by law.*

pres·er·va·tion /prèzzər váysh'n/ *n* **1.** PROTECTION FROM HARM the guarding of something from danger, harm, or injury **2.** MAINTENANCE UNCHANGED the maintenance of something, especially something of historic value, in an unchanged condition **3.** UPHOLDING OF SOMETHING the keeping of something intangible intact ○ *preservation of freedom of speech*

pres·er·va·tion·ist /prèzzər váysh'nist/ *n* somebody who tries to prevent things from being damaged, destroyed, or altered, particularly things of natural or historical interest —**pres·er·va·tion·ism** *n*

pre·ser·va·tive /pri zúrvətiv/ *adj* having the ability to protect something from decay or spoilage ■ *n* something that provides protection from decay or spoilage, e.g., a food additive

pre·serve /pri zúrv/ *vt* (**-served, -serv·ing, -serves**) **1.** MAKE SURE SOMETHING LASTS to keep something protected from anything that would cause its current quality or condition to change or deteriorate or cause it to fall out of use ○ *They are anxious to preserve the area's rural character.* ○ *We need to preserve professional standards of conduct.* **2.** MAINTAIN SOMETHING to keep up or maintain something ○ *She preserved a cool and composed manner throughout the interrogation.* **3.** TREAT FOOD FOR STORAGE to treat or store food in such a way as to protect it from decay, e.g., by pickling, drying, salting, freezing, or canning **4.** MAKE JAM FROM SOMETHING to make jelly, jam, or marmalade out of a fruit **5.** KEEP ANIMALS IN SECURE AREA to rear wild animals, especially fish and birds, in a protected area of water or land, so that they can be fished or shot for sport in the hunting season **6.** PROTECT SOMEBODY OR SOMETHING to protect somebody or something from danger, especially the danger of being killed or damaged (*formal or literary*) ○ *prayed that they would be preserved from danger* ■ *n* **1.** EXCLUSIVE AREA OF ACTIVITY something that one particular person or group regards as being his, her, or its exclusive concern, or a place kept for one person or group to enjoy exclusively ○ *The children considered the tree house their own preserve.* **2.** FRUIT JELLY OR JAM a sweet thick foodstuff made by boiling fruit in sugar and water, eaten on bread or in desserts and cakes. Preserves can be kept for several years in airtight jars, bottles, or cans. (*often used in the plural*) **3.** ENVIRON AREA WHERE WILDLIFE IS PROTECTED a piece of water or land owned by the government or a conservation group, where wildlife, plants, or geographic features are protected or where fish or wild animals are bred [14C. Via French < medieval Latin *praeservare* "guard beforehand" < Latin *servare* "keep"] —**pre·serv·a·ble** *adj*

pre·serv·er /pri zúrvər/ *n* something used to keep somebody or something safe, undamaged, or unchanged

pre·set *vt* /pree sét/ (**-set, -set·ting, -sets**) to arrange the settings of a timing device controlling an electrical appliance so that the appliance is automatically switched on at a specific time ■ *n* /prée sèt/ an electronic timing device or system that is used to make an appliance operate at a later time

pre·shrunk /pree shrúngk/ *adj* with the fabric already shrunk before being sold, so that it will not shrink when washed

pre·side /pri zíd/ (**-sid·ed, -sid·ing, -sides**) *vi* **1.** BE OFFICIALLY IN CHARGE to be the chairperson or hold a similar position of authority at a formal gathering of people **2.** HAVE CONTROL to be the most powerful person or the one everyone else obeys, usually in a specific place or situation ○ *the question of who will preside over the business once their mother retires* **3.** PERFORM AS INSTRUMENTALIST to be the featured instrumentalist in a musical performance ○ *preside at the organ* [Early 17C. Via French < Latin *praesidere* "sit in front of" < *sedere* "sit"] —**pre·sid·er** *n*

pres·i·den·cy /prézzid'nssee/ (*plural* **-cies**) *n* **1.** *also* **Pres·i·den·cy** POSITION OF PRESIDENT OF NATION the job or function of president of a republic, or a president's term of office **2.** JOB OF PRESIDENT the status, post, or function of being president of a company, society, institution, or similar body ○ *The presidency of the club turned out to be a thankless task.* **3.** LATTER-DAY SAINTS COUNCIL a three-person executive council in the Church of Jesus Christ of Latter-Day Saints **4.** LATTER-DAY SAINTS GOVERNING COUNCIL the governing body of the Church of Jesus Christ of Latter-Day Saints

pres·i·dent /prézzid'nt/, **Pres·i·dent** *n* **1.** HEAD OF STATE OF REPUBLIC the head of state, or head of state and chief political executive, of a republic. See table on next page **2.** HIGHEST-RANKING MEMBER OF ASSOCIATION the highest-ranking member of an organization or institution **3.** HEAD OF COMPANY the highest-ranking executive officer of a business or corporation **4.** HEAD OF EDUCATIONAL OR GOVERNMENTAL ESTABLISHMENT the highest-ranking executive officer of some universities, colleges, government departments, legal divisions, and other public offices **5.** SOMEBODY IN CHARGE OF MEETING somebody who is appointed or elected to oversee a meeting **6.** LATTER-DAY SAINTS LEADER in the Church of Jesus Christ of Latter-Day Saints, a man who is a member of the church's governing board. Together with counselors and the Council of the Twelve Apostles, he makes major church policy and decisions. [14C. Via French < Latin *praesident-* < present participle of *praesidere* (see PRESIDE)] —**pres·i·dent·ship** *n*

pres·i·dent-e·lect (*plural* **pres·i·dents-e·lect**) *n* an elected or appointed president who has not yet been officially installed

pres·i·den·tial /prèzzə dénshəl/ *adj* **1.** RELATING TO PRESIDENT relating to the post of president, or used or owned by a president ○ *The presidential elections dominated the news.* **2.** LIKE PRESIDENT done in the manner of a president, or having the appearance of a president ○ *appeared very presidential during the debates* **3.** LED BY PRESIDENT presided over by a president, or presiding like one —**pres·i·den·tial·ly** *adv*

Pres·i·den·tial Range /prèzzə dènshəl-/ chain of mountains in northern New Hampshire, in the White Mountains. The highest peak in the range is Mount Washington, 6,288 ft./1,917 m.

Pres·i·dents' Day *n* an official holiday commemorating the birthdays of George Washington and Abraham Lincoln. Date: third Monday in February.

pre·si·di·o /prə síddee ō/ (*plural* **-os**) *n Southwest US* a fortified settlement, especially of the type established by Spanish colonizers in the southwestern part of what is now the United States [Mid-18C. Via Spanish < Latin *praesidium* "garrison, fortification" < *praesidere* (see PRESIDE)]

pre·sid·i·um /prə síddee əm/ (*plural* **-i·a** /-ee ə/ or **-i·ums**) *n* a permanent executive committee that acted for a larger legislature in the former Soviet Union and other Communist countries [Early 20C. Via Russian < Latin *praesidium* (see PRESIDIO)]

Elvis Presley

Pres·ley /prézzlee/, **Elvis** (1935–77) US singer and actor. Renowned as a pioneer of rock and roll, he also acted in several Hollywood movies. Full name **Presley, Elvis Aron**. Known as **The King**

> "I learned very early in life that: 'Without a song, the day would never end; without a song, a man ain't got a friend; without a song, the road would never bend—without a song.' So I keep singing a song. Goodnight. Thank you."
> [Elvis Presley, *Acceptance speech, Ten Outstanding Young Men of the Year Awards*; January 16, 1971]

press[1] /press/ *v* (**pressed, press·ing, press·es**) **1.** *vti* PUSH AGAINST SOMETHING to use a steady and significant force to put weight on something, sometimes to make it move or start working ○ *press the button* **2.** *vt* SQUEEZE JUICE OUT OF SOMETHING to squeeze the juice or oil out of something using force to compress it ○ *pressing grapes* **3.** *vt* SMOOTH SOMETHING WITH HOT IRON to remove unwanted creases from a garment or piece of cloth, or make a deliberate crease in a garment or piece of cloth, using a hot iron or other device ○ *pressed a shirt* **4.** *vt* CHANGE OBJECT'S SHAPE BY SQUEEZING to change the shape of something by squeezing it or putting a steady weight on it, especially in order to make it more compact ○ *pressed the clay into a ball* **5.** *vt* FLATTEN SOMETHING TO PRESERVE IT to flatten and dry a natural object such as a flower so that it does not decompose and can be kept or used decoratively ○ *pressed flowers as a hobby* **6.** *vt* MAKE SOMETHING USING MOLD to form something in a mold, especially to make phonograph records **7.** *vt* HOLD SOMETHING TIGHTLY to grip or clasp somebody or something firmly but not roughly with the hands or arms, especially to show affection or moral support ○ *She pressed his hand in sympathy.* **8.** *vi* TRY TOO HARD to make great or greater efforts in order to achieve something, but not necessarily succeed, as an athlete under stress might ○ *Late in the crucial game, the players were obviously pressing and made one error after another.* **9.** *vt* FORCE SOMEBODY to force somebody into doing something he or she did not want or intend to do ○ *They pressed her into accepting the nomination.* **10.** *vt* TRY TO OBTAIN SOMETHING FROM SOMEBODY to ask somebody persistently or forcefully to supply, accept, or do something ○ *They pressed him for an immediate response.* **11.** *vt* EMPHASIZE SOMETHING to make sure that something is fully recognized and understood or stress its importance ○ *pressed his point* **12.** *vt* DEMAND

PRESIDENTS OF THE UNITED STATES

Term of office	President	Political party
1789–1797	George Washington	
1797–1801	John Adams	*Federalist*
1801–1809	Thomas Jefferson	*Democratic-Republican*
1809–1817	James Madison	*Democratic-Republican*
1817–1825	James Monroe	*Democratic-Republican*
1825–1829	John Quincy Adams	*Democratic-Republican*
1829–1837	Andrew Jackson	*Democrat*
1837–1841	Martin Van Buren	*Democrat*
1841	William Henry Harrison	*Whig*
1841–1845	John Tyler	*Whig*
1845–1849	James Polk	*Democrat*
1849–1850	Zachary Taylor	*Whig*
1850–1853	Millard Fillmore	*Whig*
1853–1857	Franklin Pierce	*Democrat*
1857–1861	James Buchanan	*Democrat*
1861–1865	Abraham Lincoln	*Republican*
1865–1869	Andrew Johnson	*Democrat*
1869–1877	Ulysses S. Grant	*Republican*
1877–1881	Rutherford B. Hayes	*Republican*
1881	James Garfield	*Republican*
1881–1885	Chester A. Arthur	*Republican*
1885–1889	Grover Cleveland	*Democrat*
1889–1893	Benjamin Harrison	*Republican*
1893–1897	Grover Cleveland	*Democrat*
1897–1901	William McKinley	*Republican*
1901–1909	Theodore Roosevelt	*Republican*
1909–1913	William Howard Taft	*Republican*
1913–1921	Woodrow Wilson	*Democrat*
1921–1923	Warren G. Harding	*Republican*
1923–1929	Calvin Coolidge	*Republican*
1929–1933	Herbert Hoover	*Republican*
1933–1945	Franklin Delano Roosevelt	*Democrat*
1945–1953	Harry S. Truman	*Democrat*
1953–1961	Dwight D. Eisenhower	*Republican*
1961–1963	John F. Kennedy	*Democrat*
1963–1969	Lyndon Johnson	*Democrat*
1969–1974	Richard Nixon	*Republican*
1974–1977	Gerald Ford	*Republican*
1977–1981	Jimmy Carter	*Democrat*
1981–1989	Ronald Reagan	*Republican*
1989–1993	George Bush	*Republican*
1993–2001	Bill Clinton	*Democrat*
2001–	George W. Bush	*Republican*

SOMETHING to plead or demand something insistently **13.** *vi* **MOVE AS CROWD** to move together as a body, especially in a forceful way or so as to crowd somebody or something ○ *The crowd pressed forward as the gates opened.* **14.** *vi* **REQUIRE ATTENTION** to need to be dealt with urgently (*dated or formal*) ○ *I'd like to help now, but business presses.* **15.** *vti* BASKETBALL **HARASS OPPONENT** to use a harassing and aggressive defense against an opponent in basketball ■ *n* **1. ACT OF PRESSING** an act of pressing something ○ *I gave the doorbell a few presses but nobody answered.* **2. FOOD PREPARATION DEVICE** a piece of equipment designed to crush something to release the juices or create a pulp ○ *a garlic press* **3. DEVICE FOR FLATTENING SOMETHING** a piece of equipment used to keep or make something smooth and uncreased ○ *a trouser press* **4. LINEN CLOSET** a shelved closet, usually of a large size, for storing bed or table linens or clothes **5.** RACKET GAMES **CLAMP FOR RACKETS** a clamp for holding a tennis or other racket to prevent it from warping when it is not in use **6. MACHINE FOR SHAPING MATERIALS BY MECHANICAL PRESSURE** a machine that, by applying pressure to a piece of metal or other material, can shape, form, cut, stamp, or otherwise cause a physical change to occur **7. NEWSPAPERS OR REPORTERS** the news-gathering business generally, or all the people involved in gathering and reporting on the news, especially journalists working on newspapers ○ *refused to talk to the press* **8. COMMENTS BY REPORTERS** the opinions expressed in articles or reviews in the newspapers or magazines ○ *His new musical had a lot of good press.* **9.** PRINTING same as **printing press** **10.** PUBL **PUBLISHING COMPANY** a company that publishes books (*used especially in names*) **11.** PRINTING **PROCESS OR SKILL OF PRINTING** the technical or physical process used by a printer and the skills a printer requires ○ *about to go to press* **12. CROWD** a tightly packed crowd of people **13. POWERFUL MOVEMENT** the crowding and pressing together of a lot of people or things at the same time (*literary*) ○ *He could not move because of the press of people.* **14. DEFENSE IN SPORTS** an aggressive defense, especially in basketball **15. LIFTING OF WEIGHT ABOVE HEAD** in weightlifting, a lift in which the weight is raised to shoulder height and then to above the head without moving the legs [14C. Via French < Latin *pressare* "keep on pressing" < *press-*, past participle of *premere* "press"] —**press·er** *n* ◇ **be pressed for something** to be short of something, usually time

ORIGIN The Latin word *premere* "to press," from which *press* is derived, is also the source of English *compress, depress, express, impress*[1], *oppress, repress,* and *suppress.*

press for *vt* to seek or demand something with great urgency ○ *They pressed for an immediate review of the situation.*

press on *vi* to continue in an urgent or persistent manner ○ *Night was falling but they pressed on despite their weariness.*

press[2] /press/ *vt* (**pressed, press·ing, press·es**) **1. FORCE SOMEBODY INTO MILITARY SERVICE** to forcibly recruit somebody into military service **2. USE SOMEBODY OR SOMETHING FOR NEW PURPOSE** to take somebody or something out of its intended place or function and put it to a different use ■ *n* **FORCING OF SOMEBODY INTO MILITARY SERVICE** the act of recruiting people into military service by force [Late 16C. Alteration (influenced by PRESS[1]) of obsolete *prest* "enlist by paying in advance," via French < Latin *praestare* < *stare* "to stand"]

press a·gen·cy *n* MEDIA same as **news agency**

press a·gent *n* a promoter who contacts, liaises with, and gives information to the press on behalf of a client —**press a·gent·ry** *n*

press as·so·ci·a·tion *n* **1.** MEDIA same as **news agency** **2.** *US* a national, state, or local organization of media outlets and their representatives

press·board /préss bàwrd/ *n US* **1.** a heavy glazed composition board **2.** a small ironing board used especially for pressing the sleeves of garments

press box *n* a section in a sports stadium or similar venue kept exclusively for journalists to work in

press brake *n* MECH ENG same as **brake**[4] (sense 2)

press con·fer·ence *n* a meeting to which members of the press are invited to hear a prepared statement and usually to ask questions about that statement

pressed /prest/ *adj* **1.** made compact and firm by being forced mechanically into cans or containers ○ *pressed meat* **2.** having urgent or worrying things to deal with ○ *She is particularly pressed today, so I won't ask her to help if I can avoid it.*

pressed meat, pressed souse meat, press meat *n regional* same as **headcheese**

REGIONAL NOTE See ***headcheese.***

press gal·ler·y *n* a raised gallery with seating at the back of a courtroom or legislative assembly room, where newspaper reporters and other members of the press can sit

press gang *n* formerly, a group of military personnel whose job was to find people to force into military service

press-gang *vti* to force people into military service or into doing anything that they are reluctant to do ○ *I never wanted to go to camp – my parents press-ganged me into it.*

press·ing /préssing/ *adj* **1. URGENT** needing to be attended to without delay ○ *a pressing engagement* **2. VERY PERSISTENT** persistent and demanding, and therefore difficult to ignore or refuse ○ *Her invitations were so pressing that we eventually had to accept.* ■ *n* **PHONOGRAPH RECORDS MADE AT ONE TIME** all the phonograph records produced at one time from a master mold —**press·ing·ly** *adv* —**press·ing·ness** *n*

press kit *n* a package of background and promotional material relating to a product, distributed to the media by a publicist or publicity department

press·man /présmən/ (*plural* **-men** /-mən/) *n* somebody, especially a man, who operates a printing press

press·mark /préss maark/ *n UK* same as **shelf mark**

press of can·vas *n* SAILING same as **press of sail**

press of·fi·cer *n* somebody employed by an organization or government department to provide the news media with information about the organization or department

press of sail *n* the largest amount of sail that a ship can safely carry

pres·sor /préssər/ *adj* relating to or bringing about an increase in blood pressure

press peach *n Southern US* a clingstone peach

REGIONAL NOTE ***Press peach*** is the Lower Southern counterpart of *plum peach.* Most common in lower Georgia, Alabama, Mississippi, and southwestern Louisiana, the term is also used in Florida and eastern Louisiana, although less frequently.

press·per·son /préss pùrss'n/ (*plural* **-per·sons** or **-peo·ple** /-peep'l/) *n* somebody who operates a printing press

press re·lease *n* an official statement or account of a news story that is specially prepared and issued to newspapers and other news media for them to make known to the public

press·room /préss ròom, -ròom/ *n* **1.** an enclosed area in a newspaper plant or printing establishment where the presses are located **2.** a place at a particular site, especially the White House, where reporters work when not actually covering a newsworthy event at that site

press·run /préss rùn/ *n* **1.** the continuous running of a printing press until a set number of copies is printed **2.** the number of copies run off in a continuous printing operation

press sec·re·tar·y *n* an employee responsible for managing the news media on behalf of an organization or a prominent person

press stud *n UK* same as **snap** *n* (sense 7)

press-up *n UK* FITNESS same as **pushup** (sense 1)

pres·sure /préshər/ *n* **1. PROCESS OF PRESSING STEADILY** the applying of a firm regular weight or force against somebody or something ○ *The pressure of her hand on his was comforting.* **2.** CONSTANT STATE OF WORRY AND URGENCY powerful and stressful demands on somebody's time, attention, and energy, or a demand of this sort ○ *They were under constant pressure to achieve increased output targets.* **3.** FORCE THAT PUSHES OR URGES something that affects thoughts and behavior in a powerful way, usually in the form of several outside influences working together persuasively **4.** PHYS FORCE PER UNIT AREA the force acting on a surface divided by the area over which it acts. Symbol *p* **5.** METEOROL same as **atmospheric pressure** ■ *vt* (**-sured, -sur·ing, -sures**) MAKE SOMEBODY DO SOMETHING to apply great persuasion or a strong influence on somebody in order to force him or her to do something ○ *They were pressured into selling by the rest of the family.* [14C. < Latin *pressura* < *press-* (see PRESS[1])] —**pres·sure·less** *adj*

pres·sure cab·in *n* an airtight cabin in an aircraft or spacecraft in which air pressure is maintained at a greater level than that of the outside atmospheric pressure for the comfort and safety of the occupants

pres·sure cook·er *n* **1.** a specially designed pot used to steam food at high pressure, at a higher temperature and in a shorter time than by boiling **2.** a place or situation in which people feel great stress (*slang*) ○ *The mayor's office is a real pressure cooker.* —**pres·sure-cook** *vt*

pres·sure gauge *n* a device or instrument used to measure the pressure of a gas or liquid, e.g., a gauge that measures the air pressure in the tires of a car

pres·sure group *n* a number of people who work together to make their concerns known to those in government and to influence the passage of legislation

pres·sure point *n* a point at which an artery can be compressed against a bone using a finger, stemming blood flow to the part of the body that the artery supplies

pres·sure sore *n* MED same as **bedsore**

pres·sure suit *n* an inflatable airtight suit, similar to that worn by deep-sea divers, used to protect against the effects of low pressure at very high altitude or in space

pres·sure ves·sel *n* a cylindrical or spherically shaped container designed to withstand bursting pressures

pres·sur·ize /préshə rīz/ (**-ized, -iz·ing, -iz·es**) *vt* **1.** to increase the air pressure in an enclosed space, e.g., inside an aircraft, in order to maintain air at close to normal atmospheric pressure when the external air pressure falls **2.** to increase the pressure of a gas or liquid in a container beyond normal levels —**pres·sur·i·za·tion** /prèshəri záysh'n/ *n* —**pres·sur·iz·er** *n*

press·work /préss wùrk/ *n* the operation or management of a printing press, or the work done by it

pres·ti·dig·i·ta·tion /prèstə dijə táysh'n/ *n* sleight of hand used in performing magic tricks (*formal or humorous*) [Mid-19C. < French < *prestidigitateur* "person practicing sleight of hand" < *preste* "nimble" + Latin *digitus* "finger"] —**pres·ti·dig·i·ta·tor** /prèstə díjjə taytər/ *n*

pres·tige /pre stéezh, -stéej/ *n* **1.** honor, awe, or high opinion inspired by or derived from a high-ranking, influential, or successful person or product **2.** attractiveness and importance that is very obvious or enviable, associated with wealthy or successful people ○ *It's a prestige car and its price reflects that.* [Mid-17C. Via French < Latin *praestigiae* "illusions, juggler's tricks"] —**pres·ti·gious** /pre stéejəss, -stíjjəss/ *adj*

pres·tis·si·mo /pre stíssə mō/ *adv* played or to be played as fast as possible (*used as a musical direction*) ■ *n* (*plural* **-mos**) a musical composition or passage that is to be played as fast as possible [Early 18C. < Italian, superlative of *presto* (see PRESTO)] —**pre·stis·si·mo** *adj*

pres·to /préstō/ *interj* AT ONCE used to indicate immediacy or quickness, often with an element of magic ○ *We turned the old key, and – presto! – the ancient gate creaked open.* ■ *adv* **1.** IMMEDIATELY instantly, as if magically (*informal*) **2.** VERY FAST played or to be played very fast (*used as a musical direction*) ■ *n* (*plural* **-tos**) VERY FAST MUSICAL PIECE a musical composition or passage that is to be played very fast [Late 16C. Via Italian, "quick" < Latin *praesto* "at hand"] —**pres·to** *adj*

Pres·ton /prést'n/ city and port in northwestern England. Population: 129,633 (2001).

pre·stress /pree stréss/ (**-stressed, -stress·ing, -stress·es**) *vt* to apply stress to something such as a cable or beam so that it will bear a load better when in use

pre·stressed con·crete *n* concrete that is cast over cables that are under tension, so as to increase its strength

Prest·wick /prést wìk/ town in southwestern Scotland. Population: 13,705 (1991).

pre·sum·a·bly /pri zóomәblee/ *adv* used to show that you expect that something is the case or will happen or has happened ○ *Presumably that man is her father.*

pre·sume /pri zóom/ (**-sumed, -sum·ing, -sumes**) *v* **1.** *vti* BELIEVE SOMETHING TO BE TRUE to accept that something is almost certain to be correct even though there is no proof of it, on the grounds that it is extremely likely ○ *After several days of searching, they presumed that there were no survivors.* **2.** *vt* SEEM TO PROVE SOMETHING to indicate the existence or truth of something (*formal*) ○ *Your line of reasoning presumes his being at home all evening.* **3.** *vi* BEHAVE ARROGANTLY OR OVERCONFIDENTLY to behave so inconsiderately, disrespectfully, or overconfidently as to do something without being entitled or qualified to do it (*usually used in negative statements*) ○ *I would never presume to tell you how to run your business.* **4.** *vi* TAKE ADVANTAGE to exploit or take advantage of somebody unscrupulously ○ *would not want to presume on the generosity of a stranger* [14C. Via French < Latin *praesumere* "take before, anticipate" < *sumere* "take"] —**pre·sum·a·ble** *adj* —**pre·sum·ing** *adj* —**pre·sum·ing·ly** *adv*

pre·sump·tion /pri zúmpshən/ *n* **1.** SOMETHING BELIEVED WITHOUT ACTUAL EVIDENCE a belief based on the fact that something is considered to be extremely reasonable or likely ○ *I acted on the presumption that their IDs were genuine.* **2.** LAW LEGAL INFERENCE an inference that something is the case, in the absence of evidence rebutting that assumption and on the basis of other known facts ○ *a presumption of innocence* **3.** RUDENESS OR ARROGANCE behavior that is inconsiderate, disrespectful, or overconfident [12C. Via French < Latin *praesumption-* < *praesumere* (see PRESUME)]

~~**presumptious**~~ incorrect spelling of **presumptuous**

pre·sump·tive /pri zúmptiv/ *adj* **1.** PROBABLE based on what is thought most likely or reasonable (*formal*) **2.** CAUSING PEOPLE TO PRESUME SOMETHING forming a reasonable basis for the acceptance that something exists or is true (*formal*) **3.** EXPECTED TO BECOME SOMETHING expected or thought likely to become something (*archaic or formal*) ○ *heir presumptive* [15C. Via French < late Latin *praesumptivus* < Latin *praesumere* (see PRESUME)] —**pre·sump·tive·ly** *adv* —**pre·sump·tive·ness** *n*

pre·sump·tu·ous /pri zúmpchoo əss/ *adj* inconsiderate, disrespectful, or overconfident, especially in doing something when not entitled or qualified to do it [14C. Via French < late Latin *praesumptuosus* < Latin *praesumere* (see PRESUME)] —**pre·sump·tu·ous·ly** *adv* —**pre·sump·tu·ous·ness** *n*

pre·sup·pose /prèe sə pṓz/ (**-posed, -pos·ing, -pos·es**) *vt* **1.** to make something necessary if a particular thing is to be shown to be true or false. The sentence "Fred loves his daughter" presupposes that Fred has a daughter. **2.** to believe that a particular thing is true before there is any proof of it ○ *the tendency to presuppose that everybody will understand English* —**pre·sup·po·si·tion** /prèe supə zísh'n/ *n*

prêt-à-por·ter /prèt aa pawr táy/ *n* clothing that is manufactured in standard sizes ready to be bought off the rack [Mid-20C. < French, "ready-to-wear"]

pre·teen /pree téen/, **pre·teen·ag·er** /-téen àyjər/ *adj* **1.** FOR CHILDREN BETWEEN 9 AND 12 relating to, made for, or directed at children in the few years immediately before they become teenagers ○ *preteen clothing* **2.** BETWEEN 9 AND 12 YEARS OLD describes somebody during the few years immediately before the person becomes a teenager ○ *my preteen daughter* ■ *n* CHILD BETWEEN 9 AND 12 a girl or boy in the few years before becoming a teenager

pre·tence *n* UK spelling of **pretense**

pre·tend /pri ténd/ *v* (**-tend·ed, -tend·ing, -tends**) **1.** *vti* ACT AS IF SOMETHING WERE TRUE to make believe that something is the case or that you are doing something by using your imagination or acting skills ○ *The little girl liked to pretend that she was an astronaut.* ○ *We pretended to be interested in what she was saying.* **2.** *vt* MAKE INSINCERE CLAIM ABOUT SOMETHING to claim untruthfully or exaggeratedly to be or to have a particular thing, or imply something in this way ○ *I don't pretend to be an authority on this.* **3.** *vt* MAKE SOMETHING SEEM TO BE TRUE to act in a way intended to make somebody believe something untrue or misleading ○ *pretending to be sick* **4.** *vi* CLAIM TO OWN SOMETHING to make an untruthful or dubious claim of ownership or the right to something, especially something valuable, admirable, or prestigious (*formal*) ○ *pretends to the throne* ■ *adj* IMAGINARY existing only in the imagination, not real (*informal; usually used by children*) ○ *I made a pretend house where my pretend horse lives.* [14C. Directly or via French < Latin *praetendere* "extend in front" < *tendere* "to stretch"] —**pre·tend·ed** *adj*

pre·tend·er /pri téndər/ *n* **1.** somebody who claims a disputed right to a special rank, title, or privilege, especially a royal title. Both the son and the grandson of James II of Great Britain claimed the throne and were known as the Old Pretender and the Young Pretender. **2.** somebody who intentionally gives a false impression to somebody else

pre·tend·i·an /prə téndee ən/ *n* an insulting term for somebody who is regarded as a white of European ancestry but who believes he or she is of Native American ancestry, cannot prove it, and yet wants to gain tribal membership (*insult*) [Late 20C. Blend of PRETEND and INDIAN]

pre·tense /prée tènss, pri ténss/ *n* **1.** INSINCERE OR FEIGNED BEHAVIOR something done or a way of behaving that is not genuine, but is intended to deceive somebody ○ *His display of affection was certainly a pretense.* **2.** UNWARRANTED CLAIM a claim, especially one with few facts to support it (*often used in the negative*) ○ *makes no pretense of expertise* **3.** MAKE-BELIEVE make-believe or things imagined **4.** same as **pretension**[1] (sense 1) [14C. < Anglo-Norman < medieval Latin *pretens-* "alleged" < past participle of Latin *praetendere* (see PRETEND)]

USAGE pretense or **pretext**? A ***pretext*** is a misleading or untrue reason given to mask a real reason (*came here on the pretext of offering condolences; offered several pretexts for missing the deadline*). ***Pretense*** means: "insincere behavior" (*lived a life of pretense*); "an unwarranted, factually defective claim" (*made no pretense of being an expert*); and "pretension" (*resisted conformity and pretense*).

---

pre·ten·sion[1] /pri ténshən/ *n* **1.** AFFECTED BEHAVIOR affected behavior intended to give an appearance of greater importance, status, or knowledge than is warranted **2.** QUESTIONABLE CLAIM TO SOMETHING an untruthful or dubious assertion of a right to something, especially something valuable, admirable, or prestigious (*often used in the plural and with negatives*) ○ *The book makes no pretensions to being great literature.* **3.** MAKING OF CLAIM TO SOMETHING the act of formally putting forward a claim (*formal*) [15C. < medieval Latin *praetension-* < past participle of Latin *praetendere* (see PRETEND)]

pre·ten·sion[2] /prèe ténshən/ (**-sioned, -sion·ing, -sions**) *vt* to strengthen reinforced concrete by applying tension to the reinforcing steel before the concrete has set [Mid-20C. < PRE- + TENSION]

pre·ten·tious /pri ténshəss/ *adj* **1.** SELF-IMPORTANT AND AFFECTED acting as though more important or special than is warranted, or appearing to have an unrealistically high self-image **2.** MADE TO LOOK OR SOUND IMPORTANT intended to seem to have a special quality or significance, but often seeming forced or overly clever ○ *dismissed it as yet another pretentious film* **3.** OSTENTATIOUS extravagantly and consciously showy or glamorous [Mid-19C. < French *prétentieux* < *prétention* < medieval Latin *praetension-* (see PRETENSION[1])] —**pre·ten·tious·ly** *adv* —**pre·ten·tious·ness** *n*

pre·ter- *prefix* beyond ○ *preternatural* [< Latin *praeter* < *prae* "before"]

pret·er·it /préttərit/, **pret·er·ite** *n* GRAM same as **past tense** [14C. Via French < Latin *(tempus) praeteritum* "past (tense)" < past participle of *praeterire* (see PRETERITION)] —**pret·er·it** *adj*

pret·er·i·tion /prèttə rísh'n/ *n* the act of passing over something or leaving something out (*formal*) [Late 16C. < late Latin *praeterition-* "a passing by" < Latin *praeterire* "go by" < *ire* "go"]

pre·term /pree túrm/ *adj* born before completion of a pregnancy of normal length

pre·ter·mi·nal /pree túrmən'l/ *adj* occurring at a time just before death

pre·ter·mit /prèetər mít/ (**-mit·ted, -mit·ting, -mits**) *vt* (*formal*) **1.** to overlook or ignore something deliberately, especially a natural heir from a will **2.** to leave something out or undone [15C. < Latin *praetermittere* "let go by" < *mittere* "send off"]

pre·ter·nat·u·ral /prèetər náchərəl/ *adj* **1.** exceeding what is normal in nature (*formal or literary*) **2.** supernatural or uncanny (*literary*) [Late 16C. < medieval Latin *praeternaturalis* < Latin *praeter naturam* "beyond nature"] —**pre·ter·nat·u·ral·ly** *adv*

pre·test /prée tèst/ *n* **1.** a test given to students to determine whether they are sufficiently prepared for a course of study **2.** a test of something, especially a commercial product before it is offered for sale to the public —**pre·test** /prée tést/ *vt*

pre·text /prée tèkst/ *n* a misleading or untrue reason given for doing something in an attempt to conceal the real reason [Early 16C. < Latin *praetextus* "show, display" < past participle of *praetexere* "weave before, adorn" < *texere* "weave"]

USAGE See *pretense.*

pre·tick·et /pree tíkit/ (**-et·ed, -et·ing, -ets**) *vt US* to sell somebody a ticket in advance, especially before a flight

pre·tor *n* ANCIENT HIST another spelling of **praetor**

Pre·to·ri·a /pri táwree ə/ administrative capital of South Africa, in the northeast of the country. Population: 1,985,995 (2001).

pre·to·ri·an, etc. *adj, n* ANCIENT HIST another spelling of **praetorian, etc.**

Pre·to·ri·us /pri táwree əss/, **Andries** (1798–1853) Boer general and political leader. The father of Marthinus Pretorius, he was a leader of the Great Trek, and fought the Zulus and the British. Full name **Pretorius, Andries Wilhemus Jacobus**

Pre·to·ri·us, Marthinus (1819–1901) Boer general and political leader. The son of Andries Pretorius, he was president of the Transvaal (1857–71) and of the Orange Free State (1859–63). Full name **Pretorius, Marthinus Wessels**

pret·ti·fy /príttə fì/ (**-fied, -fy·ing, -fies**) *vt* to give a person, place, or thing some added decoration, especially of a rather superficial or fussy kind —**pret·ti·fi·ca·tion** /prìttəfi káysh'n/ *n*

pret·ty /príttee/ *adj* (**-ti·er, -ti·est**) **1.** WITH PLEASANT FACE having an attractive pleasant face that is graceful and appealing rather than outstandingly beautiful **2.** NICE TO LOOK AT pleasing or charming in a delicate, gentle, or decorative way ○ *The garden looks so pretty at this time of year.* ○ *a pretty tune* **3.** UNSATISFACTORY very bad or unsatisfactory ○ *got into a pretty mess* **4.** WEAK AND SUPERFICIAL appealing or charming to hear or look at, but without any deep meaning or sincerity ○ *pretty words* **5.** LARGE large in size, extent, or value (*informal*) ○ *cost a pretty penny* ■ *adv* FAIRLY to a fairly large, noticeable, or reasonable extent (*informal*) ○ *I'm pretty sure I lost my keys.* ■ *n* (*plural* **-ties**) SOMEBODY WHO IS PRETTY a pretty person, thing, or animal (*archaic informal*) ■ **pret·ties** *npl US* LINGERIE delicate, feminine sleepwear or underwear (*informal*) ■ *vt* (**-tied, -ty·ing, -ties**) MAKE SOMEBODY OR SOMETHING PRETTY to make somebody or something pretty to look at [Old English *prættig* < Germanic, "trick"] —**pret·ti·ly** *adv* —**pret·ti·ness** *n* ◇ **pretty well** nearly completely (*informal*) ○ *I've pretty well finished reading it.*

SYNONYMS See *good-looking.*

pretty up *vt* same as **pretty**

Pret·ty Good Pri·va·cy E-COMMERCE full form of **PGP**

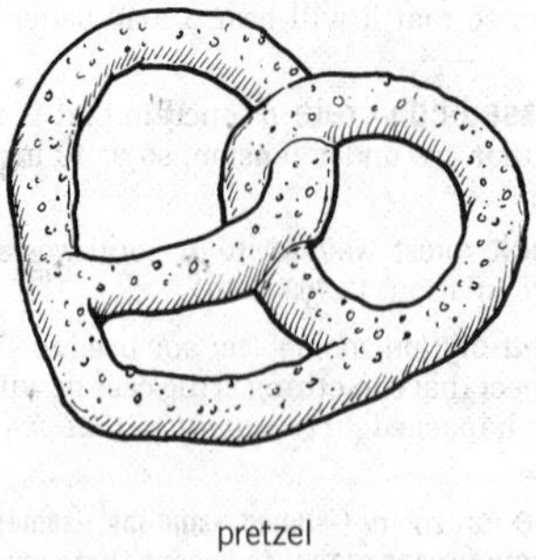

pretzel

pret·zel /préts'l/ *n* a crisp salted knot-shaped or stick-shaped biscuit with a golden brown glaze [Mid-19C. < German]

pre·vail /pri váyl/ (**-vailed, -vail·ing, -vails**) *vi* **1.** BE STRONGER to prove to be stronger and in the position of greater influence and power ○ *He prevailed over his enemies.* **2.** WIN THROUGH to prove to be effective ○ *Justice will prevail.* **3.** PREDOMINATE to predominate or be the most common or frequent ○ *Sunny skies prevail across the northeast.* **4.** BE CURRENT to remain in general use or effect (*formal*) ○ *The old customs still prevail in some parts of the country.* [14C. < Latin *praevalere* "be stronger" < *valere* "be strong"]

prevail on, prevail upon *vt* to persuade somebody to do something ○ *They prevailed on her to take part.*

pre·vail·ing /pri váyling/ *adj* **1.** found, existing, or in force at a particular time ○ *the prevailing view among modern scientists* **2.** found most commonly or having the most power or effect in an area ○ *prevailing winds* —**pre·vail·ing·ly** *adv*

prev·a·lent /prévvələnt/ *adj* occurring, accepted, or practiced commonly or widely ○ *reported a prevalent belief that the economy is structurally sound* [Late 16C. < Latin *praevalent-*, present participle of *praevalere* (see PREVAIL)] —**prev·a·lence** *n* —**prev·a·lent·ly** *adv*

SYNONYMS See *widespread.*

pre·var·i·cate /pri várrə kàyt/ (**-cat·ed, -cat·ing, -cates**) *vi* to avoid giving a direct and honest answer or opinion, or a clear and truthful account of a situation, especially by quibbling or being deliberately ambiguous or misleading [Mid-16C. < Latin *praevaricat-*, past participle stem of *praevaricari* "walk crookedly" < *varus* "crooked, knock-kneed"] —**pre·var·i·ca·tion** /pri vàrrə káysh'n/ *n* —**pre·var·i·ca·tor** *n*

USAGE prevaricate or **procrastinate**? These two verbs are sometimes confused. ***Prevaricate*** means "to evade the truth" whereas ***procrastinate*** means "to defer or put off": *Don't prevaricate – tell me exactly what happened. Don't procrastinate – the sooner you make a start, the sooner it will be finished.*

~~**prevelant, prevelent**~~ incorrect spelling of **prevalent**

pre·ven·ient /pri véenyənt/ *adj* (*formal*) **1.** coming or occurring in advance of another thing **2.** producing a sense of anticipation [Early 17C. < Latin *praevenient-*, present participle of *praevenire* "come before" (see PREVENT)]

pre·vent /pri vént/ (**-vent·ed, -vent·ing, -vents**) *vt* **1.** to cause something not to happen or not to be done ○ *Rain prevented them from playing the game.* **2.** to be the reason why somebody does not or cannot do something ○ *a sense of duty that prevented him from abandoning the project* [15C. < Latin *prevent-*, past participle of *praevenire* "come before, prevent" < *venire* "come"] —**pre·vent·a·ble** *adj*

pre·ven·ta·tive /pri véntətiv/ *adj, n* same as **preventive**

pre·ven·tion /pri vénshən/ *n* **1.** an action or actions taken to stop somebody from doing something or to stop something from happening ○ *the prevention of crime* **2.** an action that makes it impossible or very difficult for somebody to do something or for something to happen ○ *taking aspirin as a prevention against heart attacks*

pre·ven·tive /pri véntiv/ *adj* used or intended to stop something undesirable from happening or to stop somebody from doing something undesirable ○ *preventive dentistry* ■ *n* something that stops something undesirable from happening, especially something that protects against illness ○ *A good preventive against heart disease is a healthy lifestyle.* —**pre·ven·tive·ly** *adv*

pre·ven·tive de·ten·tion *n* **1.** the pretrial jailing without bail of somebody accused of a crime who is thought likely to attempt to flee, commit additional crimes, or intimidate witnesses or prosecutors, or an instance of such jailing **2.** *US* institutionalization of a psychologically disturbed patient in order to prevent him or her from committing a crime

pre·verb·al /pree vúrb'l/ *adj* **1.** at the stage of development when a child is not yet able to use speech **2.** coming before a verb

pre·view /prée vyoo/ *n* **1.** OPPORTUNITY TO SEE SOMETHING IN ADVANCE a showing of something, especially a movie, play, or exhibit, to a select audience before the general public sees it **2.** DESCRIPTION OF FORTHCOMING SHOW a piece printed in a paper or magazine or broadcast on radio or TV describing and commenting on something that is soon to be broadcast or presented to the public **3.** *also* **pre·vue** PROMOTIONAL FILM a short film shown on TV or at a movie theater promoting an upcoming movie or program **4.** *also* **pre·vue** INDICATION OF FUTURE EVENT a sample or foretaste of something likely to occur in the future ○ *polls that could provide a preview of actual election results* ■ *vt* (**-viewed, -view·ing, -views**) **1.** SHOW SOMETHING IN ADVANCE to put on a performance or showing of something for a select audience before the general public has the opportunity to see it **2.** DESCRIBE SHOW IN ADVANCE to write, print, or broadcast a short piece that describes and comments on something that is soon to be broadcast or presented to the public

pre·vi·ous /préevee əss/ *adj* **1.** COMING BEFORE SOMEBODY OR SOMETHING occurring before somebody or something of the same kind ○ *the previous edition* **2.** ALREADY ARRANGED existing, made, or settled before the one being referred to now ○ *a previous engagement* **3.** ACTING TOO HASTILY saying or doing something earlier than is appropriate (*informal*) [Early 17C. < Latin *praevius* "going before" < *via* "way"] ◇ **previous to something** before a particular thing took place

pre·vi·ous·ly /préevee əsslee/ *adv* at an earlier time or on an earlier occasion

pre·vi·ous ques·tion *n* a motion to put a question that will end a debate so that a vote on a bill can be taken without delay

pre·vise /pri víz/ (**-vised, -vis·ing, -vis·es**) *vt* (*formal or literary*) **1.** to predict or foresee something **2.** to warn somebody about something [15C. < Latin *praevis-*, past participle of *praevidere* "foresee" < *videre* "see"]

pre·vi·sion /prə vízh'n/ *n* (*formal or literary*) **1.** the ability to predict or foresee things **2.** a prediction or premonition

pre·vo·cal·ic /prée vō kállik/ *adj* describes a consonant that comes immediately before a vowel

Pre·vost /prév ost/, **Sir George** (1767–1816) British soldier and administrator. He was governor-in-chief of Canada (1811–12) and commander of British forces in North America during the War of 1812.

pre·vue /prée vyoo/ *n US* MOVIES, MEDIA another spelling of **preview** *n* (senses 3, 4)

pre·war /pree wáwr/ *adj* dating from or belonging to the period before a war, especially World War I or World War II ○ *prewar buildings*

pre·washed /pree wósht, -wáwst/ *adj* washed before being packaged and sold in the store —**pre·wash** *n, vt*

pre·writ·ing /prée rīting/ *n* the preparatory work needed before a piece of writing is begun, e.g., the formation of ideas, organization of material, and discussion

prex·y /préksee/ (*plural* **-ies**), **prex** /preks/ *n US* a president, especially of a college or university (*slang*) [Early 19C. Shortening and alteration of PRESIDENT]

prey /pray/ (*plural* **preys**) *n* **1. ANIMAL HUNTED BY OTHER ANIMALS** an animal or animals caught, killed, and eaten by another animal as food ○ *The common shrew's prey consists largely of earthworms and wood lice.* **2. SOMEBODY TREATED UNKINDLY BY OTHERS** somebody who is attacked by or receives cruel or unfair treatment from somebody else ○ *His gullibility makes him easy prey.* **3. KILLING OF OTHER ANIMALS AS FOOD** the natural practice or habit of predatory animals of hunting, killing, and eating other animals ○ *a bird of prey* [13C. Via Old French *preie* < Latin *praeda* "booty"] ◇ **be (a) prey to something** to experience something unpleasant regularly or be at risk of something unpleasant

SPELLCHECK See *pray.*

prey on, prey upon *vt* **1.** to hunt and kill other animals for food ○ *Owls prey on mice and rabbits.* **2.** to victimize or exploit somebody

prez /prez/ *n US* same as **president** (*slang*) [Late 19C. Shortening]

PRI *abbr* POL Partido Revolucionario Institucional

Pri·am /prī́ əm/ *n* in Greek mythology, the king of Troy, husband of Hecuba, and father of Hector, Paris, and Cassandra

pri·a·pic /prī áppik/ *adj* **1. OF MALE SEXUAL ACTIVITY** relating to or showing a preoccupation with male sexual activity **2. RELATING TO PHALLUS** relating to or resembling a phallus (*dated or literary*) **3.** MED **WITH PENIS PERMANENTLY ERECT** having a permanently erect penis [Late 18C. < Latin *Priapus*, Greek *Priapos* "Priapus," symbolized by the erect phallus]

pri·a·pism /prī́ ə pìzzəm/ *n* a medical disorder in which there is persistent, often painful erection of the penis in the absence of sexual interest [Early 17C. < Latin *Priapus* (see PRIAPIC)]

Pri·a·pus /prī áypəss/ *n* in Greek mythology, the god of fertility

Prib·i·lof Is·lands /príbbə làwf-/ group of islands off southwestern Alaska, in the southeastern Bering Sea. Population: 901 (1990). Area: 62 sq. mi./161 sq. km.

price /prīss/ *n* **1. COST OF SOMETHING BOUGHT OR SOLD** the amount, usually of money, that is offered or asked for when something is bought or sold **2. SOMETHING SACRIFICED TO GET SOMETHING ELSE** something lost or given in order to achieve a particular position or condition ○ *Unwanted media attention is the price of fame.* **3. SUFFICIENT BRIBE** the sum of money or other recompense in return for which somebody agrees to do something ○ *The price of her cooperation was an invitation to the gala dinner.* **4. MEASURE OF VALUE OF SOMETHING** an estimate of what somebody or something is worth, e.g., how important, useful, or irreplaceable he, she, or it is (*dated or literary*) ■ *vt* **(priced, pric·ing, pric·es) 1. DECIDE HOW MUCH SOMETHING COSTS** to state or fix the exact amount that a customer or consumer must pay for something ○ *He priced the antique clock at $700.* **2. MARK SOMETHING WITH PRICE** to show how much something costs, especially by writing on the item itself or by attaching a label or price tag ○ *spent the morning pricing merchandise* **3. FIND OUT WHAT SOMETHING COSTS** to check the price that has been set for a product, or compare the different prices charged at a variety of stores or from different companies ○ *priced a few computers before deciding which one to buy* [13C. Via Old French *pris* < Latin *pretium* "price, money"] ◇ **at any price** no matter how great the cost may be (*often used with a negative*) ◇ **at a price** at a considerable cost ◇ **beyond price** priceless ◇ **have a price on your head** to have had a reward offered for your capture or death ◇ **pay the price (for something)** to suffer the unpleasant consequences of something that you have done ◇ **what price something?** used to suggest that something such as an ideal or a promise has no value ○ *"What Price Glory?"* (Maxwell Anderson, *What Price Glory?*; 1924)

Price /prīss/, **Leontyne** (*b.* 1927) US operatic soprano. During a long career as a major international opera star (1952–85), she was especially associated with Italian opera. Full name **Price, Mary Violet Leontyne**

"Once you get on stage, everything is right. I feel the most beautiful, complete, fulfilled. I think that's why, in the case of noncompromising career women, parts of our personal lives don't work out. One person can't give you the feeling that thousands of people give you."

[Leontyne Price. Quoted in *I Dream a World: Portraits of Black Women Who Changed America*, Brian Lanker; 1989]

Leontyne Price

price con·trol *n* government control over prices of goods and services, usually introduced as an emergency measure

price-cut·ting *n* the reduction of prices below their usual level in order to sell more than competitors

price dis·crim·i·na·tion *n* the charging of different prices for the same product or service in different markets

price-earn·ings ra·tio *n* the ratio of a share's price to its earnings, which provides an indication of its value

price fix·ing *n* the setting of prices by government or by agreement between producers, instead of by free market operation

price in·dex *n* a mathematical quantity that is used to measure movements in price levels over different periods of time

price·less /prīssləss/ *adj* **1.** worth more than can be calculated in terms of money ○ *the priceless treasures of the pharaohs' tombs* **2.** extremely comic and amusing (*informal*) ○ *a priceless comment*

price point *n* the retail price of a product, especially within a range of prices of similar goods

price sup·port *n* government maintenance of price levels, e.g., by subsidies to producers

price tag *n* **1.** a small label attached to an item that is for sale, with the price written or printed on it **2.** the amount that something costs, whether in money or in something else such as emotional outlay or loss of life or health (*informal*)

price war *n* extreme competition within a market, characterized by price-cutting

pric·ey /prīssee/ (**-i·er, -i·est**), **pric·y** *adj* charging high prices or costing a great deal (*informal*) ○ *a pricey restaurant*

Prich·ard /príchərd/ city in southwestern Alabama. Population: 28,200 (2002 estimate).

prick /prik/ *v* **(pricked, prick·ing, pricks) 1.** *vt* **PIERCE SMALL HOLE IN SOMETHING** to puncture the surface of something, especially the skin, by piercing it lightly with something sharp and finely pointed ○ *pricked her finger on a cactus needle* **2.** *vti* **HURT IN STINGING WAY** to feel a slight stinging sensation, or cause something such as the eyes or the skin to hurt in this way ○ *felt his eyes prick with tears* **3.** *vt* **SUDDENLY CAUSE DISCOMFORT TO SOMEBODY** to make somebody feel a sudden strong unease, e.g., because of guilt or shame ○ *His conscience began to prick him.* **4.** *vt* **OUTLINE SOMETHING USING TINY HOLES** to make a number of small holes in or through the surface of a board, piece of card, or fabric so as to form the outline of something **5.** *vti* **RAISE EARS** to cause an animal's ears to stick up straight on hearing something, or stick up straight for this reason ○ *The dog pricked its ears at the sound of its master's voice.* **6.** *vt* **PUSH SOMEBODY INTO ACTIVITY** to force or encourage somebody to start or continue with greater speed an activity or course of action ○ *If only we could prick him into doing something.* **7.** *vt* **MAKE ANIMAL MOVE FASTER** to urge an animal, especially a horse, to gallop or move more quickly by digging the spurs or heels into its flank (*archaic or literary*) ■ *n* **1. QUICK SHARP PAIN** a sudden twinge of pain such as that caused by a fine point being pushed into the skin **2. SMALL PUNCTURE** a small puncture, hole, or indented mark, or an act of piercing that causes such a puncture **3. TABOO TERM** a highly offensive term for a penis (*taboo*) **4. TABOO TERM** a highly offensive term for a man regarded as inadequate or unpleasant (*taboo*) **5. PAINFUL THOUGHT** a sudden unpleasant thought or feeling, often one related to a past action or event **6. POINTED IMPLEMENT** a pointed implement or weapon, e.g., a goad (*archaic*) [Old English *prica* < W Germanic]

prick out *vt* to make a series of small holes in an area of soil and put young seedlings into these holes to grow

prick·er /príkər/ *n* **1.** a tool used to prick or pierce small holes in something **2.** *US* BOT same as **prickle** *n* (sense 2)

prick·et /príkət/ *n* **1.** a male deer in its second year, usually one with unbranched antlers **2.** a metal spike for sticking a candle on

prick·le /prík'l/ *n* **1. TINGLING FEELING** a tingling or stinging sensation **2. PROJECTION ON PLANT** a sharp pointed projection on the outer surface of a leaf or plant ■ *vti* **(-led, -ling, -les) HURT IN STINGING WAY** to feel a sharp stinging pain, or cause something such as the eyes or the skin to hurt in this way ■ *n* ZOOL **ANIMAL'S SPINE** a spine on an animal such as a hedgehog [Old English *pricel* "small prick" < W Germanic, "prick"]

prick·ly /príklee/ (**-li·er, -li·est**) *adj* **1. WITH SMALL SHARP SPIKES** having a surface or skin with prickles on it **2. UNCOMFORTABLE** irritating to the skin, especially because of fibers or prickles that are rough to the touch **3. OVERSENSITIVE** easily angered, offended, or upset (*informal*) ○ *a moody man with a prickly personality* **4. PROBLEMATIC OR UPSETTING** especially difficult and likely to upset people (*informal*) ○ *the prickly issue of raising taxes* —**prick·li·ness** *n*

prick·ly ash *n* **1.** an aromatic bush or small tree with prickly branches. Flowers: small, greenish, in clusters. Native to: eastern North America. Latin name: *Zanthoxylum americanum.* **2.** a spiny bush or tree with pinnately compound leaves. Native to: southern United States. Latin name: *Zanthoxylum clavaherculis.*

prick·ly heat *n* a rash of tiny raised spots, accompanied by redness and itching, appearing on the skin in hot or humid conditions. Technical name **miliaria**

prick·ly pear *n* a cactus with flattened, jointed, spiny stems and pear-shaped fruits that are edible in some species. Flowers: large, yellow or orange. Native to: North, Central, and South America. Genus: *Opuntia.*

prick·ly pop·py *n* a poppy plant with bristly stems and leaves. Flowers: yellow, lavender, or white. Use: formerly, in herbal medicine. Genus: *Argemone.*

prick-teas·er, prick-tease *n* a highly offensive term for somebody who makes sexual advances toward a man without intending to have sex with him (*taboo*)

pric·y *adj* COMM another spelling of **pricey** (*informal*)

pride /prīd/ *n* **1. SATISFACTION WITH SELF** the happy satisfied feeling somebody experiences when having or achieving something special that other people admire ○ *took great pride in his work* **2. PROPER SENSE OF OWN VALUE** the correct level of respect for the importance and value of your personal character, life, efforts, or achievements ○ *Defeat didn't damage her pride.* **3. FEELING OF SUPERIORITY** a haughty attitude shown by somebody who believes, often unjustifiably, that he or she is better than others ○ *Her pride prevented her from making many friends.* **4. SOURCE OF PERSONAL SATISFACTION** something such as an achievement or possession that somebody feels especially pleased and satisfied with ○ *His grandchildren were his pride and joy.* **5. BEST TIME** the best condition or period of something (*literary*) **6. GROUP OF LIONS** a group of lions, usually consisting of up to a dozen related adult females, their cubs and juveniles, plus from one to six adult males ■ *vr* (**prid·ed, prid·ing, prides**) **pride yourself** **BE PROUD OF SOMETHING** to obtain personal satisfaction and pleasure from a particular source, especially something accomplished or a quality possessed ○ *He prides himself on his meticulous timekeeping.* [Pre-12C. < PROUD] —**pride·ful** *adj* —**pride·ful·ly** *adv* ◇ **pride of place** the most important or prominent position

CULTURAL NOTE ***Pride and Prejudice***, a novel (1813) by the British writer Jane Austen. Through the story of the relationship between Elizabeth Bennet, the fiercely independent daughter of minor gentry, and Mr. Darcy, a wealthy and haughty nobleman, Austen reveals how both pride and prejudice create barriers to mutual understanding.

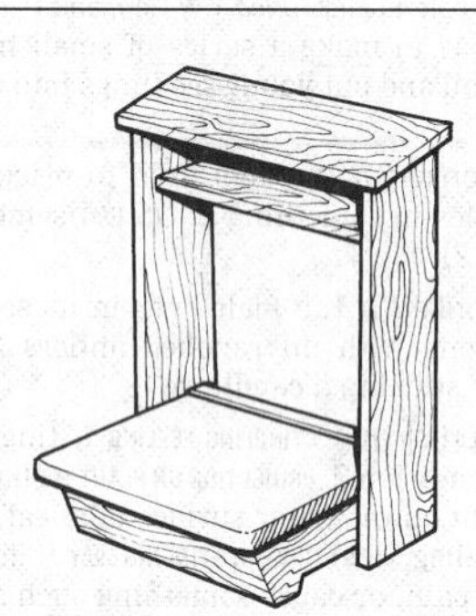
prie-dieu

prie-dieu /prēe dyṓ/ (*plural* **prie-dieux** /-dyṓ/) *n* a shelved wooden desk for use when praying, usually with a low surface for kneeling on and a higher surface for resting the elbows or a book on [Mid-18C. < French, "pray God"]

pri·er /prī́ ər/, **pry·er** *n* somebody who pries

priest /preest/ *n* **1. ORDAINED CHRISTIAN MINISTER** an ordained minister, especially in the Roman Catholic, Anglican, or Eastern Orthodox churches, responsible for administering the sacraments, preaching, and ministering to the needs of the congregation **2. MINISTER OF NON-CHRISTIAN RELIGION** a spiritual leader or teacher of a non-Christian religion **3. DESCENDANT OF FAMILY OF AARON** somebody descended from the family of Aaron of the house of Levi, appointed as priests in the Hebrew Scriptures [Old English *prēost*, via Germanic < ecclesiastical Latin *presbyter* (see PRESBYTER)]

priest·ess /prēestəss/ *n* a woman who is a spiritual leader in a pagan religion

priest·hood /prēest hòod/ *n* **1.** the official role, position, or office of a priest **2.** the priests of a particular religion, considered as a group

Priest·ley /prēestlee/, **Joseph** (1733–1804) British chemist and political radical. He isolated and described the properties of oxygen and other gases, and is considered one of the founders of modern chemistry.

> "More is owing to what we call *chance*, that is, philosophically speaking, to the observation of events arising from *unknown causes*, than to any proper *design*, or preconceived theory of the business."
> [Joseph Priestley, *Experiments and Observations of Different Types of Air*; 1775]

priest·ly /prēestlee/ *adj* **1.** used, worn, or performed exclusively by priests ○ *priestly garments* **2.** characteristic of or suitable for a priest

prig /prig/ *n* somebody who is regarded as taking pride in behaving in a very correct and proper way, and in feeling morally superior to others [Late 17C. Origin ?] —**prig·gish** *adj* —**prig·gish·ness** *n*

prill /pril/ *vt* (**prilled, pril·ling, prills**) to make a solid into granules or pellets that flow freely and do not clump together ■ *n* a granule or pellet made by prilling [Late 18C. Origin ?]

prim /prim/ (**prim·mer, prim·mest**) *adj* **1. PRUDISH** easily shocked by vulgar or obscene language or behavior **2. FORMAL AND PROPER** excessively formal and proper in manner or appearance **3. VERY NEAT** excessively neat and tidy [Early 18C. Origin ?] —**prim·ly** *adv* —**prim·ness** *n*

pri·ma bal·le·ri·na /prēemə-/ *n* the principal woman dancer in a ballet company [< Italian, "first ballerina"]

pri·ma·cy /prī́məssee/ (*plural* **-cies**) *n* **1.** the state of being the first or most important part or aspect of something ○ *the notion of the primacy of the individual* **2.** the position or office of a primate in a Christian church

pri·ma don·na /prēemə dónnə/ (*plural* **pri·ma don·nas**) *n* **1.** the principal woman soloist in an opera production **2.** somebody who is regarded as demanding and difficult to please (*insult*) [< Italian, "first lady"]

pri·ma fa·cie /prī̀mə fáyshee, -fáyshee ēe, prēemə-/ *adv* **AT FIRST GLANCE** on initial examination or consideration ○ *Prima facie, this lawsuit seems spurious.* ■ *adj* **1. APPARENT** clear from a first impression ○ *a prima facie counterexample to your hypothesis* **2. LEGALLY SUFFICIENT** sufficient in law to establish a case or fact, unless disproved [< Latin, "at first appearance"]

pri·mal /prī́m'l/ *adj* **1.** first or earliest, and often basic ○ *the primal instinct for survival* **2.** most significant and primary [Mid-16C. < medieval Latin *primalis* < Latin *primus* "first"]

pri·mal scream *n* a cry of extreme anger that somebody undergoing primal therapy is encouraged to utter

pri·mal ther·a·py *n* a style of psychotherapy in which somebody relives past traumas and unleashes repressed anger and frustration through screams, tantrums, or beating inanimate objects

pri·ma·quine /prēemə kwēen, prī́mə-, -kwin/, **pri·ma·quine phos·phate** *n* a synthetic drug derived from quinoline. Use: treatment of malaria. Formula: $C_{15}H_{21}N_3O$. [Mid-20C. < 1st element probably < form of Latin *primus* "first" + *-quine*, INN stem]

pri·mar·i·ly /prī mérrəlee/ *adv* **1.** mainly or mostly ○ *Baldness is primarily found among adult men.* **2.** originally or at first

pri·mar·y /prī mèrree, prī́mərée/ *adj* **1. MOST IMPORTANT** ranked as most important **2. FIRST IN SEQUENCE** first or earliest in a sequence ○ *the primary stage of development* **3. BASIC** essential or basic to something **4. FIRSTHAND** obtained directly from or due directly to something ○ *seeking out primary sources of information* **5. ORIGINAL** existing first, from the beginning, or before all others **6. RELATING TO EARLY EDUCATION** relating to the early years of formal education, usually for children between the ages of 6 and 12 **7. RELATING TO NATURAL RESOURCE INDUSTRY** relating to or produced by an industry such as forestry, mining, or agriculture, that collects and processes a natural resource **8.** CHEM **SUBSTITUTING ATOMS** relating to or resulting from the replacement of one or more atoms in a molecule **9.** CHEM **OF ATTACHED CARBON ATOM** describes a carbon atom in a molecule that is bonded to one other carbon atom only **10.** BIOCHEM **OF AMINO ACID SEQUENCE** describes the basic type, number, or sequence of amino acids in a polypeptide **11.** BOT **GROWN FROM EMBRYONIC TISSUE** describes growth from embryonic tissue in the tip of a root or shoot ■ *n* (*plural* **-ies**) **1.** POL **ELECTION OF CANDIDATES FOR GOVERNMENTAL POSITION** an election in which members of a party choose candidates for a governmental position **2.** POL **ELECTION OF DELEGATES TO CHOOSE CANDIDATES** an election to choose delegates who will choose the party's candidates at a political convention **3.** COLORS same as **primary color** **4.** ASTRON **BRIGHTER STAR OF BINARY STAR** the brighter or larger of two stars in a binary star **5.** ASTRON same as **primary planet** **6.** BIRDS same as **primary feather** [15C. < Latin *primarius* < *primus* "first"]

pri·mar·y ac·cent *n US* the strongest force used in pronouncing one of the syllables of a word with more than one syllable, or the mark, usually (ˈ), used to indicate this. Can term **primary stress**

pri·mar·y a·typ·i·cal pneu·mo·ni·a *n* an infectious but relatively mild form of pneumonia caused by the bacterium *Mycoplasma pneumoniae*

pri·mar·y care *n* the level of health care at which a patient is evaluated and treated by a family doctor or nurse, or, if necessary, is referred to a specialist

pri·mar·y cell *n* an electrical cell that uses an irreversible chemical reaction to generate electricity and, as a result, cannot be recharged

pri·mar·y coil *n* a coil forming part of a machine or circuit in which the current flow sets up the magnetic flux necessary for the operation of the machine or circuit

pri·mar·y col·or *n* **1.** each of the three basic colors of the spectrum, red, yellow, or blue (**primary additive colors**), from which all other colors can be blended **2.** each of the three basic colors, cyan, magenta, or yellow (**primary subtractive colors**), which, when subtracted from white, can produce all other colors

pri·mar·y con·sum·er *n* an animal that eats plants, considered in terms of its position in a food chain

pri·mar·y e·lec·tion *n* POL same as **primary** *n* (senses 1–2)

pri·mar·y feath·er *n* a main flight feather on the outer half of a bird's wing

pri·mar·y plan·et *n* a planet in direct orbit around a sun

pri·mar·y pro·duc·tion *n* the total chemical energy produced by photosynthesis

pri·mar·y school *n* same as **elementary school**

pri·mar·y stor·age *n* the main memory in a computer, including the random-access memory and the read-only memory, directly accessible by the processor

pri·mar·y stress *n Can, UK* same as **primary accent**

pri·mar·y syph·i·lis *n* the first of the three stages of syphilis, in which a painless growth (**chancre**) grows at the site of infection and the infecting bacterium (**spirochete**) spreads throughout the body

pri·mar·y tooth *n* DENT same as **milk tooth**

pri·mar·y wave *n* a seismic wave that creates vibrations parallel to its direction

pri·mate /prī́ màyt/ *n* **1.** a member of an order of mammals with a large brain and complex hands and feet, including humans, apes, and monkeys. Order: Primates. **2.** *also* **Pri·mate** an archbishop or high-ranking bishop [12C. < Latin *primat-* "of the first rank" < *primus* "first"] —**pri·ma·tial** /prī máysh'l/ *adj*

~~**primative**~~ incorrect spelling of **primitive**

pri·ma·tol·o·gy /prī̀mə tólləjee/ *n* the scientific study of primates, especially nonhuman primates —**pri·ma·to·log·i·cal** /prī̀mətə lójjik'l/ *adj* —**pri·ma·tol·o·gist** *n*

pri·ma·ve·ra[1] /prēemə vérrə/ (*plural* **-ras** or *same*) *n* **1.** the light colored wood of a Central American tree. Use: furniture-making. **2.** a tree that has yellow flowers and palmate leaves and yields primavera. Native to: Central America. Latin name: *Cybistax donnellsmithii.* [Late 19C. Via Spanish, "springtime" (because the tree flowers in spring) < late Latin *prima vera* (see PRIMAVERA[2])]

pri·ma·ve·ra[2] /prēemə vérrə/ *adj* made with an assortment of fresh spring vegetables, especially sliced as an accompaniment to pasta, meat, or seafood [Late 20C. < Italian *(alla) primavera* "(in the) spring (style)" < late Latin *prima vera* "early spring" < Latin *primum ver* "first spring"]

prime[1] /prīm/ *adj* **1. FIRST IN IMPORTANCE** of the greatest importance or the highest rank **2. BEST** of the highest quality ○ *prime grade beef* **3. EARLIEST** earliest in time or sequence **4.** MATH **NOT DIVISIBLE WITHOUT REMAINDER** describes a number that can be divided without a remainder only by one and itself **5.** MATH **LACKING COMMON FACTORS** describes a number that has no common factors with another number ○ *15 is prime to 8.* ■ *n* **1. BEST STAGE OF SOMETHING** the best state or stage of something, especially the most active and enjoyable period in adult life ○ *in the prime of life* **2. EARLIEST PERIOD OF SOMETHING** the earliest part of something, e.g., the early hours of daylight or the first season of the year **3. DISTINGUISHING MARK** a mark (′) added to a number, character, or expression in order to distinguish it from another, or as the symbol for measurement in feet or the minutes of an arc **4.** MUSIC **FIRST NOTE IN MUSICAL SCALE** the first note of a musical scale **5.** CHR **SECOND CANONICAL HOUR** in the

Roman Catholic Church, the second of the seven separate hours (**canonical hours**) that are set aside for prayer each day **6.** FENCING **FIRST PARRYING POSITION** the first of the eight parrying positions in fencing **7.** MATH same as **prime number 8.** FIN same as **prime rate** [Pre-12C. Via French < Latin *primus* "first"] —**prime·ness** *n*

CULTURAL NOTE ***The Prime of Miss Jean Brodie***, a novel (1961) by British writer Muriel Spark. The best known of Spark's novels, it is set in an Edinburgh girls' school and describes the powerful and lasting influence of an unconventional schoolteacher, Miss Jean Brodie, on a group of promising but impressionable pupils. It was adapted for the theater in 1966 and made into a movie by Ronald Neame in 1968.

prime[2] /prīm/ *v* **1.** *vt* **BRIEF SOMEBODY** to give somebody, especially a witness in a court case, information or instructions on how to behave or answer questions **2.** *vti* **MAKE OR BECOME READY** to make something ready for use, or become ready for use **3.** *vt* **PUT CHARGE IN GUN** to make a firearm ready for use by putting a charge in it **4.** *vt* **PROVIDE EXPLOSIVE WITH FUSE** to make an explosive ready for use by inserting a fuse **5.** *vt* **PREPARE SURFACE FOR PAINTING** to prepare a surface for painting or a similar process by treating it with a sealant or an undercoat of paint **6.** *vt* **PREPARE SOMETHING FOR OPERATION** to put liquid in something such as a pump or carburetor in order to get it started [Early 16C. Origin ?]

prime cost *n* the cost of the material and labor necessary to make a product

prime in·ter·est rate *n* FIN same as **prime rate**

prime me·rid·i·an *n* the 0° longitude meridian passing through Greenwich, England, from which other longitudes are calculated

prime min·is·ter *n* **1.** in a parliamentary system, the head of the cabinet and, usually, chief executive. See table on next page **2.** the chief minister appointed by the ruler of a country —**prime min·is·te·ri·al** *adj* —**prime min·is·ter·ship** *n*

prime mov·er *n* **1. MOST IMPORTANT CAUSE OF SOMETHING** somebody or something that initiates a process or activity and is usually the most important factor in its continuation **2.** PHILOSOPHY **SOURCE OF ALL MOTION** in Aristotelian philosophy, the initial source of all movement **3. NATURAL OR PHYSICAL ENERGY SOURCE** a natural or physical source of energy such as wind or electricity that can be harnessed to power a machine **4. ENERGY CONVERTER** a machine that converts energy from a natural or physical source in order to power equipment such as a windmill or turbine **5. POWERFUL VEHICLE** a sturdy, powerful truck or tractor

prime num·ber *n* a whole number that can only be divided without a remainder by itself and one

prim·er[1] /prímmər/ *n* **1.** a book used to teach young children to read, usually containing simple stories **2.** a book that provides an introduction to a topic [14C. < Anglo-Norman < Latin *primarius* (see PRIMARY)]

prim·er[2] /prímər/ *n* **1. UNDERCOAT** a paint or sealant used to prepare a surface for painting or a similar process, or a coat of this material **2. PRIMING AGENT** a person or device that primes something **3. EXPLOSIVE IGNITER** a small container or wafer of explosive material such as gunpowder, used to ignite the main explosive charge of a firearm or explosive **4.** BIOCHEM **GENETIC MATERIAL** a short sequence of RNA that is made before DNA formation can proceed [15C. < PRIME[2]]

pri·me·ra da·ma /pree mérrə daámə/ *n Hispanic* the wife of the president of the United States of Mexico [< Spanish, "first lady"]

prime rate *n* the lowest rate of interest on loans that is available from a bank at a given time

prime time *n* **1.** the hours when television audiences are usually largest, typically from 7:00 pm to 11:00 pm **2.** the busiest or most exciting period in some activity ○ *Summer is prime time for road construction.* —**prime-time** *adj*

pri·me·val /prī meév'l/ *adj* **1.** at or from the ancient original stages in the development of something **2.** primitive, or arising from instinct rather than thought ○ *a primeval urge* [Mid-17C. < Latin *primaevus* < *primus* "first" + *aevum* "age"]

prime ver·ti·cal *n* the imaginary circle around Earth that goes through the highest point of the celestial sphere directly above an observer and meets the horizon at east and west

pri·mi MUSIC plural of **primo**

pri·mi·grav·i·da /prīmi grávvidə/ (*plural* **-das** or **-dae** /-deé/) *n* a woman experiencing her first pregnancy [Late 19C. < modern Latin < *gravida* "pregnant," after PRIMIPARA]

pri·mip·a·ra /prī míppərə/ (*plural* **-ras** or **-rae** /-ree/) *n* a woman who has given birth only once, whether it was a single or a multiple birth, and whether the baby was alive or stillborn [Mid-19C. < modern Latin < Latin *primus* "first" + *-para* "bearing," form of *-parus* (see -PAROUS)] —**pri·mip·a·rous** *adj*

prim·i·tive /prímmitiv/ *adj* **1. FIRST** relating to or occurring at the first stages or form of something **2.** BIOL **DEVELOPMENTALLY EARLY** relating to or appearing in an earlier stage of biological development, particularly of an embryo or species **3. VERY SIMPLE IN DESIGN** crudely simple in design or construction (*offensive in some contexts*) ○ *built a primitive shelter from palm leaves* **4. WITH SIMPLE TECHNOLOGICAL DEVELOPMENT** not using or relying on complex modern technologies to provide comfort and efficiency (*sometimes considered offensive*) ○ *primitive camping facilities* **5. NATURAL** arising from an inherent characteristic **6.** ARTS **ARTISTICALLY UNTRAINED** created by an artist with no formal training, especially using a simple style **7.** ARTS **EARLY MEDIEVAL** created by an early medieval European artist or a folk artist **8.** LING **USED FOR DERIVING OTHER WORD** having a word form from which another word is derived ○ *The primitive root in "children" is "child."* **9.** LING **EARLIER IN LINGUISTIC DEVELOPMENT** belonging to or constituting an earlier form of a language ■ *n* **1.** ARTS **UNTRAINED ARTIST** an artist without formal training, especially one using a simple style **2.** ARTS **EARLY MEDIEVAL ARTIST** an artist or folk artist, especially a painter, whose work was characteristic of the style of early medieval Europe **3.** ARTS **WORK BY EARLY MEDIEVAL ARTIST** a painting or other work by an early medieval artist or a folk artist **4. SOMEBODY FROM CULTURE WITH SIMPLE TECHNOLOGIES** a member of a people who do not use or rely on complex modern technologies (*often considered offensive*) **5. SOMEBODY OR SOMETHING FROM ORIGINAL STAGE** somebody or something from the first stage or form of something **6.** COMPUT **BASIC ELEMENT OF COMPUTER PROGRAM** a simple element of a computer program or graphic design from which larger programs or images can be constructed [14C. Directly or via French < Latin *primitivus* < *primitus* "in the first place" < *primus* "first"] —**prim·i·tive·ly** *adv* —**prim·i·tive·ness** *n*

prim·i·tiv·ism /prímmiti vìzzəm/ *n* **1. STATE OF BEING PRIMITIVE** the state of being primitive, or the qualities associated with being primitive **2.** ARTS **SIMPLICITY OF STYLE** simplicity or naiveté of artistic style **3. OPPOSITION TO MODERN LIFE** the belief that less technologically dependent cultures and ways of living are inherently better than more technologically dependent ones —**prim·i·tiv·ist** *n, adj* —**prim·i·tiv·is·tic** /prìmmiti vístik/ *adj*

pri·mo /preémō/ *adj* **1.** *US* **FIRST** first in a sequence or series (*formal*) **2. EXCELLENT** of the finest quality or greatest value (*slang*) ○ *This pizza is primo!* ■ *n* (*plural* **-mos** or **-mi** /-mee/) **LEAD MUSICAL PART** the lead musical part in a duet, trio, or ensemble composition [Mid-18C. Via Italian and Spanish, "first, prime" < Latin *primus*]

pri·mo·gen·i·tor /prìmō jénnitər/ *n* (*formal*) **1.** the first ancestor of a people or other group **2.** an ancestor or forebear [Mid-17C. Alteration of PROGENITOR, after PRIMOGENITURE]

pri·mo·gen·i·ture /prìmō jénni choŏr/ *n* (*formal*) **1.** the right of the first-born child, usually the eldest son, to inherit the parents' entire estate **2.** the state of being the first-born child of a set of parents [Early 17C. < medieval Latin *primogenitura* < Latin *primus* "first" + *genitura* "birth"]

pri·mor·di·al /prī máwrdee əl/ *adj* **1. EXISTING FIRST** existing at the beginning of time or of the development of something **2. BASIC** essential or basic to something **3.** BIOL **OF EARLIEST STAGE OF DEVELOPMENT** relating to cells, tissues, organs, or organisms at the earliest stage of development [14C. < late Latin *primordialis* < Latin *primordium* "origin" < *primus* "first" + *ordiri* "begin"]

pri·mor·di·um /prī máwrdee əm/ (*plural* **-di·a** /-dee ə/) *n* a tissue or organ in the earliest stage of embryonic development, found when the dividing cells in the fertilized ovum first differentiate [Late 16C. < Latin (see PRIMORDIAL)]

primp /primp/ (**primped, primp·ing, primps**) *vti* to groom yourself, somebody, or something in a fussy way ○ *spending all day primping in front of the mirror* [Late 16C. Origin ?]

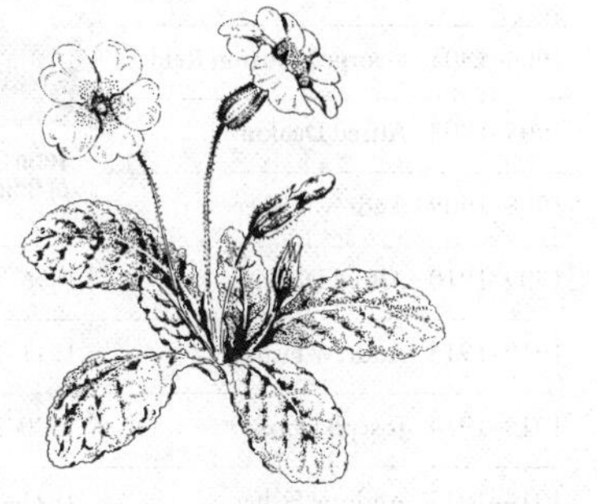

primrose

prim·rose /prím rōz/ *n* **1.** *US* a flowering plant from the family that includes the cowslip, cyclamen, and pimpernel. Native to: northern temperate regions. Family: Primulaceae. Can term **primula 2.** a small perennial plant with pale yellow flowers that appear in early spring in northern temperate regions. Native to: Europe. Latin name: *Primula vulgaris*. [14C. Via French < medieval Latin *prima rosa* "first rose," from its early flowering]

prim·rose path *n* (*literary*) **1.** an easy or pleasurable way of life **2.** an easy way or option, especially one that leads to disaster [< "the primrose path of dalliance" in Shakespeare's *Hamlet*]

prim·u·la /prímmyələ/ (*plural* **-las** or *same*) *n Can, UK* PLANTS same as **primrose** (sense 1) [Mid-18C. Via modern Latin < medieval Latin *primula (veris)* "first fruit (of spring)" < Latin *primulus* < *primus* "first"] —**prim·u·la·ceous** /prìmmyə láyshəss/ *adj*

pri·mum mo·bi·le /prīməm mṓbə leé, preéməm mṓbə lày/ *n* **1.** in Ptolemaic astronomy, the outermost sphere of the universe, thought to revolve every 24 hours, moving the inner spheres with it **2.** PHILOSOPHY same as **prime mover** (sense 2) [15C. < medieval Latin, "first moving thing"]

pri·mus in·ter pa·res /prīməss intər pér eéz/ *n* the representative or leader of a group of equals [< Latin, "first among equals"]

Pri·mus stove /prīməss-/ *tdmk* a trademark for a portable kerosene cooking stove

prince /prinss/ *n* **1. ROYAL MAN OR BOY** a man or boy in a royal family, especially a son of a reigning king or queen **2. MALE RULER** a man who rules a principality **3. EUROPEAN NOBLEMAN** a nobleman in some European countries, usually of a rank below duke **4. HIGHLY REGARDED MAN** a man or boy who is ranked highly in his field ○ *Robin Hood was the prince of thieves.* **5. GOOD MAN** a man who is outstanding, especially because of his generous or chivalrous nature (*informal*) [12C. Via French < Latin *princeps* "somebody who takes first place"] —**prince·dom** *n*

CULTURAL NOTE ***The Prince***, a political treatise (1513) by Italian writer Niccolò Machiavelli. Machiavelli based this guide to gaining and maintaining political power on his study of history and his experience of politics. The first work of its kind to present a political philosophy derived from a study of human behavior rather than traditional ethics, it gained lasting notoriety by justifying the judicious use of ruthlessness and deceit.

Prince Al·bert[1] *n US* a men's double-breasted, knee-length coat with a fitted torso and sleeves and a flared skirt [Late 19C. After Prince ALBERT]

PRIME MINISTERS OF AUSTRALIA, CANADA, NEW ZEALAND, AND THE UNITED KINGDOM AFTER 1900

Prime Ministers of Australia

Term of Office	Prime Minister
1901–1903	Edmund Barton
1903–1904	Alfred Deakin
1904	John Christian Watson
1904–1905	George Houston Reid
1905–1908	Alfred Deakin
1908–1909	Andrew Fisher
1909–1910	Alfred Deakin
1910–1913	Andrew Fisher
1913–1914	Joseph Cook
1914–1915	Andrew Fisher
1915–1923	William Morris Hughes
1923–1929	Stanley Melbourne Bruce
1929–1932	James Henry Scullin
1932–1939	Joseph Aloysius Lyons
1939	Earle Page
1939–1941	Robert Menzies
1941	Arthur William Fadden
1941–1945	John Curtin
1945	Francis Michael Forde
1945–1949	Joseph Benedict Chifley
1949–1966	Robert Menzies
1966–1967	Harold Holt
1967–1968	John McEwen
1968–1971	John Gorton
1971–1972	William McMahon

Australia . . .

1972–1975	Gough Whitlam
1975–1983	Malcolm Fraser
1983–1991	Bob Hawke
1991–1996	Paul Keating
1996–	John Howard

Prime Ministers of Canada

Term of Office	Prime Minister
1896–1911	Wilfred Laurier
1911–1920	Robert Laird Borden
1920–1921	Arthur Meighen
1921–1926	W.L. Mackenzie King
1926	Arthur Meighen
1926–1930	W.L. Mackenzie King
1930–1935	Richard Bedford Bennett
1935–1948	W.L. Mackenzie King
1948–1957	Louis St. Laurent
1957–1963	John G. Diefenbaker
1963–1968	Lester B. Pearson
1968–1979	Pierre Trudeau
1979–1980	Joseph Clark
1980–1984	Pierre Trudeau
1984	John M. Turner
1984–1993	Brian Mulroney
1993	Kim Campbell
1993–2003	Jean Chrétien
2003–	Paul Martin

Prime Ministers of New Zealand

Term of Office	Prime Minister
1893–1906	Richard John Seddon
1906	William Hall-Jones
1906–1912	Joseph George Ward
1912	Thomas Mackenzie
1912–1925	William Ferguson Masey
1925	Francis Henry Dillon Bell
1925–1928	Joseph Gordon Coates
1928–1930	Joseph George Ward
1930–1935	George William Forbes
1935–1940	Michael Joseph Savage
1940–1949	Peter Fraser
1949–1957	Sydney George Holland
1957	Keith Jacka Holyoake
1957–1960	Walter Nash
1960–1972	Keith Jacka Holyoake
1972	John Ross Marshall
1972–1974	Norman Eric Kirk
1974–1975	Wallace Edward Rowling
1975–1984	Robert David Muldoon
1984–1989	David Russell Lange
1989–1990	Geoffrey Palmer
1990	Michael Moore
1990–1997	James Bolger
1997–1999	Jenny Shipley
1999–	Helen Clark

Prime Ministers of the United Kingdom

Term of Office	Prime Minister
1902–1905	Arthur James Balfour
1905–1908	Henry Campbell-Bannerman
1908–1916	Herbert Henry Asquith
1916–1922	David Lloyd George
1922–1923	Andrew Bonar Law
1923–1924	Stanley Baldwin
1924	Ramsay MacDonald
1924–1929	Stanley Baldwin
1929–1935	Ramsay MacDonald
1935–1937	Stanley Baldwin
1937–1940	Neville Chamberlain
1940–1945	Winston Churchill
1945–1951	Clement Attlee
1951–1955	Winston Churchill
1955–1957	Anthony Eden
1957–1963	Harold Macmillan
1963–1964	Alec Douglas-Home
1964–1970	Harold Wilson
1970–1974	Edward Heath
1974–1976	Harold Wilson
1976–1979	James Callaghan
1979–1990	Margaret Thatcher
1990–1997	John Major
1997–	Tony Blair

Prince Al·bert[2] /prinss álbərt/ city in central Saskatchewan, Canada, 83 mi./140 km north of Saskatoon. Population: 34,752 (2001).

Prince Al·bert Na·tion·al Park national park in central Saskatchewan, Canada. Area: 1,496 sq. mi./3,874 sq. km.

Prince Charles Is·land /prinss chaárlz-/ largest island in Foxe Basin, west of Baffin Island, in Nunavut, Canada. Area: 3,676 sq. mi./9,521 sq. km.

prince charm·ing, **Prince Charm·ing** *n* **1.** a man who fulfills the romantic ideal of the perfect lover (*informal*) **2.** a man who actively seeks to charm people, especially women, and gain their liking [Mid-19C. After the hero of the fairy tale *Cinderella*]

prince con·sort *n* a prince who is married to a reigning queen

Prince Ed·ward Is·land /-èddwərd-/ smallest province in Canada, in the east of the country, in the Gulf of St. Lawrence, opposite New Brunswick and Nova Scotia. Capital: Charlottetown. Population: 139,900 (2002). Area: 2,185 sq. mi./5,660 sq. km. —**Prince Ed·ward Is·land·er** *n*

Prince Ed·ward Is·land Na·tion·al Park national park in eastern Canada, on the Northern shore of Prince Edward Island. Area: 8.5 sq. mi./22 sq. km.

Prince George city in central British Columbia, Canada, at the junction of the Nechako and Fraser rivers. Population: 66,239 (2001).

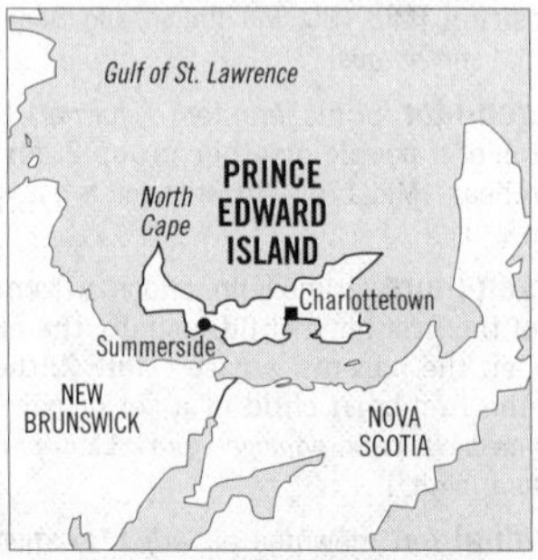

Prince Edward Island

prince·ling /prínssling/, **prince·let** /prínsslet/ *n* a prince of low rank, age, or importance

prince·ly /prínsslee/ (**-li·er, -li·est**) *adj* **1.** relating to, belonging to, or suitable for a prince **2.** generous as an amount of money, or requiring the expenditure of large sums of money ○ *a princely manor in the country* —**prince·li·ness** *n*

Prince of Wales Is·land 1. island in northern Canada, in Nunavut, between Victoria and Somerset islands. Area: 12,872 sq. mi./33,339 sq. km. **2.** island in northern Australia, in Queensland. Population: 90 (1971). Area: 69 sq. mi./180 sq. km.

prince re·gent (*plural* **prince re·gents** or **princ·es re·gent**) *n* a prince who rules in the monarch's place, e.g., when the monarch is abroad, ill, or still a child

prince roy·al (*plural* **princ·es roy·al**) *n* the eldest son of a reigning monarch

Prince Ru·pert /-ro͞opərt/ city on the northwestern coast of British Columbia, Canada. Population: 14,643 (2001).

prince's-feath·er /prìnssəz-/ (*plural* **prince's-feath·ers** or *same*) *n* **1.** a tall annual plant with reddish leaves. Flowers: red, in spikes. Native to: North America. Family: Amaranthus. **2.** a tall plant with oval leaves. Flowers: pink, in drooping spikes. Native to: Australia, Asia. Latin name: *Polygonum orientale.*

prince's pine *n* PLANTS same as **pipsissewa**

prin·cess /prínsəss, -sèss, prin séss/ *n* (*plural* **-cess·es**) **1. ROYAL WOMAN OR GIRL** a woman or girl in a royal family, especially a daughter of the reigning king or queen **2. PRINCE'S WIFE** the wife or widow of a prince **3. FEMALE RULER** a woman who rules a principality **4. EUROPEAN NOBLEWOMAN** a noblewoman in some European countries, usually of a rank below duchess **5. SPOILED YOUNG WOMAN** a rich young woman considered to be spoiled or arrogant **6. NAME FOR GIRL** a pet name for a woman or girl, especially a daughter **7. HIGHLY REGARDED WOMAN** a woman who is ranked highly in her field, or who has other outstanding qualities (*dated*) ■ *adj* **FITTED AT TOP WITH FLARED SKIRT** describes a woman's or girl's garment made with long triangular pieces of fabric that reach from neck to hem, fitted at the bodice with a flared skirt [14C. < French *princesse* < *prince* (see PRINCE)]

prin·cess roy·al (*plural* **prin·cess·es roy·al**) *n* the eldest daughter of a reigning monarch, especially of a British monarch, who confers the title on her as a special honor

prin·cess tree *n* TREES same as **paulownia** [Mid-20C. After Princess Anna Pavlovna, daughter of Tsar Paul I of Russia]

Prince·ton /prínstən/ town in west central New Jersey. It is home to Princeton University, founded in 1746. Population: 16,590 (2002 estimate).

prin·ci·pal /prínssəp'l/ *adj* **1. PRIMARY** first or among the first in importance or rank **2.** FIN **INITIALLY INVESTED** relating to the initial amount of money that was invested or borrowed ■ *n* **1. SCHOOL ADMINISTRATOR** the head administrator of a school, especially a grade school or high school **2. MOST IMPORTANT PERSON** the leading or most highly ranked person **3. SIGNIFICANT PARTICIPANT** any one of the most significant participants in an event or a situation ○ *the principals in the real-estate transaction* **4.** FIN **ORIGINAL AMOUNT INVESTED** the initial sum of money invested or borrowed, before interest or other revenue is added, or the remainder of that sum after payments have been made **5.** THEATER, ARTS **LEAD PERFORMER** a lead actor, singer, or dancer in a theatrical or musical performance **6.** MUSIC **LEAD MUSICIAN** the lead musician in a section of an orchestra, or the part played by that musician **7.** LAW **REPRESENTED PERSON** somebody for whom a representative or proxy acts in a legal matter **8.** LAW **RESPONSIBLE PARTY** somebody who is directly responsible for something **9.** LAW **CRIMINAL** the perpetrator of a crime **10.** CONSTR **MAIN SUPPORT BEAM** the main support beam, girder, or truss in a roof, bridge, or other construction [13C. Via French < Latin *principalis* < *princip-* "somebody who takes first place"] —**prin·ci·pal·ly** *adv* —**prin·ci·pal·ship** *n*

USAGE principal or **principle**? These two words, though they have the same pronunciation, have different meanings and functions. ***Principle*** is a noun only, meaning "a basic assumption," "an ethical standard," and "a way of operating or working," as in *the principles of a democratic system; a woman of principle; studied the principles of the internal-combustion engine.* By contrast, ***principal***, as a noun, means "a school administrator," "an important participant," "a lead performer," and "a monetary amount invested," as in *was sent to the principal's office; a principal in an accounting firm; a principal of $500,000.* As an adjective it means "primary": *our principal* [not *principle*] *reason for an appeal.*

prin·ci·pal ax·is *n* the line that passes through the center of curvature of a lens

prin·ci·pal di·ag·o·nal *n* in a square matrix, the diagonal line that extends from the upper left corner to the lower right corner

prin·ci·pal·i·ty /prìnssə pállətee/ (*plural* **-ties**) *n* **1. COUNTRY OR TERRITORY** a territory ruled by a prince or princess **2. POSITION OF PRINCE** the position or jurisdiction of a prince **3.** CHR **ANGEL OF THIRD-HIGHEST ORDER** an angel of the third of the nine orders of angels in the traditional Christian hierarchy

prin·ci·pal parts *npl* **1.** the basic forms of a verb, from which other forms are derived, in an inflected language such as Latin **2.** the infinitive, past tense, and participial forms of an English verb

prin·ci·pal pho·tog·ra·phy *n* the shooting of the main action and characters in a movie, as opposed to the shooting of backgrounds and crowd scenes by the second unit

Prín·ci·pe /prínssəpə, práN-/ second largest island in São Tomé and Príncipe. Population: 5,900 (1995). Area: 118 sq. mi./306 sq. km.

prin·ci·ple /prínssəp'l/ *n* **1. BASIC ASSUMPTION** an important underlying law or assumption required in a system of thought **2. ETHICAL STANDARD** a standard of moral or ethical decision-making ○ *I buy recyclable products as a matter of principle.* **3. WAY OF WORKING** the basic way in which something works **4. SOURCE** the primary source of something **5.** CHEM **CHARACTERISTIC INGREDIENT** an ingredient of a substance that gives the substance a special quality [14C. < Anglo-Norman, alteration of French *principe* < Latin *principium* < *princip-* "somebody who takes first place"] —**prin·ci·pled** *adj* ◇ **in principle** in theory or in the essentials ◇ **on principle** because of a particular ethical standard that somebody believes in

USAGE See ***principal.***

Prin·ci·ple *n* used in Christian Science to refer to God

prink /pringk/ (**prinked, prink·ing, prinks**) *vti* to dress or groom somebody or yourself in a fancy or fussy way [Late 16C. Origin ?] —**prink·er** *n*

print /print/ *n* **1. PRESSED MARK** a mark made by pressing something onto a surface ○ *left dirty paw prints on the carpet* **2. WRITING ON SURFACE** words, figures, or symbols on a surface, especially when produced by a machine ○ *books available in large print* **3. PUBLISHED STATUS** the state of being in a printed form or being published ○ *We don't want these typographical errors to make it into print.* **4. ARTWORK** a work of art made by inking a surface with a raised design and pressing it onto paper or another surface **5. FABRIC WITH DESIGN** a fabric with an ink or paint design on its surface, or the design itself (*often used before a noun*) ○ *She was wearing a new print dress.* **6. PHOTOGRAPH** a photograph, usually on paper, made from a negative **7.** MOVIES **MOTION PICTURE COPY** a copy of a motion picture **8.** ART **STAMP OR DIE** a stamp or die used to make marks on a surface **9.** CRIME same as **fingerprint** (*informal*) ■ *v* (**print·ed, print·ing, prints**) **1.** *vti* **MAKE SOMETHING WITH PRINTING MACHINE** to make a copy, document, or publication using a printing press or a computer printer ○ *These books were printed in Canada.* **2.** *vti* **PUBLISH SOMETHING** to publish information or a publication ○ *The company prints several news magazines in addition to books.* **3.** *vti* **MARK SOMETHING USING PRESSURE** to produce a mark, design, or lettering on a surface by pressing something on it ○ *A machine prints the corporate logo onto pencils.* **4.** *vti* **PRESS DESIGNS ONTO SOMETHING** to press a mark, design, or lettering onto something ○ *We printed enough T-shirts for the whole team.* **5.** *vti* **WRITE SEPARATED LETTERS** to write something by hand, using separated letters rather than script ○ *Print your name under your signature.* **6.** *vt* **MAKE IMPRESSION** to make an impression on the mind of somebody **7.** *vti* PHOTOGRAPHY, MOVIES **MAKE COPY FROM NEGATIVE** to make a positive image or copy of a photograph or motion picture from a negative **8.** *vi* PRINTING **WORK AS PRINTER** to do the work of a printer ■ *adj* **RELATING TO PUBLISHED MEDIA** produced by or relating to the published media [13C. < Old French *preinte*, form of past participle of *preindre* "press" < Latin *premere*] ◇ **in print 1.** currently available from a publisher **2.** printed in a book, newspaper, or magazine ◇ **out of print** not currently available from a publisher

print out *vt* to produce a printed copy of data from a computer

print·a·ble /príntəb'l/ *adj* **1.** sufficiently inoffensive, correct, or well-written as to be fit to be printed in a publication ○ *Some of the player's comments weren't printable.* **2.** capable of being printed or printed on ○ *This paper's too slick to be printable.* —**print·a·bil·i·ty** /prìntə bíllətee/ *n*

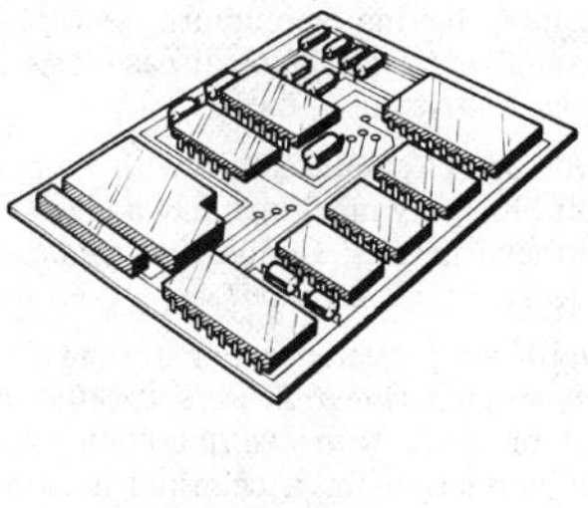

printed circuit

print·ed cir·cuit /prìntəd-/ *n* an electronic circuit in which some components and the connections between them are formed by etching a metallic coating on one or both sides of an insulating board

print·ed mat·ter *n* published material, e.g., books, newspapers, magazines, or catalogs, that qualifies for a special low postage rate

print·er /príntər/ *n* **1. PERSON OR COMPANY IN PRINTING TRADE** a person or company in the business of printing books, newspapers, or magazines **2. MACHINE FOR PRINTING** a machine that prints books, newspapers, or magazines **3. MACHINE FOR PRINTING COMPUTER DATA** a device that produces computer-generated text or graphics on paper, transparencies, or similar media **4. MACHINE FOR COPYING FILM** a machine that makes duplicates of film, normally a positive from a negative

print·er driv·er *n* a software routine that formats an application's data to print properly on a particular printer

print·er's dev·il *n* an apprentice or young assistant to a printer [< DEVIL "apprentice"]

print·head /prínt hèd/ *n* a part of a computer printer that transfers the characters to paper

print·ing /prínting/ *n* **1. PRODUCTION OF COPIES** the process or business of producing copies of documents, publications, or images **2. PRINTED CHARACTERS** typographical characters as they appear on paper or another surface ○ *The printing has washed off this bottle.* **3. LETTERS WRITTEN SEPARATELY** letters written separately or the act of writing letters separately, in contrast to script characters ○ *Her printing is easier to read than her handwriting.* **4. PRINT RUN** the process or output of one print run of a publication ○ *This book is in its eighth printing.*

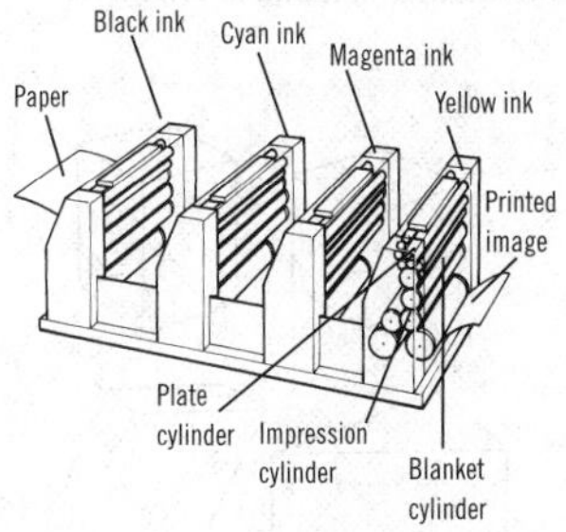

printing press

print·ing press *n* a machine that presses inked set type or etched plates onto paper or textiles that are fed through it

print·mak·er /prínt màykər/ *n* an artist who designs and makes prints —**print·mak·ing** *n*

print·out /prínt òwt/ *n* a paper copy of data from a computer

print run *n* the number of copies of a publication, document, or artwork that are printed in a single batch ○ *an initial print run of 30,000 copies*

pri·on[1] /prée òn, prī ən/ *n* an infectious particle of protein that, unlike a virus, contains no nucleic acid, does not trigger an immune response, and is not destroyed by extreme heat or cold. These particles are considered responsible for such diseases as scrapie, bovine spongiform encephalopathy, kuru, and Creutzfeldt-Jakob disease. [Late 20C. < *proteinaceous* + INFECTIOUS + -ON[1]]

pri·on[2] /prī òn/ *n* a small seabird with a serrated beak and soft blue-gray markings like a pigeon's. Native to: southern oceans. Genus: *Pachyptila*. [Mid-19C. Via modern Latin < Greek *priōn* "saw"]

pri·or[1] /prīr/ *adj* **1.** EARLIER earlier in time or sequence ○ *a prior engagement* **2.** MORE IMPORTANT more important or basic ■ *n* EARLIER CRIMINAL CONVICTION an earlier conviction for a criminal act (*informal*) ○ *Check to see whether the suspect has any priors.* [Early 18C. < Latin, "former, elder, superior," literally "more before"] ◇ **prior to somebody** *or* **something** before somebody or something in time

pri·or[2] /prīr/ *n* **1.** ABBOT'S DEPUTY an officer in a monastery of a rank below abbot **2.** MALE RELIGIOUS SUPERIOR a man who is superior in some religious communities **3.** SENIOR MEDIEVAL MAGISTRATE a senior magistrate in some medieval Italian republics, especially Florence [Pre-12C. < medieval Latin < Latin (see PRIOR[1])]

pri·or·ate /prīrət/ *n* the position or term of office of a prior or prioress

pri·or·ess /prīrəss/ *n* **1.** a woman officer in a convent of a rank below abbess **2.** a woman superior in some religious communities

pri·or·i·tize /prī áwrə tīz, prīrə tīz/ (**-tized, -tiz·ing, -tiz·es**) *vti* **1.** to order things according to their importance or urgency ○ *I must prioritize my list of things to do.* **2.** to regard something as most important or urgent ○ *I have to prioritize finding a job.* —**pri·or·i·ti·za·tion** /prī àwrəti záysh'n, prīrə-/ *n*

pri·or·i·ty /prī áwrətee/ (*plural* **-ties**) *n* **1.** GREATEST IMPORTANCE the state of having most importance or urgency ○ *Give this case priority treatment.* **2.** SOMEBODY OR SOMETHING IMPORTANT somebody or something that is ranked highly in terms of importance or urgency ○ *You've got to get your priorities right.* **3.** RIGHT OF PRECEDENCE the right to be ranked above others **4.** EARLIER OCCURRENCE the state of having preceded something else

pri·or·y /prīree/ (*plural* **-ies**) *n* a religious community or home headed by a prior or prioress, e.g., a monastery or convent

Pri·pet Marsh·es /prìp ət-/, **Pri·pyat' Marsh·es** /préepyət-/, **Po·les'ye** /pō lessyə/ swamp region in southern Belarus and northwestern Ukraine, along the Pripet River. Area: 104,000 sq. mi./270,000 sq. km.

prise *vt, n* another spelling of **prize**[2]

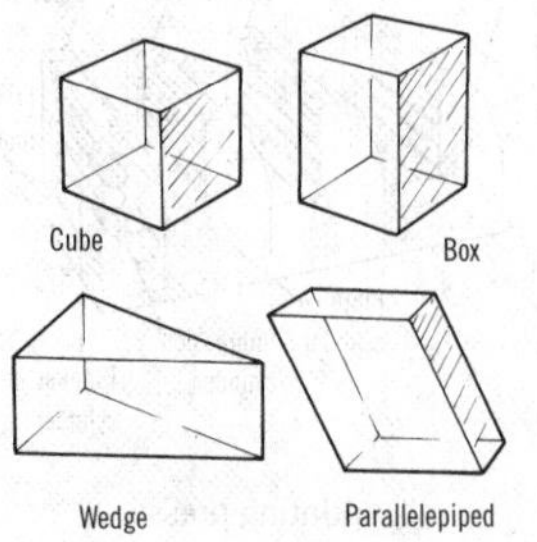

prism

pris·m /prízzəm/ *n* **1.** SOLID FOR DISPERSING LIGHT a transparent polygonal solid object with flat faces and a usually triangular cross section, used for separating white light into a spectrum of colors **2.** SOMETHING MADE OF CUT GLASS a cut-glass object, especially one that can separate white light into a spectrum **3.** CRYSTALS CRYSTAL TYPE a crystal form with faces that are parallel to a single axis **4.** MATH PARALLELOGRAM-SIDED SOLID a three-dimensional geometric figure with ends that are identical polygons and with sides that are parallelograms [Late 16C. Via late Latin < Greek *prisma* "something sawn" (because of its shape) < *prizein* "to saw"]

pris·mat·ic /priz máttik/, **pris·mat·i·cal** /-máttik'l/ *adj* **1.** RELATING TO PRISM resembling or relating to a prism **2.** SEPARATED BY PRISM describes light that shows the colors of the spectrum, as refracted by a prism **3.** COLORFUL brightly colored, like a rainbow [Early 18C. < French *prismatique* < Greek *prismat-*, stem of *prisma* (see PRISM)] —**pris·mat·i·cal·ly** *adv*

pris·ma·toid /prízmə tòyd/ *n* a polyhedron with all its vertices in one of two parallel planes [Mid-19C. < Greek *prismat-*, stem of *prisma* (see PRISM)] —**pris·ma·toi·dal** /prìzmə tóyd'l/ *adj*

pris·moid /príz mòyd/ *n* a body like a prism with sides that are parallelograms or trapezoids and equal-sided polygons as bases [Early 18C. < PRISM, after *rhomboid*] —**pris·moi·dal** /priz móyd'l/ *adj*

pris·on /prízz'n/ *n* **1.** a secure place where somebody is confined as punishment for a crime or while waiting to stand trial **2.** a place or condition of captivity or unwanted restraint ○ *His fears are a prison that he cannot escape.* ■ *vt* (**-oned, -on·ing, -ons**) same as **imprison** (*archaic or literary*) [12C. Via French < Latin *prension-* "seizing" < *prehendere* "seize"]

pris·on camp *n* **1.** a camp where prisoners of war are confined **2.** *US* a minimum security prison, where prisoners have some freedom of movement

pris·on·er /prízz'nər/ *n* **1.** SOMEBODY HELD IN PRISON somebody confined in a prison as a punishment for a crime or while waiting to stand trial **2.** SOMEBODY HELD AGAINST WILL somebody who is confined in a place ○ *He's been taken prisoner by a group of rebel soldiers.* **3.** SOMEBODY WHO IS OR FEELS TRAPPED somebody who cannot escape a situation or condition

pris·on·er of con·science *n* somebody held in a prison by a state, especially an oppressive regime, because of his or her political or religious beliefs

pris·on·er of war *n* somebody who has been captured and imprisoned by an enemy during a war

pris·on·er's base *n* a children's game in which two teams try to tag each other's members, thereby adding them to their team at their base [Alteration of *prison bars*]

pris·on fe·ver *n* same as **typhus** (*dated*)

~~prisonner~~ incorrect spelling of **prisoner**

priss /priss/ *n US* somebody who behaves prissily (*informal*) [Early 20C. Back-formation < PRISSY]

priss around *vi US* to act in an excessively fussy proper way (*informal*)

pris·sy /príssee/ (**-si·er, -si·est**) *adj* behaving in a very prudish and proper way, or reflecting prudishness and properness [Late 19C. Probably blend of PRIM + SISSY] —**pris·si·ly** *adv* —**pris·si·ness** *n*

Priš·tin·a /préeshtinə/ the largest city in the province of Kosovo in the Federal Republic of Yugoslavia. Population: 241,565 (1997).

pris·tine /prí steen, pri stéen/ *adj* **1.** IMMACULATE so clean and neat as to look as good as new ○ *The house is in pristine condition.* **2.** UNSPOILED not yet ruined by human encroachment ○ *acres of pristine forest* **3.** IN OR OF ORIGINAL STATE in or belonging to an original state or condition [Mid-16C. < Latin *pristinus* "former"]

Prit·chett /príchit/, **Sir V. S.** (1900–97) British writer. An acclaimed novelist, critic, biographer, and travel writer, he is best known for his short stories, the first collection of which was *The Spanish Virgin and Other Stories* (1930). Full name **Pritchett, Sir Victor Sawdon**

prith·ee /prí*th*ee/ *interj* used to introduce a request to somebody (*archaic*) [Late 16C. Contraction of *(I) pray thee*]

pri·va·cy /prívəssee/ *n* **1.** SECLUSION the state of being apart from other people and not seen, heard, or disturbed by them ○ *Shut the door so we can have some privacy.* **2.** FREEDOM FROM ATTENTION OF OTHERS freedom from the observation, intrusion, or attention of others ○ *If you seek celebrity, you must sacrifice privacy.* **3.** HIDDEN CONDITION the state of being kept secret

pri·vate /prīvət/ *adj* **1.** KEPT SECRET OR RESTRICTED not for other people to see or know about ○ *My salary is a private matter that I don't care to discuss.* **2.** SECLUDED sufficiently secluded for people to be alone and not watched, heard, or disturbed by others ○ *Let's find a private corner where we can talk.* **3.** PERSONAL belonging to, restricted to, or intended for an individual person ○ *The master bedroom has a private bathroom.* **4.** NOT PUBLIC not open to the public **5.** ACTING IN PERSONAL CAPACITY holding no official position in government ○ *a private citizen* **6.** NONGOVERNMENTAL not supported by government funding **7.** RESERVED AND SECRETIVE preferring not to disclose personal information or to discuss personal feelings with others ○ *She's a very private person.* **8.** NOT UNDERSTANDABLE BY EVERYONE excluding people who do not share the knowledge required to understand ○ *a private joke* **9.** LOWEST-RANKING relating to the lowest rank of Army soldier or Marine ■ *n* LOWEST-RANKING SOLDIER OR MARINE an enlisted person in the US Army or Marine Corps of the lowest rank ■ **pri·vates** *npl* ANAT same as **genitals** (*informal*) [14C. < Latin *privatus* "isolated, not in public life," past participle of *privare* (see PRIVATION)] —**pri·vate·ly** *adv* —**pri·vate·ness** *n*

pri·vate bank *n* a bank that offers individualized financial and investment advice and services to wealthy clients

pri·vate bank·ing *n* management by a bank of a customer's wealth in its entirety

pri·vate com·pa·ny *n UK* a company that is not listed on the stock market and does not issue its shares to the public

pri·vate de·tec·tive *n* a detective who is not a member of the police but is hired by individual clients or companies

pri·vate dick *n US* same as **private detective** (*dated slang*)

pri·vate en·ter·prise *n* **1.** business activities that are not regulated or owned by the government **2.** a company that is owned by a private individual or individuals and not by the government

pri·va·teer /prìvə téer/ *n* **1.** a ship that belongs to and is run by a person or company but is authorized by the government to engage in battle during war **2.** the commander or a crew member of a privateer [Mid-17C. After VOLUNTEER]

pri·vate eye *n* CRIME same as **private detective** (*informal*) [*Eye*, spelling of *I.*, abbreviation of *investigator*]

pri·vate first class (*plural* **pri·vates first class**) *n US* an enlisted person in the US Army or Marine Corps of a rank above private

pri·vate in·come *n* income from sources other than employment, e.g., from investments or allowances

pri·vate in·ves·ti·ga·tor *n* CRIME same as **private detective**

pri·vate key cryp·tog·ra·phy *n* an encryption method using a single key known to both the sender and receiver for encoding and decoding an Internet message

pri·vate la·bel card *n* a credit card for use at only one retailer that is issued and managed by a third party

pri·vate lan·guage *n* an exclusive language devised and spoken by a restricted group of people, especially twins

pri·vate law *n* the branch of law concerned with the rights and responsibilities of individual people

pri·vate means *npl* FIN same as **private income**

pri·vate parts *npl* ANAT same as **genitals**

pri·vate school *n* a school that is not run by the government and therefore charges fees for tuition, especially one below tertiary level

pri·vate sec·tor *n* the part of a free market economy that is made up of companies and organizations that are not owned or controlled by the government

pri·vate view·ing *n* a preview of a motion picture or an exhibition that is open only to invited guests

pri·va·tion /prī váysh'n/ *n* **1.** lack of the basic necessities of life such as food, housing, and heating **2.** the act of depriving somebody of something [14C. < Latin *privation-* < *privare* "deprive, isolate" < *privus* "single, isolated"]

pri·vat·ism /prīvə tìzzəm/ *n* an attitude or lifestyle in which somebody ignores all but his or her own interests —**pri·va·tist** *n, adj* —**pri·va·tis·tic** /prīvə tístik/ *adj*

priv·a·tive /prívvətiv/ *adj* **1.** RELATING TO LACK OR NEGATION indicating the absence or negation of some quality ○ *a privative term* **2.** CAUSING DEPRIVATION causing or experiencing deprivation ■ *n* AFFIX DENOTING LACK OR NEGATION an affix, word, or expression that denotes the absence or negation of some quality, e.g., English "non-" or Greek "a-" [Late 16C. Directly or via French < Latin *privativus* < *privare* (see PRIVATION)] —**priv·a·tive·ly** *adv*

pri·va·tize /prīvə tīz/ (**-tized, -tiz·ing, -tiz·es**) *vt* to transfer to private ownership an economic enterprise or public utility that has been under state ownership —**pri·va·ti·za·tion** /prīvəti záysh'n/ *n*

~~**privelage**~~ incorrect spelling of **privilege**

priv·et /prívvət/ *n* an evergreen bush commonly used for hedging. Flowers: white, in clusters. Native to: Europe, North Africa, Asia. Latin name: *Ligustrum vulgare* or *Ligustrum ovalifolium*. [Mid-16C. Origin ?]

priv·i·lege /prívvəlij, prívvlij/ *n* **1.** RESTRICTED RIGHT OR BENEFIT an advantage, right, or benefit that is not available to everyone **2.** RIGHTS AND ADVANTAGES ENJOYED BY ELITE the rights and advantages enjoyed by a relatively small group of people, usually as a result of wealth or social status ○ *a system founded on privilege* **3.** SPECIAL HONOR a special treat or honor ○ *It was a privilege to work with you.* **4.** *US* CONFIDENTIALITY OF COMMUNICATION the special right to confidentiality of communication between two parties, e.g., a lawyer and client or doctor and patient **5.** LAWMAKER'S RIGHT TO SPECIAL TREATMENT the right to or granting of special treatment or benefits such as freedom from prosecution to members of a legislative body **6.** *US* STOCK OPTION an option to buy or sell stocks over a period of time ■ *vt* (**-leged, -leg·ing, -leg·es**) **1.** GIVE SOMEBODY SPECIAL RIGHTS to grant special rights or benefits to somebody or something **2.** GRANT EXEMPTION TO SOMEBODY to exempt or release somebody or something from something [12C. Via French < Latin *privilegium* "private law" < *privus* "single, isolated" + *leg-* "law"]

priv·i·leged /prívvəlijd, prívvlijd/ *adj* **1.** ENJOYING SPECIAL ADVANTAGES enjoying privileges, especially the resources and advantages associated with the upper classes and the rich **2.** HONORED OR FORTUNATE fortunate in having a special advantage or opportunity to do something ○ *I feel privileged to be here today.* **3.** RESTRICTED available only to a select group of people ■ *npl* PEOPLE ENJOYING SPECIAL ADVANTAGES a class of people, especially the rich or the upper classes, that benefits from special rights or resources (*takes a plural verb*)

priv·i·leged com·mu·ni·ca·tion *n* **1.** a confidential conversation or correspondence that does not have to be disclosed in a court of law **2.** speech or writing that is not subject to libel or slander laws

priv·i·ty /prívvətee/ (*plural* **-ties**) *n* **1.** SHARED KNOWLEDGE OF SECRET the state of sharing knowledge of or colluding in something secret **2.** LAW LEGALLY RECOGNIZED RELATIONSHIP a legally recognized relationship between two parties, e.g., between members of a family, between an employer and employees, or between others who have entered into a contract together **3.** LAW RELATIONSHIP TO PROPERTY a successive or mutual relationship to some property [12C. Via French < medieval Latin *privitas* < Latin *privus* "single, isolated"]

priv·y /prívvee/ *adj* **1.** SHARING SECRET KNOWLEDGE sharing knowledge of something secret or private ○ *I was privy to their plans to elope.* **2.** RELATING TO SOMEBODY IN PRIVATE CAPACITY relating to somebody, especially a British monarch, as a private person, not as an official personage **3.** SECRET done or spoken secretly or privately (*archaic*) ■ *n* (*plural* **-ies**) **1.** TOILET an outhouse **2.** LAW SOMEBODY ELSE INVOLVED IN SOMETHING somebody who has an interest or agency in something that involves another party [12C. Via French *privé* < Latin *privatus* (see PRIVATE)]

priv·y cham·ber *n* an apartment reserved for private use in a royal residence

priv·y coun·cil *n* **1.** a committee that advises a ruler **2.** *US* a group of people who advise an executive —**priv·y coun·cil·or** *n*

Priv·y Coun·cil *n* the committee that advises a British king or queen. It consists mainly of present and former members of the Cabinet. —**Priv·y Coun·cil·or** *n*

Priv·y Coun·cil Of·fice *n* the Canadian government department that provides nonpartisan advice and support to the prime minister and cabinet secretariat

Priv·y Seal *n* a seal that used to be attached to documents authorized by the British king or queen

prix fixe /pree féeks/ (*plural* **prix fixes** /-féeks/) *n* **1.** a meal with several courses that is offered by a restaurant at a set price **2.** a set price for a restaurant meal with several courses [< French, "fixed price"]

prize[1] /prīz/ *n* **1.** AWARD FOR WINNER something that is given to the winner of a contest or competition **2.** SOMETHING HIGHLY VALUED something that somebody values highly, especially because it takes great skill, effort, or luck to get ■ *vt* (**prized, priz·ing, priz·es**) TREASURE SOMETHING to value something highly ○ *This award is something I'll always prize.* ■ *adj* COMPLETE perfect as an example of something, especially something undesirable ○ *I made a prize fool of myself.* [Late 16C. Variant of PRICE]

prize[2] /prīz/, **prise** *vt* (**prized, priz·ing, priz·es; prised, pris·ing, pris·es**) **1.** LEVER SOMETHING to open or part something by levering ○ *I used a screwdriver to prize the lid off the paint.* **2.** EXTRACT INFORMATION to get something, especially information, from somebody or something with difficulty ■ *n* LEVER something used as a lever [14C. Probably < Old French *prise* (see PRIZE[3])]

prize[3] /prīz/ *n* something captured and kept, especially a ship or its contents taken by another ship in wartime [13C. < Old French *prise* "something seized," form of past participle of *prendre* "take, seize" < Latin *prehendere*]

prize·fight /prīz fīt/ *n* a boxing match in which the winner receives a cash prize —**prize·fight·er** *n* —**prize·fight·ing** *n*

prize-giv·ing *n UK* a ceremony at which prizes are awarded, especially for schoolwork

prize ring *n* **1.** a boxing ring where prizefights are held **2.** the sport or business of professional boxing

prize·win·ner /prīz wìnnər/ *n* somebody or something that wins a prize in a competition —**prize·win·ning** *adj*

p.r.n. *abbr* MED as required (*used on medical prescriptions*) [< Latin *pro re nata*]

pro[1] /prō/ *n* (*plural* **pros**) **1.** SUPPORTING ARGUMENT an argument in favor of a proposal or position **2.** SIDE ARGUING FOR SOMETHING a person or side in a debate, argument, or campaign that is in favor of a proposal or proposition ■ *prep* FOR in favor of ■ *adv* IN SUPPORT OF SOMETHING on the side that favors one side of an issue [14C. < Latin, "for" (see PRO-[1])]

pro[2] /prō/ *n* (*plural* **pros**) **1.** PROFESSIONAL PERSON a professional, especially in sports (*informal*) **2.** SKILLED PERSON an experienced and skilled person (*informal*) **3.** CRIME same as **prostitute** *n* (sense 1) (*slang*) ■ *adj* PROFESSIONAL relating to or typical of an activity, especially a sport, from which somebody earns a living ■ *adv* PROFESSIONALLY as a professional [Mid-20C. Shortening]

pro[3] /prō/ *abbr* professional practice (*used in Internet addresses*) See table at **domain name**

PRO, P.R.O. *abbr* public relations officer

pro-[1] *prefix* **1.** substituting for, acting in place of ○ *proconsul* **2.** in favor of ○ *pronuclear* [Via French < Latin *pro* "for" < Indo-European, "forward, before"]

pro·a·bor·tion *adj*
pro·A·mer·i·can *adj, n*
pro·Brit·ish *adj*
pro·busi·ness *adj*
pro·cap·i·tal·ist *adj, n*
pro·Cath·o·lic *adj, n*
pro·Chi·na *adj*
pro·Chi·nese *adj*
pro·Com·mu·nist *adj*
pro·de·moc·ra·cy *adj*
pro·dem·o·crat·ic *adj*
pro·en·vi·ron·ment *adj*
pro·es·tab·lish·ment *adj*
pro·Eu·ro·pe·an *adj, n*
pro·fam·i·ly *adj*
pro·fas·cist *adj, n*
pro·fem·i·nist *adj, n*
pro·Ger·man *adj*
pro·gov·ern·ment *adj*
pro·im·pe·ri·al *adj*
pro·in·de·pend·ence *adj*
pro·in·tel·lec·tual *adj, n*
pro·Is·lam·ic *adj*
pro·la·bor *adj*
pro·man·age·ment *adj*
pro·mil·i·tar·y *adj*
pro·mon·ar·chist *adj, n*
pro·mon·ar·chy *adj*
pro·Mus·lim *adj, n*
pro·peace *adj*
pro·Prot·es·tant *adj, n*
pro·reb·el *adj*
pro·re·form *adj*
pro·res·to·ra·tion *adj*
pro·re·vi·sion *adj*
pro·rev·o·lu·tion·ar·y *adj*
pro·sep·a·ra·tist *adj, n*
pro·slav·er·y *adj*
pro·So·vi·et *adj, n*
pro·su·per·vi·sion *adj*
pro·sur·ren·der *adj*
pro·syn·di·cal·ism *n*
pro·un·ion *adj*
pro·war *adj*
pro·West·ern *adj*
pro·work·er *adj*

pro-[2] *prefix* **1.** rudimentary, precursor ○ *prothrombin* **2.** before, earlier than ○ *procambium* **3.** in front of ○ *prothoracic* [Via French < Greek *pro* "in front, before" < Indo-European "forward, before"]

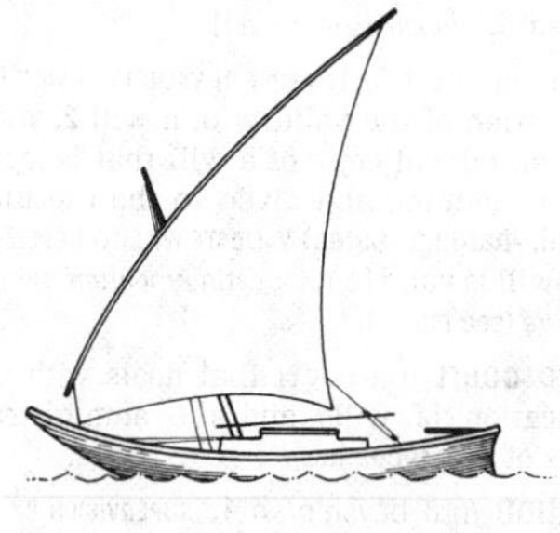

proa

pro·a /prṓ ə/ (*plural* **-as**), **prau** /prow/ (*plural* **praus**), **prah·u** /práa hoo/ (*plural* **-us**) *n* a Malayan boat with a triangular sail and a single outrigger [Late 16C. < Malay *pārāhū* "boat"]

pro·ac·tive /prō áktiv/ *adj* taking the initiative by acting rather than reacting to events [Mid-20C. After RETROACTIVE] —**pro·ac·tion** *n* —**pro·ac·tive·ly** *adv*

USAGE When people name words they despise as jargon, ***proactive*** is often on the list. ***Proactive*** does meet a need, serving as the opposite of *reactive* more naturally than, for example, *anticipatory* or *assertive* is able to. Nonetheless, it should be used sparingly.

pro-am /prō ám/ *adj* involving or composed of professional and amateur sports players ■ *n* a competition in which professional players compete against amateurs, or in which professionals and amateurs compete together [Mid-20C. < PRO[2] + *am*, shortening of AMATEUR]

prob·a·bi·lism /próbbəbə lìzzəm/ *n* **1.** the belief that certainty is impossible, and that therefore decisions must be based on probabilities **2.** the principle whereby, in moral questions in which nothing is certain, somebody may follow the probability favorable to him or her rather than a more probable, but less favorable view —**prob·a·bi·list** *n, adj* —**prob·a·bil·is·tic** /pròbbəbə lístik/ *adj* —**prob·a·bil·ist·i·cal·ly** *adv*

prob·a·bil·i·ty /pròbbə bíllətee/ (*plural* **-ties**) *n* **1.** STATE OF BEING PROBABLE the state of being probable, or the extent to which something is probable ○ *We must take into account the probability of another earthquake.* **2.** SOMETHING LIKELY TO HAPPEN something that is likely to happen or exist ○ *We must prepare for all probabilities.* **3.** STATS MATHEMATICAL LIKELIHOOD OF EVENT the likelihood that an event will occur, expressed as the ratio of the number of favorable outcomes in the set of outcomes divided by the total number of possible outcomes ◇ **in all probability** used to suggest that something is highly probable

prob·a·bil·i·ty den·si·ty func·tion *n* **1.** STATS same as **probability function** **2.** a function of a continuous variable such that the integral of the function over a specific region yields the probability that its value will fall within the region

prob·a·bil·i·ty func·tion *n* a function of a discrete random variable that yields the probability of occurrence of distinct outcomes

prob·a·bil·i·ty the·o·ry *n* the branch of mathematics that deals with quantities with random distributions, with the goal of predicting how defined systems will behave

prob·a·ble /próbbəb'l/ *adj* likely to exist, occur, or be true, although evidence is insufficient to prove or predict it ■ *n* somebody or something that is likely to be chosen for something or is likely to do something ○ *a probable for the team* [14C. Directly or via French < Latin *probabilis* "provable, plausible" < *probare* (see PROVE)]

prob·a·ble cause *n* sufficient reason to believe that an arrest or search of a suspect is warranted

prob·a·ble er·ror *n* the amount by which a statistic may vary from fact, based on chance factors

prob·a·bly /próbbəblee/ *adv* as is likely or to be expected ○ *I'll probably come tonight.*

pro·band /prṓ bànd/ *n* GENETICS same as **propositus** (sense 2) [Early 20C. < Latin *probandus-* "for testing, to be tested" < *probare* (see PROVE)]

pro·bate /prṓ bàyt/ *n* **1.** PROOF OF VALIDITY OF WILL the legal certification of the validity of a will **2.** VERIFIED COPY OF WILL an official copy of a will that is legally certified as genuine and given to the executors ■ *vt* (**-bat·ed, -bat·ing, -bates**) VALIDATE WILL to certify legally that a will is valid [14C. < Latin *probatum* "thing proved" < *probare* (see PROVE)]

pro·bate court *n* a court that deals with the legal certification of wills and the administration of estates of the deceased

pro·ba·tion /prō báysh'n/ *n* **1.** SUPERVISION BY PROBATION OFFICER the supervision of the behavior of a young or first-time criminal offender by a probation officer. During the period of supervision, the offender must regularly report to the probation officer and must not commit any further offenses. **2.** PERIOD OF TESTING SOMEBODY'S SUITABILITY a period during which somebody's suitability for a job or other role is being tested **3.** EDUC PERIOD WHEN STUDENT MUST IMPROVE a period during which a student is given a chance to improve his or her academic grades or behavior **4.** TESTING OF SOMETHING the testing or proving of something (*formal*) —**pro·ba·tion·al** *adj* —**pro·ba·tion·al·ly** *adv* —**pro·ba·tion·ar·y** *adj*

pro·ba·tion·er /prō báysh'nər/ *n* somebody on probation, especially somebody under supervision because he or she is new to a job or has just been released from prison

pro·ba·tion of·fi·cer *n* an official who supervises criminal offenders on probation

pro·ba·tive /prṓbətiv/, **pro·ba·to·ry** /prṓbə tàwree/ *adj* **1.** designed to test or prove somebody or something **2.** supplying proof or evidence [15C. < Old French *probatif* < Latin *probare* (see PROVE)]

probe /prōb/ *n* **1.** INVESTIGATION a thorough investigation, often into illegal or suspicious activities **2.** CIRCUIT-TESTING DEVICE a device with a metal tip used to test the behavior of electrical circuits **3.** SURGICAL INSTRUMENT FOR EXPLORING a long thin instrument used by doctors and dentists for exploring or examining **4.** AEROSP same as **space probe** ■ *vti* (**probed, prob·ing, probes**) **1.** INVESTIGATE SOMETHING COMPLETELY to conduct a thorough investigation of something **2.** CHECK SOMETHING USING PROBE to examine something with a probe **3.** EXAMINE AREA to search or explore a place [Mid-16C. < medieval Latin *proba* "examination" < Latin *probare* (see PROVE)] —**probe·a·ble** *adj* —**prob·er** *n* —**prob·ing·ly** *adv*

pro·ben·e·cid /prō bénnəssid/ *n* a drug that promotes the excretion of uric acid. Use: treatment of gout. [Mid-20C. Blend of PROPYL + BENZENE + ACID]

pro·bi·ot·ic /prṑ bī óttik/ *n* a substance containing live microorganisms that claims to be beneficial to humans and animals, e.g., by restoring the balance of microflora in the digestive tract

pro·bi·ty /prṓbətee/ *n* absolute moral correctness [Early 16C. Via French < Latin *probitas* < *probus* "good"]

prob·lem /próbbləm/ *n* **1.** DIFFICULTY a difficult situation, matter, or person **2.** PUZZLE TO BE SOLVED a question or puzzle that needs to be solved **3.** MATH STATEMENT REQUIRING MATHEMATICAL SOLUTION a statement or proposition requiring an algebraic, geometric, or other mathematical solution ■ *adj* HARD TO DEAL WITH difficult to discipline or deal with ○ *a problem child* [14C. Via French and Latin < Greek *problēma* "projection, obstacle," literally "thing thrown in front" < *ballein* "to throw"] ◇ **no problem** used to indicate that something will not cause any difficulty or inconvenience (*informal*)

SYNONYMS ***problem, mystery, puzzle, riddle, conundrum, enigma***

CORE MEANING: something difficult to solve or understand

problem a difficult situation, matter, or person ○ *an ongoing problem* ○ *problems with the staff* **mystery** an event or situation that is difficult to fully understand or explain, or a person about whom little is known ○ *the key to understanding the mysteries of the universe* ○ *The question of who Barry really was remains a mystery.* **puzzle** a problem or situation that is difficult or impossible to resolve, or somebody whose behavior or motives are difficult to understand ○ *The puzzle of the missing letters remained.* **riddle** something that is puzzling or confusing ○ *The DNA team announced they had solved the riddle of the unidentified human remains.* **conundrum** something that is puzzling or confusing ○ *Here's the conundrum: if advances in productivity result in more workers losing their jobs, who will be able to buy the products and services being produced?* **enigma** somebody or something that is not easily explained or understood ○ *After 20 years of marriage, Madeleine was still very much an enigma to him.*

prob·lem·at·ic /pròbblə máttik/, **prob·lem·at·i·cal** /-máttik'l/ *adj* **1.** DIFFICULT involving difficulties or problems **2.** UNCERTAIN unsettled or posing an uncertain outcome ■ *n* SOMETHING PROBLEMATIC a matter or issue that is problematic —**prob·lem·at·i·cal·ly** *adv*

~~**probly**~~ incorrect spelling of **probably**

pro bo·no /prō bṓnō/ *adj, adv* done or undertaken for the public good without any payment or compensation [Shortening of Latin *pro bono publico* "for the public good"]

pro·bos·ci·de·an /prṑ bòssi dée ən/, **pro·bos·ci·di·an** /prṑbə síddee ən/ *n* a very large mammal that has a trunk and tusks, e.g., an elephant, mammoth, or mastodon. Order: Proboscidea. [Mid-19C. < modern Latin *Proboscidea* < Latin *proboscid-*, stem of *proboscis* (see PROBOSCIS)] —**pro·bos·ci·de·an** *adj*

pro·bos·cis /prō bóssiss, -bóss kiss/ (*plural* **-bos·cis·es** or **-bos·ces** /-bos sèez/ or **-bos·ci·des** /-si dèez/) *n* **1.** LONG FLEXIBLE SNOUT the long flexible snout of some mammals such as the tapir, the elephant seal, or the proboscis monkey **2.** ELEPHANT'S TRUNK the trunk of an elephant or related extinct mammal **3.** LONG MOUTHPARTS OF INVERTEBRATE the long or tubular mouthparts of some insects, worms, and spiders, used for feeding, sucking, and other purposes **4.** LARGE NOSE a human nose, especially a large one (*humorous*) [Late 16C. Via Latin < Greek *proboskis* "elephant's trunk" < *boskein* "to feed"]

pro·bos·cis mon·key *n* a large monkey with reddish fur and a protruding bulbous nose that in older males becomes pendulous. Native to: Borneo. Latin name: *Nasalis larvatus*.

pro·caine /prṓ kàyn/ *n* a white or colorless crystalline ester. Use: local anesthetic, in the form of its hydrochloride. Formula: $C_{13}H_{20}N_2O_2$.

pro·cam·bi·um /prō kámbee əm/ *n* undifferentiated plant tissue that develops into cambium and vascular tissue —**pro·cam·bi·al** *adj*

pro·car·y·ote *n* BIOL another spelling of **prokaryote**

~~**procede**~~ incorrect spelling of **proceed**

pro·ce·dure /prə séejər/ *n* **1.** an established or correct method of doing something **2.** any means of doing or accomplishing something ○ *an extremely unorthodox procedure* **3.** COMPUT same as **routine** *n* (sense 4) **4.** COMPUT same as **subroutine** [Early 17C. < French *procédure* < *procéder* (see PROCEED)] —**pro·ce·dur·al** *adj, n*

pro·ceed /prō séed, prə-/ (**-ceed·ed, -ceed·ing, -ceeds**) *vi* **1.** BEGIN ACTION to go on to do something **2.** CONTINUE WITH ACTION to continue with a course of action **3.** PROGRESS to progress in a steady or particular manner **4.** GO IN PARTICULAR DIRECTION to go in a particular direction, especially forward **5.** DEVELOP to come from or arise from something **6.** LAW SUE to bring legal action against somebody [14C. Via French *procéder* < Latin *procedere* "go forward" < *cedere* "go"] —**pro·ceed·er** *n*

SPELLCHECK See ***precede***.

pro·ceed·ing /prō séeding, prə-/ *n* **1.** PROCEDURE an action or course of action **2.** LEGAL ACTION legal action brought against somebody (*often used in the pl*) ■ **pro·ceed·ings** *npl* **1.** SERIES OF EVENTS a series of related events occurring at one time or in one place **2.** PUBLISHED RECORDS published records of a meeting or conference

pro·ceeds /prṓ seèdz/ *npl* the money derived from a sale or other commercial transaction

proc·ess[1] /pró sèss, prṓ-/ *n* **1.** SERIES OF ACTIONS a series of actions directed toward a specific aim **2.** SERIES OF NATURAL OCCURRENCES a series of natural occurrences that produce change or development **3.** LAW LEGAL PROCEEDINGS the entire proceedings in a lawsuit **4.** LAW SUMMONS TO APPEAR IN COURT a summons or writ ordering somebody to appear in court **5.** BIOL NATURAL OUTGROWTH a part that naturally grows on or sticks out on an organism **6.** *US* HAIR same as **conk**[3] ■ *v* (**-essed, -ess·ing, -ess·es**) **1.** *vt* PREPARE SOMETHING USING A PROCESS to treat or prepare something in a series of steps or actions, e.g., using chemicals or industrial machinery **2.** *vt* TREAT FILM WITH CHEMICALS to treat light-sensitive film or paper with chemicals in order to make a latent image visible **3.** *vt* FOLLOW PROCEDURES to deal with somebody or something according to an established procedure **4.** *vti* PREPARE FOOD IN FOOD PROCESSOR to chop, mix, or otherwise prepare food in a food processor or blender **5.** *vt* COMPUT USE PROGRAM ON DATA to use a computer program to work on data in some way, e.g., to sort a database or recalculate a spreadsheet **6.** *vt* LAW SERVE SUMMONS ON SOMEBODY to serve a summons or writ on somebody **7.** *vt* LAW BRING LEGAL ACTION to bring a legal action against somebody **8.** *vt* PSYCHOL DISCUSS EMOTIONAL MEANING OF SOMETHING to discuss the interpersonal dynamics and emotional content of an event or situation **9.** *vt US* HAIR same as **conk**[3] ■ *adj* PREPARED IN A PROCESS treated or prepared using a special process [14C. Via French < Latin *processus* < *process-*, past participle of *procedere* (see PROCEED)]

proc·ess[2] /prə séss/ (**-essed, -ess·ing, -ess·es**) *vi* to move forward in a procession [Early 19C. Back-formation < PROCESSION]

proc·ess art *n* art created primarily as a physical record of the creative process. Jackson Pollock's drip paintings are perhaps the most famous works of this kind.

proc·essed /pró sèst/ *adj* treated by a chemical or industrial process

proc·essed cheese, **proc·ess cheese** *n* a blend of several types of cheese with emulsifiers added, sometimes sold in individually wrapped thin slices

proc·ess en·gi·neer·ing *n* the branch of engineering that determines the sequence of operations and the selection of tools required to manufacture a product

pro·ces·ser *n* COMPUT, HOUSEHOLD another spelling of **processor**

proc·ess in·dus·try *n* an industry in which raw materials are treated or prepared in a series of stages, e.g., using chemical processes. Process industries include oil refining, petrochemicals, water and sewage treatment, food processing, and pharmaceuticals.

pro·ces·sion /prə sésh'n/ *n* **1.** GROUP OF PEOPLE MOVING FORWARD a group of people or vehicles moving forward in a line as part of a celebration, commemoration, or demonstration **2.** FORWARD MOVEMENT the movement forward of a group of people or vehicles as part of a celebration, commemoration, or demonstration **3.** SUCCESSION a series of people or things coming one after the other [12C. Directly or via French < Latin *procession-* < *process-* (see PROCESS[1])]

pro·ces·sion·al /prə séshən'l, -séshnəl/ *adj* **1.** FOR PROCESSION used for or in a procession **2.** FORMING PROCESSION taking the form of a procession ■ *n* **1.** MUSIC FOR PROCESSION a piece of music suitable for accompanying a procession **2.** CHURCH MUSIC FOR ENTRY OF CLERGY a hymn or other piece of music that accompanies the entry of the clergy into a church **3.** BOOK OF HYMNS AND PRAYERS a book of hymns and prayers for use during a religious procession —**pro·ces·sion·al·ly** *adv*

pro·ces·sor /pró sèssər, prṓ-/, **pro·ces·ser** *n* **1.** somebody or something that processes things **2.** the central processing unit of a computer **3.** COMPUT same as **microprocessor 4.** HOUSEHOLD same as **food processor**

proc·ess print·ing *n* a method of full-color printing using multiple images from plates printed in yellow, magenta, blue, and cyan

proc·ess serv·er *n* somebody who serves a writ or summons ordering somebody to appear in court

pro·cès-ver·bal /prō sày vər ba͡al/ (*plural* **pro·cès-ver·baux** /-bṓ/) *n* a written account of official proceedings [Mid-17C. < French, "oral proceedings," originally evidence from police officers who could not write]

pro·chlor·per·a·zine /prṑ klawr pérrə zeen/ *n* a phenothiazine drug. Use: control of nausea and vomiting, to relieve symptoms of Ménière's disease, migraine, and anxiety. [Mid-20C. Blend of PROPYL + CHLOR- + PIPERAZINE]

pro-choice *adj* advocating open legal access to voluntary abortion

pro·claim /prō kláym, prə-/ (**-claimed, -claim·ing, -claims**) *vt* **1.** DECLARE SOMETHING PUBLICLY to announce something publicly or formally **2.** DECLARE SOMEBODY TO BE SOMETHING to declare publicly that somebody is something **3.** SHOW WHAT SOMETHING IS to show or reveal clearly what something is **4.** MAKE SOMETHING CLEAR to state something emphatically or openly [14C. Via French < Latin *proclamare* "cry out" < *clamare* "to cry"] —**pro·claim·er** *n* —**pro·clam·a·to·ry** /prō klámmə tàwree, prə-/ *adj*

proc·la·ma·tion /pròklə máysh'n/ *n* **1.** a public or formal announcement **2.** the act of announcing something publicly or formally [14C. Directly or via French < Latin *proclamation-* < *proclamare* (see PROCLAIM)]

pro·clit·ic /prō klíttik/ *adj* describes a reduced form of a word that is closely attached in pronunciation to the word following it and has no accent of its own, e.g., "d'" in "d'you" [Mid-19C. < modern Latin *procliticus*, after late Latin *encliticus* "enclitic"] —**pro·clit·ic** *n*

pro·cliv·i·ty /prō klívvətee/ (*plural* **-ties**) *n* a natural tendency to behave in a particular way [Late 16C. < Latin *proclivitas* < *proclivis* "inclined" < *clivus* "slope"]

~~proclomation~~ incorrect spelling of **proclamation**

Proc·ne /próknee/ *n* in Greek mythology, an Athenian princess whose husband, Tereus, raped her sister, Philomela. She avenged this act by killing their own son and feeding him to Tereus.

pro·con·sul /prō kónss'l/ *n* **1.** GOVERNOR OF ANCIENT ROMAN PROVINCE a governor of an ancient Roman province, usually a former consul **2.** GOVERNOR OF COLONY a governor or administrator of a colony or other dependency **3.** GOV, INTERNAT REL ADMINISTRATOR OF MILITARY-GOVERNED NATION a high administrator with broad powers in a nation recently invaded and under the control of the invader's armed forces, charged with pacifying the population, restoring vital services, and establishing new governance [14C. < Latin, "(person acting) for the consul"] —**pro·con·su·lar** *adj* —**pro·con·su·late** /-kónssələt/ *n* —**pro·con·sul·ship** *n*

pro·cras·ti·nate /prō krásti nàyt, prə-/ (**-nat·ed, -nat·ing, -nates**) *vti* to postpone doing something, especially as a regular practice [Late 16C. < Latin *procrastinat-*, past participle of *procrastinare* "put off until tomorrow" < *cras* "tomorrow"] —**pro·cras·ti·na·tion** /prō kràsti náysh'n, prə-/ *n* —**pro·cras·ti·na·tor** *n*

USAGE See ***prevaricate***.

pro·cre·ate /prṓkree àyt/ (**-at·ed, -at·ing, -ates**) *v* **1.** *vti* to produce offspring by reproduction **2.** *vt* to create or produce something [Mid-16C. < Latin *procreat-*, past participle of *procreare* "bring forth" < *creare* "bring forth, produce"] —**pro·cre·ant** *adj* —**pro·cre·a·tion** /prṑkree áysh'n/ *n* —**pro·cre·a·tive** *adj* —**pro·cre·a·tor** *n*

Pro·crus·te·an /prō krústee ən/, **pro·crus·te·an** *adj* trying to establish conformity by using any and all means, including violence [Mid-19C. < PROCRUSTES]

Pro·crus·tes /prō krústeez/ *n* in Greek mythology, a robber who abducted strangers and forced them to fit perfectly into a bed by either cutting off or stretching their limbs

pro·cryp·tic /prō kríptik/ *adj* describes an animal that has a coloration or pattern of shading that acts as camouflage [Late 19C. < PRO-[1] + Greek *kruptikos* (see CRYPTIC), probably after PROTECTIVE] —**pro·cryp·ti·cal·ly** *adv*

proct- *prefix* same as **procto-** (*used before vowels*)

proc·ti·tis /prok tī́tiss/ *n* inflammation of the rectum [Early 19C. < Greek *prōktos* "anus"]

procto- *prefix* anus, anal, rectum, rectal ○ *proctoscope* [< Greek *prōktos*]

proc·to·de·um /pròktə dée əm/ (*plural* **-de·a** /-dée ə/ or **-de·ums**), **proc·to·dae·um** (*plural* **-dae·a** or **-dae·ums**) *n* the exterior section of an embryo that develops into part of the anal canal [Late 19C. < modern Latin < Greek *prōktos* "anus" + *hodaios* "on the way" < *hodos* "way"]

proc·tol·o·gy /prok tóllәjee/ *n* the branch of medicine concerned with disorders of the colon, rectum, and anus —**proc·to·log·ic** /pròktə lójjik/ *adj* —**proc·tol·o·gist** *n*

proc·tor /próktər/ *n* **1.** SUPERVISOR AT EXAMINATION somebody who supervises students at an examination **2.** DORMITORY SUPERVISOR at some schools and universities, a supervisor in a dormitory ■ *vt* (**-tored, -tor·ing, -tors**) SUPERVISE EXAM to supervise an examination, especially in order to prevent cheating [14C. Contraction of PROCURATOR] —**proc·to·ri·al** /prok táwree əl/ *adj* —**proc·tor·ship** *n*

proc·to·scope /próktə skṑp/ *n* a tubular medical instrument with an integral light source, used for examining the anal canal and rectum —**proc·to·scop·ic** /pròktə skóppik/ *adj* —**proc·tos·co·py** /prok tóskəpee/ *n*

pro·cum·bent /prō kúmbənt/ *adj* **1.** lying down with the face to the ground **2.** describes a plant stem that grows along the ground without taking root [Mid-17C. < Latin *procumbent-*, present participle of *procumbere* "fall forward" < *cumbere* "lie down"]

pro·cu·ra·tion /pròkyə ráysh'n/ *n* **1.** ACQUIRING OF SOMETHING the obtaining of something, especially by effort (*formal*) **2.** CRIME PROVIDING OF PROSTITUTE the crime of providing somebody for prostitution **3.** LAW ENGAGING OF PROCURATOR the engaging of an agent to manage somebody's affairs **4.** LAW AUTHORIZING OF PROCURATOR the authorization given to somebody who acts as an agent to manage somebody else's affairs [15C. Directly or via French < Latin *procuration-* < *procurat-* (see PROCURATOR)]

proc·u·ra·tor /prókyə ràytər/ *n* **1.** in ancient Rome, an administrative official with legal or fiscal powers **2.** an agent engaged to manage somebody else's affairs [13C. Directly or via French < Latin, "agent, manager, tax-collector" < *procurat-*, past participle of *procurare* (see PROCURE)] —**proc·u·ra·to·ri·al** /pròkyərə táwree əl/ *adj* —**pro·cu·ra·tor·ship** *n*

pro·cure /prō kyŏor, prə-/ (**-cured, -cur·ing, -cures**) *v* **1.** *vt* to obtain something, especially by effort **2.** *vti* to provide somebody for prostitution [13C. Via French < Latin *procurare* "take care of, manage" < *curare* "care for"] —**pro·cur·a·ble** *adj* —**pro·cur·al** *n* —**pro·cur·ance** *n* —**pro·cure·ment** *n* —**pro·cur·er** *n*

SYNONYMS See ***get***[1].

Pro·cy·on /prṓsee òn/ *n* a binary star in the constellation Canis Minor and one of the brightest stars in the sky [< Greek, literally "before the dog," because it rises before the Dog Star, Sirius]

prod /prod/ *vti* (**prod·ded, prod·ding, prods**) **1.** POKE SOMEBODY OR SOMETHING to poke somebody or something with a finger, elbow, or pointed object **2.** INCITE SOMEBODY TO ACTION to incite or encourage somebody to take action ■ *n* **1.** A POKE a poke with a finger, elbow, or pointed object **2.** INCITEMENT TO ACTION an incitement or encouragement to do something **3.** POKING INSTRUMENT an instrument used for poking a person or animal [Mid-16C. Origin ?] —**prod·der** *n*

prod·i·gal /próddig'l/ *adj* **1.** EXTRAVAGANTLY WASTEFUL spendthrift or extravagant to a degree bordering on recklessness **2.** PRODUCING GENEROUS AMOUNTS giving or producing something in large amounts **3.** WASTING PARENTAL MONEY spending parental money wastefully, but returning home to a warm welcome (*literary*) ■ *n* SPENDTHRIFT somebody who spends money, especially money from his or her parents, wastefully [Early 16C. Via French < late Latin *prodigalis* < Latin *prodigus* "wasteful" < *prodigere* "drive away, squander" < *agere* "to drive"] —**prod·i·gal·i·ty** /pròddi gállətee/ *n* —**prod·i·gal·ly** *adv*

prod·i·gal son *n* same as **prodigal**

pro·di·gious /prə díjjəss/ *adj* **1.** great in amount, size, or extent **2.** very impressive or amazing [Mid-16C. < Latin *prodigiosus* "marvelous" < *prodigium* "prophetic sign, portent"] —**pro·di·gious·ly** *adv* —**pro·di·gious·ness** *n*

prod·i·gy /próddəjee/ (*plural* **-gies**) *n* **1.** somebody who shows an exceptional talent at an early age **2.** something very impressive or amazing [15C. < Latin *prodigium* "prophetic sign, portent"]

pro·drome /prṓ drṑm/ *n* a symptom indicating the onset of a disease [Mid-17C. Via French < Greek *prodromos* "a running before" < *dromos* "running"] —**pro·dro·mal** /prō drṓm'l/ *adj* —**pro·drom·ic** /prō drómmik/ *adj*

pro·drug /prṓ drùg/ *n* an inactive form of a drug that is converted into an active form in the body by a chemical reaction in the digestive tract. Use: chemotherapeutic agent targeting cancer cells.

pro·duce *v* /prə dŏoss/ (**-duced, -duc·ing, -duc·es**) **1.** *vti* MAKE SOMETHING to make or create something ○ *able to produce a tasty meal from the most unpromising ingredients* **2.** *vti* MANUFACTURE SOMETHING to manufacture goods for sale ○ *They produce electrical goods mainly for export.* **3.** *vt* CAUSE SOMETHING to cause something to happen or arise ○ *Marjorie's calls for silence failed to produce the desired effect.* **4.** *vti* YIELD SOMETHING to grow, bring forth, or bear something ○ *produce seeds* **5.** *vt* TAKE SOMETHING OUT to pull something out and show it ○ *He produced a pistol from his pocket and started waving it around.* **6.** *vt* PRESENT SOMETHING to put something forward for inspection or consideration ○ *produced no evidence to support her claim* **7.** *vt* ARTS ORGANIZE THE MAKING OF SOMETHING to organize and supervise the making or staging of something ○ *produce a new album* **8.** *vt* MATH EXTEND SOMETHING IN SPACE to extend the length of a line, area of a plane figure, or volume of a solid ■ *n* /prṓ dŏoss/ FARM OR GARDEN PRODUCTS products of farms or gardens, especially fruits and vegetables [15C. < Latin *producere* "lead or bring out" < *ducere* "to lead"] —**pro·duc·i·ble** *adj*

SYNONYMS See ***make***.

pro·duc·er /prə dŏossər/ *n* **1.** SOMETHING GENERATING ITEMS FOR SALE a person, company, or country that produces goods or services for sale **2.** ORGANIZER OF MOVIE OR RECORDING an organizer and administrator of the making of a movie, broadcast, or recording, or the staging of a play **3.** SOMETHING THAT PRODUCES somebody or something that produces something **4.** INDUST APPARATUS FOR PRODUCER GAS a furnace used for making producer gas **5.** ECOL ORGANISM THAT MAKES ITS FOOD an organism that manufactures its own food from simple inorganic substances, e.g., a green plant

pro·duc·er gas *n* a fuel consisting of carbon monoxide, nitrogen, and hydrogen, made by passing air and steam over hot coke in a furnace

prod·uct /pró dùkt/ *n* **1.** SOMETHING MADE OR CREATED something that is made or created by a person, machine, or natural process, especially something that is offered for sale **2.** COMPANY'S GOODS OR SERVICES the goods or services produced by a company **3.** RESULT something that arises as a consequence of something else **4.** MATH RESULT OF MULTIPLYING the result of the multiplication of two or more quantities **5.** CHEM CHEMICAL SUBSTANCE a substance produced in a chemical reaction [15C. < Latin *productus*, past participle of *producere* (see PRODUCE)]

pro·duc·tion /prə dúkshən/ *n* **1.** MAKING OF SOMETHING the making or creation of something **2.** SOMETHING

PRODUCED something that has been made or created **3. PRODUCING OF GOODS** the process of manufacturing a product for sale **4. COMPANY'S PRODUCT** the goods or services produced by a company **5. SUPERVISION OF RECORDING OR FILMING** the organization and supervision of the making of a movie, broadcast, or recording, or the staging of a play **6. MOVIE OR RECORDING** a movie, play, broadcast, or recording that has been produced for the public **7. PRESENTATION OF SOMETHING** the showing or presenting of something such as evidence or proof ■ *adj* **MASS-PRODUCED** mass-produced for sale to the general public —**pro·duc·tion·al** *adj*

pro·duc·tion line *n* a sequence of machines or processes in a factory through which the products pass until they are fully assembled

pro·duc·tion num·ber *n* a piece of music in a musical that is sung and danced by featured actors supported by the chorus ◇ **make a (great) production number out of something** to exaggerate the seriousness or importance of something by making a great fuss about it (*informal*)

pro·duc·tive /prə dúktiv/ *adj* **1. PRODUCING MUCH** producing something abundantly and efficiently **2. WORTHWHILE** producing satisfactory or useful results **3. PRODUCING SOMETHING** producing or able to produce something **4.** ECON **PRODUCING GOODS** producing goods and services of exchangeable value **5.** MED **PRODUCING MUCUS** describes a cough that produces mucus **6.** GRAM **USED TO FORM WORDS** describes a prefix or suffix that is used in forming new words —**pro·duc·tive·ly** *adv* —**pro·duc·tive·ness** *n*

pro·duc·tiv·i·ty /prō duk tívvətee/ *n* **1.** the rate at which a company produces goods or services, in relation to the amount of materials and number of employees needed **2.** the ability to be productive

prod·uct·ize /próddək tīz/ (**-ized, -iz·ing, -iz·es**) *vti* to convert something such as an idea, a process, a prototype, or an area of expertise into a marketable and salable product

prod·uct li·a·bil·i·ty *n* the liability of manufacturers and traders for damage or injury caused to purchasers or bystanders by their products

prod·uct line *n* **1.** the whole range of products marketed by a company **2.** a group of related products marketed by the same company that differ only in size or style

prod·uct place·ment *n* the practice of placing brand-name items as props in, e.g., movies, television shows, or music videos as a form of advertising

prod·uct re·call *n* the act of requesting the return of a commercial product to the retailer or manufacturer because of a defect or a safety or efficiency problem

pro·em /prṓ èm/ *n* an introduction to a literary work or a speech [14C. Via Old French *pro(h)eme* < Greek *prooimion*, literally "song before" < *oimē* "song"]

pro·en·zyme /prō én zīm/ *n* the inactive precursor of an enzyme, especially one secreted by living cells and activated by an acid, another enzyme, or other catalytic means

pro·es·trus /prō éstrəss/ *n* the period in the estrus cycle immediately preceding estrus

prof /prof/ *n* a college or university professor (*informal*) [Mid-19C. Shortening]

Prof. *abbr* EDUC Professor

pro·fane /prō fáyn, prə-/ *adj* **1. IRREVERENT** showing disrespect for God, any deity, or religion **2. SECULAR** not connected with or used for religious matters **3. UNINITIATED** not initiated into sacred or secret rites ■ *vt* (**-faned, -fan·ing, -fanes**) **TREAT SOMETHING IRREVERENTLY** to treat something sacred with disrespect [14C. Via French < Latin *profanus* "outside the temple, not sacred" < *fanum* "temple"] —**prof·a·na·tion** /pròffə náysh'n/ *n* —**pro·fan·a·to·ry** /prō fánnə tàwree, prə-/ *adj* —**pro·fane·ly** *adv* —**pro·fan·er** *n*

pro·fan·i·ty /prō fánnətee, prə-/ (*plural* **-ties**) *n* **1.** language or behavior that shows disrespect for God, any deity, or religion **2.** a word or phrase that shows disrespect for God, any deity, or religion

pro·fess /prō féss, prə-/ (**-fessed, -fess·ing, -fess·es**) *v* **1.** *vt* **DECLARE SOMETHING FALSELY** to make a statement falsely claiming that something is the case ○ *Many profess to despise what secretly they hunger after.* **2.** *vti* **DECLARE SOMETHING OPENLY** to make a statement acknowledging something openly or publicly ○ *Having professed his belief in the remedy, he had little choice but to try it.* ○ *They professed themselves delighted with the results.* **3.** *vt* RELIG **EXPRESS FAITH IN PARTICULAR BELIEF** to follow a particular religion **4.** *vti* RELIG **BECOME PRIEST OR NUN** to admit somebody into a religious order, or be admitted into a religious order [15C. < Old French *profes* "having taken religious vows" < Latin *profess-*, past participle of *profiteri* "declare publicly" < *fateri* "acknowledge"] —**pro·fessed** *adj* —**pro·fess·ed·ly** /-féssədlee/ *adv*

pro·fes·sion /prō fésh'n, prə-/ *n* **1. OCCUPATION REQUIRING EXTENSIVE EDUCATION** an occupation that requires extensive education or specialized training **2. PEOPLE IN PROFESSION** the people who practice a particular profession ○ *the legal profession* **3. DECLARATION** a public acknowledgment or declaration of something ○ *a profession of support* **4. DECLARATION OF FAITH** a declaration of belief in a religion or faith [13C. Directly or via French < Latin *profession-* < *profess-* (see PROFESS)]

pro·fes·sion·al /prō féshən'l, -féshnəl, prə-/ *adj* **1. OF PROFESSION** relating to or belonging to a profession ○ *professional people* **2. FOLLOWING OCCUPATION AS PAID JOB** engaged in an occupation as a paid job rather than as a hobby ○ *professional tennis player* **3. BUSINESSLIKE** conforming to the standards of skill, competence, or character normally expected of a properly qualified and experienced person in a work environment ○ *professional attitude* **4. VERY COMPETENT** showing a high degree of skill or competence ○ *did a very professional job* **5. DOING SOMETHING HABITUALLY** habitually, and usually annoyingly, indulging in a particular activity ○ *a professional complainer* ■ *n* **1. MEMBER OF PROFESSION** somebody whose occupation requires extensive education or specialized training **2. SOMEBODY IN SKILLED JOB** a worker in a paid occupation that usually requires a high degree of training and skill **3. SOMEBODY VERY COMPETENT** somebody with a high degree of skill or competence **4. TEACHER AT SPORTS CLUB** an expert player of a sport who is employed by a golf or other sports club to teach its members —**pro·fes·sion·al·ly** *adv*

pro·fes·sion·al as·so·ci·a·tion *n* an organization composed of members of a particular profession that regulates entry to and sets and maintains standards for that profession

pro·fes·sion·al cor·po·ra·tion *n* a business incorporated by licensed professionals such as doctors or lawyers

pro·fes·sion·al foul *n* a deliberate foul in soccer, usually committed in order to prevent the opposing team gaining a potentially crucial advantage in field position or goal-scoring opportunity

pro·fes·sion·al·ism /prō féshən'l ìzzəm, -féshnə lìzzəm, prə-/ *n* **1.** the skill, competence, or character expected of a member of a highly trained profession **2.** the use of professionals instead of amateurs

pro·fes·sion·al·ize /prō féshən'l īz, -féshnə līz, prə-/ (**-ized, -iz·ing, -iz·es**) *vti* to become professional or proceed with something in a professional way, e.g., make an activity professional by paying participants or by setting high standards that must be met —**pro·fes·sion·al·i·za·tion** /prō fèshən'li záysh'n, -fèshnəli-/ *n*

pro·fes·sor /prə féssər/ *n* **1.** EDUC **COLLEGE TEACHER OF HIGHEST ACADEMIC RANK** a teacher of the highest academic rank in a college or university **2. UNIVERSITY TEACHER** a teacher in a university or college **3. SENIOR NONACADEMIC TEACHER** a senior teacher of a nonacademic discipline in an institution other than a university, e.g., a music or drama school **4. SOMEBODY PROFESSING BELIEF** somebody who professes a religious or other belief (*formal*) [14C. Directly or via French < Latin < *profess-* (see PROFESS)] —**pro·fes·so·ri·al** /pròffə sáwree əl/ *adj* —**pro·fes·sor·ship** *n*

pro·fes·so·ri·ate /pròffə sáwree ət/, **pro·fes·so·ri·at, pro·fes·so·rate** /prə féssərət/ *n* **1.** professors as a group **2.** the status or position of professor

prof·fer /próffər/ *vt* (**-fered, -fer·ing, -fers**) **1. HOLD SOMETHING OUT** to hold something out to somebody so that he or she can take or grasp it **2. PROPOSE SOMETHING** to offer something for consideration to somebody ○ *proffer a suggestion* ■ *n* **PROPOSAL** something offered for consideration [13C. < Old French *proffrir* "offer forth" < *offrir* "to offer"]

~~**proffesor**~~ incorrect spelling of **professor**

pro·fi·cient /prə físh'nt/ *adj* having a high degree of skill in something [Late 16C. Via French < Latin *proficient-*, present participle of *proficere* "make progress" < *facere* "make"] —**pro·fi·cien·cy** *n* —**pro·fi·cient·ly** *adv*

pro·file /prṓ fīl/ *n* **1. VISIBILITY** a level or degree of noticeability ○ *kept a low profile* **2. SIDE VIEW OF FACE** the outline of somebody's face as seen from the side **3. ARTWORK OF SOMEBODY'S PROFILE** a visual representation of the outline of somebody's face as seen from the side **4. SHORT BIOGRAPHY** a short biographical account of somebody **5. BRIEF DESCRIPTION** a brief description that summarizes the characteristics of somebody or something ○ *a profile of her past philanthropy* **6.** STATS **DESCRIPTIVE DATA** a set of data, usually in graph or table form, that indicates the extent to which something matches tested or standard characteristics **7.** GEOG **VERTICAL SECTION OF PHYSICAL FEATURE** a vertical section through a physical feature, e.g., through soil, showing its development from bedrock ■ *v* (**-filed, -fil·ing, -files**) **1.** *vt* **WRITE SHORT ACCOUNT OF SOMEBODY** to write or present a short biographical account or description of somebody or something **2.** *vt* **SHOW SOMEBODY'S FACIAL PROFILE** to represent the outline of somebody's face as seen from the side **3.** *vi US* **SHOW OFF** to show off, strut, or otherwise try to attract attention (*slang*) **4.** *vt* **ANALYSE AND CLASSIFY SOMEBODY** to subject somebody to profiling, e.g., in a criminal investigation [Mid-17C. < Italian *profilo* < *profilare* "draw in outline" < *filo* "thread" < Latin *filum*] —**pro·fil·er** *n*

pro·fil·ing /prṓ fīling/ *n* the analysis and classification of somebody based on personal information such as ethnicity, shopping habits, or behavioral patterns, used, e.g., in criminal investigations or product advertising ○ *racial profiling* ○ *consumer profiling*

prof·it /próffit/ *n* **1. EXCESS OF INCOME OVER EXPENDITURE** the excess of income over expenditure, especially in business **2. INCOME FROM SOMETHING** income from an investment or transaction (*often used in the plural*) **3. ADVANTAGE** an advantage or benefit derived from an activity ■ *v* (**-it·ed, -it·ing, -its**) **1.** *vi* **MAKE MONEY ON SOMETHING** to gain financial profit from something **2.** *vti* **BENEFIT FROM SOMETHING** to gain an advantage or benefit from something, or provide an advantage or benefit [13C. Via French < Latin *profectus* "progress, profit" < past participle of *proficere* (see PROFICIENT)] —**prof·it·less** *adj*

SPELLCHECK profit or **prophet**? Do not confuse the spelling of ***profit*** and ***prophet***, which sound similar. ***Profit*** is a noun and verb referring to financial gain, benefit, or advantage: *We made a profit of $100 on the transaction. They profited from the umpire's decision.* The word ***prophet*** is only used as a noun, denoting somebody who foretells the future, as in *an Old Testament prophet, prophets of doom.*

prof·it·a·ble /próffitəb'l/ *adj* **1.** yielding a financial profit **2.** of some use, benefit, or advantage to somebody —**prof·it·a·bil·i·ty** /pròffitə bíllətee/ *n* —**prof·it·a·ble·ness** *n* —**prof·it·a·bly** *adv*

prof·it and loss *n* an account showing income and expenditure over a given period and indicating net profit or loss

prof·it cen·ter *n* an organizational unit or activity of a company for which income and expenses are reported independently

prof·it·eer /pròffi tée̱r/ (**-eered, -eer·ing, -eers**) *vi* to make excessive profits by charging high prices for scarce, necessary, or rationed goods —**prof·it·eer** *n* —**prof·it·eer·ing** *n*

pro·fit·er·ole /prə fíttə rōl/ *n* a small ball of light pastry filled with cream and usually served with chocolate sauce [Early 16C. < French, "small gain" < *profit* (see PROFIT)]

prof·it·mak·ing /próffit màyking/ *adj* operated with the primary objective of making a profit

prof·it mar·gin *n* a measure of profitability determined by dividing income after subtracting related expenses by sales, expressed as a percentage

prof·it shar·ing *n* a system by which the employees of a company receive a prearranged share of the company's profits (*hyphenated when used before a noun*)

prof·its warn·ing *n* an announcement by a company of lower than expected profits for a particular period

prof·it tak·ing *n* the selling of commodities, securities, or stocks at a time when their current market value is greater than the price at which they were purchased —**prof·it-tak·er** *n*

prof·li·gate /prófflìgət, -gàyt/ *adj* **1.** WASTEFUL extremely extravagant or wasteful **2.** WITH LOW MORALS having or showing extremely low moral standards ■ *n* **1.** SOMEBODY WASTEFUL an extremely extravagant or wasteful person **2.** SOMEBODY WITH LOW MORALS somebody with extremely low moral standards [Mid-16C. < Latin *profligatus*, past participle of *profligare* "strike down, ruin" < *fligere* "to strike"] —**prof·li·ga·cy** *n* —**prof·li·gate·ly** *adv*

pro-form *n UK* same as **substitute** *n* (sense 3)

pro for·ma /prō fáwrmə/ *adj* **1.** FORMAL OR CONVENTIONAL done or existing only as a formality **2.** PROVIDED IN ADVANCE provided in advance in order to supply descriptions of something or to serve as a model, e.g., of a later version of a document ○ *a pro forma invoice* ■ *adv* FOR CONVENTION'S SAKE for the sake of or in accordance with convention [< Latin, "for form's sake"]

pro·found /prə fównd/ *adj* **1.** GREAT very great, strong, or intense ○ *profound effect* ○ *profound regret* **2.** SHOWING GREAT UNDERSTANDING showing great perception, understanding, or knowledge ○ *profound insight* **3.** REQUIRING THOUGHTFUL STUDY containing far-reaching ideas or essential wisdom and experience that usually require serious thought to be fully appreciated ○ *a profound meditation on the human condition* **4.** VERY DEEP extending to or situated at a great depth (*literary*) [13C. Via French < Latin *profundus* "bottom forward or downward" < *fundus* "bottom"] —**pro·found·ly** *adv* —**pro·found·ness** *n*

pro·fun·di·ty /prə fúndətee/ (*plural* **-ties**) *n* **1.** INTENSE INSIGHT intense intellectual or human insight that deals seriously with the most vital aspects of any question **2.** SOMETHING SHOWING INSIGHT something that shows great perceptiveness or knowledge or requires great perceptiveness and knowledge to be properly understood **3.** INTELLECTUAL COMPLEXITY the intellectual complexity or abstruseness of something **4.** GREATNESS the greatness, strength, or intensity of something **5.** GREAT DEPTH extension to or location at a great depth (*literary*) [15C. Via French < late Latin *profunditas* < *profundus* (see PROFOUND)]

pro·fuse /prə fyóoss/ *adj* **1.** VOLUBLY EXPRESSED expressed at length, many times, and in many words ○ *profuse apologies* **2.** GENEROUS IN GIVING giving something freely and lavishly or extravagantly **3.** COPIOUS occurring or appearing in large amounts [15C. < Latin *profusus*, past participle of *profundere* "pour out" < *fundere* "pour"] —**pro·fuse·ly** *adv* —**pro·fuse·ness** *n*

pro·fu·sion /prə fyóozh'n/ *n* **1.** a large quantity of something **2.** the quality of being profuse

prog. *abbr* **1.** program **2.** progress **3.** EDUC progressive

Prog. *abbr* HIST Progressive

pro·gen·i·tor /prō jénnitər/ *n* **1.** a direct ancestor of somebody or something **2.** the originator of or original model for something [14C. < Latin, "begetter" < *progenit-*, past participle of *progignere* < *gignere* "beget"]

prog·e·ny /prójjənee/ (*plural same* or **-nies**) *n* **1.** an offspring of a person, animal, or plant **2.** something that develops or results from something else [13C. Via Old French *progenie* < Latin *progenies* "offspring" < *progignere* (see PROGENITOR)]

pro·ger·i·a /prō jéeree ə/ *n* a rare condition of premature aging that begins in childhood or early adult life and leads to death within a few years [Early 20C. < modern Latin < Greek *progērōs*, literally "aged forward" < *gēras* "old age"]

pro·ges·ta·tion·al /prò je stáyshən'l, -stáyshnəl/ *adj* **1.** relating to the stage of the menstrual cycle after ovulation when progesterone is produced **2.** relating to or resembling progesterone or its effects

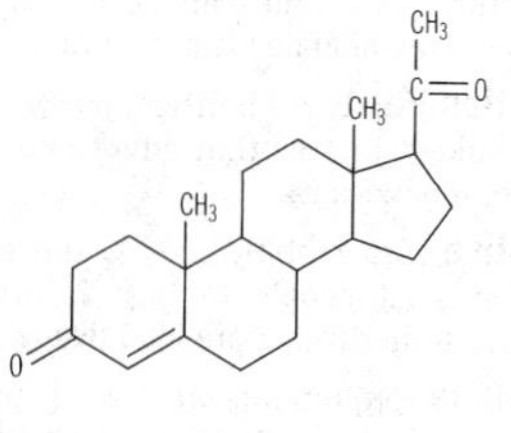

progesterone

pro·ges·ter·one /prō jéstə ròn/ *n* a sex hormone produced in women, first by the corpus luteum of the ovary to prepare the womb for the fertilized ovum, and later by the placenta to maintain pregnancy. Formula: $C_{21}H_{30}O_2$. [Mid-20C. < PRO-[1] + GESTATION + STEROL + -ONE]

pro·ges·tin /prō jéstin/ *n* a progestogen, especially progesterone [Early 20C. < PRO-[1] + GESTATION + -IN]

pro·ges·to·gen /prō jéstəjən/ *n* a steroid hormone or agent having effects similar to those of progesterone, or progesterone itself [Mid-20C. < PRO-[1] + GESTATION + -GEN]

pro·glot·tid /prō glóttid/, **pro·glot·tis** /-glóttiss/ (*plural* **-ti·des** /-ti deez/) *n* a segment of a tapeworm's body [Late 19C. < Greek *proglōttid* "tip of the tongue"]

prog·na·thous /prógnəthəss/, **prog·nath·ic** /prog náthik/ *adj* describes an animal with a jaw that sticks out markedly [Mid-19C. < PRO-[2] + Greek *gnathos* "jaw"] —**prog·na·thism** *n*

prog·no·sis /prog nṓssiss/ (*plural* **-no·ses** /-nṓ seez/) *n* **1.** a medical opinion as to the likely course and outcome of a disease **2.** a prediction about how a given situation will develop [Mid-17C. Via late Latin < Greek *prognōsis* "knowledge beforehand" < *gignōskein* "know"]

prog·nos·tic /prog nóstik/ *adj* **1.** OF DISEASE PROGNOSIS relating to or acting as a prognosis of a disease **2.** OF PREDICTION relating to or acting as a prediction ■ *n* **1.** INDICATION OF COURSE OF DISEASE an indicator used in making a prognosis concerning a disease **2.** PREDICTION a prediction as to how a given situation will develop [15C. Via French and Latin < Greek *prognōstikos* "of knowledge beforehand" < *prognōsis* (see PROGNOSIS)]

prog·nos·ti·cate /prog nósti kàyt/ (**-cat·ed, -cat·ing, -cates**) *v* **1.** *vti* to predict or foretell future events **2.** *vt* to be an indication of the likely future course of something —**prog·nos·ti·ca·tion** /-nòsti káysh'n/ *n* —**prog·nos·ti·ca·tor** *n*

pro·grade /prṓ gràyd/ *adj* moving in the same orbital or rotational direction as another astronomical body

pro·gram /prṓ gràm/ *n* **1.** BROADCAST a television or radio broadcast. UK spelling **programme 2.** PLAN OF ACTION a plan of action for achieving something ○ *The program is tennis and lunch.* UK spelling **programme 3.** SET OF ACTIVITIES WITH SPECIFIC GOAL a system of procedures or activities that has a specific purpose, e.g., to train an athletic team or provide community support ○ *an overseas aid program.* UK spelling **programme 4.** COMPUT INSTRUCTIONS OBEYED BY COMPUTER a list of instructions in a programming language that tells a computer to perform a task **5.** TECH OPERATING INSTRUCTIONS FOR MACHINE a set of coded operating instructions used to run a machine automatically **6.** SET OF CLASSES a series of classes or lectures on something. UK spelling **programme 7.** ARTS BOOKLET GIVING DETAILS OF A PERFORMANCE a booklet or leaflet giving details of a theatrical or musical performance or a ceremony. UK spelling **programme 8.** ROUTINE the established routine (*slang*) ○ *I know you're new here, but try to get with the program!* UK spelling **programme** ■ *v* (**-grammed** or **-gramed, -gram·ming** or **-gram·ing, -grams**) **1.** *vti* WRITE COMPUTER PROGRAM to write a program for a computer, or load a program into a computer **2.** *vt* TECH INSERT OPERATING INSTRUCTIONS INTO MACHINE to insert coded operating instructions into a machine **3.** *vt* SCHEDULE SOMETHING to schedule something as part of a program. UK spelling **programme 4.** *vt* TRAIN SOMEBODY TO DO SOMETHING AUTOMATICALLY to train a person or an animal to do something automatically, especially to respond automatically to a stimulus. UK spelling **programme** [Mid-17C. Via French < Greek *programma* "public notice," literally "something written publicly" < *graphein* "write"] —**pro·gram·ma·ble** /prṓ gràmməb'l/ *adj*

pro·gram di·rec·tor *n* an executive who is responsible for the selection and scheduling of television or radio programs for broadcast

pro·gram·er *n US* COMPUT another spelling of **programmer**

pro·gram e·val·u·a·tion and re·view tech·nique *n* MANAGEMT full form of **PERT**

pro·gram·ing *n US* COMPUT, BROADCAST another spelling of **programming**

pro·gram·mat·ic /prògrə máttik/ *adj* **1.** SYSTEMATIC following a plan or program **2.** RELATING TO PROGRAM relating to or consisting of a program **3.** OF PROGRAM MUSIC relating to or composed as program music —**pro·gram·mat·i·cal·ly** *adv*

pro·gramme *n, vt* ARTS, EDUC UK spelling of **program** *n* (senses 1–3, 6–7), *v* (senses 3–4)

pro·grammed in·struc·tion *n* a teaching method involving sequences of controlled steps in which a student has to learn thoroughly the material covered in one step before proceeding to the next

pro·gram·mer /prṓ gràmmər/, **pro·gram·er** *n* a writer of computer programs

pro·gram·ming /prṓ gràmming/, **pro·gram·ing** *n* **1.** the designing or writing of computer programs **2.** the selection and scheduling of television or radio programs, or the programs themselves

pro·gram·ming lan·guage *n* a unique vocabulary and set of rules for writing computer programs

pro·gram mu·sic *n* music that depicts or is inspired by a story, object, or scene

pro·gram trad·ing *n* the automatic buying and selling of large quantities of stock using computer programs that monitor price changes —**pro·gram trade** *n* —**pro·gram trad·er** *n*

pro·gress *n* /próg rèss, prṓ grèss/ **1.** POSITIVE DEVELOPMENT development, usually of a gradual kind, toward achieving a goal or reaching a higher standard ○ *making progress in the talks* **2.** ADVANCE OF HUMAN SOCIETY the general advance of human society and industry over time toward a state of greater civilization ○ *Most Victorians believed in progress.* **3.** MOTION TOWARD SOMETHING movement forward or onward **4.** ROYAL TOUR an official tour by a reigning king or queen through his or her kingdom (*archaic*) ■ *v* /prə gréss/ (**-gressed, -gress·ing, -gress·es**) **1.** *vi* IMPROVE to develop or advance continuously **2.** *vi* MOVE ALONG to move forward or onward **3.** *vt* HELP COMPLETE SOMETHING to bring something closer to completion [15C. < Latin *progressus*, past participle of *progredi* "go forward" < *gradi* "to walk"] ◇ **in progress** currently happening or being done

PRONUNCIATION The *o* in the noun ***progress*** can be pronounced two ways and both are correct: /próg rèss, prṓ grèss/. The first variant is, however, slightly more common in US English as opposed to Canadian English, which prefers the second variant.

pro·gres·sion /prə grésh'n/ *n* **1.** GRADUAL ADVANCEMENT a gradual change or advancement from one state to another **2.** FORWARD MOVEMENT movement forward or onward **3.** SERIES OF RELATED THINGS a series or succession of related things **4.** MATH SEQUENCE OF RELATED NUMBERS a sequence of numbers or terms in which each can be derived from its predecessor using a constant formula **5.** MUSIC SERIES OF NOTES OR CHORDS a movement from one musical note or chord to another [14C. Directly or via French < Latin *progression-* < *progressus* (see PROGRESS)] —**pro·gres·sion·al** *adj*

pro·gres·sive /prə gréssiv/ *adj* **1.** FAVORING REFORM advocating social, economic, or political reform **2.** PROGRESSING GRADUALLY developing gradually over a period of time ○ *a progressive decline in popularity* **3.** BECOMING MORE SEVERE describes a disease that becomes more widespread or severe over time **4.** INFORMAL AND LESS STRUCTURED EDUCATIONALLY relating to or using a more informal, less structured approach to the education of children **5. WITH HIGHER RATES FOR HIGHER INCOMES** describes a form of taxation in which the tax rate increases in proportion to the taxable income **6.** GRAM **EXPRESSING CONTINUOUS ACTION** describes an aspect or form of a verb, expressing continuous action **7.** CARDS, DANCE **HAVING CHANGES OF PARTNER** involving a change of partner at various stages of the game or dance ■ *n* **1. ADVOCATE OF REFORM** a supporter or advocate of social, political, or economic reforms **2.** GRAM **PROGRESSIVE FORM OF VERB** the progressive aspect of a verb, or a verb in the progressive aspect [Early 17C. Directly or via French < medieval Latin *progressivus* < Latin *progressus* (see PROGRESS)] —**pro·gres·sive·ly** *adv* —**pro·gres·sive·ness** *n*

Pro·gres·sive *adj* **1. OF PROGRESSIVE POLITICAL PARTY** belonging to or associated with a political party that calls itself progressive or advocates social reform **2. OF NONORTHODOX JEWISH RELIGIOUS MOVEMENT** relating to a Jewish religious movement whose members do not believe that the Torah was given literally and directly by God to Moses ■ *n* **MEMBER OF PROGRESSIVE PARTY** a member of a progressive political party

Pro·gres·sive Con·ser·va·tive *n* in Canada, a member or supporter of the Progressive Conservative Party

Pro·gres·sive Con·ser·va·tive Par·ty *n* a Canadian federal and provincial political party that became part of the Conservative Party of Canada. It originally derived its political principles from British Toryism.

pro·gres·sive ed·u·ca·tion *n* a 20th-century theory of education that stresses children's self-expression, an informal classroom atmosphere, and individual attention

pro·gres·sive jazz *n* a form of experimental, free-flowing, and improvisational jazz that uses dissonance and complex rhythms

Pro·gres·sive Par·ty *n* **1. US POLITICAL PARTY** one of three related US political parties that favored social reform and were active in the presidential elections of 1912, 1924, and 1948 **2. CANADIAN POLITICAL PARTY** a Canadian political party formed in 1920 from members of farmers' movements and dissident Liberals that was dissolved in 1942 **3. S AFRICAN POLITICAL PARTY** a South African national political party that was formed in 1959 by members of the United Party and merged again with part of the United Party in 1977 to form the Progressive Federal Party

Pro·gres·sive Rock *n* rock music originating in the early 1970s and characterized by technically elaborate and sometimes experimental arrangements

pro·gres·siv·ism /prə gréssi vìzzəm/ *n* **1.** the beliefs and practices of progressives **2.** the theories and practices of progressive education —**pro·gres·siv·ist** *n*

prog·ress pay·ment *n* a partial payment made to a contractor when a stage of a job is completed

pro·hib·it /prō híbbit/ (**-it·ed, -it·ing, -its**) *vt* **1.** to stop somebody from doing something by passing a law or rule that forbids it **2.** to prevent somebody from doing something [15C. < Latin *prohibit-*, past participle of *prohibere* "hold back" < *hibere* "to hold"]

pro·hi·bi·tion /prò ə bísh'n/ *n* **1. FORBIDDING OF SOMETHING** the act or process of forbidding something **2. ORDER THAT FORBIDS** an act or order that forbids something **3. COURT ORDER** an order from a superior court that forbids an inferior court from deciding on a matter beyond its jurisdiction **4. OUTLAWING OF TRADE IN ALCOHOLIC BEVERAGES** a policy that forbids by law the manufacture, sale, and transport of alcoholic beverages [14C. Directly or via French < Latin *prohibition-* < *prohibit-* (see PROHIBIT)]

Pro·hi·bi·tion *n* in the United States, the period between 1919 and 1933 during which the manufacture, sale, and transportation of alcoholic beverages was forbidden by the 18th Amendment

pro·hi·bi·tion·ist /prò ə bísh'nist/ *n* **1. SUPPORTER OF BANNING ALCOHOLIC BEVERAGES** somebody who supports a legal ban on the manufacture and sale of alcoholic beverages **2. Pro·hi·bi·tion·ist MEMBER OF PROHIBITION PARTY** a member or supporter of the Prohibition Party **3. SUPPORTER OF PROHIBITION** in the United States during Prohibition, a supporter of the legal ban on the manufacture, sale, and transportation of alcoholic beverages —**pro·hi·bi·tion·ism** *n* —**Pro·hi·bi·tion·ism** *n*

Pro·hi·bi·tion Par·ty *n* a political party in the United States founded in 1869 that advocated the banning of alcoholic beverages

pro·hib·i·tive /prō híbbitiv/ *adj* **1.** too expensive or costly for most people to buy **2.** prohibiting or forbidding something —**pro·hib·i·tive·ly** *adv*

pro·hib·i·to·ry /prō híbbi tàwree/ *adj* **1.** preventing or forbidding something **2.** likely to prevent or forbid something (*formal*)

pro·in·su·lin /prō ínssəlin/ *n* the inactive precursor of insulin produced in the pancreas

proj·ect *n* /pró jèkt/ **1. TASK OR PLANNED PROGRAM OF WORK** a task or planned program of work that requires a large amount of time, effort, and planning to complete (*often used before a noun*) ○ *a project to develop a faster delivery service* ○ *project management* **2. UNIT OF WORK** an organized unit of work ○ *a class project* **3. PUBLIC WORK** an extensive organized public undertaking ○ *a construction project* **4.** PUBLIC ADMIN same as **housing project** (*often used in the plural*) ■ *v* /prə jékt/ (**pro·ject·ed, pro·ject·ing, pro·jects**) **1.** *vti* **STICK OUT** to jut out beyond or farther than something, or make something jut out beyond or farther than something ○ *The balcony projected several feet.* **2.** *vt* **ESTIMATE SOMETHING** to estimate something by extrapolating data ○ *project a 3% growth rate* **3.** *vt* **DIRECT IMAGE ONTO SURFACE** to make an image appear on a surface ○ *projected the photograph onto the screen* **4.** *vt* **COMMUNICATE SOMETHING** to communicate something effectively ○ *projects himself as a confident speaker* **5.** *vti* **MAKE VOICE AUDIBLE** to make the voice heard clearly and at a distance, or be effective in making the voice heard ○ *projecting her voice to the back of the auditorium* **6.** *vt* **PROPOSE PLAN** to propose a plan of action (*often passive*) ○ *projects an extended tour next year* **7.** *vt* **IMAGINE SOMETHING** to use the imagination to see or remember something ○ *She projected herself back into the past.* **8.** *vt* PSYCHOL **BELIEVE OTHERS SHARE FEELING** to make a thought or feeling seem to have an external and objective reality, especially to ascribe a disturbing personal thought or feeling to others ○ *He had projected his fear of heights onto her.* **9.** *vt* MATH **DRAW PROJECTION OF FIGURE** to transform a geometric figure into another by drawing straight lines through every point of the figure to another plane [14C. < Latin *projectum* "something thrown forward" < *proicere* "throw forward" < *jacere* "to throw"]

pro·jec·tile /prə jékt'l, -tīl/ *n* **MISSILE OR SHELL** an object that can be fired or launched, e.g., an artillery shell or a rocket ■ *adj* **1. IMPELLED FORWARD** hurled or impelled forward **2.** ZOOL **CAPABLE OF BEING THRUST FORWARD** describes a part of an animal's body that can be thrust forward, e.g., the jaws in some types of fish

pro·jec·tion /prə jékshən/ *n* **1. SOMETHING THAT STICKS OUT** something that juts out or overhangs **2. ESTIMATE** an estimate of the rate or amount of something **3. CASTING OF SOMETHING ON SURFACE** the projecting of an image or picture on a surface **4. SOMETHING CAST ON SURFACE** an image or picture projected on a surface **5. PROTRUSION** the act or process of projecting something or the fact of projecting **6.** PSYCHOL **UNCONSCIOUS TRANSFER OF FEELING** the unconscious ascription of a personal thought, feeling, or impulse, especially one considered undesirable, to somebody else **7.** MAPS **REPRESENTATION ON SURFACE** a means of representing lines, figures, or solids on a flat surface such as a map that conforms to the viewing direction or follows particular rules **8.** MATH **DRAWN REPRESENTATION** the representation of a line, figure, or solid on a flat surface **9.** HIST **MIXING BY ALCHEMIST** in alchemy, the mixing of powdered philosopher's stone with base metals in order, supposedly, to transmute them into gold or silver —**pro·jec·tion·al** *adj*

pro·jec·tion booth *n* an enclosed compartment in a theater from which films, slides, or lights are projected onto a screen or stage

pro·jec·tion·ist /prə jékshənist/ *n* somebody whose job is to operate the projector and screen the film in a movie theater and take responsibility for the quality of the image and sound

pro·jec·tion room *n* **1.** a private room with a projector and screen in which movies are viewed **2.** *UK* MOVIES, THEATER same as **projection booth**

pro·jec·tion tel·e·vi·sion, **pro·jec·tion TV** *n* a television picture display system in which an enlarged picture is projected onto a screen

pro·jec·tive /prə jéktiv/ *adj* **1.** relating to or made by projection **2.** relating to or involving a psychological test in which something in the subject's unconscious is revealed by his or her response to specific images —**pro·jec·tive·ly** *adv*

pro·jec·tive ge·om·e·try *n* the study of those properties of plane geometric figures that do not vary when they are projected onto another plane and of the transformations of size and perspective that accompany this

pro·jec·tive test *n* a psychological test that uses images in order to evoke responses from a subject and reveal hidden aspects of the subject's mental life

pro·jec·tor /prə jéktər/ *n* a piece of equipment for projecting the image from film onto a screen and for playing back recorded sound from tracks on the film

pro·jet /prō zháy/ *n* a plan or outline, especially of a draft law or treaty [Early 19C. Via French < Latin *projectum* (see PROJECT)]

pro·kar·y·on /prō kárree òn/ *n* the nucleus of a cell or organism with no membrane separating the area containing DNA from the rest of it [Mid-20C. < Greek *pro-* "before" + *karuon* "nut"]

pro·kar·y·ote /prō kárree ōt/, **pro·car·y·ote** *n* an organism whose DNA is not contained within a nucleus, e.g., a bacterium [Mid-20C. < French < Greek *pro-* "before" + *karuōtos* "having nuts" < *karuon* "nut"] —**pro·kar·y·ot·ic** /prō kàrree óttik/ *adj*

AKG London

Sergey Sergeyevich Prokofiev

Pro·ko·fi·ev /prə káwfee ef/, **Sergey** (1891–1953) Russian composer. His symphonies, concertos, ballets, and operas include *The Love of Three Oranges* (1921), *Peter and the Wolf* (1934), and *Romeo and Juliet* (1936). Full name **Prokofiev, Sergey Sergeyevich**

pro·lac·tin /prō láktin/ *n* a pituitary hormone that stimulates lactation after childbirth

pro·la·mine /prṓləmin, -meen/ *n* a simple protein found in grains [Early 20C. < PROLINE + AMMONIA + -INE]

pro·lapse /prṓ làps, prō láps/ *n also* **pro·lap·sus** /prō lápsəss/ a slippage or sinking of a body organ or part such as a valve of the heart from its usual position ■ *vi* (**-lapsed, -laps·ing, -lapses**) /prō láps/ to slip or fall out of its proper place in the body [Late 16C. < Latin *prolaps-*, past participle of *prolabi* "fall forward" < *labi* "to fall"] —**pro·lapsed** *adj*

pro·late /prṓ làyt/ *adj* describes rock fragments that are elongated in the direction of the polar diameter [Late 17C. < Latin *prolatus*, past participle of *proferre* "carry forward" < *ferre* "carry"]

prole /prōl/ *n* SOC SCI same as **proletarian** *n* (sense 1) (*informal insult*) [Late 19C. Shortening]

pro·leg /prṓ lèg/ *n* a leg on the abdomen of a caterpillar or other insect larva

pro·le·gom·e·non /prōlə gómmə nòn, -nən/ (*plural* **-e·na** /-ənə/) *n* a preliminary discussion or introductory essay, especially to a book or treatise

[Mid-17C. < Greek < *prolegein* "say before" < *legein* "to say"]

pro·lep·sis /prō lépsiss/ (*plural* **-lep·ses** /-lép seez/) *n* **1.** INTRODUCTORY ANTICIPATION OF OBJECTION a preface intended to anticipate and answer an objection to an argument **2.** ANTICIPATORY ADJECTIVE the use after a verb of an adjective that anticipates the result of the verb's action, e.g., "to iron a shirt smooth" **3.** ANACHRONISTIC ASSUMPTION the anachronistic assumption that a future event or condition has already happened, e.g., in the phrase "precolonial United States" **4.** ANTICIPATION OF SOMETHING the assignment of something as existing or occurring before it could have done so, e.g., in the sentence "If you don't answer this letter you're a rat" [Late 16C. Via Latin < Greek *prolēpsis* < *prolambanein* "take before" < *lambanein* "take"] —**pro·lep·tic** *adj* —**pro·lep·ti·cal·ly** *adv*

pro·le·tar·i·an /pròlə térree ən/ *adj* OF WORKING CLASS relating to the working class ■ *n* **1.** WORKER a member of the working class **2.** INDUSTRIAL WAGE-EARNER in Marxist theory, a member of the industrial working class whose only asset is labor sold to an employer **3.** IMPOVERISHED ANCIENT ROMAN a member of an impoverished social class of ancient Rome that had the lowest status and possessed no property [Mid-17C. < Latin *proletarius* "low-status Roman who serves the state only by producing offspring" < *proles* "offspring"] —**pro·le·tar·i·an·ism** *n*

pro·le·tar·i·at /pròlə térree ət/ *n* **1.** WORKING CLASS the class of wage-earning workers in society **2.** CLASS OF INDUSTRIAL WAGE-EARNERS in Marxist theory, the class of industrial workers whose only asset is the labor they sell to an employer **3.** ANCIENT ROMAN SOCIAL CLASS a social class of ancient Rome that had the lowest status and possessed no property [Mid-19C. < French *prolétariat* < Latin *proletarius* (see PROLETARIAN)]

pro-life *adj* in favor of bringing the human fetus to full term, especially, involved in campaigning against open access to abortion and against experimentation on embryos —**pro-lif·er** *n*

pro·lif·er·ate /prə líffə ràyt/ (**-at·ed, -at·ing, -ates**) *v* **1.** *vi* to increase greatly in number **2.** *vti* to multiply cells in the process of reproducing new cells, offspring, or parts, as in the budding of plants, or be multiplied in this way [Late 19C. Back-formation < *proliferation* < French *prolifération* < medieval Latin *prolifer* (see PROLIFEROUS)] —**pro·lif·er·a·tion** /prə liffə ráysh'n/ *n* —**pro·lif·er·a·tive** *adj* —**pro·lif·er·a·tor** *n*

pro·lif·er·ous /prə líffərəss/ *adj* producing or growing many cells, buds, or shoots [Mid-17C. < medieval Latin *prolifer* "bearing offspring" < *proles* "offspring"]

pro·lif·ic /prə líffik/ *adj* **1.** HIGHLY PRODUCTIVE producing ideas or works frequently and in large quantities **2.** FRUITFUL producing a lot of fruit or many offspring **3.** ABUNDANT OR ABOUNDING present in large numbers, or containing large numbers of quantities of something, especially animal life ○ *a period prolific of creative achievement* [Mid-17C. < medieval Latin *prolificus* < Latin *proles* "offspring"] —**pro·lif·i·ca·cy** *n* —**pro·lif·i·cal·ly** *adv*

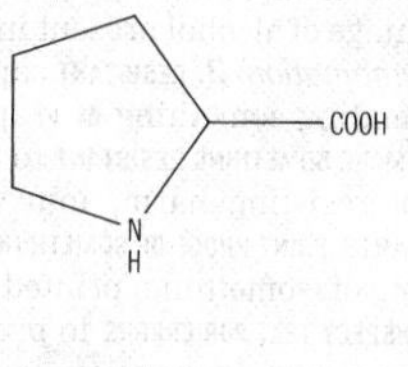

proline

pro·line /prṓ leen/ *n* an amino acid found in many proteins, particularly in collagen. Formula: $C_5H_9NO_2$. [Early 20C. Contraction of *pyrrolidine-2-carboxylic acid*]

pro·lix /prō líks, prṓ liks/ *adj* tiresomely wordy [15C. Directly or via French < Latin *prolixus* "that has flowed out" < past participle of *liquere* "flow"] —**pro·lix·i·ty** /prō líksətee/ *n* —**pro·lix·ly** *adv*

SYNONYMS See *wordy.*

pro·loc·u·tor /prō lókyətər/ *n* **1.** same as **spokesperson** (*formal*) **2.** *US* somebody who chairs a meeting (*formal*) **3.** somebody who chairs an ecclesiastical convocation in the Anglican Church [15C. Latin, "pleader, advocate" < *proloqui* "speak out" < *loqui* "speak"]

Pro·log /prṓ lòg/, **PRO·LOG** *n* a high-level programming language based on logical rather than mathematical relationships [Late 20C. < PROGRAMING + LOGIC]

pro·logue /prṓ lòg/, **pro·log** *n* **1.** INTRODUCTORY STATEMENT an introductory passage or speech before the main action of a novel, play, or long poem **2.** ACTOR INTRODUCING ACTION OF PLAY an actor who speaks introductory lines to a dramatic performance before the main action begins **3.** PRELIMINARY EVENT an event or act that leads to something more important ○ *The affair was a prologue to the complete breakdown of their marriage.* ■ *vt* (**-logued, -logu·ing, -logues; -loged, -log·ing, -logs**) PREFACE SOMETHING WITH PROLOGUE to preface something such as a novel or play with a prologue [14C. Via French and Latin < Greek *prologos*, literally "speech before" < *logos* "speech"]

pro·logu·ize /prṓlə gīz/ (**-ized, -iz·ing, -iz·es**) *vi* to speak or write the prologue to a play, speech, or long poem

pro·long /prə láwng/ (**-longed, -long·ing, -longs**) *vt* to make something go on longer [15C. Directly or via French *prolonger* < late Latin *prolongare* "lengthen out" < Latin *longus* "long"] —**pro·lon·ga·tion** /prō lawng gáysh'n/ *n* —**pro·long·er** *n*

pro·longe /prə lónj/ *n* a rope with a hook and a toggle used to tow something heavy, especially a gun carriage [Mid-19C. < French *prolonger* (see PROLONG)]

prom /prom/ *n* a formal dance for high-school or college students, usually held at the end of the school year [Late 19C. Shortening of PROMENADE]

PROM /prom/ *abbr* COMPUT programmable read-only memory

prom. *abbr* GEOG promontory

prom·e·nade /pròmmə náyd, -naád/ *n* **1.** WALK FOR PLEASURE a leisurely walk or stroll, usually in a public place, that is taken for pleasure or to be seen (*formal*) **2.** MARCHING DANCE MOVEMENT a marching movement in country dancing ■ *v* (**-nad·ed, -nad·ing, -nades**) **1.** *vi* STROLL FOR PLEASURE to walk in a slow and leisurely way, especially up and down a street or in a public place **2.** *vi* MARCH DURING DANCE to perform a marching movement in country dancing **3.** *vt* PROMENADE IN PLACE to be in a particular public place promenading [Mid-16C. < French < *se promener* "go for a walk" < late Latin *prominare* "drive forward" < *minare* "to drive"]

prom·e·nade deck *n* a covered upper deck on a passenger ship on which passengers can walk

pro·meth·a·zine /prō méthə zeen/ *n* an antihistamine drug. Use: treatment of allergies, motion sickness. [Mid-20C. < PROPYL + METHYL + AZINE]

Pro·me·the·an /prə meéthee ən/ *adj* **1.** relating to the Titan Prometheus **2.** creative and imaginatively original

Pro·me·the·us /prə meéthee əss/ *n* **1.** in Greek mythology, a Titan who became a hero to humankind because he stole fire from the gods and gave it to them **2.** a small inner natural satellite of Saturn, discovered in 1980 by Voyager 2. It is irregular in shape having a maximum dimension of 9.3 mi./150 km. [Late 16C. Via Latin < Greek *Promētheus*]

pro·me·thi·um /prə meéthee əm/ *n* a radioactive metallic element. Source: fission of uranium, thorium, or plutonium. Use: phosphorescent paints, X-ray source. Symbol **Pm**. See table at **element** [Mid-20C. After PROMETHEUS]

prom·i·nence /prómminənss/, **prom·i·nen·cy** /-nənssee/ (*plural* **-cies**) *n* **1.** CONSPICUOUS IMPORTANCE the condition or quality of being significantly important or well-known **2.** SOMETHING THAT STICKS OUT something that projects or protrudes, especially a geographic feature or a body part **3.** GAS STREAM FROM THE SUN a visible stream of glowing gas that shoots out from the Sun, seen in the upper chromosphere and lower corona

prom·i·nent /prómminənt/ *adj* **1.** WELL-KNOWN distinguished, eminent, or well-known ○ *a prominent figure in the arts* **2.** NOTICEABLE noticeable or conspicuous ○ *prominent position* **3.** STICKING OUT large and projecting ○ *prominent chin* [15C. < Latin *prominent-*, present participle of *prominere* "project forward" < *minere* "to project"] —**prom·i·nent·ly** *adv*

~~**promiscous**~~ incorrect spelling of **promiscuous**

prom·is·cu·i·ty /pròmmi skyoó ətee/ *n* **1.** behavior characterized by casual and indiscriminate sexual intercourse, often with many people **2.** confused or indiscriminate mixing (*formal*)

pro·mis·cu·ous /prə mískyoo əss/ *adj* **1.** SEXUALLY INDISCRIMINATE having many indiscriminate or casual sexual relationships **2.** CHOOSING WITHOUT DISCRIMINATING choosing carelessly or without discrimination **3.** CONFUSEDLY MIXED mixed in an indiscriminate or disorderly way (*formal*) **4.** RANDOM occurring without any set or specific pattern or time (*literary*) ○ *a sail caught by a promiscuous wind* [Early 17C. < Latin *promiscuus*, literally "mixed forward" < *miscere* "to mix"] —**pro·mis·cu·ous·ly** *adv* —**pro·mis·cu·ous·ness** *n*

prom·ise /prómmiss/ *v* (**-ised, -is·ing, -is·es**) **1.** *vti* VOW to assure somebody that something will certainly happen or be done ○ *promised to come* ○ *promised that the patient would recover* **2.** *vt* PLEDGE SOMETHING to pledge to somebody to provide or do something ○ *promised them a kitten* **3.** *vti* MAKE SOMEBODY EXPECT SOMETHING to cause somebody to expect something ○ *The sky promised rain.* **4.** *vt* ASSURE OR WARN SOMEBODY to assure or warn somebody that something is true or inevitable ○ *Things will be fine, I promise you.* **5.** *vt* AFFIANCE SOMEBODY to engage somebody to be married (*dated*) ○ *She told him that she was promised to someone else.* ■ *n* **1.** ASSURANCE OR UNDERTAKING an assurance that something will be done or not done ○ *He never keeps his promises.* **2.** INDICATION OF SUCCESS an indication that somebody or something will turn out well or successfully ○ *showed great promise* **3.** SIGNAL OF SOMETHING an indication that something is likely to happen [14C. Directly or via French < Latin *promissum* < *promiss-*, past participle of *promittere* "send forward" < *mittere* "send"] —**prom·is·ee** /pròmmi seé/ *n* —**prom·is·er** *n* —**prom·i·sor** /prómmi sàwr/ *n*

Prom·ised Land *n* **1.** the land of Canaan, according to the Bible promised by God to the descendants of Abraham **2.** *also* **prom·ised land** heaven, or a place or situation of great happiness or success

prom·is·ing /prómmissing/ *adj* likely to be successful or to turn out well —**prom·is·ing·ly** *adv*

prom·is·so·ry /prómmi sàwree/ *adj* **1.** concerning, containing, or implying a promise **2.** stating how the terms of an insurance contract will be fulfilled [15C. < medieval Latin *promissorius* < Latin *promiss-* (see PROMISE)]

prom·is·so·ry note *n* a signed agreement promising payment of a sum of money on demand or at a specific time

pro·mo /prṓmō/ (*informal*) *n* (*plural* **-mos**) something that promotes or advertises a product, e.g., a recorded announcement, commercial, or video ■ *adj* involved or engaged in the promotion or advertising of something [Mid-20C. Shortening of PROMOTION or *promotional*]

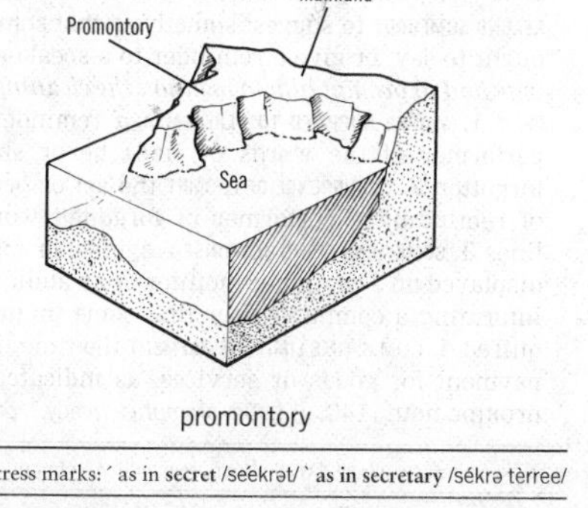

promontory

prom·on·to·ry /prómmən tàwree/ (*plural* **-ries**) *n* **1.** a point of land that juts out into the sea. See illustration on previous page **2.** a prominent or protruding part of an organ or structure in the body [Mid-16C. < medieval Latin *promontorium*, alteration of Latin *promunturium*]

pro·mote /prə mṓt/ (**-mot·ed, -mot·ing, -motes**) *vt* **1.** ADVANCE SOMEBODY IN RANK to raise somebody to a more senior job or a higher position or rank **2.** MOVE SOMEBODY TO NEXT GRADE to move a student to the next higher grade at the end of the school year **3.** SUPPORT OR ENCOURAGE SOMETHING to encourage the growth and development of something **4.** ADVERTISE SOMETHING to publicize a product so that people will buy or rent it **5.** ADVANCE SOMETHING to further something by helping to arrange or introduce it **6.** RAISE TEAM TO HIGHER DIVISION to move a soccer team or player from a lower to a higher division of a league **7.** CHESS EXCHANGE PAWN FOR MORE POWERFUL PIECE in chess, to exchange a pawn for a more powerful piece, usually a queen, when it reaches an opponent's end of the board [14C. < Latin *promot-*, past participle of *promovere* "move forward" < *movere* "to move"] —**pro·mot·a·ble** *adj*

pro·mot·er /prə mṓtər/ *n* **1.** ARRANGER OF PUBLIC EVENT a person or organization that stages an entertainment or an athletic or other public event ○ *boxing promoter* **2.** ADVOCATE a supporter or advocate of something **3.** ACQUIRER OF CAPITAL FOR VENTURE somebody who raises money for a financial or commercial undertaking **4.** PUBLICIST FOR PRODUCT somebody who tries to make a product or service more widely known or more successful **5.** GENETICS BINDING SITE IN DNA CHAIN in a DNA chain, a sequence to which the enzyme RNA polymerase binds so as to start transcription **6.** CHEM SUBSTANCE ADDED TO CATALYST a chemical additive that increases the efficiency of a catalyst

pro·mot·er gene *n* GENETICS same as **promoter** (sense 5)

pro·mo·tion /prə mṓsh'n/ *n* **1.** ADVANCEMENT IN POSITION an advancement to a more senior job or a higher rank, grade, or position **2.** ENCOURAGEMENT FOR ACTIVITY encouragement of the growth or development of something **3.** SOMETHING THAT PROMOTES something such as an advertising campaign that is designed to promote a product, cause, or organization **4.** MARKETING PROCESS OF PROMOTING the act or process of making a product, cause, or organization more widely known or more successful **5.** ADVANCE INTO HIGHER DIVISION advance by a soccer team or player into a higher division of a league **6.** CHESS EXCHANGE OF PAWN FOR SUPERIOR PIECE in chess, the act of exchanging a pawn for a more powerful piece, usually a queen, when it reaches an opponent's end of the board —**pro·mo·tion·al** *adj*

pro·mo·tive /prə mṓtiv/ *adj* tending to further or encourage something

pro·mo·to·ra /prò mō tṓrə/ *n Hispanic* an outreach worker in a Hispanic community who is responsible for raising awareness of health and educational issues [Via American Spanish < Spanish, "promoter"]

prompt /prompt/ *adj* **1.** DONE IMMEDIATELY done at once and without delay **2.** QUICK TO ACT ready, punctual, or quick to act ■ *v* (**prompt·ed, prompt·ing, prompts**) **1.** *vt* CAUSE SOMEBODY TO ACT to make somebody decide to do something ○ *What prompted him to change his mind, we don't yet know.* **2.** *vt* BRING ABOUT SOMETHING to cause something to happen ○ *Fears of inflation prompted an immediate rise in interest rates.* **3.** *vti* PROVIDE ACTOR WITH LINES to provide actors during a performance with words or lines they have forgotten ○ *She had to be prompted three times in the first scene.* **4.** *vt* REMIND SOMEBODY to suggest something that somebody ought to say, or give a reminder to a speaker ○ *His wife had to prompt him to mention the cleaning staff.* ■ *n* **1.** WORDS SUPPLIED TO PERFORMER a reminder to a performer of the words or lines he or she has forgotten **2.** OCCURRENCE OF PROMPT the act or occasion of reminding a performer of forgotten words or lines **3.** SOMETHING CUING RESPONSE a symbol or message displayed on a computer monitor or an audio signal informing a computer user that some input is required **4.** COMM TIME LIMIT FOR PAYMENT the time limit of payment for goods or services, as indicated on a prompt note [14C. < Latin *promptus* "ready," past participle of *promere*, literally "take forward" < *emere* "take"] —**prompt·ly** *adv* —**prompt·ness** *n*

prompt·book /prómpt bo͝ok/ *n* a copy of a script for a prompter to use

prompt box *n* a box situated beneath the stage in a theater in which the prompter sits

prompt·er /prómptər/ *n* somebody in a theater whose job is to prompt actors who have forgotten their words or lines

promp·ti·tude /prómpti to͞od/ *n* punctuality or quickness to act

prompt note *n* a written reminder sent to the purchaser of something, stating when payment is due

prompt side *n* the side of the stage in a theater where the prompter sits

prom·ul·gate /prómm'l gàyt, prə múl gàyt/ (**-gat·ed, -gat·ing, -gates**) *vt* (*formal*) **1.** to proclaim or declare something officially, especially to publicize formally that a law or decree is in effect **2.** to make something widely known [Mid-16C. < Latin *promulgat-*, past participle of *promulgare* "bring to public notice," literally "milk forward" < *mulgere* "to milk"] —**prom·ul·ga·tion** /pròmm'l gáysh'n/ *n* —**prom·ul·ga·tor** *n*

pron, pron. *abbr* GRAM **1.** pronominal **2.** pronoun

pron. *abbr* **1.** GRAM pronominal **2.** LANGUAGE pronounced **3.** LANGUAGE pronunciation

pro·nate /prṓ nàyt/ (**-nat·ed, -nat·ing, -nates**) *vt* (*technical*) **1.** to turn the hand or forearm so that the palm faces downward **2.** to rotate the bones of the foot so that the weight is borne mainly on the inside of the foot [Mid-19C. Back-formation < *pronation* < PRONE or its source Latin *pronus*] —**pro·na·tion** /prō náysh'n/ *n*

pro·na·tor /prṓ nàytər/ *n* a muscle that turns a part of the body so that it faces downward, e.g., one of the muscles in the forearm that rotates the hand into the palm-down position [Early 18C. < modern Latin < Latin *pronus* (see PRONE), after SUPINATOR]

prone /prōn/ *adj* **1.** DISPOSED TO SOMETHING inclined to do or be affected by something ○ *prone to exaggerate* **2.** FACE DOWN lying face down ○ *prone position* **3.** IN DOWNWARD DIRECTION sloping, leaning, or moving downward [15C. < Latin *pronus* "bent forward" < *pro* "forward"] —**prone·ness** *n*

pro·neph·ros /prō néffrəss, -né fròss/ (*plural* **-roi** /-ròy/ or **-ra** /-rə/) *n* the first of three segments of the kidney, functional in some vertebrate embryos but not in adults [Late 19C. < PRO-[2] + Greek *nephros* "kidney"] —**pro·neph·ric** *adj*

prong /prawng/ *n* **1.** SHARP POINT a thin sharp point at the end of something such as a fork **2.** RIVER a branch of a river ■ *vt* (**pronged, prong·ing, prongs**) PIERCE WITH SOMETHING SHARP to prick or stab something with a sharp pointed end [15C. < Anglo-Latin *pronga*] —**pronged** *adj*

prong·horn /práwng hàwrn/, **prong·horn an·te·lope** *n* an animal similar to an antelope that is the fastest North American mammal. Native to: Mexico, western United States. Latin name: *Antilocapra americana*.

pro·nom·i·nal /prō nómmən'l/ *adj* like or functioning as a pronoun ■ *n* a word that functions like a pronoun [Late 17C. < late Latin *pronominalis* < Latin *pronomen* (see PRONOUN)] —**pro·nom·i·nal·ly** *adv*

pro·nom·i·nal·ize /prō nómmən'l ìz/ (**-ized, -iz·ing, -iz·es**) *vt* in transformational grammars, to replace a noun or noun phrase in a sentence with a pronoun —**pro·nom·i·nal·i·za·tion** /-nòmmən'li záysh'n/ *n*

pro·noun /prṓ nòwn/ *n* a word that substitutes for a noun or a noun phrase, e.g., "I," "you," "them," "it," "ours," "who," "which," "myself," and "anybody." English pronouns differ from nouns in sometimes having an objective form, e.g., "her" for "she" and "me" for "I." [15C. < PRO-[1] + NOUN, after French *pronom*, Latin *pronomen* "something in place of a name" < *nomen* "name"]

pro·nounce /prə nówns/ (**-nounced, -nounc·ing, -nounc·es**) *v* **1.** *vti* UTTER SOUNDS OR WORDS to articulate sounds or words, especially in a way acceptable to the person to whom they are spoken or by most speakers of a language **2.** *vti* FORMALLY DECLARE SOMETHING to declare something officially to be the case **3.** *vt* GIVE JUDGMENT to render an opinion or judgment **4.** *vt* PHON SYMBOLIZE SOUND OF WORD to indicate with symbols how a word should be spoken [14C. Via Old French *pronuncier* < Latin *pronuntiare* "announce before" < *nuntiare* "announce"] —**pro·nounce·a·ble** *adj* —**pro·nounce·ment** *n* —**pro·nounc·er** *n*

pro·nounced /prə nównst/ *adj* **1.** noticeable or obvious **2.** voiced or spoken —**pro·nounc·ed·ly** /-sədlee/ *adv*

~~**pronounciation**~~ incorrect spelling of **pronunciation**

pron·to /próntō/ *adv* in a prompt or rapid way (*informal*) [Mid-19C. Via Spanish < Latin *promptus* (see PROMPT)]

pro·nu·cle·ar /prō no͞oklee ər/ *adj* **1.** in favor of using nuclear power as a source of energy, or supporting the use of nuclear weapons **2.** relating to a pronucleus —**pro·nu·cle·ar·ist** *n, adj*

pro·nu·cle·us /prō no͞oklee əss/ (*plural* **-cle·i** /-klee ì/ or **-cle·us·es**) *n* the nucleus of a fully matured ovum or spermatozoan before the nuclei are fused during fertilization

pronunc. *abbr* pronunciation

pro·nun·ci·a·men·to /prō nùnsee ə méntō/ (*plural* **-tos** or **-toes**) *n Hispanic* an announcement, proclamation, or manifesto, especially one issued by a revolutionary group [Mid-19C. < Spanish < *pronunciar* "announce" < Latin *pronuntiare* (see PRONOUNCE)]

pro·nun·ci·a·tion /prə nùnssee áysh'n/ *n* **1.** MAKING OF SOUNDS OF SPEECH the way in which a sound, word, or language is articulated, especially in conforming to an accepted standard **2.** ACT OF SPEECH the act of articulating a sound or word **3.** PHON TRANSCRIPTION OF SOUNDS a phonetic transcription of sounds [15C. Directly or via French < Latin *pronuntiation-* < *pronuntiare* (see PRONOUNCE)]

proof /proof/ *n* **1.** CONCLUSIVE EVIDENCE evidence or an argument that serves to establish a fact or the truth of something **2.** TEST OF SOMETHING a test or trial of something to establish whether it is true **3.** STATE OF HAVING BEEN PROVED the quality or condition of having been proved **4.** LAW TRIAL EVIDENCE evidence presented in a trial for consideration by the court **5.** MATH, LOGIC SEQUENCE OF STEPS TO VALIDATE SOLUTION the sequence of steps or stages used in establishing the validity of a mathematical or philosophical proposition. These steps are a logical derivation of the proposition from axioms, or explicit assumptions, and previously proved propositions. **6.** STRENGTH OF ALCOHOLIC CONTENT the relative strength of an alcoholic beverage expressed by a number that is twice the percentage of the alcohol present in the liquid **7.** PRINTING COPY USED FOR CHECKING ERRORS a printed copy used for checking corrections before the final printing of a text or image **8.** ARTS IMPRESSION FROM ENGRAVED PLATE an impression taken from an engraved plate before it is printed **9.** PHOTOGRAPHY PRINT FROM NEGATIVE a photographic print made from a negative and checked for quality prior to further reproduction **10.** COINS COIN IMPRESSION a preliminary impression of a coin, intended as a specimen for display ■ *adj* **1.** IMPERVIOUS TO SOMETHING capable of resisting something that may have a harmful or unwanted effect **2.** HAVING RELATIVE ALCOHOLIC STRENGTH having a particular alcoholic strength that is expressed by a number that is twice the percentage of alcohol present in the liquid (*often used in combination*) **3.** RESISTANT capable of resisting or withstanding something ■ *vt* (**proofed, proof·ing, proofs**) **1.** MAKE SOMETHING RESISTANT to make something capable of resisting harm, injury, or damage **2.** PRINTING, ARTS PRINT PROOF OF SOMETHING to make a trial impression of something printed or engraved **3.** PRINTING INSPECT TEXT FOR ERRORS to proofread a text, or inspect a printed impression for errors **4.** COOK ACTIVATE YEAST to cause yeast to become active by adding water and often sugar [13C. Via Old French *preve* < late Latin *proba* < Latin *probare* "prove, test"]

proof of pur·chase *n* evidence that something has been paid for, e.g., a receipt

proof·read /pro͞of rèed/ (**-read** /-rèd/, **-read·ing, -reads**) *vti* to read the proofs of a text and mark corrections to be made —**proof·read·er** *n*

proof sheet *n* a sheet of paper that has a printer's

proof on it, usually with wide margins so that corrections can be marked up easily

proof spir·it *n* an alcoholic beverage or a mixture of alcohol and water. In the United Kingdom and Canada proof spirit is 57.1 percent alcohol by volume at 10.6°C51°F, while in the United States, it is 50 percent alcohol at 15.6°C60°F. Use: formerly, as a standard for measuring alcoholic strength.

proof the·o·ry *n* the part of the theory of logic concerned with the exact nature of deriving propositions and conclusions

prop[1] /prop/ *n* **1.** RIGID SUPPORT a rigid object, e.g., a beam, stake, or pole, that supports something or holds it in place **2.** COMFORTING PERSON OR THING somebody or something that provides comfort or assistance **3.** RUGBY PLAYER AT EITHER END OF FRONT ROW in rugby, a forward at either end of the front row of a scrum ■ *vt* (**propped, prop·ping, props**) SUPPORT SOMETHING WITH PROP to use a rigid object to support something or hold it in place [15C. < Middle Dutch *proppe* "vine prop, support"]

prop up *vt* to give support or help to somebody or something

prop[2] /prop/, **Prop** *n US* a proposition placed before voters (*informal*) ○ *Prop 413 will provide money for a new library.* [Early 19C. Shortening]

prop[3] /prop/ *n* an object used during the performance of a play or film [Mid-19C. Shortening of PROPERTY]

prop[4] /prop/ *n* an aircraft propeller (*informal*) [Early 20C. Shortening]

prop. *abbr* **1.** GRAM proper **2.** properly **3.** property **4.** PHILOSOPHY, MATH proposition **5.** COMM proprietor

pro·pae·deu·tic /prṑpi dóotik/ *adj* providing preparatory instruction (*formal*) ■ *n* a preliminary course of study that precedes more advanced instruction (*often used in the plural*) [Late 18C. < PRO-[2] + Greek *paideutikē* "education," after Greek *propaideuein* "teach beforehand"]

prop·a·gan·da /pròppə gándə/ *n* **1.** information put out by an organization or government to promote a policy, idea, or cause **2.** deceptive or distorted information that is systematically spread [Early 18C. < modern Latin, in *Congregatio de propaganda fide* "Congregation for the Propagation of the Faith"] —**prop·a·gan·dism** *n* —**prop·a·gan·dist** *n, adj*

Pro·pa·gan·da *n* a committee of Roman Catholic cardinals, the Congregation for the Propagation of the Faith, in charge of supervising foreign missions and educating priests to serve in them

prop·a·gan·dize /pròppə gán dīz/ (**-dized, -diz·ing, -diz·es**) *vti* to organize or spread propaganda

prop·a·gate /próppə gàyt/ (**-gat·ed, -gat·ing, -gates**) *v* **1.** *vti* BIOL REPRODUCE ORGANISM to reproduce a plant or animal, or cause one to reproduce **2.** *vti* GARDENING CREATE NEW PLANTS to multiply plants by the use of seeds or cuttings **3.** *vt* SPREAD SOMETHING WIDELY to spread an idea or custom to many people **4.** *vti* PHYS IMPEL SOMETHING FORWARD to move or transmit something such as a sound or light wave forward through a medium such as air [Late 16C. < Latin *propagat-*, past participle of *propagare* "breed plants from shoots or layers" < *propago* "layer"] —**prop·a·ga·ble** *adj* —**prop·a·ga·tion** /pròppə gáysh'n/ *n* —**prop·a·ga·tion·al** *adj* —**prop·a·ga·tive** *adj*

prop·a·ga·tor /próppə gàytər/ *n* **1.** somebody who spreads ideas or beliefs widely **2.** a shallow box with a transparent cover used for germinating seeds or allowing cuttings to take root, especially one that can be heated

prop·a·gule /próppə gyòol/, **pro·pag·u·lum** /prə pággyələm/ (*plural* **-lums** or **-la** /-lə/) *n* a part of a plant or fungus, e.g., a bud or a spore, that becomes detached from the rest and forms a new organism [Mid-19C. < modern Latin *propagulum* "little shoot" < *propago* "layer"]

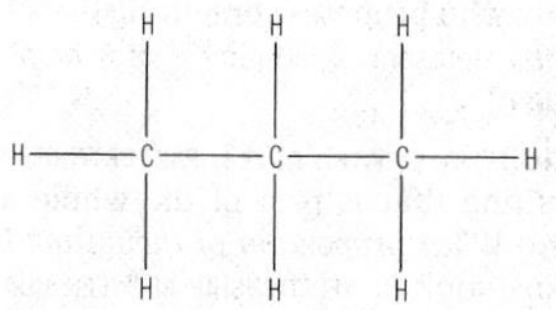

propane

pro·pane /prṓ pàyn/ *n* a flammable colorless hydrocarbon gas. Use: fuel, propellant, refrigerant. Formula: C_3H_8. [Mid-19C. < PROPIONIC]

pro·pa·no·ic ac·id /prṑpə nṓ ik-/ *n* CHEM same as **propionic acid**

pro·pa·nol /prṓpə nàwl/ *n* CHEM same as **propyl alcohol**

prop·a·none /prṓpə nōn/ *n* CHEM same as **acetone** (*technical*)

pro·par·ox·y·tone /prṑpə róksə tṑn/ *n* in classical Greek grammar, a word that has an acute accent on the third syllable from the end ■ *adj* describes a word that has an acute accent on the third syllable from the end [Mid-18C. < Greek *proparoxutonos* < *oxutonos* "having an acute accent"]

pro·pel /prə pél/ (**-pelled, -pel·ling, -pels**) *vt* **1.** to move or push somebody or something forward **2.** to impel somebody to do something or cause something to happen [15C. < Latin *propellere* "drive forward" < *pellere* "to drive"]

pro·pel·lant /prə péllənt/ *n* **1.** SUBSTANCE GIVING THRUST TO ROCKET a substance that is burned to give upward thrust to a rocket **2.** EXPLOSIVE CHARGE FOR GUN an explosive charge that projects a bullet from a gun **3.** GAS IN AEROSOL a compressed inert gas used to dispense the contents of an aerosol container when pressure is applied and released

pro·pel·lent /prə péllənt/ *adj* tending to drive or move something forward ■ *n* same as **propellant**

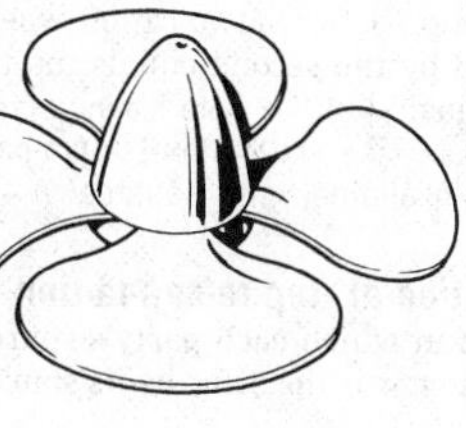

propeller

pro·pel·ler /prə péllər/ *n* a revolving shaft with spiral blades that causes a ship or an aircraft to move by the backward thrust of water or air

pro·pel·ler shaft *n* **1.** the shaft in a ship or aircraft that transmits power from the engine to the propeller **2.** MECH ENG same as **drive shaft** (sense 1)

pro·pel·ling pen·cil *n UK* same as **mechanical pencil**

~~**propellor**~~ incorrect spelling of **propeller**

pro·pene /prṓ peen/ *n* CHEM same as **propylene** [Mid-19C. < PROPYL]

pro·pen·o·ic ac·id /prṑpə nṓ ik-/ *n* CHEM same as **acrylic acid**

pro·pen·si·ty /prə pénssətee/ (*plural* **-ties**) *n* a tendency to demonstrate particular behavior [Late 16C. < obsolete *propense* "inclined, prone" < Latin *propensus*, past participle of *propendere* "hang forward" < *pendere* "hang"]

prop·er /próppər/ *adj* **1.** CORRECT appropriate or correct ○ *need to put the issue in its proper perspective* **2.** NEEDED AND APPROPRIATE fulfilling all expectations or criteria ○ *He needs proper medical care.* **3.** WITH CORRECT MANNERS behaving in a respectable or socially acceptable way **4.** CHARACTERISTIC OF SOMEBODY characteristic of or belonging exclusively to somebody or something **5.** NARROWLY IDENTIFIED strictly identified and distinguished from something else ○ *stayed in the suburbs, not the city proper* **6.** HERALDRY SHOWING NATURAL COLORS showing the natural colors in the design or device of a heraldic object **7.** CHR USED ON HOLY OCCASION reserved as a prayer, lesson, or rite for a holy day or festival **8.** GOOD-LOOKING physically handsome and admirable (*archaic*) **9.** MATH INCLUDED IN SECOND SET included as a mathematical set in a second set but not the same as it ■ *n also* **Prop·er** CHR SERVICE FOR HOLY OCCASION a Christian church service designated for use on a holy day or festival ■ *adj* EXCESSIVELY POLITE rigidly polite, or exhibiting excessive formality ○ *She's very proper, and never wears slacks in public.* [13C. Directly or via French < Latin *proprius* "your own, particular, special"] —**prop·er·ness** *n*

prop·er ad·jec·tive *n* an adjective that is formed from a proper noun, as "Canadian" is from "Canada"

prop·er frac·tion *n* a fraction in which the value of the numerator is less than the value of the denominator, e.g. $\frac{6}{8}$

prop·er·ly /próppərlee/ *adv* **1.** APPROPRIATELY in a suitable or appropriate way ○ *properly dressed for the occasion* **2.** CORRECTLY in a correct or well-mannered way ○ *If you can't behave properly, we'll have to go home.* **3.** IN REALITY in a correct and appropriate situation ○ *The chair properly belongs in the corner.* **4.** *UK* TOTALLY to the fullest degree or extent ○ *By the end of the day she was properly tired.*

prop·er noun, **prop·er name** *n* the name of a specific person or thing, normally beginning with a capital letter and not used with the indefinite article or a modifier, e.g., "York," "Sally," or "Henderson"

prop·er·ty /próppərtee/ (*plural* **-ties**) *n* **1.** SOMETHING OWNED something of value that is owned, e.g., land or a patent **2.** OWNED LAND OR REAL ESTATE a piece of land or real estate that is owned by somebody ○ *a property owner* **3.** LAW RIGHT TO OWN SOMETHING the right to own, possess, or use something **4.** TRAIT OR ATTRIBUTE a characteristic quality or distinctive feature of something (*often used in the plural*) **5.** SOMETHING AT SOMEBODY'S DISPOSAL something at the disposal of a person, a group, or the public ○ *community property* **6.** ARTS PROP a stage prop (*formal*) **7.** PHILOSOPHY DISTINCTIVE BUT NOT ESSENTIAL QUALITY in Aristotelian philosophy, an attribute or quality that is peculiar to a whole class or species, but not essential to it [13C. < Anglo-Norman *proprete*, variant of Old French *propriété* < Latin *proprietas* "ownership, appropriateness" < *proprius* "your own, particular, special"] —**prop·er·tied** *adj*

prop·er·ty tax *n* a tax based on the value of a house or other property

prop for·ward *n* RUGBY same as **prop**[1] *n* (sense 3)

pro·phage /prṓ fàyj/ *n* a stable form of virus (**bacteriophage**) that infects a bacterium with genetic material that is integrated into and replicated as part of the host bacterium's chromosome without harming the bacterium

pro·phase /prṓ fàyz/ *n* the first phase in cell division, when chromosomes condense and can be seen as two chromatids

proph·e·cy /próffəssee/ (*plural* **-cies**) *n* **1.** DIVINE PREDICTION a prediction of a future event that is believed to reveal the will of a deity **2.** PREDICTION a prediction that something will occur in the future **3.** SUPPOSED ABILITY TO PREDICT FUTURE the supposed ability to predict the future when inspired by a deity [13C. Via French *prophecie* and late Latin *prophetia* < Greek *prophēteia* < *prophētēs* (see PROPHET)]

USAGE prophecy or **prophesy**? Though spelled almost alike, these two words are pronounced differently and have different grammatical functions. ***Prophecy***, a noun only, means "a prediction or the ability to predict the future," as in *a dire economic prophecy*. ***Prophesy***, a verb, means "to predict," as in *would not go so far as to prophesy a recession just yet*.

proph·e·sy /próffə sì/ (**-sied, -sy·ing, -sies**) *v* **1.** *vti* to predict what is going to happen **2.** *vi* to supposedly reveal the will of a deity in predicting a future event [14C. < Old French *prophecier* < *prophecie* (see PROPHECY)] —**proph·e·si·able** *adj* —**proph·e·si·er** *n*

USAGE See *prophecy*.

proph·et /próffət/ *n* **1.** SOMEBODY WHO INTERPRETS DIVINE WILL somebody who claims to interpret or transmit the commands of a deity **2.** SOMEBODY PREDICTING THE FUTURE somebody who predicts the future ○ *prophets of economic doom* **3.** ADVOCATE OF SOMETHING somebody who advocates a cause or idea **4.** INSPIRED LEADER somebody considered to be an inspired leader or teacher [12C. Via French and Latin < Greek *prophētēs* "somebody who speaks beforehand" < *phētēs* "speaker"]

SPELLCHECK See *profit*.

Proph·et /próffət/ *n* **1.** Muhammad, the founder of Islam **2.** Joseph Smith, the founder of the Church of Jesus Christ of Latter-Day Saints ■ **Proph·ets** *npl* the prophetic books of the Bible. See table at **Bible**

proph·et·ess /próffətəss/ *n* a female prophet

pro·phet·ic /prə féttik/ *adj* **1.** predicting or foreshadowing something that does eventually happen **2.** relating to a prophet [15C. Via French or late Latin < Greek *prophētikos* < *prophētes* (see PROPHET)] —**pro·phet·i·cal** *adj* —**pro·phet·i·cal·ly** *adv*

Proph·et's Birth·day *n* ISLAM same as **Mawlid al-Nabi**

pro·phy /prṓfee/ (*plural* **-phies**) *n US* same as **condom** (*dated informal*) [Late 20C. Shortening of PROPHYLACTIC]

pro·phy·lac·tic /prṑfə láktik, pròffə-/ *adj* protecting against infection or disease ■ *n* **1.** HEALTH same as **condom** **2.** a drug or agent that prevents the development of disease [Late 16C. Via French *prophylactique* < Greek *prophulaktikos prophulassein*, literally "keep guard in front of" < *phulassein* "to guard"] —**pro·phy·lac·ti·cal·ly** *adv*

pro·phy·lax·is /prṑfə láksiss, pròffə-/ (*plural* **-lax·es** /-lák sèez/) *n* **1.** a treatment that prevents disease or stops it from spreading, e.g., vaccination **2.** a dental treatment to remove plaque and tartar from the teeth [Mid-19C. < modern Latin, "guarding in front of" < Greek *pro* "in front of" + *phulaxis* "guarding"]

pro·pin·qui·ty /prə píngkwətee/ *n* nearness in space, time, or relationship (*formal*) [14C. Directly or via French < Latin *propinquitas* < *prope* "near"]

pro·pi·o·nate /prṓpee ə nàyt/ *n* a chemical compound that is a salt or ester of propionic acid [Late 19C. < PROPIONIC]

pro·pi·on·ic /prṑpee ónnik/ *adj* derived from propionic acid [Mid-19C. < Greek *pro* "in front" + *piōn* "fat," because it is first in order of the fatty acids]

pro·pi·on·ic ac·id *n* a colorless liquid fatty acid. Use: manufacture of artificial flavors, perfumes, and preservatives. Formula: $C_3H_6O_2$.

pro·pi·ti·ate /prō píshee àyt/ (**-at·ed, -at·ing, -ates**) *vt* to appease or conciliate somebody or something [Late 16C. < Latin *propitiat-*, past participle of *propitiare* "make favorable" < *propitius* "favorable"] —**pro·pi·ti·a·ble** *adj* —**pro·pi·ti·a·tion** /prō pìshee áysh'n/ *n* —**pro·pi·ti·a·tive** /prō píshee àytiv/ *adj* —**pro·pi·ti·a·tor** *n* —**pro·pi·ti·a·to·ry** *adj*

pro·pi·tious /prō píshəss/ *adj* **1.** favorable and likely to lead to success **2.** kindly disposed or gracious (*formal*) [15C. Directly or via French < Latin *propitius* "favorable"] —**pro·pi·tious·ly** *adv* —**pro·pi·tious·ness** *n*

prop·jet /próp jèt/ *n* AVIAT, MECH ENG same as **turboprop** [Mid-20C. < PROP[4]]

prop·lyd /própplid/ *n* the disk of gases and dust that comprises a protoplanet [Late 20C. Contraction of *protoplanetary disk*]

prop·man /próp màn/ (*plural* **-men** /-mèn/) *n* a man who looks after stage properties

~~**propoganda**~~ incorrect spelling of **propaganda**

prop·o·lis /próppəliss/ *n* a waxy resinous substance that comes from buds, used by bees as a cement and caulking in making their hives [Early 17C. Via Latin < Greek, literally "before a city" < *polis* "city" (originally a structure around the opening of a hive)]

pro·po·nent /prə pṓnənt/ *n* **1.** ADVOCATE somebody who advocates something **2.** LAW PRESENTER OF WILL somebody who presents a will for probate **3.** PROPOSER somebody who proposes something [Late 16C. < Latin *proponent-*, present participle of *proponere* (see PROPOSITION)]

pro·por·tion /prə páwrsh'n/ *n* **1.** PART OF WHOLE a quantity of something that is part of the whole amount or number ○ *What proportion of their time is spent on administration?* **2.** RELATIONSHIP BETWEEN QUANTITIES the relationship between two or more amounts or numbers, or between the parts of a whole ○ *The proportion of trucks to cars on the road has remained the same.* **3.** RELATIVE SIZE the correct or desirable relationship of size, quantity, or degree between two or more things or parts of something ○ *An understanding of proportion is essential for an architect.* **4.** RELATIVE IMPORTANCE the importance of different aspects of a situation when compared with each other ○ *The media blew the incident all out of proportion.* **5.** MATH RATIO a relationship between two variables that remains fixed **6.** MATH EQUALITY OF TWO RATIOS a relationship of equality between two ratios, in which the first term divided by the second equals the third divided by the fourth, as in 1/2 = 3/6 ■ **pro·por·tions** *npl* **1.** SIZE OF SOMETHING the size or shape of something **2.** IMPORTANCE OF SOMETHING the importance or seriousness of something ■ *vt* (**-tioned, -tion·ing, -tions**) **1.** MAINTAIN RELATIONSHIP BETWEEN THINGS to create or maintain a relationship of size, quantity, or degree between two or more things ○ *The arms and body of the sweater had been badly proportioned.* **2.** BALANCE SOMETHING to give something a pleasing shape, appropriate dimensions, or a harmonious arrangement of parts (*usually passive*) ○ *a beautifully proportioned design* [14C. Directly or via French < Latin *proportion-* < *pro portione* "according to (each) part" < *portion-* "part, portion"] —**pro·por·tion·a·bil·i·ty** /prə pàwrsh'nə bíllətee/ *n* —**pro·por·tion·a·ble** *adj* —**pro·por·tion·a·bly** *adv* —**pro·por·tion·ment** *n*

USAGE See *percentage*.

pro·por·tion·al /prə páwrshən'l, -shnəl/ *adj* **1.** IN PROPORTION having the correct relationship of size, quantity, or degree to something else, or remaining in the same relationship when things change ○ *The rate of pay is proportional to the complexity of the task.* **2.** MATH RELATED BY RATIO related by or possessing a constant ratio ■ *n* MATH TERM IN PAIR OF EQUIVALENT RATIOS one of the four terms in a relationship of proportion between two ratios, where the first term divided by the second equals the third divided by the fourth [14C. < late Latin *proportionalis* < Latin *proportion-* (see PROPORTION)] —**pro·por·tion·al·i·ty** /prə pàwrsh'n állətee, -shə nállətee/ *n* —**pro·por·tion·al·ly** *adv*

pro·por·tion·al rep·re·sen·ta·tion *n* an electoral system in which each party's share of the seats in government is the same as its share of all the votes cast

pro·por·tion·al tax *n* a tax levied at the same rate on tax bases of different amounts

pro·por·tion·ate /prə páwrsh'nət/ *adj* having the correct relationship of size, quantity, or degree to something else, or remaining in the same relationship when things change ○ *The fall in price led to a proportionate rise in sales.* ■ *vt* (**-at·ed, -at·ing, -ates**) /prə páwrsh'n ayt/ to give two or more things the correct relationship of size, quantity, or degree [14C. < late Latin *proportionatus* < Latin *proportion-* (see PROPORTION)] —**pro·por·tion·ate·ly** *adv* —**pro·por·tion·ate·ness** *n*

pro·pos·al /prə pṓz'l/ *n* **1.** SUGGESTED IDEA OR PLAN a suggestion or intention, especially one put forward formally or officially **2.** ACT OF PROPOSING the act of making a suggestion or stating an intention **3.** REQUEST TO MARRY SOMEBODY a request for somebody to enter into marriage

pro·pose /prə pṓz/ (**-posed, -pos·ing, -pos·es**) *v* **1.** *vt* MAKE SUGGESTION to put forward something such as an idea or suggested course of action formally or officially ○ *Harsher penalties have been proposed.* **2.** *vt* STATE INTENTION to announce a plan or intended course of action ○ *What do you propose to do about it?* **3.** *vt* NOMINATE SOMEBODY to put forward somebody's name for an elected position or a promotion ○ *propose her for the new position* **4.** *vti* OFFER MARRIAGE to make an offer of marriage to somebody ○ *He proposed while we were on vacation.* **5.** *vt* SUGGEST TOAST OR VOTE OF THANKS to ask others to join in something such as a toast or a vote of thanks ○ *I propose a toast to Chris and Sarah.* [14C. < French *proposer* "put forward" < *poser* (see POSE[1]), after Latin *proponere*] —**pro·pos·a·ble** *adj* —**pro·pos·er** *n*

pro·pos·i·ta /prō pózzitə/ (*plural* **-tae** /-tee/) *n* a woman who is involved in legal proceedings [Late 20C. < Latin, form of *propositus* (see PROPOSITUS)]

pro·pos·i·ti LAW, GENETICS plural of **propositus**

prop·o·si·tion /prṑppə zísh'n/ *n* **1.** PROPOSAL an idea, offer, or plan put forward for consideration or discussion **2.** STATEMENT a statement of opinion or judgment **3.** OFFER OF SEXUAL INTERCOURSE an invitation to have sexual intercourse **4.** PRIVATE AGREEMENT a private deal or agreement **5.** SOMEBODY OR SOMETHING TO BE FACED somebody or something to be dealt with (*informal*) ○ *The news that he would be there certainly made the party a more attractive proposition.* **6.** MATH THEOREM a statement or theorem to be demonstrated **7.** PHILOSOPHY MEANING OF DECLARATIVE SENTENCE the meaning of a declarative sentence that expresses something that can be true or false **8.** *also* **Prop·o·si·tion** *US* LAW PROPOSAL FOR AMENDMENT TO LAW a proposal for an amendment to the law that is set forth to be voted on ○ *Propositions imposing term limits for politicians have been common recently.* ■ *vt* (**-tioned, -tion·ing, -tions**) **1.** OFFER SEX TO SOMEBODY to invite somebody to have sexual intercourse **2.** OFFER DEAL TO SOMEBODY to offer to make a private deal or agreement with somebody [14C. Directly or via French < Latin *proposition-* < *proposit-*, past participle of *proponere* "put forth" < *ponere* "to place"] —**prop·o·si·tion·al** *adj* —**prop·o·si·tion·al·ly** *adv*

prop·o·si·tion·al at·ti·tude *n* in philosophy, an attitude taken by somebody toward a proposition, e.g., in believing it, knowing it, or desiring it

prop·o·si·tion·al cal·cu·lus *n* the branch of deductive logic that deals with the relationships formed between propositions linked by connectives such as "and," "but," "if," or "or"

prop·o·si·tion·al func·tion *n* LOGIC same as **open sentence**

pro·pos·i·tus /prō pózzitəss/ (*plural* **-ti** /-tì/) *n* **1.** a man who is involved in legal proceedings **2.** the first person to be investigated in the genetic study of a family [Mid-18C. < Latin, past participle of *proponere* (see PROPOSITION)]

pro·pound /prə pównd/ (**-pound·ed, -pound·ing, -pounds**) *vt* to put forward a suggestion or theory for others to consider [Mid-16C. Alteration of obsolete *propone* < Latin *proponere* (see PROPOSITION)] —**pro·pound·er** *n*

propr. *abbr* COMM proprietor

pro·prae·tor /prō préetər/, **pro·pre·tor** *n* in ancient times, a Roman citizen sent to govern a province, usually after serving as a senior magistrate (**praetor**) in Rome [Late 16C. < Latin < *pro praetore* "for the praetor"]

pro·pran·o·lol /prō pránnə làwl/ *n* a drug that slows heart rate and heart output. Use: treatment of angina pectoris, irregular heart rhythms, migraine, high blood pressure. [Mid-20C. < PROPYL + *-r-* + *-olol*, INN stem]

pro·pri·e·tar·y /prə prí ə tèrree/ *adj* **1.** RELATING TO OWNERS OR OWNERSHIP relating to an owner, ownership, or something owned **2.** PRIVATELY OWNED privately owned and run **3.** EXHIBITING CHARACTERISTICS OF OWNERSHIP exhibiting characteristics that indicate ownership of somebody or something ○ *The child kept a proprietary hold on the toy.* **4.** USED WITH EXCLUSIVE LEGAL RIGHT used, manufactured, or sold by a person or company with an exclusive property right such as a patent or trademark ○ *a proprietary drug* ■ *n* (*plural* **-ies**) **1.** OWNER an owner or a group of owners **2.** PHARM PROPRIETARY AGENT a drug or other substance made and sold under the legal protection of a trademark or patent **3.** OWNERSHIP the right of ownership, or something exclusively owned **4.** HIST OWNER OF COLONY the owner of a proprietary colony [15C. Directly or via French < late Latin *proprietarius* "of a property holder" < Latin *proprietas* (see PROPERTY)] —**pro·pri·e·tar·i·ly** /prə prī̀ ə térrəlee/ *adv*

pro·pri·e·tar·y col·o·ny *n* a North American colony granted to an individual person or group by the British Crown with full ownership rights

pro·pri·e·tor /prə prī́ ətər/ *n* **1.** OWNER OF BUSINESS the owner of a commercial enterprise or establishment such as a store, hotel, or restaurant **2.** LEGAL OWNER the legal owner of something **3.** SOMEBODY WITH PARTIAL RIGHTS OVER SOMETHING a user or manager who does not have full ownership **4.** HIST same as **proprietary** *n* (sense 4) [15C. Alteration of PROPRIETARY] —**pro·pri·e·to·ri·al** /prə prī̀ ə táwree əl/ *adj*—**pro·pri·e·to·ri·al·ly** *adv*—**pro·pri·e·tor·ship** *n*

pro·pri·e·ty /prə prī́ ətee/ *n* **1.** QUALITY OF BEING SOCIALLY APPROPRIATE the quality of displaying behaviors thought to be correct or appropriate **2.** SOCIALLY CORRECT OR APPROPRIATE BEHAVIOR conformity to the standards of politeness, respect, decency, or morality conventionally accepted by a society ■ **pro·pri·e·ties** *npl* RULES OF ETIQUETTE the accepted standards of correct or appropriate social behavior [15C. < French *propriété* (see PROPERTY)]

pro·pri·o·cep·tor /prṓpree ə séptər/ *n* a sensory nerve ending in muscles, tendons, and joints that provides a sense of the body's position by responding to stimuli from within the body [Early 20C. < Latin *proprius* "your own" + RECEPTOR] —**pro·pri·o·cep·tion** *n*—**pro·pri·o·cep·tive** *adj*

prop root *n* a root that grows from the stem of a plant above the ground and helps to support it. The mangrove and corn are examples of plants with prop roots.

props mas·ter *n* somebody in charge of stage props

prop·to·sis /prop tṓssiss/ *n* the forward displacement or protrusion of an organ of the body, especially an eyeball [Late 17C. Via late Latin < Greek *proptōsis* "a falling forward" < *propiptein* "fall forward"]

pro·pul·sion /prə púlsh'n/ *n* **1.** the process by which an object such as an automobile, ship, aircraft, or missile is moved forward **2.** the force by which an object such as an automobile, ship, aircraft, or missile is moved forward [Early 17C. < obsolete *propulse* "drive away" < Latin *propulsare* < *propuls-*, past participle of *propellere* (see PROPEL)] —**pro·pul·sive** *adj* —**pro·pul·so·ry** *adj*

pro·pyl /prṓp'l/ *adj* relating to the group of atoms derived from propane after the loss of a hydrogen atom. Formula: C_3H_7. [Mid-19C. < PROPIONIC]

prop·y·lae·um /pròppə leé əm/ (*plural* **-lae·a** /-leé ə/) *n* a colonnaded gate or entrance to a building or group of buildings, especially to a temple [Early 18C. Via Latin < Greek *propulaion* < form of *propulaios* "before the gate" < *pulē* "gate"]

pro·pyl al·co·hol *n* a colorless alcohol. Use: solvent, antiseptic. Formula: C_3H_8O.

pro·pyl·ene /prṓpə leèn/ *n* a flammable gaseous hydrocarbon. Source: petroleum. Use: organic synthesis. Formula: C_3H_6.

pro·pyl·ene gly·col *n* a colorless thick sweet-tasting liquid. Source: propylene. Use: antifreeze in brake fluid, solvent, lubricant. Formula: $C_3H_8O_2$.

prop·y·lon /prṓpə lòn/ (*plural* **-lons** or **-la** /-lə/) *n* BUILDINGS same as **propylaeum** [Mid-19C. Via Latin < Greek *propulon*, literally "before the gate" < *pulē* "gate"]

pro ra·ta /prō ráytə, -raátə/ *adv, adj* in accordance with a fixed proportion [< Latin, "according to the rate"]

pro·rate /prō ráyt/ (**-rat·ed, -rat·ing, -rates**) *vti* to calculate, divide, or distribute something on a pro rata basis [Mid-19C. < PRO RATA] —**pro·rat·a·ble** *adj*—**pro·ra·tion** *n*

pro·rogue /prō rṓg, prə-/ (**-rogued, -rogu·ing, -rogues**) *v* **1.** *vti* to discontinue the meetings of a parliament or other body without formally ending the session, or be discontinued in this way **2.** *vt* to defer something to a later date or to a subsequent meeting [15C. Via French < Latin *prorogare* "prolong" *rogare* "ask"] —**pro·ro·ga·tion** /prṑrə gáysh'n/ *n*

pros. *abbr* LITERAT prosody

pro·sa·ic /prō záy ik/ *adj* **1.** LACKING IMAGINATION not having any features that are interesting or imaginative **2.** RESEMBLING PROSE characteristic of, resembling, or consisting of prose **3.** *US* STRAIGHTFORWARD lacking complications or subtleties [Late 16C. Directly or via French < late Latin *prosaicus* < Latin *prosa* (see PROSE)] —**pro·sa·i·cal·ly** *adv* —**pro·sa·ic·ness** *n*

pro·sa·ism /prō zay ìzzəm/, **pro·sa·i·cism** /prō záy ə sìzzəm/ *n* **1.** a dull or unimaginative expression or style of writing **2.** a word, phrase, or style of writing used in prose —**pro·sa·ist** /prṓ zàyist/ *n*

pros and cons *npl* the arguments for and against something

Pros. Atty. *abbr US* LAW prosecuting attorney

pro·sce·ni·um /prō seénee əm/ *n* **1.** the part of a theater stage that is in front of the curtain **2.** the stage of a theater in ancient Greece or Rome [Early 17C. Via Latin < Greek *proskēnion* "front stage" < *skēnē* "stage, scenes"]

pro·sciut·to /prō shóotō/ *n* Italian cured ham, usually served cold and uncooked in thin slices [Mid-20C. < Italian]

pro·scribe /prō skrī́b/ (**-scribed, -scrib·ing, -scribes**) *vt* **1.** BAN SOMETHING to prohibit something that is considered undesirable by those in authority **2.** CONDEMN SOMETHING to denounce or condemn something **3.** BANISH SOMEBODY to banish or exile somebody **4.** OUTLAW SOMEBODY PUBLICLY especially in ancient Rome, to state publicly that somebody is no longer protected by the law [15C. < Latin *proscribere* "publish in writing, publish somebody's name as outlawed" < *scribere* "write"] —**pro·scrib·er** *n*

pro·scrip·tion /prō skrípsh'n/ *n* **1.** BANNING OF SOMETHING the prohibition of something considered undesirable by those in authority **2.** CONDEMNATION OF SOMETHING the denunciation or condemnation of something **3.** PUBLIC OUTLAWING OF SOMEBODY especially in ancient Rome, a public statement by which somebody is no longer granted the protection of the law [14C. < Latin *proscription-* < past participle of *proscribere* (see PROSCRIBE)] —**pro·scrip·tive** *adj* —**pro·scrip·tive·ly** *adv*—**pro·scrip·tive·ness** *n*

prose /prōz/ *n* **1.** LANGUAGE THAT IS NOT POETRY writing or speech in its normal continuous form, without the rhythmic or visual line structure of poetry **2.** ORDINARY STYLE OF EXPRESSION writing or speech that is ordinary or matter-of-fact, without embellishment **3.** CHR same as **sequence** *n* (sense 6) ■ *v* (**prosed, pros·ing, pros·es**) **1.** *vti* WRITE SOMETHING IN PROSE to write something in prose **2.** *vt* REWRITE SOMETHING AS PROSE to turn poetry into prose **3.** *vi* SPEAK OR WRITE PROSAICALLY to speak or write in an ordinary, matter-of-fact, or unimaginative style [13C. Via French < Latin *prosa (oratio)* "straightforward (discourse)" < *provertere* "turn forward" < *vertere* "to turn"]

pro·sec·tor /prō séktər/ *n* somebody who prepares or dissects cadavers for anatomy demonstrations [Mid-19C. Directly or via French < late Latin, "in place of the cutter" < Latin *sector* (see SECTOR)]

pros·e·cute /próssə kyoòt/ (**-cut·ed, -cut·ing, -cutes**) *v* **1.** *vti* TAKE LEGAL ACTION AGAINST SOMEBODY to have somebody tried in a court of law for a civil or criminal offense ○ *Trespassers will be prosecuted.* **2.** *vti* PURSUE CASE IN COURT to pursue a claim or action in a court of law as the representative of the person or people bringing the action **3.** *vt* PERFORM ACTIVITY OR OCCUPATION to engage in or perform an activity or occupation (*formal*) ○ *prosecute a trade* **4.** *vt* TAKE SOMETHING TO COMPLETION to continue doing something, usually until it is finished or accomplished (*formal*) ○ *prosecute an investigation* [15C. < Latin *prosecut-*, past participle of *prosequi* "follow forward" < *sequi* "follow"] —**pros·e·cut·a·ble** *adj*

~~**prosecuter**~~ incorrect spelling of **prosecutor**

pros·e·cut·ing at·tor·ney /pràwssə kyoòting-/ *n US* a lawyer representing the state or the people in a criminal trial

pros·e·cu·tion /pròssə kyóosh'n/ *n* **1.** PURSUIT OF LEGAL ACTION the trial of somebody in a court of law for a criminal offense **2.** LAWYERS TRYING TO PROVE SOMEBODY'S GUILT the lawyers representing the person or people who are taking legal action against somebody in a court of law, especially the state or the people in a criminal trial ○ *a witness for the prosecution* **3.** PERFORMANCE OF ACTIVITY OR OCCUPATION the carrying on of an activity or occupation (*formal*) ○ *the prosecution of your duty* **4.** CONTINUATION TO COMPLETION the continuation of or perseverance in a task or activity, usually until it is finished or accomplished (*formal*)

pros·e·cu·tor /próssə kyoòtər/ *n* **1.** *US* LAW same as **prosecuting attorney** **2.** somebody who initiates a legal prosecution

Prose Ed·da *n* LITERAT same as **Edda** (sense 2)

pros·e·lyte /próssə lī̀t/ *n* a new convert to a religious faith or political doctrine ■ *vti* (**-lyt·ed, -lyt·ing, -lytes**) *US* RELIG, POL same as **proselytize** [14C. Via late Latin < Greek *prosēluthos* "somebody who comes to a place" < *proserkhesthai* "come to"] —**pros·e·lyt·ic** /pròssə líttik/ *adj* —**pros·e·ly·tism** /próssələ tìzzəm/ *n*

pros·e·ly·tize /próssələ tī̀z/ (**-tized, -tiz·ing, -tiz·es**) *vti* to try to convert somebody to a religious faith or political doctrine —**pros·e·ly·ti·za·tion** /pròssələti záysh'n/ *n* —**pros·e·ly·tiz·er** *n*

pro·sem·i·nar /prō sémmi naàr/ *n US* a course of study for graduates and advanced undergraduates, conducted in small groups under the supervision of a professor

prose po·em *n* a piece of creative writing that has the structure of prose but the style and language of poetry —**prose po·et** *n*

Pro·ser·pi·na /prō súrpənə/, **Pro·ser·pi·ne** /prō súrpi nee, -súrpin/ *n* in Roman mythology, the goddess of the Earth. Greek equivalent **Persephone**

pro·sim·i·an /prō símmee ən/ *n* a nocturnal lower primate with large eyes and ears, e.g., a lemur or bush baby. Suborder: Prosimii.

pro·sit /prōst, prṓzit/ *interj* used as a drinking toast, to wish somebody good health or good fortune [Mid-19C. Via German < Latin, "may it benefit," 3rd person present subjunctive singular of *prodesse* (see PROUD)]

pros·o·dy /próssədee/ (*plural* **-dies**) *n* **1.** STUDY OF POETIC STRUCTURE the study of the structure of poetry and the conventions or techniques involved in writing it, including rhyme, meter, and the patterns of verse forms **2.** SYSTEM OR THEORY OF WRITING VERSE a particular system or theory of writing poetry **3.** RHYTHM OF SPEECH the rhythm of spoken language, including stress and intonation, or the study of these patterns [15C. Via Latin < Greek *prosōidia* "song with an instrumental accompaniment" < *pros* "in addition to" + *ōidē* "song"] —**pro·sod·ic** /prə sóddik/ *adj*—**pro·sod·i·cal·ly** *adv*—**pros·o·dist** *n*

pro·so·ma /prō sṓmə/ (*plural* **-mas** or **-ma·ta** /-mətə/) *n* the region near the head of spiders and some related arthropods, composed of fused segments of head and thorax [Late 19C. < PRO-[2] + Greek *sōma* "body"]

pros·o·pog·ra·phy /pròssə póggrəfee/ *n* a collection of biographical sketches used by social and political historians studying a particular historical period [Mid-16C. < modern Latin *prosopographia* "writing about somebody" < Greek *prosōpon* "face, person"] —**pros·o·pog·ra·pher** *n*—**pros·o·po·graph·i·cal** /pròssəpə gráffik'l/ *adj*

pro·so·po·pe·ia /pròssəpə peé ə/, **pro·so·po·poe·ia** *n* **1.** a figure of speech that presents an imaginary or dead person as speaking **2.** a figure of speech in which human qualities are attributed to objects or abstract notions [Mid-16C. Via Latin < Greek *prosōpopoiia* "representation in human form" < *prosōpon* "face, person" + *poiein* "make"]

pros·pect /pró spèkt/ *n* **1.** POSSIBILITY OF SOMETHING HAPPENING SOON a chance or the likelihood that something will happen in the near future, especially something desirable **2.** VISION OF FUTURE something that is expected or certain to happen in the future, or a mental picture of this ○ *I don't relish the prospect of spending five months at sea.* **3.** EXTENSIVE OUTLOOK OR SCENE a view, especially one from a high position over a large expanse of land or water ○ *a pleasant prospect* **4.** DIRECTION FACED the direction in which something faces ○ *a northerly prospect* **5.** LIKELY CUSTOMER a customer who may be interested in buying something **6.** SOMEBODY OR SOMETHING WITH POTENTIAL somebody or something that is likely to succeed ○ *She's our brightest prospect.* **7.** SURVEY an act of making a survey, examination, or observation **8.** MINERAL LOCATION the location of a mineral deposit, or an area believed to have mineral deposits **9.** MINERAL DEPOSIT a probable mineral deposit or one that definitely exists **10.** MINERAL YIELD the yield that can be obtained by mining a mineral ■ **pros·pects** *npl* EXPECTATIONS OF SUCCESS the likelihood of being successful or prosperous in the future, especially in a job or career ○ *Young people who leave school early certainly narrow their prospects.* ○ *eager to improve her career prospects* ■ *v* **(-pect·ed, -pect·ing, -pects) 1.** *vti* SEARCH FOR MINERAL DEPOSITS IN AREA to explore an area in search of oil or valuable minerals, especially gold **2.** *vt* WORK MINE to work a mine to see how profitable it is **3.** *vi* LOOK FOR SOMETHING to search or watch for something ○ *prospect for business* [15C. < Latin *prospectus* "view" < past participle of *prospicere* "look forward" < *specere* "look at"] —**pros·pect·less** *adj*

pro·spec·tive /prə spéktiv/ *adj* **1.** expected or hoping to do or become something ○ *his prospective mother-in-law* **2.** likely or expected to happen ○ *prospective changes* —**pro·spec·tive·ly** *adv*

pros·pec·tor /pró spèktər/ *n* somebody who explores an area in search of oil, gold, or other mineral deposits

pro·spec·tus /prə spéktəss/ *n* **1.** an official document giving details about something that is going to happen such as a stock offering, a forthcoming publication, a new business, or a proposed project **2.** *Can, UK* a brochure or pamphlet that advertises or describes the activities, staff, and facilities of an organization or an institution such as a school, college, or university. US term **catalog** [Mid-18C. < Latin (see PROSPECT)]

pros·per /próspər/ **(-pered, -per·ing, -pers)** *vi* **1.** to be successful, especially in financial or economic terms **2.** to flourish or thrive [14C. Directly or via French < Latin *prosperare* < *prosperus* "doing well"]

pros·per·i·ty /pro spérrətee/ *n* the condition of enjoying wealth, success, or good fortune [13C. Via French < Latin *prosperitas* < *prosperus* "doing well"]

pros·per·i·ty gos·pel *n US* the doctrine taught in some Christian groups that God will grant wishes to the faithful, especially those wishes involving material wealth

pros·per·ous /próspərəss/ *adj* **1.** FINANCIALLY SUCCESSFUL successful and flourishing, especially earning or producing great wealth **2.** WEALTHY having wealth, or associated with wealthy people **3.** FULL OF GOOD FORTUNE characterized by success or good fortune ○ *wishing you a prosperous New Year* **4.** PROMISING likely to be successful or bring a good result —**pros·per·ous·ly** *adv* —**pros·per·ous·ness** *n*

pross /pross/, **pross·ie** /próssee/ *n* CRIME same as **prostitute** *n* (sense 1) (*slang*) [Early 20C. Shortening]

Pros·ser /próssər/, **Gabriel** (1776?–1800) US slave and rebel. He led an unsuccessful slave uprising near Richmond, Virginia. He and some 35 others were executed.

pross·ie *n* same as **pross**

Popperfoto

Alain Prost

Prost /prost/, **Alain** (*b.* 1955) French racing driver. He was Formula One world champion (1985, 1986, 1989, and 1993) and four times runner-up.

> "When you start off as a driver, it is a sport; but when you get into Formula One, it suddenly becomes a job."
> [Alain Prost, *Sunday Telegraph (London)*; June 18, 1989]

pros·ta·cy·clin /pròstə sī kleen/ *n* a prostaglandin that dilates blood vessels and inhibits the formation of blood clots [Late 20C. < PROSTATE + CYCLIC]

pros·ta·glan·din /pròstə glándən/ *n* an unsaturated fatty acid found in all mammals that performs a similar function to that of hormones in controlling smooth muscle contraction, blood pressure, inflammation, and body temperature [Mid-20C. < PROSTATE + GLAND[1]]

pros·tate /pró stàyt/ *n* ANAT same as **prostate gland** [Mid-17C. Via modern Latin *prostata* < Greek *prostatēs* "guardian" (of the bladder) < *proïstanai* "set before" < *histanai* "cause to stand"] —**pros·tat·ic** /pro státtik/ *adj*

pros·ta·tec·to·my /pròstə téktəmee/ (*plural* **-mies**) *n* the surgical removal of the whole or part of the prostate gland

pros·tate gland *n* an "O"-shaped gland in males that surrounds the urethra below the bladder, secreting a fluid into the semen that acts to improve the movement and viability of sperm

pros·tate-spe·cif·ic an·ti·gen *n* a protein and sugar complex (**glycoprotein**) found in the cells of the prostate of all men that is present in increased amounts when various prostate diseases, especially cancer, occur

pros·ta·tism /próstə tìzzəm/ *n* a disorder of the prostate gland, especially enlargement that blocks or inhibits urine flow

pros·ta·ti·tis /pròstə tītiss/ *n* inflammation of the prostate gland

pros·the·sis /pross théessiss/ (*plural* **-the·ses** /-thée seez/) *n* **1.** an artificial body part, e.g., an artificial limb or eye **2.** the branch of surgery concerned with replacing missing body parts with artificial devices **3.** LING same as **prothesis** (sense 1) [Mid-16C. Via late Latin < Greek, "addition" < *prostithenai* "add to" < *tithenai* "to place"] —**pros·thet·ic** /pross théttik/ *adj* —**pros·thet·i·cal·ly** *adv*

pros·thet·ic group *n* the part of a conjugated protein that is not an amino acid, e.g., the lipid group in lipoprotein

pros·thet·ics /pross théttiks/ *n* the branch of medicine dealing with the design, production, and use of artificial body parts (*takes a singular verb*) —**pros·the·tist** /prósthətist/ *n*

pros·tho·don·tics /pròsthə dóntiks/ *n* the branch of dentistry that deals with the replacement of teeth and parts of the jaw (*takes a singular verb*) [Mid-20C. < PROSTHESIS, after ORTHODONTICS] —**pros·tho·don·tic** *adj* —**pros·tho·don·tist** *n*

pros·ti·tute /próstə to͞ot/ *n* **1.** SOMEBODY PAID FOR SEXUAL INTERCOURSE somebody who is paid to provide sexual intercourse or other sex acts **2.** SOMEBODY WHO DEGRADES TALENT FOR MONEY somebody who uses a skill or ability in a way that is considered unworthy, usually for financial gain ■ *vt* **(-tut·ed, -tut·ing, -tutes) 1.** MISUSE SOMETHING FOR GAIN to use a skill or ability in a way that is considered unworthy, usually for financial gain ○ *He has been accused of prostituting his talent by appearing in TV commercials.* **2.** WORK OR OFFER SOMEBODY AS PROSTITUTE to offer somebody or yourself for sexual intercourse or other sex acts in exchange for money [Mid-16C. < Latin *prostitut-*, past participle of *prostituere* "expose publicly, offer for sale" < *statuere* "to set, place"] —**pros·ti·tu·tor** *n*

pros·ti·tu·tion /pròstə to͞osh'n/ *n* **1.** the act of engaging in sexual intercourse or performing other sex acts in exchange for money, or of offering another person for such purposes **2.** the use of a skill or ability in a way that is considered unworthy, usually for financial gain

pro·sto·mi·um /prō stōmee əm/ (*plural* **-mi·a** /-mee ə/) *n* the part of the head of some worms such as the earthworm that is in front of the mouth [Late 19C. Via modern Latin < Greek *prostomion* "something in front of the mouth" < *stoma* "mouth"] —**pros·to·mi·al** *adj*

pros·trate /pró stràyt/ *v* **(-trat·ed, -trat·ing, -trates) 1.** **pros·trate your·self** *vr* LIE FACE DOWNWARD to lie prone or stretched out with the face downward or bow very low, e.g., in worship or submission ○ *He prostrated himself before the emperor.* **2.** *vt* LAY SOMEBODY OR SOMETHING ON GROUND to lay or throw somebody or something flat on the ground ○ *was prostrated by a blow on the head* **3.** *vt* INCAPACITATE SOMEBODY to make somebody physically or emotionally weak or helpless ○ *was prostrated by illness* ■ *adj* **1.** LYING FLAT ON FACE lying prone or stretched out with the face downward, e.g., in worship or submission **2.** LYING DOWN stretched out in a horizontal position, often because of illness or injury **3.** DRAINED OF ENERGY drained of physical strength or incapacitated by overexertion or powerful emotion ○ *prostrate with grief* **4.** BOT GROWING ALONG GROUND describes a plant that grows or trails along the ground ○ *a prostrate shrub* [14C. < Latin *prostratus*, past participle of *prosternere* "throw in front of" < *sternere* "spread out, lay down"] —**pros·tra·tion** /pro stráysh'n/ *n*

pro·style /prṓ stīl/ *adj* describes a building such as a Greek temple that has a row of columns at the front [Late 17C. < Latin *prostylos* "having pillars in front" < *stilus* "pointed writing instrument, stake"]

pros·y /prṓzee/ **(-i·er, -i·est)** *adj* dull and commonplace, with no interesting, imaginative, or eloquent features —**pros·i·ly** *adv* —**pros·i·ness** *n*

Prot. *abbr* CHR Protestant

prot- *prefix* same as **proto-** (*used before vowels*)

pro·tac·tin·i·um /prō tak tínnee əm/ *n* a toxic radioactive metallic element. Source: uranium ores. Symbol **Pa**. See table at **element** [Early 20C. < PROTO- + ACTINIUM, because the most common isotope decays to give actinium]

pro·tag·o·nist /prō tággənist/ *n* **1.** MAIN CHARACTER the most important character in a novel, play, story, or other literary work **2.** MAIN CHARACTER IN ANCIENT GREEK DRAMA in ancient Greek drama, the first actor who interacted with the chorus **3.** LEADING FIGURE a main participant in an event such as a contest or dispute ○ *two protagonists in a long-running dispute* **4.** SUPPORTER an important or influential supporter or advocate of something such as a political or social issue ○ *an early protagonist of educational reform* [Late 17C. < Greek *protagōnistēs* "actor who plays the chief part" < *agōnistēs* "actor, competitor" < *agōn* "contest"] —**pro·tag·o·nism** *n*

Pro·tag·o·ras /prō tággərəss/ (480?–411? B.C.) Greek philosopher. The first of the sophists, he taught that nothing is absolutely good or bad, true or false.

> "Man is the measure of all things: of those which are, that they are; of those which are not, that they are not."
> [Protagoras, "On the Gods"; 5th century B.C.]

pro·ta·mine /prṓtə meen, -min/ *n* **1.** an arginine-rich peptide found in chromosomes that has the property of being able to condense DNA **2.** a therapeutic drug derived from protamine. Use: controlling bleeding, slow-release insulin application in diabetes treatment.

pro·ta·no·pi·a /prṑtə nṓpee ə/ *n* a form of color blindness in which the retina fails to distinguish between red and green [Early 20C. < PROTO- (red being regarded as the first of the primary colors) + AN-] —**pro·ta·nop·ic** /-nóppik/ *adj*

pro·ta·sis /próttəssiss/ (*plural* **-ta·ses** /-tə seez/) *n* **1.** the part of a conditional sentence that contains the condition, e.g., "if he asks" in "if he asks, I'll tell him" **2.** the opening section of a narrative poem or play, especially a classical drama [Mid-16C. Via Latin < Greek < *proteinein* "put forward, propose" < *teinein* "to stretch"] —**pro·tat·ic** /prō táttik/ *adj*

prote- *prefix* same as **proteo-** (*used before vowels*)

pro·te·a /prṓtee ə/ (*plural* **-as** or *same*) *n* an evergreen bush or tree, grown for its colorful bracts and dense flower heads. Native to: southern Africa. Genus: *Protea*. [Mid-18C. < modern Latin, after PROTEUS, from the variety of form in the genus] —**pro·te·a·ceous** /prṑtee áyshəss/ *adj*

pro·te·an /prṓtee ən, prō tée ən/ *adj* **1.** variable or continually changing in nature, appearance, or behavior **2.** showing great variety, diversity, or versatility [Late 16C. < PROTEUS]

pro·te·ase /prṓtee àyz, -àyss/ *n* an enzyme that breaks down proteins and peptides by catalyzing the hydrolysis of peptide bonds [Early 20C. < PROTEIN]

pro·te·ase in·hib·i·tor *n* a compound that breaks down protease, inhibiting the replication of viruses and development of some cancers. Use: treatment of AIDS.

pro·te·a·some /prṓtee ə sōm/ *n* a cluster of proteins found in the cytoplasm of living cells that degrades damaged or redundant proteins

pro·tect /prə tékt/ (**-tect·ed, -tect·ing, -tects**) *vt* **1.** to prevent somebody or something from being harmed or damaged **2.** to help the industries in a country by imposing customs duties on imports from other countries [15C. < Latin *protect-*, past participle of *protegere* "cover in front" < *tegere* "to cover"]

SYNONYMS See ***safeguard***.

pro·tect·ant /prə téktənt/ *n* a substance that prevents something from being damaged, e.g., a coating used to keep metal from rusting

pro·tect·ed /prə téktəd/ *adj* **1. ENDANGERED** legally classified as a species in danger of extinction **2. SHELTERED** sheltered from the elements **3.** COMPUT **LOCKED AGAINST UNAUTHORIZED CHANGES** locked against changes by unauthorized users of a computer program

pro·tec·tion /prə tékshən/ *n* **1. SAFEGUARDING OF SOMEBODY OR SOMETHING** the act of preventing somebody or something from being harmed or damaged, or the state of being kept safe **2. SOMETHING THAT PROTECTS SOMEBODY OR SOMETHING** something that prevents somebody or something from being harmed or damaged **3. INSURANCE COVERAGE** an agreement by an insurance company to pay compensation or costs if a specific undesirable event occurs **4. PROMISE OF SAFETY FROM CRIMINAL ATTACK** a promise made by a gangster or other person that somebody or something will not be harmed or damaged if money is paid, or the payment extorted in return for such a promise (*informal*) **5.** CRIME **CRIMINALS' BRIBERY OF LAW ENFORCEMENT OFFICIALS** the bribery of law enforcement officials by criminals in an effort to escape prosecution, or the bribe paid (*informal*) **6. CONDOM** a form of contraception, usually a condom, used during sexual intercourse to prevent sperm or disease-causing organisms from entering the body **7. GUARANTEE OF FREEDOM AND SAFETY** a document that enables somebody to travel around in freedom and safety, especially in another country or in enemy territory **8.** ECON same as **protectionism 9.** CLIMBING **SAFETY EQUIPMENT FOR CLIMBER** the safety equipment used by mountain climbers to keep them from falling, e.g., pitons, harnesses, and ropes

pro·tec·tion·ism /prə tékshə nìzzəm/ *n* the system of imposing duties on imports into a country in order to protect domestic industries —**pro·tec·tion·ist** *n, adj*

pro·tec·tion mon·ey *n* money paid to a gangster or other person who threatens to harm somebody or damage something unless the money is paid

pro·tec·tive /prə téktiv/ *adj* **1. GIVING PROTECTION** preventing somebody or something from being harmed or damaged, or designed or intended for this purpose ○ *a protective covering* **2. TAKING GREAT CARE OF SOMEBODY** anxious to protect or defend somebody or something, often excessively so ○ *She had always felt protective toward her younger brother.* **3. INTENDED TO HELP DOMESTIC INDUSTRIES** intended to give an advantage to a country's domestic industries ○ *a protective tariff* ■ *n* **SOMETHING THAT PROTECTS** something that prevents somebody or something from being harmed or damaged —**pro·tec·tive·ly** *adv* —**pro·tec·tive·ness** *n*

pro·tec·tive col·or·a·tion, pro·tec·tive col·or·ing *n* the combination of surface colors and patterns on an animal that helps it blend into its surroundings and so evade predators

pro·tec·tive cus·to·dy *n* detention by the police in order to give protection from harm by somebody

pro·tec·tor /prə téktər/ *n* **1. SOMETHING THAT PROTECTS** something that prevents somebody or something from being harmed or damaged **2. SOMEBODY WHO PROTECTS** somebody who protects or defends somebody or something **3.** *also* **Pro·tec·tor SOMEBODY RULING IN PLACE OF MONARCH** somebody in charge of a country while the monarch is absent, or too young or unfit to rule —**pro·tec·tor·al** *adj* —**pro·tec·tor·ship** *n*

Pro·tec·tor *n* the title given to the head of the Commonwealth of England, Scotland, and Ireland during the period without a monarch that lasted from 1653 to 1659. The title was held by Oliver Cromwell from 1653 to 1658 and by Richard Cromwell from 1658 to 1659.

pro·tec·tor·ate /prə téktərət/ *n* **1.** a country or region that is defended and controlled by a more powerful state, or the relationship between the two **2.** the position or term of office of a protector

pro·té·gé /prṓtə zhày, prṑtə zháy/ *n* a young person who receives help, guidance, training, and support from somebody who is older and has more experience or influence [Late 18C. < French < past participle of *protéger* "protect" < Latin *protegere* (see PROTECT)]

pro·té·gée /prṓtə zhày, prṑtə zháy/ *n* a young woman who receives help, guidance, training, and support from somebody who is older and has more experience or influence [Late 18C. < French, feminine of *protégé* (see PROTÉGÉ)]

pro·te·i MICROBIOL plural of **proteus**

pro·te·id /prṓtee id/ *n* a salamander such as a mud puppy that retains its larval form as an adult. Family: Proteidae. [Late 19C. < modern Latin *Proteus*, after PROTEUS]

pro·tein /prṓ teen/ *n* **1.** a complex natural substance that has a globular or fibrous structure composed of linked amino acids. Proteins are essential to the structure and function of all living cells and viruses. **2.** a food source that is rich in protein molecules ○ *a balanced diet of fresh vegetables, fruit, and protein* [Mid-19C. < French < Greek *prōteios* "primary" < *prōtos* "first"; from its importance to the proper functioning of the body] —**pro·tein·a·ceous** /prṑtee náyshəss, prṓt'n áyshəss/ *adj* —**pro·te·in·ic** /prṑtee ínnik/ *adj* —**pro·tein·ous** *adj*

pro·tein·ase /prṓtee nàyss, -nàyz, prṓt'n àyss, -àyz/ *n* an enzyme that splits the peptide bonds of proteins

pro·tein en·gi·neer·ing *n* the process of making changes in the sequence of a gene coding for a protein in order to bring about desirable changes in function

pro·tein·oid /prṓti nòyd/ *n* a polypeptide that is obtained by polymerization of mixtures of amino acids and that has properties thought to be similar to those of early forms of protein

pro·tein·u·ri·a /prṑtee nóoree ə, prṓt'n óo-/ *n* the presence of protein in the urine, which is usually an indication of disease

pro tem /prō tém/ *adv, adj* at the present time, but not permanently [Shortening of Latin *pro tempore* "for the time being"]

proteo- *prefix* protein ○ *proteolysis* [< PROTEIN]

pro·te·ol·y·sis /prṑtee óllәssiss/ *n* the breakdown of proteins or peptides into amino acids —**pro·te·o·lyt·ic** /prṑtee ə líttik/ *adj* —**pro·te·o·lyt·i·cal·ly** *adv*

pro·te·ome /prṓtee ōm/ *n* the set of proteins expressed by genes within an organism [Late 20C. Blend of PROTEIN + GENOME] —**pro·te·om·ic** /prṑtee ómmik/ *adj*

pro·te·om·ics /prṑtee ṓmiks/ *n* the study of proteins expressed by genes within an organism, with applications in the understanding of disease and in drug development (*takes a singular verb*) [Late 20C. Blend of PROTEIN + GENOMICS]

pro·te·ose /prṓtee ōss/ *n* a water-soluble protein derivative formed during hydrolytic processes such as digestion that does not coagulate when heated and precipitates if mixed with some sulfur-containing compounds

Prot·er·o·zo·ic /prṑtərə zṓ ik/ *n* the eon of geologic time, 2.5 billion to 570 million years ago, during which sea plants and animals first appeared. See table at **geologic time** [Early 20C. < Greek *proteros* "former" + *zōē* "life"] —**Prot·er·o·zo·ic** *adj*

pro·test *v* /prə tést, prō-, prṓ tèst/ (**-test·ed, -test·ing, -tests**) **1.** *vti* **COMPLAIN OR OBJECT STRONGLY** to express strong disapproval of or disagreement with something **2.** *vti* **COMPLAIN OR OBJECT PUBLICLY** to express strong opposition to or disapproval of something in the form of a public demonstration or other action **3.** *vt* **PROTEST AGAINST SOMETHING** to complain about or protest against something ○ *protested the outcome* **4.** *vti* **SAY FIRMLY THAT SOMETHING IS TRUE** to state or affirm something in strong or formal terms ○ *He continued to protest his innocence.* **5.** *vt* **ANNOUNCE SOMETHING** to declare or proclaim something (*archaic*) ■ *n* /prṓ tèst/ **1. STRONG COMPLAINT OR OBJECTION** an expression or display of strong disapproval of or disagreement with something **2. DEMONSTRATION OF PUBLIC OPPOSITION OR DISAPPROVAL** an expression of strong opposition to or disapproval of something in the form of a public demonstration or other action ○ *student protests* ○ *went on a protest march* **3.** LAW **CREDITOR'S FORMAL STATEMENT** a formal statement drawn up by a notary on behalf of a creditor, declaring that somebody has refused to honor a bill **4.** US **TAXPAYER'S FORMAL DECLARATION** a taxpayer's formal declaration reserving the right to contest a given tax as either illegal or excessive (*formal*) [14C. Via French < Latin *protestari* "declare publicly" < *testari* "declare"] —**prot·es·tant** *n* —**pro·test·er** *n* —**pro·test·ing·ly** *adv*

SYNONYMS See ***complain*** and ***object***.

Prot·es·tant /próttəstənt/ *n* **1.** a member or adherent of any denomination of the Western Christian church that rejects papal authority and some fundamental Roman Catholic doctrines, and believes in justification by faith. The formulation of Protestants' beliefs began with the Reformation in the 16th century. **2.** somebody who makes a protest against an action —**Prot·es·tant** *adj*

Prot·es·tant E·pis·co·pal Church *n* CHR same as **Episcopal Church**

Prot·es·tant eth·ic *n* CHR same as **Protestant work ethic**

Prot·es·tant·ism /próttəstən tìzzəm/ *n* **1. BELIEF IN PROTESTANT DOCTRINES** adherence to the principles of the Protestant religion **2. RELIGIOUS MOVEMENT OPPOSING ROMAN CATHOLICISM** a Christian religious movement originating in the 16th century from Martin Luther's attack on Roman Catholic doctrine. It grew to encompass many churches and denominations denying papal authority and believing in justification by faith. **3. ALL PROTESTANT CHURCHES** the Protestant churches considered as a whole

Prot·es·tant work eth·ic *n* a belief in the moral value of work, thrift, and the responsibility of each person for his or her actions

prot·es·ta·tion /pròttə stáysh'n/ *n* **1. FORMAL AFFIRMATION** a strong or firm declaration that something is true (*often used in the plural*) ○ *protestations of loyalty* **2. ACT OF COMPLAINING OR OBJECTING** the act of expressing strong disapproval of or disagreement with something **3. COMPLAINT OR OBJECTION** a statement expressing strong disapproval of or disagreement with something

pro·test vote *n* the casting of a vote for a candidate or party as a means of showing dissatisfaction with another candidate or party

pro·te·us /prṓtee əss/ (*plural* **-te·i** /-tee ī/) *n* a rod-shaped bacterium associated with enteritis and urinary tract infections. Genus: *Proteus.* [Early 19C. < modern Latin, after PROTEUS]

Pro·te·us /prṓtee əss/ *n* **1.** in Greek mythology, a prophetic sea god who could change his shape at will **2.** the second-largest natural satellite of Neptune, discovered in 1989 by Voyager 2. It is irregular in shape, having a maximum dimension of approximately 275 mi./440 km.

pro·tha·la·mi·on /prōthə láymee ən/ (*plural* **-mi·a** /-mee ə/), **pro·tha·la·mi·um** /-mee əm/ (*plural* **-mi·a**) *n* a song or poem celebrating a future marriage (*literary*) [Late 16C. After *epithalamion*, variant of EPITHALAMIUM]

pro·thal·lus /prō thálləss/ (*plural* **-li** /-lī/), **pro·thal·li·um** /prō thállee əm/ (*plural* **-li·a** /-lee ə/) *n* a flat green organ bearing the reproductive organs (**gametophytes**) of ferns and related plants [Mid-19C. < modern Latin Greek *thallos* "green shoot"] —**pro·thal·li·al** *adj* —**pro·thal·lic** *adj*

proth·e·sis /próthəssiss/ (*plural* **-e·ses** /-ə seez/) *n* **1.** the addition of a sound or sounds at the beginning of a word to make the word easier to pronounce **2.** in the Eastern Orthodox Church, the preparations for the offering of Communion [Late 16C. < Greek, "a placing before or in public" < *thesis* "placing"] —**pro·thet·ic** /prə théttik/ *adj* —**pro·thet·i·cal·ly** *adv*

pro·thon·o·tar·y /prō thónnə tèrree, prṑthə nṓtaree/ (*plural* **-ies**), **pro·ton·o·tar·y** /prō tónnə tèrree, prṑtə nōtəree/ *n* **1.** the chief clerk in some courts of law **2.** *also* **pro·thon·o·tar·y ap·os·tol·ic** (*plural* **pro·thon·o·tar·ies ap·os·tol·ic**) *or* **pro·ton·o·tar·y ap·os·tol·ic** (*plural* **pro·ton·o·tar·ies ap·os·tol·ic**) in the Roman Catholic Church, one of twelve officials who can act as a notary to authenticate papal proceedings, documents, and acts [15C. < medieval Latin *protonotarius* < Greek *prōtos* "first" + Latin *notarius* "notary"] —**pro·thon·o·tar·i·al** /prō thònnə térree əl, prōthənə-/ *adj*

pro·thon·o·tar·y war·bler *n* a small songbird with blue-gray wings and a bright golden yellow body. Native to: eastern North America. Latin name: *Protonotaria citrea*.

pro·tho·rac·ic gland /prōthə rássik-/ *n* a gland in insects that secretes the steroid hormone ecdysone, responsible for controlling molting and metamorphosis

pro·throm·bin /prō thrómbin/ *n* a plasma protein that is converted to thrombin during blood clotting

pro·tist /prṓtist/ *n* an organism belonging, in an older classification system, to the kingdom that includes protozoans, bacteria, and single-celled algae and fungi. Kingdom: *Protista*. [Late 19C. < modern Latin *Protista* < Greek *prōtistos* "very first" < *prōtos* "first"] —**pro·tis·tan** /prō tístən/ *adj* —**pro·tis·tol·o·gy** /prōti stólləjee/ *n*

pro·ti·um /prṓtee əm, prṓshee-/ *n* the most common and lightest isotope of hydrogen, with atomic mass 1 [Mid-20C. < Greek *prōtos* "first"]

proto- *prefix* **1.** first in time, earliest ○ *protolithic* ○ *protomartyr* **2.** original, ancestral ○ *protostar* ○ *Proto-Norse* **3.** first in a series, having the least amount of a particular element or radical ○ *protactinium* [< Greek *prōtos*]

Pro·to-Al·gon·qui·an *n* a reconstructed hypothetical language that is believed to be the ancestor of the Algonquian-Wakasan family of Native North American languages —**Pro·to-Al·gon·qui·an** *adj*

pro·to·col /prṓtə kàwl/ *n* **1.** ETIQUETTE OF FORMAL OCCASIONS the rules or conventions of correct behavior on official or ceremonial occasions **2.** CODE OF CONDUCT the rules of correct or appropriate behavior of a group, organization, or profession **3.** INTERNAT REL INTERNATIONAL AGREEMENT a formal agreement between states or nations **4.** RECORD OR DRAFT OF AGREEMENT a written record or preliminary draft of a treaty or other agreement **5.** COMPUT RULES FOR NETWORKING COMPUTERS a set of technical rules for the transmission and receipt of information between computers **6.** PHILOSOPHY same as **protocol statement** **7.** MED, SCI RESEARCH PLAN a detailed plan for a scientific experiment, medical trial, or other piece of research ■ *v* (**-coled** or **-colled**, **-col·ing** or **-col·ling**, **-cols**) **1.** *vi* PREPARE OR ISSUE PROTOCOL to draw up or issue a protocol or protocols **2.** *vt* RECORD SOMETHING IN PROTOCOL to record something in a protocol [15C. Via French and medieval Latin < Greek *prōtokollon* "first leaf of a book"]

pro·to·col state·ment *n* a statement that can be immediately verified by experience

pro·to·con·ti·nent /prṓtō kóntənənt/ *n* **1.** a large unbroken mass of land capable of becoming a major continent **2.** GEOL same as **supercontinent**

pro·to·gal·ax·y /prṓtō gálləksee/ (*plural* **-ies**) *n* a hypothetical cloud of gas believed to have been formed about 14 billion years ago from dark matter, neutral hydrogen, and helium, from which all the galaxies and stars evolved

Pro·to-Ger·man·ic *n* a reconstructed hypothetical language that is believed to be the ancestor of the Germanic branch of the Indo-European family of languages —**Pro·to-Ger·man·ic** *adj*

pro·to·hu·man /prṓtō hyoómən/ *n* an extinct hominid or primate that has some of the characteristics of modern people —**pro·to·hu·man** *adj*

Pro·to-In·do-Eur·o·pe·an *n* a reconstructed hypothetical language that is believed to be the ancestor of all the Indo-European languages —**Pro·to-In·do-Eur·o·pe·an** *adj*

pro·to·in·dus·tri·al·i·za·tion /prṓtō in dùstree əli záysh'n/ *n* the preliminary shift from an agricultural to an industrial economy, marked by the rapid spread of home-based manufacturing

pro·to·lan·guage /prṓtō làng gwij/ *n* a recorded or reconstructed language that is the ancestor of another language or family of languages

pro·to·lith·ic /prṑtə líthik/ *adj* relating to the earliest part of the Stone Age [Late 19C. After NEOLITHIC]

pro·to·mar·tyr /prṓtō maártər/ *n* **1.** St. Stephen, the first Christian martyr. **2.** the first person to die for a cause

pro·to·mor·phic /prṑtə máwrfik/ *adj* having a primitive structure

pro·ton /prṓ tòn/ *n* a stable elementary particle of the baryon family that is a component of all atomic nuclei and carries a positive charge equal to that of the electron's negative charge. Symbol **p** [Late 19C. < Greek *prōton*, form of *prōtos* "first, elementary"] —**pro·ton·ic** /prō tónnik/ *adj* —**pro·ton·i·cal·ly** *adv*

pro·to·ne·ma /prṑtə neémə/ (*plural* **-ma·ta** /-mətə/) *n* the primary thread-shaped structure of mosses and some liverworts that results from the germination of a spore and gives rise to a new plant [Mid-19C. < PROTO- + Greek *nēma* "thread"] —**pro·to·ne·mal** *adj*

pro·ton·ics /prō tónniks/ *n* the scientific study and technological application of protons in motion in conducting materials such as electrolytes (*takes a singular verb*)

pro·ton num·ber *n* PHYS same as **atomic number**

Pro·to-Norse *n* the form of the North Germanic language used in parts of Scandinavia, especially Norway and Iceland, until about the 8th century A.D. —**Pro·to-Norse** *adj*

pro·ton·o·tar·y *n* LAW, CHR another spelling of **prothonotary**

pro·ton syn·chro·tron *n* a circular, very high-energy particle accelerator that accelerates protons through the action of magnetic fields and a high-frequency electric field

pro·to-on·co·gene /prṓtō óngkə jeen/ *n* a normal gene that can mutate or be activated by a cancer-causing virus to form a cancer-producing gene

pro·to·plan·et /prṓtə plànnət/ *n* a theoretical mass of gas in the clouds of gas and dust around a star that is believed to develop into a planet —**pro·to·plan·e·tar·y** /prṑtə plánnə tèrree/ *adj*

pro·to·plasm /prṓtə plàzzəm/ *n* the colorless liquid or colloidal contents of a living cell, composed of proteins, fats, and other organic substances in water, and including the nucleus and cytoplasm [Mid-19C. < German *Protoplasma* "first created thing" < Greek *plasma* (see PLASMA)] —**pro·to·plas·mic** /prṑtə plázmik/ *adj*

pro·to·plast /prṓtə plàst/ *n* the living substance of a plant or bacterial cell, excluding the cell wall [Mid-16C. Via French and late Latin, "first created being" < Greek *prōtoplastos* < *plastos* "formed" < *plassein* "to form"] —**pro·to·plas·tic** /prṑtə plástik/ *adj*

pro·to·por·phy·rin /prṑtō páwrfərin/ *n* a purple porphyrin acid that combines with iron to form the deep red of iron-containing proteins such as hemoglobin and cytochrome

Pro·to-Ro·mance *n* the language that developed from Vulgar Latin and gave rise to the Romance languages. Some Proto-Romance forms are hypothetical and reconstructed; for others there is written evidence. —**Pro·to-Ro·mance** *adj*

Pro·to-Se·mit·ic /prṑtō sə míttik/ *n* a hypothetical reconstructed language that is believed to be the ancestor of the Semitic branch of the Afro-Asiatic family of languages —**Pro·to-Se·mit·ic** *adj*

pro·to·star /prṓtə staàr/ *n* an interstellar cloud of gas and dust thought to develop into a star when it has collapsed sufficiently for nuclear reactions to begin

pro·to·stome /prṓtə stōm/ *n* an invertebrate animal, e.g., a mollusk or arthropod, in which the mouth forms directly from the blastopore

pro·to·the·ri·an /prṑtō theéree ən/ *n* an echidna, platypus, or one of many extinct related mammals. Subclass: Prototheria. [Late 19C. < PROTO- + Greek *therion* "wild animal"]

pro·to·tro·phic /prṑtō trṓfik, -trṓffik/ *adj* describes a microorganism that has the same nutritional needs and metabolic characteristics as the wild parent strain —**pro·to·troph** /prṓtə trṑf, -tròf/ *n*

pro·to·type /prṓtə tīp/ *n* **1.** ORIGINAL USED AS MODEL the original form of something, which has the essential features and is the model for subsequent forms **2.** FULL-SIZE FUNCTIONAL MODEL a first full-size functional model to be manufactured, e.g., of a car or a machine ○ *A prototype of the solar-powered car will be on display next month.* **3.** STANDARD EXAMPLE a standard example of a particular kind, class, or group **4.** BIOL PRIMITIVE FORM a primitive form believed to be the original type of a species or group, exhibiting the essential features of the later type ■ *vti* (**-typed**, **-typ·ing**, **-types**) CREATE PROTOTYPE to develop a prototype of something [Early 17C. Via French and late Latin < Greek *prōtotypon* "primitive form" < *typos* "impression"] —**pro·to·typ·al** /prṓtə tīp'l/ *adj* —**pro·to·typ·ic** /-típpik/ *adj* —**pro·to·typ·i·cal** *adj* —**pro·to·typ·i·cal·ly** *adv*

pro·tox·ide /prō tók sīd/ *n* an oxide of an element that has the lowest proportion of oxygen of all the oxides of that element

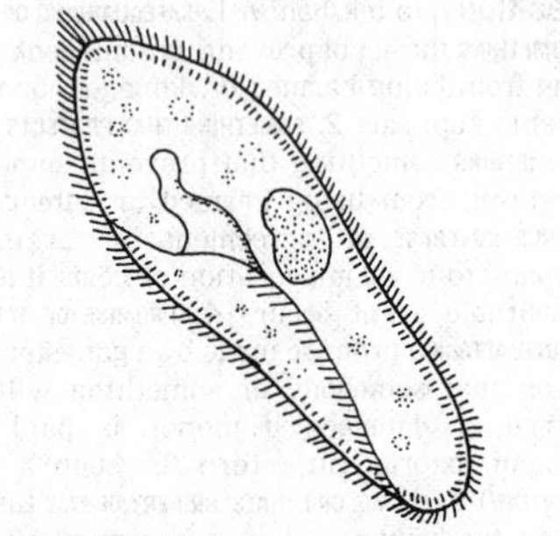

protozoan

pro·to·zo·an /prṑtə zṓ ən/, **pro·to·zo·on** /prṑtə zṓ ən/ (*plural* **-zo·ons** or **-zo·a** /-ə/) *n* a single-celled organism that can move and feeds on organic compounds of nitrogen and carbon, e.g., an amoeba. Kingdom: *Protoctista*. [Mid-19C. < modern Latin *Protozoa* "first animals" < Greek *zōia*, plural of *zōion* "animal"] —**pro·to·zo·al** *adj* —**pro·to·zo·an** *adj* —**pro·to·zo·ic** *adj*

pro·to·zo·ol·o·gy /prṑtə zō óllәjee/ *n* the branch of zoology that studies protozoans [Early 20C. < PROTOZOAN] —**pro·to·zo·o·log·i·cal** /prṑtə zṑ ə lójjik'l/ *adj* —**pro·to·zo·ol·o·gist** *n*

pro·to·zo·on *n* MICROBIOL another spelling of **protozoan**

pro·tract /prō trákt, prə-/ (**-tract·ed**, **-tract·ing**, **-tracts**) *vt* **1.** MAKE SOMETHING LAST to make something last longer **2.** PHYSIOL EXTEND BODY PART to extend or lengthen a body part **3.** MATH PLOT AND DRAW LINES to plot lines and draw them using a scale and protractor [Mid-16C. < Latin *protract-*, past participle of *protrahere* < *trahere* "draw"] —**pro·trac·tive** *adj*

pro·tract·ed /prō tráktəd, prə-/ *adj* lasting or drawn out for a long time —**pro·tract·ed·ly** *adv* —**pro·tract·ed·ness** *n*

pro·trac·tile /prō trákt'l, prə-/ *adj* **1.** capable of being thrust out **2.** ZOOL same as **protrusile**

pro·trac·tion /prō trákshən, prə-/ *n* **1.** the act of protracting something **2.** the act of drawing something such as a building or an area of land to scale, or a drawing of this kind

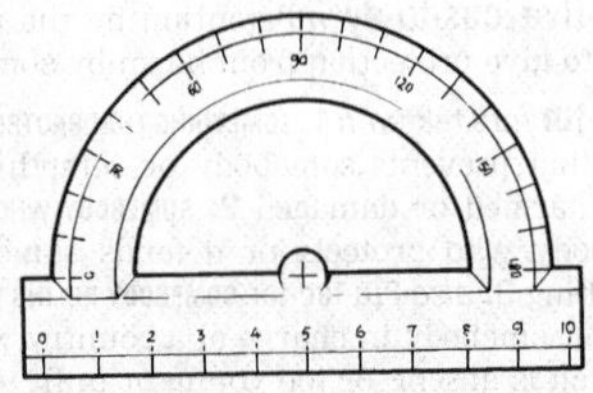

protractor

pro·trac·tor /prō tráktər, prə-/ *n* **1.** INSTRUMENT FOR MEASURING ANGLES an instrument shaped like a semicircle marked with the degrees of a circle, used to measure or mark out angles. See illustration on previous page **2.** SOMEBODY OR SOMETHING THAT LENGTHENS SOMETHING somebody or something that extends or lengthens something **3.** ANAT MUSCLE THAT EXTENDS BODY PART a muscle with the function of extending a body part

~~protray~~ incorrect spelling of **portray**

pro·trude /prō trōōd/ (**-trud·ed, -trud·ing, -trudes**) *vti* to stick out from the surroundings, or make something do this [Early 17C. < Latin *protrudere* "thrust forward" < *trudere* "thrust"] —**pro·trud·a·ble** *adj* —**pro·trud·ent** *adj*

pro·tru·sile /prō trōōss'l, -trōō sīl/, **pro·tru·si·ble** /-trōōssib'l/ *adj* used to describe an organ or appendage that can be quickly extended, e.g., the mouth of many fishes or the proboscis of nemertine worms [Mid-19C. < Latin *protrus-* (see PROTRUSION)]

pro·tru·sion /prō trōōzh'n/ *n* **1.** something that sticks out from its surroundings **2.** the act of protruding, or the state of being protruded [Mid-17C. < medieval Latin *protrusion-* < Latin *protrus-*, past participle of *protrudere* (see PROTRUDE)]

pro·tru·sive /prō trōōssiv/ *adj* **1.** jutting or sticking out **2.** having a brash forward manner [Late 17C. < Latin *protrus-* (see PROTRUSION)] —**pro·tru·sive·ly** *adv* —**pro·tru·sive·ness** *n*

pro·tu·ber·ance /prō tōōbərənss/, **pro·tu·ber·an·cy** /-rənssee/ (*plural* **-cies**) *n* **1.** something that sticks out from its surroundings ○ *the small fleshy protuberance that dangles down from the soft palate* **2.** the fact or condition of sticking out, being swollen, or bulging [Mid-17C. < PROTUBERANT]

pro·tu·ber·ant /prō tōōbərənt/ *adj* sticking out from the surroundings in a bulging rounded manner [Mid-17C. < late Latin *protuberant-*, present participle of *protuberare* "swell forward" < Latin *tuber* "lump"] —**pro·tu·ber·ant·ly** *adv*

pro·tu·ber·ate /prō tōōbə ràyt/ (**-at·ed, -at·ing, -ates**) *vi* to stick out from the surroundings in a bulging rounded manner [Late 16C. < Latin *protuberat-*, past participle of *protuberare* (see PROTUBERANT)]

pro·tyle /prṓ tīl/ *n* an imaginary substance from which the chemical elements were supposed to have been formed [Late 19C. < PROTO- + Greek *hulē* "matter"]

proud /prowd/ *adj* **1.** PLEASED AND SATISFIED feeling pleased and satisfied, e.g., about having done something or about owning something ○ *I am very proud to be here today to give you this award.* **2.** FOSTERING FEELINGS OF PRIDE characterized by feelings of pride ○ *the proudest moment in your life* **3.** HAVING SELF-RESPECT having a proper amount of self-respect **4.** ARROGANT having an exaggerated opinion of personal worth or abilities **5.** IMPRESSIVE looking magnificent and impressive, or behaving in an impressive way ○ *the proud peaks of the Rockies* **6.** *Midwest, Southern US* FEELING PLEASED feeling pleased, glad, or delighted **7.** HIGH-SPIRITED high-spirited and strong ○ *a proud horse* [Pre-12C. < Old French *prud* < Latin *prodesse* "be beneficial," literally "be for" < *esse* "be"] —**proud·ly** *adv* —**proud·ness** *n* ◇ **do somebody proud 1.** to treat somebody well and generously **2.** to bring honor or distinction to somebody

SYNONYMS ***proud, arrogant, conceited, egotistical, vain***

CORE MEANING: describing somebody who is pleased with himself or herself

proud feeling pleased and satisfied about having done something or about owning something ○ *We were very proud of our DIY project.* **arrogant** feeling or showing self-importance and contempt for others ○ *What makes this arrogant man think that I would be interested in him?* ○ *Sometimes the chairman displays not just cockiness, but an almost arrogant attitude.* **conceited** having or showing an excessively high opinion of your own qualities or abilities ○ *She was less brilliant than her sister and also, perhaps as a consequence, less conceited.* ○ *I don't know how to say this without sounding conceited, but my son is really something special.* **egotistical** having an exaggerated sense of self- importance, especially tending to speak or write about yourself excessively ○ *a documentary that portrays her as egotistical and publicity-hungry* ○ *an intensely egotistical and unfeeling man* **vain** excessively proud, especially of personal appearance ○ *He was vain about his looks, and even more vain about the state of his physique.* ○ *Being vain, she did not want to admit that her German was insufficient for a diplomatic conversation.*

Prou·dhon /prōō don/, **Pierre Joseph** (1809–65) French writer and revolutionary leader who condemned the abuses of wealth and power. His radical theories had an important influence on the development of socialism and anarchism.

"Property is theft."
[Pierre Joseph Proudhon, *Qu'est-ce que la propriété (What is Property?)*; 1840]

Proulx /proo/, **E. Annie** (*b.* 1935) US writer best known for her novel *The Shipping News* (1993) which was awarded the 1994 Pulitzer Prize for fiction

AKG London
Marcel Proust

Proust /proost/, **Marcel** (1871–1922) French novelist. He wrote a series of partly autobiographical novels, *À la recherche du temps perdu* (*Remembrance of Things Past*) (1913–27). See Cultural note at **remembrance** —**Prous·ti·an** *adj*

"It is in moments of illness that we are compelled to recognize that we live not alone but chained to a creature of a different kingdom, whole worlds apart, who has no knowledge of us and by whom it is impossible to make ourselves understood: our body."
[Marcel Proust, "Le Côté de Guermantes" ("The Guermantes Way"), *À la recherche du temps perdu (Remembrance of Things Past)*; 1913–27]

prous·tite /prōō stīt/ *n* a deep red mineral consisting of silver arsenic sulfide. Use: source of silver. [Mid-19C. After Joseph L. *Proust* (1754–1826), French chemist]

prov. *abbr* **1.** province **2.** provincial **3.** provisional

Prov. *abbr* **1.** Provençal **2.** BIBLE Proverbs **3.** EDUC, RELIG Provost

prove /proov/ (**proved, proved** or **prov·en** /prōōvən/, **prov·ing, proves**) *v* **1.** *vt* ESTABLISH TRUTH OF SOMETHING to establish the truth or existence of something by providing evidence or argument **2.** *vti* TURN OUT TO BE SOMETHING to turn out to be a particular thing or a thing of a particular character after time or testing ○ *It proved impossible to dislodge the rock.* **3. prove yourself** *vr* DEMONSTRATE COMPETENCE to show yourself to be competent and worthy ○ *eager to prove himself in his new job* ○ *proved herself more than capable of achieving excellent results* **4.** *vt* CHEM, MINERALS TEST SOMETHING TO DETERMINE CHARACTERISTICS to subject something to scientific analysis to determine its worth or characteristics **5.** *vt* MATH CHECK RESULT OF CALCULATION to verify that a mathematical result is correct **6.** *vt* MATH DEMONSTRATE TRUTH OF HYPOTHESIS to demonstrate that a hypothesis or proposition is true **7.** *vt* LAW DEMONSTRATE THAT WILL IS GENUINE to establish that a will is genuine or valid **8.** *vt* PRINTING, ARTS MAKE IMPRESSION OF SOMETHING to make a test impression of a negative, etching, or type **9.** *vi* FOOD RISE IN WARM PLACE to rise in a warm place before being baked (*refers to dough*) [12C. Via Old French *prover* < Latin *probare* "test, prove to be good" < *probus* "good"] —**prov·a·bil·i·ty** /prōōvə bíllətee/ *n* —**prov·a·ble** *adj* —**prov·a·bly** *adv*

USAGE proved or **proven**? The past participles ***proved*** and ***proven*** are both often used as verbs, with auxiliaries, and also as predicative adjectives (after *be*). Whether to say, for example, *We have proved our case* or *We have proven our case*, and *The case is proved* or *The case is proven* is a matter of choice. ***Proved*** is not, however, ordinarily employed as an adjective preceding a noun: *proven cases*; *a proven fact* are the standard forms.

ORIGIN The Latin word *probus* "good," from which ***prove*** is derived, is also the source of English *approve*, *probable*, *probe*, *probity*, *proof*, *reprobate*, and *reprove*.

prov·en /prōōvən/ *adj* **1.** done or used before and known to work or be satisfactory **2.** shown to be true beyond any doubt —**prov·en·ly** *adv*

prov·e·nance /próvvənənss, -naàns/ *n* **1.** the place of origin of something **2.** the source and ownership history of a work of art or literature or of an archaeological find [Late 18C. Via French < Latin *provenire* "arise," literally "come forth" < *venire* "come"]

SYNONYMS See ***origin***.

Pro·ven·çal /prṑvən saál, pròvv-/ *n* **1.** LANGUAGE OF SE FRANCE a Romance language spoken in southeastern France, closely related to French, Italian, and Catalan. Native speakers: 4 million. **2.** SOMEBODY FROM PROVENCE somebody who comes from Provence ■ *adj* **1.** OF PROVENCE relating to Provence, or its people or culture **2.** OF LANGUAGE OF PROVENCE relating to the Provençal language [Late 16C. Via French < Latin *provincialis* "provincial" < *provincia* (see PROVINCE), colloquial name for S Gaul during Roman rule]

Pro·ven·çale /prṑvən saál, pròvv-/ *adj* prepared with olive oil, garlic, herbs, and tomatoes [Mid-19C. < French *à la provençale* "in the Provençal manner"]

Pro·vence /prə vaánss, praw vaáNss/ region in southeastern France, bordering the Mediterranean Sea. It was an ancient Roman province.

prov·en·der /próvvəndər/ *n* **1.** food for livestock, especially hay or other dry fodder (*archaic*) **2.** food (*literary or humorous*) [14C. < Old French *provendre*, variant of *provende*, alteration (influenced by Latin *providere* "to supply") of *praebenda* "things to be given"]

pro·ve·nience /prō veényənss/ *n* US HIST same as **provenance** [Late 19C. < Latin *provenient-*, present participle of *provenire* (see PROVENANCE)]

pro·ven·tric·u·lus /prṑ ven tríkyələss/ (*plural* **-li** /-lī/) *n* **1.** PART OF BIRD'S STOMACH the first part of a bird's stomach, where digestive enzymes are mixed with food before it goes to the gizzard. It is analogous to the gizzard in insects and crustaceans. **2.** PART OF INVERTEBRATE'S STOMACH the thin-walled section of the stomach of some invertebrates **3.** PART OF INSECT'S STOMACH the part of the foregut in some insects that has teeth or plates for grinding food —**pro·ven·tric·u·lar** *adj*

prov·erb /pró vùrb/ *n* a short well-known saying that expresses an obvious truth and often offers advice [14C. Via French < Latin *proverbium* "saying, saw" < *verbum* "word"]

pro·ver·bi·al /prə vúrbee əl/ *adj* **1.** EXPRESSED AS PROVERB expressed as a proverb, or resembling a proverb either in form or because of being widely known or referred to **2.** USED IN PROVERB used to refer to a particular proverb or similar well-known phrase ○ *She was behaving like the proverbial cat on hot bricks.* **3.** WELL-KNOWN widely known and recognized, and often viewed as stereotypical ○ *their proverbial hospitality* ■ *n* WORD SUBSTITUTE used to refer to something in an expression or saying that is not being explicitly stated (*informal; often used euphemistically*) ○ *You'll find they've got you by the proverbials.* —**pro·ver·bi·al·ly** *adv*

Prov·erbs /pró vùrbz/ *n* a book of the Bible that consists of the proverbs of wise men, including Solomon (*takes a singular verb*) See table at **Bible**

pro·vide /prə vīd/ (**-vid·ed, -vid·ing, -vides**) *v* **1.** *vt* SUPPLY SOMEBODY WITH SOMETHING to supply somebody with something, or be a source of something needed or wanted by somebody **2.** *vt* MAKE SOMETHING AVAILABLE to make something available to somebody **3.** *vt* LAW REQUIRE SOMETHING AS CONDITION to require something in advance as a condition or as part of a contract (*formal*) **4.** *vi* TAKE PRECAUTIONS to take precautions to prevent harm or bring about good ○ *provide against disaster* **5.** *vi* SUPPLY MEANS OF SUPPORT to supply the material means of support for somebody ○ *provides for his children* [15C. < Latin *providere* "prepare in advance, supply," literally "see ahead" < *videre* "see"]

pro·vid·ed /prə vídəd/, **pro·vid·ed that** *conj* same as **providing** ○ *He can play provided that he has no injuries.*

prov·i·dence /próvvid'nss, -dènss/ *n* **1.** *also* **Prov·i·dence** GOD'S GUIDANCE the wisdom, care, and guidance believed to be provided by God **2.** *also* **Prov·i·dence** GOD God perceived as a caring force guiding humankind **3.** GOOD JUDGMENT AND MANAGEMENT good judgment and foresight in the management of affairs or resources [14C. Directly or via French < Latin *providentia* "foresight" < *provident-*, present participle of *providere* (see PROVIDE)]

Prov·i·dence /próvvidənss/ capital of Rhode Island and its largest city, located in the northeastern part of the state. Population: 175,901 (2002 estimate).

prov·i·dent /próvvid'nt, -dènt/ *adj* **1.** carefully preparing for future needs **2.** economical in the use of resources [15C. < Latin *provident-*, present participle of *providere* (see PROVIDE)]

prov·i·den·tial /pròvvi dénshəl/ *adj* **1.** relating to or believed to be determined by providence **2.** so favorable that it seems determined by providence

pro·vi·der /prə vídər/ *n* **1.** an organization or company that provides access to a service or system such as a cellular phone, cable, or computer network ○ *an Internet provider* ○ *a provider* **2.** somebody who provides material support for somebody or something, especially a family

pro·vid·ing /prə víding/, **pro·vid·ing that** *conj* on the understanding that another thing will also occur or be done ○ *We can save these people providing we get the equipment we need.*

prov·ince /próvvinss/ *n* **1.** POL ADMINISTRATIVE DIVISION OF NATION an administrative region or division of a country **2.** AREA OF KNOWLEDGE a sphere of knowledge or activity **3.** CHR ECCLESIASTICAL TERRITORY an ecclesiastical territory of more than two dioceses, under the jurisdiction of an archbishop or metropolitan **4.** ANCIENT HIST REGION OF ROMAN EMPIRE a country or region controlled by the ancient Roman Empire through an appointed governor **5.** ECOL AREA CHARACTERIZED BY PLANTS AND ANIMALS a biogeographical area within a region that is defined by the plants and animals that inhabit it ■ **prov·inc·es** *npl* NONMETROPOLITAN PARTS OF NATION the parts of a country exclusive of the capital and larger cities [14C. Directly or via French < Latin *provincia* "territory conquered by Rome" < *vincere* "conquer"]

Prov·ince·town /próvvinss tòwn/ town in southeastern Massachusetts, at the tip of Cape Cod, north of Dennis. It is an artists' colony, and the site of the Pilgrims' first landing in 1620. Population: 3,484 (2002 estimate).

pro·vin·cial /prə vínshəl/ *adj* **1.** OF PROVINCE belonging to or coming from a province **2.** UNSOPHISTICATED AND NARROW-MINDED unsophisticated and unwilling to accept new ideas or ways of thinking **3.** ARCHIT, FURNITURE SIMPLE AND PLAIN in a simple and plain decorative style ■ *n* **1.** SOMEBODY FROM PROVINCES somebody who comes from or lives in the provinces **2.** SOMEBODY UNSOPHISTICATED an unsophisticated or narrow-minded person **3.** CHR HEAD OF PROVINCE the head of an ecclesiastical province or of a religious order in a province [14C. Directly or via French < Latin *provincialis* < *provincia* (see PROVINCE)] —**pro·vin·ci·al·i·ty** /prə vìnshee állətee/ *n* —**pro·vin·cial·ly** *adv*

pro·vin·cial court *n* a Canadian court that deals with less serious offenses and whose judges are appointed and paid by the province

pro·vin·cial·ism /prə vínshə lìzzəm/ *n* **1.** narrow-mindedness and lack of sophistication **2.** something that originates in a province, e.g., a word, phrase, trait, or custom

pro·vin·cial po·lice *n* a Canadian police force that has jurisdiction within a province, but not in urban areas, which have their own municipal police

prov·ing ground /proōving-/ *n* a place or situation in which somebody or something new is tried out or tested

pro·vi·rus /prō vīrəss, prō vírəss/ *n* a form of a virus that is integrated into the genetic material of the host and passed on from one cell generation to the next

pro·vi·sion /prə vízh'n/ *n* **1.** SUPPLYING OF SOMETHING the act of providing or supplying something **2.** ACTION TAKEN TO PREPARE FOR SOMETHING a preparatory step taken to meet a possible or expected need ○ *No provision has been made for people with disabilities.* **3.** SOMETHING PROVIDED something provided or supplied **4.** LAW LEGAL CLAUSE STATING CONDITION a clause in a law or contract stating that a condition must be met ■ *npl* **1.** **pro·vi·sions** FOOD AND OTHER SUPPLIES supplies of food and other necessities, especially for a journey **2.** *Carib* STARCHY FRUIT AND VEGETABLES edible tubers such as eddoes, dasheen, cassava (**ground provisions**) or starchy fruit and vegetables such as breadfruit ■ *vt* (**-sioned, -sion·ing, -sions**) PROVIDE SOMEBODY WITH SUPPLIES to provide somebody with supplies, especially for a journey [14C. Via French < Latin *provision-* "foresight, preparation" < *provis-*, past participle of *providere* (see PROVIDE)] —**pro·vi·sion·er** *n*

pro·vi·sion·al /prə vízhən'l, -vízhnəl/ *adj* TEMPORARY OR CONDITIONAL temporary or conditional, pending confirmation or validation ○ *a provisional government* ■ *n* **1.** *US* HR SOMEBODY HIRED TEMPORARILY somebody hired temporarily for a job, especially before being qualified to do it permanently **2.** STAMPS TEMPORARY POSTAGE STAMP a postage stamp used temporarily until a regular stamp is issued —**pro·vi·sion·al·ly** *adv*

Pro·vi·sion·al *n* a member of an unofficial faction of the Irish Republican Army that was originally set up to strive for an independent Ireland by force of arms —**Pro·vi·sion·al** *adj*

pro·vi·sion·al li·cence *n UK* same as **learner's permit**

pro·vi·so /prə vízō/ (*plural* **-sos** or **-soes**) *n* **1.** a condition asked as part of an agreement **2.** a clause introducing a condition in a contract [15C. < medieval Latin *proviso quod* "provided that" < Latin *proviso*, form of past participle of *providere* (see PROVIDE)]

pro·vi·so·ry /prə vízəree/ *adj* **1.** stating a condition **2.** same as **provisional** [Early 17C. < medieval Latin *provisorius* "of papal provision" < Latin *provisus*, past participle of *providere* (see PROVIDE)] —**pro·vi·so·ri·ly** *adv*

pro·vi·ta·min /prō vītəmin/ *n* a chemical compound (**precursor**) that is converted to a vitamin during normal biochemical processes

Pro·vo /prṓvō/ city and county seat of Provo County in northern Utah, situated on the Provo River, southeast of Salt Lake City. A regional industrial center, it is home to Brigham Young University. Population: 105,170 (2002 estimate).

prov·o·ca·tion /pròvvə káysh'n/ *n* **1.** ACT OF PROVOKING the act of provoking somebody or something **2.** CAUSE OF ANGER something that makes somebody angry or indignant **3.** LAW REASON FOR ATTACKING SOMEBODY something that incites somebody to attack somebody else [14C. Directly or via French < Latin *provocation-* < *provocare* (see PROVOKE)]

pro·voc·a·tive /prə vókətiv/ *adj* **1.** deliberately aimed at exciting or annoying people ○ *a provocative remark* **2.** intended to arouse somebody sexually [15C. Directly or via French < late Latin *provocativus* < *provocare* (see PROVOKE)] —**pro·voc·a·tive·ly** *adv* —**pro·voc·a·tive·ness** *n*

pro·voke /prə vṓk/ (**-voked, -vok·ing, -vokes**) *vt* **1.** MAKE SOMEBODY FEEL ANGRY to make somebody feel angry or indignant **2.** ELICIT RESPONSE to be the cause or occasion of an emotion or response ○ *Her bravery provoked a lot of sympathy.* **3.** STIR SOMEBODY TO EMOTION to stir somebody to an emotion or response ○ *The article provoked me to write a letter to the editor.* **4.** INCITE SOMETHING to bring something about intentionally ○ *provoke an argument* **5.** CAUSE ACTIVITY to serve as the stimulus for an activity ○ *Her new novel should provoke a lot of discussion.* [14C. Directly or via French < Latin *provocare* "summon" < *vocare* "to call" < *vox* "voice"] —**pro·vok·er** *n* —**pro·vok·ing·ly** *adv*

pro·vo·lo·ne /prṑvə lṓnee/ *n* a smoked cheese originally made in Italy that has a mild flavor and is light in color [Mid-20C. < Italian < *provola* "buffalo's milk cheese"]

pro·vost /prṓ vòst, prṓvəst, próvvəst/ *n* **1.** a high-ranking administrative officer of a university **2.** the senior dignitary of a cathedral or collegiate church [Pre-12C. < medieval Latin *propositus*, alteration of Latin *praepositus* "somebody placed in front" < *ponere* "to place"]

pro·vost court *n* a military court set up in an occupied hostile territory for the trial of minor offenses

pro·vost guard *n US* a detail of soldiers performing police duties under the authority of the provost marshal

pro·vost mar·shal *n* the army officer in charge of a unit of military police

prow /prow/ *n* **1.** the forward part of a ship **2.** the projecting front part of something [Mid-16C. Via French *proue* and Latin *prora* < Greek *prōra* "front of a ship" < *pro* "forward"]

prow·ess /prów əss/ *n* **1.** exceptional ability or skill **2.** extraordinary valor and ability in combat [13C. < Old French *proesce* "bravery" < *prou* "brave," variant of *prud* (see PROUD)]

prowl /prowl/ *vti* (**prowled, prowl·ing, prowls**) to roam around an area stealthily in search of prey, food, or opportunity ■ *n* the act of roaming stealthily for prey, food, or opportunity [14C. Origin ?] ◇ **on the prowl** moving around stealthily looking for somebody or something

prowl car *n US* POLICE same as **squad car**

prowl·er /prówlər/ *n* **1.** somebody who moves stealthily around an area looking for an opportunity to commit a criminal act **2.** a person or animal that prowls

prox. *abbr* proximo

prox·e·mics /prok séemiks/ *n* the study of the distance individuals maintain between each other in social interaction and its significance (*takes a singular verb*) [Mid-20C. < PROXIMITY, after PHONEMICS]

prox·i·mal /próksəm'l/ *adj* **1.** nearer to the point of reference or to the center of the body than something else is. For example, the elbow is proximal to the hand. **2.** describes the surface of a tooth nearest to either the one behind it or the one in front of it [Early 18C. < Latin *proximus* (see PROXIMITY)] —**prox·i·mal·ly** *adv*

prox·i·mate /próksəmət/ *adj* **1.** PROBABLE most likely ○ *The proximate cause of the damage must be established.* **2.** NEAREST nearest in order, time, or place **3.** VERY CLOSE very close in space or time **4.** ABOUT TO HAPPEN soon to appear or take place **5.** APPROXIMATE almost accurate [Late 16C. < Latin *proximat-*, past participle of *proximare* "come near" < *proximus* (see PROXIMITY)] —**prox·i·mate·ly** *adv* —**prox·i·mate·ness** *n* —**prox·i·ma·tion** /pròksə máysh'n/ *n*

prox·im·i·ty /prok símmətee/ *n* closeness in space or time [15C. < Latin *proximitas* "nearness" < *proximus* "nearest," superlative of *prope* "near"]

prox·im·i·ty card *n* a plastic card carrying electronically coded information accessed by holding the card near a reading device. Proximity cards are often used to open doors as part of a security system.

prox·im·i·ty fuze *n* a fuze, usually part of a warhead, that will activate and cause detonation when the warhead is at a specific distance from the target

prox·im·i·ty op·er·a·tor *n* a Boolean operator separating words or phrases in a text search that directs the search engine to locate pages in which the words are near one another in any direction, the acceptable distance varying among search engines

prox·i·mo /próksə mṑ/ *adv* occurring during the next month (*archaic*) ○ *proposed a meeting for the fifth proximo* [Mid-19C. < Latin *proximo (mense)* "in the next (month)"]

prox·y /próksee/ (*plural* **-ies**) *n* **1.** AUTHORIZED CAPACITY OF SUBSTITUTE the function or power of somebody authorized to act for another person **2.** SUBSTITUTE somebody authorized to act for another person **3.** AUTHORIZATION DOCUMENT FOR STAND-IN a document authorizing somebody to act for another person **4.** LAW, FIN DOCUMENT AUTHORIZING VOTE ON ANOTHER'S STOCK a document authorizing somebody to vote on matters of corporate stock on behalf of somebody else [15C.

< medieval Latin *procuratia*, alteration of Latin *procuratio* "care, management" < *procurare* (see PROCURE)]

prox·y serv·er *n* a computer system that gives users more rapid access to popular websites by storing frequently requested and recently used items

Pro·zac /prṓ zàk/ *tdmk* a trademark for the antidepressant drug fluoxetine

prs. *abbr* pairs

prude /prood/ *n* somebody who is easily offended by matters relating to sex or nudity [Early 18C. < French, back-formation < Old French *prudefemme* (misunderstood as "virtuous woman"), feminine of *prud'homme* < assumed *pro de ome* "fine (thing) of a man"] —**prud·er·y** /proódəree/ *n* —**prud·ish** *adj* —**prud·ish·ly** *adv* —**prud·ish·ness** *n*

pru·dent /proód'nt/ *adj* **1. HAVING GOOD SENSE** having good sense in dealing with practical matters **2. CAREFULLY CONSIDERING CONSEQUENCES** using good judgment to consider likely consequences and act accordingly **3. CAREFUL IN MANAGING RESOURCES** careful in managing resources so as to provide for the future [14C. Directly or via French < Latin *prudent-*, contraction of *provident-* (see PROVIDENT)] —**pru·dence** *n* —**pru·dent·ly** *adv*

SYNONYMS See ***cautious***.

pru·den·tial /proo dénshəl/ *adj* **1.** resulting from, depending on, or marked by prudence **2.** using prudence, especially in business matters —**pru·den·tial·ly** *adv*

Prud·hoe Bay /proódhō-, prùdhō-/ bay in the Beaufort Sea, in northern Alaska. Large petroleum reserves were discovered there in 1968.

Prud·homme /proó dòm/, **Paul** (*b.* 1940) US chef and writer. He helped to introduce Creole and Cajun cuisine to a wider audience through books such as *Chef Paul's Louisiana Kitchen* (1984).

pru·i·nose /proó ə nòss/ *adj* describes something such as a fruit or a leaf that has a white powdery coating [Early 19C. < Latin *pruinosus* < *pruina* "hoar frost"]

prune[1] /proon/ *n* **1. DRIED PLUM** a plum that has been preserved by drying **2. PLUM TO BE DRIED** a plum suitable for drying (*informal*) **3. OFFENSIVE TERM** an offensive term that deliberately insults somebody's intelligence, competence, or ability to interest others (*insult*) [14C. Via French and Latin < Greek *prounon*, variant of *proumnon* "plum"]

prune[2] /proon/ *v* (**pruned, prun·ing, prunes**) **1.** *vti* **CUT BRANCHES OF PLANT** to cut branches away from a plant to encourage fuller growth **2.** *vt* **REDUCE SOMETHING BY REMOVING UNWANTED MATERIAL** to reduce something by removing whatever is unnecessary or unwanted **3.** *vt* **REMOVE SOMETHING UNNECESSARY** to remove something considered unnecessary or unwanted ■ *n* **PRUNING OF SOMETHING** an act of pruning a plant or something with unnecessary or unwanted parts [14C. < Old French *proignier* "cut in a rounded shape in front" < Latin *rotundus* "round"] —**prun·a·ble** *adj* —**prun·er** *n*

pru·nel·la /proo néllə/ *n* a wool fabric with a twill weave. Use: academic gowns, clerical robes, shoe uppers. [Mid-17C. Alteration of French *prunelle* "sloe," diminutive of *prune* "plum" (see PRUNE[1])]

pru·nelle /proo nél/ *n* **1.** a sweet French liqueur flavored with sloes **2.** TEXTILES same as **prunella** [15C. < French (see PRUNELLA)]

prun·ing hook /proóning-/ *n* a tool with a hooked blade and sometimes a long handle, used to prune trees and bushes

pru·ri·ent /proóree ənt/ *adj* having or intended to arouse an unwholesome interest in sexual matters [Mid-17C. < Latin *prurient-*, present participle of *prurire* "itch, long for"] —**pru·ri·ence** *n* —**pru·ri·ent·ly** *adv*

pru·ri·go /proō rígō/ *n* a chronic inflammatory skin disease causing small itchy swellings [Mid-17C. < Latin, "itching" < *prurire* "itch, long for"] —**pru·rig·i·nous** /proō ríjjənəss/ *adj*

pru·ri·tus /proō rítəss/ *n* an intense feeling of itchiness [Mid-17C. < Latin < "itch, long for"]

Prus·sia /prúshə/ former state and kingdom in Germany. Its capital was Berlin. —**Prus·sian** *adj, n*

Prus·sian blue *n* **1.** *also* **prus·sian blue** a water-insoluble blue iron pigment **2.** a rich dark blue color tinged with green [Because discovered in 1704 by a Prussian dyer called Diesbach] —**Prus·sian blue** *adj*

prus·si·ate /prússee ət, -àyt, prúshee-/ *n* **1.** a chemical compound that is a ferrocyanide or ferricyanide **2.** a chemical compound that is a salt of hydrocyanic acid [Late 18C. < *prussic* (see PRUSSIC ACID)]

prus·sic ac·id /prùssik-/ *n* CHEM same as **hydrocyanic acid** [< *Prussian*, because first obtained from Prussian blue]

pry[1] /prī/ *vi* (**pried, pry·ing, pries**) **BE INQUISITIVE** to inquire nosily or excessively into somebody's private affairs ■ *n* (*plural* **pries**) **1. ACT OF PRYING** the act of prying into somebody's private affairs **2. INQUISITIVE PERSON** somebody who pries into other people's private affairs [14C. Origin ?] —**pry·ing·ly** *adv*

pry[2] /prī/ *vt* (**pried, pry·ing, pries**) **1. OPEN USING LEVERAGE** to open or part something by using leverage **2. GET INFORMATION WITH DIFFICULTY** to get information from somebody with great difficulty ○ *pried the secret out of her* ■ *n* (*plural* **pries**) *US* **1. TOOL FOR APPLYING LEVERAGE** something that is used to apply leverage, e.g., a crowbar **2. LEVERAGE** leverage exerted in order to open or lift something [Early 19C. Back-formation < PRIZE[3], misunderstood as 3rd person present singular]

pry·er *n* another spelling of **prier**

pryt·a·ne·um /prìtt'n eé əm/ (*plural* **-ne·a** /-eé ə/) *n* in ancient Greece, a public building used as a meeting place [Early 17C. Via Latin < Greek *prutaneion* < *prutanis* "prince, ruler"]

Prze·wal·ski's horse /shə vaálskiz-, pùrzhə-/ *n* a wild horse with a stocky body, a chestnut coat, and an erect dark mane. Native to: Asia. Latin name: *Equus caballus przevalskii*. [Late 19C. After N. M. *Przheval'skiĭ* (1839–88), Russian explorer]

Ps. *abbr* BIBLE (Book of) Psalms

p.s. *abbr* **1.** postscript **2.** TRANSP passenger steamer

P.S. *abbr* **1.** GRAM phrase structure **2.** Police Sergeant **3.** postscript **4.** private secretary **5.** THEATER prompt side **6.** EDUC public school

PSA *abbr* **1.** MED prostate-specific antigen **2.** public service announcement

Psa. *abbr* BIBLE (Book of) Psalms

psalm /saam, saalm/, **Psalm** *n* a sacred song or poem of praise, especially one in the Book of Psalms in the Bible [12C. Via late Latin < Greek *psalmos* "harp song" < *psallein* "to pluck"] —**psalm·ic** *adj*

psalm·ist /saámist, saálm-/ *n* the author of a psalm

psalm·o·dy /saámədee, saálm-/ (*plural* **-dies**) *n* **1. PSALM SINGING** the singing of psalms in divine worship **2.** MUSIC **MUSICAL ARRANGEMENTS FOR PSALMS** the prescribed arrangements for singing individual psalms from the Book of Psalms **3. SET OF PSALMS** a collection of psalms [14C. Via late Latin < Greek *psalmōidia* < *psalmos* (see PSALM) + *ōidē* "song"] —**psalm·od·ic** /saa móddik, saal-/ *adj* —**psalm·o·dist** /saámədist, saálm-/ *n*

Psalms /saamz, saalmz/ *n* a book of the Bible that consists of 150 poems and hymns to God, traditionally attributed to King David (*takes a singular verb*) See table at **Bible**

Psal·ter /sáwltər/, **psal·ter** *n* a book containing psalms, or the Book of Psalms, used in worship [Pre-12C. < ecclesiastical Latin *psalterium* "Book of Psalms" < Latin (see PSALTERY)]

psal·te·ri·um /sawl teéree əm/ (*plural* **-ri·a** /-ree ə/) *n* ZOOL same as **omasum** [Mid-19C. < Latin, "stringed instrument" (see PSALTERY)]

psal·ter·y /sáwltəree/ (*plural* **-ies**) *n* an ancient musical instrument with numerous strings, plucked with the fingers or with a pick [13C. Via French < Latin *psalterium* "stringed instrument" < Greek *psaltērion* "stringed instrument played by plucking" < *psallein* "to pluck"]

psam·mite /sá mìt/ *n* **1.** a rock formed principally of sand **2.** a metamorphosed sandstone containing large amounts of quartz [Mid-19C. < Greek *psammos* "sand"] —**psam·mit·ic** /sa míttik/ *adj*

p's and q's /peéz ən kyoóz/ *npl* the polite manners and behavior that somebody adopts when eager to make a good impression ○ *We'd better mind our p's and q's.* [Origin ?]

PSAT *tdmk US* a trademark for a standardized test taken by high school students in the United States to prepare for the SAT™ and qualify for National Merit scholarships. Full form **Preliminary Scholastic Aptitude Test**

PSA test *n* a test for prostate cancer that detects the presence in the blood of a protein produced by prostate cells. Full form **prostate-specific antigen test**

psec. *abbr* MEASURE picosecond

pse·phol·o·gy /see fóllәjee/ *n* the statistical study of elections [Mid-20C. < Greek *psēphos* "pebble, vote"; from the Greek practice of using pebbles to vote] —**pse·pho·log·i·cal** /seéfə lójjik'l/ *adj* —**pse·pho·log·i·cal·ly** *adv* —**pse·phol·o·gist** *n*

pseud. *abbr* pseudonym

pseud- *prefix* same as **pseudo-** (*sometimes used before vowels*)

pseud·ax·is /soo dáksiss/ (*plural* **-ax·es** /-ák seéz/) *n* BOT same as **sympodium**

pseud·e·pig·ra·pha /soódə píggrəfə/ *npl* anonymous or pseudonymous writings professing to be biblical, but not included in any biblical canon [Late 17C. < Greek, form of *pseudepigraphos* "with false title" < *epigraphein* "write on" (see EPIGRAPH)] —**pseud·ep·i·graph·ic** /soód epi gráffik/ *adj* —**pseud·ep·i·graph·i·cal** *adj* —**pseud·e·pig·ra·phous** *adj*

pseu·do /soódō/ *adj* not authentic or sincere, in spite of appearances [14C. < Greek *pseudo-* < *pseudēs* (see PSEUDO-)]

pseudo- *prefix* **1.** similar ○ *pseudobulb* **2.** false, spurious ○ *pseudoscience* [< Greek *pseudēs* < *pseudein* "to lie"]

pseu·do·ar·cha·ic *adj*
pseu·do·boy·cott *n*
pseu·do·Chris·tian *n, adj*
pseu·do·code *n*
pseu·do·con·cept *n*
pseu·do·de·moc·ra·cy *n*
pseu·do·dem·o·crat·ic *adj*
pseu·do·en·quir·y *n*
pseu·do·e·qual·i·ty *n*
pseu·do·e·vent *n*
pseu·do·Goth·ic *n, adj*
pseu·do·gov·ern·ment *n*
pseu·do·her·maph·ro·dite *n*
pseu·do·his·tor·y *n*
pseu·do·i·de·al *adj*
pseu·do·in·tel·lec·tual *adj, n*
pseu·do·know·ledge *n*
pseu·do·lib·er·a·tion *n*
pseu·do·med·i·cal *adj*
pseu·do·mem·brane *n*
pseu·do·ob·struc·tion *n*
pseu·do·prob·lem *n*
pseu·do·proph·et *n*
pseu·do·ques·tion *n*
pseu·do·ra·bies *n*
pseu·do·ra·tion·al *adj*
pseu·do·re·lig·ion *n*
pseu·do·re·lig·ious *adj*
pseu·do·Re·nais·sance *adj, n*
pseu·do·state·ment *n*
pseu·do·Tu·dor *adj, n*

pseud·o·bulb /soódō bùlb/ *n* a thickened part of a stem that lies above the ground, e.g., in many orchids

pseu·do·carp /soódō kaárp/ *n* a fruit formed by combining the ripened ovary with another structure, often the receptacle, e.g., a strawberry [Mid-19C. < PSEUDO- + Greek *karpos* "fruit"] —**pseu·do·car·pous** /soódō kaárpəss/ *adj*

pseu·do·clas·sic /soódō klássik/ *adj* posing as or mistakenly believed to be classic

pseu·do·clas·si·cism /soódō klássə sìzzəm/ *n* the use in art and literature of ancient Greek and Roman styles —**pseu·do·clas·si·cal** *adj*

pseu·do·coe·lo·mate /soódō seélə màyt/ *n* an invertebrate that has a fluid-filled body cavity not lined with mesoderm tissue, e.g., a nematode or rotifer —**pseu·do·coe·lo·mate** *adj*

pseu·do·cy·e·sis /soódō sī éessiss/ (*plural* **-e·ses** /-eé seéz/) *n* MED same as **false pregnancy** (*technical*) [Mid-19C. < PSEUDO- + Greek *kuēsis* "conception"]

pseu·do·gene /soódə jeén/ *n* a nonfunctional DNA sequence that is very similar to the sequence of a functional gene

pseu·do·her·maph·ro·dit·ism /soódō hər máffrə dī tìzzəm/ *n* a condition in which somebody has either ovaries (**female pseudohermaphroditism**) or testes (**male pseudohermaphroditism**) but has external genitalia of ambiguous appearance

pseu·do·in·tran·si·tive *adj* used to describe a normally transitive verb employed when its direct object is not explicitly stated or when its direct object becomes the subject of the sentence

pseu·do·mo·nad /soódə mṓ nàd/ *n* a rod-shaped bacterium that lives in soil or decomposing organic material. Some pseudomonads are pathogenic to plants and animals. Genus: *Pseudomonas.* [Early 20C. < modern Latin *Pseudomonad-* "false monad" < late Latin *monad-* (see MONAD)]

pseu·do·morph /sóodə màwrf/ *n* **1.** a mineral that has replaced another and taken its shape **2.** an irregular or deceptive form —**pseu·do·mor·phic** /sóodə máwrfik/ *adj* —**pseu·do·mor·phism** *n* —**pseu·do·mor·phous** *adj*

pseu·do·nym /sóodə nìm/ *n* a name that is not somebody's original name, especially one used by an author in publications [Mid-19C. Via French *pseudonyme* < Greek *pseudōnumon* "false name" < *onuma* "name"] —**pseu·do·nym·i·ty** /sòodə nímmətee/ *n* —**pseu·don·y·mous** /soo dónnəməss/ *adj*

pseu·do·po·di·um /sóodə pṓdee əm/ (*plural* **-di·a** /-dee ə/), **pseu·do·pod** /sóodə pòd/ *n* a temporary cytoplasmic protrusion in amoebas and other protozoans, used for locomotion and to take up food

pseu·do·preg·nan·cy /sòodō prégnənssee/ (*plural* **-cies**) *n* MED same as **false pregnancy**

pseu·do·ran·dom /sòodō rándəm/ *adj* relating to random numbers generated by a computational process

pseu·do·sci·ence /sòodō sī ənss/ *n* a theory or method doubtfully or mistakenly held to be scientific —**pseu·do·sci·en·tif·ic** /sòodō sī ən tíffik/ *adj* —**pseu·do·sci·en·tist** *n*

pseu·do·so·phis·ti·ca·tion /sòodō sə fisti káysh'n/ *n* false or pretended sophistication

pseu·do·tu·ber·cu·lo·sis /sòodō too burkyə lṓssiss/ *n* a disease marked by the formation of nodules of inflamed tissue similar to those in tuberculosis, but not caused by the tubercle bacillus

pseu·do·vec·tor /sòodō véktər/ *n* a quantity, e.g., area or torque, that has magnitude and direction but whose component signs are unchanged if the signs of a set of coordinate axes are reversed

psf, **p.s.f.** *abbr* MEASURE pounds per square foot

Psge *abbr* Passage (*used in addresses*)

pshaw /shaw, pshaw/ *interj* used to express disbelief, impatience, or contempt [Late 17C. Natural exclamation]

psi[1] /sī, psī/ *n* the 23rd letter of the Greek alphabet, represented in the English alphabet as "ps." See table at **alphabet** [15C. < Greek *psei*]

psi[2], **p.s.i.** *abbr* MEASURE pounds per square inch

psia, **p.s.i.a.** *abbr* MEASURE pounds per square inch, absolute

psid, **p.s.i.d.** *abbr* MEASURE pounds per square inch, differential

psig, **p.s.i.g.** *abbr* MEASURE pounds per square inch, gauge

psil·o·cin /síllәssin, sīl-/ *n* a hallucinogenic compound produced in the body after eating a specific mushroom. Formula: $C_{12}H_{16}N_2O$. [Mid-20C. < Greek *psilos* "smooth"]

psil·o·cy·bin /sìllə síbin, sīlə-/ *n* a crystalline hallucinogen obtained from a specific mushroom. Formula: $C_{13}HN_2O_3P_2$. [Mid-20C. < Greek *psilos* "smooth" + *kubē* "head"]

psi·lom·e·lane /sī lómmə làyn/ *n* a mixed hydrated manganese oxide mineral occurring in dark-colored rounded masses [Mid-19C. < Greek *psilos* "smooth" + *melas* "black"]

psi par·ti·cle *n* SCI same as **J/psi particle**

psit·ta·cine /sìttə sīn/ *adj* belonging to the parrot family, or relating to, affecting, or resembling parrots or related birds ■ *n* a bird that belongs to the parrot family [Late 19C. < Latin *psittacinus* < *psittacus* "parrot" (see PSITTACOSIS)]

psit·ta·co·sis /sìttə kṓssiss/ *n* a contagious disease of parrots and related birds that can be transmitted to humans, sometimes causing serious lung infection. It is caused by the bacterium *Chlamydia psittaci.* [Late 19C. < Latin *psittacus* < Greek *psittakos* "parrot"]

PSNI *abbr* Police Service of Northern Ireland

pso·as /sṓ əss/ (*plural* **-ai** /-ī/ or **-ae** /-ee/) *n* either of two pairs of muscles that are located in the groin and help to flex the hip joint [Late 17C. < Greek, accusative plural of *psoa* "muscle of the loins"]

pso·cid /sṓssid, sóssid/ (*plural* **-cids** or *same*) *n* a tiny winged insect with reduced veins in the wings and unusual rasping mouthparts. Family: Psocidae. [Late 19C. < modern Latin *Psocus* < Greek *psōkhein* "grind"]

pso·ra·len /sáwrələn/ *n* a chemical that reacts with DNA in the presence of light and can cause mutations. Source: umbelliferous plants such as celery, carrots, parsley. Use: with ultraviolet light in treatment of severe acne and psoriasis. [Mid-20C. < modern Latin *Psoralea* < Greek *psōraleos* "itchy" < *psōra* "itch, mange"]

pso·ri·a·sis /sə rī́ əssiss/ *n* a skin disease usually marked by red scaly patches [Late 17C. Via Latin, "scurvy, mange" < Greek *psōriasis* "itching" < *psōra* "itch, mange"] —**pso·ri·at·ic** /sàwree áttik/ *adj*

P.SS., **p.ss.** *abbr* postscripts

psst /pst/ *interj* used to get the attention of somebody without alerting somebody else [Early 20C. An imitation of the sound]

PST *abbr* **1.** TIME Pacific Standard Time **2.** *Can* FIN provincial sales tax

~~**psuedonym**~~ incorrect spelling of **pseudonym**

psych /sīk/ (**psyched, psych·ing, psychs**) *vt US* (*slang*) **1.** PSYCHOL same as **psych out** (sense 1) **2.** same as **psych up** [Early 20C. Origin ?]

psych out *vt* (*slang*) **1.** INTIMIDATE SOMEBODY to intimidate somebody or undermine the confidence of somebody **2.** PUZZLE SOMETHING OUT to analyze, solve, or understand something such as a problem **3.** GUESS SOMEBODY'S THOUGHT PROCESSES to guess or anticipate correctly the intentions or thoughts of another person

psych up *vr* **psych yourself up** to prepare yourself or somebody else mentally for a task or action (*informal*) ○ *She's been psyching herself up for this interview all week.*

psych. *abbr* **1.** psychological **2.** psychology

psych- *prefix* same as **psycho-** (*used before vowels*)

psy·che /sīkee/ *n* **1.** the human spirit or soul **2.** the human mind as the center of thought and behavior [Mid-17C. Via Latin < Greek *psukhē* "breath, soul, mind" < *psukhein* "breathe"]

Psy·che /sīkee/ *n* in Roman mythology, a beautiful young woman who was loved by Cupid and ultimately made immortal by Jupiter. Cupid visited her secretly at night, forbidding her ever to look at him. When she did, he abandoned her, but they were eventually reunited.

psyched /sīkt/ *adj* extremely excited about and psychologically prepared for something (*slang*)

psy·che·de·li·a /sīkə deélee ə/ *n* the subculture of artifacts, phenomena, writings, or art associated with psychedelic drugs [Mid-20C. Back-formation < PSYCHEDELIC]

psy·che·del·ic /sīkə déllik/ *adj* **1.** RELATING TO HALLUCINOGENIC DRUGS relating to, caused by, or describing drugs that generate hallucinations, atypical psychic states, or states that resemble psychiatric disorders **2.** WILDLY DISTORTED weird, distorted, wildly colorful, or otherwise resembling images or sounds experienced by somebody under the influence of a psychedelic drug ■ *n* DRUG a psychedelic drug [Mid-20C. < Greek *psukhē* "mind" + *dēloun* "reveal, make visible" < *dēlos* "clear"] —**psy·che·del·i·cal·ly** *adv*

psy·chi·at·ric /sīkee áttrik/ *adj* relating to psychiatry or its patients —**psy·chi·at·ri·cal·ly** *adv*

psy·chi·at·ric hos·pi·tal *n* a hospital dedicated to the treatment, care, and protection of people with serious psychiatric disorders who are judged to be unfit or unsafe to live unsupervised and untreated in society

psy·chi·a·trist /si kī́ ətrist, sī-/ *n* a doctor trained in the treatment of people with psychiatric disorders

psy·chi·a·try /si kī́ ətree, sī-/ *n* a medical specialty concerned with the diagnosis and treatment of disorders that have primarily mental or behavioral symptoms and with the care of people having such disorders [Mid-19C. < French *psychiatrie* < Greek *psukhē* "mind" + *iatreia* "cure"]

psy·chic /sīkik/ *adj* **1.** OF HUMAN MIND relating to the human mind **2.** OUTSIDE SCIENTIFIC KNOWLEDGE outside the sphere of scientific knowledge **3.** SUPPOSEDLY SENSITIVE TO SUPERNATURAL FORCES claiming, or believed to have, extraordinary sensitivity to nonphysical or supernatural forces **4.** CLAIRVOYANT able, or considered able, to perceive people's unexpressed thoughts or foresee the future (*informal*) ○ *I knew you were going to say that! I must be psychic.* ■ *n* SOMEBODY SUPPOSEDLY SENSITIVE TO SUPERNATURAL somebody who is, or is believed to be, sensitive to nonphysical or supernatural forces [Late 18C. < Greek *psukhikos* "of the soul or spirit" < *psukhē* (see PSYCHE)] —**psy·chi·cal** *adj* —**psy·chi·cal·ly** *adv*

psy·cho /sīkō/ (*slang insult*) *n* (*plural* **-chos**) an offensive term for somebody who has a psychiatric or personality disorder ■ *adj* an offensive term for behaving in an uncontrolled and unpredictable way [Mid-20C. Shortening of PSYCHOPATH]

CULTURAL NOTE ***Psycho***, a movie (1960) by British director Alfred Hitchcock. A disturbing horror film with a rich vein of black comedy, it tells the story of a woman who flees her home after stealing money from her boss. Stopping at a motel run by the sinister Norman Bates and his apparently domineering mother, she is brutally murdered while taking a shower. Members of her family subsequently investigate the death. As a result of the impact of the movie, the term *Bates Motel* came to mean any rundown rooming house, motel, or structure redolent of oppressive fear and underlying horror.

psycho- *prefix* **1.** mind, mental ○ *psychoactive* **2.** psychology, psychological ○ *psychobabble* [< Greek *psukhē* (see PSYCHE)]

psy·cho·a·cous·tics /sīkō ə kóostiks/ *n* the scientific study of the psychological and physiological principles of sound perception (*takes a singular verb*)

psy·cho·ac·tive /sīkō áktiv/ *adj* describes drugs or medication having a significant effect on mood or behavior

psychoanal. *abbr* PSYCHOANAL psychoanalysis

psy·cho·an·a·lyse *vt* MED UK spelling of **psychoanalyze**

psy·cho·a·nal·y·sis /sīkō ə nállәssiss/ *n* **1.** a psychological theory and therapeutic method developed by Sigmund Freud, based on the ideas that mental life functions on both conscious and unconscious levels and that childhood events have a powerful psychological influence throughout life **2.** treatment by psychoanalysis, interpreting material presented by a patient in order to bring the processes of the unconscious into conscious awareness —**psy·cho·an·a·lyst** /sīkō ánn'list/ *n* —**psy·cho·an·a·lyt·ic** /sīkō anə líttik/ *adj* —**psy·cho·an·a·lyt·i·cal** *adj* —**psy·cho·an·a·lyt·i·cal·ly** *adv*

psy·cho·an·a·lyze /sīkō ánnə līz/ (**-lyzed, -lyz·ing, -lyz·es**) *vt* to treat a patient by applying the methods of psychoanalysis in a psychotherapeutic setting —**psy·cho·an·a·lyz·er** *n*

psy·cho·bab·ble /sīkō bàbb'l/ *n* psychological jargon used inaccurately to talk about personal problems

psy·cho·bi·og·ra·phy /sīkō bī óggrəfee/ (*plural* **-phies**) *n* a biography that focuses on the psychological profile of the subject

psy·cho·bi·ol·o·gy /sīkō bī óllәjee/ *n* the study of the biological bases of behavior —**psy·cho·bi·o·log·i·cal** /-bī ə lójjik'l/ *adj* —**psy·cho·bi·o·log·i·cal·ly** *adv* —**psy·cho·bi·ol·o·gist** *n*

psy·cho·chem·i·cal /sīkō kémmik'l/ *n* a drug that affects mood or behavior ■ *adj* relating to or acting like a psychoactive drug

~~**psychodelic**~~ incorrect spelling of **psychedelic**

psy·cho·dra·ma /sīkə draámə, -drámmə/ *n* a form of psychotherapy in which patients are required to perform roles in dramas illustrating their problems before an audience of other patients —**psy·cho·dra·mat·ic** /-drə máttik/ *adj*

psy·cho·dy·nam·ics /sīkō dī námmiks/ *n* **1.** the interaction of the emotional and motivational forces that affect behavior and mental states, especially on a subconscious level (*takes a singular or plural verb*) **2.** the study of the emotional and motivational forces that affect behavior and mental states (*takes a sin-*

gular verb) —**psy·cho·dy·nam·ic** *adj* —**psy·cho·dy·nam·i·cal·ly** *adv*

psy·cho·gen·e·sis /sīkō jénnəssiss/ *n* the psychological rather than physical cause of a disorder —**psy·cho·ge·net·ic** /-jə néttik/ *adj* —**psy·cho·ge·net·i·cal·ly** *adv*

psy·cho·gen·ic /sīkō jénnik/ *adj* originating in mental or emotional rather than in physiological processes —**psy·cho·gen·i·cal·ly** *adv*

psy·cho·his·to·ry /sīkō hìstəree, -hìstree, sīkō hístəree, -hístree/ (*plural* **-ries**) *n* the psychological analysis of somebody's life or of historical events —**psy·cho·his·tor·i·an** /sīkō hi stáwree ən/ *n* —**psy·cho·his·tor·i·cal** /sīkō hi stáwrik'l/ *adj*

psy·cho·ki·ne·sis /sīkō ki néessiss, -kī-/ *n* the supposed ability to use mental powers to make objects move or to otherwise affect them —**psy·cho·ki·net·ic** /-ki néttik, -kī-/ *adj*

psychol. *abbr* PSYCHOL **1.** psychological **2.** psychologist **3.** psychology

psy·cho·lin·guis·tics /sīkō ling gwístiks/ *n* the study of language acquisition and use in relation to the psychological factors controlling its use and recognition (*takes a singular verb*) —**psy·cho·lin·guist** /sīkō líng gwist/ *n* —**psy·cho·lin·guis·tic** /-ling gwístik/ *adj*

psy·cho·log·i·cal /sīkə lójjik'l/ *adj* **1. OF PSYCHOLOGY** relating to psychology **2. OF HUMAN MIND** relating to the mind or mental processes **3. AFFECTING HUMAN MIND** affecting or intended to affect the mind or mental processes **4. EXISTING ONLY IN HUMAN MIND** existing only in the mind, without having a physical basis ○ *His health problem is psychological.* —**psy·cho·log·i·cal·ly** *adv*

psy·cho·log·i·cal de·pend·ence *n* a strong desire for something without being physically addicted to it

psy·cho·log·i·cal mo·ment *n* the time at which the mental state of a person or group of people is most receptive or appropriate

psy·cho·log·i·cal pro·fil·ing *n* the analysis of somebody's behavior and psychological characteristics, used especially to identify and target a potential terrorist or a suspect in a criminal investigation

psy·cho·log·i·cal war·fare *n* **1.** tactics that use propaganda to try to demoralize an enemy in war, usually including the civilian population **2.** the use of psychological tactics to disconcert and disadvantage an opponent in an everyday or a business context, e.g., by causing the opponent to feel fear or anxiety

psy·chol·o·gism /sī kóllə jìzzəm/ *n* a belief in or emphasis on the importance of psychology in other fields such as history or philosophy —**psy·chol·o·gis·tic** /sī kòllə jístik/ *adj*

psy·chol·o·gist /sī kólləjist/ *n* **1.** a professional who studies behavior and experience, and who is licensed to provide therapeutic services or to work in an academic setting **2.** a student of psychology, especially as a main subject at college or university

psy·chol·o·gize /sī kóllə jīz/ (**-gized, -giz·ing, -giz·es**) *v* **1.** *vt* to interpret behavior in psychological terms or concepts **2.** *vi* to think, analyze, or reason psychologically

psy·chol·o·gy /sī kólləjee/ (*plural* **-gies**) *n* **1. STUDY OF HUMAN MIND** the scientific study of the human mind and mental states, and of human and animal behavior **2. CHARACTERISTIC MENTAL MAKEUP** the characteristic temperament and associated behavior of a person or group, or that exhibited by those engaged in an activity **3. SUBTLE MANIPULATIVE BEHAVIOR** subtle clever actions and words used to influence a person or group

psy·cho·met·rics /sīkə méttriks/ *n* a branch of psychology dealing with the measurement of mental traits, capacities, and processes (*takes a singular verb*) —**psy·cho·met·ric** /sīkə méttrik/ *adj* —**psy·cho·met·ri·cal** *adj* —**psy·cho·met·ri·cal·ly** *adv* —**psy·chom·e·tri·cian** /sī kòmmə trísh'n/ *n*

psy·chom·e·try /sī kómmətree/ *n* **1.** PSYCHOL same as **psychometrics 2.** the alleged ability to obtain information about a person or event by touching an object related to that person or event —**psy·chom·e·trist** *n*

psy·cho·mo·tor /sīkə mṓtər/ *adj* relating to bodily movement triggered by mental activity, especially voluntary muscle action

psy·cho·neu·ro·im·mu·nol·o·gy /sīkō noorō ìmmyə nólləjee/ *n* a branch of medicine concerned with how emotions affect the immune system

psy·cho·neu·ro·sis /sīkō noo rṓssiss/ (*plural* **-ros·es** /-rō sēez/) *n* PSYCHIAT same as **neurosis** —**psy·cho·neu·rot·ic** /-róttik/ *adj*

psy·cho·path /sīkə pàth/ *n* **1.** somebody affected with a personality disorder marked by aggressive, violent, antisocial thought and behavior and a lack of remorse or empathy (*technical*) **2.** an offensive term for somebody who is regarded as highly antisocial, aggressive, and lacking in empathy (*insult*) —**psy·cho·path·ic** /sīkə páthik/ *adj* —**psy·cho·path·i·cal·ly** *adv*

psy·cho·pa·thol·o·gy /sīkō pə thólləjee/ *n* the study of the causes and development of psychiatric disorders —**psy·cho·path·o·log·i·cal** /-pàthə lójjik'l/ *adj* —**psy·cho·pa·thol·o·gist** *n*

psy·chop·a·thy /sī kóppəthee/ *n* a severe personality disorder marked by antisocial thought and behavior (*not used technically*)

psy·cho·phar·ma·col·o·gy /sīkō faarmə kólləjee/ *n* the scientific study of the effects of drugs on thought and behavior —**psy·cho·phar·ma·co·log·i·cal** /-faarməkə lójjik'l/ *adj* —**psy·cho·phar·ma·col·o·gist** *n*

psy·cho·phys·ics /sīkō fízziks/ *n* a branch of psychology dealing with the effects of physical stimuli on sensory perceptions and mental states (*takes a singular verb*) —**psy·cho·phys·i·cal** *adj*

psy·cho·phys·i·ol·o·gy /sīkō fízzee ólləjee/ *n* PSYCHOL same as **physiological psychology**

psy·cho·ses plural of **psychosis**

psy·cho·sex·u·al /sīkō sékshoo əl/ *adj* relating to the mental and emotional aspects of sexuality and sexual development —**psy·cho·sex·u·al·i·ty** /-sékshoo állətee/ *n* —**psy·cho·sex·u·al·ly** *adv*

psy·cho·sis /sī kṓssiss/ (*plural* **-cho·ses** /-kṓ sēez/) *n* a psychiatric disorder such as schizophrenia or mania that is marked by delusions, hallucinations, incoherence, and distorted perceptions of reality

psy·cho·so·cial /sīkō sṓsh'l/ *adj* relating to both the psychological and the social aspects of something, or relating to something that has both of these aspects

psy·cho·so·mat·ic /sīkə sə máttik/ *adj* **1.** describes a physical illness that is caused by mental factors such as stress, or the effects related to such illnesses **2.** involving both the mind and body —**psy·cho·so·mat·i·cal·ly** *adv*

psy·cho·sur·ger·y /sīkō súrjəree/ (*plural* **-ies**) *n* surgery now performed only in rare cases to relieve severe psychotic disorder or to prevent some forms of epileptic seizure

psy·cho·syn·the·sis /sīkō sínthəssiss/ *n* **1.** a psychotherapeutic movement, opposed to psychoanalysis, that attempts to restore useful inhibitions and control **2.** a holistic form of psychotherapy involving clients in an exploration of the emotional, intellectual, physical, and spiritual aspects of the self

psy·cho·ther·a·py /sīkō thérrəpee/ *n* the treatment of mental disorders by psychological methods —**psy·cho·ther·a·peu·tic** /-thèrrə pyṓotik/ *adj* —**psy·cho·ther·a·peu·ti·cal·ly** *adv* —**psy·cho·ther·a·pist** *n*

psy·cho·thrill·er /sīkō thrìllər/ *n* an exciting book or film in which tension is generated by the psychological pressures on the characters rather than by action

psy·chot·ic /sī kóttik/ *adj* relating to, characteristic of, or affected by psychosis [Late 19C. < PSYCHOSIS] —**psy·cho·ti·cal·ly** *adv*

psy·chot·o·mi·met·ic /sī kòttō mi méttik/ *adj* describes a drug or other factor that produces a condition resembling psychosis ■ *n* a drug or other factor with a psychotomimetic effect [Mid-20C. < PSYCHOSIS + MIMETIC, after *psychotic*]

psy·cho·tro·pic /sīkə trṓpik, -tróppik/ *adj* describes drugs that are capable of affecting the mind, e.g., those used to treat psychiatric disorders —**psy·cho·tro·pic** *n*

psychro- *prefix* cold ○ *psychrophilic* [< Greek *psukhros*]

psy·chrom·e·ter /sī krómmətər/ *n* an instrument consisting of two thermometers, used to measure atmospheric humidity. The bulb of one thermometer is kept moist and the effect of evaporative cooling on it is compared to the other, which is kept dry.

psy·chro·phil·ic /sīkrō fíllik/ *adj* thriving at low temperatures ○ *psychrophilic bacteria*

~~**psycology**~~ incorrect spelling of **psychology**

psyl·li·um /síllee əm/ *n* **1.** an annual plant of the plantain family with edible seeds. Use: dietary source of fiber, mild laxative. Native to: Europe, Asia. Latin name: *Plantago psyllium.* **2.** the seeds of psyllium. Use: mild laxative, dietary source of fiber. [Mid-16C. Via Latin < Greek *psullion* "little flea" < *psulla* "flea"; because the seeds resemble fleas]

pt *abbr* ONLINE Portugal (*used in Internet addresses*) See table at **domain name**

Pt *symbol* CHEM ELEM platinum

PT *abbr* **1.** TIME Pacific Time **2.** part-time

pt. *abbr* **1.** part **2.** FIN payment **3.** MEASURE pint **4.** point **5.** port **6.** GRAM preterit *or* preterite

Pt. *abbr* (*used in place names*) **1.** Point **2.** Port

p.t. *abbr* **1.** part-time **2.** GRAM past tense **3.** pro tem

PTA, P.T.A. *abbr* EDUC Parent-Teacher Association

pta., pta *symbol* MONEY, HIST peseta

ptarmigan

ptar·mi·gan /taármigən/ (*plural same or* **-gans**) *n* a wild bird of the grouse family, that has feet covered with feathers and white plumage in the winter. Native to: mountainous regions. Genus: *Lagopus.* [Late 16C. Alteration (influenced by Greek *pt-* as in *pteron* "wing") of Gaelic *tarmachan*, literally "little ptarmigan" < *tarmach* "ptarmigan"]

PT boat *n* a highly maneuverable US Navy vessel carrying light armament, 60 to 100 feet/18 to 31 meters in length, used especially in World War II to torpedo enemy shipping

PTC *abbr* CHEM phenylthiocarbamide

pter·an·o·don /tə ránnə dòn/ *n* an extinct toothless flying reptile with a bony crest. Genus: *Pteranodon.* [Late 19C. < modern Latin < Greek *pteron* "wing"]

pter·i·dol·o·gy /tèrrə dólləjee/ *n* the branch of botany that is concerned with the study of ferns [Mid-19C. < Greek *pterid-* "fern"] —**pter·i·do·log·i·cal** /tèrrədə lójjik'l/ *adj* —**pter·i·dol·o·gist** *n*

pte·rid·o·phyte /tə ríddə fīt, térrədə-/ *n* a plant that has no flowers or seeds and reproduces by means of spores. Ferns and some mosses are pteridophytes. Division: *Pteridophyta.* [Late 19C. < Greek *pterid-* "fern"] —**pte·rid·o·phyt·ic** /tə rìddə fíttik, tèrrədə-/ *adj* —**pter·i·doph·y·tous** /tèrrə dóffətəss/ *adj*

pte·rid·o·sperm /tə ríddə spùrm, térrədə-/ *n* an extinct plant that bore seeds and resembled a fern [Early 20C. < Greek *pterid-* "fern"]

pter·o·dac·tyl /tèrrə dákt'l/ *n* an extinct flying reptile (**pterosaur**) of the Jurassic and Cretaceous periods with membranous wings and a rudimentary tail and beak. Genus: *Pterodactylus.* [Early 19C. < modern Latin *Pterodactylus* < Greek *pteron* "wing" + *daktulos* "finger"]

pter·o·pod /térrə pòd/ *n* a ocean gastropod mollusk that has a foot with wing-shaped lobes that are used as swimming organs. Order: Thecosomata or Gymnosomata. [Mid-19C. < modern Latin *Pteropoda* < Greek *pteron* "wing" + modern Latin *-poda* "foot"]

pter·o·saur /térrə sàwr/ *n* an extinct flying reptile of the Triassic, Jurassic, and Cretaceous periods that had membranous wings supported by an elongated fourth digit. Order: Pterosauria. [Mid-19C. < modern Latin *Pterosauria* < Greek *pteron* "wing" + *sauros* "lizard"]

-pterous *suffix* having wings of a particular kind or number ○ *orthopterous* ○ *dipterous* [< Greek *pteron* "wing, feather" < Indo-European, "to fly"]

pter·o·yl·glu·tam·ic ac·id /tèrrō il gloo tàmmik-/ *n* CHEM same as **folic acid** (*technical*) [< Greek *pteron* "wing" (referring to compounds occurring in insect wings) + ACYL]

pte·ryg·i·um /tə ríjjee əm/ (*plural* **-i·ums** or **-i·a** /-ee ə/) *n* a triangular patch of tissue that obstructs vision by growing over usually the inner side of the eye. It results from degeneration of the cornea and is associated with prolonged exposure to sun and wind. [Mid-17C. Via modern Latin < Greek *pterugion* "little wing" < *pterux* "wing"]

pter·y·goid proc·ess /tèrrə goyd-/ *n* either of two bony plates extending downward from the sphenoid bone of the skull [< modern Latin *pterygoides* "like a wing" < Greek *pterux* "wing"]

pter·y·la /térrələ/ (*plural* **-lae** /-lèe, -lī/) *n* a defined area on the skin of a bird from which feathers grow [Mid-19C. < modern Latin < Greek *pteron* "feather" + *hulē* "forest"]

PTFE *abbr* CHEM polytetrafluoroethylene

ptg. *abbr* printing

PTH *abbr* BIOCHEM parathyroid hormone

PTO *abbr* **1.** Parent-Teacher Organization **2.** Patent and Trademark Office

p.t.o. *abbr* please turn over

Ptol·e·mae·us /tòllə máy əss/ large walled plain on the Moon that is noticeably hexagonal in shape and has a highly cratered floor. Located northeast of Mare Imbrium, it is approximately 85 mi./140 km across.

Ptol·e·ma·ic /tòllə máy ik/ *adj* **1.** relating to the geographer and astronomer Ptolemy or to his system of planetary motion **2.** relating to the dynasty of pharaohs of ancient Egypt founded by Ptolemy I, or to Egypt during their rule

Ptol·e·ma·ic sys·tem *n* a theory of planetary motion developed by Ptolemy that held that Earth was at the center of the universe with the Sun, Moon, and planets revolving around it. The most influential of the geocentric theories, it dominated thinking for 14 centuries until the Copernican system was accepted.

Ptol·e·ma·ist /tòllə máy ist/ *n* a believer in the Ptolemaic system of planetary motion

Ptol·e·my /tólləmee/ (A.D. 100?–170?) Greek astronomer, mathematician, and geographer. His Earth-centered model of the universe prevailed until the 16th century. His writings are collected in the *Almagest*. Full name **Ptolemaeus, Claudius**

Ptol·e·my I (367?–283? B.C.) **king of Egypt.** A Macedonian by birth and general in Alexander the Great's army, he became king of Egypt in 305 B.C., thereby founding the Ptolemaic dynasty. Known as **Ptolemy Soter**

Ptol·e·my XV (47 B.C.–30 BC) **king of Egypt** He was the son of Cleopatra and the last of the Ptolemaic dynasty. His reign (44–30 B.C.) ended when he was killed by Roman forces after the defeat of his mother and Mark Antony. Known as **Caesarion**

pto·maine /tō màyn, tō máyn/ *n* one of a foul-smelling group of organic bases containing nitrogen. Source: bacteria during the decay of proteins. [Late 19C. Via French < Italian *ptomaina* < Greek *ptōma* "fallen body, corpse" < *piptein* "to fall"]

pto·maine poi·son·ing *n* food poisoning caused by bacteria, but formerly believed to be caused by ptomaines

pto·sis /tṓssiss/ (*plural* **pto·ses** /tṓ sèez/) *n* a drooping of the upper eyelid, resulting from muscle weakness or an inability to move muscles [Mid-18C. < Greek *ptōsis* "a falling" < *piptein* "to fall"]

pts. *abbr* **1.** parts **2.** FIN payments **3.** MEASURE pints **4.** points **5.** ports

PTSD *abbr* PSYCHOL post-traumatic stress disorder

PTV *abbr* MEDIA **1.** pay television **2.** public television

Pty. *abbr* *UK* BUSINESS proprietary (*used in "Pty. Ltd." to indicate a private limited company*)

pty·a·lin /tī əlin/ *n* an enzyme in saliva that catalyzes the digestion of starches [Mid-19C. < Greek *ptualon* "saliva"]

pty·a·lism /tī ə lìzzəm/ *n* excessive production of saliva [Late 17C. < Greek *ptualismos* "salivation" < *ptualon* "saliva" < *ptuein* "to spit"]

Pu *symbol* CHEM ELEM plutonium

pub /pub/ *n* *UK* a bar that may also serve food [Mid-19C. Shortening of PUBLIC HOUSE]

pub. *abbr* **1.** public **2.** publication **3.** published **4.** publisher **5.** publishing

pub-crawl (*informal*) *n* a tour in which somebody visits and drinks at several bars in succession ■ *vi* to go drinking at several bars in succession

pu·ber·ty /pyóobərtee/ *n* the stage in human physiological development when somebody becomes capable of sexual reproduction. It is marked by genital maturation, development of secondary sex characteristics, and, in girls, the first occurrence of menstruation. [14C. Directly or via French < Latin *pubertas* < *pubes* "adult"] —**pu·ber·tal** *adj*

pu·bes[1] *n* /pyóo bèez/ (*plural same*) the part of the abdomen immediately above the external genitalia that is covered with hair from puberty onward (*takes a singular verb*) ■ *npl* /pyoobz/ the hair growing on the lower abdomen from puberty onward (*takes a plural verb*) [Late 16C. < Latin *pubes* "pubic hair, genital region"]

pu·bes[2] ANAT plural of **pubis**

pu·bes·cent /pyoo béss'nt/ *adj* **1.** reaching or having attained puberty **2.** covered with down or fine hair [Mid-17C. Directly or via French < Latin *pubescent-*, present participle of *pubescere* "reach puberty" < *pubes* "adult"] —**pu·bes·cence** *n*

pu·bic /pyóobik/ *adj* relating to or located near or on the pubes or pubis ○ *pubic hair*

pu·bic bone *n* ANAT same as **pubis**

pu·bic louse *n* INSECTS same as **crab**[1] (sense 4)

pu·bis /pyóobiss/ (*plural* **pu·bes** /pyóo bèez/) *n* the bone that forms the lower front section of the hipbone in humans and is one of a pair joined at the front of the pelvis. Although a separate bone in infants, it later fuses with the ilium and the ischium to form the hipbone. [Late 16C. Shortening of Latin *os pubis* "bone of the genital region"]

publ. *abbr* **1.** publication **2.** published **3.** publisher

pub·lic /púbblik/ *adj* **1. CONCERNING ALL THE PEOPLE** relating to or concerning the people at large or all members of a community ○ *public support for the policy* **2. FOR COMMUNITY USE** provided for the use of a community ○ *public library* **3. OPEN TO ALL** open to everyone, and typically frequented by large numbers of people ○ *public spaces* **4. WELL KNOWN** known to large numbers of the community through being involved in activities such as politics or entertainment ○ *maintained a very public persona* **5. DONE OPENLY** made, done, or happening openly, for all to see ○ *a public debate* **6. KNOWN BY ALL MEMBERS OF COMMUNITY** known or potentially known by all members of a community ○ *make the information public* ○ *a public disgrace* **7. OF STATE** relating to or involving the state and governmental agencies rather than private corporations or industry ○ *working in the public sector* **8. BELONGING TO COMMUNITY** belonging to the community as a whole and administered through its representatives in government ○ *public land* **9. HAVING OPENLY PURCHASABLE SHARES** describes companies whose stock is available, or is made available, for anyone to buy ■ *n* **1. EVERYONE** the community as a whole ○ *The government has been misleading the public.* **2. PARTICULAR PART OF COMMUNITY** a section of the community, united by a common interest ○ *the reading public* **3. FANS OR FOLLOWERS** the fans or followers of a performer or author ○ *went to meet her adoring public* [15C. Directly or via French < Latin *publicus*, alteration of *poplicus* < *populus* "people"] —**pub·lic·ness** *n*

pub·lic ac·cess *n* in US law, the availability of cable broadcasting facilities for the transmission of programs produced by members of the public (*hyphenated when used before a noun*)

pub·lic-ad·dress sys·tem *n* full form of **PA**[2]

pub·lic af·fairs *npl* issues that affect people generally, or issues arising from the relationship of the public to an organization such as a government body or a financial institution (*takes a plural verb*) ■ *n* the study of issues involving the interrelationships between the public and major institutions such as government (*takes a singular verb*)

~~**publically**~~ incorrect spelling of **publicly**

pub·li·can /púbblikən/ *n* **1.** *UK* the owner or manager of a pub **2.** in ancient Rome, a collector of taxes [12C. Via French < Latin *publicanus* < *publicus* (see PUBLIC)]

pub·lic as·sis·tance *n* aid consisting of money, food, food stamps, or other benefits, given by government agencies to people on low incomes, dependent children, and others in financial distress

pub·li·ca·tion /pùbbli káysh'n/ *n* **1. ACT OF PUBLISHING** the act of making printed material, especially books, available for sale to the public (*often used before a noun*) **2. PUBLISHED ITEM** an item that has been published, especially in printed form **3. PUBLIC COMMUNICATION OF SOMETHING** the communication of information to the public [14C. Via French < Latin *publication-* < *publicare* (see PUBLISH)]

pub·lic com·pa·ny *n* *UK* same as **public corporation**

pub·lic cor·po·ra·tion *n* a company whose shares can be bought and sold on the stock market

pub·lic debt *n* ECON same as **national debt**

pub·lic de·fend·er *n* an attorney who represents defendants who cannot afford their own lawyers

pub·lic do·main *n* **1.** *US* **GOVERNMENT LAND** land that is owned and administered by a government **2. NOT IN COPYRIGHT** the condition of not being protected by patent or copyright and so freely available for use ○ *public domain software* **3. REVEALED CONDITION** the condition of being openly known or revealed as opposed to being kept a secret ○ *The information is now in the public domain.*

pub·lic en·e·my *n* a threat to the public, especially a violent criminal

pub·lic eye *n* intense scrutiny by the public ○ *The lens of the public eye is focused on the sensational trial.* ◇ **in the public eye** regularly receiving attention from the media

pub·lic fig·ure *n* somebody who is widely known to the public and whose lifestyle is the subject of great scrutiny

pub·lic health *n* the general health of a community and the practice and study of ways to preserve and improve it. Public health includes health education, sanitation, control of diseases, and regulation of pollution.

pub·lic house *n* **1.** an inn, tavern, or small hotel (*archaic*) **2.** *UK* LEISURE same as **pub** (*formal*)

pub·lic hous·ing *n* housing managed by the government and provided at a relatively low rent as a form of public assistance

pub·lic in·tel·lec·tual *n* an expert within a particular field whose opinions and published works are well known, and who frequently appears in the media to comment on newsworthy issues

pub·lic in·ter·est *n* **1.** the general benefit of the public ○ *a law that would be contrary to the public interest* **2.** the general level of interest shown by people toward an issue or event ○ *Public interest in the earnings of corporate executives is at an all-time high.*

pub·li·cist /púbblissist/ *n* a promoter who seeks to obtain media publicity for a client [Late 18C. < French *publiciste* < Latin *publicus* (see PUBLIC), after *canoniste* "canon lawyer"]

pub·lic·i·ty /pu blíssətee/ *n* **1. ACTIVITY STIMULATING PUBLIC INTEREST** activity, especially advertising and the dissemination of information, designed to increase public interest in or awareness of something or somebody (*often used before a noun*) ○ *The event was dismissed as a mere publicity stunt.* **2. INTEREST CREATED BY PUBLICITY** public or media interest gained as a result of publicizing something ○ *We got more publicity from that one newspaper photograph than from a hundred advertisements.* **3. ATTENTION-GETTING INFORMATION** information, material, or other means used to publicize something or somebody ○ *The lawsuit that turned out to be great publicity.* **4. CONDITION OF BEING PUBLIC** the condition of being known or available to the public (*formal*) [Late 18C. < French *publicité* < *public* < Latin *publicus* (see PUBLIC)]

pub·li·cize /púbbli sīz/ (**-cized, -ciz·ing, -ciz·es**) *vt* to make something generally known or known to a group, typically by advertising

pub·lic key cryp·to·gra·phy *n* in computing, an encryption method that uses two mathematically related keys for encrypting and decrypting a message

pub·lic key en·cryp·tion *n* in computing, a message encryption technique in which encoding is done using a generally available public key but decoding is done using a private key available only to the receiver

pub·lic law *n* **1.** the branch of law that deals with a state and its relationships with its citizens **2.** a law that applies to the public

pub·lic-li·a·bil·i·ty in·sur·ance *n* insurance that compensates people if they experience injury or damage resulting from lack of reasonable care by an insured business or organization

pub·lic life *n* **1.** employment as an appointed or elected official accountable to the public **2.** *UK* the part of somebody's life that is known or is of interest to the public and the media

pub·lic lim·it·ed com·pa·ny *n* a company in the United Kingdom whose shares can be bought and sold on the stock market and whose stockholders are subject to restricted liability for any debts or losses

pub·lic·ly /púbbliklee/ *adv* **1.** in a public or open manner **2.** by or in the name of the public

pub·lic nui·sance *n* **1.** somebody regarded as irritating or offensive (*insult*) **2.** an action or a thing that harms the community in general

pub·lic o·pin·ion *n* the general attitude or feeling of the public concerning an issue, especially when this has an effect on political decision-making

pub·lic pros·e·cu·tor *n* a government law official prosecuting criminal offenses on behalf of the community or the state

pub·lic re·la·tions *n* (*takes a singular or plural verb*) **1. PROMOTION OF FAVORABLE IMAGE** the practice or profession of establishing, maintaining, or improving a favorable relationship between an institution or person and the public **2. PUBLIC IMAGE** the relationship between an institution or person and the public, with respect to whether that institution or person is seen in a positive or negative light ○ *The project was a public relations disaster.* **3. DEPARTMENT MANAGING PUBLIC RELATIONS** the department in an organization that is responsible for public relations

pub·lic room *n US* a room into which the public is admitted without discrimination, e.g., the lobby in a hotel

pub·lic sale *n* an auction of goods or property

pub·lic school *n* **1.** a state-funded elementary or secondary school providing education free for children in kindergarten through the twelfth grade **2.** in England and Wales, an independent fee-charging secondary school, typically a single-sex boarding school

pub·lic sec·tor *n* the portion of a nation's affairs, especially economic affairs, that is controlled by government agencies

pub·lic ser·vant *n* an appointed or elected holder of a government position or office

pub·lic ser·vice *n* **1. GOVERNMENT EMPLOYMENT** government employment, especially within the civil service **2. PROVISION OF ESSENTIAL SERVICES** the business or activity of providing the public with essential goods or services such as electric power **3. SERVICE BENEFITING GENERAL PUBLIC** a service that is run for the benefit of the general public, e.g., the utilities, the emergency services, and public transportation

pub·lic-ser·vice cor·po·ra·tion *n US* UTIL same as **public utility**

pub·lic speak·ing *n* the skill, practice, or process of making speeches to large groups of people —**pub·lic speak·er** *n*

pub·lic spend·ing *n* the spending of money by government and governmental bodies

pub·lic-spir·it·ed *adj* motivated by or showing genuine concern for others in the community

pub·lic tel·e·vi·sion *n* noncommercial television that is funded by the government, viewers, and corporate sponsorship

pub·lic trans·por·ta·tion *n* a network of passenger vehicles for use by the public running on set routes, usually at set times and charging set fares

pub·lic trus·tee *n Can* an official who manages the estates of those who are deemed not mentally competent in law or those who die without wills but have minor heirs

pub·lic u·til·i·ty *n* a government-regulated company that provides an essential public service such as water, gas, or electricity ■ **pub·lic u·til·i·ties** *npl US* the traded shares of a public utility company

pub·lic works *npl* civil-engineering projects that are government owned or financed, and undertaken specifically for the benefit of the public

pub·lish /púbblish/ (**-lished, -lish·ing, -lish·es**) *v* **1.** *vti* **PREPARE AND PRODUCE TEXT OR SOFTWARE** to prepare and produce material in printed or electronic form for distribution and, usually, sale **2.** *vt* **DISTRIBUTE WORK OF AUTHOR** to make the work of a particular author available in printed or other form **3.** *vt* **MAKE SOMETHING PUBLIC KNOWLEDGE** to announce something publicly [14C. < Old French *publiss-*, stem of *publier* < Latin *publicare* "make public" < *publicus* (see PUBLIC)] —**pub·lish·a·ble** *adj*

pub·lish·er /púbblishər/ *n* **1.** a company or person that publishes products such as books, journals, or software **2.** the owner or representative of the owner of a newspaper, periodical, or publishing house

pub·lish·ing /púbblishing/ *n* the trade, profession, or activity of preparing and producing material in printed or electronic form for distribution to the public

pub·lish·ing house *n* an established publishing company that prepares and produces material in printed or electronic form for distribution and, usually, sale

PUC *abbr* Public Utilities Commission

Puc·ci·ni /poo cheénee/, **Giacomo** (1858–1924) Italian composer. His lyrical theatrical operas include *La Bohème* (1896), *Tosca* (1900), *Madame Butterfly* (1904), and *Turandot* (1926), left uncompleted at his death.

puc·coon /pə kóon/ (*plural* **-coons** or *same*) *n* **1.** a plant whose roots yield a reddish dye, e.g., gromwell or bloodroot. Native to: North America. Latin name: *Lithospermum canescens* or *Sanguinaria canadensis.* **2.** a dye made from puccoon [Early 17C. < Virginia Algonquian *poughkone*]

puce /pyooss/ *adj* of a brilliant purplish red color [Late 18C. Via French, "flea" (in *couleur puce* "flea-colored") < Latin *pulex*] —**puce** *n*

Pu·celle /poo sél/, **Jean** (1300–55) French manuscript illuminator. His use of perspective in *Belleville Breviary* (1325) shows the influence of the beginnings of the Italian Renaissance.

puck /puk/ *n* **1. DISK IN HOCKEY** a small disk of hard rubber that the players hit in hockey **2. STROKE AT BALL** in the Irish sport of hurling, a player's stroke at the ball ■ *vt* (**pucked, puck·ing, pucks**) **STRIKE BALL** in the Irish sport of hurling, to strike the ball [Late 19C. Origin ?]

Puck *n* **1.** *also* **puck** in English folklore, a mischievous or malevolent spirit **2.** a small natural satellite of Uranus, discovered in 1985 by the Voyager 2 planetary probe. It is approximately 154 km (96 mi.) in diameter. [Old English *pūca*, origin ?]

puck·a *adj* another spelling of **pukka**

puck·er /púkər/ *vti* (**-ered, -er·ing, -ers**) to gather something such as cloth or the skin around the lips, or be gathered, in such a way that wrinkles or small creases are formed ■ *n* a small wrinkle, fold, or crease [Late 16C. Probably < POCKET]

puck·ish /púkish/ *adj* mischievous or naughty in a playful way [Late 19C. < PUCK] —**puck·ish·ly** *adv* —**puck·ish·ness** *n*

PUD *abbr* pickup and delivery

pud·ding /pŏŏdding/ *n* **1.** a sweet cooked dessert with a smooth creamy texture, typically consisting of flour, milk, eggs, and flavoring (*often used in combination*) **2.** *UK* the dessert course of a meal [13C. Via French *boudin* "black pudding" < Latin *botellus* "sausage"]

pud·ding stone *n* a conglomerate rock in which the pebbles have a different color and texture from the material binding them together (**matrix**)

pud·dle /púdd'l/ *n* **1. SHALLOW POOL OF WATER** a shallow pool of water, e.g., one formed by rainwater in a hollow on a road **2. POOL OF LIQUID** a small pool of liquid **3.** CIV ENG **WATERPROOF LINING MATERIAL** nonporous material made from thoroughly mixed wet clay and sand and used as a waterproof lining, e.g., in constructing a canal ■ *v* (**-dled, -dling, -dles**) **1.** *vi* **SPLASH ABOUT IN SHALLOW WATER** to wade, dabble, or splash in shallow water or puddles **2.** *vt* CIV ENG **WATERPROOF SOMETHING WITH PUDDLE** to make a canal or pool waterproof by lining it with puddle **3.** *vt* CIV ENG **MIX CLAY AND SAND** to work clay and sand to make puddle **4.** *vt* METALL **PROCESS PIG IRON** to convert pig iron to wrought iron by heating it in a furnace in the presence of an oxidizing agent such as ferric oxide to remove carbon [14C. < Old English *pudd* "ditch"] —**pud·dler** *n* —**pud·dly** *adj*

pud·dle jump·er *n* a small light airplane that generally travels short distances (*informal*)

pu·den·dum /pyoo déndəm/ (*plural* **-da** /-də/) *n* the human external genital organs [Mid-17C. < Latin < *pudere* "make or feel ashamed"] —**pu·den·dal** *adj*

pudge /puj/ *n* **1.** excess body on a person (*informal insult; sometimes offensive*) **2.** an offensive term for somebody considered to be carrying more body weight than is desirable or advisable (*insult*) [Mid-19C. Origin ?]

pudg·y /pújjee/ (**-i·er, -i·est**) *adj* short and carrying more body weight than is desirable or advisable (*informal; sometimes offensive*) —**pudg·i·ly** *adv* —**pudg·i·ness** *n*

Pueb·la /pwéb laa/ **1.** state in east central Mexico. Capital: Puebla. Population: 5,076,686 (2000). Area: 13,126 sq. mi./33,995 sq. km. **2.** capital city of Puebla State in east central Mexico. It has one of the oldest cathedrals in Latin America. Population: 1,346,916 (2000).

pueb·lo /pwébblō/ (*plural* **-los**) *n* **1.** a village built by Native North or Central Americans in the southwestern United States and Central America, containing at least one, but typically a cluster of multistory stone or adobe houses **2.** *Hispanic* a town or village in a Spanish-speaking country [Early 19C. Via Spanish < Latin *populus* "people"]

Pueb·lo (*plural same* or **-los**) *n* a member of a Native North or Central American people who live or lived in pueblos. The Hopi, Taos, and Zuñi are all Pueblo peoples. —**Pueb·lo** *adj*

pu·er·ile /pyóorəl, pyoor īl, pyóo ərəl/ *adj* **1.** regarded as childishly silly or immature **2.** relating to or characteristic of childhood (*formal*) [Late 16C. Directly or via French < Latin *puerilis* < *puer* "child, boy"] —**pu·er·ile·ly** *adv* —**pu·er·il·i·ty** /pyoor ríllətee/ *n*

pu·er·il·ism /pyóorə lìzzəm, pyóo ərə-/ *n* childish or immature behavior by an adult

pu·er·per·al /pyoo úrpərəl/ *adj* relating to childbirth or the time immediately following childbirth [Mid-

18C. < Latin *puerperus* "bearing children" < *puer* "child" + *-parus* "bearing"]

pu·er·per·al fe·ver *n* MED same as **puerperal sepsis**

pu·er·per·al psy·cho·sis *n* a psychiatric disorder that may affect women in the first two weeks after giving birth. It may be depressive or schizophrenic and may involve false ideas concerning the baby.

pu·er·per·al sep·sis *n* blood poisoning following childbirth, caused by infection of the placental site

pu·er·pe·ri·um /pyoŏ ər pēeree əm/ *n* the period immediately after childbirth when the womb is returning to its normal size, lasting approximately six weeks [Early 17C. < Latin < *puerperus* (see PUERPERAL)]

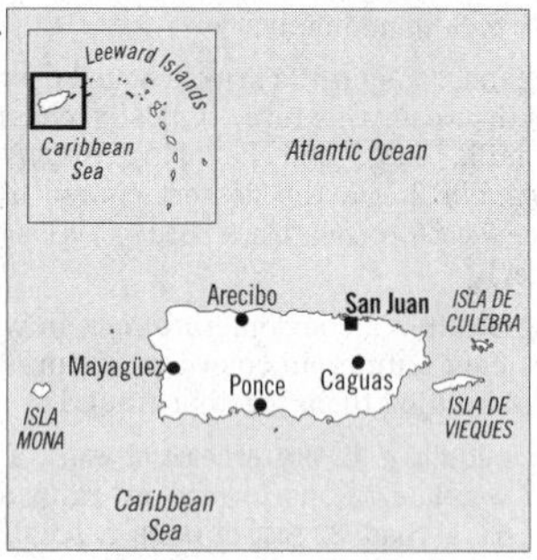

Puerto Rico

Puer·to Ri·co /pwèrtə rēekō/ commonwealth of the United States, occupying one large island and several small ones in the northern Caribbean, east of the Dominican Republic. Language: Spanish, English. Currency: US dollar. Capital: San Juan. Population: 3,937,316 (2001). Area: 3,459 sq. mi./8,959 sq. km. —**Puer·to Ri·can** *n, adj*

puff /puf/ *n* **1.** SHORT SUDDEN RUSH OF AIR a short sudden rush of air, wind, gas, or smoke **2.** SOUND OF PUFF the short sound made by a rush of air or gas **3.** AMOUNT IN PUFF the amount of substance contained in a puff **4.** SHORT EXHALATION a short blowing out of breath **5.** INHALATION FOLLOWED BY EXHALATION an inhalation followed by an exhalation, especially when smoking **6.** *US* FOOD same as **puff pastry** **7.** EXAGGERATED PRAISE OR PUBLICITY an exaggerated or flattering expression of praise, especially in publicizing something or somebody **8.** COSMETICS same as **powder puff** **9.** SWELLING a rounded swelling or projection on something **10.** GATHERED SECTION OF FABRIC a piece of fabric gathered around the edges and bulging in the middle **11.** VOLUMINOUS HAIRSTYLE hair arranged in an enlarged mass by combing, rolling, or padding it **12.** *US* QUILTED BEDSPREAD a quilted and padded covering for a bed (*dated*) **13.** GENETICS ENLARGED REGION ON CHROMOSOME an enlarged region on a chromosome resulting from active RNA synthesis ■ *v* (**puffed, puff·ing, puffs**) **1.** *vi* BREATHE QUICKLY to breathe quickly in short blasts **2.** *vti* EMIT GAS IN SHORT BLASTS to emit or blow steam, gas, or smoke in short blasts **3.** *vti* INHALE AND EXHALE SMOKE to inhale and exhale smoke from a cigarette, cigar, or pipe **4.** *vi* MOVE WHILE EMITTING SMOKE PUFFS to move in a particular direction or way emitting puffs of smoke or steam **5.** *vi* MOVE WHILE PANTING to move in a particular direction or way while panting ○ *He puffed up the hill.* **6.** *vti* SWELL UP to swell, or make something swell, e.g., with air or pride ○ *puffed out his cheeks* ○ *puffing up balloons* **7.** *vt* SPEAK HIGHLY OF SOMEBODY OR SOMETHING to praise somebody or something extravagantly, especially in publicity material [12C. Origin ?]

puff ad·der *n* **1.** a viper that inflates its body and hisses when alarmed. Genus: *Bitis.* Native to: Africa. **2.** REPT same as **hognose snake**

puff·ball /púf bàwl/ *n* a round fungus that produces a cloud of dark spores when disturbed. Many species are edible when immature. Genus: *Lycoperdon* or *Calvatia.*

puffed-up *adj* self-important or pompous

puff·er /púffər/ *n* **1.** something or somebody that puffs, especially a steam-driven train or cargo vessel **2.** **puf·fer, puf·fer·fish** /púffər fish/ (*plural same* or **-fish·es**) a tropical ocean fish, poisonous in some species, that can inflate its body with water to appear larger to predators. Although poisonous, some varieties can be eaten as food after special preparation. Family: Tetraodontidae.

puff·er·y /púffəree/ *n* exaggerated or overly flattering praise, especially in publicity (*informal*)

puffin

puf·fin /púffin/ (*plural* **-fins** or *same*) *n* a black and white diving seabird of the auk family with a short neck and a triangular, brightly colored beak. Genus: *Fratercula.* [14C. Origin ?]

puff pas·try *n* a light flaky multilayered pastry made by repeated rolling and folding of extremely rich buttery pastry dough, which then rises during baking

puff·y /púffee/ (**-i·er, -i·est**) *adj* **1.** SWOLLEN swollen, especially because of tiredness, injury, crying, or poor health **2.** SHORT OF BREATH with a tendency to puff and pant **3.** POMPOUS pompous or self-important —**puff·i·ly** *adv* —**puff·i·ness** *n*

pug

pug[1] /pug/ *n* a short compact dog with a wrinkled face, short coat, and curled tail, belonging to a breed of Asian origin [Mid-18C. Origin ?]

pug[2] /pug/ *vt* (**pugged, pug·ging, pugs**) **1.** KNEAD CLAY WITH WATER to mix clay with water to make it pliable enough to form bricks or pottery **2.** FILL GAP WITH CLAY to fill in a gap with clay or mortar **3.** *US* SOUNDPROOF SOMETHING to make something soundproof with clay or some other material ■ *n* CLAY SUITABLE FOR MOLDING clay mixed with water until it is pliable enough to form bricks or pottery [Early 19C. Origin ?] —**pug·gy** *adj*

pug[3] /pug/ *n* the print of a foot or a trail of such prints, especially when made by an animal [Mid-19C. < Hindi *pag* "footprint"]

pug[4] /pug/ *n* BOXING same as **boxer**[1] (*slang*) [Mid-19C. Shortening of *pugilist*]

Pu·get Sound /pyoŏjət-/ deep inlet of the Pacific Ocean, in northwestern Washington. Area: 217 sq. mi./561 sq. km.

pu·gi·lism /pyoŏjə lìzzəm/ *n* the practice, sport, or profession of boxing [Late 18C. < Latin *pugil* "boxer"] —**pu·gi·list** *n* —**pu·gi·lis·tic** /pyoŏjə lístik/ *adj* —**pu·gi·lis·ti·cal·ly** *adv*

pu·gil-stick /pyoŏjəl-/ *n* a long stick with padded ends used in the army to practice bayonet fighting, and in game shows involving mock combats [Probably < shortening of PUGILISM]

Pu·gin /pyoŏjin/, **Augustus** (1812–52) British architect and designer. He was leader of the Gothic revival, and his most influential work was the interior and exterior decoration of the Houses of Parliament in London, England, begun in 1836. Full name **Pugin, Augustus Welby Northmore**

> "The two great rules for design are these: first, that there should be no features about a building which are not necessary for convenience, construction or propriety; second, that all ornament should consist of enrichment of the essential construction of the building."
> [Augustus Pugin, *The True Principles of Pointed or Christian Architecture*; 1841]

pug mill *n* a machine in which materials are ground and mixed, e.g., clay with water for building or pottery-making, or cement for building [< PUG[2]]

pug·na·cious /pug náyshəss/ *adj* inclined to fight or be aggressive [Mid-17C. < Latin *pugnac-* < *pugnus* "fist"] —**pug·na·cious·ly** *adv* —**pug·na·cious·ness** *n* —**pug·nac·i·ty** /pug nássətee/ *n*

pug nose *n* a short stubby nose with a turned-up or flattened end [< PUG[1]] —**pug-nosed** *adj*

puh-leeze /pə lēez/, **puh-lease** *interj* used facetiously to express astonishment, disbelief, or indignation (*informal*) [Late 20C. Alteration of PLEASE]

puis·ne /pyoōnee, pwee nee/ *adj US* LAW **1.** junior or younger in status or rank or in age **2.** describes an associate justice of a higher court [Late 16C. < Old French, "born after" < *puis* "after" + *né* "born"]

puis·sant /pwíss'nt, pyoŏ əss'nt, pyoo íss'nt/ *adj* powerful or mighty (*literary*) [15C. < French < Latin *posse* "be able," after *potent-* "powerful"] —**puis·sance** *n* —**puis·sant·ly** *adv*

pu·ja /poŏjə/, **poo·ja** *n* **1.** in Hinduism, daily devotion consisting of a ritual offering of food, drink, and ritual actions and prayers, most commonly to an image of a deity **2.** *Carib* a Hindu prayer ceremony [Late 17C. < Sanskrit *pūjā* "worship"]

Pu·kas·kwa Na·tion·al Park /poo kaáskwə-/ national park and nature preserve beside Lake Superior in Ontario, Canada. Area: 725 sq. mi./1,878 sq. km.

puke /pyook/ (*slang*) *vti* (**puked, puk·ing, pukes**) VOMIT to vomit, or vomit something up ■ *n* **1.** SOMETHING VOMITED vomited food or other matter **2.** ACT OF VOMITING the vomiting up of something [Late 16C. Probably an imitation of the sound of vomiting]

puk·ka /púkə/, **puck·a** *adj* **1.** GENUINE genuine or authentic (*informal*) **2.** RESPECTABLE of high social status (*informal*) **3.** EXCELLENT of the highest quality or standard (*informal*) **4.** *S Asia* WELL DONE OR MADE properly done or made [Late 17C. < Hindi *pakkā* "cooked, ripe"]

pul /pool/ (*plural* **puls** or **pu·li** /poólee/) *n* a subunit of Afghan currency. See table at **currency** [Mid-19C. < Pashto]

pu·la /poólə/ (*plural same*) *n* the main unit of Botswanan currency. See table at **currency** [Late 20C. < Setswana, literally "rain"]

Pu·las·ki /pə láskee/, **Casimir** (1747–79) Polish-born American army officer. He organized and led the Pulaski Legion (1778), which fought for the colonists in the American Revolution.

pul·chri·tude /púlkrə toōd/ *n* physical beauty (*literary or humorous*) [14C. < Latin *pulchritudo* < *pulcher* "beautiful"] —**pul·chri·tu·di·nous** /pùlkrə toōd'nəss/ *adj*

pule /pyool/ (**puled, pul·ing, pules**) *vi* to whine, whimper, or cry plaintively (*archaic*) [Early 16C. Probably an imitation of the sound of whimpering] —**pul·er** *n* —**pul·ing·ly** *adv*

pu·li[1] /poŏllee, poólee, pyoólee/ (*plural* **-lis** or **-lik** /poŏlik, poólik, pyoólik/) *n* a medium-sized Hungarian sheepdog with long hair that can be combed out or left corded [Mid-20C. < Hungarian]

pu·li[2] MONEY plural of **pul**

Pu·lit·zer /poŏllitsər, pyoólitsər/, **Joseph** (1847–1911) Hungarian-born US journalist and patron of the arts. He established the Pulitzer Prizes in literature and journalism.

Pu·lit·zer prize *n* a prize awarded annually for excellence in American journalism, literature, or music [Early 20C. After Joseph *Pulitzer*]

pull /poŏl/ *v* (**pulled, pull·ing, pulls**) **1.** *vti* DRAW SOMEBODY

OR SOMETHING NEARER to apply force to somebody or something so as to draw or tend to draw that person or thing toward the origin of the force **2.** *vt* REMOVE SOMETHING FORCIBLY to remove or extract something by exerting force **3.** *vt* DRAW LOAD to draw a load such as a trailer or plow **4.** *vti* TUG AT SOMEBODY OR SOMETHING to tug at or jerk somebody or something **5.** *vt* MED STRAIN MUSCLE to strain and damage a muscle, ligament, or tendon **6.** *vt* PRESS SOMETHING TO OPERATE IT to apply force to a trigger, lever, or switch so as to operate a weapon or machine **7.** *vt* OPEN OR CLOSE CURTAINS to open or close curtains or window coverings **8.** *vti* TEAR SOMETHING to tear or rip something apart or into pieces **9.** *vt* STRETCH SOMETHING to stretch something elastic **10.** *vt* TAKE OUT WEAPON to take out a weapon in readiness to attack somebody (*informal*) **11.** *vt* ATTRACT PEOPLE to draw a large number of people, e.g., as audience members or voters (*informal*) **12.** *vt* DO SOMETHING UNDERHANDEDLY to do something undesirable or despicable in an underhand way (*informal*) ○ *How could you pull such a sneaky trick?* **13.** *vti* AUTOMOT MANEUVER VEHICLE to maneuver a vehicle in a particular direction **14.** *vi* AUTOMOT DRIFT TO ONE SIDE BECAUSE FAULTY to drift to one side or the other, usually because of a fault (*refers to motor vehicles or their steering*) ○ *My car pulls to the left.* **15.** *vi* INHALE DEEPLY to inhale deeply when smoking, or take a deep gulp at a drink **16.** *vt* COMM, PUBL REMOVE SOMETHING FROM CIRCULATION to remove something from circulation, or prevent it from ever getting into circulation (*informal*) ○ *The manufacturer pulled the product after safety questions were raised.* **17.** *vt* PRINTING MAKE PROOF FOR CORRECTION to make a printing proof **18.** *vt* HORSERACING REIN HORSE BACK to rein in a horse, especially so as to prevent it from winning a race **19.** *vt* BASEBALL HIT BALL WHERE PLAYER FACES to hit a baseball toward the direction the batter is facing after completing a swing **20.** *vt* HIT BALL TOO FAR TO SIDE to hit a ball farther left for a right-handed player or farther right for a left-handed player than intended ■ *n* **1.** ACT OF PULLING the act of pulling somebody or something, or an instance of being pulled **2.** PULLING FORCE the physical force involved in the action of pulling **3.** SUSTAINED EFFORT a sustained effort, especially under difficult circumstances **4.** SOMETHING USED FOR PULLING something used for pulling, e.g., a knob, handle, or tab (*often used in combination*) **5.** DEEP INHALATION OR GULP the inhaling or drinking of something deeply **6.** INFLUENCE special influence, usually because of personal position within an organization or society, or personal connection with somebody (*informal*) ○ *used his pull to get tickets for the final* **7.** POWER TO ATTRACT the ability or power to attract an audience or supporters (*informal*) **8.** PRINTING PROOF COPY FOR CORRECTION a printing proof made for correction **9.** HORSERACING RESTRAINT OF HORSE the restraining of a horse by its rider, especially to keep it from winning **10.** PULLING OF BALL the pulling of a ball, or a ball that is pulled **11.** ARMS RESISTANCE IN FIRING MECHANISM the amount of resistance in a firing mechanism such as a trigger or bowstring [Old English *pullian*, originally "pluck," probably < W Germanic] —**pull·er** *n*

SYNONYMS ***pull, drag, draw, haul, tow, tug, yank***

CORE MEANING: to move something toward you or in the same direction as you

pull to apply force to somebody or something so as to draw or tend to draw that person or thing toward the origin of the force ○ *They pulled their sled twenty-four kilometers without skis.* ○ *If you pull the cord, your light'll come on.* **drag** to move something, especially something that is too large, heavy, or cumbersome to carry, by pulling it along the ground or across a surface ○ *dragging the dog over to the car* ○ *a scraping sound as of something being dragged along the ground* **draw** to pull something, or lead or pull somebody, in a particular direction, especially toward or away from something ○ *We reached out and drew her into the circle.* ○ *He drew a silk handkerchief from his pocket.* **haul** to pull something with continuous and laborious movements ○ *He hauled the box up the stairs.* **tow** to pull something such as a barge or a broken-down car along by a rope or chain attached to it ○ *The two boats were towed into port.* ○ *We had to tow the damaged car back to the repair shop.* **tug** to pull at or drag somebody or something with a sharp forceful movement ○ *Frantically, I tried to tug my finger free.* ○ *The child approached and tugged at his arm, whining, "I want to go home, Daddy."* **yank** to pull somebody or something suddenly and sharply ○ *He yanked the cable from the socket.* ○ *When the elevator stopped, she yanked the gate back and stepped out.*

pull ahead *vi* to move in front of or gain a lead over somebody or something moving in the same direction

pull away *vi* **1.** MOVE AWAY to move away from somebody or something **2.** DRAW BACK to draw back from somebody or something, either physically or emotionally **3.** START TO WIN to start to win something such as a competition or race by widening the margin over an opponent

pull back *v* **1.** *vti* to withdraw, or make people, especially troops, withdraw **2.** *vi* to decide not to do something, especially in order to avoid a bad outcome

pull down *vt* **1.** DEMOLISH SOMETHING to destroy or demolish something, especially a building **2.** REDUCE SOMETHING TO LOWER LEVEL to reduce something such as a price to a lower level or value **3.** DECREASE WELL-BEING OF SOMEBODY to have a detrimental effect on the health or mental well-being of somebody **4.** COMPUT MAKE MENU APPEAR to make a menu appear on a computer screen by clicking on its heading **5.** EARN AMOUNT to earn a particular amount of money (*slang*)

pull for *vt* to hope that somebody or something will succeed in an endeavor ○ *The whole town was pulling for him in the state spelling bee.*

pull in *v* **1.** *vi* TRANSP ARRIVE to arrive and stop at a place **2.** *vt* EARN AMOUNT to earn a particular amount of money (*informal*) **3.** *vt* ARREST SOMEBODY to arrest somebody, or take somebody into a police station for questioning (*slang*)

pull off *vt* to achieve something impressive, particularly through a combination of skill and luck (*informal*)

SYNONYMS See ***accomplish***.

pull on *vt* to put on clothing or an item of clothing, especially in haste

pull out *v* **1.** *vi* WITHDRAW to withdraw from an obligation or commitment ○ *They are threatening to pull out of the deal.* **2.** *vti* RETREAT to retreat, or cause somebody to retreat ○ *The army is pulling out.* **3.** *vi* TRANSP DEPART to depart from a station or stopping place **4.** *vi* TRANSP MANEUVER INTO TRAFFIC FLOW to drive a vehicle away from the side of a road, e.g., so as to join a flow of traffic **5.** *vti* AVIAT LEVEL OUT AIRCRAFT FROM DIVE to level out, or make an aircraft level out from a dive

pull over *v* **1.** *vti* to drive a vehicle to the side of a road and stop, or make the driver of a vehicle do this **2.** *vi* to stop at a facility beside a road such as a rest stop or restaurant

pull through *vti* to recover from a period of illness or difficulties, or help somebody to do this

pull together *v* **1.** *vi* to cooperate, collaborate, or work together **2. pull yourself together** *vr* to recover your composure or self-control (*informal*)

pull up *v* **1.** *vti* TRANSP ARRIVE SOMEWHERE to arrive and stop at a place, or make a person, animal, or vehicle do this **2.** *vi* CATCH UP IN RACE to move into a closer or level position with somebody, e.g., in a race **3.** *vti* GARDENING ROOT UP SOMETHING to uproot something, e.g., in weeding, or be uprooted

pull·back /pŏŏl bàk/ *n* **1.** an act of pulling back, especially a withdrawal of troops **2.** a device for holding, restraining, or drawing something back

pull bone *n regional* same as **wishbone** (sense 1) [See WISHBONE]

REGIONAL NOTE See ***pulley bone***.

pull-down *adj* describes a software menu or another item that can be made to appear on a computer screen by clicking on its heading ■ *n* a pull-down feature on a computer screen

pul·let /pŏŏllət/ *n* a young female chicken, especially one that has not started to lay eggs [14C. < French *poulet* "little hen" < *poule* "hen" < Latin *pulla*, feminine of *pullus* "chicken, young animal"]

pul·ley /pŏŏllee/ (*plural* **-leys**) *n* **1.** a mounted rotating wheel with a grooved rim over which a belt or chain can move to change the direction of a pulling force **2.** a system of pulleys together with a

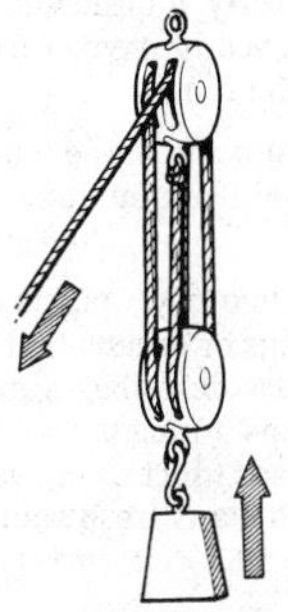

pulley

mounting block and tackle, used to improve leverage in lifting heavy weights [14C. < French *polie*, probably < Greek *polos* "pole"]

pul·ley bone *n Southern US* same as **wishbone** (sense 1) [< PULL (see WISHBONE)]

REGIONAL NOTE ***Pulley bone*** is a general-currency word used throughout the South. Other names include *breastbone, good-luck bone, lucky bone,* and *pull bone.*

pull fac·tor *n* **1.** a measure of the strength of the retail trade in an area, based on a comparison of local spending in relation to that of a wider geographic area, e.g., a state ○ *The pull factor equates sales per person in the town with sales per person in the state.* **2.** a social or environmental benefit that draws people from one region or country to another

Pull·man /pŏŏlmən/ *n* **1.** a comfortable train car for sitting or sleeping in **2.** a large suitcase [Mid-19C. After George Mortimer PULLMAN]

Pull·man /pŏŏlmən/, **George** (1831–97) US inventor and manufacturer. He designed the first railroad sleeping car (1863). Full name **Pullman, George Mortimer**

pull-on *n* a garment such as a pair of pants or a top, usually made of comfortable stretchy fabric, that can be easily pulled on

pul·lo·rum dis·ease /pə láwrəm-/ *n* a highly infectious disease of young poultry caused by the bacterium *Salmonella pullorum*, and marked by diarrhea [< modern Latin *pullorum*, "of chickens"]

pull·out /pŏŏl òwt/ *n* **1.** RETREAT a retreat from a place or military involvement **2.** WITHDRAWAL a withdrawal from an obligation or other demanding situation **3.** PUBL REMOVABLE SECTION OF PUBLICATION an object intended to be pulled out of a publication, e.g., a removable section of a magazine or a part of a book that folds out **4.** OBJECT FOR PULLING OUT an object intended to be pulled out, especially a piece of furniture that can be pulled out from a wall or opened out ○ *a pullout couch* **5.** AVIAT LEVELING-OUT MANEUVER OF AIRCRAFT an aircraft maneuver in which a dive changes to level flight

pull·o·ver /pŏŏl òvər/ *n* a garment, especially a sweater, put on by being pulled over the head

pull-tab *n* a ring or tab of metal on top of a drink can that is pulled in order to open it

pull tech·nol·o·gy *n* Internet technology that provides data or other material when a user requests an update or chooses to retrieve content from a supplier. Web browsing is an example of pull technology.

pul·lu·late /púllyə làyt/ (**-lat·ed, -lat·ing, -lates**) *vi* **1.** TEEM to teem or swarm with something (*literary*) **2.** BOT GERMINATE to germinate or sprout (*technical*) **3.** ZOOL BREED to breed freely or rapidly (*technical*) [Early 17C. < Latin *pullulat-*, past participle of *pullulare* "grow, sprout" < *pullus* "chicken, young animal"] —**pul·lu·la·tion** /pùllyə láysh'n/ *n*

pull-up *n UK* GYMNASTICS same as **chin-up**

pul·mo·nar·y /pŏŏlmə nèrree, púlmə-/ *adj* **1.** relating to or affecting the lungs **2.** ZOOL same as **pulmonate** *adj* (sense 1) [Early 18C. < Latin *pulmonarius* < *pulmo* "lung"]

pul·mo·nar·y an·thrax *n* a form of pneumonia caused by inhaling anthrax bacteria

pul·mo·nar·y ar·ter·y *n* either of two arteries that carry blood in need of oxygen from the right side of the heart to the lungs

pul·mo·nar·y vein *n* one of the four veins that carry oxygen-rich blood from the lungs to the left side of the heart

pul·mo·nate /pŏŏlmə nàyt, púlmə-/ ZOOL *adj* **1. WITH LUNGS** having lungs or organs that function as lungs **2. WITH SAC LIKE LUNG** describes a mollusk that has a sac functioning as a lung ■ *n* **MOLLUSK WITH LUNG SAC** a mollusk with a sac functioning as a lung, e.g., land snails, slugs, and many freshwater snails. Subclass: Pulmonata. [Mid-19C. < modern Latin *pulmonatus* < Latin *pulmo* "lung"]

pul·mon·ic /pŏŏl mónnik, pul-/ *adj* ANAT same as **pulmonary** (sense 1) [Mid-17C. Directly or via French < modern Latin *pulmonicus* < Latin *pulmo* "lung"]

pul·mon·ol·o·gy /pŏŏlmə nóllәjee, pùl-/ *n* the branch of medicine that deals with the structure, physiology, and diseases of the lungs —**pul·mon·o·log·i·cal** /pŏŏlmənə lójjik'l, pùl-/ *adj*—**pul·mon·ol·o·gist** *n*

pulp /pulp/ *n* **1. SOFT MATERIAL** a soft or soggy mass **2. CRUSHED WOOD FOR PAPER** crushed wood or other materials that are used to make paper **3. CHEAP BOOKS OR MAGAZINES** novels or magazines produced on cheap paper, especially crime, horror, or science fiction stories (*often used before a noun*) ○ *a prize collection of classic pulp fiction* **4. SOFT FLESHY PLANT TISSUE** soft fleshy plant tissue, e.g., the inner part of a fruit or vegetable **5. STEM PITH** the pith inside a plant stem **6.** DENT **INSIDE OF TOOTH** the sensitive tissue at the center of a tooth, consisting of nerves and blood vessels **7. PULVERIZED ORE** ore that has been mined and pulverized, especially when mixed with water ■ *v* (**pulped, pulp·ing, pulps**) **1.** *vti* **CRUSH SOMETHING** to crush something into pulp, or be crushed into pulp **2.** *vt* **REMOVE PULP FROM SOMETHING** to remove the pulp from something, especially the soft fleshy tissue from fruit or vegetables [14C. < Latin *pulpa*] —**pulp·y** *adj*

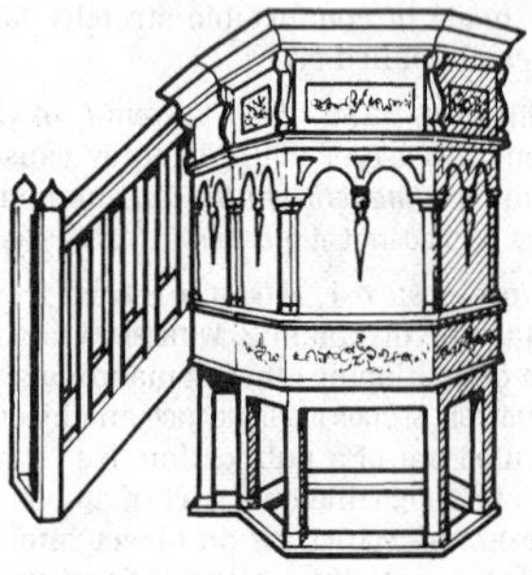

pulpit

pul·pit /pŏŏl pìt, púl-/ *n* **1. PLATFORM IN CHURCH** a raised platform or stand in a Christian church that is used by the priest or minister for preaching or leading a service **2. CHRISTIAN CLERGY** the Christian clergy considered as a group **3. GUARDRAIL ON BOAT** a metal guardrail on the bow or stern of a small boat [14C. < Latin *pulpitum* "platform, scaffold," (in late Latin) "pulpit"]

pulp·wood /púlp wŏŏd/ *n* a soft wood that is used to make paper, e.g., aspen, pine, or spruce

pul·que /pŏŏl kày, pŏŏlkee/ *n Hispanic* a thick alcoholic drink made in Mexico from the sap of the agave plant [Late 17C. Via Mexican Spanish < Nahuatl *puliúhki* "decomposed"]

pul·sar /púl saar/ *n* a small dense star that emits brief intense bursts of visible radiation, radio waves, and X-rays, and is generally believed to be a rapidly rotating neutron star [Mid-20C. Contraction of *pulsating star*, after QUASAR]

pul·sate /púl sàyt/ (**-sat·ed, -sat·ing, -sates**) *vi* **1. THROB** to vibrate or throb **2. BE FULL OF ENERGY** to be full of energy, bustling activity, or excitement ○ *The whole city is pulsating with excitement at this time of year.* **3.** PHYSIOL **EXPAND AND CONTRACT** to expand and contract with a strong regular beat (*refers to blood vessels*) [Late 18C. < Latin *pulsat-*, past participle of *pulsare* "beat repeatedly" < *pellere* "to beat"] —**pul·sa·to·ry** /púlssə tàwree/ *adj*

pul·sa·tile /púlssət'l, -tīl/ *adj* pulsating or vibrating rhythmically —**pul·sa·til·i·ty** /pùlssə tíllətee/ *n*

pul·sa·tion /pul sáysh'n/ *n* PHYSIOL **1. PULSATING** the act of pulsating **2. BEATING OF HEART** the rhythmic change in volume that takes place in the heart or an artery **3. BEAT** a single beat or pulse

pul·sa·tive /púlssə tiv/ *adj* same as **pulsatile**

pul·sa·tor /púl sàytər, pul sáytər/ *n* **1.** a device or machine that pulsates while operating **2.** a device that stimulates or maintains a rhythmic motion such as respiration

pulse[1] /pulss/ *n* **1. REGULAR BEAT OF BLOOD FLOW** the regular expansion and contraction of an artery, caused by the heart pumping blood through the body. It can be felt through an artery that is near the surface such as the one in the wrist on the same side as the thumb. **2. SINGLE BEAT OF BLOOD FLOW** a single expansion and contraction of an artery, caused by a beat of the heart **3. RHYTHMIC BEAT** a beat or throb, e.g., of a drum, or a series of rhythmic beats or throbs **4. CHANGE OR REPEATING CHANGE IN MAGNITUDE** a brief temporary change in a normally constant quantity, e.g., in a voltage, or a series of intermittent disturbances that are regular in form and frequency of occurrence **5. CURRENT ATTITUDES** the sentiments, opinions, or attitudes current in a society or group ○ *a reporter with his finger on the pulse of the nation* **6. VITALITY** energy and excitement ○ *I love the pulse of city life.* ■ *vi* (**pulsed, puls·ing, puls·es**) **1. BEAT RHYTHMICALLY** to move or throb with a strong regular rhythm **2.** PHYS **UNDERGO BRIEF SUDDEN CHANGES** to undergo a series of brief sudden changes in quantity, e.g., in voltage **3. BE ENERGETIC** to be full of energy and excitement ○ *an area pulsing with creative energy* [14C. Via French < Latin *puls-*, past participle of *pellere* "to beat"]

pulse[2] /pulss/ *n* **1.** an edible seed from a pod, e.g., a pea or bean, eaten fresh or dried **2.** a plant that has pods as fruits and roots that bear nodules containing nitrogen-fixing bacteria, e.g., the pea, the bean, alfalfa, or clover [13C. Via French < Latin *puls* "porridge"]

pulse code mod·u·la·tion *n* a technique for electronic transmission of voice signals by sampling the amplitude of the signal and converting it to a coded digital form for transmission

pulse·jet /púlss jèt/ *n* a ramjet engine in which air, admitted through movable vanes, mixes with fuel in the combustion chamber. The resulting explosion forces the vanes shut, causing a pulsating thrust.

pulse mod·u·la·tion *n* a technique for transmitting information by means of a series of electrical pulses, with the duration, amplitude, or frequency of the pulses modified to carry the information

pul·som·e·ter /pul sómmətər/ *n* a lightweight pump without a piston that works using the partial vacuum created by pulses of condensing steam being forced between two chambers [Mid-19C. < PULSE[1]]

pul·ver·ize /púlvə rīz/ (**-ized, -iz·ing, -iz·es**) *v* **1.** *vti* **CRUSH SOMETHING TO POWDER** to crush or grind something into a powder or dust, or be crushed or ground into a powder or dust **2.** *vt* **DESTROY SOMETHING** to demolish something completely (*informal*) ○ *The storm pulverized the town.* **3.** *vt* **DEFEAT SOMEBODY** to subject an opponent to a crushing defeat (*informal*) ○ *We completely pulverized the other team.* [15C. < late Latin *pulverizare* < Latin *pulver-* "powder, dust"] —**pul·ver·i·za·tion** /pùlvəri záysh'n/ *n* —**pul·ver·iz·er** *n*

pul·vi·nate /púlvə nàyt/ *adj* **1.** shaped like a cushion **2.** describes a leafstalk that has a swelling at its base

pul·vi·nus /pul vínəss/ (*plural* **-ni** /-nī/) *n* a swelling at the base of a leafstalk that causes changes in the position of the leaf as it swells and shrinks [Mid-19C. < Latin, "cushion, pillow"]

pu·ma /pŏŏmə, pyŏŏmə/ (*plural* **-mas** or *same*) *n UK* VERTEB same as **mountain lion** [Late 18C. Via Spanish < Quechua *púma*]

pum·ice /púmmiss/, **pum·i·cite** /púmmə sīt/ *n* a very light porous rock formed from solidified lava, used in solid form as an abrasive and in powdered form as a polish [15C. Via French < Latin *pumic-* "foam," because of the stone's spongy appearance] —**pu·mi·ceous** /pyoo míshəss/ *adj*

pum·mel /púmm'l/ (**-meled** or **-melled, -mel·ing** or **-mel·ling, -mels**) *vt* **1.** to hit somebody or something with repeated blows, especially using the fists **2.** to cause serious damage to something [Mid-16C. Alteration of POMMEL]

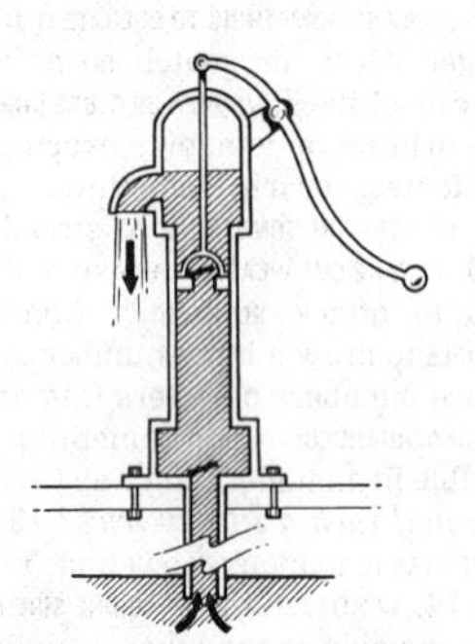

pump: cross section of a water pump

pump[1] /pump/ *v* (**pumped, pump·ing, pumps**) **1.** *vti* **MAKE LIQUID OR GAS FLOW** to force a liquid or gas to flow **2.** *vt* **MAKE SOMETHING MOVE UP AND DOWN** to move a handle, lever, or other device up and down energetically ○ *frantically pumping the brakes* **3.** *vt* **ASK SOMEBODY QUESTIONS** to try to get information from somebody by asking questions repeatedly and forcefully **4.** *vt US* **MAKE SOMEBODY EXCITED** to make somebody excited and enthusiastic about something (*informal*) ○ *The team was really pumped for the game.* **5.** *vt* MED **FLUSH OUT SOMEBODY'S STOMACH** to flush out the contents of somebody's stomach, usually to remove poison, drugs, or alcohol. A tube and a funnel are used to pour in water and allow the diluted stomach contents to run out. ■ *n* **1.** MECH ENG **DEVICE FOR MOVING LIQUID OR GAS** a device that is used to raise, compress, or transfer liquids or gases and is operated by a piston or similar mechanism **2.** PHYSIOL **WAY OF MOVING IONS OR MOLECULES** a mechanism for the active movement of ions or molecules across a cell membrane **3.** *regional* AGRIC **PILE OF VEGETABLES** a heap of vegetables, usually potatoes, covered with earth and mulch and sometimes stored in a shed [15C. Probably ultimately an imitation of the sound of pumping]

REGIONAL NOTE See *bank*[2].

pump into *vt* to supply a large quantity of something, especially money, for something ○ *pumping money into the local economy*

pump out *vt* **1.** to produce something continually and in large quantities ○ *a new radio station pumping out dance music 24 hours a day* **2.** to remove fluid from something using a pump ○ *We had to pump out the boat again because it was leaking so badly.*

pump up *vt* **1. INFLATE SOMETHING** to inflate something such as a tire or ball using a pump **2. TURN SOMETHING UP** to increase the volume of sound, especially of music, produced by amplifiers or speakers (*informal*) **3. MAKE SOMEBODY EXCITED** make somebody excited or enthusiastic (*informal*) ○ *pumped them up for the game* **4.** GYM **BUILD MUSCLE** to increase the mass of a muscle by body-building techniques (*informal*)

pump[2] /pump/ *n* **1.** a woman's shoe that is plain and cut low in front and has a moderately high heel **2.** *US* a man's patent leather slip-on shoe worn with formal attire [Mid-16C. Origin ?]

pump-and-dump, pump-'n-dump *adj US* describes a situation in which unscrupulous stockbrokers, analysts, or stockholders highly recommend their own stocks in order to drive up the price for a quick profit (*slang*)

pumped stor·age /púmpt-/ *n* a way of generating hydroelectric power during peak periods that involves pumping water up to a reservoir during periods of low demand and releasing it during peak periods

pum·per·nick·el /púmpər nìk'l/ *n* a dark dense, slightly sour bread that is made from coarse rye flour [Mid-18C. < German dialect, earlier "person regarded as loutish" < *pumpern* "break wind" + *Nickel* "goblin"]

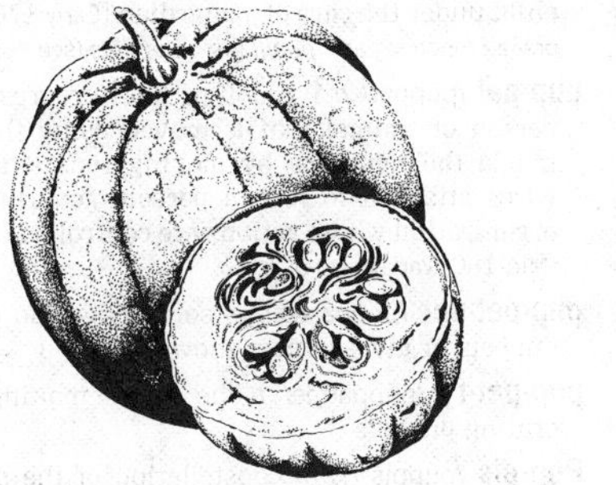

pumpkin

pump·kin /púmpkin, púmkin/ *n* **1.** a round large fruit with a thick orange-skinned rind, dry flesh, and many seeds, cooked and eaten as a vegetable or in sweet dishes **2.** the trailing or climbing plant that produces pumpkins. Genus: *Cucurbita.* [Late 17C. Alteration of obsolete *pumpion*, via obsolete French *pompon*, *popon* < Latin *pepon-*, *pepo* "pumpkin, large melon" < Greek *pepōn*, literally "ripe"]

pump·kin·seed /púmpkin sēed, púmkin-/ *n* **1.** a seed of a pumpkin **2.** a common freshwater sunfish that has an olive-colored upper body shading to yellow or orange on its belly, with one red spot on each gill cover. Native to: North America. Latin name: *Lepomis gibbosus.* [Early 19C. In sense 2 < its shape and orange color]

pump prim·ing *n* **1.** the use of investment to stimulate the economy in depressed regions and bring about self-sustaining growth **2.** the process or act of making a pump work more effectively by pouring fluid into it as it starts up

pun /pun/ *n* a humorous use of words that involves a word or phrase that has more than one possible meaning ■ *vi* (**punned, pun·ning, puns**) to make a pun or use puns [Mid-17C. Origin ?] —**pun·ny** *adj*

pu·na /pōōnə/ *n* **1.** *Hispanic* MED same as **altitude sickness 2.** a cold dry flat treeless area at a high altitude in the Andes [Early 17C. Via American Spanish < Quechua]

Pun·cak Ja·ya /pōōn chaak jaa yaa/ highest mountain in Indonesia, in the Surdiman Range, in western New Guinea. Height: 16,502 ft./5,030 m.

punch[1] /punch/ *vt* **1.** HIT SOMEBODY OR SOMETHING to hit somebody or something with the fist **2.** PRESS BUTTON to press a key or button on a computer keyboard or other device with a quick thrusting movement of the finger ○ *Punch the return key.* **3.** HIT BALL USING SHORT SWING in some sports, to hit a ball using a short sharp swing **4.** *US* POKE SOMETHING to poke or prod something **5.** AGRIC HERD CATTLE to herd cattle on horseback ■ *n* **1.** BLOW WITH FIST a blow to somebody or something with a fist **2.** VIGOR drive, energy, or power that enlivens or invigorates something ○ *The hurricane is finally losing its punch.* [14C. < Old French *poinsonner* "to prick" < *poinson, poinchon* (see PUNCHEON[2])] ◇ **not pull any** *or* **your punches, pull no punches** to use as much force and energy as necessary or possible in order to attain a goal or convey a message ◇ **pack a punch** to be very powerful or strong (*informal*) ◇ **roll with the punches** to adapt easily to a difficult situation (*informal*)

punch in *v* **1.** *vi* to arrive for work, or record the time of arrival for work, by inserting a personalized card into a time clock **2.** *vt* to enter information into a computer using the keyboard

punch out *v* **1.** *vi* to leave work, or record the time of departure from work, by inserting a personalized card into a time clock **2.** *vt* to knock somebody unconscious with a hard punch

punch up *v* (*informal*) **1.** *vt* to add force or liveliness to something ○ *Can't we do something to punch up this speech?* **2.** *Can* to input or access data on a computer or other device using a keyboard or keypad

punch[2] /punch/ *n* **1.** TOOL FOR MAKING HOLES a tool used to make holes in a material or an object **2.** TOOL FOR STAMPING OR CUTTING DESIGNS a tool that is hit to stamp a design on something or to cut something to a shape **3.** TOOL FOR DRIVING BOLTS OUT a tool used to knock a bolt or rivet out of a hole ■ *vt* (**punched, punch·ing, punch·es**) **1.** MAKE HOLE USING PUNCH to make a hole using a punch **2.** STAMP SOMETHING USING PUNCH to stamp or cut something using a punch [Early 16C. Origin ?]

punch[3] /punch/ *n* a drink made with a mixture of fruit juice and often spices and wine or liquor [Mid-17C. Origin ?]

Punch /punch/ *n* a character from traditional children's puppet shows. He is a red-cheeked hook-nosed clown who behaves in an argumentative or aggressive manner. [Late 17C. Shortening of PUNCHINELLO] ◇ **pleased as Punch** extremely pleased (*informal*)

Punch and Ju·dy, Punch-and-Ju·dy show *n* a comic children's puppet show featuring Punch and Judy, a quarrelsome couple

punch·bag /púnch bàg/ *n UK* **1.** BOXING same as **punching bag** (sense 1) **2.** same as **punching bag** (sense 2) (*informal*)

punch·ball /púnch bàwl/ *n* a version of baseball played with a rubber ball that is struck with the player's fist instead of a bat

punch·board /púnch bàwrd/ *n* a board with small holes, each containing a slip of paper. Players buy a chance to punch out a slip to see if they have won a prize.

punch·bowl /púnch bōl/ *n* a large bowl for serving punch, often with a matching ladle and cups

punch card *n* a card with patterns of holes punched in it, used to store information in early computers and telex machines

punch-drunk *adj* **1.** dazed or confused by something such as a bad experience (*informal*) **2.** showing signs of confusion and disorientation as a result of brain damage caused by blows to the head during boxing bouts

punched card /pùncht-/ *n* COMPUT same as **punch card**

pun·cheon[1] /púnchən/ *n* **1.** a large cask containing between 70 and 100 gallons **2.** a unit of capacity, equal to between 70 and 100 gallons [15C. < Old French *poinçon, poinchon*]

pun·cheon[2] /púnchən/ *n* **1.** a short upright piece of wood used for structural framing **2.** *US* a large timber with one flattened side, usually used for flooring [15C. < Old French *poinchon* < Latin *punct-*, past participle of *pungere* "prick, sting"]

Pun·chi·nel·lo /pùnchə néllō/ (*plural* **-los**) *n* **1.** a comic character who appears in Italian puppet and clown shows and is probably the source of Punch **2.** somebody who is considered silly or unintelligent (*archaic*) [Mid-17C. < Italian dialect *Pollecinella*]

punch·ing bag /púnching-/ *n* **1.** a large heavy bag, usually suspended from a rope, that boxers punch to improve their punching skills **2.** somebody who is regularly abused or treated with disrespect (*informal*)

punch·line /púnch lìn/ *n* the last part of a joke or funny story that delivers the meaning and the bulk of the humor [< PUNCH[1]]

punch-up *n Can, UK* a fistfight or brawl (*informal*)

punch·y /púnchee/ (**-i·er, -i·est**) *adj* (*informal*) **1.** forceful and concise ○ *a good punchy slogan* **2.** same as **punch-drunk** [Early 20C. < PUNCH[1]] —**punch·i·ness** *n*

punc·tate /púngk tàyt/ *adj* having tiny spots, holes, or dents ○ *a punctate leaf* [Mid-17C. < Latin *punctum* (see POINT)] —**punc·ta·tion** /pungk táysh'n/ *n*

punc·til·i·o /pungk tíllee ō/ (*plural* **-os**) *n* (*formal*) **1.** strict adherence to even the finest points of etiquette **2.** a very fine point of etiquette [Late 16C. Via obsolete Italian *puntiglio* and Spanish *puntillo* "small point" < Latin *punctum* (see POINT)]

punc·til·i·ous /pungk tíllee əss/ *adj* **1.** very careful about the conventions of correct behavior and etiquette ○ *always punctilious in his manners* **2.** showing great care in small details ○ *a punctilious execution of a complex design* [Mid-17C. < French *pointilleux* < *pointille* "small point" < *pointe* < Latin *punctum* (see POINT)] —**punc·til·i·ous·ly** *adv* —**punc·til·i·ous·ness** *n*

SYNONYMS See *careful.*

punc·tu·al /púngkchoo əl/ *adj* **1.** arriving or taking place at the arranged time ○ *a punctual start to a meeting* **2.** MATH relating to or possessing the properties of a point in space [14C. < medieval Latin *punctualis* < Latin *punctum* (see POINT)] —**punc·tu·al·i·ty** /pùngkchoo állətee/ *n* —**punc·tu·al·ly** *adv*

punc·tu·ate /púngkchoo àyt/ (**-at·ed, -at·ing, -ates**) *v* **1.** *vti* ADD PUNCTUATION TO TEXT to put punctuation marks in written work **2.** *vt* INTERRUPT SOMETHING OFTEN to interrupt a situation or activity frequently (*often passive*) ○ *a talk punctuated by humorous anecdotes* **3.** *vt* EMPHASIZE SOMETHING to do or say something in order to add emphasis [Mid-17C. < medieval Latin *punctuat-*, past participle of *punctuare* "mark with points" < Latin *punctum* (see POINT)] —**punc·tu·a·tor** *n*

punc·tu·a·ted e·qui·lib·ri·um *n* a theory of evolution holding that evolutionary change tends to be characterized by long periods of stability, or equilibrium, punctuated by episodes of very fast development

punc·tu·a·tion /pùngkchoo áysh'n/ *n* **1.** MARKS USED TO ORGANIZE WRITING the standardized nonalphabetical symbols or marks that are used to organize writing into clauses, phrases, and sentences, and in this way make its meaning clear **2.** USE OF PUNCTUATION the use of punctuation marks **3.** ACT OF PUNCTUATING WRITING the act of punctuating writing, or an occasion during which writing is punctuated

punc·tu·a·tion mark *n* a symbol that is used to organize and clarify the meaning of writing, e.g., a comma, period, or question mark

punc·ture /púngkchər/ *n* SMALL HOLE a small hole or wound made by a sharp object ■ *v* (**-tured, -tur·ing, -tures**) **1.** *vti* MAKE OR GET HOLE to sustain a small hole or wound in something such as a tire or the skin, or cause such a hole **2.** *vt* RUIN SOMEBODY'S CONFIDENCE to suddenly reduce or destroy somebody's confidence, arrogance, or conviction ○ *The interview punctured his expectation of a job offer.* [14C. < Latin *punctura* < *punct-*, past participle of *pungere* "prick, sting"]

pun·dit /púndit/ *n* **1.** a critic or authority on a subject, especially in the media ○ *The election results surprised the political pundits.* **2.** somebody with knowledge and wisdom **3.** RELIG same as **pandit** [Late 17C. Via Hindi *paṇḍit* < Sanskrit *paṇḍita-* "learned"]

Pu·ne /pōōnə/ city in Maharashtra State, west central India. Population: 3,755,525 (2001).

pung /pung/ *n New England* a low one-horse sleigh shaped like a box [Early 19C. Shortening of *tom pung* < Algonquian]

pun·gent /púnjənt/ *adj* **1.** STRONG SMELLING OR STRONG TASTING having a strong smell or a powerfully sharp or bitter taste **2.** CAUSTIC expressed in or showing a witty and biting manner ○ *pungent observations about mass culture* **3.** BIOL SHARP AND POINTED describes a plant or animal part that ends in a sharp point ○ *a plant with elongated pungent leaves* [Late 16C. < Latin *pungent-*, present participle of *pungere* "prick, sting"] —**pun·gen·cy** *n* —**pun·gent·ly** *adv*

Pu·nic /pyōōnik/ *adj* relating to the ancient Carthaginians, Carthage, or the Carthaginian language ■ *n* a Semitic language of ancient Carthage, related to Phoenician [15C. < Latin *Punicus* < *Poenus* < Greek *Phoinix* "Phoenician"]

pun·ish /púnnish/ (**-ished, -ish·ing, -ish·es**) *v* **1.** *vti* MAKE SOMEBODY UNDERGO PENALTY to subject somebody to a penalty for wrongdoing **2.** *vt* IMPOSE PENALTY ON CRIME to respond to a crime or other wrong act by imposing a penalty (*often passive*) ○ *crimes formerly punished by death* **3.** *vt* TREAT SOMEBODY OR SOMETHING ROUGHLY to treat somebody or something harshly, causing damage or pain ○ *punished the champ with some powerful body blows* **4.** *vt* TREAT SOMEBODY UNFAIRLY to treat somebody unfairly or discriminate against somebody [14C. < Old French *puniss-*, stem of *punir* < Latin *punire* < *poena* "penalty"] —**pun·ish·a·ble** *adj* —**pun·ish·er** *n*

pun·ish·ing /púnnishing/ *adj* very demanding, either physically or mentally ○ *a punishing schedule* —**pun·ish·ing·ly** *adv*

pun·ish·ment /púnnishmənt/ *n* **1. PENALTY FOR DOING SOMETHING WRONG** a penalty that is imposed on somebody for wrongdoing **2. ACT OF PUNISHING** the act or an instance of punishing **3. ROUGH USE** rough treatment or heavy use ○ *a sturdy car that can take a lot of punishment*

pu·ni·tive /pyóonətiv/ *adj* **1.** relating to, done as, or imposed as a punishment ○ *punitive air strikes* **2.** causing great difficulty or hardship ○ *punitive taxation* [Early 17C. < medieval Latin *punitivus* < Latin *punit-*, past participle of *punire* (see PUNISH)] —**pu·ni·tive·ly** *adv* —**pu·ni·tive·ness** *n*

pu·ni·tive dam·ag·es *npl* damages that are awarded by a court to punish the defendant rather than to compensate the victim

Pun·jab /pún jaab, pun jaab/ *n* **FORMER PROVINCE IN NW BRITISH INDIA** former province in the northwest of British India, divided in 1947, when the eastern part became the Indian state of Punjab (divided in 1966 into three on linguistic grounds) and the western part became the Pakistan province of Punjab ■ **1.** state in northwestern India, bordering the province of Punjab in Pakistan. Capital: Chandigarh. Population: 24,289,296 (2001). Area: 19,445 sq. mi./50,362 sq. km. **2.** province of northeastern Pakistan, bordering the Indian state of Punjab. Capital: Lahore. Population: 72,585,000 (1998). Area: 79,284 sq. mi./205,344 sq. km.

Pun·ja·bi /pun jaabee, -jábbee/, **Pan·ja·bi** *n* the official language of Punjab, belonging to the Indo-Iranian language family. Native speakers: 70 million. [Early 19C. < Urdu *Panjābī* < *Panjāb* "Punjab" < Sanskrit *pañca āpas* "five rivers"] —**Pun·ja·bi** *adj*

punk /pungk/ *n* **1. YOUTH MOVEMENT** a youth movement of the late 1970s, characterized by loud aggressive rock music, confrontational attitudes, body piercing, and unconventional hairstyles, makeup, and clothing **2. SOMEBODY BELONGING TO PUNK MOVEMENT** a member of the punk movement of the late 1970s **3.** MUSIC same as **punk rock 4. OFFENSIVE TERM** an offensive term for a young man regarded as worthless, lazy, or arrogant (*informal*) **5.** *US* **YOUNG GAY PARTNER** an offensive term for a young gay partner of an older man (*archaic; sometimes considered offensive*) **6.** *US* **DRIED WOOD** dried or decayed wood used as tinder **7. INCENSE** incense in the form of thin sticks ■ *adj* **1. NOT FEELING GOOD** feeling bad, depressed, or ill **2. NO GOOD** inferior in quality or condition (*informal*) [Late 17C. Origin ?]

pun·ka /púngkə/, **pun·kah** *n S Asia* a hand-held fan for cooling or ventilation, or, formerly, a ceiling fan operated by an attendant [Early 17C. Via Hindi *paṅkhā* < Sanskrit *pakṣakaḥ* < *pakṣaḥ* "wing"]

punk·ie /púngkee/, **punk·y** (*plural* **-ies**) *n US* a fly, almost invisible to the naked eye, that sucks the blood of animals and other insects, leaving painful itching welts. Family: Ceratopogonidae. [Mid-18C. Via assumed New York Dutch *punkje* < Delaware *pónkwas* "dust, ashes"]

punk rock *n* fast loud rock music often with confrontational lyrics that characterized the punk movement —**punk rock·er** *n*

punk·y *n* INSECTS another spelling of **punkie**

pun·ster /púnstər/ *n* somebody who frequently makes puns

punt[1] /punt/ *n* **KICK** in football or rugby, a kick in which somebody drops a ball and kicks it before it hits the ground ■ *v* (**punt·ed, punt·ing, punts**) **1.** *vti* **KICK BALL** in football or rugby, to drop a ball and then kick it before it hits the ground **2.** *vi* **GIVE UP SOMETHING** to stop doing something, especially something regarded as tedious or difficult (*informal*) ○ *I did sit down to study, but decided to punt.* [Mid-19C. Origin ?] —**punt·er** *n*

punt[2] /punt/ *n* **FLAT-BOTTOMED BOAT** a narrow open boat with square ends that has a flat bottom and is propelled by means of a long pole ■ *v* **1.** *vi* **GO IN PUNT** to travel in a punt **2.** *vti* **PROPEL PUNT** to propel a punt using a long pole [Pre-12C. < Latin *ponto*] —**punt·er** *n*

punt[3] /punt/ *UK n* a bet, especially one placed with a bookmaker (*informal*) ■ *vi* (**punt·ed, punt·ing, punts**) to bet or gamble, especially with a bookmaker [Early 18C. < French *ponter*] —**punt·er** *n*

punt

punt[4] /poont/ *n* the main unit of the former Irish currency [Late 20C. < Irish *púnt*]

Pun·ta A·re·nas /poontə ə rénnəss/ city in southern Chile, on the Strait of Magellan, the southernmost city in the world. Population: 125,631 (1998).

punt for·ma·tion *n* in football, an offensive formation in which the back making the punt stands about ten yards behind the other backs, who are in a blocking position

Punt·land /poontlənd/ autonomous region of northeastern Somalia, which is seeking independent nation status

pun·ty /púntee/ (*plural* **-ties**) *n* a long metal rod on which molten glass is turned and worked during the glass-blowing process [Mid-17C. < French *pontil* "pontil"]

Punx·su·taw·ney /pùngksə táwnee/ city in west central Pennsylvania, known for the supposed emergence of its local groundhog from hibernation every year on Groundhog Day, February 2. Population: 6,169 (2002 estimate).

pu·ny /pyóonee/ *adj* **1.** very small or thin and weak **2.** less than is required to be effective ○ *a puny attempt at an apology* [Late 16C. Anglicization of PUISNE] —**pu·ni·ness** *n*

pup /pup/ *n* **1. YOUNG DOG** a dog under a year old **2. YOUNG ANIMAL** a young animal of various species such as mice, rats, wolves, foxes, and seals **3. IMPUDENT YOUTH** an inexperienced or arrogant young person, especially a boy or young man (*informal*) ■ *vi* (**pupped, pup·ping, pups**) **BEAR PUPS** to give birth to pups [Late 16C. Shortening of PUPPY]

pu·pa /pyóopə/ (*plural* **-pae** /-pee/ or **-pas**) *n* an insect at the stage between a larva and an adult in complete metamorphosis, during which the insect is in a cocoon or case, stops feeding, and undergoes internal changes [Late 18C. < Latin, "girl, doll"] —**pu·pal** *adj*

pu·pate /pyóo pàyt/ (**-pat·ed, -pat·ing, -pates**) *vi* to develop from a larva into a pupa —**pu·pa·tion** /pyoo páysh'n/ *n*

pup·fish /púp fish/ (*plural same* or **-fish·es**) *n* a tiny killifish. Native to: streams and springs in southwestern United States and Mexico. Genus: *Cyprinodon.*

pu·pil[1] /pyóop'l/ *n* **1. STUDENT** a young student, taught at school or by a private teacher **2. FOLLOWER OR STUDENT OF SOMEBODY** a student who learns from a mentor or other person who is skilled, knowledgeable, or experienced ○ *a pupil of Jung* **3.** LAW **TRAINEE BARRISTER** somebody who trains to become a barrister in Canada or the United Kingdom [14C. < Latin *pupillus* "little boy" < *pupus* "boy"]

pu·pil[2] /pyóop'l/ *n* the dark circular opening at the center of the iris in the eye, where light enters the eye [14C. Via French < Latin *pupilla* "little doll" < *pupa* "girl, doll"; from the tiny image that you see when looking into another person's eye]

pu·pil·lage /pyóop'lij/ *n* the state of being a pupil, or the period during which somebody is a pupil

pu·pil·lar·y[1] /pyóop'l èrree/ *adj* relating to or affecting the pupil of the eye [Late 18C. < Latin *púpilla* (see PUPIL[2])]

pu·pil·lar·y[2] /pyóop'l èrree/ *adj* relating to a minor child under the care of a guardian [Early 17C. Directly or via French < Latin *pupillaris* < *pupillus* (see PUPIL[1])]

pup·pet /púppət/ *n* **1.** a doll or figure representing a person or animal that is moved using the hands inside the figure or by moving rods, strings, or wires attached to it **2.** a person, government, or organization whose actions are controlled by others [Mid-16C. Variant of POPPET]

pup·pet·eer /pùppə téer/ *n* somebody who operates puppets or gives puppet shows

pup·pet·ry /púppətree/ *n* the art of making or operating puppets

Pup·pis /púppiss/ *n* a constellation of the southern hemisphere lying partly in the Milky Way, located between Vela and Canis Major. See illustration at **constellation**

pup·py /púppee/ (*plural* **-pies**) *n* **1.** a dog under a year old **2.** an inexperienced or arrogant young person, especially a boy or young man (*informal*) [15C. Origin ?] —**pup·py·hood** *n* —**pup·py·ish** *adj*

pup·py fat *n UK* same as **baby fat** (*informal*)

pup·py love *n* the love or infatuation felt by adolescents

pup tent *n* CAMPING same as **shelter tent**

Pu·ra·na /poo raanə/ (*plural* **-nas**) *n* any of a group of sacred Hindu texts written in Sanskrit that recount the lives of deities and the creation, destruction, and recreation of the universe [Late 17C. < Sanskrit *purāṇaḥ* < *purāṇa-* "belonging to former times" < *purā* "formerly"] —**Pu·ra·nic** *adj*

Pur·bach /púr bàk/ hexagonal lunar crater visible in the southwestern quadrant of the Moon, approximately 75 mi./120 km in diameter

pur·blind /púr blīnd/ *adj* **1.** an offensive term meaning vision-impaired **2.** slow or unwilling to understand (*formal*) [13C. < PURE]

Pur·cell /pər sél/, **Henry** (1659–95) English composer. He wrote numerous instrumental and vocal pieces, including the opera *Dido and Aeneas* (1689) and incidental music for *The Tempest* (1695).

pur·chase /púrchəss/ *v* (**-chased, -chas·ing, -chas·es**) **1.** *vti* **GET SOMETHING BY PAYING MONEY** to buy something using money or its equivalent **2.** *vt* **OBTAIN SOMETHING THROUGH HARD WORK** to obtain something by hard work or sacrifice ○ *a victory purchased with great effort* **3.** *vt* **MOVE SOMETHING USING LEVER** to move, lift, or hold on to something using a device such as a lever ■ *n* **1. ACT OF BUYING** the act of buying something using money or its equivalent **2. SOMETHING BOUGHT** an item that somebody has bought **3. OBTAINING THROUGH EFFORT** the acquisition of something through hard work or sacrifice ○ *a purchase achieved at great emotional cost* **4. HOLD** a firm grip or hold on something ○ *hands too slippery to get a purchase on the rock* **5. ADVANTAGE** influence, power, or another advantage that can be exercised ○ *an attempt to gain some purchase over his rivals* **6. POWER GIVEN BY LEVER** a measure of the mechanical advantage given by a pulley or lever [13C. < Anglo-Norman *purchacer* "pursue," literally "chase eagerly" < Old French *chacier* (see CHASE[1])] —**pur·chas·a·ble** *adj* —**pur·chas·er** *n*

pur·chas·ing pow·er /púrchassing-/ *n* **1.** the ability to make purchases according to income and savings **2.** the value of a currency measured in terms of the goods and services it can buy ○ *the purchasing power of the yen*

pur·dah /púrdə/ *n* **1. KEEPING OF WOMEN FROM PUBLIC VIEW** the Hindu and Islamic custom of keeping women fully covered with clothing and apart from the rest of society **2. SCREEN** a screen or curtain used in some Hindu communities to keep women out of view **3. VEIL** a veil worn by some Hindu and Muslim women as part of purdah [Early 19C. Via Urdu *pardah* "veil" < Middle Persian *pardak*]

pure /pyoor/ (**pur·er, pur·est**) *adj* **1. NOT MIXED** not mixed with any other substance ○ *This jacket is pure wool.* **2. FREE FROM CONTAMINATION** clean and free from impurities ○ *The water from the spring is completely pure.* **3. COMPLETE** sheer or complete ○ *a look of pure terror* **4. CLEAR** describes color, sound, or light that is pleasingly clear and vivid **5. RELATING TO THEORY** relating to theory rather than practical applications

○ *pure science* **6. CHASTE** virtuous and chaste (*literary*) **7. OF UNMIXED ANCESTRY** having unmixed parentage or ancestry **8.** BIOL **PRODUCED BY CONSTANT INBREEDING** produced by continual inbreeding or self-fertilization and producing offspring with the same hereditary characteristics **9.** MUSIC, PHYS **COMPOSED OF SINGLE FREQUENCY** describes sound composed of a single frequency **10.** MUSIC **WITHOUT DISCORD** describes a musical tone without discord **11.** PHON **PRONOUNCED WITH ONE UNCHANGING SOUND** describes a vowel that is pronounced with a single unchanging sound **12.** PHON **PRONOUNCED WITHOUT ANOTHER CONSONANT** describes a consonant that is pronounced unaccompanied by any other consonant [13C. Via French < Latin *purus*] —**pure·ness** *n*

pure·blood /pyoŏr blùd/, **pure·blood·ed** /pyoŏr blùddəd, pyoŏr blúddəd/ *adj* having an ancestry that is exclusively of one type —**pure·blood** *n*

pure·bred /pyoŏr brèd/ *adj* having ancestors that belong to the same breed or variety as a result of controlled breeding ○ *a purebred Arabian stallion* ■ *n* a purebred plant or animal

pure de·moc·ra·cy *n* a form of democracy in which the people exercise direct power instead of electing representatives to govern on their behalf

pu·rée /pyoŏ ráy, pyə-/, **pu·ree** *n* a food that has been made into a thick moist paste by rubbing it through a sieve, mashing it, or blending it ■ *vti* (**-réed, -rée·ing, -rées; -reed, -ree·ing, -rees**) to become a purée, or sieve, mash, or blend food into a purée ○ *Purée the vegetables and add them to the stock.* [Early 18C. < French < form of past participle of *purer* "squeeze out," literally "make pure" < Latin *purare* < *purus* "pure"]

Pure Land Bud·dhism *n* a form of Mahayana Buddhism that worships the Buddha Amitabha as a compassionate savior and promises rebirth in paradise, known as the Pure Land, as a reward for faith [*Pure Land* is a translation of Chinese *Qingtu*]

pure·ly /pyoŏrlee/ *adv* **1. ENTIRELY** in a complete, entire, or total way ○ *a purely financial decision* **2. MERELY** solely or simply ○ *surgery for purely cosmetic purposes* **3. WITH NOTHING ADDED** in a way that is free of any added substances or of any contaminants ○ *sheep that have been purely bred from the original stock* **4. INNOCENTLY** in a way that is innocent, pure, or chaste

pur·fle /púrf'l/ *n* an ornamental border on clothing or furniture, consisting of a ruffled or curved band ■ *vt* (**-fled, -fling, -fles**) to decorate clothing or furniture with a purfle [14C. < Old French *porfil* < *porfiler* < assumed Vulgar Latin *profilare* "spin forward" < Latin *filum* "thread"] —**pur·fling** *n*

pur·ga·tion /pur gáysh'n/ *n* the act of purging or being purged (*formal*)

pur·ga·tive /púrgətiv/ (*formal*) *n* a drug or other substance that causes evacuation of the bowels ■ *adj* acting as a purgative

pur·ga·to·ri·al /pùrgə táwree əl/ *adj* (*literary*) **1.** relating to or similar to purgatory **2.** serving to rid somebody of sin

pur·ga·to·ry /púrgə tàwree/ *n* **1.** *also* **Pur·ga·to·ry** in Roman Catholic doctrine, the place where souls remain until they have expiated their sins and can go to heaven **2.** an extremely uncomfortable, painful, or unpleasant situation or experience ○ *the purgatory of lost love* [12C. Via French < medieval Latin *purgatorium* < Latin *purgare* "purify" (see PURGE)]

purge /purj/ *v* (**purged, purg·ing, purg·es**) **1.** *vt* **GET RID OF OPPONENTS** to remove opponents or people considered undesirable from a state or organization **2.** *vt* **REMOVE SOMETHING UNDESIRABLE** to get rid of something undesirable, impure, or imperfect **3.** *vt* RELIG **FREE SOMEBODY FROM GUILT OR SIN** to make somebody or something pure and free from guilt, sin, or defilement (*formal*) ○ *purge a soul of its sins* **4.** *vt* COMPUT **DELETE DATA** to delete unwanted or unneeded data from disk storage in a systematic fashion so as to remove all references to the data **5.** *vi* PSYCHOL, MED **VOMIT OR USE LAXATIVES** to rid the body of food by using laxatives or inducing vomiting **6.** *vti* MED **EMPTY BOWELS** to empty the bowels, or cause somebody to empty the bowels ■ *n* **1. GETTING RID OF OPPONENTS** the removal of opponents or people considered undesirable from a state or organization **2. GETTING RID OF SOMETHING UNDESIRABLE** the removal of something undesirable, impure, or imperfect **3.** MED **LAXATIVE** something that acts as a laxative (*archaic*) [13C. Via French < Latin *purgare* "purify" < *purus* "pure"] —**purg·er** *n*

pu·ri /poŏree/ (*plural same* or **-ris**), **poo·ri** *n* a small piece of light flat unleavened South Asian bread that is fried and served hot [Mid-20C. Via Hindi *pūrī* < Sanskrit *pūrikā*]

pu·ri·fi·ca·tor /pyoŏrəfi kàytər/ *n* a linen cloth used in some Christian churches to wipe the chalice after the celebration of Communion

pu·ri·fy /pyoŏrə fī/ (**-fied, -fy·ing, -fies**) *v* **1.** *vti* to rid something of harmful, inferior, or unwanted contaminants, or get rid of harmful, inferior, or unwanted contaminants ○ *We use special filters to purify the water.* **2.** *vt* to free somebody of sin, guilt, or defilement, e.g., in a ceremony or a ritual cleansing —**pu·ri·fi·ca·tion** /pyoŏrəfi káysh'n/ *n* —**pu·rif·i·ca·to·ry** /pyoo ríffəkə tàwree/ *adj* —**pu·ri·fi·er** *n*

Pu·rim /poŏrim, poo rím/ *n* a Jewish festival marking the Jewish people's deliverance from a plot to massacre them. Date: 14th day of Adar. [14C. < Hebrew *pū'rīm* "lots (cast)"]

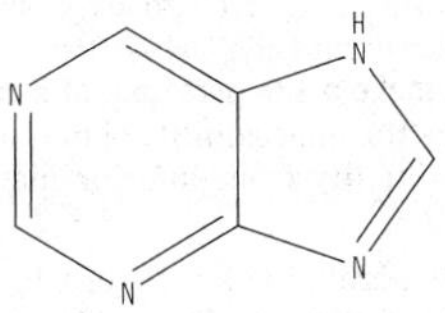

purine

pu·rine /pyoŏr èen, pyoŏrin/ *n* **1.** a nitrogen-containing substance derived from uric acid that is the precursor of several biologically important compounds. Formula: $C_5H_4N_4$. **2.** a derivative of purine, especially either of the bases adenine and guanine, which are found in RNA and DNA [Late 19C. < German *Purin* < blend of Latin *purus* "pure" + modern Latin *uricum* "uric acid"]

pur·ism /pyoŏr ìzzəm/ *n* insistence on the maintenance or observance of traditional standards in a field, especially in the use of language

pur·ist /pyoŏrist/ *n* somebody who seeks to maintain the pure or traditional form of something —**pu·ris·tic** /pyoŏ rístik/ *adj*

pu·ri·tan /pyoŏrət'n/ *n* somebody who lives by a strict moral or religious code, especially somebody who is suspicious of pleasure ■ *adj* RELIG **1.** same as **puritanical 2.** same as **puritanical** [Late 16C. < PURITAN] —**pu·ri·tan·ism** *n*

Pu·ri·tan *n* a member of a group of Protestants in 16th- and 17th-century England and 17th-century America who believed in strict religious discipline and called for the simplification of acts of worship ■ *adj* relating to Puritans or their beliefs or religious movement ○ *a Puritan form of worship* [Late 16C. < Latin *puritas* "purity" < *purus* "pure"] —**Pu·ri·tan·ism** *n*

pu·ri·tan·i·cal /pyoŏrə tánnik'l/, **pu·ri·tan·ic** /-tánnik/ *adj* adhering to strict moral or religious principles —**pu·ri·tan·i·cal·ly** *adv*

pu·ri·ty /pyoŏrətee/ (*plural* **-ties**) *n* **1. FREEDOM FROM CONTAMINANTS** the absence, or degree of absence, of anything harmful, inferior, unwanted, or of a different type ○ *tests to establish the purity of the water* **2. INNOCENCE** virtue and innocence ○ *the purity of young children* **3. CLARITY** clarity of tone or sound **4. COLOR SATURATION** the degree of saturation or lack of white in a color **5.** LING **CORRECTNESS** the observance of traditional standards of correctness in speech and writing

Pur·kin·je cell /pur kínjee-/ *n* one of the many densely branching neurons found in the middle layer of the brain's cerebellar cortex [Late 19C. After J. E. *Purkinje* (1787–1869), Bohemian physiologist]

purl[1] /purl/ HANDICRAFT *n* **1. STITCH IN KNITTING** a reverse plain knitting stitch, often combined with a plain stitch to create a ribbed effect **2.** *also* **pearl GOLD OR SILVER THREAD** sewing thread that is made from gold or silver wire **3.** *also* **pearl BORDER ON LACE OR BRAID** a decorative looped border sewn on lace or braid ■ *vti* (**purled, purl·ing, purls**) **KNIT WITH PURL** to knit something using a purl stitch [14C. Origin ?]

purl[2] /purl/ (*literary*) *vi* (**purled, purl·ing, purls**) to flow with a soft murmuring sound, producing gentle ripples (*refers to rivers and streams*) ■ *n* the soft murmuring sound and gentle rippling movement of a river or stream [15C. Probably < N Germanic]

pur·lieu /púrlyoo, púrloo/ *n* **1. OUTLYING DISTRICT** a district on the outskirts of a city or town **2. FREQUENTED PLACE** a place that somebody often visits (*formal*) **3.** *UK* **SHABBY AREA** an area or district, especially one that is old and poor (*formal*) ■ **pur·lieus** *npl* **ENVIRONS** the outer regions or boundaries of a place (*formal*) [15C. Probably alteration (influenced by LIEU) of Anglo-Norman *puralee* "king's trip around the borders" < *pur-* "forth" + *aller* "go"]

pur·lin /púrlin/ *n* a horizontal roof beam that supports the rafters [15C. Origin ?]

pur·loin /pur lóyn/ (**-loined, -loin·ing, -loins**) *vt* to steal something, especially when the theft breaks another's trust (*formal or humorous*) ○ *He purloined several small items, including a silk scarf.* [14C. < Anglo-Norman *purloigner* "move far away" < Old French *loing* "far" < Latin *longus* "long"] —**pur·loin·er** *n*

SYNONYMS See ***steal.***

pur·ple /púrp'l/ *n* **1. COLOR COMBINING RED AND BLUE** a dark color that is formed as a pigment by combining red and blue **2. PURPLE OBJECT** an object, substance, or fabric that is purple in color **3.** CLOTHING **ROBE IN COLOR PURPLE** a cloth or robe in the color purple that was formerly worn as a symbol of imperial, royal, or other high rank **4. IMPERIAL RANK** imperial power or high rank **5.** CHR **RANK OF CARDINAL OR BISHOP** the rank or office of a cardinal or a bishop **6.** CHR **BISHOPS** bishops regarded as a group ■ *adj* **1. OF DARK RED-BLUE** of a dark red-blue color **2.** LITERAT **ELABORATE OR EXAGGERATED** elaborate in style and containing too many literary effects ○ *purple prose* ■ *vti* (**-pled, -pling, -ples**) **TURN SOMETHING PURPLE** to become purple, or make something become purple ○ *His eyes narrowed and his cheeks purpled.* [Pre-12C. Alteration of Latin *purpura* < Greek *porphura* "shellfish yielding purple dye"] —**pur·ple·ness** *n* —**pur·plish** *adj* —**pur·ply** *adj*

CULTURAL NOTE ***The Color Purple***, a novel (1982) by Alice Walker. In it, Celie, an uneducated young African American woman growing up in the South after the Civil War, confides the story of her life in a series of letters to her sister, a missionary in Africa, and to God. She tells of abuse and suffering, and her gradual empowerment through friendship and love. The novel is celebrated for the emotional power of its Black vernacular language. In 1985 Steven Spielberg made it into a movie starring Whoopi Goldberg.

pur·ple finch *n* a finch, similar to the house finch, with a raspberry-red head and breast. Native to: North America. Latin name: *Carpodacus purpureus.*

pur·ple gal·li·nule *n* **1.** a large water bird with purplish feathers. Native to: North, Central and South America. Latin name: *Porphyrula martinica.* **2.** a water bird with dark bluish purple feathers and red legs. Native to: Mediterranean, Africa, Asia, North and South America, New Zealand, Pacific. Genus: *Porphyrio.*

pur·ple grack·le *n* a bird that has deep purple iridescent feathers. Native to: eastern North America. Latin name: *Quiscalus quiscula.*

pur·ple·heart /púrp'l haărt/ (*plural* **-hearts** or *same*) *n* **1.** a tree with hard brownish wood that turns purple when exposed to air. Native to: tropical South America. Genus: *Peltogyne.* **2.** the hard decorative purplish wood of the purpleheart tree

Pur·ple Heart *n* a decoration awarded to members of the US armed forces who have been wounded in action [< the silver heart and the purple ribbon from which it is suspended]

pur·ple loose·strife *n* a marsh plant with lance-shaped leaves that has naturalized in North America, sometimes driving out native plants. Flowers: purple, in spikes. Latin name: *Lystrum salicaria*.

pur·ple mar·tin *n* a large bird of the swallow family with shiny blue-black feathers, a notched tail, and, in the female, a grayish breast. Native to: North America. Latin name: *Progne subis*.

pur·port *vti* /pər páwrt/ (**-port·ed, -port·ing, -ports**) **1. CLAIM TO BE SOMETHING** to claim or seem to be something or somebody ○ *The book purports to be a series of predictions.* **2. INTEND SOMETHING** to intend to do something (*formal*) ○ *While this new measure provided money for research, it also purported to cut spending overall.* ■ *n* /púr pàwrt/ (*formal*) **1. SENSE** the meaning or significance of something ○ *The purport of the remarks was difficult to discern.* **2. INTENT** intention or purpose of something ○ *The principal purport of his letter was to inform them that he would soon be leaving the country.* [15C. Via Anglo-Norman *purporter* "carry forward" < Latin *portare* "carry"] —**pur·port·ed** *adj*

USAGE The passive form of the verb ***purport*** is often used in place of the active form with the same meaning: *The novel purports* [or *is purported*] *to be autobiographical.* Some people regard any passive use of the verb as incorrect, and it is often better to use *alleged, supposed,* or some other synonym in place of *purported*: *The president is alleged* [not *purported*] *to have vetoed the proposal.*

pur·pose /púrpəss/ *n* **1. REASON FOR EXISTENCE** the reason for which something exists or for which it has been done or made ○ *the purpose of life* **2. DESIRED EFFECT** the goal or intended outcome of something ○ *The purpose of the law is to control pollution.* **3. DETERMINATION** the desire or the resolve necessary to accomplish a goal ○ *You need to act with purpose.* ■ *vt* (**-posed, -pos·ing, -pos·es**) **SET SOMETHING AS GOAL** to intend or determine to do something [13C. < Old French *purpos* < *purposer* "intend," alteration (influenced by *poser* "put") of Latin *proponere* "put forward"] —**pur·pose·less** *adj* —**pur·pose·less·ly** *adv* —**pur·pose·less·ness** *n* ◇ **be at cross purposes 1.** to be talking about different things and so be involved in a misunderstanding **2.** in conflict with somebody else or each other, when cooperation is needed ◇ **on purpose** deliberately ◇ **to good purpose** successfully, or with good results (*formal*) ◇ **to little** *or* **no purpose** without success or achieving useful results (*formal*)

pur·pose·ful /púrpəssfəl/ *adj* **1.** showing a clear determination ○ *She set off with a purposeful stride.* **2.** having a definite purpose or aim ○ *purposeful activity* —**pur·pose·ful·ly** *adv* —**pur·pose·ful·ness** *n*

USAGE See ***purposely***.

pur·pose·ly /púrpəsslee/ *adv* deliberately or with an express purpose in mind ○ *They purposely left our names off the list.*

USAGE purposely or **purposefully**? These two adverbs are sometimes confused. Although both imply that somebody has a specific purpose in mind, they are used in different contexts and are not interchangeable. ***Purposely*** means "on purpose" or "intentionally": *I purposely left the door unlocked.* ***Purposefully*** means "in a determined way" or "with a specific goal": *She strode purposefully across the yard.*

pur·po·sive /púrpəssiv/ *adj* **1.** having a use or purpose ○ *Most human activity is purposive.* **2.** showing determination ○ *She had a purposive air about her that morning.* —**pur·po·sive·ly** *adv* —**pur·po·sive·ness** *n*

pur·pu·ra /púrpyərə/ *n* a condition in which bleeding under the skin causes purplish blotches to appear on the skin [Mid-18C. < Latin (see PURPLE)] —**pur·pu·ric** /pur pyŏŏrik/ *adj*

pur·pure /púrpyər/ *n* in heraldry, the color purple [Pre-12C. < Latin *purpura* (see PURPLE)]

pur·pu·rin /púrpyərin/ *n* a reddish orange crystalline compound. Use: manufacture of dyes, biological stain, reagent for the detection of boron. Formula: $C_{14}H_8O_5$.

purr /pur/ *n* **1. CAT'S LOW MURMURING NOISE** the characteristic soft low murmuring noise that a cat makes when it seems to be contented **2. PURRING SOUND** a sound similar to the purr of a cat ○ *the purr of the engine* ■ *v* (**purred, purr·ing, purrs**) **1.** *vi* **EMIT PURR** to make the characteristic soft low murmuring noise that a cat makes when it seems to be contented **2.** *vti* **SAY SOMETHING IN SOFT THROATY VOICE** to speak, or say something, in a soft throaty voice that suggests pleasure, contentment, or sensuality **3.** *vi* **MAKE LOW REGULAR MECHANICAL SOUND** to make the soft low vibrating noise that a machine, especially an engine, makes when it is perfectly tuned and is running well [Early 17C. An imitation of the sound] —**purr·ing·ly** *adv*

purse /purss/ *n* **1. WOMAN'S BAG FOR CARRYING EVERYDAY BELONGINGS** a bag that a woman or girl carries small personal day-to-day belongings in, such as keys, a wallet, a datebook, and pens **2.** *UK* same as **change purse 3. PRIZE MONEY** a sum of money collected as a gift or offered as a prize, especially the total sum of money offered in prizes ○ *with a purse of over $20,000* **4. AVAILABLE FUNDS** an amount of money available to spend ○ *The legislators overestimated the size of the public purse.* ■ *vt* (**pursed, purs·ing, purs·es**) **DRAW LIPS TOGETHER AT SIDES** to draw the lips together at the sides so that they wrinkle and form a circle, usually when deep in thought or to express disapproval [13C. Alteration of late Latin *bursa* < Greek, "hide, leather"] ◇ **you can't make a silk purse out of a sow's ear** used to emphasize the impossibility of making something of superior quality from inferior materials or beginnings

purse crab *n* a crab, the female of which carries its eggs in a sac. Native to: Gulf of Mexico, Caribbean. Latin name: *Persephona mediterranea* or *Persephona punctata*.

purs·er /púrssər/ *n* the officer on a merchant ship or commercial aircraft who is responsible for managing the money and who, on a passenger ship, is responsible for the well-being of the passengers

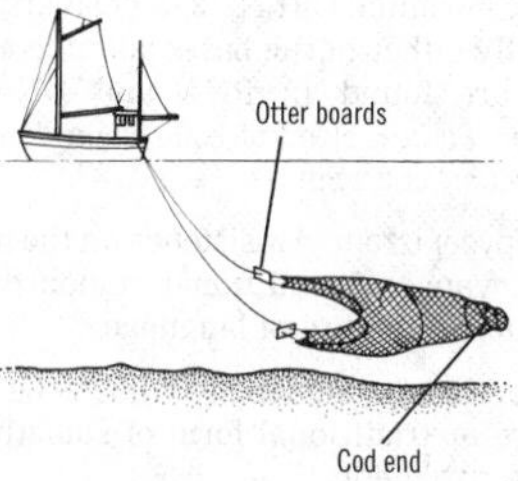

purse seine

purse seine *n* a large commercial fishing net pulled by two boats, with ends that are pulled together around a shoal of fish so that the net forms a pouch

purse strings *npl* control over the money that is available to spend

purs·lane /púrsslən, púr slàyn/ (*plural* **-lanes** or *same*) *n* a trailing weed sometimes used in salad or cooked and served as a vegetable. Native to: Asia. Genus: *Portulaca*. [14C. < Old French *porcelaine*, alteration (influenced by *porcelaine* "porcelain") of Latin *porcilaca* < *portulaca*]

pur·su·ance /pər sōō ənss/ *n* the process of doing something or carrying it out in the way that is expected or required (*formal*) ○ *in pursuance of our agreement*

pur·su·ant /pər sōō ənt/ *adj* following in order to catch [Mid-16C. < Old French *poursuiant*, present participle of *poursuir* (see PURSUE)] ◇ **pursuant to** something in accordance with something (*formal*)

pur·sue /pər sōō/ (**-sued, -su·ing, -sues**) *v* **1.** *vti* **CHASE SOMEBODY** to follow somebody, sometimes for a long time, in order to catch or capture him or her **2.** *vt* **CARRY SOMETHING OUT** to work at something or carry it out ○ *pursuing his studies* **3.** *vt* **CONTINUE WITH SOMETHING** to continue with something or follow it up ○ *pursuing a number of lines of inquiry* **4.** *vt* **SEEK SOMEBODY PERSISTENTLY FOR SEXUAL PARTNER** to make persistent attempts to start a sexual relationship with somebody **5.** *vt* **STRIVE FOR SOMETHING** to try hard to achieve or obtain something over a period of time **6.** *vt* **BE EVER-PRESENT PROBLEM FOR SOMEBODY** to be an ongoing persistent problem for a person or organization ○ *Poor investment decisions pursued the company.* **7.** *vt* **FOLLOW ROUTE** to go along a route or direction [14C. < Anglo-Norman *pursuer*, variant of Old French *poursuir, pursivre* < Latin *prosequi* "follow forward" (see PROSECUTE)] —**pur·su·a·ble** *adj* —**pur·su·er** *n*

SYNONYMS See *follow*.

pur·suit /pər sŏŏt/ *n* **1. ACT OF CHASING AFTER SOMETHING** the act of chasing after somebody or something in order to catch, attack, or overtake that person or thing ○ *in pursuit of the stolen car* **2. HOBBY** a pastime, hobby, or leisure activity **3. ACT OF STRIVING FOR SOMETHING** the effort made to try to achieve or obtain something over a period of time ○ *the pursuit of happiness* **4.** *UK* **CYCLE RACE WITH OBJECT OF OVERTAKING** a cycle race in which the riders start from points on opposite sides of a circular track and race to overtake each other rather than to reach a set finishing line first [14C. < Anglo-Norse *purseute*, variant of Old French *poursuite* < *poursuir* (see PURSUE)]

pur·suit plane *n* a fighter plane before World War II

pur·ty /púrtee/ (**-ti·er, -ti·est**) *adj regional* same as **pretty** [Early 19C. Variant of PRETTY]

pu·ru·lent /pyŏŏrələnt/ *adj* relating to, containing, or consisting of pus [15C. Via French < Latin *purulentus* "full of pus" < *pur-* "pus"] —**pu·ru·lence** *n* —**pu·ru·lent·ly** *adv*

pur·vey /pər váy/ (**-veyed, -vey·ing, -veys**) *vt* **1.** to publish or pass on news or information, especially gossip, scandal, or other kinds of information that people generally feel should not be circulated **2.** to supply goods, especially foods, commercially (*formal*) [12C. Via Anglo-Norman *purveier*, Old French *porveeir* < Latin *providere* (see PROVIDE)]

pur·vey·ance /pər váy ənss/ *n* the supplying of something, especially food (*formal*)

pur·vey·or /pər váy ər/ *n* **1.** a supplier, seller, or circulator of something, especially something that is disapproved of or ridiculed ○ *a purveyor of cheap gossip* **2.** a person or company supplying goods, especially foods (*formal*)

pur·view /púr vyōō/ *n* **1.** the scope or range of something such as a court's jurisdiction or somebody's knowledge **2.** the main body of a written piece of legislation that follows the introductory section or preamble and contains the clauses that state what the law requires [15C. < Anglo-Norman *purveii*, Old French *porveii*, past participle of *porveeir* (see PURVEY)]

pus /puss/ *n* the yellowish or greenish fluid that forms at sites of infection, consisting of dead white blood cells, dead tissue, bacteria, and blood serum [14C. < Latin]

Pu·san /poo saán/ city and port on Korea Strait in southeastern South Korea. It is the second largest city in the country. Population: 3,813,814 (1995).

Pu·sey·ism /pyōōzee ìzzəm/ *n* the teachings of Edward Pusey, leader of the Oxford Movement, who advocated a renewal of Catholic practices in the Church of England

push /pŏŏsh/ *v* (**pushed, push·ing, push·es**) **1.** *vti* **PRESS AGAINST SOMETHING TO MOVE IT** to press against somebody or something in order to move that person or object **2.** *vti* **CAUSE SOMETHING TO ADVANCE BY FORCE** to advance by using pressure or force, or make somebody or something advance in this way ○ *She pushed to the front.* **3.** *vt* **ENCOURAGE SOMEBODY STRONGLY** to urge somebody strongly to take an action or move in a particular direction ○ *pushed their children to succeed* **4.** *vt* **DEPEND ON OR EXPLOIT SOMETHING** to depend on or exploit something to the limits of what is wise or acceptable ○ *Don't push your luck.* **5.** *vt* **USE ENERGY TO ACCOMPLISH SOMETHING** to use effort or energy to promote or accomplish something ○ *push a bill through the legislative process* **6.** *vti* **EXTEND SOMETHING BEYOND LIMITS** to extend something or go beyond the usual limits ○ *pushing the boundaries of knowledge in this field* **7.** *vt* **FORCE SOMETHING TO CHANGE** to force something, especially a financial system, to change in some way ○ *a fear that increased competition will push prices down* **8.** *vt* **TRY TO SELL SOMETHING** to promote the sale or use of something, or the acceptance of an idea **9.** *vt* **SELL DRUGS** to sell drugs illegally (*slang*) **10.** *vi* MIL **ADVANCE AGAINST ENEMY** to make a sustained military advance **11.** *vt* COMPUT **ADD DATA TO PUSHDOWN LIST** to add an item at the top of a pushdown list ■ *n* **1. APPLICATION OF PRESSURE** the act of applying pressure in order to move a person or object **2. ACT OF ADVANCING** an act of advancing by using pressure or force **3. ENERGETIC EFFORT** an energetic effort used to promote or accomplish something ○ *make a push to reform the tax code* **4. DETERMINATION** vigorous energy or will to succeed ○ *dynamic graduates with plenty of push* **5. MILITARY ADVANCE** a sustained military advance ○ *a push into enemy territory* **6. STIMULUS** a stimulus or encouragement that helps the process of starting, finishing, or changing something **7.** HOCKEY **CONTINUOUS NUDGING SHOT WITH STICK** in field hockey, a shot in which the ball is moved forward along the ground to another player by the application of continuous pressure with the stick, instead of being hit **8.** COMPUT **NETWORK SERVICE TRANSMITTING DATA** a network service in which the source of the data initiates the transmission [14C. Via French *pousser* < Latin *pulsare* "drive repeatedly" < *pellere* "to drive, thrust"] ◇ **be pushing...** to be approaching a particular age (*informal*) ○ *He must be pushing 40.* ◇ **when** *or* **if push comes to shove** at the point when something must be done or a decision must be made

push ahead *vti* to carry on with, or cause the advancement of, a process or project with renewed determination or effort ○ *a pledge to push ahead with plans for closer economic and political ties*

push around *vt* to treat somebody in a domineering way, especially by making unfair demands or giving repeated orders, and generally showing no respect (*informal*)

push back *vt* **1.** to set the time at which something is to happen to a later time ○ *agreed to push back the deadline by 10 days* **2.** to force an aggressive group of people to retreat ○ *Police pushed back protesters amid a hail of rocks and bottles.*

push forward *vti* same as **push ahead**

push off *v* **1.** *vti* to move a boat out into open water, away from the place where it has been tied up **2.** *vi* to leave or go away (*informal*)

push on *vi* to continue on a journey, or carry on with an activity with renewed determination or effort

push through *vt* to get something accepted or agreed quickly, especially by using persuasion or force

push·back /po͝osh bàk/ *n* **1.** in field hockey, a stick stroke used to start a game or to restart it after a goal has been scored **2.** opposition or other resistance to something such as an initiative, plan, or strategy

push broom *n* a very wide brush designed to sweep large areas by being pushed

push but·ton *n* a button that, when pushed, mechanically opens or closes an electrical circuit, e.g., a doorbell

push-but·ton *adj* **1. OPERATED BY PUSHING BUTTON** operated by pushing a button or buttons to open or close an electrical circuit **2. EQUIPPED WITH AUTOMATIC DEVICES** equipped with modern devices that perform tasks more or less automatically ○ *the push-button kitchen* **3. INSTANTLY PROVIDED** obtained, provided, or produced easily and instantly

push·cart /po͝osh kaart/ *n* a cart light enough to be pushed by hand, e.g., one from which goods are sold

push·chair /po͝osh chèr/ *n* *UK* same as **stroller** (sense 1)

push·down /po͝osh dòwn/ *n* a method of organizing computer data in which the item most recently added to a list becomes the first item to be retrieved or removed (*often used before a noun*) ○ *a pushdown stack*

pushed /po͝osht/ *adj* (*informal*) **1.** lacking something, usually time ○ *We're pushed for time now.* **2.** *UK* able to do something only with difficulty or effort ○ *I'd be hard pushed to remember the last time I saw a good movie.*

push·er /po͝oshər/ *n* **1.** a dealer in illegal drugs (*slang*) **2.** somebody ambitious who is always trying aggressively to outdo other people (*informal*)

push·ing /po͝oshing/ *adj* **1.** showing energy, initiative, and ambition **2.** aggressively self-confident or assertive —**push·ing·ly** *adv*

Push·kin /po͝oshkin/, **Aleksandr** (1799–1837) Russian writer. He was an author of plays, novels, and short stories, and his best-known works include the verse novel *Eugene Onegin* (1831) and the tragic play *Boris Godunov* (1825). Full name **Pushkin, Aleksandr Sergeyevich**

> "With a sharp epigram it's pleasant / to infuriate a clumsy foe."
> [Aleksandr Pushkin, *Eugene Onegin*; 1831]

push·o·ver /po͝osh ōvər/ *n* (*informal*) **1.** somebody who is easily persuaded, deceived, or defeated **2.** something that is very easy to do, deal with, or accomplish with success

push·pin /po͝osh pìn/ *n* a tack with a cylindrical head, used to fix paper or other lightweight materials to a wall or bulletin board

push-pull *adj* describes an electronic circuit in which two components are arranged so that an alternating input makes them transmit a current alternately. This type of circuit is commonly used in audio amplifiers to reduce harmonic distortion.

push rod *n* a metal rod operated by a cam to open and close a valve in an internal combustion engine

push tech·nol·o·gy *n* Internet technology that provides data or other material from a supplier to a subscriber at regular intervals or whenever a new version is available, without the user needing to ask for it

Push·to, Push·tu *n, adj* PEOPLES, LANG same as **Pashto**

push·up /po͝osh ùp/ *n* **1.** a physical exercise in which, from a position of lying flat on the front with the hands under the shoulders, the body is pushed off the floor until the arms are straight **2.** a method of organizing computer data in which the first item added to a list becomes the first item to be retrieved or removed

push·y /po͝oshee/ (**-i·er, -i·est**) *adj* excessively aggressive or forceful in competing or dealing with others (*informal*) ○ *pushy sales techniques* —**push·i·ly** *adv* —**push·i·ness** *n*

pu·sil·lan·i·mous /pyo͞ossi lánniməss/ *adj* showing a contemptible lack of boldness and resolve (*formal*) [15C. < late Latin *pusillanimis* < Latin *pusillis* "very small" + *animus* "mind"] —**pu·sil·la·nim·i·ty** /pyo͞ossilə nímmətee/ *n* —**pu·sil·lan·i·mous·ly** *adv*

SYNONYMS See *cowardly.*

puss[1] /po͝oss/ *n* (*informal*) **1.** an affectionate word used for or to address a cat (*often used by or to children*) **2.** an affectionately intended word for a girl or woman (*considered offensive by many people*) [Early 16C. Probably < Middle Low German *pūs*]

puss[2] /po͝oss/ *n* somebody's face or mouth (*slang*) ○ *a familiar puss* [Late 19C. < Irish *pus* "lip, mouth"]

puss·ley /pússlee/ (*plural* **-leys** *or* *same*) *n* *US* PLANTS same as **purslane** [Early 19C. Alteration]

puss·y /po͝ossee/ (*plural* **-ies**) *n* **1. CAT** an affectionate word used for or to address a cat (*informal; often used by or to children*) **2. FURRY FLOWER** a furry hanging flower (**catkin**) of the pussy willow or other tree **3. TABOO TERM** a highly offensive term for the vulva (*taboo*) **4. OFFENSIVE TERM** an offensive term for sexual intercourse with a woman (*slang*) **5. OFFENSIVE TERM** an offensive term for women regarded as a source of sexual pleasure (*slang*) [Late 16C. < PUSS[1]]

puss·y·cat /po͝ossee kàt/ *n* **1.** an affectionate word for a cat (*often used by or to children*) **2.** a gentle and easy-going person (*informal*)

puss·y·foot /po͝ossee fo͝ot/ (**-foot·ed, -foot·ing, -foots**) *vi* (*informal*) **1.** to behave hesitantly or indecisively, or avoid speaking frankly or openly **2.** to move quietly and usually secretively

puss·y·toes /po͝ossee tòz/ (*plural same*) *n* a low-growing perennial plant with woolly leaves. Flowers: small, whitish, in clusters. Genus: *Antennaria.* [Late 19C. Because the plant resembles a cat's paw]

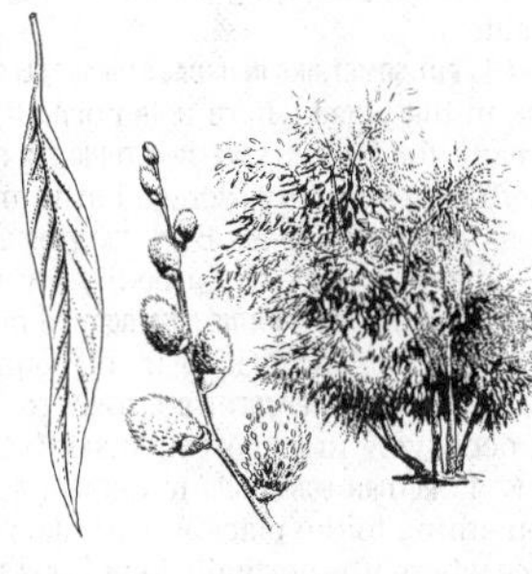

pussy willow

puss·y wil·low *n* a willow with fluffy gray clusters of flowers (**catkins**) along its branches. Native to: North America, Europe, Asia. Latin name: *Salix discolor* or *Salix caprea* or *Salix cinerea.*

pus·tu·lant /púschələnt/ *adj* causing pustules to form on the skin ■ *n* a substance that causes pustules to form on the skin

pus·tu·late *vti* /púschə làyt/ (**-lat·ed, -lat·ing, -lates**) to become covered with pustules, or cause pustules to form on the skin ■ *adj* /púschə làyt, -lət/ covered with pustules —**pus·tu·la·tion** /pùschə láysh'n/ *n*

pus·tule /púss cho͞ol/ *n* **1.** a small round raised area of inflamed skin filled with pus **2.** a small raised discolored area, especially on a plant [14C. < Latin *pustula*] —**pus·tu·lar** /púschələr/ *adj*

put /po͝ot/ *vt* (**put, put·ting, puts**) **1. PLACE SOMETHING** to move something into a particular place or position ○ *I put my arms around her.* ○ *They put the child's money into a trust fund.* **2. CAUSE SOMEBODY TO GO** to cause somebody to go to a place and stay there for a period of time ○ *put him in prison* **3. PLACE SOMEBODY IN SITUATION** to place somebody or something in a particular state or situation ○ *It put me in mind of my last visit.* **4. SET SOMEBODY TO SOMETHING** to make somebody do something ○ *She was put to work in the garden.* **5. MAKE SOMEBODY HAVE SOMETHING** to make somebody or something have or be affected by something ○ *They put pressure on him to accept the offer.* **6. EXPRESS JUDGMENT OF SOMETHING** to have a particular attitude toward somebody or something ○ *put your trust in sb* **7. USE SOMETHING** to use or apply something ○ *Put your mind to it.* **8. INVEST SOMETHING** to invest money, time, or effort in something ○ *We offered to put some money into the project.* **9. EXPRESS SOMETHING** to express or state something in a particular way ○ *How can I put this without offending you?* ○ *put your thoughts into words* **10. CREATE DISTANCE** to create a particular distance of time or space between yourself and something or somebody else **11. BRING SOMETHING UP FOR SOMEBODY** to bring something up as a question, vote, or proposal for somebody ○ *Feel free to put your questions to the president.* **12. SET WORDS TO MUSIC** to provide words with a musical form ○ *put the words to music* **13. ESTIMATE SOMETHING** to make an estimate of something such as the time ○ *I put the time at about 11 o'clock.* **14. SET RESTRICTION** to set a limit or a restriction ○ *We must put a stop to this at once!* **15. WRITE OR PRINT SOMETHING** to change or translate information from one kind of language to another **16.** GAMBLING **PLACE BET** to bet an amount of money on a race or contest **17.** TRACK AND FIELD **THROW HEAVY METAL BALL** to throw the heavy metal ball in the shot put ■ *n* **1.** TRACK AND FIELD **THROW OF HEAVY METAL BALL** in the shot put, a throw of the heavy metal ball **2.** FIN **OPTION TO SELL** an option giving the owner of an underlying asset the right to sell a set quantity at a set price during a limited time period [Assumed Old English *putian*, origin ?]

put about *v* **1.** *vti* to make a ship change course, or change course **2.** *vt* to circulate something such as news or gossip

put across *vt* to make something understood or accepted by expressing it clearly ◇ **put one across (on) somebody** *UK* to deceive or trick somebody (*informal*)

put aside *vt* **1.** SEPARATE SOMETHING FOR DISCARDING OR SAVING to separate something from something else and discard it or save it for later use **2.** IGNORE SOMETHING to disregard something ○ *They agreed to put aside their differences.* **3.** SET SOMETHING DOWN to stop holding, looking at, or concentrating on something and set it to one side

put away *vt* **1.** PUT SOMETHING IN USUAL STORAGE PLACE to put something in the place where it is normally stored or kept ready for use **2.** SAVE SOMETHING FOR FUTURE to save something, especially money, for future use **3.** VET same as **put down** (sense 6) **4.** EAT FOOD QUICKLY to eat food, especially quickly, greedily, or in large quantities (*informal*) **5.** CONFINE SOMEBODY to put somebody in prison or another form of confinement (*informal*) **6.** *US* BEAT OPPONENT DECISIVELY to beat an opponent decisively in a sporting event (*slang*)

put back *vt* **1.** RETURN SOMETHING TO WHERE IT BELONGS to return something to the place it was taken from or to the place where it is normally kept **2.** PAY SOMETHING BACK to give something back to a person or group in exchange for help or benefits received **3.** RESTORE SOMETHING TO OPERATION to restore a machine to operation **4.** RESTORE PIECES TO WHOLE to restore pieces or fragments to a unified whole ○ *putting the engine back together again* **5.** DELAY SOMETHING to delay somebody or something, or postpone something **6.** DRINK ALCOHOL to drink alcoholic drinks, especially quickly

put by *vt* to save something, especially money, for future use

put down *v* **1.** *vt* RELEASE HOLD ON SOMETHING to release a hold or grip on something and put it on a lower surface, or restore to the ground somebody who has been lifted up **2.** *vt* WRITE SOMETHING to write something on paper **3.** *vt* SUPPRESS REBELLION to use force to bring a rebellion to an end **4.** *vt* PAY DEPOSIT ON SOMETHING to pay part of the cost of a purchase as a deposit **5.** *vt* ATTRIBUTE SOMETHING TO SOMETHING to give something as or understand something to be a cause or reason for something else ○ *I put his unfriendliness down to shyness.* **6.** *vt* KILL ANIMAL HUMANELY to kill an animal in a humane way, especially because it is ill, injured, or in pain **7.** *vti* LAND AIRPLANE to land an aircraft somewhere **8.** *vt* PUT CHILD TO BED to put a baby or small child to bed **9.** *vt* DISPARAGE OR BELITTLE SOMEBODY to make somebody or something appear ridiculous or unimportant by being critical or scornful (*informal*)

put forth *v* (*formal*) **1.** *vt* MAKE SOMETHING KNOWN to make something known, e.g., by stating it, publishing it, or formally submitting it for discussion **2.** *vt* GROW LEAVES OR OTHER PARTS to send out new leaves or new growth **3.** *vt* EXERT EFFORT to exert strength or make an effort in an attempt to accomplish something **4.** *vi* START TRIP to begin a trip or voyage

put forward *vt* **1.** MAKE SOMETHING KNOWN to make something known, e.g., by stating it, publishing it, or formally submitting it for discussion **2.** OFFER SOMEBODY AS CANDIDATE to suggest somebody as a candidate for something **3.** ARRANGE FOR SOMETHING TO HAPPEN EARLIER to arrange for something to happen at a time earlier than originally planned

put in *v* **1.** *vt* GIVE TIME OR ENERGY to devote time or effort **2.** *vt* MAKE CLAIM to make a claim or application for something **3.** *vt* SAY SOMETHING to make a remark, especially to add something to a conversation **4.** *vt* MAKE TELEPHONE CALL to make a telephone call to somebody and expect that it will be returned **5.** *vi* NAUT BRING SHIP INTO PORT to bring a ship or boat into a port, especially for a short stay

put off *vt* **1.** POSTPONE SOMETHING to delay or postpone something **2.** DELAY OR HINDER SOMEBODY to delay somebody or stop somebody from acting or proceeding **3.** MAKE SOMEBODY DISGUSTED to disgust or repel somebody **4.** DISCOURAGE SOMEBODY to make somebody lose interest in or enthusiasm for something ◇ **put somebody off his** *or* **her stride** to distract somebody from what he or she is doing and make that person do it less well

put on *vt* **1.** START SOMETHING OPERATING to make something electrical or mechanical start operating, e.g., by turning a knob or pressing a switch **2.** COVER SOMETHING WITH CLOTHING to cover the body or a part of the body with clothing, headgear, footwear, or other accessories **3.** APPLY SOMETHING TO SKIN to apply something such as makeup or lotion to the skin **4.** ORGANIZE SOMETHING to organize and present an event such as a theatrical entertainment **5.** GAIN OR ADD SOMETHING to gain something that is additional or extra ○ *He's been putting on weight.* **6.** PRESCRIBE SOMETHING FOR SOMEBODY to prescribe something for somebody such as medication or a special diet ○ *put her on a low-salt diet* **7.** ADOPT FALSE BEHAVIOR to adopt an attitude or way of behaving that is false or insincere **8.** PROVIDE SOMETHING to provide something as a service or facility **9.** MAKE SOMETHING SUBJECT TO IMPOSITION to impose something such as a tax or a restriction **10.** PLACE BET to make a bet, or offer money as a stake for a bet **11.** HAND TELEPHONE TO SOMEBODY to hand a telephone to somebody so that he or she can speak to somebody on the other end ○ *I'll put her on.* **12.** TEASE SOMEBODY to make fun of somebody, especially by pretending something (*informal*) ○ *You're putting me on.*

put out *v* **1.** *vt* EXTINGUISH LIGHT OR FIRE to switch off a light or extinguish a fire **2.** *vt* ANNOY SOMEBODY to annoy, upset, or offend somebody ○ *Don't worry if they are put out by your reaction; the truth is best.* **3.** *vt* MAKE SOMETHING KNOWN to make something widely known, e.g., by announcing or broadcasting it **4.** *vt* CAUSE INCONVENIENCE to cause somebody inconvenience **5.** *vt* CAUSE INJURY TO SOMETHING to cause injury to a part of the body ○ *I put my back out.* **6.** *vt* PRODUCE SOMETHING to manufacture or produce something **7.** *vt* ELIMINATE PLAYER to eliminate a player from a game or competition ○ *The referee put the team's coach out of the game.* **8.** *vt* BASEBALL RETIRE SOMEBODY to retire a batter or base runner **9.** *vi* SET OFF IN BOAT to start sailing in a boat after a period spent at rest in harbor or on shore **10.** *vt* ANESTHETIZE SOMEBODY make somebody unconscious by means of an anesthetic **11.** *vi* AGREE TO SEX to agree to have sex (*slang; refers to women; often offensive*)

put over *vt* to make something understood by expressing it clearly ◇ **put one over (on somebody)** to make somebody believe or accept something by using deceit (*informal*)

put through *vt* **1.** MAKE SOMEBODY UNDERGO SOMETHING to make somebody experience something difficult or unpleasant **2.** CARRY SOMETHING OUT to process something or take it to a successful conclusion **3.** CONNECT SOMEBODY BY TELEPHONE to connect somebody by telephone to somebody else **4.** MAKE TELEPHONE CALL to make a telephone call to somebody

put to *v* **1.** *vt* to submit a statement or question to somebody for a response ○ *I put it to you that you are not telling us the whole truth.* **2.** *vi* to tie up a boat in a sheltered spot or harbor

put up *v* **1.** *vt* PROVIDE SOMETHING to offer or provide something, especially money **2.** *vt* BUILD SOMETHING to build or erect something **3.** *vt* FASTEN SOMETHING TO WALL to fasten something to a wall, fence, or other upright surface **4.** *vti* ACCOMMODATE SOMEBODY to give somebody accommodations, or find accommodations somewhere ○ *put us up for the night* **5.** *vt* PUT SOMETHING ON MARKET to offer something for sale ○ *The house contents were put up for sale at auction.* **6.** *vt* PILE HAIR ON TOP OF HEAD to fix long hair in a style that is coiled or piled on the top of the head and then secured, usually with hairpins **7.** *vt* ENGAGE IN SOMETHING to engage in or carry on something ○ *put up a fight* **8.** *vt* ASSEMBLE AND PACKAGE SOMETHING to assemble something, especially according to a set of instructions or specifications, and then package it appropriately for storage or transport **9.** *vt* OFFER SOMEBODY AS CANDIDATE to propose somebody as a candidate **10.** *vt* INCREASE SOMETHING to raise or increase something **11.** *vt* RETURN SOMETHING TO STORAGE place something where it belongs for storage ○ *They'll put up their tools when the project is done.* **12.** *vt* CAN FRUITS OR VEGETABLES to preserve fruits or vegetables ○ *We put up a dozen jars of apple jelly.* **13.** *vt* RETURN WEAPON TO HOLDER to return a weapon taken out for use to its holder (*archaic*) ◇ **put up or shut up** used to indicate that somebody should either do something about something or else stop talking about it (*informal*)

put upon *vt* to treat somebody badly or take advantage of somebody

put up to *vt* to encourage or persuade somebody to do something unpleasant or destructive

put up with *vt* to tolerate or accept somebody or something calmly

pu·ta·men /pyoo táymən/ (*plural* **-tam·i·na** /-támmənə/) *n* the stone inside a peach, plum, apricot, or other similar fruit (*technical*) [Mid-19C. < Latin, "shell, peel" < *putare* "to prune"]

pu·ta·tive /pyóotətiv/ *adj* **1.** generally believed to be or regarded as being something ○ *the putative father of the child* **2.** believed to exist now or to have existed at some time [15C. Directly or via French < late Latin *putativus* < *putare* "prune, think over"] —**pu·ta·tive·ly** *adv*

ORIGIN The Latin word *putare* "to prune, think over," from which ***putative*** is derived, is also the source of English *account, amputate, compute, count*[1] (of numbers), *deputy, dispute, impute, recount,* and *reputation.*

put-back *n* in basketball, an offensive rebound that consists of tipping the basketball back up toward the basket from a short distance

put·down /pŏŏt dòwn/ *n* a critical or scornful remark intended to make somebody appear ridiculous or unimportant (*informal*)

Pu·tin /pŏŏtin/, **Vladimir** (*b.* 1952) Russian politician. He worked in the KGB and local government before becoming prime minister of the Russian Federation in 1999 and president in 2000. Full name **Putin, Vladimir Vladimirovich**

put·log /pŏŏt lòg/ *n* a short horizontal beam that helps to support the planks forming the floor of a scaffold [Mid-17C. Origin ?]

put-on *adj* FALSE assumed or adopted for effect or in order to deceive ○ *a put-on accent* ■ *n* (*informal*) **1.** ACT OF TEASING SOMEBODY the act of intentionally deceiving or giving somebody the wrong impression, especially for humorous effect **2.** PRANK an instance of teasing somebody, especially as a joke **3.** FALSE OUTER APPEARANCE an exterior appearance intended to deceive or mislead somebody

Pu·tong·hua /pŏŏ tawng hwaá/ *n* LANG same as **Chinese** (sense 3) [Mid-20C. < Chinese *pǔtōnghuà* < *pǔtōng* "common" + *huà* "spoken language"] —**Pu·tong·hua** *adj*

put op·tion *n* FIN same as **put** *n* (sense 2)

put out *adj* having been inconvenienced, upset, annoyed, or offended by somebody or something ○ *I do feel a little put out that you didn't invite me.*

put·out /pŏŏt òwt/ *n* in baseball, a play in which a batter or base runner is retired ■ *vt* to cause somebody to become unconscious, especially by anesthetizing him or her

put-put /pùt pút/, **putt-putt** (*informal*) *n* **1.** SOUND OF SMALL ENGINE the sound made by a small gasoline engine, especially an old or broken one **2.** GASOLINE ENGINE a small gasoline engine **3.** VEHICLE WITH GASOLINE ENGINE a vehicle, especially a boat, fitted with a small gasoline engine ■ *vi* (**put-put·ted, put-put·ting, put-puts; putt-put·ted, putt-put·ting, putt-putts**) MOVE SLOWLY UNDER LITTLE POWER to move slowly or hesitantly under the power of a small gasoline engine [An imitation of the sound]

pu·tre·fy /pyóotrə fī/ (**-fied, -fy·ing, -fies**) *vti* to decay with a foul smell, or make something decay with a foul smell [15C. < Latin *putrefacere* < *putr-* "rotten" + *facere* "make"] —**pu·tre·fac·tion** /pyóotrə fáksh'n/ *n* —**pu·tre·fac·tive** /-fáktiv/ *adj* —**pu·tre·fi·a·ble** *adj* —**pu·tre·fi·er** *n*

pu·tres·cent /pyoo tréss'nt/ *adj* **1.** rotting **2.** relating to the process of decay [Mid-18C. < Latin *putrescent-*, present participle of *putrescere* "begin to rot" < *putr-* "rotten"] —**pu·tres·cence** *n*

pu·tres·ci·ble /pyoo tréssəb'l/ *adj* capable of decaying or rotting [Late 18C. < Latin *putrescere* (see PUTRESCENT)]

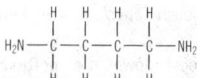

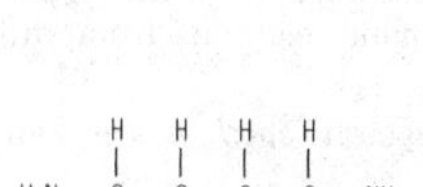

putrescine

pu·tres·cine /pyoo tré seen, pyoo tréssin/ *n* a colorless crystalline compound (**ptomaine**). Source: decaying animal tissue. Formula: $C_4H_{12}N_2$. See illustration on previous page [Late 19C. < Latin *putrescere* (see PUTRESCENT)]

pu·trid /pyóotrid/ *adj* **1. DECAYING WITH DISGUSTING SMELL** rotting and giving off a foul smell **2. DISGUSTING** physically or morally disgusting **3. WORTHLESS** worthless or contemptible (*informal*) [15C. < Latin *putridus* "rotten" < *putr-*] —**pu·trid·i·ty** /pyoo tríddətee/ *n* —**pu·trid·ly** *adv* —**pu·trid·ness** *n*

putsch /pooch/ *n* a sudden planned attempt to overthrow a government using military force [Early 20C. < Swiss German, "thrust, blow"] —**putsch·ist** *n*

putt /put/ *vti* (**putt·ed, putt·ing, putts**) to hit a golf ball with a gentle tapping stroke along the ground on a green, aiming for the hole ■ *n* a gentle tapping stroke that rolls a golf ball along the ground on a green, aiming for the hole [Mid-18C. Variant of PUT]

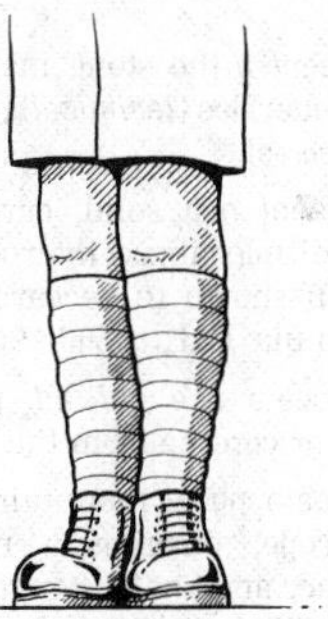

puttee

put·tee /pu tée, púttee/ *n* **1.** a strip of cloth wrapped around the lower leg from the ankle to the knee, especially one worn as part of a military uniform **2.** a leather legging or gaiter that covers the lower leg [Late 19C. Via Hindi *patti* < Sanskrit *pattika* "bandage, strip of cloth"]

put·ter[1] /púttər/ (**-tered, -ter·ing, -ters**) *vi* to do trivial or unimportant tasks in a random, leisurely way ○ *just puttering in the garden* [Late 19C. Variant of POTTER[2]] —**put·ter·er** *n*

put·ter[2] /púttər/ *n* **1.** a golf club with a flat-faced metal head, for hitting a golf ball with a gentle tapping stroke on a green **2.** a golfer who is in the process of putting [Mid-18C. < PUTT]

put·ti ARTS plural of **putto**

putt·ing green /pútting-/ *n* **1.** GOLF same as **green** *n* (sense 7) **2.** a lawn with holes for practicing putting strokes

put·to /póotō/ (*plural* **-ti** /-tee/) *n* in art especially of the baroque period, an infant boy or cherub, often portrayed with wings [Mid-17C. Via Italian < Latin *putus* "boy"]

put·ty /púttee/ *n* **1. PASTE USED IN GLAZING WINDOWS** a paste with the consistency of dough made from linseed oil and powdered chalk, used to fix glass into wooden window frames and to fill holes in wood **2. PASTE FORMING TOP COAT ON PLASTER** a thin paste of lime, water, and sand or plaster of Paris, used as a finishing coat on plaster **3.** COLORS **LIGHT GRAY COLOR** a light yellowish gray color ■ *adj* COLORS **LIGHT GRAY** of a light yellowish gray color ■ *vt* (**-tied, -ty·ing, -ties**) **FIX OR REPAIR SOMETHING WITH PUTTY** to put windows into wooden frames, or fill holes in wood, using putty [Mid-17C. < French *potée*, originally "potful" < *pot* "pot"] ◇ **be putty in somebody's hands** to be easily influenced and controlled by somebody else

put·ty knife *n* a tool similar to a knife with a blunt wide flexible blade, especially one used by glaziers to spread putty onto wooden window frames

put·ty pow·der *n* a powder consisting of tin oxide or a mixture of tin and lead oxides. Use: polishing metal and glass.

put·ty·root /púttee ròot/ *n* an orchid with only one leaf. Flowers: brown or purplish brown. Native to: North America. Latin name: *Aplectrum hyemale.* [Mid-19C. Because the substance found in the plant's corm resembles putty]

Pu·tu·ma·yo /pòotoo mī́ yō/ river that rises in the Colombian Andes and flows southeastward along the border between Colombia and Peru before joining the Amazon in Brazil. Length: 1,000 mi./1,610 km.

put un·der *vt* give somebody an anesthetic to cause unconsciousness

put-up *adj* fraudulently or dishonestly planned or done (*informal*) ○ *Was the fire a put-up job?*

put-up·on *adj* treated badly, especially by being taken advantage of or being asked to do an excessive amount of work

putz /puts/ *n* **1.** somebody regarded as very unintelligent and unpleasant (*informal insult*) **2.** an offensive term for a penis (*slang*) [Early 20C. < Yiddish *potz* "fool, penis"]

Pu·vis de Cha·vannes /poo vée də sha ván/, **Pierre** (1824–98) French painter best known for his murals. His paintings were often based on allegorical or classical subjects.

Puy de San·cy /pwee də saaN sée/ mountain in central France. It is the highest peak in the Massif Central. Height: 6,188 ft./1,886 m.

puy len·til /pwée-/ *n* a small dark blue-green lentil with a distinctive flavor [After Le *Puy*, town in the Haute-Loire region, France]

puz·zle /púzz'l/ *vt* (**-zled, -zling, -zles**) **CONFUSE SOMEBODY** to confuse somebody by being difficult or impossible to understand ■ *n* **1. GAME OF SKILL OR INTELLIGENCE** a game or toy designed to test skill or intelligence **2. DIFFICULT PROBLEM OR SITUATION** a problem or situation that is difficult or impossible to resolve **3. SOMEBODY MYSTERIOUS** somebody whose behavior or motives are difficult to understand [Late 16C. Origin ?] —**puz·zle·ment** *n* —**puz·zling** *adj* —**puz·zling·ly** *adv*

SYNONYMS See ***problem***.

puzzle out *vt* to use logic or reasoning to reach an understanding of something confusing or complicated

puzzle over *vt* to spend time thinking about and trying to understand something confusing or complicated

puz·zle game *n* a computer game that involves solving puzzles

puz·zle pal·ace *n US* a place, especially a government department, where important decisions are made in great secrecy (*slang*)

puz·zler /púzzlər/ *n* **1.** something confusing, mystifying, or testing skill or intelligence **2.** somebody who likes to solve puzzles **3.** COMPUT GAMES same as **puzzle game**

PVA *n* a colorless resin used in adhesives and paints. Full form **polyvinyl acetate**

PVC *n* a hard-wearing synthetic resin made by polymerizing vinyl chloride. Use: flooring, piping, clothing. Full form **polyvinyl chloride**

PVO *abbr US* private voluntary organization

PVS *abbr* MED **1.** persistent vegetative state **2.** post-viral syndrome

Pvt., **PVT** *abbr* MIL Private

pw *abbr* ONLINE Palau (*used in Internet addresses*) See table at **domain name**

PW *abbr* MAIL Palau

p.w. *abbr* per week

PWA[1] *n* somebody affected by AIDS. Full form **person with AIDS**

PWA[2], **P.W.A.** *abbr* GOV Public Works Administration

PWC *abbr US* SPORTS personal watercraft

PWR *abbr* INDUST pressurized-water reactor

pwt. *abbr* MEASURE pennyweight

PX *n* a store in a US military base selling goods to military personnel and their families, as well as to some authorized civilians. Full form **Post Exchange**

py *abbr* ONLINE Paraguay (*used in Internet addresses*) See table at **domain name**

py- *prefix* same as **pyo-** (*used before vowels*)

py·a /pee áa, pyaa/ *n* a subunit of currency in Myanmar. See table at **currency** [Mid-20C. < Burmese]

py·ae·mi·a *n* MED UK spelling of **pyemia**

pyc·nid·i·um /pik níddee əm/ (*plural* **-nid·i·a** /-níddee ə/) *n* an asexual flask-shaped structure in some fungi [Mid-19C. < modern Latin < Greek *puknos* "thick, dense"]

pycno- *prefix* dense, density ○ *pycnometer* [< Greek *puknos* "strong, thick, dense"]

pyc·nog·o·nid /pik nóggənid, pìknə gónnid/ *n* MARINE BIOL same as **sea spider** [Late 19C. < modern Latin *Pycnogonida* < *pycnogonum* < Greek *gonu* "knee"]

pyc·nom·e·ter /pik nómmətər/ *n* a standard container of accurately defined volume used to determine the relative density of liquids and solids —**pyc·no·met·ric** /pìknə méttrik/ *adj*

pye-dog /pī́-/ *n* a stray half-wild dog found in villages in Asia [Mid-19C. *Pye*, origin ?]

pyel- *prefix* same as **pyelo-** (*used before vowels*)

py·e·li·tis /pī̀ ə lī́tiss/ *n* inflammation of the part of the kidney (**pelvis**) from which urine drains into the tube leading to the bladder, sometimes caused by a bacterial infection that may occur during pregnancy —**py·e·lit·ic** *adj*

pyelo- *prefix* kidney, pelvis of the kidney ○ *pyelonephritis* [< Greek *puelos* "basin, trough"]

pye·lo·gram /pī́ ələ gràm/ *n* an X-ray of the urine-collecting part of the kidney. The X-ray is taken after the introduction of a contrast medium either into the bloodstream or directly into the kidney in order to highlight the internal structures.

pye·log·ra·phy /pī̀ ə lóggrəfee/ *n* the branch of radiography dealing with the kidneys and surrounding tissue, usually involving introduction of a contrast medium in order to highlight the internal structures —**pye·lo·graph·ic** /-ələ gráffik/ *adj*

py·e·lo·ne·phri·tis /pī̀ ə lō nə frítiss/ *n* inflammation of the kidney, including both the urine-forming and urine-collecting parts

py·e·mi·a /pī éemee ə/ *n* a disease caused by pus-forming microorganisms in the bloodstream [Mid-19C. < Greek *puon* "pus"]

py·gid·i·um /pī jíddee əm/ (*plural* **-gid·i·a** /-jíddee ə/) *n* **1.** the hindmost part of the body in some insects, worms, and other invertebrates **2.** a protective covering of the anal portion of the abdomen of some invertebrates [Mid-19C. < Greek *puge* "rump"] —**py·gid·i·al** *adj*

Pyg·ma·li·on /pig máylee ən/ *n* in Greek mythology, a king of Cyprus who fell in love with the goddess Aphrodite and made a statue of her that she brought to life as Galatea

pyg·my /pígmee/, **pig·my** *n* (*plural* **-mies**) **1. OFFENSIVE TERM** an offensive term for somebody who is of shorter than average height **2. OFFENSIVE TERM** an offensive term that insults somebody's importance, knowledge, or ability ■ *adj* **OF SMALL BREED** belonging to a small breed (*sometimes offensive*) ○ *a pygmy hippopotamus* [14C. Via Latin *pygmaei* (plural) < Greek *pugmaios* (singular) "dwarfish" < *pugmē* "distance from the elbow to the knuckles"]

Pyg·my (*plural* **-mies**), **Pig·my** *n* ANTHROP **1.** same as **Negrillo 2.** same as **Negrito**

pyg·my chim·pan·zee *n* VERTEB same as **bonobo**

pyin·ka·do /pyíngkə dō, pee íngkə dō/ (*plural* **-dos**) *n* a tree that yields a valuable reddish brown hardwood. Use: construction, flooring. Native to: Southeast Asia. Latin name: *Xylia xylocarpa.* [Mid-19C. < Burmese]

py·ja·mas CLOTHING Can, UK spelling of **pajamas**

Pyle /pīl/, **Ernie** (1900–45) US journalist. Known for his front-line reports during World War II, he was killed in fighting near Okinawa. Full name **Pyle, Ernest Taylor**

Pyle, Howard (1853–1911) US illustrator and writer. His work dealt chiefly with American history and medieval folklore.

pylon (sense 5)

py·lon /pī̀ lòn, pī́lən/ *n* **1.** METAL TOWER SUPPORTING HIGH-VOLTAGE CABLES a tall metal tower typically made of crisscrossing steel bars that supports high-voltage cables across a long span **2.** ROADS same as **traffic cone** **3.** AIRFIELD TOWER TO GUIDE PILOT a tower erected at an airfield to mark a course for pilots, e.g., in a race **4.** BRACKET FIXING SOMETHING TO AIRCRAFT BODY a rigid metal bracket that attaches an external aircraft part such as an engine, fuel tank, or armament to the main body of the aircraft **5.** TALL VERTICAL PART OF STRUCTURE a tall vertical structure on or forming part of a building or other construction, especially an ancient structure, e.g., a decorative gateway or a monumental pillar [Mid-19C. < Greek *pulōn* "gateway" < *pulē* "gate"]

py·lo·rec·to·my /pīlə réktəmee/ (*plural* **-mies**) *n* the surgical removal of all or part of the pylorus, sometimes including the removal of part of the stomach [Late 19C. < PYLORUS]

py·lo·rus /pī láwrəss/ (*plural* **-ri** /-rī/) *n* the thick muscular ring (**sphincter**) surrounding the outlet of the stomach into the duodenum. It closes to prevent unduly large pieces of food from leaving, thus enabling stomach acid and enzymes to break them down further. [Early 17C. Via late Latin < Greek *puloros* "gatekeeper" < *pulē* "gate"] —**py·lo·ric** *adj*

Pym /pim/, **Barbara** (1913–80) British novelist. Many of her novels e.g., *A Glass of Blessings* (1958), are satirical comedies, focusing on the ironies and intrigues of village life. Full name **Pym, Barbara Mary Crampton**

Pym, John (1583?–1643) English Parliamentary leader. He was one of the five members of parliament whom Charles I tried to arrest (1642), and was active in events leading up to the English Civil War.

Pyn·chon /pínchən/, **Thomas** (*b.* 1937) US novelist. His works, known for their intricate plots and experimental techniques, include *V* (1963) and *Gravity's Rainbow* (1973). See Cultural note at **gravity**

"Now there grows among all the rooms, replacing the night's old smoke, alcohol and sweat, the fragile, musaceous odor of Breakfast...Is there any reason not to open every window, and let the kind scent blanket all Chelsea?"
[Thomas Pynchon, *Gravity's Rainbow*; 1973]

PYO *abbr* pick your own

pyo- *prefix* pus ○ *pyoderma* [< Greek *puon* < Indo-European, "to rot"]

py·o·der·ma /pī ə dúrmə/ *n* a skin infection causing the development of pus or pustules

py·o·gen·e·sis /pī ə jénnəssiss/ *n* the formation or production of pus —**py·o·gen·ic** /-jénnik/ *adj*

Pyong·yang /pyáwng yàng/, **P'yŏng·yang** capital city of North Korea, situated on the Taedong River in the western part of the country. It is thought to be the oldest city on the Korean Peninsula. Population: 2,500,000 (1995).

py·or·rhe·a /pī ə reé ə/ *n* inflammation of the gums with a loosening of the teeth and a discharge of pus from the tooth sockets [Early 19C. < modern Latin, "flowing of pus" < Greek *puon* "pus"] —**py·or·rhe·al** *adj* —**py·or·rhe·ic** *adj*

pyr- *prefix* same as **pyro-** (*used before vowels or h*)

py·ra·can·tha /pīrə kánthə/ *n Can, UK* same as **firethorn** [Early 17C. Via modern Latin < Greek *purakantha*, an unidentified plant < *pur* "fire" + *akantha* "thorn"]

py·ral·id /pírrəlid/ *n* a small or medium-sized, slender moth with long triangular forewings. Family: Pyralidae. [Late 19C. < modern Latin *Pyralidae* < Greek *puralis* "mythical fly said to live in fire" < *pur* "fire"] —**pyral·id** *adj*

AKG London

pyramid: Chephren pyramid, Giza, Egypt

pyr·a·mid /pírrəmid/ *n* **1.** EGYPTIAN TOMB a huge stone tomb of ancient Egyptian royalty with a square base and triangular walls that slope to meet in a point at the top **2.** SOLID TRIANGULAR SHAPE a solid shape or structure that has triangular sides that slope to meet in a point and a base that is often, but not necessarily, a square. The volume of a pyramid is one-third of the product of the area of the base and the height of the vertex. **3.** SYSTEM WITH EXPANDING STRUCTURE an arrangement or system that has a small number of items at one point and expands gradually to have a large number at the opposite point **4.** POINTED BODY PART a pointed or cone-shaped body part, e.g., either of two bundles of fibers located in the brain **5.** FIN INVESTMENT METHOD a financial risk structure that spreads investments between high, medium, and low risk **6.** FIN STOCK SPECULATION METHOD stock speculation involving a series of buying and selling of shares, with paper profits as margin for more purchases **7.** CRYSTALS CRYSTALLINE FORM a crystalline form in which three or more nonparallel faces intersect all three axes of the crystal ■ *v* (**-mid·ed, -mid·ing, -mids**) **1.** *vi* TAKE ON PYRAMID SHAPE to take on the shape of a pyramid, with few items at one point or level and gradually increasing numbers toward the opposite point or level **2.** *vt* FIN SPECULATE ON STOCK to speculate on stock by engaging in a series of buying and selling, with paper profits used as margin for the purchase of more shares of stock [Mid-16C. Via Latin < Greek *puramid-*] —**py·ram·i·dal** /pi rámmidd'l/ *adj* —**py·ram·i·dal·ly** *adv* —**pyr·a·mid·ic** /pìrrə míddik/ *adj*—**pyr·a·mid·i·cal** *adj*—**pyr·a·mid·i·cal·ly** *adv*

py·ram·i·dal peak *n* a high mountain peak formed by the walls of three or more adjacent steep-sided glacial basins, e.g., the Matterhorn in Switzerland

py·ram·i·dal tract *n* either of two bundles of nerve fibers, shaped like inverted pyramids, running from each hemisphere of the cerebral cortex down the spinal cord to all voluntary muscles of the body. In the brain, they are susceptible to stroke damage that can lead to inability to move one side of the body.

pyr·a·mid scheme *n* a fraudulent scheme in which the perpetrators recruit people to pay money to those above them in a hierarchy on the expectation that they will get payments from those below. When the number of newly recruited people eventually dwindles, the payment structure collapses.

pyr·a·mid sell·ing *n* a method of distributing goods in bulk to a number of distributors, who in turn sell the goods in batches to a number of other distributors, and so on

Pyr·a·mus and This·be /pìrrəməss ən thízbee/ *n* in an ancient story, two young Babylonian lovers who were forbidden to marry and committed suicide in tragic circumstances. Pyramus, thinking Thisbe has been killed by a lion, kills himself, and Thisbe, on finding his body, kills herself.

py·ran /pī́ ràn/ *n* either of two isomers of a crystalline cyclic compound with a ring consisting of five carbon atoms and an oxygen atom with two double bonds. It is best known for its benzene derivatives, which are naturally occurring dyes that produce the colors of flowers. Formula: C_5H_6O. [Early 20C. < PYRONE]

py·rar·gy·rite /pī ráarjə rìt, pi-/ *n* a deep red to black lustrous mineral that consists of silver antimony sulfide and is a source of silver. It is commonly found associated with other silver ores. [Mid-19C. < PYRO- + Greek *arguros* "silver"]

py·ra·zole /pírrə zōl/ *n* a crystalline cyclic compound with a ring consisting of three carbon atoms and two nitrogen atoms with two double bonds. The ring system does not occur naturally, and pyrazole and its derivatives are exclusively synthetic compounds. Formula: $C_3H_4N_2$. [Late 19C. < PYRROLE + AZO-]

pyre /pīr/ *n* a pile of burning material, especially a pile of wood on which a dead body is ceremonially cremated [Mid-17C. Via Latin *pyra* < Greek *pura* < *pur* "fire"]

py·rene[1] /pī́ reèn/ *n* the stone inside some types of fruit such as cherries (*technical*) [Mid-19C. Via modern Latin < Greek *purēn*]

py·rene[2] /pī́ reèn/ *n* a solid, crystalline, colorless to yellow, multiple-ringed hydrocarbon compound that has been shown to be carcinogenic. Source: coal tar. Formula: $C_{16}H_{10}$. [Mid-19C. < Greek *pur* "fire"]

Py·re·ne·an /peèrə neé ən/ *adj* relating to, characteristic of, or coming from the Pyrenees

Pyr·e·nees /peèrə neèz/ mountain range in southwestern Europe, forming a natural boundary between France and Spain. Length: 270 mi./435 km. Area: 21,380 sq. mi./55,374 sq. km.

py·re·thrin /pī reéthrin, -réth-/ *n* either of two oily liquid complex organic compounds. Source: pyrethrum flowers. Use: insecticide. Formula: $C_{21}H_{28}O_3$ or $C_{22}H_{28}O_5$. [Early 20C. < PYRETHRUM] —**py·re·throid** *adj, n*

py·re·thrum /pī reéthrəm, -réth-/ *n* **1.** a chrysanthemum cultivated for its ornamental flowers. Genus: *Chrysanthemum*. **2.** a mixture of pyrethrins. Use: insecticide. [Mid-16C. Via Latin < Greek *purethron* "feverfew"]

py·ret·ic /pī réttik/ *adj* relating to, producing, or having a fever ■ *n* an agent that causes fever [Mid-19C. < modern Latin *pyreticos* < Greek *puretos* "fever" < *pur* "fire"]

Py·rex /pī́ rèks/ *tdmk* a trademark for a type of borosilicate glass that is resistant to heat and chemicals and is used in household kitchenware and laboratory apparatus

py·rex·i·a /pī réksee ə/ *n* same as **fever** *n* (sense 1) (*technical*) [Mid-18C. < modern Latin < Greek *purexis* < *puressein* "be feverish" < *pur* "fire"] —**py·rex·i·al** *adj* —**py·rex·ic** *adj*

pyr·he·li·om·e·ter /pìr heelee ómmətər/ *n* an instrument that measures the intensity of the Sun's radiation received at the Earth's surface [Mid-19C. < Greek *pur* "fire" + *helios* "sun"] —**pyr·he·li·o·met·ric** /-ə méttrik/ *adj*

py·ric /pī́rik, pírrik/ *adj* relating to burning, or produced as a result of burning [Mid-20C. < French *pyrique* < Greek *pur* "fire"]

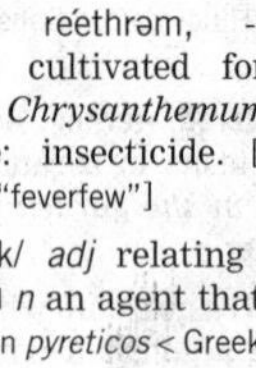

pyridine

pyr·i·dine /pírri deèn/ *n* a toxic flammable liquid with a noxious smell. Source: bone oil, coal tar. Use:

manufacture of chemicals, pharmaceuticals, and paints, textile dyeing. Formula: C_5H_5N. [Mid-19C. < Greek *pur* "fire"]

pyr·i·dox·al /pìrri dóksəl/ *n* a coenzyme derived from vitamin B_6 that is involved in the synthesis of amino acids [Mid-20C. < PYRIDOXINE]

pyr·i·dox·a·mine /pìrri dóksə meen/ *n* an amine form of vitamin B_6 derived from pyridoxine that acts as a coenzyme in protein metabolism [Mid-20C. < PYRIDINE + OXY-]

pyr·i·dox·ine /pìrri dók seen, -dóksin/ *n* a form of vitamin B_6 derived from pyrimidine, found in cereals, yeast, liver, and fish. In an organism, pyridoxine is metabolically changed to pyridoxal and pyridoxamine. Formula: $C_8H_{11}NO_3$. [Mid-20C. < PYRIDINE + OXY-]

pyr·i·form /pírrə fàwrm/ *adj* shaped like a pear [Mid-18C. < modern Latin *pyriformis* < Latin *pyrum* "pear"]

py·ri·meth·a·mine /pìrə méthə meen/ *n* a synthetic drug derived from pyrimidine. Use: treatment of malaria and toxoplasmosis. [Mid-20C. < PYRIMIDINE + ETHYLAMINE]

py·rim·i·dine /pī rímmi deen, pi-/ *n* **1.** a nitrogenous base with a six-sided ring structure **2.** a biologically significant derivative of pyrimidine, especially the bases cytosine, thymine, and uracil found in RNA and DNA [Late 19C. < PYRIDINE + IMIDE]

py·rite /pī rīt/, **py·ri·tes** /pī rīteez, pī rīts/ *n* a common iron sulfide mineral with a brassy metallic luster. Use: source of iron and sulfur. [Mid-19C. < French, or Latin *pyrites* < Greek *purites (lithos)* "fire (stone)"] —**py·rit·ic** /pī ríttik/ *adj*

pyro- *prefix* **1.** fire, heat ○ *pyromania* **2.** produced by fire or heat ○ *pyrography* **3.** fever ○ *pyrogenic* **4.** derived from an acid by loss of a molecule of water ○ *pyrophosphate* [< Greek *pur* "fire" < Indo-European]

py·ro·cat·e·chol /pìrō káttə kàwl/ *n* same as **catechol**

py·ro·cel·lu·lose /pìrō séllyə lōss, -lōz/ *n* a highly nitrated cellulose. Use: manufacture of explosives, particularly smokeless powder.

py·ro·chem·i·cal /pìrō kémmik'l/ *adj* relating to or resulting from chemical changes that take place at very high temperatures —**py·ro·chem·i·cal·ly** *adv*

py·ro·clas·tic /pìrō klástik/ *adj* describes sedimentary rock that is composed of fragments of volcanic rock produced by the explosion of a volcanic eruption (*pyroclastic flow*)

py·ro·con·duc·tiv·i·ty /pìrō kon duk tívvətee/ *n* the capacity to conduct electricity created in a solid substance by heating it to a high temperature

py·ro·e·lec·tric·i·ty /pìrō i lèk tríssətee/ *n* the production of electric charges on opposite faces of some crystals by a change in temperature —**py·ro·e·lec·tric** /-i léktrik/ *adj*

py·ro·gal·lol /pìrō gá làwl/ *n* a lustrous white crystalline organic compound that is bitter and toxic. Use: photographic developer, absorbent for oxygen in gas analysis. Formula: $C_6H_6H_3$. [PYRO- + Latin *galla* "oak apple"] —**py·ro·gal·lic** /-gállik/ *adj*

py·ro·gen /pírəjən/ *n* a substance that causes fever, especially a substance introduced into somebody's bloodstream

py·ro·gen·ic /pìrō jénnik/ *adj* **1.** causing fever or produced as a result of fever **2.** produced by igneous activity

py·rog·ra·phy /pī róggrəfee/ (*plural* **-phies**) *n* **1.** the art or technique of creating designs on wood and leather using heated tools that burn away some of the surface **2.** a design burned into wood or leather using a heated tool —**py·rog·ra·pher** *n* —**py·ro·graph·ic** /pìrə gráffik/ *adj*

py·ro·lig·ne·ous ac·id /pìrō lìgnee əss-/ *n* a reddish brown liquid of which the primary constituent is acetic acid, produced by the destructive distillation of wood. Among its impurities may be acetone, methanol, wood oils, and tars.

py·ro·lu·site /pìrə lōō sīt/ *n* a black or gray powdery metallic manganese oxide mineral. Source: deep-sea nodules. Use: source of manganese. [Early 19C. < PYRO- + Greek *lousis* "washing"; from its use in decolorizing glass]

py·rol·y·sate /pī róllə sàyt, pī rólləssət/ *n* a product of a chemical change caused by heating

py·ro·lyse *vt* CHEM UK spelling of **pyrolyze**

py·rol·y·sis /pī rólləssiss/ *n* the use of heat to break down complex chemical substances into simpler substances —**py·ro·lyt·ic** /pìrə líttik/ *adj*

py·rol·yze /pírə līz/ (**-yzed, -yz·ing, -yz·es**) *vt* to make a complex chemical substance decompose into simpler substances by heating it [Early 20C. < PYROLYSIS, after ANALYZE] —**py·rol·yz·er** *n*

py·ro·man·cy /pírə mànssee/ *n* attempting to tell the future by using fire or flames [14C. Via French and late Latin < Greek *puromanteia* < *pur* "fire"] —**py·ro·manc·er** *n* —**py·ro·man·tic** /pìrə mántik/ *adj*

py·ro·ma·ni·a /pìrō máynee ə, -máynyə/ *n* the uncontrollable urge to set fire to things —**py·ro·ma·ni·ac** *n* —**py·ro·ma·ni·a·cal** /-nī ək'l/ *adj*

py·ro·met·al·lur·gy /pìrō métt'l ùrjee/ *n* the treatment of ores and metals using high-temperature processes, or the study of these processes, which include alloying, casting, distilling, roasting, refining, sintering, smelting, and heat treating

py·rom·e·ter /pī rómmətər/ *n* an instrument that measures high temperatures, typically by converting brightness, radiation, or electric current measurements into temperature readings —**py·ro·met·ric** /pìrə méttrik/ *adj* —**py·ro·met·ri·cal** *adj* —**py·ro·met·ri·cal·ly** *adv* —**py·rom·e·try** *n*

py·ro·mor·phite /pìrə máwr fīt/ *n* a rare green, or sometimes brownish gray, white, or yellow mineral occurring as crystals in lead deposits

py·rone /pī rōn/ *n* either of two six-membered organic ring compounds containing five carbon atoms and an oxygen atom, with a second oxygen atom attached to one of the carbon atoms. The benzene derivative is used as a pharmaceutical. Formula: $C_5H_4O_2$.

py·ro·nine /pírə neen/ *n* a red dye used in biological tests, especially a test to detect the presence of RNA [Late 19C. < German]

py·rope /pī rōp/ *n* a deep red garnet containing magnesium and aluminum. Use: gems. [Early 19C. Via French and Latin < Greek *puropos* "fiery-eyed" < *pur* "fire"]

py·ro·pho·bi·a /pìrə fóbee ə/ *n* an irrational fear of fire

py·ro·phor·ic /pìrə fáwrik/ *adj* **1.** bursting into flames spontaneously when exposed to air **2.** giving off sparks when struck or scraped [Mid-19C. < Greek *purophoros* "fire-bearing" < *pur* "fire"]

py·ro·phos·phate /pìrō fóss fàyt/ *n* a salt or ester produced when pyrophosphoric acid reacts with some metals or metallic compounds

py·ro·phos·phor·ic ac·id /pìrō foss fàwrik-/ *n* a viscous liquid formed when phosphoric acid is heated and loses a water molecule. Use: catalyst. Formula: $H_4P_2O_7$.

py·ro·pho·tom·e·ter /pìrō fō tómmətər/ *n* an instrument that determines the temperature of an incandescent body as a function of the light it emits

py·ro·phyl·lite /pìrō fí līt, pī róffə līt/ *n* a silvery white or greenish mineral that is similar to talc in structure but contains hydrous aluminum silicate. Source: metamorphic rocks. [Early 19C. < German *Pyrophyllit* < Greek *pur* "fire" + *phullon* "leaf"; because it exfoliates when exposed to flame]

py·ro·sis /pī róssiss/ *n* same as **heartburn** (*technical*) [Late 18C. < Greek *purōsis* "burning" < *pur* "fire"]

py·ro·stat /pírə stàt/ *n* a thermostat that is suitable for use at very high temperatures [After THERMOSTAT] —**py·ro·stat·ic** /pìrə státtik/ *adj*

py·ro·tech·nic /pìrə téknik/, **py·ro·tech·ni·cal** /-téknik'l/ *adj* **1.** RELATING TO FIREWORKS relating to, used in, or involving fireworks **2.** BRILLIANT showing brilliance, e.g., in style or technique ■ *n* FIREWORK a firework or other explosive device [Early 19C. < modern Latin *pyrotechnia* < Greek *pur* "fire" + *tekhnē* "craft"] —**py·ro·tech·ni·cal·ly** *adv* —**py·ro·tech·nist** *n*

py·ro·tech·nics /pìrə tékniks/ *n* **1.** CRAFT OF MAKING FIREWORKS the craft or skill of making and using fireworks (*takes a singular verb*) **2.** FIREWORKS DISPLAY a display of fireworks (*takes a singular or plural verb*) **3.** SHOWY DISPLAY an extravagant display of brilliance, virtuosity, or strong emotion (*takes a singular or plural verb*)

py·rox·ene /pī rók seen/ *n* a mineral belonging to a group of dark green, brown, or black silicate minerals containing varying amounts of calcium, aluminum, iron, magnesium, and sodium. Source: igneous and metamorphic rocks. [Early 19C. < French *pyroxène* < Greek *pur* "fire" + *xenos* "stranger"; because originally thought to be a foreign substance in igneous rock] —**py·rox·en·ic** /pī rok sénnik/ *adj*

py·rox·e·nite /pī róksə nīt/ *n* an igneous rock consisting mainly of pyroxene and olivine

py·rox·y·lin /pī róksəlin/ *n* a form of cellulose nitrate. Use: manufacture of plastics and lacquers. [Mid-19C. < PYRO- + XYLO-]

pyr·rhic /pírrik/ *n* POETIC UNIT a metrical foot of two short or unaccented syllables ■ *adj* **1.** IN PYRRHICS relating to or written in pyrrhics **2.** RELATING TO WAR DANCE relating to an ancient Greek war dance [Early 17C. Via Latin < Greek *purríkhē*, after *Pyrrhikhos*, its supposed inventor]

Pyr·rhic vic·to·ry *n* a victory won at such great cost to the victor that it is tantamount to a defeat [Late 19C. < PYRRHUS]

Pyr·rho·nism /pírrə nìzzəm/ *n* **1.** the doctrine of the ancient Greek philosopher Pyrrho, who believed that it was impossible to be certain about anything and therefore suspended judgment on everything **2.** skepticism to an extreme or excessive degree [Late 17C. < Greek *Purrhōn* "Pyrrho" (360?–272? B.C.), Greek philosopher] —**Pyr·rhon·ist** *n, adj*

pyr·rho·tite /pírrə tīt/, **pyr·rho·tine** /-teen/ *n* a common yellow-brown lustrous iron sulfide mineral. Source: igneous rocks. Use: source of iron. [Mid-19C. Alteration of German *Pyrrhotin* < Greek *purrotēs* "fiery redness" < *pur* "fire"]

Pyr·rhus /pírrəss/, **king of Epirus** (318?–272 B.C.) The king of a Greek province (307–302, 297–272 B.C.), he invaded Italy and defeated the Roman army at Heraclea (280 B.C.) and Asculum (279 B.C.), but sustained huge losses to his troops

> "Such another victory and we are ruined."
> [Pyrrhus, on defeat of the Romans at Asculum 279 B.C. Quoted in "Pyrrhus," *Plutarch Parallel Lives*]

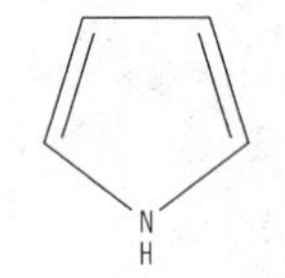

pyrrole

pyr·role /pí rōl/ *n* a colorless toxic liquid compound containing carbon, hydrogen, and nitrogen. Source: biological substances such as chlorophyll, hemoglobin, and bile pigments. Formula: C_4H_5N. [Mid-19C. < Greek *purros* "fiery red" < *pur* "fire"] —**pyr·ro·lic** /pi róllik/ *adj*

py·ru·vate /pī rōō vàyt/ *n* a chemical compound derived from pyruvic acid. It is a salt or ester of this acid. [Mid-19C. < PYRUVIC ACID]

py·ru·vic ac·id /pī rōōvik-/ *n* a colorless acid that is formed as an intermediate compound during the metabolism of carbohydrates and proteins. Formula: $C_3H_4O_3$. [Mid-19C. < PYRO- + Latin *uva* "grape"; because obtained by dry distillation from racemic acid]

Py·tha·gor·as /pi thággərəss, pī-/ (582?–500? B.C.) Greek philosopher and mathematician. He or his followers made important discoveries about number and proportion, including Pythagorean theorem, which they believed underlay everything in the universe. They also proposed that Earth is a globe, and that the planets orbit the Sun. —**Py·thag·o·re·an** /pi thàggə reé ən, pī-/ *adj, n*

Py·thag·o·re·an·ism /pi thàggə reé ə nìzzəm, pī-/ *n* the theories and teachings of Pythagoras, especially those that apply mathematics to the workings of the universe

Py·thag·o·re·an the·o·rem *n* a proved geometric proposition stating that the square of the longest side (**hypotenuse**) of a right triangle is equal to the sum of the squares of the other two sides

Pyth·i·an Games /píthee ən-/ *npl* a series of athletic contests held every four years in Delphi in ancient Greece in honor of the god Apollo [< Latin *Pythius* < Greek *Puthios* < *Puthō* "Delphi"]

py·thon /pī́ thòn/ *n* a nonvenomous constricting snake that kills its prey through suffocation and can reach lengths of over 19 ft./6 m. Native to: Asia, Africa, Australia. Family: Pythonidae. [Mid-19C. Directly or via French < Latin < Greek *Puthōn*, mythical serpent killed by Apollo]

py·tho·ness /pī́thənəss/ *n* in ancient Greek religion, a woman believed to be possessed by the spirit of an oracle, especially Apollo's priestess at Delphi [14C. < late Latin *pythonissa*, feminine of *python* (see PYTHON)]

py·u·ri·a /pī yóoree ə/ *n* the presence of pus in the urine

pyx /piks/, **pix** *n* **1.** a container in which the consecrated wafers for Communion are placed so that they can be taken to those who cannot leave home **2.** a chest in which newly minted coins are placed before being tested [14C. Via Latin < Greek *puxis* "box" (see PYXIS)]

pyx·id·i·um /pik síddee əm/ (*plural* **-id·i·a** /-íddee ə/) *n* BOT same as **pyxis** [Mid-19C. Via modern Latin < Greek *puxídion* "small box" < *puxis* (see PYXIS)]

pyx·ie /píksee/ (*plural* **-ies** or *same*) *n* a low-growing evergreen bush. Flowers: small, pink or white, star-shaped. Native to: eastern United States. Latin name: *Pyxidanthera barbulata*. [Late 19C. Shortening of modern Latin *Pyxidanthera* < *puxidium* "small box" + *anthera* "pollen"]

python

pyx·is /píksiss/ (*plural* **-i·des** /-i deèz/) *n* a seed capsule with a cap that falls off to release the seeds [Late 17C. Via Latin < Greek *puxis* "box" < *puxos* "boxwood"]

Pyx·is /píksiss/ *n* a small constellation of the southern hemisphere. See illustration at **constellation**

Qq

q /kyoo/ (*plural* **q's**), **Q** (*plural* **Q's** or **Qs**) *n* **1.** the 17th letter of the English alphabet, representing a consonant sound **2.** a written representation of the letter "q"

Q[1] (*plural* **Q's** or **Qs**) *n* something shaped like a letter "Q"

Q[2] *abbr* MONEY quetzal

Q[3] *symbol* PHYS heat

q. *abbr* **1.** MEASURE quart **2.** quarter **3.** quarterly **4.** PRINTING quarto **5.** query **6.** question **7.** MEASURE quintal **8.** PRINTING quire

Q. *abbr* **1.** MIL quartermaster **2.** quarto **3.** Quebec **4.** CHESS queen **5.** FIN quarter of a year

qa *abbr* Qatar (*used in Internet addresses*) See table at **domain name**

Qa·ba·lah /kábbələ, kə baálə/ *n* JUDAISM another spelling of **Kabbalah**

Qad·da·fi /gə daáfee, kə-/, **Gad·da·fi, Ga·daf·fi, Muammar al-** (*b.* 1942) Libyan soldier and national leader. He seized power in a coup against the Libyan monarchy (1969). He imposed Islamic and socialist policies and supported revolutionary and terrorist movements abroad.

qa·di *n* ISLAM another spelling of **cadi**

Q & A *abbr* question and answer

Qatar

Qa·tar /kaá taár, kə taár/ country in eastern Arabia, on a peninsula in the Persian Gulf, north of Saudi Arabia and the United Arab Emirates. Language: Arabic. Currency: Qatar riyal. Capital: Doha. Population: 817,052 (2003). Area: 4,412 sq. mi./11,427 sq. km. Official name **State of Qatar** —**Qa·tar·i** /kə taáree/ *adj, n*

Qat·ta·ra De·pres·sion /kə taárə-/ desert basin in northwestern Egypt. Its lowest point is 435 ft./133 m below sea level. Area: 6,950 sq. mi./18,000 sq. km.

Qay·ra·wan, Al- /kìrə waán/ ♦ **Kairouan**

qb *abbr* FOOTBALL quarterback

Q-boat *n* same as **Q-ship**

QC[1] *abbr* **1.** quality control **2.** Queen's Counsel

QC[2] *abbr* Quebec

QCD *abbr* quantum chromodynamics

QDRO /kwóddrō/ *abbr* qualified domestic relations order

q.e. *abbr* which is (*used in doctors' prescriptions*) [Latin *quod est*]

QED *abbr* PHYS quantum electrodynamics

Q.E.D. *abbr* quod erat demonstrandum

Q.E.F. *abbr* which was to be done [Latin *quod erat faciendum*]

QF *abbr* ARMS quick-firing

Q fe·ver *n* an infectious disease caused by rickettsial bacteria and characterized by fever, chills, and muscle pain [Mid-20C. Probably abbreviation of QUEENSLAND]

qi, Qi *n* PHILOSOPHY another spelling of **chi**[2]

q.i.d. *abbr* four times per day (*used in doctors' prescriptions*) [Latin *quater in die*]

qi·gong /chee góng/ *n* a Chinese practice that incorporates physical postures, breathing techniques, and mental focus, intended to improve physical and emotional health [Mid-20C. < Chinese *qi* "energy" and gong "skill"]

Qin /chin/, **Ch'in** *n* a dynasty in ancient China that ruled from 221 until 206 B.C., during which the first unified Chinese empire emerged and much of the Great Wall of China was built [Late 18C. < Chinese *Qín*]

qin·dar /kín daár/, **qin·dar·ke** /kin daárkə/ (*plural* **-ka** /*pronunc. same*/), **qin·tar** /kín taar/ *n* a subunit of Albanian currency. See table at **currency** [< Albanian *qind, qint* "hundred" < Latin *centum*]

Qing /ching/, **Ch'ing** *n* the last of the Chinese dynasties, founded by the conquering Manchu who ruled from 1644 until 1912, when the nationalist revolutionaries overthrew it [Late 18C. < Chinese *Qīng*]

Qing·dao /chìng dów/ city on the Yellow Sea, in Shandong Province, eastern China, between Beijing and Shanghai. Population: 3,140,000 (1995).

Qing·hai /chìng hí/ province in western China bounded by Xinjiang Uygur, Gansu, Sichuan, and Tibet. Capital: Xining. Population: 4,880,000 (1997). Area: 278,379 sq. mi./720,999 sq. km.

Qing·hai Hu /chìng hī hoó/ saline lake in west central China, the largest lake in the country

qin·tar *n* MONEY same as **qindar**

Qi·qi·har /cheé chee haár, -haá ər/ city and port in Heilongjiang Province, China, situated on the left bank of the Nen River 170 mi./274 km northwest of Harbin. Population: 1,520,000 (1995).

qi·vi·ut /keévee ət, -òot/ *n* the soft wool that grows beneath the long outer coat of a musk ox. Use: yarn. [Mid-20C. < Inuit]

QL *abbr* COMPUT query language

ql. *abbr* MEASURE quintal

q.l. *abbr* as much as you like (*used in doctors' prescriptions*) [Latin *quantum libet*]

Qld. *abbr* Queensland

qlty. *abbr* quality

QM *abbr* MIL quartermaster

q.m. *abbr* every morning (*used in doctors' prescriptions*) [Latin *quaque mane*]

QMC *abbr* MIL quartermaster corps

QMG *abbr* MIL Quartermaster General

qn. *abbr* question

q.n. *abbr* every night (*used in doctors' prescriptions*) [Latin *quaque nocte*]

qof *n* ALPH another spelling of **qoph**

Qom /kōm/, **Qum** /koōm/ city in central Iran, on the Qom River. It is one of the sacred cities of Iran and a center of pilgrimage for Shiite Muslims. Population: 777,677 (1996).

qoph /kof/, **qof** *n* the 19th letter of the Hebrew alphabet, represented in the English alphabet as "q." See table at **alphabet** [< Hebrew *qōph* < Semitic, "eye of a needle"]

qq. *abbr* questions

qq.v. *abbr* which (things) see (*used as a cross reference to more than one item*) [Latin *quae vide*]

qr. *abbr* **1.** quarter **2.** quarterly **3.** PRINTING quire

q.s.[1] *abbr* quarter section (*used of land*)

q.s.[2] *abbr* as much as suffices (*used in doctors' prescriptions*) [Latin *quantum sufficit*]

Q-ship *n* an armed ship disguised as a merchant ship, used to decoy or destroy enemy vessels [< the naval designation for this type of vessel]

QSO *abbr* ASTRON quasi-stellar object

qt. *abbr* **1.** quantity **2.** MEASURE quart

q.t. /kyoò teé/ *abbr* quiet (*informal*) ◇ **on the q.t.** quietly and secretly

qto. *abbr* PRINTING quarto

qty. *abbr* quantity

qu. *abbr* **1.** queen **2.** query **3.** question

qua /kway, kwaa/ *prep* in the capacity or function of (*formal*) ○*"Restrictions on trade, or on production for purposes of trade, are indeed restraints; and all restraint, qua restraint, is an evil."* (John Stuart Mill, *On Liberty*; 1859) [Mid-17C. < Latin, form of *qui* "who"]

quack[1] /kwak/ *n* **SOUND MADE BY DUCK** the harsh sound typically made by a duck ■ *vi* (**quacked, quack·ing, quacks**) **1. MAKE SOUND OF DUCK** to make the harsh sound that is characteristic of a duck **2. SPEAK IRRITATINGLY** to speak loudly and endlessly in an irritating manner (*slang*) [Early 17C. An imitation of the sound]

quack[2] /kwak/ *n* **1. FAKE DOCTOR** somebody who practices medicine without training or a valid license **2. A FRAUD** anyone who falsely claims skills and qualifications ■ *vi* (**quacked, quack·ing, quacks**) **BE QUACK** to practice medicine without training or a valid license, or to make false claims of expertise in any field [Early 17C. Shortening of QUACKSALVER] —**quack·er·y** *n* —**quack·ish** *adj*

quack grass *n* PLANTS same as **couch grass**

quack·sal·ver /kwák sàlvər/ *n* somebody who falsely claims to have medical or other skills or qualifications (*archaic*) [Late 16C. < obsolete Dutch, "salve-hawker" < Dutch *kwaken* "quack, prattle" + *zalf* "salve"]

quad[1] /kwod/ *n* same as **quadruplet** (*informal*) [Late 19C. Shortening]

quad[2] /kwod/ *n* same as **quadriceps** (*informal*) [Mid-20C. Shortening]

quad[3] /kwod/ *n* in traditional hot-metal printing, a piece of blank type metal used for spacing [Late 19C. Shortening of QUADRAT]

quad[4] /kwod/ *n* same as **quadrangle** (*informal*) [Early 19C. Shortening]

quad[5] /kwod/ *adj* same as **quadraphonic** (*informal*) [Late 20C. Shortening]

quad[6], **quad.** *abbr* MATH **1.** quadrangle **2.** quadrant **3.** quadrilateral

quadr- *prefix* same as **quadri-** (*used before vowels*)

quadra- *prefix* same as **quadri-**

Quad·ra·ges·i·ma /kwòddrə jéssimə/ *n* in the Christian liturgical calendar, the first Sunday in Lent [14C. < late Latin *quadragesima (dies)* "fortieth (day)" (before Easter) < *quadraginta* "forty"]

quad·ran·gle /kwód ràng g'l/ *n* **1. FOUR-SIDED SHAPE** a two-dimensional figure that consists of four points connected by straight lines, especially a rectangle **2. OPEN AREA SURROUNDED BY BUILDINGS** an open rectangular yard that is surrounded on all four sides by buildings **3. BUILDINGS SURROUNDING YARD** the buildings that surround an open rectangular yard **4.** *US* **AREA ON SINGLE MAP** the area of land shown on any of the map sheets produced by the US Geologic Survey [15C. Directly or via French < late Latin *quadrangulum* < Latin *quadrangulus* "having four corners"] —**quad·ran·gu·lar** /kwod ráng gyələr/ *adj*

quad·rant /kwóddrənt/ *n* **1.** MATH **QUARTER OF CIRCUMFERENCE OF CIRCLE** a 90° arc representing one fourth of the circumference of a circle **2.** MATH **QUARTER OF AREA OF CIRCLE** the area bounded by a quadrant and the two perpendicular lines that connect it to the center of the circle **3.** MATH **QUARTER OF PLANE SURFACE** any one of the four sections into which the perpendicular axes of a coordinate system divide a two-dimensional surface **4.** MATH **QUARTER OF AREA OR SURFACE** any one of the four approximately equal parts into which an area or a surface is divided by two real or imaginary perpendicular lines **5.** ASTRON **DEVICE FOR MEASURING ANGLE OF STAR** an instrument with a movable sighting mechanism attached to a 90° arc, formerly used in astronomy and navigation to measure the angles and altitudes of stars **6.** MECH ENG **DEVICE SHAPED LIKE QUARTER CIRCLE** a mechanical device or machine part in the shape of a quarter of a circle [14C. < Latin *quadrant-*, stem of *quadrans* "fourth part, quarter"]

quad·ra·phon·ic /kwòddrə fónnik/, **quad·ri·phon·ic**, **quad·ro·phon·ic** *adj* using a four-channel system to record and reproduce sound. The four separate signals may be fed to individual loudspeakers placed in the corners of a room. —**quad·ra·phon·ics** *n* —**qua·draph·o·ny** /kwo dróffənee/ *n*

quad·ra·plex /kwóddrə plèks/ *n US* same as **quadruplex** [Late 20C. < alteration of QUADRI-, after DUPLEX]

quad·rat /kwóddrət/ *n* **1.** PRINTING same as **quad**[3] **2.** a small plot of land set aside for plant and animal population studies [Late 17C. Variant of QUADRATE]

quad·rate *n* /kwód ràyt, kwóddrət/ **1. SQUARE OR CUBE** a square or cube, or a square or cubic area, space, or thing **2. JAW JOINT** in birds, fish, reptiles, and amphibians, a bony or cartilaginous part of the upper jaw that articulates with the lower jaw at the side of the skull. In mammals, this structure has evolved into the incus, a small bone of the middle ear. ■ *adj* **1. OF VERTEBRATE QUADRATE** relating to the quadrate in vertebrates **2. SQUARE OR RECTANGULAR** with four sides and four right angles ■ *vti* /kwód ràyt/ (**-rat·ed, -rat·ing, -rates**) **CONFORM OR CORRESPOND** to conform or correspond with something, or make one thing conform or correspond with another [14C. < Latin *quadratum* < *quadrum* "square"]

quad·rat·ic /kwo dráttik/ *adj* relating to or containing terms with powers no higher than the power of two ■ *n* MATH same as **quadratic equation** [Mid-17C. < QUADRATE] —**quad·rat·i·cal·ly** *adv*

quad·rat·ic e·qua·tion *n* an equation containing one or more terms raised to the power of two but no higher

quad·rat·ics /kwo dráttiks/ *n* the branch of algebra that deals with quadratic equations (*takes a singular verb*)

quad·ra·ture /kwóddrəchər, -choor/ *n* **1. MAKING SOMETHING SQUARE** the process of making something square or dividing something into squares **2.** MATH **TECHNIQUE FOR EQUATING AREAS** the construction of a square with an area equal to that of a specified surface **3.** ASTRON **90° SEPARATION OF OBJECTS** the relative position of two astronomical objects with a separation of 90° as seen from a third, especially the Sun and Moon as seen from Earth

quad·ren·ni·a TIME plural of **quadrennium**

quad·ren·ni·al /kwo drénnee əl/ *adj* **1. HAPPENING EVERY FOUR YEARS** occurring every fourth year **2. LASTING FOUR YEARS** lasting for four years ■ *n* **FOUR-YEAR PERIOD** a period of four years —**quad·ren·ni·al·ly** *adv*

quad·ren·ni·um /kwo drénnee əm/ (*plural* **-ni·ums** or **-ni·a** /-nee ə/) *n* a period of four years [Early 19C. < Latin *quadriennium* < *quadri-* "four" + *annus* "year"]

quadri- *prefix* **1.** four, fourth ○ *quadripartite* ○ *quadricentennial* **2.** square ○ *quadric* [< Latin < Indo-European, "four"]

quad·ric /kwóddrik/ *adj* MATH same as **quadratic** ■ *n* a surface or curve specified by a second degree equation [Mid-19C. < Latin *quadra*, form of *quadrum* "square"]

quad·ri·cen·ten·ni·al /kwòddrə sen ténnee əl/ *n* a 400th anniversary, or a celebration of it ■ *adj* marking or relating to a 400th anniversary

quad·ri·ceps /kwóddri sèps/ (*plural same* or **-cep·ses** /-sèpseez/) *n* a large four-part muscle at the front of the thigh that acts to extend the leg [Mid-19C. < Latin, "four-headed"] —**quad·ri·cip·i·tal** /kwòddri síppit'l/ *adj*

quad·ri·ga /kwo drígə/ (*plural* **-gae** /-jee/) *n* in ancient Greece or Rome, a two-wheeled chariot that was drawn by four horses harnessed alongside each other [Early 18C. < Latin < *quadrijuga* "team of four" < *quadri-* "four" + *jugum* "yoke"]

quad·ri·lat·er·al /kwòddri láttərəl, -láttrəl/ *n* a two-dimensional geometric figure with four sides ■ *adj* with four sides

qua·drille[1] /kwo dríl, kwə-, kə-/ *n* **1.** a French square dance in a lively duple time, popular in the 18th and 19th centuries, danced by four or more couples **2.** the music for a quadrille, often taken from a popular source and usually in a lively duple time [Mid-18C. Via French < Spanish *cuadrilla* "troop, company" < *cuadro* "square" < Latin *quadrum*]

qua·drille[2] /kwo dríl, kwə-, kə-/ *n* a card game for four players that uses a deck of 40 cards. It was popular in the 18th century. [Early 18C. < French]

quad·ril·lion /kwo drílyən/ (*plural* **-lions** or *same*) *n* **1.** the number equal to 10^{15}, written as 1 followed by 15 zeros **2.** *UK* the number equal to 10^{24}, written as 1 followed by 24 zeros (*dated*) [Late 17C. < QUADRI-, after BILLION] —**quad·ril·lion** *adj, pron* —**quad·ril·lionth** *adj, n*

quad·ri·par·tite /kwòddrə paar tìt/ *adj* **1.** made up of four parts, or divided into four **2.** involving the participation of four people or groups

quad·ri·phon·ic *adj US* RECORDING same as **quadraphonic**

quad·ri·ple·gi·a /kwòddrə pleejee ə, -pleejə/ *n* the inability to move all four limbs or the entire body below the neck —**quad·ri·pleg·ic** *n, adj*

quad·ri·plex /kwóddri plèks/ *n US* same as **quadruplex** [Late 20C. < QUADRI-, after DUPLEX]

quad·ri·va·lent /kwòddrə váylənt/ *adj* **1.** CHEM same as **tetravalent 2.** with four different valences —**quad·ri·va·lence** *n*

quad·riv·i·al /kwo drívvee əl/ *adj* **1.** with four roads or ways going in different directions and meeting at the same point **2.** relating to the quadrivium

quad·riv·i·um /kwo drívvee əm/ *n* a set of four of the seven liberal arts taught in medieval universities, consisting of arithmetic, geometry, music, and astronomy. The three lower arts (**trivium**) were grammar, rhetoric, and logic. [Early 19C. < Latin, "crossroads" < *quadri-* "four" + *via* "road"]

quad·roon /kwo droon/ *n* an offensive term for somebody with one Black and three white grandparents [Mid-17C. < Spanish *cuarterón* < Latin *quartus* "fourth"]

quad·ro·phon·ic *adj* RECORDING same as **quadraphonic**

quadru- *prefix* same as **quadri-**

quad·ru·ma·nous /kwo droomənəss/ *adj* with four feet that can also be used as hands, each having an opposable first digit. Most primates, apart from human beings, are quadrumanous. (*dated*) [Late 17C. < Latin *quadru-*, variant of *quadri-* "four" + *manus* "hand"]

quad·rum·vi·rate /kwo drúmvərət/ *n* a group of four people sharing power, especially forming a government [Mid-18C. < QUADRI-, after TRIUMVIRATE]

quad·ru·ped /kwóddrə pèd/ *n* an animal with four limbs and feet, all of which are used for walking, e.g., a lion or lizard ■ *adj* with four feet —**quad·ru·pe·dal** /kwo droopəd'l/ *adj*

quad·ru·ple /kwo droop'l/ *vti* (**-pled, -pling, -ples**) **INCREASE FOURFOLD** to multiply something by four, or become four times as great ■ *adj* **1. MULTIPLIED BY FOUR** four times as great **2. WITH FOUR PARTS** made up of four parts **3.** MUSIC **WITH FOUR BEATS PER MEASURE** describes a time or meter consisting of four beats to a measure ■ *n* **QUANTITY FOUR TIMES AS GREAT** a number or amount that is four times as great as another [14C. Via French < Latin *quadruplus* "fourfold" < *quadri-* "four"] —**quad·ru·ply** *adv*

quad·ru·plet /kwo drooplət/ *n* **1. ONE OF FOUR BABIES** any one of four babies born to the same mother from one pregnancy **2. FOUR SIMILAR THINGS** a set of four identical or very similar things **3.** MUSIC **FOUR QUICK NOTES** a group of four notes performed in the time usually occupied by three

quad·ru·plex /kwóddrə plèks/ *n* a building, especially a house, that is divided into four separate living units [Late 20C. < alteration of QUADRI-, after DUPLEX]

quad·ru·pli·cate *vti* /kwo drooplee kàyt/ (**-cat·ed, -cat·ing, -cates**) **INCREASE FOURFOLD** to multiply something by four, or be multiplied by four ■ *adj* /kwo drooplikət/ **WITH FOUR PARTS** consisting of four identical or corresponding parts ■ *n* /kwo drooplikət/ **ONE OF FOUR** any one of a set of four identical things or copies [Mid-17C. < QUADRI-, after DUPLICATE] —**quad·ru·pli·ca·tion** /kwo droopli káysh'n/ *n*

quaes·tor /kwéstər/ *n* in ancient Rome, a magistrate responsible chiefly for financial administration [14C. < Latin < *quaest-* past participle of *quaerere* "inquire"] —**quaes·to·ri·al** /kwe stáwree əl/ *adj* —**quaes·tor·ship** *n*

quaff /kwof/ (*literary or humorous*) *vti* (**quaffed, quaff·ing, quaffs**) to drink something in large gulps or with great enjoyment ■ *n* a long deep drink [Early 16C. Origin ?] —**quaff·er** *n*

quag /kwag, kwog/ *n* GEOG same as **quagmire** (sense 1) [Late 16C. Origin ?]

quag·ga /kwóggə/ (*plural* **-gas** or *same*) *n* an extinct animal of the horse family, related to the zebra, with yellowish brown coloring and stripes on the head, neck, and shoulders. Native to: South Africa. Latin name: *Equus quagga*. [Late 18C. Via Afrikaans < Nguni, an imitation of its call]

quag·gy /kwággee, kwóggee/ (**-gi·er, -gi·est**) *adj* soft and wet like a marsh or bog —**quag·gi·ness** *n*

quag·mire /kwág mìr, kwóg-/ *n* **1.** a soft marshy area of land that gives way when walked on **2.** an awkward, complicated, or dangerous situation from which it is difficult to escape

qua·hog /kwáw hàwg, -hòg, kwō-/, **qua·haug** *n* a thick-shelled edible clam, the shells of which were formerly used as money by Native North Americans. Native to: North Atlantic coast of the United States. Latin name: *Mercenaria mercenaria*. [Mid-18C. < Narraganset *poquaû hock*]

REGIONAL NOTE The ***quahog*** is also called *round clam* (especially in Connecticut) and *cohog*.

Quai d'Or·say /kee dawr sáy/ *n* **1.** the street along the south bank of the Seine River in Paris on which the French foreign office is located **2.** the French foreign office itself ○ *The Quai d'Orsay chose to make no immediate comment on the crisis.*

quail

quail[1] /kwayl/ (*plural same* or **quails**) *n* **1.** a small migratory game bird with a rounded body, mottled brown feathers, and a short tail. Native to: Europe, Asia, Africa. Genus: *Coturnix*. **2.** a small game bird related to quail, e.g., a bobwhite. Native to: North America. Family: Odontophoridae. [14C. Via French < medieval Latin *coacula* < Germanic, an imitation of its call]

quail[2] /kwayl/ (**quailed, quail·ing, quails**) *vi* to tremble with or feel fear or apprehension [Early 19C. Probably < Middle Dutch *qualen* "suffer"]

SYNONYMS See ***recoil***.

quaint /kwaynt/ *adj* **1.** with a charming old-fashioned quality ○ *a quaint little shop* **2.** strange or unusual in a pleasing or interesting way [12C. Via Old French *cointe, queinte* "clever" < Latin *cognit-*, past participle of *cognoscere* "get to know" (see COGNITION)] —**quaint·ly** *adv* —**quaint·ness** *n*

quake /kwayk/ *vi* (**quaked, quak·ing, quakes**) **1. TREMBLE WITH FEAR** to shake or tremble, especially with fear **2. SHAKE** to shake or rock, e.g., from instability or a geologic disturbance ■ *n* **1.** same as **earthquake** (*informal*) **2. SHAKING** a tremor or shake [Old English *cwacian*, origin ?] —**quak·y** *adj*

quak·er /kwáykər/, **quak·ie** /kwáykee/ *n Rocky Mountains* same as **quaking aspen**

REGIONAL NOTE As another name for the tree *quaking aspen*, ***quaker***, or occasionally ***quakie***, is common in the Middle and Upper Rocky Mountain states, especially Colorado.

Quak·er /kwáykər/ *n* a member of the Society of Friends, a Christian denomination founded in England in the 17th century that rejects formal sacraments, ministry, and creed, and is committed to pacifism. At meetings members are encouraged to speak when they feel moved to do so. [Late 17C. Probably because founder George Fox (1624–91) admonished that they should "tremble at the word of the Lord"] —**Quak·er·ism** *n* —**Quak·er·ly** *adj*

Quak·er gun *n* a dummy gun or cannon, usually made of wood, used in military training or to deceive an enemy [< Quakers' refusal to fight in wars]

quak·ing as·pen /kwàyking-/ *n* an aspen tree whose rounded flat leaves tremble in the wind. Native to: northern United States, Canada. Latin name: *Populus tremuloides*.

qual·i·fi·ca·tion /kwòlləfi káysh'n/ *n* **1. ESSENTIAL ATTRIBUTE** a skill, quality, or attribute that makes somebody suitable for a job, activity, or task **2. OFFICIAL REQUIREMENT** a condition or requirement, e.g., passing an examination, that must be met by somebody who is to be eligible for a position or privilege (*often used in the plural*) **3. MEETING OF REQUIREMENTS** the meeting of a condition or requirement to become eligible for a position or privilege **4. SOMETHING RESTRICTIVE** something that modifies, limits, or restricts **5. RESTRICTING OF SOMETHING** the modification or limitation of something, e.g., in meaning, scope, or strength

qual·i·fied do·mes·tic re·la·tions or·der *n* the awarding by a court of a part of somebody's pension or other retirement benefit to a former spouse

qual·i·fi·er /kwóllə fì ər/ *n* **1. QUALIFYING PERSON OR TEAM** a person or team that is successful in the preliminary part of a competition and earns the right to take part in the next stage **2. EARLY ROUND** a preliminary round of a competition **3. SOMEBODY WITH RIGHT OR SKILLS** somebody who has the appropriate qualifications for something **4.** GRAM **WORD MODIFYING ANOTHER** a word or phrase that restricts or modifies the meaning of another word or phrase, e.g., the word "fairly"

qual·i·fy /kwóllə fì/ (**-fied, -fy·ing, -fies**) *v* **1.** *vti* **BE OR MAKE SOMEBODY SUITABLE** to have a skill or attribute necessary for an activity, or give somebody such a skill or attribute **2.** *vti* **HAVE OR GIVE SOMEBODY ELIGIBILITY** to become legally eligible for a position or privilege, or make somebody legally eligible ○ *At 65 he automatically qualifies for a pension.* **3.** *vt* **MODIFY SOMETHING** to modify or limit something in meaning, scope, or strength **4.** *vt* **MODERATE SOMETHING** to make something less strong or extreme **5.** *vt* **DESCRIBE SOMETHING AS SOMETHING** to attribute a quality or characteristic to something **6.** *vt* GRAM **MODIFY MEANING OF WORD** to modify or restrict the meaning of a word **7.** *vi* **WIN FIRST ROUND OF COMPETITION** to complete the preliminary part of a competition successfully and earn the right to go on to the next stage [Mid-16C. Via French *qualifier* < medieval Latin *qualificare* "attribute a quality to" < Latin *qualis* "of what kind"] —**qual·i·fi·a·ble** *adj* —**qual·i·fi·ca·to·ry** /kwólləfikə tàwree/ *adj* —**qual·i·fied** *adj*

qual·i·ta·tive /kwóllə tàytiv/ *adj* relating to or based on the quality or character of something, often as opposed to its size or quantity [Early 17C. < late Latin *qualitativus* < Latin *qualitat-* (see QUALITY)] —**qual·i·ta·tive·ly** *adv*

qual·i·ta·tive a·nal·y·sis *n* identification of the chemical components of a substance

qual·i·ty /kwóllətee/ (*plural* **-ties**) *n* **1. STANDARD** the general standard or grade of something ○ *the poor quality of the air* ○ *poor-quality work* ○ *goods of the highest quality* **2. CHARACTERISTIC** a characteristic of somebody or something ○ *Honesty is one of her best qualities.* **3. ESSENTIAL PROPERTY** an essential identifying nature or character of somebody or something ○ *the soothing quality of the music* **4. EXCELLENCE** the highest or finest standard (*often used before a noun*) ○ *quality products* **5. UPPER SOCIAL CLASS** high social position or aristocratic breeding (*dated informal*) ○ *a family of quality* **6. PEOPLE OF UPPER SOCIAL CLASS** people of high social position or aristocratic breeding ○ *mixing with the quality* **7.** PHON **CHARACTER OF VOWEL SOUND** the character of a vowel sound that depends on such factors as the shape of the mouth and position of the tongue when it is uttered **8.** MUSIC **TONE OF NOTE** the distinctive tone of a musical note **9.** LOGIC **AFFIRMATIVE OR NEGATIVE CHARACTERISTIC** the positive or negative nature of a logical proposition [13C. Via French *qualité* < Latin *qualitat-* < *qualis* "of what kind"]

qual·i·ty cir·cle *n* a group of employees from different levels of a company who meet regularly to discuss ways of improving quality and to resolve any problems related to production

qual·i·ty con·trol *n* a system for achieving or maintaining the desired level of quality in a manufactured product by inspecting samples and assessing what changes may be needed in the manufacturing process

qual·i·ty fac·tor *n* a number by which a given dose of absorbed radiation is multiplied to determine the radiation's biological effect

qual·i·ty of life *n* the degree of enjoyment and satisfaction experienced in everyday life as opposed to financial or material well-being

qual·i·ty time *n* time spent with friends or family in enjoyable activities that enhance the relationship ○ *working parents determined to spend quality time with their kids*

qualm /kwaam/ *n* **1.** a sudden feeling of uncertainty or apprehension, especially a misgiving about an action or conduct **2.** a sudden pang of nausea [Early 16C. Origin ?] —**qualm·ish** *adj* —**qualm·ish·ly** *adv*

quam·ash /kwáa màsh/ (*plural* **-ash·es** or *same*) *n* PLANTS same as **camas** (sense 1) [Variant]

Qua·nah /kwáanə/ (1845?–1911) Comanche leader. He led many raids against white settlers in the southwest during the early 1870s, but after surrendering in 1875, he encouraged his people to accept assimilation. Known as **Chief Quanah**. Full name **Parker, Quanah**

quan·da·ry /kwóndəree, -dree/ (*plural* **-ries**) *n* a state of uncertainty or indecision as to what to do in a difficult situation [Late 16C. Origin ?]

quan·dong /kwón dòng/ (*plural* **-dongs** or *same*) *n* **1. RED FRUIT** a large red fruit, or its edible kernel. Use: jam. **2. SMALL AUSTRALIAN TREE** a small tree that produces quandongs. Native to: Australia. Latin name: *Santalum acuminatum*. **3. LARGE AUSTRALIAN TREE** a large lumber tree with a buttressed trunk and shiny blue fruits containing edible seeds. Native to: Australia. Latin name: *Elaeocarpus grandis*. [Mid-19C. < Wiradhuri *guwandhāng*]

~~quandry~~ incorrect spelling of **quandary**

quant /kwont/ *n* somebody skilled in computing and the analysis of quantitative data, employed by a company to make financial predictions (*slang*) [Late 20C. Shortening of QUANTITATIVE]

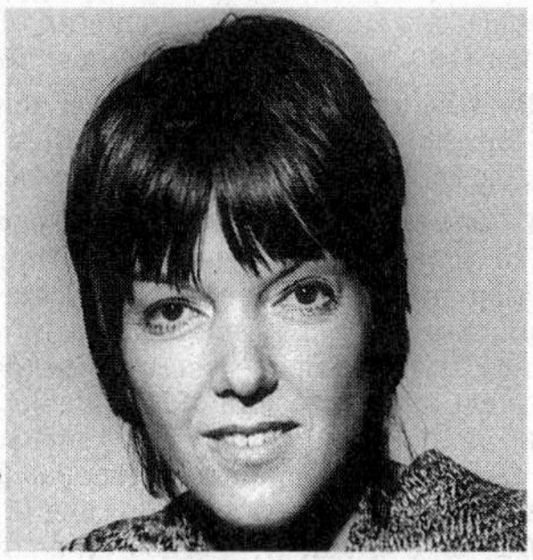

Barnaby's

Mary Quant

Quant /kwont/, **Mary** (*b.* 1934) British fashion designer. A leader of 1960s London style, she created the miniskirt and hot pants, and later expanded her business into cosmetics and textiles.

> "Legs stay throughout a woman's life."
> [Mary Quant. Quoted in *The Beautiful People*, Marilyn Bender; 1967]

quant. /kwont/ *abbr* quantitative

quan·ta PHYS, FIN plural of **quantum**

quan·tic /kwóntik/ *n* a mathematical expression with more than one variable that contains terms raised to the same power with respect to all the variables [Mid-19C. < Latin *quantus* "how much"]

quan·ti·fi·er /kwóntə fì ər/ *n* a word that indicates the range of individuals or items referred to, e.g., "all," "some," or "most," or a logical symbol with this meaning

quan·ti·fy /kwóntə fì/ (**-fied, -fy·ing, -fies**) *vt* **1.** to calculate or express the number, degree, or amount of something **2.** to use a quantifier to limit the range of individuals or items referred to in a sentence or proposition [Mid-19C. < medieval Latin *quantificare* < Latin *quantus* "how much"] —**quan·ti·fi·a·ble** /kwòntə fí əb'l/ *adj* —**quan·ti·fi·ca·tion** /-fi káysh'n/ *n*

quan·ti·tate /kwóntə tàyt/ (**-tat·ed, -tat·ing, -tates**) *vt* to estimate or determine precisely the number, degree, or amount of something [Mid-20C. Back-formation < QUANTITATIVE] —**quan·ti·ta·tion** /kwòntə táysh'n/ *n*

quan·ti·ta·tive /kwóntə tàytiv/ *adj* **1. RELATING TO QUANTITY** relating to, concerning, or based on the amount or number of something **2. MEASURABLE** capable of being measured or expressed in numerical terms **3.** LITERAT **BASED ON LENGTH OF SYLLABLES** relating or belonging to a system of poetic meter based on the length of syllables rather than on stress. Classical Latin and Greek verse uses a quantitative system. [Late 16C. < medieval Latin *quantitativus* < Latin *quantitat-* (see QUANTITY)] —**quan·ti·ta·tive·ly** *adv* —**quan·ti·ta·tive·ness** *n*

quan·ti·ta·tive a·nal·y·sis *n* determination of the relative amounts of the components of a substance

quan·ti·ta·tive dig·i·tal ra·di·og·ra·phy *n* a method of detecting thinning of the bones (**osteoporosis**) by assessing the levels of calcium present, usually in the spine and hip

quan·ti·ty /kwóntətee/ (*plural* **-ties**) *n* **1. AMOUNT** an amount or number of something **2. MEASURABLE PROPERTY** the measurable property of something ○ *a question of quantity not quality* **3. LARGE AMOUNTS** a large amount or number ○ *Foodstuffs were imported in quantity.* **4.** MATH **ENTITY WITH NUMERICAL VALUE** a mathematical entity that has a numerical value or magnitude **5.** PHYS **PARTICULAR MAGNITUDE OF SOMETHING** the product of a measurable phenomenon such as electric current or radiation intensity and the time during which the phenomenon is measured **6.** LOGIC **UNIVERSAL OR PARTICULAR NATURE OF PROPOSITION** the characteristic of a logical proposition that distinguishes it as universal or particular **7.** PHON **DURATION OF SPEECH SOUND** the length of a vowel sound or syllable [13C. Via French *quantité* < Latin *quantitat-* < *quantus* "how much"] ◇ **be an unknown quantity** to have characteristics or qualities that are not yet known and that may affect the outcome of something

USAGE See ***number***.

quan·ti·ty the·o·ry *n* the theory that prices vary with the amount of money in circulation and the rate at which it circulates

quan·tize /kwón tìz/ (**-tized, -tiz·ing, -tiz·es**) *vt* **1. EXPRESS SOMETHING IN QUANTUM NUMBERS** to express something in terms of quantum numbers **2. APPLY QUANTUM MECHANICS TO SOMETHING** to divide something into tiny discrete increments applying the rules of quantum mechanics **3.** ACOUSTICS **SEPARATE SIGNAL INTO LEVELS** to separate a continuously variable sound signal into defined levels **4.** FIN **QUOTE SOMETHING IN DIFFERENT CURRENCY** to express an asset or liability in a different currency from that normally used [Early 20C. < QUANTUM] —**quan·ti·za·tion** /kwònti záysh'n/ *n*

quant jock *n US* COMM same as **quant** (*slang*)

Quan·trill /kwóntril/, **William Clarke** (1837–65) US guerrilla leader. During the US Civil War, he led a band of Confederate desperados and outlaws in attacks on communities in Missouri and Kansas believed to be pro-Union.

quan·tum /kwóntəm/ *n* (*plural* **-ta** /-tə/) **1. SMALLEST QUANTITY OF ENERGY** the smallest discrete quantity of a physical property such as electromagnetic radiation or angular momentum **2. SMALLEST UNIT** the smallest unit used to measure a physical property. For example, the quantum of electromagnetic radiation is the photon. **3. QUANTITY** a required quantity or amount, especially an amount of money paid in recompense **4. PARTICULAR AMOUNT** a portion or allotment ■ *adj* **MAJOR** sudden, dramatic, and significant [Early 17C. < Latin, form of *quantus* "how much"] —**quan·tal** *adj*

quan·tum bit *n* PHYS full form of **qubit**

quan·tum chro·mo·dy·nam·ics *n* a quantum field theory of elementary particles that states that the color properties of quarks are bound together by gluons (*takes a singular verb*)

quan·tum com·put·er *n* a computer that uses the

quantum mechanical properties of elementary particles such as photons for transferring, processing, and storing information —**quan·tum com·put·ing** *n*

quan·tum cos·mol·o·gy *n* the cosmology of the universe during and immediately after the big bang as described through the laws of quantum mechanics —**quan·tum cos·mo·log·i·cal** *adj*

quan·tum dot *n* a small crystal containing a few hundred to several million atoms that has specific quantum-mechanical characteristics

quan·tum e·lec·tro·dy·nam·ics *n* a quantum field theory that describes the properties of electromagnetic radiation and its interaction with electrically charged particles

quan·tum field the·o·ry *n* a theory developed from quantum mechanics based on the assumption that elementary particles interact through the influence of fields around them and the exchange of energy

quan·tum foam *n* an extremely tiny hypothetical region of space-time in which numerous particles are formed and destroyed

quan·tum grav·i·ty *n* the gravitational field of subatomic physics expressed through quantum mechanics —**quan·tum grav·i·ta·tion·al** *adj*

quan·tum jump *n* **1.** the sudden transition of an atom or particle from one energy state to another **2.** same as **quantum leap**

quan·tum leap *n* a sudden, dramatic, and significant change or advance ○ *a quantum leap in our understanding of molecular science*

quan·tum me·chan·ics *n* the study and analysis of the interactions of atoms and elementary particles based on quantum theory. The study evolved in an effort to explain the behavior of atoms and subatomic particles, which do not obey the laws of classical Newtonian mechanics. (*takes a singular or plural verb*) —**quan·tum me·chan·i·cal** *adj*

quan·tum num·ber *n* any one of the set of integers or half integers that characterize the properties and energy states of an elementary particle or system

quan·tum phys·ics *n* the branch of physics that uses quantum theory

quan·tum sta·tis·tics *n* the statistical description of systems of particles that are subject to the laws of quantum physics rather than classical physics (*takes a singular verb*)

quan·tum the·o·ry *n* a theory describing the behavior and interactions of elementary particles or energy states based on the assumptions that energy is subdivided into discrete amounts and that matter possesses wave properties

quan·tum well *n* a thin layer of material with a high density of electrons whose potential energy is less than the surrounding layers and whose motion is restricted to one dimension, often used in laser and semiconducting applications

Qu'Ap·pelle /kwə pél, kə pél/ river in southern Saskatchewan, which joins the Assiniboine River east of the Manitoba border. Length: 270 mi./435 km.

quar. *abbr* **1.** quarter **2.** quarterly

quar·an·tine /kwáwrən teen/ *n* **1.** ISOLATION BECAUSE OF DISEASE enforced isolation of people or animals that may have been exposed to a contagious or infectious disease, e.g., when entering a country **2.** PLACE OF ISOLATION a place in which people or animals spend a period of isolation to prevent the spread of disease **3.** TIME OF ISOLATION the period of time during which people or animals are kept in isolation to prevent the spread of disease **4.** CONDITION OR PERIOD OF ISOLATION enforced isolation, e.g., for social or political reasons, or a period of such isolation ■ *vt* (**-tined, -tin·ing, -tines**) **1.** ISOLATE SOMEBODY to isolate a person or animal that may have been exposed to a contagious or infectious disease in order to prevent the possible spread of that disease **2.** DETAIN SOMEBODY to isolate or detain somebody, e.g., for social or political reasons [Early 17C. Via Italian *quarantina* < Latin *quadraginta* "forty"; because ships suspected of carrying disease were refused entrance to port for 40 days] —**quar·an·tin·a·ble** /kwàwrən teenəb'l/ *adj*

quar·an·tine flag *n* a yellow flag flown by a ship or boat arriving from abroad to indicate that there is no disease aboard. A second flag is flown if the vessel is not free of disease.

~~**quarentine**~~ incorrect spelling of **quarantine**

quark[1] /kwawrk/ *n* an elementary particle with an electric charge equal to one-third or two-thirds that of the electron. Quarks are believed to be the constituents of baryons and mesons. [Mid-20C. Alluding to "three quarks for Mr. Mark" in James Joyce's *Finnegans Wake*; because originally there were thought to be three quarks]

quark[2] /kwawrk/ *n* a soft cheese of German origin made from skim milk [Mid-20C. Via German < Slavic]

quar·rel[1] /kwáwrəl/ *n* **1.** ARGUMENT BETWEEN PEOPLE an angry dispute between two or more people **2.** REASON TO ARGUE a reason for a disagreement or dispute between people ○ *I have no quarrel with their proposals.* ■ *vi* (**-reled, -rel·ing, -rels**) **1.** ARGUE VEHEMENTLY to engage in an angry dispute **2.** DISAGREE WITH SOMETHING to dispute or disagree with something such as a decision **3.** FIND FAULT to complain about something [14C. Via French < Latin *querela* "complaint" < *queri* "complain"] —**quar·rel·er** *n*

quar·rel[2] /kwáwrəl/ *n* **1.** a small square or diamond-shaped pane of glass in a window **2.** a short square-headed bolt or arrow used in a crossbow [12C. Via French < assumed Vulgar Latin *quadrellus* "small square" < Latin *quadrum* "square"]

quar·rel·some /kwáwrəlssəm/ *adj* having a tendency to argue with people —**quar·rel·some·ness** *n*

quar·ri·er /kwáwree ər/ *n* a worker in a stone quarry

quar·ry[1] /kwáwree/ *n* (*plural* **-ries**) **1.** OPEN AREA FOR MINING an open excavation from which stone or other material is extracted by blasting, cutting, or drilling **2.** SOURCE a rich source of something ■ *v* (**-ried, -ry·ing, -ries**) **1.** *vti* OBTAIN SOMETHING FROM QUARRY to extract stone or other material from a quarry **2.** *vt* USE PLACE FOR EXTRACTING STONE to make a quarry in a place such as a hillside and remove material from it ○ *The area was extensively quarried in the last century.* **3.** *vti* EXTRACT SOMETHING LABORIOUSLY to obtain something such as facts or information by searching laboriously and carefully [14C. < medieval Latin *quarreia* < Old French *quarriere* < *quarre* "square-cut stone" < Latin *quadrum* "square"]

quar·ry[2] /kwáwree/ (*plural* **-ries**) *n* **1.** an animal or bird that is hunted **2.** somebody or something that is chased or hunted by another [15C. Via Anglo-Norman *couree* "entrails of an animal given to the hounds" < assumed Vulgar Latin *corata* < Latin *cor* "heart"]

quar·ry[3] /kwáwree/ (*plural* **-ries**) *n* **1.** a square or diamond shape **2.** something with a square or diamond shape, e.g., a pane of glass in a latticed window [Mid-16C. Alteration of QUARREL[2]]

quar·ry tile *n* a tile with a square or diamond shape, especially a hard-wearing unglazed clay tile used for flooring [< QUARRY[3]]

quart /kwawrt/ *n* **1.** ONE-QUARTER OF GALLON a unit of measurement for liquids equal to two pints **2.** ONE-EIGHTH OF PECK a unit of measurement for dry substances equal to two pints **3.** CONTAINER OR CONTENTS a container that holds one quart, or the contents of such a container [13C. Via French < Latin *quartus* "fourth"]

quar·tan /kwáwrt'n/ *adj* describes a fever that recurs every fourth day, e.g., in some types of malaria [13C. < Old French *quartaine* < Latin *quartus* "fourth"]

quar·ter /kwáwrtər/ *n* **1.** ONE OF FOUR PARTS one of four equal or approximately equal parts into which something is or may be divided **2.** ONE-FOURTH a number that is equal to one divided by four, represented by the symbol $\frac{1}{4}$ **3.** 25 CENTS in the United States and Canada, the sum of 25 cents **4.** COIN WORTH 25 CENTS in the United States and Canada, a coin worth 25 cents or one quarter of a dollar **5.** TIME 15 MINUTES BEFORE OR AFTER HOUR a point in time 15 minutes before or after the hour, marked on a traditional clock face at 3 and 9 **6.** CALENDAR PERIOD OF THREE MONTHS a three-month period regarded as one of four parts of a year, especially for accounting purposes **7.** *US* EDUC ACADEMIC TERM an academic term at a college or university lasting 10 or 12 weeks **8.** SPORTS PART OF SPORTS CONTEST in some sports, one of the four equal parts into which a game is divided **9.** ASTRON MOON PHASE either of the two phases of the Moon in which half of its illuminated surface can be seen from the Earth **10.** ASTRON QUARTER OF MOON'S ORBIT one-fourth of the Moon's orbital period around the Earth **11.** *also* **Quar·ter** DISTRICT OF TOWN an area in a town of a particular type or inhabited by a particular group of people ○ *the French Quarter* **12.** UNSPECIFIED SOURCE an unspecified person or group of people ○ *help from any quarter* **13.** COMPASS NORTHEAST, SOUTHEAST, SOUTHWEST, OR NORTHWEST each of the four compass points that lie midway between north, east, south, and west **14.** MERCY mercy offered to a defeated enemy **15.** MEASURE QUARTER OF STANDARD UNIT an amount or length equal to one quarter of a standard unit of measurement **16.** AGRIC, MEASURE QUARTER OF SQUARE MILE one quarter of a square mile of rural land **17.** NAUT SIDE OF REAR HALF OF VESSEL either side of the rear half of a boat or ship, usually behind the rearmost mast **18.** HERALDRY SECTION OF HERALDIC SHIELD one of the four sections into which a heraldic shield may be divided **19.** PART OF ANIMAL OR BIRD one of the four parts into which the body of an animal or bird may be divided, with a leg or wing forming part of each quarter **20.** PART OF HOOF the side of a horse's hoof ■ **quar·ters** *npl* ACCOMMODATIONS living or sleeping accommodations provided for somebody such as military personnel and their families, household employees, or members of a ship's crew ■ *adj* BEING ONE OF FOUR being one of four parts into which something is or may be divided ■ *v* (**-tered, -ter·ing, -ters**) **1.** *vt* DIVIDE SOMETHING INTO FOUR to divide something into four equal or approximately equal parts **2.** *vt* GIVE SOMEBODY LODGING to assign accommodation to somebody ○ *The soldiers were quartered in an old barn.* **3.** *vt* HIST CUT BODY INTO FOUR to cut a human body into four parts following an execution **4.** *vt* HERALDRY DIVIDE SHIELD INTO FOUR to divide a heraldic shield into four sections **5.** *vi* NAUT COME FROM REAR PART OF SIDE to come from a direction at approximately 45° to the stern of a boat or ship **6.** *vt* POSITION SOMETHING AT 90 DEGREES to locate or position a machine part at right angles to another [13C. Via French < Latin *quartarius* "fourth part" < Latin *quartus* "fourth"] ◇ **at close quarters** from very near

REGIONAL NOTE ***Quarter*** can be used with *of*, *till*, and *to* to designate fifteen minutes to the hour. Before World War II the three prepositions were characteristic of, respectively, the Northern, Midland, and Southern dialect areas, especially in the Eastern states. The pattern seems to endure, with *quarter to* gaining ground across the country.

quar·ter·age /kwáwrtərij/ *n* a sum of money paid or received every three months

quar·ter·back /kwáwrtər bàk/ *n* PLAYER IN FOOTBALL in football, a player positioned behind the center who directs the play by calling signals ■ *vt* (**-backed, -back·ing, -backs**) **1.** DIRECT TEAM to direct the offensive play of a football team **2.** BE IN CHARGE OF OPERATION to direct or mastermind an operation (*slang*)

quar·ter-bound *adj* describes a book that is bound in one material, usually leather, on the spine and in another on the covers

quar·ter·deck /kwáwrtər dèk/ *n* the rear part of the upper deck of a ship, where official ceremonies traditionally take place on a vessel

quar·ter·fi·nal /kwàwrtər fín'l, kwáwrtər fín'l/ *n* each of four contests in a tournament or competition, the winners of which go on to play each other in the semifinals [Early 20C. After SEMIFINAL] —**quar·ter·fi·nal·ist** *n*

quar·ter horse *n* a strong horse formerly bred in the United States to run short races [< *quarter-race*, a race over a quarter mile]

quar·ter hour *n* **1.** a period of 15 minutes **2.** either of the points on a clock face that indicate a time 15 minutes before or after the hour, or one of these times ○ *The clock chimes on the quarter hour.*

quar·ter-life cri·sis /kwáwrtər līf-/ *n* feelings of doubt and confusion about identity and the future experienced by some people in their twenties

quar·ter·ly /kwáwrtərlee/ *adj* **1.** HAPPENING EVERY THREE MONTHS happening, produced, or published four times a year, at three-month intervals **2.** HERALDRY DIVIDED INTO FOUR describes a heraldic shield that is divided into four sections ■ *adv* EVERY THREE MONTHS four times a year, at three-month intervals ■ *n* (*plural* **-lies**) JOURNAL PUBLISHED EVERY THREE MONTHS a magazine or journal published four times a year, at three-month intervals

quar·ter·mas·ter /kwáwrtər màstər/ *n* **1.** an army officer responsible for providing soldiers with food, clothing, equipment, and living quarters **2.** in the navy, a petty officer or ship's mate with some responsibilities for navigation and signals

quar·tern /kwáwrtərn/ *n* a fourth part of something, especially of some old weights and measures [13C. < Anglo-Norman *quartrun*]

quar·ter note *n* a musical note with one-fourth the time value of a whole note

quar·ter-phase *adj* ELEC ENG same as **two-phase** [Because the two currents are 90° out of phase]

quar·ter·pipe /kwáwrtər pīp/ *n* in snowboarding, a snow structure resembling a "U"-shaped structure (**halfpipe**) with one wall removed, used as a jumping-off place

quar·ter rest *n* a musical rest with the time value of a quarter note

quar·ter round *n* an architectural molding that, in cross section, is the shape of a quarter of a circle

quar·ter·sawn /kwáwrtər sàwn/, **quar·ter·sawed** /-sàwd/ *adj* describes wooden boards sawed from a log cut into quarters lengthwise so as to show off the grain of the wood

quar·ter sec·tion *n* a tract of land measuring 0.5 mi./800 m on each side, equal to 160 acres/65 hectares or one-fourth of a section

quar·ter·staff /kwáwrtər stàf/ (*plural* **-staves** /-stàyvz/ or **-staffs**) *n* a long heavy wooden stick tipped with iron, formerly used in hand-to-hand fighting [Mid-16C. Origin ?]

quar·ter step *n US* a difference in pitch between two tones (**intervals**) that is equal to half of a half step. Can term **quarter tone**

quar·ter tone *n Can, UK* MUSIC same as **quarter step**

quar·tet /kwawr tét/, **quar·tette** *n* **1. MUSICAL GROUP** a group of four singers or musicians **2. PIECE OF MUSIC** a piece of music written for four voices or instruments **3. GROUP OF FOUR** a group or set of four people, organizations, or things [Late 18C. Via French *quartette* < Italian *quartetto* < *quarto* "fourth" < Latin *quartus*]

Quar·tet *n* an international group of representatives from the United States, the European Union, the Russian Federation, and the United Nations that meets regularly to promote peace between Israel and the Palestinian Authority

quar·tic /kwáwrtik/ *adj* relating to or involving the fourth degree of power of an unknown quantity or variable. A quartic equation has the general form $ax^4 + bx^3 + cx^2 + dx + e = 0$. [Mid-19C. < Latin *quartus* "fourth"]

quar·tile /kwáwr tìl, kwáwrt'l/ *n* **1. STATISTICAL DIVISION** each of four equal groups into which a statistical sample may be divided **2. STATISTICAL VALUE** in statistics, each of the three values that divide a frequency distribution into four parts that each contain a quarter of the sample population **3. DISTANCE BETWEEN PLANETS** the astrological aspect of planets that are distant from each other by 90° or one-fourth of the zodiac [Early 16C. < Old French *quartil* < Latin *quartus* "fourth"]

quar·to /kwáwrtō/ (*plural* **-tos**) *n* **1.** a book with pages of a size traditionally created by folding a single sheet of standard-sized printing paper in half twice, giving four leaves or eight pages **2.** the page size of a quarto book [Late 16C. < Latin (*in*) *quarto* "in a fourth" < *quartus* "fourth"]

quartz /kwawrts/ *n* a common, hard, usually colorless, transparent crystalline mineral with colored varieties. Use: electronics, gems. [Mid-18C. < German *Quarz* < W Slavic, "hard"]

quartz clock *n* a clock in which the time-keeping mechanism is accurately controlled by a quartz crystal that vibrates at a fixed frequency in an oscillating electric circuit

quartz crys·tal *n* a small piece of quartz cut so that it vibrates at a known frequency

quartz glass *n* a clear glass made from melted silica that can withstand high or rapidly changing temperatures and is unusually transparent to ultraviolet radiation

quartz heat·er *n* a portable electric heater with heating elements sealed in quartz glass tubes

quartz·if·er·ous /kwart síffərəss/ *adj* containing or consisting of quartz

quartz-i·o·dine lamp *n* a very bright lamp with a bulb made of quartz glass that has a tungsten filament and usually contains iodine vapor. Use: automobile headlights, movie projectors.

quartz·ite /kwáwrt sìt/ *n* a pale metamorphic rock composed mainly of quartz, formed by the action of heat and pressure on sandstone. Use: construction materials. —**quartz·it·ic** /kwawrt síttik/ *adj*

quartz lamp *n* a mercury-vapor lamp with a bulb made from quartz glass that produces light rich in ultraviolet radiation and is used for street lighting and sun lamps

quartz watch *n* a watch in which the time-keeping mechanism is accurately controlled by a quartz crystal that vibrates at a fixed frequency in an oscillating electric circuit

qua·sar /kwáy zaàr/ *n* a compact object in space, usually with a large red shift indicating extreme remoteness, that emits huge amounts of energy, sometimes equal to the energy output of an entire galaxy [Mid-20C. Contraction of QUASI-STELLAR OBJECT]

quash[1] /kwosh/ (**quashed, quash·ing, quash·es**) *vt* to declare formally, especially in a court of law, that something such as an indictment or a subpoena is not valid [13C. Via French < Latin *cassare* < *cassus* "empty, void"]

quash[2] /kwosh/ (**quashed, quash·ing, quash·es**) *vt* to suppress something such as a rebellion or political protest completely by means of force [14C. Via French < medieval Latin *quassare* "shake to pieces" < *quatere* "shake"]

qua·si /kwáy zì, kwaàzee/ *adj* **1.** just as valid in law as if actual **2.** resembling somebody or something in some ways, but not exactly the same ○ *a quasi support group* [15C. Via French < Latin, "as if" < *quam* "as" + *si* "if"]

quasi- *prefix* as if, resembling ○ *quasi-judicial* [Via French < Latin *quasi* (see QUASI)]

qua·si·ab·stract *adj*
qua·si·chem·i·cal *adj*
qua·si·con·trac·tual *adj*
qua·si·crys·tal·line *adj*
qua·si·dip·lo·mat·ic *adj*
qua·si·do·mes·tic *adj*
qua·si·fas·cist *adj*
qua·si·gov·ern·men·tal *adj*
qua·si·le·gal *adj*
qua·si·leg·en·dar·y *adj*
qua·si·le·git·i·mate *adj*
qua·si·Marx·ist *adj*
qua·si·mil·i·tar·y *adj*
qua·si·mod·ern *adj*
qua·si·mys·ti·cal *adj*
qua·si·nom·i·nal *adj*
qua·si·of·fi·cial *adj*
qua·si·pe·ri·od·ic *adj*
qua·si·pri·vate *adj*
qua·si·pri·va·ti·za·tion *n*
qua·si·pri·va·tize *vt*
qua·si·pub·lic *adj*
qua·si·re·gal *adj*
qua·si·re·lig·ious *adj*
qua·si·sci·en·tif·ic *adj*
qua·si·the·at·ri·cal *adj*

qua·si·ju·di·cial *adj* **1.** describes decision-making powers that are similar to those of a court judge **2.** describes an arbitrator or inquiry with powers that are similar to those of a court judge

qua·si·leg·is·la·tive *adj* **1.** describes bodies that are empowered to make regulations having the force of law **2.** describes regulations that are not regarded as laws proper but have the force of law

qua·si·stel·lar ob·ject *n* ASTRON same as **quasar**

quass *n* BEVERAGES another spelling of **kvass**

quas·sia /kwóshə/ *n* **1. PALE WOOD** a fine-grained pale wood. Use: furniture-making. **2. INSECTICIDE** a bitter substance obtained from the bark and wood of a tropical tree. Use: insecticide. **3. TREE YIELDING QUASSIA** a bush or small tree with scarlet flowers that yields quassia. Native to: tropical America. Genus: *Quassia.* [Mid-18C. < ?]

qua·ter·cen·ten·a·ry /kwòttər sen ténnəree/ (*plural* **-ries**) *n* a four-hundredth anniversary [Late 19C. < Latin *quater* "four times"]

qua·ter·nar·y /kwóttər nèrree/ *adj* **1. OCCURRING IN FOURS** consisting of four parts, or occurring in sets of four **2. HAVING FOUR-ATOM BONDS** bonded to four other nonhydrogen atoms or groups of atoms, or containing atoms bonded in this way ■ *n* (*plural* **-ies**) **FOURTH MEMBER** the fourth member of a set [15C. < Latin *quaternarius* < *quaterni* "by fours" < *quater* "four times"]

Qua·ter·nar·y *n* the current period of geologic time, beginning 1.6 million years ago and characterized by the appearance and dominance of humans. See table at **geologic time** —**Qua·ter·nar·y** *adj*

qua·ter·nar·y am·mo·ni·um com·pound *n* a nitrogen compound regarded as a derivative of ammonium. Use: solvents, disinfectants.

qua·ter·ni·on /kwə túrnee ən/ *n* a generalized complex number that contains four terms, one real and three imaginary, and is the sum of a real number and a vector [14C. < late Latin *quaternion-* < Latin *quaterni* (see QUATERNARY)]

qua·ter·ni·ty /kwə túrnətee/ (*plural* **-ties**) *n* a set of four, especially the four beings that, in some religions, are unified in God [Early 16C. < late Latin *quaternitas* < Latin *quaterni* (see QUATERNARY)]

quat·rain /kwó tràyn/ *n* a verse of poetry consisting of four lines, especially one with lines that rhyme alternately [Late 16C. < French < *quatre* "four" < Latin *quattuor*]

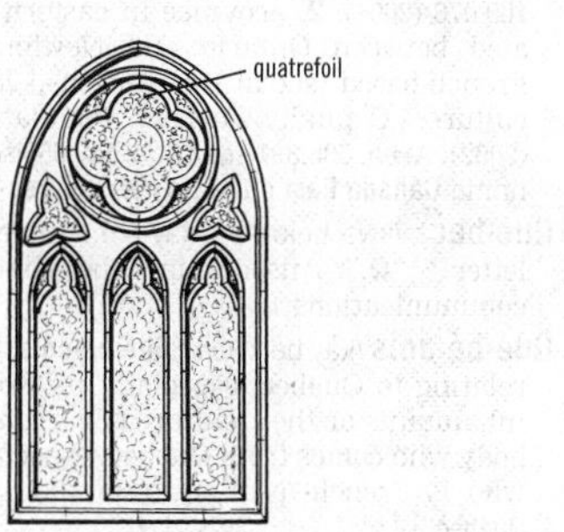

quatrefoil (sense 2)

quat·re·foil /káttər fòyl, káttrə-/ *n* **1.** a design or symbol in the shape of a flower with four petals or a leaf with four parts, often used in heraldry **2.** an architectural decoration consisting of four arcs radiating from a center like flower petals [15C. < Anglo-Norman, "four-leaf"]

quat·tro·cen·to /kwaàtrō chén tō/ *n* the 15th century in Italy, especially with reference to art and literature [Late 19C. < Italian, shortening of *mil quattrocento* "one thousand four hundred"]

qua·ver /kwáyvər/ *v* (**-vered, -ver·ing, -vers**) **1.** *vti* **SAY TREMBLINGLY** to say something or speak in a trembling voice because of nervousness or fear **2.** *vi* **SING WITH TRILL** to sing in a trilling voice **3.** *vi* **TREMBLE SLIGHTLY** to tremble because of nervousness or fear ■ *n* **1. TREMBLING SOUND** a tremble in the voice caused by nervousness or fear **2. TRILL** an alternation of a musical tone with the tone just above it **3.** *UK* MUSIC same as **eighth note** [15C. < obsolete *quave* "tremble" < Germanic] —**qua·ver·ing·ly** *adv* —**qua·ver·y** *adj*

qua·ver rest *n UK* same as **eighth rest**

quay /kee/ *n* a platform that runs along the edge of a port or harbor, where boats are loaded and unloaded [14C. Via Old N French *cai* < Gaulish *caio* "rampart"]

quay·age /kée ij/ *n* **1. FEE FOR USING QUAY** a charge that shipowners must pay to dock at a quay in order to load and unload there **2. QUAY SPACE** the space available on a quay for ships to load and unload **3. QUAY SYSTEM** a system of quays

Quayle /kwayl/, **Dan** (*b.* 1947) vice president of the United States (1989–93). As a Republican in the US Senate (1981–88) he emphasized conservative values. Full name **Quayle, James Danforth**

quay·side /kée sìd/ *n* the edge of a quay, where it meets the water

qu·bit /kyóo bìt/ *n* an elementary particle such as an electron or photon that can store data and perform computational tasks within a quantum computer's processor and memory [Late 20C. < QUANTUM + BIT[3]]

Que. *abbr* Quebec

quean /kween/ *n* an offensive term that deliberately insults a woman's morality (*archaic*) [Old English *cwene* "woman," related to QUEEN]

quea·sy /kweézee/ (**-si·er, -si·est**) *adj* **1. NAUSEATED** feeling ill in the stomach, as if on the point of vomiting **2. EASILY NAUSEATED** easily made to feel nauseated **3. CAUSING NAUSEA** causing a feeling of nausea **4. CAUSING UNEASINESS** causing a feeling of uneasiness [15C. Origin ?] —**quea·si·ly** *adv* —**quea·si·ness** *n*

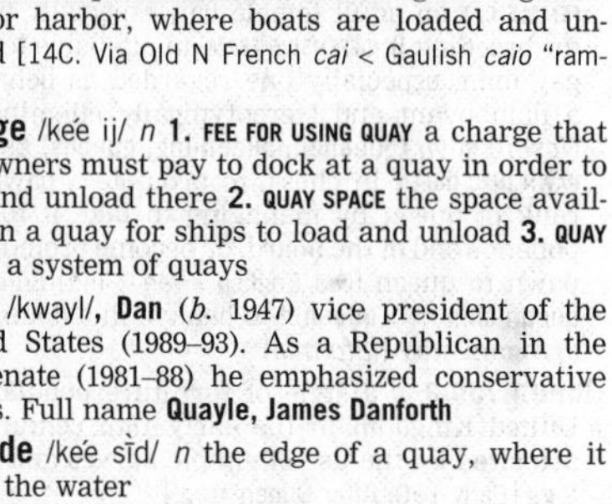

Quebec

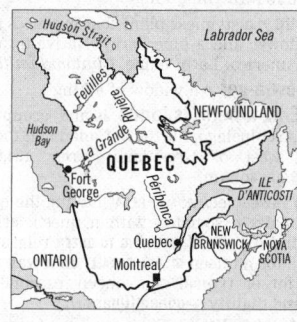

Que·bec[1] /kwi bék, ki-/, **Qué·bec** /kay-/ **1.** *also* **Que·bec Ci·ty** *or* **Qué·bec Ci·ty** capital of Quebec Province, Canada, on the St. Lawrence River. Population:

169,076 (2001). **2.** province in eastern Canada, situated between Ontario and Newfoundland, with French-based social institutions, language, and culture. Capital: Quebec. Population: 7,455,200 (2002). Area: 595,391 sq. mi./1,542,056 sq. km. Former name **Canada East** (1841–67) —**Que·bec·er** *n*

Que·bec[2] /kwə bék, kə-, kay-/ *n* a code word for the letter "Q," used in international radio communications

Qué·bé·cois /kày be kwáa/, **Qué·be·cois**, **Que·be·cois** *adj* relating to Quebec, especially its French-speaking inhabitants or their culture ■ *n* (*plural same*) somebody who comes from Quebec, especially somebody who is French-speaking [Late 19C. < French, "from Quebec"]

que·bra·cho /kay bráa chō/ (*plural* **-chos**) *n* a tree with hard tannin-rich wood. Native to: southern South America. Genus: *Schinopsis.* [Late 19C. < Spanish, alteration of *quiebrahacha* "ax-breaker" < *quebrar* "to break" + *hacha* "ax"]

Quech·ua /kéchwə/ (*plural same* or **-uas**), **Kech·ua**, **Quich·ua** /kéechwə/ *n* **1.** a member of a Native South American people living in the Andes **2.** the language of the Quechua people. Native speakers: 11 million. [Mid-19C. < Spanish] —**Quech·ua** *adj* —**Quech·uan** *adj, n*

queen /kween/ *n* **1.** FEMALE RULER a woman who rules over a country, usually by right of birth **2.** KING'S WIFE the wife or widow of a king **3.** ADMIRED WOMAN a greatly admired woman who stands out above all others ○ *the queen of blues* **4.** BEST PLACE OR THING a place or thing considered the best of its kind and personified as a woman **5.** CHESS MOST POWERFUL CHESS PIECE the most powerful piece in chess, able to move over any number of squares forward, backward, sideways, and diagonally **6.** CARDS FACE CARD a playing card with a picture of a queen on it, ranking above a jack and below a king **7.** INSECTS EGG-LAYING INSECT a large, fully developed female that lays eggs in a colony of social insects, e.g., bees or ants **8.** VERTEB FEMALE CAT an adult female cat, especially one used for breeding **9.** OFFENSIVE TERM an offensive term for a gay man, especially one regarded as behaving in a flamboyant and stereotypically effeminate way (*insult*) ■ *vti* (**queened, queen·ing, queens**) CHESS MAKE PAWN INTO QUEEN in chess, to promote a pawn to the rank of queen by managing to take it to the opponent's end of the board, or become promoted from pawn to queen [Old English *cwēn* < Indo-European] —**queen·ship** *n* ◇ **queen it** to behave in a domineering, arrogant way (*informal*)

Queen Anne *n* a style of furniture popular in the United Kingdom in the early 18th century, characterized by the use of simple curves and cabriole legs [Early 19C. After Queen ANNE]

Queen Anne's lace *n* a wild relative of the carrot with flat-topped clusters of white flowers and a thick but inedible root. Native to: Europe, Asia. Latin name: *Daucus carota.* [Late 19C. After Queen ANNE]

queen bee *n* **1.** a large, fully developed female bee that lays eggs continually **2.** a woman or girl who is treated as the most important member of her group, or who behaves as if she is (*informal*)

Queen Char·lotte Is·lands /-shaárlət-/ island group in British Columbia, Canada, northwest of Vancouver Island in the Pacific Ocean. Area: 3,705 sq. mi./9,596 sq. km. Population: 3,368 (1986).

queen con·sort (*plural* **queens con·sort**) *n* a woman married to a reigning king

queen-cup *n* a stemless plant that produces a single white flower and a blue berry. Native to: western North America. Latin name: *Clintonia uniflora.*

queen dow·a·ger *n* a widow of a king

Queen E·liz·a·beth Is·lands island group in the Arctic Archipelago, northern Canada, in the Arctic Ocean, west of Greenland. Area: 164,000 sq. mi./425,000 sq. km.

queen·ly /kweénlee/ *adj* **1.** REGAL having the qualities traditionally associated with a queen, especially grace and dignity **2.** RELATING TO QUEEN relating to or suitable for a queen ■ *adv* REGALLY in a way thought fitting for or typical of a queen, especially with grace and dignity —**queen·li·ness** *n*

Queen Maud Gulf /-màwd-/ gulf in the Arctic Ocean, between southeastern Victoria Island and the mainland of Nunavut, Canada

queen moth·er *n* the mother of a reigning king or queen and the widow of a former king

Queen of the May *n* same as **May queen**

queen of the prai·rie *n* a plant that grows in grasslands. Flowers: small, pink. Native to: central and eastern United States. Latin name: *Filipendula rubra.*

queen ol·ive *n* a large edible olive with a long flat pit

queen post *n* either of two vertical posts forming part of the triangular framework that supports a roof [After KING POST]

queen re·gent (*plural* **queens re·gent**) *n* a queen reigning on behalf of another person, especially one too young to take the throne

queen reg·nant (*plural* **queens reg·nant**) *n* a queen who reigns in her own right, as distinct from the wife of a king

Queens /kweenz/ borough of New York City, on western Long Island. Population: 2,237,815 (2002 estimate). Area: 109 sq. mi./282 sq. km.

Queen's Bench *n* a division of the High Court of Justice in England (*used when the reigning monarch is a woman or girl*)

Queens·ber·ry rules /kweénz bèrree-/ *npl* the rules that govern boxing [Late 19C. After John Sholto Douglas (1844–1900), 9th Marquess of *Queensberry,* who supervised their preparation in 1867]

Queen's Coun·sel *n* a senior barrister in England (*used when the reigning monarch is a woman or girl*)

Queen's Eng·lish *n* standard written or spoken British English, regarded as the most correct form of the language (*used when the reigning monarch is a woman or girl*)

Queen's ev·i·dence *n* in English law, evidence for the prosecution given by somebody who took part in a crime, usually in exchange for leniency (*used when the reigning monarch is a woman or girl*)

queen·side /kweén sīd/ *n* the side of a chessboard on which the queen is located at the beginning of a game

queen-size *adj* **1.** describes beds and bedclothes that are larger than the standard size but smaller than king-size ○ *a queen-size bed* **2.** describes women's clothes that are extra large [After KING-SIZE]

Queens·land /kweénz lànd, -lənd/ state in northeastern Australia. Capital: Brisbane. Population: 3,796,800 (2003). Area: 666,880 sq. mi./1,727,200 sq. km. —**Queens·land·er** *n*

Queen·stown /kweénz tòwn/ resort town in the southwestern part of the South Island, New Zealand, situated on the shore of Lake Wakatipu. Population: 8,538 (2001).

queen sub·stance *n* a pheromone secreted by a queen bee and consumed by worker bees in the same hive that prevents the worker bees from becoming fully developed and reproducing

queer /kweer/ *adj* (*dated*) **1.** NOT USUAL not usual or expected **2.** ECCENTRIC eccentric or unconventional **3.** SUSPICIOUS arousing suspicion **4.** NAUSEATED slightly unwell, especially nauseated or faint **5.** OFFENSIVE TERM an offensive term meaning gay ■ *n* OFFENSIVE TERM an offensive term for a gay man (*insult*) ■ *vt* (**queered, queer·ing, queers**) **1.** THWART SOMETHING to spoil or thwart something, especially somebody's plans **2.** COMPROMISE SOMEBODY to put somebody in an awkward situation [Early 16C. Probably < Low German *quer* "oblique, crooked"] —**queer·ly** *adv* —**queer·ness** *n*

USAGE See *insult.*

queer·core /kweér kàwr/ *n* (*slang*) **1.** a gay youth movement that rejects the stereotype of a gay person as a persecuted victim by confidently and assertively proclaiming homosexuality, especially in punk-style music **2.** a style of music similar to punk rock with lyrics that proclaim homosexuality confidently and assertively [Late 20C. < QUEER + HARD CORE]

que·le·a /kwéleeə/ (*plural* **-as** or *same*) *n* a brownish bird of the weaverbird family, the male of which has either a black face or a red head. Native to: Africa. Genus: *Quelea.*

quell /kwel/ (**quelled, quell·ing, quells**) *vt* **1.** to bring something to an end, usually by means of force ○ *using tear gas to quell the riot* **2.** to allay a disturbing feeling or thought in a reassuring way [Old English *cwellan* "kill" < Indo-European, "stab, kill"]

quench /kwench/ (**quenched, quench·ing, quench·es**) *vt* **1.** SATISFY THIRST to satisfy a thirst by drinking something **2.** EXTINGUISH FIRE to put out a fire or light **3.** SUPPRESS FEELING to suppress a feeling completely, especially enthusiasm or desire **4.** COOL METAL to cool hot metal by plunging it into cold water or other liquid [Old English *ācwencan* < Germanic] —**quench·er** *n* —**quench·less** *adj*

que·nelle /kə nél/ *n* a seasoned meat or fish dumpling poached in water and served with a sauce [Mid-19C. Via French < German *Knödel* "dumpling"]

quer·ce·tin /kwúrssitin/ *n* a yellow compound. Source: rind and bark of oak, Douglas fir, and many other plants. Use: treatment of fragile capillaries. Formula: $C_{15}H_{10}O_7$. [Mid-19C. < Latin *quercetum* "oak forest" < *quercus* "oak"]

quer·ci·tron /kwúrssitrən, -tròn, kwur síttrən/ *n* **1.** the bright orange inner bark of the black oak tree. Use: tanning, dyeing. **2.** yellow dye made from quercitron [Late 18C. < Latin *quercus* "oak" + CITRON, from the color of its bark]

que·ri·da /kay reédə/ (*plural* **-das**) *n Philippines* a man's mistress [Mid-19C. < Spanish, "darling, beloved" < *querer* "desire" < Latin *quaerere* "seek"]

que·rist /kweérist/ *n* a questioner (*archaic*) [Mid-17C. < *quere* (see QUERY)]

quern /kwurn/ *n* a simple stone mill used for grinding grain by hand [Old English *cweorn* < Indo-European, "heavy"]

quer·u·lous /kwérrələss, kwérryə-/ *adj* **1.** inclined to complain or find fault **2.** whining or complaining in tone [15C. < late Latin *querulosus* < Latin *queri* "complain"] —**quer·u·lous·ly** *adv* —**quer·u·lous·ness** *n*

que·ry /kweéree/ *n* (*plural* **-ries**) **1.** QUESTION a request for information **2.** DOUBT a doubt or criticism **3.** GRAM same as **question mark** ■ *vt* (**-ried, -ry·ing, -ries**) **1.** QUESTION SOMETHING to express doubts about, or objections to, something **2.** ASK SOMETHING to ask something as a question [Mid-17C. < obsolete *quere* "ask" (imperative), "query" < Latin *quaere* "ask" < *quaerere* "seek"] —**que·ri·er** *n*

ques. *abbr* question

que·sa·dil·la /kày sə deéyə/ *n Hispanic* a tortilla filled with cheese and other ingredients and grilled [Mid-20C. < Mexican Spanish < Spanish *queso* "cheese"]

quest /kwest/ *n* **1.** SEARCH a search for something, especially a long or difficult one **2.** ADVENTUROUS EXPEDITION a journey in search of something, especially one made by knights in medieval tales (*literary*) **3.** SOMETHING SOUGHT the object or goal of a quest (*literary*) ○ *Peace is still our quest.* **4.** COMPUT GAMES GAME OBJECTIVE an objective to be achieved in a computer game ○ *Strange things will happen if you perform quests out of sequence.* ■ *v* (**quest·ed, quest·ing, quests**) **1.** *vti* SEEK SOMETHING to seek or go in search of something (*literary*) **2.** *vi* HUNTING TRACK ANIMALS to follow the track of a bird or animal that is being hunted (*refers to hunting dogs*) [14C. Via French < Latin *quaesita* < form of past participle of *quaerere* "seek"] —**quest·er** *n*

ques·tion /kwéschən/ *n* **1.** WRITTEN OR SPOKEN INQUIRY a request for information or for a reply, which usually ends with a question mark if written or on a rising intonation if spoken ○ *Does anyone have any questions?* **2.** DOUBT a doubt or uncertainty about somebody or something **3.** ISSUE a matter that is the subject of discussion, debate, or negotiation **4.** EDUC EXAMINATION PROBLEM a problem to be discussed or solved in an examination ■ *v* (**-tioned, -tion·ing, -tions**) **1.** *vti* INTERROGATE SOMEBODY to ask somebody for information, especially formally or officially and on a specific topic **2.** *vi* INQUIRE to ask questions **3.** *vt* DOUBT SOMETHING to raise doubts about something, especially about its truth, genuineness, or usefulness [13C. Via French < Latin *quaestion-* "inquiry" < past participle of *quaerere* "seek"] —**ques·tion·er** *n* ◇ **beg the question 1.** to take for granted the very point that needs to be proved, and so fail to address an issue properly **2.** to give rise to something else that should be answered or explained ◇ **be out of the question** to be impossible or unacceptable ◇ **call something into question** to raise doubts about something ◇ **in question** used to indicate the person or thing under discussion ◇ **pop the question** to propose marriage to somebody (*informal*)

USAGE To *beg the question* is often used to mean "to raise the question" or "to avoid a direct answer," since both meanings are consistent with the form of the idiom. The basic meaning of this idiom relates to the validity of a proposition that is used as a basis of argument. For example, in an argument about the effect on the environment of gas emissions from road traffic, the proposition that a higher tax on vehicles would contribute to cleaner air ***begs the question***, because it needs to be proved that raising taxes would result in fewer road users. The fallacy implied by the notion of ***begging the question*** usually involves the omission of one stage in an argument, or a questionable assumption of its validity.

SYNONYMS ***question, quiz, interrogate, cross-examine, grill, give the third degree***

CORE MEANING: to ask for information

question to ask somebody for information, especially formally or officially and on a specific topic ○ *Patients were questioned in detail about their symptoms.* **quiz** to subject somebody to sustained close questioning ○ *Anne was being quizzed by her aunt about her many boyfriends.* **interrogate** to question somebody thoroughly, often in an aggressive or threatening manner and especially as part of a formal investigation, for example, in a police station or courtroom ○ *Police are interrogating two men and a woman arrested on Thursday.* **cross-examine** (*informal*) to ask somebody a lot of detailed questions in a persistent or aggressive way ○ *We were cross-examined about who we'd spoken to and why it had taken us so long to get home.* **grill** (*informal*) to question somebody in a persistent manner ○ *Lawyers on both sides grilled a DNA expert about his analysis of the blood found in the vehicle.* **give the third degree** (*informal*) to subject somebody to intensive interrogation, especially when accompanied by rough physical treatment ○ *My mother gave me the third degree whenever I was out late.*

ques·tion·a·ble /kwéschənəb'l/ *adj* **1.** open to doubt or disagreement **2.** not respectable or morally acceptable ○ *questionable motives* —**ques·tion·a·bly** *adv*

~~**questionaire**~~ incorrect spelling of **questionnaire**

ques·tion·ing /kwéschəning/ *n* a situation in which somebody is asked a lot of questions, especially formally or officially, or an instance of this ■ *adj* expressing a question without using words ○ *a questioning glance* —**ques·tion·ing·ly** *adv*

ques·tion·less /kwéschənləss/ *adj* **1.** same as **unquestionable 2.** same as **unquestioning**

ques·tion mark *n* the punctuation mark (?) placed at the end of a sentence or phrase intended as a direct question. It is also used after a word or phrase whose appropriateness is in doubt, or after a number or date whose accuracy is in doubt. ◇ **a question mark over something** an area of doubt and uncertainty concerning something

USAGE The ***question mark*** is used after a direct question: *"Where are you going?" "What for?"* It is not used in indirect questions: *He asked her where she was going.* It may also be used in other contexts, e.g., in creative writing, to indicate that somebody is wondering about something (*He assumed she had gone to visit her mother. But why had she taken her passport?*), or in journalism to anticipate a reader's question (*How is the tax calculated? It is based on the current market value of the property*). The question mark may also indicate uncertainty, especially when placed before or after a date: *François Rabelais (1493?–1553).* The question mark may mark a sentence that has the function but not the structure of a question: *You're from New York then?* It may be omitted from a sentence that has the structure of a question, but is not intended as such: *Will you keep quiet for a minute.*

ques·tion·naire /kwèschə nér/ *n* **1.** a set of questions used to gather information in a survey **2.** a printed paper or form that contains a questionnaire [Late 19C. < French < *questionner* "ask" < *question* (see QUESTION)]

ques·tion time *n UK* in the British Parliament, a period of time every day during which members of parliament may address questions to government ministers

Quet·ta /kwéttə/ capital of Baluchistan Province, west central Pakistan. Population: 560,307 (1998).

quet·zal /ket saál/ (*plural* **-zals** or **-za·les** /-saá làyz/) *n* **1.** a bird with brilliant green and red feathers. The male of one species, resplendent quetzal, has long streaming tail feathers. Native to: Central and South America. Genus: *Pharomachrus.* **2.** the main unit of Guatemalan currency. See table at **currency** [Early 19C. Via American Spanish < Nahuatl *quetzalli* "brilliantly colored tail feather"]

Quet·zal·co·a·tl /kèts'l kō aát'l/ *n* in Toltec and Aztec mythology, a god and the legendary ruler of Mexico, represented as a feathered serpent [Via Spanish

quetzal

< Nahuatl *Quetzalcōātl* < *quetzalli* "brilliantly colored tail feather" + *cōātl* "snake"]

queue /kyoo/ *n* **1.** COMPUT **SET OF COMPUTER TASKS** a series of messages or jobs waiting to be processed automatically one after the other by a computer system **2.** COMPUT **LIST OF DATA** a list of computer data constructed and maintained on a first in, first out basis **3.** *UK* same as **line**[1] (sense 3) **4.** HIST **MAN'S PIGTAIL** a short braid of hair worn at the back of the neck by soldiers and sailors in the late 18th and early 19th centuries ■ *v* (**queued, queu·ing** or **queue·ing, queues**) **1.** *vt* COMPUT **ADD SOMETHING TO COMPUTER'S TASKS** to add a job or message to the list of tasks being held in storage by a computer, awaiting automatic dispatching **2.** *vi UK* **FORM WAITING LINE** to form a line while waiting for something [Late 16C. Via French < Latin *cauda* "tail"]

Que·zon Cit·y /kày sawn-, -sōn-/ city in central Luzon, Philippines. It was the national capital from 1948 to 1976. Population: 2,112,722 (1999).

Quez·on y Mo·li·na /kày sawn ee mo leénə, -sōn-/, **Manuel** (1878–1944) Philippine politician. He worked for Philippine independence, and was elected the first president of the Commonwealth of the Philippines (1935–44). Full name **Quezon y Molina, Manuel Luis**

quib·ble /kwíbb'l/ *vi* (**-bled, -bling, -bles**) to argue over unimportant things and make petty objections ■ *n* **1.** an unimportant distinction or petty objection **2.** same as **pun** (*archaic*) [Early 17C. Probably < obsolete *quib* "pun, equivocation" < Latin *quibus* "whom, for whom," often used in legal documents] —**quib·bler** *n*

quiche /keesh/ *n* a pie filled with an egg-and-cream mixture and various meat or vegetable ingredients [Mid-20C. Via French < German dialect *Küche* "small cake" < German *Kuchen* "cake"]

quiche Lor·raine /-lə ráyn/ *n* a quiche made with cheese and bacon [Mid-20C. After LORRAINE, France]

Quich·ua *n, adj* PEOPLES, LANG same as **Quechua**

quick /kwik/ *adj* **1. DOING SOMETHING FAST** moving or doing something fast **2. ALERT** demonstrating alertness or sharp perception ○ *She has a very quick mind.* **3. NIMBLE** moving swiftly and with skill ○ *quick fingers* **4. DONE WITHOUT DELAY** done or doing something without delay ○ *They promised a quick delivery.* **5. EASILY ANGERED** describes a temper that is easily aroused **6. BRIEF** taking or lasting only a short time ○ *I'll take a quick look at it.* **7. HASTY** tending to be hasty ○ *Don't be too quick to blame others.* **8.** same as **alive** (sense 1) (*archaic*) ■ *n* **1. FLESH UNDER NAIL** the sensitive flesh under a fingernail or toenail **2. SOMEBODY'S SENSITIVITIES** somebody's deepest feelings or most private emotions ○ *criticisms that cut him to the quick* ■ *npl* **THE LIVING** those people who are alive (*archaic*) ○ *the quick and the dead* ■ *adv* **FAST** in a speedy manner (*informal*) ○ *Come quick!* [Old English *cwic(u)* "alive, lively" < Indo-European, "to live"] —**quick·ly** *adv* —**quick·ness** *n* ◇ **quick and dirty** produced to meet an immediate or pressing need, rather than in accordance with high standards of research or design (*informal*)

SYNONYMS See ***intelligent.***

quick as·sets *npl* cash along with other assets that can readily be converted into cash

quick bread *n* bread leavened with baking powder or soda, as opposed to yeast, and ready to bake as soon as it is mixed

quick·en /kwíkən/ (**-ened, -en·ing, -ens**) *v* **1.** *vti* **INCREASE IN SPEED** to become faster, or make something faster **2.** *vti* **STIMULATE SOMETHING** to stimulate something such as interest or enthusiasm, or be stimulated **3.** *vi* **COME TO LIFE** to begin a period of development **4.** *vi* **MOVE IN WOMB** to begin to move and be felt moving in the womb (*refers to fetuses*)

quick-fire /kwík fìr/ *adj Can, UK* **1.** ARMS same as **rapid-fire** (sense 1) **2.** same as **rapid-fire** (sense 2) (*informal*)

quick fix *n* a speedily or hastily contrived solution to a problem, often one that fails to resolve long-term issues (*informal*)

quick-freeze *vt* to freeze food rapidly in an effort to keep its full flavor and nutritional value

quick·ie /kwíkee/ *n* something that is done hurriedly, especially a hurried act of sex or a speedily consumed alcoholic drink (*informal*)

quick kick *n* in football, a punt made on the first, second, or third down, intended to take the opposing team by surprise

quick·lime /kwík lìm/ *n* CHEM same as **calcium oxide** [14C. Translation of Latin *calx viva* "living lime"]

quick·sand /kwík sànd/ *n* **1.** a deep mass of loose wet sand that sucks down any heavy object falling onto its surface **2.** a hidden trap from which escape is difficult or impossible

quick·sil·ver /kwík sìlvər/ *adj* tending to change rapidly and unpredictably ■ *n* CHEM ELEM same as **mercury** (sense 1) (*archaic or literary*) [Pre-12C. Translation of Latin *argentum vivum* "living silver," from the way it moves in its fluid state]

quick·step /kwík stèp/ *n* **1. FAST BALLROOM DANCE** a ballroom dance with fast steps **2. DANCE MUSIC** the music for a quickstep **3.** MIL **MARCHING STEP** the marching step used in the fastest marching pace (**quick time**)

quick stud·y *n* a fast learner of something

quick-tem·pered *adj* same as **short-tempered**

quick time *n* a fast military marching pace, approximately 120 paces per minute

quick-wit·ted *adj* able to think quickly and inventively —**quick-wit·ted·ly** *adv* —**quick-wit·ted·ness** *n*

quid[1] /kwid/ *n* a piece of chewing tobacco [Early 18C. Alteration of CUD]

quid[2] /kwid/ (*plural same*) *n UK* a pound sterling (*informal*) [Late 17C. Origin ?]

Quid·ditch /kwíddich/ *n* in the Harry Potter novels by J. K. Rowling, a fictional game played on broomsticks. [Late 20C. Coined by J. K. ROWLING, origin ?]

quid·di·ty /kwíddətee/ (*plural* **-ties**) *n* **1.** the real nature or essential character of something **2.** an unimportant or trifling distinction [Mid-16C. < medieval Latin *quidditas* < Latin *quid* "what"]

quid·nunc /kwíd nùngk/ *n* a nosy or gossipy person (*formal*) [Early 18C. < Latin, "what now"]

quid pro quo /kwìd prō kwṓ/ (*plural* **quid pro quos**) *n* **1.** something given or done in exchange for something else **2.** the giving of something in return for something else, often in a spirit of cooperation [Mid-16C. < Latin, "something for something"]

qui·es·cent /kwee éss'nt/ *adj* inactive or at rest [Early 17C. < Latin *quiescent-*, present participle of *quiescere* "come to rest" (see QUIET)] —**qui·es·cence** *n*

qui·et /kwī ət/ *adj* **1. NOT NOISY** making little or no noise **2. STILL** free from noise or commotion ○ *in a quiet corner of the room* **3. DONE IN PRIVATE** carried out in private, with voices not raised, in order not to be overheard ○ *I'd like a quiet word with you.* **4. UNDISTURBED** free from trouble or disturbance ○ *a quiet life* **5. RELAXING** relaxing, peaceful, and free from excitement ○ *a quiet evening at home* **6. NOT SHOWY** not grand, showy, or pretentious ○ *a quiet wedding* **7. RESTRAINED** displaying calmness and self-control and not inclined to speak much ○ *the doctor's quiet manner* **8. UNSPOKEN** not expressed in words ○ *a sense of quiet optimism* **9. NOT BUSY** not busy or active ○ *Business is a little too quiet.* **10. CALM OR MOTIONLESS** marked by very little motion ○ *a quiet sea* ■ *n* **ABSENCE OF NOISE** the absence of noise or disturbance ○ *the quiet of the forest* ■ *v* (**-et·ed, -et·ing, -ets**) **1.** *vti* **MAKE OR BECOME QUIET** to become calm and quiet, or make somebody calm and quiet ○ *He sang lullabies to quiet the baby.* ○ *Will you all just quiet down, please?* **2.** *vt* **ALLAY ANXIETY** to calm somebody's negative feelings ○ *quieting her doubts* **3.** *vt US* LAW **SECURE LEGAL CLAIM** to make a legal claim secure by resolving all possible challenges to it [14C. Via French < Latin *quiet-*, past participle of *quiescere* "come to rest" < *quies* "rest, quiet"] —**qui·et·ly** *adv* —**qui·et·ness** *n* ◇ **on the quiet** secretly

SPELLCHECK quiet or **quite**? Do not confuse the spelling of ***quiet*** and ***quite***, which sound similar. ***Quiet*** is an adjective and noun referring to lack of noise, as in *be quiet and listen, in the quiet of the evening*. ***Quite*** is an adverb meaning "entirely" or "very": *That's quite acceptable. It's quite expensive.*

SYNONYMS See ***silent***.

qui·et·en /kwī́ ət'n/ (**-ened, -en·ing, -ens**) *v UK* **1.** *vti* same as **quiet** *v* (sense 1) **2.** *vt* same as **quiet** *v* (sense 2)

qui·et·ism /kwī́ ə tìzzəm/ *n* **1.** a state of calmness, especially one arising from noninvolvement in something (*literary*) **2.** a system of Christian mysticism that requires a withdrawal from the world, a renunciation of the individual will, and passive contemplation of God and divine things [Late 17C. < Italian *quietismo* < *quieto* < Latin *quiet-* (see QUIET)] —**qui·et·ist** *adj, n* —**qui·et·is·tic** /kwī ə tístik/ *adj*

Qui·et Rev·o·lu·tion *n Can* a period of profound political, religious, social, and educational change in Quebec in the 1960s

qui·e·tude /kwī́ ə tòod/ *n* the state of being quiet, peaceful, or tranquil (*literary*) [Late 16C. Directly or via French < medieval Latin *quietudo* < Latin *quiet-* (see QUIET)]

qui·e·tus /kwī éetəss/ *n* (*literary*) **1. DEATH** death, especially when viewed as a welcome release from life **2. RELEASE** a release from a debt or duty **3. CHECK** something that brings an activity to an end [Mid-16C. < medieval Latin *quietus (est)* "(it is) at rest," acknowledging receipt or discharge of an obligation]

Quik·Clot /kwík clòt/ *tdmk* a trademark for a granular material that, when poured directly into a wound, absorbs water from the blood, thereby concentrating blood-clotting protein factors

quill /kwil/ *n* **1. LARGE FEATHER** a large stiff feather from a bird's wing or tail, or the hollow shaft of such a feather **2. PEN MADE FROM FEATHER SHAFT** an old-fashioned pen made from the shaft of a feather **3. SPINE** a sharp hollow spine on the body of a porcupine or hedgehog **4.** TEXTILES **SPINDLE OR BOBBIN** a spindle or bobbin onto which thread or yarn is wound **5.** MECH ENG **HOLLOW SHAFT** in a mechanical device, a hollow shaft in which a second independently rotating shaft is enclosed ■ *vt* (**quilled, quill·ing, quills**) **1.** TEXTILES **WIND THREAD** to wind thread or yarn onto a spindle or bobbin **2.** HANDICRAFT **MAKE FOLDS IN SOMETHING** to make small rounded folds in fabric, e.g., to make a ruff [15C. Origin ?]

quil·lai bark /kéé lày-/ *n* INDUST same as **soapbark** (sense 1) [Via modern Latin and Spanish < Araucanian, "soapbark tree" < *quillcan* "to wash"]

quill·back /kwíl bàk/ (*plural* **-backs** or *same*), **quill·back carp·suck·er** /-kaárp sukər/ *n* a freshwater fish of the sucker family with a long ray projecting from its dorsal fin. Native to: North America. Latin name: *Carpiodes cyprinus*.

quill pen *n* ART same as **quill** *n* (sense 2)

quill·work /kwíl wùrk/ *n* handicrafts decorated with porcupine quills

quill·wort /kwíl wùrt, -wàwrt/ *n* a nonflowering water plant that produces a rosette of tubular leaves, at the bases of which are spore-forming organs. Genus: *Isoetes*.

quilt /kwilt/ *n* **1. BED COVER** a bed cover made of two layers of fabric stitched together with padding held in place by decorative intersecting seams **2. SOMETHING SIMILAR TO QUILT** something that resembles a quilt or is quilted ■ *vt* (**quilt·ed, quilt·ing, quilts**) **SEW FABRIC LIKE QUILT** to sew two layers of fabric together with a filling, especially using decorative stitching [13C. Via Anglo-Norman < Latin *culcita* "cushion, mattress"] —**quilt·er** *n*

quilt·ing /kwílting/ *n* **1.** the sewing of quilted bed covers or other quilted work **2.** material that has been quilted or that is used to make quilts

Quim·per /kaN pér/ city in northwestern France. Population: 63,238 (1999).

quin /kwin/ *n UK* same as **quintuplet** (*informal*) [Mid-20C. Shortening]

quin- *prefix* same as **quino-** (*used before vowels*)

quin·a·crine hy·dro·chlo·ride /kwìnnə kreen-/ *n* same as **mepacrine** [< blend of QUINOLINE + ACRIDINE]

quin·a·liz·a·rin /kwìnnə lízzərin/ *n* a red crystalline organic compound with a green metallic luster. Use: cotton dye. Formula: $C_{14}H_8O_6$.

qui·na·ry /kwī́nəree/ (*formal*) *adj* consisting of five parts, or occurring in sets of five ■ *n* (*plural* **-ries**) a set of five, or the fifth member of a set [Early 17C. < Latin *quinarius* < *quini* "five each" < *quinque* "five"]

qui·nate /kwī́ nàyt/ *adj* describes leaves that occur in clusters of five [Early 19C. < modern Latin *quinatus* < Latin *quini* (see QUINARY)]

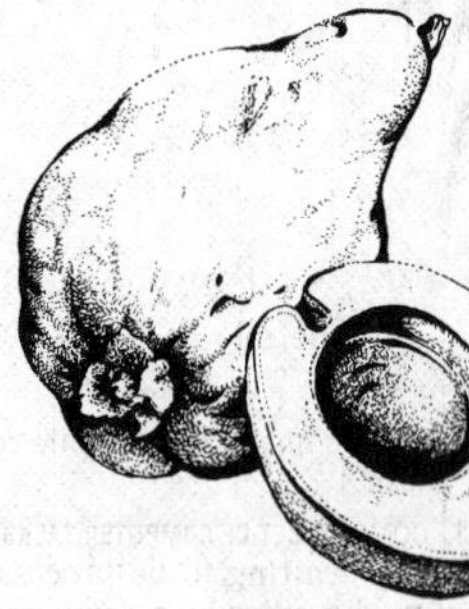

quince

quince /kwinss/ *n* **1.** an aromatic apple-shaped or pear-shaped yellow or orange fruit that is edible only when cooked. Use: preserves. **2.** a small tree that produces quinces. Native to: western Asia. Latin name: *Cydonia oblonga*. [14C. Via Old French *cooin* < Latin *(malum) cotoneum* < Greek *(mēlon) kudōnion*, literally "apple of Cydonia" (now Canea, Crete)]

quin·ce·a·ñe·ra /keen see ə nyérrə/ *n Hispanic* a Latin American celebration followed by a formal dinner-dance for a 15-year-old girl, marking her passage into adulthood. It sometimes involves a Mass at which she receives a ring from her mother as a symbol of commitment to church and family. [< Spanish, "15-year-old girl" < *quince* "15" + *año* "year"]

quin·cen·ten·a·ry /kwìn sen ténnəree/ (*plural* **-ries**), **quin·cen·ten·ni·al** /-ténnee əl/ *n* a 500th anniversary [Late 19C. < Latin *quinque* "five"] —**quin·cen·ta·ry** *adj*

Quin·cey ♦ **de Quincey, Thomas**

quin·cunx /kwín kùngks/ *n* an arrangement of five objects in a square, with four at the corners and one in the center [Mid-17C. < Latin, "five-twelfths" (from the use of this pattern on a Roman coin worth five-twelfths of a standard unit of currency) < *quinque* "five" + *uncia* "twelfth part" (see OUNCE[1])] —**quin·cun·cial** /kwin kúnsh'l/ *adj*

Quin·cy **1.** /kwínssee/ port in western Illinois. Population: 39,916 (2002 estimate). **2.** /kwínzee/ city in eastern Massachusetts. Population: 89,187 (2002 estimate).

quin·de·cen·ni·al /kwìndə sénnee əl/ *adj* **1. AT 15-YEAR INTERVALS** happening once every 15 years **2. WITH 15-YEAR DURATION** lasting for 15 years ■ *n* **ANNIVERSARY** a 15th anniversary [Late 20C. < Latin *quindecim* "fifteen," after CENTENNIAL]

Quine /kwīn/, **W. V.** (1908–2000) US philosopher. He contributed to the theory of pragmatism and to mathematical set theory. Full name **Quine, Willard Van Orman**

> "We know what it is like to be conscious, but not how to put it into satisfactory scientific terms. Whatever it may precisely be, consciousness is a state of the body, a state of nerves."
> [W. V. Quine, *Quiddities: An Intermittently Philosophical Dictionary*; 1987]

qui·nel·la /kwi néllə, kee-/, **qui·nie·la** /keen yéllə/ *n* a bet in which the bettor picks the first two finishers in a race or other sporting event without specifying their order of finish [Early 20C. < American Spanish *quiniela* < Spanish *quina* "keno" < French *quine* (see KENO)]

qui·nic ac·id /kwìnnik-, kwī́nik-/ *n* a white crystalline organic compound. Source: cinchona bark, coffee beans, leaves of many plants. Use: in medicine. Formula: $C_6H_7(OH)_4COOH$. [< Spanish *quina* "cinchona bark" (see QUINO-)]

quin·i·dine /kwínni deen/ *n* a colorless crystalline organic compound related to quinine. Source: cinchona bark. Use: treatment of malaria, heart disorders. Formula: $C_{20}H_{24}N_2O_2$.

qui·nie·la *n* GAMBLING same as **quinella**

qui·nie·la ex·act·a *n US* GAMBLING same as **exacta**

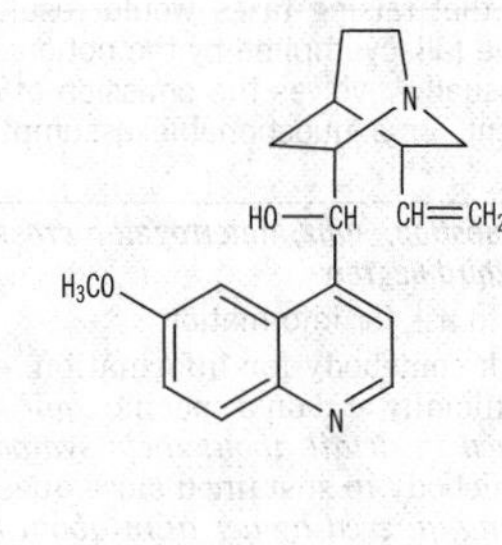

quinine

qui·nine /kwī́ nīn/ *n* a bitter-tasting drug made from cinchona bark. Use: treatment of malaria. Formula: $C_{20}H_{24}N_2O_2$. [Early 19C. < Spanish *quina* "cinchona bark" (see QUINO-)]

qui·nine wa·ter *n US* BEVERAGES same as **tonic water**

Quinn /kwin/, **Anthony** (1915–2001) Mexican-born US movie actor. His movies include *Viva Zapata!* (1952), *Lust for Life* (1956), and *Zorba the Greek* (1964). Full name **Quinn, Antonio Rudolfo Oaxaca**

quin·nat salm·on /kwínnət-/ *n* FISH same as **Chinook salmon** [< Chinook *ikwanat*]

quino- *prefix* **1.** cinchona, cinchona bark ○ *quinone* **2.** quinone ○ *quinoline* [Via Spanish *quina* "cinchona bark" < Quechua *kina*]

qui·no·a /kee nō ə, kéen waa/ *n* a plant of the goosefoot family that is cultivated for its seeds, which are ground and eaten. Native to: Andes. Latin name: *Chenopodium quinoa*. [Early 17C. Via Spanish < Quechua *kinoa*]

quin·o·line /kwínnə leen, -lin/ *n* an oily colorless substance. Source: coal tar. Use: manufacture of antiseptics and dyes. Formula: C_9H_7N.

qui·none /kwi nṓn, kwín ōn/ *n* **1.** CHEM same as **benzoquinone** **2.** an organic yellow, orange, or red compound. Source: pigments in plants, fungi, and bacteria, vitamins in animals. —**quin·o·noid** /kwínnə nòyd/ *adj, n*

quin·qua·ge·nar·i·an /kwìngkwəjə nérree ən/ (*formal*) *adj* 50 years old, or between the ages of 50 and 59 ■ *n* somebody between 50 and 59 years of age [Early 19C. < Latin *quinquagenarius* < *quinquaginta* "fifty"]

Quin·qua·ges·i·ma /kwìngkwə jéssimə/ *n* in the Christian liturgical calendar, the Sunday before Lent, seven weeks or the fiftieth day before Easter [14C. Via medieval Latin, "fiftieth (day)" < Latin *quinquagesimus* < *quinquaginta* "fifty"]

quinque- *prefix* five ○ *quinquennial* [< Latin *quinque* < Indo-European]

quin·quen·ni·um /kwing kwénnee əm/ (*plural* **-ni·ums** or **-ni·a** /-nee ə/) *n* a period of five years [Early 17C. < Latin,< *quinque* "five" + *annus* "year"] —**quin·quen·ni·al** *adj* —**quin·quen·ni·al·ly** *adv*

quin·que·va·lent /kwìngkwə váylənt/ *adj* CHEM same as **pentavalent**

quin·sy /kwínzee/ *n* a severe inflammation of the throat near a tonsil that sometimes leads to the formation of an abscess that may require surgery [14C. Directly or via French < medieval Latin *quinancia* < Greek *kunagkhē*, literally "dog-strangling" < *kuōn* "dog" + *ankhein* "to squeeze"]

quint /kwint/ *n* **1.** same as **quintuplet** (*informal*) **2.** in the card game piquet, a sequence of five cards of the same suit [Late 17C. Via French, "fifth" < Latin *quintus*]

quin·tain /kwíntən/ *n* a target used by a medieval knight for jousting practice [15C. Via French < medieval Latin *quintana (via)* "fifth (street)" (in a Roman camp) < Latin *quintus* "fifth"]

quin·tal /kwínt'l/ *n* **1.** in the metric system, a unit of weight equal to 100 kg **2.** MEASURE same as **hundredweight** [15C. Directly or via French < medieval Latin *quintale* < Arabic *ḳinṭār* < Latin *centenarius* "containing a hundred" (see CENTENARY)]

quin·tan /kwíntən/ *adj* describes a fever that flares up every fifth day [Mid-17C. Via medieval Latin *quintana* from Latin *quintus* "fifth"] —**quin·tan** *n*

quinte /kwīnt, kaaNt/ *n* in fencing, the fifth in the eight parrying or attacking positions [Early 18C. From French, feminine of *quint* (see QUINT)]

quin·tes·sence /kwin téss'nss/ *n* **1. EMBODIMENT** the purest or most perfect example of something **2.** CHEM **EXTRACT** the purest extract or essence of a substance, containing the substance's properties in their most concentrated form **3.** PHILOSOPHY **FIFTH ELEMENT** in ancient and medieval philosophy, the fifth element after earth, air, fire, and water. Heavenly bodies were said to be made of it. **4.** ASTRON **HYPOTHETICAL REPULSIVE FORCE** a hypothetical repulsive force in cosmology that permeates all of space and counteracts the force of gravity [15C. Via French < medieval Latin *quinta essentia* "fifth essence"] —**quin·tes·sen·tial** /kwìntə sénsh'l/ *adj* —**quin·tes·sen·tial·ly** *adv*

quin·tet /kwin tét/, **quin·tette** *n* **1. MUSICIANS** a group of five singers or musicians **2. MUSIC** a piece of music written for five voices or instruments **3. GROUP OF FIVE** a group or set of five people or things [Late 18C. Via French < Italian *quintetto* < *quinto* "fifth" < Latin *quintus*]

quin·tic /kwíntik/ *adj* relating to the fifth power in a mathematical expression or equation [Mid-19C. < Latin *quintus* "fifth"]

quin·tile /kwín tīl, kwínt'l/ *n* **1. STATISTICAL DIVISION** one of the five equal populations into which a statistical sample can be divided **2. STATISTICAL VALUE** in statistics, one of the values that divide a frequency distribution into five parts, each containing a fifth of the sample population **3. DISTANCE BETWEEN PLANETS** the astrological aspect of planets that are distant from each other by 72 degrees or one fifth of the zodiac [Early 17C. < Latin *quintilis* < *quintus* "fifth"]

Quin·til·ian /kwin tíllyən/ (A.D. 35?–95?) Roman rhetorician. His 12-volume *Institutio Oratoria (Training of an Orator)* had an important influence on Renaissance theories of education. Full name **Marcus Fabius Quintilianus**

> "A liar should have a good memory."
> [Quintilian, *Institutio Oratoria*; 90?]

quin·til·lion /kwin tíllyən/ *n* the number equal to 10^{18}, written as 1 followed by 18 zeros —**quin·til·lion** *adj, pron* —**quin·til·lionth** *adj, n, pron*

quin·tu·ple /kwin to͞op'l, -túpp'l/ *adj* **1. FIVE TIMES AS MUCH** five times as much or as many **2. CONSISTING OF FIVE PARTS** made up of five parts **3.** MUSIC **HAVING FIVE BEATS TO MEASURE** having five musical beats to the measure ■ *vti* (**-pled, -pling, -ples**) **MULTIPLY BY FIVE** to multiply something by five, or be multiplied by five [Late 16C. Via French < medieval Latin *quintuplus* "fivefold" < Latin *quintus* "fifth"]

quin·tu·plet /kwin túpplət, -to͞oplət/ *n* **1. ONE OF FIVE OFFSPRING** one of five offspring born to one mother from a single pregnancy **2. GROUP OF FIVE** a group of five things, especially five of the same kind **3.** MUSIC **GROUP OF FIVE MUSICAL NOTES** a group of five musical notes to be played in the time usually occupied by three or four notes

quin·tu·pli·cate *adj* /kwin to͞oplikət, -túpplikət/ **MULTIPLIED BY FIVE** multiplied by five ■ *n* /kwin to͞oplikət, -túpplikət/ **1. ONE OF FIVE** one of a set of five identical things **2. GROUP OF FIVE** a group of five usually identical things ■ *vt* /-to͞opli kàyt, -túppli-/ (**-cat·ed, -cat·ing, -cates**) **MAKE FIVE COPIES OF SOMETHING** to make five copies of something [Mid-17C. < Latin *quintus* "fifth," after DUPLICATE] —**quin·tu·pli·ca·tion** /-tùppli káysh'n, -to͞opli-/ *n*

quip /kwip/ *n* **1. WITTICISM** a witty remark, especially one made on the spur of the moment **2. PETTY DISTINCTION** a small and unimportant distinction (*archaic*) ■ *vti* (**quipped, quip·ping, quips**) **SAY SOMETHING WITTILY** to make a witty remark, especially on the spur of the moment [Mid-16C. Origin ?]

quip·ster /kwípstər/ *n* somebody who makes witty remarks

qui·pu /ke͞e po͞o/ (*plural* **-pus**) *n* a device consisting of a set of colored and knotted cords used by the Incas for conveying messages and for record-keeping [Early 18C. Via Spanish < Quechua *kipu* "knot"]

quire /kwīr/ *n* **1.** a set of 24 or 25 sheets of paper of the same size and quality, equaling one twentieth of a ream **2.** a bundle of sheets of paper folded together for binding into a book, especially a four-sheet bundle, folded once to make eight leaves or sixteen pages [15C. < Old French *qua(i)er* "copybook," literally "set of four (sheets)" < Latin *quaterni* (see QUATERNARY)]

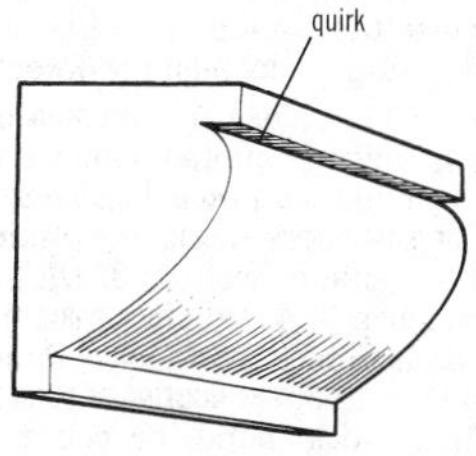

quirk (sense 4)

quirk /kwurk/ *n* **1. ODD EVENT** a strange and unexpected turn of events ○ *a strange quirk of fate* **2. ODD MANNERISM** a peculiar habit, mannerism, or aspect of somebody's character **3. CURVED SHAPE** a curved shape, pattern, or decoration, e.g., a flourish in handwriting **4.** ARCHIT **GROOVE** a continuous groove running along a molding or separating a molding from adjoining members [Mid-16C. Origin ?] —**quirk·i·ly** *adv* —**quirk·i·ness** *n* —**quirk·y** *adj*

quirt /kwurt/ *n Southwest US* a riding whip with a short handle and a braided leather lash [Mid-19C. < Mexican Spanish *cuarta* "whip"]

quis·ling /kwízzling/ *n* a traitor, especially somebody who collaborates with an occupying force [Mid-20C. After Vidkun *Quisling*, puppet premier of Norway during Nazi occupation] —**quis·ling·ism** *n*

ORIGIN Vidkun Quisling was a Norwegian politician who from 1933 led the National Union Party, the Norwegian fascist party. (Quisling was not his real name – he was originally Abraham Lauritz Jonsson.) When the Germans invaded Norway in 1940, he gave them active support, urging his fellow Norwegians not to resist them, and in 1942 he was installed by Hitler as a puppet premier. In 1945 he was shot for treason.

quit /kwit/ *v* (**quit** or **quit·ted, quit·ting, quits**) **1.** *vti* **RESIGN FROM POSITION** to give up, leave, or resign from a position or organization **2.** *vti* **STOP DOING SOMETHING** to stop doing something, especially something bad or irritating ○ *Quit complaining.* **3.** *vt* **LEAVE PLACE** to depart from a place (*archaic*) **4.** *vti* COMPUT **EXIT FROM PROGRAM** to exit from a computer program using the required exit procedure, so that the data and program configuration are saved **5.** *vti* LAW **MOVE OUT** to move out of rented property ○ *He gave his tenants notice to quit.* ■ *adj* **FREE OF SOMETHING** no longer troubled with a problem or difficult situation (*formal*) [13C. < Old French *quiter* "release, set free" < Latin *quiet-* (see QUIET)]

quitch grass /kwích-/, **quitch** *n* PLANTS same as **couch grass** [Old English *cwice*]

quit·claim /kwít klàym/ *n* **RENUNCIATION OF CLAIM** a formal statement renouncing a legal claim previously made ■ *vt* (**-claimed, -claim·ing, -claims**) **1. RENOUNCE CLAIM** to formally withdraw a legal claim previously made **2. FREE SOMEBODY FROM LIABILITY** to formally declare somebody to be no longer legally liable for something [13C. < Anglo-Norman *quiteclamer* "proclaim somebody free" < *quite* "free" + *clamer* "proclaim"]

quite /kwīt/ *adv* **1. ENTIRELY** in the highest degree or to the fullest extent ○ *not quite as bad as all that* **2. RATHER** to a considerable or great degree **3. NEARLY** used with a negative to indicate that something has almost reached a state or condition ○ *The dress is not quite finished.* **4. EMPHASIZING EXTENT** used with expressions of quantity to emphasize the great extent of something ○ *quite some time ago* **5. EMPHASIZING EXCEPTIONAL QUALITY** used to emphasize the exceptional or impressive nature of somebody or something ○ *That was quite a celebration we had yesterday.* **6.** *UK* **EXPRESSING AGREEMENT** used on its own or before "so" to express agreement or understanding ○ *"I didn't think it was up to me to say anything." "Quite."* [14C. Variant of QUIT (adj)] ◇ **be quite something** to be remarkably good, fine, attractive, or otherwise admirable or impressive (*informal*)

SPELLCHECK See *quiet*.

Qui·to /ke͞etō/ capital city of Ecuador, situated in the north of the country. Population: 1,615,809 (2000).

quit·rent /kwít rènt/ *n* in the feudal system, a rent paid by a tenant to a feudal lord in exchange for being released from some feudal obligations [15C. < QUIT (adj)]

quits /kwits/ *adj* on even terms, especially following the repayment of a debt (*informal*) [Mid-17C. Probably < QUIT (adj), influenced by medieval Latin *quittus* "freed"] ◇ **call it quits** (*informal*) **1.** to agree or decide to stop doing work or an activity **2.** to agree that an argument or dispute is over

quit·tance /kwítt'nss/ *n* **1.** release from a debt or obligation **2.** a document or statement that releases somebody from a debt or obligation [13C. < Old French *quitance* < *quiter* (see QUIT)]

quit·ter /kwíttər/ *n* somebody who gives up easily (*informal*)

quit·tor /kwíttər/ *n* an infectious disease that causes inflammation in the feet of horses and donkeys [13C. Origin ?]

quiv·er[1] /kwívvər/ *vi* (**-ered, -er·ing, -ers**) to shake rapidly with small movements ■ *n* a repeated small rapid shaking movement [15C. Probably < assumed Old English *cwifer* "active, nimble," suggestive of the movement] —**quiv·er·er** *n* —**quiv·er·y** *adj*

quiv·er[2] /kwívvər/ *n* **1.** a long narrow case for holding arrows **2.** the arrows contained in a quiver [14C. Via Anglo-Norman *quiveir* < medieval Latin *cucurum*] —**quiv·er·ful** *n*

qui vive /kee ve͞ev/ [< French, "long live who?" (i.e. "whose side are you on?"), used by sentries to challenge somebody approaching their post] ◇ **on the qui vive** alert and vigilant

quix·ot·ic /kwik sóttik/ *adj* **1. EXCESSIVELY ROMANTIC** tending to take a romanticized view of life **2. IMPRACTICAL** motivated by an idealism that overlooks practical considerations **3. IMPULSIVE** tending to act on impulses [Late 18C. < Don *Quixote*, hero of a novel by Miguel de CERVANTES] —**quix·ot·i·cal·ly** *adv* —**quix·o·tism** /kwíksə tìzzəm/ *n*

quiz /kwiz/ *n* (*plural* **quiz·zes**) **1. TEST OF KNOWLEDGE** a test of knowledge in the form of a short or rapid series of questions (*often used after nouns*) **2. TRICK** a hoax, joke, or other trick (*archaic*) ■ *vt* (**quizzed, quiz·zing, quiz·zes**) **1. TEST STUDENT OR CLASS** to give a short test to a class of pupils or students **2. INTERROGATE SOMEBODY** to subject somebody to sustained close questioning ○ *She was quizzed about the disappearance of the money.* **3. PEER AT SOMEBODY** to look intently at somebody (*archaic*) [Late 18C. Origin ?] —**quiz·zer** *n*

SYNONYMS See *question*.

~~quizes~~ incorrect spelling of **quizzes**

quiz·mas·ter /kwíz màstər/ *n* the emcee of a quiz show, who puts the questions to the contestants

quiz show *n* a television or radio program in the form of a game in which contestants compete against each other for prizes by answering questions that test their general or specialist knowledge

quiz·zi·cal /kwízzik'l/ *adj* expressing a question, puzzlement, or doubt in a mocking or amused way ○ *a quizzical glance* —**quiz·zi·cal·ly** /kwízzikəlee/ *adv*

Qum another spelling of **Qom**

quod e·rat de·mon·stran·dum /kwòd è raat dày mon stráan do͞om/ *adv* used in a formal conclusion to indicate that something such as a fact is proof of the theory that has just been been advanced [< Latin, "which was to be proved"]

quod·li·bet /kwóddli bèt/ *n* **1.** a theological question put forward as an exercise for discussion **2.** a musical performance composed largely of familiar tunes [14C. < medieval Latin *quodlibetum* < Latin *quodlibet* "whatever pleases"]

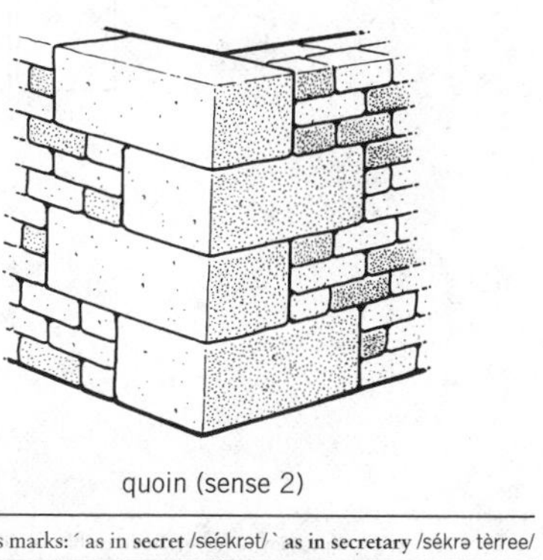
quoin (sense 2)

quoin /kwoyn, koyn/, **coign** /koyn/ *n* **1. OUTER CORNER** the outer corner of a wall **2. BLOCK FORMING CORNER** a stone block used to form a quoin, especially when it is different, e.g., in size or material, from the other blocks or bricks in the wall. See illustration on previous page **3.** ARCHIT same as **keystone** (sense 1) ■ *vt* (**quoined, quoin·ing, quoins; coigned, coign·ing, coigns**) **BUILD CORNER WITH DISTINCTIVE BLOCKS** to build an outer corner of a wall using blocks that are different, e.g., in size or texture, from the other blocks or bricks used to build the wall [Mid-16C. Variant of COIN]

quoit

quoit /kwoyt, koyt/ *n* a ring used in the game of quoits [14C. Probably via Old French *coite* "flat stone, quoit" < Latin *culcita* "cushion"]

quoits /kwoyts, koyts/ *n* a game in which players attempt to throw rings over or near a small post (*takes a singular verb*)

quok·ka /kwókə/ *n* a small short-tailed wallaby that lives in large colonies. Native to: islands off the coast of Western Australia. Latin name: *Setonix brachyurus*. [Mid-19C. < Nyungar *kwaka*]

quon·dam /kwóndəm, -dàm/ *adj* of an earlier time (*archaic or literary*) ○ *"... now torn and rent by their quondam allies"* (Jack London, *The Iron Heel*; 1907) [Mid-16C. < Latin, < *quom* "when"]

Quon·set /kwónssət/ *tdmk* a trademark for a prefabricated structure with a semicircular roof curving downward to form walls. Use: housing for military personnel.

quo·rum /kwáwrəm/ *n* a fixed minimum percentage or number of members of a legislative assembly, committee, or other organization who must be present before the members can conduct valid business [15C. < Latin, "of whom," used in requests for people to serve on committees]

quot. *abbr* quotation

quo·ta /kwṓtə/ *n* **1.** a proportional share of something that somebody should contribute or receive **2.** a maximum number or quantity that is permitted or needed [Early 17C. Via medieval Latin *quota (pars)* "how large (a part)?", feminine of *quotus* (see QUOTE)]

quot·a·ble /kwṓtəb'l/ *adj* **1.** worthy of being quoted **2.** able to be quoted in a publication such as a newspaper because the person speaking or writing has given permission —**quot·a·bil·i·ty** /kwṓtə bíllətee/ *n*

quo·ta·tion /kwō táysh'n/ *n* **1. SOMETHING QUOTED** a piece of speech or writing quoted somewhere, e.g., in a book or magazine ○ *a quotation from Henry James* **2. QUOTING OF SOMEBODY'S WORDS** the quoting of what somebody has said or written **3.** *UK* BUSINESS same as **quote** *n* (sense 3) **4.** FIN **STOCK PRICE** the prevailing price at which a stock, bond, or commodity may be purchased or sold **5.** FIN **QUOTING OF PRICES** the quoting of prevailing stock, bond, or commodity market prices **6.** ARTS **REUSE OF ARTISTIC MATERIAL** the use in an artistic work, especially music, of material taken from or alluding to somebody else's work —**quo·ta·tion·al** *adj* —**quo·ta·tion·al·ly** *adv*

quo·ta·tion mark *n* either of a pair of punctuation marks, either in double (" ") or single (' ') form, used around direct speech, quotations, and titles, or to give special emphasis to a word or phrase

USAGE ***Quotation marks*** are used to enclose direct speech and quotations: *"Where are you?" he called. Mae West said, "A man in the house is worth two in the street."* They are also used around some titles, e.g., those of poems, short stories, and articles: *Hilaire Belloc's poem "On a Sundial,"* but titles of novels, plays, films, etc., are conventionally printed in italics instead. Quotation marks are often used to make a particular word or phrase stand out from the surrounding text, usually to draw attention to it or because the author is using it self-consciously or skeptically: *compound words such as "toothbrush" and "red currant"; in a more "family-friendly" environment.* Either single (' ') or double (" ") quotation marks may be used in all these cases. Where one piece of direct speech occurs within another, or within a quotation, use quotation marks of the opposite type: *She said, "I told him to leave and he asked 'Why should I?'"* Remember that a period or comma is always placed inside the quotation mark.

quote /kwōt/ *v* (**quot·ed, quot·ing, quotes**) **1.** *vti* **REPEAT SOMEBODY'S EXACT WORDS** to repeat or copy the exact words spoken or written by somebody **2.** *vti* **REFER TO SOMETHING FOR PROOF** to refer to something as an example in support of an argument ○ *He quoted some recently published statistics.* **3.** *vti* BUSINESS **GIVE ESTIMATE FOR COST** to give an estimate of the price of providing somebody with a product or service **4.** *vt* FIN **GIVE CURRENT MARKET PRICE OF SOMETHING** to state the current market price of a stock, bond, or commodity **5.** *vt* GAMBLING **GIVE BETTING ODDS FOR SOMETHING** to give somebody or something such as a racehorse particular betting odds (*usually passive*) **6.** *vt* ARTS **REPEAT PART OF ARTISTIC WORK** to repeat an excerpt from an artistic work created by somebody else, especially a piece of music **7.** *vti* PRINTING **PUT PUNCTUATION AROUND QUOTATION** to place quotation marks around a passage of speech or writing that is being quoted ■ *n* **1.** LITERAT (*informal*) **2.** PRINTING same as **quotation mark** (*often used in the plural*) **3.** BUSINESS **ESTIMATE FOR WORK** an estimated price for a job or service ■ *interj* **INTRODUCING QUOTATION** used to show that the following words are a quotation (*often followed by "unquote"*) ○ *She told me she is, quote, "too good for him," unquote.* [14C. Via medieval Latin *quotare* "number chapters" < Latin *quotus* "of what number or amount" < *quot* "how many?"] —**quot·er** *n*

quot·ee /kwō tée/ *n* a person whose words are quoted by another person

quoth /kwōth/ *vt* said (*archaic or literary; 1st and 3rd person singular, before the subject*) ○ *"I swoon," quoth he.* [Old English *cwæð*, the past tense of *cweþan* "to say" (source of English *bequeath*)]

quo·tid·i·an /kwō tíddee ən/ *adj* **1. COMMONPLACE** of the most ordinary everyday kind (*formal*) **2. DONE DAILY** done or experienced on a daily basis (*formal*) **3.** MED **RECURRING DAILY** describes a fever that recurs or flares up every day ■ *n* MED **FEVER RECURRING DAILY** a fever, especially malaria, in which attacks of the illness recur daily [14C. Via French < Latin *quotidianus* < *cotidie* "every day"]

quo·tient /kwṓsh'nt/ *n* **1.** MATH **RESULT OF DIVISION** the number that results from the division of one number by another **2.** MATH **WHOLE NUMBER RESULT OF DIVISION** the whole number element of the result of dividing one number by another **3. AMOUNT OF QUALITY** a scale, or a point on a scale, indicating the amount, degree, or level of something (*informal*) [15C. < Latin *quotient-* "how many times?" < *quot* "how many"]

quo war·ran·to /kwṑ wə ráantō, -rántō/ (*plural* **quo war·ran·tos**) *n* a document issued by a court of law formally requiring somebody to state by what authority he or she has acted or has held a position [From Law Latin, literally "by what warrant?", words in the writ]

Qŭ·qon /kŏŏ káwn/ city in eastern Uzbekistan, in the Fergana Province. Population: 175,000 (1991).

Qur'an, **Qur·an** *n* ISLAM another spelling of **Koran**

Qut·ti·nir·paaq Na·tion·al Park /khŏŏt tee neelk paak-/ national park, established in 1988, in the northern part of Ellesmere Island situated in the Arctic Ocean, Nunavut, northeastern Canada. Area: 14,585 sq. mi./37,775 sq. km. Former name **Ellesmere Island National Park Reserve**

q.v. *abbr* which see (*used to indicate a cross reference to something within the same book or article*) [Latin, *quod vide*]

Q value *n* the energy released or absorbed during a particle or nuclear reaction

Qwa·qwa /kwaa kwaa/ former homeland in South Africa, now part of Free State Province

qwer·ty /kwúrtee/, **QWER·TY** *adj* describes an English-language typewriter or computer keyboard with keys for the Roman alphabet, the top row of alphabetical characters being the letters Q, W, E, R, T, and Y ➧ **azerty**

qy. *abbr* query

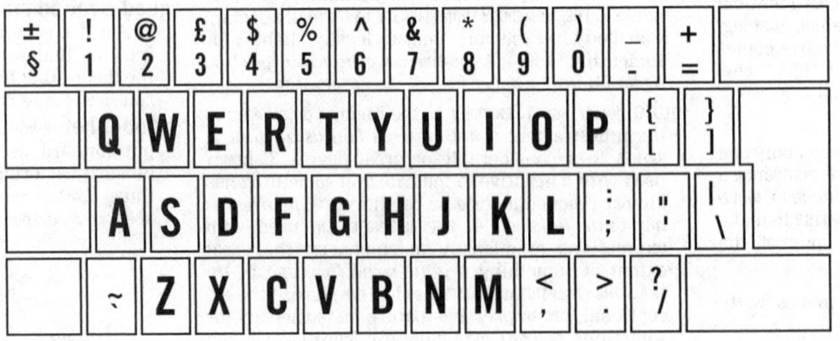

qwerty

Rr

r[1] /aar/ (*plural* **r's**), **R** (*plural* **R's** or **Rs**) *n* **1.** **18TH LETTER OF ENGLISH ALPHABET** the 18th letter of the English alphabet, representing a consonant sound **2.** **LETTER "R" WRITTEN** a written representation of the letter "r" **3.** **"R"-SHAPED OBJECT** something shaped like a letter "R" ◇ **the three R's** the basic skills of reading, writing, and arithmetic

r[2] *symbol* **1.** MATH radius **2.** ELEC ENG resistance

r[3] *abbr* PRINTING recto

R[1] *symbol* **1.** PHYS gas constant **2.** CHEM radical **3.** PHYS, MEASURE Réaumur scale **4.** ELEC ENG resistance

R[2] /aar/, **r** *v* a written form of "are" (*informal; used in e-mails or text messages*) [Because the letter *R* and *are* are pronounced the same]

R[3] /aar/ *tdmk* a trademark for a rating indicating that a movie can be seen by children under the age of 17 only if accompanied by an adult. Full form **restricted**

R[4] *abbr* **1.** MATH radius **2.** MONEY rand **3.** Regina (*used after the name of a queen*) **4.** registered trademark **5.** POL Republican **6.** CHR response (*in Christian liturgy*) **7.** Rex (*used after the name of a king*) **8.** CHESS rook **9.** BASEBALL run(s) **10.** MONEY rupee

r. *abbr* **1.** TRANSP railroad **2.** rare **3.** COMM received **4.** retired **5.** right **6.** GEOG river **7.** road **8.** MEASURE rod **9.** CARDS rubber **10.** MONEY ruble **11.** BASEBALL run(s) **12.** MONEY rupee

R. *abbr* **1.** JUDAISM rabbi **2.** TRANSP railroad **3.** GEOG range **4.** CHR rector **5.** MATH right **6.** GEOG river **7.** road **8.** royal **9.** MONEY rupee

Ra[1] /raa/, **Re** /ray/ *n* in Egyptian mythology, the Sun god, creator and controller of the universe, represented as having a human body and a hawk's head [From Egyptian *rʿ*]

Ra[2] *symbol* CHEM ELEM radium

RA *abbr* **1.** NAVY Rear Admiral **2.** ARMY Regular Army **3.** ASTRON right ascension

R.A. *abbr* **1.** NAVY Rear Admiral **2.** ARMY Regular Army **3.** Research Assistant **4.** EDUC Resident Advisor **5.** ASTRON right ascension

raas /raass/ *adj* (*slang; used in Black English*) **1.** an offensive term meaning bad **2.** an offensive term meaning lacking in intelligence [Origin ?]

Ra·bat /rə baát, raa-/ capital city of Morocco, situated in the northwest of the country, at the mouth of the Bou Regreg River, on the Atlantic coast. Population: 1,385,872 (1994).

rab·bet /rábbət/ *n* **GROOVE CUT FOR WOOD JOINT** a groove or step cut along the length of the edge of a piece of wood that is to be joined to another with a corresponding tongue or ledge cut into it (*often used before nouns*) ■ *vt* (**-bet·ed, -bet·ing, -bets**) **1.** **CUT RABBET IN SOMETHING** to cut a rabbet in a piece of wood **2.** **JOIN EDGES WITH RABBET** to join two pieces of wood at their edges by means of a rabbet [15C. < Old French *rab(b)at* "recess" < *rabattre* (see REBATE[1])]

rab·bi /rá bī/ *n* **1.** the leader of a Jewish congregation, or the chief religious official of a synagogue **2.** a scholar qualified to teach or interpret Jewish law [Pre-12C. Via late Latin and Greek < Hebrew *rabbī* "my teacher"]

rab·bin·ate /rábbə nàyt, -nət/ *n* **1.** the post or term of office of a rabbi **2.** rabbis considered as a group

rab·bin·i·cal /rə bínnik'l/, **rab·bin·ic** /rə bínnik/ *adj* relating to rabbis or to their beliefs, language, teachings, or writings —**rab·bin·i·cal·ly** *adv*

Rab·bin·ic He·brew *n* the form of Hebrew used by rabbis between the 5th and 16th centuries

rab·bin·ism /rábbə nìzzəm/ *n* the teachings of Jewish scholars, especially the scholars of the Talmudic period —**rab·bin·ist** *n, adj* —**rab·bin·is·tic** /ràbbə nístik/ *adj*

rabbit

rab·bit /rábbit/ *n* (*plural* **-bits** or *same*) **1.** ZOOL **SMALL FURRY ANIMAL** a small burrowing animal with long ears, soft fur, and a short tail. Rabbits are commonly kept as pets. Family: Leporidae. **2.** ZOOL **HARE** a word used inaccurately to refer to a hare (*informal*) **3.** INDUST **RABBIT FUR** the fur of a rabbit, used to make hats and other accessories **4.** FOOD **RABBIT FLESH** the meat of a rabbit **5.** **PACESETTER IN RACE** a long-distance runner who sets a fast pace for a stronger teammate in the early part of a race **6.** **DEVICE THAT RACING GREYHOUNDS CHASE** a mechanical device that greyhounds chase at a racetrack ■ *vi* (**-bit·ed, -bit·ing, -bits**) **HUNT RABBITS** to go hunting for wild rabbits [14C. Probably < Old French < Middle Dutch or Low German *robbe*] —**rab·bit·er** *n*

CULTURAL NOTE ***Rabbit, Run***, a novel (1960) by John Updike. It depicts the disastrous attempts of Harry Rabbit Angstrom to flee an unhappy marriage and the responsibilities of adulthood. Updike continued Harry's story in three subsequent novels, *Rabbit Redux* (1971), *Rabbit is Rich* (1981), and *Rabbit at Rest* (1990), creating a tetralogy that highlights sexual and moral confusion in late 20th-century American society.

rab·bit ears *npl* a V-shaped antenna made up of two metal rods on a base, designed to sit on top of a television set

rab·bit fe·ver *n* VET same as **tularemia**

rab·bit food *n* a vegetarian diet regarded as providing insufficient nutrition for a human being (*informal disapproving*)

rab·bit punch *n* a short sharp blow to the back of the neck —**rab·bit-punch** *vt*

rab·bit war·ren *n* ZOOL same as **warren** (sense 1)

rab·ble[1] /rább'l/ *n* **1.** **UNRULY CROWD** a noisy and unruly crowd of people **2.** **OFFENSIVE TERM** an offensive term that deliberately insults people lacking in wealth and status (*insult; takes a singular or plural verb*) **3.** **OFFENSIVE TERM** an offensive term that deliberately insults the abilities or significance of a group of people (*insult*) [14C. Origin ?]

rab·ble[2] /rább'l/ *n* a device for stirring or skimming molten metal in a furnace ■ *vt* (**-bled, -bling, -bles**) to stir or skim molten metal with a rabble [Mid-19C. Via French *râble* "fire rake" < Latin *rutabulum* < *ruere* "rake up"] —**rab·bler** *n*

rab·ble-rous·er *n* somebody who stirs up anger, violence, or other strong feelings in a crowd, especially for political reasons —**rab·ble-rous·ing** *n, adj*

Ra·be·lais /rábbə lày, ràbbə láy/, **François** (1493?–1553) French humanist and writer. His greatest works, *Pantagruel* (1532) and *Gargantua* (1534), satirized medieval scholasticism and are notable for their exuberance and earthy humor. —**Rab·e·lai·si·an** /ràbbə láyzee ən, -láyzh'n/ *adj, n*

> "Be still indebted to somebody or other, that there may be somebody always to pray for you."
> [François Rabelais, "Le Tiers Livre des faicts et dicts héroïques du bon Pantagruel (The Third Book of the Heroic Deeds and Words of Good Pantagruel)"; 1546]

Ra·bi /raábee/, **Ra·bi·a** /rə beé ə/ *n* in the Islamic calendar, either the third or the fourth month of the year. See table at **calendar** [Mid-18C. < Arabic *rabīʿ*]

Ra·bi /raábee/, **Isidor Isaac** (1898–1988) Austrian-born US physicist. He won the Nobel Prize in physics (1944) for his work on the atom.

Ra·bi·a *n* CALENDAR, ISLAM same as **Rabi**

rab·id /rábbid/ *adj* **1.** **FANATICAL** very enthusiastic about an idea, belief, or activity, often to the point of being blind to other opinions, beliefs, or preferences **2.** **INTENSE** feeling or showing an emotion or need extremely intensely ○ *a rabid lust for power* **3.** **VIOLENT** marked by ferociousness or violence **4.** MED, VET **HAVING RABIES** infected with rabies [Early 17C. < Latin *rabidus* < *rabere* "rave, be mad"] —**ra·bid·i·ty** /rə bíddətee/ *n* —**rab·id·ly** *adv* —**rab·id·ness** *n*

ra·bies /ráy beéz/ *n* an often fatal viral disease that affects the central nervous systems of most warm-blooded animals and is transmitted in the saliva of an infected animal. It causes convulsions, inability to move, and untypical behavior. [Late 16C. < Latin, "fury" < *rabere* "rave, be mad"] —**ra·bic** *adj* —**ra·bi·et·ic** /ràybee éttik/ *adj*

Ra·bin /raa beén/, **Yitzhak** (1922–95) Israeli soldier and prime minister (1974–77 and 1992–95). He was awarded the Nobel Peace Prize during his second premiership (1994), but was assassinated a year later.

> "We say to you today in a loud and clear voice: enough of blood and tears. Enough."
> [Yitzhak Rabin, *Remarks to the Palestinians, upon the signing of the Israel-Palestine Declaration, Washington, DC*; September 13, 1993]

rac·coon /ra koón/ (*plural* **-coons** or *same*), **ra·coon** *n* **1.** a small animal with grayish black fur, black patches around the eyes, and a long bushy ringed tail. Native to: forests of North and Central America. Genus: *Procyon*. See illustration on next page **2.** the fur of a raccoon [Early 17C. < Virginia Algonquian *aroughcun*]

rac·coon dog *n* a small wild dog with facial markings similar to a raccoon's and a thick yellow-brown

raccoon

coat. Native to: woodland areas of East Asia. Latin name: *Nyctereutes procyonoides.*

race[1] /rayss/ *n* **1. CONTEST OF SPEED** a contest to decide who is the fastest, e.g., between runners or horseback riders **2. CONTEST BETWEEN RIVALS** a contest between two or more people seeking to do or reach the same thing, or do or reach something first **3.** OCEANOG, GEOG **WATER CURRENT** a strong localized current in the sea or a river **4.** CIV ENG **WATER CHANNEL** a channel that carries water from one place to another, especially from a stream to a water wheel **5.** MECH ENG **GROOVE GUIDING SLIDING OBJECT** a groove along which something such as a ball bearing slides **6. NARROW PASSAGE** a narrow path or passage, e.g., one leading sheep from their enclosure to a dip **7. REGULAR COURSE** the fixed course regularly followed or traveled by something, especially the Sun or the Moon (*archaic or literary*) **8. JOURNEY** a single passage along a fixed course, especially the course that somebody's life follows (*archaic or literary*) ■ **rac·es** *npl* HORSERACING **HORSE RACES OR HORSERACING** horse races, the racetrack at which they are run, or horseracing as a spectator sport ○ *We spent the day at the races.* ■ *v* (**raced, rac·ing, rac·es**) **1.** *vti* **COMPETE AGAINST SOMEBODY IN RACE** to compete with somebody in a contest of speed **2.** *vt* **ENTER SOMETHING IN RACE** to enter, ride, or drive something such as a horse or car in a race **3.** *vti* **MOVE VERY FAST** to move somewhere with great speed or haste, or make somebody or something move in this way **4.** *vi* **BEAT FAST** to beat much faster than usual, e.g., because of nervousness or excitement (*refers to the heart*) **5.** *vti* AUTOMOT **IDLE FAST** to run at a high speed, or make an engine or motor run at a high speed [13C. < Old Norse *rás* "rush, running" < Indo-European, "be in motion"]

race[2] /rayss/ *n* **1. GROUP OF HUMANS** one of the groups into which the world's population can be divided on the basis of physical characteristics such as skin or hair color **2. FACT OF BELONGING TO GROUP** the fact of belonging to a group of humans who share the same physical features such as skin color ○ *an attempt to end discrimination on grounds of race* **3. HUMANKIND** humanity considered as a whole ○ *the fate of the race* **4.** BIOL **STRAIN OF ORGANISM** a genetically distinct population within a species that may also be geographically isolated **5.** WINE **DISTINCTIVE TASTE OF WINE** the distinctive taste of a wine, by which its grape variety or region of origin can be identified [Early 16C. Via French < Italian *razza*]

race·car /ráyss kaar/ *n* a car used, designed, or adapted for the sport of automobile racing

race card ◇ **play the race card** to use the issue of race, e.g., in legal argumentation or in a debate, to win an advantage or make a point (*informal*)

race·course /ráyss kàwrss/ *n* a course on which competitors race

race·horse /ráyss hàwrss/ *n* a horse bred and trained to run in races

rac·e·mate /rássə màyt/ *n* a chemical compound that does not deflect or absorb any of the light passing through it [Mid-19C. < RACEMIC]

ra·ceme /ray seem, rə-/ *n* a flower cluster (**inflorescence**) in which the flowers are borne on short stalks along a long main stem, as they are in the lily of the valley [Late 18C. < Latin *racemus* "bunch of grapes"]

ra·ce·mic /ray seemik, rə-, -sémmik/ *adj* describes a chemical compound that does not deflect or absorb any of the light passing through it. This is because it consists of a precise mixture of dextrorotatory and levorotatory isomers. [Late 19C. < Latin *racemus* "bunch of grapes," because the compound was originally derived from grapes]

ra·ce·mic ac·id *n* a form of tartaric acid that does not deflect or absorb any of the light passing through it. Source: grape juice.

rac·e·mi·za·tion /ràyssəmi záysh'n/ *n* the process of converting from an optically active compound or mixture to one that is racemic —**ra·ce·mize** /ráyssə mīz, ray seé-, rə seé-/ *vt*

rac·e·mose /ráyssə mòss/ *adj* **1. WITH FLOWERS CLUSTERED ALONG STEM** describes a flower cluster (**inflorescence**) in which the flowers are borne on short stalks on a long main stem, as they are in the lily of the valley **2. WITH YOUNGEST FLOWERS AT TIP** describes any pyramidal or flat-topped flower cluster in which the youngest flowers develop nearest the tip of the main stem or main side branches. Examples include the panicle, corymb, umbel, and capitulum, as well as the raceme. **3. CLUSTERED LIKE BUNCH OF GRAPES** describes glands that resemble a bunch of grapes in their structure —**rac·e·mose·ly** *adv*

rac·er /ráyssər/ *n* **1. SOMEBODY OR SOMETHING THAT RACES** a person, animal, or vehicle competing in a race **2. COMPUTER RACING GAME** a computer game that involves racing vehicles **3. THIN FAST-MOVING SNAKE** a slender fast-moving nonvenomous snake. Native to: North America. Genus: *Coluber.*

race·run·ner /ráyss rùnnər/ *n* a fast-moving lizard. Native to: North and Central America. Genus: *Cnemidophurus.*

race·track /ráyss tràk/ *n* a closed, often oval track around which cars, runners, or horses race, or the grounds in which the track is sited

race-walk *vi* to compete in the sport of race walking

race walk·ing *n* the sport of racing at a fast walking pace, with rules that require walkers to keep at least one foot on the ground at all times —**race walk·er** *n*

race·way /ráyss wày/ *n* **1. RACETRACK** a track on which races, especially harness races, are held, or the grounds in which the track is sited **2.** CIV ENG same as **race**[1] (sense 4) **3. PIPE FOR HYDRAULICS** a pipe, channel, or other means by which water is conveyed to or from hydraulic machinery **4. PROTECTIVE TUBE FOR WIRES** a tube or channel that holds, guides, and protects electric wires

Ra·chel /ráychəl/ *n* in the Bible, the daughter of Laban, wife of Jacob, and mother of Joseph and Benjamin (Genesis 29–35)

ra·chis /ráykiss/ (*plural* **ra·chis·es** or **rach·i·des** /ráki deez, ráyki-/) *n* **1.** BOT **PLANT STEM** the main stem of a flower cluster or a compound leaf **2.** BIRDS **FEATHER SHAFT** the main shaft of a feather **3.** ANAT **SPINE** the spine of a vertebrate animal (*technical*) [Late 18C. Via modern Latin < Greek *rhakhis* "spine, ridge"] —**ra·chi·al** *adj* —**ra·chid·i·al** /rə kíddee əl/ *adj*

ra·chi·tis /rə kītiss/ *n* MED same as **rickets** (*technical*) [Early 18C. < Greek *rhakhitis* "disease of the spine" < *rhakhis* "spine"] —**ra·chit·ic** /rə kíttik/ *adj*

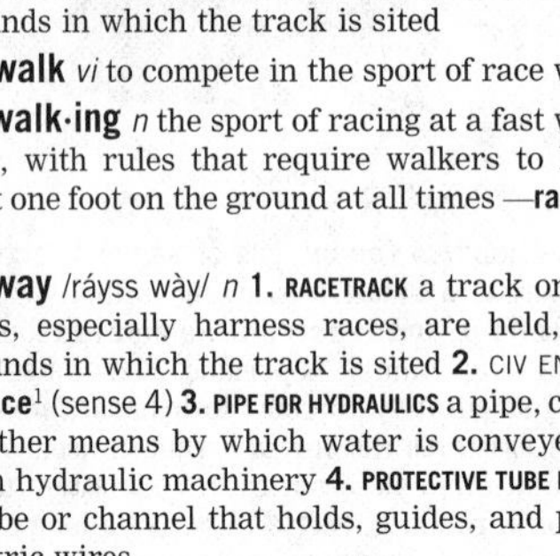

AKG London

Sergey Rachmaninoff

Rach·ma·ni·noff /raak maanə nàwf/, **Sergey** (1873–1943) Russian-born composer and pianist. His symphonies and compositions for piano are considered the last major musical expression of the Romantic era. Full name **Rachmaninoff, Sergey Vasilyevich**

ra·cial /ráysh'l/ *adj* **1.** existing or taking place between different races ○ *racial harmony* **2.** relating to or characteristic of races or a race of people —**ra·cial·ly** *adv*

ra·cial·ism /ráysh'l ìzzəm/ *n UK* SOCIOL same as **racism** (*dated*) —**ra·cial·ist** *n, adj* —**ra·cial·is·tic** /ràysh'l ístik/ *adj*

ra·cial·ize /ráysh'l īz/ (**-ized, -iz·ing, -iz·es**) *vti* **1. DISTINGUISH BY RACE** to make distinctions or classify people according to race **2. MAKE SOMETHING SEEM RACIAL** to put something into a racial context **3. SEE SOMETHING FROM RACIAL PERSPECTIVE** to view or experience something from a racial perspective

ra·cial·ly-cor·rect·ed *adj* adjusted to eliminate cultural bias or racial prejudice from something, especially a standardized test

ra·cial pro·fil·ing *n* the alleged policy of some police to attribute criminal intentions to members of some ethnic groups and to stop and question them in disproportionate numbers without probable cause

Ra·cine /rə seén/, **Jean Baptiste** (1639–99) French playwright. Considered to be the greatest French classical tragedian, he adapted Greek and Roman subjects in works such as *Andromaque* (1667) and *Phèdre* (1677). —**Ra·cin·i·an** /rə sínnee ən/ *adj*

> "Innocence has nothing to dread."
> [Jean Baptiste Racine, *Phèdre*; 1677]

rac·ing bike *n* a bicycle or motorcycle used, designed, or adapted for racing (*informal*)

rac·ing car *n UK* same as **racecar**

rac·ing form *n* a sheet giving details of the previous performances of competitors in a race, especially a horserace, for use by people wishing to place bets

ra·cism /ráy sìzzəm/ *n* **1.** prejudice or animosity against people who belong to other races ○ *"I am a Muslim and ... my religion makes me against all forms of racism."* (Malcolm X, *Speech, Prospects for Freedom*; 1965) **2.** the belief that people of different races have different qualities and abilities, and that some races are inherently superior or inferior

rac·ist /ráyssist/ *adj* **1. BASED ON RACISM** based on prejudices and stereotypes related to race **2. PREJUDICED AGAINST OTHER RACES** prejudiced against all people who belong to other races ○ *"Black power ... a call to reject the racist institutions and values of this society"* (Stokely Carmichael [Kwame Tore] and Charles Vernon Hamilton, *Black Power!*; 1967) ■ *n* **RACIST PERSON** somebody who hates others who are not of his or her own race

rack[1] /rak/ *n* **1. FRAMEWORK FOR HOLDING THINGS** a framework or stand for carrying, holding, or storing things ○ *a wine rack* **2.** AGRIC **FEED-HOLDING FRAMEWORK** a framework containing hay or other fodder for livestock **3.** AIR FORCE **BOMB-HOLDING FRAMEWORK** a framework holding bombs or rockets that is attached to an aircraft **4.** MECH ENG **TOOTHED BAR** a bar with notches, designed to engage the teeth of a pinion or worm gear and convert rotary motion to linear motion, e.g., in a vehicle's steering system **5. INSTRUMENT OF TORTURE** a torture device used to stretch the body of somebody strapped horizontally onto it **6.** ZOOL **ANTLERS** a pair of antlers **7.** CUE GAMES **BALL-PLACING FRAME** a triangular frame for grouping the balls at the beginning of a game of pool, billiards, or snooker **8.** CUE GAMES **BALLS POSITIONED BY FRAME** the target balls when in position for the start of a game of pool, billiards, or snooker **9.** CUE GAMES **GAME IN POOL** any one of the individual games that make up a match in pool, billiards, or snooker **10.** *US* **BED** a bed or a bunk (*slang*) **11.** *US* same as **sleep** *n* (sense 1) (*slang*) ○ *Time to get some rack.* ■ *vt* (**racked, rack·ing, racks**) **1. CAUSE SOMEBODY PAIN** to cause somebody great pain or stress ○ *the coughing spasms that racked his body* **2. SHAKE SOMETHING VIOLENTLY** to shake or strain something with violent force ○ *The high winds racked villages all along the coast.* **3. TRY TO USE SOMETHING TO MAXIMUM** to make a great effort to use all the resources of something such as the brain or the memory to the fullest extent ○ *I racked my brain trying to think where I'd seen him before.* **4. TORTURE SOMEBODY ON RACK** to stretch the body of somebody strapped horizontally on a rack as a means of torture **5.** PUT SOMETHING IN RACK to place something in or on a rack **6.** MECH ENG MOVE SOMETHING WITH RACK to move a device or part using a rack-and-pinion system **7.** CUE GAMES POSITION BALLS to set up the balls for a game of billiards, pool, or snooker using a rack [14C. < Dutch *rak* "framework"] —**rack·er** *n* —**rack·ful** *n* ◇ **off the rack** ready to wear, not tailor-made ◇ **on the rack** experiencing great mental anguish (*informal*)

SPELLCHECK rack or **wrack**? Do not confuse the spelling of ***rack*** and ***wrack***, which sound similar. ***Rack*** is the more common word, and the only spelling you should use for the meanings "framework for holding things" (as in *wine rack*), "toothed bar" (as in *rack and pinion*), "joint of meat" (as in *rack of lamb*), "instrument of torture" (as in *stretched on the rack*), and "accumulate" (as in *racked up 100 points*). ***Rack*** is also the usual spelling of the verb meaning "subject to great stress, pain, torture, etc.", as in *racked with guilt, rack your brains*. The noun in the phrase *rack and ruin* can be spelled ***rack*** or ***wrack***, but ***rack*** is the more common spelling. The noun ***wrack*** is chiefly used to denote a type of seaweed.

rack out *vi US* to go to bed or get some sleep (*slang*)
rack up *vt* to accumulate something such as points (*informal*) ○ *The company racked up sales of $8 million in its first year of trading.*

rack[2] /rak/ *n* a joint of meat, usually lamb, consisting of one or both sides of the front ribs, prepared for roasting, often joined end to end in a circle [Late 16C. Origin ?]

rack[3] /rak/ (**racked, rack·ing, racks**) *vt* to siphon clear wine or beer out of a barrel, leaving the sediment behind [15C. < Provençal *arracar* < *raca* "dregs"]

rack[4] /rak/ *n* in dressage, a fast walking pace for a horse in which each foot is lifted off the ground in turn ■ *vi* (**racked, rack·ing, racks**) to walk at a fast pace, lifting each foot off the ground in turn (*refers to horses*) [Late 16C. Origin ?]

rack[5] /rak/ *n* a mass of broken cloud blown fast by the wind ■ *vi* (**racked, rack·ing, racks**) to be blown fast by the wind (*refers to clouds*) [14C. Origin ?]

rack[6] /rak/ *n* a state of ruin or destruction (*archaic*) [Late 16C. Variant of WRACK[1]] ◇ **go to rack and ruin** to deteriorate into a state of neglect or ruin

SPELLCHECK See *rack*[1].

rack-and-pin·ion *adj* relating to or using a mechanical system in which a toothed wheel (**pinion**) engages a notched bar (**rack**) to convert rotary motion into linear motion

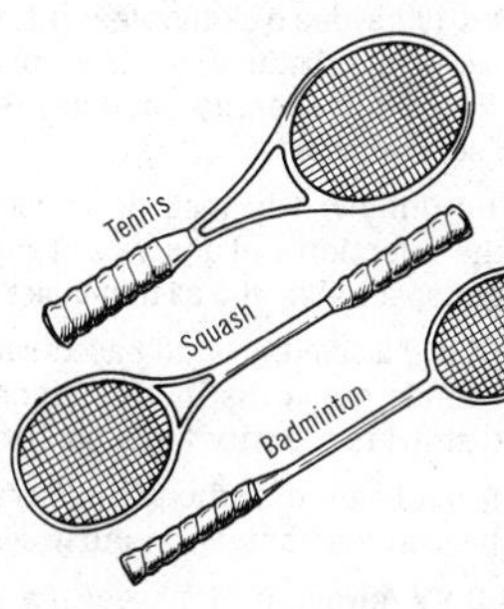

racket

rack·et[1] /rákət/, **rac·quet** *n* **1.** a lightweight bat with a network of strings, used in tennis, racquetball, badminton, squash, and similar games. The frame is usually made of a substance such as wood, aluminum, or graphite, and the strings of gut or nylon. **2.** a snowshoe in the shape of a racket [Early 16C. Via French *raquette* < Arabic *rāhat* "palm of the hand"]

rack·et[2] /rákət/ *n* **1.** NOISE a loud noise, especially when it disturbs people **2.** ILLEGAL SCHEME an illegal or dishonest money-making scheme, involving activities such as bribery, fraud, or intimidation **3.** BUSINESS a business, job, or activity of any kind (*informal*) ○ *He's in the advertising racket.* **4.** EASY LIVING an easy and very profitable way of earning a living (*informal*) [Mid-16C. Origin ?]

rack·et·ball *n* RACKET GAMES another spelling of **racquetball**

rack·et·eer /ràkə tèer/ *n* somebody who profits from illegal activities such as bribery, fraud, or intimidation ■ *vi* (**-eered, -eer·ing, -eers**) to make money from illegal activities, or operate a racket —**rack·et·eer·ing** *n*

rack·ets /rákəts/, **rac·quets** *n* a fast game similar to squash played by two or four people on a four-walled indoor court using long-handled rackets and a small hard ball. It is derived from the old game of real tennis. (*takes a singular verb*) [Early 19C. Plural of RACKET[1]]

rack·et·y /rákətee/ *adj* noisy and boisterous (*dated*)

Rack·ham /rákəm/, **Arthur** (1867–1939) British illustrator and watercolor painter. He created fanciful illustrations for editions of literary classics, as well as for children's books.

rack rail·way *n Can, UK* a mountain railway that has locomotives with a central cogwheel that engages with a toothed rack between the rails in order to pull the train up steep slopes. US term **cog railway**

rack-rent *n* an unreasonably high rent ■ *vti* to charge a tenant an unreasonably high rent [< RACK[1] "to torture"] —**rack-rent·er** *n*

ra·clette /raa klét, ra klét/ *n* **1.** a Swiss dish consisting of slices of melted cheese served on boiled potatoes or bread **2.** a hard-crusted type of Swiss cheese that melts easily, traditionally used for raclette [Mid-20C. < French < *racler* "scrape," because the cheese is melted and scraped onto a plate]

ra·con /ráy kòn/ *n* NAVIG same as **radar beacon** [Mid-20C. Blend of RADAR + BEACON]

rac·on·teur /rà kon túr/ *n* somebody who tells stories or anecdotes in an interesting or entertaining way [Early 19C. < French < Old French *raconter* "recount, retell"]

ra·coon *n* ZOOL another spelling of **raccoon**

rac·quet *n* RACKET GAMES, CLOTHING another spelling of **racket**[1]

rac·quet·ball /rákət bàwl/, **rack·et·ball** *n* a game played on a four-walled indoor court by two, three, or four players using short-handled rackets and a ball larger than the ball used in squash or rackets

rac·quets *n* RACKET GAMES another spelling of **rackets**

rac·y /ráyssee/ (**-i·er, -i·est**) *adj* **1.** MILDLY INDECENT mildly shocking because of references to or descriptions of sex **2.** LIVELY full of energy or spirit **3.** DISTINCTIVE having a distinctive quality or flavor **4.** PUNGENT sharp or piquant in taste or smell [Mid-17C. < RACE[1]] —**rac·i·ly** *adv* —**rac·i·ness** *n*

rad[1] /rad/ *n* the unit formerly used to measure the level of ionizing radiation absorbed by something, equal to 0.01 joule per kilogram of irradiated material [Early 20C. Acronym < *radiation absorbed dose*]

rad[2] /rad/ (**rad·der, rad·dest**) *adj* very good, desirable, admirable, or fashionable (*slang*) ○ *a totally rad idea* [Early 19C. Shortening of RADICAL]

rad[3] *symbol* MATH radian

rad. *abbr* **1.** MATH radical **2.** radio **3.** MATH radius **4.** MATH radix

ra·dar /ráy daar/ *n* **1.** a system that uses reflected radio waves to determine the presence, location, and speed of distant objects. The system has military, law-enforcement, and navigational applications. Examples of its uses include the locating of enemy aircraft or ships and the monitoring of vehicle speeds. **2.** the electronic equipment that transmits and receives high-frequency radio waves to detect, locate, and track distant objects [Mid-20C. Acronym < *radio detection and ranging*]

ra·dar as·tron·o·my *n* the use of radar techniques to study and map astronomical objects in the solar system

ra·dar bea·con *n* a ground-based, fixed-position radar receiver-transmitter whose signals can be received by an aircraft or ship's navigator to determine bearing and range

ra·dar gun *n* a small handheld radar device used to determine the speed of nearby objects

ra·dar·scope /ráy daar skòp/ *n* the screen on radar equipment that displays the reflected radio signal as a dot of light. In sophisticated screens, data such as speed, direction, and altitude are also shown.

radar screen ◇ **be on** *or* **off somebody's radar screen** to be of interest to somebody and receive his or her attention (*informal*)

ra·dar trap *n* ROADS same as **speed trap**

Rad·cliff /rád klìf/ city in north central Kentucky, southwest of Louisville and northeast of Elizabethtown. Population: 21,978 (2002 estimate).

rad·dle[1] /rádd'l/ (**-dled, -dling, -dles**) *vt* to twist or weave things together [Late 17C. < Anglo-Norman *reidele* "wooden pole," Old French *reddalle*]

rad·dle[2] *n, vt* MINERALS, AGRIC same as **ruddle** [Early 16C. < form of RED]

rad·dled /rádd'ld/ *adj* having a worn-out appearance that suggests long life or a life of indulgence [Late 17C. Origin ?]

ra·di·al /ráydee əl/ *adj* **1.** SPREADING FROM CENTER OUTWARD spreading out from a common center like the spokes of a wheel ○ *petals in a radial arrangement* **2.** OF RADIUS relating to a radius, especially moving along a radius **3.** ZOOL WITH BODY PARTS IN CIRCULAR ARRANGEMENT used to describe the arrangement of the bodies of invertebrate ocean animals such as the starfish and sea anemone in which parts spread out from a single center **4.** ANAT OF FOREARM BONE relating to the radius bone of the forearm ■ *n* AUTOMOT same as **radial tire** —**ra·di·al·ly** *adv*

ra·di·al en·gine *n* an internal-combustion engine that has its cylinders arranged around a central crankshaft like the spokes of a wheel, instead of in one or two straight rows

ra·di·al ker·a·tot·o·my *n* a surgical procedure for correcting nearsightedness, using a series of small radial incisions to change the shape of the cornea

ra·di·al-ply *adj* describes a tire in which the fabric cords that make up the foundation of the tire run at right angles to the circumference of the tire

ra·di·al sym·me·try *n* symmetry in which something can be divided into two identical halves by a line or plane passing through a central point or axis at any angle —**ra·di·al·ly sym·met·ri·cal** *adj*

ra·di·al tire *n* a tire in which the fabric cords that make up the foundation of the tire run at right angles to the circumference of the tire

ra·di·al ve·loc·i·ty *n* the velocity of a star or other astronomical object measured along the observer's line of sight

ra·di·an /ráydee ən/ *n* a unit of angular measurement equivalent to the angle between two radii that enclose a section of a circle's circumference (**arc**) equal in length to the length of a radius. There are 2π radians in a circle. Symbol **rad** [Late 19C. < RADIUS]

ra·di·ance /ráydee ənss/ *n* **1.** HAPPINESS OR ENERGY joy, energy, or good health discernible in somebody's face or demeanor **2.** LIGHT bright or glowing light **3.** PHYS MEASURE OF RADIANT ENERGY a measure of the amount of radiant energy emitted or received per unit area of a surface over a specific time. Symbol L_e

ra·di·ant /ráydee ənt/ *adj* **1.** SHOWING HAPPINESS expressing joy, energy, or good health in a pleasing way **2.** SHINING lit with a bright or glowing light **3.** PHYS EMITTED AS WAVES describes light, heat, or other energy emitted in the form of rays or waves ○ *radiant heat* **4.** PHYS EMITTING RADIANT ENERGY emitting light, heat, or other energy in the form of rays or waves ■ *n* **1.** HEATING ELEMENT an element in a heater that gives out radiant heat **2.** ASTRON POINT OF ORIGIN OF METEOR SHOWER a point in space from which a meteor shower appears to originate [15C. < Latin *radiant-*, present participle of *radiare* (see RADIATE)] —**ra·di·ant·ly** *adv*

ra·di·ant en·er·gy *n* energy emitted as waves, usually electromagnetic waves, through space or some other medium. Symbol Q_e

ra·di·ant flux *n* the rate of flow of radiant energy. Symbol Φ_e

ra·di·ant heat *n* heat transmitted by infrared radiation from a heat source, and not by conduction or convection

ra·di·ant heat·ing *n* heating by means of heaters such as radiators, baseboard heaters, and electric coils, not by forced hot air

ra·di·ate *v* /ráydee àyt/ (**-at·ed, -at·ing, -ates**) **1.** *vti* PHYS **EMIT ENERGY AS RAYS OR WAVES** to send out energy such as heat or light, in the form of rays or waves, or be sent out in this form **2.** *vti* **SHOW FEELING OR QUALITY** to show a feeling or quality clearly through looks, speech, behavior, or content, or be shown in this way ○ *a popular speech that radiated goodwill and commitment* **3.** *vti* **SPREAD FROM CENTER** to spread out from a central point like rays, or cause something to spread out in this way **4.** *vi* BIOL **DEVELOP AND SPREAD** to develop into several different forms capable of exploiting different resources or of living in different environments (*refers to animal and plant species*) ■ *adj* /ráydee ət/ **1. WITH RADIATING PARTS** with, or in the form of, parts spreading out from a common center **2.** BOT **WITH PETALS RADIATING FROM CENTER** describes a flower head that has petals radiating from a center, e.g., that of a daisy **3.** ZOOL **WITH RADIALLY SYMMETRICAL BODY** used to describe the bodies of starfish and other vertebrate ocean organisms with body parts radiating from a common center **4. WITH RAYS** surrounded or decorated with rays [Early 17C. < Latin *radiat-*, past participle of *radiare* "emit rays" < *radius* "ray"] —**ra·di·ate·ly** *adv* —**ra·di·a·tive** *adj*

ra·di·a·tion /ràydee áysh'n/ *n* **1. PARTICLES EMITTED BY RADIOACTIVE SUBSTANCES** energy emitted in the form of particles by substances such as uranium and plutonium, whose atoms are not stable and are spontaneously decaying. This energy can be converted into electric power, but it can also cause severe or fatal health problems to people who are exposed to it. **2.** PHYS **ENERGY EMITTED IN RAYS OR WAVES** energy emitted from a source in the form of rays or waves, e.g., heat, light, or sound **3.** PHYS **RADIATING OF ENERGY** the emission of energy in the form of rays or waves **4. EFFECT OF RADIATING** the feeling of something being radiated, e.g., heat from a hot oven **5.** MED same as **radiotherapy 6.** ECOL same as **adaptive radiation** —**ra·di·a·tion·al** *adj*

ra·di·a·tion·al cool·ing *n* loss of heat from the Earth's surface and from air near the Earth's surface, occurring mainly at night

ra·di·a·tion bi·ol·o·gy *n* BIOL same as **radiobiology**

ra·di·a·tion sick·ness *n* a medical condition caused by overexposure to X-rays or to emissions from radioactive material. Symptoms include fatigue, headache, vomiting, diarrhea, loss of hair and teeth, and in severe cases, hemorrhaging and death.

ra·di·a·tion ther·a·py *n* PHYSIOL same as **radiotherapy**

ra·di·a·tor /ráydee àytər/ *n* **1. ROOM HEATER WITH PIPES** a room-heating device that emits heat from pipes through which hot water, steam, or hot oil circulates, especially one connected to a central boiler-fed system **2.** AUTOMOT **ENGINE-COOLING DEVICE** a device that prevents a vehicle's engine from overheating, consisting of tubes through which heated water from the engine circulates to be cooled. Cool air is usually circulated around the tubes by means of a fan. **3.** PHYS **DEVICE EMITTING RADIANT ENERGY** a device that emits radiant energy, e.g., a light bulb or a television transmitter

rad·i·cal /ráddik'l/ *adj* **1. BASIC** relating to or affecting the basic nature or most important features of something ○ *a radical difference between the two* **2. PERVASIVE** far-reaching, searching, or thoroughgoing ○ *a radical reorganization of the company* **3. FAVORING MAJOR CHANGES** favoring or making economic, political, or social changes of a sweeping or extreme nature **4.** *US* **EXCELLENT** excellent, admirable, or awe-inspiring (*slang*) **5.** MED **REMOVING DISEASE SOURCE** describes medical treatment that is intended to remove the source of a disease, rather than simply treat the symptoms ○ *a radical mastectomy* **6.** BOT **GROWING FROM ROOT** growing from a root of a plant or from the base of a stem **7.** MATH **OF MATHEMATICAL ROOT** relating to the roots of numbers **8.** LING **OF WORD ROOTS** relating to the roots of words ■ *n* **1. SOMEBODY WITH RADICAL VIEWS** somebody with radical views on political, economic, or social issues ○ *the radicals in the party* **2.** MATH **MATHEMATICAL ROOT** a mathematical root of another number or quantity **3.** CHEM same as **free radical 4.** CHEM **CHEMICAL GROUP** a chemical group that behaves as a single entity in reactions (*dated*) **5.** LING same as **root**[1] (sense 10) [14C. < late Latin *radicalis* "of roots" < *radic-* "root"] —**rad·i·cal·ly** *adv* —**rad·i·cal·ness** *n*

rad·i·cal chic *n* the fashionable adoption of radical left-wing views by rich or famous people ○ *"Radical chic invariably favors radicals who seem primitive, exotic, and romantic."* (Tom Wolfe, *Radical Chic*; 1970)

rad·i·cal·ism /ráddik'l ìzzəm/ *n* **1.** POLITICS **ADVOCATING MAJOR CHANGES** political policies that advocate more sweeping political, economic, or social change than that traditionally supported by the mainstream political parties **2. POLITICALLY RADICAL ATTITUDES** support for radical political policies **3. SIGNIFICANT CHANGE** sweeping change in a context, or the attitudes of people who favor sweeping change

rad·i·cal·ize /ráddik'l ìz/ (**-ized, -iz·ing, -iz·es**) *vti* **1.** to undergo fundamental change, or introduce sweeping change in something **2.** to adopt politically radical views, or cause somebody to do this ○ *The experience of war radicalized the younger generation.* —**rad·i·cal·i·za·tion** /ràddik'li záysh'n/ *n*

rad·i·cal sign *n* the sign $\surd$ placed before a mathematical expression to denote the extraction of a square root or higher root. Roots higher than a square root are indicated by a superscript number preceding the sign.

rad·i·cand /ráddi kànd/ *n* a mathematical quantity from which a square root or higher root is to be extracted [Late 19C. < Latin *radicandus* < *radicare* "take root" < *radic-* "root"]

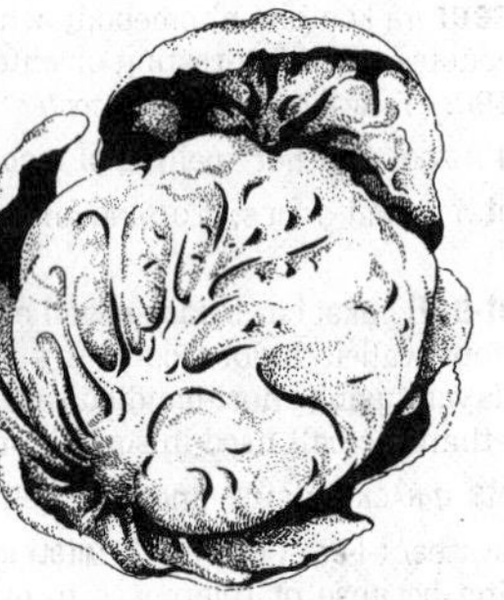

radicchio

ra·dic·chi·o /rə deékee ò, raa-/ (*plural* **-os**) *n* a variety of chicory with reddish purple and white leaves, usually eaten raw in salads. Native to: Italy. [Late 20C. Via Italian, "chicory" < Latin *radicula* (see RADICLE)]

rad·i·ces MATH, BIOL plural of **radix**

rad·i·cle /ráddik'l/ *n* **1.** the part of a plant embryo that forms the root of the young plant **2.** a small body part that superficially resembles the root of a plant, e.g., a branch of a nerve [Late 17C. < Latin *radicula* "little root" < *radic-* "root"] —**ra·dic·u·lar** /ra díkyələr/ *adj*

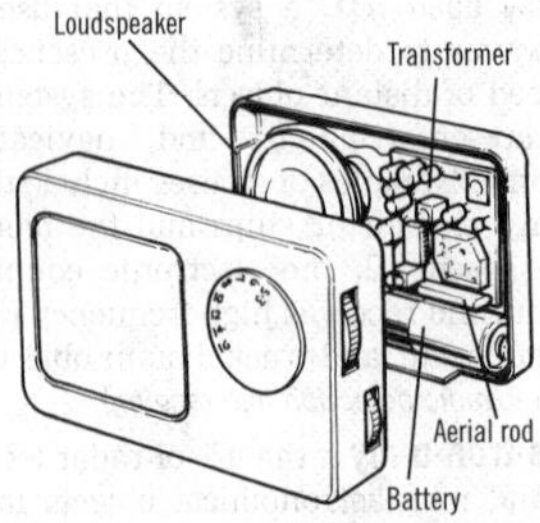

radio (sense 3)

ra·di·o /ráydee ò/ *n* (*plural* **-os**) **1. USE OF ELECTROMAGNETIC WAVES FOR COMMUNICATION** the use of electromagnetic waves to transmit and receive information, as in sound broadcasts or two-way communication, without the need for connecting wires **2. COMMUNICATION USING RADIO WAVES** communication that takes place by means of radio waves **3. DEVICE RECEIVING SOUND BROADCASTS** an electronic device for receiving sound broadcasts transmitted via radio signals **4. TWO-WAY COMMUNICATION DEVICE** an electronic device used to send and receive radio signals, used for two-way communication **5. RADIO BROADCASTS** sound broadcasts transmitted by means of radio waves **6. BROADCASTING OF PROGRAMS BY RADIO** the broadcasting by radio of programs for the public **7. SOUND BROADCASTING** radio broadcasting as an industry or profession ○ *She works in radio.* ■ *vti* (**-oed, -o·ing, -os**) **CONTACT SOMEBODY BY RADIO** to communicate by radio or send somebody a message by radio ■ *adj* PHYS **OF ELECTROMAGNETIC WAVES** relating to electromagnetic waves or electromagnetic phenomena with frequencies between 10 kHz and 300,000 MHz [Early 20C. Shortening of *radiotelegraph*]

radio- *prefix* **1.** radiation ○ *radiocarbon* **2.** radio ○ *radiolocation* [In sense 1 < shortening of words such as RADIATION, RADIOACTIVE; in sense 2 < RADIO]

ra·di·o·ac·tive /ràydee ō áktiv/ *adj* **1. EMITTING RADIATION** describes a substance such as uranium or plutonium that emits energy in the form of streams of particles, owing to the decaying of its unstable atoms. This energy can be damaging or fatal to the health of people exposed to it. **2.** PHYS **OF OR USING RADIOACTIVE SUBSTANCES** relating to or making use of radioactive substances or the radiation they emit **3. HIGHLY CONTROVERSIAL** so highly controversial that people tend to avoid the person or issue in question ○ *The topic of campaign finance reform is radioactive in many constituencies.* —**ra·di·o·ac·tive·ly** *adv*

ra·di·o·ac·tive dat·ing *n* ARCHAEOL same as **radiometric dating**

ra·di·o·ac·tive de·cay *n* PHYS same as **decay** *n* (sense 4)

ra·di·o·ac·tive se·ries *n* a series of related atom types (**nuclides**) of radioactive isotopes, each of which is transformed into the next by the emission of an elementary particle until a stable nuclide results. There are three such sequences, the thorium, the uranium-radium, and the actinium, and almost all naturally occurring radioactive isotopes belong to one of them.

ra·di·o·ac·tive trac·er *n* a substance with a radioactive isotope that can be introduced into and tracked within the body to study disease and biochemical processes

ra·di·o·ac·tive waste *n* waste material that is radioactive, particularly the waste from nuclear reactors and medical treatment and research

ra·di·o·ac·tiv·i·ty /ràydee ō ak tívvətee/ *n* **1.** the radioactive nature of a substance such as uranium or plutonium **2.** the high-energy particles emitted by radioactive substances

ra·di·o as·tron·o·my *n* a branch of astronomy that deals with the detection and analysis of radio waves received from space —**ra·di·o as·tron·o·mer** *n*

ra·di·o bea·con *n* a fixed ground-based radio transmitter that sends out a distinctive signal to help aircraft and ships to identify their position

ra·di·o beam *n* a beam of radio signals transmitted by a radio beacon for navigation purposes

ra·di·o·bi·ol·o·gy /ràydee ō bī óllajee/ *n* a branch of biology that deals with the effects of radiation on living tissues and organisms —**ra·di·o·bi·o·log·ic** /-bī ə lójjik/ *adj* —**ra·di·o·bi·o·log·i·cal** *adj* —**ra·di·o·bi·o·log·i·cal·ly** *adv* —**ra·di·o·bi·ol·o·gist** *n*

ra·di·o but·ton *n* in a computer dialogue box, any of several circles or rectangles, each with text next to it, representing a fixed set of choices, one of which must be selected

ra·di·o car *n* **1.** a car, especially a police car, equipped with a two-way radio **2.** a vehicle from which radio broadcasts are made, especially interviews

ra·di·o·car·bon /ràydee ō kaárbən/ *n* a radioactive form of carbon, especially the isotope of carbon that has a mass number of 14

ra·di·o·car·bon dat·ing *n* GEOL same as **carbon dating**

ra·di·o cas·sette, **ra·di·o·cas·sette play·er** *n* a radio and a cassette player combined in a single, usually portable machine

ra·di·o·chem·is·try /ràydee ō kémmistree/ *n* a branch of chemistry that deals with radioactive elements and their applications —**ra·di·o·chem·i·cal** *adj* —**ra·di·o·chem·i·cal·ly** *adv* —**ra·di·o·chem·ist** *n*

ra·di·o com·pass *n* a navigation device that uses incoming radio signals from radio beacons to determine the position of a ship or an aircraft

ra·di·o-con·trolled *adj* describes a device whose operation or movement is controlled from a distance using a transmitter, often handheld, that sends radio signals to the device

ra·di·o·el·e·ment /ràydee ō élləmənt/ *n* a chemical element that is radioactive

ra·di·o fre·quen·cy *n* **1.** any of the frequencies of electromagnetic radiation in the range between 10 kHz and 300 MHz, including those used for radio and television transmission **2.** a frequency on which a radio station broadcasts its programs

ra·di·o gal·ax·y *n* a galaxy that is a strong source of radio waves

ra·di·o·ge·nic /ràydee ō jénnik/ *adj* **1.** describes a substance created as a result of the spontaneous decaying of the unstable atoms of another substance ○ *a radiogenic isotope* **2.** emitted as a result of radioactive decay ○ *radiogenic heat*

ra·di·o·gram /ráydee ō gràm/ *n* **1.** a telegram sent by radio **2.** MED same as **radiograph**

ra·di·o·graph /ráydee ō gràf/ *n* an image produced on film or another sensitive surface by radiation such as X-rays or gamma rays passing through an object ■ *vt* (**-graphed, -graph·ing, -graphs**) to make a radiograph of something, especially a part of the body —**ra·di·og·ra·pher** /ràydee óggrəfər/ *n* —**ra·di·o·graph·ic** /-ō gráffik/ *adj* —**ra·di·o·graph·i·cal·ly** *adv* —**ra·di·og·ra·phy** /-óggrəfee/ *n*

ra·di·o·im·mu·no·as·say /ràydee ō ìmmyənō áss ày/ *n* the technique of measuring the levels of antibodies in the blood by introducing into the bloodstream a substance that has a radioactive tracer attached to it —**ra·di·o·im·mu·no·as·say·a·ble** *adj*

ra·di·o·i·o·dine /ràydee ō ī ə dìn/ *n* a radioactive form of iodine. Use: in medicine as a tracer.

ra·di·o·i·so·tope /ràydee ō íssə tòp/ *n* a form of a chemical element (**isotope**) that is radioactive —**ra·di·o·i·so·top·ic** /-īssə tóppik/ *adj*

ra·di·o jet *n* a stream of rapidly moving gas associated with a revolving band of matter (**accretion disk**) that emits radio waves as it traverses a magnetic field

ra·di·o·la·bel /ràydee ō láyb'l/ *n* a radioactive substance attached to another substance as a means of tracing the location or tracking the movement of that substance. The technique is used in medicine, e.g., to monitor the distribution of a drug throughout the body. ■ *vt* (**-labeled** or **-labelled, -labeling** or **-labelling, -labels**) to attach a radiolabel to a substance —**ra·di·o·la·beled** *adj* —**ra·di·o·la·bel·ing** *n*

ra·di·o·lar·i·an /ràydee ō lérree ən/ *n* a single-celled ocean organism with a round silica-containing shell that has the organs of movement radiating around it. Amoebas are radiolarians. [Late 19C. < modern Latin *Radiolaria* < *radiolus* "little staff, stick" < *radius* "staff, spoke, ray"]

ra·di·o·lo·ca·tion /ràydee ō lō káysh'n/ *n* the use of radar to detect distant objects

ra·di·ol·o·gy /ràydee ólləjee/ *n* **1.** the branch of medicine that deals with the use of X-rays and radioactive substances such as radium in the diagnosis and treatment of diseases **2.** the science of radiation and radioactive substances and their applications, e.g., in structural analysis —**ra·di·o·log·ic** /ràydee ə lójjik/ *adj* —**ra·di·o·log·i·cal** *adj* —**ra·di·o·log·i·cal·ly** *adv* —**ra·di·ol·o·gist** *n*

ra·di·o·lu·cent /ràydee ō lóoss'nt/ *adj* interfering very little or not at all with the passage of X-rays and other forms of electromagnetic radiation —**ra·di·o·lu·cen·cy** *n*

ra·di·ol·y·sis /ràydee ólləsiss/ *n* the breakdown of something into its chemical components by means of X-rays or other radiation —**ra·di·o·lyt·ic** /-ō líttik/ *adj*

ra·di·om·e·ter /ràydee ómmətər/ *n* a device used to detect and measure radiant energy, especially an instrument used to demonstrate the conversion of such energy into mechanical work —**ra·di·o·met·ric** /ràydee ə méttrik/ *adj* —**ra·di·o·met·ric·al·ly** *adv* —**ra·di·om·e·try** *n*

ra·di·o·met·ric dat·ing *n* a method of determining the age of objects or material using the decay rates of radioactive components such as potassium-argon

ra·di·o·mi·met·ic /ràydee ōmi méttik/ *adj* exerting effects similar to those of ionizing radiation ○ *the radiomimetic effects of some chemicals such as urethane*

ra·di·on·ics /ràydee ónniks/ *n* the use in alternative medicine of an electronic device that can detect vitamin and mineral deficiencies from a hair sample or can detect subtle energy changes in the body. Its results are used to determine appropriate herbal or homeopathic treatments. (*takes a singular verb*) [Mid-20C. Blend of RADIATION + ELECTRONICS]

ra·di·o·nu·clide /ràydee ə nóo klìd/ *n* a radioactive nuclide

ra·di·o·paque /ràydee ō páyk/ *adj* blocking the passage of X-rays and other forms of electromagnetic radiation —**ra·di·o·pac·i·ty** /ràydee ō pássətee/ *n*

ra·di·o·phar·ma·ceu·ti·cal /ràydee ō faàrmə sóotik'l/ *n* a radioactive drug or substance. Use: diagnosis and treatment of disease. —**ra·di·o·phar·ma·ceu·ti·cal** *adj*

ra·di·o·phone /ràydee ō fòn/ *n* TELECOM same as **radiotelephone**

ra·di·o·pho·to·graph /ràydee ō fótə gràf/, **ra·di·o·pho·to** /-fótō/ (*plural* **-tos**) *n* a photograph or another image that is sent from one location to another by means of radio waves

ra·di·o·pro·tec·tive /ràydee ō prə téktiv/ *adj* protecting or helping to protect against the harmful effects of X-rays and other radiation —**ra·di·o·pro·tec·tion** *n*

ra·di·o·re·sist·ant /ràydee ō ri zístənt/ *adj* resistant to the effects of radiant energy ○ *radioresistant tumors* —**ra·di·o·re·sis·tance** *n*

ra·di·os·co·py /ràydee óskəpee/ *n* the use of X-rays or another form of electromagnetic radiation to study the internal structure of something —**ra·di·o·scop·ic** /ràydee ō skóppik/ *adj* —**ra·di·o·scop·i·cal** *adj*

ra·di·o·sen·si·tive /ràydee ō sénssətiv/ *adj* sensitive to the biological effects of radiant energy such as X-rays —**ra·di·o·sen·si·tiv·i·ty** /-sènssətívvətee/ *n*

ra·di·o·sonde /ráydee ō sònd/ *n* an instrument carried aloft by a balloon and used to measure and transmit meteorological data by radio

ra·di·o spec·trum *n* the range of radio frequencies used for radio, television, and other electromagnetic communications, between 10 kHz and 300 MHz

ra·di·o·tel·e·phone /ràydee ō téllə fòn/ *n* a telephone that transmits sound signals by radio waves rather than through wires

ra·di·o tel·e·scope *n* an astronomical instrument used to detect and analyze radio waves from astronomical objects. It consists of an antenna, often in the form of a large dish, a detector, and an amplifier.

ra·di·o·tel·e·type /ràydee ō téllə tìp/ *n* **1.** a teletypewriter that transmits and receives by radio rather than along a cable **2.** a receiving and transmitting system that uses radioteletypes

ra·di·o·ther·a·py /ràydee ō thérrəpee/ *n* the treatment of disease using radiation X-rays or beta rays directed at the body from an external source or emitted by radioactive materials placed within the body —**ra·di·o·ther·a·peu·tic** /-thèrrə pyóotik/ *adj* —**ra·di·o·ther·a·pist** *n*

ra·di·o·tho·ri·um /ràydee ō tháwree əm/ *n* a radioactive isotope of the element thorium, with a mass number of 228

ra·di·o·tox·ic /ràydee ō tóksik/ *adj* relating to the toxic effects of radiation or radioactive substances

ra·di·o·trac·er /ràydee ō tráyssər/ *n* a radioactive substance introduced into the body as a tracer, e.g., to observe the steps in a chemical or biochemical process or locate diseased cells or tissue

ra·di·o wave *n* an electromagnetic wave whose frequency falls within the radio spectrum

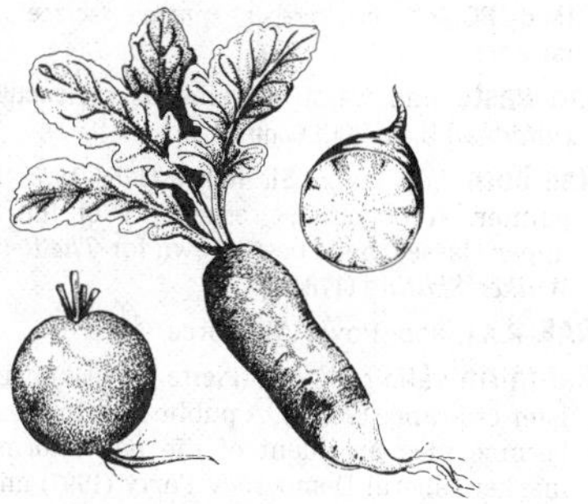

radish

rad·ish /ráddish/ *n* **1.** a crisp pungent round or bloated root, with a red or white skin, eaten raw **2.** a plant of the mustard family that produces radishes. Native to: Europe, Asia. Latin name: *Raphanus sativus.* [Pre-12C. < Latin *radic-* "root"]

Rad·is·son /ràddee sáwN/, **Pierre Esprit** (1636?–1710?) French-born Canadian explorer and fur trader. He is noted for his knowledge of Native North American life and Canadian geography.

ra·di·um /ráydee əm/ *n* a white highly radioactive metallic element. Source: pitchblende, carnotite. Use: luminous coatings, treatment of cancer. Symbol **Ra**. See table at **element** [Late 19C. < Latin *radius* "staff, spoke, ray, beam of light"; from the rays emitted by radium, which penetrate specific opaque materials]

ra·di·um ther·a·py *n* the medical use of radium to treat cancer and other diseases with radiation

ra·di·us /ráydee əss/ (*plural* **-di·i** /-dee ì/ or **-di·us·es**) *n* **1.** MATH LINE FROM CENTER a straight line extending from the center of a circle to its edge or from the center of a sphere to its surface. Symbol **r** **2.** MATH LENGTH OF RADIUS the length of a radius. Symbol **r** **3.** CIRCULAR AREA an area enclosed by a circle that has a radius of a particular length ○ *all the houses within a radius of 2 miles of the explosion* **4.** RANGE OF EFFECTIVENESS OR INFLUENCE the area or range within which somebody or something can act, work, or exert influence effectively ○ *beyond the radius of the governor's influence* **5.** ANAT BONE IN ARM OR FORELIMB the shorter and thicker of the two bones in the human forearm, the one on the thumb side, or the equivalent bone in the lower forelimbs of animals **6.** RADIATING PART a radiating line, part, or structure [Late 16C. < Latin, "staff, spoke, ray, beam of light"]

ra·di·us of ac·tion *n* **1.** a broadly circular area in which a military unit can operate or bring force to bear on an enemy **2.** the distance a vehicle, ship, or aircraft can travel and return safely to base without refueling

ra·di·us of cur·va·ture *n* the radius of the circle whose curvature matches that of a curve at a given point

ra·di·us vec·tor *n* **1.** a line connecting a fixed point or origin and a variable point, or the length of such a line **2.** a line connecting the center of an astronomical object and the center of another in orbit around it

ra·dix /ráydiks, ráddiks/ (*plural* **rad·i·ces** /ráddi seez, ráydi-/ or **ra·dix·es**) *n* **1.** the base of a number system or system of logarithms **2.** a root part or point where a plant or animal part begins [Late 16C. < Latin, "root, radish, foundation" < Indo-European]

RADM, **R.Adm.** *abbr* NAVY rear admiral

ra·dome /ráy dòm/ *n* a dome-shaped protective enclosure for a radar antenna, made from materials that do not interfere with the transmission and reception of radio waves [Mid-20C. Blend of RADAR + DOME]

ra·don /ráy dòn/ *n* a heavy gaseous radioactive element. Source: radioactive decay of radium, in small quantities in rock and soil. Use: radiotherapy.

Symbol **Rn**. See table at **element** [Early 20C. < RADIUM]

rad·u·la /rájjələ/ (*plural* **-lae** /-lee/ or **-las**) *n* a band of tissue in the mouth of some mollusks (**gastropods**) containing rows of small teeth, used in scraping off particles of food and bringing them into the mouth [Mid-18C. < Latin, "scraper" < *radere* "scrape"] —**rad·u·lar** *adj*

rad·waste /rád wàyst/ *n* same as **radioactive waste** (*informal*) [Late 20C. Contraction]

Rae·burn /ráy bùrn/, **Sir Henry** (1756–1823) Scottish painter. A portraitist, especially of the Scottish upper classes, he is best known for *The Rev. Robert Walker Skating* (1784).

RAF, **R.A.F.** *abbr* Royal Air Force

Raf·fa·rin /ràffə ráN/, **Jean-Pierre** (*b.* 1948) prime minister of France (2002–). A public relations expert, he became vice president of the newly-formed free-market Liberal Democracy Party (1997) and prime minister of the center-right coalition government (2002).

raf·fi·a /ráffee ə/, **raph·i·a** *n* **1.** fiber in the form of flexible straw-colored ribbons. Source: leaves of the raffia palm. Use: mats, baskets. **2.** TREES same as **raffia palm** [Late 19C. < Malagasy *rafia*]

raf·fi·a palm *n* a palm tree with large leaves that yield a strong fiber. Native to: Madagascar. Latin name: *Raphia ruffia*.

raf·fi·nate /ráffə nàyt/ *n* the remaining or refined part of a liquid mixture, left after other substances dissolved in it have been extracted [Early 20C. < French *raffinat* < *raffiner* "refine"]

raf·fi·nose /ráffə nōss, -nōz/ *n* a white crystalline slightly sweet sugar. Source: cottonseed meal, sugar beets, molasses. Formula: $C_{18}H_{32}O_{16}$. [Late 19C. < French *raffiner* "refine"]

raff·ish /ráffish/ *adj* **1.** displaying a charming free-spirited disregard for the conventions of society or for approved behavior ○ *a raffish politician whose engaging antics never alienated the voters* **2.** displaying an exaggerated or obtrusive showiness ○ *a raffish hotel* [Early 19C. < 2nd element of RIFFRAFF] —**raff·ish·ly** *adv* —**raff·ish·ness** *n*

raf·fle[1] /ráff'l/ *n* an event in which numbered tickets are sold, some of which are drawn at random to win prizes. The prizes in a raffle are often objects rather than money and raffles are usually held in order to raise money for some cause or organization. ■ *vt* (**-fled, -fling, -fles**) to offer or give away something as a prize in a raffle [14C. < Old French, "act of plundering"] —**raf·fler** *n*

raf·fle[2] /ráff'l/ *n* **1.** unwanted items or debris **2.** tangled ropes or other bits and pieces on a ship [Late 18C. Origin ?]

raf·fle·si·a /rə fléezhee ə, ra-, rə fléezhə, ra-/ *n* a leafless tropical plant that is a parasite of other plants and has large foul-smelling flowers that are pollinated by carrion flies. Native to: Asia. Genus: *Rafflesia*. [Early 19C. < modern Latin, after Sir Stamford *Raffles* (1781–1826), British colonial administrator]

raft[1] /raft/ *n* **1.** FLAT BOAT a flat floating structure made of wooden planks, logs, barrels, or similar materials, used as a boat or anchored in the water as a dock or diving platform **2.** INFLATABLE BOAT OR MAT an inflatable flat-bottomed rubber or plastic boat used for drifting along on a river, or an inflatable rectangular mat used for surfing or lounging in the water **3.** COLLECTION OF FLOATING OBJECTS a group of animals, especially wildfowl, or a mass of things floating or traveling together on water ○ *a raft of ducks* ■ *v* (**raft·ed, raft·ing, rafts**) **1.** *vt* MOVE SOMETHING BY RAFT to transport something by raft **2.** *vi* SAIL ON RAFT to travel on a raft **3.** *vt* FORM RAFT to form something into a raft, or make something gather together into a raft ○ *The lumberjacks rafted the logs together before sending them downstream.* [13C. < Old Norse *raptr* "log, beam"]

CULTURAL NOTE ***The Raft of the Medusa***, a painting (1819) by French artist Théodore Géricault. This monumental work is a harrowing depiction of the suffering of the survivors of an infamous 1816 shipwreck. Géricault's treatment of a contemporary subject in an epic style more traditionally associated with classical or historical themes was seen as a significant development in European art.

raft[2] /raft/ *n* a very large number or amount of something (*informal*) ○ *a whole raft of proposals* [Mid-19C. Alteration of 2nd element of RIFFRAFF, probably after RAFT[1]]

raf·ter[1] /ráftər/ *n* a sloping supporting timber, beam, or board that runs from the ridge beam of a roof to its edge [Old English *ræfter* < Germanic] —**raf·tered** *adj* —**raf·ter·ing** *n*

raft·er[2] /ráftər/ *n* **1.** a traveler on a raft **2.** a lumberjack who ties logs into a raft to transport them downstream [Early 19C. < RAFT[1]]

raft·ing /ráfting/ *n* the outdoor leisure pursuit of floating on a lake or river in a raft

rag[1] /rag/ *n* **1.** SMALL PIECE OF CLOTH a small piece or scrap of usually old or unwanted cloth used for cleaning, polishing, or applying liquid substances **2.** SMALL TATTERED PIECE a small, irregular, or tattered scrap or piece of material **3.** PIECE OF CLOTHING an item of clothing, thought of as being worn or tattered and not really fit to wear (*informal; often ironic*) **4.** INFERIOR NEWSPAPER a newspaper with low journalistic standards, or any newspaper regarded with contempt (*informal*) **5.** PAPER CLOTH FOR MAKING PAPER cloth or cloth fibers that are used in making paper ■ **rags** *npl* WORN-OUT CLOTHES clothes that are tattered, frayed, or torn [14C. Probably < Old Norse *rogg* "shaggy tuft"] ◇ **go from rags to riches** to start off in poverty and then become very wealthy ◇ **in rags** in a worn-out, tattered, and torn condition

rag[2] /rag/ (**rag·ged, rag·ging, rags**) *v* (*slang*) **1.** *vti* to subject somebody to persistent teasing or taunting **2.** *vt* to scold somebody persistently or vehemently [Mid-18C. Origin ?] —**rag·ging** *n*

rag[3] /rag/ *n* jazz in which a syncopated rhythm in the melody is accompanied by a steady beat, or a piece of music in this style ■ *vt* (**ragged, rag·ging, rags**) to compose or perform ragtime music [Late 19C. Origin ?]

rag[4] /rag/ *n* a roofing slate that has a rough surface on one side [13C. Origin ?]

ra·ga /raágə/ *n* a scale, melody, or rhythmic pattern that forms the basis of the classical music of South Asia. Particular ragas are associated with different times of the day, and are intended to create different moods. Performances may be partly or completely improvised. [Late 18C. < Sanskrit *rāga* "color, harmony"]

rag·a·muf·fin /rággə mùffən/ *n* a child dressed in worn or tattered clothes, often one allowed to roam the streets (*dated*) [14C. Origin ?]

rag·bag /rág bàg/ *n* **1.** a bag in which unwanted clothes and bits of cloth are kept for use as rags **2.** a collection of miscellaneous things (*informal*) [Early 19C. < RAG[1]]

rag doll *n* a floppy stuffed cloth doll [< RAG[1]]

rage /rayj/ *n* **1.** EXTREME ANGER sudden and extreme anger ○ *tears of rage* **2.** ANGRY OUTBURST an outburst of strong anger ○ *flew into a rage* **3.** OBJECT OF FAD something that is the object of a short-lived fascination, fashion, or enthusiasm shared by many people ○ *Those toys are all the rage for kids at the moment.* **4.** FORCE OR INTENSITY extreme or unrelenting intensity **5.** STRONG PASSION OR ENTHUSIASM a strong and sometimes overpowering desire or enthusiasm ■ *vi* (**raged, rag·ing, rag·es**) **1.** ACT WITH OR FEEL RAGE to speak or do something with sudden, extreme anger, or feel such strong anger **2.** OCCUR WITH VIOLENCE to occur, continue, move, or spread with great force and violence ○ *The storm raged for three days.* [13C. Via French < Vulgar Latin *rabia*, alteration of Latin *rabies* (see RABIES)]

SYNONYMS See ***anger***.

ra·gee *n* FOOD, PLANTS another spelling of **ragi**

~~**rageing**~~ incorrect spelling of **raging**

rag·ga /rággə/ *n* a style of reggae characterized by long rap monologues and repetitive beats [Late 20C. Shortening of RAGAMUFFIN]

rag·ged /rággəd/ *adj* **1.** TATTERED frayed or torn into irregular shapes or pieces, especially along the edge **2.** WEARING RAGS dressed in torn, tattered, or frayed clothes **3.** HAVING UNEVEN EDGE OR SURFACE having a surface, edge, or outline that is rough, uneven, or jagged **4.** UNKEMPT rough and irregular in appearance and suggesting neglect and a lack of grooming ○ *a ragged beard* **5.** OF VARYING QUALITY of unequal quality, some parts being less good than others ○ *The acting in the play was rather ragged.* **6.** NOT FIRM OR REGULAR done in an uncoordinated, hesitant, or irregular way, especially by a group who do not manage to do something all together or in unison **7.** EXHAUSTED extremely tired or anxious [13C. < RAG[1]] —**rag·ged·ly** *adv* —**rag·ged·ness** *n*

rag·ged rob·in *n* a perennial plant of the pink family. Flowers: pink or white, with ragged petals. Latin name: *Lychnis floscuculi*.

rag·ged·y /rággədee/ *adj* (*informal*) **1.** TATTERED having been torn and worn excessively **2.** BADLY DRESSED wearing worn-out torn clothes **3.** ROUGH OR UNEVEN having rough untidy ends or edges

rag·gee *n* FOOD, PLANTS another spelling of **ragi**

rag·gle-tag·gle /rágg'l tágg'l, rágg'l tàgg'l/ *adj* consisting of a mixture of strange or very different things, often with an element of messiness or scruffiness [Early 20C. Alteration of RAGTAG]

ra·gi /rággee/, **ra·gee**, **rag·gee** *n* **1.** the grain of a cereal grass used as food in South Asia and parts of Africa **2.** a cereal grass cultivated for ragi. Latin name: *Eleusine coracana*. [Late 18C. < Hindi *rāgī*]

rag·ing /ráyjing/ *adj* **1.** VERY ANGRY out of control or angry **2.** VERY STRONG done or happening with great force or intensity **3.** VERY SEVERE OR PAINFUL very severe and causing great pain or distress ○ *a raging toothache* **4.** CONSIDERABLE very good or great ○ *The play was a raging success.*

rag·lan /rágglən/ *adj* **1.** EXTENDING TO COLLAR describes a sleeve extending to the collar of a garment instead of ending at the shoulder, attached with slanting seams running from under the arm to the neck **2.** HAVING RAGLAN SLEEVES made with raglan sleeves ■ *n* GARMENT WITH RAGLAN SLEEVES an overcoat, sweater, or other garment that has raglan sleeves [Mid-19C. After Lord *Raglan* (1788–1855), British field marshal]

Rag·na·rök /raágnə ràwk/ *n* in Norse mythology, the final destruction of the gods in a great battle against the forces of evil, after which a new world will arise [Mid-18C. < Old Norse *ragnarök* "fate of the gods" < *regin* "gods" + *rok* "fate"]

ra·gout /ra góo/ *n* a rich slow-cooked stew of meat and vegetables [Mid-17C. < French < *ragoûter* "renew the appetite" < *goût* "taste" < Latin *gustus*]

rag·pick·er /rág pìkər/ *n* a gatherer and seller of old clothes and other discarded items [Mid-19C. < RAG[1]]

rag rug *n* a rug made by knotting or hooking short strips of waste fabric through a base to form a shaggy pile [< RAG[1]]

rag·stone /rág stòn/ *n* a hard sandstone or limestone that tends to break up into slabs and is used as a building material [14C. < RAG[4]]

rag·tag /rág tàg/ *adj* **1.** made up of a wide-ranging mix of people or things, often ones that are of questionable quality ○ *a ragtag team made up of friends and acquaintances* **2.** messy, unkempt, or ragged in appearance [Late 19C. < RAG[1]]

rag·tag and bob·tail *n* people who are considered members of the lowest social classes, especially when regarded as dissatisfied with their lives and likely to be disorderly or rebellious (*dated insult*)

rag·time /rág tìm/ *n* a style of US popular music of the late 19th and early 20th centuries characterized by distinctive syncopated right-hand rhythms against a regularly accented left-hand beat. Ragtime was widely popularized by the pianist and composer Scott Joplin. [Late 19C. < RAG[3]]

rag·top /rág tòp/ *n* a car with a retractable fabric roof (*slang*) [Mid-20C. < RAG[1]]

rag trade *n* the clothing industry and the various professions involved in the design, manufacture, and sale of clothing (*slang*) [< RAG[1]]

rag·weed /rág wèed/ *n* **1.** a weedy plant with small green flower heads producing large amounts of pollen that causes hay fever in many people. Native to: North America. Genus: *Ambrosia*. **2.** UK PLANTS same as **ragwort** [Mid-17C. < RAG[1]; from the raggedness of the leaves]

rag·worm /rág wùrm/ *n Can, UK* same as **clamworm** [Mid-19C. < RAG[1]; from the ragged appearance of its appendages]

rag·wort /rág wùrt, -wàwrt/ *n* a plant that has clusters of small yellow flowers with radiating petals like those of daisies. Genus: *Senecio.* [15C. < RAG[1]; from the raggedness of the leaves]

rah /raa/ *interj* used to express approval or encouragement (*informal*) [Mid-19C. Shortening of HURRAH]

Rah·man /rə maán/, **Mujibur** (1920–75) Bangladesh politician. The founding father of Bangladesh, he served as the country's first prime minister (1972–75). He was assassinated in a military coup soon after becoming president in 1975.

Rah·man, Ziaur (1935–81) president of Bangladesh (1977–81). During his presidency, he ended martial law but was assassinated in an attempted military coup.

rah-rah /raá raa/ *adj* spiritedly and often unthinkingly enthusiastic (*slang*) ○ *the rah-rah attitude of the project's supporters* [Early 20C. Doubling of RAH]

raid /rayd/ *n* **1.** SUDDEN ATTACK a sudden attack made by soldiers, aircraft, police, bandits, or any other force in an attempt to seize or destroy something **2.** BUSINESS ENTICEMENT OF VALUED PEOPLE in the business world, an attempt by an organization to hire or lure away a competitor's employees, members, or clients ○ *a raid by one advertising agency on another's clients* **3.** FIN PURCHASE OF SHARES TO CONTROL the buying of shares of a company's stock in an attempt to gain control of the company ○ *The company beat off the raid but took on debt to buy its own stock.* **4.** FIN ILLEGAL ATTEMPT TO LOWER STOCK PRICE the illegal coordinated selling of shares in a company's stock by a group of speculators in an attempt to make the stock price fall ■ *v* (**raid·ed, raid·ing, raids**) **1.** *vti* MAKE SURPRISE ATTACK to make or participate in a raid on somebody or something **2.** *vt* STEAL SOMETHING FROM SOMEWHERE to take something secretly or stealthily because it is illegal or forbidden ○ *The bank's funds had been raided by its former president.* **3.** *vt* BUSINESS LURE SOMEBODY AWAY to lure somebody away from another organization, usually from a competitor ○ *The new hockey league began to raid players from its rival.* [15C. Scots dialect form of ROAD] —**raid·er** *n*

rail[1] /rayl/ *n* **1.** LONG PIECE OF WOOD OR METAL a long horizontal or sloping piece of wood, metal, or other material that is used as a barrier, support, or place to hang things **2.** FENCE OR RAILING a structure made of a rail or rails and their supports, e.g., a fence or railing (*often used in the plural*) **3.** RAIL STEEL BAR OF RAILROAD TRACK a narrow steel bar, or a series of connected bars laid in two parallel lines, supporting and guiding the wheels of railroad locomotives and cars or anything similar **4.** TRANSP RAILROAD the railroad as a means or form of transportation ○ *We'll ship the goods by rail.* ○ *rail travel* ■ *vt* (**railed, rail·ing, rails**) PUT RAIL ON OR AROUND SOMETHING to put a rail or railing on or around something to provide a guard, barrier, or support ○ *They ought to rail off the playground.* [13C. Via Old French *reille* "bar" < Latin *regula* "straight stick, rod"] —**rail·less** /ráyl liss/ *adj* ◇ **go off the rails 1.** to begin to go wrong and lose direction **2.** to begin to behave in an unacceptable, irresponsible, or illegal way

rail[2] /rayl/ (**railed, rail·ing, rails**) *vi* to denounce, protest against, or attack somebody or something in bitter or harsh language ○ *Some people rail against the injustice of the system.* [15C. Via French *railler* "mock, tease" < Old Provençal *ralhar* "chat, joke" < late Latin *ragere* "neigh, roar"] —**rail·er** *n*

rail[3] /rayl/ (*plural* **rails** or *same*) *n* a small or medium-sized wading bird with a short tail, short wings, and long toes. Family: Rallidae. [15C. < Old French *raale* < Latin *ras-*, past participle of *radere* "scrape"]

rail·bird /ráyl bùrd/ *n* an enthusiastic fan of a sport, especially a horseracing fan who stands at the fence bordering the track in order to get close to the action (*slang*) [Late 19C. < RAIL[1] "fence bounding a racetrack," after JAILBIRD]

rail·car /ráyl kaàr/ *n* a railroad car [Mid-19C. < RAIL[1]]

rail fence *n US regional, Can* a fence made of split logs, either fastened to upright poles or laid across each other [< RAIL[1]]

REGIONAL NOTE See *zigzag fence.*

rail·head /ráyl hèd/ *n* **1.** the farthest point to which the track of a railroad line runs **2.** a place where supplies, often military materials, are unloaded from railcars for distribution to other points [Early 20C. < RAIL[1]]

rail·ing /ráyling/ *n* **1.** a structure consisting of one or more rails and their supports, used to provide a barrier or support in walking or climbing, or the upper rail of such a structure **2.** long horizontal pieces of sturdy material for making a railing [14C. < RAIL[1]]

rail·ler·y /ráylərее/ (*plural* **-ies**) *n* **1.** humorous, playful, or friendly ridiculing of somebody or something **2.** a remark that ridicules somebody or something jokingly and with good humor [Mid-17C. < French *raillerie* < *railler*]

rail·link /ráyl lìngk/ *n* a short connecting rail line, usually between a city center and an airport [Late 20C. < RAIL[1]]

rail·road /ráyl rṑd/ *n* **1.** TRACK MADE OF RAILS a track consisting of steel rails usually fastened to wood or concrete ties, designed to carry a locomotive and its cars or anything similar **2.** RAIL SYSTEM a network of railroad lines, together with the trains, buildings, equipment, and staff needed to operate a rail transport system, or the organization or company that owns or runs this ■ *v* (**-road·ed, -road·ing, -roads**) **1.** *vt* FORCE SOMETHING THROUGH QUICKLY WITHOUT DISCUSSION to push something through a legislature, committee, or other decision-making body quickly so that there is not enough time for objections to be considered (*informal*) **2.** *vt* FORCE SOMEBODY TO ACT HASTILY to force a person or group to make a decision or take action quickly, without time for consideration or discussion (*informal*) **3.** *vt* CONVICT SOMEBODY TOO QUICKLY to convict somebody on the basis of flimsy or false evidence (*informal*) **4.** *vt US* RAIL SHIP SOMETHING BY RAIL to transport or send something by rail **5.** *vi US* BE RAILROAD WORKER to work on a railroad ○ *She used to railroad for the Southern Pacific.* [Mid-18C. < RAIL[1]]

rail·road flat *n US* an apartment that has its rooms arranged in a straight line, often also lacking a hallway, so that one room can only be entered through another

rail·road·ing /ráyl rṑding/ *n US* constructing a railroad line, or operating or managing it

rail·slide /ráyl slìd/ (**-slid** /-slìd/, **-slid·ing, -slides**) *vi* in skateboarding, to slide along the top or upper edge of a ramp or obstacle using the bottom of the board rather than the wheels [Late 20C. < RAIL[1]]

rail-split·ter *n US* somebody who or a device that splits logs to make rails and posts for use in fences [< RAIL[1]]

rail·way /ráyl wày/ *n* **1.** a railroad system, especially one that uses lighter-weight equipment and operates in a limited area **2.** *Can, UK* same as **railroad** [Late 17C. < RAIL[1]] —**rail·way·man** *n*

rai·ment /ráymənt/ *n* CLOTHING same as **clothing** (sense 1) (*archaic or literary*) [14C. Shortening of *arrayment*]

rain /rayn/ *n* **1.** WATER FALLING FROM CLOUDS water condensed from vapor in the atmosphere and falling in drops from clouds **2.** PERIOD OF WET WEATHER any storm, shower, or other quantity of water falling from the sky **3.** RAINY WEATHER weather marked by heavy or persistent rainfall **4.** GREAT NUMBER OR FLOW a great number of small individual things coming in a steady flow or anything else flowing or falling like rain ○ *A rain of dust fell from the crumbling ceiling.* ■ **rains** *npl* RAINY SEASON in some countries, a season of the year when a lot of rain falls ■ *v* (**rained, rain·ing, rains**) **1.** *vi* DROP RAIN to fall from the sky or release water in the form of rain ○ *It's raining again.* **2.** *vti* COME IN GREAT NUMBER to come or fall in the form of a great number of units arriving separately but in very quick succession or in a continuous stream, or drop or deliver something in this way ○ *Missiles rained down on us from the defenders on the battlements.* ○ *Reporters rained questions on the beleaguered police chief.* **3.** *vt* GIVE SOMETHING GENEROUSLY to give somebody something in large quantities, continuously, and over a considerable period of time ○ *Generous to a fault, they positively rained gifts on all their friends.* [Old English *regn, rēn* < Germanic] —**rain·less** *adj* ◇ **(as) right as rain** perfectly all right (*informal*) ◇ **(come) rain or shine** whatever the weather or the circumstances ○ *The picnic will be held, rain or shine.*

SPELLCHECK rain, reign, or **rein**? Do not confuse the spelling of ***rain***, ***reign***, and ***rein***, which sound similar. ***Rain*** refers to water falling from the sky: *The crops need rain. It rained all afternoon.* ***Reign*** refers to the rule of a monarch, or to the dominant factor in a situation: *The castle was built during the reign of King Henry VIII. Confusion reigned in the town.* ***Rein*** refers to a strap for controlling a horse, or to any other similar means of restraint: *He pulled on the reins to stop the horse. They kept a tight rein on expenditures. She reined back her mount.*

rain off *vt UK* same as **rain out** (*usually passive*)

rain out *vt* to cause something such as a game to be canceled or postponed because of rain

rain·bird /ráyn bùrd/ *n* a bird thought to call before rainstorms, e.g., a green woodpecker or some members of the cuckoo family

rain·bow /ráyn bṑ/ *n* **1.** MULTICOLORED ARC IN SKY an arc of light separated into bands of color that appears when the Sun's rays are refracted and reflected by drops of mist or rain. The colors of the rainbow are conventionally said to be red, orange, yellow, green, blue, indigo, and violet. **2.** ARC OF BANDS OF COLOR a multicolored arc similar to a rainbow **3.** BRIGHT MULTICOLORED SIGHT an arrangement, display, or sight containing many bright colors or bright multicolored objects ○ *the rainbow of colors on an artist's palette* **4.** FALSE HOPE a goal, hope, or ideal that is unlikely to be achieved or realized **5.** VARIED ASSORTMENT a wide range or varied assortment of things, usually coexisting without clashing ■ *adj* **1.** HAVING VARIED COLORS having the colors of the rainbow or colors as varied as those of a rainbow **2.** MADE OF MANY DIFFERENT THINGS comprising a wide variety of types or elements, especially made up of people of different ethnic groups or from a variety of minority groups ○ *a rainbow coalition*

CULTURAL NOTE ***The Rainbow***, a novel (1915) by British writer D. H. Lawrence. Set in the English Midlands between 1840 and 1905, it describes the impact of contemporary social developments on the lifestyles and attitudes of succeeding generations of a provincial family, the Brangwens. The latter part of the book focuses on Ursula, the family's first independent woman, whose story is continued in a subsequent novel *Women in Love* (1920).

rain·bow cac·tus *n* a tall, cylindrical cactus, of which there are two varieties differing in flower color. Flowers: yellow or magenta. Native to: southwestern United States, Mexico. Latin name: *Echinocereus pectinatus.*

rain·bow curve *n* in baseball, a curveball with an exceptionally great arc

rain·bow trout *n* a freshwater game fish with a reddish or pinkish band along either side of its body and numerous black spots. Native to: North America, but widely introduced elsewhere. Latin name: *Salmo gairdneri.*

rain check *n* **1.** a ticket or ticket stub entitling somebody to attend an event canceled because of rain at a later rescheduled time **2.** a promise or coupon guaranteeing that an offer that cannot be fulfilled or accepted at present will be fulfilled or accepted at a later time ◇ **take a rain check (on something)** to delay doing something until a later date or time (*informal*)

rain·coat /ráyn kṑt/ *n* a coat designed to keep the wearer dry when worn in the rain, with a water-resistant or waterproof surface or coating

rain date *n* a date that an event will be rescheduled to if rainy weather forces cancellation on the intended date

rain·drop /ráyn dròp/ *n* a drop of water that falls from a cloud in the sky

rain·fall /ráyn fàwl/ *n* 1. the amount of rain that falls in a location over a period of time ○ *the annual rainfall in a city* 2. a rain shower or rainstorm

rain for·est *n* a thick evergreen tropical forest found in areas of heavy rainfall and containing trees with broad leaves that form a continuous canopy

rain gauge *n* a device used to measure the amount of rain that falls in a location

rain gut·ter *n regional* a gutter on a building

rain hat *n* a hat that provides protection from rain for the wearer's head

Rai·nier III /ray neér, rə-, rə nyáy/ (*b.* 1923) **prince of Monaco** He acceded to the throne in 1949, and in 1962 agreed to a new constitution reducing the power of the monarchy. Born **Grimaldi, Rainier Louis Henri Maxence Bertrand de**

Rai·nier, Mount /rə neér, ray-/ highest peak in Washington. It is a dormant volcano, with a permanently snow-covered summit. Height: 14,410 ft./4,392 m.

rain lil·y *n* PLANTS same as **zephyr lily**

rain·mak·er /ráyn màykər/ *n* 1. HIGH ACHIEVER an achiever of outstanding results in a profession or politics (*informal*) ○ *a rainmaker in the law firm who accrued thousands of billing hours on big clients* 2. SOMEBODY WHO CAUSES RAIN somebody whose job is cloud-seeding especially in times of severe drought (*informal*) 3. SOMEBODY MAGICALLY CAUSING RAIN somebody who is believed to have the magic powers to make rain fall —**rain·mak·ing** *n*

rain·out /ráyn òwt/ *n* an event that is canceled or postponed because of rainy weather, or the cancellation or postponement of an event because of rain ○ *The second game of today's double-header is a makeup for a March rainout.*

rain·proof /ráyn proòf/ *adj* designed or treated to prevent rain from soaking in or passing through ■ *vt* (**-proofed, -proof·ing, -proofs**) to treat something such as an item of clothing so that it becomes rainproof

rain shad·ow *n* an area on the side of a mountain barrier that is sheltered from prevailing winds and rain-bearing clouds, resulting in relatively dry conditions

rain·spout /ráyn spòwt/ *n Northeast US* a roof gutter or downspout

rain·squall /ráyn skwàwl/ *n* a sudden, brief storm of strong winds and heavy rain

rain·storm /ráyn stàwrm/ *n* a storm with heavy or steady rain

rain tree *n* a tree with pale pink flowers and long horizontal branches, whose wood is used in the manufacture of furniture. Native to: tropical America. Latin name: *Albizia saman.* [Because its leaves close up when it rains]

rain·wash /ráyn wòsh, -wàwsh/ *n* rock and soil washed away and deposited elsewhere by rainwater, or the process of erosion by rainwater

rain·wa·ter /ráyn wàwtər/ *n* water that has fallen as rain, which usually has relatively small amounts of minerals dissolved in it

rain·wear /ráyn wèr/ *n* clothing, mainly outerwear, that is waterproof and is designed to keep the wearer dry in rainy weather

rain·y /ráynee/ (**-i·er, -i·est**) *adj* characterized by or bringing rain, especially long or frequently recurring periods of rainfall —**rain·i·ly** *adv* —**rain·i·ness** *n*

rain·y day *n* a possible time of need in the future

Rai·pur /rī poór/ capital city of Chhattisgarh State in eastern India. Population: 438,639 (1991).

raise /rayz/ *v* (**raised, rais·ing, rais·es**) 1. *vt* MOVE SOMETHING HIGHER to cause somebody or something to move to a higher level or position ○ *She was too weak to raise her head from the pillow.* 2. *vt* ACT AS PARENT OR GUARDIAN TO SOMEBODY to look after somebody as or like a parent, while he or she is growing up (*often passive*) ○ *After my parents died, I was raised by my grandfather.* 3. *vt* MAKE SOMETHING LARGER OR GREATER to increase something in size, amount, value, or scope ○ *They've raised the ticket prices yet again.* 4. *vt* GROW OR BREED SOMETHING to grow vegetables or breed and care for animals, usually for profit or personal satisfaction 5. *vt* PUT SOMETHING UP to set up, erect, or build something ○ *Neighbors helped us raise a new barn on the weekend.* 6. *vt* CAUSE SOMETHING TO SWELL UP to make something rise up or swell up, e.g., on somebody's skin 7. *vt* INTENSIFY SOMETHING to increase something in degree, strength, or pitch ○ *raised their voices* 8. *vt* OFFER SOMETHING FOR CONSIDERATION to put something forward for consideration or discussion ○ *I'd like to raise a number of points that I think need clarification.* 9. *vt* START SOMETHING NOISY to start something that involves a lot of loud noise or boisterous activity ○ *Raise the alarm!* 10. *vt* DIRECT SOMETHING AT HIGHER ANGLE to direct something upward, or make something point at a higher angle ○ *She answered without raising her eyes from the book.* 11. *vt* MAKE SOMEBODY STAND OR SIT UP to move yourself or somebody else to a standing or sitting position 12. *vt* COLLECT SOMETHING TOGETHER to gather something together, collect something, or ask for something and be given it ○ *raising money for the local orphanage* 13. *vt* MATH MULTIPLY NUMBER to multiply a term or number by itself a particular number of times ○ *2 raised by the power of 4 is 16.* 14. *vti* CARDS INCREASE BET OR BID in poker and other games, to increase a bet, or bet more than another player, often specifying the amount of the increase 15. *vt* CARDS INCREASE PARTNER'S BID in bridge, to make a higher bid in the suit bid by your partner 16. *vt* COMMUNICATION CONTACT SOMEBODY BY RADIO to get into contact with somebody by radio ○ *The carrier tried to raise the overdue plane.* 17. *vt* ROUSE SOMEBODY to rouse somebody from sleep, or bring a dead person back to life ○ *They were shouting loud enough to raise the dead.* 18. *vt* MIL END SIEGE to end a siege by withdrawing the besieging force or forcing it to withdraw 19. *vt* END SOMETHING to bring a ban or restriction imposed on somebody to an end ○ *finally raised the arms embargo* 20. *vt* IMPROVE SOMETHING to make something better in some way ○ *Their visit raised his spirits.* 21. *vt* IMPROVE SOMEBODY'S CONDITION to improve somebody's situation or condition, or move somebody to a higher rank or status ○ *After three years, he was raised to the rank of sergeant.* 22. *vt* CAUSE SOMETHING to cause something to appear, arise, form, or occur ○ *The strict new rules raised a storm of protest.* 23. *vt* GIVE SIGN OF FEELING to produce a response such as a smile or cheer, or cause somebody else to produce one ○ *She obviously felt awful, but still managed to raise a faint smile.* 24. *vt* PARANORMAL CALL SOMETHING UP to attempt to cause a supernatural being to appear, e.g., by special ceremonies or magic 25. *vt* PUT SOMEBODY IN AUTHORITY to place somebody in a position of power or authority (*literary*) 26. *vt US* FIN FRAUDULENTLY INCREASE SOMETHING'S VALUE to increase the face value of something, especially a check, in an attempt to defraud somebody ○ *The embezzler was caught raising checks.* 27. *vt* STRETCH SOMETHING OUT to make something such as a crest or frill stretch out and become more visible 28. *vt* NAUT SEE LAND APPEAR ON HORIZON to sight land on the horizon after a sea voyage ○ *The ship raised Bermuda two days after leaving New York.* 29. *vt* COOK MAKE DOUGH RISE to make dough rise and swell by using yeast or a similar agent 30. *vt* PHON REPLACE VOWEL BY HIGHER VOWEL to replace a vowel by one formed with the tongue higher in the mouth 31. *vi US* same as **rise** (*nonstandard*) ○ *"Jimmy gazed at her in such consternation that he felt his hair begin to raise!"* (George Randolph Chester, *The Jingo*; 1912) ■ *n* 1. PAY INCREASE an increase in somebody's rate of pay 2. ACT OF INCREASING the raising of somebody or something, or the amount by which somebody or something is raised, e.g., in cards [12C. < Old Norse *reisa* < Germanic] —**rais·a·ble** *adj* —**rais·er** *n*

SYNONYMS ***raise, elevate, lift, hoist***

CORE MEANING: to move something to a higher position

raise to cause something to move to a higher level or position ○ *Merrill raised her wrist to peer at her watch.* ○ *He raised his eyebrows and gave her a cool stare.* **elevate** to raise something to a higher level or position (less commonly used than "raise") ○ *You might want to elevate the head of the bed at night.* **lift** to move something from one position to another, higher position ○ *She felt too exhausted even to lift the remote control off the sofa.* ○ *His colleagues had tried to lift him out with a rope and safety harness.* **hoist** to raise something, especially using a mechanical device such as a winch ○ *They made ready to hoist the sail.* ○ *An enormous crane hoisted the steel beams to the roof.*

raised /rayzd/ *adj* made so that its surface is higher than its background or what surrounds it ○ *raised lettering on an envelope*

raised beach *n* a former beach found above the present shoreline of a sea or lake following a fall in water level or a rise in land level. Raised beaches are common in areas once glaciated, which rise as the land surface readjusts to the removal of the weight of a former icecap.

raised point *n US* 1. a large half cross-stitch used in embroidery 2. embroidery done with raised point ▶ Can term **gros point**

raised work *n* embroidery stitches that produce a raised surface on the fabric or that are worked over a piece of padding

rai·sin /ráyz'n/ *n* a sweet grape that has been dried in the sun or by being processed with heat, usually to prevent spoiling and permit long-term storage [14C. Via French, "grape" < Latin *racemus* "bunch, cluster"]

rai·son d'é·tat /rày zawn day táa/ (*plural* **rai·sons d'é·tat** /*pronunc. same*/) *n* an overriding concern, usually the interests of the country concerned, that justifies political or diplomatic action that might otherwise be considered reprehensible [< French, "reason of state"]

rai·son d'ê·tre /rày zawn déttrə/ (*plural* **rai·sons d'ê·tre** /*pronunc. same*/) *n* something that gives meaning or purpose to somebody's life, or the justification for something's existence [< French, "reason for being"]

Raj /raaj/ *n* in South Asia, the period of British rule up to 1947 of what are now the countries of India, Pakistan, Bangladesh, Nepal, Bhutan, and Sri Lanka [Late 18C. Via Hindi *rāj* < Sanskrit *rājya* "kingdom, rule"]

ra·ja *n* POL another spelling of **rajah**

Raj·ab /rújjəb/ *n* in the Islamic calendar, the seventh month of the year. See table at **calendar** [Late 18C. < Arabic]

ra·jah /ráajə/, **ra·ja** *n* a Hindu king, prince, or chief in South Asia or parts of Southeast Asia [Mid-16C. Via Hindi *rājā* < Sanskrit *rājan* "king"]

Ra·ja·sthan /ráajə staán/, **Rā·ja·sthān** state in northwestern India, bordering Pakistan. Capital: Jaipur. Population: 56,473,122 (2001). Area: 132,139 sq. mi./342,239 sq. km.

Ra·jas·tha·ni /ráajə staánee/ *n* 1. an Indic group of languages spoken in northwestern India and neighboring parts of Pakistan. Native speakers: 25 million. 2. somebody who comes from Rajasthan [Early 20C. < Hindi *Rājasthānī* < *Rājasthān* "Rajasthan"] —**Ra·jas·tha·ni** *adj*

Raj·kot /ráaj kōt/ city and administrative headquarters of Rajkot District, in Gujarat State, west central India. Population: 559,407 (1991).

Raj·neesh /ráaj neésh/, **Bhaghwan Shree** (1931–90) Indian spiritual teacher. As founder of the Neo-Sannyas Movement in the late 1960s, he established meditation centers in India, Europe, and the United States. Born **Mohan, Rajneesh Chandra**

Raj·put /ráaj poòt/ *n* a member of one group of the Kshatriya caste, the second of the four Hindu castes [Late 16C. < Hindi *rājpūt* "king's son" < Sanskrit *rājan* "king" + *putra* "son"]

Raj·ya Sa·bha /ráajyə súbbə/ *n* the upper house of India's national parliament [< Sanskrit, "state assembly"]

Ra·kai·a /rə kī́ ə/ river in the South Island, New Zealand. It rises in the Southern Alps and flows into the Pacific Ocean west of the Banks Peninsula. Length: 90 mi./145 km.

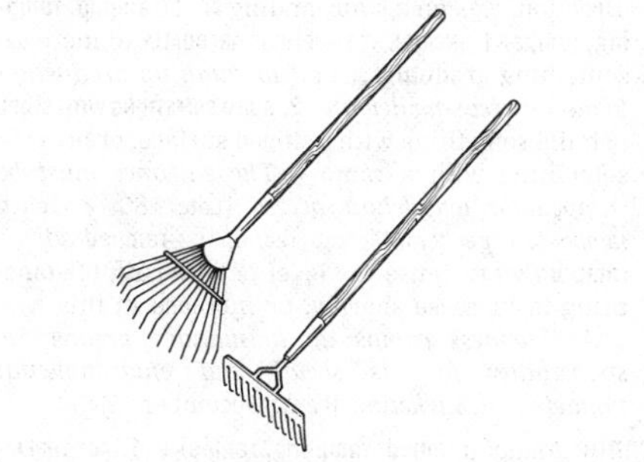

rake

rake[1] /rayk/ *n* **1. LONG-HANDLED TOOTHED GARDENING TOOL** a tool with a long handle and a head with long teeth, used for gathering leaves or cut grass, or for smoothing or loosening the surface of the soil in a garden **2. TOOL RESEMBLING GARDEN RAKE** a tool that is broadly similar to a garden rake but is used for a different purpose, e.g., digging clams or gathering money at a gambling table ■ *v* **(raked, rak·ing, rakes) 1.** *vti* **MOVE SOMETHING WITH RAKE** to gather something together, or remove or clear something, using a rake or similar implement ○ *raked up the dead leaves* **2.** *vti* **WORK WITH RAKE** to make something neat, smooth something out, or loosen something using a rake or similar tool **3.** *vti* **SEARCH THROUGH SOMETHING** to search through or examine something thoroughly, or make a search for something **4.** *vt* **USE SOMETHING LIKE RAKE** to draw or move something through or across something else like a rake ○ *She raked her fingers through her hair.* **5.** *vt* **SCRAPE OR SCRATCH SOMETHING** to claw, scrape, or scratch somebody or something with a dragging movement ○ *The cat raked my arm with its claws.* **6.** *vti* **PASS ACROSS SOMETHING** to pass across the whole length or extent of something in a continuous sweeping movement, or cause something to do this ○ *The spotlight raked around the perimeter fence.* **7.** *vti* **SHOOT ALONG LENGTH OF SOMETHING** to aim shots from a gun or guns in quick succession over the whole length or extent of something ○ *The ship's cannon raked the land battery.* [Old English *raca, racu* < Germanic] ◇ **rake somebody over the coals** to reprimand somebody severely

rake in *vt* to take in large quantities of something, especially money gained or earned with relatively little effort (*informal*)

rake together *vt* to gather people or things together with difficulty (*informal*)

rake up *vt* (*informal*) **1.** to mention or bring up for discussion something unfortunate or undesirable that happened in the past **2.** same as **rake together**

rake[2] /rayk/ *n* an unrestrained indulger in pleasures and vices, e.g., drinking and gambling [Mid-17C. Shortening of *rakehell*, by folk etymology < obsolete *rakel* "hasty, rash," origin ?]

CULTURAL NOTE ***The Rake's Progress***, a series of paintings (1735?) by British artist William Hogarth. These eight satirical scenes, which were much influenced by contemporary theater, depict the moral decline of a young city gentleman who inherits a fortune and squanders it on vice. Hogarth created engravings of the same images, which were immensely popular. In 1951, Igor Stravinsky turned the story into an opera with a libretto by W. H. Auden.

rake[3] /rayk/ *n* **1. SLANT OR SLOPE** a slant away from an upright or perpendicular position, or an incline upward from a flat or horizontal position such as that on a ship or a stage **2.** AVIAT **ANGLE OF WING OR PROPELLER** the angle that a wing or propeller blade of an aircraft makes with a perpendicular or line of symmetry ■ *vti* **(raked, rak·ing, rakes) ANGLE** to design or build something with a slant or slope away from the vertical or horizontal, or be designed or built in this way ○ *a jet with wings that rake sharply back* [Early 17C. Origin ?]

rake-and-scrape *vi Carib* to save money little by little, with great difficulty, usually for a specific purpose

rake-and-scrape band *n Carib* a rural folk-band including skin drum, accordion, rattle, and bottle or piece of iron

rake-off *n* a portion or share of a profit, fee, or something similar, especially as a bribe or other illegal or morally dubious payment (*informal*) [< RAKE[1]]

Ra·khi *n* HINDUISM same as **Raksha Bandhan**

rak·i /raákee, ráykee/ *n* an anise-flavored alcoholic drink from the eastern Mediterranean, especially a brandy made in Turkey and the Balkans from grapes, plums, or grain [Late 17C. Via Turkish *rāqī* < Arabic *araḳī*]

rak·ish[1] /ráykish/ *adj* **1.** stylish in a dashing or sporty way ○ *a hat worn at a rakish angle* **2.** having a streamlined look that suggests rapid movement through the water ○ *a rakish yacht* [Early 19C. < RAKE[3]] —**rak·ish·ly** *adv* —**rak·ish·ness** *n*

rak·ish[2] /ráykish/ *adj* having or showing a strong concern for presenting a stylish self-confident appearance [Early 18C. < RAKE[2]] —**rak·ish·ly** *adv*—**rak·ish·ness** *adv*

Rak·sha Band·han /rùk shaa búndən/, **Ra·khi** *n* a Hindu festival celebrating the bond between brother and sister. Date: middle of Sravana. [< Sanskrit, "knot of protection"]

ra·ku /raákoo/ *n* a pottery technique in which pots are raw-glazed at a low temperature then taken red-hot from the kiln and plunged in water or sawdust for reduction or carbonizing [Late 19C. < Japanese, "ease, enjoyment"]

rale /raal, ral/, **râle** *n* an intermittent crackling or bubbling sound produced by fluid in the air passages and air sacs of the lungs and heard through a stethoscope [Early 19C. < French *râle* < *râler* "make a rattling sound in the throat"]

Ra·leigh /ráwlee, raá-/ capital city of North Carolina, located in the center of the state. Population: 306,944 (2002 estimate).

Ra·leigh, Sir Walter (1554–1618) English navigator and writer. A favorite of Queen Elizabeth I, he led three expeditions to the Americas, and made the first attempt to found an English colony at Roanoke Island, North Carolina (1585). He wrote his *History of the World* (1614) while imprisoned for treason (1603–16?).

> "[History] hath triumphed over time, which besides it, nothing but eternity hath triumphed over."
> [Sir Walter Raleigh, Preface, *The History of the World*; 1614]

rall. *abbr* MUSIC rallentando

ral·len·tan·do /ràllən tándō, raàlən taándō/ *adv* with a gradual slowing of pace (*used as a musical direction*) [Early 19C. < Italian, present participle of *rallentare* "slow down"] —**ral·len·tan·do** *adj*

ral·ly[1] /rállee/ *n* (*plural* **-lies**) **1. GATHERING** a large meeting or gathering of people, usually organized by a movement or political party and intended to inspire and generate enthusiasm among those present **2. RECOVERY OR IMPROVEMENT** a sudden recovery or improvement after a setback, crisis, or period of illness, inactivity, or deterioration **3.** MIL **REASSEMBLY OF TROOPS** a regrouping of a disorganized military force and the reestablishment of command over it, or the signal calling for this ○ *The retreating hussars made a rally and drove the attackers back.* **4.** FIN **RENEWED BUYING OF STOCKS** a renewed buying of stocks after a period of selling, with a resultant rise in stock prices ○ *a rally in the industrial sector of the stock market* **5.** RACKET GAMES **EXCHANGE OF SHOTS** in tennis and other racket sports, an exchange of several shots between two opponents or sides before a point is scored **6.** MOTOR SPORTS **AUTOMOBILE RACE** an automobile race that is held on public roads using a route not known in advance by the drivers, with special rules for speed or time ■ *v* **(-lied, -ly·ing, -lies) 1.** *vti* **GATHER TOGETHER FOR SOMETHING** to come together, uniting for a common purpose or in a common cause, or call on people to do this **2.** *vti* MIL **FORM TOGETHER AGAIN** to reorganize after a setback and restore order and morale, or make people do this, especially by stopping troops retreating further ○ *The captain rallied his troops and formed a defensive line.* **3.** *vti* **REVIVE OR RECOVER** to recover or improve after a setback, crisis, or period of illness, inactivity, or deterioration, or make somebody or something do this ○ *Our spirits rallied once we had our first success.* **4.** *vi* FIN **INCREASE IN VALUE** to increase sharply in value or price owing to renewed buying by investors **5.** *vi* FIN **EXPERIENCE RENEWED BUYING OF STOCKS** to be involved in renewed buying of stocks after a period of selling ○ *The market rallied in the afternoon.* **6.** *vi* RACKET GAMES **EXCHANGE SHOTS** in tennis and other racket sports, to exchange a series of shots before a point is scored [Late 16C. < French *rallier* "reunite" < *alier* "join, ally"] —**ral·li·er** *n*

rally around *vi* to come to the aid of somebody in difficulty or need, offering either practical or moral support

ral·ly[2] /rállee/ **(-lied, -ly·ing, -lies)** *vt* to tease or ridicule somebody in a friendly or good-humored way [Mid-17C. < French *railler* (see RAIL[2])]

ral·ly·ing /rállee ing/ *n* automobile racing on public roads using a route not known in advance by the drivers and with special rules for speed or time

ralph /ralf/ **(ralphed, ralph·ing, ralphs)** *vi US* same as **vomit** (*slang*) [Late 20C. Probably < the man's first name *Ralph*, as supposedly resembling the sound of vomiting]

Ralph /ralf/ *n US* a right turn (*informal*) ○ *At the next corner, hang a Ralph.* [Late 20C. < the man's first name, as an easily understood substitute for the first sound in RIGHT]

ram /ram/ *n* **1. MALE SHEEP** a male sheep **2. BATTERING OR CRUSHING DEVICE** a device designed to batter, crush, press, or push something, e.g., a projecting underwater part of a boat's prow or the weight dropped by a pile driver **3.** ENG same as **hydraulic ram 4. WARSHIP WITH RAM** formerly, a warship equipped with a projecting underwater part on the prow that was designed to make a hole in the hull of an enemy warship ■ *v* **(rammed, ram·ming, rams) 1.** *vti* **STRIKE SOMETHING WITH GREAT FORCE** to hit or collide with something, with great force or violence, or make something do this ○ *I rammed my fist down on the table.* **2.** *vt* **COLLIDE WITH SOMETHING DELIBERATELY** to collide with another ship or vehicle deliberately in order to sink, disable, or damage it ○ *The police car rammed the getaway vehicle and pushed it off the road.* **3.** *vt* **FORCE SOMETHING INTO PLACE** to press, force, or push something into place ○ *He quickly rammed another charge down the barrel and took aim.* **4.** *vt US* POL **FORCE ACCEPTANCE OF SOMETHING** to force the passage of a bill or acceptance of a suggestion, usually despite strong objection ○ *rammed the legislation through Congress* **5.** *vt* **PRESENT SOMETHING VERY FORCEFULLY** to present something forcefully in order to impress and convince people ○ *In a series of high-profile interviews she rammed home her message.* ■ *adj Carib* same as **boar** [Old English *ram(m)*] —**ram·mer** *n*

Ram /ram/ *n* ZODIAC same as **Aries** (sense 2)

RAM *abbr* **1.** /ram/ COMPUT random-access memory **2.** PHYS relative atomic mass **3.** FIN reverse annuity mortgage **4.** ENG rocket-assisted motor **5.** *also* **R.A.M.** MUSIC Royal Academy of Music

r.a.m. *abbr* relative atomic mass

Ra·ma /raámə/ *n* in Hinduism, an incarnation (**avatar**) of the god Vishnu

Ra·ma IX /raámə/ (*b.* 1927) king of Thailand. He ascended the throne in 1950. Born **Bhumibol Adulyadej**

ra·ma·da /rə maádə/ *n Southwest US* an open porch or trellis supporting plants [Mid-19C. Via Spanish from, ultimately, Latin *ramus* "branch" (see RAMIFY)]

Ram·a·dan /raámə daán/ *n* **1.** in the Islamic calendar, the ninth month of the year. During Ramadan, Muslims fast between dawn and dusk. See table at **calendar 2.** the daily fast between sunrise and sunset practiced during Ramadan [Late 16C. < Arabic, "the hot month" < *ramaḍ* "dryness"]

Ra·ma·krish·na /raámə kríshnə/, **Sri** (1834–86) Indian religious teacher. He taught that all mystical religious experiences are equally valid and was instrumental in bringing about the 19th-century Hindu revival in India. His followers founded the Ramakrishna Mission. Born **Chatterji, Gadadhar**

Ra·man /raámən/, **Sir Chandrasekhara** (1888–1970)

Indian physicist. His work on molecular diffraction of light won him the Nobel Prize in physics (1930). Full name **Raman, Sir Chandrasekhara Venkata**

Ra·man ef·fect *n* the change in wavelength and phase exhibited by monochromatic light passing through a transparent medium. The scattering that results is used in Raman spectroscopy to obtain information about the structure of molecules. [Early 20C. After Sir Chandrasekhara Venkata RAMAN]

ra·mate *adj* BIOL same as **ramose**

Ra·ma·ya·na /raàmə yaánə/ *n* a great epic of the Hindu religion and of classical Sanskrit literature that tells of the adventures of Rama, an incarnation (**avatar**) of the god Vishnu

Dame Marie Rambert

Ram·bert /raam bér/, **Dame Marie** (1888–1982) Polish-born British ballet dancer and teacher. She founded the Ballet Rambert (1926), later called the Rambert Dance Company, which promoted the work of British choreographers. Born **Rambach, Miriam**

ram·ble /rámb'l/ *vi* (**-bled, -bling, -bles**) **1. TALK OR WRITE AIMLESSLY** to talk or write for a long time, not always keeping to the intended subject or tending to change the subject ○ *The speaker rambled on for over an hour.* **2. WALK FOR PLEASURE** to go for a walk for pleasure, usually in the countryside and sometimes without a fixed route in mind ○ *He had spent a week rambling through the villages of the Apennines.* **3. FOLLOW CHANGING COURSE** to have, follow, or proceed along a winding or often changing course ○ *The path rambled though the fields down to the river.* **4. GROW IN RANDOM WAY** to grow in random directions, usually covering a sizable area in the process ○ *Vines rambled all over the low stone wall.* ■ *n* **WALK TAKEN FOR PLEASURE** a walk for pleasure, usually in the countryside and sometimes without a fixed route in mind ○ *a ramble through the woods* [15C. Origin ?]

ram·bler /rámb'lər/ *n* **1. SOMEBODY WHO TALKS TOO MUCH** somebody who talks or writes for a long time, not always keeping to the intended subject or tending to change the subject **2. WALKER** somebody who walks in the countryside for pleasure **3. CLIMBING ROSE** a hybrid climbing rose with long flexible canes and clusters of small double flowers **4.** *US* BUILDINGS same as **ranch house** (sense 2)

ram·bling /rámb'ling/ *adj* **1. NOT TO POINT** continuing for too long and with many changes of subject ○ *a long, rambling story* **2. SPREAD OUT** built or spread over a large area and not clearly organized or regular in shape ○ *a rambling old house* **3. MEANDERING** not following a direct course ○ *a narrow rambling path through the hills* **4. GROWING AS RAMBLER** growing with long straggling shoots **5. PREFERRING TO ROAM** preferring to move from place to place rather than stay in one place or settle down —**ram·bling·ly** *adv*

SYNONYMS See ***wordy.***

Ram·bo /rámbō/ (*plural* **-bos**) *n* an aggressive or violent person who breaks rules or laws to achieve what he or she believes to be right (*slang*) [Late 20C. After John *Rambo*, aggressive protagonist in the movie *First Blood* (1982)]

Ram·bouil·let /raàmboo yáy/ town in Yvelines Department, north central France, southwest of Paris. The town's chateau is the French president's summer residence and is used for international conferences. Population: 24,758 (1999).

ram·bunc·tious /ram búngkshəss/ *adj* noisy, very active, and hard to control, usually as a result of excitement or youthful energy (*informal*) [Mid-19C. Origin ?] —**ram·bunc·tious·ly** *adv* —**ram·bunc·tious·ness** *n*

ram·bu·tan /ram bo͝ot'n/ *n* **1.** an oval red spiny fruit with a mildly acidic taste **2.** a tree that produces rambutans. Native to: Malaysia. Latin name: *Nephelium lappaceum.* [Early 18C. < Malay, < *rambut* "hair"; from the hairy skin of the fruit]

ram·e·kin /rámməkin/, **ram·e·quin** *n* **1.** a small ovenproof dish with vertical fluted sides designed to hold a single serving of a prepared food, especially one that is baked **2.** a portion of food cooked and served in a ramekin [Early 18C. Via French < Middle Dutch *rameken*, literally "little cream" < *ram* "cream"]

ra·men /ráymən/ *n* a Japanese dish of thin white noodles in small dried cakes, served in a thin well-flavored soup or stock [Late 20C. Via Japanese *rāmen* < Chinese *lāmiàn* "pulled noodles"]

ram·e·quin *n* HOUSEHOLD, FOOD another spelling of **ramekin**

Ram·e·ses II /rámmə seèz/, **Ram·ses II** /rám seèz/ (*fl* 13th century B.C.) Egyptian pharaoh. His long and prosperous reign (1279–13 B.C.), which marked the pinnacle of Egypt's power, saw the building of numerous monuments, including the sandstone temples at Abu Simbel. The Exodus of the Israelites from Egypt is thought to have occurred during his rule. Known as **Rameses the Great**

Ram·e·ses III, **Ram·ses III** (*fl* 12th century B.C.) Egyptian pharaoh. As pharaoh (1184–53 B.C.), he was a great military leader, repeatedly saving the country from invasion, notably by the Libyans.

ra·met /ráymət/ *n* a member of a collection of organisms, cells, or molecular segments (**clone**) that are genetically identical direct descendants of a single parent by asexual reproduction [Early 20C. < Latin *ramus* "branch"]

ra·mi BIOL plural of **ramus**

ram·ie /rámmee, ráymee/ *n* **1. STRONG FIBER** a lustrous soft durable fiber obtained from the bark of a bush. Use: fabric, rope. **2. CLOTH** fabric made from ramie fiber **3. ASIAN BUSH** a perennial bush whose bark yields ramie. Native to: Asia. Latin name: *Boehmeria nivea.* [Early 19C. < Malay *rami*]

ram·i·fi·ca·tion /ràmməfi káysh'n/ *n* **1. COMPLICATING RESULT** a usually unintended consequence of an action, decision, or judgment that may complicate a situation or make the desired result more difficult to achieve ○ *an unexpected ramification of the new law* **2. BRANCHING** the process of dividing or spreading out into branches **3. BRANCH** a branch or arrangement of branches

ram·i·form /rámmə fawrm/ *adj* spreading out like branches or having the form of a branch or branches [Mid-19C. < Latin *ramus* "branch"]

ram·i·fy /rámmə fī/ (**-fied, -fy·ing, -fies**) *vi* **1.** to divide into branches or similar parts **2.** to have usually unintended consequences that may complicate a situation or make the desired result more difficult to achieve [Mid-16C. Via Old French *ramifier* < medieval Latin *ramificare* < Latin *ramus* "branch"]

ram·jet /rám jèt/ *n* a jet engine in which fuel is burned in a duct with air compressed by the forward motion of the aircraft

Ra·mos /rámmōss/, **Fidel Valdez** (*b.* 1928) president of the Philippines (1992–98). He was instrumental in overthrowing President Ferdinand Marcos (1986) and introduced a wide-ranging economic reform program during his presidency.

ra·mose /ráy mōss, rə mṓss/, **ra·mous, ra·mate** /ráy màyt/ *adj* having many branches or divided into many branches [Late 17C. < Latin *ramosus* "having many branches" < *ramus* "branch"] —**ra·mose·ly** *adv*

ramp[1] /ramp/ *n* **1. SLOPING PATH OR ACCESS** a sloping surface that allows access from one level to a higher or lower level, or raises something up above floor or ground level ○ *The ship slid slowly down the ramp into the water.* **2. MOVABLE STAIRS** a movable set of stairs used for boarding or disembarking from an aircraft **3. CURVED BEND IN HANDRAIL** a curved bend or slope in a handrail or coping where it changes direction, e.g., on a stair landing ■ *vt* (**ramped, ramp·ing, ramps**) **1. INCREMENT SOMETHING GRADUALLY** to increase something gradually ○ *had to ramp up production to meet increasing demand* **2. BUILD SOMETHING WITH SLOPE** to build something with a sloped surface, or provide something with a ramp ○ *The entrance must be ramped for wheelchair access.* [Late 18C. < French *rampe* < *ramper* "crawl, creep, rear up"] —**ramped** *adj*

ramp up *vti* to cause the level or intensity of something to increase sharply, or increase in this way ○*"As business ramps up to manage greater responsibility for its social and environmental impacts..."* (*Marketing Week*; December 1998)

ramp[2] /ramp/ (**ramped, ramp·ing, ramps**) *vi* **1. ACT THREATENINGLY** to act in a threatening manner or assume a threatening stance, e.g., rearing with the forelegs ready to strike **2. MOVE VIOLENTLY OR THREATENINGLY** to move or rush violently, threateningly, or furiously **3.** HERALDRY **BE SHOWN REARING UP IN PROFILE** to be in the rampant position ○ *an old seal marked with a ramping lion on a shield* [14C. < French *ramper* "crawl, creep, rear up"]

ram·page *n* /rám pàyj/ an outburst of uncontrolled violent or riotous behavior, or a series of violent or riotous actions ■ *vi* /rám pàyj, ram páyj/ (**-paged, -pag·ing, -pag·es**) to engage in uncontrolled violent or riotous behavior, or commit a series of violent or riotous acts ○ *This weather system has rampaged up the coast, with blizzards and howling winds causing severe damage.* [Early 18C. Probably < RAMP[2]] —**ram·pa·geous** /ram páyjəss/ *adj* —**ram·pa·geous·ly** *adv* —**ram·pag·er** *n* —**ram·pag·ing** *adj* ◇ **on the rampage** behaving in a wild and uncontrolled manner

ram·pant /rámpənt/ *adj* **1. OCCURRING UNCHECKED** happening in an unrestrained manner, usually so as to be regarded as a menace ○ *rampant inflation* **2.** BOT **GROWING WILDLY** growing strongly and to a very large size, or spreading uncontrollably **3. FIERCE** exhibiting ferocious behavior or fierceness of spirit **4.** HERALDRY **ON HIND LEGS** describes a heraldic beast depicted rearing up, in profile, and with its forelegs raised, the right one above the left **5.** CONSTR **WITH UNEQUAL SUPPORTS** having a support or an abutment that is higher on one side than the other [14C. < French, present participle of *ramper* "rear up"] —**ram·pan·cy** *n* —**ram·pant·ly** *adv*

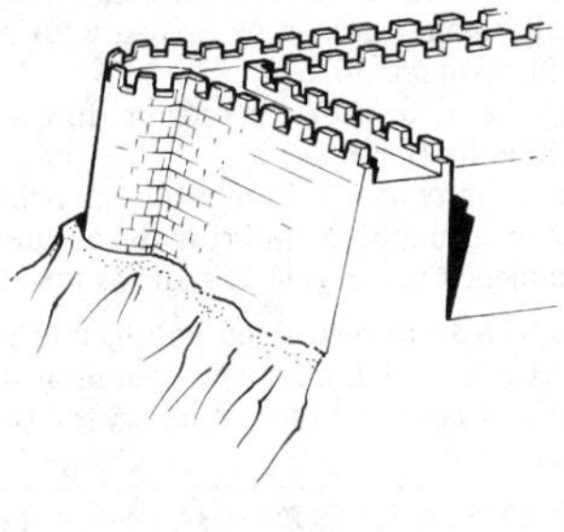

rampart

ram·part /rám paàrt/ *n* a defensive fortification made of an earthen embankment, often topped by a low protective wall ■ *vt* (**-part·ed, -part·ing, -parts**) to protect somebody or something with ramparts or something similar [Late 16C. < French *rempart* < *remparer* "defend again" < Old French *emparer* "defend"]

ramp·er /rámpər/ *n* a ground crew member at a commercial airport who operates mechanisms for onloading and offloading passengers, air crews, baggage, and provisions at parked aircraft [< RAMP[1]]

ram·pike /rám pīk/ *n* a dead tree that is still standing, especially one reduced by fire to little more than a trunk [Late 16C. Origin ?]

ram·pi·on /rámpee ən/ *n* **1.** a plant with a white edible root used in salads. Flowers: bluish, in clusters. Native to: Europe, Asia. Latin name: *Campanula rapunculus.* **2.** a plant related to the rampion. Flowers: usually blue. Genus: *Phyteuma.* [Late 16C. Probably alteration of Old French *raiponce* < Old Italian *raponzo* < Latin *rapum* "turnip"]

Ram·pur /rám po͝or/ city and administrative headquarters of Rampur District, Uttar Pradesh State, northern India. Population: 243,742 (1991).

ram·rod /rám ròd/ *n* **1.** ARMS **ROD FOR LOADING GUN** a rod for loading a charge into a muzzle-loading musket, cannon, or other gun **2.** ARMS **ROD FOR CLEANING GUN** a rod for cleaning the barrel of a firearm **3.** *US* **STERN OR STRICT OVERSEER** a stern or strict boss, commander, or other person in a position of authority ■ *adv* **RIGIDLY** rigidly or stiffly ○ *ramrod straight* ■ *vt* (**-rod·ded, -rod·ding, -rods**) *US* **1. PUSH SOMETHING THROUGH BY FORCE** to push through or achieve something by force or threat ○ *tried to ramrod the bill through the legislature* **2. CONTROL SOMEBODY STRICTLY** to exert strict control over somebody or enforce strict discipline on somebody

Ram·say /rámzee/, **Sir William** (1852–1916) British chemist. He was the first to isolate helium from terrestrial sources (1895), and discovered argon (in collaboration with Lord Rayleigh), neon, krypton, and xenon. He was awarded the Nobel Prize in chemistry (1904).

Ram·ses ➧ **Rameses II, Rameses III**

ram·shack·le /rám shàk'l/ *adj* poorly maintained or constructed and seeming likely to fall apart or collapse [Mid-19C. Back-formation < *ramshackled*, alteration of obsolete *ransackled* < RANSACK]

ram's horn *n* JUDAISM same as **shofar**

ram·sons /rámz'nz, rámss'nz/ *n* a wild garlic with round heads of white flowers and a bulbous root. Native to: Europe, Asia. Latin name: *Allium ursinum*. (*takes a singular verb*) [Mid-16C. < Old English *hram(e)san*, plural of *hramsa* < Germanic, later misinterpreted as singular]

ram·u·lose /rámmyə lōss/ *adj* having many small branches [Mid-18C. < Latin *ramulosus* "full of branching veins" < *ramus* "branch"]

ra·mus /ráyməss/ (*plural* **-mi** /-mī/) *n* a small branching body part, e.g., a stem, bone, or nerve [Early 18C. < Latin, "branch"]

ran past tense of **run**

Ran /ran/ *n* in Norse mythology, the goddess of the sea

Rance /raaNss/ river in Brittany, in northwestern France. Length: 62 mi./100 km.

ranch /ranch/ *n* **1. LIVESTOCK FARM ON RANGELAND** a farm where cattle, sheep, horses, or other livestock are raised on large tracts of open land, especially in North and South America and Australia **2. SPECIALIZED FARM** a large farm devoted to keeping a particular type of animal or growing a particular type of crop **3.** BUILDINGS same as **ranch house 4.** FOOD same as **ranch dressing** ■ *v* (**ranched, ranch·ing, ranch·es**) **1.** *vi* **WORK ON RANCH** to own, manage, or work on a ranch **2.** *vt* **RAISE ANIMALS ON RANCH** to breed, raise, or tend animals on a ranch [Early 19C. Via American Spanish *rancho* < Spanish, "group of people who eat together" < French *ranger* "arrange in position" < *rang* "row, line"] —**ranch·ing** *n*

ranch dress·ing *n* a creamy salad dressing that has a mixture of mayonnaise and buttermilk or milk as its base

ranch·er /ránchər/ *n* **1.** somebody who owns or manages a ranch **2.** BUILDINGS same as **ranch house** (sense 2)

ran·che·ra /ran chérrə/ *n Hispanic* a traditional Mexican ballad, often a love song, accompanied by a mariachi band [< American Spanish, literally "woman who runs a ranch," form of RANCHERO]

ran·che·ri·a /ràn chə rée̵ə/ *n Southwest US* a hut or a group of huts used by a Mexican shepherd or a group of shepherds [Early 17C. < American Spanish *ranchería* < *rancho* (see RANCH)]

ran·che·ro /ran chérrō/ (*plural* **-ros**) *n Southwest US* somebody who owns or manages a ranch, especially a Hispanic rancher in the southwestern United States and in Latin America [Early 19C. < American Spanish < *rancho* (see RANCH)]

ranch house *n* **1.** the building on a ranch where the owner or manager lives that usually has one story, a spread-out floor plan, and a roof that is not steeply pitched **2.** a single-story house built in a style similar to a traditional ranch house, especially one located in a suburban housing development

Ran·chi /ránchee/ capital city of Bihar State, northeastern India. Population: 862,850 (2001).

ran·cho /ránchō/ (*plural* **-chos**) *n Southwest US* **1.** AGRIC same as **ranch** *n* (senses 1–2), **ranch house** (sense 1) **2.** a hut where a ranch worker lives, or a group of such huts [Early 19C. < American Spanish (see RANCH)]

Ran·cho Cu·ca·mon·ga /ránchō ko͝okə múng gə/ city in southwestern California, west of San Bernardino. Formerly an agricultural and wine-growing region, it was rapidly developed as a residential community in the 1980s and 1990s. Population: 143,711 (2002 estimate).

ran·cid /ránssəd/ *adj* **1.** having the strong disagreeable smell or taste of decomposing fats or oils **2.** causing disgust or offense [Mid-17C. < Latin *rancidus* "stinking, rank" < *rancere* "to stink"] —**ran·cid·i·ty** /ran síddətee/ *n* —**ran·cid·ness** *n*

ran·cor /rángkər/ *n* a bitter, deeply held, and long-lasting ill will or resentment [12C. Via French < Latin, "stinking smell or offensive flavor, bitterness" < *rancere* "to stink"] —**ran·cor·ous** *adj* —**ran·cor·ous·ly** *adv* —**ran·cor·ous·ness** *n*

ran·cour *n* Can, UK spelling of **rancor**

rand /rand/ (*plural same*) *n* the main unit of South African currency. See table at **currency** [Mid-20C. After the *Rand*, gold-mining district in Transvaal, South Africa < Afrikaans *rand* "ridge of ground" < Dutch, "edge"]

Rand /rand/, **Ayn** (1905–82) Russian-born US writer and philosopher. She championed objectivism and individualism in essays, newsletters, and novels including *The Fountainhead* (1943).

> "Civilization is the process of setting man free from men."
> [Ayn Rand, *The Fountainhead*; 1943]

ran·dan /ran dán, rán dàn/ *n* **1.** a boat designed to be rowed by three people **2.** the method of rowing a randan, with one person using two oars and the other two using one oar each [Early 19C. Origin ?]

r & b /aar ən bée/, **R & B** *abbr* rhythm and blues

R & D /aar ən dée/ *abbr* research and development

Ran·dolph /rán dòlf/ town in eastern Massachusetts, northeast of Stoughton. It is a southern suburb of Boston. Population: 31,044 (2002 estimate).

Ran·dolph, A. Philip (1889–1979) US labor leader. The founding president of the Brotherhood of Sleeping Car Porters and Maids (1925–68), he unionized African American workers, campaigned for civil rights, and was a principal organizer of the great 1963 civil rights march in Washington, D.C. Full name **Randolph, Asa Philip**

> "The regnant law of the life of political parties, like all other organisms, is self-preservation. They behave in obedience to the principle of the *greatest gain for the least effort*."
> [A. Philip Randolph, *The Messenger*; October 1924]

Ran·dolph, Edmund Jennings (1753–1813) US patriot and diplomat. He was a Virginia delegate to the Constitutional Convention (1787), and served as US secretary of state (1794–95).

Ran·dolph, John (1773–1833) US politician. He served in the US House of Representatives (1799–1813, 1815–17, 1819–25, 1827–29, 1833) and Senate (1825–27), and helped draft a new constitution for Virginia. Known as **John Randolph of Roanoke**

ran·dom /rándəm/ *adj* **1. WITHOUT PATTERN** done, chosen, or occurring without an identifiable pattern, plan, system, or connection ○ *random checks* **2. LACKING REGULARITY** with a pattern or in sizes that are not uniform or regular ○ *a wall constructed of random stones* **3.** STATS **EQUALLY LIKELY** relating or belonging to a set in which all the members have the same probability of occurrence ○ *a random sampling* **4.** STATS **HAVING DEFINITE PROBABILITY** relating to or involving variables that have undetermined value but definite probability [Mid-17C. < Old French *randon* "impetuosity, rush" < *randir* "run" < Germanic] —**ran·dom·ly** *adv* —**ran·dom·ness** *n* ◇ **at random** without an identifiable pattern, plan, system, or connection

ran·dom-ac·cess *adj* relating to the capability of a computer to obtain information from any memory location without having to begin its search at the memory's starting point and work through it in sequence ○ *random-access input/output*

ran·dom-ac·cess mem·o·ry *n* the primary working memory in a computer, used for the temporary storage of programs and data and in which the data can be accessed directly and modified

ran·dom·ize /rándə mīz/ (**-ized, -iz·ing, -iz·es**) *vti* to arrange or select items so that no identifiable pattern or order determines the resulting arrangement or the selection process —**ran·dom·i·za·tion** /ràndəmi záysh'n/ *n* —**ran·dom·iz·er** *n*

ran·dom num·ber *n* a number in a series of numbers that have no pattern in their progression

ran·dom sam·ple *n* a sample of subjects that is randomly selected from a group and is therefore assumed to be representative of that group

ran·dom seg·re·ga·tion *n* a principle in genetics holding that during meiosis the two separated partners of a chromosome pair are distributed randomly to the reproductive cells (**gametes**), each gamete having an equal chance of receiving either chromosome

ran·dom var·i·a·ble *n* a variable that can have any of a range of values that occur randomly but can be described probabilistically

ran·dom walk *n* a mathematical model applicable to various processes, such as diffusion, in which the direction and sometimes the magnitude of successive steps are determined by chance

R and R, **R & R** *abbr* **1.** MIL rest and recreation **2.** rest and relaxation

ran·dy /rándee/ (**-di·er, -di·est**) *adj* having a strong desire for sex (*informal*) [Late 17C. < *rand*, Scots variant of RANT] —**ran·di·ly** *adv* —**ran·di·ness** *n*

ra·nee *n* POL another spelling of **rani**

rang past tense of **ring**[2]

range /raynj/ *n* **1. VARIETY** the number and variety of different things that something includes or can deal with ○ *dealing with a wide range of people* **2. NUMBER OF SIMILAR THINGS** a number or set of different things belonging to the same general category ○ *available in a range of styles and colors* **3. CATEGORY DEFINED BY LIMITS** a category defined by an upper and a lower limit ○ *the age range from 25 to 45* **4. AREA OF EFFECTIVE OPERATION** the area within which, or the distance over which, something can operate effectively ○ *out of range of the radar* **5.** MIL **FARTHEST DISTANCE FOR EFFECTIVE OPERATION** the farthest distance at which something can operate effectively, e.g., the farthest distance to which a gun can shoot a bullet or shell **6.** ARMS **DISTANCE BETWEEN WEAPON AND TARGET** the distance between two things, especially a gun or a tracking device and the object it is aimed at **7. PRACTICE AREA** a place where an activity is practiced or performed ○ *a shooting range* **8.** TRANSP **DISTANCE TRAVELED WITHOUT REFUELING** the farthest distance that a vehicle or aircraft can travel without needing to refuel **9.** AGRIC **OPEN LAND FOR GRAZING FARM ANIMALS** a large area of open land on which farm animals can graze **10.** MUSIC **NOTES PRODUCED BY VOICE OR INSTRUMENT** the notes, from highest to lowest, that somebody's voice or a musical instrument can produce **11.** MUSIC **REGISTER OF MUSICAL PASSAGE** the register of a musical passage, from its highest to lowest note **12.** GEOG **ROW OF MOUNTAINS** a number of mountains or hills forming a connected row or group **13. MOVEMENT OVER AREA** movement over or within an area **14.** MATH **SET OF VALUES** the set of values that can be taken by a function or a variable **15.** STATS **EXTENT OF FREQUENCY DISTRIBUTION** the difference between the smallest and the largest value in a frequency distribution **16.** HOUSEHOLD **STOVE** a cooking stove with one or more ovens and with hot plates or burners on top **17.** ECOL **AREA WHERE ORGANISM IS NORMALLY FOUND** a geographic area in which a species of organism normally lives or grows **18.** *Can, Western US* CONSTR **NORTH-SOUTH STRIP OF TOWNSHIPS** a north-south strip of townships six miles square and numbered east and west from a meridian in a public land survey ■ *v* (**ranged, rang·ing, rang·es**) **1.** *vi* **VARY BETWEEN LIMITS** to vary between a particular upper and lower limit ○ *prices ranging from $3.95 to $15.00* **2.** *vi* **DEAL WITH NUMBER OF THINGS** to include, cover, or deal with a number of different things, usually within the same context ○ *Her interests range from tennis to parachuting.* **3.** *vt* **ARRANGE THINGS IN LINE** to arrange things in a particular way, especially in a line or row (*usually passive*) ○ *Jars of pickles were ranged along the kitchen shelf.* **4.** *vt* **ALIGN OR CLASSIFY SOMEBODY OR SOMETHING** to put something or somebody into a particular group or category ○ *The cadets were ranged into platoons by height.* **5. range yourself** *vr* **GIVE PERSONAL SUPPORT** to support or side with somebody **6.** *vti* **TRAVEL FREELY AND EXTENSIVELY** to move freely across, through, or back and forth within a particular area ○ *She allowed her thoughts to range freely over the events of the previous week.* **7.** *vti* **POINT OR AIM SOMETHING** to point or aim something such as a gun, missile, or telescope at an object, or be pointed at an object **8.** *vi* ARMS **TRAVEL PARTICULAR DISTANCE** to be able to travel a particular distance (*refers to bullets or missiles*) **9.** *vi* ECOL **LIVE OR GROW** to live or grow in a particular geographic area (*refers to animals or plants*) ○ *Buffalo once ranged over the plains.* **10.** *vt* AGRIC **PUT LIVESTOCK OUT TO GRAZE** to put livestock out to graze on a large open area [13C. < Old French *rangier* "put in order" < *ranc* "row"]

range find·er /ráynj fìndər/, **range·find·er** *n* an instrument used to estimate the distance between the user and an object, especially one that is to be shot at or photographed

range·land /ráynj lànd/ *n* AGRIC same as **range** *n* (sense 9)

range pole *n* CONSTR same as **ranging pole**

rang·er /ráynjər/ *n* **1. OFFICIAL OVERSEEING COUNTRYSIDE AREA** somebody whose job is to oversee, protect, and patrol a forest or an area of natural beauty such as a national park **2.** *US* **MEMBER OF RURAL POLICE UNIT** a member of an armed law-enforcement unit in parts of the United States, especially Texas **3. WANDERER** somebody who wanders

Rang·er *n* a member of a military unit of the United States Army specially trained for commando raids

rang·ing pole /ráynjìng-/, **rang·ing rod** *n* a pole, usually held vertically, used to mark a specific position when surveying a plot of land

Ran·goon /rang go͞on/ former name for **Yangon** (until 1989)

rang·y /ráynjee/ (**-i·er, -i·est**) *adj* tall and lean, with long legs —**rang·i·ness** *n*

ra·ni /ra͈anee, raa née/, **ra·nee** *n* a Hindu queen or princess, or the wife or widow of a rajah in South Asia or parts of Southeast Asia [Late 17C. Via Hindi < Sanskrit *rājñī* < *rājan* "king"]

ra·nit·i·dine /ra nítti deen/ *n* a drug that reduces the secretion of stomach acid. Use: to treat peptic ulcers.

rank[1] /rangk/ *n* **1. OFFICIAL STATUS WITHIN ORGANIZATION** an official title or category that shows the holder's relative importance or seniority within an organization, especially a military force ○ *attained the rank of colonel* **2. STATUS IN RELATION TO OTHERS** the degree of importance or excellence of somebody or something in relation to other members of a group ○ *a political journalist of the first rank* **3. HIGH STATUS** high status or importance, especially in the military **4. LINE OF PEOPLE OR THINGS** a line of people, especially soldiers, or things standing or placed side by side **5.** CHESS **HORIZONTAL LINE OF SQUARES ON CHESSBOARD** a horizontal line of squares on a chessboard **6.** MATH **LINEARLY INDEPENDENT ROWS** in mathematics, the largest number of linearly independent rows in a matrix **7.** MUSIC **SET OF ORGAN PIPES** a set of organ pipes linked to a particular stop ■ **ranks** *npl* **1. ORDINARY SOLDIERS** members of the armed forces who are not officers, or the ordinary members of any organization who do not hold high office **2. PEOPLE IN GROUP OR CATEGORY** people belonging to a particular group or category, considered collectively and usually with the understanding that there are large numbers of them ○ *among the ranks of her supporters* ■ *v* (**ranked, rank·ing, ranks**) **1.** *vti* **HAVE OR GIVE SOMETHING RATING** to have a particular rating, position, or importance in relation to other people or things in a group, or give somebody or something such a rating ○ *This ranks fairly high on my list of desirable improvements.* **2.** *vt* **OUTRANK SOMEBODY OR SOMETHING** to have a higher rank than and take precedence over somebody or something else in a group, especially in a hierarchy ○ *A colonel ranks a major.* **3.** *vi US* **SEEM MOST IMPORTANT** to have the greatest importance or receive the best treatment among the members of a group **4.** *vti* **POSITION THINGS OR STAND IN ROWS** to place people or things in a row or rows, or stand or be placed in rows (*usually passive*) **5.** *vi* **INSULT SOMEBODY** to insult somebody in a childish way (*slang*) ○ *Quit ranking on me!* [14C. < Old French *ranc* "row" < Germanic] ◇ **break ranks 1.** to leave an ordered line of soldiers, especially when being attacked **2.** to stop supporting the policy of a group of which you are a member ◇ **close ranks 1.** to unite closely, especially when taking defensive action **2.** to form into tight disciplined lines in preparation for an expected attack (*refers to soldiers*) ◇ **pull rank (on somebody)** to assert authority over somebody in a hierarchy, especially in order to obtain personal advantage ◇ **rise (up) through the ranks** to reach a senior position in an organization by gradual promotions from an originally low position

rank[2] *adj* **1. UTTER** of the most extreme and obvious kind ○ *a rank amateur* **2. FOUL** foul-smelling or foul-tasting ○ *the rank odor of rotten eggs* **3. TOO VIGOROUS** describes vegetation that is growing too vigorously ○*"the rank ailanthus"* (T.S. Eliot, *The Dry Salvages*; 1941) **4.** same as **impudent** (*slang*; *used in Black English*) [Old English *ranc* "haughty, full-grown," of uncertain origin: perhaps ultimately from an Indo-European word meaning "to move straight ahead" that is also the ancestor of English *right*] —**rank·ly** *adv* —**rank·ness** *n*

Rank /rangk/, **Otto** (1884–1939) Austrian psychologist and psychotherapist. An early associate of Freud, he applied Freudian techniques to the interpretation of myths in *Myth of the Birth of the Hero* (1909), but later differed from Freud in ascribing neurosis to birth trauma.

rank and file *n* **1.** the majority of a group or organization, often a labor union, especially all of the members who have no power or influence ○ *the union's rank and file* **2.** the enlisted troops in a military organization, excluding officers —**rank-and-file** *adj* —**rank and fil·er** *n*

rank and yank *n* a system of reviewing employee performance by which top performers are slated for promotion and compensation increases and low performers are slated for reassignment or termination

rank cor·re·la·tion *n* an assessment of the extent to which different ways of ranking the members of a set correlate with one another

ran·kin' /rángkin/ *adj* of the best quality or the highest standard (*slang*; *used in Black English*)

Ran·kin /rángkin/, **Jeannette** (1880–1973) US politician and legislator. A prominent leader of the women's suffrage and pacifist movements, she was the first woman member of the House of Representatives (1917).

> "You no more win a war than you can win an earthquake."
> [Jeannette Rankin. Quoted in *Jeannette Rankin: First Lady in Congress*, Hannah Josephson; 1974]

Ran·kine scale /rángkin-/ *n* an absolute temperature scale in which each degree equals one degree on the Fahrenheit scale, with the freezing point of water being 491.67° and its boiling point 671.67° [Mid-19C. After the W. J. M. *Rankine* (1820–72), British physicist and engineer]

rank·ing /rángking/ *n* **1. POSITION IN RELATION TO OTHERS** the position or status held by or allocated to somebody or something in relation to others in a group **2. WORKING OUT RANKING ORDER** the work of establishing the order in which people or things should be ranked, usually according to their importance or ability ○ *Are we prepared to do a preliminary ranking of the candidates?* ■ *adj* **1. HOLDING HIGH RANK** holding a high rank in a military or other organization **2. FOREMOST** considered to be the most eminent or important of the members of a particular group ○ *the ranking diplomat at the reception*

ran·kle /rángk'l/ (**-kled, -kling, -kles**) *vi* to cause persistent feelings of bitterness, resentment, or anger [14C. < Old French *raoncler* < *raoncle* "festering sore," literally "little snake (bite)" < Latin *dracunculus* < *draco* (see DRAGON)]

Rann of Kutch /ràn əv kúch/ region of mudflats and salt marshes in western India and southern Pakistan. Area: 8,100 sq. mi./21,000 sq. km.

ran·sack /rán sàk/ (**-sacked, -sack·ing, -sacks**) *vt* **1.** to go through a place stealing some things and usually destroying or spoiling everything else **2.** to search something very thoroughly but handling things carelessly ○ *I ransacked the drawers but couldn't find my keys.* [13C. < Old Norse *rannsaka* < *rann* "house" + *-saka* "search"] —**ran·sack·er** *n*

ran·som /ránss'm/ *n* **1. MONEY DEMANDED FOR RELEASING CAPTIVE** a sum of money demanded or paid for the release of somebody who is being held prisoner **2. RELEASE OF PRISONER** the release of a prisoner in return for the payment of money **3. DELIVERANCE** the act of saving somebody from an oppressed condition or dangerous situation through self-sacrifice (*literary*) ■ *vt* (**-somed, -som·ing, -soms**) **1. PAY MONEY FOR SOMEBODY'S RELEASE** to obtain the release of somebody from captivity by paying money to the captor **2. RESCUE OR REDEEM SOMEBODY** to rescue or redeem somebody, especially by a self-sacrificing act, and especially from sin or its punishment (*literary*) [13C. Via Old French *ransoun* < Latin *redemption-* (see REDEMPTION)] —**ran·som·er** *n* ◇ **a king's ransom** a very large amount of money ◇ **hold somebody for ransom 1.** to hold somebody captive until a sum of money is paid for his or her release **2.** to use threats to try to make somebody do what you want

Ran·som /ránss'm/, **John Crowe** (1888–1974) US poet and critic. He was a leader of the southern literary renaissance in the 1920s and helped found the *Kenyon Review*.

rant /rant/ *vti* (**rant·ed, rant·ing, rants**) to speak or say something in a very loud, aggressive, or bombastic way, usually at length and repetitively ■ *n* a very loud, aggressive, or bombastic speech that is usually long and repetitive [Late 16C. < Dutch *ranten*] —**rant·er** *n* —**rant·ing** *adj, n* —**rant·ing·ly** *adv*

ran·u·la /rányələ/ *n* a cyst that forms on the underside of the tongue when the duct of a salivary or mucous gland is blocked [Mid-17C. < Latin, "little frog" < *rana* "frog"]

ra·nun·cu·lus /rə núngkyələss/ (*plural* **-lus·es** or **-li** /-lī/) *n* a plant that has divided leaves and flowers with five petals, e.g., the buttercup, clematis, and columbine. Genus: *Ranunculus*. [Late 16C. < modern Latin, < Latin, "little frog" < *rana* "frog"] —**ra·nun·cu·la·ceous** /rə nùngkyə láyshəss/ *adj*

rap[1] /rap/ *v* (**rapped, rap·ping, raps**) **1.** *vti* **HIT SOMEBODY OR SOMETHING SHARPLY** to strike somebody or something with a quick sharp blow ○ *The teacher rapped on the desk to get the students' attention.* **2.** *vt* **REBUKE SOMEBODY** to criticize or rebuke somebody harshly **3.** *vt* **SAY SOMETHING QUICKLY** to say something in a quick sharp way ○ *The sergeant rapped out an order.* **4.** *vi* **PERFORM MUSIC WITH SPOKEN RHYTHMIC VOCALS** to speak in verse using rhythm and rhyme over music with a strong beat, usually hip hop **5.** *vi US* **TALK INFORMALLY** to have an informal talk or discussion (*slang*) ○ *We rapped till dawn.* ■ *n* **1. SHARP BLOW** a quick sharp blow **2. SOUND OF KNOCKING** a quick sharp knocking sound **3. POPULAR MUSIC WITH SPOKEN RHYTHMIC VOCALS** a vocal style in which performers use rhythm and rhyme to speak in verse over music with a strong beat, usually hip hop. Rap developed from African American hip hop music and culture in the 1970s. **4. REBUKE** a harsh criticism or rebuke (*slang*) **5. CRIMINAL CHARGE** a criminal charge brought against somebody (*slang*) **6. JAIL SENTENCE** a jail sentence given to somebody found guilty of a crime (*slang*) **7.** *US* **SOMEBODY OR SOMETHING NEGATIVE** somebody or something thought of as negative or unfortunate (*slang*) ○ *You got a bum rap this time.* **8.** *US* **INFORMAL TALK** an informal talk or discussion (*slang*) [13C. Origin ?] ◇

beat the rap to avoid conviction on a charge (*slang*) ◇ **not give a rap** *US* to not care at all (*informal*) ◇ **take the rap (for something)** to take the blame or punishment for something, whether or not it was your fault (*slang*)

SPELLCHECK rap or **wrap**? Do not confuse the spelling of ***rap*** and ***wrap***, which sound similar. ***Rap*** is a verb or noun referring to a sharp blow or sound, an informal talk, or a type of popular music with spoken rhyming vocals, as in *to rap on the door, a rap singer*. ***Rap*** is also used in some fixed phrases: *I don't give a rap. She took the rap for his mistake.* ***Wrap*** is a verb meaning "cover, wind, envelop, engross" (as in *to wrap up a parcel, wrapped in thought*) or a noun meaning "shawl, cloak, or similar garment," "filled tortilla sandwich," or "completion of filming." ***Wrap*** is also used in the fixed phrase *keep under wraps*, meaning "keep secret."

rap² /rap/ *n US* the structured form or substance of something that somebody knows well and can perform at will (*slang*) ○ *You've really got the whole rap down on making quick money!*

ra·pa·cious /rə páyshəss/ *adj* **1. GRASPING** greedy and grasping, especially for money, and sometimes willing to use unscrupulous means to obtain what is desired **2. DESTRUCTIVE AND VICIOUS** engaging in violent pillaging and likely to harm or destroy things **3.** ZOOL **PREDATORY** living by eating live prey [Mid-17C. < Latin *rapac-* "tearing, grasping" < *rapere* "seize"] —**ra·pa·cious·ly** *adv* —**ra·pa·cious·ness** *n*

rape¹ /rayp/ *n* **1. FORCING OF SOMEBODY INTO SEX** the crime of using force to have sexual intercourse with somebody **2. INSTANCE OF RAPE** an instance of the crime of rape **3. VIOLENT DESTRUCTIVE TREATMENT** the violent, destructive, or abusive treatment of something ○ *the rape of a beautiful stretch of countryside* **4. ABDUCTION** an act of seizing somebody and carrying him or her away by force (*archaic*) ■ *vt* **(raped, rap·ing, rapes) 1. FORCE SOMEBODY TO HAVE SEX** to force somebody to have sexual intercourse **2. VIOLATE SOMETHING** to treat something in a violent, destructive, or abusive way ○ *rape the land for its resources* [14C. Via Anglo-Norman < Latin *rapere* "seize"]

ORIGIN The Latin word *rapere* "to seize," from which ***rape*** is derived, is also the source of English *rapacious, rapid, rapine, rapture, ravage, raven¹, ravine, ravish, surreptitious*, and *usurp*.

rape² /rayp/ *n* a commercially grown annual plant of the cabbage family. Flowers: bright yellow. Use: oil, fodder. Latin name: *Brassica napus*. [14C. < Latin *rapa* "turnip"]

rape³ /rayp/ *n* the skins and stalks of grapes after their juice has been extracted for use in winemaking [Early 17C. < French *râpe* "grape stalk" < Old French *rasper* "scrape"]

rape oil *n* an oil extracted from the seeds of the rape plant. Use: lubricant, making soap, cooking.

rape·seed /ráyp seed/ *n* the seeds of the rape plant

rape·seed oil *n* INDUST, FOOD same as **rape oil**

rape shield law *n* a law that prohibits the defense in a rape trial from questioning the victim about her or his previous sexual experiences

ra·phae ANAT, BOT plural of **raphe**

Raph·a·el /ráffee əl/ *n* in Hebrew tradition, one of the seven archangels, and the angel of healing

Raph·a·el /ráffee èl, ràaffee él/ (1483–1520) Italian artist. A master of the Italian High Renaissance, he is best known for his religious paintings. Born **Sanzio, Raffaello**

ra·phe /ráyfee/ *n* **1.** ANAT **CONNECTING RIDGE** a connecting ridge or seam between two similar parts of an organ of the body, e.g., between the two halves of the medulla oblongata or along the scrotum **2.** BOT **RIDGE ALONG SOME SEED COATS** a ridge along the coat of some seeds formed by fusion of the connecting stalk **(funiculus)** with the outer layer of the developing ovule **3.** BOT **LONGITUDINAL GROOVE** a longitudinal groove on the valve of a diatom [Mid-18C. Via modern Latin < Greek *rhaphē* "seam" < *rhaptein* "sew"]

raph·i·a *n* INDUST, TREES another spelling of **raffia**

ra·phide /ráy fīd/, **ra·phis** /ráyfiss/ (*plural* **raph·i·des** /ráffi deez/) *n* a crystal of calcium oxalate found in some plant cells as a byproduct of their metabolism [Mid-19C. Via French < Greek *rhaphid-* "needle" < *rhaptein* "sew"]

rap·id /ráppid/ *adj* acting, moving, or happening very quickly ○ *a rapid increase in turnover* ■ **rap·ids** *npl* a part of a riverbed where the water moves very fast, usually over rocks or around boulders [Mid-17C. < Latin *rapidus* "seizing" < *rapere* "seize"] —**rap·id·ly** *adv* —**rap·id·ness** *n*

Rap·id Cit·y /ràppid-/ city in western South Dakota, in the Black Hills, northwest of Pierre. Population: 60,262 (2002 estimate).

rap·id eye move·ment *n* jerky movements of the eyeballs while the eyes are closed, characteristic of somebody who is dreaming while asleep, especially during REM sleep

rap·id eye move·ment sleep *n* PHYSIOL full form of **REM sleep**

rap·id-fire *adj US* **1.** delivered or happening in very quick succession ○ *The salesman had an incredible rapid-fire delivery.* **2.** designed to fire bullets or shells in very quick succession or at a faster rate than a standard gun ▶ Can term **quick-fire**

rap·id pro·to·typ·ing *n* a method of quickly creating mechanical components, especially those with complex shapes, from a computer-based drawing that can be used to check the validity of a design

rap·id tran·sit *n* a high-speed urban public transportation system using underground or elevated trains or a combination of both

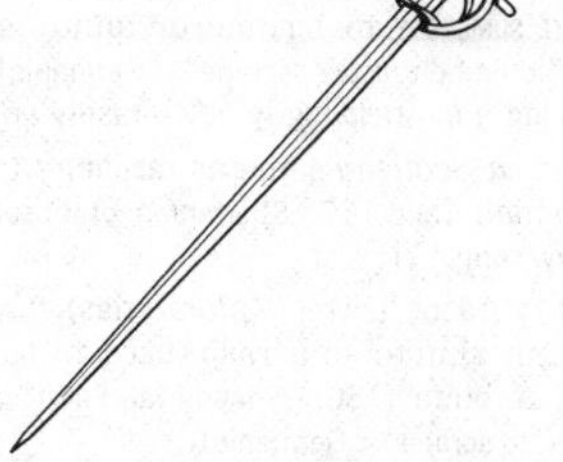

rapier

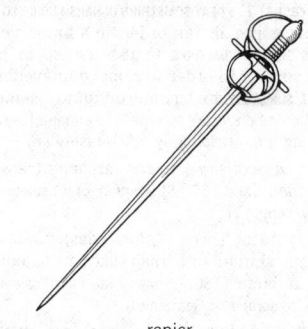

ra·pi·er /ráypee ər/ *n* a sword with a cup-shaped hilt and a long slender blade that can have two cutting edges, or only a sharply pointed tip for thrusting [Early 16C. Probably via Dutch or Low German *rappir* < French *rapière* in obsolete *espee rapière* "rapier sword"]

rap·ine /ráppən, rá pīn, ráy pīn/ *n* the use of force to seize somebody else's property (*literary*) [14C. Directly or via French < Latin *rapina* < *rapere* "seize"]

rap·i·ni /ra peénee/ *npl* the leaves of immature turnip plants, used especially in Italian and Chinese cooking [Late 20C. < Italian]

rap·ist /ráypist/ *n* somebody who uses force to have sexual intercourse with somebody else

Rapp /rap, raap/, **George** (1757–1847) German-born US religious reformer. He founded the Harmony Society, a separatist Protestant community, in Pennsylvania in 1805.

Rap·pa·han·nock /ràppə hánnək/ river in Virginia, rising in the Blue Ridge Mountains and flowing southeast into Chesapeake Bay. Length: 212 mi./341 km.

rap·pel /rə pél/ *vi* **(-pelled, -pel·ling, -pels)** to descend a steep slope or vertical face using a rope that is secured at the top and passed through a series of coils or a harness around the body ■ *n* a descent made by rappelling [Mid-20C. < French, < Old French *rapeler* "to recall" < *apeler* "to call"]

rap·pen /ráppən/ (*plural same*) *n* a Swiss centime [Mid-19C. < German, < Middle High German *rappe* "raven," referring to the depiction of a bird on a coin of the Middle Ages]

rap·per /ráppər/ *n* somebody who performs rap music

rap·port /ra páwr, rə-/ *n* an emotional bond or friendly relationship between people based on mutual liking, trust, and a sense that they understand and share each other's concerns [Mid-17C. < French, < *rapporter* "bring back" < *aporter* "bring" < Latin *portare* "carry"]

rap·por·teur /rà pawr túr/ *n* **1.** somebody who records the deliberations of a body, such as a committee, and reports them to a higher one, such as a governing body **2.** somebody who is appointed to investigate a subject and deliver a report on it [Late 15C. < French, < *rapporter* (see RAPPORT)]

rap·proche·ment /ràa prawsh maáN/ *n* the establishment or renewal of friendly relations between people or nations that were previously hostile or unsympathetic toward each other [Early 19C. < French, < *rapprocher* "bring together" < *approcher* (see APPROACH)]

rap·scal·lion /rap skállyən/ *n* (*archaic or humorous*) **1.** a mischievous and annoying child **2.** a disreputable and dishonest person [Late 17C. Alteration of *rascallion*, probably < RASCAL]

rap ses·sion *n* an informal discussion, especially between people in the same line of business or with shared concerns (*informal*)

rap sheet *n* a list of somebody's past arrests and the disposition of charges (*slang*)

rapt /rapt/ *adj* **1.** involved in, fascinated by, or concentrating on something to the exclusion of everything else ○ *staring with rapt attention at the speaker* **2.** showing or suggesting deep emotions of joy or ecstasy [14C. < Latin *raptus*, past participle of *rapere* "seize"] —**rapt·ly** *adv* —**rapt·ness** *n*

rap·tor /ráptər/ *n* BIRDS same as **bird of prey** [14C. < Latin, "robber" < *rapere* "seize"]

rap·to·ri·al /rap táwree əl/ *adj* **1. USING OTHER ANIMALS AS PREY** able to live by catching prey **2. ADAPTED FOR CATCHING PREY** specially adapted for seizing prey, as are the feet of birds of prey with their sharp talons **3. OF PREDATORY BIRDS** relating to or typical of birds of prey

rap·ture /rápchər/ *n* **1. OVERWHELMING HAPPINESS** a euphoric transcendent state in which somebody is overwhelmed by happiness or delight and unaware of anything else **2.** CHR **MYSTICAL TRANSPORTATION** a mystical experience in which somebody believes he or she is transported into the spiritual realm, sometimes applied to the second coming of Jesus Christ, when true believers are expected to rise up to join him in heaven ■ **rap·tures** *npl* **STATE OF GREAT HAPPINESS OR ENTHUSIASM** a state of great happiness or enthusiasm about something, or words and gestures that express this ○ *went into raptures about the meal they'd had* [Late 16C. Directly or via French < medieval Latin *raptura* "seizure" < Latin *raptus* (see RAPT)] —**rap·tur·ous** *adj*

rap·ture of the deep *n* MED same as **nitrogen narcosis**

ra·ra a·vis /rérrə áyviss, -ávvəss/ (*plural* **ra·rae a·ves** /rèrree áy veez/ or **ra·ra a·vis·es**) *n* somebody or something that is rarely encountered [From Latin, literally "rare bird"]

rare¹ /rer/ **(rar·er, rar·est)** *adj* **1. INFREQUENT OR UNUSUAL** not happening or found often ○ *It's rare for them to miss a meeting.* **2. VALUABLE** particularly interesting or valuable, especially to collectors or scholars, because only a few exist **3. GREAT** unusually great or excellent ○ *a rare gift for languages* **4. CONTAINING LITTLE OXYGEN** thin in density and containing so little oxygen that breathing is difficult [15C. < Latin *rarus* "having a loose texture, scarce"] —**rare·ness** *n*

rare² /rer/ **(rar·er, rar·est)** *adj* describes meat that is cooked quickly and lightly so as to remain raw and juicy inside [Mid-17C. Alteration of dialect *rear* "underdone" (describing eggs), origin ?]

rare·bit /rér bit/ (*plural same* or **-bits**) *n* FOOD same as **Welsh rarebit** [Late 18C. Alteration of RABBIT in *Welsh rabbit*, earlier form of WELSH RAREBIT]

rare earth *n* an oxide of a rare-earth element

rare-earth el·e·ment *n* a member of the lanthanide series, which contains 15 elements that have atomic numbers from 57 to 71 and share closely related chemical properties

rar·ee show /rérree-/ *n* (*archaic*) **1.** same as **peepshow**

(sense 2) **2.** a street show or spectacle with unusual or outlandish items on view [Alteration of *rare show*]

rar·e·fac·tion /rèrrə fáksh'n/, **rar·e·fi·ca·tion** /rèrrəfi káysh'n/ *n* the process of becoming or of making something such as a gas less dense [Early 17C. < medieval Latin *rarefaction-* < past participle of Latin *rarefacere* (see RAREFY)] —**rar·e·fac·tion·al** *adj*

rar·e·fied /rérrə fīd/ *adj* **1.** WITH LOW DENSITY describes an atmosphere that has a low density, especially owing to a low oxygen content **2.** ESOTERIC OR ELITE seemingly distinct or remote from ordinary reality and common people, and often purged of anything perceived as coarse or tasteless **3.** OF HIGH STANDARD showing very high quality in character or style (*literary*) ○ *Milton's rarefied prose*

rar·e·fy /rérrə fī/ (**-fied, -fy·ing, -fies**) *v* **1.** *vti* to make something, especially a gas, less dense, or become less dense **2.** *vt* to make something less connected with or typical of the ordinary [14C. Directly or via French *raréfier* < medieval Latin *rarificare* < Latin *rarefacere* "make rare" < *rarus* "scarce" + *facere* "do"] —**rar·e·fi·a·ble** /rérrə fī əb'l/ *adj*

rare gas *n* CHEM same as **noble gas**

rare·ly /rérlee/ *adv* **1.** almost never or not very often **2.** exceptionally well

rare·ripe /rér rīp/ *US adj* ripening early ■ *n* a fruit or vegetable that ripens early [Early 18C. < *rare* "early," variant of *rathe* < Old English *hræþ* "quick" < Germanic]

rar·i·fied *adj US* another spelling of **rarefied**

rar·i·fy *v US* another spelling of **rarefy**

rar·ing /rérring/ *adj* very enthusiastic and eager to start doing something (*informal*) ○ *They were raring to go.* [Early 20C. Present participle of *rare*, variant of REAR[1]]

rar·i·ty /rérrətee/ (*plural* **-ties**) *n* **1.** something that happens rarely or is particularly interesting or valuable because it is so unusual **2.** the fact of happening very seldom or of being very unusual

RAS *abbr UK* Royal Astronomical Society

Ras al-Am /raass al aam/ *n* an Islamic festival, the first day of the first month of the Hegira calendar, marking the withdrawal of Muhammad from Mecca to Medina in 622 A.D. Date: 1st of Muharram.

ra·sam /rússəm/ *n S Asia* in South Indian cuisine, a thin spicy drink or thin lentil soup, either mixed with rice or drunk by itself [Via Tamil < Sanskrit *rasa* "flavor"]

~~rasberry~~ incorrect spelling of **raspberry**

ras·bo·ra /raz báwrə, rázbərə/ *n* a tropical freshwater fish, several species of which are brightly colored and often kept in aquariums. Native to: East Africa, Asia. Genus: *Rasbora*. [Mid-20C. < modern Latin, origin ?]

ras·cal /rásk'l/ *n* **1.** somebody who behaves in a mischievous teasing way, especially a child (*humorous*) **2.** somebody, especially a man, who is dishonest or otherwise unethical [14C. < Old French *rascaille* "mob, rabble"] —**ras·cal·ly** *adj*

rase *vt* another spelling of **raze** (*literary*)

ras·gul·la /rùss gŏŏllə/ *n* in South Asian cuisine, a dessert consisting of a ball of curd cheese (**paneer**) cooked in syrup [Mid-20C. < Hindi *rasgullā* "juice ball"]

rash[1] /rash/ *adj* acting with, resulting from, or characteristic of thoughtless, impetuous behavior [14C. Probably < Germanic, "quick"] —**rash·ly** *adv* —**rash·ness** *n*

rash[2] /rash/ *n* **1.** an outbreak on the surface of the skin that is often reddish and itchy **2.** a series of events that happen in a brief period and are considered to be unusual or rare ○ *a rash of burglaries* [Early 18C. Origin ?]

rash·er /ráshər/ *n* **1.** an order or portion of slices of cooked bacon or ham **2.** a slice of bacon or ham, broiled or fried [Late 16C. Origin ?]

Ra·shîd /raa sheed/ city in Egypt, on the Mediterranean coast. Population: 52,014 (1986).

ras ma·lai /rùss mə lī/ *n* in South Asian cuisine, a dessert consisting of small balls or squares of curd cheese (**paneer**) served cold in thickened and sweetened milk [From Hindi *ras* "juice" + *malāī* "cream"]

Ras·mus·sen /rássməss'n/, **Anders Fogh** (*b.* 1953) prime minister of Denmark (2001–). A Liberal Party politician, he formed a right-wing coalition of Liberals and Conservatives in 2001 to win an election that was dominated by asylum issues.

ra·so·ri·al /rə sáwree əl/ *adj* describes a bird that is capable of or adapted for scratching the ground to look for food [Mid-19C. < late Latin *rasor* "scraper" < Latin *ras-* past participle of *radere* "scrape"]

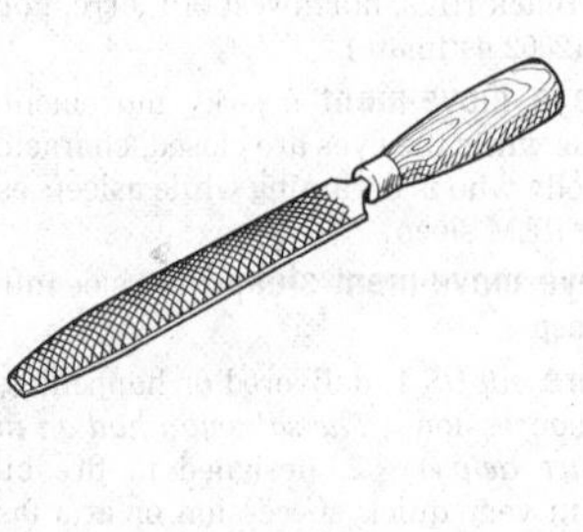

rasp (sense 2)

rasp[1] /rasp/ *n* **1.** HARSH GRATING SOUND a harsh grating sound, similar to that of a rasp or saw cutting into wood **2.** LARGE-TOOTHED FILE a tool used for scraping or smoothing wood or metal, similar to a file, but with larger teeth on its cutting surface **3.** ACT OF SMOOTHING SOMETHING the act of smoothing the surface of something such as wood or metal with a rasp ■ *v* (**rasped, rasp·ing, rasps**) **1.** *vt* SAY SOMETHING IN HARSH VOICE to utter something, especially an order, in a harsh voice **2.** *vti* FILE OR SCRAPE SOMETHING to use a rasp to file or scrape a surface in order to remove unevenness **3.** *vt* IRRITATE SOMEBODY to irritate or annoy somebody [13C. < Old French *rasper* "scrape" < Germanic] —**rasp·er** *n* —**rasp·ing** *adj* —**rasp·ing·ly** *adv* —**rasp·y** *adj*

rasp[2] /rasp/ *n Scotland* same as **raspberry** (senses 1–2) (*informal*) [Mid-16C. Shortening of obsolete *raspis* "raspberry," origin ?]

ras·pa·to·ry /ráspə tàwree/ (*plural* **-ries**) *n* a surgical instrument similar to a rasp, used to smooth the ends of a bone [15C. < medieval Latin *raspatorium* < *raspare* "to scrape" < Germanic]

rasp·ber·ry /ráz bèrree/ (*plural* **-ries**) *n* **1.** SMALL CUP-SHAPED FRUIT a small red cup-shaped fruit with a sweet taste that grows round a pithy stalk and is made up of many tiny juicy globes (**drupelets**) **2.** RASPBERRY BUSH a shrubby plant that produces raspberries. Genus: *Rubus*. **3.** *UK* same as **Bronx cheer** (*informal*) **4.** RED COLOR a deep purplish pink color [Early 17C. < RASP[2]] —**rasp·ber·ry** *adj*

rasp·ings /ráspingz/ *npl UK* fine breadcrumbs, often toasted, used to coat fish or other foods before frying or baking

Grigory Rasputin

Ras·pu·tin /rass pyoótin/, **Grigory** (1869?–1916) Russian peasant and self-proclaimed holy man. His friendship with Russia's last tsar and tsarina wrecked the Romanov dynasty's prestige and contributed to the coming of the Russian Revolution (1917). Full name **Rasputin, Grigory Yetimovich**

Ras·ta /rástə/ (*informal*) *n* **1.** PEOPLES same as **Rastafarian 2.** RELIG same as **Rastafarianism** (*used in Black English*) ■ *adj* relating to Rastafarians or Rastafarianism [Mid-20C. Shortening]

Ras·ta·far·i /ràstə faaree/ *interj* used as a greeting to another Rastafarian (*used in Black English*)

Ras·ta·far·i·an /ràstə férree ən/ *n* a member of an Afro-Caribbean religious group that venerates the former emperor of Ethiopia, Haile Selassie, forbids the cutting of hair, and stresses Black culture and identity [Mid-20C. < Amharic *Ras Tafari* "prince to be feared," name given to Haile Selassie I (1892–1975), emperor of Ethiopia (1930–36) before he came to power]

Ras·ta·far·i·an·ism /ràstə rérree ənìzəm/ *n* the belief system of Rastafarians

rast·er /rástər/ *n* the pattern of horizontal scanning lines made by an electron beam on the surface of a cathode-ray tube that create the image on a television or computer screen [Mid-20C. Via German, "screen" < Latin *rastrum* "rake" < *radere* "to scrape"]

ras·ter font *n* a bit-mapped computer font formed from pixels

ras·ter·ize /rástə rīz/ (**-ized, -iz·ing, -iz·es**) *vt* to convert a digitized image into a format suitable for display on a computer monitor or printout

rat

rat /rat/ *n* **1.** LONG-TAILED RODENT a long-tailed rodent, larger than a mouse. Genus: *Rattus*. **2.** ANIMAL LIKE RAT an animal that resembles a rat **3.** SOMEBODY UNTRUSTWORTHY somebody regarded as mean, sneaky and deceitful, especially somebody who betrays friends or confidences (*slang insult*) **4.** ARTIFICIAL HAIR a pad with tapered ends used in hairdressing to add height to the hair (*dated*) ■ *v* (**rat·ted, rat·ting, rats**) **1.** *vi* HUNT RATS to hunt and kill rats **2.** *vt US* MAKE HAIR STAND HIGH ON HEAD to use a comb to tease hair into knots with quick repeated movements, which makes it stand up high from the scalp [Old English *ræt*] ◇ **smell a rat** be suspicious that something is not right (*slang*)

rat on *vt* **1.** to betray somebody's trust, especially by revealing something told in confidence (*informal*) **2.** *UK* to abandon somebody or something, or fail to do something (*slang*)

rat·a·ble /ráytəb'l/, **rate·a·ble** *adj* **1.** able to be estimated or have a value placed on it **2.** *UK* liable for a tax —**rat·a·bil·i·ty** /ràytə bíllətee/ *n* —**rat·a·bly** *adv*

rat·a·bles /ráytəb'lz/, **rate·a·bles** *npl US* **1.** government income derived from taxes on property **2.** buildings or other property, especially those in commercial use, that supply local government with tax income

rat·a·fi·a /ràttə feé ə/ *n* **1.** a liqueur made from fruit juices or softened fruit in liquor, especially brandy, and often flavored with almonds or with peach or apricot kernels **2.** *also* **rat·a·fi·a bis·cuit** a small sweet biscuit similar to a macaroon, flavored with almond or ratafia [Late 17C. Via French < Caribbean Creole]

rat·a·plan /ráttə plàn/ *n* a noise like the rapid beating of a drum, the sound of horses' hooves striking the ground, or machine-gun fire, made up of a series of short repeated sounds [Mid-19C. < French, an imitation of the sound]

rat-a-tat-tat /ràttə tat tát/, **rat-tat-tat, rat-tat** *n* the distinctive rhythmic pattern of short loud sounds made by somebody knocking at a door ■ *interj* an imitation of the sound of somebody knocking on a door [Late 17C. An imitation of the sound]

rat·a·tou·ille /ràttə toó ee/ (*plural same* or **-illes**) *n* a dish of stewed vegetables, originally from southern France, usually consisting of tomatoes, onions, peppers, eggplant, and zucchini cooked slowly in olive oil [Late 19C. < French, alteration of *touiller* "stir" < Old French *tooiller* "drag around"]

rat-bite fe·ver *n* an infectious disease in humans caused by the bite of a rat infected with either of two bacteria, *Streptobacillus moniliformis* or *Spirillum minus*

rat-catch·er *n* somebody whose job is to rid buildings of rats and other vermin

rat cheese *n US* Cheddar cheese (*informal humorous*)

ratch·et /ráchət/ *n* **1. TURNING DEVICE MOVING IN ONE DIRECTION** a mechanism, used especially in lifting devices and some hand tools, consisting of a metal wheel operating with a catch that permits motion in only one direction **2. RATCHET WHEEL OR PAWL** either of the main parts of a ratchet device, the toothed wheel or bar, or the pawl ■ *v* (**-et·ed, -et·ing, -ets**) **1.** *vt US* **FORCE SOMETHING UP OR DOWN** to force something such as prices or political rhetoric to rise or fall in level or intensity by deliberately applying pressure in successive and irreversible stages **2.** *vti* **MOVE WITH RATCHET** to move gradually up or down by means of a ratchet, or to move something in this way [Mid-17C. < French *rochet* "spool" < Germanic]

ratch·et wheel *n* a toothed wheel in a ratchet mechanism

rate /rayt/ *n* **1. SPEED** the speed at which one measured quantity happens in relation to another measured amount such as time **2. AMOUNT IN RELATION TO STANDARD FIGURE** the amount, frequency, or speed of something expressed as a proportion of a larger figure or in relation to a whole ○ *The dropout rate at the end of the first year is around one in three.* **3.** COMM **CHARGE** the amount of money charged per unit, e.g., per hour, per page, or per thousand, for a job, service, or commodity ○ *I'm charging you the going rate for the job.* **4.** *UK* ORDINARY SAILOR a member of a navy who is not an officer ■ **rates** *npl UK* **FORMER LOCAL TAX** formerly in the United Kingdom, a tax levied by local authorities on all properties in their areas of jurisdiction, based on a fixed ratable value for each property ■ *v* (**rat·ed, rat·ing, rates**) **1.** *vt* **SET VALUE ON SOMETHING** to calculate or appraise the value of something ○ *How would you rate this gem collection?* **2.** *vti* **ASSESS SOMETHING OR BE ASSESSED** to have a particular value, position, or importance relative to other people or things, or be regarded as having this ○ *This rates as undoubtedly the worst movie I have ever seen.* **3.** *vt* **DESERVE SOMETHING** to deserve or be worthy of something ○ *Her latest book didn't even rate a review.* **4.** *vt* **CLASSIFY SOMETHING** to give a particular classification or rating to something such as a machine, identifying its performance capabilities and limits **5.** *vt* FIN **VALUE SOMETHING FOR TAX PURPOSES** to value something, especially a property, for tax purposes [15C. Via French < medieval Latin *(pro) rata (parte)* "(according to a) fixed (part)" < Latin *ratus*, past participle of *reri* "calculate"] ◇ **at any rate** used to indicate that an important point is true, whatever the other considerations

ORIGIN The Latin word *reri* "to calculate," from which ***rate*** is derived, is also the source of English *ratify, ration,* and *reason.*

rate·a·ble *adj* FIN another spelling of **ratable**

rate cap *n* a maximum interest charge permitted during the life of an adjustable-rate mortgage

rate con·stant *n* the constant in a mathematical expression relating the concentrations of the reactants and the products for a particular chemical reaction

ra·tel /ráytl, raát'l/ (*plural same* or **-tels**) *n* an aggressive carnivorous animal with short thick legs, a strong body with a thick furry coat, dark underneath and whitish on top, and a head similar to a badger's. Native to: Asia, Africa. Latin name: *Mellivora capensis.* [Late 18C. < Afrikaans]

rate·mak·ing /ráyt màyking/ *n US* the process or business of establishing rates of payment for such things as public transportation or utilities

rate of change *n* the ratio of the difference in values of a variable during a time period to the length of that time period

rate of ex·change *n* FIN same as **exchange rate**

rate of re·turn *n* the amount of income generated in a year by capital invested, expressed as a percentage of the total sum invested

rate·pay·er /ráyt pày ər/ *n* somebody who pays for the use of a utility such as electricity or water based on the amount consumed

rat·er /ráytər/ *n US* **1.** somebody who establishes rates or ratings **2.** somebody with a particular rank or level of ability (*often used in combination*) ○ *All of them are second-raters with delusions of grandeur.*

rat·fink /rát fingk/ *n* an offensive term that deliberately insults somebody's character or behavior (*insult*)

rat·fish /rát fish/ (*plural same* or **-fish·es**) *n* a cartilaginous deep-sea fish with a long narrow tail, found worldwide. Family: Chimaeridae.

rath /ruth/, **ra·tha** /rúthə/ *n S Asia* a four-wheeled chariot, especially an elaborate, carved ceremonial chariot pulled by devotees in which a representation of a deity is taken out in procession on festival days [From Sanskrit, "wagon, chariot"]

Ra·then·au /raátə nòwr/, **Walther** (1867–1922) German political economist and public servant. As foreign minister, he represented Germany at reparations conferences after World War I. He was assassinated by German nationalists.

> "There comes a painful moment in the life of every young German Jew...when he fully realizes for the first time that he has come into the world as a second-class citizen, and that no virtue and no merit can free him from this situation."
> [Walther Rathenau. Quoted in *Europe Since 1870*, James Joll; 1973]

rath·er /ráthər/ *adv* **1. SOMEWHAT** to some extent or degree ○ *rather disappointing* **2. CONSIDERABLY** to a great extent or degree ○ *I think the irises are rather attractive.* **3. MORE WILLINGLY** more readily or willingly ○ *You go to the movies; I'd rather stay home tonight.* **4. WITH MORE JUSTIFICATION** with more logic, evidence, precision, or justification ○ *You should praise rather than blame them.* **5. ON CONTRARY** in contrast or opposition to what has been claimed or expected ○ *You think she's snobbish? Rather, I'd say she's shy.* ■ *interj UK* **MOST CERTAINLY** used to express complete or enthusiastic agreement with what has just been said (*dated*) [Old English *hræþor*, originally comparative form of *hraeþ* "quick" < Germanic]

Rath·lin Is·land /ráthlin-/ island in Northern Ireland, off the northern coast of Antrim County. It is home to three lighthouses. Length: 6 mi./10 km.

rat hole *n* the entrance to a rat's nest

raths·kel·ler /raáts kèllər, ráts-/ *n* a beer hall or restaurant that serves German dishes, usually located below street level [Early 20C. < obsolete German, "council cellar" (cellar of the town hall) < *Rat* "council" + *Keller* "cellar"]

rath ya·tra /-yaátrə/ *n S Asia* a procession in which a representation of a Hindu deity is carried in a ceremonial chariot, especially the annual procession of Juggernaut in Puri [*Yatra* from Sanskrit *yātrā*, from *yā* "to travel"]

rat·i·fy /rráttə fì/ (**-fied, -fy·ing, -fies**) *vt* to give formal approval to something, usually an agreement negotiated by somebody else, in order that it can become valid or operative [14C. Via French *ratifier* < medieval Latin *ratificare* "make fixed" < Latin *ratus* (see RATE)] —**rat·i·fi·a·ble** *adj* —**rat·i·fi·ca·tion** /ràttəfi káysh'n/ *n* —**rat·i·fi·er** *n*

rat·i·né /ràttə náy,ráttə nay/, **rat·i·ne** *n* a loosely woven cloth with a coarse nubby texture [Early 20C. < French, past participle of *ratiner* "raise a nap" < *ratine* "nap, twilled fabric"]

rat·ing /ráyting/ *n* **1. ASSESSMENT** an assessment or classification of somebody or something on a scale according to how much or how little of a quality he, she, or it possesses **2.** COMM **CREDIT STANDING** an assessment of the financial status and creditworthiness of a person or company ○ *a credit rating* **3.** MECH ENG **PERFORMANCE LIMIT OF MACHINE** the performance limit of a machine or system, expressed as capacity, range, or working capability, e.g., the voltage rating on a household appliance **4.** *US* **CLASSIFICATION OF SOMEBODY BY OCCUPATION** a classification of somebody such as a member of the military or a government worker, based on his or her specialization or occupation ■ **rat·ings** *npl* MEDIA **ESTIMATE OF AUDIENCE SIZE** the estimated number of people who tuned in to a TV or radio program, used as an indication of its relative popularity

ra·tio /ráyshō, ráyshi ō/ (*plural* **-tios**) *n* **1. PROPORTIONAL RELATIONSHIP** a proportional relationship between two different numbers or quantities ○ *The ratio of teachers to students at that school is 1 to 27* **2.** MATH **ONE NUMBER DIVIDED BY ANOTHER** a quotient of two numbers or expressions arrived at by dividing one by the other **3.** *US* FIN **RELATIVE VALUE OF GOLD AND SILVER** the value of gold and silver relative to each other in a monetary system based on these two metals [Mid-17C. < Latin, "calculation" (see REASON)]

ra·ti·oc·i·nate /ràshee óss'n àyt, -ṓss'n-, rattee-/ (**-nat·ed, -nat·ing, -nates**) *vi* to think or put forward an argument about something in a strictly logical way (*formal*) [Mid-17C. < Latin *ratiocinat-*, past participle of *ratiocinari* "compute" < *ratio* (see RATIO)] —**ra·ti·oc·i·na·tion** /ràshee òss'n áysh'n, -ṑss'n-/ *n* —**ra·ti·oc·i·na·tive** *adj* —**ra·ti·oc·i·na·tor** *n*

ra·tion /rásh'n, ráysh'n/ *n* **1. FIXED AMOUNT ALLOCATED TO SOMEBODY** a fixed and limited amount of something, especially food, given or allocated to a person or group from the stocks available, especially during a time of shortage or a war **2. ADEQUATE AMOUNT** the amount of something that it seems fair or desirable for somebody to have ○ *more than your ration of bad luck* ■ **ra·tions** *npl* **AMOUNT OF FOOD OFFICIALLY ALLOCATED** food, especially an amount of food from a limited stock allocated to somebody such as a soldier or hiker ■ *vt* (**-tioned, -tion·ing, -tions**) **1. RESTRICT AVAILABLE AMOUNT OF SOMETHING** to restrict the amount of something, usually a commodity in short supply, that somebody is allowed to buy, consume, or use ○ *Gasoline was rationed, so long trips were out of the question.* **2. LIMIT QUANTITY AVAILABLE TO SOMEBODY** to allow somebody only a limited quantity of something ○ *rationed herself to one cup of coffee a day* [Early 18C. Via French < Spanish *ración* < Latin *ratio* (see RATIO)]

ration out *vt* to distribute something, especially something that is in short supply, in fixed or strictly limited quantities

ra·tion·al /rásh'n'l/ *adj* **1. REASONABLE AND SENSIBLE** governed by, or showing evidence of, clear and sensible thinking and judgment, based on reason rather than emotion or prejudice **2. ABLE TO THINK CLEARLY AND SENSIBLY** able to think clearly and sensibly, unimpaired by physical or mental condition, strong emotion, or prejudice ○ *I can't be rational when so many people give me conflicting advice.* **3. IN ACCORDANCE WITH REASON AND LOGIC** presented or understandable in terms that accord with reason and logic or with scientific knowledge ○ *a rational explanation* **4. ABLE TO REASON** endowed with the ability to reason, as opposed to being governed solely by instinct and appetite **5.** MATH **EXPRESSIBLE AS RATIO OF POLYNOMIALS** in mathematics, able to be expressed exactly as the quotient of two whole numbers or polynomials ○ *a rational function* ■ *n* MATH same as **rational number** [14C. < Latin *rationalis* < *ratio* (see RATIO)] —**ra·tion·al·ly** *adv* —**ra·tion·al·ness** *n*

SPELLCHECK Do not confuse the spelling of ***rational*** and ***rationale***, which are linked by the idea of "reason" but otherwise differ in meaning, spelling, and pronunciation. ***Rational*** is an adjective meaning "logical, sensible" (*a perfectly rational argument*), whereas ***rationale*** is a noun meaning "set of underlying reasons" (*explained the rationale behind the new guidelines*).

ra·tion·al choice the·o·ry *n* the hypothesis, derived from game theory, that there is a rational, definable, and calculable basis to human decision-making

ra·tion·ale /ràshə nál/ *n* the reasoning or principle that underlies or explains something, or a statement setting out this reasoning or principle [Mid-17C. < modern Latin, < Latin *rationalis* (see RATIONAL)]

SPELLCHECK See ***rational.***

ra·tion·al-e·mo·tive be·hav·ior ther·a·py, **ra·tion·al-e·mo·tive ther·a·py** *n* a form of cognitive-behavioral therapy in which somebody is encouraged to examine and change irrational thought patterns and beliefs in order to reduce dysfunctional behavior

ra·tion·al ho·ri·zon *n US* same as **horizon** (sense 3) (*technical*)

ra·tion·al·ism /ráshən'l ìzzəm, ráshnə lìzzəm/ *n* **1.** the belief that thought and action should be governed by reason **2.** the belief that reason and logic are the primary sources of knowledge and truth and should be relied on in searching for and testing the truth of things —**ra·tion·al·ist** *n* —**ra·tion·al·is·tic** /ràshən'l ístik, ràshnə lístik/ *adj* —**ra·tion·al·is·ti·cal·ly** *adv*

ra·tion·al·i·ty /ràshə nállətee/ (*plural* **-ties**) *n* **1.** RATIONAL ATTITUDE rational thought or behavior, or the ability to think rationally **2.** SOMETHING RATIONAL a rational belief, opinion, or action (*often used in the plural*) **3.** CONDITION OF BEING LOGICAL the condition in which values, beliefs, and techniques are believed to be based on logical, explicable principles

ra·tion·al·i·za·tion /ràshən'li záysh'n, ràshnəli-/ *n* **1.** the process of rationalizing something, or an instance of rationalizing something **2.** in psychoanalytic theory, a defense mechanism whereby people attempt to hide their true motivations and emotions by providing reasonable or self-justifying explanations for irrational or unacceptable behavior

ra·tion·al·ize /ráshən'l ìz, ráshnə lìz/ (**-ized, -iz·ing, -iz·es**) *v* **1.** *vti* OFFER REASONABLE EXPLANATION FOR SOMETHING to attempt to justify behavior normally considered irrational or unacceptable by offering an apparently reasonable explanation **2.** *vt* MAKE SOMETHING RATIONAL to make something rational, logical, or consistent **3.** *vt* INTERPRET SOMETHING RATIONALLY to interpret something from a rational or logical perspective **4.** *vt* MATH ELIMINATE IRRATIONAL NUMBERS FROM SOMETHING to eliminate irrational numbers from an expression or an equation **5.** *vti UK* MAKE SOMETHING MORE EFFICIENT AND PROFITABLE to make a business or operation more efficient and profitable, e.g., by reducing the workforce —**ra·tion·al·iz·a·ble** *adj* —**ra·tion·al·iz·er** *n*

ra·tion·al num·ber *n* a whole number or the quotient of any whole numbers, excluding zero as a denominator

ra·tio scale *n* a scale for measuring data that makes it possible to compare different values and to state the difference between them in the form of a ratio

Rat Is·lands /rát-/ group of islands in Alaska, in the western Aleutian Islands, including Kiska, Amchitka, Semisopochnoi, and Rat Island

rat·ite /rá tìt/ (*plural same* or **-ites**) *n* a flightless bird such as an ostrich or emu that has a flat breastbone without the ridge-shaped part (**keel**) to which the flight muscles are attached in a flying bird [Late 19C. < Latin *ratitus* "having the figure of a raft" < *ratis* "raft"]

rat·line /rátlən/, **rat·lin** *n* a small rope fastened horizontally between the shrouds in the rigging of a sailing ship to form a rung of a ladder for the crew going aloft [15C. Origin ?]

RATO /ráytō/ *abbr* ENG rocket-assisted takeoff

ra·toon /rə to͞on/, **rat·toon** *n* **1.** SHOOT AT BASE OF PLANT a shoot growing up from the base of a crop plant such as sugar cane or bananas after the previous growth has been cut back **2.** CROP PRODUCED ON RATOONS a crop that is produced on ratoons, e.g., sugar cane, bananas, or pineapples ■ *vti* (**-tooned, -toon·ing, -toons**) PROPAGATE SOMETHING WITH RATOONS to propagate a crop by inducing the formation of ratoons, or send up ratoons [Mid-17C. < Spanish *retoño* "new shoot"]

rat pack *n* a group of people with close ties or common interests and aims, whose activities are sometimes regarded with suspicion or disapproval (*slang insult*)

rat race *n* the struggle to survive and make progress in the competitive environment of modern life, seen as a dehumanizing and ultimately futile activity (*informal*) ○ *I'd like to get out of this rat race and retire to an isolated mountain cabin.*

rats /rats/ *interj* used to express annoyance or contempt (*informal*) [Late 19C. Plural of RAT]

rat snake *n* a large nonvenomous snake that eats rodents. Native to: North America, Asia. Genera: *Elaphe* or *Ptyas*.

rat's nest *n* **1.** something that is very messy, e.g., a room, house, or somebody's hair (*informal*) **2.** a nest in which rats live and breed

rat's tail cac·tus *n* PLANTS same as **rattail cactus**

rat-tail *n* a hairless tail on a horse ■ *adj also* **rat-tailed** looking like or having a part that resembles a rat's tail ○ *a rat-tail comb*

rat·tail cac·tus, **rat's tail cac·tus** *n* a commonly cultivated cactus with thin creeping or hanging stems. Flowers: bright crimson or pink. Native to: Mexico. Latin name: *Aporocactus flagelliformis*.

rat·tan /ra tán, rə-/ *n* **1.** STEMS USED FOR FURNITURE long thin jointed and pliable stems. Use: wickerwork, furniture, canes. **2.** TROPICAL ASIAN CLIMBING PALM a climbing palm that is the source of rattan. Native to: tropical Asia. Genera: *Calamus* or *Daemonorops* or *Plectomia*. **3.** HOUSEHOLD ARTICLES MADE OF RATTAN furniture or other things made of rattan [Mid-17C. < Malay *rotan*]

rat-tat, **rat-tat-tat** *n*, *interj* same as **rat-a-tat-tat**

rat·ted /ráttəd/ *adj* **1.** *US* describes hair with tangles combed into it in order to make it look fuller **2.** *UK* very drunk (*slang*)

rat·ter /ráttər/ *n* an animal, especially a cat or dog, that is good at catching rats

rat·tle[1] /rátt'l/ *v* (**-tled, -tling, -tles**) **1.** *vti* MAKE SHORT SHARP KNOCKING SOUNDS to make short sharp knocking sounds in quick succession, especially as a result of being moved or shaken, or make something do this ○ *The windows and doors rattled in the wind.* **2.** *vi* MOVE WITH RATTLING SOUND to move while making a rattling sound ○ *The old jalopy rattled noisily down the street.* **3.** *vt* DISCONCERT SOMEBODY to make somebody lose composure and feel frightened, worried, confused, or annoyed ■ *n* **1.** SHORT SHARP KNOCKING SOUNDS a quick succession of short sharp knocking sounds, usually caused by something being moved or shaken **2.** BABY'S TOY a baby's toy consisting of a hollow shape with small objects inside, that rattles when it is shaken **3.** NOISEMAKER an object that produces a rattling sound, e.g., a musical instrument or a tool used by a shaman **4.** REPT TIP OF RATTLESNAKE'S TAIL a set of loosely attached horny segments at the end of a rattlesnake's tail that produce a rattling or buzzing sound when shaken **5.** MED RATTLING NOISE IN THROAT a rattling or rasping noise made in the throat, caused by obstructed breathing and heard especially near death **6.** PLANTS PLANT WITH RATTLING SEEDS a plant whose seeds rattle inside the seed capsule [14C. Probably < Middle Low German *ratelen*, an imitation of the sound]

rattle around *vi* to be in a room, house, or building that is much bigger than is required (*informal*) ○ *There's just the two of us rattling around in this place.*

rattle off *vt* to say, read aloud, or perform something very rapidly or with no apparent effort

rattle on *vi* to talk rapidly and at length about something of little interest or importance to the listener

rat·tle[2] /rátt'l/ (**-tled, -tling, -tles**) *vt* to attach ratlines to the shrouds in the rigging of a ship [Early 18C. Back-formation < *ratling*, variant of RATLINE]

rat·tle·box /rátt'l bòks/ *n* a tropical plant that has inflated seed pods containing seeds that make a rattling noise when the stem moves. Genus: *Crotalaria*.

rat·tle·brained /rátt'l brāynd/ *adj US* an offensive term meaning regarded as silly and excessively talkative (*informal insult*)

rat·tler /ráttlər/ (*plural same* or **-tlers**) *n* **1.** REPT same as **rattlesnake** (*informal*) **2.** somebody or something that rattles **3.** *US* RAIL same as **freight train** (*informal*)

rattlesnake

rat·tle·snake /rátt'l snàyk/ (*plural same* or **-snakes**) *n* a large venomous snake of the pit viper family, whose tail has loosely attached horny segments that rattle or buzz when vibrated. Native to: North and South America. Genus: *Crotalis* or *Sistrurus*.

rat·tle·snake flag *n* any US flag that bears a picture of a rattlesnake in striking position and the legend "Don't Tread on Me," used during the French and Indian War and the Revolutionary War

rat·tle·snake mas·ter *n* PLANTS same as **button snakeroot** (sense 2)

rat·tle·snake plan·tain *n* an orchid with striped or mottled leaves resembling a rattlesnake's skin. Flowers: white or yellow, in spikes. Genus: *Goodyera*.

rat·tle·snake root (*plural same*) *n* a composite plant that has bitter-tasting tuberous roots and white or purple flowers resembling a strap, once believed to offer protection from rattlesnake bites. Genus: *Prenanthes*.

rat·tle·snake weed (*plural same*) *n* a plant with purple-veined leaves resembling a rattlesnake's skin. Flowers: yellow. Native to: northern America. Latin name: *Hieracium venosum*.

rat·tle·trap /rátt'l tràp/ *n* an old noisy worn-out car or other vehicle (*informal*)

rat·tling /ráttling/ *adj* moving or talking at a quick or lively pace ○ *a rattling TV debate* ■ *adv UK* extremely (*dated informal*) ○ *tells a rattling good story* —**rat·tling·ly** *adv*

rat·tly /ráttlee/ (**-tlier, -tli·est**) *adj* making a loud rattling noise ○ *a rattly air conditioner*

rat·toon *n* PLANTS another spelling of **ratoon**

rat·trap /rát tràp/ *n* **1.** a dilapidated dirty unsafe dwelling (*informal*) **2.** a trap designed to catch rats

rat·ty /rátee/ (**-ti·er, -ti·est**) *adj* **1.** MESSY having a messy and generally unkempt appearance (*informal*) ○ *a ratty old sweater* **2.** DILAPIDATED in an unsafe, rundown condition and unfit for human habitation (*informal*) **3.** INFESTED WITH RATS full of or overrun with rats **4.** OF RATS relating to or believed to be characteristic of rats **5.** *UK* IRRITABLE irritable or annoyed (*informal*) ○ *Don't get ratty: it won't take very long.* —**rat·ti·ly** *adv* —**rat·ti·ness** *n*

rau·cous /ráwkəss/ *adj* **1.** loud and harsh-sounding **2.** characterized by loud noise, shouting, and ribald laughter [Mid-18C. < Latin *raucus* "hoarse"] —**rau·ci·ty** /ráwsətee/ *n* —**rau·cous·ly** *adv* —**rau·cous·ness** *n*

raunch /ráwnch/ *n* (*slang*) **1.** SEXUAL EXPLICITNESS sexual explicitness or suggestiveness of an earthy or vulgar kind, especially as part of a performer's material or act **2.** SEXUALLY EXPLICIT MATERIAL sexually explicit or lewd material or language **3.** *US* MESSINESS lack of cleanliness or neatness [Mid-20C. Back-formation < RAUNCHY]

raun·chy /ráwnchee/ (**-chi·er, -chi·est**) *adj* **1.** sexually explicit or suggestive in an earthy or vulgar way (*informal*) **2.** lacking cleanliness or neatness (*slang*) [Mid-20C. Origin ?] —**raun·chi·ly** *adv* —**raun·chi·ness** *n*

Robert Rauschenberg

Rausch·en·berg /rówsh'n bùrg/, **Robert** (*b.* 1925) US artist. His hybrid three-dimensional works such as *Monogram* (1955–59) had a strong influence on the pop art movement of the 1960s.

> "Painting is always strongest when in spite of composition, color, etc., it appears as a fact, or an inevitability, as opposed to a souvenir or arrangement."
> [Robert Rauschenberg. Quoted in *Sixteen Americans*, Dorothy C. Miller (ed.); 1959]

Rausch·en·busch /rówsh'n bo͝osh/, **Walter** (1861–1918) US cleric. He was prominent in the Social Gospel movement, which advocated applying Christian principles to social problems.

rau·wol·fi·a /row wo͝olfee ə, raw-/ (*plural same* or **-as**) *n* **1.** a dried root with medicinal properties. Use: sedatives. **2.** the tropical tree or bush whose root has medicinal properties. Native to: Southeast Asia. Latin name: *Rauwolfia serpentina*. [Mid-18C. < modern Latin, after Leonhard *Rauwolf* (?-1596), German botanist and physician]

rav·age /rávvij/ *v* (**-aged, -ag·ing, -ag·es**) **1.** *vti* **COMPLETELY WRECK OR DAMAGE SOMETHING** to cause overwhelming damage or destruction to something (*often passive*) ○ *a war-ravaged country* **2.** *vt* **WRECK AND PLUNDER PLACE** to plunder or sack a place or area ○ *a village ravaged of all its valuables by army deserters* ■ *n* **ACT OF DESTROYING OR PLUNDERING** the destruction, damaging, or plundering of something ■ **rav·ag·es** *npl* **DAMAGING EFFECTS** the damaging or disfiguring effects of something ○ *the ravages of time* [Early 17C. < French *ravager*, alteration of *ravine* "rushing of water" < Latin *rapere* "seize"] —**rav·age·ment** *n* —**rav·ag·er** *n*

rave /rayv/ *v* (**raved, rav·ing, raves**) **1.** *vi* **GIVE HIGH PRAISE** to give praise in a very enthusiastic way ○ *All the critics raved about her performance.* **2.** *vti* **SPEAK WILDLY AND INCOHERENTLY** to speak or say something in a loud, irrational, or incoherent way **3.** *vi* **STORM** to storm and rage with intensity (*literary*) ■ *n* **1. LARGE-SCALE PARTY** a large party or club event at which pop music is played, lasting sometimes all night **2. ENTHUSIASTIC PRAISE** an expression of very enthusiastic praise (*informal*) ○ *Her performance received raves from the audience.* **3. ACT OF RAVING** an act or instance of raving **4.** *UK* **CRAZE** a craze or fad (*dated slang*) ■ *adj* **VERY ENTHUSIASTIC** expressing very enthusiastic praise (*informal*) ○ *rave reviews* [14C. < Old French *raver*]

rav·el /rávv'l/ *v* (**-eled** or **-elled, -el·ing** or **-el·ling, -els**) **1.** *vti* **FRAY** to come loose from a knitted or woven fabric, or cause threads to do this **2.** *vti* **TANGLE** to become tangled, or cause threads or fibers to tangle **3.** *vt* **UNRAVEL SOMETHING COMPLICATED** to clarify or resolve something complicated **4.** *vti* **COMPLICATE SOMETHING** to make something complicated or involved, or become complicated or involved ■ *n* **LOOSE THREAD OR FIBER** an unraveled thread or fiber [Late 16C. Probably < Dutch *ravelen*] —**rav·el·er** *n* —**rav·el·ment** *n*

Ra·vel /rə vél/, **Maurice** (1875–1937) French composer. A master of orchestration, he wrote impressionistic pieces that are classics of the 20th-century repertoire. His works include *Boléro* (1928) and *Daphnis et Chloé* (1912). Full name **Ravel, Maurice Joseph**

rav·el·in /rávv'lən/ *n* a small outwork in fortifications consisting of two embankments shaped like an arrowhead that point outward in front of a larger defense work [Late 16C. Via French < Italian *ravellina*]

Maurice Ravel

raven

ra·ven[1] /ráyvən/ *n* a large bird belonging to the crow family with glossy black feathers, a wedge-shaped tail, and a large beak. Native to: northern hemisphere. Latin name: *Corvus corax*. ■ *adj* of a deep lustrous black (*literary*) [Old English *hræfn*. Ultimately from a prehistoric Germanic word, thought to be an imitation of its croaking]

CULTURAL NOTE ***The Raven***, a poem (1845) by Edgar Allen Poe. This melancholy tale of lost love gained Poe national fame. As a young student mourns the death of his lover, a raven – a traditional symbol of doom – appears at his window. To every question that the student poses about his future and his lover, the bird responds "Nevermore."

rav·en[2] /rávvən/ (**-ened, -en·ing, -ens**) *vti* **1.** to eat something voraciously or greedily **2.** to take something away by force, especially prey or plunder [15C. Via Old French *raviner* "seize" < Latin *rapere* "seize"] —**rav·en·er** *n*

rav·en·ing /rávvəning/ *adj* living by hunting prey, especially in a greedy voracious way —**rav·en·ing·ly** *adv*

Ra·ven·na /rə vénnə/ capital city of Ravenna Province, Emilia-Romagna Region, northeastern Italy. An ancient Roman city, it contains several early Christian churches. Population: 138,122 (1999).

rav·en·ous /rávvənəss/ *adj* **1. HUNGRY** extremely hungry **2. GREEDY FOR SOMETHING** greedy for something, especially for the gratification of wants or desires **3. PREDATORY** voracious and predatory —**rav·en·ous·ly** *adv* —**rav·en·ous·ness** *n*

rav·er /ráyvər/ *n* somebody who goes to raves (*informal*)

rave-up *n UK* a wild noisy party with music, drinking, and dancing (*dated informal*)

rav·in /rávvin/ *n* the act of violently seizing something (*archaic or literary*) [14C. < Old French *ravine* (see RAVINE)]

ra·vine /rə veén/ *n* a deep narrow valley, especially one formed by running water [15C. < Old French *ravine* "rapine, violent rush" < Latin *rapere* "seize"]

rav·ing /ráyving/ *adj* **1. IRRATIONAL** wildly irrational, angry, or insulting **2. ADDS EMPHASIS** used to emphasize the sense of admiration and excitement felt for something (*informal*) ○ *a raving review of the play* ■ **rav·ings** *npl* **WILDLY IRRATIONAL SPEECH** wildly irrational, angry, or insulting utterances ○ *the ravings of a person cheated* —**rav·ing·ly** *adv*

ra·vi·o·li /ràvvee óleel/ (*plural* **-lis**) *n* a food made from small squares of pasta sealed around a meat, cheese, or vegetable filling [Mid-19C. < Italian, plural of dialectal *raviolo* "small turnip"]

rav·ish /rávvish/ (**-ished, -ish·ing, -ish·es**) *vt* **1. RAPE SOMEBODY** to force somebody to engage in sexual intercourse (*literary*) **2. CARRY SOMETHING OFF** to capture and carry off something by force (*archaic or literary*) **3. OVERWHELM SOMEBODY EMOTIONALLY** to overwhelm somebody with deep and pleasurable feelings or emotions (*usually passive*) [13C. < French *raviss-* "seize" < Latin *rapere*] —**rav·ish·er** *n* —**rav·ish·ment** *n*

rav·ish·ing /rávvishing/ *adj* extremely delightful or beautiful —**rav·ish·ing·ly** *adv*

raw /raw/ *adj* **1. UNCOOKED** not cooked **2. UNPROCESSED** not processed, refined, or treated in any way ○ *raw sewage* **3. HURT AND SORE** cut, scraped, or inflamed, often painfully so **4. INEXPERIENCED** lacking training or experience ○ *raw army recruits* ○ *raw talent* **5. COLD** extremely cold and harsh or damp ○ *a raw wind* **6. NOT SUBTLE** not subtle, restrained, or refined ○ *the raw power of the music* **7. BRUTALLY REALISTIC** factual and realistic, especially concerning unpleasant matters ○ *the raw facts* **8. NOT CHANGED OR INTERPRETED** in an original state and not yet subjected to correction or analysis ○ *raw data* **9. CRUDE** coarse and vulgar **10.** TEXTILES same as **raw-edged** (sense 1) [Old English *hrēaw*. Ultimately from an Indo-European word that also produced Latin *crudus* "raw" (source of English *crude* and *cruel*)] —**raw·ish** *adj* —**raw·ly** *adv* —**raw·ness** *n* ◇ **in the raw 1.** not wearing clothes (*informal*) **2.** in a natural state, without embellishment or refinement

Ra·wal·pin·di /raàwəl píndee/, **Rā·wal·pin·di** city of Punjab Province, northern Pakistan. Population: 1,406,214 (1998).

raw bar *n US* a seafood restaurant or a counter in a restaurant where uncooked fish and shellfish are served

raw·boned /ráw bṓnd/ *adj* having a lean body with prominent bones

raw deal *n* an arrangement, situation, or treatment that is unfair

raw-edged *adj* **1. WITHOUT HEM OR SELVAGE** with an unhemmed, sometimes frayed or scruffy cut edge **2. FRANK ABOUT UNPLEASANTNESS** brutally realistic in depicting unpleasant situations **3. CRUDE** coarse and vulgar

raw·hide /ráw hīd/ *n* **1. UNTANNED HIDE** untanned animal hide **2. WHIP OR ROPE** a whip or rope made of rawhide ■ *vt* (**-hid·ed, -hid·ing, -hides**) **BEAT SOMEBODY** to beat somebody with a rawhide

ra·win·sonde /ráywin sònd/ *n* a balloon carrying meteorological instruments that has a trackable radar target and is used to observe the velocity and direction of upper-air winds [Mid-20C. < blend of RADAR + WIND[1]]

Raw·lings /ráwlingz/, **Jerry** (*b.* 1947) president of Ghana (1992–2000). He led two military coups in 1979 and 1981 before being elected president in 1992. He also served as chair of the Economic Community of West African States (1994–96). Full name **Rawlings, Jerry John**

Raw·lings, Marjorie Kinnan (1896–1953) US writer. Most of her writing is set in rural Florida, including the Pulitzer Prize-winning novel *The Yearling* (1938).

raw ma·te·ri·al *n* **1.** a natural unprocessed material that is used in a manufacturing process **2.** somebody or something considered to have potential for use or development

raw si·en·na *n* **1.** a yellowish brown color **2.** a natural brownish yellow substance that is used as a pigment

raw silk *n* **1.** silk fibers reeled from silkworm cocoons and left untreated **2.** a fabric or yarn made from raw silk

ray[1] /ray/ *n* **1. NARROW BEAM OF LIGHT** a narrow beam of light from the Sun or an artificial light source **2. TRACE OF SOMETHING POSITIVE** a slight indication of something positive in a difficult or worrying situation ○ *a ray of hope* **3.** PHYS **BEAM OF ENERGY** a thin beam of radiant energy or particles **4.** MATH **LINE EXTENDING FROM POINT** a straight line that extends from a point infinitely in one direction **5.** ZOOL **ARM OF STARFISH** an arm of a starfish or other animal with body parts radiating from the center **6.** ASTRON **BRIGHT STREAK FROM LUNAR CRATER** a bright streak on the lunar surface that radiates from a crater **7.** BOT **RADIAL STRAND OF PLANT PITH** a distinct strand of tissue running radially through the conducting tissues in the stem of a plant ■ **rays** *npl* **SUNSHINE** hot or warm sunshine (*slang*) ○ *catch some rays* ■ *v* (**rayed, ray·ing, rays**) **1.** *vti* **EMIT LIGHT** to shine or emit rays, e.g., of light or electromagnetic particles **2.** *vi* **EXTEND IN LINES** to extend in radiating lines from a point [14C. Via French *rai* < Latin *radius* "staff, spoke, ray, beam of light"] —**rayed** *adj* ◇ **catch some rays** to go sunbathing (*slang*)

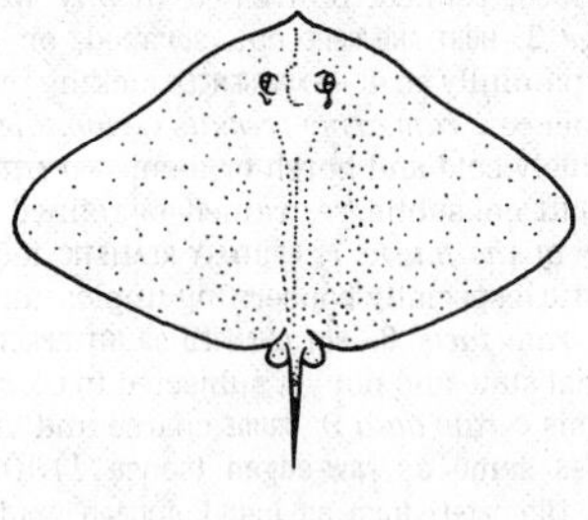

ray

ray² /ray/ *n* a fish with a cartilaginous skeleton, a horizontally flat head and body, broad pectoral fins, and a tapering tail. Order: Rajiformes. [14C. Via French < Latin *raia*]

ray³ /ray/ *n UK* MUSIC same as **re¹**

AKG London

Man Ray

Ray /ray/, **Man** (1890–1976) US artist. Founder of the New York Dada movement, he is known for his avant-garde photographs and paintings. Born **Rudnitsky, Emanuel**

Popperfoto

Satyajit Ray

Ray /rī/, **Satyajit** (1921–92) Indian movie director. His *Apu* (1955–59) and *Calcutta* (1970–75) movie trilogies won him international acclaim.

"You may suffer bereavement but life does not stop. It goes on."
[Satyajit Ray, *Deliverance*; 1981]

Ray-Bans *tdmk* a trademark for a brand of sunglasses

ray flow·er, **ray flo·ret** *n* a radiating part of the flower of a composite plant such as the dandelion or daisy, comprising either the whole flower head, as in a dandelion, or only its margin, as in a daisy

ray gun *n* in science fiction, a gun capable of firing rays of energy that stun or destroy

Ray·leigh /ráylee/, **John William Strutt, 3rd Baron** (1842–1919) British physicist. He performed research into resonance and vibration, and, with Sir William Ramsay, discovered argon (1894).

Ray·leigh scat·ter·ing *n* the scattering of electromagnetic radiation into different wavelengths by very small particles of matter, responsible for red sunrises and sunsets as well as the blue of the daytime sky [Mid-20C. After John William Strutt RAYLEIGH]

ray·less /ráyləss/ *adj* **1.** dark, gloomy, or lacking light (*literary*) **2.** lacking the ray flowers that typically form part of the flower heads of composite plants such as the daisy —**ray·less·ly** *adv* —**ray·less·ness** *n*

Ray·mond Ter·race /ràymənd-/ town in eastern New South Wales, Australia, located at the junction of the Hunter and Williams rivers. Population: 11,151 (1991).

Ray·naud's dis·ease /ray nṓz-/ *n* a disorder of the blood vessels in which somebody is affected by Raynaud's phenomenon without any identifiable underlying cause [Late 19C. After Maurice *Raynaud* (1834–81), French physician]

Ray·naud's phe·nom·e·non *n* spasms of the arteries of the fingers and toes, usually brought on by cold, causing the hands and feet to become pale, cold, numb, and sometimes painful. Causes include diseases of the arteries, rheumatoid arthritis, and repeated trauma to the fingers. [Mid-20C. See RAYNAUD'S DISEASE]

ray·on /ráy òn/ *n* **1.** a synthetic textile fiber made from cellulose **2.** a synthetic fabric or yarn made from rayon fibers [Early 20C. < RAY¹]

raze /rayz/ (**razed, raz·ing, raz·es**), **rase** (**rased, ras·ing, rases**) *vt* **1.** to destroy or level a building or settlement completely **2.** *US* to scrape or shave something off something else [Mid-16C. Via French *raser* "shave off" < Latin *radere* "scrape"] —**raz·er** *n*

Raz·nat·o·vic /raaz naátə vìch/, **Zeljko** (1952–2000) Yugoslavian paramilitary commander. An escaped bank robber, he formed the "Tigers" militia (1990), which was linked by the International War Crimes Tribunal to several massacres in Bosnia and Croatia. He was assassinated in Belgrade before he could stand trial. Known as **Arkan**

ra·zor /ráyzər/ *n* an instrument with a blade or powered cutting head that is used for shaving hair off the face or body ■ *vt* (**-zored, -zor·ing, -zors**) to shave or cut hair, or remove something else, using a razor [13C. < Old French *rasor* < *raser* "shave off" (see RAZE)]

ra·zor·back /ráyzər bàk/ *n* **1.** a feral hog that has a narrow body, ridged back, and long legs. Native to: southeastern United States. **2.** MARINE BIOL same as **finback 3.** GEOG a hill that has a sharp ridge

Ra·zor·back State *n* a nickname for Arkansas

razor-billed auk

ra·zor-billed auk /ráyzər bild áwk/, **ra·zor·bill** /ráyzər bìl/ *n* a seabird of the auk family, with black and white feathers and a sharp thick beak. Native to: North Atlantic coasts. Latin name: *Alca torda*.

ra·zor blade *n* a flat blade designed to be used in a safety razor

ra·zor clam *n* a bivalve mollusk that has a long narrow tubular shell with squared ends. It burrows rapidly downward into the sand by extending a muscular foot. Family: Solenidae.

ra·zor cut *n* a haircut that is done using a razor instead of scissors ■ *vt* to cut or style hair with a razor

ra·zor-shell *n UK* ZOOL same as **razor clam**

ra·zor wire *n* wire with sharp pieces of metal fixed along its length, used for fences and barriers

razz /raz/ (*slang*) *vt* (**razzed, razz·ing, razz·es**) to tease or make fun of somebody ■ *n* a raspberry noise [Early 20C. Shortening and alteration of RASPBERRY]

raz·zle /rázz'l/ [Early 20C. Shortening] ◇ **on the razzle** *UK* enjoying a spell of unrestrained partying or heavy drinking (*dated informal*)

raz·zle-daz·zle *n* **1.** actions intended to dazzle and confuse somebody, especially an opponent in a sport **2.** an often gaudy showiness that is designed to be impressive and exciting (*informal*) ○ *a razzle-dazzle of pairs figure skating* **3.** same as **razzle** [Late 19C. Rhyming compound < DAZZLE] ◇ **on the razzle-dazzle** same as **on the razzle** (*dated informal*)

razz·ma·tazz /rázmə táz/ *n* **1.** showiness that is designed to be impressive and exciting, especially in the context of a stage show or other spectacle **2.** language that is intended to confuse and conceal (*slang*) [Late 19C. Origin ?]

Rb *symbol* CHEM ELEM rubidium

RB *abbr* FOOTBALL running back

RBC, **rbc** *abbr* MED red blood (cell) count

RBE, **rbe** *abbr* BIOL relative biological effectiveness

RBI, **rbi** *abbr* BASEBALL runs batted in

RC *abbr* **1.** MED Red Cross **2.** MIL Reserve Corps

RCAF, **R.C.A.F.** *abbr* Royal Canadian Air Force (*dated*)

rcd. *abbr* received

RCMP, **R.C.M.P.** *abbr* Royal Canadian Mounted Police

RCN, **R.C.N.** *abbr* Royal Canadian Navy

r-col·or *n* in phonetics, the effect of an "r" sound uttered simultaneously with a vowel by constricting the oral cavity with the tongue —**r-col·ored** *adj*

R.C.P. *abbr* MED Royal College of Physicians

rcpt. *abbr* COMM receipt

R.C.S. *abbr* MED Royal College of Surgeons

rct. *abbr* recruit

RD *abbr* **1.** HEALTH SERVICES registered dietitian **2.** MAIL Rural Delivery

rd. *abbr* **1.** COMM rendered **2.** road **3.** round

Rd. *abbr* Road (*used in addresses*)

RDA *abbr* HEALTH recommended daily allowance

RDF *abbr* **1.** MEDIA radio direction finder **2.** MIL Rapid Deployment Force

RDS *abbr* MED respiratory distress syndrome

re¹ /ray/ *n* a syllable that represents the second note in a scale when singing solfeggio. In fixed solfeggio it represents the note D. [15C. Shortening of medieval Latin *resonare* "resound" in a Latin hymn to St. John the Baptist, from which names of hexachords were taken]

re² /ray, ree/ *prep* with reference to [Early 18C. < Latin, "on the matter of," form of *res* "thing, matter"]

USAGE The use of *re* meaning "with reference to" is largely restricted to the language of business, but it is also used informally as a convenient short form: *Re your recent proposal – I fully agree.*

re³ *abbr* Réunion (*used in Internet addresses*) See table at **domain name**

're *contr* are ○ *They're planning to come.*

Re¹ *n* MYTHOL same as **Ra¹**

Re² *abbr* MONEY rupee

Re³ *symbol* **1.** PHYS Reynold's number **2.** CHEM ELEM rhenium

R.E., **RE** *abbr* real estate

re- *prefix* **1.** again, anew ○ *rebuild* **2.** back, backward ○ *recall* [Via Old French from Latin]

re·ab·sorb *vt*
re·ab·sorp·tion *n*
re·ac·cept *vt*
re·ac·cept·ance *n*
re·ac·cred·i·ta·tion *n*
re·ac·cus·tom *vt*
re·ac·quaint *vt*
re·ac·quain·tance *n*
re·ac·quire *vt*
re·ac·qui·si·tion *n*
re·ac·ti·vate *vti*
re·ac·ti·va·tion *n*

re·a·dapt *vti*
re·ad·ap·ta·tion *n*
re·ad·just *vti*
re·ad·just·a·ble *adj*
re·ad·just·er *n*
re·ad·just·ment *n*
re·ad·mit *vt*
re·ad·mit·tance *n*
re·a·dopt *vt*
re·a·dop·tion *n*
re·ad·ver·tise *vti*
re·ad·ver·tise·ment *n*
re·af·firm *vti*
re·af·fir·ma·tion *n*
re·al·lo·cate *vt*
re·al·lo·ca·tion *n*
re·al·lot *vt*
re·al·lot·ment *n*
re·al·ter *vt*
re·a·nal·y·sis *n*
re·an·a·lyze *vt*
re·an·i·mate *vt*
re·an·i·ma·tion *n*
re·an·nex *vt*
re·an·nex·a·tion *n*
re·ap·pear *vi*
re·ap·pear·ance *n*
re·ap·pli·ca·tion *n*
re·ap·ply *vti*
re·ap·point *vt*
re·ap·point·ment *n*
re·ap·por·tion *vt*
re·ap·por·tion·ment *n*
re·ap·prais·al *n*
re·ap·praise *vt*
re·arm *vti*
re·ar·ma·ment *n*
re·ar·rest *vt*
re·as·sem·ble *vti*
re·as·sem·bly *n*
re·as·sert *v*
re·as·ser·tion *n*
re·as·sess *vt*
re·as·sess·ment *n*
re·as·sign *vt*
re·as·sign·ment *n*
re·as·sume *vt*
re·at·tach *vt*
re·at·tach·ment *n*
re·at·tain *vt*
re·at·tain·ment *n*
re·at·tempt *vt*
re·au·tho·ri·za·tion *n*
re·au·thor·ize *vt*
re·a·wak·en *vti*
re·badge *vt*
re·bap·tism *n*
re·bap·tize *vt*
re·bind *vt, n*
re·boil *vti*
re·book *vti*
re·bor·row *vt*
re·broad·cast *vti, n*
re·bur·i·al *n*
re·bur·y *vt*
re·buy *vti*
re·cal·cu·late *vti*
re·cal·cu·la·tion *n*
re·cal·i·brate *vt*
re·cap·i·tal·i·za·tion *n*
re·cap·i·tal·ize *vt*
re·cau·tion *vt*
re·cen·tra·li·za·tion *n*
re·cen·tral·ize *vt*
re·cer·ti·fi·ca·tion *n*
re·cer·ti·fy *vt*
re·char·ter *vt*
re·check *vti*
re·chris·ten *vt*
re·cir·cu·late *vti*
re·cir·cu·la·tion *n*
re·clas·si·fi·ca·tion *n*
re·clas·si·fy *vt*
re·col·o·ni·za·tion *n*
re·col·o·nize *vt*
re·col·or *vt*
re·com·bine *vti*
re·com·mis·sion *vt*
re·com·mit *vt*
re·com·mit·ment *n*
re·com·mit·tal *n*
re·com·pile *vt*
re·com·pose *vt*
re·com·po·si·tion *n*
re·con·duct *vt*
re·con·fig·u·ra·tion *n*
re·con·fig·ure *vt*
re·con·firm *vt*
re·con·fir·ma·tion *n*
re·con·nect *vt*
re·con·nec·tion *n*
re·con·quer *vt*
re·con·quest *n*
re·con·se·crate *vt*
re·con·se·cra·tion *n*
re·con·sid·er *vti*
re·con·sid·er·a·tion *n*
re·con·sol·i·date *vt*
re·con·sol·i·da·tion *n*
re·con·tam·i·nate *vt*
re·con·tam·i·na·tion *n*
re·con·vene *vti*
re·con·ver·sion *n*
re·con·vert *vti*
re·cook *vt*
re·cop·y *vti*
re·cross *vti*
re·crys·tal·li·za·tion *n*
re·crys·tal·lize *vti*
re·cut *vt*
re·ded·i·cate *v*
re·ded·i·ca·tion *n*
re·de·liv·er *vti*
re·de·sign *vt, n*
re·de·ter·mi·na·tion *n*
re·de·ter·mine *vti*
re·dif·fer·en·ti·ate *vti*
re·dif·fer·en·ti·a·tion *n*
re·di·gest *vt*
re·dis·count *vt*
re·dis·cov·er *vt*
re·dis·cov·er·y *n*
re·dis·so·lu·tion *n*
re·dis·solve *vti*
re·dis·till *vt*
re·dis·til·la·tion *n*
re·di·vide *vti*
re·di·vi·sion *n*
re·draw *vt*
re·ed·it *vti*
re·ed·u·cate *vt*
re·ed·u·ca·tion *n*
re·ed·u·ca·tive *adj*
re·e·lect *vt*
re·e·lec·tion *n*
re·el·i·gi·bil·i·ty *n*
re·el·i·gi·ble *adj*
re·em·bark *vti*
re·em·bar·ka·tion *n*
re·em·brace *vt*
re·e·merge *vi*
re·e·mer·gence *n*
re·e·mer·gent *adj*
re·e·mis·sion *n*
re·e·mit *vt*
re·em·pha·sis *n*
re·em·pha·size *vt*
re·em·ploy *vt*
re·em·ploy·ment *n*
re·en·act *vt*
re·en·act·ment *n*
re·en·gage *vti*
re·en·gage·ment *n*
re·en·list *vti*
re·en·list·ment *n*
re·e·quip *vt*
re·e·quip·ment *n*
re·e·rect *vt*
re·e·rec·tion *n*
re·es·ca·late *vti*
re·es·ca·la·tion *n*
re·es·tab·lish *vt*
re·es·tab·lish·ment *n*
re·e·val·u·ate *vt*
re·e·val·u·a·tion *n*
re·e·vap·o·rate *vti*
re·e·vap·o·ra·tion *n*
re·ex·am·i·na·tion *n*
re·ex·am·ine *vt*
re·ex·pe·ri·ence *vt*
re·ex·plo·ra·tion *n*
re·ex·plore *vt*
re·fash·ion *vt*
re·fight *vti*
re·file *vt*
re·fin·ish *vt*
re·fin·ish·er *n*
re·fire *vti*
re·float *vt*
re·fold *vt*
re·for·mat *vt*
re·for·mu·late *vt*
re·for·mu·la·tion *n*
re·for·ti·fi·ca·tion *n*
re·for·ti·fy *vt*
re·frame *vt*
re·freeze *vti*
re·fry *vt*
re·gath·er *vt*
re·gift *vti*
re·gild *vt*
re·glaze *vt*
re·grant *vt*
re·grind *vt*
re·grow *vti*
re·growth *n*
re·hang *vt*
re·hard·en *vti*
re·hear *vt*
re·hear·ing *n*
re·heat *vti*
re·heat·er *n*
re·ig·nite *vt*
re·ig·ni·tion *n*
re·im·port *vt, n*
re·im·por·ta·tion *n*
re·im·pose *vt*
re·im·po·si·tion *n*
re·im·press *vt*
re·im·pris·on *vt*
re·in·cor·po·rate *vt*
re·in·cor·po·ra·tion *n*
re·in·fect *vt*
re·in·fec·tion *n*
re·in·flate *vt*
re·in·fla·tion *n*
re·in·ject *vt*
re·in·jec·tion *n*
re·in·sert *vt*
re·in·ser·tion *n*
re·in·spect *vt*
re·in·spec·tion *n*
re·in·stall *vt*
re·in·stal·la·tion *n*
re·in·te·grate *vt*
re·in·te·gra·tion *n*
re·in·ter *vt*
re·in·ter·ment *n*
re·in·ter·pret *vt*
re·in·ter·pre·ta·tion *n*
re·in·ter·view *vt*
re·in·tro·duce *vt*
re·in·tro·duc·tion *n*
re·in·vade *vt*
re·in·va·sion *n*
re·in·ves·ti·gate *vti*
re·in·ves·ti·ga·tion *n*
re·in·vig·o·rate *vt*
re·in·vig·o·ra·tion *n*
re·in·vig·o·ra·tor *n*
re·is·sue *vt, n*
re·judge *vt*
re·la·bel *vt*
re·launch *vt, n*
re·learn *vt*
re·let *vt*
re·li·cense *vt*
re·light *vt*
re·line *vt*
re·load *vti*
re·mail *vt*
re·man *vt*
re·mar·ket *vt*
re·mar·riage *n*
re·mar·ry *vti*
re·meas·ure *vti*
re·meas·ure·ment *n*
re·melt *vti*
re·mend *vt*
re·mil·i·tar·i·za·tion *n*
re·mil·i·tar·ize *vt*
re·mod·i·fi·ca·tion *n*
re·mod·i·fy *vt*
re·mon·e·ti·za·tion *n*
re·mon·e·tize *vt*
re·name *vt*
re·na·tion·al·i·za·tion *n*
re·na·tion·al·ize *vt*
re·ne·go·ti·ate *vti*
re·ne·go·ti·a·tion *n*
re·nom·i·nate *v*
re·nom·i·na·tion *n*
re·oc·cu·pa·tion *n*
re·oc·cu·py *vti*
re·oc·cur *vi*
re·oc·cur·rence *n*
re·or·ches·trate *vt*
re·or·ches·tra·tion *n*
re·or·der *vti, n*
re·pack *vti*
re·pack·age *vt*
re·pack·ag·er *n*
re·pag·i·nate *vt*
re·pag·i·na·tion *n*
re·paint *vti, n*
re·pa·per *vti*
re·pass *vti*
re·pave *vt*
re·peo·ple *vt*
re·pho·to·graph *vt*
re·phrase *vt*
re·pin *vt*
re·plan *vt*
re·po·lar·ize *vt*
re·pol·ish *vt, n*
re·pop·u·late *vt*
re·pop·u·la·tion *n*
re·po·si·tion *vt*
re·pot *vt*
re·pot·ting *n*
re·price *vt*
re·pri·va·ti·za·tion *n*
re·pri·va·tize *vt*
re·pro·cess *vt*
re·pro·gram *vt*
re·pro·gram·ma·bil·i·ty *n*
re·pro·gram·ma·ble *adj*
re·pub·li·ca·tion *n*
re·pub·lish *vt*
re·pub·lish·er *n*
re·pur·chase *n, vt*
re·read *vt*
re·re·cord *vti*
re·re·cord·ing *n*
re·reg·is·ter *vti*
re·reg·is·tra·tion *n*
re·reg·u·late *vti*
re·reg·u·la·tion *n*
re·roof *vt*
re·route *vt*
re·seal *vt*
re·seal·a·ble *adj*
re·seg·re·gate *vt*
re·seg·re·ga·tion *n*
re·se·lec·tion *n*
re·sell *vti*
re·sell·er *n*
re·send *vt*
re·ship *vt*
re·show *vti*
re·site *vt*
re·size *vt*
re·sold
re·sole *vt*
re·spray *vt, n*
re·stage *vt*
re·start *n, vti*
re·start·a·ble *adj*
re·string *vt*
re·strung *adj*
re·stud·y *vt*
re·sub·mit *vt*
re·sup·ply *vt, n*
re·sur·vey *vti, n*
re·syn·the·si·za·tion *n*
re·syn·the·size *vt*
re·teach *vt*
re·test *n, vti*
re·tie *vt*
re·time *vt*
re·ti·tle *vt*
re·trans·fu·sion *n*
re·trans·late *vt*
re·trans·la·tion *n*
re·trans·mis·sion *n*
re·trans·mit *vt*
re·tune *vt*
re·type *vt*
re·up·hol·ster *vt*
re·ut·il·i·za·tion *n*
re·ut·il·ize *vt*
re·vac·ci·nate *vt*
re·vac·ci·na·tion *n*
re·val·i·date *vt*
re·val·i·da·tion *n*
re·val·or·i·za·tion *n*
re·val·or·ize *vt*
re·val·u·ate *vt*
re·val·u·a·tion *n*
re·val·ue *vt*
re·var·nish *vt*
re·vis·i·ta·tion *n*
re·vote *n, vi*
re·wake *vti*
re·wak·en *vi*
re·wash *vt*
re·weave *vt*
re·weigh *vt*
re·wrap *vt*
re·zone *vt*

reach /reech/ *v* (**reached, reach·ing, reach·es**) **1.** *vt* ARRIVE AT PLACE to arrive or come to a particular place or point **2.** *vt* ARRIVE AT STATE to get into a particular state or condition ○ *I had reached desperation point.* **3.** *vti* EXTEND AS FAR AS SOMETHING to stretch out physically or extend as far as a particular place or point ○ *I can't reach the top shelf without a chair.* **4.** *vi* MOVE TOWARD SOMETHING TO TOUCH IT to move toward something in order to touch or grasp it ○ *She reached for her coat.* **5.** *vti* INFLUENCE PEOPLE to have an influence or impact on people or on a group ○ *This campaign will reach millions of people.* **6.** *vt* CONTACT SOMEBODY to communicate with somebody ○ *I'll try to reach you at home.* **7.** *vt* PASS SOMEBODY SOMETHING to pass or hand somebody something (*informal*) ○ *Just reach me down that file, would you.* **8.** *vi* STRIVE FOR SOMETHING to strive too much to achieve or acquire something, especially without success ○ *reaching for fame* **9.** *vi* SAILING SAIL WITH WIND TO SIDE to sail on a tack with the wind blowing from the side **10.** *vi Carib* ARRIVE to arrive at a destination ○ *We reach early in the morning.* **11.** *vi Carib* GO to go as far as ○ *How far yuh reachin?* **12.** *vt Carib* BECOME to become ■ *n* **1.** EXTENT OF REACHING the extent or range that somebody or something is able to reach ○ *The top shelf is just beyond his reach.* **2.** ACT OF STRETCHING OUT the act of stretching out or extending **3.** RANGE OF POWER the extent of the power or influence exercised by somebody or something ○ *beyond the reach of the law* **4.** STRETCH OF WATER a stretch of open water, e.g., on a river **5.** NUMBER OF VIEWERS the number of viewers who visit a website or watch a television program (*informal*) ○ *Reach is one factor determining whether companies invest in the Web.* **6.** SAILING TACK SAILED BY VESSEL a tack sailed by a vessel with the wind blowing from the side ■ **reach·es** *npl* AREA OR LEVEL an area or level of something ○ *the upper reaches of the Amazon* [Old English *rǣcan.* Ultimately from a prehistoric Germanic word that also produced German *reichen* "to reach"] —**reach·a·ble** *adj* —**reach·er** *n* ◇ **out of reach 1.** beyond the grasp of somebody's outstretched hand **2.** not able to be achieved or attained by somebody ◇ **within** *or* **in reach 1.** able to be grasped by somebody with an outstretched hand **2.** achievable or attainable

re·act /ree ákt/ (**-act·ed, -act·ing, -acts**) *vi* **1.** RESPOND EMOTIONALLY to respond to something by showing the feelings or thoughts it arouses ○ *Officials reacted with guarded optimism.* **2.** RESPOND BY TAKING ACTION to respond to something by taking action ○ *The government reacted by sending in troops.* **3.** BE IN OPPOSITION to act in opposition to somebody or something ○ *children reacting against their parents* **4.** UNDERGO PHYSICAL RESPONSE to respond to the physical effects of something such as a medication or air pollution **5.** CHEM CHANGE CHEMICALLY to undergo a chemical reaction

re·ac·tance /ree áktənss/ *n* opposition to the flow of alternating current caused by the inductance and capacitance in a circuit, measured in ohms. Symbol *X*

re·ac·tant /ree áktənt/ *n* a substance that reacts with another in a chemical reaction

re·ac·tion /ree áksh'n/ *n* **1.** EMOTIONAL RESPONSE an emotional or intellectual response that something arouses ○ *My initial reaction was to laugh.* **2. ACTIVE RESPONSE** a response to something that involves taking action, or an action taken in response to something ○ *Prices jumped in reaction to rumors of a shortage.* **3. OPPOSING ACTION** an act in opposition to somebody or something ○ *a reaction against consumerism* **4. PHYSICAL RESPONSE** a response to the physical effects of something such as heat, cold, or pollution **5.** MED **BODILY RESPONSE TO SUBSTANCE** a bodily response to a foreign substance such as an infectious agent, medication, or allergen **6.** POL **STRONG CONSERVATISM** opposition to progressive social or political change **7.** PHYS **FORCES ACTING ON BODY** an equal but opposite force exerted by a body when a force acts upon it **8.** INDUST **NUCLEAR PROCESS** a nuclear process resulting in a change in the structure of atomic nuclei —**re·ac·tion·al** *adj*

re·ac·tion·ar·y /ree áksh'n èrree/ *adj* opposed to progressive social or political change ■ *n* (*plural* **-ies**) somebody who is reactionary

re·ac·tion en·gine *n* an engine such as a jet or rocket engine that produces thrust by ejecting a stream of gas at high velocity

re·ac·tion for·ma·tion *n* in psychoanalysis, a defense mechanism in which somebody condemns something that has an unconscious appeal

re·ac·tion time *n* the interval of time between the application of a stimulus and the first indication of a response

re·ac·tive /ree áktiv/ *adj* **1. REACTING** tending to react to events and situations rather than initiating or instigating them **2.** CHEM **REACTING CHEMICALLY** taking part in a chemical reaction **3.** PSYCHIAT **CAUSED BY STIMULI OR EVENTS** describes a psychiatric condition caused by situations or stimuli such as the behavior of other people or the death of a loved one —**re·ac·tive·ly** *adv* —**re·ac·tive·ness** *n* —**re·ac·tiv·i·ty** /rèe ák tívvətee/ *n*

re·ac·tor /ree áktər/ *n* **1.** somebody or something that reacts or takes part in a reaction **2.** INDUST same as **nuclear reactor 3.** ELEC a component in an electrical circuit used to create reactance, e.g., a capacitor or an inductor

read /reed/ *v* (**read** /red/, **read·ing, reads**) **1.** *vti* **INTERPRET WRITTEN MATERIAL** to identify and understand the meaning of the characters and words in written or printed material **2.** *vti* **UTTER WRITTEN WORDS** to say the words of written or printed material aloud **3.** *vti* **LEARN SOMETHING BY READING** to find something out by studying written or printed material ○ *I read it in a book.* **4.** *vt* **INTERPRET NONWRITTEN MATERIAL** to interpret the information conveyed by movements, signs, or signals ○ *We could no longer read the trail.* **5.** *vti* **INTERPRET PRINTED SIGNS** to be able to identify and understand printed or written signs or symbols ○ *to learn to read music* **6.** *vt* **BE ABLE TO READ FOREIGN LANGUAGE** to know another language well enough to be able to read in it ○ *Can you read French?* **7.** *vt* **UNDERSTAND SOMETHING INTUITIVELY** to have an understanding of something by experience or intuitive means ○ *claiming to be able to read the future* **8.** *vti* PUBL same as **proofread 9.** *vti* **GIVE PARTICULAR INTERPRETATION TO SOMETHING** to interpret something, or be interpreted, in a particular way ○ *I read this passage as being extremely optimistic.* **10.** *vi* **HAVE QUALITIES THAT AFFECT UNDERSTANDING** to have particular characteristics that affect the way something is understood ○ *In the original it reads as poetry rather than prose.* **11.** *vi* **HAVE PARTICULAR WORDS** to have a particular wording ○ *a sign that reads DANGER* **12.** *vt UK* EDUC **TAKE UNIVERSITY COURSE** to pursue a particular course of study at a university **13.** *vti* MEDIA **HEAR SOMETHING ON TWO-WAY RADIO** to receive and understand a message sent by somebody on a two-way radio **14.** *vt* **INDICATE DATA** to indicate or display data such as a temperature ○ *What does the thermometer read?* **15.** *vt* PUBL **SUBSTITUTE WORD** to substitute a word or words for others that were printed incorrectly ○ *For "peasant" read "pheasant."* **16.** *vti* COMPUT **TRANSFER DATA INTO COMPUTER MEMORY** to transfer program instructions or data from a storage device into a computer's main memory **17.** GENETICS **DECODE RNA** to recognize sections of RNA (**codons**) that are responsible for different amino acid sequences and assemble them into a protein chain (*refers to enzymes*) ■ *n* **1. READING MATERIAL** something that produces a particular reaction in the reader when read (*informal*) ○ *a thrilling read* **2. TIME SPENT READING** a period devoted to reading ○ *She settled down for a long read.* ■ *adj* /red/ **KNOWLEDGEABLE** informed or provided with knowledge through reading ○ *He was without formal education but was literate, well read, and articulate.* [Old English *rǣdan* < Indo-European] ◇ **take something as read** to assume something to be the case

SPELLCHECK read or **reed**? Do not confuse the spelling of ***read*** and ***reed***, which sound similar. ***Read*** is chiefly used as a verb, meaning "interpret written material": *I never read the sports pages of the newspaper.* It is occasionally used as a noun, meaning "something read" or "a session of reading": *Her new novel is a good read.* ***Reed*** is only used as a noun, denoting a tall plant that grows near water, or the vibrating part of musical instruments such as the clarinet or oboe.

USAGE ***read*** or ***red***? The verb ***read*** has two pronunciations. In the infinitive or present tense it rhymes with ***weed*** and as the past tense or past participle it rhymes with ***wed***. The word ***red*** denotes the color of blood and is not a variant spelling of ***read*** as a past form, which sounds the same: *I read* [not *red*] *the letter aloud. Have you read* [not *red*] *this book?* Confusion may arise because the past tense and past participle of the verb *lead* is *led*.

read into *vt* to detect meanings in speech or written text that were not necessarily intended by the speaker or writer

read out *vt* **1. READ SOMETHING ALOUD** to read written or printed material aloud **2.** COMPUT **RETRIEVE INFORMATION FROM COMPUTER** to retrieve data from the memory or a disk or other storage device of a computer **3.** *US* **EXPEL SOMEBODY FROM ORGANIZATION** to expel somebody formally from a political party, organization, or other group

read up *vti* to learn a lot about a subject by reading about it or researching it

Read /reed/, **George** (1733–98) American patriot. A delegate from Delaware, he signed the Declaration of Independence (1776).

Read, Sir Herbert (1893–1968) British art historian. A prominent advocate in his day of contemporary British art, he founded the Institute of Contemporary Arts in London, England (1947). Full name **Read, Sir Herbert Edward**

read·a·bil·i·ty /rèedə bílletee/ *n* a measure of the ease with which a passage or text may be read

read·a·ble /réedəb'l/ *adj* **1.** able to be read **2.** written in a style that is enjoyable and interesting to read —**read·a·ble·ness** *n* —**read·a·bly** *adv*

re·ad·dress /rèe ə dréss/ (**-dressed, -dress·ing, -dress·es**) *vt* **1.** to put a new address on a letter or package **2.** to return to a problem or issue with the intention of resolving it

read·er /réedər/ *n* **1. SOMEBODY WHO READS** somebody who reads something ○ *He was never much of a reader.* ○ *a reader of mysteries* **2. READING DEVICE** a device that reads, especially one connected to a computer for reading media **3.** EDUC **EDUCATIONAL BOOK** a textbook used in learning to read **4.** LITERAT **ANTHOLOGY** an anthology of literary works **5.** PUBL **SOMEBODY WHO READS FOR PUBLISHER** somebody who reads manuscripts for a publisher to assess whether they are publishable **6.** CHR same as **lay reader 7.** *UK* EDUC **LECTURER AT BRITISH UNIVERSITY** a lecturer at a British university who ranks above a senior lecturer and below a professor

read·er·ship /réedər shìp/ *n* **1.** the group or number of people who read a particular publication **2.** *UK* the position of reader in a British university

read·i·ly /rédd'lee/ *adv* **1.** with little difficulty **2.** promptly and without any hesitation

read·ing /réeding/ *n* **1. IDENTIFYING OF WRITTEN OR PRINTED WORDS** the process of identifying and understanding the meaning of the characters and words in written or printed material **2. MATERIAL THAT IS READ** written or printed material that can be read **3. OCCASION OF READING SOMETHING** an occasion during which somebody reads something to an audience or congregation ○ *a poetry reading* **4. TEXT READ TO AUDIENCE OR CONGREGATION** a piece of literature that is read to an audience, or a passage from a sacred text that is read to a congregation **5. INTERPRETATION OF SOMETHING** an interpretation or understanding of a situation or of something that has been written or said **6.** TECH **INFORMATION TAKEN FROM EQUIPMENT** a piece of information or a measurement taken from a piece of equipment or with the help of equipment

Read·ing /rédding/ **1.** city in central southern England. It is home to the University of Reading, founded in 1892. Population: 143,096 (2001). **2.** town in northeastern Massachusetts, southeast of Andover and northwest of Boston. Population: 23,680 (2002 estimate). **3.** city in southeastern Pennsylvania. Population: 80,494 (2002 estimate).

read·ing desk *n* FURNITURE same as **lectern**

read·ing frame *n* a sequence of three nucleotides on DNA or messenger RNA that indicates the starting point for translation to produce a polypeptide

README file /réedmee-/ *n* a computer text file that contains information a user may need in order to install or operate a program

read-on·ly *adj* describes computer files that can be retrieved and displayed but cannot be changed or deleted

read-on·ly mem·o·ry *n* a small computer memory for the permanent storage of data that cannot subsequently be altered or added to

read·out /réed òwt/ *n* **1. DATA RETRIEVAL** the retrieving of data from a computer's memory, disk, or other storage device **2. DATA RETRIEVED BY COMPUTER** the data retrieved from a computer's memory, disk, or other storage system **3. DEVICE DISPLAYING INFORMATION** a part of a piece of equipment that displays information

read-through *n* a reading of a play without acting, allowing actors to familiarize themselves with the dialog before full rehearsals begin

read-write head *n* a magnetic device that can both read data from and write data to a magnetic medium such as a computer floppy or hard disk

read·y /réddee/ *adj* (**-i·er, -i·est**) **1. PREPARED FOR SOMETHING** prepared for something that is going to happen ○ *Are you ready to leave?* **2. FINISHED AND AVAILABLE FOR USE** finished or completed and so able to be used immediately ○ *When will dinner be ready?* **3. ON POINT OF DOING SOMETHING** on the point of doing something or liable to do something ○ *This old roof is ready to cave in.* **4. WILLING TO DO SOMETHING** eager, willing, or prepared to do something ○ *Don't be so ready to give in!* **5. QUICKLY PRODUCED** quickly and easily given, provided, or available ○ *a ready response to questions about wrongdoing* **6. PREPARED IN ADVANCE** prepared or blended in advance, and able to be used with very little additional preparation (*often used in combination*) ○ *available ready-sliced and individually wrapped* **7. INTELLIGENT** intelligent, alert, and quick-witted ○ *a ready wit* ■ *vt* (**-ied, -y·ing, -ies**) **PREPARE SOMETHING** to prepare something, especially so that it is in a condition for something to happen to it [12C. < Old English *rǣde* "prompt" < Germanic] —**read·i·ness** *n* ◇ **at the ready** prepared for immediate use or action

read·y cash *n* cash or money that is available to be spent immediately, often as notes and coins

read·y-made *adj* **1. ALREADY PREPARED** already prepared or made for convenience **2. PRECONCEIVED** thought out in advance ○ *ready-made excuses* ■ *n* CLOTHING **READY-TO-WEAR GARMENT** an item of clothing that is offered for sale in a standard size and completely finished, as opposed to one that is made to the customer's specifications or requirements

read·y-mix *n* a correct mixture of ingredients that is preblended and able to be used with very little additional preparation —**read·y-mixed** *adj*

read·y mon·ey *n UK* same as **ready cash**

read·y-to-wear *adj* describes clothing offered for sale in a standard size and completely finished, as opposed to clothing made to the customer's specifications or requirements ■ *n UK* same as **ready-made**

Rea·gan /ráygən/, **Nancy** (*b.* 1921) US first lady (1981–89). She played an active role in campaigning against drugs. Born **Robbins, Anne Francis**

Ronald Reagan

Rea·gan, Ronald (1911–2004) 40th president of the United States (1981–89). After a career as a movie actor and then as governor of California (1967–75), he served as a Republican president for two terms. His administration was marked by improved relations with the former Soviet Union during the closing years of the Cold War. Full name **Reagan, Ronald Wilson**. See table at **president**

> "We will never forget them, nor the last time we saw them this morning, as they prepared for the journey and waved goodbye and 'slipped the surly bonds of earth' to 'touch the face of God.'"
> [Ronald Reagan, *Broadcast from the Oval Office after the loss of space shuttle* Challenger *and all its crew, Washington, D.C.*; January 28, 1986]

Rea·gan·om·ics /ràygə nómmiks/ *n* the free-market economic approach espoused by US president Ronald Reagan, involving cuts in taxes and social spending together with deregulation of domestic markets (*takes a singular verb*) [Late 20C. Blend of REAGAN + ECONOMICS]

re·a·gent /ree áyjənt/ *n* a substance taking part in a chemical reaction, especially one used to detect, measure, or prepare another substance

re·a·gin /ree áyjin/ *n* an antibody involved in allergic reactions such as hay fever. Reagins are produced following an initial exposure to an allergenic substance and they interact with allergenic substances to trigger the release of histamines, causing inflammation, swelling, and other symptoms. [Early 20C. < German, < *reagieren* "react"] —**re·a·gin·ic** /rèe ə jínnik/ *adj*

re·al[1] /rée əl/ *adj* **1. PHYSICALLY EXISTING** having actual physical existence ○ *practice medicine with real patients* **2. VERIFIABLE** verifiable as actual fact, e.g., legally or scientifically ○ *What is his real name?* **3. NOT IMAGINARY** existing as fact, rather than as a product of dreams or the imagination ○ *In the real world things are somewhat different.* **4. NOT ARTIFICIAL** genuine and original, not artificial or synthetic ○ *real leather* **5. TRADITIONAL AND AUTHENTIC** prepared or made in a traditional or authentic way, rather than being mass-produced or artificial ○ *looking for some real food* **6. UNDISPUTED** based on fact, observation, or experience and so undisputed ○ *The real success of the evening was the comedy act.* **7. ESSENTIAL** of basic, essential, or critical importance ○ *And the real question for America is: why take the risk?* **8. EMPHASIZING TRUTH** used to emphasize the accuracy or appropriateness of a particular thing ○ *He's a real professional.* **9. SINCERE** honest or sincere, not feigned or affected ○ *express your real feelings* **10.** ECON **IN TERMS OF PURCHASING POWER** regarded in terms of purchasing power rather than the actual amount **11.** LAW **RELATING TO FIXED PROPERTY** relating to land and the fixed property associated with it **12.** PHILOSOPHY **ABOUT EXISTENCE** concerned with independent objective existence **13.** MATH **INVOLVING ONLY RATIONAL OR IRRATIONAL NUMBERS** involving, relating to, or having elements of the set of rational or irrational numbers only ■ *adv* **VERY** very or extremely (*informal*) ○ *I'm real tired.* ■ *n* **1. REALITY** everything that exists in the actual world **2.** MATH same as **real number** [15C. Directly or via French < late Latin *realis* "relating to things (in law)" < Latin *res* "thing, fact"] —**re·al·ness** *n* ◇ **for real** seriously, not as a joke or as a practice (*informal*) ◇ **get real 1.** used to indicate strongly that what somebody said or thought is unrealistic or out of touch with the facts (*slang*) **2.** to begin to take a realistic view of a situation ○ *He needs to get real.* ◇ **(in) real life** in the course of normal life as opposed to imagined or fictional representations of life, e.g., in books and movies

SPELLCHECK real or **reel**? Do not confuse the spelling of ***real*** and ***reel***, which sound similar. ***Real*** is chiefly used as an adjective, meaning "existing," "factual," or "genuine," as in *the real world, her real name, real silk.* ***Reel*** is used as a noun and verb referring to a cylindrical device on which something is wound (as in *a reel of thread, reel in a fishing line*), a lively dance (as in *the Virginia reel*), or a staggering movement (as in *reeling from the shock*).

re·al[2] /ray aál, ree-/ (*plural* **-als** or **-al·es** /-aá less/) *n* **1.** the main unit of Brazilian currency. See table at **currency 2.** a former coin used in several Spanish-speaking countries [Late 16C. Via Spanish < Latin *regalis* (see ROYAL)]

re·al[3] /ray aál, ree aál/ (*plural* **re·als** or **reis** /rayss/) *n* a former unit of Portuguese currency [Mid-20C. Via Portuguese < Latin *regalis* (see ROYAL)]

re·al es·tate *n* land including all the property on it that cannot be moved and any attached rights

re·al-es·tate a·gent *n* somebody who buys, sells, and leases property on behalf of somebody else

re·al fo·cus *n* a point from which light diverges or at which it converges

re·al·gar /ree álgər, ree ál gaàr/ *n* a soft orange red arsenic sulfide mineral. Use: tanning, paints, fireworks. [14C. Via medieval Latin *realger* < Arabic *rahj al-ğār* "powder of the cave"]

re·a·lign /rèe ə lín/ (**-ligned, -lign·ing, -ligns**) *v* **1.** *vt* **STRAIGHTEN SOMETHING AGAIN** to readjust or manipulate something so that it is in a straight line or is correctly oriented **2.** *vti* **CHANGE SOMETHING TO FIT SITUATION** to alter or change something to fit different circumstances **3.** *vti* **MAKE NEW ALLIANCES** to form new alliances or associations, or cause people or groups to do this ○ *The party has realigned itself with several former ideological opponents.* —**re·a·lign·ment** *n*

re·al im·age *n* an optical image of something that is produced by reflection or refraction and can be transferred onto a surface such as the film inside a camera

re·al·ism /rée ə lìzzəm/ *n* **1. PRACTICAL UNDERSTANDING OF LIFE** a practical understanding and acceptance of the actual nature of the world, rather than an idealized or romantic view of it **2. ACCURACY OF SIMULATION** the simulation of something in a way that accurately resembles real things ○ *the increasing realism of computer graphics* **3. LIFELIKE ARTISTIC REPRESENTATION** in artistic and literary works, lifelike representation of people and the world, without any idealization **4.** PHILOSOPHY **THEORY THAT THINGS EXIST OBJECTIVELY** the theory that things such as universals, moral facts, and theoretical scientific entities exist independently of people's thoughts and perceptions **5.** PHILOSOPHY **THEORY OF OBJECTIVELY EXISTING WORLD** the theory that there is an objectively existing world, not dependent on our minds, and that people are able to understand aspects of that world through perception **6.** PHILOSOPHY **THEORY THAT STATEMENTS HAVE TRUTH VALUES** the theory that every declarative statement is either true or false, regardless of whether this can be verified

re·al·ist /rée əlist/ *n* **1.** somebody who only considers things as they are or appear to be, and avoids ideals and abstractions **2.** somebody who practices realism in the arts or believes in philosophical theories of realism

re·al·is·tic /rèe ə lístik/ *adj* **1. PRACTICAL** seeking what is achievable or possible, based on known facts ○ *Set realistic goals when looking for a new job.* **2. SIMULATING REALITY** simulating real things or imaginary things in a way that seems real ○ *computer games with realistic graphics* **3. REASONABLE** not priced or valued too low or high ○ *a realistic price* **4. REPRESENTING LIFE ACCURATELY** in the arts and literature, representing life as it really is, rather than an idealized picture of it **5.** PHILOSOPHY **RELATING TO REALISM** relating to philosophical theories of realism —**re·al·is·ti·cal·ly** *adv*

~~**realisticly**~~ incorrect spelling of **realistically**

re·al·i·ty /ree állətee/ (*plural* **-ties**) *n* **1. REAL EXISTENCE** actual being or existence, as opposed to an imaginary, idealized, or false nature **2. ALL THAT EXISTS OR HAPPENS** everything that actually does or could exist or happen in real life **3. SOMETHING THAT EXISTS OR HAPPENS** something that has real existence and must be dealt with in real life ○ *a vision that ignores the realities of the business world* **4. TYPE OF EXISTENCE** an existence or universe, either connected with or independent from other kinds ○ *fantastic notions of alternative realities* **5.** PHILOSOPHY **TOTALITY OF REAL THINGS** the totality of real things in the world, independent of people's knowledge or perception of them ◇ **in reality** in actual fact

re·al·i·ty check *n* something said or done to demonstrate the unrealistic nature of somebody's ideas or desires

re·al·i·ty prin·ci·ple *n* in Freudian psychoanalysis, the ego's ability to postpone gratification to avoid unpleasant consequences or to gain greater reward

re·al·i·ty show *n* a television or radio show that deals with real people in real situations. Reality shows range from those depicting police operations and emergency rescues to those in which people divorce, choose marriage partners, or actively deal with their personal problems on air.

re·al·i·ty tour·ism *n* travel to areas of the world deemed politically unstable or less developed, in order to experience at first hand economic disadvantage, conflict, repression, etc.

re·al·i·ty TV *n* television programs that present real people in live, though often deliberately manufactured, situations and monitor their emotions and behavior

re·al·ize /rée ə lìz/ (**-ized, -iz·ing, -iz·es**) *v* **1.** *vti* **KNOW AND UNDERSTAND SOMETHING** to know, understand, and accept something ○ *doesn't realize how lucky he is* **2.** *vti* **BE OR BECOME AWARE OF SOMETHING** to be aware or conscious of something, or to become aware of something ○ *Do you realize the problems you've caused?* **3.** *vt* **ACHIEVE SOMETHING** to fulfill a specific vision, plan, or potential **4.** *vt* **TRANSLATE SOMETHING INTO MONEY** to translate something into a particular amount of money, usually by selling it **5.** *vt* FIN **CONVERT GAIN OR LOSS INTO CASH** to convert a paper gain or loss into a cash gain or loss by closing out the original transaction ○ *realize our assets* **6.** *vt* **TURN WORK INTO PERFORMANCE** to turn something such as a play or novel into a stage or film performance **7.** *vt* MUSIC **INTERPRET PIECE OF MUSIC** to interpret a musical composition, especially the figured bass of a baroque composition [Early 17C. < REAL[1] after French *réaliser*] —**re·al·iz·a·ble** *adj* —**re·al·i·za·tion** /rèe əli záysh'n/ *n* —**re·al·iz·er** *n*

SYNONYMS See ***accomplish***.

re·al-life *adj* actual or true, as opposed to fictional or imaginary ○ *The part of the child was played by the actor's real-life daughter.*

re·al live *adj* not artificial, imagined, or invented ○ *face-to-face with a real live gangster*

re·al·ly /rée əlee, réelee/ *adv* **1. IN FACT** in fact or in reality, especially as distinct from what has been believed until now ○ *She's really going to Paris, not Bangkok.* **2. GENUINELY** used to emphasize the truthfulness or accuracy of what is being said ○ *She really is going to Paris next year.* **3. VERY** used to emphasize the extent to which something is true ○ *That's really interesting.* **4. PROPERLY** in order to act in the correct or proper manner ○ *You should really apply in writing.* ■ *interj* **EXCLAMATION OF SURPRISE** used to express surprise, doubt, or exasperation ○ *You're getting married? Really!*

realm /relm/ *n* **1. SCOPE OF SOMETHING** an area or domain, e.g., of thought or knowledge ○ *Here the scenario enters the realm of fantasy.* **2. AREA OF INTEREST** a defined area of interest or study ○ *the realm of pure mathematics* **3. KINGDOM** a country ruled by a monarch [13C. Via Old French *realme* < Latin *regimen* "government" (see REGIMEN)]

re·al num·ber *n* a number that is either rational or irrational rather than imaginary

re·al·po·li·tik /ray áal poli teék/ *n* politics based on pragmatism or practicality rather than on ethical or theoretical considerations [Early 20C. < German, "real politics"] —**re·al·po·li·tik·er** *n*

re·al pres·ence *n* in Christianity, the doctrine that the body and blood of Jesus Christ are actually present in the ritual of Communion

re·al ten·nis *n UK* same as **court tennis** [*Real* because it was the original game of tennis]

re·al time *n* **1.** the actual time during which something happens **2.** the time in which a computer system processes and updates data as soon as it is received from some external source such as an airtraffic control or antilock brake system. The time available to receive the data, process it, and respond to the external process is dictated by the time constraints imposed by the process. —**re·al-time** *adj*

Re·al·tor /reé əltər/ *tdmk* a trademark for a member of the US National Association of Realtors or the Canadian Association of Real Estate Boards

re·al·ty /reé əltee/ *n* LAW same as **real estate**

re·al-world *adj* relevant or practical in terms of everyday life

~~**realy**~~ incorrect spelling of **really**

ream[1] /reem/ *n* a quantity of paper, formerly 480 sheets but now usually 500 sheets ■ **reams** *npl* a large quantity of material, especially written material [14C. Via Old French *raime* < Arabic *rizma* "bundle"]

ream[2] /reem/ (**reamed, ream·ing, reams**) *vt* **1. FORM HOLE WITH REAMER** to form, enlarge, or shape a hole with a reamer **2. SQUEEZE CITRUS JUICE** to squeeze the juice from a citrus fruit with a reamer **3.** *US* **CHEAT SOMEBODY** to cheat or swindle somebody (*slang*) **4. REPRIMAND SOMEBODY** to reprimand somebody severely (*slang*) [Mid-18C. Origin ?]

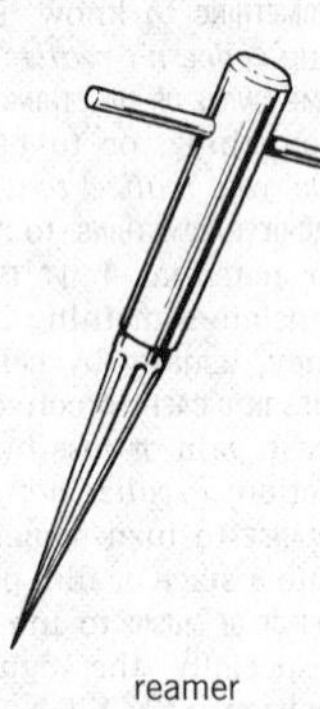

reamer

ream·er /reémər/ *n* **1.** a tool that is used to form, enlarge, or shape holes **2.** a device for extracting juice from citrus fruit, consisting of a shallow dish with a pointed ridged cone

reap /reep/ (**reaped, reap·ing, reaps**) *vt* **1.** to obtain something, especially as a consequence of previous effort or action **2.** to cut and gather a crop, especially a grain crop, from the land where it is growing [Old English *rīpan*. Origin uncertain: perhaps ultimately from an Indo-European word meaning "to tear"] —**reap·a·ble** *adj*

reap·er /reépər/ *n* somebody or something that reaps, especially, formerly, a machine for harvesting grain crops

Reap·er *n* same as **Grim Reaper**

rear[1] /reer/ (**reared, rear·ing, rears**) *v* **1.** *vt* **RAISE YOUNG ANIMALS OR CHILDREN** to bring up and care for young animals or children until they are fully grown **2.** *vt* **GROW PLANT** to raise a plant to full growth **3.** *vi* **RISE ON HIND LEGS** to rise up on the hind legs (*refers to animals*) **4.** *vi* **RISE HIGH** to rise high into the air ○ *tall office buildings rearing into the night sky* [Old English *rǣran*. Ultimately from an Indo-European word that is also the ancestor of English *raise* and *rise*] —**rear·er** *n*

rear[2] /reer/ *n* **1. BACK OF SOMETHING** the back of something, or the area near the back of something **2. PART OF ARMY FARTHEST FROM FRONT** the part of an army or a procession that is farthest from the front **3. BUTTOCKS** somebody's buttocks, or the similar part of an animal (*informal*) ■ *adj* **BACK** situated at the back ○ *Do not join the rear four carriages.* [Late 16C. Via Old French *rere* < Latin *retro* "back, behind"] ◇ **bring up the rear** to be at the back, particularly in a race or procession

rear ad·mi·ral *n* an officer in the US Navy or Coast Guard of a rank above captain, or above commodore in the British or Canadian navies

rear end *n* same as **rear**[2] *n* (senses 1, 3)

rear-end *vt* to collide with the back of another vehicle

rear-end·er *n* an accident in which one vehicle collides with the back of another (*informal*)

rear·guard /reér gaàrd/ *n* **1.** a portion of a military force on the move that is responsible for protecting against an attack from the rear **2.** members of a political party or other organization who are strongly conservative and opposed to change and progress (*disapproving*)

rear light, rear lamp *n UK* same as **taillight**

rear·most /reér mōst/ *adj* farthest toward the back

re·ar·range /reé ə ráynj/ (**-ranged, -rang·ing, -rang·es**) *vt* **1.** to change the order or position of something **2.** to reschedule the time of something such as an event —**re·ar·range·ment** *n*

rear·view mir·ror /reér vyoō-/ *n* a mirror attached to the inside of the windshield of a vehicle, allowing the driver to see behind the vehicle

rear·ward /reérwərd/ *adj* **LOCATED IN REAR** located in or near the rear or back ■ *adv also* **rear·wards** /-wərdz/ **TOWARD REAR** toward or in the rear or back ■ *n* **REAR POSITION** a position at the back, especially of an army

rea·son /reéz'n/ *n* **1. JUSTIFICATION** an explanation or justification for something ○ *refused to give a reason for her behavior* **2. MOTIVE** a motive or cause for acting or thinking in a particular way ○ *His only reason for going was that she would be there.* **3. CAUSE THAT EXPLAINS SOMETHING** a cause that explains a particular phenomenon ○ *What's the reason for grass being green?* **4. POWER OF ORDERLY THOUGHT** the power of being able to think in a logical and rational manner ○ *use reason rather than force* **5. ABILITY TO THINK CLEARLY** the ability to think clearly and coherently **6.** PHILOSOPHY **INTELLECT AS BASIS FOR KNOWLEDGE** the ability to think logically regarded as a basis for knowledge, as distinct from experience or emotions ■ *v* (**-soned, -son·ing, -sons**) **1.** *vi* **THINK IN LOGICAL WAY** to consider information and use it to reach a conclusion in a logical way **2.** *vi* **PERSUADE USING RATIONAL ARGUMENT** to try to persuade or influence somebody by means of rational argument ○ *I tried to reason with him but he insisted on going ahead.* **3.** *vt* **RESOLVE USING RATIONAL THOUGHT** to formulate or resolve something using rational means ○ *reason out a math problem* [13C. Via Old French *reisun* < Latin *ratio* "calculation, thought" < past participle of *reri* "calculate, think"] —**rea·soned** *adj* —**rea·son·er** *n* ◇ **by reason of** because of ◇ **it stands to reason** used to emphasize that something seems obvious or logical ◇ **listen to reason** to take note of sensible advice ◇ **within reason** within reasonable limits

USAGE the reason is that... or the reason is because...? The word ***reason*** is correctly followed by *that* rather than by the redundant *because* in sentences of the type *The reason I left is that* [not *because*] *I was bored.* Alternatively, simply use: *I left because I was bored.* Informally, however, and especially in conversation, *the reason is because* does occur and *that* is sometimes omitted altogether: *The reason I left is because I was bored. The reason I left is I was bored.*

SYNONYMS See ***deduce***.

rea·son·a·ble /reéz'nəb'l/ *adj* **1. RATIONAL** sensible and capable of making rational judgments ○ *He did what any reasonable person would have done in that situation.* **2. IN ACCORD WITH COMMON SENSE** acceptable and according to common sense or normal practice ○ *hoping to arrive at a reasonable time* **3. NOT EXPECTING MORE THAN IS POSSIBLE** not expecting or demanding more than is possible or achievable ○ *Come on, be reasonable!* **4. NOT EXORBITANT** fairly priced and not too expensive ○ *Three bottles for $12 is very reasonable.* **5. FAIRLY GOOD** fairly good but not excellent ○ *The food was reasonable.* **6. FAIRLY LARGE** large enough but not excessive ○ *He earns a reasonable amount of money.* —**rea·son·a·ble·ness** *n* —**rea·son·a·bly** *adv*

SYNONYMS See *valid*.

rea·son·ing /reéz'ning/ *n* **1.** the use of logical thinking in order to find results or draw conclusions **2.** an argument or other example of logical thinking ○ *Her reasoning was based on the available facts.*

re·as·sure /reé ə shoór/ (**-sured, -sur·ing, -sures**) *vt* **1.** to make somebody feel less anxious or worried **2.** INSUR same as **reinsure** —**re·as·sur·ance** *n* —**re·as·sur·er** *n*

re·as·sur·ing /reé ə shoóring/ *adj* having the effect of making people feel less anxious or worried —**re·as·sur·ing·ly** *adv*

re·a·ta *n US* AGRIC another spelling of **riata**

Ré·au·mur /ráy ō myoór, ráy ə myoór/ *adj* using or measured on the Réaumur scale [Early 19C. After René Antoine Ferchault de *Réaumur* (1683–1757), French physicist]

Ré·au·mur scale *n* an obsolete temperature scale on which water freezes at 0 degrees and boils at 80 degrees under normal atmospheric conditions

reave /reev/ (**reaved** or **reft** /reft/, **reav·ing, reaves**) *vt* (*archaic*) **1.** to plunder something or carry something off by force **2.** to rob somebody or deprive somebody of something [Old English *rēafian*. Ultimately from a prehistoric Germanic word that is also the ancestor of English *rob*] —**reav·er** *n*

Reb /reb/, **reb** *n US* same as **Johnny Reb** (*informal*) [Mid-19C. Shortening of REBEL]

re·bar·ba·tive /ri baárbətiv/ *adj* unpleasant, annoying, or forbidding (*formal*) [Late 19C. < French *rébarbatif* < *rebarber*, literally "face beard to beard" < *barbe* "beard"] —**re·bar·ba·tive·ly** *adv*

re·bate[1] *n* /reé bàyt/ money that is paid back, e.g., because somebody has overpaid a tax or is entitled to a refund ■ *vt* /reé báyt/ (**-bat·ed, -bat·ing, -bates**) to give somebody an amount of money as a rebate [15C. < French *rabattre* "beat down again" < *abattre* "beat down" < Latin *battuere* "beat"] —**re·bat·a·ble** *adj* —**re·bat·er** *n*

re·bate[2] /reé bàyt/ *UK* CONSTR *n* same as **rabbet** ■ *vt* (**-bat·ed, -bat·ing, -bates**) same as **rabbet** [Late 17C. Alteration of RABBET]

reb·be /rébbə/, **Reb·be** *n* a rabbi or spiritual leader of a Hasidic Jewish community [Late 19C. Via Yiddish < Hebrew *rabbī* "my teacher"]

reb·bet·zin /rébbitsin/, **reb·bit·zin** *n* the wife of a rabbi [Late 19C. < Yiddish < *rebbe* (see REBBE)]

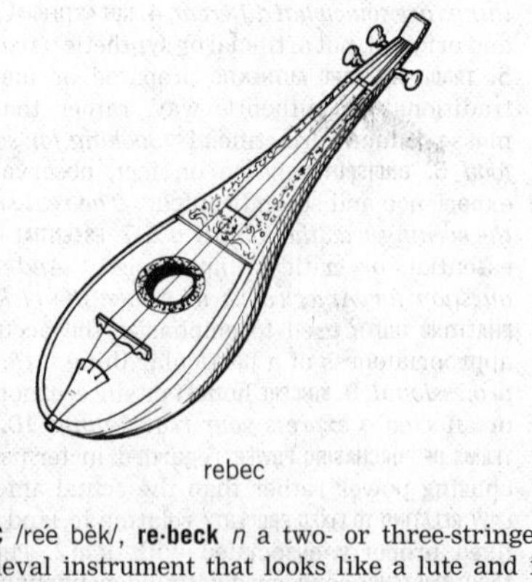

rebec

re·bec /reé bèk/, **re·beck** *n* a two- or three-stringed medieval instrument that looks like a lute and is played with a bow. It is one of the earliest bowed stringed instruments. [Early 16C. Via French < Arabic *rabāb*]

Re·bec·ca /ri békə/, **Re·be·kah** *n* in the Bible, the wife of Isaac, and mother of Jacob and Esau

re·beck *n* MUSIC another spelling of **rebec**

Re·be·kah *n* BIBLE another spelling of **Rebecca**

reb·el *n* /rébb'l/ **1. SOMEBODY UNCONVENTIONAL** somebody who rejects the codes and conventions of society **2. SOLDIER WHO OPPOSES GOVERNMENT** a soldier who belongs to a force seeking to overthrow a government or ruling power **3. PROTESTER** somebody who defiantly protests against authority ■ *vi* /ri bél/ (**re·belled, re·bel·ling, re·bels**) **1. REVOLT AGAINST GOVERNMENT** to fight to overthrow a government or ruling power **2. REFUSE TO CONFORM** to refuse to conform to the usual codes and conventions of society **3. PROTEST BY DEFYING AUTHORITY** to protest by defying a government or other form of authority ○ *students rebelling against education funding cuts* **4. HAVE DISLIKE FOR SOMETHING** to experience or express an intense dislike or distaste for something ○ *When mama went to work, grandma rebelled at the idea of taking care of the children.* [13C. Via French < Latin *rebellis* < *bellum* "war"]

~~rebelion~~ incorrect spelling of **rebellion**

re·bel·lion /ri béllyən/ *n* **1.** an organized attempt to overthrow a government or other authority by the use of violence **2.** opposition to or defiance of authority, accepted moral codes, or social conventions

re·bel·lious /ri béllyəss/ *adj* **1.** opposing or defying authority, accepted moral codes, or social conventions **2.** fighting to overthrow a government or other authority —**re·bel·lious·ly** *adv* —**re·bel·lious·ness** *n*

reb·el yell *n US* an exuberant high-pitched yell, e.g., that used during battle by soldiers of the Confederacy

re·bid *n* /reé bìd/ a further bid in an auction at bridge, especially one of the same suit as a previous one ■ *vi* /ree bíd/ (**-bid, -bid·ding, -bids**) to make a bid in an auction at bridge after previously bidding no trump or a suit, especially one in the same suit

re·birth /ree búrth, reé bùrth/ *n* **1. REGENERATION OF SOMETHING DESTROYED** the regeneration of something that has died or has been destroyed **2. REVIVAL OF IDEAS OR FORCES** the revival of important ideas or forces, usually as part of broad and significant change **3.** RELIG **REINCARNATION** the act or process of reincarnation

re·birth·ing /ree búrthing/ *n* therapy involving breathing in a way considered to reproduce the trauma of being born —**re·birth·er** *n*

re·blo·chon /rèbblə sháwN/ *n* a soft delicately flavored washed-rind cheese with a pale pinkish skin, made in the Savoy region of France [Early 20C. < French, < *reblocher* "milk for a second time"]

re·boot *v* /ree bóot/ (**-boot·ed, -boot·ing, -boots**) **1.** *vti* to restart a computer or an operating system, or be restarted **2.** *vt* COMPUT same as **warmboot** ■ *n* /reé bòot/ a restart of a computer or an operating system

re·born /ree báwrn/ *adj* recreated or regenerated, especially in order to be more effective or modern, or renewed spiritually

re·bound *v* /ree bównd/ (**-bound·ed, -bound·ing, -bounds**) **1.** *vi* **SPRING BACK** to spring back or recoil **2.** *vi* **MOVE BACK TO PREVIOUS LEVEL** to recover from a setback and move back to a previous or higher level or position **3.** *vi* **HAVE UNDESIRABLE EFFECT** to affect the person who does or creates something directly, especially in an unpleasant or unwelcome way **4.** *vti* BASKETBALL **CATCH BALL OFF BACKBOARD** in basketball, to take possession of a ball that has bounced off the backboard or rim of the basket ■ *n* /reé bòwnd/ **1. ACT OF REBOUNDING** the springing back or recoiling of something **2. UPWARD MOVEMENT** an upward movement or a recovery, especially after a setback **3.** SPORTS **BALL THAT BOUNCES** a ball that bounces back, particularly off a backboard or rim of the basket in basketball or off the goalkeeper or goalpost in hockey, soccer, or a similar sport **4.** BASKETBALL **ACT OF CATCHING REBOUND** in basketball, an act of taking possession of a rebounding ball —**re·bound·er** *n* ◇ **on the rebound** starting something new in the wake of a disappointment or setback, often the ending of a relationship, and therefore feeling uneasy or vulnerable

USAGE rebound or **redound**? In its figurative use, ***rebound*** is a metaphor based on the image of an object bouncing and returning. Just as a ball that ***rebounds*** affects the person who threw it, so an action or statement ***rebounds*** on its creator when it affects him or her directly, usually in an unpleasant or unwelcome way: *His tactic of implementing the changes without consultation rebounded on him when his team walked out in protest.* ***Redound***, a much rarer word, is sometimes used in the same way as ***rebound***, but in its primary meaning it is followed by *to* and means "to have a particular consequence," with something good or positive as the object (the opposite connotation of ***rebound***): *The offensive players' performance redounded to the benefit of the basketball team as a whole.* Note that only ***rebound*** can be used as a noun.

re·bo·zo /ri bṓssō/ (*plural* **-zos**) *n Hispanic* a long woolen or linen scarf worn over the head and shoulders, mainly by women in Mexico [Early 19C. < Spanish < *rebozar* "to muffle"]

re·buff *vt* /ri búf/ (**-buffed, -buff·ing, -buffs**) **1. REJECT OR SNUB SOMETHING** to reject or snub an offer, advance, or approach made by somebody **2. REPEL ATTACK** to beat back or repel an attack or an attacking force ■ *n* /reé bùf/ **1. REJECTION** a blunt rejection or snub of an offer, advance, or approach made by somebody else **2. SETBACK** a sudden severe setback to progress [Late 16C. Via French < Italian *ribuffare* "scold" < *buffo* "puff," an imitation of the sound]

USAGE See ***refute.***

re·build /ree bíld/ (**-built** /-bílt/, **-build·ing, -builds**) *vt* **1. BUILD STRUCTURE AGAIN** to construct a building or other structure again because it has been damaged or destroyed **2. RESTORE SOMETHING** to work to restore something that has been weakened, damaged, or ruined ○ *rebuilt her confidence* **3. MAKE MAJOR CHANGES TO SOMETHING** to make major alterations or improvements to something ○ *to rebuild society for the information age* —**re·build·er** *n*

re·buke /ri byóok/ *vt* (**-buked, -buk·ing, -bukes**) to criticize or reprimand somebody, usually sharply ■ *n* a reprimand or expression of criticism or disapproval [14C. < Anglo-Norman, Old N French *rebuker* "chop wood" < Old French *busche* "log" < Germanic] —**re·buk·er** *n*

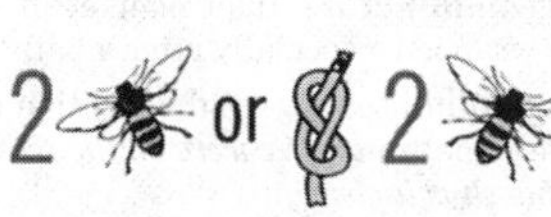

Answer: to be or not to be

rebus

re·bus /reébəss/ (*plural* **-bus·es**) *n* **1.** a puzzle in which the syllables of words and names are represented either by pictures of things that sound the same or by letters **2.** a heraldic emblem showing a picture that represents the name of the bearer, e.g., a picture of a lion for somebody named Lyon [Early 17C. Via French < Latin, literally "by things," form of *res* "thing"]

re·but /ri bút/ (**-but·ted, -but·ting, -buts**) *vti* to deny the truth of something, especially by presenting arguments that disprove it [13C. < Anglo-Norman *rebuter*, Old French *reboter* < *boter* "butt, ram"] —**re·but·ta·ble** *adj* —**re·but·tal** *n*

USAGE See ***refute.***

re·but·ter /ri búttər/ *n* **1.** somebody who rebuts something **2.** the defendant's answer in the third round of pleading in a legal action

rec /rek/ *n* LEISURE same as **recreation** (sense 1) (*informal; often used before a noun*) ○ *rec room* [Early 20C. Shortening]

rec. *abbr* **1.** COMM receipt **2.** COMM received **3.** COOK recipe **4.** recommended **5.** MAIL recorded **6.** recorder **7.** recording **8.** recreation

re·cal·ci·trant /rə kálssitrənt/ *adj* **1. RESISTING CONTROL** stubbornly resisting the authority of another person or group **2. HARD TO DO OR HANDLE** difficult to deal with or operate ○ *struggling in front of the mirror with a recalcitrant necktie* ■ *n* **STUBBORN OPPONENT** somebody who stubbornly resists authority or control ○ *A few recalcitrants refused to submit.* [Mid-19C. Directly or via French < Latin *recalcitrant-* present participle of *recalcitrare* "kick back" (used of horses) < *calcitrare* "kick (with the heels)" < *calc-* "heel"] —**re·cal·ci·trance** *n* —**re·cal·ci·trant·ly** *adv*

SYNONYMS See ***unruly.***

re·ca·lesce /reèkə léss/ (**-lesced, -lesc·ing, -lesc·es**) *vi* to exhibit or undergo a sudden increase in temperature and brightness (*refers to cooling metals*) [Late 19C. Back-formation < RECALESCENCE]

re·ca·les·cence /reèkə léss'nss/ *n* a sudden increase in the temperature and brightness of a cooling metal, caused by the release of latent heat as the metal undergoes a change in crystalline structure [Late 19C. < RE- + Latin *calescere* "grow warm" < *calere* "be warm"] —**re·ca·les·cent** *adj*

re·call *v* /ri káwl/ (**-called, -cal·ling, -calls**) **1.** *vti* **REMEMBER SOMETHING** to remember something or bring something back to mind **2.** *vt* **ORDER SOMEBODY OR SOMETHING BACK** to order something or somebody to come back or be sent back ○ *recalled the ambassador to Washington* **3.** *vt* **REVOKE SOMETHING** to revoke or cancel a previous decision or instruction ○ *The manufacturer has recalled all models built in 2003.* **4.** *vt* **BRING ATTENTION BACK** to bring somebody's attention or thoughts back to an ongoing matter **5.** *vt* **RESEMBLE SOMEBODY OR SOMETHING** to remind another person of somebody or something familiar or previously seen ○ *Her face recalls that of her grandmother.* ■ *n* /reé kàwl/ **1. REMEMBERING** the remembering of something or the calling back of somebody or something **2. MEMORY** somebody's memory or ability to remember ○ *a vague recall of the actual events* **3. REQUEST TO RETURN PRODUCT** a request by a manufacturer to return a product because of a fault or contamination **4. REVOCATION** a revocation or cancellation of a previous decision or instruction **5.** MIL **SIGNAL TO RETURN** a signal, especially a bugle call, ordering troops to return to their positions or to a rallying point **6.** POL **DISMISSAL FROM OFFICE BY VOTE** the dismissal from office of an elected official by a popular vote, or the right of the electors to do this [Late 16C. After French *rappeler* or Latin *revocare*] —**re·call·a·ble** *adj* —**re·call·er** *n* —**re·call·a·bil·i·ty** /ri kàwlə bíllətee/ *n*

re·ca·mi·er /ràykə myáy/ *n* a couch with a high headrest and low footrest, often without a back [Early 20C. After Jeanne *Récamier* (1777–1849), French hostess, portrayed reclining on a couch in a painting]

re·ca·nal·i·za·tion /ree kànn'li záysh'n/ *n* the surgical unblocking of an obstructed vessel within the body or the reconnection of a tube or duct

re·cant /ri kánt/ (**-cant·ed, -cant·ing, -cants**) *vti* to deny believing in something or withdraw something previously said [Mid-16C. < Latin *recantare* "sing back" < *cantare* "sing"] —**re·can·ta·tion** /reè kan táysh'n/ *n* —**re·cant·er** *n*

re·cap[1] /reé kàp/ *vti* (**-capped, -cap·ping, -caps**) to go over the main points of something such as an argument or a proposal again ■ *n* a summing-up of the main points of something previously put forward [Mid-20C. Shortening of RECAPITULATE]

re·cap[2] *US n* /reé kàp/ same as **retread** *n* (sense 1) ■ *vt* /ree káp/ (**-capped, -cap·ping, -caps**) to retread a tire [Mid-20C. Formed from CAP. Originally in the sense "to put a cap on something again"] —**re·cap·pa·ble** /ree káppəb'l/ *adj*

re·ca·pit·u·late /reèkə píchə làyt/ (**-lat·ed, -lat·ing, -lates**) *v* **1.** *vti* same as **recap**[1] (*formal*) **2.** *vt* to repeat stages from the evolution of the species during the embryonic period of an animal's life [Late 16C. Partly < Latin *recapitulat-*, past participle of *recapitulare* "restate by chapters" < *capitulum* "chapter"; partly back-formation < RECAPITULATION] —**re·ca·pit·u·la·tive** /reèkə píchə làytiv, -píchələtiv/ *adj* —**re·ca·pit·u·la·to·ry** *adj*

re·ca·pit·u·la·tion /reèkə pichə láysh'n/ *n* **1.** same as **recap**[1] (*formal*) **2.** BIOL the theoretical process of going through successive stages during the embryonic period of an animal's life that duplicate the evolutionary stages the species experienced **3.** MUSIC the repetition of earlier themes in a piece of music, especially in sonata form at the end of a movement [14C. Directly or via French < late Latin *recapitulation-* < Latin *recapitulat-* (see RECAPITULATE)]

re·cap·tion /ree kápsh'n/ *n* the taking back, by peaceful means, of property from somebody who has unlawfully taken it, or of a spouse or child from somebody who has unlawfully detained him or her [Early 17C. < Anglo-Latin *recaption-* "capturing back" < Latin *caption-* "capturing" < *capere* "take"]

re·cap·ture /ree kápchər/ (**-tured, -tur·ing, -tures**) *vt* **1. CAPTURE SOMEBODY OR SOMETHING AGAIN** to take back somebody or something that has escaped or has been taken away **2. EXPERIENCE SOMETHING AGAIN** to have, show, or experience again something that existed in the past or has been lost ○ *a failed attempt to recapture their youth* **3.** *US* **TAKE PART OF PROFITS** to take part of the profits, over a set amount, of a public-service corporation by law —**re·cap·ture** *n*

re·cast /ree kást/ (**-cast, -cast·ing, -casts**) *vt* **1. CAST OBJECT AGAIN** to repeat the casting process for an object formed in a mold **2. CHANGE SOMETHING** to change the form of something ○ *The experience led him to recast his philosophy of life.* **3. GIVE ROLES TO DIFFERENT ACTORS** to assign roles in something such as a play or film to different actors ○ *recast the play for a road tour*

rec·ce /rékee/ (*slang*) *n* same as **reconnaissance** (sense 1) ■ *vt* (**-ced, -ce·ing, -ces**) same as **reconnoiter** [Mid-20C. Shortening and alteration]

~~**reccommend**~~ incorrect spelling of **recommend**

recd., rec'd. *abbr* received

re·cede /ri séed/ (**-ced·ed, -ced·ing, -cedes**) *vi* **1. GO BACK** to go back or down from a point or level ○ *waiting for the flood waters to recede* **2. GET FARTHER AWAY** to become more distant or unlikely ○ *As the ship gathered speed, the island receded in the distance.* **3. SLOPE** to slope backward ○ *a receding forehead* **4. GO BALD** to gradually go bald from the front of the head backward (*refers to hair or a person*) ○ *a hairline that was slowly receding* **5. BECOME LESS** to become less in value or quality **6. WITHDRAW** to engage in a retreat [15C. Directly or via French < Latin *recedere* "go back" < *cedere* "give away"]

re·ceipt /ri séet/ *n* **1. ACKNOWLEDGMENT OF RECEIPT** a written or printed acknowledgment that things such as sums of money have been given to the person who issues the acknowledgment **2. ACT OF RECEIVING** the fact or time of receiving something ○ *The balance is payable on receipt of the goods.* **3.** COOK same as **recipe** (sense 1) (*dated*) ■ **re·ceipts** *npl* **AMOUNT RECEIVED** the amount of money or goods received, especially in business ■ *v* (**-ceipt·ed, -ceipt·ing, -ceipts**) **1.** *vt* **ACKNOWLEDGE PAYMENT** to sign a bill to acknowledge that it has been paid **2.** *vti* **GIVE RECEIPT** to give a receipt for money or goods [14C. < Anglo-Norman or Old N French *receite* "(medicinal) recipe, receipt" < Latin *recipere* (see RECEIVE)]

re·ceiv·a·ble /ri séevəb'l/ *adj* **1. SUITABLE TO BE RECEIVED** suitable to be received, especially as payment ○ *receivable notes* **2. AWAITING PAYMENT** describes a bill or account that is due to be paid ■ **re·ceiv·a·bles** *npl* **MONEY OWED** business assets consisting of amounts of money that a company is owed

re·ceive /ri séev/ (**-ceived, -ceiv·ing, -ceives**) *v* **1.** *vti* **GET SOMETHING** to take or accept something given **2.** *vti* **ACCEPT ELECTRONIC SIGNALS** to pick up electronic signals and convert them into sound or pictures **3.** *vt* **TAKE DELIVERY OF MESSAGE** to take delivery of a message such as a letter or telephone call **4.** *vt* **LEARN INFORMATION** to learn of something such as news or information **5.** *vt* **MEET WITH SOMETHING** to meet with or experience something ○ *We received a warm reception from the crowd.* **6.** *vt* **ACQUIRE SOMETHING** to come to have something, e.g., through effort ○ *the medical training students receive* **7.** *vt* **REACT TO SOMETHING** to react to something in a particular way ○ *The proposals were not well received by the members.* **8.** *vt* **BE HURT BY SOMETHING** to be subjected to something such as an injury, blow, or pressure ○ *She received the full force of the blow on her face.* **9.** *vti* **CATCH BALL** to catch, hit, or kick a ball played by an opponent **10.** *vti* **ENTERTAIN VISITORS** to be free to see or admit visitors ○ *Find out the hours during which patients can receive visitors.* **11.** *vt* **CATCH SOMETHING** to hold or take something ○ *The larger tank receives the overflow from the drainage system.* **12.** *vt* **BEAR SOMETHING** to bear or sustain something such as a burden ○ *The bridge is reinforced to receive the weight of heavy traffic.* **13.** *vt* **GREET GUESTS** to greet and admit guests ○ *We were received by the duke himself.* **14.** *vt* **HEAR AND ACKNOWLEDGE SOMETHING** to hear and acknowledge something formally ○ *The priest received her confession.* **15.** *vt* **ADMIT SOMEBODY** to allow a person entry ○ *A knight had to prove himself worthy before being received into their fellowship.* **16.** *vti UK* LAW **ACCEPT STOLEN GOODS** to accept or deal in stolen goods **17.** *vi* CHR **TAKE COMMUNION** in the Christian church, to take Communion [14C. Via Old French *receivre* < Latin *recipere* "take back" < *capere* "take"]

re·ceived /ri séevd/ *adj* generally accepted as true ○ *The received wisdom in these matters is seldom wrong.*

Re·ceived Pro·nun·ci·a·tion *n* the accent of British English that educated people from the southern part of England traditionally use, widely regarded as the least regionally modified of all British accents

re·ceiv·er /ri séevər/ *n* **1. PART OF PHONE** the part of a telephone that contains the earpiece and mouthpiece and receives and converts electronic signals into sound **2. DEVICE FOR PICKING UP SIGNALS** an electrical device that receives and converts electronic signals into sound or pictures **3.** FOOTBALL **PLAYER CATCHING FORWARD PASS** a football player on the offensive team who is eligible to catch a forward pass **4.** BASEBALL same as **catcher** (sense 1) **5.** LAW, FIN **SOMEBODY APPOINTED TO RUN BUSINESS** somebody appointed by a court to manage a business or property that is involved in a legal process such as bankruptcy **6.** LAW **SOMEBODY DEALING IN STOLEN GOODS** a dealer in stolen goods **7. SOMEBODY WHO RECEIVES SOMETHING** somebody who receives or takes delivery of something **8.** CHEM **CONTAINER USED IN DISTILLING** a container used during distillation to collect the distillate

re·ceiv·er·ship /ri séevər shìp/ *n* **1.** management by a receiver of a business or property that is involved in a legal process such as bankruptcy **2.** the office or duties of somebody appointed by a court to manage a business or property that is involved in a legal process such as bankruptcy

re·ceiv·ing blan·ket *n* a light blanket in which an infant is wrapped, especially after a bath

re·ceiv·ing end /ri séeving-/ *n* the position of having to endure something ○ *We were on the receiving end of some harsh criticism.*

re·ceiv·ing line *n* a group of people who stand in a line to greet individually the guests at a formal occasion such as a wedding reception

re·cen·sion /ri sénshən/ *n* **1.** a critical revision carried out on a literary text **2.** a literary text that has been given a critical revision [Mid-17C. < Latin *recension-* "review" < *recensere* "reassess" < *censere* "appraise, assess"]

re·cent /réess'nt/ *adj* **1.** having happened or appeared not long ago ○ *the recent birth of her daughter* **2.** from current times or the very near past ○ *recent political trends* [15C. Directly or via French < Latin *recent-*] —**re·cen·cy** *n* —**re·cent·ly** *adv* —**re·cent·ness** *n*

Re·cent /réess'nt/ *n* GEOL same as **Holocene** —**Re·cent** *adj*

re·cep·ta·cle /ri séptək'l/ *n* **1. CONTAINER** a container that holds, contains, or receives a liquid or solid **2. FLOWER-BEARING PART** the end of a flower stalk, bearing the parts of a flower or the florets of a composite flower **3. PLANT PART FOR REPRODUCTION** in a plant that reproduces through spores, e.g., an alga or liverwort, the part that bears the reproductive organs [14C. Directly or via French < Latin *receptaculum* "place in which to store something received" < *recipere* (see RECEIVE)]

re·cep·tion /ri sépshən/ *n* **1. FORMAL PARTY** a formal party to welcome somebody or celebrate an event such as a wedding **2. WAY SOMEBODY OR SOMETHING IS RECEIVED** the way in which somebody or something is received or greeted ○ *The audience gave her a warm reception.* **3.** *UK* **PLACE WHERE VISITORS ARE RECEIVED** a place in a hotel, office, or public building where visitors are first received ○ *I'll be waiting for you in reception.* **4. QUALITY OF SIGNAL** the quality of the signal received by a radio or television set ○ *We don't get very good reception on this channel.* **5. ACT OF RECEIVING** the act of receiving something given or sent **6.** ELECTRONICS **CONVERSION OF ELECTRONIC SIGNALS** the process of receiving and converting electronic signals **7.** BUILDINGS same as **reception room** **8.** FOOTBALL **CATCHING OF FORWARD PASS** in football, the catching of a pass made toward the opponent's goal [14C. Directly or via French < Latin *reception-* < *recipere* (see RECEIVE)]

re·cep·tion·ist /ri sépshənist/ *n* an employee who greets visitors, customers, or patients, answers the telephone, and makes appointments

re·cep·tion room *n* a room in which clients, patients, or visitors are received and usually wait to see somebody

re·cep·tive /ri séptiv/ *adj* **1. WILLING TO ACCEPT** ready and willing to accept something such as new ideas **2. QUICK TO LEARN** quick to take in new information **3.** PHYSIOL **RECEIVING AND TRANSMITTING STIMULI** describes a sensory organ that is capable of transmitting and receiving stimuli [15C. Directly or via French < medieval Latin *receptivus* < Latin *recipere* (see RECEIVE)] —**re·cep·tive·ly** *adv* —**re·cep·tive·ness** *n* —**re·cep·tiv·i·ty** /rèe sep tívvətee/ *n*

re·cep·tor /ri séptər/ *n* **1.** PHYSIOL **SENSITIVE NERVE ENDING** a nerve ending that is sensitive to stimuli and can convert them into nerve impulses **2.** ELECTRONICS **RECEIVING DEVICE** a device designed to receive electronic signals **3.** CHEM **SPECIFIC CELL BINDING SITE OR MOLECULE** a molecule, group, or site that is in a cell or on a cell surface and binds with a specific molecule, antigen, hormone, or antibody **4.** ENVIRON **RECEIVER OF POLLUTION** somebody or something adversely affected by a pollutant [15C. Directly or via Old French *receptour* "person who harbors criminals or stolen goods" < Latin *receptor* < *recipere* (see RECEIVE)]

re·cess /rée sèss, ri séss/ *n* **1. BREAK FROM CLASSES** a break from classes during the school day or year ○ *played hopscotch during recess* **2. BREAK FROM BUSINESS** a time during which no work or business is done, specifically a long period in which a legislative body is not sitting or a short break during court proceedings **3. REMOTE PLACE** a remote or secluded place (*often used in the plural*) ○ *A distant memory haunted the recesses of her mind.* **4. INDENTED OR HOLLOWED-OUT SPACE** an area set into a wall or other flat surface, e.g., an alcove or niche ○ *a recess large enough to hold a vase* **5.** ANAT **BODY CAVITY** a concave area or cavity in a part of the body ■ *v* (**-cessed, -cess·ing, -cess·es**) **1.** *vti* **SUSPEND PROCEEDINGS** to take a break or suspend proceedings or work ○ *The meeting was recessed at midday.* ○ *The court recessed early for the weekend.* **2.** *vt* **PUT SOMETHING IN RECESS** to put something in a recess, especially in a wall ○ *recessed lighting* **3.** *vt* **MAKE INDENTATION IN SOMETHING** to make a recess in something, especially a wall ○ *The north wall of the chamber has been recessed to form an alcove.* [Mid-16C. Directly or via French < Latin *recessus* "going back" < *recedere* "go back"]

re·ces·sion /ri sésh'n/ *n* **1. DECLINE IN ECONOMIC ACTIVITY** a period, shorter than a depression, during which there is a decline in economic trade and prosperity **2. WITHDRAWAL OF SOMEBODY IN CEREMONY** the withdrawal of the participants in a ceremony, e.g., the clergy and choir after a church service **3. RECEDING** the process of going back or becoming more distant

re·ces·sion·al /ri séshən'l, -séshnəl/ *adj* involving or typical of a recession ■ *n* **1.** CHR same as **recession** (sense 2) **2.** in Christianity, a hymn sung as the clergy and choir withdraw from a church after a service

re·ces·sive /ri séssiv/ *adj* **1. PRODUCING EFFECT IN SPECIFIC CONDITIONS** used to describe a gene that produces an effect in an organism only when its matching allele is identical. The effect is masked when the matching allele is nonidentical. **2. CONTROLLED BY RECESSIVE GENE** describes a characteristic or trait determined by a recessive gene **3. RECEDING** tending to go backward or to recede ○ *recessive flood waters* **4.** PHON **AT BEGINNING OF WORD** describes stress that is placed at or near the beginning of a word ■ *n* GENETICS **1. RECESSIVE CHARACTERISTIC** a recessive gene or trait **2. ORGANISM**

WITH RECESSIVE CHARACTERISTIC an organism that has a recessive gene or trait —**re·ces·sive·ly** *adv* —**re·ces·sive·ness** *n*

re·charge /ree chaárj/ (**-charged, -charg·ing, -charg·es**) *vt* **1.** to replenish the amount of electric power in something, especially a battery **2.** to renew something such as somebody's energy ○ *We felt recharged after the weekend.* —**re·charge·a·ble** *adj* —**re·charg·er** *n*

ré·chauf·fé /ràythō fáy/ *n* **1.** a dish of reheated leftovers **2.** a piece of work, e.g., a piece of writing, that is merely a reuse of old material [Early 19C. < French, past participle of *réchauffer* "reheat" < Latin *calere* "make or be warm"]

re·cher·ché /rə shèr sháy/ *adj* **1. RARE AND EXQUISITE** marked by such rare and exquisite quality that it is known only to connoisseurs **2. APPRECIATING FINE THINGS** having a deep appreciation of unusual or choice things ○ *a recherché taste in sculpture* **3. AFFECTED** marked by excessive refinement or exaggerated importance ○ *Some of his ideas are a little recherché for my taste.* [Late 17C. < French, past participle of *rechercher* "seek thoroughly" < *chercher* "seek"]

re·cid·i·vism /ri síddə vìzzəm/ *n* the tendency to relapse into a previous undesirable type of behavior, especially crime [Late 19C. < *recidivist*, < French *récidiviste* < Latin *recidivus* "falling back" < *recidere* "fall back" < *cadere* "fall"] —**re·cid·i·vist** *n, adj* —**re·cid·i·vis·tic** /ri sìddə vístik/ *adj*

~~**reciept**~~ incorrect spelling of **receipt**

~~**recieve**~~ incorrect spelling of **receive**

Re·ci·fe /rə seéfə/ capital city of Pernambuco State, northeastern Brazil, and the major city of the region. It is a port on the Atlantic Ocean. Population: 1,346,045 (1996).

recip. *abbr* **1.** MATH reciprocal **2.** reciprocity

rec·i·pe /réssə peè/ *n* **1. INSTRUCTIONS FOR MAKING FOOD** a list of ingredients and instructions for making something, especially a food dish **2. METHOD** a method of doing something or a combination of circumstances likely to bring something about ○ *Hard work is the recipe for success.* **3.** MED **PRESCRIPTION** a prescription for a therapeutic preparation [14C. Directly or via French < Latin, "take!", form of *recipere* (see RECEIVE)]

re·cip·i·ent /ri síppee ənt/ *n* somebody or something that receives something ■ *adj* tending or able to receive [Mid-16C. Directly or via French < Latin *recipient-*, present participle of *recipere* (see RECEIVE)] —**re·cip·i·ence** *n*

re·cip·ro·cal /ri sípprək'l/ *adj* **1. GIVEN BY EACH SIDE** given or shown by each of two sides or people to the other ○ *reciprocal compliments* **2. IN RETURN** given or done in return for something else ○ *a reciprocal exchange of gifts* **3.** MATH **MULTIPLIED TO GIVE ONE** describes a number or quality that is related to another by the fact that when multiplied together the product is one **4.** MATH **COMPLEMENTING** serving to complement one another ○ *reciprocal angles* ■ *n* **1. SOMETHING MUTUAL** something that is mutual or done in return **2.** MATH **NUMBER MULTIPLIED TO GIVE ONE** a number or quantity that is related to another by the fact that when multiplied together the product is one ○ *4 and $\frac{1}{4}$ are reciprocals.* [Late 16C. < Latin *reciprocus* "going backward and forward" < *re-* "backward" + *pro-* "forward"] —**re·cip·ro·cal·i·ty** /ri sìpprə kállətee/ *n* —**re·cip·ro·cal·ly** *adv* —**re·cip·ro·cal·ness** *n*

re·cip·ro·cal link *n* a link in both directions from one website to another as a form of bartering for advertising space

re·cip·ro·cal pro·noun *n* a word or phrase representing two or more things that mutually correspond to one another, e.g., "each other"

re·cip·ro·cate /ri síppṛə kàyt/ (**-cat·ed, -cat·ing, -cates**) *v* **1.** *vti* **GIVE MUTUALLY** to give or feel something mutually or in return ○ *I couldn't accept such a generous gift without reciprocating.* **2.** *vti* ENG **MOVE BACKWARDS AND FORWARDS** to move backward and forward in an alternating motion, or move something in this way **3.** *vi* **BE COMPLEMENTARY** to be the same or complementary [Late 16C. < Latin *reciprocat-*, past participle of *reciprocare* "move backward and forward, reciprocate" < *reciprocus* (see RECIPROCAL)] —**re·cip·ro·ca·tion** /ri sìpprə káysh'n/ *n* —**re·cip·ro·ca·tive** *adj* —**re·cip·ro·ca·tor** *n*

re·cip·ro·cat·ing en·gine /ri sípprə kayting-/ *n* an engine with one or more cylinders in which pistons move backward and forward

rec·i·proc·i·ty /rèssə próssətee/ (*plural* **-ties**) *n* **1.** a relationship between people involving the exchange of goods, services, favors, or obligations, especially a mutual exchange of privileges between trading nations or recognition of licenses between states ○ *the long-standing tariff reciprocity between our two countries* **2.** something done mutually or in return [Mid-18C. < French *réciprocité* < Latin *reciprocus* (see RECIPROCAL)]

rec·i·proc·i·ty fail·ure *n* in photography, the failure of light intensity and exposure time to act reciprocally when their values are extremely high or low, sometimes affecting the color characteristics of the resulting photograph

re·ci·sion /ri sízh'n/ *n* the cancellation or rescinding of something, especially a contract [Early 17C. < Latin *recision-* "cutting back" < *recidere* "cut back" < *caedere* "cut"]

recit. *abbr* MUSIC recitative

re·cit·al /ri sít'l/ *n* **1. SOLO PERFORMANCE** a musical or dance performance given by a soloist or small group **2. PERFORMANCE BY STUDENTS** a performance given by music or dance students to demonstrate the progress they have made **3. RECITING** the reading aloud or reciting from memory of something such as a poem **4. DETAILED ACCOUNT** a detailed account or report of something **5.** LAW **DETAILED PRESENTATION OF FACT** a statement in a judgment laying out jurisdictional facts, or a deed's preliminary part laying out the circumstances leading to its existence —**re·cit·al·ist** *n*

rec·i·ta·tion /rèssə táysh'n/ *n* **1. READING ALOUD** the public reading aloud of something or reciting of something from memory, especially poetry **2. MATTER READ ALOUD** material read aloud or recited from memory in public, especially poetry **3. ACT OF REPORTING SOMETHING** the act of listing or reporting something **4.** *US* EDUC **STUDENT'S ORAL RESPONSE** the oral response by a student to questions on previously taught material **5.** *US* EDUC **REVIEW CLASS** a class period during which previously taught material is reviewed

rec·i·ta·tive[1] /rèssətə teév/, **re·ci·ta·ti·vo** /-teévō/ (*plural* **-vos**) *n* **1.** a style of singing that is close to the rhythm of natural speech, used in opera for dialogue and narration **2.** a passage in a musical composition that is sung in the form of recitative [Mid-17C. < Italian *recitativo* < Latin *recitat-*, past participle of *recitare* (see RECITE)]

rec·i·ta·tive[2] /réssi tàytiv, ri sítətiv/ *adj* relating to recital or recitation [Mid-17C. < Italian *recitativo* (see RECITATIVE[1])]

re·ci·ta·ti·vo *n* MUSIC same as **recitative**[1]

re·cite /ri sít/ (**-cit·ed, -cit·ing, -cites**) *v* **1.** *vti* **REPEAT OR READ ALOUD** to read something aloud or repeat something from memory, either for an audience or in a class **2.** *vt* **GIVE DETAILED ACCOUNT OF SOMETHING** to give a detailed account of an occurrence or event ○ *There's no need to recite every detail of your weekend.* **3.** *vt* **LIST SOMETHING** to give a list of things ○ *He then recited all my faults.* [15C. Directly or via French *réciter* < Latin *recitare* "summon again" < *citare* "summon repeatedly"] —**re·cit·er** *n*

reck /rek/ (**recked, reck·ing, recks**) *vti* (*archaic*) **1.** to care or mind about something **2.** to matter, or matter to somebody [Old English *rēcan* < Germanic]

reck·less /rékləss/ *adj* marked by a lack of thought about danger or other possible undesirable consequences ○ *with a reckless disregard for the established safety procedures* [Old English *rec(c)elēas* < Germanic] —**reck·less·ly** *adv* —**reck·less·ness** *n*

reck·on /rékən/ (**-oned, -on·ing, -ons**) *v* **1.** *vt* **REGARD SOMEBODY OR SOMETHING AS SOMETHING** to consider somebody or something to be something (*often passive*) ○ *She's reckoned the best in her field.* **2.** *vti* **COUNT** to count or calculate something ○ *We reckoned its speed at approximately 350 mph.* **3.** *vt* **INCLUDE SOMEBODY OR SOMETHING** to include or class a person or thing as being part of a particular group ○ *I reckon him among my friends.* **4.** *vti* **THINK OR BELIEVE SOMETHING** to suppose something to be true (*informal*) ○ *I reckon we're finished now.* [Old English *gerecenian* < Germanic] —**reck·on·a·ble** *adj*

REGIONAL NOTE The informal use of ***reckon*** meaning "think, believe" and introducing a clause (with the word *that* present or suppressed), as in the sentence *I reckon you're right*, is chiefly dialectal in US English, commonly occurring in Midland and Southern US speech.

reckon on *vt* to expect with confident assurance (*informal*) ○ *You can reckon on my support.*

reckon with *vt* **1.** to deal or come to terms with somebody powerful ○ *If he lets you down, he'll have me to reckon with.* **2.** to take somebody or something into account ○ *We didn't reckon with the strength of the tide.*

reckon without *vt* to fail to take something into account ○ *The legislators reckoned without the strength of public feeling against the new law.*

reck·on·er /rékənər/ *n* a book of tables of calculations that are already worked out and are used as an aid in calculation

reck·on·ing /rékəning/ *n* **1. CALCULATION** the act or a system of calculating something ○ *By my reckoning, it shouldn't have taken them more than three hours to get there.* **2. DETERMINATION OF POSITION** calculation of an aircraft's, a spacecraft's, or a vessel's position in the air, in space, or on the sea **3. SETTLEMENT OF ACCOUNT** the settlement of an account **4. ACCOUNT** a bill or a statement of money owing **5. RETRIBUTION** punishment or vengeance for wrongs committed ○ *day of reckoning*

re·claim /ri kláym/ *vt* (**-claimed, -claim·ing, -claims**) **1. CLAIM SOMETHING BACK** to claim back something that has been taken away or temporarily given to another **2. CONVERT WASTELAND** to convert unusable land such as desert or marsh into land suitable for farming or other use **3. EXTRACT USEFUL SUBSTANCES** to extract useful substances from waste or refuse **4. MAKE SOMEBODY REFORM** to cause somebody to return to a more moral way of life **5. TAME BIRD** to tame a hawk or falcon ■ *n* **RECOVERY OR CONVERSION** the act of reclaiming something, or the state of being reclaimed [14C. Via French < Latin *reclamare* "cry out against" < *clamare* "cry out"] —**re·claim·a·ble** *adj* —**re·claim·ant** *n* —**re·claim·er** *n* —**rec·la·ma·tion** /rèklə máysh'n/ *n*

ré·clame /ray klaám/ *n* **1.** public attention or fame **2.** the capacity or gift for attracting public attention or fame [Late 19C. < French, "advertisement" < *réclamer* < Latin *reclamare* (see RECLAIM)]

rec·li·nate /réklə nàyt, -nət/ *adj* describes a leaf or stem that is bent backward or down

re·cline /ri klín/ (**-clined, -clin·ing, -clines**) *v* **1.** *vi* to lean back into a supported sloping or horizontal position, usually in order to rest or relax **2.** *vti* to tilt back from an upright position, or make something tilt back ○ *These seats are more comfortable because they recline.* [15C. Directly or via French < Latin *reclinare* "bend back or against" < *clinare* "bend"] —**re·clin·a·ble** *adj* —**re·cli·na·tion** /rèklə náysh'n/ *n*

re·clin·er /ri klínər/ *n* a chair, often one with a raisable footrest, that tilts back to a sloping or almost horizontal position to allow the person sitting in it to rest more comfortably

re·clos·a·ble /ree klṓzəb'l/ *adj* able to be closed and sealed again after being opened ○ *a reclosable package*

re·cluse /ré klooss, ri klooss/ *n* **1.** a solitary person who avoids other people **2.** somebody who lives a solitary life in prayer and meditation ■ *adj* same as **reclusive** (*archaic*) [12C. < French *reclus*, past participle of Old French *reclure* "shut up" < Latin *recludere* "shut again" < *claudere* "shut"] —**re·clu·sion** /ri kloózh'n/ *n*

re·clu·sive /ri kloóssiv, -kloóziv/ *adj* solitary and withdrawn from the rest of the world ○ *lead a reclusive existence* [Late 16C. < obsolete *recluse* "shut up" < Latin *reclus-*, past participle of *recludere* (see RECLUSE)] —**re·clu·sive·ly** *adv* —**re·clu·sive·ness** *n*

rec·og·ni·tion /rèkəg nísh'n/ *n* **1. ACT OF RECOGNIZING** the act of identifying somebody or something on the basis of a past sighting or experience, the ability to do this, or the fact of being identified through having been seen or experienced before ○ *changed beyond recognition* ○ *disguised to avoid recognition* **2.** **APPRECIATION** appreciation of the value of an achievement ○ *His pioneering work never got the recognition it deserved.* **3.** **ACKNOWLEDGMENT** acknowledgment of the existence or validity of something ○ *They'll need recognition from the committee in order to proceed.* **4.** **PERMISSION TO SPEAK** permission given by somebody chairing a meeting to somebody who has asked to speak **5.** POL **ACCEPTANCE OF COUNTRY'S EXISTENCE** the formal acceptance by one country of the independent and legal status of another **6.** **TOKEN OF ACKNOWLEDGMENT** something given or awarded as a token of acknowledgment or gratitude **7.** **SENSING OF DATA BY COMPUTER** the sensing and conversion of data into machine-readable form by a computer **8.** BIOL **COMPATIBILITY OF MOLECULES** the ability of molecules with complementary shapes to attach to one another [15C. Directly or via French < Latin *recognition-* < *recognit-*, past participle of *recognoscere* (see RECOGNIZE)] —**re·cog·ni·tive** /ri kógnitiv/ *adj* —**re·cog·ni·to·ry** /ri kógni tàwree/ *adj*

re·cog·ni·zance /ri kógniz'nss/ *n* **1.** a formal agreement made by somebody before a judge or magistrate to do something, e.g., to appear in court at a set date ○ *He was released on his own recognizance.* **2.** a sum of money pledged by somebody making a recognizance, to be forfeited if the agreed act is not carried out [14C. < Old French *reconissaunce* < *coni(s)saunce* (see COGNIZANCE)] —**re·cog·ni·zant** *adj*

rec·og·nize /rékəg nīz/ (**-nized, -niz·ing, -niz·es**) *vt* **1.** **IDENTIFY SOMEBODY OR SOMETHING SEEN BEFORE** to identify a thing or person as a result of having seen or had some other experience of him, her, or it before ○ *If you saw him again, would you recognize him?* **2.** **ACKNOWLEDGE SOMEBODY'S ACHIEVEMENT** to show appreciation of, or give credit to, another's achievement ○ *I hope you recognize their contribution to the success of the campaign.* **3.** **ALLOW SOMEBODY TO SPEAK** to allow somebody to speak to a meeting ○ *The chair recognizes the representative.* **4.** **ACCEPT STATE'S INDEPENDENCE** to accept formally the independent and legal status of a country or regime ○ *refused to recognize the military government* **5.** **REWARD SOMEBODY** to give or award something to a person as a token of acknowledgment or gratitude ○ *recognized his bravery with a medal* **6.** **SHOW ACKNOWLEDGMENT** to show in some way that somebody is personally known ○ *She recognized old friends in the crowd with a smile and a wave.* **7.** **ACCEPT SOMETHING** to accept the validity or truth of something ○ *I recognize that I am at fault.* **8.** BIOL **BIND ANOTHER MOLECULE** to bind another molecule that has a complementary structure [15C. < Old French *recon(n)iss-*, stem of *reconnaistre* < Latin *recognoscere* "know again" < *cognoscere* "know"] —**rec·og·niz·a·ble** *adj* —**rec·og·niz·a·bly** *adv* —**rec·og·nized** *adj* —**rec·og·niz·er** *n*

re·coil *vi* /ri kóyl/ (**-coiled, -coil·ing, -coils**) **1.** **MOVE BACK SUDDENLY** to move back suddenly and violently, e.g., after an impact **2.** **FEEL HORROR** to react instinctively with fear, horror, disgust, or distaste **3.** PHYS **CHANGE MOMENTUM** to experience a change in momentum as a result of a nuclear collision or the emission of an elementary particle ■ *n* /ri kóyl, rée kòyl/ **1.** **SUDDEN BACKWARD MOVEMENT** a sudden and violent backward movement, especially that of a firearm when it is fired **2.** **MOVEMENT AWAY IN HORROR** a movement back or away from something, especially in horror or disgust **3.** PHYS **CHANGE IN MOMENTUM** a change in the momentum of an atom, nucleus, or elementary particle as a result of a nuclear collision or the emission of an elementary particle [12C. < French *reculer* < Latin *culus* "buttocks"] —**re·coil·er** *n*

SYNONYMS ***recoil, flinch, quail, shrink, wince***

CORE MEANING: to react in fear or distaste

recoil to move back suddenly and violently, or react instinctively with fear, horror, disgust, or distaste ○ *As he leaned toward her, she instinctively recoiled.* ○ *She recoiled from the sight of the dead animal.* **flinch** to make an involuntary small backward movement in response to pain or something frightening or shocking ○ *He flinched at the needle's prick.* ○ *I'm not a coward, and I don't flinch from facing trouble.* **quail** to tremble with or feel fear or apprehension ○ *Her voice was strong and firm, but she quailed inwardly.* ○ *Preston quailed at the thought of being caught.* **shrink** to move back and away, especially out of disgust, fear, or horror, or be unwilling or reluctant to do something, especially something difficult or unpleasant ○ *She shrank away from the intruder in terror.* ○ *It was not the work I shrank from, but the lack of freedom that the job entailed.* **wince** to make an involuntary movement away from something because of pain or fear, or feel embarrassment ○ *He shook his head and winced as she touched the cut.* ○ *Charles winced at the thought of what he was going to do.*

re·coil·less /ri kóyl ləss/ *adj* relating to a heavy firearm such as an antitank gun, whose recoil is reduced by venting the blast to the rear

re·coil-op·er·at·ed *adj* using the movement caused by the recoil of a firearm to operate part of its mechanism

rec·ol·lect /rèkə lékt/ (**-lect·ed, -lect·ing, -lects**) *vti* to bring something back to mind [Early 16C. < Latin *recollect-*, past participle of *recolligere* "gather again," later "recall" < *colligere* (see COLLECT[1])] —**rec·ol·lec·tive** *adj* —**rec·ol·lec·tive·ly** *adv*

re-col·lect /rée kə lékt/ *vt* **1.** to regain control of something, especially of the self **2.** to collect again something that has been scattered or dispersed

rec·ol·lec·tion /rèkə lékshən/ *n* **1.** the act of remembering something, or the ability to remember something **2.** something that somebody remembers about something ○ *a recollection of having met him before*

re·com·bi·nant /ree kómbinənt/ *adj* **1.** **OF GENETIC RECOMBINATION** relating to or involved in genetic recombination ○ *a recombinant chromosome* **2.** **RELATING TO RECOMBINANT DNA** relating to recombinant DNA or produced by recombinant DNA technology ■ *n* **1.** **RESULT OF GENETIC RECOMBINATION** a cell or organism exhibiting genetic recombination **2.** **GENETIC MATERIAL FROM GENE-SPLICING** genetic material resulting from the splicing of DNA fragments

re·com·bi·nant DNA *n* DNA extracted from two or more different sources such as genes from different organisms and joined together to form a single molecule or fragment

re·com·bi·na·tion /rèe kombə náysh'n/ *n* any process that gives rise to offspring that have combinations of genes different from those of either parent, such as crossing over and independent assortment of chromosomes during gamete formation —**re·com·bi·na·tion·al** *adj*

~~**recomend**~~ incorrect spelling of **recommend**

re·com·mence /rèekə méns/ (**-menced, -menc·ing, -menc·es**) *vti* **1.** to begin again, or begin something again (*formal*) **2.** to start again or start something again [15C. < French *recommencer* "begin again" < *commencer* (see COMMENCE)]

re·com·mence·ment /rèekə ménsmənt/ *n* a beginning again, or the point at which something begins or is begun again

rec·om·mend /rèkə ménd/ (**-mend·ed, -mend·ing, -mends**) *vt* **1.** **SUGGEST SOMETHING AS GOOD IDEA** to suggest something as worthy of being accepted, used, or done ○ *You could sue, of course, although I don't really recommend it.* **2.** **ENDORSE SOMEBODY OR SOMETHING** to express approval of or support for a person or thing ○ *recommended him for promotion* **3.** **GIVE SOMETHING APPEAL** to make something worth doing or experiencing ○ *Since the legislation has little to recommend it, it is unlikely to pass.* **4.** **ENTRUST SOMEBODY TO ANOTHER** to entrust a person or thing to the care of another (*formal*) ○ *She was recommended to our care until her family returned.* [14C. < medieval Latin *recommendare* "commit thoroughly" < Latin *commendare* "entrust completely"] —**rec·om·mend·a·ble** *adj* —**rec·om·men·da·to·ry** *adj* —**rec·om·mend·er** *n*

SYNONYMS ***recommend, advise, advocate, counsel, suggest***

CORE MEANING: to put forward ideas to somebody who has to decide what to do

recommend to suggest something as worthy of being accepted, used, or done ○ *The report recommended a number of wide-ranging changes.* ○ *I would recommend that you try growing the following plant varieties for a shady garden.* **advise** to give advice to somebody on a subject or course of action, or offer a personal opinion about something to somebody ○ *Your lawyer can advise you on all the matters mentioned in this leaflet.* ○ *I would strongly advise against buying this model.* **advocate** to support or speak in favor of something ○ *They have never used nor advocated the use of violence.* ○ *We strongly advocate sustainable use of coastal resources.* **counsel** (*formal*) to advise somebody on a particular course of action ○ *The doctor counseled Anne to calm down and accept the things she could not change.* ○ *The team manager counseled caution as the best ally in the forthcoming match.* **suggest** to propose somebody or something as a possible choice, plan, or course of action for somebody else to consider ○ *I suggest that we open the subject for discussion.* ○ *This issue is suggested as an area for further research.*

rec·om·men·da·tion /rèkə men dáysh'n/ *n* **1.** **SUGGESTION RECOMMENDING SOMETHING** a suggestion as to what is a good or sensible thing to do or use in the circumstances **2.** **ENDORSEMENT** an expression of praise, approval, or support for somebody or something **3.** **ACT OF RECOMMENDING** the act of recommending something

rec·om·pense /rékəm pènss/ *vt* (**-pensed, -pens·ing, -pens·es**) **1.** **GIVE COMPENSATION** to give compensation to somebody for an injury or loss ○ *The state will recompense you for the accidental destruction of your property.* **2.** **PAY OR REWARD SOMEBODY** to pay somebody for doing work or for performing a service ○ *was recompensed for her heroism* ■ *n* **1.** **COMPENSATION** compensation for a loss or injury **2.** **REMUNERATION** payment for services or work performed [14C. Directly or via French < late Latin *recompensare* "balance out again" < Latin *compensare* "balance out"]

re·con[1] /rée kòn/ *n* reconnaissance (*informal*) [Early 20C. Shortening]

re·con[2] /rée kòn/ (**-con·ned, -con·ning, -cons**) *vt US* to transfer something from print to electronic form (*informal*) [Late 20C. Shortening of RECONFIGURE]

rec·on·cile /rékən sīl/ (**-ciled, -cil·ing, -ciles**) *v* **1.** *vti* **PUT PEOPLE BACK ON FRIENDLY TERMS** to bring two or more people back into a friendly relationship with each other after a dispute or estrangement, or return to a friendly relationship ○ *The two clans were finally reconciled after a century-long feud.* **2.** *vt* **END CONFLICT** to solve a dispute or end a quarrel ○ *reconciled their differences* **3.** *vt* **MAKE SOMEBODY ACCEPT SOMETHING** to persuade somebody or yourself to accept that something undesirable cannot be changed ○ *He reconciled himself to the fact that his football career was over.* **4.** *vti* **MAKE CONSISTENT OR COMPATIBLE** to make two or more apparently conflicting things consistent or compatible, or to become consistent or compatible ○ *trying to reconcile fitness with a penchant for fast food* [14C. Directly or via French < Latin *reconciliare* "make friendly again" < *conciliare* "make friendly" < *concilium* "meeting"] —**rec·on·cil·a·bil·i·ty** /rèkən sīlə bíllətee/ *n* —**rec·on·cil·a·ble** /rèkən sīləb'l, rékən sīləb'l/ *adj* —**rec·on·cil·a·ble·ness** *n* —**rec·on·cil·a·bly** *adv* —**rec·on·cile·ment** *n* —**rec·on·cil·er** *n*

rec·on·cil·i·a·tion /rèkən silee áysh'n/ *n* **1.** **RECONCILING OF PEOPLE** the ending of conflict or renewing of a friendly relationship between disputing people or groups ○ *a series of quarrels and reconciliations* **2.** **ACHIEVEMENT OF CONSISTENCY OR COMPATIBILITY** the making of two or more apparently conflicting things consistent or compatible ○ *the reconciliation of such action with his pacifist principles* **3.** CHR **SACRAMENT OF PENANCE** the sacrament in the Roman Catholic Church whereby a person's sins are absolved through confession and penance [14C. Directly or via French < Latin *reconciliation-* < *reconciliare* (see RECONCILE)] —**rec·on·cil·i·a·to·ry** /rèkən síllee ə tàwree/ *adj*

rec·on·dite /rékən dīt, ri kón-/ *adj* **1.** requiring a high degree of scholarship or specialist knowledge to be understood ○ *the recondite lore of the ancients* **2.** dealing with material that is too difficult to be understood by those without special knowledge ○ *recondite learning* [Mid-17C. < Latin *reconditus*, past participle of *recondere* "store away" < *condere* "store, hide"] —**rec·on·dite·ly** *adv* —**rec·on·dite·ness** *n*

SYNONYMS See *obscure.*

re·con·di·tion /rèe kən dísh'n/ (**-tioned, -tion·ing, -tions**) *vt* to bring something back into good condition, especially by repairing it and replacing worn-out parts

SYNONYMS See *renew.*

~~reconize~~ incorrect spelling of **recognize**

~~reconnaisance~~ incorrect spelling of **reconnaissance**

re·con·nais·sance /ri kónnəss'nss/ *n* **1.** MIL **EXPLORATION TO GATHER INFORMATION** the exploration or examination of an area to gather information, especially about the strength and positioning of enemy forces **2. PRELIMINARY SURVEY** a preliminary inspection of an area to obtain geographic, hydrographic, or similar data prior to a detailed survey **3. PRELIMINARY INVESTIGATION** preliminary research or investigation of something [Early 19C. < French, < *reconnaiss-*, stem of *reconnaître* "reconnoiter" < Latin *recognoscere* (see RECOGNIZE)]

re·con·noi·ter /rèekə nóytər, rèkə-/ *vti* (**-tered, -ter·ing, -ters**) to explore an area in order to gather information, especially about the strength and positioning of enemy forces ○ *reconnoiter the drop zone* ■ *n* an exploration of an area in order to gather information [Early 18C. Via obsolete French *reconnoître* < Latin *recognoscere* (see RECOGNIZE)] —**re·con·noi·ter·er** *n*

re·con·noi·tre *vti, n* MIL Can, UK spelling of **reconnoiter**

re·con·sti·tute /ree kónstə to͞ot/ (**-tut·ed, -tut·ing, -tutes**) *vt* **1.** to bring some matter or a material back to its original state, usually by adding water to a concentrated, dried, or powdered form ○ *reconstituted the orange juice* **2.** to alter the form of something ○ *reconstitute the government* —**re·con·stit·u·ent** /rèekən stíchoo ənt/ *adj, n* —**re·con·sti·tu·tion** /rèe konstə to͞osh'n/ *n*

re·con·struct /rèekən strúkt/ (**-struct·ed, -struct·ing, -structs**) *vt* **1. PUT SOMETHING BACK TOGETHER** to put something back together from its component parts, pieces, or remains **2. RE-CREATE SOMETHING FROM EVIDENCE** to show plausibly what something was like or how something happened by re-creating it on the basis of the evidence available ○ *reconstruct the culture of an ancient society* **3. REORGANIZE SOMETHING** to reorganize something, reform something, or bring somebody or something up to date **4. RESTORE NATIONAL GOVERNMENT** to restore government and the rule of law to a destroyed nation —**re·con·struc·ti·ble** *adj* —**re·con·struc·tive** *adj* —**re·con·struc·tor** *n*

re·con·struc·tion /rèekən strúksh'n/ *n* **1. RECONSTRUCTING OF SOMETHING** the act or process of reconstructing something, or of being reconstructed **2. SOMETHING RECONSTRUCTED FROM ITS PARTS** something that has been put back together from its component parts, pieces, or remains **3. SOMETHING RESTORED** something that has been reorganized, reformed, or restored **4. SOMETHING RE-CREATED** something that has been re-created from the evidence available, e.g., a re-enactment of the circumstances of a crime

Re·con·struc·tion /rèekən strúksh'n/ *n* the period of US history from 1865 through 1877, during which the states that had seceded during the Civil War were reorganized under federal control and later restored to the Union

Re·con·struc·tion·ism /rèekən strúkshə nìzzəm/ *n* **1.** support of the policies of the Reconstruction in the southern United States after the Civil War **2.** in Judaism, a movement in the United States, begun in the 1920s, emphasizing the idea that Judaism is a worldwide religious civilization and advocating continuous adaptation to contemporary conditions —**Re·con·struc·tion·ist** *n, adj*

re·con·struc·tive sur·ger·y *n* the use of surgery to restore the appearance or use of a damaged body part

re·con·vey /rèekən váy/ (**-veyed, -vey·ing, -veys**) *vt* to transfer something such as property back to a former owner or location —**re·con·vey·ance** *n*

re·cord *n* /rékərd/ **1. LASTING ACCOUNT** an account of something, preserved in a lasting form, e.g., in writing or on film ○ *She used a diary to keep a record of her life.* **2. ACCOUNT OF PROCEEDINGS** a written account of the proceedings of something ○ *the records of the Foundation* **3. WRITTEN ACCOUNT OF COURT PROCEEDINGS** an official written account of the proceedings of a court, available for use as evidence ○ *His remarks were struck from the record.* **4. DOCUMENT CONTAINING HISTORY** the document or book that bears the history of something ○ *The records are stored in the basement.* **5. BODY OF INFORMATION** a body of information or statistics, gathered over a period of time (*often used in the plural*) ○ *the hottest summer since records began* **6. EVIDENCE** something that acts as evidence or a memorial ○ *The Egyptian pyramids are a record of human engineering expertise.* **7. BEST ACCOMPLISHMENT** something that represents the greatest attainment so far, especially in sports ○ *a world record* **8. PAST PERFORMANCE** a person's accomplishments or performance to date **9. PAST CRIMES** a background of criminal convictions, or a list of the crimes committed by a person **10. MUSIC DISK** something on which sound is copied, especially a plastic disk with a groove that can be played using a phonograph **11. COPY OF MUSIC** a piece of music in a format that can be listened to repeatedly (*informal*) ○ *Their new record is only available on CD.* **12. COLLECTION OF DATA** a collection of related items of information treated as a unit by a computer, e.g., in a database ■ *v* /ri káwrd/ (**-cord·ed, -cord·ing, -cords**) **1.** *vt* **PUT SOMETHING INTO LASTING FORM** to put something into a form in which it can be kept, especially to write something down or film it ○ *Her journal records the last days of the Empire.* **2.** *vt* **NOTE SOMETHING** to make a note of something, often for official purposes or for subsequent consultation ○ *The clerk recorded their names in the register.* **3.** *vti* **INDICATE MEASUREMENT** to register or show something, usually on a scale of a measurement **4.** *vti* **COPY SOUNDS OR IMAGES** to make a copy of sounds or pictures, e.g., on magnetic tape ○ *I recorded my grandmother reminiscing about the war.* ■ *adj* /rékərd/ **GREATEST YET** exceeding any previous achievement or example in, e.g., size or speed ○ *A record crowd turned up for the game.* [12C. < French, < *recorder* "bring to mind" < Latin *recordare, recordari*, literally "bring back to the heart" < *cord-* "heart, mind"] —**re·cord·a·ble** *adj* ◇ **go on record** to make a public statement of fact ◇ **off the record** said informally or privately and not intended to be recorded or made public ◇ **on record 1.** publicly stated or known **2.** having published or having said in public ◇ **on the record** said formally or publicly with the knowledge that it may be recorded or disseminated ◇ **set the record straight** to put right a mistake or misunderstanding

re·cord·ed /ri káwrdəd/ *adj* copied to a record, tape, CD, or other form of permanent copy, rather than listened to or performed live ○ *recorded music*

re·cord·ed de·liv·er·y *n UK* same as **certified mail**

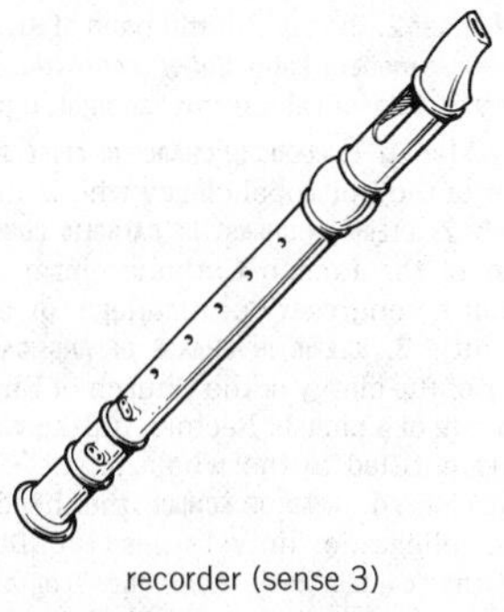

recorder (sense 3)

re·cord·er /ri káwrdər/ *n* **1. MACHINE FOR RECORDING** a machine that makes a permanent copy of sounds or pictures, e.g., a tape recorder or a videotape recorder **2. SOMEBODY NOTING SOMETHING** somebody who records something, especially official proceedings **3. MUSICAL INSTRUMENT** a wind instrument of the flute family that has finger holes and is blown through a whistle-shaped mouthpiece at one end [15C. Partly < Anglo-Norman *recordour*, Old French *recordeur* "person who records" < *recorder* (see RECORD); partly < RECORD]

re·cord·ing /ri káwrding/ *n* **1.** a permanent copy of sounds or images, e.g., a tape, CD, or videotape ○ *She was eager to buy the band's latest recording.* **2.** the act of making a record, especially a permanent copy of sounds or images

re·cord·ist /ri káwrdist/ *n* somebody who records sound during the making of a movie or broadcast

rec·ord play·er *n* a machine for reproducing the sounds recorded on records, consisting of a turntable on which the disk revolves and a needle that follows the groove to pick up sound

re·count /ri kównt/ (**-count·ed, -count·ing, -counts**) *vt* to tell the story or details of something [15C. < Anglo-Norman, Old N French *reconter* "relate again, count again" < *conter* (see COUNT[1])] —**re·count·al** *n* —**re·count·er** *n*

re·count *n* /rée kòwnt/ a second counting of the votes cast in an election, usually done because the first counting indicated a very close result ■ *vti* /ree kównt/ to count something, especially the votes cast in an election, a second time

re·coup /ri ko͞op/ (**-couped, -coup·ing, -coups**) *v* **1.** *vt* **GET SOMETHING BACK** to regain something lost or its equivalent **2.** *vi* **MAKE UP FOR LOSS** to make up for something lost ○ *It will take us years to recoup.* **3.** *vt* LAW **DEDUCT SOMETHING** to deduct legally part of what is due to a claim **4.** *vt* **REIMBURSE ANOTHER** to give another party something to make up for that which has been lost ○ *We were adequately recouped for our losses.* [Early 17C. < Old French *recouper* "cut back" < *couper* "cut" < *coup* "blow"] —**re·coup·a·ble** *adj* —**re·coup·ment** *n*

~~recouperate~~ incorrect spelling of **recuperate**

re·course /rée kàwrss, ri káwrss/ *n* **1. USE OF OTHERS FOR ASSISTANCE** the act of seeking assistance from somebody or something else in a time of difficulty ○ *Can we resolve our financial problems without recourse to further borrowing?* **2. SOURCE OF HELP OR SOLUTION** somebody, something, or a course of action to which a person turns for help or to solve a problem ○ *She felt she had no recourse but to sue.* **3.** FIN, LAW **RIGHT TO DEMAND PAYMENT** the right to demand payment of a bill of exchange from the person who draws or endorses it, when the person who accepts it fails to pay [14C. Directly or via French < Latin *recursus* "a running back" < *cursus* (see COURSE)]

re·cov·er /ri kúvvər/ (**-ered, -er·ing, -ers**) *v* **1.** *vt* **REGAIN SOMETHING** to get back something previously lost or its equivalent **2.** *vi* **RETURN TO FORMER STATE** to return to a previous state of health, prosperity, or equanimity **3. re·cov·er your·self** *vr* **CONTROL OR CORRECT YOURSELF** to return to a composed state, or make good an error ○ *He soon recovered himself sufficiently to feign a friendly welcome.* **4.** *vi* **RETURN TO RIGHT POSITION** to return to a suitable or correct state or position ○ *The goalkeeper stumbled, but recovered enough to prevent the goal.* **5.** *vt* **EXTRACT SOMETHING** to extract something from a source, e.g., to reclaim useful substances from waste or refuse **6.** *vt* LAW **OBTAIN SOMETHING THROUGH COURT** to obtain something by the ruling of a court **7.** *vi* LAW **SUCCEED IN LITIGATION** to be successful in a lawsuit [13C. Via Anglo-Norman *recoverer*, Old French *recovrer* < Latin *recuperare* "take back" < *capere* "take"] —**re·cov·er·a·bil·i·ty** /ri kùvvərə bíllətee/ *n* —**re·cov·er·a·ble** *adj* —**re·cov·er·er** *n*

re-cov·er /ree kúvvər/ *vt* **1.** to put a new cover on something **2.** to cover something again

re·cov·er·a·ble er·ror *n* a program error that can be corrected without causing a computer program to fail or data to be erased irretrievably. For example, if a user enters obviously wrong data, the program might request a different entry.

re·cov·er·y /ri kúvvəree/ (*plural* **-ies**) *n* **1. RETURN TO HEALTH** the return to normal health of somebody who has been ill or injured ○ *a speedy recovery* **2. RETURN TO NORMAL STATE** the return of something to a normal or improved state after a setback or loss ○ *an economic recovery* **3. GAINING BACK OF SOMETHING LOST** the regaining of something lost or taken away ○ *The arrests led to the recovery of large amounts of stolen property.* **4. EXTRACTION** the extraction of a substance or energy from a source, e.g., the reclamation of useful substances from waste or refuse **5. SHOT OUT OF OBSTACLE** in golf, a shot played out of the rough or an obstacle onto the green or fairway **6. RETURN TO GUARD** in fencing, a return to the guard position after making an attack **7.** BRINGING ARM FORWARD in swimming or rowing, the bringing forward of the arm to make another stroke **8.** LAW OBTAINING SOMETHING THROUGH COURT the obtaining of something by the ruling of a court [14C. < Anglo-Norman *recoverie*, Old French *reco(u)vree* < *recov(e)rer* (see RECOVER)] ◇ **in re·cov·er·y** in the process of recovering from an addiction or other destructive habit

re·cov·er·y room *n* a hospital room equipped for the care of patients who have just undergone surgery and are recovering from anesthesia

rec·re·ant /rékree ənt/ *adj* **1.** disloyal to a cause or duty **2.** same as **cowardly** (sense 1) [13C. < Old French, present participle of *recroire* "surrender" < Latin *credere* "entrust"] —**rec·re·ance** *n* —**rec·re·an·cy** *n* —**rec·re·ant** *n* —**rec·re·ant·ly** *adv*

rec·re·ate /rékree àyt/ (**-at·ed, -at·ing, -ates**) *vi* to take part in activities that are mentally or physically refreshing [15C. < Latin *recreat-*, past participle of *recreare* "bring forth again" < *creare* "bring forth"; partly back-formation < RECREATION] —**rec·re·a·tive** *adj* —**rec·re·a·tor** *n*

re-cre·ate /rèe kree áyt/ *vt* to make something that appears to be the same as something that no longer exists or that exists in a different place ○ *The decor aims to re-create a 19th-century interior.* —**re-cre·at·a·ble** *adj* —**re-cre·a·tive** *adj*

SYNONYMS See *copy.*

rec·re·a·tion /rèkree áysh'n/ *n* **1.** the refreshment of the mind and body after work, especially by engaging in enjoyable activities **2.** an activity that a person takes part in for pleasure or relaxation rather than as work ○ *She took up sketching as a recreation.*

re-cre·a·tion *n* **1.** the action or process of re-creating something **2.** something created or reproduced again

rec·re·a·tion·al /rèkree áyshən'l, -shnəl/ *adj* **1.** done or used for pleasure or relaxation rather than work **2.** describes controlled drugs taken illegally —**re·cre·a·tion·al·ly** *adv*

rec·re·a·tion·al ve·hi·cle *n* a large motor vehicle, usually with facilities for sleeping and eating, used for recreational activities such as camping

rec·re·a·tion room *n* **1.** a room set aside for games, social events, and other kinds of recreation in a public building **2.** a room used by the occupants of a house for relaxation and recreational activities ○ *a new TV for the recreation room*

re·crim·i·nate /ri krímmə nàyt/ (**-nat·ed, -nat·ing, -nates**) *vi* to accuse somebody who has already brought an accusation [Early 17C. < medieval Latin *recriminat-*, past participle of *recriminari* "accuse back or again" < Latin *criminari, criminare* "accuse"] —**re·crim·i·na·tive** *adj* —**re·crim·i·na·tor** *n* —**re·crim·i·na·to·ry** /ri krímmənə tàwree/ *adj*

re·crim·i·na·tion /ri krìmmə náysh'n/ *n* **1.** an accusation made against somebody who has brought a previous accusation ○ *It started out as a calm discussion and ended in tears and recriminations.* **2.** an accusation that somebody accused of a crime makes against the accuser

rec room *n* same as **recreation room** (*informal*)

re·cru·desce /rèe kroo déss/ (**-desced, -desc·ing, -desc·es**) *vi* to break out or become active again after a dormant period [Mid-17C. Back-formation < *recrudescence* < Latin *recrudescere* "become raw again" < *crudus* "raw, bloody"] —**re·cru·des·cence** *n* —**re·cru·des·cent** *adj*

re·cruit /ri kroót/ *v* (**-cruit·ed, -cruit·ing, -cruits**) **1.** *vti* ENROLL OR TAKE ON SOMEBODY to enroll somebody as a worker or member, or to take on people as workers or members ○ *The company has stopped recruiting.* **2.** *vti* ENLIST SOMEBODY to enlist somebody in a military force, or take part in enlisting people for a military force ○ *She was recruited by the Marines.* **3.** *vt* RAISE ARMY to establish a military force ■ *n* **1.** NEW MEMBER a new member, worker, player, or supporter **2.** NEW SOLDIER a member of a military force who has joined it recently [Mid-17C. < French *recruter* < *recrue* "new growth" < *recroître* "increase again" < Latin *crescere* "grow"] —**re·cruit·er** *n* —**re·cruit·ing** *n* —**re·cruit·ment** *n*

rec. sec. *abbr* recording secretary

rect.[1], **rec't** *abbr* COMM receipt

rect.[2] *abbr* rectangle

Rect. *abbr* CHR **1.** Rector **2.** Rectory

rec·ta ANAT plural of **rectum**

rec·tan·gle /rék tàng g'l/ *n* a two-dimensional geometric figure formed of four sides in which each angle is a right angle, especially one with adjacent sides of different length [Late 16C. Directly or via French < medieval Latin *rect(i)angulum*, < form of late Latin *rectiangulus* "straight angle" < Latin *rectus* "straight, right" + *angulus* "angle"]

rec·tan·gu·lar /rek táng gyələr/ *adj* **1.** with four sides, usually with adjacent sides of different length, and four right angles **2.** involving, having, or meeting at right angles [Early 17C. < ANGULAR after French *rectangulaire*] —**rec·tan·gu·lar·i·ty** /rek tàng gyə lárrətee/ *n* —**rec·tan·gu·lar·ly** *adv*

rec·tan·gu·lar co·or·di·nate *n* a Cartesian coordinate used in a system of axes that meet at right angles

rec·tan·gu·lar hy·per·bo·la *n* a hyperbola with asymptotes that are at right angles

rec·ti /réktə/ ANAT plural of **rectus**

rec·ti·fi·er /réktə fì ər/ *n* **1.** ELECTRONIC DEVICE an electronic device that converts alternating current to direct current, e.g., a set of semiconductor diodes connected in a bridge circuit **2.** CONDENSING APPARATUS an apparatus that condenses vapor to liquid during distillation **3.** SOMEBODY OR SOMETHING THAT RECTIFIES SOMETHING somebody or something that puts a matter or situation right

rec·ti·fy /réktə fì/ (**-fied, -fy·ing, -fies**) *vt* **1.** CORRECT SOMETHING to put something right **2.** ELECTRONICS CONVERT CURRENT to convert alternating current to direct current **3.** CHEM PURIFY SOMETHING to purify a substance, especially by distillation **4.** MATH FIND LENGTH OF CURVE to find the length of a curve [14C. Directly or via French *rectifier* < medieval Latin *rectificare* "make right" < *rectus* "straight, right"] —**rec·ti·fi·a·bil·i·ty** /rèktə fì ə bíllətee/ *n* —**rec·ti·fi·a·ble** *adj* —**rec·ti·fi·ca·tion** /rèktəfi káysh'n/ *n*

rec·ti·lin·e·ar /rèktə línnee ər/, **rec·ti·lin·e·al** /-əl/ *adj* **1.** formed or consisting of straight lines **2.** moving in a straight line [Mid-17C. < late Latin *rectilineus* < Latin *rectus* "straight, right" + *linea* "line"] —**rec·ti·lin·e·ar·ly** *adv*

rec·ti·tude /réktə tòod/ *n* **1.** RIGHTEOUSNESS strong moral integrity in character or actions **2.** CORRECTNESS correctness in judgment (*formal*) ○ *the admirable rectitude of her assessments* **3.** STRAIGHTNESS straightness in form or shape (*formal*) [15C. Directly or via French < late Latin *rectitudo* < Latin *rectus* "straight, right"] —**rec·ti·tu·di·nous** /rèktə tòod'nəss/ *adj*

rec·to /réktō/ (*plural* **-tos**) *n* **1.** the front side of a printed sheet **2.** the right-hand page of an open book [Early 19C. < modern Latin *(folio) recto* "(the page) being on the right," form of Latin *rectus* "straight, right"]

rec·tor /réktər/ *n* **1.** CLERIC IN CHARGE OF EPISCOPAL PARISH a member of the Episcopal clergy who is in charge of a parish **2.** CLERIC IN CHARGE OF CATHOLIC CONGREGATION a member of the Roman Catholic clergy who is in charge of a congregation, a college, or a religious community **3.** CLERIC IN CHARGE OF ANGLICAN PARISH a member of the clergy of the Church of England who is in charge of a parish. Rectors, unlike vicars, were formerly entitled to the whole of the tithes from their parish. **4.** HEAD OF SCHOOL the head of some schools, colleges, or universities [14C. Directly or via Old French, "captain (of a ship), head of a university" < Latin, "ruler, governor" < *regere* "rule"] —**rec·tor·ate** *n* —**rec·to·ri·al** /rek táwree əl/ *adj* —**rec·tor·ship** /réktər shìp/ *n*

rec·to·ry /réktəree/ (*plural* **-ries**) *n* **1.** the house that a rector lives in, provided by the church **2.** the post of rector and the income that goes with it [Late 16C. < Old French *rectorie* or medieval Latin *rectoria* < Latin *rector* (see RECTOR)]

rec·trix /rék triks/ (*plural* **-tri·ces** /réktri sèez, rek trí-/) *n* a tail feather of a bird [Mid-18C. < Latin, feminine of *rector* (see RECTOR)]

rec·tum /réktəm/ (*plural* **-tums** or **-ta** /-tə/) *n* the lower part of the large intestine, between the colon and the anal canal [15C. < Latin *(intestinum) rectum* "straight (intestine)" < *rectus* "straight, right"] —**rec·tal** *adj*

rec·tus /réktəss/ (*plural* **-ti** /-tì/) *n* any straight muscle, e.g., any of the muscles in the abdomen or the thigh [Early 18C. < Latin, "straight, right"]

re·cum·bent /ri kúmbənt/ *adj* **1.** LYING lying back or lying down ○ *a colossal recumbent statue* **2.** BIOL RESTING OR LEANING describes a plant or animal part that rests or leans against something else **3.** GEOL HORIZONTAL describes a geologic fold whose axis is more or less horizontal [Early 18C. < Latin *recumbent-*, present participle of *recumbere* "lie back" < *-cumbere* "lie down"] —**re·cum·bence** *n* —**re·cum·bent·ly** *adv*

re·cu·per·ate /ri kòopə ràyt/ (**-at·ed, -at·ing, -ates**) *v* **1.** *vi* to recover from an illness or injury **2.** *vt* to recover something lost, especially a sum of money ○ *recuperate investment losses* [Mid-16C. < Latin *recuperat-*, past participle of *recuperare* (see RECOVER)] —**re·cu·per·a·tion** /ri kòopə ráysh'n/ *n* —**re·cu·per·a·tive** /-ràytiv, -rətiv/ *adj* —**re·cu·per·a·to·ry** /-kòopərə tàwree/ *adj*

USAGE ***Recuperate*** is normally used intransitively, that is, without an object, as in *She needed several weeks to recuperate.* When a noun such as *health* is the object, *recover* is a better choice: *She needed several weeks to recover her health.*

re·cu·per·a·tor /ri kòopə ràytər/ *n* **1.** a device used to recover energy that would otherwise be lost, especially one that takes heat from exhaust gases and uses it to preheat incoming combustion air **2.** a device in a gun that returns it to its firing position following recoil

re·cur /ri kúr/ (**-curred, -cur·ring, -curs**) *vi* **1.** ⚠ OCCUR AGAIN to happen or appear once again or repeatedly **2.** BE REPEATED INDEFINITELY to occur as an infinitely repeated digit or series of digits at the end of a decimal fraction **3.** RETURN to return to a subject in speech, writing, or thought (*literary*) [Early 16C. < Latin *recurrere* "run back" < *currere* "run"]

USAGE As the idea of *again* is an integral part of the meaning of ***recur***, it is unnecessary to say things like "The disease recurred again." Simply say "recurred."

re·cur·rent /ri kúrrənt, ri kúr ənt/ *adj* **1.** happening or appearing again, especially repeatedly **2.** describes a blood vessel or nerve that turns back on itself and runs in the opposite direction —**re·cur·rence** *n* —**re·cur·rent·ly** *adv*

re·cur·rent fe·ver *n* MED same as **relapsing fever**

re·cur·ring dec·i·mal /ri kùrring-/ *n* UK same as **repeating decimal**

re·cur·sion /ri kúrzh'n/ *n* **1.** RETURN OF SOMETHING the return of something, often repeatedly **2.** LOGIC, MATH REPETITION OF STEPS TO GIVE RESULT the use of repeated steps, each based on the result of the one before, to define a function or calculate a number **3.** COMPUT DELEGATION AS PROGRAMMING TECHNIQUE a programming technique where a routine performs its task by delegating part of it to another instance of itself [Early 17C. < late Latin *recursion-* "a running back" < Latin *recurs-*, past participle of *recurrere* (see RECUR)]

re·cur·sive /ri kúrssiv/ *adj* **1.** repeating itself, either indefinitely or until a specific point is reached **2.** involving the repeated application of a function to its own values [Late 18C. < Latin *recurs-* (see RECURSION)] —**re·cur·sive·ly** *adv* —**re·cur·sive·ness** *n*

re·cur·vate /ri kúr vàyt, -kúrvət/ *adj* curved backward, inward, or downward

re·curve /ri kúrv/ (**-curved, -curv·ing, -curves**) *vti* to curve backward, inward, or downward, or cause something to curve in this way [Late 16C. < Latin *recurvare* "curve back" < *curvus* "curved, crooked"] —**re·cur·va·tion** /rèe kur váysh'n/ *n* —**re·curved** *adj*

rec·u·sant /rékyəz'nt, ri kyóoz'nt/ *n* **1.** CATHOLIC REFUSING TO ATTEND ANGLICAN SERVICES a Roman Catholic who broke the law by refusing to attend Church of England services in England between the 16th and 18th centuries **2.** SOMEBODY DISOBEYING AUTHORITY somebody who refuses to obey authority ■ *adj* DISOBEYING AUTHORITY refusing to obey authority —**rec·u·sance** *n*

re·cuse /ri kyóoz/ (**-cused, -cus·ing, -cus·es**) *vti* to declare yourself to be, or to render somebody, disqualified to judge something or participate in something because of possible bias or personal interest ○ *The judge recused herself because she knew the plaintiff socially.* [Early 19C. < Latin *recusare* "refuse" < *causa* "cause, case"] —**re·cus·al** *n*

re·cy·cla·ble /ree sī́k'ləb'l/ *adj* suitable or adapted for recycling ■ *n* a material or product that is able to be recycled —**re·cy·cla·bil·i·ty** /ree sī̀klə bíllətee/ *n*

re·cy·cle /ree sī́k'l/ *v* (**-cled, -cling, -cles**) **1.** *vti* PROCESS FOR REUSE to process used or waste material so that it can be used again **2.** *vti* SAVE FOR REUSE to save or collect used or waste material for reprocessing into something useful **3.** *vti* USE AGAIN DIFFERENTLY to adapt or convert something to a new use **4.** *vt* REUSE SOMETHING to use something again for the same purpose **5.** *vt* USE AGAIN UNIMAGINATIVELY to use something abstract again in the same form, often at the expense of freshness or originality ○ *recycling the same old ideas* **6.** *vti* REPEAT PROCESS to repeat a process, or pass something through a process again ■ *n* RECYCLING PROCESS the process of recycling material, especially used or waste material —**re·cy·cler** *n*

re·cy·cled /ree sī́k'ld/ *adj* **1.** manufactured from used or waste materials that have been reprocessed **2.** used again or repeatedly, often at the expense of freshness or originality

re·cy·cling /ree sī́kling/ *n* **1.** the processing of used or waste material so that it can be used again, instead of being wasted **2.** the saving or collection of used or waste material for reprocessing

red /red/ *adj* (**red·der, red·dest**) **1.** OF COLOR OF BLOOD of or near the color of blood, or of a ripe tomato or strawberry **2.** REDDISH BROWN describes hair or fur that is reddish brown, orange, or golden brown **3.** BLOODSHOT describes eyes that are bloodshot or with red rims, e.g., from tiredness **4.** WITH TEMPORARILY RED FACE blushing, e.g., from shame or embarrassment **5.** MADE FROM BLACK GRAPES describes wine made from black grapes. Pigments in the purple skins of these grapes give the wine a deep red color. **6.** REPRESENTING DEBT representing debt or financial loss **7.** *also* **Red** POL LEFT-WING socialist or communist (*informal disapproving*) **8.** *also* **Red** SOVIET relating or belonging to the former Soviet Union (*informal*) **9.** ASTRON EXHIBITING A REDSHIFT describes an astronomical object moving away from Earth and therefore showing a shift toward longer wavelengths at the red end of the spectrum ■ *n* **1.** COLOR OF BLOOD a color like that of blood, or of a ripe tomato or strawberry. Red lies at the far end of the visible spectrum and is one of the three primary colors of light and pigment. **2.** RED COLORING a pigment or dye that is of or near to the color of blood, or a ripe tomato or strawberry **3.** RED FABRIC OR CLOTHES fabric or clothing that is red in color **4.** RED THING a red object **5.** RED WINE wine made from black grapes (*informal*) **6.** SECTION OF GAMBLING TABLE in roulette and other gambling games, one of the two colored areas on the table on which players may place bets, the other being black **7.** RING ON ARCHERY TARGET in archery, a red ring immediately outside the gold disk at the center of a target **8.** RED BALL in billiards, snooker, and other cue games, a red ball **9.** *also* **Red** A SOCIALIST OR COMMUNIST somebody with socialist or communist views (*informal disapproving*) [Old English *rēad*. < Indo-European] —**red·ly** *adv* —**red·ness** *n* ◇ **in the red** in debt, e.g., to a bank ◇ **see red** to suddenly become very angry (*informal*)

USAGE See *read*.

red. *abbr* **1.** FIN redeemable **2.** reduced **3.** reduction

re·dact /ri dákt/ (**-dact·ed, -dact·ing, -dacts**) *vt* (*formal*) **1.** to edit or revise something in preparation for publication ○ *formerly classified documents that were redacted before release to protect still confidential material* **2.** to compose or draft something for publication or for an announcement [Mid-19C. < Latin *redact-*, past participle of *redigere* "reduce," literally "bring down" < *agere* "do"] —**re·dac·tion** *n* —**re·dac·tion·al** *adj* —**re·dac·tor** *n*

red ad·mi·ral *n* a brightly colored butterfly with broad orange-red bands on its forewings. Native to: Europe, North America. Latin name: *Vanessa atalanta*.

red a·lert *n* a warning or alarm that indicates a situation of the highest priority or greatest urgency, especially an imminent attack, or the state of readiness to deal with such a situation ◇ **on red alert** prepared for any trouble or danger that may occur

red al·gae *npl* ocean algae that contain a red pigment as well as chlorophyll, e.g., dulse, laver, and carrageen. Family: Rhodophyceae.

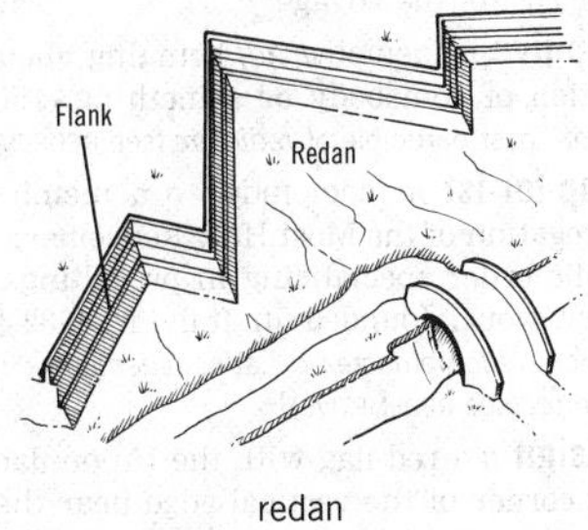

redan

re·dan /ri dán/ *n* a pair of parapets that form a V-shaped projection from the wall of a castle or other fortification [Late 17C. < French, variant of *redent* < *dent* "tooth" < Latin *dent-*]

red ant *n* **1.** a reddish ant, especially a Pharaoh ant **2.** *Carib* same as **fire ant**

Red Ar·my *n* the military organization put into place by Leon Trotsky at the time of the Russian revolution. Its members were recruited from the worker and peasant classes.

red·back /réd bàk/, **red·back spi·der** *n* a small venomous dark brown or black spider, the female of which has a red stripe or patch on the back of the abdomen. Native to: Australia, New Zealand. Latin name: *Latrodectus hasselti*.

red·bait /réd bàyt/ (**-bait·ed, -bait·ing, -baits**) *vti US* to attack or persecute somebody as a communist sympathizer (*dated*) —**red·bait·ing** *n*

red-bel·lied black snake *n* a large poisonous snake that is glossy black with an orange red underside. Native to: eastern Australian woodlands. Latin name: *Pseudechis porphyriacus*.

red·bel·ly dace /rèd bellee-/ *n* a small, brightly colored freshwater fish of the minnow family. Native to: North America. Genus: *Phoxinus*.

Red Belt *n* in France, the working-class suburban area outside Paris, historically administered by Communist mayors and populated chiefly by immigrants from North Africa and the Middle East

red·bird /réd bùrd/ *n* any bird with red feathers, e.g., a cardinal

red blood cell *n* any red-colored cell in blood that contains hemoglobin and carries oxygen to the tissues. Technical name **erythrocyte**

red-blood·ed *adj* behaving in ways stereotypically associated with men, e.g., by showing strength or active sexual desire

red·bone /réd bōn/ *n* a medium-sized hunting dog with a reddish coat, originally bred in the United States to hunt raccoons

red·breast /réd brèst/ (*plural* **-breasts** or *same*) *n* **1.** a bird with a reddish breast, especially a robin **2.** a freshwater sunfish with a reddish belly. Native to: eastern United States. Latin name: *Lepomis auritus*.

red·brick /réd brìk/ *adj* **1.** *UK* relating to British universities that were founded in the late 19th and early 20th centuries, e.g., Manchester and Leeds. The term was originally intended to emphasize their modernity in contrast to the older British universities such as Oxford and St. Andrews, and now also distinguishes them from newer universities. **2.** constructed of red bricks

Red Bri·gades *npl* a left-wing urban organization that was active in Italy during the 1970s and was responsible for the kidnapping and murder of the Italian prime minister Aldo Moro in 1978 [Translation of Italian *brigate rosse*]

red·bud /réd bùd/ (*plural* **-buds** or *same*) *n* a tree with heart-shaped leaves and small pale pink flowers. Native to: North America. Genus: *Cercis*.

red·bug /réd bùg/ *n* a red-and-black insect, some species of which are pests. Native to: tropics, subtropics. Family: Pyrrhocoridae.

red·cap /réd kàp/ *n* a porter at an airport or railroad station (*informal*) [Early 20C. < the red caps traditionally worn by such personnel]

red card *n* in soccer, a red card displayed by the referee when ejecting a player from a game for a serious infringement of the rules

red car·pet *n* **1.** a strip of red-colored carpet laid on the ground for an important visitor to walk on when arriving or departing **2.** attentive or deferential treatment given to a dignitary, celebrity, or other important person (*hyphenated when used before a noun*) ○ *Everywhere we went we got the red-carpet treatment.*

red ce·dar *n* **1.** TREE OF EASTERN N AMERICA an evergreen tree of the juniper family with reddish wood and fleshy cones. Native to: eastern North America. Latin name: *Juniperus virginiana*. **2.** TREE OF WESTERN N AMERICA an evergreen timber tree of the cypress family with reddish wood and small oval cones. Native to: western North America. Latin name: *Thuja plicata*. **3.** WOOD FROM RED CEDAR the weather-resistant close-grained wood of either of the red cedar trees. Use: building material.

red cell *n* BIOL same as **red blood cell**

red cent *n* the smallest amount of money (*informal*) [From the fact that the one-cent coin is made of copper]

Red Cloud /rèd klówd/ (1822–1909) Oglala Sioux leader. He resisted the US government's occupation of Native North American territory in present-day Wyoming and Montana, but his defeat in the Sioux War (1875–76) resulted in the relocation of his people to South Dakota.

> "...the white soldier's...presence...is...an insult to the spirits of our ancestors.... Dakotas, I am for war!"
> [Red Cloud, *Speech, council at Fort Laramie*; 1866]

red clo·ver *n* a clover often grown as a forage crop for horses or cattle. Flowers: fragrant, red. Native to: Europe, Asia, North America. Latin name: *Trifolium pratense*.

red·coat /réd kōt/ *n* a British soldier serving overseas in former times, especially during the American Revolution [Early 16C. < their bright red uniform coats]

red cor·al *n* a coral with hard deep pink skeletons. Use: ornaments, jewelry. Genus: *Corallium*.

red cor·pus·cle *n* BIOL same as **red blood cell**

Red Cres·cent *n* in Islamic countries, the name under which the Red Cross operates

Red Cross *n* an international organization founded in 1864 and dedicated to the medical care of the sick or wounded in wars and natural disasters

red cur·rant *n* **1.** a red berry with a tart flavor that grows in clusters. Use: jellies. **2.** a flowering bush that produces red currants. Native to: northern temperate regions. Latin name: *Ribes rubrum*.

redd[1] /red/ *regional vti* (**redd** or **redd·ed, redd·ing, redds**) to straighten something up, or tidy things generally ■ *n* a spell of straightening something up [15C. Origin ?] —**red·der** *n*

redd[2] /red/ *n* a hollow that is scooped out in the sand or gravel of a river bed for spawning by fish such as trout and salmon [Early 19C. Origin ?]

red deer *n* a large deer that has spreading antlers and a reddish-brown summer coat. Native to: Europe, Asia. Latin name: *Cervus elaphus*.

red·den /rédd'n/ (**-dened, -den·ing, -dens**) *v* **1.** *vti* to become red or redder, or make something red or redder **2.** *vi* to go red in the face, e.g., with embarrassment, anger, or exertion

Otis Redding

Red·ding /rédding/, **Otis** (1941–67) US singer and songwriter. He won popular and critical acclaim for his southern soul rhythm-and-blues style, an emotional blend of gospel, country, and traditional blues.

red·dish /réddish/ *adj* of a color that is a shade of red or strongly tinged with red —**red·dish·ness** *n*

red·dle *n, vt* MINERALS, AGRIC same as **ruddle**

red-dog *vt* in football, to charge directly at the quarterback the moment the ball is put into play (*informal*)

red drum *n* FISH same as **channel bass**

rede /reed/ *n* (*archaic*) **1.** same as **advice 2. EXPLANATION** a story, account, or explanation ■ *vt* (**red·ed, red·ing, redes**) **1. ADVISE SOMEBODY** to advise or counsel somebody (*archaic*) **2. INTERPRET SOMETHING** to explain, understand, or interpret something in a particular way [The noun is from Old English *rǣd*; the verb from Old English *rǣdan* (see READ)]

red·ear /réd ėer/ (*plural* **-ears** or *same*), **red·ear sun·fish** (*plural* **red·ear sun·fish·es** or *same*) *n* a freshwater sunfish with a scarlet margin around the gill cover. Native to: southern and eastern United States. Latin name: *Lepomis microlophus.*

red earth *n* a clayey soil found in tropical grasslands, colored red by the presence of iron compounds

re·dec·o·rate /ree dékə ràyt/ (**-rat·ed, -rat·ing, -rates**) *vti* to change or renew the interior decoration of a building or room —**re·dec·o·ra·tion** /-dèkə ráysh'n/ *n*

re·deem /ri dėem/ (**-deemed, -deem·ing, -deems**) *vt* **1. MAKE SOMETHING ACCEPTABLE** to make something acceptable or pleasant in spite of its negative qualities or aspects **2. RESTORE REPUTATION** to do something that changes a negative opinion to a positive one **3. ATONE FOR HUMAN SIN** to pay for the sins of humanity with death on the Cross (*refers to Jesus Christ*) **4. BUY SOMETHING BACK** to buy back an item given, e.g., to a pawnbroker, as security for a loan **5. KEEP PROMISE** to fulfill a pledge or promise **6. EXCHANGE SOMETHING FOR MONEY** to exchange or convert something such as a voucher for money or its equivalent **7. PAY SOMETHING OFF** to pay off the outstanding portion of a debt [15C. Directly or via French < Latin *redimere* "buy back" < *emere* "buy"] —**re·deem·a·ble** *adj*

re·deem·er /ri dėemər/ *n* somebody who redeems somebody or something, especially somebody who rescues another

Re·deem·er *n* Jesus Christ regarded as the savior of humanity through his death on the Cross

re·deem·ing /ri dėeming/ *adj* compensating for faults

re·de·fine /rèedi fín/ (**-fined, -fin·ing, -fines**) *vt* **1.** to interpret the meaning of something, especially a word, differently, or give something a new meaning **2.** to change the nature or scope of something or the character or role of somebody, or cause something or somebody to be understood differently ○ *The parameters of the inquiry were redefined overnight.* —**re·def·i·ni·tion** /-dèffə nísh'n/ *n*

re·demp·tion /ri démpsh'n/ *n* **1. IMPROVING OF SOMETHING** the act of saving something or somebody from a declined, dilapidated, or corrupted state and restoring it, him, or her to a better condition ○ *The house was a wreck, and the garden seemed entirely beyond redemption.* **2. REDEEMED STATE** the improved state of somebody or something saved from apparently irreversible decline **3. ATONEMENT FOR HUMAN SIN** deliverance from the sins of humanity by the death of Jesus Christ on the Cross **4. BUYING BACK OF SOMETHING** the buying back of something given, e.g., to a pawnbroker, as security for a loan **5. ENDING OF FINANCIAL OBLIGATION** the removal of a financial obligation, e.g., the repayment of a loan or promissory note [14C. Via French < Latin *redemption-* < *redempt-*, past participle of *redimere* (see REDEEM)] —**re·demp·tion·al** *adj*

re·demp·tion·er /ri démpsh'nər/ *n* an emigrant from Europe in the 18th and 19th centuries who worked as a servant on arriving in North America to pay for the cost of the voyage

re·demp·tive /ri démptiv/ *adj* bringing about the redemption of somebody or something [15C. < Latin *redempt-*, past participle of *redimere* (see REDEEM)]

Re·demp·tor·ist /ri démptərist/ *n* a member of the Congregation of the Most Holy Redeemer, a Roman Catholic order specializing in preaching and missionary work, founded in Italy in 1732 [Mid-19C. < French *rédemptoriste* < Latin *redemptor* "redeemer" < *redempt-* (see REDEMPTIVE)]

red en·sign *n* a red flag with the Union Jack in the upper corner of the vertical edge near the staff. It is flown by British merchant ships and pleasure craft.

re·de·ploy /rèedi plóy/ (**-ployed, -ploy·ing, -ploys**) *vti* to move people or equipment from one area or activity to another —**re·de·ploy·ment** *n*

re·de·vel·op /rèedi vélləp/ (**-oped, -op·ing, -ops**) *vt* to improve an area that has become run down by renovating buildings, making better use of wasteland, and encouraging inward investment —**re·de·vel·op·ment** *n*

red·eye /réd ī/ *n* **1. NIGHT FLIGHT** a late night or overnight airline service, usually a long easterly flight (*informal*) **2. PHOTOGRAPHIC FAULT** red pupils in the eyes of a subject in flash photography (*informal*) **3.** *US* **CHEAP WHISKEY** cheap inferior whiskey (*slang*)

red·eye gra·vy *n US* gravy made from the juices of baked or fried ham, often flavored with coffee [From the small bubbles of ham fat that form in it while cooking]

red·fin /réd fin/ (*plural* **-fins** or *same*), **red·fin shin·er** (*plural* **red·fin shin·ers** or *same*) *n* a small freshwater fish with reddish fins, often kept in aquariums. Native to: central North America. Genus: *Notropis.*

red fire *n* a chemical mixture, especially one containing strontium salts, that burns with a vivid red flame and is used in fireworks and flares

red·fish /réd fish/ (*plural* **-fish·es** or *same*) *n* **1.** a reddish rockfish. Native to: northern Atlantic. **2.** FISH same as **channel bass 3.** a male salmon that has recently spawned

red flag *n* **1.** *US* **INCITEMENT TO ANGER** an incitement to anger or violence. Can term **red rag 2. WARNING SIGNAL** a flag waved as a danger signal or a command to stop **3. FLAG SYMBOLIZING COMMUNISM OR SOCIALISM** a plain red flag or banner used as an international symbol of communism or socialism

Red·ford /rédfərd/, **Robert** (*b.* 1937) US actor, producer, and director. His many movies include *Butch Cassidy and the Sundance Kid* (1969). He also founded the Sundance Film Festival. Full name **Redford, Jr., Charles Robert**

red fox *n* a common fox with sharply pointed ears, a reddish orange to reddish brown coat, and a white-tipped tail. Native to: fields and open woods of Europe, Asia, and North America. Latin name: *Vulpes vulpes.*

red gi·ant *n* a red-colored star with a relatively low surface temperature and a diameter much greater than that of the Sun

Red·grave /réd gràyv/, **Sir Michael** (1908–85) British actor. One of the outstanding actors of his generation, he played both classical and contemporary roles in movies and on stage. Full name **Redgrave, Michael Scudamore**

Red·grave, Sir Steve (*b.* 1962) British rower. Between 1987 and 2000 he won nine world titles and was Olympic Games gold medalist on five consecutive occasions.

Red·grave, Vanessa (*b.* 1937) British actor. The daughter of Michael Redgrave, she is acclaimed for her sensitive and intelligent portrayals of strong-willed independent women.

red-green col·or·blind·ness *n* MED same as **deuteranopia**

Red Guard *n* **1.** the 1960s Chinese Communist youth movement that attempted to bring about the Cultural Revolution of Mao Zedong **2.** a member of the Red Guard

red gum *n* **1.** a eucalyptus tree with aromatic leaves and distinctive red wood. Native to: Australia. Latin name: *Eucalyptus camaldulensis.* **2.** TREES same as **sweet gum**

red-hand·ed *adj* in the act of committing a crime or doing something wrong ○ *was caught red-handed* [From the notion of having blood on the hands]

red·head /réd hèd/ *n* **1.** somebody, especially a woman, who has reddish-colored hair **2.** a diving duck, the male of which has a bright chestnut head. Native to: North America. Latin name: *Aythya americana.*

red·head·ed /rèd héddəd/ *adj* **1.** with reddish-colored hair **2.** describes an animal, especially a bird, with a red head

red heat *n* the temperature at which something is red-hot, or the state of being at such a temperature

red her·ring *n* **1. MISLEADING CLUE** something introduced, e.g., into a crime or mystery story, in order to divert attention or mislead **2. SMOKED HERRING** a herring salted and smoked to a reddish brown color **3.** BUSINESS **PRELIMINARY BUSINESS PROSPECTUS** a preliminary prospectus for a new stock issue, filed with the Securities and Exchange Commission, that does not include the offering price of the shares or the size of the issue. It is often issued in order to gauge the market for shares in the proposed issue. (*slang*) [< dragging smoked fish across a scent trail to teach hounds not to be distracted]

red-hot, red hot *adj* **1. GLOWING RED WITH HEAT** heated to such a high temperature as to glow red **2. VERY HOT** extremely hot **3. EXTREMELY POPULAR** in great demand (*informal*) **4. EXCITING** very exciting (*informal*) ○ *red-hot news* **5. PASSIONATE** feeling or expressing intense enthusiasm, passion, or anger (*informal*) ■ *n* FOOD **HOT DOG** a hot dog, especially one spiced with pepper

red-hot pok·er *n* a tall perennial ornamental plant. Flowers: erect spikes, red at the top and orange below. Native to: South Africa. Genus: *Kniphofia.*

re·di·a /rėedee ə/ (*plural* **-di·ae** /-dee ėe/) *n* one of the forms of the larvae of trematode worms. Rediae are found as parasites in the gut of snails. [Late 19C. < modern Latin, after Francesco *Redi* (1626–98), Italian biologist]

re·di·al /ree dī əl/ *vti* (**-aled, -al·ing, -als**) to dial a telephone number again, e.g., because the line was busy when the number was dialed earlier ■ *n* the function or button on a telephone that permits automatic redialing of a telephone number

rediculous incorrect spelling of **ridiculous**

re·did past tense of **redo**

Red In·di·an *n* an offensive term for a Native North American (*dated*)

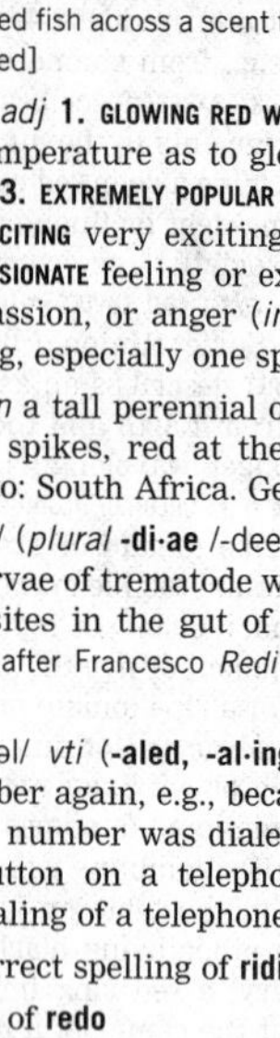
redingote (sense 1)

red·in·gote /rédding gōt/ *n* **1. WOMAN'S FULL-SKIRTED COAT** a woman's coat with an open full skirt and close-fitting top **2. WOMAN'S BELTED DRESS OR COAT** a belted woman's dress or coat of 18th-century Europe that was open at the front to show a petticoat or dress **3.** MAN'S OVERCOAT a man's double-breasted coat of 18th-century Europe that had wide flat cuffs and flared out below the waist [Late 18C. < French, alteration of English *riding-coat*]

red ink *n* a financial loss or deficit [< accountants' traditional use of red ink to record deficits and losses]

re·di·rect /reedi rékt, -dī-/ *vt* (**-rect·ed, -rect·ing, -rects**) **1.** SEND SOMETHING ELSEWHERE to send something received to a different location, e.g., because the intended recipient has moved ○ *redirecting the previous tenant's mail* **2.** REROUTE TRAFFIC to send traffic along a different route **3.** CHANGE FOCUS to focus actions or activities on a different objective ■ *n US* LAW RECALLING OF WITNESS an examination of a witness again after cross-examination is completed ○ *asked a crucial question on redirect* —**re·di·rec·tion** *n*

re·dis·trib·ute /reedi strí byoot/ (**-ut·ed, -ut·ing, -utes**) *vt* **1.** to distribute more of something previously distributed **2.** to divide something up or share something out in a different way, e.g., in more equal proportions or among a wider range of people —**re·dis·tri·bu·tion** /reedistrə byoósh'n/ *n* —**re·dis·tri·bu·tion·ist** *n* —**re·dis·trib·u·tive** /reedi stríbbyətiv/ *adj*

re·dis·trict·ing /ree dístrikting/ *n US* the redrawing of the boundaries of legislative districts for electoral purposes —**re·dis·trict** *vti*

red·i·vi·vus /rèddə vívəss, -vée-/ *adj* revived, reborn, or brought back to life (*literary*) [Late 16C. < Latin, "alive again" < *vivus* "alive"]

red lead *n* a bright red poisonous oxide of lead. Use: pigment in paints. Formula: Pb_3O_4.

red leaf *n* a plant disease that causes reddening of the leaves

red·leg /réd lèg/ *n* (*slang*) **1.** *US* MIL same as **artilleryman** **2.** *Carib* an offensive term for a white person from a lower income group

red-let·ter day *n* a very special day or occasion [< the marking of feast days in red on church calendars]

red light *n* **1.** a red warning signal, especially an instruction to drivers to stop **2.** a sign of disapproval or rejection, e.g., an instruction not to proceed with something (*informal*)

red-light *adj* relating to the part of a town or city where brothels and other commercial sex-based activities are concentrated [< the red lights traditionally displayed in the doors and windows of brothels]

red·line /réd līn/ (**-lined, -lin·ing, -lines**) *v* **1.** *vti* REFUSE FINANCIAL SERVICES IN AREA to refuse loans, insurance, or other financial services to people or businesses in a supposedly high-risk area **2.** *vt* SELECT SOMETHING FOR REMOVAL to select something such as an aircraft for removal from service **3.** *vt US* EARMARK SOMEBODY FOR DISMISSAL to select somebody for dismissal as part of employee cutbacks [Mid-20C. < the traditional use of red ink to cross out deleted items in a budget]

red man *n* an offensive term for a Native American (*dated*)

red ma·ple *n* a maple tree with red flowers and leaves that turn bright red in fall. Native to: eastern North America. Latin name: *Acer rubrum*.

red mar·row *n* the reddish bone marrow where red blood cells and some white blood cells are formed

red mass *n* a special Roman Catholic mass celebrated in red vestments for the opening of a court or congress

red meat *n* **1.** MEAT THAT IS RED WHEN RAW meat that is relatively dark red in color when raw, e.g., beef or lamb **2.** PITHY CONTENT pithy, forceful, aggressively delivered or worded content, e.g., in a speech or written presentation (*informal*) ■ *adj* COMMUNICATION FORCEFUL AND TO THE POINT pithy, forceful, aggressively delivered, and focusing sharply on contentious issues (*informal*) ○ *red meat rhetoric*

red mite *n* one of various reddish mites, e.g., the spider mite

red mul·ber·ry *n* a mulberry tree that produces clusters of small edible red to purple fruits. Native to: eastern United States. Latin name: *Morus rubra*.

red mul·let *n* **1.** FISH same as **goatfish** **2.** the flesh of a red mullet used as food

red·neck /réd nèk/ *n* **1.** an offensive term for a white farm hand in the southern United States, especially one regarded as uneducated or aggressively prejudiced **2.** an offensive term for somebody who is opposed to liberal social changes, especially somebody regarded as prejudiced [Mid-19C. < the sunburned necks of those who work outdoors in sunny climates] —**red·necked** *adj*

re·do /ree doó/ (**-did** /-díd/, **-done** /-dún/, **-do·ing, -does** /-dúz/) *vt* **1.** to do something again, e.g., in order to correct mistakes in an earlier effort **2.** to change the appearance of something such as a hairstyle or the interior decoration of a room

red oak *n* an oak tree with bristly lobed leaves that turn red in the fall. Native to: eastern North America. Genus: *Quercus*.

red o·cher *n* **1.** a rich reddish brown color used in painting **2.** a reddish earth that is rich in iron oxide. Use: red pigment in paints.

red·o·lent /rédd'lənt/ *adj* **1.** SUGGESTING suggestive or reminiscent of something ○ *redolent of corruption* **2.** HAVING PARTICULAR SMELL with a particular scent or odor ○ *redolent of pine* **3.** AROMATIC with a strong pleasant aroma (*literary*) [15C. < Old French < Latin *redolere* "smell strongly" < *olere* "to smell"] —**red·o·lence** *n*

Re·don /rə dón, rə dáwN/, **Odilon** (1840–1916) French painter and lithographer. A central figure in the symbolist movement and a forerunner of surrealism, he used dream images in lithographs such as *La Nuit (Night)* (1886).

re·done past participle of **redo**

red o·sier *n* **1.** *also* **red o·sier dog·wood** a bush of the dogwood family with red twigs and clusters of white fruits. Native to: North America. Latin name: *Cornus stolonifera*. **2.** a willow tree with reddish branches used in basketry

re·dou·ble /ree dúbb'l/ *vti* (**-bled, -bling, -bles**) **1.** INCREASE to increase something considerably, especially the amount of effort expended on something, or become much greater **2.** ECHO to echo or reecho, or cause something to echo or reecho **3.** CARDS DOUBLE DOUBLED BID in bridge, to double an opponent's double as a bid ■ *n* CARDS DOUBLING OF DOUBLE BID in bridge, a redoubling of a bid [15C. < French *redoubler* "double again" < *double* "double"]

re·doubt /ri dówt/ *n* **1.** a temporary fortification built to defend a position such as a hilltop **2.** a castle, fortress, or other stronghold (*literary*) [Early 17C. Alteration (influenced by REDOUBTABLE) of French *redoute*, via Italian *ridotto* < medieval Latin *reductus* "refuge" < Latin, past participle of *reducere* (see REDUCE)]

re·doubt·a·ble /ri dówtəb'l/ *adj* with personal qualities worthy of respect or fear [14C. < French *redoutable* < *do(u)ter* (see DOUBT)] —**re·doubt·a·bly** *adv*

re·dound /ri dównd/ (**-dound·ed, -dound·ing, -dounds**) *vi* **1.** to have a particular consequence, usually something good or positive ○ *a decision that redounded to her credit* **2.** to return to affect somebody as a repercussion or consequence (*formal*) ○ *His attempts at revenge redounded upon his own head.* [14C. Via French *redonder* < Latin *redundare* "overflow" (see REDUNDANT)]

USAGE See ***rebound***.

red·out /réd òwt/ *n* sudden headache and reddening of the field of vision experienced by pilots or astronauts during rapid deceleration and other maneuvers

re·dox /reé dòks/ *n* CHEM same as **oxidation-reduction** [Early 20C. < Contraction of REDUCTION + OXIDATION]

red pack·et *n Hong Kong, Malaysia, Singapore* money enclosed in a red envelope and given for luck by married people to unmarried young people during the first 15 days of the Chinese New Year

red pan·da *n* a reddish brown animal that resembles a raccoon in appearance. Native to: Himalayan forests and nearby areas of East Asia. Latin name: *Ailurus fulgens*.

red-pen·cil *vt* to revise, correct, or censor written material

red pep·per *n* **1.** a red pod that belongs to the capsicum family of vegetables, especially a ripe sweet pepper **2.** FOOD same as **cayenne pepper**

red pine *n* a pine tree with reddish bark and needles grouped in twos. Native to: northeastern North America. Latin name: *Pinus resinosa*.

red plan·et *n* the planet Mars (*informal*)

red·poll /réd pōl/ *n* a small bird of the finch family with a red crown and a pink breast. Native to: North America, Europe, Asia. Genus: *Carduelis*.

Red Poll, Red Polled *n* a hornless cow with short reddish hair, belonging to a breed originating in England. Raised for: beef, milk.

red puc·coon *n* PLANTS same as **bloodroot**

re·draft /ree dráft/ *vt* (**-draft·ed, -draft·ing, -drafts**) to rewrite something, making changes in it ■ *n* a second or further draft or rewriting

red rag *n Can, UK* same as **red flag** (sense 1)

re·dress *vt* /ri dréss/ (**-dressed, -dress·ing, -dress·es**) **1.** MAKE UP FOR SOMETHING to provide compensation or reparation for a loss or wrong experienced **2.** IMPOSE FAIRNESS ON SOMETHING to adjust a situation in order to make things fair or equal ■ *n* /reé drèss, ri dréss/ **1.** COMPENSATION compensation or reparation for a loss or wrong a party has experienced **2.** ACT OF COMPENSATING the compensating of a party for a loss or wrong experienced [14C. < Old French *redrecier* < *drecier* < Latin *directus* "straight" (see DIRECT)]

re·drew past tense of **redraw**

red rib·bon *n* a red-colored ribbon, badge, or other decoration awarded to somebody who comes second in a competition

Red Riv·er 1. river of the south central United States, flowing eastward along the Oklahoma-Texas border and into the Mississippi River in Louisiana. Length: 1,220 mi./1,970 km. **2.** river in the north central United States and south central Canada, flowing northward from Minnesota and emptying into Lake Winnipeg. Length: 545 mi./877 km. **3.** river in Southeast Asia, rising in southern China and emptying into the Gulf of Tonkin. Length: 500 mi./800 km.

red·root /réd root/ *n* **1.** a perennial bog plant with red roots and woolly yellow flowers. Native to: eastern North America. Latin name: *Lachnanthes caroliana*. **2.** a plant with red roots, e.g., a bloodroot or pigweed **3.** PLANTS same as **ceanothus**

red salm·on *n* FISH same as **sockeye**

Red Sea inland sea between the Arabian peninsula and northeastern Africa. It is linked to the Mediterranean in the north by the Suez Canal. Area: 169,000 sq. mi./438,000 sq. km.

red shank *n UK* same as **lady's thumb**

red·shank /réd shàngk/ *n* a large slender wading bird of the sandpiper family with red legs and a red beak. Native to: Europe, Asia. Genus: *Tringa*.

red·shift /réd shìft/ *n* a shift in the spectrum of an astronomical object toward longer wavelengths, or toward the red end of the spectrum, caused by its motion away from Earth —**red·shift·ed** *adj*

red·shirt /réd shùrt/ *n US* a college or university athlete who is kept out of competitions for one year in order to improve his or her skills and extend his or her period of eligibility [Mid-19C. < the red jerseys that customarily distinguish these players at practices] —**red·shirt** *vt*

red-should·ered hawk *n* a large hawk with reddish shoulders and a banded tail. Native to: North America. Latin name: *Buteo lineatus*.

red·skin /réd skìn/ *n* **1.** an offensive term for a Native North American (*dated*) **2.** *Carib* a light-skinned person with African features, usually of mixed European and African origin (*sometimes offensive*) —**red-skinned** *adj*

red snap·per *n* **1.** a large reddish colored fish. Native to: Atlantic coasts of North, South, and Central America. Genus: *Lutjanus*. **2.** the flesh of a red snapper used as food

red snow *n* fallen snow that is reddish in color, either from the presence of airborne dust or from red algae growing in it. It is commonly seen in Arctic and Alpine regions.

red spi·der, red spi·der mite *n* ZOOL same as **spider mite**

red spruce *n* a spruce tree with reddish brown bark and cones, and light soft wood. Native to: eastern North America. Latin name: *Picea rubens*.

Red Square *n* a large square in central Moscow, Russia, bordered by the Kremlin and Lenin's tomb. It was the site of military parades on public holidays in the former Soviet Union.

red squill *n* a squill plant with red bulbs. Use: source of rat poison. Latin name: *Urginea maritima*.

red squir·rel *n* **1.** a squirrel with reddish fur. Native to: coniferous forests of North America. Latin name: *Tamiasciurus hudsonicus*. **2.** a reddish brown squirrel with tufted ears. Native to: Europe, Asia. Latin name: *Sciurus vulgaris*.

red·start /réd staart/ *n* **1.** a bird of the warbler family, the male of which has reddish orange patches on its black and white feathers. Native to: North and South America. Latin name: *Setophaga ruticilla*. **2.** a bird of the thrush family, the male of which often has a black throat and a reddish brown tail. Native to: Europe, Asia, Africa. Genus: *Phoenicurus*. [Late 16C. < Old English *steort* "animal's tail" < Germanic]

red steen·bras /-steen bràss/ *n* same as **dentex**

red tape *n* official procedure regarded as unnecessary, overcomplicated, or obstructive (*informal*) [< the red tape once widely used to seal official documents]

red tide *n* a brownish red discoloration in seawater, caused by an increased presence of plant-based plankton that sometimes leads to the poisoning of fish and, consequently, of those who eat fish

red·top /réd tòp/ *n* a grass plant that has clusters of red flowers and is used for lawns and forage. Genus: *Agrostis*.

re·duce /ri dóoss/ (**-duced, -duc·ing, -duc·es**) *v* **1.** *vti* **DECREASE** to become smaller in size, number, extent, degree, or intensity, or make something smaller in this way **2.** *vt* **WORSEN STATE OF SOMEBODY OR SOMETHING** to bring somebody or something into a particular undesirable state ○ *Bombing had reduced the town to rubble.* ○ *reduced them to tears* **3.** *vt* **MAKE SOMETHING CHEAPER** to lower the price or cost of an item for sale **4.** *vt* **SIMPLIFY SOMETHING** to make something simpler, especially by extracting or summarizing essential components **5.** *vt* **ANALYZE SOMETHING SYSTEMATICALLY** to analyze something in terms of a system or rule, usually as an aid to explaining or understanding it **6.** *vt* **DEMOTE SOMEBODY** to place somebody officially in a lower rank or grade, e.g., as a punishment for breaking rules **7.** *vti* COOK **THICKEN** to make a sauce or stock thicker by boiling off some of the liquid, or become thicker in this way **8.** *vt* MATH **SIMPLIFY EQUATION** to simplify an expression or equation without changing its value **9.** *vti* CHEM **UNDERGO CHEMICAL REACTION** to undergo a chemical reaction in which there is a gain in hydrogen or a loss of oxygen, or cause a substance to undergo this **10.** *vti* CHEM **GAIN ELECTRONS** to undergo a chemical reaction in which there is an increase in the number of electrons, or cause a substance to undergo this **11.** *vt* PHOTOGRAPHY **DECREASE DENSITY OF NEGATIVE** to lessen the density of a photographic negative using a chemical substance **12.** *vt* **TAKE CONTROL OF PLACE OR PEOPLE** to bring a place or people under authority using force **13.** *vt* METALL **REFINE ORE** to remove the impurities from an ore in order to obtain the pure metal **14.** *vti* BIOL **UNDERGO CELL DIVISION** to undergo the type of cell division (**meiosis**) that halves the number of chromosomes in the two resultant cells, or cause cells to undergo this **15.** *vi* **LOSE WEIGHT** to lose weight, especially by dieting [14C. < Latin *reducere* "bring back" < *ducere* "to lead"] —**re·duc·i·bil·i·ty** /ri dóossə bíllətee/ *n* —**re·duc·i·ble** *adj*

re·duc·er /ri dóossər/ *n* **1.** a chemical solution that lessens the density of a photographic negative by oxidizing it **2.** a pipe fitting that connects two pipes of different diameters

re·duc·ing a·gent *n* a chemical substance that reduces the amount of oxygen in another substance and becomes oxidized in the process

re·duc·tant /ri dúktənt/ *n* CHEM same as **reducing agent** [Early 20C. < REDUCTION, after OXIDANT]

re·duc·tase /ri dúk tàyss, -tàyz/ *n* an enzyme that catalyzes the chemical reduction of an organic compound [Early 20C. < REDUCTION]

re·duc·ti·o ad ab·sur·dum /ri dùkshee ō ad əb súrdəm, -dùktee-/ *n* **1. TAKING SOMETHING TO ABSURD LENGTHS** the application of a rule or principle so strictly or literally that the result is ridiculous **2. LOGICAL DISPROOF** the disproving of a logical argument by showing that its ultimate conclusion is absurd **3. LOGICAL PROOF** the proving of a logical argument indirectly, by showing that the contradictory argument is absurd [Mid-18C. < Latin, "reduction to the absurd"]

re·duc·tion /ri dúkshən/ *n* **1. REDUCING OF SOMETHING** the decreasing of something in size, number, extent, degree, or intensity **2. AMOUNT BY WHICH SOMETHING IS REDUCED** the amount by which something is made smaller or less **3. SIMPLIFICATION** a simplification or condensation of something **4. SMALLER COPY** a copy of something made on a smaller scale, e.g., a reduced photocopy **5.** COOK **THICKENED SAUCE** a sauce or stock that has been thickened by boiling off some of the liquid **6.** MATH **MAKING FRACTION SIMPLER** the canceling of common factors in the numerator and denominator of a fraction **7.** MATH **DECIMALIZATION OF FRACTION** the converting of a fraction into decimal form **8.** BIOL same as **meiosis** (sense 1) **9.** CHEM **CHEMICAL REACTION** a chemical reaction that brings about a gain in hydrogen, a loss of oxygen, or an increase in electrons [15C. Via French < Latin *reduction-* < past participle of *reducere* (see REDUCE)] —**re·duc·tion·al** *adj*

re·duc·tion di·vi·sion *n* BIOL same as **meiosis** (sense 1)

re·duc·tion fir·ing *n* the firing of pottery in an oxygen-starved atmosphere in order to change the nature of the glaze applied

re·duc·tion gear *n* a set of gears in an engine used to reduce output speed relative to that of the engine while providing greater turning power, e.g., when climbing a hill

re·duc·tion·ism /ri dúksh'n ìzzəm/ *n* **1.** the analysis of something into simpler parts or organized systems, especially with a view to explaining or understanding it **2.** the oversimplifying of something complex, or the misguided belief that everything can be explained in simple terms —**re·duc·tion·ist** *n, adj* —**re·duc·tion·is·tic** /-dùksh'n ístik/ *adj*

re·duc·tive /ri dúktiv/ *adj* **1.** seeking to explain complex things in terms of simple structures and systems **2.** oversimplifying complex things and ignoring their subtleties or important details [Mid-16C. < medieval Latin *reductivus* < past participle of Latin *reducere* (see REDUCE)] —**re·duc·tive·ly** *adv* —**re·duc·tive·ness** *n*

re·dun·dan·cy /ri dúndənssee/ (*plural* **-cies**) *n* **1. SUPERFLUOUSNESS** the state or fact of not or no longer being needed or wanted **2. SOMETHING SUPERFLUOUS** something that is not or no longer needed or wanted ○ *eliminated the redundancies in the system* **3. USE OF SUPERFLUOUS WORDS** the use of a word or words whose meaning is already conveyed elsewhere in a passage, without a rhetorical purpose **4. DUPLICATION OF COMPONENTS** the installation of duplicate electronic or mechanical components or backup systems that are designed to come into use to keep equipment working if their counterparts fail **5.** TELECOM **DUPLICATION OF MESSAGE** duplication of information in telecommunications in order to reduce the risk of error **6.** *Can, UK* **DISMISSAL FROM WORK** dismissal from employment because the job or the worker has been deemed no longer necessary. US term **severance**

re·dun·dant /ri dúndənt/ *adj* **1. SUPERFLUOUS** not or no longer needed or wanted **2. REPEATING MEANING** with the same meaning as a word used elsewhere in a passage and without a rhetorical purpose **3. BACKUP** fitted as a backup component or system **4.** *UK* **DISMISSED FROM WORK** dismissed from employment because the job or the worker has been deemed no longer necessary [Late 16C. < Latin *redundant-*, present participle of *redundare* "overflow" < *undare* "rise in waves" < *unda* "wave"] —**re·dun·dant·ly** *adv*

re·du·pli·cate /ri dóopli kàyt/ *v* (**-cat·ed, -cat·ing, -cates**) **1.** *vti* **REPEAT OR DOUBLE** to repeat or double something, or be repeated or doubled **2.** *vt* LING **REPEAT SPEECH SOUND** to repeat a vowel, syllable, or word in order to create a new linguistic element or word such as "wishy-washy" or "goody-goody" ■ *adj* **1.** LING **REPEATED** repeated in order to create a new word or other linguistic element **2.** BOT **CURVING INWARD** describes leaves or petals that have their edges curved inward [Late 16C. < late Latin *reduplicat-*, past participle of *reduplicare* < Latin *duplicare* (see DUPLICATE)] —**re·du·pli·ca·tion** /-dòopli káysh'n/ *n* —**re·du·pli·ca·tive** *adj*

re·du·vi·id /ri dóovee id/ *n* INSECTS same as **assassin bug** [Late 19C. < modern Latin *Reduviidae* < Latin *reduvia* "hangnail"]

re·dux /ree dúks, rée dùks/ *adj* brought back, especially in being restored to former importance or prominence (*literary*) [Late 19C. < Latin < *reducere* (see REDUCE)]

red·ware[1] /réd wèr/ *n* MARINE BIOL same as **kelp** (sense 1) [Early 18C. < N English dialect *ware* "seaweed" < Germanic, "bind"]

red·ware[2] /réd wèr/ *n* reddish earthenware pottery made from clay with a high iron oxide content [Late 17C. < WARE[1]]

red wa·ter *n* a cattle disease characterized by the passage of reddish urine

red whor·tle·ber·ry *n* PLANTS same as **cowberry**

red·wing /réd wìng/ *n* **1.** a bird of the thrush family that has reddish feathers under its wings and a spotted breast. Native to: Europe, Asia. Latin name: *Turdus iliacus*. **2.** BIRDS same as **red-winged blackbird**

red-winged black·bird, red·wing black·bird *n* a blackbird, the male of which is black with scarlet and yellow patches on its wings. Native to: North America. Latin name: *Agelaius phoeniceus*.

red wolf *n* a small reddish gray wolf, nearly eliminated by overhunting and hybridization with the coyote. Native to: southeastern North America. Latin name: *Canis rufus*.

red·wood /réd wòod/ *n* **1.** a coniferous evergreen tree with fibrous reddish bark. Some California redwoods are the tallest trees in the world and can grow to 360 ft./110 m. Native to: northern coastal California, southwestern China. Latin name: *Sequoia sempervirens* or *Sequoiadendron giganteum* or *Metasequoia glyptostroboides*. **2.** durable red-colored wood, especially from a redwood

Red·wood Na·tion·al Park /rèd wòod-/ national park in Northern California. Area: 176 sq. mi./455 sq. km.

red worm *n US* ZOOL same as **bloodworm** (sense 2)

REE *abbr* CHEM rare-earth element

ree·bok *n* ZOOL another spelling of **rhebok**

re·ech·o /ree ékō/ (**-oed, -o·ing, -oes**) *v* **1.** *vi* to resound or echo back **2.** *vt* to repeat again something that has already been repeated

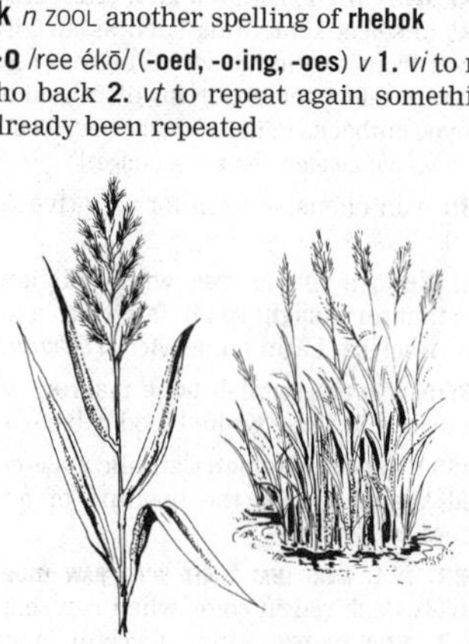

reed

reed /reed/ *n* **1. TALL WATER PLANT** a tall slender plant with jointed stalks that grows in marshes and other wet areas. Genera: *Phragmites, Arundo*. **2. STALK OF REED** a reed stalk, or a bundle of reed stalks. Use: thatching, basketry, crafts. **3.** MUSIC **VIBRATING PART OF MUSICAL INSTRUMENT** a thin piece of cane, metal, or plastic fitted inside a musical instrument that vibrates to produce sound, usually when the player blows into the instrument **4.** MUSIC **MUSICAL INSTRUMENT** a wind instrument fitted with a reed, e.g., an oboe or a clarinet (*informal*) **5.** TEXTILES **WIRES ON LOOM** a series of parallel wires on a loom that separate the threads of the warp evenly [Old English *hrēod* < Germanic]

SPELLCHECK See ***read***.

Reed /reed/, **John** (1887–1920) US writer and revolutionary. A war correspondent in Europe, he witnessed the Bolshevik Revolution in Russia (1917), described in his best-known work *Ten Days That Shook the World* (1919).

Reed, Stanley Forman (1884–1980) US Supreme Court associate justice (1938–57). He was appointed to the Supreme Court by President Franklin D. Roosevelt, and was considered a moderate.

Reed, Walter (1851–1902) US army surgeon and bacteriologist. His discovery in 1900 that yellow fever is transmitted by mosquitoes led to the near-eradication of the disease.

reed·bed /reéd bèd/ *n* an area of marshy ground where reeds grow or are grown

reed·buck /reéd bùk/ *n* a tawny antelope with long horns that curve slightly forward. Native to: sub-Saharan Africa. Genus: *Redunca*. [Mid-19C. Translation of Afrikaans *rietbok*]

reed grass *n* a tall grass plant that grows in rivers and ponds. Native to: Europe, Asia, North America. Latin name: *Glyceria maxima*.

reed·ing /reéding/ *n* **1.** a set of small convex decorative moldings on a building **2.** the narrow vertical grooves on the edge of a coin

reed·ling /reédling/ *n* a small brownish orange songbird with a long tail, the male of which has a black patch extending from the eye down the throat. Native to: Europe, Asia. Latin name: *Panurus biarmicus*.

reed mace *n* PLANTS same as **cattail**

reed·man /reédmən/ (*plural* **-men** /-mən/) *n* a musician who plays a reed instrument, especially a jazz clarinettist or saxophonist (*informal*)

reed or·gan *n* a musical instrument in which air passing over a set of reeds produces sound, e.g., a harmonica or accordion

reed pipe *n* an organ pipe containing a reed that vibrates to make the pipe sound

reed stop *n* an organ stop that controls a set of reed pipes

reed·y /reédee/ (**-i·er, -i·est**) *adj* **1. FULL OF REEDS** full of or thickly planted with reeds ○ *a reedy pond* **2. HIGH-PITCHED** thin and high-pitched, rather than deep or full-toned ○ *a reedy voice* **3. THIN** long, thin, or flexible, like a reed ○ *a reedy physique* —**reed·i·ness** *n*

reef[1] /reef/ *n* **1.** a ridge of coral or rock in a body of water, with the top just below or just above the surface **2.** a lode or vein of ore [Late 16C. < Dutch *rif*] —**reef·y** *adj*

reef[2] /reef/ *n* **PART OF SAIL** a section of a sail that can be gathered in and tied down to reduce the sail's surface ■ *vt* (**reefed, reef·ing, reefs**) **1. MAKE SAIL SMALLER BY GATHERING** to reduce the area of a sail by gathering part of it in **2. SHORTEN RIGGING PIECE** to shorten or bring in one of the pieces that support the rigging on a ship [14C. Via Dutch *reef* < Old Norse *rif* "reef (of a sail)"]

reef·er[1] /reéfər/ *n* **1.** a heavy, close-fitting double-breasted woolen jacket **2.** somebody who reefs sails [Early 19C. < REEF[2]]

reef·er[2] /reéfər/ *n* a marijuana cigarette (*slang*) [Mid-20C. Origin ?]

reef·er[3] /reéfər/ *n US* (*informal*) **1.** same as **refrigerator 2.** a refrigerated railroad car or truck trailer [Early 20C. < REFRIGERATOR]

reef knot *n Can, UK* a symmetrical knot that will not slip after tying, made by passing one end of rope over and around another first in one direction, then again in the opposite direction. US term **square knot**

reek /reek/ *v* (**reeked, reek·ing, reeks**) **1.** *vti* **SMELL STRONGLY** to have a very strong and unpleasant smell, or give off such a smell ○ *The room reeked of smoke.* **2.** *vti* **GIVE CLEAR EVIDENCE OF SOMETHING UNPLEASANT** to show very strong evidence of an unpleasant quality ○ *The document reeks of the double standard.* **3.** *vi* **GIVE OFF SMOKE** to give off smoke, steam, or fumes ○ *a reeking pile of burning tires* **4.** *vt US* **TREAT SOMETHING WITH SMOKE** to process or treat something with smoke ■ *n* **1. UNPLEASANT SMELL** a very strong unpleasant smell ○ *a reek of disinfectant* **2.** *regional* **VISIBLE VAPOR** smoke, steam, or other visible vapor [Old English *rēocan* < Indo-European]

SPELLCHECK reek or **wreak**? Do not confuse the spelling of ***reek*** and ***wreak***, which sound similar. ***Reek*** is a noun or verb referring to a strong unpleasant smell (as in *the reek of rotting vegetables; the place reeked of disinfectant*) or to smoke or fumes given off (as in *reeking heaps of burning refuse*). As a verb it can also mean "be evidence of something unpleasant," as in *the whole affair reeked of incompetence.* ***Wreak*** is a verb only meaning "cause havoc or destruction" or "inflict revenge or punishment."

SYNONYMS See ***smell***.

reel[1] /reel/ *n* **1. REVOLVING STORAGE DEVICE** a usually revolving wheel-shaped device around which something such as thread, film, or wire can be wound for storage **2. QUANTITY ON REEL** the amount of a material that a reel can hold **3.** MOVIES **SECTION OF MOVIE FILM** the amount of movie film stored on one reel **4.** FISHING **WINDER ON FISHING ROD** a winding device attached to a fishing rod that holds the fishing line and enables it to be cast and wound back ■ *vt* (**reeled, reel·ing, reels**) **WIND SOMETHING ONTO REEL** to wind something such as thread or fishing line onto or off a reel [Old English *hrēol* "spool (for winding thread)," origin ?] —**reel·er** *n*

SPELLCHECK See ***real***[1].

reel in *vt* **1.** to draw something in, especially a fish, by winding a line from a fishing rod on a reel **2.** to bring in or acquire somebody or something by using the appropriate skills or offering suitable inducements

reel off *vt* to list things in rapid succession and with no apparent effort

reel[2] /reel/ *vi* (**reeled, reel·ing, reels**) **1. STAGGER BACKWARD** to move in a sudden and uncontrolled fashion, especially backward as if struck by a blow ○ *reeled back in horror* **2. MOVE UNSTEADILY** to move unsteadily, staggering or swaying from side to side **3. FEEL GIDDY OR CONFUSED** to feel giddy or shocked and confused ○ *still reeling from the shock* **4. WHIRL AROUND AND AROUND** to move or whirl around in circles ■ *n* **STAGGERING MOTION** an unsteady or circling movement [14C. Probably < REEL[1]]

reel[3] /reel/ *n* **1.** a lively Scottish folk dance in 2/4 time for sets of two, three, or four couples **2.** same as **Virginia reel 3.** the music for a reel [Late 16C. Probably < REEL[2]] —**reel** *vi*

reel-to-reel *adj* describes magnetic tape that must be wound off a full source reel, threaded through the heads of the machine, and rewound on an empty take-up reel ■ *n* a tape recorder or player that uses reel-to-reel tape

re·en·gin·eer·ing /reè enjə neéring/ *n* **1.** a business management theory that advocates the reorganization of a business on the basis of the market value each department adds to the products produced by the business **2.** the examination and modification of an existing process or system in order to improve it —**re·en·gin·eer** *vt*

re·en·ter /ree éntər/ (**-tered, -ter·ing, -ters**), **re-en·ter** *v* **1.** *vti* **RETURN** to come back into a place again **2.** *vt* **ENTER DATA AGAIN** to key or write something in again **3.** *vti* **SIGN UP AGAIN** to decide to take part in something such as a competition again —**re·en·trance** *n*

re·en·trant /ree éntrənt/, **re-en·trant** *n* MATH same as **reentrant angle** ■ *adj* relating to a reentrant angle

re·en·trant an·gle, **re-en·trant an·gle** *n* an inward-pointing angle in a polygon that is greater than 180° when viewed or measured from inside the polygon

re·en·try /ree éntree/ (*plural* **-tries**), **re-en·try** *n* **1. ENTERING AGAIN** the act of entering again **2.** AEROSP **RETURN TO EARTH'S ATMOSPHERE** the penetration of the Earth's atmosphere by a spacecraft or missile returning from space (*often used before a noun*) ○ *a reentry vehicle* **3.** LAW **REPOSSESSION OF LAND** the repossession of land or other real-estate property under the terms of a previous agreement, e.g., where the terms of a lease have not been complied with **4.** CARDS **TAKING OF LEAD IN CARD GAME** in some card games such as bridge, the regaining of control by taking a trick, or the card played to take the trick

reeve[1] /reev/ *n* **1. DISTRICT OFFICIAL** an administrative officer in a local district or parish who usually has the responsibility of enforcing the regulations connected with a particular area of activity **2. CANADIAN TOWN COUNCIL PRESIDENT** in Ontario and some western provinces of Canada, the elected president of a town or village council **3.** HIST **REPRESENTATIVE OF KING** in Anglo-Saxon times, the representative of the monarch in a shire **4.** HIST **STEWARD OF FEUDAL MANOR** in medieval times, a steward responsible for running the everyday affairs of a feudal manor [Old English *gerēfa* "official over an assembly of soldiers" < Germanic]

reeve[2] /reev/ (**rove, reeved, reev·ing, reeves**) *vt* **1.** to thread a rope or rod through a ring or other opening **2.** to fasten a line or rope by passing it around or through some solid object [Early 17C. Origin ?]

reeve[3] /reev/ *n* a female ruff, a bird of the sandpiper family [Mid-17C. Origin ?]

re·ex·port /reè ik spáwrt, ree ék spàwrt/, **re-ex·port** *vt* (**-port·ed, -port·ing, -ports**) **EXPORT SOMETHING AFTER IMPORTING** to export goods that were previously imported from another country, especially after reprocessing them ■ *n* **1. PROCESS OF REEXPORTING** the business or process of reexporting imported goods **2. SOMETHING REEXPORTED** something that is reexported —**re·ex·por·ta·tion** /reè ek spawr táysh'n/ *n*

ref /ref/ (*informal*) *n* a sports referee ■ *vti* (**reffed, ref·fing, refs**) to referee a sport or game [Late 19C. Shortening of REFEREE]

ref. *abbr* **1.** reference **2.** referred **3.** refining **4.** reformed **5.** refunding

re·face /ree fáyss/ (**-faced, -fac·ing, -fac·es**) *vt* **1.** to restore or replace the exterior surface of a building or monument **2.** to replace the facing of a garment

re·fec·tion /ri fékshən/ *n* (*literary*) **1.** refreshment, especially in the form of food and drink **2.** a portion of food, or a light meal [14C. < Latin *refection-* "restoration" < *refect-* (see REFECTORY)]

re·fec·to·ry /ri féktəree/ (*plural* **-ries**) *n* a dining hall, especially in a monastery, convent, or college [15C. < late Latin *refectorium* "place where somebody is restored" < Latin *refect-*, past participle of *reficere* "remake" < *facere* "make"]

re·fec·to·ry ta·ble *n* a long narrow dining table with straight heavy legs

re·fer /ri fúr/ (**-ferred, -fer·ring, -fers**) *v* **1.** *vi* **MENTION** to make a comment in speech or writing that either specifically mentions somebody or something or is intended to bring somebody or something to mind ○ *referred to him by name* **2.** *vi* **GIVE DESCRIPTION** to describe somebody or something ○ *refers to her sister as "the princess"* **3.** *vi* **BE RELATED** to relate to or be connected with something ○ *This clause refers to your responsibilities as the homeowner.* **4.** *vt* **DIRECT SOMEBODY TO SOURCE OF HELP** to direct somebody to something or somebody else for information, help, treatment, or judgment ○ *referred me to a specialist* **5.** *vi* **CONSULT FOR INFORMATION** to consult a source in order to find information or assistance ○ *refer to the manual* **6.** *vt* **ATTRIBUTE SOMETHING TO CAUSE** to attribute the cause or source of something to something else ○ *They referred the high gains to the timing of their investment.* [14C. Via French < Latin *referre* "carry back" < *ferre* "carry"] —**ref·er·a·ble** /réffərəb'l, ri fúrəb'l/ *adj* —**re·fer·rer** *n*

USAGE Some people think that ***refer back*** involves redundancy, because one of the implicit meanings of *re-* is "back." But a person may ***refer*** a problem or request, for example, ***on*** to a new authority for a decision, or ***refer*** it ***back*** to the original decision-maker for reconsideration. If ***refer*** directs people to something already mentioned, for example, a text quoted, it would be better to say *In referring* [not *referring back*] *to page 321 of the book, I would like to add the following information.*

USAGE See ***allude***.

ref·e·ree /rèffə reé/ *n* **1. OFFICIAL OVERSEEING SPORT** an official who oversees the play in a sport or game, judges whether the rules are being followed, and penalizes fouls or infringements **2.** ARBITRATOR somebody not directly involved in a matter who is called in to settle disputes, make decisions, or pass judgments concerning the matter **3.** *UK* same as **reference** *v* (sense 2) **4.** LAW SOMEBODY WHO REVIEWS CASE somebody appointed by a court to review and make a report or judgment on a case ■ *vti* (**-reed, -ree·ing, -rees**) ACT AS REFEREE to act as a referee in a sport or a dispute

ref·er·ence /réffərənss/ *n* **1.** MENTION a spoken or written comment that either specifically mentions or calls attention to somebody or something or is intended to bring somebody or something to mind **2.** PROCESS OF MENTIONING the process of mentioning or alluding to somebody or something ○ *The document makes reference to three similar incidents.* **3.** HR STATEMENT OF CHARACTER AND QUALIFICATIONS a statement concerning somebody's character or qualifications, usually given to a potential employer **4.** SOMEBODY WHO RECOMMENDS ANOTHER somebody who comments on another's character and qualifications, e.g., for a job ○ *Please give the names and addresses of three references.* **5.** APPLICABILITY applicability or relevance to or connection with a particular subject or person ○ *spoke with special reference to the holiday* **6.** SOURCE OF INFORMATION a source of information, e.g., a dictionary or an encyclopedia (*often used before a noun*) ○ *a reference book* **7.** FOOTNOTE OR BIBLIOGRAPHICAL CITATION a note directing a reader's attention to another source of information **8.** PUBL same as **reference mark** **9.** IDENTIFYING CODE something, usually a set of letters or figures, that serves to identify somebody or something such as a customer, client, business letter, or a spot on a map (*often used before a noun*) ○ *a reference number* ■ *vt* (**-enced, -enc·ing, -enc·es**) **1.** COMPILE REFERENCES FOR BOOK to compile a list of references for a book, essay, or thesis **2.** USE SOMETHING AS SOURCE to use or refer to somebody or something as a source in the writing of something ○ *The author referenced some rather obscure works.*

ref·er·ence book *n* a book that is intended to be used for looking up facts, definitions, or other information

ref·er·ence mark *n* a typographical symbol used to draw the attention of a reader to a note or bibliographic entry, e.g., an asterisk or number

ref·er·en·dum /rèffə réndəm/ (*plural* **-dums** or **-da** /-də/) *n* a vote by the whole of an electorate on a specific question or questions put to it by a government or similar body [Mid-19C. < Latin, "(something) to be referred (to the Senate)," form of *referre* (see REFER)]

ref·er·ent /réffərənt/ *n* the thing or idea that a symbol, word, or phrase denotes or refers to

ref·er·en·tial /rèffə rénshəl/ *adj* **1.** relating to references or in the form of a reference **2.** describes a work of art that imitates other works or contains oblique references or homages to them, often at the expense of original content or style —**ref·er·en·ti·al·i·ty** /rèffə renshee állətee/ *n* —**ref·er·en·tial·ly** *adv*

re·fer·ral /ri fúr əl/ *n* **1.** the act or process of referring somebody or something to somebody else, especially of sending a patient to consult a medical specialist **2.** somebody or something that has been referred, especially a patient who has been sent to a medical specialist

re·ferred pain *n* pain that is felt not at its source but in another part of the body

~~referrence~~ incorrect spelling of **reference**

re·fill *vti* /ree fíl/ (**-filled, -fill·ing, -fills**) FILL AGAIN to fill a container again, or become filled again ■ *n* /reé fil/ **1.** ANOTHER FILLING OF SOMETHING a sufficient amount of something to fill a container again after it has been emptied **2.** COMM REPLACEMENT FOR CONTENTS OF CONTAINER an amount of a product packaged as a replacement for the used-up contents of a previously purchased product **3.** MED FURTHER AMOUNT OF PRESCRIBED MEDICINE a further amount of a medication prescribed on a previous occasion —**re·fill·a·ble** *adj*

re·fi·nance /ree fí nànss, reèfə nánss/ (**-nanced, -nanc·ing, -nanc·es**) *vti* to obtain new financing for something on different terms, often involving the paying off of an existing high-interest loan by means of a new lower-interest one —**re·fi·nan·cer** *n*

re·fine /ri fín/ (**-fined, -fin·ing, -fines**) *vti* **1.** REMOVE IMPURITIES to produce a purer form of something by removing the impurities from it, or become pure through such a process **2.** MAKE SOMETHING MORE EFFECTIVE to improve something through small changes that make it more effective or more subtle ○ *refining the plan* **3.** MAKE OR BECOME MORE ELEGANT to make somebody or something more cultured or elegant by eliminating less acceptable habits and tastes, or become more cultured in this way —**re·fin·a·ble** *adj* —**re·fin·er** *n*

re·fined /ri fínd/ *adj* **1.** CULTURED AND POLITE cultured and polite in habits, tastes, or appearance **2.** PURIFIED made purer by an industrial refining process **3.** SOPHISTICATED AND EFFECTIVE developed to or possessing a high degree of precision and effectiveness ○ *a refined technique*

re·fine·ment /ri fínmənt/ *n* **1.** IMPROVEMENT an addition or alteration that improves something by making it more sophisticated or effective **2.** ELEGANCE elegance, politeness, and good taste **3.** PROCESS OF REFINING the process of making something purer by industrial refining **4.** SUBTLE PRECISE POINT a subtle or precise distinction in language or point in an argument

re·fin·er·y /ri fínəree/ (*plural* **-ies**) *n* an industrial site where substances such as oil or sugar are processed and purified

re·fit *vti* /ree fít/ (**-fit·ted, -fit·ting, -fits**) to make something, especially a ship, ready for further use by repairing and reequipping it, or undergo such a process ■ *n* /reé fit, ree fít/ a thorough overhaul of something, especially a ship, in which it is repaired and reequipped

refl. *abbr* **1.** MATH reflection **2.** ANAT reflective **3.** MED reflex **4.** GRAM reflexive

re·flag /ree flág/ (**-flagged, -flag·ging, -flags**) *vt* to register a ship or plane with a different national authority

re·fla·tion /ree fláysh'n/ *n* the process of bringing an economy out of recession by increasing the amount of money in circulation within it [Mid-20C. After DEFLATION, INFLATION] —**re·flate** *vti*

re·flect /ri flékt/ (**-flect·ed, -flect·ing, -flects**) *v* **1.** *vti* SEND SOMETHING BACK to redirect something that strikes a surface, especially light, sound, or heat, usually back toward its point of origin ○ *The Moon reflects light from the Sun toward the Earth.* **2.** *vti* SHOW MIRROR IMAGE OF SOMEBODY OR SOMETHING to show a reverse image of somebody or something on a mirror or other reflective surface **3.** *vt* SHOW SOMETHING to express or be an indicator of something ○ *The election results reflect discontent among voters.* **4.** *vi* THINK SERIOUSLY to think seriously, carefully, and relatively calmly ○ *The retreat will give us time to reflect.* **5.** *vt* SAY SOMETHING TO SELF THOUGHTFULLY to have a relatively complex thought that may or may not be voiced ○ *reflected that withdrawal might be the safest option* **6.** *vti* BRING CREDIT OR DISCREDIT to bring credit, discredit, or another judgment on somebody or something ○ *an action that reflects badly on the school* [14C. Via French < Latin *reflectere* "bend back" < *flectere* "to bend"]

re·flec·tance /ri fléktənss/ *n* PHYS same as **reflectivity**

re·flect·ing tel·e·scope /ri flékting-/ *n* a telescope in which light from the object is initially focused by a concave mirror

re·flec·tion /ri flékshən/ *n* **1.** REFLECTED IMAGE the image of somebody or something that appears in a mirror or other reflecting surface **2.** ACT OF REFLECTING SOMETHING the process or act of reflecting something, especially light, sound, or heat **3.** CAREFUL THOUGHT careful thought, especially the process of reconsidering previous actions, events, or decisions **4.** CONSIDERED IDEA an idea or thought, especially one produced by careful consideration **5.** INDICATION a clear indication or result of something ○ *a reflection of your hard work* **6.** CAUSE OF BLAME OR CREDIT a cause of blame or credit to somebody or something ○ *The failure of the experiment is no reflection on you.* **7.** ANAT BENDING BACK OF STRUCTURE the bending back upon itself of a membrane or other anatomical structure **8.** MATH SYMMETRICAL TRANSFORMATION a symmetrical transformation in which a figure is reversed along an axis so that the new figure produced is a mirror image of the original one —**re·flec·tion·al** *adj*

re·flec·tive /ri fléktiv/ *adj* **1.** THOUGHTFUL characterized by deep careful thought **2.** ABLE TO REFLECT able to reflect light, sound, or other forms of energy **3.** RESULTING FROM REFLECTION produced by reflection from a surface —**re·flec·tive·ly** *adv* —**re·flec·tive·ness** *n*

re·flec·tiv·i·ty /reè flek tívvətee/ (*plural* **-ties**) *n* the ratio of the energy of a wave reflected from a surface to the energy of the incident wave. Symbol ρ

re·flec·tom·e·ter /reè flek tómmətər/ *n* an instrument used to measure the ratio of the energy of a wave after reflection to the energy of the wave before reflection

re·flec·tor /ri fléktər/ *n* **1.** an object, usually glass, plastic, or metal, that reflects light **2.** ASTRON same as **reflecting telescope**

re·flec·tor·ize /ri fléktə ríz/ (**-ized, -iz·ing, -iz·es**) *vt* **1.** to treat something, especially with chemicals, so that it reflects light **2.** to equip something with one or more reflectors

re·flet /ri fláy/ *n* a shiny or iridescent effect, especially in ceramic finishes [Mid-19C. Via French *reflet*, earlier *reflès* < Italian *riflesso* "reflection"]

re·flex /reè flèks/ *adj* **1.** AUTOMATIC AND INVOLUNTARY occurring automatically and involuntarily as a result of the nervous system's reaction to a stimulus **2.** EXTREMELY FAST very fast in reacting **3.** WITHOUT THOUGHT OR PREPARATION produced automatically, unthinkingly, and totally predictably in response to events ○ *reflex opposition* **4.** MATH OF OR OVER 180° describes an angle of between 180° and 360° **5.** BOT BENT BACK bent or folded back ○ *reflex leaves* **6.** PHYS REFLECTED involving a reflection of energy, e.g., of light or a stream of electrons ○ *reflex light* ■ *n* **1.** INVOLUNTARY BODILY REACTION an involuntary physiological reaction, e.g., a sneeze, triggered by a nerve impulse sent from a nerve center in response to a nerve receptor's reaction to a stimulus **2.** PHYS SOMETHING REFLECTED a reflected image, or a reflection of light, sound, or heat **3.** LING WORD DEVELOPED FROM EARLIER FORM a later form of a word or other linguistic element that has developed from an earlier one ■ *vti* (**-flexed, -flex·ing, -flex·es**) BEND BACK to bend back, or cause something to bend back on itself [Early 16C. < Latin *reflexus* "bent back," past participle of *reflectere* (see REFLECT)] —**re·flex·ly** *adv*

re·flex arc *n* a nerve pathway that is responsible for triggering a reflex action

re·flex cam·er·a *n* a camera with an internal mirror that reflects the actual image from the lens into the viewfinder so that the photographer can check the composition and focus exactly

re·flex·ive /ri fléksiv/ *adj* **1.** REFERRING TO PREVIOUS NOUN describes a pronoun referring to the same person or thing as another noun or pronoun in the same sentence. The reflexive pronouns in English end in "-self" or "-selves," e.g., "myself," "yourself," "ourselves." **2.** DENOTING SELF-DIRECTED ACTION describes a verb that takes a reflexive pronoun as an object, thereby indicating an action that the subject does to or for itself **3.** OF OR BY REFLEX relating to or being the product of a reflex ○ *a reflexive action in response to the explosive sound* **4.** WITHOUT THINKING automatic and involuntary or unthinking **5.** LOGIC, MATH BEING SAME describes a relation between pairs of logical objects or numbers that are the same or of the same size ■ *n* GRAM REFLEXIVE WORD a reflexive verb or pronoun —**re·flex·ive·ly** *adv* —**re·flex·ive·ness** *n*

re·flex·ol·o·gy /reè flek sóllәjee/ *n* **1.** ALTERN MED MASSAGE THERAPY a form of massage in which pressure is applied to parts of the feet and hands in order to promote relaxation and healing elsewhere in the body. See illustration on next page **2.** PHYSIOL STUDY OF REFLEXES AND BEHAVIOR the scientific study of physiological reflexes and their relation to behavior **3.** PSYCHOL BEHAVIORAL THEORY a theory that explains human behavior as complex chains of conditioned and unconditioned reflexes —**re·flex·ol·o·gist** *n*

ref·lu·ent /réffloo ənt/ *adj* flowing back (*literary*) [Late 17C. < Latin *refluent-*, present participle of *refluere* "flow back" < *fluere* "to flow"]

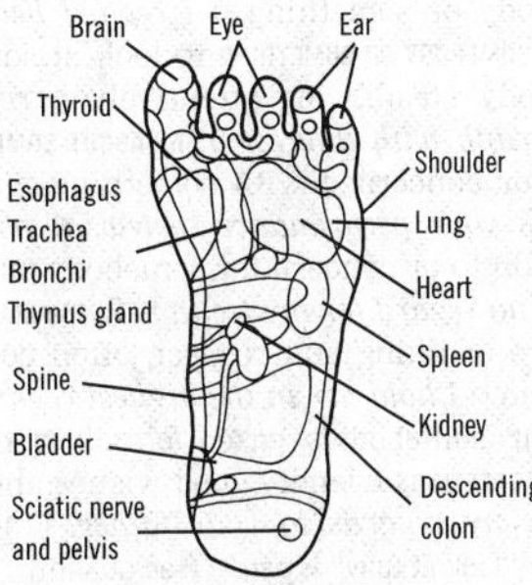

reflexology

re·flux /reé flùks/ *n* **1. BACKWARD FLOW** a returning flow of something **2.** MED **REGURGITATION OF STOMACH FLUID** a backflow of liquid in the opposite direction to its normal movement, e.g., the regurgitation of stomach and peptic juices associated with acid indigestion and hiatal hernia **3.** PHYS **HEATING WHILE CONDENSING VAPOR** a method of heating liquid so that escaping vapor is condensed and returned to the liquid ■ *vt* (**-fluxed, -flux·ing, -flux·es**) PHYS **HEAT SOMETHING WHILE CONDENSING VAPOR** to heat a liquid in a container with a condenser that catches and returns escaping vapor

re·fo·cus /ree fṓkəss/ (**-cused** or **-cussed, -cus·ing** or **-cus·sing, -cus·es** or **-cus·ses**) *vti* **1.** to change or adjust the focus of something such as a camera or telescope **2.** to concentrate attention or efforts on something different ○ *Let's refocus our discussion.*

re·for·est /ree fáwrəst/ (**-est·ed, -est·ing, -ests**) *vti* to replant an area with trees after its original trees have been cut down —**re·for·es·ta·tion** /ree fàwrə stáysh'n/ *n*

re·form /ri fáwrm/ *v* (**-formed, -form·ing, -forms**) **1.** *vt* **IMPROVE SOMETHING BY REMOVING FAULTS** to change and improve something by correcting faults, removing inconsistencies and abuses, and imposing modern methods or values **2.** *vti* **GET RID OF UNACCEPTABLE HABITS** to adopt a more acceptable way of life and mode of behavior, or persuade or force somebody else to do so **3.** *vt* INDUST **CHANGE MOLECULAR STRUCTURE OF PETROLEUM** to subject petroleum to a chemical process such as catalytic cracking, in order to convert it into gasoline ■ *n* **1. REORGANIZATION AND IMPROVEMENT** the reorganization and improvement of something such as a political institution or system that is considered to be faulty, ineffective, or unjust ○ *electoral reform* ○ *the reform candidate* **2. IMPROVING CHANGE** a change and improvement, especially in the social or political sphere ○ *reforms designed to prevent fraud* **3. CHARACTER IMPROVEMENT** the adoption by somebody of a more acceptable way of life and mode of behavior [14C. Directly or via French < Latin *reformare* "form again" < *forma* "form"] —**re·form·a·ble** *adj* —**re·for·ma·tive** *adj*

Re·form *adj* relating or belonging to Reform Judaism ■ *n* JUDAISM same as **Reform Judaism**

re-form /ree fáwrm/ *vti* to return to a previous form, or cause something to return to a previous form

ref·or·ma·tion /rèffər máysh'n/ *n* **1.** the act or process of reforming somebody or something **2.** a reformed state, especially a general improvement in somebody's behavior [15C. Directly or via French < Latin *reformation* < past participle of *reformare* (see REFORM)] —**ref·or·ma·tion·al** *adj*

Ref·or·ma·tion *n* the 16th-century religious movement in Europe that set out to reform some of the doctrines and practices of the Roman Catholic Church and resulted in the development of Protestantism

re-f·or·ma·tion *n* the process or result of returning to a previous form

re·for·ma·to·ry /ri fáwrmə tàwree/ *n* (*plural* **-ries**) a penal institution for young offenders ■ *adj* intended for the reform of somebody or something (*formal*) [Late 16C. < REFORMATION]

re·formed /ri fáwrmd/ *adj* **1.** improved by the removal of outdated, ineffective, or unjust qualities **2.** no longer behaving in an unacceptable way

Re·formed *adj* relating or belonging to a Protestant Church, especially one based on the teachings of John Calvin rather than those of Martin Luther

re·form·er /ri fáwrmər/ *n* a person or movement that reforms or tries to reform others

Re·form·er *n* an active participant in the Reformation

re·form·ism /ri fáwr mìzzəm/ *n* a philosophy or movement that advocates the reform of an existing institution

re·form·ist /ri fáwrmist/ *adj* advocating reform to an existing institution ■ *n* somebody who advocates reform

Re·form Ju·da·ism *n* the branch of Judaism that seeks to adapt religious practice to modern times and rejects the belief that Moses was literally given the Torah by God

re·form school *n* CRIME same as **reformatory**

re·fract /ri frákt/ (**-fract·ed, -fract·ing, -fracts**) *vt* **1.** PHYS **ALTER COURSE OF WAVE OF ENERGY** to alter the course of a wave of energy that passes into something from another medium, as water does to light entering it from the air **2.** OPHTHALMOL **MEASURE REFRACTION IN SOMETHING** to measure the degree of refraction in a lens or eye **3. SHOW SOMETHING DIFFERENTLY** to alter the appearance of something by viewing or showing it through a different medium [Early 17C. < Latin *refract-*, past participle of *refringere* "break off, break back" < *frangere* "to break"]

re·fract·ing tel·e·scope *n* a telescope in which a lens receives and focuses light that is then viewed through a second, magnifying lens in the eyepiece

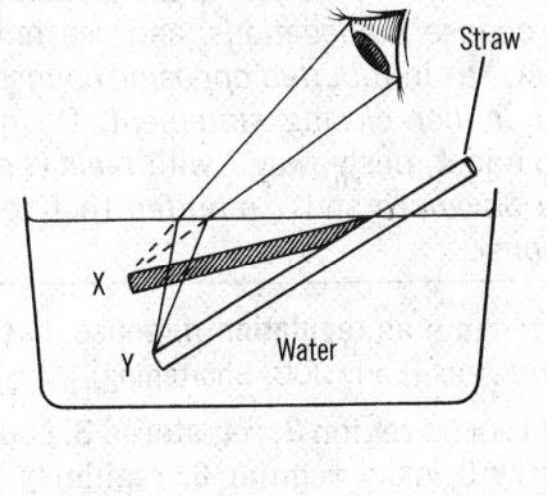

refraction

re·frac·tion /ri fráksh'n/ *n* **1.** PHYS **CHANGE OF DIRECTION OF WAVE** the change in direction that occurs when a wave of energy such as light passes from one medium to another of a different density, e.g., from air to water **2.** PHYS **DEGREE OF WAVE REDIRECTION** the degree to which a wave of energy is refracted **3.** ASTRON **DISTORTION OF POSITION OF ASTRONOMICAL OBJECT** the degree to which the apparent position of an astronomical object is distorted by the redirection of its light as it passes through the Earth's atmosphere **4.** OPHTHALMOL **ABILITY OF EYE TO BEND LIGHT** the ability of the eye to change the direction of light in order to focus it on the retina **5.** OPHTHALMOL **MEASURING OF REFRACTIVE CAPACITY OF EYE** the process of measuring the eye's ability to refract light —**re·frac·tion·al** *adj*

re·frac·tive /ri fráktiv/ *adj* relating to, involving, or capable of refraction —**re·frac·tive·ly** *adv*

re·frac·tive in·dex *n Can, UK* same as **index of refraction**

re·frac·tom·e·ter /reè frak tómmətər/ *n* an instrument that measures the index of refraction of a medium —**re·frac·to·met·ric** /ri fràktə méttrik/ *adj*

re·frac·tor /ri fráktər/ *n* **1.** ASTRON same as **refracting telescope 2.** a device that alters the direction of a beam of light by passing it between two transparent materials of different density

re·frac·to·ry /ri fráktəree/ *adj* **1. UNCONTROLLABLE** stubborn, rebellious, and uncontrollable **2.** PHYS, INDUST **HEAT-RESISTANT** resistant to high temperatures and therefore not easily melted or worked **3.** MED **NOT RESPONSIVE TO TREATMENT** unresponsive to medical treatment ○ *a refractory infection* **4.** MED **DISEASE-RESISTANT** resistant to infection or disease **5.** PHYSIOL **UNRESPONSIVE TO STIMULUS** not able to respond to a stimulus ○ *a refractory nerve* ■ *n* INDUST, PHYS **HIGHLY HEAT-RESISTANT MATERIAL** a material that is able to withstand high temperatures without melting, e.g., the fire clay used to line furnaces [Early 17C. Variant of *refractary* < Latin *refractarius* "stubborn" < *refract-* (see REFRACT)] —**re·frac·to·ri·ness** *n*

re·frac·to·ry pe·ri·od *n* the time after receiving a stimulus during which a nerve or muscle cell cannot respond to further stimuli

re·frain[1] /ri fráyn/ (**-frained, -frain·ing, -frains**) *vi* to avoid doing something or hold yourself back from doing something [14C. Via French < Latin *refrenare* "hold back, curb" < *frenum* "bridle"] —**re·frain·ment** *n*

re·frain[2] /ri fráyn/ *n* **1. RECURRING PIECE OF VERSE** a line or group of lines that recurs at regular intervals in a poem, especially at the ends of verses **2. CHORUS** the chorus in a song, or the music that accompanies it **3. MELODY** a melody or tune **4. SOMETHING REPEATED OFTEN** something that is frequently repeated, e.g., a saying or an idea [14C. < Old French, past participle of *refraindre* "repeat" < assumed Vulgar Latin *refrangere*, alteration of Latin *refringere* (see REFRACT)]

re·fran·gi·ble /ri fránjəb'l/ *adj* able to be refracted [Late 17C. < modern Latin *refrangibilis* < *refrangere*, alteration of Latin *refringere* (see REFRACT)] —**re·fran·gi·bil·i·ty** /ri frànjə bíllətee/ *n*

~~**refrence**~~ incorrect spelling of **reference**

re·fres·co /ri fréskō/ (*plural* **-cos**) *n Hispanic* a cold soft drink [< Spanish < *refrescar* "to refresh"]

re·fresh /ri frésh/ (**-freshed, -fresh·ing, -fresh·es**) *v* **1.** *vt* **RENEW SOMEBODY'S ENERGY** to make somebody feel more energetic, especially with rest, food, or drink ○ *feel refreshed after a nap* **2.** *vt* **REACTIVATE MEMORY** to prompt or reactivate the memory with a piece of information ○ *Just refresh my memory.* **3.** *vt* **REPLENISH SOMETHING** to replenish the supplies of something ○ *Can I refresh your drink?* **4.** *vt* COMPUT **UPDATE ELECTRONIC DEVICE WITH DATA** to update an electronic device, especially a visual display unit or active memory chip, with data **5.** *vti* COMPUT **UPDATE INFORMATION** to update the information on a website, or to be updated ○ *This page refreshes every two minutes.* [14C. < Old French *refreschir* "make fresh again" < *freis* "fresh"]

re·fresh·en /ri frésh'n/ (**-ened, -en·ing, -ens**) *vti* to become fresh again, or make something fresh again

re·fresh·er /ri fréshər/ *n* something that refreshes

re·fresh·er course *n* a course of instruction designed to bring somebody's knowledge and skills up-to-date

re·fresh·ing /ri fréshing/ *adj* **1.** serving to restore energy and vitality **2.** pleasingly different and exciting —**re·fresh·ing·ly** *adv*

re·fresh·ment /ri fréshmənt/ *n* **1. SOMETHING REFRESHING** something that refreshes, especially food and drink **2. ACT OF REFRESHING** the process of refreshing somebody or something, or a refreshing quality in something ■ **re·fresh·ments** *npl* **SOMETHING TO EAT AND DRINK** something to eat and drink, usually snacks or a light meal and drinks

re·fresh rate *n* the number of times per second that an image displayed on a screen needs to be regenerated to prevent flicker when viewed by the human eye. The refresh rate is dependent upon the persistence of the material used on the screen and the retina's retentivity.

~~**refridgerator**~~ incorrect spelling of **refrigerator**

re·fried beans /reé frīd-/ *npl* in Mexican and Tex-Mex cuisine, beans cooked with spices, mashed, then fried

re·frig·er·ant /ri fríjjərənt/ *n* **1. COOLING SUBSTANCE** a substance used to cool or freeze something, especially the liquid that circulates in a refrigerator **2.** MED **FEVER-REDUCING MEDICATION** a medication that alleviates fever or reduces body heat ■ *adj* **1. COOLING** having a cooling or freezing effect **2.** MED **REDUCING BODY HEAT** reducing fever or body heat [Late 16C. < Latin *refrigerant-*, present participle of *refrigerare* (see REFRIGERATE)]

re·frig·er·ate /ri fríjjə ràyt/ (**-at·ed, -at·ing, -ates**) *vt* to cool food or other heat-sensitive products to prevent deterioration in quality [Mid-16C. < Latin *refrigerare*, "chill again, cool" < *friger-*, obsolete stem of *frigus* "cold"] —**re·frig·er·a·tion** /-frìjjə ráysh'n/ *n* —**re·frig·er·a·tive** *adj*

re·frig·er·at·ed /ri fríjjə ràytəd/ *adj* **1.** describes a vehicle or container designed to keep its contents or cargo at a low temperature in order to preserve them **2.** kept or preserved at a low temperature in a refrigerator

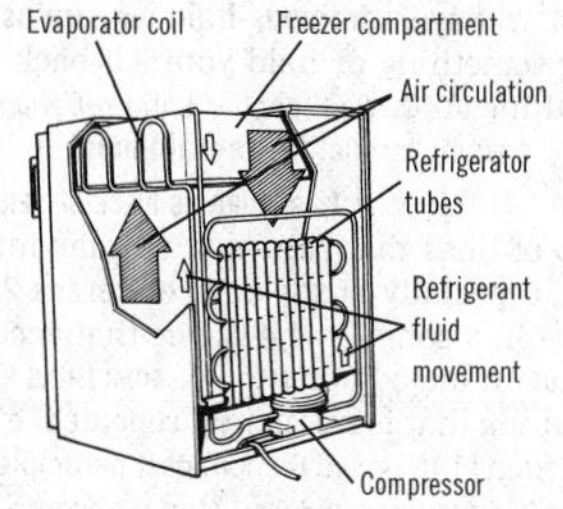

refrigerator: cross section of a refrigerator

re·frig·er·a·tor /ri fríjjə ràytər/ *n* an electrical appliance in the form of an insulated cabinet that keeps items cool through artificial means, or an insulated walk-in chamber artificially cooled for this purpose

re·frin·gent /rə frínjənt/ *adj* PHYS same as **refractive** [Late 18C. < Latin *refringent-*, present participle of *refringere* (see REFRACT)] —**re·frin·gence** *n*

reft past participle, past tense of **reave**

re·fu·el /ree fyóo əl/ (**-eled, -el·ing, -els**) *vti* **1.** to refill a vehicle's tank with fuel **2.** to provide additional material for or give a renewed impetus to something

ref·uge /ré fyooj/ *n* **1.** a sheltered or protected state safe from something threatening, harmful, or unpleasant **2.** a place, or sometimes a person, offering protection or safe shelter from something [14C. Via French < Latin *refugium* "place to flee back to" < *fugere* "flee"]

ref·u·gee /rèffyə jée/ *n* somebody who seeks or takes refuge in a foreign country, especially to avoid war or persecution (*often used before a noun*) [Late 17C. < French *réfugié*, past participle of *réfugier* "take refuge" < *refuge* (see REFUGE); assimilated to -EE]

re·fu·gi·um /ri fyóojee əm/ (*plural* **-gi·a** /-jee ə/) *n* an area whose climate remains habitable, especially for rare or endangered species, when that of the surrounding areas has changed [Mid-20C. < Latin (see REFUGE)]

re·ful·gent /ri fúljənt/ *adj* shining brilliantly or splendidly (*formal*) [Early 16C. < Latin *refulgent-*, present participle of *refulgere* "shine back, reflect" < *fulgere* "shine, flash"] —**re·ful·gence** *n* —**re·ful·gent·ly** *adv*

re·fund *vt* /ri fúnd, rée fùnd/ (**-fund·ed, -fund·ing, -funds**) RETURN MONEY TO SOMEBODY to return money to somebody, usually because he or she paid too much or did not receive what was paid for ■ *n* /rée fùnd/ **1.** RETURNED MONEY an amount of money that is returned to somebody **2.** PROCESS OF REPAYMENT the act or process of returning money [14C. Via Old French *refunder* < Latin *refundere* "pour back" < *fundere* "pour"] —**re·fund·er** *n* —**re·fund·a·ble** *adj*

re-fund /ree fúnd/ *vt* **1.** FUND SOMETHING ANEW to fund something again **2.** FIN BORROW TO REPAY DEBT to pay off a debt with new borrowing **3.** FIN REPLACE BOND ISSUE WITH NEW ISSUE to replace an existing issue of bonds with a new issue [Mid-19C. < RE- + FUND]

re·fur·bish /ree fúrbish/ (**-bished, -bish·ing, -bish·es**) *vt* to bring something back to a cleaner, brighter, or more functional state —**re·fur·bish·er** *n* —**re·fur·bish·ment** *n*

re·fus·al /ri fyóoz'l/ *n* **1.** a declaration or an attitude of unwillingness to do or accept something **2.** the chance to accept or reject something before it is offered to others

re·fuse[1] /ri fyóoz/ (**-fused, -fus·ing, -fus·es**) *v* **1.** *vti* INDICATE UNWILLINGNESS to declare a decision or intention not to do something **2.** *vt* NOT ACCEPT SOMETHING to decline to accept something offered ○ *refused the promotion* **3.** *vt* DENY SOMETHING to be unwilling to give, allow, or agree to something asked for by somebody ○ *I refused them the use of my tools.* **4.** *vti* RIDING BALK AT JUMP to stop and not jump over an obstacle (*refers to horses*) [14C. Via Old French *refuser* < assumed Vulgar Latin *refusare*, perhaps blend of Latin *recusare* "to refuse" + *refutare* "to repel"] —**re·fus·a·ble** *adj* —**re·fus·er** *n*

ref·use[2] /ré fyooss/ *n* things thrown away as being of no value or use, especially household garbage [14C. < Old French *refus*, literally "refusal" < *refuser* (see REFUSE[1])]

re·fuse·nik /ri fyóoznik/ *n* **1.** a citizen of the former Soviet Union, especially a Jew, who was not allowed by the government to emigrate **2.** somebody who refuses to agree to, take part in, or cooperate with something, especially out of principle (*informal*)

re·fute /ri fyóot/ (**-fut·ed, -fut·ing, -futes**) *vt* **1.** to prove something to be false or somebody to be in error, either through logical argument or by providing evidence to the contrary **2.** to deny an allegation or contradict a statement without disproving it ○ *military planners who tried to refute allegations of poor strategy by showing bomb-damage footage* [Early 16C. < Latin *refutare* "drive back, rebut" < *-futare* "to beat"] —**re·fut·a·bil·i·ty** /ri fyòotə bílləteе, rèffyətə-/ *n* —**re·fut·a·ble** /ri fyóotəb'l, réffyətəb'l/ *adj* —**re·fut·a·bly** *adv* —**ref·u·ta·tion** /rèffyə táysh'n/ *n*

USAGE refute, rebut, or **rebuff**? The core meaning of ***refute*** is "to prove incorrect," though a more general sense "to deny" has developed and is now widely established. It is completely acceptable to use ***refute*** and ***rebut*** interchangeably in the sense "to contradict or deny the truth of something," as in *a spokesperson who refuted/rebutted all allegations of impropriety.* Nonetheless, if you want to emphasize the idea of proving wrongness as opposed to mere denial or contradiction, then use ***refute***, as in *used unimpeachable facts to refute opposing counsel's allegations,* and use ***rebut*** to mean "contradict," as in *rebutted opposing counsel's opening statement in her closing statement.* Do not confuse ***rebuff*** ("to reject, push away") with ***rebut*** (*I rebuffed his unwanted advances* and *I rebuffed* [not *rebutted*] *his protestations*).

reg /reg/ *n* same as **regulation** *n* (sense 1) (*informal*) ○ *rules and regs* [Early 20C. Shortening]

reg. *abbr* **1.** GEOG region **2.** registered **3.** EDUC registrar **4.** registry **5.** GRAM regular **6.** regularly **7.** GENETICS regulation **8.** ENG regulator

Reg. *abbr* **1.** Regent **2.** Regina

re·gain /ri gáyn, ree-/ (**-gained, -gain·ing, -gains**) *vt* **1.** to recover something after losing it **2.** to reach a place again ○ *She regained her seat and sat down.* —**re·gain·er** *n*

re·gal /rééɡ'l/ *adj* characteristic of or suitable for a king or queen, especially in grandeur or magnificence [14C. Via < French < Latin *regalis* < *reg-* "king"] —**re·gal·i·ty** /ree gállətee/ *n* —**re·gal·ly** *adv*

re·gale /ri gáyl/ (**-galed, -gal·ing, -gales**) *vt* **1.** to entertain or amuse somebody, especially by telling stories ○ *regaled us with stories from the early days* **2.** to give somebody plenty of good things to eat and drink [Mid-17C. < French *régaler* "entertain," literally "give pleasure again" < Old French *gale* "merriment, pleasure"]

re·ga·lia /ri gáylyə/ *n* (*takes a singular or plural verb*) **1.** ROYAL INSIGNIA the ceremonial and symbolic objects and clothing used and worn by royalty or other holders of high office on formal occasions **2.** DISTINCTIVE CLOTHING the distinctive clothing or trappings showing the status of a group of people, worn especially on formal occasions **3.** SPLENDID ATTIRE splendid attire for a formal occasion ○ *The general appeared in full regalia.* [Mid-16C. < medieval Latin *regalia* "royal privileges, royal residence," form of Latin *regalis* (see REGAL)]

re·gard /ri gaárd/ *vt* (**-gard·ed, -gard·ing, -gards**) **1.** CONSIDER SOMEBODY OR SOMETHING to think of somebody or something as having a particular nature or quality or a particular role or function ○ *I regard his gift as an apology.* **2.** HAVE FEELINGS IN RELATION TO SOMETHING to have a particular feeling toward somebody or something ○ *At first they regarded the idea of early retirement with horror.* **3.** JUDGE SOMEBODY OR SOMETHING to have an opinion as to the quality or worth of somebody or something ○ *I regard her highly.* **4.** LOOK AT SOMEBODY OR SOMETHING to look at something or somebody steadily or attentively ○ *regarded the photograph with interest* **5.** BE ABOUT SOMETHING to be about or concerned with something ○ *This memo regards your performance review.* ■ *n* **1.** ATTENTION attention to or concern for somebody or something ○ *with no regard for my feelings* **2.** FAVORABLE OPINION a mixture of liking and respect, often coupled with affection ○ *I hold her in the highest regard.* **3.** GAZE a look, or somebody's gaze (*formal*) ■ **re·gards** *npl* FRIENDLY GREETINGS friendly good wishes and greetings ○ *Give my regards to your father.* [14C. < French *regarder* "look at fully" < *garder* (see GUARD)] ◇ **as regards** as far as somebody or something is concerned ◇ **in this** *or* **that regard** as far as this or that is concerned, or from this or that point of view (*formal*)

SYNONYMS ***regard, admiration, esteem, favor, respect, reverence, veneration***

CORE MEANING: appreciation of the worth of somebody or something

regard a mixture of liking and respect, often coupled with affection ○ *He is held in high regard by customers and colleagues alike.* ○ *She has little regard for other people's property.* **admiration** warm approval and appreciation of somebody or something ○ *The garden was so beautiful that Joanna gasped in admiration.* ○ *All the people who took part were very brave and I have nothing but admiration for them all.* **esteem** a high opinion and appreciation of somebody or something ○ *One of the reasons why teachers have fallen in public esteem is that the public have lost confidence in teaching methods.* ○ *Intelligence testing was held in high esteem fifty years ago, but has since gone out of fashion.* **favor** an approving, friendly, or supportive attitude ○ *struggles between board members competing for the chairman's favor* ○ *The proposals have not found favor with the public.* **respect** a feeling or attitude of admiration and deference toward somebody or something ○ *She obviously has the highest respect for her father.* ○ *Their customs and beliefs must be treated with respect.* **reverence** feelings of deep respect or devotion ○ *The prince was accustomed to being listened to with reverence.* ○ *A crucifix hangs on every classroom wall to help instill reverence for God.* **veneration** feelings of deep respect or awe ○ *A player of great distinction, he was regarded with veneration by his fellow guitarists.* ○ *My childhood experiences gave me a lasting veneration for long-established custom and ritual.*

re·gar·dant /ri gaárd'nt/ *adj* describes a heraldic figure that is looking backward over its shoulder ○ *three lions regardant* [15C. < French, present participle of *regarder* (see REGARD)]

re·gard·ful /ri gaárdfəl/ *adj* **1.** paying due attention **2.** full of esteem and often deferential respect for somebody —**re·gard·ful·ly** *adv* —**re·gard·ful·ness** *n*

re·gard·ing /ri gaárding/ *prep* about or on the subject of ○ *I'd like a word with you regarding the schedule.*

re·gard·less /ri gaárdləss/ *adv* in spite of or ignoring setbacks, hindrances, or problems ■ *adj* paying no attention, especially failing to pay proper attention —**re·gard·less·ly** *adv* —**re·gard·less·ness** *n*

USAGE See ***irregardless.***

re·gard·less of *prep* **1.** in spite of ○ *Regardless of what you were told, I cannot help you.* **2.** no matter what or taking no account of ○ *We're going on vacation regardless of the weather.*

re·gat·ta /ri gaátə, -gáttə/ *n* a sports event consisting of a series of boat or yacht races [Mid-17C. < (Venetian) Italian, "gondola race (on the Grand Canal)," originally "contest for mastery" from *regattare* "compete"]

regd. *abbr* registered

re·ge·la·tion /rèejə láysh'n/ *n* **1.** the process by which water melted by pressure beneath a glacier is refrozen **2.** reduction of the freezing point of water by force of pressure

re·gen·cy /réejənssee/ (*plural* **-cies**) *n* **1.** a group of people ruling on behalf of a monarch who is unable to rule because of youth, illness, or absence **2.** the authority and responsibilities or period in office of a regent

Re·gen·cy *n* **1. 1811–20 IN GREAT BRITAIN** the period from 1811–20 in Great Britain during which George, Prince of Wales, ruled as regent for his father King George III **2. 1715–23 IN FRANCE** the period from 1715–23 in France during which Philip, Duke of Orleans, ruled as regent on behalf of King Louis XV ■ *adj* **IN STYLE OF REGENCY** in the style prevalent and fashionable during either of the Regency periods

re·gen·er·ate *v* /ri jénnə ràyt/ (**-at·ed, -at·ing, -ates**) **1.** *vti* **FORM AGAIN** to form again, or become formed again **2.** *vti* **RECOVER FROM DECLINE** to return from a state of decline to a revitalized state, or cause something to do this **3.** *vti* BIOL **REPLACE BODY PART BY NEW GROWTH** to replace lost tissue or a lost limb or organ with a new growth, or grow again after loss **4.** *vt* RELIG **RESTORE SOMEBODY SPIRITUALLY** to restore and renew somebody morally or spiritually **5.** *vt* ELECTRONICS **RESTORE SIGNALS TO ORIGINAL WAVE SHAPE** to restore digital electrical signals to their original wave shape after transmission over long distances ■ *n* /-jénnərət/ **1. SOMEBODY SPIRITUALLY REFORMED** somebody who is spiritually reborn or renewed **2.** BIOL **REPLACEMENT TISSUE** tissue that has grown to replace lost tissue, or a regenerated part, organ, or organism ■ *adj* /-jénnərət/ **1. SPIRITUALLY REBORN OR RENEWED** spiritually reborn, renewed, or restored to health **2.** BIOL **NEWLY FORMED OR GROWN** newly formed or grown as a replacement for something lost —**re·gen·er·a·ble** *adj* —**re·gen·er·ate·ly** *adv* —**re·gen·er·a·cy** *n* —**re·gen·er·a·tion** /ri jènnə ráysh'n/ *n* —**re·gen·er·a·tive** /ri jénnə ràytiv, -rətiv/ *adj* —**re·gen·er·a·tive·ly** *adv* —**re·gen·er·a·tor** *n*

re·gen·er·a·tive med·i·cine *n* the branch of medicine that deals with repairing or replacing tissues and organs by using advanced materials and methodologies such as cloning

Re·gens·burg /ráygənz bùrg, ráygənss bòork/ city in Bavaria, southeastern Germany, on the Danube River, about 65 mi./105 km northeast of Munich. Population: 125,608 (1997).

re·gent /reéjənt/ *n* **1. SUBSTITUTE FOR MONARCH** somebody who rules on behalf of a monarch who is unable to rule because of youth, illness, or absence **2. UNIVERSITY OFFICIAL** an officer of a university, especially a member of the governing board ■ *adj* **ACTING AS REGENT** ruling as a regent ○ *the prince regent* [14C. Via French < Latin *regent-*, present participle of *regere* "rule"] —**re·gent·al** *adj*

ORIGIN The Latin word *regere* "to rule," from which ***regent*** is derived, is also the source of the English words *correct, erect, escort, realm, rector, regime, regiment,* and *region.*

reg·gae /ré gày/ *n* popular music, originally from Jamaica, that combines rock, calypso, and soul and is characterized by heavy accentuation of the second and fourth beats of a four-beat bar (*often used before a noun*) ○ *a reggae beat* [Mid-20C. Perhaps < Jamaican English *reggay*, alteration of *rege* "ragged fellow" < RAG[1]]

Reg·gio di Ca·la·bri·a /réjjee ō dee kə laábree ə/ city and administrative center of Reggio di Calabria Province in Calabria Region, southern Italy. Population: 180,353 (2001).

Reg·gio nell'E·mi·lia /réjjee ō nel e meélyə/ capital city of Reggio nell'Emilia Province in Emilia Romagna Region, northern Italy. Population: 141,877 (2001).

reg·i·cide /réjji sīd/ *n* **1.** the killing of a king **2.** somebody who kills a king [Mid-16C. < Latin *reg-* "king"] —**reg·i·ci·dal** /rèjji sīd'l/ *adj*

re·gime /ray zheém, ri-/, **ré·gime** *n* **1. FORM OF GOVERNMENT** a system or style of government **2. PARTICULAR GOVERNMENT** the government of a particular country, especially one that is considered to be oppressive **3. CONTROLLING GROUP** any controlling or managing group, or the system of control and management adopted by it **4. ESTABLISHED SYSTEM** an established system or way of doing things **5. CHARACTERISTIC CONDITIONS FOR PROCESS** the characteristic conditions under which a natural, scientific, or industrial process occurs **6.** MED same as **regimen** (sense 1) [15C. Via French < Latin *regimen* (see REGIMEN)]

re·gime change *n* **1.** the forcible overthrow of another nation's government by outside intervention, especially when the targeted nation is regarded as politically unstable (*used euphemistically*) **2.** a change in leadership, e.g., of a country or political party

reg·i·men /réjjəmən, -mèn/ *n* **1.** a prescribed or recommended program of medication, diet, exercise, or other measures intended to improve health or fitness, or stabilize a medical condition **2.** a government or form of government (*archaic*) **3.** INDUST, SCI same as **regime** (sense 5) [14C. < Latin *regimen* "rule, government" < *regere* "to rule"]

reg·i·ment *n* /réjjəmənt/ **1. ARMY UNIT** a permanent military unit usually consisting of two or three battalions of ground troops divided into smaller companies or troops under the command of a colonel **2. LARGE NUMBER OF PEOPLE OR THINGS** a large number of people or things, especially an orderly group **3. GOVERNMENTAL RULE** governmental rule or administration (*archaic*) ■ *vt* /réjjə mènt/ (**-ment·ed, -ment·ing, -ments**) **1. CONTROL SOMEBODY OR SOMETHING STRICTLY** to impose strict control or discipline on somebody or something, often to the extent of stifling flexibility, individuality, or imagination **2. GROUP SOMETHING SYSTEMATICALLY** to organize something systematically into groups **3. GROUP SOLDIERS INTO REGIMENTS** to form regiments out of a group of soldiers [14C. Via French < late Latin *regimentum* < Latin *regere* "to rule"] —**reg·i·men·tal** /rèjjə mént'l/ *adj* —**reg·i·men·tal·ly** *adv* —**reg·i·ment·ed** /réjji mèntəd/ *adj*

reg·i·men·tals /rèjjə mént'lz, réjjə ment'lz/ *npl* **1.** the uniform and insignia worn by the members of a particular regiment **2.** military dress and insignia, especially as worn for ceremonial occasions

reg·i·men·ta·tion /rèjjəmən táysh'n/ *n* the act of placing somebody or something under strict and inflexible organization or control, or the condition of being very strictly organized and controlled ○ *They are individuals and do not respond well to regimentation.*

Re·gi·na /ri jīnə/ capital city of Saskatchewan Province, Canada. Population: 178,225 (2001).

re·gion /reéjən/ *n* **1. AREA OF LAND** a large land area that has geographic, political, or cultural characteristics that distinguish it from others, whether existing within one country or extending over several **2. ADMINISTRATIVE UNIT** a large separate political or administrative unit within a country **3. ECOLOGICAL AREA** an area of the world with particular animal and plant life **4. LARGE INDEFINITE AREA** any large indefinite area of a surface **5. AREA OR ASPECT** an imprecisely defined area or part of something such as a sphere of activity **6. RANGE WITHIN WHICH FIGURE FALLS** the range within which something such as a figure, sum, or price might fall ○ *in the region of $1,000* **7.** ANAT **AREA OF BODY** an area of the body, usually an area surrounding a particular organ or part [14C. Via French < Latin *region-* "boundary, district," literally "area that is ruled" < *regere* "to rule"]

re·gion·al /reéjən'l/ *adj* **1. RELATING TO REGION** belonging to or characteristic of a geographic region **2. CONNECTED WITH ADMINISTRATIVE REGION** serving or connected with one of the administrative regions of a country ○ *a regional authority* **3. CHARACTERISTIC OF AREA** characteristic of or limited to an area of a country, especially typical of the speech and usage of a particular area and different from standard speech and usage ○ *a regional accent* —**re·gion·al·ly** *adv*

re·gion·al·ism /reéjən'l ìzzəm/ *n* **1. DIVISION INTO ADMINISTRATIVE AREAS** the policy of dividing a political territory into areas with separate administrations, or support for such a policy **2. LOYALTY TO HOME REGION** loyalty to or prejudice in favor of a region **3.** LING **LINGUISTIC FEATURE RESTRICTED TO ONE AREA** a linguistic feature, e.g., a word, pronunciation, or expression, that is found only in a particular region —**re·gion·al·ist** *n, adj*

re·gion·al·ize /reéjən'l īz/ (**-ized, -iz·ing, -iz·es**) *vt* **1.** to divide an area into administrative regions **2.** to allocate something to regional administrations —**re·gion·al·i·za·tion** /reéjən'li záysh'n/ *n*

ré·gis·seur /ràyzhee súr, rèzhee sőr/ *n* a director who is responsible for staging a theatrical work, especially a ballet [Early 19C. < French, "agent, manager" < *régir* "manage, rule" < Latin *regere*]

reg·is·ter /réjjistər/ *n* **1. OFFICIAL LIST** an official record, often in the form of a list **2. BOOK FOR OFFICIAL RECORDS** a book in which a register of names, attendance, or events is kept **3. ITEM IN OFFICIAL LIST** an item recorded in an official register **4. MEASURING DEVICE THAT RECORDS** a device that automatically records numbers, degrees, or quantities **5.** COMM same as **cash register** **6. CORRECT ALIGNMENT** correct alignment or positioning with respect to something else **7. HEATING GRATE** a closable grill or grate through which warm or cool air is forced in a household heating system **8.** COMPUT **COMPUTER MEMORY LOCATION** a memory location in a processor or microprocessor that has a particular storage capacity, is usually intended for a particular purpose, and is accessible at very high speeds **9.** MUSIC **MUSICAL RANGE** the range of a voice or instrument, or a part of this range **10.** MUSIC **ORGAN STOP** one of a group of organ stops that are similar in tonal quality **11.** LING **SITUATION-SPECIFIC LANGUAGE VARIETY** language of a type that is appropriate to a social situation or used for communicating with a particular set of people ○ *The word is informal in register.* ■ *v* (**-tered, -ter·ing, -ters**) **1.** *vti* **WRITE SOMETHING IN REGISTER** to enter something in a register, or have something entered there by an official ○ *They registered at the hotel.* **2.** *vti* **ENROLL** to record your name with an organization, e.g., to enroll for an academic course or fulfill a legal requirement ○ *register for the course in September* **3.** *vt* **MAKE RECORD OF SOMETHING** to make a record of something, or have something recorded ○ *I want to register a complaint with the manager.* **4.** *vt* **SHOW SOMETHING AS MEASUREMENT** to indicate or record a measurement on a device or scale **5.** *vti* **DISPLAY FEELING OR THOUGHT** to be visible in somebody's facial expression or body language, or to display something in this way ○ *registered her disapproval* **6.** *vt* **NOTE SOMETHING MENTALLY** to make a mental note of something ○ *I registered the time before moving on.* **7.** *vi* **BE UNDERSTOOD** to be understood or remembered by somebody ○ *The implications finally registered with me.* **8.** *vt* **ACHIEVE SOMETHING** to achieve or accomplish something ○ *The team registered several notable successes last season.* **9.** *vt* **SEND SOMETHING BY REGISTERED MAIL** to send a letter or package using a mail system that guarantees compensation if the item is lost **10.** *vi* **BE ALIGNED** to be correctly aligned [14C. Via < French < medieval Latin *registrum*, alteration of late Latin *regesta* "list," literally "things collected or brought back" < Latin *gerere* "bring"] —**reg·is·tered** *adj* —**reg·is·ter·er** *n* —**reg·is·tra·ble** *adj* —**reg·is·trant** *n*

reg·is·tered gen·er·al nurse /rèjjistərd-/ *n UK* a nurse who is qualified to practice, having undergone a three-year course of study and clinical training attached to a university

reg·is·tered mail *n* a service provided by post offices to ensure swift and secure delivery of letters and packages. Each item's route is recorded and it must be signed for on delivery.

reg·is·tered nurse *n* a nurse who has passed a qualifying examination in order to be licensed by a state government to practice

reg·is·tered post *n UK* same as **registered mail**

reg·is·tered trade·mark *n* LAW same as **trademark** *n* (sense 1)

register ton *n* MEASURE same as **ton**[1] (sense 5)

reg·is·trar /réjji straar, rèjji straar/ *n* **1. OFFICIAL RESPONSIBLE FOR STUDENT RECORDS** a university, college, or school official responsible for keeping records of such things as student enrollments and examination results **2. SOMEBODY WHO KEEPS OFFICIAL RECORDS** somebody who keeps official records **3.** *US* MED **HOSPITAL ADMISSIONS OFFICER** an administrative officer in a hospital responsible for admitting patients **4.** *US* BUSINESS **OFFICIAL RESPONSIBLE FOR STOCK RECORDS** a company official who keeps records of stock issued **5.** *UK* **RECORDER OF BIRTHS, MARRIAGES, AND DEATHS** a public official who records births, marriages, and deaths —**reg·is·trar·ship** *n*

Reg·is·trar Gen·er·al (*plural* **Reg·is·trars Gen·er·al**) *n* **1.** in Canada, an official who keeps track of births, deaths, and marriages in a province **2.** in the United

Kingdom, a senior civil servant responsible for population records and censuses

reg·is·tra·tion /rèjji stráysh'n/ *n* **1. ACT OF REGISTERING OR BEING REGISTERED** the act or an instance of registering somebody or something, or the process of being registered **2. LEGAL PROOF FOR VEHICLE** a certificate showing that a motor vehicle has been properly registered with a state's department of motor vehicles **3. ENROLLMENT PROCESS** the process of enrolling at a college or university, choosing courses, and paying fees at the beginning of an academic term **4. ENTRY IN REGISTER** an entry in a register, or somebody or something whose name or designation is entered in a register **5. PEOPLE REGISTERING TOGETHER** the number of people who register for something at a particular place at one time **6.** MUSIC **COMBINATION OF ORGAN STOPS** a combination of organ stops used to play a piece of music **7.** MUSIC **CHOICE OF COMBINATIONS OF ORGAN STOPS** the art of choosing combinations of organ stops appropriate for a piece or passage **8.** *UK* **TIME OF REGISTERING STUDENTS** the act of recording school students as present or absent at the beginning of the school day, or the time or session at which this takes place

reg·is·tra·tion doc·u·ment *n UK* an official document stating the name of the owner of a motor vehicle and giving details by which it can be identified

reg·is·tra·tion num·ber *n* a sequence of letters and numbers by which a motor vehicle can be identified, printed on plates (**license plates**) fastened to the front and back of the vehicle

reg·is·try /réjjistree/ (*plural* **-tries**) *n* **1. RECORDS OFFICE** a place where registers and other records are kept **2. REGISTERING OF SOMETHING** the act of registering somebody or something **3. SHIP REGISTRATION IN PARTICULAR COUNTRY** the nationality of a ship, as defined by where it is registered not by the nationality of its owner or its usual place of operation

reg·let /réǵglət/ *n* **1.** a flat narrow architectural molding, or a narrow strip separating moldings or panels **2.** in traditional hot metal printing, a piece of wood used to separate lines of type [Late 16C. < Old French *régelet*, literally "small rule"]

reg·nal /régnəl/ *adj* relating to a king or queen's reign, calculated from the date when he or she became the sovereign ○ *the third regnal year* [Early 17C. < Anglo-Latin *regnalis* < Latin *regnum* "kingdom"]

reg·nant /régnənt/ *adj* (*formal*) **1.** actually reigning, usually as opposed to having a royal title by marriage ○ *queen regnant* **2.** widespread, predominant, or especially fashionable ○ *according to the regnant custom* [Early 17C. < Latin *regnant-*, present participle of *regnare* "reign"]

Reg·o /ráygō/, **Paula** (*b.* 1935) Portuguese-born British painter. She was appointed first associate artist of the National Gallery, London, in 1990. An exhibition of her *Nursery Rhymes* etchings (1989) received international acclaim.

reg·o·lith /réggə lìth/ *n* the layer of loose rock particles that covers the bedrock of most land on the Earth and the Moon [Late 19C. < Greek *rhēgos* "blanket"]

re·gorge /ree gáwrj/ (**-gorged, -gorg·ing, -gorg·es**) *v* **1.** *vt* to bring up something that has been swallowed **2.** *vi* to flow or gush back along a channel or out of a pit [Early 17C. Either < Old French *regorger* < *gorge* (see GORGE) or < RE- + GORGE]

re·gress *v* /ri gréss/ (**-gressed, -gress·ing, -gress·es**) **1.** *vi* **RETURN TO EARLIER WORSE CONDITION** to return to an earlier and less advanced, less healthy, or generally worse state from a more advanced, healthier, or generally better one **2.** *vi* **GO BACK** to move backward ○ *regress in time* **3.** *vti* PSYCHOL **GO BACK TO EARLIER PERIOD PSYCHOLOGICALLY** to go back to an earlier emotional state and exhibit the type of behavior associated with it, or cause somebody to do this **4.** *vt* PARAPSYCHOL **SUPPOSEDLY MAKE SOMEBODY RECALL EARLIER LIVES** to cause somebody to think of and describe supposed earlier lifetimes while under hypnosis **5.** *vi* STATS **TEND TOWARD MEAN** to tend toward a statistical mean ■ *n* /rée grèss/ **1. MOVEMENT BACKWARD** a going backward, especially from a more advanced or better state to a less advanced or worse one **2.** LOGIC **REASONING FROM EFFECT TO CAUSE** a process of reasoning backward from effects to their causes [Early 16C. < Latin *regress-*, past participle of *regredi* "move backward" < *gradi* "to walk"] —**re·gres·sor** *n*

re·gres·sion /ri grésh'n/ *n* **1. REVERSION TO EARLIER STATE** a return to an earlier or less developed condition or way of behaving **2. MOVEMENT BACKWARD** a going backward or a backward movement or progress, especially through the earlier stages or forms of something **3.** PSYCHOL **REVERSION TO LESS MATURE STATE** reversion to an earlier, less mature, and less adaptive emotional or mental level, often involving the appearance of forms of behavior associated with childhood **4.** STATS **ASSOCIATION BETWEEN VARIABLES** a process for determining the statistical relationship between a random variable and one or more independent variables that is used to predict the value of the random variable **5.** BIOL **RETURN TO EARLIER PHYSICAL TYPE** the recurrence of an earlier, less complicated physical type among later generations of a population **6.** ASTRON **RETROGRADE MOTION** the apparent backward motion of an astronomical object, caused by the differing orbital periods of Earth and the object being observed **7.** ASTRON **MOVEMENT OF MOON'S ORBIT** the slow movement around the ecliptic of the two points where the Moon's orbit crosses it. A complete revolution happens once in about every 19 years.

re·gres·sive /ri gréssiv/ *adj* **1.** reverting to an earlier, less developed condition or way of behaving **2.** describes a tax system in which those with low incomes pay proportionally higher taxes than the wealthy —**re·gres·sive·ly** *adv* —**re·gres·sive·ness** *n*

re·gret /ri grét/ *vt* (**-gret·ted, -gret·ting, -grets**) **1. FEEL SORRY FOR SOMETHING** to feel sorry and sad about something previously done or said that now appears wrong, mistaken, or hurtful to others **2. USED POLITELY WHEN GIVING BAD NEWS** used as a polite expression of sorrow when making an apology or delivering a piece of bad or unwelcome news ○ *We regret to inform you that this service is no longer available.* ○ *We regret any inconvenience caused.* **3. MOURN FOR SOMEBODY OR SOMETHING** to feel sadness about something, or feel a sense of loss and longing for somebody or something that is no longer there (*formal*) ■ *n* **1. SAD OR DISAPPOINTED FEELING** a feeling or expression of sorrow and guilt for a past action or event that you now wish had not happened or had happened differently **2. FEELING OF SADNESS** a feeling of sadness, disappointment, or longing for somebody or something that is no longer there ■ **re·grets** *npl* **EXPRESSION OF SADNESS** a polite expression of real or pretended sadness, used especially when refusing something such as an invitation ○ *My mother sends her regrets, but she can't come to the party.* [15C. < Old French *regreter*] —**re·gret·ter** *n*

re·gret·ful /ri grétfəl/ *adj* feeling or showing regret for something —**re·gret·ful·ly** *adv* —**re·gret·ful·ness** *n*

USAGE regretful or **regrettable**? ***Regrettable*** is used of something that is a cause for regret, whereas ***regretful*** describes somebody who has feelings of regret for something: *These mistakes are regrettable. They felt regretful at missing the opportunity.* The adverbs *regrettably* and *regretfully* are even more vulnerable to confusion, but again *regrettably* relates to the cause of regret and *regretfully* to the feeling itself: *The exam results are regrettably poor. She regretfully turned down the invitation.*

re·gret·ta·ble /ri gréttəb'l/ *adj* unfortunate or blameworthy, and causing feelings of regret, embarrassment, or shame ○ *It was a regrettable lapse by a person of otherwise exemplary character.* —**re·gret·ta·ble·ness** *n* —**re·gret·ta·bly** *adv*

USAGE See ***regretful.***

re·group /ree gro͞op/ (**-grouped, -group·ing, -groups**) *v* **1.** *vti* MIL **FORM INTO ORGANIZED BODY AGAIN** to re-form into organized units or an effective fighting force, or re-form troops in this way, especially after their being dispersed or defeated **2.** *vi* **REORGANIZE** to recover, reorganize, and prepare for a further effort after receiving a setback **3.** *vi* **RECOVER COMPOSURE** to regain your composure, e.g., after a shock or a period of stress ○ *Please pardon me a minute while I regroup here.* **4.** *vt* **ARRANGE THINGS IN NEW GROUPS** to arrange people or things in new or different groups —**re·group·ment** *n*

Regt. *abbr* **1.** POL Regent **2.** MIL Regiment

reg·u·lar /réggyələr/ *adj* **1. HAVING EQUAL TIMES OR SPACES BETWEEN** occurring in a fixed, unvarying, or predictable pattern, with equal amounts of time or space between each one ○ *the regular tick-tock of the clock* **2. HAPPENING FREQUENTLY** occurring or doing something frequently enough over a period of time to establish a pattern, though not necessarily a strict one ○ *Floods are becoming a regular occurrence around here.* **3. USUAL** normally expected, or most often used or done ○ *He's not our regular mailman.* **4. FOLLOWING ROUTINE** carried out according to an established routine or schedule ○ *keep very regular hours* **5. STANDARD OR MEDIUM** of a standard or medium size or strength, as opposed to something of a larger size or greater strength ○ *regular fries* **6. SYMMETRICAL** evenly and pleasingly shaped and symmetrical ○ *a regular facial profile* **7. PROPER** conforming to the normal or accepted rules or standards **8. QUALIFIED** officially or properly qualified to perform a specific job ○ *not a regular doctor* **9. COMPLETE AND UTTER** thoroughly deserving a particular description (*informal*) ○ *a regular tyrant in the office* **10. NICE** pleasant, reliable, and thoughtful (*informal*) ○ *a regular guy* **11.** PHYSIOL **PHYSICALLY PREDICTABLE AND CONSISTENT** having predictable physical processes, especially menstruating or having bowel movements at predictable times **12.** MIL **FORMING PART OF PROFESSIONAL FORCE** belonging to or constituting a full-time professional military or police force as opposed to, e.g., the reserves ○ *an officer in the regular army* **13.** GRAM **GRAMMATICALLY NORMAL** following the normal or common grammatical patterns of a language ○ *a regular verb* **14.** CHR **OF RELIGIOUS ORDER** belonging to a religious or monastic order ○ *the regular clergy* **15.** *US* POL **POLITICALLY LOYAL** connected with or loyal to a particular political party **16.** MATH **HAVING EQUAL SIDES AND ANGLES** having both equal sides and equal angles ○ *a regular polygon* **17.** MATH **COMPOSED OF IDENTICAL POLYGONS** having faces that are congruent identical polygons and that make equal angles with each other ○ *a regular polyhedron* **18.** BOT **SYMMETRICAL** having flower parts that are similar in size and shape and are arranged symmetrically **19. WITH RIGHT FOOT FORWARD** in skateboarding and similar sports, used to describe a stance on the board in which the rider's left foot is nearer the front end (*slang*) ■ *n* **1. SOMETHING STANDARD OR MEDIUM** something of a medium or standard size or strength, as opposed to something larger, smaller, stronger, or weaker **2. FREQUENT VISITOR** a frequent visitor to a place (*informal*) **3. HABITUAL ORDER** something that somebody usually asks for or buys, e.g., a drink (*informal*) ○ *"I'll have my regular," he told the bartender.* **4.** MIL **PROFESSIONAL SOLDIER** a full-time professional soldier (*often used in the plural*) **5.** CHR **MEMBER OF RELIGIOUS ORDER** a member of a religious or monastic order **6.** *US* POL **LOYAL PARTY SUPPORTER** somebody who is loyal to a political party [14C. < Latin *regularis* < *regula* "rule" Indo-European] —**reg·u·lar·i·ty** /règgyə lárrətee/ *n* —**reg·u·lar·ly** *adv*

reg·u·lar·ize /réggyələ rīz/ (**-ized, -iz·ing, -iz·es**) *vt* to make something fit in with or conform to usual or accepted standards or practice —**reg·u·lar·i·za·tion** /règgyələri záysh'n/ *n* —**reg·u·lar·iz·er** *n*

reg·u·late /réggyə làyt/ (**-lat·ed, -lat·ing, -lates**) *vt* **1. CONTROL SOMETHING** to control something and bring it to the desired level, e.g., by adjusting the output of a machine or by imposing restrictions on the flow of something **2. ADJUST MACHINERY OR SELECT OUTPUT** to adjust a piece of machinery or a control device on it so that the machinery works correctly **3. MAKE SOMETHING REGULAR** to cause something to occur at predictable intervals or in a regular way **4. CONTROL SOMETHING BY RULES OR LAWS** to organize and control an activity or process by making it subject to rules or laws (*formal*) ○ *Governments of socialist countries regulate their nations' economies.* [15C. < late Latin *regulat-*, past participle of *regulare* Latin *regula* (see REGULAR)] —**reg·u·la·tive** *adj* —**reg·u·la·to·ry** /réggyələ tàwree/ *adj*

reg·u·la·tion /règgyə láysh'n/ *n* **1. RULE OR ORDER** an official rule, law, or order stating what may or may not be done or how something must be done (*often* *used in the plural)* **2. GOVERNMENT ORDER WITH FORCE OF LAW** an order issued by a government department or agency that has the force of law **3. REGULATING OF SOMETHING** the adjusting, organizing, or controlling of something, or the state of being adjusted, organized, or controlled **4.** BIOL **ABILITY OF EMBRYO TO GROW NORMALLY** the process or mechanism by which an embryo restores its ability to develop normally after being damaged or altered without creating new tissue ■ *adj* **1. OFFICIALLY APPROVED FOR USE** officially approved for use, or conforming to the official guidelines for something **2. STANDARD AND UNADVENTUROUS** like everyone has or does, and completely standard and unadventurous

reg·u·la·tor /réggyə làytər/ *n* **1. CONTROL MECHANISM** a mechanism that controls something such as pressure, temperature, speed, or voltage *(often used in combination)* **2. CONTROLLING OFFICIAL** an official who controls a particular activity and makes certain that regulations are complied with *(often used in combination)* ○ *the industry regulator* **3. VERY ACCURATE TIMEPIECE** a very accurate watch or clock, used as a standard by which others are set **4.** GENETICS same as **regulator gene**

reg·u·la·tor gene, reg·u·la·to·ry gene *n* a gene that regulates the expression of one or more structural genes, thereby controlling the synthesis of their corresponding proteins. In the simplest case, the regulator gene encodes a repressor molecule that binds to a site adjacent to the structural gene, so preventing transcription of the latter.

reg·u·li METALL plural of **regulus**

re·gu·lus /réggyələss/ *(plural* **-lus·es** or **-li** /-lī/) *n* **1.** the semipurified mass of metal that forms beneath the slag in the smelting of ore **2.** an impure intermediate metal product created by the smelting process [Late 16C. < Latin, diminutive of *reg-* "king;" originally in *regulus of antimony,* a metallic antimony so called because it combined readily with gold, a kingly metal] —**reg·u·line** /réggyəlin, -līn/ *adj*

Reg·u·lus /réggyələss/ *n* a bright double star in the constellation Leo

re·gur·gi·tate /ri gúrji tàyt/ (**-tat·ed, -tat·ing, -tates**) *v* **1.** *vt* **BRING FOOD UP FROM STOMACH** to bring undigested or partially digested food up from the stomach to the mouth, as some birds and animals do to feed their young **2.** *vt* **REPEAT INFORMATION MECHANICALLY** to repeat or reproduce what has been heard, read, or taught, in a purely mechanical way, with no evidence of personal thought or understanding **3.** *vi* **FLOW OUT** to flow out or be ejected, especially from the mouth *(formal)* **4.** *vi* MED **FLOW IN OPPOSITE DIRECTION TO NORMAL** to flow in the opposite direction to the normal or usual direction, especially through a faulty heart valve [Late 16C. < medieval Latin *regurgitat-,* past participle of *regurgitare,* literally "to flood back" *gurges* "whirlpool"] —**re·gur·gi·tant** *n, adj* —**re·gur·gi·ta·tion** /ri gùrji táysh'n/ *n* —**re·gur·gi·ta·tive** *adj*

re·hab /rée hàb/ *(informal) n* **1. REHABILITATION** the period or process of rehabilitation, e.g., for somebody addicted to a chemical substance *(often used before a noun)* ○ *a rehab clinic* **2. SOMETHING RESTORED** something that has been restored to good condition, especially a rehabilitated building ■ *vt* (**-habbed, -hab·bing, -habs**) **RESTORE BUILDING** to restore something, especially a building [Mid-20C. Shortening] —**re·hab·ber** *n*

re·ha·bil·i·tate /rèe ə bíllə tàyt, rèe hə-/ (**-tat·ed, -tat·ing, -tates**) *vt* **1. HELP SOMEBODY RETURN TO NORMAL LIFE** to help somebody to return to good health or a normal life by providing training or therapy **2. RESTORE SOMEBODY TO RANK OR RIGHTS** to restore somebody to a former position or rank and grant rights and privileges once more *(often passive)* **3. RESTORE SOMEBODY'S REPUTATION** to restore somebody's good reputation and standing after he or she has been disgraced or neglected **4. RESTORE PLACE TO GOOD CONDITION** to restore a building, or part of a town, to its former good condition [Late 16C. < medieval Latin *rehabilitat-,* past participle of *rehabilitare,* literally "habilitate again" (see HABILITATE)] —**re·ha·bil·i·tat·a·ble** *adj* —**re·ha·bil·i·ta·tion** /rèe ə bilə táysh'n, rèe hə-/ *n* —**re·ha·bil·i·ta·tive** *adj*—**re·ha·bil·i·ta·tor** *n*

re·hash *vt* /ree hásh/ (**-hashed, -hash·ing, -hash·es**) to repeat something or reuse and rework old material, making some changes but without introducing anything new ■ *n* /rée hàsh/ a tiresome reuse of ideas or material to which nothing new or significant has been added

re·hears·al /ri húrss'l/ *n* **1.** a session or series of sessions in which something that is to be done later, especially a public performance, is practiced **2.** a detailed listing or repetition of something *(formal)*

re·hearse /ri húrss/ (**-hearsed, -hears·ing, -hears·es**) *v* **1.** *vti* **PRACTICE SOMETHING BEFORE PERFORMING** to practice something before doing it, especially to practice something such as a play, speech, or piece of music before performing it for the public **2.** *vt* **TRAIN SOMEBODY FOR PERFORMANCE** to train or instruct somebody who is practicing before doing something, especially before giving a public performance **3.** *vt* **GO OVER LIST** to go over a list of items, often reasons, complaints, or troubles **4.** *vti* **SAY SOMETHING** to tell or repeat something such as a story *(literary)* [13C. < Old French *rehercer* "rake over" < *herce, herse* (see HEARSE)] —**re·hears·er** *n*

Rehn·quist /rén kwìst/, **William H.** (*b.* 1924) chief justice of the US Supreme Court (1986–). Appointed as an associate justice in 1971 and as chief justice in 1986, he presided over a court noted for its judicial restraint. Full name **Rehnquist, William Hubbs**

re·ho·bo·am /rèe ə bṓ əm/ *n* a large wine bottle, six times the size of a normal bottle [Mid-19C. Named for *Rehoboam,* who "fortified the strongholds, and put captains in them ... and stores of oil and wine" (2 Chronicles 11:11)]

Re·ho·bo·am /rèe ə bṓ əm/ *n* in the Bible, the son of Solomon and king of ancient Judah (922? B.C.–915? B.C.). His reign was marked by conflict with the rival kingdom of the northern tribes of Israel (1 Kings 11–14).

re·house /ree hówz/ (**-housed, -hous·ing, -hous·es**) *vt* to provide a person or group of people with a new or different place to live in, often one that is better than the previous dwelling

re·hy·drate /ree hī dràyt/ (**-drat·ed, -drat·ing, -drates**) *v* **1.** *vt* **RETURN WATER TO SOMETHING** to add water to something that has been dried in order to return it to its natural state **2.** *vi* **ABSORB WATER** to absorb water after dehydration **3.** *vt* MED **REPLENISH SOMEBODY'S BODY FLUIDS** to restore somebody's body fluids to a normal or healthy level —**re·hy·drat·a·ble** *adj* —**re·hy·dra·tion** /rèe hī dráysh'n/ *n*

Reich /rīk, rīkh/ *n* the German state or empire, especially the Holy Roman Empire (926–1806) or First Reich, the German Empire (1871–1919) or Second Reich, or the Nazi state (1933–45) or Third Reich [Early 20C. < German, "kingdom, state, empire"]

Reich /rīk/, **Steve** (*b.* 1936) US composer in minimalist style whose music has a strong steady pulse and short repeating melodic figures

reichs·mark /rīks maàrk, rīkhs-/ *(plural same* or **-marks**) *n* the basic unit of German currency from 1923 to 1948 [Mid-20C. < German < *Reich* "kingdom, state, empire" + *Mark* "mark (currency)"]

Reichs·tag /rīks taàg, rīkhs taàk/ *n* **1.** HIST **GERMAN LEGISLATIVE ASSEMBLY 1867–1919** the legislative assembly of both the North German Confederation, from 1867 to 1871, and the German Empire, from 1871 to 1919 **2.** HIST **LEGISLATIVE ASSEMBLY OF WEIMAR REPUBLIC** the sovereign legislative assembly of the Weimar Republic, from 1919 to 1933 **3. PARLIAMENT BUILDING IN BERLIN** the building in Berlin in which the Reichstag formerly met, destroyed by fire in 1933, and now rebuilt to house the parliament of the reunified German federal state [Mid-19C. < German < *Reich* "kingdom, state, empire" + *Tag* "diet, legislative assembly"]

Reich·stein /rīk stīn, rīkh-/, **Tadeus** (1897–1996) Polish-born Swiss biochemist. He shared the Nobel Prize in physiology or medicine (1950) with Edward C. Kendall and Philip Showalter Hench for their research on hormones such as cortisone.

Reid /reed/, **Whitelaw** (1837–1912) US journalist and diplomat. He served as the US minister to France (1889–92) and ambassador to Great Britain (1905–12).

re·i·fy /rée ə fī, ráy-/ (**-fied, -fy·ing, -fies**) *vt* to think of or treat something abstract as if it existed as a real and tangible object [Mid-19C. Coined from Latin *re-* (stem of *res* "thing") + -FY] —**re·i·fi·ca·tion** /rèe əfi káysh'n, rày-/ *n* —**re·i·fi·ca·to·ry** /ree íffikə tàwree, ray-/ *adj* —**re·i·fi·er** /rée i fī ər, ráy-/ *n*

Rei·gate /rī gayt, rīgit/ city in Surrey, southeastern England. Population: 64,589 (1991).

reign /rayn/ *n* **1. PERIOD OF RULE** the period of time during which somebody, especially a king or queen, rules a nation **2. CONTROL OR INFLUENCE** the fact of being the dominant or controlling power or factor in something, or the period of time during which this dominance persists ■ *vi* (**reigned, reign·ing, reigns**) **1. RULE NATION** to exercise sovereign power or a controlling influence over something, especially to rule a country as its king or queen **2. BE TITULAR SOVEREIGN** to hold a royal title and be head of state while possessing only limited powers, as in a constitutional monarchy **3. BE MOST IMPORTANT FEATURE** to be the main or most noticeable feature of a situation, place, or period of time ○ *For a while, silence reigned.* [13C. Via Old French *reignier* from Latin *regnare* "to be king," from *regnum* "kingship"]

SPELLCHECK See *rain.*

reign of ter·ror *n* a time when systematic violence is used by a government, person, or group to intimidate other people and obtain or maintain dominance over them

Reign of Ter·ror *n* the period of the French Revolution between September 1793 and July 1794, during which thousands of people were executed as enemies of the revolution

rei·ki /ráykee/ *n* in alternative medicine, a treatment in which healing energy is channeled from the practitioner to the patient to enhance energy and reduce stress, pain, and fatigue [Late 20C. < Japanese, "universal life force energy"]

re·i·mag·ine /rèe i májjin/ (**-ined, -in·ing, -ines**) *vt* **1.** to recreate something, or plan to recreate something, in a fundamentally different way ○ *to reimagine the Shakespearean corpus for television* **2.** to create a new and improved image or lifestyle for yourself

re·im·burse /rèe im búrss/ (**-bursed, -burs·ing, -burs·es**) *vt* to pay somebody back money spent for an official or approved reason or taken as a loan, or give somebody money as compensation for loss or damage [Early 17C. Formed from obsolete *imburse* "to pay, put in a purse," ultimately from Old French *borse* "purse," from medieval Latin *bursa* (source of English *purse*)] —**re·im·burs·a·ble** *adj* —**re·im·burse·ment** *n* —**re·im·burs·er** *n*

re·im·pres·sion /rèe im présh'n/ *n* a reprint of a book without any changes in the text

Reims /reemz/, **Rheims** city in Marne Department, Champagne-Ardenne Region, northeastern France. It is home to the 13th-century Cathedral of Notre Dame where the coronations of most of the French kings took place. Population: 187,206 (1999).

rein /rayn/ *n (often used in the plural)* **1. STRAP FOR CONTROLLING HORSE** a strap, or each half of a strap, by which a horse is controlled by its rider or by the driver of a coach or cart it is pulling **2. EXERCISE OF POWER** any means of guiding, controlling, or restraining somebody or something ■ **reins** *npl* **STRAP FOR GUIDING CHILD** a harness that fits around the body of a very young child, with straps attached by means of which the child can be controlled and guided, especially when out walking ■ *vt* (**reined, rein·ing, reins**) **CONTROL SOMEBODY OR SOMETHING** to guide, control, or restrain somebody or something [13C. < Old French *rene, resne*] —**rein·less** *adj* ◇ **give (free) rein to somebody** *or* **something** to allow somebody or something complete freedom, imposing no restraints or limitations ◇ **have** *or* **keep a (tight) rein on somebody** *or* **something** to maintain strict control over somebody or something ◇ **take (up) the reins** to take charge of something or somebody ○ *The new team coach will take the reins next week.*

SPELLCHECK See *rain.*

rein back *vt* to subject something or somebody to stricter control, often to reduce the amount of something or restrict somebody's freedom of action

rein in *v* **1.** *vti* to make a horse stop or slow down by pulling on the reins **2.** *vt* to bring somebody or something under control

re·in·car·nate *vt* /rēe in kaar nàyt/ (**-nat·ed, -nat·ing, -nates**) **1. GIVE SOMEBODY NEW BIRTH** in some systems of belief, to return to live another life in a different body (*often passive*) **2. PUT SOMETHING INTO NEW FORM** to present something again in a new form after it has been abandoned or discontinued ■ *adj* /rēe in kaarnət/ **1. REBORN** in some systems of belief, living again in a new body after death **2. REPACKAGED** embodied or presented in a new form

re·in·car·na·tion /rēe in kaar náysh'n/ *n* **1.** RELIG **REBIRTH OF SOUL** in some systems of belief, the cyclic return of a soul to live another life in a new body **2.** RELIG **BODY IN WHICH SOMEBODY IS REBORN** in some systems of belief, a person or animal in whose body somebody's soul is born again after he, she, or it has died **3. APPEARANCE IN NEW GUISE** a reappearance of something in a new form —**re·in·car·na·tion·ism** *n* —**re·in·car·na·tion·ist** *n*

rein·deer /ráyn dēer/ (*plural same* or **-deers**) *n* a large deer with large branched antlers in both males and females. Native to: northern and Arctic regions. Latin name: *Rangifer tarandus.* [14C. < Old Norse *hreinn* "reindeer" + *dýr* "animal"]

Rein·deer Lake /ráyn dēer-/ lake in Canada, on the Saskatchewan-Manitoba border, discharging into the Reindeer River. Area: 2,467 sq. mi./6,390 sq. km.

rein·deer moss, rein·deer li·chen *n* a gray lichen that grows in large erect branching tufts and provides food for reindeer and other animals. Native to: subarctic and Arctic regions. Latin name: *Cladonia rangiferia.*

re·in·dus·tri·al·ize /rēe in dústree ə līz/ (**-ized, -iz·ing, -iz·es**) *vti* to undergo a process of renewal, usually involving government help in the modernization of factories and equipment, or subject an industry or industrial society to such a process —**re·in·dus·tri·al·i·za·tion** /rēe in dùstree əli záysh'n/ *n*

Reines /rīnz/, **Frederick** (1918–98) US physicist. He provided evidence of the existence of the neutrino, a subatomic particle, for which he shared the Nobel Prize in physics (1995).

re·in·force /rēe in fáwrss/ (**-forced, -forc·ing, -forc·es**), **re·en·force** *vt* **1. STRENGTHEN SOMETHING** to make something stronger by providing additional external support or internal stiffening for it **2. GIVE SOMETHING SUPPORT** to give additional strength, force, or conviction to something such as an idea, opinion, or feeling, e.g., by providing further evidence to support it **3. STRENGTHEN MILITARY FORCE** to make a military force stronger by providing it with more troops or weapons **4.** PSYCHOL **INFLUENCE BEHAVIOR BY REWARD OR PUNISHMENT** to reward an action or type of behavior to increase the probability that it will be repeated or punish an action in order to discourage it [15C. Formed from ENFORCE, probably on the model of Italian *rinforzare*] —**re·in·force·a·ble** *adj*

re·in·forced con·crete /rēe in fawrst-/ *n* concrete made with metal wire or rods embedded in it to increase its strength

re·in·forced plas·tic *n* plastic with carbon or similar fibers embedded in it to make it stronger

re·in·force·ment /rēe in fáwrssmənt/ *n* **1. ADDED SUPPORT** the addition of strengthening or supporting material to make something stronger or more durable **2. SOMETHING ADDED TO INCREASE STRENGTH** something that is added to strengthen or support something else **3.** PSYCHOL **REWARD OR PUNISHMENT** the rewarding (**positive reinforcement**) or punishing (**negative reinforcement**) of actions, especially in an experimental situation, for the purpose of changing a subject's behavior ■ **re·in·force·ments** *npl* **ADDITIONAL TROOPS OR WEAPONS** additional troops, police, or weapons provided to make an existing force stronger

re·in·forc·er /rēe in fáwrssər/ *n* in behavioral psychology, a reward or stimulus used to encourage an action in order to increase the probability that it will be repeated

Re·in·ga, Cape /ree ángə/ cape at the northwestern tip of the North Island, New Zealand. In Maori folklore, it is the departure point for the souls of the dead returning to the spiritual homeland of Hawaiki.

Rein·hardt /rīn haart/, **Django** (1910–53) Belgian musician. He is generally regarded as the finest jazz guitarist of all time. He often performed with Stephane Grappelli. Born **Reinhardt, Jean-Baptiste**

reins /raynz/ *npl* the kidneys, lower abdomen, including the hips, or lower back [Pre-12C. Via French from Latin *renes*]

re·in·state /rēe in stáyt/ (**-stat·ed, -stat·ing, -states**) *vt* **1.** to give somebody back a job or position of influence that he or she once had and from which he or she was dismissed or deposed **2.** to bring something back into use or force again after it has been out of use —**re·in·state·ment** *n* —**re·in·sta·tor** *n*

re·in·sure /rēe in shóor/ (**-sured, -sur·ing, -sures**) *vt* to insure something again, especially to obtain, as an insurer, additional coverage from another insurer for a risk that a customer has been insured against —**re·in·sur·ance** *n* —**re·in·sur·er** *n*

re·in·vent /rēe in vént/ (**-vent·ed, -vent·ing, -vents**) *vt* **1.** to invent something again, or bring something back into existence, use, or popularity after a period of neglect or obscurity **2.** to change radically the appearance, form, or presentation of something or somebody —**re·in·ven·tion** *n*

re·in·vest /rēe in vést/ (**-vest·ed, -vest·ing, -vests**) *vti* **1.** to invest money again, especially to buy more shares with the income made on a previous investment **2.** to put money back into a business instead of distributing it as profit —**re·in·vest·ment** *n*

reis MONEY plural of **real**[3]

REIT *abbr* real estate investment trust

re·it·er·ate /ree íttə ràyt/ (**-at·ed, -at·ing, -ates**) *vt* ⚠ to say or do something again, once or several times, sometimes in a tiresome way —**re·it·er·ant** *adj* —**re·it·er·a·tion** /ree ìttə ráysh'n/ *n* —**re·it·er·a·tive** *adj* —**re·it·er·a·tive·ly** *adv* —**re·it·er·a·tor** *n*

USAGE The use of *again, once more, yet again,* and other such expressions with ***reiterate***, whose meaning includes the sense of "again," is unnecessary and to be avoided.

Re·iter's syn·drome /rītərz-/, **Re·iter's dis·ease** *n* a disease that begins as an infection in genetically predisposed people and is characterized by recurring bouts of arthritis, conjunctivitis, and urethritis [Early 20C. Named for Hans *Reiter* (1881–1969), German bacteriologist]

re·ject *vt* /ri jékt/ (**-ject·ed, -ject·ing, -jects**) **1. NOT ACCEPT SOMETHING** to refuse to accept, agree to, believe in, or make use of something, e.g., because it is not good enough or not the right thing **2. TURN SOMEBODY DOWN** to decide not to give somebody something asked or applied for such as a job or membership of an organization **3. BE UNKIND TO SOMEBODY** to behave in an unkind and unfriendly way toward somebody who expects or has a right to expect love, kindness, and friendship **4. NOT KEEP SOMETHING** to put something aside or throw it away ○ *rejected the faulty disk* **5.** MED **NOT ACCEPT TRANSPLANT** to fail to accept foreign tissue or an organ transplant because of immunological incompatibility **6.** MED **BRING UP FOOD** to be unable to keep food down and vomit it up again ■ *n* /rēe jèkt/ **SOMETHING OR SOMEBODY NOT WANTED** somebody or something that is refused as not meeting a required standard or is otherwise unsuitable [15C. < Latin *reject-*, past participle of *rejicere* "throw back" < *jacere* "throw"] —**re·ject·a·ble** *adj* —**re·ject·er** *n* —**re·jec·tive** *adj* —**re·jec·tor** *n*

re·jec·tion /ri jékshən/ *n* **1.** the rejecting of something or somebody, or the fact of being rejected **2.** the destruction by immune mechanisms of transplanted tissue or a transplanted organ from another individual

re·jec·tion·ist /ri jékshənist/ *n* somebody who refuses to accept a policy, proposal, or plan that others have agreed to

re·jec·tion slip *n* an official note stating that something has been rejected such as a book submitted to a publisher or a painting submitted for exhibition

re·jig /ree jíg/ (**-jigged, -jig·ging, -jigs**) *vt Can, UK* same as **rejigger** (*informal*)

re·jig·ger /ree jíggər/ (**-gered, -ger·ing, -gers**) *vt US* to alter, rearrange, or readjust something, or set it up differently, sometimes with the intention of deceiving a purchaser or user (*informal*) Can term **rejig**

re·joice /ri jóyss/ (**-joiced, -joic·ing, -joic·es**) *v* **1.** *vi* to feel very happy or show great happiness about something (*literary*) **2.** *vt* to fill somebody with happiness (*archaic*) [14C. Via Old French *rejoir* "to be most joyful" from, ultimately, Latin *gaudere* "to rejoice" (source of English *joy*)] —**re·joic·er** *n* —**re·joic·ing** *n* —**re·joic·ing·ly** *adv*

rejoice in *vt* to be lucky enough to have or own something (*often used ironically*) ○ *They rejoice in their good health.*

re·join[1] /ree jóyn/ (**-joined, -join·ing, -joins**) *vti* **1. RETURN TO SOMEBODY AFTER BEING APART** to meet up again with somebody, or go back to somebody or something, after a usually brief period of being away or apart **2. BECOME MEMBER AGAIN** to become a member again of an organization or group that you formerly belonged to **3. JOIN TOGETHER AGAIN** to join two things together again, or become joined together or merged with something again [Mid-16C. < RE- + JOIN]

re·join[2] /ri jóyn/ (**-joined, -join·ing, -joins**) *v* **1.** *vti* to say something in reply, especially to reply with a sharp, critical, angry, defensive, or clever remark (*formal*) **2.** *vi* in law, to respond to a plaintiff's reply or replication [15C. < French *rejoign-*, stem of *rejoindre* "join again" < *joindre* (see JOIN)]

re·join·der /ri jóyndər/ *n* **1.** a reply to something said, especially one that is sharp, critical, angry, defensive, or clever (*formal*) **2.** in law, the answer that a defendant makes during pleading to the plaintiff's reply or replication [15C. Via Anglo-Norman from Old French (see REJOIN[2])]

SYNONYMS See ***answer***.

---

re·ju·ve·nate /ri jóovə nàyt/ (**-nat·ed, -nat·ing, -nates**) *vt* **1. MAKE SOMEBODY YOUNG AGAIN** to make somebody become, feel, or appear young again **2. RETURN SOMETHING TO ORIGINAL CONDITION** to restore something to its condition when new, or make it more vigorous, dynamic, and effective **3.** GEOL **CAUSE RIVER TO ERODE MORE** to cause a river to start eroding the land it runs over again, usually as a result of the land being uplifted **4.** GEOL **MAKE AREA DEVELOP TOPOGRAPHICALLY YOUNG FEATURES** to cause the redevelopment of younger, more rugged topographic features in a landscape through increased erosion [Early 19C. < RE- + Latin *juvenis* "young"] —**re·ju·ve·na·tion** /-jóovə náysh'n/ *n* —**re·ju·ve·na·tive** *adj* —**re·ju·ve·na·tor** *n*

re·key /ree kēe/ (**-keyed, -key·ing, -keys**) *vt* to reenter lost text or data into a computer, or input text or data in a different form, using a keyboard

re·kin·dle /ree kínd'l/ (**-dled, -dling, -dles**) *vt* **1.** to revive or renew something such as a feeling or interest **2.** to set a fire burning again

rel. *abbr* **1.** relating **2.** GRAM relative **3.** relatively **4.** released **5.** religion **6.** religious

re·lapse *vi* /ri láps/ (**-lapsed, -laps·ing, -laps·es**) **1. GO INTO FORMER STATE** to fall back into a former mood, state, or way of life, especially a bad or undesirable one, after coming out of it for a while **2.** MED **BECOME ILL AFTER APPARENT RECOVERY** to become ill again after seeming to have made a recovery ■ *n* /rée làps, ri láps/ **1. ACT OF RETURNING TO PREVIOUS CONDITION** a return to a former mood, state, or way of life, especially a bad or undesirable one, after coming out of it for a while **2.** MED **WORSENING OF HEALTH** a sudden worsening in the condition of a patient who was ill but who seemed to have made a recovery from the illness [15C. < Latin *relaps-*, past participle of *relabi* "slip again" < *labi* "to slip"] —**re·laps·er** *n*

re·laps·ing fe·ver /ri lápsing-/ *n* an infectious disease, characterized by chills and recurring fever, caused by a bacterium transmitted to people by ticks and lice

re·late /ri láyt/ (**-lat·ed, -lat·ing, -lates**) *v* **1.** *vi* **HAVE CONNECTION WITH SOMETHING** to have a significant connection with or bearing on something ○ *How does this story relate to our conversation?* **2.** *vt* **CONNECT PEOPLE OR THINGS** to find or show a connection between two or more people or things **3.** *vi* **BE RELEVANT SPECIFICALLY** to concern, involve, or apply to somebody or something specifically ○ *These regulations relate only to imported goods.* **4.** ⚠ *vi* **FORM FRIENDLY ASSOCIATION** to have a friendly relationship with or friendly feelings toward somebody, based on an understanding of the person or on shared views or concerns **5.** *vi* **RESPOND TO SOMEBODY OR SOMETHING** to understand and respond favorably to something, or feel that it has a personal meaning or relevance (*informal*) ○ *I just can't seem to relate to the cynicism of that generation.* **6.** *vt* **TELL OR DESCRIBE SOMETHING** to tell a story or describe an event ○ *related a tale of sorrow* [15C. < French *relater* "to report" < Latin *relat-*, past participle of *referre* "carry back" < *ferre* "carry"] —**re·lat·a·ble** *adj* —**re·lat·er** *n*

USAGE The use of ***relate*** without a prepositional phrase in the context of personal dealings between people is much used in the language of sociology but in general use is sometimes regarded as jargon, as in *Children who find it hard to relate tend to be inadequately socialized.* A clearer way to express this would be *Children who find it hard to relate to their peers....*

re·lat·ed /ri láytəd/ *adj* **1. ASSOCIATED** connected by similarities or a common source **2. BELONGING TO SAME FAMILY** belonging to the same family by birth or through adoption or marriage **3.** MUSIC **HAVING CLOSE HARMONIC CONNECTION** describes a musical key or chord that, harmonically speaking, is closely connected with another, e.g., by having particular notes in common with it —**re·lat·ed·ly** *adv* —**re·lat·ed·ness** *n*

re·la·tion /ri láysh'n/ *n* **1. CONNECTION BETWEEN THINGS** a meaningful connection or association between two or more things, e.g., one based on the similarity or relevance of one thing to another **2. MEMBER OF FAMILY** a member of the same family as somebody else, by birth or through adoption or marriage **3. CONNECTION BY FAMILY** connection by birth, adoption, or marriage **4. NARRATION** the narration of a story or description of something that has happened, or what is conveyed in the narration or description (*formal*) **5.** LAW **TAKING OF SOMETHING AS DONE EARLIER** a procedure whereby an act done at a later time is, for legal purposes, deemed to have been done at an earlier time **6.** LOGIC, MATH **SHARED PROPERTY OF ASSOCIATION** a property of association, e.g., "greater than" or "less than," shared by ordered pairs of terms or objects ■ **re·la·tions** *npl* **1. CONTACTS BETWEEN GROUPS OR PEOPLE** contacts or dealings between two or more people or groups **2. SEXUAL ACTS** sexual activities between people (*euphemistic*) [14C. Directly or via French < Latin *relation-* < *relat-* (see RELATE)] ◇ **in** *or* **with relation to** with reference or regard to, or in comparison with something

re·la·tion·al /ri láyshən'l, -láyshnəl/ *adj* **1. INVOLVING RELATIONSHIP** involving or expressing a relationship **2.** GRAM **CONVEYING SYNTACTIC RELATION** expressing or relating to a syntactic relation between elements in a phrase or sentence ○ *Prepositions are relational words.* **3.** COMPUT **OF ORGANIZATION OF DATABASE** describes a way of organizing and presenting information in a database so that the user perceives it as a set of tables —**re·la·tion·al·ly** *adv*

re·la·tion·al gram·mar *n* a theory of descriptive grammar in which syntactic relationships such as subject and object are used to define grammatical processes rather than syntactic structures

re·la·tion·ship /ri láysh'n shìp/ *n* **1. CONNECTION** a significant connection or similarity between two or more things, or the state of being related to something else **2. BEHAVIOR OR FEELINGS TOWARD SOMEBODY ELSE** the connection between two or more people or groups and their involvement with one another, especially as regards the way they behave toward and feel about one another **3. FRIENDSHIP** an emotionally close friendship, especially one involving sexual activity **4. CONNECTION BY FAMILY** the way in which two or more people are related by birth, adoption, or marriage, or the fact of being related by birth, adoption, or marriage **5.** LOGIC, MATH same as **relation** (sense 6)

rel·a·tive /réllətiv/ *adj* **1. COMPARATIVE** measured or considered in comparison with each other or with something else ○ *discussing the relative merits of various methods of transportation* **2. CHANGING WITH CIRCUMSTANCES** not permanently fixed, but having a meaning or value that can only be established in relation to something else and will change according to circumstances or context ○ *"Big" and "small" are relative terms.* **3. DEPENDENT ON SOMETHING** depending on or in proportion to something else **4. CONNECTED WITH SOMETHING** connected with or referring to something **5.** GRAM **REFERRING TO PREVIOUSLY USED WORD** used to describe words or clauses that refer to a word previously used in the same sentence **6.** MUSIC **HAVING IDENTICAL KEY SIGNATURES** describes a musical key that has the same key signature as another, usually a minor key with the same sharps and flats as a major key, or vice versa ■ *n* **1. MEMBER OF FAMILY** a member of the same family by birth, marriage, or adoption **2.** BIOL **THING RELATED TO SOMETHING ELSE** one thing that is related to something else, especially a species that has developed from the same origin as another species **3.** GRAM **RELATIVE WORD** a relative word, especially a relative pronoun, or a relative clause —**rel·a·tive·ness** *n*

rel·a·tive a·tom·ic mass *n* the ratio of the average mass per atom of an element to one twelfth of the mass of a carbon-12 atom. Symbol A_r

rel·a·tive clause *n* a clause that refers to and provides additional information about a preceding noun or pronoun, often beginning with a relative pronoun such as "who," "which," or "that"

rel·a·tive den·si·ty *n* the ratio of the density of a substance to the density of a standard substance at the same temperature and pressure. For liquids and solids the standard substance is usually water, for gases, air. Symbol **d**

rel·a·tive hu·mid·i·ty *n* the ratio of the amount of water vapor in the air at a given temperature to the maximum amount air can hold at the same temperature, expressed as a percentage

rel·a·tive·ly /réllətivlee/ *adv* in comparison with other things ○ *a relatively cool day, given the summer weather*

rel·a·tive mo·lec·u·lar mass *n* same as **molecular weight**. Symbol M_r (*technical*)

rel·a·tive per·mit·tiv·i·ty *n* a measure of the resistance of a substance to an applied electric field equivalent to the ratio of the permittivity of a substance divided by that of free space. Symbol υ_r

rel·a·tive pitch *n* **1.** the pitch of a tone, determined by its position in a scale with respect to other tones **2.** the ability to identify or produce a tone by mentally comparing it to another tone recently heard

rel·a·tive pro·noun *n* a pronoun that refers to a previously used noun and introduces a relative clause, e.g., "that," "which," or "who"

rel·a·tiv·ism /rélləti vìzzəm/ *n* the belief that concepts such as right and wrong, goodness and badness, or truth and falsehood are not absolute but change from culture to culture and situation to situation —**rel·a·tiv·ist** *n*

rel·a·tiv·is·tic /rèlləti vístik/ *adj* **1.** PHYS **MOVING CLOSE TO SPEED OF LIGHT** moving at a velocity approaching the speed of light, so that properties such as mass act in accordance with the theory of relativity **2.** PHYS **RELATING TO RELATIVITY** relating to or characterized by relativity **3.** PHILOSOPHY **RELATING TO RELATIVISM** involving or characterized by relativism —**rel·a·tiv·is·ti·cal·ly** *adv*

rel·a·tiv·i·ty /rèllə tívvətee/ *n* **1.** PHYS **EQUIVALENCE OF MASS AND ENERGY** the first of two theories describing the relationship of matter, time, and space, showing that mass and energy are equivalent, and that mass, length, and time change with velocity. The theory is based on two assumptions: that the speed of light in a vacuum is constant, and that physical laws have the same mathematical form throughout the universe. **2.** PHYS **THEORY OF GRAVITATION AND ACCELERATION** the second of two theories describing the relationship of matter, time, and space, extending the principles of the first to gravitation and phenomena related to acceleration **3.** PHILOSOPHY **DEPENDENCE ON CONTEXTUALLY VARIABLE FACTOR** dependence on a factor that varies according to context **4. FACT OF BEING RELATIVE** the fact or state of being relative to something else

rel·a·tiv·ize /réllətə vìz/ (**-ized, -iz·ing, -iz·es**) *vti* to make one thing relative to something else, or regard one thing as relative to something else

re·la·tor /ri láytər/ *n* **1.** somebody who tells a story or gives an account of something **2.** *US* LAW somebody who can benefit from a legal action maintained on his or her behalf by a country or nation

re·lax /ri láks/ (**-laxed, -lax·ing, -lax·es**) *v* **1.** *vi* **SPEND TIME AT EASE** to spend time resting or doing things for pleasure, especially in contrast to or as a relief from the effort and stress of everyday life **2.** *vti* **MAKE OR BECOME LOOSER** to slacken something that is tensed or tight such as a muscle or a grip on something, or become looser, less tense, or less tight **3.** *vti* **MAKE OR BECOME LESS STRICT** to make something such as a rule less strict or less severe, or become less strict **4.** *vti* **MAKE OR BECOME LESS TENSE** to become less anxious, hostile, defensive, or formal, or make somebody or something so **5.** *vti* **MAKE OR BECOME LESS INTENSE** to become less intense and concentrated, or make something less intense and concentrated **6.** *vt* **STRAIGHTEN HAIR** to weaken or remove the curl from hair, usually by chemical means [14C. < Latin *relaxare* "loosen" < *laxus* "loose"] —**re·lax·a·ble** *adj* —**re·lax·ing** *adj*

re·lax·ant /ri láksənt/ *n* a drug that reduces tension and strain, particularly in muscles ■ *adj* causing something such as a muscle to become less tense

re·lax·a·tion /rēe lak sáysh'n/ *n* **1. ENJOYABLE ACTIVITY** a form of activity that provides a change and relief from effort, work, or tension, and gives pleasure **2. LOOSENING PROCESS** the process of becoming or making something less firm, rigid, or tight **3. LESSENING OF SEVERITY** a lessening of the strictness or severity of regulations, restrictions, or controls **4. REDUCTION IN INTENSITY** a lessening or weakening of something that was previously concentrated or intense **5.** PHYS **RETURN OF SYSTEM TO EQUILIBRIUM** the return of a system to equilibrium after it has been displaced or changed **6.** MATH **WAY OF SOLVING EQUATIONS** a way of solving equations using a series of approximate solutions, each of which reduces the number of errors contained in the previous one, until the errors fall within acceptable limits

re·laxed /ri lákst/ *adj* **1. EXPERIENCING NO STRAIN OR TENSION** under no strain or tension, and not exerting much strain or force on anything else **2. NOT FEELING ANXIOUS OR WORRIED** feeling no anxiety, tension, pressure, or sense of threat **3. ENCOURAGING INFORMALITY** encouraging informality and casual unhurried behavior **4.** CLOTHING **LOOSE-FITTING** loose-fitting and easy to wear —**re·lax·ed·ly** /ri láksədlee/ *adv* —**re·lax·ed·ness** /ri láksədnəss/ *n*

re·lax·er /ri láksər/ *n* something that slackens or loosens something else, especially a chemical used to straighten hair

re·lax·in /ri láksin/ *n* a polypeptide hormone that relaxes the pelvic ligaments of female mammals during pregnancy and is produced by the corpus luteum

re·lay *n* /rēe lày/ **1. PASSING OF SOMETHING TO SOMEBODY** the passing on of something, especially a message or information received, to somebody else, or the process of being passed on **2. REPLACEMENT TEAM** one of two or more teams of people or animals that relieve or replace each other in turn, e.g., as the previous team tires **3.** SPORTS same as **relay race** (*informal*) **4.** SPORTS **SECTION OF RELAY RACE** a section or lap of a relay race, run or swum by an individual athlete **5.** ELECTRONICS **DEVICE THAT REGULATES ANOTHER** an electronic or electromechanical switching device, typically operated by a low voltage, that controls a higher-voltage circuit and turns it on or off **6.** TELECOM **APPARATUS THAT RECEIVES AND TRANSMITS SIGNALS** an apparatus consisting of a receiver and a transmitter, used to receive and retransmit signals **7.** TELECOM **SIGNAL** a message or broadcast passed on by an apparatus that receives and retransmits signals ■ *vt* /ri láy, rēe lày/ (**-layed, -lay·ing, -lays**) **1. PASS SOMETHING ON TO SOMEBODY** to pass information or a message on to somebody **2. REPLACE TEAM WITH FRESH PEOPLE** to replace or relieve a team, squad, or crew with a new one **3. ARRANGE PEOPLE INTO TEAMS** to organize somebody or something, especially workers, into relays **4.** TELECOM **RETRANSMIT SIGNAL** to receive and retransmit a signal **5. BROADCAST SHOW** to transmit a broadcast through a transmitting station [14C. < Old French *relayer* "exchange tired horses" < Latin *relaxare* "loosen" (see RELAX)]

re-lay /ree láy/ *vt* to lay something such as a carpet again [Late 16C. < RE- + LAY[1]]

re·lay race *n* a race between teams of competitors in which each member of a team runs or swims only part of the total distance to be covered. In a running race, the current runner must pass a baton to the person running the next section.

re·lease /ri léess/ *vt* (**-leased, -leas·ing, -leas·es**) **1. LET SOMEBODY OR SOMETHING GO** to set free a person or animal who is imprisoned, trapped, or confined in some way **2. STOP CLUTCHING SOMETHING** to stop gripping or holding something **3. LET SOMETHING OUT** to let out something that has been contained or confined within something or that is pent up or latent inside somebody ○ *released a plume of smoke* **4. FREE SOMEBODY FROM OBLIGATION** to make somebody free of a debt, obligation, promise, or task **5. MAKE SOMETHING AVAILABLE** to make something available, e.g., by putting it on sale, distributing it to the press or public, or allowing access to it **6.** *US* **FIRE EMPLOYEE** to dismiss somebody from a job or position (*formal*; *used euphemistically*) **7.** ENG **OPERATE CATCH TO LET MECHANISM WORK** to take the tension off a mechanism such as a spring, brake, or catch and so allow something to move, open, or operate ○ *released the clutch* **8.** LAW **RELINQUISH SOMETHING** to relinquish something such as a right or claim to another party ■ *n* **1. LIBERATION** the act of setting somebody or something free, or the fact of being freed, from imprisonment, restraint, an obligation, or anything burdensome and oppressive **2. AUTHORIZATION FOR FREEDOM** a document or message stating that somebody is to be set free **3.** *UK* HR **LEAVE OF ABSENCE** leave of absence from a place, especially the workplace, or the granting of leave of absence, to enable somebody to do something else such as attend an educational course **4. EMISSION** the emission of something such as heat or radioactivity from the place where it is generated into the atmosphere or the environment **5. ACT OF MAKING SOMETHING AVAILABLE** the act of making something generally available or in use for the first time, or the fact of being made available in this way ○ *The release of his latest film is expected to be in the fall.* **6. SOMETHING MADE AVAILABLE TO PUBLIC** something that is made available to the public, put on show, or put on sale, e.g., a movie, recording, or item of information **7.** ENG **CONTROL MECHANISM** a mechanism, catch, or handle that is moved or pressed so that something it controls can be used or allowed to operate **8. OPERATION OF RELEASE** the moving or pressing of a mechanism so that what it controls can be used or allowed to operate **9. REMOVAL OF BURDEN** the removal of something that makes somebody feel trapped, restricted, or burdened **10.** LAW **RELINQUISHING OF CLAIM TO SOMETHING** the relinquishment of a right or claim to another party **11.** LAW **DOCUMENT CONFIRMING SURRENDER OF SOMETHING** a document stating that somebody has surrendered something such as a claim or right [13C. Via Old French *relaisser* "let go" < Latin *relaxare* "loosen" (see RELAX)] —**re·leas·a·bil·i·ty** /-lèessə bíllətee/ *n* —**re·leas·a·ble** *adj* —**re·leas·a·bly** *adv* —**re·leas·ee** /-lee sée/ *n* —**re·leas·er** *n* —**re·leas·or** *n*

re-lease /ree léess/ *vt* to lease something such as an apartment again [< RE- + LEASE]

re·leased time /ri léest-/ *n* HR same as **release time**

re·lease print *n* the version of a movie released for distribution to commercial theaters

re·lease time *n* time given to somebody by an authority or manager to allow personal matters or interests to be attended to

re·leas·ing fac·tor /ri léessing-/ *n* a hormone produced by the hypothalamus that causes the pituitary gland to secrete other hormones

rel·e·gate /réllə gàyt/ (**-gat·ed, -gat·ing, -gates**) *vt* **1. DEMOTE SOMEBODY OR SOMETHING** to move somebody or something to a less important position, category, or status **2. EXILE SOMEBODY** to banish somebody from a country or community **3. HAND SOMETHING ON** to pass something on to somebody for that person to deal with it or provide information about it (*formal*) [15C. < Latin *relegat-*, past participle of *relegare* "send away, refer" < *legare* "send as an envoy, bequeath"] —**rel·e·ga·tion** /rèllə gáysh'n/ *n*

~~releive~~ incorrect spelling of **relieve**

re·lent /ri lént/ (**-lent·ed, -lent·ing, -lents**) *vi* **1.** to become more sympathetic or amenable and do something previously ruled out or allow something previously forbidden **2.** to slacken or become less intense ○ *At last my headache relented.* [14C. < RE- + Latin *lentare* "bend, soften" < *lentus* "flexible"]

re·lent·less /ri léntləss/ *adj* **1.** never slackening, but continuing always at the same intense, demanding, or punishing level **2.** pursuing, attacking, or opposing somebody or something persistently and without mercy —**re·lent·less·ly** *adv* —**re·lent·less·ness** *n*

rel·e·vant /réllәvәnt/ *adj* **1.** having some sensible or logical connection with something else such as a matter being discussed or investigated **2.** having some bearing on or importance for real-world issues, present-day events, or the current state of society **3.** LING same as **distinctive** (sense 2) [Early 16C. < medieval Latin *relevant-*, present participle of Latin *relevare* "relieve," later "take possession of"] —**rel·e·vance** *n* —**rel·e·vant·ly** *adv*

USAGE The misspelling and mispronunciation "revelant" for ***relevant*** is increasingly common and should be avoided.

~~relevent~~ incorrect spelling of **relevant**

re·li·a·ble /ri lī́ əb'l/ *adj* **1.** able to be trusted to do what is expected or has been promised ○ *She is extremely reliable and a hard worker.* **2.** able to be trusted to be accurate or to provide a correct result ○ *That clock is not very reliable.* —**re·li·a·bil·i·ty** /-lī̀ ə bíllətee/ *n* —**re·li·a·ble·ness** *n* —**re·li·a·bly** *adv*

re·li·ance /ri lī́ ənss/ *n* **1. DEPENDENCE** dependence on another person or on something such as a service or a device, and the need for something that he, she, or it provides ○ *a reliance on painkillers* **2. CONFIDENCE** trust or confidence in the eventual fulfillment of a promise or in the eventual success of a plan **3. PRIMARY SUPPORT** somebody or something needed or depended on

re·li·ant /ri lī́ ənt/ *adj* depending on or needing somebody or something —**re·li·ant·ly** *adv*

rel·ic /réllik/ *n* **1. OLD THING SURVIVING FROM PAST** something that has survived from a long time ago, often a part of something old that has remained when the rest of it has decayed or been destroyed **2. OLD CUSTOM** a tradition, practice, or rule that dates from some time in the past, especially one that is considered out of date or inappropriate at the present time **3. KEEPSAKE** something that is kept for its interesting associations, e.g., with somebody famous or with a historic event **4.** RELIG **SOMETHING FROM DECEASED HOLY PERSON** something that is kept and venerated because it once belonged to a saint, martyr, or religious leader, especially a part of his or her body [13C. Via Old French *relique* < Latin *reliquiae* "remains" (particularly of a dead saint), plural of *reliquus* "remaining"]

rel·ict /réllikt/ *n* **1.** BIOL **SURVIVING SPECIES** a species of organism surviving long after the extinction of related species, or a once widespread natural population surviving only in isolated localities because of environmental changes **2.** GEOL **MINERAL UNALTERED BY METAMORPHISM** a mineral that did not change when the host rock metamorphosed **3.** GEOL **REMNANT OF PREEXISTING FORMATION** a remnant of a preexisting land or rock formation left behind after a destructive event has taken place **4.** LAW same as **widow** *n* (sense 1) (*archaic*) ■ *adj* BIOL **SURVIVING UNCHANGED** surviving in its original form when other related organisms have become extinct or its environment has changed completely [15C. < Latin *relictus* "left behind" < *relinquere* (see RELINQUISH)]

re·lic·tion /ri líksh'n/ *n* the gradual withdrawal of water from land, leaving it permanently dry

AKG London
relief: 9th-century Roman relief sculpture

re·lief /ri léef/ *n* **1. FREEING OF SOMEBODY FROM ANXIETY** a release from anxiety or tension, or the feeling of release, lightness, and cheerfulness that accompanies this **2. FACTOR THAT ENDS ANXIETY** a factor that ends a painful or stressful experience such as pain, hunger, or boredom **3. STARK CONTRAST CREATING DIVERSION** a factor forming a contrast to the general character of something else, especially something that breaks the monotony or tension of a longer experience **4. PROMINENCE CAUSED BY CONTRAST** uniqueness or prominence caused by contrast ○ *to bring out the differences in clear relief* **5.** SOC WELFARE **AID TO THOSE IN NEED** public help in the form of money, food, clothing, shelter, or medicine, provided to people who are temporarily unable to care for themselves **6.** HR **REPLACEMENT** somebody who assumes a task or duty when another completes his or her shift, or somebody who replaces another who is unable to work **7.** ART, SCULPTURE **PROJECTION FROM SURFACE** the elevation of figures or shapes from a flat surface, as seen in sculpture, or their apparent elevation, as seen in painting **8.** SCULPTURE, ART **WORK OF ART** a work of art with figures or shapes in relief **9.** GEOG, MAPS **ELEVATIONS OF LAND** the variations in height of a land surface and its being shaped into hills and valleys **10.** PRINTING **PRINTING PROCESS** a printing process that uses raised surfaces to apply ink to the paper, e.g., engraving **11.** MIL **LIBERATION FROM SIEGE** the freeing of a besieged town, castle, fort, or strategic position by soldiers belonging to the same side as those under siege **12.** LAW **REDRESS AWARDED BY COURT** compensation or redress for a wrong or hardship, awarded to a party by a court **13.** HIST **PAYMENT TO FEUDAL LORD** a payment made to a feudal lord by the descendant of a tenant in order to inherit a fief [14C. < Old French < *relever* (see RELIEVE)]

re·lief map *n* a map that shows variations in land height, usually by means of contour lines or different colors

re·lief pitch·er *n* in baseball or softball, a pitcher who replaces another pitcher during a game

re·lieve /ri léev/ (**-lieved, -liev·ing, -lieves**) *v* **1.** *vt* **STOP SOMETHING UNPLEASANT** to end, lessen, or provide a temporary break from something unpleasant such as pain, hunger, tension, or boredom **2.** *vt* HR **REPLACE SOMEBODY** to replace somebody on a shift or at a job **3.** *vt* HR **FIRE EMPLOYEE** to dismiss or suspend somebody from a job or position (*formal*) ○ *After the collision, the skipper was relieved of command.* **4.** *vt* **EASE SOMEBODY'S BURDEN** to remove something such as a burden or difficulty from the person on whom it is imposed ○ *They were relieved of responsibility for the children.* **5. re·lieve your·self** *vr* same as **urinate 6.** *vt* **MAKE SOMETHING PROMINENT** to make something stand out by contrast (*formal*) **7.** *vt* **HELP SOMEBODY BY REMOVING SOMETHING** to take something from somebody, usually something that the person is carrying or wearing ○ *Let me relieve you of your coat.* **8.** *vt* **TAKE AWAY THINGS FROM SOMEBODY** to take something or things away from somebody either by force of the law or by illegal means (*informal*) ○ *The police relieved the suspect of her weapon.* ○ *A thief relieved him of his wallet.* **9.** *vt* SOC WELFARE **HELP SOMEBODY** to provide help to people who are temporarily unable to care for themselves **10.** *vt* MIL **LIBERATE SOMETHING FROM MILITARY SIEGE** to liberate a besieged town, castle, fort, or strategic field position [14C. Via Old French *relever* < Latin *relevare* "raise again, help," literally "make light again" < *levis* "light"] —**re·liev·a·ble** *adj*

re·liev·er /ri léevər/ *n* **1.** somebody or something that provides relief or relieves another **2.** BASEBALL same as **relief pitcher**

re·lie·vo /rə léevō/ (*plural* **-vos**), **ri·lie·vo** *n* ARTS same as **relief** (sense 7) [Early 17C. < Italian *rilievo* < *rilevare* "to raise" < Latin *relevare* (see RELIEVE)]

relig. *abbr* religion

re·li·gion /ri líjjən/ *n* **1. BELIEFS AND WORSHIP** people's beliefs and opinions concerning the existence, nature, and worship of a deity or deities, and divine involvement in the universe and human life **2. SYSTEM** an institutionalized or personal system of beliefs and practices relating to the divine **3. PERSONAL BELIEFS OR VALUES** a set of strongly-held beliefs, values, and attitudes that somebody lives by **4. OBSESSION** an object, practice, cause, or activity that somebody is completely devoted to or obsessed by ○ *The danger is that you start to make fitness a religion.* **5.** CHR **MONK'S OR NUN'S LIFE** life as a monk or a nun, especially in the Roman Catholic Church [12C. Via French < Latin *religion-* "obligation, reverence"] —**re·lig·ion·less** *adj* ◇ **get religion** (*informal*) **1.** *US* to stop flouting the rules, regulations, customs, and expectations of society **2.** to become a believer or join a religious organization, and, usually, start to lead a life that follows its teachings

re·lig·ion·ism /ri líjjə nìzzəm/ *n* religious enthusiasm when regarded as affected or excessive (*disapproving*) —**re·lig·ion·ist** *n*

re·li·gi·ose /ri líjjee òss/ *adj* regarded as excessively, sentimentally, or affectedly pious (*disapproving*) [Mid-19C. < Latin *religiosus* (see RELIGIOUS)] —**re·lig·i·os·i·ty** /-lìjjee óssətee/ *n*

re·lig·ious /ri líjjəss/ *adj* **1. RELATING TO RELIGION** relating to belief in religion, the teaching of religion, or the practice of a religion ○ *religious freedom* **2. BELIEVING IN A HIGHER BEING** believing in and showing devotion or reverence for a deity or deities **3. THOROUGH** very thorough or conscientious ○ *a religious attention to detail* **4.** CHR **BELONGING TO MONASTIC ORDER** in Christianity, used to describe those who have committed themselves to a monastic order by taking vows, e.g., of poverty, chastity, or obedience ■ *n* (*plural same*) CHR **MONK OR NUN** a member of a monastic order [13C. Via French < Latin *religiosus* < *religio(n-)* "obligation, reverence"] —**re·lig·ious·ly** *adv* —**re·lig·ious·ness** *n*

Re·li·gious Soc·i·e·ty of Friends *n* CHR same as **Society of Friends**

~~**religous**~~ incorrect spelling of **religious**

re·lin·quish /ri língkwish/ (**-quished, -quish·ing, -quish·es**) *vt* **1. CEDE SOMETHING** to renounce or surrender something **2. ABANDON SOMETHING** to give something up or put something aside **3. LET SOMETHING GO** to let go of something physically [15C. < Old French *relinquiss-* < Latin *relinquere* "leave behind" < *linquere* "leave"] —**re·lin·quish·er** *n* —**re·lin·quish·ment** *n*

AKG London

reliquary: reliquary bust of Charlemagne

rel·i·quar·y /rélli kwèrree/ (*plural* **-ies**) *n* a container or shrine where relics such as the remains of a saint are kept [Mid-16C. < French *reliquaire* < *relique* (see RELIC)]

re·liq·ui·ae /ri líkwee èe/ *npl* the remains of something, especially fossil remains of plants or animals [Mid-17C. < Latin (see RELIC)]

rel·ish /réllish/ *vt* (**-ished, -ish·ing, -ish·es**) **1. ENJOY SOMETHING** to enjoy or take great pleasure in an experience ○ *relished every minute of their trip* **2. ENJOY EATING SOMETHING** to enjoy the taste of a particular food or drink **3. GIVE FLAVOR TO FOOD** to give a pleasing taste to food, e.g., by adding spice or relish ■ *n* **1. ENJOYMENT** a liking or appreciation of food or of an experience ○ *a relish for Spanish food* **2. SPICY SIDE DISH OR ACCOMPANIMENT** a spiced side dish or accompaniment to food, e.g., pickled or fresh vegetables with chili **3. STRONG TASTE** a pleasing sensation of strong taste or flavor **4. INTEREST OR EXCITEMENT** interest or excitement, especially when it makes something more enjoyable ○ *The incident added relish to an otherwise dull weekend.* [Early 16C. < Old French *relais* "remainder" < *relaisser* (see RELEASE)] —**rel·ish·a·ble** *adj*

re·live /ree lív/ (**-lived, -liv·ing, -lives**) *vt* to experience something again, especially as a result of thinking about it

~~**rellevant**~~ incorrect spelling of **relevant**

re·lo·cate /rée lō kàyt, rèe lō káyt/ (**-cat·ed, -cat·ing, -cates**) *vti* to move to a new place on a long-term basis, or move somebody or something to a new place, especially to change the location of a business or a residence —**re·lo·ca·tion** /rèe lō káysh'n/ *n*

re·luc·tance /ri lúktənss/ *n* **1.** unwillingness or lack of enthusiasm **2.** a measure of the resistance of a closed magnetic circuit to a magnetic flux. It is equal to the ratio of the magnetic potential difference to the magnetic flux.

re·luc·tant /ri lúktənt/ *adj* feeling or showing no willingness or enthusiasm to do something ○ *I am reluctant to drive in this weather.* [Mid-17C. < Latin *reluctant-*, present participle of *reluctari* "struggle against" < *luctari* "to struggle"] —**re·luc·tant·ly** *adv*

USAGE See ***reticent***.

SYNONYMS See ***unwilling***.

re·ly /ri lí/ (**-lied, -ly·ing, -lies**) *vi* **1.** to be dependent on somebody or something **2.** to have faith or confidence in somebody or something [14C. Via Old French *relier* < Latin *religare* "tie back" < *ligare* "to bind"]

rem /rem/ (*plural same*) *n* a unit for measuring amounts of radiation, equal to the effect that one roentgen of X-rays or gamma-rays would produce in a human being. It is used in radiation protection and monitoring. Full form **roentgen equivalent in man**

REM /rem, àar ee ém/ *abbr* MED rapid eye movement

re·made past participle, past tense of **remake**

re·main /ri máyn/ (**-mained, -main·ing, -mains**) *v* **1.** *vi* **STAY BEHIND** to stay behind or wait somewhere **2.** *vti* **CONTINUE IN SPECIFIED CONDITION** to continue in a particular state without changing **3.** *vi* **BE LEFT** to be left after everything else has gone **4.** *vi* **REQUIRE MORE WORK** to continue to need to be dealt with after everything else has been attended to ○ *The question still remains.* **5.** *vi* **ENDURE** to endure and succeed at continuing on in spite of all ○ *In spite of everything, the city remains.* [14C. < Old French *remaindre*, *remanoir* < Latin *remanere* < *manere* "to stay"]

re·main·der /ri máyndər/ *n* **1. PART OF SOMETHING LEFT** the part of something that is left after other parts have gone or been used up **2.** MATH **AMOUNT LEFT OVER AFTER DIVISION** the amount left over when a number or quantity cannot be divided exactly by another **3.** PUBL **UNSOLD BOOK** a book sold by a publisher at a reduced price after demand has fallen off **4.** LAW **INTEREST IN SOMEBODY ELSE'S ESTATE** an interest in an estate that passes to somebody only after a prior interest terminates, e.g., when the current holder of the estate dies ■ *vt* (**-dered, -der·ing, -ders**) PUBL **SELL BOOK AT REDUCED PRICE** to sell copies of a book at a reduced price after demand has fallen off [14C. < Anglo-Norman, variant of Old French *remaindre* (see REMAIN)]

re·main·ing /ri máyning/ *adj* still left or still existing

re·mains /ri máynz/ *npl* **1. ALL THAT IS LEFT** all that is left of something ○ *the remains of the barn after the fire* **2. CORPSE** a dead person's body **3. ANCIENT RUINS** the parts of something old that are still left ○ *the remains of ancient Roman baths* **4. DEAD AUTHOR'S UNPUBLISHED WRITINGS** all of an author's work that was still unpublished at the time of the author's death

re·make *n* /rée màyk/ something that has been made again or differently, especially a new version of an old movie ■ *vt* /ree máyk/ (**-made** /-máyd/, **-mak·ing, -makes**) to produce a remake of something

re·mand /ri mánd/ *vt* (**-mand·ed, -mand·ing, -mands**) **1. RETURN PRISONER TO CUSTODY** to return a prisoner or accused person to custody, or arrange for somebody to be released on bail when a court case is adjourned ○ *The judge ordered the prisoner to be remanded into custody.* **2. SEND CASE BACK TO LOWER COURT** to return a case to a lower court with instructions for further action to be taken **3. SEND SOMEBODY BACK** to send or order somebody back ■ *n* **RETURNING OF SOMEBODY UNTRIED TO PRISON** the return of a prisoner or accused person to custody, or the arrangement of bail for somebody, while waiting for trial [15C. Via French < late Latin *remandare* "send word back" < Latin *mandare* "to command"] —**re·mand·ment** *n*

re·mand cen·ter *n* in the United Kingdom and Canada, a place where accused people are detained while awaiting criminal trial

re·mand home *n UK* same as **detention home**

rem·a·nence /rémmənənss/ *n* the magnetic inductance that remains in a substance after the magnetizing field has been removed [Mid-16C. < Latin *remanent-*, present participle of *remanere* (see REMAIN)] —**rem·a·nent** *adj*

rem·a·nent mag·net·ism *n* magnetism shown by ferromagnetic minerals, which preserve the sense and direction of the Earth's magnetic field from the time of their formation

re·mark /ri maárk/ *n* **1. CASUAL COMMENT** a casual or brief observation **2. ACT OF COMMENTING** the act of making a remark about something, or an occasion on which this takes place ○ *They consumed their meal without remark.* **3. ACT OF NOTICING** an act or instance of noticing something, especially something that deserves attention (*formal*) ○ *How could such a major change take place without remark?* **4.** COMPUT same as **comment** *n* (sense 5) ■ *v* (**-marked, -mark·ing, -marks**) **1.** *vti* **MAKE COMMENT ON SOMETHING** to make a casual comment or observation about something **2.** *vt* **OBSERVE SOMETHING** to notice or observe something (*formal*) ○ *remarked the complexity of the investigation* [Late 16C. < French *remarquer* < *marquer* "to mark"] —**re·mark·er** *n*

re·mark·a·ble /ri maárkəb'l/ *adj* **1.** worth noticing or commenting on **2.** unusual or exceptional, and attracting attention because of this —**re·mark·a·ble·ness** *n*

re·mark·a·bly /ri maárkəblee/ *adv* **1.** to an extent or degree that is remarkable **2.** used to emphasize that something is worth noticing or commenting on ○ *Remarkably, no one was arrested.*

re·marque /ri maárk/ *n* **1.** a mark in the margin of an engraved plate, made to indicate its stage of production and removed before the regular printing, or the plate with the mark itself **2.** a proof of an engraving made from a plate with a remarque [Late 19C. < French < *remarquer* (see REMARK)]

Re·marque /rə maárk/, **Erich Maria** (1898–1970) German-born US writer. After he was wounded fighting for Germany in World War I, he wrote *All Quiet on the Western Front* (1929), which became a classic war novel. He lived in the United States after 1939. See Cultural note at **front**

> "Monotonously...falls the rain. It falls on our heads and on the heads of the dead up the line, on the body of the little recruit with the wound that is much too big for his hip;...it falls in our hearts."
> [Erich Maria Remarque, *All Quiet on the Western Front*; 1929]

re·mas·ter *vt* /ree mástər/ (**-tered, -ter·ing, -ters**) to make a new master copy of an earlier audio recording or movie to improve its quality of reproduction ■ *n* /rée màstər/ a new master copy of an earlier audio recording or a movie

re·match *n* /rée màch/ a second or return contest between opponents ■ *vt* /ree mách/ (**-matched, -match·ing, -match·es**) to arrange for opponents to meet in a second or return contest

Bettmann/Corbis

Rembrandt van Rijn

Rem·brandt van Rijn /rèm braant vaan rín, -bràant-/ (1606–69) Dutch artist. A major painter of the Dutch Golden Age, he imbued his portraits and religious and historical works with a moving spirituality. Full name **Rembrandt Harmenszoon van Rijn**

re·me·di·al /ri meédee əl/ *adj* **1.** ACTING AS REMEDY acting as a remedy or solution to a problem **2.** EDUC HELPING TO IMPROVE SKILLS designed to help people with learning difficulties to improve their skills or knowledge, or relating to education designed to do this **3.** MED INTENDED TO IMPROVE HEALTH intended to cure or relieve the symptoms of somebody who is ill or is physically challenged ○ *remedial exercises* —**re·me·di·al·ly** *adv*

re·me·di·a·tion /ri meèdee áysh'n/ *n* the use of remedial methods to improve skills or reverse environmental damage ○ *soil remediation*

rem·e·dy /rémmədee/ *n* (*plural* **-dies**) **1.** WAY OF PUTTING SOMETHING RIGHT a means of putting something right or getting rid of something undesirable ○ *no easy remedy for society's ills* **2.** MED TREATMENT FOR DISEASE a medication or treatment that cures a disease or disorder or relieves its symptoms **3.** ALTERN MED HOMEOPATHIC TREATMENT a substance prescribed by a homeopath, and taken in minute quantities **4.** LAW LEGAL REDRESS a legal means of enforcing a right or of providing redress **5.** COINS PERMITTED VARIATION IN COINS the legally permitted variation from an established standard in the weight or quality of a coin ■ *vt* (**-died, -dy·ing, -dies**) **1.** PUT SOMETHING RIGHT to put something right, or get rid of something undesirable **2.** MED CURE DISEASE to cure or relieve a disease or disorder [13C. Via Anglo-Norman *remedie* < Latin *remedium* "medicine"] —**re·me·di·a·ble** /ri meédee əb'l/ *adj* —**re·me·di·a·bly** *adv*

re·mem·ber /ri mémbər/ (**-bered, -ber·ing, -bers**) *v* **1.** *vti* RECALL SOMETHING FORGOTTEN to recall something to mind or become aware of something that had been forgotten **2.** *vti* KEEP SOMETHING IN MEMORY to retain an idea in the memory without forgetting it **3.** *vt* KEEP SOMEBODY IN MIND to keep somebody in mind for attention or consideration **4.** *vt* GIVE SOMEBODY A GIFT to give somebody a gift, money, or a tip ○ *She always remembered him on his birthday.* **5.** *vt* SEND SOMEBODY'S GREETINGS to mention somebody to somebody else as a way of passing on a greeting ○ *Remember me to your Mom.* **6.** *vt* COMMEMORATE SOMEBODY OR SOMETHING to commemorate somebody or something, e.g., in a ceremony or funeral service ○ *remembering our veterans on Memorial Day* [14C. Via Old French *remembrer* < late Latin *rememorari* < Latin *memor* "mindful"] —**re·mem·ber·er** *n*

re·mem·brance /ri mémbrənss/ *n* **1.** REMEMBERING the act or process of remembering people, things, or events **2.** BEING REMEMBERED the state of being remembered, or of remaining in people's minds ○ *We hold her name in fond remembrance.* **3.** ACT OF HONORING the act of honoring the memory of a person or event ○ *a service of remembrance* **4.** SOMETHING REMEMBERED something that is remembered **5.** EXTENT OF MEMORY the period of time over which memory extends **6.** MEMENTO something that reminds somebody of a thing, event, or another person **7.** FRIENDLY EXPRESSION a greeting, gift, or other expression of affection and friendship

CULTURAL NOTE ***Remembrance of Things Past***, a series of novels (1913–22) by French writer Marcel Proust. Regarded as one of the greatest works of 20th-century literature, this remarkable meditation on time and memory describes the narrator's childhood encounters with his aristocratic neighbors and his subsequent introduction to Parisian society. A series of unconscious recollections triggers the realization that the past is not lost but can be retrieved by memory and preserved as art.

Re·mem·brance Day *n Can* in Canada, a legal holiday in remembrance of those who died in World Wars I and II and subsequent conflicts. Date: November 11.

re·mex /reé mèks/ (*plural* **rem·i·ges** /rémmə jeèz/) *n* a flight feather of a bird's wing (*technical*) [Late 17C. < Latin, "oarsman" < *remus* "oar"] —**re·mig·i·al** /ri míjjee əl/ *adj*

re·mind /ri mínd/ (**-mind·ed, -mind·ing, -minds**) *vt* to cause somebody to remember or think of something or somebody else ○ *Remind me to collect the dry cleaning.* ○ *He reminds me of his grandfather.*

re·mind·er /ri míndər/ *n* **1.** a letter or message sent to remind somebody about something ○ *If they don't settle the bill next week, send them a reminder.* **2.** somebody or something that reminds a person or people of somebody or something else ○ *The monument is a reminder of their bravery.*

Rem·ing·ton /rémmingtən/, **Frederic** (1861–1909) US artist. He produced paintings and sculptures of the old American West.

~~**reminice**~~ incorrect spelling of **reminisce**

rem·i·nisce /rèmmə níss/ (**-nisced, -nisc·ing, -nisc·es**) *vi* to talk or write about events remembered from the past [Early 19C. Back-formation < REMINISCENCE] —**rem·i·nis·cer** *n*

rem·i·nis·cence /rèmmə níss'nss/ *n* **1.** RECOLLECTION OF PAST the recollection of past experiences or events in speech or writing, or the act of recalling the past **2.** SOMETHING REMEMBERED an experience or event remembered from the past **3.** REMINDER something that recalls or suggests something similar **4.** PHILOSOPHY IDEA FROM PLATO the Platonic doctrine that anything we encounter is an imperfect recollection of an idea that our souls have encountered in a previous disembodied existence **5.** PSYCHOL ABILITY TO PERFORM TASK BETTER the ability to perform a task or remember information better some time after it has been learned than was possible immediately after it was learned

rem·i·nis·cent /rèmmə níss'nt/ *adj* **1.** RESEMBLING SOMETHING OR SOMEBODY ELSE suggesting similarities or comparisons with something or somebody else **2.** SUGGESTING MEMORIES OF PAST characterized by or containing recollections of the past ○ *scenes reminiscent of her childhood* **3.** RECALLING PAST given to reminiscing about the past [Mid-18C. < Latin *reminiscent-*, present participle of *reminisci* "recollect"] —**rem·i·nis·cent·ly** *adv*

re·mise /ri míz/ *n* **1.** LAW DEEDING OF PROPERTY a transfer of property **2.** SECOND FENCING THRUST in fencing, a further thrust made on the same lunge to follow up a first thrust that has missed ■ *vi* (**-mised, -mis·ing, -mis·es**) MAKE REMISE in fencing, to make a remise when a first thrust has missed [15C. < French < Latin *remittere* "send back" (see REMIT)]

re·miss /ri míss/ *adj* careless or negligent about doing something that is expected [15C. < Latin *remissus*, past participle of *remittere* "send back" (see REMIT)]

re·mis·si·ble /ri míssəb'l/ *adj* worthy of forgiveness (*formal*) ○ *remissible sins* —**re·mis·si·bil·i·ty** /-mìssə bíllətee/ *n*

re·mis·sion /ri mísh'n/ *n* **1.** SLOWING OF DISEASE a lessening of the symptoms of a disease, or their temporary reduction or disappearance **2.** LESSENING OF SOMETHING a lessening or a reduction in the severity of something ○ *The afternoon sun beat down without remission.* **3.** RELEASE FROM SOMETHING a release from a debt, penalty, or obligation **4.** FORGIVENESS pardon or forgiveness **5.** ACT OF REMITTING an instance or the action of remitting something

re·mit *v* /ri mít/ (**-mit·ted, -mit·ting, -mits**) **1.** *vti* SEND PAYMENT to send money to pay for merchandise or services, especially by mail **2.** *vt* CANCEL SOMETHING to cancel or hold back from enforcing something **3.** *vti* REDUCE INTENSITY OF SOMETHING to reduce in intensity, or reduce the intensity of something **4.** *vt* RESTORE SOMETHING to restore something to a previous condition or position **5.** *vt* DEFER SOMETHING to postpone or defer something **6.** *vt* PARDON SOMETHING to pardon or forgive something such as a sin or other transgression **7.** *vt* LAW SEND CASE BACK TO LOWER COURT to send a case back to a lower court for further action to be taken ■ *n* /ri mít, reémit/ **1.** SOMETHING REMITTED something sent to another person or authority for consideration **2.** LAW TRANSFER OF LEGAL CASE the transfer of a legal case from a higher to a lower court for further action to be taken [14C. < Latin *remittere* "send back" < *mittere* "send"] —**re·mit·ment** *n* —**re·mit·ta·ble** *adj* —**re·mit·tal** *n* —**re·mit·tee** /ri mì teé/ *n* —**re·mit·ter** *n*

re·mit·tance /ri mítt'nss/ *n* **1.** ACT OF PAYING the sending of money to pay for merchandise or services **2.** MONEY money sent as payment for merchandise or services **3.** ACT OF REMITTING the act of remitting something

re·mit·tent /ri mítt'nt/ *adj* lessening and then intensifying again at intervals ○ *slowed down by a remittent fever* —**re·mit·tence** *n* —**re·mit·ten·cy** *n* —**re·mit·tent·ly** *adv*

re·mix *vt* /ree míks/ (**-mixed, -mix·ing, -mix·es**) to produce a new version of a piece of music by altering the emphasis of the sound and, in pop music, often adding new tracks in place of existing ones ■ *n* /reé mìks/ a recording that has been remixed

rem·nant /rémnənt/ *n* **1.** SMALL PART STILL LEFT a small part of something that remains after the rest has gone **2.** SMALL AMOUNT OF CLOTH OR CARPET a small amount of unsold cloth or flooring material left at the end of a roll, often sold at a reduced price **3.** TRACE OF SOMETHING a small amount or trace of something such as a feeling or emotion **4.** ANTHROP SMALL SURVIVING GROUP OF PEOPLE a small isolated group of people surviving from a culture or group [14C. < Old French *remanant*, present participle of *remanoir* (see REMAIN)]

re·mod·el /ree módd'l/ (**-eled, -el·ing, -els**) *vt* to renovate or alter the structure or style of something such as a building, room, or design —**re·mod·el·er** *n*

re·mon·strance /ri mónstrənss/ *n* **1.** a forceful argument in favor of or against something, or the act of making such an argument **2.** a formal protest, usually in the form of a document or petition

Re·mon·strance *n* the statement expressing Arminian Protestant principles, drawn up in 1610 in Gouda, the Netherlands. The doctrines of Jacob Arminius rejected Calvinist predestination and supported the notion of free will, and had a profound effect on Wesleyan and Methodist theology.

re·mon·strant /ri mónstrənt/ (*formal*) *n* somebody who remonstrates ■ *adj* involved in or used for a protest [Early 17C. < medieval Latin *remonstrant-*, present participle of *remonstrare* (see REMONSTRATE)] —**re·mon·strant·ly** *adv*

Re·mon·strant *n* a Dutch dissenter and supporter of the Remonstrance of 1610

re·mon·strate /ri món stràyt, rémmən stràyt/ (**-strat·ed, -strat·ing, -strates**) *vi* to reason or argue forcefully with somebody about something (*formal*) [Late 16C. < medieval Latin *remonstrat-*, past participle of *remonstrare* "demonstrate" < Latin *monstrare* "to show"] —**re·mon·stra·tion** /ri mòn stráysh'n, rèmmən-/ *n* —**re·mon·stra·tive** /ri mónstrətiv/ *adj* —**re·mon·stra·tive·ly** *adv* —**re·mon·stra·tor** *n*

SYNONYMS See ***object***.

rem·o·ra /rémmərə/ *n* a bony saltwater fish with a suction disk on the top of its head that it uses to attach itself to a larger fish or a ship's hull. Family: Echeneidae. [Mid-16C. < Latin, "hindrance"; from the belief that it slowed ships down]

re·morse /ri máwrss/ *n* a strong feeling of guilt and regret [14C. < Old French *remors* < Latin *remordere* "to torment" < *mordere* "to bite"] —**re·morse·ful** *adj* —**re·morse·ful·ly** *adv* —**re·morse·ful·ness** *n*

re·morse·less /ri máwrssləss/ *adj* **1.** showing no pity or compassion **2.** continuing without lessening in strength or intensity —**re·morse·less·ly** *adv* —**re·morse·less·ness** *n*

re·mort·gage /ree máwrgij/ *vt* (**-gaged, -gag·ing, -gag·es**) **1.** CHANGE MORTGAGE TERMS to revise the terms of a mortgage on a property **2.** MORTGAGE SOMETHING AGAIN to mortgage something again after the original mortgage has been paid off ■ *n* NEW MORTGAGE a revised or second mortgage taken out on something

re·mote /ri mṓt/ *adj* (**-mot·er, -mot·est**) **1.** FAR AWAY situated a long way away **2.** OUT-OF-THE-WAY far away from civilization, society, or any other populated area **3.** DISTANTLY RELATED distantly related by blood, adoption, or marriage **4.** LONG AGO distant in time **5.** SLIGHT faint or slight ○ *not the remotest possibility of her coming here* **6.** DISTANTLY RELEVANT distant in connection, relevance, or effect **7.** ALOOF distant in manner or behavior **8.** OPERATED FROM DISTANCE operated or performed from a distance ○ *a remote camera* ○ *a remote shopping service* ■ *n* **1.** ELEC same as **remote control** (sense 1) (*informal*) **2.** COMPUTER FAR FROM CENTRAL COMPUTER a device or computer system that is situated at a distance from a central computer and that can be accessed via a network **3.** *US* BROADCAST BROADCAST PROGRAM MADE OUTSIDE a radio or television broadcast transmitted from outside the studio [15C. < Latin *remotus*, past participle of *removere* (see REMOVE)] —**re·mote·ly** *adv* —**re·mote·ness** *n*

re·mote ac·cess *n* access that is gained to a computer by means of a separate terminal

re·mote con·trol *n* **1.** a handheld device used to operate a television set, videocassette recorder, or other electronic device from a distance **2.** the control of a device, system, or activity from a distance, usually by radio signals (*hyphenated before a noun*) ○ *a remote-control transmitter* —**re·mote-con·trolled** *adj*

re·mote sen·sor *n* an instrument that gathers information about Earth or another astronomical object from an airborne platform or from space, e.g., a radar or photographic device

ré·mou·lade /ràymoo la̅a̅d/ *n* mayonnaise with herbs, mustard, capers, and pickles added, and sometimes chopped hard-boiled egg [Mid-19C. < French]

re·mould /ree mṓld/ *UK n* same as **retread** *n* (sense 1) ■ *vt* (**-mould·ed, -mould·ing, -moulds**) same as **retread**

re·mount *v* /ree mównt/ (**-mount·ed, -mount·ing, -mounts**) **1.** *vt* PUT SOMETHING ON AGAIN to mount something again or anew **2.** *vti* GET BACK INTO SADDLE to get back on a horse or bicycle ■ *n* /rée mòwnt/ SUBSTITUTE HORSE a replacement horse to ride

re·mov·al /ri mo͞ov'l/ *n* **1.** REMOVING OF SOMETHING the taking away or getting rid of something **2.** CHANGE OF LOCATION a change in location, or in the place where somebody lives **3.** HR DISMISSAL dismissal from office or from a position

re·mo·val van *n UK* same as **moving van**

re·move /ri mo͞ov/ *v* (**-moved, -mov·ing, -moves**) **1.** *vt* TAKE SOMETHING AWAY to take something away from somebody or from a place **2.** *vti* RELOCATE OR BE RELOCATED to transfer somebody or something to another place, or change a place of residence **3.** *vt* TAKE OFF CLOTHING to take off an item of clothing ○ *removed his hat* **4.** *vt* GET RID OF SOMETHING to make something go away or disappear ○ *a detergent that can remove stains even more quickly* **5.** *vt* HR DISMISS SOMEBODY to dismiss somebody from office or from a position **6.** *vi* DEPART to leave a place **7.** *vi* BE REMOVED to go away or disappear ○ *The compound removed easily in solvent.* ■ *n* **1.** DISTANCE the degree of distance or closeness between people or things ○ *He has only experienced war at one remove.* **2.** CHANGE OF LOCATION a change of residence or business (*formal*) [14C. Via French < Latin *removere* < *movere* "to move"] —**re·mov·a·ble** *adj* —**re·mov·er** *n*

re·moved /ri mo͞ovd/ *adj* **1.** separate or distant in space, time, or character from something or somebody else **2.** separated from somebody by a particular degree of descent ○ *a first cousin twice removed* —**re·mov·ed·ness** /-ədnəss/ *n*

REM sleep /rém-/ *n* a stage of sleep that recurs several times during the night and is marked by dreaming, rapid eye movements under closed lids, and elevated pulse rate and brain activity

re·mu·da /ri mṓodə/ *n Southwest US* AGRIC same as **string** (sense 19) (*dated*) [Late 19C. < American Spanish, "change of horses" < Spanish *remudar* "to exchange"]

REGIONAL NOTE ***Remuda*** is an old-time common expression among working cattlemen in the Southwest and Rocky Mountain states. Alternative names are *caballado, cavvy,* and *caviard* (from Spanish *caballada*), and *string.*

re·mu·ner·ate /ri myṓonə ràyt/ (**-at·ed, -at·ing, -ates**) *vt* to pay somebody for goods or services, or compensate somebody financially for losses sustained or inconvenience caused [Early 16C. < Latin *remunerat-*, past participle of *remunerari* "reward" < *munus* "gift"] —**re·mu·ner·a·bil·i·ty** /-myṓonərə bíllətee/ *n* —**re·mu·ner·a·ble** *adj* —**re·mu·ner·a·tor** *n* —**re·mu·ner·a·to·ry** *adj*

re·mu·ner·a·tion /ri myṓonə ráysh'n/ *n* **1.** a payment or reward for goods or services or for losses sustained or inconvenience caused **2.** the paying or rewarding of somebody for goods or services or for losses sustained or inconvenience caused

SYNONYMS See ***wage***.

re·mu·ner·a·tive /ri myṓonə raytiv/ *adj* paying somebody or rewarding somebody with money —**re·mu·ner·a·tive·ly** *adv*

Re·mus /reéməss/ *n* in Roman mythology, the son of Mars and twin brother of Romulus, the founder of the city of Rome

ren·ais·sance /rénnə saánss, rènnə saánss, ri náyss'nss/ *n* a rebirth or revival, e.g., of culture, skills, or learning forgotten or previously ignored [Late 19C. < French *renaître* "be reborn" < Latin *renasci* < *nasci* "be born"]

Barnaby's

Renaissance: detail of the bronze doors of the Baptistery, Florence, Italy, by Lorenzo Ghiberti

Ren·ais·sance *n* **1.** END OF MIDDLE AGES the period in European history from about the 14th through 16th centuries regarded as marking the end of the Middle Ages and featuring major cultural and artistic change **2.** CLASSICAL REVIVAL the cultural and religious spirit that characterized the Renaissance, including the decline of Gothic architecture, the revival of classical culture, the beginnings of modern science, and geographic exploration ■ *adj* **1.** OF RENAISSANCE relating to the history and culture of the Renaissance **2.** IN ARCHITECTURAL STYLE OF RENAISSANCE in the architectural style of classical revival that characterized the Renaissance

Ren·ais·sance man *n* a man who has a wide range of accomplishments and intellectual interests

Ren·ais·sance wom·an *n* a woman who has a wide range of accomplishments and intellectual interests

re·nal /reén'l/ *adj* relating to or affecting the kidneys [Mid-17C. Via French < late Latin *renalis* < Latin *renes* "kidneys"]

re·nal clear·ance *n* a measure of the removal of waste products from the blood by the kidneys, expressed as the volume of blood cleared of a specific substance in one minute

re·nal pel·vis *n* the cavity in the kidney where urine collects before passing into the ureter

re·nas·cence /ri náss'nss, -náy-/ *n* same as **renaissance** [Early 18C. < RENASCENT]

Re·nas·cence *n* HIST same as **Renaissance**

re·nas·cent /ri náss'nt, -náyss'nt/ *adj* showing new life or activity [Early 18C. < Latin *renascent-*, present participle of *renasci* "be reborn" (see RENAISSANCE)]

re·na·ture /ree náychər/ (**-tured, -tur·ing, -tures**) *vt* to restore the physical and chemical properties of a denatured protein or nucleic acid —**re·nat·u·ra·tion** /ree nàychə ráysh'n/ *n*

ren·coun·ter /ren kówntər/ *n* (*archaic*) **1.** a hostile meeting between adversaries **2.** an unexpected casual meeting [Early 16C. < French *rencontrer* "have a (hostile) meeting" < *encontrer* "confront" (see ENCOUNTER)]

rend /rend/ (**rent** /rent/ or **rend·ed, rend·ing, rends**) *v* **1.** *vti* PULL SOMETHING APART to pull something apart violently, or be pulled apart violently **2.** *vt* TEAR CLOTHES to tear or pull clothes or hair, out of rage, frustration, or grief **3.** *vt* TAKE SOMEBODY OR SOMETHING AWAY FORCIBLY to tear or wrest something or somebody away **4.** *vt* SHATTER SOMETHING to disturb the silence or pierce the air with a loud sound ○ *A scream rent the air.* **5.** *vt* DISTRESS SOMEBODY to cause pain or distress to the heart or emotions [Old English *rendan* < Germanic]

SYNONYMS See ***tear***[1].

ren·der /réndər/ *v* (**-dered, -der·ing, -ders**) **1.** *vt* GIVE HELP to give help or provide a service (*formal*) **2.** *vt* TRANSLATE SOMETHING to translate something into another language (*formal*) ○ *fragments of poetry, hastily rendered into English* **3.** *vt* ARTS PORTRAY SOMETHING ARTISTICALLY to portray something or somebody in art, literature, music, or acting (*formal*) **4.** *vt* GIVE DECISION to deliver a verdict or decision officially (*formal*) **5.** *vt* COMPUT DRAW SOMETHING to draw something in computer graphics **6.** *vt* SUBMIT SOMETHING FOR ACTION to submit something for consideration, approval, or payment (*formal*) ○ *render an invoice for payment* **7.** *vt* GIVE SOMETHING AS DUE to give what is due or appropriate to somebody who has authority or power (*formal*) ○ *"Render therefore unto Caesar the things which are Caesar's"* (Matthew 22:21, *The Bible*) **8.** *vt* PUT SOMEBODY OR SOMETHING IN PARTICULAR STATE to make somebody or something be or become something (*formal*) ○ *His actions rendered her powerless.* **9.** *vt* PURIFY FAT to purify or extract something by melting, especially to heat solid fat slowly until as much liquid fat as possible has been extracted from it, leaving small crisp remains **10.** *vti* GIVE UP SOMETHING to surrender something (*formal or literary*) **11.** *vt* TRADE SOMETHING to give something in exchange for something else (*formal or literary*) **12.** *vt* RETURN SOMETHING to give something back (*formal or literary*) **13.** *vt* CONSTR COVER WALL WITH PLASTER to cover masonry with a thin coat of plaster ■ *n* **1.** CONSTR COAT OF PLASTER the first thin coat of plaster applied to masonry **2.** HIST TENANT'S PAYMENT a payment in goods, services, or money made by a tenant to a feudal lord [14C. Via French *rendre* < alteration of Latin *reddere* "give back" < *dare* "give"] —**ren·der·a·ble** *adj* —**ren·der·er** *n*

ren·der farm *n* a cluster of networked computers used to create computer graphic effects such as animation

ren·der·ing /réndəring/ *n* **1.** ARTISTIC PORTRAYAL a portrayal of somebody or something in art, music, literature, or drama **2.** TRANSLATION a translation of a literary work **3.** HEATING ANIMAL REMAINS TO EXTRACT FAT the process or business of separating fat from meat or animal remains by slow heating **4.** CONSTR COAT OF PLASTER a coat of plaster applied to masonry **5.** ARCHIT ARCHITECT'S PERSPECTIVE DRAWING an architect's representation of the inside and outside of a finished building, drawn in perspective

ren·dez·vous /raán day vo͞o, raándə-/ *n* (*plural* **-vous** /-vo͞oz/) **1.** MEETING a meeting arranged for an agreed time and place **2.** PLACE OF MEETING the location of a prearranged meeting **3.** PLACE WHERE PEOPLE MEET a popular meeting place for people ■ *vti* (**-voused** /-vo͞od/, **-vous·ing** /-vo͞o ing/, **-vouses** /-vo͞oz/) MEET SOMEBODY to meet, meet somebody, or bring people together at an agreed time and place [Late 16C. < French, literally "present yourself"]

ren·di·tion /ren dísh'n/ *n* **1.** VERSION OF MUSICAL OR THEATRICAL PIECE an interpretation or performance of a piece of music or drama **2.** WORK IN TRANSLATION a translation of a literary work **3.** TRANSLATING the act of translating something into another language (*formal*) [Early 17C. < French < *rendre* (see RENDER)]

ren·dzi·na /ren jeénə/ *n* a dark rich soil that develops beneath grassland above a layer of limestone or chalk [Early 20C. < Polish *rĕdzina*]

ren·e·gade /rénnə gàyd/ *n* **1.** somebody who abandons previously held beliefs or loyalties **2.** somebody who chooses to live outside laws or conventions [15C. < Spanish *renegado* < medieval Latin *renegatus* < past participle of *renegare* "deny" (see RENEGE)]

re·nege /ri níg, -nég, -néeg/ (**-neged, -neg·ing, -neges**) *vi* **1.** to go back on a promise or commitment **2.** in cards, to fail to follow suit when able and required to do so [Mid-16C. < medieval Latin *renegare* "deny" < Latin *negare*] —**re·nege** *n* —**re·neg·er** *n*

re·new /ri nóō/ (**-newed, -new·ing, -news**) *v* **1.** *vti* **RETURN TO DOING SOMETHING** to begin something or doing something again, or be begun again ○ *renewed their friendship after several years* ○ *renewed his calls for an investigation* **2.** *vti* **EXTEND SOMETHING** to make something such as a contract, lease, or license effective for a longer period, or be made effective for a longer period ○ *You'll need to renew your lease at the end of the year.* **3.** *vt* **REPLACE SOMETHING WORN** to replace something that is worn, broken, or no longer suitable for use **4.** *vt* **BORROW LIBRARY BOOK FOR LONGER** to extend the period of time a book or other item is borrowed from a library **5.** *vt* **REPEAT PROMISE** to reaffirm or restate a promise or commitment ○ *renewed their marriage vows* **6.** *vt* **GIVE SOMEBODY OR SOMETHING NEW ENERGY** to give somebody or something new energy, strength, or enthusiasm ○ *A day of rest renewed his strength.* **7.** *vt* **REPLACE SOMETHING USED UP** to get a new supply of something **8.** *vt* **MAKE SOMETHING NEW AGAIN** to make something new or as if new again —**re·new·al** *n* —**re·newed** *adj* —**re·new·er** *n*

SYNONYMS ***renew, recondition, renovate, restore, revamp***

CORE MEANING: to improve the condition of something

renew to replace something that is worn, broken, or no longer suitable for use ○ *He added a room and renewed the roof.* ○ *Bones should constantly renew and rebuild themselves, but in osteoporosis this doesn't happen.* **recondition** to bring something back into good condition, especially by repairing it and replacing worn-out parts ○ *Their business was reconditioning used cars.* ○ *the workshop where they reconditioned the aircraft engines* **renovate** to bring something such as a building back to a former better state by means of repairs, redecoration, or remodeling ○ *newly renovated offices* ○ *the money needed to renovate crumbling school buildings* **restore** to bring something back to an earlier and better condition ○ *a fully restored flour mill dating back to 1730* ○ *The wall hanging has been recently cleaned and restored.* **revamp** to improve the appearance, condition, or structure of something by making sometimes superficial changes ○ *a major construction program to revamp the city's shabby waterfront* ○ *As the airline revamped its business, the work force was reduced by about 900.* **overhaul** to carry out comprehensive repairs and adjustments, especially to a piece of machinery ○ *We stayed in the town while the ship was being overhauled.* ○ *Industry watchers had expected the company to overhaul its corporate structure.* **refurbish** to bring something back to a cleaner, brighter, more functional state ○ *It would cost about 1 million less to refurbish the school than to build a new one.* ○ *a major advertising campaign designed to refurbish the company's safety image.*

re·new·a·ble /ri nóō əb'l/ *adj* **1.** able to be sustained or renewed indefinitely, either because of inexhaustible supplies or because of new growth **2.** capable of being begun or done again ■ *n* ENVIRON same as **renewable resource** (*often used in the plural*) —**re·new·a·bil·i·ty** /-nòō ə bíllətee/ *n* —**re·new·a·bly** *adv*

re·new·a·ble en·er·gy *n* INDUST same as **alternative energy**

re·new·a·ble re·source *n* **1. RESOURCE THAT CAN BE SUSTAINED** a resource that can be renewed as quickly as it is used up and can, in theory, last indefinitely. Lumber, unlike mineral resources, is a renewable resource. **2. RESOURCE THAT REPLACES ITSELF** a natural resource that replaces itself unless overused, e.g., animal or plant life or fresh water **3. RENEWABLE FORM OF ENERGY** a source of alternative energy, e.g., sunlight, wind, or waves

re·newed /ri nóōd/ *adj* **1.** resuming after an interruption, usually with more intensity or energy ○ *renewed efforts to force a breakthrough* **2.** feeling stronger, or more relaxed, energetic, or enthusiastic

ren·i·form /rénnə fàwrm, réenə-/ *adj* shaped like or suggestive of a kidney [Mid-18C. < Latin *ren* "kidney"]

ren·in /rénnin/ *n* an enzyme released by the kidneys that breaks down proteins and helps regulate blood pressure [Late 19C. < Latin *ren* "kidney"]

ren·i·tent /rénnitənt, ri nī́t'nt/ *adj* (*formal*) **1.** resisting physical pressure, as opposed to being flexible or pliant **2.** reluctant to have a change of mind or concede to others [Early 18C. < Latin *renitent-*, present participle of *reniti* "struggle against"] —**ren·i·tence** *n* —**ren·i·ten·cy** *n*

ren·min·bi /rènmin bée/ (*plural same*) *n* the national currency of the People's Republic of China, equivalent in value to the yuan [Mid-20C. < Chinese < *rénmín* "people" + *bì* "currency"]

Rennes /ren/ capital city of Ile-Vilaine Department, Brittany Region, western France. It is situated about 60 mi./97 km north of Nantes. Population: 206,229 (1999).

ren·net /rénnət/ *n* **1. STOMACH LINING OF CALVES** the inner lining of the fourth stomach of calves and other young ruminants **2. SUBSTANCE FOR CURDLING MILK** a substance made from rennet that contains the enzyme rennin, used in cheese making **3. VEGETARIAN ALTERNATIVE TO RENNET** a substitute for rennet made from plants **4.** BIOCHEM same as **rennin** [15C. Probably < Germanic]

ren·nin /rénnin/ *n* a milk-curdling enzyme produced in the stomachs of young mammals [Late 19C. < RENNET]

Re·no /réenō/ city in western Nevada, located on the Truckee River, near Lake Tahoe in the Sierra Nevada Mountains. It is a resort and commercial center, and is home to the University of Nevada-Reno. Population: 190,248 (2002 estimate).

Re·no, Janet (*b.* 1938) US lawyer. She was the first woman appointed US attorney general (1993–2001).

> "Unless we are willing to invest in children early on, we will never be able to build enough prisons ever to begin to cope with the problem 13, 15, 18 years from now."
> [Janet Reno, *New York Times*; May 16, 1994]

re·no·gram /réenə gràm/ *n* **1.** a photographic record of kidney function, showing how quickly a radioactive substance injected into the bloodstream is removed when it passes through the kidneys **2.** an X-ray image of a kidney [Early 20C. < Latin *ren* "kidney"]

AKG London

Pierre Auguste Renoir

Re·noir /rén waar, rən waar/, **Auguste** (1841–1919) French painter and sculptor. One of the leading impressionists, he is noted for the harmony of his lines, the brilliance of his colors, and the intimate charm of his wide variety of subjects. Full name **Renoir, Pierre Auguste**

> "I have a predilection for a painting that lends joyousness to a wall."
> [Auguste Renoir, *Renoir*, Ambrose Vollard; 1919]

Re·noir, Jean (1894–1979) French movie director. The son of Auguste Renoir, he was a technical innovator known for the fluidity of his work. His greatest movie is *The Rules of the Game* (1939). He lived in the United States after 1941.

> "Is it possible to succeed without any act of betrayal?"
> [Jean Renoir, "Nana," *My Life and My Films*; 1974]

re·nor·mal·i·za·tion /ree nàwrm'li záysh'n/ *n* a mathematical technique used in quantum physics that eliminates infinite terms by carefully defining fundamental quantities such as mass and charge —**re·nor·mal·ize** *vt*

re·nounce /ri nównss/ *v* (**-nounced, -nounc·ing, -nounc·es**) **1.** *vt* **GIVE UP CLAIM** to give up formally a claim, title, position, or right **2.** *vt* **REJECT BELIEF** to reject or disavow a belief or theory **3.** *vt* **STOP DOING SOMETHING** to give up a habit, pursuit, or practice **4.** *vi* CARDS **NOT FOLLOW SUIT** in cards, to be unable to follow suit and be forced to play a card from a different suit ■ *n* CARDS **ACT OF NOT FOLLOWING SUIT** in cards, a failure to follow suit [14C. Via French *renoncer* < Latin *renuntiare* "report" < *nuntiare* "announce"] —**re·nounce·ment** *n* —**re·nounc·er** *n*

re·no·vas·cu·lar /réenō váskyələr/ *adj* relating to the blood vessels of the kidneys [Mid-20C. < Latin *ren* "kidney"]

ren·o·vate /rénnə vàyt/ (**-vat·ed, -vat·ing, -vates**) *vt* **1.** to bring something such as a building back to a former better state by means of repairs, redecoration, or remodeling **2.** to give new vigor to somebody or something [15C. < Latin *renovat-*, past participle of *renovare* < *novus* "new"] —**ren·o·va·tion** /rènnə váysh'n/ *n* —**ren·o·va·tive** *adj* —**ren·o·va·tor** *n*

SYNONYMS See ***renew.***

re·nown /ri nówn/ *n* widespread fame or honor [14C. < Old French *renon* < *renomer* "make famous" < *nomer* "to name" < Latin *nominare*]

re·nowned /ri nównd/ *adj* well known or famous, especially for a skill or expertise

Rens·se·laer ♦ **Van Rensselaer, Stephen**

rent[1] /rent/ *n* **1. PAYMENT BY TENANT** a regular payment made by a tenant to an owner or landlord for the right to occupy or use property **2. PAYMENT TO USE EQUIPMENT** a regular payment to the owner for the right to use equipment or personal property **3. PROFIT FROM CULTIVATED LAND** the financial return from cultivated land after production costs have been deducted **4. INCOME OF LANDOWNERS** the portion of the national income that is earned by landowners **5.** ECON same as **economic rent** ■ *vti* (**rent·ed, rent·ing, rents**) **1. PAY TO USE SOMEBODY'S PROPERTY** to occupy somebody else's property or use somebody else's equipment in return for regular payments **2. ALLOW USE OF PROPERTY FOR PAYMENT** to allow somebody to occupy property or use equipment in return for regular payments [12C. < French *rente* < alteration of Latin *reddere* "give back" (see RENDER)] —**rent·a·ble** *adj*

rent[2] /rent/ *n* **1.** an opening or hole made by tearing something **2.** a rift in a relationship, or a breach in friendly relations [Mid-16C. < obsolete variant of REND]

rent[3] /rent/ past participle, past tense of **rend**

rent·al /rént'l/ *n* **1. RENT PAYMENT** an amount paid in rent **2. RENT INCOME** an amount received in rent **3. ACT OF RENTING SOMETHING** the renting of property or equipment **4. SOMETHING RENTABLE** something rented or available to rent ○ *The car is a rental.* **5.** *US* **RENTING BUSINESS** a business that rents out property or equipment ■ *adj* **1.** *US* **FOR RENT** available to be rented **2. RELATING TO RENT** relating to property for rent or with rent payments

rent·al li·brar·y *n US* a library that lends books or other items for a fee

rent con·trol *n* government regulation of the amount charged for housing rental and sometimes of eviction procedures [< RENT[1]] —**rent-con·trolled** *adj*

rent·er /réntər/ *n* **1.** somebody who rents property or equipment from somebody else **2.** somebody who rents property or equipment to somebody else [14C. < RENT[1]]

rent-free *adj* not subject to rent payments ■ *adv* without having to pay rent [< RENT[1]]

ren·tier /rón tyày, rawN tyáy/ *n* somebody whose

income is primarily from rent and securities [Mid-19C. < French < *rente* (see RENT[1])]

rent strike *n* an organized refusal by tenants to pay their rent [< RENT[1]]

re·num·ber /ree númbər/ *vt* to number items according to a new sequence

re·nun·ci·a·tion /ri nùnssee áysh'n/ *n* **1.** a denial or rejection of something or somebody, usually for moral or religious reasons **2.** an official declaration giving up a title, office, claim, or privilege [14C. Directly or via French < Latin *renuntiation-* "announcement, (in late Latin) renunciation" < past participle of *renuntiare* (see RENOUNCE)] —**re·nun·ci·a·to·ry** /-núnssee ə tàwree/ *adj*

ren·voi /ren vóy/ *n* the referral of a case or dispute from the country or state in which it arose to the laws of another [Late 19C. < French < *renvoyer* "send back" < *envoyer* "send"]

Ren·wick /rén wìk/, **James** (1818–95) US architect. He designed the Smithsonian Institution in Washington, D.C. (1846), and St. Patrick's Cathedral in New York City (1858).

re·of·fend /reè ə fénd/ (**-fend·ed, -fend·ing, -fends**) *vi* to commit a second or subsequent offense —**re·of·fend·er** *n*

re·o·pen /ree ṓpən/ (**-pened, -pen·ing, -pens**) *vti* to open again, or cause something to be opened again ○ *I don't want to reopen old wounds.* ○ *The store will reopen in March.*

re·or·gan·i·za·tion /ree àwrgəni záysh'n/ *n* **1.** a change in the way something is organized, arranged, or done **2.** the thorough physical or financial restructuring of a business or organization —**re·or·gan·i·za·tion·al** *adj*

re·or·gan·ize /ree áwrgə nīz/ (**-ized, -iz·ing, -iz·es**) *vti* **1.** to impose organization on something again after its being disturbed **2.** to change the way that something is organized, or be changed —**re·or·gan·iz·er** *n*

re·o·ri·ent /ree áwree ənt, -ènt/ (**-ent·ed, -ent·ing, -ents**), **re·o·ri·en·tate** /ree áwree ən tàyt, -en-/ (**-tat·ed, -tat·ing, -tates**) *v* **1. re·o·ri·ent your·self** *vr* to find out where you are or where you are going after being lost **2.** *vti* to change the direction or management of something, or your behavior or ideas, to deal with a new situation —**re·o·ri·en·ta·tion** /ree àwree ən táysh'n/ *n*

re·o·vi·rus /reè ō vīrəss/ *n* a virus that contains double-stranded RNA and is associated with various infections in plants and animals. Reoviruses are often found in people with breathing and stomach disorders. [Mid-20C. < acronym < *respiratory enteric orphan*]

rep[1] /rep/, **repp** *n* a ribbed or corded silk, wool, rayon, or cotton fabric [Mid-19C. < French *reps*]

rep[2] /rep/ *n* repertory theater (*informal*) [Early 20C. Shortening of REPERTORY]

rep[3] /rep/ (*informal*) *n* COMM same as **sales representative** ■ *vi* (**repped, rep·ping, reps**) to work as a sales representative [Late 19C. Shortening of REPRESENTATIVE]

rep[4] /rep/ *n* same as **reputation** (*informal*) [Early 18C. Shortening]

rep[5] /rep/ *n* a repetition of a fitness exercise (*informal*) [Mid-19C. Shortening of REPETITION]

rep. *abbr* **1.** PUBL repair **2.** PUBL report **3.** PUBL reported **4.** LAW reporter **5.** PUBL reprint

Rep. *abbr* POL **1.** US Representative **2.** Republic **3.** US Republican

re·paid past participle, past tense of **repay**

re·pair[1] /ri páir/ *vt* (**-paired, -pair·ing, -pairs**) **1.** FIX OR MEND SOMETHING to restore something broken or damaged to good condition ○ *repair a flat tire* **2.** RESTORE RELATIONSHIP to restore a relationship or friendship by resolving a difficulty or disagreement **3.** ATONE FOR SOMETHING to make amends for something wrong ○ *How can I repair this wrong?* ■ *n* **1.** JOB OF MENDING SOMETHING the process of mending something, or the job that is done in order to achieve this ○ *carry out repairs* **2.** REPAIRED ITEM something that has been repaired **3.** CONDITION OF SOMETHING the condition of something with respect to whether it needs mending or fixing ○ *an air conditioner no longer in good repair* [14C. Via French < Latin *reparare* < *parare* "make ready"] —**re·pair·a·bil·i·ty** /ri pèrrə bíllətee/ *n* —**re·pair·a·ble** *adj* —**re·pair·er** *n*

re·pair[2] /ri páir/ *vi* (**-paired, -pair·ing, -pairs**) GO SOMEWHERE to go to a particular place (*formal*) ○ *repaired to the library after dinner* ■ *n* (*archaic*) **1.** ACT OF GOING SOMEWHERE the act of going to a particular place, especially frequently **2.** HAUNT a place where a person or animal is frequently found [14C. Via French < late Latin *repatriare* "go back home" (see REPATRIATE)]

re·pair·man /ri páir màn, -páirmən/ (*plural* **-men** /-mèn, -mən/) *n* a man whose job is making repairs to equipment or machinery

re·pair·per·son /ri páir pùrss'n/ (*plural* **-peo·ple** /-peèp'l/ or **-per·sons**) *n* somebody whose job is making repairs to equipment or machinery

re·pair·wom·an /ri páir wòommən/ (*plural* **-wom·en** /-wìmmin/) *n* a woman whose job is making repairs to equipment or machinery

re·pand /ri pánd/ *adj* with a wavy edge ○ *a repand leaf* [Mid-18C. < Latin *repandus* "curving back" < *pandere* "become curved"]

rep·a·ra·ble /réppərəb'l/ *adj* able to be repaired, recovered, or put right —**rep·a·ra·bil·i·ty** /rèppərə bíllətee/ *n* —**rep·a·ra·bly** *adv*

rep·a·ra·tion /rèppə ráysh'n/ *n* **1.** AMENDS compensation for a wrong, or something that is done to achieve this **2.** REPAIR restoration of something to good condition, or the process of doing this (*formal*) ■ **rep·a·ra·tions** *npl* COMPENSATION FOR WAR compensation demanded of a defeated nation by the victor in a war, especially that demanded of Germany by the Treaty of Versailles after World War I —**re·par·a·tive** /ri párrətiv/ *adj* —**re·par·a·to·ry** /ri párrə tàwree/ *adj*

rep·ar·tee /rèppər teé, -táy, -paar-/ *n* **1.** WITTY TALK conversation consisting of witty remarks **2.** WIT skill in making witty remarks or conversation **3.** WITTY REMARK a witty remark or reply [Mid-17C. < French *repartie* < *repartir* "set out again" < *partir* "leave"]

re·par·ti·tion /reè paar tísh'n/ *n* **1.** DISTRIBUTION distribution or division of something **2.** DIVIDING OF SOMETHING AGAIN the act of dividing or distributing something again, either in the same way or differently ■ *vt* (**-tioned, -tion·ing, -tions**) DIVIDE SOMETHING UP AGAIN to divide something up again, either in the same way or differently

re·past /ri pást/ *n* a meal, or the food eaten at a meal (*literary*) [14C. < Old French < *repaistre* "to feed" < Latin *pascere*]

re·pa·tri·ate *vt* /ree páytree àyt/ (**-at·ed, -at·ing, -ates**) **1.** SEND SOMEBODY BACK to send somebody back to his or her country of birth, the country of which he or she is a citizen, or the country from which he or she arrived **2.** SEND BACK MONEY to send money that has been earned or invested abroad back to its owner's country of origin **3.** SEND BACK ARTEFACT to send a cultural artefact or works of art back to country of origin ■ *n* /ree páytree ət, -àyt/ SOMEBODY REPATRIATED somebody who has been repatriated [Early 17C. < late Latin *repatriat-*, past participle of *repatriare* "go back home" < Latin *patria* "homeland"] —**re·pa·tri·a·tion** /ree pàytree áysh'n/ *n*

re·pay /ri páy/ (**-paid** /-páyd/, **-pay·ing, -pays**) *vt* **1.** PAY BACK MONEY TO SOMEBODY to pay back money that is owed to somebody ○ *I was repaid in full within the week.* ○ *We will repay the loan.* **2.** RETURN FAVOR TO SOMEBODY to reward somebody for his or her effort, aid, or success ○ *We can never repay your kindness.* ○ *Your hard work will be repaid with success.* **3.** RETURN SOMETHING to return something in kind ○ *repaid the visit* —**re·pay·a·ble** *adj* —**re·pay·ment** *n*

re·peal /ri peél/ *vt* (**-pealed, -peal·ing, -peals**) to officially end the validity of something such as a law ■ *n* the act of repealing something such as a law [14C. < Anglo-Norman *repeler*, variant of Old French *rapeler* < *re-* "again, back" + *apeler* (see APPEAL)] —**re·peal·a·ble** *adj* —**re·peal·er** *n*

SYNONYMS See ***nullify.***

re·peat *v* /ri peét/ (**-peat·ed, -peat·ing, -peats**) **1.** *vt* SAY SOMETHING AGAIN to say or write something again **2.** *vti* DO OR UNDERGO SOMETHING AGAIN to do, produce, or experience something again or several times ○ *She repeated the exercises every day.* **3.** *vti* ECHO SOMEBODY'S WORDS to say again what somebody else has said **4.** *vt* TELL WHAT HAS BEEN HEARD to tell another person something that was told to you, especially when it was done in confidence ○ *I'll tell you, but you mustn't repeat it to anyone else.* **5.** *vt* SAY SOMETHING MEMORIZED to recite something that has been learned **6. re·peat your·self** *vr* SAY SAME THING AGAIN to do or say something again, especially more than once ○ *You get tired of repeating yourself after a while.* **7. re·peat it·self** *vr* HAPPEN AGAIN to happen again in the same way as previously ○ *History is repeating itself.* **8.** *vti* BROADCAST BROADCAST AGAIN to broadcast a television or radio program again, or be broadcast again **9.** *vi* BE TASTED AGAIN to be tasted again after having been eaten, through wind or partial regurgitation (*informal*) ○ *Those spicy meatballs are repeating on me.* ■ *n* /reè peét/ **1.** RECURRING EVENT OR SITUATION an event or situation that is the same as a previous one **2.** SOMETHING SHOWN AGAIN something that is broadcast, shown, or performed again **3.** MUSIC RECURRING MUSICAL PASSAGE a passage of music played again within a single piece, or the notation indicating that this is to be done **4.** UNIFORMLY REPRODUCED PATTERN a pattern reproduced uniformly across a surface ○ *upholstery fabric with a large floral repeat* **5.** ACT OF REORDERING SOMETHING a reorder of the same goods or by the same customer [14C. Via French < Latin *repetere* "demand again" < *petere* "to demand"] —**re·peat·a·bil·i·ty** /ri peètə bíllətee/ *n* —**re·peat·a·ble** *adj* —**re·peat·ed** *adj*

re·peat·ed·ly /ri peétədlee/ *adv* again and again, or on several occasions

re·peat·er /ri peétər/ *n* **1.** SOMEBODY OR SOMETHING REPEATING somebody or something that repeats something **2.** ARMS GUN FIRING SEVERAL SHOTS WITHOUT RELOADING a firearm with a magazine that can fire several shots before it has to be reloaded, e.g., a rifle **3.** TIME TIMEPIECE THAT REPEATS CHIMES a clock or watch that can be made to repeat its latest chime when somebody presses a spring **4.** US EDUC STUDENT MADE TO REPEAT STUDIES a student required to repeat a course or grade after failing it **5.** US CRIME RECIDIVIST a repeat offender **6.** ELEC ENG DEVICE FOR AMPLIFYING SIGNALS an electrical device that boosts and amplifies incoming communications signals and retransmits them

re·peat·ing dec·i·mal *n* a decimal number in which one or more digits recur indefinitely after the decimal point, e.g., 3.77777... or 8.691691691...

re·peat·ing fire·arm *n* ARMS same as **repeater** (sense 2)

re·peat per·form·ance *n* an event that is the same as one that happened before

re·peat pre·scrip·tion *n Can, UK* a prescription for a regularly needed medicine that has been prescribed before and can be renewed without the doctor having to see the patient

re·pe·chage /rèppə shaázh/ *n* a heat within a competition during which runners-up in earlier heats have a final chance to qualify for the next round. Fencing, rowing, and cycling competitions often have a repechage. [Early 20C. < French < *repêcher*, literally "fish out"]

re·pel /ri pél/ (**-pelled, -pel·ling, -pels**) *v* **1.** *vti* CAUSE GREAT DISTASTE to make somebody feel intense aversion, disgust, or revulsion **2.** *vt* KEEP SOMETHING AWAY to ward something off, or keep something away ○ *a cream that is effective in repelling mosquitoes* **3.** *vt* RESIST ATTACK to ward off or force back an attack or invasion **4.** *vti* FAIL TO MIX to fail to mix or blend with something else ○ *Oil and water repel each other.* **5.** *vti* PHYS EXERT OPPOSING FORCE to exert a force that tends to push something away ○ *Particles of like charge repel each other.* **6.** *vt* SPURN SOMEBODY OR SOMETHING to reject or refuse to accept something or somebody [15C. Via French < Latin *repellere* "drive back" < *pellere* "to drive"] —**re·pel·ler** *n*

re·pel·lent /ri péllənt/, **re·pel·lant** *adj* **1.** CAUSING DISGUST making somebody feel intense dislike, disgust, or revulsion **2.** RESISTANT TO SOMETHING resistant or impervious to something (*often used in combination*) ○ *water-repellent material* **3.** PUSHING AWAY pushing something away or driving something back ■ *n* **1.** SOMETHING THAT REPELS INSECTS a substance that drives away insects **2. SUBSTANCE THAT RESISTS SOMETHING HARMFUL** a substance that is applied to a surface of something to resist water, mold, or mildew —**re·pel·lence** *n* —**re·pel·lent·ly** *adv*

USAGE Note that the adjective is usually spelled *-ent* and not *-ant*. The *-ant* variant is somewhat more commonly found for the noun (*an insect repellant*) than for the adjective.

USAGE repellent or **repulsive**? Both words mean "causing disgust," but ***repulsive*** is stronger in effect than ***repellent***. ***Repellent*** is also used in combinations such as *insect-repellent* and *water-repellent*, denoting substances that physically repel or resist a particular thing. ***Repulsive*** does not have a literal meaning corresponding to this.

re·pent[1] /ri pént/ (**-pent·ed, -pent·ing, -pents**) *vti* **1.** to recognize the wrong in something you have done and be sorry about it **2.** to feel regret about a sin or past actions and change your ways or habits [13C. < French *repentir* < *pentir* < Latin *paenitere*] —**re·pen·tance** *n* —**re·pen·tant** *adj* —**re·pent·er** *n*

re·pent[2] /reépənt/ *adj* growing or lying along the ground [Mid-17C. < Latin *repent-*, present participle of *repere* "creep"]

~~**repentence**~~ incorrect spelling of **repentance**

re·per·cus·sion /reépər kúsh'n/ *n* **1. RESULT OF ACTION** something, especially an unforeseen problem, that results from an action (*often used in the plural*) **2. REBOUND** the rebounding of a force after impact **3.** PHYS **REFLECTION** the reflection of light or sound **4.** MUSIC **POINT OF REAPPEARANCE IN FUGUE** in a fugue, the return of the theme after an episode [Mid-16C. Directly or via French < Latin *repercussion-* < past participle of *repercutere* "strike back through" < *percutere* "strike through"] —**re·per·cus·sive** *adj*

rep·er·toire /réppər twaàr/ *n* **1. MATERIAL AVAILABLE FOR PERFORMANCE** a stock of musical or dramatic material that is known and can be performed **2. BODY OF ARTISTIC WORKS** the entire body of works in a specific area of the arts **3. RANGE OF RESOURCES THAT SOMEBODY HAS** the range of techniques, abilities, or skills that somebody or something has ○ *the surgeon's repertoire* [Mid-19C. Via French < late Latin *repertorium* (see REPERTORY)] ◇ **in repertoire** used to refer to performances of different plays or ballets given on different days

rep·er·to·ry /réppər tàwree/ (*plural* **-ries**) *n* **1.** *Can, UK* a system by which a permanent theater company presents a set of works during a season, usually in its own theater. US term **stock 2. USER OF STOCK SYSTEM** a theater or company that uses the stock system **3.** ARTS same as **repertoire** (senses 1–2) **4. COLLECTION OF AVAILABLE THINGS** a store or stock of available items ○ *a comedian with a large repertory of jokes* [Late 16C. < late Latin *repertorium* "inventory" < Latin *reperire* "get completely" < *parire* "get"] —**rep·er·to·ri·al** /rèppər táwree əl/ *adj*

rep·er·to·ry com·pa·ny *n Can, UK* same as **stock company** (sense 2)

rep·e·tend /réppə tènd/ *n* **1.** the part of a repeating decimal that is repeated infinitely, e.g., "37" in "0.373737" **2.** something that is repeated [Early 18C. < Latin *repetendum* "thing to be repeated" < *repetere* "demand again"]

ré·pé·ti·teur /ri pèttee túr/ *n* a musician in an opera company who coaches the singers and accompanies them on the piano in rehearsal [Mid-20C. < French, "somebody who repeats"]

rep·e·ti·tion /rèppə tísh'n/ *n* **1. REPEATING OF SOMETHING** an act of doing something again **2. SOMETHING SAME AS BEFORE** an event or situation that is the same as one that happened previously **3. PROCEDURE OF STATING SOMETHING AGAIN** the act or process of saying or writing something again **4. REPEATED WORDS** something that is repeated, especially unnecessary words [Early 16C. Via French < Latin *repetition-* < *repetere* "demand again"]

rep·e·ti·tious /rèppə tíshəss/ *adj* full of repetition, especially unnecessary or tiresome repetition —**rep·e·ti·tious·ly** *adv* —**rep·e·ti·tious·ness** *n*

re·pet·i·tive /ri péttitiv/ *adj* full of or involving repetition ○ *a boring repetitive task* —**re·pet·i·tive·ly** *adv* —**re·pet·i·tive·ness** *n*

re·pet·i·tive mo·tion dis·or·der *n US* MED same as **cumulative trauma disorder**

re·pet·i·tive strain in·ju·ry, re·pet·i·tive stress in·ju·ry *n* MED same as **cumulative trauma disorder**

re·pine /ri pīn/ (**-pined, -pin·ing, -pines**) *vi* to feel dissatisfied or fretful about something and complain or grumble about it (*literary*) [Early 16C. < PINE[2] "fret," after REPENT[1]] —**re·pin·er** *n*

~~**repitition**~~ incorrect spelling of **repetition**

re·place /ri pláyss/ (**-placed, -plac·ing, -plac·es**) *vt* **1. SUBSTITUTE FOR SOMETHING** to take the place of or substitute for somebody or something ○ *The new ways rapidly replaced the old.* **2. SUPPLANT SOMEBODY OR SOMETHING** to fill the place of somebody or something with somebody or something else ○ *You can be replaced.* **3. PUT SOMETHING IN ANOTHER'S PLACE** to provide or find a substitute for something ○ *can't afford to replace his car* **4. PUT SOMETHING BACK IN ITS PLACE** to put an object back in its usual place ○ *She replaced the receiver slowly.* —**re·place·a·ble** *adj* —**re·plac·er** *n*

USAGE replace or **substitute**? The constructions involving these two words are different, although the resulting meaning is usually the same. You ***replace*** item B *with* (or less often *by*) item A, but ***substitute*** item A *for* item B.

re·place·ment /ri pláyssmənt/ *n* **1. SUBSTITUTION** the act or process of taking the place of or substituting for somebody or something **2. SUBSTITUTE** somebody or something that replaces another **3.** CHEM **CHANGE OF ONE MINERAL TO ANOTHER** the partial or complete transformation of one mineral into another in response to changing conditions such as the presence of water **4.** *US* MIL **SOMEBODY FILLING MILITARY VACANCY** somebody who fills a vacancy in a military force

re·plant /ree plánt/ (**-plant·ed, -plant·ing, -plants**) *vt* **1. TRANSFER PLANT TO NEW PLACE** to transfer a plant or part of a plant into new soil or a new area **2. PROVIDE PLACE WITH NEW PLANTS** to put new plants in a place or container to replace previous plants ○ *replant the flower boxes every spring* **3.** MED, DENT **REATTACH OR REINSERT BODY PART** to reattach or reinsert a severed body part such as a limb or tooth —**re·plan·ta·tion** /reè plan táysh'n/ *n*

re·play *vt* /ree pláy/ (**-played, -play·ing, -plays**) **1. PLAY RECORDING AGAIN** to play again something that has been recorded on tape, video, or film **2. PLAY MATCH AGAIN** to play a game, match, or contest again ■ *n* /reè plày/ **1. CONTEST PLAYED AGAIN** a game, match, or contest that is played again **2. RECORDED MATERIAL REPLAYED** something recorded on tape, video, or film that is played again **3. REPEAT OF PREVIOUS EVENT** an event that repeats or appears to repeat something in the past ○ *The latest business failure was a replay of the previous one.*

re·plen·ish /ri plénnish/ (**-ished, -ish·ing, -ish·es**) *vt* **1. REPLACE USED ITEMS** to restock depleted items or material ○ *time for the campers to replenish their supplies* **2. NOURISH SOMEBODY OR SOMETHING** to fill somebody or something with needed energy or nourishment **3. REFUEL FIRE** to resupply a fire with fuel [Early 17C. < Old French *repleniss-*, stem of *replenir* "fill again" < *plenir* "fill" < Latin *plenus* "full"] —**re·plen·ish·er** *n* —**re·plen·ish·ment** *n*

re·plete /ri pleét/ *adj* **1.** amply, completely, or fully supplied with something ○ *a kitchen replete with all the latest gadgets* **2.** having eaten enough to be fully satisfied [14C. Directly or via French < Latin *repletus*, past participle of *replere* "fill up" < *plere* "fill"] —**re·plete·ness** *n*

re·ple·tion /ri pleésh'n/ *n* **1.** a condition of being overfull after eating too much **2.** the condition of being fully satisfied

re·plev·in /ri plévvin/ *n* an act or writ to recover goods by somebody who claims to own them and who promises to have the claim later tested in court ■ *vt* (**-ined, -in·ing, -ins**) LAW same as **replevy** [14C. < Anglo-Norman < *replevir* (see REPLEVY)]

re·plev·y /ri plévvee/ *vt* (**-ied, -y·ing, -ies**) to seize goods on the grounds of ownership after promising to test the claim in court ■ *n* (*plural* **-ies**) a seizure of claimed goods after a promise that the claim will be tested in court later [Late 16C. < Anglo-Norman *replevir* "recover thoroughly" < *plevir* "recover"] —**re·plev·i·a·ble** *adj*

rep·li·ca /répplikə/ *n* **1.** an accurate reproduction of an object **2.** a scrupulous copy of a work of art, especially one made, authorized, or supervised by the original artist [Early 19C. < Italian, "repeat" < Latin *replicare* (see REPLICATE)]

rep·li·cant /répplikənt/ *n* especially in science fiction, an imaginary being that has been constructed from organic and computerized components to look like a human being

rep·li·case /réppli kàyss, -kàyz/ *n* a polymerase enzyme, especially one that uses RNA molecules as a template to make new RNA molecules in RNA virus replication [Mid-20C. < REPLICATE]

rep·li·cate *v* /réppli kàyt/ (**-cat·ed, -cat·ing, -cates**) **1.** *vt* **DO SOMETHING AGAIN** to make an identical version of something repeatedly and exactly, or do something again in exactly the same way **2.** *vi* **BE DONE AGAIN** to undergo a repetition or reproduction **3.** *vt* BIOL **COPY CELLULAR OR GENETIC MATERIAL** to reproduce exactly an organism, genetic material, or a cell ■ *adj* /répplikət/ BOT **BENT BACK** describes a leaf or other part that is folded back on itself [Mid-16C. < Latin *replicat-*, past participle of *replicare* "fold back" < *plicare* "to fold"] —**rep·li·ca·tive** *adj*

SYNONYMS See ***copy***.

rep·li·ca·tion /rèppli káysh'n/ *n* **1. PROCESS OF REPEATING** the process of repeating, duplicating, or reproducing something **2.** BIOL **MAKING OF CELLULAR OR GENETIC COPY** the production of exact copies of molecules, genetic material, or cells **3.** LAW **REPLY OF PLAINTIFF** a plaintiff's reply to the plea of a defendant (*dated*) **4.** BOT **FOLD** a fold or folding back of a leaf or other part **5. REPLY TO ANSWER** something said in reply to an answer

rep·li·con /réppli kòn/ *n* a segment of DNA or RNA that replicates itself as a unit, distinct from adjacent segments in a chromosome or other genetic element [Mid-20C. < REPLICATION]

re·ply /ri plí/ *v* (**-plied, -ply·ing, -plies**) **1.** *vti* **RESPOND TO WHAT SOMEBODY SAYS** to say or write something in response to what somebody else has said or written ○ *replied that she wouldn't be available to take the job* **2.** *vi* **RESPOND WITH ACTION OR GESTURE** to respond to somebody's action with a countering action or gesture **3.** *vi* LAW **ANSWER DEFENDANT'S PLEA** to speak in response to the plea of a defendant in a court of law **4.** *vi* **ECHO** to echo or return a sound ■ *n* (*plural* **-plies**) **1. SPOKEN OR WRITTEN RESPONSE** a reaction, usually written or spoken, to a question, letter, or situation **2. ACTION PERFORMED AS RESPONSE** something done as a response to somebody else's action ○ *Her only reply was to turn on her heel and leave.* **3.** LAW **ANSWER TO DEFENDANT'S PLEA** a statement made in response to the plea of a defendant in a court of law [14C. Via Old French *replier* < Latin *replicare* (see REPLICATE)] —**re·pli·er** *n*

SYNONYMS See ***answer***.

re·ply-paid *adj UK* MAIL same as **postpaid**

re·po /reépō/ (*plural* **-pos**) *n* (*informal*) **1.** property that is repossessed because payments have not been made wholly or in part **2.** a repurchase agreement for something [Late 20C. Shortening of REPOSSESS]

re·point /ree póynt/ (**-point·ed, -point·ing, -points**) *vt* to repair a brick wall by putting new mortar or cement between the bricks

re·po·lar·i·za·tion /reè pōlərə záysh'n/ *n* the restoration of the normal electrical polarity of a nerve or muscle cell membrane following reversal of its polarity (**depolarization**) during passage of a nerve impulse or muscle contraction —**re·po·lar·ize** *vt*

re·port /ri páwrt/ *v* (**-port·ed, -port·ing, -ports**) **1.** *vti* **TELL ABOUT WHAT HAPPENED** to give information about something that has happened ○ *reported that negotiations were proceeding slowly* **2.** *vti* **TELL PEOPLE NEWS USING MEDIA** to find out facts and tell people about them in print or a broadcast **3.** *vt* **INFORM AUTHORITIES ABOUT SOMETHING OR SOMEBODY** to inform somebody in authority about something that has happened, especially a crime or an accident, or about somebody who has done something wrong ○ *reported him missing two days ago* ○ *reported the break-in to the police* **4.** *vti* TELL ABOUT RESEARCH to give detailed information about research or an investigation ○ *The committee will report their findings early next week.* **5.** *vti* MAKE OFFICIAL STATEMENT to make a formal statement regarding something **6.** *vt* RECORD COURT PROCEEDINGS to record the proceedings of a court of law **7.** *vi* INFORM ABOUT ARRIVAL to let somebody know you have arrived ○ *Guests should report to reception on arrival.* **8.** *vi* BE UNDER SOMEBODY'S AUTHORITY to be subordinate and responsible to somebody or something ○ *You'll be reporting to me from now on.* ■ *n* **1.** ACCOUNT OF SOMETHING an account of an event, situation, or episode **2.** NEWS ITEM an account of news presented by a journalist, in a print or broadcast medium **3.** DOCUMENT GIVING INFORMATION a document that gives information about an investigation or a piece of research, often put together by a group of people working together **4.** UNCONFIRMED ACCOUNT a widely-known account of something that may be true but has not been confirmed ○ *Report had it that the company was approaching bankruptcy.* **5.** BUSINESS PERIODIC STATEMENT OF COMPANY'S FINANCES a detailed periodic account of a company's activities, financial condition, and prospects that is made available to stockholders and investors ○ *a quarterly report* **6.** *UK* EDUC same as **report card** **7.** SHARP LOUD NOISE a very sharp loud noise, especially that of an explosion or gunshot **8.** REPUTATION reputation or perceived character ■ **re·ports** *npl* LAW ACCOUNTS OF COURT CASES written accounts of a court's adjudication, summarizing arguments and findings [14C. Via French < Latin *reportare* "carry back" < *portare* "carry"] —**re·port·a·ble** *adj*

re·port·age /rèppər taázh, ri páwrtij/ *n* **1.** PROCESS OF TELLING NEWS the use of print and electronic media to inform people about news and current events **2.** THINGS REPORTED a body of reported news **3.** WAY OF GIVING NEWS a particular way of gathering and presenting news [Late 19C. < REPORT, after French *reportage*]

re·port card *n* a record of a child's performance at school over a specific period, prepared by teachers and given to the child's parents

re·port·ed·ly /ri páwrtədlee/ *adv* according to an unconfirmed report ○ *Reportedly he lost all his money.*

re·port·ed speech *n* GRAM same as **indirect speech**

re·port·er /ri páwrtər/ *n* **1.** SOMEBODY WHO REPORTS NEWS somebody whose job is to find out facts and use the print or broadcast media to tell people about them **2.** SOMEBODY WHO REPORTS somebody who makes a report about something that has happened or the results of research or an investigation **3.** LAW same as **court reporter** **4.** POL RECORDER OF LEGISLATIVE PROCEEDINGS an official who makes a written record of the proceedings of a legislature —**rep·or·to·ri·al** /rèppər táwree əl, reèpər-/ *adj* —**rep·or·to·ri·al·ly** *adv*

re·pose[1] /ri pṓz/ *n* **1.** REST a state of rest or inactivity **2.** TRANQUILLITY a condition of peacefulness and tranquillity, e.g., in a place **3.** PEACE OF MIND freedom from troubles or stress **4.** COMPOSURE calmness and composure of manner ■ *v* (**-posed, -pos·ing, -pos·es**) (*formal*) **1.** *vti* LIE RESTING to lie at rest, or lay something at rest **2.** *vi* LIE RESTING ON TOP OF SOMETHING to lie while resting on or supported by something **3.** *vi* BE DEAD to lie dead (*used euphemistically*) **4. re·pose your·self** *vr* SETTLE SELF AT REST to settle yourself in a relaxed or restful position **5.** *vi* TAKE SUPPORT FROM SOMETHING to be supported or based on something ○ *Your argument reposes on false analogies.* [15C. Via French *reposer* < Latin *repausare* "rest completely" < *pausare* "to rest"] —**re·pos·al** *n* —**re·pos·er** *n*

re·pose[2] /ri pṓz/ (**-posed, -pos·ing, -pos·es**) *vt* to place faith, confidence, or trust in somebody or something (*formal*) ○ *reposed a great deal of confidence in him* [Mid-16C. < Latin *repos-*, stem of *reponere* "place again" < *ponere* "to place"]

re·pose·ful /ri pṓzfəl/ *adj* showing or giving rise to restfulness or calm —**re·pose·ful·ly** *adv* —**re·pose·ful·ness** *n*

re·pos·i·to·ry /ri pózzə tàwree/ (*plural* **-ries**) *n* **1.** PLACE FOR STORAGE a place or container in which something is stored **2.** POSSESSOR OF EXTENSIVE KNOWLEDGE somebody with, or something such as a book that contains, extensive detailed knowledge of something ○ *She was a repository of information about the history of the island.* **3.** CONFIDANT somebody in whom something is confided **4.** *UK* WAREHOUSE FOR COMMODITIES a place where goods are stored prior to sale **5.** TOMB a burial vault or sepulcher [15C. Directly or via French < Latin *repositorium* < past participle of *reponere* (see REPOSE[1])]

re·pos·sess /reèpə zéss/ (**-sessed, -sess·ing, -sess·es**) *vt* to take back goods or property from a buyer who has failed to keep up payments on them —**re·pos·ses·sion** *n* —**re·pos·ses·sor** *n*

re·pous·sé /rə poo sáy/ *adj* **1.** FORMING PATTERN IN RELIEF formed as a raised pattern on a thin piece of metal by having been hammered through from the reverse side **2.** DECORATED WITH HAMMERED PATTERN decorated with a raised pattern that has been hammered through from the reverse side ■ *n* **1.** HAMMERED DESIGN a repoussé design on metal **2.** TECHNIQUE OF HAMMERING DESIGN the technique of producing repoussé designs [Mid-19C. < French, past participle of *repousser* "push back" < *pousser* "push"]

repp *n* TEXTILES another spelling of **rep**[1]

repr. *abbr* **1.** representative **2.** represented **3.** representing **4.** PUBL reprint

rep·re·hend /rèppri hénd/ (**-hend·ed, -hend·ing, -hends**) *vt* to criticize or reprove somebody or something [14C. < Latin *reprehendere* "seize again" < *prehendere* "seize"] —**rep·re·hend·a·ble** *adj* —**rep·re·hen·der** *n*

rep·re·hen·si·ble /rèppri hénssəb'l/ *adj* highly unacceptable and deserving censure [14C. < late Latin *reprehensibilis* < past participle of Latin *reprehendere* (see REPREHEND)] —**rep·re·hen·si·bil·i·ty** /-henssə bíllətee/ *n* —**rep·re·hen·si·bly** *adv*

rep·re·hen·sion /rèppri hénshən/ *n* reproof or criticism for wrongdoing [14C. < Latin *reprehension-* < past participle of *reprehendere* (see REPREHEND)] —**rep·re·hen·sive** *adj* —**rep·re·hen·sive·ly** *adv*

rep·re·sent /rèppri zént/ (**-sent·ed, -sent·ing, -sents**) *v* **1.** *vt* ACT OR SPEAK FOR ANOTHER to act or speak on behalf of somebody or something **2.** *vt* GO SOMEWHERE ON BEHALF OF ANOTHER to go or be present somewhere, or participate in a competition, on behalf of a person, constituency, organization, or other group **3.** *vt* ACT FOR ANOTHER OFFICIALLY to speak and act for somebody else in an official way ○ *Who will be representing France at the conference?* **4.** *vt* EXPRESS OR EXPLAIN SOMETHING to express or explain what is happening or what people think ○ *Her views represent those of the majority of the community.* **5.** *vt* BE EQUIVALENT OF SOMETHING to be a sign or equivalent of something **6.** *vt* SYMBOLIZE SOMETHING to symbolize or stand for something ○ *The bear is often used to represent Russia.* **7.** *vt* DEPICT SOMETHING OR SOMEBODY to portray or present an image of somebody or something as being something in particular **8. rep·re·sent your·self** *vr* UNTRUTHFULLY CLAIM TO BE SOMETHING to describe yourself as something you are not ○ *He was arrested at the airport despite trying to represent himself as a tourist.* **9.** *vt* THEATER DEPICT SOMEBODY ON STAGE to portray or perform a character or role on stage [14C. Directly or via French < Latin *repraesentare,* literally "show back" < *praesentare* "to show"] —**rep·re·sent·a·bil·i·ty** /-zèntə bíllətee/ *n* —**rep·re·sent·a·ble** *adj* —**rep·re·sent·er** *n* ◇ **be represented** to be present somewhere to a particular degree ○ *Women are now well represented in all levels.*

USAGE See *denote.*

re-pre·sent /reè pri zént/ *vt* to send, offer, or present something again

rep·re·sen·ta·tion /rèppri zen táysh'n/ *n* **1.** PICTURE a visual depiction of somebody or something **2.** FACT OF BEING SERVED BY REPRESENTATIVE the fact or right of being represented by somebody, especially of having a member in a legislature with power to vote or speak for an electorate **3.** VOTING SYSTEM OR BODY OF ELECTORS the system by which electors vote for people to represent them as legislators, administrators, or judges, or the group of people so elected **4.** SOMETHING SPOKEN OR DONE FOR ANOTHER an action done or speech made on behalf of another, especially as an agent or deputy **5.** SOMETHING DESCRIBED OR STATED a description, account, or statement of something real or alleged, especially one meant to induce a response from authority (*often used in the plural*) **6.** LAW STATEMENT INDUCING SOMEBODY TO MAKE CONTRACT a statement, real or implied, that encourages somebody to make an agreement **7.** THEATER PERFORMANCE a theatrical performance or production

rep·re·sen·ta·tion·al /rèppri zen táyshən'l, -táyshnəl/ *adj* **1.** relating to or characterized by representation **2.** depicting something in a physically recognizable form, especially in art —**rep·re·sen·ta·tion·al·ly** *adv*

rep·re·sen·ta·tion·al·ism /rèppri zen táyshən'l ìzzəm, -táyshnə lìzzəm/, **rep·re·sen·ta·tion·ism** /rèppri zən táysh'n ìzzəm/ *n* **1.** the practice or principle of depicting objects in recognizable form, especially in art **2.** the theory that the mind directly apprehends external objects only through ideas or data provided by the senses —**rep·re·sen·ta·tion·al·ist** *n* —**rep·re·sen·ta·tion·al·is·tic** /-tayshən'l ístik, -tayshnə-/ *adj*

rep·re·sen·ta·tive /rèppri zéntətiv/ *n* **1.** SOMEBODY WHO SPEAKS FOR OTHERS somebody who speaks, acts, or votes on behalf of others **2.** MEMBER OF LEGISLATURE a member of a legislative assembly **3.** *also* **Rep·re·sen·ta·tive** *US* MEMBER OF HOUSE OF REPRESENTATIVES a member of the House of Representatives in the US Congress, or of a state legislature **4.** COMMERCIAL AGENT OR SALESPERSON an agent or salesperson for a company **5.** EXAMPLE an example or type of something ■ *adj* **1.** CHARACTERISTIC characteristic of something, especially of a class or kind **2.** MADE UP OF ELECTED PEOPLE composed of elected or authorized people ○ *a representative assembly* **3.** LETTING PEOPLE ELECT SOMEBODY allowing people to vote for somebody to represent them in a legislative body such as the Congress in the United States or the House of Commons in the United Kingdom ○ *a representative form of government* **4.** MADE UP OF ALL TYPES including a complete range of examples of something ○ *a representative sample* **5.** ACTING ON SOMEBODY'S BEHALF acting as somebody's agent, deputy, or delegate —**rep·re·sen·ta·tive·ly** *adv* —**rep·re·sen·ta·tive·ness** *n*

~~**representitive**~~ incorrect spelling of **representative**

re·press /ri préss/ (**-pressed, -press·ing, -press·es**) *vt* **1.** CURB ACTIONS THAT SHOW FEELINGS to check or restrain an action that would reveal feelings ○ *He had to repress a smile.* **2.** SUPPRESS SOMETHING BY FORCE to control a population or an expression of people's freedom by force or military means ○ *repressed any uprising* **3.** PSYCHOL BLOCK SOMETHING FROM MIND in Freudian psychology, to block unacceptable or painful impulses, desires, or memories from the conscious mind [14C. < Latin *repress-*, past participle of *reprimere* "press back" < *premere* "to press"] —**re·press·i·bil·i·ty** /ri prèssə bíllətee/ *n* —**re·press·i·ble** *adj*

re-press /ree préss/ *vt* to press something again, especially to manufacture another issue of a recording

re·pres·ser /ri préssər/ *n* another spelling of **repressor**

re·pres·sion /ri présh'n/ *n* **1.** the process of suppressing a population, or the condition of having political, social, or cultural freedom controlled by force or military means **2.** in Freudian psychology, a mechanism by which people protect themselves from threatening thoughts by blocking them out of the conscious mind

re·pres·sive /ri préssiv/ *adj* exerting strict control on the freedom of others —**re·pres·sive·ly** *adv* —**re·pres·sive·ness** *n*

re·pres·sor /ri préssər/, **re·press·er** *n* **1.** a means of repressing something or somebody **2.** a protein that stops gene transcription

re·prieve /ri preév/ *vt* (**-prieved, -priev·ing, -prieves**) **1.** STOP OR POSTPONE SOMEBODY'S PUNISHMENT to halt or delay the punishment of somebody, especially when the punishment is death (*often passive*) **2.** OFFER RESPITE TO SOMEBODY to provide somebody with temporary relief from something harmful, especially danger or pain ■ *n* **1.** STOPPING OR POSTPONEMENT OF PUNISHMENT the halting or delay of somebody's punishment, especially when the punishment is death **2.** WARRANT HALTING OR POSTPONING PUNISHMENT a warrant giving the authority to stop or postpone somebody's punishment, especially when the punishment is death **3.** RESPITE FROM SOMETHING HARMFUL a relief from something harmful, especially danger or pain [Mid-17C. Alteration of obsolete *repry* "take back to prison, escape the death sentence" < Old French *repris* "taken back" < Latin *reprehendere* (see REPREHEND)] —**re·priev·a·ble** *adj* —**re·priev·er** *n*

rep·ri·mand /réppre mànd/ *vt* (**-mand·ed, -mand·ing, -mands**) to rebuke somebody for a wrongdoing ■ *n* a rebuke given for having done something wrong [Mid-17C. Via French *réprimande* < Latin *reprimenda* "that is to be suppressed" < *reprimere* "press back"]

re·print *vt* /ree prínt/ (**-print·ed, -print·ing, -prints**) **PRINT SOMETHING AGAIN** to print something again, especially with few or no changes ■ *n* /rée prìnt/ **1. COPY OF SOMETHING ALREADY PUBLISHED** a printed copy of something that has already been in print **2.** PUBL same as **offprint 3. REISSUE OF PRINTED WORK** a book or other printed work that is the same as or has only minor changes from one that was previously issued **4. IMPRESSION OF POSTAGE STAMP** an impression of a postage stamp made from the original plates but after the stamp has been withdrawn from circulation —**re·print·er** *n*

re·pri·sal /ri príz'l/ *n* **1. RETALIATION IN WAR** a violent military action, e.g., the killing of prisoners or civilians, carried out in retaliation for an enemy's action **2. STRONG OR VIOLENT RETALIATION** a strong or violent retaliation for an action that somebody has taken **3. RETALIATORY SEIZURE FROM ANOTHER COUNTRY** the forcible seizure of property or people from another country as retaliation for some injury [15C. Via Anglo-Norman *reprisaille* < medieval Latin *reprisalia, represalia*, contraction of *reprehensalia* < Latin *reprehendere* (see REPREHEND)]

re·prise /ri préez/ *n* **1. REPEAT OF MUSICAL PASSAGE** a repeated passage of music, or a return to an earlier musical theme **2.** MUSIC same as **chorus** *n* (sense 1) **3. REPETITION** a repetition or recurrence of something ■ *vt* (**-prised, -pris·ing, -pris·es**) **1. REPEAT MUSIC** to repeat a passage of music or return to an earlier theme **2. REPEAT ACTION** to repeat an action or performance ○ *reprised her role as Gertrude in the New York production* [Mid-20C. < French < past participle of *reprendre* "take again" < *prendre* "take" < Latin *prehendere*]

re·pro /réeprō/ *n* (*informal*) **1.** a reproduction, especially of a painting or piece of furniture **2.** PRINTING same as **reproduction proof** [Mid-20C. Shortening]

re·proach /ri prṓch/ *v* (**-proached, -proach·ing, -proach·es**) **1.** *vt* **CRITICIZE SOMEBODY** to criticize somebody for doing something wrong **2. re·proach your·self** *vr* **FEEL BLAMEWORTHY** to feel ashamed because you know you have done something wrong ■ *n* **1. CRITICISM** criticism or disapproval for having done something wrong, or an expression of this **2. SOMETHING DISGRACEFUL** something that reflects badly on somebody who has failed to improve or deal with it **3. DISCREDIT** shame or disgrace that somebody or something incurs ○ *actions that brought reproach upon his family* [15C. < Old French *reprochier* < Latin *prope* "near"] —**re·proach·a·ble** *adj* —**re·proach·a·ble·ness** *n* —**re·proach·a·bly** *adv* —**re·proach·er** *n* —**re·proach·ing·ly** *adv* ◇ **above** *or* **beyond reproach** so good that no criticism can be made

re·proach·ful /ri prṓchfəl/ *adj* expressing disapproval or blame —**re·proach·ful·ly** *adv* —**re·proach·ful·ness** *n*

rep·ro·bate /réppre bàyt/ *n* **1. SOMEBODY IMMORAL** a disreputable or immoral person **2.** RELIG **SOMEBODY DAMNED** somebody whose soul is believed to be damned ■ *adj* **1. DISREPUTABLE** disreputable or immoral **2.** RELIG **DAMNED** having a soul that is believed to be damned ■ *vt* (**-bat·ed, -bat·ing, -bates**) **1. CENSURE SOMEBODY** to censure or condemn somebody (*formal*) **2.** RELIG **DENY SALVATION TO SOMEBODY** to condemn somebody to supposed eternal damnation [Mid-16C. < late Latin *reprobatus* < Latin *reprobat-*, past participle of *reprobare* "prove to be unworthy" < *probare* "prove"] —**rep·ro·bat·er** *n* —**rep·ro·ba·tive** *adj*

rep·ro·ba·tion /rèppre báysh'n/ *n* **1.** strong condemnation or disapproval of somebody or something **2.** the supposed condemnation of somebody's soul to eternal damnation [15C. Directly or via French < Latin *reprobation-* < *reprobat-* (see REPROBATE)] —**rep·ro·ba·tion·ar·y** *adj*

re·pro·duce /rèepre dóoss/ (**-duced, -duc·ing, -duc·es**) *v* **1.** *vti* **MAKE DUPLICATE OF SOMETHING** to copy something by photographing, scanning, printing, or another process, or be copied in this way **2.** *vi* BIOL **PRODUCE OFFSPRING** to produce offspring or new individuals through a sexual or asexual process **3.** *vt* **REPEAT SOMETHING** to do something in the same way as before **4.** *vt* **REMEMBER SOMETHING** to remember or imagine something again —**re·pro·duc·er** *n* —**re·pro·duc·i·bil·i·ty** /rèepre doosse bílletee/ *n* —**re·pro·duc·i·ble** *adj* —**re·pro·duc·i·bly** *adv*

SYNONYMS See ***copy***.

re·pro·duc·tion /rèepre dúkshən/ *n* **1. ACT OF REPRODUCING SOMETHING** the act or process of reproducing something **2. PRODUCTION OF OFFSPRING** the production of offspring or new individuals through a sexual or asexual process **3. COPY OF OBJECT** a copy of something in an earlier style, especially a painting or a piece of furniture **4. PRINT, ELECTRONIC, OR PHOTOGRAPHIC DUPLICATE** a copy of something printed, scanned, photographed, or produced by other means **5. RECORDING OF SOUND** the recording of sound, or the quality of recorded sound [Mid-17C. < REPRODUCE, after *production*]

re·pro·duc·tion proof *n* a printed proof, usually on glossy paper, of such high quality that it can be photographed for making a printing plate

re·pro·duc·tive /rèepre dúktiv/ *adj* relating to, taking part in, or enabling the production of new offspring or individuals ○ *reproductive organs* [Mid-18C. < REPRODUCE, after *productive*] —**re·pro·duc·tive·ly** *adv* —**re·pro·duc·tive·ness** *n*

re·pro·duc·tive clon·ing *n* the use of cloning to produce a new genetically identical human or animal from the cells of another animal or human. ◊ **therapeutic cloning**

re·pro·duc·tive sys·tem *n* the combination of bodily organs and tissues used in the process of producing offspring

re·prog·ra·phy /ri próggrəfee/ *n* the reproduction of something printed, e.g., by offset printing, microfilming, photography, or xerography [Mid-20C. < German *Reprographie*, blend of *Reproduktion* "reproduction" + *Photographie* "photography"] —**re·pro·graph·ic** /rèepre gráffik, rèpprə-/ *adj*

re·proof /ri próof/ (*plural* **-proofs** *or* **-prov·als**) *n* the act of criticizing somebody for having done something wrong, or something said as a rebuke [14C. < Old French *reprove* < *reprover* (see REPROVE)]

re·prove /ri próov/ (**-proved, -prov·ing, -proves**) *vt* to speak to somebody in a way that shows disapproval of something he or she has done [14C. Via Old French *reprover* < Latin *reprobare* "prove to be unworthy" (see REPROBATE)] —**re·prov·a·ble** *adj* —**re·prov·er** *n* —**re·prov·ing·ly** *adv*

rept. *abbr* report

rep·tant /réptənt/ *adj* creeping or lying along the ground [Mid-17C. < Latin *reptant-*, present participle of *reptare* "keep creeping" < *repere* "to creep"]

rep·tile /rép tìl, rept'l/ *n* **1. COLD-BLOODED SCALY VERTEBRATE** an air-breathing cold-blooded egg-laying vertebrate with an outer covering of scales or plates and a bony skeleton, e.g., the crocodile, tortoise, snake, or lizard. Class: Reptilia. **2. OFFENSIVE TERM** an offensive term that deliberately insults somebody whose behavior or character is regarded as suspicious, untrustworthy, or sickeningly ingratiating (*insult*) ■ *adj* **BEING REPTILE** belonging to the class of reptiles [14C. Via French < late Latin *reptilis* "creeping" < Latin *rept-*, past participle of *repere* "creep"] —**rep·til·i·an** /rep tíllee ən/ *adj, n*

Rep·ton /réptən/, **Humphry** (1752–1818) British landscape architect. He designed many parks of English country houses, working in the picturesque style.

Repub. *abbr* POL **1.** Republic **2.** Republican

re·pub·lic /ri púbblik/ *n* **1. POLITICAL SYSTEM WITH ELECTED REPRESENTATIVES** a political system or form of government in which people elect representatives to exercise power for them **2.** *also* **Re·pub·lic STATE WITH ELECTED REPRESENTATIVES** a country or other political unit whose government or political system is that of a republic **3.** *also* **Re·pub·lic UNIT WITHIN LARGER COUNTRY** a constituent political and territorial unit of a national federation or union **4. GROUP WITH COLLECTIVE INTERESTS** a group of people who are considered to be equals and who have a collective interest, objective, or vocation (*formal*) ○ *the republic of letters* [Late 16C. Via French *république* < Latin *res publica* "public matter"]

CULTURAL NOTE ***The Republic***, a political treatise (early 4th century B.C.) by the Greek philosopher Plato. Presented in the form of a series of dialogues between Socrates and his pupils, it begins with a discussion of the nature of justice that leads in turn to an attempt to define the ideal society. For Plato, this would consist of an aristocracy run by a class of legislators groomed for leadership by a state education system.

re·pub·li·can /ri púbblikən/ *n* somebody who believes that the best government is one in which supreme power is vested in an electorate ■ *adj* relating to, belonging to, or characteristic of a republic

Re·pub·li·can[1] *adj* **1.** belonging to or supporting the republican party in the United States **2.** *UK* supporting the idea that Northern Ireland should be united politically with the Republic of Ireland and should cease to form part of the United Kingdom —**Re·pub·li·can** *n*

Re·pub·li·can[2] /ri púbblikən/ river that flows from Colorado into Kansas, where it unites with the Smoky Hill River to form the Kansas River. Length: 445 mi./716 km.

re·pub·li·can·ism /ri púbblikə nìzzəm/ *n* **1.** the belief that the supreme power of a country should be vested in an electorate **2.** the theory and principles of republican government

Re·pub·li·can·ism *n* **1.** support for the Republican Party in the United States **2.** *UK* support for the idea of uniting Northern Ireland politically with the Republic of Ireland

re·pub·li·can·ize /ri púbblikə nìz/ (**-ized, -iz·ing, -iz·es**) *vt* to make a state or other political unit into a republic —**re·pub·li·can·i·za·tion** /ri pùbblikəni záysh'n/ *n*

Re·pub·li·can Par·ty *n* in the United States, a political party at state and national level, founded in 1854–56

re·pu·di·ate /ri pyóodee àyt/ (**-at·ed, -at·ing, -ates**) *vt* **1. DISOWN SOMETHING** to disapprove of something formally and strongly and renounce any connection with it ○ *She repudiated the committee's actions.* **2. DENY SOMETHING** to state that something is untrue **3. REJECT SOMETHING** to reject something that is offered **4. DISOWN LOVED ONE** to disown a family member or lover **5. REJECT SOMETHING AS INVALID** to refuse to accept the validity of something **6. REFUSE TO PAY DEBT** to refuse to acknowledge or pay a debt [Mid-16C. < Latin *repudiat-*, past participle of *repudiare* "to divorce" < *repudium* "divorce"] —**re·pu·di·a·ble** *adj* —**re·pu·di·a·tive** *adj* —**re·pu·di·a·tor** *n*

re·pug·nance /ri púgnənss/, **re·pug·nan·cy** *n* a very strong feeling of disgust about something

SYNONYMS See ***dislike***.

re·pug·nant /ri púgnənt/ *adj* **1.** offensive and completely unacceptable **2.** making somebody feel physically repelled ○ *a repugnant odor* [Late 18C. Via Old French, "contrary" < Latin *repugnant-*, present participle of *repugnare* "fight back" < *pugnare* "to fight"] —**re·pug·nant·ly** *adv*

re·pulse /ri púlss/ *vt* (**-pulsed, -puls·ing, -puls·es**) **1. FORCE BACK MILITARY ATTACK** to repel an attacking military force **2. DISGUST SOMEBODY** to cause disgust or revulsion in somebody (*informal*) **3. SPURN SOMEBODY** to reject or rebuff an approach from somebody ■ *n* **1. REJECTION** a refusal or rejection of somebody **2. ACT OF FORCING BACK ATTACK** the forcing back of an attacking military force [Mid-16C. < Latin *repuls-*, past participle of *repellere* "drive back" (see REPEL)] —**re·puls·er** *n*

re·pul·sion /ri púlshən/ *n* **1. FACT OF BEING REPULSED** the act or condition of being repulsed **2. REVULSION** a feeling of disgust or very strong dislike **3. REPELLING FORCE** a force between two bodies of the same electric charge or magnetic polarity that tends to repel or separate them. It is this repulsive force between atoms and molecules at very short distances that tends to keep them separated.

re·pul·sive /ri púlssiv/ *adj* **1.** making somebody feel disgust or very strong dislike **2.** tending to repel —**re·pul·sive·ly** *adv* —**re·pul·sive·ness** *n*

USAGE See ***repellent***.

re·pur·chase a·gree·ment *n* **1.** an agreement between a dealer and an investor in which the investor agrees to sell purchased securities back to the dealer on a fixed date for a specific profit **2.** an agreement between a buyer and a seller in which the seller agrees to buy back the purchased item at the end of a fixed period

rep·u·ta·ble /réppyətəb'l/ *adj* known to be honest, reliable, or respectable [Late 17C. Directly or via French < medieval Latin *reputabilis* < Latin *reputare* (see REPUTE)] —**rep·u·ta·bil·i·ty** /rèppyətə bíllətee/ *n* —**rep·u·ta·bly** *adv*

rep·u·ta·tion /rèppyə táysh'n/ *n* **1.** GENERAL OPINIONS the views that are generally held about somebody or something **2.** GOOD OPINION a high opinion that people hold about somebody or something **3.** SOMETHING THAT SOMEBODY IS KNOWN FOR the generally accepted estimation of somebody or something as having particular qualities or attributes ○ *The new manager has a reputation for being a stickler for details.* [14C. < Latin *reputation-* "consideration" < *reputare* (see REPUTE)]

re·pute /ri pyóot/ *n* (*formal*) **1.** estimation or character according to what people in general think **2.** good reputation or standing [Mid-16C. Directly or via French < Latin *reputare* "think repeatedly" < *putare* "think"]

re·put·ed /ri pyóotəd/ *adj* widely believed, although not necessarily established as fact [Late 16C. < REPUTE used as a verb]

re·put·ed·ly /ri pyóotədlee/ *adv* according to popular belief

req. *abbr* **1.** request **2.** require **3.** required **4.** requirement **5.** requisition

re·quest /ri kwést/ *vt* (**-quest·ed, -quest·ing, -quests**) **1.** ASK POLITELY FOR SOMETHING to ask formally or courteously for something to be given or done ○ *requested that he be excused* ○ *requested her favorite song* **2.** ASK SOMEBODY FOR SOMETHING to ask somebody to do something ○ *requested Father Peter to perform their marriage ceremony* ■ *n* **1.** ACT OF EXPRESSING WISH the act of asking or petitioning for something to be done or given **2.** EXPRESSION OF POLITE WISH an act of politely or formally asking that something be done or given **3.** MUSIC THAT IS ASKED FOR a piece of music played on a radio program, at a live performance, or at a club because somebody asks for it ○ *We'll be playing requests later tonight.* [14C. < Old French *requeste* < Latin *requisit-*, past participle of *requirere* (see REQUIRE)] —**re·quest·er** *n*

req·ui·em /rékwee əm/, **Req·ui·em** *n* **1.** ROMAN CATHOLIC SERVICE FOR DEAD a Roman Catholic mass held to offer prayers for somebody who has died **2.** MUSIC FOR REQUIEM a piece of music written to accompany a requiem mass **3.** COMMEMORATIVE MUSIC a piece of music written to commemorate somebody who has died [14C. < Latin, "rest," in *Requiem aeternam dona eis Domine* "Grant them eternal rest, O Lord"]

req·ui·em shark *n* a voracious gray or brownish shark with a slender body and rounded snout. Tiger sharks and blue sharks are requiem sharks. Native to: tropical waters. Family: Carcharhinidae. [By folk etymology < French *requin* "shark"]

req·ui·es·cat /rèkwee é skaàt/ *n* a prayer asking that the soul of a dead person might be at rest [Early 19C. < Latin, "may he or she rest"]

re·quire /ri kwír/ (**-quired, -quir·ing, -quires**) *vt* **1.** NEED SOMETHING OR SOMEBODY to be in need of something or somebody for a purpose ○ *The recipe requires a cup of milk.* **2.** MAKE SOMETHING NECESSARY to have something as a necessary precondition ○ *A password is required for entry to the system.* **3.** DEMAND SOMETHING BY LAW to demand something by a law or regulation (*often passive*) ○ *Notification was required by law.* **4.** INSIST ON SOMETHING to insist that somebody do something ○ *All applicants are required to pass a medical exam.* [14C. < Old French *requ(i)er-*, stem of *requere* < Latin *requirere* "seek in return" < *quaerere* "seek"] —**re·quir·a·ble** *adj* —**re·quire·ment** *n* —**re·quir·er** *n*

re·quired /ri kwírd/ *adj* **1.** necessary or appropriate for a specific purpose ○ *He lacks the required degree of expertise.* **2.** insisted upon or imposed as a condition ○ *required reading for a course*

req·ui·site /rékwizit/ *adj* necessary or appropriate for a specific purpose (*formal*) ○ *the requisite skills for the job* ■ *n* something that is necessary or indispensable [15C. < Latin *requisitus*, past participle of *requirere* (see REQUIRE)] —**req·ui·site·ly** *adv* —**req·ui·site·ness** *n*

SYNONYMS See ***necessary***.

req·ui·si·tion /rèkwi zísh'n/ *n* **1.** DEMAND FOR SOMETHING a demand for something that is required **2.** OFFICIAL FORM a written or printed request for something that is needed **3.** FACT OF MAKING FORMAL DEMAND the act or process of making a formal demand for something **4.** REQUEST FOR FUGITIVE a request by a government that another government return a fugitive from the law ■ *vt* (**-tioned, -tion·ing, -tions**) **1.** TAKE SOMETHING OFFICIALLY to demand and take something that is needed, especially for official or military use **2.** OBTAIN SOMEBODY FOR JOB to require and obtain the services of somebody to do something ○ *requisitioned a few friends for the weekend to help paint the house* [Mid-16C. Directly or via French < Latin *requisition-* < past participle of *requirere* (see REQUIRE)] —**req·ui·si·tion·ar·y** *adj*

re·quite /ri kwít/ (**-quit·ed, -quit·ing, -quites**) *vt* **1.** to return in kind a kindness or hurt that somebody has done **2.** to pay somebody back for a service performed [Early 16C. < RE- + earlier form of QUIT "pay up"] —**re·quit·a·ble** *adj* —**re·quit·al** *n* —**re·quite·ment** *n* —**re·quit·er** *n*

re·ra·di·ate /ree ráydee àyt/ (**-at·ed, -at·ing, -ates**) *vt* to emit radiation after absorbing incident radiation —**re·ra·di·a·tion** /ree ràydee áysh'n/ *n*

reredos

re·re·dos /rérrə dòss, rírrə-, reér dòss/ *n* **1.** an artistic decoration behind the altar in a church, e.g., a wood or stone screen or a wall-hanging **2.** the back of an open fireplace [14C. Via Anglo-Norman < Old French *areredos* < *arere* "behind" + *dos* "back" < Latin *dorsum*]

re·re·lease /reé ri leéss/ *vt* (**-leased, -leas·ing, -leas·es**) to release a music recording or a movie again for distribution to the public ■ *n* a music recording or a movie that has been released again to the public

re·run *vt* /ree rún/ (**-ran** /-rán/, **-run, -run·ning, -runs**) **1.** SHOW SOMETHING AGAIN to show or broadcast a TV series, video, or movie again **2.** REPEAT RACE to run a race again, or cause a race to be run again, after the result on the first occasion has been disallowed because of an infraction of the rules ■ *n* /reé rùn/ (*plural* **-runs**) **1.** REPEAT OF PROGRAM a repeat showing of recorded entertainment, especially a TV series **2.** REPEAT OF RACE the repeat running of a race after an infraction of the rules

res /rayss, reez/ (*plural same*) *n* in law, a matter or thing [< Latin, "thing, legal matter"]

res. *abbr* **1.** research **2.** reservation **3.** reserved **4.** reservoir **5.** residence **6.** resident **7.** resolution

res ad·ju·di·ca·ta *n* LAW same as **res judicata**

re·sale /reé sàyl/ *n* **1.** the selling of something again ○ *Not for resale.* **2.** the selling of something secondhand —**re·sal·a·bil·i·ty** /ree sàylə bíllətee/ *n* —**re·sal·a·ble** /ree sáyləb'l/ *adj*

re·scale /ree skáyl/ (**-scaled, -scal·ing, -scales**) *vt* to modify the scale of something, especially to reduce it ○ *rescale a budget* ○ *rescale a drawing*

re·sched·ule /ree skéjjool, -skéjjəl/ (**-uled, -ul·ing, -ules**) *vt* **1.** to arrange a new time slot for something **2.** to extend the payment schedule of a loan

re·scind /ri sínd/ (**-scind·ed, -scind·ing, -scinds**) *vt* **1.** to remove the validity or authority of something **2.** to declare a decision or enactment null and void [Mid-16C. < Latin *rescindere* "cut back" < *scindere* "to cut"] —**re·scind·a·ble** *adj* —**re·scind·er** *n* —**re·scind·ment** *n*

re·scis·sion /ri sízh'n/ *n* the act of rescinding something [Early 17C. < late Latin *rescission-* < Latin *resciss-*, past participle of *rescindere* (see RESCIND)]

re·score /ree skáwr/ (**-scored, -scor·ing, -scores**) *vt* to write new instrumentation for a piece of music

re·script /reé skript/ *n* **1.** REWRITE an act of rewriting something **2.** ECCLESIASTICAL RULING a formal reply by the pope or some other high dignitary of the Roman Catholic Church on a matter of doctrine or discipline **3.** ROMAN EMPEROR'S LEGAL RULING a formal reply by an ancient Roman or Holy Roman emperor on a point of law [14C. < Latin *rescriptum*, form of past participle of *rescribere* "write back" < *scribere* "write"]

res·cue /réskyoo/ *v* (**-cued, -cu·ing, -cues**) **1.** *vt* REMOVE SOMEBODY FROM DANGER to save somebody or something from a dangerous or harmful situation ○ *The boys had to be rescued from the rocks by helicopter.* **2.** SAVE SOMETHING to prevent something from being discarded, rejected, or put out of operation ○ *At the last minute the factory was rescued from closure.* **3.** *vt* LAW GET SOMEBODY OUT OF JAIL to release somebody from legal custody by force **4.** *vt* LAW TAKE FORCIBLE POSSESSION OF SOMETHING to seize property or goods by force ■ *n* **1.** REMOVAL FROM DANGER OR HARM an act or instance of saving somebody or something from a dangerous or harmful situation (*often used before a noun*) ○ *a daring rescue attempt* **2.** PROVISION OF HELP an instance of helping somebody in an awkward or difficult situation ○ *I couldn't think what to say, but luckily he came to my rescue.* **3.** LAW RELEASE FROM JAIL the release of somebody from legal custody by force **4.** LAW SEIZURE OF GOODS the seizure of property or goods by force [14C. < Old French *rescourre* "shake loose" < *escourre* "shake" < Latin *escutere* < *ex-* "out" + *quatere* "to strike"] —**res·cu·a·ble** *adj* —**res·cu·er** *n*

res·cue grass *n* a grass cultivated for hay. Native to: South America. Latin name: *Bromus unioloides*.

res·cue work·er *n* a member of a medical or emergency service

re·search *n* /reé sùrch, ri súrch/ methodical investigation into a subject in order to discover facts, to establish or revise a theory, or to develop a plan of action based on the facts discovered ■ *vti* /ri súrch, reé sùrch/ (**-searched, -search·ing, -search·es**) to carry out research into a subject [Late 16C. < obsolete French *recerche* < Old French *recercher* "search closely" < *cerchier* "explore"] —**re·search·a·ble** *adj* —**re·search·er** *n*

re·search and de·vel·op·ment *n* in business and industry, the work of investigating improved processes, products, and services and of developing new ones

re·seat /ree seét/ (**-seat·ed, -seat·ing, -seats**) *vt* **1.** SEAT SOMEBODY ELSEWHERE to seat somebody in another place **2.** SEAT SOMEBODY AS BEFORE to return somebody to the seat previously occupied **3.** REPLACE SEATS IN BUILDING to fit new seats in an auditorium or hall **4.** PUT NEW MATERIAL ON SEAT to replace the material on a seat **5.** ENG REPLACE VALVE SEATING to return the seating of a valve to good condition

re·seau /ray zṓ, rə-/ (*plural* **-seaux** /-zṓz, -zṓ/ or **-seaus** /-zṓz/) *n* **1.** a mesh foundation on which lace is made **2.** a grid of lines photographed onto or cut into a glass plate and used as a reference for astronomical observations [Late 16C. < French *réseau* "network," later form of Old French *reseuil* "little net" < *raiz* "net" < Latin *rete*]

re·sect /ri sékt/ (**-sect·ed, -sect·ing, -sects**) *vt* to cut through and surgically remove part of an organ, bone, or other body part [Mid-17C. < Latin *resect-*, past participle of *resecare* "cut back" < *secare* "to cut"]

re·sec·tion /ri sékshən/ *n* **1.** the surgical removal of part of an organ, bone, or other body part **2.** the establishment of the location of a point when surveying by sighting from that point to two other points whose locations are known

re·sec·to·scope /ri séktə skōp/ *n* a surgical instrument that allows a resection to be made without a bigger incision than that caused by the instrument itself

reseda

re·se·da /ri sēedə, séddə/ (*plural* **-das** *or* same) *n* **1.** a plant that has small dense spikes of grayish green flowers with divided petals. Native to: Mediterranean. Genus: *Reseda.* **2.** a grayish green color [Mid-18C. Via modern Latin genus name < Latin] —**re·se·da** *adj*

re·seed /ree sēed/ (**-seed·ed, -seed·ing, -seeds**) *v* **1.** *vt* to plant seeds on an area of land again **2.** *vti* to grow a plant from seed dropped by the previous generation, or grow in this way

re·sem·blance /ri zémblənss/ *n* **1.** SIMILARITY similarity in appearance or quality to somebody or something else **2.** DEGREE OF SIMILARITY the extent to which somebody or something resembles somebody or something else ○ *The resemblance between them is remarkable.* **3.** POINT OF SIMILARITY a respect in which somebody or something resembles somebody or something else **4.** SOMETHING SIMILAR something that resembles something else

re·sem·ble /ri zémb'l/ (**-bled, -bling, -bles**) *vt* to be similar to somebody or something in appearance or behavior [14C. < Old French *resembler* "be very like" < *sembler* "seem" < Latin *simulare* (see SIMULATE)] —**re·sem·bler** *n*

~~**resemblence**~~ incorrect spelling of **resemblance**

re·sent /ri zént/ (**-sent·ed, -sent·ing, -sents**) *vt* to feel aggrieved about something or toward somebody, often because of a perceived wrong or injustice [Late 16C. < obsolete French *ressentir* "feel strongly" < *sentir* "feel" < Latin *sentire*]

re·sent·ful /ri zéntfəl/ *adj* annoyed about having been badly treated, or characterized by such a feeling of annoyance —**re·sent·ful·ly** *adv* —**re·sent·ful·ness** *n*

re·sent·ment /ri zéntmənt/ *n* aggrieved feelings caused by a sense of having been badly treated [Early 17C. < obsolete French *ressentiment* "strong feeling" < *ressentir* (see RESENT)]

SYNONYMS See *anger.*

res·er·va·tion /rèzzər váysh'n/ *n* **1.** ARRANGEMENT MADE BEFOREHAND an advance booking, e.g., of a seat, hotel room, or ticket **2.** PLACE ARRANGED BEFOREHAND something booked in advance, e.g., a seat, hotel room, or ticket **3.** ACT OF ARRANGING BEFOREHAND the act of booking something in advance **4.** LAND SET ASIDE an area of land set aside for a special purpose, especially in North America for the use of a Native North American people **5.** KEEPING SOMETHING BACK the act of withholding something, or an instance of so doing **6.** LIMITING CONDITION a limiting condition to an agreement **7.** LAW RETAINED LEGAL INTEREST a clause in a deed by which somebody retains an interest in something being granted or leased, or such an interest itself **8.** CHR PRESERVATION OF CONSECRATED ELEMENTS FOR LATER the practice of retaining part of the consecrated bread and wine after celebrating Communion for later use, e.g., when visiting the sick ■ **res·er·va·tions** *npl* MISGIVINGS doubts that prevent wholehearted agreement to or approval of something —**res·er·va·tion·ist** *n*

re·serve /ri zúrv/ *vt* (**-served, -serv·ing, -serves**) **1.** SET SOMETHING ASIDE to keep something back for future use or for some specific purpose **2.** BOOK PLACE BEFOREHAND to make arrangements in advance to secure a place such as a seat, ticket, table, or hotel room **3.** RETAIN SOMETHING FOR YOUR OWN BENEFIT to retain the option of future action on somebody's or your own behalf ○ *I reserve the right to change my mind.* **4.** POSTPONE DECISION to defer making a decision until all the issues have been considered ○ *reserve judgment* ■ *n* **1.** EMERGENCY SUPPLY something kept back for later use, especially in an emergency **2.** COOLNESS OF MANNER emotional restraint, resulting in a reticent or composed manner **3.** INACTIVE PART OF ARMED SERVICES the part of a country's armed services that is not on active service at a given time **4.** REINFORCEMENT FORCE the part of an armed force that is not initially committed during a military engagement but supplies reinforcements as necessary **5.** MEMBER OF RESERVE a member of a military reserve **6.** SUBSTITUTE PLAYER a team member called to play when a member of the original team withdraws, either before or during a game **7.** NEXT RUNNER-UP a competitor or exhibit, e.g., an animal at an agricultural show, that places immediately after the prizewinners and will receive a prize if a prizewinner is disqualified **8.** *Can* LAND USED AS RESERVATION an area of land set aside as a reservation for use by a Native North American people **9.** ECON NATIONAL FUNDS a country's supply of gold and foreign currency that is held by the central bank against future liabilities or to support the currency when the exchange rates fluctuate **10.** FIN MONEY RETAINED FOR FUTURE USE an amount of capital or revenue retained by a company or financial institution to meet future contingencies (*often used in the plural*) **11.** GEOL UNEXPLOITED NATURAL RESOURCE a supply of a natural resource such as a mineral or petrochemical that is estimated to exist from geologic data but is not yet utilized **12.** *UK* ENVIRON same as **preserve** *n* (sense 3) ■ **re·serves** *npl* EXTRA STAMINA, USABLE IN EMERGENCY additional personal resources of energy or strength that can be called upon in an emergency [14C. Directly or via French *réserver* < Latin *reservare* "keep back" < *servare* "keep"] —**re·serv·a·ble** *adj* —**re·serv·er** *n* ◇ **have** *or* **keep something in reserve** to use only part of something, keeping some of it back in case it is needed at a later time

re·serve bank *n* any of the 12 banks in the US Federal Reserve system

re·serve clause *n* in former times, a clause in the contract of a professional athlete stating that the club, not the athlete, has the exclusive right to renew the contract

re·serve cur·ren·cy *n* foreign currency that is acceptable for settling international transactions and that is held in reserve for that purpose by a central bank

re·served /ri zúrvd/ *adj* **1.** BOOKED booked in advance **2.** EARMARKED FOR SPECIFIC USE set aside for a specific purpose **3.** HAVING COOL MANNER having a tendency to emotional restraint and so appearing reticent or composed —**re·serv·ed·ly** /ri zúrvədlee/ *adv* —**re·serv·ed·ness** *n*

re·serve price *n* the lowest price that a seller is willing to accept for something being sold at auction. ◊ **upset price**

re·serv·ist /ri zúrvist/ *n* a member of a military force not on active service at a given time

res·er·voir /rézzər vwaar/ *n* **1.** LAKE OR TANK FOR STORING WATER a large tank or natural or artificial lake used for collecting and storing water for human consumption or agricultural use **2.** LARGE BACKUP SUPPLY a substantial reserve supply of something intangible **3.** LIQUID STORE IN DEVICE a part of a machine or device where liquid is stored for use by the machine or device **4.** UNDERGROUND SUPPLY OF GAS OR OIL a natural chamber in porous rock where a supply of natural gas or crude oil collects **5.** BIOL PARASITE CARRIER an organism in which a parasite lives and develops without damaging it, but from which the parasite passes to another species that is damaged by it **6.** ANAT same as **cisterna** [Mid-17C. < French < *réserver* (see RESERVE)]

re·set /ree sét/ (**-set, -set·ting, -sets**) *vt* **1.** to set something again **2.** to change the reading of a dial or counter to zero or a different number [Mid-17C. < RE- + SET[1]] —**re·set·ta·ble** *adj* —**re·set·ter** *n*

re·set·tle /ree sétt'l/ (**-tled, -tling, -tles**) *vt* to provide a group or population with a new place to live and transfer it there —**re·set·tle·ment** *n*

~~**resevoir**~~ incorrect spelling of **reservoir**

res ges·tae /ràyss gé stī, rēez jé stēe/ *npl* circumstances and facts that may be admitted as evidence in a lawsuit because they shed light on the matters in question [< Latin, "things done"]

resh /resh/ *n* the 20th letter of the Hebrew alphabet, represented in the English alphabet as "r." See table at **alphabet** [Early 19C. < Aramaic *rēš* "head"]

re·shape /ree sháyp/ (**-shaped, -shap·ing, -shapes**) *vt* **1.** to alter or restore the shape of something **2.** to change the form or organization of something

re·shuf·fle /ree shúff'l/ *n* **1.** REDISTRIBUTION OF JOBS a reorganization of the jobs of a group of people, especially a change by a president or prime minister of the positions or personnel of a cabinet **2.** SHUFFLING OF CARDS AGAIN an act of shuffling playing cards again ■ *vt* (**-fled, -fling, -fles**) **1.** REDISTRIBUTE JOBS to carry out a reshuffle of jobs **2.** SHUFFLE CARDS AGAIN to shuffle playing cards again

re·sid /ri zíd/ *n US* same as **residual oil** (*informal*) [Mid-20C. Shortening]

re·side /ri zīd/ (**-sid·ed, -sid·ing, -sides**) *vi* **1.** LIVE SOMEWHERE to have a home in a particular place **2.** BE PRESENT to be present in or belong to somebody or something **3.** BE VESTED to be vested or placed in somebody or something [15C. Probably via French *résider* < Latin *residere* "remain behind" < *sedere* "sit"]

res·i·dence /rézzid'nss/ *n* **1.** HOME the house, apartment, or other dwelling in which somebody lives **2.** LARGE HOUSE a grand and imposing dwelling **3.** *US* BUSINESS CORPORATION'S HEADQUARTERS the official headquarters of a corporation **4.** LIVING SOMEWHERE the fact of living in a place **5.** TIME LIVED IN PLACE the period of time that somebody lives in a place **6.** *US* MED same as **residency** (sense 1) ◇ **in residence 1.** living in a place at a particular time **2.** employed as a creative artist by an educational or other institution to foster interest in a subject

res·i·den·cy /rézzid'nssee/ (*plural* **-cies**) *n* **1.** MEDICAL TRAINING a period of specialized training in clinical medicine or surgery in a hospital on completion of an internship **2.** PERFORMING AND TEACHING ENGAGEMENT an engagement at a university or conservatory for a performer or group of performers, usually for at least a semester, that involves performance, teaching, and master classes **3.** RESIDENCE OF INDIAN GOVERNOR in former times, the official residence of a governor in India **4.** *UK* TERRITORY ADMINISTERED BY RESIDENT AGENT formerly, a territory that was administered by the resident agent of a protecting state, e.g., the East Indies **5.** same as **residence** (senses 4–5)

res·i·dent /rézzid'nt/ *n* **1.** SOMEBODY LIVING IN PLACE a permanent or long-term dweller in a place **2.** DOCTOR COMPLETING RESIDENCY a doctor or surgeon engaged in a residency **3.** SOMEBODY LIVING IN RESIDENTIAL SITUATION somebody who lives in a nursing home, children's home, retirement home, or other communal housing **4.** DIPLOMAT a diplomatic official based in a foreign country **5.** *US* LOCAL ORGANIZER OF INTELLIGENCE AGENCY a member of a government intelligence-gathering agency who lives in and oversees operations for the agency in a foreign country **6.** NONMIGRATORY ANIMAL a bird or other animal that does not migrate seasonally **7.** *UK* BRITISH COLONIAL OFFICIAL a representative of the British government in a British colony or protectorate ■ *adj* **1.** LIVING IN A PLACE living permanently or for a considerable period in a place **2.** LIVE-IN living somewhere as part of a particular job **3.** INHERENT present or inherent in something **4.** NONMIGRATORY not migrating seasonally **5.** COMPUT PERMANENTLY INSTALLED IN A COMPUTER'S MEMORY describes a computer program or data intentionally retained in random-access memory after being loaded so that it can be accessed quickly [14C. Directly or via French < Latin *resident-*, present participle of *residere* (see RESIDE)] —**res·i·dent·ship** *n*

res·i·dent com·mis·sion·er *n* in the United States, a representative from a dependency who is allowed to speak but not vote in the US House of Representatives

res·i·den·tial /rèzzi dénshəl/ *adj* 1. RELATING TO HOUSING relating to or consisting of private housing rather than offices or factories 2. FOR LONG-TERM LIVING used as a place to live for the long term 3. WITH LIVING ACCOMMODATIONS providing living accommodations ○ *a residential post* [Mid-17C. < RESIDENCE] —**res·i·den·tial·ly** *adv*

res·i·den·tial school *n* a government-run school providing education and living accommodations for children who are physically or mentally challenged

res·i·den·ti·ar·y /rèzzi dénshee èrree, -dénsharee/ *adj* 1. requiring the incumbent to live in an official residence 2. residing in an official residence

re·sid·u·al /ri zíjjoo əl/ *adj* 1. LEFT OVER remaining after the majority of something has been removed ○ *residual dampness* 2. GEOL RELATING TO WEATHERED ROCK RESIDUE relating to the material left after the weathering of a rock has removed its soluble constituents ■ *n* 1. SOMETHING LEFT OVER something that remains after part of something has been removed 2. STATS DIFFERENCE BETWEEN ACTUAL AND THEORETICAL the difference between results obtained through theoretical calculation and those obtained through observation 3. MOVIES, MEDIA REPEAT FEE a payment to performers, directors, or writers when their filmed work is shown again, especially on television —**re·sid·u·al·ly** *adv*

re·sid·u·al oil *n* the low-grade hydrocarbons that remain after the process of petroleum distillation. Use: in asphalt, furnace fuel.

re·sid·u·al un·em·ploy·ment *n* unemployment remaining during times of full employment, made up of people unable to work because of poor physical or mental health

re·sid·u·ar·y /ri zíjjoo èrree/ *adj* 1. entitled to the residue of a deceased person's estate after debts have been paid and bequests distributed 2. remaining after a process has been gone through [Early 18C. < RESIDUUM]

res·i·due /rézzi do͞o/ *n* 1. something that remains after a process involving the removal of part of the original has been completed 2. the remainder of a deceased person's estate after debts have been paid and bequests distributed [14C. Via French < Latin *residuum* "something remaining" < *residere* (see RESIDE)]

re·sid·u·um /ri zíjjoo əm/ (*plural* **-u·a** /-oo ə/) *n* LAW same as **residue** (sense 2) [Late 17C. < Latin (see RESIDUE)]

re·sign /ri zín/ (**-signed, -sign·ing, -signs**) *v* 1. *vti* LEAVE JOB to give up a paid or unpaid position voluntarily 2. **re·sign your·self** *vr* ACCEPT SOMETHING RELUCTANTLY to come to terms with something and acquiesce in it reluctantly ○ *He resigned himself to giving up work.* 3. *vt* RELINQUISH CLAIM to give up a right or claim to something [14C. Via French < Latin *resignare* "unseal, cancel, give back" < *signare* "to seal" < *signum* "mark"] —**re·signed** *adj* —**re·sign·er** *n*

re-sign *v* 1. *vti* to sign another contract, or cause a player to sign another contract 2. *vt* to sign a document again

res·ig·na·tion /rèzzig náysh'n/ *n* 1. NOTIFICATION OF LEAVING JOB a formal notification of leaving a paid or unpaid position ○ *I've handed in my resignation.* 2. DEPARTURE FROM JOB an instance of leaving a paid or unpaid position 3. UNPROTESTING ACCEPTANCE OF SOMETHING agreement to something, usually given reluctantly but without protest

re·sile /ri zíl/ (**-siled, -sil·ing, -siles**) *vi* (*formal*) 1. to spring back into the same shape or position 2. to jump or leap back [Early 16C. Directly or via French < Latin *resilire* (see RESILIENT)]

re·sil·ience /ri zíllyənss/, **re·sil·ien·cy** /-zíllyənssee/ *n* 1. the ability to recover quickly from setbacks 2. the ability of matter to spring back quickly into shape after being bent, stretched, or deformed

re·sil·ient /ri zíllyənt/ *adj* 1. able to recover quickly from setbacks 2. able to spring back quickly into shape after being bent, stretched, or squashed [Mid-17C. < Latin *resilient-*, present participle of *resilire* "jump back" < *salire* "to jump"] —**re·sil·ient·ly** *adv*

res·in /rézzin/ *n* 1. SUBSTANCE FROM PLANTS a semisolid substance secreted in the sap of some plants and trees. It is used in varnishes, paints, adhesives, inks, and medicines. 2. SYNTHETIC RESEMBLING RESIN a synthetic polymeric compound physically resembling natural resin, e.g., polyvinyl, polystyrene, or epoxy. Use: manufacture of petrochemicals and plastics. ■ *vt* (**-ined, -in·ing, -ins**) TREAT SOMETHING WITH RESIN to coat or rub something with resin [14C. Via Old French *resine* and Latin *resina* < Greek *rhētinē*] —**res·in·oid** *adj, n* —**res·in·ous** *adj* —**res·in·ous·ly** *adv* —**res·in·ous·ness** *n*

res·in·ate /rézzə nàyt/ (**-at·ed, -at·ing, -ates**) *vt* to impregnate, saturate, or flavor something with resin

res ip·sa lo·qui·tur /ràyss ìpsə lókwə to͝or, rèez-/ *n* a rule of evidence that allows that mere proof that an injury occurred establishes a presumption of negligence on the part of the defendant [< Latin, "the thing speaks for itself"]

re·sist /ri zíst/ *v* (**-sist·ed, -sist·ing, -sists**) 1. *vti* FIGHT AGAINST SOMEBODY OR SOMETHING to oppose and stand firm against somebody or something 2. *vt* REFUSE TO GIVE IN TO SOMETHING to refuse to accept or comply with something ○ *resisted all attempts to force them out of their homes* 3. *vt* BE UNHARMED BY SOMETHING to remain unaltered by the damaging effect of something ○ *ability to resist infection* 4. *vti* SAY NO TO SOMETHING TEMPTING to refrain from something in spite of being tempted ○ *I couldn't resist taking a peek.* ■ *n* INDUST PROTECTIVE COATING a protective coating used to prevent corrosion or oxidation, provide electrical insulation in a printed circuit, or prevent part of a fabric from accepting dye [14C. Directly or via French < Latin *resistere* "stand against" < *sistere* "make stand" < *stare* "to stand"] —**re·sis·ter** *n* —**re·sist·i·bil·i·ty** /ri zìstə bíllətee/ *n* —**re·sist·i·ble** *adj* —**re·sist·i·bly** *adv*

re·sis·tance /ri zístənss/ *n* 1. OPPOSITION opposition to somebody or something 2. REFUSAL TO GIVE IN refusal to accept or comply with something 3. ABILITY TO WITHSTAND DAMAGING EFFECT the ability to remain unaltered by the damaging effect of something, e.g., an organism's ability not to succumb to disease or infection 4. ABILITY TO SAY NO TO TEMPTATION the ability to refrain from something in spite of being tempted 5. PHYS FORCE OPPOSING ANOTHER FORCE a force that opposes or slows down another force. Symbol *R*, **r** 6. ELEC OPPOSITION TO ELECTRIC CURRENT the opposition that a circuit, component, or substance presents to the flow of electricity. Symbol *R* 7. ELEC SOURCE OF RESISTANCE something that is a source of opposition to the flow of electricity, e.g., a resistor. Symbol *R* 8. PSYCHOANAL REPRESSION OF THOUGHTS in psychology, the process by which the ego keeps repressed thoughts and feelings from the conscious mind

Re·sis·tance *n* an illegal secret organization that fights for national freedom against an occupying power, especially one that fought in France, the Netherlands, Denmark, or Italy during World War II

re·sis·tant /ri zístənt/ *adj* 1. RESISTING offering resistance to something ○ *resistant to change* 2. NOT DAMAGED BY SOMETHING unaltered by or impervious to the damaging effect of something (*often used in combination*) ○ *moisture-resistant* ■ *n* SOMEBODY OR SOMETHING THAT RESISTS somebody or something that offers resistance

~~resistence~~ incorrect spelling of **resistance**

re·sist·in /ri zístin/ *n* a hormone that increases the resistance of cells to insulin, so causing levels of sugar in the bloodstream to rise

re·sis·tive /ri zístiv/ *adj* 1. same as **resistant** 2. having the property of electrical resistance —**re·sis·tive·ly** *adv* —**re·sis·tive·ness** *n*

re·sis·tiv·i·ty /ri zìs tívvətee/ *n* 1. the electrical resistance of a substance of a standard length and cross section. Symbol ρ 2. the capacity to resist something

re·sist·less /ri zístləss/ *adj* 1. not able to be resisted 2. not able to resist something

re·sis·tor /ri zístər/ *n* a component of an electrical circuit that has resistance and is used to control the flow of electric current

res ju·di·ca·ta /ràyss joodi kaátə, rèez-/, **res ad·ju·di·ca·ta** /-ə joodi-/ *n* an issue already decided by a court [< Latin, "judged matter"]

re·skill /ree skíl/ (**-skilled, -skill·ing, -skills**) *vt* to teach somebody new skills, especially with a view to his or her finding or changing employment —**re·skill·ing** *n*

Res·nais /re náy/, **Alain** (*b.* 1922) French movie director. Among his noted movies are *Hiroshima mon amour* (1959) and *Last Year at Marienbad* (1961).

re·sol·u·ble[1] /ri zóllyəb'l/ *adj* able to be resolved or analyzed [Early 17C. Directly or via French < Latin *resolubilis* < *resolvere* (see RESOLVE)] —**res·ol·u·bil·i·ty** /-zòllyə bíllətee/ *n* —**re·sol·u·ble·ness** *n*

re·sol·u·ble[2] /ree sóllyəb'l/ *adj* able to be dissolved again [15C. < RE- + SOLUBLE] —**re·sol·u·bil·i·ty** /-sòllyə bíllətee/ *n* —**re·sol·u·ble·ness** *n*

res·o·lute /rézzə lo͞ot/ *adj* 1. possessing determination and purposefulness 2. motivated by or displaying determination and purposefulness [15C. < Latin *resolutus*, past participle of *resolvere* (see RESOLVE)] —**res·o·lute·ly** *adv* —**res·o·lute·ness** *n*

res·o·lu·tion /rèzzə lo͞osh'n/ *n* 1. PROCESS OF RESOLVING the process of resolving something such as a problem or dispute ○ *the resolution of a difficulty* 2. DECISION a firm decision to do something 3. DETERMINATION firmness of mind or purpose 4. SOLUTION an answer to a problem 5. EXPRESSION OF COLLECTIVE OPINION a formal expression of the consensus at a meeting, arrived at after discussion and usually as the result of a vote 6. QUALITY OF DETAIL IN IMAGE the quality of detail offered by a TV or computer screen or a photographic image 7. PHYS, CHEM SEPARATION INTO CONSTITUENT PARTS the process or act of separating something such as a chemical compound or a source of light into its constituent parts 8. MED SUBSIDING OF SYMPTOMS the disappearance or coming to an end of a medical symptom or condition 9. MUSIC HARMONIC PROGRESSION the musical progression from a dissonant to a consonant chord or note 10. MUSIC FINAL NOTE the musical note or chord to which the harmony moves when progressing from dissonance to consonance 11. THEATER, LITERAT PART OF NARRATIVE WHEN CONFLICT IS RESOLVED the point in a literary work when the conflict is resolved 12. PHYS same as **resolving power** 13. LITERAT SYLLABLE REPLACEMENT the substitution of a long syllable for two short ones in the rhythm of a line of poetry [14C. Directly or via French < Latin *resolution-* < past participle of *resolvere* (see RESOLVE)]

re·solve /ri zólv/ *v* (**-solved, -solv·ing, -solves**) 1. *vti* MAKE DECISION to come to a firm decision about something, or cause somebody to do this ○ *He resolved to leave.* 2. *vt* SOLVE DIFFICULTY to find a solution to a problem 3. *vt* SETTLE ARGUMENT to bring a disagreement to an end 4. *vt* DISPEL DOUBTS to dispel doubts or anxieties 5. **re·solve it·self** *vr* CHANGE to change into something else ○ *"O! that this too too solid flesh would melt,/Thaw, and resolve itself into a dew"* (William Shakespeare, *Hamlet*) 6. *vt* EXPRESS JOINT OPINION FORMALLY to express the opinion of a meeting formally as a consensus, after discussion and usually as the result of a vote 7. *vti* MED MAKE OR BECOME LESS SWOLLEN to subside, or cause an inflammation, swelling, or tumor to subside 8. *vti* SPLIT INTO CONSTITUENT PARTS to cause something to separate into its constituent elements, or become separated into constituent parts 9. *vt* CHEM SEPARATE RACEMIC MIXTURE to separate a racemic compound or mixture into its two components 10. *vti* MUSIC MOVE FROM DISSONANT TO CONSONANT to move from dissonant to consonant, or cause a chord or note to move from dissonant to consonant 11. *vt* PHYS MAKE PARTS OF IMAGE DISTINCT to make parts of an image distinct, e.g., in a microscope or telescope 12. *vt* MATH SPLIT VECTOR INTO DIRECTIONAL COMPONENTS to separate a vector into its directional components ■ *n* 1. DETERMINATION firmness of purpose 2. DECISION a firm decision to do something [14C. Directly or via French < Latin *resolvere* "loosen up" < *solvere* "loosen, dissolve"] —**re·solv·a·bil·i·ty** /-zòlvə bíllətee/ *n* —**re·solv·a·ble** *adj* —**re·solv·a·ble·ness** *n* —**re·solv·er** *n*

re·solved /ri zólvd/ *adj* determined in purpose —**re·sol·ved·ly** /-zólvədlee/ *adv*

re·sol·vent /ri zólvənt/ *adj* 1. CAUSING SEPARATION INTO CONSTITUENT PARTS causing or capable of causing something to separate into its constituent parts 2. MED

ANTI-INFLAMMATORY able to cause reduction in inflammation or swelling ■ *n* **1.** SOMETHING CAUSING SEPARATION INTO CONSTITUENT PARTS a substance that causes or is capable of causing something to separate into its constituent parts **2.** MED ANTI-INFLAMMATORY MEDICINE a medicine that reduces inflammation or swelling

re·solv·ing pow·er /ri zólving-/ *n* the ability of an optical system such as a telescope or microscope to distinguish objects separated by small angular distances

res·o·nance /rézzənənss/ *n* **1.** UNDERLYING MEANING the effect of an event or work of art beyond its immediate or surface meaning **2.** AMPLIFIED SOUND an intense and prolonged sound produced by sympathetic vibration **3.** RINGING QUALITY OF INSTRUMENT OR VOICE an amplification of a sound, e.g., that of an instrument or the human voice, caused by sympathetic vibration in a chamber such as an auditorium or a singer's chest **4.** PHYS LARGE OSCILLATION AT NATURAL FREQUENCY increased amplitude of oscillation of a mechanical system when it is subjected to vibration from another source at or near its own natural frequency **5.** ELEC OSCILLATION IN ELECTRICAL CIRCUIT a state of oscillation that occurs at a very specific frequency in an electrical circuit consisting of inductive and capacitive components **6.** MED SOUND WHEN BODY CAVITY IS TAPPED the sound heard during tapping (**percussion**) of a healthy chest or abdomen **7.** CHEM PROPERTY OF SOME CHEMICAL COMPOUNDS the property of some chemical compounds of having simultaneously the characteristics of two or more structures that differ in the arrangement of electrons

res·o·nant /rézzənənt/ *adj* **1.** DEEP IN SOUND deep and rich in sound **2.** RESOUNDING continuing to sound for some time **3.** CAUSING ECHOES producing or increasing amplification of sound or echoes, usually by sympathetic vibration [Late 16C. Directly or via French < Latin *resonant-*, present participle of *resonare* (see RESONATE)] —**res·o·nant·ly** *adv*

res·o·nate /rézzə nàyt/ (**-nat·ed, -nat·ing, -nates**) *v* **1.** *vti* RESOUND to echo, or cause something to echo **2.** *vi* HAVE EXTENDED EFFECT to have an effect or impact beyond that which is immediately apparent **3.** *vti* PRODUCE RESONANCE to produce or exhibit chemical, mechanical, or electrical resonance, or cause a chemical compound or a electrical system to produce or exhibit resonance **4.** *vi* BE FAMILIAR to produce a response in somebody, especially by reminding that person of something or prompting feelings of support or approval [Late 19C. < Latin *resonat-*, past participle of *resonare* "resound" < *sonare* "to sound" < *sonus* "sound"]

res·o·na·tor /rézzə nàytər/ *n* **1.** a device or part that resonates, especially one that produces sound or microwaves **2.** a part of a musical instrument designed to produce resonance, e.g., the hollow body of a violin or the tubes in a vibraphone

re·sorb /ri sáwrb, -záwrb/ (**-sorbed, -sorb·ing, -sorbs**) *vt* to absorb something again [Mid-17C. < Latin *resorbere* "drink in again" < *sorbere* "suck in"] —**re·sor·bent** *adj*

res·or·cin·ol /ri záwrssi nàwl/ *n* a colorless crystalline phenol. Use: manufacture of dyes, resins, drugs, in tanning. Formula: $C_6H_6O_2$. [Late 19C. < RESIN + *orcin*, crystalline substance obtained from orchils]

re·sorp·tion /ri sáwrpsh'n, -záwrpsh'n/ *n* **1.** the process or state of resorbing or being resorbed **2.** the partial fusion of a crystal in a magma in response to changing conditions of temperature and pressure [Early 19C. < RESORB, after *absorption*] —**re·sorp·tive** *adj*

re·sort /ri záwrt/ *n* **1.** VACATION PLACE a place that is popular for recreation and vacations and provides accommodations and entertainment **2.** SOURCE OF HELP a person, place, or course of action seen as a source of help in dealing with a problem ○ *As a last resort we could sell the car.* **3.** ACT OF HAVING RECOURSE TO SOMETHING the act of turning to somebody or something for help in dealing with a problem **4.** FREQUENT VISITING the act of going somewhere frequently or in large numbers **5.** MUCH-VISITED PLACE a place frequently visited [14C. < Old French *resortir* "come back" < *sortir* "go out"]
resort to (**resorted to, resorting to, resorts to**) *vt* **1.** to turn to something, sometimes something extreme, for help in dealing with a problem **2.** to go somewhere that is frequently visited, or go somewhere in large numbers

re-sort *vt* to sort things into categories or a sequence

re·sort·er /ri záwrtər/ *n* somebody who spends a lot of time at a resort

re·sort·wear /ri záwrt wèr/ *n* casual, lightweight, easy-care clothing designed for vacation wear

re·sound /ri zównd/ (**-sound·ed, -sound·ing, -sounds**) *v* **1.** *vi* BE FILLED WITH REVERBERATING SOUND to be filled with a long reverberating sound ○ *The hall resounded to the cheers of the audience.* **2.** *vi* MAKE REVERBERATING SOUND to produce a long reverberating sound **3.** *vi* BE EXTREMELY WELL KNOWN to be extremely well known, especially over a long period or a wide area **4.** *vt* US SAY SOMETHING SO THAT IT ECHOES to say something loudly and in echoing tones **5.** *vt* PRODUCE ECHO to cause a sound to reverberate [14C. Alteration (after SOUND[1]) of Old French *resoner* < Latin *resonare* (see RESONATE)]

re·sound·ing /ri zównding/ *adj* **1.** clear and unequivocal ○ *a resounding defeat* **2.** making a loud noise that echoes —**re·sound·ing·ly** *adv*

re·source /rée sàwrss, ri sáwrss/ *n* **1.** SOURCE OF HELP somebody or something that is a source of help or information **2.** BACKUP SUPPLY a reserve supply of something such as money, personnel, or equipment **3.** ABILITY TO FIND SOLUTIONS adeptness at finding solutions to problems **4.** ECOL same as **natural resource** ■ **re·sour·ces** *npl* **1.** TALENT DRAWN ON WHEN NECESSARY an inner ability or capacity that is drawn on in time of need, or such abilities considered collectively **2.** NATION'S NATURAL, ECONOMIC, OR MILITARY ASSETS the natural, economic, political, or military assets enjoyed by a nation, e.g., mineral wealth, labor, capital, or military personnel **3.** COMM CORPORATE ASSETS any or all of the sources drawn on by a company for making profit, e.g., personnel, capital, machinery, or stock ■ *vt* (**-sourced, -sourc·ing, -sour·ces**) PROVIDE SOMETHING WITH RESOURCES to provide something with monetary or other resources ○ *not adequately resourced to carry out their responsibilities* [Early 17C. < French *ressource* < Latin *resurgere* "rise again, be replenished" < *surgere* "rise up from below"] —**re·source·less** *adj*

re·source·ful /ri sáwrssfəl/ *adj* full of initiative and good at problem-solving, especially in difficult situations —**re·source·ful·ly** *adv* —**re·source·ful·ness** *n*

re·sourc·ing *n* the work of finding and providing the material, financial, or human resources required for a task

resp. *abbr* **1.** respective **2.** respectively **3.** BIOL respiration **4.** LAW respondent

re·spect /ri spékt/ *n* **1.** ESTEEM a feeling or attitude of admiration and deference toward somebody or something ○ *He has no respect for authority.* **2.** STATE OF BEING ADMIRED the state of being admired deferentially **3.** THOUGHTFULNESS consideration or thoughtfulness **4.** CHARACTERISTIC an individual characteristic or point ○ *satisfactory in every respect* ■ **re·spects** *npl* REGARDS polite greetings offered to somebody ■ *vt* (**-spect·ed, -spect·ing, -spects**) **1.** ESTEEM SOMEBODY OR SOMETHING to feel or show admiration and deference toward somebody or something **2.** NOT GO AGAINST OR VIOLATE SOMETHING to pay due attention to and refrain from violating something ○ *respect the law* ○ *respect another's privacy* **3.** BE CONSIDERATE TOWARD SOMEBODY OR SOMETHING to show consideration or thoughtfulness in relation to somebody or something [14C. Via French < Latin *respectus*, past participle of *respicere* "regard, look back at" < *specere* "look at"] —**re·spect·ed** *adj* —**re·spect·er** *n*

SYNONYMS See ***regard***.

re·spect·a·ble /ri spéktəb'l/ *adj* **1.** MORALLY ABOVE REPROACH in accordance with accepted standards of correctness or decency ○ *a respectable district* **2.** SATISFACTORY meeting an adequate standard ○ *a respectable piece of work* **3.** LARGE ENOUGH sufficiently large ○ *a respectable salary* **4.** ACCEPTABLE IN APPEARANCE tidy and fit to be seen by others, especially in public (*informal*) —**re·spect·a·bil·i·ty** /-spèktə bíllətee/ *n* —**re·spect·a·ble·ness** *n* —**re·spect·a·bly** *adv*

re·spect·ful /ri spéktfəl/ *adj* showing appropriate deference and respect —**re·spect·ful·ness** *n*

re·spect·ful·ly /ri spéktfəlee/ *adv* with respect or in a respectful manner

USAGE respectfully or **respectively**? ***Respectfully*** means "with respect; with all due respect; in a respectful manner," as in the complimentary close of a letter (*Respectfully, Jane Doe*), and in *We respectfully* [not *respectively*] *reserve the right to disagree with the ruling.* ***Respectively*** matches one list with another in the order given for both, as in *The captain and the first officer have 20 and 15 years' experience, respectively* [not *respectfully*].

re·spect·ing /ri spékting/ *prep* with reference to or concerning somebody or something

re·spec·tive /ri spéktiv/ *adj* varying according to each of the people or things concerned ○ *They returned to their respective homes.* —**re·spec·tive·ness** *n*

re·spec·tive·ly /ri spéktivlee/ *adv* matching one list with another in the order given for both ○ *Mr. Jones and his wife are aged 52 and 51, respectively.*

USAGE See ***respectfully***.

re·spell /ree spél/ (**-spelled, -spell·ing, -spells**) *vt* to spell something again or in a different way, especially using a different alphabet in order to give guidance on pronunciation —**re·spell·ing** *n*

res·pi·ra·ble /résperəb'l, ri spírəb'l/ *adj* fit or able to be breathed —**res·pi·ra·bil·i·ty** /rèspərə bíllətee, ri spírə bíllətee/ *n*

res·pi·ra·tion /rèspə ráysh'n/ *n* **1.** PHYSIOL BREATHING the act of breathing air in and out **2.** PROCESS OF SUPPLYING OXYGEN TO CELLS the chemical and physical process in which oxygen is delivered to tissues or cells in an organism and carbon dioxide and water are given off (**external respiration**) **3.** ENERGY-PRODUCING PROCESS IN CELLS a metabolic process in cells leading to the production of energy by the breakdown of organic substances (**internal respiration**) —**res·pi·ra·tion·al** *adj*

res·pi·ra·tor /réspə ràytər/ *n* **1.** a machine used in hospitals to maintain breathing for patients unable to breathe unaided **2.** a device placed over the nose and mouth to filter out noxious particles and fumes from inhaled air or to warm chilled air before it is inhaled

res·pi·ra·to·ry /résperə tàwree, ri spírə-/ *adj* relating to or used in breathing or the system in the body that takes in and distributes oxygen

res·pi·ra·to·ry dis·tress syn·drome *n* a respiratory disease of newborns, especially premature infants, caused by the inability of the lungs to take in oxygen and marked by cyanosis and difficult breathing

res·pi·ra·to·ry pig·ment *n* a protein that can bind with oxygen, e.g., hemoglobin

res·pi·ra·to·ry quo·tient *n* the ratio of the volume of carbon dioxide released to the volume of oxygen absorbed by an organism, cell, or tissue over a given time period

res·pi·ra·to·ry sys·tem *n* the system of organs in the body responsible for the intake of oxygen and the expiration of carbon dioxide. In mammals it consists of the lungs, bronchi, bronchioles, trachea, diaphragm, and nerve supply.

re·spire /ri spír/ (**-spired, -spir·ing, -spires**) *v* **1.** *vti* to breathe air in and out **2.** *vi* to breathe again in a normal way after anxiety or exertion (*literary*) [14C. Directly or via French < Latin *respirare* "breathe again" < *spirare* "breathe"]

res·pi·rom·e·ter /rèspə rómmətər/ *n* an instrument for measuring and studying the process in which oxygen is taken into the body, delivered to tissues and cells, and used by them [Late 19C. < RESPIRATION] —**res·pi·ro·met·ric** /rèsperō méttrik/ *adj* —**res·pi·rom·e·try** *n*

res·pite /réspit/ *n* **1.** BRIEF INTERVAL OF REST a brief period of rest and recovery between periods of exertion or after something disagreeable **2.** DELAY a temporary delay **3.** LAW REPRIEVE a temporary stay of execution of a criminal [13C. Via Old French, "refuge" < Latin *respectus*, past participle of *respicere* (see RESPECT)]

~~resplendant~~ incorrect spelling of **resplendent**

re·splen·dent /ri spléndənt/ *adj* having a dazzlingly impressive appearance ○ *resplendent in his dress uniform* [15C. < Latin *resplendent-*, present participle of *resplendere* "shine brightly" < *splendere* "shine"] —**re·splen·dence** *n* —**re·splen·dent·ly** *adv*

re·spond /ri spónd/ *v* (**-spond·ed, -spond·ing, -sponds**) **1.** *vti* **PROVIDE ANSWER** to say or write something in reply **2.** *vi* **REACT** to act or do something in reaction to something else ○ *was unsure of how to respond to his moods* **3.** *vi* MED **HAVE POSITIVE MEDICAL REACTION** to react positively to medical treatment ■ *n* **1.** ARCHIT **PILASTER OR PILLAR SUPPORTING ARCH** a pilaster or pillar that supports an arch **2.** CHR, MUSIC **CHORAL PART OF ANTHEM** the choral part in an anthem for priest and choir in a church service [Mid-16C. Via French < Latin *respondere* "promise in return" < *spondere* "to pledge"] —**re·spon·dence** *n* —**re·spon·der** *n*

~~respondant~~ incorrect spelling of **respondent**

re·spon·dent /ri spóndənt/ *n* **1. ANSWERER** somebody who replies to something **2.** LAW **DEFENDANT** the person against whom a divorce petition or an appeal is brought ■ *adj* **1. RESPONDING** giving a response **2.** LAW **DEFENDING IN DIVORCE** acting as the defendant in a divorce petition or appeal

re·spon·sa JUDAISM plural of **responsum**

~~responsability~~ incorrect spelling of **responsibility**

re·sponse /ri spónss/ *n* **1. REPLY GIVEN TO A QUESTION** something said or written in reply to a statement or question from somebody else **2. REACTION** something done in reaction to something else **3.** CARDS **BID IN BRIDGE** in bridge, a bid that is in reply to a partner's bid or double **4.** CHR **REPLY MADE BY CHURCH CHOIR** a phrase sung or spoken by the choir or congregation in reply to the officiant during a church service **5.** MED **BODY'S REACTION TO STIMULUS** the reaction of an organism or any of its parts to a stimulus [14C. Directly or via French < Latin *responsum* < past participle of *respondere* (see RESPOND)]

SYNONYMS See *answer.*

re·spon·si·bil·i·ty /ri spònssə bíllətee/ (*plural* **-ties**) *n* **1. ACCOUNTABILITY** the state, fact, or position of being accountable to somebody or for something **2. SOMETHING TO BE RESPONSIBLE FOR** somebody or something for which a person or organization is responsible **3. BLAME** the blame for something that has happened ○ *took full responsibility for the mix-up* **4. AUTHORITY TO ACT** authority to make decisions independently

re·spon·si·ble /ri spónssəb'l/ *adj* **1. ANSWERABLE TO SOMEBODY** accountable to somebody for an action or for the successful carrying out of a duty ○ *Jo was responsible for that phase of the project.* **2. BEING TO BLAME FOR SOMETHING** being the cause of something, usually something wrong or disapproved of ○ *Who's responsible for this mess?* **3. IMPORTANT** conferring the authority to make decisions independently and requiring conscientiousness and trustworthiness ○ *in a responsible position* **4. RELIABLE** able to be counted on owing to qualities of conscientiousness and trustworthiness ○ *very responsible for his age* **5.** FIN **FINANCIALLY SOUND** having adequate means to meet financial obligations [Late 16C. < obsolete French, "corresponding" < Latin *respons-*, past participle of *respondere* (see RESPOND)] —**re·spon·si·ble·ness** *n* —**re·spon·si·bly** *adv*

re·spon·sive /ri spónssiv/ *adj* **1. SHOWING POSITIVE RESPONSE** reacting quickly, strongly, or favorably to something, especially a suggestion or proposal **2. RESPONDING TO TREATMENT** reacting positively to medical treatment **3. DONE IN RESPONSE** serving to respond to something **4.** CHR **CONSISTING OF CHOIR'S OR CONGREGATION'S RESPONSES** consisting of responses by a choir or congregation in a church service —**re·spon·sive·ly** *adv*—**re·spon·sive·ness** *n*

re·spon·so·ry /ri spónssəree/ (*plural* **-ries**) *n* an anthem consisting of short verses sung or spoken by the officiant and responses sung or spoken by the choir, especially after the lesson in a church service —**re·spon·so·ri·al** /-spòn sáwree əl/ *adj*

re·spon·sum /ri spónssəm/ (*plural* **-sa** /-sə/) *n* in Judaism, definitive written reply by a rabbinical authority to a question on religion [Late 19C. < Latin, form of past participle of *respondere* (see RESPOND)]

res pub·li·ca /ràyss póobli kàa, rèez púbblikə/ *n* **1.** the state, a republic, or the commonwealth as a concept **2.** the public or common good [From Latin, literally "public matter"]

res·sen·ti·ment /rə sàaNtee màaN/ *n* a feeling of resentment and hostility characterized by an inability to act to change the situation [Mid-20C. Directly or via German < French, < *ressentir* "feel strongly" < *sentir* "feel"]

rest[1] /rest/ *n* **1. STOPPING OF WORK OR ACTIVITY** a state or period of refreshing freedom from exertion **2. SLEEP** the repose of sleep that is refreshing to body and mind and is marked by a reduction in metabolic activity **3. ABSENCE OF MOVEMENT** the cessation of movement or action ○ *The boat lay at rest in the harbor.* **4. DEATH** death perceived as freedom from earthly toil ○ *He is now at rest.* **5. FREEDOM FROM ANXIETY** freedom from mental or emotional anxiety ○ *I put her mind at rest.* **6. PLACE TO STOP AND RELAX** a stopping place for shelter and relaxation **7. SUPPORT** something used for support, especially on a piece of furniture **8.** MUSIC **PAUSE IN MUSIC** a rhythmic pause between musical notes, or the mark indicating a musical pause **9.** LITERAT same as **caesura** (sense 1) ■ *v* (**rest·ed, rest·ing, rests**) **1.** *vi* **SLEEP OR RELAX** to restore your energy by means of relaxation or sleep ○ *Put your feet up and rest.* **2.** *vt* **LET SOMEBODY SLEEP OR RELAX** to allow a person or animal to regain energy by means of relaxation or sleep, or allow a limb or body part to be inactive to restore its strength ○ *rest the sled dogs* ○ *sat down to rest my feet* **3.** *vi* **BE TRANQUIL** to be in a state of tranquillity **4.** *vi* **BE DEAD** to be dead, and so free from earthly concerns **5.** *vti* **STOP MOVING** to cease activity, or cause something to cease activity **6.** *vi* **BE LEFT ALONE** to be subject to no further discussion or attention ○ *Let the matter rest.* **7.** *vi* **LIE FALLOW** to lie unfarmed **8.** *vti* **SUPPORT OR BE SUPPORTED** to support something on or against something, or be supported on or against something ○ *The ornament was resting on a narrow ledge.* **9.** *vi* **COME TO STOP** to allow the eyes to come to a stop on somebody or something **10.** *vi* **BE VESTED** to be vested or placed in somebody or something ○ *The authority rests with him.* **11.** *vi* **DEPEND ON SOMEBODY OR SOMETHING** to depend on somebody or something for action or as a burden or responsibility **12.** *vi* **BE BASED ON SOMETHING** to rely on something for proof or explanation **13.** *vti* LAW **CONCLUDE A LEGAL CASE** to conclude the presentation of evidence in a case ○ *I rest my case.* [Old English *ræst* (noun), *ræstan* (verb) < Germanic] —**rest·ed** *adj* —**rest·er** *n*

rest[2] /rest/ *n* something left as a remainder (*takes a singular or plural verb*) ■ *vi* (**rest·ed, rest·ing, rests**) to remain or continue to be (*usually used as a command*) ○ *Rest assured that we're doing everything possible.* [15C. < French *reste* "remnant" < *rester* "remain" < Latin *restare* "stay behind" < *stare* "to stand"]

~~restaraunt~~ incorrect spelling of **restaurant**

rest ar·e·a *n* an area at the side of a major road where motorists can rest

re·state /ree stáyt/ (**-stat·ed, -stat·ing, -states**) *vt* to say something again, especially in order to clarify or summarize what has already been said ○ *time to restate our goals* —**re·state·ment** *n*

res·tau·rant /réstərənt, -rònt/ *n* a place where meals and drinks are sold and served to customers [Early 19C. < French, < present participle of *restaurer* < Latin *restaurare* "set upright again"]

res·tau·rant car *n UK* same as **dining car**

res·tau·ra·teur /rèstərə túr/, **res·tau·ran·teur** /rèstə raan-/ *n* an owner or manager of a restaurant [Late 18C. < French, "restorer" < *restaurer* (see RESTAURANT)]

rest cure *n* a treatment involving complete rest, e.g., as a remedy for stress

rest·ful /réstfəl/ *adj* **1.** giving, promoting, or involving rest ○ *a restful vacation* **2.** at rest or tranquil —**rest·ful·ly** *adv* —**rest·ful·ness** *n*

rest·har·row /rést hàrrō/ *n* a pod-bearing plant with three-lobed leaves and woody stems and roots. Flowers: white, purple, or pink, in clusters. Native to: Europe, Asia. Latin name: *Ononsis repens* or *Ononsis spinosa.* [Because its tough roots can stop, or "arrest," the progress of a harrow]

rest home *n* a place where senior citizens and chronically ill people live and are cared for

rest·ing /résting/ *adj* **1.** *US* **DEAD** having recently died (*often used euphemistically*) **2.** BIOL **IMMOBILE** describes organisms that are not moving or active **3.** BIOL **NOT DIVIDING** not undergoing cell division **4.** BOT **DORMANT** describes spores, seeds, and eggs that are dormant before germination

res·ti·tu·tion /rèsti tóosh'n/ *n* **1. GIVING BACK** the return of something to its rightful owner **2. PAYING BACK** compensation for a loss, damage, or injury **3. RESTORATION** the return of something to the condition it was in before it was changed [13C. Directly or via French < Latin *restitution-* < past participle of *restituere* "restore" < *statuere* "set up"] —**res·ti·tute** /résti tòot/ *vt*—**res·ti·tu·tive** /résti tòotiv/ *adj*—**res·ti·tu·to·ry** *adj*

res·tive /réstiv/ *adj* **1. UNEASY** uneasy and on the verge of resisting control ○ *The people grew restive under the rule of the occupying force.* **2. IMPATIENT** having little patience and unwilling to tolerate annoyances **3. OBSTINATE OR AWKWARD** unwilling to be guided or controlled ○ *a restive horse* [Late 16C. Alteration of *restiff* < Old French *restif* < Latin *restare* "to rest"] —**res·tive·ly** *adv* —**res·tive·ness** *n*

rest·less /réstləss/ *adj* **1. CONSTANTLY MOVING** constantly moving, or unable to be still ○ *Some waited patiently but others were restless.* **2. DISCONTENTED** seeking a change because of discontent ○ *He began to feel restless after only a few weeks in the job.* **3. SLEEPLESS** lacking rest or sleep ○ *She spent a restless night worrying.* —**rest·less·ly** *adv* —**rest·less·ness** *n*

rest·less leg syn·drome *n* a condition of the legs characterized by a painful discomfort when inactive that can cause interrupted sleep and fatigue

rest mass *n* the mass a body has when it is not moving, as opposed to the additional mass it gains as a result of its movement, according to the theory of relativity

re·stock /ree stók/ (**-stocked, -stock·ing, -stocks**) *vti* to replace or refill something after it has been used or its contents emptied —**re·stock·able** *adj*

res·to·ra·tion /rèstə ráysh'n/ *n* **1. RESTORING OF SOMETHING REMOVED** the return of something that was removed or abolished ○ *calls for the restoration of curfews* **2. RESTORING OF SOMETHING TO FORMER CONDITION** the restoring of something such as buildings or furniture to an earlier and usually better condition ○ *Restoration work will begin next week.* **3. THING RESTORED** something, especially a building, that has been brought back to an earlier and usually better condition **4. MODEL** a model made to resemble or represent something in its original condition ○ *a restoration of a Neandertal dwelling*

Res·to·ra·tion *n* the reestablishment of monarchy in Great Britain under Charles II in 1660, or the period of his reign

re·stor·a·tive /ri stáwrətiv/ *adj* tending or meant to give somebody new strength or vigor ○ *restorative properties of a vacation* ■ *n* something that gives somebody new strength or vigor, especially an activity or medication —**re·stor·a·tive·ly** *adv* —**re·stor·a·tive·ness** *n*

re·store /ri stáwr/ (**-stored, -stor·ing, -stores**) *vt* **1. GIVE SOMETHING BACK** to return something to its proper owner or place **2. RETURN SOMETHING TO PREVIOUS CONDITION** to bring something back to an earlier and better condition ○ *techniques used to restore old oil paintings* **3. ENERGIZE SOMEBODY** to give somebody new strength or vigor ○ *I felt restored after my weekend away.* **4. RETURN SOMEBODY TO PREVIOUS POSITION** to return somebody to a previously held rank, office, or position ○ *restore the ousted governor to his office* **5. PUT SOMETHING BACK** to reestablish or put back something that was once but is no longer there ○ *restore order in the capital* [13C. Via French < Latin *restaurare* "set upright again"] —**re·stor·a·ble** *adj* —**re·stor·er** *n*

SYNONYMS See *renew.*

re·strain /ri stráyn/ (**-strained, -strain·ing, -strains**) *vt* **1. STOP SOMEBODY FROM DOING SOMETHING** to prevent somebody or yourself from doing something ○ *I couldn't restrain myself from calling out.* **2.** CONTROL SOMETHING to keep somebody or something under control or within limits ○ *finally able to restrain the violence* ○ *barriers to restrain the crowds* **3.** CONTROL SOMEBODY to physically control the movements of a person or animal ○ *Restrain him before he hurts someone.* **4.** IMPRISON SOMEBODY to put somebody in prison or otherwise take away his or her freedom [14C. Via Old French *restreindre* < Latin *restringere* "bind fast, confine" < *stringere* "draw tight"] —**re·strain·a·ble** *adj*

SYNONYMS See *hinder*[1].

re·strained /ri stráynd/ *adj* characterized by control, especially in not being excessively emotional or aggressive ○ *the artist's restrained use of color* —**re·strain·ed·ly** /-stráynədlee/ *adv*

re·strain·ing or·der *n* **1.** a court order that commands somebody to have no contact or communication with another person **2.** a preliminary court order that prohibits an action that might cause harm to the person seeking the order. A restraining order can be granted immediately without a hearing and often stays in effect pending a hearing and decision on the granting of an injunction.

re·straint /ri stráynt/ *n* **1.** HOLDING BACK an act or the quality of holding back, limiting, or controlling something ○ *Although severely provoked, she showed admirable restraint in not retaliating.* **2.** RESTRAINING THING something that controls or limits somebody or something ○ *impose trade restraints* **3.** HOLDING DEVICE something that is fastened to limit somebody's freedom of movement [14C. < Old French *restreinte*, form of past participle of *restreindre* (see RESTRAIN)]

re·straint of trade *n* the limiting of commercial competition by means such as price-fixing or monopolistic practices

~~**restraunt**~~ incorrect spelling of **restaurant**

re·strict /ri stríkt/ (**-strict·ed, -strict·ing, -stricts**) *vt* to keep something within fixed limits ○ *Entry is restricted to members only.* [15C. < Latin *restrict*, past participle of *restringere* (see RESTRAIN)]

re·strict·ed /ri stríktəd/ *adj* **1.** LIMITED limited or made smaller or less than might be desired ○ *It's difficult to turn the vehicle in such a restricted space.* **2.** SUBJECT TO CONTROLS subject to controls or limits, e.g., of time or availability ○ *restricted use of the facilities* **3.** REQUIRING AUTHORIZATION intended only for authorized people ○ *That information is restricted.* —**re·strict·ed·ly** *adv* —**re·strict·ed·ness** *n*

re·stric·tion /ri stríkshən/ *n* **1.** something that limits or controls something else ○ *There are restrictions on the use of the photocopier.* **2.** a restricting of something, or the condition of being restricted ○ *the restriction of a person's freedom*

re·stric·tion en·zyme, res·tric·tion en·do·nu·cle·ase *n* an enzyme that splits DNA into segments at precise locations. Use: genetic engineering.

re·stric·tion frag·ment *n* a specific portion of DNA produced by a restriction enzyme

re·stric·tion frag·ment length pol·y·mor·phism *n* a variation between individuals in the length of the DNA fragments produced by a specific restriction enzyme. They are caused by mutations and can be used to detect genetic anomalies.

re·stric·tive /ri stríktiv/ *adj* **1.** acting as a limit or control on something **2.** limiting the range of reference or application of a word, phrase, or clause —**re·stric·tive·ly** *adv* —**re·stric·tive·ness** *n*

re·stric·tive cov·e·nant *n* a stipulation on a party buying or leasing land to refrain from something such as reselling or subletting it

re·stric·tive prac·tice *n UK* **1.** something done customarily by a group of workers, especially a union, that places limits on the work of others or the freedom of operation of employers **2.** something done by companies in trade that is against the public interest, e.g., price-fixing

re·strike /rée strīk/ *n* a coin struck at a later date from a die that has already been used to produce the original issue —**re·strike** /ree strīk/ *vt*

rest·room /rést ro͝om, -ro͞om/ *n* a room that includes a toilet, especially in a building used by the public

re·struc·ture /ree strúkchər/ (**-tured, -tur·ing, -tures**) *v* **1.** *vti* to change the way in which something is organized or arranged ○ *restructure the company* **2.** *vt* to alter the terms of a loan, especially to relieve its burden on the debtor

re·struc·tur·ing /ree strúkchəring/ *n* the process or an instance of changing the way in which something is organized or arranged

rest stop *n* **1.** ROADS same as **rest area** **2.** a break in a journey for the use of a restroom or for refreshment

re·style /ree stíl/ (**-styled, -sty·ling, -styles**) *vt* **1.** to give something a new design or shape **2.** to give somebody or something a new name or designation —**re·style** *n*

re·sult /ri zúlt/ *n* **1.** CONSEQUENCE something that follows as a consequence of another action, condition, or event **2.** SCORE an outcome, especially the final score in a sports competition or the grade awarded to somebody who has taken a test ○ *The results were in Saturday's paper.* **3.** NUMBER a number arrived at by a calculation ■ **re·sults** *npl* DESIRED OUTCOME the desired outcome from an action ○ *The new policy is already showing results.* ■ *vi* (**-sult·ed, -sult·ing, -sults**) **1.** FOLLOW AS CONSEQUENCE to follow as a consequence of a particular action, condition, or event ○ *This kind of error results from inattention.* **2.** CAUSE OUTCOME to produce a particular outcome ○ *Overgrazing results in soil erosion.* [15C. < Latin *resultare* "spring back, reverberate" ("result" in medieval Latin) < *saltare* "to jump"]

re·sul·tant /ri zúltn't/ *adj* RESULTING FROM happening as a consequence of something else ■ *n* **1.** OUTCOME OF SOMETHING ELSE something that is an outcome of something else such as a calculation **2.** SINGLE VECTOR EQUIVALENT TO OTHERS ADDED a single vector that is equivalent to two or more other vectors

re·sul·tant tone *n* a tone that is created by the sounding together of two other tones but is different from both of them

re·sume /ri zo͞om/ (**-sumed, -sum·ing, -sumes**) *v* **1.** *vti* to continue with something after a temporary halt, or be continued **2.** *vt* to take, assume, or occupy a position again ○ *She came in and resumed her place at the head of the table.* [15C. Directly or via French *résumer* < Latin *resumere* "take up again" < *sumere* "take"] —**re·sum·a·ble** *adj*

ré·su·mé /rézzə mày/, **re·su·mé, re·su·me** *n* **1.** a summary of somebody's educational and work experience, for the information of possible future employers. A résumé is typically used by people in all professions except academia and medicine. **2.** a summary of something such as events that have happened ○ *a résumé of the afternoon's activities* [Early 19C. < French, past participle of *résumer* (see RESUME)]

re·sump·tion /ri zúmpshən/ *n* the act or an instance of continuing with something that has been stopped for a while ○ *hoping for a resumption of negotiations* [15C. Directly or via French < Latin *resumption-* < past participle of *resumere* (see RESUME)]

re·su·pi·nate /ri so͞opə nàyt, -so͞opənət/ *adj* describes a plant part, especially the flower of an orchid, that grows upside down or appears to do so [Late 18C. < Latin *resupinatus*, past participle of *resupinare* "bend back" < *supinus* "turned upward"] —**re·su·pi·na·tion** /ri so͞opə náysh'n/ *n*

re·sur·face /ree súrfəss/ (**-faced, -fac·ing, -fac·es**) *v* **1.** *vi* COME TO SURFACE AGAIN to come back to the surface of a body of water after having submerged **2.** *vi* APPEAR AGAIN to appear again after having disappeared or been absent ○ *He resurfaced in Bangkok after the war.* **3.** *vt* PUT NEW SURFACE ON SOMETHING to put a new surface on something, especially a road

re·surge /ri súrj/ (**-surged, -surg·ing, -surg·es**) *vi* **1.** to rise or grow strong again (*formal*) **2.** to sweep forward or back in a powerful way ○ *watched the waves dissipate and resurge along the rocky shore* [Late 16C. < Latin *resurgere* (see RESURGENT)]

re·sur·gence /ri súrjənss/ *n* the act or process of rising again or becoming stronger again ○ *a resurgence of patriotism*

re·sur·gent /ri súrjənt/ *adj* rising or becoming stronger again [Late 18C. < Latin *resurgent-*, present participle of *resurgere* "rise again" < *surgere* "rise up from below"]

res·ur·rect /rèzzə rékt/ (**-rect·ed, -rect·ing, -rects**) *v* **1.** *vti* to come back to life after apparent death, or bring somebody back to life **2.** *vt* to bring back into use something that had been stopped or discarded ○ *resurrect an old argument* [Late 18C. Back-formation < RESURRECTION]

res·ur·rec·tion /rèzzə rékshən/ *n* **1.** in some systems of belief, a rising from or raising of somebody from the dead, or the state of having risen from the dead **2.** the revival of something old or long disused ○ *the resurrection of a youthful dream* [13C. Via French < late Latin *resurrection-* < Latin *resurrect-*, past participle of *resurgere* (see RESURGENT)] —**res·ur·rec·tion·al** *adj*

Res·ur·rec·tion *n* **1.** in Christian belief, the rising of Jesus Christ from the dead after his crucifixion and entombment **2.** in Christianity, Judaism, and Islam, the rising of the dead on Judgment Day

res·ur·rec·tion plant *n* a plant that survives well in hot dry conditions, e.g., the rose of Jericho

re·sus·ci·tate /ri sússi tàyt/ (**-tat·ed, -tat·ing, -tates**) *v* **1.** *vti* to revive somebody from unconsciousness or apparent death, or be revived **2.** *vt* to revive waning interest in something such as a style or project [Early 16C. < Latin *resuscitat-*, past participle of *resuscitare* < *suscitare* "raise" < *citare* "summon repeatedly"] —**re·sus·ci·ta·ble** *adj* —**re·sus·ci·ta·tion** /ri sùssi táysh'n/ *n* —**re·sus·ci·ta·tive** *adj* —**re·sus·ci·ta·tor** *n*

res·ver·a·trol /ress vérrə tràwl/ *n* an antioxidant present in many plants and plant products, especially in red grape skins [Late 20C. < RESORCINOL + Latin *veratrum* "hellebore"]

ret /ret/ (**ret·ted, ret·ting, rets**) *vti* to soak plant fibers such as flax or hemp so that they become easier to separate, or be soaked and become easier to separate [15C. < Middle Dutch *reeten*]

ret. *abbr* **1.** LAW retain **2.** retired **3.** LAW return **4.** COMM returned

re·ta·ble /rée tàyb'l, réttəb'l/ *n* a shelf or setting behind an altar for holding candles, flowers, or religious images [Early 19C. Via French *rétable* and Spanish *retablo* < medieval Latin *retrotabulum* < Latin *retro-* "back" + *tabula* "table"]

re·tail /rée tàyl, ree táyl/ *n* SALE TO CONSUMERS the selling of goods directly to customers, e.g., in stores ○ *She works in retail.* ■ *adv* NOT WHOLESALE from an ordinary store or at the regular customer price and in small amounts rather than in bulk ○ *I bought it retail.* ■ *v* (**-tailed, -tail·ing, -tails**) **1.** *vti* SELL GOODS to sell goods to customers in small amounts and without a discount, or be sold in this way ○ *This item usually retails at a much higher price.* **2.** *vt* REPEAT SOMETHING HEARD to repeat regularly what is heard, especially gossip [14C. < Old French *retaille* "piece cut off" < *taillier* "to cut"] —**re·tail·er** *n*

re·tail price in·dex *n UK* a list of the prices of essential consumer goods that is published each month by the government to show how much prices in general have risen or fallen

re·tail ther·a·py *n* shopping for enjoyment (*humorous*)

re·tain /ri táyn/ (**-tained, -tain·ing, -tains**) *vt* **1.** KEEP SOMETHING to keep possession of something ○ *Despite losing the court case he retains all rights to the magazine article.* **2.** REMEMBER THINGS to be able to keep ideas or information in the memory **3.** KEEP SOMETHING IN POSITION to keep or hold something in a place or position ○ *water retained by a dam* **4.** HOLD SOMETHING WITHIN to be able to hold or accumulate something, especially liquid **5.** PAY SOMEBODY TO DO WORK to pay somebody regularly to do work **6.** HIRE PROFESSIONAL PERSON to pay a preliminary fee to reserve the services of an attorney, accountant, or other professional whenever needed [14C. Via Anglo-Norman *retaign-* < Latin *retinere* "hold back" < *tenere* "hold"] —**re·tain·a·bil·i·ty** /-tàynə bíllətee/ *n* —**re·tain·a·ble** *adj* —**re·tain·ment** *n*

re·tained ob·ject /ri tàynd-/ *n* the direct or indirect object of a passive verb, e.g., "letter" in "She was sent a letter by her brother"

re·tained prof·its *npl* the part of the after-tax profits of a business that is not distributed to stockholders

re·tain·er /ri táynər/ *n* **1. FEE RESERVING PROFESSIONAL SERVICES** a fee paid to reserve the services of a professional, especially an attorney or accountant, whenever needed **2. HOLDER** a device for holding something in place **3.** DENT **DEVICE HOLDING TEETH IN POSITION** a device for holding a tooth or teeth in position after orthodontic treatment **4.** HR **SERVANT** a paid servant, especially one who has been employed for many years **5.** HIST **FOLLOWER** in former times, a soldier or other person who supported or was dependent on somebody of high rank ◇ **on (a) retainer** paid regularly in order to be consulted whenever necessary, rather than being paid for each job

re·tain·ing wall /ri táyning-/ *n* a wall built to keep earth or water in place

re·take *vt* /ree táyk/ (**-took** /-to͝ok/, **-tak·en** /-táykən/, **-tak·ing, -takes**) **1. RECAPTURE SOMETHING** to recapture a place that has been captured by an enemy **2.** RECORDING, MOVIES **FILM SOMETHING AGAIN** to record, photograph, or film something again in order to get it right **3.** SPORTS **TAKE SHOT AGAIN** to take a shot in a game again because of an infringement of the rules during the first attempt **4.** EDUC **TAKE EXAM AGAIN** to take an examination again ■ *n* /rée tàyk/ RECORDING, MOVIES **ACT OF RECORDING SOMETHING AGAIN** an instance of recording, photographing, or filming something again, or the product that results from this

re·tal·i·ate /ri tállee àyt/ (**-at·ed, -at·ing, -ates**) *vi* to deliberately harm somebody in response or revenge for a harm he or she has done [Early 17C. < Latin *retaliat-*, past participle of *retaliare* "pay back in kind" < *talio* "punishment in kind"] —**re·tal·i·a·tion** /ri tàllee áysh'n/ *n* —**re·tal·i·a·tive** *adj* —**re·tal·i·a·tor** *n* —**re·tal·i·a·to·ry** /ri tállee ə tàwree/ *adj*

re·tard /ri taárd/ *vt* (**-tard·ed, -tard·ing, -tards**) **SLOW SOMETHING DOWN** to slow or delay the progress of something ■ *n* **1.** /ri taárd/ **SLOWING OF TEMPO** in music, a slowing down of a previously quick tempo **2.** /rée taárd/ **OFFENSIVE TERM** an offensive term that deliberately insults somebody with a learning disability or somebody regarded as unintelligent (*slang insult*) [15C. Via French < Latin *retardare* < *tardus* "slow"]

re·tar·dant /ri taárd'nt/ *n* something designed to slow down a particular process or change, especially a chemical substance that inhibits change (*often used in combination*) ■ *adj* capable of making something move or happen more slowly ○ *flame-retardant fabric*

re·tar·da·tion /rée taar dáysh'n/ *n* **1. SLOWING** the process or fact of slowing down **2. DELAY** something that acts as a delay or obstacle to progress **3. DECELERATION** deceleration, or the rate of deceleration **4. DEVELOPMENTAL DISABILITIES** the condition of being mentally challenged (*dated; sometimes considered offensive*)

re·tard·ed /ri taárdəd/ *adj* **1.** not fully developed ○ *the retarded growth of the plant* **2.** an offensive term meaning intellectually or emotionally challenged

retch /rech/ *v* (**retched, retch·ing, retch·es**) **1.** *vi* **EXPERIENCE A VOMITING SPASM** to experience a spasm of vomiting without bringing anything up **2.** *vti* **VOMIT** to vomit, or vomit something ■ *n* **VOMITING SPASM** a spasm of vomiting without bringing anything up [Mid-16C. Variant of obsolete *reach* "spit, vomit" < Old English *hræcan* < Germanic, an imitation of the sound]

SPELLCHECK retch or **wretch**? Do not confuse the spelling of ***retch*** and ***wretch***, which sound similar. ***Retch*** is a noun or verb referring to a spasm of vomiting or trying to vomit, as in *a foul smell that made him retch.* ***Wretch*** is a noun denoting a person who arouses pity, irritation, or contempt: *The poor wretch had nowhere else to go.*

retd. *abbr* **1.** LAW retained **2.** retired **3.** COMM returned

re·te /réetee/ (*plural* **-ti·a** /-tee ə, -shə/) *n* a network of veins, arteries, or nerve fibers in the body [14C. < Latin, "net"] —**re·tial** /réesh'l/ *adj*

re·tell /ree tél/ (**-told** /-tṓld/, **-tell·ing, -tells**) *vt* to tell something such as a story or joke again, especially in a different form or to somebody who has not heard it

re·tell·ing /ree télling/ *n* a repeating of an account or story that has been told before, often in a different form ○ *a modern retelling of an ancient fable*

re·tene /rée teèn, ré-/ *n* a yellow crystalline hydrocarbon. Source: pine tar, some fossil resins. Formula: $C_{18}H_{18}$. [Mid-19C. < Greek *rhētinē* "resin" + -ENE]

re·ten·tion /ri ténsh'n/ *n* **1. KEEPING OR HOLDING OF SOMETHING** the act of retaining something or the condition of being retained **2. MEMORY** the ability to remember things **3.** PHYSIOL **HOLDING IN OF WASTE** the holding in the body of waste that is normally excreted [14C. Directly or via French < Latin *retention-* < past participle of *retinere* (see RETAIN)]

re·ten·tive /ri téntiv/ *adj* **1.** able to or tending to hold something ○ *a soil that is highly retentive of rainwater* **2.** able to remember a great deal of information [14C. Directly or via French < medieval Latin *retentivus* < Latin *retent-*, past participle of *retinere* (see RETAIN)] —**re·ten·tive·ly** *adv* —**re·ten·tive·ness** *n*

re·ten·tiv·i·ty /rèe ten tívvətee/ *n* **1.** the power or condition of retaining something **2.** the capacity of a material to remain magnetized after the force that magnetized it has been taken away

re·think *vti* /ree thíngk/ (**-thought** /-tháwt/, **-think·ing, -thinks**) to think about something again, especially using new information or in order to produce a better result ■ *n* /rée thìngk/ an attempt to rethink something, or an occasion on which something is rethought ○ *Let's have a rethink before we proceed.* —**re·think·er** *n*

re·ti·a ANAT plural of **rete**

ret·i·cent /réttiss'nt/ *adj* **1.** unwilling to communicate very much, talk freely, or reveal all the facts about something ○ *rather reticent on the subject of her finances* **2.** ⚠ unwilling to do something —**ret·i·cence** *n* —**ret·i·cent·ly** *adv*

USAGE In its traditional sense, ***reticent*** means unwilling to communicate. Thus it is more nearly a synonym for *silent* than it is for *reluctant*: *He was never reticent about wanting the job.* It is, however, increasingly seen in contexts in which it conveys other kinds of reluctance: *He was reticent to travel so much.* Many regard this as a misuse, and in fact such usages tend to convey nothing that *reluctant* would not convey better.

SYNONYMS See ***silent.***

ret·i·cle /réttik'l/ *n* a grid of fine lines in the focus of an optical instrument, used for determining the scale or position of what is being looked at [Mid-17C. < Latin *reticulum* (see RETICULUM)]

re·tic·u·la BIOL plural of **reticulum**

re·tic·u·lar /ri tíkyələr/ *adj* **1.** relating to, involving, or structurally resembling a net or network **2.** having a complicated intricate structure [Late 16C. < modern Latin *reticularis* < Latin *reticulum* (see RETICULUM)]

re·tic·u·lar for·ma·tion *n* a formation of neurons in the brainstem that regulates many body functions, including respiration, blood pressure, sleeping and waking, and transmission of stimuli

re·tic·u·late *adj* /ri tíkyələt, -tíkyə làyt/ same as **reticular** (sense 1) ■ *v* /ri tíkyə làyt/ (**-lat·ed, -lat·ing, -lates**) **1.** *vti* to form a network, or be formed into a network **2.** *vt* to mark something with lines so that it looks like a network [Mid-17C. < Latin *reticulatus* < *reticulum* (see RETICULUM)] —**re·tic·u·late·ly** *adv* —**re·tic·u·la·tion** /-tìkyə láysh'n/ *n*

ret·i·cule /rétti kyo͞ol/ *n* **1.** a small fabric purse, usually closed with a drawstring, carried by women in the late 18th and early 19th centuries **2.** OPTICS same as **reticle** [Early 18C. Via French < Latin *reticulum* (see RETICULUM)]

re·tic·u·lo·cyte /ri tíkyələ sìt/ *n* an immature red blood cell containing a network of fibers of ribosomal remains that show up with laboratory staining [Early 20C. < RETICULUM] —**re·tic·u·lo·cyt·ic** /-tìkyələ síttik/ *adj*

re·tic·u·lum /ri tíkyələm/ (*plural* **-la** /-lə/) *n* **1.** a network, or something resembling a network in structure **2.** the second stomach or stomach compartment in cows, sheep, and other ruminants [Mid-17C. < Latin, "little net" < *rete* "net"]

Re·tic·u·lum *n* a small constellation of the southern hemisphere lying between Dorado and Horologium near to the Large Magellanic Cloud

retin- *prefix* same as **retino-** (*used before vowels*)

ret·i·na /rétt'nə/ (*plural* **-nas** or **-nae** /-nee/) *n* a light-sensitive membrane in the back of the eye containing rods and cones that receive an image from the lens and send it to the brain through the optic nerve [14C. < medieval Latin < Latin *rete* "net"; from the network of blood vessels]

ret·i·nac·u·lum /rètt'n ákyələm/ (*plural* **-la** /-lə/) *n* a part of the forewings of moths and butterflies that connects to the bristle (**frenulum**) on the hind wings that keeps the wings together in flight [Mid-18C. < Latin, "band," literally "little thing that holds back" < *retinire* (see RETAIN)] —**ret·i·nac·u·lar** *adj*

ret·i·nae ANAT plural of **retina**

ret·i·nal[1] /rétt'nəl/ *adj* involving or in the retina [Mid-19C. < RETINA + -AL[1]]

ret·i·nal[2] /rétt'n'l/, **ret·i·nene** /rétt'n èen/ *n* a derivative of vitamin A that forms part of the light-sensitive pigment in the eye [Mid-20C. < RETINA + -AL[2]]

ret·i·nite /rétt'n ìt/ *n* a fossil resin, especially one in which the plant matter has not formed a hard coal [Early 19C. < French < Greek *rhētinē* "resin"]

ret·i·ni·tis /rètt'n ítiss/ *n* inflammation of the retina

ret·i·ni·tis pig·men·to·sa /-pigmən tṓzə/ *n* an inherited disorder of the eye involving progressive disintegration of the retina and optic nerve and leading eventually to tunnel vision or inability to see [*Pigmentosa* from modern Latin, "pigmented"]

retino- *prefix* retina ○ *retinoblastoma* [From RETINA]

ret·i·no·blas·to·ma /rètt'nō bla stṓmə/ (*plural* **-mas** or **-ma·ta** /-mətə/) *n* a malignant tumor of the eye, usually resulting from a genetic disorder and appearing in early childhood

ret·i·no·ic ac·id /rètt'n ṓ ik-/ *n* PHARM same as **tretinoin** ["Retinoic" formed from RETINOL]

ret·i·nol /rét'n àwl/ *n* BIOCHEM same as **vitamin A** [Mid-20C. < RETINA]

ret·i·nop·a·thy /rètt'n óppəthee/ (*plural* **-thies**) *n* a disease of the retina, especially one that is noninflammatory and associated with damage to the blood vessels of the retina ○ *diabetic retinopathy* —**ret·i·no·path·ic** /rètt'nō páthik/ *adj*

ret·i·no·scope /rétt'nə skṑp/ *n* an instrument for identifying refractive errors in the eye by measuring the angle of a beam of light reflected from the retina and back out through the pupil

ret·i·nos·co·py /rètt'n óskəpee/ *n* a method of measuring refractive errors in the eye using a retinoscope —**ret·i·no·scop·ic** /rètt'nə skóppik/ *adj* —**ret·i·no·scop·i·cal·ly** *adv* —**ret·i·nos·cop·ist** *n*

ret·i·nue /rétt'n o͞o/ *n* a group of people who travel with and attend an important person [14C. < Old French, "retained (in service)" < past participle of *retenir* < Latin *retinere* (see RETAIN)]

re·tire /ri tír/ (**-tired, -tir·ing, -tires**) *v* **1.** *vi* **STOP WORKING WILLINGLY** to leave a job or career voluntarily, at or near the usual age for doing so **2.** *vi* **GO TO BED** to stop engaging in daily activities and go to bed **3.** *vi* **WITHDRAW** to leave a place, position, or way of life and go to a place of less activity ○ *retire from public life* **4.** *vt* **MAKE SOMEBODY STOP WORKING** to stop a person or animal performing some activity because of illness or an inability to continue ○ *injuries so extensive that the horse was retired* **5.** *vt* **WITHDRAW SOMETHING FROM SERVICE** to take a machine or piece of equipment out of service **6.** *vti* MIL **GO BACK OR MOVE TROOPS BACK** to fall back, or move troops away from a position, action, or danger **7.** *vt* BASEBALL **PUT SOMEBODY OUT** to end a batter's or team's turn at bat by getting batters out ○ *The pitcher retired eight batters in a row.* **8.** *vti* SPORTS **WITHDRAW FROM SPORTS CONTEST** to withdraw from a sports contest, or withdraw somebody from a sports contest, because of an inability to continue **9.** *vt* FIN **WITHDRAW SOMETHING FROM CIRCULATION** to take a loan, stock, bond, or other financial instrument out of circulation by paying for it [Mid-16C. < French *retirer* "retreat" < *tirer* "draw"] —**re·tir·er** *n*

re·tired /ri tírd/ *adj* **1.** NO LONGER WORKING having stopped working, typically after having worked many years ○ *a retired bus driver* **2.** HAVING WITHDRAWN having withdrawn from a busy way of life ○ *a retired lifestyle* ■ *n* RETIRED PEOPLE used to refer to retired people as a group (*takes a plural verb*)

re·tir·ee /ri tī rée/ *n* somebody who has retired from a job or career

re·tire·ment /ri tírmənt/ *n* **1.** LEAVING OF JOB OR CAREER the act of leaving a job or career at or near the usual age for doing so, or the state of having left a job or career **2.** TIME AFTER HAVING STOPPED WORKING the time that follows the end of somebody's working life **3.** BEING AWAY FROM BUSY LIFE a state of being withdrawn from the rest of the world or from a former busy life ○ *He lives in retirement in the country.*

re·tir·ing /ri tíring/ *adj* **1.** avoiding social contact with other people **2.** at, involving, or undergoing retirement from a job or career ○ *The retiring chairman made an emotional speech.* —**re·tir·ing·ly** *adv* —**re·tir·ing·ness** *n*

re·told *vt* past participle, past tense of **retell**

re·took past tense of **retake**

re·tool /ree to͞ol/ (**-tooled, -tool·ing, -tools**) *vti* **1.** to reorganize something in order to make it more efficient or powerful ○ *The company will have to retool if it's to remain competitive.* **2.** to replace the tools or machinery in a factory, or obtain new tools or machinery

re·tor·sion /ri táwrsh'n/ (*plural* **-sions** or **-tions**) *n* an act of retaliation by a government against citizens of another country for a similar offense committed by the other country [Mid-17C. < French *rétorsion* < Latin *retort-* (see RETORT[1])]

re·tort[1] /ri táwrt/ *vt* (**-tort·ed, -tort·ing, -torts**) **1.** RESPOND SHARPLY to say something sharp, angry, witty, or insulting in quick response to something somebody else has said **2.** ARGUE SOMETHING IN REPLY to put forward something as an argument in reply to somebody else's argument ■ *n* SHARP ANSWER something sharp, angry, witty, or insulting said quickly in response to something somebody else has said [15C. < Latin *retort-*, past participle of *retorquere* "twist again, twist back" < *torquere* "twist"] —**re·tort·er** *n*

SYNONYMS See *answer.*

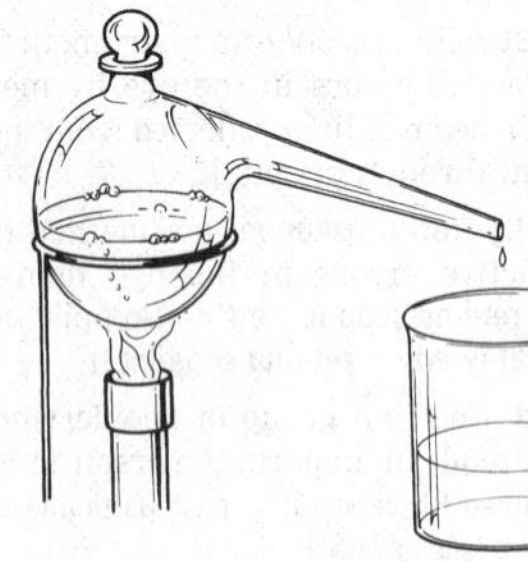

retort

re·tort[2] /ri táwrt/ *n* **1.** GLASS VESSEL a glass vessel with a long downward-pointing tapering spout, used for distilling by heat **2.** CLOSED CONTAINER FOR HEATING SUBSTANCES a closed container in which large quantities of a substance are heated to extract something such as metal from ore ■ *vt* (**-tort·ed, -tort·ing, -torts**) HEAT SOMETHING IN RETORT to heat or distill something in a retort [Early 17C. Via French < medieval Latin *retorta* < Latin *retorquere* "twist back" (see RETORT[1]), from the shape of the neck]

re·tor·tion *n* INTERNAT REL same as **retorsion**

re·touch *vt* /ree túch/ (**-touched, -touch·ing, -touch·es**) **1.** IMPROVE SOMETHING to make small finishing, correcting, or improving changes to something **2.** PHOTOGRAPHY ALTER PHOTOGRAPH to alter a photographic negative or print by removing imperfections or adding details **3.** COLOR HAIR to color new hair growth to match hair that is already bleached, tinted, or dyed ■ *n* /rée tùch, ree túch/ **1.** ACTIVITY OF RETOUCHING the process of retouching something, or an occasion on which something is retouched **2.** SOMETHING ALTERED something that has been retouched, especially a photograph **3.** IMPROVING CHANGE a small finishing, correcting, or improving change to something —**re·touch·er** *n*

re·trace /ri tráyss/ (**-traced, -trac·ing, -trac·es**) *vt* **1.** to go back over a path or route again **2.** to review something in the mind such as an argument, account, or series of events ○ *retraced the events leading up to the war* —**re·trace·a·ble** *adj* —**re·trac·er** *n*

re·tract /ri trákt/ (**-tract·ed, -tract·ing, -tracts**) *v* **1.** *vti* MOVE, OR MOVE SOMETHING, BACK INSIDE to draw something in from an extended position, or be drawn in ○ *Cats can retract their claws but dogs can't.* **2.** *vti* WITHDRAW STATEMENT to withdraw or deny something previously said, published, or promised ○ *She has since retracted her earlier statement.* **3.** *vi* MOVE BACK to move back from something **4.** *vt* PHON CHANGE VOWEL SOUND to alter a vowel sound by drawing the tongue inward from the lips [15C. < Latin *retract-*, past participle of *retrahere* "draw back" < *trahere* "pull"] —**re·tract·a·bil·i·ty** /-tràktə bíllətee/ *n* —**re·tract·a·ble** *adj* —**re·trac·ta·tion** /rèe trak táysh'n/ *n*

re·trac·tile /ri trákt'l/ *adj* capable of being retracted —**re·trac·til·i·ty** /ri tràk tíllətee/ *n*

re·trac·tion /ri tráksh ən/ *n* **1.** ACT OF RETRACTING the act of retracting something, or the condition of being retracted **2.** RETRACTING STATEMENT a statement, sometimes formal, that withdraws or denies a previous statement **3.** SOMETHING RETRACTED something that has been denied or taken back **4.** POWER TO RETRACT the ability or authority to draw back or be drawn back

re·trac·tor /ri tráktər/ *n* **1.** a surgical instrument used to hold back skin or tissue during surgery **2.** a muscle that retracts a body part, e.g., one that closes the jaw

re·train /ree tráyn/ (**-trained, -train·ing, -trains**) *vti* to teach somebody new skills, or learn new skills —**re·train·a·ble** *adj*

re·train·ing /ree tráyning/ *n* the process or activity of learning new skills or of updating existing skills

re·tread *n* /rée trèd/ **1.** AUTOMOT TIRE WITH NEW TREAD a secondhand tire with a new tread bonded to it **2.** REMAKE a revised or remade version of something **3.** RETRAINED WORKER a worker who has been retrained for a new position (*informal*) **4.** *US* RETURNING WORKER somebody who returns to a job previously given up (*informal*) ■ *vt* /ree tréd/ (**-tread·ed, -tread·ing, -treads**) INDUST ADD LAYER TO TIRE to add a new tread to a worn tire

re-tread /ree tréd/ *vt* to walk again on a route that has already been walked over

re·treat /ri tréet/ *n* **1.** MOVEMENT BACK a movement away from danger or a confrontation, back along the original route ○ *The bear had the hunters in full retreat.* **2.** WITHDRAWAL FROM POSITION a withdrawal from a position or point of view to one intended to lessen conflict ○ *their retreat from a previously inflexible position* **3.** TROOP WITHDRAWAL a withdrawal of military forces following a defeat or preceding a change of position **4.** SIGNAL TO MOVE BACK a signal, usually a bugle call or drumbeat, telling soldiers to perform a retreat **5.** QUIET TIME a period of quiet rest and contemplation in a secluded place **6.** QUIET PLACE a quiet secluded place where people go for rest and privacy **7.** SAFE PLACE a place where people or animals go to avoid danger or capture **8.** SPECIAL HOSPITAL a place for the long-term care and treatment of people who are incapable of caring for themselves (*dated*) **9.** RELIG PERIOD OF SECLUSION a period away from normal activities, devoted to prayer and meditation, often spent in a religious community **10.** MIL FLAG-LOWERING CEREMONY the ceremony of lowering the flag at a military institution, or the signal given to lower the flag ■ *v* (**-treat·ed, -treat·ing, -treats**) **1.** *vi* MOVE BACK to move back away from danger or a confrontation **2.** *vi* WITHDRAW FROM POSITION to withdraw from a position or point of view to one intended to lessen conflict **3.** *vi* MAKE MILITARY WITHDRAWAL to withdraw following a defeat or prior to a change of position **4.** *vi* RECEDE to recede or fall back from a previous position ○ *when the glaciers retreated* **5.** *vt* CHESS MOVE PIECE BACK to move a chesspiece back to an earlier position [13C. < Old French *retret* < past participle of *retraire* < Latin *retrahere* (see RETRACT)] —**re·treat·er** *n* ◇ **beat a (hasty) retreat 1.** to leave, especially in a hurry **2.** *US* to back down or take something back that was said

re·treat·ant /ri tréet'nt/ *n* a participant in a spiritual or religious retreat

re·trench /ri trénch/ (**-trenched, -trench·ing, -trench·es**) *v* **1.** *vti* ECONOMIZE to reduce something such as costs **2.** *vt* CUT SOMETHING OUT to cut out, cut back, or omit something **3.** *vi* REORGANIZE to stop doing something in order to reorganize or rethink something ○ *We retrenched and began reorganizing when we realized the plan wasn't working.* [Late 16C. < French *retrancher* "cut again" < *trenchier* "to cut"] —**re·trench·er** *n* —**re·trench·ment** *n*

re·tri·al /ree trí əl/ *n* a second trial in a court of law replacing a prior one that was flawed or ended in a hung jury

ret·ri·bu·tion /rèttrə byo͞osh'n/ *n* something done or given to somebody as punishment or vengeance for something he or she has done ○ *a just retribution for their crime* [14C. < Latin *retribution-* < past participle of *retribuere* "hand back, repay" < *tribuere* "allot"] —**re·trib·u·tive** /ri tríbbyətiv/ *adj* —**re·trib·u·tive·ly** *adv* —**re·trib·u·to·ry** /ri tríbbyə tàwree/ *adj*

re·triev·al /ri tréev'l/ *n* **1.** RECOVERY OF SOMETHING the act of getting something back, or a particular occasion on which this is done **2.** POSSIBILITY OF BEING RESTORED the possibility of something being brought back, saved, or restored to an original condition ○ *Their business seemed beyond retrieval.* **3.** COMPUT DATA ACCESS the process of reading data from a storage device and returning it to the program or device that requested it

re·trieve /ri tréev/ *v* (**-trieved, -triev·ing, -trieves**) **1.** *vt* GET SOMETHING BACK to get something back **2.** *vt* SAVE SOMETHING to save something from being lost, damaged, or destroyed **3.** *vt* REMEDY SOMETHING to set something right or make it better ○ *attempt to retrieve the situation before it worsens* **4.** *vt* RESTORE SOMETHING to revive or restore something to its original condition ○ *She quickly retrieved her sense of humor.* **5.** *vt* REMEMBER SOMETHING to recall something from memory **6.** *vt* COMPUT GET DATA to read data from a storage device and return it to the program or device that requested it **7.** *vti* RACKET GAMES RETURN SHOT in a game such as tennis or badminton, to return a difficult shot **8.** *vti* HUNTING FETCH GAME to fetch small game that has been shot by a hunter ■ *n* RETRIEVING OF SOMETHING the act of retrieving something ○ *a successful retrieve* [15C. < Old French *retroev-*, stem of *retrover* "find again" < *trover* "to find"] —**re·triev·a·bil·i·ty** /ri trèevə bíllətee/ *n* —**re·triev·a·ble** *adj* —**re·triev·a·bly** *adv*

retriever

re·triev·er /ri tréevər/ *n* **1.** a large dog belonging to a breed originally used to fetch game shot by a hunter **2.** somebody or something that retrieves something

ret·ro /réttrō/ *adj* modeled on something from the past such as a style of fashion or music ○ *retro clothing* ■ *n* (*plural* **-ros**) **1.** the practice of modeling things such as clothes or music on styles from the past, or an example of such a practice ○ *The band is heavily into sixties retro.* **2.** AEROSP same as **retrorocket** [Late 20C. < French *rétro*, shortening of *rétrograde* "retrograde" < Latin *retrogradus* (see RETROGRADE); influenced by RETRO-]

retro- *prefix* **1.** back, backward, after ○ *retrorocket* ○ *retrofit* **2.** behind ○ *retrochoir* [< Latin *retro*]

ret·ro·ac·tion /rèttrō áksh ən/ *n* **1.** APPLICABILITY TO PAST the applicability of something to past circumstances or events **2.** ACTION REACTING TO PAST SITUATION an action that responds or reacts to something in the past **3.** COUNTERACTION an action that goes against or balances a previous action

ret·ro·ac·tive /rèttrō áktiv/ *adj* relating or applying to things that have happened in the past as well as the present ○ *retroactive pay increases*

ret·ro·ac·tive in·hi·bi·tion *n* the tendency of recently gained knowledge or skills to degenerate when new learning in a similar area is acquired

ret·ro·cede /réttrō sèed/ (**-ced·ed, -ced·ing, -cedes**) *v* **1.** *vi* to go back or return **2.** *vt* to give something such as land or a territory back to somebody [Mid-17C. < French *rétrocéder* < *céder* "give way"] —**ret·ro·ce·dent** /rèttrō sèed'nt/ *adj* —**ret·ro·ces·sion** /-sésh'n/ *n* —**ret·ro·ces·sive** /-séssiv/ *adj*

ret·ro·choir /réttrō kwīr/ *n* the area behind the high altar in a large church or cathedral [Mid-19C. After medieval Latin *retrochorus* "back choir"]

ret·ro·en·gine *n* AEROSP same as **retrorocket**

ret·ro·fire /réttrō fīr/ (**-fired, -fir·ing, -fires**) *vti* to fire a retrorocket in order to decelerate, or be fired to cause deceleration

ret·ro·fit /réttrō fìt/ *vt* (**-fit·ted, -fit·ting, -fits**) **1.** MODIFY SOMETHING WITH NEW PARTS to modify something such as a machine or a building by adding newly developed parts or devices that were not available when the machine or building was made ○ *older cars retrofitted with catalytic converters* **2.** INSTALL NEW PARTS to install newly developed parts or devices into a machine or building, that were not available when the machine or building was made ○ *retrofit a microchip in the alarm system* ■ *n* **1.** NEW PART, OR SOMETHING WITH ONE something that has been equipped with a newly developed component, or such a component designed for something that is already in use **2.** PROCESS OF ADDING NEW PART the process or an instance of modifying something such as a machine or a building by adding newly developed parts or devices

ret·ro·flec·tion /rèttrō fléksh'n/, **ret·ro·flex·ion** *n* **1.** BENT CONDITION the condition of bending or being bent backward **2.** PHON PRONUNCIATION WITH TONGUE BENT BACK the pronunciation of a letter or sound with the tongue raised and bent backward **3.** PSYCHOL INABILITY TO EXTERNALIZE EMOTION in Gestalt therapy, the act of directing a difficult emotion such as anger at yourself rather than at somebody who has provoked the emotion [Early 19C. < RETRO- after REFLECTION]

ret·ro·flex /réttrō flèks/, **ret·ro·flexed** /-flèkst/ *adj* **1.** bent or curved backward **2.** describes speech sounds that are pronounced with the tip of the tongue raised and bent backward [Late 18C. < Latin *retroflex-*, past participle of *retroflectere* "bend back" < *flectere* "bend"]

ret·ro·flex·ion *n* PHON, PSYCHOL another spelling of **retroflection**

ret·ro·grade /réttrō gràyd/ *adj* **1.** MOVING BACKWARD moving backward in space or time **2.** GETTING WORSE worsening or returning to an earlier worse condition **3.** INVERSE in writing, inverse or reversed, especially in syntactic order **4.** ASTRON HAVING CONTRARY ORBIT orbiting in a direction opposite to that of Earth's orbit around the Sun, or of the Moon's orbit around the Earth **5.** ASTRON MOVING EAST TO WEST moving or appearing to move from east to west in the sky, counter to the direction of most astronomical objects **6.** MUSIC REVERSING NOTES reversing the sequence of notes of an earlier version of a musical composition ■ *vi* (**-grad·ed, -grad·ing, -grades**) **1.** GO BACKWARD to go back or appear to be moving backward in space or time **2.** same as **retrogress** (sense 1) [14C. < Latin *retrogradus* "going backward" < *gradus* "step"] —**ret·ro·gra·da·tion** /rèttrō gray dáysh'n/ *n* —**ret·ro·grade·ly** *adv*

ret·ro·gress /rèttrō gréss/ (**-gressed, -gress·ing, -gress·es**) *vi* **1.** REVERT OR DEGENERATE to return to an earlier and usually worse condition **2.** GO BACKWARD to move or travel backward **3.** BIOL HAVE LESS COMPLEX FEATURES to show or develop the less complex features of simpler organisms [Early 19C. < RETRO- after PROGRESS] —**ret·ro·gres·sive** *adj* —**ret·ro·gres·sive·ly** *adv*

ret·ro·gres·sion /rèttrə grésh'n/ *n* **1.** the process of returning to an earlier and usually worse condition **2.** the development of less complex features usually associated with simpler organisms

ret·ro·len·tal /rèttrō lént'l/ *adj* located behind the lens of the eye or the lens of an optical instrument [Mid-20C. < RETRO- + modern Latin *lent-* "lens" < Latin, "lentil"]

ret·ro·nym /réttrō nìm/ *n US* a term that distinguishes a subclass from members of a superclass, e.g., "snail mail" is a retronym coined by those for whom "mail" is likely to mean "e-mail" [< RETRO- after SYNONYM]

ret·ro·pack /réttrō pàk/ *n* an array of retrorockets on a spacecraft, used for slowing down or for changing direction

ret·ro·pul·sion /rèttrō púlshən/ *n* a tendency to walk backward involuntarily, associated with Parkinson's disease [Late 18C. < RETRO- after PROPULSION]

ret·ro·rock·et /réttrō ròkət/ *n* a small rocket engine on a spacecraft or missile that produces thrust to act against the main engines, used for decelerating

re·trorse /ri tráwrss/ *adj* describes plant parts that are turned back or down [Early 19C. < Latin *retrorsus*, contraction of *retroversus* "turning backward" < *versus* "turning"] —**re·trorse·ly** *adv*

ret·ro·spect /réttrə spèkt/ *n* the remembering of past events [Early 17C. < RETRO- after PROSPECT] —**ret·ro·spec·tion** /rèttrə spékshən/ *n* ◇ **in retrospect** thinking about or reviewing the past, especially from a new perspective or with new information

ret·ro·spec·tive /rèttrə spéktiv/ *adj* **1.** REVIEWING PAST looking back over things in the past **2.** APPLYING TO PAST EVENTS applying to things that have happened in the past as well as the present ○ *a retrospective ruling* **3.** ARTS CONTAINING PAST WORKS containing examples of work from many periods of an artist's life ○ *a retrospective exhibition* ■ *n* ARTS EXHIBITION OF PAST WORKS an exhibition of the work of an artist or artistic movement that shows examples from all periods or styles ○ *a Degas retrospective* —**ret·ro·spec·tive·ly** *adv*

re·trous·sé /rèttroo sáy/ *adj* describes a nose that is turned up at the end [Early 19C. < French, "turned up"]

ret·ro·ver·sion /rèttrə vúrzh'n/ *n* **1.** the act or condition of being turned backward **2.** the turning or tilting backward of a body part such as the uterus, but without folding [Late 16C. < Latin *retroversus* (see RETRORSE)] —**ret·ro·verse** *adj* —**ret·ro·vert·ed** *adj*

ret·ro·vi·rus /rèttrō vīrəss, réttrə vīrəss/ *n* a virus whose genetic information is contained in RNA rather than DNA. Some retroviruses cause AIDS and cancer and they contain the enzyme reverse transcriptase for generating DNA from RNA. —**ret·ro·vi·ral** /-vīrəl/ *adj*

re·try /ree trī/ *v* (**-tried, -try·ing, -tries**) **1.** *vt* TRY SOMEBODY AGAIN to try a person or case again in a court of law **2.** *vti* ATTEMPT SOMETHING AGAIN to try to do something again ■ *n* (*plural* **-tries**) SECOND ATTEMPT another attempt to do something

ret·si·na /rétsinə, ret séenə/ *n* a Greek wine flavored with pine resin [Early 20C. < modern Greek < Greek *rhētinē* "pine resin"]

re·turn /ri túrn/ *v* (**-turned, -turn·ing, -turns**) **1.** *vi* COME OR GO BACK to come or go back to a place after leaving it, or come or go back to a former condition **2.** *vi* MENTION OR CONSIDER SOMETHING AGAIN to go back to something that has already been mentioned or considered, especially in order to deal with it more thoroughly or conclusively ○ *Let's return to the matter at hand.* **3.** *vi* APPEAR AGAIN to appear or happen again **4.** *vt* SAY SOMETHING to say something in reply ○ *"Do it yourself!" she returned.* **5.** *vt* PUT SOMETHING BACK to put, bring, send, or take something back to where it came from **6.** *vt* REPAY SOMETHING to give back something of equivalent value ○ *I hope that some day I'll be able to return the favor.* **7.** *vt* YIELD PROFIT to yield something as a profit on an investment ○ *returns 6% annually* **8.** *vt* REELECT SOMEBODY TO OFFICE to reelect somebody to an office or position ○ *returned her to Congress for a second term* **9.** *vt* PRODUCE VERDICT to give a particular verdict in a court of law ○ *return a guilty verdict* **10.** *vt* REFLECT SOMETHING to send back or reflect something such as an echo ○ *The cliff wall returned the sound of their laughter.* **11.** *vt* SUBMIT OFFICIAL REPORT to give an official report, usually in response to a request or legal requirement **12.** *vt* COMPUT GIVE RESPONSE of a computer, to give a particular response to a command, routine, or subroutine ○ *returns zero if the condition is false* **13.** *vti* SPORTS HIT BALL BACK in sports such as tennis, to hit a ball, especially a serve, back to an opponent **14.** *vt* FOOTBALL RUN FOOTBALL BACK UP FIELD to run a football back up the field after it has been kicked, punted, fumbled, or intercepted **15.** *vt* CARDS LEAD SAME SUIT to lead the same suit as a partner in a card game such as bridge or pinochle **16.** *vt* ARCHIT BUILD SOMETHING TO FACE OPPOSITE DIRECTION to construct part of a building such as a wall or decoration so that it turns away from its original direction ■ *n* **1.** INSTANCE OF GOING BACK an instance of going or coming back to a place after having left it or to a former condition **2.** REPLACEMENT an instance of putting, taking, sending, or bringing back something to where it came from **3.** SOMETHING GIVEN BACK something that has come or been brought back, especially unsold merchandise ○ *Returns go in that container over there.* **4.** REAPPEARANCE a reappearance or recurrence of something **5.** RECIPROCATION a response to something done or given ○ *If you are kind to your puppy it will give you love in return.* **6.** ANSWER something said in response to something else ○ *If you ask her an absurd question you can expect an angry return.* **7.** FIN PROFIT a profit made on an investment or business venture (*often used in the plural*) **8.** FIN same as **tax return** **9.** FIN FINANCIAL REPORT a periodic financial report of an organization **10.** COMPUT same as **return key** **11.** SPORTS BALL PLAYED BACK an instance of hitting or playing the ball back to an opponent in a sport such as tennis **12.** LAW LEGAL REPORT a report on a legal document previously issued by a court, prepared by an officer of that court **13.** CARDS LEAD OF SAME SUIT an instance of leading the same suit as a partner in a card game such as bridge or pinochle **14.** ARCHIT ANGLED PART part of a building, e.g., a wall or decoration, built so that it turns away from its original direction ■ **re·turns** *npl* ELECTION RESULTS the results from an election or election district ○ *We sat up late waiting for the election returns.* ■ *adj* **1.** CONNECTED WITH GOING BACK AGAIN relating to an act of going or coming back to an earlier place or position ○ *I hope the return flight isn't delayed.* **2.** *Can, UK* TRAVEL same as **round-trip** **3.** HAPPENING AGAIN given or done again ○ *We enjoyed the resort so much that we decided to make a return visit the next year.* [14C. < Old French *reto(u)rner* "turn again" < *to(u)rner* "to turn" < Latin *tornare*] —**re·turn·a·ble** *adj, n* —**re·turn·ee** /ri tùr née/ *n* ◇ **in return (for something)** as an exchange for something ◇ **many happy returns (of the day)** a conventional way of expressing good wishes to somebody whose birthday it is, often as an exclamation

re·turn·er /ri túrnər/ *n UK* somebody who returns to work or rejoins the workforce of a particular organization after a prolonged break, e.g., after bringing up a family

return key *n* the key on a computer or typewriter keyboard, usually marked with an angled arrow, that can be used to execute an instruction or create a new line

re·turn tick·et *n* **1.** the portion of a ticket for the trip back to your point of departure **2.** *Can, UK* same as **round-trip ticket**

re·tuse /ri tόoss/ *adj* describes leaves that have a blunt notched apex [Mid-18C. < Latin *retusus*, past participle of *retundere* "beat back" < *tundere* "beat"]

Reu·ben[1] /rόobən/, **Reu·ben sand·wich** *n* a grilled sandwich of rye bread filled with corned beef, sauerkraut, Swiss cheese, and thousand island dressing [Mid-20C. < ?]

Reu·ben[2] /rόobən/ *n* in the Bible, a Hebrew patriarch and the eldest son of Jacob and his first wife Leah. He was the ancestor of one of the tribes of Israel.

re·u·ni·fy /ree yόonə fī/ (**-fied, -fy·ing, -fies**) *vti* to come together, or bring people or factions together again, after they have been divided —**re·u·ni·fi·ca·tion** /-yòonəfi káysh'n/ *n*

re·un·ion /ree yόonyən/ *n* **1.** a gathering of old friends, relatives, or colleagues ○ *a high-school class reunion* **2.** the coming together again of things or people that have been divided, or the condition of having come together in this way

Ré·un·ion /ree yo͞onyən, rayoo nyáwN/ island in the Indian Ocean, south-east of Madagascar. It is an overseas department of France. Population: 653,000 (1995). Area: 970 sq. mi./2,512 sq. km.

re·un·ion·ist /ree yo͞onyənist/ *n* a supporter of reunion between divided groups or parties, especially somebody who seeks reunion between the Anglican and Roman Catholic churches —**re·un·ion·ism** *n* —**re·un·ion·is·tic** /ree yo͞onyə nístik/ *adj*

re·u·nite /rèe yoo nīt/ (**-nit·ed, -nit·ing, -nites**) *vti* to bring people together after a separation, or come together after a separation

re-up (**re-upped, re-up·ping, re-ups**) *v* (*informal*) **1.** *vi US* to sign up for another tour of duty in a military service **2.** *vti* to renew something such as an employment contract, membership in an organization, or subscription

re·up·take /ree úp tàyk/ *n* the reabsorption of neurotransmitters by the nerve cells that produced them. Prozac™ and similar drugs work by inhibiting reuptake of the neurotransmitter serotonin so that circulating levels are high and depression is eased.

re·use *vt* /ree yo͞oz/ (**-used, -us·ing, -us·es**) to use something again, often for a different purpose and usually as an alternative to throwing it out ■ *n* /ree yo͞oss/ the use of something again, often for a different purpose and usually as an alternative to throwing it out —**re·us·a·bil·i·ty** /ree yo͞ozə bíllətee/ *n* —**re·us·a·ble** *adj*

Reu·ter /róytər/, **Paul Julius, Baron von** (1816–99) German-born British journalist. In 1851, he established the pioneer Reuters Telegrams, now Reuters, the first news agency in the world. Born **Josaphat, Israel Beer**

Reu·ters /róytərz/ *n* a London news agency providing international news reports [Mid-19C. After Paul Julius, Baron von REUTER]

Reu·ther /ro͞othər/, **Walter Philip** (1907–70) US labor leader. An automobile factory worker, he organized sit-down strikes for wage increases and social welfare programs, and became president of the United Automobile Workers (1946–70).

rev /rev/ *vti* (**revved, rev·ving, revs**) to increase a vehicle's engine speed by pressing down on the gas pedal or advancing the throttle, especially while the vehicle is stationary, or undergo this process ■ *n* a single revolution of a vehicle's engine (*informal; usually pl*) [Early 20C. Shortening of REVOLUTION]
rev up *vt* (*informal*) **1.** to increase the tempo, intensity, or amount of something ○ *We'd better rev up production if we're going to meet our deadline.* **2.** to stir up intense feelings in somebody, usually feelings of excitement, desire, or anger

rev. *abbr* **1.** revenue **2.** FIN reverse **3.** MIL review **4.** PUBL revised **5.** EDUC revision **6.** revolution

Rev. *abbr* CHR Reverend

re·vamp /rèe vámp/ *vt* (**-vamped, -vamp·ing, -vamps**) to improve the appearance, condition, or structure of something by making sometimes superficial changes ■ *n* a change made in something in order to improve its appearance or functioning [Mid-19C. < RE- + VAMP[2]]

SYNONYMS See *renew.*

re·vanche /ri vaánch/ *n* a nation's or an ethnic group's policy of regaining lost territory [Mid-19C. < French < Old French *revancher* "avenge" < *vengier*] —**re·vanch·ism** *n* —**re·vanch·ist** *adj, n*

Revd. *abbr* CHR Reverend

re·veal[1] /ri vèel/ (**-vealed, -veal·ing, -veals**) *vt* **1.** MAKE SOMETHING KNOWN to disclose something that was unknown or secret **2.** EXPOSE SOMETHING to make something visible that had been hidden or covered **3.** RELIG MAKE KNOWN DIVINE TRUTH to make something known by what is believed to be divine or supernatural means [14C. Via French < Latin *revelare* "unveil" < *velum* "sail, curtain, veil"] —**re·veal·er** *n*

re·veal[2] /ri vèel/ *n* the vertical section of wall that lies between a doorframe or window frame and the outer wall [Late 17C. Alteration of obsolete *revale* "lower, bring down" < Old French *revaler* < *val* "valley"]

re·vealed re·lig·ion *n* a religion based on what its adherents believe to be the word of a supreme deity

re·veal·ing /ri vèeling/ *adj* **1.** SHOWING BODY exposing part of the body that would normally be kept covered **2.** DISCLOSING INFORMATION giving away new, surprising, or valuable information **3.** FRANK exposing true emotions or intentions —**re·veal·ing·ly** *adv*

re·veg·e·tate /ree véjjə tàyt/ (**-tat·ed, -tat·ing -tates**) *vti* to provide eroded or otherwise barren land with new plant life —**re·veg·e·ta·tion** /-vèjjə táysh'n/ *n*

rev·eil·le /révvəlee/ *n* **1.** WAKE-UP CALL the sounding of a bugle to awaken and summon military personnel in a camp **2.** TIME OF REVEILLE the time of day at which reveille is sounded **3.** EARLY-MORNING MILITARY FORMATION the military formation that begins the day **4.** SIGNAL TO AWAKE any signal that tells somebody it is time to get out of bed [Mid-17C. Alteration of French *réveillez* "wake up!" < Old French *resveiller* "awaken" < *esveiller* < Latin *vigil* "awake, alert"]

rev·el /révv'l/ *vi* (**-eled** or **-elled, -el·ing** or **-el·ling, -els**) **1.** TAKE PLEASURE to take great pleasure in something **2.** ENJOY PARTY to have an enjoyable time in the company of others, especially at a party ■ *n* NOISY CELEBRATION an uproarious party or celebration (*often used in the plural*) [14C. Via Old French *reveler* "rebel, carouse" < Latin *rebellare* "to rebel" < *bellum* "war"] —**rev·el·er** *n*

~~**revelant**~~ incorrect spelling of **relevant**

rev·e·la·tion /rèvvə láysh'n/ *n* **1.** INFORMATION REVEALED information that is newly disclosed, especially surprising, or valuable **2.** SURPRISING THING a surprisingly good or valuable experience **3.** DISCLOSURE the revealing of something previously hidden or secret **4.** CHR DEMONSTRATION OF DIVINE WILL a showing or revealing of what is believed to be divine will or truth [14C. < French < Latin *revelat-* past participle of *revelare* (see REVEAL[1])] —**rev·e·la·tion·al** *adj* —**rev·e·la·to·ry** /révvələ tàwree, ri véllə-/ *adj*

Rev·e·la·tion, Rev·e·la·tions /rèvvə láysh'nz/ *n* a book of the Bible that includes a description of the end of the world. See table at **Bible**

rev·e·la·tor /révvə làytər/ *n* somebody or something believed to reveal divine will or truth [15C. < late Latin < Latin *revelat-* past participle of *revelare* (see REVEAL[1])]

rev·el·ry /révv'lree/ (*plural* **-ries**) *n* lively enjoyment or celebration, usually involving eating, drinking, dancing, and noise (*often used in the plural*)

rev·e·nant /révvənənt/ *n* a dead person believed to have come back as a ghost (*formal*) [Early 19C. < French < present participle of *revenir* "return" (see REVENUE)]

re·venge /ri vénj/ *n* **1.** PUNISHMENT the punishment of somebody in retaliation for harm done **2.** RETALIATION ACT something done to get even with somebody else who has caused harm **3.** DESIRE FOR RETALIATION the desire or urge to get even with somebody ■ *vt* (**-venged, -veng·ing, -veng·es**) PUNISH SOMEBODY FOR SOMETHING to punish somebody who has harmed you or harmed a friend ○ *Those who seek to revenge themselves often regret the effort.* [14C. < Old French *revengier* < *vengier* "avenge" < late Latin *vindicare* "claim, set free, avenge"] —**re·venge·ful** *adj* —**re·venge·ful·ly** *adv* —**re·veng·er** *n*

rev·e·nue /révvə no͞o/ *n* **1.** INCOME FROM BUSINESS money that comes into a business from the sale of goods or services **2.** GOVERNMENT INCOME the income of a government from all sources, used to pay for a nation's expenses **3.** PERSONAL INCOME income or salary received from employment **4.** FIN YIELD ON INVESTMENT the total return produced by an investment **5.** GOV TAX-COLLECTING DEPARTMENT the department of a nation's government that is responsible for collecting taxes [15C. < French *revenu* < past participle of *revenir* "return" < Latin *revenire* "come back" < *venire* "come"]

rev·e·nue bond *n* a bond issued by a government agency in order to build or improve a public property. The income from the property pays for the bond.

rev·e·nue cut·ter *n* a small lightly armed boat used to patrol coastlines, enforce customs regulations, and prevent smuggling

rev·e·nu·er /révvə no͞o ər/ *n* (*informal*) **1.** a government agent who is in charge of collecting revenue, especially those in charge of stopping the illegal manufacture of alcoholic beverages **2.** same as **revenue cutter**

rev·e·nue shar·ing *n* the practice of distributing a portion of federal income to state and city governments

rev·e·nue stamp *n* a stamp put on something that proves a government tax has been paid

rev·e·nue tar·iff *n* a tax or duty imposed to produce public revenue, as distinct from one imposed to protect a domestic economy

re·verb /ri vúrb/ *n* **1.** ECHO IN MUSIC an echoing effect produced in live or recorded music by electronic means **2.** ECHO-PRODUCING DEVICE an electronic device used to produce an echoing effect in live or recorded music ■ *vi* (**-verbed, -verb·ing, -verbs**) PRODUCE ELECTRONIC ECHO to produce an echoing effect in live or recorded music [Early 17C. Shortening of REVERBERATE]

re·ver·ber·ate /ri vúrbə ràyt/ (**-at·ed, -at·ing, -ates**) *v* **1.** *vi* ECHO to echo repeatedly **2.** *vi* HAVE CONTINUING EFFECT to have a far-reaching or lasting impact, especially as a result of being circulated widely **3.** *vi* PHYS BOUNCE BACK to be reflected repeatedly off different surfaces (*refers to heat, light, or sound waves*) **4.** *vt* CAUSE SOUND TO ECHO to cause sound to bounce back from a surface **5.** *vt* METALL HEAT OR REFINE METAL to treat metal in a furnace (**reverberatory furnace**) that reflects flame or heat [15C. < Latin *reverberat-*, past participle of *reverberare* "beat again" < *verberare* "beat" < *verber* "scourge"] —**re·ver·ber·ant** *adj* —**re·ver·ber·a·tion** /ri vùrbə ráysh'n/ *n* —**re·ver·ber·a·tive** *adj* —**re·ver·ber·a·tor** *n*

re·ver·ber·a·tion time *n* the time it takes for a sound in a room to be reduced by 60 decibels

re·ver·ber·a·to·ry /ri vúrbərə tàwree/ *adj* produced or functioning by the process of deflection of sound, light, or heat

re·ver·ber·a·to·ry fur·nace *n* a furnace in which material is heated by heat reflected from above

re·vere /ri vèer/ (**-vered, -ver·ing, -veres**) *vt* to regard somebody with admiration and deep respect [Mid-17C. Via French < Latin *revereri* < *vereri* "be in awe of"]

Re·vere /ri vèer/ city in eastern Massachusetts, east of Medford. It is a northeastern suburb of Boston. Population: 47,496 (2002 estimate).

Re·vere, Paul (1735–1818) American patriot. A leading Boston silversmith, he made an historic midnight ride, on April 18, 1775, from Boston to Concord to warn of an impending British attack.

> "[We agreed] that if the British went out by water, we would show two lanterns in the North Church steeple; and if by land, one as a signal...."
> [Paul Revere, *on signals to be used if British troops moved out of Boston, in plans made with the Charlestown Committee of Safety*, April 16, 1775]

rev·er·ence /révvərənss, révvrənss/ *n* **1.** RESPECT FELT feelings of deep respect or devotion **2.** RESPECT GAINED the respect or devotion that others show somebody or something **3.** *also* **Rev·er·ence** CHR USED TO ADDRESS CHRISTIAN CLERGY used as a form of address for some members of the Christian clergy ■ *vt* (**-enced, -enc·ing, -enc·es**) RESPECT SOMEBODY OR SOMETHING DEEPLY to regard somebody or something with deep respect (*formal*)

SYNONYMS See *regard.*

rev·er·end /révvərənd, révvrənd/ *adj* **1.** ⚠ OF CLERGY relating or belonging to the Christian clergy **2.** RESPECTED deserving to be shown respect (*formal*) ■ *n* CHRISTIAN CLERIC a member of the Christian clergy (*informal*) [15C. Directly or via French < Latin *reverendus* "to be revered" < *revereri* (see REVERE)]

USAGE reverend or **reverent**? Care should be taken in distinguishing between ***reverend***, a noun and adjective referring to a member of the clergy, and ***reverent***, which is a descriptive adjective meaning "feeling or expressing reverence," not restricted to religious contexts.

Rev·er·end *n* used as a title and form of address for some members of the clergy in many Christian churches

Rev·er·end Moth·er *n* used as a title of respect to address the nun in charge of a convent

rev·er·ent /révvərənt, révvrənt/ *adj* ⚠ feeling or expressing profound respect or awe [14C. < Latin *reverent-*, present participle of *revereri* (see REVERE)] —**rev·er·ent·ly** *adv*

USAGE See *reverend.*

rev·er·en·tial /rèvvə rénshəl/ *adj* **1.** feeling or expressing deep respect or awe **2.** worthy of deep respect or awe —**rev·er·en·tial·ly** *adv*

rev·er·ie /révvəree/ (*plural* **-ies**) *n* a state of idle and pleasant contemplation [Early 17C. < French < *rêver* "to dream"]

re·vers /ri veér, -vér/ (*plural* **-vers** /-veérz, -vérz/) *n* a part of a garment turned back so that the reverse side shows, e.g., a lapel [Mid-19C. < French (see REVERSE)]

re·ver·sal /ri vúrss'l/ *n* **1.** CHANGE TO OPPOSITE DIRECTION a change to an opposite direction or state **2.** REVERSING OF SOMETHING the act or process of changing something to an opposite direction or state **3.** PROBLEM an unfortunate experience or setback, particularly in business or financial affairs **4.** LAW CHANGE OF JUDICIAL DECISION a ruling made by a higher court that sets aside the decision of a lower court

re·verse /ri vúrss/ *v* (**-versed, -vers·ing, -vers·es**) **1.** *vt* CHANGE SOMETHING TO OPPOSITE to change something to the opposite direction, order, or position ○ *reversing the trend of population growth* **2.** *vti* GO BACKWARD to go backward, or move something in a backward direction ○ *reverse the car* **3.** *vt* TURN SOMETHING INSIDE OUT to change something so that the opposite side or part shows ○ *You can reverse the cloak and wear it with the lining on the outside.* **4.** *vt* LAW REVOKE RULING to overturn a previous ruling made by a lower court **5.** *vt* PRINTING PRINT SOMETHING WHITE AGAINST DARK BACKGROUND to print text or graphics in white against a dark or colored background **6.** *vt* MIL TURN WEAPON UPSIDE DOWN to turn a weapon upside down, especially as a sign of mourning ■ *n* **1.** GEAR FOR BACKWARD MOVEMENT the gear in a vehicle or machine that makes it run backward ○ *It's easier to get out of here in reverse.* **2.** THE OPPOSITE the contrary of something ○ *She always does the reverse of what I tell her.* **3.** BACK SIDE the rear or back side of something ○ *The names are written on the reverse of the photo.* **4.** CHANGE TO OPPOSITE DIRECTION a change or turn to the opposite direction, position, or condition **5.** SETBACK a change for the worse ○ *a military reverse* **6.** COINS BACK SIDE OF COIN the side of a coin, medal, or seal on which the primary design does not appear ○ *The reverse of some coins carries the national motto.* **7.** FOOTBALL OFFENSIVE PLAY IN FOOTBALL in football, a move in which a back receives the handoff from the quarterback and then hands the ball to another back running in the opposite direction ■ *adj* **1.** OPPOSITE TO USUAL OR PREVIOUS ARRANGEMENT opposite to what is usual or what was previously said or arranged ○ *announce the results in reverse order* **2.** ON BACK SIDE on the other side or the back side of something **3.** FOR BACKWARD MOVEMENT used to make a machine or vehicle go backward ○ *reverse gear* [14C. Via Old French *revers* "reversed" < Latin *reversus*, past participle of *revertere* "turn back" < *vertere* "turn"] —**re·verse·ly** *adv* —**re·vers·er** *n*

re·verse bi·as *n* a voltage applied to a semiconductor or a junction in a semiconductor in a direction such that little or no current flows

re·verse-charge *adj UK* same as **collect**[1]

re·verse charg·es *adv UK* same as **collect**[1]

re·verse com·mut·ing *n* the practice of traveling regularly between a home in a city and a job in the suburbs —**re·verse com·mut·er** *n*

re·verse dis·crim·i·na·tion *n* discrimination against a member of a social group generally regarded as dominant or privileged, e.g., in employment or admission to a university

re·verse en·gi·neer·ing *n* the pirating of a competitor's technology by dismantling an existing product and reproducing its parts and construction to manufacture a replica —**re·verse-en·gi·neer** *vt* —**re·verse-en·gi·neered** *adj*

re·verse ge·net·ics *n* the process of discovering the biological function of a gene by modifying or deleting it and then looking for the effect the change has on the organism carrying the gene

re·verse mort·gage *n* a financial document in which a residential mortgage is transferred to a bank, which then pays an annuity to the homeowner

re·verse os·mo·sis *n* a process of purifying water or other liquids such as fruit juices by passing them through a semipermeable membrane that filters out unwanted substances

re·verse take·o·ver *n* the sale of a company to another company in order to avoid takeover by an unwanted predatory company

re·verse tran·scrip·tase *n* an enzyme, found naturally in retroviruses, that assists in the formation of DNA in genetic engineering, using RNA as a template

re·verse vid·e·o *n* the reversal of the usual character and background color combination on a computer display, used in highlighting

re·ver·si /ri vúrssee/ *n* a board game for two players, played on a checkerboard, in which captured pieces are turned upside down [Early 19C. < French, alteration of *reversin* < Italian *rovescina* "reversal" < Latin *reversus* (see REVERSE)]

re·vers·i·ble /ri vúrssəb'l/ *adj* **1.** able to be changed or undone **2.** made so that either side can be used as the outer or upper side —**re·vers·i·bil·i·ty** /-vùrssə bíllətee/ *n* —**re·vers·i·ble·ness** *n* —**re·vers·i·bly** *adv*

re·vers·ing light *n UK* same as **backup light**

re·vers·ing prism *n* a prism that reverses the positions of parallel rays by a combination of refraction and internal reflection

re·ver·sion /ri vúrzh'n/ *n* **1.** RETURN TO FORMER CONDITION a return to an earlier condition often perceived as less desirable or inferior **2.** REVERSAL a change to the opposite direction **3.** GENETICS RETURN TO ORIGINAL CHARACTERISTICS the restoration of the normal genetic constitution in a mutant organism, e.g., by means of a second mutation that cancels out the effects of an earlier one **4.** GENETICS REVERTED ORGANISM an organism that has reverted to ancestral genetic characteristics **5.** LAW RETURN TO FORMER OWNER the return of property to its former owner or his or her heirs at the end of a specific period, usually when the present owner dies **6.** LAW PROPERTY RETURNED TO FORMER OWNER property that has been returned to its former owner or his or her heirs **7.** LAW RIGHT TO INHERIT PROPERTY the right to succeed to property, granted to somebody by the former owner ■ *vti* MAKE DIFFERENT VERSION OF SOMETHING to make a new or different version of an existing thing, especially a radio or television program or piece of software —**re·ver·sion·al** *adj* —**re·ver·sion·al·ly** *adv* —**re·ver·sion·ar·y** *adj*

re·ver·sion·er /ri vúrzh'nər/ *n* somebody to whom ownership of property will be returned after a specific period of time

re·vert /ri vúrt/ (**-vert·ed, -vert·ing, -verts**) *vi* **1.** GO BACK TO PREVIOUS STATE to return to a former state, often one perceived as less desirable or inferior **2.** RETURN IN DISCUSSION to return to an earlier topic in the course of a discussion **3.** RETURN TO OLD HABITS to return to a former pattern of behavior, usually something less acceptable **4.** GENETICS REACQUIRE ORIGINAL FEATURES to acquire or develop original genetic features again **5.** LAW BE RETURNED TO OWNER to become once again the property of the former owner or his or her heirs [14C. Via French < Latin *revertere* (see REVERSE)] —**re·vert·er** *n* —**re·vert·i·ble** *adj*

re·ver·tant /ri vúrt'nt/ *adj* describes an organism or part of an organism that has reacquired features that are original or simpler ■ *n* a revertant organism or part

re·vest /ree vést/ (**-vest·ed, -vest·ing, -vests**) *vt* **1.** to reinstate somebody in a position or office **2.** to restore power or property to somebody

re·vet /ri vét/ (**-vet·ted, -vet·ting, -vets**) *vti* to give a structure additional support by adding a facing of bricks, stone, or concrete [Early 19C. Via French *revêtir* < late Latin *revestire* "clothe again" < Latin *vestire* "clothe" < *vestis* "clothing, garment"]

re·vet·ment /ri vétmənt/ *n* **1.** a facing added to a structure such as a wall or building that provides additional support **2.** a barricade constructed to protect against damage or injury from explosives

re·view /ri vyóo/ *v* (**-viewed, -view·ing, -views**) **1.** *vt* LOOK AT SOMETHING CRITICALLY to examine something to make sure that it is adequate, accurate, or correct ○ *They need to review their sales strategy.* **2.** *vt* GIVE OPINION ON SOMETHING to write a journalistic report on the quality of a new play, book, movie, concert, or other public performance ○ *He reviews movies for a newspaper.* **3.** *vt* CONSIDER SOMETHING AGAIN to consider, study, or check something again **4.** *vi* EDUC STUDY FOR TEST to study for a test by looking over notes and course materials **5.** *vt* LOOK BACK ON SOMETHING to discuss or examine something again ○ *She's writing an article reviewing the company's history.* **6.** *vt* LAW RECONSIDER JUDICIAL DECISION to reexamine a judicial decision made in a lower court in order to consider whether it should be overturned **7.** *vt* MIL SUBJECT TROOPS TO INSPECTION to make a formal inspection of a military force ■ *n* **1.** SURVEY OF PAST a report or survey of past actions, performance, or events ○ *a review of stock market performance during the past five years* **2.** ARTICLE GIVING OPINION a journalistic article giving an assessment of a book, play, movie, concert, or other public performance ○ *The book got unexpectedly bad reviews.* **3.** PUBLICATION FEATURING REVIEWS a magazine or journal that publishes reviews ○ *the Literary Review* **4.** REEXAMINATION OF SOMETHING another look at or consideration of something **5.** EDUC DISCUSSION OF MATERIAL ALREADY LEARNED a brief discussion of subject matter already learned, in preparation for a test ○ *This professor always has a review before a big test.* **6.** MIL INSPECTION a formal military inspection **7.** MIL FORMAL CEREMONY a formal military ceremony staged to honor a person or an occasion **8.** LAW JUDICIAL REEXAMINATION a critical examination by a higher court of a decision taken by a lower court **9.** THEATER same as **revue** [15C. < obsolete French *reveue* "inspection," < *revoir* "inspect" < Latin *revidere* "see again" < *videre* "see"] —**re·view·a·ble** *adj* —**re·view·er** *n*

USAGE review or **revue**? ***Review*** is the only spelling for the verb, meaning "to examine again," "to write a critique of," etc., and for most noun senses: *The novel had both good and bad reviews in the popular press.* The spelling ***revue*** is restricted to the noun denoting a form of theatrical entertainment.

re·view cop·y *n* a copy of a new book that a publisher sends to potential critics and reviewers to encourage published reviews

re·vile /ri víl/ (**-viled, -vil·ing, -viles**) *v* **1.** *vt* to make a fierce or abusive verbal attack on somebody or something **2.** *vi* to use insulting or abusive language [14C. < Old French *reviler* < *vil(e)* (see VILE)] —**re·vile·ment** *n* —**re·vil·er** *n*

re·vise *v* /ri víz/ (**-vised, -vis·ing, -vis·es**) **1.** *vt* RETHINK SOMETHING to come to different conclusions about somebody or something after thinking again **2.** *vt* GIVE UPDATED VERSION OF SOMETHING to change a previous estimate in order to make it more accurate or realistic **3.** *vt* ALTER TEXT to amend a text in order to correct, update, or improve it **4.** *vti UK* same as **review** *v* (sense 4) ■ *n* /reé vìz, ri víz/ **1.** SOMETHING REVISED something that has been revised **2.** PUBL STAGE OF PRINTED PROOF a late stage of a printed proof that incorporates corrections to earlier proofs (*often used in the plural*) [Mid-16C. Via French < Latin *revisere* "look over again" < *visere* "keep watching" < *videre* "see"] —**re·vis·a·ble** *adj* —**re·vis·er** *n* —**re·vi·so·ry** *adj*

Re·vised Stan·dard Ver·sion /ri vízd-/ *n* a modern US revision of the American Standard Version of the Bible, published in full in 1953

Re·vised Ver·sion *n* a 19th-century British revision of the King James' Bible

re·vi·sion /ri vízh'n/ *n* **1.** ACT OF CHANGING TEXT the amendment of a text in order to correct, update, improve, or adapt it **2.** NEW EDITION a revised and republished version of a text **3.** *UK* STUDY FOR EXAM study that involves looking over notes and course materials, in preparation for a test —**re·vi·sion·ar·y** *adj*

re·vi·sion·ism /ri vízh'n ìzzəm/ *n* **1.** the re-examining of long-established practices, views, or beliefs, especially when such re-examination is regarded as unnecessary or misguided **2.** a socialist movement arguing against revolutionary Marxist theory and believing in the peaceful achievement of social progress through reforms —**re·vi·sion·ist** *adj, n*

re·vis·it /ree vízzit/ *vt* (**-it·ed, -it·ing, -its**) **1.** GO TO PLACE AGAIN to visit a place again **2.** RECONSIDER SOMETHING to reconsider something such as an issue of public policy or a course of action, especially when additional facts indicate that an earlier decision was inappropriate ■ *n* SUBSEQUENT VISIT another visit to a place

re·vi·tal·ize /ree vít'l ìz/ (**-ized, -iz·ing, -iz·es**) *vt* to give new life or energy to somebody or something —**re·vi·tal·i·za·tion** /-vìt'li záysh'n/ *n*

re·viv·al /ri vív'l/ *n* **1.** RENEWAL OF INTEREST a renewal of interest in something that results in its becoming popular once more **2.** NEW PRODUCTION a new production of a play or opera that has not been performed recently **3.** PROCESS OF REVIVING SOMEBODY the process of bringing somebody back to life, consciousness, or full strength **4.** RECOVERY the recovering of life, consciousness, or full strength **5.** RELIG RENEWED RELIGIOUS INTEREST a new interest in religion, or the reawakening of such interest **6.** CHR EVANGELICAL CHRISTIAN MEETING a meeting or a series of meetings of evangelical Christians intended to awaken religious fervor in those who attend **7.** LAW REESTABLISHING OF LEGAL VALIDITY the renewal of the validity of a contract or the effect of a judicial decision

re·viv·al·ism /ri vív'l ìzzəm/ *n* **1.** a desire or tendency to renew interest in something old such as old customs or beliefs **2.** the efforts of a religious movement, especially an evangelical Christian movement, to reawaken religious commitment

re·viv·al·ist /ri vív'list/ *n* **1.** RELIG EVANGELIST a promoter, organizer, or preacher at a religious revival meeting, especially one for evangelical Christians **2.** ADVOCATE OF PAST CUSTOMS somebody who wishes to revive customs, ideas, or institutions ■ *adj* RELIG REAWAKENING RELIGIOUS FAITH dedicated to reawakening or stimulating religious fervor in evangelical Christians —**re·viv·al·is·tic** /ri vìv'l ístik/ *adj*

re·vive /ri vív/ (**-vived, -viv·ing, -vives**) *v* **1.** *vti* RECOVER CONSCIOUSNESS to come back to life, consciousness, or full strength, or bring somebody back to life, consciousness, or full strength **2.** *vti* FLOURISH AGAIN to become active, accepted, or popular once more, or make something active, accepted, or popular once more **3.** *vt* CAUSE EXPERIENCE TO RETURN to cause something to be experienced again as a memory or feeling **4.** *vt* STAGE SOMETHING AGAIN to stage a new production of an old play or opera [15C. Directly or via French < late Latin *revivere* "make live again" < Latin *vivere* "live"] —**re·viv·a·ble** *adj* —**re·viv·er** *n*

re·viv·i·fy /ree vívvə fì/ (**-fied, -fy·ing, -fies**) *vt* to impart new life, energy, or spirit to something or somebody —**re·viv·i·fi·ca·tion** /ree vìvvəfi káysh'n/ *n*

rev·o·ca·ble /révvəkəb'l, ri vṓk-/ *adj* able to be revoked or canceled —**rev·o·ca·bil·i·ty** /rèvvəkə bíllətee, ri vṓkə-/ *n* —**rev·o·ca·bly** *adv*

re·voke /ri vṓk/ *v* (**-voked, -vok·ing, -vokes**) **1.** *vt* LAW FORMALLY CANCEL SOMETHING to make something null and void by withdrawing, recalling, or reversing it **2.** *vt* SUMMON SOMEBODY BACK to call somebody back, e.g., from exile or from an overseas position **3.** *vi* CARDS NOT FOLLOW SUIT in a card game, to fail to follow suit when able to do so ■ *n* CARDS FAILURE TO FOLLOW SUIT failure to follow suit in a card game when able to do so [14C. Via French < Latin *revocare* "call back" < *vocare* "call"] —**rev·o·ca·tion** /rèvvə káysh'n, ree vō-/ *n* —**re·vok·er** *n*

re·volt /ri vṓlt/ *v* (**-volt·ed, -volt·ing, -volts**) **1.** *vi* REBEL AGAINST STATE to try to overthrow an existing government **2.** *vi* DEFY AUTHORITY to resist authority or rules **3.** *vti* FEEL DISGUST to feel disgust or repulsion, or cause somebody to feel disgust or repulsion ■ *n* **1.** UPRISING AGAINST GOVERNMENT an uprising that attempts to overthrow a government **2.** DEFIANCE OF AUTHORITY a protest against authority or rules [Mid-16C. Via French < Italian *revoltare* < Latin *revolvere* "roll back" (see REVOLVE)] —**re·volt·er** *n*

re·volt·ing /ri vṓlting/ *adj* **1.** arousing feelings of disgust, nausea, or repulsion **2.** unattractive or otherwise unpleasant (*informal*) —**re·volt·ing·ly** *adv*

rev·o·lute /révvə lòot/ *adj* describes leaves and other plant parts that are rolled backward and downward from the tip or edge [Mid-18C. < Latin *revolutus*, past participle of *revolvere* (see REVOLVE)]

rev·o·lu·tion /rèvvə lóosh'n/ *n* **1.** OVERTHROW OF GOVERNMENT the overthrow of a ruler or political system **2.** MAJOR CHANGE a dramatic change in ideas or practice **3.** COMPLETE CIRCULAR TURN one complete circular movement made by something round or cylindrical, e.g., a wheel, around a fixed point **4.** CIRCLE AROUND SOMETHING a complete circle made around something, e.g., the orbit made by a planet or satellite around another body **5.** GEOL PERIOD OF MAJOR GEOLOGIC CHANGE a period during which the Earth's crust changes considerably and major features such as mountain ranges may emerge [14C. Directly or via French < late Latin *revolution-* < Latin *revolut-*, past participle of *revolvere* (see REVOLVE)]

rev·o·lu·tion·ar·y /rèvvə lóosh'n èrree/ *adj* **1.** OF POLITICAL REVOLUTION relating to or involving a political or social revolution **2.** STIRRING REBELLION causing, supporting, or advocating revolution **3.** NEW AND DIFFERENT so new and different as to cause a major change in something ■ *n* (*plural* **-ies**) REBEL somebody committed to a political or social revolution —**rev·o·lu·tion·ar·i·ly** *adv* —**rev·o·lu·tion·ar·i·ness** *n*

Rev·o·lu·tion·ar·y *adj* **1.** *US* relating to the war with Great Britain fought by the American colonists **2.** relating to a particular revolution that has taken place such as the Russian Revolution or the French Revolution

Rev·o·lu·tion·ar·y Cal·en·dar *n* HIST same as **French Republican Calendar**

rev·o·lu·tion·ist /rèvvə lóosh'nist/ *n* POL same as **revolutionary**

rev·o·lu·tion·ize /rèvvə lóosh'n ìz/ (**-ized, -iz·ing, -iz·es**) *vt* **1.** CHANGE SOMETHING RADICALLY to cause a radical change in something such as a method or approach **2.** INCITE PEOPLE TO REBELLION to inspire people with revolutionary ideas **3.** CAUSE REBELLION IN COUNTRY to bring about a revolution in a country —**rev·o·lu·tion·iz·er** *n*

re·volve /ri vólv/ *v* (**-volved, -volv·ing, -volves**) **1.** *vti* MOVE IN CIRCULAR FASHION to move in a circular movement, or send something in a circular movement, either around an object or on a central axis **2.** *vi* BE FOCUSED to have something as a primary focus or theme **3.** *vi* RECUR to happen in cycles or regular periodic intervals ■ *n* THEATER TURNING STAGE a circular part of a stage that can be turned mechanically in order to change a scene [14C. < Latin *revolvere* "roll back" < *volvere* "to roll"] —**re·volv·a·ble** *adj*

re·volv·er /ri vólvər/ *n* a handgun with a revolving cylinder of chambers, allowing several shots to be fired without reloading

re·volv·ing cred·it /ri vòlving-/ *n* a credit plan that imposes regular repayments and a predetermined spending limit

re·volv·ing door *n* **1.** a door, usually in a large building, consisting of four panels that intersect at right angles and turn on a central pivot **2.** any system in which people frequently enter and leave, e.g., a corporation that repeatedly hires and fires staff or a criminal justice system that returns offenders to society (*hyphenated when used before a noun*)

re·volv·ing door syn·drome *n* **1.** the phenomenon of adult children returning to live with their parents, often for financial reasons, after a period of living away from home (*humorous informal*) **2.** the phenomenon of people joining or attending something such as an educational institution or a drug treatment program, leaving, and then returning later (*informal*)

re·volv·ing fund *n* a fund that can be drawn upon and repaid repeatedly from the revenue of the projects that it finances

re·vue /ri vyóo/ (*plural* **-vues**) *n* a musical variety show consisting of skits, dance routines, and songs that often satirize current events and personalities [Late 19C. < French < *revoir* "inspect" (see REVIEW)]

USAGE See ***review***.

re·vulsed /ri vúlst/ *adj US* disgusted or appalled by something

re·vul·sion /ri vúlsh'n/ *n* **1.** FEELING OF DISGUST a sudden violent feeling of disgust **2.** WITHDRAWAL a pulling back or turning back (*formal*) **3.** MED DIVERSION OF BLOOD the diversion of blood or disease from one part of the body to another [Mid-16C. < French < Latin *revuls-* past participle of *revellere* "pull back" < *vellere* "tear, pull"] —**re·vul·sive** *adj*

SYNONYMS See ***dislike***.

Rev. Ver. *abbr* BIBLE Revised Version

re·ward /ri wáwrd/ *n* **1.** THING GIVEN IN RETURN something desirable given in return for what somebody has done **2.** MONEY OFFERED IN RETURN money offered for information about the whereabouts of a criminal or the return of something lost or stolen **3.** BENEFIT RECEIVED a benefit obtained as a result of an action taken or a job done **4.** PSYCHOL SOMETHING REINFORCING DESIRED BEHAVIOR something positive that follows a desired response and acts to encourage desired behavior ■ *vt* (**-ward·ed, -ward·ing, -wards**) **1.** GIVE SOMEBODY SOMETHING AS REWARD to give somebody something in return, especially in thanks for kindness or help **2.** REPAY EFFORT to be worth the effort or attention that is given [14C. < Anglo-Norman, variant of Old French *reguard* "regard"] —**re·ward·a·ble** *adj* —**re·ward·er** *n*

re·ward·ing /ri wáwrding/ *adj* **1.** providing somebody with personal satisfaction or great pleasure **2.** intended as a reward for something —**re·ward·ing·ly** *adv*

re·wind *vt* /ree wínd/ (**-wound** /-wównd/, **-wind·ing, -winds**) WIND SOMETHING BACK to wind something such as video or audio tape back onto its original spool or back to an earlier point ■ *n* /rée wìnd/ **1.** REWINDING PROCESS the process of rewinding something **2.** REWINDING FUNCTION a function that rewinds film or tape, e.g., on a camera or video recorder

re·wire /ree wír/ (**-wired, -wir·ing, -wires**) *vt* to install new electrical wiring in a building, vehicle, or electrical device

re·word /ree wúrd/ (**-word·ed, -word·ing, -words**) *vt* to change the wording of something written or spoken

re·work /ree wúrk/ *vt* (**-worked, -work·ing, -works**) **1.** MAKE IMPROVEMENTS TO SOMETHING to alter something in order to improve or update it **2.** AMEND SOMETHING FOR REUSE to alter something in order to reuse it in a different context ■ *n US* REVISED VERSION a new version of something, especially a spoken or written text. Can term **reworking**

re·work·ing /rée wùrking/ *n Can, UK* same as **rework**

re·writ·a·ble /ree rítəb'l/ *adj* describes a magnetic disk that can be written on repeatedly

re·write *vt* /ree rít/ (**-wrote** /-rṓt/, **-writ·ten** /-rítt'n/, **-writ·ing, -writes**) **1.** AMEND WORDING to redraft a text by changing the wording or structure **2.** EDIT SOMETHING FOR PUBLICATION to edit a reporter's copy for publication in a newspaper or magazine **3.** ALTER INTERPRETATION to change the way the past is perceived or known about ■ *n* /rée rìt/ AMENDED TEXT an amended version of a written document —**re·writ·er** *n*

Rex /reks/ *n* a word used in the formal title of a reigning king, especially on coins and official documents [Early 17C. < Latin, "king"]

Rex·burg /réks bùrg/ city in northeastern Idaho, northeast of Idaho Falls. Population: 17,558 (2002 estimate).

Reye's syn·drome /ríz-/ *n* a rare and serious childhood disease, usually following a respiratory infection, causing vomiting, fatty deposits in the liver, disorientation, and swelling of the kidneys and brain [After Ralph Douglas *Reye* (1912–78), Australian pediatrician]

Rey·kja·vik /ráykyə vìk/ capital city of Iceland, situated on Faxaflói Bay, in the southwest of the country. Population: 108,351 (1998).

Rey·nolds /rénn'ldz/, **Burt** (*b.* 1936) US actor. In his early movies such as *Deliverance* (1972), he played action roles, but later moved on to comedies. Full name **Reynolds Jr., Burton Leon**

Rey·nolds, Sir Joshua (1723–92) British painter. He painted portraits of many notable people of his day, and was the founding president of the Royal Academy of Arts (1768).

> "He who resolves never to ransack any mind but his own, will be soon reduced, from mere barrenness, to the poorest of all imitations; he will be obliged to imitate himself, and to repeat what he has before often repeated."
> [Sir Joshua Reynolds, *Discourse to the students of the Royal Academy*, December 10, 1774]

Reyn·old's num·ber *n* a number used to indicate the flow of fluid through a pipe or around an obstruction. Symbol **Re** [After Osborne *Reynolds* (1842–1912), Irish physicist]

Rf[1] *symbol* CHEM ELEM rutherfordium

Rf[2] *abbr* MONEY rufiyaa

RF *abbr* **1.** MEDIA radio frequency **2.** AIR FORCE reconnaissance fighter **3.** MIL regular forces **4.** GENETICS releasing factor **5.** MAPS representative fraction **6.** République Française **7.** MIL Reserve Force **8.** CHEM retention factor **9.** BASEBALL right fielder

rf. *abbr* **1.** GEOG reef **2.** COMM refund

r.f. *abbr* **1.** MEDIA radio frequency **2.** MIL rapid fire **3.** PAPER rough finish

R fac·tor *n* a combination of genes that makes some bacteria resistant to antibiotics. It can be transferred to other bacteria through conjugation. [< abbreviation of RESISTANCE]

RFC *abbr* **1.** Reconstruction Finance Corporation **2.** Rugby Football Club

RFD *abbr* **1.** MEDIA radio-frequency device **2.** MIL reporting for duty **3.** MAIL rural free delivery

RFLP *abbr* BIOTECH restriction fragment length polymorphism

Rfn. *abbr* MIL Rifleman

RG *abbr* FOOTBALL right guard

RGB *abbr* red, green, blue (*used to describe a color monitor or color value*)

RGS *abbr* Royal Geographical Society

Rgt. *abbr* MIL regiment

Rh[1] *symbol* CHEM ELEM rhodium

Rh[2] *adj* relating to or involving the Rh factor ○ *presence of the Rh antigen*

RH *abbr* **1.** METEOROL relative humidity **2.** right hand **3.** Royal Highness

r.h. *abbr* **1.** METEOROL relative humidity **2.** right hand

rhab·dom /rábdəm, ráb dòm/ *n* a transparent rod-shaped part of the compound eye of insects, spiders, and other arthropods [Late 19C. < late Greek *rhabdōma* < Greek *rhabdos* "rod"]

rhab·do·man·cy /rábdə mànssee/ *n* the use of a divining rod to locate underground water or mineral ores [Mid-17C. < Greek *rhabdomanteia* < *rhabdos* "rod"] —**rhab·do·man·cer** *n*

rhab·do·vi·rus /rábdə vìrəss/ *n* a rod-shaped virus that contains RNA, e.g., the virus that causes rabies [Mid-20C. < Greek *rhabdos* "rod"]

Rhad·a·man·thus /ràddə mánthəss/ *n* in Greek mythology, the son of Zeus and Europa, who became one of the three judges of the dead in the underworld

Rhae·tian /réeshee ən, réesh'n/ *n* LANG same as **Rhaeto-Romance** ■ *adj* **1.** relating to Rhaeto-Romance **2.** relating to Rhaetia, an Alpine province of ancient Rome, or the section of the Alps in this area [Late 16C. < *Rhaetia*, province of ancient Rome]

Rhae·to-Ro·mance /réetō-/ *n* a group of Romance dialects spoken in some Alpine regions of Switzerland and Italy, including Romansch, Ladin, and Friulian —**Rhae·to-Ro·mance** *adj*

rham·nose /rám nòss/ *n* a white crystalline sugar found in plant cells and the protective cell wall of some bacteria. Formula: $_6H_{12}O_5$. [Late 19C. < modern Latin *Rhamnus*, genus name of the buckthorn (in whose berries the substance is found) < Greek *rhamnos*]

rhap·sode /ráp sōd/ *n* ANCIENT HIST same as **rhapsodist** (sense 2) [Mid-19C. < Greek *rhapsōidēs* < *rhapsōidein* "recite" (see RHAPSODY)]

rhap·sod·ic /rap sóddik/, **rhap·sod·i·cal** /-ik'l/ *adj* **1.** relating to a rhapsody, or with the emotional and improvisational qualities of a rhapsody **2.** joyfully enthusiastic or ecstatic about something —**rhap·sod·i·cal·ly** *adv*

rhap·so·dist /rápsədist/ *n* **1.** somebody who is joyfully enthusiastic or ecstatic about something (*literary*) **2.** an ancient Greek poet who recited epic poetry professionally

rhap·so·dize /rápsə dìz/ (**-dized, -diz·ing, -diz·es**) *v* **1.** *vi* to speak or write in an enthusiastic or ecstatic manner **2.** *vti* to write or recite a rhapsody

rhap·so·dy /rápsədee/ (*plural* **-dies**) *n* **1.** ENTHUSIASTIC TALK an expression of intense enthusiasm (*often used in the plural*) ○ *went into rhapsodies about the garden* **2.** MUSIC FREEFORM MUSICAL COMPOSITION a composition that is often irregular in form, emotional in effect, and improvisational in nature **3.** LITERAT ANCIENT GREEK RECITED POEM in ancient Greece, an epic poem recited by a professional reciter **4.** LITERAT EXALTED LITERARY COMPOSITION a literary work written in an intense or exalted style [Mid-16C. Via Latin < Greek *rhapsōdia* < *rhapsōidein* "recite poems" < *rhaptein* "stitch together" + *ōidē* "song"]

CULTURAL NOTE ***Rhapsody in Blue***, a musical composition (1924) by US composer George Gershwin. Originally written for piano and jazz band, it was later rearranged for orchestra by Ferde Grofé. One of the first classical works to incorporate jazz influences such as syncopated rhythms, it was inspired by the vibrancy of contemporary urban life, particularly that of New York City.

rhat·a·ny /rátt'nee/ (*plural same* or **-nies**) *n* **1.** the dried root of a South American bush. Use: toothpaste, mouthwash. **2.** a bush with spiny globular fruits and thick roots that are dried as rhatany. Native to: South America. Genus: *Krameria*. [Early 19C. Via modern Latin *rhatania* < Quechua *ratánya*]

rhe·a /rée ə/ (*plural* **-as** or *same*) *n* a large flightless bird that looks like an ostrich but is slightly smaller. Native to: South America. Family: Rheidae. [Early 19C. < modern Latin]

Rhe·a /rée ə/ *n* **1.** in Greek mythology, a Titan who was the wife of Cronus and mother of the gods. Roman equivalent **Cybele 2.** a large natural satellite of Saturn

rhe·bok /rée bòk/ (*plural* **-boks** or *same*), **ree·bok** *n* a straight-horned antelope with brownish gray woolly hair. Native to: southern Africa. Latin name: *Pelea capreolus*. [Late 18C. < Dutch *reebok* "roebuck"]

Rhee /ree/, **Syngman** (1875–1965) president of South Korea (1948–60). He led the fight for Korean independence from Japan and served as South Korea's first president.

Rheims another spelling of **Reims**

rheme /reem/ *n* the part of a sentence, often the predicate, that adds the greatest amount of new information to what is already available in the discourse [Late 19C. < Greek *rhēma* "what is said"]

Rhen·ish /rénnish/ *adj* coming from or relating to the Rhineland area of Germany [14C. < Anglo-Norman *reneis* < Latin *Rhenus* "the Rhine"]

rhe·ni·um /réenee əm/ *n* a rare heavy silvery white metallic element with a high melting point. Source: molybdenite. Use: catalyst, with tungsten in thermocouples. Symbol **Re**. See table at **element** [Early 20C. < German < Latin *Rhenus* "the Rhine"]

rheo- *prefix* flow, current ○ *rheometer* [< Greek *rheos* "stream, current" < *rhein* "to flow" < Indo-European]

rhe·o·base /rée ō bàyss/ *n* the minimum electrical nerve impulse necessary to cause a twitch in a muscle

rhe·ol·o·gy /ree óllәjee/ *n* a branch of physics dealing with the way matter flows and changes shape —**rhe·o·log·i·cal** /rèe ə lójjik'l/ *adj* —**rhe·o·log·i·cal·ly** *adv* —**rhe·ol·o·gist** *n*

rhe·om·e·ter /ree ómmətər/ *n* an instrument that measures the flow of thick liquids such as blood —**rhe·o·met·ric** /rèe ə méttrik/ *adj* —**rhe·om·e·try** *n*

rhe·o·mor·phism /rèe ə máwr fìzzəm/ *n* the liquefying of rock

rhe·o·stat /rée ə stàt/ *n* a resistor designed to allow variation in resistance without breaking the electrical circuit of which it is a part —**rhe·o·stat·ic** /rèe ə státtik/ *adj*

rhe·o·tax·is /rèe ə táksiss/ *n* the motion of an organism toward or away from a current of water or air —**rhe·o·tac·tic** /-táktik/ *adj*

rhe·ot·ro·pism /ree óttrə pìzzəm/ *n* growth of a plant, or of an immobile animal such as a coral, in the direction of a flow of water

Rhe·sus /réessəss/ *n* in Greek mythology, one of the kings of Thrace

Rhe·sus fac·tor *n* MED same as **Rh factor** [Because the antigens were first discovered in the blood of rhesus monkeys]

rhe·sus mon·key /réessəss-/ *n* a common brownish monkey of the macaque family. Native to: South Asia. Latin name: *Macaca mulatta*. [< modern Latin, arbitrarily after RHESUS]

Rhe·sus neg·a·tive *adj* MED same as **Rh negative**

Rhe·sus pos·i·tive *adj* MED same as **Rh positive**

rhet·o·ric /réttərik/ *n* **1.** PERSUASIVE SPEECH OR WRITING speech or writing that communicates its point persuasively **2.** PRETENTIOUS WORDS complex or elaborate language that only succeeds in sounding pretentious **3.** EMPTY TALK fine-sounding but insincere or empty language **4.** SKILL WITH LANGUAGE the ability to use language effectively, especially to persuade or influence people **5.** STUDY OF WRITING OR SPEAKING EFFECTIVELY the study of methods employed to write or speak effectively and persuasively [14C. Via Old French *rethorique* < Greek *rhētorikē (tekhnē)* "(art) of public speaking" < *rhētor* "speaker"]

rhe·tor·i·cal /ri táwrik'l/ *adj* **1.** relating to the skill of using language effectively and persuasively **2.** relating to or using language that is elaborate or fine-sounding but insincere —**rhe·tor·i·cal·ly** *adv*

rhe·tor·i·cal ques·tion *n* a question asked for effect that neither expects nor requires an answer

rhet·o·ri·cian /rèttə rísh'n/ *n* **1.** SKILLED SPEAKER OR WRITER a skilled and effective speaker or writer **2.** PRETENTIOUS SPEAKER OR WRITER a speaker or writer of elaborate or fine-sounding but insincere language **3.** EDUC RHETORIC TEACHER a teacher of the effective and persuasive use of language

rheum /room/ *n* watery discharge coming from the eyes, nose, or mouth [14C. Via French < Greek *rheuma* "flow, bodily humor"] —**rheum·y** *adj*

rheu·mat·ic /roo máttik/ *adj* relating to or affected with rheumatism ■ *n* somebody who is affected with rheumatism

rheu·mat·ic fe·ver *n* an acute infectious disease that causes fever and swelling in the joints, and often damage to the heart valves

rheu·mat·ic heart dis·ease *n* damage to the valves or muscular tissue of the heart caused by rheumatic fever

rheu·ma·tism /róomə tìzzəm/ *n* **1.** a painful condition of the joints or muscles in which neither infection nor injury is a contributing cause **2.** MED same as **rheumatoid arthritis** (*not in technical use*)

rheu·ma·toid /róomə tòyd/ *adj* relating to or affected with rheumatism or rheumatoid arthritis

rheu·ma·toid ar·thri·tis *n* a chronic disease of joints that causes stiffness, swelling, weakness, loss of mobility, and leads to damage and eventual destruction of the joints

rheu·ma·toid fac·tor *n* an antibody found in the blood serum of many people who have rheumatoid arthritis

rheu·ma·tol·o·gy /ròomə tóllәjee/ *n* the branch of medicine dealing with the study and treatment of rheumatic diseases —**rheu·ma·tol·og·i·cal** /ròomətə lójjik'l/ *adj* —**rheu·ma·tol·o·gist** *n*

Rh fac·tor /aar áych-/ *n* a group of antibody-producing substances (**antigens**) present in most people's red blood cells. Rh compatibility is important in matching blood for transfusions and between pregnant women and their fetuses. [Abbreviation of RHESUS FACTOR]

rhin- *prefix* same as **rhino-** (*used before vowels*)

rhi·nal /rín'l/ *adj* relating to the nose

Rhine /rīn/ river in western Europe, flowing northwestward from southeastern Switzerland through Germany and the Netherlands, emptying into the North Sea. Length: 820 mi./1,320 km.

Rhine, Joseph Banks (1895–1980) US psychologist. He was a pioneer in the field of parapsychology, including the study of extrasensory perception.

Rhine·land /rín lànd/ region in western Germany, west of the Rhine

rhi·nen·ceph·a·lon /rìn en séffə lòn, -séffələn/ (*plural* **-lons** or **-la** /-lə/) *n* the area of the forebrain that controls the sense of smell

rhine·stone /rín stōn/ *n* a small piece of paste or glass used as an imitation diamond [Late 19C. Translation of French *caillou du Rhin*; because the stones were first made in the city of Strasbourg, on the Rhine]

rhi·ni·tis /rī nítiss/ *n* inflammation of the mucous membranes of the nose, usually accompanied by a discharge of mucus

rhi·no /rínō/ (*plural same* or **-nos**) *n* same as **rhinoceros** (*informal*) [Late 19C. Shortening]

rhino- *prefix* nose, nasal ○ *rhinoplasty* [< Greek *rhin-*, stem of *rhis* "nose"]

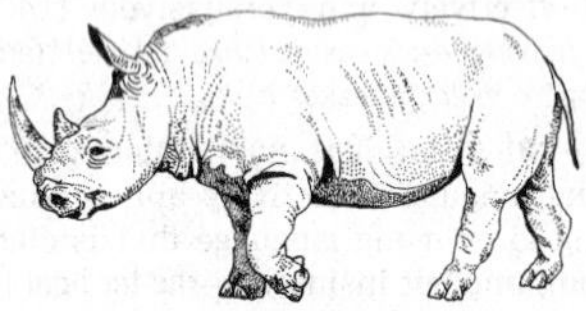

rhinoceros

rhi·noc·er·os /rī nóssərəss/ (*plural* **-os·es** or *same* or **-i** /-ər ī/) *n* a very large herbivorous animal with very thick skin and one or two horns on its snout. Native to: Africa, Asia. Family: Rhinocerotidae. [13C. Via Latin < Greek *rhinokerōs* < *rhin-* "nose" + *keras* "horn"]

rhi·noc·er·os bee·tle *n* a large tropical scarab beetle that has horns on its head and thorax

rhi·noc·er·os bird *n* BIRDS same as **oxpecker**

~~**rhinocerous**~~ incorrect spelling of **rhinoceros**

rhi·nol·o·gy /rī nólləjee/ *n* the branch of medicine dealing with conditions and structures of the nose —**rhi·nol·og·i·cal** /rìnə lójjik'l/ *adj* —**rhi·nol·o·gist** *n*

rhi·no·phar·yn·gi·tis /rì nō fàrrən jítiss/ *n* inflammation of the mucous membranes in the nose and pharynx

rhi·no·plas·ty /rínō plàstee, rínə-/ (*plural* **-ties**) *n* plastic surgery performed on the nose, whether for medical or cosmetic reasons —**rhi·no·plas·tic** /rìnō plástik, rìnə-/ *adj*

rhi·no·scope /rínə skōp/ *n* a device used by physicians to examine the nasal passages —**rhi·nos·co·py** /rī nóskəpee/ *n*

rhi·no·vi·rus /rìnō vīrəss/ *n* a virus containing RNA that causes infections of the upper respiratory system, including the common cold

rhiz- *prefix* same as **rhizo-** (*used before vowels*)

rhizo- *prefix* root ○ *rhizosphere* [< Greek *rhiza* "root"]

rhi·zo·bi·um /rī zṓbee əm/ (*plural* **-bi·a** /-bee ə/) *n* a soil bacterium that forms nodules on the roots of legumes and takes up nitrogen from the atmosphere. Genus: *Rhizobium*. [Early 20C. < modern Latin < Greek *rhiza* "root" + *bios* "life"]

rhi·zo·car·pous /rìzō kaárpəss/ *adj* describes plants that produce their fruit underground

rhi·zo·ceph·a·lan /rìzō séffələn/ *n* a small crustacean that lives in water as a parasite on crabs. Order: Rhizocephala. [Late 19C. < modern Latin *Rhizocephala* < Greek *rhiza* "root" + *kephalē* "head"]

rhi·zo·fil·tra·tion /rìzō fil tráysh'n/ *n* the use of plant roots to absorb or precipitate ground-water contaminants

rhi·zo·gen·ic /rìzō jénnik/, **rhi·zo·ge·net·ic** /rìzō jə néttik/, **rhi·zog·e·nous** /rī zójjənəss/ *adj* describes plant cells and tissues from which roots develop

rhi·zoid /rí zòyd/ *n* a slender outgrowth on mosses, liverworts, and the reproductive cells of ferns that absorbs nourishment in much the same way as a root —**rhi·zoi·dal** /rī zóyd'l/ *adj*

rhi·zome /rí zōm/ *n* a thick underground horizontal stem that produces roots and has shoots that develop into new plants [Mid-19C. < Greek *rhizōma* "mass of roots" < *rhiza* "root"] —**rhi·zom·a·tous** /rī zómmətəss, -zṓmə-/ *adj*

rhi·zo·morph /rízə màwrf/ *n* a structure in some pathogenic fungi that allows them to move from host to host —**rhi·zo·mor·phous** /rìzə máwrfəss/ *adj*

rhi·zoph·a·gous /rī zóffəgəss/ *adj* feeding on roots

rhi·zo·plane /rízə plàyn/ *n* the part of a plant's root that lies at the surface of the soil, where many microorganisms adhere to it

rhi·zo·pod /rízə pòd/ *n* a single-celled organism (**protozoan**) that moves and eats by means of filaments that it can extend temporarily. Subphylum: Rhizopoda. —**rhi·zop·o·dous** /rī zóppədəss/ *adj*

rhi·zo·pus /rízōpəss, rízə-/ *n* a mold that causes decay, e.g., the common bread mold. Genus: *Rhizopus*. [Late 19C. < modern Latin < Greek *rhiza* "root" + *pous* "foot"; because of its shape]

rhi·zo·sphere /rízə sfeer/ *n* the area of soil that immediately surrounds and is affected by a plant's roots

rhi·zot·o·my /rī zóttəmee/ (*plural* **-mies**) *n* surgery in which spinal nerves are cut in order to relieve pain or high blood pressure

Rh neg·a·tive /aar aych-/ *adj* lacking the Rh factor in the blood

rho /rō/ (*plural* **rhos**) *n* the 17th letter of the Greek alphabet, represented in the English alphabet as "r." See table at **alphabet** [14C. < Greek *rhō* < Phoenician]

rhod- *prefix* same as **rhodo-** (*used before vowels*)

rho·da·mine /rṓdə meen/ *n* a red or pink fluorescent dye. Use: coloring wool and silk, as a biological stain. [Late 19C. < Greek *rhodon* "rose"]

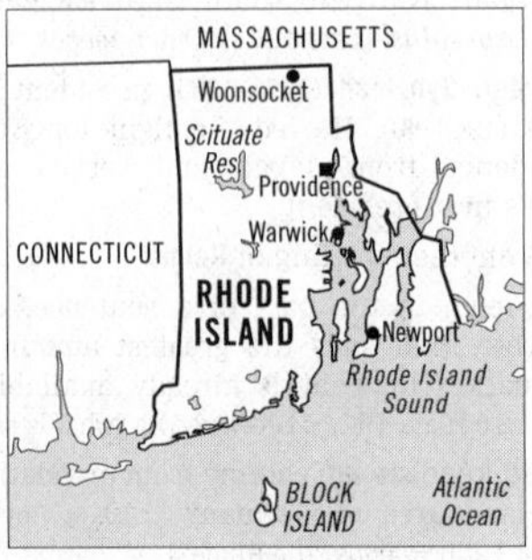

Rhode Island

Rhode Is·land /ròd-/ state in the northeastern United States, bordered by Massachusetts, the Atlantic Ocean, and Connecticut. Capital: Providence. Population: 1,069,725 (2002 estimate). Area: 1,231 sq. mi./3,188 sq. km. Official name **State of Rhode Island and Providence Plantations** —**Rhode Is·land·er** *n*

Rhodes /rōdz/ **1.** largest island of the Dodecanese, Greece. Population: 87,831 (1981). Area: 540 sq. mi./1,400 sq. km. **2.** capital of Rhodes, Greece. Population: 43,619 (1991).

Rhodes, Cecil (1853–1902) British financier and colonial administrator. He made a fortune mining diamonds in South Africa before serving as prime minister of Cape Colony (1890–96). He later helped to develop the area that became modern-day Zimbabwe. Full name **Rhodes, Cecil John**

Rho·de·sia /rō deezhə/ former name for **Zimbabwe** (1964–79) —**Rho·de·sian** *adj, n*

Rho·de·sian man *n* an early human being sharing features with the Neandertals and with modern human beings and living in Africa in the late Pleistocene period. Latin name: *Homo sapiens rhodesiensis*. [Early 20C. Because the fossils were first found in Rhodesia (Zimbabwe)]

Rho·de·sian ridge·back *n* a large dog with a ridge of hair growing down its back, belonging to a breed originally developed in Africa

Rhodes schol·ar *n* a student from the United States, South Africa, or another Commonwealth country who holds a scholarship founded by Cecil Rhodes to study at Oxford University in the United Kingdom [Early 19C. After Cecil RHODES] —**Rhodes schol·ar·ship** *n*

rho·di·nal /rṓd'n àl/ *n* CHEM same as **citronellal** [Early 20C. < German < Greek *rhodinos* "of roses" < *rhodon* "rose"]

rho·di·um /rṓdee əm/ *n* a hard, silvery white, corrosion-resistant metallic element. Source: platinum and nickel ores. Use: alloys, in plating other metals. Symbol **Rh**. See table at **element** [Early 19C. < Greek *rhodon* "rose," from the pink color of its compounds]

rhodo- *prefix* red, rosy ○ *rhodolite* [< Greek *rhodon* "rose"]

rho·do·chro·site /rṓdə krṓ sīt/ *n* a pink, red, brown, or gray manganese carbonate mineral. Use: source of manganese. [Mid-19C. < Greek *rhodokhrōs* "rose-colored"]

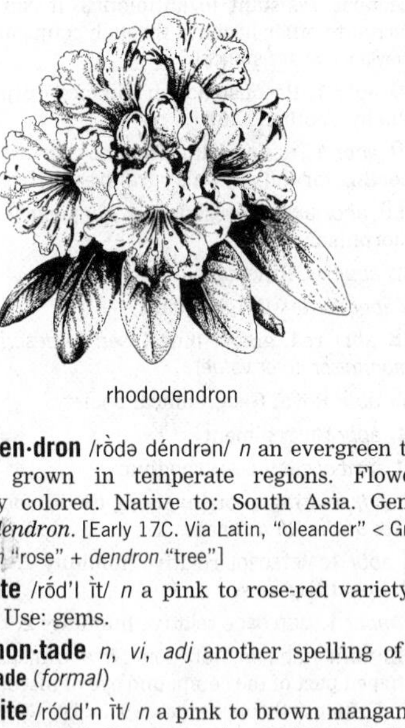

rhododendron

rho·do·den·dron /rṓdə déndrən/ *n* an evergreen tree widely grown in temperate regions. Flowers: brightly colored. Native to: South Asia. Genus: *Rhododendron*. [Early 17C. Via Latin, "oleander" < Greek < *rhodon* "rose" + *dendron* "tree"]

rho·do·lite /rṓd'l īt/ *n* a pink to rose-red variety of garnet. Use: gems.

rhod·o·mon·tade *n, vi, adj* another spelling of **rodomontade** (*formal*)

rho·do·nite /rṓdd'n īt/ *n* a pink to brown manganese silicate mineral. Source: metamorphic rock. Use: ornamental stone. [Early 19C. < Greek *rhodon* "rose"]

Rhod·o·pe Moun·tains /ròddəpee-/ mountain range in southwestern Bulgaria and northern Greece. Highest peak: Musala 9,596 ft./2,925 m.

rho·dop·sin /rō dópsin/ *n* a reddish light-sensitive pigment found in the rod cells of the retina [Late 19C. < RHODO- + Greek *opsis* "sight"]

rho·do·ra /rō dáwrə/ *n* a marshland bush of the rhododendron family that blooms in spring before the leaves emerge. Flowers: deep pink. Native to: northeastern North America. Latin name: *Rhododendron canadense*. [Late 18C. < modern Latin < Greek *rhodon* "rose"]

rhomb /rom, romb/ *n* MATH same as **rhombus** [Late 16C. Directly or via French *rhombe* < Latin *rhombus* (see RHOMBUS)]

rhom·ben·ceph·a·lon /ròmb en séffə lòn, -lən/ (*plural* **-lons** or **-la** /-lə/) *n* ANAT same as **hindbrain** [Late 19C. < RHOMBUS]

rhom·bi MATH plural of **rhombus**

rhom·bo·he·dron /ròmbō héé drón/ (*plural* **-drons** or **-dra** /-drə/) *n* a prism with six faces, each one a rhombus [Mid-19C. < RHOMBUS, after POLYHEDRON] —**rhom·bo·he·dral** *adj*

rhom·boid /róm bòyd/ *n* **PARALLELOGRAM WITH UNEQUAL SIDES** a parallelogram with adjacent sides that are not equal ■ *adj* **1. RHOMBOID-SHAPED** shaped like a rhomboid **2. RELATING TO RHOMBUS** relating to or characteristic of a rhombus [Late 16C. < Greek *rhomboeidēs* "lozenge-shaped" < *rhombos*]

rhom·bus /rómbəss/ (*plural* **-bus·es** or **-bi** /-bī/) *n* a parallelogram that has four equal sides and oblique angles [Mid-16C. Via Latin < Greek *rhombos*] —**rhom·bic** *adj*

rhon·chus /róngkəss/ (*plural* **-chi** /-kī/) *n* a harsh rattling or whistling sound heard through a stethoscope on examination of the chest, caused by partial obstruction of the airways [Early 19C. Via Latin, "snoring" < Greek *rhegkhos* < *rhegkein* "to snore"]

Rhon·dda /róndə/ community in southern Wales, formerly an important coalmining center. Population: 56,059 (2001).

Rhône /rōn/ river in Switzerland and France, flowing southwestward from the Alps into the Mediterranean Sea. Length: 505 mi./813 km.

rho·ta·cism /rṓtə sìzzəm/ *n* unusual pronunciation of the letter "r," or too much emphasis on this sound [Mid-19C. < modern Latin *rhotacismus* < Greek *rhōtakizein* "make wrong use of the letter *r*" < *rhō*]

rho·tic /rṓtik/ *adj* pronouncing the letter "r" when it occurs after a vowel or at the end of a syllable ○ *a rhotic accent* [Mid-20C. < RHOTACISM]

rhp, **r.h.p.** *abbr* MEASURE rated horsepower

Rh pos·i·tive /áar aych-/ *adj* containing the Rh factor in the blood, or having blood that contains the Rh factor

rhubarb

rhu·barb /ro͞o baarb/ *n* **1. STALKS COOKED AS FRUIT** the pink stalks of a cultivated perennial plant, cooked as fruit **2. PLANT WITH EDIBLE STALKS** a perennial plant with poisonous leaves that produces rhubarb. Genus: *Rheum*. **3.** PHARM **MEDICINAL ASIAN PLANT** a medicinal rhubarb plant native to central and eastern Asia. Use: dried underground stems as laxative. [14C. Via Old French *reubarbe* < Latin *rha barbarum* "barbarian rhubarb" < Greek *Rha*, the Volga River]

ORIGIN The Greeks had two words for ***rhubarb***: *rhēon* (which evolved into Latin *rheum*, now the plant's scientific name) and *rha*, which is said to have come from *Rha*, an ancient name of the river Volga, in allusion to the fact that ***rhubarb*** was once grown on its banks (***rhubarb*** is native to China, and was once imported to Europe via Russia). In medieval Latin ***rhubarb*** became known as *rha barbarum* "barbarian rhubarb, foreign rhubarb," again with reference to the plant's exotic origins; and in due course association with Latin *rheum* altered this to *rheubarbarum*.

rhumb /rum, rumb/ *n* **1.** NAVIG same as **rhumb line** (sense 2) **2.** any of the 32 points of a compass [Late 16C. < French *rumb* "compass point," probably < Dutch *ruim* "space, room"]

rhum·ba *n* DANCE, MUSIC another spelling of **rumba**

rhumb line *n* **1.** an imaginary line on the surface of the Earth intersecting all meridians at the same angle **2.** a steady course along one compass setting taken by a ship or aircraft

rhyme /rīm/ *n* **1. SIMILARITY IN SOUND** a similarity in the sound of word endings, especially in poetry **2. WORD SOUNDING SAME AS ANOTHER** a word with an ending that sounds similar to the ending of another word **3. POEM** a poem, or poetry generally, of a lighthearted kind with a pattern of similar sounds at the ends of the lines ■ *v* (**rhymed, rhym·ing, rhymes**) **1.** *vi* **SOUND SIMILAR** to have an ending that sounds similar to the ending of another word or line of poetry, or have endings that sound similar ○ *"Rough" rhymes with "cuff."* **2.** *vt* **CHOOSE RHYMING WORD** to find or choose a particular word and use it with another because its ending sounds similar **3.** *vti* **WRITE POETRY** to write rhyming poetry, or express something in rhyme [12C. Via French *rime* < medieval Latin use of Latin *rhythmus* (see RHYTHM); because accented verse usually rhymed] —**rhyme·less** *adj* ◇ **without rhyme or reason** without any rational explanation or apparent sense

rhym·er /rímər/ *n* LITERAT same as **rhymester**

rhyme roy·al *n* **1.** a form of poetry using verses with seven lines of iambic pentameter with a rhyme scheme ababbcc **2.** a verse written in rhyme royal [Mid-19C. Because the form was used by James I of Scotland]

rhyme scheme *n* the pattern of rhyming lines in a poem or in a verse of a poem

rhyme·ster /rímstər/ *n* a writer of poems with rhyming lines, especially popular or amateur verse

rhym·ing /ríming/ *adj* with lines that end in similar sounding words, forming a pattern

rhym·ing slang *n* a form of slang that replaces a word with an expression that rhymes with the word but has no meaningful connection with it, used especially in Cockney

rhyn·cho·ce·pha·lian /rìngkō sə fáylyən/ *adj* relating to an order of primitive reptiles resembling lizards with only one living representative, the tuatara of New Zealand. Order: Rhynchocephalia. ■ *n* a member of the rhynchocephalian order [Mid-19C. < modern Latin *Rhyncocephalia* < Greek *rhugkhos* "snout" + *kephalē* "head"]

rhy·o·lite /rí ə līt/ *n* a fine-grained acid rock that is the volcanic form of granite [Mid-19C. < Greek *rhuax* "stream (of lava)" < *rhein* "to flow"] —**rhy·o·lit·ic** /rī ə líttik/ *adj*

Rhys /reess/, **Jean** (1894–1979) Caribbean-born British writer. Her work reflects her Caribbean background and often reveals a pessimistic view of the world. Pseudonym of **Rees Williams, Ellen Gwendolen**

> "We can't all be happy, we can't all be rich, we can't all be lucky—and it would be so much less fun if we were.... Some must cry so that others may be able to laugh more heartily."
> [Jean Rhys, *Good Morning, Midnight*; 1939]

rhythm /ríthəm/ *n* **1. PATTERN OF BEATS IN MUSIC** the regular pattern of beats and emphasis in a piece of music ○ *The audience clapped in rhythm as we sang.* **2. PARTICULAR MUSIC PATTERN** a pattern of beats in a piece or a particular kind of music ○ *boogie-woogie rhythm* **3. PATTERN OF STRESS IN POETRY** in poetry, the pattern formed by stressed and unstressed syllables **4. PARTICULAR POETRY PATTERN** a pattern of stress in a poem or a particular kind of poetry **5. REGULAR PATTERN** a regularly recurring pattern of activity, e.g., the cycle of the seasons, night and day, or repeated functions of the body **6. CHARACTERISTIC PATTERN** the characteristic pattern of an activity **7.** ARTS **PATTERN IN ART** a pattern suggesting movement or pace in something such as a work of art **8.** LANGUAGE **SOUND PATTERN** the pattern of sound that characterizes a language, dialect, or accent **9.** MOVIES, LITERAT **PATTERN FROM REPETITION** a mood or effect in a book, play, or movie created from repetition [Mid-16C. Via Latin *rhythmus* < Greek *rhuthmos* < Indo-European, "to flow"]

rhythm and blues *n* a style of music combining blues and jazz, originally developed by African American musicians

rhythm gui·tar *n* a chordal accompaniment from a guitar that does not play the melody

rhyth·mic /ríthmik/, **rhyth·mi·cal** /ríthmik'l/ *adj* **1.** with a regularly recurring pattern or beat **2.** relating to rhythm —**rhyth·mi·cal·ly** *adv* —**rhyth·mic·i·ty** /rith míssətee/ *n*

rhyth·mic gym·nas·tics *n* a sport in which athletes combine gymnastic dance movements with the use of apparatuses such as ribbons and hoops (*takes a singular or plural verb*)

rhyth·mics /ríthmiks/ *n* the study of rhythms and rhythmic forms (*takes a singular verb*)

rhyth·mist /ríthmist/ *n* a student or creator of rhythm

rhythm meth·od *n* a method of contraception in which sexual intercourse is avoided at the times when a woman is most likely to conceive

rhythm sec·tion *n* the instruments in a band that provide the basic rhythm, e.g., the drums, bass, piano, or guitar

rhythm stick *n* either of a pair of wooden sticks, often with notches, used as a simple percussion instrument

rhy·ti·dec·to·my /rìtti déktəmee/ (*plural* **-mies**) *n* MED same as **facelift** (*technical*) [Mid-20C. < Greek *rhutid-* "wrinkle"]

rhy·ton /rí tòn/ *n* a drinking vessel in ancient Greece with a hole in the bottom through which to drink [Mid-19C. < Greek *rhuton* < *rhutos* "flowing"]

RI, **R.I.** *abbr* **1.** EDUC religious instruction **2.** Rhode Island

RIA *abbr* MED radioimmunoassay

ri·al /ree áal/ *n* the main unit of currency in Iran and Oman. See table at **currency** [Mid-20C. Via Persian, Arabic *riyāl* < Spanish *real* (see REAL[2])]

ri·al·to /ree áltō/ (*plural* **-tos**) *n* **1.** *also* **Ri·al·to** *US* the part of a town or city where its theaters are located **2.** a market or marketplace [Mid-16C. After *Rialto*, district of Venice in which the market was located]

ri·a·ta /ree áatə/, **re·a·ta** *n* a lasso or lariat [Mid-19C. < Spanish *reata* < *reatar* "retie" < *atar* "tie" < Latin *aptare* "join" < *apere* "tie"]

rib /rib/ *n* **1. CURVED BONE OF CHEST** any of the curved bones extending from the vertebrae and in some cases meeting the sternum, forming a cavity housing vital organs in many vertebrates **2.** FOOD **MEAT** a cut of meat that contains ribs **3.** HANDICRAFT **RIDGED KNITTING** a portion of knitted material with raised vertical lines of stitches, made by alternating purl stitches with plain stitches **4.** BOT **LEAF VEIN** a raised vein on a leaf **5.** ARCHIT **MOLDING ON VAULT** a ridge or molding on the underside of a vault or arched ceiling **6.** NAUT **PART OF SHIP'S HULL** a beam extending from the keel to the top of the hull of a ship, giving it its shape **7.** AVIAT **PART OF AIRCRAFT'S WING** a part of an aircraft's wing crossing from the leading to the trailing edge of the wing **8. PIECE RESEMBLING RIB** a bar, rod, or other supporting part that has the shape or function of a rib ○ *a broken rib on the umbrella* **9. TEASING COMMENT** a comment or action meant as a joke or to tease somebody (*informal*) ■ **ribs** *npl* **RIBS WITH LITTLE MEAT** the ribs of an animal from which most of the meat has been removed, eaten as food ■ *v* (**ribbed, rib·bing, ribs**) **1.** *vti* **TEASE** to make playful teasing remarks to somebody (*informal*) ○ *They ribbed me about my haircut.* **2.** *vt* **PROVIDE SOMETHING WITH RIBS** to provide or strengthen something with ribs **3.** *vti* HANDICRAFT **KNIT PLAIN AND PURL STITCHES** to knit plain stitches alternately with purl stitches to make raised lines, or form a piece of knitting in this way [Old English *ribb* < Germanic, "covering (of the chest cavity)"] ◇ **stick to your ribs** to be substantial, nourishing, or hearty as a meal (*informal*)

rib·ald /ríbb'ld, rí bàwld/ *adj* humorous but rude and vulgar, often involving jokes about sex [14C. < Old French *ribau(l)t* < *riber* "sleep around" < Germanic]

rib·ald·ry /ríbbəldree, ríbəl-/ *n* language or behavior that is humorous but rude and vulgar, often involving jokes about sex

rib·and /ríbbənd/, **rib·band** *n* a ribbon, especially one that is used for decorative purposes [14C. < Old French *riban*]

Ri·bault /rí bṓ/, **Jean** (1520?–65) French-born American explorer and colonizer. He explored the Florida coast and settled Port Royal, South Carolina (1562).

ri·ba·vi·rin /rībə vīrin/ *n* a synthetic antiviral agent that inhibits the synthesis of viral DNA and RNA. Use: treatment of viral diseases. [Late 20C. < *riba-* < ?]

rib·band *n* another spelling of **riband**

ribbed /ribd/ *adj* **1. KNITTED INTO PATTERN OF VERTICAL LINES** knitted to form a pattern of raised vertical lines, giving a stretchy fabric **2. STRIPED** with a surface marked by raised, roughly parallel bands **3. HAVING RIBS** with structural support or decoration in the form of ribs

Rib·ben·trop /ríbbən tròp/, **Joachim von** (1893–1946) German Nazi official. As Germany's ambassador to Britain (1936) and foreign minister (1938–43), he helped promote the expansionist program of the Nazis. After World War II he was tried at Nuremberg and executed.

rib·bing /ríbbing/ *n* **1. SECTION OF RIB IN KNITTING** a section of knitting in a pattern of raised vertical lines, making a stretchy fabric **2. RIB FRAMEWORK** a supporting structure or framework of ribs, e.g., in the hull of a boat **3. TEASING** playful or friendly teasing (*informal*)

rib·bon /ríbbən/ *n* **1. DECORATIVE STRIP OF FABRIC** a strip of fabric used to tie something or for decoration **2. RIBBON AS AWARD OR BADGE** a decorative strip of fabric given to somebody as an award or worn as a sign of rank, membership, or support for a cause **3. LONG NARROW STRIP** something that is long, narrow, and thin, in the shape of a ribbon **4.** COMM **STRIP OF INKED MATERIAL** a strip of material with ink on it, used in some printers and typewriters **5.** COMPUT **FLAT CABLE** a flat cable in which all the wires are parallel to one another in a single plane **6.** CONSTR same as **ledger board** (sense 2) ■ **rib·bons** *npl* **1. BADLY DAMAGED STATE** a damaged state in which something is cut or torn very badly ○ *My shirt was in ribbons.* **2.** RIDING **REINS** reins for controlling a horse (*informal*) ■ *vt* (**-boned, -bon·ing, -bons**) **1. DECORATE SOMETHING WITH RIBBONS** to decorate something by attaching ribbons to it **2. TEAR SOMETHING INTO STRIPS** to tear something into long thin strips [Early 16C. Variant of RIBAND] —**rib·bon·y** *adj*

Rib·bon Falls /ríbbən-/ falls in eastern California. Height: 1,612 ft./491 m.

rib·bon·fish /ríbbən fish/ (*plural same* or **-fish·es**) *n* a fish with a long tapering ribbon-shaped body and, typically, a dorsal fin extending from head to tail. Some species can exceed 32 ft./10 m in length. Native to: deeper parts of oceans. Family: Trachypteridae.

rib·bon grass *n* a grass that is grown as an ornamental in northern temperate regions for its drooping cream-striped leaves. Native to: Europe, North America. Latin name: *Phalaris arundinacea picta.*

rib·bon snake *n* a nonvenomous snake with longitudinal reddish or yellow stripes that gives birth to live young and feeds on frogs and worms. Native to: North America. Latin name: *Thamnophis sauritus.*

rib·bon worm *n* a worm with a long flat unsegmented body that burrows in the mud covered by ocean tides. Phylum: Nemertea.

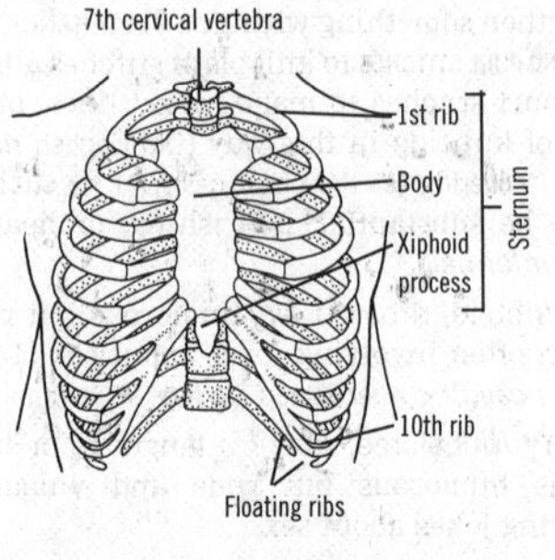

rib cage

rib cage *n* the ribs as a whole, forming a protective bony enclosure surrounding the heart and lungs

rib eye *n US* a cut of meat, especially beef, taken from the outer side of the rib

rib·grass /ríb gràss/ (*plural* **-grass·es** or *same*) *n* a plant with long slender ribbed leaves that grows as a weed. Flowers: small, white, in a rounded head. Native to: Europe, Asia. Latin name: *Plantago lanceolata.* [Early 16C. Because the leaves are ribbed]

rib·let /ríbblət/ *n* **1.** a piece of veal or lamb cut from the end of a rib **2.** one of a series of tiny grooves incorporated into a material that can be applied to the exterior surface of aircraft or boats to reduce drag

ribo- *prefix* ribose ○ *riboflavin* [< RIBOSE]

ri·bo·fla·vin /rībə flàyvin/ *n* vitamin B_2, the yellow component of the B complex group, an important coenzyme in many biochemical processes. Formula: $C_{17}H_{20}N_4O_6$.

ri·bo·nu·cle·ase /rìbō nóoklee àyss, -àyz/ *n* BIOCHEM full form of **RNase**

ri·bo·nu·cle·ic ac·id /rìbō noo klée ik-/ *n* BIOCHEM full form of **RNA**

ri·bo·nu·cle·o·pro·tein /rìbō nooklee ō prṓ teen/ *n* a complex of RNA and a protein formed during the synthesis of RNA

ri·bo·nu·cle·o·side /rìbō nóoklee ə sīd/ *n* a nucleoside in which the sugar group is ribose

ri·bo·nu·cle·o·tide /rìbō nóoklee ə tīd/ *n* a nucleotide that contains the sugar ribose, making up units in important molecules such as RNA and ATP

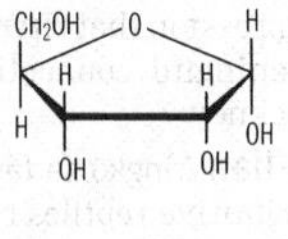

ribose

ri·bose /rī bōss/ *n* a white crystalline sugar found in all living cells as a constituent of RNA and many other metabolically important compounds, including ribonucleotides, nucleic acids, and riboflavin. Formula: $C_5H_{10}O_5$. [Late 19C. < German, alteration of ARABINOSE]

ri·bo·so·mal /rībə sṓm'l/ *adj* relating to ribosomes

ri·bo·so·mal RNA *n* an RNA that is a structural and functional component of ribosomes

ri·bo·some /rībə sōm/ *n* a submicroscopic cluster of proteins and RNA, occurring in great numbers in the cytoplasm of living cells, that takes part in the manufacture of proteins [Mid-20C. < RIBONUCLEIC ACID]

ri·bo·zyme /rībə zīm/ *n* an RNA that can catalyze changes to its own structure [Late 20C. Blend of RIBONUCLEIC ACID + ENZYME]

rib roast *n* a large cut of red meat that includes the part along the outer edge of the rib

rib-tick·ler *n* a very funny joke or story (*informal*) —**rib-tick·ling** *adj*

rib·u·lose /ríbbyə lōss/ *n* a sugar that occurs in plants and is used in photosynthesis. Formula: $C_5H_{10}O_5$. [Mid-20C. < RIBOSE + -ULE]

Ri·car·do /ri kaárdō/, **David** (1772–1823) British economist. He introduced the concept of an "economic model" in his major work *Principles of Political Economy and Taxation* (1817).

> "The natural price of labor is that price which is necessary to enable the laborers, one with another, to subsist and perpetuate their race, without either increase or diminution."
> [David Ricardo, *Principles of Political Economy and Taxation*; 1817]

Ric·ci /réechee/, **Matteo** (1552–1610) Italian priest. A Jesuit missionary, he lived in China from 1583, and provided the West with early descriptions of the country.

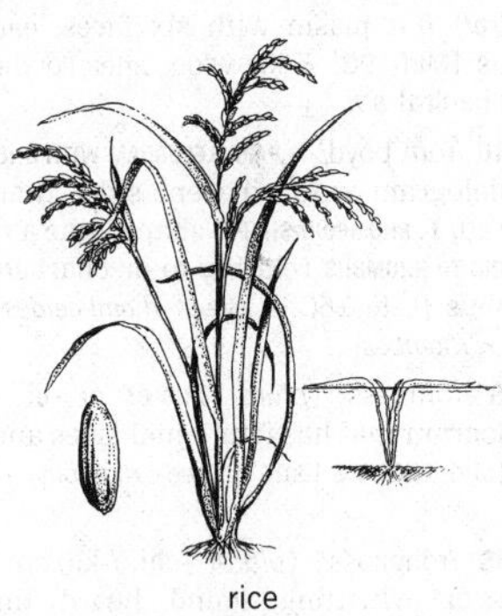

rice

rice /rīss/ *n* **1. EDIBLE GRAINS** the edible grains of a cereal plant of South Asian origin. Rice is served hot or cold after cooking in water or other liquid. **2. CEREAL PLANT** a cereal plant that produces rice, cultivated in tropical and warm regions of the world. Native to: South Asia. Latin name: *Oryza sativa.* ■ *vt* (**riced, ric·ing, ric·es**) **SIEVE FOOD** to push food through a sieve or ricer to make it into a coarse purée [13C. Via Old French *ris* and Italian *riso* < Greek *oruza* < Indo-Iranian]

UPI/Corbis-Bettmann

Anne Rice

Rice /rīss/, **Anne** (*b.* 1941) US writer. She is best known for the Vampire Chronicles, beginning with *Interview with the Vampire* (1976). Born **O'Brien, Howard Allen**

Rice, Condoleezza (*b.* 1954) US national security adviser. A former provost of Stanford University, in 2002 she became the first woman to be appointed national security adviser.

Rice, Elmer (1892–1967) US playwright. He won a Pulitzer Prize for the play *Street Scene* (1929), and is also known for *The Adding Machine* (1923). Born **Reizenstein, Elmer**

rice·bird /rīss bùrd/ *n* a bird that is commonly seen in rice fields, especially a bobolink

rice pa·per *n* **1.** a thin brittle edible paper made from the rice-paper plant and other plant sources, used to undercoat baked food that would otherwise stick to the pan during baking **2.** a thin artist's paper made from the pith of the rice-paper plant

rice-pa·per plant *n* a bush grown for its fiber. Use: rice paper. Native to: China. Latin name: *Tetrapanax papyriferus.*

ric·er /rīssər/ *n* a kitchen utensil consisting of a perforated plate in one end of an open cylinder through which foods can be pressed to form long strings

rice rat *n* a rat that inhabits the marshes where rice fields are located. Native to: southern United States, Central and South America. Genus: *Oryzomys.*

ri·cer·ca·re /reechər kaá ràyl/ (*plural* **-ri** /-reel/) *n* a fugal composition for musical instruments, analogous to a motet for voices, involving lines of melody interwoven in an often complicated pattern [Late 18C. < Italian, "seek out"]

rice wee·vil *n* an insect of the weevil family that infests stored rice, wheat, and other grains. Latin name: *Sitophilus oryzae.*

rich /rich/ *adj* **1. WEALTHY** owning a lot of money or expensive property **2. WORTH MUCH** worth a great deal of money ○ *a rich endowment* 3. COSTLY AND FINE made from or consisting of things of the highest quality ○ *rich fabrics* 4. WITH GOOD SUPPLY OF SOMETHING with a good supply of a resource or substance ○ *an area rich in minerals* ○ *a city rich in culture* ○ *cotton-rich fabric* 5. PLENTIFUL existing in large quantities and in plentiful supply ○ *a rich covering of new growth* 6. PRODUCTIVE productive and so potentially very profitable 7. FERTILE very fertile and able to produce strong healthy plants 8. WITH FATTY INGREDIENTS containing a high proportion of foods such as cream, eggs, or butter that are full of fat ○ *a very rich chocolate cake* 9. STRONG AND SMOOTH-FLAVORED with a pleasantly strong, smooth flavor ○ *rich coffee* 10. WITH STRONG PLEASANT SMELL having a strong and pleasant smell 11. STRONGLY COLORED deep or fully saturated in color ○ *a rich shade of brown* 12. WITH DEEP FULL SOUND with a deep smooth full sound 13. WITH TOO MUCH FUEL IN MIXTURE with a higher than normal proportion of fuel to air in the mixture supplied to an engine 14. UNLIKELY hard to believe because ridiculous (*informal*) ○ *That's rich, coming from her!* ■ *npl* WELL-OFF wealthy people in general ○ *a playground for the rich and famous* [Old English *rīce* "strong, powerful" and Old French *riche*, via Germanic < Indo-European, "king"] —**rich·ness** *n*

Rich·ard I /ríchərd/ (1157–99) **king of England** He spent most of his reign (1189–99) overseas, fighting in the Third Crusade and against Philip II of France. Known as **Richard the Lionheart**

Rich·ard II (1367–1400) **king of England** His reign (1377–99) was marked by national disunity and civil strife that culminated in his being deposed

Rich·ard III (1452–85) **king of England** He usurped the throne while protector of the young Edward V (1483), but was defeated at the Battle of Bosworth Field (1485) in a rebellion led by the future King Henry VII

Rich·ard Roe /rìchərd rṓ/ *n US* a name used for a second unknown man in legal proceedings, the first unknown man being called John Doe

Rich·ards /ríchərdz/, **I. A.** (1893–1979) British critic, poet, and teacher. He founded the New Criticism movement, which was influential in the teaching of English literature in colleges and universities. Full name **Richards, Ivor Armstrong**

Rich·ards, Maxwell (*b.* 1931) president of Trinidad and Tobago (2003–). A chemical engineer, he held posts in industry and academia before becoming the country's second elected president. Full name **Richards, George Maxwell**

Rich·ard·son /ríchərdss'n/, **H. H.** (1838–86) US architect. He was a leader of the Romanesque revival movement in the United States, which led to a distinctively American style of architecture. Full name **Richardson, Henry Hobson**

Rich·ard·son, John (1796–1852) Canadian writer. He is known for his historical and autobiographical novels.

Rich·ard·son, Sir Ralph (1902–83) British actor. He appeared in many Shakespearean and classical stage roles, and in numerous movies. Full name **Richardson, Sir Ralph David**

Rich·ard·son, Robert C. (*b.* 1937) US physicist. With David M. Lee and Douglas D. Osheroff he shared the Nobel Prize in physics (1996) for research into the superfluidity of helium-3.

Rich·ard·son, Samuel (1689–1761) British novelist. He wrote *Pamela* (1740), *Clarissa* (1747–48), and other novels in epistolary form, and had a major influence on the early development of the English novel.

Rich·ard·son's ground squir·rel /rìchərdss'nz-/ *n* a ground squirrel that can be a pest of grain crops. Native to: northwestern United States and Canadian prairies. Latin name: *Citellus richardsoni*. [Mid-20C. After Sir John *Richardson* (1787–1865), Scottish naturalist]

Rich·e·lieu /ríshə lo͝o, reeshə lyṓ/, **Armand Jean du Plessis, Duc de** (1585–1642) French cardinal and royal minister. As chief minister to Louis XIII after 1624, he wielded supreme power in France. He strengthened the monarchy and made France the pre-eminent military power in Europe. Known as **Cardinal Richelieu**

MEASURING EARTHQUAKES USING THE RICHTER SCALE

The Richter scale measures the magnitude of an earthquake based on how much the ground shakes at a distance of 100 km (60 miles) from the epicenter of the earthquake (the site on the Earth's surface directly above its origin). Other systems used by seismologists to measure earthquakes include the Modified Mercalli scale, a 12-point scale that measures intensity at different locations.

Richter number	Increase in the motion of the ground	Results
1	1	Generally not felt, but recorded on seismometers
2	10	
3	100	
4	1,000	Felt by many people; trees sway
5	10,000	Poorly built structures damaged
6	100,000	Specially designed structures damaged; others collapse
7	1,000,000	Many structures destroyed; cracks in ground
8+	10,000,000	Severe destruction; very wide cracks in ground

"Authority compels people to obedience, but reason persuades them to it."
[Armand Jean du Plessis Richelieu, *Testament politique*; 1688]

rich e-mail *n* an e-mail that has a voice message attached to it

rich·es /ríchəz/ *npl* 1. great wealth or many valuable possessions 2. things occurring naturally in abundance ○ *enjoy the riches of the forest* [12C. Variant of obsolete *richesse* (singular) "wealth" < Old French *richeise* < *riche* (see RICH), misunderstood as plural]

Rich·ler /ríchlər/, **Mordecai** (1931–2001) Canadian writer. He has drawn on his working-class Jewish background in *The Apprenticeship of Duddy Kravitz* (1959) and other works.

"Remember this, Griffin. The revolution eats its own. Capitalism re-creates itself."
[Mordecai Richler, *Cocksure*; 1968]

rich·ly /ríchlee/ *adv* 1. ELABORATELY beautifully and elaborately ○ *richly decorated* 2. WITH DEEP COLOR with a deep, fully saturated color 3. COMPLETELY completely and suitably ○ *a richly deserved award* 4. PLENTIFULLY plentifully or very fully

Rich·mond /ríchmənd/ 1. capital of Virginia, in the eastern part of the state. Population: 197,456 (2002 estimate). 2. city in eastern Indiana, west of the Indiana-Ohio border, on the East Fork River, east of Indianapolis. Population: 38,470 (2002 estimate). 3. city in central Kentucky. Population: 28,093 (2002 estimate).

Rich·ter scale /ríktər-/ *n* a scale from 1 to 10 used to measure the severity of earthquakes according to the amount of energy released, with a higher number indicating stronger tremors [Mid-20C. After Charles Francis *Richter* (1900–85), US seismologist]

rich text *n* computer text that includes formatting codes, e.g., for bold or italic

Richt·ho·fen /ríkt hṓfən, ríkht-/, **Manfred, Baron von** (1892–1918) German aviator. As the leader of a German air squadron during World War I, he is thought to have shot down 80 Allied aircraft. Known as **the Red Baron**

ri·cin /ríss'n, ríss'n/ *n* a highly toxic protein. Source: seeds of the castor oil plant. Use: destruction of cancer cells in treatments such as bone marrow transplants. [Late 19C. < Latin *ricinus* "castor oil plant"]

ric·in·o·le·ic ac·id /rìss'n ō lée ik-/ *n* an unsaturated fatty acid that is the main constituent of castor oil. Use: soap, plastics, textile finishing. Formula: $C_{18}H_{34}O_3$. [< Latin *ricinus* "castor oil plant" + OLEIC]

rick /rik/ *n* a large quantity of hay or straw stacked into a rectangular shape for storage and covered at the top to protect it from the weather ■ *vt* (**ricked, rick·ing, ricks**) to stack hay or straw to form a rick [Old English *hrēac*, origin ?]

Rick·en·back·er /ríkən bàkər/, **Eddie** (1890–1973) US aviator and business executive. He was one of the most decorated US combat pilots of World War I, and later had a long career in the airline industry. Full name **Rickenbacker, Edward Vernon**

rick·ets /ríkits/ *n* a disease, especially of children, caused by a deficiency in vitamin D that makes the bones become soft and prone to bending and structural change. Technical name **rachitis** [Mid-17C. Origin ?]

rick·ett·si·a /ri kétsee ə/ (*plural* **-as** or **-ae** /-see/ or *same*) *n* a parasitic bacterium that typically lives inside ticks and can be transmitted to humans, causing Rocky Mountain spotted fever, forms of typhus, and other diseases. Order: Rickettsiales. [Early 20C. < modern Latin, after H. T. *Ricketts* (1871–1910), US pathologist] —**rick·ett·si·al** *adj*

rick·et·y /ríkətee/ (**-i·er, -i·est**) *adj* 1. UNSTABLE in bad condition, unstable, and likely to collapse ○ *a rickety chair* 2. INFIRM weakened by the aging process or illness 3. MED WITH RICKETS affected by rickets 4. MED RELATING TO RICKETS relating to or resembling rickets [Late 17C. < RICKETS, from the unsteadiness that the disease causes]

rick·ey /ríkee/ (*plural* **-eys**) *n* a cocktail made from soda water, lime or lemon juice, sugar, and gin or vodka [Late 19C. Probably < a surname]

Rick·o·ver /rík ōvər/, **Hyman** (1900–86) Russian-born US admiral. He supervised the design and construction of the first nuclear-powered submarine, the USS *Nautilus* (1954). Full name **Rickover, Hyman George**

rick·rack /rík ràk/, **ric·rac** *n* a narrow decorative braid in a zigzag shape [Late 19C. Doubling of RACK[1]]

rick·shaw /rík shàw/, **rick·sha** *n* 1. a small vehicle with two wheels and a seat for passengers, pulled along by somebody walking in front of it, used especially in South and East Asia 2. a small three-wheeled vehicle, like a tricycle with a seat at the back for passengers, that is driven by somebody sitting at the front and pedaling [Late 19C. Shortening of Japanese *jinrikisha* < *jin* "man" + *riki* "strength" + *sha* "vehicle"]

RICO /reekō/ *abbr* Racketeer Influenced and Corrupt Organizations (Act)

ric·o·chet /ríkə shày, rìkə sháy/ *vi* (**-cheted** /ríkə shàyd, rìkə sháyd/, **-chet·ing** /-shày ing, -sháy ing/, **-chets** /-shàyz, -sháyz/) to hit a surface and bounce, traveling away in a different direction ■ *n* the rebounding action of something that hits a surface and bounces off in a different direction [Mid-18C. < Old French, "give-and-take, repetition"]

ri·cot·ta /ri kóttə/ *n* a soft white mild-tasting Italian cheese made from whey and used mostly in cooking, or a cheese made to resemble this [Late 19C. Via Italian, "recooked" < Latin *recocta*, form of past participle of *recoquere* "recook" < *coquere* "cook"]

ric·rac *n* HANDICRAFT another spelling of **rickrack**

ric·tus /ríktəss/ (*plural same* or **-tus·es**) *n* 1. a fixed open-mouthed grin or grimace, especially an expression of horror 2. the gape of a bird's beak

[Mid-18C. < Latin < past participle of *ringi* "gape"] —**ric·tal** *adj*

rid /rid/ (**rid** or **rid·ded** *archaic*, **rid·ding**, **rids**) *vt* **1.** to free, relieve, or empty a place or thing of something, usually something undesirable ○ *an attempt to rid the town of crime* **2.** to free somebody or yourself from something undesirable ○ *trying to rid myself of the habit* [12C. < Old Norse *ryðja* "to clear land" < *hrjóða* "to strip"] ◇ **be well rid of somebody** *or* **something** to be in a better position because you no longer have to deal with somebody or something burdensome, unpleasant, or unnecessary ◇ **get rid of somebody** *or* **something** to make somebody or something burdensome, unpleasant, or unnecessary go away

rid·dance /rídd'nss/ *n* the removal or destruction of something unwanted ◇ **good riddance (to somebody** *or* **something)** used to show that you are glad to be free of somebody or something

rid·den past participle of **ride**

rid·dle[1] /rídd'l/ *n* **1.** WORD PUZZLE a puzzle in the form of a question or rhyme that contains clues to its answer **2.** PUZZLING THING something that is puzzling or confusing ■ *v* (**-dled, -dling, -dles**) **1.** *vti* ANSWER RIDDLE to find or explain the answer to a riddle **2.** *vi* TALK IN RIDDLES to speak in an intentionally obscure way [Old English *rǣdels* < Indo-European] —**rid·dler** *n*

SYNONYMS See ***problem***.

rid·dle[2] /rídd'l/ *vt* (**-dled, -dling, -dles**) **1.** MAKE HOLES IN SOMETHING to damage something by making a large number of small holes in it **2.** AFFECT EVERY PART to affect every part of something, e.g., by spreading throughout **3.** SIFT SOIL OR STONES to put soil or stones through a sieve to separate the large pieces from the small ones **4.** SHAKE ASHES FROM FIRE to shake ashes from the bottom of a fire by poking it with a metal rod or moving a mechanism under the grate ■ *n* SIEVE a large flat shallow sieve for sifting soil or stones [Old English *hriddel* "sieve," alteration of *hridder* < Indo-European, "to sort"] —**rid·dler** *n*

rid·dling /rídd'ling/ *adj* communicating in riddles, or in a deliberately obscure and confusing way

ride /rīd/ *v* (**rode** /rōd/, **rid·den** /rídd'n/, **rid·ing**, **rides**) **1.** *vti* SIT ON AND CONTROL HORSE to sit on a horse or other animal and control it as it moves along **2.** *vti* TRAVEL ON BIKE to travel mounted on a bicycle or motorcycle **3.** *vt* USE SPORTS EQUIPMENT to support your weight and move on a skateboard, surfboard, or other piece of gliding or rolling sports equipment **4.** *vti* TRAVEL AS PASSENGER to travel as a passenger in a vehicle **5.** *vti* US TRAVEL IN ELEVATOR to travel in an elevator **6.** *vt* TRAVEL OVER AREA to travel across an area of land ○ *ride the range* **7.** *vt* BE IN RACE to take part in a race or other event on a horse or bike **8.** *vi* APPEAR TO BE FLOATING to appear to be floating in the sky or moving like a floating object ○ *riding the air currents* **9.** *vi* DO SOMETHING EFFORTLESSLY to do something successfully and apparently effortlessly, as if carried along by a wave ○ *riding on a tide of sympathy* **10.** *vi* DEPEND ON SOMETHING to depend on something for success ○ *Her future rides on this interview.* **11.** *vi* BE ALLOWED TO CONTINUE to continue without intervention or alteration ○ *Let it ride for now.* **12.** *vi* HANDLE WELL OR BADLY to function in a particular way while moving ○ *a car that rides well over rough ground* **13.** *vt* AUTOMOT PARTIALLY DEPRESS CLUTCH OR BRAKE to put your foot on the clutch or brake, partially depressing it, while driving **14.** *vt* NAUT, SWIMMING, SURFING RISE ON TOP OF WAVE to rise up on a wave and move forward with it **15.** *vti* NAUT ANCHOR to be moored with the anchor down, or moor a ship by dropping its anchor ○ *a ship riding at anchor* **16.** *vi* ENG BE SUPPORTED BY SOMETHING to be supported by something such as a pivot or an axle ○ *Most of the weight rides on the central shaft.* **17.** *vt* TEASE OR TORMENT SOMEBODY to tease or torment somebody with criticism or mockery (*informal*) ○ *riding me about my hair* ■ *n* **1.** JOURNEY BY VEHICLE OR ANIMAL a journey or outing in a motor vehicle or on an animal ○ *Let's go for a ride.* **2.** TRANSPORTATION IN VEHICLE a means of transportation as a passenger in a vehicle, especially when this is offered to somebody who would otherwise have to walk or use public transportation **3.** AUTOMOT QUALITY OF TRAVEL the quality of travel in a motor vehicle ○ *The new model offers a very smooth ride.* **4.** LEISURE FAIRGROUND ENTERTAINMENT an entertainment at an amusement park or carnival that offers a physically thrilling experience, e.g., a roller coaster **5.** RIDING, ROADS PATH FOR HORSES a broad grassy path where horses can be ridden **6.** MUSIC JAZZ CYMBAL one of the three cymbals in a drum set, used to keep time and mark rhythmic accents in jazz [Old English *rīdan* < Indo-European] —**rid·a·ble** *adj* ◇ **be riding high** to be enjoying a period or feeling of success ◇ **ride roughshod over somebody** to treat somebody very arrogantly without justice or consideration for his or her feelings ◇ **ride roughshod over something** to disregard a rule, law, or agreement ◇ **ride shotgun** to sit in the front passenger seat of a car (*informal*) ◇ **take somebody for a ride** to cheat or deceive somebody

ride down *vt* **1.** to hit and knock down somebody while riding, especially on horseback **2.** to catch up with or overtake somebody

ride out *vt* to manage to deal with a difficult situation successfully and survive without too much harm ○ *ride out the storm*

ride up *vi* to gradually move up out of the correct position ○ *Her skirt was riding up.*

Ride /rīd/, **Sally** (*b.* 1951) US astronaut. She was the first US woman to fly in space (1983). Full name **Ride, Sally Kirsten**

Ri·deau Hall /ri dṓ-/ *n* the official residence of the governor-general of Canada, in Ottawa

rid·er /rídər/ *n* **1.** SOMEBODY ON HORSE OR BIKE somebody who rides on an animal or a vehicle **2.** ADDITIONAL COMMENT an extra comment or clause added to a document or statement **3.** LAW ADDITIONAL CLAUSE TO BILL an extra clause added to a legislative bill, often not directly related to the main issue **4.** STRENGTHENING ELEMENT something that rests on or strengthens something else, e.g., the horizontal rail of a fence or additional timbers in the frame of a ship **5.** SPORTS SNOWBOARDER somebody riding a snowboard

rid·er·ship /rídər shìp/ *n* the number of passengers using a public transportation system

ride·shar·ing /rīd shèrring/ *n* an arrangement in which commuters take turns using their cars for going to work, taking one another as passengers to cut down the number of cars on the roads

ridge /rij/ *n* **1.** RAISED LAND FORMATION a long narrow hilltop or range of hills **2.** RAISED AREA ON OCEAN FLOOR an elevation on the ocean floor resembling a ridge on land and resulting from volcanic eruption along the fissures between tectonic plates **3.** RAISED STRIP a long narrow raised area of something **4.** TOP OF ROOF the line along the top of a roof or a tent where the two sloping sides meet **5.** METEOROL AREA OF HIGH PRESSURE a long area of high pressure in a weather system **6.** ANAT RAISED PART ON BONE a long narrow protuberance or crest, e.g., on a bone **7.** ZOOL BACKBONE OF ANIMAL the backbone of an animal, especially a whale ■ *v* (**ridged, ridg·ing, ridg·es**) **1.** *vt* FORM SOMETHING INTO RIDGES to mark or provide something with ridges, or make something into the shape of a ridge **2.** *vi* FORM A RIDGE to form or rise up into a ridge or series of ridges [Old English *hrycg* < Germanic, "back, spine"] —**ridg·y** *adj*

ridge·back /ríj bàk/ *n* ZOOL same as **Rhodesian ridgeback**

ridge·line /ríj lìn/ *n* GEOG same as **ridge** *n* (sense 1)

ridge·ling /ríjjling/, **ridg·ling** *n* a male animal in which one or both testes fail to descend into the scrotum at the usual time [Mid-16C. < dialect *ridgel* < ?]

ridge·pole /ríj pòl/ *n* **1.** a long beam of wood that runs along the ridge of a roof, supporting the upper ends of the rafters **2.** the horizontal pole supporting the top of a tent

ridge tent *n* a tent with rectangular sides that stands chiefly by suspension from a supported horizontal pole

ridg·ling *n* ZOOL another spelling of **ridgeling**

Ridg·way /ríj wày/, **Matthew Bunker** (1895–1993) US general. He commanded an airborne assault on Normandy (1944) during World War II and was supreme commander of United Nations ground forces in Korea (1951–52).

rid·i·cule /ríddi kyòol/ *vt* (**-culed, -cul·ing, -cules**) to reduce or dismiss the importance or quality of somebody or something in a contemptuous way ■ *n* mocking laughter, mimicry, or comments intended to make fun of somebody in a contemptuous way [Late 17C. Directly or via French < Latin *ridiculum* "joke" < *ridiculus* (see RIDICULOUS)]

SYNONYMS ***ridicule, deride, laugh, mock, make fun of, send up***

CORE MEANING: to belittle somebody or something by making them appear ridiculous

ridicule to reduce or dismiss the importance or quality of somebody or something in a contemptuous way ○ *His feat has been ridiculed by reporters, who question whether he really swam most of the way or actually came aboard his support boat.* **deride** to show contempt for somebody or something ○ *Critics have derided his recent works, but he still commands huge advances.* **laugh** to make scornful fun of somebody or something ○ *He laughed at our old-fashioned journalistic methods and called our newspapers "country sheets."* **mock** to treat somebody or something with scorn or contempt ○ *The emcee delights in mocking her narcissistic celebrity guests.* **make fun of** to make somebody or something appear ridiculous ○ *The children made fun of his shoes.* **send up** (*informal*) to make somebody or something appear ridiculous by humorous imitation ○ *We'd mercilessly send up Dad's complete incompetence with tools.*

ri·dic·u·lous /ri díkyələss/ *adj* **1.** completely unreasonable and not at all sensible or acceptable **2.** silly and amusing [Mid-16C. < Latin *ridiculus* "laughable" < *ridere* "to laugh"] —**ri·dic·u·lous·ly** *adv* —**ri·dic·u·lous·ness** *n*

rid·ing[1] /ríding/ *n* **1.** BEING ON HORSE the sport or hobby of sitting on a horse and controlling it as it moves along **2.** TRAVELING ON ANIMAL OR VEHICLE the act of traveling on an animal or vehicle ■ *adj* USED ON HORSEBACK used while riding a horse ○ *riding breeches* [13C. < RIDE]

rid·ing[2] /ríding/ *n* **1.** in Canada, a constituency represented by either a federal member of parliament or a member of the provincial legislature **2.** *also* **Rid·ing** one of the three administrative districts into which the former British county of Yorkshire was split [Pre-12C. < Old Norse *þriðungr* "third part" < *þriði* "third"]

rid·ing coat *n* a coat with cutaway front and tails worn in the 19th century for riding

rid·ing crop *n* a straight short riding whip with a loop at the end

rid·ing hab·it *n* an outfit worn for horseback riding

Rid·ing Moun·tain Na·tion·al Park /ríding-/ national park in southwestern Manitoba, Canada. Area: 1,148 sq. mi./2,973 sq. km.

rid·ley /ríddlee/ (*plural* **-leys**) *n* a small turtle, especially the gray-shelled Kemp's ridley found in the Atlantic, or the larger greenish olive ridley found in the Pacific [Early 20C. Origin ?]

ri·dot·to /ri dóttō/ (*plural* **-tos**) *n* a musical entertainment with dancing, popular in England in the 18th century [Early 18C. Via Italian, "retreat, entertainment" < medieval Latin *reductus* < past participle of Latin *reducere* (see REDUCE)]

rie·beck·ite /reébə kìt, reé be-/ *n* a blue-black silicate mineral of the amphibole group containing iron and sodium. Source: acidic igneous rocks, schists. [Late 19C. After Emil *Riebeck* (1853–85), German explorer]

Rief·en·stahl /reéf'n staal, -shtaal/, **Leni** (1902–2003) German movie director and photographer. Her documentaries of a Nazi rally and of the 1936 Berlin Olympic Games glorified the Nazis, but are nevertheless masterpieces of cinematic technique. Born **Riefenstahl, Helena Bertha Amalie**

ri·el /ree él/ *n* the main unit of Cambodian currency. See table at **currency** [Mid-20C. < Khmer]

Ri·el /ree él/, **Louis David** (1844–85) Canadian political leader. He headed provisional governments of Manitoba (1869, 1885), and led the North West Rebellion.

Rie·mann /reémən, reé maan/, **Georg Friedrich Bernhard** (1826–66) German mathematician. He studied function theory and developed a system of geometry relevant to modern theoretical physics.

Rie·mann·ian ge·om·e·try /ree maánee ən-/ *n* a non-Euclidean geometry in which it is assumed that in a plane all pairs of straight lines intersect

rien incorrect spelling of **rein**

Ries·ling /réezling, réessling/ *n* **1.** a fruity dry to sweet white wine made from a variety of white grape grown mainly in Germany, Austria, Alsace, and Australia **2.** a white grape that is used to make Riesling [Mid-19C. < German]

Ries·man /réessmən/, **David** (1909–2002) US sociologist. His controversial work *The Lonely Crowd* (1950) describes a US society evolving from individualism to conformism.

rif /rif/ (**rif·fed, rif·fing, rifs**) *vt* to lay off members of a workforce or to be laid off (*informal*) [< RIF]

RIF *n US* the laying off of members of a workforce. Full form **reduction in force**

ri·fam·pin /ri fámpin/, **ri·fam·pi·cin** /ri fámpissin/ *n* a semisynthetic derivative of rifamycin that works by interfering with RNA synthesis in the infecting bacteria Use: treatment of bacterial infections, especially tuberculosis [Mid-20C. Blend of RIFAMYCIN + PIPERAZINE]

rif·a·my·cin /riffə mīss'n/ *n* an antibiotic belonging to a group originally isolated from the soil bacterium *Streptomyces mediterranei.* Use: treatment of leprosy, tuberculosis, other bacterial infections. [Mid-20C. Probably < Italian *riformare* "to reform" < *formare* "to form" < Latin (see REFORM)]

rife /rīf/ *adj* **1.** found widely, or frequently ○ *areas where poverty is rife* ○ *Rumors were rife that the factory was about to be closed down.* **2.** full of something undesirable, or experiencing a widespread and very frequent occurrence of something, especially something undesirable ○ *an organization rife with corruption* [Old English *rȳfe* < Germanic] —**rife·ly** *adv* —**rife·ness** *n*

SYNONYMS See ***widespread.***

riff /rif/ *n* **1. SERIES OF NOTES** a short, often repeated series of notes in pop music or jazz that forms a distinctive part of the accompaniment **2. QUIP** a quick, witty remark, especially one that is part of a rapid exchange ■ *vi* (**riffed, riff·ing, riffs**) **USE RIFFS** to play or make use of riffs as a musical accompaniment to something [Early 20C. Probably shortening of RIFFLE]

Rif·fi·an /ríffee ən/ *n* a dialect of Berber spoken in Morocco, especially in the Riff Mountains of northern Morocco [Mid-19C. < the *Riff*, Mountains] —**Rif·fi·an** *adj*

rif·fle /ríff'l/ *v* (**-fled, -fling, -fles**) **1.** *vti* **FLICK THROUGH PAGES** to flick through the pages of a book, magazine, or newspaper, glancing casually at the contents **2.** *vt* **SHUFFLE CARDS** to shuffle playing cards by halving the deck, lifting the corners, and flicking the cards so that they overlap as they fall **3.** *vi* **BECOME CHOPPY** to become rough and choppy when passing over submerged rocks (*refers to water*) ○ *Water riffles over the rocks.* ■ *n* **1. QUICK LOOK AT BOOK** a quick flick through the pages of a book, magazine, or newspaper **2. SHUFFLING OF CARDS** the shuffling of playing cards **3.** *US* **SUBMERGED ROCKS OR SANDBAR** an area of rocks or a sandbar lying just below the surface of the water **4. ROUGH WATER** an area of rough water caused by submerged rocks or a sandbar **5. GROOVED PART OF SLUICE** the bottom part of a sluice that has grooves for collecting gold or other mineral particles [Mid-18C. < ?]

rif·fler /rífflər/ *n* a curved file for smoothing concave surfaces [Late 18C. < French *rifloir* < *rifler* "to scratch"]

riff·raff /ríf ràf/ *n* **1.** an offensive term that deliberately insults somebody's social status, importance, and manners (*insult*) **2.** rubbish or worthless objects (*informal*) [15C. < French *rif et raf* "pieces of plunder of small value" < *rifler* "plunder" and *raffler* "snatch"]

ri·fle[1] /rīf'l/ *n* **1. LONG GUN** a gun with a long barrel that is fired from the shoulder. Spiral grooves inside the barrel make the bullet spin, improving its accuracy over a long distance. **2. CANNON** a large cannon with spirals cut into the bore ■ **ri·fles, Ri·fles** *npl* **SOLDIERS WITH RIFLES** a unit of soldiers armed with rifles ■ *vt* (**-fled, -fling, -fles**) **1. CUT GROOVE IN GUN BARREL** to cut spiral grooves on the inside of a gun barrel **2. THROW VERY FAST BALL** to hit or throw a ball hard, making it travel very fast [Late 17C. < French *rifler* "scratch"]

ri·fle[2] /rīf'l/ (**-fled, -fling, -fles**) *v* **1.** *vti* to search through something, e.g., a drawer or room, vigorously, hurriedly, and recklessly, often leaving things in disorder, sometimes with the intent to steal **2.** *vt* to rob or plunder somebody or something [14C. < French *rifler* "plunder, scratch"] —**ri·fler** *n*

ri·fle·bird /rīf'l bùrd/ *n* a bird of paradise, the male of which performs an elaborate courtship dance. Native to: Australia, New Guinea. Genus: *Ptiloris.* [Mid-19C. *Rifle* < ?]

ri·fle gre·nade *n* a grenade propelled to its target by a rifle-fired bullet, requiring special adapting hardware

ri·fle·man /rīf'lmən/ (*plural* **-men** /-mən/) *n* **1.** a soldier, especially a man, who has been trained to use a rifle, or who is a member of a unit armed with rifles **2.** somebody, especially a man, skilled in the use of a rifle

ri·fle range *n* an area with targets where people can practice shooting rifles

ri·fle·ry /rīf'lree/ *n US* **1.** the skill or practice of firing rifles **2.** fire from rifles

ri·fle·scope /rīf'l skōp/ *n* a telescopic sight designed to be used on a rifle [Mid-20C. < RIFLE[1] + TELESCOPE]

ri·fle·wom·an /rīf'l wòomman/ (*plural* **-wom·en** /-wìmmin/) *n* **1.** a woman skilled in the use of a rifle **2.** a female soldier who has been trained to use a rifle, or who is a member of a unit armed with rifles

ri·fling /rīfling/ *n* **1.** the cutting of spiral grooves in the barrel of a gun **2.** a series of spiral grooves cut in the barrel of a gun

rift[1] /rift/ *n* **1. GAP OR BREAK** a gap or break in something where it has split apart **2. DISAGREEMENT** a serious disagreement that disrupts good relations **3.** GEOL same as **fault** *n* (sense 6) ■ *vti* (**rift·ed, rift·ing, rifts**) **SPLIT APART** to split apart, or make something split apart [14C. < N Germanic]

rift[2] /rift/ *n US* **1.** a shallow, often rapidly flowing area of water **2.** the backward flow of water caused by a wave when it breaks [Early 18C. Probably < Dutch *rif* "ridge"]

rift val·ley *n* a valley formed by geologic faulting, where the land between two parallel faults drops down to give a broad central plain with steep sides

rift zone *n* an area of Earth's surface, often associated with the margins of continental plates, that is especially heavily faulted and may be subject to earth tremors

rig[1] /rig/ *vt* (**rigged, rig·ging, rigs**) **1. EQUIP VESSEL WITH RIGGING** to fit out a boat or its mast with sails and rigging **2. ERECT SOMETHING** to erect, set up, or assemble something so that it is ready for use ○ *rig the antenna* **3. MAKE SOMETHING HASTILY** to construct something temporary but serviceable, usually in haste and without the proper materials ○ *rigged up a makeshift shelter* **4.** same as **rig out** (*informal*) ■ *n* **1. ARRANGEMENT OF SAILS AND MASTS** the arrangement of sails and masts on a boat **2. DRILLING STRUCTURE FOR OIL** a structure and the apparatus used for drilling for oil and gas **3. SPECIALIST EQUIPMENT** the special equipment used for an activity, especially fishing tackle or the radio equipment used by an amateur radio operator **4. CLOTHES** an outfit that somebody is wearing (*informal*) **5. BIG TRUCK** a tractor-trailer, or a tractor without a trailer (*informal*) **6.** *US* **HORSE CARRIAGE** in former times, a carriage or cart pulled by one or more horses [15C. Probably < N Germanic]

rig out *vt* (*informal*) **1.** to put a special kind of clothing on somebody ○ *rigged himself out for a heavyweight bout* **2.** to fit a person, place, or object with proper or necessary equipment ○ *rigged out for a long mountain biking trip*

rig[2] /rig/ (*informal*) *vt* (**rigged, rig·ging, rigs**) to affect the outcome of something by intervening dishonestly or unfairly to gain an advantage ○ *tried to rig the election* ■ *n* a trick or swindle [Early 18C. < ?]

rig[3] /rig/ *n* a male animal in which one or both testes fail to descend into the scrotum at the usual time. The condition is most common in horses and pigs. (*informal*) [15C. Variant of RIDGE]

Ri·ga /réegə/ capital city of Latvia, in the east of the country, on the Baltic Sea. Population: 764,328 (2000).

rig·a·doon /riggə dóon/, **rig·au·don** /rée gaw dáwN/ *n* **1.** a French dance for couples in duple or quadruple time. Originally a traditional dance from the Provence region, it became popular in the 17th and 18th centuries at the French court, where it was danced in a more dignified manner. **2.** the music for a rigadoon [Late 17C. < French *rigaudon*]

rig·a·ma·role *n* same as **rigmarole**

rig·a·to·ni /riggə tónee/ *n* short rounded tubes of pasta with narrow ridges running along them [Mid-20C. < Italian < *rigato* "ridged," past participle of *rigare* "draw a line" < *riga* "line"]

rig·au·don *n* DANCE, MUSIC same as **rigadoon**

Ri·gel /rījəl/ *n* a blue-white double star in the constellation Orion [< Arabic *rijl* "foot," because it appears at the base of the constellation]

rig·ger /ríggər/ *n* **1. RIGGED SHIP** a ship with a specific kind of rigging (*usually used in combination*) ○ *square-rigger* **2. SOMEBODY WHO RIGS BOATS** somebody whose job is to rig a sailboat **3. BRACKET ON ROWBOAT** a bracket supporting an oarlock on a rowboat **4. SCAFFOLDING WORKER** somebody whose job is to erect and maintain scaffolding and lifting equipment **5. OIL-RIG WORKER** a worker on an oil or gas rig **6. LARGE CRANE FOR LIFTING** a mechanized crane used for hoisting very large and heavy construction materials to great heights [Early 17C. < RIG[1]]

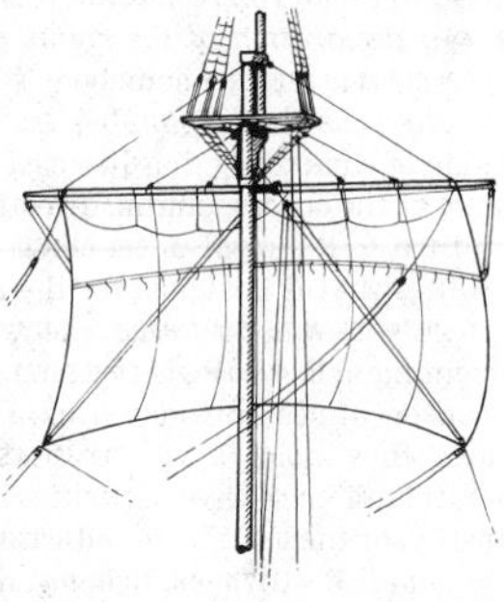

rigging

rig·ging /rígging/ *n* **1. ROPES, WIRES, AND PULLEYS** the ropes, wires, and pulleys that support the masts and control the sails of a boat **2. THEATER EQUIPMENT** the system of ropes, pulleys, and other equipment used to shift scenery on a stage **3. SUPPORTING EQUIPMENT** a system of ropes, pulleys, or other equipment used as a support for something, e.g., construction scaffolding [15C. < RIG[1]]

rig·ging loft *n* **1.** a raised area or gallery in a boatyard where workers stand while fitting rigging **2.** an area above a stage equipped with lifting gear for raising and lowering scenery

right /rīt/ *adj* **1. CORRECT** accurate, or consistent with the facts or general belief ○ *gave the right answer* **2. HAVING CORRECT OPINION** holding a correct opinion about somebody or something ○ *hard to tell who's right in this situation* **3. PROPER** correct with regard to use, function, or operation ○ *You're not holding the thing by the right end.* ○ *It has to be stored right side up.* **4. MORALLY GOOD** morally justified and correct, or consistent with generally held ideas of morality and proper conduct ○ *I only wanted to do what is right.* **5. USUAL** in the usual or expected state, or in a desirable state for good functioning or good relations ○ *Something didn't seem right when I walked in.* ○ *You can't expect to put everything right overnight.* **6. BEST** most suitable or desirable ○ *waiting for the right offer to come along* **7. HEALTHY** in good physical and mental health ○ *hasn't felt right in weeks* **8. PROMINENT** prominent in business, society, or some other sphere ○ *knows all the right people* **9. EAST WHEN FACING NORTH** on the side of the body that is east when you face north, or on the corresponding side of an object **10. FITTING RIGHT HAND OR FOOT** designed to fit the right hand, foot, arm, or leg **11.** *also* **Right RIGHT-WING** holding generally conservative political views and tending to be cautious about social change **12.** MATH **PERPENDICULAR** being perpendicular or forming an angle of 90° **13.** *UK* **TOTAL** complete and utter (*informal*) ○ *felt a right fool* ■ *adv* **1. PROPERLY** in the best and most effective way, or a way that will be successful ○ *You didn't do it right.* **2. CORRECTLY** accurately with regard to fact ○ *If you'd answered right you would have won $100.* **3. MORALLY AND APPROPRIATELY** in a way that is morally good or acceptable, or conducive to somebody's benefit or happiness ○ *treat sb right* **4. DESIRABLY** desirably or advantageously ○ *afraid that it won't turn out right* **5. COMPLETELY** used to emphasize how completely something happens, or that something is situated at, or moves or extends to, an extreme point ○ *went right through the wall* ○ *right at the end of the book* ○ *reaches right across the room* **6. IMMEDIATELY** used to emphasize the immediacy with which something happens or should happen ○ *You'll do it right this minute.* **7. EXACTLY** used to emphasize the preciseness of something ○ *right in the middle* ○ *right at that moment* **8. DIRECTLY** without deviating from a course ○ *Keep right on down this road.* **9. TOWARD EAST WHEN FACING NORTH** in or toward the east when you are facing or moving north, and correspondingly for other directions ○ *turn right at the church* **10. USED AS PART OF TITLE** used as part of a title of respect ○ *Right Reverend* **11.** *regional* same as **very** ○ *a right good deal* ■ *n* **1. MORALLY APPROPRIATE THING** that which is morally good or in accordance with accepted principles of justice, fairness, and honesty ○ *She's too young to know right from wrong.* ○ *Right will prevail!* **2. ENTITLEMENT OR FREEDOM** a justified claim or entitlement, or the freedom to do something (*often used in the plural*) ○ *You're within your rights to complain.* ○ *a declaration of the rights of civilized people* **3.** LAW **CLAIM TO PROPERTY** somebody's interest in a property (*often used in the plural*) **4. EAST WHEN FACING NORTH** the side of something that lies east when it is facing north, or the corresponding direction **5. RIGHT-HAND TURN** a turn to the right **6. ONE OF PAIR** the one of a pair of things that is designed for the right hand or foot **7. BLOW MADE WITH RIGHT HAND** a blow delivered with the right hand **8.** *also* **Right CONSERVATIVES AS GROUP** political conservatives considered as a group, or the opinions they hold **9.** FIN **SECURITIES OPTION** an option to purchase or receive securities not offered for sale openly, or the certificate indicating it (*often used in the plural*) ■ *v* (**right·ed, right·ing, rights**) **1.** *vti* **MAKE OR BECOME UPRIGHT** to put something upright, or return to an upright position ○ *I righted the vase and mopped up the water.* **2.** *vt* **IMPROVE SOMETHING** to return something to its normal, well-functioning state, or bring it to a better or more equitable one ○ *She did everything she could to right the situation.* **3.** *vt* **MAKE AMENDS FOR WRONG** to redress an error or misdeed ■ *interj* (*informal*) **1. OK** used to indicate assent or understanding ○ *Right, I'm with you now.* **2. IS THAT SO?** used to ask for confirmation of a statement ○ *You just got here, right?* [Old English *riht* < Indo-European, "go straight"] —**right·a·ble** *adj* —**right·er** *n* —**right·ness** *n* ◇ **by rights** if things were justly or correctly done ○ *By rights, he should be head teacher by now.* ◇ **have** *or* **catch somebody dead to rights** to catch a criminal in the act of committing a crime (*informal*) ◇ **in the right** correct in what you say or do, especially legally or morally justified in saying or doing it ◇ **in your own right** because of your birth, ability, or other entitlement, without reference to anyone else ◇ **set** *or* **put somebody right 1.** to restore somebody to good health **2.** to make the true facts or the truth of a situation clear to somebody ◇ **set** *or* **put something to rights** to put something into a correct or well-ordered state

SPELLCHECK right, rite, or **write**? Do not confuse the spelling of ***right, rite,*** and ***write,*** which sound similar. ***Right*** has the widest range of usage, meaning "correct, true, proper" (as in *the right answer*), "not left" (as in *turn right at the church*), "entitlement" (as in *human rights, right of way*), or "make upright, correct, just, etc." (as in *righting wrongs*). ***Rite*** is only used as a noun, denoting a ceremonial or formal procedure, as in *religious rites such as baptism and marriage, the rites of passage that mark the transition from childhood to adulthood.* ***Write*** is only used as a verb, meaning "form letters or words" or "create a piece of text or music": *Write your address on the back. She's writing her autobiography.*

right·a·bout /rítə bòwt/ *n* a turn through 180° to face in the opposite direction ■ *adj, adv* facing in the opposite direction

right an·gle *n* an angle of 90° —**right-an·gled** *adj* ◇ **at right angles** placed at an angle of 90° to something or forming an angle of 90° with something

right-an·gled tri·an·gle *n UK* same as **right triangle**

right as·cen·sion *n* one of the two reference points in the equatorial coordinate system for specifying the position of an astronomical object on the celestial sphere. Corresponding to longitude on the Earth, it is measured in hours, minutes, and seconds eastward from the vernal equinox, the point where the ecliptic intersects the celestial equator.

right a·tri·o·ven·tric·u·lar valve *n* ANAT same as **tricuspid valve**

right a·way *adv* immediately, without waiting or any delay

Right Bank /rīt-/ a residential and commercial area north of the Seine River in central Paris, near the Champs-Élysées

right-brain *adj* relating to or involving the emotions or creative ability, these being believed to be associated with the right half of the cerebrum

right cir·cu·lar cone *n* MATH same as **cone** *n* (sense 2)

right-click *vi* to press and release the right-hand button of a computer mouse

right·eous /ríchəss/ *adj* **1. STRICTLY OBSERVANT OF MORALITY** always behaving according to a religious or moral code **2. JUSTIFIABLE** considered to be correct or justifiable **3. RESPONDING TO INJUSTICE** arising from the perception of great injustice or wrongdoing ○ *righteous indignation* **4.** *US* **GREAT** good or outstanding (*dated slang*) ■ *npl* **MORALLY UPRIGHT PEOPLE** righteous people viewed as a group ○ *believing that the righteous will prevail* [Old English *rihtwīs* < earlier forms of RIGHT + -WISE] —**right·eous·ly** *adv* —**right·eous·ness** *n*

right face *US n* a military command to turn 90° to the right ■ *interj* used as a military command to turn 90° to the right

right field *n* **1.** the right side of the outfield on a baseball field, when looking from home plate **2.** in baseball, the position of the player responsible for fielding balls hit to right field —**right field·er** *n*

right-foot·ed *adj* **1.** having a natural tendency to lead with or use the right foot, especially in playing sports such as soccer **2.** performed using the right foot ○ *a right-footed shot onto the goal*

right·ful /rítfəl/ *adj* **1. HAVING CLAIM** with a legal or moral claim to something ○ *the rightful owner* **2. OWNED BY SOMEBODY WITH RIGHT** owned by somebody who has a right to it ○ *rightful property* **3. FAIR** considered to be right and fair ○ *a rightful objection* —**right·ful·ly** *adv* —**right·ful·ness** *n*

right hand *n* **1.** the side of something that lies east when it is facing north, or the corresponding direction **2.** somebody who is of invaluable help to another person

right-hand *adj* **1. ON OR TO RIGHT** on the right or leading toward the right **2. FOR RIGHT HAND** designed for or done with the right hand **3. MOST IMPORTANT AND TRUSTED** most important and trusted, and relied upon to the greatest extent

right-hand·ed *adj* **1. PREFERRING TO USE RIGHT HAND** using the right hand in preference to the left for writing, throwing, and other activities that require skill and careful control **2. DONE WITH RIGHT HAND** carried out with the right hand **3. DESIGNED FOR RIGHT HAND** designed to be done with or used by the right hand **4. MOVING TOWARD RIGHT** turning toward the right in a clockwise direction **5.** BASEBALL **SWINGING BAT TO LEFT** swinging a bat or other implement to the left ■ *adv* **1. WITH RIGHT HAND** using the right hand **2. TOWARD LEFT** with a swing or direction toward the left ○ *hit a ball right-handed* —**right-hand·ed·ly** *adv* —**right-hand·ed·ness** *n*

right-hand·er *n* **1.** a right-handed person, especially an athlete **2.** a blow delivered with the right hand

Right Hon·our·a·ble *n Can* a title of respect used to refer to the governor general, prime minister, or chief justice of Canada, and other eminent Canadians

right·ist /rítist/ *adj* favoring or relating to political conservatism ■ *n* somebody with politically conservative views —**right·ism** *n*

right·ly /rítlee/ *adv* **1. CORRECTLY** correctly, properly, and appropriately ○ *As you quite rightly said, we agreed to this at the last meeting.* **2. UNDERSTANDABLY** with very good reason ○ *She was furious, and quite rightly so!* **3. CERTAINLY** certainly or positively (*informal*) ○ *I don't rightly know.*

right-mind·ed *adj* with opinions and attitudes considered to be sensible and fair —**right-mind·ed·ly** *adv* —**right-mind·ed·ness** *n*

right·most /rít mōst/ *adj* in the position that is farthest to the right

right off *adv* immediately, without waiting or any delay

right of search *n* the right of a country at war to stop and search the merchant ships of neutral nations to determine if they are carrying forbidden goods that may be seized

right of way *n* **1. PERMISSION TO GO FIRST** the legal or accepted right of a vehicle or craft to proceed ahead of another **2. RIGHT TO CROSS PROPERTY** the right to cross somebody else's property by a specific route, e.g., as a means of accessing your own property **3. LAWFUL ROUTE ACROSS SOMEBODY'S PROPERTY** a lawful route that may be taken across somebody else's property **4. LAND USED FOR ROAD OR LINE** a narrow length of land used for the route of a railroad, electric power line, or public road

right on *interj* used to show enthusiastic agreement with something said or done (*dated informal*)

right-on *adj* **1.** socially and politically fashionable and forward-looking, particularly in a way that corresponds to the attitudes of the political left (*dated informal*) **2.** perfectly true (*informal*)

Right Rev·er·end *n* a form of address for a Roman Catholic, Anglican, or Episcopal bishop, or for a Roman Catholic abbot or cleric with the title "M"

right shoul·der arms *n* the command or act of bringing a weapon to rest on the right shoulder during a military drill

rights is·sue *n* an instance of an organization offering stock to existing holders on favorable terms so that they can maintain their percentage share of ownership

right-size *vi* to bring a company to what is considered to be its optimal size, usually by dismissing some of its employees —**right-siz·ing** *n*

right stuff *n* exactly the psychological and physical characteristics called for by a task (*informal*)

right-think·ing *adj* same as **right-minded**

right-to-life *adj* SOC SCI same as **pro-life**

right-to-work *adj* relating to the right of workers to gain or keep a job regardless of whether they belong to a union

right tri·an·gle *n* a triangle having one angle that is a right angle

right·ward /rítwərd/ *adj* moving toward or positioned on the right ■ *adv also* **right·wards** /-wərdz/ in a direction toward the right

right whale *n* a large-headed whale with a deeply curved jawline and notched tail. Native to: North Atlantic, Pacific Ocean. Family: Balaenidae. [Early 18C. Because once regarded as the "right" whale to harpoon and kill]

right wing *n* **1. CONSERVATIVE** those members of a group or political party who hold more conservative views than the others **2. PLAYER OR POSITION AT RIGHT** in some team games, the space or position on the right-hand side of a playing area when facing an opponent, or a player who plays in this area **3. RIGHT-HAND SECTION OF MILITARY FORCE** the right-hand part or position of a military force while facing the enemy

right-wing *adj* **1.** POL **CONSERVATIVE** conservative in conviction or temperament **2.** SPORTS **POSITIONED ON RIGHT FACING OPPONENT** in some games, occupying the right-hand part of a playing area when facing an opponent **3.** MIL **OCCUPYING RIGHT DURING MILITARY ENGAGEMENT** occupying the right-hand part or position of a military force when it is facing the enemy —**right-wing·er** *n*

right·y /rítee/ *US* (*informal*) *n* (*plural* **-ies**) **1.** RIGHT-HANDED PERSON somebody who is right-handed **2.** POL RIGHT-WING PERSON somebody with right-wing views ■ *adv* WITH RIGHT HAND using the right hand

rig·id /ríjjid/ *adj* **1.** FIRM AND STIFF not bending or easily moved into a different shape or position ○ *lengths of rigid plastic pipe* **2.** INFLEXIBLE applied or carried out strictly, with no allowances or exceptions ○ *a rigid set of rules* **3.** INFLEXIBLY ADHERED TO kept unchanged and strictly adhered to ○ *rigid opinions* **4.** REFUSING TO CHANGE unwilling to change or adapt behavior, opinions, or attitudes ○ *Despite arguments to the contrary, she remained rigid in her stand.* [15C. < Latin *rigidus* < *rigere* "be stiff"] —**ri·gid·i·ty** /ri jíddətee/ *n* —**rig·id·ly** *adv* —**rig·id·ness** *n*

rig·id des·ig·na·tor *n* in philosophy, a name that stands for the same thing in every possible world as opposed to a description that could stand for somebody or something else in some possible world

ri·gid·i·fy /ri jíddi fī/ (**-fied, -fy·ing, -fies**) *vti* to become stiff and inflexible, or cause something to become stiff and inflexible

rig·ma·role /rígmə rōl/, **rig·a·ma·role** /ríggəmə-/ *n* **1.** an irritating, tedious, or confusing sequence of tasks, especially tasks that seem unnecessary or absurd **2.** a tediously long, complicated, or unhelpful explanation [Mid-18C. Probably alteration of *ragman roll*, parchment scroll used in the gambling game of *ragman*]

ORIGIN A *ragman roll* was a parchment scroll used in a medieval gambling game. The roll had things such as names written on it, with pieces of string attached to them, and participants had to select a string at random. The word *ragman* may have been a contraction of *ragged man*, perhaps in allusion to the appearance of the scroll, with all its bits of string hanging from it. *Ragman roll* eventually came to be used for any list or catalog, and *ragman* itself denoted a "long rambling discourse" in 16th-century Scottish English – a meaning that seems to have transferred itself eventually to ***rigmarole***.

rig·or /ríggər/ *n* **1.** SEVERITY OR HARSHNESS unrelenting strictness or toughness in dealing with people or things and an unwillingness to make allowances **2.** USE OF DEMANDING STANDARDS the application of precise and exacting standards in the doing of something **3.** HARDSHIP an experience of great hardship or difficulty (*usually used in the plural*) ○ *the rigors of life on the battlefront* **4.** SEVERE WEATHER harshness of weather or climate **5.** RIGIDITY OF BODY stiffness and lack of response to stimuli in body organs or tissues **6.** SUDDEN FEELING OF CHILLINESS an abrupt attack of shivering and coldness, typically marking a rise in body temperature, e.g., at the onset of fever **7.** BOT INERTIA IN PLANTS insensitivity of a plant arising from unfavorable conditions **8.** MED same as **rigor mortis** (*informal*) [14C. Directly or via French < Latin, "stiffness" < *rigere* "be stiff"]

rig·or·ism /ríggə rìzzəm/ *n* **1.** great strictness or severity **2.** in Roman Catholic philosophy, the theory that in matters of moral choice the stricter course should be taken —**rig·or·is·tic** /riggə rístik/ *adj*

rig·or mor·tis /-máwrtiss/ *n* the progressive stiffening of the body that occurs several hours after death as a result of the coagulation of protein in the muscles. It usually starts to wane after about 24 hours. [< Latin, "stiffness of death"]

rig·or·ous /ríggərəss/ *adj* **1.** STRICT, HARSH, OR UNRELENTING characterized by unrelenting demands, and allowing little or no scope for variation or relaxation ○ *a rigorous training program* **2.** EXACTING extremely precise and exacting ○ *rigorous standards of cleanliness* **3.** SEVERE experienced as severe or extreme ○ *climbing in rigorous conditions* **4.** LOGIC PRECISE precise and formalized ○ *a rigorous proof* —**ri·gor·ous·ly** *adv* —**rig·or·ous·ness** *n*

rig·our *n* Can, UK spelling of **rigor**

Rig-Ve·da /rig váydə, rig véedə/ *n* a large collection of Hindu hymns dating from 2,000 B.C. or earlier [Late 18C. < Sanskrit *ṛgvedaḥ* < *ṛc* "verse" + *vedaḥ* "knowledge" (see VEDA)]

Riis /reess/, **Jacob** (1849–1914) Danish-born US journalist and social reformer. He reported on life in overcrowded areas of US cities.

Ri·je·ka /ree yékə/ city and port in northwestern Croatia, situated on the Gulf of Kvarner, on the Adriatic Sea. Population: 167,964 (1991).

rijst·ta·fel /rī́ss taaf'l/, **rijs·ta·fel** *n* a Dutch meal of Indonesian origin based on rice with many small side dishes such as Indonesian-style curry, seafood, satay, soups, sauces, and condiments [Late 19C. < Dutch < *rijs* "rice" + *tafel* "table"]

ri·ki·shi /ríki shée/ (*plural same*) *n* a sumo wrestler [Early 20C. < Japanese, "strength warrior"]

rile /rīl/ (**riled, ril·ing, riles**) *vt* **1.** to irritate somebody enough that it provokes anger (*informal; often passive*) **2.** to stir up water or other liquid violently [Early 19C. Variant of ROIL]

Ri·ley /rílee/ [Early 20C. < ?] ◇ **the life of Riley** a comfortable well-off life with no worries

Ri·ley /rílee/, **Bridget** (*b.* 1931) British painter. She was a leading figure in the 1960s art movement known as op art. Full name **Riley, Bridget Louise**

Ri·ley, James Whitcomb (1849–1916) US poet. Best known for his Hoosier dialect and whimsical sense of humor, he published several collections of poems.

> "The ripest peach is highest on the tree."
> [James Whitcomb Riley, "The Ripest Peach"]

ri·lie·vo *n* ARTS another spelling of **relievo**

Ril·ke /rílkə/, **Rainer Maria** (1875–1926) Bohemian-born German poet. The mystic lyricism and precise imagery of his verse exerted a profound influence on 20th-century poetry. His works include *Duino Elegies* and *Sonnets to Orpheus* (both 1923).

> "We need in love to practice only this: letting each other go. For holding on comes easily; we do not need to learn it."
> [Rainer Maria Rilke, *Requiem für eine Freundin (Requiem for a Friend)*; 1908]

rill /ril/ *n* **1.** STREAM a little stream or brook **2.** GROOVE IN SOIL a small channel cut in soil **3.** *also* **rille** TRENCH ON MOON a long narrow valley on the Moon's surface **4.** GARDEN FEATURE an artificial channel, often a straight and narrow one, along which water is made to flow, used in landscaping a garden ■ *vt* FORM CHANNELS IN FIELD to form small channels in a plowed field as a result of the runoff of rainwater [Mid-16C. < Low German *rille* < Indo-European, "run"]

rill·et /rílət/ *n* **1.** a little brook or stream **2.** a short narrow valley on the Moon's surface

ril·lettes /ri léts/ *n* seasoned pork or goose cooked in its own fat until very tender and potted as a type of soft spreadable pâté (*takes a singular or plural verb*) [Late 19C. < French, "small pieces of pork" < *rille* "piece of pork," variant of *reille* "board" < Latin *regula* "straight stick, standard"]

rim /rim/ *n* **1.** OUTER EDGE OF SOMETHING CIRCULAR an outer edge, often slightly raised, that runs along the outside of something curved or circular **2.** PART AROUND WHEEL'S EDGE the curved outer edge of a wheel of a motor vehicle or bicycle **3.** PART OF GLASSES FRAME a usually curved part that holds and forms an edge to lenses in a pair of glasses **4.** HOOP FOR BASKETBALL NET the metal hoop to which a basketball net is attached **5.** LIMIT the farthest limit of something (*literary*) ○ *a novel that probes the rim of human imagination* ■ *vt* (**rimmed, rim·ming, rims**) FORM OUTER EDGE to form an edge, usually a slightly raised edge, along the edge of something curved or circular [Old English *rima* "border, coast" < ?] —**rimmed** *adj*

ri·maye /ri máy/ *n* GEOG same as **bergschrund** [Early 20C. < French, "group of fissures" < Latin *rima* (see RIMOSE)]

Rim·baud /ram bō, raN-/, **Arthur** (1854–91) French poet. Although he stopped writing at only 19 years of age, his poems were an important influence upon symbolism. Full name **Rimbaud, Jean Nicholas Arthur**

> "I have bathed in the Poem / Of the Sea, immersed in stars, and milky, / Devouring the green azures."
> [Arthur Rimbaud, *Le Bateau ivre (The Drunken Boat)*; 1871]

rime[1] /rīm/ *n* a thin coating of frost formed on cold objects exposed to fog or cloud ■ *vt* (**rimed, rim·ing, rimes**) to cover something with a thin frost or with something resembling it (*often passive*) [Old English *hrīm* < Germanic] —**rim·y** *adj*

rime[2] /rīm/ LITERAT (*archaic*) *n* same as **rhyme** ■ *vti* (**rimed, rim·ing, rimes**) same as **rhyme** *v* [Early variant]

rime riche /reém réesh/ *n* the use of rhyme in which stressed syllables or words are identical in pronunciation, as in "weigh" and "away" [< French, "rich rhyme"]

rim·fire /rím fīr/ *adj* describes a firearm designed for or using a cartridge with its primer located in the rim of the base, rather than in the center

Ri·mi·ni /rímmənee/ city and port in Forli Province, Emilia-Romagna Region, northern Italy, on the Adriatic Sea. Population: 128,656 (2001).

ri·mose /rī móss, rī mòss/ *adj* covered with cracks, fissures, or crevices [Early 18C. < Latin *rimosus* < *rima* "fissure" < Indo-European, "to scratch"] —**ri·mose·ly** *adv* —**ri·mos·i·ty** /rī móssətee/ *n*

Ri·mous·ki /ri mo͞oskee/ town in Canada, in Quebec State, on the St. Lawrence River, northeast of Quebec City. Population: 35,561 (2001).

rim·rock /rím ròk/ *n* a layer of rock that forms a vertical boundary to a plateau, valley, or deposit of gravel

Rim·sky-Kor·sa·kov /rìmskee káwrssə kàwf/, **Nikolay** (1844–1908) Russian composer. He was renowned as a consummate orchestrator. His works, often inspired by Russian folk music, include *Scheherazade* (1888). Full name **Rimsky-Korsakov, Nikolay Andreyevich**

rind /rīnd/ *n* **1.** the thick tough outer skin of a fruit **2.** a tough outer protective layer of a food product such as a cheese [Old English *rind(e)* "something torn off" < Indo-European, "to tear"]

rin·der·pest /ríndər pèst/ *n* a sometimes fatal viral disease mainly affecting cattle, sheep, and goats that occurs chiefly in central Africa and Asia and is marked by fever, hemorrhage, and diarrhea. Animals can be vaccinated against rinderpest, and importation of animals from affected regions is strictly controlled. [Mid-19C. < German < *Rinder* "cattle" + *Pest* "plague"]

Rine·hart /rīn haart/, **Mary Roberts** (1876–1958) US writer. She wrote mystery stories and coauthored the play *The Bat* (1920).

rin·for·zan·do /reén fawr tsaán dō/ *adj, adv* loud and with emphasis (*used as a musical direction*) [Early 19C. < Italian, "getting stronger"]

ring[1] /ring/ *n* **1.** BAND a durable circular band of something, especially a small band made of a particular material or for some special use **2.** CIRCULAR PIECE OF JEWELRY a band, usually made of precious metal and often engraved or mounted with gemstones, worn as an ornament, especially around a finger **3.** ENCIRCLING MARK an outline, mark, or figure in the shape of a circle (*often used in the plural*) **4.** CIRCLE a circular arrangement of people or objects ○ *a ring of chairs* **5.** CIRCULAR MOTION a movement of steps, especially by people skipping or dancing, that goes around in a continuous circle ○ *dancing in a ring* **6.** GROUP OF PEOPLE OPERATING DISHONESTLY an organized group of people who work together in a dishonest or unethical way ○ *a gambling ring* **7.** CIRCULAR AREA FOR PERFORMANCE a round stage or piece of ground, usually surrounded by seating, on which a spectator event such as a circus or a theatrical performance takes place ○ *a small circus of only one ring* **8.** PLATFORM FOR BOXING OR WRESTLING a raised square roped platform on which a boxing or wrestling match takes place **9.** BOXING the sport of boxing ○ *choose the ring as a career* **10.** SPORTS same as **bullring** **11.** COMPETITION a competition or contest, especially a political one ○ *still debating whether to enter the ring* **12.** AGRIC ENCLOSURE FOR LIVESTOCK AT FAIR an enclosure at a fair in which livestock are shown, paraded, or auctioned **13.** ASTRON BAND OF MATTER CIRCLING PLANET a band of dust, particles, and small bodies revolving around a planet. Such bands are known to circle Saturn, Jupiter, Uranus, and Neptune. **14.** TREES same as **growth ring** **15.** TURN OF SPIRAL a single turn of a spiral **16.** CHEM CLOSED LOOP OF ATOMS a collection of bound atoms represented graphically in cyclic form **17.**

MATH **SET OF MATHEMATICAL ELEMENTS** a set of elements that is associative under multiplication and distributive under addition **18.** MATH **SPACE BETWEEN CIRCLES** a space between two concentric circles ■ **rings** *npl* **GYMNASTIC APPARATUS** a pair of metal rings that are suspended from a ceiling and used to perform gymnastic routines ■ *vt* **(ringed, ring·ing, rings) 1. ENCIRCLE SOMETHING** to form a circle, or move in a circle, around something (*often passive*) ○ *We were ringed by the herd of cattle.* **2.** *US* LEISURE **ENCIRCLE SOMETHING WITH RING** to throw a ring or horseshoe so that it encircles a peg or stake [Old English *hring* < Indo-European, "to curl"] ◇ **run rings around somebody** to be effortlessly superior in intelligence, skill, or performance to somebody else (*informal*)

SPELLCHECK ring or **wring**? Do not confuse the spelling of ***ring*** and ***wring***, which sound similar. ***Ring***, the more common of the two words, is used as a noun or verb referring to something circular (as in *a diamond ring on her finger, ring the correct answer*) or to the sound of a bell: *The telephone is ringing. His story had a familiar ring.* ***Wring*** means "twist or extract forcefully," as in *wring the wet towels, wringing his hands in despair, wring the truth out of her.*

CULTURAL NOTE *The Ring of the Nibelung*, a series of musical dramas by German composer Richard Wagner. Based on Teutonic legends, this massive tetralogy — *The Rhinegold* (1869), *The Valkyrie* (1870), *Siegfried* (1876), and *The Twilight of the Gods* (1876) — a full performance of which lasts up to 15 hours, recounts the complex chain of events triggered by the theft of a magical gold ring. It represents Wagner's most successful attempt to create a new form of theater in which poetic drama is set to a musical score unified by recurring themes or leitmotifs.

ring[2] /ring/ *v* **(rang** /rang/, **rung** /rung/, **ring·ing, rings) 1.** *vti* **MAKE SOUND OF BELL** to make a metallic sound when struck or played, or cause something such as a bell to make this sound **2.** *vti* **MAKE SOUND TO ALERT SOMEBODY** to produce a continuous or regular high-pitched sound to alert somebody, or make something produce such a sound **3.** *vi* **ECHO LOUDLY** to be full of a loud, high-pitched, or reverberating sound, especially laughter or applause ○ *The hall rang with applause.* **4.** *vi* **MAKE CALL FOR SOMETHING** to call for somebody or something by sounding a bell or buzzer ○ *You rang, sir?* **5.** *vi* **IMPRESS SOMEBODY AS SOMETHING** to make a particular impression on somebody ○ *His excuse didn't ring true.* **6.** *vti UK* **TELEPHONE SOMEBODY** to make a telephone call to somebody ○ *He rang me to cancel the appointment.* **7.** *vi* **HAVE SENSATION OF HIGH-PITCHED SOUNDS** to have a sensation of a repeated or continuous high-pitched sound ○ *It made my ears ring.* ■ *n* **1. ACT OF SOUNDING BELL** the act of making a bell sound **2. BELL SOUND** the sound of a bell or something like a bell **3. PHONE CALL** a call on the telephone (*informal*) ○ *She gave us a ring about noon.* **4. GENERAL IMPRESSION** a general impression made by somebody or something ○ *It had a familiar ring to it.* **5. REPEATED SOUND** a loud continuous repeated or reverberating sound **6. SET OF BELLS** a set of bells in a tower or belfry [Old English *hringan*, probably < Germanic, "make a noise"]

ring back *vti* to make a return telephone call to somebody (*informal*) ○ *I left several messages but she never rang back.*

ring in *vt* to celebrate the beginning of something by or as if by ringing bells ○ *rang in the New Year in Times Square*

ring off *vi* to finish speaking on the telephone and break the connection, usually by replacing the receiver

ring out *v* **1.** *vi* to be heard loudly and clearly **2.** *vt* to celebrate the end of something by or as if by ringing bells

ring up *v* **1.** *vt* **ACCOMPLISH** to accomplish or achieve something **2.** *vt* **ENTER SUM PAID FOR SOMETHING** to press keys on a cash register to record the amount of money being paid for something (*dated*) **3.** *vti UK* **PHONE SOMEBODY** to make a telephone call to somebody

ring-a-le·vi·o /rìng ə léevee ō/ *n* a children's game in which members of one team hide and the other team tries to find and capture them. A captured player must stand inside a circle drawn on the ground until tagged by a free teammate. [Early 20C. Alteration of *ring relievo* < RING[1] + RELIEVE]

ring-a·round-the-ros·y, ring-a·round-a-ros·y *n* a young children's game in which players sing while moving around in a circle and abruptly squat when the words "all fall down" are sung [Late 19C. < ?]

ring-bill *n* BIRDS same as **ring-necked duck**

ring-billed gull *n* a white gull that nests by inland lakes and lives on the coast in winter, and has a black ring around its beak. Native to: North America. Latin name: *Larus delawarensis.*

ring bind·er *n* a stiff cover with metal rings inside the spine that snap open for insertion or removal of punched loose-leaf paper

ring·bolt /ríng bōlt/ *n* a bolt with a ring fitted through the eye at its head

ring·bone /ríng bōn/ *n* **1.** a condition of a horse's pastern bone in which bony outgrowths develop, sometimes leading to pain and lameness. It is treated with rest, medication, or surgery. **2.** a bony outgrowth characteristic of ringbone [Because the outgrowths encircle the bone]

ring dance *n* DANCE same as **round dance** (sense 1)

ring·dove /ríng dùv/ *n* BIRDS same as **wood pigeon**

ringed /ringd/ *adj* **1. WEARING RING** wearing one or more rings **2. ENCIRCLED** encircled by a ring **3. HAVING MARKS THAT FORM RING** having markings that form a ring around the neck, bill, or other body part

ringed seal *n* a seal that has a dark grayish coat with lighter markings that encircle the body. Native to: Arctic and subarctic regions. Latin name: *Pusa hispida.*

rin·gent /rínjənt/ *adj* having an opening bordered by parts resembling the lips of a gaping mouth, as in the flower of a snapdragon [Mid-18C. < Latin *ringent-*, present participle of *ringi* "gape"]

ring·er[1] /ríngər/ *n* **1.** a horseshoe or quoit thrown skillfully so that it encircles a peg or stake **2.** *also* **ring·ers** /ríngərz/ *US* a game in which marbles are formed like a cross inside a circle and each player uses a marble to shoot the laid out marbles outside the circle [Late 17C. < RING[1]]

ring·er[2] /ríngər/ *n* somebody or something fraudulently substituted in a competition (*informal*) [15C. < RING[2]]

ring·ers *n US* LEISURE same as **ringer**[1] (sense 2) (*takes a singular verb*)

Ring·er's so·lu·tion, Ring·er so·lu·tion *n* a solution of inorganic salts used to sustain cells, tissues, or organs outside the body [Late 19C. After Sydney *Ringer* (1834–1910), British physician]

ring·ette /ring ét/ *n Can* a game with rules similar to hockey played with a straight stick and a rubber ring instead of a puck. Intentional physical contact is forbidden. [Late 20C. < RING[1]]

ring fin·ger *n* the third finger of the hand, especially the left hand, on which an engagement or wedding ring is traditionally worn

ring·git /ríng git/ *n* the main unit of currency of Malaysia. See table at **currency** [Mid-20C. < Malay]

ring·hals /ríng hàlss/ (*plural same* or **-hals·es**) *n* a snake related to the cobra that has a small rough-skinned black or brown body and can spit jets of venom from its fangs at an aggressor. Native to: southern Africa. Latin name: *Hemachatus hemachatus.* [Late 18C. < Afrikaans, "ring-neck," from the one or two white rings across the snake's neck]

ring·ing /ríngging/ *n* a clear, continuing, usually high-pitched sound ■ *adj* expressed in a definite, unrestrained way —**ring·ing·ly** *adv*

ring·lead·er /ríng lèedər/ *n* the member of a circle or gang who organizes and encourages others, especially in unlawful or rebellious activities [Early 16C. < *lead the ring* "go first"]

ring·let /rínglət/ *n* **1.** a spiral curl of hair **2.** a small ring or circle —**ring·let·ed** *adj*

ring·mas·ter /ríng màstər/ *n* **1.** a presider over a circus show who announces and comments on performances **2.** somebody who starts, maintains, or is responsible for verifying the links on a web ring

Ring Neb·u·la *n* a ring-shaped nebula in the constellation Lyra

ring-necked /ríng nèkt/, **ring-neck** /-nèk/ *adj* with markings resembling a ring around the neck in a color that contrasts with adjacent feathers, scales, or hair

ring-necked duck *n* a diving duck found on woodland ponds that has coppery ring neck markings and two white rings on the bill. Native to: North America. Latin name: *Aythya collaris.*

ring-necked pheas·ant *n* a pheasant widely introduced to the United States and Europe as a game bird, the male of which has a white neck collar, a red head, and lustrous coppery red and green plumage. Native to: Asia. Latin name: *Phasianus colchicus.*

ring·neck snake, ring-necked snake *n* a small nonvenomous snake that has a yellowish or orange neck band. Native to: North America. Genus: *Diadophis.*

ring ou·zel *n* BIRDS same as **ouzel**

ring-po·rous *adj* describes a tree or wood with annual rings marked by prominent bands of large pores. These rings are readily apparent when a cross section of a trunk or branch is examined.

ring-pull *n UK* same as **pull-tab**

ring road *n UK* same as **beltway**

ring·side /ríng sīd/ *n* **1.** the row of seats or area directly in front of a boxing, wrestling, or circus ring **2.** a place or location offering a clear and close view of something (*informal*) —**ring·sid·er** *n*

ring spot *n* **1.** a pale or yellowish ring-shaped discoloration occurring in plants infected with a virus disease **2.** a fungus disease affecting members of the cabbage family, with brown spots appearing on the leaves

ring·tail /ríng tàyl/ *n* **1.** a ring-tailed mammal, especially a member of the family that includes the cacomistle and raccoon. Family: Procyonidae. **2.** ZOOL same as **ringtail possum**

ring-tailed *adj* with a tail encircled by colored bands or markings in a color that contrasts with adjacent feathers, scales, or hair

ring-tailed lemur *n* a lemur with a gray coat and a long tail with black and white bands. Latin name: *Lemur catta.*

ring·tail pos·sum *n* an opossum with a curly-tipped striped tail that it uses for grasping branches and carrying objects. Native to: Australasia, New Guinea. Family: Pseudocheiridae.

ring·tone /ríng tōn/ *n* the sound that notifies somebody of an incoming call on a cell phone, e.g., a series of beeps or a musical tune

ring·toss /ríng tòss/ *n* a game in which rope or metal rings are thrown to encircle a peg, popular at carnivals

ring·worm /ríng wùrm/ *n* a fungal disease of the skin, scalp, or nails in which intensely itchy ring-shaped patches develop. Infection is transmitted to humans from pets or livestock, or from infected bedding.

rink /ringk/ *n* **1. AREA OF ICE USED FOR SPORTS** a smooth, enclosed, and often artificially prepared ice surface used for ice-skating, hockey, or curling **2. SURFACE USED FOR ROLLER-SKATING** a smooth, enclosed, usually wooden surface used for roller- or in-line skating **3. BUILDING FOR ICE SPORTS** a building or arena in which ice-skating, hockey, or curling takes place **4. PLAYING SIDE** a team of players in curling, bowls, or quoits [14C. < ?]

rin·ky-dink /ríngkee dìngk/ (*informal*) *adj* **1. OUT-OF-DATE** broken down or no longer useful **2. OLD-FASHIONED** old-fashioned or outmoded **3. INSIGNIFICANT** small and insignificant ■ *n US* **INFERIOR PERSON OR THING** something or somebody considered shoddy and inferior [Late 19C. < ?]

Ri·no /rī́nō/ (*plural* **-nos**) *n* a member of the Republican Party, especially a member of Congress, who usually does not vote the party line and who disagrees with colleagues on issues (*slang*) [Acronym of *Republican in name only.*]

rinse /rinss/ *vt* **(rinsed, rins·ing, rins·es) 1. LIGHTLY CLEAN SOMETHING IN LIQUID** to wash something lightly by dipping it in a liquid, especially clean water, or by running liquid over it **2. FLUSH MOUTH WITH WATER** to flush the mouth or teeth with clean water **3. DIP**

SOMETHING INTO DYE to dip fabrics or garments into a dye solution ■ *n* 1. GENTLE WASH the act of washing something lightly by running a liquid, usually clean water, over or around it 2. COSMETIC TREATMENT FOR HAIR a solution that is applied to somebody's wet hair to alter or enhance its color or condition temporarily 3. CLEANSING LIQUID a liquid, usually water or a water-based solution, used to wash away something lightly [13C. < Old French *reincier*] —**rins·a·ble** *adj* —**rins·er** *n* —**rins·i·ble** *adj*

Ri·o de Ja·nei·ro /rèe ō day zhə nérrō, -neérō/ city and port in Brazil, in the southeast of the country. It is the capital of Rio de Janeiro State, and the former capital of the country. Population: 5,857,904 (2000).

Rí·o de la Pla·ta /rèe ō də la plaàtə/ estuary of the Paraná and Uruguay rivers, lying between Uruguay and Argentina. Length: 190 mi./300 km.

Ri·o Gran·de /rèe ō gránd, -grándee/ river of North America, rising in Colorado, flowing through New Mexico and along the Texas-Mexico boundary, and emptying into the Gulf of Mexico. Length: 1,900 mi./3,100 km.

Ri·o·ja /ree ṓ haà/ *n* a dry red or white wine with a distinctive flavor, produced in northern Spain [Early 20C. After a district in N Spain]

Rí·o Mu·ni /rèe ō moónee/ mainland region of Equatorial Guinea, in western central Africa. Population: 240,804 (1983). Area: 10,045 sq. mi./26,017 sq. km.

ri·ot /rī́ ət/ *n* 1. VIOLENT DISTURBANCE a public disturbance during which a group of angry people becomes noisy and out of control, often damaging property and acting violently. In law, a riot is typically defined as a group of three or more persons disturbing the peace for private purposes. 2. GREAT DISPLAY a spectacular visual display 3. SOMETHING EXTREMELY ENJOYABLE a social occasion, event, or experience that people enjoy in a wild, noisy, and energetic way (*informal*) 4. FUNNY PERSON OR EVENT an extremely amusing person or event (*informal*) 5. UNCONTROLLED WAY OF LIFE behavior that shows complete lack of control, especially financially or sexually (*archaic*) ■ *vi* (**-ot·ed, -ot·ing, -ots**) 1. CAUSE PUBLIC DISTURBANCE to get out of control and act in an unruly, violent, and destructive way, especially so as to cause a public disturbance 2. BE WILD AND SELF-INDULGENT to behave with a complete lack of personal restraint, especially in financial or sexual matters (*archaic*) [12C. < Old French, "quarrel" < *rioter* "to quarrel"] —**ri·ot·er** *n* ◇ **read (somebody) the riot act** to reprimand somebody severely for doing something, often including a threat of punishment if the offending behavior does not stop ◇ **run riot** 1. to behave in a wild and uncontrolled way 2. to grow in profusion

Ri·ot Act *n* an English law, passed in 1713, providing that persons making a public disturbance had to disperse within one hour of having had the act read to them by a magistrate

ri·ot gun *n* a short-barrelled gun used to disperse crowds. It fires plastic or rubber bullets.

ri·ot·ous /rī́ ətəss/ *adj* 1. loud, conspicuous, and unrestrained 2. involved in or taking part in serious public unrest (*formal*) —**ri·ot·ous·ly** *adv* —**ri·ot·ous·ness** *n*

ri·ot po·lice *n* a police reserve specially equipped for controlling a rioting crowd

rip[1] /rip/ *v* (**ripped, rip·ping, rips**) 1. *vti* TEAR OR BE TORN to roughly tear something apart or off, or become torn in this way 2. *vt* USE FORCE TO REMOVE SOMETHING to forcibly and carelessly remove something from a place where it has been firmly set ○ *Most of the original features of the house were ripped out.* 3. *vt* TAKE SOMETHING FROM SOMEBODY to take something from somebody, or remove somebody from a place in a way that seems unjust ○ *families ripped from their communities* 4. *vi* MOVE WITH EXTREME SPEED to move with dangerous or destructive speed ○ *The tornado ripped through northern Nebraska.* 5. *vt* WOODWORK DIVIDE WOOD LENGTHWISE to split or saw a piece of wood along its grain ■ *n* 1. ROUGHLY TORN PLACE a rough tear or split 2. same as **ripsaw** (*informal*) [14C. < ?] ◇ **let it** *or* **her rip** to proceed without hesitation or restraint (*informal*) ◇ **let rip** to speak rapidly and without restraint, especially with a series of curses (*informal*)

SYNONYMS See *tear*[1].

rip into *vt* to attack somebody or something, especially with a sudden and damaging criticism (*informal*)

rip off *vt* (*informal*) 1. to charge somebody an unfair price, or cheat somebody financially 2. to rob somebody, or steal something

rip up *vt* to tear something up into pieces or strips

rip[2] /rip/ *n* 1. an area of rough water caused by waves meeting opposing currents 2. OCEANOG same as **rip current** [Late 18C. Probably < RIP[1]]

rip[3] /rip/ *n* (*archaic informal*) 1. somebody considered to be corrupt and dissolute 2. something, especially a horse, that is old and of no value [Late 18C. < ?]

R.I.P. *abbr* rest in peace [Latin *requiescat in pace* or *requiescant in pace*]

ri·par·i·an /ri pérree ən, rī-/ *adj* situated or taking place along or near the bank of a river ■ *n* an owner of land along a river [Mid-19C. < Latin *riparius* (see RIVER)]

rip·cord /ríp kàwrd/ *n* 1. a cord that, when pulled, opens a parachute 2. a cord used to release gas from a hot air balloon during an emergency [Early 20C. < RIP[1]]

rip curl *n* a large and powerful wave with a curling crest that is particularly good for surfers to ride on

rip cur·rent *n* a strong narrow subsurface current flowing away from shore, visible as a band of agitated water [< RIP[2]]

ripe /rīp/ (**rip·er, rip·est**) *adj* 1. READY TO EAT mature and ready to be picked and eaten ○ *a ripe plum* 2. READY TO HARVEST having developed to the stage for harvesting ○ *fields of ripe wheat* 3. MATURE AND MELLOW matured or aged enough to have developed the best flavor and body ○ *ripe cheese* 4. EXACTLY READY at the most suitable stage of preparation or development ○ *The occasion was ripe for asking for a raise.* 5. ADVANCED IN YEARS representing or constituting a long life ○ *a ripe old age* 6. EXPERIENCED AND KNOWLEDGEABLE showing maturity and judgment acquired by experience and study 7. FULL AND RED full and ruddy, suggesting ripe fruit 8. SMELLY giving off a strong and unpleasant smell, especially caused by sweat from part of the body (*informal*) 9. IMPOLITE OR LEWD containing offensive language and sexual references (*informal*) [Old English *rīpe* < Germanic] —**ripe·ly** *adv* —**ripe·ness** *n*

rip·en /rīpən/ (**-ened, -en·ing, -ens**) *vti* 1. to become ripe for eating or harvesting, or make a fruit or crop ripe 2. to become fully developed, mature, or ready, or make something fully developed, mature, or ready (*often passive*) —**rip·en·er** *n*

ri·pie·no /ri pyáynō/ *n* in a baroque concerto, the full ensemble, as contrasted with the soloist or group of soloists (**concertino**) [Mid-18C. < Italian, "filled up" < *pieno* "full"]

Rip·ken /rípkən/, **Cal Jr.** (*b.* 1960) US baseball player. He broke Lou Gehrig's major league record of 2,130 consecutive games played (1995), and voluntarily ended his playing streak at 2,632 games in 1998. Full name **Ripken Jr., Calvin Edward**

rip-off *n* (*informal*) 1. UNFAIRLY PRICED ITEM something that is not worth the price asked or paid 2. ACT OF BEING DISHONESTLY TREATED an act or example of being cheated, tricked, or exploited 3. INEXPENSIVE COPY an inexpensive imitation of a prestigious product [< RIP[1]]

ri·poste /ri pṓst/ *n* 1. a quick or witty reaction to something, usually spoken 2. in fencing, a quick deft thrust made after parrying the lunge of an opponent [Early 18C. Via French < Italian *risposta*, past participle of *rispondere* "respond" < Latin *respondere* (see RESPOND)]

SYNONYMS See *answer*.

ripped /ript/ *adj* intoxicated by alcohol or drugs (*slang*) [Early 19C. < RIP[1]]

rip·per /ríppər/ *n* 1. a murderer who uses a knife to kill and mutilate people (*informal*) 2. a program used to copy digital music from a compact disk onto a computer before converting it into a format storable as a computer file [Early 17C. < RIP[1]]

rip·ping /rípping/ *n* the process of copying digitized music as a stored computer file ■ *adj UK* wonderful or excellent (*dated informal*) [Mid-16C. < RIP[1]] —**rip·ping·ly** *adv*

rip·ple[1] /rípp'l/ *v* (**-pled, -pling, -ples**) 1. *vti* HAVE OR GIVE SOMETHING WAVY FLOW to flow or move in tiny gentle waves, or disturb a surface with such waves ○ *a breeze rippled the water* 2. *vti* APPEAR WAVY ON SURFACE to have a wavy appearance or form, or make something have a wavy appearance or form ○ *shiny black rippled hair* 3. *vi* MAKE LAPPING SOUND to make a gentle lapping sound 4. *vi* RISE AND FALL IN VOLUME to pass through a group or place, increasing and decreasing in loudness ○ *Laughter rippled around the room.* ■ *n* 1. TINY WAVE OR SERIES OF WAVES a small wave or series of gentle waves across a surface 2. GENTLE WAVY SHAPE OR MARK something that resembles a ripple in its smooth undulating shape 3. SOUND RISING AND FALLING IN VOLUME a sound that passes through a group or place, increasing and decreasing in loudness ○ *a ripple of scorn* 4. GEOL SHALLOW BROKEN RIVER WATER an area of shallow water in a river broken by rocks or sand bars 5. ELEC OSCILLATION OF CURRENT a small oscillation of electrical current ■ **rip·ples** *npl* CONSEQUENCES a series of repercussions or consequences ○ *The ripples of the sector's downturn continue to be felt.* ■ *adj* FOOD WITH SECOND FLAVOR MIXED IN with a second flavor partly combined or marbled through ○ *raspberry ripple ice cream* [Late 17C. < ?] —**rip·pler** *n* —**rip·ply** *adj*

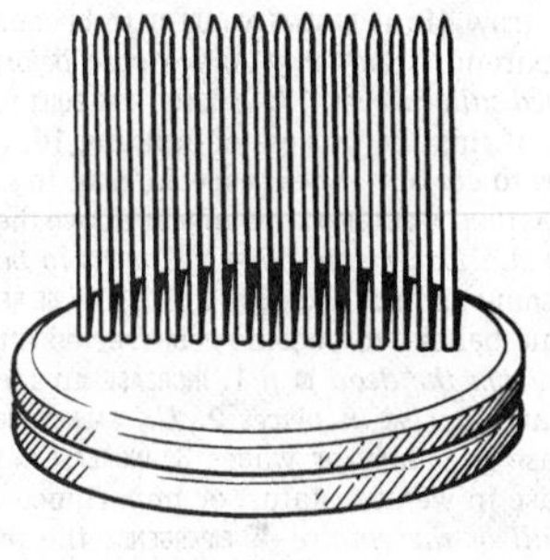

ripple

rip·ple[2] /rípp'l/ *vt* (**-pled, -pling, -ples**) to remove seeds from a plant with a comb-shaped tool ■ *n* a comb-shaped tool used to remove seeds from a plant [Mid-17C. < ?]

rip·ple ef·fect *n* a spreading series of effects or consequences caused by a single event [< RIPPLE[1] from the ripples that spread across the surface of a pool when something is dropped into the water]

rip·ple mark *n* a series of small wavy ridges created in sand or silt by wind or water. Ripple marks can be preserved in sedimentary rocks. [< RIPPLE[1]] —**rip·ple-marked** *adj*

rip·pling /rípling/ *adj* 1. IN SMOOTH GENTLE WAVES moving in or resembling the flow of small gentle waves 2. SOUNDING LIKE SOFTLY FLOWING WATER moving with a gentle lapping sound ■ *n* SOUND OF SOFTLY FLOWING WATER the lapping sound of gently flowing water [Mid-17C. < RIPPLE[1]]

rip·rap /ríp ràp/ *n* 1. SOMETHING BUILT OF LOOSE STONE a stabilizing foundation or embankment of loose and broken stone in or along the edge of water 2. STONE USED IN RIPRAP loose and broken stone used for riprap ■ *vt* (**-rapped, -rap·ping, -raps**) CONSTRUCT SOMETHING WITH BROKEN STONE to build or stabilize something with riprap [Late 16C. Doubling of RAP[1]]

rip-roar·ing *adj* boisterous, lively, and exciting (*informal*) [Mid-19C. < RIP[1] + UPROARIOUS] —**rip-roar·ing·ly** *adv*

rip·saw /ríp sàw/ *n* a saw with coarse teeth used to cut along the grain of wood [Mid-19C. < RIP[1]]

rip·snort·er /ríp snàwrtər/ *n* something or somebody exceptionally impressive (*informal*) [Mid-19C. < RIP[1] + slang *snorter* "something big and impressive"]

rip·stop /ríp stòp/ *adj* woven with extra threads at regular intervals to make tearing less likely ○ *ripstop nylon* [Late 20C. < RIP[1]]

rip·tide /rip tīd/ *n* same as **rip current** [< RIP[2]]

Rip·u·ar·i·an /rìppyoo érree ən/ *adj* relating to the Frankish people who lived beside the Rhine in the 4th century B.C. [Late 18C. < medieval Latin *Ripuarius*]

RISC /risk/ *abbr* reduced-instruction-set computer

rise /rīz/ *v* (**rose** /rōz/, **ris·en** /rízz'n/, **ris·ing, ris·es**) **1.** *vi* STAND UP to assume a standing or nearly vertical position after sitting, kneeling, or lying **2.** *vi* ASCEND to go up to a higher position or location ○ *Disturbed by our footsteps, the birds rose above the trees.* **3.** *vi* GET HIGHER to gain a greater height or level ○ *After heavy rains the river rose dangerously.* **4.** *vi* GROW LARGER to increase in amount, degree, or quantity ○ *Prices are rising.* **5.** *vi* ACHIEVE GREATER SOCIAL PROMINENCE to achieve higher wealth, status, or importance ○ *rose through the ranks* **6.** *vi* EXTEND UPWARD to become elevated, or extend upward ○ *The church tower rose above the village.* **7.** *vi* GROW LOUDER OR MORE INTENSE to increase in volume or intensity of sound ○ *Their voices rose.* **8.** *vi* INTENSIFY EMOTIONALLY to become emotionally more intense or powerful ○ *Tempers were rising.* **9.** *vi* DEVELOP to develop or intensify, especially until a particular state is reached ○ *By morning a blizzard had risen.* **10.** *vi* SWELL to swell and puff out, e.g., in the manner of dough containing yeast ○ *The bread is rising.* **11.** *vi* REBEL OR REVOLT to make an organized rebellion against something or somebody ○ *The entire region rose up against the authorities in protest.* **12.** *vi* END MEETING to adjourn after a meeting or assembly **13.** *vi* BECOME ERECT to become stiff and erect ○ *felt the hairs rise on the back of his neck* **14.** *vi* ORIGINATE to have an origin or beginning ○ *The stream rises a few miles back.* **15.** *vi* GROW to spring up or grow **16.** *vi* BECOME APPARENT to become visible or apparent ○ *Suddenly Africa rose before the astonished sailors' eyes.* **17.** *vi* CONSTR BE BUILT to become larger during the process of building **18.** *vi* GET UP IN MORNING to get out of bed, especially in the morning **19.** *vi* ASTRON APPEAR IN SKY to appear above the horizon ○ *The sun was rising when we went to bed.* **20.** *vt* NAUT same as **raise** *v* (sense 28) **21.** *vi* BE RESURRECTED in some beliefs, to become resurrected after death ○ *rise from the dead* ■ *n* **1.** INCREASE an increase in amount ○ *a rise in prices* **2.** *UK* SALARY INCREASE an increase in salary or wages **3.** INCREASE IN STATUS an increase in wealth, status, or importance ○ *the rise and fall of the empire* **4.** EMERGENCE the process of becoming noticed and successful ○ *the rise of a new talent* **5.** UPWARD SLOPE an upward slope or gradient ○ *a rise in the road* **6.** HIGHER GROUND a hill or piece of raised or rising ground **7.** UPWARD MOVEMENT an ascent or upward movement **8.** INTENSIFICATION an increase in degree, intensity, or force ○ *a rise in her fever* **9.** INCREASE OF SOUND an increase in loudness or pitch **10.** HEIGHT the vertical extent of something **11.** ASTRON APPEARANCE IN SKY the appearance of the Sun, Moon, or other astronomical object above the horizon **12.** ORIGIN a beginning or origin of something **13.** REBELLION a rebellion against authority **14.** CLOTHING DISTANCE BETWEEN CROTCH AND WAIST the length between the crotch and the waist of a pair of pants [Old English *rīsan* < Germanic] ◇ **give rise to something** to cause something ◇ **take** *or* **get a rise out of somebody** to produce a desired response, usually anger or annoyance, by teasing or taunting somebody (*informal*)

rise above *vt* to overcome something unpleasant by not letting it become too important

rise to *vt* to behave well in response to a challenge or difficulty (*informal*) ○ *rose to the occasion*

ris·er /rízər/ *n* **1.** SOMEBODY WHO RISES FROM BED somebody who gets out of bed at a particular time ○ *We are late risers on weekends.* **2.** HEIGHT OF STEP the vertical part of a step or stair **3.** CONSTR VERTICAL PIPE a vertical pipe, duct, or conduit **4.** SOMEBODY RISING somebody who or something that rises

ris·i·ble /rízzəb'l/ *adj* **1.** causing or capable of causing laughter **2.** able or inclined to laugh (*formal*) [Mid-16C. < late Latin *risibilis* < Latin *ris-*, past participle of *ridere* "laugh"] —**ris·i·bil·i·ty** /rìzzə bíllətee/ *n* —**ris·i·bly** *adv*

ris·ing /rízing/ *adj* **1.** GETTING MORE IMPORTANT becoming increasingly respected or significant in an occupation or activity **2.** BECOMING POWERFUL becoming more influential and powerful **3.** GETTING HIGHER going up or becoming higher ■ *n* **1.** UPRISING a rebellion or revolt **2.** SOMETHING GETTING HIGHER something that rises in height **3.** UPWARD MOVEMENT the process of moving upward or to a higher level **4.** ACTION OF STANDING UP the act of assuming a standing or nearly vertical position after sitting, kneeling, or lying **5.** LEAVENING PROCESS the process of leavening in bread

ris·ing damp *n* moisture that is absorbed from the ground into walls, resulting in structural damage

ris·ing diph·thong *n* a diphthong in which the second of two sounds has more stress or sonority than the first

ris·ing rhythm *n* a rhythmic pattern produced by a succession of metrical feet, each foot having an accented syllable preceded by one or more syllables that are unaccented

ris·ing trot *n* a horse-riding technique used while trotting, in which the rider rises from the saddle every second beat

risk /risk/ *n* **1.** CHANCE OF SOMETHING GOING WRONG the danger that injury, damage, or loss will occur **2.** HAZARD somebody or something likely to cause injury, damage, or loss **3.** INSUR CHANCE OF LOSS TO INSURER the probability of loss to an insurer, or the amount that an insurer is in danger of losing **4.** FIN POSSIBILITY OF INVESTMENT LOSS the possibility of loss in an investment or speculation **5.** STATISTICAL ODDS OF DANGER the statistical chance of danger from something, especially from the failure of an engineered system ■ *vt* (**risked, risk·ing, risks**) **1.** ENDANGER SOMEBODY OR SOMETHING to expose somebody or something to harm, danger, or loss **2.** INVITE BAD CONSEQUENCE to incur the chance of something harmful, dangerous, or detrimental ○ *risked imprisonment by their action* [Mid-17C. Via French *risque* < obsolete Italian *rischo* < *rischiare* "run into danger"] —**risk·er** *n* —**risk·less** *adj* —**risk·y** *adj* ◇ **at risk 1.** in danger of injury, damage, or loss ○ *needlessly putting lives at risk* **2.** SOC SCI in danger of being harmed or of harming others ◇ **run** *or* **take a risk** to do something that involves the possibility of injury, damage, or harm

risk ar·bi·trage *n* the technique of using price discrepancies in a market in order to profit, e.g., by buying shares in a company being acquired while selling shares in the acquiring company —**risk ar·bi·tra·geur** *n*

risk-a·verse *adj* **1.** wanting to avoid risk in an investment or speculation **2.** having an investment strategy that is designed to preserve capital

risk-ben·e·fit *adj* studying or testing whether the benefits of a procedure, process, or treatment outweigh the risks involved

risk cap·i·tal *n* FIN same as **venture capital**

risk fac·tor *n* a feature of somebody's habits, genetic makeup, or personal history that increases the probability of disease or harm to health

risk man·age·ment *n* the profession or technique of determining, minimizing, and preventing accidental loss in a business, e.g., by taking safety measures and buying insurance

Ri·sor·gi·men·to /ree sàwrjə méntō/ *n* the movement for, and period of, political unification in Italy beginning about 1750 and culminating in the occupation of Rome by Italian troops in 1870 [Late 19C. < Italian, "resurgence"]

ri·sot·to /ri zóttō/ *n* a dish of short-grained rice and other ingredients cooked in stock [Mid-19C. < Italian < *riso* (see RICE)]

ris·qué /ri skáy/ *adj* alluding to sexual conduct in a way that verges on indecency or bad taste [Mid-19C. < French, past participle of *risquer* "risk" < *risque* (see RISK)]

Riss /riss/ *n* one of the four major glacial periods in Europe, at its peak 150,000 years ago [Early 20C. After the *Riss* River in Germany, where signs of the glaciation were observed]

ris·sole /ri sṓl, ríssōl/ *n* a small fried cake of minced seasoned meat or poultry, coated with breadcrumbs [Early 18C. Via French < late Latin *russeolus* "reddish" < Latin *russus* "red"]

ri·sus sar·don·i·cus /reéssəss saàr dónnikəss/ *n* a distorted grinning expression caused by involuntary prolonged contraction of the facial muscles, especially as a result of tetanus [< modern Latin, "sardonic grin"]

rit. *abbr* MUSIC **1.** ritardando **2.** ritenuto

ri·tar·dan·do /reè taar daándō/ *adj, adv* becoming gradually slower (*used as a musical direction*) [Early 19C. < Italian, present participle of *ritardare* "slow down" < Latin *retardare* (see RETARD)]

rite /rīt/ *n* **1.** CEREMONIAL ACT a solemn ceremony or procedure customary to a community, especially a religious group (*often used in the plural*) ○ *the rite of baptism* **2.** SET PROCEDURE a formal and established observance or practice (*often used in the plural*) ○ *rites of courtship* **3.** CEREMONIAL WAY OF PROCEEDING a system of ceremonial procedures ○ *the Roman rite* **4.** *also* **Rite** CHR LITURGICAL PROCEDURE a liturgy or version of a liturgy, especially of a Communion service **5.** *also* **Rite** CHR DIVISION OF CHURCHES a historical division of Christian churches based on their liturgies [14C. Directly or via French < Latin *ritus* < Indo-European, "fit together"]

SPELLCHECK See *right.*

ri·te·nu·to /reètə nṓotō/ *adj, adv* played slightly slower than the rest of a piece of music (*used as a musical direction*) [Early 19C. < Italian, "held back"]

rite of pas·sage *n* **1.** an event or act that marks a significant transition in a human life **2.** a ceremony that marks somebody's passage from one stage of life to another, e.g., from childhood to puberty or from unmarried to married life [Translation of French *rite de passage*]

ri·tor·nel·lo /reè tawr néllō/ (*plural* **-los** *or* **-li** /-lee/) *n* **1.** a short musical passage used as an orchestral refrain between verses of a song or aria **2.** in a concerto grosso, the return of full orchestral music after a solo [Late 17C. < Italian, "little return"]

rit·u·al /ríchoo əl/ *n* **1.** ESTABLISHED FORMAL BEHAVIOR an established and prescribed pattern of observance, e.g., in a religion **2.** PERFORMANCE OF FORMAL ACTS the observance of actions or procedures in a set, ordered, and ceremonial way (*often used before a noun*) ○ *a ritual dance* **3.** SYSTEM OF RITES the system of set procedures and actions of a group ○ *Orthodox ritual* **4.** UNCHANGING PATTERN a pattern of actions or words followed regularly and precisely (*informal*) ○ *the weekend car-washing ritual* **5.** BIOL SET FORM OF COMMUNICATION a set sequence of actions that an animal uses to communicate information or to reinforce social cohesion ○ *mating rituals* **6.** PSYCHOL REPETITIVE BEHAVIOR an inflexible, stylized, and often repetitive sequence of actions, e.g., repeated handwashing, that may indicate an obsession **7.** BOOK OF CEREMONIES a book containing rites or ceremonial procedures, especially religious rites ■ *adj* **1.** FOLLOWING PATTERN done regularly and in precisely the same way each time ○ *her ritual morning exercises* **2.** OF RITE relating to or done as a ceremonial rite ○ *ritual observance* [Late 16C. < Latin *ritualis* < *ritus* (see RITE)] —**rit·u·al·ly** *adv*

rit·u·al a·buse *n* the physical abuse of children believed by some to exist as part of supposed satanic rituals

rit·u·al·ism /ríchoo ə lìzzəm/ *n* devotion or adherence to rituals

rit·u·al·is·tic /rìchoo ə lístik/ *adj* forming part of or adhering to a ritual —**rit·u·al·is·ti·cal·ly** *adv*

rit·u·al·i·za·tion /rìchoo əli záysh'n/ *n* **1.** the act of making something into a ritual **2.** the process in which different forms of behavior are modified and combined to form a ritual

rit·u·al·ize /ríchoo ə līz/ (**-ized, -iz·ing, -iz·es**) *v* **1.** *vt* to make a ritual of something **2.** *vi* to promote the use of rituals —**rit·u·al·ized** *adj*

rit·u·al mur·der *n* **1.** a human sacrifice, especially to appease a deity **2.** a murder performed in a methodical, formalized, or ritualistic way

ritz /rits/ *n* an extravagant or ostentatious display of something (*informal*) [Early 20C. Back-formation < RITZY] ◇ **put on the ritz** to make a show of wealth and extravagance (*dated informal*)

ritz·y /rítsee/ (**-i·er, -i·est**) *adj* expensively stylish and elegant (*informal*) [Early 20C. < *Ritz*, name given to luxurious hotels established by César Ritz (1850–1918), Swiss-born entrepreneur] —**ritz·i·ly** *adv* —**ritz·i·ness** *n*

riv. *abbr* river

ri·val /rī́v'l/ *n* **1. COMPETING PERSON OR GROUP** a person or group that competes with another **2. EQUAL OR BETTER COMPETITOR** somebody or something that can equal or surpass another in a specific respect ■ *v* **(-valed, -val·ing, -vals) 1.** *vt* **BETTER SOMEBODY OR SOMETHING** to equal or surpass somebody or something **2.** *vti* **COMPETE WITH SOMEBODY** to engage in competition with somebody **3.** *vt* **TRY TO BETTER SOMEBODY** to try to equal or surpass somebody or something ■ *adj* **COMPETING** in competition with somebody or something [Late 16C. < Latin *rivalis* "using the same stream" < *rivus* "stream"] —**ri·val·rous** *adj*

CULTURAL NOTE ***The Rivals***, a play (1775) by Irish dramatist Richard Brinsley Sheridan. This lively comedy of manners portrays the attempts of Captain Jack Absolute to woo Lydia Languish, the idealistic niece and ward of Mrs. Malaprop. The latter's habit of misusing similar-sounding words created one of the most memorable characters in English drama and gave rise to a new term: *malapropism*.

ri·val·ry /rī́v'lree/ (*plural* **-ries**) *n* **1.** the condition or fact of competing with somebody or something **2.** an act of competitiveness

rive /rīv/ (**rived, riv·en** /rívvən/ or **rived, riv·ing, rives**) *v* **1.** *vt* to tear something apart (*literary*) **2.** *vti* to split a material such as wood by striking it, or become split in this way [12C. < Old Norse *rífa* < Indo-European, "to cut"]

riv·en /rívvən/ *adj* torn apart (*literary*) ○ *a political party riven by dissent* [Past participle of RIVE]

WORLD'S LONGEST RIVERS

1		Nile
	Length	[4,160 mi. / 6,695 km]
	Location	Africa
2		Amazon
	Length	[4,000 mi. / 6,400 km]
	Location	South America
3		Yangtze (Chang Jiang)
	Length	[3,900 mi. / 6,300 km]
	Location	Asia
4		Mississippi-Missouri
	Length	[3,710 mi. / 5,970 km]
	Location	North America
5		Huang He (Yellow River)
	Length	[3,395 mi. / 5,464 km]
	Location	Asia
6		Ob'-Irtysh
	Length	[3,362 mi. / 5,410 km]
	Location	Asia
7		Lena
	Length	[2,730 mi. / 4,400 km]
	Location	Asia
8		Congo
	Length	[2,718 mi. / 4,374 km]
	Location	Africa
9		Amur
	Length	[2,700 mi. / 4,345 km]
	Location	Asia
10		Mekong
	Length	[2,610 mi. / 4,200 km]
	Location	Asia
11		Niger
	Length	[2,600 mi. / 4,180 km]
	Location	Africa

riv·er /rívvər/ *n* **1.** a natural stream of water that flows through land and empties into a body of water such as an ocean or lake **2.** a large flow or stream of something (*often used in the plural*) ○ *a river of mud* [13C. Via Anglo-Norman *rivere*, Old French *rivière* < Latin *riparius* < *ripa* "riverbank" < Indo-European, "to cut"] ◇ **sell somebody down the river** to betray or desert somebody, usually for a selfish or mercenary motive (*informal*)

Ri·ve·ra /ri vérrə/, **Diego** (1886–1957) Mexican artist. He is known for his murals portraying Mexican social issues, influenced by Native American art.

CORBIS/Bettmann

Diego Rivera

riv·er·bank /rívvər bàngk/ *n* a piece of sloping ground at the edge of a river

riv·er ba·sin *n* an area of land drained by a river and its tributaries

riv·er·bed /rívvər bèd/ *n* the usually water-covered ground between the banks of a river

riv·er birch *n* a tree with a fissured reddish brown lower trunk and smooth pinkish upper trunk, grown as an ornamental and for its wood. Native to: riverbanks of eastern United States. Latin name: *Betula nigra*.

riv·er blind·ness *n* MED same as **onchocerciasis**

riv·er·boat /rívvər bṑt/ *n* a boat built with a flat bottom or shallow draft, used on rivers

riv·er catch·ment *n* GEOG same as **river basin**

riv·er dol·phin *n* a dolphin that is found in rivers and coastal waters. Family: Platanistidae.

riv·er·front /rívvər frùnt/ *n* the property or land along the edge of a river (*often used before a noun*) ○ *a riverfront park*

riv·er·head /rívvər hèd/ *n* the source of a river and the land surrounding it

Ri·ve·ri·na /rìvvə reénə/ region of south central New South Wales, Australia. It is heavily irrigated and predominantly agricultural. Area: 26,509 sq. mi./68,658 sq. km.

riv·er·ine /rívvə rīn, -reen/ *adj* **1. OF RIVER** relating to or resembling a river **2. BESIDE RIVER** located or living beside a river ○ *a riverine people* **3. OPERATING ON RIVER** operating or capable of operating on a river

riv·er red gum *n* a large eucalyptus tree with pale smooth bark and durable dark red wood. Native to: inland waterways of Australia. Latin name: *Eucalyptus camaldulensis*.

Riv·ers /rívvərz/, **Larry** (1923–2002) US artist. A versatile painter and sculptor, he was both an early exponent of pop art, a realist, and an abstract expressionist. Born **Grossberg, Yitzroch Loisa**

riv·er·side /rívvər sīd/ *n* the area of land beside a river ■ *adj* located beside a river

Riv·er·side /rívvər sīd/ city in southwestern California, on the Santa Ana River. It is a citrus-growing center, and is home to the University of California-Riverside. Population: 274,226 (2002 estimate).

riv·er·ward /rívvərwərd/ *adj* moving toward or facing a river (*literary*) ■ *adv also* **riv·er·wards** /-wərdz/ toward a river

riv·er·weed /rívvər weéd/ *n* a small many-branched freshwater plant that clings to rock with roots that function as suckers. Genus: *Podostema*.

riv·et /rívvit/ *n* **SHORT METAL FASTENER** a fastener with a head attached to a metal shaft that is passed through a hole in a material and flattened on the other side ■ *vt* (**-et·ed, -et·ing, -ets**) **1. FIRMLY FIX ATTENTION** to fix or direct the attention completely (*informal; often passive*) ○ *Jurors appeared riveted by the testimony.* **2. FASTEN SOMETHING WITH RIVET** to fasten something using a rivet or rivets **3. HOLD SOMEBODY'S GAZE** to attract and hold onto somebody's gaze or attention firmly (*informal*) ○ *"Old Grannis dared not move, but sat rigid, his eyes riveted on his empty soup plate."* (Frank Norris, *McTeague – A Story of San Francisco*; 1899) **4. FIX SOMETHING FIRMLY** to fix or secure something firmly [14C. < Old French < *river* "fasten"]

riv·et·er /rívvitər/ *n* a worker or machine that joins metal plates together with rivets

riv·et·ing /rívviting/ *adj* completely fixing and holding the attention (*informal*) —**riv·et·ing·ly** *adv*

Ri·vette /ri vét/, **Jacques** (*b.* 1928) French movie director. He is one of the most experimental and influential directors of the French new wave, and his movies include *Paris Nous Appartient (Paris Belongs to Us)* (1960) and *La Belle Noiseuse (Beautiful Troublemaker)* (1991).

~~**rivetting**~~ incorrect spelling of **riveting**

riv·i·er·a /rìvvee érrə/ *n* a coastal beach area with a warm climate and fashionable resorts [Mid-18C. < ITALIAN]

Riv·i·er·a /rìvvee érrə/ coastal region of southeastern France and northwestern Italy, bordering the Mediterranean Sea

ri·vière /rìvvee ér, ri vyér/ *n* a necklace made of a string of precious gemstones [Mid-19C. < French (see RIVER)]

Riv·ière-du-Loup /reev yèr doo lóo/ city in Quebec, Canada, on the southern bank of the St. Lawrence River. Population: 14,994 (2001).

riv·u·let /rívvyələt/ *n* **1.** a small quick-flowing stream of something **2.** a small stream or river (*literary*) [Late 16C. Alteration of obsolete *riveret* < earlier form of French *rivièrette*, diminutive of *rivière* (see RIVER)]

rix-dol·lar /ríks-/ *n* a silver coin formerly used in Denmark, the Netherlands, and Germany [Late 16C. < obsolete Dutch *rijksdaler* "dollar of the realm"]

Ri·yadh /ree yaád/ capital city of Saudi Arabia, located in the east central part of the country. Population: 3,180,000 (1999).

ri·yal /ri yaál/ *n* the main unit of currency in Qatar, Saudi Arabia, and Yemen. See table at **currency** [Mid-20C. Via Arabic < Spanish *real* (see REAL[2])]

RJ *abbr* ROADS road junction

Rm *abbr* BIBLE Romans

RM *abbr* MED Registered Midwife

rm. *abbr* **1.** MEASURE ream **2.** room

rms *abbr* MATH root mean square

RMS *abbr* **1.** *also* **R.M.S.** Railway Mail Service **2.** *also* **R.M.S.** MAIL Royal Mail Service **3.** MAIL Royal Mail Ship

Rn *symbol* CHEM ELEM radon

RN *abbr* **1.** *also* **R.N.** MED registered nurse **2.** *also* **R.N.** NAVY Royal Navy

RNA *n* a nucleic acid containing ribose found in all living cells, essential for protein synthesis. RNA also acts instead of DNA as the genetic material in some viruses. Full form **ribonucleic acid**

RNA pol·y·mer·ase *n* a polymerase that catalyzes the synthesis of RNA

R·N·ase /aár en áyz, -áyss/ *n* an enzyme that splits or degrades RNA. Full form **ribonuclease**

RNA vi·rus *n* a virus in which the core of nucleic acid consists of RNA

R'n'B, R & B *abbr* MUSIC rhythm and blues

rnd, rnd. *abbr* round

RNP *abbr* BIOCHEM ribonucleoprotein

ro *abbr* **1.** PUBL recto **2.** ONLINE Romania (*used in Internet addresses*) See table at **domain name**

ro. *abbr* MEASURE rood

roach[1] /rōch/ (*plural same* or **roach·es**) *n* **1.** a small sunfish resembling a European roach. Native to: eastern North America. Latin name: *Hesperoleucus symmetricus*. **2.** a freshwater fish of the carp family with an olive green or gray green back and reddish fins, popular as a game fish. Native to: northern Europe. Latin name: *Rutilus rutilus*. [12C. < Old French *roche*]

roach[2] /rōch/ *n* **1.** INSECTS same as **cockroach** (*informal*) **2.** the end of a marijuana cigarette after the rest of it has been smoked (*slang*) [Mid-19C. Shortening of COCKROACH]

roach[3] /rōch/ *n* the upward curve at the foot of a square sail ■ *vt* (**roached, roach·ing, roach·es**) to cut a horse's mane short so that the hairs stand up [Late 18C. < ?]

road /rōd/ *n* **1. HARD TRACK FOR VEHICLES** a long surfaced route broad enough for vehicles to be driven on it **2.** COURSE OF ACTION a course of action or behavior that leads to a particular outcome ○ *the road to financial success* **3.** RAIL same as **railroad** *n* (sense 1) **4.** MIN EXTRACT **MINE TUNNEL** a tunnel used for hauling coal or ore in a mine **5.** NAUT same as **roadstead** (*often used in the plural*) [Old English *rād* "act of riding" < Indo-European, "ride"] ◇ **down the road** in the future ◇ **one for the road** an alcoholic drink taken just before leaving a place (*informal*) ◇ **on the road** traveling from place to place ○ *The band has been on the road all summer.*

CULTURAL NOTE ***On the Road***, a novel (1957) by Jack Kerouac. A thinly disguised memoir, it describes a series of cross-country trips undertaken by a group of people united by their quest for new experiences and disregard for traditional values. It is both an engaging chronicle of the Beat generation and a lyrical evocation of the energy and passion of youth.

road·a·bil·i·ty /rṓdə bíllətee/ *n US* the ability of a motor vehicle to maintain a steady, balanced, and comfortable ride over a variety of routes

road ap·ple *n* a round piece of horse manure on a road (*informal*)

road·bed /rṓd bèd/ *n* a foundation of soil, cinders, or crushed rock that supports a road or railroad

road·block /rṓd blòk/ *n* **1.** a temporary barrier used to stop vehicles on a road, so they can be checked or their drivers questioned by authorities **2.** a hindrance or obstacle to something

road com·pa·ny *n US* a group of actors who tour with a show

road·e·o /rṓdee ō/ (*plural* **-os**) *n* a competition in driving skill for professional truck drivers [Mid-20C. Alteration of RODEO]

road hock·ey *n Can* a game that uses the rules of ice hockey and is played on a road or street by children wearing shoes or in-line skates

road hog *n* an inconsiderate motorist who obstructs traffic, especially one who refuses to let other drivers pass or go first, or forces them to move out of the way (*informal*)

road·house /rṓd hòwss/ (*plural* **-hous·es** /-hòwzəz/) *n* a hotel or tavern located beside a main road

road·ie /rṓdee/ *n* somebody who is responsible for the equipment used by a musical or theatrical group on tour, especially a rock band —**road·ie** *vi*

road·kill /rṓd kìl/ *n* an animal that has been killed by a motor vehicle on a road

road map, road·map /rṓd màp/ *n* **1.** a map or atlas that shows routes, mileage, and often other features of interest to travelers **2.** a plan or guide for something (*informal*) ○ *a road map for the months ahead* ○ *a road map to the Internet*

road met·al *n* the cinders, crushed rock, and other materials used in the construction of roads

road mov·ie *n* a movie that depicts the adventures of a person or people who leave home and travel from place to place by road, often to find or escape from something

road race *n* a competitive event in which participants race on foot, bicycles, or in motorized vehicles on public roads instead of on a track —**road-race** *vi*

road rac·ing *n* the sport of racing motor vehicles or bicycles on public roads temporarily reserved for the purpose or on speedways resembling public roads

road rage *n* uncontrollable anger experienced by a driver in difficult road conditions, often leading to violent behavior

road·roll·er /rṓd rōlər/ *n* a machine with wide heavy wheels used to roll flat a new or repaired road

road·run·ner /rṓd rùnnər/ *n* a swift-running bird of the cuckoo family with streaked brown-and-white feathers, a head crest, small round wings, and a long tail. Native to: deserts of western United States, and Mexico. Latin name: *Geococcyx californianus.*

road·show /rṓd shō/ *n* **1.** TRAVELING BROADCAST a live radio or television show that travels to a series of locations **2.** PERFORMANCE BY TRAVELING ACTORS a show

roadrunner

staged by a touring company of entertainers, or the company performing such a show **3.** TRAVELING CAMPAIGN a traveling promotional or political campaign

road·side /rṓd sìd/ *n* an area along or bordering a road

road sign *n* a sign by the side of the road giving directions or instructions

road·stead /rṓd stèd/ *n* a partly sheltered area for anchored vessels

road·ster /rṓdstər/ *n* **1.** a small open-topped car with a single seat in front and often an additional folding seat (**rumble seat**) at the back (*dated*) **2.** formerly, a sturdy horse for riding on a road

road test *n* **1.** AUTOMOT **PRACTICAL DRIVING TEST** a driving test to determine whether a driver of a motor vehicle is competent to be issued a license to drive **2.** TEST OF VEHICLE OR TIRE PERFORMANCE a test of a motor vehicle or tire under actual operating conditions **3.** MANUF **TEST OF HOW WELL SOMETHING WORKS** a series of tests to determine how well a new product or design performs during actual use —**road-test** *vt*

road·way /rṓd wày/ *n* the part of a road intended to be driven on

road·work /rṓd wùrk/ *n* **1.** ROADS **REPAIR OF ROADS** construction or repair work being carried out on a section of public road, or on the utilities located near it, creating a temporary obstruction for road users **2.** SPORTS **TRAINING EXERCISE** a form of exercise consisting of long runs on roads, done especially as part of a training program **3.** MUSIC **WORK OF TOURING** the activity of taking a band, especially a rock band, on a lengthy tour of performances ■ **road·works** *npl UK* ROADS same as **roadwork** (sense 1)

road·wor·thy /rṓd wùrthee/ *adj* in a safe condition to be driven on public roads [Early 19C. After SEAWORTHY] —**road·wor·thi·ness** *n*

roam /rōm/ *vti* (**roamed, roam·ing, roams**) to move over a large area, especially without a specific purpose or definite destination ■ *n* an act of roaming [14C. < ?] —**roam·er** *n*

roam·ing /rṓming/ *n* the use of a cell phone outside the local calling area

roan /rōn/ *adj* WITH LIGHT SPECKLES IN DARK COAT having a reddish brown, brown, or black coat speckled with white or gray hairs ■ *n* **1.** ROAN HORSE an animal, especially a horse, with a roan coat **2.** COLORS **ROAN COLOR** the color of a roan animal **3.** INDUST **FINE-GRAINED LEATHER** a soft pliable sheepskin leather used in bookbinding [Early 16C. Via French < Old Spanish *roano*]

Ro·a·noke /rō ə nōk/ **1.** river in the United States, rising in western Virginia and flowing through eastern North Carolina to Albemarle Sound. Length: 380 mi./610 km. **2.** city in southwestern Virginia, on the Roanoke River. Population: 93,873 (2002 estimate).

Ro·a·noke Is·land island off eastern North Carolina. Expeditions sent out by the English explorer Sir Walter Raleigh twice attempted to establish colonies. The first returned to England in 1586, the second disappeared between 1587 and 1591.

roar /rawr/ *v* (**roared, roar·ing, roars**) **1.** *vi* GROWL LOUDLY to make a loud growling noise (*refers to large animals*) **2.** *vti* SHOUT LOUDLY to utter a loud shout or cry, or utter something with a loud shout or cry **3.** *vi* LAUGH LOUDLY to laugh loudly and without restraint **4.** *vi* BURN NOISILY to burn noisily and intensely ○ *a roaring fire* **5.** *vi* CRASH OR BLOW LOUDLY to produce a crashing or blowing noise ○ *The storm roared through the area causing extensive damage.* **6.** *vi* PRODUCE HARSH NOISE to move or operate with a loud harsh or droning noise ○ *Jets roared overhead.* **7. roar your·self** *vr* BECOME SOMETHING BY ROARING to cause your voice to be in a particular condition, e.g., by shouting or cheering ○ *roared themselves hoarse* **8.** *vi* VET **BREATHE NOISILY** to breathe with difficulty, making a rasping or wheezing noise (*refers to horses*) ■ *n* **1.** LOUD SHOUT a loud shout or cry ○ *the roar of the fans* **2.** LOUD LAUGH a loud unrestrained laugh **3.** LOUD GROWL a loud growling noise made by a large animal, especially a lion **4.** NOISE OF FIRE a loud noise made by an intense fire **5.** CRASHING NOISE a loud crashing or blowing noise ○ *the roar of the tempest* [Old English *rārian*, origin ?] —**roar·er** *n*

roar·ing /ráwring/ *adj* **1.** BURNING INTENSELY describes a fire that is burning brightly and with extreme heat **2.** VERY GREAT extreme, or extremely great or good ○ *a roaring success* **3.** WITH ROAR making or characterized by a roar ■ *n* **1.** ACT OF MAKING ROAR an act of making a roar **2.** VET **BREATHING DIFFICULTIES IN HORSES** noisy breathing in horses, especially when caused by loss of function of the recurrent laryngeal nerve ■ *adv* EXCEEDINGLY to an extreme degree ○ *roaring drunk* —**roar·ing·ly** *adv*

Roar·ing Twen·ties *npl* the 1920s, thought of as being a time of exuberance, hedonism, and prosperity in contrast to the hardship of World War I

roast /rōst/ *v* (**roast·ed, roast·ing, roasts**) **1.** *vti* COOK IN OVEN to cook meat or vegetables by dry heat, usually in an oven **2.** *vti* PREPARE BY DRYING OR BROWNING to heat something until it is dry or brown, or be heated in this way ○ *roast coffee beans* **3.** *vt* METALL **HEAT ORE IN FURNACE** to heat ore in a furnace without fusing in order to concentrate, dehydrate, or purify it or to cause a chemical change that will facilitate smelting **4.** *vti* OVERHEAT to become too warm, or make something or somebody too warm ○ *roasting in front of the log fire* **5.** *vt* CRITICIZE SOMEBODY to subject somebody to harsh criticism (*informal*) **6.** *vt* MOCK SOMEBODY to make fun of somebody (*informal*) ■ *n* **1.** OVEN-COOKED MEAT a piece of meat that is suitable for roasting, or that has been roasted **2.** OPEN-AIR MEAL an outside gathering or party with food cooked on an open fire **3.** CELEBRATION a gathering, party, or other celebration at which the guest of honor is the subject of speeches that alternate between praise and humorous criticism ■ *adj* OVEN-COOKED cooked by dry heat, usually in an oven [13C. < Old French *rostir* < Germanic]

roast·er /rṓstər/ *n* **1.** EQUIPMENT FOR ROASTING FOOD a pan, dish, or oven for roasting food in **2.** SOMEBODY WHO ROASTS somebody who roasts something **3.** FOOD FOR ROASTING an item of food, especially a chicken, that is suitable for roasting

roast·ing /rṓsting/ (*informal*) *adj* VERY HOT feeling or causing somebody to feel very hot ■ *n* HARSH CRITICISM a harsh criticism of somebody ■ *adv* EXTREMELY to a high degree of temperature ○ *roasting hot*

rob /rob/ (**robbed, rob·bing, robs**) *v* **1.** *vt* DEPRIVE SOMEBODY ILLEGALLY to take something illegally from a person or place, especially by using force, threats, or violence **2.** *vt* DEPRIVE SOMEBODY UNFAIRLY to deprive somebody of something due, expected, or wanted ○ *Many claimed the team was robbed of another title.* **3.** *vt* DEPRIVE SOMEBODY OR SOMETHING INJURIOUSLY to deprive somebody or something of something, causing harm ○ *Excessive stress robs the body of nutrients.* **4.** *vi* COMMIT ROBBERY to commit robbery, especially habitually **5.** *vt* CRIME same as **steal** *v* (sense 1) ○ *They broke in and robbed the TV and video.* [12C. < Old French *rober* < Germanic]

ro·ba·lo /rō baálō/ (*plural* **-los** or *same*) *n* a fish belonging to a large diverse family that ranges from large ocean fish such as the snook to the tiny glass fish kept in aquariums. Family: Centropomidae. [Late 19C. < Spanish *robalo*, probably < *lobo* "wolf" < Latin *lupus*]

ro·band /rṓbənd, rṓ bànd/ *n* a piece of rope used to attach a sail to a spar [15C. Probably < Dutch *raband* < *ra* "yard for a sail" + *band* "band"]

Ro·bards /rō baárds/, **Jason** (1922–2000) US actor. Primarily a stage actor known especially for his roles in plays by Eugene O'Neill, he also won an Academy Award for his role in the movie *All the President's Men* (1976). Full name **Robards, Jr., Jason Nelson**

Robbe-Gril·let /ràwb gree yáy/, **Alain** (*b.* 1922) French novelist and screenwriter. He was one of the leading experimental writers in France in the 1950s and wrote the screenplay of *Last Year in Marienbad* (1961).

"The true writer has nothing to say, just a way of saying it."
[Alain Robbe-Grillet, *Pour un nouveau roman (Towards a New Novel)*; 1963]

Rob·ben Is·land /róbb'n-/ island 12 km/7 mi. off the coast of Cape Town, used for centuries as a place for isolating the sick or confining criminals and political prisoners. During the apartheid era many political activists were imprisoned there, including Nelson Mandela, Govan Mbeki, and Walter Sisulu. It was declared a World Heritage Site by UNESCO in 1999.

rob·ber /róbbər/ *n* somebody who commits robbery

rob·ber bar·on *n* **1.** a wealthy industrialist or businessman of the late 19th century who used unscrupulous business practices **2.** a land-holding nobleman who, in feudal Europe, habitually stole from people traveling through his lands

rob·ber fly *n* a predatory fly that catches other insects in its long bristly legs and pierces them with its sharp mouthparts. Family: Leptidae.

rob·ber·y /róbbəree/ (*plural* **-ies**) *n* the act or an instance of illegally taking something that belongs to somebody else, especially by using force, threats, or violence

Rob·bi·a ♦ **Della Robbia, Luca**

Rob·bins /róbbinz/, **Jerome** (1918–98) US dancer and choreographer. Among the Broadway musicals he choreographed are *The King and I* (1951), *West Side Story* (1957), and *Fiddler on the Roof* (1964). Born **Rabinowitz, Jerome**

robe /rōb/ *n* **1.** same as **bathrobe** **2.** CEREMONIAL DRESS a long loose garment worn on ceremonial occasions or as a symbol of authority, especially by the judiciary, academics, and members of the clergy (*often used in the plural*) **3.** WOMAN'S OUTER DRESS in Europe in the 17th and 18th centuries, a woman's outer dress, especially a heavy brocade or ornately decorated one worn over a plainer one **4.** MATERIAL FOR KEEPING LEGS WARM a fur or fabric covering put over the lap to keep the lower part of the body warm ■ *v* (**robed, rob·ing, robes**) **1.** *vti* DRESS IN ROBE to dress somebody in a robe, or be dressed in a robe **2.** *vt* COVER SOMETHING to cover or adorn something ○ *robed in glory* [13C. < Old French, "(clothes taken as) booty, spoil" < Germanic]

robe de cham·bre /rōb də shaámbrə, -shaáNbrə/ (*plural* **robes de cham·bre** /*pronunc. same*/) *n* CLOTHING same as **dressing gown** [Mid-18C. < French, "chamber robe, dressing gown"]

Rob·ert I /róbbərt-/ (1274–1329) king of Scotland. During his reign (1306–29) he fought successfully for Scottish independence from the English, whom he defeated at the Battle of Bannockburn (1314). Known as **Robert the Bruce**

Rob·ert II (1316–90) king of Scotland. The grandson of Robert I, he founded the Stuart dynasty.

Rob·ert III (1337–1406) king of Scotland. The son of Robert II and father of James I of Scotland, he ruled Scotland (1390–1406) during a time of civil strife and war with England.

Rob·erts /róbbərts/, **Sir Charles George Douglas** (1860–1943) Canadian poet. He wrote poems about New Brunswick and Nova Scotia.

Rob·erts, Julia (*b.* 1967) US movie actor. She is best known for her roles in *Pretty Woman* (1990) and *Erin Brockovich* (2000) for which she won the Academy Award for best actress.

Rob·erts, Owen Josephus (1875–1955) US Supreme Court associate justice (1930–45). He was a leading exponent of conservatism in jurisprudence.

AKG London
Paul Robeson

Robe·son /rṓbssən/, **Paul** (1898–1976) US singer and actor. He acted in both stage and movie productions of *Show Boat* (1928, 1936) and in other musical and Shakespearean roles including Othello. He stood against racism and racial segregation, and his socialist sympathies led to his being driven from the stage during the McCarthy era. Full name **Robeson, Paul Bustill**

"No barriers can stand against the mightiest river of all, the people's will for peace and freedom now surging in floodtide throughout the world!"
[Paul Robeson, *Here I Stand*; 1958]

Robes·pierre /rṓbz pee èr, -pyèr/, **Maximilien** (1758–94) French lawyer and revolutionary. He was elected as first deputy for Paris to the National Convention after the fall of the monarchy in 1792. As commissioner of public safety (1793) he instituted the Reign of Terror and was later guillotined. Full name **Robespierre, Maximilien François Marie Isidore de**

"Any law which violates the inalienable rights of man is in essence unjust and tyrannical; it is no law."
[Maximilien Robespierre, *Article 6, Déclaration des droits de l'homme (Declaration of the Rights of Man)*; 1793]

rob·in /róbbin/ *n* **1.** LARGE N AMERICAN THRUSH a large thrush with a rust-colored breast and dark gray or brown upper parts. Native to: North America. Latin name: *Turdus migratorius.* **2.** EUROPEAN SONGBIRD a small thrush, the adult male of which has a reddish orange breast and head. Native to: Europe. Latin name: *Erithacus rubecula.* **3.** BIRD WITH REDDISH BREAST LIKE ROBIN a bird with a reddish breast that is similar to the European or North American robin, especially one of numerous Australian species [14C. < the name *Robin*, diminutive of *Robert*; originally in ROBIN REDBREAST]

Rob·in Good·fel·low /ròbbin go͝od féllō/ *n* same as **Puck**

rob·ing room /rṓbing-/ *n* a room set aside for putting on ceremonial or official robes, e.g., in a court, church, or other building

rob·in red·breast *n* BIRDS same as **robin** (senses 1–2)

rob·in's-egg blue *n* a pale greenish blue color —**rob·in's-egg blue** *adj*

Rob·in·son /róbbinss'n/, **Arthur** (*b.* 1926) prime minister (1986–91) and president (1997–2003) of Trinidad and Tobago. He was the country's first elected president. Full name **Robinson, Arthur Napoleon Raymond**

Rob·in·son, Brooks (*b.* 1937) US baseball player. He played 23 seasons with the Baltimore Orioles, and was the American League's most valuable player (1964). Full name **Robinson, Brooks Calbert Jr.**

Rob·in·son, Edward G. (1893–1973) Romanian-born US actor. He is best known as the tough-talking gangster in the movie *Little Caesar* (1930). Born **Goldenberg, Emanuel**

Rob·in·son, Edwin Arlington (1869–1935) US poet. His collection *Captain Craig and Other Poems* (1902) attracted the attention of Theodore Roosevelt. He won Pulitzer Prizes (1922, 1925, and 1928) for subsequent works.

"Miniver Cheevy, child of scorn, / Grew lean while he assailed the seasons; / He wept that he was ever born, / And he had reasons."
[Edwin Arlington Robinson, "Miniver Cheevy," *The Town Down the River*; 1907]

Rob·in·son, Jackie (1919–72) US baseball player and civil rights activist. He broke baseball's color barrier, stole home 19 times, and was elected to the Baseball Hall of Fame (1962). Full name **Robinson, Jack Roosevelt**

"Baseball is a poker game. Nobody wants to quit when he's losing; nobody wants you to quit when you're ahead."
[Jackie Robinson. Quoted in *Giants of Baseball*, Bill Gutman; 1975]

Express Newspapers
Mary Robinson

Rob·in·son, Mary (*b.* 1944) president of the Republic of Ireland (1990–97). She was the first woman to serve as Irish president, and later became the United Nations High Commissioner for Human Rights (1997–). Born **Bourke, Mary Terese Winifred**

Rob·in·son, Sugar Ray (1921–89) US boxer. He was the world welterweight champion (1946–51) and five times world middleweight champion between 1951 and 1960. Born **Smith, Walker**

"I can hurt anybody. The question is, can I hurt him enough?"
[Sugar Ray Robinson, *The Black Lights: Inside the World of Professional Boxing*, Thomas Hauser; 1987]

Rob·in's plan·tain *n* a plant with rayed purple flower heads. Native to: eastern North America. Latin name: *Erigeron pulchellus.* [Late 18C. < ?]

ro·ble /rṓ blày/ *n Southwest US* **1.** an oak with a short trunk, leathery leaves, and thin tapering acorns. Native to: California. Latin name: *Quercus lobata.* **2.** an oak that resembles or is related to the roble. Native to: California, Mexico. [Mid-19C. Via Spanish and Portuguese < Latin *robur* "oak tree, hardness, strength"]

ro·bo·call /rṓbō kàwl/ (*informal*) *n* a telephone call made using a computer that plays a voice recording, used in election campaigning and telemarketing ■ *vti* (**-called, -call·ing, -calls**) to place a telephone call to somebody using a computer that plays a voice recording, in election campaigning or telemarketing [Late 20C. < ROBOT]

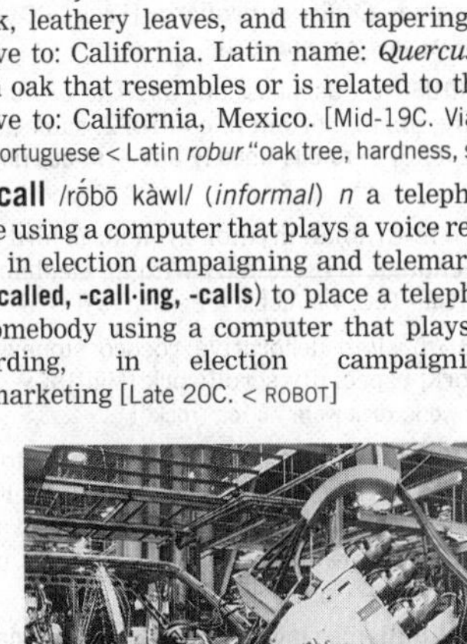
Popperfoto
robot: part of an automated car assembly line

ro·bot /rṓ bòt, rṓbət/ *n* **1.** PROGRAMMABLE MACHINE FOR PERFORMING TASKS a mechanical device that can be programmed to carry out instructions and perform complicated tasks usually done by people. **2.** IMAGINARY MACHINE a machine that resembles a human in appearance and can function like a human, especially in science fiction **3. PERSON LIKE MACHINE** somebody who works or behaves mechanically and emotionlessly **4.** *S Africa* **TRAFFIC LIGHT** a set of automatic traffic lights (*informal*) [Early 20C. Via German < Czech, < *robota* "forced labor"; coined by Karel Čapek in his play *R.U.R.* (Rossum's Universal Robots) (1920)] —**ro·bot·ic** /rō bóttik/ *adj* —**ro·bot·i·cal·ly** *adv*

ro·bot bomb *n* a jet-propelled bomb whose flight to a target is governed by a gyroscopic guidance system, e.g., the V-1 used by Germany against London in World War II

ro·bot·ics /rō bóttiks/ *n* the science and technology relating to computer-controlled mechanical devices such as the automated tools commonly found on automobile assembly lines (*takes a singular verb*)

ro·bot·ize /rṓbə tīz/ (**-ized, -iz·ing, -iz·es**) *vt* **1.** to introduce automation into something, especially a factory or factory process **2.** to make somebody act in an automated and unemotional or insensitive fashion —**ro·bot·i·za·tion** /rōbəti záysh'n/ *n*

Rob Roy /ròb róy/ *n* a cocktail made with Scotch whisky, sweet vermouth, and a dash of bitters [Mid-19C. After ROB ROY]

Rob Roy /ròb róy/ (1671–1734) Scottish brigand. Forced into life as an outlaw by debts, he led raids against both the English and the Scots. His life was romanticized in a novel by Sir Walter Scott. Born **MacGregor, Robert**

ro·bust /rō bússt, rṓ bùst/ *adj* **1. STRONG AND HEALTHY** strong, healthy, and hardy in constitution **2. STRONGLY CONSTRUCTED** built, constructed, or designed to be sturdy, durable, or hard-wearing **3. NEEDING PHYSICAL STRENGTH** involving or requiring great physical strength and stamina ○ *Football is a robust sport.* **4. DETERMINED** characterized by firmness and determination and a refusal to make concessions ○ *a robust defense* **5. STRAIGHTFORWARD** showing clear thought and common sense **6. BLUNT OR CRUDE** rough and direct or crude **7. FULL-FLAVORED** rich, strong-tasting, and full-bodied **8.** COMPUT **CAPABLE OF RECOVERY** describes a computer program or system that is able to recover from unexpected conditions during operation ○ *a robust operating system* [Mid-16C. < Latin *robustus* "made of oak, hard, strong" < *robur* "oak tree, hardness, strength"] —**ro·bust·ly** *adv* —**ro·bust·ness** *n*

ro·bus·ta /rō bústə/ *n* **1.** beans from a widely cultivated coffee bush, or coffee made from them **2.** a widely cultivated species of coffee bush that produces robusta beans. Native to: west central Africa. Latin name: *Coffea canephora.* [Early 20C. < Latin, form of *robustus* (see ROBUST)]

ro·bus·tious /rō búschəss/ *adj* (*archaic or humorous*) **1.** rowdy, unruly, or out of control **2.** same as **robust** (senses 1, 6) —**ro·bus·tious·ly** *adv* —**ro·bus·tious·ness** *n*

roc /rok/ *n* in Arabian mythology, a large bird of prey strong enough to lift and fly with an elephant in its talons [Late 16C. Via Arabic < Persian *ruk*]

ro·caille /rō kī́/ *n* decorative rococo stonework or shellwork, especially scrollwork [Mid-19C. < French, "pebble work, rock work" < *roc* "rock"]

roc·am·bole /rókəm bṑl/ *n* a plant related to garlic sometimes used to flavor food. Native to: Europe, Asia. Latin name: *Allium scorodoprasum.* [Late 17C. Via French < German *Rockenbolle* "distaff bulb" (from its shape) < *Rocken* "distaff" + *Bolle* "bulb"]

Ro·cham·beau /rōshaaN bṓ/, **Jean-Baptiste Donatien de Vimeur, Comte de** (1725–1807) French general. He commanded French forces in the American Revolution and played an important part in the British defeat at Yorktown (1781).

Roch·dale /róch dàyl/ city in Lancashire, northwestern England. Population: 207,563 (1996).

Roche ➧ **de la Roche, Mazo**

Roche lim·it /ráwsh-, rṓsh-/ *n* the closest a satellite can come to the astronomical object it is orbiting before being destroyed by tidal forces generated by gravity. The distance varies with relative density but is approximately 2.45 times the radius of the primary object. [Late 19C. After Édouard *Roche* (1820–83), French astronomer]

Ro·chelle salt /rə shél-, rō shél-/ *n* PHARM same as **potassium sodium tartrate** [Mid-18C. After LA ROCHELLE]

roche mou·ton·née /ròsh moot'n áy, ràwsh moo tón ay/ (*plural* **roches mou·ton·nées** /*pronunc. same*/) *n* an elongated mound of bare rock, modified by glacial erosion, that is smooth and striated on one side and shattered rubble on the other [Mid-19C. < French, "fleecy rock," because rounded like a sheep's back]

Roch·es·ter /róchistər/ **1.** city and port in western New York, south of Lake Ontario and northeast of Buffalo. Population: 217,158 (2002 estimate). **2.** city on the Zumbro River in southeastern Minnesota. It is the site of the Mayo Clinic, founded in 1914. Population: 90,515 (2002 estimate).

roch·et /róchət/ *n* a white linen garment, similar to a surplice but with tight-fitting sleeves, worn on ceremonial occasions by bishops and other high-ranking members of the clergy [14C. < Old French, "little mantle" < *roc* "mantle" < Germanic]

rock[1] /rok/ *n* **1. HARD MINERAL AGGREGATE** any consolidated material consisting of more than one mineral and, sometimes, organic material, e.g., granite or limestone **2.** *also* **Rock PROJECTING MASS OF ROCK** a large mass of mineral material, especially an isolated or projecting one (*often used in place names*) ○ *Ayers Rock* **3. BOULDER** a large stone or boulder **4. DEPENDABLE PERSON** a stable, dependable, or supportive person or thing, especially in times of trouble **5. GEM** a large gemstone, especially a diamond (*informal*) **6.** DRUGS **CRACK COCAINE** crack cocaine, or a small piece of crack cocaine (*slang*) **7.** *UK* **HARD CANDY** a hard, often brightly colored candy made from boiled sugar, usually in the form of a long cylindrical stick and sometimes with the name of a seaside resort through it **8.** *UK* FISH same as **rockfish** (sense 3) ■ **rocks** *npl* **1.** *US* same as **money** (*informal*) **2. OFFENSIVE TERM** an offensive term for the testicles (*slang*) [14C. < Old French *ro(c)que*] ◇ **between a rock and a hard place** faced with a choice between two equally unpleasant or undesirable alternatives ◇ **get your rocks off** (*slang*) **1.** an offensive phrase meaning to have an orgasm (*refers to men*) **2.** an offensive phrase meaning to get a great deal of pleasure or excitement from some activity ◇ **on the rocks 1.** in great difficulties and heading for ruin or disaster, especially financially or emotionally (*informal*) **2.** served with ice cubes

rock[2] /rok/ *v* (**rocked, rock·ing, rocks**) **1.** *vti* **SWAY TO AND FRO** to swing or sway backward and forward or from side to side, or cause something or somebody to swing or sway in this way, especially with a slow gentle rhythm **2.** *vt* **BRING TO STATE BY ROCKING** to cause somebody to be in a particular condition by rocking ○ *rocked the child to sleep* **3.** *vti* **SHAKE OR TREMBLE** to move or shake violently, or cause somebody or something to move or shake violently ○ *A tremor rocked the city.* **4.** *vt* **SHOCK SOMEBODY** to disturb, upset, or shock somebody (*informal*) ○ *The ruling rocked the legal profession.* **5.** *vi* **PLAY MUSIC OR DANCE** to sing, play, or dance to music, especially to rock music (*informal*) **6.** *vi* **BE FILLED WITH ROCK MUSIC** to contain people performing or enjoying music, especially rock music (*informal*) ○ *The joint was really rocking.* **7.** *vi* MUSIC **HAVE STRONG BEAT** to have or play music with a strong solid beat (*informal*) **8.** *vi* **TRAVEL** to advance steadily or quickly (*informal*) ○ *rocking along at 60 miles an hour* **9.** *vti* MIN EXTRACT **WASH ORE IN CRADLE** to wash gold-bearing or gem-bearing sands or gravel in a pivoting cradle **10.** *vt* ART **ROUGHEN COPPER PLATE** in engraving a mezzotint, to prepare a copper plate with a tool with a short curved jagged blade (**rocker**) ■ *n* **1. ACT OF ROCKING** an act or the process of rocking somebody or something **2.** MUSIC **TYPE OF POP MUSIC** a style of pop music, derived from rock and roll, usually played on electric or electronic instruments and equipment [Old English *roccian*, probably < Germanic, "move"]

Rock[1] /rok/ *n* (*informal*) **1.** *US* Alcatraz **2.** *Can* Newfoundland [< ROCK[1]]

Rock[2] /rok/ river rising in Wisconsin, flowing through Illinois and into the Mississippi River. Length: 300 mi./480 km.

rock·a·bil·ly /rókə bìllee/ *n* a style of pop music, originating in the late 1950s, that combines rock and roll with country music [Mid-20C. Blend of ROCK AND ROLL + HILLBILLY]

rock·a·bye /rókə bī/, **rock·a·by** *interj* used to encourage a baby or child to go to sleep [Early 19C. < ROCK[2] + LULLABY]

rock and roll, **rock'n'roll** /ròkən rṓl/ *n* **1. POP MUSIC WITH HEAVY BEAT** pop music derived from blues music that has heavily stressed beats. It is usually played on electric instruments and has simple, often repetitive, lyrics. **2. DANCE DONE TO ROCK AND ROLL** dancing done to rock and roll music ■ *vi* (**rocked and rolled, rock·ing and roll·ing, rocks and rolls; rock'n'rolled, rock'n'roll·ing, rock'n'rolls**) **DANCE TO ROCK AND ROLL** to do a rock and roll dance —**rock and roll·er** *n*

rock and rye *n* a rye whiskey that contains pieces of rock candy and, occasionally, fruits

rock·a·way /rókə wày/ *n US* a light, four-wheeled, horse-drawn carriage for two or four passengers that usually has a fixed top and open sides [Mid-19C. After a town in N New Jersey]

rock bass /-bàss/ *n* a sunfish with a dark olive back, white undersides, and red eyes. Native to: central and eastern North America. Latin name: *Ambloplites rupestris.*

rock bot·tom *n* the lowest level or price possible —**rock-bot·tom** *adj*

rock·bound /rók bòwnd/ *adj* **1.** entirely, or almost entirely, surrounded by rocks **2.** so rocky as to be inaccessible

rock brake *n* a fern that has compound fronds and grows on rocky ground. Genus: *Crytogramma.*

rock can·dy *n* a hard candy consisting of dissolved sugar that is cooled to form large crystals. It is sometimes made on a piece of string or a stick.

rock climb *n* **1. ACT OF CLIMBING ROCK FACE** an act or instance of scaling a rock face, usually using ropes and other specialized equipment **2. ROCK CLIMB ROUTE** the route followed on a rock climb ■ *vi* **ENGAGE IN ROCK CLIMBING** to practice rock climbing

rock climb·ing *n* the activity of scaling rock faces, usually using ropes and other specialized equipment and often in a team —**rock-climb·er** *n*

Rock Cor·nish *n* a small chicken belonging to a breed developed by crossbreeding Cornish and white Plymouth Rock fowls. Raised for: food. Native to: North America.

rock crab *n* a fast-moving crab. Native to: rocky coastal areas of North America. Genus: *Cancer.*

rock crys·tal *n* a colorless transparent variety of quartz. Use: electronic and optical instruments.

rock dove *n* a bluish gray dove from which domestic and wild pigeons are descended. Native to: Europe, southern Asia. Latin name: *Columba livia.*

Rock·e·fel·ler /rókə fèllər/, **John D.** (1839–1937) US industrialist and philanthropist. He founded Standard Oil and established the Rockefeller Foundation (1913). Full name **Rockefeller, John Davison**

> "I believe it is my duty to make money and still more money and to use the money I make for the good of my fellow man according to the dictates of my conscience."
> [John D. Rockefeller, *Interview*; 1905]

Rock·e·fel·ler, John D., Jr. (1874–1960) US industrialist and philanthropist. The son of John D. Rockefeller, he donated the land for the United Nations headquarters in New York. Full name **Rockefeller, John Davison, Jr.**

> "Good management consists in showing average people how to do the work of superior people."
> [Attributed to John D. Rockefeller, Jr.]

Rock·e·fel·ler, Nelson A. (1908–79) vice president of the United States (1974–77). The son of John D. Rockefeller, Jr., he replaced Vice President Gerald Ford, who had become President when Richard Nixon resigned in 1974.

rock elm *n* **1.** a deciduous tree with corky branches. Native to: eastern North America. Latin name: *Ulmus thomasii.* **2.** the wood of the rock elm tree

rock·er /rókər/ *n* **1. ROCKING DEVICE** a device that functions by way of a rocking movement **2. FURNITURE STAND** an upwardly curved piece of wood or metal that allows something such as a rocking chair or baby's cradle to move backward and forward or from side to side **3.** FURNITURE same as **rocking chair** **4.** MIN EXTRACT same as **cradle** *n* (sense 8) **5.** ART **ENGRAVER'S TOOL** a tool with a short curved jagged blade used in the engraving of mezzotints for roughening the copper plates **6.** ICE SKATING **TYPE OF ICE SKATE** an ice skate with a curved blade, or the curved blade itself (*often used in the plural*) **7.** MUSIC **ROCK MUSICIAN** a rock singer or musician (*informal*) **8.** MUSIC **ROCK FAN** a fan of rock music or rock and roll (*informal*) **9.** MUSIC **ROCK SONG** a rock music song ◇ **off his** *or* **her rocker** an offensive term that deliberately insults somebody's state of mental balance

rock·er arm *n* a pivoted lever, e.g., in an internal-combustion engine, that transmits motion from a cam or push rod at one end to open and close a valve at the other

rock·er cam *n* a cam that oscillates or rocks but does not revolve

rock·er pan·el *n* on a passenger vehicle, the exterior panel located below the doorsill of the passenger compartment

rock·er·y /rókəree/ (*plural* **-ies**) same as **rock garden** (sense 1)

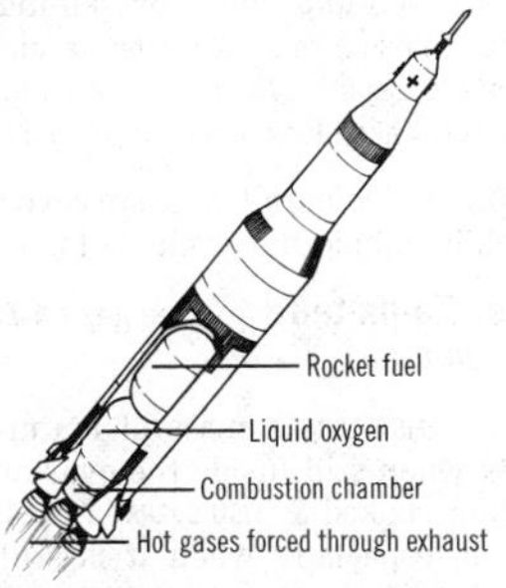

rocket

rock·et[1] /rókət/ *n* **1.** **SELF-PROPELLED FIREWORK OR FLARE** a firework, flare, or similar device, usually cylindrical in shape, containing combustible propellants **2.** AEROSP **SPACE VEHICLE** a vehicle designed for space travel, propelled by a rocket engines **3.** AEROSP same as **rocket engine** **4.** ARMS **ROCKET-PROPELLED WEAPON** a weapon consisting of an explosive, nuclear, or other warhead that is propelled by a rocket engine ■ *v* (**-et·ed, -et·ing, -ets**) **1.** *vi* **MOVE FAST** to move or begin to move at great speed **2.** *vti* **ATTAIN SOMETHING QUICKLY** to get to a particular condition or position very quickly, or cause somebody or something to do this (*informal*) ○ *They rocketed to fame with their first single.* **3.** *vi* **INCREASE QUICKLY** to increase very quickly and dramatically (*informal*) ○ *House prices have rocketed in the last year or so.* **4.** *vt* MIL, AEROSP **POWER SOMETHING USING ROCKET ENGINE** to send something, especially a spacecraft, warhead, or missile, into the air or atmosphere by means of a rocket engine or rocket engines **5.** *vt* **BOMBARD SOMETHING WITH ROCKET** to fire a rocket at a target **6.** *vi* **FLY UP QUICKLY** to fly up vertically at speed (*refers to game birds*) [Early 17C. < Italian *rocchetta* "small distaff" (from its shape) < *rocca* "distaff" < Germanic]

rock·et[2] /rókət/ *n* **1.** a fast-growing plant with pale-yellow flowers, typically growing on waste ground. Genus: *Sisymbrium.* **2.** PLANTS same as **dame's violet** **3.** PLANTS same as **sea rocket** **4.** *UK* PLANTS, FOOD same as **arugula** [Early 16C. Via French *roquette* < Italian *ruchetta* "small ruca" (a cabbage) < Latin *eruca* "caterpillar, cole"]

rock·et·eer /ròkə tëer/ *n* **1.** a scientist or engineer who designs space rockets **2.** somebody who launches, operates, or travels in a space rocket

rock·et en·gine *n* a device that carries both fuel and oxidizer, which it burns in a combustion chamber, producing thrust by expelling the expanding hot gases through a nozzle. The fuel and oxidizer may be liquefied gases such as oxygen and hydrogen, or solids such as powdered aluminum and ammonium perchloride.

rock·et-launched gre·nade *n* ARMS same as **rocket-propelled grenade**

rock·et plane *n* **1.** an aircraft that is powered by a rocket engine or engines **2.** an aircraft that is designed to carry and launch rockets, missiles, or warheads

rock·et-pro·pelled gre·nade *n* a heavy grenade with a rocket attachment that is fired from a launching tube, usually against armored vehicles or helicopters

rock·et·ry /rókətree/ *n* the science and technology of the design, construction, operation, flying, and maintenance of rockets

rock·et sci·ence *n* a complex and intellectually demanding activity (*informal*) ○ *Using the Internet isn't exactly rocket science.* [Late 20C. Because the province of a few highly qualified specialists]

rock·et sci·en·tist *n* an extremely intelligent person (*informal*) ○ *It doesn't take a rocket scientist to figure that one out!*

rock·et ship *n* a spaceship powered by rocket engines (*dated*)

rock·et sled *n* a rocket-propelled vehicle that runs on a rail or rails and can be accelerated rapidly to high speeds, used in aeronautical applications such as crash and G-force tolerance testing

rock·et·sonde /rókət sònd/ *n* an instrument transported by rocket to the upper atmosphere to carry out weather observations

rock·fall /rók fàwl/ *n* **1.** a collection or mass of fallen rocks **2.** an avalanche of falling rocks

rock·fish /rók fish/ (*plural same* or **-fish·es**) *n* **1.** a fish that lives among rocks. Native to: Pacific Ocean. **2.** *US* FISH same as **striped bass** **3.** *UK* the flesh of a dogfish or catfish as food

rock flour *n* fine powdery rock produced by grinding or abrasion, e.g., by the movement of a glacier

Rock·ford /rókfərd/ city in northern Illinois, south of the Wisconsin border, east of Freeport and northwest of Chicago. Population: 151,068 (2002 estimate).

rock gar·den *n* **1.** a garden or area of a garden in which plants, especially low-growing colorful hardy ones, grow between carefully arranged large stones **2.** a rocky area in which plants suited to the habitat are grown

Rock·hamp·ton /rok hámptən/ city in eastern Queensland, Australia, on the Fitzroy River. Population: 59,410 (2002 estimate).

Rock Hill city in northern South Carolina, north of Columbia and southwest of Charlotte, North Carolina. Population: 45,606 (2002 estimate).

rock·hop·per /rók hòppər/ *n* a small penguin with a short bill and a yellow crest. Native to: Antarctica, New Zealand, Falkland Islands. Latin name: *Eudyptes crestatus.*

rock hound *n* (*informal*) **1.** a collector of rocks and minerals **2.** an expert in or student of geology — **rock·hound·ing** /rók hòwnding/ *n*

rock hy·rax *n* a small plant-eating hyrax that lives in large colonies in rocky outcrops. Native to: Africa. Genus: *Procavia.*

Rock·ies /rókeez/ ➧ **Rocky Mountains**

rocking chair

rock·ing chair /róking-/ *n* a chair that is set on a pair of curved pieces of wood so that somebody sitting in it can be rocked backward and forward

Rock·ing·ham /rókingəm/ coastal town in southwestern Western Australia, near Perth. Population: 76,262 (2002 estimate).

Rock·ing·ham, Charles Watson-Wentworth, 2nd Marquess (1730–82) British prime minister (1765–66, 1782). His government is best known for its repeal of the Stamp Act and sympathetic attitude toward Britain's colonies in America.

rock·ing horse *n* a small model horse fitted with reins and a saddle and set on a pair of rockers, on which a child can sit and rock backward and forward

rock·ing stone *n UK* a large stone or boulder that is so finely balanced, e.g., on another stone or stones, that it can be made to rock backward and forward with little effort

Rock Is·land city in northwestern Illinois, on the eastern bank of the Mississippi River. It forms the Illinois-Iowa border southwest of Moline. Population: 39,045 (2002 estimate).

rock·ling /rókling/ (*plural* **-lings** or *same*) *n* a small fish of the cod family. Native to: northern Atlantic. Family: Gadidae.

rock lob·ster *n* MARINE BIOL same as **spiny lobster**

rock ma·ple *n* TREES same as **sugar maple**

rock me·chan·ics *n* the study of the physical properties of rocks such as density, elasticity, and strength, especially with relation to their behavior in tunnels and mines and when subjected to environmental forces (*takes a singular verb*)

rock music *n* same as **rock**[2] *n* (sense 2)

Rock·ne /róknee/, **Knute Kenneth** (1888–1931) Norwegian-born US college football coach. As coach at Notre Dame University, he used offensive tactics such as the forward pass that called for speed and agility and markedly changed the sport.

> "Win this one for the Gipper."
> [Knute Kenneth Rockne, *Derived from Knute Rockne's quote from George Gipp, halftime, game with Army*; 1928]

rock'n'roll *n, vi* MUSIC, DANCE same as **rock and roll**

rock·oon /ro ko͞on/ *n* an upper-atmosphere research system consisting of a large plastic balloon, launched at a high altitude, that carries a small rocket fitted with scientific equipment [Mid-20C. Blend of ROCKET[1] + BALLOON]

rock pi·geon *n* BIRDS same as **rock dove**

rock plant *n UK* a plant that has adapted to living on rocks or rocky ground

rock rab·bit *n* ZOOL **1.** same as **rock hyrax** **2.** same as **pika**

rock-ribbed *adj* **1.** rigid and inflexible in beliefs or principles **2.** characterized by rocks or rocky outcrops

rock·rose /rók rōz/ *n* a low-growing woody bush or perennial plant. Flowers: small, white, light-yellow or reddish, resembling wild roses. Native to: warm regions. Genera: *Cistus* or *Helianthemum.*

rock salt *n* MINERALS same as **halite**

rock·slide /rók slīd/ *n* **1.** a collection or mass of rocks that have slipped downward **2.** an avalanche of rocks that occurs as a result of surface movement

rock-sol·id *adj* **1.** firm and unshakable **2.** extremely hard and unlikely to break

rock stead·y *n* Jamaican reggae of the early 1960s, popular as dance music

rock-stead·y *adj* firm, unshaking, and calm

rock·u·men·ta·ry /ròkyə méntəree, -méntree/ (*plural* **-ries**) *n* a documentary movie about rock music in general or a particular rock band or musician, containing film footage of relevant performances (*informal*) [Late 20C. Blend of ROCK AND ROLL + DOCUMENTARY]

Rock·ville /rók vil/ city in west central Maryland, south of Gaithersburg. It is a northwestern suburb of Washington, D.C. Population: 52,573 (2002 estimate).

Rock·ville Cen·tre /-séntər/ village on Long Island, southeastern New York, directly east of the New York City borough of Queens. Population: 24,573 (2002 estimate).

rock wal·la·by *n* a medium-sized marsupial with

large padded hind feet, found in open rocky country. Native to: Australia. Genus: *Petrogale.*

rock·weed /rók wèed/ *n* a coarse brown seaweed that grows on coastal rocks. Genera: *Fucus* or *Ascophyllum.*

Rock·well /rók wèl/, **Norman** (1894–1978) US illustrator. He is best known for his magazine covers and illustrations of everyday small-town life, published in US periodicals such as *The Saturday Evening Post* and the *Ladies' Home Journal.*

rock wool *n* INDUST same as **mineral wool**

rock·work /rók wùrk/ *n* **1.** artificial or decorative stonework designed to resemble the irregularity of natural rocks **2.** a collection or mass of large stones or rocks

rock wren *n* a gray wren commonly found in rocky barrens and canyons. Native to: western North America. Latin name: *Salpinctes obsoletus.*

rock·y[1] /rókee/ (**-i·er, -i·est**) *adj* **1. WITH ROCKS** consisting of or covered with rocks ○ *rocky terrain* **2. HARD** resembling rock in its hardness or firmness **3. UNEMOTIONAL** unyielding, unwavering, or lacking in human emotions —**rock·i·ness** *n*

rock·y[2] /rókee/ (**-i·er, -i·est**) *adj* **1. DIFFICULT** characterized by difficulties, obstacles, or troubles ○ *a rocky start* ○ *a rocky reception* **2. UNSTEADY** wobbly and unsteady **3. UNWELL** unwell, especially feeling sick or dizzy (*informal*) —**rock·i·ly** *adv* —**rock·i·ness** *n*

Rock·y Moun·tain col·um·bine *n* a rare species of columbine. Flowers: blue and white. Native to: Rocky Mountains, USA. Latin name: *Aquilegia caerules.*

Rock·y Moun·tain goat *n* ZOOL same as **mountain goat**

Rock·y Moun·tain mag·pie *n regional* BIRDS same as **camp robber**

REGIONAL NOTE See *camp robber.*

Rock·y Moun·tain Na·tion·al Park /ròkee-/ national park in Northern Colorado, in the heart of the Rocky Mountains, established in 1915. Area: 415 sq. mi./1,075 sq. km.

Rock·y Moun·tains major mountain system of North America. Its highest point is Mount Elbert, at 14,433 ft./4,399 m. Length: 2,000 mi./3,200 km.

Rock·y Moun·tain spot·ted fe·ver *n* an acute infectious disease transmitted by the bite of ticks infected with the microorganism *Rickettsia rickettsi.* Symptoms include chills, fever, muscle and joint pain, skin rash, and prostration. [Because first reported in the area of the ROCKY MOUNTAINS]

~~**rococco**~~ incorrect spelling of **rococo**

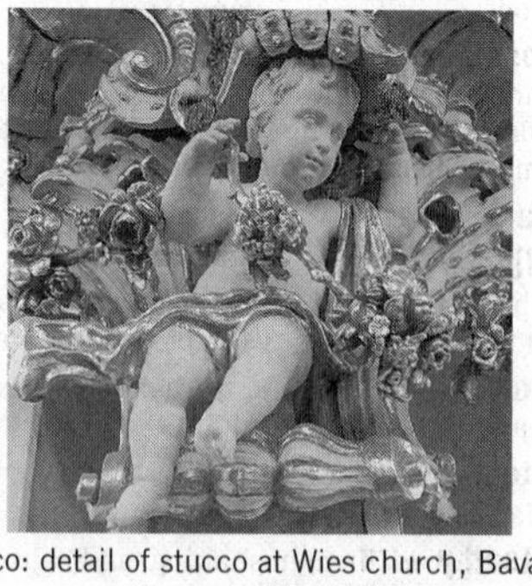

AKG London

rococo: detail of stucco at Wies church, Bavaria, Germany (1745–54)

ro·co·co /rə kṓkō, rō-, rōkə kṓ/ *n* **1.** *also* **Ro·co·co ORNATE 18C ART STYLE** a style of architecture and the decorative arts characterized by intricate ornamentation that was popular throughout Europe in the early 18th century **2.** *also* **Ro·co·co ORNATE 18C MUSIC STYLE** a style of music characterized by the use of ornamentation and embellishment that was popular in Europe in the 18th century **3. ORNATE STYLE** any very ornate style ■ *adj* **1.** *also* **Ro·co·co** ARTS **IN STYLE OF ROCOCO** belonging to, relating to, or in the style of 18th-century rococo **2. ORNATE** very ornate in style [Mid-19C. < French, fanciful alteration of *rocaille* (see ROCAILLE)]

rod /rod/ *n* **1. THIN STICK** a narrow, usually cylindrical length of wood, metal, plastic, or other material **2.** FISHING same as **fishing rod 3. WHIPPING STICK** a stick, or bundle of sticks tied together, used for whipping somebody as a punishment **4. SURVEYING POLE** a graduated pole used by surveyors for sighting with a leveling instrument to determine elevation differences **5.** same as **lightning rod** (sense 1) **6. STAFF OF OFFICE** a staff, especially one that indicates somebody's standing, office, authority, or power **7. POWER WIELDED** tyrannical or oppressive power **8. PLANT STEM** a straight stem or shoot that has been cut from, or that is growing on, a woody plant **9.** RAIL **METAL BAR SUPPORTING RAILROAD CAR** one of the metal bars that form the framework of the underside of a railroad car, especially one on a freight car (*often used in the plural*) **10.** ANAT **RECEPTOR CELL IN EYE** a rod-shaped receptor in the retina of the eye that is sensitive to dim light but not color **11.** MICROBIOL **BACTERIUM** a rod-shaped bacterium **12. BOARD MARKED WITH FULL-SCALE JOINERY PATTERN** a board on which the dimensions of a joinery assembly such as a window or door frame are marked in full scale **13.** MEASURE **UNIT OF LENGTH** a unit of length equal to $5\frac{1}{2}$ yd./5.03 m, now largely obsolete **14.** MEASURE **UNIT OF AREA** a unit of area equal to $30\frac{1}{4}$ sq. yd./25.3 m^2, now largely obsolete **15. PISTOL** a gun, especially a pistol (*slang*) [Old English *rodd* "pole, rod", origin ?] —**rod·less** *adj* —**rod·like** *adj*

Rod·bell /ród bèl/, **Martin** (1925–98) US biochemist. He shared a Nobel Prize in physiology or medicine (1994) for discovering a chemical transducer.

Rod·chen·ko /rod chénkō/, **Aleksandr** (1891–1956) Russian painter, designer, and photographer. He was a central figure of the constructivist movement in Revolutionary Russia.

rode[1] past tense of **ride**

rode[2] /rōd/ *n* a rope or chain, especially one attached to an anchor [Early17C. < ?]

ro·dent /rṓd'nt/ *n* a small animal of an order with large gnawing incisor teeth that continue growing throughout the animal's life, e.g., a mouse, rat, squirrel, or marmot. Rodents make up more than a third of all living mammal species and are adapted to all terrestrial habitats. Order: Rodentia. [Mid-19C. < modern Latin *Rodentia* < Latin *rodent-*, present participle of *rodere* "gnaw"]

ro·den·ti·cide /rō déntə sīd/ *n* a substance designed to kill rodents, especially rats and mice

ro·dent ul·cer *n* a persistent, usually cancerous ulcer of the skin, especially of the face [< RODENT as adjective, "gnawing"]

ro·de·o /rṓdee ō, rō dáy ō/ *n* (*plural* **-os**) **1.** *Southwest US* **COMPETITION IN COWBOY SKILLS** a competition or display of lassoing, bronco-riding, calf-roping, and steer-wrangling **2. MOTORCYCLING COMPETITION** a competition or display of motorcycle riding that often includes stunts **3.** *Southwest US* **CATTLE ROUND-UP** an occasion when cattle are rounded up, especially so that they can be branded, counted, or have their health checked **4.** *Southwest US* **CATTLE PEN** a pen for rounded-up cattle ■ *vi* (**-od, -o·ing, -os**) *Southwest US* AGRIC, SPORTS **PARTICIPATE IN RODEO** to take part in a rodeo [Mid-19C. < Spanish, "cattle ring" < *rodear* "go round, surround" < Latin *rotare* (see ROTATE)]

Rodg·ers /rójjərz/, **Richard** (1902–79) US composer. His collaborations with Lorenz Hart and Oscar Hammerstein II produced popular musicals such as *Pal Joey* (1940) and *Oklahoma!* (1943).

Ro·din /rō dáN/, **Auguste** (1840–1917) French sculptor. Among his bronze sculptures are *The Thinker* (1880), *The Kiss* (1880), and *The Burghers of Calais* (1886). Full name **Rodin, François Auguste René**

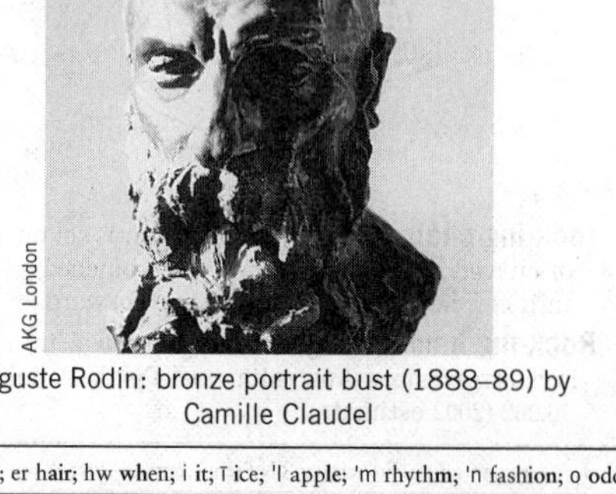

AKG London

Auguste Rodin: bronze portrait bust (1888–89) by Camille Claudel

> "What is ugly in Art is only that which is without character, that is, that which offers no truth at all, either exterior or interior."
> [Attributed to Auguste Rodin]

rod·man /ródmən, ród màn/ (*plural* **-men** /-mən, -mèn/) *n* a surveyor's assistant, especially a man, whose job is to hold the graduated pole, or rod

Rod·ney /ródnee/, **Caesar** (1728–84) American patriot. A delegate from Delaware to the first and second continental congresses, he was a signatory of the Declaration of Independence (1776). He later served as president, or chief executive, of Delaware (1778–81).

rod·o·mon·tade /ròddəmən táyd, -mon-, -taad/, **rhod·o·mon·tade** (*literary*) *n* **BOASTFULNESS** pretentious, self-important, or self-indulgent boasting, speech, or behavior ■ *vi* (**-tad·ed, -tad·ing, -tades**) **BOAST** to boast or speak in a pretentious, self-important, or self-indulgent way ■ *adj* **BOASTFUL** boastful in a pretentious, self-important, or self-indulgent way [Early 17C. Via French < obsolete Italian *rodomontada* < *rodomonte* "braggart" < *Rodomonte*, boastful Saracen king in 15 and 16C Italian long romantic poems]

rod·per·son /ród pùrss'n/ *n* a surveyor's assistant whose job is to hold the graduated pole, or rod

Ro·drí·guez Za·pa·te·ro /ro drèe gez-/ ➧ **Zapatero, José Luis Rodríguez**

roe[1] /rō/ *n* **1. FISH EGGS** a mass of mature fish eggs, especially when still inside the ovarian sac, sometimes eaten cooked **2. FISH SPERM** a mass of mature fish sperm, especially when it is still inside the testicular sac **3. CRUSTACEAN EGGS** a mass of mature eggs of some crustaceans, e.g., lobsters, especially when still inside the ovarian sac [15C. < Middle Dutch or Middle Low German *roge*]

roe[2] /rō/ (*plural same* or **roes**) *n* ZOOL same as **roe deer** [Old English *rā* < Germanic]

Roeb·ling /rṓbling/, **Emily** (1843–1903) US civil engineer. Married to civil engineer Washington Roebling, she supervised the completion of the Brooklyn Bridge after her husband, the engineer in charge, became paralyzed.

Roeb·ling, John Augustus (1806–69) German-born US civil engineer. A pioneer of the construction of suspension bridges, he designed the Brooklyn Bridge (1869), which was later built by his son Washington Augustus Roebling (1837–1926).

roe·buck /rṓ bùk/ (*plural same* or **-bucks**) *n* a male roe deer, especially an adult one

roe deer *n* a medium-sized reddish brown deer. Native to: deciduous woodlands of Europe and Asia. Latin name: *Capreolus capreolus.*

roent·gen /réntgən, réntjən/, **rönt·gen** *n* a unit of radiation, used to measure the exposure of somebody or something to X-rays and gamma rays, defined in terms of the ionization effect on air. It is equal to the quantity of radiation that produces ionization equal to one electrostatic unit of charge at 0° and standard atmospheric pressure. Symbol **R** [Late 19C. After W. C. ROENTGEN]

Roent·gen /réntgən, réntjən/, **Wilhelm Conrad** (1845–1923) German physicist. He discovered X-rays, originally known also as "Roentgen rays." He was awarded the Nobel Prize (1901).

> "All bodies are transparent to this agent ...For brevity's sake I shall use the expression 'rays'; and to distinguish them from others of this name I shall call them 'X-rays.'"
> [Wilhelm Conrad Roentgen. Quoted in *William Conrad Roentgen and the Early History of the Roentgen Rays*, Otto Glasser; 1933]

Roes·lare·e /ro͝ossə laarə/ city in West Flanders Province, western Belgium, 18 mi./29 km south of Bruges. Population: 54,002 (1999).

Roeth·ke /rétkee, rétkə/, **Theodore** (1908–63) US poet. His volume of poetry, *The Waking: Poems* (1953), won a Pulitzer Prize.

> "In a dark wood I saw / I saw my several selves / Come running from the leaves, / Lewd, tiny, careless lives / That scuttled under stones, / Or broke, but would not go."
> [Theodore Roethke, "The Exorcism"; 1958]

ro·gal·lo /rə gállō/ (*plural* **-los**), **ro·gal·lo wing** *n* a fabric-covered delta-shaped wing that can be folded compactly. Use: hang-gliders, ultralight aircraft. [Mid-20C. After Francis M. *Rogallo* (1912–), US engineer]

ro·gan josh /rōgən jósh/ *n* in South Asian cuisine, a dish of curried meat, usually lamb, in a thick tomato-based sauce [Mid-20C. < Urdu]

ro·ga·tion /rō gáysh'n/ *n* **1.** in the Christian Church, a solemn prayer or supplication, especially one made as part of the observation of the three days preceding Ascension Day **(Rogation Days)** (*often used in the plural*) **2.** in ancient Rome, the submission of a law by a consul or tribune to the people for their approval, or a law so submitted [14C. < Latin *rogation-* < *rogat-*, past participle of *rogare* "ask, beg"]

Ro·ga·tion Day *n* any of the three days preceding Ascension Day (*often used in the plural*)

Ro·ga·tion Sun·day *n* the Sunday before the Christian festival of Ascension Day. Date: five weeks after Easter.

ro·ga·to·ry /róggə tàwree/ *adj* requesting information, especially information that might be pertinent to a court case [Mid-19C. Via French < medieval Latin *rogatorius* < Latin *rogat-* (see ROGATION)]

rog·er /rójjər/ *interj* **1.** MESSAGE RECEIVED indicates that the speaker has received and understood a transmitted message (*in telecommunications*) **2.** OK used to indicate the speaker's agreement to something (*informal*) ■ *vti* **(-ered, -er·ing, -ers)** OFFENSIVE TERM an offensive term meaning to have sexual intercourse with somebody (*dated slang*) [Mid-20C. < the name *Roger*, used in radio communications for the letter *r*, for "received"]

Rog·ers /rójjərz/ city in northwestern Arkansas, west of Beaver Lake and north of Springdale. Population: 41,545 (2002 estimate).

Rog·ers, Ginger (1911–95) US dancer and actor. She was Fred Astaire's dance partner in many Hollywood musicals (1933–49), including *Top Hat* (1935). Born **McMath, Virginia Katherine**

Rog·ers, Sir Richard George, Baron Rogers of Riverside (*b.* 1933) British architect. A prominent exponent of postmodernism, he developed a high-tech style, exemplified by the Lloyd's Building, London, England (1986).

Rog·ers, Will (1879–1935) US humorist. He was known for his vaudeville performances and rope tricks. Full name **Rogers, William Penn Adair**

> "You can't say civilization don't advance, however, for in every war they kill you a new way."
> [Will Rogers, *New York Times*; December 23, 1929]

Rog·ers Moun·tain mountain in southwestern Virginia, near the North Carolina border. It is the highest point in the state. Height: 5,729 ft./1,746 m.

Ro·get /rō zháy/, **Peter Mark** (1779–1869) British scholar and doctor. He compiled the *Thesaurus of English Words and Phrases* (1852), now known as *Roget's Thesaurus.*

rogue /rōg/ *n* **1.** SOMEBODY DISHONEST an unscrupulous or dishonest person, especially somebody who is also likable **2.** SOMEBODY MISCHIEVOUS a mischievously playful person, especially a naughty child **3.** DANGEROUS SOLITARY ANIMAL a vicious or uncontrolled animal that lives apart from the rest of its herd or group **4.** BOT BIOLOGICALLY INFERIOR VARIANT a plant that is a biologically inferior variant of its type ■ *adj* **1.** UNORTHODOX AND UNPREDICTABLE acting independently and using unorthodox methods that are unpredictable and are likely to cause trouble ○ *a rogue trader* **2.** DANGEROUS AND SOLITARY describes an animal that is vicious and uncontrolled and lives apart from the rest of the herd or group ○ *a rogue male* **3.** BOT STRAY describes a plant that is inferior and unwanted ■ *vt* **(rogued, rogu·ing, rogues)** AGRIC, PLANTS CLEAR PLANTS to remove inferior plants from a crop or a group of plants [Mid-16C. < ?] —**rogu·er·y** /rōgəree/ *n*

Rogue /rōg/ river in southwestern Oregon, rising in the Cascade Mountains and emptying into the Pacific Ocean. Length: 200 mi./322 km.

rogues' gal·ler·y *n* a set of photographs of known criminals that the police show to witnesses to crimes for possible identification (*informal*)

rogue site *n* website that acquires visitors by having a domain name similar to that of a popular site

rogue state *n* a nation whose leadership intentionally refuses to adhere to the conventions of international law, does not honor established treaties, and may engage in terrorism and warfare

rogu·ish /rōgish/ *adj* **1.** unscrupulous or dishonest in the manner of a rogue **2.** mischievously playful —**rogu·ish·ly** *adv* —**rogu·ish·ness** *n*

Ro·he ♦ **Mies van der Rohe, Ludwig**

Roh Moo-hyun /rōmoo hyún/ (*b.* 1946) president of South Korea. A human rights lawyer, he entered politics in 1988 and was elected president in 2002.

Ro·hyp·nol /rō híp nàwl/ *tdmk* a trademark for flunitrazepam, a powerful sedative sometimes associated with date rape

ROI *abbr* FIN return on investment

'roid /royd/ *n* same as **steroid** (*slang*) [Late 20C. Shortening]

'roid rage *n* an outburst of violent or aggressive behavior supposedly caused by taking too many anabolic steroids to improve athletic performance (*slang*)

roil /royl/ **(roiled, roil·ing, roils)** *v* **1.** *vti* to stir up a liquid so that the sediment becomes dispersed through the liquid and makes it cloudy, or become cloudy with sediment by being stirred **2.** *vt* to anger or annoy somebody [Late 16C. < ?] —**roil·y** *adj*

Roi·sín Dubh /ro sheen do͞ov/ *n Ireland* Ireland personified as a woman (*literary*) [< Irish, "black rose"]

rois·ter /róystər/ **(-tered, -ter·ing, -ters)** *vi* **1.** to take part in loud rowdy partying or celebrations (*dated*) **2.** to behave in a loud bragging manner (*archaic*) [Mid-16C. Probably < Old French *ru(i)stre* "boor, churl" < Latin *rusticus* "rustic"] —**rois·ter·er** *n* —**rois·ter·ous** *adj* —**rois·ter·ous·ly** *adv*

ro·jak /rō jàk/ *n Malaysia, Singapore* **1.** a mixed salad of fruit and vegetables **2.** an offensive term for a person of mixed ethnic background (*slang*) [Late 20C. < Malay, "mixed"]

Ro·land /rōlənd/ [After the legendary nephew of Charlemagne and comrade of Oliver in medieval romance] ◇ **a Roland for an Oliver** an equally good retort, response, or retaliation (*archaic*)

role /rōl/, **rôle** *n* **1.** ACTING PART an individual part in a play, movie, opera, or other performance **2.** SPECIFIC FUNCTION the usual or expected function of somebody or something, or the part somebody or something plays in an action or event **3.** PART PLAYED IN SOCIAL CONTEXT the part played by somebody in a given social context, with any characteristic or expected pattern of behavior that it entails [Early 17C. < French *rôle* "(paper) roll on which an actor's part is written" < Old French *rol(l)e* (see ROLL)]

SPELLCHECK role or **roll**? Do not confuse the spelling of ***role*** and ***roll***, which sound similar. ***Role*** is a noun denoting a part played by somebody or something: *She has a leading role in the movie. What was the role of the president in this affair? Teachers are role models for their students. We engaged in role-playing exercises.* ***Roll*** is a noun or verb referring to a round shape or movement (as in *roll into a ball, roll down the hill, a roll of film*) or an official list (as in *call the roll, on the electoral roll*).

role mod·el *n* a worthy person who is a good example for other people

role-play *n* **1.** ACTING OUT OF PART the acting out of a part, especially that of somebody with a particular social role, in order to understand it better **2.** GAME SESSION INVOLVING TAKING ON ROLES in a computer or other game, a session during which players take on the roles of characters ■ *v* **1.** *vti* ACT OUT PART to engage or act out a part in role-playing **2.** *vt* PLAYING CHARACTER IN GAME in a computer or other game, to take on the role of a character in a game

role-play·ing *n* the acting out of a part, especially as a learning aid in language learning, or as an aid to better understanding a well-defined social role in psychotherapy

role-play·ing game COMPUT GAMES full form of **RPG**

Rolfe /rolf/, **John** (1585–1622) English-born American colonist. He devised a method for curing tobacco and was married to the Native North American princess, Pocahontas (1614).

Rolf·ing /rólfing/ *n* a service mark for a therapy using vigorous massage to alleviate physical or psychological tension

roll /rōl/ *v* **(rolled, roll·ing, rolls) 1.** *vti* TURN OVER AND OVER to move with repeated turning or rotating motions, or cause something to move in this way **2.** *vti* MOVE ON WHEELS to move on wheels or rollers, or cause something to move on wheels or rollers **3.** *vi* DRIVE IN VEHICLE to move in a wheeled vehicle **4.** *vti* ROTATE to turn in a complete or partial rotation, or cause something to turn in this way **5.** *vi* ASTRON ORBIT to revolve in an orbit (*refers to astronomical objects*) **6.** *vti* AVIAT ROTATE AIRCRAFT to cause an aircraft to perform a single complete rotation about its lengthwise axis while maintaining the same altitude and direction, or perform such a rotation **7.** *vi* WRITHE to lie on the back and move about or from side to side, but without moving very far, often with a writhing motion (*refers to animals*) **8.** *vi* BE CARRIED BY RIVER to be transported by river **9.** *vti* THROW DICE to throw a die or dice **10.** *vt* SCORE NUMBER BY THROWING DICE to achieve a particular number, position, or score by throwing a die or dice **11.** *vt* FLATTEN SOMETHING WITH ROLLER to flatten or spread something, especially by using a roller or rolling pin **12.** *vti* FORM INTO ROUND SHAPE to form something into a ball, tube, cylinder, or other rounded shape, or be formed into such a shape **13.** *vt* TURN BETWEEN OR ON SOMETHING to revolve something between two surfaces or on a coating material ○ *Roll the chocolates in powdered sugar.* **14.** *vi* STRETCH OUT OR AWAY IN UNDULATIONS to have or take the form of a succession of gentle slopes ○ *green hills rolling away into the distance* **15.** *vti* MOVE WITH UNDULATIONS to move in a steady flowing motion, or cause something to move in a steady flowing motion **16.** *vti* ROCK FROM SIDE TO SIDE to move with a sideways swaying or rocking motion on waves or a swell, or cause something, especially a ship, to move in this way **17.** *vi* WALK UNSTEADILY to walk with an unsteady or staggering motion **18.** *vi* WALK WITH SWAY to sway rhythmically in walking **19.** *vti* OPERATE SOMETHING to function, or cause something to function, especially a movie camera or printing press **20.** *vti* MOVIES, MEDIA SEND OR GO UP ON SCREEN to cause credits, titles, or other captions to move in a continuous upward direction on a cinema or television screen, or move in this way **21.** *vi* ELAPSE to go by or elapse, especially uneventfully or imperceptibly (*refers especially to time*) **22.** *vi* TRAVEL AROUND to travel from place to place **23.** *vi* BE UNDER WAY to proceed or continue successfully (*informal*) ○ *Now this project is finally rolling.* ○ *We're ready to roll.* **24.** *vi* MOVE AS CROWD to move or arrive in large numbers or in a crowd **25.** *vi* REVERBERATE LOUDLY to make a low prolonged rumbling noise **26.** *vi* BEAT DRUM to make a series of quick beats on a drum **27.** *vt* MUSIC PLAY CHORD WITH SPREAD NOTES to play a chord sounding its notes in rapid succession **(arpeggio)** rather than simultaneously **28.** *vt* ROB SOMEBODY to take money or belongings from somebody who cannot offer any resistance (*informal*) **29.** *vt* PHON TRILL SOUND to pronounce a sound, especially an "r," with a trill **30.** *vt* PRINTING INK SOMETHING WITH ROLLER to apply ink to type or a plate with a roller **31.** *vti* HAVE SEX to have sexual intercourse or engage in sexual foreplay with somebody (*informal; sometimes offensive*) ■ *n* **1.** SOMETHING TUBE-SHAPED a tube, cylinder, or coil of something, especially something that is wrapped around itself **2.** EQUIPMENT HOLDER WITH POCKETS a length of fabric or leather that has pockets to hold tools, medical instruments, or other equipment and can usually be wrapped around itself and tied up **3. WAD OF MONEY** a cylindrical wad of bills formed by coiling the wad around itself (*informal*) **4. BREAD ROLL** a small individual bread, usually round or long in shape, or a sandwich made from one **5. FILLED FOOD** a food made by wrapping pastry around a filling or by spreading a filling on something such as sponge cake and wrapping it around itself (*usually used in combination*) **6. REPEATED TURN** a repeated turning or rotating motion **7. TOSS OF DICE** a throw of a dice **8.** AVIAT **ROTATION OF AIRCRAFT** a midair flight maneuver in which an aircraft maintains the same height and direction while doing a single complete rotation about its lengthwise axis **9.** GYMNASTICS **SOMERSAULT** a gentle somersault **10. MOVEMENT ON WHEELS** a movement on wheels or rollers **11. SINGLE TURN** a complete or partial rotation **12. WRITHING MOTION** an action that involves writhing while turning backward and forward or from side to side, but without moving very far **13. MOVEMENT FROM SIDE TO SIDE** a swaying or rocking motion, especially by a ship **14. SWAYING WALK** a rhythmic sway in walking **15. OFFICIAL LIST** an official register or list of names, especially of school pupils, members of a club, or people entitled to vote **16. TOTAL ON OFFICIAL LIST** the total number of people registered on a school, club, or electoral roll **17. ROUNDED LAYER** a thick rounded layer of something, especially of flesh **18.** ARCHIT **SPIRAL SCROLL** in Greek architecture, a spiral scroll on an Ionic column **19. ACT OF FLATTENING** an act of flattening or spreading something, especially by using a roller or rolling pin **20. SOMETHING UNDULATING** a gentle rounded hump on a surface, often one of a series **21. UNDULATING MOVEMENT** a steady, flowing, undulating movement **22. RHYTHMIC STREAM OF WORDS** a continuous stream of words with a rhythmic quality **23. ROLLER FOR METAL** a cylinder or roller used for pressing, shaping, or flattening something, especially one used for shaping metal in a rolling mill **24. BOOKBINDER'S TOOL** a bookbinder's tool for embossing decorative lines on book covers **25. TRILLING SOUND** a trilling noise, especially the sound of a trilled "r" or the song of a canary **26. RUMBLING NOISE** a low prolonged rumbling noise **27. DRUM BEATS** a series of quick beats on a drum **28.** MUSIC **CHORD WITH SPREAD NOTES** a chord with its notes played in rapid succession (**arpeggio**) rather than simultaneously **29. ACT OF ROBBERY** an act or the process of taking money or belongings from somebody who cannot offer any resistance (*slang*) **30. SEX ACT** an act of sexual intercourse or foreplay (*informal; sometimes offensive*) [12C. Via Old French *rolle* "scroll" < Latin *rotul-* "little wheel" < Latin *rota* "wheel"] ◇ **a roll in the hay** an instance of having sex with somebody (*slang*) ◇ **be rolling in it** to be very rich (*informal*) ◇ **on a roll** enjoying a period of good luck or of doing something well (*informal*) ◇ **rolled into one** forming a single unit consisting of a number of different aspects or qualities

SPELLCHECK See *role*.

roll back *vt* **1. DECREASE SOMETHING** to cause something, especially prices or wages, to decrease **2. FORCE TO WITHDRAW** to cause somebody or something to retreat **3. PUT STOP TO SOMETHING** to reduce or nullify the influence or effectiveness of something

roll in *vi* **1.** to come home or arrive at a destination, especially in a leisurely way, often later than expected **2.** to arrive or attend in large numbers or quantities

roll off *vi* **1.** to flow, especially with ease or in large numbers **2.** to display a gradually decreasing response in the upper and lower portions of the amplitude-frequency range (*refers to an electronic system or transducer*)

roll on *vi UK* used in interjections to express a wish that a time or occasion may arrive soon (*informal*) ○ *Roll on summer!*

roll out *v* **1.** *vt* **FLATTEN PASTRY** to flatten pastry, dough, or other uncooked food by shaping it with a rolling pin **2.** *vt* **UNCOIL SOMETHING** to unfold or uncoil something **3.** *vi* FOOTBALL **RUN TOWARD SIDELINE** in football, to perform a play in which a quarterback runs toward either sideline **4.** *vt* **SHOW SOMETHING TO PUBLIC** to put a new product on public display for the first time **5.** *vt* MARKETING **LAUNCH PRODUCT GRADUALLY** to launch a new product or service by gradually increasing the number of outlets where it is available to the public

roll over *v* **1.** *vi* **CAPSIZE** to capsize, tip over, or overturn **2.** *vt* **DEFEAT SOMEBODY** to defeat a person or team overwhelmingly (*informal*) **3.** *vti* **ACCUMULATE PRIZE MONEY** to add the amount of prize money not won on one occasion to the prize money available on a subsequent occasion, or be added to future prize money in this way **4.** *vt* FIN **EXTEND LOAN** to allow a loan to be paid at a later date **5.** *vt* FIN **NEGOTIATE NEW FINANCIAL TERMS FOR SOMETHING** to achieve new terms for a financial contract through discussion **6.** *vt* FIN **REINVEST FUNDS** to transfer funds from one investment to a similar investment

roll up *v* **1.** *vt* **PRODUCE CYLINDER SHAPE** to turn something into a cylindrical form **2.** *vt US* **ACCUMULATE SOMETHING** to accumulate something, especially money **3.** *vi* **ARRIVE** to come to a place or destination, often in a vehicle and especially when later than expected or when not expected at all

roll·a·way /rṓlə wày/ *adj* fitted with wheels or casters so as to be easily moved or stored

roll·back /rṓl bàk/ *n* **1.** a decrease in something, especially in something such as prices and wages **2.** a reduction or nullification of the influence or effectiveness of something

roll bar *n* a reinforcing bar across the top of a vehicle, especially an open-top sports car or rally car, to protect the occupants if the vehicle overturns

roll cage *n* **1.** a protective network of metal bars enclosing the driver of a racing car **2.** a reinforcing framework, usually built into the bodywork of a car, around and over the passenger cabin to protect the occupants if the vehicle turns over

roll call *n* **1.** a check on attendance, especially in a school or military establishment, by calling out the names of those expected to be present, with each of those present responding **2.** a time when a roll call is read out, especially one that is fixed at a regular time of day

roll down *n* in financial markets, the closure of one option position and the opening of another one of the same class, but with a lower strike price

rolled gold *n Can, UK* a thin layer of gold bonded to a backing layer of brass or other base metal. It is used in the manufacture of inexpensive and costume jewellery. US term **filled gold**

rolled oats *npl* oats that have had the husks removed and been flattened and are used in making oatmeal

rolled steel *n* steel produced to a desired thickness by being passed through a set of rollers

roll·er[1] /rṓlər/ *n* **1. DEVICE FOR APPLYING PAINT** a painting tool in the form of a revolving tube with a soft absorbent covering and a handle, used for applying paint to large surface areas **2. SMALL SOLID WHEEL** a small wheel without spokes, especially on a skate or a piece of heavy furniture **3. DEVICE FOR FLATTENING LAWNS** a large heavy revolving cylinder or pair of cylinders with a handle, used for flattening a lawn or green **4. HAIR CURLER** a short tube around which hair is wrapped in order to make it curly or wavy **5. COILED BANDAGE** a long bandage that is rolled up tightly upon itself to form a dense cylinder. The required amount is then cut off for use. **6. HEAVY WAVE** a long heavy wave that does not break until it reaches the shoreline **7.** PRINTING **INKED TUBE** a hard tube, usually of compressed rubber, on which ink is spread and rolled over type or an engraved plate before printing **8.** ENG **CYLINDER THAT TRANSMITS FORCE AND MOTION** a cylindrically shaped rotating device that transmits force and motion via its rotation, often used in sets or pairs and machine-operated **9.** RIDING **BELT FOR HORSE BLANKET** a strap around the belly of a horse to hold a blanket in place **10.** *US* BASEBALL **WEAKLY HIT BASEBALL** in baseball, a batted ball that rolls along the ground slowly **11. SOMEBODY OR SOMETHING THAT ROLLS** somebody or something that rolls [14C. < ROLL]

rol·ler[2] /rṓlər/ *n* a blue and brown bird that performs rolling dives and flies erratically during the breeding season. Native to: Europe. Family: Coraciidae. [Late 17C. < German < *rollen* "to roll"]

roll·er·ball /rṓlər bàwl/ *n* a device containing a freely rotating ball that is moved by the fingers to control a cursor on a computer screen

roll·er bear·ing *n* a set of rotating cylindrically shaped parallel steel rollers contained within a closed track, used to prevent friction between machine parts

Roll·er·blade /rṓlər blàyd/ *tdmk* a trademark for a type of roller skate on which the wheels are arranged in one straight line

roll·er blind *n* a blind consisting of a length of fabric rolled around a pole and fitted to the top of a window. It unrolls when lowered and rolls up when raised.

roll·er chain *n* a power transmission chain consisting of freely rotating hollow cylindrical rollers mounted on pins that connect the plates that link adjacent rollers

roll·er coast·er *n* **1.** an amusement park ride consisting of a narrow rail track on a metal framework shaped into extreme peaks and troughs and sharp bends **2.** a situation that is characterized by sudden, extreme, and often repeated changes (*hyphenated when used before a noun*)

roll·er der·by *n* competition between two teams of roller skaters

roll·er hock·ey *n* hockey played on a roller rink or other hard surface by players wearing roller skates

roll·er rink *n* a place where people can go to roller-skate

roll·er skate *n* **1.** a metal or plastic frame with wheels attached, usually one pair at the front and another at the back, fastened onto a shoe and used for skating **2.** a specially designed shoe or boot to which a roller skate is attached —**roll·er-skate** *vi* —**roll·er skat·er** *n* —**roll·er skat·ing** *n*

roll·er tow·el *n* a continuous roll of material housed inside a metal box and used for drying the hands. Each user pulls down a fresh section of towel.

roll film *n* a length of film rolled around a spool and put inside a protective case ready to be loaded into a camera

roll for·ward *n* the closure of one financial option position and the opening of another one of the same class, but with a later expiration date

rol·lick /róllik/ (**-licked, -lick·ing, -licks**) *vi* to have fun, especially in a loud, rowdy way [Early 19C. Probably blend of ROLL or ROMP + FROLIC] —**rol·lick** *n* —**rol·lick·some** *adj* —**rol·lick·y** *adj*

rol·lick·ing /rólliking/ *adj* loud and rowdy —**rol·lick·ing·ly** *adv*

roll·ing /rṓling/ *adj* **1. UNDULATING** characterized by undulating slopes **2. GRADUALLY DEVELOPING** proceeding in successive phases and usually gaining in momentum, intensity, or effectiveness ○ *a rolling program of reform* **3. REVERBERATING** characterized by a low, prolonged, rumbling noise **4. RICH** very well-off (*informal*) ■ *adv* **EXTREMELY** to the extent of staggering (*informal*) ○ *rolling drunk*

roll·ing con·tract *n* a contract for a period of more than one year that is renewed annually for the initial period, subject to a favorable review

roll·ing hitch *n* a knot used for joining two pieces of rope together or shortening a length of rope, or for attaching a rope to a spar

Roll·ing Mead·ows /rṓling mèddōz/ city in northeastern Illinois, northeast of Hoffman Estates. It is a northwestern suburb of Chicago. Population: 24,582 (2002 estimate).

roll·ing mill *n* **1.** a factory, or part of a factory, where metal, usually in ingot form, is processed by being rolled into sheets or bars of the desired shape and size **2.** a machine with rollers that press metal into sheets or bars of the desired shape and size

roll·ing pa·per *n* a small piece of fine paper used for rolling a handmade cigarette (*often used in the plural*)

roll·ing pin *n* a cylinder, sometimes with small handles at either end, used for rolling out and flattening dough, pastry, or other uncooked food

roll·ing stock *n* **1.** railroad vehicles, e.g., locomotives, passenger cars, and freight cars, thought of collectively, especially those belonging to a particular company **2.** road vehicles thought of collectively, especially those belonging to a particular company

roll·ing stone *n* somebody who is incapable of staying in the same job or place for very long [Originally in the proverb, "a rolling stone gathers no moss"]

Rol·ling Stones /rṓling stṓnz/ British rock group, formed in 1962, that rivaled the popularity of the group's early contemporaries, the Beatles. The group was formed by Mick Jagger, Keith Richards, Brian Jones, Charlie Watts, and Bill Wyman, who left the band in late 1992. After Jones' death (1968), Mick Taylor replaced him until 1975, when Ron Wood took his place.

roll·mops /rṓl mòps/ *n* a fillet of raw herring wrapped around a slice of onion or a pickle and left to marinate in spiced vinegar. It is usually served as an hors d'oeuvre. [Early 20C. < German < *rollen* "to roll" + *Mops* "pug dog"]

roll·neck /rṓl nèk/ *n* **1.** a garment neck that is loose-fitting and worn folded down **2.** a garment, especially a sweater, with a rollneck —**roll·necked** *adj*

roll-on *adj* applied to the skin by means of a rotating ball in the top of the container ■ *n* a deodorant, cosmetic, or other product that comes in a container with a rotating ball in its top

roll·out /rṓl òwt/ *n* **1.** SHOWING OF NEW PRODUCT the first public display of a new product **2.** GRADUAL LAUNCH OF NEW PRODUCT a launch of a new product that involves gradually increasing the number of outlets where it is available to the public **3.** PASSING PLAY IN FOOTBALL in football, a play in which a quarterback runs with the ball toward the side of the field in order to pass it

roll·o·ver /rṓl ṑvər/ *n* **1.** ACCUMULATION OF PRIZE MONEY the addition of prize money not won on one occasion to the prize money available on a subsequent occasion **2.** FIN TRANSFER OF FUNDS a transfer of funds from one investment to another similar investment, often without taking possession of the funds **3.** CAPSIZING INCIDENT an act or the process of capsizing, tipping over, or overturning **4.** ACCIDENT WHERE VEHICLE OVERTURNS a road accident involving a vehicle that has overturned

roll-top desk, roll-top *n* a desk with a rounded cover consisting of connected parallel wooden slats that can be pulled down over the writing area and, usually, locked

roll-up *n UK* same as **roll-your-own** (*informal*)

roll·way /rṓl wày/ *n* **1.** a natural or artificial sloping area along which cylindrical objects are rolled, especially a slope used by lumberjacks to move felled timber to water for transportation **2.** a series of parallel rollers used to facilitate the transportation of heavy loads

roll-your-own *n* a hand-rolled cigarette made using a cigarette paper and loose tobacco (*informal*)

Ro·lo·dex /rṓlə dèks/ *tdmk* a trademark for a desktop card-index system in which cards containing names, addresses, and telephone numbers are attached to but removable from a central cylinder

Röl·vaag /rṓl vaàg/, **O. E.** (1876–1931) Norwegian-born US writer and educator. He wrote epic novels about Norwegian settlers in the United States. Full name **Rölvaag, Ole Edvart**

ro·ly-po·ly /rṓlee pṓlee/ *adj* of greater body weight than is considered desirable (*sometimes offensive*) [Early 17C. Probably rhyming compound of ROLL + POLL]

Rom /rōm/ (*plural same* or **Ro·ma** /rṓmə/) *n* **1.** a member of a nomadic people who migrated from South Asia to Europe in the 15th century and now live throughout the world **2.** a man belonging to the Roma [Mid-19C. < Romany, "married man"] —**Ro·ma** *adj*

ROM /rom/ *abbr* COMPUT read-only memory

rom., rom *abbr* PRINTING roman

Rom. *abbr* **1.** Roman **2.** LANG Romance **3.** Romania **4.** LANG Romanian **5.** BIBLE Romans

Ro·ma PEOPLES plural of **Rom**

Ro·ma·gna /rō maányə/ historical region of north central Italy. It was under Byzantine rule between the 6th and the 8th centuries, when it became incorporated into the Papal States.

ro·maine /rō máyn/, **ro·maine let·tuce** *n* a variety of lettuce with a long slender head and loose leaves. Latin name: *Latuca sativa longifolia.* [Early 20C. < French, form of *romain* "Roman"]

ro·ma·ji /rṓmajee/ *n* the Roman alphabet as used for transliterating Japanese [Late 19C. < Japanese < *roma* "Roman" + *ji* "character"]

ro·man[1] /rṓmən/ *adj* relating to a typeface with upright as opposed to slanting characters that is the standard type used in printing books, newspapers, and magazines ■ *n* roman type or characters [Early 16C. Because it imitates the style of Roman inscriptions]

ro·man[2] /rō maáN/ *n* **1.** a novel, especially a French one or one in a French genre (*literary*) **2.** a medieval French narrative poem, especially one that has heroic exploits as its main theme [Mid-18C. < French, "romance, romantic narrative"]

Ro·man /rṓmən/ *adj* **1.** OF MODERN ROME relating to the modern city of Rome and its inhabitants **2.** ANCIENT HIST OF ANCIENT ROME relating to the ancient city of Rome and its territories and inhabitants **3.** ARCHIT OF ANCIENT ROMAN ARCHITECTURAL STYLE relating to, or built in, a style characteristic of the buildings of ancient Rome, especially in having rounded arches, vaults, and domes **4.** CHR OF ROMAN CATHOLIC CHURCH belonging to or characteristic of the Roman Catholic Church ■ *n* **1.** SOMEBODY FROM MODERN ROME somebody who comes from the modern city of Rome **2.** ANCIENT HIST SOMEBODY FROM ANCIENT ROME somebody who came from ancient Rome **3.** CHR OFFENSIVE TERM an offensive term for a member of the Roman Catholic Church [Pre-12C. < Latin *Romanus* "Roman, a Roman" < *Roma* "Rome"; later reinforced by French *Romain*]

ro·man à clef /rō maáN a kláy/ (*plural* **ro·mans à clef** /*pronunc. same*/) *n* a novel in which some or all of the characters are based on real people and that usually includes clues to the characters' true identities [< French, "novel with a key"]

Ro·man al·pha·bet *n* the writing system that represents sounds by 26 letters from A to Z, used for most languages in Western Europe and many elsewhere. It is based on the alphabet developed in ancient Rome.

ro·man à thèse /rō maáN aa táyz/ (*plural* **ro·mans à thèse** /*pronunc. same*/) *n* a novel in which the author focuses on an injustice and suggests how it might be rectified, especially by putting forward a political message or social theory [< French, "novel with a thesis"]

Ro·man cal·en·dar *n* the lunar calendar, comprising 10 months and an intercalated month, that was used by the ancient Romans until the introduction of the Julian calendar in 46 B.C.

Ro·man can·dle *n* a short cylindrical firework that when placed on the ground and lit produces showers of sparks and occasional colored balls or stars of fire

Ro·man Cath·o·lic *adj* relating to the Roman Catholic Church, its members, or its beliefs ■ *n* a member of the Roman Catholic Church

Ro·man Cath·o·lic Church *n* a Christian church that has a pope as the head of a hierarchy of bishops and priests and is administered from the Vatican City in Rome

Ro·man Ca·thol·i·cism *n* the system of beliefs, practices, and organization of the Roman Catholic Church

ro·mance *n* /rō mánss, rṓ mànss/ **1.** LOVE AFFAIR a love affair, especially a brief and intense one ○ *This is more than just a holiday romance.* **2.** PHYSICAL LOVE sexual love, especially when the other person or the relationship is idealized or when it is exciting and intense **3.** SPIRIT OF ADVENTURE a spirit or feeling of adventure, excitement, the potential for heroic achievement, and the exotic ○ *the romance of cruising down the Nile* **4.** FASCINATION WITH SOMETHING a fascination or enthusiasm for something, especially of an uncritical or inexplicable kind ○ *his lifelong romance with football* **5.** STORY OF LOVE a novel, movie, or play with a love story as its main theme ○ *a writer of cheap romances* **6.** LOVE STORIES COLLECTIVELY love stories considered as a genre **7.** MEDIEVAL ADVENTURE STORY a story of the adventures of chivalrous heroes written in verse or prose in a vernacular language in the Middle Ages **8.** MEDIEVAL ADVENTURE STORIES COLLECTIVELY the genre of medieval adventure stories ○ *Arthurian romance* **9.** NARRATIVE OF ADVENTURES a fictional narrative dealing with exciting and extravagant adventures ○ *a romance of piracy on the high seas* **10.** FICTITIOUS ACCOUNT an extravagant or absurd fictitious account of something **11.** MUSIC SHORT LYRICAL PIECE a short lyrical song or instrumental composition, usually expressing or evoking tender emotions ■ *v* /rō mánss/ (**-manced, -manc·ing, -manc·es**) **1.** *vi* TELL ADVENTUROUS STORIES to tell or write extravagant or idealized fictitious accounts **2.** *vi* TELL LOVE STORIES to tell or write stories about love **3.** *vi* THINK ROMANTICALLY to think or behave in a romantic way **4.** *vt* TREAT SOMEBODY ROMANTICALLY to treat somebody in a special way during a love relationship or with a view to entering on one **5.** *vt* HAVE AFFAIR WITH SOMEBODY to have a love affair with somebody [13C. < Old French *romanz* "(work composed) in French" < assumed Vulgar Latin *romanice* "in the vernacular," form of Latin *romanicus* "Roman" < *Roma* "Rome"] —**ro·manc·er** /rō mánsər/ *n*

Ro·mance *n* the branch of Indo-European languages that includes French, Italian, Portuguese, Romanian, and Spanish, all of which are descended from Latin. Native speakers: 500 million. —**Ro·mance** *adj*

Ro·man col·lar *n* CLOTHING, CHR same as **clerical collar**

Ro·man Em·pire *n* **1.** the territories ruled by ancient Rome under its emperors, from 27 B.C. to B.C. 395. In 395, these territories were split into the Byzantine or Eastern Roman Empire and the Western Roman Empire. **2.** the rule or form of government of ancient Rome under its emperors

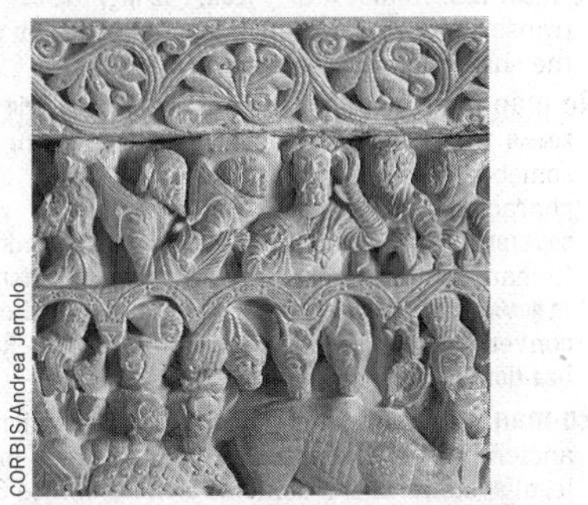

Romanesque: carved stone capital (1127–45), Pamplona cathedral, Spain

Ro·man·esque /rṓmə nésk/ *adj* **1.** TYPICAL OF EARLY EUROPEAN ARCHITECTURAL STYLE relating to or built in the style characteristic of European architecture in the 11th and the 12th centuries, especially in having rounded arches and barrel vaults **2.** RELATING TO EARLY EUROPEAN ART WORKS characteristic of or relating to the style of European painting, sculpture, or decorative arts contemporary with Romanesque architecture. Romanesque works of art show a Byzantine influence and often feature elaborate ornamentation. ■ *n* ROMANESQUE STYLE the Romanesque style in architecture or art

ro·man-fleuve /rō maáN flṓv/ (*plural* **ro·mans-fleuves** /*pronunc. same*/) *n* a long novel or series of novels telling the stories of a linked group of people over many years [< French, "river-novel"]

Ro·man hol·i·day *n* **1.** an entertainment in which people are killed, e.g., a gladiatorial contest **2.** a feeling of pleasure derived from watching other people be maimed or killed

Rom·a·ni *n, adj* LANG, PEOPLES another spelling of **Romany**

Ro·ma·ni·a /rō máynee ə/ country in southeastern Europe, bordered by Ukraine, Moldova, the Black Sea, Bulgaria, Yugoslavia, and Hungary. Language: Romanian. Currency: Romanian leu. Capital: Bucharest. Population: 22,271,839 (2003). Area: 91,700 sq. mi./237,500 sq. km. See map on next page

Ro·ma·ni·an /rō máynee ən, -máynyən/ (*plural* **Ro·ma·ni·ans** or **Ru·ma·ni·ans**) *n* **1.** somebody who comes from Romania **2.** the official language of Romania, belonging to the Romance group of Indo-European

Romania

languages that developed from Latin —**Ro·ma·ni·an** *adj*

Ro·man·ic /rō mánnik/ *adj* **1.** OF ANCIENT ROME belonging or relating to ancient Rome or the ancient Romans **2.** OF ROMANCE LANGUAGES relating to the Romance family of languages ■ *n* ROMANCE LANGUAGES COLLECTIVELY the Romance family of languages as a group

Ro·man·ism /rṓmə nìzzəm/ *n* an offensive term for Roman Catholicism, especially its rituals

Ro·man·ist /rṓmənist/ *n* **1.** OFFENSIVE TERM an offensive term for a member of the Roman Catholic Church **2.** STUDENT OF ANCIENT ROME a student of or expert in ancient Roman history or law ■ *adj* **1.** OFFENSIVE TERM an offensive term meaning belonging or relating to the Roman Catholic Church **2.** OF ANCIENT ROMAN HISTORY relating to or involving ancient Roman history or law —**Ro·man·is·tic** /rṑmə nístik/ *adj*

ro·man·ize /rṓmə nīz/ (**-ized, -iz·ing, -iz·es**) *vt* to transcribe something such as a language or text in the characters of the Roman alphabet

Ro·man·ize (**-ized, -iz·ing, -iz·es**) *v* **1.** *vti* MAKE OR BECOME ROMAN to take on Roman characteristics, or make somebody or something take on Roman characteristics ○ *the Romanized Celts* **2.** *vt* MAKE SOMETHING ROMAN CATHOLIC to make something take on a Roman Catholic character or influence **3.** *vti* CONVERT TO ROMAN CATHOLICISM to become a Roman Catholic, or convert somebody to Roman Catholicism —**Ro·man·i·za·tion** /rṑməni záysh'n/ *n*

Ro·man law *n* **1.** the system of law established in ancient Rome, forming the basis of many modern legal systems **2.** LAW same as **civil law** (sense 3)

Ro·man mile *n* a measure of distance used in ancient Rome, approximately equal to 1,620 yards/1,481 m

Ro·man nose *n* a nose with a high and prominent bridge

Ro·man nu·mer·al *n* a letter or sequence of letters used by the ancient Romans to represent cardinal numbers, including I for 1, V for 5, and X for 10

Ro·ma·no /rō maánō/ *n* a hard sharp-tasting Italian cheese similar to Parmesan [Early 20C. Via Italian, "Roman" < Latin *Romanus* < *Roma* "Rome"]

Ro·ma·no /rō maánō/ ➧ **Giulio Romano**

Ro·mans /rṓmənz/ *n* a book of the Bible, originally a letter addressed to the Church in Rome and traditionally attributed to St. Paul. Written in about A.D. 58, it explains his theory of religious thinking. (*takes a singular verb*) See table at **Bible**

Ro·mansch /rō maánsh, -mánsh/, **Ro·mansh** *n* a Rhaeto-Romance language that is one of the official languages of Switzerland. Native speakers: 50,000. [Mid-17C. < Romansch < assumed Vulgar Latin *romanice* (see ROMANCE)] —**Ro·mansch** *adj*

ro·man·tic /rō mántik/ *adj* **1.** INVOLVING SEXUAL LOVE involving or characteristic of a love affair or sexual love, especially when the relationship is idealized or exciting and intense ○ *I don't think there's any romantic attachment between them.* **2.** SUITABLE FOR LOVE characterized by or suitable for lovemaking or the expression of tender emotions ○ *a romantic candlelit dinner for two* **3.** IDEALISTIC characterized by or arising from idealistic or impractical attitudes and expectations ○ *a romantic dreamer* **4.** IMAGINARY imaginary or fictitious in an extravagant or glamorizing way ○ *a romantic version of the events of her life* **5.** INVOLVING ADVENTURE relating to or characterized by adventure, excitement, the potential for heroic achievement, or the exotic ○ *a romantic tale about life in the outback* **6.** ARTS another spelling of **Romantic** ■ *n* **1.** SOMEBODY ROMANTIC somebody who has a romantic personality or outlook **2.** ARTS another spelling of **Romantic** [Mid-17C. < obsolete *romaunt* "romance, romantic narrative" < Old French, variant of *romanz* (see ROMANCE)] —**ro·man·ti·cal·ly** *adv*

Ro·man·tic *adj* relating to a movement in late 18th- and early 19th-century music, literature, and art that departed from classicism and emphasized sensibility, the free expression of feelings, nature, and interest in other cultures ■ *n* a writer, composer, or artist who was involved in the Romantic movement during the late 18th and early 19th centuries

ro·man·tic com·e·dy *n* **1.** a humorous movie, play, or novel about a love story that ends happily **2.** the genre of romantic comedies

ro·man·ti·cism /rō mánti sìzzəm/ *n* the quality of being romantic or having romantic inclinations

Ro·man·ti·cism *n* in the arts, the style and theories of the Romantic movement, or the movement itself —**Ro·man·ti·cist** *n*

ro·man·ti·cize /rō mánti sīz/ (**-cized, -ciz·ing, -ciz·es**) *v* **1.** *vt* to make something seem or believe something to be more glamorous or ideal than it really is ○ *The movie tends to romanticize a rather sordid period in history.* **2.** *vi* to think or express something in an amorous, idealistic, or sentimental way —**ro·man·ti·ci·za·tion** /-màntissi záysh'n/ *n*

Rom·a·ny /rómmənee, rṓmənee/ (*plural* **-nies**), **Rom·a·ni** *n* **1.** the Indic language of the Roma people. Native speakers: 250,000. **2.** a member of the Roma people (*dated*) [Early 19C. < Romany *Romani*, form of *Romano* "Roma" (adjective) < *Rom* "man"] —**Rom·a·ny** *adj*

Rom·berg /róm bùrg/, **Sigmund** (1887–1951) Hungarian-born US composer. His operettas include *The Student Prince* (1924), *The Desert Song* (1926), and *Up in Central Park* (1945).

rom·com /róm kòm/ *UK* same as **romantic comedy** (*informal*) [Late 20C. Contraction]

Rome /rōm/ **1.** capital city of Italy, located in the center of the country. The former capital of the Roman Empire, it includes within its boundaries the independent state of Vatican City. Population: 2,546,804 (2001). **2.** town in New York, on the Mohawk River, northwest of Utica and northeast of Syracuse. Population: 34,709 (2002 estimate). ◇ **fiddle while Rome burns** to occupy yourself with unimportant things when there are extremely important things requiring to be done ◇ **when in Rome (do as the Romans do)** used to indicate the advisability of adopting the behavior and customs of the place or circumstances in which you find yourself

Ro·me·o /rṓmee ṑ/ (*plural* **-os**) *n* **1.** a man with a reputation for having or seeking romantic or sexual involvement with a large number of women **2.** a code word for the letter "R," used in international radio communications [Mid-18C. After the lover of Juliet in William Shakespeare's play *Romeo and Juliet* (1594)]

Rom·ish /rṓmish/ *adj* an offensive term meaning belonging to, characteristic of, or influenced by the Roman Catholic Church —**Rom·ish·ly** *adv* —**Rom·ish·ness** *n*

Rom·mel /rómm'l/, **Erwin** (1891–1944) German general. He is renowned for his victories in the North African deserts during World War II. Known as **the Desert Fox**

Rom·ney /rómnee, rúmnee/, **George** (1734–1802) British painter. He is noted for his portraits of British aristocrats in neoclassical settings, especially Emma, Lady Hamilton, whom he depicted in more than 50 portraits.

Rom·ney Marsh /rómnee-/ *n* a sheep that has long wool and produces mutton, belonging to a breed originating in southern England [After a region in S Kent, England]

romp /romp/ *vi* (**romped, romp·ing, romps**) **1.** PLAY BOISTEROUSLY to run around or play in a boisterous way ○ *kids romping in the playground* **2.** RUN EASILY to run or move forward easily and smoothly ○ *The horse romped toward the finishing line.* **3.** MAKE EASY PROGRESS to progress swiftly and effortlessly ○ *romped through her final exam* **4.** WIN WITH EASE to win a contest easily (*informal*) ○ *Their team just romped all over us.* ■ *n* **1.** BOISTEROUS ACTIVITY boisterous or playful activity ○ *The dogs had a romp in the park.* **2.** LIGHTHEARTED WORK a book, play, or movie that is lighthearted and lively as opposed to serious or weighty (*informal*) ○ *The novel is an exhilarating romp through the pages of recent history.* **3.** CASUAL SEX a casual or lighthearted sexual encounter (*informal*) **4.** EASY VICTORY a victory that is remarkably or unexpectedly easy (*informal*) **5.** EASY PACE an easy smooth pace [Early 18C. Origin ?]

romp·ers /rómpərz/ *npl* a one-piece suit usually with short pants and a bib held up by shoulder straps, worn by babies and small children

Ro·mu·lo /rómmyə lṑ/, **Carlos Pena** (1899–1985) Filipino politician. He served as president of the United Nations General Assembly (1949–50), and was ambassador to the United States (1952–3, 1955–62).

Rom·u·lus /rómmyələss/ *n* in Roman mythology, the founder of the city of Rome. He was the son of Mars and twin brother of Remus, whom he is said to have killed.

Rom·u·lus Au·gus·tu·lus /ròmmyələss aw gúschələss/ (461?–476?) Roman emperor. He was the last Roman emperor in the West, and his deposition by Odoacer in 475–476 marked the end of the Western Roman Empire.

ROM·ve·lope /rómvə lṑp/, **rom·ve·lope** *n* a protective cardboard or similar cover for a CD [Late 20C. < ROM + ENVELOPE]

RONA *abbr* ACCT return on net assets

ron·deau /róndō, ron dṓ/ (*plural* **-deaux** /-dōz, -dṓz/) *n* **1.** a poem of 13 or 10 lines in 3 stanzas, with 2 rhymes and with the opening phrase repeated twice as an unrhymed refrain **2.** a medieval French song, especially a trouvère song with a two-part refrain [Early 16C. < French, later form of *rondel* (see RONDEL)]

ron·del /rónd'l, ron dél/, **ron·delle** /ron dél/ *n* a poem, similar to a rondeau, that has 13 or 14 lines in 3 stanzas, with 2 rhymes and with the opening 2 lines repeated as a refrain [14C. < Old French, "small round" (from the repetition of the opening two lines) < *ro(u)nd-* (see ROUND[1])]

ron·de·let /róndə lèt, ròndə lét/ *n* a short form of rondeau, with 5 or 7 lines and the first line repeated as a refrain. The first line is of 4 syllables and is repeated as line 3 and, in the longer form, line 7, while the other lines have 8 syllables.

ron·delle *n* LITERAT same as **rondel**

ron·do[1] /róndō/ (*plural* **-dos**) *n* a piece of instrumental music or movement in which the principal theme is repeated between at least two sections that contrast with it, often forming the last movement of a sonata [Late 18C. Via Italian < French *rondeau* (see RONDEAU)]

ron·do[2] /róndō/ (*plural* **-dos**) *n* a condominium unit that has been converted from a rental apartment [Late 20C. Blend of RENTAL + CONDO]

rönt·gen *n* MEASURE another spelling of **roentgen**

roo /roo/ (*plural* **roos**) *n* same as **kangaroo** (*informal*) [Early 20C. Shortening]

rood /rood/ *n* **1.** CRUCIFIX a crucifix, especially one mounted at the entrance to the choir or chancel of a church **2.** JESUS CHRIST'S CROSS the cross on which Jesus Christ was crucified (*archaic*) **3.** QUARTER OF ACRE a unit of area equal to 0.25 acre/0.10117 hectares [Old English *rōd* "cross, pole" < Germanic]

rood screen *n* a partition separating the choir or chancel of a church from the nave or main part

roof /roof, rŏŏf/ *n* **1.** UPPER COVERING OF BUILDING the outside covering of the top of a building, or the framework supporting this. See illustration on next page **2.** TOP PART the top part of something, forming a covering, e.g., the top of a vehicle ○ *a blue car with a black roof* **3.** TOP OF INSIDE CAVITY the top of the inside of a hollow structure ○ *the roof of the cave* **4.** STRUCTURE COVERING BODY CAVITY the upper covering structure of a body part, especially one with a vaulted structure such as the mouth **5.** HIGHEST POINT the highest point or upper limit of something ■ *vt* (**roofed, roof·ing, roofs**) INSTALL ROOF ON SOMETHING to put a top covering onto something, especially a building ○ *The house*

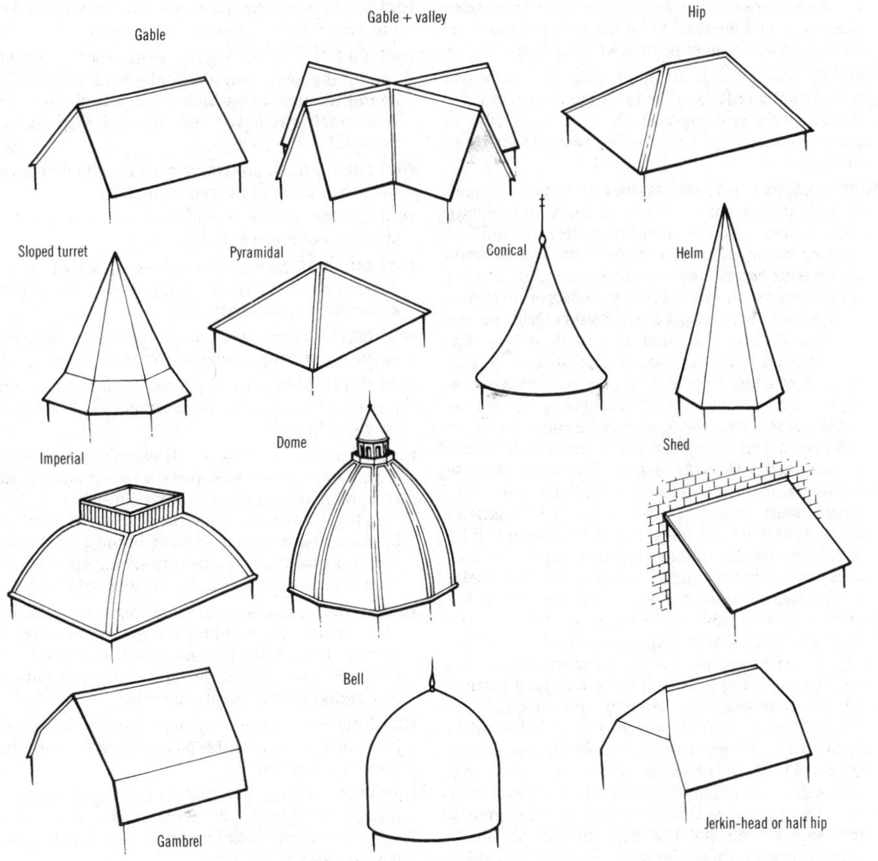

roof: types of roofs

is roofed with slate tiles. [Old English *hrōf* "roof, ceiling, top" < Germanic] —**roof·less** *adj* —**roof·like** *adj* ◇ **go through the roof** to rise to an extremely high level (*informal*) ◇ **hit the roof** to be extremely angry (*informal*)

CULTURAL NOTE ***Cat on a Hot Tin Roof***, a play (1955) by Tennessee Williams. Set in the US South, it depicts the Pollitt family gathering to celebrate the 65th birthday of patriarch Big Daddy. The simmering conflicts between Daddy and sons Gooper and Buck and their wives reflect the lies and deceit that underpin many family relationships. It was made into a movie by Richard Brooks in 1958. One of its best-known lines is the last one from Act III: "Nothing's more determined than a cat on a tin roof – is there? Is there, baby?".

roof·er /ro͝ofər, ro͝offər/ *n* somebody whose job is to build or repair the roofs of buildings

roof gar·den *n* **1.** a garden on the flat roof of a building **2.** *US* a restaurant, bar, or public area at the top of a building, usually with access to an outdoor area

roof·ie /ro͝ofee, ro͝ofee/ *n* flunitrazepam, or a dose of flunitrazepam, especially when used as a date-rape drug (*slang*) [Late 20C. Probably alteration of ROHYPNOL]

roof·ing /ro͝ofing, ro͝offing/ *n* **1.** MATERIAL FOR ROOF material used to make a roof **2.** TOP OF SOMETHING something forming a top or roof **3.** OCCUPATION OF ROOFER the business or occupation of making or repairing roofs

roof·line /ro͝of līn, ro͝of-/ *n* the outline of the roof of a building or a series of roofs

roof rack *n Can, UK* a frame attached to the top of a motor vehicle, used for carrying things, especially luggage. US term **luggage rack**

roof rat *n* ZOOL same as **black rat**

roof·top /ro͝of tòp, ro͝of-/ *n* the outer surface of the roof of a building ◇ **shout something from the rooftops** to make something publicly known or announce something to everybody, often in a jubilant manner

roof·tree /ro͝of trèe, ro͝of-/ *n* CONSTR same as **ridgepole** (sense 1)

rook

rook[1] /ro͝ok/ *n* **1.** BIRD OF CROW FAMILY a large bird of the crow family with black feathers and a pale area at the base of its beak, that nests in colonies in treetops. Native to: Europe, Asia. Latin name: *Corvus frugilegus*. **2.** SWINDLER a swindler or cheat, especially at cards (*slang*) ■ *vt* (**rooked, rook·ing, rooks**) CHEAT SOMEBODY to overcharge, swindle, or cheat somebody (*slang*) ○ *If you paid that amount you've been rooked.* [Old English *hrōc* < Germanic] —**rook·y** *adj*

rook[2] /ro͝ok/ *n* any of four chess pieces that begin a game in the corner squares and that can move in a straight line in any direction over any number of unoccupied squares [13C. Via French < Arabic *rukk*]

rook·er·y /ro͝okəree/ (*plural* **-ies**) *n* **1.** GROUP OF ROOKS a colony of rooks nesting in treetops **2.** GROUP OF PENGUINS a colony of nesting penguins **3.** ANIMALS' COLLECTIVE BREEDING PLACE a breeding or living area for large numbers of animals, especially birds or mammals, that come together in colonies to nest or breed [Early 18C. < ROOK[1]]

rook·ie /ro͝okee/ *n* (*informal*) **1.** somebody who is new to an activity or job **2.** a player, especially a professional athlete, who is in the first year of participation in a sport [Late 19C. Origin ?]

room /room, ro͝om/ *n* **1.** SPACE space that may or may not be filled with something or where something can happen ○ *no room to move* ○ *need more room* ○ *room for another chair* **2.** PART OF BUILDING an area within a building that is enclosed by a floor, walls, and a ceiling ○ *a hotel room* **3.** PEOPLE IN ROOM the people in a room considered as a group ○ *Her entrance silenced the room.* **4.** SCOPE the scope, opportunity, or possibility for something to exist, happen, or be done ○ *There's room for improvement.* ■ **rooms** *npl* ACCOMMODATIONS part of a house or hotel that may be rented as separate accommodations ○ *I managed to find myself rooms in town.* ■ *vi* (**roomed, room·ing, rooms**) SHARE LIVING QUARTERS to occupy or share living quarters with one person or several people ○ *She rooms with her aunt.* [Old English *rūm* < Germanic, "spacious"] —**room·ful** *n* ◇ **not enough room to swing a cat** very little space

room and board *n* accommodations with all meals provided, sometimes paid for and sometimes given in return for work ○ *Do you prefer bed and breakfast or room and board?*

~~roomate~~ incorrect spelling of **roommate**

room·er /ro͝omər, ro͝ommər/ *n* same as **lodger** (sense 1) (*dated*)

room·ette /roo mét, ro͝o-/ *n* a private single compartment in a railroad sleeping car

room·ie /ro͝omee, ro͝ommee/ *n* same as **roommate** (*informal*)

room·mate /ro͝om màyt, ro͝om-/ *n* somebody with whom a person shares a room, apartment, or house

room ser·vice *n* **1.** a service providing food and drinks served to hotel guests in their rooms ○ *Room service is available 24 hours a day.* **2.** the staff or department of a hotel responsible for serving food and drinks to guests in their rooms ○ *Call room service and order lunch.*

room tem·per·a·ture *n* the average normal temperature of a living room, usually thought of as around 20°C/68°F or slightly above ○ *This cheese should be served at room temperature.*

room·y /ro͝omee, ro͝ommee/ (**-i·er, -i·est**) *adj* having plenty of space in which to move around —**room·i·ly** *adv* —**room·i·ness** *n*

roor·back /ro͝or bàk/ *n US* a false and defamatory story made public to gain a political advantage [Mid-19C. < Baron von *Roorback*, fictitious author of a nonexistent work supposedly quoted in an attack on US presidential candidate James K. Polk in 1844]

Roo·se·velt /rṓzə vèlt, rṓz-, ro͝oz-/, **Edith** (1861–1948) US first lady (1901–09). She married Theodore Roosevelt in 1886 and is credited with institutionalizing the role of first lady. Full name **Roosevelt, Edith Kermit Carow**

Eleanor Roosevelt

Roo·se·velt, Eleanor (1884–1962) US first lady (1933–45), social activist, and writer. As the wife of President Franklin D. Roosevelt, she made national broadcasts and wrote a syndicated newspaper column, establishing her reputation as a campaigner for progressive social causes. She was a US delegate to the United Nations (1945–53) and chaired the commission that drafted the Universal Declaration of Human Rights. Born **Roosevelt, Anna Eleanor**

"No one can make you feel inferior without your consent."
[Eleanor Roosevelt, *Catholic Digest*, August 1960]

Franklin D. Roosevelt

Roo·se·velt, Franklin D. (1882–1945) 32nd president of the United States. A Democrat, he served longer than any other president (1933–45), with an unprecedented election to four terms. He held office during the Great Depression of the 1930s and World War II. Full name **Roosevelt, Franklin Delano**. See table at **president**

> "We look forward to a world founded upon four essential human freedoms. The first is freedom of speech and expression—everywhere in the world. The second is freedom of every person to worship God in his own way—everywhere in the world. The third is freedom from want—everywhere in the world. The fourth is freedom from fear—anywhere in the world."
> [Franklin D. Roosevelt, *Speech to Congress, Public Papers*; January 6, 1941]

Theodore Roosevelt

Roo·se·velt, Theodore (1858–1919) 26th president of the United States (1901–09). During his Republican presidency he expanded US involvement in world affairs, established domestic reforms, and promoted conservation. Famed for his exploits in the Spanish-American War, he served as governor of New York (1899–1900). As William McKinley's vice president (1901), he assumed the presidency after McKinley's assassination, and during his presidency the Panama Canal was built. He won the Nobel Peace Prize (1906) for mediating the end of the Russo-Japanese War. Known as **Teddy Roosevelt**. See table at **president**

> "We have room in this country for but one flag, the Stars and Stripes...We have room for but one loyalty, loyalty to the United States...We have room for but one language, the English language."
> [Theodore Roosevelt, *Message to the American Defense Society*; January 3, 1919]

> "There is a homely adage which runs 'Speak softly and carry a big stick, you will go far.'"
> [Theodore Roosevelt, *Speech at Minnesota State Fair*; September 2, 1901]

roost /roost/ *n* **1. PLACE WHERE BIRDS SLEEP** a place where a bird rests or sleeps, e.g., a perch or a building with perches for domestic fowl **2. BIRDS SHARING ROOST** a group of birds sharing a roost **3. TEMPORARY ACCOMMODATIONS** a place where somebody may rest or sleep temporarily (*slang*) ■ *vi* (**roost·ed, roost·ing, roosts**) **GO TO SLEEP** to rest or sleep on or in a roost ○ *Starlings were roosting in the trees.* [Old English *hrōst*, origin ?] ◇ **rule the roost** to be the person who is in charge and who must be obeyed (*informal*)

roost·er /ro͝ostər/ *n* **1.** an adult male of a domestic fowl, usually only kept for breeding. Roosters have a distinctive crowing call. **2.** *US* a man who is regarded as cocky, vain, or posturing (*sometimes offensive*)

root^{1} /root, ro͝ot/ *n* **1. UNDERGROUND BASE OF PLANT** the part of a plant that has no leaves or buds and usually spreads underground, anchoring the plant and absorbing water and nutrients from the soil **2. UNDERGROUND EDIBLE PART OF PLANT** an underground plant part that is used as a vegetable, e.g., a carrot or turnip ○ *diced roots* ○ *root crops* **3. ATTACHMENT OF BODY PART** the portion of a body part such as a tooth or hair that is embedded in tissue **4. BASE OF SOMETHING** the bottom or base of something, or the part by which something is attached to the body ○ *the root of the tongue* **5. CAUSE OF SOMETHING** the fundamental cause, basis, or essence of something, or the source from which something derives ○ *the roots of discontent* **6. ANCESTOR** an ancestor or progenitor, especially one from whom many people are descended **7.** MATH **NUMBER MULTIPLIED BY ITSELF** a number that when multiplied by itself a particular number of times equals another number ○ *2 is the square root of 4.* **8.** MATH **NUMBER SUBSTITUTABLE FOR VARIABLE** a number that can take the place of the variable in an equation and solve the equation **9.** LING **BASIC PART OF WORD** the basic meaningful part of a word that is left when any affixes are removed and that cannot be analyzed further **10.** LING **ORIGINAL FORM OF WORD** the original reconstructed form from which a recorded word is derived, e.g., by phonetic change or the addition of affixes **11.** MUSIC **FOUNDATION OF CHORD** the note that forms the foundation of a chord **12.** ANAT **END OF NERVE** the end of a nerve that is nearer to the center of the body ■ **roots** *npl* **1. ORIGINS** cultural or family origins, especially as the basis for a feeling of belonging in a particular place or environment ○ *I live in the city but my roots are in the country.* **2. SOMEBODY'S GENETIC ORIGIN** somebody's genetic origins or ancestry ■ *v* (**root·ed, root·ing, roots**) **1.** *vti* **GROW ROOTS** to develop a root or roots, or cause a plant to grow roots **2.** *vti* **BE FIXED** to become fixed, embedded, or immobile, or cause somebody or something to become fixed, embedded, or immobile ○ *news that rooted me to the spot* **3.** *vi* **BE BASED** to have a basis or origin in something ○ *herbal remedies that are rooted in folk medicine* [Pre-12C. < Old Norse *rót* < Indo-European, "branch, root"] —**root·er** *n* ◇ **root and branch** in every respect, or to the fullest extent ○ *reformed the system root and branch* ◇ **take root** to become established and accepted

SYNONYMS See ***origin***.

root up *vt* to pull or dig up a whole plant, including its roots

root^{2} /root, ro͝ot/ (**root·ed, root·ing, roots**) *v* **1.** *vti* to dig in the surface of the ground with the snout or nose out of curiosity or in search of food ○ *The pigs were rooting for beech nuts.* **2.** *vi* to move things about unsystematically while looking for something ○ *rooting in the drawer for a pencil* [Old English *wrōtan* < Germanic; influenced by ROOT^{1}] —**root·er** *n*

root out *vt* **1.** to eradicate or remove somebody or something completely ○ *He ruthlessly rooted out all opposition.* **2.** to find or remove something after rummaging for it ○ *I'll root out some old photos of him.*

root^{3} /root, ro͝ot/ (**root·ed, root·ing, roots**) *vi* **1.** to cheer, shout, or applaud in support of a contestant or team **2.** to provide support to or be actively in favor of somebody or something [Late 19C. Origin ?] —**root·er** *n*

Root /root/, **Elihu** (1845–1937) US lawyer and politician. He won the Nobel Peace Prize (1912) for his work with the League of Nations.

root·age /ro͝otij/ *n* **1. PLANT ROOTS** a system of plant roots **2. GROWTH OF ROOTS** the developing of roots **3. BECOMING FIXED** the act or process of becoming rooted or established [Late 19C. < ROOT^{1}]

root ball *n* the tightly packed mass of roots and soil produced by a plant, especially when grown in a container

root beer *n* a sweet carbonated soft drink made from the extracts of various roots and herbs

root ca·nal *n* **1.** the cavity in the root of a tooth, containing pulp, nerves, and blood vessels **2.** a dental treatment in which the diseased tissue in a root canal is removed and replaced with an inert material

root cap *n* a thick protective mass of cells that covers the growing tip of the root of a plant

root cel·lar *n* a pit or underground cellar used for storing root crops and vegetables

root climb·er *n* a vine that climbs up a structure by developing small roots on its stems that grip the structure. Ivy is a root climber.

root crop *n* a crop grown for its edible underground parts, e.g., turnips, potatoes, or sugar beets

root di·rec·to·ry *n* the top-level directory in a computer's filing system, represented by a backslash (\), as in C:\

root·ed /ro͝otəd, ro͝otəd/ *adj* **1. HAVING ROOTS** on which strong roots have developed ○ *a rooted plant* **2. WELL ESTABLISHED** arising from firmly held beliefs or long-standing traditions or practices ○ *a rooted conviction* **3. UNABLE TO MOVE** unable to move because of shock or fear **4. HAVING STRONG TIES** having strong emotional or cultural roots [14C. < ROOT^{1}] —**root·ed·ness** *n*

root hair *n* a fine growth from the outer cells of a plant root that resembles a hair and absorbs nutrients. Root hairs are elongated epidermal cells that increase the surface area of roots to improve absorption of water and minerals.

root knot *n* a disease of plants caused by nematodes in which the roots become enlarged and plant growth is stunted

root·less /ro͝otləss, ro͝ot-/ *adj* **1.** lacking close ties to people or places **2.** with roots cut off or underdeveloped [14C. < ROOT^{1}] —**root·less·ly** *adv* —**root·less·ness** *n*

root·let /ro͝otlət, ro͝ot-/ *n* a small root or part of a root [Late 18C. < ROOT^{1}]

root mean square *n* the square root of the mean of the squares of a set of numbers. Sometimes the root mean square is a more useful measure of central tendency than the mean or the median.

root nod·ule *n* a swelling on the roots of leguminous plants such as alfalfa, soybeans, and peas, caused by symbiotic bacteria that can fix nitrogen in the soil

root pres·sure *n* the pressure that forces water upward through the conducting tissues of a plant, caused by the water potential in the stem being lower than in the root. Root pressure causes exudation of sap from cut stems and secretion of water droplets from leaves.

root rot *n* a disease of plants that causes the roots to break or decay, often caused by fungi

root·stock /ro͝ot stòk, ro͝ot-/ *n* **1.** BOT same as **rhizome** **2.** a root or piece of root used as a stock in propagation by grafting **3.** a source or origin of something [Mid-19C. < ROOT^{1}]

root sys·tem *n* the network of roots that a plant develops

root veg·e·ta·ble *n* a vegetable such as a carrot, turnip, or beet that is grown for its fleshy edible underground parts. Some are also used in cooking for their young leaves.

root·worm /ro͝ot wùrm, ro͝ot-/ *n* a beetle whose larvae feed on the roots of crops, including corn. Genus: *Diabrotica.* [Late 19C. < ROOT^{1}]

root·y /ro͝otee, ro͝ottee/ (**-i·er, -i·est**) *adj* **1.** full of or having many roots **2.** resembling a root or roots [15C. < ROOT^{1}] —**root·i·ness** *n*

ro·pa·ble /rṓpəb'l/, **rope·a·ble** *adj* able to be caught or restrained using a rope ○ *ropable steers*

rope /rōp/ *n* **1. STRONG CORD** a strong cord made by twisting together strands of hemp or other fibers or wire **2. STRING OF THINGS** a row of things strung or twisted together ○ *a rope of pearls* **3. STRAND OF STICKY MATERIAL** a stringy strand of a sticky substance ○ *a rope of saliva* **4. CORD FOR HANGING SOMEBODY** a cord with a noose at one end that is used for hanging people **5. DEATH BY HANGING** execution by hanging **6. FREEDOM**

freedom or latitude to do something ■ **ropes** *npl* **1.** LASSO a lasso or lariat **2.** CORDS OF RING USED FOR FIGHTING the cords used to enclose a boxing or wrestling ring **3.** USUAL PROCEDURES the appropriate means and procedures for doing something or for functioning in an environment (*informal*) ○ *Her task was to show the new employee the ropes.* ■ *v* (**roped, rop·ing, ropes**) **1.** *vt* SECURE SOMETHING WITH ROPE to tie, link, or bind somebody or something with rope ○ *The two climbers were roped together for the ascent.* **2.** *vt* ENCLOSE AREA to enclose or partition an area using ropes as barriers ○ *The museum staff had roped off the area.* **3.** *vt* LASSO ANIMAL to catch an animal with a lasso ○ *rope a steer* **4.** *vi* FORM STRANDS to form strands that resemble rope in shape or texture [Old English *rāp* < Germanic] —**rop·er** *n* ◇ **give somebody enough rope** *US* to allow somebody enough freedom or latitude to accomplish something or do something well ◇ **give somebody enough rope to hang himself** *or* **herself** to give somebody enough freedom to make mistakes or reveal his or her shortcomings ◇ **on the ropes** in a desperate or hopeless position and likely to fail (*informal*)

rope in *vt* (*informal*) **1.** to involve somebody in an activity, especially somebody who was initially reluctant or unwilling ○ *We got roped in to help with the cleaning up.* **2.** *US* to trick or deceive somebody into doing something

rope·a·ble *adj* another spelling of **ropable**

rope-a-dope *adj* describes a strategy in which somebody feigns weakness until an opponent becomes exhausted in an effort to win, then defeats the opponent decisively (*slang*)

rope·danc·er /rṓp dànssər/ *n* an acrobat who dances or performs feats on a rope, especially a tightrope, stretched above the ground —**rope·danc·ing** *n*

rope tow *n* SKIING same as **ski tow**

rope·walk·er /rṓp wàwkər/ *n* an acrobat who performs on a rope stretched above the ground, especially a tightrope walker [Early 17C]

rope·way /rṓp wày/ *n* a system of cables strung from high supports and used to carry heavy objects such as logs from one place to another through the air

rop·y /rṓpee/ (**-i·er, -i·est**), **rop·ey** *adj* **1.** resembling a rope or ropes **2.** forming into sticky, stringy strands —**rop·i·ly** *adv* —**rop·i·ness** *n*

roque /rōk/ *n* a game developed from croquet and played on a hard court with a surrounding wall from which the ball can rebound and still be in play [Late 19C. Alteration of CROQUET]

Roque·fort /rṓkfərt/ *n* a moist, strongly flavored, blue-veined cheese made from ewes' milk and matured in caves [Mid-19C. After ROQUEFORT-SUR-SOULZON]

Roque·fort-sur-Soul·zon /rṑkfərt syoor sòò zàwN/ town in Aveyron Region, in south central France, famous for its blue cheese. Population: 679 (1999).

ro·que·laure /ròkə láwr, rṑkə-/ *n* a knee-length hooded cloak worn by men in Europe in the 18th and 19th centuries [Early 18C. After Antoine-Gaston (1656–1738), Duc de *Roquelaure* and Marshal of France]

ro·quet /rō káy/ *vti* (**-queted** /-kayd, -kid/, **-quet·ing** /-kay ing, -ki ing/, **-quets** /-kiz/) in croquet, to strike another player's ball with your own ball ■ *n* in croquet, a stroke that makes the player's ball strike that of another player [Mid-19C. Probably alteration of CROQUET]

ror·qual /ráwrkwəl/ *n* a large streamlined baleen whale that has a small pointed dorsal fin and longitudinal grooves on the throat, e.g., the blue whale or the humpback whale. Genus: *Balaenoptera.* [Early 19C. Via French < Norwegian *røyrkval* < Old Norse *reyðarhvalr* < *reyðr* "rorqual" (< *rauðr* "red") + *hvalr* "whale"]

Ror·schach test /ráwr shaak-, -shaakh-/ *n* a projective test of personality or mental state based on somebody's interpretation of a series of standard inkblots [Early 20C. After Hermann *Rorschach* (1884–1922), Swiss psychiatrist]

Ro·sa /rṓzə/ ➧ **Monte Rosa**

ro·sa·ce·a /rō záyshee ə/ *n* a recurring inflammatory disorder of the skin of the nose, cheeks, and forehead that is characterized by swelling, dilation of capillaries, pimples, and a reddened appearance [Late 19C. < modern Latin *(acne) rosacea* "rose-colored (acne)" < form of Latin *rosaceus* < *rosa* (see ROSE[1])]

ro·sa·ceous /rō záyshəss/ *adj* **1.** belonging or relating to the rose family **(Rosaceae)** of flowering plants **2.** resembling a rose flower [Mid-18C. < Latin *rosaceus* < *rosa* (see ROSE[1])]

Ro·sa·lind /rózzə lind, rṓzə-/ *n* a small inner natural satellite of Uranus, discovered in 1986 by the Voyager 2 planetary probe. It is approximately 58 km (36 mi.) in diameter.

ros·an·i·line /rō zánn'lin/, **ros·an·i·lin** *n* a brownish red crystalline compound. Source: aniline. Use: dye, dye manufacture, antifungal drug, in Schiff's reagent. Formula: $C_{20}H_{21}N_3O$. [Mid-19C. < ROSE[1]]

ro·sar·i·an /rō zérree ən/ *n* a cultivator of or expert in the growing of roses [Mid-19C. < Latin *rosarium* "rose garden" < form of *rosarius* "of roses" < *rosa* (see ROSE[1])]

Ro·sa·ri·o /rō zaaree ō, -saaree-/ city in east central Argentina, situated on the Parana River. Population: 1,157,372 (1991).

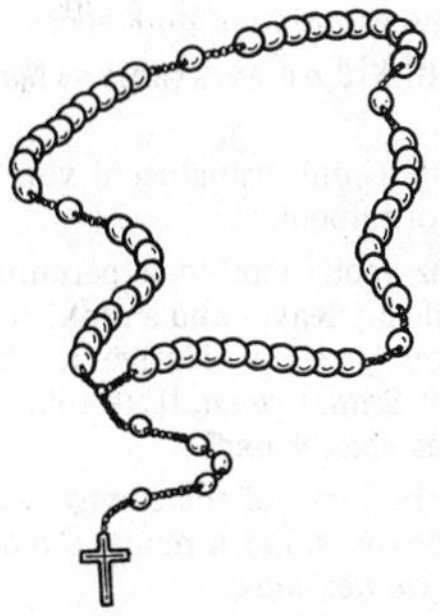

rosary (sense 2)

ro·sa·ry /rṓzəree/ (*plural* **-ries**) *n* **1.** SERIES OF PRAYERS a series of Roman Catholic prayers, usually made up of five or 15 decades of Hail Marys, each decade beginning with an Our Father and ending with a Gloria **2.** CATHOLIC PRAYER BEADS a string of beads used in counting the prayers said in a rosary **3.** *also* **ro·sa·ry bead** NON-CATHOLIC PRAYER BEADS a string of beads used in praying by members of religions or denominations other than Roman Catholicism [15C. < Latin *rosarium*, Anglo-Latin *rosarius* "rose garden" (see ROSARIAN)]

ORIGIN It was a common stylistic device in the Middle Ages to name collections of verse or similar short pieces after bunches of flowers (*anthology* comes from the Greek word for "flower," and a similar inspiration underlies *florilegium*). This was the background against which a collection of Roman Catholic prayers came to be known as a ***rosary***. The metaphor was probably encouraged by the symbolic association of roses and rose gardens with, respectively, the Virgin Mary and paradise.

ro·sa·ry pea *n* **1.** a tropical vine naturalized in Florida that produces scarlet and black poisonous seeds. Use: seeds: beads, roots: licorice substitute. Latin name: *Abrus precatorius.* **2.** a seed of the rosary pea

Ros·com·mon /ross kómmən/ **1.** county in Connacht province, west central Republic of Ireland. Population: 51,975 (2002). Area: 951 sq. mi./2,463 sq. km. **2.** town and administrative center of County Roscommon, in the Republic of Ireland. Population: 3,427 (1991).

rose[1] /rōz/ *n* **1.** PRICKLY BUSH WITH ORNAMENTAL FLOWERS a prickly bush with compound leaves that is cultivated in many varieties and hybrids for its flowers. Genus: *Rosa.* **2.** FLOWER OF ROSE a flower of the rose. Roses are usually red, pink, yellow, or white and are often fragrant. The wild rose has five petals, but cultivated varieties are usually double or partly double. **3.** PLANT SIMILAR TO ROSE a member of the family of flowering plants that includes the rose, or a plant that resembles it, especially in having similar flowers. Family: Rosaceae. **4.** REDDISH COLOR a reddish pink color **5.** ORNAMENT RESEMBLING ROSE a representation of a rose flower as an emblem or decoration, or an ornament or design resembling a rose flower **6.** SPRINKLER NOZZLE a perforated nozzle on a watering can or hose for producing a spray **7.** HANDICRAFT, MANUF same as **rose cut 8.** MINERALS FORM OF MINERAL a mineral form that is round and resembles a rose **9.** GEOG same as **compass card** ■ **ros·es** *npl* **1.** PINK COLORING pink coloration, especially in the cheeks ○ *a baby with roses in his cheeks* **2.** EASY CIRCUMSTANCES favorable, comfortable, or easy circumstances (*informal*) ○ *She thinks the exam will be roses, but is she ever wrong!* ■ *adj* **1.** REDDISH PINK of a reddish pink color **2.** HAVING OR RESEMBLING ROSES containing or resembling rose plants or blossoms, or smelling like rose blossoms **3.** RELATING TO ROSES relating to or used for roses [Old English *rōse*, via Germanic < Latin *rosa*, probably < Greek *rhodon* < Iranian] ◇ **everything's coming up roses** everything is going very well (*informal*)

rose

rose[2] past tense of **rise**

ro·sé /rō záy/ *n* a pink-colored wine, especially one made by fermenting red grapes and removing the skins from the juice before all the color has been extracted [Late 19C. < French < *(vin) rosé* "pink (wine)"]

Rose /rōz/, **Pete** (*b.* 1941) US baseball player and manager. He had a record-breaking 4,256 career hits, but was banned from baseball for betting (1989). Full name **Rose, Peter Edward**

rose a·ca·cia *n* a prickly bush. Flowers: pale purple or rose-pink, in clusters. Native to: southeastern United States. Latin name: *Robinia hispida.*

rose ap·ple *n* **1.** a rose-scented oval fruit. Use: jellies, confections. **2.** an evergreen tree with decorative flowers, that produces rose apples. Native to: South-east Asia. Latin name: *Syzygium jambos.*

ro·se·ate /rṓzee àyt, -ee ət/ *adj* **1.** having plumage of a reddish pink color **2.** optimistic or idealistic, especially to an absurd degree [15C. < Latin *roseus* "rosy" < *rosa* (see ROSE[1])] —**ro·se·ate·ly** *adv*

ro·se·ate spoon·bill *n* a wading bird that has pink feathers and a spoon-shaped beak. Native to: southern North America, Central America. Latin name: *Ajaia ajaja.*

Ro·seau /rō zṓ/ coastal town and capital of Dominica, in the southwestern part of the island. Population: 15,853 (1991).

rose·bay /rṓz bày/ *n* PLANTS **1.** same as **rosebay rhododendron 2.** same as **fireweed 3.** same as **oleander**

rose·bay rho·do·den·dron *n* a rhododendron with rose-pink bell-shaped flowers. Native to: eastern United States. Latin name: *Rhododendron maximum.*

rose·bay wil·low herb *n UK* PLANTS same as **fireweed**

rose bee·tle *n* INSECTS same as **rose chafer**

Rose·ber·y /rṓz bèrree/ lake in the center of the North Island, New Zealand, originally formed by a volcanic eruption. It is a major tourist attraction. Area: 31 sq. mi./80 sq. km.

Rose·ber·y, Archibald Philip Primrose, 5th Earl of (1847–1929) British prime minister (1894–95). He served twice as foreign secretary before succeeding W. E. Gladstone as Liberal Party leader and prime minister.

rose-breast·ed gros·beak *n* a woodland finch with a heavy beak, the male of which is black and white with a rose-red patch on its breast. Native to: North America. Latin name: *Pheucticus ludovicianus.*

rose·bud /rṓz bùd/ *n* the unopened flower of a rose

rose bug *n US* INSECTS same as **rose chafer**

rose·bush /rṓz bòòsh/ *n* a rose growing as a bush rather than as a climber or as ground cover

rose cam·pi·on *n* a plant with white woolly down on its stems and leaves. Flowers: pink. Native to: Europe, Asia. Latin name: *Lychnis coronaria.*

rose cha·fer *n* a beetle that feeds on the roots, leaves, and flowers of roses and other garden plants. Native to: North America. Latin name: *Macrodactylus subspinosus.*

rose cold *n* MED same as **rose fever**

rose-col·ored *adj* **1.** a reddish pink color **2.** optimistic or idealistic, especially to an unjustifiable degree ○ *He tends to take a rose-colored view of things.*

Rose·crans /rṓz kràηz/, **William Starke** (1819–98) US Union general. His miscalculation at the Battle of Chickamauga (September 1863) during the US Civil War led to a Confederate victory and heavy casualties on both sides, and he was relieved of his command.

rose cut *n* a way of cutting gemstones that gives them a flat base and a hemispherical crown with facets rising to a low point —**rose-cut** *adj*

rose fe·ver *n* hay fever experienced in the spring or early summer, caused by pollen, usually of grasses, that is airborne when roses are in bloom

rose·fish /rṓz fìsh/ (*plural same* or **-fish·es**) *n* **1.** a spiny-finned red fish. Native to: northern Atlantic. Latin name: *Sebastes marinus.* **2.** FISH same as **redfish** (sense 1)

rose ge·ra·ni·um *n* a pelargonium with scented leaves. Flowers: pink. Use: leaves: flavoring, perfumes. Latin name: *Pelargonium graveolens.*

rose·hip /rṓz hìp/ *n* the fleshy fruit of a rose, resembling a berry. Use: jelly, herbal tea, medicinal syrups.

ro·selle /rō zél/ *n* a hibiscus that has flowers with yellow petals and a red calyx from which jelly and beverages are made. Latin name: *Hibiscus sabdariffa.* [Mid-19C. < ?]

Ro·selle /rō zél/ town in northeastern Illinois, south of Schaumburg. It is a western suburb of Chicago. Population: 23,383 (2002 estimate).

rose mal·low *n* **1.** a tall plant that grows in marshy areas and has downy leaves. Flowers: pink or white. Native to: eastern North America. Genus: *Hibiscus.* **2.** *US* PLANTS same as **hollyhock**

rosemary

rose·mar·y /rṓz mèrree/ *n* **1.** aromatic gray green needle-shaped leaves. Use: food flavoring, perfume. **2.** an aromatic bush with gray green needle-shaped leaves that are rosemary. Native to: southern Europe. Latin name: *Rosmarinus officinalis.* [14C. By folk etymology < obsolete *rosmarine* < Latin *rosmarinus* < *ros* "dew" + *marinus* "of the sea"; from its growth near seacoasts and its blossom's resemblance to dew]

rose moss *n* PLANTS same as **portulaca**

Ro·sen·berg /rṓz'n bùrg/, **Julius** (1918–53) US Soviet spy. He and his wife Ethel Rosenberg (1915–53), both members of the Communist Party, were convicted in 1951 of passing nuclear weapons information to the Soviets during World War II. They were the first US civilians to be executed for espionage.

Ro·sen·wald /rṓz'n wàwld/, **Julius** (1862–1932) US merchant and philanthropist. He financed various educational projects, including the Museum of Science and Industry (1929) in Chicago.

rose of Jer·i·cho *n* a plant that curls up into a ball in dry conditions and unfolds and grows in wet conditions. Native to: desert regions. Latin name: *Anastatica hierochuntica* or *Selaginella lepidophylla.*

rose of Shar·on /-shárrən/ *n* **1.** a bush widely grown as an ornamental. Flowers: large, red, purple, or white. Native to: Syria. Latin name: *Hibiscus syriacus.* **2.** a creeping bush, widely grown as ground cover. Flowers: large, yellow. Native to: southern Europe. Latin name: *Hypericum calycinum.* [Early 17C. < *Sharon*, fertile plain south of Mount Carmel, Israel]

rose oil *n* an essential oil. Source: rose flowers. Use: in perfumes, flavorings, medicines.

ro·se·o·la /rōzee ṓlə, rō zeé ələ/ *n* a red rash on the skin, seen in diseases such as measles, scarlet fever, and syphilis [Early 19C. < Latin *roseus* "rosy" < *rosa* (see ROSE[1]), after RUBEOLA] —**ro·se·o·lar** *adj*

ro·se·o·la in·fan·tum /-in fántòom/ *n* a mild disease of young children, typically involving a three-day fever and the eruption of pink spots

rose per·i·win·kle *n* PLANTS same as **Madagascar periwinkle**

rose quartz *n* a pink translucent variety of quartz. Use: gems, ornaments.

rose·root /rṓz ròot, -ròot/ *n* a perennial mountain plant with fleshy leaves and a pinkish underground stem. Flowers: yellow. Native to: Europe, Asia. Latin name: *Sedum rosea.* [Late 16C. Because its root smells of roses when bruised]

rose slug *n* the larva of the sawfly, which feeds on the leaves of roses. Latin name: *Claudius isomerus* or *Endelomyia aethiops.*

rose to·paz *n* a pink form of topaz made by applying heat to yellowish brown topaz

Ro·set·ta /rō zéttə/ ◆ **Rashîd**

Ro·set·ta stone *n* a stone tablet found in 1799 near Rashîd in Egypt that contained the same text repeated in Egyptian hieroglyphics, Egyptian demotic script, and Greek. It supplied the key to deciphering hieroglyphics.

ro·sette /rō zét/ *n* **1.** ROSE-SHAPED BADGE a circular badge made from gathered loops of ribbon or pleated material, worn to demonstrate support for a team or political party or to indicate having won a prize **2.** ORNAMENT RESEMBLING ROSE a carved or painted ornament resembling the open flower of a rose **3.** ZOOL MARKING RESEMBLING ROSE a patch of color or a marking resembling the open flower of a rose, especially a cluster of spots on the fur of a leopard **4.** BOT CLUSTER OF LEAVES a circular or spiral cluster of leaves at the base of the stem of a plant [Mid-18C. < French, "small rose" < *rose* < Latin *rosa* (see ROSE[1])]

rose wa·ter *n* a fragrant liquid made by distilling or steeping rose petals in water. Use: toilet water, in cooking.

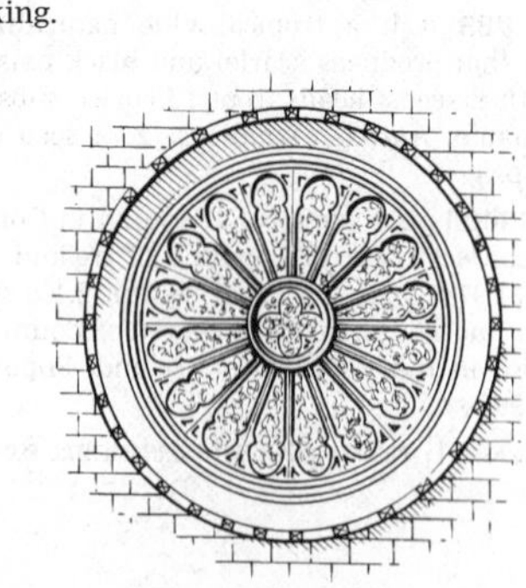

rose window

rose win·dow *n* a round window with tracery radiating from the center in a pattern that resembles a rose and often made of stained glass

rose·wood /rṓz wòod/ *n* **1.** the dark, heavy, rose-scented wood of various tropical trees, especially those belonging to the genus *Dalbergia.* Use: furniture. **2.** a tree that yields rosewood. Genus: *Dalbergia.*

Rosh Cho·desh /ràwsh kháwdəsh/ *n* the first day of a new month in the Jewish religious calendar [< Hebrew *rō'š ḥōdeš* "head of the month"]

Rosh Ha·sha·nah /ràwsh hə sháwnə, -shaánə/, **Rosh Ha·sha·na, Rosh Ha·sho·na, Rosh Ha·sho·nah** *n* the festival that marks the Jewish New Year and the beginning of the Days of Awe. Date: 1st and 2nd of Tishri in the autumn. [Mid-18C. < Hebrew *rō'š haššānāh* "head of the year"]

Ro·si·cru·cian /rṑzi kròosh'n, ròzzi-/ *n* a member of an international organization concerned with esoteric wisdom derived from ancient mystical and philosophical doctrines [Early 17C. < modern Latin *rosa crucis* "rose of the cross," translation of German *Rosenkreuz*, after Christian *Rosenkreuz*, the organization's reputed founder] —**Ro·si·cru·cian·ism** *n*

ros·in /rózzin/ *n* a hard translucent resin ranging in color from amber to dark brown. Source: sap, stumps, or other parts of pine trees. Use: varnishes and other products, to increase friction, e.g., between the bow and strings of some stringed instruments. ■ *vt* (**-ined, -in·ing, -ins**) to treat something with rosin, especially to rub rosin on the bow of a stringed instrument to increase friction [13C. Alteration of Old French *raisine*, variant of *resine* < Latin *resina*; also via Anglo-Latin *rosina* < Latin *resina*] —**ros·in·y** *adj*

Ros·i·nan·te /ròzz'n ántee, rṑz'n-/ *n* **1.** the bony old horse that belongs to Don Quixote, the hero of the novel by Cervantes published in 1605 **2.** a worn-out old horse (*literary*)

ros·in oil *n* a thick yellowish sticky liquid distilled from rosin. Use: manufacture of varnishes and inks.

ros·in·weed /rózzin weèd/ *n* a plant such as the compass plant that smells of resin or has resinous juice. Native to: North America. Genera: *Silphium* or *Grindelia.*

Ros·kil·de /ròoss keèlə/ town in Denmark, in eastern Sjaelland, situated about 15 mi./24 km west of Copenhagen. Population: 42,739 (1999).

Ross /rawss, ross/, **Betsy** (1752–1836) US seamstress. She is credited with sewing the first flag of the United States of America (1776). Born **Griscom, Elizabeth**

Diana Ross

Ross, Diana (*b.* 1944) US pop singer. Known for her seductive vocal style and glamorous appearance, she helped her 1960s female group the Supremes become one of the most successful acts in the history of popular music before pursuing a solo career. Born **Ross, Diane Ernestine**

> "I've always said if one person believes in me, I will try to move mountains."
> [Diana Ross, *Secrets of a Sparrow*; 1993]

Ross, George (1730–79) American patriot. A member of the Continental Congress (1774–77) from Delaware, he was a signatory of the Declaration of Independence (1776).

Ross, Sir James Clark (1800–62) British explorer. He determined the position of the north magnetic pole (1831) and discovered Victoria Land, Ross Island, and the Ross Sea (1839–43).

Ross, John (1790–1866) Cherokee leader. He led his people on the Georgia–Oklahoma "Trail of Tears" to a new home (1838–39) and became chief of the United Cherokee nation.

Ross, Nellie Tayloe (1876–1977) governor of Wyoming (1925–27). She was the first woman to be elected governor of a US state when she completed her late husband's term of office.

Ros·sel·li·ni /ròssə léenee/, **Roberto** (1906–77) Italian movie director. He directed several neorealist movies after World War II, including *Rome, Open City* (1945) and historical movies for television.

Ros·set·ti /rō zéttee/, **Dante Gabriel** (1828–82) British painter and poet. A founder of the Pre-Raphaelite Brotherhood (1848), he brought medieval and Italianate influences to bear on idealized, emotionally charged paintings such as *The Annunciation* (1850) and *Proserpina* (1874). His last volume of verse was *Ballads and Sonnets* (1881). Full name **Rossetti, Gabriel Charles Dante**

Ros·si·ni /rō séenee/, **Gioacchino** (1792–1868) Italian composer. The most successful operatic composer of his time, he was a master of the bel canto style and excelled in comedy. His 37 operas, all written before 1831, include *The Barber of Seville* (1816) and *William Tell* (1829). Full name **Rossini, Gioacchino Antonio**

> "Give me a laundry list and I'll set it to music."
> [Attributed to Gioacchino Rossini]

Ross Sea /ràwss-, ròss-/ southern extension of the Pacific Ocean, bordering Antarctica. A large part of its surface is frozen, forming the Ross Ice Shelf. Ross Island, in the Ross Sea, is the location of the volcano Mount Erebus.

Ros·tand /ràwss taáN/, **Edmond** (1868–1918) French playwright. He is best known for the romantic verse play *Cyrano de Bergerac* (1898).

> "My nose is huge!...let me inform you that I am proud of such an appendage, since a big nose is the proper sign of a friendly, good, courteous, witty, liberal, and brave man, such as I am."
> [Edmond Rostand, *Cyrano de Bergerac*; 1898]

> "The dream, alone, is of interest. What is life, without a dream?"
> [Edmond Rostand, *La Princesse Lointaine*; 1895]

ros·tel·lum /rò stélləm/ (*plural* **-la** /-lə/) *n* a part of an animal or plant that resembles a beak, e.g., the hooked projection from the head of a tapeworm [Mid-18C. < Latin, "small beak" < *rostrum* (see ROSTRUM)] —**ros·tel·lar** *adj* —**ros·tel·late** /róstə làyt, ro stéllət/ *adj*

ros·ter /róstər/ *n* **1. LIST OF NAMES** a list of personnel, especially employees, athletes, or members of the armed forces, often detailing their duties and the times when they are to be carried out **2. PEOPLE ON LIST** the people listed on a roster ■ *vt* (**-tered, -ter·ing, -ters**) **PUT SOMEBODY ON ROSTER** to name somebody on a roster [Early 18C. < Dutch *rooster* "gridiron," (from the resemblance of its pattern to lines on paper) "list" < *roosten* "roast"]

rös·ti /róstee/ *n* a Swiss fried potato cake made from thinly sliced or grated potatoes, sometimes with added onions and bacon [Mid-20C. < Swiss German]

Ros·tock /róst òk, ráwst àwk/ city and port in northeastern Germany, in the state of Mecklenburg-Western Pomerania, on the Baltic Sea. Population: 232,634 (1997).

Ros·tov /rə stáwf/ city in southwestern European Russia, on the Don River. Population: 1,127,339 (1995).

ros·tra FURNITURE, ARCHIT plural of **rostrum**

ros·trum /róstrəm/ (*plural* **-trums** or **-tra** /-trə/) *n* **1. PLATFORM FOR PUBLIC SPEAKING** a platform or raised area where somebody stands to address an audience **2.** MUSIC **CONDUCTOR'S PLATFORM** a platform on a stage or in front of an orchestra where the conductor stands **3.** ANCIENT HIST **PROW OF ROMAN SHIP** the beak-shaped prow of an ancient Roman ship, especially a war galley **4.** BIOL **BEAK-SHAPED PART** a beak or beak-shaped part of an organism [Mid-16C. < Latin, "beak, ship's prow," in plural "platform" (because ships' prows decorated the orator's platform in the Roman forum) < *rodere* "gnaw"] —**ros·tral** *adj* —**ros·tral·ly** *adv* —**ros·trate** *adj*

Ros·well /róz wèl, rózwəl/ town in southeastern New Mexico, directly west of the Pecos River and southeast of Albuquerque. Population: 44,058 (2002 estimate).

ros·y /rṓzee/ (**-i·er, -i·est**) *adj* **1. ROSE-COLORED** of the reddish pink color of roses ○ *the sunset turning the sky a rosy hue* **2. HAVING PINKISH COMPLEXION** having a pinkish complexion that is regarded as indicating good health in white people **3. PROMISING** likely to be characterized by success or happiness ○ *predicts a rosy future for the business* **4. OPTIMISTIC** optimistic, especially to an unreasonable degree ○ *takes a rosy view of things* **5. LOOKING OR SMELLING LIKE ROSES** resembling roses, characteristic of roses, or full of roses —**ros·i·ly** *adv* —**ros·i·ness** *n*

rot /rot/ *v* (**rot·ted, rot·ting, rots**) **1.** *vti* **DECOMPOSE** to be broken down by the action of bacteria or fungi, or break something organic down in this way ○ *The fruit rotted quickly in the heat.* **2.** *vti* **CHANGE BY DECOMPOSITION** to be reduced, damaged, or broken by the action of bacteria or fungi, or affect something organic in this way ○ *allow the compost to rot* **3.** *vi* **LANGUISH** to endure the effects of complete neglect ○ *thrown into prison and left to rot* ■ *n* **1. PROCESS OF DECAYING** the process or condition of decaying, or decayed matter **2. NONSENSE** irrelevant or ridiculous talk (*informal*) **3.** VET, FUNGI **FUNGAL DISEASE** a disease caused by fungi, e.g., foot rot of sheep, dry rot of timber and plants, and wet rot of timber **4. ANIMAL DISEASE** infestation with liver flukes **5. BACTERIAL PLANT DISEASE** a plant disease in which the tissue is broken down by the action of bacteria ■ *interj* **EXPRESSION OF DISAGREEMENT** used to disagree with what somebody has said or to express annoyance or exasperation (*informal*) [Old English *rotian* (verb) < Germanic]

rot. *abbr* MATH rotation

ro·ta /rṓtə/ *n UK* a list of people's names and the order in which they are to carry out duties [Mid-17C. < Latin, "wheel"]

ORIGIN The Latin word *rota* "wheel," from which ***rota*** is derived, is also the source of English *control, rodeo, roll, rondo*[1], *rotate, rotund, roué*, and *round*[1].

Ro·ta *n* the supreme ecclesiastical tribunal of the Roman Catholic Church

Ro·tar·i·an /rō térree ən/ *n* a member of a Rotary Club [Early 20C. < ROTARY CLUB] —**Ro·tar·i·an·ism** *n*

ro·ta·ry /rṓtəree/ (*plural* **-ries**) *n* **1.** a machine or part of a machine that rotates around an axis or a fixed point **2.** ROADS same as **traffic circle** [Mid-18C. < medieval Latin *rotarius* < Latin *rota* "wheel"]

Ro·ta·ry Club *n* a local club that is a member of an international organization of business and professional people that encourages service to the community [From the organization's early practice of holding meetings in rotation at members' business premises]

ro·ta·ry cul·ti·va·tor *n* AGRIC same as **rototiller**

ro·ta·ry en·gine *n* **1.** an internal-combustion engine with cylinders that rotate about a fixed crankshaft **2.** an engine that produces torque or power entirely by a rotating mechanism rather than by a crankshaft and reciprocating piston arrangement

Ro·ta·ry In·ter·na·tion·al *n* an international organization of business and professional people formed in the United States in 1905 to encourage service to the community [See ROTARY CLUB]

ro·ta·ry mow·er *n* a lawn mower with a single blade attached in the middle and sharpened at both ends that rotates as the mower is moved

ro·ta·ry plough *n UK* same as **rototiller**

rotary plow *n* AGRIC same as **rototiller**

ro·ta·ry press *n* a printing press that prints from curved plates mounted on a revolving cylinder, often onto a continuous roll of paper

ro·ta·ry pump *n* a pump that imparts motion by internal sets of rotating vanes or screws, used to move water or other fluids

ro·ta·ry til·ler *n* AGRIC same as **rototiller**

ro·ta·ry-wing air·craft *n* an aircraft, especially a helicopter, that is lifted or propelled by rotating airfoils

ro·tate /rṓ tàyt/ *vti* (**-tat·ed, -tat·ing, -tates**) **1. TURN AROUND AXIS** to turn like a wheel around an axis or a fixed point, or make something turn around an axis or a fixed point ○ *Earth rotates around the axis through its poles.* ○ *The windmill's sails are rotated by the wind.* **2. FOLLOW IN ORDER** to follow in a sequence, taking turns, or make things follow in such a sequence ○ *Rotate the plates in the pile so that they all get used.* **3.** HR **REPLACE PERSONNEL** to be replaced by somebody else, or replace one person or group by another, e.g., in a sports team or military unit ○ *The manager rotates first-string players with promising newcomers in less important games.* **4.** AGRIC **VARY CROPS** to vary the crops grown on the same piece of ground so as not to exhaust the soil or make it susceptible to disease, or be varied in this way ■ *adj* **WHEEL-SHAPED** having parts that radiate from a central point [Late 17C. Either < Latin *rotat-*, past participle of *rotare* < *rota* "wheel"; or back-formation < ROTATION] —**ro·tat·a·ble** *adj* —**ro·ta·tive** *adj* —**ro·ta·to·ry** /rṓtə tàwree/ *adj*

ro·ta·tion /rō táysh'n/ *n* **1. TURNING MOTION** a turning motion like that of a wheel around an axis or a fixed point, or the act or process of turning in such a way ○ *the rotation of the Earth* **2. SINGLE REVOLUTION** a single turn of something around an axis or a fixed point ○ *one full rotation of the wheel* **3. REGULAR VARIATION** a regular or planned recurrent sequence of events or changes of position ○ *The families use the vacation home in strict rotation.* **4.** AGRIC same as **crop rotation** **5.** MATH **MATHEMATICAL TRANSFORMATION** a mathematical transformation in which axes are rotated by a fixed angle while the origin remains unchanged **6.** CUE GAMES **WAY OF PLAYING POOL** a way of playing pool in which the balls are shot in ascending numerical order [15C. Directly or via French < Latin *rotation-* < *rotat-* (see ROTATE)] —**ro·ta·tion·al** *adj*

ro·ta·tor /rṓ tàytər/ *n* **1.** somebody or something that rotates or causes rotation **2.** (*plural* **ro·ta·tor·es** /rṓtə táwr èez/) a muscle that rotates part of the body on an axis

ro·ta·tor cuff *n* the deep muscles of the shoulder and their tendons that connect the arm to the shoulder joint, encircle it, and provide strength and stability while permitting rotation of the arm

ro·ta·vi·rus /rṓtə vìrəss/ *n* a wheel-shaped RNA virus that causes gastroenteritis, especially in infants [Late 20C. < modern Latin < Latin *rota* "wheel" + *virus* "poison, virus"]

ro·tax·ane /rō ták sàyn/ *n* a chemical compound consisting of two unbonded portions, a long thin molecule that is encircled by a molecule held in its position by large end groups

ROTC /rótsee/ *abbr* Reserve Officers' Training Corps

rote[1] /rōt/ *n* mechanical repetition of something so that it is remembered, often without real understanding of its meaning or significance ○ *learned it by rote* [13C. < ?]

rote[2] /rōt/ *n* the noise of waves breaking on the shore [Early 17C. < ?]

rote[3] /rōt/ *n* a medieval stringed instrument played by plucking [14C. < Old French, probably < late Latin *chrotta* "British musical instrument" < Welsh *crwth* "crowd (Celtic stringed instrument)" or Old Irish *crot* "harp, cithara"]

ro·te·none /rṓt'n ṑn/ *n* a white crystalline insecticide. Source: roots of derris. Formula: $C_{23}H_{22}O_6$. [Early 20C. < Japanese *roten* "derris"]

rot·gut /rót gùt/ *n* cheap and rough alcoholic drink (*informal*)

Roth /rawth/, **Philip** (*b.* 1933) US writer. His novels, which often concern American Jewish life, include *Goodbye, Columbus* (1959) and *Portnoy's Complaint* (1969). Full name **Roth, Philip Milton**

> "Just like those who are incurably ill, the aged know everything about their dying except exactly when."
> [Philip Roth, "Opening letter to Zuckerman," *The Facts*; 1988]

Roth·er·ham /róthərəm/ city in South Yorkshire, northern England. Population: 248,175 (2001).

Roth·ko /róth kṑ/, **Mark** (1903–70) Russian-born US artist. He is known for large color-field abstract expressionist paintings, often in somber tones.

> "It is a widely accepted notion among painters that it does not matter what one paints

as long as it is well painted. This is the essence of academism. There is no such thing as good painting about nothing." [Mark Rothko, *Letter to Edwin A. Jewell, New York Times*; June 13, 1943]

Roth·schild /róth chīld, róths-/, **Lionel Nathan** (1808–79) British financier. The eldest son of Nathan Mayer Rothschild, he was the manager of the London branch of the family business and the first Jewish member of the British Parliament.

Roth·schild, Mayer Amschel (1743–1812) German financier. The father of Nathan Mayer Rothschild, he was a financial agent of the British government.

Roth·schild, Salomon (1774–1855) German financier. The son of Mayer Amschel Rothschild, he established a branch of the House of Rothschild in Vienna.

ro·ti /rṓtee/ (*plural* **-tis**) *n* an unleavened bread made from wheat flour and cooked on a griddle, originally from northern South Asia but also eaten in the Caribbean [Early 20C. < Hindi *roṭī*]

ro·ti·fer /rṓtəfər/ *n* a microscopic invertebrate that has a wheel-shaped crown of projecting threads (**cilia**) at the anterior end and lives mostly in freshwater habitats. Phylum: Rotifera. [Late 18C. < modern Latin, "wheel-bearing, wheel-bearer" < Latin *rota* "wheel"] —**ro·tif·er·al** /rō tíffərəl/ *adj* —**ro·tif·er·ous** /rō tíffərəss/ *adj*

ro·tis·se·rie /rō tíssəree/ *n* **1.** a cooking appliance for roasting meat using a rotating spit **2.** a shop or restaurant where meat is roasted and sold [Mid-19C. < French *rôtisserie* < *rôtir* "to roast" < Germanic]

rot·l /rótt'l/ (*plural* **ar·tal** /áar taal/) *n* in many Islamic countries, a unit of weight varying from approximately 1 to 5 lb./0.45 to 2.25 kg [Early 17C. < Arabic *raṭl*]

ro·to·gra·vure /rṓtəgrə vyo͝or/ *n* **1.** a printing process in which images are etched photomechanically onto copper cylinders mounted in a rotary press, from which they are printed onto a moving web of paper **2.** something printed using rotogravure, e.g., a magazine or a photographic section of a newspaper [Early 20C. < German *Rotogravur*, corporation name]

ro·tor /rṓtər/ *n* **1.** ROTATING AIRFOILS ON HELICOPTER an assembly consisting of several flat blades attached to a hub, which rotates either horizontally to give lift and thrust to a helicopter, or vertically to help control it **2.** ROTOR BLADE a blade or airfoil of a rotor (*informal*) **3.** ROTATING PART OF MACHINE a rotating part of an electrical apparatus, e.g., the armature of a generator, or of a mechanical device **4.** METEOROL WAVE OF AIR a wave of air in which air rotates around a horizontal axis [Late 19C. Contraction of ROTATOR]

ro·tor·craft /rṓtər kràft/ (*plural same*) *n* AVIAT same as **rotary-wing aircraft**

Ro·to·ru·a /rṑtə ro͞o ə/ city in the center of the North Island, New Zealand, noted for its volcanic activity and thermal springs. Population: 52,608 (2001).

ro·to·till /rṓtə til/ (**-tilled, -till·ing, -tills**) *vt* to break up or till soil using a rototiller [Mid-20C. Back-formation < ROTOTILLER]

ro·to·till·er /rṓtə tìllər/ *n* a machine for breaking up and tilling soil, consisting of a series of blades mounted on a revolving power-driven shaft [Early 20C. < Latin *rota* "wheel" + TILLER[2]]

rot·ten /rótt'n/ *adj* **1.** DECAYED affected by rot or decay ○ *a rotten apple* **2.** CORRUPT characterized by a lack of honesty or moral principles ○ *The administration was rotten to the core.* **3.** NASTY mean and nasty in attitude and behavior toward others (*informal*) ○ *He's been rotten to his sister.* **4.** FOUL extremely unpleasant or unfortunate (*informal*) ○ *They've had rotten luck.* ○ *rotten weather* **5.** INFERIOR bad, incompetent, or substandard (*informal*) ○ *He's a rotten driver.* **6.** UNWELL generally unwell, usually without a specific complaint (*informal*) ○ *I woke up feeling rotten the morning after the party.* **7.** UNHAPPY unhappy or uncomfortable, especially through guilt or embarrassment (*informal*) ○ *I feel rotten about letting you down.* ■ *adv* TO GREAT DEGREE to a great degree, especially so much as to be disapproved of (*informal*) ○ *spoils those kids rotten* [13C. < Old Norse *rotinn*] —**rot·ten·ly** *adv* —**rot·ten·ness** *n*

rot·ten bor·ough *n* a political constituency with few electors but the same right to elect a representative as a more populous constituency

rot·ten·stone /rótt'n stṑn/ *n* a form of silica-rich limestone that has been decomposed by weathering and is used in powdered form for polishing metal

rot·ter /róttər/ *n UK* somebody considered to be nasty or unpleasant (*dated informal*) [Early 17C. < ROT]

Rot·ter·dam /róttər dàm, ráwtər daàm/ city and port in Zuid-Holland Province, southwestern Netherlands. Population: 593,321 (2000).

rott·wei·ler /rót wīlər, -vīlər/ *n* a large powerful dog belonging to a breed that has a black smooth coat with tan markings [Early 20C. After *Rottweil*, town in SW Germany]

ro·tund /rō túnd/ *adj* **1.** having a rounded body shape and, usually, a greater body weight than is advisable **2.** having a full, rich sound [15C. Directly or via Italian *rotondo* < Latin *rotundus* "round" < *rotare* "rotate" < *rota* "wheel"] —**ro·tun·di·ty** *n*

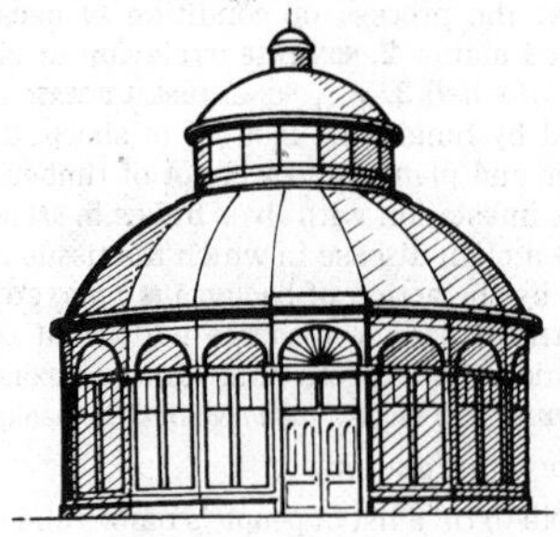

rotunda

ro·tun·da /rō túndə/ *n* **1.** ROUND BUILDING a round building, usually covered with a dome **2.** ROUND ROOM a large round hall or room **3.** OPEN AREA IN PUBLIC BUILDING a large open area at an airport, railroad station, or other public building [Early 17C. < Italian *rotonda* < Latin *rotunda*, form of *rotundus* "round" (see ROTUND); altered after the Latin]

Rou·baix /roo báy/ city in Nord Department, Nord-Pas-de-Calais Region, northern France, situated northeast of Lille. Population: 96,984 (1999).

rou·é /roo áy/ *n* a man who regularly engages in drinking, gambling, and womanizing (*literary*) [Early 19C. < French < past participle of *rouer* "break on the wheel" (a medieval instrument of torture) < Latin *rotare* (see ROTATE)]

ORIGIN The term ***roué*** is thought to stem from Philip, duke of Orléans and regent of France (1715–23), who humorously designated his debauched companions as *roués*, either to suggest that they deserved to be broken upon the wheel or because their behavior was so exhausting that they felt they had undergone this torture. See also ***rota***.

Rou·en /roo áan, -áaN/ capital of Seine-Maritime Department, Haute-Normandie Region, northwestern France. Population: 106,592 (1999).

rouge /roozh/ *n* **1.** REDDISH MAKEUP FOR CHEEKS red or pink makeup in powder or cream form used to add color to the cheeks or lips or to accentuate the shape of the cheekbones (*dated*) **2.** POLISH IN POWDER FORM a polish in powder form containing metallic oxides, especially a polish for metal (**crocus**) that contains ferric oxide ■ *vt* (**rouged, roug·ing, roug·es**) COLOR SOMETHING WITH ROUGE to put rouge on the cheeks or lips (*dated*) [Mid-18C. Via French < Latin *rubeus* "red"]

rouge et noir /-ay nwaár/ *n* a card game played on a table marked with two red and two black diamonds, with all betting against the house at even money [< French, "red and black"]

rough /ruf/ *adj* **1.** NOT SMOOTH OR FLAT having a bumpy, knobby, or uneven surface rather than being smooth, flat, and regular **2.** NOT SOFT not soft and smooth, but rather coarse in texture ○ *a dog with a rough bristly coat* **3.** WINDY OR TURBULENT stormy, or unpleasantly turbulent as a result of stormy conditions ○ *Rough seas washed some boats onto the beach.* **4.** NOT GENTLE characterized by or done with a lot of force or violence ○ *toys that will stand up to rough handling* **5.** BOORISH not refined or polite in manner and behavior, but tending to be noisy and rowdy ○ *rough talk* **6.** FREQUENTED BY UNSAVORY PEOPLE frequented or inhabited by people who tend to be noisy, rowdy, or violent ○ *a rough part of town* **7.** HARSH harsh in sound or to the taste **8.** GENERAL not exact, precise, or detailed, but broadly correct ○ *a rough estimate* **9.** THROWN TOGETHER made quickly and without using proper or good-quality materials, or providing for only the most basic needs ○ *a rough shelter made from branches* **10.** CRUDE hastily or incompletely made ○ *a rough wooden carving* **11.** DIFFICULT TO TRAVEL OVER in a wild and natural state and difficult to travel across ○ *marching over rough terrain* **12.** SEVERE OR UNPLEASANT severe, unfair, or generally unpleasant ○ *They felt they had received rough treatment at the hands of the judge.* ○ *It's rough on the children when the parents split up.* ■ *n* **1.** UNMOWN PART OF GOLF COURSE the area of a golf course on which grass and other vegetation is allowed to grow higher than on the fairway **2.** PRELIMINARY OUTLINE a preliminary version of something, e.g., a sketch giving the broad layout of an artwork **3.** *UK* VIOLENT PERSON a violent or brutal person, especially a hired thug ■ *vt* (**roughed, rough·ing, roughs**) **1.** ROUGHEN SOMETHING to make something rough **2.** *US* USE VIOLENCE ON OPPOSING PLAYER in football and ice hockey, to treat an opposing player with unnecessary violence [Old English *rūh* < Germanic] —**rough·ish** *adj* —**rough·ness** *n* ◇ **in the rough** in a crude, unfinished, or uncultivated state ◇ **rough it** to live in a less comfortable or less sophisticated way than usual (*informal*) ◇ **rough or smooth** used as a call when spinning a racket in a game of tennis or squash to decide which player should serve first or choose the end to serve from ◇ **take the rough with the smooth** to accept the disadvantages of a situation as well as the advantages

SPELLCHECK rough or **ruff**? Do not confuse the spelling of ***rough*** and ***ruff***, which sound similar. ***Rough*** is chiefly used as an adjective, meaning "coarse," "bumpy," "harsh," or "approximate," as in *a rough surface*, *a rough flight*, *rough treatment*, *a rough draft.* It is occasionally used as a noun or verb, as in *take the rough with the smooth*, *roughing it in makeshift accommodations.* ***Ruff*** is a noun denoting a stiff pleated collar worn in the 16th and 17th centuries, or a bird with neck feathers resembling such a collar.

rough out *vt* to prepare a rough model, plan, or sketch of something ○ *roughed out a scene-by-scene narrative*

rough up *vt* **1.** to subject somebody to a violent beating (*informal*) **2.** to make something, e.g., somebody's hair, look messy by rubbing it carelessly

rough·age /rúffij/ *n* MED same as **fiber** (sense 5)

rough-and-read·y *adj* **1.** not elegant or stylish and often hastily made or improvised, but practical or usable ○ *rough-and-ready accommodations in a hostel* **2.** crude and vigorous in behavior rather then gentle, polite, or well-mannered, but not malicious

rough-and-tum·ble *n* **1.** a situation characterized by aggressive tactics and a disregard for rules and conventions **2.** a bout of rough physical horseplay or free-for-all fighting —**rough-and-tum·ble** *adj*

rough blue·grass *n* a yellowish green grass that grows in thick patches, naturalized and considered a weed in the United States. Latin name: *Poa trivialis.* Native to: Europe, Asia, northern Africa.

rough breath·ing *n* in ancient Greek, a sound like that of the English "h," occurring with an initial vowel or the letter ρ and indicated by the symbol ʻ

rough·cast /rúf kàst/ *n* **1.** PEBBLED SURFACE ON WALLS a surface of coarse plaster covered with pebbles on the outside walls of a building (*often used before a noun*) ○ *roughcast walls* **2.** ROUGH MODEL a preliminary form or model of something ○ *made a roughcast in clay before starting to work the marble* ■ *vt* (**-cast, -cast·ing, -casts**) **1.** COVER WALL WITH ROUGHCAST to cover the surface of a wall or the walls of a building with roughcast **2.** FORM SOMETHING ROUGHLY to shape or form something in a crude fashion or as a preliminary to more polished work

rough col·lie *n* a longhaired collie dog that is black and white or black, white, and tan and has a band of thick hair around its neck and shoulders

rough cop·y *n* a preliminary draft of a piece of writing, usually raw and unedited

rough cut *n* the preliminary version of a movie, with only basic editing done to put the scenes together in sequence

rough-cut *adj* **1.** NOT SMOOTHED cut or shaped only roughly, with the surface and the edges not smoothed ○ *rough-cut planks* **2.** UNREFINED lacking polish or finesse in manner ■ *vt* CUT ROUGHLY to cut or carve something roughly without smoothing the surface or edges ○ *rough-cut timbers for the barn*

rough di·a·mond *n UK* same as **diamond in the rough**

rough-dry *vt* to dry washed laundry but not iron it —**rough-dry** *adj*

rough·en /rúffən/ (**-ened, -en·ing, -ens**) *vti* to make something rough, or become rough

rough en·do·plas·mic re·tic·u·lum *n* endoplasmic reticulum containing ribosomes that give its surface an uneven appearance, involved in the synthesis of proteins in plant and animal cells

rough fish *n* a species of fish that is neither caught for food nor fished for by anglers

rough-hew *vt* **1.** to cut or carve something roughly without smoothing the surface or edges ○ *He rough-hewed the wood to make a crude table.* **2.** to shape or form something crudely

rough-hewn *adj* **1.** NOT SMOOTHED cut or shaped only roughly, with the surface and the edges not smoothed ○ *blocks of rough-hewn sandstone* **2.** CRUDELY MADE crudely shaped or formed **3.** UNREFINED uncouth and unrefined in character

rough·house /rúf hòwss/ (*informal*) *vti* (**-housed, -hous·ing, -hous·es** /-hòwzəz/) to behave or treat somebody in a rough boisterous way ○ *letting the kids roughhouse in the basement* ■ *n* a situation characterized by rough behavior or excessively boisterous play

rough·ly /rúfflee/ *adv* **1.** APPROXIMATELY as a fairly close estimate, or in a manner that is broadly correct but without any claim to exactness ○ *Roughly one-third of the funding comes from government.* **2.** VIOLENTLY OR RUDELY in a violent way or a manner lacking in gentleness and politeness ○ *shoved him roughly to one side* **3.** CRUDELY in a crude, preliminary, or incomplete way ○ *sketched the design out roughly on a scrap of paper*

rough·neck /rúf nèk/ *n* **1.** a rough, bad-mannered person (*informal*) **2.** an unskilled worker on an oil-drilling rig or at an oil well (*slang*)

rough·rid·er /rúf rīdər/ *n* a breaker or trainer of wild or untrained horses

Rough Rid·er *n* a soldier in the 1st US Volunteer Cavalry recruited by Theodore Roosevelt to fight in the Spanish-American War

rough·shod /rúf shòd/ *adj* **1.** fitted with horseshoes that have short spikes to prevent slipping in wet weather **2.** displaying great forcefulness and a lack of consideration ◇ **ride roughshod over somebody** *or* **something** to dispose of somebody or something forcefully and inconsiderately

rough sled·ding *n US* a hard or difficult time or experience (*informal*)

rough stuff *n* violent behavior or acts (*informal*)

rough trade *n* an offensive term for a man whose physicality and lack of refinement are found sexually attractive by a gay man from a higher social class (*slang*)

rough-winged swal·low *n* a small brown bird of the swallow family commonly found near water. Native to: North America. Genus: *Stelgidopteryx*. [< the barb-shaped hooks on the outer feathers]

rou·ille /roo ee/ *n* a sauce made from chilies, garlic, and olive oil served as an accompaniment to Provençal foods such as bouillabaisse [Mid-20C. Via French, "rust" (from its color) < Latin *robigo*]

rou·lade /roo laad/ *n* **1.** a dish in which a piece of food is coated with a sauce or filling and rolled up before being cooked, so that each slice has a spiral appearance **2.** a run of several musical notes sung rapidly to one syllable [Early 18C. < French < *rouler* "to roll"]

rou·leau /roo lṓ/ (*plural* **-leaux** /-lṓ/ or **-leaus** /-lṓz/) *n* **1.** a stack of coins wrapped in a paper cylinder **2.** a rolled or folded ribbon used as decorative piping or trimming [Late 17C. Via French, "small roll" < Latin *rotula* "small wheel" < *rota* "wheel"]

rou·lette /roo lét/ *n* **1.** GAMBLING GAME WITH WHEEL a game in which a ball is rolled onto a spinning horizontal wheel divided into compartments, with players betting on which compartment the ball will come to rest in (*often used before a noun*) **2.** TOOL WITH TOOTHED WHEEL a tool with a toothed wheel used for making dots, e.g., in engraving, or for making perforations in paper, e.g., on a sheet of postage stamps **3.** SLITS CUT IN PAPER a line of slits or perforations made by a cutting tool on a sheet of paper ■ *vt* (**-lett·ed, -lett·ing, -lettes**) MARK SOMETHING WITH DOTS OR PERFORATIONS to use a roulette to mark a surface with a line of dots or make perforations in a sheet of paper [Mid-18C. < French, "small wheel" < late Latin *rotella* < Latin *rota* "wheel"]

round[1] /rownd/ *adj* **1.** CIRCULAR OR SPHERICAL shaped like a circle or a ball ○ *a big, perfectly round bowl* **2.** CURVED curved rather than square or angular **3.** IN CIRCULAR MOTION done with or involving a circular motion **4.** COMPLETE not less or more than ○ *a round dozen* **5.** EXPRESSED BY INTEGER expressed as an approximate value, especially to the nearest integer or power of ten ○ *use 1,500 as a round number* **6.** CONSIDERABLE large in amount or size ○ *a round sum* **7.** PLUMP full and plump, especially in facial features ○ *kindly eyes in a round face* **8.** SONOROUS mellow and rich in tone **9.** BRISK lively and rather fast ○ *We set off at a round pace.* **10.** STRAIGHTFORWARD plain and outspoken ○ *"I said in good round English 'I'm going to knock the stuffing out of you'."* (John Buchan, *Greenmantle*; 1916) **11.** PHON PRONOUNCED WITH ROUNDED LIPS describes speech sounds articulated with the lips forming an oval opening ○ *a round vowel sound* ■ *n* **1.** ROUND SHAPE a round shape or object **2.** SESSION a session or instance of an event, usually in a series of similar or related events ○ *the first round of talks* **3.** STAGE OF COMPETITION a game, or series of games, forming a stage in a competition ○ *lost to the reigning champion in the third round* **4.** DIVISION OF BOXING OR WRESTLING MATCH one the periods of actual fighting, usually three minutes in length, into which a boxing or wrestling match is divided **5.** GAME OF GOLF a session of golf in which all the holes on a golf course are played once **6.** PERIOD OF PLAY IN CARDS a period of play, especially in a game of cards, during which each player takes his or her turn **7.** CHARGE OF AMMUNITION FOR ONE SHOT an item of ammunition, e.g., a cartridge, or the quantity of ammunition required to fire one shot ○ *hundreds of mortar rounds* **8.** GUN DISCHARGE a single discharge by a gun or guns ○ *fired a few rounds* **9.** SERIES OF VISITS a series of visits made on a regular basis to different places or people (*often used in the plural*) **10.** APPLAUSE an outburst of applause or cheering **11.** SET OF DRINKS a number of drinks bought, one for each person in a group **12.** PART SONG a song sung by several voices in which each voice sings the same tune at the same pitch, but the voices enter one after the other so that they end up singing different parts of the song at the same time **13.** CIRCULAR DANCE a dance with a sequence of movements in a circle **14.** *UK* SLICE OF BREAD a slice of bread or toast, or a sandwich made from two slices of bread **15.** CUT OF BEEF a cut of beef from between the rump and the shank ■ *v* (**round·ed, round·ing, rounds**) **1.** *vt* MOVE PAST OBSTACLE to move in a curve past the edge or corner of something **2.** *vti* EXPRESS AS ROUND NUMBER to express a number containing several units as the nearest significant number above or below it, e.g., treating 5,753 as 6,000, or 6.375 as 6 ○ *The estimate was rounded to the nearest dollar.* **3.** *vt* PRONOUNCE SOUNDS to pronounce a sound with rounded lips ○ *Try to round your vowels.* **4.** *vt* PURSE LIPS to purse the lips [13C. < Old French *ro(u)nd-* < Latin *rotundus* (see ROTUND)] —**round·ish** *adj*—**round·ness** *n* ◇ **in the round 1.** THEATER having a stage in the center and the audience seated around it (*refers to a theater or performance*) **2.** SCULPTURE free-standing and viewable from all sides, rather than being carved from a background **3.** considered from a variety of different perspectives and as a whole ◇ **make** *or* **do** *or* **go the rounds 1.** to circulate and become widespread ○ *a new rumor making the rounds* **2.** to go from place to place in a regular pattern

round down *vt* to express a number as a smaller, less exact, but more manageable number for ease of calculation

round off *vt* **1.** FINISH SOMETHING IN PLEASING WAY to bring something to a pleasant or satisfactory end by doing or adding one last thing **2.** MAKE SOMETHING MORE ROUNDED to make the edges, sides, or corners of something less straight or angular and more rounded **3.** EXPRESS SOMETHING AS ROUND NUMBER to express a number as the nearest significant number above or below it for ease of calculation

round on *vt* to attack somebody suddenly, either physically or verbally, in a fit of anger

round out *vti* to achieve a more complete or satisfactory form, or cause something to achieve this

round up *vt* **1.** to gather people or animals together in one place **2.** to express a number as a larger, less exact, but more manageable number for ease of calculation

round[2] /rownd/ CORE MEANING: a grammatical word used to indicate that a circle of people, a place, or an object surrounds or encloses something ○ (prep) *She sat clasping her hands round her knees.* ○ (prep) *an area of green belt round the town* ○ (adv) *A crowd soon gathered round.*

1. *prep, adv* SURROUNDING so as to surround or be on all sides of ○ (adv) *gathered round to watch* ○ (prep) *put his arm round her* **2.** *prep* TO OTHER SIDE OF moving or looking to the other side of ○ *The truck came round the bend at breakneck speed.* **3.** *prep, adv* TURNING ON AXIS revolving around a center or axis ○ (prep) *the movement of the planets round the Sun* ○ (adv) *propellers going round at 1,000 revolutions per minute.* **4.** *prep, adv UK* same as **around** (senses 13–14) [14C. Partly < ROUND[1]; partly shortening of AROUND] ◇ **round about 1.** approximately ○ *round about midnight* **2.** surrounding somebody or something on all sides

USAGE round or **around**? In British English, ***round*** and ***around*** are interchangeable in many contexts: *She wore a silver chain round* [or *around*] *her neck. There was nothing but sand for miles around* [or *round*]. ***Round*** is often preferred, especially where circular movement is involved, as in *He spun round to face me*, and in fixed phrases such as *the wrong way round* and *round and round*. In US English *around* is the usual form, and it may be regarded as an Americanism by some British people. ***Round*** and ***around*** can sometimes be replaced by ***about*** in British English: *children running about in the garden.* ***About*** and ***around*** can also be used to mean "approximately": *We left at about* [or *around*] *midnight.*

round·a·bout /równdə bòwt/ *adj* proceeding in a way that is not direct or straightforward ○ *went by a roundabout route* ○ *answered in a roundabout way* ■ *n UK* **1.** same as **merry-go-round** (sense 2) **2.** same as **traffic circle**

round clam *n* ZOOL same as **quahog**

round dance *n* **1.** FOLK DANCE a folk dance in which several dancers or couples form a circle **2.** BALLROOM DANCE a ballroom dance in which couples revolve as they move around the room, as in a waltz **3.** BEE'S MOVEMENT a more or less circular sequence of movements that a honeybee performs in or near the hive to show other bees that food is nearby

round·ed /równdəd/ *adj* **1.** CURVED having curved, not straight or angular, surfaces or edges ○ *a frame with rounded corners* **2.** COMPLEX OR DIVERSE having many different features or aspects that together form a whole that is complete and interestingly complex or diverse ○ *received a rounded education* **3.** PHON PRONOUNCED WITH PURSED LIPS pronounced with the lips pursed to form a round shape —**round·ed·ness** *n*

roun·del /równd'l/ *n* **1.** ROUND PART a round part or piece, e.g., a round section in a stained-glass window or a round panel in a section of wood paneling **2.** LITERAT MODIFIED FORM OF RONDEAU an English form of the rondeau that has eleven lines arranged in three stanzas of three lines and a one-line refrain after the first and third stanzas **3.** LITERAT TYPE OF RONDEL a modified form of the rondel that has ten lines arranged in two stanzas of three lines and one of four lines, with the opening line repeated as a refrain **4.**

DANCE same as **roundelay** (sense 2) [13C. < Old French *rondel* "small circle" < *ro(u)nd-* (see ROUND[1])]

roun·de·lay /równdə lày, róndə lày/ *n* **1.** a simple song in which one of the verses is repeated at intervals, or the music for such a song **2.** a slow medieval dance performed by a group who form a circle [15C. Anglicization of French *rondelet* "small roundel" < *rondel* "small circle" < *ro(u)nd-* (see ROUND[1])]

round·er /równdər/ *n* **1.** TOOL MAKING THINGS ROUND a tool that makes edges or surfaces round **2.** BOXING MATCH a boxing match that lasts for a particular number of rounds (*usually used in combination*) ○ *fighting a ten-rounder* **3.** COMPLETE CIRCUIT IN ROUNDERS a score in the game of rounders made when the batter runs around all four bases after a single hit of the ball

round·ers /równdərz/ *n* a British ball game in which batters score a point, or rounder, if they run around all four marked fielding positions or bases after a single hit of the ball (*takes a singular verb*)

round hand *n* handwriting with broad rounded letters

Round·head /równd hèd/ *n* a supporter of Oliver Cromwell and the Parliamentarians against King Charles I during the English Civil War [Mid-17C. < their close-cropped hair (contrasted with that of the Cavaliers)]

round·house /równd hòwss/ (*plural* **-hous·es** /-hòwzəz/) *n* **1.** BUILDING FOR LOCOMOTIVES a circular building in which railroad locomotives are stored or repaired, consisting of a central turntable with several sections of track radiating from it **2.** CABIN ON SAILING SHIP a large cabin or set of cabins at the rear of an old-fashioned sailing ship **3.** PINOCHLE MELD in pinochle, a meld of four kings and four queens in all suits **4.** PUNCH DELIVERED WITH CIRCULAR SWING a punch made with a wide circular swing of the arm (*slang*)

round·let /równdlət/ *n* a small circular or disk-shaped object (*formal*)

round lot *n* a regular number of stocks or bonds as a trading unit, usually 100 shares of stock or 5 bonds

round·ly /równdlee/ *adv* **1.** forcefully and thoroughly ○ *was roundly criticized* **2.** so as to form a circle or sphere (*dated*)

round rob·in *n* **1.** TOURNAMENT WITH EVERYONE PLAYING ONE ANOTHER a tournament in which each player or team plays against every other player or team in turn **2.** DOCUMENT EACH PERSON PASSES ON a letter or other document circulated in turn to all members of a group, with each of them adding comments if they wish **3.** PETITION WITH SIGNATURES IN CIRCLE a letter, especially a petition or letter of protest, on which the signatures are arranged in a circle in order to hide the identity of the first person to sign [< the man's first name *Robin*]

round-shoul·dered *adj* with the shoulders hunched or drooping and the upper back bent forward slightly

round steak *n* a lean cut of beef from between the rump and shank

round·ta·ble /równd tàyb'l/ *n* a discussion or negotiation between several parties or groups who all take part on equal terms [< ROUND TABLE]

Round Ta·ble *n* **1.** in Arthurian legend, the table at which King Arthur and his knights sat, made round so that no one would appear to have precedence **2.** the knights of King Arthur as a group

round-the-clock *adj* lasting or operating throughout the day and night ○ *round-the-clock nursing care*

round-the-world tick·et *n* an airline ticket that entitles a passenger to travel to various destinations around the world, returning to the point of departure

round trip *n* **1.** a trip to a place and back again, usually returning by the same route **2.** CARDS same as **roundhouse** (sense 3)

round-trip *adj* involving a journey to somewhere and back again

round-trip tick·et *n* a ticket that entitles a passenger to travel both to and back from a place

round·up /równd ùp/ *n* **1.** a gathering together of people or animals, e.g., suspects in a criminal investigation or livestock on a farm or ranch **2.** a gathering together of things of any kind, especially information or news ○ *a news roundup on the hour*

round·worm /równd wùrm/ *n* a parasitic round-bodied worm (**nematode**) that infests the intestines of people and some animals. Latin name: *Ascaris lumbricoides.*

roup /roop/ *n* an infectious respiratory disease that affects poultry [14C. Probably < N Germanic]

rouse /rowz/ (**roused, rous·ing, rous·es**) *v* **1.** *vti* WAKE to wake somebody, or to awaken, from sleep or unconsciousness **2.** *vt* SHAKE SOMEBODY OUT OF APATHY to stir somebody into action or a more active state, or become more active ○ *He roused even the most apathetic students to something like enthusiasm for the subject.* **3.** *vt* CAUSE EMOTION to cause a particular emotion to be felt ○ *the feelings of guilt that the whole affair roused in us* [15C. < ?] —**rous·er** *n*

rous·ing /rówzing/ *adj* **1.** filling people with passion, emotion, and enthusiasm ○ *a rousing speech* **2.** full of energy and vigor ○ *a rousing chorus* —**rous·ing·ly** *adv*

Rous sar·co·ma /rówss-/ *n* a cancerous tumor found in chickens, caused by a tumor-producing RNA virus [Early 20C. After Francis Peyton *Rous* (1879–1970), US physician]

Rous·seau /roo só/, **Henri** (1844–1910) French painter. He painted in a bold primitive style, and is especially known for dreamscapes and jungle landscapes, painted after his retirement from a post as a customs official. Full name **Rousseau, Henri Julien Félix**. Known as **Le Douanier Rousseau**

Rous·seau, Jean Jacques (1712–78) French philosopher and writer. He was one of the great authors of the Age of Enlightenment. His works include *The Social Contract* (1762), *The New Heloise* (1761), and *Émile* (1762).

> "The passing from the state of nature to the civil society produces a remarkable change in man; it puts justice as a rule of conduct in place of instinct, and gives his actions the moral quality they previously lacked."
> [Jean Jacques Rousseau, *The Social Contract*; 1762]

Rous·seau, Théodore (1812–67) French painter. Best known for his naturalistic landscapes, he was the leader of the Barbizon School and a forerunner of impressionism. Full name **Rousseau, Pierre Étienne Théodore**

roust /rowst/ *vt* (**roust·ed, roust·ing, rousts**) **1.** FORCE SOMEBODY TO GET UP to make somebody get up, make a move, or take action, especially abruptly or roughly **2.** HARASS SOMEBODY to bother, annoy, or jostle somebody (*slang*) ■ *n US* HARASSING a harassing of somebody (*slang*) [Mid-17C. Probably alteration of ROUSE]

roust·a·bout /rówstə bòwt/ *n* an unskilled laborer, especially on an oil-drilling rig, on a ship or wharf, or in a circus

roust·er /rówstər/ *n* a deck hand or longshoreman

rout[1] /rowt/ *n* **1.** DEFEATED ARMY'S RETREAT a swift and disorderly retreat by a defeated army **2.** CRUSHING DEFEAT a severe and humiliating defeat ○ *The game quickly turned into a rout.* **3.** RABBLE a noisy and disorganized group of people ■ *vt* (**rout·ed, rout·ing, routs**) **1.** FORCE ARMY TO RETREAT to defeat an army completely and force it to make a swift and disorderly retreat **2.** DEFEAT SOMEBODY THOROUGHLY to subject an opponent to a thorough and humiliating defeat [13C. < Anglo-Norman *rute*, Old French *route* "dispersed group" < Latin *rupta* (see ROUTE)]

rout out *vt* **1.** to drive a person or animal from a place, especially by the use of force **2.** to reveal or uncover something, especially after a search ○ *routed out his true motives*

rout[2] /rowt/ (**rout·ed, rout·ing, routs**) *v* **1.** *vt* to cut a groove in wood or metal, especially with a router **2.** *vti* to search for something by poking around or digging through something, as pigs do with their snouts [Mid-16C. Variant of ROOT[2]]

route /root, rowt/ *n* **1.** COURSE a sequence of roads or paths taken, or places passed through, in traveling from one place to another, or a plan of these **2.** PROGRESSION the course that something follows, or the way it progresses or develops ○ *My career might have taken an entirely different route.* **3.** REGULAR JOURNEY a journey somebody regularly makes, especially a set sequence of stops made, e.g., by somebody delivering something ○ *Their store wasn't on my usual route.* ■ *vt* (**rout·ed, rout·ing, routes**) SEND SOMEBODY OR SOMETHING ALONG ROUTE to direct or arrange for somebody or something to follow a particular course ○ *All phone calls were routed through my office.* [12C. < Old French *route* < Latin *rupta*, form of past participle of *rumpere* "break"]

route march *n* a long march over rough ground, often used as training in physical endurance for soldiers —**route-march** *vti*

rout·er[1] /rówtər/ *n* a tool that cuts shaped grooves and hollows in wood or metal, originally a hand tool but now usually a power tool [Early 19C. < ROUT[2]]

rout·er[2] /róotər, rówtər/ *n* **1.** somebody who arranges routes, especially an organizer of deliveries **2.** a computer switching program that transfers incoming messages to outgoing links via the most efficient route possible, e.g., over the Internet [Late 20C. < ROUTE]

route step *n* a mode of marching in military formation where there is no requirement to keep in step and talking and singing are allowed

rou·tine /roo tééen/ *n* **1.** USUAL PATTERN OF ACTIVITY the usual sequence for a set of activities **2.** SOMETHING REPETITIVE something that is unvarying or boringly repetitive ○ *a life of mindless routine* **3.** REHEARSED PERFORMANCE a rehearsed set of movements, actions, or speeches that make up a performance ○ *her gymnastic routine on the parallel bars* **4.** PART OF COMPUTER PROGRAM a part of a computer program that performs a task ○ *a dump routine* ■ *adj* **1.** USUAL OR STANDARD regular or standard and not out of the ordinary ○ *carrying out routine maintenance* **2.** REPETITIVE boringly predictable, monotonous, and unchanging ○ *found the work pretty routine* [Late 17C. < French < *route* (see ROUTE)] —**rou·tine·ly** *adv*

SYNONYMS See ***habit***.

rou·tin·ize /róot'n ìz, roo téé nìz/ (**-ized, -iz·ing, -iz·es**) *vt* to arrange or plan something so that it follows a regular or unchanging pattern —**rou·tin·i·za·tion** /ròot'ni záysh'n, roo tèèni-/ *n*

roux /roo/ *n* a mixture of flour and fat that is cooked briefly and used as the thickening base of a sauce or soup [Early 19C. Via French, "browned" < Old French *rous* "reddish brown" < Latin *russus* "red"]

Rou·yn /róo in, roo áN/ city in eastern Quebec, Canada. Population: 23,635 (2001).

rove[1] /rōv/ (**roved, rov·ing, roves**) *v* **1.** *vti* to wander or travel with no definite purpose, often over a wide area, or travel over an area in this way **2.** *vi* to move, especially to look, in changing directions ○ *as his gaze roved around the room* [Early 16C. < ?]

rove[2] /rōv/ *vt* (**roved, rov·ing, roves**) to twist fibers slightly before they are spun into yarn or thread ■ *n* wool, cotton, or other fibers twisted slightly in preparation for spinning [Late 18C. < ?]

rove[3] NAUT past participle, past tense of **reeve**[2]

rove bee·tle *n* a carnivorous or scavenging beetle with a long body and short wing covers. Family: Staphylinidae. [< ?]

rov·er[1] /rṓvər/ *n* **1.** WANDERER somebody who wanders from place to place, never settling anywhere for long **2.** VEHICLE FOR EXPLORING PLANET a small vehicle launched from a lander and used to explore the surface of the moon or a planet **3.** ARCHERY TARGET a mark or object selected randomly as a target in archery [15C. < ROVE[1]]

rov·er[2] /rṓvər/ *n* a machine or attachment for twisting fibers slightly in preparation for spinning [Mid-18C. < ROVE[2]]

rov·er[3] /rṓvər/ *n* a pirate or pirate ship (*archaic*) [14C. < Middle Low German or Middle Dutch *rōver* < *rōven* "rob"]

rov·ing /rṓving/ *adj* **1.** moving or traveling from one place or thing to another ○ *a roving ambassador* **2.** tending to wander or waver rather than settle or concentrate on one thing ○ *a roving mind*

rov·ing eye *n* a wide and often promiscuous sexual interest

row[1] /rō/ *n* **1. THINGS OR PEOPLE PLACED IN LINE** a group of things or people arranged in a line that is usually straight ○ *a row of cabbages* **2. LINE OF THINGS OR PEOPLE** a line along which things or people are placed next to one another ○ *arranged us in rows* **3. LINE OF SEATS** a line of seats in a theater, lecture hall, or similar public place ○ *the second row in the balcony* **4. NARROW STREET BETWEEN LINES OF HOUSES** a narrow street that is lined with houses or other buildings on both sides **5.** MUSIC same as **tone row** [Old English *rāw* < Germanic] ◇ **in a row** one after the other in succession ◇ **a tough** *or* **hard row to hoe** something difficult to do

row[2] /rō/ (**rowed, row·ing, rows**) *v* **1.** *vti* to propel a boat across water by using oars **2.** *vi* to take part in the sport of rowing [Old English *rōwan* < Germanic, "to steer"] —**row·er** *n*

row back *vi UK* to moderate or modify a previous assertion, claim, or opinion, or retreat from a previous position on an issue (*informal*)

row[3] /row/ *n* **1. LOUD FIGHT** a noisy quarrel or dispute **2. RACKET** an unpleasant or excessively loud noise ■ *vi* (**rowed, row·ing, rows**) **ARGUE NOISILY** to make a lot of noise, especially during an argument [Mid-18C. < ?]

row·an /rṓ ən, rów ən/ *n* **1.** same as **mountain ash 2.** a deciduous tree with grayish compound leaves, clusters of white flowers, and bright red berries. Native to: Europe, Southwest Asia, North Africa. Latin name: *Sorbus aucuparia*. [Early 19C. < N Germanic < Indo-European, "red"]

row·boat /rṓ bṑt/ *n* a small lightweight boat designed to be propelled through the water by one or more people rowing with oars

row·dy /rówdee/ *adj* (**-di·er, -di·est**) noisy and disorderly ○ *The debate was a pretty rowdy affair.* ■ *n* (*plural* **-dies**) a rough and noisy person who often causes disturbances ○ *local rowdies hanging out on the streets* [Early 19C. Probably < ROW[3]] —**row·di·ly** *adv* —**row·di·ness** *n* —**row·dy·ism** *n*

row·el /rów əl, rowl/ *n* a small spiked revolving wheel on the end of a horse rider's spur ■ *vt* (**-eled, -el·ing, -els**) to urge a horse on by digging rowels into its sides [14C. Via Old French *roel(e)* "small wheel" < late Latin *rotella* (see ROULETTE)]

row·en /rów ən/ *n New England* a second mowing of hay or grass in the same season [14C. < Old N French, variant of Old French *regain* "till again" < *gaignier* "till" < Germanic]

REGIONAL NOTE The word ***rowen*** is the one commonly used in New England, extending across upstate New York and the northernmost counties of Pennsylvania. See also ***aftermath***.

row house /rṓ-/, **row home** /rṓ-/ *n* one of a line of houses joined to each other by their side walls

row·ing /rṓ ing/ *n* the propelling of a small boat through the water using oars, especially the sport of racing in specially designed lightweight boats (*often used before a noun*) ○ *a member of the rowing team*

row·ing boat *n UK* same as **rowboat**

row·ing ma·chine *n* a fitness machine that imitates the action of rowing a boat

Row·land /rṓlənd/, **F. Sherwood** (*b.* 1927) US chemist. He shared the Nobel Prize in chemistry (1995) for his research into chlorofluorocarbons and the depletion of the ozone layer. Full name **Rowland, Frank Sherwood**

Row·ling /rṓling/, **J. K.** (*b.* 1965) British author of the *Harry Potter* series of children's books. Full name **Joanne Kathleen Rowling**

row·lock /rṓ lòk/ *n UK* same as **oarlock** [Mid-18C. < ROW[2] + OARLOCK]

Roy /roy/, **Arundhati** (*b.* 1961) Indian writer. She achieved success with her first novel, *The God of Small Things* (1997), which won the British Booker Prize.

Roy, Gabrielle (1909–83) Canadian writer. She wrote novels about poverty among the working classes.

roy·al /róy əl/ *adj* **1. OF KINGS AND QUEENS** relating to, belonging to, or consisting of a king, queen, or other member of a monarch's family ○ *the royal palace* **2. ENJOYING MONARCH'S PATRONAGE** used in the titles of organizations and societies established by a monarch or a member of a monarch's family, or given his or her formal approval and support **3. EXCELLENT** of the most excellent kind ○ *given a royal welcome* **4. EXTREMELY BAD** used to emphasize how extremely bad something is (*informal*) ○ *a royal pain in the neck* **5.** SAILING **ABOVE TOPGALLANT** located in the area of a sailing ship's rigging that is above the topgallant ■ *n* **1. MONARCH OR MEMBER OF MONARCH'S FAMILY** a monarch, or a member of a monarch's family, especially his or her immediate family (*informal*) **2. STAG WITH LARGE ANTLERS** a stag with large antlers that have 12 or more points on them **3.** SAILING **SAIL ABOVE TOPGALLANT SAIL** the sail above the topgallant sail on a full-rigged ship **4.** PRINTING **SIZE OF PAPER** a size of printing paper 20 x 25 in./508 x 635 mm [13C. Via Old French *roial* < Latin *regalis* (see REGAL)]

Popperfoto
Arundhati Roy

roy·al blue *adj* of a bright deep blue color —**roy·al blue** *n*

Roy·al Brit·ish Le·gion *n UK* same as **British Legion**

Roy·al Ca·na·di·an Mount·ed Po·lice *n* a police force that operates throughout Canada except in cities and provinces with their own police forces

roy·al fern *n* a deep-rooted fern with branched stems. Native to: worldwide. Latin name: *Osmunda regalis.*

roy·al flush *n* in poker, a hand that consists of a ten, jack, queen, king, and ace of the same suit

Roy·al High·ness *n* a title used when speaking or referring to a member of a royal family other than a king or queen

roy·al·ist /róy əlist/ *n* a supporter of a monarch or the monarchic system of government (*often used before a noun*) —**roy·al·ism** *n*

Roy·al·ist *n* **1.** a Cavalier or supporter of Charles I during the English Civil War **2.** HIST same as **Tory** (sense 1) **3.** in France, a supporter of the Bourbon dynasty after the Revolution

roy·al jel·ly *n* a protein-rich substance that worker bees secrete and feed to larvae in the early stages of their development and to the larvae of queen bees in all stages of their development

roy·al·ly /róy əlee/ *adv* **1. GENEROUSLY** with impressive generosity and hospitality ○ *royally entertained* **2. EXPENSIVELY** with great magnificence or at great expense ○ *paid royally for their front-row seats* **3. WITH DIGNITY** in a stately or dignified manner as befits a king or queen ○ *swept royally through the crowd*

roy·al mast *n* the highest section of a sailing ship's mast that is immediately above the topgallant

roy·al palm *n* a palm tree with a tall naked trunk. Native to: tropical America. Genus: *Roystonea.*

roy·al poin·ci·an·a *n* a tropical tree widely grown for ornament. Flowers: bright red, in clusters. Native to: Madagascar. Latin name: *Delonix regia.*

roy·al pre·rog·a·tive *n* the power or right of a monarch to do something or be exempt from something, especially as formerly exercised by British monarchs

roy·al pur·ple *adj* of a deep vivid reddish purple color —**roy·al pur·ple** *n*

roy·al·ty /róy əltee/ (*plural* **-ties**) *n* **1. ROYAL PERSON OR PEOPLE** a king, queen, or other member of a monarch's family, or members of a royal family generally ○ *an adviser to royalty and prime ministers* **2. ROYAL PERSON'S STATUS** the status or authority of a king, queen, or other member of a monarch's family **3. PERCENTAGE OF INCOME PAID TO CREATOR** a percentage of the income from a book, piece of music, or invention that is paid to the author, composer, or inventor (*often used in the plural*) ○ *still living on the royalties from her first novel* **4. MINING COMPANY'S PAYMENT TO LANDOWNER** money paid to a landowner by a company taking minerals, oil, or gas from his or her land (*often used in the plural*)

Royce /royss/, **Josiah** (1855–1916) US philosopher and teacher. A proponent of idealism, he wrote many philosophical works, including *The Religious Aspect of Philosophy* (1885).

RP *abbr* **1.** LING Received Pronunciation **2.** role-play

RPG[1] *n* a high-level computer language used primarily for business reports. Full form **report program generator**

RPG[2] *n* a computer or other game in which the participants assume roles, often as fantasy characters such as heroes or elves, in a scenario that develops as the game progresses. Full form **role-playing game**

RPG[3] *abbr* ARMS rocket-propelled grenade

rpm, r.p.m. *abbr* RECORDING, MECH ENG revolutions per minute

rps, r.p.s. *abbr* MECH ENG revolutions per second

rpt. *abbr* **1.** repeat **2.** report

RPV *abbr* MIL remotely piloted vehicle

R.Q. *abbr* MED respiratory quotient

RR *abbr* **1.** TRANSP railroad **2.** CHR Right Reverend **3.** MAIL rural route

RRB *abbr* Railroad Retirement Board

-rrhagia *suffix* unusual or excessive flow or discharge ○ *metrorrhagia* [< Greek < *rhag-* stem of *rhēgnunai* "burst out"]

-rrhea, -rrhoea *suffix* flow, discharge ○ *pyorrhea* [< modern Latin < Greek *rhein* "to flow"]

rRNA *abbr* BIOCHEM ribosomal RNA

RRSP *abbr* Registered Retirement Savings Plan

RS *abbr* **1.** recording secretary **2.** right side **3.** *also* **R.S.** Royal Society

RSA *n* in computing, a system of encryption based on the difficulty of factoring very large numbers [< *RSA Security Inc.*]

RSC *abbr* Royal Society of Canada

RSFSR, R.S.F.S.R. *abbr* Russian Soviet Federated Socialist Republic

RSI *n Can, UK* a painful condition affecting some people who overuse muscles as a result of activities such as regularly operating a computer keyboard and mouse or playing the piano. Full form **repetitive strain injury.** US term **cumulative trauma disorder**

RSM *abbr* MIL regimental sergeant major

RSV, R.S.V. *abbr* BIBLE Revised Standard Version

R.S.V.P., r.s.v.p. *v* used on an invitation to request a response to it [Abbreviation of French *répondez s'il vous plaît*]

RT *abbr* **1.** TELECOM radiotelephone **2.** real time **3.** MED respiratory therapy **4.** FOOTBALL right tackle **5.** room temperature **6.** TRAVEL round trip

rt. *abbr* right

RTA *abbr* ready to assemble

RTDS *abbr* COMPUT real-time data system

Rte. *abbr* MAIL route

rtf[1] *n* **1.** a format for a computer file that contains rich text **2.** a computer file in rich text format [Abbreviation of *rich text format*]

rtf[2] *abbr* a file extension for an rtf file

RTFM *v* a highly offensive term used as a response in e-mail communications to an obvious technical question (*taboo*) Full form **read the fucking manual**

Rt. Hon. *abbr* POL Right Honorable

RTM *abbr* read the manual (*used in e-mails or text messages*)

Rt. Rev. *abbr* CHR Right Reverend

RTS *n* in computer gaming, a strategy game in which the action is continuous rather than turn-based [Abbreviation of real-time strategy]

RTW *abbr* CLOTHING ready-to-wear

ru *abbr* Russian Federation (*used in Internet addresses*) See table at **domain name**

Ru *symbol* CHEM ELEM ruthenium

RU *abbr* are you (*used in e-mails or text messages*)

Ru·a·hi·ne Range /ròo ə hée nay-/ mountain range in the south of the North Island, New Zealand. Its highest point is Mount Mangaweka, 5,686 ft./1,733 m.

ru·a·na /roo áanə/ *n* a cape or poncho worn in Peru and Colombia [Mid-20C. Via American Spanish < Spanish, "woolen fabric" < Latin *ruga* "wrinkle"]

Ru·an·da-U·run·di /roo áandə oo róondee/ former name for **Burundi** (until 1962)

Ru·a·pe·hu /ròo ə páyhoo/ active volcano in the central part of the North Island, New Zealand. It last erupted in 1996. Height: 9,177 ft./2,797 m.

rub /rub/ *v* (**rubbed, rub·bing, rubs**) **1.** *vt* **PRESS AND MOVE HAND ON SOMETHING** to move the hand or an object over the surface of something, pressing down with a repeated circular or backward and forward motion ○ *rubbed his aching shoulders with ointment* **2.** *vi* **TOUCH WITH DRAGGING PRESSURE** to make dragging contact with a surface ○ *metal parts rubbing against one another* **3.** *vti* **CLEAN WITH REPEATED STROKES** to clean, dry, or polish something, or be able to be cleaned, dried, or polished, by moving a cloth, sponge, or other implement over the surface repeatedly ○ *rubbed the stain from the tablecloth* **4.** *vti* **CAUSE ABRASION ON SKIN** to cause discomfort or pain by repeatedly scraping the skin ○ *These shoes are rubbing my heels.* ■ *n* **1. RUBBING ACTION** a rubbing motion, or a rubbing of something with or against something else **2. MASSAGE** a massaging of part of the body ○ *a soothing back rub* **3. DIFFICULTY** a problem or difficulty ○ *That's the rub: too little time.* **4. IRRITATING THING** something that somebody does or says that irritates or offends somebody else [14C. < ?] ◇ **rub somebody the wrong way** *US* to irritate or annoy somebody

rub down *vt* **1.** to massage somebody or part of the body vigorously **2.** to dry a person's or animal's body by vigorous rubbing with a towel

rub in *vt* to keep referring to something that the hearer does not want to be reminded of, usually because it is embarrassing (*informal*)

rub off *vi* to be passed to somebody, or be an influence on somebody who is exposed to it

rub out *v* **1.** *vti* to remove or obliterate something, e.g., by rubbing or wearing away, or be removed or obliterated **2.** *vt* to murder somebody (*slang*)

rub up *vti* same as **brush up**

ru·bab /ròo báb/ *n* a short-necked lute played in Afghanistan [Via Afghan Persian or Pashto < Arabic *rabāb*]

Rub al-Kha·li /ròob al káalee/ desert in the Arabian Peninsula. Also called the "Empty Quarter," it extends from central Saudi Arabia into Yemen, the United Arab Emirates, and Oman. Area: 250,000 sq. mi./650,000 sq. km.

ru·basse /roo báss, ròo báss/ *n* a ruby-red variety of quartz containing iron oxide [Late 19C. < French *rubace* < *rubis* "ruby" < Latin *rubeus* "red"]

ru·ba·to /roo báatō/ *n* rhythmic freedom in musical performance, often against a steady accompaniment ■ *adj, adv* performed with rubato [Late 18C. < Italian *(tempo) rubato* "robbed (time)," past participle of *rubare* "rob"]

rub·ber[1] /rúbbər/ *n* **1. NATURALLY OCCURRING ELASTIC SUBSTANCE** a strong elastic material made by drying the sap from various tropical trees, especially the American rubber tree **2. ELASTIC SYNTHETIC SUBSTANCE** a strong elastic synthetic substance made either by improving the qualities of natural rubber or by an industrial process using petroleum and coal products **3.** CLOTHING **WATERPROOF OVERSHOE** a waterproof overshoe worn over normal shoes to protect them in wet weather (*usually used in the plural*) **4.** BASEBALL **SPOT PITCHER STANDS ON** in baseball, the rectangle of hard rubber on the mound that the pitcher stands on to throw the ball **5. RUBBING OR POLISHING CLOTH** a cloth or pad used for rubbing or polishing something, especially the pad that a cabinetmaker uses to apply varnish or polish **6. DEVICE THAT RUBS SOMETHING** any machine or device that rubs a surface **7. CONDOM** a contraceptive sheath that fits over a man's penis (*slang; sometimes offensive*) **8.** *UK* same as **eraser** [Mid-16C. < RUB] ◇ **burn rubber** to drive very fast (*informal*)

rub·ber[2] /rúbbər/ *n* **1. BRIDGE MATCH OF THREE GAMES** a match of three or five games in cards, especially bridge and whist **2. DECIDING GAME IN CARDS MATCH** in some card games, an extra game played to decide a tied match **3. SESSION OF PLAY IN CARD GAME** a match or session of playing in a card game (*informal*) **4. SET OF GAMES** a series of games in some sports (*informal*) [Late 16C. Origin ?]

rub·ber band *n* a loop of thin rubber that is wrapped around objects to hold them together

rub·ber bridge *n* a form of contract bridge in which a new hand is dealt for each round

rub·ber bul·let *n* a cylindrical block of hard rubber fired by police officers or troops during crowd-control operations, designed as a deterrent but capable of inflicting serious injury

rub·ber ce·ment *n* an adhesive made by dissolving rubber in an organic solvent

rub·ber check *n* a check that is returned by a bank because the person who wrote it has insufficient funds in his or her account to cover it (*informal humorous*) [Because it bounces]

rub·ber-chick·en cir·cuit *n* a series of events that people feel obliged to attend, especially lunches or dinners for politicians or other public figures (*informal*) [Because the food served is usually unappetizing]

rub·ber·ize /rúbbə rìz/ (**-ized, -iz·ing, -iz·es**) *vt* to coat or impregnate something, especially fabric, with rubber

rub·ber·neck /rúbbər nèk/ (*informal*) *vi* (**-necked, -neck·ing, -necks**) to stare at somebody or something in an excessively inquisitive or insensitive way ■ *n UK* same as **rubbernecker** [Late 19C. < craning or turning the neck as if it were made of rubber] —**rub·ber·neck·ing** *n*

SYNONYMS See *gaze*.

rub·ber·necked /rúbbər nèkt/ *adj* staring insensitively or in an excessively inquisitive way (*informal*) ○ *a crowd of rubbernecked onlookers*

rub·ber·neck·er /rúbbər nèkər/ *n* somebody who stares at somebody or something in an excessively inquisitive, stupid, or insensitive way (*informal*)

rub·ber plant *n* **1.** a tropical plant with thick glossy leaves and a rubbery sap, widely grown as a houseplant but growing as a full-size tree in Southeast Asia. Latin name: *Ficus elastica*. **2.** any plant that produces a rubbery sap

rub·ber stamp *n* **1. STAMPING DEVICE** a device for stamping words or numbers on paper, consisting of an embossed flat rubber pad that is inked **2. AUTOMATIC AUTHORIZATION** authorization or approval that is given automatically **3. SOMEBODY GIVING APPROVAL AUTOMATICALLY** a person or group who gives authorization or approval automatically, without thinking, questioning, or dissenting

rub·ber-stamp *vt* **1.** to authorize or approve something automatically, without thinking, questioning, or dissenting **2.** to mark a document with an imprint from a rubber stamp

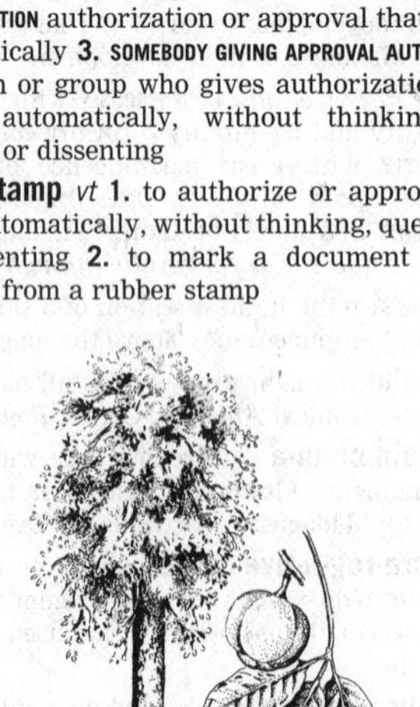

rubber tree

rub·ber tree *n* **1.** a tree whose sap is the main source of natural rubber. Native to: tropical America. Latin name: *Hevea brasiliensis*. **2.** any tree whose sap is made into rubber

rub·ber·y /rúbbəree/ *adj* **1.** with the elastic or tough texture of rubber **2.** lacking firmness or stiffness ○ *Suddenly, my legs felt rubbery.*

rub·bing /rúbbing/ *n* an impression of a textured surface, e.g., a raised design on a tombstone, made by placing paper over the surface and rubbing with a drawing implement

rub·bing al·co·hol *n* a liquid, usually consisting of 70% denatured ethyl alcohol or isopropanol, used for massaging and as an antiseptic

rub·bish /rúbbish/ *n* **1. TRASH** trash, garbage, or other unwanted things (*often used before a noun*) **2. WORTHLESS THINGS** things that are worthless or of very poor quality ○ *Most of what he's written is utter rubbish.* **3. NONSENSE** foolish things said or written, or things dismissed as wrong or not to be believed ○ *Don't talk rubbish!* [14C. < Anglo-Norman *rubbous*] —**rub·bish·y** *adj*

rub·ble /rúbb'l/ *n* **1. FRAGMENTS OF BROKEN BUILDINGS** broken stones, bricks, and other materials from buildings that have fallen down or been demolished **2. ROUGH STONES AS FILLER OR BULK** rough unfinished stones used to fill space between walls or to build the bulk of a wall that will have a finishing surface of dressed stone **3.** *also* **rub·ble·work** /rúbb'l wùrk/ **MASONRY OF ROUGH STONES** masonry that is constructed using rough unfinished stones [14C. Origin ?] —**rub·bly** *adj*

rub·down /rúb dòwn/ *n* a brisk rubbing down, usually of a person's or animal's body after exercising

rube /roob/ *n* an offensive term for somebody who is regarded as naive or unsophisticated, especially somebody from a rural area who is not used to city ways (*slang*) [Late 19C. Shortening of the forename *Reuben*]

ru·be·fa·cient /ròobə fáysh'nt/ *adj* causing the skin to become red (*formal*) ■ *n* a substance that causes the skin to become red, especially a cream or ointment used as a counterirritant [Early 19C. < Latin *rubefacient-*, present participle of *rubefacere* "make red" < *rubeus* "red" + *facere* "make"] —**ru·be·fac·tion** /-fáksh'n/ *n*

ru·be·fy /ròobə fì/ (**-fied, -fy·ing, -fies**) *vt* to use a rubefacient on skin [14C. < Old French *rubifier* "make red" < Latin *rubeus* "red"]

Rube Gold·berg /ròob gṓld bùrg/ *adj* unnecessarily intricate and complicated [Mid-20C. After Reuben "*Rube*" *Goldberg* (1883–1970), US cartoonist known for depictions of complex devices performing elementary tasks]

ru·bel·la /roo béllə/ *n* a highly contagious viral disease, especially affecting children, that causes swelling of the lymph glands and a reddish pink rash on the skin. It can be harmful to the unborn baby of a pregnant woman who contracts it. (*technical*) [Late 19C. < modern Latin, "rash" < form of Latin *rubellus* "reddish" < *rubeus* "red"]

ru·bel·lite /ròobə lìt, roo bé-/ *n* a red variety of tourmaline. Use: jewelry. [Late 18C. < Latin *rubellus* (see RUBELLA)]

Ru·bens /ròobənz/, **Peter Paul** (1577–1640) Flemish painter. He is considered one of the most important artists of the 17th century, and his style has come to define the sensuous aspects of baroque painting.

ru·be·o·la /roo bée ələ, ròobee ṓlə/ *n* same as **measles** (*technical*) [Late 17C. < modern Latin < Latin *rubeus* "red"] —**ru·be·o·lar** *adj*

ru·bes·cent /roo béss'nt/ *adj* turning red or reddish, e.g., by blushing (*literary*) [Mid-18C. < Latin *rubescent-*, present participle of *rubescere* "redden" < *rubeus* "red"] —**ru·bes·cence** *n*

Ru·bi·con /ròobi kòn/, **ru·bi·con** *n* a point at which any action taken commits the person taking it to a further course of action that cannot be avoided [Early 17C. After the stream in N Italy that Julius Caesar crossed illegally with his army in 49 B.C., making civil war inevitable] ◇ **cross the Rubicon** to do something that commits you to a particular course of action

ru·bi·cund /ròobikənd/ *adj* with the reddish skin color that is widely regarded as a sign of good health in people with white skin (*literary*) [15C. < Latin *rubicundus* < *rubeus* "red"] —**ru·bi·cun·di·ty** /ròobi kúndətee/ *n*

ru·bid·i·um /roo bíddee əm/ *n* a soft silvery white radioactive element of the alkali metal group that reacts strongly with water and bursts into flame when exposed to air. Source: lepidolite, carnallite. Use: photocells. Symbol **Rb**. See table at **element** [Mid-19C. < modern Latin < Latin *rubidus* "red" < *rubere* "be red" < *ruber* "red"; from the two red lines in its spectrum]

Ru·bik's cu·be /ro͞obiks-/ *tdmk* a trademark for a puzzle that is a cube composed of smaller rotating colored cubes, the aim being to rotate them to make each of the large cube's faces a uniform color

Ru·bin·stein /ro͞obin stīn/, **Anton** (1829–94) Russian composer and pianist. He is best known for his small piano pieces, e.g., *Melody in F* (1859). Full name **Rubinstein, Anton Grigoryevich**

Ru·bin·stein, Arthur (1887–1982) Polish-born US pianist. He is known for his interpretations of works by the romantic composers, notably Frédéric Chopin.

> "Sometimes, I think, not so much am I a pianist, but a vampire. All my life I have lived off the blood of Chopin."
> [Attributed to Arthur Rubinstein]

ru·ble /ro͞ob'l/, **rou·ble** *n* the main unit of currency in Russia, Belarus, and Tajikistan. See table at **currency** [Mid-16C. Via French < Russian *rubl'*]

ru·bric /ro͞obrik/ *n* **1.** TITLE OR HEADING a printed title or heading, usually distinguished from the body of the text in some way, especially the heading of a section of a legal statute, originally underlined in red **2.** SET OF PRINTED INSTRUCTIONS a set of printed rules or instructions, e.g., the rules governing how Christian services are to be conducted, often printed in red in a prayer book **3.** ESTABLISHED CUSTOM a well-established custom or tradition that provides rules for conduct **4.** CATEGORY a class or category of things ■ *adj* IN RED printed or marked in red [13C. Directly or via French < Latin *rubrica* "red ocher" < *ruber* "red"] —**ru·bri·cal** *adj* —**ru·bri·cal·ly** *adv*

ru·bri·cate /ro͞obri kàyt/ (**-cat·ed, -cat·ing, -cates**) *vt* (*formal*) **1.** ADD HEADINGS TO TEXT to add titles or heading to a text, or print them in red **2.** MARK SOMETHING IN RED to print or mark something in red **3.** REGULATE SOMETHING to apply a set of rules to something —**ru·bri·ca·tion** /ro͞obri káysh'n/ *n* —**ru·bri·ca·tor** *n*

ru·bri·cian /roo brísh'n/ *n* an expert in the way religious services should be conducted

ru·by /ro͞obee/ (*plural* **-bies**) *n* **1.** a red precious stone that is a form of corundum. Use: jewelry, manufacture of watches, precision instruments. **2.** a deep glowing purplish red color like that of a ruby [14C. Via Old French *rubi* < medieval Latin *rubinus* < Latin *rubeus* "red"] —**ru·by** *adj*

ru·by port *n* a port that is matured for a minimal period in the barrel and then bottled for immediate drinking

ru·by spi·nel *n* a red transparent form of the mineral spinel. Use: jewelry.

ru·by-throat·ed hum·ming·bird *n* a common hummingbird with a red throat and a shiny green back. Native to: North America. Latin name: *Archilochus colubris.*

ruche /roosh/ *n* a decorative strip of gathered, pleated, or frilled fabric on a garment ■ *vt* (**ruched, ruch·ing, ruch·es**) to decorate the edges of a garment with ruches [Early 19C. Via French < medieval Latin *rusca* "tree bark" < Celtic]

ruch·ing /ro͞oshing/ *n* decorative edges of gathered, pleated, or frilled fabric

ruck[1] /ruk/ *n* **1.** LARGE NUMBER a large number of people or things **2.** ORDINARY PEOPLE OR THINGS the great mass of unexceptional people or things **3.** FOLLOWERS the group of competitors behind the leader in a race [13C. Probably < N Germanic, "pile of combustible material"]

ruck[2] /ruk/ *vti* (**rucked, ruck·ing, rucks**) to become creased, or cause something, especially fabric, to become creased ○ *The carpet is rucked up under your chair.* ■ *n* a crease, especially in a fabric [Late 18C. < Old Norse *hrukka* "wrinkle"]

ruck·sack /rúk sàk, ro͝ok-/ *n* a large bag, usually with two straps and often with a supporting frame, carried on the back and used especially by walkers and climbers [Mid-19C. < German, "back sack"]

ruck·us /rúkəss/ *n* a noisy and unpleasant disturbance [Late 19C. < ?]

ruc·tion /rúkshən/ *n* a noisy, often violent, quarrel or fight [Early 18C. < ?]

rud·beck·i·a /rud békee ə, rood-/ (*plural* **-as** or *same*) *n* a plant with alternate leaves and showy yellow flowers that have green or black centers. Native to: North America. Genus: *Rudbeckia.* [Mid-19C. < modern Latin, after Olof *Rudbeck* the elder (1630–1702) and the younger (1660–1740), Swedish botanists]

rudd /rud/ (*plural* **rudds** or *same*) *n* a freshwater fish of the carp family with a thin greenish brown body and red fins. Native to: Europe. Latin name: *Scardinius erythrophthalmus.* [Early 16C. Variant of obsolete *rud* "redness" < Germanic, "red"]

rud·der /rúddər/ *n* **1.** MEANS OF STEERING BOAT OR SHIP a means of steering a boat or ship, usually in the form of a pivoting blade under the water, mounted at the stern and controlled by a wheel or handle (**tiller**) **2.** AIRFOIL FOR STEERING AIRPLANE an airfoil, usually on the tail of an airplane, that pivots vertically and controls left-to-right movement **3.** CONTROLLING FORCE a guiding or controlling force or influence [Old English *rōþer* < Germanic] —**rud·der·less** *adj*

rud·dle /rúdd'l/, **red·dle** /rédd'l/, **rad·dle** /rádd'l/ *n* a red ocher. Use: dye, formerly, to mark sheep. ■ *vt* (**-dled, -dling, -dles**) to dye or mark something such as a sheep with ruddle [Mid-16C. < obsolete *rud* "redness" < Germanic, "red"]

rud·dy /rúddee/ *adj* (**-di·er, -di·est**) **1.** ROSY WITH HEALTH with a healthy reddish glow ○ *ruddy cheeks* **2.** REDDISH red or reddish in color ○ *ruddy sky* ■ *adj, adv UK* SWEARWORD used as a swearword to emphasize how good, bad, or severe something is (*slang; sometimes offensive*) [Old English *rudig* < Germanic, "red"] —**rud·di·ly** *adv* —**rud·di·ness** *n*

rud·dy duck *n* a duck with a broad beak, upright tail, and white cheeks, the male of which is brownish red with a black crown and blue beak during the mating season. Native to: North America. Latin name: *Oxyura jamaicensis.*

rude /rood/ (**rud·er, rud·est**) *adj* **1.** ILL-MANNERED disagreeable or discourteous in manner or action ○ *Don't be rude!* **2.** INDECENT offensive to accepted standards of decency ○ *rude words* **3.** UNREFINED lacking refinement or social skills **4.** SUDDEN AND UNPLEASANT happening with unexpected suddenness and unpleasantness ○ *a rude awakening* **5.** ROUGHLY MADE in a rough or incomplete state ○ *a rude wooden bench* **6.** UNSKILLED showing a lack of skill or training ○ *rude paintings* **7.** INEXPERIENCED without schooling or experience ○ *a rude youth raised in the wilderness* **8.** RAW in a raw or unprocessed state ○ *rude fibers* **9.** VAGUE lacking precision ○ *a rude guess* **10.** UNDEVELOPED technologically or economically undeveloped **11.** ROBUST strong and energetic ○ *in rude health* [13C. Via French < Latin *rudis* "raw, rough"] —**rude·ly** *adv* —**rude·ness** *n*

rude·boy /ro͞od bòy/ *n Carib* a member of an anti-establishment street gang, often involved in violent crime. Rudeboys originated in Jamaica in the 1960s. (*informal*)

ru·der·al /ro͞odərəl/ *adj* describes a plant growing in wasteland, trash, or disturbed ground [Mid-19C. < Latin *ruder-* "rubble"] —**ru·der·al** *n*

ru·di·ment /ro͞odəmənt/ *n* **1.** SOMETHING BASIC TO SUBJECT a basic principle or skill, especially in a particular field or subject (*often used in the plural*) ○ *the rudiments of computer programming* **2.** BEGINNING an early stage in the development of something such as a plan (*often used in the plural*) **3.** BIOL UNDEVELOPED BODY PART a body part that does not develop fully and performs no useful function. The mammary gland in males is a rudiment. **4.** BIOL EMBRYO OF ORGAN an embryonic stage of an organ or body part [Mid-16C. Directly or via French < Latin *rudimentum* < *rudis* "raw, rough"]

ru·di·men·ta·ry /ro͞odə méntəree/, **ru·di·men·tal** /-mént'l/ *adj* **1.** BASIC existing at an elementary or basic level ○ *a rudimentary knowledge of French* **2.** DEVELOPING in an early or partially developed stage **3.** BIOL UNDEVELOPED not fully developed ○ *a rudimentary tail* **4.** BIOL IN FORM OF EMBRYO in an embryonic state —**ru·di·men·tar·i·ly** *adv* —**ru·di·men·ta·ri·ness** *n*

Ru·dolf /ro͞o dòlf/, **archduke and crown prince of Austria** (1858–89) The son of Franz Josef of Austria, he was a well-traveled patron of the arts

Ru·dolf I (1218–91) **king of Germany and Holy Roman Emperor** His acquisition of Bohemian territories in 1278 greatly strengthened the house of Hapsburg. He is considered the founder of the Hapsburg dynasty.

Ru·dolf, Lake /ro͞o dòlf/ former name for **Turkana, Lake**

Ru·dolph /ro͞o dòlf/, **Wilma Glodean** (1940–94) US athlete. She was the first American woman to win three Olympic gold medals in running events: 100 meters, 200 meters, and 400-meters relay (1960).

rue[1] /roo/ *vti* (**rued, ru·ing, rues**) to feel regret or sorrow for something in the past ○ *I rue the day I offered to help.* ■ *n* a feeling of regret or sorrow (*archaic*) [Old English *hrēowan* < Germanic]

rue[2] /roo/ (*plural* **rues** or *same*) *n* a woody plant with bitter, strongly scented leaves that yield an oil formerly used in medicines. Flowers: small, yellow. Native to: Europe, Asia. Latin name: *Ruta graveolens.* [14C. Via French and Latin *ruta* < Greek *rhutē*]

rue·ful /ro͞of'l/ *adj* **1.** feeling, showing, or causing regret **2.** causing people to feel pity —**rue·ful·ly** *adv* —**rue·ful·ness** *n*

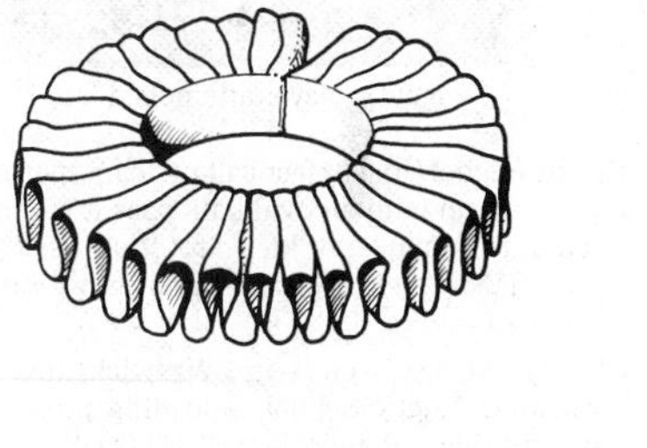

ruff

ruff[1] /ruf/ *n* **1.** FANCY PLEATED COLLAR a separate collar of starched pleated linen or lace worn by men and women in the 16th and 17th centuries **2.** NECK HAIR OR FEATHERS a growth of long, colorful, or bushy hair or feathers on the neck of a bird or other animal **3.** (*plural* **ruffs** or *same*) BIRD WITH ELABORATE RUFF a bird of the sandpiper family, the male of which, in spring, grows a ruff of feathers that are raised during courtship displays. Native to: Europe, Asia. Latin name: *Philomachus pugnax.* [Early 16C. Probably < variant of ROUGH] —**ruffed** *adj*

SPELLCHECK See *rough*.

ruff[2] /ruf/ *n* **1.** PLAYING OF TRUMP CARD in bridge or whist, the act of playing a trump card **2.** CARD GAME an old card game similar to whist ■ *vti* (**ruffed, ruff·ing, ruffs**) PLAY TRUMP ON DIFFERENT SUIT in bridge or whist, to play a trump card on a card from a different suit [Late 16C. < Old French *roffle*, a card game]

ruf·fi·an /rúffee ən/ *n* a rough, bullying, or violent person, often a member of a gang of thugs (*dated*) [15C. Via French < Italian *ruffiano* < Germanic] —**ruf·fi·an·ism** *n* —**ruf·fi·an·ly** *adj*

ruf·fle[1] /rúff'l/ *v* (**-fled, -fling, -fles**) **1.** *vt* MAKE FEATHERS ERECT to erect feathers, e.g., in defense, as a display, or for warmth or grooming (*refers to birds*) **2.** *vti* MAKE WAVES IN SURFACE to disturb or ripple something, especially a surface, or become disturbed or rippled **3.** *vti* ANNOY SOMEBODY to bother or fluster somebody, or become bothered or flustered ○ *gets ruffled so easily* **4.** *vt* GATHER OR PLEAT FABRIC to draw a strip of material into pleats or gathers to use as trim **5.** *vt* GLANCE QUICKLY THROUGH SOMETHING to flip rapidly through the pages of a book or magazine (*dated*) **6.** *vt* SHUFFLE CARDS to shuffle playing cards (*dated*) ■ *n* **1.** WAVE IN SURFACE a disturbance or ripple in something, especially a surface **2.** IRRITATING THING a source of irritation or annoyance **3.** TRIM OF PLEATED FABRIC a strip of closely pleated or gathered material used as trim **4.** ZOOL same as **ruff**[1] (sense 2) [14C. < ?] —**ruf·fled** *adj* —**ruf·fly** *adj*

ruf·fle[2] /rúff'l/ *n* a low continuous drumbeat ■ *vt* (**-fled, -fling, -fles**) to play a ruffle on a drum [Early 18C. Probably an imitation of the sound]

ru·fi·yaa /roo fée yaa, ro͝o fee yáa/ (*plural same*) *n* the main unit of currency in the Maldives. See table at **currency** [Late 20C. Via Divehi < Hindi *rūpiyā* (see RUPEE)]

rug /rug/ *n* **1. FABRIC FLOOR COVERING** a thick heavy fabric covering for a floor, especially one that is smaller than a carpet **2. ANIMAL SKIN MAT** an animal skin used as a mat or small carpet **3. BLANKET** a thick blanket, especially one formerly used by car or carriage passengers to cover their legs and feet **4. HAIRPIECE** a toupee or wig (*informal*) [Mid-16C. Probably < N Germanic]

ru·ga /ro͞ogə/ (*plural* **-gae** /-gee, -gī/) *n* a natural crease or ridge in a body part, especially in the internal organs (*often used in the plural*) [Late 18C. < Latin, "wrinkle"] —**ru·gate** /-gàyt/ *adj*

rugby: a player attempts a kick

rug·by /rúgbee/, **rug·by foot·ball** *n* a team sport in which players run with an oval ball, pass it laterally from hand to hand, and kick it (*often used before a noun*) [Mid-19C. After RUGBY School, where it was reputedly invented]

Rug·by /rúgbee/ city in Warwickshire, central England. Rugby School, a leading prep school, is located there. Population: 87,453 (2001).

rug·by league *n* a form of rugby that has teams of 13 players. Throughout the history of the game, rugby league players have always been allowed to turn professional.

rug·by un·ion *n* a form of rugby that has teams of 15 players. Rugby union players have only been allowed to turn professional since 1995.

rug·ged /rúggəd/ *adj* **1. WITH IRREGULAR SURFACE** with a sharply rising and falling, rough, or jagged surface ○ *over rugged terrain* **2. STRONG-FEATURED** with furrowed facial features thought to suggest physical strength or strength of character, especially in men ○ *their rugged faces* **3. PHYSICALLY RESILIENT** physically strong enough to endure harsh conditions, or used to enduring them **4. SEVERE IN MANNER** harsh and forbidding in manner **5. LACKING REFINEMENT** coarse or unrefined in behavior **6. TESTING** requiring strength, skill, or endurance **7. STRONGLY BUILT** designed and manufactured to withstand hard use or harsh environments **8. STORMY** affected by violent and dangerous storms ■ *n* COMPUT **DURABLE DEVICE** a device such as a laptop that is made of durable materials resistant to extreme conditions such as heat, cold, liquids, and impact [13C. Probably < N Germanic] —**rug·ged·ly** *adv* —**rug·ged·ness** *n*

rug·ged·ize /rúggə dīz/ (**-ized, -iz·ing, -iz·es**) *vt* to make something such as a piece of computer equipment capable of withstanding rough treatment —**rug·ged·i·za·tion** /rùggədi záysh'n/ *n* —**rug·ged·ized** *adj*

ru·go·sa rose /roo gṓssə-/ *n* a common wild hedge rose. Flowers: fragrant, pink or white. Native to: eastern North America. Latin name: *Rosa rugosa*. [< Latin, form of *rugosus* (see RUGOSE)]

ru·gose /ro͞o gṓss/, **ru·gous** /ro͞ogəss/ *adj* **1.** with creases, wrinkles, or ridges **2.** describes a leaf or other plant part that has a surface of alternating depressions and ridges [15C. < Latin *rugosus* < *ruga* "wrinkle"] —**ru·gose·ly** *adv* —**ru·gos·i·ty** /roo góssətee/ *n*

rug rat *n* a young child, especially an infant or toddler (*informal humorous*)

Ruhr /roor/ **1.** river in western Germany. It rises near Winterberg and flows northwest and west to join the Rhine River at Duisburg. Length: 146 mi./235 km. **2.** region of western Germany, comprising the valley of the Ruhr River and adjacent areas, and including the cities of Düsseldorf and Dortmund. It contains the largest coalfield and industrial region in western Europe. Area: 1,737 sq. mi./4,500 sq. km.

ru·in /ro͞o in/ *n* **1. BROKEN REMAINS** the physical remains of something such as a building or city that has decayed or been destroyed (*often used in the plural*) **2. COMPLETE DEVASTATION** a state of complete destruction, decay, collapse, or loss (*often plural*) ○ *The buildings had gone to ruin.* **3. COMPLETE FAILURE** complete moral, social, or economic failure ○ *facing financial ruin* **4. SOMEBODY OR SOMETHING DESTROYED** somebody or something completely lost or destroyed **5. CAUSE OF DESTRUCTION** a cause of complete loss or destruction ○ *Alcohol was their ruin.* **6. LOSS OF VIRGINITY** a woman's loss of virginity to a man other than her husband (*archaic*) ■ **ru·ins** *npl* **COMPLETE DEVASTATION** a state of complete destruction, decay, collapse, or loss ○ *Her dreams lay in ruins.* ■ *v* (**-ined, -in·ing, -ins**) **1.** *vt* **DESTROY SOMETHING** to cause something to be destroyed or lost **2.** *vt* **DESTROY SOMEBODY FINANCIALLY** to bring about somebody's financial demise **3.** *vt* **DAMAGE SOMETHING BEYOND REPAIR** to spoil something so severely that it cannot be restored **4.** *vi* **DECLINE** to fall into a state of complete destruction or loss (*literary*) **5.** *vt* **SEDUCE THEN ABANDON WOMAN** to induce a woman to engage in sex before marriage, then abandon her (*archaic*) [14C. Via French < Latin *ruina* < *ruere* "to fall"] —**ru·ined** *adj* —**ru·in·er** *n*

ru·in·a·tion /ro͞o i náysh'n/ *n* **1.** the destruction or loss of something **2.** something that brings about destruction or loss

ru·in·ous /ro͞o inəss/ *adj* **1.** causing severe damage or complete destruction or loss **2.** decayed or deteriorated beyond repair —**ru·in·ous·ly** *adv* —**ru·in·ous·ness** *n*

rule /rool/ *n* **1. PRINCIPLE GOVERNING CONDUCT** an authoritative principle set forth to guide behavior or action ○ *the rules of the game* **2. USUAL CONDITION** a prevailing condition or quality **3. GOVERNING POWER** a governing or reigning power ○ *under Communist rule* **4. PERIOD OF GOVERNING** a period during which a person or group reigns or governs **5. RELIGIOUS PRINCIPLES** a body of principles governing a religious order or group ○ *the Benedictine rule* **6. METHOD OF CALCULATING** a mathematical procedure for performing an operation or solving a problem **7.** PRINTING **LINE BETWEEN PRINTED COLUMNS** a thin strip or design used for borders or for separating columns of type **8.** LAW **LAW GOVERNING COURT PROCEDURE** a law made to govern procedure in court **9.** LAW **COURT ORDER** an order issued by a court of law or by a judge **10.** MEASURE same as **ruler** (sense 2) ■ *v* (**ruled, rul·ing, rules**) **1.** *vti* **GOVERN** to exercise controlling authority over somebody or something ○ *She ruled for almost 50 years.* **2.** *vt* **CONTROL SOMETHING** to subject something to control, or restrain something **3.** *vti* LAW **MAKE LEGAL DECISION** to issue a legal decision or order ○ *The judge ruled against the plaintiff.* **4.** *vti* **DOMINATE** to prevail, or be the prevailing influence over something ○ *He let his heart rule his head.* **5.** *vt* **MARK SOMETHING WITH LINES** to make a straight line or mark something with straight lines [13C. Via French *riule* < Latin *regula* "straight stick, standard"] —**rul·a·ble** *adj*

rule out *vt* **1.** to exclude something, or take a decision not to consider something **2.** to make something impossible

rule·book /ro͞ol bo͝ok/ *n* **1.** a book or pamphlet containing the official rules of a game, sport, or organization, or job **2.** the strictly correct or orthodox way of doing something ○ *doing everything by the rulebook*

rule·book slow·down *n US* a labor protest in which workers make a point of adhering strictly to the rules of the workplace so that work will slow down. Can term **work-to-rule**

rule of thumb *n* **1.** a way of proceeding based on experience or sound judgment **2.** any practical, though not entirely accurate, method that can be relied on for an acceptable result [Probably < the practice of using the thumb as a rough measure] —**rule-of-thumb** *adj*

rul·er /ro͞olər/ *n* **1.** somebody who governs a state or nation, e.g., a sovereign **2.** a strip of plastic, wood, or metal with at least one straight edge and units of length marked on it. It is used for measuring and for drawing straight lines.

rul·ing /ro͞oling/ *adj* **1. IN POWER** exercising controlling or governing authority ○ *the ruling party* ○ *joined the ruling body* **2. MOST POWERFUL** exerting the strongest influence ○ *a ruling passion* ■ *n* **DECISION BY AUTHORITY** an official or binding decision such as one made by a court or judge

rum[1] /rum/ *n* **1.** an alcoholic liquor made from sugar cane or molasses. It can be clear but is usually colored brownish red by storage in oak casks or by the addition of caramel. **2.** *US* any intoxicating liquor [Mid-17C. Shortening of obsolete *rumbullion*, origin ?]

rum[2] /rum/ (**rum·mer, rum·mest**) *adj UK* out of the ordinary (*informal dated*) [Late 18C. Origin ?]

Ru·ma·ni·an /roo máynee ən/ *n, adj* LANG, PEOPLES another spelling of **Romanian** (*dated*) [Variant] —**Ru·ma·ni·an** *adj*

rum·ba /rúmbə, ro͝om-, ro͞om-/, **rhum·ba** *n* **1. CUBAN DANCE** a rhythmically complex Cuban dance **2. RHYTHMIC BALLROOM DANCE** a ballroom dance based on the Cuban rumba, with exaggerated swinging of the hips **3. MUSIC** the music for a rumba ■ *vi* (**-baed** /-bəd/, **-ba·ing, -bas**) **DANCE RUMBA** to dance a Cuban rumba or the ballroom dance based on it [Early 20C. Via American Spanish < Spanish *rumbo* "course, direction" < Latin *rhombus* "rhombus"]

rum·ble /rúmb'l/ *v* (**-bled, -bling, -bles**) **1.** *vi* **MAKE DEEP SOUND** to make a deep rolling sound ○ *thunder rumbling in the distance* **2.** *vi* **MOVE NOISILY** to travel, e.g., along a road, with a deep rolling sound ○ *Trucks rumbled past.* **3.** *vt* **UTTER SOMETHING WITH RUMBLE** to say something in a deep continuous voice **4.** *vi* **FIGHT** to be involved in a street fight, especially one between members of rival gangs (*slang*) **5.** *vt UK* **FIND OUT ABOUT SOMEBODY OR SOMETHING** to discover the truth about somebody or something (*informal*) ○ *We've been rumbled!* **6.** *vt* MINERALS, MECH ENG **CLEAN STONES OR METAL** to polish stones or metal in a rotating drum (**tumbling barrel**) ■ *n* **1. DEEP SOUND** a deep rolling sound **2. MURMUR OF DISSATISFACTION** a feeling of dissatisfaction quietly expressed by several people (*informal*) **3. STREET FIGHT** a street fight, especially one fought by members of rival gangs (*slang*) **4.** MINERALS, MECH ENG same as **tumbling barrel** [14C. Probably < obsolete Dutch *rommelen*, an imitation of the sound] —**rum·bler** *n* —**rum·bly** *adj*

rum·ble seat *n* a folding passenger seat on the back of some early automobiles

rum·ble strip *n* a strip of textured road surface that alerts drivers by vibration or tire noise of an approaching intersection, speed restriction, or hazard

rum·bling /rúmbling/ *n* **1. DEEP SOUND** a deep rolling sound **2. FIRST INDICATION** an early sign of growing discontent, or an indication of an unpleasant event that is about to happen (*often used in the plural*) ■ *adj* **MAKING DEEP SOUND** making a deep rolling sound ○ *rumbling stomach*

rum·bus·tious /rum búschəss/ *adj* full of noisy uncontrollable exuberance [Late 18C. Probably alteration of archaic *robustious* < ROBUST] —**rum·bus·tious·ly** *adv* —**rum·bus·tious·ness** *n*

ru·men /ro͞o men, ro͞omən/ (*plural* **-mi·na** /-mənə/ or **-mens**) *n* the large first chamber of a ruminant animal's stomach in which microorganisms break down plant cellulose before the food is returned to the mouth as cud for additional chewing [Early 18C. < Latin] —**ru·mi·nal** *adj*

Ru·mi /ro͞omee/, **Jalal ad-Din Muhammad Din ar-** (1207–73) Persian mystic and poet. His works, which include the six-volume *Masnavi-ye Manavi* (*Spiritual Couplets*), had an important influence on Islamic literature and thought.

ru·mi·na ZOOL plural of **rumen**

ru·mi·nant /ro͞omənənt/ *n* **HOOFED ANIMAL THAT CHEWS CUD** any cud-chewing hoofed mammal with an even number of toes and a stomach with multiple chambers, e.g., cattle, camels, and giraffes. Suborder: Ruminantia. ■ *adj* **1. OF RUMINANTS** relating or belonging to the suborder of animals that chew the cud **2. THOUGHTFUL** inclined to be thoughtful and reflective [Mid-17C. < Latin *ruminant-*, present participle of *ruminare* (see RUMINATE)] —**ru·mi·nant·ly** *adv*

ru·mi·nate /ro͞omə nàyt/ (**-nat·ed, -nat·ing, -nates**) *v* **1.** *vti* to think carefully and at length about something **2.** *vi* to regurgitate partially digested food and chew it again (*refers to ruminants*) [Mid-16C. < Latin *ruminat-*, past participle of *ruminare* < *rumen* "rumen"] —**ru·mi·na·tion** /ro͞omə náysh'n/ *n* —**ru·mi·na·tive** *adj* —**ru·mi·na·tive·ly** *adv*

rum·mage /rúmmij/ *v* (**-maged, -mag·ing, -mag·es**) **1.** *vti* **SEARCH THROUGH THINGS** to make a rapid search for or through something by carelessly moving and disarranging things **2.** *vt* **FIND SOMETHING** to find something by searching ■ *n* **1. THOROUGH SEARCH** a thorough search for or through something **2.** *US* **SECONDHAND ARTICLES** articles sold at a rummage sale **3. GROUP OF THINGS** a miscellaneous collection of items [15C. < Old French *arrumage* "arrangement of cargo in a ship" < *run* "ship's hold" < Dutch *ruim* "space"] —**rum·mag·er** *n*

rum·mage sale *n* a sale of miscellaneous donated items to raise money for charity

rum·mer /rúmmər/ *n* a large drinking glass, especially one with a short stem [Mid-17C. Directly or via German *Römer* < Dutch *roemer* < *roemen* "praise"]

rum·my[1] /rúmmee/ *n* a card game in which the players try to get three or more cards of the same rank or a sequence of three or more cards of the same suit [Early 20C. Origin ?]

rum·my[2] /rúmmee/ *adj* tasting or smelling of rum, or similar to rum in smell or taste ■ *n* (*plural* **-mies**) same as **drunkard** (*slang*) [Mid-19C. < RUM[1]]

ru·mor /ro͞omər/ *n* **1. UNVERIFIED REPORT** a generally circulated story, report, or statement without facts to confirm its truth **2. IDLE SPECULATION** general talk or opinions of uncertain reliability ■ *vt* (**-mored, -mor·ing, -mors**) **TO PASS ON RUMORS** to pass along information by rumor (*usually passive*) ○ *It is rumored that they are leaving the company.* [14C. Via French < Latin, "noise, rumor"]

ru·mor mill *n* the process by which rumors are started and spread

ru·mor·mon·ger /ro͞omər mùng gər, -mòng-/ *n* somebody who habitually spreads rumors ■ *vi* (**-gered, -ger·ing, -gers**) to participate actively in spreading rumors

ru·mour *n, vt* Can, UK spelling of **rumor**

rump /rump/ *n* **1. ANIMAL'S HINDQUARTERS** the fleshy hindquarters of a four-legged mammal, not including its legs **2. BEEF FROM HINDQUARTERS** a cut of beef that is tender and contains some fat, taken from the animal's rump ○ *rump steak* **3. BOTTOM** the buttocks (*informal*) **4.** LAW **REMAINS OF LEGISLATURE** the remnant of a legislative body after the majority of its members have resigned or been expelled **5. BIRD'S TAIL END** the lower part of a bird's back nearest the tail that is sometimes colored distinctively [15C. Probably < N Germanic]

rum·ple /rúmp'l/ *vti* (**-pled, -pling, -ples**) to take on a disheveled appearance, or make clothes or hair untidy, e.g., by creasing clothes or pulling hair out of style ■ *n* a wrinkle or crease [Early 16C. Origin ?]

rum·pus /rúmpəss/ *n* an outcry or noisy disturbance [Mid-18C. < ?]

rum·pus room *n* a room in a house for recreational activities such as parties and children's play

rum·run·ner /rúm rùnnər/ *n* **1.** a smuggler of alcoholic beverages across a border **2.** a boat used to smuggle liquor across a border

run /run/ *v* (**ran** /ran/, **run, run·ning, runs**) **1.** *vi* **GO AT FAST PACE** to move rapidly on foot so that both feet are momentarily off the ground in each step **2.** *vi* **GALLOP** to go at a fast pace in which all four feet are momentarily off the ground in each stride (*refers to four-footed animals*) **3.** *vt* **TRAVEL DISTANCE BY RUNNING** to cover a particular distance while running **4.** *vti* **PARTICIPATE IN RACE** to compete in a race on foot or on a horse or other animal **5.** *vt* **ENTER ANIMAL IN RACE** to enter a horse or other animal in a race **6.** *vti* **CAMPAIGN IN ELECTION** to be a candidate in an election, or enter somebody as a candidate in an election ○ *will be running for president* **7.** *vi* **BE IN RELATIVE POSITION** to be or end in a particular position, e.g., in a race, election, or contest ○ *running behind until the last lap* **8.** *vt* **PERFORM SOMETHING** to carry out or accomplish something ○ *run a test* **9.** *vi* **LEAVE QUICKLY** to leave a place quickly or in a hurry, usually in order to escape notice or capture ○ *take the money and run* **10.** *vi* **MOVE FREELY** to move around without restraint ○ *allow the cats to run* **11.** *vt* **SPEED ACROSS SOMETHING** to travel quickly across, over, or through something ○ *ran the rapids* **12.** *vt* **TRANSPORT SOMEBODY OR SOMETHING** to take or transport somebody or something, usually by motor vehicle ○ *ran me into town* **13.** *vi* **GO FOR HELP** to turn to somebody for assistance, especially in desperation or as a dependant to a protector ○ *ran to his brother for money* **14.** *vi* **VISIT** to make a brief trip or visit somewhere ○ *ran out to the mountains for the weekend* **15.** *vti* **MOVE SMOOTHLY** to pass quickly or smoothly through or over something, or cause something to pass quickly or smoothly through or over something ○ *ropes running easily through the pulleys* **16.** *vi* **ENTER CONDITION** to enter into a particular state or condition ○ *Supplies were running low.* **17.** *vti* **OPERATE** to be functioning, or put or leave something in a functioning mode ○ *Let the engine run.* **18.** *vt* **CONTROL SOMETHING** to direct the activities, affairs, or operation of something ○ *responsible for running the whole department* **19.** *vti* **POUR OR FLOW** to flow, or cause water or another liquid to flow from or to something ○ *run a faucet* **20.** *vi* **RELEASE MUCUS** to discharge a fluid such as pus or mucus ○ *a nose that was constantly running* **21.** *vti* **GO BACK AND FORTH** to travel regularly over a set route, or cause somebody or something to travel regularly over a set route ○ *runs a shuttle between stations* **22.** *vi* **ROLL FREELY** to roll unhindered or unchecked ○ *could only stand and watch it run down the hill* **23.** *vti* **GO OR TAKE OFF COURSE** to deviate from the usual or proper course, or allow something such as a ship or automobile to deviate from the usual or proper course ○ *run a car off the road* **24.** *vi* **SPREAD OR LEAK UNDESIRABLY** to spread as a result of unwanted dissolving or mixing ○ *The red stripes ran into the white.* **25.** *vi* **RANGE** to range between particular limits ○ *The work ran from difficult to impossible.* **26.** *vi* **KEEP COMPANY** to associate with a particular person or group **27.** *vti* **EXTEND SOMETHING** to route something in a particular direction or for a particular distance, or be routed in this way ○ *They plan to run the cable under the road.* **28.** *vt* **CONTINUE** to continue for a particular length or period ○ *a report running ten pages* **29.** *vt* **EXPERIENCE SOMETHING** to experience, undergo, or be subject to something ○ *a child running a high temperature* **30.** *vti* **TOTAL** to total a particular amount ○ *The bill runs to four figures.* **31.** *vt* **BREACH SOMETHING** to break through a barrier of some kind ○ *ran a checkpoint* **32.** *vi* **BE WORDED** to be worded in a particular way ○ *in a statement that runs as follows* **33.** *vi* **EXHIBIT TENDENCY** to tend or be inclined in a particular direction ○ *His tastes in art run to abstractions.* **34.** *vi* **RECUR** to appear recurrently as a feature or quality ○ *Stubbornness runs in the family.* **35.** *vi* **BE COMMUNICATED** to be communicated from person to person ○ *a story running around the office* **36.** *vti* **UNRAVEL** to unravel, or cause the stitching in a garment such as a stocking to come undone, and cause damage **37.** *vi* **REMAIN LEGALLY VALID** to continue to have force in law ○ *The contract has a year to run.* **38.** *vt* **TRADE GOODS ILLEGALLY** to import or export goods illegally ○ *running guns to the rebels* **39.** *vi* **GO UPSTREAM TO SPAWN** to migrate in large numbers, usually upstream, to spawn (*refers to fish*) **40.** *vti* PUBL, BROADCAST **SHOW PUBLICLY** to print, broadcast, or exhibit something, or be printed, broadcast, or exhibited ○ *run a news story* **41.** *vti* FOOTBALL **CARRY FOOTBALL DOWNFIELD** in football, to advance the ball while running as opposed to passing **42.** *vt* METALL **PRODUCE METAL BY CASTING** to cast or mold molten metal ■ *n* **1. FAST PACE** a rapid pace faster than a walk or jog **2. GALLOPING PACE** an animal's fastest pace **3. SPELL OF RUNNING** a spell of running, especially for pleasure or exercise **4. RACE** a race in which the competitors run **5. REGULAR TRIP** a regular or scheduled trip or route ○ *the run to work each day* **6. DISTANCE OR TIME COVERED** a distance or period covered while traveling or running **7. ERRAND** a brief trip made in order to get something ○ *a quick run to the store* **8. FREE USE OF PLACE** unrestricted access to, use of, and movement around a place ○ *given the run of the whole house* **9. UNINTERRUPTED PERIOD** an extended period during which a particular condition or circumstance prevails ○ *a run of bad luck* **10. QUANTITY MANUFACTURED** an amount of something produced in a period of continuous operation of a machine or factory ○ *an initial print run of five thousand copies* **11. OPERATING PERIOD** a period of continuous operation of a machine or factory **12.** CARDS **SEQUENCE OF CARDS** in card games, a sequence of playing cards in one suit **13.** CUE GAMES **SUCCESSIVE SHOTS** in billiards and some other cue games, a series of successful shots **14.** ARTS **SERIES OF PERFORMANCES** a series of continuous showings or performances **15. URGENT REQUIREMENT** a sudden large demand for something such as goods or payment ○ *Rumors of a shortage led to a run on coffee.* **16. FLOW** a flow of liquid **17. PIPE FOR LIQUID** a channel or pipe in which a liquid flows **18. PERIOD OF FLOW** a period during which a liquid flows **19. AMOUNT OF LIQUID** an amount of liquid in a flow **20. STEEP ROUTE** a sloping course or track for a particular activity ○ *a ski run* **21. PASSAGE DOWN TRACK** a single trip along a course or down a slope **22. DIRECTION OF PATTERN** the natural direction of a pattern in something such as wood grain **23. TENDENCY** the general direction in which things or events are moving ○ *the usual run of things* **24. SOMETHING ORDINARY** an average or typical kind of person or thing ○ *the general run of merchandise* **25. TRIP FOR PLEASURE** a trip in a vehicle, especially for pleasure ○ *went for a run along the coast road* **26. UNRAVELING OF STITCHES** a damaged section of a stocking or other knitted garment caused by unraveling stitches **27. ANIMAL ENCLOSURE** an outdoor enclosure for domestic animals, often one attached to or used as a temporary break from a standard enclosure that allows less freedom of movement **28. ANIMAL TRAIL** a trail followed regularly by a group or herd of animals **29.** POL **ELECTION CAMPAIGN** a campaign for election to public office ○ *a run for Congress* **30.** MUSIC **RAPID MUSICAL PASSAGE** a rapid musical scale or melodic passage, especially one for the piano **31.** FOOTBALL **GAIN WHILE RUNNING** in football, an offensive player's advance of the ball while running **32.** BASEBALL **SCORE IN BASEBALL** a score in baseball made by traveling around all the bases to home plate ■ *adj* **1. MELTED** in a melted state **2. WORN OUT** exhausted or out of breath, especially from running [Old English *rinnan* < Germanic] ◇ **be on the run** to be fleeing from something, especially the law ◇ **give somebody a run for his** *or* **her money** to provide somebody with some serious, sometimes unexpected, competition ◇ **in the long run** eventually or finally ◇ **in the short run** in the near future ◇ **run yourself** *or* **somebody ragged** to work yourself *or* somebody else to the point of exhaustion

REGIONAL NOTE *Run*, a small fast-flowing stream, is a South Midland and Southern term, common from Pennsylvania south to Virginia, as in *Bull Run*. Terms such as Northern *creek* and Southern *branch* identify larger streams.

run about *vi* to move hurriedly from place to place

run across *vt* to meet somebody or find something unexpectedly

run after *vt* **1.** to chase after somebody or something **2.** to pursue somebody romantically or sexually (*informal*)

run along *vi* to go away (*usually used as a command*)

run around *vi* (*informal*) **1.** to behave promiscuously **2.** to spend a lot of time with somebody ○ *running around with a bad crowd*

run away *vi* to escape or flee from somebody or something

run away with *vt* **1. TAKE SOMETHING AND LEAVE** to steal something and escape with it **2. ELOPE WITH SOMEBODY** to leave secretly with a lover, especially in order to marry **3. TAKE CONTROL OF SOMEBODY** to cause somebody to lose self-control ○ *His excitement ran away with him.* **4. WIN SOMETHING EASILY** to win a competition, contest, or election easily

run by *vt* to tell somebody about something in order to find out his or her opinions or ideas about it ○ *Could I run these figures by you before I send them out?*

run down *v* **1.** *vti* **STOP FUNCTIONING** to lose power and cease to function, or allow a device to lose its power **2.** *vt* **HIT SOMEBODY WITH VEHICLE** to knock somebody or something to the ground with a vehicle **3.** *vti* **REDUCE**

to shrink in size or amount, or reduce the size or amount of something **4.** *vt* BELITTLE SOMEBODY to speak of somebody in a disparaging or critical manner **5.** *vt* CATCH SOMEBODY EVENTUALLY to find or capture somebody after a long search or chase **6.** *vt US* TRACE SOMETHING to find the source of something ○ *run down a lead* **7.** *vt* READ SOMETHING QUICKLY to read or review something quickly **8.** *vt* NAUT CAUSE SHIP TO SINK to collide with a ship and cause it to sink **9.** *vt* BASEBALL REMOVE BASEBALL PLAYER in baseball, to chase and tag out a base runner trapped between two bases

run in *v* **1.** *vt* ARREST SOMEBODY to take somebody into police custody (*informal*) **2.** *vi US* VISIT to pay somebody a quick visit (*informal*) **3.** *vt* PRINTING ADD SOMETHING AS TEXT to insert additional text in printed matter

run into *v* **1.** *vt* MEET SOMEBODY BY CHANCE to meet somebody unexpectedly **2.** *vti* COLLIDE WITH SOMETHING to collide with somebody or something, or cause something to collide with somebody or something **3.** *vt* ENCOUNTER SOMETHING to encounter something unanticipated, usually problems or trouble **4.** *vt* AMOUNT TO SOMETHING to add up to something, or be approximately equal to something ○ *left debts running into millions*

run off *v* **1.** *vi* LEAVE IN HASTE to leave quickly without notifying anyone **2.** *vt* MAKE COPIES to produce or print copies, e.g., on a photocopier **3.** *vt* FORCE SOMEBODY TO LEAVE to force trespassers off property **4.** *vt* SETTLE TIED CONTEST to settle a tied competition or election by running a final deciding contest

run off with *vt* **1.** to steal and escape with something **2.** to leave secretly with a lover, especially in order to marry

run on *v* **1.** *vi* TALK AT LENGTH to talk at length, especially about trivial things **2.** *vi* CONTINUE to continue without interruption, often boringly or frustratingly **3.** *vt* PRINTING PRINT TEXT WITHOUT PARAGRAPH BREAK to print or typeset following text without a paragraph break

run out *v* **1.** *vi* COME TO END to be consumed completely ○ *Time is running out.* **2.** *vi* EXHAUST SUPPLIES to consume all of a supply of something ○ *We've run out of milk.* **3.** *vi* BECOME INVALID to become invalid because of time restrictions **4.** *vt US* CHASE SOMEBODY AWAY to expel somebody using force

run out on *vt* to leave somebody or something in a helpless state or at a time when support is needed (*informal*)

run over *v* **1.** *vt* KNOCK SOMEBODY DOWN WITH VEHICLE to hit somebody or something with a vehicle while driving it **2.** *vi* OVERFLOW to overflow the limits or capacity of a container **3.** *vti* TAKE LONGER THAN PLANNED to go beyond a limit or time previously set **4.** *vt* REVIEW SOMETHING to examine or consider something again, especially reviewing its main points

run past *vt* same as **run by**

run through *vt* **1.** USE SOMETHING UP to exhaust a supply of something, especially money, quickly and without much consideration **2.** REVIEW SOMETHING to examine or consider something again, especially reviewing its main points **3.** REHEARSE SOMETHING QUICKLY to read or perform at speed the whole or part of a play, script, piece of music, lecture, or other prepared text in order to rehearse it **4.** STAB SOMEBODY WITH SWORD to push a sword all the way through somebody's body (*literary*)

run to *vt* to have a particular length ○ *The report runs to 500 pages.*

run up *vt* **1.** INCUR EXPENSE to amass or accumulate a large expense **2.** SEW SOMETHING to make something, usually a garment, by means of fast sewing **3.** RAISE FLAG to hoist a flag on a flagpole

run up against *vt UK* to suddenly encounter an unexpected problem

run·a·bout /rúnnə bòwt/ *n* **1.** a small car, motorboat, or aircraft, especially one used for short trips **2.** somebody who wanders from place to place

run·a·round /rúnnə ròwnd/ *n* **1.** inconvenience deliberately engineered in order to mislead or delay somebody (*informal*) ○ *They've been giving me the runaround.* **2.** an arrangement of printed type in which lines are shortened to leave room for an illustration or symbol

run·a·way /rúnnə wày/ *n* SOMEBODY WHO ESCAPES somebody who escapes from something such as confinement or harm (*often used before a noun*) ■ *adj* **1.** OUT OF CONTROL moving too fast to be stopped or controlled **2.** EASILY WON OR ACHIEVED won by an overwhelming margin, or achieved to an impressive degree (*informal*) ○ *a runaway success*

Run·a·way, Cape /rúnnə wày/ cape on the northeastern coast of the North Island, New Zealand, situated at the eastern end of the Bay of Plenty

run·back /rún bàk/ *n* a run made in football after catching an opponent's kick or intercepting a pass

run·ci·ble spoon /rùnssəb'l-/ *n* a fork with three curved prongs, one of which is sharp [< nonsense word coined by Edward Lear in *The Owl and the Pussy Cat* (1871)]

run·down /rún dòwn/ *n* **1.** a summary of the main points of a subject **2.** in baseball, a play in which a runner is tagged out after being chased back and forth between two bases

run-down *adj* **1.** EXHAUSTED tired out, e.g., from overwork or poor health **2.** SHABBY in poor repair from neglect or hard use **3.** OUT OF POWER depleted of energy or power and unable to operate

Rund·stedt /rŏont shtèt/, **Karl von** (1875–1953) German military commander. He led the German offensives on the western front (1942–44) during World War II. Full name **Rundstedt, Karl Rudolf Gerd von**

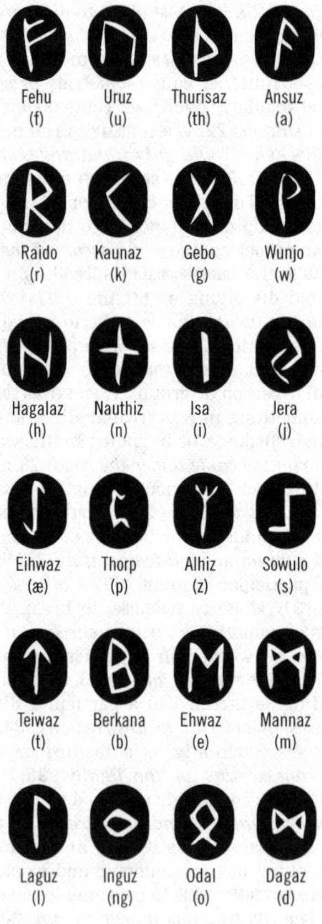

rune

rune /roon/ *n* **1.** OLD GERMANIC ALPHABET CHARACTER a character in an ancient Germanic alphabet used between the 3rd and the 13th centuries **2.** MAGICAL SYMBOL OR SPELL a mysterious symbol, inscription, or incantation, especially one with supposed magical power **3.** POEM IN FINNISH a Finnish poem or stanza [Old English *rūn* < Germanic] —**run·ic** *adj*

rung[1] /rung/ *n* **1.** LADDER STEP a step of a ladder **2.** CROSSPIECE OF CHAIR a horizontal bar used to strengthen the legs of a chair or stool **3.** LEVEL IN HIERARCHY a position in a hierarchy, e.g., of a profession **4.** NAUT PART OF SHIP'S WHEEL a spoke or handle on the wheel of a ship by which the wheel is turned [Old English *hrung* < Germanic]

rung[2] past participle of **ring**[2]

run-in *n* **1.** a heated argument or quarrel (*informal*) **2.** a section of text added to a page that has already been typeset or printed

~~**runing**~~ incorrect spelling of **running**

run·let /rúnnlət/ *n regional* a small river or stream

run·nel /rúnn'l/ *n* **1.** a small brook or stream **2.** any narrow channel for water, e.g., a gutter [Late 16C. Alteration of obsolete *rindle* < Germanic, "run"]

run·ner /rúnnər/ *n* **1.** RACER somebody or something that runs, especially an athlete or a horse in a race **2.** DOOR OR DRAWER SLIDE a guide on which a drawer or door slides **3.** SLED BLADE either of the long blades that a sled or sleigh slides on **4.** SKATE BLADE the blade of an ice skate **5.** SMUGGLER somebody involved in smuggling (*often used in combination*) ○ *gun runner* **6.** SMUGGLER'S VESSEL a boat or ship used for smuggling (*often used in combination*) **7.** MESSENGER a messenger or undertaker of errands for a bank, brokerage firm, or other business **8.** CARPET STRIP a long narrow piece of carpet **9.** FABRIC STRIP a strip of fabric, often linen or lace, used to protect or decorate the top of a piece of furniture such as a dresser **10.** CREEPING STEM THAT GROWS ROOTS a thin horizontal plant stem that grows roots from nodes at regular intervals **11.** PLANT GROWING FROM STEM NODES a plant that has runners or grows by runners, e.g., a strawberry **12.** CLIMBING PLANT any plant that climbs and twists, e.g., a bean plant **13.** *UK* CANDIDATE somebody entered as a candidate in an election **14.** OPERATOR a manager or operator of something such as a business or a machine **15.** BASEBALL same as **base runner** **16.** FOOTBALL same as **ball carrier** **17.** ANCHORING LOOP in mountaineering, a continuous loop of webbing used to provide an anchor to a rock, tree, or other point **18.** DEEP-WATER OCEAN FISH a swift streamlined deep-water sea fish of the jack family, especially either of two edible bluish species. Latin name: *Caranx crysos* or *Elagatis bipinnulata*.

run·ner bean *n UK* same as **scarlet runner**

run·ner-up (*plural* **run·ners-up**) *n* a contestant or competitor who comes second, e.g., in a sports event or an election

run·ning /rúnning/ *n* **1.** FAST MOVEMENT rapid movement on foot, with long strides and both feet momentarily off the ground **2.** RUNNING AS EXERCISE the sport or exercise of running **3.** MANAGEMENT the managing of a business or organization ■ **run·nings** *npl* (*slang; used in Black English*) **1.** GOINGS-ON events or activities **2.** BUSINESS same as **running** (sense 3) ■ *adj* **1.** FLOWING flowing continuously in a stream **2.** FUNCTIONING in operation or in working order **3.** FOR USE OR WEAR BY RUNNERS relating to or intended for the sport or exercise of running ○ *running shoes* **4.** WHILE RUNNING begun with a run, or performed during a run ○ *a running jump* **5.** LONG-STANDING begun long ago and still continuing ○ *a running joke* **6.** MADE DURING EVENT made while something is operating or happening ○ *a running commentary* **7.** MED OPEN open and discharging fluid or pus ○ *a running sore* **8.** BOT CREEPING growing by means of horizontal stems that creep along the ground **9.** FOOTBALL GAINING YARDS WHILE RUNNING in football, advancing the ball while running rather than passing ■ *adv* CONSECUTIVELY in succession ○ *for five days running* ◇ **be in** *or* **out of the running** to have *or* not have a chance of success

run·ning back *n* in football, an offensive back who advances the ball in running plays

run·ning board *n* a narrow step beneath the doors of some motor vehicles, typically vintage cars

run·ning hand *n* handwriting done without lifting the pen or pencil from the writing surface

run·ning head *n* a heading printed on every page or every other page of a book

run·ning light *n* a light displayed on a ship or aircraft at night to show its location and size

run·ning mate *n* **1.** a candidate for the lesser of two associated political offices, e.g., a vice-presidential candidate **2.** in horseracing, a horse that is entered in a race for the purpose of setting the pace for a stronger horse from the same stable

run·ning start *n* SPORTS same as **flying start**

run·ning stitch *n* a simple sewing stitch that goes down and up evenly through cloth without being looped

run·ning ti·tle *n* PUBL same as **running head**

run·ny /rúnnee/ (**-ni·er, -ni·est**) *adj* **1. OF LIQUID CONSISTENCY** of a liquid or semiliquid consistency that pours or flows **2. WATERY** of a consistency that is too thin **3. RELEASING MUCUS** producing excessive flowing mucus ○ *a runny nose* —**run·ni·ness** *n*

Run·ny·mede /rúnnee meed/ meadow on the southern bank of the Thames River, near Windsor, southeastern England. King John granted the Magna Carta there in 1215.

run·off /rún àwf, -òf/ *n* **1.** GEOG **WATER NOT ABSORBED BY SOIL** rainfall that does not soak into the soil but flows into surface waters **2.** ENVIRON **WATER POLLUTION** agricultural or industrial waste products that are carried by rainfall and melting snow into surface waters **3.** SPORTS, POL **SECOND CONTEST TO DETERMINE WINNER** an election, race, or other contest held after an earlier one that produced no clear winner

run-of-the-mill *adj* with no exceptional or distinguishing qualities

run-on *adj* PRINTING **ON SAME LINE** added to a line of text without a line break ■ *n* **1.** PRINTING **TEXT ADDED WITHOUT LINE BREAK** an added section of text that continues a line, without a line break **2.** LING **WORD UNDERSTOOD BUT UNDEFINED** an undefined word appearing at the end of a dictionary entry, whose meaning can be understood from the previous defined senses

runs /runz/ *n* an attack of diarrhea (*informal; takes a singular or plural verb*) ○ *have the runs*

runt /runt/ *n* **1.** an animal that is considerably smaller than others of the same kind, especially the smallest or weakest animal in a litter **2.** an offensive term that deliberately insults somebody's stature as short or physical strength as lacking (*insult*) [Mid-16C. < ?] —**runt·i·ness** *n* —**runt·ish** *adj* —**runt·y** *adj*

run-through *n* **1.** a practice or rehearsal of something, especially a dramatic performance **2.** a brief review of something such as an agenda or report

run-time *n* **1.** the time during which a computer program runs **2.** a version of a computer program that allows a user to perform some, but not all, of the program's functions (*hyphenated before a noun*) ○ *a run-time module* **3.** COMPUT same as **execution time**

run-up *n* **1.** *US* **SUDDEN RISE** a sudden increase in something such as price, sales, or value **2. PREPARATORY RUN** a run taken to gather momentum, e.g., for a jump or kick in an athletic event **3.** *UK* **TIME IMMEDIATELY BEFORE SOMETHING** the period of time that leads up to an important event

run·way /rún wày/ *n* **1. STRIP FOR AIRCRAFT LANDINGS AND TAKEOFFS** a long wide level roadway or other strip of land on which aircraft land and take off **2. EXTENSION OF STAGE INTO AUDIENCE** a narrow ramp or platform that is part of a stage and extends into the auditorium, especially as used in fashion shows **3. CHUTE FOR LOGS** a chute down which logs are slid **4. TRACK** a track, passageway, or channel along which something runs

Damon Runyon

Run·yon /rúnnyən/, **Damon** (1884–1946) US journalist and short-story writer. His writings, mainly about gangsters, are distinguished by their use of slang and colorful characterizations. His collected stories include *Guys and Dolls* (1932), which formed the basis of the Broadway musical of the same name (1950). Full name **Runyon, Alfred Damon**

> "A freeloader is a confirmed guest."
> [Damon Runyon, "Freeloading Ethics," *Short Takes*; 1946]

ru·pee /roo peé, róopee/ *n* the main unit of currency in India, Mauritius, Nepal, Pakistan, the Seychelles, and Sri Lanka. See table at **currency** [Early 17C. Via Hindi *rūpiyā* < Sanskrit *rūpya* "wrought silver" < *rūpa* "shape"]

Ru·pert (of the Rhine) /róopərt-/ (1619–82) German prince. A nephew of Charles I of England, he commanded Royalist troops in the English Civil War and was a founder of the Hudson's Bay Company.

Ru·pes Rec·ta /róopez réktə/ fault on the surface of the Moon running north-south for 75 mi./120 km along the eastern edge of Mare Nubium

ru·pi·ah /roo peé ə/ (*plural* **-ahs** or *same*) *n* the main unit of Indonesian currency. See table at **currency** [Mid-20C. Via Malay < Hindi *rūpiyā* (see RUPEE)]

ru·pic·o·lous /roo píkʹləss/ *adj* describes organisms that live or grow on or among rocks [Mid-19C. < Latin *rupes* "rock" + *-cola* "inhabitant"]

rup·ture /rúpchər/ *n* **1. BROKEN STATE** a break in something, or a breaking apart of something ○ *a rupture in a water main* **2. BREACH IN RELATIONS** a breakdown in a friendly or peaceful relationship **3.** MED **TORN TISSUE** a tear in bodily tissue, or a tearing of bodily tissue ○ *the rupture of a blood vessel* **4.** MED same as **hernia** ■ *vti* (**-tured, -tur·ing, -tures**) **1. BREAK, BURST, OR TEAR SOMETHING** to break, burst, or tear something, or become broken, burst, or torn **2. CAUSE RIFT IN RELATIONSHIP** to cause a breakdown in a friendly or peaceful relationship, or undergo such a breakdown **3.** MED **TEAR TISSUE** to cause a tearing of body tissue, or experience it **4.** MED **PRODUCE OR HAVE HERNIA** to cause a hernia, or be affected by a hernia [15C. Via French < Latin *ruptura* < *rupt-*, past participle of *rumpere* "break"] —**rup·tur·a·ble** *adj*

ORIGIN Latin *rumpere* "to break," from which ***rupture*** is derived, is also the source of English *corrupt, disrupt, erupt, rout*[1], *route*, and *routine*.

ru·ral /róorəl/ *adj* **1. OUTSIDE CITY** found in or living in the country **2. TYPICAL OF COUNTRY** relating to or characteristic of the country or country living **3. AGRICULTURAL** relating to, characteristic of, or involving farming [15C. Via French < Latin *rural-* < *rur-* "country, countryside"] —**ru·ral·i·ty** /roo rállətee/ *n* —**ru·ral·ly** *adv*

ru·ral free de·liv·er·y *n US* free mail delivery in rural areas

ru·ral·ist /róorəlist/ *n* **1.** somebody who lives in the countryside **2.** a supporter or promoter of a rural lifestyle and rural interests

ru·ral·ize /róorə lìz/ (**-ized, -iz·ing, -iz·es**) *v* **1.** *vt* to make something rural in character or habit **2.** *vi* to live or pass time in the country after having lived in a city or town —**ru·ral·i·za·tion** /ròorəli záysh'n/ *n*

ru·ral route *n* a route for mail delivery in rural areas

Ru·rik /róorik/ (*d.* AD 879) Scandinavian military leader. He established the first kingdom and royal dynasty of Russia, which continued until 1598.

Ru·ri·tan /róorətən/ *n US* a member of the Ruritan National club, a service organization with emphasis on education for underprivileged people

Ru·ri·ta·ni·a /ròorə táynee ə/ *n* a place of romance, adventure, and intrigue [Late 19C. After a fictional central European kingdom in novels by Anthony Hope (1863–1933)] —**Ru·ri·ta·ni·an** *adj, n*

ruse /rooz, rooss/ *n* a clever trick or plot used to deceive others [15C. Old French *ruser* "repulse, retreat, dodge"]

Ru·se /róo sày/ city in Ruse Province, northern Bulgaria. Population: 168,051 (1996).

Ru·sed·ski /roo sétskee/, **Greg** (*b.* 1973) Canadian-born British tennis player. Known for his fast serve, he has won 11 singles titles and was runner-up in the US Open (1997). Full name **Rusedski, Gregory**

rush[1] /rush/ *v* (**rushed, rush·ing, rush·es**) **1.** *vi* **MOVE FAST** to move, act, or proceed quickly **2.** *vt* **HURRY SOMEBODY OR SOMETHING ALONG** to make somebody or something move, act, or proceed quickly ○ *Don't rush me.* **3.** *vt* **TAKE SOMEBODY OR SOMETHING URGENTLY** to take or send somebody or something to a place quickly and urgently ○ *We rushed him to the airport to catch his flight.* **4.** *vt* **DO SOMETHING HASTILY** to do something in a hurry and without careful thought ○ *rushed the job* **5.** *vi* **GO RECKLESSLY** to proceed in a quick and reckless way ○ *We mustn't rush into things.* ○ *"For fools rush in where angels fear to tread."* (Alexander Pope, *An Essay on Criticism*; 1711) **6.** *vi* **FLOW FAST** to flow quickly and in quantity **7.** *vt* **CAPTURE ENEMY QUICKLY** to seize a position or overcome an enemy by a sudden quick attack **8.** *vt* **ENCOURAGE SOMEBODY TO JOIN SOMETHING** to encourage somebody to become a member of something, especially a fraternity or sorority, with parties and entertainment **9.** *vt* **SEEK TO JOIN ASSOCIATION** to seek to become a member of something, especially a fraternity or sorority, by, e.g., attending its parties ○ *I'm rushing Sigma Chi, what about you?* **10.** *vti* FOOTBALL **CARRY FOOTBALL** in football, to carry ball forward in a running play **11.** *vt* FOOTBALL **CHARGE PASSER OR KICKER** in football, to move aggressively toward the opposing passer or kicker to try to prevent the the ball from being passed or kicked ■ *n* **1. GREAT HURRY** a hurry, or a need for hurry ○ *Slow down; you're always in a rush!* ○ *There's no great rush for it.* **2. SUDDEN FAST MOVEMENT BY CROWD** a sudden and quick movement of a person or group of people toward a place or objective ○ *There was a rush to the door.* **3. BUSY TIME** a very busy period, e.g., a time when large numbers of people try to do something at the same time ○ *a rush during the store's sale* **4. SUDDEN ATTACK** a sudden quick forward movement in an attack **5. SUDDEN FLOW** a sudden quick flow or movement of something **6. SUDDEN FEELING** a sudden powerful onset of an emotion **7. SUDDEN PLEASURABLE SENSATION** a sudden feeling of elation and pleasure (*informal*) **8.** FOOTBALL **FOOTBALL PLAY WITHOUT PASS** in football, a play in which the ball is carried rather than passed **9.** FOOTBALL **DEFENSIVE PLAY** in football, a defense in which linemen move aggressively toward the opposing passer or kicker to try to block the ball or tackle the player before the ball is passed or kicked **10. GREEK-LETTER RECRUITMENT DRIVE** a concentrated effort by a fraternity or sorority to recruit new members ○ *a rush party* ■ **rushes** *npl* MOVIES **UNEDITED PRINTS OF MOVIE SCENES** the first unedited prints of a scene or scenes shot for a movie ■ *adj* **1. DONE QUICKLY** done or needing to be done quickly ○ *a rush job* **2. VERY BUSY** very busy, especially with many people traveling at the same time [14C. < Old French *re(h)usser* "repel"] —**rushed** *adj* —**rush·er** *n*

rush into *vt* to do or agree to something with little consideration of the consequences, or cause somebody to do this

rush through *vt* **1.** to get something approved or put in place hurriedly, often without allowing time for full consideration ○ *The plans for the new building were rushed through.* **2.** to do something quickly and with little thought or preparation

rush[2] /rush/ *n* **1.** the cylindrical and sometimes hollow stem of a marsh plant. Use: weaving baskets and mats, caning chairs. (*often used before a noun*) ○ *a rush mat* **2.** a marsh plant with stems that are rushes and leaves that resemble blades of grass. Genus: *Juncus.* [Old English *rysc* < Germanic] —**rush·y** *adj*

Rush·die /rúshdee, róosh-/, **Salman** (*b.* 1947) Indian-born British novelist. A master of the magic realist style, his novels include *Midnight's Children* (1981), which won the Booker Prize, *The Satanic Verses* (1988), and *The Ground Beneath Her Feet* (1999). Full name **Rushdie, Ahmed Salman**

> "I call upon the intellectual community in this country and abroad to stand up for freedom of the imagination, an issue much larger than my book or indeed my life."
> [Salman Rushdie, *Public statement*; February 14, 1989]

rush·ee /ru sheé/ *n* a college or university student who is being rushed by a fraternity or sorority

rush hour *n* a period of heavy traffic in the morning and evening during which people are traveling to and from work

Mount Rushmore

Russia

Rush·more, Mount /rúsh màwr/ mountain in the Black Hills, western South Dakota, carved with the faces of the US presidents George Washington, Thomas Jefferson, Abraham Lincoln, and Theodore Roosevelt. Height: 5,725 ft./1,745 m.

Rus·kin /rúskin/, **John** (1819–1900) British art and social critic. He argued for the moral and religious significance of art in works such as *Modern Painters* (1843–60) and *The Stones of Venice* (1851–53).

> "Life without industry is guilt, and industry without art is brutality."
> [John Ruskin, "The Relation of Art to Morals," *Lectures on Art*; 1870]

Rus·sell /rúss'l/, **Bertrand, 3rd Earl Russell** (1872–1970) British philosopher and mathematician. A pacifist, he wrote many highly influential philosophical works. He was awarded a Nobel Prize in literature (1950). Full name **Russell, Bertrand Arthur William**

> "Mathematics may be defined as the subject in which we never know what we are talking about, nor whether what we are saying is true."
> [Bertrand Russell, *Mysticism and Logic*; 1918]

> "Fear is the main source of superstition, and one of the main sources of cruelty."
> [Bertrand Russell, "An Outline of Intellectual Rubbish," *Unpopular Essays*; 1950]

Rus·sell, Bill (*b.* 1934) US basketball player. He played for the Boston Celtics (1957–69), during which time the team won 11 National Basketball Association (NBA) championships. Full name **Russell, William Felton**

Rus·sell, Charles Taze (1852–1916) US religious leader. He founded the International Bible Students Association, now known as Jehovah's Witnesses (1872). Known as **Pastor Russell**

Rus·sell, Henry Norris (1877–1957) US astronomer. He studied the evolution of stars by plotting them on a special graph, which became known as the Hertzsprung-Russell diagram.

Rus·sell, Ken (*b.* 1927) British movie director. His vivid adaptation of D. H. Lawrence's *Women in Love* (1969) and biographies of composers have often attracted controversy. Full name **Russell, Henry Kenneth Alfred**

Rus·sell, Lillian (1861–1922) US singer. Her most famous roles included leading parts in the operettas of Gilbert and Sullivan. Born **Leonard, Helen Louise**

Rus·sell's vi·per *n* a venomous snake that has a yellowish brown body with black markings. Native to: South Asia. Latin name: *Vipera russelli.* [Early 20C. After Patrick *Russell* (1727–1805), Scottish naturalist and physician]

rus·set /rússət/ *n* **1. REDDISH BROWN** a reddish brown color **2.** BOT **POTATO** a usually small reddish brown potato **3.** *also* **rus·set ap·ple APPLE WITH ROUGH SKIN** an apple with a rough brownish skin, a deep sweet-sharp flavor, and a firm texture **4. HOMESPUN FABRIC** a coarse homespun fabric with a reddish brown color [13C. < Old French *rousset,* literally "small red" < *rous* "red" < Latin *russus*] —**rus·set** *adj*

LANGUAGE HERITAGE ***Russian*** Much of English is made up of words from other languages, and Russian is a small but significant contributor in this respect. English absorbed many words relating to prerevolutionary Russian life, from ***muzhik*** (peasant), through ***kulak*** (land-owning peasant) and ***boyar*** (member of the higher nobility), to ***tsar,*** the ***dacha***, ***samovar,*** and ***troika***, and, alas, the ***pogrom***. The word ***ukase***, an order from the tsar with the force of law, developed in English to refer to any decree by a self-styled expert. Soviet politics also provided a vocabulary able to travel beyond its original boundaries: the unquestioningly loyal ***apparatchik*** is found outside its ruling Communist Party; ***agitprop*** can be disseminated under other regimes; the ***gulag*** is available for dissenters anywhere, whether in totalitarian nations or unsavory work environments. The end of the Soviet Union gave the world ***glasnost*** (greater accountability, openness, discussion, and freer disclosure of information) and ***perestroika***, which became able to refer to any political, economic, or bureaucratic restructuring.

Keen interest in – and often hostility to – Soviet politics and society led to many other Russian words becoming familiar to English speakers: ***Bolshevik***, ***commissar,*** ***kremlin***, ***nomenklatura***, ***samizdat***, and ***soviet*** itself, to name a few. Early Soviet successes in space gave us the ***sputnik*** (literally "fellow traveler") and ***cosmonaut***, not in itself a Russian form, but modeled on Russian *kosmonavt*. Russia's vast landscapes have provided ***steppe*** (via German) and ***tundra*** (ultimately from Sami). Soil science is indebted to Russian for ***chernozem***, ***podzol***, ***solonchak***, and other terms.

Translations of Russian literature, as well as travels and Russian émigrés, have brought awareness and enjoyment of Russian food and cuisine: ***blini***, ***borscht***, ***kvass***, ***pirozhki***, ***shashlik*** (ultimately from Crimean Turkish), and ***zakuski***, for instance; ***knish*** and ***latke*** came via Yiddish. Russian also gave us ***vodka*** and ***beluga*** caviar. The dish ***bitok*** (fried ground beef patties served with a sour cream sauce) has come a complete linguistic circle: English *beefsteak* passed into French as *bifteck* then into Russian as *bitok*, only to be returned to English in a new guise.

Names of the many peoples and languages of European and Asian Russia have naturally come to English via Russian: ***Cossack*** (ultimately from Turkic), ***Evenki*** (via Russian from Evenki, a language of parts of eastern Asia), ***Kalmyck***, ***Ostyak*** (via Russian from Tatar), ***Osset*** (via Russian from Georgian), ***Udmurt***, and ***Yakut*** (via Russian from Yakut, a Turkic language), for example. Some names are formed from Russian words combined with English suffixes, as ***Ugrian*** and ***Ugric*** (from *Ugry* "Hungarians") and ***Zyrian*** (from *Zyryanin*).

Russian words appear in many places in English, expected and unexpected: the ***balalaika*** is a Russian string instrument and the ***borzoi*** a Russian dog; ***babushka***, a word for "grandmother," applies also to a headscarf; ***parka*** came from Russian via Aleut; ***mammoth*** derives from an obsolete Russian word (the first remains were found in Siberia); ***shaman*** goes back through Tungus to Sanskrit, but was adopted into English from Russian. The suffix ***-nik***, now thoroughly Anglicized, came from Russian, either directly or through Yiddish. Self-conscious awareness of Russian – and a Soviet stereotype – is manifested in the hybrid form ***nyetwork***, "computer network that is not functional," from *nyet* "no."

Rus·sia /rúshə/ country in eastern Europe and northern and western Asia. In the past the term referred to the Russian Empire, a state that included several republics that are now independent. Russia was also the largest part of the former Soviet Union. Language: Russian. Currency: ruble. Capital: Moscow. Population: 144,526,280 (2003). Area: 6,592,770 sq. mi./17,075,200 sq. km. Official name **Russian Federation**

Rus·sia leath·er *n* a smooth brownish red leather impregnated with oil from birch bark. Use: binding books.

Rus·sian /rúsh'n/ *n* **1. SOMEBODY FROM RUSSIA** somebody who comes from Russia **2. OFFICIAL LANGUAGE OF RUSSIA** the official Balto-Slavic language of Russia, also spoken elsewhere in the world. Native speakers: 160 million. Other speakers: 110 million. ■ *adj* **1. OF RUSSIA** relating to Russia, or its people, language, or culture **2. OF SOVIET UNION** relating to the former Soviet Union, or its peoples or cultures (*dated*)

Rus·sian dress·ing *n* a salad dressing with a mayonnaise or vinaigrette base and sometimes added chili sauce or pickles

Rus·sian Fed·er·a·tion ➧ **Russia**

Rus·sian·ize /rúsh'n ìz/ (**-ized, -iz·ing, -iz·es**) *vti* to become Russian in style, character, or appearance, or make somebody or something do this —**Rus·sian·i·za·tion** /rùsh'ni záysh'n/ *n*

Rus·sian ol·ive *n* BOT same as **oleaster** (sense 2)

Rus·sian Or·tho·dox Church *n* the national church of Russia, an independent branch of the Orthodox Church with the Patriarch of Moscow at its head

Rus·sian rou·lette *n* **1.** a deadly game in which people take turns firing a revolver loaded with only one bullet at their own heads, after spinning the cylinder **2.** a dangerous or reckless action or activity [Because reportedly played by Russian officers in Romania in 1917]

Rus·sian this·tle, Rus·sian tum·ble·weed *n* a saltwort with narrow spiny leaves that has become a troublesome weed in western North America. Native to: Europe. Latin name: *Salsola kali.*

Rus·sian wolf·hound *n* BREED same as **borzoi**

Rus·ski /rúskee, ròoskee/ (*plural* **-skis**), **Rus·sky** (*plural* **-skies**) *n* an offensive term for a Russian person (*slang*) [Mid-19C. < Russian *russkiĭ*]

Russo- *prefix* Russia, Russian ○ *Russo-Japanese* [< RUSSIA]

Rus·so-Jap·a·nese War /rùssō-, ròossō-/ *n* a war fought in 1904–05 between Russia and Japan, mainly over control of Korea, in which Russia was unexpectedly defeated

Rus·so·lo /ru sólō/, **Luigi** (1885–1947) Italian painter and composer. He was one of the leading figures in the futurist movement.

rust /rust/ *n* **1. REDDISH BROWN COATING ON METAL** a reddish brown coating of iron oxide on the surface of iron or steel that forms when the metal is exposed to air and moisture **2. SOMETHING RESEMBLING RUST** something that resembles rust, especially in color, e.g., another type of corrosion or a stain **3.** COLORS **REDDISH BROWN** a reddish brown color **4.** BOT **PLANT DISEASE** a plant disease caused by fungus in which reddish brown spots form on the leaves and stems **5.** FUNGI same as **rust fungus** ■ *v* (**rust·ed, rust·ing, rusts**) **1.** *vti* **CORRODE WITH RUST** to cause something to corrode with rust, or become corroded with rust **2.** *vi* **DETERIORATE** to deteriorate from neglect or lack of use ○ *His knowledge of German had rusted over the years.* [Old English *rūst* < Germanic, "red"] —**rust** *adj*

rust belt, Rust Belt *n US* an area of heavy industry where unprofitable factories have closed down or are closing down

rust buck·et *n* a car that is badly affected by rust (*slang humorous*)

rust fun·gus *n* a fungus that lives as a parasite on many plants, causing reddish brown spots on the plant parts. Order: Uredinales.

rus·tic /rústik/ *adj* **1. OF COUNTRY LIFESTYLE** relating to, characteristic of, or appropriate to the country or country living **2. PLAIN AND SIMPLE** lacking excessive refinement or elegance **3. MADE OF ROUGH BRANCHES** made of rough wood, especially branches with the bark left on them ○ *rustic chairs on the patio* **4.** CONSTR **HAVING ROUGH SURFACE** with a rough finish ○ *rustic bricks* ■ *n* **1. SOMEBODY LIVING IN COUNTRY** somebody who lives in the country, especially somebody who is unsophisticated (*dated; sometimes offensive*) **2.** CONSTR **BRICK WITH ROUGH FINISH** brick or stone with a rough finish [15C. < Latin *rusticus* < *rus* "country, countryside"] —**rus·ti·cal·ly** *adv* —**rus·tic·i·ty** /ru stíssətee/ *n*

rus·ti·cate /rústi kàyt/ (**-cat·ed, -cat·ing, -cates**) *v* **1.** *vi* **MOVE TO COUNTRY** to go to the country to live **2.** *vt* **SEND SOMEBODY TO COUNTRY** to send somebody to the country to live **3.** *vti* **MAKE SOMEBODY OR SOMETHING APPEAR RUSTIC** to become rustic in appearance or quality, or cause somebody or something to do this **4.** *vt* CONSTR **FINISH WALL WITH ROUGH MASONRY** to finish the outside of a wall with large blocks of masonry that are left with a rough surface, beveled, and have deep joints between them **5.** *vt UK* EDUC **SUSPEND STUDENT FROM UNIVERSITY** to suspend a student from a university for a set time as a punishment —**rus·ti·ca·tion** /rùsti káysh'n/ *n* —**rus·ti·ca·tor** *n*

rus·ti·cle /rústik'l/ *n* a long structure that is formed as iron rusts underwater, consisting of iron compounds produced as waste by a complex community of microorganisms that use the rusting metal as a source of food

rus·tic·work /rústik wùrk/ *n* CONSTR same as **rustic** *n* (sense 2)

rus·tle /rúss'l/ *v* (**-tled, -tling, -tles**) **1.** *vti* **MAKE SWISHING SOUND** to make a swishing or soft crackling sound such as that made by dry leaves rubbing together, or cause something to make such a sound **2.** *vi* **MOVE WITH SWISHING SOUND** to move with a swishing or soft crackling sound **3.** *vti* **STEAL LIVESTOCK** to steal livestock, especially cattle or horses **4.** *vi* **MOVE QUICKLY AND ENERGETICALLY** to move or work quickly and energetically ■ *n* **RUSTLING SOUND** a swishing or soft crackling sound ○ *the rustle of paper money* [14C. An imitation of the sound] —**rus·tler** *n* —**rus·tling·ly** *adv*
rustle up *vt* (*informal*) **1.** to prepare a meal or snack quickly using any food that is immediately available **2.** to quickly find and bring together things or people

rust mite *n* a gall mite that produces brown spots on leaves and fruit by burrowing into them

rust·proof /rúst proof/ *adj* not susceptible to rust, or treated so as not to be susceptible to rust ■ *vt* (**-proofed, -proof·ing, -proofs**) to treat metal to prevent it from rusting —**rust·proof·ing** *n*

rust·y /rústee/ (**-i·er, -i·est**) *adj* **1. CORRODED** covered with or corroded by rust **2. OUT OF PRACTICE** out of practice or impaired because of advanced age, neglect, or lack of use ○ *My German is very rusty.* **3.** COLORS same as **rust** *n* (sense 3) **4. DISCOLORED** faded and threadbare from wear and age **5.** BOT **INFECTED WITH RUST FUNGUS** affected by rust fungus —**rust·i·ly** *adv* —**rust·i·ness** *n*

rut[1] /rut/ *n* **1. NARROW GROOVE** a narrow channel or groove in something, especially one made by the wheels of vehicles **2. BORING SITUATION** a routine procedure, situation, or way of life that has become uninteresting and tiresome ○ *I felt I was in a rut.* ■ *vt* (**rut·ted, rut·ting, ruts**) **MAKE RUTS IN SOMETHING** to make ruts in a road, track, or other surface [Late 16C. Probably < Old French *route* (see ROUTE)]

rut[2] /rut/ *n* a period of sexual excitement that recurs annually in male ruminants, especially deer ■ *vi* (**rut·ted, rut·ting, ruts**) ZOOL to be in a state of sexual excitement (*refers to male ruminants*) [12C. < Old French, "bellowing, roaring (of a stag in rut)" < late Latin *rugitus* "roaring" < Latin *rugire* "to roar"] —**rut·tish** *adj*

ru·ta·ba·ga /rootə bàygə/ *n* **1.** a large rounded yellowish root cooked as a vegetable **2.** a European turnip plant that produces rutabagas. Latin name: *Brassica napus napobrassica.* [Late 18C. < Swedish dialect *rotabagge* < *rot* "root" + *bagge* "bag"]

ruth /rooth/ *n* (*archaic*) **1.** pity for another person's troubles **2.** sorrow or remorse for having done something wrong [12C. < RUE[1] after words like TRUTH]

Ruth /rooth/ *n* **1.** in the Bible, a Moabite widow who left her own people to live with her mother-in-law Naomi, married Boaz, and was an ancestor of King David **2.** a book of the Bible that tells the story of Ruth. See table at **Bible**

Ruth /rooth/, **Babe** (1895–1948) US baseball player. When he played for the New York Yankees in the 1920s and 1930s, his legendary home run hitting dominated the sport and made him one of the most popular players in the history of baseball. Born **Ruth, George Herman**

> "All I can tell them is pick a good one and sock it. I get back to the dugout and they ask me what it was I hit and I tell them I don't know except it looked good."
> [Babe Ruth. Quoted in *The American Treasury, 1455–1955*, Clifton Fadiman; 1955]

Ru·the·ni·a /roo theénee ə/ former region of central Europe, corresponding to present-day Zakarpats'ka Oblast, Ukraine —**Ru·the·ni·an** *n, adj*

ru·then·ic /roo thénnik, -theénik/ *adj* relating to or containing ruthenium, especially with a high valence [Mid-19C. < RUTHENIUM]

ru·the·ni·ous /roo theénee əss/ *adj* relating to or containing ruthenium, especially with a low valence [Mid-19C. < RUTHENIUM]

ru·the·ni·um /roo theénee əm/ *n* a brittle white metallic element. Source: platinum ores. Use: hardening of platinum and palladium alloys. Symbol **Ru**. See table at **element** [Mid-19C. After RUTHENIA]

Ruth·er·ford /rúthərfərd/, **Ernest, 1st Baron Rutherford of Nelson and Cambridge** (1871–1937) New Zealand-born British physicist. He discovered the nuclear structure of the atom (1909), and was awarded the Nobel Prize in chemistry (1908).

> "All science is either physics or stamp collecting."
> [Ernest Rutherford. Quoted in *Rutherford at Manchester*, J. B. Birks; 1962]

National Screen Service Ltd

Dame Margaret Rutherford

Ruth·er·ford, Dame Margaret (1892–1972) British actor. A character and comic actor in movies and on stage, she is best known for her role as Miss Marple in movie adaptations of novels by Agatha Christie.

ruth·er·ford·i·um /rùthər fáwrdee əm/ *n* a radioactive element. Source: produced artificially in high-energy atomic collisions. Symbol **Rf**. See table at **element** [Mid-20C. After Ernest RUTHERFORD]

ruth·less /roóthləss/ *adj* having or showing no pity or mercy —**ruth·less·ly** *adv* —**ruth·less·ness** *n*

ru·tile /roo teél, -tīl/ *n* a dark reddish brown or lustrous black titanium dioxide mineral forming needle-shaped crystals. Source: igneous and metamorphic rocks. Use: source of titanium. [Early 19C. Via French and German < Latin *rutilus* "reddish"]

Rut·land /rútlənd/ county in the eastern Midlands, central England. Population: 34,563 (2001). Area: 152 sq. mi./394 sq. km.

Rut·ledge /rúttlij/, **Edward** (1749–1800) American politician. A signatory of the Declaration of Independence (1776), he was governor of South Carolina (1798–1800).

Rut·ledge, John (1739–1800) chief justice of the US Supreme Court (1795)

rut·ting /rútting/ *adj* describes male ruminants, especially deer, that are in a state of sexual excitement

Ru·wen·zo·ri Range /roo ən záwree/ mountain range in central Africa, on the northeastern border of the Democratic Republic of the Congo and the southwestern border of Uganda, between Edward and Albert lakes

RV *abbr* **1.** CAMPING recreational vehicle **2.** AEROSP reentry vehicle **3.** *also* **Rv., R.V.** BIBLE Revised Version

r.v. *abbr* STATS random variable

R-val·ue *n* a measure of the ability of a material such as insulation to retard heat flow. A higher number indicates better insulating properties. [Mid-20C. < R[1] "resistance"]

rw *abbr* Rwanda (*used in Internet addresses*) See table at **domain name**

Rwan·da[1] /roo aándə/ *n* a Bantu official language of Rwanda, also spoken in other parts of east central Africa. Native speakers: 15 million. [Early 20C. < Bantu] —**Rwan·da** *adj*

Rwanda

Rwan·da[2] /roo aándə/ country in east central Africa bordered by Uganda, Tanzania, Burundi, Lake Kivu, and the Democratic Republic of the Congo. During the civil war that broke out between the Hutu and Tutsi peoples in 1994, an estimated quarter of the population was either killed or displaced to neighboring countries. Language: Rwanda, French. Currency: Rwanda franc. Capital: Kigali. Population: 7,810,056 (2003). Area: 10,169 sq. mi./26,338 sq. km. Official name **Rwandese Republic** —**Rwand·an** *n, adj* —**Rwand·ese** /roo aan deéz, -deéss/ *n, adj*

RWD *abbr* TRANSP rear-wheel drive

rwy., Rwy. *abbr* TRANSP railway

Rx *n* a prescription [Early 20C. Alteration of a symbol at the beginning of prescriptions, abbreviation of Latin *recipe* "take"]

ry., Ry. *abbr* TRANSP railway

-ry *suffix* same as **-ery**

ry·a /reé ə/ *n* **1.** a handwoven Scandinavian rug with a deep pile and a colorful pattern **2.** the weaving pattern or style used in making a rya [Mid-20C. After *Rya*, Sweden]

Ry·an /rī ən/, **Nolan** (*b.* 1947) US baseball player. Considered one of the greatest pitchers in major league history, he retired in 1993 with the record for most career strike-outs (5,714) and most career no-hitters (7). Born **Ryan, Lynn Nolan, Jr.**

Ry·der /rídər/, **Albert Pinkham** (1847–1917) US painter. His idiosyncratic style of painting, often seen in depictions of the sea, involved the application of several layers of paint.

> "Imitation is not inspiration, and inspiration only can give birth to a work of art. The least of man's original emanation is better than the best of a borrowed thought."
> [Albert Pinkham Ryder. Quoted in *Albert Pinkham Ryder*, John Sherman; 1920]

rye[1] /rī/ *n* **1.** the light brown grain of an annual cereal grass. Use: to make flour and whiskey, as fodder. **2.** a tall hardy annual cereal plant that has bluish green leaves and is widely cultivated for its grain. Latin name: *Secale cereale*. **3.** BEVERAGES same as **rye whiskey** **4.** FOOD same as **rye bread** [Old English *ryge* < Germanic]

CULTURAL NOTE ***Catcher in the Rye***, a novel (1951) by J. D. Salinger. A moving and realistic account of a young boy's attempt to come to terms with encroaching adulthood, it describes two days in the life of disaffected teenager Holden Caulfield. Holden absconds to New York, then resolves to leave home for good; his failure to accomplish this results in his mental collapse.

rye[2] /rī/ *n* same as **gentleman** (*used by Roma people*) [Mid-19C. Via Romany *rai* < Sanskrit *rājan* "king"]

rye bread *n* a dark or light bread made using rye flour, often flavored with caraway seed

rye grass *n* a grass that is widely cultivated as forage, as a cover crop, and for lawns. Native to: Europe. Latin name: *Lolium perenne*.

Ry·er·son /rírss'n/, **Adolphus Egerton** (1803–82) Canadian cleric and educator. As superintendent of education for Canada West (1844–76), he promoted universal and compulsory education.

rye whis·key *n* whiskey distilled from fermented rye

Ryle /rīl/, **Sir Martin** (1918–84) British astronomer. As Astronomer Royal (1972–82) he developed aperture synthesis in radio astronomy. He received the Nobel Prize in physics (1974).

~~ryme~~ incorrect spelling of **rhyme**

ry·o·kan /ree ṓkən/ *n* a traditional Japanese establishment providing food and lodging for travelers [Mid-20C. < Japanese < *ryo-* "travel" + *kan-* "building"]

rye

RYS *abbr* ONLINE read your screen (*used in e-mails or text messages*)

~~rythmn~~ incorrect spelling of **rhythm**

ry·u /ree óo/ (*plural same* or **-us**) *n* a style or method of practicing a Japanese art, especially a martial art [Early 19C. < Japanese]

Ry·u·kyu Is·lands /ree óokoo-/ chain of islands in southwestern Japan, between Kyushu and Taiwan. Population: 1,222,458 (1990). Area: 873 sq. mi./2,260 sq. km.

Ss

s[1] (*plural* **s's**), **S** (*plural* **S's** or **Ss**) *n* **1.** the 19th letter of the English alphabet, representing a consonant sound **2.** a written representation of the letter "s"

s[2] *symbol* TIME, MATH second

s[3] *abbr* **1.** MEASURE stere **2.** QUANTUM PHYS strange quark

S[1] /ess/ (*plural* **S's** or **Ss**) *n* something shaped like a letter "S"

S[2] *symbol* **1.** QUANTUM PHYS entropy **2.** PHYS siemens **3.** CHEM ELEM sulfur

S[3] *abbr* **1.** BIBLE Samuel **2.** EDUC satisfactory **3.** MONEY schilling **4.** CLOTHING small (*used in clothes sizes*) **5.** ONLINE smile (*used in e-mails or text messages*) **6.** ONLINE smiling (*used in e-mails or text messages*) **7.** COMPASS south **8.** QUANTUM PHYS strangeness **9.** BASEBALL strike

s. *abbr* **1.** semi- **2.** MONEY shilling **3.** GRAM singular **4.** sire **5.** sister **6.** small **7.** MUSIC solo **8.** son **9.** MUSIC soprano **10.** FIN stock **11.** GRAM substantive

S. *abbr* **1.** Sabbath **2.** Saint **3.** Saturday **4.** Saxon **5.** Sea **6.** September **7.** South **8.** Sunday

-'s *suffix* used to form the possessive of nouns ○ *school's* ○ *person's* ○ *men's* [Old English *-es*]

-s, -es *suffix* **1.** used to form the plural of many regular nouns ○ *dogs* ○ *bananas* **2.** used to form the 3rd person present singular of regular verbs and most irregular verbs ○ *speaks* [Old English *-as*]

sa *abbr* ONLINE Saudi Arabia (*used in Internet addresses*) See table at **domain name**

SA *abbr* CHR Salvation Army

s.a.[1] *abbr* **1.** semiannual **2.** COMM subject to approval

s.a.[2] *abbr* without date [Latin *sine anno*]

SAA *abbr* COMPUT systems application architecture

Saa·di another spelling of **Sadi**

Saa·di·a ben Jo·seph /saadee ə ben jṓzif/ (882–942) Arabian philosopher and scholar. His *Book of Opinions and Beliefs* (933) is a classic exegesis of Jewish traditions and laws.

saag /saag/ *n S Asia* green leaf vegetables, especially spinach [Mid-20C. < Hindi]

Saa·kash·vi·li /saakash víllee/, **Mikhail** or **Mikheil** (*b.* 1967) president of Georgia (2004–). A US-trained lawyer, he formed the National Movement that forced the resignation of President Eduard Shevardnadze in 2003.

Saa·mi /saamee/ (*plural same* or **-mis**) *n* **1.** a member of an indigenous people of Lapland **2.** the Finno-Ugric language of the Saami people. Native speakers: 80,000. [Late 18C. < Saami *Sabme*] —**Saa·mi** *adj*

Saar /saar, zaar/ river in eastern France and western Germany. It rises in the Vosges Mountains and flows north to join the Moselle River. Length: 150 mi./241 km. French name **Sarre**

Saar·brück·en /zaar bróokən, saar-/ capital city of Saarland State, in southwestern Germany. Population: 189,012 (1997).

Saa·ri·nen /saarənən/, **Eero** (1910–61) Finnish-born US architect. He is known for his innovative and elegant buildings such as the TWA terminal at New York's Kennedy International Airport (1962). He was the son of Eliel Saarinen.

Saa·ri·nen, Eliel (1873–1950) Finnish-born US architect. His most admired work was the Helsinki Railroad Station (1904–14). He emigrated to the United States (1923), where he headed the Cranbrook Academy of Art (1932–48). He often worked in collaboration with his son, Eero Saarinen. Full name **Saarinen, Gottlieb Eliel**

Sab. *abbr* JUD-CHR Sabbath

sab·a·dil·la /sàbbə díllə, -dée yə/ (*plural* **-las** or *same*) *n* **1.** the seeds of a plant of the lily family that contain veratrine. Use: insecticides, source of veratrine. **2.** a plant of the lily family whose seeds are sabadilla. Flowers: long spikelets. Native to: Mexico. Latin name: *Schoenocaulon officinale*. [Early 19C. < Spanish *cebadilla*, diminutive of *cebada* "barley" < Latin *cibus* "food"]

Sa·bah /saa baa/ second largest state in Malaysia, on the northeast of the island of Borneo. Capital: Kota Kinabalu. Population: 2,593,400 (1997). Area: 28,425 sq. mi./73,620 sq. km. Former name **North Borneo** (until 1963)

Sa·ba·tier /saa baa tyáy/, **Paul** (1854–1941) French chemist. His research on the catalytic hydrogenation of oils made possible the manufacture of margarine. He shared the Nobel Prize in chemistry (1912).

sab·bat /sábbət/ *n* PARANORMAL same as **witches' Sabbath** [Via French < Latin *sabbatum* (see SABBATH)]

Sab·ba·tar·i·an /sàbbə téeree ən/ *n* **1.** STRICT OBSERVER OF SABBATH a believer in the strict observance of a designated day of worship and rest **2.** OBSERVER OF SATURDAY AS SABBATH somebody who observes the Sabbath on Saturday, e.g., in Judaism ■ *adj* OF SABBATH OR SABBATARIANS relating to the Sabbath or its observance, or to Sabbatarians [Early 17C. < late Latin *Sabbatarius* < Latin *sabbatum* (see SABBATH)] —**Sab·ba·tar·i·an·ism** *n*

Sab·bath /sábbəth/ *n* **1.** Sunday, observed by most Christians as the day of worship and rest from work **2.** Saturday, observed as a day of religious worship and rest from work in Judaism and some Christian denominations **3.** PARANORMAL same as **witches' Sabbath** [Pre-12C. Via Latin *sabbatum* < Greek *sabbaton* < Hebrew *šabbāṯ* "rest" < *šāḇaṯ* "to rest"]

Sab·bath school *n* in the tradition of the Seventh-Day Adventists, a school for religious teaching held on Saturday

sab·bat·i·cal /sə báttik'l/ *n* a period of leave from work for research, study, or travel, often with pay and usually granted to college professors every seven years ■ *adj* relating to a sabbatical [Late 16C. < late Latin *sabbaticus* < Greek *sabbatikos* "of the Sabbath" < *sabbaton*, (see SABBATH)]

Sab·bat·i·cal /sə báttik/, **Sab·bat·ic** *adj* relating to or suitable for the Sabbath

sab·bat·i·cal year, sab·bat·i·cal leave *n* EDUC same as **sabbatical**

Sab·bat·i·cal Year *n* in biblical times, every seventh year, during which the ancient Israelites allowed their land to lie fallow

sa·ber /sáybər/ *n* **1.** HEAVY SWORD WITH CURVED BLADE a heavy cavalry sword with a slightly curved blade that is sharp on one edge **2.** FENCING SWORD WITH TAPERING BLADE a light sword with a guard to cover the hand and a tapering flexible blade, used in fencing **3.** FENCING WITH SABER the sport or technique of fencing with a saber ■ *vt* (**-bered, -ber·ing, -bers**) INJURE SOMEBODY WITH SABER to jab, injure, or kill somebody with a saber [Late 17C. Via French *sabre* < obsolete German *Sabel*]

sa·ber-rat·tling *n* an aggressive display or threat of force, especially military force

sa·ber-toothed ti·ger *n* an extinct animal of the cat family that lived in the Oligocene and Pleistocene epochs and had long curving upper canine teeth. Genus: *Smilodon*.

sa·bin /sáybin/ *n* a unit of sound absorption equal to the absorption of one square foot of a perfectly absorbing surface [Mid-20C. After Wallace Clement Ware *Sabine* (1868–1919), US physicist]

Sa·bin /sáybin/, **Albert** (1906–93) Polish-born US microbiologist and immunologist. Best known for developing an oral live-virus polio vaccine (1960), he also developed vaccines against dengue and sandfly fever. Full name **Sabin, Albert Bruce**

Sa·bine[1] /sáy bīn, -been/ *n* **1.** a member of an ancient people who lived in central Italy. By the 3rd century B.C., after centuries of rivalry and fighting, the Romans had defeated them. **2.** the Italic language of the Sabine people [14C. < Latin *Sabinus*] —**Sa·bine** *adj*

Sa·bine[2] /sə béen/ river rising in Texas, forming the Texas-Louisiana border, flowing into the Gulf of Mexico. Length: 380 mi./610 km.

Sa·bin vac·cine *n* an oral vaccine used to immunize against poliomyelitis and containing live poliovirus [Mid-20C. After Albert SABIN]

sab·ji /súbjee/ *n S Asia* a raw or cooked vegetable dish [Early 19C. < Urdu *sabzī* "greenness" < *sabz* "green" < Persian *sebz*]

sa·ble /sáyb'l/ *n* (*plural* **-bles** or *same*) **1.** INDUST BROWN FUR the soft dark fur of a marten (*often used before a noun*) **2.** CLOTHING SABLE GARMENT a garment made of sable fur **3.** ZOOL N ASIAN MARTEN a short-tailed marten whose fur is sable. Native to: northern Asia. Latin name: *Martes zibellina*. **4.** ART ARTIST'S BRUSH an artist's brush made with the hairs of a sable **5.** HERALDRY COLOR BLACK IN HERALDRY in heraldry, the color black ■ *npl* MOURNING CLOTHES black clothes worn in mourning (*archaic*) ■ *adj* (*literary*) **1.** COLORS, HERALDRY OF BLACK COLOR of the color black, e.g., in heraldry **2.** DARK very dark or gloomy [15C. Via French < medieval Latin *sabelum*, probably < Lithuanian *sàbalas* or Russian *sobol'*]

sa·ble an·te·lope *n* a large antelope with long backward-curving horns. The male has a black coat. Native to: Africa. Latin name: *Hippotragus niger*.

sa·ble·fish /sáyb'l fish/ (*plural same* or **-fish·es**) *n* a large dark-colored fish that is important for commercial fisheries. Native to: North American Pacific coast. Latin name: *Anaplopoma fimbria*.

sa·bot /sa bṓ, sábbō/ *n* **1.** WOODEN SHOE a wooden shoe, or a shoe with a wooden sole, formerly worn in Belgium, France, the Netherlands, and Germany **2.** *US* SANDAL OR STRAP a strap across the instep of a sandal, or a sandal with a strap across the instep **3.** SUPPORT FOR PROJECTILE IN WEAPON a sleeve placed around a projectile so that it can be fired from a weapon with a larger bore. The sabot drops away shortly after the projectile is fired. [Early 17C. < French]

sab·o·tage /sábbə taazh/ *n* **1.** DELIBERATE DESTRUCTION the deliberate damaging or destroying of property or equipment, e.g., by resistance fighters, enemy agents, or disgruntled workers **2.** ACTION TO HINDER an action taken to undermine or destroy somebody's efforts or achievements ■ *vt* (**-taged, -tag·ing, -tag·es**) **1.** DAMAGE SOMETHING to damage, destroy, or disrupt something deliberately, especially in a war **2.** HINDER SOMETHING to undermine or destroy somebody's efforts or achievements [Mid-19C. < French < *saboter* "clatter in sabots," hence "act clumsily, work badly, ruin" < *sabot* "sabot"]

sab·o·teur /sàbbə túr/ *n* somebody who commits sabotage [Early 20C. < French, < *saboter* (see SABOTAGE)]

sa·bra /saábrə/ *n* a Jew who was born in Israel [Mid-20C. Directly or via colloquial modern Hebrew *ṣābrāh* < Arabic *ṣabr* "prickly pear"]

sa·bre *n, vt* ARMS, FENCING Can, UK spelling of **saber**

sab·u·lous /sábbyə ləss/, **sab·u·lose** /-lòss/ *adj* having a gritty texture like sand [Mid-19C. < Latin *sabulum* "sand"] —**sab·u·los·i·ty** /sàbbyə lóssətee/ *n*

sac /sak/ *n* a small bag or pouch, especially one that contains a fluid, formed by a membrane in an animal or plant [Mid-18C. Via French < Latin *saccus* (see SACK[1])] —**sac·cate** *adj*

SPELLCHECK sac or **sack**? Do not confuse the spelling of ***sac*** and ***sack***, which sound similar. The word ***sac*** is largely restricted to scientific contexts, denoting a small bag or pouch inside an animal or plant, as in *air sac, yolk sac*. It is also found in *cul-de-sac*, meaning "a road with no exit at one end." ***Sack*** is a more common word, denoting a large cloth or paper bag, as in *a sack of potatoes*. It is also used as a noun or verb referring to dismissal from a job: *She threatened to give him the sack. They will sack anybody who is persistently late for work.*

Sac *n, adj* PEOPLES, LANG same as **Sauk**

SAC /sak/ *abbr* AIR FORCE Strategic Air Command

Sac·a·ga·we·a /sàkəjə weé ə/ (1784–1812 or 1884) Shoshone interpreter and guide. She was the guide and interpreter for the Lewis and Clark expedition (1805–06). Born **Boinaiv**

sac·a·ton /sákə tòn/ *n* a coarse perennial grass grown in dry alkaline areas. Use: hay, pasture. Native to: southwestern United States, Mexico. Latin name: *Sporobolus wrightii*. [Mid-19C. < American Spanish *zacatón* "large coarse grass" < *zacate* "coarse grass" < Nahuatl *zacatl* "straw"]

sac·cade /sa kaád, sə-/ *n* a rapid irregular movement of the eye as it changes focus moving from one point to another, e.g., while reading [Early 18C. < French, "twitch" < *sac* "sack" < Latin *saccus* (see SACK[1])] —**sac·cad·ic** *adj* —**sac·cad·i·cal·ly** *adv*

sacchar- *prefix* same as **saccharo-** (*used before vowels*)

sac·cha·rase /sákə ràyss, -ràyz/ *n* BIOCHEM same as **invertase**

sac·cha·rate /sákə ràyt, -rət/ *n* a compound that is a salt or ester of saccharic acid [Early 19C. < SACCHARIC ACID]

sac·char·ic ac·id /sə kàrrik-, sa-/ *n* a white soluble solid formed by the oxidation of sugar or starch. Formula: $COOH(CHOH)_4COOH$.

sac·cha·ride /sákə rìd/ *n* a sweet-tasting, water-soluble carbohydrate based on a ring of four or five carbon atoms and one oxygen atom

sac·char·i·fy /sə kárrə fì, sa-/ (**-fied, -fy·ing, -fies**) *vt* to convert a starch into simple sugars [Mid-19C. < SACCHARINE] —**sac·char·i·fi·ca·tion** /sə kàrrəfə káysh'n, sa-/ *n*

sac·cha·rim·e·ter /sàkə rímmətər/ *n* an instrument used to measure the concentration of sugar in a solution, e.g., a polarimeter —**sac·cha·rim·e·try** *n*

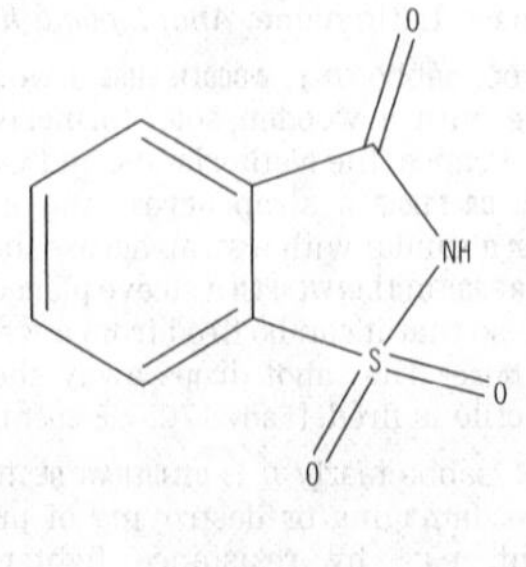

saccharin

sac·cha·rin /sákərin/ *n* a white crystalline compound that is several hundred times sweeter than sugar. Use: sugar substitute. Formula: $C_7H_5NO_3S$.

sac·cha·rine /sákərin, -reen/ *adj* **1.** OF OR LIKE SUGAR relating to, resembling, or containing sugar **2.** TOO SWEET excessively sweet and ingratiating ○ *a saccharine smile* **3.** TOO SENTIMENTAL excessively sentimental and cloying —**sac·cha·rine·ly** *adv* —**sac·cha·rin·i·ty** /sàkə rínnətee/ *n*

saccharo- *prefix* sugar ○ *saccharometer* [Via Latin and Greek < Sanskrit *śarkarā* "sugar"]

sac·cha·roid /sákə ròyd/, **sac·cha·roi·dal** /sàkə róyd'l/ *adj* describes rocks and minerals that have a texture resembling loaf sugar

sac·cha·rom·e·ter /sàkə rómmətər/ *n* a hydrometer used to determine the strength of a sugar solution by measuring its density —**sac·cha·rom·e·try** *n*

sac·cha·ro·my·cete /sàkərō mí seet/ (*plural* **-my·cetes** /-mí seets, -mì seéteez/) *n* a single-celled yeast that has no mycelium, reproduces asexually, and ferments sugar. Genus: *Saccharomyces*. [Late 19C. < SACCHARO- + Greek *mukētes* "mushrooms, fungi"]

sac·cha·rose /sákə ròss, -ròz/ *n* CHEM same as **sucrose**

Sac·co /sákō/, **Nicola** (1891–1927) Italian-born US anarchist. With Bartolomeo Vanzetti, he was convicted of murder in 1921 and executed in 1927 despite international protests at the unfairness and political bias of his trial. Both men's names were cleared by proclamation in 1977. Full name **Sacco, Ferdinando Nicola**

sac·cu·lar /sákyələr/ *adj* resembling a sac or saccule [Mid-19C. < Latin *sacculus* (see SACCULE)]

sac·cule /sá kyool, **sac·cu·lus** /sákyələss/ (*plural* **-li** /-lì, -lee/) *n* **1.** a small membranous bag or pouch in an animal or plant **2.** the smaller of two sacs in the vestibule of the inner ear [Mid-19C. < Latin *sacculus* "little sack" < *saccus* (see SACK[1])] —**sac·cu·late** *adj*

sac·er·do·tal /sàssər dót'l, sàkər-/ *adj* relating to or characteristic of a priest or the priesthood [14C. Via French < Latin *sacerdotalis* "priestly" < *sacerdot-* "priest"] —**sac·er·do·tal·ly** *adv*

sac·er·do·tal·ism /sàssər dót'l ìzzəm, sàkər-/ *n* **1.** the beliefs or methods of priests **2.** the belief that a priest is able to mediate between God and human beings —**sac·er·do·tal·ist** *n*

SACEUR *abbr* MIL Supreme Allied Commander, Europe

sac fun·gus *n* FUNGI same as **ascomycete**

sa·chem /sáychəm/ *n* **1.** a chief of a Native North American people or confederation, especially of the Algonquian people **2.** POL, HIST a leader or official of Tammany Hall [Early 17C. < Algonquian] —**sa·chem·ic** /say chémmik/ *adj*

sa·cher torte /saákər tàwrt, zaákhər tàwrtə/ *n* a dark rich chocolate cake covered with glossy chocolate frosting [Early 20C. < German, after Franz *Sacher*, German pastry chef]

sa·chet /sa sháy/ *n* a small bag containing perfumed powder or potpourri, used to perfume clothes in closets or drawers [15C. < Old French, "little sack" < *sac* "sack" < Latin *saccus* (see SACK[1])]

sack[1] /sak/ *n* **1.** LARGE BAG a large bag, especially one that is made from coarse cloth or thick heavy-duty paper **2.** AMOUNT IN BAG the amount that a sack will hold **3.** JOB DISMISSAL dismissal from a job (*informal*) ○ *got the sack* **4.** BED a bed as a place to sleep (*slang*) ○ *in the sack trying to get some shut-eye* **5.** FOOTBALL TACKLE OF PASSER in football, a tackle of the quarterback behind the line of scrimmage during the quarterback's attempt to pass the ball **6.** BASEBALL BASE IN BASEBALL a base on a baseball diamond (*informal*) **7.** CLOTHING WOMAN'S DRESS a woman's loose-fitting dress that narrows below the knee **8.** CLOTHING, HIST 18C WOMAN'S GOWN a gown worn by women in the 18th century that had a bodice with loose pleats at the back ■ *vt* (**sacked, sack·ing, sacks**) **1.** FIRE SOMEBODY to dismiss somebody from a job (*informal*) **2.** PUT SOMETHING IN SACK to put something into a sack, e.g., for storage or transportation **3.** FOOTBALL TACKLE PASSER BEHIND LINE OF SCRIMMAGE in football, to tackle the quarterback behind the line of scrimmage during the quarterback's attempt to pass the ball [Pre-12C. < Latin *saccus* "bag, wallet" < Greek *sakkos* "packing material" < Semitic] —**sack·er** *n* ◇ **hit the sack** to go to bed (*slang*)

SPELLCHECK See *sac*.

sack out *vi* to go to sleep or to bed (*informal*)

sack[2] /sak/ *vt* (**sacked, sack·ing, sacks**) to destroy a captured town or city and plunder its goods and valuables ■ *n* the destruction of a captured town or city and the plundering of its goods and valuables [Mid-16C. < Old French *(a) sac*, call to plunder, literally "(to the) sack" < Latin *saccus* (see SACK[1])]

sack[3] /sak/ *n* dry white wine from Spain, Portugal, or the Canary Islands (*archaic*) [Early 16C. < French *(vin) sec* "dry (wine)" < Latin *siccus* "dry"]

sack·but /sák bùt/ *n* a medieval wind instrument with a long slide like a trombone [Early 16C. < Old French *saqueb(o)ute* "hooked lance for pulling riders from their horses"]

sack·cloth /sák klàwth, -klòth/ *n* **1.** a coarse cloth made from goat or camel's hair or cotton, hemp, or flax. Use: sacks. **2.** clothes made from sackcloth, formerly worn as a sign of mourning or penitence [14C. < SACK[1]] ◇ **sackcloth and ashes** a show of mourning or repentance (*dated*)

sack·ing /sáking/ *n* a coarse cloth woven from hemp or jute. Use: sacks. [Late 16C. < SACK[1]]

sack race *n* a race in which each competitor stands in a sack and jumps toward the finish line while holding up the sack [< SACK[1]]

E. O. Hoppe/Corbis
Vita Sackville-West

Sack·ville-West /sàk vil wést/, **Vita** (1892–1962) British writer. She is remembered for poems such as "The Land" (1926) and novels including *The Edwardians* (1930). Virginia Woolf celebrated their friendship in her novel *Orlando* (1928). Full name **Sackville-West, Victoria Mary**

> "For observe, that to hope for Paradise is to live in Paradise, a very different thing from actually getting there."
> [Vita Sackville-West, *Passenger to Tehran*; 1926]

Sa·co /sáykō/ town in southwestern Maine, on the northern shore of the Saco River, opposite Biddeford. Population: 17,634 (2002 estimate).

sa·cra ANAT plural of **sacrum**

~~sacrafice~~ incorrect spelling of **sacrifice**

sa·cral[1] /sákrəl, sáyk-/ *adj* relating to or near the sacrum at the base of the spine [Mid-18C. < SACRUM]

sa·cral[2] /sákrəl, sáyk-/ *adj* relating to or used in sacred rites [Late 19C. < Latin *sacr-* "sacred"]

sac·ra·ment /sákrəmənt/ *n* **1.** RELIGIOUS RITE OR CEREMONY in Christianity, a rite that is considered to have been established by Jesus Christ to bring grace to those participating in or receiving it. In the Protestant Church, the sacraments are baptism and Communion. The Roman Catholic and Eastern Orthodox Churches also include penance, confirmation, holy orders, matrimony, and the anointing of the sick. **2.** *also* **Sac·ra·ment** CONSECRATED ITEMS the bread and wine consecrated at Communion **3.** SOMETHING SACRED something considered to be sacred or to have a special significance [12C. Via French < Latin *sacramentum* "soldier's oath, solemn obligation," later "rite, mystery, revelation" < *sacr-* "sacred"]

sac·ra·men·tal /sàkrə mént'l/ *adj* **1.** USED IN SACRAMENT relating to or used in a Christian sacrament **2.** SACRED bound by a sacrament or in a way considered inviolable ■ *n* **RITUAL ACTION OR SIGN** in the Roman Catholic Church, an object, act, or ritual that is used to show religious devotion, e.g., the sign of the cross —**sac·ra·men·tal·i·ty** /sàkrəmən tálləteе, -men-/ *n* —**sac·ra·men·tal·ly** *adv*

sac·ra·men·tal·ism /sàkrə mént'l ìzzəm/ *n* in Christianity, the belief in the necessity of the sacraments to attain salvation and God's grace —**sac·ra·men·tal·ist** *n*

Sac·ra·men·tar·i·an /sàkrəmən térree ən, sàkrə men-/ *n* in Christianity, a believer that the consecrated bread and wine of the Communion merely symbolize the body and blood of Jesus Christ ■ *adj* relating to or characteristic of Sacramentarians —**Sac·ra·men·tar·i·an·ism** *n*

Sac·ra·men·to /sàkrə méntō/ **1.** river in California, rising near Mount Shasta and flowing south into San Francisco Bay. Length: 377 mi./607 km. **2.** capital city of California, at the confluence of the Sacramento and American rivers. Population: 435,425 (2002 estimate).

Sac·ra·men·to Moun·tains mountain range in southern New Mexico, between the Pecos River and the Rio Grande

sa·crar·i·um /sə krérree əm/ (*plural* **-i·a** /-ee ə/) *n* **1.** a Christian church's sanctuary or sacristy **2.** CHR same as **piscina** (sense 1) [Early 18C. < Latin, "shrine" < *sacr-* "sacred"]

sa·cred /sáykrid/ *adj* **1. DEVOTED TO DEITY** dedicated to a deity or religious purpose **2. OF RELIGION** relating to or used in religious worship **3. WORTHY OF WORSHIP** worthy of or regarded with religious veneration, worship, and respect **4. DEDICATED TO SOMEBODY** dedicated to or in honor of somebody **5. INVIOLABLE** not to be challenged or disrespected [14C. < past participle of obsolete *sacre* "consecrate," via French < Latin *sacrare* < *sacr-* "sacred"] —**sa·cred·ly** *adv* —**sa·cred·ness** *n*

ORIGIN The Latin word *sacer, sacr-* "holy, sacred," from which ***sacred*** is derived, is also the source of English *consecrate, execrate, sacrament, sacrifice, sacrilege, sacristan*, and *sexton*.

sa·cred ba·boon *n* VERTEB same as **hamadryas baboon** [Late 19C. Because sacred to the ancient Egyptians]

sa·cred cow *n* somebody or something exempt from any criticism or interference [Because cattle are sacred to Hindus]

Sa·cred Heart *n* **1.** in the Roman Catholic Church, the heart of Jesus Christ, seen as a symbol of his love **2.** an image representing the Sacred Heart, often shown as bleeding

sa·cred mush·room *n* a hallucinogenic mushroom. Native to: Americas. Genus: *Psilocybe*. [Because formerly eaten in Native American rituals]

~~sacreligious~~ incorrect spelling of **sacrilegious**

sac·ri·fice /sákrə fìss/ *n* **1. GIVING UP OF SOMETHING VALUED** a giving up of something valuable or important for somebody or something else considered to be of more value or importance **2. SOMETHING VALUED AND GIVEN UP** something valuable or important given up as a sacrifice **3. LOSS IN GIVING UP SOMETHING VALUED** a loss incurred by giving away or selling something below its value **4.** RELIG **OFFERING TO GOD** an offering to honor or appease a god, especially of a ritually slaughtered animal or person **5.** RELIG **SOMETHING OR SOMEBODY OFFERED TO GOD** something or somebody offered to honor or appease a god **6.** CHESS **STRATEGIC GIVING UP OF CHESS PIECE** in chess, an act or instance of allowing or forcing an opponent to take one of your pieces or pawns so that you can gain an advantage position ■ *v* (**-ficed, -fic·ing, -fic·es**) **1.** *vt* **GIVE UP SOMEBODY OR SOMETHING VALUED** to give up somebody or something important or valued in exchange for somebody or something else that is considered more important or valuable **2.** *vt* **ABANDON SOMEBODY OR SOMETHING FOR ADVANTAGE** to allow somebody or something to be hurt, killed, or destroyed for your own advantage **3.** *vti* RELIG **MAKE OFFERING TO GOD** to make an offering of a ritually slaughtered animal or person to a god **4.** *vt* CHESS **STRATEGICALLY GIVE UP CHESS PIECE** in chess, to allow or force one of your pieces or pawns to be taken by an opponent so that you can gain an advantage in position **5.** *vi* BASEBALL **HIT SACRIFICE BUNT** in baseball, to bunt the ball, expecting to be put out, in order to advance a base runner [13C. Via French < Latin *sacrificium* "making sacred" < *sacr-* "sacred"] —**sac·ri·fice·a·ble** *adj* —**sac·ri·fic·er** *n*

sac·ri·fice bunt *n* in baseball, an act of bunting the ball, expecting to be put out, in order to advance a base runner

sac·ri·fice fly *n* in baseball, a fly ball that is caught in the outfield and on which a runner scores

sac·ri·fice hit *n* BASEBALL same as **sacrifice bunt**

sac·ri·fi·cial /sàkrə físh'l/ *adj* relating to, used in, or offered as a sacrifice —**sac·ri·fi·cial·ly** *adv*

sac·ri·lege /sákrəlij/ *n* **1.** the violation, desecration, or theft of something considered holy or sacred **2.** the disrespectful or irreverent treatment of something other people consider worthy of respect or reverence [14C. Via French < Latin *sacrilegium* "temple robbery" < *sacrilegus* "collector of sacred things" < *sacr-* "sacred" + *legere* "collect"] —**sac·ri·le·gious** /sàkrə líjjəss/ *adj* —**sac·ri·le·gist** /-leejist/ *n*

sac·ris·tan /sákristən/ *n* **1.** somebody in charge of the contents of a Christian church, especially objects kept in the sacristy **2.** CHR same as **sexton** (*dated*) [14C. < medieval Latin *sacristanus* < *sacrista* "keeper of sacred things" < Latin *sacr-* "sacred"]

sac·ris·ty /sákristee/ (*plural* **-ties**) *n* a room in a Christian church in which sacred objects such as vessels and vestments are kept [15C. Via French < medieval Latin *sacristia* < *sacrista* (see SACRISTAN)]

sac·ro·il·i·ac /sàkrō íllee àk/ *adj* relating to the sacrum and the upper portion of the hip bone (**ilium**), or to the joint between the sacrum and ilium ■ *n* the joint in the back where the sacrum and the ilium meet [Mid-19C. < SACRUM]

sac·ro·sanct /sákrō sàngkt/ *adj* **1.** very holy and sacred **2.** not to be criticized or tampered with [Early 17C. < Latin *sacrosanctus*, "made holy through religious rites" < *sacr-* "sacred" + *sanctus*, past participle of *sacrare* "make holy"] —**sac·ro·sanc·ti·ty** /sàkrō sángktətee/ *n*

sa·crum /sáykrəm, sák-/ (*plural* **-crums** or **-cra** /-krə/) *n* a triangular bone at the base of the spine that joins to a hip bone on each side and forms part of the pelvis. In human beings it consists of five fused vertebrae. [Mid-18C. < Latin *(os) sacrum*, translation of Greek *hieron (osteon)* "sacred (bone)"; from the belief that the soul resided there]

sad /sad/ (**sad·der, sad·dest**) *adj* **1. UNHAPPY** feeling or showing unhappiness, grief, or sorrow ○ *a sad expression* **2. CAUSING UNHAPPINESS** causing or containing unhappiness ○ *sad news* **3. REGRETTABLE** unfortunate or to be deplored ○ *The sad fact is that there are not enough funds available to support this project.* **4. PITIABLE OR CONTEMPTIBLE** uninteresting and pitiable or contemptible (*slang*) ○ *wearing a really sad shirt* **5. DULL IN COLOR** dull or dark in color [Old English *sæd* "weary, heavy, sated" < Indo-European] —**sad·ly** *adv* —**sad·ness** *n*

SAD *abbr* MED seasonal affective disorder

Anwar al-Sadat

Sa·dat /sə daát/, **Anwar al-** (1918–81) president of Egypt (1970–81). He was the first Arab leader to recognize Israel and, together with Israeli prime minister Menachem Begin, negotiated a historic peace treaty in 1978, for which they shared the Nobel Peace Prize. He was assassinated by members of his own army.

"Most people seek after what they do not possess and they are enslaved by the very things they want to acquire."
[Anwar al-Sadat, *In Search of Identity*, 1978]

Sa·dat, Jehan (*b.* 1933) Egyptian social activist and educator

Sad·dam /sa daám, sáddəm/ ➧ **Hussein, Saddam**

sad·den /sádd'n/ (**-dened, -den·ing, -dens**) *vti* to become sad, or cause somebody to become sad (*often passive*)

sad·dhu *n* HINDUISM another spelling of **sadhu**

sad·dle /sádd'l/ *n* **1. SEAT FOR RIDING ANIMAL** a seat, usually made of leather, used by a rider on the back of an animal such as a horse or donkey **2. SEAT ON BICYCLE OR MOTORCYCLE** a padded seat for a rider on a vehicle such as a bicycle, motorcycle, or tractor **3. PART OF ANIMAL'S BACK** the part of an animal where a saddle is placed **4. PART OF HARNESS** a pad that forms part of a harness and fits across the back of an animal carrying or pulling something **5. SOMETHING RESEMBLING SADDLE** something that looks like or is used like a saddle **6.** GEOG **LOW POINT OF RIDGE** a low point of a ridge connecting two peaks **7.** FOOD **CUT OF MEAT** a cut of meat that includes part of the backbone and both loins **8.** FOOD **BACK PART OF CHICKEN** the back part of a chicken or other fowl nearest its tail ■ *v* (**-dled, -dling, -dles**) **1.** *vt* **STRAP SADDLE ONTO ANIMAL** to put a saddle onto a horse or other animal **2.** *vi* **MOUNT ANIMAL** to mount a horse, or other animal, that has a saddle on it [Old English *sadol* < Indo-European, "sit"] ◇ **in the saddle** in control of something

saddle up *vti* to put a saddle on a horse to prepare for riding it

saddle with *vt* to give somebody an unwelcome or unpleasant task or responsibility

sad·dle·back /sádd'l bàk/ *n* **1.** an animal, e.g., a bird, fish, or other vertebrate, that has a saddle-shaped marking on its back **2.** ARCHIT same as **saddle roof** **3.** GEOG same as **saddle** *n* (sense 6)

sad·dle-backed *adj* **1.** with its back curved into a shape like a saddle **2.** with a saddle-shaped marking on its back

sad·dle·bag /sádd'l bàg/ *n* a bag, sometimes one of a pair, carried near or attached to an animal's saddle or attached to a frame over a wheel of a bicycle or motorcycle

sad·dle-billed stork /sádd'l bìl/, **sad·dle·bill** (*plural* **-bills** or *same*) *n* a stork with black and white feathers, black legs with red joints, and a red beak with a black band. Native to: sub-Saharan Africa. Latin name: *Ephippiorhynchus senegalensis*.

sad·dle blan·ket *n* a blanket or other pad placed under a saddle to prevent it from chafing the animal's back

sad·dle·bow /sádd'l bō/ *n* the high arch or raised part (**pommel**) at the front of a horse's saddle

sad·dle·cloth /sádd'l klàwth, -klòth/ *n* a cloth placed under or over a racehorse's saddle that shows the horse's number

sad·dle horn *n* a projection like a horn on the arch at the front of a horse's saddle

sad·dle horse *n* a horse that is used or trained for riding

sad·dler /sáddlər/ *n* a maker, repairer, or seller of saddlery

sad·dle roof *n* a roof that has two gables and a ridge

sad·dler·y /sáddləree/ (*plural* **-ies**) *n* **1. EQUIPMENT FOR HORSES** saddles, harnesses, and other equipment for horses **2. JOB OF SADDLER** the work done by a saddler **3. SADDLER'S SHOP** a shop that sells equipment for horses **4. PLACE FOR STORING SADDLES** a room in or near a stable used for making, repairing, or storing equipment for horses

sad·dle shoe *n* a white or light-colored laced shoe with a band of contrasting leather across the instep

sad·dle soap *n* a mild soap containing neat's-foot oil. Use: cleaning, softening, and preserving leather.

sad·dle sore *n* **1.** a sore on the buttocks, groin, or inner thighs of a rider, caused by the rubbing of the saddle **2.** a sore on a horse's body, caused by the rubbing of an ill-fitting saddle

sad·dle-sore *adj* **1.** sore from having ridden a horse, bicycle, or other mode of transport with a saddle **2.** sore, or affected by sores, from the wearing of a saddle

sad·dle stitch *n* **1.** a long running stitch, usually made with a contrasting color for ornamentation **2.** in bookbinding, a method of binding the pages of a small book or magazine together by folding it in half and stitching along the line of the fold —**saddle-stitch** *vti*

sad·dle·tree /sádd'l trèe/ *n* the frame of a saddle

Sad·du·cee /sájjəssee, sáddyəssee/ *n* a member of an ancient Jewish group of priests and aristocrats who accepted the literal interpretation of the Torah but rejected Oral Law and belief in the afterlife. Sadducees favored accommodation with the Roman occupiers of Palestine. [Pre-12C. Via late Latin < late Greek *Saddoukaios* < post-biblical Hebrew *Ṣĕdūqī* "follower of Zadok" < *Ṣādōq* "Zadok," high priest who supposedly founded the group] —**Sad·du·ce·an** /sàjjə sée ən, sàddyə-/ *adj* —**Sad·du·cee·ism** *n*

sa·de *n* another spelling of **sadhe**

Sade /saad/, **Marquis de** (1740–1814) French philosopher and novelist. His own cruel sexual practices, for which he was imprisoned, were reflected in novels such as *Juliette* (1797). Full name **Donatien Alphonse François, Comte de Sade**

sa·dhe /saádee, saádə/, **sa·de, tsa·de** /tsaádee, tsaádə/ *n* the 18th letter of the Hebrew alphabet, represented in the English alphabet as "s" or "ts." See table at **alphabet** [Late 19C. < Hebrew *ṣādhē*]

sa·dhu /saá dòo/, **sad·dhu** *n* a Hindu holy man who lives by begging [Mid-19C. < Sanskrit *sādhu-* "good, holy"]

Sa·di /saa dée/, **Saa·di** (1200?–92) Persian poet. His contributions to classical Persian literature include the *The Rose Garden* (1258). Full name **Musilh-ud-Din**

sad·i·ron /sád ìrn/ *n* a heavy iron that curves to a point at both ends, has a removable handle, is heated on an external source, and is used for pressing clothes and linens [Mid-18C. < SAD in the obsolete sense "solid, heavy"]

sa·dism /sáy dìzzəm/ *n* **1.** HURTING OTHERS FOR SEXUAL PLEASURE the gaining of sexual gratification by causing physical or mental pain to other people, or the acts that produce such gratification **2.** BEING CRUEL FOR FUN the gaining of pleasure from causing physical or mental pain to people or animals **3.** CRUELTY great physical or mental cruelty [Late 19C. < French *sadisme*, after the Marquis de SADE] —**sa·dist** *n* —**sa·dis·tic** /sə dístik/ *adj* —**sa·dis·ti·cal·ly** *adv*

sa·do·mas·o·chism /sàydō mássə kìzzəm, sàddō-/ *n* **1.** the gaining of sexual gratification by alternately or simultaneously enduring pain and causing pain to somebody else, or the acts that produce such gratification **2.** a combination of sadistic and masochistic sexual tendencies within an individual person, who may derive sexual pleasure both from inflicting and from enduring pain and cruelty [Mid-20C. < SADISM] —**sa·do·mas·o·chist** *n* —**sa·do·mas·o·chis·tic** /sàydō massə kístik, sàddō-/ *adj*

sad sack *n* somebody, especially a soldier, who means well but is hopelessly inept (*informal*) [Mid-20C. < a melancholy cartoon GI created by US cartoonist George Baker]

SAE *abbr* AUTOMOT Society of Automotive Engineers

s.a.e., SAE *abbr* MAIL stamped addressed envelope

Sa·far /sə faár/, **Sa·phar** *n* in the Islamic calendar, the second month of the year. See table at **calendar** [Late 18C. < Arabic *safar*]

sa·fa·ri /sə faáree/ *n* **1.** a journey across a stretch of land, especially in Africa, for the purpose of hunting or observing wild animals ○ *go on safari* **2.** a group of people on a safari, together with the animals or vehicles that transport them [Late 19C. Via Kiswahili < Arabic *safar* "journey"]

sa·fa·ri jack·et *n* a casual jacket with four large pockets and a belt

sa·fa·ri park *n* a large enclosed area of land where wild animals wander relatively freely and people pay to drive around and observe them

sa·fa·ri suit *n* a short-sleeved safari jacket with matching pants, shorts, or skirt

Sa·fa·vid dy·nas·ty /sə faá wìd-/ *n* a Persian dynasty that ruled from 1500 to 1722 and established the Shiite branch of Islam as the state religion [Early 20C. < Arabic *ṣafawī*, < *Ṣfī* al-Din Isḥaq, the dynasty's founder]

safe /sayf/ *adj* (**saf·er, saf·est**) **1.** NOT DANGEROUS unlikely to cause or result in harm, injury, or damage ○ *Have a safe journey!* **2.** NOT IN DANGER in a position or situation that offers protection, so that harm, damage, loss, or unwanted tampering is unlikely ○ *You'll be safe with me.* ○ *It's hidden in a safe place.* **3.** UNHARMED OR UNDAMAGED in an unharmed, uninjured, or undamaged condition ○ *They're safe, but the car's been totaled.* **4.** SURE TO BE SUCCESSFUL certain to be successful or profitable, and not at risk of failure or loss ○ *a safe investment* **5.** UNLIKELY TO CAUSE TROUBLE unlikely to cause trouble or controversy ○ *Is it safe to talk about politics with them?* **6.** PROBABLY CORRECT unlikely to be wrong ○ *It's safe to assume that the weather will be good.* **7.** CAUTIOUS AND CONSERVATIVE cautious with regard to risks or unforeseen problems, conservative with regard to estimates, or unadventurous with regard to choices and decisions ○ *The safe option is just to put the money in the bank.* **8.** DEPENDABLE able to be trusted or depended on ○ *Don't worry, your child's in safe hands.* **9.** HAVING REACHED BASE SUCCESSFULLY in baseball, having reached a base or home plate without being put out ■ *n* **1.** CONTAINER FOR VALUABLES a strong metal container, often with a complex locking system, for the storage of money and other valuables **2.** STORAGE CONTAINER a container for storage or protection, especially a ventilated box or small cupboard for keeping food cool or fresh **3.** same as **condom** (*slang*) **4.** *regional* PLACE FOR STORING MILK a storage house or shed for storing milk and other perishables [13C. Via Old French *sauf* < Latin *salvus*] —**safe·ly** *adv* —**safe·ness** *n*

REGIONAL NOTE See *dairy*.

safe·break·er /sáyf bràykər/ *n UK* same as **safecracker** —**safe·break·ing** *n*

safe-con·duct *n* **1.** official protection from harm or immunity from arrest for somebody passing through a dangerous area such as enemy territory in wartime **2.** a document or escort providing safe-conduct

safe·crack·er /sáyf kràkər/ *n* somebody who breaks into a safe, with or without the use of force, so that the contents can be stolen —**safe·crack·ing** *n*

safe-de·pos·it *n* the placement of money and other valuables in storage without risk of loss or damage by fire or theft, e.g., in a bank vault

safe-de·pos·it box *n* a strong metal container for valuables such as jewelry or documents, usually kept in a bank vault

safe·guard /sáyf gaàrd/ *n* **1.** PROTECTIVE MEASURE something intended to prevent undesirable consequences from happening, e.g., a safety device or measure, or a proviso in a legal document **2.** SAFE-CONDUCT DOCUMENT a document providing safe-conduct ■ *vt* (**-guard·ed, -guard·ing, -guards**) KEEP SOMETHING SAFE to prevent something or somebody from being harmed, damaged, badly treated, or lost [14C. < Anglo-Norman *salve garde*, French *sauve garde* < *sauf* (see SAFE) + *garde* (see GUARD)] —**safe·guard·er** *n*

SYNONYMS ***safeguard, protect, defend, guard, shield***

CORE MEANING: to keep something or somebody safe from actual or potential damage or attack

safeguard to prevent something or somebody from being harmed, damaged, badly treated, or lost ○ *their promise to continue a free market approach while safeguarding local industry.* ○ *measures to safeguard our citizens against terrorism* **protect** to prevent somebody or something from being harmed or damaged ○ *protect your skin from direct sunlight* ○ *efforts to protect our national parks from overuse* **defend** to protect somebody or something from attack, harm, or danger ○ *The stallion will defend his mares against the attentions of other males.* ○ *Charlie defended himself well, using the ropes and corner as he ducked and dived.* **guard** to protect somebody or something against danger or loss by being vigilant and taking defensive measures ○ *The main prison was guarded by armed officers.* ○ *Guard against identity theft.* **shield** to prevent harm or damage to somebody or something by using a physical barrier or by intervening in a protective way ○ *His broad-brimmed hat shielded his eyes from the sun.* ○ *The president's children are protectively shielded from the public spotlight at home.*

safe ha·ven *n* a place guaranteed safe from danger or attack

safe house *n* a house or other place of refuge where people in danger can hide or meet in secret

safe·keep·ing /sàyf kéeping, sáyf kèeping/ *n* **1.** protection from harm, damage, loss, or theft ○ *I put the documents in my desk for safekeeping.* **2.** *US* a system whereby banks keep checks that people write, rather than returning them to the account holder with the monthly statement

safe·light /sáyf lìt/ *n* a light used in darkrooms to filter out the rays that are harmful to sensitive film and photographic paper

safe room *n* a room in a building reinforced against intruders, attack, or severe weather

safe sex *n* sexual activity in which precautions are taken to avoid spreading sexually transmitted diseases, e.g., intercourse using a condom

safe·ty /sáyftee/ (*plural* **-ties**) *n* **1.** FREEDOM FROM DANGER protection from, or not being exposed to, the risk of harm or injury ○ *a safety device* ○ *The captain is responsible for the safety of the crew.* **2.** LACK OF DANGER inability to cause or result in harm, injury, or damage ○ *People are beginning to question the safety of the medication.* **3.** SAFE PLACE a place or situation where harm, damage, or loss is unlikely ○ *She led the passengers to safety.* **4.** BEING UNHARMED OR UNDAMAGED the fact of being or remaining unharmed, uninjured, or undamaged ○ *There are fears for their safety.* **5.** DEVICE PREVENTING UNINTENTIONAL OPERATION a device designed to prevent a mechanism from being operated unintentionally, e.g., one that keeps a gun from being fired by accident or an elevator from falling **6.** DEFENSIVE BACK in football, a player defending the back of the field **7.** PLAY GIVING POINTS TO DEFENSIVE TEAM in football, a play in which a member of the offensive team downs the ball intentionally or unintentionally in his own end zone, resulting in the defensive team being awarded two points **8.** *US* HEALTH same as **condom** (*slang*) [14C. Via French *sauveté* < medieval Latin *salvitas* < Latin *salvus* "safe"]

safe·ty belt *n* **1.** TRANSP same as **seat belt** **2.** a strong strap attached to a fixed point, worn by somebody in danger of falling such as somebody working in a high place

safe·ty-crit·i·cal *adj* describes an electronic, electromechanical, or computer feature or system whose failure may cause injury or death to human beings ○ *a workshop on safety-critical software and systems*

safe·ty cur·tain *n* a fireproof curtain that can be lowered at the front of the stage in a theater to isolate the auditorium from the stage in the event of fire

safe·ty film *n* nonflammable movie film made with a cellulose acetate or polyester base. Formerly, film was made with cellulose nitrate and was prone to catch fire upon aging.

safe·ty glass *n* **1.** strong laminated glass designed not to shatter, made with a layer of clear plastic sandwiched between two glass sheets **2.** glass that, if it breaks, forms rounded fragments rather than sharp splinters

safe·ty har·ness *n* an arrangement of straps or belts designed to restrain or support somebody at risk of falling or injury

safe·ty is·land *n US* an area within a road that is marked off and from which vehicular traffic is prohibited, used especially for the safety of pedestrians

safe·ty lamp *n* a miner's lamp in which the flame is enclosed in fine wire gauze to prevent the combustion of flammable gases

safe·ty·man /sáyftee màn/ (*plural* **-men** /-mèn/) *n* FOOTBALL same as **safety**

safe·ty match *n* a match that will only produce a flame if it is struck against a specially prepared surface

safe·ty net *n* **1.** a net installed below a high place such as a circus tightrope or trapeze from which somebody might fall or jump **2.** something intended to help people in the event of hardship or misfortune, especially something providing financial security, e.g., insurance or welfare payments

safe·ty pin *n* **1.** a loop-shaped pin that fastens into itself with its point under a protective cover to prevent accidental opening or injury **2.** a pin that when properly seated prevents accidental or premature detonation, e.g., in a grenade

safe·ty ra·zor *n* a razor in which the blade is partially covered to minimize the risk of accidental injury

safe·ty valve *n* **1.** a valve that will automatically open and release a fluid when the pressure in a chamber, e.g., the boiler of a steam engine, approaches a dangerous level **2.** something that enables people to get rid of strong feelings such as anger, grief, anxiety, or excitement without harming themselves or others

saf·flow·er /sá flòwr/ *n* **1.** PLANT YIELDING OIL AND DYE an annual composite plant. Flowers: orange or red. Use: dye, cooking oil, paints, medicines. Native to: South Asia. Latin name: *Carthamus tinctorius.* **2.** DRIED FLOWERS the dried flowers of the safflower plant. Use: red dye. **3.** RED DYE a red dye made from the dried flowers of the safflower plant. Use: colorant for fabric, food, and cosmetics. [15C. Via Dutch or German < Old French *saffleur,* via Italian < Arabic *asfar* "yellow plant"]

saf·fron /sáffrən/ (*plural* **-frons** or *same*) *n* **1.** COOKING SPICE the deep orange-colored stigmas of a type of crocus, sometimes ground to a powder. Use: food colorant, flavoring. **2.** SPICE-PRODUCING CROCUS a crocus thought to have originated from the Greek island of Crete whose flowers produce saffron. Native to: Europe, South and Southwest Asia. Flowers: showy, purple or white. Latin name: *Crocus sativus.* **3.** BRIGHT ORANGE-YELLOW COLOR a bright orange-yellow color [Pre-12C. Via French *safran* and medieval Latin *safranum* < Arabic *za'farān*] —**saf·fron** *adj*

Sa·fi /saa fée/ capital city of Safi Province and a port on the Atlantic Ocean, in western Morocco. Population: 376,038 (1994).

S. Afr. *abbr* South Africa

saf·ra·nine /sáffrə neèn, -nin/, **saf·ra·nin** /sáffrənin/ *n* a red organic azine. Use: textile color, biological stain. [Mid-19C. < French < *safran* (see SAFFRON)]

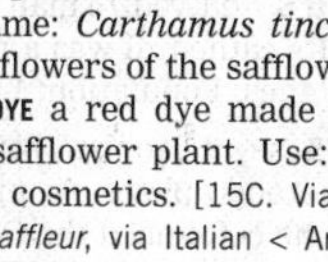

safrole

saf·role /sá frōl/ *n* a colorless or yellow poisonous oily liquid. Source: sassafras, camphor oils. Use: manufacture of perfumes and soaps. Formula: $C_{10}H_{10}O_2$. [Mid-19C. < SASSAFRAS]

~~saftey~~ incorrect spelling of **safety**

sag /sag/ *v* (**sagged, sag·ging, sags**) **1.** *vti* BEND UNDER WEIGHT to bend downward in the middle, hang, or droop instead of remaining firm or level, usually through having to support excessive weight, or make something bend in this way ○ *The skirt's hem sags in the back.* **2.** *vi* BECOME WEAKER OR LOSE INTENSITY to become weaker or lose intensity or enthusiasm **3.** *vi* FALL IN VALUE to decrease in value **4.** *vi* NAUT DRIFT LEEWARD to drift to leeward ■ *n* **1.** PLACE WHERE SOMETHING SAGS a bend, depression, or slackness in something where it has sagged **2.** DECLINE IN STRENGTH a decline in strength, intensity, or value ○ *a sag in the stock market* **3.** NAUT LEEWARD DRIFT a tendency of a boat or ship to drift to leeward [14C. < Middle Low German *sacken* "to sink"] —**sag·gy** *adj*

sa·ga /saágə/ *n* **1.** SERIES OF EVENTS a complicated series of events or personal experiences stretching over a considerable period of time, or a detailed account of such a series of events or experiences (*informal*) ○ *Have you heard the saga of our coast-to-coast relocation?* **2.** LONG NOVEL OR SERIES OF NOVELS a long story or novel, or a series of stories or novels, often following the lives of a family or community over several generations **3.** NORSE LITERARY GENRE an epic tale in Old Norse literature, usually in prose, recounting events in the lives of historical and mythological figures from medieval Iceland and Norway [Early 18C. < Old Icelandic]

CULTURAL NOTE ***The Forsyte Saga***, a series of novels (1906–22) by British writer John Galsworthy. Set in early 20th-century England, it charts the decline of traditional Victorian values in upper-middle-class society through the story of three generations of the Forsyte family. It was made into a popular television series in 1967 and again in 2002.

sa·ga·cious /sə gáyshəss/ *adj* having or based on a profound knowledge and understanding of the world combined with intelligence and good judgment [Early 17C. < Latin *sagac-* "of quick perception"] —**sa·ga·cious·ly** *adv* —**sa·ga·cious·ness** *n*

sa·gac·i·ty /sə gássətee/ *n* profound knowledge and understanding, coupled with foresight and good judgment [15C. Via French < Latin *sagacitas* < *sagac-* "of quick perception"]

sag·a·more /sággə màwr/ *n* among the Native North American Algonquian people, a subordinate chief [Early 17C. < Algonquian *sangman* "he overcomes," "chief"]

Françoise Sagan

Sa·gan /saa gaáN, -gaáN/, **Françoise** (*b.* 1935) French writer. Among her best known novels are *Bonjour Tristesse* (1954) and *A Certain Smile* (1956). Pseudonym of **Quoirez, Françoise**

> "To jealousy, nothing is more frightful than laughter."
> [Françoise Sagan, *La Chamade (Heartbeat)*; 1965]

sa·ga nov·el *n* LITERAT same as **roman-fleuve**

sage[1] /sayj/ (*literary*) *n* somebody who is regarded as knowledgeable, wise, and experienced, especially a man of advanced years revered for his wisdom and good judgment ■ *adj* having or showing great wisdom, especially that gained from long experience of life [14C. < French. < Latin *sapere* "be wise, have taste"] —**sage·ly** *adv* —**sage·ness** *n*

sage[2] /sayj/ (*plural* **sag·es** or *same*) *n* **1.** a plant or bush with aromatic grayish green leaves. Use: flavoring food. Latin name: *Salvia officinalis.* **2.** PLANTS same as **sagebrush 3.** COLORS same as **sage green** [14C. Via French *sauge* < Latin *salvia* "healing plant" < *salvus* "healthy, uninjured"] —**sage** *adj*

sage·brush /sáyj brùsh/ (*plural* **-brush·es** or *same*) *n* a bush of dry regions with silvery wedge-shaped leaves and large flower clusters. Native to: western North America. Genus: *Artemisia.*

Sage·brush Re·bel·lion *n* a populist campaign in the late 1970s waged in the western states by ranchers and farmers with mining and timber interests, who protested the imposition of more federal regulations on land management

Sage·brush State *n* a nickname for Nevada

sage green *adj* of a grayish green color, like sage leaves —**sage green** *n*

sage grouse *n* a large grouse with mottled plumage, a black belly, and a long pointed tail that it spreads during courtship. Native to: western North America. Latin name: *Centrocercus urophasianus.*

sage thrash·er *n* a grayish brown thrasher that nests in sagebrush and other low-growing desert plants. Native to: western North America. Latin name: *Oreoscoptese montanus.*

sag·gar /sággər/, **sag·ger** *n* a clay box into which delicate ceramic objects are placed to protect them in the kiln during firing. It is now seldom used. [Mid-18C. Probably contraction of SAFEGUARD]

Sa·git·ta /sə jíttə/ *n* a small prominent constellation of the northern hemisphere. See illustration at **constellation**

sag·it·tal /sájjət'l/ *adj* **1.** relating to or situated on the imaginary plane that divides a human or animal body into right and left halves **2.** resembling an arrow or an arrowhead in shape [Mid-16C. < medieval Latin *sagittalis* < Latin *sagitta* "arrow"] —**sag·it·tal·ly** *adv*

Sag·it·tar·i·us /sàjjə térree əss/ *n* **1.** CONSTELLATION IN SOUTHERN HEMISPHERE a zodiacal constellation of the southern hemisphere. See illustration at **constellation 2.** 9TH SIGN OF ZODIAC the ninth sign of the zodiac, represented by an archer and lasting from approximately November 22 to December 21. Sagittarius is classified as a fire sign and its ruling planet is Jupiter. **3.** SOMEBODY BORN UNDER SAGITTARIUS somebody whose birthday falls between November 22 and December 21 [Pre-12C. < Latin, "archer" < *sagitta* "arrow"] —**Sag·it·tar·i·an** *adj, n* —**Sag·it·tar·i·us** *adj*

sag·it·tate /sájjə tàyt/, **sag·it·ti·form** /sə jíttə fàwrm/ *adj* describes a leaf that is shaped like an arrowhead [Mid-18C. < Latin *sagitta* "arrow"]

sa·go /sáygō/ *n* a powdery substance obtained from the pith of the sago palm. Use: cooking, fabric stiffener. [Mid-16C. < Malay *sagu*]

sa·go palm *n* a tall palm tree that yields sago. Native to: Asia. Genus: *Metroxylan.*

sa·gua·ro /sə gwaárō, -waárō/ (*plural* **-ros** or *same*), **sa·hua·ro** /sə waárō/ *n* a large cactus growing up to 60 ft./18 m tall, with upward-curving branches and edible red fruit. Flowers: white, nocturnal. Native to: southwestern United States, Mexico. Latin name: *Carnegiea gigantea.* [Mid-19C. < Mexican Spanish]

Sa·gua·ro Na·tion·al Park /sə gwaárō-/ national park near Tucson in southern Arizona, established in 1994. Area: 143 sq. mi./370 sq. km.

Sa·hap·tin /sə háptin/ (*plural same* or **-tins**) *n* **1.** a member of a group of Native North American peoples who once lived in a wide area around the Columbia River and who now mainly live in its basin **2.** the language of the Sahaptin peoples, in some classifications belonging to the Penutian group of Native American languages. Native speakers: 4,000. [Mid-19C. < Salish *S?aptnx*] —**Sa·hap·tin** *adj*

Sa·hap·tin-Chi·nook *n* in some language classifications, a northern branch of the Penutian family of Native American languages consisting of Sahaptin and Chinook —**Sa·hap·tin-Chi·nook** *adj*

Sa·har·a /sə hárrə, -hérrə/ the largest desert in the world, covering much of northern Africa between the Atlantic Ocean and the Red Sea. Area: 3,500,000 sq. mi./9,100,000 sq. km. —**Sa·har·an** *adj, n*

sa·heb *n S Asia* same as **sahib**

Sa·hel /sə háyl, sá hil/ a dry zone, extending from Sudan in the east to Senegal in the west, and separating the Sahara from the tropical regions of western and central Africa

sa·hib /saá ìb, -eeb, -hìb/, **sa·heb** /saab, saá heb/ *n S Asia* a respectful form of address for men, formerly widely used to address white men during the colonial period. The term is also used as a title, placed after the man's name. [Late 17C. Via Urdu and Persian < Arabic *ṣāḥib* "friend, lord"]

sa·hit·ya /saa híttyə/ *n S Asia* **1.** literature **2.** song lyrics, especially for songs in Hindi movies [Mid-20C. < Sanskrit *sāhitya* "composition"]

Sahl /saal/, **Mort** (*b.* 1927) Canadian-born US comedian. He was known for his satirical monologues based on current events.

sa·hua·ro *n* PLANTS same as **saguaro**

said[1] /sed/ *v* past participle, past tense of **say** ■ *adj* previously named or mentioned ○ *The said car was later found abandoned.* ○ *discovered the said car*

sa·id[2] *n* ISLAM another spelling of **sayyid**

sai·ga /sīgə/ (*plural* **-gas** or *same*) *n* an antelope with a thick tawny coat and enlarged snout. Native to: steppes of Central Asia. Genus: *Saiga*. [Early 19C. < Russian]

Sai·gon /sī gón/ former name for **Ho Chi Minh City** (until 1975)

sail /sayl/ *n* **1.** FABRIC CATCHING WIND ON BOAT a large piece of strong fabric, usually triangular or rectangular in shape, fixed by rigging, masts, and booms to catch the wind and propel a vessel forward **2.** JOURNEY IN VESSEL a trip in a boat or ship, especially a sailing vessel ○ *a pleasant sail across the bay* **3.** SAILS OF VESSEL the sails of a boat or ship considered collectively ○ *a ship under full sail* **4.** SAILING SHIPS COLLECTIVELY ships and boats with sails considered collectively or as a means of transport ○ *Steam gives way to sail.* **5.** THING OR PART RESEMBLING SAIL something that resembles a sail of a boat or ship in form, function, or position **6.** BLADE OF WINDMILL a long flat structure on the outside of a windmill that is designed to be turned by the wind in order to drive machinery **7.** PART OF SUBMARINE the conning tower of a submarine **8.** (*plural same*) VESSEL WITH SAILS a boat or ship with sails (*archaic*) ○ *a fleet of 200 sail* ■ *v* (**sailed, sail·ing, sails**) **1.** *vti* GO BY VESSEL ON WATER to be transported in a boat or ship across a stretch of water ○ *We sailed to Shanghai on a large cruise ship.* **2.** *vti* MOVE ON WATER to move across the surface of water, or across a particular stretch of water, driven by wind or engine power ○ *pirate ships that sailed the high seas* **3.** *vt* DRIVE BOAT OR SHIP to control the movement of a boat or ship, especially one with sails ○ *She sailed the boat into the harbor.* **4.** *vi* BEGIN SEA JOURNEY to depart in a boat or ship, or to leave a harbor, mooring, or anchorage ○ *The ferry sails at noon.* **5.** *vi* MOVE SMOOTHLY to move smoothly or swiftly and usually in a graceful way ○ *The ball sailed over the fence.* [Old English *segl* < Germanic] —**sail·a·ble** *adj* ◇ **set sail** to depart in a boat or ship, or to leave a harbor, mooring, or anchorage ◇ **under sail** with sails hoisted, and not propelled by an engine

SPELLCHECK sail or **sale**? Do not confuse the spelling of ***sail*** and ***sale***, which sound similar. A ***sail*** is something that catches the wind, as in *the sails of a boat, the sails of a windmill.* ***Sail*** is also used as a verb, meaning "be transported by a boat or ship" or "move smoothly and swiftly," as in *sailing down the river, sailing through the air.* The word ***sale*** is only used as a noun, referring to the selling of goods or services, as in *houses for sale, a sale of secondhand books, the sales manager of the company.*

sail into *vt* (*informal*) **1.** to make a violent physical or verbal attack on somebody ○ *She sailed into me for forgetting to mail the letter.* **2.** to start to do something with vigor and enthusiasm ○ *He sailed into the task of redesigning the building.*

sail through *vti* to do something, especially to pass a test, with ease ○ *He sailed through the exam.*

sail·board /sáyl bàwrd/ *n* a large surfboard with a keel and a mast and a sail mounted on it that is operated by one person standing up ■ *vi* to ride on a sailboard —**sail·board·er** *n* —**sail·board·ing** *n*

sail·boat /sáyl bōt/ *n* a boat with one or more masts and sails that is propelled by the wind, chiefly used for sport and leisure. Larger sailboats often have an engine as well.

sail·cloth /sáyl klàwth, -klòth/ *n* **1.** any strong fabric used to make sails, originally a heavy cotton canvas **2.** a lightweight cotton fabric with a texture like that of canvas. Use: clothes.

sail·er /sáylər/ *n* a boat or ship, especially a sailing vessel, that has particular sailing characteristics

sail·fish /sáyl fish/ (*plural same* or **-fish·es**) *n* a warm-water ocean fish with a large high dorsal fin resembling a sail and an elongated upper jaw that projects forward like a spear. Genus: *Istiophorus*.

sail·ing /sáyling/ *n* **1.** TRAVELING IN VESSEL WITH SAILS the sport, leisure activity, or occupation of traveling in or operating a boat or ship propelled by sails **2.** SKILL OF OPERATING VESSEL the art or a method of controlling a boat or ship, especially one with sails ○ *Expert sailing is required in such conditions.* **3.** SHIP'S DEPARTURE OR DEPARTURE TIME the departure of a ship, or the time at which a ship is scheduled to leave port ○ *The next sailing is at noon.*

sail·ing boat *n UK* same as **sailboat**

sail·ing ship *n* a ship with masts and sails that is propelled by the wind, formerly used for transporting passengers and goods

sail·or /sáylər/ *n* **1.** somebody who works aboard a boat or ship, especially a low-ranking member of the crew of a merchant or naval ship **2.** somebody who frequently sails or travels on a boat or ship, especially with reference to his or her susceptibility to seasickness ○ *I'm not a good sailor.*

sail·or col·lar *n* a collar that is V-shaped in front and has a broad square shape at the back, traditionally worn by sailors

sail·or hat *n* a hat with a flat top, a low crown, and wide brim that is either straight or rolled upward all around

sail·or's-choice *n* a small fish such as the pinfish or pigfish. Native to: North American Atlantic coast.

sail·or suit *n* an outfit for children resembling the traditional sailor uniform, consisting of a top with a sailor collar and pants or a skirt, usually in dark blue and white

sail·plane /sáyl plàyn/ *n* a light glider particularly well adapted to making use of rising air currents, used for soaring ■ *vi* (**-planed, -plan·ing, -planes**) to travel in a sailplane —**sail·plan·er** *n*

Sai·maa, Lake /sī maa/ lake in southeastern Finland. Area: 500 sq. mi./1,300 sq. km.

sain·foin /sáyn fòyn/ (*plural* **-foins** or *same*) *n* a forage plant with feathery leaves. Flowers: pink, in clusters. Native to: Europe, Asia. Latin name: *Onobrychis viciifolia*. [Early 17C. Via obsolete French < modern Latin *sanctum foenum* "holy hay," alteration of *sanum foenum* "wholesome hay"]

saint /saynt/; *often in French names* /saN/ *n* **1.** SOMEBODY HONORED BY CHURCH AFTER DEATH a member of a religion who after death is formally designated as having led a life of exceptional holiness **2.** SOMEBODY IN HEAVEN somebody who goes to heaven after death **3.** VIRTUOUS PERSON a particularly good or holy person, or one who is exceptionally kind and patient in dealing with difficult people or situations ■ *vt* (**saint·ed, saint·ing, saints**) RECOGNIZE SOMEBODY AS SAINT to declare somebody officially to be a saint of a Christian church [Pre-12C. < Latin *sanctus* "holy," past participle of *sancire* "confirm, consecrate"] —**saint·dom** *n*

St Ag·nes's Eve /-ágnəssəz-/ *n* the eve of St. Agnes's Day, on which, according to British folklore, people dream of their future partners if they have performed special rituals before going to sleep. Date: January 20.

St. Al·bans /-áwlbənz/ city in Hertfordshire, southeastern England. Nearby are the ruins of the Roman town of Verulamium. Population: 129,005 (2001).

St. An·drews /-ándrooz/ university city in Fife, Scotland. It is famous for its historic connections with the game of golf. Population: 69,181 (1991).

St. An·drew's cross /-àn drooz-/ *n* a diagonal cross with arms of equal length, especially a white one on a blue background, as on the flags of St. Andrew and Scotland.

St. An·tho·ny's cross *n* same as **tau cross**

St. Au·gus·tine /saynt áwgə steen/ city and tourist resort in northeastern Florida, on the Matanzas and San Sebastian rivers, near the Atlantic coast. Population: 11,795 (2002 estimate).

St. Bar·thol·o·mew's Day Mas·sa·cre /-baar thòllə myooz-/ *n* a massacre of Huguenots that began in Paris on St. Bartholomew's Day, August 24, 1572.

St. Ber·nard /-bər naárd/ *n* a very large working dog belonging to a breed developed in Switzerland to rescue lost mountain travelers [Mid-19C. After the Hospice of the Great ST. BERNARD PASS]

St. Ber·nard Pass either of two mountain passes running between Italy and Switzerland

St. Cath·a·rines /-káthərənz/ city in Ontario, Canada, on the Welland Canal, across Lake Ontario from Toronto. Population: 299,935 (2001).

St. Charles /-chaárlz/ city in eastern Missouri, on the Missouri River, near its confluence with the Mississippi River. It is a suburb of St. Louis. Population: 60,755 (2002 estimate).

St. Clair, Lake /-klér/ lake in central North America, on the border between Michigan and Ontario. Area: 430 sq. mi./1,114 sq. km.

St. Clair Shores /-klèr-/ city in southeastern Michigan, on Lake St. Clair, near Detroit. Population: 62,737 (2002 estimate).

St. Cloud /-klówd/ city in central Minnesota, on the Mississippi and Sauk rivers. Since 1870, it has been an important center for quarrying and polishing granite. Population: 59,752 (2002 estimate).

St. Croix /-króy/ largest island of the US Virgin Islands. Population: 50,139 (1990). Area: 80 sq. mi./207 sq. km.

St. Da·vid's /-dáyvədz/ small city in Pembrokeshire, Wales. Its cathedral was a pilgrimage center in the Middle Ages. Population: 1,589 (1999).

St. Den·is /saynt dénniss/, **Ruth** (1878–1968) US dancer and choreographer. A pioneer of 20th-century dance, she cofounded the Denishawn Dance School (1915) with her husband, Ted Shawn. Born **Dennis, Ruth**

St.-De·nis /saN də neé/ city in north central France, in Seine-St-Denis Department, on the Seine River. It is a northern suburb of Paris. Population: 85,832 (1999).

saint·ed /sáyntəd/ *adj* **1.** RECOGNIZED AS SAINT officially declared to be a saint of a Christian church **2.** IN HEAVEN dead and thought to be in heaven **3.** VIRTUOUS exceptionally good, virtuous, or holy (*literary*)

Sainte-Foy /saynt fóy, sant fwaá/ city in the southern part of the province of Quebec, Canada, located on the St. Lawrence and Cap-Rouge rivers. Population: 72,547 (2001).

St. E·li·as, Mount /-ə lī əss/ second highest mountain in Canada, on the Alaska-Yukon Territory border, in the St Elias Range. Height: 18,008 ft./5,489 m.

St. El·mo's fire /-élmōz-/ *n* a luminous region of electrical discharge that appears during stormy weather around a narrow pointed object such as a church spire or the mast of a ship [Early 19C. After *St. Elmo* (d. A.D. 303), patron saint of sailors]

St-É·mil·ion /sàN tay meélyən/ *n* a prestigious red wine from the Bordeaux region of southwestern France

St.-É·tienne /sàN tay tyén/ city and administrative center of Loire Department, Rhône-Alpes Region, east central France. Population: 180,210 (1999).

Saint-Ex·u·pé·ry /sàN teg zoo pay reé/, **Antoine** (1900–44) French aviator and writer. He wrote novels, essays and autobiographical works, but is chiefly remembered for his much-loved children's story, *The Little Prince* (1943). Full name **Saint-Exupéry, Antoine Marie Roger de**

> "Although human life is precious, we always act as if something had an even greater price than life... But what is that something?"
> [Antoine Saint-Exupéry, *Vol de Nuit (Night Flight)*, 1931]

St. Fran·cis river rising in southeastern Missouri and flowing south through Arkansas to join the Mississippi River. Length: 425 mi./684 km.

St. Gal·len /-gaálən/, **St. Gall** /-gáwl/ capital of St. Gallen Canton, northeastern Switzerland, situated about 40 mi./64 km east of Zurich. Population: 69,747 (1998).

Saint-Gau·dens /saynt gáwd'nz/, **Augustus** (1848–1907) Irish-born US sculptor. His works, mostly in bronze, include various US public monuments such as the Shaw Memorial in Boston, Massachusetts (1897) and *Grief* in Washington, D.C. (1891).

St. Geor·ge's capital, main port, and tourist center of Grenada, in the southwest of the island. Population: 30,000 (1994).

St. Geor·ge's Chan·nel sea passage between southeastern Ireland and southwestern Wales

St. Geor·ge's cross /-jàwrjəz-/ *n* a red cross on a white background, as on the flags of St. George and England.

St. Gott·hard Pass /-góttərd-/ pass through the central Alps between southern Switzerland and Italy. Length: 16 mi./26 km.

St. He·le·na /-hə léenə/ volcanic island in the South Atlantic Ocean off the western coast of Angola. It was the site of Napoleon's death in exile in 1821 and became a British dependency in 1834. Language: English. Capital: Jamestown. Population: 7,367 (2003). Area: 47 sq. mi./122 sq. km.

St. Hel·ens, Mount /-héllənz/ active volcano in southwestern Washington State, in the Cascade Range. Its last major eruption was in 1980. Height: 8,365 ft./2,550 m.

St. He·li·er /-héllee ər/ port and chief town of Jersey, in the Channel Islands. Population: 27,083 (1991).

saint·hood /sáynt hòod/ *n* **1.** the condition or status of being a saint or saintly **2.** saints regarded as a group

St. John /-jón/ **1.** river in east central North America. It rises in northwestern Maine, flows northeastward into New Brunswick, and empties into the Atlantic Ocean. It forms part of the border between the United States and Canada. Length: 418 mi./673 km. **2.** largest city and principal port of New Brunswick, Canada, situated on the Bay of Fundy. Population: 72,494 (1996).

St. John, Lake /-jón/ lake in south central Quebec Province, Canada. It drains into the St. Lawrence River via the Saguenay River. Area: 414 sq. mi./1,070 sq. km.

St. Johns /-jónz/ river flowing in eastern Florida to Jacksonville, emptying into the Atlantic Ocean. Length: 285 mi./459 km.

St. John's /-jónz/ **1.** capital city and principal port of Newfoundland, Canada, situated on the Atlantic Ocean. Population: 122,709 (2001). **2.** capital of Antigua and Barbuda. It is situated in the northwestern part of Antigua, on an inlet of the Caribbean Sea. Population: 25,000 (1999).

St. John's bread *n* FOOD same as **carob** (sense 2)

St. John's day *n* CALENDAR same as **Midsummer Day**

St. John's-wort /-jónz wùrt, -wàwrt/ *n* an herb or bush with five-petaled yellow flowers. Genus: *Hypericum.* [Because it is said to flower on the feast of St. JOHN the Baptist]

St. Jo·seph /-jṓzəf, -jṓssəf/ city in Buchanan County, northwestern Missouri, on the Missouri River. Population: 73,148 (2002 estimate).

St. Kil·da /-kíldə/ group of small, now uninhabited islands in the Outer Hebrides, Scotland. They are home to a seabird sanctuary and a National Nature Reserve.

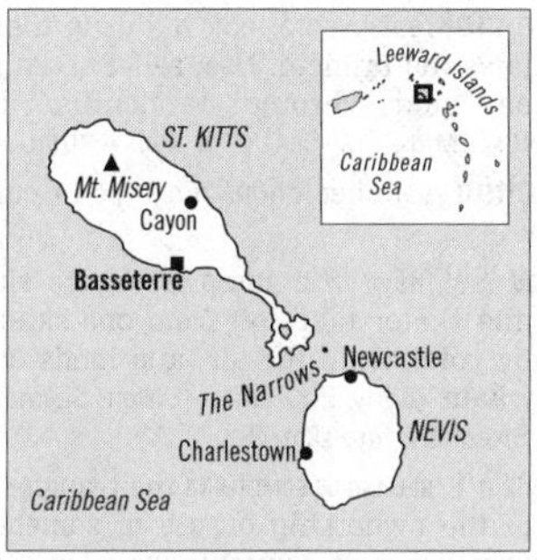

St. Kitts and Nevis

St. Kitts and Ne·vis /-kìts ənd néeviss/ independent state in the Caribbean, comprising two islands that are part of the Leeward Islands group. It became an independent member of the British Commonwealth in 1983. Capital: Basseterre. Population: 38,763 (2003). Area: 104 sq. mi./269 sq. km. Official name **Federation of St. Kitts and Nevis**

St. Lau·rent /sàN law ráaN/, **Louis** (1882–1973) prime minister of Canada (1948–57). A prominent member of the Liberal Party of Canada, he was instrumental in establishing the United Nations before becoming prime minister. See table at **prime minister**. Full name **St Laurent, Louis Stephen**

Saint-Lau·rent /sànt law rént, sàN law ráaN/ city in le-de-Montreal County, in southern Quebec Province, Canada, on Montreal Island. Population: 77,391 (2002).

St. Law·rence /saynt láwrənss/ river in southeastern Canada, flowing northeastward from Lake Ontario into the Gulf of St. Lawrence. Length: 800 mi./1,300 km.

St. Law·rence, Gulf of deep inlet of the Atlantic Ocean between Newfoundland and the Canadian mainland. Area: 100,000 sq. mi./259,000 sq. km.

St. Law·rence Is·lands Na·tion·al Park national park in Ontario, Canada, incorporating part of the shore of the St. Lawrence River and 13 of the Thousand Islands. Area: 3.09 sq. mi./8 sq. km.

St. Law·rence Sea·way system of canals bypassing unnavigable sections of the St. Lawrence River and allowing oceangoing vessels to reach the Great Lakes, sometimes also including the canals between the Great Lakes.

Saint-Lé·o·nard /saynt lénnərd, sàN lay ō náar/ city in le-de-Montreal County, in southern Quebec Province, Canada, on Montreal Island. Population: 69,604 (2001).

St.-Lô /saN lṓ/ town and administrative center of Manche Department, Basse-Normandie Region, northwestern France. Population: 20,090 (1999).

St. Lou·is /-lòo iss/ city in eastern Missouri, extending along the western bank of the Mississippi River. It is one of the principal industrial and cultural centers of the Midwest. Population: 338,353 (2002 estimate).

St.-Lou·is /sàN loo ée/ city and port in northwestern Senegal, situated 110 mi./177 km northeast of Dakar. Population: 132,499 (1994).

St. Lou·is en·ceph·a·li·tis /-lòo iss-/ *n* a viral inflammation of the brain, found in parts of North America and transmitted by mosquitoes [Mid-20C. After ST. LOUIS, Missouri]

St. Lou·is Park city in southeastern Minnesota, on Minnehaha Creek. It is a residential and industrial suburb of Minneapolis. Population: 44,123 (2002 estimate).

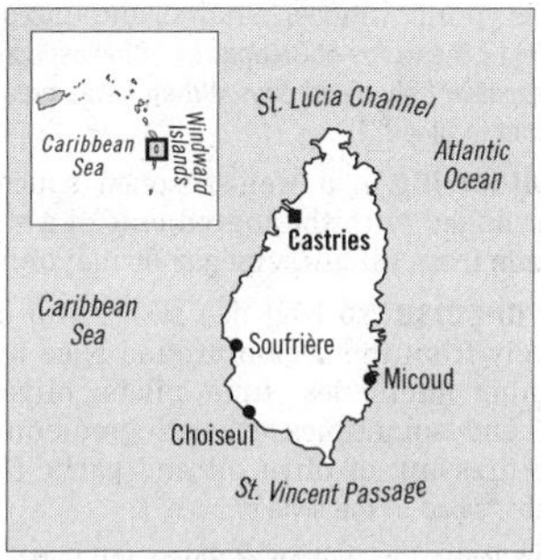

St. Lucia

St. Lu·cia /saynt lóoshə/ independent island state in the Caribbean, one of the Windward Islands. It became an independent member of the British Commonwealth in 1979. Capital: Castries. Population: 162,157 (2003). Area: 238 sq. mi./616 sq. km.

saint·ly /sáyntlee/ (**-li·er, -li·est**) *adj* **1.** characteristic of or associated with a saint of a Christian church **2.** very good, virtuous, or holy —**saint·li·ness** *n*

St. Mar·tin /-máart'n/ one of the Leeward Islands, divided between a dependency of Guadeloupe in the north and part of the Netherlands Antilles in the south. Area: 20 sq. mi./52 sq. km. Population: 65,774 (1994).

St. Mar·ys /-mérreez/ **1.** river rising in the Okefenokee Swamp in the US state of Georgia, winding eastward into the Atlantic Ocean. Length: 175 mi./282 km. **2.** river in North America connecting Lake Superior with Lake Huron, forming part of the border between the United States and Canada. Length: 63 mi./101 km.

St. Mat·thews /-máth yooz/ town in northern Kentucky, south of the Illinois border. It is an eastern suburb of Louisville. Population: 17,414 (2002 estimate).

St. Mo·ritz /sàN mə ríts/ spa town in southeastern Switzerland, situated 9 mi./14 km from the Italian border. Population: 5,600 (1994).

St.-Na·zaire /sàN na zér/ city and port in Loire-Atlantique Department, Pays de la Loire Region, western France. Population: 65,874 (1999).

St. Pat·rick's Day /-páttriks-/ *n* the day commemorating St. Patrick, the patron saint of Ireland. Date: March 17.

St. Paul /-páwl/ capital city of Minnesota, in the southeastern part of the state on the banks of the Mississippi River, and near Minneapolis. Population: 284,037 (2002 estimate).

saint·pau·lia /sàynt páwlyə/ (*plural* **-lias** or *same*) *n UK* PLANTS same as **African violet** [Late 19C. After Baron Walter von *Saint-Paul* (1860–1910), German explorer]

St. Paul's Ca·the·dral /-pàwlz-/ *n* a large domed baroque cathedral in the City of London, England

St. Pe·ter's /-péetərz/ *n* a large baroque basilica in the Vatican City, Rome, Italy

St. Pe·ters·burg /-péetərz bùrg/ **1.** second largest city in Russia, located in the northwestern part of the country. Situated at the head of the Gulf of Finland, an arm of the Baltic Sea, it is also the country's largest port. It was the capital of Russia from 1712 until 1918. Population: 4,695,400 (1999). Former name **Petrograd** (1914–24), **Leningrad** (1924–90) **2.** city in western Florida, located on Pinellas Peninsula between Tampa Bay and the Gulf of Mexico. Population: 248,546 (2002 estimate).

St.-Pi·erre /-pee ér/ town and tourist center on Martinique Island in the eastern Caribbean, near the base of the volcano Montagne Pelée. Population: 4,453 (1999).

St.-Pi·erre and Mi·que·lon /san péer ən méekə lòn, saN pyèr ən mée klòN/ overseas territory of France, in the North Atlantic Ocean, off the coast of Newfoundland, Canada. It consists of two small groups of islands. The capital is St. Pierre on the island with that name. The islands' proximity to the Grand Banks makes them a base for fishing vessels. Population: 6,976 (2003). Area: 93 sq. mi./242 sq. km.

Saint-Saëns /saN sáaNss/, **Camille** (1835–1921) French composer. His works, including symphonies, church music, concertos, songs, and operas, are in the classical French tradition. Full name **Saint-Saëns, Charles Camille**

saint's day *n* a day of the year on which a specific saint is remembered or honored. Some saint's days are marked by traditional festivities or associated with popular superstitions.

St. Si·mons Is·land /-sīmənz-/ island in the Atlantic Ocean off southeastern Georgia, in the United States. It is home to Fort Frederica, a national monument that commemorates the Battle of Bloody Marsh in 1742, when a colonial force led by James Oglethorpe successfully repelled a Spanish attack. Area: 36 sq. mi./93 sq. km.

St. Thom·as /-tómməss/ island of the US Virgin Islands. Population: 48,166 (1990). Area: 28 sq. mi./73 sq. km.

St.-Tro·pez /sàN trō páy/ resort town on the Mediterranean coast, southern France. It is situated 60 mi./155 km east of Marseille. Population: 5,444 (1999).

St. Val·en·tine's Day /saynt vállən tīnz-/ *n* CALENDAR same as **Valentine's Day**

St. Vin·cent, Cape /saynt vínsənt/ cape at the most southwesterly point of Portugal

St. Vin·cent, Gulf of gulf in southern Australia, located between the Yorke and Fleurieu peninsulas

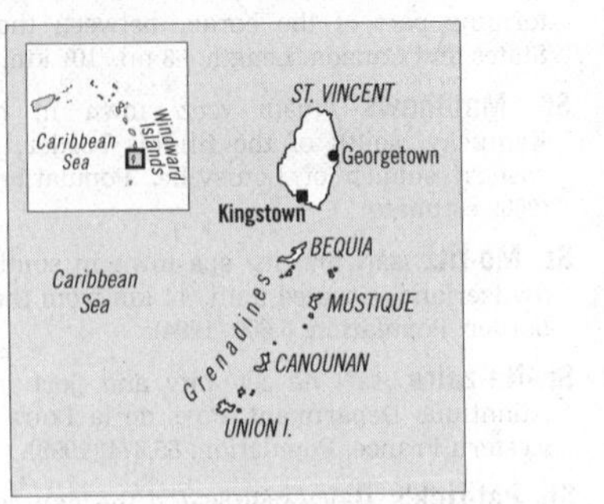

St. Vincent and the Grenadines

St. Vin·cent and the Gren·a·dines /-vìnsənt ənd t͟hə grènnə deénz/ independent state in the Caribbean comprising the island of St. Vincent and 32 of the islands of the Grenadine group. It became an independent member of the British Commonwealth in 1979. Capital: Kingstown. Population: 116,812 (2003). Area: 150 sq. mi./389 sq. km.

St. Vi·tus·'s dance /-vītəssəz-/ *n* former name for **Sydenham's chorea** (*not in technical use*) [Early 17C. After *St. Vitus* (3C), patron saint of those affected by this condition]

Sai·pan /sī pán, -paán/ largest island, seat of government, and main port of the Northern Mariana Islands, in the western Pacific Ocean. Capital: Tanapeg. Population: 38,896 (1990). Area: 47 sq. mi./122 sq. km.

Sai·va /sívə/ *n* a member of a Hindu religious group that worships Shiva [Late 18C. < Sanskrit *śaiva-* "sacred to Shiva"] —**Sai·va** *adj* —**Sai·vism** *n* —**Sai·vite** *n*

sa·kai /saá kī/ *n* a member of an aboriginal people who live in the forests of Malaysia [Mid-19C. < Malay, "dependent, subject"]

Sa·kai /saá kī/ southern suburb of Osaka, situated on Osaka bay in Osaka Prefecture, on western Honshu, Japan. Population: 787,833 (2002).

sake[1] /sayk/ *n* **1.** the good, benefit, or welfare of somebody or something ○ *I hope you're right, for all our sakes!* **2.** the purpose of doing, obtaining, achieving, or maintaining something ○ *It's not worth risking your life for the sake of getting there a few minutes earlier.* [Old English *sacu* < Germanic, "seeking," hence "accusation, cause"]

sa·ke[2] /saákee/, **sa·ki** *n* a Japanese alcoholic beverage made from fermented rice and usually served warm [Late 17C. < Japanese]

sa·ker /sáykər/ *n* a large falcon with brown feathers on its body and a pale-colored head, used in falconry. Native to: central Asia, eastern Europe. Latin name: *Falco cherrug.* [15C. Via French < Arabic *ṣakr* "hawk, falcon"]

Sa·kha·lin /sàkə leén, sàk͟hə lyeén/ island off eastern Russia, lying in the Sea of Okhotsk north of the Japanese island of Hokkaido. Area: 29,500 sq. mi./76,400 sq. km. Population: 660,000 (1983).

Sa·kha·rov /saákə ràwf/, **Andrei** (1921–89) Soviet physicist and political dissident. His research led to the development of the Soviet hydrogen bomb, but he became a spokesman for civil liberties and international disarmament, and was exiled to Gorky (1980). He was awarded the Nobel Peace Prize (1975). Full name **Sakharov, Andrei Dmitriyevich**

sa·ki *n* BEVERAGES another spelling of **sake**[2]

Sak·ka·ra /sə kaárə/ village near Cairo, Egypt. It is the site of a stepped pyramid built by King Zoser between 2737 and 2717 B.C., the first monumental royal tomb, and one of the oldest stone structures in Egypt.

Sak·ta /shaáktə/, **Shak·ta** *n* a member of a Hindu religious group who particularly worship the female principle or the female gods [Early 19C. < Sanskrit *śākta* (see SAKTI)]

Sak·ti /saáktee/, **Shak·ti** /shúktə, shaáktee/ *n* in Hinduism, the vital generative and creative principle at work in the universe, typically associated with the feminine component of the divine, often embodied as a goddess [Early 19C. < Sanskrit *śaktiḥ* "power" < *śak-* "be strong"]

Sak·ya·mu·ni /saákyə moónee/ *n* one of the names of the Buddha, deriving from Sakya, the name of his clan

sal /sal/ *n* in pharmacy, salt (*usually used in combination*) ○ *sal ammoniac* [14C. < Latin]

sa·laam /sə laám/ *n* **1.** DEEP BOW WITH HAND ON FOREHEAD a deeply respectful or deferential gesture of greeting or acknowledgment, used especially in Islamic countries, made by bowing low with the palm of the right hand against the forehead **2.** RESPECTFUL GREETING the word "salaam," meaning "peace," used as a respectful greeting ■ *vti* (**-laamed, -laam·ing, -laams**) MAKE SALUTATION OF GREETING OR RESPECT to perform a salaam, or greet somebody with a salaam [Early 17C. < Arabic *salām* "peace"]

sal·a·ble /sáyləb'l/, **sale·a·ble** *adj* suitable for selling or capable of being sold —**sal·a·bil·i·ty** /sàylə bíllətee/ *n* —**sal·a·ble·ness** *n* —**sal·a·bly** *adv*

sa·la·cious /sə láyshəss/ *adj* **1.** intended to titillate or arouse people sexually, usually by having an explicit erotic content **2.** having or showing explicit or crude sexual desire or interest [Mid-17C. < Latin *salac-* < *salire* "to leap"] —**sa·la·cious·ly** *adv* —**sa·la·cious·ness** *n*

sal·ad /sálləd/ *n* **1.** MIXTURE OF RAW VEGETABLES a cold dish consisting mainly of a mixture of raw vegetables, whole, sliced, chopped, or in pieces, usually served with a dressing for flavor. Many other ingredients may be incorporated into a salad, which can be served as a separate course or as an accompaniment to other food. **2.** DISH OF COLD INGREDIENTS a cold dish consisting of a particular type of food such as a single vegetable or a selection of fruit, cut into pieces or slices, and served usually with a dressing ○ *potato salad* **3.** LEAFY VEGETABLES any leafy vegetable commonly used to make a green salad, typically the many types of lettuce, watercress, chicory, and endive **4.** CONFUSED MIXTURE a confused or varied mixture ○ *a salad of ideas* [14C. < French *salade* < Latin *sal* "salt"]

sal·ad bar *n* a counter in a restaurant or grocery store where salads of various types are available, set up as a buffet where customers can choose their own ingredients

sal·ad bird *n regional* same as **goldfinch** [Because it feeds on lettuce seeds]

sal·ad days *npl* the period of a person's life when he or she is young, innocent, naive, and inexperienced (*literary*) [< the words of Cleopatra in Shakespeare's *Antony and Cleopatra*: "My salad days, When I was green in judgment, cold in blood"]

sal·ad dress·ing *n* a well-seasoned sauce poured over or mixed with the ingredients of a salad, e.g., one made from oil and vinegar or mayonnaise

sal·ade ni·çoise /sə laád nee swaáz/ *n* a cold dish originally from the region around Nice in France, containing anchovies, tuna fillets, olives, green beans, and sometimes other ingredients, served with a dressing of olive oil and garlic [Early 20C. < French, "salad in the style of Nice"]

Sal·a·din /sállədin/, **sultan of Egypt and Syria** (1138–93) During his sultanate (1174–93), he led the Muslims successfully against the Christian crusaders in Palestine until he was defeated and captured at Acre (1191). Full name **Salah ad-din Yussuf ibn Ayub**

sal·ad spin·ner *n* a kitchen utensil for draining washed greens consisting of a perforated basket able to revolve inside a circular container. The basket is turned by a handle, and the water forced out through the perforations.

Sa·laf·ism /sə laáfizzəm/ *n* an Islamic movement associated with Wahhabism that in its radical form emphasizes strict interpretation of religious texts and opposition to non-Islamic influences [Early 20C. < Arabic *as-salaf as-salah* "pious forebears"] —**Sa·laf·ist** *n, adj*

sa·lal /sə lál/ (*plural* **sal·als** or **sal·al**) *n* an evergreen bush with leathery leaves and edible purple berries. Flowers: pink or white, in clusters. Native to: coast of western North America. Latin name: *Gaultheria shallon.* [Early 19C. < Chinook Jargon *sallal*]

Sa·lam /saa laám/, **Abdus** (1926–96) Pakistani physicist. He was noted for his study of the interactions of elementary particles, in particular his formulation of the electroweak theory. He shared the Nobel Prize in physics (1979).

Sal·a·man·ca /sàllə mángkə/ city in the autonomous region of Castile-León, west central Spain. It is the site of the University of Salamanca, founded in 1218. Population: 156,006 (2002).

salamander

sal·a·man·der /sállə màndər/ *n* **1.** SMALL ANIMAL RESEMBLING LIZARD an amphibian that resembles a lizard but has porous moist skin instead of scales, and that lives in water as a larva and on land as an adult. Order: Caudata. **2.** MYTHICAL REPTILE LIVING IN FIRE a mythical lizard that can live in fire **3.** PORTABLE STOVE a stove that is used on construction projects to heat or dry out buildings or to thaw frozen water pipes [14C. Directly or via French < Latin *salamandra* < Greek] —**sal·a·man·drine** /sàllə mándrin, sállə màndrin/ *adj*

sa·la·mi /sə laámee/ *n* a large, thick, highly seasoned, and often cured type of sausage, Italian in origin and usually served cold in thin slices [Mid-19C. < Italian, plural of *salame* < Latin *sal* "salt"]

Sal·a·mis /sálləmiss/ island in eastern Greece 8 mi./13 km west of the port of Piraeus. It was the location of a major sea battle in 480 B.C. in which the Greeks defeated the Persians. Population: 28,574 (1981). Area: 40 sq. mi./104 sq. km.

sal am·mo·ni·ac /sàl ə mṓnee àk/ *n* CHEM same as **ammonium chloride** [< Latin *sal ammoniacus* (see AMMONIA)]

sal·a·ry /sálləree/ (*plural* **-ries**) *n* a fixed annual sum, paid at regular intervals, usually monthly, to an employee, especially for professional or clerical work [13C. Directly or via French < Latin *salarium* "money given to a Roman soldier to buy salt" < *sal* "salt"] —**sal·a·ried** *adj*

SYNONYMS See ***wage.***

sa·la·ry·man /sálləree màn/ (*plural* **-men** /-mèn/) *n* in Japan, a loyal and unambitious employee of a large corporation

sal·bu·ta·mol /sal byoótə mòl/ *n* a drug that relaxes and dilates the bronchi. Use: relief of asthma, emphysema, and chronic bronchitis. Formula: $C_{13}H_{21}NO_3$. [Mid-20C. < SALICYLIC ACID + BUTYL + AMINE]

sal·chi·chón /sàl chee chón/ *n* a type of cured pork sausage

sal·chow /sál kòw/ *n* a jump in figure skating in which the skater takes off from one skate, does a complete rotation in the air, and lands on the opposite skate [Early 20C. After Ulrich *Salchow* (1877–1949), Swedish figure skater]

sale /sayl/ *n* **1.** SELLING OF SOMETHING the transfer of something to the ownership or use of somebody else, or the provision of something, e.g., a service, in exchange for an agreed amount of money ○ *The sale of alcohol to children is illegal.* **2.** OPPORTUNITY TO BUY GOODS AT DISCOUNT a period of time when a store sells goods at reduced prices, often in order to clear its stock ○ *We always look for bargains at the after-Christmas sales.* **3.** OPPORTUNITY TO BUY SECONDHAND GOODS an event at which personal possessions or other secondhand items are sold, usually at low prices, sometimes to raise money for a charitable or other cause **4.** AUCTION an event at which goods are sold to the highest bidder **5.** AMOUNT SOLD OR RATE OF SELLING a quantity of things sold, or the rate at which they are sold ○ *disappointed by the slow sale of the new model* **6.** MARKET OR DEMAND demand that creates an opportunity to sell something ○ *found no sale for the goods at that price* ■ **sales** *npl* (*often used before a noun*) **1.** DEPARTMENT SELLING THINGS the department of a company involved with selling its products or services ○ *sales manager* **2.** THINGS SOLD the total number or value of items sold ○ *Sales fell by 10 percent last month.* [Pre-12C. < Old Norse *sala* < Germanic] ◇ **for sale** available for purchase ◇ **on sale** available for purchase, especially at a reduced price

SPELLCHECK See *sail.*

Sa·lé /saa láy/ city on the Atlantic coast of Morocco. Population: 289,391 (1982).

sale·a·ble *adj* another spelling of **salable**

sale and lease·back *n* the sale of an asset that the vendor rents back from the buyer immediately after the sale, thereby raising cash and allowing a tax deduction

Sa·leh /saa lékh/, **Ali Abdullah** (*b.* 1942) Yemeni soldier and politician. He became president of the Yemen Arab Republic, or North Yemen, in 1978 and in 1990 unified the country with the People's Democratic Republic of Yemen, or South Yemen, as the Republic of Yemen.

Sa·lem /sáyləm/ **1.** city in northeastern Massachusetts, on Massachusetts Bay, northeast of Boston. It was the site of witchcraft trials and executions in 1692. Population: 42,149 (2002 estimate). **2.** capital city of Oregon, on the Willamette River, in the northwest of the state. Population: 140,977 (2002 estimate).

sal·ep /sálləp/ *n* a starchy powder produced from ground dried tubers of various orchids. Use: food thickener. [Mid-18C. Via French < Turkish *sālep*, < Arabic *ta'lab*, shortening of *kuṣat-ta'lab* "orchid," literally "fox's testicles"]

Sa·ler·no /sə lúrnō/ capital city and port in Salerno Province, Campania Region, southern Italy. Population: 138,188 (2001).

sale·room /sáyl ro͝om, -ro͞om/ *n UK* same as **salesroom** (sense 2)

~~**salery**~~ incorrect spelling of **salary**

sales check *n* same as **sales slip**

sales·clerk /sáylz klùrk/ *n* somebody who is employed to assist and sell goods to customers in a retail store

sales force *n* the body of salespeople employed by a company to sell its goods and services

Sa·le·sian /sə lée̱zh'n/ *n* a member of the Roman Catholic order of St. Francis de Sales founded in Turin, Italy, in 1845 and dedicated to educational and missionary work. [Mid-19C. < French *salésien* < St. Francis de Sales] —**Sa·le·sian** *adj*

sales·man /sáylzmən/ (*plural* **-men** /-mən/) *n* a man who sells goods or services, either in a store or by contacting potential customers

CULTURAL NOTE ***Death of a Salesman,*** a play (1949) by Arthur Miller. The tragic story of Willy Loman, an ageing salesman tormented by an overwhelming sense of failure, highlights the false values of contemporary consumer society and questions traditional ideas of success and failure. It was made into a movie by Volker Schlöndorff in 1985. As a result of the power of the play, the term *Willy Loman* came to mean a man who has tragically sacrificed or sold his own life, and that of his family, in pursuit of the so-called American Dream.

sales·man·ship /sáylzmən shìp/ *n* the skills, techniques, and tactics involved in persuading people to buy goods or services

sales·per·son /sáylz pùrss'n/ (*plural* **-peo·ple** /-peep'l/ or **-per·sons**) *n* somebody who sells goods or services, either in a store or by contacting potential customers

sales pitch *n* the statements made, arguments used, and assurances given by somebody trying to sell something

sales rep·re·sen·ta·tive *n* somebody employed by a company to visit prospective customers with a view to selling them the company's products

sales re·sis·tance *n* reluctance or refusal to buy, especially when aggressive selling techniques are used

sales·room /sáylz ro͝om, -ro͞om/ *n* **1.** a large room where goods for sale are put on display **2.** a large room where goods are sold by auction

sales slip *n* a record of a purchase or sale made in a store, usually given to the customer as a receipt

sales tax *n* a tax on retail merchandise that is levied by the federal, state, or local government and collected at the point of sale by the retailer

sales·wom·an /sáylz wo͝omman/ (*plural* **-wom·en** /-wìmmin/) *n* a woman who sells goods or services, either in a store or by contacting potential customers

Sal·ford /sáwlfərd/ city in Lancashire, northwestern England. It is adjacent to Manchester, from which it is separated by the River Irwell. Population: 216,103 (2001).

Sa·li·an /sáylee ən, sáylyən/ *n* a member of an ancient Frankish people who settled in the Rhine valley in the Netherlands during the 4th century A.D. They subsequently spread into and conquered large parts of Northern Gaul. [Early 17C. < late Latin *Salii* "Salian Franks"]

Sal·ic /sáylik, sállik/, **Sal·ique** /sáylik, sállik, sə léek, sa-/ *adj* **1.** relating to Salic law **2.** relating to the Salian people or their culture [Mid-16C. < French *salique* or medieval Latin *Salicus* < late Latin *Salii* "Salian Franks"]

sal·i·ca·ceous /sàlli káyshəss/ *adj* describes trees or woody shrubs that have catkins, e.g., the willow and poplar. Family: Salicaceae. [Mid-19C. < modern Latin *salicaceus* < Latin *salic-* "willow"]

sal·i·cin /sállissin/ *n* a colorless crystalline substance obtained from the bark of willow trees. Use: formerly, as an analgesic. [Mid-19C. < French *salicine* < Latin *salic-* "willow"]

sa·li·cion·al /sə líshən'l, -líshnəl/ *n* a stop and pipes on an organ that produce a soft, gentle tone [Mid-19C. < German < Latin *salic-* "willow"]

Sal·ic law *n* a law excluding women from the right to succeed to the throne that formerly applied in France and some other European monarchies. The prohibition was supposedly founded on a law of the Salians that prevented women from inheriting land in some areas.

sa·lic·y·late /sə lísse làyt, -lət/ *n* a salt or ester of salicylic acid [Mid-19C. < French *salicyle* < Latin *salictum* < *salic-* "willow"]

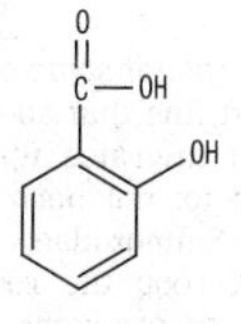

salicylic acid

sal·i·cyl·ic ac·id /sàlli sìllik-/ *n* a white crystalline acid. Use: as a preservative, in the manufacture of aspirin and dyes. Formula: $C_7H_6O_3$. [< French *salicyle* (see SALICYLATE)]

sa·li·ent /sáy lee ənt, sáylyənt/ *adj* **1.** NOTICEABLE OR STRIKING particularly noticeable, striking, or relevant **2.** PROJECTING sticking out from a surface **3.** MATH PROJECTING OUTWARD describes an angle that projects outward from a polygon **4.** HERALDRY JUMPING in heraldry, represented as a jumping or leaping animal ■ *n* **1.** MIL PROJECTING PART OF DEFENSIVE ALIGNMENT a part of a military front, line, or fortification that projects outward into enemy-held territory or toward the enemy **2.** MATH SALIENT ANGLE an angle that projects outwards from a polygon [Mid-17C. < Latin *salient-*, present participle of *salire* "leap"] —**sa·li·ence** *n* —**sa·li·ent·ly** *adv*

ORIGIN The Latin word *salire* "to jump, leap," from which ***salient*** is derived, is also the source of English *assail, assault, desultory, insult, salacious, sally,* and *sauté.*

sa·li·en·tian /sàylee énsh'n/ *adj* AMPHIB same as **anuran** [Mid-20C. < modern Latin *Salientia* < Latin *salient-* (see SALIENT)]

Sal·i·er·i /sàllee éree/, **Antonio** (1750–1825) Italian composer. As a successful writer of operas and church music in Vienna, he was a rival of Mozart.

sa·lim·e·ter /sa límmətər/ *n* CHEM same as **salinometer** [Mid-19C. < Latin *sal* "salt"] —**sal·i·met·ric** /sàllə méttrik/ *adj* —**sa·lim·e·try** *n*

sa·li·na /sə léenə, -línə/ *n* a salt marsh, lake, pond, or spring [Late 16C. Via Spanish < medieval Latin, "salt pit" < *sal* "salt"]

Sa·li·na /sə línə/ city in central Kansas, on the Smoky Hill River, southwest of Abilene and north of McPherson. Population: 45,969 (2002 estimate).

Sa·li·nas /sə léenəss/ river in western California, rising in the Santa Lucia Mountains and flowing into Monterey Bay. Length: 150 mi./241 km.

Sa·li·nas de Gor·ta·ri /-də gawr táaree/, **Carlos** (*b.* 1948) president of Mexico (1988–94). He signed the North American Free Trade Agreement (NAFTA) with the United States and Canada in 1992.

sa·line /sáy leen, -līn/ *adj* **1.** CONTAINING SALT containing or impregnated with salt **2.** CHEM CONTAINING SALTS relating to or containing alkali metal salts or magnesium salt ■ *n* MED SOLUTION OF SALT AND DISTILLED WATER a solution of common salt (**sodium chloride**) and distilled water, especially one having the same concentration as body fluids. It is used as a diluent for drugs and as a plasma substitute. [15C. < Latin *salinum* "saltcellar" < *sal* "salt"] —**sa·lin·i·ty** /sə línnətee/ *n*

sa·line so·lu·tion *n* MED same as **saline**

Sal·in·ger /sállinjər/, **J. D.** (*b.* 1919) US writer. After great success with *The Catcher in the Rye* (1951) and his short stories, in the mid-1960s he became a recluse. Full name **Salinger, Jerome David**. See Cultural note at **rye**[1]

> "What really knocks me out is a book that, when you're all done reading it, you wish the author that wrote it was a terrific friend of yours and you could call him up on the phone whenever you felt like it."
> [J. D. Salinger, *The Catcher in the Rye*; 1951]

Sal·in·ger·esque /sàllinjə résk/ *adj* relating or similar to the writings of J.D. Salinger [Mid-20C. Surname of US writer J.D. Salinger (*b.* 1919) + -ESQUE]

sal·i·nize /sállə nīz/ (**-nized, -niz·ing, -niz·es**) *vt* to treat or contaminate something with salt —**sal·i·ni·za·tion** /sàlləni záysh'n/ *n*

sal·i·nom·e·ter /sàllə nómmətər/, **sa·lom·e·ter** /sə lómmətər/ *n* an instrument used to measure the concentration of salt in solutions —**sal·i·no·met·ric** /sàllənə méttrik/ *adj* —**sal·i·nom·e·try** *n*

Sa·lique *adj* PEOPLES, HIST another spelling of **Salic**

Salis·bur·y /sáwlz bèrree, -bree/ **1.** city in Wiltshire, southwestern England. Salisbury Cathedral dates from the 12th century and has the highest spire in the country at 404 ft./125 m. Population: 114,613 (2001). Former name **Sarum 2.** city and port in southeastern Maryland, on the Delmarva Peninsula, on the Wicomico River. Population: 24,645 (2002 estimate).

Salis·bur·y, Robert Arthur Talbot Gascoyne-Cecil, 3rd Marquess of (1830–1903) British prime minister. As foreign secretary (1878–80) and prime minister (1885–86, 1886–92, 1895–1902) he extended British influence abroad, especially in Africa.

Salis·bur·y Plain area of rolling chalky downs in Wiltshire, southwestern England. Stonehenge is located there. Area: 300 sq. mi./775 sq. km.

Salis·bur·y steak /sáwlz bèrree-/ *n* a mixture of ground beef, egg, bread crumbs, onion, and seasoning that is formed into a flat round cake, cooked by broiling or frying, and usually served with gravy [Late 19C. After J. H. *Salisbury* (1823–1905), US physician]

Sa·lish /sáylish/ *n* **1.** a small family of Native North American languages spoken in the northwestern United States and British Columbia. Native speakers: 2,000. **2.** a member of a Salish-speaking Native North American people who live in British Columbia [Mid-19C. < Salish *sé?liš* "Flatheads"] —**Sa·lish·an** *adj, n*

sa·li·va /sə lívə/ *n* the clear liquid secreted into the mouth by the salivary glands, consisting of water, mucin, protein, and enzymes. It moistens food and starts the breakdown of starches. [15C. < Latin]

sal·i·var·y /sállivəri/ *adj* relating to saliva or the salivary glands

sal·i·var·y gland *n* any gland in mammals that produces and secretes saliva into the mouth

sal·i·vate /sállə vàyt/ (**-vat·ed, -vat·ing, -vates**) *v* **1.** *vi* PRODUCE SALIVA to produce saliva in the mouth, especially at an increased rate, e.g., when food is seen, smelled, or expected **2.** *vt* CAUSE ANIMAL TO DROOL to cause an animal in an experiment to produce large amounts of saliva **3.** *vi* LONG FOR SOMETHING to feel or show an immense desire for or appreciation of something (*informal*) ○ *I'm practically salivating over that set of golf clubs in the shop window.* [Mid-17C. Back-formation < *salivation* < Latin *salivation-* < past participle of *salivare* "salivate" < *saliva* "saliva"] —**sal·i·va·tion** /sàllə váysh'n/ *n*

AKG London

Jonas Salk

Salk /sawlk/, **Jonas** (1914–95) US physician and epidemiologist. He developed the first vaccine against poliomyelitis. Full name **Salk, Jonas Edward**

Salk vac·cine *n* a vaccine against poliomyelitis, containing a form of the virus causing the disease made inactive by treatment with a solution of formaldehyde

sal·let /sállət/, **sal·et** *n* a light helmet protecting the head and the back of the neck, worn in the late Middle Ages [15C. Via French *salade* < Latin *caelata* "engraved (helmet)" < *caelum* "chisel"]

Sal·lie Mae /sàllee máy/ *n* in the United States, the Student Loan Marketing Association, the US government agency providing liquidity to the student loan market (*informal*) [< pronunciation of the abbreviation *SLMA*]

sal·low[1] /sállō/ *adj* unnaturally pale and yellowish ○ *a sallow complexion* ■ *vt* (**-lowed, -low·ing, -lows**) to make something unnaturally pale and yellowish ○ *The illness had sallowed her skin.* [Old English *salo* "dark, dusky" < Germanic] —**sal·low·ly** *adv* —**sal·low·ness** *n*

sal·low[2] /sállō/ (*plural* **-lows** or *same*) *n* a willow tree with large catkins that yields a hard wood used to produce charcoal. Native to: Europe. Latin name: *Salix caprea.* [Old English *salh* < Indo-European] —**sal·low·y** *adj*

Sal·lust /sálləst/ (86–35? B.C.) Roman historian. His histories of Catiline's conspiracy and the Romans' war with the African king Jugurtha, written after he retired from holding colonial governorships, influenced the work of later historians. Full name **Gaius Sallustius Crispus**

"To like and dislike the same things, that is indeed true friendship."
[Sallust, *Bellum Catilinae*; 43 B.C.]

sal·ly /sállee/ *vi* (**-lied, -ly·ing, -lies**) **1.** SET OUT to set out on a journey or excursion ○ *Ena sallied forth to face the day, her gait determinedly nonchalant.* **2.** RUSH OUT SUDDENLY to rush or spring out suddenly **3.** MIL MAKE SALLY to make an offensive thrust from a defensive position ■ *n* (*plural* **-lies**) **1.** WITTY REMARK a witty remark, reply, or retort **2.** SUDDEN RUSH FORWARD a sudden rush or spring forward **3.** SUDDEN ACTION a sudden burst of activity or springing into action **4.** SUDDEN EXPRESSION a sudden outburst of speech or expression of emotion **5.** EXPEDITION an expedition or excursion **6.** MIL ATTACK FROM DEFENSIVE POSITION an offensive thrust from a defensive position, especially, formerly, a sudden attack by the defenders of a besieged position on the people besieging them [Mid-16C. < French *saillie* < past participle of *saillir* "leap" < Latin *salire*]

Sal·ly Lunn /sàllee lún/ *n* a sweet bread leavened with yeast that is typically baked in a round pan with a hole in the center and served warm in slices with butter [Late 18C. Probably < the name of a woman who sold cakes in Bath, England]

sal·ly port *n* an opening in a fortification from which the defenders can make sallies

sal·ma·gun·di /sàlmə gúndee/ *n* **1.** a mixed salad of various ingredients such as meat, poultry, fish, and vegetables, arranged in rows on a platter **2.** a mixture of different types of things (*literary*) [Late 17C. < French *salmagondis*, originally "seasoned salt meats"]

Sal·man·a·zar /sàlmə názzər/, **sal·man·a·zar** *n* a large wine bottle that holds the equivalent of 12 standard bottles, used especially for champagne [Mid-20C. After *Salmanasar* or *Shalmaneser*, a king of Assyria in the Bible]

sal·mi /sálmee/, **sal·mis** (*plural same*) *n* a dish made from pieces of partly roasted game stewed with mushrooms and served with a rich wine sauce [Mid-18C. Shortening of French *salmagondis* (see SALMAGUNDI)]

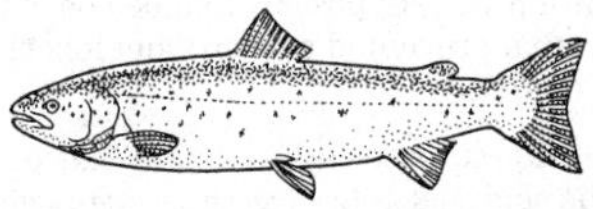

salmon

salm·on /sámmən/ (*plural same* or **-ons**) *n* **1.** a large food fish with soft fins that spends most of its life in the ocean but migrates up freshwater rivers to spawn. Native to: northern Atlantic, northern Pacific. Family: Salmonidae; Genera: *Salmo* or *Oncorhynchus.* **2.** FOOD the red or pink flesh of salmon as food **3.** COLORS same as **salmon pink** [13C. Via French < Latin *salmon-*] —**salm·on** *adj*

Salm·on /sámmən/ river in Idaho flowing into the Snake River on the Washington border. Length: 420 mi./680 km.

salm·on·ber·ry /sámmən bèrree/ (*plural* **-ries**) *n* **1.** a salmon-pink raspberry **2.** a plant that produces salmonberries. Flowers: red. Native to: Pacific coast of North America. Latin name: *Rubus spectabilis.*

sal·mon day *n* a day on which continuous and strenuous efforts produce no progress and no worthwhile result (*humorous*)

sal·mo·nel·la /sàlmə néllə/ (*plural* **-lae** /-lee/) *n* **1.** a rod-shaped bacterium found in the intestine that can cause food poisoning, gastroenteritis, and typhoid fever. Genus: *Salmonella.* **2.** MED same as **salmonellosis** [Early 20C. < modern Latin, after Daniel Elmer *Salmon* (1850–1914), US veterinarian]

sal·mo·nel·lo·sis /sàlmə ne lóssiss/ *n* food poisoning caused by infection with salmonella organisms, usually characterized by gastrointestinal upset, diarrhea, fever, and occasionally death. It is usually contracted by eating undercooked contaminated food.

salm·o·nid /sámmənid, sálmənid/ *n* a bony soft-finned fish of the family that includes salmon, trout, whitefish, and char. Family: Salmonidae.

salm·on pink *n* a pale orange-pink color, like salmon flesh —**salm·on-pink** *adj*

Sa·lo·me /sə lṓmee, sállə mày/ *n* in the Bible, the daughter of Herodias who demanded and received John the Baptist's head as reward for dancing before her stepfather, Herod Antipas (Matthew 14:6–11 and Mark 6:21–28)

sa·lom·e·ter /sə lómmətər/ *n* CHEM same as **salinometer** [Mid-19C. < Latin *sal* "salt"]

sa·lon /sə lón, sa láwN/ *n* **1.** GRAND SITTING ROOM an elegantly furnished room in a large house where guests are received and entertained **2.** SOCIAL GATHERING OF INTELLECTUALS a regular gathering of prominent people from the worlds of literature, art, music, or politics, especially one held at the home of a wealthy woman. Salons were especially popular in the 17th, 18th, and 19th centuries. **3.** PLACE FOR HAIRDRESSING OR BEAUTY TREATMENTS a commercial establishment where hairdressers or beauticians work, sometimes part of a larger store or a hotel **4.** EXPENSIVE CLOTHES SHOP a shop selling elegant or fashionable women's clothes, especially expensive designer clothes **5.** ART EXHIBITION OR GALLERY an art exhibition, especially one devoted to the work of living artists, or the hall in which the exhibits are displayed [Late 17C. Via French < Italian *salone* "large hall" < *sala* "hall" < Germanic]

Sa·lo·ni·ka /sə lónnikə, sàllə néekə/ ♦ **Thessaloníki**

sa·lon mu·sic *n* light classical music for easy listening

sa·loon /sə lóon/ *n* **1.** a commercial establishment serving alcoholic drinks to the general public **2.** *UK* LEISURE same as **lounge bar** **3.** *UK* same as **sedan** **4.** a large room on a ship where passengers can sit and relax [Early 18C. Alteration of SALON]

sa·loon bar *n UK* LEISURE same as **lounge bar**

sa·lo·pettes /sàllə péts/ *npl UK* a garment worn by skiers, comprising a pair of usually padded, water-resistant pants that reach up to the chest with straps passing over the shoulders [Late 20C. < French]

salp /salp/, **sal·pa** /sálpə/ (*plural* **-pae** /-pee/ or **-pas**) *n* a tiny free-swimming organism (**tunicate**) that has a transparent barrel-shaped body. Native to: warm seas. Genus: *Salpa.* [Mid-19C. Via French < modern Latin *salpa*, < Greek *salpē* "fish"] —**sal·pi·form** /sálpə fàwrm/ *adj*

sal·pi·glos·sis /sàlpə glóssiss/ (*plural* **-glos·ses** /-gló sèez/ or *same*) *n* a tall annual plant. Flowers: large, funnel-shaped. Native to: Chile. Genus: *Salpiglossis.* [Early 19C. < modern Latin < Greek *salpigx* "trumpet" + *glossa* "tongue"; from the plant's shape]

sal·pin·gec·to·my /sàlpin jéktəmee/ (*plural* **-mies**) *n* the severing or surgical removal of a fallopian tube [Late 19C. < Greek *salpigg-* "trumpet"]

sal·pin·gi·tis /sàlpin jítiss/ *n* inflammation of a fallopian tube [Mid-19C. < Greek *salpigg-* "trumpet"] —**sal·pin·git·ic** /-jíttik/ *adj*

sal·sa /saálssə/ *n* **1.** SPICY SAUCE a spicy sauce of finely chopped vegetables including tomatoes, onions, and chilies, eaten with tortilla chips and other Mexican foods **2.** LATIN AMERICAN DANCE MUSIC Latin American dance music combining aspects of jazz and rock with African-Cuban melodies **3.** DANCE TO SALSA MUSIC a dance performed to salsa music [Late 20C. < Spanish, "sauce" < Latin, "salted," form of past participle of *sallere* "to salt" < *sal* "salt"]

sal·sa ver·de /-vúrdee/ *n* a sauce based on tomatillos blended with cilantro, peppers, onions and spices, served as a dip or as a condiment or sauce with meat or fish [< Spanish, "green sauce"]

sal·si·fy /sálssəfee, -fī/ (*plural* **-fies** or *same*) *n* **1.** a long earth-colored edible root of a plant of the daisy family, which is said to have a taste resembling oysters, cooked as a vegetable **2.** a plant of the daisy family with long thin leaves and roots that are salsify. Native to: Europe. Latin name: *Tragopogon porrifolius.* [Early 18C. Via French *salsifis* < Italian *salsefica*]

sal so·da *n* CHEM same as **washing soda**

salt /sawlt/ *n* **1. WHITE CRYSTALS USED IN FOOD PREPARATION** small white tangy-tasting crystals consisting largely of sodium chloride. Source: seawater, mineral deposits. Use: food seasoning and preservative. **2. SALT CONTAINER** a container of salt, especially one for use at the table ○ *Please pass the salt.* **3. CRYSTALLINE CHEMICAL COMPOUND** a crystalline compound formed from the neutralization of an acid by a base containing a metal or group acting like a metal **4. SOMETHING THAT ADDS ZEST** something that adds zest, piquancy, liveliness, or vigor **5. DRY WIT** sharp or dry wit **6.** NAUT same as **old salt** ■ **salts** *npl* **SUBSTANCE RESEMBLING SALT** a chemical or crystalline solution used for a particular purpose ○ *smelling salts* ■ *adj* **1. PRESERVED WITH SALT** preserved with salt or a salt solution ○ *salt cod* **2. CONTAINING SALT** containing or consisting of salt ○ *salt tears* **3. CONTAINING OR ASSOCIATED WITH SALT WATER** containing, covered with, or growing near salt water ○ *a salt marsh* **4. TASTING OF SALT** tasting or smelling of salt ■ *vt* (**salt·ed, salt·ing, salts**) **1. SEASON FOOD WITH SALT** to add salt to food, during or after preparation, to emphasize its flavor **2. PRESERVE FOOD WITH SALT** to preserve food by treating it with salt or a salt solution **3. PUT SALT ON COLD GROUND** to scatter salt over a road or sidewalk to melt ice or prevent it from forming **4. ADD ZEST TO SOMETHING** to add a more lively or entertaining quality to something ○ *She salted her speech with jokes.* **5. ENRICH ORE SAMPLE** to enrich a mining area or sample with a valuable ore artificially introduced in order to increase its apparent value [Old English *sealt* < Indo-European] —**salt·ness** *n* ◇ **rub salt in the wound** to add to somebody's distress, embarrassment, or sense of shame, often deliberately ◇ **take something with a grain** *or* **pinch of salt** to listen to something without fully believing it ◇ **the salt of the earth** a very good, worthy person or group of people ◇ **worth your salt** efficient and doing the job well

ORIGIN The Indo-European word from which *salt* is ultimately derived is also the ancestor of English *halogen, salad, salami, salary, saline, sauce, sausage,* and *souse.*

salt away *vt* to save money for future use, often carefully over time [Probably < the practice of preserving food in salt]

salt out *vt* to separate a dissolved substance from a solution by adding a salt

SALT /sawlt/ *abbr* Strategic Arms Limitation Talks (or Treaty)

salt-and-pep·per *adj* describes hair flecked with dark and light colors

sal·ta·rel·lo /saàltə réllō, sàwltə-/ (*plural* **-los** or **-li** /-lee/) *n* **1.** a dance in triple time originating in medieval times and especially popular in Spain and Italy **2.** the music for a saltarello [Late 16C. < Italian < Latin *saltare* "to dance" (see SALTATION)]

sal·ta·tion /sal táysh'n, sawl-/ *n* **1. JUMPING OR JUMP** leaping or jumping, or a sudden jump or leap (*formal*) **2. SUDDEN CHANGE** development or transition that takes place in jumps or leaps (*formal*) **3.** BIOL **ABRUPT EVOLUTIONARY DEVELOPMENT** the abrupt evolutionary development of a new species or property, especially as a result of genetic mutation **4.** GEOL **JUMPING MOTION OF PARTICLES** the transportation of particles of soil or sand in the wind or in running water, characterized by bouncing movements [Early 17C. < Latin *saltation-* < *saltare* "keep leaping, dance" < *salire* "to leap"]

sal·ta·to·ri·al /sàltə táwree əl, sàwltə-/, **sal·ta·to·ry** /sáltə tàwree, sáwltə-, sóltə-/ *adj* **1. RELATING TO JUMPING** relating to or adapted for jumping ○ *an insect with saltatorial legs* **2. ASSOCIATED WITH JUMPING OR DANCING** associated with or involving jumping, leaping, or dancing **3. DEVELOPING IN JUMPS OR LEAPS** involving or characterized by sudden change rather than gradual transition

salt ba·con *n regional* same as **fatback**

REGIONAL NOTE See ***fatback.***

salt·box /sáwlt bòks/ *n* **1.** a box in which salt is stored, especially one with a sloping lid **2.** a wood-frame house that has two floors at the front but only one in the back, and with a long, typically broken rear slope to the roof

salt·bush /sáwlt bòosh/ (*plural* **-bush·es** or *same*) *n* PLANTS same as **orach**

salt cake *n* an impure form of sodium sulfate. Use: manufacture of glass, paper pulp, soap, and ceramic glazes.

salt·cel·lar /sáwlt sèllər/ *n* a small container for salt, especially one used at the table to season food after it is served

salt·chuck /sáwlt chùk/ *n Can* a stretch of salt water flowing into a freshwater lake or river

salt·chuck·er /sáwlt chùkər/ *n Can* an angler who fishes in salt water

salt dome *n* a dome-shaped structure formed in sedimentary rock when buried salt deposits move up through overlying rocks, owing to their low density and high buoyancy

salt·ed /sáwltəd/ *adj* **1.** with salt added for seasoning, preservation, or some other purpose **2.** hardened or experienced, e.g., in a trade or profession

salt·er /sáwltər/ *n* **1.** a producer or seller of salt **2.** a preserver of food by using salt

salt·ern /sáwltərn/ *n* **1.** a place where salt is produced commercially **2.** a place where salt is produced naturally when pools of sea water evaporate [Pre-12C. < SALT + Old English *ærn* "building"]

salt·fish /sáwlt fìsh/ *n Carib* cod or other fish preserved with salt

salt flat *n* a broad flat area in hot deserts encrusted with salt left after the evaporation of water from shallow saline lakes (*often used in the plural*)

salt gland *n* a gland in some ocean birds or reptiles, used to excrete excess ingested salt

salt glaze *n* a glaze formed by throwing salt into a kiln during the firing process

salt grass *n* any grass native to salt marshes or alkaline regions

salt hay *n* hay produced from salt grass, used as fodder

Sal·ti·llo /sal téelyō/ capital of Coahuila State in northern Mexico, founded in 1575. Population: 577,372 (2000).

sal·tim·boc·ca /saàltim bókə, sàwl-, -bókə/ *n* a dish consisting of thin slices of veal rolled up with prosciutto ham and fresh sage leaves, lightly fried and braised in white wine [Mid-20C. < Italian < *saltare* "to leap" + *in* "into, in" + *bocca* "mouth"]

sal·tine /sawl téen/ *n* a thin crisp cracker sprinkled with salt

sal·tire /sál tìr, sáwl-/ *n* in heraldry, one of the basic designs used on coats of arms, consisting of a diagonal cross [15C. Via Old French *sau(l)toir* "stirrup, stile" < medieval Latin *saltatorium* < Latin *saltare* (see SALTATION)]

salt-kind *n Carib* salted meat or meat soaked in brine, including pig's feet and oxtails, used in making soup or cooking beans

salt lake *n* a lake with no outlet and having a high salt content as a result of evaporation, e.g., the Dead Sea

Salt Lake Ci·ty /sàwlt-/ capital city of Utah, located in the north central part of the state, 15 mi./24 km east of the Great Salt Lake. Population: 181,266 (2002 estimate).

salt lick *n* **1.** a place where animals go to lick salt deposits that occur naturally **2.** a block of salt or other preparation that livestock lick in order to supplement their salt intake. It may also contain other essential minerals such as magnesium or iodine.

salt marsh *n* a marshy grassland area regularly flooded with salt water

salt meat *n regional* same as **fatback**

REGIONAL NOTE See ***fatback.***

Sal·ton Sea /sàwlt'n-/ saltwater lake in southern California, formed when the Colorado River flooded in 1905. Area: 364 sq. mi./943 sq. km.

salt·pan /sáwlt pàn/ *n* a basin in a semiarid region where salts are precipitated after saline floodwaters evaporate

salt·pe·ter /sàwlt péetər/ *n* CHEM **1.** same as **Chile saltpeter 2.** same as **potassium nitrate** [14C. Directly or via French < medieval Latin *salpetra* < Latin *sal* "salt" + *petra* "rock"; from its appearance as a crust on rock]

salt·pe·tre /sàwlt péetər/ *n* CHEM Can, UK spelling of **saltpeter**

salt pork *n* a fat cut of pork from the belly, back, or sides, cured by salting

salt·shak·er /sáwlt shàykər/ *n* a small container with holes in the top for sprinkling salt over food at the table

salt wa·ter *n* **1.** water containing a lot of salt **2.** the water of the sea and coastal inlets

salt·wa·ter /sáwlt wàwtər/ *adj* **1.** containing or involving salt water **2.** living or growing in salt water

salt·wa·ter croc·o·dile *n* a large crocodile that inhabits coastal waterways and feeds on fish, birds, reptiles, and small mammals. Native to: northern Australia, Southeast Asia. Latin name: *Crocodylus porosus.*

salt·works /sáwlt wùrks/ *n* a place or factory where salt is produced commercially (*takes a singular or plural verb*)

salt·wort /sáwlt wùrt, -wàwrt/ (*plural* **-worts** or *same*) *n* a prickly leaved seashore plant. Native to: Europe, Asia. Genus: *Salsoa.*

salt·y /sáwltee/ (**-i·er, -i·est**) *adj* **1. TASTING OF SALT** containing or tasting of salt **2. OF SEA OR SAILORS** associated with the sea or with nautical life **3. LIVELY AND AMUSING** lively, amusing, and sometimes mildly indecent ○ *salty jokes* —**salt·i·ly** *adv* —**salt·i·ness** *n*

sa·lu·bri·ous /sə lóobree əss/ *adj* beneficial to or promoting health or well-being [Mid-16C. < Latin *salubris* < *salus* "health"] —**sa·lu·bri·ous·ly** *adv* —**sa·lu·bri·ous·ness** *n* —**sa·lu·bri·ty** *n*

Sa·lu·da /sə lóodə/ river in South Carolina, rising in the Blue Ridge Mountains and flowing into the Congaree River. Length: 200 mi./322 km.

sa·lu·ki /sə lóokee/ *n* a tall slender dog with a smooth coat and long fur on the ears and tail, belonging to a breed originally developed in Arabia and Egypt [Early 19C. < Arabic *salūķī* < *Salūķ*, town in Yemen]

sal·u·tar·y /sállyə tèrree/ *adj* **1.** of value or benefit to somebody or something ○ *We asked if military service had been a salutary experience for him.* **2.** promoting good health (*formal*) [15C. Via French < Latin *salutaris* < *salut-*, stem of *salus* "health"] —**sal·u·tar·i·ly** /sállyə tèrralee, sàllyə térralee/ *adv* —**sal·u·tar·i·ness** *n*

sal·u·ta·tion /sàllyə táysh'n/ *n* **1. SIGN OF GREETING** a gesture or phrase that is used to greet, welcome, or recognize somebody **2. ACT OF GREETING SOMEBODY** the expression of greetings, welcome, or recognition **3. OPENING GREETING** the opening phrase of a letter or speech, used to address the recipient or audience, e.g., "Dear Sir or Madam" or "Ladies and Gentlemen" ■ *npl, interj* **sal·u·ta·tions GREETINGS** greetings or regards (*formal*) ○ *Salutations from us all!* —**sal·u·ta·tion·al** *adj*

sa·lu·ta·to·ri·an /sə lòotə táwree ən/ *n* in the United States, a student in a graduating class who is second highest in academic ranking and is usually required to give a salutatory at the graduation ceremony

sa·lu·ta·to·ry /sə lóotə tàwree/ *adj* expressing or conveying greetings ■ *n* (*plural* **-ries**) a welcoming speech, especially one given at a graduation ceremony [Mid-17C. < Latin *salutatorius* < *salutare* (see SALUTE)]

sa·lute /sə lóot/ *v* (**-lut·ed, -lut·ing, -lutes**) **1.** *vti* **GIVE FORMAL SIGN OF RESPECT** to formally signal respect to another member of the armed forces or to a flag, usually by raising the right hand to the forehead or by presenting arms **2.** *vt* **GREET SOMEBODY** to greet, welcome, or acknowledge somebody, either with a gesture or in words **3.** *vt* **FORMALLY PRAISE OR HONOR SOMEBODY** to praise or honor somebody for something, especially in a formal ceremony ○ *We salute you for your contribution.* ■ *n* **1. GESTURE OF RESPECT** a gesture used by members of the armed forces and some other organized groups as a formal sign of respect **2.** FIRING GUNS AS MILITARY HONOR a military display of honor for a dignitary or on a special occasion, e.g., the firing of guns into the air at the funeral of an officer ○ *a 21-gun salute* **3.** ACT OF SALUTING an act or an occasion of saluting [14C. < Latin *salutare* < *salut-*, stem of *salus* "health"] —**sa·lut·er** *n*

Sal·va·dor /sálvə dàwr/ port and capital city of Bahia State in eastern Brazil, on the Atlantic Ocean. Population: 2,211,539 (1996). Former name **Bahia**

Sal·va·dor, El ◆ **El Salvador**

Sal·va·do·ran /sàlvə dáwrən/, **Sal·va·do·ri·an** /-dáwree ən/, **Sal·va·do·re·an** *n* somebody who comes from El Salvador ■ *adj* relating to El Salvador or its people or culture

sal·vage /sálvij/ *vt* (**-vaged, -vag·ing, -vag·es**) **1.** SAVE SOMETHING FOR FURTHER USE to save used, damaged, or rejected goods for recycling or further use ○ *Maybe we can salvage some spare parts from your old car.* **2.** RESCUE SOMETHING FROM BAD SITUATION to save something of worth or merit from a situation or event that is otherwise a failure ○ *Diplomats are meeting to consider ways to salvage the peace process.* **3.** SAVE SOMETHING FROM DESTRUCTION to save a ship, cargo, crew, or other property or goods from destruction or loss (*often passive*) ○ *They salvaged what they could from the wreckage.* ■ *n* **1.** RESCUE OF PROPERTY FROM DESTRUCTION the rescue of property or goods from destruction or loss, e.g., because of a flood or fire **2.** RESCUE OF SHIP FROM SEA the rescue of a ship, its cargo, or crew from loss at sea **3.** RESCUED GOODS something that has been saved from destruction or loss ○ *a salvage yard* **4.** SOMETHING REUSED something that would otherwise be destroyed or discarded but is recycled or put to further use **5.** COMPENSATION FOR RESCUERS compensation to volunteers who help in the rescue of ships, property, or goods from destruction or loss **6.** MONEY FROM SALE OF RESCUED GOODS money from the sale of property or goods that have been salvaged [Mid-17C. Via French (noun) < medieval Latin *salvgium* < late Latin *salvare* "save" < Latin *salvus* "safe"] —**sal·vage·a·bil·i·ty** /sàlvijə bíllətee/ *n* —**sal·vage·a·ble** *adj* —**sal·vag·er** *n*

sal·va·tion /sal váysh'n/ *n* **1.** ACT OF SAVING FROM HARM the saving of somebody or something from harm, destruction, difficulty, or failure ○ *The business was clearly beyond salvation.* **2.** MEANS OF SAVING SOMEBODY OR SOMETHING somebody or something that protects or delivers another from harm, destruction, difficulty, or failure ○ *Those long walks were my salvation.* **3.** CHR DELIVERANCE FROM SIN THROUGH JESUS CHRIST in the Christian religion, deliverance from sin or the consequences of sin through Jesus Christ's death on the cross **4.** CHRISTIAN SCIENCE PHILOSOPHY OF LIFE in the Christian Science religion, belief in the supremacy of life, truth, and love, and in their destruction of such illusions as sin, illness, and death [13C. Via French < ecclesiastical Latin *salvation-* < late Latin *salvare* "save" (see SALVAGE)] —**sal·va·tion·al** *adj*

Sal·va·tion Ar·my *n* a worldwide evangelical Christian organization that provides aid to those in need. It was founded by William Booth in London, England, in 1865.

sal·va·tion·ist /sal váysh'nist/ *n* a Christian who preaches the doctrine that Jesus Christ died on the cross to save people from sin or the consequences of sin —**sal·va·tion·ism** *n*

Sal·va·tion·ist *n* a member of the Salvation Army

salve[1] /sav, salv/ *n* **1.** SOOTHING OINTMENT an ointment that soothes and heals **2.** SOMETHING CALMING something that eases pain or anxiety ○ *Her forgiveness was a salve to my conscience.* ■ *vt* (**salved, salv·ing, salves**) EASE PAIN OR WORRY to soothe or ease pain or anxiety ○ *salve your wounded pride* [Old English *salf* < Germanic]

salve[2] /salv/ (**salved, salv·ing, salves**) *vt* to save something from destruction or loss [Early 18C. Back-formation < SALVAGE] —**sal·vor** *n*

sal·ver /sálvər/ *n* a tray, especially a silver one, used to serve food or drinks, or to present things such as letters or visiting cards [Mid-17C. Via French *salve* "tray for presenting things to the king" < Spanish *salva* < late Latin *salvare* "save" (see SALVAGE)]

sal·ver·form /sálvər fàwrm/ *adj* describes the corolla of a flower with joined petals that is long and tube-shaped with a spreading upper part

sal·vi·a /sálvee ə/ (*plural* **-as** or *same*) *n* an ornamental plant with opposite leaves. Flowers: red, whorled, with two-lipped corolla. Latin name: *Salvia splendens.* [Mid-19C. Via modern Latin, genus name < Latin, "sage (plant)" < *salvus* "safe"]

sal·vo[1] /sálvō/ (*plural* **-vos** or **-voes**) *n* **1.** SIMULTANEOUS DISCHARGE OF WEAPONS the firing of several weapons simultaneously, especially at a formal military ceremony **2.** HEAVY BURST OF FIRING OR BOMBING a concentrated burst of firing or bombing from several different sources during a battle **3.** NUMBER OF BOMBS RELEASED AT ONCE a number of bombs or projectiles released simultaneously **4.** OUTBURST a sudden burst of applause or cheering **5.** VERBAL ATTACK a vigorous written or spoken attack ○ *a blistering salvo* [Mid-17C. Alteration of obsolete *salva* < Italian, "greeting" < Latin *salvus* "safe"]

sal·vo[2] /sálvō/ *n* something that is used to save a reputation or soothe somebody's conscience or wounded pride [Early 17C. < Latin, form of *salvus* "safe"]

sal vo·la·ti·le /sàl və látt'lee/ *n* **1.** CHEM same as **ammonium carbonate 2.** a solution of ammonium carbonate in alcohol and ammonia in water, often mixed with aromatic oils. Use: smelling salts. [Mid-17C. < modern Latin, "volatile salt"]

sal·war /shál vaàr/, **shal·war** *n* a pair of loose-fitting pleated trousers tapering to the ankle, worn by women from northern India and Pakistan, especially in the Punjab region, usually under a long tunic (**kameez**) [Early 19C. < Persian, Urdu *šalwār*]

Sal·ween /sál wèen/ river in Southeast Asia, flowing through China, including Tibet, and Myanmar (Burma). Length: 1,740 mi./2,800 km.

Salz·burg /sálts bùrg, zaálts-/ capital city of Salzburg Province in western Austria. The Salzburg Festival, which concentrates on the music of Mozart, who was born in the city, is held there annually. Population: 143,991 (1999).

Salz·git·ter /zaálts gìttər/ city in Lower Saxony State, north central Germany, situated 105 mi./169 km south of Hamburg. Population: 117,842 (1997).

SAM /sam, èss ay ém/ *abbr* ARMS surface-to-air missile

Sam. *abbr* BIBLE Samuel

sa·ma·dhi /su maádee/ *n* in Buddhism and Hinduism, a state of intense meditation believed to lead to spiritual enlightenment [Late 18C. < Sanskrit *samādhiḥ*]

sa·man /sə maán/ (*plural same* or **-mans**) *n Carib* same as **rain tree** [Late 19C. Via American Spanish *samán* < Carib *zamang*]

sam·a·ra /sámmərə, sə márrə, sə maárə/ *n* BOT same as **key**[1] *n* (sense 26) (*technical*) [Late 16C. < Latin, "elm seed"]

Sa·mar·i·a /sə mérree ə/ ancient city and state in Palestine, located north of present-day Jerusalem, east of the Mediterranean Sea —**Sam·ar·i·an** *n, adj*

Sa·mar·i·tan /sə márrətən/ *n* **1.** somebody who came from ancient Samaria **2.** same as **Good Samaritan** [Pre-12C. < late Latin *Samaritanus* < Greek *Samareitēs* < *Samareia* "Samaria"] —**Sa·mar·i·tan·ism** *n*

sa·mar·i·um /sə mérree əm/ *n* a silvery gray metallic element. Source: monazite, bastnaesite. Use: strong magnets, carbon-arc lighting, laser materials, neutron absorber. Symbol **Sm**. See table at **element** [Late 19C. < SAMARSKITE]

Sa·mar·qand /sámmər kànd/, **Sa·mar·kand** capital city of Samarqand Oblast, central Uzbekistan. Located in the valley of the Zeravshan River, it is the oldest city in Central Asia. Population: 368,000 (1994).

sa·mar·skite /sə maár skìt, sámmər-/ *n* a black mineral containing uranium and rare-earth elements. Source: pegmatite. [Mid-19C. After V. E. *Samarskii*-Vykhovets (1803–70), Russian mining engineer]

Sa·ma-Ve·da /saámə váydə/ *n* one of the four collections of chants (**Vedas**) used during Hindu sacrifices, containing songs based on the Rig-Veda with instructions on their recitation [Late 18C. < Sanskrit < *sāman* "chant" + *vedaḥ* "knowledge"]

sam·ba /sámbə, saámbə/ *n* **1.** BRAZILIAN DANCE a lively Brazilian ballroom dance with strong African influences in 4/4 time **2.** BRAZILIAN MUSIC the music for a samba ■ *vi* (**-baed, -ba·ing, -bas**) DANCE SAMBA to dance the samba [Late 19C. < Portuguese]

sam·bal /saám baál, saam baál/, **sam·bol** *n* a spicy condiment or relish of Southeast Asia made of chili, spices, tomato, and vegetables [Early 19C. < Malay]

sam·bar /sámbər, saámbər/ (*plural* **-bars** or *same*), **sam·bur** (*plural* **-burs** or *same*) *n* a large deer that has a reddish brown coat and three-pronged antlers. Native to: Southeast Asia. Latin name: *Cervus unicolor*. [Late 17C. Via Hindi < Sanskrit *śambaraḥ*]

samb·har /súm baár/ *n* in southern Indian cuisine, a stew of highly spiced lentils and vegetables eaten mixed with rice [Mid-20C. Via Tamil < Sanskrit *sambhāra* "collection"]

sam·bo /sámbō/, **sam·bo wres·tling** *n* a form of wrestling based on judo that originated in the former Soviet Union and is now practiced internationally [Mid-20C. Acronym < Russian *samozashchita bez oruzhiya* "unarmed self-defense"] —**sam·bo wres·tler** *n*

Sam Browne belt /sàm brówn-/, **Sam Browne** *n* a wide belt supported by a diagonal strap that passes from the left-hand side over the right shoulder, worn as part of military or police uniforms [After Sir *Samuel Browne* (1824–1901), British military commander]

sam·bu·ca /sam bóokə, -byóokə/ *n* an Italian liqueur made from elderberries and flavored with licorice or aniseed [Late 20C. Via Italian < Latin *sambucus* "elder tree"]

same /saym/ CORE MEANING: a word indicating that one thing or person is involved rather than two or more different things or people ○ (adj) *I can't drive and talk at the same time.* ○ (adj) *He lives on the same street as I do.*

1. *adj, pron, adv* IDENTICAL identical, or alike in every significant respect ○ (adj) *They turned up at the party wearing the same dress.* ○ (adj) *All the houses looked exactly the same.* ○ (adj) *Look – their curtains are the same as ours!* ○ (pron) *All the experts say the same.* **2.** *adj, pron* PREVIOUSLY MENTIONED previously mentioned, or as previously described or identified (*used as a pronoun without "the" in business and legal contexts; see Usage note below*) ○ (adj) *She left because she was bored, and I left two months later for the same reason.* ○ (pron) *Wool should always be washed carefully. The same applies to silk.* ○ (pron) *"Are you Lee Smith?" – "The same."* **3.** *adj* UNCHANGED not changed or changing ○ *After the accident, he just wasn't the same person.* ○ *The house looked the same as always.* ○ *I want things to stay the same.* [12C. < Old Norse *samr* < Indo-European, "one"] —**same·ness** *n* ◇ **all** *or* **just the same 1.** despite a particular situation or comment ○ *All the same, I wish she hadn't said it.* ○ *They tried to stop us but we took it just the same.* **2.** nevertheless ◇ **same old, same old** used to say that a situation is unchanged or unexciting (*informal*) ◇ **the same as** in the identical way that (*informal*) ○ *He wants to win, the same as I do.*

USAGE The use of ***same*** as a pronoun as in *We have received your order and have pleasure in completing same* is characteristic of commercial and legal language; it is not normally found in general use, except with special or humorous effect: *The dog excavated a huge bone and consumed same.*

sa·mekh /saá mèk, -mèkh/ *n* the 15th letter of the Hebrew alphabet, represented in the English alphabet as "s." See table at **alphabet** [Early 19C. < Hebrew *sāmekh* "a support"]

same-sex *adj* relating to gays or lesbians ○ *involved in a same-sex relationship*

Sam Hill /sàm híl/, **sam hill** *n* used for emphasis, especially in questions, as a euphemism for "hell" (*slang*) ○ *What the Sam Hill is wrong with my computer?* [Mid-19C. Origin ?]

Sa·mi·an /sáymee ən/ *n* somebody who comes from the Greek island of Samos [Late 16C. < Latin *Saniius* "Samos"] —**Sa·mi·an** *adj*

sam·i·sen /sámmi sèn/ *n* a Japanese three-stringed musical instrument that has a long fretless neck and is plucked with a plectrum. See illustration on next page [Early 17C. Via Japanese < Chinese *sānxián* "three strings"]

sam·ite /sá mìt, sáy-/ *n* a heavy silk fabric, often interwoven with gold or silver threads. Use:

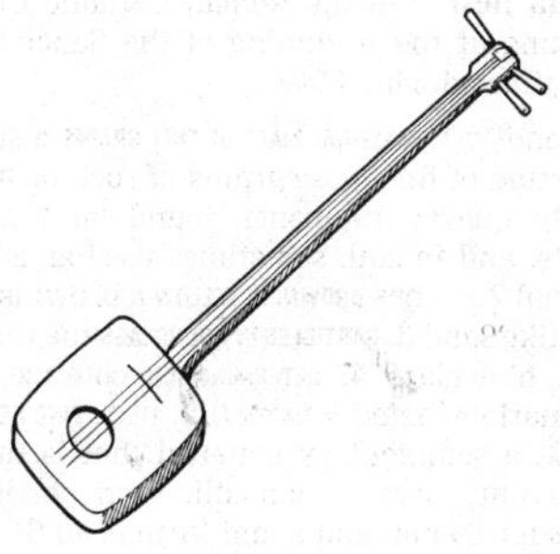

samisen

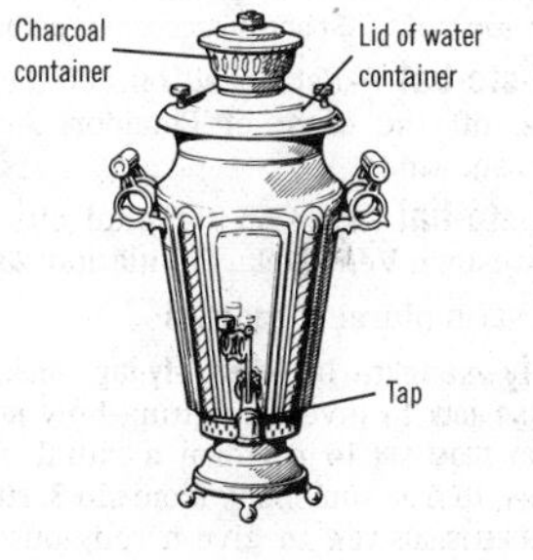

samovar

formerly, clothing. [12C. Via Old French *samit* < medieval Latin *examitum* < Greek *hexamiton* "six threads"]

sam·i·ti /súmmitee/, **sam·i·thi** *n S Asia* same as **committee** [Mid-20C. < Sanskrit *samitiḥ* "assembly"]

sa·miz·dat /saámiz dàt, -daàt/ *n* **1. SOVIET UNDERGROUND PUBLISHING** in the former Soviet Union, the printing and distribution of secret or banned literature **2. BANNED LITERATURE** literature produced by the samizdat system **3. SECRET PRINTING PRESS** a secret printing press, especially in the former Soviet Union [Mid-20C. < Russian < *sam-* "self" + shortening of *izdatel'stvo* "publishing house"]

Sam·ma·ri·nese /sa màrrə neéz/ (*plural* **-ne·si** /-náyzee/) *n* somebody who comes from San Marino [Mid-20C. < Italian < SAN MARINO] —**Sam·ma·ri·nese** *adj*

Sam·nite /sám nīt/ *n* a member of an ancient people who lived in central and southern Italy in the 4th and 3rd centuries B.C. They repeatedly tried to spread into territory held by Rome and were eventually defeated by the Romans around 290 B.C. ■ *adj* relating to the Samnites, or their culture or empire ○ *the Samnite wars* [14C. < Latin *Samnites* "the Samnites"]

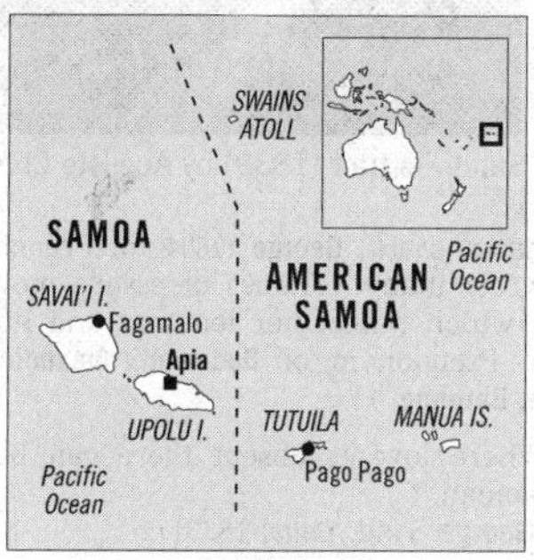

Samoa

Sa·mo·a /sə mṓ ə/ independent island state in the southern Pacific Ocean, situated west of American Samoa. It became an independent member of the British Commonwealth in 1970. Language: Samoan, English. Currency: tala. Capital: Apia. Population: 178,173 (2003). Area: 1,093 sq. mi./2,831 sq. km. Official name **Independent State of Samoa**. Former name **Western Samoa** (until 1997)

Sa·mo·an /sə mṓ ən/ *n* **1.** somebody who comes from American Samoa or the Independent State of Samoa **2.** the Polynesian language of the Independent State of Samoa. Native speakers: 300,000. —**Sa·mo·an** *adj*

Sa·mos /sáy moss, sámmōss, saá-/ Greek island in the Aegean Sea, separated from the southwestern coast of Turkey by the narrow Samos Strait. Population: 41,965 (1991). Area: 184 sq. mi./477 sq. km.

sa·mo·sa /sə mṓssə, sə mṓssə/ (*plural* **-sas** or *same*) *n* a South Asian snack consisting of a thin pastry case filled with spiced vegetables or meat and then deep-fried [Mid-20C. < Urdu]

Sam·o·set /sámmə sèt/ (1590?–1655?) Abenaki Algonquin leader. He was friendly to the Pilgrims in the Plymouth Colony and became the first Native American to sell land to an English settler (1625).

Sam·o·thrace /sámmə thràyss/ Greek island in the northeastern Aegean Sea, situated 25 mi./40 km from mainland Greece. Population: 2,871 (1981). Area: 69 sq. mi./178 sq. km.

sam·o·var /sámmə vaàr/ *n* a large and often ornate Russian tea urn, originally heated by a built-in charcoal burner [Mid-19C. < Russian < *samo-* "self" + *varit'* "boil"]

Sam·o·yed /sámmə yèd, sá moy èd/ *n* **1.** (*plural* **Sam·o·yeds** or *same*) **MEMBER OF SIBERIAN PEOPLE** a member of a people living in northeastern European Russia and western Siberia **2. LANGUAGE OF SAMOYEDS** the group of Uralic languages spoken by the Samoyed people, related to Finno-Ugric. Native speakers: 35,000. **3. SIBERIAN DOG** a dog with a thick creamy white coat, distinctive ruff, and tightly-curled tail, belonging to a Siberian breed [Late 16C. < Russian] —**Sam·o·yed** *adj*

samp /samp/ *n* **1.** *New England* same as **mush**[1] *n* (sense 3) **2.** *S Africa* coarsely crushed corn, frequently cooked with dried beans as a staple food by Black South Africans [Mid-17C. < Algonquian *nasàump*]

sampan

sam·pan /sám pàn/ *n* a small flat-bottomed boat (**skiff**) propelled by two oars or a single rear-mounted oar (**scull**), used in East Asia [Early 17C. < Chinese (Cantonese) *saam-paán* "three-board (boat)"]

sam·phire /sám fīr/ (*plural* **-phires** or *same*) *n* **1.** a coastal plant with fleshy leaves that are used in pickles. Flowers: small, white. Native to: Europe. Latin name: *Crithmum maritimum*. **2.** PLANTS same as **glasswort** [Mid-16C. Contraction of French *herbe de Saint Pierre* "St. Peter's herb"]

sam·ple /sámp'l/ *n* **1. EXAMPLE** a small amount or part of something, used as an example of the character, features, or quality of the whole ○ *a free sample of the new shampoo* **2. SPECIMEN FOR ANALYSIS** a small part or quantity of something such as blood or soil, for scientific or medical examination or analysis ○ *took a blood sample* **3.** RECORDING **PIECE OF RECORDED SOUND** a piece of recorded sound or a musical phrase taken from an existing recording, especially in digital form, and used as part of a new recording ○ *a CD of drum samples* **4.** STATS **GROUP SELECTED FOR TESTING** a representative selection of a population that is examined to gain statistical information about the whole ■ *vti* (**-pled, -pling, -ples**) **1. GET SAMPLE OF SOMETHING** to take a sample of something, especially in order to determine its character, features, or quality ○ *sample the river water* **2.** RECORDING **CONVERT SOUND INTO DIGITAL INFORMATION** to convert sound into digital information in order to store or manipulate it electronically **3.** RECORDING **TAKE SAMPLE OF SOMETHING FOR RECORDING** to take a sample of recorded music, especially in order to use it in another recording ○ *sampled whatever albums happened to be lying around* [13C. Shortening of Anglo-Norman *assample* "example" < Latin *exemplum* (see EXAMPLE)]

sam·pler /sámplər/ *n* **1. EMBROIDERED CLOTH** a piece of embroidered cloth containing rows of different stitches, either as a practice piece or, originally, as a demonstration of the embroiderer's skill **2. REPRESENTATIVE SELECTION** a selection that is intended to represent what is available in a range **3. SOMEBODY WHO ANALYZES SAMPLES** somebody who samples small quantities of something, especially to determine quality **4. DEVICE FOR TAKING SAMPLES** a machine or device used to take and analyze samples **5.** RECORDING **ELECTRONIC EQUIPMENT FOR SAMPLING MUSICAL PHRASES** an electronic device that can record sounds or take short musical phrases from an existing recording and allow them to be manipulated digitally before being used to make a new recording **6.** RECORDING **MACHINE CONVERTING SOUND TO DIGITAL INFORMATION** an electronic device that converts sound to digital information for electronic storage or manipulation

sam·ple space *n* the set of all possible outcomes of a statistical experiment, represented by points

sam·pling /sámpling/ *n* **1. PROCESS OF SELECTING SAMPLE GROUP** the process of selecting a group of people or products to be used as a representative or random sample **2. SOMETHING USED AS SAMPLE** a small part, number, or quantity of something that has been taken or selected as a sample **3.** RECORDING **REUSE OF RECORDED MUSICAL PHRASES** the process of taking a short musical phrase from one recording and using it in another recording, often in repeated sequences and sometimes in an adapted or edited form ○ *recent advances in sampling technology*

Pete Sampras

Sam·pras /sámprəss/, **Pete** (*b.* 1971) US tennis player. At 19, he became the youngest man to win the US Open. His many Grand Slam titles include seven Wimbledon trophies. Full name **Peter Sampras**. Known as **Pistol Pete**

sam·sa·ra /səm saárə/ *n* **1.** in Hinduism, the endless cycle of birth, life, death, and rebirth **2.** in Buddhism, somebody's rebirth [Late 19C. < Sanskrit *saṃsaraḥ* < *sam* "together" + *sarati* "it flows"]

sam·ska·ra /səm skaárə/ *n* a Hindu purification ceremony that marks a transition in a person's life [Early 19C. < Sanskrit *saṃskārāḥ* "preparation, making perfect"]

Sam·son /sámss'n/ *n* **1.** in the Bible, an Israelite judge and warrior. He used his enormous strength to fight the Philistines, to whom he was ultimately betrayed by his mistress, Delilah (Judges 13–16). **2.** any very strong man —**Sam·so·ni·an** /sam sṓnee ən/ *adj*

Sam·u·el /sámmyoo əl/ *n* **1.** in the Bible, the leader of the Israelites in the 11th century B.C. He was the first prophet after Moses. **2.** either of two books of the Bible that describe the history of the Israelites from the birth of Samuel to the end of the reign of King David, traditionally attributed to Samuel. See table at **Bible**

Sam·u·el·son /sámmyoo əlss'n, sámmyəlss'n/, **Joan Benoit** (*b.* 1957) US athlete. She won the first Olympic marathon ever held for women (1984).

Sam·u·el·son, Paul (*b.* 1915) US economist, who is best known for his widely used and constantly updated textbook, *Economics*, first published in 1948. He won the Nobel Prize in economics (1970). Full name **Samuelson, Paul Anthony**

sam·u·rai /sámmə rī/ (*plural same* or **-rais**) *n* an aristocratic Japanese warrior of a class that dominated the military aristocracy between the 11th and the 19th centuries [Early 18C. < Japanese]

san /saan/, **-san** *n* used in Japanese after somebody's first name, last name, or title, as a polite form of address [Late 19C. < Japanese]

San[1] /san/ *n* used as a title, usually in place names, before the name of a man who has been made a saint [< Spanish and Italian, form of *Santo* (see SANTO) used before vowels]

San[2] /saan/ (*plural same* or **Sans**) *n* **1.** a member of a people living in southern Africa. The San traditionally live in small nomadic groups as hunters and gatherers. **2.** the group of Khoisan languages spoken by the San people [Late 19C. < Nama] —**San** *adj*

San Andreas Fault

San An·dre·as Fault /sàn an drày əss-/ *n* a geologic fault zone between two tectonic plates that runs from San Francisco south to San Diego in California. It is an area of frequent earthquakes caused by the plates sliding past each other. Length: 600 mi./1,000 km. [Because it runs along the San Andreas valley]

San An·ge·lo /san ánjəlō/ city in western Texas, on the Concho River. Population: 87,423 (2002 estimate).

San An·to·ni·o /-an tṓnee ō/ city in south central Texas. It is the cultural and commercial center of the Rio Grande Valley, and was the site of the battle of the Alamo in 1836. Population: 1,194,222 (2002 estimate).

san·a·tive /sánnətiv/ *adj* able to restore health (*archaic formal*) [15C. Via French < late Latin *sanativus* < Latin *sanare* "heal" (see SANATORIUM)]

san·a·to·ri·um /sànnə táwree əm/ (*plural* **-ri·ums** or **-ri·a** /-ree ə/), **san·i·ta·ri·um** /sànnə térree əm/ *n* **1.** a medical facility where people affected by long-term illnesses can receive treatment and those recovering from severe illnesses can recuperate **2.** a resort for maintaining or improving health (*dated*) [Mid-19C. < modern Latin < Latin *sanat-*, past participle of *sanare* "heal" < *sanus* "healthy"]

san·be·ni·to /sànbə neétō/ (*plural* **-tos**) *n* a sackcloth garment worn by those declared heretics by the Spanish Inquisition. Penitent heretics wore a yellow one with a red cross on it and impenitent heretics wore a black one decorated with flames and devils. [Mid-16C. < Spanish *sambenito*, alteration of *San Benito* "St. Benedict," because it resembles the scapular of a Benedictine monk]

San Ber·nar·di·no /-bərnər deénō/ city in southern California, situated at the foot of the San Bernardino Mountains at the eastern edge of the large metropolitan region surrounding Los Angeles. Population: 191,631 (2002 estimate).

San Ber·nar·di·no Moun·tains mountain range in southern California. The highest peak is San Gorgonio Mountain, 11,485 ft./3,506 m. Length: 100 mi./161 km.

San Bru·no /-brōōnō/ city in San Mateo County, western California, on San Francisco Bay. Population: 39,366 (2002 estimate).

San Car·los /-kaárləss/ city in San Mateo County, western California, on the San Francisco Peninsula. Population: 27,165 (2002 estimate).

San Cle·men·te /-klə méntee/ city and tourist resort in Orange County, southwestern California, on the Pacific Ocean. Population: 55,986 (2002 estimate).

san·coche /sang kóch, -kósh, -kóchee/ *n Carib* a Caribbean soup made with a variety of vegetables, split peas, and meat [Mid-20C. Alteration of American Spanish *sancocho* < Spanish *sancochar* "parboil"]

San Cri·sto·bal /-krístə baál/ one of the Galapagos Islands, off the coast of Ecuador. Area: 195 sq. mi./505 sq. km.

San Cri·stó·bal /-kri stṓb'l/ capital city of Táchira State, western Venezuela. Population: 238,670 (1992).

sanc·ta RELIG plural of **sanctum**

sanc·ti·fy /sángktə fī/ (**-fied, -fy·ing, -fies**) *vt* **1.** MAKE SOMETHING HOLY to give something holy status **2.** FREE SOMEBODY FROM SIN to perform a ritual or other act intended to free somebody from sin **3.** BLESS SOMETHING THROUGH RELIGIOUS VOW to give a religious blessing to something such as a marriage, usually through an oath or vow ○ *sanctified the marriage* **4.** OFFICIALLY APPROVE SOMETHING to give social, moral, or official approval to something ○ *rules sanctified by tradition* **5.** MAKE SOMETHING ROUTE TO HOLINESS to make something a means of achieving holiness or a source of grace [14C. < Old French *saintifier*, later *sanctifier* < Latin *sanctus* "holy" (see SAINT)] —**sanc·ti·fi·a·ble** *adj* —**sanc·ti·fi·ca·tion** /sàngktəfi káysh'n/ *n* —**sanc·ti·fi·er** *n*

sanc·ti·mo·ni·ous /sàngktə mṓnee əss/ *adj* making an exaggerated show of holiness or moral superiority [Early 17C. < Latin *sanctimonia* "sanctity" < *sanctus* "holy" (see SAINT)] —**sanc·ti·mo·ni·ous·ly** *adv* —**sanc·ti·mo·ni·ous·ness** *n* —**sanc·ti·mo·ny** /sángktə mōnee/ *n*

sanc·tion /sángksh'n/ *n* **1.** AUTHORIZATION official permission or approval for a course of action ○ *unable to proceed without the sanction of the board* **2.** SUPPORT something that serves as approval or encouragement, e.g., social acceptance or custom **3.** LAW a law or rule that leads to a penalty being imposed when it is disobeyed **4.** PENALTY IMPOSED FOR BREAKING RULE a punishment imposed as a result of breaking a law or rule **5.** INTERNAT REL PUNITIVE MEASURE TO PRESSURE COUNTRY a measure taken by one or more nations to apply pressure on another nation to conform to international law or opinion (*often used in the plural*) ○ *imposed trade sanctions* **6.** ETHICS PRINCIPLE DETERMINING BEHAVIOR an ethical principle or consideration that determines or influences somebody's conduct ■ *vt* (**-tioned, -tion·ing, -tions**) **1.** AUTHORIZE SOMETHING to grant official approval or permission for something ○ *The county government refused to sanction the proposed design.* **2.** TACITLY APPROVE OF SOMETHING to allow something to be tolerated or accepted ○ *The school's inaction further sanctions this behavior.* [15C. Via French < Latin *sanction-* < *sanctus* "holy" (see SAINT)] —**sanc·tion·a·ble** *adj* —**sanc·tion·er** *n* —**sanc·tion·less** *adj*

sanc·ti·ty /sángktətee/ (*plural* **-ties**) *n* **1.** the condition of being considered sacred or holy, and therefore entitled to respect and reverence **2.** something considered holy or sacred (*formal*) [14C. Via French < Latin *sanctitas* < *sanctus* "holy" (see SAINT)]

sanc·tu·ar·y /sángkchoo èrree/ (*plural* **-ies**) *n* **1.** REFUGE a safe place, especially for people being persecuted **2.** PLACE WHERE WILDLIFE IS PROTECTED a place or area of land where wildlife is protected from predators and from being destroyed or hunted by human beings ○ *a bird sanctuary* **3.** RELIG HOLY PLACE a holy place, e.g., a church, mosque, or temple **4.** RELIG MOST SACRED PART OF HOLY BUILDING the most sacred part of a consecrated building, e.g., the area around the altar in a Christian church **5.** CHR CHURCH PROTECTING FUGITIVES in medieval times, a holy place, usually a church, that provided immunity from the law **6.** JUDAISM same as **holy of holies** [14C. Via French < Latin *sanctuarium* < *sanctus* "holy" (see SAINT)]

sanc·tum /sángktəm/ (*plural* **-tums** or **-ta** /-tə/) *n* **1.** a sacred place inside a church, temple, or mosque **2.** a quiet private place where somebody is free from interference or interruption [Late 16C. < late Latin < form of Latin *sanctus* "holy" (see SAINT)]

sanc·tum sanc·to·rum /sàngktəm sangk táwrəm/ (*plural* **sanc·ta sanc·to·rum** /sàngktə-/ or **sanc·tum sanc·to·rums**) *n* **1.** JUDAISM same as **holy of holies** (sense 1) **2.** same as **sanctum** (sense 2) [14C. < late Latin, "holy of holies"]

Sanc·tus /sángktəss/ *n* **1.** in some Christian churches, a hymn praising the power and holiness of God that is part of the Mass **2.** a musical setting for the Sanctus [14C. < Latin, "holy" (see SAINT), the first word of the hymn]

Sanc·tus bell *n* in the Roman Catholic Church, a bell rung at the beginning of the Sanctus and at other times during Mass

sand /sand/ *n* **1.** MATERIAL MADE OF TINY GRAINS a substance consisting of fine loose grains of rock or minerals, usually quartz fragments, found on beaches, in deserts, and in soil, sometimes used as a building material **2.** COLORS BROWNISH YELLOW a brownish yellow color like sand **3.** PARTICLES IN HOURGLASS the tiny grains in an hourglass **4.** DETERMINATION courage and determination (*dated informal*) **5.** GEOL FINE SEDIMENTARY MATERIAL a sedimentary material that is finer than gravel but coarser than silt, with particle sizes between 0.06 mm and 2 mm (*technical*) **6.** GEOG AREA OF SAND an area covered with or made up of sand, e.g., a beach or a desert ○ *playing on the sand and swimming in the sea* ■ **sands** *npl* MOMENTS moments remaining or allotted (*literary*) ○ *The sands of time are running out for the old king.* ■ *v* (**sand·ed, sand·ing, sands**) **1.** *vt* SMOOTH SOMETHING USING SANDPAPER to rub a surface with sandpaper or sand to make it smoother **2.** *vt* SPRINKLE SOMETHING WITH SAND to cover or sprinkle something such as an icy road with sand **3.** *vt* MIX SAND WITH SOMETHING to add sand to something, e.g., to a mixture of materials when making mortar **4.** *vti* FILL WITH SAND to become filled with sand, or fill something with sand [Old English < Germanic] —**sand** *adj* ◇ **kick sand in somebody's face** to show contempt for or dominance over somebody less strong or powerful

AKG London

George Sand: portrait (1839) by Auguste Charpentier

Sand /sand, saaN/, **George** (1804–76) French writer. She wrote many volumes of essays, novels, and plays, which reflect her feminist and libertarian ideals. Pseudonym of **Dudevant, Amandine Aurore Lucille, Baronne**

> "Where love is absent there can be no woman."
> [George Sand, *Lelia*; 1833]

san·dal /sánd'l/ *n* **1.** a light open shoe that is held on by straps across the instep or around the heel or ankle, usually worn during warm weather **2.** a strap for going around the ankle or across the instep to keep a shoe on a foot [14C. Via Latin < Greek *sandalion*, diminutive of *sandalon*] —**san·daled** *adj*

san·dal·wood /sánd'l wòod/ *n* **1.** PALE YELLOW FRAGRANT WOOD a fragrant close-grained pale yellow wood. Use: furniture-making, carving, incense. **2.** AROMATIC OIL OF SANDALWOOD an aromatic oil extracted from sandalwood. Use: perfumes, incense, aromatherapy oil. **3.** TROPICAL EVERGREEN TREE a parasitic tropical evergreen tree that produces sandalwood. Native to: South Asia, Australia. Latin name: *Santalum album*. **4.** TREE RESEMBLING SANDALWOOD TREE a tree that resembles true sandalwood and is harvested for wood. Native to: South Asia, Australia. Genera: *Adenanthera* or *Myroporum* or *Pterocarpus*.

san·da·rac /sándə ràk/ *n* **1.** BRITTLE RESIN a brittle yellowish translucent resin exuded by a coniferous tree. Use: varnishes, incense. **2.** WOOD FOR BUILDING a hard dark aromatic wood. Use: building material. **3.** EVERGREEN TREE a coniferous tree with flat branches and leaves with overlapping scales, which produces sandarac. Native to: northwestern Africa, Spain. Latin name: *Tetraclinis articulata*. [Mid-17C. Via Latin < Greek *sandarakē*]

sand·bag /sánd bàg/ *n* **1.** SACK OF SAND a sealed bag full of sand, used in building defenses against gunfire or flooding, or as ballast in hot air balloons **2.** BAG

OF SAND USED AS WEAPON a small bag filled with sand and used as a weapon in the same way as a blackjack ■ *v* (**-bagged, -bag·ging, -bags**) **1.** *vt* PROTECT SOMETHING WITH SANDBAGS to put sandbags in or around something as protection **2.** *vt* KNOCK SOMEBODY OR SOMETHING DOWN to attack or hit somebody or something with a sandbag (*informal*) **3.** *vti* DELAY NEGOTIATIONS to delay negotiations or a business deal in the hope of receiving a more favorable offer from somebody else (*slang*) **4.** *vt* COERCE SOMEBODY to force somebody to do something by using coercive or crude tactics (*dated slang*) —**sand·bag·ger** *n*

sand·bank /sánd bàngk/ *n* a mound, hillside, or shoal of sand formed by the action of wind or water

sand·bar /sánd baàr/ *n* a long ridge of sand formed in a body of water by currents or tides

sand·blast /sánd blàst/ *vti* (**-blast·ed, -blast·ing, -blasts**) POLISH WITH SAND to clean, polish, or mark the surface of glass, metal, or stone by applying a jet of pressurized air or steam mixed with sand ■ *n* **1.** JET OF SAND FIRED UNDER PRESSURE a jet of pressurized air or steam mixed with sand or grit that is used for sandblasting **2.** MACHINE FOR SANDBLASTING a machine that produces a jet of pressurized air or steam mixed with sand or grit for sandblasting —**sand·blast·er** *n*

sand-blind *adj* having reduced ability to see (*archaic or literary*) [15C. Alteration of Old English *samblind*, literally "half blind"] —**sand-blind·ness** *n*

sand·board /sánd bàwrd/ *n* a board similar to a surfboard or snowboard used for riding down sand dunes or performing stunts on a course covered in sand —**sand·board·er** *n* —**sand·board·ing** *n*

sand·box /sánd bòks/ *n* an area of sand for children to play in, usually contained in a box or frame

sand·box tree *n* a spiny tree with woody seed capsules that explode when ripe. Native to: tropical America. Latin name: *Hura crepitans*. [Because the seed capsules formerly served as boxes for sand]

sand·bur /sánd bùr/ *n* **1.** a grass with a single-grained spikelet that is enclosed by a spiny bur. Native to: eastern United States, tropical America. Genus: *Cenchrus*. **2.** a bur of the sandbur plant

Sand·burg /sánd bùrg/, **Carl** (1878–1967) US poet, folklorist, and historian. He wrote poems, collected and sang American folksongs, and won a Pulitzer Prize for his six-volume biography *Abraham Lincoln* (1926–39).

> "Slang is a language that rolls up its sleeves, spits on its hands and goes to work."
> [Carl Sandburg, *New York Times*; February 13, 1959]

sand-cast *vt* to make a casting by pouring molten metal into a sand mold

sand cast·ing *n* a casting made by pouring molten metal into a sand mold

sand·cas·tle /sánd kàss'l/ *n* a small model of a castle that is made out of damp sand, usually by children on a beach

sand crack *n* a crack in a horse's hoof that starts at the top (**coronet**) and extends vertically toward the sole

sand dab *n* a small flatfish caught for food. Native to: North American Pacific coast. Genus: *Citharichthys*.

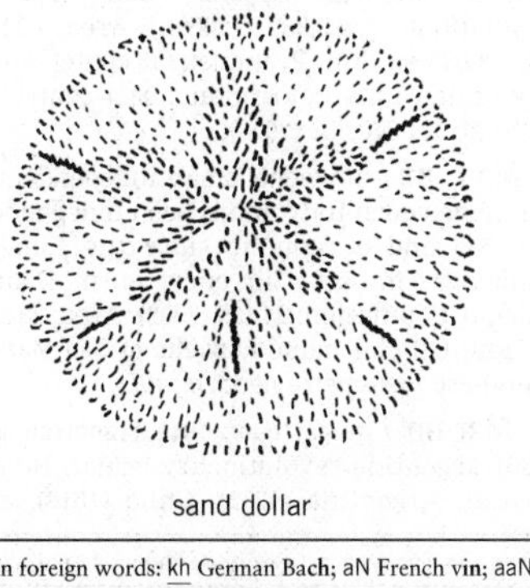

sand dollar

sand dol·lar *n* a flat circular sea animal related to the starfish and sea urchin, that is enclosed in white shell with an imprint that resembles a flower. Native to: shallow sandy coastal waters of North America. Genus: *Citharichthys*.

sand eel *n* FISH same as **sand lance**

sand·er /sándər/ *n* **1.** POWER TOOL FOR SMOOTHING SURFACES an electric power tool that is used to smooth wooden or metal surfaces **2.** TRUCK THAT SPREADS SAND ON ROADS a truck or a truck attachment that spreads sand on roads **3.** SOMEBODY WHO SANDS SOMETHING somebody who sands something or operates a sander

sand·er·ling /sándərling/ (*plural* **-lings** or *same*) *n* a small bird of the sandpiper family with gray and white plumage in winter. Native to: coastal regions worldwide. Latin name: *Calidris alba*. [Early 17C. Origin ?]

sand flea *n* **1.** INSECTS same as **chigoe 2.** a tiny jumping crustacean that lives on sandy tidal beaches. Genus: *Orchestia*.

sand fly *n* a hairy fly that resembles a moth. Blood-sucking females transmit several tropical diseases. Native to: tropics. Genus: *Phlebotomus*.

sand·fly fe·ver /sánd flī-/ *n* a mild viral illness transmitted by the bite of a female sand fly. It causes fever, headaches, eye pain, and general discomfort.

sand·glass /sánd glàss/ *n* TIME same as **hourglass**

sand·grouse /sánd gròwss/ (*plural* **-grouses** or *same*) *n* a bird related to the pigeon that has long pointed wings and a short beak and feet. Native to: dry and semiarid regions of Europe and Asia. Genus: *Pterocles*.

S & H *abbr* COMM shipping and handling

san·dhi /sándee, saán-, sún-/ *n* the modification of the sound or form of a word under the influence of a preceding or following sound. The variation between "a" and "an" for the indefinite article in English is a form of sandhi. [Early 19C. < Sanskrit *saṃdhiḥ* "combination"]

sand·hill crane /sánd hìl-/ *n* a crane with gray drooping feathers and a bald red crown. Native to: North America, northeastern Siberia. Latin name: *Grus canadensis*. [Because commonly found among sand dunes]

sand·hog /sánd hàwg, -hòg/ *n* a worker inside a caisson in underwater building projects such as tunnels (*slang*)

sand hop·per *n* MARINE BIOL same as **sand flea**

San Di·e·go /-dee áygō/ city and major port of entry in southwestern California, on San Diego Bay. It is the second largest city in California, and the sixth largest in the United States. Population: 1,259,532 (2002 estimate).

San Di·mas /-deéməss/ city in Los Angeles County, southwestern California, 25 mi./40 km east of Los Angeles. Population: 35,876 (2002 estimate).

San·din·is·ta /sàndə neéstə, saàndə-/ *n* a member of a socialist movement in Nicaragua that successfully overthrew the government of President Anastasio Somoza in 1979 and fought a US-backed insurgent force in the 1980s [Early 20C. < Spanish, after Augusto César Sandino (1893–1934), Nicaraguan revolutionary leader]

S & L *abbr* BANKING savings and loan association

sand lance *n* a small slender ocean fish resembling an eel. Genus: *Ammodytes*.

sand lil·y *n* a low-growing stemless plant with long thin leaves. Flowers: fragrant, white, star-shaped. Native to: western North America. Latin name: *Leucocrinum montanum*.

sand·lot /sánd lòt/ *n* a vacant lot used by children for playing games, especially baseball (*informal*) —**sand·lot·ter** *n*

S & M *abbr* sadism and masochism

sand·man /sánd màn/ *n* in folklore and fairy tales, a character personifying drowsiness, who makes children go to sleep by sprinkling sand in their eyes

sand paint·ing *n* **1.** a ceremonial practice of the Navajo and Pueblo peoples, in which different colors of sand are distributed over a flat surface to create symbolic pictures and designs **2.** a picture or design made by sand painting

sand·pa·per /sánd pàypər/ *n* strong paper coated on one side with sand or another abrasive. Use: smoothing surfaces. ■ *vt* (**-pered, -per·ing, -pers**) to rub a surface such as a piece of wood or a wall with sandpaper —**sand·pa·per·y** *adj*

sand pear *n US* FOOD, TREES same as **Asian pear** (sense 1)

sand·pi·per /sánd pīpər/ (*plural* **-pers** or *same*) *n* a shorebird with a long slender beak that it uses to catch insects, worms, and soft mollusks in sand and mud. Family: Scolopacidae. [Late 17C. < its piping voice]

sand·pit /sánd pìt/ *n* **1.** a large deep pit from which sand is excavated **2.** *UK* same as **sandbox**

sand shark *n* a shark of mainly shallow waters. Native to: central and southern Atlantic, western Pacific coasts. Genus: *Carcharias*.

sand·shoe /sánd shoō/ *n UK* a light low-cut canvas shoe with a rubber sole

sand·stone /sánd stōn/ *n* a sedimentary rock made up of particles of sand bound together with a mineral cement. Use: building material.

sand·storm /sánd stàwrm/ *n* a strong windstorm, especially in the desert, that carries clouds of sand or dust, reducing visibility

sand ta·ble *n* **1.** a table covered with a layer of sand molded to imitate the relief of a battleground terrain, used to plan military tactics **2.** a table whose top is a shallow box filled with sand for children to play with

sand trap *n* a depression on a golf course that is partly filled with sand, usually located near a green as a hazard

sand ver·be·na *n* a low trailing plant of the four-o'clock family. Flowers: fragrant, usually red, yellow, or white. Native to: western North America. Genus: *Abronia*.

sand vi·per *n* REPT same as **horned viper**

sand wedge *n* a golf club with a face angle of more than 50° that is used for chipping the ball out of a sand trap

sand·wich /sándwich, sámwich/ *n* **1.** BREAD SLICES WITH FILLING IN BETWEEN a snack or light meal made of two slices of bread or a split roll with a filling, or a single slice of bread with a topping **2.** SOMETHING LIKE SANDWICH something resembling a sandwich, especially something in which various things are squashed together or arranged in layers ■ *vt* (**-wiched, -wich·ing, -wich·es**) SQUEEZE SOMEBODY OR SOMETHING BETWEEN OTHERS to fit something or somebody tightly between two other things in space or time ○ *I'll see if I can sandwich you in on Tuesday.* [Mid-18C. After John Montague (1718–92), 4th Earl of *Sandwich*]

ORIGIN The Earl of Sandwich is said to have been so addicted to the gambling table that in order to sustain him through an entire 24-hour session uninterrupted, he had a portable meal of cold beef between slices of toast brought to him. The idea was not new, but the earl's patronage ensured that it became a vogue, and by the early 1760s we have the first evidence of his name being attached to it: the historian Edward Gibbon recorded in his diary in 1762 how he dined at the Cocoa Tree and saw "twenty or thirty of the best men in the kingdom ... supping at little tables ... upon a bit of cold meat, or a ***Sandwich***."

Sand·wich /sánd wìch/ market town in southern Kent, England. It was one of the original Cinque Ports. Population: 4,164 (1991).

sand·wich board *n* **1.** a pair of boards, usually displaying advertisements or notices, joined by straps and hung from the shoulders with one displayed in front and one behind **2.** either of the two boards that make up a sandwich board [Because the boards sandwich the person wearing them]

sand·wich coin *n* a three-layered coin that has a middle layer made of a different metal from the outside layers, e.g., a US twenty-five-cent piece

sand·wich man *n* a man who carries a sandwich board

~~sandwitch~~ incorrect spelling of **sandwich**

sand·worm /sánd wùrm/ *n* a segmented worm living in coastal sand or mud, often used as fishing bait. Genera: *Nereis* or *Anicola.*

sand·wort /sánd wùrt, -wàwrt/ (*plural* **-worts** or *same*) *n* a plant that grows in thick tufts close to the ground on sandy soil. Flowers: single, white or pink. Genus: *Arenaria.*

sand·y /sándee/ (**-i·er, -i·est**) *adj* **1.** FULL OF SAND made up of, covered in, or full of sand **2.** LIKE SAND having a grainy texture or consistency similar to that of sand **3.** OF COLOR OF SAND of a reddish or brownish yellow color ○ *sandy hair* —**sand·i·ness** *n*

sane /sayn/ (**san·er, san·est**) *adj* **1.** mentally healthy and able to make rational decisions **2.** based on sensible, reasonable, or rational thinking ○ *a sane and practical solution to the problem* [Early 17C. < Latin *sanus* "healthy"] —**sane·ly** *adv* —**sane·ness** *n*

San Fer·nan·do Val·ley /-fər nándō-/ residential and industrial region in southern California, north of Los Angeles. It is bounded by the Transverse Range on the north, the Santa Susana Mountains on the west, and the Santa Monica Mountains on the south. Population: 1,300,000 (1998).

San·ford /sánfərd/ city in southwestern Maine, southwest of Biddeford and Saco. Population: 21,550 (2002 estimate).

San Fran·cis·co /-frən sískō/ city in western California, the largest West Coast US port, located on San Francisco Bay. The famous Golden Gate Bridge, a suspension bridge that connects Marin County with San Francisco, was opened there in 1937. Population: 764,049 (2002 estimate). —**San Fran·cis·can** *n, adj*

San Fran·cis·co Bay inlet in California, linked to the Pacific Ocean by the Golden Gate Strait. Length: 60 mi./100 km.

sang past tense of **sing**

San Gab·ri·el /-gáybree əl/ city in Los Angeles County, southwestern California, a residential community near Los Angeles. Population: 40,784 (2002 estimate).

san·ga·ree /sàng gə reé/ *n* **1.** a chilled drink of wine mixed with fruit juice, nutmeg, and sometimes a hard liquor **2.** BEVERAGES same as **sangria** [Mid-18C. Alteration of Spanish *sangría* (see SANGRIA)]

Sang·er /sángər/, **Frederick** (*b.* 1918) British biochemist. He was noted for his work on insulin, the structure of proteins, and the nucleotide sequence of nucleic acids. He twice won the Nobel Prize in chemistry (1958, 1980).

Margaret Sanger

Sang·er, Margaret (1883–1966) US social reformer. She founded and led the US birth control movement in the 1910s and 1920s. Born **Higgins, Margaret Louise**

sang-froid /sàng frwaá, saáng-/ *n* self-possession or calmness, especially in a dangerous or stressful situation [Mid-18C. < French, "cold blood"]

San·gi·o·vese /sànjō váyzee/ *n* **1.** a red wine made from a black grape grown mainly in Italy **2.** a black grape variety. Use: to make Sangiovese. [Early 20C. < Italian]

San·greal /san gráyl/, **San·graal** /san graál/ *n* CHR same as **Grail** [15C. < Old French *saint graal* "Holy Grail"]

San·gre de Cris·to Moun·tains /sàng gree dee krístō-/ range of the Rocky Mountains in southeastern Colorado and northern New Mexico. Its highest peak is Blanca Peak, 14,345 ft./4,372 m. Length: 220 mi./354 km.

san·gri·a /sang gréé ə/ *n* a chilled Spanish drink of red wine, fruit juice, carbonated water, sugar, and brandy or another liquor, usually served in a jug with pieces of fruit [Mid-20C. < Spanish *sangría* "act of bleeding" < Latin *sanguis* "blood"]

san·gui·nar·i·a /sàng gwə nérree ə/ *n* **1.** PLANTS same as **bloodroot 2.** the dried rhizome and roots of the bloodroot plant. Use: antiplaque agent in toothpaste, formerly, internally as medicine. [Early 19C. < modern Latin < Latin *sanguis* "blood"]

san·gui·nar·y /sáng gwə nèrree/ *adj* (*formal*) **1.** INVOLVING BLOODSHED involving death or bloodshed **2.** BLOODTHIRSTY bloodthirsty or eager to kill **3.** BLOODIED consisting of or stained with blood [15C. < Latin *sanguinarius* < *sanguis* "blood"] —**san·gui·nar·i·ly** *adv*

san·guine /sáng gwin/ *adj* **1.** CONFIDENT cheerfully optimistic **2.** RUDDY flushed with a healthy rosy color ○ *a sanguine complexion* **3.** BLOOD RED of a blood red color **4.** BLOODTHIRSTY eager to shed blood (*archaic*) **5.** PHYSIOL, HIST HAVING BLOOD AS DOMINANT HUMOR in medieval physiology, having blood as the dominant humor and therefore characterized by a ruddy complexion and a courageous, optimistic, and romantic temperament [14C. Via French < Latin *sanguin-*, stem of *sanguis* "blood"] —**san·guine·ly** *adv* —**san·guine·ness** *n* —**san·guin·i·ty** /sang gwínnətee/ *n*

san·guin·e·ous /sang gwínnee əss/ *adj* **1.** relating to or containing blood, especially mixed with other fluids (*often used in combination*) ○ *a sero-sanguineous discharge* **2.** COLORS same as **sanguine** (sense 3) **3.** involving or enjoying bloodshed (*literary*) [Early 16C. < Latin *sanguineus* < *sanguin-* (see SANGUINE)]

San·hed·rin /san heédrin, -héddrin/ *n* the supreme Jewish judicial, ecclesiastical, and administrative council in ancient Jerusalem before A.D. 70, having 71 members from the nobility and presided over by the high priest [Late 16C. Via Hebrew < Greek *sunedrion* "council" < *sun* "together" + *hedra* "seat"]

san·i·cle /sánnik'l/ *n* a widely distributed plant with oval fruits and hooked bristles. Flowers: small, variously colored, in clusters. Use: formerly, astringent. Genus: *Sanicula.* [15C. Via French < medieval Latin *sanicula*]

san·i·dine /sánni deen, -din/ *n* a glassy high-temperature form of the mineral orthoclase. Source: lavas. [Early 19C. < Greek *sanid-* "board"; from the shape of the mineral's crystals]

sanit. *abbr* **1.** sanitary **2.** sanitation

san·i·tar·i·a MED plural of **sanitarium**

san·i·tar·i·um *n* HEALTH SERVICES another spelling of **sanatorium**

san·i·tar·y /sánnə tèrree/ *adj* **1.** relating to public health, especially general hygiene and the removal of human waste through the sewage system **2.** clean and free from agents that cause disease or infection [Mid-19C. < French *sanitaire* < Latin *sanitas* "health" < *sanus* "healthy"] —**san·i·tar·i·an** /sànnə térree ən/ *adj, n* —**san·i·tar·i·ly** /sànnə térrəlee/ *adv* —**san·i·tar·i·ness** *n*

san·i·tar·y en·gi·neer·ing *n* the branch of civil engineering concerned with the building, maintenance, and development of water and sewage systems and other public health services —**san·i·tar·y en·gi·neer** *n*

san·i·tar·y land·fill *n* ENVIRON same as **landfill** (*dated*)

san·i·tar·y pad, san·i·tar·y nap·kin *n* a disposable or cotton pad worn by women to absorb the blood flow during menstruation

san·i·tar·y pro·tec·tion *n* sanitary pads and tampons as means of absorbing the blood flow during menstruation

san·i·ta·tion /sànnə táysh'n/ *n* **1.** the study and maintenance of public health and hygiene, especially the water supply and sewage systems ○ *sanitation laws* **2.** conditions or procedures related to the collection and disposal of sewage and garbage [Mid-19C. < SANITARY]

san·i·ta·tion work·er *n US* OCCUPATIONS same as **garbageman**

san·i·tize /sánnə tīz/ (**-tized, -tiz·ing, -tiz·es**) *vt* **1.** to clean something thoroughly by disinfecting or sterilizing it **2.** to make something more likely to be acceptable by removing anything that might be considered offensive or controversial (*usually passive*) ○ *a sanitized version of the article* [Mid-19C. < SANITARY] —**san·i·ti·za·tion** /sànnəti záysh'n/ *n* —**san·i·tiz·er** *n*

~~sanitorium~~ incorrect spelling of **sanatorium**

san·i·ty /sánnətee/ *n* **1.** the condition of being mentally healthy and able to make rational decisions **2.** common sense, reasonableness, and predictability ○ *to restore a little sanity to the situation* [Early 17C. < Latin *sanitas* < *sanus* "healthy"]

San Ja·cin·to /-jə síntō/ river flowing from southeastern Texas into the Gulf of Mexico at Galveston Bay. Length: 85 mi./137 km.

San Joa·quin /-waw keén/ river in central California flowing from the Sierra Nevada Mountains into the Sacramento River. Length: 350 mi./560 km.

San Jo·se /-hō sáy/ city and county seat of Santa Clara county in western California, situated in Santa Clara Valley, south of San Francisco Bay. Historically an agricultural center, it is now regarded as the capital of Silicon Valley. Population: 900,403 (2002 estimate).

San Jo·sé /-hō sáy/ capital city of Costa Rica, and of San José Province, situated in the center of the country. It is the country's largest city and its economic and political hub. Population: 309,672 (2000).

San Jo·se scale *n* a scale insect that is destructive to fruit trees and other fruit-bearing plants. Native to: Asia. Latin name: *Quadraspidiotus perniciosus.* [Late 19C. After SAN JOSE]

San Juan /-waán, -hwaán/ **1.** river flowing from Colorado into New Mexico and back into Colorado, before joining the Colorado River in Utah. Length: 360 mi./580 km. **2.** capital city and port of Puerto Rico, situated in the northeast of the island. Population: 421,958 (2000).

San Juan Cap·is·tra·no /-kàppi straánō/ city in Orange County, southwestern California. It is the site of a Spanish mission. Population: 34,637 (2002 estimate).

San Juan Is·lands group of 172 islands in Washington State, between Haro and Rosario straits, east of Vancouver Island. Population: 14,565 (2002 estimate).

San Juan Moun·tains mountain range in the southwestern United States, in southwestern Colorado and northern New Mexico. Volcanic in origin, it is part of the Rocky Mountains. The highest peak is Uncompahgre Peak, 14,309 ft./4,361 m.

sank past tense of **sink**

USAGE See *sink.*

San·khya /saángkyə/ *n* one of six systems of orthodox Hindu philosophy, based on the perpetual interaction of spirit and matter [Late 18C. < Sanskrit *sāṁkhya-* "relating to number"]

San Le·an·dro /-lee ándrō/ city in Alameda County, western California, on San Francisco Bay, near Oakland. Population: 80,609 (2002 estimate).

San Lu·is Ob·is·po /-loò iss ə bíspō/ city in western California, on San Luis Obispo Creek, near the Pacific coast. Population: 44,259 (2002 estimate).

San Lu·is Po·to·sí /-loo eéss pòttō seé/ **1.** state in east central Mexico. Capital: San Luis Potosí. Population: 2,299,360 (2000). Area: 24,339 sq. mi./63,038 sq. km. **2.** industrial center and capital city of San Luis Potosí State, east central Mexico. Population: 670,532 (2000).

San Ma·ri·no /-mə reénō/ small independent enclave in northeastern Italy. It has been independent since A.D. 885 and a republic since the 14th century. Language: Italian. Currency: euro. Capital: San Marino. Population: 28,119 (2003). Area: 23 sq. mi./61 sq. km. Official name **Republic of San Marino** —**San Ma·ri·nese** /san mèrrə neéz/ *n, adj*

San Mar·tín /-maar teén/, **José Francisco de** (1778–1850) Argentine revolutionary leader. He helped to liberate Argentina (1812), Chile (1818), and Peru

San Marino

(1821) from Spanish rule. Frustrated by political quarrels, he retired to France in 1824.

San Ma·te·o /-mə táy ō/ city in San Mateo County, western California, on San Francisco Bay. Population: 91,935 (2002 estimate).

San Mig·uel de Tu·cu·mán /-mi gèl də tookoo maán/ capital city of Tucumán Province, northwestern Argentina, on the Río Salí. Population: 470,809 (1991).

san·nup /sánnəp/ *n US* a married Native North American man [Early 17C. < Massachusetts Algonquian *sanomp*]

sann·ya·si /sun yaássee/ (*plural* **-sis**), **sann·ya·sin** /-yaássin/ *n* in Hinduism, a Brahmin who has reached the fourth and final stage of life as a mendicant [Early 17C. < Sanskrit *saṃnyāsī* "somebody who renounces"]

S-A node *abbr* ANAT sinoatrial node

San Pe·dro Su·la /-pèddrō sóo laa/ capital city of Cortés Department, northwestern Honduras, in the Sula Valley. Population: 383,900 (1995).

san·pro /sán prō/ *n* same as **sanitary protection** (*informal*) [Late 20C. Contraction]

San Ra·fael /san rə fél/ city in western California, on San Francisco Bay, near San Francisco. Population: 56,288 (2002 estimate).

San Re·mo /-reémō/ city and port in Imperia Province, Liguria Region, northwestern Italy. Population: 50,608 (2001).

sans /sanz, saaN/ *prep* same as **without** (*archaic or literary or humorous*) ○ *looking forward to a well-earned break sans children* [13C. < Old French *sanz* < alteration of Latin *sine* "without"]

San Sal·va·dor 1. capital city of El Salvador and of San Salvador Department, located in central El Salvador. Population: 415,346 (1992). **2.** island of the Bahamas, in the Atlantic Ocean, near Cat Island. Population: 465 (1990). Area: 60 sq. mi./155 sq. km.

sans-cu·lotte /sànz kyə lót, sàn kyə-/ *n* **1.** during the French Revolution, a revolutionary either from the poorer classes or with extreme republican sympathies **2.** a revolutionary in any country who has extremist views (*formal*) [Late 18C. < French, "without breeches"] —**sans-cu·lot·tism** *n*

San Se·bas·tián /-sə báschən/ city and administrative center of Guipúzcoa Province in the Basque Country, northern Spain. It is the site of an annual international film festival. Population: 178,229 (1998).

San·sei /saán sày, saan sáy/ (*plural* **-seis** or *same*) *n* somebody born in North America whose grandparents immigrated from Japan (*used mainly by Japanese Americans*) [Mid-20C. < Japanese, "third generation"]

san·ser·if *n* PRINTING another spelling of **sans serif**

san·se·vie·ri·a /sànssə veéree ə/ (*plural* **-as** or *same*) *n* a tropical plant with thick variegated blade-shaped leaves, commonly grown as a houseplant. Use: bowstring hemp. Native to: Africa, Asia. Genus: *Sansevieria*. [Early 19C. After Raimondo de Sangro, prince of *Sanseviero* (1710–70), Italian patron of horticulture]

San·skrit /sánskrit/ *n* an Indo-European language that is the ancestor of most of the languages of northern South Asia and of Sri Lanka. The language of the Vedas and other Hindu scriptures, classical literature, and a vast body of scientific, philosophical, and religious scholarship, it is now used by a tiny minority, but its cultural influence far outstrips its tiny base of speakers. [Early 17C. < Sanskrit *saṃskṛta-* "perfected"] —**San·skrit** *adj* —**San·skrit·ic** /san skríttik/ *n, adj* —**San·skrit·ist** *n*

LANGUAGE HERITAGE ***Sanskrit*** Much of English is made up of words from other languages, and Sanskrit, an ancient language of South Asia, is an important contributor in this respect. Sanskrit is the ancestor of modern languages including Hindi, Urdu, Gujarati, Sinhalese, Punjabi, Bangla (formerly called Bengali), and Romany, but it also survives as the language of classical literary and religious texts. Trade brought Europeans into contact with South Asia early, but scholarly interest in Sanskrit blossomed from the late 18th century, especially with the development of comparative and historical linguistics during the 19th, and most words of direct Sanskrit origin are recognizably émigrés and arrived in or after this period. However migrants that took a circuitous route are often fully naturalized.

The familiar foodstuffs ***pepper***, ***sugar***, and the ***orange***, for example, are ultimately from Sanskrit. ***Pepper*** existed in Old English as *piper*, and comes from a prehistoric West Germanic word itself ultimately, through Latin and Greek, from Sanskrit *pippalī* "berry, peppercorn." ***Sugar*** arrived in the 13th century, via French, medieval Latin, and Arabic from Sanskrit *śarkarā* "grit, ground sugar." ***Orange*** is from the same century, having reached English from Sanskrit through Old French, Italian, Arabic, and Persian.

Some well-established words also arrived through Sanskrit's descendants – via Hindi, for example, ***cheetah***, ***chit*** ("official note"), ***jungle***, ***pundit***, and ***thug***; via Bangla ***jute***; and via English Romany ***pal*** (ultimately from Sanskrit *bhrātṛ* "brother").

Nevertheless words of Eastern religion, philosophy, scholarship, and society dominate the Sanskritic émigré community. Religious migrants include: Hindu deities such as ***Kali***, ***Krishna***, ***Shiva***, and ***Vishnu***; texts, for example, ***Bhagavadgita***, ***Veda***, and ***Upanishad***; terms of the practice of Hinduism, including ***ashram***, ***avatar*** (now also transformed into a computer game persona), and ***saddhu***; terms of Buddhism, including its forms ***Hinayana*** and ***Mahayana***, the name ***Buddha*** itself, and the sacred syllable ***Om***; terms of Sikhism, including ***Sikh*** itself and its principal scripture the ***Adi Granth***; terms of Jainism, including ***Jain*** and ***Tirthankara*** ("traditional holy man"); and terms shared by several of the subcontinent's religions, for example, ***ahimsa*** ("the philosophy of revering all life"), ***dharma***, ***guru***, ***karma***, ***mantra***, ***nirvana***, and ***sutra***. Closely associated with Hindu philosophy is ***yoga***, with its various forms, for example, ***hatha yoga*** (literally "force yoga"); yoga terms used in English include ***asana*** ("a posture"), ***chakra*** ("a center of spiritual power"), and ***prana*** ("inhaling, holding the breath, and exhaling"). Sanskrit also provided names for the four great Hindu castes: ***Brahman***, ***Kshatriya***, ***Vaisya***, and ***Sudra***, with the untouchables below these (***Dalit***, which came via Hindi, with the alternative name ***Harijan*** directly from Sanskrit). Sanskrit scholarship has given linguists ***bahuvrihi*** (a type of compound word) and ***sandhi*** ("modification of a word under the influence of a preceding or following sound"), the ***Devanagari*** alphabet, and ***Sanskrit*** itself (Sanskrit *saṃskṛta-* "perfected").

In the 20th century Sanskrit emerged in social movements in South Asia, where Mahatma Gandhi (***mahatma*** is from Sanskrit, literally "great soul") and his followers sought a new social order (***Sarvodaya***) through the doctrine of nonviolent resistance (***satyagraha***). It also emerged, in a totally different way, in Europe, where the ancient religious symbol the ***swastika*** (Sanskrit *svastikaḥ* "good-luck sign") was appropriated by the German Nazi party, with its perverted ideal of ***Aryan*** (from Sanskrit *ārya* "of good family") superiority.

Other terms that have traveled through Sanskrit's descendants include, for example, in social and cultural life ***rajah***, ***rupee***, ***sari***, and ***wallah*** from Hindi; trees, ***deodar*** and ***pipal*** from Hindi, the ***bo tree*** from Sinhalese, the ***banyan*** from Gujarati (via Portuguese); animals, ***cheetah***, ***langur***, ***nilgai***, and ***sambar*** from Hindi. However a few words of Sanskrit origin – again mostly with a spiritual or religious theme – have migrated to English by less expected routes, for example, ***shaman*** (via Russian and Tungus), ***wat*** ("Buddhist monastery or temple," via Thai), and ***Zen*** (via Japanese and Chinese).

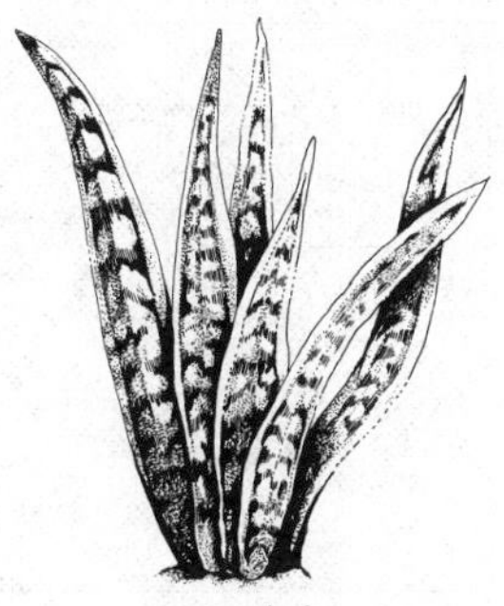

sansevieria

sans ser·if /san sérrif/, **san·ser·if** *n* a typeface in which there are no fine lines (**serifs**) at the ends of the main strokes of the characters

San·ta[1] /sántə/ *n* used as a title, usually in place names, before the name of a woman who has been made a saint [< Spanish and Italian, form of *Santo* (see SANTO)]

San·ta[2] /sántə/ *n* same as **Santa Claus** (*informal*) [Early 20C. Shortening]

San·ta An·a[1] /-ánnə/ *n* a strong hot dry wind that blows from the deserts of California toward the Pacific coast during the winter months [After the *Santa Ana* Mountains, S California]

San·ta An·a[2] /sàntə ánnə/ city in Orange County, southwestern California, in the south of the large metropolitan region surrounding Los Angeles. Population: 343,413 (2002 estimate).

San·ta An·na /sàntə ánnə/, **Antonio Lopez de** (1794–1876) general and president of Mexico (1833–36, 1844, 1847, and 1853–55). He led Mexican forces against the Texan revolt of 1835–36, first winning at the battle of the Alamo before himself being defeated and captured. Alternately viewed as a national hero and national scapegoat, he was a dictatorial president who was several times overthrown.

San·ta Bar·ba·ra /-baárbərə/ city and county seat of Santa Barbara County in southwestern California, situated on the Pacific coast northwest of Los Angeles. A resort and industrial center, it is home to the University of California-Santa Barbara. Population: 89,380 (2002 estimate).

San·ta Bar·ba·ra Is·lands group of eight US islands in the Pacific Ocean, off the southern coast of California

San·ta Cat·a·li·na Is·land /-kàttə leénə-/ island off the coast of California in the Pacific Ocean, south of Long Beach. It is one of the Santa Barbara Islands. Population: 2,918 (1990).

San·ta Cla·ra /-klárrə/ city in Silicon Valley, western California, on the Guadalupe River, near San Jose. Population: 101,867 (2002 estimate).

San·ta Cla·ri·ta /-klə reétə/ city in southern California, in Los Angeles County, situated on a valley floor and in canyons reaching into the San Gabriel and Santa Susanna mountains. Population: 160,554 (2002 estimate).

San·ta Claus /sántə klàwz/ *n* Christmas personified as a jolly old man with a white beard and a red suit who brings presents to children [Late 18C. < Dutch dialect *Sante Klaas* "St. Nicholas"]

San·ta Cruz /-króoz/ **1.** river in southern Argentina that flows eastward out of Lake Argentino in western Santa Cruz Province, and empties into the Atlantic Ocean at the port of Santa Cruz. Length: 250 mi./400 km. **2.** city in Santa Cruz Department, central Bolivia, on the Piray River, in the tropical plains region east of the Andes Mountains. Population: 914,795 (1997). **3.** city and tourist center in Santa Cruz County, western California, on Monterey Bay. Population: 53,836 (2002 estimate).

San·ta Cruz de Te·ne·ri·fe /-də tènnə reé fay/ capital

city and port of Tenerife Island and of Santa Cruz de Tenerife Province, in the Canary Islands, Spain. Population: 217,415 (2002).

San·ta Fe /-fáy/ **1.** capital city of New Mexico, on the Santa Fe River, in the north of the state. Population: 65,127 (2002 estimate). **2.** capital city of Santa Fe Province in northeastern Argentina. It is a port on the River Salado. Population: 353,063 (1991). —**San·ta Fe·an** /-fáy ən/ *n, adj*

San·ta Fe Trail *n* an important route from Independence, Missouri, to Santa Fe in what is now New Mexico for wagons and stagecoaches prior to the opening of the railroad during the 19th century

San·ta Ger·tru·dis /-gər tróodəss/ (*plural* **San·ta Ger·tru·dis·es** or *same*) *n* a large red beef cow that is highly resistant to heat and insects, belonging to a breed developed in Texas from Brahman and shorthorn cattle [After a section of the King Ranch in Kingsville, Texas, where the breed was developed]

San·ta Ma·ri·a /-mə reé ə/ city in Santa Barbara County, southwestern California. Population: 80,006 (2002 estimate).

San·ta Mar·ta /-maártə/ port and capital city of Magdalena Department in northern Colombia, on the Caribbean Sea. Population: 343,038 (1997).

San·ta Mo·ni·ca /-mónnikə/ city near Los Angeles in southwestern California, on Santa Monica Bay. It is chiefly a resort and residential city. Population: 86,799 (2002 estimate).

San·tan·der /saàntaan dér/ port and capital city of Cantabria Province in the autonomous region of Cantabria, northern Spain. Population: 184,661 (2002).

San·ta Pau·la /-páwlə/ city in Ventura County, southern California, situated on the Santa Clara River, northwest of Los Angeles. Population: 28,835 (2002 estimate).

San·ta Ro·sa /-rṓzə/ city in Sonoma County, northwestern California. Population: 153,489 (2002 estimate).

San·ta·ya·na /sàntee yánnə/, **George** (1863–1952) Spanish-born US philosopher. He maintained that reality is external to consciousness, and that all beliefs about the external world rest on "animal faith." His major work is *Realms of Being* (1927–40).

> "For an idea ever to be fashionable is ominous, since it must afterwards be always old-fashioned."
> [George Santayana, "Modernism and Christianity," *Winds of Doctrine*; 1913]

San·tee[1] /san teé/ (*plural same* or **-tees**) *n* a member of the eastern branch of the Sioux people, who now mainly live in Nebraska, Minnesota, North and South Dakota, and Canada —**San·tee** *adj*

San·tee[2] /sántee/ river flowing from southern South Carolina into the Atlantic Ocean, south of Georgetown. Length: 143 mi./230 km.

San·t'El·ia /san téllyə/, **Antonio** (1888–1916) Italian architect. His futurist drawings of buildings with sheer vertical lines and external lifts were a major influence on modern architecture.

San·te·rí·a /sàntə reé ə, saànta-/, **san·te·ri·a** *n* a religion that combines the West African Yoruba religion with Roman Catholicism. The religion recognizes a supreme God as well as other spirits. Originally developed in Cuba by West African slaves, it is now practiced in the Caribbean and the United States. [Mid-20C. < Spanish *santería* "holiness" < Latin *sanctus* "holy" (see SAINT)]

San·ti·a·go /sàntee aágō/ capital and largest city of Chile, on the Mapocho River, in the central part of the country. Population: 5,493,062 (2000).

San·ti·a·go de Com·po·ste·la /-də kompo stéllə/ capital city of the autonomous region of Galicia, northwestern Spain. Its cathedral has been a major place of pilgrimage since medieval times. Population: 93,273 (2002).

San·ti·a·go de Cu·ba /-kóobə/ second largest city in Cuba, situated in the southeast of the country. It is a major port. Population: 432,396 (1996).

san·tim /sán teem/ *n* a subunit of Latvian currency. See table at **currency** [Late 20C. < Latvian *santims* < French *centime* (see CENTIME)]

San·to /sántō/ (*plural* **-tos**) *n* used as a title, usually in place names, before the name of a man who has been made a saint [< Spanish and Italian < Latin *sanctus* "holy" (see SAINT)]

San·to Do·min·go /-də míng gō/ capital and largest city of the Dominican Republic, situated in the south of the country. Population: 2,677,056 (2001).

san·ton·i·ca /san tónnikə/ (*plural* **-cas** or *same*) *n* **1.** the dried unopened flower heads of a wormwood plant. Use: source of santonin. **2.** a wormwood plant with twin needle-shaped leaves grown for its abundant flower heads, which when dried are santonica. Native to: Europe, Asia. Genus: *Artemisia*. [Mid-17C. < modern Latin < form of Latin *santonicus* < *Santoni*, tribe of the Gauls]

san·to·nin /sántənin/ *n* a white crystalline compound. Source: extracted from santonica flower heads. Use: formerly, to eradicate parasitic worms. Formula: $C_{15}H_{18}O_3$. [Mid-19C. < SANTONICA]

San·tor·in·i /sàntə reénee/ ➧ **Thera**

San·tos /sántəss, saán tóoss/ city and port in São Paulo State, in southeastern Brazil, situated on the Atlantic island of São Vicente. Population: 412,243 (1996).

San·us·i /sə nóossee/ *n* a member of an Islamic Sufi religious group in Arabia and North Africa [Late 19C. After Sīdī Muḥammad ibn 'Alī as-*Sanūsī* (*d.* 1859), the group's founder]

São Mi·guel /sòw mi gél/ largest island of the Azores, located in the North Atlantic Ocean 740 mi./1,200 km from the western coast of Portugal. Population: 126,388 (1991). Area: 288 sq. mi./746 sq. km.

Saône /sōn/ river in east central France. It is a tributary of the Rhône. Length: 298 mi./480 km.

São Pau·lo /-pówlō/ capital of São Paulo State in southeastern Brazil. It is the largest city in South America, and an industrial and commercial metropolis. Population: 9,839,436 (1996).

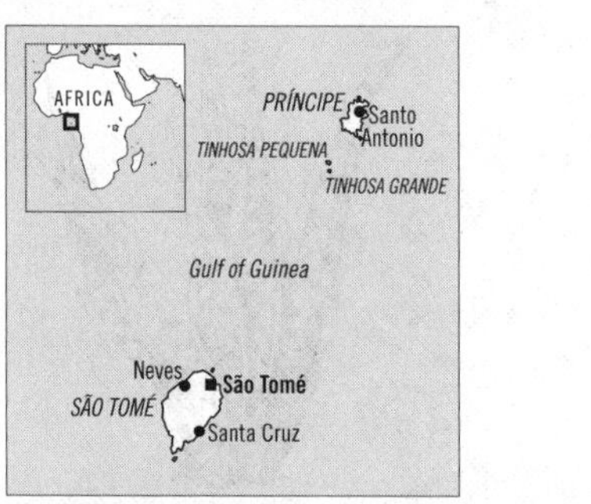

São Tomé and Príncipe

São To·mé and Prín·ci·pe /-tō mày ənd prínssəpə/ island country in the Gulf of Guinea, approximately 180 mi./290 km west of Gabon, West Africa. Formerly Portuguese, the territory became an independent republic in 1975. Language: Portuguese. Currency: dobra. Capital: São Tomé. Population: 175,883 (2003). Area: 386 sq. mi./1,001 sq. km. Official name **Democratic Republic of São Tomé and Príncipe**

sap[1] /sap/ *n* **1.** PLANT FLUID a watery liquid containing mineral salts, sugars, and other nutrients that circulates through the conducting tissues of a plant **2.** BODY FLUID any essential body fluid **3.** ENERGY bodily strength or vitality ○ *feel the sap rising* **4.** OFFENSIVE TERM an offensive term that deliberately insults somebody's intelligence and judgment (*slang insult*) **5.** *US* SMALL CLUB a weapon such as a blackjack ■ *vt* (**sapped, sap·ping, saps**) **1.** DRAW SAP FROM PLANT to drain a plant of sap **2.** *US* HIT SOMEBODY WITH SAP to hit or knock somebody out with a sap [Old English *sæp* < Germanic] —**sap·less** *adj*

sap[2] /sap/ *n* TUNNEL LEADING TO ENEMY a covered trench, dug to approach or get inside enemy territory ■ *v* (**sapped, sap·ping, saps**) **1.** *vi* DIG SAP to dig a covered trench to approach or get inside enemy territory **2.** *vt* TUNNEL UNDER FORTIFICATIONS to weaken the foundations of an enemy fortification with a tunnel **3.** *vt* TAKE AWAY SOMEBODY'S ENERGY to gradually weaken or reduce something, especially somebody's strength or energy ○ *The long hours were sapping his strength.* [Late 16C. Via French and Italian < late Latin *sappa*]

sap·a·jou /sáppə jòo, sàppə zhóo/ (*plural* **-jous** or *same*) *n* ZOOL same as **capuchin** (sense 1) [Late 17C. < French]

sa·pe·le /sə peélee/ (*plural* **-les** or *same*) *n* **1.** a wood that resembles mahogany. Use: furniture-making. **2.** a tall rain-forest tree that produces sapele. Native to: West Africa. Genus: *Entandrophragma*. [Early 20C. After *Sapele*, port in Nigeria]

Sa·phar *n* CALENDAR, ISLAM another spelling of **Safar**

sap·head /sáp hèd/ *n* an offensive term that deliberately insults somebody's intelligence and judgment (*slang insult*) [Late 18C. < SAP[1]] —**sap·head·ed** *adj*

sa·phe·na /sə feénə/ (*plural* **-nae** /-nee/) *n* ANAT same as **saphenous vein** —**sa·phe·nous** *adj*

sa·phe·nous vein /sə feénəss-/ *n* either of two major veins in the leg that run from the foot to the thigh near the surface of the skin [< medieval Latin *saphena* "vein"]

~~**saphire**~~ incorrect spelling of **sapphire**

sap·id /sáppəd/ *adj* (*formal*) **1.** having a strong and pleasant taste **2.** engaging or pleasant to think about [Early 17C. < Latin *sapidus* < *sapere* "to taste"] —**sa·pid·i·ty** /sə píddətee/ *n* —**sap·id·ness** *n*

sa·pi·ent /sáypee ənt/ *adj* wise or learned [15C. Via French < Latin *sapient-*, present participle of *sapere* "be wise"] —**sa·pi·ence** *n* —**sa·pi·ent·ly** *adv*

Sa·pir-Whorf hy·poth·e·sis /sə peér wáwrf-/ *n* the theory that the structure of a language helps determine how its native speakers perceive and categorize experience [Mid 20C. After Edward *Sapir* (1884–1939) and Benjamin Lee *Whorf* (1897–1941), US linguists]

sap·ling /sápling/ *n* **1.** a young tree with a slender trunk **2.** a young person (*literary*) [14C. < SAP[1]]

sap·o·dil·la /sàppə díllə, -deé yə/ *n* **1.** *also* **sap·o·dil·la plum** a brown rough-skinned fruit with sweet yellowish pulp **2.** an evergreen tree that produces chicle and sapodillas. Native to: Mexico, Central America, Caribbean. Latin name: *Manilkara zapota*. [Late 17C. Alteration of Spanish *zapotillo* < *zapote* (see SAPOTE)]

sa·pon·i·fy /sə pónnə fī/ (**-fied, -fy·ing, -fies**) *vti* to be converted into soap, or convert a fat into soap, especially by reaction with an alkali [Early 19C. < French *saponifier* < Latin *sapon-*, stem of *sapo* "soap" < Germanic] —**sa·pon·i·fi·a·ble** /sə pònnə fī́əb'l/ *adj* —**sa·pon·i·fi·ca·tion** /sə pònnifə káysh'n/ *n* —**sa·pon·i·fi·er** *n*

sap·o·nin /sáppənin, sə pṓnin/ *n* a glucoside extracted from plants that forms a soapy lather when mixed with water. Use: detergents. [Mid-19C. < French *saponine* < Latin *sapon-* (see SAPONIFY)]

sap·o·nite /sáppə nīt/ *n* a soft soapy clay mineral. Source: veins and cavities of rocks altered by hot water. [Mid-19C. < Latin *sapon-* (see SAPONIFY)]

sa·po·te /sə pṓtee, -pō tay/ *n* **1.** an oval brown sweet fruit **2.** a tree that produces sapotes. Native to: Mexico, Central America. Latin name: *Poulteria sapota*. [Mid-16C. Via modern Latin < Spanish *zapote* < Nahuatl *tzapotl*]

sap·pan·wood /sə pán wòod/ *n* **1.** a wood from which a red dye is obtained **2.** the leguminous tree whose wood is sappanwood. Native to: tropical Asia. Latin name: *Caesalpina sappan*. [Early 17C. < obsolete *sappan*, via Dutch < Malay *sapang*]

sap·per /sápper/ *n* **1.** a military engineer who specializes in fortifications, especially tunnels dug under enemy territory **2.** a military engineer who lays, detects, and disarms mines [Early 17C. < SAP[2]]

Sap·phic /sáffik/ *adj* **1.** relating to the Greek poet Sappho or her poetry, largely written in 11-syllable lines, with stanzas of three such lines and a shorter fourth line **2.** same as **lesbian** (*literary*) ■ *n* a Sapphic line, stanza, or poem

sap·phire /sá fīr/ *n* **1.** a clear hard precious stone that is a variety of the mineral corundum and is usually deep blue in color **2.** a brilliant blue color like that of a sapphire [13C. Via French and Latin < Greek *sappheiros*] —**sap·phire** *adj*

sap·phi·rine /sáffə rīn, -reèn, -rin/ *adj* resembling a sapphire, especially in being a brilliant blue color ■ *n* a rare blue or green aluminum magnesium silicate mineral

sap·phism /sá fìzzəm/ *n* same as **lesbianism** (*literary*) [Late 19C. After SAPPHO]

Sap·pho /sáffō/ (*fl* 7th century B.C.) Greek poet. She wrote odes, wedding songs, and hymns notable for their depth of feeling. Few fragments of her work remain.

Sap·po·ro /sa páwrō/ commercial center and capital of Hokkaido Prefecture, on western Hokkaido Island, Japan. Population: 1,822,992 (2002).

sap·py /sáppee/ (**-pi·er, -pi·est**) *adj* **1. FULL OF SAP** containing a large quantity of sap **2. OVERLY SENTIMENTAL** expressing or portraying emotion in an excessively sentimental way (*slang*) ○ *a sappy movie* **3. OFFENSIVE TERM** an offensive term meaning silly or unintelligent (*slang insult*) [Pre-12C. < SAP[1]] —**sap·pi·ly** *adv*

sapr- *prefix* same as **sapro-** (*used before vowels*)

sapro- *prefix* **1.** death, decay, putrefaction ○ *saprozoic* **2.** dead or decaying organic matter ○ *saprophagous* [< Greek *sapros* "rotten"]

sap·robe /sáp rōb/ *n* an organism that gets its nourishment from inorganic or decaying organic matter [Mid-20C. < SAPRO-, after MICROBE] —**sap·ro·bic** /sa prōbik/ *adj*

sap·ro·bi·ol·o·gy /sàpprō bī óllajee/ *n* the study of environments that support organisms (**saprobes**) that feed on decaying organic matter —**sap·ro·bi·o·log·i·cal** /-bī ə lójjik'l/ *adj* —**sap·ro·bi·ol·o·gist** *n*

sap·ro·gen·ic /sàpprə jénnik/ *adj* causing or resulting from decay —**sap·ro·ge·nic·i·ty** /sàpprəjə níssətee/ *n*

sap·ro·lite /sápprə līt/ *n* soft disintegrating igneous rock that remains where it was located when solid, formed by heavy weathering in a humid environment —**sap·ro·lit·ic** /sàpprə líttik/ *adj*

sap·ro·pel /sápprə pèl/ *n* a soft black layer of decaying organic matter at the bottom of a body of water [Early 20C. < German < Greek *sapros* "rotten" + *pēlos* "mud"] —**sap·ro·pel·ic** /sàpprə péllik, -peélik/ *adj*

sa·proph·a·gous /sa próffəgəss/ *adj* feeding on or obtaining food from decaying organic matter

sap·ro·phyte /sápprə fīt/ *n* an organism, especially a fungus or bacterium, that obtains food from dead or decaying organic matter —**sap·ro·phyt·ic** /sàpprə fíttik/ *adj* —**sap·ro·phyt·i·cal·ly** *adv*

sap·ro·phyt·ism /sápprō fīt ìzzəm/ *n* the process of obtaining nourishment from dissolved decaying organic matter

sap·ro·zo·ic /sàpprə zō ik/ *adj* getting nourishment by absorbing dissolved organic matter and salts

sap·sa·go /sap sáygō, sápsə gō/ *n* a hard green Swiss cheese made with sour skim milk and flavored with sweet clover [Mid-19C. Alteration of German *Schabzieger* < *schaben* "scrape" + *zieger* "curd cheese"]

sap·suck·er /sáp sùkər/ *n* a small woodpecker that drills holes in trees in order to drink the sap and eat insects attracted by the sap. Native to: North America. Genus: *Sphyrapicus*. [Early 19C. < SAP[1]]

sap·wood /sáp wŏŏd/ *n* the soft wood of a tree between the inner bark and the heartwood [Late 18C. < SAP[1]]

SAR[1] *n* the rate at which a mass, especially human tissue, absorbs radiated electrical energy, e.g., that produced by a cell phone, measured in watts or milliwatts per kilogram. Full form **specific absorption rate**

SAR[2] *abbr* **1.** search and rescue **2.** *US* Sons of the American Revolution

sar·a·band /sárrə bànd/, **sar·a·bande** *n* **1.** a dignified Spanish dance of the 17th and 18th centuries in triple time **2.** the music for a saraband [Early 17C. Via French < Spanish *zarabanda*]

Sar·a·cen /sárrəss'n/ *n* **1. MUSLIM OPPOSING CHRISTIAN CRUSADES** a Muslim who fought against the Christian Crusaders in the Middle Ages **2. MEMBER OF ANCIENT DESERT PEOPLE** a member of an ancient desert people of Syria and Arabia living on the fringes of the Roman Empire **3.** same as **Arab** (*archaic*) ■ *adj* **RELATING TO SARACENS** relating to the ancient or medieval Saracens or their culture [Pre-12C. Via French < late Latin *Saracenus* < late Greek *sarakēnos*] —**Sar·a·cen·ic** /sàrrə sénnik/ *adj* —**Sar·a·cen·i·cal** *adj*

Sar·a·gos·sa /sàrrə góssə/ ♦ **Zaragoza**

Sa·rah /sérrə/ *n* in the Bible, the wife and half-sister of Abraham, and mother of Isaac (Genesis 17:15–22)

Sa·ra·je·vo /sàrrə yáyvō/ capital city of Bosnia-Herzegovina, in the east central part of the country. Population: 360,000 (1997).

sa·ran /sə rán/ *n* a thermoplastic resin produced from a vinyl compound. Use: fabrics, plastic wrap. [Mid-20C. Originally a trademark]

Sa·ran·don /sə rándən/, **Susan** (*b.* 1946) US movie actor. She won an Academy Award for *Dead Man Walking* (1995). Born **Susan Abigail Tomalin**

sar·an·gi /sə ráng gee/ (*plural* **-gis**) *n* a musical instrument of South Asia that resembles a violin, with a rectangular soundbox and three playing strings that have sympathetic strings [Mid-19C. < Sanskrit *sārangī*]

sa·ra·pe *n* CLOTHING another spelling of **serape**

Sa·ra·so·ta /sàrrə sṓtə/ city and county seat of Sarasota County in western Florida, situated on Sarasota Bay, south of Tampa. It is a resort and a commercial and agricultural center. Population: 53,321 (2002 estimate).

Sar·a·to·ga Springs /sàrrə tṓgə-/ city in eastern New York, in the foothills of the Adirondack Mountains, north of Albany. Two battles were fought in its vicinity during the American Revolution. A major health resort and horseracing center, it is home to Skidmore College. Population: 27,014 (2002 estimate).

Sar·a·to·ga trunk /sàrrə tṓgə-/ *n* a large traveling trunk with a rounded top, once widely used by women [After SARATOGA SPRINGS]

Sa·ra·wak /sə raá waák/ state in Malaysia, in the northwestern portion of the island of Borneo. Capital: Kuching. Population: 1,954,300 (1997). Area: 48,050 sq. mi./124,449 sq. km.

Sa·ra·zen /sárrəz'n/, **Gene** (1902–99) US golfer. He was the first golfer to win the four championships that comprise the grand slam of golf. Born **Saraceni, Eugene**

sarc- *prefix* same as **sarco-** (*used before vowels*)

sar·casm /saár kàzzəm/ *n* remarks that mean the opposite of what they seem to say and are intended to mock or deride [Mid-16C. Directly or via French < late Latin *sarcasmus* < Greek *sarkazein* "tear flesh" < *sarx* "flesh"]

sar·cas·tic /saar kástik/ *adj* **1.** characterized by words that mean the opposite of what they seem to say and are intended to mock or deride **2.** fond of or habitually using sarcasm —**sar·cast·ic·al·ly** *adv*

SYNONYMS ***sarcastic, ironic, sardonic, satirical, caustic***

CORE MEANING: used to describe remarks that are designed to hurt or mock

sarcastic characterized by words that mean the opposite of what they seem to say and are intended to mock or deride ○ *She cared little for his sarcastic jokes.* ○ *As a politician, he is eloquent and sometimes bitingly sarcastic.* **ironic** deliberately stating the opposite of the truth, usually with the intention of being amusing ○ *The nickname Charles the Bald may not have been descriptive but ironic, implying Charles was exceptionally hairy.* ○ *songs bristling with ironic observation and vivid imagery* **sardonic** disdainfully or cynically mocking ○ *a sardonic smile* ○ *He gradually evolved into a more polished politician – his sardonic humor emerged, his views became more refined.* **satirical** using wit, especially irony, sarcasm, and ridicule, to criticize faults, particularly in the arts or politics ○ *a satirical TV show* ○ *He was a sharp, satirical observer of the social scene.* **caustic** very sarcastic and intended to mock, offend, or belittle somebody ○ *a barrage of caustic editorials* ○ *His caustic style made him the most controversial broadcaster of his time.*

sar·ce·net /saárssnət/, **sar·se·net** *n* a soft delicate silk cloth. Use: formerly, veils, linings, ribbons. [15C. < Old French *sarzinet*]

sarco- *prefix* **1.** striated muscle ○ *sarcolemma* **2.** flesh ○ *sarcoid* [< Greek *sark-*, stem of *sarx* "flesh" < Indo-European, "cut, tear"]

sar·co·din·i·an /saàrkə dínnee ən/ *adj* belonging to the class of protozoans that includes amoebas ■ *n* a protozoan that belongs to the same class as amoebas [< modern Latin *Sarcodina* < Greek *sarkōdēs* "fleshy" < *sarx* "flesh"]

sar·coid /saár kòyd/ *n* a small area of chronic infection in the body of a person affected by sarcoidosis ■ *adj* relating to or resembling flesh

sar·coi·do·sis /saàr koy dṓssiss/ *n* a disease in which lumps of fibrous tissue and collections of cells (**granulomas**) appear on the skin and internal organs

sar·co·lac·tic ac·id /saàrkə làktik-/ *n* a form of lactic acid produced by muscle tissue during anaerobic activity

sar·co·lem·ma /saàrkə lémmə/ *n* a thin clear membrane that covers a striated muscle fiber

sar·co·ma /saar kṓmə/ (*plural* **-mas** or **-ma·ta** /-mətə/) *n* a malignant tumor that begins growing in connective tissue such as muscle, bone, fat, or cartilage. Sarcomas may occur in any part of the body, and are typically fast-growing and quick to spread. —**sar·co·ma·toid** *adj* —**sar·co·ma·to·sis** /saar kṓmə tṓssiss/ *n* —**sar·co·ma·tous** *adj*

sar·co·mere /saàrkə meèr/ *n* a segment of a fibril of striated muscle

sar·coph·a·gus /saar kóffəgəss/ (*plural* **-gi** /-gī/ or **-gus·es**) *n* an ancient stone or marble coffin, often decorated with sculpture and inscriptions [Early 17C. Via Latin < Greek *sarkophagos* "flesh-eater"]

sar·co·plasm /saàrkə plàzzəm/ *n* the cytoplasm of a striated muscle fiber —**sar·co·plas·mic** /saàrkə plázmik/ *adj* —**sar·co·plas·mous** /saàrkə plázməss/ *adj*

sar·co·plas·mic re·tic·u·lum *n* the endoplasmic reticulum of a striated muscle fiber that regulates the concentration of calcium ions in the cell cytoplasm

sar·cop·tic mange /saar kòptik-/ *n* a form of mange caused by a parasitic mite that burrows into the skin [< modern Latin *Sarcoptes*, genus of mites < Greek *sarx* "flesh" + *koptein* "cut"]

sar·cous /saárkəss/ *adj* consisting of or relating to flesh or muscle tissue

sard /saard/ *n* a deep orange red variety of chalcedony. Use: jewelry. [15C. < Latin *sarda* < Greek *sardios*]

sar·dar /súr daár, sər daár/ *n* POL, MIL same as **sirdar** [Late 16C. < Persian, Urdu *sardār*, "holding the position of chief"]

sar·dine /saàr deén/ *n* **1.** a small ocean fish related to the herring, especially the European pilchard. Sardines are netted in large numbers for food and preserved in cans, packed tightly in oil. Latin name: *Sardinia pilchardus*. **2.** the flesh of a sardine as food, usually preserved in cans, packed tightly in oil [15C. Via French < Latin *sardina* < Greek *Sardō* "Sardinia"] ◇ **be packed like sardines** to be crowded closely together

Sar·din·i·a /saar dínnee ə/ Italian island in the Mediterranean Sea. It is the second largest island in the Mediterranean after Sicily. Capital: Cagliari. Population: 1,659,466 (1995). Area: 9,194 sq. mi./23,813 sq. km. —**Sar·din·i·an** *adj, n*

Sar·dis /saárdiss/ ancient city of Asia Minor, in present-day Turkey. It was the capital city of Lydia and an early seat of Christianity.

sar·di·us /saárdee əss/ *n* CRYSTALS same as **sard** [15C. < Latin < *sarda* (see SARD)]

sar·don·ic /saar dónnik/ *adj* disdainfully or cynically mocking [Mid-17C. < French *sardonique*, alteration of obsolete *sardonien* < Latin *sardonius* < Greek *sardanios* "scornful"] —**sar·don·i·cal·ly** *adv* —**sar·don·i·cism** *n*

SYNONYMS See ***sarcastic***.

sar·don·yx /saar dónniks/ *n* a variety of onyx with alternating bands of light orange brown and white chalcedony. Use: formerly, cameos. [14C. Via Latin < Greek *sardonux*, literally "sard onyx"]

sa·ree *n* CLOTHING another spelling of **sari**

sar·gas·so /saar gássō/ *n* MARINE BIOL same as **gulfweed** [Late 16C. < Portuguese *sargaço*]

Sar·gas·so Sea /saar gàssō-/ section of the North Atlantic Ocean, between the Greater Antilles and the Azores. It is noted for its predominantly still waters. Area: 2,000,000 sq. mi./5,200,000 sq. km.

sar·gas·so weed *n* PLANTS same as **gulfweed**

sar·gas·sum /saar gássəm/ *n* PLANTS same as **gulfweed** [Early 20C. < modern Latin < SARGASSO]

sar·gas·sum fish *n* a brown and black fish that lives in floating gulfweed. Native to: Atlantic and western Pacific oceans. Latin name: *Histrio histrio.*

sarge /saarj/ *n* a sergeant in the armed forces or police (*informal*) [Mid-19C. Shortening]

Library of Congress
John Singer Sargent

Sar·gent /saárjənt/, **John Singer** (1856–1925) Italian-born US artist. Possessing a brilliant technique, he was known for oil portraits of well-known people, e.g., *Madame Gautreau* (1883–84). He later turned to watercolors.

> "Every time I paint a portrait I lose a friend."
> [John Singer Sargent, *Treasury of Humorous Quotations*, N. Bentley and E. Esar; 1951]

Sar·go·dha /saar gṓdə/ city in Punjab Province, Pakistan, about 110 mi./177 km northwest of Lahore. Population: 291,361 (1981).

Sar·gon II /saár gòn/ (763?–705 B.C.) king of Assyria. During his reign (721–705 B.C.) he extended the Assyrian empire through a series of military campaigns and deported thousands of Israelites.

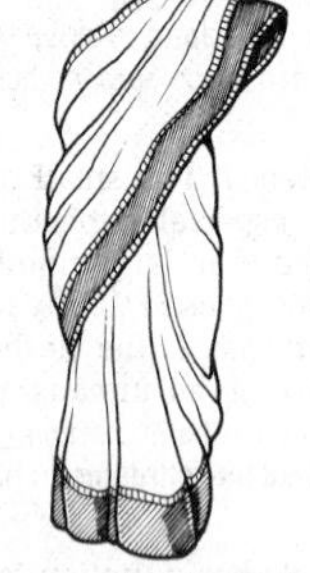
sari

sa·ri /saáree/, **sa·ree** *n* a garment, traditionally worn by South Asian women, consisting of a long rectangle of fabric reaching the feet, wrapped and pleated around the waist over an underskirt and short-sleeved fitted top (**choli**), and draped over the shoulder [Late 18C. Via Hindi *sarī* < Sanskrit *śaṭī* "garment"]

sar·in /saárin/ *n* an extremely toxic gas that attacks the central nervous system, causing convulsions and death. It has been used for chemical warfare. Formula: $C_4H_{10}FO_2P$. [Mid-20C. < German]

Sark /saark/ one of the Channel Islands, in the English Channel, forming a dependency of Guernsey. It comprises Great Sark and Little Sark, linked to each other by a narrow isthmus. Population: 550 (1996). Area: 2 sq. mi./5 sq. km.

sar·men·tose /saar méntōss/, **sar·men·tous** /-təss/ *adj* producing long slender stems that reach out and take root along the ground [Mid-18C. < Latin *sarmentosus* "full of twigs" < *sarmentum* "twig"]

Sar·ni·a /saárnee ə/ city at the southern tip of Lake Huron, on the St. Clair River, Ontario, Canada. Population: 78,577 (2001).

Sar·noff /saár nàwf/, **David** (1891–1971) Russian-born US broadcasting executive. A pioneer in radio and television, he headed RCA (Radio Corporation of America) (1930–70) and established the National Broadcasting Company (1926).

> "Freedom is the oxygen without which science cannot breathe."
> [David Sarnoff, "Electronics—Today and Tomorrow"; 1954]

sa·rod /sə rṓd/ *n* a stringed instrument of northern South Asia that resembles a lute with two resonating gourds [Mid-19C. Via Urdu < Persian *sarūd*]

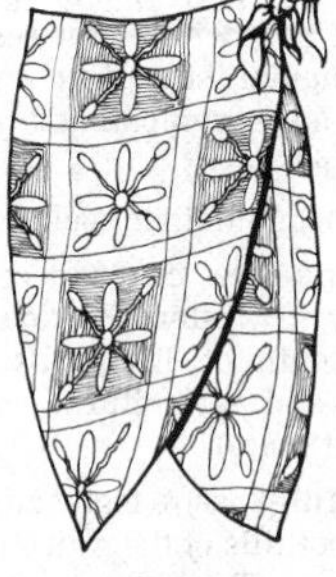
sarong

sa·rong /sə ráwng/ *n* **1. TRADITIONAL MALAYSIAN GARMENT** a traditional Malayan and Javanese garment for men or women, consisting of a length of fabric wrapped and tied around the body at the waist or under the arms **2. FASHION VERSION OF SARONG** a fashion version of the sarong worn by a woman as a wrapped skirt, often for the beach **3. CLOTH FOR MALAYSIAN GARMENTS** cloth for a sarong, often brightly colored [Mid-19C. < Malay, "covering"]

Sa·ron·ic Gulf /sə rónnik-/ gulf of the Aegean Sea, on the coast of southeastern Greece

sa·ros /saárōss/ *n* the cycle of 6,585.32 days, or approximately 18 years 11 days, after which a sequence of eclipses of the Sun and Moon repeats itself. It was known to the Babylonians and some other ancient civilizations. [Early 19C. Via Greek < Babylonian *sāru* "the number 3,600"] —**sa·ron·ic** /sə rónnik/ *adj*

Sa·roy·an /sə róy ən/, **William** (1908–81) US playwright and novelist, whose often flamboyant works include the play *The Time of Your Life* (1938). He refused a Pulitzer Prize because he disapproved of such awards.

> "If you give to a thief he cannot steal from you, and he is then no longer a thief."
> [William Saroyan, *The Human Comedy*; 1943]

sar·ra·ce·ni·a /sàrrə seénee ə/ (*plural* **-as** or *same*) *n* a pitcher plant with hollow tubular leaves that trap insects. Native to: eastern North America. Genus: *Sarracenia*. [Mid-18C. < modern Latin, after D. *Sarrazin*, 17C North American botanist]

sar·ru·so·phone /sə roózə fōn/ *n* a woodwind musical instrument resembling a bassoon but made of brass [Late 19C. After Pierre-Auguste *Sarrus* (1813–76), French bandleader]

SARS /saarz/ *n* a serious respiratory illness that is caused by a coronavirus and often develops into pneumonia. It was first reported in Asia in 2003 and includes symptoms such as high fever and aching limbs. Full form **severe acute respiratory syndrome**

sar·sa·pa·ril·la /saàspə rílla/ (*plural* **-las** or *same*) *n* **1. MEDICINAL ROOT** the dried root of a tropical creeper or temperate plant. Use: traditional or herbal medicine, soft drink. **2. SOFT DRINK** a carbonated drink flavored with sarsaparilla root, similar to root beer **3. TROPICAL VINE** a tropical vine with aromatic roots and heart-shaped leaves. Native to: America. Genus: *Smilax*. **4. PLANT LIKE SARSAPARILLA VINE** a plant similar to the sarsaparilla vine. Genera: *Aralia* or *Smilax*. [Late 16C. < Spanish *zarzaparrilla* < *zarza* "bramble" + *parra* "vine"]

sar·sen /saárss'n/ *n* any large sedimentary rock that has been broken into blocks by frost action and is found on the chalk downs of southern England [Late 17C. Alteration of SARACEN]

sar·sen·et *n* TEXTILES another spelling of **sarcenet**

sar·tor /saártər/ *n* same as **tailor** (*archaic*) [Mid-17C. < Latin < *sart-* past participle of *sarcire* "patch"]

sar·to·ri·al /saar táwree əl/ *adj* **1.** relating to tailoring or clothing in general **2.** relating to the sartorius muscle in the thigh

sar·to·ri·us /saar táwree əss/ (*plural* **-ri·i** /-ree ī/) *n* a flat narrow muscle that extends from the hip to the inner thigh and helps rotate the leg to a cross-legged position. It is the longest muscle in the human body. [Early 18C. < modern Latin *musculus sartorius* "tailor's muscle" < *sartor* (see SARTOR)]

AKG London
Jean-Paul Sartre

Sar·tre /saártrə, saart/, **Jean-Paul** (1905–80) French philosopher, playwright, and novelist. The principal exponent of existentialism, he wrote *Being and Nothingness* (1943) and the novel *Nausea* (1938).

> "Hell is other people."
> [Jean-Paul Sartre, *Huis Clos (In Camera)*; 1944]

> "The one and only basis of the moral life must be spontaneity, that is, the immediate, the unreflective."
> [Jean-Paul Sartre, *Notebooks for an Ethics*; 1983]

Sa·rum /sérrəm/ former name for **Salisbury** (sense 1)

Sar·vo·day·a /saar vṓdə yə/ *n* the name that Mahatma Gandhi and his followers gave to the new social order that they sought to establish in India [Early 20C. < Sanskrit, "prosperity for all"]

SAS *n* a British army regiment that is specially trained to undertake dangerous clandestine operations. Full form **Special Air Service**

SASE *abbr* MAIL self-addressed stamped envelope

sash /sash/ *n* **1. FABRIC BELT** a strip of cloth tied around the waist, e.g., as part of ceremonial dress **2. WIDE RIBBON WORN ACROSS CHEST** a band of cloth draped over one shoulder and across the chest as a symbol of rank or office **3. FRAME FOR GLASS** a frame holding the glass panes of a window or door [Late 17C. < Arabic *šāš* "muslin"]

sa·shay /sa sháy/ *vi* (**-shayed, -shay·ing, -shays**) **1. FLOUNCE GRACEFULLY** to walk in a way that is intended to attract attention, especially by swaying the hips or swinging the elbows (*humorous*) **2. PERFORM STEPS IN SQUARE DANCING** to dance a sequence of gliding or sideways steps in square dancing ■ *n* **1.** DANCE same as **chassé 2. PATTERN IN SQUARE DANCING** a figure in square dancing in which partners circle each other using sideways steps [Mid-19C. Alteration of French *chassé* "chasing, chase"]

sa·shi·mi /saa sheémee/ *n* a Japanese dish consisting of slices of raw fish, usually served with a dipping sauce, e.g., a seasoned soy sauce. Small quantities of other ingredients such as finely shredded white radish or pickles may also be added as garnishes and palate-refreshing accompaniments. [Late 19C. < Japanese]

sash saw *n* a small saw with a thin blade, used in making window sashes

sash win·dow *n* a window that consists of two frames, one above the other in vertical grooves, allowing either to be opened or shut by sliding it up or down

Sask. *abbr* Saskatchewan

Sas·katch·e·wan /sa skáchəwən/ **1.** river in Canada, rising in central Saskatchewan and flowing into Lake Winnipeg, in Manitoba. Length: 340 mi./550 km. **2.** the central Prairie Province of Canada, between Alberta and Manitoba. Capital: Regina. Population: 1,011,800 (2002). Area: 251,366 sq. mi./651,036 sq. km. —**Sas·katch·e·wa·ni·an** /sa skàchə wáanee ən/ *n, adj*

sas·ka·toon /sàskə tóon/ *n* **1.** a sweet purplish black fruit **2.** a bush that produces saskatoons. Flowers: white. Native to: northwestern North America. Latin name: *Amelanchier alnifolia.* [Early 19C. < Cree *misaaskwatoomin* "amelanchier berry"]

Sas·ka·toon /sàskə tóon/ second largest city in Saskatchewan, Canada, 150 mi./242 km northwest of Regina. Population: 196,211 (2001).

sas·quatch /sáss kwòch, -kwàwch/ *n* same as **Bigfoot** [Early 20C. < Salish]

sass /sass/ (*informal*) *vt* (**sassed, sass·ing, sass·es**) to talk disrespectfully or impudently to somebody, especially somebody who is older or in authority ■ *n* disrespectful or impudent remarks, especially in reply to an older person or somebody in authority [Mid-19C. Back-formation < SASSY[1]]

sas·sa·by /sássəbee/ (*plural* **-bies**) *n* an antelope that is a type of topi. Native to: southern Africa. Latin name: *Damaliscus lunatus lunatus.* [Early 19C. Alteration of Tswana *tsessébi*]

sas·sa·fras /sássə fràss/ (*plural same*) *n* **1.** a deciduous tree with aromatic bark, lobed leaves, and small bluish fruits. Native to: eastern North America. Latin name: *Sassafras albidum.* **2.** the dried root bark of the sassafras tree. Use: flavoring, perfumes, medicines. [Late 16C. < Spanish *sasafrás*]

~~sassafrass~~ incorrect spelling of **sassafras**

Sas·sa·nid /sássənid/ *n* a member of a Persian dynasty that ruled from A.D. 224–651. The dynasty superseded the Parthian Empire, and challenged Roman power in the East. It was the last line of Persian kings before the Arab conquests. [Late 18C. After *Sasan*, Persian monarch and grandfather of the first Sassanid] —**Sas·sa·ni·an** /sə sáynee ən/ *adj*

Sas·sa·ri /sássə rée/ capital of Sassari Province, Sardinia, Italy, situated near the northwestern coast of the island. Population: 120,729 (2001).

Sas·soon /sə sóon/, **Siegfried** (1886–1967) British poet and novelist. He is known for his searing poems about the horrors of World War I and for his semiautobiographical fictional trilogy, collected as *The Complete Memoirs of George Sherston* (1937). Full name **Sassoon, Siegfried Lorraine**

> "And when the war is done and youth stone dead / I'd toddle safely home and die—in bed."
> [Siegfried Sassoon, "Base Details"; 1918]

sass·wood /sáss wòod/ *n* TREES same as **sassy**[2] [Late 19C. < shortening of SASSY[2]]

sas·sy[1] /sássee/ (**-si·er, -si·est**) *adj* **1.** IMPUDENT impudent or disrespectful **2.** HIGH-SPIRITED lively and high-spirited ○ *The show has refreshingly sassy hoedown-style choreography.* **3.** *US* STYLISH stylish or fashionable ○ *a sassy look for spring* [Mid-19C. Alteration of SAUCY]

sas·sy[2] /sássee/ (*plural* **-sies**) *n* a tree with poisonous bark and insect-resistant wood used for building. Native to: West Africa. Latin name: *Erythrophleum suaveolens.* [Mid-19C. Probably < an African language]

sas·tra *n* HINDUISM another spelling of **shastra**

sas·tru·ga /sass tróogə, sástrəgə/ *n* a long wave-shaped ridge of hard snow formed by the wind, common in polar regions [Mid-19C. Via German < Russian *zastruga*]

sat past participle, past tense of **sit**

USAGE See *sit.*

SAT *tdmk* a trademark for a standardized test taken by applicants to colleges in the United States. Full form **Scholastic Assessment Test**

Sat. *abbr* CALENDAR Saturday

~~satalite~~ incorrect spelling of **satellite**

Sa·tan /sáyt'n/ *n* in Christianity, the enemy of God, the lord of evil, and the tempter of human beings. He is sometimes identified with Lucifer, the leader of the fallen angels. [Pre-12C. Via Latin and Greek < Hebrew *śāṭān* "adversary" < *śāṭan* "accuse"]

sa·tang /sə táang/ (*plural same*) *n* a subunit of Thai currency. See table at **currency** [Late 19C. Via Thai < Pali *sata* "hundred"]

sa·tan·ic /sə tánnik/ *adj* **1.** relating to Satan or the worship of Satan **2.** extremely evil or cruel —**sa·tan·i·cal·ly** *adv*

Sa·tan·ism /sáyt'n ìzzəm/ *n* the worship of Satan, especially as a parody of Christian rites

sa·tay /saá tay/ *n* a popular Indonesian and Malaysian dish consisting of marinated pieces of meat, chicken, or fish grilled on wooden skewers and served with peanut sauce [Mid-20C. < Malay]

SATB *abbr* MUSIC soprano, alto, tenor, bass

satch·el /sáchəl/ *n* a small bag, especially one with shoulder straps used for carrying schoolbooks [14C. Via Old French *sachel* < Latin *sacellus* < *saccus* "bag"]

sate /sayt/ (**sat·ed, sat·ing, sates**) *vt* **1.** to satisfy completely somebody's hunger or some other desire **2.** to provide somebody with more than enough, to the point of exhaustion or disgust [Old English *sadian* < Indo-European]

sa·teen /sə téen/ *n* a cotton or polyester fabric with a shiny side intended to look like satin [Late 19C. Alteration of SATIN, after VELVETEEN]

~~satelite~~ incorrect spelling of **satellite**

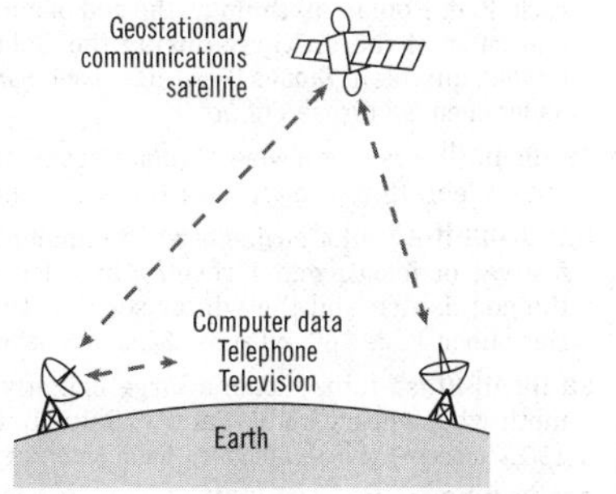

satellite

sat·el·lite /sátt'l ìt/ *n* **1.** DEVICE THAT ORBITS PLANET an object put into orbit around Earth or another planet in order to relay communications signals or transmit scientific data **2.** MOON ORBITING OTHER BODY an astronomical object that orbits a larger one **3.** COUNTRY DEPENDENT ON ANOTHER COUNTRY a nation or political unit that is dependent economically and politically on another more powerful nation **4.** SUBURB a town or small city located near and dependent on a larger city **5.** ATTENDANT an attendant of an important person [Mid-16C. Via French < Latin *satellit-* "attendant"]

sat·el·lite broad·cast·ing *n* the global transmission of television programs via satellite

sat·el·lite cell *n* one of the cells forming the capsule that encloses the nerve cells in many spinal ganglia

sat·el·lite dish *n* a dish-shaped device for receiving television signals broadcast via satellite

sat·el·lite DNA *n* a component of an animal's DNA that differs in density from surrounding DNA, consists of short repeating sequences of nucleotide pairs, and does not undergo transcription

sat·el·lite link *n* a communications signal or link from a transmitting Earth station to a satellite and back to a receiving Earth station

sat·el·lite phone *n* a wireless phone that connects callers via a communications satellite that receives transmissions, then relays them back to Earth

sat·el·lite sta·tion *n* a radio or television station that receives programs from another station and rebroadcasts them immediately on a different wavelength

sat·el·lite tel·e·phone *n* a cell phone that can send voice messages over extremely long distances via links to communications satellites

sat·el·lite tel·e·vi·sion *n* a television service for which the signal is relayed via satellite to be broadcast to customers who have appropriate receiving equipment

sat·el·li·ti·um /sàttə líttee əm/ *n* in astrology, a group of planets in one sign of the zodiac

sa·tem /saátəm/ *adj* relating to Indo-European languages in which the consonant sounding like "k" developed into the sound "s" or "sh" [Early 20C. < Avestan, "hundred"]

~~Saterday~~ incorrect spelling of **Saturday**

sa·ti *n* RELIG same as **suttee**

sa·ti·ate /sáyshee àyt/ *vt* (**-at·ed, -at·ing, -ates**) **1.** GRATIFY DESIRE to satisfy hunger or another appetite completely **2.** GLUT SOMEBODY to provide somebody with too much of something desirable, to the point of overindulgence (*often passive*) ■ *adj* HAVING TOO MUCH having had enough or too much [15C. < Latin *satiat-*, past participle of *satiare* < *satis* "enough"] —**sa·tia·ble** *adj* —**sa·ti·a·tion** /sàyshee áysh'n/ *n*

Sa·tie /saa tée/, **Erik** (1866–1925) French composer. His light, innovative ballets, dramas, and piano pieces influenced Maurice Ravel, Claude Debussy, and the composers known as Les Six. Full name **Satie, Erik Alfred Leslie**

sa·ti·e·ty /sə tí ətee/ *n* a state in which somebody has had enough or too much [Mid-16C. Via French < Latin *satietas* < *satis* "enough"]

sat·in /sátt'n/ *n* GLOSSY SILK OR RAYON FABRIC a fabric woven of silk or rayon, with a smooth glossy finish and a dull back ■ *adj* **1.** OF SATIN made of satin fabric **2.** GLOSSY LIKE SATIN smooth and glossy like satin [14C. Via French < Arabic *zaytūnī* "of Zaytun," probably the Chinese city of Quangzhou] —**sat·in·y** *adj*

sat·in·et /sàtt'n ét/, **sat·in·ette** *n* **1.** an imitation satin made from cotton and wool **2.** thin or inferior satin

sat·in flow·er *n* **1.** an annual plant with lance-shaped leaves that is a common garden plant. Flowers: red. Native to: Pacific coast of North America. Latin name: *Clarkia amoena.* **2.** PLANTS same as **honesty** (sense 3)

sat·in spar *n* a fibrous variety of gypsum

sat·in stitch *n* an embroidery stitch that is worked in close parallel lines to fill in an area or form a solid line

sat·in wal·nut *n* the wood of the sweet gum tree. Use: furniture.

sat·in weave *n* a weave in which the face of the fabric is covered entirely with warp threads, producing a smooth finish

sat·in·wood /sátt'n wòod/ *n* **1.** WOOD FROM S ASIAN TREE a smooth hard yellow brown wood. Use: furniture making. **2.** S ASIAN TREE a deciduous tree with hard yellow brown wood. Native to: South Asia. Latin name: *Chloroxylon swietenia.* **3.** CARIBBEAN TREE an evergreen tree with smooth lustrous wood. Native to: Caribbean. Latin name: *Zanthoxylum flavum.*

sat·ire /sá tìr/ *n* **1.** the use of wit, especially irony, sarcasm, and ridicule, to criticize faults **2.** a literary work that uses satire, or the branch of literature made up of such works [Early 16C. Directly or via French < Latin *satira* "poetic medley, satire"]

sa·tir·i·cal /sə tírrik'l/, **sa·ti·ric** /-tírrik/ *adj* using wit, especially irony, sarcasm, and ridicule, to criticize faults —**sa·tir·i·cal·ly** *adv*

SYNONYMS See *sarcastic.*

sat·i·rist /sáttərist/ *n* a writer or performer of satires

sat·i·rize /sáttə rìz/ (**-rized, -riz·ing, -riz·es**) *vt* to attack or criticize somebody or something by means of satire —**sat·i·ri·za·tion** /sàttəri záysh'n/ *n* —**sat·i·riz·er** *n*

sat·is·fac·tion /sàttəss fáksh'n/ *n* **1.** GRATIFICATION the feeling of pleasure that comes when a need or desire is fulfilled ○ *job satisfaction* **2.** HAPPINESS WITH ARRANGEMENT happiness with the way that something has been arranged or done ○ *was organized to her satisfaction* **3.** COMPENSATION compensation for an injury or loss ○ *demanded satisfaction for their mistreatment* **4.** FULFILLMENT the fulfillment of a need, claim, or desire ○ *the satisfaction of their hunger*

[14C. Via French < Latin *satisfaction-* < past participle of *satisfacere* (see SATISFY)]

sat·is·fac·to·ry /sàttəss fáktəree/ *adj* good enough to meet a requirement or to be considered acceptable [15C. Directly or via French < medieval Latin *satisfactorius* < past participle of Latin *satisfacere* (see SATISFY)] —**sat·is·fac·to·ri·ly** *adv*

sat·is·fy /sáttəss fī/ (**-fied, -fy·ing, -fies**) *v* **1.** *vt* **CONTENT SOMEBODY** to do or offer enough to make somebody feel pleased or content **2.** *vti* **FULFILL NEED** to fulfill a need or gratify a desire **3.** *vt* **MEET CONDITION** to achieve or be of sufficient standard to meet a requirement or condition **4.** *vt* MATH **SOLVE MATHEMATICAL PROBLEM** to make both sides of an equation equal by finding the values of the unknown variables **5.** *vt* LAW **PAY DEBT** to pay a debt in full **6.** *vt* **COMPENSATE SOMEBODY** to compensate somebody for an injury or loss [15C. Via Old French *satisfier* < Latin *satisfacere* < *satis* "enough" + *facere* "make"] —**sat·is·fied** *adj* —**sat·is·fi·er** *n* —**sat·is·fy·ing·ly** *adv*

Sa·to Ei·sa·ku /saàtō áyss aakoo/ (1901–75) prime minister of Japan (1964–72). He was awarded the Nobel Peace Prize (1974) for his role in negotiating a nuclear nonproliferation pact.

sa·to·ri /saa táwree/ *n* in Zen Buddhism, a state of spiritual enlightenment that is a spiritual objective [Early 18C. < Japanese, "awakening"]

SAT phone /sát-/ *n* TELECOM same as **satellite telephone** (*informal*)

sa·trap /sá tràp, sáy-/ *n* **1.** in ancient Persia, the governor of a province **2.** a subordinate official, especially a self-important one [15C. Via French and Latin < Old Persian *kšathrapāvā* "protector of the country"]

sa·tra·py /sáttrəpee, sáy-/ (*plural* **-pies**) *n* in ancient Persia, a province or territory governed by a satrap

sat·su·ma /sat so͝omə/ *n* **1.** a cultivated variety of mandarin orange, with a thin orange skin **2.** a citrus tree that bears satsumas. Native to: Japan. Latin name: *Citrus reticulata*. [Late 19C. After *Satsuma*, province in Kyushu, Japan]

Sat·su·ma ware, Sat·su·ma *n* cream-colored Japanese pottery [After a province in Kyushu, Japan]

~~**sattelite**~~ incorrect spelling of **satellite**

sat·u·rant /sáchərənt/ *n* a substance that is used to saturate another substance ■ *adj* causing saturation [Mid-18C. < Latin *saturant-*, present participle of *saturare* (see SATURATE)]

sat·u·rate *vt* /sáchə ràyt/ (**-rat·ed, -rat·ing, -rates**) **1. MAKE SOMETHING WET** to soak something with liquid **2. FILL SOMETHING COMPLETELY** to fill something with so many people or things that no more can be added **3.** COMM **SUPPLY MARKET FULLY** to supply a market fully, so that all existing demand for a product is met **4.** CHEM **FILL SOLUTION WITH ANOTHER SUBSTANCE** to add as much of a liquid, solid, or gas to a solution as it can absorb at a given temperature **5.** MIL **BOMB ENEMY HEAVILY** to overwhelm an enemy with intensive bombing ■ *adj* /sáchərət/ **SATURATED** saturated with liquid (*archaic*) [Mid-16C. < Latin *saturat-*, past participle of *saturare* < *satur* "satiated"] —**sat·u·ra·ble** *adj*

sat·u·rat·ed /sáchə ràytəd/ *adj* **1. WET** soaked with liquid **2. PACKED FULL** completely packed or full so that no more can be added **3.** CHEM **CONTAINING MAXIMUM SOLUTE** containing the maximum amount of solute that can be absorbed at a given temperature **4.** CHEM **CONTAINING SINGLE BONDS BETWEEN CARBON ATOMS** containing only single bonds between carbon atoms

SYNONYMS See *wet*.

sat·u·rat·ed fat *n* a fat in which the carbon atoms are fully hydrogenated, found in animal products. A diet heavy in saturated fat is thought to raise cholesterol in the bloodstream.

sat·u·ra·tion /sàchə ráysh'n/ *n* **1. STATE OF TOTAL WETNESS** a state in which something is completely soaked with liquid **2. STATE OF BEING PACKED FULL** a state in which something is so full or packed that no more can be added **3.** MIL **HEAVY BOMBING** intensive bombing of a military target in order to overwhelm an enemy **4.** COMM **FULL SUPPLYING OF MARKET** the full supplying of a commercial market, to the point where all existing demand for a product is met **5.** CHEM **MAXIMUM ABSORPTION** the absorption of the greatest possible amount of a liquid, solid, or gas by a solution at a given temperature **6.** PHYS **STATE OF MAGNETIZATION** a state of complete magnetization **7.** METEOROL **100 PERCENT HUMIDITY** the condition of the atmosphere when it contains as much water vapor as it can hold at a specific temperature **8.** PHYS **COLOR INTENSITY** the intensity of a color **9.** ELECTRONICS **CONDITION OF STABLE OUTPUT CURRENT** a condition where the output current of an electronic device is substantially constant and no longer increases as a function of increasing input ■ *adj* **COMPREHENSIVE** comprehensive in the use of outlets or other resources ○ *The event had saturation coverage in the press.*

sat·u·ra·tion div·ing *n* a method of diving in which the diver's bloodstream is saturated with an inert gas so that the time required for decompression is unaffected by the duration of the dive

sat·u·ra·tion point *n* **1.** the point at which no more can be added **2.** the point at which the greatest possible amount of a substance has been absorbed by a solution at a given temperature

sat·u·ra·tion zone *n* the zone below the water table that is saturated with ground water

Sat·ur·day /sáttər dày, -dee/ *n* the day of the week after Friday and before Sunday [Pre-12C. Contraction of *Saturn's day*, translation of Latin *Saturni dies*]

Sat·ur·day night spe·cial *n US* a small cheap handgun that is easy to obtain and conceal (*informal*) [Because the guns are most often used in the types of crime that typically occur on a Saturday night]

Sat·ur·days /sáttər dàyz, -deez/ *adv* every Saturday

Sat·urn /sáttərn/ *n* **1.** the second-largest planet in the solar system and the sixth planet from the Sun. It has bright rings made up of orbiting fragments of rock. **2.** in Roman mythology, the god of agriculture and ruler of the universe during the Golden Age. Greek equivalent **Cronus** [Pre-12C. < Latin *Saturnus*] —**Sa·tur·ni·an** /sa túrnee ən/ *adj*

sat·ur·na·li·a /sàttər náylee ə/ (*plural* **-as** or *same*) *n* a wild celebration or orgy [Late 18C. < SATURNALIA]

Sat·ur·na·li·a /sàttər náylee ə/ *npl* an ancient Roman festival of feasting and revelry in celebration of the god Saturn and the winter solstice. Date: mid-December. [Late 16C. < Latin < *Saturnus* "Saturn"]

sa·tur·ni·id /sa túrnee id/ *n* a large brightly colored moth with a hairy body. Family: Saturniidae. [Late 19C. < modern Latin *Saturniidae* < Latin *Saturnus* "Saturn"]

sat·ur·nine /sáttər nīn/ *adj* **1.** gloomy and morose **2.** caused by the absorption of lead or suffering from lead poisoning (*archaic*) [15C. Directly or via French < medieval Latin *saturninus* < Latin *Saturnus* "Saturn"] —**sat·ur·nine·ly** *adv*

sa·tya·gra·ha /sə tyaágrəhə/ *n* the doctrine of nonviolent resistance originated by Mohandas Gandhi and used in the opposition to British rule in India [Early 20C. < Sanskrit *satyāgrahaḥ* "force born out of truth"]

sa·tya·gra·hi /sə tyaágrəhee/ *n* a practitioner of nonviolent resistance or satyagraha [Early 20C. < Sanskrit *satyāgrahī*]

sa·tyr /sáytər, sáttər/ *n* **1. HALF-MAN, HALF-GOAT** in Greek mythology, a wood-dwelling creature with the head and body of a man and the ears, horns, and legs of a goat. Satyrs were characterized as being fond of lechery and drunken merriment. Roman equivalent **faun 2. MAN DISPLAYING INAPPROPRIATE SEXUAL BEHAVIOR** a man who displays inappropriate or excessively sexual behavior **3.** INSECTS **BUTTERFLY** a brown or gray butterfly with spotted wings. Family: Satyridae. [14C. Via French < Latin *satyrus* < Greek *saturos*] —**sa·tyr·ic** /say tírik, sə-/ *adj* —**sa·tyr·i·cal** *adj*

sa·ty·ri·a·sis /sàytə rī́ əssiss, sàttə-/ *n* excessive and uncontrollable sexual desire in a man

sa·tyr·id /sáytərid, sáttə-/ *n* a small brown butterfly. Family: Satyridae.

sa·tyr play *n* in ancient Greece, a comic play that mocked a mythological subject and included a chorus of satyrs

sauce /sawss/ *n* **1. FLAVORING LIQUID FOR FOOD** a thick liquid that is served with food to add extra flavor **2. STEWED FRUIT** stewed fruit served with a meal ○ *cranberry sauce* **3. ZEST** something that adds zest or excitement **4. IMPUDENT REMARKS** impudent or disrespectful remarks (*informal*) **5. ALCOHOL** alcoholic drinks (*slang*) ■ *vt* (**sauced, sauc·ing, sauc·es**) **1. ADD SAUCE TO FOOD** to add flavor to food using a sauce **2. ENLIVEN SOMETHING** to add zest or interest to something **3. SPEAK TO SOMEBODY DISRESPECTFULLY** to make impudent or disrespectful remarks to somebody (*informal*) [14C. Via French < Latin *salsus*, past participle of *sallere* "to salt" < *sal* "salt"]

sauce·boat /sáwss bōt/ *n* a low boat-shaped pitcher used for serving sauce or gravy

sauce·pan /sáwss pàn/ *n* a cooking pot with a handle, used on top of a stove

sauce·pot /sáwss pòt/ *n US* a cooking pot with two handles and a close-fitting lid

sau·cer /sáwssər/ *n* **1.** a small shallow dish designed to hold a matching cup **2.** anything circular and shallow like a saucer

sauc·y /sáwssee/ (**-i·er, -i·est**) *adj* **1. IMPUDENT** showing a lack of respect **2. PERT** cheerfully pert ○ *a hat at a saucy angle* **3. SEXUALLY EXPLICIT** intended to be amusingly vulgar, especially in sexual innuendo —**sau·ci·ly** *adv* —**sau·ci·ness** *n*

Sa·ud[1] /saa o͞od/ ➧ **Ibn Saud, Abdul Aziz**

Sa·ud[2] (1902–69) king of Saudi Arabia. The son of King Ibn Saud, he ruled (1953–64) until he was peacefully deposed and replaced by his brother Faisal.

Sau·di /sówdee/ *n* somebody who comes from Saudi Arabia ■ *adj* relating to Saudi Arabia or its people or culture [Mid-20C. After the *Saud* family, the ruling dynasty]

Saudi Arabia

Sau·di A·ra·bi·a /sòwdee ə ráybee ə/ country in Southwest Asia, on the Arabian Peninsula. Language: Arabic. Currency: riyal. Capital: Riyadh. Population: 24,293,844 (2003). Area: 864,900 sq. mi./2,240,000 sq. km. Official name **Kingdom of Saudi Arabia** —**Sau·di A·ra·bi·an** *n, adj*

sau·er·bra·ten /sów ər braàt'n/ *n* a German dish of beef roast marinated and cooked in vinegar [Late 19C. < German, "sour roast meat"]

sau·er·kraut /sów ər kròwt/ *n* a German dish of shredded cabbage fermented in its own juice with salt [Mid-17C. < German, "sour cabbage"]

sau·ger /sáwgər/ *n* a freshwater fish similar to but smaller than a walleyed pike and valued in sport fishing. Native to: North America. Latin name: *Stizostedion canadense*. [Late 19C. Origin ?]

Sau·gus /sáwgəss/ town in northeastern Massachusetts, on the Saugus River. It is a northeastern suburb of Boston. Population: 26,415 (2002 estimate).

Sauk /sawk/ (*plural same* or **Sauks**), **Sac** /sak, sawk/ (*plural same* or **Sacs**) *n* **1.** a member of a Native North American people who lived in Wisconsin, Illinois, and Iowa and who now live mainly in Oklahoma. The Sauk joined with the Fox to fight in the Black Hawk War of 1832, following US attempts to move the Fox from their lands in Illinois. **2.** the Algonquian language of the Sauk people, related to Fox [Early 18C. Via Canadian French *Saki* < Ojibwa *osākì*] —**Sauk** *adj*

Saul /sawl/ (*fl* 11th century B.C.) Israelite monarch, mentioned in the Bible (1 Samuel 8–15). He defeated the Philistines but later died in battle against them. He was succeeded by his son-in-law, David.

sault /soo/ *n* a waterfall or rapids [14C. Via French < Latin *saltus* "leap" < *salire* "to leap"]

Sault Sainte Ma·rie /so͞o sàynt mə ree/ **1.** city in

northern Michigan, between lakes Superior and Huron, on the St. Marys River. Population: 14,264 (2002 estimate). **2.** city in Ontario, Canada, opposite Sault Saint Marie, Michigan. Population: 67,384 (2001).

Sault Sainte Ma·rie Ca·nals series of ship canals in North America, comprising two in the United States and one in Canada, on the St. Marys River, between lakes Superior and Huron.

sau·na /sáwnə, sównə/ *n* **1.** a bath involving a spell in a hot steamy room followed by a plunge into cold water or a light brushing with birch or cedar boughs **2.** a room designed or prepared for having a sauna [Late 19C. < Finnish]

saunf /sawNf/ *n S Asia* aniseed used as a flavoring, snack, or mouth freshener after food [< Hindi *saūṇph*]

saun·ter /sáwntər/ *vi* **(-tered, -ter·ing, -ters)** STROLL to walk at an easy unhurried pace ■ *n* **1.** EASY PACE an easy unhurried pace ○ *walk at a saunter* **2.** SLOW WALK a slow leisurely walk ○ *go for a saunter around the grounds* [Mid-17C. Origin ?] —**saun·ter·er** *n*

sau·rel /sáwrəl, saw rél/ *n US* FISH **1.** same as **jack mackerel** **2.** same as **horse mackerel** [Late 19C. < French < late Latin *saurus* < Greek *sauros* "lizard, horse mackerel"]

sau·ri·an /sáwree ən/ *n* any of a former suborder of reptiles that included all lizards. Suborder: Sauria. ■ *adj* relating to or resembling a lizard [Early 19C. < modern Latin *Sauria* < Latin *saurus* "lizard" < Greek *sauros*]

saur·is·chi·an /saw rískee ən/ *n* a dinosaur that had a pelvis like that of a modern lizard. Order: Saurischia. ■ *adj* relating to the saurischians [Late 19C. < modern Latin *Saurischia* "lizard hip-joint"]

~~**saurkraut**~~ incorrect spelling of **sauerkraut**

sau·ro·pod /sáwrə pòd/ *n* a gigantic plant-eating dinosaur that had a long neck and tail and a small head. Suborder: Sauropoda. ■ *adj* relating to the sauropods [Late 19C. < modern Latin *Sauropoda* "lizard foot"] —**sau·rop·o·dous** /saw róppədəss/ *adj*

sau·ry /sáwree/ (*plural* **-ries**) *n* a small offshore fish resembling a needlefish but with shorter jaws and a series of small fins behind the dorsal and anal fins. Native to: tropical and temperate seas. Family: Scomberosocidae. [Late 18C. < modern Latin *saurus* "lizard" < Greek *sauros*]

sau·sage /sáwssij/ *n* a tube of animal intestine or another tube-shaped casing stuffed with finely chopped pork or other meat [15C. Via Old French *saussiche* < medieval Latin *salsicius* "made by salting" < Latin *salsus* (see SAUCE)]

sau·sage tree *n* a tree with long hard-shelled fruits that hang down on very long stalks. Flowers: large, red, bell-shaped. Native to: tropical Africa. Latin name: *Kigelia pinnata*.

Saus·sure /sō sóor, -syóor/, **Ferdinand de** (1857–1913) Swiss linguist. His masterwork, *Course in General Linguistics* (1916), was assembled from his students' lecture notes. He is considered the founder of structural linguistics, structuralism, and semiotics.

sau·té /sō táy/ *vt* **(-téed, -té·ing, -tés)** FRY SOMETHING LIGHTLY to cook food quickly and lightly in a little butter, oil, or fat ■ *n* SAUTÉED DISH a dish consisting of food, usually meat, that has been sautéed and prepared with a sauce ■ *adj* COOKED LIGHTLY cooked by being sautéed [Early 19C. < French, past participle of *sauter* "leap" < Latin *salire*]

Sau·ternes /sō túrn/ (*plural same*), **sau·ternes** *n* **1.** a sweet white wine from southwestern France **2.** a sweet white wine similar to Sauternes [Early 18C. After a French region]

Sau·vé /sō váy/, **Jeanne-Mathilde Benoit** (1922–93) Canadian journalist and politician. She was the first woman governor-general of Canada (1984–90). Born **Benoit, Jeanne-Mathilde**

sauve qui peut /sōv kee pṓ/ *n* a disordered or panicked escape [< French, "save who can"]

Sau·vi·gnon Blanc /sòvi nyōn blaángk/ *n* **1.** a typically light white wine made from a white grape originally grown in west central France **2.** a white grape variety. Use: to make Sauvignon Blanc. [< French, "white Sauvignon"]

sav·age /sávvij/ *adj* **1.** VIOLENT unrestrained, violent, or vicious **2.** BRUTAL brutal and severe ○ *savage cuts in funding* **3.** UNDOMESTICATED living wild, beyond the control of people ○ *savage beasts* **4.** OFFENSIVE TERM an offensive term meaning relating to a culture that is unfamiliar and perceived as inferior, especially one not using complex modern technologies ■ *n* **1.** VICIOUS OR VIOLENT PERSON somebody who enjoys treating people and animals cruelly and violently **2.** OFFENSIVE TERM an offensive term for a member of a people considered inferior to or not as advanced as your own group ■ *vt* **(-aged, -ag·ing, -ag·es)** **1.** ATTACK SOMEBODY OR SOMETHING VIOLENTLY to attack somebody or something violently, viciously, and without restraint **2.** CRITICIZE SOMEBODY OR SOMETHING CRUELLY to criticize somebody or something cruelly and unrestrainedly ○ *The same critics who praised her first book savaged her second.* [13C. Via French *sauvage* < Latin *silvaticus* "wild" < *silva* "forest"] —**sav·age·ly** *adv* —**sav·age·ness** *n*

USAGE The use of ***savage*** to refer to peoples not using complex modern technologies and with an unfamiliar culture was a feature of 19th-century and earlier English (*Vouchsafe to show the sunshine of your face, that we, like savages, may worship it*, Shakespeare, *Love's Labour's Lost* Act 5, Scene 2) but is regarded as inappropriate and offensive in current use.

Sav·age /sávvij/, **Michael Joseph** (1872–1940) Australian-born prime minister of New Zealand (1935–40). He won a landslide victory to become the country's first Labour Party prime minister. See table at **prime minister**

sav·age·ry /sávvijəree/ *n* **1.** barbarity or violent cruelty **2.** an offensive term for a culture perceived to be inferior to or less advanced than your own

sa·van·na /sə vánnə/, **sa·van·nah** *n* a flat grassland, sometimes with scattered trees, in a tropical or subtropical region [Mid-16C. Via Spanish *zavana* < Taino]

Sa·van·nah /sə vánnə/ **1.** river rising in northeastern South Carolina and emptying into the Atlantic Ocean below Savannah, Georgia. Length: 314 mi./505 km. **2.** city and seaport in southeastern Georgia on the Savannah River near its mouth on the Atlantic Ocean. Population: 127,691 (2002 estimate).

sa·vant /sa vaánt/ *n* a wise or scholarly person [Early 18C. < French, present participle of *savoir* "know" < Latin *sapere* "be wise"]

sa·vate /sə vát, sə vaát/ *n* a form of boxing in which kicking as well as hitting is allowed [Mid-19C. < French, originally a kind of shoe]

save[1] /sayv/ *v* **(saved, sav·ing, saves)** **1.** *vt* RESCUE SOMEBODY OR SOMETHING to rescue somebody or something from harm or danger ○ *The entire crew was saved.* **2.** *vti* ACCUMULATE MONEY to set aside money for later use, often adding to the sum periodically ○ *She's saving for a new computer.* **3.** *vt* CONSERVE SOMETHING to avoid wasting something or using something unnecessarily ○ *take a shortcut to save time* ○ *switched it off to save the batteries* **4.** *vt* KEEP SOMETHING BACK FOR LATER to set something aside, keep something back, or protect something so that it can be used later ○ *Save some of the pie for tomorrow.* **5.** *vti* REDUCE EXPENSE to reduce or limit the expense of something ○ *Extra insulation helps us to save on fuel.* **6.** *vt* COLLECT ITEMS FOR LATER to collect as many items of a particular kind as possible, usually in order to do something with them later ○ *She saves old jars for when she makes jelly.* **7.** *vt* SPARE SOMEBODY FROM SOMETHING to make it possible for somebody to be spared from a situation or activity ○ *It will save me from having to decide.* **8.** *vt* PRESERVE SOMETHING to treat something carefully or stop using it in order to keep it from being used up or worn out ○ *Turn the radio off to save the batteries.* **9.** *vti* COMPUT COPY DATA FOR STORAGE to store a copy of a data file on a storage medium such as a hard drive or disk **10.** *vt* SPORTS PREVENT GOAL to prevent a goal from being scored by an opponent **11.** *vt* BASEBALL MAINTAIN LEAD SUCCESSFULLY in baseball, to maintain the lead in completing a game started by another pitcher **12.** *vt* RELIG REDEEM SOMEBODY in some beliefs, to free somebody from the consequences of sin ■ *n* **1.** SPORTS BLOCK an action that keeps an opponent from scoring **2.** BASEBALL MAINTENANCE OF LEAD in baseball, the successful maintenance of a team's lead by a relief pitcher [13C. Via French < late Latin *salvare* < Latin *salvus* "safe"]

save[2] /sayv/ *prep, conj* same as **except** (sense 1) ○ *Everyone agreed save one.* [13C. Via Old French *sauf, sauve* < form of Latin *salvus* "safe"]

save-all *n* **1.** a receptacle for catching waste products so that they can be reused **2.** something that prevents waste or loss

sav·e·loy /sávvə lòy/ *n UK* a spicy smoked pork sausage [Mid-19C. Via French *cervelas* < Italian *cervellata* "sausage"]

sav·er /sáyvər/ *n* **1.** somebody who saves money, especially in a bank account ○ *The fall in interest rates is not such good news for savers.* **2.** something that avoids wasting resources or using them unnecessarily (*used in combination*) ○ *E-mail is a great time-saver.*

Sa·ver·y /sáyvəree/, **Thomas** (1650?–1715) English engineer and inventor. He patented a method of paddle-wheel propulsion for vessels and a steam pump, and, with Thomas Newcomen, developed a steam piston engine.

Save the Chil·dren Fund *n* an organization in the United Kingdom that provides international aid directed toward children's well being

sav·in /sávvin/, **sav·ine** *n* an evergreen bush that yields an oil formerly used medicinally and in perfumes. Native to: Europe, northern Asia, North America. Latin name: *Juniperus sabina*. [Pre-12C. Via Old French *savine* < Latin *herba Sabina* "Sabine plant"]

sav·ing /sáyving/ *n* **1.** SOMETHING KEPT FROM BEING USED an amount of time or money that is not spent or used ○ *a saving of ten percent* **2.** AMOUNT SAVED a particular amount of money saved by buying the equivalent at a lower rate **3.** RESCUE FROM DANGER rescue of somebody or something from harm or danger **4.** LAW LEGAL EXCEPTION an exception or reservation in law ■ *prep, conj* same as **except** (sense 1) (*literary*)

USAGE Saving or savings? ***Savings*** means "money saved," as in *Substantial savings help provide a secure retirement.* In this sense it takes a plural verb. On the other hand, ***savings*** is commonly used with a singular verb to mean "a particular amount of money saved by buying the equivalent at a lower rate," as in *A savings of $3,000 was gained during the transaction.* This usage undoubtedly has its origins in the well-established expressions *a savings and loan association, a savings bank,* and *a savings account*. However, some people still prefer ***saving*** in the singular in this context: *A saving of $3,000 was gained during the transaction.*

sav·ing grace *n* a quality or feature that redeems a person or situation

sav·ings /sáyvings/ *n* same as **saving** *n* (sense 2) (*takes a singular verb*) ■ *npl* money set aside for future use (*takes a plural verb*)

USAGE See ***saving***.

sav·ings ac·count *n* a bank account that earns interest on money deposited

sav·ings and loan as·so·ci·a·tion *n US* a financial institution that issues shares to members who deposit savings and invests the money mainly in home mortgage loans. Members receive interest on their savings in the form of dividends.

sav·ings bank *n* a bank that invests the savings of depositors and pays interest on the deposits

sav·ings bond *n* **1.** a registered bond issued by the US government in denominations of $50 to $10,000. It allows people to earn interest on the savings they entrust to the government in exchange for the bond. **2.** *Can* a bond issued by the Canadian government in denominations of $100 to $100,000. The bond is offered to most working Canadians through a payroll deduction plan.

sav·ings meth·od *n US* a method of testing memory by assessing how much faster somebody can learn information already previously learned, seen, or read

sav·ings ra·tio *n* the ratio of national disposable income to consumer spending, used as a measure of national saving

sav·ior /sáyvyər/ *n* somebody who rescues somebody or something from harm or danger [13C. Via Old French *sauveour* < ecclesiastical Latin *salvator* < late Latin *salvare* (see SAVE[1])]

Sav·ior *n* used by Christians as a name for Jesus Christ

sav·iour *n* Can, UK spelling of **savior**

sa·voir-faire /sàv waar fér/ *n* the ability to act appropriately and adroitly in any situation [Early 19C. < French, "know how to do"]

Sa·vo·na·ro·la /sàvvənə rṓlə/, **Girolamo** (1452–98) Italian religious leader and martyr. He criticized the corruption of the Medici family and Pope Alexander VI and was excommunicated (1497), declared guilty of heresy, and hanged (1498).

> "Art cannot imitate nature entirely, even if the artist is perfect, because, even if a painter makes something similar to man in everything, yet it will not have life."
> [Girolamo Savonarola, *Sermon on the Psalm Quam Bonus*; 1493]

sa·vor /sáyvər/ *v* (**-vored, -vor·ing, -vors**) **1.** *vt* ENJOY SOMETHING UNHURRIEDLY to enjoy something with unhurried appreciation ○ *savor the moment* **2.** *vt* RELISH SOMETHING to enjoy the taste or smell of something **3.** *vi* SHOW TRACES to show traces of something ○ *something in his manner that savored of deceit* ■ *n* **1.** ENJOYMENT enjoyment and relish **2.** TASTE OR SMELL SOMETHING HAS the way that something tastes or smells **3.** DISTINCTIVE QUALITY a quality that identifies or distinguishes something [12C. Via Old French *savour* < Latin *sapor* "taste" < *sapere* "have a taste"] —**sa·vor·less** *adj* —**sa·vor·ous** *adj*

sa·vor·y[1] /sáyvəree/ *n* an herb with aromatic leaves. Use: flavoring food. Latin name: *Satureja hortensis.* [14C. Via Old French *sarree* < Latin *satureia*]

sa·vor·y[2] /sáyvəree/ *adj* **1.** APPETIZING having an appetizing taste or smell **2.** NOT SWEET salty or sharp-tasting rather than sweet **3.** RESPECTABLE respectable or morally acceptable ○ *not a very savory character* ■ *n* (*plural* **-ies**) *UK* DISH THAT ADDS RELISH a light salty or spicy dish served before or at the end of a meal [13C. < Old French *savoure*, past participle of *savourer* "taste" < Latin *sapor* (see SAVOR)] —**sa·vor·i·ly** *adv* —**sa·vor·i·ness** *n*

sa·vour, sa·vour·y UK spelling of **savor, savory**. Can spelling of **savor, savory**

sa·voy /sə vóy/ *n* a winter cabbage with crinkled leaves [16C. After *Savoy*, region of SE France]

Sa·voy·ard /sàv oy àard/ *n* **1.** somebody who comes from the Savoy region of southeastern France **2.** a performer, producer, or admirer of the operettas of W. S. Gilbert and Arthur Sullivan. [Early 17C. < French < *Savoie* "Savoy"; in sense 2, after the *Savoy* Theatre in London, England]

sa·voy cab·bage *n* PLANTS, FOOD same as **savoy**

Sa·voy o·pe·ra *n* an operetta by Gilbert and Sullivan or a work composed in the same style

sav·vy /sávvee/ (*informal*) *n* SHREWDNESS shrewdness and practical knowledge ■ *adj* SHREWD shrewd and well informed ■ *vti* (**-vied, -vy·ing, -vies**) COMPREHEND SOMETHING to understand something, especially what somebody has said [Late 18C. < Spanish *sabe (usted)?* "you know?"]

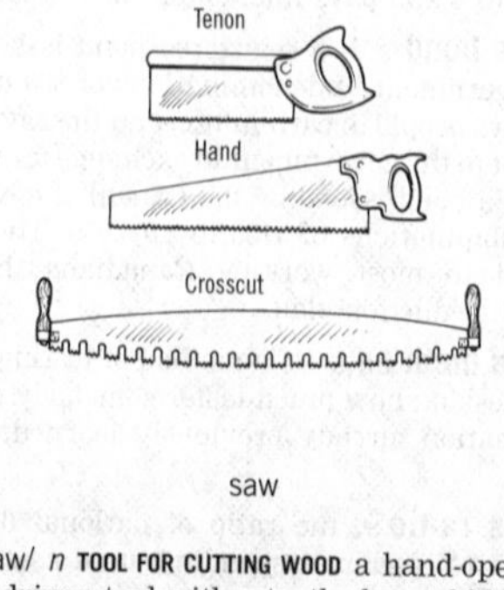

saw

saw[1] /saw/ *n* TOOL FOR CUTTING WOOD a hand-operated or power-driven tool with a toothed metal blade, used to cut wood or other hard materials ■ *v* (**sawed, sawed** or **sawn** /sawn/, **saw·ing, saws**) **1.** *vti* CUT SOMETHING WITH SAW to cut something using a saw **2.** *vt* MOVE FORWARD AND BACK to make back-and-forth motions through something such as the air, as if using a handsaw [Old English *saga* < Indo-European]

saw[2] /saw/ *n* an old saying, especially a cliché [Old English *sagu* < Germanic]

saw[3] /saw/ past tense of **see**[1]

SAW *abbr* ELECTRONICS surface acoustic wave

saw·bones /sáw bṑnz/ (*plural same* or **-bones·es**) *n* a surgeon or physician (*slang*) [Mid-19C. < early surgeons' role as amputators]

saw·buck /sáw bùk/ *n* **1.** CONSTR same as **sawhorse 2.** a ten-dollar bill (*slang*) [Mid-19C. < Dutch *zaagbok*; in sense 2, from the resemblance between the X-shaped end of a sawhorse and the Roman numeral for "ten"]

saw·dust /sáw dùst/ *n* tiny particles of wood produced when wood is sawed

sawed-off *adj* **1.** describes a firearm that has the barrel cut short so that it is less cumbersome or obtrusive and its field of fire is increased ○ *a sawed-off shotgun* **2.** an offensive term meaning of small stature (*slang*)

sawfish

saw·fish /sáw fìsh/ (*plural same* or **-fish·es**) *n* a ray having a long snout with projections resembling teeth that it uses as a weapon. Native to: tropical oceans. Family: Pristidae.

saw·fly /sáw flì/ (*plural* **-flies**) *n* an insect in which the female has a prominent, often serrated appendage at the tip of its abdomen, for boring holes and laying eggs in wood and plants. Family: Tenthredinidae.

saw grass *n* any one of various sedges that have serrated leaves. Genus: *Cladium.*

saw·horse /sáw hàwrss/ *n* a support for wood during sawing

saw·ine /sáy wìn, saa-/ *n Carib* a Trinidadian dessert consisting of milk with fried vermicelli, spiced with cinnamon, raisins, and other additions, usually made and shared with others during the Muslim festival of Eid al-Fitr [< Urdu, Hindi, contraction of *sivaiyām* "noodles"]

saw log *n* a log of sufficient size to be suitable for sawing

saw·mill /sáw mìl/ *n* **1.** a factory in which wood is sawed into planks or boards by machine **2.** a powerful sawing machine

sawn past participle of **saw**[1]

sawn-off *adj UK* ARMS same as **sawed-off**

saw pal·met·to *n* a palm tree with spiny-toothed leafstalks. Native to: southeastern United States. Latin name: *Serenoa repens.*

saw-scaled vi·per *n* a small venomous snake that lives in dry areas and is believed to have the most powerful venom of all the vipers. Native to: North Africa, central Asia. Latin name: *Echis carinaus.*

saw set *n* an instrument that bends alternating teeth of a saw in opposite directions

Saw·tell /saw tél/ coastal town in northeastern New South Wales, Australia. Population: 10,810 (1991).

saw·tooth /sáw tòoth/ *n* (*plural* **-teeth** /-tèeth/) any of the teeth of a saw ■ *adj* in a zigzag shape, like the teeth of a saw

saw-toothed *adj* **1.** having notched teeth like a saw **2.** DESIGN same as **sawtooth**

saw-whet owl *n* a small owl with a call that is a long series of short whistles. Native to: North America. Latin name: *Aegolius acadicus.* [Because its call was considered to resemble the sound of a saw being sharpened]

saw·yer /sáwyər/ *n* **1.** somebody who saws wood for a living **2.** a horned beetle whose larvae bore into coniferous trees. Genus: *Monochamus.* [13C. < SAW[1] + *-yer*, variant of -IER]

sax /saks/ *n* MUSIC same as **saxophone** (*informal*) [Early 20C. Shortening]

sax·a·tile /sáksə tìl, sáksət'l/ *adj* growing on or living in rocks [Mid-17C. < Latin *saxatilis* < *saxum* "rock"]

saxe blue /sàks-/ *adj* of a light grayish blue color [Via French < German *Sachsen* "Saxony"] —**saxe blue** *n*

sax·horn /sáks hàwrn/ *n* a valved brass wind instrument, often used in military brass bands [Mid-19C. After Charles Joseph *Sax* (1791–1865) and his son Antoine Joseph *Sax* (1814–94) (known as "Adolphe"), Belgian instrument makers]

sax·ic·o·lous /sak síkələss/, **sax·ic·o·line** /-síkə lìn/ *adj* BIOL same as **saxatile** [Mid-19C. < modern Latin *saxicola* < Latin *saxum* "rock" + *colere* "inhabit"]

sax·i·frage /sáksi frìj, -fràyj/ (*plural* **-frages** or *same*) *n* a plant that grows on rocky ground. Flowers: small, white, yellow, purple, or red. Genus: *Saxifraga.* [14C. Via French < Latin *saxifraga* "rock-breaking" < *saxum* "rock, stone"]

sax·i·tox·in /sàksi tóksin/ *n* a strong neurotoxin found in plankton (**dinoflagellates**) and concentrating in shellfish, causing food poisoning in humans. It is found in red tides. [Mid-20C. < modern Latin *Saxodomus*, genus of clams]

Sax·on /sáks'n/ *n* **1.** MEMBER OF ANCIENT GERMANIC PEOPLE a member of a West Germanic people who started to spread west during Roman times, establishing powerful kingdoms with the Angles in southern Britain in the 7th century A.D. **2.** LANGUAGE OF ANCIENT SAXONS the group of West Germanic dialects spoken by the ancient Saxons **3.** SOMEBODY FROM SAXONY somebody who comes from Saxony [12C. Via French < Latin *Saxones* "Saxons" < Germanic] —**Sax·on** *adj*

Sax·on blue *n* a dye made from a solution of indigo in sulfuric acid

Sax·on·ism /sáksə nìzzəm/ *n* a word, phrase, or idiom in English supposedly from an Anglo-Saxon rather than Latin source

sax·o·ny /sáks'nee/ *n* **1.** a fine three-ply knitting yarn **2.** a fine woolen fabric. Use: coats. [Mid-19C. After SAXONY]

Sa·xo·ny /sáks'nee/ state in eastern Germany. It was a kingdom until 1918, although part of the North German Confederation from 1866. Between 1945 and 1989 the area was part of East Germany. Capital: Dresden. Population: 4,489,415 (1998). Area: 7,078 sq. mi./18,337 sq. km.

sax·o·phone /sáksə fṑn/ *n* a metal wind instrument with keys and a reed that comes in several sizes and registers and is particularly associated with jazz music. The alto and tenor saxophones are the most popular. [Mid-19C. After Antoine Joseph *Sax* (see SAXHORN)] —**sax·o·phon·ic** /sàksə fónnik/ *adj* —**sax·o·phon·ist** *n*

sax·tu·ba /sáks tòobə/ *n* a large bass saxhorn [Mid-19C. < SAXHORN + TUBA]

say /say/ *v* (**said** /sed/, **say·ing, says** /sez/) **1.** *vt* UTTER SOMETHING to utter something in a normal voice, not singing, shouting, or whispering **2.** *vti* EXPRESS VERBALLY to convey information or express feelings in spoken words **3.** *vt* STATE SOMETHING to utter something as a matter of fact, belief, or prediction ○ *was said to be the largest in captivity* **4.** *vt* INDICATE SOMETHING to convey information in written or printed words, numbers, or symbols ○ *The clock said midnight.* ○ *The rules say that you may not kick your opponent.* **5.** *vt* MAKE CASE FOR OR AGAINST SOMETHING to utter something by way of argument, explanation, or excuse ○ *There's much to be said for a dress code.* **6.** *vt* COMMAND SOMETHING to utter something as an instruction ○ *said to go* **7.** *vt* SUPPOSE SOMETHING to assume something for the sake of argument, or take something as a suitable example ○ *Let's say we can't get* *there in time.* **8.** *vt* **RECITE SOMETHING** to utter something that has a formula or set form of words ○ *says his prayers* **9.** *vt* **CONVEY SOMETHING INDIRECTLY** to convey something over and above the immediate words or superficial sound or appearance ○ *Your clothes say a lot about you.* **10.** *vt* **CONVEY SOMETHING IMPORTANT** to convey something substantial or significant in what is spoken or written ○ *We talked for hours but didn't really say anything.* ■ *n* **1. CHANCE TO SPEAK** a chance or turn to say something, especially to give an opinion ○ *You've already had your say.* **2. RIGHT TO GIVE OPINION** the right to express an opinion and have it considered by others ○ *had no say in the decision* ■ *adv* **APPROXIMATELY** approximately, or as a possibility or example ○ *if we get, say, three gallons* ■ *interj* (*informal*) **1. EXPRESSING SURPRISE** used to express surprise, admiration, or protest **2. ATTRACTING ATTENTION** used to attract somebody's attention [Old English *secgan* < Germanic] —**say·er** *n* ◇ **easier said than done** used to describe something that is more difficult than it sounds ◇ **enough said, 'nuff said** used to indicate that nothing more need be said for a situation to be understood ◇ **I say** *UK* (*dated*) **1.** used to express surprise, admiration, or protest **2.** used to attract somebody's attention ◇ **it goes without saying** used to emphasize that there should be no doubt concerning something ◇ **say when** used to ask somebody to indicate when enough drink has been poured or food served (*informal*) ◇ **that is to say** used to indicate that you are repeating something more clearly or in other words ◇ **there's no saying** used to emphasize the uncertainty of a situation ◇ **you can say that again** used to indicate complete agreement with what has just been said (*informal*)

Say·da ➧ **Sidon**

Dorothy L. Sayers

Say·ers /sáy ərz/, **Dorothy L.** (1893–1957) British writer. She wrote detective stories, including *Whose Body?* (1923) and *Gaudy Night* (1936). Full name **Sayers, Dorothy Leigh**

> "The worst sin—perhaps the only sin—passion can commit, is to be joyless."
> [Dorothy L. Sayers, *Gaudy Night*; 1936]

say·est /sáy əst/, **sayst** /sayst/ 2nd person singular present of **say** (*archaic*)

say·ing /sáy ing/ *n* a frequently offered piece of advice or information, or a frequently heard reflection on the way things are

sa·yo·na·ra /sī ə naárə/ *interj US* same as **goodbye** (*informal*) [Late 19C. < Japanese, "if it be so"]

say-so *n* (*informal*) **1. ASSERTION** a mere assertion by somebody that something is so **2. AUTHORIZATION** permission or authorization from somebody **3. AUTHORITY** the right to decide something

say·yid /saáyid, sī yid/, **say·id, sa·id** /saá id/ *n* **1.** a Muslim who claims to be descended from Muhammad's grandson Husain **2.** an Islamic title of respect for a man [Mid-17C. < Arabic, "prince"]

sb *abbr* ONLINE Solomon Islands (*used in Internet addresses*) See table at **domain name**

Sb *symbol* CHEM ELEM antimony [Abbreviation of Latin *stibium*]

SB *abbr* **1.** BROADCAST simultaneous broadcast **2.** BASEBALL stolen base

S.B. *abbr US* Bachelor of Science [Latin *Scientiae Baccalaureus*]

SBA[1] *n* a system of radio navigation that provides an aircraft with lateral guidance and marker beam indicators at set points during its landing approach. Full form **standard beam approach**

SBA[2] *abbr* Small Business Administration

SbE *abbr* south by east

SBS *abbr* HEALTH sick building syndrome

SbW *abbr* south by west

sc[1] *abbr* Seychelles (*used in Internet addresses*) See table at **domain name**

sc[2], **s.c.** *abbr* PRINTING small capital

Sc *symbol* CHEM ELEM scandium

SC *abbr* **1.** POL Security Council **2.** MIL Signal Corps **3.** South Carolina

sc. *abbr* **1.** LITERAT, THEATER scene **2.** scilicet **3.** MEASURE scruple

S.C. *abbr US* **1.** South Carolina **2.** Supreme Court

scab /skab/ *n* **1. CRUST OVER HEALING WOUND** a hard crust of dried blood, serum, or pus that forms over a wound during healing **2. STRIKEBREAKER** somebody who continues to work or replaces a worker during a strike (*disapproving*) **3.** VET **SKIN DISEASE OF SHEEP** a skin disease of sheep and other animals that resembles mange **4.** BOT **PLANT DISEASE CAUSING CRUSTY SPOTS** a fungal plant disease causing crusty spots on the affected parts **5.** BOT **CRUSTY SPOT ON PLANT** a crusty spot on a plant caused by a fungal disease **6. DISLIKABLE PERSON** somebody regarded as despicable or dislikable (*slang insult*) ■ *vi* (**scabbed, scab·bing, scabs**) **1. BECOME COVERED WITH SCAB** to become covered with a scab during healing **2. WORK DURING STRIKE** to continue to work during a strike, or do a striker's job during a strike (*disapproving*) [13C. < Old Norse *skabb* < Indo-European, "to scrape"]

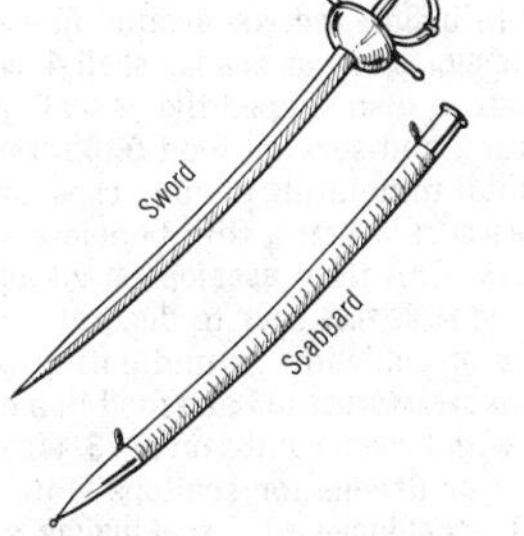

scabbard

scab·bard /skábbərd/ *n* a sheath, hanging from a belt, for a sword, dagger, or bayonet ■ *vt* (**-bard·ed, -bard·ing, -bards**) to put a sword, dagger, or bayonet into a sheath [13C. < Anglo-Norman *escauberge*]

scab·bard fish *n* an ocean fish with an elongated body and long sharp teeth. Family: Trichiuridae.

scab·ble /skább'l/ (**-bled, -bling, -bles**) *vt* to give a rough shape to stone [Early 17C. Alteration of obsolete *scapple* < Old French *escapeler* "shape timber" < *capler* "to cut"]

scab·by /skábbee/ (**-bi·er, -bi·est**) *adj* **1.** having or covered in scabs **2.** despicable or dislikable (*slang*) —**scab·bi·ness** *n*

sca·bies /skáybeez/ *n* a contagious skin disease marked by intense itching, inflammation, and red papules [14C. < Latin < *scabere* "to scratch"]

sca·bi·ous /skáybee əss, skábbee əss/ *adj* having scabs or scabies ■ *n* (*plural* **-ous·es** or *same*) a plant with blue, pink, or white dome-shaped flowers. Genera: *Scabiosa* or *Knautia*. [14C. Directly or via French < Latin *scabiosus* < *scabies* (see SCABIES)]

scab·lands /skáb làndz/ *npl* tracts of elevated land with bare rock, thin soil, and sparse vegetation, crossed by dry channels formed by glacial floodwaters

scab·rous /skábbrəss, skáybrəss/ *adj* **1. WITH ROUGH SURFACE** having a rough surface because of scales or short stiff hairs **2. REQUIRING TACT** having to be handled with tact and care **3. OBSCENE** dealing with or referring to sex in an obscene way (*literary*) [Late 16C. < late Latin *scabrosus* < Latin *scaber* "scurfy, scaly"]

scad /skad/ (*plural same* or **scads**) *n* **1.** a fish with a long body and sharp bony plates on either side of the narrow point of the tail. Native to: tropical and subtropical seas. Family: Caringidae. **2.** FISH same as **horse mackerel** [Early 17C. Origin ?]

scads /skadz/ *npl* large numbers or quantities (*informal*) ○ *scads of money* [Mid-19C. Origin ?]

scaf·fold /skáff'ld, -fōld/ *n* **1. FRAMEWORK TO SUPPORT WORKERS** a temporary framework of poles and planks that is used to support workers and materials during the erection, repair, or decoration of a building **2. PLATFORM FOR EXECUTIONS** a raised platform on which somebody is executed by hanging or beheading **3. DEATH BY HANGING** death by hanging or beheading as a form of punishment **4. SUPPORT** a supporting framework ■ *vt* (**-fold·ed, -fold·ing, -folds**) **ERECT SCAFFOLD AROUND BUILDING** to put up a scaffold around or against a building [13C. Via Old French *(e)schaffaut* < Vulgar Latin *catafalcum*] —**scaf·fold·er** *n*

scaf·fold·ing /skáff'lding, ská fōlding/ *n* **1.** a scaffold or system of scaffolds around or against a building **2.** the poles and planks used to build a scaffold

scag /skag/, **skag** *n* DRUGS same as **heroin** (*slang*) [Early 20C. Origin ?]

scagl·io·la /skal yṓlə/ *n* imitation marble made of gypsum mixed with glue, with a polished surface of marble or granite dust [Late 16C. < Italian, "tiny scale, chip of marble" < Germanic]

scal·a·ble /skáyləb'l/ *adj* **1. CLIMBABLE** able to be climbed up or over **2. VARIABLE** describes computer graphics fonts generated by an algorithm that permits the size to vary proportionately over a wide range **3. EXPANDABLE** describes a computer, component, or network that can be expanded to meet future needs —**scal·a·bil·i·ty** /skàylə bíllətee/ *n* —**scal·a·ble·ness** *n*

scal·age /skáylij/ *n US* **1.** an allowance in the form of a percentage deducted from the cost of goods to reflect loss in amount or size during storage or shipping **2.** the estimated yield of lumber from a log

sca·lar /skáylər/ *n* PHYS, MATH a quantity that has magnitude but no direction, e.g., mass or time ■ *adj* describes a quantity that has magnitude but no direction [Mid-17C. < Latin *scalaris* < *scala* "staircase, ladder"]

sca·la·re /skə lérree, -laáree/ (*plural same* or **-res**) *n* FISH same as **angelfish** (sense 1) [Early 20C. < Latin *scalaris* "of a ladder" (from its markings) < *scala* "staircase, ladder"]

sca·lar·i·form /skə lérrə fàwrm/ *adj* describes the walls of a cell that have parallel structural formations resembling the rungs of a ladder [Mid-19C. < Latin *scalaris* (see SCALAR)]

sca·lar prod·uct *n* a number (**scalar**) equal to the product of the magnitudes of any two vectors and the cosine of the angle formed between them

scal·a·wag /skállə wàg/, **scal·ly·wag** /skállee-/ *n* **1.** a rascal or scamp (*dated informal*) **2.** a white person in the South who worked with the federal government during the Reconstruction period after the Civil War [Mid-19C. Origin ?]

ORIGIN *Scalawag* is thought variously to derive from the name *Scallaway* of Scotland's Shetland Islands, or from an obsolete Scots word *scallag*, "a farm servant." Its first recorded appearance in the United States is understood to be 1848, with the spelling *scalaway.* In western New York State a *scalaway* meant "a mean rascal." During Reconstruction a *scalawag* referred to a Caucasian southern operative who assisted the federal government in implementing its policies throughout the South, often profiteering in the process. But its earlier political meaning, first recorded in 1862, was "an intriguer, especially in politics."

scald /skawld/ *vt* (**scald·ed, scald·ing, scalds**) **1. BURN SOMEBODY WITH HOT LIQUID** to burn somebody or a part of the body with hot liquid or steam **2. HEAT LIQUID TO NEAR BOILING POINT** to heat a liquid to just below the boiling point **3. TREAT SOMETHING WITH BOILING LIQUID** to subject something to the action of boiling liquid or steam ■ *n* **1. BURN CAUSED BY HOT LIQUID** a burn caused by hot liquid or steam **2.** BOT **PLANT DISEASE** a plant disease or condition that produces brownish discoloration of leaves and fruit [12C. Via Anglo-Norman *escalder* < late Latin *excaldere* "bathe in hot water" < Latin *calidus* "hot"]

scald·ing /skáwlding/ *adj* **1.** extremely hot, especially hot enough to scald somebody **2.** severely critical ○ *a scalding remark*

scale[1] /skayl/ *n* **1.** WEIGHING MACHINE a device on which something or somebody can be weighed (*sometimes used in the plural*) **2.** PAN OF BALANCE either of the dishes or pans of a balance ■ *vt* (**scaled, scal·ing, scales**) **1.** WEIGH SO MUCH to have a particular weight when put on a scale **2.** WEIGH SOMETHING OR SOMEBODY to weigh something or somebody with a scale [12C. < Old Norse *skál* "bowl, scales" < Germanic, "shell"] ◇ **tip the scales at** to weigh a particular amount

scale[2] /skayl/ *n* **1.** MEASURING SYSTEM a system of measurement based on a series of marks laid down at regular intervals and representing numerical values **2.** SIZE RATIO a ratio representing the size of an illustration or reproduction, especially a map or a model, in relation to the object it represents ○ *The scale of the map is 1:50,000.* **3.** MEASURING INSTRUMENT an instrument or apparatus with graduated markings for measuring something **4.** SYSTEM OF CLASSIFICATION a system of classification in which people or things are ranked progressively according to a specific criterion ○ *rated their satisfaction on a scale of 1 to 5* **5.** LEVEL the extent or relative size of something ○ *the scale of the devastation* **6.** *US* MINIMUM PAYMENT the minimum payment for work, as agreed on during labor negotiations **7.** SERIES OF MUSICAL NOTES a series of musical notes, usually sequential, arranged in ascending or descending order of pitch ■ *v* (**scaled, scal·ing, scales**) **1.** *vt* CLIMB SOMETHING to climb up something, especially a steep incline, often using a ladder **2.** *vt* MAKE SOMETHING IN DIFFERENT SIZE to make a model or draw a map of something in a regular proportion to the size of the original **3.** *vi* RISE IN STAGES to go upward in stages or steps [14C. < Latin *scala* "staircase, ladder"] —**scal·a·ble** *adj* ◇ **to scale** with the same proportion of reduction or enlargement throughout, e.g., in a map or model

scale down, scale back *vt* to reduce something in size, amount, or extent

scale up *vt* to increase something in size, amount, or extent

scale[3] /skayl/ *n* **1.** BONY PLATE ON FISH any of the small flat bony or horny overlapping plates that cover the bodies of fish and some reptiles and mammals **2.** INSECTS COVERING OF BUTTERFLY WING a small structure that overlaps others to form the covering of the wings of butterflies and moths **3.** FLAKE a thin flat piece or flake of something such as dead skin **4.** METALL FLAKY OXIDE ON HEATED METAL a flaky oxide that forms on the surface of some metals undergoing heat treatment, especially the black oxide that forms on iron or steel at high temperatures **5.** DEPOSIT INSIDE KETTLE OR BOILER a white deposit sometimes formed on the inside of a kettle or boiler by the action of heat on the water **6.** DENT same as **tartar** (sense 1) **7.** BOT same as **scale leaf 8.** BOT PLANT DISEASE the diseased condition of plants caused by scale insects **9.** INSECTS same as **scale insect** ■ *v* (**scaled, scal·ing, scales**) **1.** *vt* CLEAN SCALES OR SCALE FROM SOMETHING to remove the scales or scale from something ○ *scaling the fish* **2.** *vi* FLAKE OFF to come off in scales **3.** *vt* THROW FLAT OBJECT to throw a thin flat object through the air, especially a flat stone in order to make it skip across a surface of water **4.** *vt* DENT SCRAPE TOOTH to remove the tartar from a tooth by scraping the surface with a sharp instrument **5.** *vi* REPT SHED SCALES to shed scales from the body [13C. < Old French *escale* < Germanic, "husk"] —**scale·less** *adj*

scale in·sect *n* a plant-sucking insect that covers itself with a waxy secretion resembling scales. Superfamily: Coccoidea. [< SCALE[3]]

scale leaf *n* a leaf that protects a plant bud before the bud expands [< SCALE[3]]

scale moss *n* a liverwort with leaves resembling scales. Order: Jungermanniales. [< SCALE[3]]

sca·lene /skáy leen, skay léen/ *adj* describes a triangle in which each side is a different length [Mid-17C. Via Latin < Greek *skalenos* "unequal"]

scal·er /skáylər/ *n* an electronic circuit that produces an output pulse for every specific number of input pulses received [Mid-20C. < SCALE[2]]

Scales /skaylz/ *npl* ZODIAC same as **Libra** (sense 2) [Plural of SCALE[1]]

Sca·li·a /skə lée ə/, **Antonin** (*b.* 1936) associate justice of the US Supreme Court (1986–)

scal·ing /skáyling/ *n* in social research, the creation of a measurement system for such qualities as attitudes and strength of feeling, where there is no existing scale [< SCALE[2]]

scal·ing lad·der *n* a ladder used to climb high walls, especially those of a besieged fortress

scal·lion /skállyən/ *n* an onion with a small bulb and long green leaves, e.g., a green onion or shallot [13C. Via Anglo-Norman *scal(o)un* < Old French *esc(h)aloigne* < Latin *Ascalonia (caepa)* "(onion) of Ascalon," port in ancient Palestine]

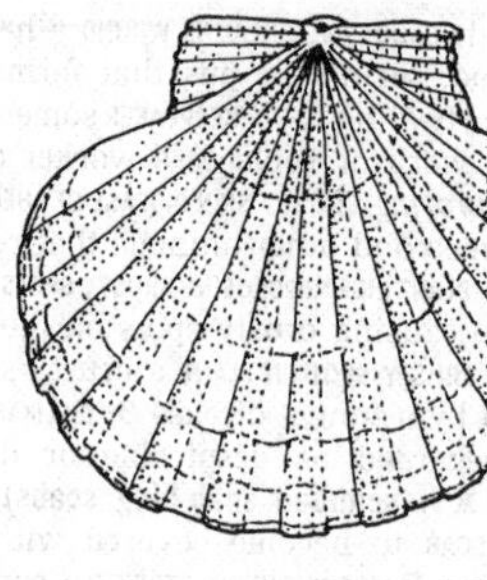

scallop

scal·lop /skólləp, skáll-/ *n* **1.** SEA MOLLUSK a sea bivalve mollusk that has a fan-shaped shell with radial ribs and wavy edges. Family: Pectinidae. **2.** SCALLOP AS FOOD the round white edible muscle of a scallop, often with bright red roe around one side, as food **3.** MARINE BIOL same as **scallop shell 4.** DISH SHAPED LIKE SCALLOP SHELL a dish shaped like a scallop shell, used for cooking and serving food **5.** DECORATIVE EDGING an ornamental undulating edging, especially in fabric **6.** *US* THIN SLICE OF MEAT a thin boneless slice of meat or poultry. Can term **escalope** ■ *v* (**-loped, -lop·ing, -lops**) **1.** *vt* MAKE EDGE WAVY to decorate the edge of a fabric or object with an undulating pattern **2.** *vt* COOK FOOD IN CREAM SAUCE to bake food in a cream sauce, usually with breadcrumbs on top **3.** *vi* COLLECT SCALLOPS to gather or dredge for scallops [14C. < Old French *escalope*] —**scal·loped** *adj* —**scal·lop·ing** *n*

scal·lop shell *n* either of the fan-shaped shell valves of the scallop, with radial ribs and a wavy edge

scal·ly·wag *n* same as **scalawag**

scal·o·gram /skáylə gràm/ *n* a test of attitudes or opinions in which the questions are ranked so that the answer to one implies the same answer to all questions lower on the scale [Mid-20C. < SCALE[2], probably after CARDIOGRAM]

scalp /skalp/ *n* **1.** SKIN ON TOP OF HEAD the skin and underlying tissues covering the dome of the skull **2.** SCALP CUT OFF AS TROPHY the scalp of an enemy cut off as a trophy **3.** TROPHY a trophy or achievement ■ *vt* (**scalped, scalp·ing, scalps**) **1.** RESELL SOMETHING FOR QUICK PROFIT to resell something quickly or at an inflated price in order to make a quick profit ○ *scalping tickets* **2.** CUT OFF SOMEBODY'S SCALP to cut off the scalp of an enemy as a trophy [14C. Probably < N Germanic] —**scalp·er** *n*

scal·pel /skálpəl/ *n* a surgical knife with a short, very sharp blade [Mid-18C. Directly or via French < Latin *scalpellum* "small cutting tool"]

scalp lock *n* a tuft or braid of hair left on the otherwise shaven scalp by the men among some Native North American peoples

scal·y /skáylee/ (**-i·er, -i·est**) *adj* covered in scales or flakes [15C. < SCALE[3]] —**scal·i·ness** *n*

scal·y ant·eat·er *n* ZOOL same as **pangolin**

scam /skam/ (*slang*) *n* a scheme for making money by dishonest means ■ *vt* (**scammed, scam·ming, scams**) to obtain money or other goods from somebody by dishonest means [Mid-20C. Origin ?] —**scam·mer** *n*

scam·mo·ny /skámmənee/ (*plural* **-nies** or *same*) *n* **1.** a twining plant with arrow-shaped leaves. Flowers: white, pink, or purple, funnel-shaped. Native to: Asia. Latin name: *Convulvulus scammonia.* **2.** a resin obtained from the roots of the scammony or similar plants. Use: purgative. [Pre-12C. Via French and Latin < Greek *skammōnia*]

scamp[1] /skamp/ *n* **1.** MISCHIEVOUS CHILD a mischievous person, especially a child who misbehaves in harmless or humorous ways (*informal*) **2.** ROGUE a rascally or dishonest person (*dated informal*) **3.** *Carib* WICKED PERSON a wicked or immoral person, or a criminal [Mid-18C. Probably < Middle Dutch *schampen* (see SCAMPER)]

scamp[2] /skamp/ (**scamped, scamp·ing, scamps**) *vt* to do something hastily, carelessly, or in a perfunctory manner [Mid-19C. Origin ?]

scam·per /skámpər/ *vi* (**-pered, -per·ing, -pers**) to run quickly or playfully ■ *n* a quick or playful run [Late 17C. Probably via Middle Dutch *schampen* "slip away, decamp" < Old French *esc(h)amper* < Latin *campus* "field"] —**scam·per·er** *n*

scam·pi /skámpee/ *n* shrimp cooked in a very garlicky sauce with lemon [Mid-20C. < Italian, plural of *scampo*, kind of lobster < Greek *kampē* "bending"; from its shape]

scan /skan/ *v* (**scanned, scan·ning, scans**) **1.** *vt* EXAMINE SOMETHING IN DETAIL to subject something to a thorough examination ○ *scanning the horizon* **2.** *vt* LOOK THROUGH SOMETHING QUICKLY to look through or read something quickly **3.** *vt* MED OBTAIN IMAGE OF BODY to obtain an image of internal organs with any of various devices, especially in order to make a diagnosis without the need for exploratory surgery **4.** *vt* COMPUT EXAMINE SOMETHING WITH BEAM OF LIGHT to direct a light-sensitive device over a surface in order to convert an image into digital or electronic form for further storage, retrieval, and transmission ○ *scanned the document* **5.** *vt* COMPUT EXAMINE STORED DATA to make an automatic search of a computer storage medium such as a magnetic disk or tape for data in anticipation of retrieving that data **6.** *vti* ELECTRONICS SEARCH AREA USING RADAR to search a region for something, e.g., aircraft, by systematically sweeping a radar or sonar beam across it **7.** *vi* LITERAT CONFORM TO VERSE RULES to conform to the rules of meter ○ *That line doesn't scan.* **8.** *vt* LITERAT ANALYZE VERSE to analyze verse according to the rules of meter ■ *n* **1.** IMAGE OF BODY an image of an internal body part taken using a scanner **2.** BRIEF PERUSAL a quick look at or through something **3.** ACT OF SCANNING the act or process of scanning something **4.** SWEEP OF RADAR BEAM a single sweep of a radar or sonar beam across a region [14C. < Latin *scandere* "climb, (in late Latin) scan a verse"] —**scan·na·ble** *adj*

scan·dal /skánd'l/ *n* **1.** SOMETHING CAUSING PUBLIC OUTRAGE a situation or event that causes public outrage or censure **2.** PUBLIC OUTRAGE an outburst of public outrage or censure as a consequence of an event **3.** MALICIOUS TALK malicious talk, especially about other people's private lives [12C. Via French < Latin *scandalum* "trap, temptation" < Greek *skandalon*]

CULTURAL NOTE ***School for Scandal***, a play (1777) by Irish dramatist Richard Brinsley Sheridan. In this satire on contemporary middle-class mores, Sir Oliver Surface attempts to spy on his nephews Charles and Joseph in order to discover their true characters. Among the play's many targets are the hypocrisy and vindictiveness of gossipmongers, personified by the characters of Lady Sneerwell, Sir Benjamin Backbite, and Mrs. Candour.

scan·dal·ize /skánd'l ìz/ (**-ized, -iz·ing, -iz·es**) *vt* to shock somebody by outrageous or improper behavior

scan·dal·mon·ger /skánd'l mùng gər, -mòng-/ *n* a spreader of malicious talk about other people's private lives —**scan·dal·mon·ger·ing** *n*

scan·dal·ous /skánd'ləss/ *adj* **1.** causing or deserving to cause public outrage or censure **2.** causing or having the potential to cause damage to somebody's reputation —**scan·dal·ous·ly** *adv*

scan·dal sheet *n* a periodical publication that features scandalous stories about people's private lives (*disapproving*)

scan·dent /skándənt/ *adj* describes a plant that climbs as it grows [Late 17C. < Latin *scandent-*, present participle of *scandere* "climb"]

LANGUAGE HERITAGE ***Scandinavian*** Much of English is made up of words from other languages, and the languages of Scandinavia are important contributors in this respect, especially in their shared early form Old Norse, the language of the Vikings. This North Germanic language is closely related to English, which belongs to the West Germanic group. Vikings settled in much of England, and between 1016 and 1042 part of the country was ruled by Danish kings, and indeed words from the early period are so integral to English that they are hardly regarded as borrowings: words such as ***anger, bag, call, dirt, husband, ill, law, near, odd, sale, seem, want, window,*** and two of the commonest verbs ***get*** and ***take***. The penetration of Norse is such that it provides some of the "grammatical" or "functional" words of English, for example, ***both*** and the preposition ***like***, and most notably the personal pronouns ***their, them,*** and ***they,*** which replaced their Old English equivalents, which began with *h-*. Other forms from Old Norse that have ousted related native English words include ***egg*** (Old English had the sound *y* as in *yes*), ***ankle***, and ***gate***. Sometimes both Anglo-Saxon and Viking forms survive, either with differences in dialectal distribution, for example, Scottish ***kirk*** alongside standard English ***church***, or with differentiation of meaning, as with ***shirt*** (English) alongside ***skirt*** (from Old Norse). Native and Norse elements have combined freely, for example, in ***awkward*** (from obsolete *awk* "turned the wrong way," from Old Norse *afugr* "turned backwards" + the English suffix *-ward*) and ***blackmail*** (from *black* + obsolete *mail* "tribute, tax" from Old Norse *mál* "speech, agreement"), and English idiom has modeled itself on Norse, as in ***afoot***, partly based on Old Norse *á fótum* "on foot," and ***upon***, based on Old Norse *upp á*.

Some relatively modern words also trace their ancestry to Old Norse. ***Berserk***, for instance, is recorded only from the early 19th century, but derives from a Norse word meaning "wild warrior," which is probably formed from the stem of *bjorn* "bear" with *serkr* "shirt."

The modern Scandinavian languages such as Norwegian, Danish, and Swedish have provided in particular terms reflecting occupations and activities of northern peoples: seafaring, fisheries, and winter sports. The ***minke whale, narwhal, rorqual*** (via French from Norwegian *røyrkval*, from an Old Norse word meaning literally "red whale"), and ***sei whale*** may feed on ***krill***, and whalers might ***flense*** (strip the skin or blubber from) them (from Danish). Other ocean creatures with North Germanic names include the ***auk, brisling, eider*** (from Icelandic), ***fulmar***, and ***kraken***, a huge sea monster shaped like a giant squid, periodically reported by Norwegian fishermen since the 16th century; from the land come the ***lemming, mink***, and, perhaps surprisingly, the ***vole***. In winter sports Norwegian has provided ***ski, slalom***, and ***skijoring***, a sport in which a skier is towed across a frozen surface by a horse or vehicle. Swedish has made its sporting contribution with ***orienteering*** (an Anglicization of Swedish *orientering*) and ***fartlek*** (literally "speed play"), another name for interval training.

Scandinavian foods have inevitably been welcomed into English: ***gravlax, rutabaga***, and the Swedish ***smorgasbord*** (literally "bread-and-butter table"), which has become familiar enough to develop a figurative meaning, "a wide variety." Adopted geographic features include the ***fjord*** and the ***geyser*** (named for *Geysir*, a hot spring in Iceland). In science Scandinavia has provided the name for the element ***tungsten***, and the prefixes for units ***atto-*** and ***femto-***, from words meaning "eighteen" and "fifteen" respectively. In cultural life Sweden has made the significant contribution of the ***ombudsman***.

One word of individual interest is ***gauntlet*** (the kind that you "run"). Its Scandinavian origin has been concealed by identification with the completely different word (from French) for a long glove with a wide cuff. The ***gauntlet*** was a punishment formerly used in the military in which a soldier was forced to run between two lines of men armed with weapons who beat him as he passed; its earlier form in English was *gantlope*, which came from Swedish *gatlopp* "passageway."

scan·dic /skándik/ *adj* relating to or containing the element scandium

Scan·di·na·vi·a /skàndə náyvee ə/ region in northern Europe comprising Norway, Sweden, Denmark, Finland, Iceland, and the Faroe Islands

Scan·di·na·vi·an /skàndə náyvee ən/ *n* **1.** somebody who comes from one of the countries of Scandinavia **2.** LANG same as **North Germanic** —**Scan·di·na·vi·an** *adj*

scan·di·um /skándee əm/ *n* a rare silvery white metallic element. Source: wolframite. Use: tracer. Symbol **Sc**. See table at **element** [Late 19C. < Latin *Scandia*, shortening of *Scandinavia*; because found in various minerals there]

~~**scandle**~~ incorrect spelling of **scandal**

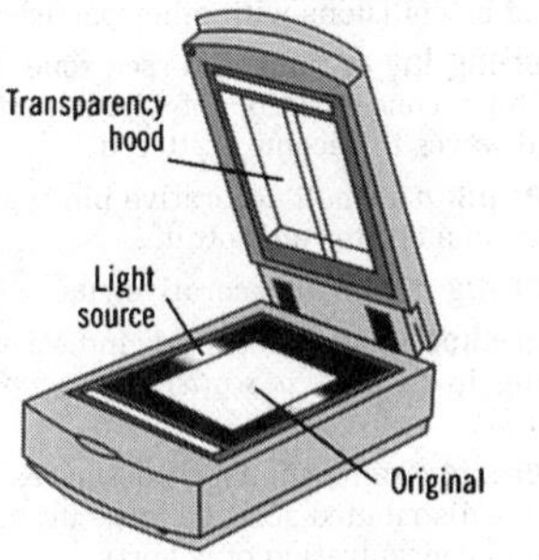

scanner

scan·ner /skánnər/ *n* **1.** DEVICE PUTTING SOMETHING INTO DIGITAL FORM an input device used to convert an image or text into digital form for storage or display **2.** DATA-SCANNING DEVICE a device for examining written or recorded data, e.g., for reading a product bar code for inventory and pricing purposes **3.** BODY-SCANNING DEVICE a device used to obtain information about the internal parts of the body without the need for surgery, or the contents of something without the need for opening it **4.** RADIO RECEIVER a receiver that continuously broadcasts radio signals it picks up from specific frequencies ○ *a police scanner* **5.** RADAR SEARCHING DEVICE a rotating directional radar antenna that emits a beam to search for or locate objects **6.** SOMEBODY WHO SCANS TEXTS somebody who scans texts, e.g., for errors or in poetic analysis

scan·ning e·lec·tron mi·cro·scope /skànning-/ *n* a microscope that uses a beam of electrons to scan an object and produce an enlarged image of it on a cathode-ray tube —**scan·ning e·lec·tron mi·cros·co·py** *n*

scan·ning tun·nel·ing mi·cro·scope *n* a microscope used to study surfaces in which a very small probe is moved across a sample and quantum mechanical effects give information about the surface structure —**scan·ning tun·nel·ing mi·cros·co·py** *n*

scan·sion /skánshən/ *n* **1.** the analysis of verse according to the rules of meter **2.** the way that a line, verse, or poem scans [Mid-17C. < Latin *scansion-* "climbing, (in late Latin) scansion" < *scandere* "to climb"]

scant /skant/ *adj* **1.** not sufficient **2.** just about or just below a particular amount ○ *a scant twenty votes* [14C. < Old Norse *skamt*, form of *skammr* "short"] —**scant·ly** *adv*

scant·ies /skánteez/ *npl* very brief panties for women (*dated informal*) [Early 20C. < SCANTY after PANTIES]

scant·ling /skántling/ *n* **1.** THIN PIECE OF TIMBER a piece of timber with a small cross section, e.g., a rafter **2.** SIZE the dimension of a building material or a structural part of a ship **3.** SMALL AMOUNT a small amount or quantity [Early 16C. Alteration of obsolete *scantillon* "gauge" < late Latin *scandaculum* "ladder" < Latin *scandere* "to climb"]

scant·y /skántee/ (-i·er, -i·est) *adj* **1.** INADEQUATE not much, and less than is needed ○ *can't tell much from the scanty evidence* **2.** MEAGER only just enough ○ *found the remains of a scanty meal* **3.** REVEALING not covering much of the part of the body that it is worn on —**scant·i·ly** *adv* —**scant·i·ness** *n*

Scap·a Flow /skaàpə flṓ/ anchorage in the Orkney Islands, Scotland. It was used as a base for Britain's home fleet during both world wars. Area: 120 sq. mi./310 sq. km.

scape[1] /skayp/ *n* **1.** BOT LEAFLESS FLOWER STALK a leafless flower stalk rising directly from the root **2.** ZOOL PART OF FEATHER OR ANTENNA a shaft of a feather or other animal part, or a segment of an antenna **3.** ARCHIT ARCHITECTURAL COLUMN the shaft of an architectural column [Early 17C. Via Latin < Greek *skapos* "rod"]

scape[2] /skayp/ (**scaped, scap·ing, scapes**) *vti* same as **escape** (*archaic*) [13C. Shortening]

-scape *suffix* a scene or view ○ *seascape* [< LANDSCAPE]

scape·goat /skáyp gṑt/ *n* somebody who is made to take the blame for others ■ *vt* (**-goat·ed, -goat·ing, -goats**) to force somebody to take the blame for others [Mid-16C. < SCAPE[2]; because in Jewish ritual the goat, having had the sins of the people symbolically laid on it, was allowed to "escape" into the desert]

scape·grace /skáyp gràyss/ *n* a lazy, mischievous, or irresponsible person, especially a child (*archaic*) [Early 19C. < SCAPE[2]]

scaph·oid /ská fòyd/ *adj* same as **navicular** ■ *n* the navicular bone in the wrist [Mid-18C. Via modern Latin < Greek *skaphoeidēs* < *skaphē* "boat"]

scap·o·lite /skáppə lìt/ *n* a variously colored aluminosilicate mineral. Source: metamorphic rocks, weathered basic igneous rocks. Use: semiprecious gems. [Early 19C. < Greek *skapos* "rod"]

scap·u·la /skáppyələ/ (*plural* **-lae** /-lee/ or **-las**) *n* **1.** either of two large flat triangular bones that form the back of the shoulder in humans **2.** a bone in vertebrates that corresponds to the human shoulder blade [Late 16C. < late Latin, singular < Latin *scapulae* "shoulder blades"]

scap·u·lar[1] /skáppyələr/ *n* any of the feathers on a bird's shoulder ■ *adj* relating to or associated with the shoulder blade [Late 17C. < SCAPULA]

scap·u·lar[2] /skáppyələr/, **scap·u·lar·y** /skáppyə lèrree/ (*plural* **-ies**) *n* **1.** a loose sleeveless garment worn by Christian monks **2.** two small pieces of cloth joined together and worn over the shoulder and back underneath other garments to signify membership in a Christian religious order or some other devotional purpose [15C. < late Latin *scapulare* < *scapula* (see SCAPULA)]

scar[1] /skaar/ *n* **1.** MARK ON SKIN AFTER DAMAGE a mark left on the skin after a wound, burn, or sore has healed over **2.** MENTAL EFFECT OF DISTRESSING EXPERIENCE a lasting effect left on somebody's mind by a personal misfortune or unpleasant experience **3.** MARK ON SURFACE a mark on a surface caused by damage **4.** BOT MARK OF FORMER ATTACHMENT ON PLANT the mark on a plant indicating the place where a part such as a leaf was formerly attached ■ *v* (**scarred, scar·ring, scars**) **1.** *vt* MARK SOMEBODY OR SOMETHING WITH SCARS to leave somebody or something with a physical or emotional scar **2.** *vi* FORM SCAR to form or become marked by a scar [14C. Directly or via French < late Latin *eschara* "scab" < Greek *eskhara* "brazier, scab formed after a burn"]

scar[2] /skaar/ *n* **1.** a steep bare rocky cliff **2.** a rock submerged or partly submerged in the ocean [14C. < Old Norse *sker* "low reef" < Germanic, "something cut off"]

scar·ab /skárrəb/ *n* **1.** a beetle regarded as sacred by the ancient Egyptians. Family: Scarabaeidae. **2.** a representation of a beetle used on amulets and signets by the ancient Egyptians [Late 16C. < Latin *scarabaeus* < Greek *karabos* "crab, beetle"]

scar·a·bae·id /skàrrə beé id/, **scar·a·bae·an** /-ən/ *n* INSECTS same as **scarab** (sense 1) [Mid-19C. < modern Latin *Scarabaeidae* < Latin *scarabaeus* (see SCARAB)]

Scar·a·mouch /skárrə mòoch, -mòosh/, **Scar·a·mouche** *n* a boastful and cowardly man (*literary*) [Mid-17C. Via French < Italian *Scaramuccia*, character in the commedia dell'arte]

Scar·bor·ough /skaár bùr ō, -bərə/ city in northeastern England, on the North Sea. A market center in the Middle Ages, it is now primarily a resort. Population: 116,243 (2001).

scarce /skerss/ *adj* (**scar·cer, scar·cest**) **1.** being in insufficient supply ○ *scarce resources* **2.** rarely found or rarely occurring ○ *Elephants are becoming scarce.* ■ *adv* same as **scarcely** (*archaic or literary*) [13C. < Anglo-Norman *(e)scars* < Latin *excerpere* "pick out" < *carpere* "pluck"] —**scarce·ness** *n* ◇ **make yourself**

scarce to go or stay away, often in order to avoid some kind of trouble or difficulty (*informal*)

scarce·ly /skérsslee/ *adv* **1.** HARDLY only just ○ *scarcely arrived when she was put to work* **2.** HARDLY AT ALL only to the slightest degree ○ *scarcely slept all night* **3.** SURELY NOT surely or almost certainly not ○ *scarcely a good reason*

USAGE See *hardly*.

scar·ci·ty /skérssətee/ (*plural* **-ties**) *n* **1.** an insufficient supply of something **2.** an infrequency of occurrence of something

scare /sker/ *v* (**scared, scar·ing, scares**) **1.** *vt* FRIGHTEN SOMEBODY to make somebody afraid or alarmed **2.** *vi* BE FRIGHTENED to be or become frightened ■ *n* **1.** FRIGHT a sudden fright or feeling of fear **2.** SOMETHING THAT FRIGHTENS a situation causing general fear or alarm ○ *another food scare* [12C. < Old Norse *skirra* "frighten" < *skjarr* "timid"]

scare off, scare away *vt* to frighten a person or an animal into going away

scare up *vt* to manage to find something or put something together with difficulty or skill (*informal*)

scare·crow /skér krō/ *n* **1.** OBJECT FOR SCARING BIRDS AWAY an object in the shape of a person dressed in old clothes, set up in a field to scare birds away from the crops **2.** SOMETHING FRIGHTENING BUT NOT DANGEROUS somebody or something that may have a frightening effect but is not dangerous **3.** POORLY DRESSED PERSON a wearer of ragged clothes (*informal*)

scared /skerd/ *adj* feeling full of worry or fear

scare·dy-cat /skérrdee kàt/ *n Can, UK* somebody who is unusually timid and frightened (*informal*) US term **fraidy-cat**

scare·mon·ger /skér mùng gər, -mòng-/ *n* a spreader of alarming rumors —**scare·mon·ger·ing** *n*

scarf[1] /skaarf/ *n* (*plural* **scarfs** or **scarves** /skaarvz/) **1.** CLOTH WORN AROUND NECK a piece of cloth worn around the neck or on the head for warmth, decoration, or concealment **2.** CLOTH COVERING FOR SURFACE a cloth covering a surface such as a table or a piano **3.** MILITARY SASH an official sash, usually indicating military rank ■ *vt* (**scarfed, scarf·ing, scarfs**) WRAP SOMETHING IN SCARF to wrap a scarf around something (*literary*) [Mid-16C. Shortened < Old N French *escarpe*, probably variant of Old French *escherpe* "bag hung around the neck" < Frankish *skirpja* "bag woven from rushes" < Latin *scirpus* "rush"]

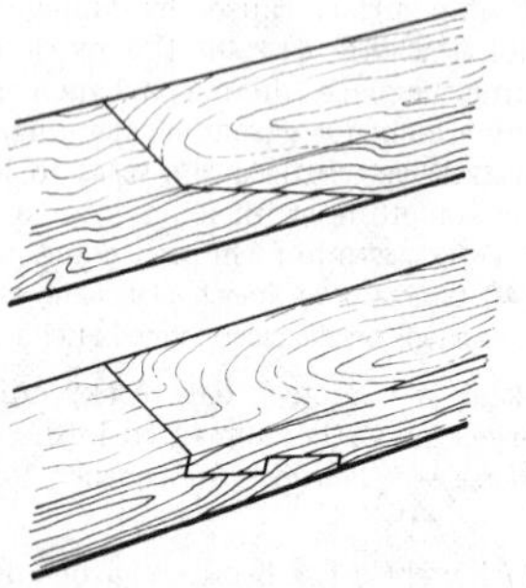

scarf

scarf[2] /skaarf/ *n* **1.** JOINT MADE BETWEEN NOTCHED ENDS a joint made by joining two notched boards together **2.** NOTCHED END either of the notched ends of a scarf joint ■ *vt* (**scarfed, scarf·ing, scarfs**) JOIN BOARDS USING NOTCHES to join boards together by means of a scarf joint [13C. Probably via French < N Germanic]

scarf[3] /skaarf/ *vt* to eat or drink something greedily or noisily (*slang*) ○ *scarfed down the food* [Mid-20C. Variant of SCOFF[2]]

scarf joint *n* CONSTR same as **scarf**[2] *n* (sense 2)

scarf·skin /skaárf skìn/ *n* the outermost layer of skin, especially the cuticle of a nail [Early 16C. Probably < SCARF[1]]

scar·i·fy[1] /skárrə fī/ (**-fied, -fy·ing, -fies**) *vt* **1.** MAKE SCRATCHES ON SKIN to make scratches on or superficial incisions in the skin, as a traditional cosmetic practice in some cultures or as a medical procedure **2.** LOOSEN SOIL to break up and loosen the surface of soil **3.** SCRATCH SEEDS to break the outer cover of hard seeds to aid germination [14C. Via French *scarifier* < late Latin *skarificare* < Greek *skariphasthai* "scratch an outline" < *skariphos* "stylus"] —**scar·i·fi·ca·tion** /skàrrəfi káysh'n/ *n* —**scar·i·fi·er** *n*

scar·i·fy[2] /skérrə fī/ (**-fied, -fy·ing, -fies**) *vt* to make somebody afraid or alarmed (*informal*) [Late 18C. < SCARE, probably after TERRIFY]

scar·i·ous /skérree əss/, **scar·i·ose** /-ōss/ *adj* describes parts of plants that have a thin dry membranous appearance [Late 18C. Directly or via French < modern Latin *scariosus*]

scar·la·ti·na /skaàrlə teénə/ *n* MED same as **scarlet fever** (*technical*) [Early 19C. Via modern Latin < Italian *scarlattina* "little scarlet things" < *scarlatto* "scarlet" < Arabic *siqillāt* (see SCARLET)]

Scar·lat·ti /skaar laátee/, **Alessandro** (1659–1725) Italian composer. The father of Domenico Scarlatti, he was a major contributor to the establishment of the Neapolitan style of opera. Full name **Scarlatti, Pietro Alessandro Gaspare**

Scar·lat·ti, Domenico (1685–1757) Italian composer. The son of Alessandro Scarlatti, he composed operas and church music, but is best known for over 550 sonatas for harpsichord. Full name **Scarlatti, Giuseppe Domenico**

scar·let /skaárlət/ *n* **1.** a bright orange-tinged red color **2.** scarlet clothing or cloth, especially the traditional red uniforms of the British army [13C. Via Old French *escarlate* < Arabic *siqillāt*, a rich red cloth < Latin *sigillatus* "decorated with raised figures" < *signum* "sign"] —**scar·let** *adj*

scar·let fe·ver *n* a contagious bacterial infection marked by fever, a sore throat, and a red rash, mainly affecting children

scar·let let·ter *n* a scarlet letter "A" that a woman convicted of adultery was formerly made to wear, especially among the Puritans of 17th-century New England

CULTURAL NOTE ***The Scarlet Letter***, a novel (1850) by Nathaniel Hawthorne. The title of this eloquent plea for tolerance refers to the red letter "A" that Hester Prynne, a woman living in mid-17th-century New England, is forced to wear as punishment for an adulterous affair. While her husband and lover are consumed by anger and guilt respectively, Hester's honesty and strength of character help her to survive the scandal.

scar·let pim·per·nel *n* a common pimpernel whose flowers close in cloudy weather. Flowers: small, scarlet, purple, or white. Latin name: *Anagallis arvensis.*

scar·let run·ner *n* a climbing bean plant that has long flat green pods containing edible seeds. Latin name: *Phaseolus coccineus.*

scar·let tan·a·ger *n* a medium-sized songbird, the male of which is bright red with black wings and tail during the breeding season. Native to: eastern United States. Latin name: *Piranga olivacea.*

scar·let wom·an *n* an offensive term for a woman believed to be an adulterer or prostitute or to engage excessively in sexual activity (*literary*) [< Revelations 17:1–6 in the Bible, in which a sinful woman appears "in purple and scarlet color"]

scarp /skaarp/ *n* **1.** a steep slope or cliff, formed by erosion or faulting **2.** a steep slope in front of a fortification, e.g., the inner wall of a ditch [Late 16C. < Italian *scarpa*]

scarp·er /skaárpər/ (**-ered, -er·ing, -ers**) *vi UK* to leave a place quickly (*slang*) [Mid-19C. Probably < Italian *scappare* "to escape"]

scar tis·sue *n* dense fibrous tissue that forms the scar over a healed wound

scarves CLOTHING plural of **scarf**[1]

scar·y /skérree/ (**-i·er, -i·est**) *adj* (*informal*) **1.** causing fear or alarm **2.** easily frightened —**scar·i·ly** *adv* —**scar·i·ness** *n*

scat[1] /skat/ (**scat·ted, scat·ting, scats**) *vi* to leave immediately and quickly (*informal; usually used as a command*) [Mid-19C. Origin ?]

scat[2] /skat/ *n* a style of jazz singing that uses nonsense syllables to approximate the sound of a solo instrument ■ *vi* (**scat·ted, scat·ting, scats**) to sing in scat style [Early 20C. Probably an imitation of the sound]

scat[3] /skat/ (*plural* **scats** or *same*) *n* a small tropical ocean fish, often kept in aquariums because of its bright color. Native to: Indian and Pacific oceans. Family: Scatophagidae. [Mid-20C. Shortening of modern Latin *Scatophagidae* < Greek *scatophagos* "dung-eating"; because it frequents sewage outlets]

scat[4] /skat/ *n* a fecal dropping of an animal [Mid-20C. < Greek *skat-* (see SCATO-)]

scathe /skayth/ *vt* (**scathed, scath·ing, scathes**) **1.** CRITICIZE SOMEBODY to subject somebody to severe criticism (*literary*) **2.** DAMAGE SOMETHING BY BLASTING to damage something by blasting or scorching it (*archaic*) ■ *n* HARM injury or harm (*archaic*) [12C. < Old Norse *skaða* "harm, damage"]

scath·ing /skáything/ *adj* severely critical and scornful —**scath·ing·ly** *adv*

scato- *prefix* excrement ○ *scatology* [< Greek *skat-*, stem of *skōr* "excrement" < Indo-European, "cut off"]

sca·tol·o·gy /ska tóllәjee, skə-/ *n* **1.** VULGAR LANGUAGE vulgar language related to excretory functions **2.** OBSESSION WITH EXCREMENT a preoccupation with excrement or obscenity **3.** STUDY OF EXCREMENT the scientific study of excrement, especially for diagnostic purposes —**scat·o·log·i·cal** /skàtt'l ójjik'l/ *adj* —**sca·tol·o·gist** *n*

scat·ter /skáttər/ *v* (**-tered, -ter·ing, -ters**) **1.** *vt* THROW THINGS AROUND to throw things around so that they land with an irregular distribution over a relatively wide area ○ *scatter seeds* **2.** *vt* SCATTER SOMETHING OVER AREA to cover an area by throwing things around over it **3.** *vti* DISPERSE to separate and move suddenly in different directions, or cause people or animals to move in this way **4.** *vti* PHYS DEVIATE to cause waves or a beam of particles to be irregularly deflected, dispersed, or reflected, or be turned aside in this way ■ *n* THINGS SCATTERED AROUND a number of things spread messily around an area (*literary*) [12C. Probably variant of SHATTER] —**scat·ter·a·ble** *adj* —**scat·ter·er** *n*

scat·ter·brain /skáttər bràyn/ *n* a person regarded as unable to think seriously or systematically or to remember important things —**scat·ter·brained** *adj*

scat·ter cush·ion *n UK* same as **throw pillow**

scat·ter di·a·gram *n* a graph that represents the joint relationship of two variables by depicting the data as points along two axes at right angles to each other

scat·tered /skáttərd/ *adj* **1.** in a number of different places far away from each other ○ *scattered communities* **2.** few in number and far apart in distance or time ○ *scattered showers*

scat·ter·gun /skáttər gùn/ *n* same as **shotgun**

scat·ter·ing /skáttəring/ *n* **1.** a small amount or number of things irregularly spread over a large area **2.** the deflection of a wave or beam of particles caused by collisions with other particles

scat·ter·ing lay·er *n* an undersea zone where there is a high concentration of plankton that causes sound waves to become scattered

scat·ter pin *n* a small decorative pin typically worn as part of a cluster on clothing

scat·ter rug *n* a small decorative rug

scat·ter·shot /skáttər shòt/ *adj* indiscriminate and lacking in focus ○ *a scattershot approach to the operation*

scat·ter·site /skáttər sīt/ *adj US* describes low-income housing distributed across a large urban area so as to avoid concentration of poverty

scat·ty /skáttee/ (**-ti·er, -ti·est**) *adj Can, UK* lacking in serious or organized thought, forgetful, and often eccentric in behavior (*informal*) [Early 20C. Probably < shortening of *scatterbrained*] —**scat·ti·ly** *adv* —**scat·ti·ness** *n*

scaup /skawp, skaap/ (*plural* **scaups** or *same*), **scaup duck** *n* a diving duck, the male of which has a black and white body. Native to: Europe, North America. Genus: *Aythya.* [Late 17C. Variant of *scalp* "shellfish bed," origin ?]

scav·enge /skávvənj/ (**-enged, -eng·ing, -eng·es**) *vti* **1.** LOOK FOR SOMETHING USABLE to search for or through discarded material in order to find something usable **2.** FEED ON CARRION OR SCRAPS to feed on dead and rotting flesh or discarded food scraps **3.** CLEAN PLACE UP to remove waste material and dirt from an area **4.** CHEM GET RID OF IMPURITIES to neutralize or remove impurities in a chemical reaction or mixture [Mid-17C. Back-formation < SCAVENGER]

scav·en·ger /skávvənjər/ *n* **1.** ANIMAL FEEDING ON CARRION OR SCRAPS an animal, bird, or other organism that feeds on dead and rotting flesh or discarded food scraps **2.** SOMEBODY LOOKING FOR SOMETHING USABLE somebody who seeks or looks through discarded items in the hope of finding something usable **3.** CHEM SUBSTANCE REMOVING IMPURITIES something that is added to a chemical reaction or mixture to neutralize or remove impurities [Mid-16C. Alteration of *scavager*, former official whose responsibilities included street-cleaning < Anglo-Norman *scawager* < Flemish *scauwen* "look at"]

ORIGIN The term *scavager* was originally, in the Middle Ages, an official who collected taxes levied on overseas merchants. Later the term came to denote a street-cleaner, and by the time it had metamorphosed into ***scavenger*** (by the same process as produced *messenger* from *messager* and *passenger* from *passager*) it had completed its descent to its modern meaning.

scav·en·ger bee·tle *n* a dark oval-shaped beetle that lives in water and feeds on decaying vegetation. Family: Hydrophilidae.

scav·en·ger hunt *n* a game in which people must obtain items on a list within a time limit and without buying them

scav·en·ger moth *n* a small moth that is commonly found scavenging stored food such as grains and oils. Family: Tineidae.

Sc.B. *abbr* EDUC Bachelor of Science [Latin *Scientiae Baccalaureus*]

SCC *abbr* storage connecting circuit

Sc.D. *abbr* EDUC Doctor of Science [Latin *Scientiae Doctor*]

~~**scedule**~~ incorrect spelling of **schedule**

~~**sceince**~~ incorrect spelling of **science**

~~**sceme**~~ incorrect spelling of **scheme**

sce·na /sháynə/ (*plural* **-ne** /-nay/) *n* **1.** a division of an opera that is equivalent in length or structure to a scene in a play **2.** a dramatic concert piece written and performed in the style of an operatic scena [Early 19C. Via Italian < Latin *scaena* (see SCENE[1])]

sce·nar·i·o /sə nárree ō, -nérree-, -naáree-/ (*plural* **-os**) *n* **1.** POSSIBLE SITUATION an imagined sequence of possible events, or an imagined set of circumstances ○ *the worst-case scenario* **2.** LITERAT, MUSIC PLOT OUTLINE an outline of the plot of a play or opera **3.** MOVIES SCREENPLAY a screenplay for a movie [Late 19C. < Italian, < *scena* "scene" < Latin *scaena* (see SCENE[1])]

sce·nar·ist /sə nárrəst, -nérrəst/ *n* a writer of movie scripts [Early 20C. < SCENARIO]

scend /send/, **send** *n* the upward movement of a ship that is moving up and down in heavy seas ■ *vi* (**scend·ed, scend·ing, scends; send·ed, send·ing, sends**) to rise up high under the force of a strong wave (*refers to boats*) [15C. Probably shortening of DESCEND or ASCEND]

scene[1] /seen/ *n* **1.** DIVISION OF ACT OF PLAY a division of an act of a play or opera, presenting continuous action in one place **2.** ARTS SHORT SECTION OF PLAY OR MOVIE a short section of a play, movie, opera, or work of literature that presents a single event ○ *the love scene* **3.** VIEW OR PICTURE a view of a place or an activity, especially one presented in a painting or photograph **4.** PLACE WHERE SOMETHING HAPPENS a location at which an event or action happens ○ *the scene of many battles* **5.** ARTS SETTING IN DRAMATIC WORK a setting for the whole or a part of a play, movie, opera, or work of literature **6.** ARTS SCENERY FOR DRAMATIC WORK the backgrounds, sets, or props for a play, movie, or opera (*often used before a noun*) ○ *a couple of quick scene changes* **7.** EMBARRASSING PUBLIC DISPLAY an embarrassing or disconcerting public display of emotion ○ *Don't make a scene, but I think they lost your coat.* **8.** MILIEU the characteristic environment in which an activity or pursuit is carried out ○ *new to the fashion scene* **9.** *US* SITUATION a set of circumstances of any kind (*informal*) ○ *a bad scene* [Mid-16C. Via Latin *scaena* < Greek *skēnē* "tent, stage"] ◇ **behind the scenes 1.** in private and away from public view **2.** out of sight of the audience at a performance or spectacle ◇ **it's not somebody's scene** it is not the kind of thing that somebody likes to do or takes an interest in ◇ **set the scene 1.** to create the circumstances in which something can or does happen **2.** to describe a situation or the background to an event

sce·ne[2] /sháynay/ MUSIC plural of **scena**

scen·er·y /seénəree/ *n* **1.** landscape or natural surroundings, especially when regarded as picturesque ○ *admired the scenery from the hotel balcony* **2.** the set or decorated background for a play, movie, or opera [Mid-18C. Alteration of obsolete *scenary* "scenario of a play or opera" < Italian *scenario* (see SCENARIO)]

scene-steal·er *n* a performer who, by his or her performance or personal qualities, takes the audience's attention away from another performer who is supposedly the focus of the scene

sce·nic /seénik, sénnik/ *adj* **1.** PICTURESQUE with attractive or impressive natural scenery **2.** OF NATURAL SCENERY relating to the natural scenery of an area ○ *famous for its scenic beauty* **3.** ARTS OF DRAMATIC SCENES relating to scenes in a play, movie, or opera **4.** THEATER OF STAGE SCENERY relating to the scenery for a play or opera —**sce·ni·cal·ly** *adv*

sce·nic rail·road, sce·nic rail·way *n* **1.** *US* a railroad that has been restored for passenger use, especially for tourists, because of its passage through attractive scenery **2.** a miniature railroad that carries customers past artificial scenery in an amusement park or other place of entertainment

sce·nog·ra·phy /see nóggrəfee/ *n* **1.** the artistic representation of objects according to the rules of perspective **2.** the painting of theatrical scenery —**sce·nog·raph·er** *n* —**sce·no·graph·ic** /seénə gráffik/ *adj*

scent /sent/ *n* **1.** PLEASANT SMELL a pleasant sweet smell such as that of a flower ○ *the scent of jasmine* **2.** SMELL USED AS TRAIL the characteristic smell given off by a person or animal and used especially for tracking ○ *They followed the scent deep into the forest.* **3.** PERFUME cosmetic liquid worn on the skin, especially women's perfume **4.** SMELLING SENSE the sense of smell **5.** HINT a faint indication that something is likely to happen ○ *There was the scent of danger in the air.* ■ *v* (**scent·ed, scent·ing, scents**) **1.** *vt* IMBUE SOMETHING WITH PLEASANT SMELL to fill something with a distinctive odor, especially a pleasant one ○ *Roses scented the room.* **2.** *vti* SMELL SOMEBODY OR SOMETHING to perceive somebody or something by smelling **3.** *vt* DETECT SOMETHING AS IMMINENT to sense that something is likely to happen ○ *They could scent victory.* [14C. Via French *sentir* "to sense" < Latin *sentire* "feel"] —**scent·less** *adj* ◇ **put** *or* **throw somebody off the scent** to divert somebody from finding or discovering something

SYNONYMS See *smell.*

scent gland *n* a specialized skin gland that enables an animal to secrete a scent designed to send social or sexual signals or serve as a deterrent

scent strip *n* a strip of perfumed paper used to advertise a commercially available perfume to potential customers

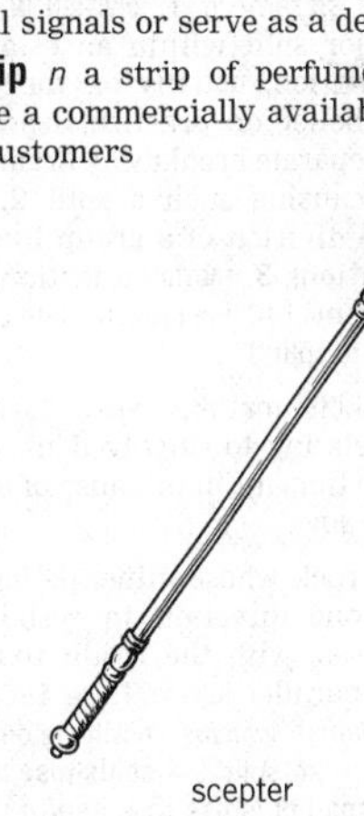

scepter

scep·ter /séptər/ *n* **1.** STAFF USED AS ROYAL EMBLEM a ceremonial staff, rod, or wand used as an emblem of a monarch's authority **2.** ROYAL AUTHORITY royal or imperial power or authority ■ *vt* (**-tered, -ter·ing, -ters**) GIVE SOMEBODY ROYAL AUTHORITY to endow somebody with royal power or authority [13C. Via French and Latin < Greek *skēptron* "staff" < *skēptein* "lean on"] —**scep·tered** *adj*

scep·tic *n, adj* RELIG, PHILOSOPHY another spelling of **skeptic**

Scep·tic *n, adj* PHILOSOPHY, ANCIENT HIST another spelling of **Skeptic**

scep·ti·cal *adj* another spelling of **skeptical**

scep·tre *n, vt* POL Can, UK spelling of **scepter**

sch. *abbr* school

scha·den·freu·de /shaád'n fròydə/, **Scha·den·freu·de** *n* malicious or smug pleasure taken in somebody else's misfortune [Late 19C. < German < *Schaden* "harm" + *Freude* "joy"]

Schaff·hau·sen /shaáf hòwzən/ town in north central Switzerland, on the Rhine River. Population: 33,789 (1998).

schappe /shap, shaápə/, **schappe silk** *n* yarn or fabric made from the waste products of silk [Late 19C. < German]

Schaum·burg /shaám bùrg/ village in northeastern Illinois. Population: 74,919 (2002 estimate).

schav /shav, shchaav/ *n US* a chilled soup made from sorrel or spinach, to which chopped egg, sour cream, lemon juice, and chopped green onions are sometimes added [Via Yiddish *shtshav* < Polish *szczaw*]

sched·ule /skéjjool, skéjjəl/ *n* **1.** LIST OF MEETINGS, COMMITMENTS, OR APPOINTMENTS an outline description of the things somebody is to do and the times at which they are to be done ○ *Her busy work schedule didn't permit us to meet for lunch.* **2.** WORK PLAN a plan of work to be done, showing the order in which tasks are to be carried out and the amounts of time allocated to them ○ *The project was completed ahead of schedule.* ○ *draw up a production schedule* **3.** LIST OF ARRIVALS AND DEPARTURES a list of the times of arrivals and departures, e.g., of buses or trains **4.** *US* EDUC LIST OF CLASSES a list of the classes and the times at which they occur for a student or teacher in a given period **5.** LIST OF ITEMS a table of items of information ○ *a schedule of tariffs* **6.** *US* DRUGS LIST OF RESTRICTED DRUGS a list of drugs subject to the same legal restrictions **7.** SUPPLEMENTARY LIST a list of details, often in the form of an appendix to a legal or legislative document ■ *vt* (**-uled, -ul·ing, -ules**) **1.** PLAN SOMETHING FOR A PARTICULAR TIME to plan something to happen at a particular time ○ *They are scheduled to arrive at noon.* **2.** MAKE A LIST OF THINGS to put together a table of items of information, or place an item in the table [14C. Via French < late Latin *schedula* "small piece of paper" < Greek *skhedē* "page"] —**sched·u·lar** *adj* —**sched·u·ler** *n*

Sched·uled Castes /skéjjoold-, skéjjəld-/ *npl* in India, castes that are officially considered disadvantaged and granted special treatment, including Dalits [Because listed in a "schedule" of the Indian constitution, 1950]

sched·uled ter·ri·to·ries *npl UK* FIN same as **sterling area**

Sched·uled Tribes *npl* in India, the indigenous rural communities who are officially considered disadvantaged and granted special treatment

Schee·le /sháylə/, **Carl Wilhelm** (1742–86) Swedish chemist. He discovered many elements, compounds, and chemical reactions, and isolated oxygen before the British chemist Joseph Priestley.

schee·lite /sháy lìt, sheé-/ *n* a variously colored calcium tungstate mineral. Use: source of tungsten. [Mid-19C. After Carl Wilhelm SCHEELE]

schef·fle·ra /shef leérə, shéfflərə/ (*plural* **-ras** or *same*) *n* a tropical tree or bush with glossy leaves, often cultivated as a house plant. Genus: *Schefflera.* [Mid-20C. After J. C. *Scheffler* (1742–86), German botanist]

Schel·ling /shélling/, **Friedrich** (1775–1854) German philosopher. He was one of the leading exponents of idealism and the Romantic tendency in German philosophy. Full name **Schelling, Friedrich Wilhelm Joseph von**

Schel·te /skéltə/ river in Europe that flows through France, Belgium, and the Netherlands. Length: 270 mi./435 km.

sche·ma /skeéma/ (*plural* **-ma·ta** /skee maáta, ski mátta/) *n* **1.** DIAGRAM a diagram or plan showing the basic outline of something **2.** MENTAL PATTERN an organizational or conceptual pattern in the mind **3.** KANTIAN PHILOSOPHICAL PRINCIPLE in the philosophy of Kant, a method that allows the understanding to apply concepts to the evidence of the senses **4.** DUMMY EXPRESSION IN LOGIC in logic, a dummy expression indicating where particular words should appear, e.g., in "S and R," "S" and "R" are schemata for sentences [Late 18C. Directly or via German < Greek *skhēma*]

sche·mat·ic /skee máttik, ski-/ *adj* showing the basic form or layout of something ○ *a schematic drawing* ■ *n* a diagram, especially of electrical circuits

sche·ma·tism /skeéma tìzzam/ *n* the basic arrangement or layout of parts in a complex object or system

sche·ma·tize /skeéma tīz/ (**-tized, -tiz·ing, -tiz·es**) *vt* to arrange or organize something according to a system —**sche·ma·ti·za·tion** /skeémati záysh'n/ *n*

scheme /skeem/ *n* **1.** SECRET PLOT a secret and cunning plan, especially one designed to cause damage or harm ○ *Luckily, we got wise to their little scheme.* **2.** PLAN OF ACTION a systematic plan of action ○ *money-making schemes* **3.** SYSTEM a systematic and coherent arrangement of parts **4.** DIAGRAM OF SOMETHING a diagram, chart, or map **5.** ASTROLOGER'S CHART an astrological chart of the sky **6.** *UK* GOVERNMENT OR BUSINESS PROGRAM a plan, policy, or program carried out by a government or business ○ *a training scheme* ■ *vi* (**schemed, schem·ing, schemes**) MAKE A SECRET PLAN to devise plots and plans, especially secret or cunning ones intended to cause damage or harm [Mid-16C. Via Latin *schema* "form" < Greek *skhēma*] —**schem·er** *n*

schem·ing /skeéming/ *adj* continually devising plots and plans, especially cunning or underhand ones, or using them to achieve objectives —**schem·ing·ly** *adv*

Sche·nec·ta·dy /ska néktadee/ city in eastern New York, on the Mohawk River, northwest of Albany. Population: 61,420 (2002 estimate).

Schep·isi /skép seé/, **Fred** (*b.* 1939) Australian moviemaker. He directed *The Chant of Jimmie Blacksmith* (1978). After the 1980s he made movies in Hollywood, including *Six Degrees of Separation* (1994). Full name **Schepisi, Frederick Alan**

Scher·er·ville /shérrar vìl/ town in northwestern Indiana, near the Indiana-Illinois border, southeast of Chicago. Population: 25,576 (2002 estimate).

scher·zan·do /sker tsaándō/ *adj, adv* performed in a playful musical style and tempo (*used as a musical direction*) ■ *n* (*plural* **-dos** or **-di** /-dee/) a scherzando piece or passage of music [Early 19C. < Italian, < *scherzare* "to joke"]

scher·zo /skértsō/ (*plural* **-zos** or **-zi** /-tsee/) *n* **1.** a lively and often playful or humorous movement in a musical composition, usually the third of four **2.** an independent musical work in a lively and often playful or humorous style [Mid-19C. < Italian, < *scherzare* "to joke"]

Sche·ven·in·gen /skáyvan ìngan/ resort town in the western Netherlands, on the North Sea. It is now a district of The Hague.

Elsa Schiaparelli

Schia·pa·rel·li /skee aápa réllee, skàppa-/, **Elsa** (1896–1973) Italian fashion designer. Her designs were often extravagant with deliberately overstated effects.

> "A dress has no life of its own unless it is worn, and as soon as this happens another personality takes over from you and animates it, or tries to, glorifies or destroys it, or makes it into a song of beauty."
> [Elsa Schiaparelli, *A Shocking Life*; 1954]

Schick test /shík-/ *n* an injection of nontoxic diphtheria under the skin, used to determine whether a patient is immune to diphtheria. A patch of reddened skin at the point of injection indicates no immunity. [Early 20C. After Bela *Schick* (1877–1967), Hungarian-born US pediatrician]

Schie·le /sheéla/, **Egon** (1890–1918) Austrian painter. His depictions of the human figure, in the expressionist style, have a strongly erotic quality.

Schiff's re·a·gent /shiffs-/, **Schiff re·a·gent** *n* an acid solution of fuchsin. Use: test for aldehydes. [Late 19C. After Hugo *Schiff* (1834–1915), German chemist]

schil·ler /shíllar/ *n* an iridescent luster in some minerals [Early 19C. < German, "iridescence"]

Schil·ler /shíllar/, **Friedrich von** (1759–1805) German poet, dramatist, historian, and philosopher. Regarded as Germany's greatest playwright, he wrote works in praise of the freedom of the human spirit, including the dramas *Wallenstein* (1799), *Maria Stuart* (1800), and *Wilhelm Tell* (1804). Full name **Schiller, Johann Christoph Friedrich von**

> "Kings are only slaves of their own position who may not follow their own heart."
> [Friedrich von Schiller, *Maria Stuart*; 1800]

schil·ling /shílling/ *n* the main unit of the former Austrian currency [Mid-18C. < German]

schipperke

schip·per·ke /shíppar keé/ (*plural* **-kes** or *same*) *n* a small black tailless dog belonging to a breed with pointed ears and a thick coat [Late 19C. < Dutch dialect, diminutive of Dutch *schipper* (see SKIPPER[1])]

schism /skízzam, sízzam/ *n* **1.** DIVISION IN RELIGIOUS DENOMINATION a major split within an established religious denomination, usually on the grounds of differences in belief or practice, leading to the setting up of a separate breakaway organization, or the offense of causing such a split **2.** DIVISIVE UNPLEASANT SPLIT the division of a group into mutually antagonistic factions **3.** FACTION a faction formed as a result of a schism [14C. Via French < late Latin *schisma* < Greek *skhizein* "to split"]

schis·mat·ic /skiz máttik, siz-/, **schis·mat·i·cal** /-máttik'l/ *adj* relating to, involved in, or causing schism ■ *n* a participant in or cause of a schism —**schis·mat·i·cal·ly** *adv*

schist /shist/ *n* a rock whose minerals have aligned themselves in one direction in response to deformation stresses, with the result that the rock can be split in parallel layers [Late 18C. Via French *schiste* < Latin *(lapis) schistos* "fissile (stone)" < Greek *skhistos* < *skhizein* "to split"] —**schis·tose** /shíss tōss, -tōz/ *adj* —**schis·tos·i·ty** /shiss tóssatee/ *n*

schis·to·cyte /shísta sīt/ *n* a red blood cell undergoing fragmentation, or any one of the fragments that are formed as a result

schis·to·some /shísta sōm/ *n* a tiny flatworm that often lives as a parasite in the blood of birds and mammals. In humans, it causes the disease schistosomiasis.

schis·to·so·mi·a·sis /shìstasō mī́ assiss/ *n* an often chronic illness that results from infection of the blood with a parasitic flatworm (**schistosome**). It causes debilitation and can cause liver and intestinal damage. It is most common in Asia, Africa, and South America, especially in areas where the water is contaminated by freshwater snails that carry the parasite.

schiz- *prefix* same as **schizo-** (*used before vowels*)

schiz·o /skítsō/ (*slang insult*) *n* (*plural* **-os**) an offensive term for somebody who has schizophrenia ■ *adj* an offensive term meaning having characteristics thought of, though often erroneously, as symptomatic of schizophrenia [Mid-20C. Shortening of SCHIZOPHRENIC]

schizo- *prefix* **1.** split, cleft ○ *schizocarp* **2.** cleavage, fission ○ *schizogony* **3.** schizophrenia ○ *schizothymia* [< modern Latin, < Greek *skhizein* "to split" < Indo-European]

schiz·o·carp /skítsa kaàrp/ *n* a dry fruit that splits into individually seeded parts (**carpels**) when ripe —**schiz·o·car·pic** /skìtsa kaárpik/ *adj* —**schiz·o·car·pous** /-kaárpass/ *adj*

schi·zog·o·ny /ski zóggonee, skit sóggonee/ *n* a form of asexual reproduction that occurs in some single-celled organisms (**protozoans**), in which the nucleus of an individual divides many times before the cytoplasm divides to form the daughter cells. This process enables some parasites, including the malaria parasite, to undergo rapid proliferation in the body tissues of an infected host.

schiz·oid /skít sòyd/ *adj* **1.** showing some of the symptoms of schizophrenia such as withdrawal into the self and a tendency to fantasize (*technical*) ○ *exhibits a schizoid personality* **2.** an offensive term describing a personality that suggests inner conflicts and exhibits outer contradictions (*insult*)

schiz·ont /skíz ònt, skít sònt/ *n* a cell formed during the asexual phase of the life cycle of some single-celled organisms (**protozoans**)

schiz·o·phre·ni·a /skìtsa freénee a/ *n* **1.** a severe psychiatric disorder with symptoms of emotional instability, detachment from reality, and withdrawal into the self **2.** an offensive term for a state characterized by contradictory or conflicting attitudes, behavior, or qualities (*insult*) [Early 20C. < SCHIZO- + Greek *phrēn* "mind"]

schiz·o·phren·ic /skìtsa frénnik/ *adj* **1.** relating to or resulting from schizophrenia **2.** an offensive term meaning characterized by conflicts and contradictions (*insult*) —**schiz·o·phren·ic** *n*

schiz·o·phyte /skítsa fīt/ *n* a microorganism that reproduces by fission. Bacteria and bluish green algae are schizophytes. —**schiz·o·phyt·ic** /skìtsa fíttik/ *adj*

schiz·o·pod /skítsa pòd, skízza-/ (*plural* **-pods** or *same*) *n* a crustacean resembling a shrimp, e.g., a krill. Order: Mysidacea or Euphausiacea.

schiz·o·thy·mi·a /skìtsa thīmee a/ *n* an introverted psychiatric condition that resembles a mild form of schizophrenia (*technical*) [Mid-20C. < SCHIZO- + Greek *thumos* "soul, mind"] —**schiz·o·thy·mic** *adj*

schiz·y /skítssee/ (**-i·er, -i·est**) *adj* an offensive term for somebody regarded as emotionally sensitive or moody to a degree that makes others feel uneasy (*slang insult*) [Mid-20C. Shortening of SCHIZOPHRENIC or SCHIZOID with alteration]

schle·miel /shla meél/, **schle·mihl** *n* an offensive term that deliberately insults somebody's ability to cope or do things or somebody's failure to experience good fortune (*slang insult*) [Late 19C. < Yiddish *shlemiel*]

schlep /shlep/, **shlep** *v* (**schlepped, schlep·ping, schleps; shlepped, shlep·ping, shleps**) (*informal*) **1.** *vt* MOVE SOMETHING WITH DIFFICULTY to lug or haul something from one place to another **2.** *vi* GO WITH DIFFICULTY to move slowly, clumsily, or tediously ■ *n* **1.** TEDIOUS JOURNEY a long, tedious, or difficult journey (*informal*) ○ *It's such a schlep all the way across town.* **2.** OFFENSIVE TERM an offensive term that deliberately insults somebody's intelligence or physical coordination (*informal insult*) [Early 20C. Via Yiddish < German *schleppen* "to drag"] —**schlep·per** *n*

Schles·in·ger /shléssinjər/, **Arthur Meier, Jr.** (*b.* 1917) US historian, writer, and educator. An adviser to President John F. Kennedy, he received a Pulitzer Prize for *A Thousand Days* (1965), a history of the Kennedy administration, a book that also won a National Book Award.

"The Kennedy presidency began with incomparable dash. The young president, the old poet, the splendid speech, the triumphant parade, the brilliant sky and the shining snow, it was one of the most glorious of inaugurals."
[Arthur M. Schlesinger, Jr., *A Thousand Days*; 1965]

Schles·wig-Hol·stein /shlèzvig hólstīn/ state in northern Germany occupying the southern part of the Jutland peninsula. Capital: Kiel. Population: 2,766,057 (1998). Area: 6,088 sq. mi./15,769 sq. km.

Schlie·mann /shleé maan/, **Heinrich** (1822–90) German archaeologist who discovered and excavated the remains of ancient Troy (1870–80)

schlie·ren /shleérən/ *npl* **1.** zones of different density and refraction in a transparent fluid, visible as streaks and caused by pressure or temperature variations **2.** a texture observed in some igneous rocks where the darker, more basic minerals form linear aggregates in the paler host rock [Late 19C. < German, "streaks"]

schlie·ren pho·tog·ra·phy *n* a form of flash photography that records schlieren present in a fluid

schli·ma·zel /shli maázəl/ *n US* an offensive term for somebody regarded as prone to making mistakes and having bad luck (*slang insult*) [Mid-20C. < Yiddish, < Middle High German *slim* "crooked" + Hebrew *mazzāl* "luck"]

schlock /shlok/ (*slang*) *n* something that has no value and is shoddily made ■ *adj* cheap and lacking any redeeming quality ○ *a schlock horror film* [Early 20C. Probably via Yiddish *shlak* "evil blow" < Middle High German *slag*] —**schlock·y** *adj*

schlock·meis·ter /shlók mīstər/ *n US* a dealer in shoddy goods of little value (*slang*) [Mid-20C. < SCHLOCK + German *Meister* "master"]

schlub /shlub/ *n, adj* same as **zhlub** (*slang insult*) [Via Yiddish < Polish *zhŁób*, literally "trough"]

schm-, shm- *prefix* somebody or something purported or purporting to be genuine, real, or of the expected high quality but really not (*used dismissively in rhyming compounds*) ○ *doctor-schmoctor* [< Yiddish]

schmaltz /shmaalts, shmawlts/, **schmalz, shmaltz** *n* **1.** cloying or exaggerated sentimentality (*informal*) **2.** melted chicken fat used for cooking [Mid-20C. Via Yiddish *shmalts* "melted fat" < German *Schmalz*] —**schmaltz·i·ly** *adv* —**schmaltz·i·ness** *n* —**schmaltz·y** *adj*

schmat·te /shmaátə/, **shmat·te** *n* a rag or worthless thing (*informal*) [Late 20C. Via Yiddish < Polish *szmata* "rag"]

schmeer /shmeer/, **schmear, shmeer** *n* **1.** WHOLE SET an entire set or group of related things (*slang*) ○ *the whole schmeer* **2.** *US* BRIBE a bribe (*slang*) **3.** *US* FOOD SPREAD OR PASTE something spread on a roll or bagel, e.g., cream cheese [Mid-20C. < Yiddish *schmirn* "to smear" < Middle High German *smiren*]

Schmidt /shmit/, **Helmut** (*b.* 1918) chancellor of West Germany (1974–82). He was a prominent leader of the European Union, and, from 1983, publisher of the weekly newspaper *Die Zeit*. Full name **Schmidt, Helmut Heinrich Waldemar**

Schmidt cam·er·a /shmít-/ *n* ASTRON same as **Schmidt telescope**

Schmidt sys·tem *n* an optical system that uses a special concave spherical mirror to correct optical aberrations [Mid-20C. After Bernhard Voldemar *Schmidt* (1879–1935), Estonian-born German specialist in optics]

Schmidt tel·e·scope *n* a wide-angle photographic telescope used in astronomy. It has a special internal mirror to correct optical aberrations. [Mid-20C. Because it uses a Schmidt system]

Schmitt trig·ger /shmít-/ *n* an electronic circuit that produces an output when the input exceeds a predetermined turn-on or threshold level. The output is maintained until the input falls below the threshold level. [Mid-20C. After Otto H. *Schmitt* (b. 1913), US electronics engineer]

schmo /shmō/ (*plural* **schmoes**), **shmo** (*plural* **shmoes**) *n* an offensive term that deliberately insults somebody's character or perceptiveness (*slang insult*) [Mid-20C. Alteration of SCHMUCK]

schmooze /shmooz/ (*slang*) *v* (**schmoozed, schmooz·ing, schmooz·es**) **1.** *vi* CHAT INFORMALLY to chat socially and agreeably **2.** *vt* BE INGRATIATING TOWARD SOMEBODY to talk persuasively to somebody, often to gain personal advantage ■ *n* INFORMAL CHAT an informal chat about trivial matters [Late 19C. Via Yiddish *schmuesn* "talk" < Hebrew *šĕmūʽāh* "rumor"] —**schmooz·er** *n*

schmuck /shmuk/, **shmuck** *n* a highly offensive term that deliberately insults somebody's personal worth (*slang insult*) [Late 19C. < Yiddish *shmok* "penis"]

Schna·bel /shnaáb'l/, **Artur** (1882–1951) Austrian pianist and composer. He was known for his interpretations of Beethoven, Schubert, and Mozart. His own compositions include chamber music and piano works. After 1938 he settled in the United States.

"When a piece gets difficult make faces."
[Artur Schnabel. Quoted in *The Unimportance of Being Oscar*, Oscar Levant; 1968]

schnapps /shnaps/ (*plural same*) *n* **1.** a strong liquor in which flavoring such as peppermint is distilled in rather than added later **2.** a glass or measure of schnapps [Early 19C. Via German < Low German or Dutch *snaps* "mouthful"]

~~schnaps~~ incorrect spelling of **schnapps**

schnau·zer /shnówzər, shnówtsər/ *n* a wiry-coated dog with bushy eyebrows and whiskers that grow like a beard, belonging to any one of three breeds (giant, standard, and miniature) that originated in Germany [Early 20C. < German, < *Schnauze* "snout"]

schneck·en /shnékən/ *npl US* sweet bread rolls flavored with layers of butter, chopped nuts, and cinnamon between the spiraled strands [< German, "snails"]

schnit·zel /shníts'l/ *n* a piece of meat, typically veal, beaten flat and served fried, usually coated in egg and breadcrumbs [Mid-19C. < German, < Old High German *snidan* "to cut"]

Schnitz·ler /shnítslər/, **Arthur** (1862–1931) Austrian doctor, playwright, and novelist. His works, inspired by psychoanalysis and focusing on human relationships, include *Reigen* (1897), later staged and filmed as *La Ronde*.

schnook /shnŏŏk/ *n US* an offensive term for somebody who is regarded as easily duped or unimportant (*slang insult*) [Mid-20C. Origin ?]

schnor·rer /shnáwrər/ *n* an offensive term for somebody who is regarded as unduly dependent on or parasitic upon other people (*slang insult*) [Late 19C. Via Yiddish < German *Schnurrer* < Middle High German *snurren* "to hum"; from the practice of playing a musical instrument while begging]

schnoz·zle /shnózz'l/, **schnoz** /shnoz/ (*plural* **schnoz·es**) *n US* a nose, especially a large one (*slang*) [Mid-20C. < Yiddish *shnoytsl*, diminutive of *shnoyts* "snout" < German *Schnauze*]

Schoen·berg /shúrn bùrg, shőn bèrk/, **Arnold** (1874–1951) Austrian composer. He is best known for his revolutionary 12-tone, or serial, system, which broke with traditional harmony. Full name **Schoenberg, Arnold Franz Walter**

"If it is art, it is not for the masses."
[Arnold Schoenberg, *Letter to W. S. Schlamm*; July 1, 1945]

schol·ar /skóllər/ *n* **1.** LEARNED PERSON a learned person, especially an academic specialist in one area of knowledge **2.** SCHOLARSHIP STUDENT a student who receives a scholarship **3.** STUDENT a student, especially one who earns high grades (*formal*) [Pre-12C. < late Latin *scholaris* < Latin *schola* (see SCHOOL[1])]

schol·ar·ly /skóllərlee/ *adj* **1.** LEARNED possessing or showing a great deal of knowledge, especially knowledge of an academic subject **2.** OF SCHOLARS relating to scholars or to formal study ○ *scholarly journals* **3.** ACCORDING TO PRINCIPLES OF FORMAL STUDY in keeping with a rigorous and systematic approach to acquiring knowledge or to setting out the results of study —**schol·ar·li·ness** *n*

schol·ar·ship /skóllər shìp/ *n* **1.** FINANCIAL HELP FOR STUDENT a sum of money awarded to a student to help with living expenses, study, or travel **2.** FORMAL STUDY academic learning or achievement **3.** ACADEMIC WORKS a body of learning on an academic subject ○ *a review of German scholarship on the topic*

SYNONYMS See ***knowledge***.

scho·las·tic /skə lástik, sko-/ *adj* **1.** OF SCHOOLS OR STUDYING relating to students, schools, or studying **2.** PEDANTIC too concerned with details or fine distinctions and too ready to criticize minor errors (*disapproving*) **3.** OF SCHOLASTICISM relating to the medieval movement of religious and philosophical learning known as scholasticism ■ *n* **1.** STUDENT OR TEACHER UNDER SCHOLASTICISM a student or teacher in the medieval intellectual movement known as scholasticism **2.** PEDANT a person regarded as pedantic or quibbling (*disapproving*) **3.** CHR SOMEBODY UNDERGOING ROMAN CATHOLIC SCHOLASTICATE a probationer in a scholasticate at a Roman Catholic seminary [Late 16C. Via Latin < Greek *skholastikos* "learned" < *skholē* "learned discussion, school"] —**scho·las·ti·cal·ly** *adv*

Scho·las·tic Ap·ti·tude Test *n* EDUC full form of **SAT**

scho·las·ti·cate /skə lásti kàyt, -lástikət/ *n* **1.** a probationary period of study for a Jesuit student at a Roman Catholic seminary **2.** a seminary where a scholasticate is undertaken

scho·las·ti·cism /skə lásti sìzzəm, sko-/ *n* **1.** a medieval theological and philosophical system of learning based on the authority of St. Augustine and other leaders of the early Christian Church, and on the works of Aristotle. It sought to bridge the gap between religion and reason. **2.** narrowly traditional learning, or adherence to traditional educational methods

scho·li·a LITERAT plural of **scholium**

scho·li·ast /skőlee àst, -əst/ *n* a medieval scholar who wrote commentaries on ancient Greek and Latin texts [Late 16C. < medieval Greek *skholiastēs* < *skholion* (see SCHOLIUM)] —**scho·li·as·tic** /skòlee ástik/ *adj*

scho·li·um /skőlee əm/ (*plural* **-li·a** /-lee ə/) *n* a medieval annotation or commentary written on an ancient Greek or Latin text [Mid-16C. < Greek *skholion* "interpretation" < *skholē* "learned discussion, school"]

school[1] /skool/ *n* **1.** INSTITUTION FOR TEACHING CHILDREN an institution in which children and teenagers are taught, usually up to the age of 17, or a building housing such an institution (*often used before a noun*) **2.** EDUC UNIVERSITY-LEVEL INSTITUTION a college or university **3.** DEPARTMENT SPECIALIZING IN AN ACADEMIC SUBJECT a faculty, department, or institution that offers specialized instruction in an academic subject ○ *medical school* **4.** INSTITUTION TEACHING A NON-ACADEMIC SKILL an institution that specializes in teaching a particular skill, especially a practical or sports skill ○ *tennis school* **5.** STAFF AND STUDENTS all the staff and students of an educational institution (*often used before a noun*) **6.** DAY IN SCHOOL the part of a day spent teaching or being taught in a school ○ *School was over for another day.* **7.** YEARS SPENT AT SCHOOL the part of somebody's life spent being taught in a school ○ *After school, he went abroad for two years.* **8.** INSTRUCTIVE PLACE OR PERIOD a place or period of activity regarded as providing knowledge or experience ○ *the school of life* **9.** ARTISTS OR WRITERS SHARING SAME APPROACH a group of people, especially artists, writers, or philosophers, who share the same principles, methods, ideals, or style ○ *the Impressionist school* ○ *the Aristotelian school* ■ *vt* (**schooled, school·ing, schools**) **1.** INSTRUCT SOMEBODY to train somebody in a particular skill or area of expertise in a thorough and detailed way ○ *were schooled in the art of debate* **2.** EDUCATE SOMEBODY IN SCHOOL to educate a child or teenager formally in a school **3.** DISCIPLINE SOMEBODY to exert control or discipline over somebody or yourself **4.** RIDING TRAIN A HORSE to train a horse, especially for riding and dressage [Pre-12C. Via Latin *schola* < Greek *skholē* "learned discussion, school"]

SYNONYMS See ***teach***.

school[2] /skool/ *n* a group of fish, whales, porpoises, or other ocean animals of a single type ■ *vi* (**schooled, school·ing, schools**) to congregate in a school or swim in a school [14C. < Middle Dutch *schole* < W Germanic]

school age *n* the age at which a child is required legally to attend school —**school-age** *adj*

school board *n* in the United States, a group of people elected or appointed in each county or local school system to make decisions about education in public schools

school·book /skōol bo͝ok/ *n* a textbook or other book used in school

school·boy /skōol bòy/ *n* a boy who attends school ■ *adj* at a level of maturity regarded as characteristic of, or designed to appeal to, boys of school age ○ *schoolboy clothes*

school bus *n* a large motor vehicle that takes children to and from school or on school-related trips

school·child /skōol chīld/ (*plural* **-chil·dren** /-childrən/) *n* a child who attends school

School·craft /skōol kràft/, **Henry Rowe** (1793–1864) US ethnologist. His studies of Native North American life included *Historical and Statistical Information Respecting the Indian Tribes of the United States* (1851–57). In 1832 he discovered the source of the Mississippi River in Minnesota.

school day *n* **1. DAY OF SCHOOL OR SCHOOLING** a day on which school is conducted, or the hours of instruction in that day **2. PORTION OF DAY IN SCHOOL** the part of a day spent at school ■ **school days** *npl* **YEARS SPENT AT SCHOOL** the period of time in somebody's life spent attending school

school dis·trict *n* an area that includes a number of public schools that are administered together

school fig·ure *n* in figure skating, one of a number of basic movements that used to be required as a part of competition (*often used in the plural*)

school·girl /skōol gùrl/ *n* a girl who attends school ■ *adj* at a level of maturity regarded as characteristic of, or designed to appeal to, girls of school age ○ *schoolgirl clothes*

school·house /skōol hòwss/ (*plural* **-houses** /-hòwzəz/) *n* a building that houses a school, especially a rural elementary school

school·ing /skōoling/ *n* **1. EDUCATION AT SCHOOL** the education or skills acquired in school **2. INSTRUCTION** instruction or training in something, carried out systematically and in a disciplined way **3. TRAINING OF HORSE** the training of a horse, especially for riding and dressage

school·kid /skōol kìd/ *n* a child or teenager who attends school (*informal*)

school-leav·er *n UK* a student who has quit school or is about to do so, especially one who quits at the minimum age and does not go on to further or higher education

School·man /skōol màn/ (*plural* **-men** /-mèn/) *n* a university teacher, philosopher, or theologian in the late medieval period who espoused scholasticism

school·marm /skōol maàrm/ *n* **1.** an offensive term for a woman thought to live in a way regarded as old-fashioned (*insult*) **2.** an offensive term for a woman schoolteacher, especially one considered too proper and old-fashioned (*dated insult*) —**school·marm·ish** *adj*

school·mas·ter[1] /skōol màstər/ *n* a man who teaches school, especially in a private school as a headmaster (*dated*) [13C. < SCHOOL[1]]

school·mas·ter[2] /skōol màstər/ (*plural same*) *n* a fish of the snapper family that has yellow fins. Native to: Caribbean, tropical Atlantic. Latin name: *Lutjanus apodus*. [Mid-19C. < SCHOOL[2]]

school·mate /skōol màyt/ *n* a friend or companion at school

school·mis·tress /skōol mistrəss/ *n* a woman who teaches school, especially in a private school (*dated*)

school of hard knocks *n* difficult or challenging experiences that are considered to be instructive

school of thought *n* a way of thinking about something, or a group of people who share the same attitude or opinion

school psy·chol·o·gist *n* a psychologist who specializes in the assessment and problems of schoolchildren

school·room /skōol ro͝om, -rōom/ *n* a classroom in a school

school·teach·er /skōol teèchər/ *n* a teacher in a school —**school·teach·ing** *n*

school·work /skōol wùrk/ *n* the work that a student does in or after school

school·yard /skōol yaàrd/ *n* a playground adjacent to a school

school year *n* **1.** the months during which instruction is given at a school, college, or university **2.** a period of 12 months, beginning usually in late August or early September, throughout which students are assigned to the same class

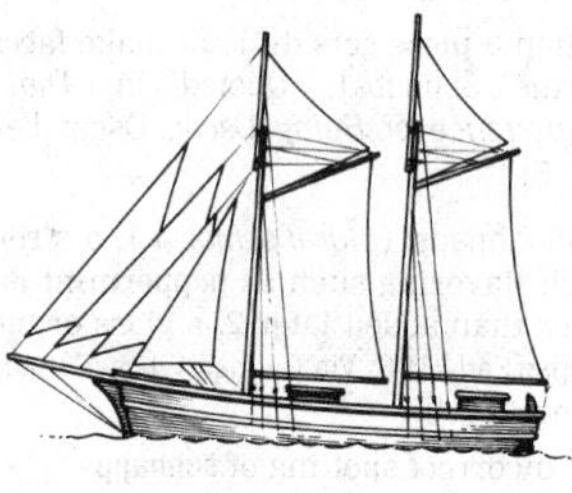

schooner

schoo·ner /skōonər/ *n* **1.** a fast sailing ship with at least two masts and with sails set lengthwise (**fore-and-aft**) **2.** HIST same as **prairie schooner 3.** a tall slim glass for beer [Early 18C. Origin ?]

schoo·ner rig *n* an arrangement of masts and sails (**rig**) in which the mainmast is taller than the foremast —**schoo·ner-rigged** *adj*

Scho·pen·hau·er /shōpən hòw ər/, **Arthur** (1788–1860) German philosopher. His atheistic, deeply pessimistic philosophy was most fully expounded in *The World as Will and Idea* (1819).

> "I cannot here withhold the statement that *optimism*...seems to me to be not merely an absurd, but also a really *wicked*, way of thinking, a bitter mockery of the unspeakable sufferings of mankind."
> [Arthur Schopenhauer, *The World as Will and Idea*; 1819]

schorl /shawrl/ *n* a black opaque form of the mineral tourmaline, often occurring in needle-shaped radiating crystals [Late 18C. < German *Schörl*] —**schor·la·ceous** /shawr láyshəss/ *adj*

schot·tische /shóttish, sho teésh/ *n* **1.** a round dance of German origin, resembling a slow polka **2.** the music for a schottische [Mid-19C. < German *schottische (Tanz)* "Scottish dance"]

Schott·ky ef·fect /shótkee-/ *n* a reduction in the energy needed to remove an electron from a solid surface caused by the application of an electric field [Mid-20C. After Walter *Schottky* (1886–1976), German physicist]

schrod *n US* FISH, FOOD another spelling of **scrod**

Schrö·der /shrúrdər/, **Gerhard** (*b.* 1944) chancellor of Germany (1998–). A former lawyer, and member of the center-left Social Democratic Party since 1963, he ended 16 years of government by the Christian Democratic Union when he won the general election in 1998.

Schroe·der /shrōdər/, **Patricia** (*b.* 1940) US lawyer and politician. She served as a US representative from Colorado (1972–96) and subsequently as the president and chief executive officer of the Association of American Publishers (AAP) (1997–).

schtetl *n* another spelling of **shtetl**

schtick *n* another spelling of **shtick** (*informal*)

Franz Schubert

Schu·bert /shōobərt/, **Franz** (1797–1828) Austrian composer. He is particularly noted for his songs and chamber works, although he also wrote choral and orchestral music. Full name **Schubert, Franz Peter**

schul *n* JUDAISM another spelling of **shul**

Schulz /sho͝olts/, **Charles** (1922–2000) US cartoonist. He created the successful *Peanuts* comic strip (1950), featuring Snoopy and Charlie Brown. Full name **Schultz, Charles Monroe**

Schu·mach·er /shōo maàkər/, **Michael** (*b.* 1969) German racecar driver. He was Formula One world champion six times between 1994 and 2003.

Schu·man /shōomən/, **William** (1910–92) US composer. He is known for his Pulitzer Prize-winning *Secular Cantata, No. 2 (A Free Song)* (1943). He headed the Juilliard School of Music in New York City (1945–62). Full name **Schuman, William Howard**

Schu·mann /shōo maàn, shōomən/, **Robert** (1810–56) German composer. He was a major exponent of the romantic style, noted for his songs, piano music, and orchestral and chamber works. Full name **Schumann, Robert Alexander**

> "Music owes as much to Bach as religion to its founder."
> [Attributed to Robert Schumann]

Schum·pe·ter /shōom pàytər/, **Joseph** (1883–1950) Austrian-born US economist. A professor at Harvard University (1932–50), he promoted entrepreneurship for the "creative destruction" by which it drives economies forward. Full name **Schumpeter, Joseph Alois**

Schurz /shurts, shoorts/, **Carl** (1829–1906) German-born US politician and journalist. He was a US senator from Missouri (1869–75) and secretary of the interior (1877–81). He continued to advocate for progressive policies as an editor and journalist.

schuss /sho͝oss, shooss/ *vi* (**schussed, schuss·ing, schuss·es**) to ski straight downhill at high speed ■ *n* a straight fast downhill run on skis [Mid-20C. < German, "shot"]

schuss·boom·er /sho͝oss bōomər, sho͝oss-/ *n* a skier adept at making fast straight downhill runs (*informal*)

Schüs·sel /sho͝oss'l/, **Wolfgang** (*b.* 1945) chancellor of Austria. A former lawyer, he became leader of the Austrian People's Party in 1995, chancellor in 2000.

schwa /shwaa, shvaa/, **shwa** *n* an unstressed vowel, e.g., "a" in "above" or "e" in "sicken." It is represented in the International Phonetic Alphabet by the symbol ə. [Late 19C. Via German < Hebrew *šəwā*]

Schwann cell /shwaán-, shvaán-/ *n* a cell of the peripheral nervous system that wraps around a nerve fiber and forms the myelin sheath [Early 20C. After Theodor *Schwann* (1810–82), German physiologist]

Schwarz·en·eg·ger /shwáwrtsə nèggər/, **Arnold** (*b.* 1947) Austrian-born US body builder, movie actor and politician. He has appeared in numerous movies, usually in action roles such as in *The Terminator* (1984). In 2003 he was elected governor of California in a gubernatorial recall.

> "I'll be back."
> [Arnold Schwarzenegger, line in *The Terminator*; 1984]

Schwarz·kopf /shwáwrts kòpf/, **Dame Elisabeth** (*b.* 1915) German soprano. She was noted for her operatic roles, especially in operas by Wolfgang Amadeus Mozart and Richard Strauss, and for her interpretation of lieder. Full name **Schwarzkopf, Olga Maria Elisabeth Friederike**

Schwarz·kopf, H. Norman (*b.* 1934) US general and commander of the Allied Forces during the Gulf War. Full name **Schwarzkopf, Herbert Norman**

Schwarzs·child ra·di·us /shwáwrts chīld-, shvaárts shīlt-/ *n* the critical radius within which the gravitational force of a gravitationally collapsing astronomical object becomes so great that neither matter nor energy can escape, creating a black hole [Mid-20C. After Karl *Schwarzschild* (1873–1916), German astronomer]

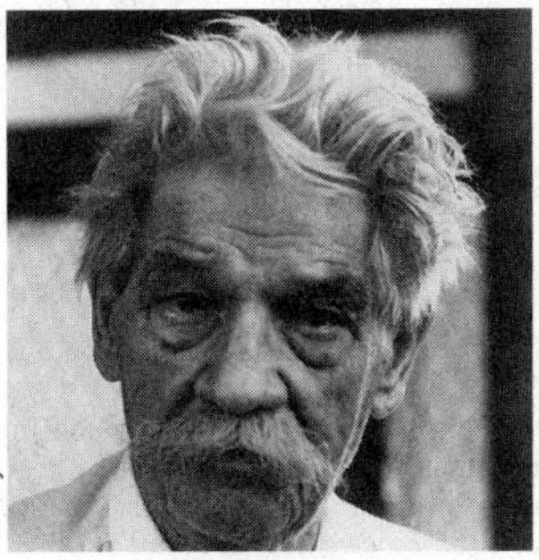

Barnaby's

Albert Schweitzer

Schweit·zer /shwítsər/, **Albert** (1875–1965) German-born theologian, musicologist, and missionary. He wrote important works on J.S. Bach and theology before setting up a hospital in 1913 at Lambaréné, in present-day Gabon, where he spent most of the rest of his life. He was awarded the Nobel Peace Prize (1952).

> "Pain is a more terrible lord of mankind than even death himself."
> [Albert Schweitzer, *On the Edge of the Primeval Forest*; 1922]

sci. *abbr* **1.** science **2.** scientific

s.c.i. *abbr* PRINTING single column inch

sci·am·a·chy /sī ámmәkee, skī-/ (*plural* **-chies**), **ski·am·a·chy** /skī ámmәkee/ *n* the activity of fighting or arguing against imaginary opponents, usually for practice, or a fight or argument against an imagined opponent (*literary*) [Early 17C. < Greek *skiamakhia* < *skia* "shadow" + *makhē* "fight"]

sci·at·ic /sī áttik/ *adj* **1.** relating to or affecting the back of the human hip or the sciatic nerve **2.** causing sciatica or caused by sciatica [Early 16C. Via French < medieval Latin *sciaticus* < Greek *iskhion* "hip joint"]

sci·at·i·ca /sī áttikә/ *n* pain and tenderness extending from the back of the hip down to the calf, usually caused by a protrusion of vertebral disk substance pressing on the roots of the sciatic nerve [15C. < medieval Latin, form of *sciaticus* (see SCIATIC)]

sci·at·ic nerve *n* either of two nerves, one in each leg, that run from the back of the hip down the thigh to the calf and have the largest diameter of any nerves in the human body

SCID *abbr* MED severe combined immunodeficiency

sci·ence /sī әnss/ *n* **1. STUDY OF PHYSICAL WORLD** the study of the physical and natural world and phenomena, especially by using systematic observation and experiment (*often used before a noun*) **2. BRANCH OF SCIENCE** a particular area of study or knowledge of the physical world ○ *the life sciences* **3. SYSTEMATIC BODY OF KNOWLEDGE** a systematically organized body of knowledge about a particular subject ○ *the behavioral sciences* **4. SOMETHING STUDIED OR PERFORMED METHODICALLY** an activity that is the object of careful study or that is carried out according to a developed method ○ *the science of dressing for success* **5. KNOWLEDGE GAINED FROM SCIENCE** the knowledge gained by the study of the physical world [14C. Via French < Latin *scientia* < *scient-*, present participle of *scire* "know, discern" < Indo-European, "cut"] ◇ **blind somebody with science** to confuse or overwhelm somebody by giving an impenetrable explanation using technical terms and concepts

sci·ence fic·tion *n* a form of fiction, usually set in the future, that deals with imaginary scientific and technological developments and contact with other worlds —**sci·ence-fic·tion** *adj*

sci·ence park *n* an area, usually associated with a university, where scientific research is carried out by commercial companies

sci·en·ter /sī éntәr/ *adv* in law, with full knowledge or awareness [Early 19C. < Latin, "knowingly" < *scient-* (see SCIENCE)]

sci·en·tial /sī énsh'l/ *adj* **1.** relating to science or knowledge **2.** possessing considerable knowledge or skill (*formal*)

sci·en·tif·ic /sī әn tíffik/ *adj* **1.** relating to, using, or conforming to science or its principles **2.** proceeding in a systematic and methodical way —**sci·en·tif·i·cal·ly** *adv*

sci·en·tif·ic meth·od *n* the system of advancing knowledge by formulating a question, collecting data about it through observation and experiment, and testing a hypothetical answer

sci·en·tif·ic no·ta·tion *n* a way of expressing a given number as a number between 1 and 10 multiplied by 10 to the appropriate power. 5,743.6 expressed in scientific notation is 5.7436 ± 10^3.

sci·en·tif·ic rev·o·lu·tion *n* the period of advances in science that was at its height in the 17th century and produced widespread change in traditional beliefs held since the Middle Ages

sci·en·tism /sī әn tìzzәm/ *n* **1.** the use of the scientific method of acquiring knowledge, whether in the traditional sciences or in other fields of inquiry **2.** the belief that science alone can explain phenomena, or the application of scientific methods to fields unsuitable for it ○ *"We feel that the attitude that predominates in science at present is arrogance, which has fostered dogmatism and scientism."* (Brian D. Josephson, Beverly A. Rubik, *The Challenge of Consciousness Research*; 1992) —**sci·en·tis·tic** /sī әn tístik/ *adj*

sci·en·tist /sī әntist/ *n* somebody who has scientific training or works in one of the sciences ○ *a forensic scientist*

Sci·en·tist *n* **1.** in Christian Science belief, Jesus Christ as the paramount spiritual healer **2.** a member of the Church of Christ, Scientist

sci-fi /sī fī/ *n* same as **science fiction** (*informal*) [Mid-20C. Shortening]

scil·i·cet /sílli sèt, skeéli kèt/ *adv* used to introduce a word or phrase of clarification, or a missing word or phrase (*formal*) [14C. < Latin, contraction of *scire licet* "it is permitted to know"]

Scil·ly Isles /síllee-/ group of about 150 islands, only four of which are inhabited, in the Atlantic Ocean off Cornwall, southwestern England. Population: 2,153 (2001). Area: 6.2 sq. mi./16 sq. km.

scimitar

scim·i·tar /símmәtәr, -taar/, **sim·i·tar** *n* an Arab or Turkish sword with a curved blade that broadens out as it nears the point [Mid-16C. < French *cimeterre* or Italian *scimitarra*]

scin·dap·sus /skin dápsәss/ (*plural* **-sus·es** or *same*) *n* a climbing plant with heart-shaped, often variegated leaves that is popular as a house plant. Native to: Asia. Genus: *Scindapsus*. [Mid-20C. Via modern Latin < Greek *skindapsos*, plant like ivy]

scin·ti·gram /sínti gràm/ *n* a two-dimensional image of the distribution of a radioactive tracer in a body organ such as the brain or a kidney, obtained using a special scanner (**scintiscanner**) [Mid-20C. < SCINTILLATION]

scin·til·la /sin tíllә/ *n* a tiny amount of something ○ *There's not a scintilla of truth in what he said.* [Late 17C. < Latin, "spark"]

scin·til·late /síntʼl àyt/ (**-lat·ed, -lat·ing, -lates**) *vi* **1. SPARKLE AND FLASH BRIGHTLY** to give off or reflect light in sparks or flashes **2. BE CLEVER OR WITTY** to be very lively, exciting, and entertaining, especially by saying brilliantly clever or witty things **3.** PHYS **EMIT LIGHT FLASHES** to produce sparks of light when hit by particles or photons [Early 17C. < Latin *scintillat-*, past participle of *scintillare* < *scintilla* "spark"] —**scin·til·lant** *adj* —**scin·til·lant·ly** *adv* —**scin·til·la·tor** *n*

scin·til·lat·ing /síntʼl àyting/ *adj* possessing or displaying a dazzlingly impressive liveliness, cleverness, or wit —**scin·til·lat·ing·ly** *adv*

scin·til·la·tion /sìntʼl áysh'n/ *n* **1. FLASH** a bright flash of light or spark **2. EMISSION** the emission of flashes and sparks of light **3.** ASTRON **TWINKLING OF STARS** the twinkling of stars, caused by refraction of light rays from the stars because of different densities in the Earth's atmosphere **4.** PHYS **FLASH OF LIGHT** a flash of light caused by the impact of particles or photons **5. LIVELINESS** dazzling liveliness, cleverness, or wit (*formal*)

scin·til·la·tion count·er *n* a device that detects and measures high-energy radiation through flashes of light produced when ionizing radiation impacts on a phosphorescent substance

scin·ti·scan /sínti skàn/ *n* MED same as **scintigram** [Mid-20C. < SCINTILLATION]

scin·ti·scan·ner /sínti skànnәr/ *n* an apparatus used in diagnosing some diseases that produces an image (**scintigram**) of the distribution in the body of a radioactive tracer that has been administered to the patient

sci·o·lism /sī ә lìzzәm/ *n* displays of sham learning designed to deceive or impress [Early 19C. < late Latin *sciolus*, diminutive of *scius* "having knowledge" < *scire* "know"] —**sci·o·list** *n* —**sci·o·lis·tic** /sī ә lístik/ *adj*

sci·on /sī әn/ *n* **1.** a child or descendant of a family, especially a rich, famous, or important family **2.** a living shoot or twig of a plant used for grafting to a stock [13C. < Old French *ciun*]

Scip·i·o /síppee ō, skíppee ō/, **Publius Cornelius** (*d.* 211 B.C.) Roman general. He was the father of Scipio Africanus the Elder. Although he failed to defeat the Carthaginians in northern Italy and Spain, he helped to check their advances on Rome.

Scip·i·o Af·ri·ca·nus (the El·der) /-afri kaánәss/ (234?–183 B.C.) Roman general. He was the grandfather by adoption of Scipio Africanus the Younger. His defeat of Hannibal in 202 B.C. ended the Second Punic War. Full name **Publius Cornelius Scipio**

Scip·i·o Af·ri·ca·nus (the Youn·ger) (185?–129 B.C.) Roman general. He was the grandson by adoption of Scipio Africanus the Elder. A successful military commander, he destroyed Carthage to end the Third Punic War (146 B.C.). As a government official in Rome, he opposed the populist Gracchi brothers. Full name **Publius Cornelius Scipio Aemilianus**

sci·re fa·ci·as /sīree fáyshee әss/ *n* **1.** a writ that requires a defendant to appear in court and show why the plaintiff should not be permitted to take a specific legal step **2.** the judicial proceeding that produces a writ of scire facias [< Latin, "you should cause (him or her) to know"]

sci·roc·co *n* METEOROL another spelling of **sirocco**

scir·rhous /skírrәss, sírrәss/ *adj* describes a cancerous tumor (**carcinoma**) that is hard and fibrous [Mid-16C. < modern Latin *scirrhosus* < *scirrhus* "hard growth," alteration of Latin *scirrus* < Greek *skirros* "hard"] —**scir·rhos·i·ty** /ski róssәtee, si-/ *n*

scis·sel /síss'l, sízz'l/ *n* metal clippings left over after disks, especially coins, have been punched out of sheets of metal [Early 17C. < French *cisaille* < *cisailler* "clip with shears"]

scis·sile /síss'l, sí sìl/ *adj* capable of being easily and smoothly cut, separated, or divided (*technical*) [Early 17C. < Latin *scissilis* < *sciss-* (see SCISSION)]

scis·sion /sízh'n, sísh'n/ *n* the act or process of cutting, separating, or dividing (*technical*) [15C. Via French < Latin *scission-* < *sciss-*, past participle of *scindere* "cut"]

scis·sor /sízzər/ (**-sored, -sor·ing, -sors**) *vti* **1.** to use scissors to cut something **2.** to move the legs, arms, or body in a way that resembles the opening and shutting of the blades of a pair of scissors ○ *The swimmer scissored through the water.* [Early 17C. Back-formation < SCISSORS]

scis·sors /sízzərz/ (*plural same*) *n* **1.** INSTRUMENT FOR CUTTING SOMETHING a hand-held cutting instrument made up of two crossed connected blades, each with a ring-shaped handle, that pivot on each other and cut as they come together (*takes a plural verb*) **2.** GYMNASTICS MOVEMENT in gymnastics, a movement of the legs that resembles the opening and closing of scissors **3.** TECHNIQUE IN HIGH-JUMPING in the high jump, a simple technique of clearing the bar sideways with a leading leg and then the other in a fast separating and closing movement. This technique is now rarely used. **4.** WRESTLING same as **scissors hold** [14C. Via French *cisoires* < late Latin *cisoria* "cutting tool" < Latin *cis-*, past participle of *caedere* "cut"]

scis·sors hold *n* a wrestling hold in which the legs are wrapped and the feet locked around an opponent's head or body

scis·sors kick *n* in swimming, a kicking motion that resembles the opening and closing of scissors, used especially when doing the sidestroke

scis·sor·tail /sízzər tàyl/ (*plural* **-tails** or *same*) *n* a bird with a long forked tail

sci·u·rine /sí yoo rìn/, **sci·u·rid** /sí yoo rìd/ *n* a rodent belonging to the family that includes squirrels, marmots, and chipmunks. Family: Sciuridae. ■ *adj* relating to or belonging to the squirrel family of rodents [Mid-19C. < Latin *sciurus* (see SQUIRREL)]

sclaff /sklaf/ *vti* (**sclaffed, sclaff·ing, sclaffs**) in golf, to scrape the ground with the club head in making a stroke, or hit the ball after scraping the ground with the club head ■ *n* a golf stroke in which the ground and ball are sclaffed [Early 19C. Probably an imitation of the sound] —**sclaff·er** *n*

SCLC *abbr US* Southern Christian Leadership Conference

scler- *prefix* same as **sclero-** (*used before vowels*)

scle·ra /skléerə/ *n* the dense outer coating of the eyeball that forms the white of the eye [Late 19C. < modern Latin, < Greek *sklēros* "hard"]

scler·e·id /sklérree ìd/ *n* a short thick-walled plant cell that makes up a plant's supporting tissue (**sclerenchyma**) [Late 19C. < SCLERENCHYMA]

scle·ren·chy·ma /sklə réngkəmə/ *n* strengthening or supporting walls of plant tissue made up of long cells or fibers and short cells (**sclereids**) [Mid-19C. < SCLERO- after PARENCHYMA] —**scle·ren·chym·a·tous** /skleerən kímmətəss/ *adj*

scle·ri·a·sis /sklə rí əssiss/ *n* MED same as **scleroderma**

scle·rite /skléer ìt/ *n* a hard plate or layer of chitin or calcium on the outer skeleton of an arthropod —**scle·rit·ic** /sklə ríttik/ *adj*

scle·ri·tis /sklə rítiss/ *n* inflammation of the tough outer coat of the eyeball that forms the white of the eye (**sclera**)

sclero- *prefix* **1.** hard ○ *scleroderma* **2.** hardness ○ *sclerometer* **3.** sclera ○ *scleritis* [< Greek *sklēros* "hard" < Indo-European, "dried up"]

scle·ro·der·ma /skleerə dúrmə/ *n* a disease in which the skin becomes progressively hard and thickened

scle·ro·der·ma·tous /skleerə dúrmətəss/ *adj* **1.** describes an organism having a hard external covering of scales or plates **2.** relating to or characteristic of the skin disease scleroderma

scle·rom·e·ter /sklə rómmətər/ *n* an instrument that determines the hardness of a metal or mineral by measuring the force required to scratch or pierce it —**scle·ro·met·ric** /skleerə méttrik/ *adj*

scle·ro·phyll /skléerə fil/ *n* a woody plant of dry areas with thick leathery evergreen foliage that retains water —**scle·ro·phyl·lous** /skleerə fílləss/ *adj*

scle·ro·pro·tein /skleerō prō teen/ *n* any of a group of fibrous insoluble proteins that are found in body tissue, e.g., keratin, elastin, and collagen

scle·ro·sis /sklə rōssiss/ (*plural* **-ro·ses** /-rō seez/) *n* **1.** the hardening and thickening of body tissue as a result of unwarranted growth, degeneration of nerve fibers, or deposition of minerals, especially calcium **2.** the hardening and thickening of a plant cell wall that occurs as lignin is deposited, turning young green growth woody —**scle·ro·sal** *adj* —**scle·rosed** /sklə rōst, -rōzd/ *adj*

scle·ro·ti·a FUNGI plural of **sclerotium**

scle·rot·ic /sklə róttik/ *adj* **1.** OF PLANT CELL WALL HARDENING relating to the hardening and thickening of plant cell walls that turns young green growth woody **2.** OF WHITE OF THE EYE relating to the dense outer coating of the eyeball that forms the white of the eye (**sclera**) **3.** OF SCLEROSIS OF BODY TISSUE relating to or suffering from sclerosis of body tissue **4.** INFLEXIBLE having become unresponsively rigid, especially from longevity ○ *a political party grown sclerotic from too many years in power* ■ *n* ANAT same as **sclera** [Mid-16C. < Greek *sklēros* "hard" + -OTIC]

scler·o·tin /skléerətin, sklérrətin/ *n* an insoluble protein that hardens and darkens the chitin on the outer skeleton of arthropods [Mid-20C. < SCLERO- after words such as KERATIN]

scle·ro·ti·um /sklə rōshee əm, -shəm/ (*plural* **-ti·a** /-shee ə/) *n* a compact hard mass in a fungus that contains stored food [Mid-19C. < modern Latin, genus of fungi < Greek *sklērotēs* "hardness" < *sklēros* "hard"] —**scle·ro·ti·al** *adj* —**scle·ro·ti·oid** *adj*

scle·ro·tize /sklérrə tìz/ (**-tized, -tiz·ing, -tiz·es**) *vt* to harden and darken an arthropod's outer skeleton [Mid-20C. < SCLEROTIC] —**scler·o·ti·za·tion** /sklèrrəti záysh'n/ *n*

scle·rot·o·my /sklə róttəmee/ (*plural* **-mies**) *n* a surgical operation in which the outer coat (**sclera**) of the eyeball is cut, e.g., in order to remove an underlying tumor

scle·rous /skléerəss, sklérrəss/ *adj* **1.** describes animal parts that are bony or scaly **2.** describes body tissue or body parts that have become especially hardened, as a result of the deposition of minerals

Sc.M. *abbr* EDUC Master of Science

SCN *abbr* ANAT suprachiasmatic nucleus

scoff[1] /skof, skawf/ *vi* (**scoffed, scoff·ing, scoffs**) BE DERISIVE OR SCORNFUL to express derision or scorn about somebody or something ○ *She scoffed at all our suggestions.* ■ *n* **1.** EXPRESSION OF SCORN an expression of derision or scorn **2.** OBJECT OF SCORN somebody or something that is derided or scorned [14C. Probably < N Germanic] —**scoff·er** *n* —**scoff·ing·ly** *adv*

scoff[2] /skof, skawf/ (**scoffed, scoff·ing, scoffs**) *vti* to eat food quickly and hungrily or greedily (*informal*) [Late 18C. Origin ?]

scoff·law /skóf làw, skáwf-/ *n* a flouter of the law [Early 20C. < SCOFF[1]]

Sco·field /skō feeld/, **Sir Paul** (*b.* 1922) British actor. He won an Academy Award for *A Man for All Seasons* (1966) and is known for his versatility in numerous stage and screen roles, from Shakespeare to contemporary drama. Full name **Scofield, Sir David Paul**

scold /skōld/ *v* (**scold·ed, scold·ing, scolds**) **1.** *vt* TELL SOMEBODY OFF to rebuke somebody angrily **2.** *vi* SPEAK HARSHLY to use harsh language, especially when complaining or finding fault ■ *n* **1.** PERSON WHO REBUKES OTHERS an insistent rebuker of others **2.** OFFENSIVE TERM an offensive term for a woman regarded as making a habit of using abusive language, especially when constantly reminding a man to do something (*archaic*) [13C. Probably < Old Norse *skáld* "poet, bard"; from the poet's role of satirizing people] —**scold·er** *n* —**scold·ing·ly** *adv*

scol·e·cite /skáwlə sìt, skōlə-/ *n* a white zeolite mineral consisting of hydrated calcium aluminum silicate and found in both crystalline and massive forms [Early 19C. < Greek *skōlēk-*, stem of *skōlēx* "worm"]

sco·lex /skō lèks/ (*plural* **-li·ces** /-li seez/ or **-le·ces** /-lə seez/) *n* the head of a tapeworm, with suckers or hooks that enable the parasitic worm to attach itself to its host [Mid-19C. Via modern Latin < Greek *skōlēx* "worm"]

sco·li·o·sis /skōlee ōssiss/ *n* an excessive sideways curvature of the human spine [Early 18C. Via modern Latin < Greek *skoliōsis* < *skolios* "bent, curved"] —**sco·li·ot·ic** /skōlee óttik/ *adj*

scol·lop *n* MARINE BIOL another spelling of **scallop**

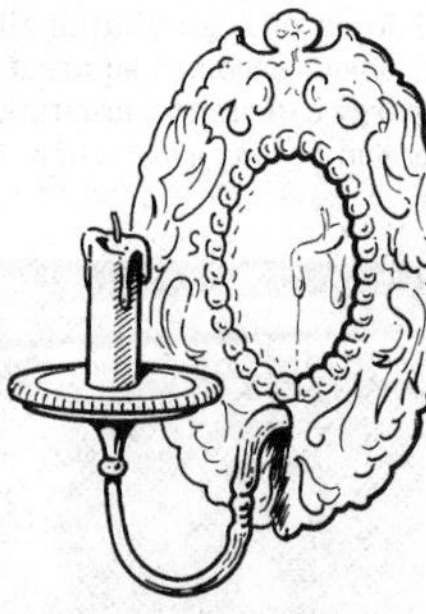

sconce

sconce[1] /skonss/ *n* a wall bracket for holding candles or, sometimes, electric light bulbs [14C. < Old French *esconse* < medieval Latin *absconsa (laterna)* "hidden (lantern)" < *abscondere* (see ABSCOND)]

sconce[2] /skonss/ *n* a small defensive fort or earthwork [Late 16C. < Dutch *schans* "brushwood, earthwork"]

scone /skōn/ *n* **1.** a small baked quick bread, similar to a rich biscuit and traditionally served split and buttered. Plain scones are served with jam and clotted cream as part of the traditional British cream tea. **2.** *regional* in Utah, rich fried dough served with butter, honey, or tasty fillings [Early 16C. Origin ?]

Scone /skoon/ village in central Scotland, near the Tay River. It is famous for the Stone of Destiny on which Scottish kings were crowned, which was originally located there. The stone was moved to Westminster Abbey, London, England, by Edward I in 1296 then returned to Edinburgh Castle in 1996. Population: 4,533 (1991).

scoop /skoop/ *n* **1.** UTENSIL RESEMBLING A TROWEL a utensil with a short handle and deep rounded sides, used for shoveling or ladling grain, flour, or other dry or semisolid substances **2.** LADLE FOR SERVING LIQUIDS a utensil with a long handle and round bowl, used for transferring liquids **3.** UTENSIL WITH A BOWL-SHAPED HEAD a utensil with a long handle and a small hemispherical bowl, used for serving such things as ice cream and mashed potatoes or making melon balls **4.** DIGGING PART the part of a dredge or digging machine that is used for excavating **5.** QUANTITY LIFTED BY SCOOP the quantity that is taken by a scoop ○ *three scoops of ice cream* **6.** DIGGING MOTION a curving digging movement made with a scoop or the hand **7.** CAVITY a shallow cavity, hole, or other hollow area in something **8.** AUTOMOT OPENING TO TAKE IN A SUBSTANCE an opening that allows a substance to flow or be sucked inside, e.g., an air intake on the hood of a hot rod **9.** ACT OF SLIDING TO PITCH in vocal and instrumental music, a sliding up to a pitch **10.** EXCLUSIVE a news story that is published by a newspaper, magazine, or news program before its rivals (*informal*) ○ *the scoop of the year* **11.** QUICK PROFIT a large amount of money made quickly (*informal*) **12.** NEWS the latest news or gossip (*informal*) ○ *What's the scoop?* ■ *v* (**scooped, scoop·ing, scoops**) **1.** *vt* HOLLOW SOMETHING OUT to create a shallow hole in something with a scoop or similar object, or a cupped hand ○ *He scooped out a hole in the ground.* **2.** *vt* REMOVE SOMETHING to remove an amount of a liquid or solid substance with a scoop or similar object, or a cupped hand ○ *scooping up water with a ladle* **3.** *vt* LIFT SOMEBODY OR SOMETHING SWIFTLY to pick somebody or something up swiftly and without ceremony ○ *She scooped the tiny puppy up in her arms.* **4.** *vti* HIT BALL UPWARD to hit a ball upward from underneath so that it rises into the air **5.** *vt* PUBLISH OR BROADCAST SOMETHING FIRST to publish or broadcast an item of news before any other newspaper, magazine, or news program (*informal*) ○ *The newspaper scooped its rivals for the second time in a week.* ○ *scooping the hottest story of* *the year* **6.** *vt* GET A GREAT DEAL OF MONEY to win or otherwise obtain a large amount of money (*informal*) ○ *scoop the jackpot* [14C. < Middle Low German, Middle Dutch *schōpe* "bucket for bailing, bucket of a water wheel"] —**scoop·er** *n*

scoop neck *n* a low curved neckline on an article of women's clothing

scoot /skoot/ (*informal*) *v* (**scoot·ed, scoot·ing, scoots**) **1.** *vi* LEAVE FAST to go away quickly (*often used as a command*) **2.** *vi* MOVE QUICKLY to move, run, or go somewhere quickly **3.** *vt* SEND QUICKLY to move or send something quickly ○ *Scoot that file to me as soon as you can.* ■ *n* SWIFT MOVEMENT a swift movement or trip ○ *a quick scoot to the supermarket* [Mid-18C. Origin ?]

scoot·er /skóotər/ *n* **1.** a child's toy consisting of handlebars attached by a long rod to a footboard on two wheels. One foot is placed on the board and the other pushes against the ground to propel the scooter along. **2.** AUTOMOT same as **motor scooter 3.** *US* a sailboat that can be used on water or ice

scop /skop/ *n* a bard or poet in Anglo-Saxon England [Old English *sc(e)op* < Germanic]

scope[1] /skōp/ *n* **1.** ROOM TO ACT freedom, space, or capacity to act ○ *not much scope for originality* **2.** RANGE COVERED the range covered by an activity, subject, or topic ○ *a question that is beyond the scope of this lecture* **3.** MENTAL CAPACITY the extent of somebody's mental capacity **4.** NAUT MOORING CABLE the length of a ship's mooring cable **5.** LOGIC RANGE OF LOGICAL OPERATOR the range of application or boundaries of a logical operator, usually indicated by parentheses. The scope of "and" in "(p and q) or r" is limited to "p" and "q." ■ *vt* (**scoped, scop·ing, scopes**) LOOK AT SOMETHING to look at or examine something (*slang*) ○ *Let's send the biopsy to the lab to be scoped.* [Mid-16C. Via Italian *scopo* "aim, purpose" < Greek *skopos* "target"] ◇ **scope out** to investigate or study something (*informal*)

scope[2] /skōp/ *n* an optical device or tool for viewing something (*informal*) ○ *a hunting rifle with a high-powered scope* [Early 17C. < -SCOPE]

-scope *suffix* an instrument for viewing or observing ○ *nephroscope* ○ *periscope* [< modern Latin *-scopium* < Greek *skopein* "look, see" < Indo-European] —**-scopic** *suffix* —**-scopy** *suffix*

Scopes /skōps/, **John T.** (1900–70) US teacher and subject of a controversial court case. He was prosecuted (1925) for violating a Tennessee law that forbade the teaching of the theory of evolution in public schools because it contradicted the account of creation in the Bible. Full name **Scopes, John Thomas**

sco·pol·a·mine /skə póllə meen, -mən/ *n* a colorless thick liquid poisonous alkaloid found in some plants of the nightshade family and used as a truth serum, to prevent motion sickness, and as a sedative. Formula: $C_{17}H_{21}NO_4$. [Late 19C. < modern Latin *Scopolia japonica*, the Japanese belladonna, after G. A. Scopoli (1723–88), Italian naturalist]

scop·u·la /skóppyələ/ (*plural* **-las** or **-lae** /-lee/) *n* a tuft of dense hairs on the back of the legs of some insects or spiders [Early 19C. < late Latin, "little broom"]

scor·bu·tic /skawr byóotik/, **scor·bu·ti·cal** /-byóotik'l/ *adj* relating to, affected with, or causing scurvy [Mid-17C. < modern Latin *scorbuticus* < medieval Latin *scorbutus* "scurvy"] —**scor·bu·ti·cal·ly** *adv*

scorch /skawrch/ *v* (**scorched, scorch·ing, scorch·es**) **1.** *vti* BURN SURFACE to burn the surface of something, or be burned so as to cause pain, injury, or discoloring ○ *scorched the handkerchief with the iron* **2.** *vti* DRY OUT to dry or parch something with intense heat, or become dried out or parched because of intense heat ○ *The plains had been scorched by the Sun.* **3.** *vt* CRITICIZE SOMEBODY to subject somebody to severe criticism (*informal*) ■ *n* **1.** SURFACE BURN a burn, or burn mark on the surface of something ○ *The iron left a slight scorch on the blouse.* **2.** DISCOLORATION ON PLANTS a brown marking on plants or vegetables caused by disease, insecticide, or heat [12C. Probably < N Germanic]

scorched /skawrcht/ *adj* dried out or parched from the intense heat of the Sun

scorched-earth pol·i·cy *n* **1.** a policy of destroying crops or buildings, especially by burning, or of removing anything that might be useful to an advancing enemy in wartime **2.** a strategy adopted by a company facing a hostile takeover whereby it makes itself appear a financially less attractive acquisition until the threat has gone

scorch·er /skáwrchər/ *n* **1.** SOMETHING THAT BURNS somebody or something that scorches **2.** HOT DAY an extremely hot day (*informal*) ○ *Yesterday was fairly warm but today is a scorcher!* **3.** CRITICAL REMARK a severely critical remark (*informal*)

scorch·ing /skáwrching/ *adj* extremely hot (*informal*)

score /skawr/ *n* **1.** POINTS MADE the total number of points made by a player or team at the end of or during a match or game **2.** TALLY OF POINTS MADE a record of the number of points made by a player or team in a match or game ○ *Who's keeping score?* **3.** GAINING OF POINT an action that leads to the gaining of a point or points in a match or game **4.** EXAM RESULT the result of a test or examination, usually presented in numerical form **5.** (*plural same* or **scores**) GROUP OF 20 a group of twenty things or people (*often used in combination*) ○ *A score or more people showed up.* **6.** PRINTED MUSIC a written or printed copy of a musical composition ○ *distributed copies of the score to the chorus* **7.** MUSIC COMPOSED the music that has been composed for a movie, play, or musical ○ *a movie with a breathtaking score* **8.** COPY OF CHOREOGRAPHIC NOTATION a written record of the choreography for a dance or ballet **9.** NOTCH CUT ONTO SURFACE a notch or incision cut into the surface of something **10.** PARTIAL CUT a crease or superficial cut made in something such as a piece of paper to enable it to be folded or separated easily **11.** RECORD OF MONEY OWED a record of an amount of money due for payment **12.** MONEY OWED an amount of money due for payment **13.** FESTERING GRUDGE a grievance that is not resolved and incurs resentment ○ *settling old scores* **14.** PRESENT SITUATION the present state or actual facts of a situation (*informal*) ○ *What's the score? Are you coming or not?* **15.** SUCCESS a successful result or achievement, especially one that is significant (*slang*) ○ *made a big score on the stock market* **16.** DRUG DEAL a purchase of illegal drugs (*slang*) **17.** ROBBERY the successful theft of something (*slang*) **18.** SEXUAL CONQUEST a successful seduction of somebody or the sexual encounter itself (*slang*) **19.** NAUT GROOVE FOR ROPE a groove cut in wood to hold a rope ■ **scores** *npl* MANY a great many ○ *Scores of members protested at the decision.* ■ *v* (**scored, scor·ing, scores**) **1.** *vti* MAKE POINTS to make a point or points in a match or game ○ *scored twice in the second half* **2.** *vt* AMASS POINTS TOTAL to make a particular number of points in total during a match, game, or other competition **3.** *vti* RECORD POINTS to keep a record of the number of points made in a match, game, or other competition ○ *Who's scoring?* **4.** *vt* ASSIGN SOMEBODY POINTS to award a particular number of points to somebody in a match, game, or other competition ○ *Three of the judges scored the skater perfect 6.0s.* **5.** *vt* BE WORTH POINTS IN A GAME to count for a particular number of points in a match, game, or other competition ○ *Hitting the red area scores ten.* **6.** *vt US* EDUC EXAM GRADE to grade or evaluate a test or examination **7.** *vti* GET POINTS IN EXAM to achieve a particular number of points in a test or examination **8.** *vt* CUT LINES IN SOMETHING to make notches, cuts, or lines in a surface **9.** *vt* CUT SOMETHING SUPERFICIALLY TO SEPARATE IT to make a superficial cut or crease in something such as a piece of paper in order to fold, tear, or break it easily **10.** *vt* WRITE SOMETHING BY MAKING INCISIONS to write something by means of notches, incisions, or lines cut into a surface ○ *names scored on the back of the bench with a pocketknife* **11.** *vti* CROSS SOMETHING OUT to draw a line through something in order to mark it as canceled or deleted **12.** *vt* RECORD MONEY OWED to keep a record of an amount of money owed by somebody by making a series of marks next to his or her name **13.** *vt* ORCHESTRATE SOMETHING to orchestrate or arrange a piece of music **14.** *vt* COMPOSE THE MUSIC FOR SOMETHING to write the music for a movie, play, or musical **15.** *vt* WRITE THE CHOREOGRAPHY FOR SOMETHING to write out the choreography for a dance or ballet **16.** *vi* DO WELL to secure an advantage (*slang*) ○ *She scores because she can communicate.* **17.** *vt* GET SOMETHING to succeed in getting something (*slang*) ○ *scored front-row tickets for the concert* **18.** *vti* DRUGS BUY DRUGS to buy illegal drugs (*slang*) **19.** *vi* HAVE SEX to succeed in having sex with somebody, especially a new sexual partner (*slang*) **20.** *vt* CRITICIZE SOMEBODY to subject somebody to severe criticism (*informal*) [Pre-12C. < Old Norse *skor* "notch, tally, 20"] ◇ **on this** *or* **that score** as far as this or that is concerned ○ *Her health is fine, so there's no need to worry on that score.*

score·board /skáwr bàwrd/ *n* a board at a sporting venue on which the score of a game, match, or other competition in progress is displayed

score·card /skáwr kaàrd/ *n* **1.** a small card used by a player to keep a record of his or her own score, e.g., in golf **2.** a card listing the players in a game or match that enables a spectator to identify who is who and to keep a record of the progress of play

score·keep·er /skáwr keepər/ *n* somebody who keeps a record of the score in a game, match, or other competition —**score·keep·ing** *n*

score·less /skáwrləss/ *adj* having no points scored ○ *The game remained scoreless at the half.*

scor·er /skáwrər/ *n* **1.** SOMEBODY SCORING POINT somebody who scores a point or points in a game or match **2.** SPORTS, LEISURE same as **scorekeeper 3.** *US* EDUC SOMEBODY SCORING POINTS IN AN EXAM a student who gets a particular score in a test or examination ○ *a consistently high scorer in math* **4.** CUTTING DEVICE a device for cutting a notch or incision into something

Scores·by Sound /skàwrzbee-/ arm of the Norwegian Sea touching eastern Greenland. It is the largest fjord in the world. Length: 280 mi./451 km.

sco·ri·a /skáwree ə/ *n* **1.** loose rubbly porous solidified lava that is ejected from a volcano and builds up around the crater **2.** METALL same as **slag** *n* (sense 1) [14C. Via Latin < Greek *skōria* "refuse, dross" < *skōr* "dung"] —**sco·ri·a·ceous** /skàwree áyshəss/ *adj*

sco·ri·fy /skáwrə fī/ (**-fied, -fy·ing, -fies**) *vt* to purify ore by separating it out into metal and slag —**sco·ri·fi·ca·tion** /skàwrəfi káysh'n/ *n* —**sco·ri·fi·er** *n*

scorn /skawrn/ *n* **1.** DISDAIN a strong feeling of contempt ○ *poured scorn on my attempts at writing* **2.** OBJECT OF CONTEMPT somebody or something that is held in contempt ○ *Their behavior made them the scorn of the entire community.* ■ *v* (**scorned, scorn·ing, scorns**) **1.** *vt* DISDAIN SOMEBODY OR SOMETHING to hold somebody or something in contempt **2.** *vti* REJECT SOMETHING CONTEMPTUOUSLY to reject something with contempt ○ *They had scorned our attempts at peace.* [12C. < Old French *escarn* < *escharnir* "mock, despise" < Germanic] —**scorn·er** *n*

scorn·ful /skáwrnfəl/ *adj* feeling or expressing great contempt for somebody or something —**scorn·ful·ly** *adv* —**scorn·ful·ness** *n*

Scor·pi·o /skáwrpee ō/ *n* **1.** ASTRON same as **Scorpius 2.** the eighth sign of the zodiac, represented by a scorpion and lasting from approximately October 23 to November 21. Scorpio is classified as a water sign and its ruling planets are Mars and Pluto. **3.** somebody whose birthday falls between October 23 and November 21 [14C. < Latin (see SCORPION)] —**Scor·pi·an** *n* —**Scor·pi·o** *adj*

scor·pi·oid /skáwrpee òyd/ *adj* **1.** relating to or resembling a scorpion **2.** having the main stem curled at the end ○ *a scorpioid inflorescence* [Mid-19C. < Greek *skorpioeidēs* < *skorpios* "scorpion"]

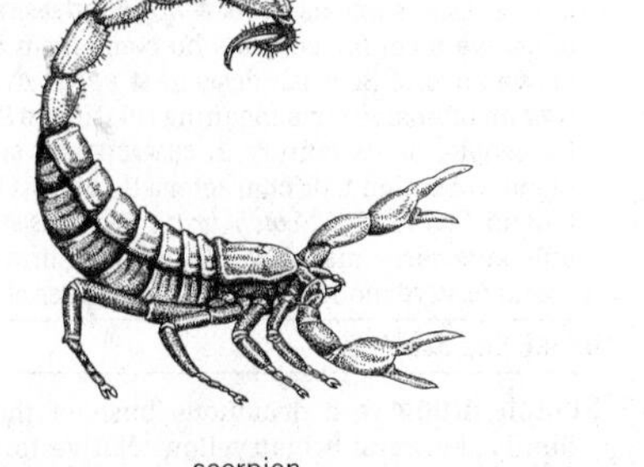

scorpion

scor·pi·on /skáwrpee ən/ *n* a nocturnal arachnid of warm dry regions that has a long body with pincers in front and a thin segmented upturned tail tipped with a venomous sting. Order: Scorpionida. [12C.

Via French < Latin *scorpion-*, stem of *scorpio*, alteration of *scorpius* < Greek *skorpios* "scorpion, scorpion fish"]

Scor·pi·on *n* **1.** ASTRON same as **Scorpius 2.** ZODIAC same as **Scorpio** (sense 2)

scor·pi·on fish *n* a small brightly colored fish with venomous spines in its fins. Family: Scorpaenidae.

scor·pi·on fly *n* a nonvenomous insect that has downward-pointing mouthparts and a reproductive organ in the male resembling the sting of a scorpion. Order: Mecoptera.

scor·pi·on grass *n* PLANTS same as **forget-me-not**

Scor·pi·us /skáwrpee əss/ *n* a zodiacal constellation of the southern hemisphere. See illustration at **constellation** [15C. < Latin *scorpius* (see SCORPION)]

Scor·se·se /skawr sáyssee, -sézzee/, **Martin** (*b.* 1942) US movie director. His movies, including *Taxi Driver* (1976) and *Goodfellas* (1990), often depict urban violence.

> "I don't think there is any difference between fantasy and reality in the way these should be approached in a film. Of course if you live that way you are clinically insane."
> [Martin Scorsese, "Mean Streets—Alice Doesn't Live Here Anymore—Taxi Driver," *Scorsese on Scorsese*; 1989]

scot /skot/ *n* money assessed or paid for something, e.g., as a tax or fine (*archaic*) [Pre-12C. Partly < Old Norse *skot* "shot," partly < Old French *escot* < Germanic]

Scot /skot/ *n* **1.** ⚠ somebody who comes from Scotland or who has Scottish ancestry **2.** a member of a people who lived in Ireland and who settled in northern Britain during the 6th century [Pre-12C. < late Latin *Scottus*]

USAGE Scot, Scotch, Scots, or **Scottish**? All these words make a direct connection to Scotland, but they are used in different ways. ***Scottish*** is the most generally used adjective to describe the country and people of Scotland (*Scottish history; a Scottish poet; Scottish Gaelic; a Scottish accent*), whereas ***Scots*** is particularly applied to people from the Lowlands or to a language related to English spoken there (*the Scots Guards; a Scots speaker*). A ***Scot*** is a person who comes from Scotland or who has Scottish ancestry; more specific words are *Scotsman* and *Scotswoman*. ***Scotch*** as an adjective is a literary word more closely associated with the writings of Robert Burns and Sir Walter Scott and has fallen out of general use, usually being considered offensive except in fixed expressions such as *Scotch-Irish, Scotch pine,* and *Scotch mist.*

Scot. *abbr* **1.** Scotch **2.** Scotland **3.** Scottish

scotch[1] /skoch/ *vt* (**scotched, scotch·ing, scotch·es**) **1.** STOP SOMETHING to put a stop to something such as an idea, plan, or rumor **2.** DISABLE SOMEBODY to disable somebody by wounding (*archaic*) **3.** GASH SOMETHING to make a gash or score in something (*archaic*) ■ *n* (*archaic*) **1.** CUT OR SCORE a cut or score in something **2.** LINE a line drawn on the ground, especially one used to mark out a grid for hopscotch [15C. Origin ?]

scotch[2] /skoch/ *n* a wedge used to prevent something from moving ■ *vt* (**scotched, scotch·ing, scotch·es**) to wedge something in order to prevent it from moving [Early 17C. Origin ?]

Scotch /skoch/ *n* **1.** WHISKEY whiskey produced in Scotland **2.** LANG same as **Scots** ■ *npl* ⚠ OFFENSIVE TERM an offensive term for people who come from Scotland or who are of Scottish descent ■ *adj* **1.** ⚠ OFFENSIVE TERM an offensive term meaning relating to Scotland, its people, or its culture **2.** CHARACTERISTIC OF SCOTLAND made in Scotland, or characteristic of a style prevalent in Scotland ○ *Scotch broth* **3.** OFFENSIVE TERM an offensive term meaning regarded as unwilling to spend or give money [Late 16C. Contraction of SCOTTISH]

USAGE See ***Scot.***

Scotch broom *n* a deciduous bush of the broom family. Flowers: bright yellow. Native to: western Europe. Latin name: *Cytisus scoparius.*

Scotch catch *n* MUSIC same as **Scotch snap**

Scotch egg *n* a hard-boiled egg wrapped in sausage meat, coated with breadcrumbs, and deep fried. It is served cut in half, either hot or cold.

Scotch-I·rish, Scots-I·rish *npl* Irish people of Scottish descent or US citizens descended from these people —**Scotch-I·rish** *adj*

Scotch·man /skóchmən/ (*plural* **-men** /-mən/) *n* an offensive term for a Scotsman (*archaic*)

Scotch mist *n* **1.** a fine, damp mist **2.** a figment of somebody's imagination (*humorous*)

Scotch pine *n* **1.** a pine with a reddish trunk, twisted needles, and yellowish wood. Native to: Europe, Asia. Latin name: *Pinus sylvestris.* **2.** the wood of the Scotch pine, valuable as timber

Scotch snap *n* in music, a rhythmic figure consisting of a dotted note preceded by a note the value of the dot

Scotch tape *tdmk* a trademark for a type of transparent adhesive tape

Scotch ter·ri·er *n* BREED same as **Scottish terrier**

Scotch ver·dict *n US* **1.** a verdict of "not proven" in a case in which there is insufficient evidence to prove the defendant's guilt **2.** a judgment or statement that is inconclusive

Scotch whis·key *n* BEVERAGES same as **Scotch** *n* (sense 1)

Scotch·wom·an /skóch wŏŏmən/ (*plural* **-wom·en** /-wìmmin/) *n* an offensive term for a Scotswoman (*archaic*)

Scotch wood·cock *n* a snack or light meal of toast spread with an anchovy paste and topped with scrambled eggs [Fanciful]

sco·ter /skṓtər/ (*plural* **-ters** or *same*) *n* a large sea duck, the male of which has black feathers with white spots on its head. Native to: northern coasts of North America, southern Asia, and Europe. Genus: *Melanitta.* [Late 17C. Origin ?]

scot-free *adv* without punishment being exacted or payment being made

sco·tia /skṓshə/ *n* a deep concave molding, especially on the base of a column [Mid-16C. Via Latin < Greek *skotia* < *skotos* "darkness" (from the shadow inside the molding)]

Sco·tia /skṓshə/ *n* a former name for Scotland, still sometimes used in literary contexts (*archaic or literary*) [Early 17C. < medieval Latin] —**Sco·tian** *adj*

Sco·tism /skṓ tìzzəm/ *n* the philosophical tenets of, or school of scholastic philosophy founded by, the 13th-century Scottish philosopher and theologian Duns Scotus —**Sco·tist** *adj* —**Sco·tis·tic** /skə tístik/ *adj*

Scot·land /skóttlənd/ country forming the northernmost part of Great Britain and of the United Kingdom. It became united with England by the Act of Union in 1707, though the crowns had been united since 1603. Following a referendum in 199, a separate Scottish Parliament was established in 1999 giving the country a limited degree of self-government. Capital: Edinburgh. Population: 5,062,011 (2001). Area: 30,420 sq. mi./78,790 sq. km.

Scot·land Yard *n* the headquarters of the Metropolitan Police in London, from which national criminal investigations are coordinated. The headquarters moved to new premises in 1890 and 1967 and is officially known as New Scotland Yard. [Because originally located in *Great Scotland Yard,* where the palace used by visiting kings of Scotland once stood]

sco·to·ma /skə tṓmə/ (*plural* **-mas** or **-ma·ta** /-mətə/) *n* a permanent or temporary area of diminished sight in the field of vision [Mid-16C. Via late Latin < Greek *skotōma* "dizziness" < *skotos* "darkness"] —**sco·to·ma·tous** *adj*

sco·to·pi·a /skə tṓpee ə, skō-/ *n* the ability to see in poor light or in the dark [Early 20C. < Greek *skotos* "darkness"] —**sco·to·pic** /-tóppik/ *adj*

Scots /skots/ *adj* **1.** OF SCOTLAND relating to Scotland, especially the Lowlands **2.** OF LANGUAGE OF SCOTS relating to the Germanic language, closely related to English, spoken in parts of Scotland, especially the Lowlands ■ *n* LANGUAGE OF SCOTS a Germanic language closely related to English, spoken in parts of Scotland, especially the Lowlands. See panel on next page [14C. Contraction of SCOTTISH]

Scots Gael·ic *n* LANG same as **Scottish Gaelic**

USAGE See ***Scot.***

Scots·man /skótsmən/ (*plural* **-men** /-mən/) *n* a man who comes from Scotland or who has Scottish ancestry

USAGE See ***Scot.***

Scots pine *n UK* **1.** TREES same as **Scotch pine** (sense 1) **2.** FORESTRY same as **Scotch pine** (sense 2)

Scots·wom·an /skóts wŏŏmmən/ (*plural* **-wom·en** /-wìmmin/) *n* a woman who comes from Scotland or who has Scottish ancestry

USAGE See ***Scot.***

Scott /skot/, **Dred** (1795–1858) US slave. He sued for his freedom in 1846. The case came before the United States Supreme Court (1856–57) and was among the causes of the American Civil War.

Scott, George C. (1927–99) US actor. He specialized in tough-guy roles such as the title role in *Patton* (1970), for which he won an Academy Award, but refused to accept it. Full name **Scott, George Campbell**

Scott, Robert Falcon (1868–1912) British naval officer and explorer. On his second expedition to Antarctica (1910–12) he was beaten to the South Pole by Roald Amundsen. He died on the return journey. Known as **Scott of the Antarctic**

Sir Walter Scott

Scott, Sir Walter (1771–1832) Scottish novelist and poet. His ballads and historical novels, which mainly dealt with Scottish subjects, made him one of the most popular writers of his day and did much to establish widespread European interest in Scottish history and culture. See Cultural note at **heart**

> "O Caledonia! stern and wild, / Meet nurse for a poetic child! / Land of brown heath and shaggy wood, / Land of the mountain and the flood, / Land of my sires! what mortal hand / Can e'er untie the filial band / That knits me to thy rugged strand!"
> [Sir Walter Scott, *The Lay of the Last Minstrel*; 1805]

> "O what a tangled web we weave, / When first we practice to deceive!"
> [Sir Walter Scott, *Marmion*; 1808]

Scott, Winfield (1786–1866) US general. A veteran of the War of 1812, he conducted a masterful campaign in the Mexican War (1846–48). He unsuccessfully ran for US president (1852). Known as **Old Fuss and Feathers**

> "Say to the seceded states: 'Wayward sisters, depart in peace!'"
> [Winfield Scott, *Letter to William Henry Seward*; March 3, 1861]

Scot·ti·cism /skótti sìzzəm/ *n* a word, phrase, or idiom that is characteristic of the Scots language or the English spoken in Scotland

Scot·tie /skóttee/, **Scot·ty** (*plural* **-ties**) *n* (*informal*) **1.** BREED same as **Scottish terrier 2.** an offensive term for somebody, especially a man, who is Scottish

Scot·tish /skóttish/ *adj* relating to Scotland or its people or culture ■ *n* LANG same as **Scots** ■ *npl* people who come from Scotland [12C. < SCOT] —**Scot·tish·ness** *n*

WORLD ENGLISH ***Scots*** is the Germanic speech of the Scottish Lowlands, in contrast to Gaelic, the traditional Celtic speech of the Highlands. It is regarded by some as a dialect of English, by others as a distinct language. Many scholars regard Scots of the period before the Union of the Crowns (1603) as a language in its own right and after that date as a more limited vernacular. It is, however, listed alongside languages such as Basque, Catalan, and Gaelic by the European Bureau of Lesser Used Languages (an institution of the European Union). Scots has its own dialects, from the Borders (linked with the dialects of northern England) to Orkney and Shetland (mixed with elements of Old Norse). Its literature includes two medieval epic poems, copious 16th-century verse, the works of Robert Burns, and more recent poetry and fiction.

Though there has been a massive mixing with English for over 200 years, its major characteristics remain clear-cut, including (1) the pronunciation of *r* as a trill in words such as *art, door,* and *worker*; (2) the use of the \kh\ sound (as in German *machen*) in words such as *nicht* "night," *sicht* "sight," *ach* "ah," and *och* "oh"; (3) verbs like *tell* and *sell* have distinctive past forms (*tellt* and *sellt* for *told* and *sold*); (4) some "double modal" verbs, as in *Ah micht could dae it* ("I might could do it"), are used to mean "I could probably do it"; (5) the vocabulary is large and distinctive: e.g., *tae blether* "to talk nonsense," *a blether* "someone who talks nonsense," *tae dicht* "to wipe clean," *tae ken* "to know," *tae loup* "to leap," *a loup* "a leap," *an ashet* "a serving dish" (from French *assiette*), *a dwam* "a hazy mental condition," *a howf(f)* "a favorite spot, a pub," *glaikit* "stupid-looking," *fantoosh* "flashy," and *tapselteerie* "topsy-turvy."

WORLD ENGLISH ***Scottish English*** is the variety of English used in Scotland, considered by some to include traditional (Lowland) Scots, and by others to be distinct from it, despite overlap. A compromise with the English of England began to emerge after the Act of Union in 1707, when many among the upper and middle classes began to take on the pronunciation, grammar, and vocabulary of so-called refined London. The Scottish aristocracy became socially and linguistically indistinguishable from their peers in England, while the middle class developed a shaky compromise.

USAGE See *Scot.*

Scot·tish deer·hound *n* ZOOL same as **deerhound**

Scot·tish Eng·lish *n* a variety of English spoken in Scotland

Scot·tish Ex·e·cu·tive *n* the devolved government of Scotland. See panel on next page

Scot·tish Gael·ic *n* the Celtic language spoken in parts of the Highlands and Western Isles of Scotland

Scot·tish-I·rish *npl UK* same as **Scotch-Irish** —**Scot·tish-I·rish** *adj*

Scot·tish rite *n US* a Masonic rite

Scottish terrier

Scot·tish ter·ri·er *n* a terrier belonging to a breed with short sturdy legs, pointed ears, and thick, wiry, usually black hair

Scotts·bor·o /skóts bərō/ city in northeastern Alabama, on the western bank of the Tennessee River, southeast of Huntsville. Population: 14,811 (2002 estimate).

Scotts·dale /skóts dàyl/ city in southern Arizona, on the Salt River, east of Phoenix. Population: 215,779 (2002 estimate).

scoun·drel /skówndrəl/ *n* a dishonorable or unprincipled person [Late 16C. Origin ?] —**scoun·drel·ly** *adj*

scour[1] /skowr/ *v* (**scoured, scour·ing, scours**) **1.** *vti* **CLEAN SOMETHING BY RUBBING** to clean or brighten something by rubbing it with an abrasive substance or material **2.** *vti* **REMOVE SOMETHING BY RUBBING** to remove something by rubbing with an abrasive substance or material **3.** *vt* **FREE SOMETHING FROM DIRT** to remove dirt or impurities from something by washing **4.** *vt* **FLUSH SOMETHING OUT** to clear something out by passing water through it **5.** *vi* VET **HAVE DIARRHEA** to be affected by diarrhea (*refers to cattle*) ■ *n* **1. SCOURING** a scouring of something **2. CLEANING SUBSTANCE** a substance or tool that can be used for scouring **3. PLACE SCOURED** a place that has been scoured, especially by water **4.** VET same as **scours** [12C. Via Middle Low German, Middle Dutch *schūren* < late Latin *excurare* "clean out, take care of" < Latin *cura* "care"] —**scour·er** *n*

scour[2] /skowr/ (**scoured, scour·ing, scours**) *vti* **1.** to search something thoroughly and quickly for somebody or something ○ *They scoured the countryside for him, but to no avail.* **2.** to move quickly over or through an area [15C. Probably < N Germanic] —**scour·er** *n*

scourge /skurj/ *n* **1. TORMENTOR** somebody or something that is perceived as an agent of punishment, destruction, or severe criticism ○ *the scourge of my childhood* **2. WHIP** a whip that is used for inflicting punishment ■ *vt* (**scourged, scourg·ing, scourg·es**) **1. PUNISH SOMEBODY** to punish or criticize somebody severely **2. WHIP SOMEBODY** to whip somebody severely [12C. < Old French *escorgier* "to whip" < Latin *corrigia* "thong, whip"] —**scourg·er** *n*

scour·ing rush /skówring-/ *n* a horsetail with a rough stem. Use: formerly, scouring. Genus: *Equisetum.*

scour·ings /skówringz/ *npl* the material removed or left after scouring something, especially that left after scouring grain

scours /skowrz/ *n* diarrhea affecting cattle and pigs (*takes a singular or plural verb*)

scouse /skowss/ *n UK regional* a stew made from leftover meat with potatoes and vegetables [Mid-19C. Shortening of LOBSCOUSE]

Scouse /skowss/ *UK* (*informal*) *n* the dialect spoken in Liverpool, England ■ *adj* relating to Liverpool, England, its people, or its dialect [Mid-20C. < SCOUSE]

scout /skowt/ *n* **1. SOLDIER SENT TO GATHER INFORMATION** somebody, especially a soldier, who is sent to gather information about an enemy's position or movements **2.** SPORTS, ARTS same as **talent scout** **3.** *US* **SOMEBODY SENT TO EVALUATE OPPOSING TEAM** somebody sent to discover and evaluate the performance, tactics, and players of an opposing team **4. RECONNAISSANCE CRAFT OR VEHICLE** a ship, aircraft, or vehicle designed and used by the armed forces for reconnaissance purposes **5. SEARCH** a search for somebody or something ○ *have a scout around for the missing keys* **6. RECONNOITERING** a gathering of information concerning an enemy's position or movements **7. PERSON** a person, usually a boy or man (*dated informal*) ○ *Be a good scout and give me a hand here.* ■ *v* (**scout·ed, scout·ing, scouts**) **1.** *vti* **SEARCH AREA** to make a search of an area for somebody or something ○ *scouting around for a place to camp* **2.** *vi* **GATHER INFORMATION** to seek out information about somebody or something, especially about an enemy's position or movements **3.** *vti* SPORTS, ARTS **SEEK OUT NEW TALENT** to look for talented players for a sports team, or talented performers for a show or group **4.** *vt* **EVALUATE OPPOSING TEAM** to discover and evaluate the performance, tactics, and players of an opposing team [14C. < Old French *escouter* "to listen" < Latin *auscultare*] —**scout·er** *n*

Scout *n* a member of the Boy Scouts or Girl Scouts

Scout·ing /skówting/ *n* the activities of the Boy Scouts or Girl Scouts

scout·mas·ter /skówt màstər/ *n* a man who is in charge of a troop of Boy Scouts

scow /skow/ *n* **1.** a barge for transporting freight **2.** a flat-bottomed sailboat [Mid-17C. < Dutch *schouw*]

scowl /skowl/ *n* **FROWN** an expression of anger, displeasure, or menace made by drawing the eyebrows together toward the middle of the forehead ■ *v* (**scowled, scowl·ing, scowls**) **1.** *vi* **FORM FROWN** to draw the eyebrows together toward the middle of the forehead in an expression of anger, displeasure, or menace **2.** *vt* **REVEAL NEGATIVE FEELING** to give expression to an emotion by means of a scowl [14C. Probably < N Germanic] —**scowl·er** *n*

SCPO *abbr* NAVY Senior Chief Petty Officer

scrab·ble /skrább'l/ *v* (**-bled, -bling, -bles**) **1.** *vi* **SCRATCH AT SOMETHING** to scrape or scratch at something with small, hurried movements of the fingers, toes, or claws ○ *The cat was scrabbling at the door.* **2.** *vi* **FEEL WITH FINGERS** to grope around frantically in an effort to find something ○ *She scrabbled around trying to find the flashlight.* **3.** *vi* **CLIMB OVER SOMETHING** to climb hastily or clumsily up or over something **4.** *vi* **STRUGGLE TO GET SOMETHING** to struggle desperately to get something ○ *scrabbling for enough money to make ends meet* **5.** *vt* **PRODUCE SOMETHING WITH DIFFICULTY** to produce something hastily and with difficulty from scarce resources ○ *scrabble together a meal* **6.** *vti* **SCRIBBLE** to scribble something ■ *n* **1. ACT OF SCRATCHING** a scraping or scratching at something with short hurried movements of the fingers, toes, or claws **2. A SEARCH WITH FINGERS** a frantic groping around in an effort to find something **3. HASTY CLIMB** a climb up or over something, performed hastily or clumsily **4. DESPERATE STRUGGLE** a desperate struggle to acquire or gain something **5. SCRIBBLING** a scribbling of something **6. SOMETHING SCRIBBLED** something that somebody has scribbled [Mid-16C. < Middle Dutch *schrabbelen* "scratch repeatedly" < *schrabben* "scratch, scrape"] —**scrab·bler** *n*

scrab·bly /skrábblee/ (**-bli·er, -bli·est**) *adj* **1.** characterized by a scratching sound **2.** *US* thinly covered with vegetation

scrag /skrag/ *n* **1. THIN PERSON OR ANIMAL** an unattractively thin person or animal **2. BONY CUT OF MUTTON** the bony neck joint, especially of mutton, usually cut up and used in soups and stews **3. NECK** somebody's neck (*informal*) ■ *vt* (**scragged, scrag·ging, scrags**) **STRANGLE SOMEBODY** to throttle or strangle somebody (*informal*) [Mid-16C. Probably < dialect *crag* "neck" < Middle Dutch *crāghe* "throat"]

scrag·gly /skrágglee/ (**-gli·er, -gli·est**) *adj* messy and uneven in appearance or shape [Mid-19C. < SCRAG] —**scrag·gli·ness** *n*

scrag·gy /skrággee/ (**-gi·er, -gi·est**) *adj* **1.** *US* having sharp points or edges **2.** bony and thin ○ *a scraggy little cat* —**scrag·gi·ly** *adv* —**scrag·gi·ness** *n*

SYNONYMS See *thin.*

scram /skram/ *v* (**scrammed, scram·ming, scrams**) **1.** *vi* **LEAVE QUICKLY** to get out or leave quickly (*informal; often used as a command*) **2.** *vti* INDUST **SHUT DOWN NUCLEAR REACTOR** to shut down a nuclear reactor rapidly in an emergency, or be shut down rapidly ■ *n* INDUST **REACTOR SHUTDOWN** a rapid shutdown of a nuclear reactor in an emergency [Early 20C. Origin ?]

scram·ble /skrámb'l/ *v* (**-bled, -bling, -bles**) **1.** *vi* **CLAMBER** to climb or advance over something using hands and feet ○ *We managed to scramble over the fence.* **2.** *vi* **HURRY** to move in haste and with a sense of urgency **3.** *vi* **COMPETE FRANTICALLY** to struggle or compete frantically in order to get something ○ *Everyone was scrambling for the best seats.* **4.** *vt* **JUMBLE THINGS TOGETHER** to mix or gather a number of things together haphazardly **5.** *vt* COOK **BEAT AND COOK EGGS** to beat eggs, usually with some milk, and cook while stirring in a pan until set **6.** *vi US* FOOTBALL **RUN WHEN UNABLE TO PASS** in football, to run with the ball after the pass protection breaks down, trying to avoid being tackled and pass the ball, or to gain yardage (*refers to a quarterback*) **7.** *vt* TELECOM **ENCODE TRANSMITTED SIGNALS** to render a telecommunications or broadcast signal unintelligible by means of an electronic device **8.** *vti* AIR FORCE **LAUNCH AIRCRAFT AGAINST ATTACK** to launch a large number of aircraft in a short space of time in response to an impending attack, or be launched in these circumstances ■ *n* **1. HARD CLIMB** a difficult climb or walk that involves using the hands as well as the feet but no ropes **2. DASH OR STRUGGLE** a hasty, undignified, or disorganized struggle for something or in order to do something **3. CONFUSED MASS** a jumbled mass of people or things **4.** MOTORCYCLES **MOTORCYCLE RACE** a motorcycle race over rough terrain **5.** AIR FORCE **LAUNCH OF AIRCRAFT** the scrambling of military aircraft [Late 16C. Probably to suggest the action]

scram·bled eggs *n* (*takes a singular or plural verb*) **1.** a dish made by beating eggs and often milk together and cooking them in a pan **2.** gold braid attached to the peak of the cap of a senior military officer (*slang*)

scram·bler /skrámblər/ *n* an electronic device that renders telecommunications or broadcast signals unintelligible without a special receiver

scram·jet /skrám jèt/ *n* a ramjet aircraft in which fuel is burned in air that is moving at supersonic speeds [Mid-20C. < initial letters of SUPERSONIC and COMBUSTION + RAMJET]

Scran·ton /skránt'n/ city in northeastern Pennsylvania. A mining town until the 1940s, it is now a manufacturing center. Population: 74,712 (2002 estimate).

scrap[1] /skrap/ *n* **1. FRAGMENT** a small piece or remnant that has been detached from or torn off a larger piece **2. WASTE MATERIAL** waste material, especially metal awaiting reprocessing **3. SMALL PIECE** a very small piece of something ○ *There's not a scrap of evidence to prove it.* **4. BIT OF WRITTEN OR PRINTED MATERIAL** a short piece of writing, or a cutting from something printed ■ **scraps** *npl* **1. LEFTOVERS** pieces of leftover food ○ *table scraps* **2.** *US* FOOD **CRACKLINGS** the crisp remains of animal fat after the oil has been rendered ■ *vt* (**scrapped, scrap·ping, scraps**) **1. GET RID OF SOMETHING** to discard or discontinue something because it is considered useless or ineffective **2. CONVERT SOMETHING TO SCRAP** to convert something into scrap material ○ *scrapping old warships* [14C. < Old Norse *skrap* "scraps, trifles"]

scrap[2] /skrap/ (*informal*) *n* a minor fight or disagreement ■ *vi* (**scrapped, scrap·ping, scraps**) to have a minor fight or disagreement with somebody [Late 17C. Origin ?]

scrap·book /skráp bòok/ *n* a blank book or album for pasting in photos, pictures, cuttings, or other material

scrape /skrayp/ *v* (**scraped, scrap·ing, scrapes**) **1.** *vti* **RUB SURFACE** to move something hard, sharp, or rough across a surface, especially in order to clean it ○ *scraping the wall to remove the paint* **2.** *vt* **TAKE SOMETHING OFF** to remove something by drawing or rubbing a hard or sharp edge over it ○ *My efforts to scrape the paint off failed.* ○ *scraped out the contents of the pot* **3.** *vt* **SCRATCH SOMETHING** to scratch, cut, or damage something by bringing it into contact with a rough or abrasive surface ○ *fell and scraped my knees* **4.** *vti* **MAKE GRATING NOISE** to make a harsh grating sound, or cause something to make such a sound ○ *scraping his chair along the floor* **5.** *vi* **SCRIMP** to live economically in an effort to save money ○ *scraping by on a single income* **6.** *vti* **BARELY DO SOMETHING** to barely manage to do or achieve something ○ *He just scraped through law school.* ■ *n* **1. SCRAPING** a scraping of something ○ *I'll give the paint a quick scrape.* **2. LIGHT SCRATCH** a light cut, graze, or area of damage caused by contact with a rough or abrasive surface **3. GRATING SOUND** a sharp grating sound ○ *the scrape of chairs on the bare floor* **4. DANGEROUS SITUATION** a dangerous, difficult, or awkward situation (*informal*) **5. MINOR FIGHT** a minor fight or disagreement (*informal*) [Old English *scrapian* "to scratch" < Germanic] —**scrap·er** *n*

scrape together, scrape up *vt* to manage with difficulty to collect together an amount of something, especially money, or a number of people or things

scrap·er·board /skráypər bàwrd/ *n* *UK* ART same as **scratchboard**

scrap·heap /skráp hèep/ *n* **1.** a large pile of unwanted or discarded items, especially those being used as scrap material **2.** an imagined place to which people and things regarded as worn out and useless are consigned (*informal*) ○ *workers who are relegated to the scrapheap at 50*

scra·pie /skráypee/ *n* a usually fatal disease affecting the nervous system of sheep and goats that is marked by intense itching and loss of muscular control. It is now thought to be one of the diseases caused by a prion, and is similar to bovine spongiform encephalopathy in cattle and Creutzfeldt-Jakob disease in humans. [Early 20C. < SCRAPE, because the animals rub against objects to alleviate itching]

scrap·per /skráppər/ *n* an enthusiastic, determined fighter, especially a boxer (*slang*) [Late 19C. < SCRAP[2]]

scrap·ple /skrápp'l/ *n* *US* pork trimmings cooked with cornmeal and seasonings, formed into a loaf, and cooled. It is sliced and fried before serving. [Mid-19C. < SCRAP[1]]

scrap·py[1] /skráppee/ (**-pi·er, -pi·est**) *adj* **1.** consisting of scraps or fragments **2.** poorly held together or structured —**scrap·pi·ly** *adv* —**scrap·pi·ness** *n*

scrap·py[2] /skráppee/ (**-pi·er, -pi·est**) *adj* (*informal*) **1.** plucky, determined, and willing to fight or argue **2.** *US* too ready to fight or quarrel —**scrap·pi·ly** *adv* —**scrap·pi·ness** *n*

scratch /skrach/ *v* (**scratched, scratch·ing, scratch·es**) **1.** *vt* **SCRAPE SURFACE** to make a slight mark on the surface of something with something sharp or rough ○ *He scratched the tabletop with the knife.* **2.** *vti* **TEAR SKIN** to make a thin tear in the surface of the skin of a person or animal ○ *The cat scratched me.* **3.** *vti* **RELIEVE ITCHING** to rub the skin with nails or claws, especially to relieve itching or discomfort **4.** *vti* **MAKE SCRAPING MOVEMENT** to rub or scrape a surface, e.g., with claws or a scraping instrument ○ *The cat was scratching at the door.* **5.** *vi* **MAKE HARSH NOISE** to make a scraping sound **6.** *vt* **DRAG SOMETHING ALONG SURFACE** to drag something along a rough surface so that the object is scraped **7.** *vti* **CAUSE ITCHING** to irritate the surface of the skin by being rough or prickly ○ *a wool sweater that scratches* **8.** *vt* **WRITE SOMETHING WITH SHARP INSTRUMENT** to write or draw something by marking a surface with a pointed or sharp instrument ○ *names scratched on the tree* **9.** *vti* **PEN QUICKLY** to write or draw something hastily **10.** *vt* **DELETE SOMETHING** to delete or erase something by scraping it off, crossing it out, or rendering it illegible **11.** *vt* **CANCEL SOMETHING** to cancel or abandon a project, plan, or proposal completely **12.** *vi* **SEARCH AIMLESSLY** to search for something in an unsystematic way by picking through things or looking on the ground ○ *scratching around for evidence* **13.** *vti* **JUST GET BY** to make a barely adequate living ○ *scratching out a living* **14.** *vti* MUSIC **PRODUCE SCRAPING SOUND FROM RECORD** to run a record backward and forward on a turntable in order to repeat and distort the original sound of the record **15.** *vti* **WITHDRAW FROM COMPETITION** to withdraw a person or team from a race or competition **16.** *vi* CUE GAMES **INCUR PENALTY** to make a billiard shot that incurs a penalty, e.g., by hitting the cue ball into a pocket **17.** *vi* CUE GAMES **MAKE FLUKE SHOT** in billiards, to make a mishit that produces a score ■ *n* **1. MARK ON SURFACE** a slight mark on a surface made with something sharp or rough **2. TEAR IN SKIN** a thin cut or tear in the surface of the skin of a person or animal **3. SCRAPING SOUND** a scraping sound, especially one made with the claws or nails **4. ACTION TO RELIEVE ITCHING** a rubbing of the skin with the nails or claws, especially to relieve itching or discomfort **5. SCRIBBLY WRITING** something written hastily or illegibly **6. MONEY** money or cash (*slang*) **7.** SPORTS same as **scratch line** (sense 1) **8.** SPORTS **WITHDRAWN COMPETITOR** a person or team withdrawn from a race or competition **9.** GOLF **HANDICAP OF ZERO** in golf, a zero handicap **10.** CUE GAMES **SHOT INCURRING PENALTY** a billiard shot that incurs a penalty **11.** CUE GAMES **FLUKE SHOT** in billiards, a mishit that produces a score **12.** MUSIC **TYPE OF POP MUSIC** music produced by running a record backward and forward on a turntable, repeating and distorting the original sound. Scratch is performed especially by disk jockeys in clubs. ■ *adj* **1. FOR JOTTED NOTES** used for making quick or preliminary notes ○ *scratch paper* **2.** SPORTS **DONE RANDOMLY** done randomly or by chance ○ *a scratch shot* **3. ASSEMBLED HASTILY** assembled hastily from available resources ○ *a scratch team* **4.** GOLF **WITH NO HANDICAP** playing golf with a handicap of zero [14C. Probably blend of dialect *scrat* "scratch" (< ?) + dialect *cratch* "scratch" (< ?)] ◇ **from scratch** (*informal*) **1.** right from the beginning, or with nothing having been done previously **2.** using basic ingredients instead of a prepared mix ◇ **up to scratch** of or up to a satisfactory standard (*informal*) ○ *exam results that aren't really up to scratch*

scratch together, scratch up *vt* same as **scrape together**

scratch-and-sniff *adj* designed to release a smell when scratched, especially as a complement to a visual experience

scratch·board /skrách bàwrd/ *n* a drawing board that is covered with a layer of white clay on top of which is a layer of black that can be scraped away to make line drawings

scratch·book /skrách bòok/ *n* a tiny notepad encased in a cardboard cover resembling that of a matchbook. These are given out to customers of some establishments in jurisdictions where smoking in public places is forbidden. [Early 21C. Modeled on MATCHBOOK]

scratch card *n* a card containing one or more sections covered in an overlay that can be scratched off to reveal a possible prize printed beneath

scratch line *n* **1.** a starting line in a race **2.** a line that a competitor may not step over without committing a foul

scratch·pad /skrách pàd/ *n* **1.** a pad of paper for making rough notes **2.** a high-speed temporary storage area in a computer memory

scratch·proof /skrách pròof/ *adj* resistant to being scratched

scratch sheet *n* *US* in horseracing, a program listing horses withdrawn from races and giving odds on those horses still entered

scratch test *n* a test to discover if somebody is allergic to a substance (**allergen**), in which a small amount of the substance is rubbed into a lightly scratched area of skin. A reaction, e.g., the formation of a welt, indicates an allergy to the substance.

scratch·y /skráchee/ (**-i·er, -i·est**) *adj* **1. ITCHY** causing or feeling itchiness on the skin ○ *a scratchy sweater* **2. WITH SCRAPING SOUND** making a scratching or scraping sound ○ *a scratchy recording* **3. PENNED QUICKLY** written or drawn hastily or illegibly **4.** *US* **IRREGULAR** done haphazardly or not smoothly —**scratch·i·ly** *adv* —**scratch·i·ness** *n*

scrawl /skrawl/ *vti* (**scrawled, scrawl·ing, scrawls**) to write or draw something untidily or hastily, especially in large letters that are difficult to read ■ *n* messy or hurried-looking handwriting or drawing [Early 17C. Origin ?] —**scrawl·er** *n* —**scrawl·y** *adj*

scraw·ny /skráwnee/ (**-ni·er, -ni·est**) *adj* unpleasantly or unhealthily thin and bony [Mid-19C. Variant of dialect *scranny*, origin ?] —**scraw·ni·ly** *adv* —**scraw·ni·ness** *n*

SYNONYMS See *thin.*

screak /skreek/ *US* *vi* (**screaked, screak·ing, screaks**) **1. MAKE SCREECHING SOUND** to produce a screech **2. MAKE CREAKING SOUND** to produce a creak ■ *n* **1. SCREECH** a screeching sound **2. CREAK** a creaking sound [15C. < Old Norse *skrækja*, an imitation of the sound] —**screak·y** *adj*

scream /skreem/ *n* **1. PIERCING CRY** a loud, piercing, high-pitched cry, uttered in fear, pain, excitement, or amusement **2. HIGH-PITCHED NOISE** a very loud, high-pitched sound, e.g., that of a siren or jet engine **3. SOMEBODY OR SOMETHING HIGHLY AMUSING** an extremely funny or entertaining person, event, or activity (*informal*) ■ *v* (**screamed, scream·ing, screams**) **1.** *vi* **CRY** to utter a loud, piercing, high-pitched cry, especially in fear, pain, or excitement ○ *He screamed for help.* **2.** *vt* **SHOUT SOMETHING IN PIERCING VOICE** to utter something in a loud, piercing, high-pitched voice, especially in fear, panic, desperation, or excitement ○ *"Get out!" he screamed.* **3.** *vi* **LAUGH LOUDLY** to laugh shrilly and loudly **4.** *vi* **MAKE HIGH-PITCHED SOUND** to make a loud high-pitched sound ○ *The ambulance went by, sirens screaming.* **5.** *vi* **MOVE AT SPEED** to move extremely quickly while producing a loud high-pitched sound ○ *The police car screamed by.* **6.** *vi* **BE OBVIOUS** to be extremely obvious or noticeable ○ *The* *mistakes just scream out at you.* [13C. Origin ?] —**scream·ing·ly** *adv*

CULTURAL NOTE ***The Scream,*** a painting (1893) by the Norwegian painter Edvard Munch. Painted in a bold, expressionist style, it depicts a panic-stricken human figure standing on a bridge or pier. The skull-like face appears to emit a cry that reverberates through the surrounding landscape. A powerful symbol of despair, it is one of the best-known icons of modern art.

scream·er /skreémər/ *n* **1.** **SOMETHING THAT SCREAMS** somebody or something that screams **2.** BIRDS **BIRD RESEMBLING GOOSE** a water bird that resembles a goose, but has a smaller beak and a harsher call. Native to: South America. Family: Anhimidae. **3.** *US* MEDIA **SENSATIONAL HEADLINE** a sensational headline set in large letters (*slang*) **4.** PRINTING same as **exclamation point** (*slang*)

scream·ing ab·dabs /-áb dàbz/, **scream·ing hab·dabs** /-háb dàbz/ *npl UK* same as **screaming meemies** (*informal*) [*Abdabs*, origin ?]

scream·ing mee·mies /-meémeez/ *n* an attack of nervous anxiety (*informal; takes a singular or plural verb*) [*Meemies*, origin ?]

scree /skree/ *n* **1.** an accumulation of rock debris at the base of a cliff, hill, or mountain slope, often forming a heap **2.** a slope covered with a layer of scree [Early 18C. < Old Norse *skriða* "landslide"]

screech /skreech/ *n* **1.** **SHRILL SCREAM OR CRY** a high-pitched grating cry or scream ○ *the screech of an owl* **2.** **HIGH-PITCHED SOUND** a loud high-pitched grating sound ○ *a screech of brakes* **3.** *Can* BEVERAGES **DARK RUM** a dark rum bottled in Newfoundland, Canada ■ *v* (**screeched, screech·ing, screech·es**) **1.** *vi* **UTTER SHRILL SCREAM** to utter a high-pitched grating cry or scream ○ *They screeched with delight.* **2.** *vt* **SHRIEK SOMETHING** to utter something in a high-pitched and grating tone of voice **3.** *vi* **MAKE SCREECHING SOUND** to make a loud high-pitched grating sound **4.** *vi* **PRODUCE SCREECHING SOUND BY MOVING FAST** to move, usually extremely fast, while producing a screeching sound ○ *The car screeched to a stop.* [Mid-16C. Alteration of archaic *scritch*, ultimately an imitation of the sound] —**screech·er** *n* —**screech·i·ness** *n* —**screech·y** *adj*

screech owl *n* a small owl with a high-pitched whistling call and feather tufts on the head that resemble ears. Native to: North America. Genus: *Otus*.

screed /skreed/ *n* **1.** **LENGTHY PIECE OF WRITING** a long and often tedious piece of writing or speech **2.** CONSTR **GUIDE FOR PLASTERING** a strip of plaster, wood, or other material placed on a surface as a guide to the correct thickness of plaster or concrete to be applied there **3.** CONSTR **BOARD FOR LEVELING** a board or tool used to level a layer of concrete, sand, or other loose material **4.** CONSTR **TOP LAYER** a smooth top layer on a concrete floor or other surface [14C. Variant of SHRED "torn strip"]

screel /skreel/ (**screeled, screel·ing, screels**) *vi Carib* **1.** to complain **2.** to squeal or scream [Late 19C. An imitation of the sound, or related to SKIRL]

screen /skreen/ *n* **1.** **PARTITION OR SHELTER** a fixed or movable partition or frame that is used to conceal, divide, separate, or provide shelter ○ *You may change your clothes behind the screen.* **2.** **DECORATIVE FRAME** a decorative frame or partition, e.g., in a church choir ○ *a rood screen* **3.** **MESH FRAME OR MESH** a frame with a fine wire or plastic mesh designed to prevent the entry of mosquitoes or other insects, or the mesh itself **4.** **SIEVE** a sieve used to filter out fine particles, e.g., of sand or gravel **5.** **SOMETHING THAT CONCEALS** anything that serves to conceal, divide, separate, or provide shelter ○ *A screen of leaves protected her from the sun.* **6.** **CONCEALMENT** a measure taken to conceal something ○ *This report is just a screen for the government's inaction.* **7.** **SELECTION SYSTEM** a system for selecting suitable people, e.g., for a job, membership in an organization, or tenancy **8.** COMPUT, MEDIA **ELECTRONIC DISPLAY SURFACE** the broad flat end of a cathode-ray tube or liquid crystal display on which images are displayed, e.g., in a television set or computer monitor **9.** COMPUT **DATA DISPLAYED ON MONITOR** the data displayed on the screen of a computer monitor ○ *to print the screen* **10.** MOVIES, PHOTOGRAPHY **SURFACE FOR PROJECTING MOVIE ONTO** a large flat white or silver surface onto which a movie or slide is projected **11.** MOVIES **MOVIES** the movie industry **12.** PHOTOGRAPHY **CAMERA PLATE FOR FOCUSING** a ground-glass plate in a camera that is used in focusing an image before photographing it **13.** MIL **ADVANCE DETACHMENT** a military detachment sent in advance of a main force to protect it from the enemy or give warning of an enemy approach **14.** PRINTING **GLASS PLATE FOR HALF-TONE REPRODUCTIONS** a glass plate marked with very fine lines and used in producing half-tone reproductions **15.** SPORTS **BLOCKING TACTIC** a tactic in a team game in which players of one team block a player from the opposing team **16.** *US* FOOTBALL same as **screen pass** **17.** PSYCHOANAL **EMOTIONAL BLOCK** something that prevents somebody from understanding his or her real feelings ■ *v* (**screened, screen·ing, screens**) **1.** *vt* **CONCEAL OR SHELTER SOMEBODY OR SOMETHING** to provide somebody or something with shelter, protection, or concealment from somebody or something **2.** *vt* **PARTITION SOMETHING OFF** to partition, separate, or divide something off from something else ○ *They had screened the area into cubicles.* **3.** *vt* **FIT SOMETHING WITH SCREEN** to provide something with a screen **4.** *vt* **PROTECT SOMEBODY** to protect somebody from something unpleasant or dangerous **5.** *vt* **SIFT SOMETHING** to filter something through a sieve **6.** *vti* **TEST FOR DISEASE** to test somebody or something for an illness or disease **7.** *vti* **SELECT BY WEEDING OUT** to examine a candidate or candidates for something such as a post, membership in an organization, or renting an apartment as part of a selection process **8.** *vti* MOVIES **SHOW IN MOVIE THEATER** to project a movie onto a screen in a theater, or be projected in a theater **9.** *vti* MEDIA **SHOW ON TELEVISION** to broadcast a movie, program, or other item on television, or be broadcast on television **10.** *vt* PRINTING **PHOTOGRAPH FOR HALF-TONE REPRODUCTION** to photograph something through a glass plate to make a half-tone reproduction **11.** *vti* **BLOCK OPPONENT** to block a member of an opposing team so that he or she cannot see or respond to a move [14C < Old N French *escren*] —**screen·er** *n* —**screen·ful** *n*

screen·ag·er /skreén àyjər/ *n* a young person who has grown up watching TV and playing with computers and is knowledgeable about and skilled in operating electronic devices (*informal*)

screen dump *n* the process of printing or saving the contents of a computer display screen

screened shot /skreénd-/ *n* COMPUT same as **screen shot**

screen font *n* a font used to display text on a computer screen

screen·ing /skreéning/ *n* **1.** **A SHOWING IN CINEMA** a projection of a movie on a screen in a cinema **2.** **A SHOWING ON TELEVISION** a showing of a movie, program, or other item on television **3.** **TEST FOR DISEASE** a test or testing carried out routinely on supposedly healthy people in order to establish, as early as possible, whether or not they have an illness or disease **4.** **WIRE MESH** fine wire or plastic mesh used on a door or window to prevent the entry of mosquitoes or other insects **5.** **PROTECTING SCREENS** screens for providing shelter, protection, or concealment, or for separating or dividing ■ **screen·ings** *npl* **SIFTED MATERIAL** waste material that has been screened from something

screen mem·o·ry *n* an early childhood memory that is used subconsciously to mask another related, often distressing, memory

screen pass *n US* in football, a forward pass to a player who is protected from being tackled by a screen of members of his or her own team

screen·play /skreén plày/ *n* a script or scenario for a film

screen-print *n* a print produced by silk-screen printing —**screen-print** *vti* —**screen-print·ing** *n*

screen rage *n* extreme anger and frustration experienced by a computer user who encounters difficulties (*slang*)

screen sav·er *n* a computer utility that automatically makes the screen go blank or display a preselected image after a given period of time

screen shot *n* a photograph or printout showing what appears on a computer screen, especially for the purposes of demonstrating a program

screen test *n* an audition for a movie role in which an actor is filmed, or the film made of the audition —**screen-test** *vti*

screen·writ·er /skreén rìtər/ *n* the writer of a script that is intended to be filmed —**screen·writ·ing** *n*

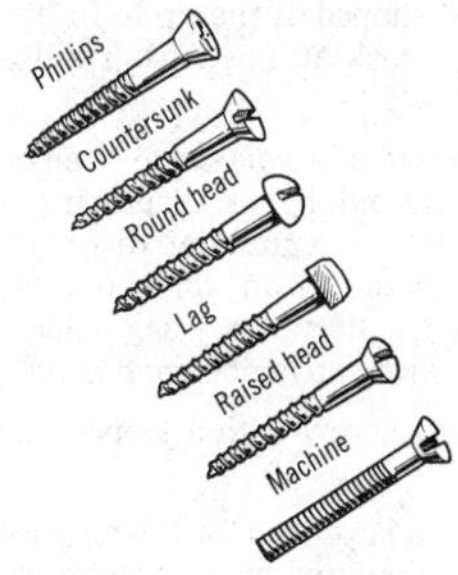

screw

screw /skroo/ *n* **1.** **THREADED FASTENER INSERTED INTO MATERIAL** a piece of metal with a tapering threaded body and grooved head by which it is turned into something in order to fasten things together **2.** **SCREW FOR NUT** a screw with a blunt end onto which a nut is fitted to hold two objects together **3.** **DEVICE SIMILAR TO SCREW** anything that has a form similar to a tapering metal screw, e.g., a corkscrew **4.** **TWISTING ACTION** a turn of a screw or of a device like a screw **5.** **OFFENSIVE TERM** an offensive term for an act or instance of sexual intercourse (*slang*) **6.** **OFFENSIVE TERM** an offensive term for a sexual partner considered with regard to his or her sexual performance (*slang*) **7.** **GUARD** a prison guard (*slang*) **8.** ENG same as **propeller** ■ *v* (**screwed, screw·ing, screws**) **1.** *vti* **FASTEN WITH SCREWS** to fasten or tighten something with a screw or screws, or be fastened or tightened in this way ○ *He screwed the shelf to the wall.* **2.** *vti* **FASTEN BY ROTATING** to rotate something along a thread in order to fasten or tighten it, or be rotated in this way ○ *screwed the bulb in carefully* **3.** *vt* **CRUSH SOMETHING** to crumple or crush something into a tight ball ○ *screwed up the letter and threw it away* **4.** *vti* **CONTORT THE FACE** to contort or crumple a part or all of the face, or be contorted or crumpled ○ *She screwed her eyes up against the glare.* **5.** *vti* **OFFENSIVE TERM** an offensive term meaning to have sexual intercourse with somebody (*slang*) **6.** *vt* **CHEAT SOMEBODY** to cheat or swindle somebody (*slang*) **7.** *vt* **EXTORT SOMETHING** to get something out of somebody with great difficulty (*slang*) ○ *We managed to screw some money out of him in the end.* **8.** *vt* **OFFENSIVE TERM** an offensive term expressive of anger or frustration with somebody or something (*slang*) [15C. < Old French *escroue*, directly or via Germanic < Latin *scrofa* "sow" (from its curly tail)] —**screw·er** *n* ◇ **have a screw** *or* **few screws loose** to be irrational or lack common sense or good judgment (*informal*) ◇ **put the screws on somebody** to use force or pressure on somebody (*slang*)

screw around *vi* (*slang*) **1.** an offensive term meaning to have sex with a number of different people, especially when married or in an established relationship **2.** an offensive term meaning to waste time in trivial or pointless activities

screw up *v* **1.** **MUSTER SOMETHING** to gather courage or nerve before doing something **2.** *vti* **OFFENSIVE TERM** an offensive term meaning to mismanage, disrupt, or make a mess of something (*slang*) **3.** *vt* **OFFENSIVE TERM** an offensive term meaning to disturb somebody psychologically or emotionally (*slang*)

screw·ball /skroó bàwl/ *n* **1.** **OFFENSIVE TERM** an offensive term for somebody who is regarded as behaving in an unconventional, irrational, or strange way (*slang insult*) **2.** **PITCH IN OPPOSITE DIRECTION TO CURVE BALL** in baseball, a pitch that curves in a direction opposite to that of a regular curveball, traveling instead to the same side as the hand with which it is thrown ■ *adj* **OFFENSIVE TERM** an offensive term meaning regarded as unconventional, irrational, or strange (*slang insult*)

screw·ball com·e·dy *n* a movie, especially a Hollywood comedy of the 1930s, featuring the amusing antics of appealing characters in a glamorous world. These films often feature an emancipated and strong-willed heroine.

screw bean *n* **1.** a bush of the legume family that produces twisted pods. Native to: southwestern

United States, Mexico. Latin name: *Prosopis pubescens.* **2.** a pod of the screw bean plant. Use: fodder.

screw·driv·er /skróo drìvər/ *n* **1.** a tool for driving screws that consists of a handle or power tool with a metal rod shaped at the tip to fit into the head of a screw **2.** a cocktail made from vodka and orange juice

screwed up /skróod-/ *adj* (*slang*) **1.** an offensive term meaning affected by or displaying symptoms of psychological or emotional disorder (*hyphenated before a noun*) **2.** an offensive term meaning mismanaged, disrupted, or made a mess of (*hyphenated when used before a noun*)

screw eye *n* a screw with a looped instead of a flat head

screw jack *n* a jack used for lifting heavy items such as vehicles, operated by a screw mechanism

screw pine *n* TREES same as **pandanus**

screw pro·pel·ler *n* ENG, NAUT same as **propeller**

screw tap *n* same as **tap**[2] *n* (sense 5)

screw thread *n* **1.** the continuous helical outer surface of a screw or the inner surface of a nut **2.** a full turn of a screw thread

screw-up /skróo ùp/ *n* (*slang*) **1.** an offensive term for a mess, blunder, or bungled event **2.** an offensive term for somebody who habitually messes up, blunders, or bungles things

screw·worm /skróo wùrm/ *n* the larva of the screwworm fly that grows under the skin of livestock and other mammals, causing injury and death [Late 19C. < the spiny hairs of the larva, which encircle each segment]

screw·worm fly *n* a bluish blowfly whose eggs, laid on the skin of livestock and other large mammals, hatch as larvae (**screwworms**) that grow under the skin. Latin name: *Cochliomyia hominivorax.*

screw·y /skróo ee/ (**-i·er, -i·est**) *adj* **1.** an offensive term meaning regarded as irrational, unconventional, or strange (*slang insult*) **2.** not quite right or correct, especially in being improper or illegal (*informal*) —**screw·i·ly** *adv* —**screw·i·ness** *n*

scrib·ble /skríbb'l/ *v* (**-bled, -bling, -bles**) **1.** *vti* **WRITE MESSILY** to write something hastily or untidily, often in smallish letters **2.** *vti* **MAKE MEANINGLESS MARKINGS** to write or draw meaningless or undecipherable marks on something ○ *Don't scribble on the wall!* **3.** *vi* **BE WRITER** to be a writer, especially one of little merit (*humorous*) ■ *n* **1.** **MESSY HANDWRITING** messy or careless handwriting **2.** **HASTY NOTE** something written messily or hastily **3.** **DOODLES** meaningless marks written or drawn on something [15C. < medieval Latin *scribillare* < Latin *scribere* "write"] —**scrib·bler** *n* —**scrib·bly** *adj*

scribe /skrīb/ *n* **1.** **BOOK COPIER** a copier or transcriber of documents, especially somebody who copied manuscripts in medieval times **2.** **COPIER OF JEWISH RELIGIOUS DOCUMENTS** a copier of the Sefer Torah and other Jewish religious documents using a quill pen on parchment **3.** **CLERK** an official public clerk **4.** **JOURNALIST** a writer, especially a journalist (*humorous*) **5.** same as **scriber** ■ *vti* (**scribed, scrib·ing, scribes**) CONSTR **MARK LINES ON SOMETHING** to mark something such as wood or metal with a line using a pointed instrument, especially as a guide for cutting [12C. < Latin *scriba* "official or public writer" < *scribere* "write"] —**scrib·al** *adj*

scrib·er /skrībər/ *n* a sharp instrument for marking lines on wood or other material

scrim /skrim/ *n* **1.** a drop curtain in a theater that appears opaque to the audience when lit from the front but transparent when lit from behind **2.** a durable open-weave cotton or linen fabric. Use: curtains, clothing, upholstery lining. [Late 18C. Origin ?]

scrim·mage /skrímmij/ *n* **1.** SPORTS **PRACTICE GAME** a practice game between two squads, often from the same team **2.** FOOTBALL **PLAY IN FOOTBALL** in football, the action from the moment the ball is snapped to the moment the ball is dead **3.** **STRUGGLE** a rough or confused struggle **4.** **FIGHT** a skirmish or minor battle ■ *vti* (**-maged, -mag·ing, -mag·es**) **TAKE PART IN SCRIMMAGE** to engage in a scrimmage or play a scrimmage against somebody [15C. Alteration of SKIRMISH]

scrim·mage line *n* FOOTBALL same as **line of scrimmage**

scrimp /skrimp/ (**scrimped, scrimp·ing, scrimps**) *v* **1.** *vi* **ECONOMIZE** to economize drastically or be extremely frugal ○ *scrimp on food* **2.** *vt* **LIMIT SOMEBODY'S PROVISIONS** to severely limit provision to somebody **3.** *vt* **MAKE SOMETHING TOO SMALL** to make something too small or scanty [Mid-18C. < obsolete *scrimp* "scant, meager," origin ?] —**scrimp·i·ly** *adv* —**scrimp·i·ness** *n* —**scrimp·y** *adj*

scrim·shand·er /skrím shàndər/ *n* a carver or engraver of objects made from the teeth or bones of whales [Mid-19C. < variant of SCRIMSHAW]

scrim·shaw /skrím shàw/ *n* **1.** **CARVED WHALE IVORY** a carved or engraved object made originally by North American whalers from the teeth and bones of whales, or such objects collectively **2.** **MAKING OF SCRIMSHAW** the skill or pastime of making scrimshaw ■ *v* (**-shawed, -shaw·ing, -shaws**) **1.** *vi* **MAKE SCRIMSHAW** to make scrimshaw **2.** *vt* **CARVE OR ENGRAVE SOMETHING** to carve or engrave something into scrimshaw [Mid-19C. Origin ?]

scrip[1] /skrip/ *n* **1.** *US* **TEMPORARY PAPER CURRENCY** paper currency issued for temporary emergency use, e.g., by an occupying force **2.** **BRIEF PIECE OF WRITING** a list, receipt, or other short piece of writing **3.** *US* **PRESCRIPTION** a doctor's prescription (*slang*) [Late 16C. Alteration of SCRIPT, influenced by SCRAP[1]]

scrip[2] /skrip/ *n* a document or certificate representing a fraction of a share or stock [Mid-18C. Contraction of obsolete *subscription receipt* "receipt for stock"]

scrip[3] /skrip/ *n* a wallet or small satchel or bag [14C. < Old French *escrep(p)e* "alms purse" < *escherpe* (see SCARF[1])]

Scripps /skrips/, **E. W.** (1854–1926) US newspaper publisher. He gradually acquired newspapers and in 1894 established what became the Scripps-Howard newspaper chain. In 1897 he founded a news service that became the United Press Association. Full name **Scripps, Edward Wyllis**

script /skript/ *n* **1.** **TEXT OF PLAY OR BROADCAST** the printed version of a stage play, movie screenplay, or radio or television broadcast, including the words to be spoken and often also technical directions **2.** **TEXT INSTRUCTING SOMEBODY WHAT TO SAY** a real or imagined piece of text setting out what somebody is to say or do on a specific occasion ○ *The president stuck to his script and refused to comment on side issues.* **3.** **MANUSCRIPT** an original document or manuscript **4.** **HANDWRITING** characters written by hand, especially in cursive form **5.** **SYSTEM OF WRITING** any system of characters used in writing **6.** **PRINTED TYPE RESEMBLING WRITING** printed type designed to imitate handwriting **7.** **SERIES OF COMMANDS IN COMPUTER PROGRAM** a sequence of automated computer commands embedded in a program that tells the program to execute a specific procedure when a Web page is opened or a hypertext link is clicked ■ *vt* (**script·ed, script·ing, scripts**) **1.** **WRITE SCRIPT FOR SOMETHING** to write or prepare a script for something, especially a play, film, or broadcast **2.** **DIRECT SOMEBODY TO SAY OR DO SOMETHING** to make or arrange something as if according to a script ○ *carefully scripted comments* [14C. Via French < Latin *scriptus* < *scribere* "write"] —**script·ed** *adj*

Script. *abbr* RELIG, BIBLE Scripture

script doc·tor *n* a writer who revises an unsatisfactory script for a movie or play

scrip·to·ri·um /skrip táwree əm/ (*plural* **-ri·ums** or **-ri·a** /-ree ə/) *n* a room in a monastery for storing, copying, illustrating, or reading manuscripts [Late 18C. < medieval Latin, < Latin *script-* (see SCRIPTURE)]

scrip·ture /skrípchər/, **Scrip·ture** *n* **1.** **BIBLICAL WRITINGS** the sacred writings of the Bible **2.** **BIBLICAL TEXT** a passage from the Bible **3.** **SACRED WRITING** any sacred writing or book ○ *Buddhist scripture* **4.** **AUTHORITATIVE STATEMENT** a statement regarded as authoritative [14C. < Latin *scriptura* "what is written" < *script-*, past participle of *scribere* "write"] —**scrip·tur·al** *adj*

script·writ·er /skrípt rītər/ *n* a writer of scripts for broadcasts or movies

scriv·en·er /skrívvənər/ *n* **1.** in former times, somebody whose job involved writing or making handwritten copies of documents, books, or other texts **2.** LAW same as **notary public** (*archaic*) [14C < Old French *escrivein* < Latin *scriba* (see SCRIBE)]

scro·bic·u·late /skrō bíkyə làyt, -lət/ *adj* with a grooved or pitted surface [Early 19C. < late Latin *scrobiculus* "groove" < Latin *scrobis* "trench"]

scrod /skrod/, **schrod** *n* a young cod or haddock [Mid-19C. Origin ?]

scrof·u·la /skróffyələ/ *n* tuberculosis of the lymph glands, especially of the neck. If untreated, the glands burst through the skin to form running sores. [14C. < medieval Latin, "swelling of glands" < *scrofa* "breeding sow"; because sows were thought to be subject to the disease]

scrof·u·lous /skróffyələss/ *adj* **1.** **HAVING OR RESEMBLING SCROFULA** affected with or characteristic of scrofula **2.** **SHABBY IN APPEARANCE** run-down, diseased, or shabby in appearance **3.** **MORALLY CORRUPT** morally corrupt and degenerate —**scrof·u·lous·ly** *adv* —**scrof·u·lous·ness** *n*

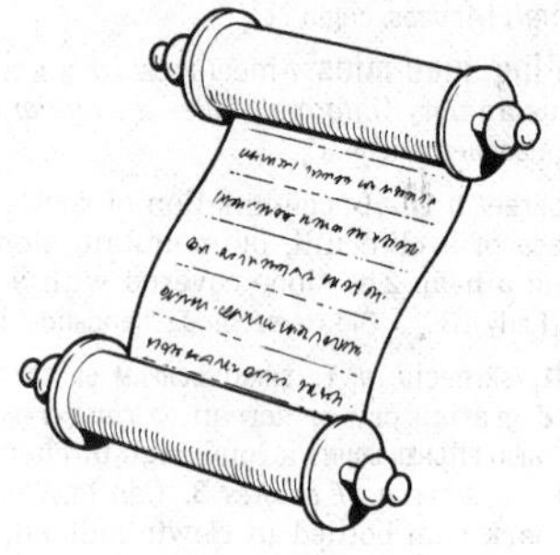

scroll

scroll /skrōl/ *n* **1.** **ROLL OF PARCHMENT** a roll of paper, parchment, leather, or other material, used for a written document, or a document written on such a roll **2.** **LIST** a list, roll, or roster **3.** **ORNAMENTAL DESIGN RESEMBLING ROLL OF PAPER** an ornamental design shaped like a rolled or partially rolled piece of paper **4.** **CURVED HEAD OF STRINGED INSTRUMENT** the curved head of a stringed musical instrument where the tuning pegs are set **5.** **HERALDIC RIBBON WITH MOTTO** in heraldry, a ribbon with rolled ends inscribed with a motto ■ *vti* (**scrolled, scroll·ing, scrolls**) COMPUT **MOVE TEXT ON COMPUTER SCREEN** to move, or move text or graphics, smoothly up, down, or across a computer display [15C. Alteration (after ROLL) of obsolete *scrow*, via Old French *escroe* "strip of parchment" < medieval Latin *scroda* "strip" < Germanic, "something cut"]

scroll bar *n* a narrow horizontal or vertical bar on a computer display, used to make text or graphics move up, down, or across

scroll saw *n* a saw with a narrow blade used for cutting curved ornamental designs

scroll·work /skrṓl wùrk/ *n* ornamental designs characterized by scrolls, especially in wood

scrooch /skrooch/ (**scrooched, scrooch·ing, scrooch·es**) *vi US* to crouch or bend down [Mid-19C. Alteration of dialect *scruze* "to squeeze," probably blend of SCREW + SQUEEZE]

scrooge /skrooj/, **Scrooge** *n* same as **miser** (*informal*) [Mid-19C. After Ebenezer *Scrooge*, character in *A Christmas Carol* (1843), by Charles Dickens]

scro·ta ANAT plural of **scrotum**

scro·tum /skrṓtəm/ (*plural* **-tums** or **-ta** /-tə/) *n* the external pouch of skin and muscle containing the testes in mammals. It allows sperm to develop at a temperature lower than that of the body. [Late 16C. < Latin] —**scro·tal** *adj*

scrounge /skrownj/ (**scrounged, scroung·ing, scroung·es**) *vti* (*informal*) **1.** to acquire something from somebody by begging or borrowing without intending to make repayment or return **2.** to seek and acquire something from any available source, e.g., by foraging [Early 20C. Alteration of dialect *scringe* "prowl around," alteration of CRINGE] —**scroung·er** *n*

scroung·y /skrównjee/ (**-i·er, -i·est**) *adj US* shabby, dirty, and neglected (*informal*) ○ *a scroungy hovel*

scrub[1] /skrub/ *v* (**scrubbed, scrub·bing, scrubs**) **1.** *vti* **CLEAN BY RUBBING** to clean something by rubbing hard **2.** *vt* **REMOVE DIRT BY RUBBING** to remove dirt by rubbing hard, usually with a brush **3.** *vt* REMOVE IMPURITIES FROM GAS to remove impurities or pollutants from a gas **4.** *vi* CLEANSE FOR SURGERY to cleanse the arms and hands in preparation for performing surgery **5.** *vt* CANCEL SOMETHING to cancel or postpone something (*informal*) ○ *The launch was scrubbed with only 3 seconds to go.* ■ *n* ACT OF SCRUBBING the act of cleaning something by rubbing hard ■ **scrubs** *npl* CLOTHING WORN WHILE PERFORMING SURGERY the clothing, usually a matching green shirt and pants, worn by surgeons and nurses in an operating room (*informal*) [13C. Probably < Middle Low German or Middle Dutch *schrubben*]

scrub up *vi* to look good, attractive, or elegant with proper care and attention, e.g., when groomed and well dressed or when cleaned and polished (*informal*) ○ *Out of his work clothes, he scrubs up well, doesn't he?*

scrub[2] /skrub/ *n* **1.** STUNTED TREE a stunted tree or bush **2.** AREA OF LOW VEGETATION low, stunted, or straggly vegetation or an area of such vegetation **3.** MONGREL a domestic animal of mixed breeding **4.** OFFENSIVE TERM an offensive term for somebody regarded as small or insignificant (*slang*) **5.** PLAYER NOT ON FIRST STRING a player not on the first string or a team made up of such players [14C. Alteration of SHRUB[1]]

scrub·ber /skrúbbər/ *n* **1.** somebody or something such as an appliance or brush that cleans by rubbing hard **2.** a device for removing impurities or pollutants from a gas [Mid-19C. < SCRUB[1]; in sense 3 perhaps partly < SCRUB[2]]

scrub·by /skrúbbee/ (**-bi·er, -bi·est**) *adj* **1.** SHABBY shabby, messy, or wretched in appearance **2.** STUNTED OR STRAGGLY inferior in size or quality **3.** COVERED WITH LOW TREES covered with or consisting of low or undersized shrubs or trees —**scrub·bi·ness** *n*

scrub fowl (*plural* **scrub fowls** or *same*) *n* BIRDS same as **megapode**

scrub·land /skrúb lànd/ *n* land covered with low trees and shrubs

scrub nurse *n* a nurse who helps a surgeon in the operating room

scrub oak *n* a small oak of scrubland. Native to: North America. Latin name: *Quercus ilicifolia.*

scrub pine *n* a stunted, straggly, or undersized pine tree that is unsuitable for use as lumber

scrub ty·phus *n* a common infectious disease in East Asia that is caused by the microorganism *Rickettsia tsutsugamushi* and spread by a biting mite. Symptoms include fever, painful swollen lymph nodes, and a skin rash.

scruff[1] /skruf/ *n* the back of the neck ○ *got hold of him by the scruff of the neck* [Late 18C. Alteration of *scuff* < Old Norse *skoft* "hair of the head"]

scruff[2] /skruf/ *n UK* an untidy or disreputable person (*informal*) [Old English *scruf*, variant of SCURF]

scruff·y /skrúffee/ (**-i·er, -i·est**) *adj* messy, shabby, or run-down in appearance [Mid-17C. < SCRUFF[2]] —**scruf·fi·ly** *adv* —**scruf·fi·ness** *n*

scrum /skrum/ *n* a formalized contest for possession of the ball during a rugby game between the two sets of forwards who each assemble in a tight-knit formation with bodies bent and arms clasped around each other and push forward together against their opponents ■ *vi* (**scrummed, scrum·ming, scrums**) to form a scrum in rugby [Late 19C. Shortening of SCRUMMAGE]

scrum·mage /skrúmmij/ *n* RUGBY same as **scrum** [Early 19C. Variant of SCRIMMAGE] —**scrum·mag·er** *n*

scrump·tious /skrúmpshəss/ *adj* very pleasing, especially to the taste (*informal*) [Mid-19C. Probably alteration of SUMPTUOUS] —**scrump·tious·ly** *adv* —**scrump·tious·ness** *n*

scrunch /skrunch/ *v* (**scrunched, scrunch·ing, scrunch·es**) **1.** *vt* SQUEEZE SOMETHING to crumple, crush, or squeeze something together tightly **2.** *vi* MOVE WITH CRUNCHING SOUND to move with or make a crunching sound **3.** *vi* HUNKER DOWN to hunker down, hunch, or crouch ■ *n* CRUNCHING SOUND a rustling crunching sound [Late 18C. An imitation of the sound]

scrunch up *vt* same as **scrunch** *v* (sense 1)

scrunch-dry *vt* to dry hair while squeezing it together tightly in your hand to shape it and add volume

scrunch·ie /skrúnchee/ *n* a thick elasticized band loosely covered with fabric for fastening back hair [Late 20C. < SCRUNCH, because of its crumpled appearance]

scrunt /skrunt/ (**scrunt, scrunt·ing, scrunts**) *vi Carib* to be in a poor financial situation [Late 20C. Perhaps < Scottish and northern English dialect, "scratch, scrub"]

scru·ple /skróop'l/ *n* **1.** MORAL OR ETHICAL CONSIDERATION a moral or ethical consideration that tends to restrain action or behavior **2.** UNIT OF WEIGHT a unit of apothecaries' weight equal to 20 grains/or about 1.3 g **3.** VERY SMALL AMOUNT a minute amount or portion of something (*archaic*) ■ *vi* (**-pled, -pling, -ples**) HESITATE BECAUSE OF MORAL CONSIDERATIONS to hesitate to act, or refrain from taking action, because of moral or ethical considerations ○ *She wouldn't scruple to cheat.* [15C. Via French < Latin *scrupulus* "small sharp stone, uneasiness" < *scrupus* "sharp stone"]

scru·pu·lous /skróopyələss/ *adj* **1.** having or showing careful regard for what is morally right ○ *He was too scrupulous to falsify even the slightest detail.* **2.** rigorously precise or thorough ○ *scrupulous cleanliness* —**scru·pu·los·i·ty** /skròopyə lóssətee/ *n* —**scru·pu·lous·ly** *adv* —**scru·pu·lous·ness** *n*

SYNONYMS See ***careful.***

scru·ta·ble /skróotəb'l/ *adj* capable of being understood by careful observation, examination, or study [Late 16C. Back-formation < INSCRUTABLE] —**scru·ta·bil·i·ty** /skròotə bíllətee/ *n*

scru·ti·neer /skròot'n éer/ *n* an inspector or examiner of something [Mid-16C. < SCRUTINY]

scru·ti·nize /skróot'n ìz/ (**-nized, -niz·ing, -niz·es**) *vt* to examine somebody or something closely and carefully [Late 17C. < SCRUTINY] —**scru·ti·niz·er** *n*

scru·ti·ny /skróot'nee/ (*plural* **-nies**) *n* **1.** CAREFUL INSPECTION close, careful, and thorough examination or inspection **2.** OBSERVATION careful study or surveillance **3.** GAZE a searching look [15C. < Latin *scrutinium* "inquiry" < *scrutinari* "examine" < *scruta* "trash"]

SCSI /skúzzee/ *n* a specification for a high-speed computer interface used to connect peripheral devices to a computer. Full form **small computer systems interface**

scu·ba /skóobə/ *n* an apparatus for breathing underwater consisting of a portable canister of compressed air and a mouthpiece [Mid-20C. Acronym < *self-contained underwater breathing apparatus*]

scu·ba div·er *n* an underwater swimmer using scuba equipment —**scu·ba div·ing** *n*

scud /skud/ *vi* (**scud·ded, scud·ding, scuds**) **1.** MOVE SWIFTLY to move swiftly and smoothly ○ *clouds scudding across the sky* **2.** SAIL BEFORE GALE to sail with a gale or strong wind blowing from behind ■ *n* **1.** SWIFT MOVEMENT a swift smooth movement **2.** CLOUDS DRIVEN BY WIND low clouds that are driven swiftly by the wind **3.** SUDDEN SHOWER OR GUST a sudden shower of rain or gust of wind [Mid-16C. Origin ?]

scu·di MONEY plural of **scudo**

Scud mis·sile /skúd-/ *n* a surface-to-surface missile that can take a nuclear, conventional, or chemical warhead [< NATO code name < SCUD]

scu·do /skóodō/ (*plural* **-di** /-dee/) *n* a former gold or silver coin in various Italian states, or a modern commemorative coin issued occasionally by the republic of San Marino [Mid-17C. Via Italian < Latin *scutum* "shield"]

scuff /skuf/ *vti* (**scuffed, scuff·ing, scuffs**) **1.** SCRAPE OR RUB to scrape, rub, or wear away the surface of something, or become scraped, rubbed, or worn with use **2.** SCRAPE FEET WHILE WALKING to scrape the feet on the ground while standing or walking, or walk in a manner that makes the feet scrape **3.** *US* POKE FOOT to move or shift the foot tentatively in embarrassment or exploration ■ *n* **1.** ACT OF SCUFFING a scraping or shuffling movement or sound **2.** MARK FROM SCRAPING OR RUBBING a mark or scratch made by scuffing **3.** FLAT SHOE a flat-soled shoe with no strap or back [Late 16C. Probably < N Germanic]

scuf·fle[1] /skúff'l/ *n* DISORDERLY FIGHT a confused and disorderly fight or struggle between people at close quarters, usually one regarded as minor and not resulting in serious harm ■ *vi* (**-fled, -fling, -fles**) **1.** FIGHT IN CONFUSION to struggle or fight in a disorderly way at close quarters **2.** SHUFFLE QUICKLY to shuffle along hurriedly [Late 16C. Probably < SCUFF "dodge repeatedly"] —**scuf·fler** *n*

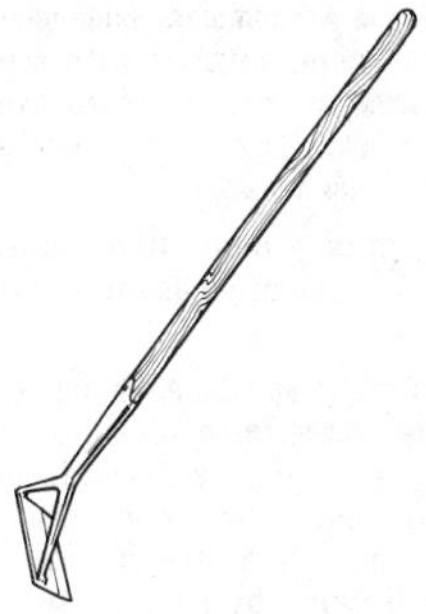

scuffle

scuf·fle[2] /skúff'l/, **scuf·fle hoe** *n US* a hoe that is pushed back and forth across the surface of the ground [Late 18C. < Dutch *schoffel*]

scull /skul/ *n* **1.** EITHER OF PAIR OF OARS either one of a pair of relatively short oars used by a single rower **2.** LIGHT RACING BOAT a light narrow racing boat propelled by one, two, or four rowers using sculls **3.** SINGLE OAR AT BACK OF BOAT a single oar that is moved from side to side at the stern of a boat to propel the boat forward ■ *vti* (**sculled, scull·ing, sculls**) PROPEL BOAT WITH SCULLS to propel a boat using a scull or sculls [14C. Origin ?] —**scull·er** *n*

scul·ler·y /skúlləree/ (*plural* **-ies**) *n* a small room for washing and storing dishes and utensils and doing other kitchen chores [15C. < French *escuelerie* "duty of a servant in charge of plates" < *escuelle* "dish" < Latin *scutella* "serving platter"]

scul·lion /skúllyən/ *n* a servant employed to perform menial kitchen chores (*archaic*) [15C. < Middle French *escouillon* "swab, washcloth" < *escouve* "broom" < Latin *scopae*]

sculp. *abbr* ARTS sculptor

scul·pin /skúlpin/ (*plural same* or **-pins**) *n* **1.** a fish, mostly bottom-dwelling, with a large flat head, large pectoral fins, and spines. Native to: North American coasts. Family: Cottidae. **2.** a scorpion fish with venomous spines, caught for food and for sport. Native to: southern California coast. Latin name: *Scorpaena guttata.* [Late 17C. Origin ?]

sculpt /skulpt/ (**sculpt·ed, sculpt·ing, sculpts**) *v* **1.** *vti* MAKE SCULPTURE to carve, model, cast, or otherwise create a three-dimensional representation of something as a work of art **2.** *vt* CARVE OR MODEL MATERIAL to use a material in sculpting **3.** *vi* BE SCULPTOR to create three-dimensional works of art as a profession or pastime **4.** *vt* SHAPE SOMETHING NATURALLY to change the shape or contours of something by natural processes such as erosion [Mid-19C. < French *sculpter* < *sculpteur* "sculptor" < Latin *sculpt-* (see SCULPTURE)]

~~**sculpter**~~ incorrect spelling of **sculptor**

sculp·tor /skúlptər/ *n* an artist who creates three-dimensional works of art, especially by carving, modeling, or casting [Mid-17C. < Latin, < *sculpt-* (see SCULPTURE)]

Sculp·tor *n* a faint constellation of the southern hemisphere. See illustration at **constellation**

~~**sculptur**~~ incorrect spelling of **sculpture**

sculp·ture /skúlpchər/ *n* **1.** CREATION OF THREE-DIMENSIONAL ART the creation of a three-dimensional work of art, especially by carving, modeling, or casting **2.** THREE-DIMENSIONAL WORK OF ART a work of art created by sculpture, or such works collectively **3.** NATURAL MARKING ON PLANT OR ANIMAL a natural indentation or other marking on a plant or animal, e.g., a ridge on a seashell ■ *v* (**-tured, -tur·ing, -tures**) **1.** *vti* ARTS same as **sculpt** (senses 1–3) **2.** *vt* GEOL same as **sculpt** (sense 4) [14C. < Latin *sculptura* < *sculpt-*, past participle of *sculpere* "carve, scratch"] —**sculp·tur·al** *adj* —**sculp·tur·al·ly** *adv*

sculp·tur·esque /skùlpchə résk/ *adj* resembling sculpture —**sculp·tur·esque·ly** *adv*

scum /skum/ *n* **1.** FILMY LAYER ON SURFACE OF LIQUID a filmy layer of extraneous matter or impurities that rises to, or is formed on, the surface of a liquid **2.** OFFENSIVE TERM an offensive term for a person or group of people regarded as contemptible or worthless (*slang insult*) **3.** REFUSE refuse or worthless material **4.** METALL REFUSE FROM MOLTEN METAL dross or refuse from molten metals ■ *v* (**scummed, scum·ming, scums**) **1.** *vi* HAVE SCUM to become covered with scum **2.** *vt* CLEAR SOMETHING OF SCUM to remove scum from something [14C. < Middle Dutch *scūme* "foam, froth" < Germanic] —**scum·mer** *n* —**scum·my** *adj*

scum·bag /skúm bàg/ *n* an offensive term for somebody who is seen as unpleasant or malicious (*slang insult*)

scum·ble /skúmb'l/ *vt* (**-bled, -bling, -bles**) **1.** SOFTEN SOMETHING WITH OPAQUE COLOR to soften the colors or outlines of a painting or drawing by covering it with a film of opaque or semiopaque color **2.** SOFTEN COLORS BY RUBBING to soften the colors or outlines of a painting or drawing by rubbing ■ *n* **1.** TECHNIQUE OF SCUMBLING the technique or effect of scumbling **2.** SCUMBLING MATERIAL a material used for scumbling [Late 17C. Origin ?]

scun·der /skúndər/ *n Ireland* an unreasonable or extreme dislike [Variant of SCUNNER]

scun·gil·li /skoon jíllee/ *n* conch eaten as food [Mid-20C. < Italian]

scup /skup/ (*plural* **scups** or *same*) *n* a fish of the porgy family. Native to: eastern Atlantic coast of the United States. Latin name: *Stenotomus chrysops*. [19C. < Narraganset *mishcup* "big and close together"; because of the shape of the fish's scales]

scup·per[1] /skúppər/ *n* **1.** an opening in the bulwarks of a ship that allows water on the deck to drain overboard **2.** an opening allowing water to drain from the roof or floor of a building [15C. Origin ?]

scup·per[2] /skúppər/ (**-pered, -per·ing, -pers**) *vt* **1.** to wreck, defeat, or ruin something **2.** to sink a ship, especially to sink your own vessel intentionally [Late 19C. Origin ?]

scup·per·nong /skúppər nàwng, -nòng/ *n* **1.** a cultivated variety of the muscadine grape that has sweet yellowish green fruit **2.** a sweet amber-colored wine made from scuppernong grapes [Early 19C. After the *Scuppernong* River in North Carolina]

scurf /skurf/ *n* **1.** DANDRUFF thin dry flaking scales of skin, usually as a result of a skin condition such as dandruff **2.** FLAKY ENCRUSTATION a flaky or scaly encrustation on a surface **3.** SCALY DEPOSIT ON PLANT a scaly deposit or covering on a plant **4.** PLANT DISEASE a plant disease characterized by scurf [Old English *sceorf* < W Germanic] —**scurf·y** *adj*

scur·ril·i·ty /skə ríllətee/ (*plural* **-ties**) *n* **1.** coarseness, vulgarity, or a lack of refinement **2.** language that is coarse and vulgar, or a remark made in coarse vulgar language

scur·ri·lous /skúrrələss, skúr ə-/ *adj* **1.** ABUSIVE OR DEFAMATORY containing abusive language or defamatory allegations **2.** FOUL-MOUTHED OR VULGAR using or containing coarse, vulgar, or obscene language **3.** WICKED behaving in ways thought to be evil or immoral [Late 16C. < archaic *scurrile*, via French < Latin *scurrilis* < *scurra* "buffoon"] —**scur·ri·lous·ly** *adv* —**scur·ri·lous·ness** *n*

scur·ry /skúrree, skúr ee/ *vi* (**-ried, -ry·ing, -ries**) **1.** MOVE BRISKLY to move at a hurried pace, usually with small fast steps **2.** MOVE AROUND AGITATEDLY to move around in an agitated manner or with a swirling motion ■ *n* (*plural* **-ries**) SCURRYING MOVEMENT a hurried, agitated, or swirling movement [Early 19C. Origin ?]

Scur·ry /skúrree, skúr ee/, **Briana** (*b.* 1971) US soccer player. She was goalkeeper on the US women's national soccer team that won a gold medal in the 1996 Olympics and won the World Cup championship in 1999. Full name **Scurry, Briana Collette**

scur·vy /skúrvee/ *n* a disease caused by insufficient vitamin C, the symptoms of which include spongy gums, loosening of the teeth, and bleeding into the skin and mucous membranes ■ *adj* (**-vi·er, -vi·est**) behaving in ways thought to be mean or contemptible [15C. < SCURF] —**scur·vi·ly** *adv* —**scur·vi·ness** *n*

scut /skut/ *n* a short erect tail, e.g., that of a rabbit [15C. Origin ?]

scu·ta ZOOL, ARMS plural of **scutum**

scu·tage /skyóotij/ *n* in feudal times, a tax paid by a knight or vassal to his lord that freed him from military service [15C. < medieval Latin *scutagium* "shield tax" < Latin *scutum* "shield"]

scu·tate /skyóo tàyt/ *adj* **1.** shaped like a shield ○ *a scutate leaf* **2.** covered or protected by external bony or horny plates or scales [Early 19C. < SCUTUM] —**scu·ta·tion** /skyoo táysh'n/ *n*

scutch /skuch/ *vt* (**scutched, scutch·ing, scutch·es**) to beat flax, cotton, or hemp in order to separate the valuable fibers from the woody parts ■ *n* a tool or machine for scutching flax, cotton, or hemp [Late 17C. Via Old French *escoucher* < Latin *excutere* "shake"]

scutch grass *n* PLANTS same as **Bermuda grass**

scute /skyoot, skoot/ *n* an external bony or horny plate or scale in some animals, especially snakes and other reptiles [14C. < Latin *scutum* "shield"]

scu·tel·lum /skyoo télləm/ (*plural* **-la** /-lə/) *n* **1.** a hard plate or scale, e.g., on the thorax of an insect or a toe of a bird **2.** the shield-shaped embryonic leaf (**cotyledon**) of a grass seed [Mid-18C. < modern Latin, alteration of Latin *scutella* "dish, tray" as if meaning "small shield" and < Latin *scutum* "shield"] —**scu·tel·lar** *adj* —**scu·tel·late** /skyoo téllət, skyóot'l àyt/ *adj* —**scu·tel·la·tion** /skyòotə láysh'n/ *n*

scut·ter /skúttər/ (**-tered, -ter·ing, -ters**) *vi* to move hastily in a scurrying manner [Late 18C. Alteration of SCUTTLE[3]]

scut·tle[1] /skútt'l/ *n* **1.** SMALL HATCH a small hatchway with a cover in the deck or hull of a ship or in some part of a building such as the roof or a wall **2.** SCUTTLE COVER ON SHIP the cover for a scuttle on a ship ■ *vt* (**-tled, -tling, -tles**) **1.** DESTROY SOMETHING to destroy or bring something to an end ○ *had effectively scuttled his plans* **2.** SINK SHIP BY LETTING WATER IN to sink a ship by making or opening holes in its bottom [15C. Via French *escoutille* < Spanish *escotilla* "hatchway" < *escotar* "cut out" < Germanic]

scuttle

scut·tle[2] /skútt'l/ *n* **1.** HOUSEHOLD same as **coal scuttle** **2.** an open shallow basket used to carry foods or small items [Pre-12C. < Old Norse *skutill*, via Germanic < Latin *scutella* "dish, tray"]

scut·tle[3] /skútt'l/ *vi* (**-tled, -tling, -tles**) to run or move quickly with short steps ■ *n* a hurried pace or scuttling movement [15C. Origin ?]

scut·tle·butt /skútt'l bùt/ *n* **1.** rumors about somebody's activities, often of an intimate and scandalous nature (*slang*) **2.** a drinking fountain on a ship [Early 19C. < SCUTTLE[2] + BUTT[4]]

scu·tum /skyóotəm/ (*plural* **-ta** /-tə/) *n* **1.** ZOOL same as **scute** **2.** a large shield used by legionaries in ancient Rome [Late 18C. < Latin, "shield"]

Scu·tum *n* a small faint constellation of the southern hemisphere

scut·work /skút wùrk/ *n* routine and monotonous or menial work (*informal*) [Mid-20C. Origin ?]

scuzz /skuz/ *n* **1.** something dirty, disgusting, or disreputable (*slang*) **2.** an offensive term for somebody regarded as unpleasant and contemptible (*slang insult*) [Mid-20C. Origin ?] —**scuzz·i·ly** *adv*—**scuz·zi·ness** *n* —**scuz·zy** *adj*

scuzz·bag /skúz bàg/, **scuzz·ball** /skúz bàwl/, **scuzz·buck·et** /skúz bùkət/ *n* same as **scuzz** (sense 2)

Scyl·la /síllə/ *n* in Greek mythology, a sea monster who attacked sailors. In later times, Scylla was thought to be a rock on the Italian side of the Straits of Messina. ◇ **be between Scylla and Charybdis** to be faced with the necessity of choosing between two equally undesirable or unpleasant things

scy·phis·to·ma /sī fístəmə/ (*plural* **-mae** /-mee/ or **-mas**) *n* the form taken by a jellyfish or other scyphozoan during the stage in its life cycle when it remains fixed in one place and reproduces asexually to produce free-swimming offspring [Late 19C. < Latin *scyphus* "large cup" < Greek *skuphos*]

scy·pho·zo·an /sìfə zō ən/ *n* a member of a class of marine invertebrate animals that are generally free-swimming and only sedentary when reproducing, especially a jellyfish [Early 20C. < modern Latin *Scyphozoa* < Greek *skuphos* "cup" + *zōa* "animals"]

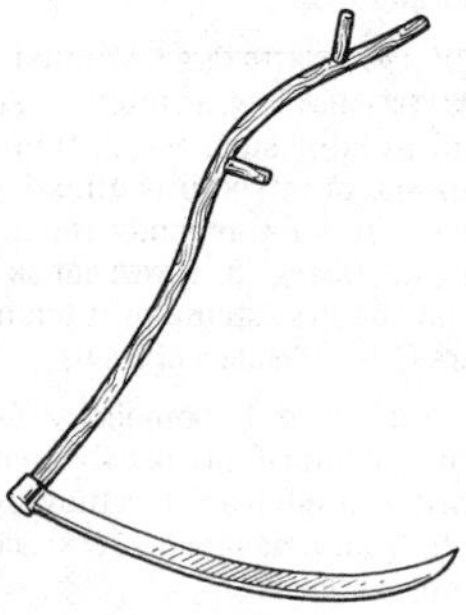

scythe

scythe /sīth/ *n* an implement with a long handle and a long curved single-edged blade, used to cut grass, crops, or similar plants by swinging the blade horizontally close to the ground ■ *vti* (**scythed, scyth·ing, scythes**) to cut or reap something with or as if with a scythe ○ *scythed grass* [Old English *siþe* < Indo-European, "to cut"]

Scyth·i·a /síthee ə, sīthee ə/ ancient region in what is now Moldova, Ukraine, and eastern Russia

Scyth·i·an /síthee ən, sīthee-/ *n* a member of an ancient people who lived in Scythia ■ *adj* relating to ancient Scythia or its people or culture

sd *abbr* Sudan (*used in Internet addresses*) See table at **domain name**

SD *abbr* **1.** South Dakota **2.** special delivery **3.** STATS standard deviation

S.D. *abbr* **1.** South Dakota **2.** special delivery

S. Dak. *abbr* South Dakota

SDI, **S.D.I.** *abbr* MIL, POL Strategic Defense Initiative

SDR, **SDRs** *abbr* ECON special drawing rights

SDRAM *abbr* COMPUT synchronous dynamic random-access memory

SDS *abbr* US HIST, POL Students for a Democratic Society

se *abbr* Sweden (*used in Internet addresses*) See table at **domain name**

Se *symbol* CHEM ELEM selenium

SE *abbr* COMPASS **1.** southeast **2.** southeastern

sea /see/ *n* **1.** SALT WATERS OF EARTH the great body of salt water that covers a large portion of Earth ○ *swimming in the sea* ○ *sea air* ○ *a sea fish* **2.** BODY OF SALT WATER a body of salt water that is surrounded by land on all or most sides, or that is part of one of the oceans ○ *the Caribbean Sea* **3.** LARGE LAKE a large inland body of fresh water **4.** ASTRON same as **mare**[2] **5.** TURBULENCE OF OCEAN the motion and disturbance of a large body of water such as the ocean, or the waves themselves ○ *big seas* **6.** SEAFARER'S JOB OR LIFE the occupation or way of life of a sailor ○ *ran away to sea* **7.** VAST BODY a large area or great number of something ○ *a sea of faces* [Old English *sǣ* < Germanic] ◇ **at sea 1.** traveling on the ocean **2.** bewildered and confused

SPELLCHECK sea or **see**? Do not confuse the spelling of ***sea*** and ***see***, which sound similar. ***Sea*** denotes a large body of water, as in *the Mediterranean Sea*, and is used figuratively in such phrases as *a sea of faces*. ***See*** is chiefly used as a verb, meaning "perceive with the eyes," "have a clear understanding," etc.: *She couldn't see him anywhere. I see what you mean.* There is also a different word ***see***, a noun, referring to the area of jurisdiction of a bishop or archbishop.

sea an·chor *n* a device, e.g., a conical canvas bag, that is thrown overboard and dragged behind a ship to control its speed or heading

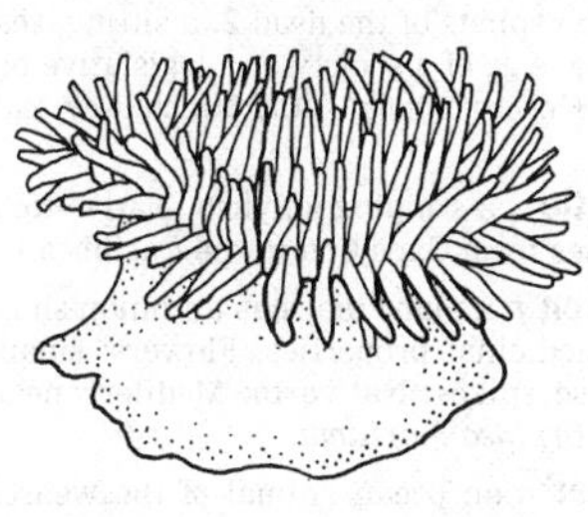

sea anemone

sea a·nem·o·ne *n* a solitary and often colorful sea animal with a squat cylindrical body topped by a ring of tentacles that attaches itself to rock or other nonliving material. Order: Actiniaria.

sea bass /-bàss/ *n* a bony sea fish that has a long body, large mouth, and spiny dorsal fin and is a popular game fish. Native to: Atlantic coast of North America. Latin name: *Centropristis striata.*

sea·bed /seé bèd/ *n* the ground at the bottom of the ocean

Sea·bee /seé beè/ *n* a member of one of the construction battalions of the US Navy that build naval shore facilities in combat zones [Mid-20C. < pronunciation of *CB*, abbreviation of *construction battalion*]

sea·bird /seé bùrd/ *n* a bird that frequents the open ocean, e.g., a gull, albatross, or petrel

sea bis·cuit *n* FOOD same as **hardtack**

sea·blite /seé blìt/ *n* an annual plant that grows in salt marshes. Latin name: *Suaeda maritima.* [Mid-18C. < *blite* "plant of the goosefoot family," via Latin < Greek *bliton*]

sea·board /seé bàwrd/ *n* **1.** same as **seacoast 2.** land near a seacoast ○ *the Eastern Seaboard*

sea·bor·gi·um /see báwrgee əm/ *n* a very unstable chemical element produced by high-energy collisions of atoms. Symbol **Sg**. See table at **element** [Late 20C. After Glenn T. *Seaborg* (1912–99), US nuclear chemist]

sea·borne /seé bàwrn/ *adj* **1.** transported by ship across the sea **2.** carried on or in the sea

sea bream *n* **1.** a porgy. Native to: Atlantic coastal waters. Latin name: *Archosargus rhomboidalis.* **2.** an ocean fish that resembles a freshwater bream. Native to: European waters. Family: Sparidae.

sea breeze *n* a cooling breeze that blows inland from the sea during the daytime when the land is warmer than the surface of the water

Sea·bur·y /seé bèrree, -bəree/, **Samuel** (1729–96) US cleric. He served as a Loyalist under the British during the Revolution (1776–83). Afterward he became the first Episcopal bishop of Connecticut and Rhode Island (1784).

sea cap·tain *n* somebody in charge of a ship, especially a merchant ship

sea change *n* a substantial transformation ○ *a sea change in attitudes about legalized gambling*

sea chest *n* a large box or trunk in which a sailor's personal belongings are stored

sea·coast /seé kòst/ *n* the land that borders the sea or ocean

sea·cock /seé kòk/ *n* a valve in the hull of a ship used to let water in or out

Sea·cole /seé kòl/, **Mary Jane** (1805–81) Jamaican nurse. She worked in the Crimean War and received honors from the British, French, and Turkish governments for her courage on the battlefields.

sea cow *n* MARINE BIOL same as **sirenian**

sea cray·fish *n* ZOOL same as **spiny lobster**

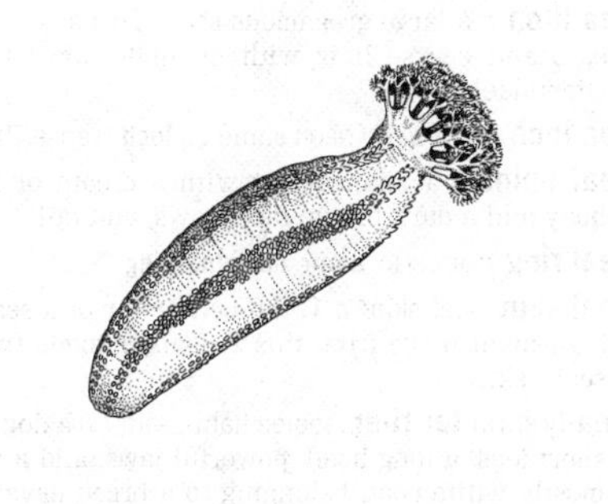

sea cucumber

sea cu·cum·ber *n* an invertebrate (**echinoderm**) that has a long tough muscular body and a mouth encircled by tentacles, and lives on the seabed. Class: Holothuroidea.

sea de·vil *n* FISH same as **devilfish**

sea dog *n* a sailor of long experience

sea·dog /seé dòg/ *n* METEOROL same as **fogbow**

sea ea·gle *n* a fish-eating eagle that lives near the ocean. Genus: *Haliaeetus.*

sea el·e·phant *n* MARINE BIOL same as **elephant seal**

sea fan *n* a coral with a fan-shaped skeleton. Native to: Florida, Caribbean. Genus: *Gorgonia.*

sea·far·er /seé fèrrər/ *n* somebody who travels by sea

sea·far·ing /seé fèrring/ *adj* **1.** REGULARLY GOING TO SEA regularly traveling by sea or working at sea **2.** OF SEA TRAVEL OR TRANSPORTATION relating to travel or transportation by sea ■ *n* SAILOR'S WAY OF LIFE the work and way of life of a sailor

sea fire *n* light that is produced by ocean organisms

sea·floor /seé flàwr/ *n* OCEANOG same as **seabed**

sea·floor spread·ing *n* a process in which molten material from the Earth's mantle rises up at ocean ridges, causing volcanic and seismic activity, spreads out, and creates a new seafloor

sea·food /seé food/ *n* fish and shellfish from the sea eaten as food

sea·fowl /seé fòwl/ (*plural same* or **-fowls**) *n* BIRDS same as **seabird**

sea·front /seé frùnt/ *n* land or property along the edge of the sea

sea·girt /seé gùrt/ *adj* encircled by the sea (*literary*)

sea·go·ing /seé gō ing/ *adj* **1.** same as **oceangoing 2.** NAUT same as **seafaring** *adj* (sense 1)

sea grape *n* a tree with large rounded leaves and clusters of purple-to-whitish berries. Native to: sandy shores from Florida to South America. Latin name: *Coccoloba uvifera.*

sea·grass /seé gràss/ *n* an underwater ocean grass with long thick blades that is harvested and processed into a material, similar to twine or jute, used for making baskets and matting

sea green *n* a blue-green color in which the green is predominant —**sea-green** *adj*

sea·gull /seé gùl/ *n* BIRDS same as **gull**[1]

CULTURAL NOTE ***The Seagull***, a play (1896) by the Russian writer Anton Chekhov. The plot centers on the young writer Triplev's love for the aspiring actress Nina, who, to Triplev's dismay, allows herself to be seduced by an older, more famous writer, Trigorin. One of Chekhov's most successful plays, it typically eschews melodrama for social and psychological analysis.

sea·gull man·ag·er *n* a manager whose interaction with the work force consists solely in arriving, criticizing everything and everybody harshly, and leaving again (*slang*)

sea hare *n* a large ocean mollusk that has an arched back, a reduced or absent external shell, and two tentacles resembling rabbit ears. Genus: *Aplysia.*

sea hog *n* MARINE BIOL same as **porpoise** (sense 1)

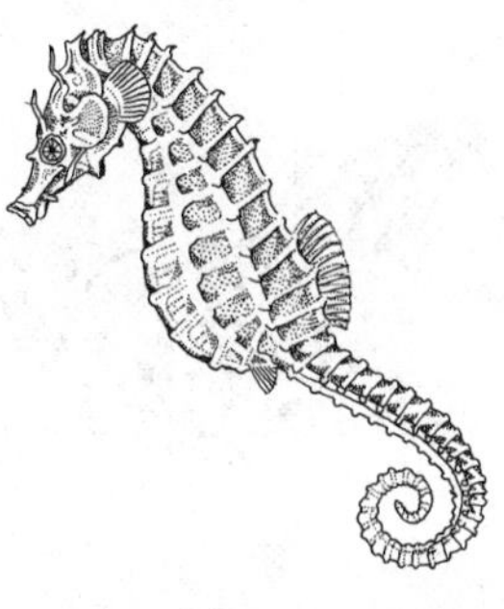

sea horse

sea horse *n* **1.** a small bony fish with a head shaped like that of a horse, a vertical swimming position, and a tail that it uses to cling to seaweed. Genus: *Hippocampus.* **2.** a mythological creature with the head and forelegs of a horse and the body of a fish **3.** MARINE BIOL same as **walrus** (*archaic*)

sea-is·land cot·ton *n* a cotton with long silky fibers, grown chiefly in the Caribbean. Latin name: *Gossypium barbadense.* [After the SEA ISLANDS]

Sea Is·lands chain of several hundred low islands in the southern United States, lying in the Atlantic Ocean off the coast of South Carolina, Georgia, and Florida. The main islands include Parris and Hilton Head in South Carolina and Amelia in Florida. The Sea Islands are a popular tourist destination and home to the Gullah people.

sea kale *n* a plant related to the cabbage, with edible leaves and shoots. Native to: seashores of Europe and Asia. Latin name: *Crambe maritima.*

sea king *n* a Norse pirate chief of the early Middle Ages

seal[1] /seel/ *n* **1.** TIGHT OR PERFECT CLOSURE a tight closure that prevents the entrance or escape of, e.g., air or water, or a substance or device that forms such a closure **2.** SPECIAL CLOSURE THAT REVEALS TAMPERING a closure for a package or container that must be broken when the package or container is opened and can therefore reveal tampering **3.** AUTHENTICATING STAMP a ring or stamp with a raised or engraved symbol or emblem that is pressed into wax in order to certify a signature or authenticate a document **4.** WAX MARKED WITH SEAL a piece of wax bearing the mark of a seal **5.** SYMBOL OF OFFICE a device, emblem, or symbol that is a mark of office **6.** ORNAMENTAL ADHESIVE STAMP an ornamental adhesive stamp used to close a letter or package **7.** SOMETHING GIVING CONFIRMATION something that gives confirmation or assurance ○ *Mother gave our plans for the party her seal of approval.* ■ *vt* (**sealed, seal·ing, seals**) **1.** CLOSE SOMETHING FIRMLY to close something tightly or securely with a seal **2.** MAKE SOMETHING WATERTIGHT OR AIRTIGHT to make something watertight, airtight, or nonporous, e.g., by filling gaps or applying a coating **3.** ATTACH AUTHENTICATING SEAL TO SOMETHING to affix a marked piece of wax to something in order to authenticate or certify it **4.** CONFIRM SOMETHING to confirm a decision or come to an agreement on something ○ *seal a contract* **5.** SETTLE SOMETHING to determine something irrevocably ○ *His fate was sealed when his lies were discovered.* **6.** SOLEMNIZE MARRIAGE OR ADOPTION in the Church of Jesus Christ of Latter-Day Saints, to solemnize a marriage or adoption [12C. Via Anglo-Norman < Latin *sigillum* "little mark" < *signum* "sign, token"] —**seal·a·ble** *adj* ◇ **set the seal on something 1.** to be the thing that ensures that something happens or that completes and perfects something **2.** to give final approval or authorization for something ◇ **set your seal on something** to have a decisive influence on the character of something

seal off *vt* to prevent people or things from entering or leaving a place, e.g., by surrounding it or closing it securely ○ *Police sealed off the area.*

seal[2] /seel/ *n* **1.** FISH-EATING OCEAN MAMMAL a carnivorous ocean mammal with a sleek body adapted for swimming and living in cold regions and webbed feet modified as flippers. Families: Otariidae or Phocidae. See illustration on next page **2.** SEAL'S PELT the pelt or fur of a seal **3.** LEATHER FROM SEAL'S SKIN leather made from the skin of a seal ■ *vi* (**sealed, seal·ing,**

seal

seals) HUNT SEALS to hunt seals, usually for their skins or blubber [Old English *seol-*, stem of *seolh* < Germanic]

SEAL /seel/ *abbr US* NAVY sea, air, land (team)

sea lam·prey *n* a large eel-shaped jawless ocean fish that swims up rivers to spawn and lives as a parasite on other fish. Native to: Atlantic coast of North America. Latin name: *Petromyzon marinus.*

sea-lane *n* an established and commonly used sea route for large ships

seal·ant /seélənt/ *n* a substance used to seal something, e.g., by filling gaps or making a surface nonporous

sea lav·en·der *n* a perennial plant of the thrift family with a rosette of slender leaves at the base. Flowers: bluish purple, in branching spikes. Native to: temperate salt marshes. Genus: *Limonium.*

sea law·yer *n* an argumentative sailor (*informal*)

sealed-beam head·light /seeld-/ *n* a vehicle headlight with a prefocused reflector and lens sealed in one unit

sealed or·ders *npl* written instructions not to be opened or read before a specific time

sea legs *npl* the ability to maintain balance and not experience motion sickness from the rolling and pitching of a boat (*informal*)

seal·er[1] /seélər/ *n* **1.** a person, substance, or device that seals something, e.g., a substance used to make a surface nonporous **2.** an official who inspects and certifies weights and measures [14C. < SEAL[1]]

seal·er[2] /seélər/ *n* a hunter of seals, or a boat used by such hunters [Mid-18C. < SEAL[2]]

seal·er·y /seéləree/ (*plural* **-ies**) *n* **1.** BREEDING PLACE FOR SEALS a place where seals are raised or where seals congregate and breed **2.** HUNTING GROUND FOR SEALS a place where seals are hunted **3.** HUNTING OF SEALS the occupation or practice of hunting seals [Late 19C. < SEAL[2]]

sea let·tuce *n* a seaweed sometimes used as food in salads. Genus: *Ulva.*

sea lev·el *n* the level of the surface of the ocean relative to the land, halfway between high and low tide, used as a standard in calculating elevation

sea·lift /seé lìft/ (**-lift·ed, -lift·ing, -lifts**) *vt* to transport people or cargo by ship, especially at short notice

sea lil·y *n* an invertebrate that has a stalk anchored to the seabed and a flower-shaped body. Class: Crinoidea.

seal·ing wax /seéling-/ *n* a resinous substance that is soft when heated and used for sealing letters, documents, batteries, or jars

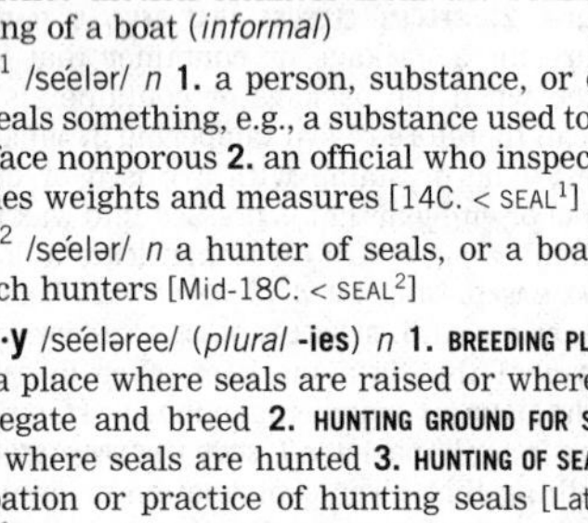

sea lion

sea li·on *n* a large gregarious seal that has external ears and coarse hair with no underfur. Family: Otariidae.

sea loch *n Scotland* GEOG same as **loch** (sense 2)

seal point *n* a Siamese cat with a cream or fawn body and a dark brown face, paws, and tail

seal ring *n* JEWELRY same as **signet ring**

seal·skin /seél skìn/ *n* **1.** the pelt or fur of a seal, or a garment made from this **2.** leather made from a seal's skin

Sea·ly·ham ter·ri·er /seélee hàm-, -əm-/ *n* a dog with short legs, a long head, powerful jaws, and a wiry, mostly white coat, belonging to a breed developed in Wales for catching rabbits and similar animals [Late 19C. After a village in South Wales]

seam /seem/ *n* **1.** PLACE WHERE PIECES JOIN the line along which pieces of cloth or leather are joined by sewing **2.** STITCHES FORMING SEAM the stitches used to form a seam **3.** LINE FORMED BY ADJACENT SECTIONS any line, groove, or ridge formed by joining or fitting together two sections along their edges **4.** LINEAR INDENTATION a scar, wrinkle, or other linear indentation **5.** GEOL THIN LAYER OF ROCK a thin layer of a rock or mineral such as a coal deposit occurring between different strata of bedrock ■ *v* (**seamed, seam·ing, seams**) **1.** *vt* JOIN THINGS ALONG EDGES to join two parts or pieces along their edges, e.g., by sewing them together **2.** *vti* MARK WITH LINES to mark something with wrinkles, scars, furrows, or other lines, or become marked in this way [Old English *sēam* < Germanic, "sew"] ◇ **bulging** *or* **bursting at the seams** extremely full ◇ **come** *or* **fall apart at the seams** to show signs of imminent failure or collapse

SPELLCHECK Do not confuse the spelling of ***seam*** and ***seem***, which sound similar. ***Seam*** is usually a noun, denoting a line, layer, or ridge where things join, as in *sewed a seam, a rock seam.* ***Seem*** is a verb, meaning "give a particular impression or sensation": *He seemed to be looking for someone. They seem very pleasant.*

sea·man /seémən/ (*plural* **-men** /-mən/) *n* **1.** somebody, especially a man, who works aboard a boat or ship, especially a low-ranking member of the crew of a merchant or naval ship **2.** an enlisted person in the US Navy or Coast Guard of a rank above seaman apprentice —**sea·man·ship** *n*

sea·man ap·pren·tice *n* an enlisted person in the US Navy or Coast Guard of a rank above seaman recruit

sea·man re·cruit *n* an enlisted person in the US Navy or Coast Guard of the lowest rank

sea·mark /seé maàrk/ *n* an object on land easily visible from the sea that serves as an aid to navigation

sea mat *n* MARINE BIOL same as **bryozoan**

seam·er /seémər/ *n* a person or machine that makes seams, or the operator of such a machine

sea mile *n* MEASURE same as **nautical mile**

sea milk·wort *n* a plant of the primula family. Flowers: small, pink. Native to: northern temperate coasts. Latin name: *Glaux maritima.*

seam·less /seémləss/ *adj* **1.** WITHOUT SEAMS having no seams **2.** PERFECTLY SMOOTH free from awkward transitions and creating perfectly smooth continuity **3.** COMPUT FULLY INTEGRATED characterized by integration into an existing software or hardware system without causing any disruption, as if the new item were part of the original design —**seam·less·ly** *adv* —**seam·less·ness** *n*

sea·moss /seé màwss, -mòss/ *n Carib* a drink popular in the Caribbean, made of seaweed that is boiled until it dissolves and then mixed with milk and spices

sea·mount /seé mòwnt/ *n* an isolated undersea mountain of volcanic origin that rises from the seabed to a height of up to 3,300 ft./1,000 m, usually 3,300 ft./1,000 m to 6,500 ft./2,000 m below the surface of the sea

sea mouse *n* a large sea worm with a broad flat body covered in bristles resembling hair. Genus: *Aphrodite.*

seam·stress /seémstrəss/ *n* a woman who sews or whose occupation is sewing [Late 16C. < archaic *seamster* "tailor, somebody who sews" < SEAM]

seam·y /seémee/ (**-i·er, -i·est**) *adj* having unpleasant qualities associated with a degraded or degenerate way of living —**seam·i·ness** *n*

se·ance /sáy aànss, -aàNss/ *n* **1.** a meeting at which a spiritualist attempts to receive communications from the spirits of the dead **2.** a sitting, session, or meeting, e.g., of a society or a legislative body [Late 18C. < French, "sitting" < Old French *seoir* "sit" < Latin *sedere*]

sea net·tle *n* a stinging jellyfish. Native to: Atlantic estuaries from Cape Cod to the Caribbean.

sea on·ion *n* a plant that has an onion-shaped bulb with medicinal properties. Flowers: small, white, in dense spikes. Native to: Mediterranean. Latin name: *Urginea maritima.*

sea ot·ter *n* an ocean animal of the weasel family that has a thick brown coat and feeds mainly on shellfish. Native to: northern Pacific coasts. Latin name: *Enhydra lutris.*

sea pen *n* an ocean organism related to coral that forms feathery colonies. Native to: warm seas. Genus: *Pennatula.*

sea pink *n* PLANTS same as **thrift** (sense 3)

sea·plane /seé plàyn/ *n* a plane designed in such a way that it can take off from and land on water

sea poach·er *n* a small slender ocean fish that has an armor of bony plates and is found near the bottom of the North Pacific and other cold waters. Family: Agonidae.

sea·port /seé pàwrt/ *n* a port, town, or harbor that can accommodate oceangoing ships

sea pow·er *n* **1.** a nation that has formidable naval strength **2.** the military power that a nation can deploy to fight on water

sea purse *n* the egg pouch of a shark or ray that often has curly tendrils so that it can attach itself to seaweed

sea·quake /seé kwàyk/ *n* an earthquake occurring under the sea

sear[1] /seer/ *v* (**seared, sear·ing, sears**) **1.** *vt* BURN SOMETHING to burn or scorch something with intense heat **2.** *vt* HAVE UNPLEASANT EFFECT to have a sudden painful or unpleasant effect on somebody or something **3.** *vti* WITHER to wither, shrivel, or dry up, or cause something to wither, shrivel, or dry up ■ *n* BURN OR SCORCH MARK a mark or scar made by searing [Old English *sēarian* "wither away" < Germanic]

sear[2] /seer/ *n* the catch that holds a gunlock cocked or at half-cock [Mid-16C. < French *serre* "grasp, lock" < *serrer* "to grasp" < Latin *sera* "bar for a door"]

sear[3] /seer/ *adj* another spelling of **sere**[1] (*archaic or literary*)

sea rav·en *n* a fish that swallows air and blows up like a balloon when removed from the water. Native to: Atlantic coast of North America. Latin name: *Hemitripterus americanus.*

search /surch/ *v* (**searched, search·ing, search·es**) **1.** *vti* EXAMINE SOMETHING THOROUGHLY to look into, over, or through something carefully in order to find somebody or something ○ *searched his pockets for some change* ○ *searching through the pile of papers on the desk* **2.** *vt* EXAMINE SOMEBODY FOR CONCEALED ITEMS to examine the clothing, personal effects, or body of somebody in order to discover something such as weapons or illegal drugs that have been deliberately concealed **3.** *vt* DISCOVER SOMETHING BY EXAMINATION to discover, come to know, or find something by examination ○ *searched out the relevant file* **4.** *vt* COMPUT EXAMINE COMPUTER FILE to examine a computer file, disk, database, or network for information ■ *n* **1.** THOROUGH EXAMINATION a careful and thorough examination in order to find somebody or something **2.** COMPUT EXAMINATION OF COMPUTER FILE the examination of a computer file, disk, database, or network in order to find information **3.** LAW ACT OF BOARDING SHIP TO SEARCH the act of boarding a ship in accordance with international law in order to search it, especially during wartime [14C. Via Anglo-Norman *sercher*, Old French *cerchier* "explore" < Latin *circare* "go around in circles" < *circus* "circle"] —**search·a·ble** *adj* —**search·er** *n* ◇ **search me**

used for emphasizing your lack of knowledge about something (*informal*)

search and res·cue *n* **1.** EMERGENCIES a rapid coordinated response to an emergency situation involving human casualties by volunteer or professional personnel ○ *trained in search and rescue* **2.** a voluntary or professional organization that provides search and rescue facilities

search di·rec·to·ry *n* a website in which links to information are organized into a categorical, alphabetical hierarchy to provide the broadest response to a query

search dog *n* a dog that is trained to find people who are lost or have become trapped after an accident or disaster, or to uncover specific substances such as drugs

search en·gine *n* a computer program that searches for specific words and returns a list of documents in which they were found, especially a commercial Internet service

search·ing /súrching/ *adj* observing acutely or examining thoroughly —**search·ing·ly** *adv*

search·light /súrch lìt/ *n* **1.** an apparatus for projecting a high-intensity beam of light in any direction **2.** the light from a searchlight

search par·ty *n* a group of volunteers or professionals organized to search for a missing person

search war·rant *n* a court order authorizing entry to somebody's property to look for unlawful possessions

sear·ing /séering/ *adj* **1.** extremely intense or strong ○ *felt a searing pain* **2.** extremely critical of something ○ *wrote a searing criticism of the performance* —**sear·ing·ly** *adv*

sea rob·in *n Can* FISH same as **gurnard** (sense 1)

sea rock·et *n* a plant of the mustard family that grows along seashores and has sharp-tasting leaves. Flowers: white or lavender. Native to: North America, Europe, Asia, Australia. Genus: *Cakile.*

sea·room /seé ròom, -ròom/ *n* open space at sea in which to turn or maneuver a ship

sea rov·er *n* a pirate or a pirate ship (*literary*)

sea salt *n* coarse salt obtained from the evaporation of seawater

sea·scape /seé skàyp/ *n* a painting or picture of the sea, or a view of the sea

Sea Scout *n* a member of a scouting organization who learns sailing, boating, canoeing, and other water activities

sea ser·pent *n* **1.** a giant snake often reported to have been seen at sea, but never proven to exist **2.** REPT same as **sea snake** (sense 1)

sea·shell /seé shèl/ *n* the empty shell of a sea organism, especially a mollusk

sea·shore /seé shàwr/ *n* **1.** the land lying next to the ocean **2.** in law, the land lying between the usual high and low water marks

sea·sick /seé sìk/ *adj* nauseated or dizzy as a result of the rocking movement of a vessel on water —**sea·sick·ness** *n*

sea·side /seé sìd/ *n* the area of land bordering the sea ■ *adj* situated or taking place at the seaside ○ *a seaside cottage*

sea·side spar·row *n* a small sparrow. Native to: Atlantic coast of North America. Latin name: *Ammodramus maritimus.*

sea slug *n* a marine invertebrate animal that resembles a sea snail with no shell and is often brightly colored. Order: Nudibranchia.

sea snail *n* a small marine organism with a spiral shell resembling that of a snail, e.g., a whelk or periwinkle. Class: Gastropoda.

sea snake *n* **1.** a venomous snake that swims by means of an oar-shaped tail and bears live young. Native to: tropical waters. Family: Hydrophidae. **2.** MYTHOL same as **sea serpent** (sense 1)

sea·son /seéz'n/ *n* **1.** TRADITIONAL DIVISION OF YEAR a traditional division of the year based on distinctive weather conditions. In temperate regions, there are four seasons, spring, summer, fall, and winter, while in tropical countries there are often only two, a dry season and a rainy season. **2.** PERIOD FOR PARTICULAR ACTIVITY a period of the year during which a particular activity usually takes place in the human world or among plants and animals ○ *planting season* ○ *mating season* **3.** PERIOD SET ASIDE FOR ACTIVITY a fixed period of every year during which particular activities, especially sports, take place or are permitted ○ *baseball season* **4.** PLAYER'S OR TEAM'S PERFORMANCE the performance of a player or team during a sporting season in relation to others ○ *had his best season ever* **5.** TIME FOR FOOD the time of year when something, especially a kind of food, is abundant and at its best ○ *asparagus season* **6.** HIGH SEASON AT RESORTS the time of year at which resorts receive most visitors and charge their highest rates ○ *the height of the season* **7.** SOCIAL SEASON the time during which the important social events of the year involving members of high society take place **8.** TIME AROUND HOLIDAY the period of time just before, after, and including a holiday ○ *the Christmas season* **9.** PERIOD OF TIME a period of time of unspecified length ○ *a brief season* **10.** SUITABLE TIME an appropriate time for something (*literary*) **11.** *UK* ARTS CONNECTED SERIES OF PERFORMANCES a period of time during which artistic works of a particular kind are shown or performed ■ *v* (**-soned, -son·ing, -sons**) **1.** *vti* ADD FLAVORINGS to add flavorings such as salt, spices, or herbs to food **2.** *vt* ENLIVEN SOMETHING to liven up something such as a speech or piece of writing by inserting exciting or amusing material ○ *a speech seasoned with wit* **3.** *vti* DRY OUT BEFORE USE to allow wood to dry out fully before use, or become fully dried out before being used **4.** *vt* PREPARE NEW PAN FOR USE to prepare a new frying pan or wok for use by rubbing vegetable oil into the heated cooking surface **5.** *vt* CAUSE SOMEBODY TO GAIN EXPERIENCE to cause or enable somebody to gain experience and become more skilled, or to gain toughness and strength ○ *seasoned troops* **6.** *vt* MODERATE SOMETHING to temper something such as a strong emotion (*literary*) [14C. Via Old French < Latin *sation-* "sowing" < *sat-*, past participle of *serere* "sow"] —**sea·son·er** *n* ◇ **in season 1.** plentifully available and at a peak of quality ○ *Strawberries are in season now.* **2.** allowed to be hunted, caught, or killed **3.** VET sexually receptive to males **4.** at an appropriate time (*literary*) ◇ **out of season 1.** not widely available or not of good quality because of the time of year ○ *Tulips are out of season at this time of year.* **2.** not allowed to be hunted, caught, or killed because of the time of year **3.** at an inappropriate time (*literary*)

CULTURAL NOTE ***The Four Seasons***, a violin concerto (1725) by the Italian composer Antonio Vivaldi. Vivaldi's best-known work (Opus 8) consists of four movements, each of which describes a season with appropriate music. The section called "Spring," for example, features birdsong, while "Autumn" incorporates sounds that suggest rustling leaves. Vivaldi provided a commentary on each movement in a series of sonnets he wrote to accompany the concerto.

sea·son·a·ble /seéz'nəb'l/ *adj* **1.** typical of or appropriate for the time of year **2.** done, given, or occurring at a time when needed or appropriate —**sea·son·a·ble·ness** *n* —**sea·son·a·bly** *adv*

sea·son·al /seézən'l, seéznəl/ *adj* **1.** dependent on or determined by the time of year **2.** available or employed only during one season or at specific times of the year —**sea·son·al·ly** *adv*

sea·son·al af·fec·tive dis·or·der, sea·son·al af·fec·tive dis·or·der syn·drome *n* medical depression associated with the onset of winter and thought to be caused by decreasing amounts of daylight

sea·son·ing /seéz'ning/ *n* **1.** salt, pepper, or any herb or spice used to give additional flavor to food **2.** the process of treating lumber to reduce its moisture sufficiently so that it is suitable for the function for which it will be used

sea·son·ing meat *n regional* same as **fatback**

REGIONAL NOTE See ***fatback.***

sea·son tick·et *n* a ticket, or one of a set of tickets, valid for a specific period of time for use of leisure facilities or attendance at sporting or cultural events (*often used in the plural*)

sea spi·der *n* a marine organism resembling a spider, with a fairly small body and four to six pairs of long jointed legs. Class: Pycnogonida.

sea squill *n UK* same as **sea onion**

sea squirt *n* a marine invertebrate animal that has a transparent sac-shaped body with openings through which water passes in and out. It squirts out a stream of water when disturbed. Class: Ascidiacea.

sea star *n* ZOOL same as **starfish**

sea swal·low *n* a bird of the tern family, especially a common tern. Latin name: *Sterna hirundo.*

seat /seet/ *n* **1.** PLACE TO SIT something for sitting on, especially something designed for this, e.g., a chair or bench **2.** PART OF CHAIR SAT ON the usually horizontal part of a chair or other seat that takes most of the weight of the person sitting on it **3.** VIEWER'S OR TRAVELER'S SITTING PLACE a place to sit and watch an event or travel in a vehicle, for which a ticket is usually required ○ *We reserved seats in the front row.* **4.** PART OF GARMENT COVERING BUTTOCKS the part of a garment that covers the buttocks **5.** MEMBERSHIP IN OFFICIAL GROUP a position as a member of an official body or group, especially in an elected legislature ○ *won a seat in the legislature* **6.** BASE a place where something is located or based (*formal*) ○ *the seat of consciousness* **7.** *US* CENTER OF POWER a place from which administrative power is exercised ○ *a county seat* **8.** RESIDENCE a residence, especially a large house associated with a specific family **9.** OBJECT ON WHICH SOMETHING RESTS an object, part, or space on which something rests or into which it fits **10.** RIDER'S POSITION the position in which a rider sits on a horse ■ *v* (**seat·ed, seat·ing, seats**) **1.** *vt* PLACE SOMEBODY IN SEAT to place somebody or yourself in a chair or other seat **2.** *vt* PROVIDE SEATS FOR PEOPLE to have or provide seats for a particular number of people ○ *The hall seats five hundred.* **3.** *vti* REST OR FIT SECURELY to rest something securely on or fit something firmly into another thing, or be firmly resting on or fitted into something ○ *The valve isn't seating properly.* **4.** *vt* INSTALL SOMEBODY IN POWERFUL POSITION to establish somebody in a position of power or authority (*literary*) **5.** *vt* FIT SEAT ON SOMETHING to put or refurbish a seat in or on something [12C. < Old Icelandic *sæti* < Germanic, "sit"] ◇ **by the seat of your pants 1.** using intuition and guesswork rather than theory or specialized knowledge **2.** without the help of any instruments or technical aids

seat·back /seét bàk/ *n* the part of a seat against which the back rests

seat belt *n* a strong strap or harness designed to keep the wearer securely in a seat in a vehicle or aircraft

-seater *suffix* a venue, vehicle, or piece of furniture that can seat a particular number of people ○ *a three-seater sofa* ○ *drove up in a two-seater*

seat·ing /seéting/ *n* **1.** SEATS the places provided for people to sit, especially in a public building or a vehicle **2.** ARRANGEMENT OF SEATS OR SITTERS the way in which seats or people sitting are arranged ○ *a seating plan* **3.** ACT OR TIME OF SITTING a time or instance when everyone sits down and an activity such as meal service begins ○ *a restaurant with two seatings for dinner* **4.** SOMETHING THAT OBJECT RESTS ON something on which an object rests or into which it fits **5.** UPHOLSTERING MATERIAL material for upholstering the seat of a chair

seat·mate /seét màyt/ *n* somebody in an adjacent seat, e.g., on an airplane

SEATO /seétō/ *abbr* Southeast Asia Treaty Organization

seat-of-the-pants *adj* relying on intuition or guesswork rather than mechanical aids, rules and procedures, or planning (*slang*) [Because pilots claim to feel an aircraft's motion through the seat]

sea·train /seé tràyn/ *n US* a ship carrying loaded railroad freight cars

sea trout *n* **1.** a sea fish of the croaker family resembling a trout. Native to: Atlantic coast of North America. Latin name: *Cynoscion regalis.* **2.** a large silvery colored trout living mainly in the sea but returning to fresh water to spawn. Native to: Europe, North Africa. Latin name: *Salmo trutta.*

Se·at·tle /see átt'l/ city in west central Washington, between Puget Sound and Lake Washington. The most important city in the Pacific Northwest, it is a major seaport and commercial center. Population: 570,426 (2002 estimate).

sea tur·tle *n* a large turtle with limbs shaped like paddles. Native to: tropical and subtropical seas. Family: Cheloniidae or Dermochelyidae.

seat·work /séet wùrk/ *n* tasks to be done by students while sitting at their desks in the classroom

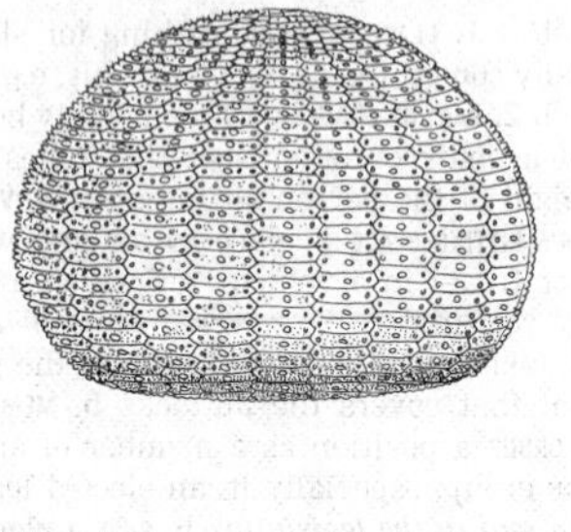

sea urchin

sea ur·chin *n* a small marine invertebrate animal with a soft body enclosed in a spherical shell, spiny when the animal is alive. Class: Echinoidea.

sea wall *n* a wall built to prevent flooding or coastal erosion by the sea

sea·ward /séeward/ *adj* **1.** TOWARD OCEAN moving toward or facing the ocean **2.** BLOWING FROM OCEAN describes wind that blows in toward the shore from the ocean ■ *adv also* **sea·wards** /-wardz/ TOWARD OCEAN in a direction toward the ocean

sea·ware /sée wèr/ *n* seaweed collected from the shore and used as fertilizer

sea wasp *n* a jellyfish that has a cube-shaped body with tentacles hanging from the lower corners. Its sting is very venomous and sometimes fatal. Order: Cubomedusae.

sea·wa·ter /sée wàwtar/ *n* salt water in or from the sea

sea·way /sée wày/ *n* **1.** INLAND CHANNEL FOR SHIPS an inland canal, passage, or channel large enough for ocean-going ships to navigate ○ *the St. Lawrence Seaway* **2.** ROUTE ACROSS OCEAN a shipping route across an ocean **3.** SHIP'S PROGRESS the progress of a ship through the ocean **4.** ROUGH OCEAN CONDITIONS ocean conditions that are moderate to rough

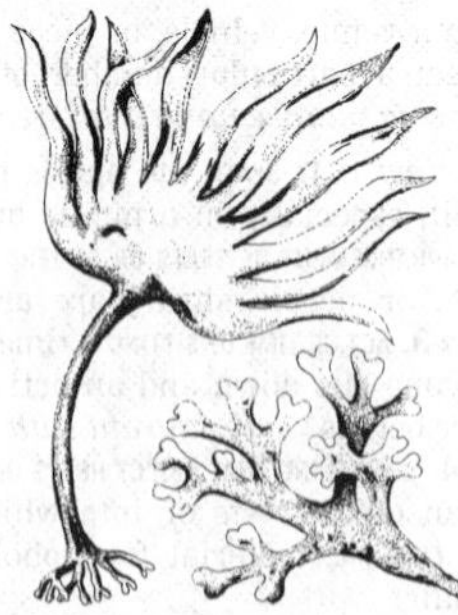

seaweed

sea·weed /sée wèed/ *n* plants that grow in the ocean, e.g., kelp

sea whip *n* a coral that forms long flexible structures with few or no branches and is common on Atlantic reefs. Class: Anthozoa.

sea·wom·an /sée wòomman/ (*plural* **-wom·en** /-wìmmin/) *n* a woman who works aboard a boat or ship, especially a low-ranking member of the crew of a merchant or naval ship

sea·wor·thy /sée wùrthee/ *adj* suitable or in a fit state to sail safely on the ocean —**sea·wor·thi·ness** *n*

sea wrack *n* seaweed, especially clumps of the larger varieties, found cast up on shore

se·ba·ceous /sa báyshass/ *adj* relating to or producing a waxy yellowish body secretion (**sebum**) [Early 18C. < Latin *sebaceus* < *sebum* "grease, tallow"]

se·ba·ceous gland *n* a gland that secretes sebum into hair follicles to lubricate the hair and skin. Sebaceous glands are found all over the human body except for the palms of the hands and the soles of the feet.

se·bac·ic ac·id /sa bàssik-, -bàysik-/ *n* a white crystalline acid. Use: manufacture of synthetic resins, rubbers, plasticizers. Formula: $COOH(CH_2)_8COOH$. [< SEBACEOUS]

Se·bas·tian /si báschan/, **St.** (*fl* 3rd century) Roman Christian martyr. He is said to have survived execution by archers ordered by the emperor Diocletian, who then had him beaten to death.

Se·bas·to·pol /sa bástə pòl/, **Se·vas·to·pol** /-vástə-/ city and port on the Black Sea, in southern Ukraine, on the southern coast of the Crimean Peninsula. Population: 356,000 (1998).

SEbE *abbr* southeast by east

seb·or·rhe·a /sèbba rée a/ *n* excessively oily skin caused by heavy discharge from the sebaceous glands [Late 19C. < SEBUM] —**seb·or·rhe·al** *adj* —**seb·or·rhe·ic** *adj*

seb·or·rhoe·a /sèbba rée a/ *n* MED UK spelling of **seborrhea**

SEbS *abbr* southeast by south

se·bum /séebam/ *n* an oily substance secreted by the sebaceous glands that lubricates the hair and skin and gives some protection against bacteria [Late 19C. < Latin, "grease, tallow"]

sec[1] /sek/ *n* a very short period of time (*informal*) [Late 19C. Shortening of SECOND[2]]

sec[2] /sek/ *adj* describes a wine, especially champagne, that is dry in taste [Mid-19C. Via French < Latin *siccus* "dry"]

sec[3] *abbr* MATH secant

SEC *abbr* Securities and Exchange Commission

sec. *abbr* **1.** secondary **2.** BUSINESS, GOV, FURNITURE secretary **3.** section **4.** sector **5.** security

SECAM /sée kàm/ *n* a broadcasting system for color television used in France, Russia, and a number of other countries. Full form **séquentiel couleur à mémoire**

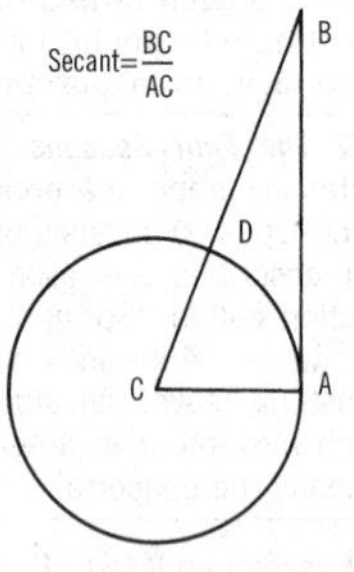

secant

se·cant /séekant/ *n* **1.** a straight line that intersects with a curve in two or more places **2.** the ratio of the hypotenuse to the side adjacent to a given angle in a right triangle [Late 16C. < Latin *secant-*, present participle of *secare* "cut"]

se·ca·teurs /sékə tùrz/ *npl UK* a gardening tool used for pruning that has two short heavy blades with a spring mechanism [Mid-19C. < French < Latin *secare* "to cut"]

sec·co /sékō/ *n* (*plural* **-cos**) **1.** ART WALL PAINTING TECHNIQUE the technique of wall painting on dry plaster using tempera or pigments ground in limewater **2.** ART PICTURE PAINTED ON WALL a painting on a wall made by the secco method **3.** MUSIC RECITATIVE STYLE a style of vocal recitative in which the natural stress of the words is paramount and, if accompanied at all, is supported only by occasional chords of continuo instruments ■ *adj* MUSIC **1.** ACCOMPANIED ONLY BY CONTINUO INSTRUMENTS used to refer to vocal recitatives that are unaccompanied or accompanied only by occasional chords of continuo instruments **2.** STACCATO played and released quickly and lacking resonance (*used as a musical direction*) ■ *adv* MUSIC IN STACCATO MANNER with the notes played and released quickly and without resonance (*used as a musical direction*) [Mid-19C. Via Italian < Latin *siccus* "dry"]

se·cede /si séed/ (**-ced·ed, -ced·ing, -cedes**) *vi* to make a formal withdrawal of membership from an organization, state, or alliance [Early 18C. < Latin *secedere* "go apart" < *cedere* "give way"] —**se·ced·er** *n*

~~**seceed**~~ incorrect spelling of **secede**

se·ces·sion /si sésh'n/ *n* a formal withdrawal from an organization, state, or alliance [Mid-16C. Directly or via French < Latin *secession-* < *secedere* (see SECEDE)] —**se·ces·sion·al** *adj*

Se·ces·sion *n* the withdrawal from the Union of 11 Southern States in 1860–61 that led to the formation of the Confederacy and the beginning of the Civil War

se·ces·sion·ism /sə sésh'n ìzzəm/ *n* a belief or policy in favor of withdrawal from a nation, state, or organization, or alliance —**se·ces·sion·ist** *n, adj*

Seck·el pear /sék'l-/ *n* a small sweet variety of pear with a reddish skin, cultivated in North America [Early 19C. After an early grower from Philadelphia]

se·clude /sa klóod/ (**-clud·ed, -clud·ing, -cludes**) *vt* **1.** to remove somebody from contact with others **2.** to make a place private and quiet by screening or isolating it [15C. < Latin *secludere* "shut out" < *claudere* "shut"]

se·clud·ed /sa klóodad/ *adj* **1.** cut off from other places and therefore private and quiet **2.** having or involving little or no contact with others —**se·clud·ed·ly** *adv* —**se·clud·ed·ness** *n*

se·clu·sion /sa klóozh'n/ *n* **1.** CONDITION OF BEING SECLUDED the condition of being cut off from others, or from other places **2.** ACT OF SECLUDING an act of setting somebody or something apart from others **3.** SECLUDED PLACE a quiet place removed from activity and people [Early 17C. < Latin *seclusion-* < past participle of *secludere* (see SECLUDE)]

se·clu·sive /sa klóossiv/ *adj* preferring to be solitary [Mid-19C. < SECLUDE, after INCLUSIVE] —**se·clu·sive·ly** *adv* —**se·clu·sive·ness** *n*

sec·o·bar·bi·tal /sèkō baárbi tàwl/ *n* a controlled barbiturate used in its sodium salt form. Use: sedative, treatment of insomnia. Formula: $C_{12}H_{18}N_2O_3$. [Mid-20C. < contraction of SECONDARY]

sec·ond[1] /sékand/ *adj* **1.** COMING AFTER FIRST coming after the first in a series **2.** ANOTHER additional to, repeating, or following one that came before or was previously mentioned ○ *I need to take a second look at those numbers.* **3.** ADDITIONAL AND LESS IMPORTANT additional to and less important than the first or main one ○ *a second home* **4.** SIMILAR TO PREDECESSOR similar or comparable in many respects to a particular renowned personality or event ○ *a second Watergate* **5.** INFERIOR inferior to or less important than somebody or something else ○ *second only to the President* **6.** MUSIC PERFORMING LOWER OR LESS IMPORTANT PART singing or playing a lower or less important part ■ *n* **1.** 2 IN SERIES the ordinal number assigned to item number two in a series **2.** ANOTHER PERSON OR THING another person or thing of the same kind as one previously mentioned **3.** COMPETITOR'S OR DUELIST'S ASSISTANT an official assistant to a contestant in a boxing match or a participant in a duel **4.** SECONDER a seconder for a proposal, a motion, or nomination in a debate **5.** ITEM WITH FAULT an imperfectly manufactured item that is sold at a discount **6.** AUTOMOT FORWARD GEAR a forward gear of a transmission that is higher than first gear and lower than third gear **7.** BASEBALL same as **second base** (sense 1) **8.** MUSIC INTERVAL OF TWO NOTES in a standard musical scale, the interval between one note and another that lies one note above or below it. In the scale of C major, C and D form a second. **9.** MUSIC NOTE SECOND AWAY FROM ANOTHER in a standard musical scale, a note that is a second away from another note **10.** BALLET same as **second position** ■ **sec·onds** *npl* ANOTHER HELPING OR SERVING another helping or serving of a dish or type of food (*informal*) ■ *vt* (**-ond·ed, -ond·ing, -onds**) **1.** ACT AS SECONDER to state support officially for a proposal, motion, or nomination introduced by somebody else, so that discussion or voting can take place **2.** EXPRESS AGREEMENT AND SUPPORT to express agreement and support for something that somebody has just said (*informal*) ○ *I second that.* **3.** ACT AS COMPETITOR'S OR DUELIST'S SECOND to act as second to a contestant in a boxing match or duel **4.** ASSIST OR SUPPORT to assist or support somebody or something (*formal*) ○ *seconded her efforts* ■ *adv* **1.** EXCEPT FOR ONE the one that exceeds all the rest, except for one, in a particular way (*used to qualify a superlative*) ○ *the second-highest mountain in the world* **2.** same as **secondly** [14C. Via French < Latin *secundus* "following" < *sequi* "follow"] ◇ **second to none** better than anyone or anything else

sec·ond² /sékənd/ *n* **1.** 60TH OF MINUTE a unit of time that is equal to 1/60th of a minute. Symbol **s** **2.** UNIT OF MEASUREMENT OF ANGLES a unit of measurement of angles equal to 1/60th of a minute or 1/360th of a degree. Symbol **"** **3.** VERY SHORT TIME a very short period of time [14C. Via French < medieval Latin *secunda* < *secunda pars minuta* "second diminished part"]

se·cond³ /sə kónd/ (**-cond·ed, -cond·ing, -conds**) *vt UK* to transfer an employee, official, or soldier temporarily to other duties [Early 19C. < French *en second* "in the second rank"] —**se·cond·ment** *n*

Sec·ond Ad·vent *n* CHR same as **Second Coming**

sec·ond·ar·y /sékən dèrree/ *adj* **1.** NOT PRIMARY OR MAJOR subordinate to something else ○ *matters of secondary importance* **2.** DERIVED FROM SOMETHING ORIGINAL derived from or reliant on something original ○ *a secondary source* **3.** MED HAPPENING AS RESULT OF OTHER ILLNESS happening as a result of another disorder or condition ○ *secondary tumors* **4.** EDUC OCCURRING AFTER PRIMARY SCHOOL intended for students who have completed their primary education, usually for children in grades 7 to 12 ○ *a secondary school* **5.** BIRDS GROWING ALONG INNER EDGE OF WING describes feathers that grow along the trailing edge of the inner segment of a bird's wing **6.** ELEC ELECTRICALLY INDUCED describes a circuit or coil that has an electric current produced by induction **7.** INDUST INVOLVED IN MANUFACTURING involved in the manufacture of goods from raw materials ○ *a secondary industry* **8.** CHEM ORGANIC CARBON COMPOUND describes an organic compound that has a carbon atom attached to three organic groups, at least one of which is chemically active **9.** CHEM RELATING TO ORGANIC NITROGEN COMPOUND describes an amine that has two alkyl groups and one hydrogen atom attached to a nitrogen atom **10.** BOT OF RAPIDLY DIVIDING TISSUE relating to or derived from rapidly dividing tissue (**cambium**) that gives rise to increased girth, not increased length ■ *n* (*plural* **-ies**) **1.** SOMEBODY OR SOMETHING SECONDARY somebody or something that is secondary or subordinate **2.** MED SECONDARY TUMOR a cancerous growth at a site remote from that of the original malignant tumor **3.** BIRDS SECONDARY FEATHER a feather that grows along the trailing edge of the inner segment of a bird's wing **4.** ELEC INDUCED COIL OR CIRCUIT a coil or circuit in which an induced current flows [14C. < Latin *secondarius* < *secundus* (see SECOND¹)] —**sec·ond·ar·i·ly** /sèkən dérrəlee/ *adv* —**sec·ond·ar·i·ness** *n*

sec·ond·ar·y ac·cent *n* **1.** *US* an accentuation on a syllable that is weaker than that on the syllable receiving the main accent. For example, in the word "secondary," the main accent falls on the first syllable and the secondary accent on the third. Can term **secondary stress** **2.** a mark used to indicate where a secondary accent is placed in a word

sec·ond·ar·y bat·ter·y *n US* ELEC ENG same as **storage battery**

sec·ond·ar·y boy·cott *n US* a strike or boycott against a company that is a supplier or customer of a company involved in a labor dispute

sec·ond·ar·y cell *n* an electric cell in which electricity is produced by a reversible chemical reaction. It is therefore rechargeable and able to store electrical energy.

sec·ond·ar·y col·or *n* a color produced by mixing two primary colors in roughly equal quantities, e.g., orange, green, or purple

sec·ond·ar·y e·lec·tron *n* an electron released by secondary emission

sec·ond·ar·y e·mis·sion *n* the emission of electrons from the surface of a substance bombarded with electrons or ions

sec·ond·ar·y in·fec·tion *n* an infection that is acquired during the course of a separate initial infection

sec·ond·ar·y of·fer·ing *n US* the sale of securities to dealers outside the stock exchange

sec·ond·ar·y school *n* a school for students who have completed their primary education, usually attended by children in grades 7 to 12

sec·ond·ar·y sex·u·al char·ac·ter·is·tic *n* a characteristic that develops at puberty but is not directly concerned with reproduction, e.g., a woman's breasts or a man's facial hair

sec·ond·ar·y stress *n Can, UK* same as **secondary accent**

sec·ond·ar·y syph·i·lis *n* the second, highly infectious stage of syphilis that appears several weeks or months after primary infection and is marked by a faint skin rash, fever, and muscular pain

sec·ond bal·lot *n* a second round of voting in an election in which no candidate obtained a winning majority in the first round. In a second ballot, the candidates who received the fewest votes in the first round are usually left out.

sec·ond ba·nan·a *n* (*slang*) **1.** an assistant or subordinate to somebody else **2.** a straight man or stooge to a comedian in burlesque or vaudeville

sec·ond base *n* **1.** the base opposite home plate in the baseball diamond, or the position of the infielder playing nearest to second base on the first-base side **2.** BASEBALL same as **second baseman**

sec·ond base·man *n* in baseball, the player positioned closest to second base, on the first-base side of it

sec·ond best *n* **1.** SOMEBODY OR SOMETHING NEXT TO BEST somebody or something that is next in quality to, or surpassed only by, the best **2.** SOMEBODY OR SOMETHING INFERIOR TO BEST somebody or something inferior to the best or the favorite ■ *adj* (*hyphenated when used before a noun*) **1.** NEXT IN QUALITY TO BEST next in quality to, or surpassed only by, the best ○ *my second-best suit* **2.** INFERIOR TO BEST inferior to the best or the favorite ○ *had to make do with a second-best alternative*

sec·ond child·hood *n* an offensive term for a condition associated with aging that manifests itself in behavior regarded as resembling that of a child

sec·ond class *n* **1.** CATEGORY AFTER BEST the category or standard of something, especially of accommodations or travel, that comes immediately below the best **2.** MAIL SERVICE a mail delivery service for newspapers and periodicals ■ *adj* (*hyphenated when used before a noun*) **1.** BELONGING TO SECOND CLASS belonging to or meeting the standards of second class, especially regarding mail service or travel accommodations ○ *second-class cabins* **2.** INFERIOR inferior to, or less important than, somebody or something else ○ *treated as second-class citizens*

sec·ond-class *adv* by second-class mail delivery service or travel accommodations ○ *traveled second-class*

sec·ond-class cit·i·zen *n* somebody who does not have the same rights, privileges, or opportunities as a full citizen

Sec·ond Com·ing *n* in Christian belief, the anticipated and prophesied return of Jesus Christ to judge humanity at the end of the world

sec·ond cous·in *n* a child of a first cousin of either of your parents

sec·ond crop *n Southern US* AGRIC same as **second cutting**

sec·ond cut·ting, sec·ond crop *n Southern US* a second crop or growth of grass in the same season, after the first harvest or mowing

sec·ond-de·gree burn *n* a burn that causes blistering on the skin but does not damage the deeper layers of the skin or require grafting

se·conde /sə kónd/ *n* the second of the eight classic parrying positions in fencing [Early 18C. < French, "second (in order)"]

Sec·ond Em·pire *n* **1.** the reign or the government of the Emperor Napoleon III of France, lasting from 1852 until 1870 **2.** the weighty, grandiose, and highly ornamented style of architecture, furnishing, and decoration typical of the Second Empire

sec·on·der /sékəndər/ *n* somebody who states support for a proposal, motion, or nomination introduced by somebody else, so that discussion or voting can take place

sec·ond es·tate *n* the nobility, as one of the three broad traditional classes of people within a monarchic state

sec·ond fid·dle *n* a less important or less prominent role, or somebody or something in such a role

sec·ond gen·er·a·tion *n* **1.** the children of immigrants **2.** a later stage in the development of something that benefits from what was learned from the first stage of development —**sec·ond-gen·er·a·tion** *adj*

sec·ond growth *n* the trees and plants that grow back naturally in an area of forest after the original trees have been removed by cutting or fire

sec·ond-guess *vti* **1.** to criticize, assess, or correct somebody or something after an event is over and the outcome is known **2.** to predict a course of events, an outcome, or somebody's intentions from a position of relative ignorance ○ *no point in trying to second-guess what they'll do* —**sec·ond-guess·er** *n*

sec·ond hand *n* the hand of a clock or watch that shows time passing second by second and rotates once around the dial in the space of a minute

sec·ond·hand /sèkənd hánd/ *adj* **1.** PREVIOUSLY OWNED previously owned or used **2.** SELLING USED GOODS selling or dealing in used goods **3.** NOT ORIGINAL received from or reliant on somebody or something other than the original source ○ *secondhand accounts of the incident* ■ *adv* **1.** IN USED CONDITION after being owned or used by somebody else ○ *bought it secondhand* **2.** THROUGH INTERMEDIARY from or through somebody or something else and not by direct experience or personal effort ○ *acquires the information secondhand* ◇ **at secondhand, at second hand** from or through somebody or something else

sec·ond·hand smoke *n* tobacco smoke unintentionally inhaled by people who do not smoke

se·con·di MUSIC plural of **secondo**

sec·ond-in-com·mand *n* a person ranking next below somebody in command

Sec·ond In·ter·na·tion·al *n* an international socialist association established in 1889 in Paris and lasting until World War I

sec·ond lan·guage *n* **1.** a language learned by somebody after the first language he or she learns at home (*hyphenated before a noun*) **2.** a language in widespread use in a country, sometimes having official status (*hyphenated when used before a noun*)

sec·ond lieu·ten·ant *n* an officer in the US and Canadian armies or air forces, the US Marine Corps, or the British Royal Marines of the lowest rank above chief warrant officer

sec·ond·ly /sékəndlee/ *adv* used to introduce the second point in an argument or discussion

sec·ond mate *n* the officer on a merchant ship next in the line of command after the first mate, usually the third-highest-ranking officer on board

sec·ond mort·gage *n* an additional mortgage on a property that has been mortgaged once already, secondary to the main loan that is secured on the property

sec·ond na·ture *n* a habit or tendency so well-developed and long-practiced that it seems to be done unconsciously

se·con·do /si kóndō/ (*plural* **-di** /-dee/) *n* the second or lower part in a piece of music for two players, especially a piano duet [Late 18C. < Italian, "second (in order)"]

sec·ond o·pin·ion *n* an opinion, especially one of a professional nature, from somebody other than the usual or first person consulted

sec·ond per·son *n* **1.** the form of a verb or pronoun used when addressing somebody. In English, the second-person singular and plural pronoun is "you." **2.** the grammatical set containing the forms indicating the second person

sec·ond po·si·tion *n* in ballet, a position in which the feet are turned outward with the feet slightly apart

sec·ond-rate *adj* inadequate in quality or performance ○ *a second-rate pianist* —**sec·ond-rat·er** *n*

sec·ond read·ing *n* the second presentation of a bill to a legislature as part of the process of turning the bill into law. In the US Congress, it follows the committee stage and precedes a full debate and opportunity for amendment.

Sec·ond Re·pub·lic *n* the period of the Republican government in France from 1848 to 1852

sec·ond sight *n* the supposed ability to see things that the physical eye cannot see, especially events taking place in the future or elsewhere —**sec·ond-sight·ed** *adj* —**sec·ond-sight·ed·ness** *n*

sec·ond-strike *adj* relating to, involving, or intended for use in a retaliatory nuclear attack with weapons designed to survive a first nuclear strike by an enemy ○ *second-strike capabilities*

sec·ond string, sec·ond team *n* a lineup of players, any of whom may substitute for a starting player during the course of the game, but who do not play at the beginning of a game —**sec·ond-string** *adj* —**sec·ond-string·er** *n*

sec·ond team *n* SPORTS same as **second string**

sec·ond thought *n* a reconsideration of something tentatively decided, e.g., in light of new developments or something not previously taken into account (*often used in the plural*) ○ *having second thoughts about getting married* ◇ **on second thought** after reconsideration

sec·ond wind /-wind/ *n* a renewal of energy following a period of effort and exertion

Sec·ond World War *n* HIST same as **World War II**

Se·cord /seé kàwrd/, **Laura** (1775–1868) Massachusetts-born Canadian patriot. She became a hero in British Canada during the War of 1812 when she walked a substantial distance to warn the British after overhearing plans for a US attack. Born **Ingersoll, Laura**

~~secratary~~ incorrect spelling of **secretary**

se·cre·cy /seékrəssee/ *n* **1. STATE OF CONCEALMENT** the state of being concealed or secret ○ *talks held in secrecy* **2. KEEPING OF SECRET** the keeping of a secret ○ *sworn to secrecy* **3. SECRETIVENESS** a tendency to keep things secret [Late 16C. < SECRET]

se·cret /seékrət/ *adj* **1. NOT WIDELY KNOWN** known by only a few people and intentionally withheld from general knowledge **2. UNDERCOVER** working or operating without the knowledge of the general public **3. UNADMITTED** acting or feeling in a particular way without admitting to it ○ *a secret admirer* **4. PRIVATE AND SECLUDED** known to very few people and consequently quiet and secluded **5. SECRETIVE** tending by nature to keep things secret (*informal*) **6. MYSTERIOUS** mysterious and often beyond common understanding ■ *n* **1. INFORMATION NOT WIDELY KNOWN** a piece of information that is known only to a few people and is intentionally withheld from general knowledge **2. MYSTERY** something that is unknown, hidden, or not understood ○ *still trying to unravel the secrets of the atom* **3. SOMETHING ENSURING SUCCESS** a little-known technique, approach, or piece of information that is the key to success in an endeavor ○ *the secret of making a good soufflé* [14C. Via French < Latin *secretus* "separate, hidden" < *secernere* "separate apart" < *cernere* "to separate"] —**se·cret·ly** *adv* ◇ **in secret** without anyone else's knowledge ○ *meet in secret*

SYNONYMS ***secret, clandestine, covert, furtive, stealthy, surreptitious, secretive***

CORE MEANING: conveying a desire or need for concealment

secret known by only a few people and intentionally withheld from general knowledge ○ *was supported by a majority in a secret ballot* ○ *The find was kept secret until it had been properly excavated by the archaeological department.* **clandestine** needing to be concealed, usually because it is illegal or unauthorized ○ *clandestine arms deals* ○ *It appeared he was having a clandestine relationship with the owner, from whom he had received the information.* **covert** not intended to be known, seen, or found out ○ *a covert police operation* ○ *a covert intelligence and sabotage campaign* **furtive** done in a way that is intended to escape notice ○ *Sandra was whispering to her neighbor, with occasional furtive glances in Edward's direction.* ○ *The stranger looked about him, then walked in an unexpectedly furtive manner toward the gate.* **stealthy** done quietly, slowly, and cautiously in order to escape notice ○ *Casting a stealthy glance around, he leaned forward and lowered his voice.* **surreptitious** done in a concealed or underhand way to escape notice, especially disapproval ○ *surreptitious methods for getting your own way* ○ *If she did a little surreptitious investigating she might find something, she thought.* **secretive** unwilling to reveal or share information ○ *Even as a child he had a very secretive nature.*

Se·cret /seékrət/, **se·cret** *n* formerly, the Prayer over the Gifts in the Roman Catholic Mass (*dated*) [14C. < ecclesiastical Latin *secreta oratio* "concealed speech"; from the low voice used]

se·cret a·gent *n* somebody engaged in espionage for a government or organization

se·cre·ta·gogue /sə kreétə gòg/ *n* a substance that causes or stimulates secretion, e.g., a hormone [Early 20C. < SECRETE[1]] —**se·cre·ta·gog·ic** /sə kreétə gójjik/ *adj*

se·cré·taire /sèkrə tér/ *n Can, UK* same as **secretary** (sense 3) [Late 18C. Via French < late Latin *secretarius* (see SECRETARY)]

sec·re·tar·i·at /sèkrə térree ət/ *n* **1. ADMINISTRATIVE DEPARTMENT** a department that carries out the administrative and clerical work of an organization or legislature **2. SECRETARIAL STAFF** the secretarial staff under the direction of a secretary-general **3. BUILDING HOUSING SECRETARIAT** the headquarters or offices of a secretariat [Early 19C. Via French < medieval Latin *secretariatus* < late Latin *secretarius* (see SECRETARY)]

sec·re·tar·y /sékrə tèrree/ (*plural* **-ies**) *n* **1. CLERICAL WORKER** an employee who does clerical and administrative work in an office for a person or organization **2. OFFICER OF ORGANIZATION** somebody elected or appointed to keep the records of the meetings of an organization such as a club, society, or committee, and to write or answer letters on its behalf **3.** *also* **Sec·re·tar·y** *US* **CABINET MEMBER** a cabinet-level official of a national government **4.** *US* FURNITURE **CABINET INCORPORATING WRITING DESK** a large cabinet with a fold-down desktop, usually with drawers below and an enclosed bookcase above. Can term **secretaire 5.** *UK* GOV same as **Secretary of State** (sense 2) **6.** *UK* **SENIOR CIVIL SERVANT** a senior civil servant who advises a government minister [14C. < late Latin *secretarius* "confidential officer" < *secretus* (see SECRET)] —**sec·re·tar·i·al** /sèkrə térree əl/ *adj* —**sec·re·tar·y·ship** *n*

secretary bird

sec·re·tar·y bird *n* a large long-legged bird of prey that has gray-and-black feathers and a crest projecting from the back of its head and which feeds mainly on snakes. Native to: Africa. Latin name: *Sagittarius serpentarius.* [< the resemblance of the bird's crest to quill pens stuck behind a secretary's ear]

sec·re·tar·y-gen·er·al (*plural* **sec·re·tar·ies-gen·er·al**) *n* the chief executive officer of a large organization such as the United Nations, who oversees a secretariat

sec·re·tar·y of state *n* a state government official with administrative responsibilities that vary from state to state

Sec·re·tar·y of State *n* **1.** the US government official and cabinet member who is in charge of foreign affairs **2.** a member of the British government and cabinet who is in charge of a major department such as Education or Defense

se·cret bal·lot *n* a situation in which people cast votes secretly in order to determine the outcome of an election or some other decision

se·crete[1] /sə kreét/ (**-cret·ed, -cret·ing, -cretes**) *vti* to produce and discharge a substance [Early 18C. < Latin *secret-*, past participle of *secernere* (see SECRET)] —**se·cret·or** *n* —**se·cre·to·ry** *adj*

se·crete[2] /sə kreét/ (**-cret·ed, -cret·ing, -cretes**) *vt* to conceal somebody or something [Mid-18C. Alteration of SECRET in the obsolete sense "to hide"]

se·cre·tin /sə kreét'n/ *n* a hormone secreted in the duodenum that stimulates the pancreas and the bowel to produce digestive enzymes and the liver to produce bile [Early 20C. < SECRETION[1]]

se·cre·tion[1] /sə kreésh'n/ *n* **1.** the process of producing a substance from the cells and fluids within a gland or organ and discharging it **2.** a substance formed and discharged by a cell, tissue, gland, or organ [Mid-17C. Directly or via French < Latin *secretion-* < past participle of *secernere* (see SECRET)] —**se·cre·tion·ar·y** *adj*

se·cre·tion[2] /si kreésh'n/ *n* the act of concealing somebody or something [Mid-20C. < SECRETE[2]]

se·cre·tive /seékrətiv/ *adj* unwilling to reveal information —**se·cre·tive·ly** *adv* —**se·cre·tive·ness** *n*

SYNONYMS See *secret.*

se·cret part·ner *n* a partner whose involvement in a business is kept secret

se·cret po·lice *npl* a police force that operates in secret and whose function is to prevent subversion or suppress political opposition to a regime

se·cret ser·vice *n* a government department that carries out secret investigations and covert operations

Se·cret Ser·vice *n* a branch of the US Treasury Department whose main function is the protection of the president and vice president and their families

se·cret so·ci·e·ty *n* an organization that requires its members to keep all or some of its activities secret from nonmembers

sect /sekt/ *n* **1. NONMAINSTREAM RELIGIOUS GROUP** a religious group with beliefs and practices at variance with those of the more established main groups **2. RELIGIOUS DENOMINATION** a denomination of a larger religious group **3. CLOSE-KNIT GROUP** a small close-knit group with strongly held views that are sometimes regarded as extreme by the majority [14C. Via French < Latin *secta* "school of thought" < *sequi* "follow"]

-sect *suffix* **1.** to cut or divide ○ *quadrisect* **2.** cut, divided ○ *pinnatisect* [< Latin *sectus*, past participle of *secare* "cut"]

sec·tar·i·an /sek térree ən/ *adj* **1. OF RELIGIOUS GROUP** relating to or involving relations between religious groups or denominations **2. OF SINGLE RELIGIOUS GROUP** relating to, involved with, or devoted to a single religious group or denomination **3. DOGMATIC AND INTOLERANT** rigidly adhering to a set of doctrines and intolerant of other views ■ *n* **1. MEMBER OF RELIGIOUS GROUP** a member of a religious group or denomination **2. SOMEBODY DOGMATIC AND INTOLERANT** somebody who rigidly adheres to a set of doctrines and is intolerant of other views —**sec·tar·i·an·ism** *n*

sec·tar·i·an·ize /sek térree ə nìz/ (**-ized, -iz·ing, -iz·es**) *vt* to cause somebody or something to become sectarian

sec·ta·ry /séktəree/ (*plural* **-ries**) *n* a member of a religious group or denomination (*archaic*)

sec·tile /sékt'l/ *adj* describes minerals that can be cut so as to leave a smooth surface [Early 18C. < Latin *sectilis* < *sect-* (see SECTION)] —**sec·til·i·ty** /sek tíllətee/ *n*

sec·tion /séksh'n/ *n* **1. DISTINCT PART** a distinct part that can be separated or considered separately from the whole of something **2. UNIT OF PEOPLE** a group of people forming a unit within a larger group, e.g., a subdivision of a military unit, or the musicians playing a particular kind of instrument in an orchestra **3. SUBDIVISION OF DOCUMENT** a major subdivision of a written work such as a book or newspaper, or of an official or legal document, often numbered **4. VIEW OF SOMETHING CUT THROUGH** a view or representation of something cut through to show its internal structure or workings **5.** *US* GEOG **FUNCTIONAL AREA** an area of a country, county, city, or town, usually characterized by the type of activity mainly carried on there ○ *a residential section of the city* **6.** URBAN PLAN **AREA OF ONE SQUARE MILE** an area of land, for purposes of land surveying, equal to one square mile, 2.59 square kilometers, or one thirty-sixth of a township **7.** SCI **VERY THIN SLICE** a very thin slice of something removed for examination under a microscope ○ *a tissue section* **8.** SURG **SURGICAL CUT** a surgical incision **9.** RAIL **LENGTH OF TRACK** a length of railroad track maintained by a single crew **10.** BOT **SEGMENT OF CITRUS FRUIT** a segment of an orange, grapefruit, or other citrus fruit **11.** PRINTING same as **section mark** ■ *vt* (**-tioned, -tion·ing, -tions**) **1. DIVIDE SOMETHING** to divide something up into separate parts **2. CUT SOMETHING SURGICALLY** to make a surgical incision in something [14C. Via French < Latin *section-* < *sect-*, past participle of *secare* "cut"]

ORIGIN The Latin word *secare* "to cut," from which ***section*** is derived, is also the source of the English words *bisect, dissect, insect, intersect, secateurs, sector,* and *segment.*

sec·tion·al /sékshən'l, sékshnəl/ *adj* **1. OF SECTION** relating to a group or section **2. INVOLVING DIFFERENT SECTIONS** involving different groups or sections **3. CONSISTING OF SECTIONS** divided into or made up of sections ■ *n* **FURNITURE IN PARTS** a piece of furniture made up of coordinated sections that can be used together or apart —**sec·tion·al·ly** *adv*

sec·tion·al·ism /sékshən'l ìzzəm, sékshnə lìzzəm/ *n* excessive concern for the interests of one group or area to the detriment of the whole —**sec·tion·al·ist** *n, adj*

sec·tion·al·ize /sékshən'l ìz, sékshnə lìz/ (**-ized, -iz·ing, -iz·es**) *vt* to divide something, especially a geographic area, into sections —**sec·tion·al·i·za·tion** /sèkshən'li záysh'n, sèkshnəli-/ *n*

Sec·tion Eight *n US* **1.** a discharge from military service on physical or psychological grounds **2.** a soldier discharged under Section Eight regulations

sec·tion gang *n* a gang of railroad workers responsible for maintaining a section of track

sec·tion hand *n* a worker on a section gang

sec·tion mark *n* a symbol (§) sometimes used in printing to mark the beginning of a section of a book or one of a series of footnotes, and for various other purposes

sec·tor /séktər/ *n* **1. COMPONENT PART** a component of an integrated system such as an economy or a society **2.** MIL **PART OF AREA OF MILITARY OPERATIONS** a part of an area where military forces are operating or in control **3.** MATH **PART OF CIRCLE** a part of a circle bounded by two radii and the part of the circumference that lies between them **4.** MATH **MEASURING INSTRUMENT** a measuring instrument consisting of two arms marked with graduations, hinged together at one end **5.** COMPUT **UNIT OF MAGNETIC STORAGE DEVICE** the smallest addressable unit of a magnetic storage device ■ *vt* (**-tored, -tor·ing, -tors**) **DIVIDE SOMETHING** to divide something into sectors [Late 16C. < late Latin, "something that cuts" < Latin *sect-* (see SECTION)] —**sec·tor·al** *adj*

sec·to·ri·al /sek táwree əl/ *adj* **1.** relating to a sector or consisting of sectors **2.** adapted or specialized for cutting ○ *sectorial teeth*

sec·u·lar /sékyələr/ *adj* **1. NOT CONCERNED WITH RELIGION** not controlled by a religious body or concerned with religious or spiritual matters ○ *secular education* **2. NOT RELIGIOUS** not religious or spiritual in nature ○ *secular music* **3. NOT MONASTIC** not belonging to a monastic order ○ *secular clergy* **4. OCCURRING ONCE IN CENTURY** occurring only once in the course of an age or century ○ *a secular change* **5.** ASTRON, GEOL **OCCURRING OVER LONG PERIOD** taking place over an extremely or indefinitely long period of time ■ *n* **1. MEMBER OF SECULAR CLERGY** a member of the secular clergy **2. LAY PERSON** a member of the laity [14C. Via French < Latin *saecularis* < *saeculum* "world, generation"] —**sec·u·lar·i·ty** /sèkyə lárrətee/ *n* —**sec·u·lar·ly** *adv*

sec·u·lar hu·man·ism *n* a philosophy or world view that stresses human values without reference to religion or spirituality

sec·u·lar·ism /sékyələ rìzzəm/ *n* **1.** the belief that religion and religious bodies should have no part in political or civic affairs or in running public institutions, especially schools **2.** the rejection of religion or its exclusion from a philosophical or moral system —**sec·u·lar·ist** *n* —**sec·u·lar·is·tic** /sèkyələ rístik/ *adj*

sec·u·lar·ize /sékyələ rìz/ (**-ized, -iz·ing, -iz·es**) *vt* **1.** to transfer something from a religious to a nonreligious use, or from control by a religious body to control by the state or a lay body **2.** to remove the religious dimension or element from something, or otherwise make it secular —**sec·u·lar·i·za·tion** /sèkyələri záysh'n/ *n* —**sec·u·lar·iz·er** *n*

se·cund /sée kùnd, sé-, sə kúnd/ *adj* arranged on or curving toward only one side of an axis [Late 18C. < Latin *secundus* (see SECOND[1])] —**se·cund·ly** *adv*

se·cure /sə kyóor/ *adj* **1. FIRMLY FIXED** firmly fixed or placed in position and unlikely to come loose or give way ○ *made the rope secure* **2. NOT WORRIED** untroubled by feelings of fear, doubt, or vulnerability **3. RELIABLE** reliable and unlikely to fail or be lost ○ *a secure investment* **4. WELL GUARDED AND FORTIFIED** well guarded and strongly fortified or protected **5. SAFE** safe, especially against attack or theft **6. SAFE FOR SECRET COMMUNICATIONS** safe to use for secret or confidential communication ○ *a secure line* **7. ASSURED** certain to be achieved or gained ○ *Just when victory seemed secure, we let it slip from our grasp.* ■ *v* (**-cured, -cur·ing, -cures**) **1.** *vt* **ATTACH SOMETHING FIRMLY** to attach something firmly in position **2.** *vti* **MAKE SAFE** to make a building or area safe to occupy, usually by ensuring that all internal sources of danger are removed or that it is defended against attack **3.** *vt* **ACQUIRE SOMETHING** to obtain something, especially after using considerable effort to persuade somebody to grant or allow it ○ *secure an agreement* **4.** *vt* FIN **ENSURE PAYMENT FOR SOMETHING** to provide security for something or otherwise guarantee payment ○ *a loan secured against your house* **5.** *vti* **GUARANTEE** to guarantee or ensure something **6.** *vt* **PREVENT SOMEBODY FROM ESCAPING** to ensure that somebody cannot escape ○ *secure a prisoner* **7.** *vt* **MAKE SOMETHING SAFE FOR SECRET COMMUNICATIONS** to ensure that a means of communication can be safely used for secret or confidential messages ○ *secure a telephone line* **8.** *vt* **MAKE SOMETHING SAFE ON SHIP** to make sure that everything on board a ship or aircraft is safely stowed and that openings are covered or doors closed ○ *secure a ship* ○ *secure the cargo* [Mid-16C. < Latin *securus* "without care" < *cura* "care"] —**se·cur·a·ble** *adj* —**se·cure·ly** *adv* —**se·cure·ment** *n* —**se·cure·ness** *n* —**se·cur·er** *n*

SYNONYMS See ***get***[1].

Se·cure E·lec·tron·ic Trans·ac·tion *tdmk* a trademark for a standard protocol for secure Internet credit card transactions (*used in e-commerce*)

se·cure serv·er *n* an Internet server that allows for the encryption of data and thus is suitable for use in e-commerce

Se·cu·ri·ties and Ex·change Com·mis·sion *n* an agency of the US government set up to regulate transactions in securities and protect investors against malpractice

se·cu·ri·ti·za·tion /sə kyòorəti záysh'n/ *n* the preparation of readily marketable securities representing an ownership interest in an asset such as credit card loans or timberland that is not otherwise conveniently traded

se·cu·ri·ty /sə kyóorətee/ (*plural* **-ties**) *n* **1. STATE OR FEELING OF SAFETY** the state or feeling of being safe and protected **2. FREEDOM FROM WORRIES OF LOSS** the assurance that something of value will not be taken away ○ *job security* **3. SOMETHING GIVING ASSURANCE** something that provides a sense of protection against loss, attack, or harm ○ *the security of knowing that the vehicle has been thoroughly checked* **4. SAFETY** protection against attack from without or subversion from within ○ *a matter of national security* **5. PRECAUTIONS TO MAINTAIN SAFETY** precautions taken to keep somebody or something safe from crime, attack, or danger ○ *security measures* **6. GUARDS** people or an organization entrusted with the job of protecting somebody or something, especially a building or institution, against crime ○ *If you don't leave, I'll call security.* **7. ASSET DEPOSITED TO GUARANTEE REPAYMENT** something pledged to guarantee fulfillment of an obligation, especially an asset guaranteeing repayment of a loan that becomes the property of the creditor if the loan is not repaid **8. GUARANTOR** somebody who pledges to fulfill somebody else's obligation should that person fail to do so **9. FINANCIAL INSTRUMENT** a tradable document that shows evidence of debt or ownership, e.g., a stock certificate or bond

se·cu·ri·ty blan·ket *n* a familiar blanket, toy, or other object that a child carries around for the feeling of security it gives, or any object that fulfills the same function for an adult

se·cu·ri·ty clear·ance *n* official permission for somebody to have access to a secure facility or to information that has been classified for reasons of national security

Se·cu·ri·ty Coun·cil *n* the permanent committee of the United Nations that oversees its peacekeeping operations throughout the world. The Security Council has five permanent members, Great Britain, China, France, Russia, and the United States, and ten other members chosen in rotation from among the other member states.

se·cu·ri·ty guard *n* somebody employed by a private organization to guard and protect a building or other property

se·cu·ri·ty risk *n* somebody or something considered a threat to security, especially somebody whose behavior is thought likely to compromise the security of a country

secy., **sec'y.** *abbr* secretary

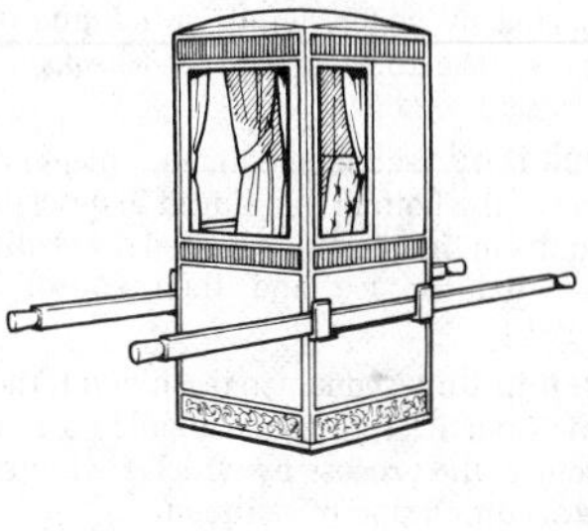

sedan

se·dan /sə dán/ *n* **1.** a car with a fully enclosed passenger compartment, a permanent roof, two or four doors, front and rear seats, and a separate trunk **2.** in the 17th and 18th centuries, an enclosed chair carried by porters at the front and rear on two long poles passed through handles on the sides of the box [Mid-17C. Origin ?]

Se·dan /sə dán, sə daáN/ town in northeastern France. It was the location of a decisive French defeat in 1870 during the Franco-Prussian war. Population: 20,548 (1999).

Se·dar·im JUDAISM plural of **Seder**

se·date[1] /sə dáyt/ *adj* dignified, subdued, and lacking any sense of hurry or urgency [Mid-17C. < Latin *sedatus*, past participle of *sedare* "to calm" < *sedere* "sit"] —**se·date·ly** *adv* —**se·date·ness** *n*

se·date[2] /sə dáyt/ (**-dat·ed, -dat·ing, -dates**) *vt* to administer a sedative to somebody [Mid-20C. Back-formation < SEDATIVE or SEDATION]

se·da·tion /sə dáysh'n/ *n* **1.** the use of a sedative or tranquilizing drug to induce a state of calm, restfulness, or drowsiness **2.** a state of calm, restfulness, or drowsiness, especially as induced by a sedative or tranquilizing drug [Mid-16C. Directly or via French < Latin *sedation-* < *sedatus* (see SEDATE[1])]

sed·a·tive /séddətiv/ *n* a drug or other agent that induces sedation ■ *adj* inducing sedation, especially by means of a tranquilizing drug ○ *a sedative effect* [15C. Directly or via French < medieval Latin *sedativus* < Latin *sedatus* (see SEDATE[1])]

Sed·don /sédd'n/, **Richard** (1845–1906) British-born prime minister of New Zealand (1893–1906). A Liberal politician, he was New Zealand's longest-serving premier. Full name **Seddon, Richard John**. Known as **King Dick**. See table at **prime minister**

sed·en·tar·y /sédd'n tèrree/ *adj* **1.** INVOLVING SITTING involving a lot of sitting and correspondingly little exercise ○ *sedentary work* **2.** USUALLY SITTING tending to sit most of the time and getting little exercise ○ *a sedentary person* **3.** MARINE BIOL NOT MOVING describes shellfish that remain in one place, usually attached to a rock, for most of their lives **4.** BIRDS NONMIGRATORY describes birds that remain in the same area throughout the year and do not migrate [Late 16C. Via French < Latin *sedentarius* < *sedere* "sit"] —**sed·en·tar·i·ness** *n*

Se·der /sáydər/ (*plural* **-ders** or **-dar·im** /sə daárim/) *n* in Judaism, a ceremonial meal eaten on either of the first two nights of Passover, commemorating the exodus of the Jews from Egypt [Mid-19C. < Hebrew *sēḏer* "order, procedure"]

sedge /sej/ *n* a wetland plant that resembles grass and has a triangular stem, leaves growing in three vertical rows, and inconspicuous spikes of flowers. Genus: *Carex*. [Old English *secg* < Indo-European, "to cut"] —**sedg·y** *adj*

sedge wren *n* a bird of the wren family that lives in grassy meadows and sedge marshes. Native to: eastern North America. Latin name: *Cistothorus platensis*.

se·di·lia /sə díllyə, -díllee ə/ *npl* a set of three seats placed near the altar of a Christian church and often recessed into the wall, used by priests celebrating Mass or Communion [Late 18C. < Latin, plural of *sedile* "seat" < *sedere* "sit"]

sed·i·ment /séddimənt/ *n* **1.** material, originally suspended in a liquid, that settles at the bottom of the liquid when it is left standing for a long time **2.** material eroded from preexisting rocks that is transported by water, wind, or ice and deposited elsewhere [Mid-16C. < Latin *sedimentum* "settling" < *sedere* "sit"]

sed·i·men·ta·ry /sèddə méntəree, -méntree/ *adj* **1.** forming at the bottom of a liquid **2.** describes rocks formed from material deposited as sediment by water, wind, or ice and then consolidated by pressure

sed·i·men·ta·tion /sèddəmən táysh'n/ *n* **1.** the process by which particles in suspension in a liquid form sediment **2.** the process by which rocks are formed by the accumulation of sediment

sed·i·men·ta·tion tank *n* a tank in which sewage is left in order to allow its solid constituents to separate out

sed·i·men·tol·o·gy /sèddəmən tólləjee/ *n* the branch of geology concerned with the nature and formation of sedimentary rocks —**sed·i·men·to·log·ic** /sèddə ment'l ójjik/ *adj* —**sed·i·men·tol·o·gist** *n*

se·di·tion /sə dísh'n/ *n* actions or words intended to provoke or incite rebellion against government authority, or actual rebellion against government authority [14C. Via French < Latin *sedition-* "coming apart" < *se(d)-* "apart" + *ition-* "going" < *ire* "go"]

se·di·tious /sə díshəss/ *adj* **1.** involving or encouraging rebellion against a government or other authority **2.** taking part in activities that are directed against a government or other authority [15C. Via French < Latin *seditiosus* < *sedition-* (see SEDITION)] —**se·di·tious·ly** *adv* —**se·di·tious·ness** *n*

se·duce /sə dóoss/ (**-duced, -duc·ing, -duc·es**) *vt* **1.** ENCOURAGE SOMEBODY TO HAVE SEX to persuade somebody to have sex, especially by using a romantic or deceptive approach **2.** LEAD SOMEBODY ASTRAY to persuade somebody to do something by making it seem desirable or exciting **3.** WIN SOMEBODY OVER to persuade somebody into giving support or agreement [15C. < Latin *seducere* "lead astray" < *se(d)-* "apart" + *ducere* "to lead"] —**se·duc·er** *n*

se·duce·ment /sə dóossmənt/ *n* something that tempts or persuades ○ *"ere any flattering seducement, or vain principle seize them"* (John Milton, *Civil War Polemic, part I*)

se·duc·tion /sə dúksh'n/ *n* **1.** LURING OF SOMEBODY INTO SEX the act of persuading somebody to have sex, especially by using a romantic or deceptive approach **2.** LEADING ASTRAY OF SOMEBODY the act of persuading somebody to do something wrong ○ *their easy seduction into a life of crime* **3.** TEMPTING THING something that tempts, persuades, or attracts [15C. Directly or via French < Latin *seduction-* < *seduct-*, past participle of *seducere* "lead astray" (see SEDUCE)]

se·duc·tive /sə dúktiv/ *adj* **1.** aiming to be or regarded as being sexually inviting ○ *his seductive smile* **2.** serving to tempt, persuade, or attract ○ *made me a very seductive offer* [Mid-18C. < SEDUCTION] —**se·duc·tive·ly** *adv* —**se·duc·tive·ness** *n*

se·duc·tress /sə dúktrəss/ *n* a woman who seduces people [Early 19C. < obsolete *seductor* "seducer" < Latin *seduct-* (see SEDUCTION)]

sed·u·lous /séjjələss/ *adj* (*literary*) **1.** working with great zeal and persistence **2.** carried out with great care, concentration, and commitment ○ *sedulous attention to detail* [Mid-16C. < Latin *sedulus* < *se* "without" + *dolus* "deception"] —**se·du·li·ty** /sə dóolətee/ *n* —**sed·u·lous·ly** *adv* —**sed·u·lous·ness** *n*

se·dum /seédəm/ *n* a low-growing herbaceous plant that grows naturally in rocky places and has fleshy leaves. Flowers: white, yellow, or pink, in clusters. Genus: *Sedum*. [Mid-16C. < Latin, "houseleek"]

see[1] /see/ (**saw** /saw/, **seen** /seen/, **see·ing, sees**) *v* **1.** *vti* PERCEIVE WITH EYES to perceive, or perceive something, with the eyes **2.** *vi* HAVE VISION to have the faculty of sight ○ *sees fine without his glasses* **3.** *vti* VIEW OR WATCH SOMETHING to examine, look at, or watch somebody or something using the eyes ○ *He asked to see my passport.* **4.** *vti* COMPREHEND SOMETHING to have a clear understanding of something ○ *I'm not sure I see what you mean.* **5.** *vti* REALIZE SOMETHING BY SEEING to realize that something is true or exists by using the eyes, e.g., by reading about it ○ *I see from his letter that he's worked here before.* **6.** *vt* PERCEIVE SOMETHING AS PLEASING OR GOOD to perceive or find a trait in somebody, especially one that is interesting or pleasing ○ *I don't understand what she sees in him.* **7.** *vt* MEET OR CONSULT WITH SOMEBODY to meet somebody or spend time with somebody, either socially or professionally ○ *I'm seeing an old friend for lunch.* **8.** *vt* HAVE RELATIONSHIP WITH SOMEBODY to meet with somebody in a romantic context, or have a romantic or sexual relationship with somebody ○ *Is he seeing anyone at the moment?* **9.** *vt* HAVE INTERVIEW WITH SOMEBODY to meet with somebody in order to raise or discuss an issue such as a complaint ○ *She asked to see the manager.* **10.** *vt* RECEIVE SOMEBODY FOR INTERVIEW to admit or receive somebody who has come for a visit or an interview ○ *The doctor can't see you until next week.* **11.** *vt* IMAGINE SOMETHING to picture something in the mind ○ *I couldn't see someone like him in a jacket and tie.* **12.** *vt* BELIEVE SOMETHING to regard it as likely that somebody will do something ○ *We couldn't see them agreeing to that.* **13.** *vt* CONSIDER SOMEBODY OR SOMETHING to regard somebody or something in a particular way ○ *see her as a potential rival* **14.** *vt* UNDERGO SOMETHING to experience something firsthand ○ *saw active service* **15.** *vt* ESCORT SOMEBODY to go somewhere with somebody, usually as a guide, for company, or for protection ○ *Would you see me to my car?* **16.** *vt* MAKE SURE THAT SOMETHING HAPPENS to be sure to do something, or make sure that somebody does something ○ *See that they wash their hands.* **17.** *vt* REFER TO SOMETHING to consult or refer to something for information ○ *See our main advertisement on page 25.* **18.** *vti* ASCERTAIN SOMETHING to act to find something out ○ *see what he wants* **19.** *vi* WAIT UNTIL LATER TO DECIDE to allow time to elapse, either in order to be better able to judge what the outcome will be or in order to delay making a decision ○ *I don't know; we'll have to see.* **20.** *vt* GAMBLING MATCH BET to match an opponent's bet by staking the same amount [Old English *sēon* < Germanic] —**see·a·ble** *adj* ◇ **what you see is what you get** used to emphasize that nothing is disguised, hidden, or insincere

SPELLCHECK See *sea*.

see about *vt* **1.** to take care of a matter **2.** to make inquiries about a particular matter

see after *vt US* to take care of somebody or something, especially children or animals

see into *vt* **1.** to discern the true nature or content of something hidden such as somebody's thoughts **2.** to be able to predict future events

see off *vt* to accompany somebody to a place of departure and say goodbye

see out *vt* **1.** to accompany somebody who is leaving a room, building, or other place **2.** to stay in a place or stay committed to something until the end

see through *vt* **1.** PERCEIVE TRUTH BENEATH EXTERIOR to discern the true nature of somebody or something beneath a facade or disguise ○ *I saw through his bravado.* **2.** FINISH SOMETHING to continue with something until it is completed ○ *a professional who sees every job through personally* **3.** HELP SOMEBODY THROUGH DIFFICULTY to provide somebody with help, advice, and support, especially in times of trouble ○ *He's seen me through some bad times.*

see to *vt* to do what is required in order to deal with something or take care of somebody successfully ○ *We need an usher to see to guests as they arrive.* ○ *I'll see to it immediately.*

see[2] /see/ *n* **1.** the area that is under the jurisdiction of a bishop or archbishop **2.** the position or authority of a bishop or archbishop [13C Via Old French *se* < Latin *sedes* "seat" < *sedere* "sit"]

SPELLCHECK See *sea*.

See·beck ef·fect /seé bèk-/ *n* the production of an electric current in a circuit containing junctions between different metals or semiconductors kept at different temperatures [Early 20C. After Thomas J. Seebeck (1770–1831), Russian-born German physicist]

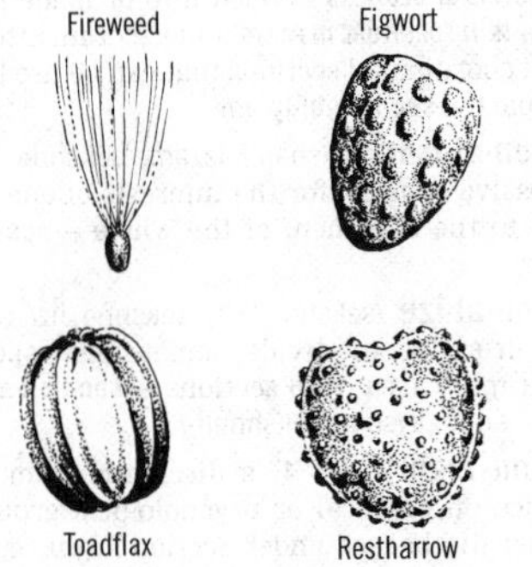

seed

seed /seed/ *n* **1.** PLANT PART CONTAINING EMBRYO a plant part produced by sexual reproduction that contains the embryo and gives rise to a new individual. In flowering plants it is enclosed within the fruit. **2.** FRUIT OF GRASS PLANT the small dry hard fruit produced by cereal plants or grasses **3.** PROPAGATIVE PART OF PLANT a compact part of a plant that is used for propagation, e.g., a bulb, tuber, or spore **4.** PROPAGATIVE PLANT PARTS COLLECTIVELY propagative plant parts as a whole, including seeds, tubers, rhizomes, spores, and bulbs ○ *a dry place to store seed* **5.** SOURCE something that is the source of a significant change in outlook or action ○ *the seeds of doubt* **6.** SOMETHING RESEMBLING SEED something that resembles a seed in shape, size, or function **7.** SPORTS GRADED COMPETITOR a competitor who is graded according to the perceived likelihood of his or her winning a specific tournament **8.** CHEM CRYSTAL a small crystal added to a supersaturated or supercooled solution to induce crystallization **9.** SPERM sperm or semen as a vehicle of reproduction (*literary*) **10.** DESCENDANTS a person's children or descendants (*literary*) ○ *the seed of Abraham* **11.** MARINE BIOL same as **seed oyster** ■ *v* (**seed·ed, seed·ing, seeds**) **1.** *vt* PLANT SEEDS IN PLACE to plant seeds in the soil of a place, or plant an area by sowing seeds ○ *The lower field was seeded with barley.* **2.** *vr* DROP SEEDS to shed seeds that develop into new plants (*refers to plants*) ○ *Those poppies have seeded themselves everywhere.* **3.** *vt* REMOVE SEEDS FROM SOMETHING to take the seeds out of a fruit or vegetable before eating or cooking **4.** *vt* SPORTS RANK PLAYER to rank a player according to the perceived likelihood of his or her winning a specific tournament **5.** *vt* SPORTS STRUCTURE TOURNAMENT to arrange the draw of a tournament so that the best players meet in the later rounds **6.** *vt* METEOROL SPRINKLE CLOUD WITH CRYSTALS to release silver iodide into clouds to encourage precipitation **7.** *vt* CHEM ADD CRYSTAL TO SOLUTION to add a small crystal to a supersaturated or supercooled solution to induce crystallization **8.** *vt* BUSINESS ENCOURAGE ENTERPRISE to give financial or other assistance to something such as a business during the early stages of its development ○ *"Big venture capital funds have helped seed a start-*

up culture..." (*Newsweek*; November 1998) ■ *adj* AGRIC **RESERVED FOR USE AS SEED** reserved for planting to grow the next crop ○ *seed potatoes* [Old English *sǣd* < Germanic, "to sow"] —**seed·less** *adj* ◇ **go to seed 1.** to become shabby or unhealthy from lack of proper care or attention **2.** to reach the stage of producing seeds and stop flowering or become unusable

SPELLCHECK See ***cede***.

seed·bed /séed bèd/ *n* **1.** a plot of ground in which seeds and seedlings are cultivated before being transplanted **2.** a place where conditions encourage the development of a significant change in outlook or action ○ *Small business is the seedbed of job creation.*

seed·cake /séed kàyk/ *n* a cake or cookie flavored with seeds, usually caraway seeds

seed cap·i·tal *n UK* same as **seed money**

seed coat *n* BOT same as **testa**

seed·eat·er /séed èetər/ *n* a bird that relies on seeds for its food and usually has a strong conical bill adapted to cracking the seeds open. Finches are seedeaters.

seed·er /séedər/ *n* **1. MACHINE FOR SOWING SEEDS** a mechanical device designed to scatter seed on the surface of the ground. Seeders are usually either pulled by a tractor or have wheels and a handle that is pushed. **2. DEVICE FOR REMOVING SEEDS** a kitchen device used to remove the seeds from fruit and vegetables **3. SOMEBODY OR SOMETHING THAT SEEDS** somebody or something that seeds, especially somebody who seeds clouds

seed fern *n* PLANTS same as **pteridosperm**

seed leaf *n* BOT same as **cotyledon** (sense 1)

seed·ling /séedling/ *n* a young developing plant that has been grown from a seed

seed mon·ey *n* money provided to enable a business venture to be developed

seed oys·ter *n* a small young oyster, especially one that is transplanted to a commercial oyster bed

seed pearl *n* a very small round pearl, natural or cultured, weighing less than one quarter of a grain

seed plant *n* BOT same as **spermatophyte**

seed·pod /séed pòd/ *n* BOT same as **pod**[1] *n* (sense 1)

seed stock *n* **1.** a supply of seed for planting **2.** a supply of animals kept or provided for breeding purposes, capable of founding a new population or sustaining an existing population

seed tick *n* the tiny larva of a tick

seed·time /séed tìm/ *n* **1.** the time of the year when seeds are planted **2.** a period of new development or growth

seed wee·vil *n* an insect of the weevil family that lays its eggs in seeds, where the larvae then develop. There are several species.

seed·y /séedee/ (**-i·er, -i·est**) *adj* **1. SHABBY** shabby, dirty-looking, and often disreputable ○ *a seedy hotel* **2. HAVING SEEDS** containing many seeds ○ *seedy raspberry jam* **3. UNWELL** somewhat ill, especially with a stomach complaint (*informal*) —**seed·i·ly** *adv* —**seed·i·ness** *n*

See·ger /séegər/, **Alan** (1888–1916) US poet. He died during World War I.

> "I have a rendezvous with Death / At some disputed barricade, / When spring comes back with rustling shade / And apple blossoms fill the air."
> [Alan Seeger, "I Have a Rendezvous with Death"; 1916]

See·ger, Pete (*b.* 1919) US singer and songwriter. He led the 1960s folk music revival with songs including "Where Have All the Flowers Gone?" (1956).

> "Where have all the flowers gone? / Young girls picked them every one."
> [Pete Seeger, "Where Have All the Flowers Gone?"; 1956]

see·ing /sée ing/ *n* **1. VISION** vision or perception with the eyes ○ *My seeing isn't too good.* **2.** ASTRON **ATMOSPHERIC CONDITIONS** the clarity of the Earth's atmosphere for astronomical observations using an optical telescope **3.** ASTRON **QUALITY OF ASTRONOMICAL IMAGES** the quality of the images obtained using an optical telescope ■ *conj* **see·ing that, see·ing as (how)** *informal* ⚠ **IN VIEW OF** used to introduce a statement that takes into account something mentioned before or after ○ *Seeing that you're an old friend, I'll give you a special price.*

USAGE The use of ***seeing that*** as a conjunction not grammatically attached to a particular subject is established in current English and conforms to a pattern used also in *given that, granted that*, and others, as in the sentence: *Perhaps a vacation would be in order, seeing that you have been working so hard.* The alternate forms ***seeing as*** and ***seeing as how*** are highly informal; *since* is an acceptable substitute in contexts where ***seeing that*** sounds inappropriate.

seek /seek/ (**sought** /sawt/, **seek·ing, seeks**) *v* **1.** *vti* **SEARCH FOR SOMETHING** to try to find a person, thing, or place **2.** *vt* **STRIVE FOR SOMETHING** to try to achieve or obtain something ○ *candidates seeking election* **3.** *vt* **ASK FOR SOMETHING** to consult somebody in order to obtain something such as help or advice **4.** *vt* **HEAD FOR SOMETHING** to go to or toward a place or thing ○ *As the water rose, they sought higher ground.* **5.** *vt* **ATTEMPT SOMETHING** to try to do something ○ *seeking to exploit the rift between them* [Old English *sēcan* < Indo-European, "seek out"] —**seek·er** *n*

seek out *vt* to find somebody or something as a result of active searching

seel /seel/ (**seeled, seel·ing, seels**) *vt* to sew shut the eyelids of a hawk or falcon in order to make it tame [15C. Via Old French *siller* < medieval Latin *ciliare* < Latin *cilium* "eyelid"]

seem /seem/ (**seemed, seem·ing, seems**) *v* **1.** *vti* to give a particular impression or sensation, either of a quality or of something happening ○ *It's not as easy as it seems.* ○ *It seems that I was wrong.* **2.** *vt* used to lessen the force of a following statement, usually by suggesting uncertainty or mitigating criticism, often for the sake of politeness ○ *We seem to have a misunderstanding.* [12C. < Old Norse *sœma* "conform to" < *sœmr* "fitting"]

SPELLCHECK See ***seam***.

seem·ing /séeming/ *adj* apparent to the senses or to the mind, but not necessarily true or real ○ *her seeming joy at his return* —**seem·ing·ly** *adv*

seem·ly /séemlee/ (**-li·er, -li·est**) *adj* in keeping with accepted standards and appropriate to the circumstances [12C. < Old Norse *sœmiligr* < *sœmr* "fitting."] —**seem·li·ness** *n*

seen past participle of **see**[1]

seep /seep/ *vi* (**seeped, seep·ing, seeps**) **1. PASS THROUGH** to pass or escape through an opening very slowly and in small quantities (*refers to liquids or gases*) ○ *water seeping out of the cracks* **2. DISAPPEAR** to diminish slowly but steadily ○ *with her resistance gradually seeping away* **3. GO SLOWLY** to enter or escape slowly but inexorably ○ *new sensations seeping into his consciousness* ■ *n* **1.** GEOL **PLACE WHERE LIQUID ESCAPES** a small pool or spring where liquid escapes from the ground **2.** same as **seepage** [Late 18C. Variant of dialect *sipe*, origin ?]

seep·age /séepij/ *n* **1.** a slow discharge or escape of liquid **2.** the amount of a liquid that has seeped

seer /seer, sée ər/ *n* **1.** somebody believed to be able to predict the future **2.** somebody with supposed supernatural powers [14C. < SEE[1]]

seer·suck·er /séer sùkər/ *n* a lightweight cotton, linen, or synthetic fabric with a pattern of alternate puckered and smooth stripes [Early 18C. Via Hindi < Persian *šīr o šakar* "milk and sugar"]

see·saw /sée sàw/ *n* **1. PLAYGROUND TOY** a playground toy in which two people sit at either end of a bar balanced in the middle and take turns riding up into the air **2. SEESAW RIDING** the game of riding a seesaw **3. UP-AND-DOWN MOVEMENT** an up-and-down, back-and-forth, or otherwise alternating movement, e.g., in the popularity of one political party over another ■ *vi* (**-sawed, -saw·ing, -saws**) **1. RIDE SEESAW** to ride up and down on a seesaw **2. MOVE LIKE SEESAW** to move in an alternating fashion, especially back and forth or up and down **3. ALTERNATE** to change regularly and repeatedly from one thing to another, e.g., one state of mind to another [Mid-17C. Probably to suggest the repetitive action of a two-handled saw]

seethe /seeth/ *vi* (**seethed, seeth·ing, seethes**) **1. BE ANGRY** to be in a state of extreme emotion, especially unexpressed anger ○ *I sat in my office quietly seething.* **2. BE BUSY** to be full of bustling activity, especially with crowds of people moving in many different directions **3. MAKE BOILING MOVEMENTS** to boil, or churn or foam as if boiling **4. BEGIN BOILING** to come to a boil (*archaic*) ■ *n* **ACT OF SEETHING** a seething movement or action [Old English *sēothan* < Germanic]

seeth·ing /séething/ *adj* **1. ANGRY** full of anger, especially pent-up anger **2. BUSTLING** moving in all directions, busily or frantically ○ *"the seething crowd of Paris"* (Baroness Orczy, *The Scarlet Pimpernel*; 1905) **3. BOILING** boiling and bubbling or foaming —**seeth·ing·ly** *adv*

see-through *adj* made of transparent material, especially so as to reveal clothes or skin underneath

Se·fer Tor·ah /sáyfər táwrə/ (*plural* **Se·fer Tor·ahs** or **Si·frei Tor·ah** /sì fray-/) *n* a parchment scroll on which the Pentateuch is handwritten [Mid-17C. < Hebrew *sēpēr tōrāh* "book of (the) Law"]

seg·ment *n* /ségmənt/ **1. COMPONENT PART** any of the parts or sections into which an object or group is divided **2.** ZOOL **ORGANISM'S BODY PART** any of the individual units that make up the body or part of the body of some animals **3.** MATH **PART OF GEOMETRIC FIGURE** the portion of a line or curve between any two of its points, or the portion of a solid cut by a plane **4.** LING **SPEECH SOUND** any of the individual speech sounds that make up a longer string of sounds ■ *vt* /ségmənt, seg mént/ (**-ment·ed, -ment·ing, -ments**) **SPLIT SOMETHING INTO SEGMENTS** to divide an object or group into segments [Late 16C. < Latin *segmentum* < *secare* "to cut"] —**seg·men·tal** /seg mént'l/ *adj* —**seg·men·tar·y** /ségmən tèrree/ *adj*

seg·men·ta·tion /sèg men táysh'n, -mən-/ *n* **1. SPLITTING INTO SEGMENTS** the dividing of something into segments **2. SEGMENTED STRUCTURE** the structure of something that is made up of a series of similar segments **3.** ZOOL **BODY STRUCTURE** the structure of the body of an organism such as a worm or centipede that consists of a linear series of similar subunits

seg·men·ta·tion cav·i·ty *n* BIOL same as **blastocoel**

se·gno /sáynyō/ (*plural* **-gnos** or **-gni** /sáynyee/) *n* a symbol used on sheet music to mark the beginning or end of a repeated section [Early 20C. Via Italian < Latin *signum* "sign"]

se·go lil·y /séegō-/ *n* a lily with an edible bulb. Flowers: mottled, variously colored. Native to: western United States. Latin name: *Calochortus nuttallii.* [Early 20C. < Southern Paiute *sigho'o*]

Sé·gou /sáygoo/ capital of Ségou Region, southwestern Mali. Population: 107,000 (1998).

Se·go·vi·a /sə gṓvee ə/ capital of Segovia Province, central Spain. Population: 54,945 (2002).

Se·go·vi·a /si gṓvee ə, say gáwvyaa/, **Andrés** (1893–1987) Spanish guitarist. His successful international career revived interest in the classical guitar.

Seg·re /sé gràyl/, **Emilio** (1905–89) Italian-born US physicist. He discovered the antiproton with physicist Owen Chamberlain (1955) and they shared the Nobel Prize in physics (1959) for their research into atomic nuclei. Full name **Segre, Emilio Gino**

seg·re·gant /séggrəgənt/ *adj* describes an organism having a genetic makeup that differs from that of either parent because of genetic segregation —**seg·re·gant** *n*

seg·re·gate /séggrə gàyt/ (**-gat·ed, -gat·ing, -gates**) *v* **1.** *vt* **SEPARATE PEOPLE OR THINGS** to separate one person or group from the rest, or divide a group into smaller units that are kept apart **2.** *vti* SOCIOL **KEEP GROUPS SEPARATE** to keep different groups within a population separate, especially different ethnic, racial, religious, or gender groups **3.** *vti* GENETICS **UNDERGO GENETIC SEGREGATION** to undergo genetic segregation, or cause cells to undergo genetic segregation [Mid-16C. < Latin *segregat-*, past participle of *segregare* "separate from the flock" < *grex* "flock"] —**seg·re·ga·ble** *adj* —**seg·re·gate** /séggrəgət, -gàyt/ *n* —**seg·re·ga·tive** *adj* —**seg·re·ga·tor** *n*

seg·re·ga·tion /sèggrə gáysh'n/ *n* **1. ENFORCED SEPARATION**

OF GROUPS the practice of keeping ethnic, racial, religious, or gender groups separate, especially by enforcing the use of separate schools, transportation, housing, and other facilities, and usually discriminating against a minority group **2.** SEGREGATED STATE the state or position of somebody or something kept separate from others **3.** ACT OF SEGREGATING the separating of one person, group, or thing from others, or the dividing of people or things into separate groups kept apart from each other **4.** GENETICS GENE SEPARATION the separation of the two versions (**alleles**) of each gene and their distribution to separate sex cells during the formation (**meiosis**) of these cells in organisms with paired chromosomes —**seg·re·ga·tion·al** *adj*

seg·re·ga·tion·ist /sèggrə gáysh'nist/ *n* an advocate or enforcer of segregation, especially racial segregation —**seg·re·ga·tion·ist** *adj*

se·gue /sé gwày, sáy-/ *vi* (**-gued, -gue·ing, -gues**) **1.** MOVE SMOOTHLY to make a smooth, almost imperceptible transition from one state, situation, or subject to another ○ *segued into a discussion of the playoffs without missing a beat* **2.** MUSIC CONTINUE PLAYING in music, to continue by playing the following piece or passage without a pause ■ *n* **1.** SMOOTH TRANSITION the act of making a smooth transition from one state, situation, or subject to another **2.** MUSIC CONTINUATION OF MUSIC the act of moving without a pause from one musical piece or passage into another **3.** MUSIC INSTRUCTION TO CONTINUE an instruction to a musician to begin playing a following piece or passage without a pause [Mid-18C. < Italian < *seguire* "follow" < Latin *sequi*]

se·gui·dil·la /sèggə dée yə, sàygə-, -déelyə/ *n* **1.** DANCE SPANISH DANCE a Spanish dance in triple time, usually accompanied by castanets and guitars **2.** MUSIC SPANISH MUSIC the music for a seguidilla **3.** LITERAT SPANISH VERSE FORM a Spanish verse form with either four or seven very short lines that makes use of assonance rather than rhyme [Mid-18C. < Spanish < *seguida* "sequence" < *seguir* "follow" < Latin *sequi*]

sei·cen·to /say chéntō/ *n* the 17th century, with reference to Italian art and literature [Early 20C. < Italian, shortening of *milseicento* "one thousand six hundred"]

seiche /saysh, seech/ *n* a movement on the surface of an enclosed body of water such as a lake, usually caused by intense storm activity [Mid-19C. < Swiss French]

sei·del /sīd'l, zīd'l/ *n* a large beer glass [Early 20C. Via German < Latin *situla* "bucket"]

seif dune /sáyf-, sīf-/ *n* a sand dune with curved edges, found in hot deserts in a series of parallel ridges and often reaching several miles in length and up to 300 ft./100 m in height [Early 20C. < Arabic *sayf* "sword"]

seige incorrect spelling of **siege**

seign·eur /sayn yúr/ *n* **1.** HIST same as **seignior 2.** in French Canada until 1854, the owner of an estate originally granted by the king of France and farmed by tenants holding a form of feudal tenure over the land [Late 16C. < French, later form of *seignor* (see SEIGNIOR)]

seign·eur·y /sáynyəree, sén-/ (*plural* **-ies**) *n* **1.** the estate of a seigneur **2.** the rank or authority of a seigneur

seign·ior /sàyn yáwr/ *n* a feudal lord, especially in medieval England [13C. Via Anglo-Norman *segnour*, Old French *seignor* < Latin *senior* "older"] —**sei·gnio·ri·al** *adj*

seign·ior·age /sáynyərij/ *n* the profit represented by the difference between the value of bullion and the face value of the coins minted from it

seign·ior·y /sáynyəree/ (*plural* **-ies**), **sign·ior·y** /séen-/, **sign·or·y** *n* **1.** the estate of a seignior **2.** the rank or authority of a seignior

seine /sayn/ *n* a large commercial fishing net that is weighted so that it hangs vertically in the water ■ *vti* (**seined, sein·ing, seines**) to catch fish with a seine [Old English *segne*, via W Germanic < Latin *sagena* "net" < Greek *sagēnē*] —**sein·er** *n*

Seine /sayn, sen/ river rising in eastern France and flowing northwestward through Paris into the English Channel. Length: 482 mi./776 km.

Sein·feld /sīn fèld/, **Jerry** (*b.* 1954) US comedian. His comedy series *Seinfeld* (1989–98) was one of the most popular television shows of its time.

seise /seez/ (**seised, seis·ing, seis·es**) *vt* LAW same as **seize** (sense 11) [Early 17C. Variant of SEIZE]

sei·sin /séezin/, **sei·zin** *n* **1.** LAND OWNERSHIP the legal freehold possession of land **2.** ACT OF TAKING POSSESSION OF LAND the act of taking legal freehold possession of land **3.** OWNED LAND land that is wholly and legally owned, especially land taken possession of legally [13C. < Anglo-Norman *sesine* < Old French *saisir* (see SEIZE)]

seism /sízəm/ *n* same as **earthquake** (sense 1) (*technical*) [Late 19C. < Greek *seismos* (see SEISMO-)]

seism- *prefix* same as **seismo-** (*used before vowels*)

seis·mic /sízmik/ *adj* **1.** relating to or caused by an earthquake or earth tremor **2.** extremely large or great (*informal*) ○ *had a seismic impact* —**seis·mi·cal·ly** *adv*

seis·mic ar·ray *n* a network of seismometers positioned to maximize the sensitivity of each of them and best monitor seismic activity in a specific region of the world

seis·mic·i·ty /sīz míssətee/ *n* the distribution and frequency of seismic events

seis·mic wave *n* a shock wave traveling through the Earth from the epicenter of an earthquake

seismo- *prefix* earthquake ○ *seismograph* [Late 19C. < Greek *seismos* "earthquake" < *seiein* "to shake"]

seis·mo·gram /sízmə gràm/ *n* a record of an earthquake made by a seismograph

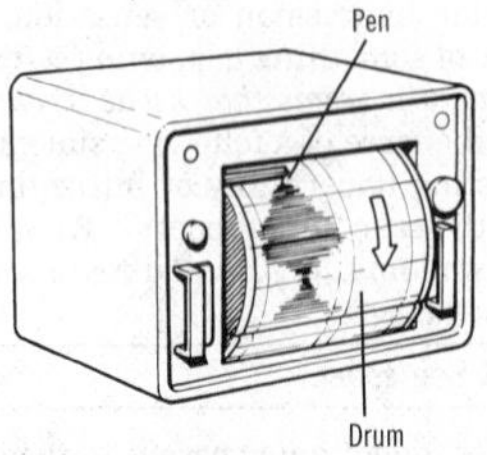

seismograph

seis·mo·graph /sízmə gràf/ *n* an instrument that detects the presence of an earthquake and measures and records its magnitude —**seis·mog·ra·pher** /sīz mógrəfər/ *n* —**seis·mo·graph·ic** /sīzmə gráffik/ *adj* —**seis·mog·ra·phy** /sīz mógrəfee/ *n*

seis·mol·o·gy /sīz móllәjee/ *n* the scientific study of earthquakes —**seis·mo·log·i·cal** /sīzmə lójjik'l/ *adj* —**seis·mo·log·i·cal·ly** *adv* —**seis·mol·o·gist** *n*

seis·mom·e·ter /sīz mómmətər/ *n* an instrument used to measure vibrations caused by an earthquake —**seis·mom·e·try** *n*

seive incorrect spelling of **sieve**

sei whale /sáy-/ *n* a dark bluish gray whale similar to the blue whale but smaller and more streamlined. It lives in all but the polar oceans and belongs to the rorqual family of whales. Latin name: *Balaenoptera borealis*. [Early 20C. < Norwegian *sejhval* < *sei* "coalfish" + *hval* "whale"]

seize /seez/ (**seized, seiz·ing, seiz·es**) *v* **1.** *vt* TAKE HOLD OF SOMETHING to take a hold of an object quickly and firmly ○ *seized the letter from his hand* **2.** *vt* EXPLOIT SOMETHING IMMEDIATELY to take advantage of something such as a chance eagerly and immediately ○ *seize an opportunity* **3.** *vt* AFFECT SOMEBODY SUDDENLY to overwhelm the mind or emotions suddenly ○ *seized by panic* **4.** *vt* AFFECT SOMEBODY PHYSICALLY to overwhelm somebody physically ○ *Yet another spasm seized him.* **5.** *vt* APPROPRIATE SOMETHING to take official or legal possession of something, often something held illegally such as arms, drugs, or stolen goods ○ *The shipment was seized by customs officials.* **6.** *vt* ARREST SOMEBODY to take somebody into custody ○ *seized the suspects after a chase* **7.** *vti* COMPREHEND SOMETHING to understand an idea or concept, especially quickly **8.** *vi* STOP WORKING to become jammed, especially as a result of great heat, pressure, or friction, often arising from lack of lubrication ○ *The engine seized up.* **9.** *vi* STIFFEN UP to become painfully stiff and immobile ○ *My leg's just seized up.* **10.** *vi* STOP to come to a sudden and sometimes permanent halt ○ *The negotiations seized up after the most recent incident.* **11.** *vt* LAW GIVE LEGAL POSSESSION TO SOMEBODY to make somebody the legal owner of property or goods ○ *The families were seized of all the relevant documentation.* **12.** *vt* NAUT LASH SOMETHING to tie or secure something by lashing it using several turns of thin rope or wire [13C. Via Old French *saisir* < medieval Latin *sacire* "to claim" < Germanic] —**seiz·a·ble** *adj* —**seiz·er** *n* ◇ **seized of 1.** LAW in control of **2.** engaged with and interested in (*formal*)

sei·zin *n* LAW another spelling of **seisin**

seiz·ing /séezing/ *n* a knot or lashing made using thin rope or wire, e.g., to join two ropes or to secure an item of ship's gear

sei·zure /séezhər/ *n* **1.** the seizing of something, especially the taking of something by force or the official or legal appropriation of something **2.** a sudden attack of an illness or condition, especially of the kind experienced by people with epilepsy

se·jant /séejənt/, **se·jeant** *adj* in heraldry, used to describe a figure on a coat of arms that is in a sitting position [15C. < French *séant* < Latin *sedere* "sit"]

Sek·on·di-Ta·ko·ra·di /sekən dée takə raádee/ capital of Western Region, southwestern Ghana, situated 120 mi./193 km southwest of Accra. Population: 116,500 (1990).

se·la·chi·an /sə láykee ən/ *n* a fish of the order that includes all sharks, rays, and skates. Order: Selachii. [Mid-19C. < modern Latin *selachii* < Greek *selakhē* "shark"] —**se·la·chi·an** *adj*

se·lag·i·nel·la /sə làjjə néllə/ *n* a mossy plant with branching stems and small leaves bearing spores. Genus: *Selaginella*. [Mid-19C. < modern Latin < Latin *selago*, herb similar to savin]

se·lah /séelə, -laá/ *interj* used to perform a punctuating function between verses of the Bible. It is an ancient Hebrew word of unknown meaning and uncertain grammatical status that appears in some books of the Bible and is therefore, when included in English translations, left untranslated. [Mid-16C. < Hebrew *selāh*]

sel·dom /séldəm/ *adv* not often [Old English *seldum*, *seldan* < Germanic]

se·lect /sə lékt/ *vti* (**-lect·ed, -lect·ing, -lects**) CHOOSE FROM OTHERS to choose somebody or something from among several ○ *selected a chocolate from the box* ■ *adj* **1.** OF GOOD QUALITY chosen on grounds of particularly high quality **2.** HAVING LIMITED MEMBERSHIP admitting only a few carefully chosen members ○ *one of the more select country clubs* **3.** SPECIALLY CHOSEN chosen from several others and given special treatment or a special privilege ○ *advance copies sent to a select few* **4.** DISCRIMINATING showing care and discernment when choosing ○*"foreign films which generally attract a select audience"* (James Berardinelli, *Review: Deception*; 1993) **5.** *US* FOOD LEAN describes meat with a relatively low amount of fat (**marbling**) ■ *n* SOMEBODY OR SOMETHING CHOSEN somebody or something chosen from among others, often on the basis of high quality (*often used in the plural*) [Mid-16C. < Latin *select-*, past participle of *seligere* < *legere* "pick out"] —**se·lect·a·ble** *adj* —**se·lect·ness** *n*

se·lect com·mit·tee *n* a small group of members of Congress instructed by either the Senate or the House of Representatives to investigate and report on a specific matter

se·lec·tion /sə léksh'n/ *n* **1.** ACT OF CHOOSING an act of choosing somebody or something from a wide variety of others **2.** SOMEBODY OR SOMETHING CHOSEN somebody or something chosen from among others ○ *among the judges' final selection* **3.** AVAILABLE CHOICE the range from which somebody or something can be selected ○ *a fantastic selection of carpets* **4.** GENETICS SURVIVAL OF FITTEST the process by which organisms that adapt well to their environment produce offspring, while those that do not adapt die out, resulting in gradual changes in a species. Selection may take place naturally (**natural selection**) or as the result of breeding for specific characteristics (**artificial selection**). [Early 17C. < Latin *selection-* < *select-* (see SELECT)]

se·lec·tion·ist /sə léksh'nist/ *n* a believer or promoter of the theory that natural selection is the chief or only force governing biological development

se·lec·tion rule *n* a rule derived from quantum mechanics that governs whether changes may or may not occur in quantized systems such as molecules, atoms, or nuclei

se·lec·tive /sə léktiv/ *adj* **1. DISCERNING** tending to make careful choices **2. NOT UNIVERSAL** applying to some but not others **3.** ELECTRONICS **RECEIVING ON SOME FREQUENCIES ONLY** describes an electronic receiver capable of selecting some frequencies or frequency bands and blocking out all others, and therefore eliminating interference in reception —**se·lec·tive·ly** *adv* —**se·lec·tive·ness** *n*

se·lec·tive at·ten·tion *n* the ability to pay attention to those things that are considered important and to ignore those that are not

se·lec·tive se·ro·to·nin re·up·take in·hib·i·tor *n* a drug that increases serotonin levels in synapses, resulting in elevation of mood. Use: antidepressant.

se·lec·tive ser·vice *n* a system for calling up men for US military service, which requires almost all men aged 18 through 25 to register with the relevant agency. In the event of a draft, men will be called in a sequence determined by a random lottery number and year of birth.

se·lec·tiv·i·ty /sə lèk tívvətee/ *n* **1.** the choosing of only some, not all, and the exercising of judgment in making the choice **2.** the degree to which an electronic device or circuit can distinguish a desired frequency from other adjacent frequencies

se·lect·man /si lékt màn, -mən/ (*plural* **-men** /-mèn, -mən/) *n* in most New England communities, somebody, especially a man, who is a member of an elected administrative board that manages local affairs

se·lec·tor /sə léktər/ *n* a person or device that selects

se·lect·per·son /si lékt pùrss'n/ (*plural* **-per·sons** or **-peo·ple** /-peep'l/) *n* in most New England communities, a member of an elected administrative board that manages local affairs

se·lect·wom·an /si lékt wòomən/ (*plural* **-women** /-wìmmin/) *n* in most New England communities, a woman who is a member of an elected administrative board that manages local affairs

selen- *prefix* same as **seleno-** (*used before vowels*)

sel·e·nate /séllə nàyt/ *n* a salt or ester of selenic acid [Early 19C. < SELENIUM]

Se·le·ne /sə leenee/ *n* in Greek mythology, the goddess of the Moon. Roman equivalent **Luna**

se·le·nic /sə lénnik, -leenik/ *adj* relating to or containing selenium, especially with a valence of six [Early 19C. < SELENIUM]

se·le·nic ac·id *n* a highly corrosive acid usually found in the form of a whitish solid. Formula: H_2SeO_4.

sel·e·nif·er·ous /sèllə nífərəss/ *adj* containing or producing selenium [Early 19C. < SELENIUM]

se·le·ni·ous /sə leenee əss/ *adj* relating to or containing selenium, especially with a valence of two or four [Early 19C. < SELENIUM]

sel·e·nite /séllə nīt/ *n* a transparent colorless variety of gypsum that cleaves to reveal lustrous crystal faces [Mid-16C. Via Latin < Greek *selēnitēs lithos* "moon stone" < *selēnē* (see SELENIUM)]

se·le·ni·um /sə leenee əm/ *n* a nonmetallic element that occurs in several forms ranging from a red powder to gray black crystals and is an essential trace element, although toxic in excess. Source: copper refining. Use: photocells, photocopiers. Symbol **Se**. See table at **element** [Early 19C. < modern Latin < Greek *selēnē* "moon" < *selas* "light"]

se·le·ni·um cell *n* a photoelectric cell based on the light-sensitive properties of selenium and containing a strip of selenium mounted between two metal electrodes

seleno- *prefix* the moon ○ *selenography* [< Greek *selēnē* "moon" (see SELENIUM)]

sel·e·nog·ra·phy /sèllə nóggrəfee/ *n* the branch of astronomy that is concerned with mapping the surface features of the Moon —**sel·e·no·graph·ic** /sèllənə gráffik, sə leenə-/ *adj*

sel·e·nol·o·gy /sèllə nóllәjee/ *n* the branch of astronomy concerned with the origin and physical characteristics of the Moon —**sel·e·no·log·i·cal** /sèllənə lójjik'l, sə leenə-/ *adj* —**sel·e·nol·o·gist** *n*

Sel·es /sél ess/, **Monica** (*b.* 1973) Yugoslavian-born US tennis player. She has won numerous Grand Slam tennis championships since turning professional at age 15. Her career was interrupted for two years after she was stabbed by a spectator in 1993.

Se·leu·cid /sə lòossid/ *n* a member of a dynasty of rulers who ruled Asia Minor from 312 to 64 B.C., after the death of Alexander the Great [Mid-19C. < Latin *Seleucides* < Greek *Seleukidēs* < *Seleukos*, the dynasty's founder] —**Se·leu·cid** *adj*

Se·leu·cus I /sə lòokəss/ (358?–280 B.C.) Macedonian general. One of Alexander the Great's successors, he founded the Seleucid dynasty. He became king of Babylonia in 312 B.C. and gained control of territory from India to Asia Minor, but died trying to seize the throne of Macedonia. Known as **Seleucus Nicator**

Se·leu·cus II (265?–226? B.C.) Syrian monarch. During his reign over the Seleucid kingdom (247–226 B.C.), the Bactrians and Parthians won independence.

self /self/ *n* (*plural* **selves** /selvz/) **1. PERCEIVED PERSONALITY** somebody's personality, or an aspect of somebody's personality, especially as perceived by others ○ *not his usual self* **2. SELF-INTEREST** somebody's own individual interests and welfare, especially when placed before those of other people **3. COMPLETE PERSONALITY** a complete and individual personality, especially one that somebody recognizes as his or her own and with which there is a sense of ease ○ *develop a sense of self* **4.** IMMUNOL **OWN BODY PARTS** the set of organs and tissues that the body recognizes as its own and does not attack with antibodies ■ *pron* **ONESELF** myself, yourself, himself, or herself (*informal*) ○ *not enough to sustain self and family* ■ *adj* **1. SELF-COLORED** having the same color all over **2. OF SAME FABRIC** made of the same material as the garment it is worn with ○ *a self belt* [Old English < Indo-European]

USAGE The two main uses of ***-self*** compounds such as *himself, herself*, and *myself* are, first, to serve as a reflexive pronoun when the object of the verb is the same as the subject (*He saw himself in the mirror*), and, second, to reinforce or emphasize a noun (*Jane herself had wanted to go with them*). In formal contexts, compounds with ***-self*** should not be used simply as alternatives for other pronouns such as *him, her, me*, and *I*: *It was up to her* [not *herself*] *whether she came or not. This is between him and me* [not *myself*]. The plural of *-self* is *-selves*, and *themself* is not acceptable in standard English (see ***themself***).

self- *prefix* **1.** of, by, for, to, or in somebody's own self or a thing itself ○ *self-adhesive* ○ *self-control* **2.** automatic ○ *self-winding* [< SELF]

self-a·ban·doned *adj*
self-a·ban·don·ment *n*
self-a·base·ment *n*
self-ab·ne·gat·ing *adj*
self-ab·ne·ga·tion *n*
self-ac·cep·tance *n*
self-ac·cu·sa·tion *n*
self-ac·cus·ing *adj*
self-act·ing *adj*
self-ac·tion *n*
self-ac·tu·al·i·za·tion *n*
self-ac·tu·al·ize *vi*
self-ad·just·ing *adj*
self-ad·min·is·ter *vt*
self-ad·min·is·tered *adj*
self-ad·min·is·trat·ing *adj*
self-ad·min·is·tra·tion *n*
self-ad·mi·ra·tion *n*
self-ad·vance·ment *n*
self-ad·ver·tise·ment *n*
self-ag·gran·dize·ment *n*
self-ag·gran·diz·er *n*
self-ag·gran·diz·ing *adj*
self-a·noint·ed *adj*
self-ap·prov·al *n*
self-ap·proved *adj*
self-a·vowed *adj*
self-be·tray·al *n*
self-bet·ter·ment *n*
self-cen·sor·ship *n*
self-clos·ing *adj*
self-com·mand *n*
self-com·pla·cen·cy *n*
self-com·pla·cent *adj*
self-con·ceit *n*
self-con·cept *n*
self-con·cep·tion *n*
self-con·cern *n*
self-con·cerned *adj*
self-con·dem·na·tion *n*
self-con·demned *adj*
self-con·duct·ed *adj*
self-con·sis·tent *adj*
self-con·sum·ing *adj*
self-con·tempt *n*
self-con·tent *adj, n*
self-con·tra·dict·ing *adj*
self-con·tra·dic·tion *n*
self-con·tra·dic·to·ry *adj*
self-cre·at·ed *adj*
self-crit·i·cal *adj*
self-crit·i·cal·ly *adv*
self-crit·i·cism *n*
self-cul·ti·va·tion *n*
self-de·base·ment *n*
self-de·ceit *n*
self-de·ceived *adj*
self-de·ceiv·ing *adj*
self-de·cep·tion *n*
self-de·cep·tive *adj*
self-de·cep·tive·ly *adv*
self-de·fin·ing *adj*
self-def·i·ni·tion *n*
self-de·lud·ed *adj*
self-de·lud·ing *adj*
self-de·lu·sion *n*
self-dep·re·cat·ing *adj*
self-dep·re·cat·ion *n*
self-de·pre·ci·a·tion *n*
self-de·scribed *adj*
self-de·vel·op·ment *n*
self-de·vour·ing *adj*
self-di·ag·no·sis *n*
self-di·rect·ed *adj*
self-di·rect·ing *adj*
self-di·rec·tion *n*
self-dis·gust *n*
self-dis·trust *n*
self-dis·trust·ful *adj*
self-ed·u·cat·ed *adj*
self-ed·u·ca·tion *n*
self-e·lect·ed *adj*
self-en·closed *adj*
self-en·grossed *adj*
self-en·rich·ment *n*
self-e·val·u·a·tion *n*
self-ex·plain·ing *adj*
self-flat·ter·y *n*
self-for·get·ful *adj*
self-for·get·ful·ly *adv*
self-for·get·ful·ness *n*
self-gen·er·at·ing *adj*
self-giv·ing *adj*
self-grat·i·fi·ca·tion *n*
self-gui·dance *n*
self-guid·ed *adj*
self-hate *n*
self-hat·ing *adj*
self-ha·tred *n*
self-heal·ing *adj*
self-hu·mil·i·a·tion *n*
self-hyp·no·sis *n*
self-i·den·ti·fi·ca·tion *n*
self-i·den·ti·fy *vi*
self-i·den·ti·ty *n*
self-ig·nite *vi*
self-im·prove·ment *n*
self-in·i·ti·at·ed *adj*
self-in·struct·ed *adj*
self-in·volved *adj*
self-in·volve·ment *n*
self-la·beled *adj*
self-liq·ui·da·tion *n*
self-loath·ing *n*
self-love *n*
self-lov·ing *adj*
self-man·age·ment *n*
self-mas·ter·y *n*
self-med·i·ca·tion *n*
self-med·i·ca·tor *n*
self-mock·er·y *n*
self-mov·ing *adj*
self-ob·ser·va·tion *n*
self-ob·sessed *adj*
self-oc·cu·pied *adj*
self-or·dained *adj*
self-par·o·dy *n*
self-penned *adj*
self-per·cep·tion *n*
self-pow·ered *adj*
self-praise *n*
self-pro·duced *adj*
self-pro·fessed *adj*
self-pro·mot·er *n*
self-pro·mo·tion *n*
self-prop·a·gat·ing *adj*
self-pro·pelled *adj*
self-pro·pel·ling *adj*
self-pro·pul·sion *n*
self-pub·lished *adj*
self-pun·ish·ment *n*
self-pu·ri·fi·ca·tion *n*
self-ques·tion·ing *adj*
self-re·cord·ing *adj*
self-re·crim·i·na·tion *n*
self-re·flec·tion *n*
self-re·li·ance *n*
self-re·li·ant *adj*
self-re·new·al *n*
self-re·nun·ci·a·tion *n*
self-rep·li·cat·ing *adj*
self-rep·li·ca·tion *n*
self-re·spect·ful *adj*
self-re·veal·ing *adj*
self-rev·e·la·tion *n*
self-rid·i·cule *n*
self-sat·i·riz·ing *adj*
self-sat·is·fac·tion *n*
self-sat·is·fied *adj*
self-scru·ti·ny *n*
self-stud·y *n*
self-sup·port *n*
self-sup·port·ed *adj*
self-sup·port·ing *adj*
self-sus·tain·ing *adj*
self-tor·ment *n*
self-tor·ture *n*
self-trans·for·ma·tion *n*
self-treat·ment *n*
self-trust *n*
self-un·der·stand·ing *n*
self-val·i·dat·ing *adj*

self-ab·sorbed *adj* excessively concerned with your own life and interests

self-ab·sorp·tion *n* **1.** excessive concern with your own life and interests **2.** a radioactive material's absorption of part of the radiation that it emits

self-a·buse /-ə byòoss/ *n* **1.** masturbation when viewed as being detrimental to character (*dated; sometimes humorous*) **2.** somebody's deprecation or deliberate misuse of his or her talents and abilities —**self-a·bus·er** *n*

self-ad·dressed *adj* addressed to the sender for return by mail ○ *enclose a self-addressed envelope*

self-ad·he·sive *adj* having adhesive on one side and able to stick in a position without needing to be moistened or to have adhesive applied

self-a·nal·y·sis *n* a systematic attempt to try and gain insight into your own personality and emotions

self-an·ni·hi·la·tion *n* **1.** loss of awareness of being an individual person, achieved through meditation or other mystical means **2.** an act or instance of suicide

self-ap·point·ed *adj* assuming a role personally, rather than being given it or being regarded as worthy of it by others ○ *a self-appointed arbiter of good taste*

self-as·sem·bly *n* the construction by the purchaser of something such as a piece of furniture sold in kit form

self-as·ser·tive *adj* tending to be aggressively confident in making your views heard and your presence felt —**self-as·sert·ing** *adj* —**self-as·ser·tion** *n* —**self-as·ser·tive·ly** *adv* —**self-as·ser·tive·ness** *n*

self-as·sured *adj* behaving in a relaxed manner that displays confidence that your views and abilities are of value —**self-as·sur·ance** *n* —**self-as·sur·ed·ly** *adv* —**self-as·sur·ed·ness** *n*

self-a·ware *adj* having a balanced and honest view of your own personality, and often an ability to interact with others frankly and confidently —**self-a·ware·ness** *n*

self-bast·ing *adj* commercially prepared with added fat to prevent drying out when cooked in an oven ○ *a self-basting turkey*

self-ca·ter·ing *adj* UK describes accommodations, especially for vacationers or students, in which meals are not provided but cooking facilities are

self-cen·tered *adj* tending to concentrate selfishly on your own needs and affairs and to show little or no interest in those of others —**self-cen·tered·ness** *n*

self-clean·ing *adj* designed to stay clean when being used, usually by virtue of being coated with materials that shed dirt ○ *a self-cleaning oven*

self-col·ored *adj* **1.** UNIFORM IN COLOR of the same color all over or throughout **2.** BOT RETAINING NATURAL COLOR describes a flower whose color has not been artificially changed by hybridization **3.** TEXTILES UNDYED describes cloth that has not been dyed and so retains its natural color

self-com·pat·i·ble *adj* describes a plant that is capable of pollinating itself

self-con·fessed *adj* admitting freely to having a particular characteristic, quality, or behavior —**self-con·fess·ed·ly** *adv*

self-con·fi·dence *n* confidence in yourself and your own abilities —**self-con·fi·dent** *adj*

self-con·grat·u·la·tion *n* the frequent mentioning of personal achievements and the displaying of the smug satisfaction taken in them —**self-con·grat·u·la·to·ry** *adj*

self-con·scious *adj* **1.** feeling acutely and uncomfortably aware of your failings and shortcomings when in the company of others and believing that others are noticing them too ○ *too self-conscious to speak in public* **2.** highly conscious of the impression made on others and tending to act in a way that reinforces this impression ○ *swinging his car keys in a self-conscious manner* —**self-con·scious·ly** *adv* —**self-con·scious·ness** *n*

self-con·tained *adj* **1.** HAVING EVERYTHING REQUIRED possessing all the features and facilities required to function independently **2.** KEEPING FEELINGS PRIVATE able or tending to keep feelings and opinions private or to control feelings and reactions in front of others **3.** HAVING OWN FACILITIES AND ENTRANCE describes accommodations that have their own kitchen, bathroom, and entrance ○ *All of our units are self-contained.* —**self-con·tain·ment** *n*

self-con·ten·ted *adj* feeling contented with personal achievements and good fortune

self-con·trol *n* the ability to control your own behavior, especially in terms of reactions and impulses —**self-con·trolled** *adj*

self-cor·rect·ing *adj* **1.** describes a word processor that automatically corrects typing errors as they occur **2.** able or tending to notice personal mistakes and correct them

self-deal·ing *n* the benefiting or attempting to benefit from a financial transaction carried out on behalf of somebody else

self-de·feat·ing *adj* defeating the very objective or purpose it is designed to serve

self-de·fense *n* **1.** LEGAL RIGHT TO DEFEND SELF the use of reasonable force to defend yourself, your family, and your property against physical attack, or the right to do this **2.** FIGHTING TECHNIQUES fighting techniques used to defend yourself against physical attack, especially unarmed combat techniques such as any of the martial arts **3.** JUSTIFYING OF SELF the defending of your own ideas, principles, or actions —**self-de·fen·sive** *adj*

self-de·ni·al *n* the setting aside of your own wishes, needs, or interests, whether voluntary, altruistic, or enforced by circumstances —**self-de·ny·ing** *adj*

self-de·struct /-di strúkt/ *vi* **1.** DESTROY ITSELF AUTOMATICALLY to destroy itself by means of a built-in mechanism **2.** RUIN OWN LIFE to behave in a way that destroys any chance of your success, credibility, or effectiveness ■ *adj* CAUSING DESTRUCTION OF ITSELF causing a device or machine to destroy itself if given conditions are met

self-de·struc·tion *n* **1.** AUTOMATIC DESTRUCTION OF DEVICE the automatic destruction of a device fitted with a self-destruct mechanism **2.** RUINING OF OWN LIFE the ruining of your own life or an aspect of it such as your health, happiness, or career **3.** SUICIDE an act or instance of suicide

self-de·struc·tive *adj* causing or tending to cause harm to yourself

self-de·ter·mi·na·tion *n* **1.** the ability or right to make your own decisions without interference from others **2.** the right of a people to determine its own form of government without interference from outside —**self-de·ter·min·ing** *adj*

self-dis·ci·pline *n* the ability to do what is necessary or sensible without needing to be urged by somebody else —**self-dis·ci·plined** *adj*

self-dis·cov·er·y *n* the process of learning about your true personality and motives

self-di·vin·i·za·tion *n* PHILOSOPHY the elevation by human beings, philosophically, of humankind to godlike status

self-doubt *n* feelings of doubt about your own worth and abilities

self-ef·fac·ing *adj* tending to be modest about your achievements and to avoid drawing attention to yourself in company —**self-ef·face·ment** *n* —**self-ef·fac·ing·ly** *adv*

self-em·ployed *adj* earning a living by working independently of an employer, either freelance or by running a business —**self-em·ploy·ment** *n*

self-es·teem *n* confidence in your own merit as an individual person

self-ev·i·dent *adj* obvious without explanation or proof —**self-ev·i·dent·ly** *adv*

self-ex·am·i·na·tion *n* **1.** careful reflection on your own thoughts, beliefs, behavior, and circumstances **2.** the regular examination of parts of your own body for signs of disease

self-ex·cit·ed *adj* describes an electrical device with a field system that is excited by a current the device generates for itself

self-ex·e·cut·ing *adj* legally effective without intervention ○ *self-executing clauses in the contract*

self-ex·ile *n* **1.** a person who leaves his or her own country voluntarily to live elsewhere, especially for political reasons **2.** a voluntary state of exile —**self-ex·iled** *adj*

self-ex·plan·a·to·ry *adj* clear and easy to understand with no need for explanation

self-ex·pres·sion *n* the expressing of your own ideas, emotions, or individuality through behavior or an activity such as painting, music, or writing

self-feed·er *n* a machine or device that automatically supplies or replaces materials as they are needed, e.g., a device for feeding animals

self-fer·tile *adj* describes a plant or organism that uses its own pollen or sperm to fertilize itself

self-fer·til·i·za·tion *n* fertilization of a plant or animal ovum using pollen or sperm from the same individual —**self-fer·til·ized** *adj* —**self-fer·til·iz·ing** *adj*

self-fi·nanced *adj* describes a business or venture that is paid for or run using its own money, rather than being supported by somebody else

self-fi·nanc·ing *adj* paid for or run without outside financial support

self-flag·el·la·tion *n* **1.** very strong or harsh self-criticism **2.** severe self-administered physical punishment, formerly used as an act of penance, often in the form of beatings or floggings

self-fo·cus·ing *adj* focusing automatically rather than manually ○ *a camera with a self-focusing lens*

self-ful·fill·ing *adj* **1.** brought about or proved true because of having been expected or predicted **2.** providing satisfaction or pleasure through personal labor, initiative, or talent

self-ful·fill·ment *n* contentment or happiness as a result of personal work, initiative, or talent

self-glo·ri·fi·ca·tion *n* promotion of your own qualities and abilities, especially beyond what is true or appropriate

self-gov·erned *adj* **1.** INDEPENDENT run by the people who live or work in an area or place rather than by external government **2.** NOT INFLUENCED BY OTHERS not needing or wanting the advice or influence of others **3.** USING SELF-CONTROL capable of exercising self-control

self-gov·ern·ing *adj* **1.** US able to control your own actions and behavior **2.** run by its own members, employees, or citizens, rather than being run from outside

self-gov·ern·ment *n* **1.** the ability or right of the citizens of a region to choose their own government rather than having it imposed from outside **2.** the ability to exercise self-control (*archaic*)

self-hard·en·ing *adj* becoming harder without special treatment after being heated above a specific temperature

self-harm *n* the practice of injuring yourself, especially by cutting, in order to relieve emotional distress —**self-harm** *vti* —**self-harm·ing** *n*

self·heal /sélf heėl/ *n* a low-growing creeping mint that grows as a weed in North America. Flowers: purple-blue, in small spikes. Native to: Europe, Asia. Latin name: *Prunella vulgaris.* [14C. Because it is believed to have medicinal properties]

self-help *n* **1.** GROUP HELP AND SUPPORT the practice of meeting or working with others who share a common problem rather than relying on professional or government help **2.** ACTION OUTSIDE LEGAL SYSTEM an action that is usually left to the legal authorities and may not be permitted by law, but that is undertaken by an individual person to protect a legal or moral right **3.** SOLVING PROBLEMS WITHOUT OTHERS' HELP the practice of dealing with your own problems and challenges without seeking outside help

self·hood /sélf hŏŏd/ *n* **1.** INDIVIDUALITY the possession of a unique identity, distinct from others **2.** SOMEBODY'S CHARACTER OR PERSONALITY all the qualities and characteristics that make up somebody's character or personality **3.** COMPLETE SENSE OF SELF the possession of a fully developed personality and sense of identity

self-i·den·ti·fied *adj* **1.** having somebody or something particular as the focus of a sense of self **2.** having voluntarily acknowledged your true identity without coercion ○ *a self-identified thief*

self-im·age *n* the opinion that you have of your own worth, attractiveness, or intelligence

self-im·mo·la·tion *n* suicide, usually by burning, as an act of sacrifice or protest

self-im·por·tance *n* an unrealistically high evaluation of your own importance or worth —**self-im·por·tant** *adj* —**self-im·por·tant·ly** *adv*

self-im·posed *adj* chosen willingly as a burden or limit ○ *a self-imposed deadline*

self-in·crim·i·na·tion *n* speech or action that suggests your own guilt, especially during court testimony —**self-in·crim·i·nat·ing** *adj* —**self-in·crim·i·na·to·ry** *adj*

self-in·duced *adj* **1.** brought on by your own actions **2.** produced by the process of self-induction

self-in·duc·tion *n* induction of an electromotive force in a circuit by means of a changing current in that circuit —**self-in·duc·tive** *adj*

self-in·dul·gence *n* **1.** lack of self-control in pursuing your own pleasure or satisfaction **2.** something that reveals lack of self-restraint —**self-in·dul·gent** *adj* —**self-in·dul·gent·ly** *adv*

self-in·flict·ed *adj* caused or done by your own actions ○ *a self-inflicted wound*

self-in·sur·ance *n* the saving of money to protect against a loss instead of buying an insurance policy

self-in·ter·est *n* **1.** the placing of your own needs or desires before those of others **2.** your own needs and desires —**self-in·ter·est·ed** *adj* —**self-in·ter·est·ed·ness** *n*

self·ish /sélfish/ *adj* **1.** concerned with your own interests, needs, and wishes while ignoring those of others **2.** showing that personal needs and wishes are thought to be more important than those of other people —**self·ish·ly** *adv* —**self·ish·ness** *n*

self·ish DNA *n* a segment of DNA that increases itself, e.g., as repeated sequences, within the total genetic material of a population over successive generations without apparent benefit to the organisms concerned

self·ish gene *n* a gene that exploits the organism in which it occurs as a vehicle for its self-perpetuation. Posited by the biologist Richard Dawkins in 1976, it overturns the traditional concept of the gene serving as a vehicle of inheritance for the organism.

self-jus·ti·fi·ca·tion *n* **1.** an attempt to explain your own behavior or actions by making excuses **2.** something that somebody does or says in an attempt to explain personal behavior or actions

self-jus·ti·fy·ing *adj* **1.** ATTEMPTING TO EXPLAIN making excuses in an attempt to explain your own behavior or actions **2.** AUTOMATICALLY MAKING TEXT UNIFORM ON MARGIN automatically providing an even right or left margin for text printed on a page **3.** LOGICALLY COMPLETE describes an argument or rule that justifies or explains itself without referring to something else because of being regarded as completely logical or obvious

self-knowl·edge *n* awareness or understanding of your own motives and behavior

self·less /sélfləss/ *adj* putting other people's needs, interests, or wishes before your own —**self·less·ly** *adv* —**self·less·ness** *n*

self-lim·it·ed, **self-lim·it·ing** *adj* **1.** limited by internal or personal characteristics rather than by outside influences **2.** used to describe a disease that lasts for a specific length of time time whether or not it is treated

self-lim·it·ing *adj* **1.** imposing personal limitations or restrictions **2.** same as **self-limited** —**self-lim·i·ta·tion** *n*

self-liq·ui·dat·ing *adj* **1.** describes a loan to fund a transaction that is expected to make money before the loan is due to be repaid **2.** describes a business transaction that makes enough money to cover its costs

self-load·ing *adj* describes a firearm that automatically ejects a spent cartridge and puts a new round into the chamber each time it is fired —**self-load·er** *n*

self-lock·ing *adj* describes a window or door that locks automatically when closed

self-lu·bri·cat·ing *adj* not requiring external application of lubrication to parts that experience friction because the lubricant is self-contained

self-made *adj* **1.** successful or wealthy through your own efforts, rather than through birth or from the work of others **2.** made without the help of others

self-mor·ti·fi·ca·tion *n* self-administered punishment, often as prescribed by religious precepts, because of some perceived fault or flaw

self-mo·ti·vat·ed *adj* energetic and ambitious, and so able to make plans and get things done without being directed by others —**self-mo·ti·va·tion** *n*

self-mu·ti·la·tion *n* self-inflicted injury, especially with a sharp object

self-o·pin·ion *n* a very high opinion of your own abilities or worth

self-o·pin·ion·at·ed *adj* **1.** confident of holding the correct opinions **2.** very conceited

self-per·pet·u·at·ing *adj* continuing because of having the power to preserve or renew itself indefinitely —**self-per·pe·tu·a·tion** *n*

self-pit·y *n* the self-indulgent belief that your life is harder and sadder than everyone else's —**self-pit·y·ing** *adj* —**self-pit·y·ing·ly** *adv*

self-pol·li·na·tion *n* pollination that takes place within a flower through the transfer of pollen from its anthers to its stigmas —**self-pol·li·nate** *vi* —**self-pol·li·nat·ing** *adj*

self-por·trait *n* a visual image, sculpture, or written description of somebody, produced by that person —**self-por·trai·ture** *n*

self-pos·sessed *adj* confident and in control of your own emotions

self-pos·ses·sion *n* the ability to remain calm and confident, especially in difficult or emotional circumstances

self-pres·er·va·tion *n* the instinctive need to do what is necessary to survive danger

self-pro·claimed *adj* claiming to be something, often without justification

self-pro·tec·tion *n* action taken to protect against attack on or injury to yourself —**self-pro·tect·ing** *adj* —**self-pro·tec·tive** *adj*

self-rais·ing *adj UK* same as **self-rising**

self-re·al·i·za·tion *n* fulfillment of personal potential

self-ref·er·en·tial *adj* describes an art form that employs references to the art itself or to personal experience or character —**self-ref·er·ence** *n* —**self-ref·er·en·tial·ly** *adv*

self-re·gard *n* **1.** self-interest rather than concern for the well-being of others **2.** belief in your own worth and dignity —**self-re·gard·ing** *adj*

self-reg·u·lat·ing, **self-reg·u·la·to·ry** *adj* **1.** regulating its own affairs rather than being regulated by an outside organization or by law **2.** capable of regulating its functions automatically —**self-reg·u·la·tion** *n*

self-reg·u·la·tion *n* the system by which an organization or institution deals with its own disciplinary and legal problems, often in private, rather than being publicly regulated by somebody else

self-re·proach *n* self-criticism or blame —**self-re·proach·ful** *adj* —**self-re·proach·ful·ly** *adv*

self-re·spect *n* belief in your own worth and dignity —**self-re·spect·ing** *adj*

self-re·straint *n* the ability to restrain the urge to do or say something

self-right·eous *adj* sure of the moral superiority of personal beliefs and actions, usually to an irritating degree —**self-right·eous·ly** *adv* —**self-right·eous·ness** *n*

self-right·ing *adj* able to right itself after being capsized

self-ris·ing *adj* having a leavening agent added so that baking powder is not needed when making cakes ○ *self-rising flour*

self-rule *n* POL same as **self-government** (sense 1)

self-sac·ri·fice *n* the giving up of personal wants and needs, either from a sense of duty or in order to benefit others —**self-sac·ri·fic·ing** *adj* —**self-sac·ri·fic·ing·ly** *adv*

self·same /sélf sàym/ *adj* being the very same

self-scan·ner *n* a hand-held electronic device that supermarket customers can use to scan the prices of goods they intend to buy and add up their total bill in order to save time at the checkout

self-seal·ing *adj* **1.** describes an envelope that has a flap coated with adhesive that can be closed without being moistened **2.** describes a tire that can seal itself after being punctured. The tire contains a compound that hardens in contact with air.

self-seed·ed *adj* BOT same as **self-sown**

self-seek·ing *adj* interested only in gaining an advantage over others, not in sharing or cooperating ■ *n* behavior intended to secure an advantage over others —**self-seek·er** *n*

self-se·lec·tion *n* **1.** COMM same as **self-service** **2.** the choosing of yourself for something, or the choosing of something for yourself —**self-se·lect·ed** *adj* —**self-se·lec·tive** *adj*

self-ser·vice *adj* describes a retail outlet or device used by customers or users helping themselves ○ *a self-service gas station* ○ *a self-service drink dispenser* —**self-ser·vice** *n*

self-serv·ing *adj* putting personal concerns and interests before those of others

self-sown *adj* describes plants that grow from seeds that have fallen to the soil naturally, without being deliberately planted

self-start·er *n* **1.** somebody with the initiative and motivation to work without needing help or supervision **2.** an electrically operated device for starting an internal-combustion engine —**self-start·ing** *adj*

self-ster·ile *adj* describes organisms that are unable to fertilize their female sex cells using their own male sex cells, as flowering plants are

self-stick, **self-stick·ing** *adj US* coated with adhesive so as to adhere to something without being moistened. Can term **self-adhesive**

self-stor·age *n* a property divided into storage units of varying sizes that are rented to people who store their personal property there

self-styled *adj* using a particular name or title or professing knowledge of a subject without having training or independent proof

USAGE See *so-called.*

self-suf·fi·cient, **self-suf·fic·ing** *adj* **1.** able to provide what is needed, e.g., by making enough money or growing enough food, without having to borrow or buy from others **2.** able to live independently of others —**self-suf·fi·cien·cy** *n* —**self-suf·fi·cient·ly** *adv*

self-sug·ges·tion *n* PSYCHOL same as **autosuggestion**

self-talk *n* the things that an individual says to himself or herself mentally

self-tan·ner *n* an ointment or lotion that can be applied to the skin in order to produce the effect of a suntan

self-taught *adj* having learned a skill, job, or subject without formal instruction

self-ten·der *n* an offer made by a company to buy back shares from its shareholders, e.g., to avoid a hostile takeover bid

self-test *n* **1.** SELF-ADMINISTERED TEST a diagnostic test that you give yourself to determine your health, e.g., for blood pressure **2.** TEST OF KNOWLEDGE a test you give yourself to find out how well you know a subject ■ *v* (**self-test·ed, self-test·ing, self-tests**) **1.** *vti* TEST YOUR HEALTH to perform a diagnostic test of something on yourself in order to determine your health **2.** *vi* TEST YOURSELF ON KNOWLEDGE to test yourself on a subject to find out how well you know it

self-will *n* stubborn determination to hold to personal views and behavior —**self-willed** *adj*

self-wind·ing *adj* not needing to be wound ○ *a self-winding watch*

self-worth *n* confidence in personal value and worth as an individual person

Sel·juk /sél jo͝ok, sel jo͝ok/ *n* a member of one of the Turkish dynasties that ruled large areas of central and western Asia between the 11th and 13th centuries before the Ottoman Empire [Mid-19C. < Turkish *Selčük*, the dynasty's reputed founder] —**Sel·juk** *adj*

Sel·kirk Moun·tains /sél kurk-/ mountain range in southeastern British Columbia, Canada, west of the Rocky Mountains. The highest point is Mount Sandford, 11,555 ft./3,522 m.

sell /sel/ *v* (**sold** /sōld/, **sell·ing, sells**) **1.** *vti* EXCHANGE FOR MONEY to exchange a product or service for money, or be exchanged for money **2.** *vt* OFFER SOMETHING FOR SALE to offer a particular product or range of products for sale **3.** *vi* BE BOUGHT IN QUANTITY to be bought in large numbers ○ *The book is selling well.* **4.** *vt* MAKE PEOPLE WANT TO BUY SOMETHING to increase the sale of or the demand for a product ○ *Advertising sells products.* **5.** *vt* PERSUADE SOMEBODY OF SOMETHING to make an idea or proposal acceptable to somebody ○ *You've convinced me but now you have to sell it to the stockholders.* **6.** *vt* GIVE SOMETHING UP FOR MONEY to sacrifice an important personal quality in order to obtain wealth or success ○ *He's sold his integrity for a long-term contract.* **7. sell your·self** *vr* to work hard to persuade others that you are talented, pleasant, well-qualified, or suitable for a particular job ■ *n* PROCESS OF SELLING the activity or process of persuading people to buy a product or service (*informal*) ○ *use an aggressive sell* [Old English *sellan* "hand over" < Germanic] —**sell·a·ble** *adj* ◇ **sell somebody** *or* **something short 1.** to make an estimate of the quality and worth of somebody or something that is too low ○ *You've a lot in your favor – don't sell yourself short.* **2.** to sell goods or securities without owning them, expecting to buy them at a price lower than the selling price ◇ **sold on something** enthusiastic about something (*informal*)

sell off *vt* to sell something, especially at a low price, in order to get rid of it

sell on *vt* to convince somebody that a plan or product is the best (*usually passive*)

sell out *v* **1.** *vi* to sell the entire stock of a product or range **2.** *vti* to be disloyal to personal principles or to another person for reasons of short-term advantage (*informal*)

sell·back /séll bàk/ *n US* the act of selling something back to the person it was bought from

sell-by date *n* a date displayed on food and pharmaceutical products, after which they should not be sold

sell·er /séllər/ *n* **1.** a person, store, or company that offers something for sale **2.** a product that sells in a particular way, especially well or badly

Sel·lers /séllərz/, **Peter** (1925–80) British actor. A member of the Goons radio comedy team (1952–60), he was later a screen actor. He played the eccentric detective Inspector Clouseau in the hugely successful Pink Panther movies (1964–82).

"There used to be a me behind the mask, but I had it surgically removed."
[Attributed to Peter Sellers]

sell·er's mar·ket *n* a situation or market in which the demand for something is greater than the supply, so that its price can be forced up

sell·ing cli·max /sélling-/ *n* a large volume of trading at the end of a downturn in the stock markets (*informal*)

sell·ing plate *n UK* HORSERACING same as **selling race**

sell·ing point *n* a feature of something such as a product or an idea that makes people more likely to want to buy or support it

sell·ing race *n* a horse race in which the winner is auctioned and sold

sell·out /sél òwt/ *n* **1.** EVENT WITHOUT AVAILABLE TICKETS a show, concert, or athletic event for which all the tickets are sold **2.** BETRAYAL betrayal of personal principles or of another person (*informal*) **3.** TRAITOR TO PRINCIPLE a betrayer of a principle or cause for money or something else (*informal*)

Sel·ma /sélmə/ city in central Alabama, northwest of Montgomery, on the northern bank of the Alabama River. Population: 19,991 (2002 estimate).

sel·syn /sél sìn/ *n* a system used to transmit angular rotation or position in a generator to a motor [Early 20C. Blend of SELF + SYNCHRONOUS]

selt·zer /séltsər/ *n* **1.** mineral water that contains naturally occurring dissolved gases that make it slightly fizzy, often used for medicinal purposes **2.** BEVERAGES same as **soda water** (sense 1) (*dated*) [Mid-18C. Alteration of German *Selterser* "from Selters" < *Nieder-Selters*, village near Wiesbaden with mineral springs]

sel·va /sélvə/ *n* a dense tropical rain forest, especially in the Amazon basin [Mid-19C. Via Spanish or Portuguese < Latin *silva* "wood"]

sel·vage /sélvij/, **sel·vedge** *n* **1.** NONFRAYING EDGE OF FABRIC an edge of a piece of fabric that is woven so that it will not fray **2.** STRIP OF MATERIAL an edge or strip of material included when manufacturing something such as a metal or plastic object or a sheet of postage stamps that allows it to be handled **3.** LOCK PLATE a slotted plate or surface through which the bolt of a lock passes **4.** RUG FRINGE a decorative fringe on the ends of an Oriental rug [15C. Contraction of SELF + EDGE; because it "edges" itself and does not need hemming] —**sel·vaged** *adj*

selves plural of **self**

Popperfoto
David O. Selznick

Selz·nick /sélznik/, **David O.** (1902–65) US movie producer. His many classic productions included *Gone With the Wind* (1939). Full name **Selznick, David Oliver**

SEM *abbr* PHYS scanning electron microscope

se·man·teme /sə mán tèem/ *n* the smallest possible unit of meaning in language, expressing a single image or idea, e.g., cat, sit, or non- [Early 20C. < French *sémantème* < Greek *semantikos* (see SEMANTIC), after *morphème* "morpheme"]

se·man·tic /sə mántik/ *adj* **1.** LING RELATING TO WORD MEANINGS relating to meaning or the differences between meanings of words or symbols **2.** LING OF SEMANTICS relating to semantics **3.** LOGIC RELATING TO TRUTH relating to the conditions in which a system or theory can be said to be true [Mid-17C. Via French < Greek *sēmantikos* "significant" < *sēmainein* "signify" < *sēma* "sign, mark"] —**se·man·ti·cal·ly** *adv*

se·man·tics /sə mántiks/ *n* (*takes a singular verb*) **1.** STUDY OF MEANING IN LANGUAGE the study of how meaning in language is created by the use and interrelationships of words, phrases, and sentences **2.** STUDY OF SYMBOLS the study of the relationship between symbols and what they represent **3.** STUDY OF LOGIC the study of ways of interpreting and analyzing theories of logic —**se·man·ti·cist** /sə mántissist/ *n*

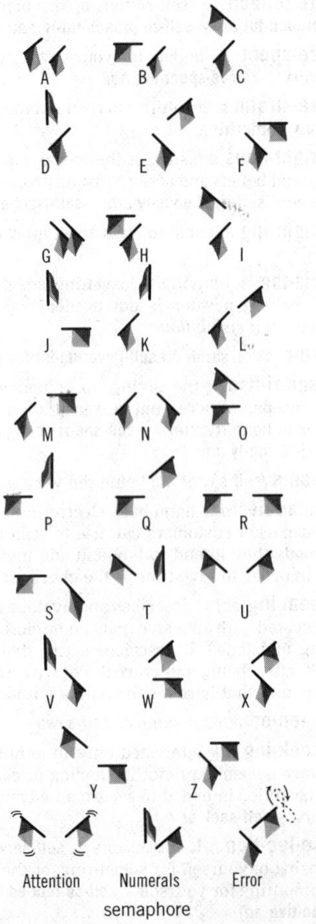

semaphore

sem·a·phore /sémmə fàwr/ *n* **1.** SYSTEM OF SIGNALING a system for sending messages using hand-held flags that are moved to represent alphabetical letters **2.** MECHANICAL SIGNALING DEVICE a signaling device for sending information over distances using mechanically operated arms or flags mounted on a post, especially on a railroad ■ *vti* (**-phored, -phor·ing, -phores**) USE SEMAPHORE TO SIGNAL to send messages using semaphore [Early 19C. Via French *sémaphore* "sign-bearer" < Greek *sēma* "sign, mark"] —**sem·a·phor·ic** /sèmmə fáwrik/ *adj* —**sem·a·phor·i·cal·ly** *adv*

Se·ma·rang /sémmə ráng/ city and port on the island of Java, Indonesia, located east of Jakarta. Population: 812,979 (1997).

se·ma·si·ol·o·gy /sə màyssee óllәjee, -màyzee-/ *n* LING, LOGIC same as **semantics** (senses 1–2) [Mid-19C. < German *Semasiologie* "science of meaning" < Greek *sēmasia* "meaning" < *sēmainein* (see SEMANTIC)] —**se·ma·si·o·log·i·cal** /sə màyssee ə lójjik'l, -màyzee-/ *adj* —**se·ma·si·o·log·i·cal·ly** *adv* —**se·ma·si·ol·o·gist** *n*

se·mat·ic /sə máttik/ *adj* describes bright colorings on animals that act as a warning to predators, e.g., because the animals are poisonous [Late 19C. < Greek *sēmat-*, stem of *sēma* "sign, mark"]

sem·bla·ble /sémbləb'l/ *adj* resembling or similar to something or somebody else (*formal*) ■ *n* somebody or something that closely resembles another (*archaic*) [13C. < Old French < *sembler* (see SEMBLANCE)] —**sem·bla·bly** *adv*

sem·blance /sémbləns/ *n* **1.** TRACE OF SOMETHING a small amount of something ○ *a semblance of dignity* **2.** LOOK OF BEING SOMETHING an outward appearance or imitation of something ○ *a semblance of competence* **3.** COPY a representation, likeness, or copy (*literary*) [14C. < Old French < *sembler* "seem" < Latin *simulare* (see SIMULATE)]

se·mé /sə máy, sé mày/ *adj* covered with many small dots or delicate designs [15C. < French, past participle of *semer* "sow" < Latin *semere*]

se·meme /sée meem/ *n* the meaning that a morpheme has in a linguistic system [Early 20C. < Greek *sēma* "sign, mark," after MORPHEME]

se·men /séemən/ *n* the thick white fluid containing sperm that a male ejaculates [14C. < Latin, "seed"]

se·mes·ter /sə méstər/ *n* especially in the United States, either of two periods of 15 to 18 weeks into which the academic year is divided in some universities and colleges [Early 19C. Via German < Latin *semestris* "of six months" < *sex* "six" + *mensis* "month"] —**se·mes·tral** *adj*

sem·i /sémmee, sémmī/ *n* **1.** VEHICLES same as **tractor-trailer 2.** VEHICLES same as **semitrailer** (sense 1) **3.** SPORTS same as **semifinal** (*informal*) [Early 20C. Shortening]

semi- *prefix* **1.** partial, partially, somewhat ○ *semisweet* ○ *semiterrestrial* **2.** half ○ *semicircle* **3.** resembling, having some characteristics of something ○ *semitropical* ○ *semivowel* **4.** occurring twice during a particular period ○ *semiweekly* [< Latin, "half" < Indo-European]

sem·i·a·cous·tic *adj*
sem·i·al·le·gor·i·cal *adj*
sem·i·al·pha·bet·i·cal *adj*
sem·i·an·i·mate *adj*
sem·i·an·tique *adj*
sem·i·ar·bo·re·al *adj*
sem·i·at·tached *adj*
sem·i·a·ware *adj*
sem·i·a·ware·ness *n*
sem·i·base·ment *n*
sem·i·civ·i·lized *adj*
sem·i·co·lo·nial *adj*
sem·i·col·o·ny *n*
sem·i·com·mer·cial *adj*
sem·i·con·tin·u·ous *adj*
sem·i·crys·tal·line *adj*
sem·i·cu·bist *adj*
sem·i·cyl·in·der *n*
sem·i·cy·lin·dri·cal *adj*
sem·i·de·i·ty *n*
sem·i·de·po·nent *adj, n*
sem·i·der·e·lict *adj*
sem·i·dic·ta·to·ri·al *adj*
sem·i·dom·i·nant *adj*
sem·i·dou·ble *adj*
sem·i·dry·ing *adj*
sem·i·du·ra·ble *adj*
sem·i·e·lec·tron·ic *adj*
sem·i·em·pir·i·cal *adj*
sem·i·e·rect *adj*
sem·i·ev·er·green *adj*
sem·i·fab·ri·cat·ed *adj*
sem·i·feu·dal *adj*
sem·i·fic·tion·al *adj*
sem·i·fit·ted *adj*
sem·i·flex·i·ble *adj*
sem·i·formed *adj*
sem·i·free *adj*
sem·i·gov·ern·men·tal *adj*
sem·i·hard·y *adj*
sem·i·his·tor·i·cal *adj*
sem·i·hu·mid *adj*
sem·i·in·va·lid *n*
sem·i·leg·en·dar·y *adj*
sem·i·liq·uid *adj, n*
sem·i·liq·uid·i·ty *n*
sem·i·lus·trous *adj*
sem·i·ma·jor *adj*
sem·i·mat *adj*
sem·i·mi·nor *adj*

sem·i·mo·dal *n*
sem·i·moist *adj*
sem·i·mol·ten *adj*
sem·i·mo·nas·tic *adj*
sem·i·mon·o·coque *adj*
sem·i·mys·ti·cal *adj*
sem·i·myth·i·cal *adj*
sem·i·nat·u·ral *adj*
sem·i·o·pac·i·ty *n*
sem·i·o·paque *adj*
sem·i·o·pen *adj*
sem·i·op·e·ra *n*
sem·i·phil·o·soph·i·cal *adj*
sem·i·po·lit·i·cal *adj*
sem·i·pop·u·lar *adj*
sem·i·por·no·graph·ic *adj*
sem·i·prone *adj*
sem·i·pub·lic *adj*
sem·i·pu·ri·fied *adj*
sem·i·quan·ti·ta·tive *adj*
sem·i·re·fined *adj*
sem·i·re·lig·ious *adj*
sem·i·round *adj, n*
sem·i·sa·cred *adj*
sem·i·sed·en·tar·y *adj*
sem·i·shrub·by *adj*
sem·i·spher·i·cal *adj*
sem·i·staged *adj*
sem·i·stag·ger *vti*
sem·i·ster·ile *adj*
sem·i·sub·ter·ra·ne·an *adj*
sem·i·syn·thet·ic *adj*
sem·i·trained *adj*
sem·i·trans·lu·cent *adj*
sem·i·trans·par·ent *adj*
sem·i·un·con·scious *adj*
sem·i·un·con·scious·ness *n*
sem·i·wild *adj*

sem·i·ab·stract /sèmmee áb stràkt, sèmmī-/ *adj* describes art that has heavily stylized but still recognizable subject matter —**sem·i·ab·strac·tion** *n*

sem·i·an·nu·al /sèmmee ánnyoo əl, sèmmī-/ *adj* **1.** happening or issued every six months or twice a year **2.** lasting for half a year —**sem·i·an·nu·al·ly** *adv*

sem·i·a·quat·ic /sèmmee ə kwóttik, sèmmī-/ *adj* growing or living near water as well as in it

sem·i·ar·id /sèmmee árrid, sèmmī-/ *adj* with little rainfall and scrubby vegetation —**sem·i·a·rid·i·ty** /sèmmee ə ríddətee, sèmmī-/ *n*

sem·i·au·to·bi·o·graph·i·cal /sèmmee àwtō bī ə gráffik'l, sèmmī-/ *adj* describes something such as a novel or movie that is based in part on the life or experiences of its author

sem·i·au·to·mat·ic /sèmmee àwtə máttik, sèmmī-/ *adj* **1.** RELOADING AUTOMATICALLY automatically ejecting a spent shell from a weapon's chamber and replacing it with another round each time the weapon is fired **2.** PARTIALLY AUTOMATED operated partly automatically and partly manually ■ *n* SEMIAUTOMATIC WEAPON a weapon that is semiautomatic —**sem·i·au·to·mat·i·cal·ly** *adv*

sem·i·au·ton·o·mous /sèmmee aw tónnəməss, sèmmī-/ *adj* **1.** ruled partly by its own citizens or rulers and partly by another country or region **2.** self-governing but remaining within a larger organization of which it is part —**sem·i·au·ton·o·mous·ly** *adv* —**sem·i·au·ton·o·my** *n*

sem·i·bold /sèmmee bṓld, sèmmī-/ *adj* darker than ordinary type but not as dark as bold type

sem·i·breve /sémmee brēev, sémmī-/ *n UK* same as **whole note**

sem·i·breve rest *n UK* same as **whole rest**

sem·i·cen·ten·ni·al /sèmmee sen ténnee əl, sèmmī-/ *adj* marking the date or year that is 50 years after an event ■ *n* the 50th anniversary of an important event

sem·i·cir·cle /sémmi sùrk'l/ *n* **1.** half of the area or circumference of a circle **2.** a curved or crescent-shaped line of things or people in the shape of a semicircle [Early 16C. < Latin *semicirculus* < *circulus* "small circle"] —**sem·i·cir·cu·lar** /sèmmi súrkyələr/ *adj*—**sem·i·cir·cu·lar·ly** *adv*

sem·i·cir·cu·lar ca·nal *n* each of three tubes in the inner ear, semicircular in shape and set at right angles to one another, that help to maintain balance

sem·i·clas·si·cal /sèmmee klássik'l, sèmmī-/ *adj* classical in musical style, pleasant, easy to listen to, and usually written relatively recently —**sem·i·clas·si·cal·ly** *adv*

sem·i·co·lon /sémmi kṓlən/ *n* a punctuation mark (;) used to separate parts of a sentence or list and indicate a pause longer than a comma but shorter than a period

USAGE A *semicolon* is used to separate two parts of a sentence that have a relationship to each other in terms of meaning when each part could stand alone as a sentence in its own right: *The building is chiefly a tourist attraction; it is rarely used as a church these days. There is no proof that the disease is caused by agricultural use of this chemical; however, experts admit that there could be a link.* Semicolons may also separate parts of a complex list when it would be confusing to use commas for this purpose: *We invited Jack and Kate, who live next door; Maria, my sister-in-law; Tom, an old school friend of my husband's; and some of our colleagues from work.* Like commas, semicolons are sometimes used to break up a lengthy complicated sentence, but it is often better and clearer to split the sentence up into smaller units.

sem·i·co·ma /sèmmee kṓmə, sèmmī-/ *n* a partial or light comatose state from which it is sometimes possible to rouse people by stimulating them

sem·i·co·ma·tose /sèmmee kṓmə tṑss, sèmmī-/ *adj* **1.** bordering on being unconscious but capable of being awakened **2.** almost unconscious or half asleep

sem·i·con·duc·tor /sèmmee kən dúktər, sèmmī-/ *n* a solid material that has electrical conductivity between that of a conductor and an insulator —**sem·i·con·duct·ing** *adj* —**sem·i·con·duc·tion** *n* —**sem·i·con·duc·tive** *adj* —**sem·i·con·duc·tiv·i·ty** /sèmmee kòndək tívvətee, sèmmī-/ *n*

sem·i·con·scious /sèmmee kónshəss, sèmmī-/ *adj* only partly conscious —**sem·i·con·scious·ly** *adv* —**sem·i·con·scious·ness** *n*

sem·i·con·ser·va·tive /sèmmee kən súrvətiv, sèmmī-/ *adj* relating to the replication of a nucleic acid molecule such as DNA in which a double stranded molecule separates into two templates for the formation of complementary strands —**sem·i·con·ser·va·tive·ly** *adv*

sem·i·dark·ness /sèmmee daárknəss, sèmmī-/ *n* a state in which it is neither fully dark nor fully light

sem·i·des·ert /sèmmee dézzərt, sèmmī-/ *n* a region that is not completely dry, usually one lying between desert and a more heavily vegetated area

sem·i·de·tached /sèmmee di tácht, sèmmī-/ *adj* joined to a neighboring building by a shared wall ■ *n* a house with a wall in common with the next house

sem·i·di·am·e·ter /sèmmee dī ámmətər, sèmmī-/ *n* half of the angular diameter of the visible disk of an astronomical object as measured by an observer

sem·i·di·ur·nal /sèmmee dī úrn'l, sèmmī-/ *adj* **1.** continuing or happening over half a day **2.** happening approximately once every twelve hours

sem·i·di·vine /sèmmee də vīn, sémmī-/ *adj* having some of the characteristics or powers of a deity, or existing on a higher spiritual plane than ordinary mortals but not wholly divine

sem·i·doc·u·men·ta·ry /sèmmee dòkyə méntəree, sèmmī-/ (*plural* **-ries**) *n* a movie or TV program that is fictional but makes use of or is based on factual details or events

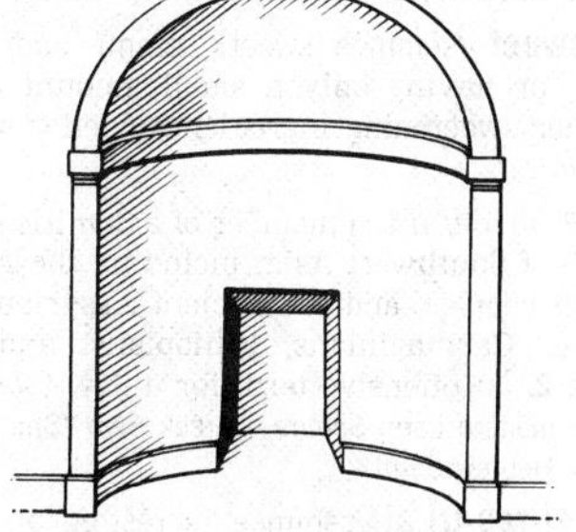

semidome

sem·i·dome /sémmee dṓm, sémmī-/ *n* a half dome, especially one used as the roof for a semicircular space or recess

sem·i·do·mes·ti·cat·ed /sèmmee də mésti kàytəd, sèmmī-/ *adj* describes animals that are wild but live near or with humans to mutual benefit —**sem·i·do·mes·ti·ca·tion** /-də mèsti káysh'n/ *n*

sem·i·dry /sèmmee drī, sèmmī-/ *adj US* describes wine that is partially or moderately dry

sem·i·dwarf /sèmmee dwáwrf, sèmmī-/ *adj* describes plants that grow to heights greater than true dwarf plants but less than regular specimens

sem·i·el·lip·ti·cal /sèmmee i líptik'l, sèmmī-/ *adj* resembling half an ellipse in shape, especially one that is divided along its major axis

sem·i·fi·nal /sèmmee fīn'l, sèmmī-/ *n* either of two matches or games, the winners of which will play each other in the final round of a competition —**sem·i·fi·nal** *adj* —**sem·i·fi·nal·ist** *n*

sem·i·fin·ished /sèmmee fínnisht, sèmmī-/ *adj* partially finished, treated, or processed

sem·i·flu·id /sèmmee flōō id, sèmmī-/ *adj* having properties between those of a fluid and a solid —**sem·i·flu·id** *n* —**sem·i·flu·id·i·ty** /sèmmee floo íddətee, sèmmī-/ *n*

sem·i·for·mal /sèmmee fáwrm'l, sèmmī-/ *adj* designed to be worn on moderately formal occasions ■ *n* a dance to which people, often students, wear semiformal attire

sem·i·gloss /sèmmee gláwss, sèmmī-/ *n* a paint or varnish with a finish that is midway between gloss and matte when it dries

sem·i·group /sémmee grōōp, sémmī-/ *n* a mathematical set for which there is a closed and associative binary operation

sem·i·hard /sèmmee haárd, sèmmī-/ *adj* describes cheese that has a consistency firm enough to slice but that is moist and pliable

sem·i·in·fi·nite *adj* unbounded in one dimension or direction

sem·i·le·thal /sèmmee lēeth'l, sèmmī-/ *adj* lethal in more than 50 percent but fewer than 100 percent of cases

sem·i·lit·er·ate /sèmmee líttərət, sèmmī-/ *adj* **1.** unable to read or write properly **2.** having only limited understanding of a particular subject, especially a technical one —**sem·i·lit·er·a·cy** *n* —**sem·i·lit·er·ate** *n*

Sé·mil·lon /sáy meel yòN/, **Se·mil·lon** *n* **1.** a white wine made from a variety of white grape originally grown in southwestern France **2.** a white grape variety. Use: to make Sémillon. [Mid-19C. < French < Latin *semen* "seed"]

sem·i·log·a·rith·mic /sèmmee lòggə ríthmik, sèmmī-/ *adj* having one logarithmic scale and one arithmetic scale

sem·i·lu·nar /sèmmee lōōnər, sèmmī-/ *adj* shaped like a crescent or a half moon

sem·i·lu·nar car·ti·lage *n* either of two crescent-shaped pieces of cartilage in the knee joint

sem·i·lu·nar valve *n* either of two crescent-shaped valves in the heart that prevent blood from flowing back into the ventricles. The two valves are called the aortic valve and the pulmonary valve.

sem·i·met·al /sémmee mètt'l, sémmī-/ *n* CHEM same as **metalloid** —**sem·i·me·tal·lic** /sémmee mə tállik, sémmī-/ *adj*

sem·i·month·ly /sèmmee múnthlee, sèmmī-/ *adj* HAPPENING TWICE IN MONTH happening or published twice each month, usually at equal intervals ■ *adv* TWICE DURING MONTH twice each month, usually at equal intervals ■ *n* (*plural* **-lies**) SEMIMONTHLY PUBLICATION a publication that appears twice each month, usually at equal intervals

sem·i·nal /sémmin'l/ *adj* **1.** INFLUENTIAL highly original and influential **2.** CAPABLE OF DEVELOPMENT containing an idea or set of ideas that forms a basis for later developments **3.** OF SEMEN OR SEEDS relating to, containing, or carrying semen or seeds [14C. Via French < Latin *seminalis* < *semin-*, stem of *semen* "seed"] —**sem·i·nal·i·ty** /sèmmee nállətee/ *n* —**sem·i·nal·ly** *adv*

sem·i·nal flu·id *n* ANAT same as **semen**

sem·i·nal ves·i·cle *n* either of a pair of glands that secrete the fluid component of semen into the ejaculatory duct in males

sem·i·nar /sémmə naar/ *n* **1.** MEETING ON SPECIALIZED SUBJECT a single session or short, often one-day meeting devoted to presentations on and discussion of a specialized topic, usually at an advanced or professional level ○ *a seminar on the industrial applications of biotechnology* **2.** SPECIALIZED EDUCATIONAL CLASS a course of specialized graduate or undergraduate study under faculty supervision, in which ideas, approaches, and advances are regularly shared among participants **3.** MEETING OF STUDENTS AND

ACADEMIC SUPERVISOR a meeting of university or college students for study or discussion with an academic supervisor, or the group that participates in it [Late 19C. Via German, "advanced class" < Latin *seminarium* "seed plot, breeding ground" < *semin-* (see SEMINAL)]

sem·i·nar·y /sémmə nèrree/ (*plural* **-ies**) *n* a school for the training of priests, ministers, or rabbis [15C. < Latin *seminarium* "seed plot, breeding ground" < *semin-* (see SEMINAL)] —**sem·i·nar·i·an** /sèmmə nérree ən/ *n*

sem·i·nif·er·ous /sèmmee níffərəss/ *adj* **1.** carrying, containing, or producing semen **2.** bearing or producing seeds [Late 17C. < Latin *semin-* (see SEMINAL)]

Sem·i·nole /sémmə nōl/ *n* (*plural same* or **-noles**) **1.** NATIVE NORTH AMERICAN PEOPLE a member of a Native North American people who lived in Georgia and Florida, and now live mainly in Oklahoma and Florida. The Seminole were one of the Five Civilized Nations who, under the Removal Act of 1830, were forced to settle in Indian Territory. **2.** SEMINOLE LANGUAGE the Muskogean language of the Seminole people ■ *adj* HANDICRAFT **PATCHWORK STYLE** describes a type of patchwork, originally developed by the Seminole, in which long strips of fabric are joined together, then cut up and reformed to create new patterns [Mid-18C. < Creek *simanó:li*, alteration of *simaló:ni*, alteration of American Spanish *cimarrón* "wild, untamed"] —**Sem·i·nole** *adj*

sem·i·no·ma /sèmmə nṓmə/ (*plural* **-mas** or **-ma·ta** /-mətə/) *n* a malignant tumor of the sperm-producing tissue in the testicle [Early 20C. < modern Latin *seminoma* < Latin *semin-* (see SEMINAL)]

sem·i·no·mad·ic /sèmmee nō máddik, sèmmī-/ *adj* belonging or relating to an ethnic group or people who migrate seasonally and cultivate crops during periods of settlement

sem·i·nude /sèmmee no͞od, sèmmī-/ *adj* only partly clothed, usually in underclothes or skimpy outer clothing ■ *n* the state of being only partly clothed, usually in underclothes or skimpy outer clothing —**sem·i·nu·di·ty** /-no͞odətee/ *n*

se·mi·o·chem·i·cal /seemee ō kémmik'l, sèmmee-/ *n* an organic chemical that plays a role in animal communication, e.g., pheromone [Late 20C. < Greek *sēmeion* "sign" (see SEMIOLOGY)]

sem·i·of·fi·cial /sèmmee ə físh'l, sèmmī-/ *adj* with only some degree of authority or official status and therefore not completely reliable —**sem·i·of·fi·cial·ly** *adv*

se·mi·ol·o·gy /seemee óllәjee, sèmmee-/ *n* LING, MED same as **semiotics** [Late 17C. < Greek *sēmeion* "sign"] —**se·mi·o·log·ic** /seemee ə lójjik, sèmmee-/ *adj* —**se·mi·o·log·i·cal** *adj* —**se·mi·o·log·i·cal·ly** *adv* —**se·mi·ol·o·gist** *n*

se·mi·ot·ics /seemee óttiks, sèmmee-/ *n* (*takes a singular verb*) **1.** the study of signs and symbols of all kinds, what they mean, and how they relate to the things or ideas they refer to **2.** the study of identifying the ways that various symptoms indicate the diseases that underlie them —**se·mi·ot·ic** *adj* —**se·mi·o·ti·cian** /seemee ə tísh'n, sèmmee-/ *n*

sem·i·pal·mate /sèmmee pál màyt, -paa-, sèmmī-/, **sem·i·pal·mat·ed** /sèmmee pál màytəd, -paa-, sèmmī-/ *adj* with feet or toes that are partially webbed. Some shore birds have semipalmate feet.

sem·i·per·ma·nent /sèmmee púrmənənt, sèmmī-/ *adj* set up or arranged to last quite a long time but not indefinitely ○ *Dozens of refugees have taken up semipermanent residence in the grounds of the embassy.* —**sem·i·per·ma·nent·ly** *adv*

sem·i·per·me·a·ble /sèmmee púrmee əb'l, sèmmī-/ *adj* describes a membrane or tissue that allows some types of particles to pass through, but not others —**sem·i·per·me·a·bil·i·ty** /sèmmee pùrmee ə bíllətee, sèmmī-/ *n*

sem·i·po·lar bond /sèmmee pṓlər-, sèmmī-/ *n* CHEM same as **coordinate bond**

sem·i·por·ce·lain /sèmmee páwrsslən, sèmmī-/ *n* a durable glazed ceramic material widely used for tableware. It resembles porcelain but is opaque.

sem·i·post·al /sèmmee pṓst'l, sèmmī-/ *n* a postage stamp sold for more than its face value, with the consequent proceeds going to a charity

sem·i·pre·cious /sèmmee préshəss, sèmmī-/ *adj* describes stones, gems, and minerals that have commercial value but are not valued as highly as those called precious

sem·i·pri·vate /sèmmee prī́vət, sèmmī-/ *adj* shared with at least one other person, e.g., with another patient ○ *She had a semiprivate room in the hospital.*

sem·i·pro /sèmmee prṓ, sèmmī-/ (*informal*) *n* (*plural* **-pros**) same as **semiprofessional** ■ *adj* relating to or being semiprofessional

sem·i·pro·fes·sion·al /sèmmee prə féshən'l, sèmmī-/ *adj* **1.** PAID BUT NOT FULL-TIME participating in a sport or artistic activity for pay but not as a full-time professional **2.** FOR SEMIPROFESSIONAL ATHLETES played in or contested by semiprofessional athletes **3.** LIKE PROFESSIONAL displaying some aspects of a professional ■ *n* PART PROFESSIONAL somebody, especially an athlete or performing artist, who is intermediate between an amateur and a professional —**sem·i·pro·fes·sion·al·ly** *adv*

sem·i·qua·ver /sémmee kwàyvər, sémmī-/ *n UK* same as **sixteenth note**

sem·i·qua·ver rest *n UK* same as **sixteenth rest**

sem·i·re·tired /sèmmee ri tī́rd, sèmmī-/ *adj* working only part-time following the end of a full-time career —**sem·i·re·tire·ment** *n*

sem·i·rig·id /sèmmee ríjjid, sèmmī-/ *adj* **1.** partly rigid, or rigid only in some parts **2.** describes an airship with a rigid keel that maintains its shape

sem·i·rug·ged /sèmmee rúggəd, sèmmī-/ *adj* **1.** designed and made to be resilient enough to withstand a moderate amount of rough treatment or fairly harsh environmental conditions **2.** moderately rough or moderately difficult to walk or drive over ○ *semirugged terrain* —**sem·i·rug·ged** *n*

sem·i·ru·ral /sèmmee ro͝orəl, sèmmī-/ *adj* intermediate between rural and urban

sem·i·se·cret /sèmmee seekrət, sèmmī-/ *adj* intended or supposedly intended to be secret but actually known about

sem·i·skilled /sèmmee skíld, sèmmī-/ *adj* with or requiring relatively few skills or little training ○ *semiskilled workers* ○ *a semiskilled job*

sem·i·soft /sèmmee sáwft, sèmmī-/ *adj* softer than most things, especially foods, of its type

sem·i·sol·id /sèmmee sólləd, sèmmī-/ *adj* not quite solid or liquid, but somewhere in between, like a gel ■ *n* a substance that has most of the qualities of a solid but can also flow, e.g., a gel

sem·i·sub·mers·i·ble /sèmmee səb múrssəb'l, sèmmī-/, **sem·i·sub·mers·i·ble rig** *n* a self-propelled oil-drilling platform resting on vertical pontoons that can be flooded for stability in deep water

sem·i·sweet /sèmmee sweet, sèmmī-/ *adj* slightly sweet, or having only a small amount of sugar or other sweetening ingredient added ○ *semisweet chocolate*

Sem·ite /sé mīt/ *n* **1.** a member of a Semitic-speaking people of Southwest Asia, including the Arab and Jewish peoples, and the ancient Assyrians, Babylonians, Carthaginians, Ethiopians, and Phoenicians **2.** an offensive term for a Jew (*slang*) [Mid-19C. < modern Latin *Semita* < Greek *Sēm* "Shem," son of Noah < Hebrew *Šēm*]

sem·i·ter·res·tri·al /sèmmee tə réstree əl, sèmmī-/ *adj* living partly on land but requiring a watery environment

Se·mit·ic /sə míttik/ *n* LANGUAGES SPOKEN BY SEMITES a group of languages belonging to the Afro-Asiatic family and spoken in North Africa and Southwest Asia, including Hebrew, Arabic, Aramaic, Maltese, and Amharic ■ *adj* **1.** OF SEMITIC in or relating to Semitic **2.** OF SEMITIC-SPEAKING PEOPLES relating to the peoples who speak Semitic languages

Se·mit·ics /sə míttiks/ *n* the study of the Semitic peoples, languages, and culture (*takes a singular verb*) —**Se·mit·i·cist** /sə míttissist/ *n*

Sem·i·tism /sémmi tìzzəm/ *n* **1.** the customs, traditions, and characteristics of Semitic people **2.** a word or other language feature of Semitic origin, especially one occurring in a non-Semitic language

Sem·i·tist /sémmitist/ *n* an expert in or student of Semitics

sem·i·tone /sémmee tōn, sémmī-/ *n* the smallest interval of the diatonic scale, half of a whole tone. It is the difference in pitch between adjacent frets on fretted string instruments such as guitars, or between adjacent black or white notes on the piano. [15C. Via French < medieval Latin *semitonus* < Latin *tonus* (see TONE)] —**sem·i·ton·al** /sèmmee tṓn'l, sèmmī-/ *adj* —**sem·i·ton·al·ly** *adv* —**sem·i·ton·ic** /sèmmee tónnik, sèmmī-/ *adj*

sem·i·trail·er /sémmee tràylər, sémmī-/ *n* **1.** a large rectangular vehicle with wheels only at the rear and a hitch at the front that attaches to a tractor or other towing vehicle **2.** a tractor with an attached semitrailer

sem·i·trop·i·cal /sèmmee tróppik'l, sèmmī-/ *adj* GEOG same as **subtropical** —**sem·i·trop·ics** *npl*

sem·i·vow·el /sémmee vòw əl, sémmī-/ *n* a sound that is like a vowel in involving no major obstruction of the airflow but that functions as a consonant in preceding vowels that form the nucleus of syllables. Examples in English are initial "w" and "y."

sem·i·week·ly /sèmmee weeklee, sèmmī-/ *adj* happening or published twice each week ■ *adv* twice each week

sem·i·year·ly /sèmmee yeerlee, sèmmī-/ *adj* happening or published twice each year ■ *adv* twice each year

sem·o·li·na /sèmmə leenə/ *n* gritty ground grains of wheat that are a byproduct of flour milling. Use: pasta, couscous, other foods. [Late 18C. Alteration of Italian *semolino* "small bran" < *semola* "bran" < Latin *simila* "fine wheat flour"]

sem·per fi·del·is /sèmpər fi dáyliss/ *adj* "always faithful," the motto of the US Marine Corps [< Latin]

sem·per par·a·tus /sèmpər pə raatəss, -ráytəss/ *adj* "always prepared," the motto of the United States Coast Guard [< Latin]

sempervivum

sem·per·viv·um /sèmpər vī́vəm/ *n* a widely grown ornamental garden plant that has rosettes of fleshy leaves. Flowers: pink, in clusters on stems. Genus: *Sempervivum.* [Late 16C. < modern Latin < form of Latin *sempervivus* "ever-living" < *semper* "ever" + *vivus* (see VIVID)]

sem·pi·ter·nal /sèmpi túrn'l/ *adj* lasting forever (*literary*) [15C. Via French < late Latin *sempiternalis* < Latin *sempiternus* < *semper* "always" + *-ternus*, suffix of time] —**sem·pi·ter·nal·ly** *adv* —**sem·pi·ter·ni·ty** *n*

sem·pli·ce /sémplə chày/ *adv* in a simple manner, without rubato (*used in musical directions*) [Mid-18C. < Italian, "simple"]

sem·pre /sém pray/ *adv* to be played or sung throughout in the manner indicated (*used in musical directions*) ○ *sempre largo* [Early 19C. < Italian, "always"]

semp·stress /sémpstrəss, sémstrəss/ *n* OCCUPATIONS same as **seamstress** (*archaic*) [Mid-17C. < *sempster*, variant of *seamster* (see SEAMSTRESS)]

sen /sen/ (*plural same*) *n* a subunit of currency in several countries in East and Southeast Asia. See table at **currency** [Early 18C. Via Japanese < Chinese *qián* "money, coin"]

Sen. *abbr* **1.** POL senate **2.** POL senator **3.** senior

Se·na·na·ya·ke /sènnə nī́ yəkə/, **D. S.** (1884–1952) prime minister of Ceylon (1947–52). As the country's first prime minister, he presided over its transition to independence (1948). Full name **Senanayake, Don Stephen**

sen·ate /sénnət/ *n* **1. LEGISLATIVE BODY** the sole or upper law-making chamber of government in many countries or states, past or present **2. US STATE LEGISLATURE** the higher of two elected legislative bodies in many states of the United States **3. ANCIENT ROMAN ASSEMBLY** the highest council of the ancient Roman Republic and of the Roman Empire **4. SENATE BUILDING** the building where a senate meets **5. UNIVERSITY BODY** the main faculty governing body in some universities and colleges [12C. Via French < Latin *senatus* "assembly of elders" < *senex* "male elder"]

Sen·ate *n* **1.** the upper of the two elected legislative bodies of the United States government. It is made up of two senators from each state. **2.** the upper chamber of the federal parliament of Canada. It is made up of 104 senators appointed by the ruling government. **3.** POL another spelling of **senate** (sense 1)

sen·a·tor /sénnətər/ *n* an elected or appointed member of a senate, e.g., in the United States, Australia, or ancient Rome [13C. Via French < Latin, related to *senatus* (see SENATE)]

sen·a·to·ri·al /sènnə táwree əl/ *adj* **1.** relating to or characteristic of a senate or the post of senator ○ *senatorial privileges* **2.** made up of senators —**sen·a·to·ri·al·ly** *adv*

sen·a·to·ri·al cour·te·sy *n* a custom in the US Senate allowing it to refuse to approve a presidential appointment if objections are raised by either the senior senator in the president's party from the appointee's state, or both senators from that state

sen·a·to·ri·al dis·trict *n* a state electoral district in the United States, represented in a state senate by a senator

send[1] /send/ *v* (**sent** /sent/, **send·ing, sends**) **1.** *vt* **CAUSE SOMEBODY OR SOMETHING TO GO** to cause somebody or something to be moved or taken to another place **2.** *vt* **COMMUNICATE SOMETHING** to transmit information or a message to somebody who is somewhere else **3.** *vt* **COMMAND SOMEBODY TO GO** to ask or command somebody to come or go **4.** *vt* **ENABLE SOMEBODY TO GO** to enable somebody to go somewhere special ○ *Let's send the children to camp this summer.* **5.** *vt* **REFER SOMEBODY SOMEWHERE** to suggest that somebody go somewhere or see somebody, usually for a specific kind of information ○ *He sent the student to his colleague for advice.* **6.** *vt* **BRING SOMETHING ABOUT** to make something happen ○ *Our blessings were sent by a higher power.* **7.** *vt* **PROPEL SOMETHING** to make something move or travel by pushing it or hitting it ○ *A gust of wind sent the papers swirling around the office.* **8.** *vt* **DRIVE SOMEBODY INTO PARTICULAR STATE** to make somebody enter a particular condition ○ *The delay is sending her into fits of frustration.* **9.** *vt* **EXCITE SOMEBODY GREATLY** to excite or thrill somebody intensely (*dated slang*) **10.** *vi* COMPUT **BE TRANSMITTED** to be transmitted or transmittable ○ *This e-mail won't send.* **11.** *vi* TELECOM **BROADCAST INFORMATION** to transmit information by telecommunication ○ *The operator was still sending when the power was cut off.* ■ *n* COMPUT **COMMAND TO TRANSMIT COMPUTER DATA** a command, key, or icon on a computer monitor or keyboard that is used to start the transmission of data [Old English *sendan* < Germanic, "cause to go"] —**send·er** *n* ◇ **send flying** to make somebody or something fly through the air by force of impact ◇ **send somebody packing** to dismiss or send somebody away in a firm, not very polite way (*informal*)

send away for *vt* to order something by mail or through a mail order catalog

send for *vt* to request the delivery, dispatch, or appearance of somebody or something ○ *send for reinforcements*

send forth *vt* to give out or produce somebody or something (*archaic or literary*) ○ *sent forth a cry of joy*

send in *vt* to mail something such as an application form for processing along with those sent by other people

send off *vt* **1. DISPATCH SOMETHING** to dispatch something in the mail **2. SEND SOMEBODY AWAY** to send somebody away, either on an errand or by way of dismissal ○ *We sent him off to buy some things.* **3. BID SOMEBODY FAREWELL** to say goodbye or good luck to somebody who is leaving ○ *Who was there to send her off?*

send on *vt* **1.** to send something such as mail or belongings to a second place for somebody or ahead of somebody or yourself **2.** to send something received to a subsequent place or person

send out for *vt* to order food by telephone, to be delivered to you and paid for when it arrives (*informal*) ○ *Let's send out for a pizza.*

send up *vt* **1. RAISE SOMETHING** to make something rise or climb, especially a scale or index such as on a thermometer or a listing of stock market values **2. SEND SOMEBODY TO PRISON** to imprison somebody following conviction (*informal*) ○ *He was sent up for armed robbery.* **3. MOCK SOMEBODY OR SOMETHING BY IMITATION** to make somebody or something appear ridiculous by humorous imitation (*informal*)

SYNONYMS See *ridicule*.

send[2] /send/ *n, vi* NAUT another spelling of **scend**

Sen·dai /sen dī/ capital city of Miyagi Prefecture, on northeastern Honshu Island, Japan. Population: 986,713 (2002).

Sen·dak /sén dàk/, **Maurice** (*b.* 1928) US writer and illustrator best known for the popular children's book *Where the Wild Things Are* (1963)

send·off /sénd àwf, -òf/ *n* an occasion when people gather to give good wishes to somebody who is leaving, e.g., at an airport ◇ **give somebody a good sendoff** to have a good party after somebody's funeral (*informal*)

send·up /sénd ùp/ *n* a parody done as a joke (*informal*)

se·ne /sáy nay/ (*plural same*) *n* a subunit of Samoan currency. See table at **currency** [Mid-20C. < Samoan, "cent"]

Sen·e·ca /sénnəkə/ (*plural same* or **-cas**) *n* **1.** a member of an Iroquois people who lived in western New York and who now mainly live there and in southern Ontario, Canada. The Seneca were one of the five peoples who formed the Iroquois Confederacy, which later became known as the Six Nations. **2.** the Iroquoian language of the Seneca people. It now has few speakers. [Mid-17C. < Dutch *Sennecaas* "the Upper Iroquois peoples"] —**Sen·e·ca** *adj* —**Sen·e·can** *adj*

Sen·e·ca /sénnəkə/ (4? B.C.–A.D. 65) Spanish-born Roman philosopher and writer. He was Nero's tutor, and influenced the early years of his reign. He committed suicide after being condemned for conspiracy against the state. His writings as a dramatist, rhetorician, and Stoic moralist were influential in shaping the thought and literature of the European Renaissance. Full name **Seneca, Lucius Annaeus**

Sen·e·ca Lake /sènnəkə-/ lake in New York. It is one of the Finger Lakes. Area: 67 sq. mi./174 sq. km.

Sen·e·ca snake·root *n* a flowering plant that has roots with various medicinal uses. Flowers: small, white. Native to: eastern North America. Latin name: *Polygala senega*. [< the plant's use by the Seneca people]

se·ne·ci·o /si neéshee ō, -neéshō/ (*plural* **-os**) *n* PLANTS same as **ragwort** [Mid-16C. < Latin, "groundsel" < *senex* "male elder"; from the plant's white hairs]

sen·e·ga /sénnəgə/ *n* PLANTS same as **Seneca snakeroot** [Mid-18C. Probably alteration of SENECA (Iroquois people)]

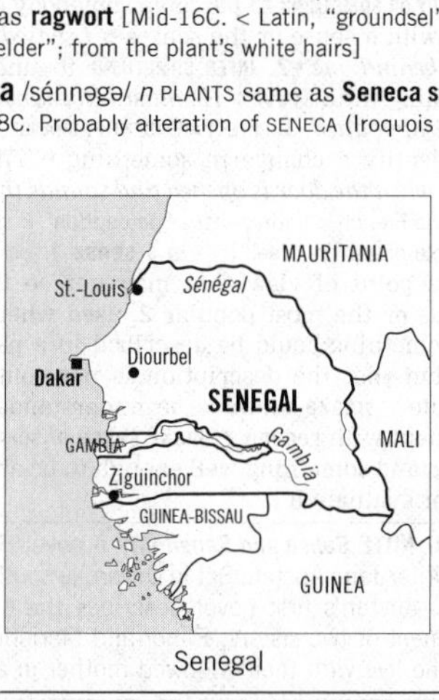

Senegal

Sen·e·gal /sènni gáwl, -gaál/ **1.** country in West Africa. Formerly a French territory, it became an independent republic in 1960. Language: French. Currency: C.F.A. franc. Capital: Dakar. Population: 10,580,307 (2003). Area: 75,955 sq. mi./196,722 sq. km. Official name **Republic of Senegal 2.** river in western Africa that forms the border between Senegal and Mauritania and empties into the Atlantic Ocean near St-Louis, Senegal. Length: 1,000 mi./1,610 km. —**Sen·e·gal·ese** /sènni gaw leéz, -gə-, -leéss/ *n, adj*

~~senery~~ incorrect spelling of **scenery**

se·nes·cent /sə néss'nt/ *adj* approaching an advanced age (*literary*) [Mid-17C. < Latin *senescent-*, present participle of *senescere* < *senex* "advanced in age"] —**se·nes·cence** *n*

sen·e·schal /sénnəshəl/ *n* in medieval times, a steward who managed the domestic staff of a noble house [14C. Via French < medieval Latin *seniscalcus* < Germanic]

Sen·ghor /seng gáwr, saaN-/, **Léopold Sédar** (1906–2001) Senegalese president and writer. He was the first president of Senegal (1960–80) and a leading African intellectual. He promoted the cultural heritage of Africans, developing the idea of negritude.

sen·hor /sayn yáwr, sin-/ (*plural* **-hors** or **-hor·es** /-yáw rayss/) *n* a Portuguese title equivalent to English "Mr." [Late 18C. Via Portuguese < medieval Latin *senior* "lord, superior" < Latin (see SENIOR)]

sen·ho·ra /sayn yáwrə, sin-/ *n* a Portuguese title equivalent to English "Mrs." [Early 19C. < Portuguese < *senhor* (see SENHOR)]

sen·ho·ri·ta /sàynyə reétə, sènnyə-/ *n* a Portuguese title equivalent to English "Miss" [Late 19C. < Portuguese < *senhor* (see SENHOR)]

se·nile /seé nīl, sé-/ *adj* **1.** forgetful, confused, or otherwise mentally less acute in later life **2.** occurring in or believed to be characteristic of later life, especially the period after the age of 65 years ○ *senile dementia* [Mid-17C. < Latin *senilis* "advanced in age" < *senex* "old"] —**se·nile·ly** *adv* —**se·nil·i·ty** /sə níllətee/ *n*

se·nile de·men·tia *n* a form of brain disorder marked by progressive and irreversible mental deterioration, memory loss, and disorientation, known to affect some people in later life

sen·ior /seényər/ *adj* **1. MORE ADVANCED IN AGE** of a more advanced age **2. HIGHER IN RANK** of higher rank or having longer service or employment than another ○ *Everyone on the committee is senior to me.* **3.** *also* **Sen·ior BELONGING TO EARLIER GENERATION** used to distinguish the elder of two members of the same family with the same name from the younger person of that name ■ *n* **1. PERSON OF GREATER AGE** somebody who is older than somebody else **2. HIGHER-RANKING PERSON** somebody who ranks higher than somebody else or has worked in the same place longer ○ *She is my only senior in the department.* **3. FINAL-YEAR STUDENT** a student in the last year of high school or college **4.** same as **senior citizen** [14C. < Latin, "elder, older" < *senex* "old"]

sen·ior chief pet·ty of·fi·cer *n* a noncommissioned officer in the US Navy or Coast Guard of a rank above chief petty officer

sen·ior cit·i·zen *n* somebody of retirement age or beyond

sen·ior debt *n* an indebtedness with no claims ahead of it and the first in line to be paid off

sen·ior ex·ec·u·tive of·fi·cer *n US* **1.** any of the most important managers in an organization **2.** the most important manager in an organization

sen·ior high school *n* a school for the last three or four years of secondary education grades 9 or 10 through 12

sen·ior·i·ty /seen yáwrətee/ (*plural* **-ties**) *n* **1.** status accorded to greater age, higher rank, or longer service or employment ○ *Days off will be awarded on the basis of seniority.* **2.** the state of being of greater age or higher rank than somebody else

sen·ior mas·ter ser·geant *n* a noncommissioned officer in the US Air Force of a rank above master sergeant

sen·ior mo·ment *n* a temporary lapse in memory or performance, which may be characteristic of an older person (*informal*)

sen·i·ti /sénnee tee/ (*plural same*) *n* a subunit of Tongan currency. See table at **currency** [Mid-20C. Via Tongan < CENT]

sen·na /sénnə/ *n* **1.** a leguminous plant. Flowers: yellow, in clusters. Native to: temperate regions. Genus: *Cassia*. **2.** dried plant leaves or pods of the senna plant. Use: purgative, laxative. [Mid-16C. Via modern Latin *senna* < Arabic *sanā'*]

Ayrton Senna

Sen·na /sénnə/, **Ayrton** (1960–94) Brazilian racing driver. One of the most celebrated Brazilian sportsmen of the 20th century, he won the World Grand Prix Formula One championship three times (1988, 1990, 1991). Full name **Senna da Silva, Ayrton**

> "To survive in grand prix racing, you need to be afraid. Fear is an important feeling. It helps you to race longer and live longer."
> [Ayrton Senna, *Times (London)*; May 3, 1994]

Sen·na·che·rib /sə nákə rìb/ (*d.* 681 B.C.) king of Assyria. During his reign (705–681 B.C.) he conquered Babylon (689 B.C.) and rebuilt Nineveh.

sen·net[1] /sénnət/ *n* a trumpet call that announced the exits and entrances of actors in Elizabethan drama [Late 16C. Probably alteration of SIGNET in obsolete sense "signal"]

sen·net[2] /sénnət/ *n* a barracuda that is found in the waters of the western Atlantic Ocean. Latin name: *Sphyraena borealis*. [Late 17C. Origin ?]

Sen·nett /sénnit/, **Mack** (1880–1960) Canadian-born US movie director. A leading director of silent movies, he was known for slapstick movies featuring Charlie Chaplin and the Keystone Cops. Born **Sinnott, Mikall (or Michael)**

sennit

sen·nit /sénnət/ *n* **1.** braided cord in flat strands, used on ships **2.** braided straw, reeds, or leaves, used to make hats [Mid-18C. Origin ?]

se·ñor /sen yáwr, sin-/ (*plural* **-ñors** or **-ñor·es** /-yáwress/) *n* a Spanish title equivalent to English "Mr." [Early 17C. Via Spanish < medieval Latin *senior* "lord, superior" < Latin (see SENIOR)]

se·ño·ra /sen yáwrə, sin-/ *n* a Spanish title equivalent to English "Mrs." [Late 16C. < Spanish < *señor* (see SEÑOR)]

se·ño·ri·ta /sàynyə reétə, sènnyə-/ *n* a Spanish title equivalent to English "Miss" [Early 19C. < Spanish < *señora* (see SEÑOR)]

sen·ry·u /sénnree ŏŏ/ (*plural same*) *n* a three-line ironic or satirical Japanese poem, similar in structure to a haiku [Mid-20C. After Karai *Senryu* (1718–90), Japanese poet]

sen·sate /sén sàyt/ *adj* **1.** perceived through any of the senses **2.** able to feel sensation [15C. < late Latin *sensatus* "equipped with senses" < Latin *sensus* (see SENSE)] —**sen·sate·ly** *adv*

sen·sa·tion /sen sáysh'n/ *n* **1.** PHYSICAL FEELING a physical feeling caused by having one or more of the sense organs stimulated ○ *a burning sensation in my mouth and throat* **2.** POWER TO PERCEIVE the capacity to receive impressions through the sense organs ○ *He has lost all sensation in his legs.* **3.** MENTAL IMPRESSION a vague or general feeling, especially one not attributable to an obvious cause ○ *a sensation of falling* **4.** PUBLIC INTEREST a state of avid public interest in a phenomenon ○ *Her speech caused a sensation.* **5.** INTERESTING PHENOMENON a phenomenon that creates avid public interest [Early 17C. Via French < medieval Latin *sensation-* "perception" < Latin *sensus* (see SENSE)]

sen·sa·tion·al /sen sáyshən'l/ *adj* **1.** OUTSTANDING exceptionally good ○ *sensational results* **2.** EXTRAORDINARY attracting a great deal of attention and interest ○ *a sensational defeat* **3.** EMPHASIZING LURID DETAILS giving too much emphasis to the most shocking and lurid aspects of something ○ *sensational coverage of the murder trial* **4.** PHYSIOL, PHILOSOPHY SENSORY connected with the senses or sense impressions —**sen·sa·tion·al·ly** *adv*

sen·sa·tion·al·ism /sen sáyshən'l ìzzəm/ *n* **1.** the practice of emphasizing the most lurid, shocking, and emotive aspects of something under discussion or investigation, especially by the media **2.** the belief that all knowledge is obtained only through the senses —**sen·sa·tion·al·ist** *n, adj* —**sen·sa·tion·al·is·tic** /sen sàyshən'l ístik/ *adj*

sen·sa·tion·al·ize /sen sáyshən'l ìz/ (**-ized, -iz·ing, -iz·es**) *vt* to place excessive emphasis on the most shocking and emotive aspects of a subject —**sen·sa·tion·al·i·za·tion** /sen sàyshən'li záysh'n/ *n*

sense /senss/ *n* **1.** PHYSICAL FACULTY any of the faculties by which a person or animal obtains information about the physical world, e.g., sight or taste **2.** FEELING DERIVED FROM SENSES a feeling derived from multiple or subtle sense impressions ○ *a sense of security* **3.** ABILITY TO APPRECIATE SOMETHING the faculty whereby somebody appreciates a particular quality ○ *a sense of humor* **4.** MORAL DISCERNMENT the ability to perceive and be motivated by moral or ethical principles ○ *instill a sense of right and wrong in the children* **5.** INTELLIGENCE the ability to make intelligent decisions or sound judgments ○ *He's got no sense at all.* **6.** POINT useful purpose or good reason ○ *There's no sense in waiting any longer.* **7.** REASONED OPINION an opinion arrived at through reflection or perception, often as a consensus ○ *The sense of the meeting was clearly to go ahead.* **8.** MAIN IDEA the essence or gist of something ○ *What was the sense of her argument?* **9.** MEANING a single meaning of a word or phrase that may have many **10.** LOGIC MEANING OF TERM the meaning as opposed to the reference of a word or sentence ■ **sens·es** *npl* RATIONAL MIND a sensible, rational state of mind ○ *I came to my senses in time to cancel the purchase.* ■ *vt* (**sensed, sens·ing, sens·es**) **1.** PERCEIVE SOMEBODY OR SOMETHING to perceive somebody or something with a sense or the senses ○ *I sensed a movement behind me.* **2.** INFER SOMETHING to understand something intuitively ○ *He must have sensed that I was disappointed.* **3.** DETECT AND IDENTIFY CHANGE to detect and identify a change in something ○ *The device senses when the door is opened and sounds the alarm.* [14C. Via French < Latin *sensus* "perception" < *sens-*, past participle of *sentire* "feel"] ◇ **in a sense 1.** considered from a point of view that may not be the most obvious or the most popular **2.** used when saying that something could be described in a particular way, but that the description is not complete or accurate ◇ **make sense** to be understandable and consistent with reason ◇ **make sense of something** to understand something well enough to be able to act on it or evaluate it

CULTURAL NOTE ***Sense and Sensibility***, a novel (1811) by British writer Jane Austen. Set in Devon, in southwestern England, Austen's first novel describes the emotional development of two sisters, Elinor and Marianne Dashwood, who live with their widowed mother in a modest cottage. Outwardly, Elinor appears dull and practical, Marianne sensitive and passionate, but the story of their involvement with two seemingly appropriate suitors warns against simplistic character judgments.

ORIGIN The Latin word *sentire* "to feel," from which ***sense*** is derived, is also the source of English *assent, consensus, consent, dissent, resent, sensible, sensual, sentence*, and *sentiment*.

sense da·tum *n* in the philosophical doctrine of phenomenalism, a sensation

sen·seh fowl /sénsse-/ *n Carib* same as **frizzle fowl** [< Twi *asense* "hen without a tail"]

sen·sei /sen sáy/ (*plural same*) *n* **1.** a teacher of a martial art such as karate or tai chi **2.** used as a title to address somebody who is a teacher, especially in the martial arts [Late 19C. Via Japanese < Middle Chinese *senshiaj* "first person"]

sense·less /sénssləss/ *adj* **1.** WITH NO APPARENT PURPOSE apparently or really without purpose or meaning ○ *a senseless activity* ○ *a senseless crime* **2.** UNCONSCIOUS unconscious, or unable to perceive anything ○ *was knocked senseless by the blow* **3.** WITHOUT INTELLIGENCE demonstrating a lack of reason and intelligence ○ *a senseless decision* —**sense·less·ly** *adv* —**sense·less·ness** *n*

sen·se·mil·la *n* DRUGS, PLANTS same as **sinsemilla**

sense or·gan *n* an organ such as an eye or ear that is specialized to receive stimuli from the physical world and transmit them via nerve impulses to the brain

sen·si·bil·i·a /sènssə bíllee ə/ *npl* things that can be sensed, considered collectively [Mid-19C. < late Latin < Latin *sensibilis* (see SENSIBLE)]

sen·si·bil·i·ty /sènssə bíllətee/ *n* **1.** ⚠ CAPACITY TO RESPOND the capacity to respond emotionally or aesthetically ○ *a literary sensibility* **2.** CAPACITY TO FEEL the capacity to perceive or feel **3.** BOT CAPACITY OF PLANTS FOR RESPONSE the sensitivity of plants to external stimuli ■ **sen·si·bil·i·ties** *npl* MORAL SCRUPLES sensitivity about moral or ethical issues ○ *careful not to offend their sensibilities*

USAGE sensibility or **sensitivity**? ***Sensitivity*** is used in ways corresponding to the meanings of the adjective *sensitive*, and is mainly concerned with physical or emotional reactions of various kinds: *a sensitivity to bright light*. ***Sensibility*** is less closely related in meaning to *sensible* than ***sensitivity*** is to *sensitive*, and chiefly denotes somebody's capacity to respond emotionally or aesthetically, as in *poetry that appealed to his sensibility*.

sen·si·ble /sénssəb'l/ *adj* **1.** SHOWING GOOD SENSE having or demonstrating sound reason and judgment ○ *a sensible decision* ○ *She's not very sensible.* **2.** PRACTICAL practical, usually comfortable and hard-wearing, and not worn as an adornment ○ *a pair of sensible shoes* **3.** SUBJECT TO PERCEPTION able to be perceived through the senses ○ *sensible objects in the world around us* **4.** CONSCIOUS awake or conscious, and having the capacity to understand **5.** ⚠ AWARE OF SOMETHING very aware of something, emotionally or intellectually (*formal*) ○ *not sensible of the tragic mistake he'd made* [14C. Via French < Latin *sensibilis* "perceptible by the senses, able to perceive" < *sens-* (see SENSE)] —**sen·si·ble·ness** *n* —**sen·si·bly** *adv*

USAGE sensible or **sensitive**? The two words overlap in meaning to some extent in the sense illustrated by the sentence *I am sensible of your difficult situation* ("I can appreciate your difficult situation"). In this meaning, ***sensible*** is normally used to express emotional or intellectual awareness. In a comparable use, ***sensitive*** is followed by *to* and denotes a tactful and sympathetic feeling about or for something: *He was always sensitive to their needs.*

SYNONYMS See ***aware***.

sen·si·ble ho·ri·zon *n* ASTRON same as **horizon** (sense 2)

sen·sil·lum /sen síllәm/ (*plural* **-la** /-lə/) *n* a simple sense organ made up of one or a few cells connected by a nerve cell, often found in insects [Early 20C. < modern Latin < Latin *sensus* (see SENSE)]

sen·si·tive /sénssətiv/ *adj* **1. THOUGHTFUL AND SYMPATHETIC** tactful and sympathetic in relation to the feelings of others **2. TOUCHY** easily offended or annoyed if something is spoken about ○ *He's very sensitive about his driving.* **3. SECRET OR CONFIDENTIAL** not to be mentioned or divulged ○ *sensitive matters of national security* **4. REQUIRING TACTFULNESS** needing to be dealt with tactfully to avoid embarrassment ○ *a sensitive issue* **5. ABLE TO SENSE** with the capacity to perceive via the sense organs **6. DELICATE** easily damaged or irritated physically ○ *a toothpaste for people with sensitive teeth* **7. ACUTELY PERCEPTIVE** unusually responsive to physical stimuli or emotional cues ○ *a sensitive nose* **8. AFFECTED BY EXTERNAL STIMULUS** affected in some way by a particular external stimulus such as an allergen (*often used in combination*) ○ *sensitive to light* ○ *a touch-sensitive screen* **9. ABLE TO MEASURE SMALL DIFFERENCES** capable of detecting minute changes in levels, conditions, or amounts ○ *a sensitive scientific instrument* **10.** FIN **FLUCTUATING** volatile and subject to fluctuation ○ *a sensitive market* **11.** PHOTOGRAPHY **RESPONSIVE TO LIGHT** extremely responsive to radiation, especially to light of a specific wavelength ○ *light-sensitive film* ■ *n* **PSYCHIC PERSON** a person with supposedly clairvoyant or psychic powers [14C. Via French < medieval Latin *sensitivus* < Latin *sens-* (see SENSE)] —**sen·si·tive·ly** *adv* —**sen·si·tive·ness** *n*

USAGE See ***sensible***.

sen·si·tive plant *n* a plant that recoils when touched. Flowers: purplish. Native to: tropical Americas. Latin name: *Mimosa pudica*.

sen·si·tive site ex·ploi·ta·tion *n* MIL full form of **SSE**[1]

sen·si·tiv·i·ty /sènssi tívvitee/ *n* **1. CONSIDERATION** care and understanding of needs and requirements ○ *sensitivity to different cultural traditions* **2. RESPONSIVENESS** capacity for physical sensation or response ○ *sensitivity to heat* **3.** ELECTRONICS **RESPONSIVENESS TO RADIO SIGNALS** the ability of a radio or other receiver to respond to transmitted signals ■ **sen·si·ti·vi·ties** *npl* **FEELINGS** somebody's feelings, especially feelings that might be offended

USAGE See ***sensibility***.

sen·si·tize /sénssə tìz/ (**-tized, -tiz·ing, -tiz·es**) *vt* **1. MAKE SOMEBODY SENSITIVE** to make somebody sensitive, especially to a situation **2. MAKE SOMEBODY ALLERGIC** to induce undue sensitivity in somebody to a substance such as a food ingredient or drug so that subsequent exposure to the substance triggers an allergic reaction **3.** PHOTOGRAPHY **MAKE FILM SENSITIVE TO LIGHT** to make a photographic film, plate, or other medium sensitive to light by coating it with an emulsion [Mid-19C. < SENSITIVE] —**sen·si·ti·za·tion** /sènssəti záysh'n/ *n* —**sen·si·tiz·er** *n*

sen·si·tom·e·ter /sènssə tómmətər/ *n* an instrument for measuring degrees of sensitivity, especially one used on photographic materials [Late 19C. < SENSITIVE] —**sen·si·tom·e·try** *n*

sen·sor /sénssər/ *n* a device capable of detecting and responding to physical stimuli such as movement, light, or heat [Mid-20C. < SENSE or Latin *sens-* (see SENSE)]

sen·so·ri·a PHYSIOL plural of **sensorium**

sen·so·ri·al /sen sáwree əl/ *adj* relating to sensation and the sense organs [Mid-18C. < SENSORIUM] —**sen·so·ri·al·ly** *adv*

sen·so·ri·mo·tor /sènssərə mṓtər/ *adj* **1.** relating to both the motor and sensory functions in the brain or the neurological structures underlying these functions **2.** relating to motor functions arising from sensory stimuli

sen·so·ri·mo·tor stage *n* the first major stage in Jean Piaget's theory of cognitive development, from birth to approximately two years, in which children begin to understand their world through sensory and motor experience

sen·so·ri·neu·ral /sènssərə nóorəl/ *adj* involving or relating to sensory nerves

sen·so·ri·um /sen sáwree əm/ (*plural* **-ri·a** /-ree ə/) *n* **1.** the sensory components of the brain and nervous system that deal with the receiving and interpreting of external stimuli **2.** all the sensory functions in the body, considered as a single unit [Mid-17C. < late Latin, "organ of sensation" < Latin *sens-* (see SENSE)]

sen·so·ry /sénssəree/ *adj* relating to sensation and the sense organs ○ *heightened sensory awareness* [Mid-18C. < SENSE or Latin *sens-* (see SENSE)]

sen·so·ry ad·ap·ta·tion *n* the tendency of a sensory system to adjust as a result of repeated exposure to a specific type of stimulus such as low levels of light

sen·so·ry dep·ri·va·tion *n* the elimination of or a sharp reduction in sensory stimulation, usually as part of an experiment in psychology or as part of repressive interrogation procedures or brainwashing

sen·so·ry in·te·gra·tion dys·func·tion *n* a neurological disorder of children caused by the inability of the brain to process sensory information correctly, making them either oversensitive or not sensitive enough to touch, taste, and sound, and resulting in inappropriate behavior

sen·so·ry reg·is·ter, sen·so·ry store *n US* a memory store for each sense such as touch, vision, or hearing. It is presumed to hold large quantities of information, but only for milliseconds.

sen·so·ry thresh·old *n* the minimum intensity of a stimulus at which it can be detected

sen·su·al /sénshoo əl/ *adj* **1. CARNAL** relating to physical or, especially, sexual pleasure **2. VOLUPTUOUS** suggesting a great deal of physical or, especially, sexual pleasure ○ *sensual lips* **3. SENSORY** relating to the body or the senses as opposed to the mind or the intellect [15C. < late Latin *sensualis* "equipped with feeling or sensation" < Latin *sensus* (see SENSE)] —**sen·su·al·ly** *adv* —**sen·su·al·ness** *n*

USAGE sensual or **sensuous**? Both words are connected with gratification of the human senses. ***Sensual*** is the older word, and in the 17th century it developed special meanings associated with the bodily appetites, especially eating and above all sexual satisfaction: *Her mouth looked sensual and inviting. They enjoyed the sensual pleasures of the table.* About this time the poet John Milton seems to have invented the word ***sensuous*** to refer more specifically to the aesthetic and spiritual senses (seeing, hearing, thinking), and it was taken up by Samuel Taylor Coleridge in the 19th century. In current use, it is almost impossible to keep the two sets of meanings apart, since the senses cannot readily be compartmentalized in this way, but it is prudent to have regard for the main distinction when using these words. ***Sensuous***, for example, is the word to use in connection with music or poetry: *The conductor relished the sensuous parts of Ravel's score.*

sen·su·al·ism /sénshoo ə lìzzəm/ *n* **1.** devotion to sensual gratification **2.** PHILOSOPHY, ETHICS same as **sensationalism** (sense 2) —**sen·su·al·ist** *n* —**sen·su·al·is·tic** /sènshoo ə lístik/ *adj*

sen·su·al·i·ty /sènshoo állətee/ *n* **1.** the capacity for enjoying the pleasures of the senses **2.** the quality of being pleasing to the senses

sen·su·ous /sénshoo əss/ *adj* **1. OF SENSE STIMULATION** relating to stimulation of the senses **2. APPRECIATING STIMULATION** enjoying or appreciating pleasurable stimulation of the senses ○ *a sensuous lover* **3. CAUSING STIMULATION** causing pleasurable stimulation of the senses ○ *a sensuous experience* [Mid-17C. < Latin *sensus* (see SENSE)] —**sen·su·ous·ly** *adv* —**sen·su·ous·ness** *n*

USAGE See ***sensual***.

sent[1] /sent/ past participle, past tense of **send**[1]

sent[2] /sent/ (*plural* **sen·ti** /séntee/) *n* a subunit of Estonian currency. See table at **currency** [Late 20C. Via Estonian < CENT]

~~**sentance**~~ incorrect spelling of **sentence**

sen·te /séntee/ (*plural* **li·sen·te** /li séntee/) *n* a subunit of currency in Lesotho. See table at **currency** [Late 20C. Via Sesotho < CENT]

sen·tence /sént'nss/ *n* **1.** GRAM **MEANINGFUL LINGUISTIC UNIT** a group of words or a single word that expresses a complete thought, feeling, or idea. It usually contains an explicit or implied subject and a predicate containing a finite verb. **2.** LAW **JUDGMENT** a judgment by a court specifying the punishment of somebody convicted of a crime **3.** LAW **JUDICIAL PUNISHMENT** the punishment imposed by a court on somebody convicted of a crime ○ *a sentence of 15 years in prison* **4.** LOGIC **WELL-FORMED EXPRESSION** a well-formed expression in a symbolic language ■ *vt* (**-tenced, -tenc·ing, -tenc·es**) LAW **ALLOCATE SOMEBODY PUNISHMENT** to allocate a punishment to somebody convicted of a crime, usually stating its nature and its duration ○ *was sentenced to 90 hours of community service* [13C. Via French < Latin *sententia* "feeling, opinion" < *sentient-*, present participle of *sentire* "feel"] —**sen·tenc·er** *n*

sen·tence ad·verb *n* an adverb that modifies an entire sentence

USAGE Many English adverbs can be used to modify whole sentences; for example: *Obviously there must be some mistake. Regrettably I will be away that week. Financially it was a disaster. I've never liked him, frankly.* They are known as sentence adverbs. Sentence adverbs are concise; they allow you to express in a single word what you might otherwise have to say in several words. Sentence adverbs form a completely standard aspect of English grammar, but there are a few, for example, *hopefully*, that give rise to widespread criticism as they express the user's attitude to the sentence content rather than modify the sentence as a whole. Others that may incur criticism in the same way are *mercifully, thankfully*, and *truthfully*. In formal contexts, writers are advised to avoid all these and simply recast their sentences accordingly.

sen·tence sub·sti·tute *n* a single word that, when used in the proper context, meets all the semantic requirements of a sentence. Words such as "yes" and "no" are sentence substitutes.

sen·tenc·ing /sént'nssing/ *n* **1.** the phase of a court trial in which a sentence is arrived at and pronounced **2.** the act of pronouncing a judicial sentence on a defendant

sen·ten·tial /sen ténsh'l/ *adj* relating to sentences in natural language or logic

sen·ten·tial cal·cu·lus *n* LOGIC same as **propositional calculus**

sen·ten·tious /sen ténshəss/ *adj* **1. FULL OF APHORISMS** tending to use, or full of, maxims and aphorisms **2. OVERLY MORALIZING** inclined to moralize more than is merited or appreciated **3. PITHY** expressing much in few words [15C. Via French < Latin *sententiosus* "meaningful" < *sententia* (see SENTENCE)] —**sen·ten·tious·ly** *adv* —**sen·ten·tious·ness** *n*

sen·ti MONEY plural of **sent**[2]

sen·tient /sénshənt, sénshee ənt/ *adj* **1.** capable of feeling and perception ○ *a sentient being* **2.** capable of responding emotionally rather than intellectually [Mid-17C. < Latin *sentient-*, present participle of *sentire* "feel"] —**sen·tience** *n*

sen·ti·ment /séntəmənt/ *n* **1. MENTAL FEELING** a thought or idea based on a feeling or emotion **2. GENERAL FEELING** a feeling or opinion prevailing among a group of people ○ *The sentiment emerged that we were acting too soon.* **3. UNDERLYING FEELING** an underlying feeling, as distinct from the action that it brings about ○ *His speech was awkward, but the sentiment was real.* **4. APPEAL TO FEELING** a calculated appeal to feeling or emotion, especially one that is excessive and unreasoning ○ *The book ends on a note of cheap sentiment.* **5. DEEP FEELING** refined or tender feeling, especially when expressed in a work of art (*formal*) ■ **sen·ti·ments** *npl* **OPINION** a point of view or judgment on something ○ *What are her sentiments on the matter?* [14C. Via French < medieval Latin *sentimentum* "opinion, feeling" < Latin *sentire* "feel"]

sen·ti·men·tal /sèntə ménť'l/ *adj* **1. MAWKISH IN FEELING** affected acutely by emotional matters, often to the point of mawkishness **2. MAWKISH IN EXPRESSION** displaying too much uncontrolled or self-indulgent emotion **3. APPEALING TO TENDER FEELINGS** experiencing, appealing to, or expressing tender, often romantic or nostalgic, feelings ○ *a sentimental portrait of our town* **4. EXPRESSING DEEP FEELING** expressing deep, refined feeling (*formal*) —**sen·ti·men·tal·ly** *adv*

CULTURAL NOTE ***A Sentimental Journey***, a novel (1768) by British writer Laurence Sterne. Sterne's second and last novel was intended as a riposte to Tobias Smollett's ill-tempered *Travels Through France and Italy* (1766) and even features a Smollett-like curmudgeon called Smellfungus. A rambling account of a trip through

France from Calais to Lyons, it is transformed into an engaging work of art by the author's wit, sensitivity, and sharp social observation. Not surprisingly, the word *smellfungus* came to mean a carping faultfinder in general parlance.

sen·ti·men·tal·ism /sèntə mént'l ìzzəm/ *n* **1.** a tendency to express or use obvious or powerful feelings or emotions without appealing to reason **2.** something that expresses excessive emotion, especially something that is self-indulgent or nostalgic —**sen·ti·men·tal·ist** *n*

sen·ti·men·tal·i·ty /sèntəmən tállətee/ *n* the tendency or practice of indulging in emotion or nostalgia

sen·ti·men·tal·ize /sèntə mént'l ìz/ (**-ized, -iz·ing, -iz·es**) *v* **1.** *vi* to indulge excessively in emotion or nostalgia **2.** *vt* to treat somebody or something, or express something, with undue emphasis on feeling —**sen·ti·men·tal·i·za·tion** /sèntə mènt'li záysh'n/ *n*

sen·ti·men·tal val·ue *n* a value placed on something because of its emotional associations rather than its monetary worth

sen·ti·nel /séntən'l, sént'nəl/ *n* SENTRY a guard or lookout ■ *vt* (**-neled, -nel·ing, -nels**) **1.** GUARD SOMETHING to stand guard over something or a group of people **2.** PROVIDE GUARD FOR SOMETHING to provide a guard for something or for a group of people [16C. Via French < Italian *sentinella*]

sen·try /séntree/ (*plural* **-tries**) *n* somebody who is assigned to keep watch and to warn of danger, especially a member of the armed services who guards entrances and exits [Early 17C. Origin ?]

sen·try box *n* a covered shelter for a sentry, typically at an entrance or crossing

sen·za /séntsə, sénzə/ *prep* without something indicated by a following Italian noun (*used in musical directions*) ○ *senza ritenuto* [Early 18C. < Italian]

Seoul /sōl/ capital and largest city of South Korea, in the northwest of the country, on the Han River. Population: 9,895,217 (2000).

SEP /sep/ *abbr US* simplified employee pension

Sep. *abbr* **1.** CALENDAR September **2.** Septuagint

se·pal /seép'l, sépp'l/ *n* a modified leaf in the outermost whorl **(calyx)** of a flower that encloses the petals and other parts [Early 19C. Via French < modern Latin *sepalum*, blend of Greek *skepē* "covering" + Latin *petalum* "petal"]

se·pal·oid /seéppə lòyd, séppə-/ *adj* resembling or functioning as a sepal

sep·a·ra·ble /séppərəb'l/ *adj* capable of being divided, taken apart, or removed, either from each other or from something else —**sep·a·ra·bil·i·ty** /sèppərə bíllətee/ *n* —**sep·a·ra·bly** *adv*

sep·a·rate *adj* /séppərət/ **1.** APART not touching or connected, not together, or not in the same place ○ *They slept in separate rooms.* **2.** UNRELATED distinct from or unrelated to something else ○ *treated it as a separate issue* **3.** DIFFERENT not shared with somebody or something else ○ *offers an apartment with a separate entrance* ■ *v* /séppə ràyt/ (**-rat·ed, -rat·ing, -rates**) **1.** *vt* MOVE OR KEEP SOMETHING APART to move two or more people or things away from each other, or prevent people or things from coming into contact with each other ○ *Somehow we got separated in the crowd.* **2.** *vt* BE BETWEEN THINGS to stand or lie between one person or thing and another **3.** *vi* COME APART to come apart or stop being attached or connected **4.** *vt* DISTINGUISH PEOPLE OR THINGS to be the factor that makes two people or things different from one another ○ *His ready wit separated him from his classmates.* **5.** *vi* PART COMPANY to leave one another and go off in different directions ○ *The group separated soon after lunch.* **6.** *vi* CEASE LIVING AS COUPLE to stop living together as a couple **7.** *vt* CATEGORIZE SOMEBODY OR SOMETHING to put somebody or something into different categories or groups **8.** *vt* SHOW HOW THINGS DIFFER to see or show that two or more things are different or not ○ *Try to separate the issues and establish priorities.* **9.** *vti* DIVIDE to split something into component parts, or be split into component parts **10.** *vti* MAKE OR BECOME INDEPENDENT to leave a larger group and become independent, or cause part of a larger group to leave and form an independent unit **11.** *vt* RELEASE OR FIRE SOMEBODY to dismiss somebody from a job, or release somebody from military service ■ **sep·a·rates** /séppərəts/ *npl* CLOTHING INDIVIDUAL ITEMS OF CLOTHING articles of women's clothing that can be bought as individual items and worn in various combinations, e.g., blouses, skirts, jackets, and pants [15C. < Latin *separat-*, past participle of *separare*, literally "arrange apart" < *parare* "make ready"] —**sep·a·rate·ly** *adv* —**sep·a·rate·ness** *n* —**sep·a·ra·tor** /-ràytər/ *n*

separate out *v* **1.** *vti* to split something into component parts, or be split into component parts **2.** *vt* to be the factor that makes two people or things different from one another

sep·a·rat·ed /séppə ràytəd/ *adj* **1.** LIVING APART WHILE MARRIED no longer living together as a couple but still legally married **2.** POSITIONED APART moved apart so as not to be touching or connected, not together, or not in the same place ○ *geographically separated families* **3.** DIVIDED split into component parts ○ *separated eggs*

sep·a·rate school *n Can* a school run according to the beliefs of a denomination or religion, especially Roman Catholicism, that receives public funding

sep·a·rat·ing fun·nel /séppə rayting-/ *n* a large funnel that has a valve in its output tube. Use: separation of liquids that do not mix.

sep·a·ra·tion /sèppə ráysh'n/ *n* **1.** KEEPING OF THINGS APART the act or process of separating things or people **2.** STATE OF BEING APART the state or duration of being apart from other things or people **3.** PLACE OF MEETING OR SPACE BETWEEN a place, line, or mark that shows where two things meet, or the gap between them **4.** AGREEMENT NOT TO LIVE TOGETHER the act of stopping living together as husband and wife while remaining married, or a formal agreement to do so, especially one made in a court of law **5.** DEPARTURE FROM GROUP dismissal from a job, or release from military service [15C. Via French < Latin *separation-* < *separat-* (see SEPARATE)]

sep·a·ra·tion anx·i·e·ty *n* a state of anxiety caused in somebody, especially a young child, by the thought or fact of being separated from his or her mother or primary caregiver

sep·a·ra·tion·ist /sèppə ráysh'nist/ *n, adj* POL same as **separatist**

sep·a·ra·tion of pow·ers *n* the constitutional requirement that each of the three branches of the US government, executive, judicial, and legislative, be autonomous and distinct from the others

sep·a·ra·tist /séppərətist/ *n* **1.** somebody who breaks away from or who is in favor of breaking away from a group, organization, or country **2.** somebody who favors keeping members of racial, religious, gender, or cultural groups separate —**sep·a·ra·tism** *n* —**sep·a·ra·tist** *adj*

Sep·a·ra·tist *n Can* somebody who favors the secession of a province, especially Quebec, from Canada

sep·a·ra·tive /séppərətiv/ *adj* tending to become separate or make something become separate

sepd. *abbr US* separated

~~seperate~~ incorrect spelling of **separate**

Se·phar·di /sə fáar dee/ (*plural* **-dim** /-dim/) *n* a Jew of Spanish or Portuguese origin, or one who is not of German or eastern European descent **(Ashkenazi)** [Mid-19C. < modern Hebrew < *sěpāraḏ*, land of exile mentioned in the Bible] —**Se·phar·dic** /-dik/ *adj*

se·pi·a /seépee ə/ *n* **1.** REDDISH BROWN PIGMENT made from the dark liquid in the ink sacs of various species of cuttlefish, or an artificial form of it, used in painting **2.** ARTS SEPIA DRAWING OR PHOTOGRAPH a drawing done in sepia, or a photograph with a brownish tone **3.** COLORS DARK BROWN a dark brown color tinged with yellow or red **4.** PHOTOGRAPHY BROWNISH COLOR IN PHOTOGRAPHS a brownish tone produced by some photographic processes, especially seen in early photographs [14C. Via Latin < Greek *sēpia* "cuttlefish"] —**se·pi·a** *adj*

Se·pik /sépik/ river on eastern New Guinea. Length: 700 mi./1,100 km.

se·pi·o·lite /seépee ə lìt/ *n UK* MINERALS same as **meerschaum** (sense 1) [Mid-19C. < German *Sepiolith* < Greek *sēpion* "cuttlefish bone" < *sēpia* "cuttlefish"]

se·poy /seé pòy/ *n* in former British India, an Indian soldier under British command, especially one who served in the British East India Company [Early 18C. < Persian, Urdu *sipāhī* "horseman, soldier"]

sep·pu·ku /se pòòkoo, séppə koo/ *n* CULTL ANTHROP same as **hara-kiri** [Late 19C. < Japanese < *setsu* "to cut" (< Middle Chinese *tshet*) + *fuku* "abdomen" (< Middle Chinese *fuwk*)]

sep·sis /sépsiss/ *n* the condition or syndrome caused by the presence of microorganisms or their toxins in the tissue or the bloodstream [Late 19C. < Greek *sēpsis* < *sēpein* "make rotten"]

sept /sept/ *n* **1.** a section of a people that believes itself to be descended from one particular ancestor **2.** a branch of a Scottish or Irish clan [Early 16C. Probably alteration of SECT]

Sept. *abbr* **1.** CALENDAR September **2.** BIBLE Septuagint

sep·ta ANAT, ENG plural of **septum**

sep·tar·i·um /septérree əm/ (*plural* **-i·a** /-ee ə/) *n* a nodule of mineral containing cracks filled with crystalline material [Late 18C. < modern Latin < Latin *septum* (see SEPTUM)] —**sep·tar·i·an** *adj*

Sep·tem·ber /sep témbər/ *n* in the Gregorian calendar, the ninth month of the year, lasting 30 days. See table at **calendar** [Pre-12C. Via French < Latin < *septem* "seven"; because September was the 7th month of the Roman year]

Sep·tem·ber 10th *adj* so petty, shallow, or outmoded as to be irrelevant

Sep·tem·ber 11 *n* September 11, 2001, the day on which terrorists attacked the Pentagon and the twin New York City World Trade Center towers using passenger-carrying commercial jet aircraft, which the terrorists crashed into the buildings, killing thousands

Sep·tem·ber Mas·sa·cre *n* the massacre of hundreds of prisoners by mobs in Paris in September 1792, during the French Revolution. The killings were caused by fears of a counterrevolution by royalist prisoners, but most of those who were killed were ordinary criminals.

Sep·tem·brist /sep témbrist/ *n* a member of the Paris mob that carried out the September Massacre in 1792

sep·te·na·ry /sép teénaree/ *adj* **1.** OF 7 relating to the number seven **2.** CONTAINING 7 made up of seven people or things ■ *n* (*plural* **-ries**) **1.** NUMBER 7 the number seven **2.** GROUP OF 7 a group of seven people or things **3.** 7 YEARS a period of seven years **4.** LITERAT LINE OF VERSE CONTAINING 7 FEET a line of verse consisting of seven metrical feet [15C. < Latin *septenarius* < *septeni* "seven each" < *septem* "seven"]

septennia plural of **septennium**

sep·ten·ni·al /sep ténnee əl/ *adj* **1.** FOR 7 YEARS lasting seven years **2.** HAPPENING EVERY 7 YEARS occurring once every seven years ■ *n* SEPTENNIAL EVENT something that happens every seven years [Mid-17C. < Latin *septennium* (see SEPTENNIUM)] —**sep·ten·ni·al·ly** *adv*

sep·ten·ni·um /sep ténnee əm/ (*plural* **-ni·ums** or **-ni·a** /-nee ə/) *n* a period of seven years [Mid-19C. < Latin < *septem* "seven" + *annus* "year"]

sep·tet /sep tét/, **sep·tette** *n* **1.** a group of seven instrumentalists or singers **2.** a musical piece composed for seven instrumentalists or singers [Early 19C. < German *Septett* < Latin *septem* "seven"]

septi- *prefix* seven ○ *septivalent* [< Latin *septem*]

sep·tic /sép tik/ *adj* **1.** full of or generating pus **2.** relating to, involving, or causing sepsis [Early 17C. Via Latin < Greek *sēptikos* < *sēpein* "make rotten"] —**sep·tic·i·ty** /sep tíssətee/ *n*

sep·ti·cae·mi·a *n* MED UK spelling of **septicemia**

sep·ti·ce·mi·a /sèptə seémee ə/ *n* a disease caused by toxic microorganisms in the bloodstream [Mid-19C. < Latin *septicus* (see SEPTIC)] —**sep·ti·ce·mic** *adj*

sep·ti·ci·dal /sèptə síd'l/ *adj* describes a fruit that splits open along a septa, dividing the component carpels [Early 19C. < SEPTUM + Latin *-cidere* "to cut" < *caedere*]

sep·tic tank *n* a tank, usually underground, in which human waste matter is decomposed by bacteria

Sept-Îles /se teél/ city in southeastern Quebec,

Canada, on the St. Lawrence River. Population: 23,636 (2001).

sep·til·lion /sep tíllyən/ (*plural* **-lions** or *same*) *n* **1.** *US* the number equal to 10^{24}, written as 1 followed by 24 zeros **2.** *UK* the number equal to 10^{42}, written as 1 followed by 42 zeros (*dated*) [Late 17C. < French < *sept* "seven" + *-illion* as in *million*] —**sep·til·lion** *adj* —**sep·til·lionth** *adj, n*

sep·time /sep teém/ *n* in fencing, the seventh of eight positions from which a parry or attack can be made [Late 19C. Via French < Latin *septimus* "seventh" < *septem* "seven"]

sep·tu·a·ge·nar·i·an /sèp too əjə nérree ən, sèp choo-/ *n* a person between 70 and 79 years of age ■ *adj* between 70 and 79 years old [Early 18C. < Latin *septuaginarius* < *septuaginta* "seventy"]

Sep·tu·a·ges·i·ma /sèp too ə jéssimə, sèp choo-/ *n* in the Christian calendar, the third Sunday before Lent [14C. < Latin *septuagesima (dies)* "seventieth (day)" < *septuaginta* "seventy"]

Sep·tu·a·gint /sép too ə jìnt, sép choo-/ *n* a Greek translation of the Hebrew Bible made in the 3rd and 2nd centuries B.C. to meet the needs of Greek-speaking Jews outside Palestine. The Septuagint contains some books not in the Hebrew canon. [Mid-16C. < Latin *septuaginta* "seventy"; because about seventy translators were said to have worked on it]

sep·tum /séptəm/ (*plural* **-ta** /-tə/) *n* **1.** a thin partition or membrane dividing something into two or more cavities. Examples include the tissue separating the nostrils, each of the muscular membranes separating the chambers of the heart, and the internal dividing walls in the seed heads of poppies. **2.** a thin partition that separates components in a machine [Mid-17C. < Latin, "partition" < *sepire* "enclose" < *sepes* "hedge"] —**sep·tal** *adj* —**sep·tate** *adj*

sep·tu·ple /sèp tóop'l, -túp'l/ *adj* **1.** 7 TIMES AS MUCH seven times as many or as much as something else **2.** HAVING 7 PARTS consisting of seven parts ■ *vti* (**-pled, -pling, -ples**) INCREASE BY 7 TIMES to multiply something by seven, or become seven times as much or as many (*formal*) [Early 17C. < late Latin *septuplus* < Latin *septem* "seven"]

sep·tu·plet /sep túpplət, -tóoplət/ *n* **1.** ONE OF 7 BORN TOGETHER one of seven people or animals born to the same mother at one time **2.** GROUP OF 7 a group of seven people or things **3.** MUSIC GROUP OF 7 NOTES a group of seven notes to be played or sung in the time of four, six, or eight of the same notated value [Late 19C. < SEPTUPLE, after TRIPLET]

sep·ul·cher /sépp'lkər/ *n* **1.** BURIAL PLACE a vault in which a corpse is buried **2.** *US* CONTAINER FOR RELICS a container for sacred relics, especially one in an altar ■ *vt* (**-chered, -cher·ing, -chers**) PUT CORPSE IN BURIAL VAULT to put a corpse into a sepulcher (*literary*) [12C. Via French < Latin *sepulc(h)rum* < *sepult-*, past participle of *sepelire* "bury"]

se·pul·chral /sə púlkrəl, -póolkrəl/ *adj* **1.** suggesting or possessing characteristics associated with the grave, e.g., gloominess **2.** relating to burial vaults or funerals and burials (*formal*)

sep·ul·chre *n, vt* BUILDINGS, CHR Can, UK spelling of **sepulcher**

seq. *abbr* sequel

se·qua·cious /si kwáyshəss/ *adj* **1.** argued, or developing an argument, in a logically consistent and coherent way (*formal*) **2.** too willing to follow a leader uncritically (*archaic*) [Mid-17C. < Latin *sequax* "inclined to follow" < *sequi* "follow"]

se·quel /seékwəl/ *n* **1.** a movie, novel, or play that continues a story begun in a previous movie, novel, or play **2.** something that happens after something else, especially as a consequence of it [15C. Via French < Latin *sequel(l)a* < *sequi* "follow"]

se·quel·a /si kwéllə/ (*plural* **-quel·ae** /-kwéllee/) *n* a disease or disorder that is caused by a preceding disease or injury in the same individual [Late 18C. < Latin (see SEQUEL)]

se·quel·i·tis /seékwəl ítiss/ *n* the tendency of authors and moviemakers to continue to produce sequels to their works as long as they are financially successful

se·quence /seékwənss/ *n* **1.** SERIES OF THINGS a number of things, actions, or events arranged or happening in a specific order or having a specific connection **2.** ORDER OF THINGS the order in which things are arranged, actions are carried out, or events happen ○ *a chronological sequence* **3.** MOVIES SECTION OF MOVIE a section of a movie showing a single incident or set of related actions or events ○ *a chase sequence* **4.** CARDS CARDS OF CONSECUTIVE VALUES three or more consecutive playing cards, usually of the same suit **5.** MUSIC REPEATED MUSICAL PHRASE a musical passage or chant consisting of three or more related short phrases repeated several times at successively higher or lower pitch levels **6.** CHR HYMN in the Roman Catholic Church, a hymn sung or said between the gradual and the gospel **7.** MATH ORDERED SET OF ELEMENTS in mathematics, an ordered set of elements that can be put into a one-to-one correspondence with the set of positive integers **8.** BIOCHEM ORDER DETERMINING BIOLOGICAL PROPERTIES the order of the amino acids in a protein or of the nucleotides in a nucleic acid ■ *vt* (**-quenced, -quenc·ing, -quenc·es**) **1.** PUT OR DO THINGS IN ORDER to arrange things or perform actions in a definite order **2.** BIOCHEM DETERMINE MOLECULE'S SEQUENCE to determine the sequence of a protein or nucleic acid [14C. < late Latin *sequentia* "what follows" < Latin *sequent-*, present participle of *sequi* "follow"]

ORIGIN The Latin word *sequi* "to follow," from which ***sequence*** is derived, is also the source of English *consecutive, consequence, ensue, obsequious, persecute, prosecute, pursue, second*[1] in a series, *sect, sequel, set*[2], *subsequent, sue,* and *suit.*

se·quence of tens·es *n* the grammatical relationship that causes the tense of a verb in a subordinate clause to be influenced or dictated by the tense of the verb in the related main clause

se·quenc·er /seékwənssər/ *n* **1.** ELECTRONICS DEVICE FOR SORTING DATA an instrument for sorting information into the correct order for data processing **2.** MUSIC ELECTRONIC DEVICE FOR STORING MUSIC an electronic device or piece of software that digitally stores sequences of musical notes, chords, or rhythms that can be transmitted to an electronic musical instrument **3.** BIOCHEM DEVICE FOR DETERMINING SEQUENCES an apparatus for automatically determining the sequence of a protein or nucleic acid

se·quence tagged site *n* a short DNA sequence, usually 200 to 500 base pairs, that has a single occurrence in the human genome and whose location and base sequence are known

se·quent /seékwənt/ *adj* **1.** CONSEQUENT following as a consequence or result (*formal*) **2.** FOLLOWING following one after another (*formal or archaic*) ■ *n* **1.** CONSEQUENCE a consequence or result (*formal*) **2.** LOGIC FORMAL LOGICAL REPRESENTATION in logic, a formal representation of an argument showing that an element is a theorem [Mid-16C. < Latin *sequent-* (see SEQUENCE)] —**se·quent·ly** *adv*

se·quen·tial /si kwénsh'l/ *adj* **1.** happening in chronological order, or forming a sequence **2.** being a consequence or result of something else [Early 19C. < SEQUENCE, after CONSEQUENCE, CONSEQUENTIAL] —**se·quen·ti·al·i·ty** /si kwènshee állətee/ *n* —**se·quen·tial·ly** *adv*

se·quen·tial ac·cess *n* a way of accessing and reading a computer file by starting at the beginning

se·quen·tial scan·ning *n* a system that scans a television picture using lines in a numerical sequence

se·ques·ter /si kwéstər/ (**-tered, -ter·ing, -ters**) *vt* **1.** PUT SOMEBODY INTO ISOLATION to put somebody in an isolated or lonely place away from other people, the pressures of everyday life, or possible disturbances (*formal*) **2.** LAW TAKE PROPERTY TO COVER OBLIGATION to take legal possession of somebody's property temporarily until a debt that person owes is paid, a dispute is settled, or a court order is obeyed **3.** LAW TAKE ENEMY'S PROPERTY to demand or seize the property of an enemy [14C. Via French < late Latin *sequestrare* "place in safe keeping" < *sequester* "follower, trustee"]

se·ques·trant /seé kwəss trənt, sék-/ *n* a chemical that in effect removes ions from a solution. Use: soil treatment to correct mineral deficiencies.

se·ques·trate /seékwə stràyt, sékwə-/ (**-trat·ed, -trat·ing, -trates**) *vt UK* to take legal possession of somebody's property temporarily until a debt that person owes is paid, a dispute is settled, or a court order obeyed [15C. < late Latin *sequestrat-*, past participle of *sequestrare* (see SEQUESTER)] —**se·ques·tra·tor** *n*

se·ques·tra·tion /seèkwə stráysh'n, sèkwə-/ *n* **1.** CONFISCATING OR BEING CONFISCATED the act or process of legally confiscating somebody's property temporarily until a debt that person owes is paid, a dispute is settled, or a court order obeyed **2.** LAW SEIZING OR BEING SEIZED the seizing of an enemy's property, or the fact or process of being seized **3.** GOING INTO OR BEING IN ISOLATION the act of going into or putting somebody in an isolated place, away from people or everyday pressures, or the fact of being in such a place (*formal*) **4.** CHEM ION-BINDING PROCESS the chemical process of binding an ion, especially a metallic ion, in a coordination complex

se·ques·trum /si kwésstrəm/ (*plural* **-tra** /-trə/) *n* a fragment of dead tissue, usually bone, that separates from surrounding living tissue [Mid-19C. < medieval Latin *sequestrum* "sequestration" < late Latin *sequester* "follower, trustee"] —**se·ques·tral** *adj*

se·quin /seékwin/ *n* **1.** a small round flat piece of shiny metal or plastic that is sewn onto clothing as a decoration, usually in large numbers **2.** a gold coin that was used in Venice and Turkey between the 16th and 18th centuries [Late 16C. Via French < Italian *zecchino* < *zecca* "mint" < Arabic *sikka* "coin, die for making coins"] —**se·quined** *adj*

se·quoi·a /si kwóy ə/ (*plural same* or **-as**) *n* **1.** a large redwood tree that grows in California. Latin name: *Sequoia sempervirens* or *Sequoiadendron giganteum.* **2.** same as **giant sequoia** [Mid-19C. < modern Latin, after SEQUOYA]

Se·quoi·a another spelling of **Sequoya**

Se·quoi·a Na·tion·al Park /si kwòy ə-/ park in south central California, established in 1890. It includes Mount Whitney, and is noted for its giant sequoia trees. Area: 629 sq. mi./1,629 sq. km.

Se·quoy·a /si kwóy ə/, **Se·quoi·a** (1770?–1843) Cherokee leader. He tried to integrate Native North American and European culture, and invented the Cherokee alphabet. Known as **Gist, George.** Also known as **Guess, George**

se·ra BIOL plural of **serum**

se·rac /sə raák, say-/, **sé·rac** *n* a ridge, pinnacle, or block of ice in the crevasses or slope of a glacier [Mid-19C. < Swiss French *sérac*, originally "kind of firm white cheese"]

se·ra·glio /sə rállyō, sə raályō/ (*plural* **-glios**) *n* **1.** ISLAM same as **harem** (senses 1–2) **2.** a Turkish palace, especially the Ottoman sultan's palace at Istanbul [Late 16C. < Italian *serraglio*, alteration of Turkish *saray* "palace" < Persian *sarāī* "inn"]

se·rai /sə rī/ *n* **1.** BUILDINGS same as **caravanserai** (sense 1) **2.** HIST same as **seraglio** (sense 2) [Early 17C. < Turkish *saray* (see SERAGLIO)]

se·ra·pe /sə raápee, -ráppee/, **sa·ra·pe** *n* a usually brightly colored woolen blanket worn as a cloak by some men in Mexico and Central and South America [Early 19C. < Mexican Spanish *sarape*]

ser·aph /sérrəf/ (*plural* **-aphs** or **-a·phim** /-əffim/) *n* an angel of the highest rank of nine orders of angels in the traditional Christian hierarchy [Pre-12C. Via late Latin *seraphim* (plural) < Hebrew *sĕrāpīm*] —**se·raph·ic** /sə ráffik/ *adj*

Serb /surb/ *n* a member of a Slavic people living mainly in Serbia, as well as other parts of the Balkan region [Early 19C. < Serbo-Croatian *Srb*]

Ser·bi·a /súrbee ə/ larger constituent republic of Serbia and Montenegro, in southeastern Europe. Capital: Belgrade. Population: 9,979,752 (2002). Area: 34,116 sq. mi./88,361 sq. km.

Ser·bi·a and Mon·te·ne·gro country in the Balkans, southeastern Europe, consisting of Serbia and Montenegro, two of the six republics that made up the former Federal People's Republic of Yugoslavia. Language: Serbian. Currency: Yugoslav dinar, euro. Capital: Belgrade. Population: 10,655,774 (2003). Area: 39,449 sq. mi./102,173 sq. km. Former name **Yugoslavia, Federal Republic of.** See map on next page

Serbia and Montenegro

Ser·bi·an /súrbee ən/ *n* **1.** PEOPLES **SOMEBODY FROM SERBIA** somebody who comes from Serbia **2.** LANG **DIALECT OF SERBO-CROATIAN** the Slavic language of Serbia, written in the Roman or Cyrillic alphabet and closely related to Bosnian and Croatian ■ *adj* **OF SERBIA** relating to Serbia or its language, people, or culture

Ser·bo-Cro·a·tian /sùrbō-/, **Ser·bo-Cro·at** *n* **1.** the Slavic language spoken by the Serbians and Croatians, now considered as Bosnian, Croatian, and Serbian **2.** somebody whose native language is Serbo-Croatian —**Ser·bo-Cro·a·tian** *adj*

sere[1] /seer/, **sear** *adj* dry and withered (*literary*) [Old English *sēar* "withered" < Indo-European]

SYNONYMS See ***dry***.

sere[2] /seer/ *n* the series of different communities of plants and animals that occupy a specific site and create a stable system during the process of ecological succession [Early 20C. < Latin *serere* "join, connect"] —**ser·al** *adj*

se·rein /sə rán/ *n* in the tropics, a very fine rain that falls from a clear sky at dusk [Late 19C. Via French < Latin *serum* "evening" < *serus* "late"]

ser·e·nade /sèrrə náyd, sérrə nàyd/ *n* **1.** **LOVE SONG** a song used to court somebody, traditionally sung by a man in the evening outside a woman's window, or the performance of such a song **2.** **INSTRUMENTAL COMPOSITION FOR SMALL ENSEMBLE** an instrumental work similar to a sonata, designed for evening outdoor performance by a small ensemble of musicians **3.** *regional* same as **shivaree** ■ *vti* (**-nad·ed, -nad·ing, -nades**) **PERFORM LOVE SONG** to sing or play a serenade for somebody ○ *A mockingbird serenades us every evening.* [Mid-17C. Via French *sérénade* < Italian *serenata* < *sereno* "clear, calm, serene" < Latin *serenus*] —**ser·e·nad·er** *n*

ser·e·na·ta /sèrrə naátə/ *n* **1.** a choral work popular during the 18th century, often based on a religious text and having solos and duets **2.** MUSIC same as **serenade** *n* (senses 1–2) [Mid-18C. < Italian (see SERENADE)]

ser·en·dip·i·ty /sèrrən díppətee/ *n* **1.** the accidental discovery of something pleasant, valuable, or useful **2.** a natural gift for making pleasant, valuable, or useful discoveries by accident [Mid-18C. < *The Three Princes of Serendip*, Persian story about three princes who had this ability] —**ser·en·dip·i·tous** *adj* —**ser·en·dip·i·tous·ly** *adv*

SYNONYMS See ***lucky***.

se·rene /sə réen/ *adj* **1.** without worry, stress, or disturbance **2.** bright and without clouds [15C. < Latin *serenus* "clear, calm"] —**se·rene·ly** *adv* —**se·ren·i·ty** /sə rénnətee/ *n*

Se·rene *adj* used in the titles of members of some European royal families, e.g., that of Monaco ○ *His Serene Highness*

Se·ren·ge·ti Na·tion·al Park /sèrrəng gèttee-/ national park on the plains of western Tanzania. Established in 1941, it is home to many species of large mammals and other wildlife. Area: 5,695 sq. mi./14,750 sq. km.

serf /surf/ *n* **1.** an agricultural worker, especially in feudal Europe, who cultivated land belonging to a landowner, and who was bought and sold with the land **2.** a laborer legally bound to and obliged to serve a lord [15C. Via French < Latin *servus* "slave"] —**serf·dom** *n*

~~sergant~~ incorrect spelling of **sergeant**

serge /surj/ *n* a strong cloth, usually made of wool, used especially to make coats, jackets, and pants [14C. Via Old French *sarge* < Latin *serica lana* "silken wool" < *sericus* "silken" < Greek *sērikos* (see SILK)]

ser·geant /saárjənt/ *n* **1.** a noncommissioned officer of a rank above corporal in the US Army or Marine Corps, in the British or Canadian armies and air forces, or in the British Royal Marines **2.** a police officer of a rank below a lieutenant [12C. Via Old French *sergent* "servant" < Latin *servient-*, present participle of *servire* (see SERVE)] —**ser·gean·cy** *n*

ser·geant at arms (*plural* **ser·geants at arms**) *n* somebody appointed to keep order within an organization such as a legislative body or court of law, and to perform various other duties such as making arrests

ser·geant first class (*plural* **ser·geants first class**) *n* a noncommissioned officer in the US Army of a rank above staff sergeant

ser·geant fish *n* FISH **1.** same as **cobia** **2.** same as **snook**[1] [Because of the stripes on its body]

ser·geant ma·jor (*plural* **ser·geants ma·jor** or **ser·geant ma·jors**) *n* **1.** *US* **MILITARY ADMINISTRATIVE OFFICER** a title for the highest-ranking noncommissioned officer at a US Army or Marine Corps headquarters **2.** **ARMY RANK** a noncommissioned officer in the US Army or Marine Corps of a rank above master sergeant, or a noncommissioned warrant officer of the highest rank in the British Army **3.** (*plural* **ser·geant ma·jors**) FISH **LARGE TROPICAL FISH** a large damselfish ranging from blue-green to yellow in color with black vertical stripes. Native to: tropical Atlantic waters. Latin name: *Abudefduf saxatilis*.

se·ri·al /séeree əl/ *n* **1.** **STORY IN PARTS** a story that is published or broadcast in parts, normally at regular intervals **2.** PUBL **REGULAR NEWSPAPER OR MAGAZINE** a magazine or newspaper published at regular intervals, especially weekly or monthly ■ *adj* **1.** **IN SERIES** in, forming, or done repeatedly in a series **2.** **PRODUCED IN PARTS** published or broadcast in parts, usually at regular intervals **3.** COMPUT **SENDING COMPUTER INFORMATION SEQUENTIALLY** describes a form of data communication in which the individual bits that comprise each byte or character travel one after another through a single wire **4.** MUSIC **OF MUSIC WITH ALL CHROMATIC TONES** describes a method of musical composition in which all 12 chromatic tones of the octave appear in strict order with no note repeated before the sequence is completed [Mid-19C. < SERIES] —**se·ri·al·ly** *adv*

SPELLCHECK See ***cereal***.

se·ri·al·ism /séeree əlìzzəm/ *n* a method of musical composition in which all 12 chromatic tones of the octave appear in strict order with no note repeated before the sequence is completed —**se·ri·al·ist** *n*

se·ri·al·ize /séeree ə lìz/ (**-ized, -iz·ing, -iz·es**) *v* **1.** *vti* to publish or broadcast a story in parts at intervals **2.** *vt* to adapt a work to a form suitable for publishing or broadcasting as a serial —**se·ri·al·i·za·tion** /sèeree əli záysh'n/ *n*

se·ri·al kill·er *n* a murderer who kills a number of people over a period of time, especially somebody who uses the same method each time —**se·ri·al kill·ing** *n*

se·ri·al mo·nog·a·my *n* the idea or practice of having only one sexual partner at a time and entering another relationship when one comes to an end

se·ri·al num·ber *n* any of a set of identifying numbers assigned to, and usually marked on, each of a series of identical products such as television sets, cars, paper money, or computers

se·ri·al port *n* a computer socket used to connect a peripheral device such as a mouse, a keyboard, an external modem, or a monitor

se·ri·ate /sírree àyt, -it/ *adj* arranged in rows or a series [Mid-20C. < SERIES]

se·ri·a·tim /sèerree áytəm, -áttim/ *adv* one after another, or in a series [15C. < medieval Latin < Latin *series* (see SERIES)]

se·ri·ceous /sə ríshəss/ *adj* **1.** covered with small soft silky hairs **2.** having the soft smooth feel of silk (*formal*) [Late 18C. < Latin *sericus* "silken" < Greek *sērikos* (see SILK)]

ser·i·cin /sérrəssin/ *n* a gelatinous protein that binds together the filaments of a silk fiber [Mid-19C. < Latin *sericum* "silk," form of *sericus* < Greek *sērikos* (see SILK)]

ser·i·cul·ture /sérrə kùlchər/ *n* the commercial breeding of silkworms for their silk [Mid-20C. Shortening of French *sériciculture* < Latin *sericum* "silk," form of *sericus* < Greek *sērikos* (see SILK)] —**ser·i·cul·tur·al** /sèrrə kúlchərəl/ *adj*

ser·i·e·ma /sèrree éemə/ (*plural same* or **-mas**) *n* either of two large, crested, mainly ground-dwelling birds with long tails and legs. Native to: South America. Family: Cariamidae. [Mid-19C. Via Spanish < Tupi *siriema*]

se·ries /séer eez/ (*plural same*) *n* **1.** **THINGS ONE AFTER ANOTHER** a number of similar or related things coming one after another ○ *a series of lectures on modern philosophy* **2.** BROADCAST **SET OF BROADCAST PROGRAMS** a set of regularly broadcast programs, each of which is complete in itself **3.** PUBL **SIMILAR PUBLICATIONS FROM ONE ORGANIZATION** a number of books, pamphlets, or periodicals brought out by one company or organization on the same or related topics or in the same format **4.** SPORTS **SET OF GAMES BETWEEN SAME TEAMS** in some sports such as baseball and cricket, a set of games between the same teams **5.** COLLECTING **RELATED ITEMS PRODUCED AT ONE TIME** a number of related items brought out at one time, e.g., stamps or coins of different values **6.** CHEM **RELATED CHEMICALS** a group of related chemicals that are similar in structure or properties **7.** MATH **SUM OF SEQUENCE OF TERMS** in mathematics, the indicated sum of a finite or infinite sequence of terms, each term being added to those that precede it **8.** GEOL **ROCK LAYER** a succession of rock strata deposited during a particular period of geologic time **9.** ELECTRONICS **ARRANGEMENT OF ELECTRIC COMPONENTS** a set of two or more electronic components through which current flows in sequence **10.** MUSIC **SET OF 12 NOTES** a set of 12 notes, the 12 chromatic pitches of an octave, in which no pitch is repeated **11.** GRAM **TWO OR MORE COORDINATE ELEMENTS** a sequence of two or more parts in a sentence that have the same grammatical structure [Early 17C. < Latin < *serere* "join, connect"] ◇ **in series** **1.** arranged to form a series **2.** connected in an electrical circuit so that the same current flows through each component in sequence

USAGE ***Series*** can be a singular or a plural noun, depending on its meaning. When it is used to refer to a single set of things, it takes a singular verb even if it is followed by the preposition *of* and a plural noun: *A series of medical tests is planned for next week.* When ***series*** refers to two or more sets of things, it takes a plural verb: *Three series of medical tests are planned for next week.*

ORIGIN The Latin word *serere* "to join or connect," from which ***series*** is derived, is also the source of English *assert* and *insert*.

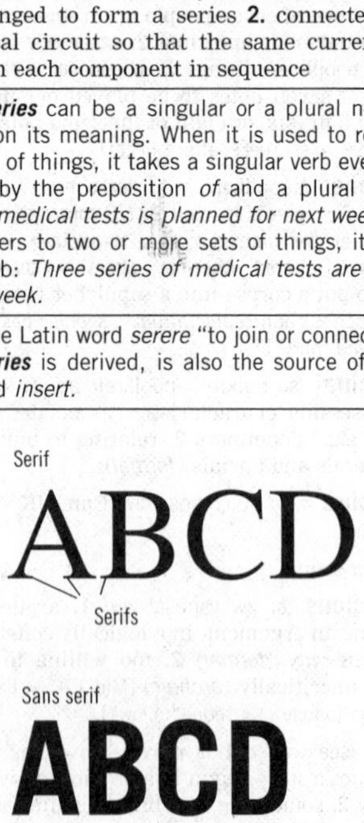

ser·if /sérrif/ *n* a short decorative line at the start or finish of a stroke in a letter [Mid-19C. Origin ?]

ser·i·graph /sérrə gràf/ *n* same as **silk-screen** *n* (sense 1) [Late 19C. < Latin *sericum* "silk," form of *sericus* < Greek *sērikos* (see SILK)] —**se·rig·ra·phy** /sə ríggrəfee/ *n*

ser·in /sérrin/ (*plural* **-ins** or *same*) *n* a yellowish or grayish finch, e.g., a canary. Native to: North Africa, Mediterranean. Genus: *Serinus*. [Mid-16C. < French, "canary"]

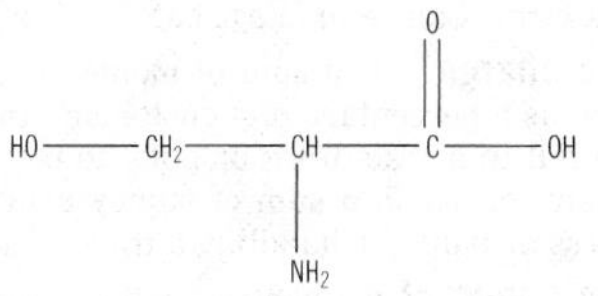

serine

ser·ine /sə reen/ *n* an amino acid produced in the hydrolysis of proteins that is a precursor of a number of biochemically important molecules. Formula: $C_3H_7O_3N$. [Late 19C. < German *Serin* < Latin *sericum* "silk," form of *sericus* < Greek *sērikos* (see SILK)]

se·rin·ga /sə ríng gə/ *n* a tree that yields rubber. Native to: Brazil. Genus: *Hevea*. [Mid-18C. Via French and Portuguese < Latin *syring-* < Greek *surigg-* "pipe, tube"]

se·ri·o·com·ic /séeree ō kómmik/, **se·ri·o·com·i·cal** /-kómmik'l/ *adj* with both serious and comic aspects [Late 18C. < SERIOUS] —**se·ri·o·com·i·cal·ly** *adv*

se·ri·ous /séeree əss/ *adj* **1. VERY BAD OR GREAT** very great, bad, dangerous, harmful, or difficult to handle **2. IMPORTANT** important or grave enough to require thought and attention ○ *a serious difference of opinion* **3. THOUGHTFUL OR THOUGHT-PROVOKING** discussing or dealing with matters in a thoughtful or thought-provoking way, as opposed to in a superficial or merely entertaining manner ○ *a serious discussion of the issues* **4. NOT LIGHTHEARTED** quiet, thoughtful, not laughing or making jokes very often, and always being sensible **5. MEANING SOMETHING LITERALLY** not joking, pretending, or exaggerating about something ○ *Do you think she's serious about helping us out?* **6. DEDICATED TO SOMETHING** showing great interest in or commitment to an endeavor, skill, or pastime ○ *a serious stamp collector* **7. LIKELY TO SUCCEED** having a possibility of success, or showing an intention to succeed ○ *serious candidates for the job* **8. SUBSTANTIAL** substantial or sustained rather than trivial or insignificant (*informal*) ○ *I've invested serious money in this venture.* [15C. Via French < late Latin *seriosus* < Latin *serius*] —**se·ri·ous·ness** *n*

se·ri·ous·ly /séeree əsslee/ *adv* **1. BADLY** in a great, bad, dangerous, harmful, or problematic way ○ *seriously ill* **2. GRAVELY** in a grave and thoughtful way, without being lighthearted or dismissive ○ *We have to take this threat seriously.* **3. TRULY** in a true or literal way, without exaggeration or deceit ○ *Do you seriously expect me to go along with this?* **4. EXTREMELY** to a great or remarkable extent (*informal*) ○ *I'm getting seriously fed up with her attitude.*

se·ri·ous-mind·ed *adj* earnest and taking an interest in matters that are weighty and important

Ser·kin /súrkin/, **Rudolf** (1903–91) Czechoslovakian-born US pianist. He was known especially for his interpretations of the classical Austro-German repertoire.

ser·mon /súrmən/ *n* **1.** a talk on a religious or moral subject given by a member of the clergy as part of a religious service **2.** a long and tedious talk, especially one telling somebody how or how not to behave [12C. Via Anglo-Norman < Latin *sermon-* "talk, conversation"] —**ser·mon·ic** /sur mónnik/ *adj*

ser·mon·ette /sùrmə nét/ *n* a short and usually unwelcome sermon or scolding

ser·mon·ize /súrmə nīz/ (**-ized, -iz·ing, -iz·es**) *vti* to give somebody a long tedious talk about how or how not to behave —**ser·mon·iz·er** *n*

Ser·mon on the Mount *n* a collection of Jesus Christ's religious and moral teachings recorded in Matthew's Gospel in the Bible, much of which Jesus Christ set out in a speech to his disciples from a hillside

sero- *prefix* serum ○ *serology* [< SERUM]

se·ro·con·vert /sèerōkən vúrt/ (**-vert·ed, -vert·ing, -verts**) *vi* to produce specific antibodies in response to the presence of an antigen such as a bacterium or virus —**se·ro·con·ver·sion** *n*

se·ro·group /séerə groop/ *n* a group of bacteria that have the same antigens. A serogroup may contain more than one serotype.

se·rol·o·gy /si róllәjee/ *n* the branch of medicine concerned with the study of blood serum and its constituents, especially its role in protecting the human body against disease —**se·ro·log·ic** /sèerə lójjik/ *adj* —**se·rol·o·gist** *n*

se·ro·neg·a·tive /sèerō néggətiv/ *adj* after a blood test, showing no immunological evidence of infection, either current or previous, with a specific bacterium, virus, or other infective agent

se·ro·pos·i·tive /sèerō pózzətiv/ *adj* after a blood test, showing immunological evidence of infection, either current or previous, with a specific bacterium, virus, or other agent

se·ro·pu·ru·lent /sèerō pyóorələnt/ *adj* consisting of a mixture of blood serum and pus

se·ro·sa /sə rṓssə, -zə/ (*plural* **-sae** /-see, -zee/ or **-sas**) *n* ANAT same as **serous membrane** [Late 19C. < modern Latin *(membrana) serosa* "serous (membrane)"]

se·ro·sta·tus /sèerō stáytəss, -státəss/ *n* somebody's condition with regard to being seropositive or seronegative

ser·o·tine /sérrətin, -tīn/ *n* a small brown bat. Native to: Europe, Asia. Genus: *Eptesicus*. [Late 18C. Via French < Latin *serotinus* "belated, late flowering, (in late Latin) in or of the evening" < *serus* "late"]

se·ro·to·ner·gic /sèrrətə núrjik/, **se·ro·to·ni·ner·gic** /sèrrə tōnə núrjik/ *adj* describes neurons or nerves that are capable of releasing serotonin as a neurotransmitter at their endings [Mid-20C. < SEROTONIN]

se·ro·to·nin /sèrrə tṓnin/ *n* a chemical derived from the amino acid tryptophan and widely distributed in tissues. It acts as a neurotransmitter, constricts blood vessels at injury sites, and may affect emotional states. Formula: $C_{10}H_{12}N_2O$. [Mid-20C. < SERO- + TONIC]

se·ro·to·ni·ner·gic *adj* ANAT same as **serotonergic**

se·ro·type /séerə tīp/ *n* same as **serovar** ■ *vt* (**-typed, -typ·ing, -types**) to analyze bacteria, in order to assign them to particular serotypes

se·rous /séerəss/ *adj* relating to, resembling, or producing serum [15C. < French *séreux* or medieval Latin *serosus*, both < Latin *serum* "whey, watery fluid"]

se·rous flu·id *n* a bodily fluid that resembles serum

se·rous mem·brane *n* a thin moist transparent membrane that lines the body cavities and surrounds the internal organs, e.g., the peritoneum that lines the abdomen

se·ro·var /séerə vaar/ *n* a group of bacteria that share a characteristic set of antigens [Late 20C. < *var*, shortening of VARIETY or VARIANT]

se·row /sérrō, sə rṓ/ (*plural* **-rows** or *same*) *n* a goat antelope with short horns, long hair, and a beard. Native to: mountains of tropical and subtropical eastern Asia. Genus: *Capricornus*. [Mid-19C. Probably < Lepcha *sā-ro*]

SERPACWA /sur pák waa/ *n* a cream containing Teflon-like compounds that, when spread on the skin, reduces or delays the effects of exposure to chemical agents such as mustard gas [Late 20C. Acronym < *skin exposure reduction paste against chemical warfare agents*]

Ser·pens /súr penz/ *n* a constellation near the celestial equator. See illustration at **constellation** [Late 17C. < Latin, "serpent"]

ser·pent /súrpənt/ *n* **1.** REPT same as **snake** *n* (sense 1) (*literary*) **2.** a sly or treacherous person **3.** a large medieval woodwind instrument shaped like a curving snake [13C. Via French < Latin *serpent-*, present participle of *serpere* "creep"]

Ser·pent *n* **1.** in the Bible, the reptile said to have tempted Eve **2.** BIBLE same as **Satan** (*literary*) **3.** ASTRON same as **Serpens**

ser·pen·tine /súrpən teen, -tīn/ *adj* **1. WINDING** winding and twisting, with many bends and curves **2. RESEMBLING SNAKE** like a snake in motion or shape (*literary*) **3. CUNNING** untrustworthy and cunning, as a snake is conventionally thought to be (*literary*) **4.** MATH **CURVING** relating to or being a complex curve that is symmetrical about the x-axis and has a convex central part ■ *n* MINERALS **GREEN OR BROWN MINERAL** a dull green or brownish mineral consisting of hydrous magnesium silicate. Use: ornamental stone. [14C. Via French < late Latin *serpentinus* < Latin *serpent-* (see SERPENT)]

Ser·pen·tine Ridge /sùrpən tīn-/ low ridge on the Moon running north to south across the eastern side of the Mare Serenitatis, or Sea of Tranquillity

ser·pul·id /súrpyəlid/ *n* a round segmented ocean worm with a crown of tentacles and a flat coiled shell, typically found on rocks and seaweed. Family: Serpulidae. [Late 19C. < modern Latin *Serpulidae* < late Latin *serpula* "small serpent"]

Ser·ra /sérrə/, **Junípero** (1713–84) Spanish-born North American missionary. He was a Franciscan who established Roman Catholic missions throughout California, beginning in San Diego in 1769. Born **Serra, Miguel José**

ser·rate /sé ràyt/ *adj also* **ser·rat·ed** /sə ráytid/ edged with notches or with projections resembling the teeth of a saw ■ *vt* (**-rat·ed, -rat·ing, -rates**) to give something a notched or toothed edge [14C. < late Latin *serratus*, past participle of *serrare* "to saw" < Latin *serra* "saw"]

ser·ra·tion /sə ráysh'n/ *n* **1. NOTCHES LIKE SAW TEETH** a row of notches and projections similar to the teeth of a saw **2. TOOTH OR NOTCH** an individual tooth or notch in a serration **3. STATE OF BEING NOTCHED** the state of having a sharp notched edge

ser·ried /sérreed/ *adj* crowded together with little space between each (*literary*) ○ *serried ranks* [Mid-17C. Past participle of obsolete *serry* "close ranks" < French *serrer* "press close together" < Latin *sera* "bolt"]

ser·ri·form /sérrə fàwrm/ *adj* having pointed projections resembling the teeth of a saw [Early 19C. < Latin *serra* "saw"]

ser·ru·late /sérryələt, -làyt/, **ser·ru·lat·ed** /sérryə làytəd/ *adj* having an edge with tiny projections resembling the teeth of a saw [Late 18C. < modern Latin *serrulatus* < Latin *serrulus* "small saw" < *serra* "saw"] —**ser·ru·la·tion** /sèrryə láysh'n/ *n*

se·rum /séerəm/ (*plural* **-rums** or **-ra** /-rə/) *n* **1.** the fluid that separates from clotted blood, similar to plasma but without clotting agents **2.** a clear watery body fluid, especially that exuded by serous membranes **3.** MED same as **antiserum** [Late 17C. < Latin, "whey, watery fluid"] —**se·rum·al** *adj*

se·rum al·bu·min *n* a protein abundant in blood serum that helps regulate the osmotic pressure of blood

se·rum glob·u·lin *n* a globular protein or mixture of proteins in the blood that contains many antibodies

se·rum hep·a·ti·tis *n* MED same as **hepatitis B**

se·rum sick·ness *n* an adverse reaction to an injection of serum, with symptoms such as swelling, fever, or a rash. It is the result of a reaction between the recipient's antibodies and antigens in the injected serum.

ser·val /súrv'l/ (*plural* **-vals** or *same*) *n* a wild cat that has a reddish brown coat with black spots, long legs, a long neck, and a relatively small head with large ears. Native to: sub-Saharan Africa. Latin name: *Felis serval*. [Late 18C. Via French < Portuguese *lobo cerval* "lynx," literally "wolf resembling a deer"]

ser·vant /súrvənt/ *n* **1.** an employee who serves somebody else, especially an employee hired to do household tasks or be a personal attendant to somebody **2.** PUBLIC ADMIN same as **public servant** [12C. < Old French, present participle of *servir* (see SERVE)]

serve /surv/ *v* (**served, serv·ing, serves**) **1.** *vti* **WORK FOR SOMEBODY** to work, or work for somebody ○ *She's decided to step down after serving on the committee for 18 years.* **2.** *vt* **PROVIDE CUSTOMERS WITH GOODS** to attend to customers, especially in a store, and provide them with goods, supplies, or services ○ *Are you being served, madam?* **3.** *vi* **BE IN ARMED FORCE** to be a member of an armed force, especially in wartime ○ *My father served in the Korean War.* **4.** *vti* **WORK AS SERVANT** to work, or work for somebody, as a domestic servant **5.** *vti* **BE USED FOR SOMETHING** to be useful for a particular purpose ○ *A box with a piece of wood on top served as a table.* ○ *It serves no purpose at all.* **6.** *vti* ASSIST SOMEBODY IN PARTICULAR WAY to assist or help somebody in a particular way, either well or badly ○ *His previous experience served him well.* **7.** *vti* HAVE PARTICULAR EFFECT to have a particular effect or result ○ *This letter will serve to remind you of our appointment.* **8.** *vti* GIVE SOMEBODY FOOD OR DRINK to bring food or drink to somebody, or give somebody a serving of a particular food ○ *Can I serve you with some potatoes?* **9.** *vt* PREPARE AND SUPPLY FOOD to present food or drink in a particular way, e.g., with a particular accompaniment, or make it available at a particular time ○ *This chicken dish is delicious served with rice and a green salad.* ○ *Ladies and gentlemen, dinner is served.* **10.** *vi* ASSIST DURING MASS OR LITURGY to assist a Roman Catholic, Anglican, or Eastern Orthodox priest in the celebration of Mass or a liturgy **11.** *vti* CRIME SPEND TIME IN PRISON to spend a particular length of time in a house of corrections ○ *served ten years for armed robbery* **12.** *vti* PUT BALL OR SHUTTLECOCK IN PLAY in racket games, to hit a ball or shuttlecock toward an opponent as a way of beginning play for a point **13.** *vt* LAW DELIVER LEGAL DOCUMENT TO SOMEBODY to deliver a legal document, especially a summons, writ, or warrant, to somebody ○ *He's been served with a writ.* **14.** *vt* WORSHIP SOMEBODY OR SOMETHING to admire or follow somebody or something worshipfully (*formal*) ○ *They serve only the icon of greed.* **15.** *vt* ZOOL COPULATE WITH FEMALE to copulate with a female to breed **16.** *vt* NAUT BIND ROPE TO PREVENT FRAYING to bind a rope with something such as fine wire or cord to keep it from wearing or fraying ■ *n* **1.** HIT THAT STARTS POINT in racket games, the shot used to begin every point ○ *It's almost impossible to return her serve.* **2.** GAME in racket games, a game in which a particular player serves ○ *He's lost his serve three times in a row.* [12C. Via French *servir* < Latin *servire* < *servus* "slave"] —**serv·a·ble** *adj* ◇ **serve somebody right** to be a deserved punishment for doing something wrong

ORIGIN The Latin word *servire* "to serve," from which ***serve*** is derived, is also the source of English *deserve*, *dessert*, *sergeant*, and *serviette* (but not of *conserve*, *observe*, *preserve*, and *reserve*, which come from the unrelated Latin *servare* "to watch, pay attention, keep").

serv·er /súrvər/ *n* **1.** SOMEBODY WHO SERVES somebody, especially a member of a wait staff, who serves food to patrons at a meal **2.** SOMEBODY WHO STARTS GAME in racket games, the player who starts a point or game by hitting the ball or shuttlecock across the net to an opponent **3.** TRAY FOR SERVING SOMETHING a tray for serving food or drinks on **4.** FOOD UTENSIL a utensil for serving food **5.** CHR ASSISTANT AT MASS OR LITURGY an assistant to a Roman Catholic, Anglican, or Eastern Orthodox priest during Mass or a liturgy **6.** COMPUT same as **file server**

serv·er farm *n* **1.** a group of networked servers that distributes tasks in a way that maximizes the efficiency of the computers and minimizes the risk of losing data **2.** E-COMMERCE same as **web server farm**

~~**servicable**~~ incorrect spelling of **serviceable**

ser·vice[1] /súrvəss/ *n* **1.** WORK DONE FOR SOMEBODY ELSE work done by somebody for somebody else as a job, duty, punishment, or favor ○ *After 25 years of service to the company, all I got was a watch.* **2.** HELPFUL ACTION an action done to help somebody or as a favor to somebody ○ *Would you do me one small service?* **3.** WORK FOR CUSTOMERS work done for the customers of a store, restaurant, hotel, or similar establishment, often with regard to whether it pleases them or not ○ *The service in this restaurant is lousy.* ○ *You can never get any service in this place!* **4.** HOUSE SERVANT'S WORK work done as a servant in a private house **5.** USE the use that can be had from a machine or piece of equipment ○ *Treat it carefully, and it'll give you years of good service.* **6.** USE OR OPERATION current use or operation ○ *The number you have dialed is not in service at this time.* **7.** MECH ENG MAINTENANCE OF MACHINERY the act of cleaning, checking, adjusting, or making minor repairs to a piece of machinery, especially a motor vehicle, to make sure that it works properly ○ *take the car in for a service* **8.** MEETING OF PUBLIC NEED a system or organization that provides people with something that they need, e.g., public transportation or a utility ○ *the tourist information service* ○ *a bus service* **9.** GOVERNMENT AGENCY a body of people who carry out work for the public benefit within an organization run by local or national government ○ *the diplomatic service* ○ *the police service* **10.** ONE OF ARMED FORCES the armed forces of a country, or one of its branches ○ *Which branch of the service is your daughter in?* **11.** FORM OF PUBLIC WORSHIP a religious ceremony usually involving specific forms for worship and prayer ○ *a memorial service* **12.** RELIG RELIGIOUS RITUAL the prescribed form for a particular act of public worship or religious ceremony ○ *the marriage service* **13.** SET OF DISHES a set of dishes and cups for use in serving a particular meal ○ *dinner service* **14.** RACKET GAMES same as **serve** **15.** SERVING OF LEGAL DOCUMENT TO SOMEBODY the delivery of a legal document such as a writ or summons **16.** NAUT MATERIAL USED TO BIND ROPE something used to bind a rope to prevent it from fraying, e.g., fine wire or cord ■ *npl* **1.** SKILLS AND WORK the work that somebody can do or does by virtue of their job, profession, or training ○ *You seem to need the services of a plumber.* ○ *I'm afraid we've decided to dispense with your services.* **2.** WORK THAT DOES NOT MAKE ANYTHING jobs and businesses that provide something for other people but do not produce tangible goods, e.g., banking and insurance **3.** THINGS PROVIDED BY GOVERNMENT things that are provided by national or local government and paid for by taxation, e.g., education, health care, and roads **4.** FACILITIES FOR TRAVELERS facilities for travelers available at intervals along a highway, e.g., stores, restaurants, toilets, and a service station ○ *There are no services at the next exit.* ■ *vt* (**-viced, -vic·ing, -vic·es**) **1.** PROVIDE SOMETHING FOR COMMUNITY to provide a community or organization with something that it needs ○ *The electric company services all nine counties.* **2.** MECH ENG CLEAN AND ADJUST MACHINERY to clean, check, adjust, and make minor repairs to a piece of machinery in order to make sure that it works properly ○ *It's time to have my car serviced.* **3.** PAY INTEREST ON DEBT to pay interest on a debt **4.** ZOOL MATE WITH FEMALE to copulate with a female (*refers to male animals*) ■ *adj* **1.** PROVIDING SERVICE NOT GOODS relating to jobs or businesses that provide services but do not manufacture goods **2.** FOR MAINTENANCE AND REPAIR providing maintenance and repair for manufactured products ○ *automotive service technicians* **3.** USED BY EMPLOYEES OR FOR DELIVERIES intended for employees or deliveries rather than for members of the public (*often used before a noun*) ○ *a service elevator* [Pre-12C. Via French < Latin *servitium* "servitude" < *servus* "slave"] —**ser·vic·er** *n* ◇ **press somebody** *or* **something into service** to use something or somebody for an unusual purpose, especially in an emergency situation ○ *At the last minute, she was pressed into service as the organist at her brother's wedding.*

ser·vice[2] /súrvəss/ *n* TREES same as **service tree** [Mid-16C. Plural of obsolete *serve* < Latin *sorbus* "service tree"]

Ser·vice /súrvəss/, **Robert W.** (1874–1958) British-born Canadian writer. He is remembered for the popular poems such as "The Shooting of Dan McGrew" (1907) that gained him the epithet "the Canadian Kipling." Full name **Service, Robert William**

> "This is the Law of the Yukon, that only the strong shall thrive; /That surely the weak shall perish, and only the Fit survive."
> [Robert W. Service, "The Law of the Yukon," *Songs of a Sourdough*; 1907]

ser·vice·a·ble /súrvəssəb'l/ *adj* **1.** MADE TO WEAR WELL suitable for everyday use and hard wear **2.** WORKING in working condition **3.** EFFECTIVE useful or effective —**ser·vice·a·ble·ness** *n* —**ser·vice·a·bly** *adv*

ser·vice ar·e·a *n* **1.** a place beside a highway where there are facilities for travelers such as a shops, cafés, toilets, and a service station **2.** the area over which a radio or television broadcasting station can transmit a satisfactory signal for reception

ser·vice·ber·ry /súrvəss bèrree/ (*plural* **-ries**) *n* **1.** a small round dark blue edible fruit from a small North American tree **2.** a commonly cultivated small tree or bush that produces serviceberries. Flowers: white, in clusters. Native to: North America. Genus: *Amelanchier*. [< SERVICE[2]]

ser·vi·ce break *n* in racket games, a game won by a player when an opponent was serving

ser·vice cap *n US* a round, flat-topped military cap with a visor. Can term **forage cap**

ser·vice charge *n* **1.** a sum of money, usually calculated as a percentage of a customer's bill, added to the bill in a restaurant or hotel to pay the staff for their service **2.** a sum of money charged by a business or bank for handling a transaction

ser·vice con·tract *n* a contract with a company or manufacturer to maintain equipment in working order at an agreed price over a fixed period

ser·vice court *n* in tennis, badminton, and similar games, the marked-out area on the opposite side of the net into which a ball or shuttlecock must be served for play to continue

ser·vice dog *n US* a dog that has been specially trained to assist people with disabilities, e.g., by opening doors and retrieving needed objects

ser·vice in·dus·try *n* an industry that provides a service rather than goods, or such industries as a whole

ser·vice learn·ing *n US* a school program that integrates citizenship values into education by involving students in community service, often as a requirement for graduation

ser·vice line *n* in racket games and volleyball, a line on a court that the server must not cross before serving

ser·vice·man /súrvəssmən/ (*plural* **-men** /-mən/) *n* **1.** a man serving in the armed forces **2.** *also* **ser·vice man** a man whose job is repairing and servicing equipment

ser·vice mark *n* a sign or symbol used by people or companies who provide a service to identify themselves and set them apart from other companies

ser·vice·mem·ber /súrvəss mèmbər/ *n* a member of the US armed forces ○ *a speech delivered to all servicemembers stationed at the Pentagon* [20C.]

ser·vice mod·ule *n* the section of an Apollo spacecraft in which parts of the propulsion and navigation systems are kept and which is jettisoned when the craft reenters the Earth's atmosphere

ser·vice·per·son /súrvəss pùrss'n/ (*plural* **-peo·ple** /-peèp'l/ or **-per·sons**) *n* **1.** MIL same as **servicemember** **2.** *also* **ser·vice per·son** somebody whose job is maintaining and servicing equipment

ser·vice pro·vid·er *n* **1.** a company that provides people and businesses with access to the Internet, usually charging a monthly fee **2.** a company that provides a specific service or services, e.g., health or life insurance

ser·vice road *n* a minor road that runs alongside a main road, especially a major highway, giving access to houses, stores, offices, and other businesses

ser·vice sta·tion *n* a place where gasoline, oil, and other requirements for motor vehicles can be bought, and often where maintenance and repair work are also done

ser·vice stripe *n* a stripe worn on the sleeve of somebody's uniform indicating the number of years that he or she has been a member of the armed forces

ser·vice tree *n* tree that has leaves consisting of numerous toothed leaflets and produces fruits (**serviceberries**) sometimes used for cider-making. Native to: central and southern Europe. Latin name: *Sorbus domestica*.

ser·vice·wom·an /súrvəss wòommən/ (*plural* **-wom·en** /-wìmmin/) *n* **1.** a woman serving in the armed forces **2.** *also* **ser·vice wom·an** a woman whose job is repairing and servicing equipment

ser·vi·ette /sùrvee ét/ *n UK* HOUSEHOLD same as **napkin** [15C. < French < *servir* (see SERVE)]

ser·vile /súrv'l, -vìl/ *adj* **1.** TOO OBEDIENT too willing to agree with somebody or to do anything, however demeaning, that somebody wants **2.** MENIAL relating to work that is considered menial or degrading ○ *servile tasks* **3.** RELATING TO SLAVERY relating to slaves or the condition of slavery [14C. < Latin *servilis* < *servus* "slave"] —**ser·vile·ly** *adv* —**ser·vile·ness** *n* —**ser·vil·i·ty** /sur vílləteе/ *n*

serv·ing /súrving/ *n* a portion of food, or of a particular type of food, served to one person

serv·ing dish *n* a large dish used to serve food at table, especially vegetables or rice

serv·ing hatch *n UK* same as **pass-through** (sense 1)

serv·ing spoon *n* a large spoon used to serve food, especially liquids such as gravy, and vegetables

ser·vi·tor /súrvitər, -tàwr/ *n* a servant or attendant (*archaic*) [14C. Via French < late Latin < Latin *servire* (see SERVE)]

ser·vi·tude /súrvi to͞od/ *n* **1. STATE OF SLAVERY** the state of being a slave **2. SUBJECTION** the state of being ruled or dominated by somebody or something **3. WORK IMPOSED AS PUNISHMENT** work imposed as a punishment for a crime **4.** LAW **RESTRICTION OR OBLIGATION ON PROPERTY** a restriction or obligation attached to a property that entitles somebody other than the owner to a specific use of it such as the right to cross it [15C. Via French < Latin *servitudo* < *servus* "slave"]

ser·vo /súrvō/ *adj* relating to, forming part of, or activated by a servomechanism ■ *n* (*plural* **-vos**) MECH ENG **1.** same as **servomechanism 2.** same as **servomotor** [Late 19C. Shortening of French *servo-moteur* "auxiliary motor" < Latin *servus* "slave"]

ser·vo·mech·a·nism /súrvō mèkə nìzzəm/ *n* a closed-circuit device in which a small input power controls a much larger power, as in a radio telescope —**ser·vo·me·chan·i·cal** /sùrvōmə kánnik'l/ *adj*

ser·vo·mo·tor /súrvō mōtər/ *n* a motor that supplies the initial power in a servomechanism

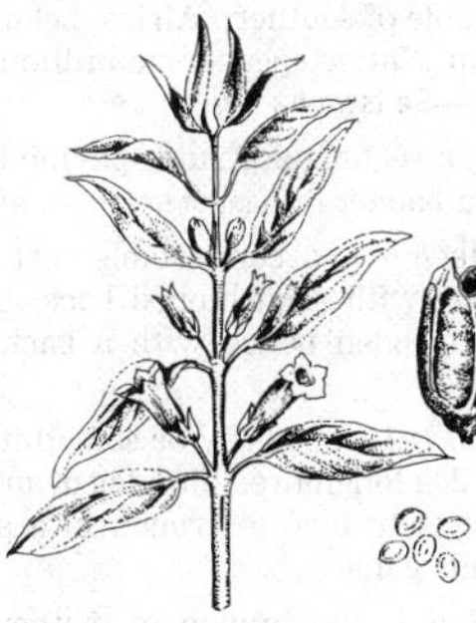

sesame

ses·a·me /séssəmee/ (*plural* **-mes** or *same*) *n* **1.** the small oval white seeds of the sesame plant. Use: cooking, oil extraction. **2.** an annual plant cultivated for its oil-rich seeds. Native to: tropical and subtropical Asia. Latin name: *Sesamum indicum*. [15C. Via Latin < Greek *sēsamon*]

ses·a·me oil *n* a strongly flavored oil from sesame seeds, widely used in East and Southeast Asian cooking

ses·a·moid /séssə mòyd/ *n* a small, roughly spherical bone lying within a tendon to assist in its mechanical action or to bear pressure ■ *adj* relating to or being various small bones or cartilages in a tendon or joint such as the knee [Late 17C. < SESAME]

Se·so·tho /sə sōtō, sə so͞o to͞o/ *n* the dialect of Sotho spoken by the Basotho people in Lesotho [Mid-19C. < Sesotho] —**Se·so·tho** *adj*

sesqui- *prefix* one and a half ○ *sesquicentennial* [< Latin < *semis* "half" + *-que* "and"]

ses·qui·cen·ten·ni·al /sèskwi sen ténnee əl/, **ses·qui·cen·ten·ar·y** /-ténnəree/ *n* (*plural* **-als;** *plural* **-ies**) **1. 150TH ANNIVERSARY** a 150th anniversary or the celebration of one **2. 150 YEARS** a period of 150 years ■ *adj* **OCCURRING EVERY 150 YEARS** relating to or happening after a period of 150 years —**ses·qui·cen·ten·ni·al·ly** *adv*

ses·qui·pe·da·lian /sèskwipə dáylee ən/, **ses·quip·e·dal** /se skwíppəd'l, sèskwi pédd'l/ (*literary*) *adj* **1. USING LONG WORDS** characterized by the use of long words **2. LONG** containing a great many letters or syllables ■ *n* **LONG WORD** a word with many letters or syllables [Early 17C. < Latin *sesquipedalis* "measuring one and one-half feet" < *sesqui-* (see SESQUI-) + *ped-* "foot"] —**ses·qui·pe·da·lian·ism** *n*

sess. *abbr* session

ses·sile /sé sīl, séss'l/ *adj* **1.** describes a leaf or flower that has no stalk but is attached directly to the stem **2.** describes an animal that is permanently attached to something rather than free-moving, e.g., a barnacle [Early 18C. < Latin *sessilis* "lying close to the ground" < *sess-*, past participle of *sedere* "sit"] —**ses·sil·i·ty** /sə síllətee/ *n*

ses·sion /sésh'n/ *n* **1. MEETING** a meeting of an official body, especially a court or legislature **2. PERIOD OF MEETING** a period during which an official body meets or does business **3. SERIES OF MEETINGS** a series of meetings of an official body **4. TEACHING PERIOD** the time of year or the time of day during which a school or university holds classes **5. PERIOD OF DOING SOMETHING** a period of time during which people are involved in an activity together **6. PERIOD OF PLAYING MUSIC** a period during which musicians play together, especially in a recording studio **7. GOVERNING BODY OF PRESBYTERIAN CONGREGATION** the governing body of a Presbyterian congregation, consisting of the minister and elders ■ **ses·sions** *npl* LAW **SITTINGS OF ENGLISH JUSTICE OF PEACE** in England, the sittings of a justice of the peace in court ■ *adj* **1. RELATING TO FREELANCE MUSICIAN** relating to or being a musician paid to play or sing on recordings in a studio but not a permanent member of a band **2. RELATING TO FREELANCE MUSIC** relating to playing or singing done by a session musician [14C. Via French < Latin *session-* "a sitting" < *sess-* (see SESSILE)] —**ses·sion·al** *adj*

ORIGIN The Latin word *sedere* "to sit," from which ***session*** is derived, is also the source of English *assess, assiduous, assize, hostage, insidious, obsess, reside, seance, sedentary, sediment, sessile, size*[1], *subsidy*, and *supersede*.

Ses·sions /sésh'nz/, **Roger** (1896–1985) US composer. He is known for his 12-tone compositions. He won two Pulitzer Prizes. Full name **Sessions, Roger Huntington**

ses·terce /séss tùrss/, **ses·ter·ti·us** /se stúrshəss, -shee əss/ (*plural* **-ti·i** /-shə, -shee ə/) *n* an ancient Roman coin, originally silver but later bronze, worth a quarter of a denarius [Late 16C. < Latin *sestertius* "two and one-half times as great" < *semis* "half" + *tertius* "third"]

ses·ter·tium /se stúrshəm, -shee əm/ (*plural* **-tia** /-shə, -shee ə/) *n* an ancient Roman unit of currency equal to 1,000 sesterces [Mid-16C. < Latin *(mille) sestertium* "(a thousand) sesterces" (see SESTERCE)]

ses·tet /se stét/ *n* a stanza or poem of six lines, especially the last six lines of a Petrarchan sonnet [Early 19C. < Italian *sestetto* < *sesto* "sixth" < Latin *sextus*]

ses·ti·na /se steénə/ *n* a poem of six six-line stanzas and a three-line envoy, with the last words of the first six lines repeated, in different order, at the ends of the other lines [Mid-19C. < Italian < *sesto* (see SESTET)]

set[1] /set/ *v* (**set, set·ting, sets**) **1.** *vt* **PLACE SOMETHING** to put somebody or something somewhere ○ *Set the books on the table.* **2.** *vt* **CAUSE SOMEBODY TO BE SOMETHING** to put somebody or something into a particular condition ○ *finally set the hostages free* **3.** *vt* **INITIATE ACTION OR PROCESS** to cause something or somebody to begin doing something, or begin to do something ○ *set my heart thumping* ○ *set to work* **4.** *vt* **APPLY FIRE** to apply something to an object or material that will cause it to burn ○ *set fire to the house* **5.** *vt* **CONCENTRATE MIND** to focus your mind on a goal or task ○ *Once he sets his mind to it, he can usually come up with a solution.* **6.** *vti* **SOLIDIFY** to become, or cause something to become, solid or hard ○ *Let the concrete set.* **7.** *vi* **BECOME PERMANENT** to become permanent or fast (*refers to dyes or colors*) **8.** *vt* **ARRANGE SOMETHING FOR USE** to arrange, place, or prepare something to be used ○ *set a trap* ○ *set the table* **9.** *vt* **ADJUST MEASURING DEVICE** to adjust a mechanical or electronic device such as a clock to a desired time, level, or position ○ *set the counter at zero* **10.** *vt* **DECIDE ON SOMETHING** to reach a decision about something such as a price or time ○ *We've set a date for the wedding.* **11.** *vt* **IMPOSE SOMETHING** to establish or impose something that determines the scope or direction of future action ○ *set a limit to government spending* ○ *set a course for home* **12.** *vt* **ESTABLISH EXAMPLE OR STANDARD** to establish something that others have to emulate, follow, or try to beat ○ *tried to set an example for her younger siblings* ○ *set a precedent* **13.** *vt* **CONSIDER AS HAVING VALUE** to consider something as having a particular value ○ *set a high value on his own work* **14.** *vt* **ASSIGN SOMETHING FOR STUDY** to make something, usually a particular book or subject, an obligatory object of study for a course or examination **15.** *vt* **INSTRUCT SOMEBODY TO DO SOMETHING** to assign a task to somebody or give somebody instructions to do something ○ *set homework for the children* ○ *set two men to guard the gate* **16.** *vt* **ARRANGE HAIR** to arrange hair by using styling products or clips **17.** *vt* **PUT BROKEN BONE IN POSITION** to put a broken bone back in its normal position so it can heal properly **18.** *vi* **HEAL** to heal up and become solid after being broken (*refers to bones*) **19.** *vt* **PROVIDE MUSIC FOR SOMETHING** to provide the music that a particular text is to be sung to ○ *set his words to music* **20.** *vt* **PORTRAY IN PARTICULAR SETTING** to portray something as happening in a particular place or time period (*usually passive*) ○ *The play is set in the 19th century.* **21.** *vt* **PUT SCENERY ON STAGE** to place scenery on a stage **22.** *vt* **ARRANGE TYPE** to arrange type for printing **23.** *vt* **PUT GEM IN SETTING** to put a gem or stone in a metal setting **24.** *vt* **ADORN** to adorn something with decorations ○ *set a gown with sequins* **25.** *vti* **POSITION SAIL** to rig a sail to catch the wind, or be rigged in this way **26.** *vi* **GO BELOW HORIZON** to move below the horizon (*refers to the Sun and Moon*) ○ *watched the sun set* **27.** *vi* **COME TO GRADUAL END** to come to a gradual end and pass into eclipse or obscurity (*literary*) ○ *a glorious writing career that has at last begun to set* **28.** *vi* **FIT WELL OR POORLY** to fit in a particular way (*refers to clothes*) ○ *The skirt sets well.* **29.** *vi* SPORTS **GET READY TO START RACE** to get into a position ready to start a race ○ *Ready, get set, go!* **30.** *vt* **LET DOUGH RISE** to place dough aside to allow it to rise **31.** *vt* **SHARPEN SOMETHING** to sharpen a blade **32.** *vt* **DISPLACE TEETH ON SAW** to bend the teeth of a saw alternately to either side of the blade **33.** *vt* **DRIVE NAIL HEAD BELOW SURFACE** to drive the head of a nail below the surface **34.** *vti* PLANTS **PRODUCE FRUIT OR SEEDS** to produce fruit or seeds after being pollinated, or be produced in this way **35.** *vt* AGRIC, GARDENING **PLANT** to plant something **36.** *vti* AGRIC **SIT OR MAKE SIT ON EGGS** to sit on eggs, or put a hen to sit on eggs, to keep them warm **37.** *vti* HUNTING **INDICATE GAME** to indicate the presence of game by turning toward it and holding that position (*refers to hunting dogs*) **38.** *vt* **BEAT IN BRIDGE** in bridge, to prevent an opponent from meeting the contract **39.** *vi* METALL **BECOME BENT** to become bent from strain **40.** *vt regional* **SIT SOMEBODY** to cause somebody to sit somewhere ○ *Set yourself here.* ■ *n* **1. CONDITION OF SOLIDITY** the condition of being solid **2. POSTURE** the particular position, angle, or posture of a part of the body, often considered suggestive of a character trait or emotion ○ *the set of his shoulders* **3. FIT OF CLOTHES** the way something hangs when worn **4. DIRECTION OF WIND OR MOVING WATER** the direction of a wind, tide, or current **5. ARRANGEMENT OF SAILS** the way the sails and other rigging are arranged on a sailboat **6. THEATRICAL SCENERY** an arrangement of scenery for a scene in a play or movie **7. PLACE WHERE SCENE IS FILMED** the place or area where the actors perform when a scene in a movie is shot **8. HAIR-STYLING TECHNIQUE** a method of styling hair that involves giving it a particular shape when wet and then drying it so that it retains that shape **9. PREFERENCE** a preference for or increased ability in a particular activity **10. BIAS INFLUENCING REACTION TO STIMULUS** the psychological state that causes a living being to react to a stimulus in a particular way **11.** PRINTING **WIDTH OF PIECE OF TYPE** the width of a piece of type **12.** PRINTING **WIDTH OF LINE OF TYPE** the width of a column or a page of type **13.** AGRIC, GARDENING **SEEDLING READY FOR PLANTING** a plant that is ready to be planted, e.g., a seedling **14.** AGRIC **CLUTCH OF EGGS** the number of eggs that a hen lays at one time **15.** METALL **DISTORTION UNDER STRESS** a distortion or bending that occurs in metal as a result of stress **16.** INDUST, ZOOL same as **sett** ■ *adj* **1. ESTABLISHED** previously established, arranged, or decided upon ○ *There's no set way of doing this.* ○ *a set menu* **2. ACCORDING TO STEREOTYPE** conforming to an established, often conventional formula ○ *rattled off a set speech* **3. ASSIGNED TO STUDY** assigned for students to study ○ *a set text* **4. READY** prepared for somebody or something, or to do something ○ *We're all set to go.* **5. DETERMINED** determined to do something ○ *We're set on the idea and won't consider changing.* [Old English *settan* "cause to sit" < Germanic, "sit"] ◇ **set in your ways**

unwilling to change your habitual ways of doing things ○ *Living alone he's become more set in his ways.*

set about *vt* to begin doing something

set against *vt* **1.** to consider something in relation to something else, or consider something as being offset by something else ○ *Set against her previous good work, this is only a minor lapse.* **2.** to make people or groups start to fight with or be hostile to people who used to be their friends ○ *The civil war set brother against brother and father against son.*

set apart *vt* **1.** to keep something for a specific use or purpose **2.** to make somebody conspicuous or different ○ *Her knowledge sets her apart.*

set aside *vt* **1. RESERVE SOMETHING** to keep something, especially time or money, for a specific purpose **2. PUT SOMETHING TO ONE SIDE** to put something to one side **3. REJECT PREVIOUS DECISION** to discard, reject, or annul a previous decision or judgment

set back *vt* **1.** to block or delay the progress of something or somebody **2.** to cost somebody a lot of money (*informal*)

set down *vt* **1. LAY SOMETHING ON HORIZONTAL SURFACE** to put something down on a surface **2. WRITE SOMETHING DOWN** to write something down, especially on paper **3. SUSPEND COMPETITOR** to take somebody such as a jockey out of competition as a punishment **4. ASSESS SOMEBODY OR SOMETHING** to judge somebody or something as being a particular thing ○ *set the whole thing down as a failure* ○ *set her down as very ambitious* **5. ATTRIBUTE SOMETHING TO CAUSE** to attribute an event or quality to a cause ○ *set his mistake down to inexperience* **6.** *US* **CAUSE SOMEBODY TO SIT** to cause or allow somebody to sit down **7.** *UK* **SCOLD SOMEBODY** to snub or rebuke somebody **8. LAND AIRCRAFT** to land an aircraft or a space shuttle

set forth *v* **1.** *vt* to state or present an argument or a set of figures in speech or writing **2.** *vi* to leave on a journey (*literary*)

set in *v* **1.** *vi* **BEGIN** to begin and become established ○ *once the winter snows set in* **2.** *vt* **ADD ON SOMETHING TO GARMENT** to add a separately made part to a garment **3.** *vi* **MOVE SHOREWARD** to move in a shoreward direction (*refers to winds, tides, or currents*)

set off *v* **1.** *vi* **START OUT ON TRIP** to start out on a journey **2.** *vt* **MAKE SOMETHING WORK** to make something such as an alarm or a firework operate or explode **3.** *vt* **MAKE SOMEBODY START DOING SOMETHING** to make somebody start doing something such as laughing, crying, or complaining ○ *When she started giggling, it set us all off too.* **4.** *vt* **START SOMETHING** to make something start happening ○ *set off a chain of events that eventually led to war* **5.** *vt* **MAKE SOMETHING LOOK ATTRACTIVE** to provide a contrast to something in a way that makes it look more attractive ○ *The new frame really sets off the painting.* **6.** *vt* ACCT **COUNTERBALANCE CREDIT** to counterbalance a credit in the accounts of one person or organization against a debit in those of another

set on *vt* **1.** to attack somebody, or encourage a person or animal to attack somebody or something **2.** to encourage somebody to do something

set out *v* **1.** *vi* **BEGIN TRIP** to begin something, especially a journey ○ *The caravan set out across the desert.* **2.** *vi* **PLAN TO DO SOMETHING** to plan or intend to do something, or take action to realize a deliberate plan or intention to do something ○ *set out to ruin the performance* **3.** *vt* **DISPLAY SOMETHING** to arrange or display something ○ *merchants setting out their wares* **4.** *vt* **LAY SOMETHING OUT IN PLAN** to lay out something in a planned way ○ *The gardens are beautifully set out.* **5.** *vt* **PRESENT SOMETHING FULLY** to present or explain something, especially in a well-planned way ○ *a book that clearly sets out the author's philosophy* **6.** *vt US* GARDENING **PUT PLANT IN DIRT** to place small plants into dirt

set to *vi* **1.** to start doing something, especially work **2.** to start fighting

set up *v* **1.** *vt* **ERECT SOMETHING** to erect something or put something in an upright or usable position ○ *set up road blocks* **2.** *vti* **PREPARE EQUIPMENT FOR EVENT** to prepare the equipment needed for an event ○ *The band is setting up on stage.* **3.** *vt* **ESTABLISH SOMETHING** to establish something, or bring something into being ○ *The charity set up a fund for the refugees.* **4.** *vt* **PLAN SOMETHING** to make necessary arrangements for something such as a meeting or conference ○ *Please set up a meeting for the five of us early next week.* **5.** *vti* **START BUSINESS** to start a business, or give somebody everything needed to start a business ○ *His family set him up in business.* **6.** *vt* **PRODUCE LOUD SOUND** to start making a loud noise or giving voice to something ○ *The spectators set up a howl of protest.* **7.** *vt* **PRESENT AS MODEL** to give prominence to something or somebody and present it, him, or her as an example to a group ○ *They've set him up as a model for the younger generation.* **8.** *vti* **CLAIM TO BE EXPERT** to claim to be something, or claim somebody to be something, especially an expert or authority in a particular area ○ *She set herself up as an expert on childcare.* **9.** *vt* **MAKE HEALTHY** to make somebody feel healthy or invigorated, especially after having been ill **10.** *vt* **CAUSE SOMEBODY TO BE BLAMED** to cause somebody to be caught and blamed for something (*informal*) ○ *claims he was set up* **11.** *vt* **GIVE DRINKS** to buy or provide an alcoholic drink for somebody (*informal*) ○ *asked the bartender to set up another two beers*

set upon *vt* to attack somebody violently

set[2] /set/ *n* **1. COLLECTION CONSIDERED AS UNIT** a collection of people or things considered together and usually having something in common **2. SOCIAL GROUP** a group of people who form a social group ○ *They were the first in our set to have kids.* **3. DEVICE RECEIVING SIGNALS** a device that receives radio or television signals **4. PART OF TENNIS MATCH** a part of a tennis match that is won when one player or couple wins a minimum of six games **5. SONGS PLAYED IN ONE SESSION** a number of songs or acts that an entertainer or band performs on a single occasion **6. NUMBER OF REPETITIONS OF EXERCISE** a number of repetitions of an exercise done at one time **7. COLLECTION OF ELEMENTS** a collection of elements in mathematics or logic, e.g., numbers or terms **8. COUPLES REQUIRED FOR DANCE** a number of couples required for a dance ○ *We need another couple to complete our set.* ■ *vi* (**set, set·ting, sets**) **DANCE FACING PARTNER** to perform a series of moves while facing another dancer [14C. Via Old French *sette* < Latin *secta* (see SECT)]

SET *abbr* E-COMMERCE Secure Electronic Transaction

se·ta /séetə/ (*plural* **-tae** /-tee/) *n* a slender, usually rigid bristle or hair [Late 18C. < Latin, "bristle"] —**se·tal** *adj*

se·ta·ceous /si táyshəss/ *adj* having bristles or made up of bristles [Mid-17C. < modern Latin *setaceus* < Latin *seta* "bristle"]

set·back /sét bàk/ *n* **1. SOMETHING THAT DELAYS PROGRESS** something that reverses or delays the progress of somebody or something **2. SHELF OR RECESS IN WALL** a place in the wall of a building where there is a shelf or recess **3.** MECH ENG **THERMOSTAT REDUCTION** an automatic adjustment made by a thermostat to reduce a temperature, e.g., in a domestic heating system at night **4.** LAW **DISTANCE FROM BUILDING TO PROPERTY LINE** the distance required by law between the edge of a building and the property line

se ten·ant /sə ténnənt, sə tə naáN/ *adj* describes two stamps that are joined together but have different values or designs ■ *n* a pair of stamps that are joined together but have different values or designs [Early 20C. < French, "holding together"]

SETI /séttee/ *n* a scientific attempt to detect or communicate with intelligent beings from beyond Earth, especially using radio signals. Full form **search for extraterrestrial intelligence**

se·tif·er·ous /sə tíffərəss/, **se·tig·er·ous** /sə tíjjərəss/ *adj* describes an organism that has bristles or projections that resemble bristles [Early 19C. < SETA]

set-in *adj* **1.** *US* built or inserted into a space in something else **2.** describes a part of a garment that is made separately and stitched in

set·line /sét līn/ *n* a fishing line suspended over a stream or between buoys with shorter hooked and baited lines hanging down from it into the water

set·off /sét àwf, -òf/ *n* **1. COUNTERBALANCE TO SOMETHING ELSE** something that compensates for something else **2. FEATURE IMPROVING APPEARANCE** a quality or feature that contrasts with something else and in that way improves its appearance **3.** PRINTING same as **offset** *n* (sense 4) **4.** ACCT **COUNTERBALANCING CLAIM** a claim brought by a debtor against a creditor that counterbalances the debt owed

Se·ton /séet'n/, **Ernest Thompson** (1860–1946) British-born US writer and illustrator. He was one of the founders of the Boy Scouts of America (1910). He is known for his stories about animals for young people such as *Wild Animals I Have Known* (1898). Born **Seton-Thompson, Ernest**

Se·ton, St. Elizabeth Ann (1774–1821) US educator and religious leader. She established a religious community, the Sisters of Charity (1809), and in 1975 became the first US-born saint of the Roman Catholic Church. Known as **Mother Seton**

se·tose /sée tōss/ *adj* covered with bristles [Mid-17C. < Latin *setosus* < *seta* "bristle"]

set phrase *n* a phrase which does not vary and whose meaning is different from the literal combination of its parts, e.g., "the apple of somebody's eye" or "make waves"

set piece *n* **1. PLANNED ACTION** a carefully planned and rehearsed performance or action, especially a military or diplomatic operation **2. FORMAL WORK OF ART** a work of art with a formal theme, undertaken to show the artist's skill **3. PIECE OF SCENERY** a piece of stage scenery that can stand unsupported

set point *n* **1.** a situation in a tennis or paddle tennis match when a player can win a set by winning the next point, or the point he or she has to win **2.** the natural weight that somebody's body will assume if provided with a balanced diet

set·screw /sét skroo/ *n* **1.** a screw that attaches one part of a mechanism to another and prevents it moving relative to the part to which it is fixed **2.** *US* a screw that regulates the tension in a spring or the opening of a valve

set square *n UK* same as **triangle** (sense 3)

Se·tswa·na /set swaanə/ *n* the Bantu language of the Tswana people of southern Africa, belonging to the Sotho group. Native speakers: 3 million. [Early 19C. < Setswana] —**Se·tswa·na** *adj*

sett /set/ *n* **1.** a rectangular stone paving block **2.** the burrow of a badger [Variant of SET[1]]

set·tee /se tée/ *n* **1.** a comfortable seat for two or more people, with a cushioned back and arms **2.** *US* a long wooden bench with a back [Early 18C. Origin ?]

set·ter /séttər/ *n* **1.** somebody or something that sets something **2.** a longhaired bird dog of any of several breeds that is trained to crouch in a set position when it finds game

set the·o·ry *n* **1.** the branch of mathematics that deals with the properties and relationships of sets **2.** the system of axioms for sets

set·ting /sétting/ *n* **1. SURROUNDINGS** the surroundings or environment in which something exists or takes place ○ *a lovely setting for the wedding* **2. OPERATIONAL LEVEL OF DEVICE** something, often represented by a mark on a dial or scale, that determines how a machine will operate, e.g., at what temperature or speed ○ *Put the stove on its highest setting.* **3. SURROUNDINGS OF JEWEL** the metal fixture into which a jewel is fixed **4. UTENSILS** the utensils, napkin, table mat, and any other items placed on a table to be used by one person during a meal **5. PERIOD OR PLACE OF STORY** the period in time or the place in which the events of a story are said to occur **6. SET FOR PERFORMANCE** the set, including props and scenery, where actors perform for a movie or play **7. MUSIC FOR POEM** the music composed for a text such as a poem or hymn **8. CLUTCH OF EGGS** a batch of eggs in a bird's nest, especially a hen's

set·ting cir·cle *n* a scale on the mounting of an equatorial telescope, used to show right ascension or declination

set·tle /sett'l/ *v* (**-tled, -tling, -tles**) **1.** *vti* **DECIDE ON SOMETHING** to come to a decision or agreement about something, usually so that further arrangements can be made ○ *That's settled then.* ○ *Can we settle on a date for the meeting first?* **2.** *vti* **SOLVE** to solve a problem or end a dispute **3.** *vti* **MAKE OR BECOME RESIDENT** to become a resident of a place, or cause somebody to become a resident of a place ○ *Her family settled in Minnesota in the 1890s.* **4.** *vt* **COLONIZE PLACE** to populate an area with permanent residents **5.** *vti* **STOP FLOATING** to stop floating and sink to the bottom or the ground, or cause something to do so ○ *waited for the dust to settle before opening their eyes* **6.** *vti* **PAY WHAT IS OWED** to pay a bill, debt, or claim ○ *She* *settled the lunch bill and left the restaurant.* ○ *Our client settled up with us yesterday.* **7.** *vi* **MOVE DOWNWARD** to move downward and spread over something ○ *A blanket of mist settled over the field.* **8.** *vi* **SUBSIDE** to sink slowly to a lower level ○ *Cracks sometimes appear in a new building as the foundations settle.* **9.** *vi* **STOP MOVING** to stop moving and come to rest somewhere **10.** *vti* **MAKE OR BECOME CLEAR** to cause a cloudy liquid to become clear after a sediment has sunk to the bottom, or become clear in this way **11.** *vti* **END LEGAL DISPUTE** to end a legal dispute by mutual agreement out of court **12.** *vti* **MAKE OR BECOME CALM** to become calm, quiet, or stable, or cause somebody or something to become calm, quiet, or stable **13.** *vt* **PUT DETAILS IN ORDER** to put all the details of a piece of business in order or into a desired arrangement ○ *settle your affairs* **14.** *vti* **MAKE SOMEBODY COMFORTABLE** to make somebody feel comfortable in a particular position, or get yourself into a position where you feel comfortable ○ *Father settled back in his chair and sighed.* **15.** *vt* **PUT SOMETHING IN PLACE** to put something in a place firmly or permanently **16.** *vti* **ESTABLISH OR BECOME ESTABLISHED** to establish somebody in a place, occupation, or way of life, or become established in this way **17.** *vt* **COMPACT SOMETHING FIRMLY** to press something such as loose soil down and make it firm **18.** *vt* LAW **ASSIGN PROPERTY** to give something, especially property or money, to somebody legally and formally ○ *settled her with a substantial inheritance* **19.** *vti* VET **IMPREGNATE OR BE IMPREGNATED** to make an animal pregnant, or become pregnant ■ *n* **LONG WOODEN SEAT WITH HIGH BACK** a long wooden seat with a high back, and often with storage space inside the box-shaped seat [Old English *setlan* < *setl* "chair, bench" < Indo-European, "sit"] —**set·tle·a·ble** *adj*

settle down *v* **1.** *vti* **MAKE OR BECOME CALM** to become calm, quiet, or orderly, or cause somebody or something to become calm, quiet, or orderly **2.** *vi* **LIVE ORDERLY LIFE** to begin a stable, orderly, and often conventional way of life **3.** *vi* **DO SOMETHING DILIGENTLY** to begin doing something in a diligent and orderly way ○ *settled down to her morning's work*

settle for *vt* to accept or agree to something that is not ideal or exactly what was wanted

settle in *v* **1.** *vti* to adapt to a new environment, or cause somebody to adapt to a new environment ○ *settling in at a new school* **2.** *vi* to get comfortable in a place because the intention is to stay there for a long time ○ *decided to settle in for the night*

set·tle·ment /sétt'lmənt/ *n* **1.** **ACT OR STATE OF SETTLING** an act of settling, or the state of being settled **2.** **ACT OF POPULATING** the act of populating a place with permanent residents or becoming a permanent resident in a place **3.** **COLONY** a place that has recently been populated with permanent residents **4.** **OUT-OF-COURTAGREEMENT** an agreement reached without completing legal proceedings **5.** **AGREEMENT** an agreement reached after discussion or negotiation **6.** **PAYMENT** the payment of a bill, debt, or claim **7.** **SMALL COMMUNITY** a small group of dwellings or small community **8.** *UK* CONSTR **SUBSIDENCE** subsidence in a building **9.** LAW **SETTLING OF PROPERTY ON SOMEBODY** a conveyance of property to somebody or to the trustees for somebody **10.** LAW **CONVEYANCE DOCUMENT** a document recording a conveyance of property **11.** SOC WELFARE same as **settlement house**

set·tle·ment house *n* a public building in which social workers provide services to an underprivileged area, especially an urban area

set·tler /séttlər/ *n* a new resident of a place, especially a place that is unpopulated or populated by people of a different race or civilization

set·tlings /séttlingz/ *npl* solid material that has sunk to the bottom of a liquid

set·tlor /séttlər/ *n* somebody who creates a trust or settlement

set-to (*plural* **set-tos**) *n* a brief and hot-tempered argument or fight (*informal*)

Se·tú·bal /se to͝ob'l/, **Se·tú·bal** city and port in western Portugal, situated 20 mi./32 km southeast of Lisbon. Population: 104,270 (1995).

set·up /sét ùp/ *n* **1.** **ORGANIZATION OF SOMETHING** the way that something is organized or arranged **2.** **SET OF PREPARED OBJECTS FOR TASK** a set of the tools or apparatus required to perform a task, properly assembled and prepared for its performance **3.** **POSITION OF CAMERA FOR SCENE** the position of a camera at the beginning of a movie scene **4.** BEVERAGES **SET OF REQUIREMENTS FOR COCKTAIL** a glass, mixer, ice, or soda water provided to customers who provide their own liquor **5.** *US* **TABLE SETTING** a table setting for a single person **6.** *US* **STRATEGY** a planned course of action **7.** **SOMETHING DELIBERATELY MADE EASY** a task or contest that is deliberately made easy to accomplish or win (*informal*) **8.** **DISHONEST PLAN OR TRICK** something that is planned to bring about a desired result dishonestly (*informal*)

set width *n* PRINTING same as **set**[1] *n* (senses 11–12)

AKG London

Georges Seurat: portrait drawing (1890?) by Maximilien Luce

Seu·rat /sə rάa/, **Georges** (1859–91) French painter. He developed the theory and practice of pointillism, seen in works such as *A Sunday Afternoon on the Island of La Grande Jatte* 1884–86.

Seuss /sooss/, **Dr.** (1904–91) US writer and illustrator. His children's books, replete with fanciful word play and illustrated with his own drawings, include *Horton Hatches the Egg* (1940) and *The Cat in the Hat* (1957). Pseudonym of **Geisel, Theodor Seuss**

Se·van, Lake /se vάan/ largest lake in Armenia, in the north of the country, in the Caucasus Mountains. It is drained by the Razdau River. Area: 540 sq. mi./1,397 sq. km.

Se·vas·to·pol another spelling of **Sebastopol**

sev·en /sévvən/ *n* **1.** **7** the number 7 **2.** **SOMETHING WITH VALUE OF 7** something in a numbered series, e.g., a playing card, with a value of 7 ○ *the seven of clubs* ○ *to play the seven* **3.** **GROUP OF 7** a group of seven objects or people [Old English *seofon* < Indo-European] —**sev·en** *adj, pron*

sev·en dead·ly sins *npl* CHR same as **deadly sins**

sev·en·fold /sévvən fòld/ *adj* **1.** **BEING SEVEN TIMES AS MUCH** relating to something that is seven times as much as something else **2.** **CONSISTING OF SEVEN PARTS** relating to something that is made up of seven parts ■ *adv* **BY SEVEN TIMES** by seven times as much or as many

Se·ven Hills of Rome the Capitoline, Quirinal, Viminal, Esquiline, Caelian, Aventine, and Palatine hills surrounding the center of ancient Rome

sev·en seas *npl* all the oceans of the world. They are the North and South Atlantic, North and South Pacific, Arctic, Antarctic, and Indian oceans.

Sev·en Sis·ters *n* ASTRON, MYTHOL same as **Pleiades**

sev·en·teen /sèvvən téen/ *n* **1.** the number 17 **2.** a group of 17 objects or people [Old English *seofontīene* < *seofon* "seven" + - *tīene* "ten more than"] —**sev·en·teen** *adj, pron*

sev·en·teenth /sèvvən téenth/ *n* one of 17 equal parts of something —**sev·en·teenth** *adj, adv*

sev·en·teen-year lo·cust *n* a cicada that spends most of its 17 years of life as an underground nymph, living as a winged adult for only a few weeks. Native to: eastern North America. Latin name: *Magicicada septendec.*

sev·enth /sévvənth/ *n* **1.** **ONE OF 7 PARTS OF SOMETHING** one of seven equal parts of something **2.** **INTERVAL OF SEVEN NOTES** in a standard musical scale, the interval between one note and another that lies six notes above or below it. In the scale of C major, C and B form a seventh. **3.** **NOTE SEVENTH AWAY FROM ANOTHER** in a standard musical scale, a note that is a seventh away from another note **4.** MUSIC same as **seventh chord** —**sev·enth** *adj, adv*

sev·enth chord *n* a chord with a seventh note above the base note

Sev·enth-Day Ad·vent·ist *n* a member of a Protestant denomination that believes in the imminent Second Coming of Jesus Christ and observes Saturday as the Sabbath

sev·enth heav·en *n* **1.** a state of extreme happiness (*informal*) **2.** in Islamic and Talmudic belief, the highest of the seven heavens

sev·en·ti·eth /sévvəntee əth/ *n* one of 70 equal parts of something —**sev·en·ti·eth** *adj, adv*

sev·en·ty /sévvəntee/ *n* (*plural* **-ties**) **1.** **70** the number 70 **2.** **GROUP OF 70** a group of 70 objects or people ■ **sev·en·ties** *npl* **1.** **NUMBERS 70 TO 79** the numbers 70 to 79, particularly as a range of Fahrenheit temperatures ○ *in the low seventies* **2.** **YEARS FROM 70 TO 79** the years from 70 to 79 in a century **3.** **PERIOD FROM AGE 70 TO 79** the period of somebody's life from the age of 70 to 79 [Old English *hundseofontig* < *hund* (origin ?) + *seofon* "seven" + *-tig* "ten"] —**sev·en·ty** *adj, pron*

sev·en·ty-eight, **78** *n* a phonograph record designed to be played at 78 revolutions per minute, a former standard speed

sev·en-up *n* a card game in which the first person to reach seven points wins the game

Sev·en Years' War *n* a war fought from 1756 to 1763 by Prussia, assisted by British subsidies and Hanoverian troops, against France and Austria

sev·er /sévvər/ (**-ered, -er·ing, -ers**) *vti* **1.** **CUT THROUGH OR OFF** to cut through something or cut something off, or be cut through or off **2.** **BREAK OFF RELATIONSHIP** to break off a relationship or tie with somebody, or become broken off ○ *severed her relationship with him* **3.** **SEPARATE** to separate or put things or people apart, or become separated or put apart [14C. Via Anglo-Norman *severer* < Latin *separare* (see SEPARATE)] —**sev·er·a·ble** *adj*

sev·er·al /sévvərəl/ CORE MEANING: a grammatical word indicating a small number ○ (pron) *Several of the apples were bruised.*

1. *adj, pron* **FEW** a small number, though more than two or three ○ *several years later* ○ *several of the children* **2.** *adj* **VARIOUS** various or separate ○ *They all went their several ways.* **3.** *adj* LAW **SEPARATE** relating to separate persons ○ *joint and several liability* [15C. Via Anglo-Norman < medieval Latin *separalis*, < Latin *separare* (see SEPARATE)]

sev·er·al·fold /sévvərəl fòld/ *adj* **1.** **BEING SEVERAL TIMES AS MUCH** amounting to several times as much as something else **2.** **CONSISTING OF SEVERAL PARTS** relating to something that is made up of several parts ■ *adv* **BY SEVERAL TIMES** by several times as much or as many

sev·er·al·ly /sévvərəlee/ *adv* (*formal or literary*) **1.** in a separate or individual way **2.** in turn or respectively

sev·er·al·ty /sévvərəltee/ *n* *US* the state of being several or separate

sev·er·ance /sévvərənss/ *n* **1.** **ACT OF SEVERING** an act of severing, or the state of being severed **2.** *US* BUSINESS **LOSS OF EMPLOYMENT** loss of employment because of lack of available work. Can term **redundancy 3.** BUSINESS same as **severance pay 4.** LAW **ACT OF SPLITTING SOMETHING** the act or process of splitting into separate parts something that was held jointly, e.g., an estate

sev·er·ance pay *n* money paid as compensation, on the basis of length of service, to an employee whose job ceases to exist

sev·er·ance tax *n* a tax imposed by a state on natural resources such as oil or gas extracted for use in another state

se·vere /sə véer/ *adj* **1.** **HARSH** very harsh or strict ○ *a severe punishment* **2.** **DANGEROUS** extremely bad or dangerous ○ *severe injuries* **3.** **STERN** looking stern or serious **4.** **EXTREMELY UNPLEASANT** causing great discomfort by being extreme ○ *a severe frost* **5.** **DIFFICULT** difficult to do or endure ○ *severe hardship* **6.** **EXACTING** having standards or other criteria that are difficult to meet ○ *a severe test* **7.** **PLAIN** plain or austere in style, with little or no decoration ○ *severe clothing* [Mid-16C. < Latin *severus* "serious"] —**se·vere·ly** *adv* —**se·vere·ness** *n*

Se·ve·ri·ni /sèvvə réenee/, **Gino** (1883–1966) Italian artist. One of the founders of futurism, his painting shows strong cubist influences, as in *Dynamic Hieroglyphic of the Bal Tabarin* (1912).

se·ver·i·ty /sə vérrətee/ *n* **1.** STATE OR EXTENT OF BADNESS the state of being very bad, or the extent to which something is bad **2.** STRICTNESS OR STERNNESS the state of being very strict or stern **3.** PLAINNESS the plainness or austerity of something such as a building or style of dress **4.** (*plural* **se·ver·i·ties**) HARSH ACT OR CRITICISM an instance of harsh treatment or censure

Sev·ern /sévvərn/ **1.** longest river in Britain, rising in Wales and flowing into the Bristol Channel. Its estuary is crossed by two suspension bridges. Length: 220 mi./354 km. **2.** river that originates in lakes in western Ontario, Canada, and flows northeast into Hudson Bay. Length: 610 mi./982 km.

Se·ver·sky ➧ **de Seversky, Alexander Procofieff**

Se·ve·rus /sə veérəss/, **Lucius Septimus** (146–211) North African-born Roman emperor. As emperor (193–211), he was noted for his civil, judicial, and military reforms and his military expeditions to maintain his control of the Roman Empire.

Se·ve·so /se váyzō/ town situated near Milan, in northern Italy. It was the scene of an industrial accident in 1976, when the poisonous gas dioxin escaped into the atmosphere.

se·vi·che *n* FOOD another spelling of **ceviche**

Se·ville /sə víl/ city and river port in the autonomous region of Andalusia, southwestern Spain. Population: 704,114 (2002).

Se·ville or·ange *n UK* same as **bitter orange**

~~**sevral**~~ incorrect spelling of **several**

Sè·vres /sévvrə/ *n* a highly decorated French porcelain [Mid-18C. After a suburb of Paris, France (formerly a separate town)]

sew /sō/ (**sewed, sewn** /sōn/ or **sewed, sew·ing, sews**) *vti* to join things or repair or make something by using a needle to pass thread repeatedly through material [Old English *siowan* < Indo-European] —**sew·a·ble** *adj*

SPELLCHECK sew, **so**, or **sow**? Do not confuse the spelling of ***sew***, ***so***, and ***sow***, which sound similar. Both ***sew*** and ***sow*** are verbs: ***sew*** means "to join things or repair or make something using a needle and thread" and ***sow*** means "plant seed." ***So*** is an adverb or conjunction introducing a reason, consequence, etc.: *Put your coat on so that you won't get cold. He asked me outright, so I had to tell him.* ***So*** is also used in numerous fixed phrases, as in *office equipment, stationery, and so on; so many things to do; so be it; so what?*

sew up *vt* to finish a business deal or other endeavor successfully

sew·age /sóo ij/ *n* human and domestic waste matter from buildings, especially houses, that is carried away through sewers [Mid-19C. < SEWER[1]]

sew·age farm *n UK* same as **sewage plant**

sew·age plant *n* a place where sewage is treated to make it nontoxic, and especially to make it into manure

Sew·all /sóo əl/, **Samuel** (1652–1730) British-born US judge. He was a primary judge in the witchcraft trial in Salem, Massachusetts (1692). In 1697 he confessed his error, and in 1700 he wrote one of the earliest antislavery tracts. His diary remains a revealing picture of his times.

> "The Numerousness of Slaves at this day in the Province, and the Uneasiness of them under their Slavery, hath put many upon thinking whether the Foundation of it be firmly and well laid...all Men...have equal Right unto Liberty, and all other outward Comforts of Life."
> [Samuel Sewall, *The Selling of Joseph*; 1700]

Sew·ard /sóo ərd/, **William H.** (1801–72) US secretary of state (1861–69). Serving under presidents Abraham Lincoln and Andrew Johnson, he negotiated foreign policy during the Civil War, and in 1867 purchased Alaska from Russia for $7.2 million, an act widely derided at the time as "Seward's folly." Full name **Seward, William Henry**

> "I know, and all the world knows, that revolutions never go backward."
> [William H. Seward, *Speech, Rochester*; October 1858]

Sew·ard Pen·in·su·la peninsula in western Alaska projecting into the Bering Sea. Length: 180 mi./290 km.

Sew·ell /sóo əl/, **Anna** (1820–78) British writer. Her only book, *Black Beauty* (1877), was written to advocate humane treatment of animals and became a children's classic.

se·wel·lel /sə wéləl/ *n* ZOOL same as **mountain beaver** [Early 19C. < Chinook *šwalál* "robe made of mountain beaver skin"]

sew·er[1] /sóo ər/ *n* a pipe or drain, usually underground, that carries away waste or rainwater [15C. Via Anglo-Norman *sever* < Vulgar Latin *exaquare* "remove water" < Latin *ex-* "out" + *aqua* "water"]

sew·er[2] /sóo ər/ *n* a medieval servant who served meals [14C. < Anglo-Norman *asseour* < French *asseoir* "place a seat for" < Latin *sedere* "sit"]

sew·er[3] /sō ər/ *n* somebody or something that sews [14C. < SEW]

sew·er·age /sóo ərij/ *n* **1.** a system of sewers **2.** the removal of waste by means of sewers **3.** INDUST same as **sewage**

sew·ing /sō ing/ *n* **1.** the act or work of using a needle and thread to join or repair material **2.** a piece of material that somebody is sewing

sew·ing cir·cle *n* a group of people who meet regularly to sew items, often for charity

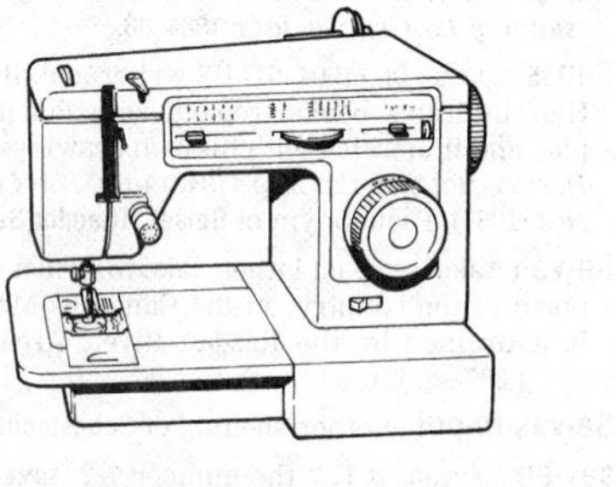

sewing machine

sew·ing ma·chine *n* a machine for sewing material

sewn HANDICRAFT past participle of **sew**

sex /seks/ *n* **1.** same as **sexual intercourse 2.** SEXUAL BEHAVIOR sexual activity, or behavior leading to it **3.** MALE OR FEMALE GENDER either of the two reproductive categories, male or female, of animals and plants **4.** ANAT same as **genitals** (*literary*) **5.** BIOL REPRODUCTIVE CHARACTERISTICS the set of characteristics that determine whether the reproductive role of an animal or plant is male or female ■ *adj* OF SEX relating to sexual matters or to the sexes ■ *vt* (**sexed, sex·ing, sex·es**) DETERMINE SEX OF SOMETHING to determine the sex of an animal or plant [14C. Directly or via French < Latin *sexus*]

USAGE See *gender*.

sex up *v* **1.** *vti US* SEXUALLY AROUSE to arouse somebody sexually, or become aroused **2.** *vt US* MAKE SOMEBODY OR SOMETHING APPEALING to make somebody or something more appealing or stimulating, especially sexually **3.** *vt* MAKE SOMETHING INTERESTING to make changes to something such as a piece of writing or artistic production so that it appears more interesting, exciting, or significant than before (*slang*) ○ *the report had been sexed-up for the media*

sex- *prefix* six ○ *sexennial* [< Latin *sex* < Indo-European]

sex·a·ge·nar·i·an /sèksəjə nérree ən/, **sex·ag·e·nar·y** /sek sájjə nèrree/ *n* somebody aged between 60 and 69 —**sex·a·ge·nar·i·an** *adj*

Sex·a·ges·i·ma /sèksə jéssimə/ *n* in the Christian calendar, the second Sunday before Lent, eight weeks before Easter [14C. < ecclesiastical Latin < Latin *sexagesimus* (see SEXAGESIMAL)]

sex·a·ges·i·mal /sèksə jéssim'l/ *adj* relating to or based on the number 60 ■ *n* a fraction in which the denominator is a power of 60 [Late 17C. < Latin *sexagesimus* "sixtieth" < *sexaginta* "sixty"]

sex ap·peal *n* **1.** the quality of being sexually attractive **2.** *US* attractiveness in general ○ *Their new product has real sex appeal.*

sex·a·va·lent /sèksə váylənt/ *adj* CHEM same as **hexavalent**

sex cell *n* GENETICS same as **gamete**

sex·cen·te·nar·y /sèk sen ténnəree, sek sént'n èrree/ *adj* **1.** OF 600 relating to the number 600 or a period of 600 years **2.** OF 600TH ANNIVERSARY relating to a 600th anniversary ■ *n* (*plural* **-ies**) 600TH ANNIVERSARY a 600th anniversary, or the celebration of one

sex change *n* an operation with accompanying hormonal treatment that changes somebody's physical characteristics from those of one sex to those of the other

sex chro·ma·tin *n* GENETICS same as **Barr body**

sex chro·mo·some *n* a chromosome that determines the sex of an organism, e.g., the X and Y chromosomes in human beings and other mammals. In each cell nucleus, a male mammal has one X and one Y chromosome, and a female has two X chromosomes.

sex·duc·tion /seks dúksh'n/ *n* the transfer of a fragment of chromosome from one bacterial cell to another by its incorporation into a special DNA particle (**plasmid**) that initiates sexual conjugation between the cells [Mid-20C. < SEX + TRANSDUCTION]

sexed /sekst/ *adj* **1.** having a particular degree of interest in sex ○ *highly sexed* **2.** possessing sexual characteristics

sex·en·ni·al /sek sénnee əl/ *adj* happening every six years or over a period of six years ■ *n* something that happens every six years or over a period of six years [Mid-17C. < Latin *sexennium* "period of six years" < *sex* "six" + *annus* "year"] —**sex·en·ni·al·ly** *adv*

sex fac·tor *n* a genetic element found in some bacteria that enables the cell to put out a fine tube to another bacterial cell and transfer some of its genetic material

sex gland *n* ANAT same as **gonad**

sex hor·mone *n* a hormone that affects the development of the reproductive organs and sexual characteristics

sex in·dus·try *n* prostitution or the provision of sexual services considered as a business or an area of employment (*often used euphemistically*)

sex·ism /sék sìzzəm/ *n* **1.** discrimination against women or men because of their sex **2.** the tendency to treat people as cultural stereotypes of their sex

sex·ist /séksist/ *adj* **1.** BELIEVING ONE SEX IS INFERIOR believing that one sex is inferior to the other in a variety of attributes ○ *sexist coworkers* **2.** OF BELIEF IN ONE SEX'S INFERIORITY resulting from or relating to the belief that one sex is inferior to the other in a variety of attributes ○ *a sexist employment policy* ■ *n* SOMEBODY SEXIST somebody who believes that one sex is inferior to the other

sex·i·va·lent /sèksi váylənt/ *adj* CHEM same as **hexavalent**

sex kit·ten *n* an offensive term for a young woman perceived as sexually appealing

sex·less /séksləss/ *adj* **1.** WITHOUT SEXUAL ACTIVITY living without sexual intercourse or interest in sex **2.** NOT SEXY sexually unattractive **3.** WITHOUT SEXUAL CHARACTERISTICS describes an animal or plant that has no, or no obvious, sexual characteristics —**sex·less·ly** *adv* —**sex·less·ness** *n*

sex-lim·i·ted *adj* describes genetically inherited traits or conditions that appear in one sex only, although the genes themselves may be found in either sex

sex-linked *adj* relating to a gene located on a sex chromosome, typically the X chromosome, or to inheritance determined by such a gene —**sex-link·age** *n*

sex ob·ject *n* somebody treated or seen as worthy of notice solely because of characteristics perceived as sexually appealing

sex of·fend·er *n* somebody who has committed a crime involving a sexual act

sex·ol·o·gy /sek sólləjee/ *n* the study of human sexual behavior —**sex·o·log·i·cal** /sèksə lójjik'l/ *adj* —**sex·ol·o·gist** *n*

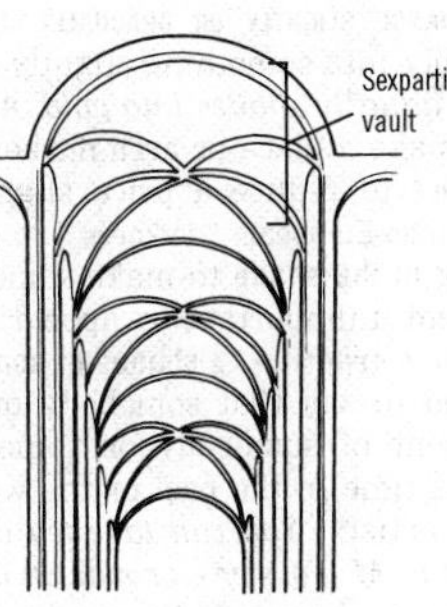

sexpartite

sex·par·tite /seks paár tīt/ *adj* **1.** divided into or made up of six parts ○ *a sexpartite vault* **2.** involving six participants [Mid-18C. < SEX-]

sex·ploi·ta·tion /sèks ploy táysh'n/ *n* the deliberate use of sexual material to make a product, especially a movie, commercially successful [Mid-20C. Blend of SEX + EXPLOITATION]

sex·pot /séks pòt/ *n* an offensive term for a woman who appears to radiate sexuality

sex role *n* a set of behaviors characteristic of or expected of members of one sex or the other

sex se·lec·tion *n* sex determination before conception by separating spermatozoa carrying Y chromosomes from those carrying X chromosomes

sex shop *n* a shop that sells items intended to aid sexual arousal or add to the pleasure of sexual intercourse

sex-starved *adj* frustrated by an absence of sexual activity

sex sym·bol *n* somebody whose fame is linked to a widely perceived sex appeal

sext /sekst/ *n* in the Roman Catholic Church, the fourth of the seven separate hours (**canonical hours**) that are set aside for prayer each day. This was originally the sixth hour of the day, midday. [14C. < Latin *sexta (hora)* "sixth (hour)"]

Sex·tans /sék stànz/ *n* a faint constellation near the celestial equator. See illustration at **constellation**

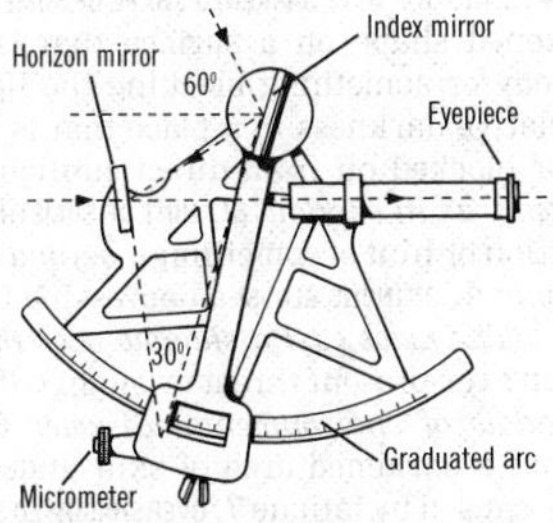

sextant

sex·tant /sékstənt/ *n* a navigational instrument incorporating a telescope and an angular scale that is used to work out latitude and longitude. An astronomical object is viewed through the telescope and its angular distance above the horizon is read off the scale. The data is then used to calculate the viewer's position. [Late 16C. < Latin *sextant-* "sixth part (of a circle)" (from the arc on which the scale is marked) < *sextus* "sixth"]

sex·tet /sek stét/, **sex·tette** *n* **1.** a group of six musicians or singers, or a piece of music composed for them **2.** any group of six people or things [Mid-19C. Alteration of SESTET after Latin *sex* "six"]

sex ther·a·py *n* the treatment of sexual problems through counseling and psychotherapy —**sex ther·a·pist** *n*

sex·tile /sékst'l, -stīl/ *n* **1.** STATISTICAL DIVISION any of the six equal groups into which a statistical sample can be divided **2.** STATISTICAL VALUE any of the five statistical values that divide a frequency distribution into six parts, with each containing a sixth of the sample population **3.** ANGLE BETWEEN PLANETS a position of two astronomical objects in which they are 60° apart as viewed from Earth [Mid-16C. < Latin *sextilis* < *sextus* "sixth"] —**sex·tile** *adj*

sex·til·lion /sek stíllyən/ (*plural* **-lions** or *same*) *n* **1.** the number equal to 10^{21}, written as 1 followed by 21 zeros **2.** *UK* the number equal to 10^{36}, written as 1 followed by 36 zeros (*dated*) [Late 17C. < French < Latin *sex* "six," after MILLION] —**sex·til·lion** *adj, pron* —**sex·til·lionth** *n, adj*

sex·to·dec·i·mo /sèkstō déssi mō/ (*plural* **-mos**) *n* a size of book page traditionally created by folding a single sheet of standard-sized printing paper four times, giving 16 leaves or 32 pages [Mid-17C. < Latin *sexto decimo*, form of *sextus decimus* "sixteenth"]

sex·ton /sékstən/ *n* the caretaker of a church and its graveyard whose duties often include ringing the bell and digging graves [14C. Via Anglo-Norman *segerstein* < medieval Latin *sacristanus* (see SACRISTAN)]

Sex·ton /sékstən/, **Anne** (1928–74) US poet. Much of her intense poetry dealt with the psychiatric disorder that led to her suicide. Born **Anne Harvey**

> "I'm no more a woman/than Christ was a man."
> [Anne Sexton, *Consorting with Angels*; February 1963]

sex tour·ism *n* travel undertaken or organized to take advantage of the relatively lax laws on prostitution and sexual activities in some countries —**sex tour·ist** *n*

sex·tu·ple /sek sto͝op'l, sek stúpp'l, sék stùpp'l/ *n* NUMBER SIX TIMES ANOTHER a number or quantity that is six times another number or quantity ■ *adj* **1.** BEING SIX TIMES ANOTHER relating to or being a number or quantity that is six times greater than another number or quantity **2.** CONSISTING OF SIX PARTS made up of six parts or members **3.** MUSIC HAVING SIX BEATS TO BAR describes a time or rhythm in which there are six beats to the bar ■ *vti* (**-pled, -pling, -ples**) MULTIPLY BY SIX to multiply something by six, or be multiplied by six [Early 17C. < medieval Latin *sextuplus* < Latin *sex* "six"]

sex·tup·let /sek stúpplət, -sto͝oplət, sék stùpplət/ *n* **1.** ONE OF SIX OFFSPRING BORN TOGETHER one of six babies or young animals born in a single birth **2.** GROUP OF SIX a group of six things **3.** MUSIC GROUP OF SIX NOTES in music, a group of six notes played in a time normally given to four [Mid-19C. < SEXTUPLE, after TRIPLET]

sex·tu·pli·cate /sek sto͝oplikət, -stúpplikət/ *n* SET OF SIX THINGS a set of six things, especially identical copies ■ *adj* BEING SIX TIMES ANOTHER relating to or being a number or quantity that is six times greater than another number or quantity ■ *v* (**-cat·ed, -cat·ing, -cates**) **1.** *vti* MULTIPLY BY SIX to multiply something by six, or be multiplied by six **2.** *vt* COPY SOMETHING SIX TIMES to make six copies of something [Mid-17C. < medieval Latin *sextuplicat-*, past participle of *sextuplicare* "increase sixfold" < *sextuplus* (see SEXTUPLE)]

sex-typed *adj* intended for or conventionally perceived as appropriate for one sex and not the other —**sex-typ·ing** *n*

sex·u·al /sékshoo əl, séksh'l/ *adj* **1.** OF SEX relating to sex, sexuality, or the sexual organs ○ *a sexual disease* **2.** RELATING TO EITHER SEX relating to the two sexes or to either of them ○ *sexual differences* **3.** BIOL INVOLVING REPRODUCTIVE UNION relating to the union of male and female gametes in reproduction [Mid-17C. < late Latin *sexualis* < Latin *sexus* "sex"] —**sex·u·al·ly** *adv*

sex·u·al as·sault *n* an incident that involves sexual contact that is forced on somebody

sex·u·al di·mor·phism *n* the existence of differences in the appearance of the male and female of a species

sex·u·al ha·rass·ment *n* unwanted sex-related behavior toward somebody, e.g., touching somebody or making suggestive remarks, especially by somebody with authority toward a subordinate

sex·u·al in·ter·course *n* an act carried out for reproduction or pleasure involving penetration, especially one in which a man inserts his erect penis into a woman's vagina

sex·u·al·i·ty /sèkshoo állətee/ *n* **1.** STATE OF BEING SEXUAL the state of being sexual **2.** INVOLVEMENT IN SEXUAL ACTIVITY involvement or interest in sexual activity **3.** SEXUAL APPEAL sexual appeal or potency **4.** same as **sexual orientation**

sex·u·al·ize /sékshoo ə līz/ (**-ized, -iz·ing, -iz·es**) *vt* to impose a sexual interpretation or perception on something or somebody

sex·u·al·ly trans·mit·ted in·fec·tion, sex·u·al·ly trans·mit·ted dis·ease *n* a disease that is normally passed from one person to another through sexual activity, e.g., syphilis or genital herpes

sex·u·al o·ri·en·ta·tion *n* the direction of somebody's sexual desire, toward people of the opposite sex, people of the same sex, or people of both sexes

sex·u·al re·la·tions *npl* same as **sexual intercourse**

sex·u·al re·pro·duc·tion *n* reproduction that involves the union of male and female gametes, each contributing half of the genetic makeup of the resulting zygote

sex·u·al se·lec·tion *n* the choice by a female animal of a mate on the basis of a characteristic such as a bird song or bright plumage

sex·va·lent /sèks váylənt/ *adj* CHEM same as **hexavalent**

sex work *n* the work of somebody in one of the sex industries such as pornography or prostitution —**sex work·er** *n*

sex·y /séksee/ (**-i·er, -i·est**) *adj* **1.** AROUSING DESIRE arousing or intended to arouse sexual desire **2.** AROUSED sexually aroused **3.** APPEALING appealing because of being new, interesting, or trendy (*informal*) ○ *a sexy new slogan* —**sex·i·ly** *adv* —**sex·i·ness** *n*

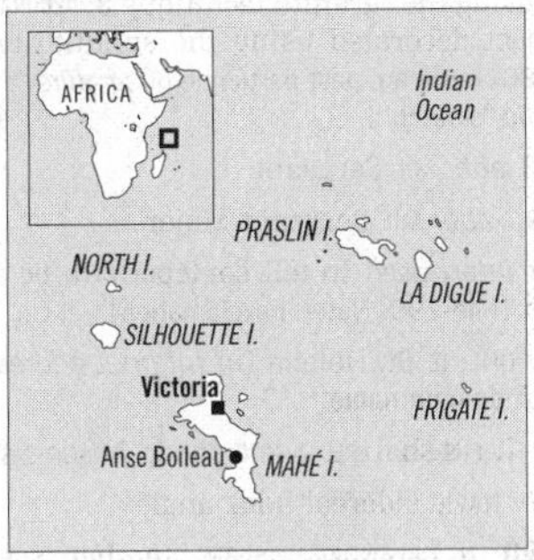

Seychelles

Sey·chelles /say shélz/ island country in the western Indian Ocean. It contains four main islands and many islets. It became an independent member of the British Commonwealth in 1976. Language: Creole, English, French. Currency: Seychelles rupee. Capital: Victoria. Population: 79,715 (2001). Area: 175 sq. mi./454 sq. km. Official name **Republic of Seychelles** —**Sey·chell·ois** /sày shel waá/ *adj, n*

Sey·fert gal·ax·y /seéfərt-, sīfərt-/ *n* a small spiral galaxy that varies in brightness and emits radio waves and X-rays [Mid-20C. After Carl K. *Seyfert* (1911–60), US astronomer]

Sey·mour /seé màwr/, **Jane** (1509?–37) queen of England and Ireland. She was the third wife of Henry VIII of England, and died shortly after giving birth to Edward VI, Henry's only male heir.

Se·zer /sé zer/, **Ahmet Necdet** (*b.* 1941) president of Turkey. A former chief justice of the Constitutional Court (1998–2000), he became president in 2000.

sf *abbr* **1.** LITERAT science fiction **2.** MUSIC sforzando

SF *abbr* **1.** BASEBALL sacrifice fly **2.** LITERAT science fiction **3.** FIN sinking fund

Sfax /sfaks/ port and capital city of Safaqis Governorate, east-central Tunisia. Population: 230,900 (1994).

SFC *abbr US* MIL Sergeant First Class

sfer·ics *npl* METEOROL another spelling of **spherics**

sfor·zan·do /sfawrt saándō/ *adv* with a sudden strong accent (*used as a musical direction*) ■ *n* (*plural* **-dos** or **-di** /-dee/) a note or chord that is to be played with a sudden strong accent, or a symbol indicating this [Early 19C. < Italian < *sforzare* "use force" < Latin *fortis* "strong"] —**sfor·zan·do** *adj*

sfu·ma·to /sfoo maátō/ *n* the gradual blending of one area of color into another without a sharp outline [Mid-19C. < Italian, past participle of *sfumare* "tone down," < Latin *fumus* "smoke"]

sfz. *abbr* MUSIC sforzando

sg *abbr* ONLINE Singapore (*used in Internet addresses*) See table at **domain name**

Sg[1] *symbol* CHEM ELEM seaborgium

Sg[2] *abbr* BIBLE Song of Songs

SG *abbr* **1.** EDUC senior grade **2.** GRAM singular **3.** LAW solicitor general **4.** PHYS specific gravity **5.** SURG Surgeon General

S.G. *abbr* LAW **1.** Secretary General **2.** solicitor general

sgd. *abbr* signed

SGHWR *abbr* ENG steam-generating heavy-water reactor

SGM *abbr* *US* MIL Sergeant Major

SGML *n* an international standard markup system for the definition of system-independent methods of representing texts in electronic form by describing the relationship between a document's form and its structure. SGML is used widely to manage large documents that are subject to frequent revisions and need to be printed in different formats. Full form **Standard Generalized Markup Language**

SGR *abbr* ASTRON soft gamma repeater

sgraf·fi·to /zgraa feétō, skraa feétō/ (*plural* **-ti** /-tee/) *n* **1.** DECORATION TECHNIQUE a technique used to decorate ceramics or plaster walls, in which the top layer has patterns scratched into it, revealing the different-colored layer beneath **2.** DECORATION a decoration made using the sgraffito technique **3.** DECORATED OBJECT an object decorated using the sgraffito technique [Mid-18C. < Italian, past participle of *sgraffire* "to scratch" < *sgraffio* "scratch"]

Sgt., **SGT** *abbr* MIL Sergeant

Sgt. Maj. *abbr* MIL Sergeant Major

sh[1], **shh** *interj* used to tell somebody to be silent or quieter [Mid-19C. Natural exclamation]

sh[2] *abbr* ONLINE St. Helena (*in Internet addresses*) See table at **domain name**

sh. *abbr* **1.** FIN share **2.** AGRIC sheep **3.** AGRIC sheet

SHA *abbr* NAVIG sidereal hour angle

Shaa·ban *n* CALENDAR, ISLAM another spelling of **Sha'ban**

Shaan·xi /shaán sheé/ province in China bordered by Ningxia Hui, Nei Monggol, Shanxi, Henan, Hubei, Sichuan, and Gansu. Capital: Xi'an. Population: 35,430,000 (1997). Area: 75,598 sq. mi./195,799 sq. km.

Sha'ban /shə baán, shaa-/, **Sha·ban**, **Shaa·ban** *n* in the Islamic calendar, the eighth month of the year. See table at **calendar** [Mid-18C. < Arabic *ša'bān*]

Shab·bat /shə baát/ *n* the Jewish Sabbath, celebrated on Saturday [Mid-19C. < Hebrew *šabbāṯ* "day of rest"]

shab·by /shábbee/ (**-bi·er**, **-bi·est**) *adj* **1.** WORN AND THREADBARE worn out, frayed, or threadbare after long use **2.** WEARING WORN CLOTHES wearing worn-out clothing and perceived as being unappealing to the eye **3.** INCONSIDERATE inconsiderate and unfair ○ *won't put up with shabby treatment* **4.** INFERIOR IN QUALITY inferior in quality ○ *shabby goods* **5.** RUN DOWN poorly maintained and thus falling apart or dirty ○ *a shabby section of town* [Mid-17C. < obsolete *shab* "disreputable person" < Old English *sceabb* "scab" < Indo-European, "to scrape"] —**shab·bi·ly** *adv* —**shab·bi·ness** *n*

sha·bu /shaáboo/ *n Philippines* the recreational drug methamphetamine hydrochloride [Late 20C. < Japanese, literally "swish"]

sha·bu·sha·bu /shaáboo shaá boo/ *n* a Japanese dish in which thinly sliced beef and vegetables are cooked at table in a pot of simmering stock, then dipped into a sauce and eaten [Late 20C. < Japanese, literally "swish swish," an imitation of the sound of bubbling water]

Sha·cha·ris /shaákhriss/ *n* the Jewish morning liturgy [< Hebrew *šaḥărīṯ* "morning time"]

shack /shak/ *n* a small crude building typically made of boards or sheets of material, usually without a foundation [Late 19C. Origin ?]

shack up (**shacked up, shacking up, shacks up**) *vi* to live with a lover without being married (*informal disapproving*)

shackle (sense 3)

shack·le /shák'l/ *n* **1.** METAL BAND ON PRISONER a round metal band that can be opened or locked in order to hold the wrist or ankle of a captive, usually attached by chains in pairs or fours (*often used in the plural*) **2.** BINDER FOR ANIMAL LEGS a device used to hold together the legs of horses and other animals **3.** U-SHAPED FASTENER a U-shaped bar that is fastened with a straight pin or bolt to hold something securely **4.** RESTRAINT ON FREEDOM an oppressive restraint on something or somebody (*often used in the plural*) ○ *mental shackles* ■ *vt* (**-led, -ling, -les**) **1.** RESTRICT SOMEBODY to restrict the freedom of somebody or something ○ *felt shackled by the inflexible rules* **2.** RESTRAIN SOMEBODY WITH SHACKLES to restrain somebody or an animal using shackles **3.** SECURE SOMETHING WITH SHACKLE to connect or secure something with a shackle [Old English *sceacul* < Germanic, "fastening"] —**shack·ler** *n*

Shack·le·ton /shák'ltən/, **Sir Ernest** (1874–1922) Irish explorer. He was the leader of an expedition that almost reached the South Pole (1907–09). He was the first to cross South Georgia (1916), but died there on his fourth expedition. Full name **Shackleton, Sir Ernest Henry**

shad /shad/ (*plural* **shads** or *same*) *n* a fish similar to herring that spawns upstream in rivers. Native to: northern Atlantic. Genus: *Alosa*. [Old English *sceadd*. Origin ?]

shad·ber·ry /shád bèrree/ (*plural* **-ries**) *n* TREES same as **serviceberry** (sense 1) [Mid-19C. Because it flowers when shad appear in rivers to spawn]

shad·blow /shád blō/ *n* TREES same as **serviceberry** (sense 2) [Mid-19C. < BLOW[3]]

shad·bush /shád bo͝osh/ *n* TREES same as **serviceberry** (sense 2)

shad·chan /shaádkhən/ (*plural* **-cha·nim** /-khənim/ or **-chans**), **shad·khan** (*plural* **-kha·nim** or **-khans**) *n* a marriage broker for Jewish couples [Mid-19C. Via Yiddish *shadkhn* < medieval Hebrew *šaddĕkān* < *šiddēk* "make marriage proposals"]

shad·dock /sháddək/ *n* TREES, FOOD same as **pomelo** (senses 1–2) [Late 17C. After a 17C English ship captain named *Shaddock*]

shade /shayd/ *n* **1.** AREA OUT OF DIRECT SUNLIGHT an area of relative darkness where direct sunlight is blocked or obscured **2.** SLIGHTLY DIFFERENT COLOR a color that is a variation on a basic color, e.g., by being more or less bright or dark ○ *a pretty shade of blue* **3.** SOMETHING THAT BLOCKS LIGHT something used to block a direct light source, e.g., a lampshade **4.** WINDOW DEVICE a flexible piece of material mounted on a window that can be rolled down to block light or rolled up to admit light **5.** DARK PARTS OF PAINTING the darker areas of a painting, drawing, or photograph **6.** SMALL AMOUNT a slight degree or amount ○ *a shade too close* **7.** VARIATION a slight variation on something similar ○ *different shades of opinion* **8.** OBSCURITY a position of relative obscurity **9.** GHOST a ghost or phantom (*literary*) ■ **shades** *npl* same as **sunglasses** (*see* **sunglass**) (*informal*) ■ *v* (**shad·ed, shad·ing, shades**) **1.** *vt* PROTECT SOMETHING FROM SUNLIGHT to protect something or block it off from direct light, particularly from direct sunlight ○ *The awning shades the porch well.* **2.** *vt* DARKEN PART OF PICTURE to darken part of a drawing or picture using pencil, ink, or some other dark medium ○ *He shaded in the trees in the background.* **3.** *vi* CHANGE SLIGHTLY OR GRADUALLY to change imperceptibly into something slightly different ○ *The cream gradually shades into gold.* **4.** *vt* DARKEN SOMETHING to make a place or area darker **5.** *vt* BUSINESS REDUCE PRICE to reduce a price slightly [Old English *sceadu* < Indo-European, "darkness"] ◇ **put somebody** *or* **something in the shade** to make somebody or something seem unimportant by appearing much more special or attractive ◇ **shades of somebody** *or* **something** used to say that somebody or something is reminiscent of somebody or something else, especially a time in the past or the work of a writer or other artist ○ *You can take tea on the terrace – shades of E. M. Forster – or ride on an elephant.*

Shades /shaydz/ *npl* MYTHOL same as **underworld** (*literary*)

shade tree *n* a tree planted to provide shade

shad·fly /shád flī/ (*plural* **-flies**) *n US* INSECTS same as **mayfly** (sense 1) [Early 19C. Because it appears when shad appear in rivers to spawn]

shad·ing /sháyding/ *n* **1.** an area of relatively dark tone or close lines, dots, or hatching that produces darkness or shadow in a drawing or picture **2.** a subtle difference or variation

shad·khan *n* JUDAISM another spelling of **shadchan**

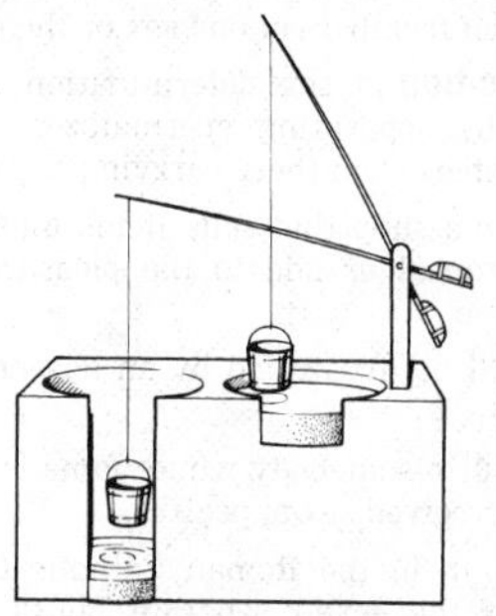

shadoof

sha·doof /shə do͞of, shaa-/, **sha·duf** *n* in ancient Egypt, a water-raising device consisting of a suspended pivoting pole with a bucket on one end and a counterweight on the other [Mid-19C. < Egyptian Arabic *šādūf*]

shad·ow /sháddō/ *n* **1.** DARKENED SHAPE OF SOMETHING IN LIGHT a darkened shape on a surface that falls behind somebody or something blocking the light **2.** DARKNESS relative darkness in a place that is being screened or blocked off from direct sunlight ○ *Part of the room was in shadow.* **3.** HINT OF SOMETHING a slight suggestion or hint of something ○ *beyond the shadow of a doubt* **4.** OMINOUS GLOOM a depressing or ominous gloom ○ *The news cast a shadow over the party.* **5.** THREAT an ever-present threat or blight ○ *living under the shadow of environmental disaster* **6.** DARK AREA UNDER EYES a darkened area of skin under the eyes, usually caused by fatigue **7.** OVERSHADOWED STATE a state in which somebody is always overshadowed by another person ○ *grew up in his brother's shadow* **8.** REGULAR COMPANION somebody who is the invariable companion of somebody else **9.** PERSON SECRETLY TRAILING ANOTHER somebody who secretly follows somebody, e.g., a detective or spy **10.** INFERIOR REMNANT a remnant of somebody or something formerly greater or more important ○ *now a shadow of her former self* **11.** COPY an imitation or copy of something ○ *the shadow of the stars in the dark lake* **12.** SHELTER something that provides protection **13.** BUSINESS SOMEBODY LEARNING BY OBSERVATION somebody who learns a job by observing the person who regularly does the job **14.** MED ATYPICAL AREA IN X-RAY an atypical area showing up on an X-ray **15.** PSYCHOANAL JUNGIAN ARCHETYPE in Jungian psychology, the archetype that represents sexual and aggressive instincts inherited from a more primitive stage of humanity ■ *vt* (**-owed, -owing, -ows**) **1.** PROTECT SOMETHING FROM LIGHT to shade something from the light ○ *Her face was shadowed by a wide-brimmed straw hat.* **2.** FOLLOW SOMEBODY to go everywhere that somebody else goes in order to watch what they are doing, especially secretly ○

The police had been shadowing him for days. **3.** BUSINESS **LEARN JOB BY FOLLOWING WORKER** to accompany and observe somebody who is doing a job in order to learn how it is done **4. REPRESENT SOMETHING VAGUELY** to represent something vaguely or in outline ■ *adj UK* POL **IN CAPACITY OF OPPOSITION COUNTERPART** describes a member of the largest opposition party who speaks on a particular area of policy and would hold a ministerial job if that party were in government ○ *the shadow cabinet* [Old English *sceaduwe*, form of *sceadu* (see SHADE)] —**shad·ow·er** *n*

SYNONYMS See *follow*.

shad·ow box *n* a shallow box consisting of a frame and a glass front in which small objects can be displayed and protected

shad·ow·box /sháddō bòks/ *vi* to practice boxing moves by sparring with an imaginary partner —**shad·ow·box·er** *n* —**shad·ow·box·ing** *n*

shad·ow dance *n* a dance performance in which the dancers' shadows are seen on a screen

shad·ow e·con·o·my (*plural* **shad·ow e·con·o·mies**) *n* ECON same as **black economy**

shad·ow·graph /sháddō gràf/ *n* **1.** an image of a shape made by casting a shadow onto a surface, e.g., by shaping the hands so that their shadow resembles the silhouette of an animal **2.** MED same as **radiograph**

shad·ow mask *n* a perforated metal sheet mounted close to the rear of the phosphor dot faceplate of a three gun color picture tube. The shadow mask is used to direct the electron beam to the desired phosphor color element.

shad·ow play *n* a theatrical performance in which the audience views a screen on which the shadows of puppets or performers are cast by a light source behind them

shad·ow price *n* the estimated price of goods or a service for which no market price exists

shad·ow sen·a·tor *n* a nonvoting representative of the District of Columbia in the Senate

shad·ow·y /sháddō ee/ (**-i·er, -i·est**) *adj* **1. FULL OF SHADOWS** full of shadows or shade **2. NOT CLEARLY SEEN** seen only vaguely **3. MYSTERIOUS** mysteriously little-known or obscure —**shad·ow·i·ness** *n*

sha·duf *n* AGRIC another spelling of **shadoof**

shad·y /sháydee/ (**-i·er, -i·est**) *adj* **1. HAVING SHADE** having little natural light, often giving shelter from harsh sunlight ○ *a shady corner of the park* **2. DISHONEST** probably dishonest or illegal ○ *shady dealings with foreign investors* **3. PROVIDING SHADE** providing shade ○ *a shady tree* —**shad·i·ly** *adv* —**shad·i·ness** *n*

SHAEF /shayf/ *abbr* MIL Supreme Headquarters Allied Expeditionary Forces

shaft /shaft/ *n* **1. LONG HANDLE** the long slender handle on various instruments and tools such as golf clubs and hammers **2. BODY OF PROJECTILE** a long narrow rod that forms the body of a spear, arrow, harpoon, or other projectile **3. POLE FOR HARNESSING HORSE** either of the two parallel bars by which an animal is harnessed to a cart or wagon **4. ROTATING ROD IN MACHINE** a rotating rod that provides motion or power for a machine **5. VERTICAL PASSAGE** a vertical passage, especially one in which an elevator travels or one that gives access to a mine **6. PASSAGE FOR VENTILATION IN BUILDING** a small passageway in a building, particularly in a wall, ceiling, or floor, to allow for air circulation **7. LIGHT BEAM** a beam of light ○ *a shaft of sunlight* **8. SHARP COMMENT** a sharp or barbed comment directed at somebody ○ *a shaft of wit* **9. HARSH TREATMENT** unkind or harsh treatment or dismissal (*informal*) ○ *His girlfriend gave him the shaft.* **10.** ARMS same as **arrow** *n* (sense 1) (*literary*) **11.** ANAT **MIDDLE OF LONG BONE** the middle part of a long bone **12.** ANAT **BODY OF PENIS** the cylindrical body of the penis **13.** ANAT **MAIN PART OF HAIR** the part of a hair that is visible above the skin **14.** ARCHIT **BODY OF COLUMN** the main body of a column, between the capital and base **15.** ARCHIT **COLUMN** a column, especially one of a pair supporting an arch **16.** BIRDS **FEATHER RIB** the central rib of a feather **17.** TREES **TRUNK** the trunk of a tree **18. UPRIGHT PART OF CROSS** the upright bar in a cross ■ *vt* (**shaft·ed, shaft·ing, shafts**) **TREAT SOMEBODY UNFAIRLY** to cheat somebody or treat somebody unfairly (*slang*) ○ *She got shafted on her book contract.* [Old English *sceaft* < Germanic]

Shaftes·bur·y /sháfts bèrree, -bəree/, **Anthony Ashley Cooper, 7th Earl of** (1801–85) British philanthropist. An influential figure of the social reform movement, he established schools for the poor and a ten-hour day for factory workers (1847).

shag[1] /shag/ *n* **1. LONG-PILED CARPET** a carpet or rug with a long thick pile **2. LONG PILE ON TEXTILE** a long rough nap or pile on a textile **3. SHREDDED TOBACCO** a strong coarse tobacco that is finely shredded **4. LAYERED HAIRCUT** a hairstyle with layers that are cut progressively shorter from base to crown **5. MATTED TANGLE OF HAIR** a rough matted tangle of hair or wool ■ *vt* (**shagged, shag·ging, shags**) **1. PROVIDE SOMETHING WITH SHAFT** to provide something such as a tool with a shaft **2. MAKE SOMETHING ROUGH** to cause something to be rough-looking and shaggy [Old English *sceacga* < Germanic]

shag[2] /shag/ (**shagged, shag·ging, shags**) *vt US* **1. RETRIEVE** to run and retrieve something **2. CATCH FLY BALLS** to chase, catch, and return fly balls in baseball practice **3. CHASE AWAY** to chase somebody or something away [Early 20C. Origin ?]

shag[3] /shag/ *n* a small crested cormorant. Native to: Europe, North Africa. Latin name: *Phalacrocorax aristotelis.* [Mid-16C. Origin ?]

shag[4] /shag/ (**shagged, shag·ging, shags**) *vti UK* an offensive term meaning to have sexual intercourse with somebody (*slang*) [Late 18C. Origin ?]

shag[5] /shag/ *n* **1. 1930S DANCE** a 1930s dance step involving hopping alternately on each foot **2. DANCE FOR COUPLES** a lively dance for couples that is similar to the swing and is popular in the southeastern United States ■ *vi* (**shagged, shag·ging, shags**) **DANCE SHAG** to dance the shag [Early 20C. Origin ?]

shag·bark /shág baàrk/, **shag·bark hick·o·ry** *n* **1. HICKORY WITH SHAGGY BARK** a hickory that has gray shaggy bark, hard wood, and bears edible nuts. Native to: eastern North America. Latin name: *Carya ovata.* **2. HICKORY NUT** the round hard-shelled sweet nut of the shagbark **3. SHAGBARK WOOD** the valuable hard light-colored wood of the shagbark

shag·gy /shággee/ (**-gi·er, -gi·est**) *adj* **1. LONG AND TANGLED** growing long and unevenly **2. HAVING COARSE LONG FIBERS** covered with or resembling coarse, long, and usually uneven hair, wool, or similar fibers **3. ROUGH NAPPED** having a rough, relatively long nap or pile **4.** *US* **DONE WITHOUT PLANNING** done in a haphazard way, with little thought or planning

shag·gy cap *n* FUNGI same as **shaggymane**

shag·gy-dog sto·ry *n* a long drawn-out absurd story or joke, often with an ending or punchline that is anticlimactic [< one such anecdote involving a shaggy dog]

shag·gy·mane /shággee màyn/ *n* a common edible mushroom with shaggy scales on its cap that contain black spores. Latin name: *Coprinus comatus.*

sha·green /shə greén/ *n* **1.** the rough skin of some sharks and rays, used as an abrasive or as leather **2.** rough untanned leather with a grainy surface, made from the hide of various animals and often dyed green [Late 17C. Via French *chagrin* "untanned leather," < Turkish *sağri* "back of a horse"]

shah /shaa/ *n* in former times, the hereditary monarch of some Southwest Asian nations, especially Iran [Mid-16C. < Persian *šāh*] —**shah·dom** *n*

Shah Ja·han /shaà jə haán/ (1592–1666) emperor of India. The fifth Mughal emperor (1628–58), he made Delhi the capital of India and built the Taj Mahal and Pearl Mosque in Agra.

Shahn /shaan/, **Ben** (1898–1969) Lithuanian-born US artist. He is known for employing bold colors and a poster style in paintings that often had political themes.

> "Fame is like a smudge on your nose. You can't see it. Other people can."
> [Ben Shahn, *Christian Science Monitor*; November 11, 1972]

shaikh *n* POL another spelling of **sheik**

shai·kha *n* POL another spelling of **sheika**

shai·tan /shī taán, shày-/ *n* in Islamic countries, an evil spirit or person [Late 17C. < SHAITAN]

Shai·tan /shī taán, shày taán/ *n* in Islamic belief, the devil [Mid-17C. Via Arabic < Hebrew *śāṭān* (see SATAN)]

shake /shayk/ *v* (**shook** /shoŏk/, **shak·en** /sháykən/, **shak·ing, shakes**) **1.** *vti* **MOVE BACK AND FORTH** to move back and forth or up and down in short quick movements, or make something or somebody move in this way ○ *I shook my coat to see if my keys were in the pockets.* **2.** *vi* **TREMBLE** to tremble uncontrollably ○ *shaking with fright* **3.** *vti* **BECOME SOMETHING BY SHAKING** to achieve a particular state by shaking, or shake something in order to achieve a particular state ○ *The door finally shook free of its hinges.* ○ *We shook the apples from the tree.* **4.** *vi* **QUAVER WITH EMOTION** to sound uncertain, nervous, angry, or distressed ○ *Her voice was shaking.* **5.** *vt* **SHOCK AND UPSET SOMEBODY** to shock and upset or disturb somebody ○ *He was badly shaken by the accident.* **6.** *vt* **MAKE SOMEBODY LESS CONFIDENT** to cause somebody to lose confidence or certainty ○ *Nothing could shake his faith.* **7.** *vti* **CLASP HANDS AS GREETING** to grasp another person's hand and move it up and down as a greeting or sign of trust **8.** *vt* **GET RID OF SOMETHING** to get rid of something undesired ○ *I can't shake this cold.* **9.** *vt* **MIX INGREDIENTS BY SHAKING** to mix ingredients together in a container by shaking the container **10.** *vt* **MOVE HEAD TO EXPRESS "NO"** to move the head from side to side in order to express disagreement, disbelief, commiseration, or sorrow **11.** *vt* **WAVE SOMETHING THREATENINGLY** to wave something in the air in a threatening way ○ *She shook her fist at them.* **12.** *vti* **RATTLE DICE BEFORE THROWING** to rattle a dice in the hand or in a dice cup before throwing **13.** *vti* MUSIC **TRILL** to trill a note ■ *n* **1. ACT OF SHAKING** a shaking of something ○ *She gave the bag a good shake.* **2. VIBRATION** a trembling motion or vibration ○ *The device moves smoothly along the track without shake.* **3. MOMENT** a brief moment (*informal*) ○ *I'll do it in two shakes.* **4.** BEVERAGES same as **milk shake** (sense 1) **5. SHAKEN BEVERAGE** a beverage made without milk or ice cream but blended or shaken like a milk shake ○ *a fruit and yogurt shake* **6. HANDSHAKE** an act of grasping somebody's hand as a greeting **7.** *US* **REASONABLE CHANCE** reasonable treatment or a reasonable opportunity to succeed ○ *give everybody a fair shake* **8.** GEOL, FORESTRY **FISSURE OR CRACK** a fissure or crack in a rock or timber **9.** MUSIC **TRILL** a trilled note **10.** SEISMOL same as **earthquake** (sense 1) (*informal*) **11.** CONSTR **WOODEN SHINGLE** a rough wooden shingle cut with a hatchet ■ **shakes** *npl* **UNCONTROLLABLE TREMBLING** uncontrollable trembling, especially caused by fear or illness [Old English *sceacan* < Germanic] —**shak·a·ble** *adj*
◇ **no great shakes** not very good or not very important (*informal*)

shake down *v* **1.** *vt* **EXTORT MONEY FROM SOMEBODY** to extort money from somebody (*slang*) **2.** *vt US* **SEARCH FOR SOMETHING** to search somebody or a place, especially for contraband (*informal*) **3.** *vt US* **TAKE SOMETHING FOR TRIAL RUN** to subject a ship or aircraft to a trial run in order to look for faults or train the crew **4.** *vi* **BECOME ACCUSTOMED** to become comfortable in a new setting (*informal*) **5.** *vi* **SLEEP IN MAKESHIFT BED** to go to bed in a makeshift bed

shake off *vt* **1.** *UK* same as **shake** *v* (sense 8) **2.** to get away from a pursuer

shake out *vt* to open something, spread something, or dislodge things from something by holding it and shaking it

shake up *vt* **1. MAKE MAJOR CHANGES** to make major changes in an organization or institution, especially with the intention of improving or modernizing it **2. UPSET SOMEBODY** to make somebody feel upset and disturbed **3. MIX SOMETHING BY SHAKING** to mix something by shaking it in a container

shake·down /sháyk dòwn/ *n* **1. ACT OF EXTORTION** an act of extorting money from somebody using threats (*slang*) **2. THOROUGH SEARCH** a thorough search of somebody or a place (*informal*) **3. TRIAL RUN OF VESSEL** a trial run of a ship or aircraft carried out in order to locate and fix problems or to familiarize the crew with their duties (*informal*) **4. MAKESHIFT BED** a makeshift bed, e.g., a pile of blankets on a floor

shak·en past participle of **shake**

shak·en ba·by syn·drome, **shak·en in·fant syn·drome** *n* in young babies, a series of often life-threatening internal head injuries sustained through being shaken violently

shake·out /sháyk òwt/ *n* a major change in an organization or system resulting in some streamlining ○ *a shakeout in the voluntary sector*

shak·er /sháykər/ *n* **1. CONTAINER FOR DISPERSING PARTICLES** a container with small holes in its lid that can be shaken to disperse the contents **2. CONTAINER FOR MIXING DRINKS** a container with a lid in which drinks are mixed by shaking the container **3. SOMEBODY CAUSING CHANGE** somebody who is active in something, especially somebody who brings about change (*informal*) ○ *a real shaker in the industry* **4. SOMETHING THAT SHAKES** somebody or something that shakes, or shakes something ■ *adj* HANDICRAFT another spelling of **Shaker** *adj* (sense 2)

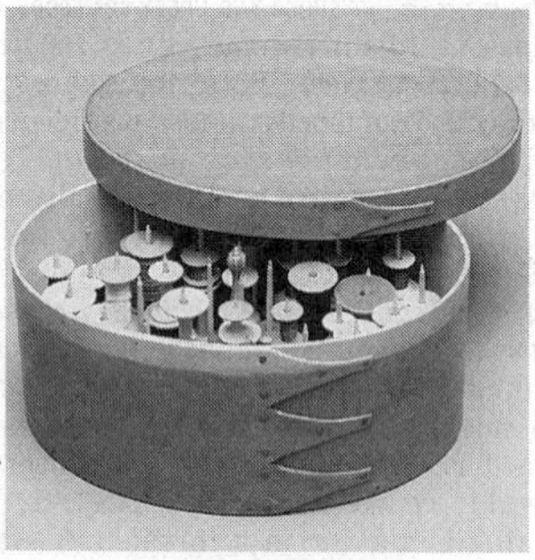
Philadelphia Museum of Art/Corbis
Shaker: wooden Shaker box

Shak·er *n* **MEMBER OF ASCETIC DENOMINATION** a member of a Christian denomination related to the Quakers who live communally, simply, and celibately. The denomination originated in England in the 18th century but settled in the United States. ■ *adj* **1. SIMPLE AND FUNCTIONAL** designed or made in the simple, functional style that originated with the Shakers **2. PARALLEL RIBBED** knit in a large gauge in thin parallel ribs [Late 18C. < shaking movements in their ritual dances]

Shak·er Heights /shàykər-/ city near Cleveland in northeastern Ohio. It is named for a Shaker religious community that was located there between 1822 and 1889. Population: 28,854 (2002 estimate).

~~Shakespear~~ incorrect spelling of **Shakespeare**

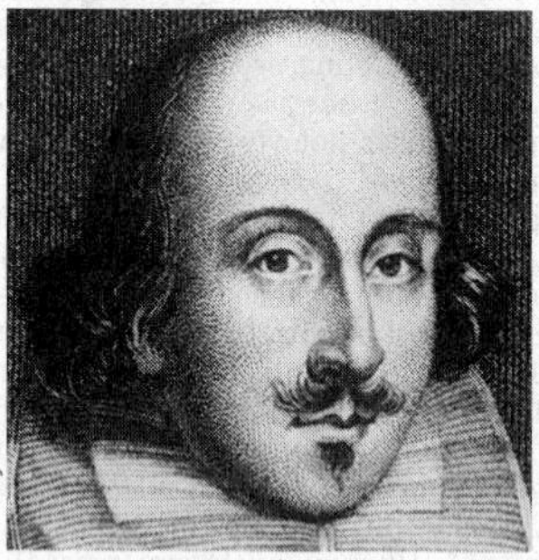
Barnaby's
William Shakespeare

Shake·speare /sháyks peer/, **William** (1564–1616) English poet and playwright. He is widely recognized as the greatest dramatist in the English-speaking world. Although much about his life is obscure, it is known that he was born in Stratford-upon-Avon, England, and was established as an actor-playwright in London by about 1590. Over the next 23 years he wrote 36 tragedies, histories, and comedies, including *Hamlet* (1601?), *Richard III* (1593?), and *Twelfth Night* (1600?). His poetry includes over 150 sonnets. See Cultural note at **ado, labor, like**[2], **measure, merchant, merry, midsummer, shrew, tempest, Twelfth Night** —**Shake·spear·e·an** /shayk speeree ən/ *adj, n*

"JAQUES All the world's a stage, / And all the men and women merely players; / They have their exits and their entrances; / And one man in his time plays many parts, / His acts being seven ages."
[William Shakespeare, *As You Like It*; 1599]

"HAMLET To be, or not to be—that is the question; / Whether 'tis nobler in the mind to suffer / The slings and arrows of outrageous fortune, / Or to take arms against a sea of troubles, / And by opposing end them? To die, to sleep—/ No more; and by a sleep to say we end / The heart-ache and the thousand natural shocks / That flesh is heir to, 'tis a consummation / Devoutly to be wish'd. To die, to sleep; / To sleep, perchance to dream. Ay, there's the rub; / For in that sleep of death what dreams may come, / When we have shuffled off this mortal coil, / Must give us pause."
[William Shakespeare, *Hamlet*; 1601?]

"Shall I compare thee to a summer's day? / Thou art more lovely and more temperate. / Rough winds do shake the darling buds of May, / And summer's lease hath all too short a date."
[William Shakespeare, *Sonnet 18*; 1609]

Shake·spear·e·an·a /shayk speeree ánnə, -aánə/, **Shake·spear·i·an·a** *n* collectively, things relating to William Shakespeare

Shake·spear·e·an son·net *n* a sonnet in iambic pentameter composed of three quatrains followed by a couplet. The rhyme pattern is abab cdcd efef gg. This is the form perfected by William Shakespeare.

Shake·spear·i·an·a *n* LITERAT another spelling of **Shakespeareana**

shake-up *n* a major reorganization or change

shak·ing pal·sy *n* MED same as **Parkinson's disease** (*dated informal*)

shak·o /shákō, sháykō/ (*plural* **-os** or **-oes**) *n* a tall cylindrical military hat made of stiff material with a short visor and a plume at the front [Early 19C. Via French *schako* < Hungarian *csákós (süveg)* "peaked (cap)"]

Shak·ta /shúktə, shaáktə/, **Sak·ta** /súktə, saáktə/ *n* a Hindu who worships Sakti, the female consort of Shiva [Early 19C. < Sanskrit *śāktaḥ* < *śaktiḥ* (see SAKTI)] —**Shak·tism** *n* —**Shak·tist** *n*

Shak·ti *n* HINDUISM another spelling of **Sakti**

sha·ku·ha·chi /shaàkoo haáchee/ (*plural* **-chis**) *n* a Japanese bamboo flute [Late 19C. < Japanese]

shak·y /sháykee/ (**-i·er, -i·est**) *adj* **1. TREMBLING** trembling or unsteady **2. NOT STURDY** not sturdy or firm and likely to collapse **3. WEAK AND NOT LIKELY TO LAST** weak or wavering and unlikely to last long or to be successful ○ *a shaky financial venture* **4. UNRELIABLE** unreliable or uncertain ○ *made us a pretty shaky promise* —**shak·i·ly** *adv* —**shak·i·ness** *n*

shale /shayl/ *n* a dark fine-grained sedimentary rock composed of layers of compressed clay, silt, or mud [Mid-18C. Ultimately < Germanic, "split"] —**shal·y** *adj*

shale oil *n* crude oil distilled from heated shale

shall *stressed* /shal/; *unstressed* /shəl/ CORE MEANING: will happen in the future, or intended to happen ○ *I shall as president promote measures that keep families whole.*

modal v **1. FUTURE EVENTS** indicates that something will or ought to happen in the future **2. DETERMINATION** used especially in formal speech and writing to indicate determination on the part of the speaker that something will happen or somebody will do something ○ *If you want to behave like that you shall certainly not do it here.* **3. RULES AND LAWS** indicating that something must happen or somebody is obliged to do something because of a rule or law ○ *The department shall issue an account number to the vehicle owner.* **4. OFFERS AND SUGGESTIONS** used to make offers and suggestions or to ask for advice (*used in questions*) ○ *Shall I arrange it for you?* ○ *What shall I do next?* **5. CERTAINTY** indicating the certainty or inevitability of something happening in the future ○ *If you want a new outfit that badly then you shall have one.* [Old English *sceal* < Germanic, "owe"]

USAGE shall or **will**? The traditional rule, often stated in grammars and usage books, is that to express a simple future tense ***shall*** is used after *I* and *we* (*I shall leave promptly at noon*) and ***will*** in other cases, i.e., the second and third persons (*Will you leave at noon? They will leave at noon*). To express intention, command, or wish their roles are reversed: *I will do this right or die trying. Passengers shall present two photo IDs prior to ticketing.* It is unlikely that this rule has ever been regularly observed, however, and many examples in the printed works of the best writers contradict it. Though ***will*** and, occasionally, ***shall*** are used as auxiliary verbs referring to a future action or state, other ways of expressing this are often preferred as more natural, for example, *am going to.* When ***shall*** and ***will*** are used in conversation, they are normally contracted to *'ll*, so that the difference between the two words becomes irrelevant. In all parts of the English-speaking world other than England, ***shall*** has been more or less replaced by ***will***. It survives mostly in usages such as *Shall we go?* and the contracted negative form *shan't*, but this is rarely if ever used in modern-day US English. In US English, ***shall*** is still sometimes used in official and quasi-legal contexts such as *These precincts shall recount the votes as per the state election regulations* (a command), but this sounds old-fashioned. ***Shall*** is also a part of well-established expressions in US English such as *We shall overcome.*

shal·loon /shə lóon/ *n* a light wool twill. Use: garment lining. [Mid-17C. < French *chalon*]

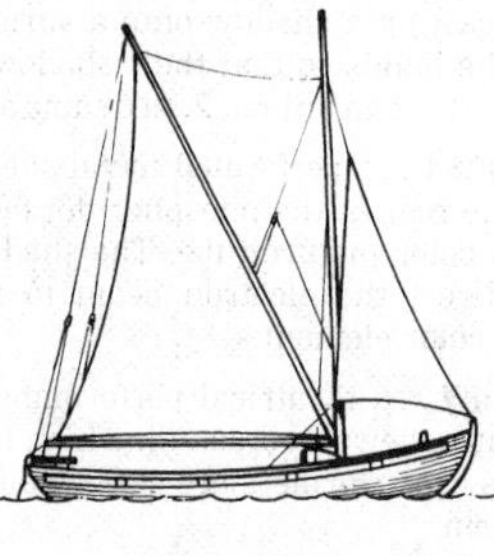
shallop

shal·lop /shálləp/ *n* a light boat with oars, sails, or both, used in shallow waters [Late 16C. < French *chaloupe*]

shal·lot /shə lót/ *n* **1.** an edible bulb with a delicate onion flavor **2.** a cultivated plant of the onion family that produces shallots. Latin name: *Allium ascalonicum.* [Mid-17C. < French *échalotte*, alteration of Old French *esc(h)aloigne* (see SCALLION)]

shal·low /shállō/ *adj* **1. NOT DEEP** with little space between the bottom and the surface or top **2. NOT THINKING OR FEELING DEEPLY** having or displaying little intellectual or emotional complexity or value **3. TAKING IN LITTLE AIR** characterized by the inhaling and exhaling of only a small amount of air ■ **shal·lows** *npl* **SHALLOW WATER** an area of shallow water ■ *vti* (**-lowed, -low·ing, -lows**) **MAKE OR BECOME SHALLOW** to become less deep, or make water less deep [15C. Origin ?] —**shal·low·ly** *adv* —**shal·low·ness** *n*

shal·low wa·ter black·out *n* the sudden loss of consciousness by a diver upon resurfacing caused by oxygen starvation

sha·lom /shaa lṓm/ *interj* used as a greeting or leave-taking among Jews [Late 19C. < Hebrew *šālōm* "peace"]

shalt /shalt/ 2nd person singular present of **shall**. 2nd person plural present of **shall** (*archaic*)

shal·war *n S Asia* CLOTHING another spelling of **salwar**

sham /sham/ *n* **1. SOMETHING FAKE** something that is presented as genuine but that is not **2. IMPOSTOR** somebody who pretends to be something that he or she is not **3.** HOUSEHOLD same as **pillow sham** ■ *adj* **NOT GENUINE** not genuine and used for deception ○ *sham credentials* ■ *vti* (**shammed, sham·ming, shams**) **FEIGN SOMETHING** to pretend to be experiencing a condition such as illness or an emotion in order to deceive ○ *He shammed a migraine to avoid the exam.* ○ *Is the patient really ill or just shamming?* [Late 17C. Probably variant of SHAME] —**sham·mer** *n*

sha·man /shaámən, sháymən/ *n* a spiritual leader who is believed to have special powers such as prophecy and the ability to heal [Late 17C. Via Russian < Tungus *šaman* < Sanskrit *śramanáḥ* "Buddhist ascetic" < *śrámas* "religious exercise"] —**sha·man·ic** /shə mánnik, shay-/ *adj*

sha·man·ism /shaáma nìzzəm, sháymə-/ *n* **1.** a religion of northern Asia, in which shamans are believed to be able to intercede between humanity and powerful good and evil spirits **2.** an animistic belief system involving shamans

sha·mash *n* JUDAISM another spelling of **shammash**

sham·ble /shámb'l/ *vi* (**-bled, -bling, -bles**) to walk clumsily keeping the feet close to the ground ■ *n* a shuffling awkward walking style [Late 16C. Probably < obsolete *shamble legs* "ungainly legs"]

sham·bles /shámb'lz/ (*plural same*) *n* **1. DISORGANIZED FAILURE** a failure caused by inadequate planning or organization (*takes a singular verb*) **2. MESSY DISORDER** a state of messy disorder or chaos (*takes a singular verb*) **3. PLACE OF CARNAGE** a place of great destruction and carnage (*literary*; *takes a singular verb*) **4.** same as **slaughterhouse** (*archaic*) **5. MEAT MARKET** a meat or fish market (*archaic*) [15C. < obsolete *shamble* "stool, table, meat vendor's stall," via W Germanic < Latin *scamellum* "small bench"]

ORIGIN The Old English ancestor of *shamble*, the source of ***shambles***, meant simply "stool, table." It gradually acquired the specialized meaning "meat table," being applied to meat sellers' stalls at markets (a street in the old butchers' quarter of York in northern England is still known as the Shambles). By a natural extension the plural form ***shambles*** came to denote a "slaughterhouse," and hence metaphorically any "place of carnage," but the milder modern sense "state of disorder or chaos" did not emerge until as recently as the early 20th century.

sham·bol·ic /sham bóllik/ *adj UK* poorly organized and in a messy or chaotic state (*informal*) [Late 20C. < SHAMBLES]

shame /shaym/ *n* **1. NEGATIVE EMOTION** a negative emotion that combines feelings of dishonor, unworthiness, and embarrassment **2. CAPACITY TO FEEL UNWORTHY** the capacity or tendency to feel shame ○ *He has no shame.* **3. STATE OF DISGRACE** a state of disgrace or dishonor ○ *bring shame on the family* **4. CAUSE FOR REGRET** a cause for regret or disappointment ○ *It's a shame you couldn't stay for lunch.* **5. CAUSE OF SHAME** somebody or something that causes somebody else to feel shame ■ *vt* (**shamed, sham·ing, shames**) **1. MAKE SOMEBODY FEEL ASHAMED** to make somebody feel the negative emotion of shame ○ *It shamed her that she had cheated.* **2. FORCE SOMEBODY THROUGH SHAME** to make somebody do something by exploiting the fact that he or she would be ashamed not to do it ○ *He shamed us into making higher donations to the ministry.* **3. MAKE SOMEBODY FEEL INFERIOR** to be so much better or more successful than others as to expose their comparative inadequacy ■ *interj* **EXPRESSING SYMPATHETIC REACTION** used to react sympathetically to something disappointing ○ *Shame, old friend, we would have invited you if we'd known you were free.* [Old English *sceamu* < Germanic] ◇ **put somebody** *or* **something to shame** to make somebody or something seem inferior or of inferior quality by comparison

shame·faced /sháym fàyst/ *adj* **1.** showing a feeling of shame or embarrassment **2.** timid or easily embarrassed [Mid-16C. Alteration of obsolete *shamefast* "bashful"] —**shame·fac·ed·ly** /-fàyssədlee, -fàystlee/ *adv*—**shame·fac·ed·ness** /-fàysədnəss/ *n*

shame·ful /sháymf'l/ *adj* bad enough to inspire shame in those responsible —**shame·ful·ly** *adv* —**shame·ful·ness** *n*

shame·less /sháymləss/ *adj* **1.** untroubled or unaffected by shame, especially in situations where others would be ashamed **2.** done without shame, especially where others would feel shame —**shame·less·ly** *adv*—**shame·less·ness** *n*

sha·mi·a·na /shàmmee aánə/ *n S Asia* a decorative circus-style tent used for outdoor entertaining or weddings [Early 17C. < Persian, Urdu *shāmiyāna*]

Sha·mir /shə meér/, **Yitzhak** (*b.* 1914) Polish-born prime minister of Israel (1983–84, 1986–92). He has held many other government positions, including foreign minister (1980–92) and leader of the Likud Party (1983–93). Born **Jazernicki, Yitzhak**

sham·mash /shaáməss/ (*plural* **-ma·shim** /shaa maássim/), **sha·mash, sham·mes** (*plural* **-mo·sim** /shaa mṓssim/) *n* **1.** the sexton of a synagogue **2.** a candle used to light the candles in a Hanukkah candlestick [Mid-17C. Via Yiddish *shames* < Hebrew *šammaš* "attendant" < *šimmēš* "serve"]

sham·my /shámmee/ (*plural* **-mies**) *n* INDUST, HOUSEHOLD same as **chamois** (senses 2–3) [Early 18C. Representing the pronunciation]

sham·poo /sham poó/ *n* **1. HAIR-CLEANING SOAP** soap for cleaning the hair and scalp, usually in liquid or gel form **2. SUDSY DETERGENT** sudsy detergent for cleaning upholstery and carpets **3. USE OF SHAMPOO** a cleaning of the hair with shampoo ■ *vt* (**-pooed, -poo·ing, -poos**) **CLEAN SOMETHING WITH SHAMPOO** to clean the hair and scalp, upholstery, or a carpet with shampoo [Mid-18C. < Hindi *cāpō* < *cāpnā* "knead, massage"]

shamrock

sham·rock /shám ròk/ *n* a three-leafed clover or a plant similar to clover that serves as the national emblem of Ireland [Late 16C. < Irish *seamróg* "small clover" < *seamar* "clover"]

sha·mus /sháyməss/ *n* (*slang*) **1.** *US* a police officer **2.** same as **private detective** [Early 20C. Origin ?]

Shan /shaan, shan/ (*plural same* or **Shans**) *n* **1.** a member of a people living mainly in northeastern Myanmar and also in neighboring parts of China, Laos, and Thailand **2.** the Tai language of the Shan people. Native speakers: 2.5 million. [Early 19C. < Burmese] —**Shan** *adj*

Shan·dong /shaán dóong/ province on the eastern coast of China, bordered by Hebei, the Yellow Sea, Henan, and Jiangsu. Capital: Jinan. Population: 87,380,000 (1997). Area: 59,190 sq. mi./153,300 sq. km.

shan·dy /shándee/ (*plural* **-dies**) *n* **1.** a drink made of beer and lemon-lime soda **2.** BEVERAGES same as **shandygaff** [Late 19C. Shortening of SHANDYGAFF]

shan·dy·gaff /shándee gàf/ *n US* a drink made of beer and ginger beer [Mid-19C. Origin ?]

Shang /shaang/ *n* a Chinese dynasty that ruled from about 1766 to about 1027 B.C., a period that coincided with the development of China's system of handwriting and work in bronze (*often used before a noun*) [Mid-17C. < Chinese *Shāng*]

Shan·gaan /shàng gaán/ (*plural same* or **-gaans**) *n* PEOPLES, LANG same as **Tsonga** [Late 19C. < Bantu] —**Shan·gaan** *adj*

shang·hai /shang hī́, shang hī́/ (**-haied, -hai·ing, -hais**) *vt* **1.** to trick or force somebody to do something or go somewhere **2.** to recruit somebody forcibly into a navy [Late 19C. After SHANGHAI, typical destination of ships with enforced crews]

Shang·hai /shàng hī́/ city and port on Huang-pu River in eastern China. Population: 13,580,000 (1995). —**Shang·hai·nese** /shàng hī neéz/ *npl, adj*

Shan·go /shaáng gṓ/ *n Carib* an African-based religion based on the worship of numerous deities, who also have Catholic counterparts. Worship includes animal sacrifice, spirit possession, drumming, dancing, and chanting. [Mid-20C. < Yoruba, the god of thunder]

Shan·gri-la /shàng gree laá/ *n* an imaginary and remote paradise [Mid-20C. After an imaginary land in *The Lost Horizon* (1933) by English novelist James Hilton]

shank /shangk/ *n* **1. LONG NARROW PART** the long narrowest part of something such as a key or pipe, especially when it connects two functional parts **2. CUT OF MEAT** a cut of meat from the leg of cattle, hogs, or sheep **3. BOTTOM OF ANIMAL LEG** the lower part of an animal's leg, between the bottom and middle joints **4. LOWER LEG** the lower part of the human leg, from ankle to knee **5. LEG** a human leg (*informal*) **6.** MECH ENG **BODY OF PIN OR NAIL** the long narrow part of a pin, nail, screw, or bolt, between the head and the pointed or threaded part **7.** MECH ENG **PART CONNECTING TOOL HEAD TO HANDLE** a part sticking out from the head of a tool, by which it can be fitted into a handle **8.** JEWELRY **RING BAND** the plain band part of a ring, not including any jewels and their settings **9.** CLOTHING **NARROW PART OF SHOE SOLE** the narrow part of the sole of a shoe, beneath the arch of the foot, or any fitting at this part of a shoe **10.** *US* CLOTHING same as **shankpiece 11.** NAUT **ANCHOR'S STEM** the stem of an anchor **12.** PRINTING **PART OF PRINTING TYPE** the body of a piece of type, between the foot and shoulder **13.** CLOTHING **BUTTON STEM** a loop or stem at the back of a button, by which it is sewn to the cloth **14.** *regional* **EARLY PART** the early part of a period of time **15.** *regional* **LATER PART** the later or remaining part of a period of time **16.** CRIME **HOMEMADE DAGGER** a makeshift dagger, e.g., one made from a shard of glass, especially one made by a prisoner (*slang*) ■ *v* (**shanked, shank·ing, shanks**) **1.** *vt* GOLF **MISHIT GOLF BALL** to hit a golf ball with the heel of the club, sending it in the wrong direction **2.** *vt US* FOOTBALL **MISKICK FOOTBALL** to kick a football so that it goes in the wrong direction **3.** *vi* BOT **SHOW DISEASE FROM BASE UP** to shrivel, or show other signs of disease spreading upward from the base of the stem (*refers to plants*) [Old English *sceanca* "shinbone" < W Germanic]

Popperfoto

Ravi Shankar

Shan·kar /shángk aar/, **Ravi** (*b.* 1920) Indian sitarist, composer, and teacher. His international tours popularized Indian music in the West. His compositions include movie scores and sitar concertos.

shank·piece /shángk peéss/ *n US* a shoe insert that supports the arch of the foot

shan·na·chie /shánna kheé/ *n Ireland* a traditional Irish storyteller [Mid-16C. < Irish *seanchaidhe*]

Shan·non /shánnən/ longest river in the British Isles. It rises in northwestern County Cavan, north central Republic of Ireland, and empties into the Atlantic Ocean. Length: 230 mi./370 km.

shan't /shant/ *contr* shall not

shan·tey *n* MUSIC, NAUT another spelling of **chantey**

shan·tung /shan túng/ *n* **1.** heavy silk cloth with a nubby uneven weave **2.** cotton or synthetic fabric made to resemble silk shantung [Late 19C. After SHANDONG]

shan·ty[1] /shántee/ (*plural* **-ties**) *n* a crudely built shack or hut [Early 19C. Probably < Canadian French *chantier* "lumberjack's hut," via French, "timberyard" < Latin *cant(h)erius* "rafter"]

shan·ty[2] /shántee/ (*plural* **-ties**) *n* MUSIC, NAUT UK spelling of **chantey**

shan·ty·town /shántee tòwn/ *n* a settlement consisting of shacks

Shan·xi /shaán sheé/ agricultural province in northeastern China, bordered by Nei Monggol, Hebei, Henan, and Shaanxi. Capital: Taiyuan. Population: 31,090,000 (1997). Area: 60,656 sq. mi./157,099 sq. km.

shape /shayp/ *n* **1. OUTLINE** the outline of something's form ○ *His face has a square shape.* **2. SOMETHING NOT CLEARLY SEEN** something that has bulk but is not clearly seen in outline ○ *She could see a shape through the fog.* **3.** MATH **GEOMETRIC FORM** a geometric form, e.g., a square, triangle, cone, or cube **4. GENERAL CHARACTER OF SOMETHING** the broad character that something has ○ *the overall shape of the proposals* **5.**

ORIGINAL FORM the original or optimal form of something ○ *The pleats lost their shape in the wash.* **6. HEALTH** the condition of somebody's health or fitness ○ *She exercises regularly and is in pretty good shape.* **7. SOMETHING'S CONDITION** the condition that something is in ○ *The lawn is in great shape.* **8. MOLD FOR SOMETHING** a mold or pattern for making something or giving something its form **9. GHOST** a ghostly form or phantom ■ *vt* (**shaped, shap·ing, shapes**) **1. INFLUENCE SOMETHING GREATLY** to have a profound or crucial influence over something ○ *His beliefs were shaped by his upbringing.* **2. PLAN FOR NATURE OF SOMETHING** to plan or decide on what the character of something should be ○ *They are meeting to shape the nation's future.* **3. GIVE SHAPE TO SOMETHING** to mold something into a different shape ○ *She shapes the clay into little animals.* **4.** PSYCHOL **TRAIN WITH REWARD AND PUNISHMENT** to change somebody's behavior gradually using reward as the person comes closer to the desired behavior, and punishment for moving away from it [Old English *gesceap* "creation" < Germanic, "cut out"] —**shaped** *adj* —**shap·er** *n* ◇ **knock** *or* **lick** *or* **whip somebody** *or* **something into shape** to bring somebody or something to a desired state quickly, roughly, or haphazardly (*informal*) ◇ **take shape** to take a definite form

shape up *vi* **1. REACH ACCEPTABLE STANDARD** to reach an acceptably high standard of behavior, skill, or attitude **2. DEVELOP IN PARTICULAR WAY** to seem to be developing in a particular way ○ *It's shaping up to be an environmental disaster.* **3. IMPROVE** to improve or develop in the way that is wanted (*informal*)

shape·less /sháypləss/ *adj* **1.** with an indefinite or imprecise shape **2.** put together in a very haphazard way —**shape·less·ly** *adv* —**shape·less·ness** *n*

shape·ly /sháyplee/ (**-li·er, -li·est**) *adj* having a shape that is visually appealing —**shape·li·ness** *n*

shape mem·o·ry al·loy *n* a metallic alloy that has the ability when it is heated to return to a previously defined shape or size after deformation

shape-up /sháyp ùp/, **shape·up** *n US* a method of hiring dock workers in which those seeking work arrive at the docks in the morning and employers select from among them

shard /shaard/, **sherd** /shurd/ *n* **1. BROKEN PIECE OF GLASS** a sharp broken piece of glass or metal **2.** ARCHAEOL same as **potsherd** **3.** ZOOL **ANIMAL'S SCALE OR SHELL** an animal's scales, shell, or other tough outer covering **4.** INSECTS **BEETLE'S OUTER WING** the outer wing covering of a beetle [Old English *sceard* "cut, notch" < Indo-European, "to cut"]

share[1] /sher/ *v* (**shared, shar·ing, shares**) **1.** *vti* **USE SOMETHING ALONG WITH OTHERS** to have or use something in common with other people ○ *We shared an apartment.* **2.** *vti* **TAKE RESPONSIBILITY TOGETHER** to take equal responsibility for something along with other people ○ *We shared the blame.* **3.** *vti* **LET SOMEBODY USE SOMETHING** to allow somebody to use something or have part of something ○ *I shared my ice cream with him.* **4.** *vt* **DIVIDE SOMETHING EQUALLY BETWEEN PEOPLE** to allocate equal parts of something to different people or groups ○ *She shared out the money among her six grandchildren.* **5.** *vt* **HAVE SIMILAR FEELING OR EXPERIENCE** to have something the same as or in common with somebody else ○ *He shared my view that the plan would not work.* **6.** *vt* **TELL SOMEBODY SOMETHING** to express something to another person rather than keeping silent ○ *Do you want to share your feelings?* ■ *n* **1. PART OF SOMETHING ALLOTTED** a part of something that is owned by, paid for by, done by, or set aside for each of several people ○ *He hasn't had his share of the cake.* **2.** FIN **PART OF COMPANY'S STOCK** any of the equal, usually small, parts into which a company's capital stock is divided ○ *100 shares of General Motors* **3. REASONABLE OR APPROPRIATE PORTION** the portion that somebody deserves or should be responsible for ○ *She does more than her share of the work.* [Old English *scearu* "division, portion" < Indo-European, "to cut"] —**shar·er** *n*

SYNONYMS ***share, divide up, allocate, allot, distribute, dispense, dole out***

CORE MEANING: to give something to or divide it between different people or groups

share to divide something, especially equally, between different people or groups ○ *Occasionally the role of chairperson may be shared between several people.* ○ *The new agreement calls for added revenue to be shared equally among the players.* **divide up** to divide something into several parts ○ *There is no way of dividing up the work that will satisfy everybody.* **allocate** to divide something and give it for a specific purpose, or to divide something between different people or groups ○ *allocate funds for recurrent expenditures* ○ *Warranties serve as a means of allocating business risk between the vendor and the purchaser.* **allot** to give something to somebody as a share of what is available or what has to be done ○ *We rejected the plan, which would allot us control of 49 percent of the undertaking.* ○ *Some tasks now allotted to local government might more efficiently be handled by the state* **distribute** to give things to a number of people ○ *The remaining funds will be distributed among good causes around the world.* ○ *The premier's speech was distributed to reporters beforehand.* **dispense** to give a service or advice to several recipients ○ *the agency responsible for dispensing nonmilitary foreign aid* ○ *The prime role of the law courts is to dispense justice.* **dole out** (*informal*) to give something to each of a group of people ○ *Dad began to dole out the oatmeal from the saucepan.* ○ *a need to dole out sympathy to the losers of today's game*

share[2] /sher/ *n* AGRIC same as **plowshare** [Old English *scear* < Indo-European, "to cut"]

share cer·tif·i·cate *n UK* same as **stock certificate**

share·crop·per /shér kròppər/ *n US* a tenant farmer who farms land for the owner and is paid a share of the value of the yielded crop —**share·crop** *vti*

share·hold·er /shér hòldər/ *n UK* FIN same as **stockholder**

share op·tion *n UK* same as **stock option, stockholder**

share·ware /shér wèr/ *n* software made available for free trial with the understanding that users will voluntarily pay a fee to the author or publisher for continued use

sha·ri·a /shaa reé ə/, **sha·ri'·a, sha·ri'·ah** *n* Islamic religious law, based on the Koran (*often used before a noun*) [Mid-19C. < Arabic *šarī'īya* "lawfulness" < *aš-šar'* "Islamic law"]

sha·rif /shə reéf/, **she·rif, she·reef** *n* **1. DESCENDANT OF MUHAMMAD** a descendant of the prophet Muhammad through his daughter Fatima **2. GOVERNOR OF MECCA** the governor or chief magistrate of Mecca during the years of Ottoman Turkish rule **3. ARAB RULER** an Arab prince or ruler [Late 16C. < Arabic *šarīf* "illustrious"] —**sha·rif·i·an** *adj*

Shar·jah /shaárjə/ one of the seven member states of the United Arab Emirates. Capital: Sharjah. Population: 200,000 (1989). Area: 1,000 sq. mi./2,590 sq. km.

shark

shark /shaark/ *n* **1. CARNIVOROUS FISH** a carnivorous fish with a long body, two dorsal fins, sharp teeth, a cartilaginous skeleton, and thick, rough skin. Class: Chondrichthyes. **2. RUTHLESS PERSON** a ruthless greedy person (*informal*) **3.** same as **loan shark** (*informal*) **4.** *US* **ESPECIALLY TALENTED PERSON** somebody with a particular talent ■ *vi* (**sharked, shark·ing, sharks**) **CHEAT OTHERS PROFESSIONALLY** to make a living as a cheater or fraud [Mid-16C. Origin ?] ◇ **jump the shark** to do something atypical or out of place that seems to mark the beginning of an inevitable decline in quality or popularity (*informal*)

shark bait *n US* a swimmer or surfer who swims out far from shore (*slang humorous*)

Shark Bay /shaárk-/ bay on the coast of Western Australia

shark·skin /shaárk skìn/ *n* **1.** a smooth glossy fabric made from a mixture of acetate and rayon **2.** leather made from a shark's skin

shark·suck·er /shaárk sùkər/ *n* FISH same as **remora** [Mid-19C. < its habit of attaching itself to sharks]

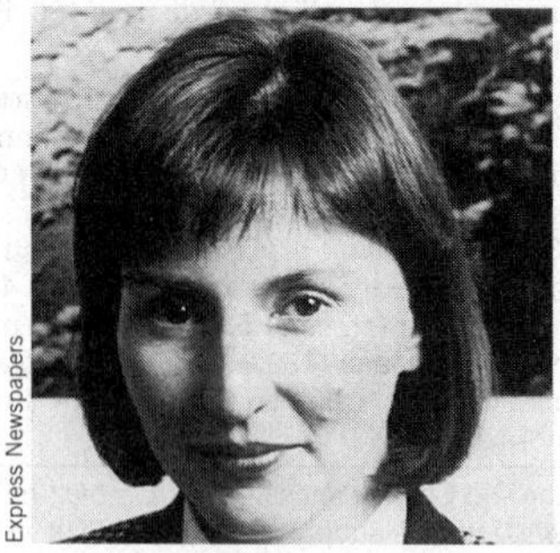

Express Newspapers

Helen Sharman

Shar·man /shaármən/, **Helen** (*b.* 1963) British astronaut. With her participation in the Anglo-Soviet scientific space mission Project Juno, she became Britain's first astronaut (1991). Full name **Sharman, Helen Patricia**

Shar·on, Plain of /shárrən/ plain between the Mediterranean coast and the Samarian foothills in western Israel. It extends southward from Haifa to Tel Aviv and is the most densely populated region of the country.

Sha·ron /sha rón/, **Ariel** (*b.* 1928) Israeli soldier and prime minister (2001–). A prominent member of the Likud Party, he became party leader in 1999 and prime minister in 2001.

sharp /shaarp/ *adj* **1. ABLE TO CUT** having an edge or point that is very acute and able to cut or puncture things ○ *a sharp blade* **2. POINTED** ending in a point or sharp angle ○ *a sharp nose* **3. ABRUPT IN CHANGING DIRECTION** making a change in direction that forms an acute angle ○ *a sharp turn* **4. QUICK-WITTED** quick-witted and intelligent or quick to notice and understand **5. CRITICAL** critical and unsympathetic ○ *a sharp rebuke* **6. IRRITABLE** irritable or angry ○ *a sharp temper* **7. SUDDEN** sudden and significant or noticeable ○ *a sharp rise in prices* ○ *a sharp intake of breath* **8. DISTINCT** clearly and definitely distinct ○ *Her soft voice was in sharp contrast to her forbidding expression.* **9. CLEARLY DETAILED** with the detail clear and distinct ○ *a sharp image* **10. PIERCING** loud, piercing, and abrupt or unexpected ○ *a sharp cry* **11. STRONG IN TASTE** strong and slightly bitter in taste ○ *a sharp cheese* **12. INTENSE** penetrating and intense ○ *a sharp frost* **13.** MUSIC **HIGHER BY HALF STEP** higher in pitch by a half step ○ *F sharp* **14.** MUSIC **TOO HIGH PITCHED** a little too high in pitch and therefore slightly out of tune **15. STYLISH** neat, stylish, and fashionable (*informal*) ○ *a sharp dresser* **16. FRAUDULENT** deceitful or fraudulent ○ *sharp business practice* ■ *adv* **1. PRECISELY** exactly and not before or after ○ *at 9 o'clock sharp* **2.** MUSIC **AT SLIGHTLY TOO HIGH PITCH** at higher than the usual pitch and therefore slightly out of tune ○ *She's singing sharp.* ■ *n* **1.** MUSIC **NOTE HIGHER BY HALF STEP** a note or tone that is a half step higher in pitch than the natural or unmodified pitch. Symbol ♯ **2.** MUSIC **SHARP SYMBOL** the symbol for a sharp note **3.** HANDICRAFT **LONG SEWING NEEDLE** a long thin needle for hand sewing **4.** MED **SHARP MEDICAL INSTRUMENT** a pointed or cutting medical instrument that requires careful disposal, e.g., a hypodermic needle or surgical blade (*usually used in the plural*) ○ *a container labeled "sharps only"* **5. SKILLED CHEATER** somebody who is skilled at cheating others, especially in gambling and at cards (*informal*) **6. EXPERT** somebody expert at something (*informal*) [Old English *scearp* < Indo-European, "to cut"] —**sharp·ly** *adv* —**sharp·ness** *n*

Sharp /shaarp/, **Phillip** (*b.* 1944) US molecular biologist. He shared the Nobel Prize in physiology or medicine (1993) for his research on the genetic structure of DNA. Full name **Sharp, Phillip Allen**

sharp·bill /shaárp bìl/ *n* a small fruit-eating bird with a straight sharp beak, green and yellow feathers, and a red crest. Native to: rain forests of Central and South America. Latin name: *Oxyruncus cristatus.*

shar-pei /shaar páy/, **Shar-Pei** *n* a medium-sized dog with a squarish snout, blue tongue, short hair, and loose skin that falls in folds over its body, especially when young. It belongs to a breed originating in China. [Late 20C. < Chinese *shā pi* "sand skin"]

sharp·en /shaárpən/ (**-ened, -en·ing, -ens**) *v* **1.** *vti* to become sharp or sharper, or make something sharp or sharper **2.** *vt* to improve something so that it is more efficient or stylish than before —**sharp·en·er** *n*

sharp·er /shaárpər/ *n* GAMBLING same as **sharp** *n* (sense 5) (*informal*)

Sharpe·ville /shaárp vìl/ township near Vereeniging, South Africa. It was the scene of a massacre of antiapartheid demonstrators in 1960. Population: 42,000 (1972).

sharp-eyed *adj* **1.** alert and able to notice detail **2.** with very keen eyesight

sharp·ie /shaárpee/, **sharp·y** (*plural* **-ies**) *n* **1.** *US* a long narrow fishing boat with a flat bottom and one or two masts with triangular sails **2.** a quick-witted and alert person **3.** *US* GAMBLING same as **sharp** *n* (sense 5) (*informal*)

sharp-nosed puff·er *n* an ocean fish that is a puffer and can inflate its body like other puffers but also has a long snout with prominent nostrils. Native to: tropics. Family: Canthigasteridae.

Sharps·burg /shaárps bùrg/ village in northwestern Maryland, northwest of Antietam. During the Civil War, it was the site of one of the bloodiest days of fighting, on September 17, 1862, an engagement often referred to in the North as the Battle of Antietam.

sharp-shinned hawk *n* a small bird-hunting hawk with short wings, a long square tail, and gray feathers with a brown underside. Native to: North America. Latin name: *Accipiter striatus.* [< its slender legs]

sharp·shoot·er /shaárp shòotər/ *n* **1.** somebody who can shoot a firearm extremely accurately **2.** *US* an accurate finder of a target, e.g., a basketball player who can make baskets

sharp-sight·ed *adj* same as **sharp-eyed** —**sharp-sight·ed·ly** *adv* —**sharp-sight·ed·ness** *n*

sharp-tailed grouse *n* a light-colored grouse with a narrow tapered tail and dark breast markings. Native to: prairies and scrubland of northwestern United States and Canada.

sharp-tailed spar·row *n* a sparrow with tail feathers that have pointed ends. Native to: marshes of North America. Latin name: *Ammodramus caudacutus.*

sharp-tongued *adj* critical or sarcastic and unsympathetic in speech

sharp-wit·ted *adj* quick to think, understand, or react —**sharp-wit·ted·ly** *adv* —**sharp-wit·ted·ness** *n*

sharp·y *n* another spelling of **sharpie** (*informal*)

shash·lik /shaásh lìk, shaash lík/, **shash·lick** *n* FOOD same as **shish kebab** [Early 20C. Via Russian *shashlyk* < Crimean Turkish *şişlik* "small skewer" < *şiş* "skewer"]

Shas·ta /shástə/ (*plural same* or **-tas**) *n* **1.** a member of a group of Native North American peoples of the highlands of northern California **2.** the Hokan language of the Shasta people, which is nearly extinct [Mid-19C. Origin ?] —**Shas·ta** *adj*

Sha·sta, Mount /shástə/ mountain and extinct volcano in the Cascade Range, northern California. It has five glaciers. Height: 14,162 ft./4,317 m.

Shas·ta dai·sy *n* a chrysanthemum with large white flower heads. Latin name: *Chrysanthemum maximum.*

shas·tra /shaástrə/, **sas·tra** *n* in Hinduism, a sacred text [Mid-17C. < Sanskrit *śāstra* "lesson" < *śās-* "instruct"]

shat past participle, past tense of **shit** (*taboo offensive*)

Shatt al-Ar·ab /shàt al árrəb, shaát-/ river in Southwest Asia. It rises at the confluence of the Tigris and Euphrates rivers, flows along the border between Iran and Iraq, and empties into the Persian Gulf, near Kuwait. Length: 110 mi./170 km.

Shat·ten /shátt'n/, **Gerald P.** (*b.* 1949) US developmental biologist. He led the research team that produced the first genetically modified monkey.

shat·ter /sháttər/ *v* (**-tered, -ter·ing, -ters**) **1.** *vti* SMASH INTO PIECES to break suddenly into many small brittle pieces, or cause something to break in this way **2.** *vt* DESTROY HOPE OR BELIEF to destroy something that somebody believed in or hoped for **3.** *vt* SHOCK SOMEBODY to shock and distress somebody badly **4.** *vi US* AGRIC SHED PLANT PARTS to drop petals, ripe fruit, or leaves ■ **shat·ters** *npl* FRAGMENTS fragments made by shattering something [14C. Ultimately < Indo-European, "split apart"] —**shat·ter·er** *n*

shat·ter cone *n* a cone-shaped rock piece that has stripes running from its point, created by volcanic pressure or meteoric impact

shat·ter·proof /sháttər pròof/ *adj* made to resist shattering

shave /shayv/ *v* (**shaved, shaved** or **shav·en** /sháyvən/, **shav·ing, shaves**) **1.** *vti* REMOVE HAIR WITH RAZOR to remove hair from the body using a razor **2.** *vt* REDUCE AMOUNT SLIGHTLY to reduce an amount, price, or time taken by a very slight amount ○ *shaved two seconds off her best time* **3.** *vt* BARELY TOUCH SOMETHING to barely touch something when passing **4.** *vt* REMOVE THIN LAYER to remove a thin layer from something using a razor, rasp, or similar tool **5.** *vt* TRIM SOMETHING to trim something closely ■ *n* **1.** ACT OF SHAVING the act, process, or result of shaving **2.** same as **shaving** (sense 1) **3.** SHAVING TOOL a tool for shaving or scraping [Old English *sceafan* < Indo-European, "to scrape, scratch"]

shav·en /sháyvən/ past participle of **shave** ■ *adj* (*often used in combination*) **1.** with the beard or the hair shaved off **2.** trimmed or cropped

shav·er /sháyvər/ *n* **1.** a device that is used to shave the beard or hair, especially an electric razor (*often used before a noun*) **2.** a boy who is not old enough to shave (*dated informal*)

Sha·vi·an /sháyvee ən/ *adj* **1.** BY OR LIKE G. B. SHAW written by or in the style of the work of the playwright George Bernard Shaw **2.** OF G. B. SHAW relating to or studying George Bernard Shaw or his works ■ *n* STUDENT OF G. B. SHAW an admirer or student of George Bernard Shaw or his works [Early 20C. < modern Latin *Shavius* "Shaw"]

shav·ing /sháyving/ *n* **1.** a thin slice shaved off **2.** the removing of hair or a beard with a razor (*often used before a noun*)

Sha·vu·oth /shə vòo ōt, -ōth/, **Sha·vu·ot** /-ōt/ *n* a Jewish festival marking the Law being given by God to Moses on Mount Sinai. Date: 6th of Sivan, in May or June. [Late 19C. < Hebrew *šāḇū'ōt* "weeks" (between Passover and Pentecost)]

shaw /shaw/ *n Midwest, UK* a thicket of shrubs or small trees [Old English *sceaga* < Germanic, "something sticking out"]

Shaw /shaw/, **Anna Howard** (1847–1919) British-born US social reformer. One of the first women to be ordained as a Methodist minister, she campaigned around the world for social justice, women's suffrage, and peace.

Barnaby's

George Bernard Shaw

Shaw, George Bernard (1856–1950) Irish playwright. His plays, including *Pygmalion* (1913) and *Heartbreak House* (1919), established him as the leading English-language playwright of his time. He promoted socialism in works such as *The Intelligent Woman's Guide to Socialism and Capitalism* (1928).

"All professions are conspiracies against the laity."
[George Bernard Shaw, *The Doctor's Dilemma*, Act I; 1911]

"I don't want to talk grammar, I want to talk like a lady."
[George Bernard Shaw, *Pygmalion*, Act II; 1913]

Sha·wa·no *n, adj* PEOPLES, LANG same as **Shawnee**[1]

Sha·win·i·gan /shə wínnigən/ town in southern Quebec, Canada, northwest of Trois Rivières on the St. Maurice River. Population: 48,366 (2001).

shawl /shawl/ *n* a fabric square worn by women over the shoulders or head and shoulders or used to wrap a baby in ■ *vt* (**shawled, shawl·ing, shawls**) to cover somebody or something with a shawl or with something performing a similar function [Early 17C. < Persian, Urdu *šāl*]

shawm /shawm/ *n* a woodwind instrument of the Middle Ages and Renaissance that has a double reed and was the predecessor of the modern oboe [14C. Via Old French *chalemie* < Latin *calamus* "reed"]

Shawn /shawn/, **Ted** (1891–1972) US dancer and choreographer. He founded the Denishawn Dance School (1915) with his wife, Ruth St. Denis, and they were leading exponents of modern dance. Born **Shawn, Edwin Myers**

Shaw·nee[1] /shaw née/ (*plural same* or **-nees**), **Sha·wa·no** /shə waánō/ (*plural same* or **-nos**) *n* **1.** a member of an Algonquian people who lived along the Ohio, Cumberland, and Tennessee rivers, and now live mainly in Oklahoma **2.** the Algonquian language of the Shawnee people. Few people now speak Shawnee. [Late 17C. < Delaware *ša:wano:w*] —**Shaw·nee** *adj*

Shaw·nee[2] /shaw née/ city in northeastern Kansas. It is a western suburb of Kansas City. Population: 52,715 (2002 estimate).

Shaw·wal /shə waál/ *n* in the Islamic calendar, the tenth month of the year. See table at **calendar** [Late 18C. < Arabic *shawwāl*]

Shays /shayz/, **Daniel** (1747–1825) US revolutionary soldier who led a rebellion against the government in Massachusetts in 1787

she *stressed* /shee/; *unstressed* /shi/ *pron* (*used as the subject of a verb*) **1.** PREVIOUSLY MENTIONED FEMALE PERSON OR ANIMAL used to refer to a female person or animal who has been previously mentioned or whose identity is known ○ *Ms. Jones continues to enjoy high approval ratings as she starts her third year in office.* **2.** OBJECT PERCEIVED AS FEMALE used to refer to something previously mentioned or known that has been traditionally thought of as female, e.g., a nation, car, machine, boat, or ship ○ *Brazil stated that she is ready to start talks on the issue.* ○ *The tanker is 25 years old but she is still very seaworthy.* ■ *n* FEMALE ANIMAL OR GIRL a female animal or person, sometimes used of a new baby ○ *Is it a he or a she?* [12C. Probably alteration of Old English *hēo*, feminine form of HE[1]]

s/he /shée awr hée/ *pron* used in writing as a pronoun to mean "she or he" (*intended to avoid sexism in writing*) ○ *If a student wishes to change courses s/he should consult me before the end of next week.*

shea /shee, shay/ *n* TREES same as **shea tree** [Late 18C. < Mande *si*]

shea but·ter *n* a white fat obtained from the seeds of the shea tree. Use: food, soap and candle manufacture.

sheaf /sheef/ *n* (*plural* **sheaves** /sheevz/) **1.** a bundle of the harvested stalks of a plant, especially wheat or another cereal, with the heads still containing their seeds **2.** a bundle of objects gathered or tied together ■ *vt* (**sheafed, sheaf·ing, sheafs**) AGRIC same as **sheave**[1] [Old English *sceaf* < Germanic]

shear /sheer/ *v* (**sheared, sheared** or **shorn** /shawrn/, **shear·ing, shears**) **1.** *vti* CUT SOMETHING OFF to remove something with a sharp tool **2.** *vti* CUT HAIR OR FOLIAGE FROM SOMETHING to cut hair, fleece, or foliage from the surface of something using a sharp tool **3.** *vt* DEPRIVE SOMEBODY OF SOMETHING VALUABLE to take something valuable or prized away from somebody ○ *sheared of all self-respect* **4.** *vti* MOVE SMOOTHLY THROUGH SOMETHING to move quickly and cleanly through something **5.** *vti*

DEFORM BY TWISTING FORCE to cause something to deform or break by applying a twisting force, or deform or break in this way ■ *n* **1.** REMOVAL OF FLEECE a cutting off of a sheep's wool, often used as a measure of the age of a sheep **2.** WOOL CUT OFF a quantity of wool cut off a sheep **3.** PHYS, ENG same as **shear strain 4.** PHYS, ENG same as **shear stress 5.** CUTTING TOOL a cutting tool with blades like scissors [Old English *sceran* < Indo-European, "to cut"] —**shear·er** *n*

SPELLCHECK shear or **sheer**? Do not confuse the spelling of ***shear*** and ***sheer***, which sound similar. ***Shear*** is chiefly used as a verb, meaning "remove something with a sharp tool," "deprive somebody of something valuable" (as in *shear them of their self-respect*), or "deform or break by a twisting force": *The head of the bolt has sheared off.* ***Shears*** is a plural noun denoting a cutting tool. The most commonly used word spelled ***sheer*** is chiefly used as an adjective, meaning "complete and utter," "vertical," or "thin and almost transparent" (as in *sheer folly, a sheer drop, sheer fabric*). Another ***sheer*** is primarily a verb, meaning "swerve from a course": *The boat sheered away, narrowly avoiding a collision.* A third ***sheer*** is a nautical term referring to the upward curve of a boat's hull.

shear force *n* a force, or a component of a force, that acts parallel to a plane

shear·legs *n* ENG another spelling of **sheerlegs**

shear·ling /shéerling/ *n* **1.** a young sheep, usually between six and twelve months old, after its first shearing **2.** the tanned skin of a recently sheared lamb or sheep, with the short wool that remains after shearing still attached

shear mod·u·lus *n* the ratio of the shear stress to the shear strain, taken as an indication of the strength of a material under shear forces

shear pin *n* a pin inserted in a machine as a safety device. If safe loads are exceeded, the pin breaks and the machine shuts down.

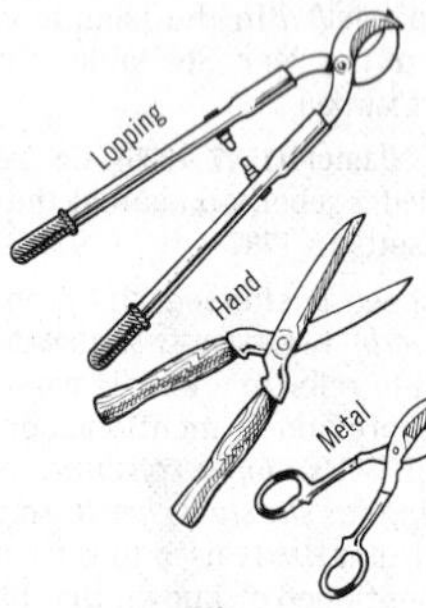

shear

shears /sheerz/ (*plural same*) *n* (*takes a singular or plural verb*) **1.** a tool like a large pair of scissors, used for cutting or trimming **2.** ENG same as **sheerlegs**

shear strain *n* the angular deformation of a body, quantitatively taken to be the sideways displacement of two adjacent planes divided by the distance between them

shear stress *n* the forces acting on a body that produce shear strain

shear·wa·ter /sheér wáwtər/ (*plural* **-ters** or *same*) *n* a long-winged seabird with a short hooked beak, that flies low over the water in search of food. Genus: *Puffinus.* [< the impression when the bird flies that its wings are shearing the water]

sheath /sheeth/ *n* (*plural* **sheaths** /shee*th*z, sheeths/) **1.** CASE FOR BLADE a case for the blade of a knife, sword, or other cutting implement **2.** CLOSE-FITTING COVERING a covering or case that fits closely around something in the way that a sheath covers a blade **3.** CLOSELY FITTING DRESS a woman's closely fitting dress, originally floor-length, but now also knee-length **4.** *UK* HEALTH same as **condom 5.** BIOL PROTECTIVE TUBE a tubular covering that protects some body parts, e.g., some of the nerves and blood vessels, and plant parts, e.g., leaf stems in some grasses ■ *vt* (**sheathed, sheath·ing, sheaths**) same as **sheathe** [Old English *scǣð* < Germanic, "to divide, split"]

sheath·bill /sheéth bil/ *n* an all-white shorebird resembling a pigeon, which has a horny sheath on its face, around the beak, and is a scavenger. Native to: rocky Antarctic and subantarctic coasts. Latin name: *Chionis alba* or *Chionis minor.*

sheathe /shee*th*/ (**sheathed, sheath·ing, sheathes**) *vt* **1.** PUT INTO SHEATH to put a knife, sword, or other cutting implement into a sheath **2.** ENCLOSE SOMETHING to enclose something in a covering or case ○ *PVC-sheathed cable* ○ *sheathed in a tight silk dress* **3.** RETRACT CLAWS to retract the claws, in the way a cat does **4.** THRUST CUTTING IMPLEMENT to thrust a knife or sword into somebody's flesh (*literary*) [14C. < SHEATH]

sheath·ing /sheé*th*ing/ *n* something that encloses and protects, e.g., a covering of boards on a building's framework or a protective material applied to the underwater surfaces of a boat's hull

sheath knife *n* a knife with a fixed blade that is carried in a sheath

shea tree *n* a tropical tree with seeds from which shea butter is obtained. Native to: West Africa. Latin name: *Vitellaria paradoxa* or *Butytrospermum parkii.*

sheave[1] /sheev/ (**sheaved, sheav·ing, sheaves**) *vt* to gather something, especially the cut stalks of a cereal crop, into a sheaf [Late 16C. Back-formation < SHEAVES]

sheave[2] /sheev/ *n* a wheel with a grooved rim for a rope, cable, or belt, especially one used as a pulley [13C. Ultimately < Germanic, "disk, slice of bread"]

sheaves AGRIC plural of **sheaf**

She·ba /sheébə/ ancient kingdom of southwestern Arabia, in present-day Yemen. It reached the height of its wealth and power in the 8th century B.C. In the Bible, it is the meeting place of Solomon and the Queen of Sheba (1 Kings 10:1–13).

she·bang /shə báng/ *n* a situation, an event, or a particular thing (*slang*) ○ *When does this black-tie shebang start?* [Mid-19C. Origin ?] ◇ **the whole shebang** the entirety of something (*slang*) ○ *They sold their house, car, furniture, and boat – the whole shebang.*

She·bat *n* CALENDAR, JUDAISM another spelling of **Shevat**

she·been /shə beén/ *n* a small establishment that sells alcoholic beverages illegally or without a license, traditionally operating in the poorer regions of Ireland, Scotland, and South Africa [Late 18C. < Irish *síbín* "little mug" < *séibe* "mug"]

She·chi·na /shə k͟heénə, -keénə, -kīnə/, **She·chi·nah, She·khi·nah** *n* in the theology of Judaism, God's presence in and throughout the world [Mid-17C. < late Hebrew *šĕk͟īnāh* < *šākan* "rest, dwell"]

she·chi·ta /shə k͟heétə/, **sche·chi·ta** *n* under Jewish dietary laws, the prescribed method of slaughter of animals and birds. The act is performed by a trained and licensed slaughterer (**shochet**) who draws a very sharp knife across the animal's throat and allows the blood to drain out. [Late 19C. < Hebrew *šĕḥīṭāh* "slaughter" < *šāḥaṭ* "to slaughter"]

shed[1] /shed/ *v* (**shed, shed·ding, sheds**) **1.** *vt* CAUSE SOMETHING TO FLOW to cause tears or blood to pour out **2.** *vt* RADIATE SOMETHING to radiate or disperse something, especially light **3.** *vti* BIOL LOSE GROWING PART NATURALLY to cast off a growing part such as hair or leaves as a result of a natural process such as molting **4.** *vt* GET RID OF UNDESIRABLE to get rid of somebody or something that is unwanted or unnecessary **5.** *vti* REPEL OR BE REPELLED to flow off or drop off, or cause something, especially water, to flow off or drop off **6.** *vt UK* LOSE LOAD ACCIDENTALLY to have a transported load accidentally fall off onto the road **7.** *vt Scotland* PART HAIR to put a part in the hair ■ *n Scotland* DIVISION IN HAIR a part in the hair [Old English *scēadan* "divide, separate" < Germanic]

shed[2] /shed/ *n* **1.** SMALL BUILDING a small structure, either free-standing or attached to a larger building, used especially for storage or shelter **2.** LARGE OPEN BUILDING a large building with an open interior and sometimes no walls, used for storage or shelter or as a work area **3.** LARGE ENCLOSED BUILDING a large rectangular enclosed building containing an open space, used especially for commercial and retail purposes [15C. Probably variant of SHADE]

she'd /sheed/ *contr* **1.** she had **2.** she would

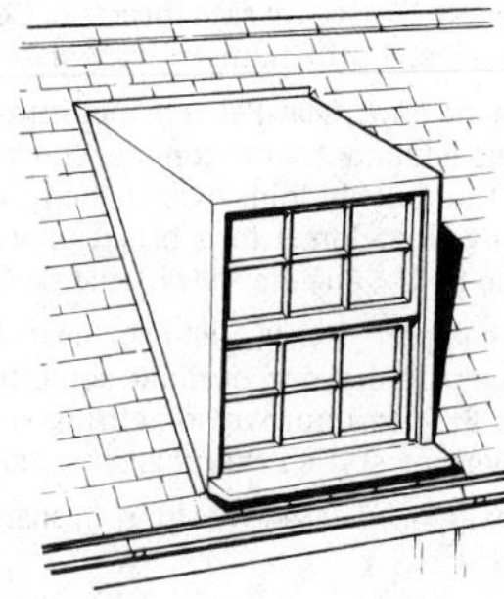

shed dormer

shed dor·mer *n* a dormer with a flat roof that slopes in the same direction as the main roof that surrounds it [< SHED[2]]

she-dev·il *n* an offensive term for a woman who is regarded as treating people with cruelty or gross contempt (*insult*)

shed·load /shéd lōd/ *n UK* a very large amount or number of something (*informal; often used in the plural*) ○ *He always turns up with shedloads of gear, even if we're only camping for the weekend.*

Sheel·er /sheélər/, **Charles** (1883–1965) US painter and photographer. He is known for his images of urban and rural structures, combining abstractionism and realism.

sheen /sheen/ *n* **1.** a bright, softly shining surface or appearance **2.** fine or brightly colored clothing (*literary*) [14C. < archaic *sheen* "beautiful" < Germanic, "to see"]

shee·ny /sheénee/ (*plural* **-nies**) *n* a highly offensive term for a Jew (*slang insult*) [Early 19C. Origin ?]

sheep

sheep /sheep/ (*plural same*) *n* **1.** DOMESTICATED MAMMAL a stocky hooved animal, with ribbed horns in the male. Raised for: wool, meat. Genus: *Ovis.* **2.** LEATHER FROM SHEEP leather made from the skin of a sheep **3.** OFFENSIVE TERM an offensive term that deliberately insults somebody's courage, self-assertion or leadership qualities (*insult*) [Old English *scēap* < Germanic] ◇ **separate the sheep from the goats** to distinguish good or competent members of a group from the bad or incompetent

sheep·ber·ry /sheép bèrree/ (*plural* **-ries**) *n* a bush or tree of the honeysuckle family with edible black berries. Native to: North America. Latin name: *Viburnum lentago.* [< from the berry's supposed resemblance to a sheep dropping]

sheep-dip *n* **1.** a disinfectant in which sheep are immersed to rid them of external parasites such as mites, ticks, and flies **2.** a bath containing a disinfectant in which sheep are immersed to rid them of external parasites

sheep·dog /sheép dàwg, -dòg/ *n* a dog that is used to herd sheep, or belongs to a breed traditionally used to herd sheep. See illustration on next page

sheep·fold /sheép fōld/ *n* an enclosure or shelter for sheep

sheep·herd·er /sheép hùrdər/ *n* a herder of sheep, especially a flock on the open range

sheep·ish /sheépish/ *adj* **1.** showing embarrassment as a result of having done something awkward or wrong **2.** showing the meekness popularly as-

sheepdog

sociated with sheep —**sheep·ish·ly** *adv* —**sheep·ish·ness** *n*

sheep ked /-kèd/ *n* INSECTS same as **sheep tick** [< *ked* "sheep tick," origin ?]

sheep lau·rel *n* a low-growing evergreen bush with leaves that are poisonous to young grazing animals. Flowers: crimson or pink. Native to: eastern United States, Canada. Latin name: *Kalmia angustifolia.*

sheep's eyes *npl* shy glances full of love and longing (*dated*) [< the large size and the docile appearance of the eyes of sheep]

sheep·shank /shéep shàngk/ *n* a knot used to shorten a rope in which the rope is doubled up upon itself

sheeps·head /shéeps hèd/ (*plural same* or **-heads**) *n* **1.** an ocean fish with a deep body marked with dark vertical bands. Native to: Atlantic coastal waters of North America. Latin name: *Archosargus rhomboidalis.* **2.** a freshwater fish of the drum family. Native to: eastern North America. Latin name: *Aplodinotus grunniens.* [Mid-16C. < a supposed resemblance of its head to that of a sheep]

sheep·skin /shéep skìn/ *n* **1.** SHEEP LEATHER WITH OR WITHOUT WOOL the skin of a sheep used as leather, with or without the wool still attached (*often used before a noun*) **2.** SHEEPSKIN GARMENT OR RUG a rug or a garment, especially a coat or jacket, made from sheepskin with the wool attached **3.** PARCHMENT a parchment made from the skin of a sheep (*often used before a noun*) **4.** DIPLOMA a diploma, traditionally made of sheepskin parchment (*informal*)

sheep tick *n* a wingless fly that lives as a blood-sucking parasite on sheep and can cause serious skin irritations. Latin name: *Melophagus ovinus.*

sheer[1] /sheer/ *adj* **1.** COMPLETE AND UTTER used to emphasize the unlimited extent or unmitigated quality of something ○ *That explanation is sheer nonsense.* **2.** EXCLUSIVE OF ANYTHING ELSE considered by itself without reference to anything else, or acting by itself without help from anything else ○ *She won the race by sheer endurance.* **3.** PURE OR UNADULTERATED free of any impurities, or not mixed with anything else **4.** VERTICAL rising nearly straight up or falling nearly straight down over a long distance ○ *They looked over the edge and there was a sheer drop.* **5.** THIN AND ALMOST TRANSPARENT so thin and fine as to be almost transparent ○ *a sheer summer blouse* ■ *adv* **1.** VERTICALLY with an almost vertical rise or fall **2.** COMPLETELY completely and utterly ■ *n* NEARLY TRANSPARENT FABRIC a fabric or piece of clothing that is very thin and fine and almost transparent [Mid-16C. Origin ?] —**sheer·ly** *adv* —**sheer·ness** *n*

SPELLCHECK See *shear.*

sheer[2] /sheer/ *vti* (**sheered, sheer·ing, sheers**) SWERVE FROM COURSE to swerve from a course, or cause a vehicle or vessel to swerve from its course ■ *n* **1.** CHANGE OF COURSE an abrupt or sudden change of course **2.** POSITION OF SHIP AT ANCHOR the position of a ship in relation to its anchor [Early 17C. Origin ?]

SPELLCHECK See *shear.*

sheer[3] /sheer/ *n* the upward curve of a boat's hull as seen from the side, or the degree to which the hull curves upward [Late 17C. Origin ?]

SPELLCHECK See *shear.*

sheer·legs /shéer lègz/, **shear·legs** *n* a lifting device consisting of two poles tied together at the top and spread apart at the bottom with a pulley suspended from the apex (*takes a singular or plural verb*) [Mid-19C. < variant of SHEAR]

sheet[1] /sheet/ *n* **1.** CLOTH USED ON BED a large rectangular piece of cloth that is used to cover the mattress of a bed or somebody sleeping on the mattress **2.** FLAT THIN RECTANGULAR PIECE a broad flat thin piece of a material, especially a rectangular piece of paper, metal, or glass **3.** BROAD THIN EXPANSE a broad flat thin expanse of a substance, especially ice or water **4.** EXPANSE OF SOMETHING MOVING a broad expanse of something that is in motion, e.g., falling water **5.** HOUSEHOLD FLAT BAKING PAN a large flat metal rectangle with very shallow sides or none at all, used for baking **6.** STAMPS PAGE OF STAMPS an entire rectangular page of postage stamps that were printed as a unit **7.** PUBL NEWSPAPER a newspaper or periodical, especially one dismissed as trivial ■ *v* (**sheet·ed, sheet·ing, sheets**) **1.** *vt* PUT SHEET OVER SOMETHING to cover or wrap something in a sheet **2.** *vt* COVER SOMETHING WITH THIN LAYER to cover something with a thin layer of a material **3.** *vt* FORM SOMETHING INTO THIN PIECES to form something, especially metal, into broad flat thin pieces **4.** *vi* FALL OVER BROAD EXPANSE to fall, flow, or spread out over a broad area ○ *Rain sheeted over the parking lot.* ■ *adj* **1.** BROAD, FLAT, AND THIN made in broad flat thin, usually rectangular pieces **2.** COVERING THINLY covering a broad area thinly [Old English *scēte* "cloth" < Germanic, "to project"]

sheet[2] /sheet/ *n* a rope or line attached to a bottom corner of a sail and used to change the sail's position ■ **sheets** *npl* the spaces in the bow and stern of an open boat that are not occupied by the seats [Old English *scēata* "corner, lower part of a sail" < Germanic]

sheet an·chor *n* **1.** a large anchor that is dropped only in emergencies **2.** a personal source of help in a time of crisis or danger [Origin ?]

sheet bend *n* a knot used for tying one rope to a loop formed in another [< SHEET[2]]

sheet·ing /shéeting/ *n* **1.** wide cotton or linen cloth. Use: sheets. **2.** thin material for lining and covering surfaces [Early 18C. < SHEET[1]]

sheet light·ning *n* lightning that appears in a broad sheet as a result of being diffused by cloud cover [< SHEET[1]]

sheet met·al *n* metal that has been formed into a sheet by being pressed between rollers until it is thinner than plate but thicker than foil [< SHEET[1]]

sheet mu·sic *n* music printed on folded or unfolded sheets of paper that have not been bound into a book

sheet pile *n* a vertical column of steel, wood, or concrete driven into the ground alongside others to form an underground barrier impeding the movement of earth or water [< SHEET[1]]

Sheet·rock /shéet ròk/ *tdmk* a trademark for a type of dry-wall

Shef·field /shé feeld/ city in South Yorkshire, northern England. It was for many years the center of the British steel industry. Population: 513,234 (2001).

she·getz /sháygəts/ (*plural* **shkotz·im** /shkáwtsim/) *n* an offensive term for a boy or man who is not Jewish (*insult*) [Early 20C. Via Yiddish *sheygets* < Hebrew *šeqeṣ* "abomination, detested thing"]

sheik /sheek, shayk/, **sheikh, shaikh** *n* **1.** ARAB CHIEF the leader of an Arab family or village **2.** ISLAMIC RELIGIOUS LEADER a senior official in an Islamic religious organization **3.** PHYSICALLY APPEALING MAN a handsome and physically appealing man (*dated informal*) [Late 16C. < Arabic *šayk* "man of advanced years" < *šāka* "be aged"] —**sheik·dom** *n*

shei·ka /sháy kaa/, **shei·kha, shai·kha** *n* the wife of a sheik [Mid-19C. < Arabic *šayka*]

sheikh, etc. ISLAM another spelling of **sheik, etc.**

~~**sheild**~~ incorrect spelling of **shield**

shei·tel /sháyt'l/ *n* a wig worn by a married Orthodox Jewish woman to avoid showing her natural hair in accordance with Orthodox belief [Late 19C. Via Yiddish *sheytl* < Middle High German *scheitel* "crown of the head"]

shek·el /shék'l/ *n* **1.** ISRAELI CURRENCY UNIT the main unit of Israeli currency. See table at **currency 2.** ANCIENT JEWISH UNIT OF WEIGHT an ancient Jewish unit of weight equivalent to approximately 0.5 oz/16 g **3.** ANCIENT JEWISH COIN an ancient Jewish coin that was a unit of currency between 66 A.D. and 130 A.D. ■ **shek·els** *npl* MONEY money or cash (*slang*) [Mid-16C. < Hebrew *šeqel* < *šaqal* "weigh"]

She·khi·nah *n* JUDAISM another spelling of **Shechina**

shel·drake /shél dràyk/ (*plural* **-drakes** or *same*) *n* a male shelduck [14C. Origin ?]

shel·duck /shél dùk/ (*plural* **-ducks** or *same*) *n* a large thick-set, often brightly colored or variegated duck with a thick beak. Native to: Europe, Asia. Genus: *Tadorna.* [Early 18C. Alteration of SHELDRAKE after DUCK[1]]

shelf /shelf/ (*plural* **shelves** /shelvz/) *n* **1.** FLAT SURFACE FOR HOLDING OBJECTS a flat, usually rectangular board on which things are stored or displayed. It can be attached to a wall or can form part of a cabinet. **2.** CONTENTS OF SHELF the contents of a shelf, or the quantity of something that a shelf holds **3.** GEOG LEDGE ON LANDSCAPE a ledge of rock, ice, or sand **4.** MIN EXTRACT LAYER OF UNDERGROUND ROCK a layer of underground rock encountered when sinking a shaft **5.** ARCHERY HEEL OF HAND the part of the heel of the hand on which the back end of an arrow is supported before being fired from a bow [14C. < Low German *schelf*] —**shelf·ful** *n* ◇ **be (left) on the shelf 1.** to be thought too old to have any chance of marrying (*sometimes offensive*) **2.** to be no longer wanted, used, or taken account of

shelf fun·gus *n* FUNGI same as **bracket fungus**

shelf ice *n* a large plate of floating ice that has broken off from an ice shelf

shelf life *n* **1.** the length of time a product may be stored before it begins to lose its freshness or effectiveness **2.** the length of time that somebody or something is popular or lasts (*informal*)

shelf mark *n UK* a series of numbers or letters on a book indicating its location in a library

shell /shel/ *n* **1.** COVERING OF TURTLE OR CRAB the hard protective outer covering of turtles, crabs, and other mollusks and crustaceans, or the calcium-based material this covering is made of **2.** COVERING OF INSECT'S BODY the hard outer covering (**exoskeleton**) of an insect's body **3.** COVERING OF EGG the hard or tough protective outer covering of the eggs of birds, reptiles, and a few mammals **4.** OUTER COVERING OF NUT the hard or fibrous protective outer covering of some seeds and fruits such as nuts **5.** PROTECTIVE CASING a hard casing or covering that protects or holds its contents, e.g., a sunglasses case **6.** CONSTR FRAMEWORK OF BUILDING the basic framework of a building, especially while under construction or after damage by fire **7.** NAUT HULL OF SHIP the outer hull of a ship **8.** COOK PASTRY CASE a casing of pastry that has a filling put into it **9.** SOMETHING HOLLOW OR EMPTY an external form that contains nothing ○ *a mere shell of her former self* **10.** RESERVED MANNER a reserved manner behind which a shy person hides feelings or thoughts ○ *eventually came out of her shell and joined in* **11.** ARMS LARGE EXPLOSIVE PROJECTILE an explosive projectile fired from a large-bore gun such as a field gun or tank gun **12.** ARMS GUN CARTRIDGE a piece of ammunition fired by a gun, especially a shotgun cartridge, which holds the shot and explosive powder **13.** INDUST FIREWORK CARTRIDGE the cartridge that forms the outside of a firework and contains the explosive powder **14.** *US* HOUSEHOLD SMALL GLASS a small beer glass **15.** CLOTHING UNLINED JACKET an unlined, usually lightweight jacket **16.** *US* CLOTHING SLEEVELESS BLOUSE a sleeveless blouse or sweater for a woman **17.** BUSINESS same as **shell company 18.** ROWING NARROW RACING BOAT a narrow light boat used for racing, rowed by one or more persons **19.** PHYS GROUP OF ELECTRONS IN SIMILAR ORBITS a group of electrons with the same principal quantum number that orbit the nucleus of an atom **20.** COMPUT COMMAND PROGRAM a computer program that simplifies the interface between a user and the operating system by allowing the user to pick from a set of menus instead of entering commands ■ *v* (**shelled, shell·ing, shells**) **1.** *vti* TAKE SOMETHING OUT OF SHELL to take something out of a shell, or be taken out of a shell ○ *shell peas* **2.** *vti* SEPARATE KERNELS FROM COB to separate kernels from a cob, or be separated from a cob ○ *shell sweet corn* **3.** *vti* MIL BOMBARD TARGET to fire artillery shells at something **4.** *vi* FLAKE OFF to fall off in thin scales **5.** *vi* **COLLECT SEASHELLS** to look for and gather shells at the seashore **6.** *vt* BASEBALL **MAKE MANY HITS AGAINST** in baseball, to make many hits against an opposing pitcher and score many runs [Old English *scell* < Germanic]

shell out *vti* to pay out money, especially a great deal of money (*informal*)

she'll /sheel/ *contr* **1.** she shall **2.** she will

shel·lac /shə lák/, **shel·lack** *n* **1. PURIFIED RESIN** yellowish orange flakes of a resin (**lac**) secreted by a tropical insect **2. VARNISH** a thin varnish made of purified lac dissolved in alcohol. Use: formerly, as a coating on wooden items. **3. 78 RPM PHONOGRAPH RECORD** an old type of phonograph record originally made from a material containing purified lac, played at 78 rpm ■ *vt* (**-lacked, -lack·ing, -lacs; -lacked, -lack·ing, -lacks**) **1. APPLY SHELLAC TO SOMETHING** to coat something with shellac varnish **2. HIT SOMEBODY REPEATEDLY** to beat somebody repeatedly with hard blows (*slang*) **3. DEFEAT SOMEBODY EASILY** to defeat somebody easily or decisively (*slang*) [Mid-17C. < SHELL + LAC[1], after French *laque en écailles* "lac (melted) in thin plates"]

shel·lack·ing /shə láking/ *n* (*slang*) **1.** a severe physical beating **2.** an easy or decisive defeat

shell·back /shél bàk/ *n* **1.** a sailor who has crossed the equator, especially one whose crossing was marked by a traditional initiation ceremony **2.** an experienced sailor or somebody who has been a sailor for many years [< the idea that limpets and barnacles have grown on the sailor's back during the long time at sea]

shell bean *n* **1.** *US* a bean plant that is grown for its seeds not its pods **2.** a seed of a shell bean plant, used as food

shell com·pa·ny *n* a company that has no independent assets or operations of its own, but is used by its owners to conduct specific business dealings or maintain control of other companies

Popperfoto

Mary Shelley

Shel·ley /shéllee/, **Mary** (1797–1851) British writer. Her most famous work is *Frankenstein* (1818). She was the daughter of Mary Wollstonecraft and the wife of Percy Bysshe Shelley. Born **Godwin, Mary Wollstonecraft**

Shel·ley, Percy Bysshe (1792–1822) British poet. His lyric poetry was at the forefront of the English romantic movement and included odes such as "To a Skylark" (1819) and an elegy on Keats, "Adonais" (1821). He was the husband of Mary Shelley.

> "Hail to thee, blithe Spirit! / Bird thou never wert, / That from Heaven, or near it, / Pourest thy full heart / In profuse strains of unpremeditated art."
> [Percy Bysshe Shelley, "To a Skylark"; 1819]

> "Poets are...the trumpets which sing to battle and feel not what they inspire...Poets are the unacknowledged legislators of the world."
> [Percy Bysshe Shelley, *A Defence of Poetry*; 1821]

shell·fire /shél fīr/ *n* **1.** artillery shells or projectiles fired at a target **2.** the firing or exploding of artillery shells or projectiles

shell·fish /shél fish/ (*plural* **same** or **-fish·es**) *n* an invertebrate water animal with a shell, especially an edible mollusk or crustacean such as an oyster, shrimp, or lobster

shell game *n* **1.** a form of the game thimblerig in which spectators bet on the final location of an object hidden under one of three walnut shells or cups that have been shuffled **2.** a scheme for defrauding or deceiving people

shell jack·et *n* a tight-fitting military jacket that extends only to the waist and is worn on semiformal occasions

shell-like *n UK* somebody's ear (*slang humorous*)

shell pink *adj* of a pale pink color (*hyphenated when used before a noun*) —**shell pink** *n*

shell shock *n* a psychiatric disorder caused by exposure to warfare, especially shellfire (*dated*)

shell-shocked *adj* **1.** stunned, upset, or exhausted as a result of a stressful experience (*informal*) **2.** experiencing severe psychological effects from exposure to warfare, especially shellfire (*dated*)

shell star *n* a star that is thought to have a surrounding shell of gas

shell steak *n US* a cut of steak from the short loin area

shell·work /shél wùrk/ *n* seashells stuck on furniture and other items to give a decorative finish

Shel·ta /shéltə/ *n* an ancient secret language used by the Roma and other traveling people in the Republic of Ireland and the United Kingdom, based on Gaelic [Late 19C. Origin ?] —**Shel·ta** *adj*

shel·ter /shéltər/ *n* **1. STRUCTURE THAT PROTECTS OR COVERS** a structure or building that provides cover from weather or protection against danger **2. REFUGE** an establishment providing temporary accommodations and food for people in need or without a home **3. REFUGE FOR ANIMALS** an establishment that takes in and looks after lost or unwanted animals **4. PROTECTION OR COVER** the protection, cover, refuge, or safety that a shelter provides **5. DWELLING OR HOUSING** a place to live, considered as one of life's necessities ■ *v* (**-tered, -ter·ing, -ters**) **1.** *vt* **PROVIDE SOMEBODY OR SOMETHING WITH PROTECTION** to provide somebody or something with protection, cover, refuge, or safety **2.** *vi* **FIND PROTECTION** to find protection, cover, refuge, or safety **3.** *vi Carib* **FIND DRY PLACE** to find protection from the rain **4.** *vt* **INVEST MONEY TO AVOID TAXES** to put money into an investment that is subject to a lower tax rate or is free from taxes [Late 16C. Origin ?]

shel·tered /shéltərd/ *adj* **1.** protected from the adverse effects of the weather, especially wind **2.** protected from the unpleasant, upsetting, or testing experiences of life

shel·tered work·shop *n* a workplace specially designed to provide a noncompetitive environment where people who are physically or mentally challenged can acquire job skills and experience

shel·ter tent *n US* a small tent for two people usually made from two similar pieces of waterproof fabric

shel·tie /shéltee/, **shel·ty** (*plural* **-ties**) *n* (*informal*) **1.** ZOOL same as **Shetland pony 2.** BREED same as **Shetland sheepdog** [Early 16C. Probably < Old Norse *Hjalti* "Shetlander"]

shelve[1] /shelv/ (**shelved, shelv·ing, shelves**) *vt* **1. PUT SOMETHING ON SHELF** to put or store something on a shelf **2. SET SOMETHING ASIDE** to put something off until later, or set something aside **3. DISMISS SOMEBODY OR SOMETHING** to dismiss or withdraw somebody or something from active service [Late 16C. Back-formation < SHELVES]

shelve[2] /shelv/ (**shelved, shelv·ing, shelves**) *vi* to descend with a flat, usually gradual slope [Late 16C. Origin ?]

shelves plural of **shelf**

shelv·ing /shélving/ *n* **1.** the shelves in a place, or shelves in general **2.** material used for making shelves

She·ma /shə maá/ *n* the confession of faith made in Jewish religious practice [Early 18C. < Hebrew *šəma* "hear!"]

she·moz·zle /shə mózz'l/ *n* (*dated informal*) **1.** a confused or muddled situation **2.** a noisy quarrel or argument [Late 19C. Via Yiddish, "crooked luck" < Middle High German *slim* "crooked" + *mazzāl* "luck"]

Shen·an·do·ah Na·tion·al Park /shènnən dō ə-/ national park in the Blue Ridge Mountains, northern Virginia, established in 1935. Area: 310 sq. mi./802 sq. km.

Shen·an·do·ah Riv·er /shènnən dō ə-/ river in Virginia. Length: 140 mi./225 km., flowing through the Shenandoah Valley between the Allegheny and Blue Ridge mountains, southwest of Harpers Ferry, West Virginia

she·nan·i·gan /shə nánnigən/ *n* (*informal*) **1.** something that is deceitful, underhanded, or otherwise questionable (*usually used in the plural*) **2.** a playful trick, mischievous prank, or other display of high spirits [Mid-19C. Origin ?]

Shen·yang /shèn yaáng/ city in Liaoning Province, northeastern China. Population: 5,120,000 (1995).

She·ol /shée ōl, shee ṓl/ *n* in ancient Hebrew theology, the dwelling place of the dead [Late 16C. < Hebrew *šə'ōl*]

~~**shepard**~~ incorrect spelling of **shepherd**

Shep·ard /shéppərd/, **Alan, Jr.** (1923–98) US astronaut. He was the first US astronaut in space (May 5, 1961) and the fifth person to walk on the moon (1971). Full name **Shepard, Alan Bartlett Jr.**

Shep·ard, Sam (*b.* 1943) US playwright and actor. His offbeat plays include the Pulitzer Prize-winning *Buried Child* (1978). Full name **Rogers, Samuel Shepard, Jr.**

> "In this business we make movies, American movies. Leave the films to the French."
> [Sam Shepard, *True West*; 1980]

shep·herd /shéppərd/ *n* **1. SOMEBODY TENDING SHEEP** somebody who looks after sheep **2. SOMEBODY PROVIDING GUIDANCE** somebody who is responsible for caring for and guiding a group of people, especially a Christian minister ■ *v* (**-herd·ed, -herd·ing, -herds**) **1.** *vti* **TEND SHEEP** to look after sheep **2.** *vt* **GUIDE** to guide a group of people somewhere **3.** *vt* **TAKE CARE OF OTHERS** to look after the well-being of a group of people [Old English *scēaphirde* < *scēap* "sheep" + *hierde* "herder"]

shep·herd·ess /shéppərdəss/ *n* a girl or woman who looks after sheep (*dated*)

shep·herd's check *n* (*often used before a noun*) **1.** a pattern of small black and white squares **2.** a fabric in a shepherd's check pattern

shep·herd's pie *n* a baked dish made of cooked ground meat, traditionally lamb or mutton, in gravy with a topping of mashed potato

shep·herd's purse *n* an annual plant that has heart-shaped seed pods and is a common garden weed. Latin name: *Capsella bursa-pastoris*. [< the pod's resemblance to a bag used by shepherds to carry food]

Shep·par·ton /shéppərtən/ city in northern Victoria, Australia. It is an industrial, agricultural, and food-processing center. Population: 17,001 (1991).

Popperfoto

Sheraton: a Sheraton chair

Sher·a·ton /shérrət'n/ *adj* describes furniture designed by or in the simple graceful style of Thomas Sheraton, who favored straight lines, understated classical ornamentation, and light thin legs

Sher·a·ton /shérrət'n/, **Thomas** (1751–1806) British cabinetmaker. He wrote *The Cabinet-Maker and Upholsterer's Drawing Book* (1793–94), which was influential in formulating the neoclassical style in English furniture.

sher·bert /shúrbərt/ *n* FOOD another spelling of **sherbet** (sense 1)

sher·bet /shúrbət/ *n* **1.** FROZEN DESSERT a frozen dessert made with fruit syrup, milk and the white of an egg, whisked until smooth and opaque **2.** *UK* FIZZY POWDER a fruit-flavored sweet powder that fizzes when moistened on the tongue and is eaten as a confection or is stirred into water to make a fizzy drink (*often used before a noun*) **3.** *UK* FRUIT DRINK a drink made from fruit juice, water, and sugar and served chilled [Early 17C. Via Turkish *şerbet* and Persian *šerbet* < Arabic *šarbat* "drink" < *šariba* "to drink"]

Sher·brooke /shúr brŏŏk/ city situated south of the St. Lawrence River in Quebec, Canada, 100 mi./160 km east of Montreal. Population: 127,354 (2001).

sherd *n* ARCHAEOL same as **shard**

she·reef *n* ISLAM, POL, HIST same as **sharif**

Sher·i·dan /shérrid'n/, **Philip Henry** (1831–88) US Union general. His victory at the Battle of Five Forks (1865) led to the surrender of the Confederate commander.

Sher·i·dan, Richard Brinsley (1751–1816) Irish-born British playwright. His comedies of manners include *The Rivals* (1775) and *The School for Scandal* (1777). He was a Whig member of Parliament (1780–1812). See Cultural note at **rival, scandal**

> "MRS. MALAPROP If I reprehend any thing in this world, it is the use of my oracular tongue, and a nice derangement of epitaphs!"
> [Richard Brinsley Sheridan, *The Rivals*; 1775]

she·rif *n* ISLAM, POL, HIST same as **sharif**

sher·iff /shérrif/ *n* **1.** US COUNTY LAW ENFORCEMENT OFFICER in the United States, the chief law enforcement officer for a county, whose duties are sometimes restricted to the enforcement of the orders of the courts **2.** SENIOR OFFICIAL OF ENGLISH COUNTY in England and Wales, the senior representative of the monarch in a county, who performs ceremonial and some judicial duties **3.** SCOTTISH JUDGE in Scotland, a judge who presides over one of the lower courts for civil and criminal cases **4.** CANADIAN COURT OFFICER in Canada, an officer of the courts who assists with the administration of the justice system, e.g., by serving writs **5.** AUSTRALIAN COURT OFFICIAL in Australia, a court official charged with managing juries and implementing orders from the Supreme Court [Old English *scīrgerēfa* "reeve of the shire" < *scīr* "shire" + *gerēfa* "reeve"] —**sher·iff·dom** *n*

sher·iff court *n* in Scotland, the lower court for civil and criminal cases

sher·iff of·fi·cer *n* in Scotland, a court official who carries out warrants and serves writs

Sher·lock Holmes /shùr lok hṓmz/ *n* **1.** somebody with exceptional powers of deduction or perception (*humorous*) **2.** CRIME same as **private detective** (*informal*) [Early 20C. After the detective in the stories of Sir Arthur Conan Doyle]

Sher·man /shúrmən/, **Cindy** (*b.* 1954) US photographer. Her carefully staged and composed photographs, featuring herself in various roles, gained widespread notice in the 1980s.

Sher·man, James S. (1855–1912) vice president of the United States. He was William Howard Taft's vice president (1909–12). Full name **Sherman, James Schoolcraft**

Sher·man, John (1823–1900) US politician. The brother of General William T. Sherman, he served as secretary of the treasury (1877–81) and secretary of state (1897–98). As a Republican US senator (1861–77, 1881–97), he wrote the Sherman Antitrust Act (1890) and the Sherman Silver Purchase Act (1890).

Sher·man, Roger (1721–93) American patriot. He was a signatory of the Declaration of Independence (1776) and represented Connecticut at the Constitutional Convention (1787).

Sher·man, William T. (1820–91) US Union general. A Mexican War veteran, he rejoined the army in 1861 as the Civil War broke out and became one of the Union army's most aggressive and successful generals, marching on Atlanta and then to the sea (1864). Full name **Sherman, William Tecumseh**

> "There is many a boy here today who looks on war as all glory, but, boys, it is all hell."
> [William T. Sherman, *Speech, Columbus, OH*; August 11, 1880]

sher·pa /shúrpə/ *n* CLIMBING another spelling of **Sherpa** (senses 2–3) [Mid-20C. < SHERPA]

Sher·pa /shúrpə/ (*plural* **-pas** or *same*) *n* **1.** MEMBER OF HIMALAYAN PEOPLE a member of a people originally from Tibet who live on the southern slopes of the Himalayan range in Nepal and Sikkim. Sherpas are noted for their mountaineering skills. **2.** HIMALAYAN GUIDE a Sherpa who works as a guide for mountaineers in the Himalayan range **3.** EXPERT POLITICAL AIDE an expert who helps a government leader prepare for a summit meeting [Mid-19C. < Tibetan *sharpa* "inhabitant of an eastern country"]

~~**sherrif**~~ incorrect spelling of **sheriff**

sher·ry /shérree/ *n* a wine, especially one made near Jerez de la Frontera, Spain, that has a higher alcohol content as a result of adding brandy, and ranges from very sweet to very dry [Late 16C. Alteration of archaic *sherris*, interpreted as plural, after *Xeres* (now JEREZ DE LA FRONTERA)]

sher·wa·ni /shər wáanee/ (*plural* **-nis**) *n* a knee-length formal coat without lapels that buttons up to the neck, worn by men in and from South Asia [Early 20C. < Urdu, Persian *širwānī* "from Shirvan," town in NE Persia]

Sher·wood /shúr wŏŏd/, **Robert E.** (1896–1955) US playwright. His Pulitzer Prize-winning plays include *Idiot's Delight* (1936). Full name **Sherwood, Robert Emmet**

Sher·wood For·est ancient forest in Nottinghamshire, central England, now reduced to a small fraction of its former extent. According to legend it was the haunt of Robin Hood.

she's /sheez/ *contr* **1.** she has **2.** she is

Shet·land /shéttlənd/ *n* **1.** ZOOL same as **Shetland pony 2.** BREED same as **Shetland sheepdog 3.** TEXTILES same as **Shetland wool 4.** CLOTHING an item of clothing made of Shetland wool, especially a sweater ■ *adj* made of Shetland wool

Shet·land Is·lands /shétlənd-/ group of about 150 islands lying 130 mi./209 km north of mainland Scotland. The islands serve as a base for the North Sea oil industry. Mainland is the chief island. Capital: Lerwick. Population: 22,522 (2001). Area: 555 sq. mi./1,438 sq. km. —**Shet·land·er** *n*

Shetland pony

Shet·land po·ny *n* a small sturdy pony with a long shaggy mane and tail, belonging to a breed that originated in the Shetland Islands

Shet·land sheep·dog *n* a small herding dog with a heavy coat that resembles a collie, belonging to a breed that originated in the Shetland Islands

Shet·land wool *n* a fine wool from sheep raised in the Shetland Islands, or a yarn spun from this wool

Shev·ard·na·dze /shèvvərd náadzə/, **Eduard** (*b.* 1928) Georgian chairman (1992–96) and president (1995–2003). As foreign minister of the former Soviet Union, he helped to implement democratic reforms. After his native Georgia became an independent republic, he became its head of state, but was forced to resign following election disputes. Full name **Shevardnadze, Eduard Amvrosiyevich**

She·vat /shə váat/, **She·bat** /-báat, -váat/ *n* in the Jewish calendar, the 11th month of the religious year, lasting 30 days and falling about the same time as January to February. See table at **calendar** [Mid-16C. < Hebrew *šəḇaṭ*]

shew /shō/ (**shewed, shewed** or **shewn** /shōn/, **shew·ing, shews**) *vti* same as **show** (*archaic*) [Variant]

shew·bread /shṓ brèd/ *n* in the Bible, the twelve loaves of bread placed in the tabernacle every Sabbath by the Hebrew priests of ancient Israel (*archaic*)

SHF, shf *abbr* PHYS superhigh frequency

shh *interj* another spelling of **sh**

Shi·a /shée ə/, **Shi·'a, Shi·'ah** *n* (*plural same* or **-as;** *plural same* or **-'as;** *plural same* or **-'ahs**) **1.** the branch of Islam that considers Ali, the cousin of Muhammad, and his descendants as Muhammad's true successors **2.** ISLAM same as **Shiite** ■ *adj* ISLAM same as **Shiite** [Early 17C. < Arabic *šīʿa* "faction, party"]

shi·at·su /shee áat sŏŏ/, **shi·at·zu** *n* a form of healing massage in which the hands are used to apply pressure at acupuncture points on the body in order to stimulate and redistribute energy. Originating in Japan, it is used to treat various conditions such as back pain, migraine, insomnia, depression, and digestive problems. [Mid-20C. < Japanese, "finger pressure"]

shib·bo·leth /shíbbə lèth/ *n* **1.** CATCHWORD OR SLOGAN a word or phrase frequently used, or a belief strongly held, by members of a group that is usually regarded by outsiders as meaningless, unimportant, or misguided **2.** COMMON SAYING OR BELIEF a saying that is widely used or a belief that is widely held, especially one that interferes with somebody's ability to speak or think about things without preconception **3.** IDENTIFYING WORD OR CUSTOM a unique pronunciation, word, behavior, or practice used to distinguish one group of people from another and to identify somebody as either a member of the group or an outsider [Mid-17C. < Hebrew *šibbōleṯ* "stream"]

ORIGIN According to the Bible, the people of Gilead used the word *šibbōleṯ* as a password, because they knew their enemies the Ephraimites could not pronounce the "sh" properly ("And it was so, that when those Ephraimites which were escaped said, Let me go over; that the men of Gilead said unto him, Art thou an Ephraimite? If he said, Nay, then they said unto him, Say now Shibboleth; and he said Sibboleth: for he could not frame to pronounce it right") (Judges 12:5–6).

shid·duch /shíddək/ (*plural* **-duch·im** /shíddəkim/) *n* a Jewish marriage, in former times usually arranged by a professional matchmaker (**shadchan**) [Late 19C. Via Yiddish < Hebrew *šiddūḵ* "negotiation"]

~~**shiek**~~ incorrect spelling of **sheik**

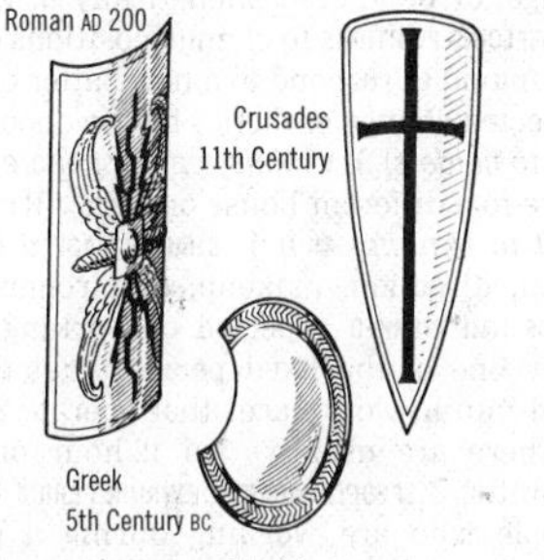

shield

shield /sheeld/ *n* **1.** PIECE OF ARMOR CARRIED ON ARM a flat or convex piece of armor carried on the arm and used as a protection against weapon blows, arrows, bullets, or projectiles **2.** PROTECTION OR DEFENSE somebody or something that serves as protection or acts as a defense **3.** COAT OF ARMS a shield or a shield-shaped insignia that contains somebody's coat of arms **4.** PRIZE OR TROPHY a prize or trophy, especially in a sports competition, that is made in the shape of a shield **5.** DECORATIVE OFFICIAL EMBLEM a decorative device used as an official emblem by a government or organization, usually containing symbolic images associated with the government's territory or the organization's purpose **6.** US POLICE OFFICER'S BADGE the official badge that a US law enforcement officer wears or carries **7.** CLOTHING same as **dress shield** **8.** ARMS **PROTECTIVE PLATE ATTACHED TO ARTILLERY** a steel plate attached to a piece of artillery to protect those operating the artillery from bullets and shrapnel **9.** MECH ENG **MACHINE'S SAFETY BARRIER** a protective barrier around the moving parts of a piece of machinery, e.g., a screen or housing **10.** ELEC ENG **ANTISTATIC OR ANTIMAGNETIC SCREEN** a screen used to protect equipment or people from unwanted electric or magnetic fields **11.** PHYS **WALL PROTECTING FROM RADIATION** an encasing structure or wall, usually made of lead or concrete that is put around a nuclear reactor or other source of radiation to prevent the release of radiation **12.** GEOL **FLAT AREA OF ROCK** a broad flat area of exposed Precambrian basement rock that lies at the center of each continent **13.** ZOOL **PROTECTIVE PART COVERING ANIMAL** a protective part covering an animal, e.g., a shell, scale, or plate **14.** BOT same as **apothecium** ■ *v* (**shield·ed, shield·ing, shields**) **1.** *vt* **PROTECT SOMEBODY OR SOMETHING WITH SHIELD** to prevent harm or damage to somebody or something by using a physical barrier or by intervening in a protective way **2.** *vi* **ACT AS SHIELD** to serve or act as a protection or defense **3.** *vt* **HIDE SOMEBODY OR SOMETHING** to conceal or shelter somebody or something from view [Old English *scield* < Germanic] —**shield·er** *n*

SYNONYMS See ***safeguard***.

shield·ing /sheélding/ *n* the use of material such as lead or concrete around a source of radiation to prevent the harmful release of radiation

shield law *n* in North America, a law that protects a journalist from being forced to reveal the name of a source who provided information confidentially

Shield of Da·vid *n* JUDAISM same as **Star of David**

shiel·ing /sheéling/ *n Scotland* **1.** a mountain hut used by a cowherd **2.** a mountain pasture that is used by cattle in the summer [Mid-16C. < *shiel* "shieling," origin ?]

shift /shift/ *v* (**shift·ed, shift·ing, shifts**) **1.** *vti* **MOVE** to move somebody or something to a different position, or be moved to a different position **2.** *vti* **CHANGE OR EXCHANGE** to change or exchange something for something else of the same group, set, or class, or be changed or exchanged in this way ○ *I've shifted jobs three times in the last year.* **3.** *vti* **OPERATE GEARS OF VEHICLE** to put a car or other vehicle into a different gear **4.** *vi* **PROVIDE FOR OWN NEEDS** to provide for your own personal needs or manage your personal affairs ○ *You need to learn to shift for yourself.* **5.** *vi* **GET BY WITH DECEIT** to get by through the use of deceit, tricks, or underhanded methods **6.** *vi* **PRESS SHIFT KEY** to press the shift key on a computer or typewriter keyboard in order to produce capital letters or other characters **7.** *vti* LING **ALTER PHONETICALLY** to alter a sound phonetically in the course of the development of a language, or be altered phonetically **8.** *vi* BASEBALL **CHANGE FIELDING POSITIONS** to change positions on a baseball diamond to respond to a new batter or forestall an expected change of tactics by the opposing team (*refers to fielders*) **9.** *vi Malaysia, Singapore* **MOVE HOUSE** to move to a different house or area ○ *We are going to shift to Penang.* ■ *n* **1. CHANGE MADE** a change in position, direction, makeup, or circumstances **2. PERIOD OF TIME WORKED** a period of working time, especially one of the fixed periods that the day is divided into in workplaces that operate 24 hours a day. There are usually two 12-hour or three 8-hour shifts. **3. PEOPLE WORKING DURING PERIOD** the group of people who are working during a particular period of time **4.** COMPUT same as **shift key** **5.** CLOTHING **DRESS** a loose-fitting dress that hangs down from the shoulders **6.** CLOTHING **WOMAN'S UNDERGARMENT** a woman's shirt-shaped undergarment of the 17th and 18th centuries **7. TRICK** a deceitful or underhanded scheme or plan **8.** BASEBALL **CHANGE IN FIELDERS' POSITION** a change in the positions of the fielders on a baseball diamond to respond to a new batter or forestall an expected change of tactics by the opposing team **9.** FOOTBALL **CHANGE IN PLAYERS' POSITION** in football, a change in the position of a player or players on the field after the teams have lined up but before the ball is snapped **10.** GEOL **ROCK DISPLACEMENT AT FAULT** a displacement of rocks on a fault line **11.** MUSIC **CHANGE IN HAND POSITION** a change in hand position in order to play a different set of notes in a different register on a keyboard or stringed instrument **12.** LING **CHANGE IN PRONUNCIATION** a change in the pronunciation of a sound in the course of the development of a language **13.** PHYS **CHANGE IN FREQUENCY** a change in the position of a spectral line representing a change of frequency, e.g., that caused by the Doppler effect [Old English *sciftan* "divide, arrange" < Germanic]

SYNONYMS See ***change***.

shif·ta /shíftə/ (*plural same* or **-tas**) *n* in parts of Africa, somebody who commits a robbery, usually of a traveler, on or near a public road [Mid-20C. Via Somali *shúfto* "bandit" < Amharic]

shift key *n* a key on a computer or typewriter keyboard that is pressed to produce capital letters or other characters

shift·less /shíftləss/ *adj* **1.** unwilling to make the effort to be successful or do something properly **2.** lacking the abilities or knowledge required to do something successfully or properly —**shift·less·ly** *adv* —**shift·less·ness** *n*

shift work /shíft wùrk/ *n* a system of working in which people work one of a set of usually two 12-hour or three 8-hour shifts in a 24-hour period (*often used before a noun*)

shift·y /shíftee/ (**-i·er, -i·est**) *adj* **1. UNTRUSTWORTHY** likely to try to deceive or avoid responsibility **2. CHANGING DIRECTION OR POSITION** changing direction or position often or quickly, or able to do so **3. RESOURCEFUL** having the abilities and knowledge needed to do something successfully —**shift·i·ly** *adv* —**shift·i·ness** *n*

shi·gel·la /shi géllə/ (*plural* **-lae** /-lee/ or **-las**) *n* a rod-shaped bacterium that lives in the intestinal tracts of human beings and animals and causes dysentery. There are four species, all causing dysentery, but with varying degrees of severity. Genus: *Shigella*. [Mid-20C. < modern Latin, after Kiyoshi *Shiga* (1870–1957), Japanese bacteriologist]

shig·el·lo·sis /shìggə lṓssiss/ (*plural* **-lo·ses** /-lṓ seez/) *n* a highly infectious form of dysentery caused by the shigella bacterium. It occurs mainly in tropical countries, especially under unsanitary conditions and among children and people with weakened immune systems.

shih tzu /sheé tsóo/ (*plural same* or **shih tzus**) *n* a small short-legged dog with a short muzzle, long dense coat, and a tail that curls over its back, belonging to a breed developed in Tibet [Early 20C. < Chinese *shīzigǒu* "lion dog"]

Shi·ism /sheé ìzzəm/, **Shi·'ism** *n* the Shiite branch of the Islamic religion [Late 19C. < SHIA or SHIITE]

shi·i·ta·ke /shi taákee/, **shi·i·ta·ke mush·room, shi·ta·ke, shi·ta·ke mush·room** *n* a dark-colored mushroom with an edible fleshy cap. Native to: East Asia. Latin name: *Lentinus edodes*. [Late 19C. < Japanese, "oak-tree mushroom"]

Shi·ite /sheé ìt/, **Shi·'ite** *n* a follower of the Shia branch of Islam, which considers Ali, the cousin of Muhammad, and his descendants as Muhammad's true successors ■ *adj* relating to Shiites or the Shia branch of Islam —**Shi·it·ic** /shee íttik/ *adj*

Shi·jia·zhuang /sheéjyaá jwaáng/ industrial center and capital of Hebei Province, southwest of Beijing, in northeastern China. Population: 1,600,000 (1995).

shi·ka·ri /shi kaáree/ (*plural* **-ris** or **-rees**) *n S Asia* a big-game hunter, especially a professional hunter who works as a guide [Early 19C. Via Urdu < Persian *šikārī* "of hunting" < *šikār* "hunting"]

Shi·ko·ku /shee kókoo/ smallest of the four main islands of Japan. Area: 7,259 sq. mi./18,800 sq. km. Population: 4,195,000 (1990).

shik·sa /shíksə/, **shik·se** *n* an offensive Jewish term for a girl or woman who is not Jewish (*insult*) [Late 19C. < Yiddish *shikse*, feminine of *sheygets* (see SHEGETZ)]

shill /shil/ *n* **1. PRETENDED CUSTOMER OR GAMBLER** an accomplice who pretends to be an interested customer or gambler in order to lure others into buying or gambling **2. SELF-INTERESTED PROMOTER** somebody who promotes somebody else or makes a sales pitch for something for reasons of self-interest ■ *v* (**shilled, shill·ing, shills**) **1.** *vi* **BE SHILL** to be or work as a shill **2.** *vt* **PROMOTE SOMEBODY OR SOMETHING AS SHILL** to promote somebody or make a sales pitch for something using the tactics of a shill [Early 20C. Origin ?]

shil·le·lagh /shə láylee, -láylə/, **shil·la·lah** *n Ireland* a stick or club, traditionally made of oak or blackthorn wood [Late 18C. After *Shillelagh*, town in east central Ireland, famous for oaks]

shil·ling /shílling/ *n* **1. FORMER BRITISH COIN** a former subunit of British currency **2. FORMER US COIN** any of various former US coins **3. UNIT OF CURRENCY IN EAST AFRICA** the main unit of currency in several East African countries. See table at **currency** **4.** *Malaysia, Singapore* COINS same as **coin** (*informal*) [Old English *scilling* < Germanic]

Shil·long /shi lóng/ capital of Meghalaya State, northeastern India. Population: 267,881 (2001).

Shil·luk /shi lóok/ (*plural same* or **-luks**) *n* **1.** a member of a people who live in northeastern Africa, mainly along the western bank of the Nile River in southern Sudan **2.** the Nilo-Saharan language of the Shilluk people. Native speakers: 110,000. [Late 18C. < Shilluk] —**Shil·luk** *adj*

shil·ly-shal·ly /shíllee shàllee/ *vi* (**shil·ly-shal·lied, shil·ly-shal·ly·ing, shil·ly-shal·lies**) **1. HESITATE OR VACILLATE** to be unable to make a choice or decision when one is needed **2. WASTE TIME** to waste time on unimportant things ■ *adv* **IRRESOLUTELY** with hesitation or a lack of decision ■ *adj* **LACKING DECISIVENESS** feeling or showing a lack of decisiveness ■ *n* (*plural* **shil·ly-shal·lies**) **HESITATION** a failure or inability to make a choice or decision [Early 18C. Alteration of *shall I? shall I?*] —**shil·ly-shal·li·er** *n*

Shi·loh /shílō/ site near Pittsburg Landing in southwestern Tennessee, situated on the Tennessee River, north of Savannah. A major Civil War battle fought there on April 6–7, 1862 ended inconclusively after heavy casualties.

shim /shim/ *n* a thin, usually wedge-shaped piece of wood, metal, plastic, or other material that is used to help position something properly, usually by adjusting a level or filling a gap ■ *vt* (**shimmed, shim·ming, shims**) to position or adjust something using a shim [Early 18C. Origin ?]

shim·mer /shímmər/ *vti* (**-mered, -mer·ing, -mers**) **1. SHINE WITH WAVERING LIGHT** to shine softly with a wavering or flickering light, or make something do this **2. BE VISIBLE AS WAVERING IMAGE** to be visible as a wavering or flickering and sometimes distorted image, or make something do this ■ *n* **1. WAVERING LIGHT OR GLOW** a wavering or flickering soft light or glow **2. WAVERING IMAGE OR APPEARANCE** a wavering or flickering and sometimes distorted image such as that caused by hot air rising from the ground [Old English *scymrian* < Germanic, "shine"] —**shim·mer·y** *adj*

shim·my /shímmee/ *n* **1. WOBBLING OF VEHICLE** a wobbling motion or vibration, especially in the front wheels of a motor vehicle **2. POPULAR 1920S DANCE** a 1920s jazz dance in which the body was held straight and shaken rhythmically and rapidly from the shoulders down **3. QUICK SIDEWAYS MOVEMENT** a quick movement of the body to the side **4.** CLOTHING same as **chemise** (*informal*) ■ *vi* (**-mied, -my·ing, -mies**) **1. MOVE WITH WOBBLE** to wobble or be shaken with a wobbling motion, especially in the front wheels (*refers to vehicles*) **2. DANCE SHIMMY** to dance the shimmy **3. MOVE WITH SHAKE** to move the body in a shaking or swaying way **4. MOVE QUICKLY SIDEWAYS** to make a quick movement of the body to the side [Early 20C. Origin ?]

Shi·mo·no·se·ki /shìmmənō sékee/ city and seaport in Yamaguchi Prefecture on southwestern Honshu Island, Japan, across the Shimonoseki Strait from Kitakyushu. Population: 246,924 (2002).

shin[1] /shin/ *n* **1. FRONT OF LOWER LEG** the front part of the leg from below the knee to above the ankle **2.** ANAT same as **shinbone** **3. CUT OF BEEF** the lower portion of the foreleg in cattle, used as a cut of beef in stews ■ *v* (**shinned, shin·ning, shins**) **1.** *vti UK* same as **shinny**[1] **2.** *vt* **KICK SOMEBODY IN SHIN** to kick or hit somebody in the shin **3.** *vi US* **WALK BRISKLY OR RUN** to walk at a fast pace or run [Old English *scinu* < Germanic]

shin[2] /shin/ *n* the 22nd letter of the Hebrew alphabet, represented in the English alphabet as "sh." See table at **alphabet** [Early 19C. < Hebrew *šīn*]

shin·bone /shín bṑn/ *n* the flat bone immediately under the skin on the front of the lower leg. Technical name **tibia** (sense 1)

shin·dig /shín dìg/ *n* (*informal*) **1.** a noisy and festive party or celebration **2.** same as **shindy** (sense 1) [Late 19C. Probably alteration of SHINDY]

shin·dy /shíndee/ (*plural* **-dies**) *n* (*informal*) **1.** a disturbance or commotion **2.** same as **shindig** (sense 1) [Early 19C. Probably variant of SHINTY]

shine /shīn/ *v* (**shone** /shōn/, **shin·ing, shines**) **1.** *vi* EMIT LIGHT to give out light **2.** *vi* BE BRIGHT to be bright or reflect light **3.** *vt* DIRECT LIGHT OF SOMETHING to direct the light emitted by something ○ *Shine the flashlight over here.* **4.** *vi* EXCEL to be very good at or do very well in an activity **5.** *vi* BE OBVIOUS to appear clearly **6.** *vi* HAVE RADIANT QUALITY to appear to have a specially bright or radiant quality as a result of good health or a strong positive emotion ○ *Her face shone with happiness.* **7.** (*past and past participle* **shined**) *vt* POLISH SOMETHING to make something bright and gleaming by polishing it ■ *n* **1.** BRIGHTNESS FROM LIGHT SOURCE brightness or radiance emitted by a source of light **2.** BRIGHT SURFACE the bright or gleaming surface of something **3.** ACT OF POLISHING SOMETHING an act of polishing something to make it shiny **4.** *US* BEVERAGES same as **moonshine** (sense 1) (*informal*) ■ **shines** *npl US* TRICKS mischievous or amusing tricks played on somebody (*slang*) [Old English *scīnan* < Indo-European, "to glimmer"] ◇ **come rain or shine** whatever the weather or other attending circumstances ◇ **take a shine to somebody** to develop a liking for somebody (*informal*)

shin·er /shīnər/ *n* **1.** MED same as **black eye** (*informal*) **2.** a small silvery freshwater fish. Native to: North America. Genus: *Notropis.* **3.** something that shines or makes something shine

shin·gle[1] /shíng g'l/ *n* **1.** ROOF OR WALL TILE a small flat tile, especially one made of wood or asphalt, used in overlapping rows to cover a roof or wall **2.** SIGN OR NAMEPLATE a nameplate or a small sign giving the name of a doctor, lawyer, or other professional person, fixed outside that person's office **3.** HAIRSTYLE a short hairstyle for women, popular in the 1920s, in which the back hair was cut to taper at the nape of the neck ■ *vt* (**-gled, -gling, -gles**) **1.** COVER SOMETHING WITH TILES to cover something with small overlapping tiles **2.** TAPER HAIR AT BACK to cut hair so that it is tapered at the nape of the neck [12C. Alteration of late Latin *scindula*, variant of Latin *scandula*] —**shin·gler** *n* ◇ **hang out your shingle** to begin working as a professional from your own office (*informal*)

shin·gle[2] /shíng g'l/ *n* **1.** small round pebbles on a beach **2.** an area of beach covered in shingle [Mid-16C. Origin ?] —**shin·gly** *adj*

shin·gle[3] /shíng g'l/ (**-gled, -gling, -gles**) *vt* to remove the slag from iron by hammering or squeezing it in the process of making wrought iron [Late 17C. Via French *cingler* < German *zängeln* < *Zange* "tongs"]

shin·gles /shíng g'lz/ *n* a disease of adults caused by the reactivation of chickenpox viruses in a nerve ganglion and resulting in inflammation, pain, and a rash of small skin blisters. Technical name **herpes zoster, zoster** (sense 1) [14C. Alteration of Latin *cingulum* "girdle" < *cingere* "gird"]

shin·ing /shīning/ *adj* having a bright or radiant quality

shin·leaf /shín lèef/ (*plural* **-leafs** or **-leaves** /-lèevz/) *n* a plant of the wintergreen family with a low cluster of evergreen leaves. Flowers: white, on a long stem. Native to: Canada and northeastern USA. Latin name: *Pyrola elliptica.* [Early 19C. Because it was used to treat sore shins]

shin·ney *n, vi* FIELD HOCKEY another spelling of **shinny**[2]

shin·ny[1] /shínnee/ (**-nied, -ny·ing, -nies**) *vi* to climb up or down something using the hands and legs [Late 19C. < SHIN[1]]

shin·ny[2] /shínnee/, **shin·ney** *n* (*plural* **-nies**; *plural* **-neys**) **1.** N AMERICAN GAME RESEMBLING FIELD HOCKEY in the United States and Canada, an informal game similar to field hockey, played with a small hard ball and curved wooden sticks **2.** STICK USED IN SHINNY the stick that is used to play shinny ■ *vi* (**-nied, -ny·ing, -nies; -neyed, -ney·ing, -neys**) PLAY SHINNY to play the game of shinny [Late 17C. Variant of SHINTY]

shin·plas·ter /shín plàstər/ *n* a piece of low-value paper money, especially one issued in the United States during the Civil War [Early 19C. Because it resembled plaster used for leg plasters]

shin splints *n* a painful inflammation of the muscles surrounding the shinbone, often caused by running or jogging on hard roads (*takes a singular or plural verb*)

shin·tai·do /shin tīdō/ *n* a form of exercise based on the movements used in Japanese martial arts, performed by a group [Late 20C. < Japanese *shintaidō* < *shintai* "Shinto object"+ *dō* "art"]

Shin·to /shíntō/ *n* a Japanese religion in which devotees worship and make offerings to numerous gods and spirits associated with the natural world [Early 18C. < Japanese *shintō* < *shin* "gods" (< Middle Chinese) + *tō* "way" (< Middle Chinese *daw'*)] —**Shin·to·ism** *n* —**Shin·to·ist** *n, adj*

shin·ty /shíntee/ *n* (*plural* **-ties**) **1.** SCOTTISH GAME RESEMBLING FIELD HOCKEY a game resembling field hockey traditionally played in the Highlands of Scotland **2.** STICK USED IN SHINTY the stick that is used to play shinty ■ *vi* (**-tied, -ty·ing, -ties**) PLAY SHINTY to play the game of shinty [Late 17C. Probably < *shin (t')ye!*, uttered by players of the game]

shin·y /shīnee/ (**-i·er, -i·est**) *adj* **1.** BRIGHT AND POLISHED bright or highly polished, with a glossy or glistening surface **2.** WORN SMOOTH AND GLOSSY smooth and glossy on the surface through too much wear ○ *a shiny patch on the seat of his pants* **3.** SUNNY bright with sunlight **4.** *US* LIGHT filled with light —**shin·i·ness** *n*

ship /ship/ *n* **1.** LARGE BOAT a large wind-driven or engine-powered vessel designed to carry passengers or cargo over water, especially across the ocean **2.** LARGE SQUARE-RIGGED SAILBOAT a large sailing vessel with three, four, or five square-rigged masts **3.** SHIP'S CREW the crew of a ship **4.** AIRCRAFT OR SPACECRAFT a large aircraft or spacecraft ■ *v* (**shipped, ship·ping, ships**) **1.** *vti* TRANSPORT SOMETHING OVER WATER to transport something by ship **2.** *vt* TRANSPORT SOMETHING OVERLAND OR BY AIR to send or transport something overland or by air, using a common carrier **3.** *vt* SEND SOMEBODY to send somebody to a place ○ *shipped the children off to summer camp* **4.** *vti* COMM SEND OR BE SENT TO STORES to send a product to stores and make it available for purchase, or be sent in this way ○ *If all goes well, the new software will be shipping early next year.* **5.** *vt* TAKE IN WATER to take in water over the sides of a ship or boat ○ *We're shipping water.* **6.** *vt* BRING OARS INSIDE BOAT to bring oars inside a boat and lay them down **7.** *vi* GO ON VOYAGE to travel on a ship **8.** *vi* WORK ON SHIP to take a job aboard a ship [Old English *scip* < Germanic] —**ship·pa·ble** *adj* ◇ **desert** *or* **leave a sinking ship** to leave an organization that is having difficulties ◇ **when your ship comes in** when you become rich

-ship *suffix* **1.** condition, state, quality ○ *companionship* **2.** skill, art, craft ○ *musicianship* **3.** office, title, position, profession ○ *governorship* **4.** group of people collectively ○ *membership* **5.** something showing a particular quality or condition ○ *township* **6.** somebody holding a particular title ○ *ladyship* [Old English *-scipe* < Germanic]

ship bis·cuit *n* FOOD same as **hardtack**

ship·board /shíp bàwrd/ *adj* used, intended for, or occurring on board a ship ◇ **on shipboard** on board a ship

ship·borne /shíp bàwrn/ *adj* transported by ship

ship·build·er /shíp bìldər/ *n* a person or business that constructs ships —**ship·build·ing** *n*

ship ca·nal *n* a canal that is wide and deep enough for ships to pass through

ship chan·dler *n* a person, store, or company that sells supplies for ships or boats —**ship chan·dler·y** *n*

ship fit·ter *n* **1.** an assembler of the structural parts of a ship **2.** a sailor in the US Navy who maintains a ship's metal fittings

ship·load /shíp lōd/ *n* the quantity of cargo carried by a ship

ship·mas·ter /shíp màstər/ *n* the captain or master of a ship

ship·mate /shíp màyt/ *n* a sailor or passenger on the same ship as another

ship·ment /shípmənt/ *n* **1.** a quantity of goods that are shipped together as part of the same cargo **2.** the act of shipping something

ship of the line *n* in former times, a sailing warship large enough to be in the line of battle

ship·own·er /shíp ōnər/ *n* a person or company owning one or more ships

ship·per /shíppər/ *n* a person or company that sends or receives goods by sea, land, or air

ship·ping /shípping/ *n* **1.** the act or business of transporting goods **2.** ships considered collectively, especially those belonging to a single port, country, or industry, and often referred to in terms of their tonnage

ship·ping clerk *n* an employee who prepares, sends, receives, and records shipments of goods

ship·ping lane *n* a route regularly used by ships when crossing a body of water

ship-rigged *adj* describes a sailing ship with three, four, or five masts and square sails set at right angles to the hull

ship·shape /shíp shàyp/ *adj* neat and in good order ■ *adv* in a neat and orderly way [Mid-17C. Shortening of obsolete *shipshapen* "made appropriate for use aboard ship"]

ship·side /shíp sīd/ *n* the area, especially at a dock, beside a ship

ship's pa·pers *npl* documents stating the ownership, nationality, cargo, and destination of a ship or boat, required by international law to be carried by all vessels

ship·way /shíp wày/ *n* **1.** a structure on which a ship is built and down which it slides when it is launched **2.** NAUT same as **ship canal**

ship·worm /shíp wùrm/ *n* a burrowing sea mollusk that drills into wood, damaging wharves and ships. Family: Teredinidae.

ship·wreck /shíp rèk/ *n* **1.** SINKING OR DESTRUCTION OF SHIP the sinking, destruction, or damaging of a ship while at sea **2.** SUNKEN SHIP a ship that has been sunk or destroyed **3.** DESTRUCTION the destruction or failure of something ■ *v* (**-wrecked, -wreck·ing, -wrecks**) **1.** *vti* INVOLVE SOMEBODY IN SHIPWRECK to experience the sinking or destruction of a ship, or cause somebody to experience this (*usually passive*) ○ *was shipwrecked on a desert island* **2.** *vti* SINK SHIP to sink or destroy a ship, or be sunk or destroyed at sea (*usually passive*) **3.** *vt* RUIN SOMETHING to ruin or destroy something utterly (*literary*)

ship·wright /shíp rīt/ *n* somebody who builds or repairs ships [Pre-12C. < SHIP + Old English *wyrhta, wryhta* "maker, builder" < W Germanic]

ship·yard /shíp yaàrd/ *n* a place where ships are built or repaired

Shi·raz /shi raáz/ *n* **1.** a red wine made from a variety of black grape grown mainly in Australia and South Africa **2.** a black grape variety. Use: to make Shiraz. [Mid-17C. After *Shiraz*, port in Iran]

shire /shīr/ *n* **1.** *UK* a county in England or Wales **2.** *also* **Shire** ZOOL same as **shire horse** [Old English *scīr* "administrative office, district." Origin ?]

Shi·re /sheér ay/ river flowing from Malawi to Mozambique in south central Africa. Length: 250 mi./402 km.

Shi·re High·lands plateau in southern Malawi, east of the Shire River. Height: 2,953 ft./900 m.

shire horse, Shire horse *n* a large heavy cart horse with long hair growing from its fetlocks, belonging to a breed originating in the Midlands of England

shirk /shurk/ (**shirked, shirk·ing, shirks**) *v* **1.** *vt* to avoid having to carry out something such as an obligation, task, or responsibility through lack of initiative, cowardice, or distaste for it **2.** *vi* to lack initiative, or deliberately avoid work or duty [Mid-17C. Origin ?] —**shirk·er** *n*

Shir·ley pop·py /shúrlee-/ *n* an annual poppy. Flowers: red, pink, or white, single or double. [Late 19C. After a district in Croydon, Surrey, England]

shirr /shur/ (**shirred, shirr·ing, shirrs**) *v* **1.** *vti* to gather fabric into two or more parallel rows for decoration on a garment such as a skirt, usually using elasticized thread **2.** *vt* to bake an egg without its shell, e.g., in a ramekin dish [Mid-19C. Origin ?]

shirt /shurt/ *n* **1.** an item of clothing for the upper part of the body, usually made of a fairly light material and fitted with a collar, sleeves, and buttons down the front **2.** a usually loose linen garment for the upper body with sleeves that was worn by men as underwear until the early 20th century **3.** CLOTHING same as **nightshirt** [Old English *scyrte* < Indo-European, "to cut"] ◇ **keep your shirt on** to keep your temper (*informal; usually used as a command*) ◇ **lose your shirt** to lose everything you have, especially as a result of losing a bet (*informal*)

shirt·dress /shúrt drèss/ *n* a woman's dress that is tailored to resemble a shirt, with buttons fastening down the front

shirt·front /shúrt frùnt/ *n* the front part of a shirt, especially the stiffened fabric on the front of a dress shirt

shirt·ing /shúrting/ *n* plain or striped cotton fabric. Use: men's shirts.

shirt·sleeve /shúrt slèev/ *n* the part of a shirt that covers all or part of the arm ■ *adj* sufficiently warm or sufficiently informal for a shirt without a jacket to be the appropriate wear ○ *shirtsleeve weather* ◇ **in (your) shirtsleeves** not wearing a jacket

shirt·tail /shúrt tàyl/ *n* **1.** BOTTOM PART OF SHIRT the lower part of a shirt, usually cut in a curved shape, that extends below the waist at the back and is usually tucked into pants **2.** *US* PIECE AT END OF NEWSPAPER ARTICLE a short additional and related piece of writing at the end of a newspaper article ■ *adj* **1.** TOO SMALL small and inadequate ○ *living on a shirttail allowance* **2.** *US* YOUNG very young

shirt·waist /shúrt wàyst/ *n* **1.** a woman's blouse styled like a man's shirt **2.** same as **shirtdress**

shirt·waist·er /shúrt wàystər/ *n UK* same as **shirtdress**

shirt·y /shúrtee/ (**-i·er, -i·est**) *adj UK* aggressive or bad-tempered because of being annoyed about something (*informal*) [Mid-19C. < taking shirts off to fight] —**shirt·i·ly** *adv* —**shirt·i·ness** *n*

shi·shi·to /shə shèetō/ *n* in Japanese cuisine, a mild, sweet pepper used, e.g., in tempura

shish ke·bab /shísh-/ *n* a dish of cubes of marinated meat and vegetables grilled and served on a skewer [Early 20C. Via Armenian < Turkish *şiş kebabıu* < *şiş* "skewer" + *kebab* "roast meat"]

shi·so /shèessō/ *n* in Japanese cuisine, an aromatic herb in the mint-basil family, used as seasoning in salads and sushi. Latin name: *Perilla frutescens.*

shit /shit/ *n* **1.** a highly offensive term for human or animal excrement (*taboo*) **2.** a highly offensive term for an act of defecating (*taboo*) **3.** a highly offensive term for somebody regarded as unpleasant or malicious (*taboo insult*) **4.** a highly offensive term for something that is unpleasant, of no value, or of inferior quality (*taboo*) **5.** a highly offensive term for useless or unnecessary things (*taboo*) **6.** a highly offensive term for nonsense or lies (*taboo*) **7.** a highly offensive term for difficulty or trouble (*taboo*) **8.** a highly offensive term for criticism perceived as unhelpful or mean-spirited (*taboo*) **9.** a highly offensive term for illegal drugs, especially cannabis (*taboo*) ■ **shits** *npl* a highly offensive term for an attack of diarrhea (*taboo*) ■ *interj* a highly offensive term used as a swearword (*taboo*) ■ *v* (**shit** or **shat** /shat/, **shit·ting, shits**) (*taboo*) **1.** *vti* a highly offensive term meaning to eliminate waste from the body via the rectum **2.** *vi* a highly offensive term meaning to behave toward or criticize somebody with arrogant contempt and a total disregard for his or her feelings, especially from a position of power **3.** *vt US* a highly offensive term meaning to tease somebody or deceive somebody for amusement ■ *adj* a highly offensive term meaning very bad or inferior (*taboo*) [Old English *scitte* < Indo-European, "to cut, split"] ◇ **get your shit together** a highly offensive phrase meaning to get organized (*taboo*) ◇ **in deep shit** a highly offensive phrase meaning in trouble or in a difficult situation (*taboo*) ◇ **no shit** a highly offensive term indicating surprise, disbelief, or sarcasm (*taboo*) ◇ **tough shit** a highly offensive phrase indicating in an unfriendly way that there is no alternative to a difficult or undesirable situation (*taboo*) ◇ **when the shit hits the fan** a highly offensive phrase meaning when trouble starts (*taboo*)

shi·ta·ke *n* FUNGI, FOOD another spelling of **shiitake**

shit·faced /shít fàyst/ *adj* a highly offensive term meaning extremely intoxicated by alcohol (*taboo*)

shit·head /shít hèd/ *n* a highly offensive term that deliberately insults somebody's intelligence or character (*taboo*)

shit·house /shít hòwss/ *n* a highly offensive term for a toilet (*taboo*)

shit·less /shítləss/ *adv* a highly offensive term meaning to a very great extent (*taboo*) [Mid-20C. < the tendency to lose control of the bowels when terror-stricken]

shit·list /shít lìst/ *n* a highly offensive term meaning a list of people who are out of favor, especially in the view of somebody in authority (*taboo*)

shit·load /shít lòd/ *n* a highly offensive term meaning an undesirably large amount or quantity of something (*taboo*)

shit·tah /shíttə/ (*plural* **-tahs** or **-tim** /shíttim/) *n* the tree that yielded the shittimwood of the Bible, probably a species of acacia [Early 17C. < Hebrew *šiṭṭāh*]

shit·tim·wood /shíttim wòod/ (*plural* **-woods** or *same*) *n* **1.** the wood of the shittah tree that according to the Bible was used to make the Ark of the Covenant **2.** a tree that has hard dense wood and black fruit. Native to: North America. Genus: *Bumelia.*

shit·ty /shíttee/ *adj* (*taboo*) **1.** a highly offensive term meaning regarded as inferior, unpleasant, or unenjoyable **2.** a highly offensive term meaning wretched or miserable **3.** a highly offensive term meaning of very poor quality **4.** a highly offensive term meaning covered with excrement —**shit·ti·ly** *adv* —**shit·ti·ness** *n*

shiv /shiv/ (*slang*) *n* a pocketknife, often a switchblade or razor, used as a weapon ■ *vt* (**shivved, shiv·ving, shivs**) to slash or stab somebody with a shiv [Late 17C. Origin ?]

shiv·a /shívə/, **shiv·ah** *n* seven days of formal mourning observed by close relatives of a deceased Jew during which they sit on low stools and do not go out, work, bathe, or shave [Late 19C. Via Yiddish < Hebrew *šib'āh* "seven"]

Shi·va /shèevə/, **Si·va** /sèevə/ *n* in Hinduism, an important deity, worshipped as the god of destruction [Late 18C. < Sanskrit, "the auspicious one"]

shiv·ah *n* JUDAISM another spelling of **shiva**

Shi·va·Ra·tri /-raátree/ *n* a Hindu festival honoring the god Shiva. Date: middle of Magha. [*Ratri* < Hindi, "night"]

shiv·a·ree /shìvvə rèe, shívvə rèe/ *n* a noisy mock-serenade to wish newlyweds well, involving the banging of saucepans, kettles, and other objects [Mid-19C. Alteration of French *charivari*]

shiv·er[1] /shívvər/ *v* (**-ered, -er·ing, -ers**) **1.** *vi* TREMBLE to tremble or shake slightly because of cold, fear, or illness **2.** *vti* FLAP OR MAKE SAIL FLAP to flap, or make a sail flap, when a sailing vessel is too close to the wind ■ *n* BODY TREMOR a tremor or shudder in the body caused by fear, cold, or illness ■ **shiv·ers** *npl* ATTACK OF SHIVERING an attack of shivering caused by fear, cold, or illness (*informal*) [13C. Origin ?] —**shiv·er·er** *n* —**shiv·er·ing·ly** *adv*

shiv·er[2] /shívvər/ *vti* (**-ered, -er·ing, -ers**) to splinter into fragments, or cause something to splinter into fragments ■ *n* a very small piece of something such as glass that has splintered off a larger piece [12C. < assumed Old English *scifer* < Indo-European, "to split"]

shiv·er·y /shívvəree/ *adj* trembling from cold, fear, or illness [Mid-18C. < SHIVER[1]]

Shi·zu·o·ka /shèezoo ṓkə/ city on southeastern Honshu Island, Japan, west of Suruga Bay. Population: 468,775 (2002).

shkotz·im JUDAISM plural of **shegetz** (*offensive insult*)

shle·miel *n* JUDAISM another spelling of **schlemiel** (*informal*)

shlep *vti, n* another spelling of **schlep** (*informal*)

Shluh /shloo/ (*plural same* or **Shluhs**) *n* **1.** a member of a Berber people who live mainly in the Atlas Mountains of Morocco and Algeria **2.** the Berber dialect of the Shluh people [Early 18C. < Berber] —**Shluh** *adj*

SHM *abbr* PHYS simple harmonic motion

shm- *prefix* another spelling of **schm-** (*used dismissively in rhyming compounds*)

shmaltz *n* another spelling of **schmaltz** (*informal*)

shmat·te *n* another spelling of **schmatte** (*informal*)

shmeer *n* another spelling of **schmeer**

shme·geg·ge /shmə géggə/ *n* an offensive term for a person who is regarded variously as petty, humorless, dull, clumsy, or sycophantic (*slang insult*) [Yiddish SH- + *megege* "dawdler, idler"]

shmo *n* another spelling of **schmo** (*slang insult*)

shmuck *n* another spelling of **schmuck** (*slang offensive*)

Sho·ah /shṓ ə, -aá/ *n* HIST same as **Holocaust** (*used by Jews*) [Mid-20C. < Hebrew *šōāh* "catastrophe"]

shoal[1] /shōl/ *n* **1.** GROUP OF FISH a large group of fish or other sea animals swimming together **2.** GROUP OF PEOPLE a large group of similar people or things ○ *a shoal of reporters* ■ *vi* (**shoaled, shoal·ing, shoals**) FORM SHOAL to group together to form a shoal [Late 16C. < Middle Dutch *scōle* or Middle Low German *schōle* (see SCHOOL[2])]

shoal[2] /shōl/ *n* **1.** SHALLOW WATER an area of shallow water in a larger body of water **2.** UNDERWATER SANDBANK an underwater sandbank or sandbar that is visible at low water ■ *v* (**shoaled, shoal·ing, shoals**) **1.** *vti* MAKE OR BECOME SHALLOW to become shallow or shallower, or make something shallow **2.** *vi* ENTER SHALLOWER WATER to enter a shallower area of water ■ *adj also* **shoal·y** /shṓlee/ SHALLOW describes water that is shallow [Old English *sceald* "shallow" < Germanic]

shoat /shōt/, **shote** *n* a young pig that has just been weaned [15C. Origin ?]

shoch·et /shṓkət, shṓkhət/ (*plural* **-et·im** /-ətim/) *n* somebody licensed to perform the ritual kosher slaughter of animals for food (**shechita**) [Late 19C. < Hebrew *šōḥēṭ*, present participle of *šāḥaṭ* "slaughter"]

shock[1] /shok/ *n* **1.** SOMETHING SURPRISING AND UPSETTING an unexpected, intense, and distressing experience that has a sudden and powerful effect on somebody's emotions or physical reactions ○ *The news of her death came as a great shock to us all.* **2.** DISTRESSING FEELINGS AFTER SHOCK the feeling of distress or numbness experienced by somebody who has had a shock **3.** MED PHYSIOLOGICAL COLLAPSE a state of physiological collapse, marked by a weak pulse, coldness, sweating, and irregular breathing, and resulting from a situation such as blood loss, heart failure, allergic reaction, or emotional trauma ○ *in shock* **4.** PHYSICAL IMPACT a sudden and violent impact, collision, or blow **5.** SOMETHING THREATENING OR DAMAGING an unexpected event that threatens or damages a system, organization, or conventional situation ○ *the announcement was a shock to international markets* **6.** ELEC same as **electric shock** **7.** MECH ENG same as **shock absorber** ■ *v* (**shocked, shock·ing, shocks**) **1.** *vt* UPSET SOMEBODY to make somebody feel suddenly and acutely distressed or upset **2.** *vti* OFFEND OR BE OFFENDED to make somebody feel deeply offended or disgusted, or be likely to feel offended or disgusted ○ *He shocks easily.* **3.** *vt* GIVE SOMEBODY ELECTRIC SHOCK to give an electric shock to a person or animal **4.** *vt* MED PUT SOMEBODY INTO SHOCK to cause a state of shock in somebody [Mid-16C. < French *choc* < French *choquer* "to strike"] —**shock·a·ble** *adj*

shock[2] /shok/ *n* a group of sheaves of grain or corn set upright in a field for drying ■ *vt* (**shocked, shock·ing, shocks**) to arrange sheaves of grain or corn in a shock [14C. Origin ?]

shock[3] /shok/ *n* a large amount of thick shaggy hair [Early 19C. Origin ?]

shock ab·sorb·er *n* a device on a vehicle designed to absorb jarring or jolting such as that caused by wheels moving over a rough surface. See illustration on next page [< SHOCK[1]]

shock and awe *n* MIL a very rapid, selective strike against an enemy's military command-and-control networks, political hierarchy, and economic assets, designed to paralyze the nation's counteroffensive options and to render the decision-making structure psychologically inoperative [Late 20C. Possibly from a

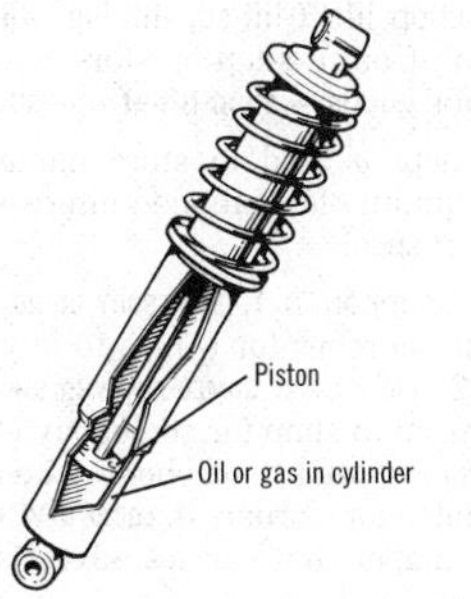

shock absorber

1996 National Defense University study titled "Shock and Awe: Achieving Rapid Dominance" by Harlan K. Ullman, James P. Wade, et al.] —**shock and awe** *adj*

shock·er /shókər/ *n* (*informal*) **1.** a difficult, troublesome, or unpleasant experience, thing, or person **2.** a story, play, or movie that is particularly lurid and intended to shock people [Early 19C. < SHOCK[1]]

shock-hor·ror *adj* lurid, sensational, and apparently intended to cause a shocked or horrified reaction (*informal; used ironically*) [< SHOCK[1]]

shock·ing /shóking/ *adj* **1. DISTRESSING** emotionally distressing or horrifying **2. OUTRAGEOUS** provoking a deeply offended or outraged response **3. VERY BAD** very bad or unpleasant (*informal*) ■ *adj, adv* **VERY BRIGHT** very bright or glaring in shade of color [Early 18C. < SHOCK[1]] —**shock·ing·ly** *adv*

shock·ing pink *adj* of a garish pink color —**shock·ing pink** *n*

shock jock *n* a DJ or radio host who uses provocative language and broadcasts his or her extreme views (*slang*) [< SHOCK[1]]

Shock·ley /shóklee/, **William B.** (1910–89) US physicist. He codeveloped the transistor (1948) and shared the Nobel Prize in physics (1956). He went on to promote controversial theories about intelligence and race. Full name **Shockley, William Bradford**

shock·proof /shók proof/ *adj* designed or able to withstand the effects of jarring or impact [Early 20C. < SHOCK[1]]

shock tac·tics *npl* methods that are likely to shock people, deliberately used in order to achieve a goal [< SHOCK[1]]

shock ther·a·py, shock treat·ment *n* a method of treating patients affected with psychiatric disorders that involves passing an electric current through the brain [< SHOCK[1]]

shock troops *npl* soldiers who are specially trained and equipped to be in the forefront of an attack [< SHOCK[1]; translation of German *Stosstruppen*]

shock wave *n* **1.** a wave of increased temperature or pressure as a result of an explosion or earthquake or the movement of a supersonic body **2.** a widespread reaction of shock or distress caused by an event or piece of news (*often used in the plural*) [< SHOCK[1]]

shod CLOTHING past participle, past tense of **shoe**

shod·dy /shóddee/ *adj* (**-di·er, -di·est**) **1. POORLY MADE** poorly or carelessly made or done **2. OF INFERIOR MATERIAL** made from inferior material **3. DISHONEST** dishonest or disgraceful ○ *shoddy treatment* ■ *n* (*plural* **-dies**) **1. CLOTH MADE WITH OLD WOOL** cloth made using a mixture of old unraveled woolen cloth and new wool **2. SOMETHING INFERIOR** something that is of inferior quality, especially if it is imitating something better [Mid-19C. Origin ?] —**shod·di·ly** *adv*—**shod·di·ness** *n*

shoe /shoo/ *n* **1. STIFF OUTER COVERING FOR FOOT** an outer covering for the foot, usually made of leather, fabric, or plastic, with a stiff sole and usually not reaching above the ankle **2.** same as **horseshoe** *n* (sense 1) **3.** MECH ENG **DEVICE TO SLOW SOMETHING DOWN** a device that slows or stops the movement of an object, e.g., the part of a brake that presses against the drum **4.** MECH ENG **PROTECTIVE PART IN ENGINE** a lining or part in an engine or machine that protects another part from being worn down **5.** RAIL **POWER COLLECTOR ON ELECTRIC TRAIN** the part of an electric train or streetcar that connects with the electrified rail from which it draws power ■ *vt* (**shoed, shod** /shod/ or **shoed, shoe·ing, shoes**) **1. PROVIDE HORSE WITH HORSESHOES** to fix a horseshoe on a horse **2. SUPPLY SOMEBODY WITH SHOES** to provide somebody with shoes (*usually passive*) **3.** MECH ENG **PUT PROTECTIVE COVERING ON SOMETHING** to cover something with a hard, especially metal plate to protect against wear [Old English *scōh* < Germanic] —**shoe·less** *adj* ◇ **be in somebody's shoes** to be in somebody else's position (*informal*)

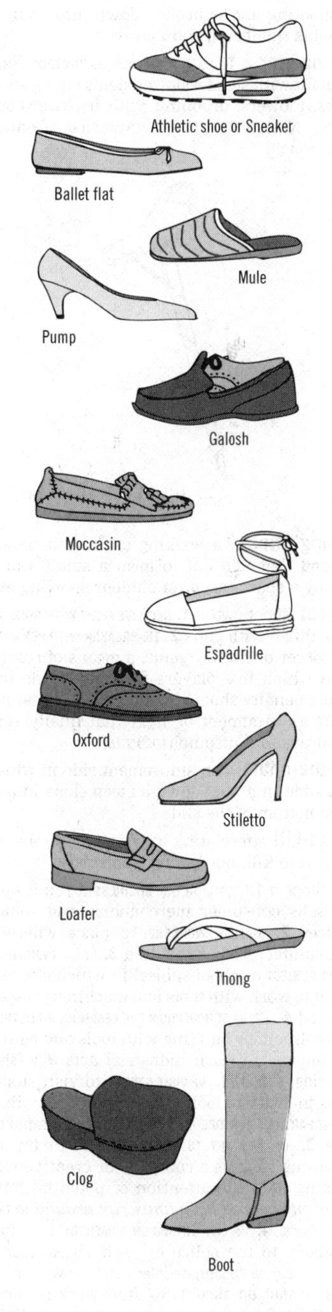

shoe

shoe·bill /shoo bil/ *n* a large tropical wading bird with shaggy gray feathers, a large head, black legs, and a broad hooked beak. Native to: East Africa. Latin name: *Balaeniceps rex.*

shoe·box /shoo bòks/ *n* **1.** a box, usually made of cardboard, in which shoes are packed for sale **2.** a small and cramped living or working space (*informal*)

shoe·horn /shoo hàwrn/ *n* a curved piece of plastic, metal, or horn used to help ease the heel into a tight-fitting shoe or boot ■ *vt* (**-horned, -horn·ing, -horns**) to squeeze somebody or something into a space that is barely large enough

shoe·lace /shoo làyss/ *n* a thin cord of leather or fabric, used as a shoe fastener

shoe·mak·er /shoo màykər/ *n* a maker or repairer of footwear —**shoe·mak·ing** /shoo màyking/ *n*

Shoe·ma·ker /shoo màykər/, **Willie** (1931–2003) US jockey. He won 8,833 horseraces during his 42-year career. Full name **Shoemaker, William Lee**

shoe·pac /shoo pàk/, **shoe·pack** *n* a heavy laced waterproof boot [Mid-18C. Alteration of pidgin Delaware *seppock* "shoes" < Unami Delaware *čipahko* "moccasins"]

shoe·shine /shoo shìn/ *n* **1.** the act of giving a clean or shiny finish to shoes by polishing them **2.** a polished finish on shoes

shoe·string /shoo strìng/ *adj* **1.** consisting of or running on a very limited amount of money ○ *operates on a shoestring budget* **2.** *US* FOOD cut or made long and narrow in shape ○ *shoestring licorice* ■ *n US* CLOTHING same as **shoelace** ◇ **on a shoestring** using very little money

shoe·string catch *n* in baseball, a catch made near the ground by a running player

shoe·tree /shoo tree/ *n* a wooden or metal block that is inserted into a boot or shoe to stretch it or help it to keep its shape when not being worn

sho·far /shṓ faar, shṓfər/ (*plural* **sho·fars** or **sho·froth** /shō frṓt/) *n* a horn, usually a ram's horn, blown by the ancient Hebrews in battle and during religious ceremonies, now sounded in a synagogue on Rosh Hashanah and Yom Kippur [Mid-19C. < Hebrew *šōpār* "ram's horn"]

sho·gi /shṓgee/ *n* a Japanese board game for two players that resembles chess [Mid-19C. Via Japanese < Chinese *jiàng qí* < *jiàng* "commander in chief" + *qí* "board game, chess"]

sho·gun /shṓgən, shō gùn/ *n* a hereditary military commander in feudal Japan who ruled the country under the nominal rule of an emperor between the years 1192 and 1867 [Mid-17C. Via Japanese < Chinese *jiāng jūn* "general"] —**sho·gun·al** *adj*

sho·gun·ate /shṓgənət, -nàyt/ *n* the office, period in office, or rule of a shogun

sho·ji /shṓ jee/ (*plural same* or **-jis**) *n* a rice-paper screen in a wooden frame used as a sliding partition or door in traditional Japanese houses [Late 19C. < Japanese *shōji* < *shō* "screen, barrier" (< Middle Chinese *tsiang*) + *-ji* "seed" (< Middle Chinese *tsz*)]

Sho·la·pur /shṑlə poor/ city in west central India. Population: 604,215 (1991).

~~**sholder**~~ incorrect spelling of **shoulder**

Sho·na /shṓnə/ (*plural same* or **-nas**) *n* **1.** a member of a people living in parts of southern central Africa, mainly in Zimbabwe and Mozambique **2.** the Bantu language of the Shona people. Native speakers: 8 million. [Mid-20C. < Bantu] —**Sho·na** *adj*

shone past participle, past tense of **shine**

shoo /shoo/ *interj* used to tell a child or animal to go away ■ *vti* (**shooed, shoo·ing, shoos**) to say shoo and gesture to a child or animal to go away ○ *shooed the pigeons away* [15C. Natural exclamation]

shoo·fly /shoo flì/ (*plural* **-flies**) *n US* a child's rocker with the seat between two flat sides cut in the shape of an animal [Late 19C. < obsolete *shoo-fly*, expressing annoyance]

shoo·fly pie *n* a pie made with a filling of crumbs, butter, and brown sugar or molasses [< its sweet filling, which is apt to attract flies]

shoo-fly plant *n US* PLANTS same as **apple of Peru** [Because it is supposed to repel flies]

shoo-in *n* a certain winner

shook[1] /shòok/ past tense of **shake**

shook[2] /shòok/ *n* **1.** AGRIC same as **shock**[2] **2.** a set of timber parts for assembling a barrel or box [Late 18C. Origin ?]

shook-up *adj* disturbed and upset (*informal*)

shoot /shoot/ *v* (**shot** /shot/, **shoot·ing, shoots**) **1.** *vti* **FIRE WEAPON OR PROJECTILE** to fire a projectile such as a bullet, missile, or arrow from a weapon, or make a weapon fire a projectile ○ *Don't shoot!* **2.** *vt* **HIT SOMEBODY OR**

SOMETHING WITH BULLET to fire a weapon at and hit, injure, or kill a person or animal ○ *She shot herself.* **3.** *vti* **HUNT ANIMALS WITH GUN** to hunt animals with a gun for sport **4.** *vti* **MOVE FAST** to move quickly and suddenly, or cause something to move quickly and suddenly ○ *She shot out her hand to catch the ball.* **5.** *vt* **TRAVEL OVER SOMETHING FAST** to travel quickly over a stretch of water where the current is fast ○ *shoot the rapids* **6.** *vi* **PROGRESS VERY RAPIDLY** to make extremely rapid progress, or undergo a startlingly rapid change of state ○ *She shot to fame.* **7.** *vti* **SEND SOMETHING OUT RAPIDLY** to send out something rapidly or forcefully or in a beam or ray, or be sent out in this way **8.** *vt* **ASK OR SAY SOMETHING RAPIDLY** to say something or ask a question rapidly **9.** *vti* SPORTS **KICK BALL TO GET POINT** in a sport such as soccer or basketball, to kick, hit, or throw a ball in an attempt to score a goal or point **10.** *vt* SPORTS **SCORE POINT** in a sport, to score a goal or point **11.** *vt* SPORTS, LEISURE **MAKE PARTICULAR SCORE** in a game such as golf or dice, to score a particular amount ○ *shot a 72* **12.** *vt* SPORTS, LEISURE **PLAY GAME** to play a game such as pool, golf, or dice **13.** *vti* MOVIES, PHOTOGRAPHY, MEDIA **RECORD SOMETHING ON FILM** to record a shot, scene, movie, or program on film with a camera **14.** *vt* **MOVE BOLT INTO PLACE** to move something such as a bolt into or out of a fastening **15.** *vi US* **STRIVE TO ACHIEVE SOMETHING** to try to achieve something difficult (*informal*) ○ *shooting for a five percent increase in productivity* **16.** *vt* DRUGS same as **shoot up** (sense 4) (*slang*) **17.** *vi* BOT **GERMINATE** to germinate or begin to grow **18.** *vt* ASTRON **MEASURE DISTANCE TO ASTRONOMICAL OBJECT** to measure the altitude of a star or other astronomical object ■ *n* **1. NEW PLANT GROWTH** a newly grown aerial part of a plant, e.g., a leaf bud or branch **2. OCCASION FOR PHOTOGRAPHING OR FILMING** an occasion when a professional photographer or filmmaker is photographing or filming something **3. ACT OF FIRING** an act of firing a weapon **4.** *UK* **HUNTING PARTY** a party of people gathered together to hunt animals with guns for sport **5.** *UK* **HUNTING AREA** an area where people shoot animals with guns for sport **6.** GEOL **VEIN OF ORE** a narrow vein of ore ■ *interj* (*informal*) **1. USED TO TELL SOMEBODY TO START** used to tell somebody to go ahead and start talking **2. USED TO EXPRESS ANNOYANCE** used as an exclamation of annoyance or disappointment [Old English *scēotan* < Germanic]

SPELLCHECK See *chute*[1].

shoot down *vt* **1. BRING DOWN AIRCRAFT** to bring down an aircraft while it is in the air by firing a weapon or missile **2. KILL SOMEBODY OR SOMETHING BY SHOOTING** to fire a weapon at and hit, injure, or kill a person or animal **3. DESTROY ARGUMENT** to destroy somebody's argument, theory, or idea by disproving, criticizing, or discrediting it

shoot up *v* **1.** *vi* **INCREASE SUDDENLY** to increase suddenly by a large amount **2.** *vi* **GET TALLER** to grow considerably taller in a short space of time **3.** *vt* **HARM SOMEBODY OR SOMETHING BY GUNFIRE** to cause serious injuries to somebody or damage to something with gunfire **4.** *vti* DRUGS **INJECT DRUG** to inject an illegal drug (*slang*)

shoot·down /sho͞ot dòwn/ *n* the process or an instance of destroying an aircraft in flight by means of a gun or missile attack

shoot-'em-up *n* **1.** a video or computer game in which a player scores points by shooting at figures on the screen **2.** a movie or television show featuring a large amount of shooting and bloodshed (*dated*)

shoot·er /sho͞otər/ *n* **1. SOMEBODY SHOOTING** somebody or something that shoots **2. PLAYER WHO SHOOTS BALL** in a sport such as soccer or basketball, a player who shoots a ball to score a goal or point ○ *a reliable free-throw shooter* **3. GUN** a pistol or other gun (*informal*)

shoot·ing gal·ler·y /sho͞oting-/ *n* **1.** a place used for target practice using guns or rifles **2.** a place where addicts inject drugs, e.g., an abandoned building (*slang*)

shoot·ing i·ron *n US* ARMS same as **handgun** (*informal*)

shoot·ing match ◇ **the whole shooting match** everything, or everything connected with the thing or issue in question (*informal*) ○ *They're planning to demolish the factory, the warehouse, the offices – the whole shooting match.*

shoot·ing script *n* the final screenplay for a feature movie or television movie that includes directions for shooting and is broken down into scenes with the shots numbered consecutively

shoot·ing star *n* **1.** ASTRON same as **meteor** (sense 2) **2.** a plant with slender flower stems rising above the leaves. Flowers: drooping, with backward-curving petals. Native to: North America. Genus: *Dodecatheon.*

shooting stick

shoot·ing stick *n* a walking stick with handles at one end that fold out to form a small seat, often used by a spectator at an outdoor sporting event

shoot·out /sho͞ot òwt/ *n* **1. DECISIVE FIGHT WITH GUNS** a fight to the finish with guns **2. TIE-BREAKER WITH PENALTY SHOTS** in a soccer or hockey game, a means of resolving a tie in which five players from each side take alternate penalty shots at the goal **3.** *US* **FIGHT TO SETTLE DISPUTE** an argument or fight that finally settles a long-drawn-out dispute (*informal*)

shoot-the-chute *n* an amusement ride in which visitors slide in a boat down a steep slope into a pool at the bottom of the slide

shoot-to-kill *adj* relating to or involving the aiming of a gun to kill, not wound, somebody

shop /shop/ *n* **1.** COMM **RETAIL BUSINESS** a retail business that sells consumer merchandise and sometimes services **2.** MANUF **WORKSHOP** a place where goods are manufactured or repaired **3.** EDUC **INDUSTRIAL ARTS SCHOOL SUBJECT** a school subject in which students are taught to work with tools and machinery, especially on wood **4.** EDUC **SCHOOLROOM FOR LEARNING INDUSTRIAL ARTS** a schoolroom or building with tools and equipment for students to learn industrial arts ■ *v* (**shopped, shop·ping, shops**) **1.** *vi* **VISIT STORES** to visit stores and shops in order to look at and usually buy things **2.** *vt* **VISIT PARTICULAR STORE** to buy goods from a particular store **3.** *vt US* **TRY TO SELL SOMETHING** to try to sell something such as a company or creative work by bringing it to the attention of potential buyers ○ *His agent shopped his manuscript around to various publishers.* **4.** *vt UK* **INFORM ON SOMEBODY** to inform on somebody to the police or authorities (*slang*) [Old English *sceoppa* "booth, peddler's stall" < W Germanic] ◇ **close** *or* **shut up shop 1.** to stop working or doing something **2.** to close down a business ◇ **talk shop** to talk about your work or some other specialized activity

shop around *vi* **1.** to look around for the best deal or bargain **2.** to review a number of possibilities before making a choice

shop·a·hol·ic /shòppə háwlik/ *n* a compulsive shopper (*informal*)

shop as·sis·tant *n UK* same as **salesclerk**

shop·bot /shóp bòt/ *n* an automated device that allows potential customers to search the Internet for specific products and compare prices and specifications

shop-bought *adj UK* COMM same as **store-bought**

shop floor *n UK* **1.** the area in a factory where goods are manufactured **2.** the manual workers in a factory

shop·front /shóp frùnt/ *n UK* same as **storefront** *n* (sense 1)

shop·house /shóp hòwss/ *n Malaysia, Singapore* a two-story building with a store on the ground level and the proprietor's home on the upper level

shop·keep·er /shóp kēèpər/ *n UK* same as **storekeeper** (sense 1)

shop·lift /shóp lìft/ (**-lift·ed, -lift·ing, -lifts**) *vti* to steal something from a shop or store while pretending to shop for goods —**shop·lift·er** *n* —**shop·lift·ing** *n*

shoppe /shop/ *n* used in store names in order to create a quaint old-fashioned impression [Early 20C. Alteration of SHOP]

shop·per /shóppər/ *n* **1. SOMEBODY DOING SHOPPING** somebody who searches for things to buy, especially in a store **2.** *US* COMM **SOMEBODY WHO SHOPS FOR OTHERS** a person hired to shop for somebody else **3.** *US* **SOMEBODY FILLING MAIL ORDERS** somebody whose job is to fill mail or telephone orders **4. LOCAL NEWSPAPER** a usually free newspaper that carries advertising and some local news

shop·ping /shópping/ *n* **1.** the activity of visiting shops and stores to look at and buy things **2.** *UK* goods bought in a shop or shops, especially food and household items

shop·ping a·gent *n* a computer program used to browse websites searching for a product or service

shop·ping bag *n* a large strong bag with handles used for carrying purchases when shopping

shop·ping bas·ket *n* **1.** a basket used to carry purchases **2.** *UK* same as **shopping cart**

shop·ping cart *n* **1.** a basket mounted on wheels with a push handle that is supplied by supermarkets and other stores for shoppers to collect their purchases in **2.** a storage area on a seller's website in which a customer lists the items that he or she intends to buy

shop·ping cen·ter *n* **1.** a group of stores, usually with restaurants and other businesses, built around a shared parking area **2.** *UK* same as **mall** (sense 1)

shop·ping ex·pe·ri·ence *n* the virtual environment in which a buyer browses a retailer's website, places items in a virtual shopping cart, and sends the order to the merchant

shop·ping list *n* **1.** a list of all the things somebody wants to buy when shopping **2.** a list of demands, requirements, or things wanted

shop·ping mall *n* **1.** a pedestrianized shopping area with enclosed walkways in a town **2.** COMM same as **mall** (sense 1)

shop·ping trol·ley *n UK* same as **shopping cart**

shop·soiled /shóp sòyld/ *adj UK* same as **shopworn**

shop stew·ard *n* a worker elected by fellow union members as their representative in dealings with the management

shop·talk /shóp tàwk/ *n* **1.** conversation about work or another specialized activity at a time when more lighthearted chat is the norm, especially outside working hours **2.** *US* jargon used in a specific field, job, or profession

shop·walk·er /shóp wàwkər/ *n UK* same as **floorwalker**

shop·worn /shóp wàwrn/ *adj* **1.** faded, tarnished, or otherwise slightly spoiled from being on display in a shop **2.** describes trite or stale ideas or language

sho·ran /sháw ràn/ *n* a short-range navigational system in which a ship's or aircraft's precise location is determined by the time taken for a signal to travel to two fixed stations and back [Mid-20C. Contraction of *short-range (navigation)*]

shore[1] /shawr/ *n* **1. LAND AT EDGE OF WATER** the land that runs along the edge of the ocean, a sea, or lake **2. DRY LAND** dry land as opposed to water ○ *on shore* **3. COUNTRY** a land or country (*literary; often used in the plural*) ○ *on the shores of Tripoli* **4.** *UK* LAW **COAST BETWEEN LOW AND HIGH TIDES** the area of land that lies between normal low and high tide marks [Old English *scora* < Indo-European, "to cut"]

shore[2] /shawr/ *vt* (**shored, shor·ing, shores**) **1. PROP UP STRUCTURE** to stop something such as a wall from falling down or over by propping a support against it **2. HELP TO STOP SOMETHING FAILING** to give support or help in order to stop something failing ○ *took measures to shore up the exchange rate* ■ *n* **PROP TO SUPPORT SOMETHING** a beam or other prop set at an angle to support something such as a wall or tree [14C. < Middle Low German, Middle Dutch *schōre* "prop"]

shore·bird /sháwr bùrd/ *n* a bird that lives and feeds near the shores of coastal or inland waters, e.g., a plover, sandpiper, or avocet. Suborder: Charadrii. [Late 17C. < SHORE[1]]

shore din·ner *n* a meal consisting mainly of fish and seafood [< SHORE[1]]

shore·front /sháwr frùnt/ *n* land situated immediately next to a body of water [< SHORE[1]]

shore ice *n* a large sheet of sea ice attached to a shore [< SHORE[1]]

shore leave *n* **1.** permission for a member of a ship's crew to go ashore **2.** a period of time spent ashore by a member of a ship's crew [< SHORE[1]]

shore·less /sháwrləss/ *adj* having no flat shore on which a boat can land [Early 17C. < SHORE[1]]

shore·line /sháwr lìn/ *n* the land where a body of water, especially the ocean, meets the shore [Mid-19C. < SHORE[1]]

shore pa·trol *n* the military police of the the US Navy, Coast Guard, or Marine Corps while on duty on shore [< SHORE[1]]

shore·ward /sháwrwərd/ *adj* facing or near the shore ■ *adv also* **shore·wards** /-wərdz/ toward the shore [Late 16C. < SHORE[1]]

shor·ing /sháwring/ *n* **1.** a structure or arrangement designed to shore something up **2.** the act or process of shoring something up with a support [15C. < SHORE[2]]

shorn /shawrn/ past participle of **shear** ■ *adj* **1.** with hair cut short **2.** having had something removed or taken away ○ *shorn of all the trappings of power*

short /shawrt/ *adj* **1.** NOT LONG having little or relatively little length or distance ○ *short hair* **2.** NOT TALL having little or relatively little height ○ *shorter than her sister* **3.** NOT LASTING LONG lasting for only a small amount of time ○ *a short stay* **4.** NOT SEEMING LONG IN DURATION seeming or imagined not to last very long ○ *in a few short weeks* **5.** CONCISE expressed economically and briefly ○ *a short summary* **6.** ABBREVIATED expressed in fewer words or using fewer letters or characters than the full form ○ *Typo is short for typographical error.* ○ *the short form of the word* **7.** HAVING LESS THAN NEEDED having less than the amount needed, expected, or thought to be sufficient ○ *The proposal sounded good, but it was short on specifics.* **8.** INSUFFICIENTLY LONG OR TALL not long or tall enough by a particular amount ○ *All the beams are six inches short.* **9.** NOT REMEMBERING MORE DISTANT EVENTS unable or unwilling to recall events that happened before the comparatively recent past ○ *a short memory* **10.** DISCOURTEOUS rude and abrupt when speaking to somebody ○ *She was very short with the cashier.* **11.** FULL OF FAT made with lots of fat so as to be flaky or crumbly when baked ○ *short pastry* **12.** FIN SOLD WITHOUT POSSESSING SHARES SOLD involving a seller who, at the time of sale, does not possess the shares he or she is selling and has to borrow them before being able to deliver. Once the share price has fallen, the short seller buys the shares and returns them to the person from whom they were borrowed, resulting in a gain on the deal. **13.** FIN MATURING SOON being due for payment or repayment within a comparatively short space of time ○ *a short bond* **14.** PHON PRONOUNCED WITH RELATIVELY BRIEF SOUND describes phonemes or syllables that, when spoken, are comparatively brief in duration or are categorized as being of this type. The vowel "a" in the word "pat" is short compared with the similar vowel in the word "part." ■ *adv* **1.** ABRUPTLY abruptly and unexpectedly ○ *stop short* **2.** NOT REACHING TARGET before reaching a goal, target, or destination ○ *The pass fell three yards short.* **3.** FIN WITHOUT ACTUAL POSSESSION without actually possessing the things being sold when the sale is agreed on ○ *sell short* ■ *n* **1.** MOVIE OF SHORT DURATION a movie whose running time is approximately 30 minutes or less **2.** ELEC ENG same as **short-circuit 3.** BASEBALL same as **shortstop 4.** GARMENT SIZE a size of garment for a short person **5.** *UK* SMALL DRINK a drink consisting of a small measure of spirits in a small glass (*informal*) ■ **shorts** *npl* **1.** SHORT PANTS pants that end somewhere between the upper thigh and the knee **2.** UNDERPANTS men's underpants **3.** AGRIC MIXTURE OF BRAN AND COARSE FLOUR a mixture of bran and coarse flour left over from the milling of wheat **4.** FIN SHORT-DATED ITEMS bills or securities that are due to mature within a comparatively short space of time ■ *v* (**short·ed, short·ing, shorts**) **1.** *vti* ELEC same as **short-circuit** (sense 1) **2.** *vt* PROVIDE WITH LESS to give somebody less than expected or due [Old English *sceort* < Indo-European, "to cut"] —**short·ness** *n* ◇ **for short** as an abbreviation or shortened form ◇ **go short** to have insufficient money or food ◇ **in short** used to introduce a rephrasing of something in a more concise form ◇ **short and sweet** pleasant or bearable because brief ◇ **short of 1.** not having something, or not having enough of something **2.** less than ○ *Nothing short of an apology will do.* **3.** without actually doing something ○ *praised the candidate, but stopped short of endorsing him*

short-act·ing *adj* effective for a short period

short·age /sháwrtij/ *n* an absence of something that is needed or required

---

SYNONYMS See *lack.*

---

short back and sides *n UK* a hairstyle in which the hair at the back and sides of the head is cut short

short-billed marsh wren *n* same as **sedge wren**

short·bread /sháwrt brèd/ *n* a rich crumbly cookie made with a high proportion of butter to flour and a comparatively small proportion of sugar

short break *n* a vacation away from home lasting a few days, but usually less than a week

short·cake /sháwrt kàyk/ *n* **1.** a dessert consisting of a sponge-cake or biscuit base topped with fruit and cream **2.** a round, spongy cake that serves as a base for a shortcake dessert

short·change /shàwrt cháynj/ (**-changed, -chang·ing, -chang·es**) *vt* **1.** to give somebody less change than is due to him or her **2.** to behave unfairly toward somebody by giving him or her less of something than he or she deserves or expects —**short·chang·er** *n*

short cir·cuit *n* a failure in an electrical circuit caused by an accidental flow of excessive current

short-cir·cuit *v* **1.** *vti* HAVE OR CAUSE FAILURE IN CIRCUIT to have a failure in an electrical circuit by creating a connection of low resistance across which an excessive current flows, or cause such a failure in a circuit **2.** *vt* AVOID STANDARD PROCEDURE to ignore or bypass a standard procedure by using a much quicker or more direct method to achieve something ○ *short-circuited the legislative process by issuing an executive order* **3.** *vt* FRUSTRATE OR HINDER PLANS to hinder a plan or project by erecting obstacles ○ *An injury short-circuited his career in the major leagues.*

short·com·ing /sháwrt kùmming/ *n* a failure or flaw in somebody's character or in a system or organization (*often used in the plural*)

short·cut /sháwrt kùt/ *n* **1.** SHORTER ROUTE a route that is shorter or more direct than the usual one **2.** TIMESAVER a way of saving time and effort in doing something **3.** COMPUT QUICK WAY OF PERFORMING COMPUTER FUNCTION a means of quickly ordering a computer to perform a complicated function, e.g., an icon on a computer screen or a short series of keystrokes —**short·cut** *vti*

short-day *adj* able to flower only upon exposure to relatively short periods of sunlight, e.g., during spring or autumn

short·en /sháwrt'n/ (**-ened, -en·ing, -ens**) *v* **1.** *vti* BECOME OR MAKE SHORTER to make something shorter, or become shorter **2.** *vti* GAMBLING MAKE ODDS SHORTER to reduce the odds on a bet, or be reduced **3.** *vt* SAILING REDUCE SAIL to reduce the area of a sail **4.** *vt* COOK MAKE PASTRY MORE SHORTER to make pastry more crumbly by adding more shortening —**short·en·er** *n*

short·en·ing /sháwrt'ning/ *n* **1.** FAT fat that is solid at room temperature, e.g., lard, used for making pastry **2.** ABBREVIATION an abbreviated form of a word consisting of its first few letters, often ending with a final period, e.g., *cont.* for *continued.* **3.** ACT OF MAKING SOMETHING SHORTER the act or process of making something shorter, or of becoming shorter

short·fall /sháwrt fàwl/ *n* **1.** an amount by which something falls short of what is required **2.** a failure to meet a goal or requirement

short fuse *n* a tendency to get angry quickly and with little provocation (*informal*)

short·hair /sháwrt hèr/ *n* a medium-sized muscular domestic cat with a short thick coat

short·haired /shàwrt hèrd/ *adj* describes an animal with a coat of short hair ○ *a shorthaired cat*

short·hand /sháwrt hànd/ *n* **1.** QUICK WAY OF TAKING NOTES a fast method of writing, using symbols to represent letters, words, or phrases **2.** SHORTER WAY OF SAYING SOMETHING a shorter or quicker way of referring to something **3.** SYSTEM OF E-MAIL SYMBOLS the smileys, emoticons, abbreviations, and acronyms used in e-mail, chat rooms, instant messaging, and newsgroup postings

short-hand·ed *adj* having fewer than the usual or required number of staff, helpers, or players — **short-hand·ed·ness** *n*

short·hand typ·ist *n UK* same as **stenographer** (sense 2)

short haul *n* **1.** a short period of time **2.** a short journey or distance

short-haul *adj* traveling or used for traveling a short distance ○ *a short-haul flight*

short·horn /sháwrt hàwrn/ (*plural* **-horns** or *same*) *n* a reddish brown or white cow with short curved horns, belonging to a breed developed in northern England. Raised for: beef, milk.

short-horned grass·hop·per *n* a winged grasshopper with short antennae belonging to the family that includes the locust and many other common crop pests. Family: Acrididae.

short hun·dred·weight *n* MEASURE same as **hundredweight** (sense 1)

short·ie *n* another spelling of **shorty** (*informal*)

short in·ter·est *n* the number of shares in a security that have been borrowed and sold and must eventually be returned to the lender

short·leaf pine /shàwrt leef-/ *n* **1.** a pine tree with reddish bark and short needles grouped in twos. Native to: southeastern United States. Latin name: *Pinus echinata.* **2.** the yellow wood of the shortleaf pine. Use: construction.

short list *n* a list of the best candidates for a position or award after all others have been eliminated

short-list *vt* to put somebody or something on a final list of candidates for a position or award

short-lived /-lívd, -lívd/ *adj* lasting or living for only a short period of time

---

SYNONYMS See *temporary.*

---

short·ly /sháwrtlee/ *adv* **1.** SOON soon or in a short time ○ *The guests will arrive shortly.* **2.** CURTLY in a curt or discourteous manner ○ *"I wish you'd stop interrupting me," he said shortly.* **3.** BRIEFLY using only a few words

short or·der *n* food in a restaurant that is prepared and served quickly (*hyphenated before a noun*) ○ *a short-order cook*

short po·si·tion *n* an open position in a security in which the investor borrowed the security from somebody, sold it, and promised to replace the borrowed security at a later time

short ra·di·us *n* the perpendicular distance or line from the center of a regular polygon to one of its sides

short-range *adj* **1.** designed for or capable of traveling or operating only over a short distance **2.** concerned with the near future ○ *short-range plans*

short ribs *npl* a cut of beef consisting of tough fatty meat on rib ends from between the rib roast and plate

short sale *n* the sale of a borrowed security in anticipation that the security price will fall and can be paid back from the profits earned after repurchasing it at the lower price

short score *n* a condensed orchestra score omitting some of the less important instruments and often combining several parts on one staff

short shrift *n* brief and inconsiderate or unsympathetic treatment ○ *The proposal got short shrift.* ◇ **make short shrift of something** to deal with a matter quickly, giving it little attention

short sight *n* an inability to see distant objects clearly

short-sight·ed *adj* **1.** *UK* OPHTHALMOL same as **near-**

sighted 2. done or determined without taking the future into account —**short-sight·ed·ly** *adv* —**short-sight·ed·ness** *n*

short-spo·ken *adj* inclined to speak abruptly

short-staffed *adj* lacking the normal or required number of staff

short·stop /sháwrt stòp/ *n* **1.** in baseball, the position of the infielder playing closest to second base on the side toward third base **2.** the baseball player playing at shortstop

short sto·ry *n* a work of prose fiction that is shorter than a novel

short sub·ject *n* a short movie of approximately 30 minutes or less, sometimes a documentary, shown before a full-length feature movie (*dated*)

short-tem·pered *adj* easily made angry or impatient

short term *n* the period of time extending from the present only a short time into the future

short-term *adj* **1. NOT LASTING LONG** lasting for or affecting a relatively short period of time **2.** FIN **MATURING OR DUE SOON** maturing or payable within a relatively short period of time ○ *a short-term bond* **3.** FIN **FROM ASSETS HELD BRIEFLY** realized from assets held for a short time and then sold ○ *short-term profits*

short-term mem·o·ry *n* the part of the mind used for retaining temporary information over a short period

short ton *n* MEASURE same as **ton**[1] (sense 1)

short-waist·ed *adj* unusually short between the shoulders and the waist

short wave *n* a radio wave with a wavelength between 10 and 100 m

short·wave /sháwrt wàyv/ *adj* transmitting or receiving radio wavelengths shorter than 100 m ■ *n* a radio capable of transmitting or receiving short waves

short-wind·ed *adj* **1.** experiencing shortness of breath, especially after mild exertion **2.** expressed in few words

short·y /sháwrtee/ (*plural* **-ies**), **short·ie** *n* somebody or something very short or shorter than average (*informal*) —**short·y** *adj*

Sho·sho·ne /shō shṓnee/ (*plural* **-nes** or *same*), **Sho·sho·ni** (*plural* **-nis** or *same*) *n* **1.** a member of a Native North American people living mainly in Nevada, Idaho, Wyoming and Utah **2.** the group of Uto-Aztecan languages spoken by the Shoshone people. Native speakers: 3,000. [Early 19C. Origin ?] —**Sho·sho·ne** *adj* —**Sho·sho·ne·an** *n, adj*

Sho·sho·ne, Lake /shō shṓnee/ lake in NW Wyoming. Length: 12 mi./19 km.

Sho·sho·ne Falls falls in S Idaho, on the Snake River. Height: 212 ft./65 m.

Sho·sho·ni *n* PEOPLES, LANG another spelling of **Shoshone**

Shos·ta·ko·vich /shòstə kṓvich/, **Dmitri** (1906–75) Russian composer. A major figure in 20th-century music, he wrote prolifically in many different forms despite repeated criticism of his work by the Soviet government. His works include 15 symphonies and 15 string quartets. Full name **Shostakovich, Dmitri Dmitrievich**

> "You have to treat everything with irony, especially the things you hold dear. There's more of a chance then that they'll survive. That is perhaps one of the greatest secrets of our life."
> [Dmitri Shostakovich, *Testimony: The Memoirs of Shostakovich*; 1979]

shot[1] /shot/ *n* **1. SHOOTING OF GUN** a firing of a gun or other weapon **2. SOMEBODY WHO SHOOTS** somebody who shoots in a particular way ○ *a good shot* **3. SHOOTING OF PROJECTILE AT TARGET** an aimed discharge of a projectile, e.g., a bullet from a gun **4.** ARMS **BULLET OR CANNONBALL** a single solid metal missile for a gun or cannon, e.g., a bullet or cannonball **5.** ARMS **SMALL METAL PELLETS** small steel or lead pellets used in shotgun shells **6.** SPORTS **ATTEMPT TO SCORE** in a sport, an attempt to score points by throwing, hitting, kicking, or shooting something ○ *Jordan's foul shot went right into the hoop.* **7.** SPORTS **ACT OF HITTING BALL** in sports such as golf, tennis, or pool, an act of hitting the ball ○ *a long shot from the fairway* **8.** TRACK AND FIELD same as **shot put 9.** PHOTOGRAPHY **PARTICULAR VIEW ON FILM** a view recorded on film with a camera ○ *got a clear shot of the damaged wheels* **10.** MOVIES **CONTINUOUS UNINTERRUPTED FILM SEQUENCE** a continuous action or image on the screen that appears to be the result of a single uninterrupted operation of the camera **11.** AEROSP **ROCKET LAUNCH** the launching of a rocket or probe to a particular destination **12. ATTEMPT** an opportunity to attempt something ○ *had a shot at repairing the vacuum cleaner* **13. SHARP COMMENT** an angry or critical remark **14. GUESS** a wild guess or speculation, usually based on little or no information (*informal*) **15.** MED **INJECTION** an injection of a medication or vaccine (*informal*) **16.** BEVERAGES **SMALL AMOUNT OF ALCOHOL** a small glass or drink of a strong alcoholic beverage (*informal*) **17.** GAMBLING **CHANCE AT WINNING** something to bet on at particular odds, e.g., a racehorse (*informal*) ○ *The horse was a 3-to-1 shot.* **18.** MEASURE **MEASUREMENT IN FATHOMS** a unit of chain length equal to 15 fathoms in the United States and 12.5 fathoms in the United Kingdom ■ **shots** *npl US* **SMALL CANDIES** small candies sprinkled on something such as ice cream or cake [Old English *sceot, gesceot* "act of shooting" < Germanic, "to project"] ◇ **a shot in the arm** something that has a sudden good effect on somebody or something ◇ **a shot in the dark 1.** a guess made without any information **2.** an attempt made in desperation but with little hope of success ◇ **deliver** *or* **fire a shot across somebody's bows** to give somebody a warning of what might happen ◇ **like a shot** very eagerly and quickly

shot[2] /shot/ past participle, past tense of **shoot** ■ *adj* **1. TWO-TONE IN COLOR** woven of two colors in such a way that when the fabric is viewed from different angles the visible colors change **2. MARKED WITH VARYING COLOR** streaked or flecked with a different color **3. FILLED WITH PARTICULAR QUALITY** filled with or permeated by a particular emotion or quality ○ *stories shot through with pathos* **4. MADE USELESS** brought to a state of ruin or exhaustion (*informal*) ○ *I've been so stressed my nerves are shot.* **5. USED UP** no longer full or operating properly (*informal*) ○ *This tube of toothpaste is shot.*

shot clock *n* a clock used in basketball to limit the time a team may take before it must either shoot or lose possession of the ball [< SHOT[1]]

shote *n* AGRIC another spelling of **shoat**

shot·fir·er /shót fīrər/ *n* somebody who fires a charge used in blasting, e.g., in a mine [Late 19C. < SHOT[1]]

shot·gun /shót gùn/ *n* **1. GUN THAT SHOOTS PELLET LOAD** a short-range smoothbore gun that discharges a load of small pellets **2. FORMATION IN FOOTBALL** in football, an offensive formation, usually used when passing, in which the quarterback receives the snap a few yards behind the line of scrimmage ■ *adj* **1. INVOLVING INTIMIDATION** brought about by pressure, threats, or force **2.** *US* **HIT-OR-MISS** having no clear design, purpose, or objective [Early 19C. < SHOT[1]]

shot·gun clon·ing *n* the cloning of a gene segment by dividing the original into many random fragments and then mapping and sequencing the fragments to reconstruct the segment or genome

shot·gun house *n US* a one-story house with all the rooms in a line, usually from front to back, found especially in the southern United States

shot·gun wed·ding, shot·gun mar·riage *n* a marriage that takes place at short notice, usually because the bride is pregnant [Because the parties are compelled as if at gunpoint]

shot hole *n* **1.** a hole bored into rock in which an explosive charge is placed **2.** a small hole made in wood or leaves by insects or parasites (*informal*) [< SHOT[1]]

shot put *n* **1.** a track-and-field event in which contestants compete to throw a heavy metal ball as far as possible **2.** a heavy metal ball used in the shot put [< SHOT[1]] —**shot-put·ter** *n*

shot·ten /shótt'n/ *adj* describes a fish that has recently spawned and is therefore less valuable as food ○ *a shotten fish* [15C. Old past participle of SHOOT]

shot tow·er *n* a tower formerly used for making lead shot, in which molten lead was dropped from the top into water at the bottom in which the drops solidified [< SHOT[1]]

Barnaby's

shot put

should *stressed* /shŏŏd/; *unstressed* /shəd/ CORE MEANING: modal verb indicating that something is the right thing for somebody to do ○ *You should get more exercise.* ○ *I should have told her I was leaving.* ○ *The report recommended that children should be tested regularly.*

modal v **1. EXPRESSING DESIRABILITY** expresses desirability or rightness ○ *You should work less.* **2. EXPRESSING LIKELIHOOD OR PROBABILITY** to be scheduled or expected to be or do something ○ *I should be back by 12.* ○ *The scissors should be in the second drawer down.* ○ *They should have arrived at Grandma's by now.* **3. EXPRESSING CONDITIONS OR CONSEQUENCES** used to express the conditionality of an occurrence and suggest it is not a given, or to indicate the consequence of something that might happen (*used in conditional clauses*) ○ *If anything should happen to my car, I'd be heartbroken.* ○ *Should you have any questions, our staff will be available to help.* ○ *"If I should die, think only this of me..."* (Rupert Brooke, *The Soldier*; 1887–1915) **4. WOULD** used to mean the same thing as the verb would (*used with "I" or "we"*) ○ *If we spent that much every month, we should soon run out of money.* ○ *I should love to meet her.* **5. REPORTING PAST VIEWPOINT ABOUT FUTURE** used when reporting something such as somebody's words or thoughts from a past perspective about a future event ○ *It was intended that the library should be for the use of everyone.* ○ *He was eager that I should meet his publisher friend.* **6. USED TO SOFTEN HARSH WORDS** used to soften a blunt statement or make one more polite ○ *I should hope you're sorry now.* ◇ **I should** used to advise somebody to do something ○ *I should take him up on his offer, if I were you.*

USAGE should or **would**? The same general pattern is true here as for *shall* and *will*. As an auxiliary verb, ***would*** is more usual than ***should*** when stating a condition or proposition and is the only choice when asking a question (*They would like to come. I would think so. Would you like to go to the movies?*). ***Should*** has the special role of denoting obligation, validity, or likelihood (*I should stay until they arrive. Should you be lifting that? That should be our visitors now.*) and must be used in inverted constructions expressing a condition: *Should it rain, the party will be held indoors.* ***Would*** is required when referring to habitual past action: *On Wednesdays I would go to the library.* In conversational English, the contracted forms *I'd, you'd*, etc., are regularly used instead of the full forms in making simple statements (*They'd like to come*), but these cannot be used in place of ***should*** in its senses of obligation or likelihood.

shoul·der /shṓldər/ *n* **1. PLACE WHERE ARM ATTACHES TO TRUNK** either of the two parts of the human body immediately below and at each side of the neck, where the arm joins the trunk **2. JOINT ATTACHING FORELIMB TO TRUNK** the part of the body of a vertebrate animal equivalent to the shoulder, where the forelimb joins the pectoral girdle **3. PART OF GARMENT FITTING SHOULDER** a part of a piece of clothing that covers the shoulder **4. MEAT FROM SHOULDER** a fairly fatty cut of meat consisting of the upper part of a foreleg of an animal **5. SOMETHING SLOPED LIKE SHOULDER** something resembling a shoulder in position or slope, e.g., the part of a stringed instrument between the neck and body or the slope near the top of a hill **6.** ROADS **LAND BESIDE ROAD** a strip of land along the side of a road **7.** PRINTING **TYPE SURFACE THAT IS NOT LETTER** a flat surface of printers' type below the base of the raised letter or character **8.** ENG **WIDER PORTION OF SHAFT** any portion of a shaft or other instrument for transmitting force that has an increase in diameter to withstand thrust ■ **shoul·ders** *npl* **1. UPPER AREA OF BACK** the upper back, including both shoulders and the area between them **2. CAPACITY TO HANDLE RESPONSIBILITY** the capacity to carry responsibility for something, especially something unpleasant or worrying, or the fact of being responsible for it ○ *The blame rests on her shoulders.* ■ *v* (**-dered, -der·ing, -ders**) **1.** *vt* **CARRY OR PLACE SOMETHING ON SHOULDERS** to carry, lift, or place something on the shoulders **2.** *vt* **ACCEPT RESPONSIBILITY** to accept and bear a burden or responsibility **3.** *vti* **MOVE SOMETHING WITH SHOULDER** to push something or make way using a shoulder ○ *She successfully shouldered her way to the front of the crowd.* [Old English *sculdor* < Germanic] ◇ **put your shoulder to the wheel** to work hard ◇ **rub shoulders with somebody** to associate with somebody of a particular type or social class ◇ **shoulder to shoulder 1.** side by side **2.** in a cooperative effort ○ *They fought shoulder to shoulder to prevent the measure being adopted.* ◇ **straight from the shoulder** in a frank or blunt way

shoul·der bag *n* a bag carried by a long strap hung over the shoulder

shoul·der belt *n* AUTOMOT same as **shoulder harness**

shoul·der blade *n* either one of two large flat triangular bones over the upper outer parts of the ribs at the top of the back that joins with the upper arm bone. Technical name **scapula** (sense 1)

shoul·der board *n US* one of a pair of stiff cloth patches worn on the shoulders of a military uniform to indicate rank. Can term **shoulder strap**

shoul·der gir·dle *n* an incomplete ring of bones formed by the two shoulder blades (**scapulas**), the two collar bones (**clavicles**), and the upper edge of the breastbone (**sternum**)

shoul·der har·ness, shoul·der belt *n* a safety belt in a motor vehicle that is worn diagonally across the shoulder and chest and is attached at the waist to the seat belt

shoul·der hol·ster *n* a holster hung from a shoulder strap and worn under the arm, used to hide a gun under a coat or jacket

shoul·der knot *n* a decoration of braided cord worn on the shoulder of a uniform

shoul·der pad *n* a pad inserted into the shoulder of a piece of clothing to improve its shape, often making it appear larger

shoul·der patch *n* a cloth patch with an identifying emblem on it, worn on the upper part of the sleeve of a uniform

shoul·der rest *n* a support for a firearm that rests on or against a person's shoulder

shoul·der strap *n* **1.** a strap that goes over a shoulder for carrying a bag or holding up a garment **2.** *Can, UK* CLOTHING, MIL same as **shoulder board**

should·n't /shŏŏd'nt/ *contr* should not

shouldst /shŏŏdst/ 2nd person singular present of **should** (*archaic*)

should've /shŏŏdəv/ *contr* should have (*informal*)

USAGE See ***of.***

shout /showt/ *v* (**shout·ed, shout·ing, shouts**) **1.** *vt* **SAY SOMETHING LOUDLY** to say or utter something very loudly **2.** *vi* **SPEAK LOUDLY** to speak in a loud or angry voice **3.** *vi* ONLINE **TYPE SOMETHING IN CAPITALS** to type a sentence or paragraph entirely in capital letters as the netiquette equivalent of raising the voice in anger or for emphasis **4.** *vti* **PAY FOR FOOD OR DRINK** to buy something for somebody else, especially a drink in a bar or a meal in a restaurant (*informal*) ■ *n* **1. LOUD CRY** a loud call or cry **2.** *UK* **TURN TO PAY** somebody's turn to buy something, especially a drink or meal (*informal*) ○ *"It's my shout. What would you like to drink?"* [14C. Origin ?] —**shout·er** *n* ◇ **be all over bar the shouting** *UK* used for saying that something is almost over, and the outcome is clear ◇ **nothing to shout about** not good enough to speak of with pride (*informal*) ◇ **send a shout out to somebody** *US* to say hello to a viewer or listener during a broadcast (*slang*)

shout down *vt* to prevent somebody from being heard by shouting loudly

shout·ing match *n* an argument in which the participants shout at one another or try to shout each other down (*informal*)

shout·out /shówt òwt/ *n* (*slang*) **1.** a shouted aside on a rap recording, usually paying tribute to somebody **2.** a statement acknowledging or thanking somebody

shove /shuv/ *vti* (**shoved, shov·ing, shoves**) **1. MOVE SOMETHING WITH FORCE** to push somebody or something along or forward with force **2. PUSH SOMEBODY OR SOMETHING ROUGHLY** to push somebody or something in a rude or careless way ■ *n* **PUSH** a strong push [Old English *scufan* "push away" < Germanic] —**shov·er** *n*

shove off *vi* **1.** to leave (*informal; sometimes used as a command*) **2.** to move from shore or a mooring in a boat

shovel

shov·el /shúvv'l/ *n* **1. LONG-HANDLED SCOOP** a hand tool consisting of a broad, usually curved blade attached to a long handle, used for lifting and moving loose material **2. MACHINE FOR DIGGING** a power-driven machine that operates with a scooping motion, especially one used for digging or moving soil **3. AMOUNT HELD BY SHOVEL** the amount that a shovel is capable of holding ■ *v* (**-eled, -el·ing, -els**) **1.** *vti* **DIG WITH SHOVEL FOR SOMETHING** to lift, move, or clear something with a shovel **2.** *vt* **THROW SOMETHING CARELESSLY** to move large amounts of something from one place to another in a careless or clumsy way [Old English *scofl* < Germanic] —**shov·el·ful** *n*

shov·el·er /shúvvələr/ *n* **1.** somebody or something that uses a shovel to move or throw something **2.** a small freshwater duck with a broad and very long beak. Native to: marshes in the northern hemisphere. Latin name: *Anas clypeata.*

shov·el hat *n* a black felt hat with a low crown and a wide brim turned up at the sides, formerly worn by some English clergymen

shov·el·head /shóvv'l hèd/ (*plural* **-heads** or *same*) *n* a common hammerhead shark with a broad shovel-shaped head. Native to: shallow Atlantic and Pacific waters. Latin name: *Sphyrna tiburo.*

shov·el·ler /shúvv'lər/ *n* UK spelling of **shoveler** (sense 1)

shov·el-nosed *adj* having a broad shovel-shaped head, snout, or bill

shov·el-nosed stur·geon *n* a freshwater sturgeon with a broad shovel-shaped snout. Native to: North America. Latin name: *Scaphirhynchus platorhynchus.*

shov·el·ware /shúvv'l wèr/ *n* software or material that is put on the Web or on a CD-ROM indiscriminately without regard for its appearance or usefulness (*informal*)

show /shō/ *v* (**showed, shown** /shōn/, **show·ing, shows**) **1.** *vt* **MAKE SOMETHING VISIBLE** to cause or allow something to come into view, or present something to be looked at ○ *Show me your hand.* **2.** *vti* **BE VISIBLE** to be visible, or allow something to be seen easily, often inadvertently or against inclination ○ *Does the spot on my shirt show?* **3.** *vti* **EXHIBIT** to put on an exhibition or performance, or be presented for the public to see ○ *She's showing her paintings all over the world now.* ○ *A new movie is showing.* **4.** *vti* **PRESENT SOMETHING TO PUBLIC** to display something publicly, e.g., in a sale, exhibition, or competition, or be displayed publicly ○ *His work was showing at the Museum of Modern Art.* **5.** *vt* **DEMONSTRATE SOMETHING FOR INSTRUCTION** to give a demonstration of something in order to teach others ○ *She showed us how to apply the glaze to the pot.* **6.** *vt* **ESTABLISH SOMETHING USING REASON** to explain, demonstrate, or prove something in a logical way ○ *The teacher showed them the solution.* **7.** *vt* **GIVE INFORMATION** to register information ○ *This chart shows the sudden increase in temperature.* **8.** *vt* **GUIDE SOMEBODY** to guide or accompany somebody ○ *Show them to the office.* **9.** *vt* **POINT SOMETHING OUT TO SOMEBODY** to call somebody's attention to something ○ *She showed him the mistake.* **10.** *vt* **DEMONSTRATE QUALITIES** to make fundamental qualities or characteristics evident ○ *He has shown that he is honest.* **11.** *vt* **DISPLAY ATTITUDE** to display a personal feeling or attitude ○ *She's never shown much interest in art.* **12.** *vi* **HAVE A PARTICULAR APPEARANCE** to have a particular appearance when being viewed ○ *The horse shows well.* **13.** *vi* **ARRIVE** to put in an appearance at a place (*informal*) ○ *They never showed.* **14.** *vi* **COME IN THIRD** to finish at least third in a race, especially a horse race or a dog race **15.** *vt* LAW **PLEAD SOMETHING IN LAWSUIT** to allege or plead something in a legal document ■ *n* **1. PUBLIC PRESENTATION** a public entertainment, e.g., a theater performance, movie, or radio or television program ○ *Shall we go to a show tonight?* **2. EXHIBITION** an exhibition, e.g., of art, flowers, animals, or an industry's products ○ *a flower show* **3.** *UK* LEISURE, AGRIC same as **fair**[2] (sense 1) **4. DEMONSTRATION** an expression or demonstration of something ○ *a show of force* **5. APPEARANCE** an appearance given, either as an outward display of an emotion or trait, or as a demonstration of falseness and pretense ○ *a show of diligence* **6. SIZABLE VENTURE** an undertaking or task, especially one of some size and complexity (*informal*) ○ *You decide – it's your show!* **7. IMPRESSIVE DISPLAY** an extravagant or impressive display ○ *Their lawyers put on quite a show!* **8. THIRD PLACE** a third place finish in a race, especially a horse race or a dog race **9.** *US* **OPPORTUNITY** a chance or opportunity (*informal*) ○ *no show of winning* **10. INDICATION** a trace of something indicating its presence, e.g., oil in the ground **11.** MED **BLOOD INDICATING START OF LABOR** a bloody mucous discharge indicating the onset of labor in childbirth [Old English *scēawian* "look at" < W Germanic, "to look"] —**show·a·ble** *adj* ◇ **get the** *or* **this show on the road** to begin an activity or start an event (*informal*) ◇ **steal the show** to attract the most attention or admiration

show off *v* **1.** *vi* **ATTRACT ATTENTION OF OTHERS** to try to impress others by behaving in a way that attracts attention **2.** *vt* **PRESENT SOMETHING FOR APPROVAL** to display somebody or something proudly for others to admire **3.** *vt* **PRESENT SOMETHING IN APPEALING WAY** to display something in a way that enhances it

show up *v* **1.** *vi* **ARRIVE** to arrive or put in an appearance (*informal*) **2.** *vt* **BRING SOMETHING TO LIGHT** to expose or reveal something, especially an error or personal shortcoming **3.** *vi* **BE SEEN** to be easily seen **4.** *vt* **EMBARRASS SOMEBODY BEFORE OTHERS** to embarrass or humiliate somebody publicly **5.** *vt* **MAKE SOMEBODY LOOK BAD** to perform in a superior way and make somebody look inferior by comparison

show-and-tell *n* **1.** a classroom activity for children in which each child brings an object to school and tells the other children about it **2.** an informative meeting or presentation to which the public is invited (*informal*)

show bill *n* a poster advertising or publicizing something

show biz *n* ARTS same as **show business** (*informal*)

show·boat /shō bōt/ *n* **1. RIVERBOAT THEATER** a river steamboat equipped with a theater and carrying an acting company that performs for communities along the river **2. SHOW-OFF** a flamboyant person who seeks attention (*informal*) ■ *vi* (**-boat·ed, -boat·ing, -boats**) **SHOW OFF FOR ATTENTION** to behave flamboyantly in order to attract attention (*informal*)

show busi·ness *n* the entertainment industry, including movies, radio, television, theater, and music recording

show·case /shō kàyss/ *n* **1. GLASS CASE FOR DISPLAYING OBJECTS** a box or case, usually one made of glass, used to display objects, especially in a museum or shop **2. MOST FAVORABLE SETTING** an event, setting, or medium in which something or somebody is presented to advantage ■ *vt* (**-cased, -cas·ing, -cas·es**) PRESENT SOMETHING TO ADVANTAGE to present something or somebody in a way that is designed to attract attention and admiration

show·down /shṓ dòwn/ *n* **1.** a confrontation to settle a conflict or dispute **2.** in poker, the moment at the end of a round when the players show their cards to see who has the best hand

show·er[1] /shów ər/ *n* **1.** BATH UNDER SPRAY a method of washing in which somebody stands upright under a spray of water from a nozzle **2.** PLACE AND EQUIPMENT FOR SHOWER an enclosure or the plumbing apparatus for a shower **3.** PERIOD OF PRECIPITATION a short period of rain, snow, hail, or sleet **4.** SOMETHING LIKE RAIN a sudden spray or fall of something such as meteors, sparks, or bullets ○ *a meteor shower* **5.** LARGE AMOUNT OF SOMETHING something that somebody receives all at once in quantity **6.** PARTY WITH GIFTS a party given by friends, especially in honor of a woman who is about to be married or is expecting a baby, at which gifts are given **7.** *UK* DISAGREEABLE GROUP a group of people considered unpleasant, worthless, or inferior (*informal*) **8.** PHYS IONIZING PARTICLES CAUSED BY COSMIC RAY a large number of ionizing particles and photons caused by the collision of a cosmic-ray particle with the upper atmosphere ■ *v* (**-ered, -er·ing, -ers**) **1.** *vi* WASH UNDER SHOWER to wash using a shower **2.** *vti* RAIN DOWN ON SOMEBODY to fall in a spray, or make things fall in a spray **3.** *vt* GIVE SOMEBODY SOMETHING PLENTIFULLY to give somebody something in abundance ○ *They were showered with gifts.* [Old English *scūr* < W Germanic] —**show·er·y** *adj*

show·er[2] /shṓ ər/ *n* somebody or something that shows, especially an exhibitor at a public exhibition [Old English *scēawere* "scout, watchman" < *scēawian* (see SHOW)]

show·er bath *n* HOUSEHOLD same as **shower**[1] *n* (sense 1) (*dated*)

show·er gel *n* a liquid soap with the consistency of a gel, used especially when in the shower and often scented

show·er·head /shów ər hèd/ *n* a spray nozzle that is part of an overhead plumbing fixture used in a shower

show·girl /shṓ gùrl/ *n* a young woman who performs in the chorus of a stage show, usually a musical, as a dancer or singer

show house, show home *n UK* same as **model home**

show·ing /shṓ ing/ *n* **1.** DISPLAY a presentation or exhibition, e.g., of a movie or artwork **2.** TYPE OF PERFORMANCE the way a person, group, or team performs **3.** PRESENTATION OF FACTS a presentation of facts

show jump·ing /shṓ jùmping/ *n* a competitive sport in which riders on horseback take turns jumping over a series of obstacles on a set course and are judged on speed and ability —**show·jump** *vi* —**show·jump·er** *n*

show·man /shṓmən/ (*plural* **-men** /-mən/) *n* **1.** GIFTED ENTERTAINER somebody, especially a man, who is naturally talented in dramatic presentation or entertainment **2.** PRODUCER OF SHOW a producer or promoter of commercial entertainment ventures, especially in musical theater **3.** SHOWER OF LIVESTOCK a man who exhibits livestock in competition at fairs —**show·man·ship** *n*

Show Me State *n* a nickname for Missouri

shown past participle of **show**

show-off *n* a flamboyant person who seeks attention (*informal*)

show of hands *n* a form of voting that involves counting the hands raised by people to vote for or against a proposal

show·per·son /shṓ pùrss'n/ (*plural* **-peo·ple** /-pēep'l/ or **-per·sons**) *n* **1.** somebody who exhibits livestock in competition at fairs **2.** somebody who is in show business

show·piece /shṓ pēess/ *n* something considered or offered as a fine example of something

show·place /shṓ plàyss/ *n* **1.** a place visited for its beauty or historical significance **2.** a place that is considered or offered as an example of beauty

show·room /shṓ ro͞om, -ro͝om/ *n* a room in which goods for sale, especially cars or electrical appliances, are displayed

show·stop·per /shṓ stòppər/ *n* **1.** a performance receiving so much applause from an audience that the show is interrupted **2.** somebody or something so spectacular as to attract and hold everyone's attention

show·time /shṓ tīm/ *n* **1.** the scheduled time for an entertainment such as a movie or play to begin **2.** the scheduled time for any event or activity to begin (*informal*)

show tri·al *n* a trial with a predetermined verdict held for propaganda purposes

show win·dow *n* a window in a store used to display merchandise

show·wom·an /shṓ wo͝ommən/ (*plural* **-wom·en** /-wìmmin/) *n* **1.** a woman who is naturally talented in dramatic presentation or entertainment **2.** a woman who exhibits livestock in competition at fairs

show·y /shṓ ee/ (**-i·er, -i·est**) *adj* **1.** making an attractive or impressive display **2.** appearing tasteless and ostentatious —**show·i·ly** *adv* —**show·i·ness** *n*

sho·yu /shṓ yo͞o/ *n* a Japanese variety of soy sauce [Early 18C. < Japanese]

shp, s.h.p. *abbr* MECH ENG shaft horsepower

shpil·kes /shpílkəss/ *npl* a state of great nervousness or anxiety [< Yiddish]

shpt. *abbr* shipment

shr. *abbr* FIN share

shrad·dh *n* CULTL ANTHROP another spelling of **sraddhaa**

shrank past tense of **shrink**

shrap·nel /shrápnəl/ *n* **1.** metal balls or fragments that are scattered when a shell, bomb, or bullet explodes **2.** an artillery shell designed to explode before impact producing a shower of metal balls and fragments [Early 19C. After General Henry *Shrapnel* (1761–1842), British artillery officer]

shred /shred/ *n* **1.** LONG TORN STRIP a ragged scrap or strip cut or torn from something **2.** SMALL PART a very small amount or fragment of something ■ *v* (**shred·ded, shred·ding, shreds**) **1.** *vt* TEAR SOMETHING INTO SHREDS to cut or tear something into shreds **2.** *vt* PUT DOCUMENT THROUGH SHREDDER to reduce a document to unreadable strips in a shredder **3.** *vti* SURF OR SNOWBOARD EXPERTLY to ride a wave on a surfboard or descend a slope on a snowboard with expert skill (*informal*) [Old English *scrēade* < W Germanic, "to cut"]

shred·der /shréddər/ *n* **1.** an office machine used to destroy documents by cutting them into very small pieces so that they cannot be read **2.** an expert surfer or snowboarder (*informal*)

Shreve·port /shrēev pàwrt/ city in northwestern Louisiana, on the western bank of the Red River, east of the Texas border. The city is an important producer of oil, natural gas, and cotton. Population: 199,033 (2002 estimate).

shrew

shrew /shroo/ *n* **1.** a small nocturnal animal that resembles a mouse but is an insectivore, with velvety fur, a long pointed snout, and small eyes and ears. Native to: found worldwide, except New Guinea, Australia, and New Zealand. Family: Soricidae. **2.** an offensive term for a woman who is regarded as quarrelsome, nagging, or ill-tempered [Old English *scrēawa*. Origin ?]

CULTURAL NOTE *The Taming of the Shrew*, a play (1593–94?) by English dramatist William Shakespeare. The central story of this play within a play is set in Verona and describes Petruchio's attempts to woo the wealthy but haughty and temperamental Katharina (the "shrew" of the title). The rounded and convincing protagonists make this an intriguing character study as well as a boisterous farce. The expression "Kiss me, Kate" comes from Act II, scene i: "Kiss me, Kate, we will be married o' Sunday.".

shrewd /shrood/ *adj* **1.** GOOD AT JUDGING PEOPLE OR SITUATIONS showing or possessing intelligence, insight, and sound judgment, especially in business or politics **2.** CLEVER AND PROBABLY ACCURATE based on good judgment and probably correct ○ *a shrewd assessment of the situation* ○ *a shrewd guess* **3.** CRAFTY inclined to deal with others in a clever underhanded way **4.** SHARP piercing or sharp (*archaic*) [13C. < SHREW in the obsolete sense "wicked person"] —**shrewd·ly** *adv* —**shrewd·ness** *n*

shrew·ish /shro͞o ish/ *adj* with a quarrelsome ill-tempered disposition —**shrew·ish·ly** *adv* —**shrew·ish·ness** *n*

Shrews·bur·y /shro͞oz bèrree/ town in central Massachusetts, southeast of Leominster and northeast of Worcester. Population: 32,751 (2002 estimate).

Shri *n* same as **Sri**

shriek /shreek/ *v* (**shrieked, shriek·ing, shrieks**) **1.** *vi* MAKE SHRILL SOUND to make a loud high-pitched piercing sound **2.** *vt* SAY SOMETHING IN SHRILL VOICE to utter something in a loud high-pitched piercing voice ■ *n* SHRILL CRY a loud high-pitched piercing cry or sound [15C. < N Germanic] —**shriek·er** *n*

shrie·val·ty /shrēev'ltee/ (*plural* **-ties**) *n UK* **1.** SHERIFF'S OFFICE the office or position of sheriff **2.** SHERIFF'S TERM the term of office of a sheriff **3.** SHERIFF'S JURISDICTION the jurisdiction of a sheriff [Early 16C. < obsolete *shrieve* "sheriff"]

shrift /shrift/ *n* (*archaic*) **1.** SHRIVING SOMEBODY the act of shriving or of being shriven **2.** CONFESSION confession to a priest **3.** ABSOLUTION absolution granted by a priest. ◊ **short shrift** [Old English *scrift* < *scrīfan* (see SHRIVE)]

shrike

shrike /shrīk/ (*plural* **shrikes** or *same*) *n* a brown or gray songbird with a screeching call and a hooked beak that eats insects and small animals that it impales on sharp objects such as thorns. Family: Laniidae. [Mid-16C. Origin ?]

shrill /shril/ *adj* **1.** PENETRATINGLY HIGH-PITCHED with a high-pitched penetrating quality **2.** MAKING SHRILL SOUND making a high-pitched penetrating sound **3.** INSISTENT with an obtrusive insistent quality **4.** STRIDENT having a harsh intense quality perceived as unpleasant ■ *v* (**shrilled, shrill·ing, shrills**) **1.** *vi* MAKE SHRILL SOUND to make a high-pitched penetrating sound (*literary*) **2.** *vt* SAY SOMETHING IN PIERCING VOICE to utter something in a high-pitched penetrating voice [13C. Origin ?] —**shrill·ness** *n* —**shril·ly** *adv*

shrimp /shrimp/ *n* (*plural same* or **shrimps**) **1.** SMALL OCEAN CRUSTACEAN a small, mainly ocean-dwelling crustacean with ten legs, belonging to a suborder that includes several edible species. A shrimp has a long thin semitransparent body, five pairs of jointed legs, a tail resembling a fan, and a pair of pincers. Suborder: Natantia. See illustration on next page **2.** SOMETHING UNDERSIZED somebody or something very small or considered insignificant

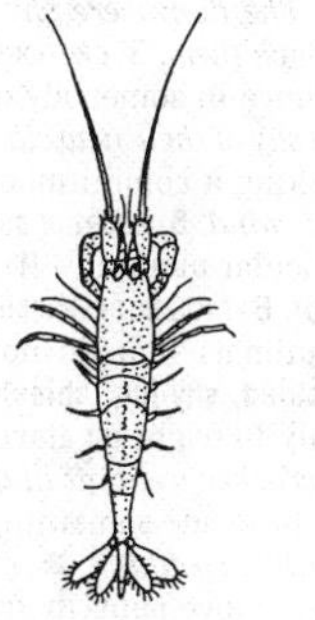
shrimp

(*informal*) ■ *vi* (**shrimped, shrimp·ing, shrimps**) FISH FOR SHRIMP to fish for shrimp [14C. Origin ?] —**shrimp·er** *n*

shrimp plant *n* an ornamental plant with long curving flower spikes within overlapping pink bracts. Native to: tropical America. Latin name: *Beloperone guttata*.

shrine /shrīn/ *n* **1.** HOLY PLACE OF WORSHIP a sacred place of worship associated with a holy person or event **2.** CONTAINER FOR HOLY RELICS a case or other container for sacred relics such as the bones of a saint **3.** TOMB OF HOLY PERSON the tomb of a saint or other revered figure **4.** NICHE FOR RELIGIOUS ICON a ledge or alcove for a religious icon, e.g., in a church **5.** SOMETHING REVERED an object or place revered for its associations or history ■ *vt* (**shrined, shrin·ing, shrines**) same as **enshrine** (sense 2) (*literary*) [Pre-12C. < Latin *scrinium* "case for books or papers"]

Shrin·er /shrínər/ *n* a member of a secret fraternal non-Masonic organization whose members are Knights Templars and 32nd-degree Masons

shrink /shringk/ *v* (**shrank** /shrangk/ or **shrunk** /shrungk/, **shrunk** or **shrunk·en** /shrúngkən/, **shrink·ing, shrinks**) **1.** *vti* MAKE OR BECOME SMALLER to become smaller, or cause something to become smaller, e.g., when exposed to cold, heat, or damp **2.** *vti* REDUCE SIZE to decrease in amount, extent, value, or weight, or cause something to decrease in this way **3.** *vi* DRAW AWAY FROM SOMETHING to move back and away, especially out of disgust, fear, or horror ○ *shrinking back in revulsion* **4.** *vi* BE DISINCLINED TO DO SOMETHING to be unwilling or reluctant to do something, especially something difficult or unpleasant ○ *She does not shrink from tackling tough problems.* ■ *n* **1.** same as **psychiatrist** (*slang; considered offensive by some people*) **2.** ACT OF SHRINKING AWAY an act of shrinking away from something **3.** AMOUNT SOMETHING SHRINKS the amount by which something shrinks [Old English *scrincan* "to wither" < Indo-European, "to turn, bend"] —**shrink·a·ble** *adj* —**shrink·er** *n*

SYNONYMS See ***recoil***.

shrink·age /shríngkij/ *n* **1.** DECREASE AFTER SHRINKING the amount lost when something is decreased or reduced, or when it shrinks **2.** ACT OF SHRINKING the shrinking of something **3.** MERCHANDISE STOLEN OR BROKEN the loss of goods through theft or breakage **4.** LOSS OF VALUE the decrease in value of something **5.** WEIGHT REDUCTION IN CARCASSES the loss in body weight of livestock carcasses during shipping, storage, and preparation for sale **6.** REDUCED SIZE OF CLAY ITEM the reduction in size of a clay object when it is fired in a kiln, caused by the moisture burning off

shrink fit *n* the fit of two interlocking parts in which the outer is heated and therefore expands before being put in position, the contraction during cooling ensuring that it is tight

shrink·ing vi·o·let /shrìngking-/ *n* a shy or retiring person (*informal*)

shrink-wrap *n* a clear thermoplastic film that is wrapped around a product and shrunk to its original smaller size using heat, thereby forming a tightly sealed package ■ *vt* to wrap goods in shrink-wrap

shrive /shrīv/ (**shrove** /shrōv/ or **shrived, shriv·en** /shrívvən/ or **shrived, shriv·ing, shrives**) *v* **1.** *vt* ABSOLVE SOMEBODY OF SINS in Christianity, to hear somebody's confession of sins and give the person absolution **2.** *vt* IMPOSE PENANCE in Christianity, to impose a penance on a sinner **3.** *vi* CONFESS to confess sins to a priest (*archaic*) [Old English *scrīfan*, via Germanic < Latin *scribere* "write"] —**shriv·er** *n*

shriv·el /shrívv'l/ (**-eled, -el·ing, -els**) *vti* **1.** SHRINK to become shrunken or wrinkled, or cause somebody or something to become shrunken or wrinkled, especially from drying out or aging **2.** WEAKEN to become useless or ineffectual, or cause somebody to become useless or ineffectual **3.** BECOME OR MAKE SMALLER to become gradually smaller or less, or cause something to become gradually smaller or less [Mid-16C. Origin ?]

shriv·en CHR past participle of **shrive**

Shriv·i·jay·a HIST another spelling of **Sri Vijaya**

shroff /shrof, shrawf/ *n* **1.** SOUTH ASIAN BANKER in South Asia, a banker or moneychanger **2.** EXPERT IN COUNTERFEIT COINS somebody employed in eastern Asia to separate counterfeit from real coins ■ *vt* (**shroffed, shroff·ing, shroffs**) SEPARATE COUNTERFEIT COINS to separate counterfeit from real coins [Early 17C. Alteration of Hindi *śarāf* < Arabic *ṣarrāf*]

Shrop·shire[1] /shróp sheer, -shər/ *n* a dark-faced sheep belonging to a breed raised for wool and meat [Mid-18C. After SHROPSHIRE[2]]

Shrop·shire[2] /shróp sheer, -shər/ county on the Welsh border in the Midlands, England. It is mainly agricultural, and was an early center of the iron industry. Shrewsbury is the county town. Population: 283,173 (2001). Area: 1,348 sq. mi./3,490 sq. km.

shroud /shrowd/ *n* **1.** BURIAL CLOTH a cloth in which a dead body is wrapped before burial **2.** COVERING something that covers or conceals something or somebody **3.** PROTECTIVE COVERING a protective covering, e.g., a guard for a piece of machinery **4.** NAUT MAST STAY any one of the supporting ropes or wires that extend down from the top of a mast to the deck **5.** AEROSP PROTECTIVE COVERING FOR SPACECRAFT a shield that protects a spacecraft from heat during launch **6.** AEROSP PART OF AIRFOIL SURFACE a rearward extension of a fixed airfoil surface covering the leading edge of a movable surface hinged to it **7.** CONSTR CABLE TO STOP SWAY a supporting cable that extends from the top of a tall structure such as a smokestack to the ground **8.** AVIAT PARACHUTE LINE any one of the lines by which the harness of a parachute is attached to the canopy ■ *vt* (**shroud·ed, shroud·ing, shrouds**) **1.** COVER OR CONCEAL SOMETHING to cover or conceal somebody or something **2.** WRAP CORPSE to wrap a dead body in a cloth [Old English *scrūd* "garment" < W Germanic, "to cut"]

shroud-laid *adj* describes a rope that is made up of four twisted strands

shroud-wav·ing *n UK* the calculated use of distressing events or statistics to publicize issues or gain political advantage (*slang*) —**shroud-wav·ing** *adj*

shrove CHR past tense of **shrive**

Shrove·tide /shrṓv tīd/ *n* in the Christian calendar, the three-day period preceding Ash Wednesday and the season of Lent

Shrove Tues·day /shrṑv-/ *n* in the Christian calendar, the last day before the beginning of Lent [< past tense of SHRIVE; from the practice of going to confession at the beginning of Lent]

shrub[1] /shrub/ *n* a woody plant without a trunk but with several stems growing from the base [Old English *scrybb* "shrubbery" < Indo-European, "to cut"]

shrub[2] /shrub/ *n* a drink made with fruit juice, sugar, spices, and rum or other alcohol [Early 18C. < Arabic *surb* "a drink"]

shrub·ber·y /shrúbbəree/ (*plural* **-ies**) *n* **1.** a part of a garden where shrubs grow **2.** shrubs considered collectively

shrub·by /shrúbbee/ (**-bi·er, -bi·est**) *adj* **1.** planted or covered with shrubs **2.** resembling a shrub in size or in having little or no trunk —**shrub·bi·ness** *n*

shrug /shrug/ *vti* (**shrugged, shrug·ging, shrugs**) to raise and drop the shoulders briefly, especially to indicate indifference or lack of knowledge ■ *n* a gesture of raising and dropping the shoulders briefly [14C. Origin ?]

shrug off *vt* **1.** DISMISS SOMETHING to reject or disregard something as unimportant **2.** GET FREE OF SOMETHING to become free of something such as a disease **3.** REMOVE CLOTHING to get out of clothing by wriggling

shrunk past participle, past tense of **shrink**

shrunk·en past participle of **shrink**

sht. *abbr* sheet

shtetl /shtétt'l, shtáyt'l/ (*plural* **shtetls** or **shtet·lach** /shtét laakh, shtáyt-/), **schtetl** (*plural* **schtetls** or **schtet·lach**) *n* in former times, a small Jewish town or village in Eastern Europe [Mid-20C. < Yiddish, "little town" < German *Stadt* "town"]

shtg. *abbr* shortage

shtick /shtik/, **schtick**, **shtik** *n* **1.** SPECIAL ATTRIBUTE OF SOMEBODY something that especially characterizes somebody, e.g., an interest, talent, trait, job, or hobby (*slang*) **2.** ENTERTAINER'S ROUTINE a comedian's or entertainer's act or gimmick (*informal*) **3.** EXAGGERATION an exaggerated complaint or extreme position (*humorous*) [Mid-20C. Via Yiddish, "piece, routine" < Old High German *stucki*]

shuck /shuk/ *n* **1.** OUTER COVERING OF GRAIN OR FRUIT the husk, pod, or shell of something such as a nut, pea, or ear of corn **2.** OYSTER OR CLAM SHELL the shell of a clam or oyster ■ **shucks** *npl* SOMETHING WITH LITTLE VALUE something of little or no value (*dated informal*) ■ *vt* (**shucked, shuck·ing, shucks**) **1.** TAKE SOMETHING FROM HUSK to remove the husk, pod, or shell from something **2.** GET RID OF SOMETHING to get rid of or remove something or throw something off (*informal*) [Late 17C. Origin ?] —**shuck·er** *n*

shucks /shuks/ *interj* used to express disappointment, bashfulness, or irritation (*dated informal*) [Mid-19C. < *shucks* "worthless things"]

shud·der /shúddər/ *vi* (**-dered, -der·ing, -ders**) **1.** SHIVER VIOLENTLY to shake or tremble uncontrollably from a reaction such as cold, fear, or disgust **2.** VIBRATE to vibrate rapidly and heavily ■ *n* **1.** VIOLENT SHAKING MOVEMENT an uncontrolled shaking or trembling movement **2.** VIBRATION a rapid heavy vibrating movement [12C. Probably < Middle Low German *schōderen* or Middle Dutch *shūderen* "keep on shuddering"] —**shud·der·y** *adj*

Shu·dra *n* HINDUISM same as **Sudra**

shuf·fle /shúff'l/ *v* (**-fled, -fling, -fles**) **1.** *vi* WALK WITHOUT LIFTING FEET to walk slowly without picking up the feet **2.** *vt* DRAG FEET to move the feet without picking them up **3.** *vi* MOVE AWKWARDLY to move in an awkward clumsy way **4.** *vi* DANCE BY SHUFFLING FEET to slide the feet in a dance step **5.** *vt* CHANGE WHERE SOMETHING IS LOCATED to move things around from one place to another **6.** *vt* MIX THINGS UP to mix things together carelessly **7.** *vti* REARRANGE ORDER OF PLAYING CARDS to rearrange playing cards randomly so that the order is not known **8.** *vi* BEHAVE EVASIVELY to be deliberately evasive or shifty in addressing an issue ■ *n* **1.** FOOT-DRAGGING WALK a slow walk while dragging the feet **2.** SLIDING DANCE STEP a dance or dance step in which the feet drag or slide on the floor **3.** JUMBLE OF THINGS a careless mixture of things **4.** REORDERING OF CARDS a random reordering of playing cards **5.** SOMEBODY'S CHANCE TO SHUFFLE SOMETHING a player's turn to shuffle playing cards **6.** EVASION a deliberate evasion of an issue [Mid-16C. Origin ?] —**shuf·fler** *n*

shuf·fle·board /shúff'l bàwrd/ *n* **1.** a game in which players use a long pronged cue to push disks along a smooth hard surface into numbered scoring areas **2.** the surface on which shuffleboard is played [Mid-19C. Alteration of *shovelboard*, alteration of obsolete *shove-board*, earlier name for the game]

shul /shool/, **schul** *n* JUDAISM same as **synagogue** (sense 1) [Late 19C. Via Yiddish < German *Schule* "school"]

Shull /shul/, **Clifford G.** (1915–2001) US physicist. He shared the Nobel Prize (1994) for his research on shattering neutrons and atomic structure.

shun /shun/ (**shunned, shun·ning, shuns**) *vt* to avoid somebody or something intentionally [Old English *scunian*. Origin ?] —**shun·ner** *n*

shun·pike /shún pīk/ *n US* a secondary road taken to avoid traffic or to avoid paying a toll on a main highway or turnpike

shunt /shunt/ *v* (**shunt·ed, shunt·ing, shunts**) **1.** *vt* MOVE SOMEBODY OR SOMETHING ELSEWHERE to move somebody or something to a different place, especially for convenience rather than fairness or kindness **2.** *vti*

CHANGE TRACKS to move rolling railroad cars from one track to another, either by using a locomotive or by means of an automatic switch, especially when assembling trains, or be moved in this way **3.** *vt* **GET RID OF RESPONSIBILITY** to avoid something by ignoring it or shifting responsibility for it to somebody else **4.** *vt* ELECTRONICS **DIVERT CURRENT** to use an electrical device to divert electrical current from an instrument **5.** *vt* **SURGICALLY DIVERT FLOW** to use an artificially created passage to redirect the circulation of blood or cerebrospinal fluid ■ *n* **1. DIVERSION OF SOMETHING** a turning aside, or a means of turning something aside **2. SORTING OF RAILROAD VEHICLES** the act of a locomotive pushing railroad vehicles in the process of sorting them **3.** ELECTRONICS **DEVICE FOR DIVERTING ELECTRIC CURRENT** a component in an electric circuit that is connected in parallel with an instrument and diverts the majority of current from the instrument **4. BYPASS FOR BODILY FLUID** a passage in the body that diverts the flow of blood or other bodily fluid from one channel to another, created either as a result of disease or injury or artificially by surgery. Artificial shunts are used to facilitate regular connection to a kidney dialysis machine or to relieve the pressure of cerebrospinal fluid on the brain in the condition of hydrocephalus. [13C. Origin ?]

shush /shŏŏsh, shush/ *interj* used to tell somebody to be quiet ■ *vti* (**shushed, shush·ing, shush·es**) to silence somebody, or become silent (*informal*) [Early 20C. Natural exclamation]

shu-shu /shŏŏ shŏŏ/ *n Carib* whispering or gossip [Origin ?]

Shus·wap /shŏŏss wòp/ (*plural same* or **-waps**) *n* **1.** a member of a Native North American people of southern British Columbia **2.** the Salishan language of the Shuswap people. Native speakers: 500. [Mid-19C. < Shuswap] —**Shus·wap** *adj*

shut /shut/ *v* (**shut, shut·ting, shuts**) **1.** *vti* **CLOSE OPENING** to move something into a position that blocks or covers an opening, or move into such a position ○ *leaned over to shut the window* **2.** *vt* **STOP ACCESS OR EXIT** to prevent entrance to or exit from something, e.g., by locking doors ○ *Rising water levels meant that they had to shut the tunnel.* **3.** *vt* **FOLD PARTS CLOSED** to close something by bringing its covering or parts together ○ *had to shut her eyes against the light* **4.** *vt* **LOCK SOMETHING** to secure something with a lock or latch ○ *The gate had not been shut properly.* **5.** *vti* **STOP OPERATION** to discontinue operation temporarily or permanently, or cause something to discontinue operation ○ *Another factory shut because it was losing money.* ■ *adj* **SECURED** closed or fastened against entrance or exit ■ *n* METALL **CONNECTION BETWEEN WELDED PIECES** the region of connection between pieces of metal that are welded together [Old English *scyttan* < Germanic]

shut down *v* **1.** *vti* **STOP OPERATION** to cease operation or activity, or cause something to cease operation or activity **2.** *vi* **SETTLE OVER PLACE** to settle over and blanket a place **3.** *vt* **CUT REACTOR OUTPUT** to reduce the power output of a nuclear reactor by maintaining it at its lowest possible level

shut in *vt* to confine or enclose somebody or something

shut off *v* **1.** *vti* **STOP SOMETHING FROM WORKING** to stop operating, or cause something to stop operating **2.** *vt* **CUT OFF FLOW** to stop the passage, flow, or supply of something **3.** *vt* **BLOCK SOMETHING OFF** to impede the flow or progress of something **4.** *vt* **ISOLATE SOMEBODY** to put somebody or something into a state of isolation

shut out *vt* **1. EXCLUDE SOMEBODY** to exclude somebody or something **2. STOP SOMEBODY FROM ENTERING** to prevent somebody or something from entering a place **3. HIDE SOMETHING** to hide something from sight **4. KEEP SOMEBODY FROM SCORING** to prevent an opponent from scoring in a game

shut up *v* **1.** *vi* **STOP TALKING** to be quiet or stop talking (*informal*) ○ *I shut up before saying something I would regret.* **2.** *vt* **SILENCE SOMEBODY** to cause somebody to be quiet or stop talking (*informal*) ○ *She shot me a look that shut me up instantly.* **3.** *vt* **CONFINE SOMEBODY** to confine or imprison somebody or something ○ *She shut the dog up in the pen.* **4.** *vt* **CLOSE SOMETHING** to close or prevent entrance to something ○ *The building is all shut up.*

shut·down /shút dòwn/ *n* **1.** the cessation or suspension of activities at a business, factory, or plant **2.** the reduction of power in a nuclear reactor by maintaining the core at the lowest level possible

shut·eye /shút ī/ *n* a short sleep (*informal*)

shut-in *n* somebody who is rarely or never able to leave home, especially because of illness or lack of physical mobility (*informal*)

shut·off /shút àwf, -òf/ *n* **1.** a device, usually a valve, that shuts something off **2.** an interruption or stoppage, e.g., in flow or supply

shut·out /shút òwt/ *n* **1.** a game in which one team does not score **2.** MANAGEMT same as **lockout**

shut·ter /shúttər/ *n* **1. DOOR OR WINDOW COVER** a hinged cover for a door or window, often with louvers and usually fitted in pairs **2. CAMERA DEVICE** a mechanical part of a camera that opens and closes the lens aperture to expose the film or plate to light ■ *vt* (**-tered, -ter·ing, -ters**) **1. CLOSE SOMETHING USING SHUTTERS** to close or protect something by means of shutters **2. FIT SOMETHING WITH SHUTTERS** to equip something with shutters

shut·ter·bug /shúttər bùg/ *n* an active and enthusiastic amateur photographer (*informal*)

shut·tle /shútt'l/ *n* **1. ROUTE TAKEN OR VEHICLE USED** the route taken or the aircraft, bus, or train used to travel frequently between two places, often relatively near each other **2.** AEROSP same as **space shuttle** **3. GOING BACK AND FORTH** frequent travel by vehicle between two places **4.** RACKET GAMES same as **shuttlecock** **5. WEAVING DEVICE** a device in weaving that holds the weft thread and is used to pass it between the warp threads **6. SPINDLE OR BOBBIN** a thread holder, e.g., in tatting or netting or for the lower thread in a sewing machine ■ *vti* (**-tled, -tling, -tles**) **1. GO BACK AND FORTH** to move between two places frequently, or cause somebody or something to move in this way **2. GO BY SHUTTLE** to transport somebody or something by a shuttle, or be transported by a shuttle [Old English *scytel* "arrow, dart" < Germanic, "shoot"]

shuttlecock

shut·tle·cock /shútt'l kòk/ *n* a small rounded piece of cork or rubber attached to a cone of feathers that is hit back and forth in badminton and in the old game of battledore ■ *vt* (**-cocked, -cock·ing, -cocks**) to toss or send something back and forth [Early 16C. *Shuttle* probably < its going back and forth, like the shuttle in a loom; *cock* < the feathers, like a bird's crest]

shut·tle·craft /shútt'l kràft/ (*plural same*) *n* a reusable spacecraft for carrying astronauts or material between Earth and space or between objects in space

shut·tle di·plo·ma·cy *n* diplomatic negotiations carried on between countries by a mediator who travels back and forth between the countries

shvart·se /shvaártsə/ *n US* an offensive term for somebody of African ancestry (*slang*) [Mid-20C. < Yiddish < German *schwarz* "black"]

shwa *n* PHON another spelling of **schwa**

Shwe /shə wáy/, **Than** (*b.* 1933) national leader of Myanmar (1992–). A senior general and specialist in psychological warfare, he became head of the State Law and Order Restoration Council (1992) and refuses to transfer power to the National League for Democracy, despite its election victory in 1990.

shy[1] /shī/ *adj* (**shi·er** or **shy·er, shi·est** or **shy·est**) **1. UNCOMFORTABLE WITH OTHERS** reserved, diffident, and uncomfortable in the company of others **2. TIMID** easily frightened ○ *The deer were shy and ran when we tried to approach them.* **3. CAUTIOUS** unwilling to trust or put confidence in somebody or something ○ *The children were shy of their new classmates.* **4. RELUCTANT** fearful of making a commitment ○ *Don't be shy of speaking your mind.* **5. SHORT OF SOMETHING** short of the full or a particular amount ○ *We are $100 shy of the down payment.* **6.** BIOL **NOT REPRODUCING EASILY** describes plants and animals that do not breed readily or freely ■ *vi* (**shied, shy·ing, shies**) **1. MOVE SUDDENLY** to move suddenly in fright or alarm ○ *The horse shied when the firecracker went off in the next field.* **2. STAY AWAY** to avoid or evade something ○ *He always shies away from public speaking.* ■ *n* (*plural* **shies**) **SUDDEN MOVE** a sudden movement in fright or alarm [Old English *sceōh* < Germanic] —**shy·er** *n* —**shy·ly** *adv* —**shy·ness** *n*

shy[2] /shī/ *vt* (**shied, shy·ing, shies**) to toss something quickly and suddenly ■ *n* (*plural* **shies**) a quick sudden throw of something [Late 18C. Origin ?] —**shy·er** *n*

shy·lock /shī lòk/ *n* a ruthless and demanding moneylender or creditor ■ *vi* (**-locked, -lock·ing, -locks**) to charge exorbitant interest on borrowed money [Late 18C. After *Shylock*, a moneylender in Shakespeare's play *The Merchant of Venice*]

shy·ster /shīstər/ *n* an unscrupulous person, especially a lawyer or political representative (*slang insult*) [Mid-19C. Origin ?]

si[1] /see/ *n* MUSIC same as **ti** [Early 18C. < the initial letters of Latin *Sancte Iohannes* "St. John," the words sung to this note in the hymn for St. John's day]

si[2] *abbr* ONLINE Slovenia (*used in Internet addresses*) See table at **domain name**

Si *symbol* CHEM ELEM silicon

SI *abbr* MEASURE International System of Units [< French *Système International (d'Unités)*]

si·al /sī àl/ *n* rocks rich in silicon and aluminum that form the crust of the continental masses (*dated*) [Early 20C. Blend of *silicon* + *aluminum*] —**si·al·ic** /sī állik/ *adj*

si·al·a·gogue /sī állə gòg/, **si·al·o·gogue** *n* a drug or agent that stimulates the flow of saliva [Late 18C. < Greek *sialon* "saliva"] —**si·al·a·gog·ic** /sī állə gójjik, -góggik/ *adj*

si·al·ic ac·id *n* an amino sugar found in animal tissues [< Greek *sialon* "saliva"]

Si·al·kot /see ál kòt/ city in Punjab Province, northeastern Pakistan, situated about 60 mi./97 km north of Lahore. Population: 302,009 (1981).

si·a·loid /sī ə lòyd/ *adj* resembling saliva [< Greek *sialon* "saliva"]

Si·am /sī ám/ former name for **Thailand** (until 1939)

Si·am, Gulf of former name for **Thailand, Gulf of**

si·a·mang /seé ə màng, -maàng/ *n* the largest species of gibbon, with a large throat sac that inflates during calls. Native to: Sumatra, Malaysia. Latin name: *Hylobates syndactylus.* [Early 19C. < Malay]

si·a·mese /sī ə meéz, -meéss/ *adj US* connecting two or more hoses or pipes into a Y-shaped adapter that permits a discharge in a single stream

Si·a·mese /sī ə meéz, -meéss/ *adj* **THAI** relating to Siam, now Thailand, or to its people or culture (*dated*) ■ *n* (*plural same*) **1.** BREED same as **Siamese cat** **2. SOMEBODY FROM THAILAND** somebody who comes from Thailand (*dated*) **3. THAI** the Thai language (*dated*)

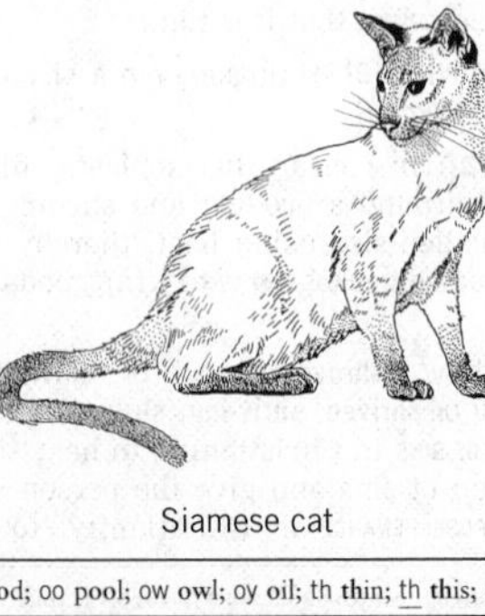

Siamese cat

Si·a·mese cat *n* a shorthaired domestic cat belonging to a breed that originated in Thailand (formerly Siam) with blue eyes and a long cream-colored body with dark ears, paws, face, and tail. See illustration on previous page

Si·a·mese fight·ing fish *n* a brightly colored long-finned freshwater fish often kept in aquariums, the male of which is very aggressive. Native to: Thailand, Malaysia. Latin name: *Betta splendens.*

Si·a·mese twins *npl* same as **conjoined twins** (*informal*) [After twins, Chang and Eng (1811–74), born in Siam (Thailand)]

sib /sib/ *n* **1. BROTHER OR SISTER** a brother or sister **2.** GENETICS **INDIVIDUAL WITH SAME PARENTS AS ANOTHER** an individual that has the same parents as another individual **3.** ANTHROP **GROUP WITH SINGLE COMMON ANCESTOR** a group of persons who trace their descent lineally from a single real or presumed ancestor ■ **sibs** *npl* **WIDER FAMILY** members of an extended family considered as a group ■ *adj* **CLOSELY RELATED** with the same parents or closely related [Old English *sib(b)*, origin ?]

Jean Sibelius

Si·be·li·us /sə báylee əss, -báylyəss/, **Jean** (1865–1957) Finnish composer. One of the leading symphonic composers of the 20th century, his works are much influenced by the culture and landscape of his native Finland. Born **Sibelius, Johan Julius Christian**

> "My heart sings, full of sadness—the shadows lengthen."
> [Jean Sibelius, *Diary entry*; October 1914]

Si·be·ri·a /sī beéree ə/ vast region of eastern Russia, extending from the Ural Mountains in the west to the Pacific Ocean in the east, and from the Arctic Ocean in the North to China, Mongolia, and Kazakhstan in the south. Much of it is frozen for over half the year. Sparsely populated, it was used during Soviet rule (1917–91) as a place of exile. —**Si·be·ri·an** *n, adj*

Si·be·ri·an hus·ky *n* a medium-sized dog with a thick soft coat, erect ears, and a bushy tail, belonging to a breed originally developed in Siberia for pulling sleds

sib·i·lant /síbbilənt/ *adj* **1. PRONOUNCED WITH HISSING SOUND** describes consonants that are pronounced with a hissing sound **2. PRODUCING HISSING SOUND** producing a hissing sound ○ *the sibilant sound of air escaping from a tire* ■ *n* **SIBILANT CONSONANT** a consonant that is pronounced with a hissing sound [Mid-17C. < Latin *sibilant-*, present participle of *sibilare* "hiss," probably an imitation of the sound] —**sib·i·lance** *n* —**sib·i·lant·ly** *adv*

sib·i·late /síbbə làyt/ (**-lat·ed, -lat·ing, -lates**) *vti* to pronounce sounds with a hiss [Mid-17C. < Latin *sibilat-*, past participle of *sibilare* (see SIBILANT)]

sib·ling /síbbling/ *n* **1.** a brother or sister (*often used before a noun*) **2.** a member of a group of persons who trace their descent from a single real or presumed ancestor [Old English < *sib(b)* (see SIB)]

sib·ling spe·cies *n* a species that closely resembles another in appearance and other characteristics but cannot interbreed with it

sib·yl /síbb'l/ *n* **1.** a woman of ancient Greece and Rome believed to be an oracle or a prophet **2.** a female prophet or fortune teller [13C. Via French and Latin < Greek *Sibulla*] —**si·byl·lic** /si bíllik/ *adj* —**syb·il·line** /síbbə lìn, -leèn/ *adj*

sic[1] /sik/ *adv* thus or so, used within brackets to indicate that what precedes it is written intentionally or is copied verbatim from the original, even if it appears to be a mistake [Late 19C. < Latin] ◇ **sic passim** /sìk pássim/ used to indicate that a word or term is used in the same form throughout a printed work ◇ **sic transit gloria mundi** "thus passes the glory of the world," used, e.g., when a distinguished person dies or an important era comes to an end

sic[2] /sik/ (**sicced, sic·cing, sics**), **sick** (**sicked, sick·ing, sicks**) *vt* **1.** to attack somebody physically, usually used as a command to a dog **2.** to urge a person or animal, especially a dog, to attack somebody physically [Mid-19C. Dialect variant of SEEK]

Si·ca ▶ **De Sica, Vittorio**

sic·ca·tive /síkətiv/ *n* a substance added to liquids to speed drying ■ *adj* absorbing moisture to promote drying [15C. < late Latin *siccativus* < past participle of Latin *siccare* "to dry" < *siccus* "dry"]

Si·chuan /si chwaán/, **Sze·chwan** /se-/ province in southern China bordered by Qinghai, Gansu, Shaanxi, Hubei, Hunan, Guizhou, Yunnan, and Tibet. Capital: Chengdu. Population: 114,300,000 (1997). Area: 220,000 sq. mi./569,000 sq. km.

Si·chuan pep·per /si chwaán-/ *n* a spice with a hot aniseed flavor, one of the ingredients of Chinese five-spice powder

si·cil·i·a·no /si sìllee aánō/ (*plural* **-nos**), **si·cil·i·a·na** /si sìllee aánə/ *n* **1.** an old Sicilian folk dance **2.** the music for a siciliano, in a minor key with six or twelve beats to the bar [Early 18C. < Italian, "Sicilian"]

Si·ci·ly /síss'lee/ largest island in the Mediterranean Sea, in southern Italy. Population: 5,082,697 (1995). Area: 9,927 sq. mi./25,710 sq. km. —**Si·cil·ian** /si síllee ən/ *n, adj*

sick[1] /sik/ *adj* **1. ILL** affected by an illness **2. RELATING TO ILLNESS** relating to illness or to people who are ill ○ *The company gives employees five sick days a year.* **3. LIKELY TO VOMIT** feeling on the point of vomiting **4. OFFENSIVE TERM** an offensive term for somebody thought to have a psychiatric disorder that makes him or her dangerous to others **5. DISTRESSED** spiritually or emotionally distraught ○ *sick with worry* **6. VERY BORED WITH SOMETHING** utterly tired of something because of having had too much of it ○ *I am sick of watching television.* **7. YEARNING** feeling a deep or passionate longing for something or somebody ○ *sick for my family* **8. DISGUSTED** filled with disgust or repulsion ○ *Such rudeness makes me sick.* **9. IMPAIRED** in need of repair or improvement ○ *a sick economy* **10. SUGGESTING ILLNESS** pale and unhealthy-looking **11. IN BAD TASTE** dealing with subjects regarded by most people as bizarre, gruesome, or otherwise unsuitable for lighthearted treatment (*informal*) **12.** AGRIC **UNPRODUCTIVE** unable to produce a profitable crop ○ *a sick field* **13.** MED **FORMING UNHEALTHFUL ENVIRONMENT** describes a building or other location that is seen as an unhealthful environment for people **14.** EXTREME SPORTS **EXCELLENT** in snowboarding, so brilliantly performed as to cause envy (*slang*) ○ *sick tricks* ■ *npl* **ILL PEOPLE** people who are ill [Old English *sēoc*, origin ?]

sick[2] /sik/ *vt* another spelling of **sic**[2]

sick·bay /sík bày/ *n* **1.** a place for treating the sick or injured **2.** a hospital and dispensary on a ship

sick·bed /sík bèd/ *n* a bed on which a sick person lies

sick build·ing syn·drome *n* a group of symptoms typically including headaches, skin rashes, and respiratory problems that affect workers in office buildings and are attributed to toxic building materials or poor ventilation

sick call *n* a daily lineup or formation for military personnel in need of medical attention, or the scheduled time at which they may receive medical attention

sick·en /síkən/ (**-ened, -en·ing, -ens**) *vti* **1. MAKE OR BECOME NAUSEATED** to become ill or nauseated, or make somebody feel ill or nauseated ○ *I sicken at the sight of blood.* **2. MAKE OR FEEL DISGUSTED** to feel disgust for something or somebody, or inspire disgust in somebody **3. MAKE OR BECOME BORED** to grow weary of somebody or something, or make somebody weary ○ *We soon sickened of their chatter.*

sick·en·er /síkənər/ *n* a widely distributed poisonous mushroom with a fragile red cap. Latin name: *Russula emetica* or *Russula fragilis.*

sick·en·ing /síkəning/ *adj* **1.** inspiring feelings of disgust or repulsion ○ *sickening cruelty* **2.** bringing on illness ○ *sickening toxic fumes* —**sick·en·ing·ly** *adv*

sick head·ache *n* a headache accompanied by feelings of nausea

sick·ie /síkee/ *n* same as **sicko** (*slang offensive*) ◇ **throw a sickie** *UK* to take a day of sick leave for reasons other than genuine illness (*informal*)

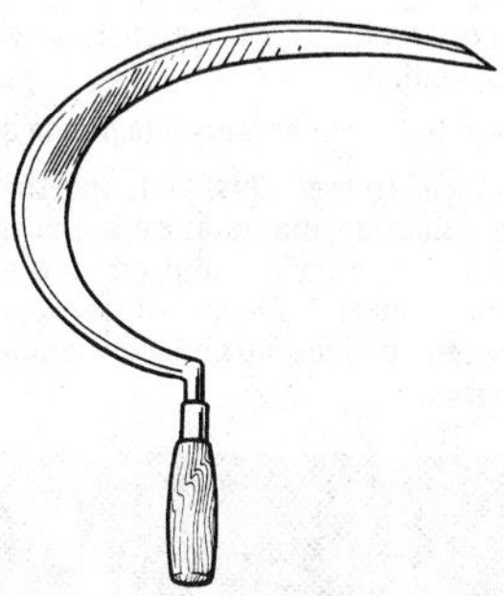
sickle

sick·le /sík'l/ *n* **1. TOOL FOR CUTTING GRASS** a short-handled implement with a curved blade used for cutting tall grass or grain **2. BLADES OF FARM IMPLEMENT** the cutting mechanism of a combine harvester, reaper, or mower ■ *v* (**-led, -ling, -les**) **1.** *vt* **CUT SOMETHING WITH SICKLE** to cut something using a sickle **2.** *vti* BIOL **DEFORM RED BLOOD CELL** to change a red blood cell into a sickle cell, or become a sickle cell ■ *adj* **CURVED** curved in shape like a sickle (*literary*) ○ *by the light of a sickle moon* [Old English *sicol*, via Germanic < Latin *secula* < *secare* "to cut"]

sick leave *n* absence from work for reasons of illness

sick·le·bill /sík'l bìl/ *n* a bird of paradise, the male of which has glossy black feathers, a long down-curved beak, and a long tail. Native to: New Guinea. Genus: *Epimachus.*

sick·le cell *n* a red blood cell that is crescent-shaped as a result of an inherited mutation in the cell's hemoglobin

sick·le-cell a·ne·mi·a *n* a chronic hereditary form of anemia that occurs mainly in people of African descent. It is caused by a gene inherited from both parents.

sick·le cell trait *n* a hereditary condition of the blood in which some red cells become sickle-shaped, but there are not enough affected cells to cause anemia. This trait, which usually gives some resistance to malaria, occurs when the responsible gene is inherited from only one parent.

sick·le feath·er *n* either of two long curving feathers in the tail of a rooster

sick·le med·ic, sick·le med·ick *n* a small plant with three-lobed leaves, yellow flowers, and curved pods. Native to: Europe, Asia. Latin name: *Medicago falcata.*

sick·le·mi·a /sìkə leémee ə/ *n US* MED same as **sickle cell trait**

sick list *n* a list of people who are sick, especially in the military

sick·ly /síklee/ *adj* (**-li·er, -li·est**) **1. OFTEN ILL** unhealthy, or tending to be frequently ill ○ *a sickly child* **2. STEMMING FROM ILLNESS** produced by or related to illness ○ *a sickly complexion* **3. BRINGING ILLNESS** causing or conducive to illness ○ *a sickly climate* **4. CAUSING DISGUST** provoking feelings of disgust or nausea ○ *a sickly smell* **5. FEEBLE** lacking in strength or intensity ○ *a sickly winter sun* **6. OVERLY SENTIMENTAL** sentimental to a degree that inspires disgust or scorn ○ *a sickly display of affection* ■ *adv* **FEEBLY** in a weak or feeble way —**sick·li·ness** *n*

sick·ly-sweet *adj* excessively sweet or sentimental ○ *a sickly-sweet smile*

sick·ness /síknəss/ *n* **1. ILLNESS** an illness or a disease **2. NAUSEA** feelings of nausea **3. IMPAIRED CONDITION** an unsound or corrupt condition

sick note *n UK* HR same as **excuse** *n* (sense 4)

sick·o /síkō/ (*plural* **-os**), **sick·ie** /síkee/ *n* an offensive term for somebody thought to have a psychiatric disorder that makes him or her dangerous to others (*slang*)

sick-out *n US, Carib* an organized absence from work by employees on the pretext of illness in an effort to force an employer to grant demands

sick pa·rade *n UK* MIL same as **sick call**

sick pay *n* wages paid to an employee who is absent from work due to illness

sick·room /sík ro͝om, -ro͞om/ *n* a room to which an ill person is confined

SID *abbr* MED full form **sensory integration dysfunction**

sid·dhi /síddee/ (*plural* **-dhis**) *n* **1.** in Hinduism, the complete spiritual understanding and insight that is the goal of meditation and other practices **2.** a paranormal power believed to be acquired by a Hindu ascetic who has attained enlightenment [Late 19C. < Sanskrit]

Sarah Siddons

Sid·dons /sídd'nz/, **Sarah** (1755–1831) British actor. An acclaimed tragic stage actor, she was noted particularly for her role as Lady Macbeth. Born **Kemble, Sarah**

sid·dur /sí do͝or, síddər/ (*plural* **-du·rim** /si do͝orim/ or **-durs**) *n* a Jewish daily and Sabbath prayer book [Mid-19C. < Hebrew *siddūr* "arrangement, order"]

side /sīd/ *n* **1. PERIMETER OF FIGURE** a line segment that forms part of the perimeter of a plane geometric figure ○ *A square has four sides.* **2. SURFACE OF FIGURE** a surface of a solid geometric figure ○ *A cube has six sides.* **3. SURFACE OF SOMETHING FLAT** either of the two surfaces of a flat object **4. LEFT OR RIGHT OF SOMETHING** the left or right of an object as opposed to the top, bottom, front, or back **5. EITHER DIVISION** either of two parts or areas into which something can be divided relative to the observer ○ *The playing field is on the far side of the park.* **6. PLACE RELATIVE TO CENTER** a location, place, or direction relative to a central point ○ *We live on the east side of the city.* **7. PLACE SEPARATED BY BARRIER** either of the areas separated by a barrier or boundary ○ *We live on the east side of the river.* **8. VERTICAL SURFACE** a vertical surface of something ○ *the side of a building* **9. EDGE OF SOMETHING** the area at the edge of something ○ *the side of the road* **10. HALF OF BODY** either half of the body of an animal or person, especially the area of a person's body between the shoulder and the hip ○ *My side aches.* **11. HALF OF CARCASS** half of a meat carcass ○ *a side of pork* **12. NEARBY POSITION** the place next to somebody or something ○ *Come stand at my side.* **13. PARTY IN CONTEST** any one of two or more opposing persons, teams, groups, or factions **14. OPINION IN DISPUTE** any one of the positions or opinions held in a dispute **15. SUPPORTERS** the group of people who support a particular party in a dispute ○ *I'm on your side.* **16. ASPECT** an aspect or view of an issue or event ○ *the funny side of a situation* **17. PART OF FAMILY** a line of descent ○ *He gets his red hair from his father's side.* **18.** FOOD same as **side dish** **19.** *UK* **ARROGANCE** an air of pretentiousness, arrogance, or superiority (*informal*) ○ *You wouldn't think he was a high court judge – there's no side to him.* **20.** *UK* CUE GAMES same as **English** *n* (sense 5) ■ *adj* **1. AT SIDE** situated at or on a side ○ *The side door is open.* **2. FROM SIDE** directed to or from the side ○ *a side blow* ○ *a side view* ■ *v* (**sid·ed, sid·ing, sides**) **1.** *vi* **ALIGN WITH OR AGAINST SOMEBODY** to align with or against one or other of the persons, teams, groups, or factions in a contest or dispute ○ *We all sided with the home team.* **2.** *vt* **FIT BUILDING WITH OUTER WALLS** to fit a building with boards (**siding**) that form an outer skin ○ *side the barn* [Old English *sīde* < Germanic] ◇ **be on the safe side** to take as few risks, or eliminate as many risks, as possible ◇ **be on the wrong side of a particular age** to be older than a particular age (*informal*) ◇ **get** *or* **keep on the right side of somebody** to get into or remain in somebody's favor ◇ **get on the wrong side of somebody** to make yourself disliked by somebody ◇ **look on the bright side** to make a deliberate attempt to see the positive aspects of a situation instead of the negative ones ◇ **on the side 1.** illegally or secretly **2.** in addition to a main job or activity **3.** FOOD as an additional separate dish ◇ **side by side** close beside each other ◇ **take sides** to support one person or group against another ◇ **the other side of the coin** the contrasting or contrary aspect of something ◇ **the wrong side of the tracks** the less affluent and socially advantaged part of a town or area (*informal*) ◇ **this side of** almost at or just short of ○ *The negotiations stalled just this side of an agreement.* ◇ **to one side** out of the focus of attention for the moment, to be dealt with later

side arm *n* a weapon that is worn at the waist, usually on a belt, e.g., a pistol

side·arm /sīd aarm/ *adj US* in baseball, used to describe a throw made by sweeping the arm out to the side while keeping it below shoulder height ○ *a sidearm pitch* —**side·arm** *adv*

side·band /sīd bànd/ *n* in telecommunications, the band of frequencies on either side of the carrier frequency, produced by modulation of a carrier wave

side·bar /sīd baar/ *n* **1.** a short news story containing supplementary information that is printed alongside a featured story **2.** *US* a conversation between a judge and lawyers at a trial that those on the jury cannot hear

side·board /sīd bawrd/ *n* a piece of dining room furniture with a flat top, drawers, and cupboards to store tableware and linens

side·burns /sīd burnz/ *npl* hair grown down the side of a man's face in front of his ears [Late 19C. Alteration of *burnsides*, after Ambrose E. *Burnside* (1824–81), US general]

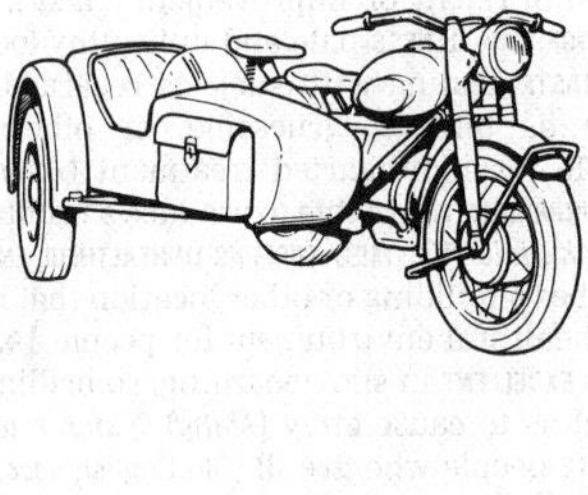
sidecar

side·car /sīd kaar/ *n* **1.** a one-wheeled passenger vehicle attached to the side of a motorcycle **2.** a cocktail of brandy, orange liqueur, and lemon juice

side chain *n* a group of atoms attached to an atom in a principal chain or ring

side chair *n* a straight-backed chair with no arms, especially at a dining table

side deal *n* a mutually beneficial agreement made between two people aside from an agreement negotiated by them on behalf of the parties or organizations they represent

side dish *n* accompanying food served with the main dish of a meal, e.g., vegetables or salad

side-dress *vt* to fertilize plants by applying nutrients to the soil near the roots

side-dress·ing *n* **1.** fertilizer that is put into the soil near the roots of a growing crop **2.** the adding of fertilizer near the roots of growing crops

side drum *n* MUSIC same as **snare drum**

side ef·fect *n* **1.** an undesirable secondary effect of a drug or other form of medical treatment **2.** a usually undesirable secondary effect produced by something

side-glance *n* **1.** a glance directed sideways **2.** a casual or indirect reference or allusion

side-im·pact *adj* describes features of vehicles that are designed to protect the occupants from an impact from the side

side is·sue *n* an incidental minor matter that tends to distract attention from the important issue

side·kick /sīd kìk/ *n* an associate or companion who is sometimes considered subordinate (*informal*) [Early 20C. < obsolete *side-kicker*, in same sense]

side·light /sīd līt/ *n* **1. INCIDENTAL INFORMATION** incidental information, usually additional to what is known already **2. LIGHT FROM SIDE** light coming from the side **3.** *UK* AUTOMOT same as **parking light** **4.** ARCHIT **SIDE WINDOW** a window at the side of a door **5.** NAUT **SHIP'S LIGHT** either of a ship's two navigational running lights, red on the left and green on the right

side·line /sīd līn/ *n* **1. SIDE BOUNDARY OF SPORTS FIELD** either of two lines marking the side limits of a playing field **2. SUPPLEMENTARY SOURCE OF INCOME** a job or activity that supplements income from a primary job ○ *He does television repairs as a sideline.* **3.** COMM **ADDITIONAL RANGE OF MERCHANDISE** a supplementary line of merchandise ■ **side·lines** *npl* **1. AREA OF SPORTS FIELD** the area of a playing field outside the lines marking its limits **2. PLACE FOR UNINVOLVED PEOPLE** a place for people who are not involved in something, or the condition of being uninvolved (*informal*) ○ *You can always get opinions on any subject from the sidelines.* ■ *vt* (**-lined, -lin·ing, -lines**) **1.** *US* **KEEP PLAYER OUT OF GAME** to remove or keep a player from a game ○ *sideline a player for injuries* **2. EXCLUDE SOMEBODY** to keep somebody from participating in an activity

side·long /sīd làwng, -lòng/ *adj* **1. TO SIDE** directed to the side **2. SLOPING** slanting to one side **3. INDIRECT** not direct or straightforward ○ *a sidelong remark* ■ *adv* **OBLIQUELY** toward an area that lies at the side

side·man /sīd màn/ (*plural* **-men** /-mèn/) *n* a member of a jazz or dance band who is neither the leader nor a soloist

side meat *n US regional, Can* salt pork or bacon

REGIONAL NOTE See ***fatback***.

side mir·ror *n* a mirror attached to the side of the windshield or the outside of a front door of a vehicle, allowing the driver to see behind the vehicle

side or·der *n* a portion of food ordered as an accompaniment to the main dish in a restaurant or other food outlet

side·piece /sīd peess/ *n* a part attached to or forming the side of something

sider- *prefix* same as **sidero-** (*used before vowels*)

side re·ac·tion *n* a chemical reaction that occurs as a secondary or subsequent reaction to the primary one

si·de·re·al /sī deeree əl/ *adj* relating to the stars, especially measured with reference to the apparent motion of the stars [Mid-17C. < Latin *sidereus* < *sidus* "star"]

si·de·re·al day *n* the time it takes for Earth to make one complete revolution in relation to a specific star, equal to 23 hours, 56 minutes, 4.1 seconds

si·de·re·al hour *n* a 24th part of a sidereal day

si·de·re·al month *n* the time it takes for the Moon to make one revolution around the Earth in relation to a given star, equal to 27 days, 7 hours, 43 minutes, 4.5 seconds

si·de·re·al time *n* time measured by the daily rotation of the Earth in relation to a given star, rather than to the Sun

si·de·re·al year *n* the time it takes the Sun to make one revolution with reference to a given star, equal to 365 days, 6 hours, 9 minutes, 9.5 seconds

sid·er·ite /síddə rīt/ *n* **1.** a yellow-brown mineral consisting of iron carbonate. Source: sedimentary rocks. Use: source of iron. **2.** a dense metallic meteorite, chiefly iron alloyed with nickel [Late 18C. < Greek *sidēros* "iron"] —**sid·er·it·ic** /síddə ríttik/ *adj*

sidero- *prefix* iron ○ *siderolite* [< Greek *sidēros* "iron"]

side·road /sīd rōd/ *n* **1.** a secondary road off the main road **2.** *Can* a road along the side boundary of a concession road

sid·er·o·lite /síddərə līt/ *n* a meteorite that is made up of approximately equal amounts of iron and stone

sid·e·roph·i·lin /sìddə róffəlin/ *n* BIOCHEM same as **transferrin**

sid·er·o·sis /sìddə róssiss/ *n* **1.** a chronic lung disease caused by inhaling dust particles of iron or other metals. It is a form of pneumoconiosis. **2.** an accumulation of iron in the blood and tissues —**sid·er·ot·ic** /-róttik/ *adj*

sid·er·o·stat /síddərə stàt/ *n* an astronomical instrument consisting of a plane mirror driven by a clock mechanism that keeps an astronomical object within the same field of view of a telescope [Mid-19C. < Latin *sider-* "star"] —**sid·er·o·stat·ic** /sìddərə státtik/ *adj*

side·sad·dle /sīd sàdd'l/ *n* a saddle designed for women wearing long skirts so that the rider sits with both legs on the same side of the horse ■ *adv* seated with both legs on the same side of a horse

side scroll·er *n* a computer game in which the screen scrolls from side to side as you move along to show changes of scene and there is little or no vertical movement involved

side·show /sīd shō/ *n* **1.** SMALLER SHOW a minor attraction offered in addition to the main entertainment at a circus or fair **2.** SOMETHING OUTRAGEOUS an action or behavior that is outrageous or bizarre (*informal*) ○ *that sideshow that they call a professional relationship* **3.** MINOR EVENT a subordinate event or spectacle

side·slip /sīd slìp/ *vi* (**-slipped, -slip·ping, -slips**) **1.** SLIDE SIDEWAYS to skid or slide sideways **2.** AVIAT SLIP SIDEWAYS IN AIRPLANE to move sideways and downward while banking steeply in an airplane **3.** SKIING SLIDE SIDEWAYS DOWN SLOPE in skiing, to slide at an angle down a slope ■ *n* **1.** SIDEWAYS SKID a skid to the side ○ *The car went into a sideslip.* **2.** AVIAT SIDEWAYS MOVEMENT OF AIRPLANE a sideways and downward movement made by a steeply banking aircraft **3.** SKIING ANGLED SLIDE DOWN SLOPE in skiing, a sideways slide at an angle down a slope

side·split·ting /sīd splìtting/ *adj* extremely funny —**side·split·ting·ly** *adv*

side·step /sīd stèp/ *vti* (**-stepped, -step·ping, -steps**) **1.** STEP ASIDE to step aside or out of the way of somebody or something ○ *I sidestepped to avoid the running children.* **2.** EVADE SOMETHING to avoid saying or discussing something ○ *sidestep the question* ■ *n* SIDEWAYS MOVEMENT a movement to one side —**side·step·per** *n*

side-strad·dle hop *n US* LEISURE, SPORTS same as **jumping jack**

side·stream smoke /sīd streem-/ *n US* smoke from a cigarette or cigar that the smoker does not inhale

side street *n* a secondary street, often off a main street

side·stroke /sīd strōk/ *n* a swimming stroke performed on the side by thrusting the arms alternately forward and downward while doing a scissors kick

side·swipe /sīd swīp/ *n* **1.** GLANCING BLOW a glancing blow from or on the side **2.** GIBE a critical or insulting remark made in passing (*informal*) ○ *They were all taking sideswipes at my golfing skills.* ■ *vt* (**-swiped, -swip·ing, -swipes**) STRIKE SIDE OF SOMETHING to strike a glancing blow to or from the side of something ○ *sideswiped a car in the parking lot* —**side·swip·er** *n*

side·track /sīd tràk/ *v* (**-tracked, -track·ing, -tracks**) **1.** *vt* DISTRACT SOMEBODY to divert somebody from the original subject or activity ○ *The interruption sidetracked the discussion.* **2.** *vti* DIVERT TRAIN to divert a train to a railroad siding, or run into a siding ■ *n* **1.** CAUSE OF DIVERSION something that causes a diversion from the original subject or activity **2.** RAIL SIDING OF RAILROAD a railroad siding

side·walk /sīd wàwk/ *n* a paved path for pedestrians alongside a street

side·walk su·per·in·ten·dent *n US* somebody, often a passing pedestrian, who watches or gives unsolicited advice to workers on a construction site

side·wall /sīd wàwl/ *n* the side surface of a vehicle's tire, between the edge of the tread and the rim

side·ward /sīdwərd/ *adj* toward one side or at one side ■ *adv also* **side·wards** /-wərdz/ toward one side

side·ways /sīd wàyz/, **side·wise** /-wīz/ *adj, adv* **1.** TO SIDE to or toward one side ○ *a sideways jump* **2.** FROM SIDE from one side ○ *a sideways approach* **3.** WITH SIDE FACING FRONT with or into a position with the side toward the front ○ *See if it will fit in sideways.* **4.** INTO NEW BUT EQUAL POSITION into a job or position with the same rank or status as previously held ○ *not a promotion but more of a sideways move into another department*

side·wheel /sīd weel, -hweel/ *n* either of the paddle wheels on the sides of a sidewheeler ■ *adj* propelled by a paddle wheel on each side ○ *a sidewheel steamboat*

side·wheel·er /sīd weelər, -hweelər/ *n* a steamboat propelled by a paddle wheel on each side

side whis·kers *npl* sideburns, especially long ones

side·wind·er /sīd wīndər/ *n* **1.** RATTLESNAKE a small rattlesnake that moves forward with a diagonal looping motion. Native to: southwestern United States, northern Mexico. Latin name: *Crotalus cerastes.* **2.** SOMEBODY SNEAKY a sneaky or treacherous person (*slang*) **3.** *US* HARD PUNCH a hard swinging punch from the side

side·wise /sīd wīz/ *adj, adv* same as **sideways**

Si·di-bel-Ab·bès /seedee bel ə béss/ capital of Sidi-bel-Abbès Province, northwestern Algeria, situated 50 mi./80 km south of Oran. Population: 152,778 (1987).

sid·ing /sīding/ *n* **1.** sheets of wood, vinyl, aluminum, or other material used to surface the outside of a building **2.** a short stretch of railroad track that connects with the main track

si·dle /sīd'l/ *v* (**-dled, -dling, -dles**) **1.** *vi* MOVE FURTIVELY to edge along in a furtive way ○ *I sidled to the door in the hope that no one would notice me.* **2.** *vti* MOVE SIDEWAYS to move sideways, or move something sideways ■ *n* SIDLING MOVEMENT a sideways or furtive movement [Late 17C. Probably back-formation < archaic *sideling* "sideways"]

Sid·ney /sídnee/, **Sir Philip** (1554–86) English soldier, courtier, and poet. He was a favorite of Elizabeth I and an accomplished diplomat and soldier. His *Arcadia*, posthumously published in 1590, became the model for later English pastoral poetry.

Si·don /sīd'n/, **Say·da** /sáydə/ town and seaport in southwestern Lebanon, on the Mediterranean Sea south of Beirut. It was a Phoenician city-state in the 3rd millennium B.C. Population: 38,000 (1998).

Sid·ra, Gulf of /síddrə/ arm of the Mediterranean Sea that forms a bay on the coast of Libya, northern Africa

SIDS /sidz/ *abbr* MED sudden infant death syndrome

siege /seej/ *n* **1.** MILITARY OPERATION a military or police operation in which troops or the police surround a place and cut off all outside access to force surrender (*often used before a noun*) ○ *siege warfare* **2.** PROLONGED EFFORT a prolonged effort to gain or overcome something **3.** TIRESOME PERIOD a prolonged and tedious period ■ *vt* (**sieged, sieg·ing, sieg·es**) MIL SUBJECT PLACE TO SIEGE to assail or besiege an enemy's fortifications ○ *a town sieged with troops* [12C. < Old French *sege* "seat" < Latin *sedere* "sit"] ◇ **lay siege to something 1.** to besiege a place **2.** to make a persistent attempt to gain something

Siege Per·il·ous *n* the seat at King Arthur's Round Table that was fatal to all except Sir Galahad, the knight who was to find the Holy Grail

Sieg·fried /seeg freed, síg-/ *n* in medieval Germanic mythology, a prince who kills the dragon guarding the treasure of the Nibelungs, and wins Brunhild for Gunther

Sieg·fried line *n* the line of fortifications constructed by Germany before and during World War II on its western frontier, facing the Maginot line in France

Sieg Heil /seeg hīl/ *interj* a Nazi salute usually accompanied by the right arm raised with the palm facing downward [Mid-20C. < German, "hail victory!"]

sie·mens /seemənz/ (*plural same*) *n* the SI unit of electrical conductance equal to one ampere per volt. Symbol **S** [Mid-20C. After Werner von *Siemens* (1816–92), German inventor]

Si·en·a /see énnə/ capital of Siena Province, Tuscany Region, in north central Italy. Population: 52,625 (2001). —**Si·e·nese** /seè ə neez/ *n, adj*

~~**sience**~~ incorrect spelling of **science**

~~**siene**~~ incorrect spelling of **scene**

si·en·na /see énnə/ *n* **1.** artists' paint made with iron-rich soil **2.** an iron-rich soil. Use: paint pigment. [Late 18C. After SIENA] —**si·en·na** *adj*

si·er·ra /see érrə/ *n* **1.** a range of mountains with jagged peaks, or the country surrounding such a range **2.** *US* a large Spanish mackerel valued as a game fish and for food. Genus: *Scomberomorus.* [Mid-16C. Via Spanish < Latin *serra* "saw"] —**si·er·ran** *adj*

Si·er·ra *n* a code word for the letter "S," used in international radio communications

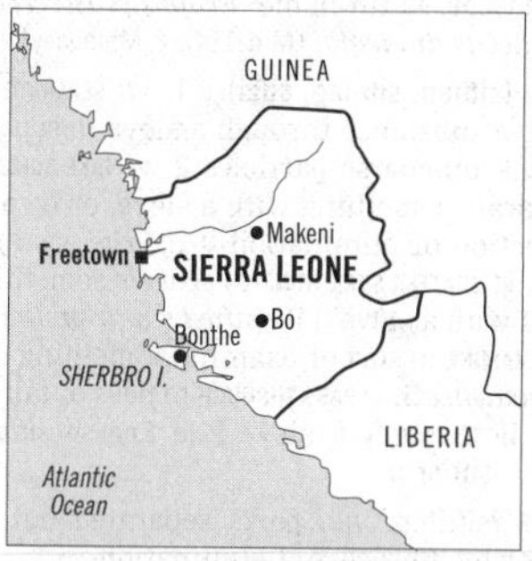

Sierra Leone

Si·er·ra Le·one /see èrrə lee ōn/ country in West Africa, bordered by Guinea, Liberia, and the Atlantic Ocean. It became an independent member of the British Commonwealth in 1961. Language: English. Currency: leone. Capital: Freetown. Population: 5,732,681 (2003). Area: 27,699 sq. mi./71,740 sq. km. Official name **Republic of Sierra Leone** —**Si·er·ra Le·on·e·an** *n, adj*

Si·er·ra Ma·dre /-maá dray/ mountain system in Mexico that stretches southeastward from the US border in the north to the border with Guatemala in the south. Its highest peak is Orizaba, 18,406 ft./5,610 m. Length: 680 mi./1,100 km.

Si·er·ra Ne·va·da /-nə vaádə/ **1.** mountain range in eastern California, extending from the Mojave Desert to the Coast Range. Its highest peak is Mount Whitney, 14,491 ft./4,417 m. Length: 400 mi./600 km. **2.** mountain range in southeastern Spain. Its highest peak is Cerro de Mulhacén, 11,411 ft./3,480 m.

Si·er·ra Vis·ta /see èrrə veestə/ town in southeastern Arizona, north of the Mexican border and southeast of Tucson. Population: 38,999 (2002 estimate).

si·es·ta /see éstə/ *n* an early afternoon rest or nap [Mid-17C. Via Spanish < Latin *sexta (hora)* "sixth (hour of the day), noon"]

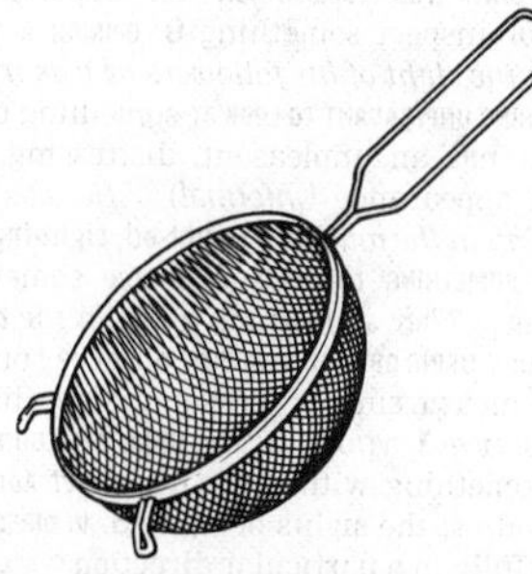

sieve

sieve /siv/ *n* a utensil consisting of a round frame surrounding a mesh and used to separate solids from liquids or large particles from small particles, or to purée foods ■ *vt* (**sieved, siev·ing, sieves**) to pass something through a sieve [Old English *sife* < Germanic]

sieve el·e·ment *n* BOT same as **sieve tube element**

sieve plate *n* an area of perforations in the end walls of the cells that make up a sieve tube in plants

siev·ert /séevərt/ *n* the SI unit measuring the probability that a specific dose of a particular radiation type will cause a biological effect. 1 sievert is equal to 1 joule per kilogram. Symbol **Sv** [Mid-20C. After R. M. *Sievert* (1896–1966), Swedish radiologist]

sieve tube *n* a sap-conducting tube within the phloem tissue of a plant. It is composed of numerous cells (**sieve tube elements**) connected end to end and separated by porous sieve plates.

sieve tube el·e·ment *n* any one of the numerous cells connected end to end and separated by porous sieve plates in a sieve tube

~~sieze~~ incorrect spelling of **seize**

si·fa·ka /si fáakə/ *n* a large rare tree-dwelling lemur that has a black face and long soft fur variously patterned in white, black, or brown. Native to: Madagascar. Latin name: *Propithecus verreauxi* or *Propithecus diadema*. [Mid-19C. < Malagasy]

sift /sift/ (**sift·ed, sift·ing, sifts**) *v* **1.** *vti* SEPARATE PARTICLES to pass a substance through a sieve to separate out or break up coarse particles **2.** *vt* TAKE SOMETHING OUT to separate something with a sieve, or by a process of selection or elimination ○ *sift the good from the bad* **3.** *vt* SCATTER SOMETHING to scatter something with or as if with a sieve ○ *We sifted sugar on the candies.* **4.** *vti* EXAMINE to sort or examine something carefully ○ *sift evidence* **5.** *vi* PASS THROUGH to pass or fall through or as if through a sieve [Old English *siftan* < Germanic] —**sift·er** *n*

sift·ings /síftingz/ *npl* parts separated out using a sieve or by a process of elimination

SIG *abbr* special-interest group

sig. *abbr* **1.** signal **2.** signature **3.** signor **4.** signore

Sig. *abbr* Signor

sig file *n* ONLINE same as **signature file** (*informal*)

sigh /sī/ *v* (**sighed, sigh·ing, sighs**) **1.** *vi* BREATHE LONG AND LOUD to take in and let out a deep audible breath in relief or weariness **2.** *vi* MAKE EXHALING SOUND to make a sound like the exhalation of a deep breath ○ *The wind sighed in the trees.* **3.** *vi* YEARN to long for somebody or something ○ *sigh for simpler times* **4.** *vt* EXPRESS FEELING IN SIGHS to express an emotion by sighs ○ *She sighed her relief when she found us.* ■ *n* **1.** EXHALATION an audible exhalation of a deep breath **2.** SOUND OF EXHALING a sound like that of somebody exhaling a deep breath [13C. Probably back-formation < past tense of Old English *sīcan*, origin ?]

sight /sīt/ *n* **1.** FACULTY OF SEEING the ability to see using the eyes **2.** ACT OF SEEING the perception of something using the visual sense **3.** RANGE OF SEEING the range or field of vision ○ *By now the coastline was out of sight.* **4.** SOMETHING SEEN something that somebody sees **5.** SOMETHING WORTH SEEING something that is worth seeing, especially the landmarks of a place (*often used in the plural*) ○ *the sights of the city* **6.** ALIGNMENT DEVICE an alignment device on a gun or surveying instrument used to guide the eye in aiming or determining direction **7.** AIM a determination of direction made with a gun or surveying instrument **8.** OPPORTUNITY FOR OBSERVATION an opportunity to observe or inspect something **9.** OPINION a point of view ○ *In the sight of his followers he was infallible.* **10.** SOMETHING UNPLEASANT TO LOOK AT something or somebody that has an unpleasant, distressing, or disarranged appearance (*informal*) ○ *He was a sight after falling in the mud.* ■ *v* (**sight·ed, sight·ing, sights**) **1.** *vt* SEE SOMETHING to see or notice somebody or something ○ *They sighted the plane in the distance.* **2.** *vti* OBSERVE USING OPTICAL DEVICE to observe something, or take measurements of something, using an optical device **3.** *vti* AIM AT SOMETHING WITH GUN to take aim at something with a firearm **4.** *vt* ADJUST GUN'S SIGHTS to adjust the sights of a gun **5.** *vi* DIRECT EYES to look carefully in a particular direction ○ *sight down a line* [Old English *(ge)siht* < W Germanic] —**sight·ed** *adj* ◇ **a sight** a great deal or quantity (*informal*) ○ *He's feeling a far sight better today.* ◇ **a sight for sore eyes** a very welcome sight ◇ **at** *or* **on sight** as soon as something or somebody is able to be seen ◇ **in sight 1.** able to be seen **2.** likely to happen in the near future ◇ **know somebody by sight** to be able to recognize somebody whom you have never actually met or spoken to ◇ **out of sight 1.** no longer able to be seen **2.** used as an exclamation to express approval and surprise (*slang*) ◇ **out of sight, out of mind** it is easy to forget or ignore somebody or something not present or visible ◇ **set** *or* **have your sights on something** to decide to try to get something ◇ **sight unseen** without seeing or inspecting first ○ *buy something sight unseen*

SPELLCHECK See ***cite***.

sight draft *n US* a written order for the payment of money that is payable upon presentation

sight gag *n* a joke or comic episode whose humor depends on its being seen (*informal*)

sight·ing /síting/ *n* an occasion on which something is seen, usually something unusual or searched for ○ *alleged sightings of the long-dead superstar*

sight·less /sítləss/ *adj* **1.** without the faculty of sight **2.** invisible (*literary*) ○*"heaven's cherubim, hors'd upon the sightless couriers of the air"* (William Shakespeare, *Macbeth*; 1623) —**sight·less·ly** *adv* —**sight·less·ness** *n*

sight·line /sít līn/ *n* a line of vision between a person and an object, especially between a member of an audience and the stage in a theater

sight·ly /sítlee/ (**-li·er, -li·est**) *adj* **1.** pleasing to look at **2.** *US* affording a fine view

sight-read /sít reed/ *vti* to read or perform something such as music or a foreign language without having seen or practiced it beforehand —**sight-read·er** *n*

sight rhyme *n* LITERAT same as **eye rhyme**

sight·see /sít see/ (**-saw** /-sàw/, **-seen** /-seen/, **-see·ing, -sees**) *vi* to visit a place's interesting sights —**sight·se·er** *n*

sight·see·ing /sít see ing/ *n* visiting places of interest (*often used before a noun*) ○ *a sightseeing tour*

sight·seen past participle of **sightsee**

sig·il /síjjəl/ *n* **1.** a seal or signet **2.** a sign or image that is supposed to have magical power [15C. < late Latin *sigillum* "sign, trace, (in medieval Latin) seal," singular < Latin *sigilla* "small images" < *signum* "mark, sign"] —**sig·il·la·ry** /si jílləree/ *adj*

sig·int /síggint/, **SIGINT** *n* intelligence data acquired electronically. Full form **signals intelligence**

Sig·is·mund /síggissmənd/ (1368–1437), king of Hungary and Holy Roman Emperor. As king of Hungary (1387–1437), he conquered much Balkan territory. He was Holy Roman Emperor from 1411 to 1437. His rule over Bohemia (1419–37) was constantly challenged by Bohemians opposed to his role in the execution of John Huss (1415).

> "Only do always in health what you have often promised to do when you are sick."
> [Sigismund, *Biographiana*; 14th-15th century]

sig·ma /sígmə/ *n* **1.** the 18th letter of the Greek alphabet, represented in the English alphabet as "s." See table at **alphabet 2.** MATH the symbol (σ) indicating the addition of the numbers or quantities indicated **3.** PHYS same as **sigma hyperon** [Early 17C. Via Latin < Greek] —**sig·mate** *adj*

sig·ma hy·per·on, sig·ma par·ti·cle *n* an unstable elementary particle of the baryon group with a positive, negative, or neutral electric charge and mass of 2,328 to 2,343 times that of an electron

sig·moid /síg mòyd/ *adj* **1.** shaped like the letter "S" **2.** relating to the sigmoid colon of the large intestine

sig·moid co·lon *n* the final S-shaped portion of the large intestine leading to the rectum

sig·moid flex·ure *n* **1.** ANAT same as **sigmoid colon 2.** an S-shaped curve or bend, e.g., in the neck of a bird or turtle

sig·moid·o·scope /sig móydə skōp/ *n* a fiber-optic tubular instrument inserted through the anus for examining the interior of the rectum and sigmoid colon —**sig·moid·o·scop·ic** /sig mòydə skóppik/ *adj* —**sig·moid·os·co·py** /sig moy dóskəpee/ *n*

sign /sīn/ *n* **1.** THING REPRESENTING SOMETHING ELSE something that indicates or expresses the existence of something else not immediately apparent ○ *a sign of wealth* **2.** SOMETHING CONVEYING IDEA an action or gesture used to convey an idea, information, a wish, or a command ○ *His kick under the table was a sign that we should leave.* **3.** ADVERTISING NOTICE a publicly displayed structure carrying lettering or designs intended to advertise a business or product, e.g., a painted board or neon lights **4.** INFORMATION NOTICE a publicly displayed notice or board bearing directions, instructions, or warnings ○ *a highway sign* **5.** INDICATION something that indicates the presence of something or somebody ○ *no sign of life* **6.** TRACE LEFT BY ANIMAL a trace of a wild animal, e.g., the droppings, scent, or footprints **7.** OMEN something interpreted as being an omen **8.** ASTROL DIVISION OF ZODIAC any one of the 12 equal parts into which the zodiac is divided, each represented by a symbol **9.** MED EVIDENCE OF DISEASE an indication of the presence of a disease or disorder, especially one observed by a doctor but not apparent to the patient ○ *Fever is a sign of an infection.* **10.** MATH, LOGIC SYMBOL USED IN MATH OR LOGIC a symbol indicating an operation or relation in mathematics or logic ○ *the plus sign* **11.** MUSIC MUSICAL NOTATION SYMBOL a symbol used in musical notation **12.** COMMUNICATION same as **sign language** ■ *v* (**signed, sign·ing, signs**) **1.** *vti* WRITE NAME to write a signature on something **2.** *vti* APPROVE DOCUMENT to affirm or approve a document formally by affixing a signature or seal ○ *sign a bill into law* **3.** *vti* HIRE SOMEBODY to engage the services of somebody by written agreement ○ *The college signed him to coach the team.* **4.** *vi* AGREE TO TAKE JOB to agree to be hired by writing a signature on a contract **5.** *vti* SIGNAL INFORMATION to convey information using a signal or signals **6.** *vt* PORTEND SOMETHING to be an omen of something to come ○ *That signs danger.* **7.** *vti* COMMUNICATION COMMUNICATE IN SIGN LANGUAGE to use sign language to communicate a message ○ *She signed "yes."* **8.** *vt* CHR GIVE BLESSING TO SOMEBODY to bless somebody or something by making the sign of the cross [13C. Via French < Latin *signum* "mark, sign"] —**sign·er** *n*

SPELLCHECK Do not confuse the spelling of ***sign*** and ***sine***, which sound similar. The general and commoner word is ***sign***, which usually refers to something that indicates or expresses something or that provides information (*a sign of the times, a highway sign*), and is also used as a verb (*sign a document*). ***Sine*** is a specialized noun referring to a trigonometric function.

ORIGIN The Latin word *signum* "mark," from which **sign** is derived, is also the source of English *assign, consign, design, designate, ensign, insignia, resign, seal*[1], *signal, signature, signet*, and *significant*.

sign away *vt* to convey rights or property to somebody by signing a document ○ *He signed away his property to pay his debts.*

sign in *vi* to write a signature in a register, usually as a way of recording presence or attendance

sign off *v* **1.** *vi* to bring to an end a communication or transmission such as a radio or TV program, a letter, or an e-mail message, by announcing its conclusion **2.** *vt* to give written approval or authorization for something (*informal*) ○ *Several members have not yet signed off on the proposed changes.*

sign on *v* **1.** *vi* to agree to do some activity, especially by signing a contract **2.** *vt* to take somebody on as an employee or to do a particular job

sign out *v* **1.** *vi* to write a signature as a record of having left somewhere, especially a workplace **2.** *vt* to sign your name as an acknowledgment of having received something, especially as being temporarily in possession of it

sign over *vt* to transfer possession of something to somebody else by writing a signature on a document

sign up *vti* **1.** to agree to participate in something, or get somebody to agree to participate in something, especially by way of a signature **2.** to enlist for military service, or enlist somebody for military service

signa., Signa. *abbr* signorina

Si·gnac /seen yaák/, **Paul** (1863–1935) French painter. In his earlier years he was a major exponent of divisionism, which he developed to produce an effect resembling mosaic.

sign·age /sínij/ *n* **1.** signs collectively ○ *the signage along a highway* **2.** the design and display of signs

sig·nal /sígn'l/ *n* **1.** MEANS OF COMMUNICATION an action, gesture, or sign used as a means of communication **2.** COMMUNICATED INFORMATION a piece of information communicated by an action, gesture, or sign **3.** INCITEMENT something that incites somebody to action ○ *The threat of a shortage was a signal to hoard.* **4.** ELECTRONICS TRANSMITTED INFORMATION information transmitted by means of a modulated current or an electromagnetic wave and received by telephone, telegraph, radio, television, or radar ■ *adj* NOTABLE of considerable importance ○ *a signal accomplishment* ■ *v* (**-naled, -nal·ing, -nals**) **1.** *vti* SEND MESSAGE USING SIGNAL to communicate a message to somebody using a signal or signals **2.** *vt* COMMUNICATE SOMETHING to communicate something with an action or gesture ○ *She signaled her impatience.* **3.** *vt* INDICATE SOMETHING to be a sign that something has happened or is about to happen ○ *This event signaled the end of the conflict.* [14C. Via French < medieval Latin *signale* < Latin *signum* "mark, sign"] —**sig·nal·er** *n*

sig·nal box *n UK* RAIL same as **signal tower**

sig·nal gen·er·a·tor *n* a device used to test electronic equipment by generating a signal whose frequency, wave shape, and amplitude are independently adjustable over a wide range of settings

sig·nal·ize /sígnə lìz/ (**-ized, -iz·ing, -iz·es**) *vt* **1.** MAKE SOMETHING STAND OUT to make something conspicuous or remarkable **2.** POINT SOMETHING OUT to indicate something distinctly **3.** *US* PROVIDE TRAFFIC SIGNALS to provide a place with traffic signals —**sig·nal·i·za·tion** /sìgnəli záysh'n/ *n*

sig·nal·ly /sígnə'lee/ *adv* completely and unmistakably

sig·nal·man /sígnəlmən/ (*plural* **-men** /-mən/) *n* **1.** a member of the armed forces who sends and receives signals **2.** a railroad employee who is in charge of operating signals

sig·nal·ment /sígn'lmənt/ *n US* a detailed physical description of somebody for purposes of identification [Late 18C. < French *signalement* < *signaler* "mark out" < *signal* (see SIGNAL)]

sig·nal-to-noise ra·tio *n* the ratio of the strength of a signal carrying information to unwanted interference in an electronic circuit

sig·nal tow·er *n US* an electrically and semiautomatically operated control point for a large system of railroad track

sig·na·to·ry /sígnə tàwree/ *n* (*plural* **-ries**) a person, government, or organization that has signed a treaty or contract and is bound by it ■ *adj* bound by the terms of a treaty or contract ○ *a signatory nation*

sig·na·ture /sígnəchər, -choor/ *n* **1.** SIGNED NAME somebody's name written by him or her in a characteristic way **2.** SIGNING OF NAME the act of signing your name **3.** DISTINCTIVE CHARACTERISTIC a distinctive mark, characteristic, or thing that identifies somebody (*often used before a noun*) ○ *The interior design had her signature all over it.* **4.** MED DIRECTIONS ON PRESCRIPTION the part of a doctor's prescription that contains the directions for use **5.** MUSIC same as **key signature** **6.** MUSIC same as **time signature** **7.** PRINTING MARK INDICATING PAGE ORDER a letter or mark printed on what will become the first page of a section of a book, indicating its order in binding **8.** PRINTING SHEET FORMING SECTION OF BOOK a sheet of paper printed with several pages that, when folded and cut, makes up a section of a book ■ *adj* MOST CLOSELY ASSOCIATED distinctive and closely associated with or identifying somebody or something ○ *the marathon, signature race of the Olympics* [Mid-16C. Via French < medieval Latin *signatura* < Latin *signare* "to sign" < *signum* "mark, sign"]

sig·na·ture file *n* a short text file with information such as the user's name and address, serving as a signature at the end of e-mails and Usenet messages

sig·na·ture tune *n UK* same as **theme song**

sign·board /sín bàwrd/ *n* a board carrying a notice or advertisement

signed /sínd/ *adj* **1.** bearing a signature, e.g., for authentication or as an autograph **2.** with a positive or negative value, as indicated by a plus or minus sign

signed-ranks test *n* STATS same as **Wilcoxon test**

sig·net /sígnət/ *n* **1.** SMALL SEAL a small seal, e.g., one that is engraved on a ring **2.** STAMP FOR DOCUMENTS a seal used to stamp official documents **3.** IMPRESSION MADE BY SEAL an impression made on a document by a seal ■ *vt* (**-net·ed, -net·ing, -nets**) STAMP DOCUMENT WITH SEAL to stamp a document with a seal [14C. Via French < medieval Latin *signetum* "small seal" < Latin *signum* "mark, sign"]

sig·net ring *n* a finger ring containing a small seal

sig·nif·i·cance /sig níffikənss/, **sig·nif·i·can·cy** /-kənssee/ *n* **1.** IMPORTANCE the quality of having importance or being regarded as having great meaning **2.** MEANING implied or intended meaning **3.** STATS VALUE AS STATISTICAL POINTER status as a statistical value that is not accidental or random (*often used before a noun*)

sig·nif·i·cant /sig níffikənt/ *adj* **1.** MEANINGFUL having or expressing a meaning **2.** COMMUNICATING SECRET MEANING having a hidden or implied meaning ○ *a significant nod of the head* **3.** MOMENTOUS AND INFLUENTIAL having a major or important effect ○ *a significant idea* **4.** SUBSTANTIAL relatively large in amount ○ *Her work was a significant contribution to the project.* **5.** STATS OCCURRING NOT MERELY BY CHANCE relating to the occurrence of events or outcomes that are too closely linked statistically to be mere chance [Late 16C. < Latin *significant-*, present participle of *significare* (see SIGNIFY)]

sig·nif·i·cant dig·its *npl* the digits necessary in a decimal number to express accuracy, beginning with the first nonzero digit to the right of the decimal and ending with the digit farthest to the right

sig·nif·i·cant·ly /sig níffikəntlee/ *adv* **1.** to a large extent or degree ○ *significantly higher* **2.** in an important or fundamental way ○ *Your ideas will contribute significantly.*

sig·nif·i·cant oth·er *n* **1.** a spouse or somebody with whom a person has a long-term sexual relationship **2.** an influential or supportive person in somebody's life

sig·ni·fi·ca·tion /sìgnəfi káysh'n/ *n* **1.** the meaning of something such as a word, event, or other phenomenon **2.** the signifying or indicating of something [13C. Via French < Latin *signification-* "indication, sign" < past participle of *significare* (see SIGNIFY)]

~~significent~~ incorrect spelling of **significant**

sig·ni·fy /sígni fì/ (**-fied, -fy·ing, -fies**) *v* **1.** *vt* MEAN SOMETHING to have something as a particular meaning **2.** *vt* BE SIGN OF SOMETHING to be a sign or symbol of something **3.** *vi* BE IMPORTANT to be important or significant **4.** *vi US* EXCHANGE INSULTS to exchange insults with somebody playfully (*slang*) [13C. Via French *signifier* < Latin *significare* < *signum* "mark, sign"] —**sig·ni·fi·a·ble** *adj* —**sig·nif·i·ca·tive** /sig níffi kàytiv/ *adj* —**sig·ni·fi·er** *n*

sign·ing /síning/ *n* COMMUNICATION same as **sign language**

sign·ing bo·nus *n* an extra amount paid to somebody when he or she signs a contract, especially in entertainment and sports

si·gnior *n* another spelling of **signor**

si·gnio·ry *n* HIST same as **seigniory**

sign lan·guage *n* communication, or a system of communication, by gestures as opposed to written or spoken language, especially the highly developed system of hand signs used by or to people who are hearing-impaired

sign man·u·al (*plural* **signs man·u·al**) *n* in law, somebody's signature, especially that of a king or queen on an official document [Translation of Anglo-Latin *signum manuale* "sign made with the hand"]

sign-off *n* **1.** the end of a transmission period or communication **2.** *US* approval or agreement (*informal*)

sign of the cross *n* in Christianity, a movement of the hand as if tracing a cross in the air or on the body, usually by touching the forehead, chest, and shoulders in turn. The gesture is made, e.g., by Roman Catholics, in order to invoke the blessing of God or as a declaration of Christian faith.

si·gnor /seen yáwr/ (*plural* **-gnors** or **-gno·ri** /-ree/), **si·gnior** (*plural* **-gniors** or **-gnio·ri**), **Si·gnor, Si·gnior** *n* the usual Italian form of title or address for a man. It is the equivalent of English "Mr." [Late 16C. < Italian, shortened form of *signore* (see SIGNORE[1])]

si·gno·ra /seen yáwrə/ (*plural* **-ras** or **-re** /-ray/), **Si·gno·ra** *n* the usual Italian form of title or address for a married or older woman. It is equivalent to English "Mrs." or "madam." [Mid-17C. < Italian, feminine form of *signore* (see SIGNORE[1])]

si·gno·re[1] /seen yáw ray/ (*plural* **-ri** /-ree/) *n* the Italian form of title or address for a highly respected man or a man of advanced age. It is equivalent to English "sir." [Late 16C. Via Italian < medieval Latin *senior* "lord, superior" < Latin (see SENIOR)]

si·gno·re[2] plural of **signora**

si·gno·ri plural of **signor, signore**

si·gno·ri·na /sèenyə réenə/ (*plural* **-nas** or **-ne** /-nay/) *n* the usual Italian form of title or address for a young or unmarried woman. It is equivalent to English "Miss." [Early 19C. < Italian < *signora* (see SIGNORA)]

si·gno·ry *n* HIST same as **seigniory**

sign-out *n US* the act or an instance of signing out, or of signing somebody or something out

sign paint·ing *n* the activity or profession of designing and painting signs, especially for advertising —**sign paint·er** *n*

sign·post /sín pòst/ *n* **1.** INFORMATION SIGN a pole with a sign on it, especially one that gives directions or similar information **2.** SOMETHING THAT INDICATES SOMETHING something that gives a clue, indication, hint, or guide ■ *vt* (**-post·ed, -post·ing, -posts**) DIRECT SOMEBODY TO PLACE to direct somebody or mark the way to a place with signposts or similar indications ○ *a series of notices signposting patients to the X-ray department*

sign·writ·ing /sín rìting/ *n UK* same as **sign painting**

sigra., Sigra. *abbr* signora

sig·ri /sèegree/ (*plural* **-ris**) *n S Asia* a brazier usually burning charcoal and used for cooking [Mid-20C. < Punjabi *sagrī*]

Sig·urd /síggərd/ *n* in Norse mythology, a warrior with a cursed hoard of gold whom Brynhild contrives to have killed after he has woken her from an enchanted sleep

Si·ha·nouk /sée ə nòok/, **Norodom** (*b.* 1922) king of Cambodia. As king of Cambodia (1941–55) and intermittently prime minister and head of state, he helped win independence from French rule (1954) and protested the Vietnamese occupation (1975–82). He was restored to the throne after negotiating a political settlement in 1993.

Sikh /seek/ *n* a member of a religious group that broke away from Hinduism during the 16th century and advocated a monotheistic doctrine, incorporating some aspects of Islam ■ *adj* belonging or relating to the Sikhs or their religion, beliefs, customs, or history [Late 18C. Via Punjabi or Hindi < Sanskrit *śiṣya* "disciple"] —**Sikh·ism** *n*

Sik·kim /síkim/ mountainous state in northeastern India, in the eastern Himalaya range, bordered by Tibet, Bhutan, and Nepal. Capital: Gangtok. Population: 540,493 (2001). Area: 2,740 sq. mi./7,096 sq. km. —**Sik·kim·ese** /sìki méez, -méess/ *n, adj*

Si·kor·sky /si káwrskee/, **Igor** (1889–1972) Russian-born US aeronautical engineer and corporate executive. He built the first multiengine airplane (1913) and produced the first helicopter that could be controlled during sustained flight (1939). He founded an aircraft company bearing his name. Full name **Sikorsky, Igor Ivanovich**

si·la /séelə/ *n* in Buddhism, morality, representing three aspects of the eightfold path, right speech, right action, and right livelihood [Mid-20C. < Pali]

si·lage /sílij/ *n* animal fodder that is made by storing green plant material in a silo where it is preserved by partial fermentation [Late 19C. < French *ensilage* < Spanish *ensilar* "store in a silo" < *silo* (see SILO)]

si·lane /sí làyn/ *n* a compound of silicon and hydrogen belonging to a group analogous to the paraffin hydrocarbons. Formula: Si_nH_{2n+2}. [Early 20C. < SILICON]

sild /sild/ (*plural* **silds** or *same*) *n* an immature herring, especially one that has been processed and canned [Early 20C. Via Danish and Norwegian < Old Norse *síld* "herring"]

sil·den·a·fil cit·rate /sil dènnəfil-/ *n* a drug used to treat impotence [Late 20C. < *sil-* + *-denafil*, informal INN stem]

si·lence /sīlənss/ *n* **1. QUIETNESS** the absence or lack of noise **2. NOT SPEAKING** a refusal, failure, or inability to speak **3. IGNORING OF SOMETHING** a failure to notice or acknowledge something ○ *Most remarkable was the statement's silence about the recent policy change.* ■ *vt* (**-lenced, -lenc·ing, -lenc·es**) **1. STOP SOMEBODY OR SOMETHING MAKING NOISE** to stop somebody or something from making a noise **2. SUPPRESS SOMETHING** to suppress the expression of something, or stop a person or group from speaking out ○ *silence criticism* **3. END HOSTILE BEHAVIOR OF SOMEBODY** to cause somebody to stop hostile or aggressive behavior [13C. Via French < Latin *silentium* < *silent-* (see SILENT)]

si·lenc·er /sīlənssər/ *n* **1.** ARMS a device that muffles the noise of a gun **2.** somebody or something that causes silence or lessens noise **3.** *UK* same as **muffler** (sense 1)

si·lent /sīlənt/ *adj* **1. UTTERLY QUIET** lacking any noise or sound ○ *a silent country lane* **2. NOT SPEAKING** not speaking or communicating at a particular time, especially through choice ○ *The children all remained silent.* **3. SAYING LITTLE** not inclined to say much ○ *the strong silent type* **4. UNSPOKEN** communicated without words or sound ○ *a silent warning* ○ *rolled her eyes in silent disbelief* **5. INACTIVE** currently inactive or not operating ○ *a silent volcano* **6. NOT PRONOUNCED** describes a letter that appears in a word but is not pronounced, e.g., the "k" in "knight" or the "b" in "debt" **7.** MOVIES **WITHOUT SOUNDTRACK** describes movies made without sound, especially those made before 1927 **8.** RELIG **NOT ALLOWED TO SPEAK** not allowed to speak because of a religious vow of silence ○ *a silent order of monks* ■ *n* MOVIES **SILENT MOVIE** a motion picture made without sound [15C. < Latin *silent-*, present participle of *silere* "be silent"] —**si·lent·ly** *adv* —**si·lent·ness** *n*

CULTURAL NOTE ***Silent Spring***, (1962) by Rachel Carson. In passionate prose it presented to a popular audience evidence that the indiscriminate use of pesticides like DDT was killing wildlife. It foresaw an eerie future: "A spring without voices. On the mornings that had once throbbed with the dawn chorus of scores of bird voices there was now no sound; only silence lay over the fields and woods and marsh." *Silent Spring* was fiercely attacked by the chemical industry, but its findings were endorsed by a Presidential Commission, and its publication is credited with launching the environmental movement in the United States.

SYNONYMS ***silent, quiet, reticent, taciturn, uncommunicative***

CORE MEANING: not speaking or not saying much

silent not speaking or communicating at a specific time, especially through choice, or not inclined to speak much ○ *Both girls fell silent for a moment.* ○ *He's a rather silent type where women are concerned.* **quiet** displaying calmness and self-control and not inclined to speak much, or not speaking or communicating at a specific time ○ *Jed, who was coming up to five years old, was very bright, but very quiet.* ○ *Keep quiet and sit still for a minute, please!* **reticent** unwilling to communicate very much, talk freely, or reveal all the facts about something ○ *On Tuesday, the usually reticent athlete even ventured some fighting talk.* ○ *The boss of the lucrative cosmetics empire had been reticent in the past when it came to revealing details of his bank account.* **taciturn** habitually uncommunicative or reserved in speech and manner ○ *Both men were taciturn and found it difficult to put ideas into words.* ○ *The team's coach, never particularly talkative, has been even more taciturn than usual.* **uncommunicative** not willing to say much, especially not to reveal information, or tending not to say much ○ *Fred was somewhat reserved and uncommunicative concerning his recent experiences.* ○ *Luke stopped trying to salvage the relationship, becoming increasingly uncommunicative.*

si·lent auc·tion *n* an auction that is conducted by submitting bids in sealed envelopes before the sale

si·lent but·ler *n* a small container, usually with a hinged lid, for crumbs from the table and the contents of ashtrays (*dated*)

si·lent ma·jor·i·ty *n* a significant proportion of a population who choose not to express their views, often because of apathy or because they do not believe their views matter

si·lent part·ner *n* somebody who invests capital in a business but who takes no part in managing it

si·lent ser·vice *n US* the submarine service of the US Navy (*informal*)

si·lent treat·ment *n* a prolonged spell of refusing to communicate as a way of expressing contempt, anger, disapproval, or some other negative emotion (*informal*)

si·le·nus /sī lēenəss/ (*plural* **-ni** /-nī/) *n* in Greek mythology, a spirit of woodlands and forests, usually depicted as an elderly satyr [Early 18C. Via Latin < Greek *Silēnos* "Silenus"]

Si·le·nus /sī lēenəss/ *n* in Greek mythology, an aged woodland god who was in charge of Dionysus' education. In art, Silenus is often depicted as a drunken old man.

si·le·sia /sī lēezhə, -shə/ *n* a hard-wearing cotton twill fabric. Use: pockets, linings. [Late 17C. After SILESIA]

Si·le·sia /sī lēezhə, -shə/ historic region in east central Europe, lying mostly within present-day southwestern Poland —**Si·le·sian** *n, adj*

si·lex /sī lèks/ *n* **1.** powdered silica or tripoli, used as a filter material **2.** a heat-resistant glass with high quartz content [Late 16C. < Latin, "flint"]

silhouette

sil·hou·ette /sìlloo ét/ *n* **1. SHADOWED CONTOUR** an outline of somebody or something filled in with black or a dark color on a light background, especially when done as a likeness or work of art **2. SOMETHING DARK ON LIGHT BACKGROUND** something lit in such a way as to appear dark, but surrounded by light, or the effect produced by such lighting ○ *silhouettes dancing in front of the bonfire* ■ *vt* (**-et·ted, -et·ting, -ettes**) **MAKE SOMETHING APPEAR AS SILHOUETTE** to cause somebody or something to appear surrounded by light (*often passive*) ○ *The buildings were silhouetted against the rising sun.* [Late 18C. < French, after Étienne de *Silhouette* (1709–67), French finance minister]

ORIGIN As French finance minister in the late 1750s, Étienne de Silhouette gained a reputation for stinginess, and ***silhouette*** came to be used for anything skimped. One account of the application of the word to a simple picture showing a dark shape against a light background is that it carries on this notion of "simplicity" or "lack of finish," but an alternative theory is that Silhouette himself was in the habit of making such pictures.

silic- *prefix* same as **silici-** (*used before vowels*)

sil·i·ca /síllikə/ *n* silicon dioxide found naturally in various crystalline and amorphous forms, e.g., quartz, opal, sand, flint, and agate. Use: manufacture of glass, abrasives, concrete. [Early 19C. Via modern Latin < Latin *silic-*, stem of *silex* "flint"] —**si·li·ceous** /sə líshəss/ *adj*

sil·i·ca gel *n* gelatinous silica in a form that readily absorbs water from the air. Use: drying agent, carrier for catalysts, anticaking agent.

sil·i·ca glass *n* glass made from fused silica, which expands minimally when heated

sil·i·cate /sílli kàyt, -kət/ *n* a common rock-forming mineral belonging to a group formed from silicon and oxygen combined with various elements and classified by their crystalline structures

silici- *prefix* **1.** silica ○ *silicosis* **2.** silicon ○ *silicate* [< SILICON, SILICA]

si·lic·ic /sə líssik/ *adj* relating to or containing silica or silicon

si·lic·ic ac·id *n* a weak gelatinous acid obtained by adding an acid to sodium silicate

sil·i·cide /síllə sīd/ *n* a binary compound of silicon with another element

sil·i·cif·er·ous /sìllə síffərəss/ *adj* containing or yielding silica

si·lic·i·fy /sə líssə fī/ (**-fied, -fy·ing, -fies**) *vti* to convert something into silica, or become converted into silica —**si·lic·i·fi·ca·tion** /sə lìssəfi káysh'n/ *n*

sil·i·cle *n* BOT same as **silicula**

sil·i·con /síllikən, -kòn/ *n* an abundant brittle nonmetallic element. Source: sand, granite, clay, many minerals. Use: alloys, semiconductors, building materials. Symbol **Si**. See table at **element** [Early 19C. < SILICA]

sil·i·con car·bide *n* an extremely hard bluish black crystalline compound. Use: abrasive, refractory, semiconductor. Formula: SiC.

sil·i·con chip *n* a small wafer of silicon forming the base on which an integrated circuit is laid out, or such a wafer together with its integrated circuit

sil·i·con di·ox·ide *n* a colorless transparent solid that melts at a very high temperature. Use: manufacture of microchips. Formula: SiO_2.

sil·i·cone /sílli kōn/ *n* a heat-resistant silicon-based synthetic substance in the form of a grease, oil, or plastic. Use: lubricants, insulators, water-repellents, resins, adhesives, coatings, paints, prosthetics.

Sil·i·con Val·ley /síllikən-, -kon-/ region in Santa Clara County, western California, that is an important center for electronics and computer manufacturing industries

sil·i·co·sis /sìlli kóssiss/ *n* a lung disease caused by prolonged inhalation of dust containing silica and marked by the development of fibrous tissue in the lungs and a resultant chronic shortness of breath —**sil·i·cot·ic** /-kóttik/ *adj*

sil·i·cu·la /si líkyələ/ (*plural* **-lae** /-lèe/ or **-las**), **sil·i·cule** /sílli kyo͞ol/, **sil·i·cle** /síllik'l/ *n* a dry fruit consisting of a broad flat pod divided by a membrane into two seed chambers, e.g., that of honesty [Mid-18C. < modern Latin, "little pod" < Latin *siliqua* "seed pod"]

si·lique /si léek, síllik/, **si·li·qua** /síllikwə/ (*plural* **-quae** /-kwèe/ or **-quas**) *n* a long dry seed capsule of plants of the mustard family that has two valves that open, leaving a central partition to which seeds are attached [Late 18C. Via French < Latin *siliqua* "seed pod"] —**si·li·qua·ceous** /sìlli kwáyshəss/ *adj* —**si·li·quose** /sílli kwōss/ *adj* —**si·li·quous** /-kwəss/ *adj*

silk /silk/ *n* **1. THREAD FROM SILKWORMS** the fine fiber that silkworms secrete to make their cocoons. Use: threads, fabrics. **2.** TEXTILES **SILK FABRIC** fabric woven from spun silk **3.** ZOOL **THREAD FROM SPIDERS** a fine fiber that spiders secrete and use to make their webs, nests, and cocoons **4.** PLANTS same as **corn silk 5.** *UK* LAW **KING'S OR QUEEN'S COUNSEL** a lawyer who has the right to practice as a King's or Queen's Counsel in British courts (*informal*) **6.** *UK* LAW **HIGH BARRISTER'S GARMENT** the gown worn by a King's or Queen's Counsel in British courts ■ **silks** *npl* HORSERACING **JOCKEY'S SILK GARMENTS** the distinctively colored silk clothes worn by a jockey as a mark of identification [Old English *seoloc*, via Slavic or Latin < Greek *sērikos* "silken" < *Sēres* "people from E Asian countries producing silk"] ◇ **hit the silk** *US* to jump from an aircraft with a parachute

silk·a·line /sílkə lèen/, **silk·a·lene** *n* a fine cotton fabric with a glossy finish [Late 19C. < SILK]

silk cot·ton *n* TEXTILES same as **kapok**

silk-cot·ton tree *n* a large tropical tree whose seed

pods yield the silky fiber kapok. Latin name: *Ceiba pentandra.*

silk·en /sílkən/ *adj* **1.** MADE OF SILK made or consisting of silk **2.** LIKE SILK IN TEXTURE OR APPEARANCE resembling silk, especially in smoothness, softness, or shininess ○ *Spaniels have lovely silken ears.* **3.** IN SILK CLOTHES dressed in garments made of silk **4.** SOFT OR GENTLE pleasingly soft, gentle, or delicate ○ *silken phrases* **5.** LUXURIOUS luxurious or opulent (*dated*)

silk gland *n* a salivary gland of a cocoon-spinning insect or an abdominal gland of a web-spinning spider that produces a viscous liquid that is expelled in a thread and polymerizes into a filament

silk hat *n* a man's top hat with an outer covering made of silk or a similar fabric

silk-screen *vti* to print a design on paper or fabric using the silk-screen printing technique ■ *n* **1.** a print made using the silk-screen printing technique **2.** PRINTING same as **silk-screen printing**

silk-screen print·ing *n* a method of printing on paper or fabric in which ink is forced through areas of a silk screen that are not blocked out with an impermeable substance

silk-stock·ing *adj* affluent, wealthy, or aristocratic

silk tree *n* a widely cultivated tree of the mimosa family. Flowers: showy, pink, with silky filaments. Native to: Asia. Latin name: *Albizia julibrissin.*

silk·weed /sílk wèed/ *n* PLANTS same as **milkweed**

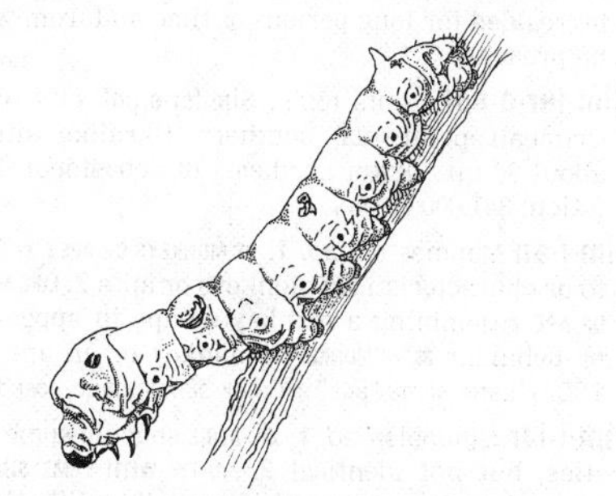

silkworm

silk·worm /sílk wùrm/ *n* **1.** a yellowish caterpillar, the larva of an Asian moth, that feeds on mulberry leaves and is a commercial source of silk. Latin name: *Bombyx mori.* **2.** a moth larva that excretes a substance resembling silk. Family: Bombycidae.

silk·worm moth *n* a moth with larvae that spin silk for cocoons. Family: Bombycidae.

silk·y /sílkee/ (**-i·er, -i·est**) *adj* **1.** LOOKING OR FEELING LIKE SILK resembling silk, especially in smoothness, softness, or shininess ○ *silky hair* **2.** MADE OF SILK made of silk or a similar fiber or fabric ○ *a silky blouse* **3.** SMOOTH IN MANNER smooth, refined, elegant, or sophisticated, often to the extent of being unctuous ○ *a silky manner* **4.** COVERED WITH FINE HAIRS covered with delicate downy hairs or feathers —**silk·i·ly** *adv* —**silk·i·ness** *n*

silk·y oak *n* an ornamental evergreen tree with feathery leaves and smooth silky wood. Flowers: orange. Native to: Australia. Latin name: *Grevillea robusta.*

silk·y ter·ri·er *n* a small slender terrier with a long silky gray or gray-and-tan coat, belonging to a breed developed from a cross between the Australian terrier and the Yorkshire terrier

sill /sil/ *n* **1.** WINDOW LEDGE a ledge below a window, especially one on the inside of a building **2.** BOTTOM OF FRAME the horizontal part at the bottom of a window or door frame **3.** GEOL LAYER OF IGNEOUS ROCK a more or less horizontal layer of igneous rock forced between layers of sedimentary rock or older volcanic beds [Old English *syll* "foundation of a wall" < Germanic]

sil·li·man·ite /síllәmә nīt/ *n* a white or greenish brown fibrous mineral consisting of aluminum silicate. Source: metamorphic rocks. [Mid-19C. After Benjamin *Silliman* (1779–1864), US geologist]

Sil·li·toe /síllitō/, **Alan** (*b.* 1928) British novelist, short-story writer, and poet. The theme of social exclusion and of the individual's rebellion against society runs through much of his work, including *Saturday Night and Sunday Morning* (1958).

Sills /silz/, **Beverly** (*b.* 1929) US soprano. Known for her coloratura voice, she joined the New York City Opera in 1955, and was its manager (1979–91). Born **Silverman, Belle Miriam**

sil·ly /síllee/ *adj* (**-li·er, -li·est**) **1.** FOOLISH lacking common sense **2.** TRIVIAL unworthy of serious concern **3.** DAZED OR HELPLESS in or into a stunned, dazed, or helpless condition ○ *be scared silly* ■ *n* (*plural* **-lies**) FOOLISH PERSON somebody regarded as lacking in common sense (*informal*) [Old English *sælig* "happy" < W Germanic, "luck, happiness"] —**sil·li·ly** *adv* —**sil·li·ness** *n*

ORIGIN *Silly* has undergone one of the most astonishing semantic about-faces in the history of the English lexicon. In a thousand years it has gone from "blessed, happy" to "foolish." The transformation began with "blessed" becoming "pious." This led on via "innocent, harmless," "pitiable," and "feeble" to "feeble in mind, foolish." The related German *selig* retains its original meaning "happy, blessed."

sil·ly sea·son *n* a period in summer when newspapers print frivolous articles because there is a lack of political news

si·lo /sīlō/ *n* (*plural* **-los**) **1.** CONTAINER FOR GRAIN OR ANIMAL FEED a tall cylindrical tower used for storing grain, animal feed, or other material, or for making silage **2.** MISSILE SAFETY CHAMBER a reinforced protective underground chamber where a missile or missiles can be stored and from which they can be launched ■ *vt* (**-loed, -lo·ing, -los**) STORE SOMETHING IN SILO to store something in a silo, e.g., grain, animal feed, or a missile [Mid-19C. Via Spanish < Latin *sirus* < Greek *siros* "storage pit for grain"]

~~**silouette**~~ incorrect spelling of **silhouette**

si·lox·ane /si lók sàyn, sī-/ *n* a compound containing alternating silicon and oxygen atoms in which the silicon atoms are attached to organic groups or hydrogen [Early 20C. Blend of SILICON + OXYGEN + METHANE]

silt /silt/ *n* a fine-grained sediment, especially of mud or clay particles at the bottom of a river or lake ■ *vti* (**silt·ed, silt·ing, silts**) to become full or obstructed with silt, or fill or obstruct something with silt [15C. Probably < N Germanic] —**sil·ta·tion** /sil táysh'n/ *n* —**silt·y** *adj*

silt·stone /sílt stōn/ *n* a form of fine-grained sandstone consisting of compressed silt

Sil·u·res /síllyә rèez/ *npl* an ancient people who lived in western Britain, especially South Wales, and who strongly resisted the invading Romans during the 1st century A.D. [Late 19C. < Latin]

Si·lu·ri·an /si lòoree әn, sī-/ *n* **1.** the period of geologic time, 435 million to 410 million years ago, during which the first air-breathing animal and land plants appeared. See table at **geologic time 2.** a member of the Silures [Early 18C. < Latin *Silures*; from the discovery of rocks of this period in SE Wales, home of the ancient people the Silures] —**Si·lu·ri·an** *adj*

si·lu·rid /si lòorid, sī-/ *n* a freshwater catfish with an elongated scaleless body, a short dorsal fin, and a long anal fin. Native to: Europe, Asia. Family: Siluridae. ■ *adj* relating to or belonging to the silurids [< modern Latin *Siluridae* (plural) < Latin *silurus*, type of catfish < Greek *silouros*]

sil·va /sílvә/ (*plural* **-vas** or **-vae** /-vèe/), **syl·va** *n* **1.** the forests or trees of a region **2.** a book or treatise on the forests or trees of a region

Sil·va /sílvә/, **Luis Inacio Lula da** (*b.* 1945) president of Brazil. A former union activist, he helped to organize the Workers' Party (1980) and in 2002 became the first left-wing leader to be elected president of Brazil. Known as **Lula**

sil·van *adj* another spelling of **sylvan**

Sil·va·nus /sil váynәss/, **Syl·va·nus** *n* in Roman mythology, the god of fields and forests, protector of flocks and cattle. He later came to be identified with the gods Pan and Faunus.

Sil·vas·sa /sil vússә/ capital of the Union Territory of Dadra and Nagar Haveli, western India. Population: 11,720 (1991).

sil·ver /sílvәr/ *n* **1.** SHINY GRAYISH ELEMENT a shiny grayish white metallic element that has the highest thermal and electric conductivity of any substance. Use: coins, ornaments, jewelry, dental materials, solders, photographic chemicals, conductors. Symbol **Ag**. See table at **element 2.** HOUSEHOLD SILVER ARTICLES items of tableware or other household goods that are made of silver, coated with silver plate, or made of a silver-colored metal **3.** COINS COINS money, especially coins made of silver or a silver-colored metal **4.** COLORS LUSTROUS GRAYISH WHITE a lustrous grayish white color **5.** PHOTOGRAPHY SILVER COMPOUND a compound of silver used in photography, e.g., to make paper sensitive to light **6.** same as **silver medal** (*informal*) ■ *adj* **1.** MADE OF SILVER made of, plated with, or containing silver ○ *a silver bracelet* **2.** WITH COLOR OF SILVER of the color silver **3.** SHINY shining like silver ○ *silver moonlight* **4.** OF 25TH ANNIVERSARY relating to the 25th anniversary of something ○ *silver wedding anniversary* **5.** RESONANT pleasingly resonant and clear in tone **6.** FLUENT fluent or persuasively eloquent ○ *a silver tongue* ■ *v* (**-vered, -ver·ing, -vers**) **1.** *vt* COAT SOMETHING WITH SILVER to coat something with a layer of silver or a similar shiny material **2.** *vti* MAKE OR BECOME LIKE SILVER to become like silver in color or sheen, or cause something to do this ○ *Frost silvered the trees.* [Old English *siolfor* < Germanic] —**sil·ver·er** *n* —**sil·ver·ing** *n*

Sil·ver Age *n* in classical mythology, the epoch following the Golden Age that was characterized by a refusal to serve the gods and a love of luxury

sil·ver·back /sílvәr bàk/ *n* an older adult male gorilla with grayish white hair on its back

sil·ver·bell /sílvәr bèl/, **sil·ver·bell tree** *n* a deciduous tree or bush with toothed leaves. Flowers: drooping, white, bell-shaped. Native to: southeastern United States, Asia. Genus: *Halesia.*

sil·ver·ber·ry /sílvәr bèrree/ (*plural* **-ries**) *n* **1.** a bush with silvery leaves and berries. Native to: North America. Latin name: *Elaeagnus commutata.* **2.** PLANTS same as **oleaster** (sense 2)

sil·ver birch *n* a deciduous tree with peeling silvery white bark. Native to: Europe, Asia. Latin name: *Betula pendula.*

sil·ver bro·mide *n* a yellowish powder that darkens when exposed to light. Use: photographic emulsions. Formula: AgBr.

sil·ver bul·let *n* a magical solution to a problem, e.g., a cure for cancer (*informal*) [< the idea that silver possesses magical qualities]

sil·ver ceil·ing *n* discrimination in the workplace against employees and job applicants who are no longer considered young

sil·ver cer·tif·i·cate *n* a bill redeemable for a fixed quantity of silver. Such bills were issued as legal tender by the US government under the former silver standard.

sil·ver chlo·ride *n* a white powder that darkens when exposed to light. Use: photographic emulsions. Formula: AgCl.

sil·ver cord *n* the mutual bond that unites a mother and child (*dated or literary*) [< the title of a play (1926) by Sidney Howard]

sil·ver dol·lar *n* **1.** a one-dollar coin with a high silver content, minted from time to time in the United States **2.** *Can* a commemorative Canadian dollar coin issued annually **3.** *US* PLANTS same as **honesty** (sense 3)

sil·ver dol·lar fish *n* a freshwater fish with a flattened round silver body. Native to: tropical Central and South America. Genera: *Metynnis* or *Myleus.*

sil·ver fir *n* a fir tree with leaves that have a white or silvery underside. Genus: *Abies.*

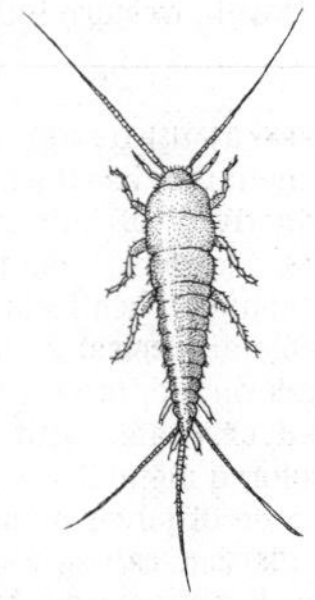

silverfish

sil·ver·fish /sílvər fìsh/ (*plural same* or **-fish·es**) *n* **1.** a small silvery wingless insect with three long tail bristles and two long antennae that feeds on the starch of books, wallpaper, food, and other materials. Latin name: *Lepisma saccharina*. **2.** a silvery fish, e.g., a tarpon

sil·ver fox *n* **1.** a North American red fox in the color phase in which the black fur is silver-tipped **2.** the pelt of the silver fox, once valued for making fur coats and other articles

sil·ver-gilt *n* **1.** silver that has been coated with a very thin layer of gold **2.** a decorative coating of silver leaf

silver-gray *n* a pale lustrous gray color —**silver-gray** *adj*

sil·ver hake *n* a fish resembling a cod with silvery scales. Native to: North American Atlantic coastal waters. Latin name: *Merluccius bilinearis*.

sil·ver i·o·dide *n* a yellow powder that darkens when exposed to light. Use: photographic emulsions, antiseptics, seeding of clouds to make rain. Formula: AgI.

sil·ver lin·ing *n* something that offers hope or benefit in a situation that is generally adverse [< the proverb "Every (dark) cloud has a silver lining"]

sil·ver ma·ple *n* **1.** the hard wood of a maple tree **2.** a common maple tree with deeply cut five-lobed leaves that are silvery white underneath. Native to: North America. Latin name: *Acer saccharinum*.

sil·ver med·al *n* an award for taking second place in a race or other competition, usually in the form of a silver disk on a ribbon —**sil·ver med·al·ist** *n*

sil·vern /sílvərn/ *adj* made of or resembling silver (*archaic or literary*) [Old English *silfren* < *siolfor* (see SILVER)]

sil·ver ni·trate *n* a white poisonous compound that turns black when it is exposed to light while in contact with organic matter. Use: photographic emulsion, reagent, antiseptic, astringent. Formula: $AgNO_3$.

sil·ver perch *n* **1.** a silvery fish resembling a perch, e.g., a white crappie **2.** a drum fish. Native to: southern Atlantic coast of the United States. Latin name: *Bairdiella chrysoura*.

sil·ver plate *n* **1.** a thin layer of silver, especially one that is used to coat a base metal **2.** items, especially of tableware, that are made from a base metal coated with a thin layer of silver

sil·ver-plate *vt* to coat something, especially a base metal, with a thin layer of silver, usually by electroplating

sil·ver·point /sílvər pòynt/ *n* **1.** a drawing technique that involves using a silver-tipped pencil on specially prepared paper or parchment **2.** a drawing made using the silverpoint technique

sil·ver sal·mon *n* FISH same as **coho salmon**

sil·ver screen *n* **1.** movies or the movie industry in general **2.** the screen that a movie is projected onto

sil·ver ser·vice *n* a silver tray, coffee pot, teapot, sugar bowl, and cream pitcher used in formal entertaining

sil·ver·side /sílvər sīd/ *n* a small bony fish with a broad silvery stripe along each side of its body. Family: Atherinidae.

sil·ver·smith /sílvər smìth/ *n* somebody who makes or repairs silver or silver-plated objects —**sil·ver·smith·ing** *n*

sil·ver spoon *n* inherited wealth and high social status [< the expression "be born with a silver spoon in your mouth"]

sil·ver·spot /sílvər spòt/ *n* a butterfly that has silver-colored spots on its wings. Native to: northern temperate areas. Family: Nymphalidae.

sil·ver stan·dard *n* a basis for currency consisting of a reserve of silver for which issued bills are redeemable at a fixed rate

Sil·ver Star, **Sil·ver Star Med·al** *n* a US military decoration for gallantry in combat

sil·ver·tip /sílvər tìp/ *n US* ZOOL same as **grizzly bear** [Late 19C. < the white tips of its hairs]

sil·ver-tongued *adj* having the gift of persuading or complimenting people eloquently and with charm

sil·ver·ware /sílvər wèr/ *n* **1.** metal knives, forks, and other items of tableware **2.** items made of silver or silver plate, especially tableware

sil·ver·weed /sílvər wèed/ *n* a creeping plant that has leaves with silvery undersides, used in herbal medicine for its mildly astringent properties. Flowers: yellow. Native to: northern temperate regions. Latin name: *Potentila anserina*.

sil·ver·y /sílvəree/ *adj* **1.** LIKE SILVER resembling silver, especially in color or sheen **2.** WITH SILVER containing silver or coated with a thin layer of silver **3.** CLEAR AND RESONANT clear and ringing in tone ○ *silvery peals of laughter* —**sil·ver·i·ness** *n*

sil·vex /síl vèks/ *n* an herbicide used to control woody plants that is toxic to animals. Its use is now widely banned or severely restricted. Formula: $C_9H_7Cl_3O_3$. [Mid-20C. < Latin *silva* "a wood" + *-ex*, as in EXTERMINATE]

sil·vic·o·lous /sil víkləss/ *adj* describes plants and animals that grow or live in woods or forests [< Latin *silvicola* "living in woods" < *silva* "a wood"]

sil·vi·cul·ture /sílvi kùlchər/, **syl·vi·cul·ture** *n* the study, cultivation, and management of forest trees [Late 19C. < French < Latin *silva* "a wood" + French *culture* "cultivation"] —**sil·vi·cul·tur·al** /sìlvi kúlchərəl/ *adj* —**sil·vi·cul·tur·ist** *n*

sim /sim/ *n* COMPUT GAMES same as **simulation** (sense 5) (*informal*) [Shortening]

sim. *abbr* similar

si·ma[1] /sèemə/ *n* an area consecrated for the ordination of Buddhist monks, and for other formal monastic activities [< Sanskrit *sīmā*, "border, boundary"]

si·ma[2] /símə/ *n* the rocks that form the lower part of the Earth's crust, lying beneath the oceans and the continents and consisting mainly of silica and magnesia [Early 20C. < SILICA + MAGNESIUM]

sim·a·rou·ba /sìmmə ro͝obə/, **sim·a·ru·ba** *n* a tree of the quassia family whose bark has medicinal properties. Native to: tropical America. Genus: *Simaruba*. [Mid-18C. Via French and Portugese < Galibi *simaruppa*]

~~**simbol**~~ incorrect spelling of **symbol**

SIM card *n* a smart card inserted into a cell phone that holds personal information relating to the subscriber such as the subscriber's PIN number or stored phone numbers. Full form **Subscriber Identity Module card**

Sim·chat To·rah /sìm khaat-/, **Sim·chas To·rah** /-khaass-/, **Sim·chath To·rah** /-khaat-/ *n* a Jewish festival marking the end of the annual cycle of reading from the Torah. Date: end of Sukkoth. [Late 19C. < Hebrew *śimḥath tōrā* "rejoicing of the Torah"]

Sim·coe /símkō/, **John Graves** (1752–1806) British military officer. He was lieutenant governor of Upper Canada (1791–96).

Georges Simenon

Si·me·non /seemə náwN/, **Georges** (1903–89) Belgian-born French writer. He published more than 400 novels under a variety of pseudonyms, but is best known for the 80 crime novels featuring his tough and intuitive sleuth, Inspector Maigret. Full name **Simenon, Georges Joseph Christian**

> "Writing is not a profession but a vocation of unhappiness."
> [Georges Simenon, *Interview, Paris Review*; Summer 1955]

Sim·e·on Sty·li·tes /sìmmee ən stī lít eez/, **St.** (390?–459) Syrian ascetic. He was the first "pillar saint," so called for the stone pillar near Antakya on which he resided for long periods of time and from which he preached.

Sim·fer·o·pol /sìmfə rŏp'l/, **Sim·fer·o·pol'** city on the Crimean peninsula, southern Ukraine, situated about 30 mi./48 km northeast of Sebastopol. Population: 341,000 (1998).

sim·i·an /símmee ən/ *adj* **1.** OF MONKEYS OR APES relating to or characteristic of monkeys or apes **2.** LIKE MONKEY OR APE resembling a monkey or ape in appearance or behavior ■ *n* MONKEY a monkey or an ape [Early 17C. < Latin *simia* "ape" < Greek *simos* "snub-nosed"]

sim·i·lar /símmələr/ *adj* **1.** ⚠ ALIKE sharing some qualities, but not identical **2.** MATH WITH SAME SHAPE OR ANGLES describes geometric figures that differ in size or proportion but not in shape or angular measurements **3.** *Malaysia, Singapore* IDENTICAL exactly the same [Late 16C. Via French < medieval Latin *similaris* < Latin *similis* "like, similar"]

USAGE In its meaning "sharing some qualities," *similar* is followed by *to*: *My own experience has been similar to yours.* Usage of it with *as*, though occasionally found, is incorrect: *I had a similar experience as yours.*

sim·i·lar·i·ty /sìmmə lárrətee/ (*plural* **-ties**) *n* **1.** the possession of one or more qualities or features in common **2.** a quality or feature that two or more people or things have in common

sim·i·lar·ly /símmələrlee/ *adv* **1.** so as to share some qualities but not exactly identical **2.** used to indicate that something corresponds to or is similar to something else

sim·i·le /símmələe/ *n* a figure of speech that draws a comparison between two different things, especially a phrase containing the word "like" or "as," e.g., "as white as a sheet" [14C. < Latin, "like thing" < *similis* "like, similar"]

~~**similer**~~ incorrect spelling of **similar**

~~**similie**~~ incorrect spelling of **simile**

si·mil·i·tude /si mílli to͞od/ *n* **1.** CONDITION OF BEING SIMILAR likeness or resemblance (*formal*) **2.** SOMEBODY OR SOMETHING RESEMBLING ANOTHER somebody or something that is like somebody or something else **3.** SHARED CHARACTERISTIC a quality or feature shared by two or more people or things (*formal*) **4.** FORM OR SEMBLANCE a form or semblance of somebody or something (*formal or literary*) [14C. Via French < Latin *similitudo* "likeness" < *similis* "like,similar"]

Si·mi Val·ley /see mèe-/ city near Los Angeles between the Santa Susana Mountains and the Simi Hills in southwestern California. It is the site of the Ronald Reagan Presidential Library. Population: 116,562 (2002 estimate).

Sim·la /símmlə/ capital city of Himachal Pradesh

State, northwestern India. Population: 110,360 (1991).

SIMM /sim/ *n* a module plugged into the motherboard of a computer to add memory. Full form **single inline memory module**

Sim·men·tal /zímmən taal/ (*plural* **-tals** or *same*), **Sim·men·thal** (*plural* **-thals** or *same*) *n* a large cow with a yellowish brown or reddish coat, a white head, and white legs. It belongs to a breed originating in Switzerland and is bred for beef and milk. [Early 20C. After a valley in Switzerland]

sim·mer[1] /símmər/ *v* (**-mered, -mer·ing, -mers**) **1.** *vti* COOK **COOK JUST BELOW BOIL** to cook something gently just below boiling point, usually with the occasional bubble breaking on the surface, or be cooked in this way **2.** *vti* COOK **STAY OR KEEP SOMETHING BELOW BOIL** to keep a liquid just below boiling point, or be kept at this point **3.** *vi* **GROW ANGRY** to have anger or another strong emotion building up inside ○ *simmering with rage* **4.** *vi* **BUILD UP** to build up inside somebody, often without being expressed (*refers to strong emotions*) ○*"with grief and rage and laughter all simmering within me like a boiling pot"* (Arthur Conan Doyle, *The Lost World*; 1912) ■ *n* COOK **GENTLE COOKING TEMPERATURE** a cooking temperature that cooks food or keeps liquid at just below boiling point [Mid-17C. Alteration of obsolete *simper*, probably an imitation of the sound]

simmer down *v* **1.** *vi* to become calm, e.g., after an outburst of anger or a state of excitement **2.** *vti* to condense something by simmering it gently, or be condensed in this way

sim·mer[2] /símmər/ *n* somebody who plays computer or video simulation games [< SIM.]

si·mo·le·on /sə mólee ən/ *n US* same as **dollar** (sense 2) (*dated slang*) [Late 19C. Origin ?]

Si·mon /símən/ (*fl* A.D. 1st century) one of the 12 apostles of Jesus Christ in the Bible, he is traditionally believed to have been martyred in Persia with St. Jude. Known as **Simon the Zealot**

Si·mon, Neil (*b.* 1927) US playwright. Plays such as *The Odd Couple* (1965) and *Sweet Charity* (1966) made him the country's most successful writer of comedies. He later wrote more serious works including *Lost in Yonkers* (1991), which won a Pulitzer Prize. Full name **Simon, Marvin Neil**

Express Newspapers

Nina Simone

Si·mone /si mṓn/, **Nina** (1933–2003) US jazz singer and composer. She wrote and sang protest songs against racism in the 1960s, using her smoky contralto voice to great dramatic effect. Born **Waymon, Eunice Kathleen**

> "Getting stardom and, once you've got it, keeping it, is like fighting a war. You plan your campaign, recruit your troops, equip them properly, and then fight until you've stormed the cities you want. Then you dig in and defend your position."
> [Nina Simone, *I Put a Spell On You: The Autobiography*; 1991]

si·mo·ni·ac /sī mónee àk, si-/ *n* somebody who buys and sells sacred Christian objects ■ *adj also* **si·mo·ni·a·cal** /sīmə nī ək'l, sìmmə-/ relating to the buying or selling of sacred Christian objects [14C. < French *simoniaque* < late Latin *simonia* (see SIMONY)]

Si·mon Le·gree /-lə grée/ *n US* a hard taskmaster who insists on discipline [After the brutal owner of enslaved people in Harriet Beecher Stowe's *Uncle Tom's Cabin* (1852)]

si·mon-pure *adj* completely genuine or authentic, often used to describe somebody who is an amateur as opposed to a professional [Late 18C. After *Simon Pure*, character in Susannah Centlivre's play *A Bold Stroke for a Wife* (1717)]

Si·mons /sīmənss/, **Menno** (1496–1591) Dutch religious reformer who believed in adult baptism and pacifism. The Protestant sect of Mennonites takes its name from him.

Si·mon's Town /símənz-/ town and naval base in Western Cape Province, South Africa, situated about 20 mi./32 km south of Cape Town. Population: 6,500 (1997).

si·mo·ny /símənee/ *n* the buying or selling of sacred Christian objects [13C. Via French < late Latin *simonia* < *Simon* Magus, Samaritan who tried to buy the power of conferring the Holy Spirit] —**si·mo·nist** *n*

si·moom /si móom/, **si·moon** /si móon/ *n* a hot dry wind that blows across northern Africa and the Arabian Peninsula, carrying dust and sand particles [Late 18C. < Arabic *samūm* < *samma* "poison"]

simp /simp/ *n* an offensive term that deliberately insults somebody's intelligence or common sense (*slang*) [Early 20C. Shortening of SIMPLETON]

sim·pa·ti·co /sim páatikō, -pátti-/ *adj* **1.** sharing similar temperaments or interests and, therefore, able to get along well together **2.** easy to like because pleasant and friendly [Mid-19C. < Spanish or Italian, "sympathetic" < Latin *sympathia* (see SYMPATHY)]

sim·per /símpər/ *v* (**-pered, -per·ing, -pers**) **1.** *vt* **SAY SOMETHING COYLY** to say something while smiling in an affected, coy, and usually irritating way **2.** *vi* **SMILE COYLY** to smile in an affected, coy, and usually irritating way ■ *n* **COY SMILE** an affected, coy, and usually irritating smile [Mid-16C. Origin ?] —**sim·per·er** *n* —**sim·per·ing** *adj, n* —**sim·per·ing·ly** *adv*

sim·ple /símp'l/ *adj* (**-pler, -plest**) **1. EASY** able to be done or understood quickly, or with very little effort ○ *a simple task* **2. NOT ELABORATE** lacking decoration or embellishment and therefore plain in appearance ○ *a simple black dress* **3. NOT COMPLEX** made up of or having only one part or element ○ *a simple organism* **4. WITHOUT COMPLICATIONS** having no complications, luxuries, or embellishments ○ *the simple life* **5. STRAIGHTFORWARD** ordinary or straightforward ○ *It's a simple case of the flu and I should be back to work in a couple of days.* **6. OFFENSIVE TERM** an offensive term meaning having an intellectual capacity that does not permit the performance of higher-level cognitive processes **7. NAIVE** naive and lacking in depth and detail **8. HUMBLE** humble and unsophisticated ○ *simple folk* **9. GUILELESS** direct, sincere, or lacking any form of deceitfulness **10.** CHEM **CONTAINING ONE COMPOUND ONLY** consisting of a single chemical compound **11.** BIOL **NOT DIVIDED** not divided, either totally or partially, into separate segments ○ *a simple leaf* ■ *n* **HERBAL MEDICINE** an herbal medicine, or an herb that yields medicine (*archaic*) [Pre-12C. Via French < Latin *simplus*] —**sim·ple·ness** *n*

USAGE See ***simplistic***.

SYNONYMS See ***easy***.

sim·ple closed curve *n* a plane curve that is closed and does not intersect itself, e.g., a circle or ellipse

sim·ple e·qua·tion *n* MATH same as **linear equation**

sim·ple frac·tion *n* a fraction that consists of two whole numbers separated by a horizontal or slanting line, as opposed to a decimal fraction

sim·ple frac·ture *n* e. Same as **closed fracture**

sim·ple fruit *n* a fruit that forms from a single pistil, e.g., a pea pod or a tomato

sim·ple har·mon·ic mo·tion *n UK* PHYS same as **harmonic motion**

sim·ple-heart·ed *adj* honest, open, and lacking deceit or deviousness

sim·ple in·ter·est *n* interest on an investment that is calculated once per period, usually annually, on the amount of the capital alone and not on any interest already earned

sim·ple ma·chine *n* each of the six devices formerly considered to be the basic components from which all machines were composed. They were the inclined plane, lever, pulley, screw, wedge, and wheel and axle.

sim·ple-mind·ed *adj* **1. LACKING DUE THOUGHT** showing a lack of intelligent thinking or proper consideration **2. OFFENSIVE TERM** an offensive term meaning regarded as having limited intellectual ability **3. UNSOPHISTICATED** lacking guile or complexity —**sim·ple-mind·ed·ly** *adv* —**sim·ple-mind·ed·ness** *n*

sim·ple pro·tein *n* a protein such as globulin that yields only amino acids on complete hydrolysis

sim·ple sen·tence *n* a sentence that takes the form of a single main clause with no relative or subordinate clauses, e.g., "I read the book"

Sim·ple Si·mon *n* an offensive term for somebody, especially a man or boy, who is perceived as lacking intelligence or sophistication (*insult*) [After a character in a nursery rhyme]

sim·ple sug·ar *n* CHEM same as **monosaccharide**

sim·ple tense *n* a grammatical form of a verb that expresses a relationship of time without using any auxiliary or modal verbs. In English, there are only two simple tenses, the simple present, as in "I walk," and the simple past, as in "I walked."

sim·ple time *n* a musical tempo in which the main beats are divisible by two, e.g., 2/2 or 4/4 time

sim·ple·ton /símp'ltən/ *n* an offensive term for somebody regarded as lacking intelligence or common sense (*insult*)

sim·plex /sím plèks/ *adj* **1. SIMPLE** containing, using, or designed for a single element or component **2.** TELECOM **ALLOWING TRANSMISSION IN ONE DIRECTION** allowing transmission of signals or communication in only one direction at a time ■ *n* **1.** *US* **APARTMENT ON ONE FLOOR** an apartment with all rooms on one floor **2.** LING **ROOT FORM OF WORD** a word in its base form, without any inflections, prefixes, or suffixes, and not formed by putting two distinct words together. The words "book" and "mark" are simplexes, whereas "bookmark," "books," "marked," and "remark" are not. **3.** MATH **GEOMETRIC FIGURE OR ELEMENT** a geometric element in a Euclidean space that exhibits the minimum number of dimensions of the space, e.g., a line in one-dimensional space or a triangle in two-dimensional space [Late 16C. < Latin (see SIMPLICITY)]

~~simpley~~ incorrect spelling of **simply**

sim·plic·i·ty /sim plíssətee/ (*plural* **-ties**) *n* **1.** a lack of complexity, complication, embellishment, or difficulty **2.** a simple quality or thing [14C. Via French < Latin *simplicitas* < *simplic-*, stem of *simplex* < *simplus* "simple"]

sim·pli·fy /símplə fī/ (**-fied, -fy·ing, -fies**) *vt* **1.** to make something less complicated or easier to understand **2.** to convert a mathematical expression such as a fraction or equation to a simpler form by removing common factors or regrouping elements [Mid-17C. Via French *simplifier* < medieval Latin *simplificare* < Latin *simplus* "simple"] —**sim·pli·fi·ca·tion** /sìmpləfi káysh'n/ *n* —**sim·pli·fic·a·tive** /símpləfi kàytiv/ *adj* —**sim·pli·fi·er** *n*

sim·plism /sím plìzzəm/ *n* a tendency to avoid or ignore the complexities of something —**sim·plist** *n*

sim·plis·tic /sim plístik/ *adj* **1.** tending to oversimplify, especially by avoiding or ignoring complexities **2.** ⚠ characterized by simplicity —**sim·plis·ti·cal·ly** *adv*

USAGE simple or **simplistic**? ***Simplistic*** is normally a derogatory word, implying that something is oversimplified rather than naturally simple: *He argued that it was simplistic to reject these methods as unscientific.* It should not be used as an alternative or supposedly stronger word for ***simple***: *A simple* [not *simplistic*] *approach would be helpful here.*

Sim·plon Pass /sìm plon-/ mountain pass in the Swiss Alps, between Brig in Switzerland, and Iselle in northern Italy. Height: 6,590 ft./2,009 m.

sim·ply /símplee/ *adv* **1. NOTHING OTHER THAN** with nothing else involved ○ *It was simply a misunderstanding.* **2. PLAINLY** in an uncomplicated, straightforward, or plain way ○ *To put it simply, I can't afford it.* **3. ABSOLUTELY** absolutely or utterly ○ *simply astonishing*

○ *This kind of behavior simply won't be tolerated.* **4.** FRANKLY frankly and without embellishment ○ *It was, quite simply, the best they had in stock.* **5.** NAIVELY without full understanding

Simp·son /símps'n/, **Sir George** (1787?–1860) British-born Canadian administrator and explorer. He was the governor of the Hudson's Bay Company from 1821 to 1856. In 1841–42 he traveled overland around the world. Known as **Little Emperor**

Simp·son, Sir James Young (1811–70) British obstetrician and the founder of gynecology. He pioneered the use of ether in childbirth, later replacing it with chloroform (1847).

Simp·son, O. J. (*b.* 1947) US football player, sportscaster, and actor. He was one of the National Football League's greatest running backs in a ten-year career, mostly with the Buffalo Bills. He was acquitted of murdering his wife after a controversial criminal trial (1995), but deemed guilty in a civil trial (1997). Full name **Simpson, Orenthal James**

Simp·son Des·ert desert in central Australia, at the junction of the South Australia, Northern Territory, and Queensland borders. Area: 40,000 sq. mi./100,000 sq. km.

sim·u·la·crum /sìmmyə láykrəm, -lákrəm/ (*plural* **-cra** /-krə/) *n* **1.** a representation or image of something **2.** something that has a vague, tentative, or shadowy resemblance to something else [Late 16C. < Latin < *simulare* (see SIMULATE)]

sim·u·lant /símmyələnt/ *adj* serving to imitate or reproduce the essential features of something (*formal*) ■ *n* ENG same as **simulator** (sense 1) [Mid-18C. < Latin *simulant-*, present participle of *simulare* (see SIMULATE)]

sim·u·late /símmyə làyt/ (**-lat·ed, -lat·ing, -lates**) *vt* **1.** REPRODUCE FEATURES OF SOMETHING to reproduce the essential features of something, e.g., as an aid to study or training ○ *a computer model simulating the process of continental drift* **2.** FAKE SOMETHING to feign or pretend to experience something ○ *simulating enjoyment* **3.** MIMIC SOMEBODY OR SOMETHING to mimic or imitate somebody or something [15C. < Latin *simulat-*, past participle of *simulare* < *similis* "like, similar"] —**sim·u·la·tive** *adj* —**sim·u·la·tive·ly** *adv*

sim·u·lat·ed /símmyə làytəd/ *adj* **1.** REPRODUCED BY SIMULATION reproduced or realized by simulation, especially computer simulation **2.** NOT GENUINE artificial, especially made in imitation of a genuine article, fabric, or other substance **3.** FALSE feigned or faked

sim·u·la·tion /sìmmyə láysh'n/ *n* **1.** REPRODUCTION OF FEATURES OF SOMETHING the reproduction of the essential features of something, e.g., as an aid to study or training **2.** FALSE APPEARANCE the imitation or feigning of something **3.** FAKE an artificial or imitation object **4.** COMPUT CONSTRUCTION OF MATHEMATICAL MODEL the construction of a mathematical model to reproduce the characteristics of a phenomenon, system, or process, often using a computer, in order to infer information or solve problems **5.** COMPUT GAMES COMPUTER GAME a computer game that simulates a real activity such as flying

sim·u·la·tor /símmyə làytər/ *n* **1.** DEVICE THAT SIMULATES SOMETHING a device, instrument, or piece of equipment designed to reproduce the essential features of something, e.g., as an aid to study or training **2.** COMPUT COMPUTER PROGRAM SIMULATING REAL WORLD a computer program that simulates something else such as a board game, a vehicle, or a complex system like a city or railway system **3.** SOMEBODY WHO SIMULATES SOMETHING somebody who feigns or imitates something —**sim·u·la·to·ry** *adj*

si·mul·cast /sím'l kàst, símm'l-/ *n* **1.** SIMULTANEOUS TV AND RADIO BROADCAST a program that is broadcast simultaneously on both television and radio, on multiple channels, or in multiple languages **2.** LIVE BROADCAST a live broadcast of an event on closed-circuit television ■ *vt* (**-cast, -cast·ing, -casts**) MAKE SIMULTANEOUS BROADCAST to broadcast a program as a simulcast [Mid-20C. Blend of SIMULTANEOUS + BROADCAST]

si·mul·ta·ne·ous /sìm'l táynee əss, sìmm'l-/ *adj* **1.** done, happening, or existing at the same time **2.** describes equations that are satisfied by the same values of the variables [Mid-17C. < medieval Latin *simultaneus* < Latin *simul* "at the same time," probably after late Latin *momentaneus* "momentary"] —**si·mul·ta·ne·i·ty** /sìm'ltə née ətee, sìmm'l-/ *n* —**si·mul·ta·ne·ous·ly** *adv* —**si·mul·ta·ne·ous·ness** *n*

~~simultanious~~ incorrect spelling of **simultaneous**

sim·va·stat·in /sìmvə státtin/ *n* a drug that lowers lipid levels in the blood. Use: treatment of high cholesterol. [Late 20C. < *sim-*, perhaps alteration of SYN- + *vastatin*, INN stem]

sin[1] /sin/ *n* **1.** TRANSGRESSION OF THEOLOGICAL PRINCIPLES an act, thought, or way of behaving that goes against the law or teachings of a religion, especially when the person who commits it is aware of this **2.** SHAMEFUL OFFENSE something that offends a moral or ethical principle **3.** ESTRANGEMENT FROM GOD in Christian theology, the condition of being denied God's grace because of a sin or sins committed ■ *vi* (**sinned, sin·ning, sins**) **1.** KNOWINGLY DO WRONG to commit a sin, especially by knowingly violating the law or teachings of a religion **2.** COMMIT SHAMEFUL OFFENSE to commit a serious moral or ethical offense [Old English *synn* < Indo-European] —**sin·less** *adj* —**sin·less·ly** *adv* —**sin·less·ness** *n* ◇ **live in sin** to live together as husband and wife without being married (*dated or humorous*)

sin[2] /seen, sin/ *n* the 21st letter of the Hebrew alphabet, represented in the English alphabet as "s." See table at **alphabet** [< Hebrew *śīn*, after *šīn* "shin (the 22nd letter)"]

sin[3] /sīn/ *abbr* MATH sine

Si·nai /sī nī/ peninsula of northeastern Egypt bounded on the east by the Gulf of Aqaba, on the north by the Mediterranean Sea, and on the west by the Gulf of Suez. A sparsely populated wilderness, it has long been the land bridge between Africa and Asia. Area: 23,500 sq. mi./60,900 sq. km.

Si·nai, Mount mountain in northeastern Egypt on the south central Sinai Peninsula, about 7,500 ft./2,888 m high. According to the Bible, it is the place where Moses received the Ten Commandments (Exodus 19).

si·na·may /sènə mī, sínnə mī/ *n* a stiff open-weave fabric spun from the fibers of the banana plant. Use: hats. [Mid-20C. < Tagalog]

Sin·an·thro·pus /sin ánthrəpəss/ *n* the original scientific name for Peking man [Early 20C. < modern Latin < late Latin *Sinae* "the Chinese" + Greek *anthrōpos* "person"]

Frank Sinatra

Si·na·tra /si naátrə/, **Frank** (1915–98) US singer and actor. He won an Academy Award for *From Here to Eternity* (1953), and is generally recognized as the supreme master of the popular song. Full name **Sinatra, Francis Albert**

sin bin *n* same as **penalty box** (sense 1) (*slang*)

since /sinss/ CORE MEANING: a grammatical word used to indicate that a situation has continued from a particular time or event in the past ○ (prep) *Karen has lived in London since 1988.* ○ (adv) *She left the firm in 1980 and has since been self-employed.* ○ (conj) *He has been on a high since he got married in January.*

1. *prep, conj* HAPPENING AFTER happening at some point or points after the period of time or event mentioned ○ *The rate of job growth is higher than any administration since 1920.* ○ *Since Ryland became commissioner in 1994, all complaints are investigated fully.* **2.** *adv* SUBSEQUENTLY at some point between then and now ○ *The department had an engineer, who has since retired.* **3.** *conj* BECAUSE because, seeing that ○ *Since it was still light, they were allowed to play in the park.* [15C. Contraction of obsolete *sithence* "then, afterward" < Old English *siððan* (< Germanic) + *-s* forming adverbs]

USAGE See *ago* and *because*.

---

sin·cere /sin sèer/ (**-cer·er, -cer·est**) *adj* **1.** honest and unaffected in a way that shows what is said is really meant **2.** based on what is truly and deeply felt [Mid-16C. < Latin *sincerus* "pure, whole"] —**sin·cere·ness** *n*

sin·cere·ly /sin sèerlee/ *adv* in an honest and unaffected way ○ *He sincerely told her everything that was in his heart.* ◇ **yours sincerely** used immediately before the signature to end a letter that is addressed to somebody by name ○ *Yours sincerely, John Smith*

sin·cer·i·ty /sin sérrətee/ *n* honesty in the expression of true or deep feelings

~~sincerly~~ incorrect spelling of **sincerely**

sin·ci·put /sínssəpət/ (*plural* **-ci·puts** or **-cip·i·ta** /sin síppətə/) *n* the part of the skull that includes the forehead and the area above it [Late 16C. < Latin, "half head"] —**sin·cip·i·tal** /sin síppət'l/ *adj*

Sin·clair /sin klér, sing-/, **Upton** (1878–1968) US writer and reformer. His social and political novels include *The Jungle* (1906). He ran unsuccessfully for several public offices including governor of California (1934). Full name **Sinclair, Upton Beall**

Sind /sind/ region of southeastern Pakistan in the lower Indus valley. A province of British India from 1843, it became part of Pakistan after partition in 1947. Capital: Karachi. Population: 29,991,000 (1998). Area: 54,407 sq. mi./140,914 sq. km.

Sind·bis vi·rus /síndbiss-/ *n* a virus found in Africa, Asia, Australia, and Europe that can be transmitted by mosquitoes from mammals and birds to human beings, causing rash, joint pain, and headache [Mid-20C. After a village in Egypt]

Sin·dhi /síndee/ (*plural same* or **-dhis**) *n* **1.** somebody who comes from Sind **2.** the Indic language of the people of Sind. Native speakers: 14 million. [Early 19C. < Persian, Urdu *sindī* < *Sind* "the Indus River" < Sanskrit *sindhu*] —**Sin·dhi** *adj*

sine /sīn/ *n* **1.** for a given angle in a right triangle, a trigonometric function equal to the length of the side opposite the angle divided by the hypotenuse **2.** a mathematical function equal to the vertical coordinate of a circumference point divided by the radius of a circle with its center at the origin of a Cartesian coordinate system [Late 16C. < Latin *sinus* "curve, fold"]

SPELLCHECK See *sign*.

---

si·ne·cure /sīnə kyoor/ *n* **1.** a job or position that provides a regular income, but requires little or no work **2.** a church office whose holder is paid, but is not required to do pastoral work [Mid-17C. < medieval Latin *beneficium sine cura* "benefice without care (of souls)"]

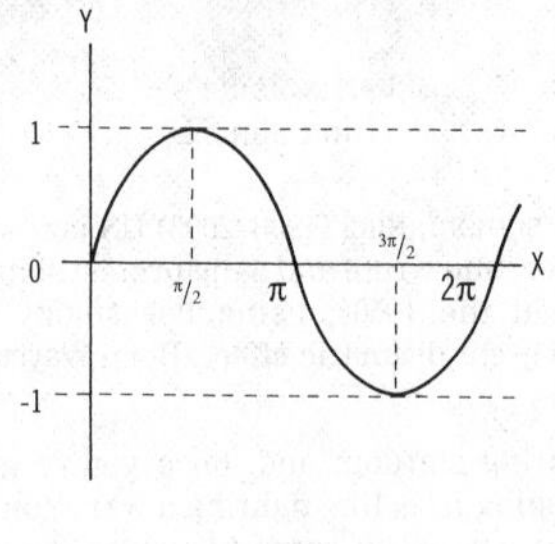

sine curve

sine curve *n* a graph of the sine equation "y = a sin bx," with "a" and "b" being constants

si·ne di·e /sīni dī ee, sìn ay dée ay/ *adv* without a day being fixed for a further meeting ○ *The committee was adjourned sine die.* [< Latin, "without a day"]

si·ne pro·le /sīni prō lee, sìn ay prō lay/ *adv* without offspring ○ *She died in 1985, aged 59, sine prole.* [< Latin, "without offspring"]

si·ne qua non /sìnni kwaa nón, -nōn, sīni-, sīnee kway nón/ *n* an essential condition or prerequisite ○ *The*

WORLD ENGLISH ***Singapore English*** is the variety of English used in the city-state of Singapore, where it has been co-official since 1965 with Mandarin Chinese, Malay, and Tamil, having already been a regional lingua franca since the early 19th century. As the key language of government, business, and education, it has uniquely acquired a large fully native-speaking community of non-Western origin. There are two varieties: educated, more formal usage, and a patois influenced by Chinese and Malay. Singapore English does not pronounce *r* in words such as *art, door,* and *worker.* It tends to have full vowels in all syllables (e.g., *seven* is pronounced "seh-ven" not "sev'n"). Words ending in *k, p,* and *t,* e.g., *kick, stop,* and *put,* are generally pronounced with "glottal stops." Those words ending in clusters such as *-st* and *-ld* are reduced to the vowel and the first of the last two consonants e.g., "fas" for *fast,* "sol" for *sold.* Colloquial usage diverges considerably from the standard, as in: *You come or not?* for *Are you coming?*; *My dad, he come from Penang* for *My dad comes from Penang*; *This hotel cheap* for *This hotel is cheap.*

suspension of industrial activity is considered a sine qua non for talks to proceed. [< Latin, "without which (cause) not"]

sin·ew /sínnyoo/ *n* **1.** ANAT same as **tendon 2. STRENGTH** strength, power, or resilience (*literary*) **3. SOURCE OF POWER** a source of strength or power (*literary; often used in the plural*) ■ *vt* (**-ewed, -ew·ing, -ews**) **STRENGTHEN SOMEBODY OR SOMETHING** to give added strength to somebody or something [Old English *sin(e)we* < Germanic] —**sin·ew·less** *adj*

sine wave *n* a waveform with the shape of a sine curve, representing a single frequency indefinitely repeated in time

sin·ew·y /sínnyoo ee/ *adj* **1. THIN AND STRONG** lean, tough, and muscular ○ *a sinewy 20-year-old* **2. CONTAINING OR RESEMBLING TENDONS** consisting of or containing tendons or stringy parts resembling tendons ○ *a rather sinewy steak* **3. FORCEFUL** vigorous and forceful (*literary*) ○ *rich, sinewy prose* —**sin·ew·i·ness** *n*

sin·fo·ni·a /sin fōnee ə/ (*plural* **-ni·as** *or* **-ni·e** /-nee ày/) *n* **1.** a piece of orchestral music used as an overture or interlude in an opera **2.** a complex instrumental composition, usually for a group of stringed instruments or an orchestra [Late 18C. Via Italian < Latin *symphonia* "sound of instruments, harmony" (see SYMPHONY)]

sin·fo·ni·et·ta /sìnfən yéttə, sìnfōn-/ *n* **1.** an orchestral piece that resembles a symphony but is shorter or written for fewer instruments, often for strings only **2.** a small symphony orchestra, often composed of stringed instruments only [Early 20C. < Italian, "little sinfonia" < *sinfonia* (see SINFONIA)]

sin·ful /sínf'l/ *adj* **1.** engaging in or characterized by behavior that goes against the law or teachings of a religion **2.** morally or ethically wrong ○ *a sinful waste of an expensive education* —**sin·ful·ly** *adv* —**sin·ful·ness** *n*

sing /sing/ *v* (**sang** /sang/, **sung** /sung/, **sing·ing, sings**) **1.** *vti* **MAKE MUSIC WITH VOICE** to use the voice to produce words or sounds in a musical way ○ *Sing me that song again.* ○ *Paul was sitting in a chair singing to himself.* **2.** *vti* **PERFORM SONGS PROFESSIONALLY** to perform songs as a trained or professional singer **3.** *vti* **MAKE TUNEFUL ANIMAL SOUND** to make the melodious sound that is characteristic of an animal species ○ *I could hear a nightingale singing in the distance.* **4.** *vi* **MAKE CONTINUOUS MUSICAL SOUND** to make a continuous whistling, humming, or ringing sound ○ *A strong wind was making the wires sing.* **5.** *vi* **MAKE BRIEF SPEEDING SOUND** to make a brief whistling or whizzing sound **6.** *vi* **EXPERIENCE RINGING OR HUMMING IN HEAD** to experience a continuous ringing or humming sound in the head **7.** *vt* **INTONE SOMETHING** to chant something, especially a religious text, on a single note or a small range of notes **8.** *vt* **AFFECT SOMEBODY BY SINGING** to bring somebody to a particular condition by singing ○ *sing the baby to sleep* **9.** *vti* **TELL ABOUT SOMETHING** to praise somebody or proclaim something, especially in verse **10.** *vi* **BE HAPPY** to rejoice or be extremely happy ○ *Her heart was singing.* **11.** *vi* **CONFESS** to confess to or implicate others in a crime (*slang*) ■ *n* **SINGING SESSION** a session of singing, especially by a group gathered for this purpose (*informal*) [Old English *singan* < Indo-European] —**sing·a·bil·i·ty** /sìngə bíllətee/ *n* —**sing·a·ble** *adj* —**sing·ing·ly** *adv*

sing along *vi* to join in a song that somebody else is singing

sing out *vi* to call out in a loud voice, especially to warn somebody (*informal*)

sing. *abbr* GRAM singular

sing-a-long *n* a meeting of a group of people to sing songs together for fun, or an impromptu session of singing

Singapore

Sin·ga·pore /síng gə pàwr, síngə-/ city-state in Southeast Asia, comprising one major island and several islets, situated south of Malaysia. It became an independent member of the British Commonwealth in 1965. Language: Chinese, Malay, Singapore English, Tamil. Currency: Singapore dollar. Population: 4,608,595 (2003). Area: 250 sq. mi./648 sq. km. Official name **Republic of Singapore** —**Sin·ga·por·e·an** /sìng gə páwree ən, sìngə-/ *n, adj*

Sing·a·pore Eng·lish *n* a variety of English spoken in Singapore

singe /sinj/ *v* (**singed, singe·ing, sing·es**) **1.** *vti* **SCORCH SOMETHING SLIGHTLY** to burn something slightly so that only the surface, edge, or tip is affected, or be burned in this way **2.** *vt* **REMOVE FEATHERS OR HAIR WITH FLAME** to expose the carcass of a bird or animal to a flame in order to remove unwanted feathers, bristles, or hair **3.** *vt* **BURN ENDS OF CLOTH FIBERS** to burn the short fuzzy ends of fibers from cloth in the manufacturing process ■ *n* **SCORCH** a superficial burn [Old English *sencgan* < W Germanic]

sing·er /síngər/ *n* **1.** somebody who sings, especially professionally **2.** a bird that sings **3.** LITERAT same as **poet** (*literary*)

Sing·er /síngər/, **Isaac Bashevis** (1904–91) Polish-born US writer. His novels often concern Polish-Jewish subjects, and, like most of his works, were written first in Yiddish. He won the Nobel Prize in literature (1978).

> "It seems that the analysis of character is the highest human entertainment. And literature does it, unlike gossip, without mentioning real names."
> [Isaac Bashevis Singer, *Interview, New York Times Magazine*; November 26, 1978]

> "Originality is not seen in single words or even sentences. Originality is the sum total of a man's thinking on his writing."
> [Isaac Bashevis Singer, *Interview, New York Times Magazine*; December 3, 1978]

Sing·er, Isaac M. (1811–75) US inventor and entrepreneur. He patented a home sewing machine (1851) and founded the Singer Manufacturing Company. Full name **Singer, Isaac Merritt**

Singh /sing/ *n* a title adopted as a surname by a Sikh boy when he is initiated at puberty into the fraternity of warriors [Early 17C. Via Punjabi *siṅgh* "lion" < Sanskrit *siṃha*]

Singh /sing/, **Manmohan** (*b.* 1932) economist and prime minister of India (2004–). As finance minister for the Congress Party (1991–96) he instituted wide-ranging economic reforms. He is the first non-Hindu prime minister of India.

Singh. *abbr* Singhalese

Sin·gha·lese *n, adj* PEOPLES, LANG same as **Sinhalese**

sing·ing /sínging/ *n* **1. USE OF VOICE TO PRODUCE SONGS** the technique of producing musical sounds with the voice, or the performance of songs **2. MELODIC SOUNDS** the melodic or other sounds made by somebody or something that sings ■ *adj* **MAKING MUSICAL SOUND** performing songs or making a melodic, whistling, humming, or ringing sound

sing·ing tel·e·gram *n* a message sung by a messenger paid to do so, or the service of providing sung messages

sin·gle /síng g'l/ *adj* **1. ONE** only or even one ○ *in the space of a single day* ○ *didn't get a single reply* **2. CONSIDERED INDIVIDUALLY** considered separately as something distinct or unique ○ *Every single piece must be accurately measured.* **3. WITHOUT PARTNER** unmarried or unattached or characteristic of this state ○ *decided to give up the single life and get married* **4. FOR ONE PERSON** suitable or designed for one person ○ *a single bed* **5. CONSISTING OF ONE THING** consisting of one part, element, or quality ○ *single malt whiskey* **6. BETWEEN ONLY TWO PEOPLE** taking place as a contest or competition between two persons only, one to each side ○ *single combat* **7. FORMING ONE UNDIVIDED UNIT** forming a whole and left undivided or unbroken ○ *carved the sculpture from a single block of ice* **8. UNIFORM** sole and the same for all ○ *a single tax rate* **9.** BOT **WITH ONE PETAL ROW** describes a flower that has only one whorl or row of petals ■ *n* **1. ACCOMMODATION FOR ONE** a room, cabin, or bed for one person **2. RECORDING OF ONE SONG** a recording of one individual song released for sale on its own, or of one featured song together with another less publicized one **3. BASEBALL HIT** a hit in baseball that allows the batter to reach first base **4.** *US* **ONE DOLLAR** a one-dollar bill **5. TWO-PLAYER GOLF MATCH** a match between two golfers **6.** *UK* **OUTWARD-BOUND TICKET** a ticket that covers the outward-bound part of a journey to a destination but not the return ■ *vti* (**-gled, -gling, -gles**) **HIT BASEBALL SINGLE** in baseball, to hit a single, or advance a runner by hitting a single ◊ **singles** [13C. Via French < Latin *singulus* < *simplus* "simple"] —**sin·gle·ness** *n*

single out *vt* to select an individual from a group for special attention

sin·gle-ac·tion *adj* requiring the hammer of a firearm to be cocked by hand before each shot can be fired ■ *n* a firearm that cannot be fired until the hammer is cocked by hand

sin·gle-blind *adj* describes an experiment or clinical trial in which the subjects are not told whether the tested substance or procedure they receive is active, in order to avoid subjective bias in the results

sin·gle bond *n* a covalent bond between two atoms formed through the sharing of a pair of electrons

sin·gle-breast·ed *adj* with a small overlap at the front and fastened with a single row of buttons

sin·gle-cell pro·tein *n* a protein derived from one-celled organisms grown in various cultures

sin·gle cross *n* the first generation of offspring resulting from hybridization between two inbred lines

sin·gle-cut file *n* a metal file that has all its teeth pointing in one direction

sin·gle en·try *n* a system of bookkeeping in which the amounts owed and due are kept in a single account (*hyphenated before a noun*)

sin·gle-fam·i·ly *adj* designed or suitable for one family ○ *single-family homes*

sin·gle file *n* a line of people, animals, or vehicles standing or moving one behind another ■ *adv* moving in a line, one behind another

sin·gle-foot RIDING *n* same as **rack**[4] ■ *vti* same as **rack**[4] *v*

sin·gle-hand·ed *adj* **1. UNAIDED** accomplished alone and unaided ○ *the first single-handed circumnavigation of the world* **2. WITH ONE HAND ONLY** made with only one hand or the use of one hand ○ *a single-handed shot* **3. FOR ONE HAND ONLY** using or requiring only one hand ■ *adv* **WITHOUT HELP** without any help from anyone ○ *sailed around the world single-handed* —**sin·gle-hand·ed·ly** *adv*

sin·gle-heart·ed *adj* sincere, faithful, and straightforward [< SINGLE in the obsolete sense "honest"] —**sin·gle-heart·ed·ly** *adv*

sin·gle-is·sue *adj* concerned with only a single public issue ○ *single-issue environmental groups*

sin·gle knot *n* same as **overhand knot**

sin·gle-lens re·flex *n* a camera in which the light passes through one lens to the film and, by means of a mirror and prism system, to the focusing screen

sin·gle-mind·ed *adj* concentrated on attaining only one goal or accomplishing only one task ○ *their single-minded attention to quality* —**sin·gle-mind·ed·ly** *adv* —**sin·gle-mind·ed·ness** *n*

sin·gle nu·cle·o·tide pol·y·mor·phism *n* a commonly found change in a single nucleotide base in a DNA sequence, occurring about every 1,000 bases. It is of significance in biomedical research.

sin·gle par·ent *n* a parent who brings up a child or children alone, usually because he or she is unmarried, widowed, or divorced (*hyphenated before a noun*) —**sin·gle-par·ent·ing** *n*

sin·gle-phase *adj* with, generating, or powered by a single alternating voltage

sin·gle pho·ton e·mis·sion com·put·ed to·mog·ra·phy *n* a technique used in diagnosing some diseases that generates a three-dimensional computer image of the distribution of a radioactive tracer in an organ

sin·gle-player *adj* describes computer games that are played alone —**sin·gle-play·er** *n*

sin·gles /síng g'lz/ *n* (*plural same*) a game of tennis or badminton between two people ○ *played singles* ■ *npl* unmarried or unattached people considered as a group

sin·gles bar *n* a bar frequented by men and women, usually unmarried or unattached, who are seeking romance, companionship, or sex

sin·gle-serve *adj* packaged in small amounts intended for one person ○ *available in single-serve sizes*

sin·gle-sex *adj* restricted to either men or to women

sin·gle-shot *adj* describes a firearm that needs to be reloaded after each shot is fired

sin·gle-space *vt* to type or print text without a blank space between the lines

sin·gle·stick /síng g'l stìk/ *n* **1.** a stick fitted with a hand guard, formerly used in fencing **2.** the former sport or skill of fencing with a singlestick

sin·gle sup·ple·ment *n* an additional charge made to somebody on a package tour who is not sharing a hotel room

sin·glet /síng glət/ *n* **1.** a sleeveless shirt worn with shorts in sports such as basketball or amateur boxing **2.** *UK* a sleeveless undershirt [Mid-18C. < SINGLE after DOUBLET, because originally an unlined one-layered garment]

sin·gle tax *n* **1.** a taxation system in which all revenue is raised from a tax on one thing, usually the value of land **2.** a tax applied to one thing only, especially the value of land

sin·gle·ton /síng g'ltən/ *n* **1.** somebody or something that occurs singly and not as part of a group, e.g., the only child in a family **2.** a playing card that is the only one of its suit in a hand

sin·gle-tongue *vti* to articulate notes on a wind instrument by raising the tip of the tongue against the palate, temporarily obstructing the flow of air

sin·gle-track *adj* **1.** fixed on one thought or idea only **2.** with only one track and passing places for trains coming from opposite directions

sin·gle·tree /síng g'l trèe/ *n US* AGRIC same as **whiffletree** [Mid-19C. Alteration of SWINGLETREE, after DOUBLETREE]

Sing·lish /síng glish/ *n* the variety of English spoken by many people in Singapore, showing the influence of Malay and Chinese (*informal*) [Mid-20C. Blend of SINGAPORE + ENGLISH] —**Sing·lish** *adj*

sin·gly /síng glee/ *adv* **1.** INDIVIDUALLY IN SEQUENCE one at a time or one by one **2.** WITHOUT HELP alone and by unaided efforts **3.** SEPARATELY solely and separately

sing·song /síng sàwng/ *adj* WITH REPEATEDLY RISING AND FALLING INTONATION having an intonation that regularly rises and falls in pitch ■ *n* **1.** RISING AND FALLING INTONATION a way of speaking in which the voice rises and falls regularly in pitch **2.** SINGSONG VERSE RHYTHMS OR RHYMES a verse marked by a singsong rhythm or rhyme **3.** *UK* same as **sing-along**

sing·spiel /síng spèel, zíng-/, **Sing·spiel** *n* an 18th-century German comic opera in which folk songs, or arias written mainly in a simple popular style, are interspersed with spoken dialogue [Late 19C. < German, "singing play"]

sin·gu·lar /síng gyələr/ *adj* **1.** EXCEPTIONAL especially great or remarkable ○ *He had the singular misfortune of encountering a man-eating tiger on a day when he had left his gun at home.* **2.** UNUSUAL unusual, odd, or striking **3.** SOLE being only one, or the only one of a kind ○ *He had hitherto thought of himself as singular, as Rachael's only son.* **4.** GRAM NOT PLURAL referring to one person or thing **5.** LOGIC STANDING FOR INDIVIDUAL THING used to describe a term intended to stand for an individual thing, or a proposition containing such a term ■ *n* **1.** SINGULAR FORM OF WORD the form of a word that is used when referring to one person or thing **2.** LOGIC THING IN ISOLATION something considered solely by itself [14C. Via French < Latin *singularis* "alone of its kind" < *singulus* (see SINGLE)] —**sin·gu·lar·ly** *adv*

sin·gu·lar·i·ty /sìng gyə lárrətee/ (*plural* **-ties**) *n* **1.** SINGULAR QUALITY a singular, exceptional, or unusual quality **2.** SOMETHING UNIQUE OR UNUSUAL something that is unique, distinctive, or remarkable **3.** CHARACTERISTIC a distinguishing trait **4.** ASTRON HYPOTHETICAL POINT IN SPACE a hypothetical region in space in which gravitational forces cause matter to be infinitely compressed and space and time to become infinitely distorted **5.** MATH FUNCTION THAT IS NOT DIFFERENTIABLE in mathematics, a point at which a complex function is undefined because it is neither differentiable nor single-valued while the function is defined in every neighborhood of the point [13C. Via French < late Latin *singularitas* < Latin *singularis* (see SINGULAR)]

sin·gu·lar·ize /síng gyələ rīz/ (**-ized, -iz·ing, -iz·es**) *v* **1.** *vti* to make a word singular, or become singular **2.** *vt* to distinguish somebody or something or make somebody or something stand out from the rest (*formal*) —**sin·gu·lar·i·za·tion** /sìng gyələri záysh'n/ *n*

sin·gu·lar point *n* MATH same as **singularity** (sense 5)

Sin·ha·la /sin haalə/ *n* LANG same as **Sinhalese** (sense 2) [Early 20C. < Sanskrit *Siṁhala* (see SINHALESE)] —**Sin·ha·la** *adj*

Sin·ha·lese /sìnhə léez/ (*plural same*), **Sin·gha·lese** /sìng gə-, sìngə-/ *n* **1.** a member of a people who live mainly in Sri Lanka **2.** the Indic language of the Sinhalese people. Native speakers: 13 million. [Late 18C. < Portuguese *Singhalez* < Sanskrit *Siṁhala*, variant of *Siṁhala* "Sri Lanka"] —**Sin·ha·lese** *adj*

Si·ni·cize /sínə sīz, sínnə-/ (**-cized, -ciz·ing, -ciz·es**) *vti* to acquire a Chinese idiom, form, or cultural trait, or give somebody or something a Chinese idiom, form, or cultural trait (*often passive*) [Late 16C. < obsolete *Sinic* "Chinese" < late Latin *Sinae* (see SINO-)]

sin·is·ter /sínnəstər/ *adj* **1.** threatening or suggesting malevolence, menace, or harm **2.** on the left side of a heraldic shield as seen by the holder ○ *a bend sinister* [15C. Via French < Latin, "left"; from the superstition that the left side is unlucky] —**sin·is·ter·ly** *adv*

sin·is·tral /sínnistrəl, si nístrəl/ *adj* **1.** relating to or located on the left side, especially the left side of the body (*archaic*) **2.** same as **left-handed** (*archaic*) **3.** MARINE BIOL describes gastropod shells coiling in a clockwise direction from the apex to the aperture —**sin·is·tral·ly** *adv*

sin·is·trorse /sínnə stràwrss/ *adj* describes plants growing upward in a clockwise spiral [Mid-19C. < Latin *sinistrorsus* < *sinister* "left"] —**sin·is·trorse·ly** *adv*

Si·nit·ic /si níttik, sī-/ *n* the branch of the Sino-Tibetan language group that includes the Chinese languages [Late 19C. < late Latin *Sinae* "the Chinese" (see SINO-)]

sink /singk/ *v* (**sank** /sangk/ or **sunk** /sungk/, **sunk, sink·ing, sinks**) **1.** *vti* GO BENEATH SURFACE OF LIQUID to descend, or cause something to descend, beneath the surface of a liquid or a soft substance and become partly or wholly submerged ○ *We think the ship was sunk by a freak wave.* **2.** *vi* FALL TO LOWER LEVEL to descend, or appear to descend, from a higher position or level to a lower one ○ *The water level has sunk because of drought.* ○ *The sun was sinking in the west.* **3.** *vi* SUBSIDE to become gradually more deeply embedded in something, e.g., the ground or mud ○ *This corner of the foundation is sinking.* **4.** *vi* BE ABSORBED to become absorbed in something ○ *Smear a little oil on the surface and leave it to sink in.* **5.** *vi* FALL GENTLY to fall or collapse slowly ○ *sank to his knees* **6.** *vi* LIE BACK ON SOMETHING to lower yourself gently or luxuriously ○ *She sank back into the cushions.* **7.** *vi* SUBSIDE to diminish in degree, volume, or strength ○ *The wind sank toward evening.* **8.** *vi* BECOME LESS AUDIBLE to become quieter or weaker in sound ○ *voice sank to a whisper* **9.** *vi* LOSE STANDING to pass to a less desirable condition, e.g., a lower social status ○ *sink into obscurity* **10.** *vi* PASS INTO SPECIFIC STATE to pass to a less active, quieter, or less healthy state ○ *sink into a coma* **11.** *vi* FEEL DISCOURAGEMENT to pass into a condition of hopelessness, dejection, or despair ○ *His heart sank.* **12.** *vi* DECLINE IN VALUE to decline in value or amount ○ *The dollar sank again yesterday.* **13.** *vi* BE DYING to be approaching death ○ *The old lady was sinking fast.* **14.** *vi* DISAPPEAR to be no longer in existence, come to an end, or disappear, often as a result of failure ○ *I don't know what happened to the project, it seems to have sunk without trace.* **15.** *vti* PENETRATE OR MAKE PENETRATE to penetrate something, or cause something to penetrate something ○ *sank its fangs into her leg* **16.** *vt* DRILL SOMETHING INTO GROUND to drill a well, tunnel, or shaft in the ground **17.** *vt* DRIVE SOMETHING INTO GROUND to force something into the ground ○ *sinking piles for a dock* **18.** *vt* INVEST IN SOMETHING to invest or lose money in a business or project ○ *He must have sunk millions into these theaters.* **19.** *vt* BRING SOMEBODY OR SOMETHING TO RUIN to defeat, undo, or ruin somebody or something ○ *If they won't accept our offer, we're sunk.* **20.** *vt* DEFEAT SOMEBODY IN CONTEST to defeat an opponent easily in a game or contest (*informal*) **21.** *vt* SHOOT OR HIT SOMETHING SUCCESSFULLY to take aim at something and make a successful shot or stroke (*informal*) ○ *sink a critical putt* **22.** *vt UK* DRINK SOMETHING to drink something, usually quickly (*informal*) ○ *sink a pint* ■ *n* **1.** BASIN FOR WASHING SOMETHING a basin that is fixed or mounted against a wall, and has a piped water supply and drainage **2.** CESSPOOL a cesspool, drain, or sewer **3.** BAD OR CORRUPT PLACE a place considered to be wicked and corrupt (*dated*) **4.** POORLY DRAINED LAND an area of low-lying, poorly drained land in which water collects, sometimes in the form of a salt lake, and evaporates or sinks into the ground **5.** GEOG same as **sinkhole** (sense 1) **6.** PHYS DEVICE ABSORBING ENERGY a device or component of a system in which a physical entity such as energy or neutrons is absorbed [Old English *sincan* < Germanic] —**sink·a·ble** *adj* ◇ **sink or swim** to have no alternative but to succeed or fail without help from anyone else

---

SPELLCHECK sink or **synch**? Do not confuse the spelling of ***sink*** and ***sync***, which sound similar. ***Sink*** is a common verb referring to movement to a lower or deeper level (*The ship sank beneath the waves. Her success hasn't sunk in yet.*). It is also a noun denoting a basin with piped water. ***Sync*** is an informal word relating to synchronization: *out of sync*.

USAGE sank, sunk, or **sunken**? The inflections of the verb ***sink*** have been variable over many centuries of use. In current usage, the preferred past tense is ***sank***, although ***sunk*** is also used and is not incorrect (*The submarine sank* [or *sunk*] *in 3,000 feet of water*). For the past participle, ***sunk*** is used (*Six enemy ships were sunk on a single day*); the old form ***sunken*** is now used only as an adjective: *a sunken garden*.

---

sink in *vi* **1.** to become absorbed **2.** to become fully understood ○ *I don't think the news of her death has sunk in yet.*

sink·age /síngkij/ *n* the process of sinking or the extent to which something sinks

sink·er /síngkər/ *n* **1.** a weight used to take a fishing line or net to the bottom **2.** in baseball, a pitched ball that curves sharply downward as it reaches the plate **3.** *US* FOOD same as **doughnut** (sense 1) (*informal*)

sink·hole /síngk hōl/ *n* **1.** a natural depression in the land surface, especially in limestone, where a stream flows underground into a passage or cave **2.** a sunken area where waste collects

sink·ing fund /síngking-/ *n* a fund created by setting aside regular sums for investment, usually in bonds, in order to repay a debt that will fall due at a future date

sin·ner /sínnər/ *n* somebody who commits a sin or who habitually does wrong

Sinn Féin /shìn fáyn/ *n* a nationalist Irish republican party founded in 1905 [Early 20C. < Irish *sinn féin* "we ourselves"] —**Sinn Féin·er** *n* —**Sinn Féin·ism** *n*

Sino- *prefix* China or Chinese ○ *Sino-American* [< late Latin *Sinae* "the Chinese" < Arabic *Sīn* "China"]

si·no·a·tri·al /sīnō áytree əl/ *adj* relating to the sinus venosus and the right atrium of the heart

si·no·a·tri·al node *n* a small mass of specialized cardiac muscle fibers in the wall of the right atrium of the heart which originates the regular electrical impulses that stimulate the heartbeat

Si·nol·o·gy /sī nólləjee/ *n* the study of Chinese civilization, literature, and language —**Si·no·log·i·cal** /sīnə lójjik'l, sìnnə-/ *adj* —**Si·nol·o·gist** *n*

Si·no·pe /si nōpee/ *n* a small natural satellite of Jupiter

Si·no-Ti·bet·an /sīnō tə bétt'n/ *n* a family of languages of East and Southeast Asia, including two main branches, Chinese (**Sinitic**) and Tibeto-Burman. Native speakers: 1,200 million. —**Si·no-Ti·bet·an** *adj*

sin·se·mil·la /sìnssə mée yə, -míllə/, **sen·se·mil·la** /sènssə-/ *n* a very strong form of marijuana obtained from unpollinated female hemp plants [Late 20C. < American Spanish, "seedless"]

sin tax *n* a tax on something such as tobacco, alcoholic beverages, or gambling that is considered to have harmful personal and social effects

sin·ter /síntər/ *vti* (**-tered, -ter·ing, -ters**) **BOND METAL PARTICLES** to use pressure and heat below the melting point to bond and partly fuse masses of metal particles, or be bonded in this way ■ *n* **1. BONDED METAL PARTICLES** a mass of metal particles bonded and partly fused by the use of pressure and heat below the melting point **2. POROUS MINERAL SEDIMENT** a whitish chemical sediment consisting of porous silica or calcium carbonate deposited by a mineral spring [Late 18C. < German, "cinder"]

Sin·tra /síntrə/ resort town in western Portugal. Population: 20,000 (1981).

Sin·tu /sín too/ *n* LANG same as **Bantu** (sense 1) [Mid-20C. < Bantu *(i)si-* "language, culture" + *-ntu* "person"] —**Sin·tu** *adj*

sin·u·ate *adj* /sínnyoo ət, -àyt/ *also* **sin·u·at·ed** /-àytəd/ describes a leaf with a wavy indented edge ■ *vi* /sínnyoo àyt/ (**-at·ed, -at·ing, -ates**) to wind in and out [Late 16C. < Latin *sinuat-*, past participle of *sinuare* "to bend, curve" < *sinus* "curve"] —**sin·u·ate·ly** *adv*

sin·u·os·i·ty /sìnnyoo óssətee/ (*plural* **-ties**) *n* **1.** the condition of being winding or curving in shape or movement **2.** a winding bend or curving movement

sin·u·ous /sínnyoo əss/ *adj* **1. SUPPLE AND GRACEFUL** lithe and graceful, especially making graceful winding or curving movements ○ *the dancer's sinuous gestures* **2. WINDING OR SERPENTINE** full of bends and curves ○ *the sinuous course of a stream* **3. DEVIOUS** indirect and devious **4.** BOT same as **sinuate** [Late 16C. < Latin *sinuosus* < *sinus* "curve"] —**sin·u·ous·ly** *adv* —**sin·u·ous·ness** *n*

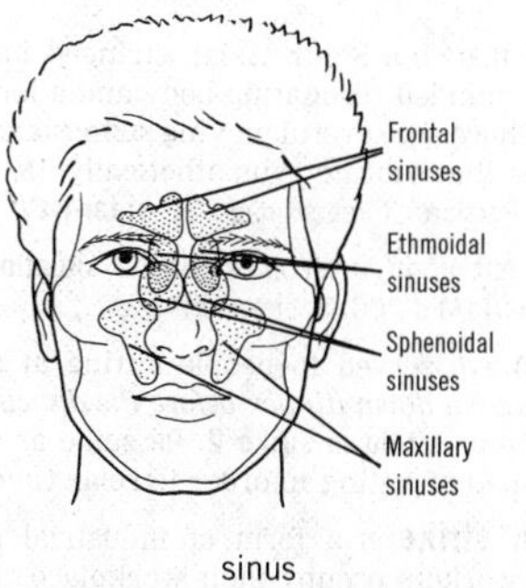

sinus

si·nus /sínəss/ *n* **1. CAVITY IN BONE OF SKULL** a cavity filled with air in the bones of the face and skull, especially one opening into the nasal passages **2. CHANNEL FOR BLOOD** a widened channel containing blood, especially venous blood **3. CHANNEL LEADING FROM BODY CAVITY** an elongated tract leading from a pus-filled region of the body to the exterior or to the cavity of a hollow organ **4. NOTCH BETWEEN LEAVES** a cleft or indentation between the lobes of a leaf or the fused petals of a corolla [15C < Latin, "curve, fold, hollow"]

Si·nus I·rid·um /sínəss írridəm/ *n* a large half-crater on the Moon adjoining the northwestern side of Mare Imbrium. Its walled perimeter forms the Montes Jura and it is approximately 160 mi./260 km in diameter.

si·nus·i·tis /sīnə sītiss/ *n* inflammation of the membrane lining a sinus of the skull

si·nus node *n* ANAT same as **sinoatrial node**

si·nu·soid /sīnə sòyd/ *n* **1.** a small blood vessel or cavity in the tissue of an organ such as the liver, heart, or pancreas **2.** MATH same as **sine curve** ■ *adj* resembling a sinus in shape or function —**si·nu·soi·dal** /sīnə sóyd'l/ *adj* —**si·nus·oi·dal·ly** *adv*

si·nu·soi·dal pro·jec·tion *n* a map projection on which equal areas appear equal, the parallels of latitude are regularly spaced straight lines, and all the lines of longitude except the prime meridian are curved

si·nus ve·no·sus /-və nōssəss/ (*plural* **si·nus ve·no·si** /-see/) *n* an enlarged pouch attached to the heart of fish, amphibians, and reptiles through which blood from the veins is forced into the atrium [< modern Latin, "veined sinus"]

Siou·an /sóo ən/ *n* **1.** a family of Native North American languages that includes Dakota, Omaha, and Choctaw. Native speakers: 30,000. **2.** a speaker of a Siouan language —**Siou·an** *adj*

Sioux /soo/ (*plural same*) *n* a member of a group of Native North American peoples who lived throughout the Great Plains, and now live mainly in North and South Dakota [Early 18C. < North American French, shortening of *Nadouessioux* < Ojibwa (Ottawa dialect) *natowēssiwak*] —**Sioux** *adj*

Sioux Cit·y /sóo-/ city in western Iowa, across the Missouri River from South Dakota and Nebraska. Population: 84,131 (2002 estimate).

Sioux Falls city in southeastern South Dakota, on the Big Sioux River. Population: 130,491 (2002 estimate).

sip /sip/ *vti* (**sipped, sip·ping, sips**) to drink something slowly, taking only a small amount at a time ■ *n* a very small amount of liquid taken into the mouth [14C. Probably variant of SUP[1]] —**sip·per** *n*

SIPC *abbr US* Securities Investor Protection Corporation

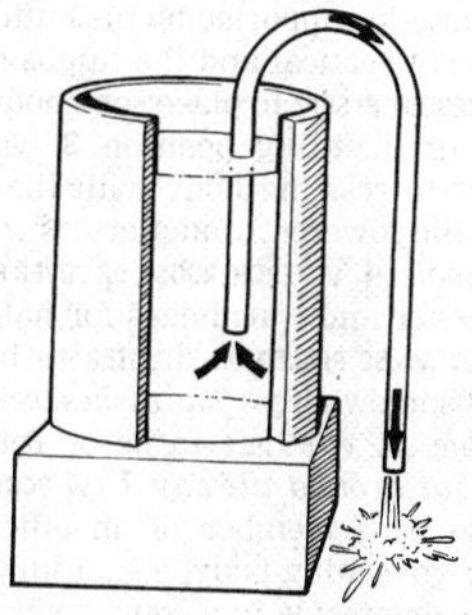

siphon

si·phon /sífən/, **sy·phon** *v* (**-phoned, -phon·ing, -phons**) **1.** *vt* **DRAW LIQUID THROUGH TUBE** to transfer liquid from one container to another through a tube using atmospheric pressure to make it flow **2.** *vti* **ILLEGALLY TAP FUNDS OR RESOURCES** to convey or draw money or resources from something, especially illegally ■ *n* **1. BENT TUBE FOR DRAWING OFF LIQUID** a bent tube or pipe used to transfer liquid from one container to another using atmospheric pressure to make it flow **2.** BEVERAGES, HOUSEHOLD same as **siphon bottle 3. TUBULAR ORGAN** a tubular organ, especially of arthropods and mollusks, by which water is taken in or expelled [14C. Via Latin *siphon-* < Greek *siphōn* "pipe, tube"] —**si·phon·age** *n* —**si·phon·al** *adj* —**si·phon·ic** /sī fónnik/ *adj*

si·phon bot·tle *n* a heavy sealed bottle fitted with a valve and nozzle at the top and containing pressurized carbonated water

si·phon·o·phore /sī fónnə fàwr, sīffənə-/ *n* an ocean hydrozoan that forms floating or swimming transparent or lightly-colored colonies, e.g., the Portuguese man-of-war. Order: Siphonophora. —**si·pho·noph·o·rous** /sīfə nóffərəss/ *adj*

sip·pet /síppət/ *n UK* a small piece of toast or fried bread cut in a triangle or small neat shape and usually eaten with stews or dishes served with sauce (*archaic*) [Mid-16C. < alteration of SOP]

Si·quei·ros /si káyrōss/, **David Alfaro** (1896?–1974) Mexican painter and political activist. He was a major figure among Mexican mural painters. His works include *The March of Humanity* (1968).

sir *stressed* /sur/; *unstressed* /sər/ *n* **1.** a form of address to a man often used in speech as a sign of respect ○ *Excuse me, sir, do you know what time it is?* **2.** *UK* a form of address to a man teacher, mainly used by his students [13C. Variant of SIRE] ◇ **yes** *or* **no sir** used to emphasize emphatic confirmation or denial of something

Sir *n* **1.** a title of honor used before the name of a knight or baronet **2.** used at the beginning of a formal letter to a man, especially one whose name is not known to you (*formal*) ○ *Dear Sir*

Si·raj-ud-Daw·lah /sə raáj ŏŏd dówlə/, **Si·raj-ud-Dau·la** (1729?–57) Bengali ruler. In his attack on the British settlement of Fort William in India, he lethally imprisoned people in a tiny room, known as the Black Hole of Calcutta (1756). He was defeated by the British at the Battle of Plassey and executed (1757). Born **Muhammad, Mirza**

sir·dar /súr daar, sər daár/ *n* **1. HIGH-RANKING LEADER** in India or Pakistan, a political or military leader of high rank **2. TITLE FOR SIKH MAN** a title of respect for a Sikh man **3. FORMER BRITISH COMMANDER OF EGYPTIAN ARMY** formerly, the title given to the British commander of the Egyptian army [Early 17C. Via Hindi *sardār* < Persian, "head holder"]

sire /sīr/ *vt* (**sired, sir·ing, sires**) **FATHER OFFSPRING** to father young, especially animals ■ *n* **1. MALE PARENT OF FOUR-LEGGED ANIMAL** the male parent of a four-legged animal, especially a domesticated animal such as a stallion or bull **2.** *also* **Sire ADDRESS TO KING OR LORD** a respectful form of address for a king or lord (*archaic*) [12C. Via French < Latin *senior* (see SENIOR)]

si·ren /sīrən/ *n* **1. STATIONARY WARNING DEVICE** a warning device that produces a loud wailing sound when a current of compressed air or steam is forced through a rotating perforated disk **2. PORTABLE WARNING DEVICE** an electronic warning device, often mounted or placed on a moving vehicle, that produces a loud wailing sound **3. SEA NYMPH LURING SAILORS ONTO ROCKS** in Greek mythology, a sea nymph, half-woman and half-bird, who was believed to sing beguilingly to passing sailors in order to lure them to their doom on the rocks she sat on **4. OFFENSIVE TERM** an offensive term for a woman whose sexual attractiveness is considered dangerous **5. SALAMANDER RESEMBLING EEL** a salamander with a long thin body and tail, permanent external gills, lungs, small forelegs, and no hind limbs. Family: Sirenidae. [14C. Via French < Latin *Siren* "sea nymph" < Greek *Seirēn*]

si·ren call *n* same as **siren song**

si·re·ni·an /sī reénee ən/ *n* a herbivorous placental sea mammal that has forelimbs like paddles, no hind limbs, and a broad flat tail. The dugong and manatee are sirenians. Order: Sirenia. [Late 19C. < modern Latin *Sirenia* < Latin *Siren* (see SIREN)] —**si·re·ni·an** *adj*

si·ren song *n* an alluring appeal, possessed by something or made by somebody, that has the power to tempt people, though yielding to the temptation may have unfortunate effects ○ *She yielded to the siren song of a higher salary.*

Sir·i·us /sírree əss/ *n* a binary star in the constellation Canis Major, the brightest star in the sky

sir·loin /súr lòyn/ *n* an expensive prime cut of beef used for roasting or steaks, taken from the lower part of the ribs or the upper loin [15C. < Old French, "above the loin"]

ORIGIN One of the most persistent of etymological fictions is that the ***sirloin*** got its name because a particular English king found the joint of beef so excellent that he knighted it. The monarch in question has been variously identified as Henry VIII, James I, and Charles II, but none of these is chronologically possible, and in fact the story has no truth in it at all. The spelling *sir-*, which began to replace the original *sur-* (from Old French *sur* "above") in the 18th century, no doubt owes something to the "knighting" story.

si·roc·co /sə rókō/ (*plural* **-cos**), **sci·roc·co** *n* a hot dusty humid southeast wind in southern Europe that begins in the Sahara and picks up moisture as it crosses the Mediterranean [Early 17C. Via French < Italian *scirocco* < Arabic *sharūq* "east"]

sir·rah /sírrə/ *n* a form of address for a man or boy that was used to express contempt (*archaic*) [Early 16C. Alteration of SIRE]

sir·ree /sə rée/ *n* sir, used to express emphasis [Early 19C. Alteration of SIR] ◇ **yes** *or* **no sirree** *US* used to emphasize agreement *or* disagreement (*informal*)

sir·up *n* FOOD another spelling of **syrup**

sis /siss/ *n* a form of address for a sister (*informal*) [Mid-17C. Shortening]

si·sal /síss'l, síz'l/, **si·sal hemp** *n* **1.** a strong white fiber obtained from the leaves of an agave plant. Use: rope, rugs. **2.** an agave plant that produces sisal. Native to: Mexico. Latin name: *Agave sisalana*. [Mid-19C. After *Sisal*, port in Yucatán, Mexico]

sis·kin /sískin/ *n* **1.** a yellow-and-black finch related to the goldfinch. Native to: Europe, Asia, North Africa. Latin name: *Carduelis spinus*. **2.** BIRDS same as **pine siskin** [Mid-16C. < Middle Dutch *siseken*, early Flemish *sijsken* "little siskin"]

Sis·ley /sísslee, síz-/, **Alfred** (1839–99) French painter. He was one of the early impressionist painters, noted for his landscapes and village scenes of northern France.

sis·si·fied /síssə fīd/ *adj* same as **sissy**

~~sissors~~ incorrect spelling of **scissors**

sis·sy /síssee/, **cis·sy** *n* (*plural* **-sies**) an offensive term for a boy or man who is considered not to exhibit stereotypical masculine behavior, especially by other boys or men (*informal offensive insult*) ■ *adj* an offensive term referring to a boy, man, behavior, or object that is considered not to exhibit or be characteristic of stereotypical masculinity (*informal*) [Mid-19C. < SIS]

sis·sy bar *n* a U-shaped bar that chiefly acts as a backrest for the rider or passenger of a motorcycle or bicycle

sis·ter /sístər/ *n* **1.** FEMALE SIBLING a girl or woman who has the same parents as another person **2.** STEPSISTER OR HALF-SISTER a girl or woman who has one parent in common with another person **3.** *also* **Sis·ter** NUN a female member of a Christian religious community **4.** *also* **Sis·ter** WAY TO ADDRESS NUN a form of address to a female member of a Christian religious community **5.** AFRICAN AMERICAN WOMAN a form of address or way of referring to an African American woman, used especially by other African Americans **6.** WOMAN SUPPORTER OF FEMINISM a woman who advocates or supports feminist principles **7.** CLOSE WOMAN FRIEND a close woman friend, especially of another woman **8.** WOMAN MEMBER OF SAME ORGANIZATION a woman who belongs to the same organization as another, especially a sorority ■ *adj* **1.** CLOSELY LINKED belonging to or closely associated with something ○ *her sister ship, The Princess* **2.** GENETICS WITH PAIRED CELL describes either of an identical pair of cells or cell components formed by division of a parent cell or component [Old English *sweostor* < Indo-European]

CULTURAL NOTE ***The Three Sisters***, a play (1900) by the Russian dramatist Anton Chekhov. Set in rural Russia, this powerful and compassionate study of the quiet desperation of bourgeois life centers on the three Pozarov sisters. Stifled by the dreariness of local society, they look to the officers of the local garrison for romance and entertainment. But when the army departs, the sisters are left with only their dreams and each other.

sis·ter·hood /sístər hòod/ *n* **1.** SOLIDARITY AMONG WOMEN the empathy and loyalty that women feel for other women who have shared goals, experiences, or viewpoints **2.** WOMEN'S GROUP a group of women who have shared goals, experiences, or viewpoints **3.** STATUS AS SISTER the status of a sister or the relationship of sisters **4.** COMMUNITY OF NUNS a religious community of Christian nuns

sis·ter-in-law (*plural* **sis·ters-in-law**) *n* **1.** the sister of somebody's husband or wife **2.** the wife of somebody's brother

sis·ter·ly /sístərlee/ *adj, adv* relating to, coming from, or characteristic of a sister, especially in an affectionate, kind, or caring way

Sis·tine /síss tèen, si stéen/ *adj* **1.** relating to any of the popes named Sixtus, especially Sixtus IV, who was pope 1471–84 **2.** relating to the Sistine Chapel in the Vatican [Late 18C. < Italian *Sistino* "of Sixtus"]

sis·tra MUSIC plural of sistrum

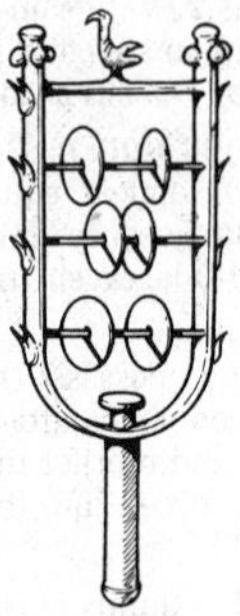

sistrum

sis·trum /sístrəm/ (*plural* **-tra** /-trə/) *n* an ancient Egyptian percussion instrument consisting of a thin metal frame with rods or loops attached that jingle when shaken [14C. Via Latin < Greek *seistron* < *seiein* "shake"]

Si·su·lu /si sòoloo/, **Walter** (1912–2003) South African political activist. He served a prison sentence (1963–89) for his membership in the African National Congress, and was later the party's deputy president (1991–94).

Sis·y·phe·an /sìssə fée ən/ *adj* **1.** involving endless but futile labor **2.** relating to Sisyphus [Late 16C. < Latin *Sisypheius* < Greek *Sisuphos* "Sisyphus"]

Sis·y·phus /síssəfəss/ *n* in Greek mythology, a cruel king of Corinth who was condemned for eternity to roll a boulder up a hill only to have it roll down again just before it reached the top

sit /sit/ *v* (**sat** /sat/, **sit·ting, sits**) **1.** *vi* REST WITH WEIGHT ON BUTTOCKS to assume a position of rest in which the weight is largely supported by the buttocks, usually with the body vertical and the thighs horizontal **2.** *vt* PLACE SOMEBODY IN SEAT to place somebody or yourself in a seat or a sitting position **3.** *vi* REST BODY ON HINDQUARTERS to rest the body with the weight supported by the lowered hindquarters (*refers to four-legged animals*) **4.** *vi* PERCH, ROOST, OR COVER EGGS to perch, roost, or cover and warm eggs for hatching (*refers to birds*) **5.** *vi* BE PLACED OR SITUATED to be located or positioned somewhere ○ *The dishes were still sitting on the table.* **6.** *vi* BE IDLE to be or remain idle or unused ○ *sat around all day* **7.** *vi* OCCUPY POSITION OF AUTHORITY to be a member of an official decision-making or governing body, e.g., a jury, council, or committee, or preside in a court ○ *sits on the House Appropriations Committee* **8.** *vi* MEET IN OFFICIAL SESSION to hold an official session or be in session (*refers to a legislative or judicial body*) ○ *The court will sit tomorrow to hear appeals.* **9.** *vi* POSE FOR SOMETHING to pose for a portrait or picture ○ *She sat for an official portrait.* **10.** *vti* same as **baby-sit** (sense 1) (*informal*) **11.** *vt* HAVE SEATS FOR NUMBER OF PEOPLE to have seats or seating space for a particular number of people ○ *We can sit ten around the dining table.* **12.** *vi* REST OR WEIGH IN PARTICULAR WAY to rest, weigh, or lie in a particular way ○ *The responsibility sat heavily on his shoulders.* **13.** *vi* BE REGARDED IN PARTICULAR WAY to be accepted or considered by somebody in a particular way ○ *The news didn't sit well with her.* **14.** *vi* BE DIGESTIBLE to be digestible (*informal*) **15.** *vi* BE COMPATIBLE to accord with or seem appropriate in conjunction with something ○ *It was not, they thought in those days, a role that sat well with motherhood.* **16.** *vi* FIT OR HANG to fit or hang on somebody in a particular way ○ *a gown that sat beautifully on her* ■ *n* **1.** TIME SPENT BEING SEATED a period of being seated, especially while waiting **2.** CLOTHING WAY GARMENT FITS the way a garment hangs on somebody [Old English *sittan* < Indo-European] ◇ **sit tight** to refrain from moving or acting until the right time (*informal*) ○ *I'll be right there – just sit tight.* ○ *advised shareholders to sit tight* ◇ **sitting pretty** in a good or favorable position (*informal*)

USAGE sat or **sitting**? ***Sat***, the past participle of the verb *sit*, is sometimes wrongly used in place of the present participle ***sitting*** in sentences like this: *I was sitting* [not *sat*] *by the telephone, waiting for it to ring.* The only correct use of *I was sat* is as the passive form of *sit* in the sense "place somebody in a seat," as in *I asked for a seat near the president, but I was sat at the opposite end of the table.* The same mistake sometimes occurs with *stood* and *standing*, the past and present participles of the verb *stand*: *I've been standing* [not *stood*] *here for almost an hour.*

sit back *vi* to take no action ○ *sat back and watched the crisis develop*

sit down *vti* to become seated, or make somebody become seated ○ *time to sit him down and tell him the truth*

sit in *vi* **1.** ATTEND WITHOUT TAKING PART to attend something but not take an active part in it ○ *Do you mind if I sit in on your meeting?* **2.** TEMPORARILY REPLACE SOMEBODY to do a job for the person who normally does it ○ *sitting in for the regular announcer* **3.** OCCUPY BUILDING AS PROTEST to take part in a sit-in

sit on *vt* (*informal*) **1.** DELAY DEALING WITH SOMETHING to fail to take action on or reveal something over a period of time, although in a position to do so ○ *The government sat on the information for weeks.* **2.** SUPPRESS SOMETHING to put a stop to something or prevent it from going ahead **3.** NAG SOMEBODY to nag somebody continually ○ *You'll have to sit on him if you want this done on time.* **4.** QUELL SOMEBODY to prevent somebody from saying or doing anything more, especially by means of a crushing remark or rebuke

sit out *vt* **1.** to remain seated during something and not join in ○ *I think I'll sit this one out.* **2.** to remain until the end of something, especially something unpleasant

sit up *vi* **1.** SIT STRAIGHT to sit upright or rise from lying down **2.** BECOME ALERT to become alert or interested **3.** STAY UP LATE to stay up past the usual time of going to bed

Si·ta /séetə, sée taa/ *n* in Hinduism, an incarnation of the goddess Lakshmi

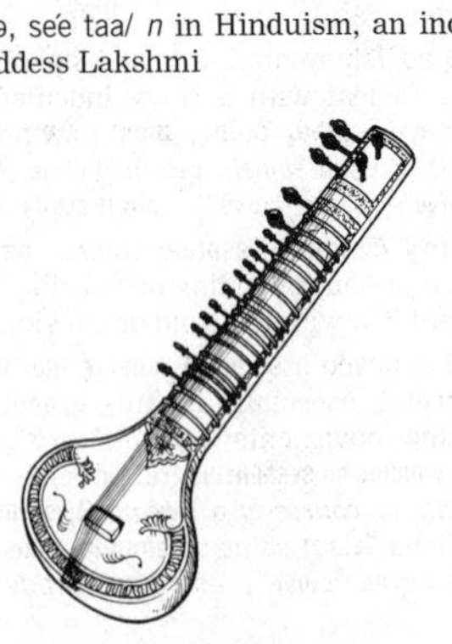

sitar

si·tar /si taár/ *n* a South Asian stringed instrument with a rounded resonating body and a long fretted neck. There are several playing strings and a larger number that vibrate sympathetically. [Mid-19C. Via Hindi < Persian, "three-stringed"] —**si·tar·ist** *n*

sit·com /sít kòm/ *n* MEDIA same as **situation comedy** (*informal*) [Mid-20C. Shortening]

sit-down *adj* served to people sitting at a table ○ *There's a sit-down dinner before the dancing.* ■ *n* **1.** HR same as **sit-down strike 2.** HR same as **sit-in 3.** a short spell of sitting in order to relax (*informal*)

sit-down strike *n* a form of industrial action in which workers occupy their workplace and refuse to leave it until their demands are granted or negotiated

site /sīt/ *n* 1. PLACE WHERE SOMETHING STANDS an area or piece of land where something was, is, or will be located ○ *The whole block has become one vast building site.* ○ *the site of an ancient temple* 2. PLACE OF SIGNIFICANT EVENT a place where something important happened ○ *the site of last summer's championships* 3. ONLINE same as **website** ■ *vt* (**sit·ed, sit·ing, sites**) POSITION SOMETHING to locate something in a particular place or position ○ *The plan is to site all further malls in the suburbs.* [14C. Via Anglo-Norman < Latin *situs* "place, position" < *sinere* "put"]

SPELLCHECK See *cite*.

si·tel·la *n* BIRDS another spelling of **sittella**

site-spe·cif·ic *adj* designed, built, or intended for one individual site

sit-in *n* 1. a form of protest in which people occupy a building or public place and refuse to leave until their demands have been met or negotiated 2. a protest against racial discrimination in which people occupy the seats or an area of a segregated business or place and refuse to leave

Sit·ka /sítkə/ city in southeastern Alaska, on the west coast of Baranof Island, in the Alexander Archipelago. Population: 8,829 (2002 estimate).

sit·ka spruce /sìtkə-/ *n* a spruce tree with reddish brown bark and silvery white needles, widely planted for timber. Native to: northwestern coast of North America. Latin name: *Picea sitchensis.* [Late 19C. After SITKA]

sit spin *n* a spin on one ice skate made in a squatting position with one leg stretched out in front of the body

sit·tel·la /si téllə/, **si·tel·la** *n* a small gregarious songbird, similar to a nuthatch in its build, short tail, and habit of hopping up and down trees. Native to: New Guinea, Australasia. Family: Neosittidae. [Mid-19C. < modern Latin *Sittella*, literally "little nuthatch" < Greek *sittē* "nuthatch"]

sit·ter /síttər/ *n* 1. BABY-SITTER somebody who baby-sits a child 2. HIRED MINDER somebody hired to take care of something or somebody (*often used in combination*) ○ *a house-sitter* 3. POSER FOR PICTURE an artist's or photographer's model, especially for a portrait 4. BROODING HEN a hen or other bird sitting on eggs to hatch them

sit·ting /sítting/ *n* 1. TURN TO EAT a period when a meal is served in a place where there is insufficient room for everyone to eat at the same time ○ *The first sitting is at 12 o'clock.* 2. PERIOD OF BEING SEATED a period of being seated while engaged in an activity ○ *read the book in three sittings* 3. SESSION OF PUBLIC BODY a meeting or session of an official body such as a legislature or court 4. TIME FOR POSING a period of time during which somebody is posing for a portrait 5. SET OF EGGS a clutch of eggs under a brooding bird 6. INCUBATION OF EGGS the period of time during which a hen sits on eggs to hatch them ■ *adj* 1. SEATED seated or for being seated ○ *a sitting area* 2. DONE SEATED done or performed while seated ○ *prescribed some simple sitting exercises* 3. IN OFFICE holding office at the present time ○ *a sitting judge*

USAGE See *sit*.

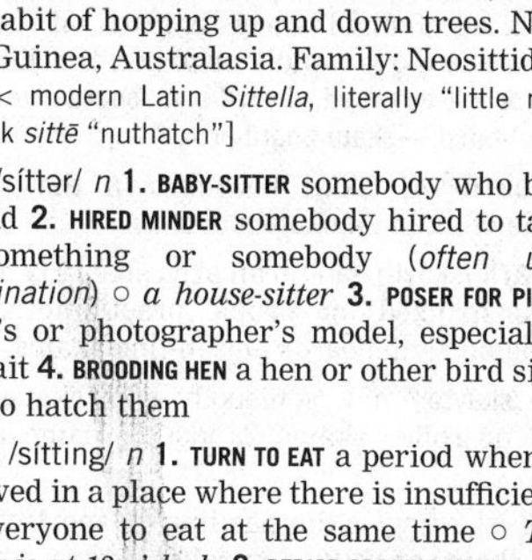

Library of Congress

Sitting Bull

Sit·ting Bull /sítting bòol/ (1831?–90) Sioux leader. He defeated General George Custer at the Battle of Little Big Horn (1876). He was killed during a later outbreak of hostilities.

> "What treaty that the white man ever made with us have they kept? Not one."
> [Attributed to Sitting Bull]

sit·ting duck *n* somebody or something that is defenseless, exposed to danger, and easy to attack or exploit (*informal*)

sit·ting room *n* a small room in a house, apartment, or office that is used for sitting, especially one that forms part of a connecting suite

sit·ting trot *n* a horse-riding technique used while trotting in which the rider does not rise from the horse's saddle

sit·u·ate /síchoo àyt/ (**-at·ed, -at·ing, -ates**) *vt* 1. to put something in a particular place or position 2. to place something in a context or set of circumstances and show its connections [15C. < late Latin *situat-*, past participle of *situare* "place" < Latin *situs* (see SITE)]

sit·u·at·ed /síchoo àytəd/ *adj* (*often used in combination*) 1. located in a place or position ○ *a conveniently situated building* 2. in a particular financial condition ○ *comfortably situated, living off their investments*

sit·u·a·tion /sìchoo áysh'n/ *n* 1. STATE OF AFFAIRS a particular set of circumstances existing in a particular place or at a particular time ○ *Kaye assessed the situation and decided to call you.* ○ *a situation where they didn't have a formal planning process* 2. CURRENT CIRCUMSTANCES the current conditions that characterize somebody's life or events in a particular place, country, or society ○ *destabilized the political situation* 3. LOCATION the location of a property ○ *a pleasing situation with a view* 4. COMBINATION OF DIFFICULT CIRCUMSTANCES a difficult or problematic set of circumstances ○ *I'm afraid we have a situation on our hands.* 5. *UK* JOB a job or position of employment (*formal*) —**sit·u·a·tion·al** *adj*

sit·u·a·tion·al eth·ics *pron, n* PHILOSOPHY same as **situation ethics**

sit·u·a·tion com·e·dy *n* a television or radio comedy series in which a regular cast of characters, usually working or living together, respond to everyday situations in a humorous way

sit·u·a·tion eth·ics, **sit·u·a·tion·al eth·ics** *n* a system of ethics in which moral judgments are thought to depend on the context in which they are to be made, rather than on general moral principles (*takes a singular verb*)

sit-up *n* an exercise in which you lie flat on your back with your legs bent and then raise the upper part of your body to a sitting position

si·tus /sítəss/ (*plural* **-tus·es** *or same*) *n* 1. the position of an organ or part of the body, especially the normal position 2. the place where a thing or a right properly belongs [Early 18C. < Latin (see SITE)]

si·tus in·ver·sus /-in vúrsəss/ *n* an uncommon reversal of organs in the body in which the apex of the heart points to the right and the liver and appendix are on the left side [< Latin, shortening of *situs inversus viscerum* "inverted position of the internal organs"]

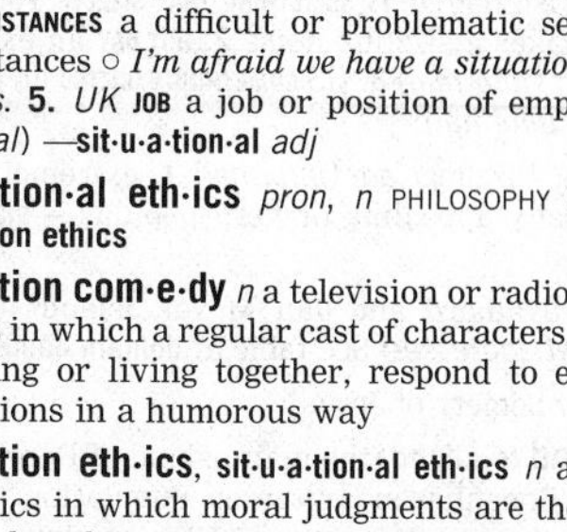

Popperfoto

Dame Edith Sitwell

Sit·well /sít wèl, síttwəl/, **Dame Edith** (1887–1964) British writer. Unconventional in her writing, behavior, and dress, she is best known for her poetic work *Façade* (1922), which was set to music by Sir William Walton. She was the sister of Osbert and Sacheverell Sitwell. Full name **Sitwell, Dame Edith Louisa**

Sit·well, Sir Osbert, 5th Baronet Sitwell (1892–1969) British writer. He wrote satirical and serious poetry and five volumes of memoirs (1944–50). He was the brother of Edith and Sacheverell Sitwell. Full name **Sitwell, Sir Francis Osbert Sacheverell**

Sit·well, Sir Sacheverell, 6th Baronet Sitwell (1897–1988) British writer. He was known for his biographies and studies in baroque art, which included *Sacred and Profane Love* (1940). He was the brother of Osbert and Edith Sitwell.

sitz bath /síts-, zíts-/ *n* 1. a bathtub shaped like a chair in which the bather sits immersed up to the waist in water 2. an act of immersion in a sitz bath, especially for therapeutic purposes [Partial translation of German *Sitzbad* "sitting bath"]

sitz·krieg /síts krèeg, zíts-/ *n* a period in a war during which there is little offensive activity or change in the positions of the combatants [Mid-20C. < German *sitzen* "sit," after BLITZKRIEG]

sitz·mark /síts maark, zíts-/ *n* a depression in the snow made by a skier who has fallen backward [Mid-20C. < German *Sitzmarke* "sitting mark"]

SI u·nit *n* a unit adopted for international use under the Système International d'Unités in science and technology. The seven fundamental units are the meter, kilogram, second, ampere, kelvin, candela, and mole.

Si·va *n* HINDUISM another spelling of **Shiva**

Si·van /sívvən/ *n* in the Jewish calendar, the third month of the religious year, lasting 30 days and falling about the same time as May to June. See table at **calendar** [14C. < Hebrew *sīwān*]

Si·wash /sī wòsh, -wàwsh/ *n Can, Northwest US* an offensive term for an Aboriginal, or Native North American, person [Mid-19C. Via Chinook Jargon < French *sauvage* (see SAVAGE)]

Si·wash sweat·er *n Can* a heavy sweater made from unbleached wool, originally by the Native North Americans of British Columbia, decorated with symbolic designs

six /siks/ *n* 1. 6 the number 6 2. SOMETHING WITH VALUE OF 6 something in a numbered series, e.g., a playing card, with a value of 6 3. GROUP OF SIX a group of six objects or people, e.g., an ice hockey team 4. SOMETHING WITH SIX PARTS something with six parts, especially a car or an engine with six cylinders [Old English *si(e)x* < Indo-European] —**six** *adj, pron* ◇ **at sixes and sevens** (*informal*) 1. disorganized or in disarray 2. in disagreement ◇ **six of one and half-a-dozen of the other** used when there is not much difference between two choices

Six MUSIC ➧ **Les Six**

Six-Day War *n* a war between Israel and the states of Egypt, Jordan, and Syria that lasted six days in June 1967

six-eight time *n* a time signature in which there are six beats to the measure and each beat is a eighth note

six·fold /síks fòld/ *adj* 1. SIX TIMES GREATER with six times as much or as many 2. WITH SIX PARTS with six parts ■ *adv* MULTIPLIED BY SIX by six times as much or as many

six-foot·er *n* somebody who is six feet tall or taller (*informal*)

six-gun *n US* ARMS same as **six-shooter**

Six Na·tions *n* a confederacy of six Iroquois peoples, the Cayuga, Mohawk, Oneida, Onondaga, Seneca, and Tuscarora, that was formed in 1722

six-pack *n* 1. six cans or bottles, usually of beer, sold together in a pack 2. a well-developed block of abdominal muscles (*informal*)

six·pence /síkspənss, síks pènss/ *n* a small silver-colored coin used in Britain between 1550 and 1980, worth 6 old pennies or 2.5 new pence

six·pen·ny nail /síks pènnee-/ *n* a nail that is 2 in./5 cm long [< the original price of a hundred such nails]

six-shoot·er *n* a handgun whose bullets are loaded

into a revolving cylinder containing six chambers (*informal*)

sixte /sikst/ *n* in fencing, the sixth of the eight basic defensive positions [Late 19C. < French, "sixth"]

six·teen /siks teén/ *n* **1.** 16 the number 16 **2.** SOMETHING WITH VALUE OF 16 something in a numbered series with a value of 16 **3.** GROUP OF 16 a group of sixteen objects or people [Old English *si(e)xtiene* < Germanic, "ten more than six"] —**six·teen** *adj, pron*

six·teen·mo /siks teénmō/ (*plural* **-mos**) *n* PRINTING same as **sextodecimo**

six·teenth /siks teénth/ *n* **1.** one of 16 equal parts of something **2.** one-sixteenth of an ounce of a drug such as cannabis (*slang*) —**six·teenth** *adj, adv*

six·teenth note *n* a musical note with the time value of one-sixteenth of a whole note. It is written as a filled note-head with a stem and two tails.

six·teenth rest *n* a musical rest with the time value of a sixteenth note

sixth /siksth/ *n* **1.** ONE OF 6 PARTS OF SOMETHING one of six equal parts of something **2.** INTERVAL OF SIX NOTES in a standard musical scale, the interval between one note and another that lies five notes above or below it. In the scale of C major, C and A form a sixth. **3.** NOTE SIXTH AWAY FROM ANOTHER in a standard musical scale, a note that is a sixth away from another note **4.** ONE NOTE IN SIXTH one of the two notes in a sixth **5.** HARMONY OF SIXTH the harmony created by playing two notes a sixth apart —**sixth** *adj, adv*

sixth chord *n* a musical chord made up of a note plus a note a third above and a note a sixth above

sixth sense *n* a supposed special ability to perceive something not using any of the five senses of sight, hearing, touch, smell, and taste

six·ti·eth /síkstee əth/ *n* one of 60 equal parts of something —**six·ti·eth** *adj, adv*

Six·tus V /síkstəss/, **Pope** (1521–90) As pope (1585–90) he reformed the administration of the Roman Catholic Church, ordered the construction of public buildings in Rome, and supported missions abroad

six·ty /síkstee/ *n* (*plural* **-ties**) **1.** 60 the number 60 **2.** GROUP OF 60 a group of sixty objects or people ■ **six·ties** *npl* **1.** NUMBERS 60 TO 69 the numbers 60 to 69, particularly as a range of Fahrenheit temperatures ○ *in the low sixties* **2.** YEARS FROM 60 TO 69 the years from 60 to 69 in a century **3.** PERIOD FROM AGE 60 TO 69 the period of somebody's life from the age of 60 to 69 [Old English *sixtig* < SIX + *-tig* "ten"] —**six·ty** *adj, pron*

64-bit key /síkstee fawr bit-/ *n* an industry standard encryption key length for e-commerce transactions

six·ty-four·mo /-fáwrmō/ (*plural* **six·ty-four·mos**) *n* a size of book page traditionally created by folding a single sheet of standard-sized printing paper 6 times, giving 64 leaves or 128 pages

six·ty-fourth note *n* a musical note with the time value of one-64th that of a whole note. It is written as a filled note-head with a stem and four tails.

six·ty-four thou·sand dol·lar ques·tion, $64,000 question, 64,000 dollar question *n* a question whose answer is not yet known but is significant and important (*informal*) ○ *Yes, but will it actually work? That's the sixty-four thousand dollar question!* [< the top prize in a popular TV quiz show of the 1950s]

six·ty-nine *n* an offensive term for a sexual activity in which two people simultaneously stimulate each other's genitals orally (*slang*) [< the position of the couple]

siz·a·ble /sízəb'l/, **size·a·ble** *adj* fairly large —**siz·a·bly** *adv*

size[1] /sīz/ *n* **1.** HOW BIG SOMETHING IS the dimensions, extent, amount, or degree of something, in terms of how large or small it is ○ *I think this table is about the right size for our dining room.* **2.** BIGNESS the fact of being large, often very large, in dimensions or degree ○ *Did you see the size of that fish?* **3.** STANDARD MEASUREMENT OF MANUFACTURED ITEM a set of measurements used when making or classifying articles such as clothing or shoes that are produced and sold ■ *vt* (**sized, siz·ing, siz·es**) **1.** SORT THINGS ACCORDING TO SIZE to put things into different groups according to their size **2.** MAKE SOMETHING TO PARTICULAR SIZE to cut, shape, or manufacture goods so that they have the necessary or chosen measurements [13C. < Old French *sise*, shortening of *assise* (see ASSIZE)] —**sized** *adj* ◇ **cut somebody down to size** to make somebody be less self-important and arrogant ◇ **that's about the size of it** used to indicate that something describes a situation very well (*informal*) ◇ **try something (on) for size 1.** to put something on to see whether it fits you or not **2.** to find out how much you like something

size up *vt* to assess a person or situation and form a judgment

size[2] /sīz/ *n* a gelatinous mixture made from glue, starch, or varnish. Use: filling pores in the surface of paper, textiles, or plaster. ■ *vt* (**sized, siz·ing, siz·es**) to coat a porous surface such as paper, textile, or plaster with size [15C. Origin ?]

size·a·ble *adj* another spelling of **sizable**

size·ism /sī zìzzəm/ *n* discrimination against somebody on the basis of the person's size, especially the person's unusual tallness, shortness, fatness, or thinness —**size·ist** *adj*

siz·ing /sízing/ *n* **1.** INDUST, ARTS same as **size**[2] **2.** the process of coating something with size

siz·zle /sízz'l/ *v* (**-zled, -zling, -zles**) **1.** *vti* MAKE NOISE OF FOOD FRYING to make the hissing and spattering sound typical of frying food, or cook food so that it makes a hissing sound **2.** *vi* BE HOT to be extremely hot (*informal*) **3.** *vi* BE PHYSICALLY APPEALING to be physically appealing or very popular (*informal*) **4.** *vi* BE FURIOUS to show or feel great anger (*informal*) ■ *n* **1.** PHYSICAL APPEAL appeal based on physical attributes (*informal*) **2.** FRYING NOISE the hissing and splattering sound of something frying, or a sound resembling this [Early 17C. An imitation of the sound]

siz·zler /sízzlər/ *n* **1.** SOMETHING THAT SIZZLES something that makes a sizzling noise **2.** HOT DAY an extremely hot day (*informal*) **3.** *US* SOMETHING EXCITING an exciting event (*informal*)

siz·zling /sízzling/ *adj* (*informal*) **1.** extremely hot **2.** physically appealing or very popular —**siz·zling·ly** *adv*

sj *abbr* Svalbard and Jan Mayen Islands (*used in Internet addresses*) See table at **domain name**

S.J. *abbr* Society of Jesus

Sjæl·land /syéllənd/ the main island of Denmark, on which Copenhagen is situated. Population: 2,159,260 (1994). Area: 2,715 sq. mi./7,031 sq. km. English name **Zealand**

sjam·bok /sham bók, -búk/ *n S Africa* a sturdy whip or riding crop made from the hide of a rhinoceros or hippopotamus [Late 18C. Via Afrikaans < Malay *chambuk* < Persian *chābuk* "whip"]

S.J.D. *abbr* Doctor of Juridical Science [Latin *Scientiae Juridicae Doctor*]

sk *abbr* Slovakia (*used in Internet addresses*) See table at **domain name**

SK *abbr* Saskatchewan

ska /skaa/ *n* dance music in 4/4 time, marked by emphasis on the second and fourth beats, originating in Jamaica in the late 1950s. It combines traditional Caribbean music and jazz, and was a predecessor of reggae. [Mid-20C. Origin ?]

skag *n* DRUGS another spelling of **scag** (*slang*)

Skag·er·rak /skággə ràk/ arm of the North Sea between Norway and the Jutland Peninsula, Denmark. Length: 130 mi./210 km.

skald /skawld/, **scald** *n* a medieval Scandinavian poet or traveling minstrel (*archaic or literary*) [Mid-18C. < Old Norse *skáld*] —**skald·ic** *adj*

Skån·e /skṓnə/ province forming the southern tip of Sweden. It consists of the counties of Kristianstad and Malmöhus. Population: 1,120,038 (1998). Area: 4,241 sq. mi./10,984 sq. km.

skank /skangk/ *vi* (**skanked, skank·ing, skanks**) to dance to reggae music, especially in a jerky way ■ *n* an offensive term for a girl or woman who is regarded as unpleasant-looking and sexually promiscuous (*slang insult*) [Late 20C. Origin ?]

skan·ky /skángkee/ *adj* disgusting or unpleasant (*slang*) [Late 20C. Origin ?]

skat /skat/ *n* a card game for three players played with 32 cards and involving bids, contracts, and the taking of tricks [Mid-19C. Via German < Italian *scarto* "discarded card" < Latin *c(h)arta* (see CARD[1])]

skate[1] /skayt/ *n* **1.** ICE SKATING same as **ice skate 2.** ROLLER-SKATING same as **roller skate 3.** METAL BLADE FOR ICE SKATE a steel runner that is fastened to the sole of a boot or shoe to make an ice skate **4.** TIME SPENT SKATING a period of time spent skating ■ *v* (**skat·ed, skat·ing, skates**) **1.** *vi* MOVE AROUND ON SKATES to glide along a surface wearing ice skates or roller skates **2.** *vi* SLIDE SMOOTHLY to slide along a slippery surface **3.** *US* BEHAVE IDLY OR IRRESPONSIBLY to behave in an idle, irresponsible manner (*informal*) ○ *Instead of studying, he's skating.* [Mid-17C. < Dutch *schaats* "skate, stilt" < Old French *eschasse* "stilt"]

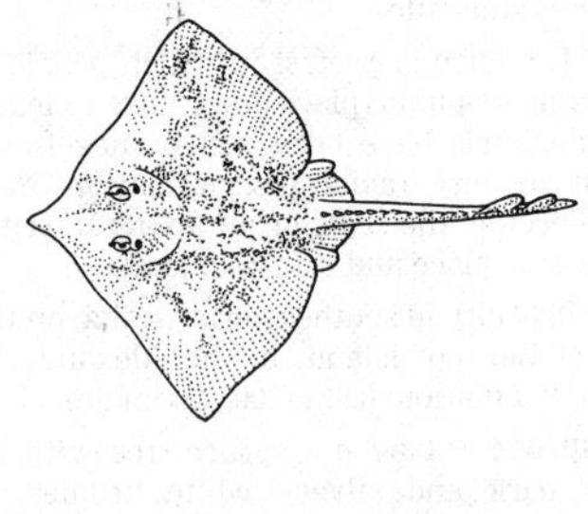

skate

skate[2] /skayt/ (*plural* **skates** or *same*) *n* **1.** a bottom-dwelling cartilaginous ocean fish with a flat body, very large flat pectoral fins, two small dorsal fins, a long snout, and short slender tail. Family: Rajidae. **2.** the flesh of a skate as food [14C. < Old Norse *skata*]

skate·board /skáyt bàwrd/ *n* a short narrow board to which a set of small wheels is fitted on the underside, used to move rapidly or to perform jumps and stunts ■ *vi* (**-board·ed, -board·ing, -boards**) to ride on a skateboard —**skate·board·er** *n*

skate·board·ing /skáyt bàwrding/ *n* the sport or pastime of riding a skateboard

skate·park /skáyt paàrk/ *n* an area specially designed and constructed for people practicing and performing on skateboards and in-line skates

skat·er /skáytər/ *n* **1.** somebody who skates on ice skates or roller skates **2.** INSECTS same as **water strider**

skat·ing /skáyting/ *n* the pastime or sport of sliding on ice skates or rolling on roller skates

skat·ole /ská tōl, -tàwl/ *n* an organic crystalline solid that has a strong fecal odor. Source: feces, beetroot, coal tar. Use: perfume fixative. Formula: C_9H_9N. [Late 19C. < Greek *skat-* (see SCATO-)]

skean /skeen/ *n* a dagger with a double-edged blade formerly used in Scotland and Ireland [Early 16C. Via Gaelic < Old Irish *scían*]

ske·dad·dle /skə dádd'l/ (*slang*) *vi* (**-dled, -dling, -dles**) to run away quickly ■ *n* a very quick or agitated departure [Mid-19C. Origin ?] —**ske·dad·dler** *n*

skeet /skeet/, **skeet shoot·ing** *n* a form of sport shooting in which clay targets are tossed into the air at speeds and angles intended to simulate the flight of birds [Early 20C. Invented word, supposedly archaic form of SHOOT]

skeet·er /skeétər/ *n* same as **mosquito** (*slang*) [Mid-19C. Shortening and alteration of MOSQUITO]

skeet·er hawk *n Southern US* same as **dragonfly**

REGIONAL NOTE See *snake doctor.*

---

skeet shooting *n* SPORTS same as **skeet**

skeg /skeg/ *n* **1.** a part of the keel of a ship, near the stern, that connects the keel with the rudder post **2.** the short stabilizing fin on the rear underside of a surfboard or sailboard [Early 17C. Via Dutch < Old Norse *skegg* "beard, point of a ship's stern"]

skein /skayn/ *n* **1.** BUNDLE OF YARN a length of yarn or thread wound loosely and coiled together **2.** TANGLE a tangled or complex mass of material **3.** GROUP OF GEESE IN FLIGHT a flock of wild birds flying across the sky in a line [15C. < Old French *escaigne*]

skel·e·tal /skéllət'l/ *adj* **1.** relating to a skeleton **2.** extremely thin or emaciated —**skel·e·tal·ly** *adv*

skel·e·ton /skéllət'n/ *n* **1.** BONES OF PERSON OR ANIMAL the rigid framework of interconnected bones and cartilage that protects and supports the internal organs and provides attachment for muscles in humans and other vertebrate animals **2.** SUPPORTIVE PROTECTIVE STRUCTURE OF INVERTEBRATES something that provides support, gives protection, or maintains shape in an invertebrate animal, e.g., the shell of a snail or the cuticle of a crab **3.** BASIC FRAME SOMETHING IS BUILT AROUND a structure that is needed to support and hold something together as an internal framework, onto which the connecting or covering parts are attached **4.** SOMETHING WITH ONLY ESSENTIAL PARTS LEFT a plan, organization, or structure that has been reduced so that only its most basic and necessary parts are still functioning or in place **5.** OUTLINE OR LAYOUT OF SOMETHING a description that gives the main points but no details of something such as a book or plan **6.** SOMEBODY VERY THIN an emaciated person or animal (*informal*) **7.** RACING SLED a small sled used for high-speed racing, on which the driver lies head first [Late 16C. Via modern Latin < Greek *skeleton (sōma)* "dried up (body)" < *skellein* "dry up"] ◇ **a skeleton in the closet** a closely kept secret that is a source of shame or embarrassment

skel·e·ton·ize /skéllət'n īz/ (**-ized, -iz·ing, -iz·es**) *vt* **1.** CUT SOMETHING BACK TO BASICS to reduce something until only its most basic structure or outline remains **2.** CREATE OUTLINE OF SOMETHING to create something in basic outline **3.** REDUCE SOMETHING TO SKELETAL FORM to reduce something to a skeleton

skel·e·ton key *n* a key with the usually serrated part that connects with the lever of a lock (**bit**) filed down so that it can open many different unsophisticated locks [< its basic cut-back shape]

skell /skel/ *n US* a homeless or jobless person who lives on the street (*slang*) [Late 20C. Origin ?]

skep·tic /sképtik/, **scep·tic** *n* **1.** a doubter of accepted beliefs **2.** a doubter of religious doctrines and principles **3.** PHILOSOPHY another spelling of **Skeptic** [Early 17C. < SKEPTIC]

SYNONYMS See ***doubtful.***

Skep·tic /sképtik/, **Scep·tic** *n* a member of an ancient Greek school of philosophy holding the doctrine that real knowledge is impossible, or a later follower of this doctrine [Late 16C. Via Latin < Greek *skeptikos* "follower of the Greek philosopher Pyrrho" < *skeptesthai* "look about"] —**Skep·tic** *adj*

skep·ti·cal /sképtik'l/, **scep·ti·cal** *adj* **1.** tending not to believe or accept things but to question them **2.** marked by a doubting attitude —**skep·ti·cal·ly** *adv*

SYNONYMS See ***doubtful.***

skep·ti·cism /sképti sìzzəm/ *n* **1.** an attitude marked by a tendency to doubt what others accept to be true **2.** a doubting attitude toward religious beliefs **3.** PHILOSOPHY another spelling of **Skepticism**

Skep·ti·cism *n* the doctrine that holds that true knowledge is not possible

Sker·rit /skérrət/, **Pierre** (*b.* 1972?) prime minister of Dominica (2004–). A member of the Dominican Labor Party, he served as minister for education before becoming the country's youngest ever prime minister.

sker·ry /skérree/ (*plural* **-ries**) *n Scotland* a rocky islet or reef [Early 17C. < Old Norse *sker* "reef"]

sketch /skech/ *n* **1.** PICTURE DONE QUICKLY AND ROUGHLY a drawing or painting that is done quickly without concern for detail. A sketch might be made to capture the general mood of a scene, or to help the artist work out an idea for a finished composition. **2.** SHORT PERFORMANCE a quick comic routine or piece of acting that is part of a variety show or comedy revue **3.** ROUGH DESCRIPTION OR EXPLANATION a short written or spoken account that conveys just a general outline or idea, with little detail **4.** SHORT PIECE OF WRITING a short, often descriptive piece of writing **5.** SHORT MUSICAL COMPOSITION a short piece of instrumental music, often for piano ■ *vti* (**sketched, sketch·ing, sketch·es**) MAKE SKETCH to create a sketch of something [Mid-17C. Via Dutch *schets* or German *Skizze* < Italian *schizzo* < Vulgar Latin *schediare* "do hastily" < Latin *schedius* < Greek *skhedios* "on the spur of the moment"] —**sketch·a·ble** *adj* —**sketch·er** *n*

sketch·book /skéch bo͝ok/, **sketch·pad** /-pàd/ *n* a book of plain paper for making sketches on

sketch·y /skéchee/ (**-i·er, -i·est**) *adj* **1.** SUPERFICIAL lacking in substance, depth, or finality **2.** GIVING ONLY ROUGH IDEA giving only the main points, with little detail **3.** DRAWN LIKE A SKETCH drawn or painted quickly without concern for detail —**sketch·i·ly** *adv* —**sketch·i·ness** *n*

skew /skyoo/ *v* (**skewed, skew·ing, skews**) **1.** *vti* SLANT, OR CAUSE SOMETHING TO SLANT to make something uneven, sloping, or unsymmetrical, or be in this state **2.** *vt* DISTORT SOMETHING to misrepresent the true meaning or nature of something **3.** *vi* SQUINT to look sideways at something ■ *adj* **1.** IN SLANTED POSITION OR LINE being in a slanted or unsymmetrical position **2.** MATH NOT PARALLEL OR INTERSECTING describes a line that is neither parallel nor intersecting ■ *n* **1.** TILTED OR INACCURATE POSITION a position that is not straight but that slants or twists out of correct alignment **2.** MECH ENG SLANTING DIRECTION a slanting movement, line, or direction [14C. Shortening of Old N French *eskiuer*, variant of Old French *eschiver* "eschew"]

skew arch *n* an arch with sides that are not at right angles to the span, e.g., on a bridge or tunnel

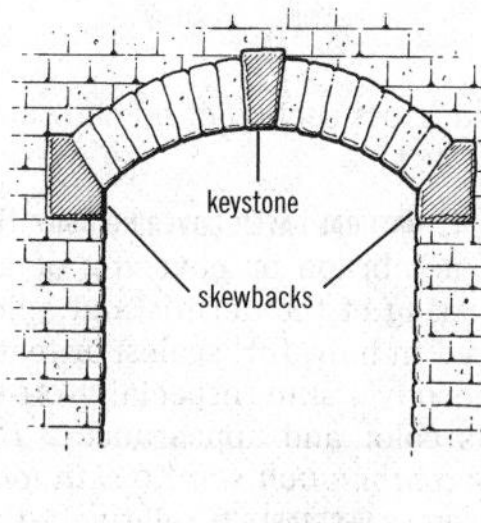

skewback

skew·back /skyo͞o bàk/ *n* either of the sloping surfaces on which the sides of a segmental arch abut

skew·bald /skyo͞o bàwld/ *adj* describes a horse that has a spotted coat consisting of white and another color other than black, generally brown ■ *n* a skewbald horse [Mid-17C. Blend of obsolete *skewed* "having mixed colors" (origin ?) + PIEBALD]

skew·er /skyo͞o ər/ *n* **1.** THIN ROD TO COOK FOOD ON a thin metal or wooden rod with a sharp end used to hold meat or meat and vegetables during cooking **2.** SOMETHING SIMILAR TO SKEWER a thin pointed object used to pierce something or hold it in place ■ *vt* (**-ered, -er·ing, -ers**) **1.** PIERCE SOMETHING WITH SKEWER to pierce somebody or something with a skewer or with something else that is thin and sharp **2.** CRITICIZE POINTEDLY to criticize somebody pointedly and effectively [15C. Origin ?]

skew lines *npl* two straight lines that do not lie in the same plane, are not parallel, and do not intersect, the distance between them being the unique segment perpendicular to both lines

skew·ness /skyo͞onəss/ *n* **1.** the way or amount that something is tilted or distorted from the true or straight position **2.** in statistics, a lack of symmetry about the mean in a frequency distribution

ski /skee/ *n* (*plural* **skis**) **1.** BOARD USED TO SLIDE ACROSS SNOW either of a pair of long thin boards made of wood, metal, or other material that curve up at the front and are used to slide across snow **2.** WATER SKIING same as **water ski 3.** RUNNER FOR VEHICLES TRAVELING ON SNOW a runner fitted to vehicles such as snowmobiles and airplanes for landing or traveling on snow and ice ■ *vti* (**skied, ski·ing, skis**) MOVE ALONG ON SKIS to glide over the surface of snow or water wearing skis, as a means of travel or as a leisure pursuit or sport [Mid-18C. Via Norwegian < Old Norse *skíð* "piece of split wood, snowshoe"] —**ski·a·ble** *adj* —**ski·er** *n*

ski·board /skée bàwrd/ *n* either of a pair of boards, shorter and wider than standard skis and often with sharp edges, worn and used like skis —**ski·board·er** *n*

ski·board·ing /skée bàwrding/ *n* the sport of traveling over snow or performing stunts on skiboards

ski·bob /skée bòb/ *n* a vehicle similar to a bicycle that has skis instead of wheels and is used to travel over snow [Mid-20C. < SKI + *bob*, shortening of BOBSLED] —**ski·bob·ber** *n* —**ski·bob·bing** *n*

skid /skid/ *n* **1.** UNCONTROLLED SLIDE an uncontrolled slide across a surface in a wheeled vehicle **2.** AIRCRAFT RUNNER a runner on the underside of an aircraft, used as part of its landing gear **3.** PALLET a low pallet on which goods are loaded for handling or transport **4.** POLE USED TO FORM TRACK one of two or more logs or poles used to form a track for sliding or rolling something along, e.g., from a truck to the ground **5.** MECH ENG BLOCK USED TO PREVENT WHEEL TURNING a shoe or block used to prevent a wheel from turning, e.g., when a vehicle is descending a hill **6.** NAUT SHIP'S FENDER a wooden structure hung over the side of a ship to protect the ship in loading and unloading cargo ■ *v* (**skid·ded, skid·ding, skids**) **1.** *vti* SLIDE DANGEROUSLY ACROSS SURFACE to slide across a surface, or make a vehicle slide across a surface, usually unintentionally, so that the wheels lose their grip and control is lost **2.** *vi* SLIDE OVER SURFACE WITHOUT ROLLING to slide across a surface without turning around and gripping it in the proper way **3.** *vti* SLIDE SIDEWAYS to slide sideways, or make an aircraft slide sideways away from the center of curvature when it is insufficiently banked in making a turn **4.** *vt* DRAG LOGS to move logs by dragging them **5.** *vt* MOVE SOMETHING ON SKIDS to lift or move something along using a track made of poles or logs [Early 17C. Origin ?] —**skid·dy** *adj* ◇ **on the skids** in difficulties and heading for failure (*slang*)

Ski-Doo /ski do͞o/ *tdmk* a trademark for a snowmobile

skid·proof /skíd pro͞of/ *adj* designed to prevent skidding

skid road *n* **1.** same as **skid row** (*informal*) **2.** a road with logs embedded in it, along which timber is hauled to a mill or loading area

skid row /-ró/ *n* an area of a city that has cheap bars and rundown hotels and is frequented by members of the city's underclass (*informal*) [Alteration of *skid road*, originally an area of a town frequented by loggers]

skied[1] /skeed/ SPORTS past participle, past tense of **ski**

skied[2] /skīd/ SPORTS past participle, past tense of **sky**

skiff /skif/ *n* a small flatbottom boat of shallow draft that can be propelled with oars, a sail, or a motor [15C. Via French *esquif* < Italian *schifo*, probably < Old High German *schif*]

skif·fle /skíff'l/ *n* music popular in the 1950s, usually played by a small group on guitars with improvised instruments such as a washboard used as percussion [Early 20C. Origin ?]

skiing

ski·ing[1] /skée ing/ *n* the activity, sport, or pastime of traveling on skis [< SKI]

ski·ing[2] /skée ing/ *n* the spending by retirees of their savings for their own enjoyment, rather than leaving the money to their children when they die (*humorous*) [< acronym < *spending the kids' inheritance*]

ski·jor·ing /skée jàwring/ *n* a sport in which a skier is towed across a frozen surface by a horse or vehicle [Early 20C. < Norwegian *skikjøring* "ski driving"] —**ski·jor·er** *n*

ski jump *n* **1.** TRACK FOR SKIERS TO JUMP FROM a steep artificial slope with a sharp upturn at the bottom. People ski down this and then leap into the air, competing to travel the longest distance before landing. **2.** JUMP MADE FROM SKI JUMP a jump made by a skier from a ski jump ■ *vi* (**ski jumped, ski jump·ing, ski jumps**) **EXECUTE SKI JUMP** to perform a ski jump —**ski-jump** *vi* —**ski jump·er** *n*

Skik·da /skík daˈa/ city and port in northeastern Algeria, situated about 220 mi./354 km east of Algiers. Population: 128,747 (1987).

skil·ful *adj* Can, UK spelling of **skillful**

ski lift *n* a motor-driven apparatus consisting of a continuously moving cable with seats, gondolas, or tow bars suspended from it, built to transport skiers to the top of a ski run

skill /skil/ *n* **1.** the ability to do something well, usually gained through training or experience **2.** something that requires training and experience to do well, e.g., an art or trade [12C. < Old Norse *skil* "discernment"] —**skilled** *adj* —**skill-less** *adj* —**skill-less·ness** *n*

SYNONYMS See ***ability.***

skil·let /skíllit/ *n* **1.** HOUSEHOLD same as **frying pan 2.** *UK* in former times, a small shallow pan with a long handle and usually legs, used for frying or braising food [15C. Probably < Old French *escuelete* "small platter" < *escuele* "platter" < Latin *scutella* "flat dish"]

skill·ful /skílf'l/ *adj* **1.** with special ability and dexterity in doing something **2.** requiring or done with specialized techniques and abilities developed over a period of time —**skill·ful·ly** *adv* —**skill·ful·ness** *n*

~~**skillfull**~~ incorrect spelling of **skillful**

skim /skim/ *v* (**skimmed, skim·ming, skims**) **1.** *vt* **SCOOP SOMETHING FROM TOP OF LIQUID** to remove a substance such as fat forming a layer on the surface of a liquid, usually with a large shallow spoon **2.** *vt* **RID LIQUID OF FLOATING MATERIAL** to rid a liquid of material accumulating on its surface **3.** *vti* **PASS CLOSELY OVER SURFACE OF SOMETHING** to pass quickly across and just above the surface of something, or make something pass in this way, sometimes touching it lightly and briefly **4.** *vt* **GLANCE THROUGH BOOK OR PAPER** to read something very quickly, looking only at occasional lines or words, in order to get a general idea of its contents **5.** *vt* **SEND SOMETHING BOUNCING ALONG** to throw something so that it bounces lightly along the surface of water **6.** *vt* **TREAT SOMETHING IN CURSORY WAY** to deal with something in a superficial way **7.** *vti* **COAT OR BECOME COATED WITH LAYER** to develop a thin surface layer of something, or coat an object so that its surface is covered in a thin layer of something **8.** *vti* **EMBEZZLE** to embezzle some of the proceeds from a business (*informal*) **9.** *vt* **HIDE PROFITS TO AVOID TAXES** to hide earnings or profits in order to avoid paying taxes on them (*informal*) ■ *n* **1. THIN FILM** a thin layer of something on a surface **2. CURSORY LOOK** a cursory look at or treatment of something ○ *a quick skim over the main topics on the agenda* **3. SUBSTANCE REMOVED FROM SURFACE OF SOMETHING** the matter that forms a layer on a surface and is skimmed off **4. SKIMMING PROCESS** the process of removing a substance from a surface [15C. < Old French *escumer* < *escume* "scum"]
skim off *vt* to cull the best people or items from a group

ski mask *n* a covering for the face and head, usually made of knitted material and having openings for the eyes, the mouth, and sometimes the nose, worn by skiers as protection against the cold

skimmed milk /skìmd-/ *n UK* BEVERAGES same as **skim milk**

skim·mer /skímmər/ *n* **1. SOMEBODY OR SOMETHING THAT SKIMS** a person, object, or device that skims **2. FLAT STRAW HAT** a flat hat usually made of straw **3. LONG-WINGED FRESHWATER BIRD** a long-winged freshwater bird that has a beak with the lower half longer than the upper, used for skimming food from the surface of water while in flight. Native to: South America, Africa, Asia. Genus: *Rynchops*. **4. UTENSIL USED FOR SKIMMING** a broad flat spoon with small perforations in it, used to skim something such as fat from the surface of a liquid

skim milk *n* milk with most or all of its fat content removed. Same as **skim milk**

skim·ming /skímming/ *n* the crime of fraudulently reusing the electronic information from a swiped credit card or payment card ■ **skim·mings** *npl* the floating fat or debris skimmed off the surface of a liquid

skimp /skimp/ (**skimped, skimp·ing, skimps**) *v* **1.** *vti* **USE TOO LITTLE OF SOMETHING** to use or provide hardly enough of something **2.** *vt* **DO SOMETHING IMPROPERLY** to carry out a piece of work poorly, without spending enough time, trouble, or materials on it **3.** *vt* **NOT PROVIDE SOMEBODY WITH ENOUGH** to give or allow somebody only an inadequate amount of money, food, or other necessary items [Late 18C. Origin ?]

skimp·y /skímpee/ (**-i·er, -i·est**) *adj* **1.** made or done using barely enough of the necessary materials **2.** not giving somebody enough of something through meanness —**skimp·i·ly** *adv* —**skimp·i·ness** *n*

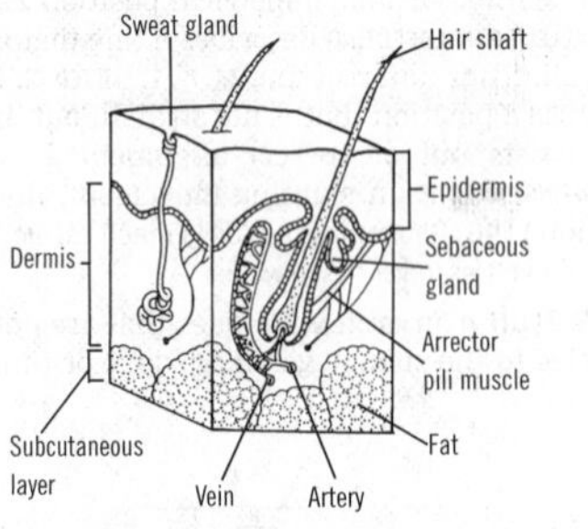

skin: cross section of human skin

skin /skin/ *n* **1. NATURAL LAYER COVERING BODY** the external protective membrane or covering of an animal's body, consisting of the dermis and epidermis and often covered in hair, fur, scales, or feathers **2. SKIN ON FACE** somebody's skin, especially on the face, in terms of its color and appearance ○ *Do you have oily, dry, or combination skin?* ○ *skin tone* **3. NATURAL COVERING OF FRUIT OR VEGETABLE** a relatively thin but protective layer closely surrounding the flesh of a fruit or vegetable **4. FUR OR LEATHER FROM DEAD ANIMAL** skin or a piece of skin removed from an animal's body, especially once it has been cleaned and treated to use as fur or leather **5. SOLID SURFACE LAYER ON LIQUID** a thin pliant surface that forms on the top of some liquids, e.g., on hot milk left to cool **6. TIGHT-FITTING COVERING** a thin tough casing or cover that fits closely around something such as a sausage to hold in, protect, or preserve the enclosed material **7. OUTER COVERING OF STRUCTURE** the outer protective covering of a structure such as an aircraft **8. SMALL LEATHER SACK** a bag made from animal hide used to hold liquid such as wine or water **9.** COMPUT **SOFTWARE FOR EDITING IMAGES** a piece of software that enables the user to change the appearance of images produced by existing software without changing their function **10.** COMPUT **APPEARANCE OF COMPUTER IMAGE** a specific visual appearance given to an image produced on a computer screen ■ **skins** *npl* MUSIC **JAZZ DRUMS** drums, especially in a jazz band (*informal*) ■ *v* (**skinned, skin·ning, skins**) **1.** *vt* **TAKE SKIN OFF FRUIT OR VEGETABLE** to remove the skin from a fruit or vegetable, or from an animal or person, especially by cutting or ripping it **2.** *vt* **SCRAPE SKIN** to make the skin on a part of the body red, sore, and broken, especially by falling on it or scraping it **3.** *vt* **REMOVE OUTSIDE LAYER OF SOMETHING** to strip off an outer, covering layer of something that resembles a skin **4.** *vi* **ACQUIRE LAYER LIKE SKIN** to become covered with a layer that resembles a skin **5.** *vti* COMPUT **ALTER SOFTWARE IMAGES** to change the appearance of images produced by existing software, without changing their function **6.** *vt* CRIME **SWINDLE SOMEBODY** to trick somebody out of money or property (*slang*) ■ *adj US* **PORNOGRAPHIC** relating to or containing pornographic material (*informal*) [12C. < Old Norse *skinn*] —**skin·less** *adj* ◇ **be no skin off somebody's back** to be a matter that does not harm somebody at all and therefore may be of little interest (*informal*) ◇ **by the skin of your teeth** by a very narrow margin, or only just (*informal*) ◇ **get under somebody's skin** (*informal*) **1.** to annoy or irritate somebody **2.** to make somebody feel great interest or attraction ◇ **jump out of your skin** to get a bad fright or a shock (*informal*) ◇ **save somebody's skin** to prevent somebody from suffering hurt, loss, or punishment by giving vital help (*informal*)

skin·care /skín kèr/ *adj* intended to keep the skin healthy, supple, or young-looking

skin-deep *adj* appearing to be important, meaningful, or valuable but having little deep or lasting importance ■ *adv* in a superficial way

skin div·ing *n* the sport of underwater diving using flippers, a mask, and a snorkel —**skin-dive** *vi* —**skin div·er** *n*

skin ef·fect *n* the tendency of a high-frequency alternating current to flow near the surface of the conductor rather than in its interior

skin flick *n* a pornographic movie (*slang*)

skin·flint /skín flìnt/ *n* same as **miser** (sense 1) [Late 17C. < the idea of somebody so miserly as to try to remove the skin from a piece of flint]

skin fric·tion *n* a frictional force that acts on the surface of an airfoil or other object immersed in and moving through a fluid

~~**sking**~~ incorrect spelling of **skiing**

skin game *n* a confidence trick or scheme used to cheat people of their money (*slang*) [< SKIN "swindle"]

skin graft *n* a piece of skin taken from part of the body and used to replace lost or damaged skin

skin·head /skín hèd/ *n* (*slang*) **1.** somebody whose hair is very short or whose head is shaved **2.** one of a group of young white men with closely-cropped or shaven hair, characterized by extreme right-wing views and aggressive behavior

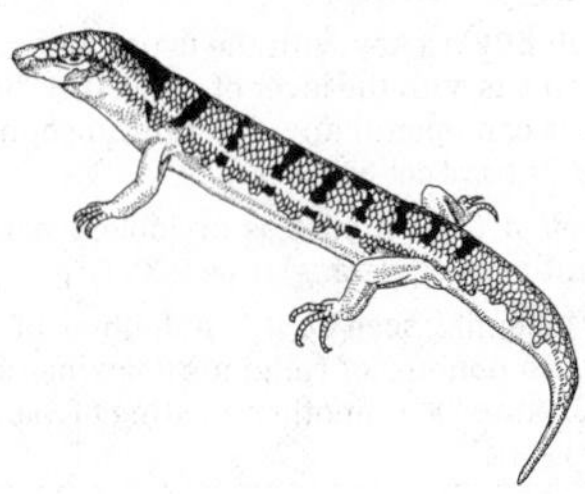

skink

skink /skingk/ *n* a small smooth insect-eating lizard with a long thin body and small limbs. It lives in temperate and tropical regions, especially in Asia and Africa. Family: Scincidae. [Late 16C. Via Latin *scincus* < Greek *skigkos*]

skin·ner /skínnər/ *n* **1. SOMEBODY WHO SKINS** somebody who skins animals, or deals in animal skins **2. CHANGER OF COMPUTER IMAGES** somebody who creates software to change the appearance of images on a computer screen **3.** *Western US* **MULE DRIVER** a driver of a team of mules [14C. < SKIN]

Skin·ner /skínnər/, **B. F.** (1904–90) US behavioral psychologist. His stimulus-response experiments and behaviorist theories profoundly influenced methods of education and behavior therapy. His works include *Beyond Freedom and Dignity* (1971). Full name **Skinner, Burrhus Frederic** —**Skin·ner·i·an** /ski néeree ən/ *adj, n*

> "The real problem is not whether machines think but whether men do."
> [B. F. Skinner, *Contingencies of Reinforcement*; 1969]

Skin·ner, Cornelia Otis (1901–79) US writer and actor. Known for her one-woman shows, she was coauthor of *Our Hearts Were Young and Gay* (1942).

> "Woman's virtue is man's greatest invention."
> [Attributed to Cornelia Otis Skinner]

Skin·ner box *n* an enclosure for isolating an animal during studies of learning behavior or operant conditioning that contains a device the animal may operate to receive a reward or avoid punishment [Mid-20C. After B. F. SKINNER]

skin·ny /skínnee/ *adj* (**-ni·er, -ni·est**) **1. VERY THIN** thin, especially in an unappealing or unhealthy way **2. LOW-FAT** made with skim milk (*slang*) ○ *One skinny* *latte to go.* ■ *n US* RELIABLE INFORMATION the truth about something (*slang*) [Mid-16C. < SKIN] —**skin·ni·ness** *n*

SYNONYMS See *thin.*

skin·ny-dip (*informal*) *vi* to go swimming in the nude ■ *n* a swim in the nude [< SKINNY "of the skin"] —**skin·ny-dip·per** *n* —**skin·ny-dip·ping** *n*

skin-pop *vti* to take narcotic drugs by inserting the needle under the skin, not straight into a vein (*slang*)

skin test *n* a test in which a substance is applied to the skin to determine somebody's allergic sensitivity or immunity to it

skin·tight /skìn tī́t/ *adj* fitting tightly to the body

skip[1] /skip/ *v* (**skipped, skip·ping, skips**) **1.** *vi* MOVE WITH SMALL HOPPING STEPS to move along by hopping from one foot to the other **2.** *vti* JUMP REPEATEDLY OVER CIRCLING ROPE to jump repeatedly over a rope as it is swung around over the head and under the feet **3.** *vt* JUMP OVER SOMETHING to jump nimbly over something **4.** *vti* OMIT SOMETHING to pass over or leave out something that should properly follow as part of a sequence or a complete work **5.** *vi* DEAL WITH SOMETHING CURSORILY to deal with or look at something in a cursory way ○ *Can we just skip through the draft document before we break for lunch?* **6.** *vt* NOT ATTEND SOMETHING to decide to miss an event or activity (*informal*) **7.** *vt* OMIT SCHOOL GRADE to promote a student to a grade that is one beyond the next in succession, or omit a grade in this way **8.** *vi* NOT PLAY CORRECTLY to fail to play properly by jumping from one place to another (*refers to CDs or records*) **9.** *vti* LEAVE SOMEWHERE SECRETLY to make a secret getaway from a place, especially for some dishonest reason, e.g., to avoid being punished for something (*informal*) ○ *He skipped town.* **10.** *vti* MOVE IN SERIES OF SMALL HOPS to move lightly across a surface in a series of small hops, or make something move in this way ■ *n* **1.** SMALL HOPPING STEP a small forward hopping step **2.** ACT OF OMITTING SOMETHING an act of omitting part of something [13C. Probably < Old Norse] —**skip·pa·ble** *adj*

skip[2] /skip/ (*slang*) *n* NAUT same as **skipper**[1] *n* (sense 1) ■ *vi* (**skipped, skip·ping, skips**) to be the skipper of a vessel [Early 19C. Shortening]

ski pants *npl* **1.** *UK* same as **stirrup pants 2.** lined, windproof, water-resistant pants that are worn for skiing and other cold weather activities

skip dis·tance *n* the shortest distance between a radio transmitter and receiver that permits waves of a specific frequency to be sent and received by reflection from the ionosphere

skip·jack /skíp jàk/ (*plural* **-jacks** or *same*) *n* **1.** LEAPING SEA FISH a sea fish that leaps out of the water, e.g., the bonito, ladyfish, or bluefish **2.** *also* **skip·jack tu·na** SEA FISH a tropical ocean fish of the tuna family that is blue and silver with dark stripes on its abdomen. Latin name: *Euthynnus pelamus.* **3.** *US* SAILBOAT a sailboat with straight sides and a V-shaped bottom

ski·plane /skée plàyn/ *n* an aircraft equipped with skis for taking off from and landing on snow

ski pole *n* either of a pair of lightweight poles held by skiers for balance and control. The bottom end has a point surrounded by a disk for gaining a hold on the snow.

skip·per[1] /skíppər/ *n* **1.** SOMEBODY IN CHARGE OF SHIP somebody in charge of a ship or boat **2.** LEADER OF TEAM somebody in charge of a squad or group of others, especially the captain or coach of a sports team (*informal*) ■ *vt* (**-pered, -per·ing, -pers**) BE SKIPPER OF SOMETHING to be in charge of a ship, team, or aircraft (*informal*) [14C. < Middle Dutch *schipper* < *schip* "ship"]

skip·per[2] /skíppər/ *n* **1.** somebody or something that skips **2.** a quick-flying insect that has a hairy body and clubbed antennae with hooked tips, and is closely related to true butterflies. Families: Hesperiidae or Megathymidae. **3.** FISH same as **saury** [Mid-18C. < SKIP[1]]

skip·ping rope *n Can, UK* a piece of rope, often with handles at either end, for skipping over. US term **jump rope**

skirl /skurl/ *Scotland n* the high-pitched wailing sound that bagpipes typically make ■ *vti* (**skirled, skirl·ing, skirls**) to produce a high-pitched wailing sound on the bagpipes [14C. Probably < N Germanic]

skir·mish /skúrmish/ *n* **1.** BRIEF FIGHT BETWEEN TWO ARMED GROUPS an incident where fighting breaks out briefly between two small groups, sometimes as part of a larger battle **2.** SCUFFLE a brief fight or disagreement between people ■ *vi* (**-mished, -mish·ing, -mish·es**) ENGAGE IN MINOR BATTLE to become involved in a skirmish [14C. < Old French *eskermiss-* "to fence" < Germanic, "defend"] —**skir·mish·er** *n*

SYNONYMS See *fight.*

skirr /skur/ *n* a whirring sound [Mid-16C. Origin ?]

skir·ret /skúr ət/ *n* a plant with sweetish edible roots resembling carrots. Native to: East Asia. Latin name: *Sium sisarum.* [14C. Origin ?]

skirt /skurt/ *n* **1.** GARMENT THAT HANGS FROM WAIST a piece of clothing that hangs from the waist and does not divide into two separate legs, usually worn by women and girls **2.** AREA OF GARMENT FALLING FROM WAISTLINE the section from the waist to the hem on a dress, coat, or robe **3.** SOMETHING SIMILAR TO SKIRT an attachment shaped like a skirt, or covering the lower part of something like a skirt **4.** OFFENSIVE TERM an offensive term for a girl or woman, or women in general (*slang*) **5.** *UK* FOOD CUT OF BEEF a stewing cut of beef taken from the flank, below the sirloin and rump, and cut from the inside of flank steak **6.** ENG FLAP AROUND BOTTOM OF HOVERCRAFT the lower outer section of a rocket or the flap around the bottom of a hovercraft **7.** RIDING FLAP ON SADDLE one of a pair of leather flaps that hang from a saddle ■ *v* (**skirt·ed, skirt·ing, skirts**) **1.** *vti* BE AROUND OUTSIDE OF SOMETHING to form a border along the edge of an area or object **2.** *vti* MOVE AROUND OUTSIDE OF SOMETHING to travel along the edge of something such as an area, structure, or geographic feature **3.** *vt* NOT DEAL WITH SOMETHING to avoid dealing with a subject in any depth, usually because it is tricky or unpleasant **4.** *vt* GIVE EDGE TO SOMETHING to provide something with an attachment shaped like a skirt or border [13C. < Old Norse *skyrta* "shirt" < Germanic, "cut"] —**skirt·er** *n*

skirt-chas·er *n* an offensive term for a man who is regarded as being excessively interested in pursuing women sexually (*slang*) —**skirt-chas·ing** *n*

skirt·ing /skúrting/ *n* **1.** material used to make skirts **2.** *UK* CONSTR same as **baseboard** (sense 2)

skirt·ing board *n UK* CONSTR same as **baseboard** (sense 2)

skirt steak *n US* a thin cut of beef taken from the plate or diaphragm

ski run *n* a snow-covered slope or course used for skiing

ski stick *n UK* SKIING same as **ski pole**

skit /skit/ *n* **1.** a short comic sketch **2.** a short piece of comic writing that satirizes somebody or something [Early 18C. Origin ?]

ski tour·ing *n* traveling over long distances on skis, especially in wilderness areas

ski tow *n* an apparatus consisting of a motor-driven rope that skiers hang onto to be towed up a mountain

skit·ter /skíttər/ (**-tered, -ter·ing, -ters**) *v* **1.** *vi* to move about or run off quickly with small scampering steps **2.** *vti* to pass quickly across something, touching its surface very lightly and briefly, or send something skidding rapidly over the surface of something [Mid-19C. Origin ?]

skit·tish /skíttish/, **skit·ter·y** /skíttəree/ *adj* **1.** NERVOUS easily agitated or alarmed **2.** SILLY AND IRRESPONSIBLE with moods or ideas that constantly change, in a frivolous and unreliable way **3.** LIVELY tending to dash about in an energetic or restless way [14C. Origin ?] —**skit·tish·ly** *adv* —**skit·tish·ness** *n*

skit·tle /skítt'l/ *n UK* same as **ninepin** [Mid-17C. Origin ?]

skive /skīv/ (**skived, skiv·ing, skives**) *vt* to scrape thin slices off leather in preparing it [Early 19C. < N Germanic]

skiv·er /skívər/ *n* **1.** a thin soft tanned leather taken from the outer side of a skin **2.** somebody or something that skives leather [Early 19C. < SKIVE]

skiv·vy /skívvee/ *n* (*plural* **-vies**) **1.** MAN'S UNDERSHIRT a man's short-sleeved undershirt (*slang*) **2.** *US* LONG-SLEEVED COTTON TOP a long-sleeved, usually cotton piece of clothing with a rolled neck worn on the upper part of the body ■ **skiv·vies** *npl* MEN'S UNDERWEAR men's underwear consisting of an undershirt and shorts (*slang*) [Mid-20C. Origin ?]

ski·wear /skée wèr/ *n* clothing designed for skiers to wear

skoal /skōl/ *interj* used as a drinking toast [Early 17C. Via Danish, Swedish, and Norwegian < Old Norse *skál* "bowl"]

Sko·bel·ev /skáwbi lèv/ former name for **Fergana** (1907–24)

Sko·kie /skṓkee/ village in northeastern Illinois, south of Wilmette, on the northern border of Chicago. Population: 63,126 (2002 estimate).

Sko·mer /skṓmər/ islet in St. Bride's Bay, off the Pembrokeshire coast, Wales.

skoo·kum /skóokəm/ *adj Can, Northwest US* very large and impressive [Mid-19C. < Chinook Jargon]

Skop·je /skóp yee/ capital of the Former Yugoslav Republic of Macedonia, situated in the north central part of the country. Population: 440,577 (1994).

skosh /skōsh/ *n US* a little bit (*slang*) ○ *I'd like just a skosh more, please.* [Mid-20C. < Japanese *sukoshi*]

Skr., **Skt.** *abbr* LANG Sanskrit

SKU /èss kay yóo, skyoo/, **Sku** *n* a unique code, consisting of numbers or letters and numbers, assigned to a product by a retailer for identification and inventory control. Full form **stockkeeping unit**

sku·a /skyóo ə/ *n UK* same as **jaeger** [Late 17C. Via modern Latin < variant of Faeroese *skugvur* < Old Norse *skúfr*]

skul·dug·ger·y *n* another spelling of **skullduggery** (*humorous*)

skulk /skulk/ *vi* (**skulked, skulk·ing, skulks**) **1.** MOVE FURTIVELY to move about in a furtive way **2.** HIDE SOMEWHERE to hide, especially in order to do something sinister **3.** *UK* SHIRK to avoid work or responsibilities ■ *n* **1.** SOMEBODY WHO SKULKS a furtive person, or somebody who conceals a sinister purpose **2.** GROUP OF FOXES a pack of foxes [12C. < N Germanic]

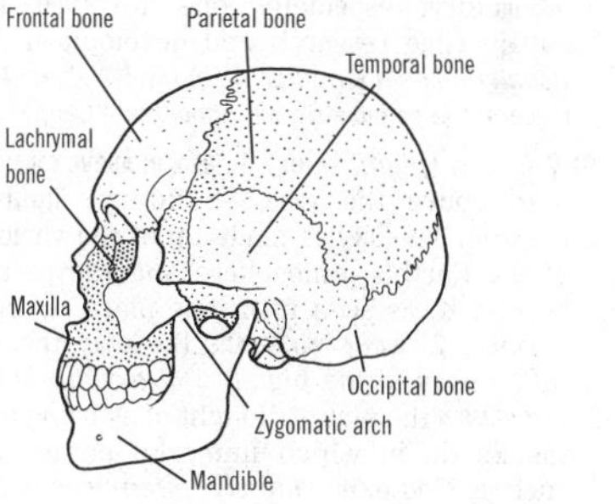

skull

skull /skul/ *n* **1.** the skeletal part of the head in humans and other vertebrates, consisting of the cranium, which encases the brain, and the bones of the face and jaws **2.** a person's head or mind (*informal*) ○ *tried to drum the principles of thermodynamics into his skull* [13C. Probably < N Germanic] —**-skulled** *suffix*

skull and cross·bones *n* **1.** a representation of a human skull above two human thighbones crossed over each other, used as a symbol of danger or death **2.** same as **Jolly Roger**

skull·cap /skúl kàp/ *n* **1.** SMALL ROUND BRIMLESS HAT a simple hat consisting of a small circle of fabric shaped to fit over the crown of the head **2.** CLOTHING same as **yarmulke 3.** PERENNIAL MINT PLANT a perennial plant of the mint family. Flowers: blue or pinkish, with helmet-shaped calyx. Genus: *Scutellaria.* **4.** TOP OF SKULL the top part of the skull

skull·dug·ger·y /skul dúggəree/, **skul·dug·ger·y** *n* unfair and dishonest practices carried out in a secretive way in order to trick other people (*humorous*) [Mid-19C. Alteration of *sculduddery* "sexual impropriety, indecency," origin ?]

skull ses·sion *n US (informal)* **1.** a meeting to talk over and think about policies and procedures **2.** a meeting for a coach to instruct team members on strategy

skunk

skunk /skungk/ *n (plural* **skunks** *or same)* **1.** BLACK-AND-WHITE MAMMAL a black-and-white animal of the weasel family that ejects a foul-smelling liquid from an anal gland as a defensive action. Native to: North, South America. **2.** OFFENSIVE TERM an offensive term for a person considered to be despicable *(slang insult)* **3.** DRUGS same as **skunkweed** (sense 2) *(slang)* ■ *vt* **(skunked, skunk·ing, skunks)** *(slang)* **1.** DEFEAT SOMEBODY SOUNDLY to defeat an opponent soundly, especially by not allowing him or her to score any points in a sports competition **2.** CHEAT to cheat somebody out of something [Mid-17C. < Massachusett]

skunk cab·bage *n* **1.** a foul-smelling broad-leaved perennial herb with small flowers enclosed in greenish spathes. Native to: swampy areas of eastern North America. Latin name: *Symplocarpus foetidus.* **2.** a plant similar to skunk cabbage that has a large yellow spathe. Native to: western North America. Latin name: *Lysichitum americanum.*

skunk·weed /skúngk weed/ *(plural* **-weeds** *or same) n* **1.** an annual plant with an unpleasant smell. Native to: southern United States. Latin name: *Croton texensis.* **2.** marijuana with a pungent smell *(slang)* **3.** PLANTS same as **skunk cabbage**

skunk·works /skúngk wùrks/ *n US* a department or laboratory, especially one involved in secret cutting-edge research and development *(informal; usually takes a singular verb)* [Mid-20C. < *Skonk Works,* place in the comic strip *L'il Abner* by Al Capp]

sky /skī/ *n (plural* **skies)** **1.** REGION ABOVE EARTH the area high above the trees, buildings, landscape, or horizon. The sky is made up of the various layers of the Earth's atmosphere and the part of space beyond it, as seen from one place on the Earth's surface. **2.** WAY SKY APPEARS the way the sky looks *(often used in the plural)* ○ *clear blue skies* **3.** *also* **Sky** HEAVEN the plane, thought of as being high above the Earth, in which immortal powers or beings such as God exist *(literary; often used in the plural)* **4.** HIGHEST LIMIT the topmost limit or the best and most it is possible to achieve ○ *reach for the sky* ■ *vti* **(skied, sky·ing, skies)** MAKE BALL GO VERY HIGH to hit or throw a ball high up into the air [13C. < Old Norse *ský* "cloud"] ◇ **praise somebody** *or* **something to the skies** to praise somebody *or* something very highly ◇ **the sky's the limit** there is no upper limit on something *(informal)*

sky blue *n* a pale blue color like that of the sky on a clear day —**sky blue** *adj*

sky·box /skī bòks/ *n* a raised room or balcony area in a stadium, which is private and separate from the main seating areas

sky·cap /skī kàp/ *n US* a porter who works at an airport [Mid-20C. After REDCAP]

sky·dive /skī dīv/ **(-dived** or **-dove** /-dōv/, **-div·ing, -dives)** *vi* to jump from an airplane and descend in free fall, sometimes performing acrobatic maneuvers, before pulling the ripcord of a parachute —**sky·div·er** *n* —**sky·div·ing** *n*

Skye /skī/ largest island in the Inner Hebrides, in Scotland. Portree is the chief town and port. Population: 8,843 (1991). Area: 647 sq. mi./1,676 sq. km.

Skye ter·ri·er *n* a small terrier with short legs, a long body, and a long straight coat, belonging to a breed originating in Scotland

sky-high *adv, adj* up to or at the highest level ○ *They charge sky-high prices.* ■ *adv* high into the air or in all directions, forcefully and often in pieces

sky-hook *n* a helicopter that is specially configured with a hook-and-cable apparatus in its fuselage, used to lift, drop, and transport heavy objects

sky·jack /skī jàk/ **(-jacked, -jack·ing, -jacks)** *vt* to use force to take over control of an aircraft, especially a commercial aircraft, when it is in the air [Mid-20C. After HIJACK] —**sky·jack·er** *n* —**sky·jack·ing** *n*

sky·lark /skī laark/ *n* a lark with streaked brown-and-white feathers that is noted for singing melodiously while hovering high in the air. Native to: Europe, Asia. Latin name: *Alauda arvensis.* ■ *vi* **(-larked, -lark·ing, -larks)** to take part in lively physical playful behavior *(informal)* —**sky·lark·er** *n*

sky·light /skī līt/ *n* an opening in a roof or ceiling that is fitted with glass to let in daylight

sky·light fil·ter *n* a photographic filter that is slightly pink and is used to filter out ultraviolet light and reduce blueness

sky·line /skī līn/ *n* **1.** the pattern of shapes made by the various features of a landscape, e.g., hills or buildings, against the sky **2.** the place where the ground appears to join the sky

sky mar·shal *n US* a US federal law enforcement officer providing in-flight security on commercial passenger aircraft

sky pi·lot *n* an offensive term for a priest or chaplain, associated especially with the armed forces *(slang)*

sky·rock·et /skī ròkət/ *vti* **(-et·ed, -et·ing, -ets)** to rise suddenly to a very high level or value, or make something do this *(informal)* ■ *n* INDUST same as **rocket**[1] *n* (sense 1)

Sky·ros /skīrəss, skee ràwss/ largest and most easterly of the Greek Sporades Islands, in the Aegean Sea. Population: 2,757 (1981). Area: 79 sq. mi./205 sq. km.

sky·sail /skī sàyl, skīss'l/ *n* a small light square sail that goes above the royal on a square-rigged sailing vessel

sky·scape /skī skàyp/ *n* a scene or picture showing chiefly sky, especially an artistic study of a section of sky

sky·scrap·er /skī skràypər/ *n* a modern building, especially a block of city offices or apartments, that is extremely tall

sky·surf·ing /skī sùrfing/ *n* the sport of jumping from an airplane and performing a series of moves before descending by parachute —**sky·surf** *vi* —**sky·surf·er** *n*

sky·walk /skī wàwk/ *n* a raised walkway, usually joining two buildings

sky·ward /skīwərd/ *adj* heading toward the sky ■ *adv also* **sky·wards** /-wərdz/ in the direction of the sky

sky wave *n* a radio wave that is transmitted around the curved surface of the Earth by being reflected back to Earth by the ionosphere

sky·way /skī wày/ *n* **1.** a route used by aircraft **2.** an elevated highway, supported by tall spans ○ *the Chicago Skyway* **3.** ARCHIT same as **skywalk**

sky·writ·ing /skī rīting/ *n* **1.** the use of an aircraft releasing colored smoke to form letters in the sky **2.** letters or a message formed in the sky by colored smoke released from an aircraft —**sky·write** *vti* —**sky·writ·er** *n*

sl *abbr* Sierra Leone *(used in Internet addresses)* See table at **domain name**

SL *abbr* **1.** GEOG sea level **2.** LING source language **3.** GEOG south latitude

slab /slab/ *n* **1.** THICK PIECE a thick flat broad piece of something, especially when cut or trimmed **2.** STONE BASE FOR SOMETHING a flat rectangular base or foundation of concrete or stone **3.** GEOL SHEET OF ROCK a smooth flat sheet of rock sharply angled to the horizontal **4.** WASTE FROM LOG any large outer section of a log that is sawed off in manufacturing lumber ■ *vt* **(slabbed, slab·bing, slabs)** **1.** COVER AREA WITH SLABS to cover something by laying stone or concrete slabs on it **2.** MAKE SOMETHING INTO SLABS to cut or make something into slabs **3.** TRIM SOMETHING BY SAWING to saw off the rough outer parts of a log [13C. Origin ?]

slab·bing /slábbing/ *n* **1.** the laying of stone or concrete slabs to form a surface such as a pathway **2.** stone or concrete slabs, collectively

slab pot·ter·y *n* pottery made by hand using rolled-out sheets of clay

slab-sid·ed *adj US* **1.** having long, flat sides **2.** tall and thin *(informal)*

slack /slak/ *adj* **1.** NOT TIGHT not tight or stretched taut, but hanging loosely or having a good deal of give ○ *The reins are too slack.* **2.** NOT SHOWING ENOUGH CARE not showing enough care, attention, or rigor ○ *They've been rather slack about keeping to performance targets.* **3.** NOT BUSY not busy or active, or less busy than usual ○ *the slack period following the main tourist season* **4.** MOVING SLOWLY moving slowly or sluggishly **5.** PHON same as **lax** (sense 4) ■ *adv* LOOSELY in a loose or limp way ○ *His clothes hung slack on him.* ■ *n* **1.** LOOSENESS looseness or give in something such as a rope, or the extra length or fullness in it that needs to be taken in to make it taut **2.** UNUSED POTENTIAL productive potential in an organization or system that is not being fully made use of ○ *take in some of the slack in the administrative division* **3.** QUIET TIME a period of time that is not busy **4.** STILL WATER a stretch of water that is still or moving only slowly ■ **slacks** *npl* PANTS casual pants, especially loose-fitting ones ■ *v* **(slacked, slack·ing, slacks)** **1.** *vi* AVOID WORK to be lazy, avoid work, or work with insufficient vigor or concentration **2.** *vt* NEGLECT SOMETHING to neglect something such as duty, or leave something undone **3.** *vti* same as **slacken** (sense 1) **4.** *vti* CHEM same as **slake** (sense 2) [Old English *slæc* < Indo-European, "be loose"] —**slack·ly** *adv* —**slack·ness** *n*

slack·en /slákən/ **(-ened, -en·ing, -ens)** *vti* **1.** to become less intense, vigorous, or fast, or make something become less intense, vigorous, or fast **2.** to become looser or more relaxed, or make something become looser or more relaxed

slack·er /slákər/ *n* **1.** somebody who avoids doing something, especially work or military service **2.** an offensive term for a young educated person who is regarded as being disaffected or apathetic and underachieving *(slang)*

slack wa·ter *n* the period of time during which the tide is turning and the water is still or slow-moving because of this

slag /slag/ *n* **1.** WASTE MATERIAL FROM SMELTING fused glassy material that is produced when a metal is separated from its ore during smelting **2.** COAL WASTE the mixture of coal dust and mineral waste produced after coal has been mined **3.** GEOL same as **scoria** (sense 1) ■ *vti* **(slagged, slag·ging, slags)** TURN SOMETHING INTO SLAG to convert something into slag, or become slag [Mid-16C. < Middle Low German *slagge* < Germanic, "strike"]

slag heap *n* a large mound of waste material from a coal mine or factory

slain past participle of **slay**

slake /slayk/ **(slaked, slak·ing, slakes)** *v* **1.** *vt* to satisfy a desire for something, especially a drink **2.** *vti* to treat lime with water to produce calcium hydroxide, or undergo this process [Old English *slacian* "relax" < Germanic] —**slak·a·ble** *adj*

slaked lime /slàykt-/ *n* CHEM same as **calcium hydroxide**

Popperfoto

slalom

sla·lom /slaáləm/ *n* **1. ZIGZAG SKI RACE** a downhill ski race in which competitors follow a winding course and zigzag through flags on poles or other obstacles. See illustration on previous page **2. ZIGZAG RACE** any race that involves following a zigzag course through obstacles ■ *vi* (**-lomed, -lom·ing, -loms**) **FOLLOW ZIGZAG COURSE** to follow a zigzag or winding course, especially in a race. See illustration on previous page [Early 20C. < Norwegian *slalåm* "sloping track"]

slam[1] /slam/ *v* (**slammed, slam·ming, slams**) **1.** *vti* **CLOSE FORCEFULLY** to close something forcefully and noisily, or be closed in this way **2.** *vti* **PUT SOMETHING DOWN VIOLENTLY** to put something down violently and noisily, or be put down in this way **3.** *vti* **HIT SOMETHING VIOLENTLY** to hit something with sudden or violent force ○ *The waves slammed into the dock.* **4.** *vt* **CRITICIZE SOMEBODY OR SOMETHING** to criticize somebody or something forcefully (*informal*) ○ *The press slammed the President's performance.* **5.** *vt US* TELECOM **CHANGE SOMEBODY'S PHONE SERVICE** to change the telephone service provider of a customer without his or her consent or authorization (*informal*) ■ *n* **1. IMPACT** a heavy, noisy, or violent blow or impact **2. CRITICISM** a forceful piece of criticism or critical remark [Late 17C. Origin ?]

slam[2] /slam/ *n* **1.** the winning of all, or all but one, of the tricks in a hand of bridge or whist **2.** LITERAT same as **poetry slam** [Mid-17C. Origin ?]

slam-bang (*informal*) *adv* **1. VIOLENTLY** in a sudden, noisy, or violent way **2. CARELESSLY** in a careless and reckless way **3. EXCITINGLY** in an exciting and vigorous way ○ *The novel ended slam-bang with a fight to the finish.* ■ *adj* **1. SUDDEN AND NOISY** sudden, noisy, or violent ○ *a slam-bang fight* **2. CARELESS AND RECKLESS** careless and reckless ○ *a slam-bang approach to his work* **3. EXCITING** exciting and vigorous ○ *slam-bang action scenes*

slam danc·ing *n* boisterous dancing to rock music in which young people hurl their bodies against one another, more out of enthusiasm than aggression —**slam dance** *vi*

slam dunk *n* **1.** in basketball, a dunk shot carried out with great force **2.** something dramatically successful and effective (*informal*)

slam-dunk *vt* **1. SLAM BALL INTO BASKET** in basketball, to jam or slam the ball through the hoop from above with great force **2.** *US* **TREAT SOMEBODY HARSHLY** to speak of or treat somebody in a dramatic, hostile, or disrespectful way (*slang*) **3.** *US* **DEFEAT SOMEBODY COMPLETELY** to defeat a person or a group of people completely (*slang*) ■ *adj US* **CERTAIN OF SUCCESS** without risk and sure to be successful ○ *a slam-dunk scenario*

slam·mer /slámmər/ *n* CRIME same as **prison** *n* (sense 1) (*slang*) [Mid-20C. < the idea of the doors slamming shut]

s.l.a.n. *abbr* PUBL without place, year, or name [Latin *sine loco, anno, vel nomine*]

slan·der /slándər/ *n* **1. SAYING OF SOMETHING FALSE AND DAMAGING** the act or offense of saying something false or malicious that damages somebody's reputation **2. FALSE AND DAMAGING STATEMENT** a false and malicious statement that damages somebody's reputation ■ *vt* (**-dered, -der·ing, -ders**) **UTTER SLANDER AGAINST SOMEBODY** to make a false and malicious oral statement about somebody [13C. Via Old French *esclandre* < ecclesiastical Latin *scandalum* "cause of offense" (see SCANDAL)] —**slan·der·er** *n* —**slan·der·ous** *adj* —**slan·der·ous·ly** *adv* —**slan·der·ous·ness** *n*

SYNONYMS See *malign*.

slang /slang/ *n* **1. VERY CASUAL SPEECH OR WRITING** words, expressions, and usages that are casual, vivid, racy, or playful replacements for standard ones, are often short-lived, and are usually considered unsuitable for formal contexts **2. LANGUAGE OF EXCLUSIVE GROUP** a form of language used by a particular group of people, often deliberately created and used to exclude people outside the group ○ *a word that came from surfers' slang* ■ *adj* **IN SLANG** belonging to, expressed in, or containing slang ○ *a slang dictionary* ■ *vti* (**slanged, slang·ing, slangs**) **USE ABUSIVE LANGUAGE** to use abusive language, usually slang, or use this to attack somebody verbally [Mid-18C. Origin ?] —**slang·i·ly** *adv* —**slang·i·ness** *n* —**slang·y** *adj*

SYNONYMS See *jargon*[1].

slant /slant/ *v* (**slant·ed, slant·ing, slants**) **1.** *vti* **BE OR SET SOMETHING AT ANGLE** to be at an angle, or set something at an angle **2.** *vt* **CAUSE SOMETHING TO HAVE PARTICULAR APPEAL** to make something appeal to a particular group of people ○ *a magazine slanted toward the youth market* **3.** *vt* **PRESENT INFORMATION WITH BIAS** to present something in a way that is biased toward a particular person, group, or viewpoint ○ *The news report was slanted in favor of the nationalists.* ■ *n* **1. ANGLED POSITION** an angled position or a direction that is at an angle to something else ○ *the roof was built on a slant* **2. BIASED PERSPECTIVE** a particular bias, or a perspective on something that is likely to appeal to a particular group ○ *The news was given a pro-government slant.* **3. POINT OF VIEW** a point of view or way of looking at something ○ *Her diaries give us a new slant on the events of the time.* **4.** FOOTBALL **RUNNING PLAY** in football, a play in which an offensive player runs forward with the ball at an angle to the line of scrimmage ■ *adj* **SLOPING** sloping, or at an angle (*informal*) [15C. Variant of dialect *slent* < N Germanic] —**slan·ted** *adj* —**slant·ing** *adj* —**slant·ing·ly** *adv*

slant·wise /slánt wìz/, **slant·ways** /-wàyz/ *adv* at an angle to something else

slant·y /sláantee/ *adj* sloping, or at an angle (*informal*)

slap /slap/ *n* **1. BLOW MADE WITH OPEN HAND** a blow made with the open hand or a flat object **2. NOISE OF SLAP** the noise made by a slap, or something that sounds like it ○ *the slap of a wave on the side of the boat* **3. REBUKE** something that rebukes, insults, or hurts ■ *v* (**slapped, slap·ping, slaps**) **1.** *vt* **HIT SOMEBODY WITH OPEN HAND** to hit somebody or something with an open hand or flat object **2.** *vi* **STRIKE SHARPLY** to strike sharply and noisily, as if with a slap ○ *water slapping against the hull* **3.** *vt* **PUT SOMETHING DOWN SHARPLY** to put something down sharply or noisily on something else ○ *He slapped the money on the table and walked away.* **4.** *vt* **APPLY SOMETHING CARELESSLY** to put something on, make something, or do something, quickly and carelessly ○ *I slapped on some makeup and ran for the car.* **5.** *vt* **APPLY SOMETHING AS PENALTY** to apply something as a punishment, penalty, or restriction to somebody or something (*informal*) ○ *The company was slapped with a fine.* ○ *They slapped me with a fine.* ■ *adv* (*informal*) **1. FORCEFULLY** forcefully, and often with the sound or effect of a slap ○ *landed slap on the floor* **2. EXACTLY** exactly, and usually with suddenness and force ○ *slap in the middle of the target* [Mid-17C. An imitation of the sound] —**slap·per** *n*
◇ **a slap in the face** a rebuke or rebuff (*informal*) ◇ **a slap on the back** congratulations (*informal*) ◇ **a slap on the wrist** a mild rebuke or punishment (*informal*)
slap down *vt* (*informal*) **1.** to rebuke somebody sharply or cruelly **2.** to suppress or check something thought to be unacceptable ○ *Any disrespect is slapped down immediately.*

slap-bang *adv* (*informal*) **1.** *UK* same as **smack-dab 2.** *UK* same as **slam-bang**

slap·dash /sláp dàsh/ *adj* careless, hasty, and unskillful ■ *adv* in a careless, hasty, and unskillful way

slap·hap·py /sláp hàppee/ *adj* (*informal*) **1.** irresponsible or careless in a cheerful way **2.** dazed or disoriented, like a boxer who has been hit in the head too many times

slap·jack /sláp jàk/ *n* **1.** same as **pancake 2.** a card game in which players compete to be first in slapping a hand on a face-up jack [Early 19C. Alteration of FLAPJACK]

slap shot *n* in hockey, a shot in which the player swings the stick with a fast powerful stroke [< the loud sound made when the stick hits the ice]

slap·stick /sláp stìk/ *n* comedy with the emphasis on fast physical action, farcical situations, and obvious jokes that do not depend on language (*often used before a noun*) ○ *slapstick comedy* [Early 20C. < *slapstick*, a device made of two flat linked pieces of wood, formerly used in comic performances to simulate the sound of a blow]

slash /slash/ *vt* (**slashed, slash·ing, slash·es**) **1. MAKE CUTS IN SOMETHING** to make long deep cuts in something **2. ATTACK SOMEBODY WITH SHARP OBJECT** to cut or attack somebody with the sharp sweeping strokes of a sword, knife, stick, or whip **3.** *US* **CRITICIZE SOMEBODY** to criticize somebody or something severely **4. REDUCE OR CUT SOMETHING SHORT** to reduce or shorten something greatly ○ *All prices slashed!* **5.** CLOTHING **SLIT FABRIC** to make a slit in fabric or a garment to reveal the lining **6.** FORESTRY **CLEAR GROWTH BY CUTTING** to cut bushes and undergrowth from a wooded area ■ *n* **1. SHARP SWEEPING STROKE** a sharp sweeping stroke of a sword, knife, stick, or whip **2. LONG AND DEEP CUT** a long deep cut or wound **3.** CLOTHING **SLIT IN FABRIC** a slit in fabric or a garment, made to reveal the lining **4.** FORESTRY **DEBRIS FROM CUT TREES** the debris left after trees have been cut down **5.** PRINTING **PRINT CHARACTER** a punctuation mark (/) that is used to separate optional items in a list or to express fractions or division, and that has various uses in computer programming. Technical name **virgule 6.** *US* **SWAMPY GROUND** swampy ground covered with bushes and small trees (*often used in the plural*) [Late 16C. Probably < French *esclachier* "break"] —**slash·er** *n*

USAGE A *slash* is used between optional or alternate elements: *He refused to work with children and/or animals. Please place unwanted clothes/toys/books in the box.* It may also mean "to" or "between": *the academic year 2001/2002*; *the parent/child relationship.* Slashes are used to separate numbers in fractions: *33/140 of the total weight*; dates: *your invoice of 9/12/04*; to stand for "per": *at the rate of 2 mm/sec*; and in some abbreviations, e.g., *c/o* meaning "care of." They are also used to indicate line breaks when quoting poetry, when they are usually followed (and sometimes preceded) by a space: *The weight of the world/ is love* (Allen Ginsberg). In computing the slash (/) is called a *forward slash* to distinguish it from the *backslash* (\), which is used for specific purposes, e.g., to show the location of a computer file or document: *c:\letters\surfclub.doc.* Internet locations usually have forward slashes.

slash-and-burn *adj* **1.** describes a form of agriculture characterized by the cutting down and burning of trees and vegetation in order to plant crops **2.** having or showing the intention to deal with somebody or something drastically and ruthlessly or to destroy somebody or something completely (*informal*) ○ *her slash-and-burn approach to budget cuts*

slash·er mov·ie *n* a horror movie featuring gory effects such as people being slashed with blades (*slang*)

slash·ing /sláshing/ *n* **1.** SPORTS **ILLEGAL ACT IN HOCKEY AND LACROSSE** the illegal striking or swinging of a stick at an opposing player in hockey or lacrosse **2. CUTTING ATTACK** an act of attacking and cutting somebody with a blade ■ *adj* **1. CRITICAL** aggressively critical **2. REDUCING** severely reducing or shortening something ○ *make slashing cuts to the budget* —**slash·ing·ly** *adv*

slash neck *n* a wide shallow neckline in a sweater, blouse, or dress

slash pine *n* **1.** a pine of swampy regions that yields turpentine, pulp, and lumber. Native to: southeastern United States. Latin name: *Pinus caribaea.* **2.** the hard durable wood of the slash pine [< *slash* "swamp." Origin ?]

slash pock·et *n* a pocket in a garment fitted with a diagonal slit for easy access

slat /slat/ *n* **1. THIN STRIP** a light thin narrow strip of wood or metal **2. AIRFOIL ON AIRCRAFT WING** an auxiliary airfoil fixed to the leading edge of a wing to give extra lift ■ *vt* (**slat·ted, slat·ting, slats**) **ADD SLATS TO SOMETHING** to put slats in something [Mid-18C. < Old French *esclat* "splinter, piece broken off"]

slate /slayt/ *n* **1. LAYERED ROCK** a fine-grained metamorphic rock that splits easily into layers and is widely used as a roofing material **2. ROOFING TILE** a roofing tile made of slate **3. WRITING TABLET** a small square piece of slate formerly used for writing on, especially by school students. It could be wiped clean and reused indefinitely. **4. IDENTIFYING BOARD ON MOVIE SET** a board used on a movie set to give information identifying something such as the number of the scene being shot **5. DARK GRAY** a dark gray color **6.** POL **LIST OF CANDIDATES** a list of the candidates in an election ■ *vt* (**slat·ed, slat·ing, slates**) **1. TILE ROOF WITH SLATE** to cover a roof with tiles made of slate **2.** POL **INCLUDE SOMEBODY IN LIST OF CANDIDATES** to put somebody's name on a list of candidates for election **3.** DESIGNATE SOMEBODY to choose or schedule somebody or something for a particular job or time ○ *You've been slated to be our next director.* ○ *The satellite is slated for launch in December.* **4.** *UK* SUBJECT SOMEBODY TO HARSH CRITICISM to criticize somebody or something severely (*informal*) ○ *His last play was slated by the critics.* [14C. < Old French *esclate,* feminine of *esclat* "splinter, piece broken off"] —**slate** *adj* —**slat·y** *adj* ◇ **a clean slate** an imaginary record of somebody's past, with no bad marks recorded on it or with all previous bad marks forgotten (*informal*) ◇ **wipe the slate clean** to forget about what has happened and make a fresh start (*informal*)

slate black *adj* having a purplish black color —**slate black** *n*

slate blue *adj* having a dark bluish gray color —**slate blue** *n*

slat·er /sláytər/ *n* somebody whose job is to lay roofing tiles made of slate

Slat·er /sláytər/, **Samuel** (1768–1835) British-born US engineer and entrepreneur. He founded the first North American cotton mill in Pawtucket, Rhode Island (1790), after emigrating there and reconstructing British textile machinery from memory.

slath·er /sláthər/ *vt* (**-ered, -er·ing, -ers**) **1.** SPREAD SOMETHING THICKLY to spread something thickly or excessively on something else ○ *slather jelly on toast* **2.** SQUANDER SOMETHING to use something wastefully (*informal*) ■ **slath·ers** *npl US* LARGE AMOUNT a large or generous quantity (*informal*) [Mid-19C. Origin ?]

slat·ing /sláyting/ *n* **1.** the process of covering something with slates, or slates collectively as a covering material **2.** *UK* harsh criticism, or a severe reprimand (*informal*)

slat·tern /sláttərn/ *n* (*dated*) **1.** an offensive term that deliberately insults a woman's standards of hygiene and grooming **2.** an offensive term that deliberately insults a woman for the number of her supposed sexual partners [Mid-17C. Origin ?] —**slat·tern·li·ness** *n* —**slat·tern·ly** *adj*

slaugh·ter /sláwtər/ *n* **1.** KILLING OF PEOPLE the brutal killing of a person or large numbers of people **2.** KILLING OF ANIMALS the killing of animals for their meat **3.** MAJOR DEFEAT an overwhelming defeat (*slang*) ■ *vt* (**-tered, -ter·ing, -ters**) **1.** KILL PEOPLE BRUTALLY to kill a person or large numbers of people brutally **2.** KILL ANIMAL FOR MEAT to kill an animal or animals, usually for their meat **3.** DEFEAT SOMEBODY CONVINCINGLY to defeat a person or a group of people overwhelmingly (*slang*) [13C. < Old Norse *slátr* "meat, butchery"] —**slaugh·ter·er** *n* —**slaugh·ter·ous** *adj*

SYNONYMS See ***kill***[1].

slaugh·ter·house /sláwtər hòwss/ (*plural* **-hous·es** /-hòwzəz/) *n* a place where animals are killed for their meat

CULTURAL NOTE ***Slaughterhouse-Five,*** a novel (1970) by Kurt Vonnegut. In this highly original blend of realism and science fiction, World War II veteran Billy Pilgrim is kidnapped by aliens who enable him to revisit his past. He subsequently relives the Allied firebombing of Dresden in 1945, an event witnessed by Vonnegut himself and here presented as a symbol of the unending cruelty and suffering of humanity.

Slav /slaav/ *n* a member of any of the peoples of eastern Europe and northwestern Asia who speak a Slavic language [14C. < medieval Latin *S(c)lavus,* same as *s(c)lavus* (see SLAVE); because the Slavs were reduced to an enslaved state in the 9C]

slave /slayv/ *n* **1.** SOMEBODY FORCED TO WORK FOR ANOTHER somebody who is forced to work for somebody else for no payment and is regarded as the property of that person **2.** DOMINATED PERSON somebody who is dominated by somebody or by something **3.** SOMEBODY ACCEPTING ANOTHER'S RULE somebody who meekly accepts being ruled by somebody else **4.** VERY HARD WORKER somebody who works hard, in bad conditions, and for low pay **5.** DEVICE CONTROLLED BY ANOTHER an electronic or mechanical device that is controlled by another (*often used before a noun*) ■ *vi* (**slaved, slav·ing, slaves**) WORK VERY HARD to work very hard ○ *I've been slaving away over this manuscript all day.* ■ *adj* **1.** USING SLAVES using or relating to enslaved workers **2.** HARSH very harsh and unfair ○ *slave conditions* [13C. Shortening of Old French *esclave* < medieval Latin *s(c)lavus* "captive," *S(c)lavus* "Slav" < Slavic]

slave ant *n* an ant captured and forced to work for an ant colony of another species

slave driv·er *n* **1.** somebody who makes employees work unduly hard **2.** formerly, somebody who was employed to make sure that enslaved people worked hard

slave·hold·er /sláyv hòldər/ *n* somebody who owns enslaved workers

slave la·bor *n* **1.** a work force consisting of people who are forced to work against their will **2.** hard or demanding work, in poor conditions, that is not well paid (*informal*)

slave-mak·ing ant, slave-mak·er ant *n* an ant of a species that raids the colonies of other ant species, capturing larvae and pupae to be used in its own colony

slav·er[1] /sláyvər/ *n* **1.** an owner of or dealer in enslaved workers **2.** HIST same as **slave ship** [Early 19C. < SLAVE]

slav·er[2] /slávvər, sláyvər/ *vi* (**-ered, -er·ing, -ers**) **1.** DRIBBLE SALIVA to dribble saliva from the mouth **2.** BEHAVE OBSEQUIOUSLY to fawn or behave obsequiously to somebody ■ *n* DRIPPING SALIVA saliva that drips from somebody's mouth [14C. Probably < N Germanic]

slav·er·y /sláyvəree/ *n* **1.** SYSTEM BASED ON ENSLAVED LABOR the practice of, or a system based on, using the enforced labor of other people **2.** CONDITION OF BEING ENSLAVED LABORER the state or condition of being held in involuntary servitude as the property of somebody else **3.** HARD WORK very hard work, especially for low pay and under bad conditions **4.** STATE OF BEING DOMINATED a state of being completely dominated by another

slave ship *n* a ship used to carry captured people, especially from Africa, to countries where they were bought as enslaved workers

slave state *n* any of the 15 states in which slavery was legal until the Civil War

slave trade *n* the business of capturing people and buying and selling them as enslaved workers

Slav·ic /slaávik/ *n* a branch of the Indo-European family of languages that includes Bulgarian, Russian, and Polish ■ *adj* relating to Slavic or the people who speak a language belonging to Slavic

slav·ish /sláyvish/ *adj* (*sometimes offensive*) **1.** showing total unquestioning obedience or devotion ○ *slavish loyalty to the cause* **2.** showing a complete lack of originality or independence of thought ○ *a slavish copy* —**slav·ish·ly** *adv* —**slav·ish·ness** *n*

Slav·ism /slaá vìzzəm/ *n* a feature or characteristic of the Slavs or Slavic languages

slav·oc·ra·cy /slay vókrəssee/ *n* owners of slaves considered collectively as a ruling group, or rule by owners of slaves

Sla·von·ic /slə vónnik/ *n, adj* LANG same as **Slavic** [Early 17C. < medieval Latin *S(c)lavonicus* < *S(c)lavonia* "country of the Slavs" < *S(c)lavus* (see SLAVE)]

Slav·o·phile /slaávə fìl/, **Slav·o·phil** /-fil/ *n* (*often used before a noun*) **1.** an admirer of Slavic culture or people **2.** somebody who, in 19th-century Russia, advocated the supremacy of Slavic culture over European culture —**Sla·voph·i·lism** /slə vóffə lìzzəm/ *n*

slaw /slaw/ *n* FOOD same as **coleslaw** [Late 18C. < Dutch *sla,* contraction of French *salade* (see SALAD)]

slay /slay/ (**slew** /sloo/, **slain** /slayn/, **slay·ing, slays**) *vt* **1.** to kill a person or animal (*formal or literary*) ○ *slew the beast with one stroke of his sword* **2.** (*past* **slayed,** *past participle* **slayed** or **slain**) to amuse somebody very much (*informal*) [Old English *slēan* < Germanic, "strike"] —**slay·er** *n*

SPELLCHECK Do not confuse the spelling of ***slay*** and ***sleigh,*** which sound similar. ***Slay*** is a verb meaning "kill"; ***sleigh*** is a noun denoting "a horse-drawn vehicle used on snow and ice" ("a one-horse open sleigh"), or a verb meaning "move in a sleigh."

SYNONYMS See ***kill***[1].

slay·ing /sláy ing/ *n* a killing or murder

SLBM *abbr* ARMS submarine-launched ballistic missile

SLCM *abbr* ARMS sea-launched cruise missile

SLE *abbr* MED systemic lupus erythematosus

sleaze /sleez/ *n* **1.** corruption, dishonesty, or scandal, especially among public figures **2.** same as **sleazebag** (*slang insult*) [Mid-20C. Back-formation < SLEAZY]

sleaze·bag /sleéz bàg/, **sleaze·ball** /sleéz bàwl/ *n* an offensive term for somebody whose behavior is perceived as immoral, unethical, or despicable (*slang insult*)

slea·zy /sleézee/ (**-zi·er, -zi·est**) *adj* **1.** dirty, disreputable, or sordid in character or appearance **2.** dishonest or immoral ○ *You get some pretty sleazy types in here.* [Mid-17C. Origin ?] —**slea·zi·ly** *adv* —**slea·zi·ness** *n*

sled /sled/ *n* **1.** SMALL VEHICLE SLIDING OVER SNOW a small low vehicle on ski-style or other runners, designed to be pulled over snow or ice by people or dogs **2.** CHILD'S TOY VEHICLE FOR SNOW a child's toy vehicle on runners, used for sliding down snowy hills ■ *vti* (**sled·ded, sled·ding, sleds**) MOVE BY SLED to ride, travel, or transport something by sled [14C. < Middle Low German *sledde* < Germanic, "slip, slide"] —**sled·der** *n*

sled·ding /slédding/ *n* **1.** USE OF SLED the use of a sled for work or recreation **2.** *US* CONDITIONS FOR USING SLED conditions in which a sled may be used ○ *The sledding is good right now.* **3.** PROGRESS a particular kind of progress ○ *It was hard sledding for a while, but now things are easier.*

sled dog *n* a dog trained to pull a sled, especially as part of a dog team

sledge[1] /slej/ *n* **1.** a large sled pulled by animals, used for transporting loads across snow or ice **2.** VEHICLES same as **sled** *n* (sense 1) ■ *vti* (**sledged, sledg·ing, sledg·es**) to travel or transport something by sledge [Late 16C. < Dutch dialect *sleedse*]

sledge[2] /slej/ *n* same as **sledgehammer** [Old English *slecg* < Germanic, "strike"]

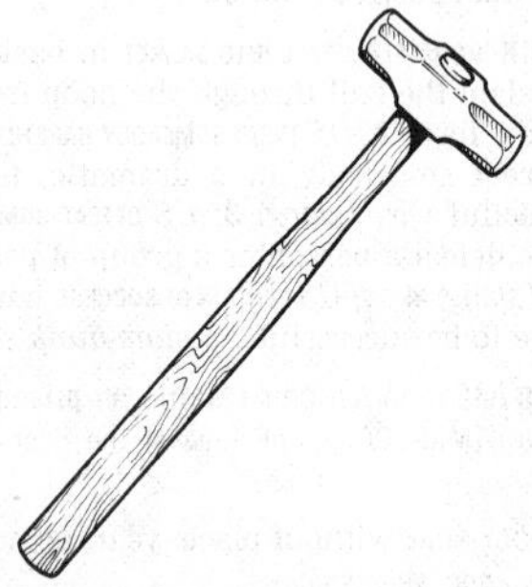

sledgehammer

sledge·ham·mer /sléj hàmmər/ *n* LARGE HAMMER a large heavy hammer swung with both hands ■ *vt* (**-mered, -mer·ing, -mers**) STRIKE SOMETHING WITH SLEDGEHAMMER to hit something with a sledgehammer or with the force of one ■ *adj* VERY FORCEFUL delivered with tremendous force and power ○ *sledgehammer blows*

sleek /sleek/ *adj* **1.** SMOOTH AND SHINY attractively smooth and shiny **2.** WELL-GROOMED well-groomed and healthy looking **3.** SUAVE smooth and polished in behavior or speech, often insincerely or suspiciously so ○ *a sleek sales pitch* ■ *vt* (**sleeked, sleek·ing, sleeks**) MAKE SOMETHING SLEEK to make something appear smooth or shiny [Late 16C. Variant of SLICK] —**sleek·ly** *adv* —**sleek·ness** *n*

sleep /sleep/ *n* **1.** STATE OF NOT BEING AWAKE a state of partial or full unconsciousness in people and animals, during which voluntary functions are suspended and the body rests and restores itself, or a period spent in this state **2.** STATE RESEMBLING SLEEP any state that is inactive or dormant, like sleep **3.** same as **death** (sense 1) (*literary; also euphemistic*) **4.** MUCUS IN EYES small amounts of dried mucus that collect in the eyes during sleep (*informal*) **5.** BOT same as **nyctitropism** ■ *v* (**slept** /slept/, **sleep·ing, sleeps**) **1.** *vi* BE IN STATE OF SLEEP to be in or go into a state of sleep

2. *vt* SPEND TIME IN SLEEP to spend a period of time sleeping ○ *We slept the night in a hotel.* **3.** *vt* PROVIDE BEDS FOR PEOPLE to provide sleeping accommodations for a particular number of people ○ *The yacht sleeps eight.* **4.** *vi* BE INACTIVE to be in an inactive or dormant state ○ *a city that never sleeps* **5.** *vi* BE DEAD to be dead (*literary; also euphemistic*) ○ *He sleeps in the bosom of Abraham.* **6.** *vi* BOT CHANGE POSITION AT NIGHT in plants, to assume a position at night that is different from the daytime position [Old English *slǣp* (noun), *slǣpan* (verb) < Germanic] ◇ **get** *or* **go to sleep** to begin sleeping ◇ **in your sleep 1.** while you are sleeping **2.** with ease, as if not having to be fully awake (*informal*) ○ *I could find my way there in my sleep, I've been so often.* ◇ **not lose (any) sleep over something** to not worry about something because it is thought to be trivial or irrelevant ◇ **put something to sleep** to kill an animal in a humane way, especially because it is ill, injured, or in pain ◇ **put somebody to sleep** to anesthetize somebody ◇ **sleep on it** to postpone a decision until at least the next day in order to give it more thought ◇ **sleep rough** *UK* to sleep outdoors, especially in the street, usually as a result of being homeless

SYNONYMS See ***kill***[1].

sleep around *vi* to have a lot of casual sexual relationships with different people (*informal*)
sleep in *vi* **1.** to sleep longer than you usually do **2.** *US* to sleep at the place where you are employed
sleep off *vt* to recover from something such as an illness or hangover by sleeping
sleep out *vi* **1.** to sleep out of doors **2.** *US* to sleep somewhere other than the place where you are employed
sleep over *vi* to sleep at somebody else's house as part of a visit
sleep together *vi* to have sex (*used euphemistically*)
sleep with *vt* to have sex with somebody (*used euphemistically*)

sleep ap·ne·a *n* a temporary cessation of breathing during sleep, experienced by some people

sleep·er /sléepər/ *n* **1.** SOMEBODY WHO SLEEPS somebody who is sleeping, or somebody who sleeps in a particular way ○ *a light sleeper* **2.** TRAIN CAR WITH BEDS a train car or compartment with beds for passengers **3.** *UK* same as **tie** *n* (sense 5) **4.** HEAVY BEAM a heavy beam used as a sill, footing, or support **5.** BELATED SUCCESS somebody who or something that is not an immediate success but, often surprisingly, later becomes one **6.** SPY INACTIVE UNTIL CALLED INTO ACTION a spy or secret agent who lives an ordinary life until called into action **7.** TROPICAL FISH a sea or freshwater tropical fish related to the goby that often lies immobile. Family: Eleotridae. **8.** *US* FURNITURE CONVERTIBLE BED a piece of furniture that converts into a bed **9.** WRESTLING WRESTLING HOLD INDUCING UNCONSCIOUSNESS a wrestling hold in which pressure is applied to the sides of an opponent's neck so as to induce real or simulated unconsciousness ■ **sleep·ers** *npl* CHILDREN'S PAJAMAS children's one-piece pajamas with feet

sleep·er cell *n* a cell of trained terrorists who are awaiting instructions to commit a terrorist act against the country in which they are living seemingly ordinary lives

sleep-in *adj US* living in the house of an employer ○ *a sleep-in maid* Can term **live-in**

sleep·ing bag /sléeping-/ *n* a long padded or lined fabric bag, often zippered, for sleeping in, especially when camping

sleep·ing car *n* a railroad car that has bunks or compartments in which passengers can sleep

sleep·ing part·ner *n UK* same as **silent partner**

sleep·ing pill *n* a pill containing a drug that is meant to induce sleep

sleep·ing sick·ness *n* **1.** a disease in tropical Africa caused by parasitic protozoans that are carried by tsetse flies. Affected people and animals experience fever, weight loss, and lethargy. **2.** an epidemic form of encephalitis causing lethargy, muscular weakness, and impaired vision

sleep-learn·ing *n* a method of learning something that involves the continuous playing of recordings of it to a sleeping learner

sleep·less /sléepləss/ *adj* **1.** without sleep, or unable to sleep ○ *a sleepless night* **2.** always awake, active, or busy —**sleep·less·ly** *adv* —**sleep·less·ness** *n*

sleep mode *n* an energy-saving state that a device may go into automatically if it is not used over a period of time, in which some of its functions shut down

sleep-out *n* a night or period spent sleeping outdoors

sleep·o·ver /sléep òvər/ *n* a children's party that includes an overnight stay at somebody's house (*informal*)

sleep·suit /sléep sòot/ *n UK* a one-piece sleeping garment for a baby or child, usually with feet

sleep ter·ror dis·or·der *n* a condition of persistent nightmares from which the sleeper awakens in a state of terror and disorientation but remembers nothing of the episode in the morning

sleep·walk /sléep wàwk/ (**-walked, -walk·ing, -walks**) *vi* **1.** to walk while asleep **2.** to do something in an inattentive or lethargic way (*informal*) —**sleep·walk·er** *n* —**sleep·walk·ing** *n*

sleep·wear /sléep wèr/ *n* clothes for people to wear while sleeping

sleep·y /sléepee/ (**-i·er, -i·est**) *adj* **1.** DROWSY feeling drowsy and wanting to sleep **2.** QUIET AND WITHOUT MUCH ACTIVITY quiet and not very lively or exciting ○ *a sleepy mining town* **3.** CAUSING SLEEP tending to make somebody fall asleep —**sleep·i·ly** *adv* —**sleep·i·ness** *n*

sleep·y·head /sléepee hèd/ *n* somebody who is drowsy and is nearly falling asleep or has just woken up (*informal*) —**sleep·y·head·ed** *adj*

sleet /sleet/ *n* **1.** PARTLY FROZEN RAIN partly frozen rain **2.** THIN COATING OF ICE the thin coating of ice formed when rain freezes on something ■ *vi* (**sleet·ed, sleet·ing, sleets**) FALL AS SLEET to have sleet falling from the sky [13C. Probably ultimately < Germanic]

sleeve /sleev/ *n* **1.** COVERING FOR ARM either of the two parts of a garment that wholly or partially cover the arms **2.** *UK* RECORDING same as **jacket** *n* (sense 4) **3.** ENG TUBULAR PIECE a tubular piece designed to fit inside or over a cylinder ■ *vt* (**sleeved, sleev·ing, sleeves**) FIT WITH SLEEVE to provide something with a sleeve [Old English *slēfe* < Indo-European, "slide, slip"] —**sleeve·less** *adj* ◇ **roll up your sleeves** to get ready to do something energetically (*informal*) ◇ **up your sleeve** kept hidden or secret but available for use

sleeve notes *npl UK* same as **liner notes**

sleeve valve *n* a valve for an internal-combustion engine, fitted and reciprocating inside a cylinder

sleev·ing /sléeving/ *n Can, UK* flexible, tubular insulation inside which wires that carry electric current can be fitted. US term **spaghetti**

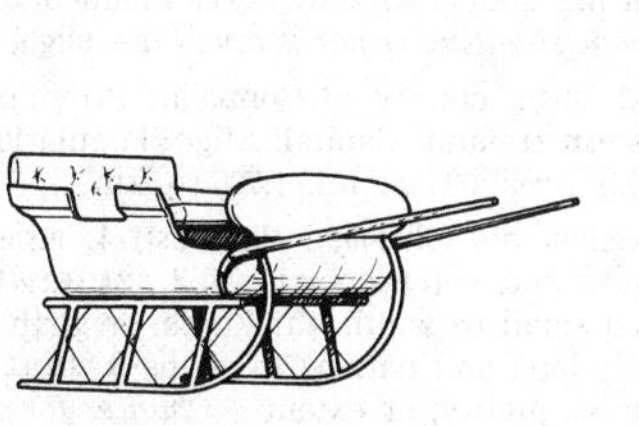

sleigh

sleigh /slay/ *n* an open, usually horse-drawn vehicle on runners, used for travel on snow and ice ■ *vi* (**sleighed, sleigh·ing, sleighs**) to move over snow or ice in a sleigh [Early 18C. < Dutch *slee*, later form of Middle Dutch *slēde* < Germanic, "slip, slide"]

SPELLCHECK See ***slay***.

sleigh·bell /sláy bèl/ *n* a small bell attached to a sleigh or to the harness of horses pulling it. Sometimes a number of them are used together as a musical instrument.

sleight /slīt, slayt/ *n* (*archaic*) **1.** dexterity or skill in doing something **2.** cunning or trickery [13C. < Old Norse *slœgð* "cunning" < *slœgr* "crafty"]

sleight of hand *n* **1.** skill or dexterity with the hands in performing magic tricks, card tricks, or juggling **2.** any kind of skill by which something happens without it being obvious how it is done

slen·der /sléndər/ *adj* **1.** SLIM thin in a graceful way **2.** SMALL IN WIDTH small or slight in width in proportion to height or length ○ *a flower with a slender stem* **3.** LIMITED small or limited in degree, extent, or size ○ *The home team won by a slender margin.* [13C. Origin ?] —**slen·der·ly** *adv* —**slen·der·ness** *n*

SYNONYMS See ***thin***.

slen·der·ize /sléndə rīz/ (**-ized, -iz·ing, -iz·es**) *vti US* to become slender, or make somebody or something slender

slen·der lo·ris *n* a small tailless slow-moving primate. Native to: rain forests of India and Sri Lanka. Latin name: *Loris tardigradus*.

slept past participle, past tense of **sleep**

Sles·sor /sléssər/, **Kenneth** (1901–71) Australian poet. His work, mostly written between 1919 and 1939, includes "Five Bells" (1939). Full name **Slessor, Kenneth Adolf.** See Cultural note at **bell**[1]

sleuth /slooth/ *n* **1.** same as **detective** (*informal*) **2.** BREED same as **sleuthhound** (sense 1) (*dated*) ■ *v* (**sleuthed, sleuth·ing, sleuths**) **1.** *vi* to make investigations as, or in a similar way to, a detective (*informal*) **2.** *vt* to track or find somebody or something [Early 19C. Shortening of SLEUTHHOUND]

sleuth·hound /slóoth hòwnd/ *n* **1.** a dog used for tracking people, especially a bloodhound (*dated*) **2.** same as **detective** (*dated informal*) [14C. < Old Norse *slóð* "track, trail"]

slew[1] /sloo/ past tense of **slay**

slew[2] /sloo/, **slue** *n* a large quantity or number of something (*informal*) ○ *They hit us with a whole slew of complaints.* [Mid-19C. < Irish *sluagh* "multitude," later form of Old Irish *slúag* "host, army"]

slew[3] /sloo/ *vti* another spelling of **slue**[1] *v* (sense 2) ■ *n* UK spelling of **slue**[1] *n* (sense 1)

slew[4] /sloo/ *n* GEOG same as **slough**[1] (sense 2) [Early 18C. Alteration]

slice /slīss/ *n* **1.** PIECE CUT FROM SOMETHING a thin broad piece cut from something larger ○ *a slice of ham* **2.** SHARE a part, portion, or share of something ○ *a slice of the profits* **3.** SERVING UTENSIL a utensil with a thin flat triangular blade, used for cutting and serving food, especially cake **4.** OBLIQUE WAY OF HITTING BALL a stroke in which the ball is hit off-center so that it follows a curving path **5.** FLIGHT OF BALL the flight of a ball that has been hit with a slice **6.** TENNIS SHOT a tennis shot that makes the ball spin and stay low when it bounces in the opponent's court ■ *v* (**sliced, slic·ing, slic·es**) **1.** *vti* CUT SOMETHING INTO PORTIONS to cut something into slices or portions, or be cut into slices or portions ○ *slice the ham* **2.** *vti* CUT CLEANLY to cut something cleanly and effortlessly, or be cut in this way ○ *The sword sliced the rope in half.* **3.** *vi* MOVE SWIFTLY AND CLEANLY to move swiftly and cleanly, especially through a medium such as air or water **4.** *vti* CUT SOMETHING OFF to cut a slice or piece off something else, or be cut off in a slice or piece ○ *The spinning blade sliced off log after log.* **5.** *vt* SET BALL ON CURVING PATH to hit a ball off-center so that it follows a curving path, whether intentionally or as a result of a bad swing or stroke **6.** *vti* HIT BALL WITH CHOPPING ACTION to hit a tennis shot with a chopping stroke so that the ball spins and stays low when it bounces in the opponent's court **7.** *vt* PUT OAR IN WATER AT ANGLE to put the blade of an oar into the water at an angle [15C. < Old French *esclice* "splinter" < *esclicier* "to splinter" < Germanic] —**slice·a·ble** *adj* —**slic·er** *n*

slice of life *n* a realistic portrayal of life, especially a harsh or unpleasant life, e.g., in literature or a movie [< the idea of cutting into something to see inside]

slick /slik/ *adj* **1.** SLIPPERY having a smooth, glossy, or slippery surface ○ *a slick runway* **2.** CRAFTY clever and resourceful but not entirely trustworthy **3.** GLIB superficially impressive or persuasive but lacking substance or sincerity ○ *a slick sales pitch* **4.** EFFORTLESS done with great skill and apparently effortless ease and smooth continuity, or able to do things in this way ○ *a slick presentation* **5.** SUAVE smooth or refined in manners or behavior ■ *n* **1.**

SLIPPERY PATCH a thinly spread or slippery patch of something, especially of oil floating on water **2.** TREADLESS TIRE a wide treadless tire used in auto racing **3.** PUBL EXPENSIVE MAGAZINE a magazine, especially a fashion magazine, containing high-quality color photographs, printed on smooth-coated paper **4.** AVIAT, MIL UNARMED AIRCRAFT an aircraft carrying no armaments ■ *vt* (**slicked, slick·ing, slicks**) SMOOTH SOMETHING to make something smooth, glossy, or presentable ○ *He wears his hair slicked back.* [14C. Ultimately < Indo-European, "slippery"] —**slick·ly** *adv* —**slick·ness** *n*

slick·en·side /slíkən sìd/ *n* a rock surface that is smooth and marked with fine scratches caused by friction with another rock surface [Early 19C. < dialect variant of SLICK + SIDE]

slick·er /slíkər/ *n* **1.** RAINCOAT a shiny raincoat, often made of a plastic or rubber material **2.** SOPHISTICATED BUT UNTRUSTWORTHY PERSON an apparently sophisticated, stylish, or clever person who is not honest or trustworthy (*informal*) **3.** SMOOTHING TOOL a tool used for smoothing something

slide /slīd/ *v* (**slid** /slid/, **slid·ing, slides**) **1.** *vti* MOVE SMOOTHLY to move, or make something move, in an uninterrupted glide across a smooth surface, remaining in continuous contact with it but experiencing little friction or unable to get a grip on it ○ *The car slid for 50 yards when the brakes locked.* **2.** *vti* MOVE UNOBTRUSIVELY to move unobtrusively, or move something unobtrusively ○ *He slid the letter into his pocket.* **3.** *vi* SLIP to lose your grip or secure footing on a surface ○ *It seemed to slide right off the window ledge.* **4.** *vi* TO CHANGE TO DIFFERENT CONDITION to change to a different, usually worse, state or condition ○ *unable to stop the economy from sliding into recession* **5.** *vi* DECREASE to decrease in value or quantity ○ *Stock prices are sliding for the third straight day.* **6.** *vi* MUSIC PLAY GLIDE BETWEEN NOTES to make a gliding change from one note to another **7.** *vti* BASEBALL APPROACH BASE HORIZONTALLY in baseball or softball, to approach a base while skidding feet first, low to the ground ○ *The runner avoided the tag with a beautiful hook slide.* ■ *n* **1.** STRUCTURE THAT CHILDREN PLAY ON a structure with a sloping surface that children slide down for fun **2.** SLIDING MOVEMENT a swift, gliding, and often uncontrollable movement across a smooth surface **3.** FALL OF ROCK, MUD, OR EARTH a downhill displacement of rock, mud, or earth, often caused by rainfall or erosion **4.** SMALL POSITIVE PHOTOGRAPH a positive photograph reproduced on a small piece of film that can be viewed by projection on a screen or through a magnifying device **5.** SPECIMEN HOLDER a small glass plate on which a specimen is mounted for viewing under a microscope **6.** CLOTHING SHOE WITH NO HEEL OR TOE a slip-on shoe with an open heel and often an open toe **7.** SLIDING MACHINE PART a machine part that slides, or the track on which it slides **8.** ROWING same as **sliding seat** **9.** TROMBONE MECHANISM the U-shaped tube of a trombone that is pushed in and out to allow for changes in pitch **10.** MUSIC MUSICAL FEATURE a sliding change from one note to another [Old English *slīdan* < Germanic] ◇ **let things** *or* **something slide** to let a situation gradually deteriorate ◇ **on the slide** in the process of becoming worse (*informal*)

slide-ac·tion *adj* describes a shotgun or rifle with a lever that ejects the case of a spent round and loads a new one

slide gui·tar *n* a method of playing a guitar by which the player moves a metal or glass object along the strings to produce a gliding effect between notes

Sli·dell /slī dél/ city in southeastern Louisiana, on the northeastern shore of Lake Pontchartrain, opposite New Orleans. Population: 26,466 (2002 estimate).

Sli·dell, John (1793–1871) US politician and diplomat. He was the Confederacy's commissioner to France during the Civil War.

slid·er /slídər/ *n* **1.** SLIDING CONTROL a control knob or lever that moves horizontally or vertically, e.g., to change the volume of a radio or CD player **2.** SOMETHING THAT SLIDES somebody or something that slides **3.** FAST REVERSE CURVE a fast pitch in baseball that curves outward from the side of the pitcher's throwing arm as it reaches the batter

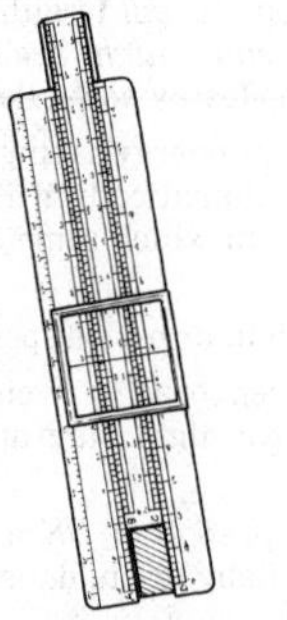

slide rule

slide rule *n* a manual calculating device, now largely obsolete, consisting of two rulers marked with graduated logarithmic scales, one sliding inside the other

slide show *n* a sequence of photographic slides projected on a screen or wall as education or entertainment

slide tack·le *n* in soccer, an aggressive tackle in which the tackler slides in, feet first, on the ground

slide trom·bone *n* a trombone with a slide that is moved to select different pitches as distinct from a trombone fitted with valves

slid·ing /slíding/ *adj* **1.** varying according to changing conditions **2.** moved by sliding ○ *a sliding door*

slid·ing scale *n* a scale that varies according to changes in some other factor, e.g., a scale of wages, costs, or fees

slid·ing seat *n* a seat in a rowboat that slides back and forth, allowing a rower to lengthen the stroke of the oars

slieght incorrect spelling of **sleight**

slight /slīt/ *adj* **1.** VERY SMALL very small in size, degree, amount, or importance ○ *a slight resemblance* **2.** THIN having a slim body that does not look very strong **3.** INSUBSTANTIAL not very substantial or convincing ○ *an assertion made without the slightest evidence* ■ *vt* (**slight·ed, slight·ing, slights**) **1.** SNUB SOMEBODY to treat somebody rudely, e.g., by deliberately ignoring him or her **2.** TREAT SOMETHING AS UNIMPORTANT to think of or treat something as unimportant **3.** *US* DO SOMETHING CARELESSLY to handle duties or responsibilities carelessly ■ *n* IMPOLITE ACT an action that shows contempt for somebody or something [14C. Probably partly < Old Norse *sléttr* "level, smooth," partly < Middle Dutch *slicht* "simple, defective," both < Germanic] —**slight·ly** *adv* —**slight·ness** *n* ◇ **not in the slightest** *UK* not at all (*informal*)

slight·ing /slíting/ *adj* showing contempt or disrespect ○ *made slighting remarks about it* —**slight·ing·ly** *adv*

Sli·go /slígō/ county in Connacht Province, northwestern Ireland. Capital: Sligo. Population: 55,821 (2002). Area: 693 sq. mi./1,796 sq. km.

slim /slim/ *adj* (**slim·mer, slim·mest**) **1.** PLEASINGLY THIN slender and well-proportioned **2.** SMALLER IN WIDTH THAN HEIGHT small in width, thickness, or girth and generally long and narrow in shape **3.** SMALL small in degree, quality, or extent ○ *Chances for their survival were slim.* ■ *v* (**slimmed, slim·ming, slims**) **1.** *vi* LOSE WEIGHT to lose weight, especially by dieting **2.** *vt* REDUCE SOMETHING IN EXTENT to reduce the size or scope of something ○ *slim down the bloated bureaucracy* [Mid-17C. < Dutch, "inferior, small" < Germanic] —**slim·ly** *adv* —**slim·mer** *n* —**slim·ness** *n*

SYNONYMS See *thin*.

Slim /slim/, **William Joseph, 1st Viscount** (1891–1970) British general. He led the British forces to victory in Burma (Myanmar) during World War II and was governor-general of Australia (1952–60).

slime /slīm/ *n* **1.** SLIPPERY LIQUID a fluid that is thick and slippery, especially one that is unpleasant to touch **2.** MUCOUS SECRETION OF SOME LIVING THINGS a mucous substance secreted by some living things such as fish, snails, and fungi ■ *v* (**slimed, slim·ing, slimes**) **1.** *vt* COVER SOMETHING WITH SLIME to cover or smear something with slime **2.** *vt* MIL USE CHEMICAL OR BIOLOGICAL WEAPONS to attack enemy troops with chemical or biological weapons, or be so attacked (*slang*) **3.** *vt* REMOVE SLIME FROM SOMETHING to remove slime from something such as a fish before preparing it for cooking **4.** INSULT SOMEBODY to make malicious or abusive statements about somebody (*slang*) [Old English *slīm* < Indo-European, "slippery"]

slime·ball /slím bàwl/ *n* an offensive term that deliberately insults somebody's character or appearance (*slang insult*)

slime mold *n* a simple organism that forms a small slimy amoeboid mass, e.g., on fallen logs, and produces spore-bearing reproductive organs similar to those of a fungus

slim·sy /slímzee/ (**-si·er, -si·est**), **slimp·sy** /slímpzee/ *adj US* both slight and flimsy (*informal*) [Mid-19C. Blend of SLIM + FLIMSY]

slim·y /slímee/ (**-i·er, -i·est**) *adj* **1.** LIKE SLIME covered with or having the consistency of slime ○ *a slimy secretion* **2.** DISGUSTING extremely unpleasant, especially to the touch ○ *a slimy mess* **3.** OFFENSIVE TERM an offensive term meaning thought to behave in an excessively ingratiating way (*insult*) —**slim·i·ly** *adv* —**slim·i·ness** *n*

sling[1] /sling/ *n* **1.** SUPPORTING BANDAGE a wide bandage suspended from somebody's neck to support an injured arm or hand **2.** CARRYING STRAP a carrying strap attached to something such as a rifle **3.** LOOP FOR CARRYING SOMETHING HEAVY a loop of rope, leather, chain, or net used to lift, lower, or carry something heavy **4.** LOOP USED AS WEAPON a weapon used for throwing a stone or other object, consisting of a loop of leather or other material in which the missile is twirled before being released **5.** *US* ARMS same as **slingshot** **6.** NAUT SUPPORT FOR YARD a rope or chain that supports a ship's beam ■ **slings** *npl* CLIMBING ANCHORING LOOP a fixed loop of webbing used to provide an anchor to a rock, tree, or other point ■ *v* (**slung** /slung/, **sling·ing, slings**) **1.** *vt* THROW WITH FORCE to throw something with a lot of force **2.** CARRY OR MOVE SOMETHING IN SLING to attach something to, carry something with, or hang something from a sling ○ *sling a hammock* **3.** *vt UK* PASS OR PUT SOMETHING CASUALLY to throw, pass, or put something somewhere in a casual or careless way (*informal*) **4.** *vt* HANG SOMETHING LOOSELY to hang or suspend something loosely, e.g., a piece of clothing from a part of the body (*often passive*) ○ *with his coat slung over one arm* **5.** *vt* SERVE FOOD OR DRINK to prepare or serve food or drink in a bar or diner (*slang*) [13C. Origin ?] —**sling·er** *n*

sling[2] /sling/ *n* a mixed alcoholic drink made with liquor, sugar, lemon or lime juice, and water [Mid-18C. Origin ?]

sling·back /slíng bàk/ *n* a woman's shoe that is open at the heel and is held on the foot by a strap (*often used before a noun*)

sling·shot /slíng shòt/ *n* a Y-shaped weapon with a loop of elastic attached to the two prongs, used to propel stones or other objects

slink /slingk/ *v* (**slunk** /slunk/ *or* **slinked, slink·ing, slinks**) **1.** *vi* MOVE FURTIVELY to move or behave quietly and secretively ○ *I could see her trying to slink away through the back door.* **2.** *vi* MOVE SEXILY to walk in a sexually alluring way **3.** *vt* VET BEAR PREMATURE YOUNG to give birth to young prematurely, especially to a calf ■ *n* VET PREMATURE ANIMAL a prematurely born animal, especially a calf ■ *adj* VET BORN EARLY describes an animal, especially a calf, that is born prematurely [Old English *slincan* < Germanic, "slide, throw"]

slink·y /slíngkee/ (**-i·er, -i·est**) *adj* **1.** having a seductive appearance or way of moving **2.** close-fitting and emphasizing the curves of the body ○ *a slinky outfit* —**slink·i·ly** *adv* —**slink·i·ness** *n*

slip[1] /slip/ *v* (**slipped, slip·ping, slips**) **1.** *vti* MOVE SMOOTHLY to move smoothly and easily and usually with a sliding motion, or make something move in this way ○ *It slips easily in and out of its case.* **2.** *vti* PUT ON OR TAKE OFF to put something on or take something off quickly and easily, or be put on or taken off in this way **3.** *vi* LOSE YOUR FOOTING to lose your footing or grip on a slippery surface ○ *I slipped and fell.* **4.** *vi* MOVE FROM PROPER POSITION to slide or move accidentally out of the proper or desired position ○ *This strap keeps slipping off my shoulder.* **5.** *vti* BE FORGOTTEN to escape from somebody's memory or mind and be forgotten or overlooked ○ *It slipped my mind.* **6.** *vi*

GO QUIETLY to go somewhere in a quiet, furtive, or unnoticed way ○ *He slipped out while nobody was looking.* **7.** *vt* PASS SOMETHING SECRETLY to give somebody something furtively or secretly ○ *I saw the man slip her an envelope.* **8.** *vi* GET WORSE to decline from a previous standard, e.g., a standard of performance or awareness ○ *He's slipping – two years ago he would have spotted that mistake at once.* ○ *She's in danger of slipping back into her bad old ways.* **9.** *vt* DISLOCATE BONE to dislocate or displace a bone, especially in the spine **10.** *vti* RELEASE to release an animal from a restraint, or be released in this way **11.** *vti* AUTOMOT DISENGAGE CLUTCH to disengage the clutch of a motor vehicle, or be disengaged **12.** *vi* MECH ENG FAIL TO ENGAGE to fail to engage properly, usually because of wear (*refers to mechanical parts*) **13.** *vt* NAUT LET RESTRAINING CABLE GO to release a line or cable that is securing a vessel to a mooring or anchor ■ *n* **1.** ACT OF SLIPPING an act of slipping, especially a sudden slide on a slippery surface **2.** ERROR a minor mistake, especially one caused by carelessness **3.** LAPSE a moral lapse or an instance of misconduct **4.** CLOTH COVERING a cloth covering for something **5.** CLOTHING UNDERGARMENT a light sleeveless woman's undergarment worn under a dress **6.** NAUT SHIP BERTH a place between two piers for a ship to dock **7.** NAUT same as **slipway 8.** CRYSTALS DEFORMATION OF CRYSTAL the deformation of a metallic crystal by shearing along a plane **9.** AVIAT same as **sideslip** *n* (sense 2) [13C. Probably < Middle Dutch, Middle Low German *slippen* < Germanic] ◇ **give somebody the slip** to get away from somebody who is pursuing you ◇ **let slip 1.** to say something without meaning to, or reveal something that should be kept secret **2.** to allow somebody or something to escape ◇ **slip one over on somebody** to trick or deceive somebody (*informal*)

SYNONYMS See ***mistake***.

slip up *vi* to make a mistake (*informal*) ○ *Somebody slipped up and forgot to put your name on the guest list.*

slip[2] /slip/ *n* **1.** PLANT CUTTING a stem or branch of a plant broken off and used to grow a new plant **2.** NARROW PIECE a narrow strip of something ○ *a slip of paper* **3.** DELICATE YOUNG PERSON a young and slightly built person ○ *a slip of a girl* **4.** SMALL DOCUMENT a small form, document, or record of a transaction ○ *a deposit slip* **5.** *US* NARROW CHURCH PEW a church pew that is narrow ■ *vt* (**slipped, slip·ping, slips**) REMOVE SLIP to remove a slip from a plant in order to grow a new plant [15C. Probably < Middle Dutch, Middle Low German *slippe* "flap, split"]

slip[3] /slip/ *n* a mixture of clay and water used as a decorative layer on pottery or for casting in molds to form an actual piece [Old English *slipa, slyppe* "slime"]

SLIP /slip/ *n* the older of two protocols for dial-up access to the Internet using a modem. It has now been largely replaced by a higher-level protocol (**PPP**). Full form **serial line Internet protocol**

slip·case /slíp kàyss/ *n* a box for protecting a book or set of books, usually made of sturdy cardboard, with one or more open ends

slip·cov·er /slíp kùvvər/ *n* a fitted protective cover for a piece of upholstered furniture, usually made of cloth ■ *vt* (**-ered, -er·ing, -ers**) to provide a piece of furniture with a slipcover

slip·knot /slíp nòt/ *n* **1.** a knot that slips easily along the rope or cord around which it is tied **2.** a knot that can be unfastened by pulling

slip-on *n* a shoe or piece of clothing that is easy to put on or remove ■ *adj* easy to put on and take off

slip·o·ver /slíp ὸvər/ *n* CLOTHING same as **pullover**

slip·page /slíppij/ *n* **1.** SLIDE the process or an instance of slipping, especially from a stable or desired position ○ *Recent thunderstorms have caused slippage in the banks along rivers.* **2.** AMOUNT OF SLIPPING an amount or extent that something slips **3.** DECLINE a decrease in the quality, performance, or production of something **4.** MECH ENG LOSS OF POWER a loss of power or forward motion caused by the slipping of a mechanical part

slipped disk *n* one of the disks of cartilage separating the bones of the spine that has become displaced or protrusive and causes pain by pressing on a nerve

slip·per /slíppər/ *n* a flat shoe of soft or lightweight material, usually worn indoors —**slip·pered** *adj*

slip·per flow·er *n US* PLANTS same as **calceolaria**

slip·per·wort /slíppər wùrt, -wàwrt/ *n* PLANTS same as **calceolaria**

slip·per·y /slíppəree/ (**-i·er, -i·est**) *adj* **1.** CAUSING SLIDING likely to cause somebody or something to slip **2.** HARD TO HOLD FIRMLY sliding easily from the grasp or from a position **3.** PRECARIOUS unstable and liable to change ○ *We're in a slippery situation; things could go either way.* **4.** UNTRUSTWORTHY behaving in a devious or deceitful way ○ *a slippery character* —**slip·per·i·ly** *adv* —**slip·per·i·ness** *n*

slip·per·y elm *n* **1.** the moist sticky inner bark of an elm. Use: natural remedy in alternative medicine to relieve inflammation in the digestive tract. **2.** a deciduous hardwood tree that yields slippery elm. Native to: North America. Latin name: *Ulmus rubra.*

slip·pery slope *n* a dangerous situation that can lead to ultimate downfall

slip ring *n* a metal ring in a generator or motor to which current is delivered or from which it is removed by brushes

slip·sheet /slíp shèet/ *n* a sheet of blank paper placed between newly printed sheets to prevent wet ink on the printed sheets from rubbing off or smearing ■ *vt* (**-sheet·ed, -sheet·ing, -sheets**) to place a blank sheet of paper between newly printed papers on which the ink is still wet

slip·shod /slíp shòd/ *adj* **1.** done in a sloppy way without attention to details **2.** not neat in appearance [Late 16C. < SLIP[1] "slide" + SHOD "wearing shoes"] —**slip·shod·di·ness** *n*

slip stitch *n* a hidden stitch used to connect two layers of fabric —**slip stitch** *vt*

slip·stream /slíp strèem/ *n* **1.** AREA BEHIND FAST-MOVING VEHICLE an area of reduced air pressure and forward suction that is directly behind and caused by a rapidly moving vehicle **2.** AIR FROM PROPELLER a stream of air driven backward by an aircraft's propeller ■ *vi* (**-streamed, -stream·ing, -streams**) FOLLOW IN SLIPSTREAM to follow in another vehicle's slipstream, taking advantage of the decreased air resistance

slip-up *n* an accidental mistake or blunder (*informal*)

slip·ware /slíp wèr/ *n* pottery that has been coated or decorated with slip

slip·way /slíp wày/ *n* a sloping surface used to build or repair boats before returning them to the water

slit /slit/ *vt* (**slit, slit·ting, slits**) **1.** SLICE SOMETHING to make a long straight cut in something ○ *She slit the bag open with a knife.* **2.** CUT SOMETHING INTO STRIPS to cut something into thin strips ■ *n* NARROW OPENING a long narrow cut or opening [12C. < Old English *slitan* "cut up" < Germanic] —**slit·ter** *n*

SYNONYMS See ***tear***[1].

slith·er /slíthər/ *v* (**-ered, -er·ing, -ers**) **1.** *vti* SLIDE OR CAUSE SOMETHING TO SLIDE to move along a slippery or uneven surface, or make something slide along ○ *We slithered down the muddy river bank.* **2.** *vi* GLIDE to slide along easily, using friction to move forward, as a snake does ■ *n* GLIDING MOVEMENT a gliding, effortless movement [12C. Alteration of Old English *slidrian* "slide repeatedly" < SLIDE]

sli·ther·y /slíthəree/ *adj* **1.** moving with a slithering motion ○ *slithery snake* **2.** having a smooth and slippery surface ○ *slithery surface*

slit trench *n* a narrow trench dug as protection against shelling during a battle

sliv·er /slívvər/ *n* **1.** SPLINTER a thin piece of something that has been split, cut, or broken off **2.** SMALL PIECE a small narrow portion or piece of something **3.** LOOSE FIBER a loose strand of wool, cotton, or some other material prepared for drawing and twisting by carding ■ *vti* (**-ered, -er·ing, -ers**) BREAK INTO SPLINTERS to break something into splinters, or become splintered [14C. < obsolete *slive* "cleave, split" < Germanic]

sliv·o·vitz /slívvə vìts/ *n* a dry colorless plum brandy made in eastern Europe [Late 19C. < Serbo-Croatian *šljivovica* "plum brandy" < *šljiva* "plum"]

Sloan /slōn/, **John** (1871–1951) US artist. A member of the group of artists called The Eight, he is known for his realistic paintings of urban life, which gave rise to the name "the Ashcan School." Full name **Sloan, John French**

> "Painting without drawing is just 'coloriness,' color excitement. To think of color for color's sake is like thinking of sound for sound's sake. Who ever heard of a musician who was passionately fond of B-flat?"
>
> [John Sloan, *The Gist of Art: Principles and Practice Expounded in the Classroom and Studio*; 1939]

slob /slob/ *n* an offensive term that deliberately insults somebody regarded as having an unhealthy lifestyle or poor standards of hygiene or manners (*insult*) [Late 18C. Via Irish *slab* "mud" < English *slab* "bog" < N Germanic] —**slob·bish** *adj*

slob·ber /slóbbər/ *v* (**-bered, -ber·ing, -bers**) **1.** *vti* DRIBBLE SALIVA to allow saliva or a liquid to run from the mouth **2.** *vi* EXPRESS EXTREME EMOTION to be overly sentimental or emotional **3.** *vt* SMEAR SOMETHING WITH SALIVA to soak or cover something with saliva or liquid from the mouth ■ *n* **1.** SALIVA saliva or liquid that has been drooled from the mouth **2.** SENTIMENTAL WRITING OR TALK overemotional or sentimental talk or writing ○ *I can't stand to read such slobber.* [14C. Probably < Middle Dutch *slobberen* "feed noisily, walk through mud"] —**slob·ber·er** *n* —**slob·ber·y** *adj*

slob ice *n Can* floating ice in slushy masses

sloe /slō/ (*plural* **sloes** or *same*) *n* **1.** SOUR BLUE-BLACK FRUIT a small sour blue-black fruit of the blackthorn **2.** DARK RED OR YELLOW FRUIT a dark purple fruit, or a red or yellow fruit, produced by different species of North American plum trees **3.** TREES same as **blackthorn** (sense 1) **4.** N AMERICAN PLUM TREE a plum tree that bears sloes. Native to: eastern North America. Latin name: *Prunus alleghaniensis* or *Prunus americana.* [Old English *slah* < Indo-European, "bluish"]

sloe-eyed *adj* with dark almond-shaped eyes [Because of the blue-black color of the fruit]

sloe gin *n* a liqueur made of gin flavored with sloes

slog /slog/ *v* (**slogged, slog·ging, slogs**) **1.** *vi* PLOD to walk slowly with great effort ○ *How long did it take us to slog up that mountain?* **2.** *vi* WORK LONG AND HARD to work at something for a long time with little progress ○ *They've all been down at the office, slogging through endless reams of paperwork.* **3.** *vt* MAKE YOUR WAY to make your way through something with great difficulty ○ *We had to slog our way through several muddy fields.* **4.** *vt* HIT SOMEBODY OR SOMETHING HARD to hit somebody or something with great force ○ *It was like being slogged by a heavyweight boxer.* ■ *n* **1.** LONG HARD WALK a long difficult trip or walk ○ *It was quite a slog from the station to the hotel.* **2.** HARD WORK a long period of hard work ○ *It was a hard long slog during law school* **3.** HARD HIT a hard blow or swipe [Early 19C. Origin ?] —**slog·ger** *n*

slo·gan /slṓgən/ *n* **1.** MOTTO a short distinctive phrase used to identify a company or organization or its goals **2.** ADVERTISING PHRASE a short catchy phrase used in advertising to promote something **3.** *Scotland* SCOTTISH BATTLE CRY the battle cry of a Highland clan (*archaic*) [Early 16C. < Gaelic *sluagh-ghairm* < *sluagh* "army" + *gairm* "cry"]

slo·gan·eer /slὸgə néer/ *n* a creator or frequent user of slogans ○ *the kind of politician who is little more than a clever sloganeer* ■ *vi* (**-eered, -eer·ing, -eers**) to create or use slogans

slo·gan·ize /slṓgə nīz/ (**-ized, -iz·ing, -iz·es**) *vt* to express something in a slogan, or make a slogan of something ○ *the sloganizing of political ideals* —**slo·gan·iz·er** *n*

slo-mo /slṓ mṑ/ *adj* same as **slow-motion** (sense 1) (*informal*) [Mid-20C. Shortening]

sloop /sloop/ *n* a single-masted sailing boat, rigged fore-and-aft, with one headsail extending from the foremast to the bowsprit [Early 17C. < Dutch *sloep*]

sloop of war *n* a small armed sailing ship that is

larger than a gunboat and carries guns on only one deck

slop[1] /slop/ *n* **1. SOMETHING SPILLED** a liquid that has spilled or overflowed ○ *Look at all the slop on the floor!* **2. MUD OR SLUSH** soft mud or slushy snow ○ *How far do we have to wade through this slop?* **3. UNAPPEALING FOOD** poor-quality unappetizing or watery food (*often used in the plural*) **4. HUMAN WASTE** human waste, e.g., urine **5. OVERLY SENTIMENTAL WRITING OR SPEECH** overly emotional or sentimental speech or writing without any literary value (*informal*) ○ *He has gotten rich by writing pure slop and is proud of it.* **6.** FOOD INDUST **MASH** what remains of the mash after an alcoholic beverage has been distilled (*often used in the plural*) ■ **slops** *npl* **HOG FEED** leftover food, especially kitchen waste, that is fed to hogs ■ *v* (**slopped, slop·ping, slops**) **1.** *vti* **SPILL LIQUID** to spill a liquid, or be spilled on or over somebody or something **2.** *vi* **WALK THROUGH MUD OR WATER** to trudge or splash through water, mud, or slush **3.** *vt* **SERVE FOOD MESSILY** to serve food in a careless and unappetizing way **4.** *vt* **FEED ANIMALS SLOPS** to feed kitchen waste to hogs and other livestock **5.** *vi* **WRITE GUSHILY** to write or speak about something in an overly emotional or sentimental way (*informal*) [14C. < Old English *sloppe* "dung" < Germanic]

slop[2] /slop/ (*archaic*) *n* a loose smock or overalls ■ **slops** *npl* clothes and personal articles that are sold from the ship's store to sailors on a merchant ship [14C. Probably < Middle Dutch]

slop bowl *n* a bowl or other container into which tea or coffee dregs are emptied at the table

slope /slōp/ *n* **1. SLANTED GROUND** ground that inclines slightly **2. SIDE OF HILL OR MOUNTAIN** the part of a hill or mountain that is at an angle ○ *thousands of skiers hitting the slopes this weekend* **3. SLANT** a slant upward or downward, or the degree of such a slant **4. SOMETHING SLANTED** a line, surface, direction, or plane that is inclined **5.** *US* **TABOO TERM** a highly offensive term that deliberately insults somebody of East or Southeast Asian, particularly Vietnamese, descent (*taboo*) **6.** MATH **TANGENT** the tangent of the angle between a straight line and the x-axis **7.** MATH **FIRST DERIVATIVE OF CURVE** the first derivative of a curve at a point ■ *v* (**sloped, slop·ing, slopes**) **1.** *vti* **GO UP OR DOWN** to ascend or descend, or make something ascend or descend ○ *From here, the road slopes gently down to the valley.* **2.** *vi* **BE AT SLANT** to be at or have an angle that deviates from horizontal ○ *Does the floor in this room slope?* **3.** *vt* **TAKE SOMETHING UP OR DOWN** to make something rise or descend gradually ○ *We had a landscaper slope the path through our yard.* [Late 16C. < *slope* "so as to slope, on a slope," shortening of *aslope*, origin ?] —**slop·er** *n* —**slop·ing** *adj*

slo-pitch *n* SPORTS another spelling of **slow-pitch**

slop·py /slóppee/ (**-pi·er, -pi·est**) *adj* **1. MESSY** lacking order or tidiness **2. WET** slushy, muddy, or very wet **3. WATERY** cooked or prepared in a way that results in excessive wateriness **4. DIRTY** splashed or covered with liquid **5. NOT DONE WELL** carelessly or badly done (*informal*) **6. GUSHY** overly sentimental or emotional (*informal*) **7.** CLOTHING **BAGGY** loose-fitting so as to be casual and comfortable ○ *a big sloppy sweater*

slop·py joe *n* ground beef cooked in a spicy tomato sauce and served on a bun

slop·work /slóp wùrk/ *n* **1.** any kind of work that has been done quickly and carelessly **2.** clothing that is cheap and of inferior quality, or the manufacture of such clothing (*dated*) —**slop·work·er** *n*

slosh /slosh/ *v* (**sloshed, slosh·ing, slosh·es**) **1.** *vt* **SPILL LIQUID CLUMSILY** to spill or splash a liquid on or over something **2.** *vi* **WADE IN LIQUID** to wade or splash around in water, mud, or slush (*informal*) **3.** *vti* **STIR SOMETHING IN LIQUID** to move or splash something, or move or splash in a liquid (*informal*) ○ *Slosh the shirt in some warm water before the stain sets.* ■ *n* **1. SLUSH** wet snow or mud **2. LIQUID SPLASHING** liquid splashing, or its sound ○ *We could hear the slosh of water against the docks all night because of the storm.* [Early 19C. Probably blend of SLOP[1] "bog" + SLUSH] —**slosh·y** *adj*

sloshed /slosht/ *adj* thoroughly intoxicated (*slang*)

slot[1] /slot/ *n* **1. OPENING** a narrow vertical or horizontal opening into which something can be inserted ○ *Put the coin in the slot.* **2. SCHEDULED TIME** an assigned place and time in a sequence or schedule ○ *The station is moving the new comedy to a prime-time slot next month.* **3. JOB** a position in a company or organization **4.** AVIAT **AIR PASSAGE** an air passage in an airfoil that directs air from the lower to the upper surface **5.** ELEC ENG same as **expansion slot** ■ *v* (**slot·ted, slot·ting, slots**) **1.** *vti* **ASSIGN PLACE TO SOMETHING** to put something in a place, position, or time, or be put in a place ○ *We've slotted your appointment for three o'clock tomorrow afternoon.* **2.** *vt* **MAKE SLOT IN SOMETHING** to cut a slot or slots in something [14C. < Old French *esclot* "hollow of the breastbone"]

slot in *vti* to find a suitable time or place for somebody or something in a plan, organization, or series of events, or be found a time or place ○ *The doctor is busy this morning but she could slot you in at 2 o'clock.*

slot[2] /slot/ *n* the track of an animal, especially a deer [Late 16C. < Old French *esclot* "horse's hoofprint"]

slot car *n US* an electric toy racing car that is operated by a rheostat and has a pin underneath that fits into a groove on a slotted track

sloth

sloth /slawth, slōth, sloth/ *n* **1.** a slow-moving mammal that uses its long claws to hang upside down from tree branches. Native to: Central, South America. Genera: *Bradypus* or *Choloepus*. **2.** a dislike of work or any kind of physical exertion [12C. < SLOW + *-th*, suffix forming nouns < Indo-European]

sloth bear *n* a bear with long shaggy fur and a long snout that enables it to feed on plants and insects. Native to: India, Sri Lanka. Latin name: *Melursus ursinus*.

sloth·ful /sláwthf'l, slṓthf'l, slóthf'l/ *adj* disliking work or any form of physical exertion —**sloth·ful·ly** *adv* —**sloth·ful·ness** *n*

slot ma·chine *n* **1.** a gambling machine in which a player inserts coins or bills in a slot and pulls a lever that spins symbols on a dial to generate combinations that determine winnings **2.** a coin-operated vending machine

slot rac·ing *n US* the racing of slot cars

slot·ter /slóttər/ *n US* a gambler who plays a slot machine (*informal*)

slouch /slowch/ *v* (**slouched, slouch·ing, slouch·es**) **1.** *vti* **WALK OR SIT IN LAZY WAY** to stand, sit, or walk in a careless drooping way, or make a part of the body droop carelessly ○ *He slouched his back and shoulders and leaned against the wall.* **2.** *vi* **DROOP** to hang casually, often at an angle ○ *That child slouched all over the chair, watching TV all day.* ■ *n* **1. EXTREMELY CASUAL POSTURE** an extremely relaxed or ungainly way of sitting, standing, or walking **2. LAZY OR INEPT PERSON** somebody who will not or cannot do something well (*informal; usually used in negative statements*) ○ *very good with children and no slouch around the house either* [Early 16C. Probably < N Germanic] —**slouch·er** *n* —**slouch·i·ly** *adv* —**slouch·i·ness** *n* —**slouch·y** *adj*

slouch hat *n* a hat made of a soft material such as felt that has a broad drooping brim

slough[1] /sloo, slow/ *n* **1. DEEP MUDDY HOLE** a hole or low area in the ground filled with mud or water **2. SWAMPY AREA** a stagnant area of water connected to a larger body of water such as a marsh, inlet, bayou, or backwater **3. ESTUARY** a saltwater estuary **4. HOLE FILLED WITH WATER** on the prairies, a low area filled with water, especially from melting snow **5. SPIRITUAL LOW POINT** deep despair or disgrace [Old English *slōh*, origin ?] —**slough·y** *adj*

slough[2] /sluf/, **sluff** *n* **1. SOMETHING CAST OFF** something discarded or shed **2.** ZOOL **DEAD OUTER COVERING** the dead outer skin shed by a reptile or an amphibian **3.** MED **DEAD TISSUE LAYER** a layer of dead skin that separates from healthy skin after an infection or inflammation **4.** CARDS **DISCARDED CARD** in card games, a card that has been discarded ■ *v* (**sloughed, slough·ing, sloughs; sluffed, sluff·ing, sluffs**) **1.** *vti* **CAST SOMETHING OFF** to shed something, or be shed ○ *Snakes slough off their dead skins.* **2.** *vt* **DISCARD SOMETHING OR SOMEBODY** to get rid of somebody or something that is no longer wanted or needed ○ *She sloughs off friends when she no longer has a use for them.* **3.** *vt* **IGNORE SOMETHING** to pay no attention to something **4.** *vt regional* **SKIP SOMETHING UNWANTED** to skip something unwanted, especially school **5.** *vi* MED **SEPARATE FROM HEALED TISSUE** to separate from surrounding healthy skin (*refers to dead skin*) **6.** *vti* CARDS **DISCARD CARD** to get rid of an unwanted card [14C. Origin ?]

REGIONAL NOTE The use of ***slough*** to mean "skip something unwanted," as in *sloughing school*, is a Nevada usage.

Slough /slow/ city in south central England. Population: 119,067 (2001).

slough of de·spond /slōō-, slòw-/ *n* a state of extreme despair and depression [After the deep bog in *Pilgrim's Progress, Part 1* (1678) by John Bunyan (1628–88)]

Slo·vak /slṓ vàk/ (*plural* **-vaks** or **-va·ki·ans**) *n* **1.** somebody who comes from Slovakia **2.** the Slavic national language of Slovakia. Native speakers: 5 million. [Early 19C. < Slovak, Czech, Russian] —**Slo·vak** *adj*

Slovakia

Slo·va·ki·a /slō vaákee ə/ country in east central Europe. It was part of Czechoslovakia until 1993 and became a member of the European Union in 2004. Language: Slovak. Currency: Slovak koruna. Capital: Bratislava. Population: 5,430,033 (2003). Area: 18,933 sq. mi./49,035 sq. km. Official name **Slovak Republic**

Slo·va·ki·an /slō vákee ən/ *n* PEOPLES, LANG same as **Slovak** —**Slo·va·ki·an** *adj*

slov·en /slúvv'n/ *n* an offensive term that deliberately insults somebody whose standards of personal hygiene and tidiness are considered too low [15C. Probably < Middle Flemish *sloovin* "a scold"]

Slo·vene /slṓ veen/ *n* **1.** somebody who comes from Slovenia **2.** the Slavic national language of Slovenia. Native speakers: 2 million. [Late 19C. Via German < Slovene *Sloven(ec)* < Slavic] —**Slo·vene** *adj*

Slovenia

Slo·ve·ni·a /slō veénee ə/ country in eastern Europe, on the Balkan Peninsula. It was part of Yugoslavia until 1991. It became a member of the European Union in 2004. Language: Slovene. Currency: tolar. Capital: Ljubljana. Population: 1,935,677 (2003). Area: 7,820 sq. mi./20,253 sq. km. See map on previous page. Official name **Republic of Slovenia**

Slo·ve·ni·an /slō veénee ən/ *n* PEOPLES, LANG same as **Slovene** —**Slo·ve·ni·an** *adj*

slov·en·ly /slúvvənlee/ (**-li·er, -li·est**) *adj* an offensive term meaning not concerned about conventional standards of personal hygiene and tidiness —**slov·en·li·ness** *n*

slow /slō/ *adj* **1.** NOT FAST not moving at a fast pace **2.** LENGTHY taking a long time to do or create something ○ *Writing software is a slow process.* **3.** TAKING TOO MUCH TIME requiring more time than is usual or expected **4.** NOT KEEPING ACCURATE TIME showing a time that is earlier than the correct time ○ *I was late for my appointment because my watch was slow.* **5.** HESITANT doing something hesitantly or unwillingly ○ *Why were you so slow to answer my question?* **6.** SLUGGISH lacking the usual volume of sales or customers ○ *Business is usually slow during the summer months.* **7.** DULL lacking in interest or activity ○ *The acting was good but the plot was terribly slow.* **8.** REDUCING SPEED OF BALL OR RUNNER tending to reduce the speed or ability to travel of a ball, runner, or other competitor ○ *a slow track* **9.** UNINTELLIGENT lacking in intelligence or mental sharpness (*informal insult*) **10.** COOK WARM operating at a low temperature that ensures thorough cooking throughout ○ *A turkey should be cooked in a slow oven.* ■ *adv* **1.** BEHIND behind the correct time or pace ○ *My watch seems to be running slow.* **2.** ⚠ AT LOW SPEED at a reduced speed or pace ○ *The law requires motorists to drive slow through school zones.* ■ *vti* (**slowed, slow·ing, slows**) **1.** MAKE OR BECOME SLOW to make somebody or something slow or slower, or become slow or slower ○ *Could you slow your speed a little on those sharp turns?* **2.** DELAY OR BE DELAYED to reduce the speed or progress of something, or become reduced in speed or progress ○ *slowed down the company's rate of expansion* [Old English *slaw* "sluggish" < Indo-European] —**slow·ly** *adv* —**slow·ness** *n*

USAGE slowly or **slow**? The standard adverb is ***slowly***: *The car went slowly up the hill.* ***Slow***, although usually an adjective, is used as an adverb of keeping time (*My watch is running slow*), and also more generally in highly informal contexts, on signs (*Go Slow*), and as an element of compound words like *slow-moving*.

slow burn, **slow boil** *n* a state of steadily becoming angrier (*informal*) ○ *doing a slow burn*

slow·coach /slṓ kōch/ *n UK* same as **slowpoke** (*informal*)

slow·down /slṓ dòwn/ *n* an intentional reduction in pace or production by workers in order to win demands from their employer

slow-foot·ed *adj* happening or proceeding at an extremely slow pace ○ *Congress has been slow-footed in passing the bill.* —**slow-foot·ed·ness** *n*

slow lo·ris *n* a small slow-moving primate that has a rounded, almost tailless body. Native to: Indonesia. Latin name: *Nycticebus coucang*.

slow match *n* a match or fuse that burns without a flame very slowly or at a known rate and is used to set off explosives

slow mo·tion *n* a method of filming action at a rate faster than the normal projection rate, so that it appears on the screen at a slower than normal rate

slow-mo·tion *adj* **1.** photographed or shown in slow motion **2.** taking place at a slower pace than normal ○ *her slow-motion reaction*

slow neu·tron *n* a relatively slow-moving neutron that possesses less than 100 electron volts of kinetic energy and is capable of bringing about nuclear fission

slow-pitch, **slo-pitch** *n* softball game in which there are ten players on a team and the pitched ball must travel in an arc from three to ten feet high

slow·poke /slṓw pōk/ *n* somebody who moves, acts, responds, or works very slowly (*informal*) [Mid-19C. < POKE[1] "dawdling person"]

slow vi·rus *n* any virus, or any agent resembling a virus, that causes diseases with very long incubation periods. Technical name **lentivirus**

slow-wave sleep *n* a state of dreamless sleep characterized by slow brain waves and lowered heart rate, respiration, and blood pressure

slow·worm /slṓ wùrm/ *n* a legless lizard with a smooth body resembling that of a snake. Native to: Europe, North Africa, western Asia. Latin name: *Anguis fragilis*. [< WORM "snake"]

SLR *abbr* PHOTOGRAPHY single-lens reflex

slub /slub/ *n* **1.** KNOT IN YARN a lump in yarn or fabric that is sometimes an imperfection, but is often made to provide a knobby effect **2.** TWISTED THREAD a loosely twisted roll of fiber, e.g., of silk or cotton, prepared for spinning ■ *vt* (**slubbed, slub·bing, slubs**) PREPARE FIBER FOR SPINNING to draw out and twist a strand of fiber to prepare it for spinning [Early 19C. Origin ?]

sludge /sluj/ *n* **1.** SOLID WASTE the solids in sewage that separate out during treatment **2.** SLUSH wet material, especially watery mud or snow **3.** SEDIMENT a solid deposit found at the bottom of a liquid **4.** BROKEN ICE a layer of broken or half-formed ice on a body of water, especially the sea **5.** MED MASS OF BLOOD CELLS a sticky grouping of blood cells that form a mass and hinder the circulation of blood [Mid-17C. Origin ?] —**sludg·y** *adj*

slue[1] /sloo/, **slew** *vti* (**slued, slu·ing, slues; slewed, slew·ing, slews**) **1.** *US* PIVOT AROUND AXIS to pivot or turn around an axis, or cause something to pivot or turn **2.** VEER OR SKID to swerve or skid sideways, or cause something to swerve or skid sideways off course ■ *n* **1.** VEERING OR SKIDDING an act of swerving or skidding sideways **2.** *US* POSITION AFTER SOMETHING SLUES a position in which something stops after it slues [Variant of SLOUGH[1] and SLEW[3] "turn"]

slue[2] /sloo/ *n* GEOG same as **slough**[1] (sense 2) [Variant]

sluff *n, vti* ZOOL, MED, CARDS another spelling of **slough**[2]

slug[1] /slug/ *n* **1.** BULLET a metal projectile that is fired from a gun or rifle **2.** DISK USED AS ILLEGAL COIN a small metal disk, made in the shape and size of a coin, used to purchase something illegally, especially from a vending machine **3.** DRINK OF SOMETHING a single shot of a strong alcoholic drink (*informal*) **4.** PRINTING TYPE METAL a strip of type metal, less than type-high, used for spacing in traditional hot-metal printing **5.** PRINTING LINE OF TYPE a strip of cast type in a single strip of metal in traditional hot-metal printing **6.** PRINTING TEMPORARY TYPE LINE a temporary type line inserted in copy that carries identifying marks or a compositor's instructions **7.** MANUF METAL OR GLASS BLANK FOR PROCESSING a metal or glass blank that will receive further processing to make it into a finished object **8.** MEASURE UNIT OF MASS a foot-pound-second unit of mass equal to 32.17 pounds that will acquire an acceleration of one foot per second per second when acted on by a one pound force ■ *vt* **1.** DRINK SOMETHING QUICKLY to gulp down a drink (*informal*) **2.** PRINTING ADD SLUGS TO COPY to add printers' slugs to copy in traditional hot-metal printing [Early 17C. Origin ?]

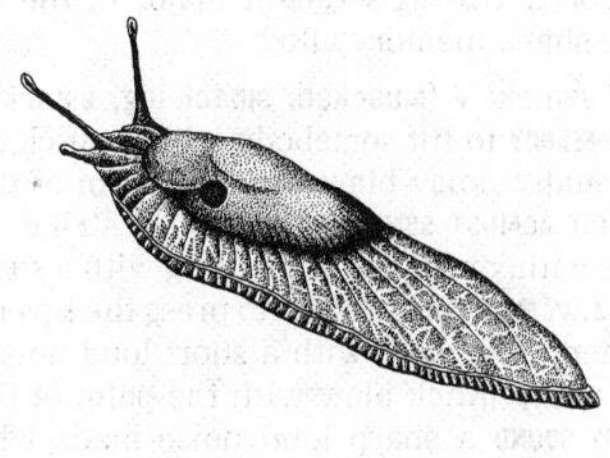

slug

slug[2] /slug/ *n* **1.** MOLLUSK WITHOUT SHELL a small slow-moving terrestrial mollusk that resembles a snail but has no shell, or only a rudimentary one. Order: Stylommatophora. **2.** SOFT INSECT LARVA a soft smooth larva of some insects such as the sawfly **3.** OFFENSIVE TERM an offensive term that deliberately insults somebody's level of energy or activity **4.** BIOL CELLS THAT DEVELOP INTO SPORE-BEARING STRUCTURE a sticky mass of cells from which the sporophore of a slime mold develops [15C. Probably < N Germanic]

slug[3] /slug/ *vt* (**slugged, slug·ging, slugs**) to strike somebody or something very hard with the fist or a bat ■ *n* a hard strike or blow [Mid-19C. Variant of SLOG] ◇ **slug it out** to fight to a conclusion (*informal*)

slug[4] /slug/ *n* a commuter who is not a member of an organized car pool and who hitches rides at established pickup points, hoping for an empty seat (*slang*) [Late 20C. Origin ?]

slug·fest /slúg fèst/ *n* **1.** BASEBALL GAME WITH MANY HITS a baseball game in which both teams make a large number of hits and score a large number of runs **2.** HEATED ARGUMENT an intense debate or dispute **3.** BRAWL a long fight in which many heavy blows are exchanged (*slang*) [Early 20C. < SLUG[3]]

slug·gard /slúggərd/ *n* somebody who avoids work or physical exertion (*archaic*) ■ *adj* sluggishly lazy [14C. < SLUG[2]] —**slug·gard·li·ness** *n* —**slug·gard·ly** *adj* —**slug·gard·ness** *n*

slug·ger /slúggər/ *n* **1.** a fighter who delivers hard blows **2.** a baseball player who hits many extra-base hits [< SLUG[3]]

slug·ging av·er·age, **slug·ging per·cent·age** *n US* the total number of bases reached on hits by a baseball player divided by the number of official times at bat, expressed as a three-digit decimal

slug·gish /slúggish/ *adj* **1.** NOT MOVING MUCH inactive and moving slowly or very little **2.** NOT VERY RESPONSIVE slow to react or respond to stimulation **3.** LACKING ALERTNESS AND ENERGY not alert and showing little energy or vitality —**slug·gish·ly** *adv* —**slug·gish·ness** *n*

sluice

sluice /slooss/ *n* **1.** WATER CHANNEL an artificial channel for a flow of water that is controlled by a valve or gate **2.** FLOODGATE a valve or floodgate that controls the water in a sluice **3.** WATER BEHIND FLOODGATE a body of water contained by a floodgate **4.** DRAINAGE CHANNEL a channel for carrying away excess water **5.** TROUGH a long inclined trough used to separate gold ore from sand or gravel **6.** CHANNEL TO MOVE LOGS an artificial stream or channel for floating logs ■ *v* (**sluiced, sluic·ing, sluic·es**) **1.** *vt* FLUSH SOMETHING WITH WATER to flood or clean something with a sudden heavy flow of water **2.** *vt* WASH GOLD to wash gold or other minerals in water flowing in a sluice **3.** *vti* RELEASE SOMETHING FROM SLUICE to flow from a sluice, or let something out of a sluice **4.** *vt* MOVE SOMETHING IN SLUICE to float something, especially logs, down a sluice [14C. < Old French *escluse* < Latin *exclus-*, past participle of *excludere* (see EXCLUDE)]

sluice·gate /slooss gàyt/ *n* ENG same as **sluice** *n* (sense 2)

sluice·way /slooss wày/ *n* an artificial channel into which water flows from a sluice

slum /slum/ *n* POOR AREA an overcrowded area of a city in which the housing is typically in very bad condition (*often used in the plural*) ■ *v* (**slummed, slum·ming, slums**) **1.** *vti* ACCEPT LOWER STANDARDS THAN USUAL to stay in or go to a place that you would usually consider unacceptable (*often used humorously*) ○ *We'll have to slum it and stay here until we can find a better place.* **2.** *vi* VISIT SLUMS to go into a slum out of curiosity [Mid-19C. < *back slum* "street housing poor people" < obsolete *slum* "room," origin ?] —**slum·mer** *n*

slum·ber /slúmbər/ *vi* (**-bered, -ber·ing, -bers**) **1.** SLEEP to be asleep **2. BE IN QUIET STATE** to be in a state of inactivity or rest ■ *n* **1. SLEEPING** the state of being asleep, or a period of sleep ○ *A loud noise disturbed my slumber.* **2. INACTIVITY** a state of being dormant or quiet [14C. Alteration of obsolete *sloom* "light sleep" < Germanic] —**slum·ber·less** *adj*

slum·ber·ous /slúmbərəss/ *adj* **1. DROWSY** feeling sleepy **2. INACTIVE** characterized by inactivity or sluggishness ○ *A slumberous atmosphere seemed to stifle sound and motion in the town.* **3. CAUSING SLEEP** inducing lethargy or sleep ○ *She dozed in the slumberous heat of the afternoon.* —**slum·ber·ous·ly** *adv* —**slum·ber·ous·ness** *n*

slum·ber par·ty *n* a party at which a group of girls, wearing nightgowns or pajamas, talk, eat, and stay overnight at one of the girls' homes

slum·gul·lion /slum gúllyən, slúm gùllyən/ *n US* a watery meat stew (*informal*) [Mid-19C. Origin ?]

slum·lord /slúm làwrd/ *n* somebody who owns housing in slum areas, especially a neglectful landlord who overcharges tenants [Mid-20C. < SLUM + LANDLORD]

slump /slump/ *vi* (**slumped, slump·ing, slumps**) **1. COLLAPSE** to sink or fall suddenly and heavily **2. SLOUCH** to have a hunched drooping posture ○ *She was slumped over her desk.* **3. DECREASE** to decline suddenly and sharply in value ○ *stock prices slumped* ■ *n* **1. SLOUCHED POSTURE** a drooping or hunched posture **2. ECONOMIC RECESSION** a sudden decline in business, stock prices, or productivity ○ *an economy fluctuating between boom and slump* **3.** *US* **PERIOD OF POOR PERFORMANCE** a relatively long period of time during which somebody or something such as an employee, athlete, or team fails to perform well ○ *If he doesn't pull out of his slump, his job may be in jeopardy.* [Mid-17C. Origin ?]

slump·fla·tion /slùmp fláysh'n/ *n* an economic situation in which an economic depression is accompanied by increasing inflation [Late 20C. < SLUMP + INFLATION]

slung past participle, past tense of **sling**[1]

slung·shot /slúng shòt/ *n* a weight or weights attached to the end of a cord and used as a weapon

slunk past participle, past tense of **slink**

slur /slur/ *v* (**slurred, slur·ring, slurs**) **1.** *vti* **SPEAK INDISTINCTLY** to pronounce sounds or words so that they cannot be distinguished, or be pronounced in this way **2.** *vt* **DEMEAN SOMEBODY** to speak of somebody in an insulting or demeaning way **3.** *vt* **GLOSS OVER SOMETHING** to ignore something or treat it superficially ○ *The committee slurred over my protests.* **4.** *vti* **SMEAR OR BE SMEARED** to blur or smear wet ink on a page, or be blurred or smeared **5.** *vt* MUSIC **PERFORM MUSIC SMOOTHLY** to play musical notes in a smooth, uninterrupted way ■ *n* **1. INSULT** an insulting or demeaning statement about somebody **2. SLURRED PRONUNCIATION** an indistinct pronunciation or sound **3. BLURRED IMAGE** an image that has been smeared or blurred **4.** MUSIC **MUSIC SYMBOL** a curved line that connects two or more notes on a score, indicating that they are to be performed smoothly [Early 17C. Origin ?]

slurb /slurb/ *n US* an ugly suburban area in which the housing is crowded or badly built (*informal*) [Mid-20C. Blend of SLUM + SUBURB]

slurp /slurp/ *vti* (**slurped, slurp·ing, slurps**) **DRINK SOMETHING NOISILY** to make a loud sucking sound while drinking or eating something ○ *Would you stop slurping your milk shake?* ■ *n* **1. SUCKING SOUND** a loud sucking sound made while drinking or eating **2. LIQUID MOUTHFUL** a mouthful of a liquid (*informal*) ○ *Can I have a slurp of your soda?* [Mid-17C. < Dutch *slurpen*] —**slurp·ing·ly** *adv*

slur·ry /slúr ee/ *n* a liquid mixture of water and an insoluble solid material such as cement or clay [15C. < English dialect *slur* "thin mud," origin?]

slush /slush/ *n* **1. MELTING SNOW OR ICE** snow or ice that has begun to melt **2. SEMILIQUID SUBSTANCE** a solid substance that has become wet and sloppy, e.g., mud **3. OVERLY SENTIMENTAL EXPRESSION** extremely sentimental speech or writing **4. ICE DRINK** a drink made of finely crushed ice with a flavored syrup poured over it **5. GREASE** a greasy substance used to lubricate machine parts **6.** NAUT **GREASE FROM SHIP'S GALLEY** the waste grease or fat produced by a ship's galley ■ *v* (**slushed, slush·ing, slush·es**) **1.** *vt* **SOAK SOMETHING WITH SLUSH** to splash or cover something with mud or slush **2.** *vi* **WALK THROUGH SLUSH** to walk through wet snow or mud ○ *It had been raining so hard we had to slush through mud to get there.* **3.** *vi* **MAKE SPLASHING SOUND** to make a splashing or squelching sound **4.** *vt* ENG **GREASE MACHINERY** to lubricate the parts of a machine **5.** *vt* CONSTR **PUT MORTAR IN JOINTS** to fill masonry joints with mortar, or cover a surface with cement [Mid-17C. Origin ?]

slush fund *n* **1. MONEY FOR ILLEGAL ACTIVITIES** money set aside by a business or other organization for corrupt activities such as the bribery of public officials **2. MONEY FOR ENTERTAINMENT** money set aside to use for fun or entertainment expenses **3. LUXURY FUND FOR SHIP'S CREW** money raised by selling refuse from a ship to pay for small luxuries for the crew [< SLUSH "grease collected in a ship's galley (and sold)"; from the idea of "greasing" somebody's palm with money]

slush pile *n* a pile of unsolicited manuscripts accumulated in a publisher's office (*informal*)

slush·y /slúshee/ (**-i·er, -i·est**) *adj* **1. FULL OF SLUSH** covered with or full of melting snow and ice **2. RESEMBLING SLUSH** with the consistency of slush **3. OVERLY SENTIMENTAL** filled with or expressing excessive sentiment ○ *a slushy love story* —**slush·i·ness** *n*

slut /slut/ *n* **1.** an offensive term for a woman thought to be sexually promiscuous **2.** an offensive term for a woman who charges for engaging in sexual activities **3.** an offensive term for a woman who is regarded as not concerned about conventional standards of domestic cleanliness (*dated*) [15C. Origin ?] —**slut·tish** *adj* —**slut·tish·ly** *adv* —**slut·tish·ness** *n* —**slut·ty** *adj*

Slu·ter /slóotər/, **Claus** (1350?–1406) Dutch sculptor noted for the intense facial expressions of his figures. His best-known work is *Well of Moses* (1395–1403).

SLV *abbr* AEROSP space launch vehicle *or* standard launch vehicle

sly /slī/ (**sli·er, sli·est**) *adj* **1. CRAFTY** cleverly skillful and cunning **2. EVASIVE** lacking honesty or straightforwardness **3. MISCHIEVOUS** full of playful mischief [13C. < Old Norse *slœgr* "clever, crafty"] —**sly·ly** *adv* —**sly·ness** *n* ◇ **on the sly** without the knowledge or permission of others

sly·boots /slī boots/ *n* somebody considered to be cunning or devious (*insult; takes a singular verb*)

slype /slīp/ *n* a covered passage in a cathedral or church that joins the transept to a chapter house [Mid-19C. Origin ?]

sm *abbr* San Marino (*used in Internet addresses*) See table at **domain name**

Sm *symbol* CHEM ELEM samarium

SM[1] *abbr* **1.** *also* **S.M.** sergeant major **2.** COMM service mark **3.** *also* **S.M.** Soldier's Medal **4.** THEATER stage manager **5.** RAIL station master

SM[2] *abbr* EDUC Master of Science [Latin *Scientiae Magister*]

sm. *abbr* small

S/M, S-M *abbr* sadomasochism

SMA *abbr* **1.** *US* MIL sergeant major of the army **2.** METALL shape memory alloy

smack[1] /smak/ *v* (**smacked, smack·ing, smacks**) **1.** *vti* **SLAP SOMEBODY** to hit somebody with a quick stinging and usually noisy blow with the palm of the hand **2.** *vi* **HIT AGAINST SOMETHING NOISILY** to strike against, collide with, or land in something with a sharp loud noise **3.** *vt* **PRESS LIPS TOGETHER** to press the lips together and then open them with a short loud noise ■ *n* **1. SLAP** a sharp quick blow with the palm of the hand **2. NOISY SOUND** a sharp loud noise made when one thing strikes another **3. LOUD KISS** a brief noisy kiss ■ *adv* **1. WITH LOUD NOISE** with a sharp loud noise or collision **2. DIRECTLY** directly or precisely ○ *I was smack in the middle of getting ready to leave when you called.* [Mid-16C. < Middle Low German *smacken* "open the lips noisily," an imitation of the sound]

smack[2] /smak/ *n* **1. DISTINCTIVE TASTE** a unique flavor or taste of something **2. HINT** a small amount or trace ■ *vi* (**smacked, smack·ing, smacks**) **1. BE DISTINCTIVELY FLAVORED** to have a unique flavor or taste **2. EXPRESS SOMETHING INDIRECTLY** to suggest or hint at something ○ *an editorial that smacked of snobbery* [Old English *smæc* "taste" < Germanic]

smack[3] /smak/ *n* a sailing vessel used for fishing, usually for carrying the catch to market [Early 17C. < Dutch *smak*]

smack[4] /smak/ *n* DRUGS same as **heroin** (*slang*) [Mid-20C. Probably alteration of slang *schmeck* < Yiddish, "a sniff" < Middle High German *smecken* "to smell"]

smack-dab *adv* straight or directly (*informal*) ○ *I landed smack-dab in a huge mud puddle.*

smack·er /smákər/ *n* (*informal*) **1.** a noisy smacking kiss **2.** MONEY same as **dollar**

smack·ing /smáking/ *adj* very brisk or lively ○ *a smacking breeze*

small /smawl/ *adj* **1. LITTLE** of a relatively little size ○ *a small animal* **2. NOT MUCH** little in quantity or value ○ *a small sum of money* **3. INSIGNIFICANT** unimportant or trivial ○ *a small matter* **4. LIMITED** operating on a limited scale ○ *small businesses* **5. MINOR** lacking in power, influence, or status ○ *a small fish in a big pond* **6. NOT YET MATURE** young or not fully grown ○ *small children* **7. ORDINARY** humble or modest ○ *He came from small beginnings.* **8. MEAN** petty and mean-spirited ○ *He's too small to apologize.* **9. LOWERCASE** in lowercase rather than capitals ○ *small letters* **10. WITHOUT SELF-RESPECT** humiliated or feeling little self-worth ○ *Her criticisms and ridicule made me feel very small.* ■ *adv* **1. IN SMALL PIECES** in or into little pieces ○ *Cut it up small.* **2. IN SMALL WAY** in a moderate or limited way ○ *start out small* **3. QUIETLY** quietly or softly (*archaic*) ■ *n* **1. NARROW PART** a part of something that is narrower or smaller than the rest of it ○ *the small of the back* **2. SIZE FOR SOMEBODY SMALL** a size that fits somebody who is of less than average proportions, or a garment in that size ■ **smalls** *npl* **1. LITTLE THINGS** small things or products (*informal*) **2.** *UK* **UNDERGARMENTS** items of underwear (*informal or humorous*) [Old English *smæl* "slender, small" < Germanic, "small animal"] —**small·ish** *adj* —**small·ness** *n*

small ad *n UK* same as **classified advertisement** (*informal; usually used in the plural*)

small arms *npl* firearms that can be held in one or both hands while firing, e.g., pistols and rifles

small beer *n* **1.** something of little or no importance (*informal*) ○ *A thousand dollars is small beer to folks like him.* **2.** weak or inferior beer (*dated*)

small-bore *adj* describes .22-caliber firearms or ammunition.

small cal·o·rie *n* MEASURE same as **calorie** (sense 1)

small cap·i·tal *n* a capital letter that is the same height as a lowercase letter

small change *n* **1.** coins that have a low denomination **2.** something considered to be comparatively insignificant

small cir·cle *n* the circumference of a plane that cuts a sphere but does not pass through its center

small-claims court *n* a local court that has jurisdiction to try civil actions involving claims worth only a small sum of money

Smal·ley /smáwlee/, **Richard E.** (*b.* 1943) US chemical physicist. Together with Robert Curl and Harold Kroto, he discovered the family of carbon molecules called fullerenes, and shared the Nobel Prize in chemistry (1996).

small fry *npl* **1. TRIVIAL THINGS** people, events, or issues that are thought to be of little importance **2. CHILDREN** a young child or young children (*informal*) **3. YOUNG FISH** young, immature, or small fish

small game *n* small animals and birds that are hunted for sport

small hours *npl* the early morning hours after midnight

small in·tes·tine *n* the part of the intestine between the stomach and the large intestine, consisting of the duodenum, jejunum, and ileum, where digestion of food and most absorption of nutrients takes place

small is·land *n Carib* any of the small Caribbean islands northwest of Trinidad such as St. Vincent and Grenada. (*disapproving*)

small-mind·ed *adj* petty and intolerant of the ideas

and beliefs of others —**small-mind·ed·ly** *adv* —**small-mind·ed·ness** *n*

small·mouth bass /smáwl mowth bàss/ *n* a greenish brown freshwater bass found in clear streams and lakes that is a popular game fish. Native to: North America. Latin name: *Micropterus dolomieu.*

small po·ta·toes *npl* somebody or something considered to be unimportant or trivial (*informal*) ○ *A thousand dollars is small potatoes to him.* [< the idea of potatoes too small to be worth cleaning or peeling]

small·pox /smáwl pòks/ *n* a highly contagious disease caused by a poxvirus and marked by high fever and the formation of scar-producing pustules. A worldwide inoculation program has almost eradicated the smallpox virus from the human population. Technical name **variola**

small print *n UK* same as **fine print**

small-scale *adj* **1.** limited in scope or size ○ *small-scale businesses* **2.** made or constructed on a small scale ○ *She built a small-scale replica of the ship.*

small screen *n* the medium of television, especially as distinct from the movies (*informal*)

small slam *n* CARDS same as **little slam**

small stores *npl* small items sold on a ship or at a naval base, e.g., clothing

small stuff *n* somebody or something that is regarded as unimportant or trivial (*informal*) ○ *Forget what she thinks; don't sweat the small stuff.*

small·sword /smáwl sàwrd/ *n* a light sword used in the 17th and 18th centuries for dueling and fencing (*archaic*)

small talk *n* polite conversation about matters of little importance, especially between people who do not know each other well

small-time *adj* of minor importance or influence (*informal*) ○ *He's just a small-time crook.*

smalt /smawlt/ *n* **1.** silica glass that has been colored a deep blue by cobalt oxide **2.** a deep blue pigment made by crushing smalt [Mid-16C. Via French < Italian *smalto* (see SMALTO)]

smalt·ite /smáwl tìt/ *n* a blue-gray cobalt nickel arsenide mineral. Use: source of cobalt.

smal·to /smáwltō/ *n* small bits of pottery, glass, and tiles used in mosaics [Early 18C. < Italian < Germanic]

sma·rag·dite /smə rág dìt/ *n* a fibrous green amphibole mineral [Early 19C. < Latin *smaragdus*, via Greek < Hebrew *bāreqeṯ* "emerald" < *bāraq* "flash, sparkle"]

smarm /smaarm/ *n* (*informal*) **1.** ingratiating or servile flattery **2.** charm that is distastefully self-conscious or insincere [Early 20C. Origin ?]

smarm·y /smaármee/ (**-i·er, -i·est**) *adj* excessively earnest and ingratiating in manner —**smarm·i·ly** *adv* —**smarm·i·ness** *n*

smart /smaart/ *adj* **1.** CLEVER showing intelligence and mental alertness ○ *smart students* **2.** KEEN shrewd and calculating in business and other dealings ○ *a smart dealer* **3.** WITTY AND AMUSING amusingly clever and possessing a quick wit **4.** INSOLENT disrespectful or impertinent ○ *Whatever you say to him, he has some smart answer.* **5.** WELL-GROOMED having a neat and well-cared-for appearance **6.** FASHIONABLE fashionable and stylish ○ *smart restaurants* **7.** LIVELY vigorous and brisk ○ *a smart pace* **8.** STINGING causing a sharp stinging sensation ○ *a smart slap* **9.** MIL LASER- OR RADIO-GUIDED describes a missile or weapon that is guided to its target by laser or radio beams **10.** ELECTRONICS ELECTRONIC fitted with a built-in microprocessor ○ *smart traffic signals* **11.** DISCRIMINATING selective in application or effect ○ *smart sanctions* ■ *vi* (**smart·ed, smart·ing, smarts**) **1.** CAUSE OR HAVE SHARP PAIN to feel, cause, or be the site of a sharp stinging pain ○ *My hand smarts.* **2.** BE EMBARRASSED to feel acute embarrassment, shame, or remorse ○ *She still smarted when she remembered his criticism.* **3.** BE PUNISHED to be punished severely ■ *adv* SMARTLY in a smart manner ■ *n* **1.** PAIN a sharp stinging localized pain **2.** EMBARRASSMENT OR MENTAL DISCOMFORT a feeling such as acute embarrassment, shame, or remorse ■ **smarts** *npl* INTELLIGENCE practical intelligence or expertise (*informal*) ○ *She has the smarts to succeed.* [Old English *smeortan* "be painful," origin ?] —**smart·ly** *adv* —**smart·ness** *n*

SYNONYMS See ***intelligent.***

smart al·eck /-àllik/, **smart al·ec** *n* somebody who makes an annoying show of knowing something or of being cleverer than others (*informal*) [Mid-19C. Origin ?] —**smart-al·eck** *adj*

smart·ass /smaárt àss/, **smart-ass** *n* same as **smart aleck** (*slang offensive*)

smart bomb *n* a missile that is guided to its target by laser or radio beams

smart card *n* a small plastic card containing a microchip that can store personal data such as bank-account details, used for identification and for payment of purchases

smart·en /smaárt'n/ (**-ened, -en·ing, -ens**) *vt* **1.** to improve the appearance of somebody or something **2.** to increase the speed of something

smarten up *vti* **1.** IMPROVE APPEARANCE to improve your appearance, or the appearance of somebody or something else **2.** MAKE OR BECOME LIVELIER to make somebody or something brighter or livelier, or become brighter or livelier **3.** MAKE OR BECOME WISER to make somebody wiser or more knowing, or become wiser or more knowing

smart growth *n* economic growth that consciously seeks to avoid wastefulness and damage to the environment and communities

smart·ish /smaártish/ *adv UK* without delay or quickly (*informal*) ○ *You'd better make up your mind smartish!*

smart mon·ey *n* **1.** WISE INVESTMENT OR BET money invested in or bet on something likely to yield a good profit **2.** WISE INVESTORS people who know what to invest in or bet on to make a good profit **3.** *US* LAW DAMAGES AWARDED TO PUNISH DEFENDANT damages awarded to a plaintiff in excess of the usual level of compensation to punish a defendant in cases of serious negligence or willful misconduct

smart·siz·ing /smaárt sìzing/ *n* the process of reducing the size of a work force by eliminating staff positions (*slang*)

smart ter·mi·nal *n* a network terminal that carries out processing but uses another computer for data and program storage

smart·weed /smaárt weèd/ *n* a plant of the buckwheat family that grows in marshy temperate regions and has acidic juice that can irritate the skin. One variety of smartweed is water pepper, a plant with peppery-tasting leaves. Genus: *Polygonum.* [Late 18C. Because its acidic juice causes smarting]

smart·y pants /smaártee-/ (*plural same*), **smart·y** (*plural* **-ies**) *n* same as **smart aleck** (*informal*)

smash /smash/ *v* (**smashed, smash·ing, smash·es**) **1.** *vti* BREAK SOMETHING INTO PIECES to break something into many small pieces, or be broken in this way **2.** *vti* BREAK SOMETHING WITH FORCE to break something with great force or violence, or move violently so as to break something **3.** *vti* HIT SOMETHING FORCEFULLY to hit something with great force, or make something do this **4.** *vt* DEFEAT OR DESTROY SOMETHING to ruin, defeat, or put an end to somebody or something completely **5.** *vt* RACKET GAMES HIT BALL WITH OVERHEAD STROKE in racket games, to hit a ball or shuttlecock downward with great force with an overhead stroke ■ *n* **1.** LOUD NOISE the loud sound of something hitting or being hit by something else and breaking into pieces ○ *The mirror hit the floor with a smash.* **2.** HEAVY BLOW a blow delivered with great force **3.** COLLISION a crash or collision ○ *There's been a bad smash on the freeway.* **4.** BUSINESS, THEATER GREAT SUCCESS an unqualified success (*often used before a noun*) ○ *The new show was a smash hit.* **5.** BUSINESS BIG FAILURE a major failure, especially one involving finances **6.** RACKET GAMES OVERHEAD STROKE in racket games, an overhead stroke hit downward with great force **7.** VOLLEYBALL same as **spike** (sense 12) **8.** BEVERAGES COCKTAIL a cocktail made with sugar, seltzer, mint leaves, and usually brandy ■ *adv* WITH SMASH with the sound of a smash [Late 17C. Origin ?] —**smash·a·ble** *adj* —**smash·er** *n*

smash up *v* **1.** *vti* to damage something severely in a collision with something solid, or be damaged in this way **2.** *vt* to damage or destroy something by breaking

smashed /smasht/ *adj* very drunk or under the influence of drugs (*informal*)

smash·ing /smáshing/ *adj* **1.** *US* crushing or serving to smash something ○ *a smashing blow to the jaw* **2.** *UK* extremely good or pleasing (*dated informal*)

smash·up /smásh ùp/ *n* **1.** a collision between vehicles in which all the machines involved are badly damaged **2.** *US* complete ruin, collapse, or destruction

smat·ter /smáttər/ *vt* (**-tered, -ter·ing, -ters**) **1.** to study a subject or language in a not very serious way **2.** to speak a language badly ■ *n* same as **smattering** [15C. Origin ?] —**smat·ter·er** *n*

smat·ter·ing /smáttəring/ *n* **1.** SLIGHT KNOWLEDGE a slight knowledge of something such as a subject or language **2.** SMALL AMOUNT a small amount or number ○ *a smattering of rain* ■ *adj* SUPERFICIAL concerned only with surface issues and not going into depth or substance [Mid-16C. < *smatter* "dabble, speak without proper knowledge," origin?]

SMATV *abbr* satellite master antenna television

SME *abbr* small and medium-sized enterprise

smear /smeer/ *v* (**smeared, smear·ing, smears**) **1.** *vti* SPREAD SOMETHING OVER SURFACE to spread something liquid or greasy over a surface, or be spread over a surface ○ *This lipstick is made not to smear.* **2.** *vt* SAY BAD THINGS ABOUT SOMEBODY to deliberately spread damaging rumors about somebody **3.** *vt US* DEFEAT SOMEBODY to severely defeat a competitor or enemy (*informal; usually passive*) ○ *We got smeared.* ■ *n* **1.** PATCH OF SMEARED SUBSTANCE an act of smearing, or a smeared patch of something **2.** HARMFUL RUMOR a damaging rumor about somebody **3.** MED SAMPLE OF CELLS a sample of cells taken from body tissue or a bodily secretion or discharge and smeared on a microscope slide for examination [Old English *smeirwan* (verb), *smeoru* (noun) < Germanic] —**smear·er** *n*

smear cam·paign *n* a concerted effort to damage somebody's reputation by spreading harmful rumors about him or her

smear·case /smeér kàyss/ *n regional* same as **cottage cheese** [Early 19C. < German *Schmierkäse* < *schmieren* "spread" + *Käse* "cheese"]

REGIONAL NOTE Although the term ***smearcase*** is mainly used in eastern Pennsylvania, it has spread with migrations throughout Appalachia into the western Carolinas and East Tennessee.

smear·y /smeéree/ (**-i·er, -i·est**) *adj* **1.** smeared on, easily smeared, or likely to smear **2.** having or covered with smears

smec·tic /sméktik/ *adj* describes materials such as liquid crystals whose liquid phase consists of elongated molecules arranged in layers and with their axes parallel to each other [Late 17C. Via Latin < Greek *smēktikos* < *smēkhein* "rub, cleanse"]

smec·tite /smék tìt/ *n* a clay mineral belonging to the group that swell in water. Use: ion exchange materials. [Early 19C. < Greek *smēktis* "fuller's earth"]

smeg·ma /smégmə/ *n* a secretion of the sebaceous glands that collects under the foreskin or around the clitoris [Early 19C. Via Latin < Greek *smēgma* "soap" < *smēkhein* "rub, cleanse"]

smell /smel/ *v* (**smelled** or **smelt** /smelt/, **smell·ing, smells**) **1.** *vti* DETECT SOMETHING USING NOSE to detect or recognize something by means of sensitive nerves in the nose **2.** *vt* USE NOSE TO ASSESS SOMETHING to use the sensitive nerves in the nose to assess something ○ *Smell that and see if it's still good.* **3.** *vi* BE DETECTED WHEN BREATHED IN to seem to be in a particular condition or give a particular impression, when judged by somebody breathing in through the nose ○ *Something smells good.* **4.** *vi* GIVE UNPLEASANT IMPRESSION WHEN BREATHED IN to be considered unpleasant when breathed in through the nose ○ *That really smells!* **5.** *vi* GIVE IMPRESSION to give off a suggestion or impression of something ○ *It smells dangerous.* **6.** *vt* FEEL OR DETECT SOMETHING to detect the presence or existence of something, usually something bad ○ *I smell trouble here.* **7.** *vi US* SEEM DISHONEST to seem dishonest or illegal ○ *Her excuse really smells.* ■ *n* **1.** SENSE BASED ON NERVES IN NOSE the sense based on the sensitive nerves in the nose that distinguish odors **2.** QUALITY DETECTED BY NOSE the quality of something that can be detected by the sensitive nerves in the nose **3.** UNPLEASANT ODOR the unpleasant impression that something gives when breathed in through the nose ○ *What's that smell?* **4.** ACT OF SMELLING an act or instance of breathing something in through the nose in order to make a judgment about it **5.** SUGGESTION OF SOMETHING a suggestion or impression of something [12C. Origin ?] —**smell·er** *n*

SYNONYMS ***smell, odor, aroma, bouquet, scent, perfume, fragrance, stink, stench, reek***

CORE MEANING: the way something smells

smell a neutral, pleasant, or unpleasant quality detected by the nerves of the nose ○ *the smell of newly mown grass* ○ *a black substance that had the most awful smell* **odor** a smell, whether pleasant or unpleasant ○ *the rank odor of sweat* ○ *Horses can smell dry oats, which for us have no strong odor.* **aroma** a distinctive pleasant smell, especially one related to cooking or food ○ *the appealing aroma of fresh coffee* **bouquet** the characteristic pleasant smell of a wine ○ *There is seldom much of a bouquet from Pinot Blanc wines.* **scent** a pleasant sweet smell such as that of a flower, or the characteristic smell given off by a particular animal or person and used as a trail ○ *The air was heavy with the scent of flowers.* ○ *Badgers can sometimes become nervous if they catch the scent of a stranger.* **perfume** a sweet, pleasant, and heady smell, especially the smell of flowers or plants ○ *the heady perfume of the old roses* **fragrance** a pleasant sweet smell, especially a delicate or subtle one ○ *the faint, elusive fragrance of his cologne* ○ *The jasmine filled the evening air with its fragrance.* **stink** a strong and unpleasant smell ○ *the stink of sewage* **stench** a very strong unpleasant smell, especially a lingering smell associated with death or decay ○ *The stench of rotting fish hung in the air.* ○ *Rescue workers wore face masks to guard against the foul stench.* **reek** a strong unpleasant smell ○ *the pungent reek of stable manure*

smell up *vt US* to fill something with an unpleasant smell

smell·fun·gus /sméll fùng gəss/ (*plural* **-gi** /-jī, -gī/ or **-guses**) *n* a carping faultfinder (*archaic*) [Early 19C. After *Smellfungus*, name given to Tobias Smollett by Laurence Sterne in *A Sentimental Journey* (1768), because of the ill-tempered tone of Smollett's *Travels through France and Italy* (1766)]

smell·ing salts /smélling-/ *npl* a mixture of ammonium carbonate and perfume. Use: especially formerly, to revive somebody who felt faint or had fainted.

smell·y /smélle̅e̅/ (**-i·er, -i·est**) *adj* giving off a strong or unpleasant smell —**smell·i·ness** *n*

smelt[1] /smelt/ (**smelt·ed, smelt·ing, smelts**) *v* **1.** *vt* to melt ore in order to get metal from it, or produce metal in this way. The separation of the metal usually requires a chemical change. **2.** *vi* to undergo fusing or melting in the process of smelting [Mid-16C. < Middle Low German *smelten*]

smelt[2] /smelt/ (*plural* **smelts** or *same*) *n* **1.** a small silvery sea or freshwater fish. Native to: northern waters. Family: Osmeridae. **2.** the oily flesh of a smelt as food [Pre-12C. Origin ?]

smelt[3] past participle, past tense of **smell**

smelt·er /sméltər/ *n* **1.** SOMEBODY WHO SMELTS ORE somebody who smelts ore or who owns a place where ore is smelted **2.** SMELTING FACTORY a place where smelting is carried out **3.** SMELTING APPARATUS an apparatus used for smelting

Smet ♦ **De Smet, Pierre Jean**

Smet·a·na /sméttənə/, **Bedřich** (1824–84) Czech composer. The founder of Czech nationalist music, he is best known for his opera *The Bartered Bride* (1866) and the six symphonic poems *Ma Vlast* (My Homeland) (1874–79).

smew /smyoo/ (*plural* **smews** or *same*) *n* a sub-Arctic duck with a hooked serrated beak, the male of which has predominantly white feathers with black markings. Native to: Europe, Asia. Latin name: *Mergus albellus.* [Late 17C. Probably ultimately < W Germanic]

smid·gen /smíjjən/, **smid·gin, smid·geon, smidge** /smij/ *n* a small amount (*informal*) [Mid-19C. Origin ?]

smi·lax /smī lὰks/ *n* **1.** a climbing plant with red or bluish black berries and often prickly stems. Flowers: small, white or yellowish. Native to: temperate and tropical regions. Genus: *Smilax.* **2.** a vine prized by florists for its glossy bright green leaves. Native to: southern Africa. Latin name: *Asparagus asparagoides.* [Late 16C. Via Latin < Greek, "bindweed"]

smile /smīl/ *v* (**smiled, smil·ing, smiles**) **1.** *vti* MAKE PLEASANT EXPRESSION WITH MOUTH to raise the corners of the mouth in an expression of amusement, pleasure, or approval **2.** *vt* EXPRESS SOMETHING BY SMILING to express something by or while smiling ○ *smiled his agreement* **3.** *vi* HAVE PLEASANT APPEARANCE to appear to be in a state of happiness or enjoying good fortune or pleasure **4.** *vi* BE FAVORABLE to be favorably disposed to somebody or something ○ *Fortune smiled on their trip.* ■ *n* **1.** PLEASANT EXPRESSION a facial expression in which the corners of the mouth are raised, usually expressing amusement, pleasure, or approval **2.** PLEASANT APPEARANCE an appearance of pleasure or approval (*often used in the plural*) ○ *They were all smiles when we left.* **3.** SIGN OF FAVOR an expression or sign of favor [13C. Probably < N Germanic] —**smil·er** *n* —**smil·ing·ly** *adv*

smil·ey /smíle̅e̅/ *adj* (**-i·er, -i·est**) smiling or often smiling ■ *n* (*plural* **-eys**) a symbol (**emoticon**), often in the form :-), keyed in e-mails and text messages to communicate feelings such as pleasure, approval, or humor

Smil·ey /smíle̅e̅/, **Jane** (*b.* 1949) US writer. Her novels include *A Thousand Acres* (1991) and *Moo* (1995).

smil·ey face *n* **1.** a round yellow image representing a smiling face, generally consisting of two dots and an upward-curving arc, representing eyes and a mouth **2.** ONLINE same as **smiley**

smi·lo·don /smílə dòn/ *n* a large saber-toothed tiger existing during the Pleistocene epoch, between about 2 million and 10,000 years ago. Genus: *Smilodon.* [Mid-19C. < modern Latin, "knife-toothed" < Greek *smilē* "knife"]

smirch /smurch/ *vt* (**smirched, smirch·ing, smirch·es**) **1.** DAMAGE REPUTATION to damage somebody's or something's reputation or good name **2.** DIRTY SOMETHING to make something dirty by smearing or staining it (*archaic or literary*) ■ *n* **1.** DIRTY STAIN a dirty stain or smear (*archaic or literary*) **2.** SOMETHING DAMAGING something that damages a reputation [15C. Origin ?]

smirk /smurk/ *n* INSOLENT SMILE an insolent smile expressing feelings such as superiority, self-satisfaction, or conceit ■ *v* (**smirked, smirk·ing, smirks**) **1.** *vi* SMILE INSOLENTLY to smile in an insolent, smug, or contemptuous way **2.** *vt* EXPRESS SOMETHING WITH SMIRK to express something with a smirk [Old English *smearcian* "smile" < Germanic]

smite /smīt/ (**smote** /smōt/, **smit·ten** /smítt'n/ or **smote, smit·ing, smites**) *v* **1.** *vti* HIT SOMEBODY OR SOMETHING HARD to hit somebody or something with a hard blow (*archaic or literary*) **2.** *vt* AFFECT OR AFFLICT SOMEBODY to affect somebody strongly or disastrously, or afflict somebody with something (*literary; often passive*) **3.** *vt* FILL SOMEBODY WITH LOVE to fill somebody with love or longing (*literary; usually passive*) [Old English *smītan* "smear, pollute" < Germanic] —**smit·er** *n*

smith /smith/ *n* **1.** somebody who makes or repairs metal objects **2.** OCCUPATIONS same as **blacksmith** [Old English *smiþ* < Germanic, "coppersmith"]

Smith /smith/, **Adam** (1723–90) British philosopher and economist. He articulated his theory of free trade in *The Wealth of Nations* (1776).

> "The chief enjoyment of riches consists in the parade of riches."
> [Adam Smith, *The Wealth of Nations*; 1776]

Smith, Bessie (1894–1937) US singer. The leading blues singer of her day, she recorded widely with major jazz bands.

> "It's mighty strange, without a doubt, Nobody knows you when you're down and out."
> [Bessie Smith, "Nobody Knows You When You're Down and Out," *Harlem: The Great Black Way*, Jervis Anderson; 1982]

Smith, David (1906–65) US sculptor. Originally inspired by Picasso, his abstract sculptures of the 1930s, made of iron and steel, greatly influenced later 20th-century sculptors. Full name **Smith, David Roland**

Smith, Donald Alexander, 1st Baron Strathcona and Mount Royal (1820–1914) Scottish-born Canadian business executive and diplomat who was a financial backer of the Canadian Pacific Railway (1885), governor of Hudson's Bay Company (1889), and Canadian high commissioner in Britain (1896)

Smith, Ian (*b.* 1919) prime minister of Rhodesia (now Zimbabwe; 1964–79). He led the ruling white minority of Rhodesia to declare unilateral independence from the United Kingdom in 1965. Full name **Smith, Ian Douglas**

> "I don't believe in Black majority rule in Rhodesia...not in a thousand years."
> [Ian Smith, *Speech*; March 1976]

Smith, Jedediah Strong (1799–1831) US explorer and fur trader. He was an early explorer of the Far West, including California and Oregon (1826–30).

Smith, John (1579–1631) English-born North American colonist. He was president of the Virginia colony at Jamestown (1608–09) and claimed to have been rescued from Native North Americans by Pocahontas. His explorations and accounts influenced many English people to settle in North America.

> "Two great stones were brought before *Powhatan*: then as many as could layd hands on him...to beate out his braines, *Pocahontas* the Kings dearest daughter...got his head in her armes, and laid her owne upon his to save him."
> [John Smith, *The Generall History of Virginia, New-England, and the Summer Isles*; 1624]

Smith, Joseph (1805–44) US religious leader. He was the visionary founder of the Church of Jesus Christ of Latter-Day Saints (1830). Amid local controversy, he established communities in Missouri and Illinois. He was killed by a mob opposed to his philosophy.

> "He called me by name, and said unto me that he was a messenger sent from the presence of God to me, and that...God had a work for me to do."
> [Joseph Smith, *In His Own Words*; 1844]

Express Newspapers

Dame Maggie Smith

Smith, Dame Maggie (*b.* 1934) British actor. Her work in classical theater was complemented by her comedy performances and extensive movie appearances. Full name **Smith, Dame Margaret Nathalie**

Smith, Margaret Chase (1897–1995) US representative (1940–48) and senator (1948–72). She was the first woman to be elected to both houses of Congress.

Smith, Stevie (1902–71) British poet and novelist. Her works include the autobiographical *Novel on Yellow Paper* (1936) and collections of sharp, wry verse such as *Not Waving but Drowning* (1957). Her *Collected Poems* (1975) was published posthumously. Born **Smith, Florence Margaret**

> "Nobody heard him, the dead man, / But still he lay moaning: / I was much further out than you thought / And not waving but drowning."
> [Stevie Smith, "Not Waving But Drowning"; 1957]

smith·er·eens /smìthə reénz/ *npl* very small broken pieces (*informal*) [Early 19C. Probably < Irish *smidirín* "small fragment" < *smiodar* "fragment"]

smith·er·y /smíthəree/ (*plural* **-ies**) *n* **1.** the work or craft of a smith **2.** MANUF same as **smithy** (sense 1)

Smith·son /smíths'n/, **James** (1765–1829) British mineralogist and chemist. His legacy helped to establish the Smithsonian Institution (1846).

Smith·son, Robert (1938–73) US sculptor. He reshaped large areas of land into earthworks such as *Spiral Jetty* (1970). Full name **Smithson, Robert Irving**

> "Size determines an object, but scale determines art."
> [Robert Smithson, "The Spiral Jetty," *Robert Smithson: Collected Writings*; 1996]

Smith·so·ni·an In·sti·tu·tion /smith sṑnee ən-/, **Smith·so·ni·an** *n* a government trust founded in Washington, D.C., by an act of Congress in 1846 to promote research and education. It sponsors scientific research and publications and maintains the national collections. The fourteen museums it administers include the National Museum of American History and the National Air and Space Museum in Washington, D.C., and the National Museum of the Native American in New York City. [Early 19C. After James SMITHSON]

smith·son·ite /smíthsə nìt/ *n* a white or yellow-to-brown zinc carbonate mineral. Use: source of zinc. [Mid-19C. After James SMITHSON]

smith·y /smíthee, smíthee/ (*plural* **-ies**) *n* **1.** the place where a blacksmith works **2.** *US* OCCUPATIONS same as **blacksmith**

smit·ten past participle of **smite** (*archaic or literary*)

SMN *abbr* seaman

smock /smok/ *n* **1.** OVERSHIRT a loose garment worn to protect the clothes **2.** UNDERGARMENT a woman's loose-fitting undergarment or chemise of a type used until the 18th century ■ *vt* (**smocked, smock·ing, smocks**) SEW SOMETHING WITH GATHERED STITCHES to sew or decorate something with decorative gathered stitches [Old English *smoc* < Germanic, "creep"]

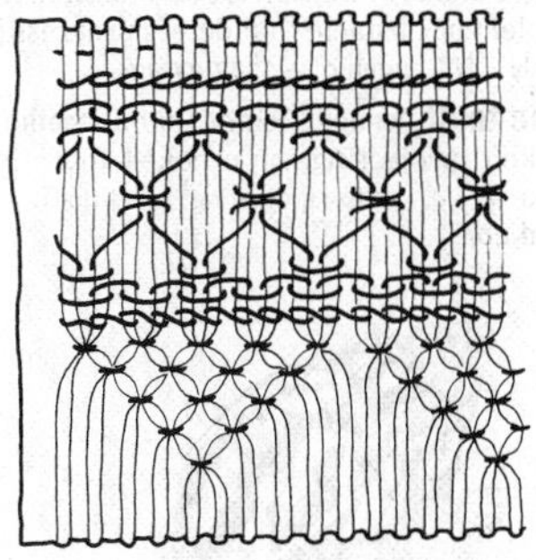

smocking

smock·ing /smóking/ *n* decorative stitching in a honeycomb or zigzag pattern, used to gather fabric evenly

smog /smog/ *n* a mixture of fog and smoke or other airborne pollutants such as exhaust fumes [Early 20C. Blend of SMOKE + FOG] —**smog·gy** *adj*

smoke /smōk/ *n* **1.** CLOUD OF TINY PARTICLES a mass of tiny particles in the air that rises up from something burning **2.** VAPOR RESEMBLING SMOKE something that resembles smoke, usually consisting of minute particles suspended in a gas ○ *a white, stinging smoke of chemical fumes* **3.** INHALING OF BURNING TOBACCO FUMES an act of smoking a cigarette, cigar, or pipe **4.** CIGARETTE a cigarette or other tobacco product (*informal*) **5.** SMOKABLE SUBSTANCE something that can be smoked, e.g., tobacco (*informal*) ○ *picked up some great smoke last week* **6.** SOMETHING THAT OBSCURES something that obscures or obstructs information, understanding, or awareness **7.** SOMETHING TRANSIENT something transient or illusory **8.** COLORS GRAY COLOR a gray color tinged with blue or brown ■ *v* (**smoked, smok·ing, smokes**) **1.** *vti* USE TOBACCO to inhale and exhale the smoke of burning tobacco or a drug, or smoke from a cigarette, cigar, or pipe **2.** *vti* INHALE VAPORS to inhale the smoke of any substance that can burn and be inhaled **3.** *vi* GIVE OFF SMOKE to give off smoke, often in a way that indicates a malfunction **4.** *vt* FUMIGATE SOMETHING WITH SMOKE to fumigate, clean, or clear something with smoke **5.** *vt* STUPEFY SOMETHING to stupefy something with smoke ○ *smoke a hive* **6.** *vt* HANDICRAFT DARKEN SOMETHING to darken something so as to give it the color of smoke ○ *smoked glass* **7.** *vt* FOOD CURE FOOD WITH WOOD SMOKE to cure or treat food such as meat, fish, or cheese with wood smoke **8.** *vt US* BEAT SOMEBODY EASILY to defeat somebody heavily, or outclass a competitor (*informal*) [Old English *smoca* < Germanic] —**smok·a·ble** *adj*—**smoke** *adj* ◇ **go up in smoke 1.** to fail completely to happen as planned or hoped **2.** to be destroyed by burning **3.** to get into a very bad temper

smoke out *vt* **1.** to drive a person or animal from a hiding place by using smoke **2.** to bring something to light by clever or assertive inquiry

smoke a·larm *n UK* same as **smoke detector**

smoke and mir·rors *n* something that is intended to draw attention away from something else that somebody would prefer remain unnoticed [< the use of smoke and mirrors in magic acts]

smoke bomb *n* a device that gives off dense clouds of irritating chemical smoke, used to drive people or animals out of a place

smoke de·tec·tor *n* a device that sets off an alarm when it becomes aware of smoke

smoke-dried *adj* cured with or dried in smoke

smoked rub·ber /smṑkt-/ *n* crude rubber prepared by drying coagulated latex sheets in smokehouses before they are packed into bales. The smoking process hinders the formation of bacteria and molds, and aids in the preservation of the rubber against oxidation.

smoke-filled room *n* a room where deals are negotiated in private, traditionally considered to be filled with the smoke of the negotiators' cigarettes, cigars, or pipes

smoke hood *n* a plastic head covering with a breathing apparatus

smoke·house /smṓk hòwss/ (*plural* **-hous·es** /-hòwzəz/) *n* a small building where meat, fish, or other materials are cured in smoke

smoke·jack /smṓk jàk/ *n* a device that turns a roasting spit and is powered by rising gases in a chimney

smoke·jump·er /smṓk jùmpər/ *n* a firefighter who parachutes into inaccessible areas to extinguish forest fires —**smoke·jump·ing** *n*

smoke·less /smṓkləss/ *adj* producing little or no smoke

smoke·less pow·der *n* a nitrocellulose-based explosive or propellant that produces little smoke

smoke·less to·bac·co *n* tobacco in a form that is not smoked but used in some other way such as chewing tobacco or snuff

smok·er /smṓkər/ *n* **1.** SOMEBODY WHO SMOKES somebody who smokes something, especially tobacco products **2.** GATHERING OF MEN a social gathering of men **3.** RAIL RAILROAD CAR DESIGNATED FOR SMOKING a railroad car or compartment where smoking is permitted **4.** HOUSEHOLD APPARATUS FOR SMOKING FOOD an apparatus for smoking food

smok·er's cough *n* a hacking cough, often accompanied by phlegm, caused by excessive smoking

smoke screen *n* **1.** an action taken to mislead somebody or obscure something **2.** a mass of smoke produced to conceal the movements of ships, troops, or equipment

smoke·stack /smṓk stàk/ *n* **1.** a funnel mounted to the boiler of a locomotive or steamboat that provides draft to the firebox and draws off the combustion gases from the cylinders of an engine **2.** a tall, often cylindrical industrial chimney, often attached to a factory

smoke tree *n* a bush or small tree whose clusters of small flowers resemble puffs of smoke. Genus: *Cotinus*.

Smok·ey /smṓkee/ *n* the highway police (*slang*) [Late 20C. < *Smokey the Bear*, fictional character used in a fire-prevention campaign]

smok·ing gun /smṑking-/ *n* conclusive evidence or proof, especially of wrongdoing [< the idea of finding a recently fired gun in a suspect's hand]

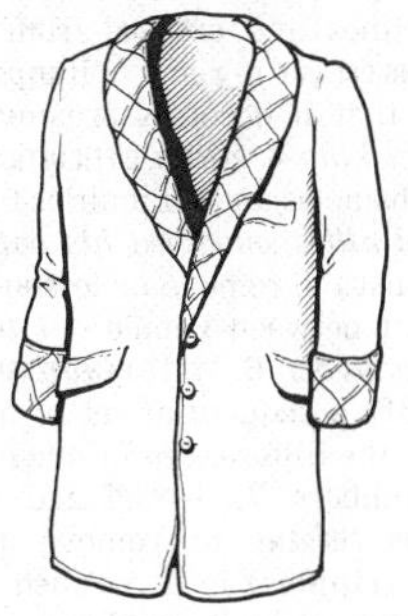

smoking jacket

smok·ing jack·et *n* a loose-fitting jacket made of a rich fabric such as velvet or silk, worn in the past by men while smoking or relaxing

smok·ing room *n* a room designated as a place where people may smoke

smok·y /smṓkee/ (**-i·er, -i·est**) *adj* **1.** FILLED WITH SMOKE filled with or smelling of smoke **2.** GIVING OFF EXCESSIVE SMOKE giving off smoke, especially excessively **3.** AFFECTED BY SMOKE discolored or marked with smoke **4.** FOOD TASTING OF SMOKE having or suggesting a taste imparted by smoke or an open flame **5.** COLORS COLORED LIKE SMOKE of a gray color, like smoke —**smok·i·ly** *adv* —**smok·i·ness** *n*

Smok·y Hill /smṑkee-/ river rising in eastern Colorado and flowing eastward into the Kansas River, in eastern Kansas. Length: 540 mi./870 km.

smok·y quartz *n* MINERALS same as **cairngorm**

smol·der /smṓldər/, **smoul·der** *vi* (**-dered, -der·ing, -ders**) **1.** BURN SLOWLY to burn slowly and gently, usually with some smoke, but without a flame **2.** HAVE SUPPRESSED EMOTION to have or show a strong emotion that is suppressed, but liable to flare up at any time **3.** EXIST IN BACKGROUND to exist in the background, liable to appear or reappear at any moment ■ *n* **1.** THICK SMOKE thick smoke from a slow-burning fire **2.** SMOKY FIRE a slow-burning fire [14C. Origin ?]

Smo·lensk /smō lénsk, smə-/ city in western Russia, on the Dnieper River. It is the capital of Smolensk Oblast. Population: 398,405 (1995)..

Smol·lett /smóllət/, **Tobias** (1721–71) British novelist whose picaresque novels, including *The Adventures of Roderick Random* (1748) and *The Expedition of Humphry Clinker* (1771), successfully combined adventure, comedy, and satire. Full name **Smollett, Tobias George**

> "Some folk are wise, and some are otherwise."
> [Tobias Smollett, *The Adventures of Roderick Random*; 1748]

smolt /smōlt/ *n* a young salmon before it has swum to the sea. It is characterized by physiological changes undergone in preparation for living in salt water, e.g., silver coloration. [15C. Origin ?]

smooch /smooch/ (*informal*) *vti* (**smooched, smooch·ing, smooch·es**) to kiss and caress somebody ■ *n* an act of kissing [Mid-20C. An imitation of the sound of kissing] —**smooch·y** *adj*

smooth /smooth/ *adj* **1.** NOT ROUGH OR BUMPY not having a rough or uneven surface ○ *The sea was calm and as smooth as glass.* **2.** WITHOUT LUMPS having no lumps or pieces of solid matter ○ *Beat the mixture to a smooth paste.* **3.** WITHOUT UPHEAVAL OR DIFFICULTIES proceeding without interruption, upheaval, or problems **4.** WITHOUT JERKS OR JOLTS in a steady flowing motion, without jolts or interruptions **5.** NOT HARSH having no harshness ○ *spoke in smooth tones* **6.** NOT SHARP OR SOUR not tasting sharp, sour, or unpleasant **7.** NOT EASILY UPSET not easily ruffled or upset ○ *a smooth and serene personality* **8.** INSINCERELY CONVINCING using insincere flattery and pleasantness, especially in order to persuade somebody to do something ○ *his smooth talk* **9.** HAIRLESS having no beard or mustache ○ *a smooth-faced young man* **10.** WITHOUT FRICTION offering no apparent resistance to sliding **11.** PHON UN-

ASPIRATED spoken without audible breath ■ *vt* (**smoothed, smooth·ing, smoothes**) **1.** **EVEN OUT ROUGHNESS OF SOMETHING** to remove bumps, unevenness, or roughness from something **2.** **PRESS OUT CREASES IN SOMETHING** to remove lines and creases from something **3.** **MAKE SOMETHING CREAMY** to remove lumps from a liquid mixture so that it becomes creamy ○ *smooth the gravy by whisking* **4.** **REMOVE DIFFICULTIES FROM SOMETHING** to remove obstacles and difficulties from something ○ *Influential allies smoothed his path to power.* **5.** **LESSEN BAD FEELINGS** to remove or lessen bad feeling or disagreement between people ○ *I tried to smooth things over with her.* **6.** STATS **REMOVE IRREGULARITIES FROM DATA** to modify a sequential set of numerical data by reducing the differences in magnitude between adjacent numbers **7.** PHYS, ELEC ENG **REMOVE IRREGULARITIES IN CURRENT** to remove the slight irregularities (**ripples**) in a rectified current ■ *adv* **WITHOUT PROBLEMS** without problems or difficulties ○ *The path of true love never did run smooth.* ■ *n* **1.** **ACT OF SMOOTHING** the action of smoothing something **2.** **SOMETHING SMOOTH** a smooth part of something [Old English *smōþ*, origin ?] —**smooth·a·ble** *adj* —**smooth·er** *n* —**smooth·ly** *adv* —**smooth·ness** *n*

smooth down *v* **1.** *vti* to make something flat by a smoothing action, or become flat in this way **2.** *vt* to calm or placate somebody

smooth out *vti* **1.** to make something smooth by the removal of lines and creases, or become smooth in this way **2.** to make something easier or calmer after a period of difficulty, or become easier or calmer in this way

smooth over *vt* to remove or lessen difficulties or tensions

smooth·bore /smo͞o*th* bàwr/ *adj* having a barrel without ridges or grooves in the bore. Early firearms and modern shotguns and mortars are characterized by smooth bores. ■ *n* a firearm that has a barrel without ridges or grooves in the bore

smooth breath·ing *n* a mark (') written over some initial Greek vowels to show that they are not aspirated

smooth col·lie *n* a dog belonging to a breed of collie with a thick shorthaired coat

smooth·en /smo͞o*th*ən/ (**-ened, -en·ing, -ens**) *vti* to make something smooth, or become smooth

smooth en·do·plas·mic re·tic·u·lum *n* endoplasmic reticulum that stores key enzymes in plant and animal cells and is involved in various processes including the synthesis of fatty acids and the detoxification of chemicals such as drugs and alcohol

smooth fox ter·ri·er *n* a dog belonging to a breed of English fox terrier with a mostly white short coat

smooth hound *n* a small bottom-dwelling shark. Native to: Atlantic from southern Brazil to northern Gulf of Mexico. Latin name: *Mustelus norrisi.*

smooth·ie /smo͞o*th*ee/ *n* **1.** a drink made from puréed fruit, sometimes with milk, yogurt, or ice cream **2.** *also* **smooth·y** (*plural* **-ies**) an attractive and charming man perceived as being insincere (*informal*)

smooth·ing cir·cuit /smo͞o*th*ing-/ *n* a circuit used to remove the alternating current component from a direct current power source

smooth mus·cle *n* a muscle found in the viscera that functions by slow contraction and is made up of layers of spindle-shaped cells lacking cross striations. Smooth muscle is not under voluntary control and is activated by the autonomic nervous system, hormones, or drugs.

smooth-tongued *adj* speaking or spoken skillfully and persuasively

smooth·y *n* another spelling of **smoothie** (sense 2) (*informal*)

smor·gas·bord /smáwrgəss bàwrd/ *n* **1.** **BUFFET MEAL** a meal served buffet style, consisting of a large variety of hot and cold dishes **2.** **RESTAURANT SERVING BUFFET** a restaurant featuring a smorgasbord **3.** **VARIETY** a wide variety (*informal*) [Late 19C. < Swedish *smörgåsbord*, literally "bread-and-butter table"]

smote past tense, past participle of **smite** (*archaic or literary*)

smoth·er /smú*th*ər/ *v* (**-ered, -er·ing, -ers**) **1.** *vti* **ALLOW OR GET TOO LITTLE AIR** to deprive somebody or something of air, or be deprived of air **2.** *vti* **SUFFOCATE** to kill somebody or something by suffocation, or die by suffocation **3.** *vt* **OVERWHELM SOMEBODY WITH AFFECTION** to give somebody too much love or affection with the effect that he or she feels restricted **4.** *vti* **PUT OUT FIRE** to extinguish something such as a fire, or go out from lack of oxygen **5.** *vt* **SUPPRESS OR HIDE SOMETHING** to suppress or hide the expression of something **6.** *vt* **COVER SOMETHING THICKLY** to cover something with a thick layer of something else ■ *n* **1.** **DENSE SMOKE** dense smoke or gas **2.** **THICK COATING** a thick coating of something [12C. < Old English *smorian* "suffocate, choke (with smoke)"] —**smoth·er·er** *n* —**smoth·er·ing·ly** *adv* —**smoth·er·y** *adj*

smoul·der *vi, n* another spelling of **smolder**

smri·ti /smríttee/ *n* a group of Hindu scriptures giving instruction on social and domestic matters [< Sanskrit, "what is remembered"]

SMS *n* a service that allows short text messages to be sent, e.g., between cellular phones and pagers. Full form **short message service**

SMSA *abbr* standard metropolitan statistical area

S.M.Sgt., **SMSGT** *abbr US* Senior Master Sergeant

SMTP *n* the main protocol used to send electronic mail on the Internet, consisting of rules for how programs sending mail should interact with programs receiving mail. Full form **Simple Mail Transfer Protocol**

smudge /smuj/ *n* **1.** **SMEARED INK OR PAINT** a patch of smeared ink or paint blurring what has been written or painted **2.** **DIRTY MARK** a dirty or greasy mark **3.** **INDISTINCT AREA** something visible, but blurred or indistinct, and not easily identifiable **4.** AGRIC **SMOKE OR FIRE** smoke produced to protect trees from frost or insect damage, or a fire that produces such smoke ■ *v* (**smudged, smudg·ing, smudg·es**) **1.** *vti* **SMEAR OR BE SMEARED** to smear or blur something by rubbing it, or become smeared or blurred by being rubbed **2.** *vti* **MAKE OR BECOME DIRTY** to smear something with dirt or grease, or become smeared with dirt or grease **3.** *vt* AGRIC **PROTECT TREES WITH SMOKE** to fill an orchard with smoke to protect the trees from frost or insects [15C. Origin ?] —**smudg·i·ly** *adv* —**smudg·i·ness** *n* —**smudg·y** *adj*

smug /smug/ (**smug·ger, smug·gest**) *adj* conceited and self-satisfied [Mid-16C. Origin ?] —**smug·ly** *adv* —**smug·ness** *n*

smug·gle /smúgg'l/ (**-gled, -gling, -gles**) *v* **1.** *vti* to carry goods into a country secretly because they are illegal or in order to avoid paying duty on them **2.** *vt* to take, bring, or carry somebody or something secretly into or out of a place [Late 17C. < Low German *smukkelen* or Dutch *smokkelen*] —**smug·gler** *n*

smut /smut/ *n* **1.** **OBSCENE MATERIAL** obscene jokes, stories, or pictures **2.** **SMALL PIECE OF SOOT** a speck of dirt or soot **3.** PLANTS **PLANT DISEASE** a plant disease, especially of cereals and other grasses, caused by fungi and characterized by sooty black masses of spores forming on leaves and other parts **4.** FUNGI **FUNGUS CAUSING DISEASE** a parasitic fungus that causes smut. Order: Ustilaginales. ■ *v* (**smut·ted, smut·ting, smuts**) **1.** *vt* **MAKE SOMETHING DIRTY** to mark or dirty something with smuts **2.** *vi* BOT **BECOME AFFECTED WITH SMUT** to become affected with smut [15C. Ultimately < Germanic]

smutch /smuch/ *n* a smudge of something dirty or greasy ■ *vt* (**smutched, smutch·ing, smutch·es**) to mark something with a smudge of something dirty or greasy [Mid-16C. Origin ?] —**smutch·y** *adj*

Smuts /smuts, smöts/, **Jan** (1870–1950) South African general and prime minister (1919–24, 1939–48). He was instrumental in forming the Union of South Africa (1910) and, as prime minister, was sometimes unpopular for his pro-British policies. Full name **Smuts, Jan Christiaan**

smut·ty /smúttee/ (**-ti·er, -ti·est**) *adj* **1.** **OBSCENE** obscene or pornographic **2.** **MARKED WITH SMUTS** covered with sooty marks of dirt **3.** BOT **AFFECTED BY SMUT** affected by the disease smut —**smut·ti·ly** *adv* —**smut·ti·ness** *n*

SMV *abbr* slow-moving vehicle

Smyr·na /smúrnə/ former name for **Izmir**

sn *abbr* Senegal (*used in Internet addresses*) See table at **domain name**

Sn *symbol* CHEM ELEM tin

SN *abbr US* NAVY seaman

SNA *abbr* COMPUT systems network architecture

snack /snak/ *n* **1.** **SMALL MEAL** a small meal of prepared or easy-to-prepare food eaten in place of a main meal or between main meals **2.** **FOOD FOR SNACK** a food suitable for eating between meals or instead of a main meal ■ *vi* (**snacked, snack·ing, snacks**) **EAT BETWEEN MEALS** to eat between the times that meals are usually served, or eat a snack instead of a main meal ○ *I've been snacking all afternoon.* [15C. < Middle Dutch *snac* "bite"]

snack bar *n* a small restaurant or food outlet that sells snacks

snaf·fle /snáff'l/ *n* **BIT FOR HORSES** a bit for a horse that is jointed in the middle and has rings on either end where the reins are attached ■ *vt* (**-fled, -fling, -fles**) **1.** **FIT HORSE WITH BIT** to fit a horse or pony with a snaffle bit **2.** *UK* **STEAL SOMETHING** to steal or take something, usually something worth relatively little (*informal*) [Mid-16C. < Low Dutch]

sna·fu /sna fo͝o/ (*informal*) *n* a mishap or mistake generally caused by incompetence and resulting in delay or confusion ■ *vti* (**-fued, -fu·ing, -fus**) to cause a situation or process to become confused or delayed, generally by incompetence, or become confused or delayed in this way [Mid-20C. < SNAFU]

SNAFU *abbr* situation normal all fouled up

snag /snag/ *n* **1.** **SMALL PROBLEM** a minor problem or obstacle to progress **2.** **INCONVENIENT SHARP PROJECTION** a sharp projection on which something may catch and tear **3.** **HOLE IN FABRIC** a hole in a fabric resulting from catching it on something sharp **4.** NAUT **NAVIGATIONAL OBSTRUCTION** an object underwater that may obstruct boats, e.g., a tree stump ■ *v* (**snagged, snag·ging, snags**) **1.** *vti* **CATCH ON SNAG** to catch on or collide with a sharp projection, or be caught or struck in this way ○ *snagged my sleeve on a nail* **2.** *vt US* **OBSTRUCT SOMETHING** to obstruct the progress of something **3.** *vt* **OBTAIN SOMETHING** to obtain something by luck or skillful maneuvering **4.** *vt US* **CLEAR SOMETHING OF OBSTRUCTIONS** to clear a river or lake of underwater obstructions **5.** *vi US* **MEET PROBLEM** to come up against a problem or obstacle that deters progress [Late 16C. Probably < N Germanic] —**snag·gy** *adj*

snag·gle·tooth /snágg'l to͞oth/ (*plural* **-teeth** /-teeth/) *n* a broken, projecting, or crooked tooth [Early 19C. < SNAG + *-le*, suffix indicating repetition] —**snag·gle·toothed** *adj*

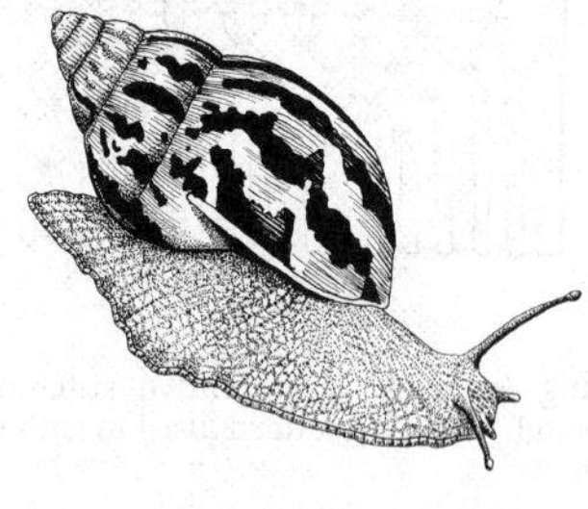

snail

snail /snayl/ *n* **1.** a small organism with a coiled shell and a retractable muscular foot on which it crawls. Class: Gastropoda. **2.** somebody or something that moves very slowly (*informal*) [Old English *snægel* < Germanic, "to crawl"]

snail dart·er *n* a small snail-eating fish. Native to: eastern Tennessee. Latin name: *Percina tanasi.*

snail fe·ver *n* MED same as **schistosomiasis**

snail·fish /snáyl fish/ (*plural same or* **-fish·es**) *n* a small elongated flabby bottom-dwelling ocean fish, often with ventral fins modified to form a sucking disk. Native to: cold oceans, especially northern Pacific. Family: Liparidae. [Origin ?]

snail kite *n* a bird of prey that has a sharp hooked beak, travels in flocks, and feeds on snails. Native to: tropical America. Latin name: *Rostrhamus sociabilis.*

snail mail *n* mail sent through the postal service, as distinct from the faster electronic mail (*informal*)

snail's pace *n* a speed that is thought unbearably or unaccountably slow —**snail-paced** *adj*

snake /snayk/ *n* **1. LEGLESS REPTILE** a legless reptile with a scaly tubular body tapering toward the tail, lidless eyes, and often venomous fangs. Suborder: Serpentes. **2. OFFENSIVE TERM** an offensive term that deliberately insults somebody's reliability and honesty, especially in personal dealings (*insult*) **3. PLUMBER'S TOOL** a plumber's tool consisting of a long flexible wire that can be inserted into and rotated inside drains to unblock them ■ *v* (**snaked, snak·ing, snakes**) **1.** *vi* **MOVE LIKE SNAKE** to move or lie like a snake, with many bends or twists **2.** *vt US* **DRAG SOMETHING** to drag something by a rope or chain **3.** *vt US* **TUG SOMETHING** to pull or jerk something suddenly [Old English *snaca* < Germanic, "to crawl"] ◇ **a snake in the grass** an offensive term for somebody perceived as betraying or deceiving others

Snake /snayk/ river in the northwestern United States, rising in Wyoming and flowing into the Columbia River in Washington State. Length: 1,040 mi./1,670 km.

snake·bird /snáyk bùrd/ *n* BIRDS same as **anhinga**

snake·bite /snáyk bìt/ *n* the bite of a poisonous snake, or illness resulting from this

snake charm·er *n* an entertainer who elicits a swaying movement from snakes, especially cobras, by means of music and rhythmic body movements

snake dance *n* **1.** a ritual dance of some Native North American peoples in which live snakes are handled **2.** a group dance in which a single file follows the leader, often holding the person in front and sometimes zigzagging

snake doc·tor *n Southern US* same as **dragonfly**

REGIONAL NOTE ***Snake doctor***, the Piedmont term for "dragonfly," has spread across the Upper and Middle South, from Virginia to Arkansas and Texas. The Pennsylvania term *snake feeder* endures in eastern sections of Kentucky and Tennessee and the western parts of the Carolinas. Elsewhere, along the Atlantic and Gulf coasts, *mosquito hawk* prevails, with the clipped form *skeeter hawk*. See also ***darning needle***.

snake eyes *n* a throw of two dice that turns up one spot on each die (*slang*)

snake feed·er *n regional* same as **dragonfly**

REGIONAL NOTE See ***snake doctor***.

snake fence *n regional* same as **worm fence**

REGIONAL NOTE See ***zigzag fence***.

snake·fish /snáyk fìsh/ (*plural same* or **-fish·es**) *n* an elongated predatory fish such as a lizardfish or cutlass fish. Native to: eastern Pacific and western Atlantic coasts. Latin name: *Trachinocephalus myops*.

snake·head /snáyk hèd/ *n* **1. TROPICAL FISH WITH PROTRUDING LOWER JAW** a freshwater fish that has a protruding lower jaw and possesses an accessory organ for breathing atmospheric air in oxygen-depleted water. Many snakeheads are valued as food and others are kept as aquarium fish. Native to: Africa, Asia. Family: Channidae. **2. INVASIVE BANNED FISH** a large predatory fish, capable of surviving out of water for several days and moving over land by wriggling. It is regarded as an injurious species and banned in the United States. Native to: China. Latin name: *Channa argus*. **3.** *Hong Kong* **SMUGGLER** somebody who smuggles illegal immigrants from mainland China into Hong Kong **4.** PLANTS same as **turtlehead**

snake liz·ard *n* a legless lizard, resembling a snake except that its tongue is flat and fleshy like a lizard's. Native to: Australia, New Guinea. Family: Pygopodidae.

snake oil *n* **1.** any worthless liquid preparation sold as a medicine, especially in the past by traveling peddlers **2.** something said or written with the intention of deceiving, pacifying, or persuading others

snake pit *n* **1.** a place or situation of aggression and destruction (*informal*) **2.** *US* an offensive term for a place used to house and care for people judged to have a psychiatric disorder

snake·root /snáyk ròot/ *n* a plant with roots used in folk medicine to treat snakebite, or the root of any of these plants used as medicine

snake·skin /snáyk skìn/ *n* **1.** the skin of a snake **2.** the skin of a snake or snakes made into leather, e.g., for shoes

snake·weed /snáyk wèed/ *n* a plant, especially bistort, used in folk medicine to cure snakebite

snak·y /snáykee/ (**-i·er, -i·est**) *adj* **1.** resembling a snake in being long and narrow with bends or coils, or like a snake's twisting and turning movements **2.** treacherous and deceitful —**snak·i·ly** *adv* —**snak·i·ness** *n*

snap /snap/ *v* (**snapped, snap·ping, snaps**) **1.** *vti* **BREAK WITH SHARP NOISE** to break suddenly with a sharp cracking sound, or make something do this **2.** *vti* **DO SOMETHING WITH SHARP NOISE** to move, strike, or operate something in a way that makes a sharp noise, or be moved, struck, or operated in this way **3.** *vti* **BREAK UNDER PRESSURE** to break something by excessive force or pressure, or be broken in this way ○ *The rope snapped under the weight of the log.* **4.** *vi* **LOSE CONTROL OF EMOTIONS** to lose control or erupt in anger suddenly **5.** *vti* **SPEAK ANGRILY** to say something or reply in anger or irritation **6.** *vt* **PHOTOGRAPH SOMEBODY OR SOMETHING** to take a photograph of somebody or something, especially in a casual way (*informal*) **7.** *vti* **BITE SOMEBODY OR SOMETHING** to bite or try to bite somebody or something with a quick movement or movements ○ *He ran off, with the little dog snapping and yapping behind him.* **8.** *vti US* **TAKE SOMETHING** to take or grasp something eagerly, or take something away from somebody suddenly ○ *She suddenly snapped the paper away from me.* **9.** *vti* **MOVE SHARPLY** to move something quickly and sharply, or be moved quickly and sharply ○ *The sentries snapped to attention.* **10.** *vi* **APPEAR ANGRY** to flash, especially in anger (*refers to eyes*) **11.** *vt US* **FLICK SOMETHING AWAY** to flick something away with a finger coming forward sharply from the thumb **12.** *vt* FOOTBALL **PLAY BALL** in football, to put the ball into play by passing it back to the quarterback behind the line of scrimmage ■ *n* **1. SHARP SOUND** a short sharp sound, e.g., of something brittle suddenly breaking or of something clicking shut **2. SWEET COOKIE** a crisp thin sweet cookie **3. SHORT TIME** a short period of time, especially one with cold weather ○ *a sudden cold snap* **4.** CARDS **CARD GAME** a game where players lay cards face up in a pile and try to be the first to shout "snap" when two identical cards are played one after the other. The object of the game is to win the whole deck of cards. **5.** PHOTOGRAPHY same as **snapshot** (sense 1) **6. LIVELINESS** liveliness and vigor ○ *His campaign needs more snap.* **7. FASTENER THAT CLICKS TOGETHER** a circular fastener consisting of two halves that close when pressed together and open when pulled apart **8. SOMETHING EASY** something easily done ○ *The test was a snap.* **9. FOOTBALL PLAY** in football, the action required to start play, when the ball is passed to the quarterback behind the line of scrimmage ■ *adj* **1. DECIDED WITHOUT REFLECTION** arrived at quickly and without reflection ○ *a snap decision* **2. COMING WITHOUT WARNING** coming suddenly and without warning ○ *a snap election* **3. OPERATING WITH SHARP SOUND** operating with interlocking parts that snap when being shut ○ *a snap lid* **4.** *US* **EASILY DONE** easily done with success ○ *a snap job* ■ *adv* **WITH SNAP** in such a way as to make a sharp sound [15C. Partly an imitation of the sound, partly < Middle Dutch *snappen* "seize"]

snap up *v* **1.** *vt* to quickly buy or take up something offered or available **2.** *vti US* to make something go faster, or go faster (*informal*) ○ *Snap it up or we'll be late.*

snap bean *n* an edible bean with long tubular pods that are harvested and eaten when immature [< its crispness, or because the pods are broken in pieces before being cooked]

snap-brim, snap-brim hat *n US* a man's hat with a flexible brim all around that is usually turned up in back and down in front

snap·drag·on /snáp dràggən/ *n* a common perennial plant with spikes of flowers of various colors. Genus: *Antirrhinum*. [Late 16C. Because the flowers are said to be similar to a dragon's mouth]

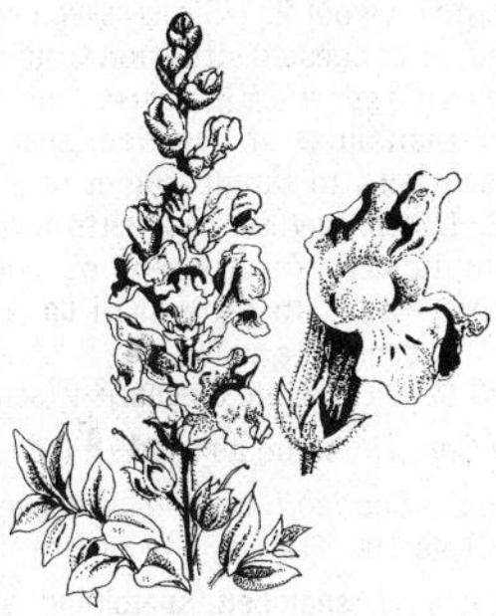

snapdragon

snap-on *adj* designed to attach to something quickly and easily, especially with a click when pressed into position, or designed to take attachments of this kind ○ *snap-on cover*

snap·per /snáppər/ *n* **1.** (*plural* **snap·pers** or *same*) **CARNIVOROUS FISH** a carnivorous reddish ocean fish. Native to: tropical waters. Family: Lutjanidae. **2. SNAPPER AS FOOD** the flesh of a snapper as food **3. SNAPPING PERSON OR THING** somebody or something that snaps **4.** ZOOL same as **snapping turtle**

snap·ping be·etle /snàpping-/ *n US* INSECTS same as **click beetle**

snap·ping tur·tle *n* a freshwater turtle with a large head and powerful hooked jaws. Native to: North America. Family: Chelydridae.

snap·pish /snáppish/ *adj* **1.** showing a sharpness or curtness caused by irritation or impatience **2.** describes an animal that tends to snap at people —**snap·pish·ly** *adv* —**snap·pish·ness** *n*

snap·py /snáppee/ (**-pi·er, -pi·est**) *adj* **1. STYLISH** fashionable and stylish (*informal*) ○ *a snappy dresser* **2. INTERESTING** interesting and to the point, or able to write something interesting and to the point (*informal*) **3. SHOWING IMPATIENCE** expressing or showing impatience or irritation **4. HASTY** done or produced without delay —**snap·pi·ly** *adv* —**snap·pi·ness** *n* ◇ **make it snappy** to do something quickly (*informal*)

snap ring *n* CLIMBING same as **carabiner**

snap roll *n* an aerial maneuver in which an airplane turns a complete circle longitudinally while maintaining altitude and direction of flight

snap·shot /snáp shòt/ *n* **1.** a photograph, especially one taken by an amateur with simple equipment **2.** a record or view of a particular point in a sequence of events or a continuing process [Early 19C. < SNAP "quick, sudden"]

snare[1] /sner/ *n* **1. ANIMAL TRAP** a trap for small animals that operates like a noose **2. TRAP FOR UNWARY** a situation that is both alluring and dangerous **3.** SURG **SURGICAL DEVICE** a surgical instrument consisting of a wire loop that can be tightened like a noose around the base of polyps or tumors to sever and remove them ■ *vt* (**snared, snar·ing, snares**) **1. CATCH IN TRAP** to catch somebody or something in a snare **2. ENTRAP SOMEBODY** to entrap somebody by alluring deception [Pre-12C. < Old Norse *snara*] —**snar·er** *n*

snare[2] /sner/ *n* a gut or wire cord stretched across the bottom skin of a drum to create a rattling sound when the drum is hit (*often used in the plural*) [Late 17C. Probably < Dutch *snaar* "string"]

snare drum *n* a drum fitted with snares to produce a rattling effect

snarf /snaarf/ (**snarfed, snarf·ing, snarfs**) *vt US* to eat or drink something noisily or greedily (*informal*) [Mid-20C. Probably an imitation of the sound]

snark·y /snáarkee/ (**-i·er, -i·est**) *adj* sarcastically critical or mocking and malicious (*informal*) ○ *a snarky remark*

snarl[1] /snaarl/ *v* (**snarled, snarl·ing, snarls**) **1.** *vi* **GROWL** to growl threateningly **2.** *vti* **SAY SOMETHING ANGRILY** to speak or say something angrily or threateningly ■ *n* **GROWLING NOISE** the sound of somebody or something snarling [Late 16C. < obsolete *snar* "to snarl" (ultimately an imitation of the sound) + *-le*, suffix indicating repetition] —**snarl·er** *n* —**snarl·ing·ly** *adv*

snarl[2] /snaarl/ *n* **1. TANGLE** a tangled mass of something such as hair or wool **2.** *US* **CONFUSION** a complicated, disordered, or congested situation from which there is no easy exit ○ *got stuck in a rush-hour traffic snarl* Can term **snarl-up** ■ *vti* **(snarled, snarl·ing, snarls) 1. TANGLE SOMETHING** to tangle something, or become tangled **2.** *US* **GET CONFUSED OR JUMBLED** to make something complicated, disordered, or congested, or become this way. Can term **snarl up** [14C. Probably < SNARE[1] + *-le*, diminutive suffix]

snarl up *vti Can, UK* same as **snarl**[2] *v* (sense 2)

snarl-up *n Can, UK* same as **snarl**[2] *n* (sense 2)

snash /snash/ *n Scotland* abusive language or insolent behavior [Late 18C. Probably an imitation of the sound]

snatch /snach/ *vt* **(snatched, snatch·ing, snatch·es) 1. TAKE SOMETHING QUICKLY** to grab or grasp somebody or something hastily **2. MOVE SOMETHING QUICKLY** to move or remove something quickly **3. TAKE SOMETHING WHEN OPPORTUNITY ARISES** to take or get something while there is an opportunity ○ *snatched a few hours of sleep* **4.** same as **kidnap** (*informal*) ■ *n* **1. GRABBING** an instance of grabbing or grasping somebody or something **2. SMALL AMOUNT** a small incomplete bit or short period of something **3.** same as **kidnapping** (*informal*) **4.** *US* **TABOO TERM** a highly offensive term for the outer sexual organs of a woman (*taboo*) **5.** GYM **LIFTING FEAT** a weightlifting feat in which the barbell is raised from the floor over the lifter's head in one motion [12C. Origin ?] —**snatch·er** *n*

snatch block *n* a block that can be opened on one side to insert a rope, thereby avoiding the necessity of threading the rope through from one end

snatch squad *n* **1.** a group of police officers trained to find and arrest ringleaders in situations of public disorder **2.** a special operations unit trained to capture targeted individuals and disable enemy sentries or patrols

snatch·y /snáchee/ **(-i·er, -i·est)** *adj* occurring or done in short spells

snath /snath/, **snathe** /snayth/ *n* the handle of a scythe [Late 16C. Variant of dialect *snead*, origin ?]

snaz·zy /snázzee/ **(-zi·er, -zi·est)** *adj* attractively new, bright, or fashionable (*informal*) [Mid-20C. Origin ?] —**snaz·zi·ly** *adv* —**snaz·zi·ness** *n*

SNCC /snik/ *abbr US* Student Nonviolent Coordinating Committee

SNCF *n* the national railroad system in France. Full form **Société Nationale des Chemins de Fer**

Snead /sneed/, **Sam** (1912–2002) US golfer. He won 84 Professional Golfers' Association (PGA) tournaments. Born **Snead, Samuel Jackson**. Known as **Slammin' Sammy**

sneak /sneek/ *v* **(sneaked** or **snuck** /snuk/, **sneak·ing, sneaks) 1.** *vi* **MOVE AROUND STEALTHILY** to go or move in a stealthy, secretive way **2.** *vt* **DO SOMETHING FURTIVELY** to do something stealthily, furtively, and without being noticed ○ *He sneaked a look over the wall.* **3.** *vt* **BRING STEALTHILY** to bring, take, or carry somebody or something secretly and furtively ○ *sneak friends into the house for a surprise party* ■ *n* **1. STEALTHY DEPARTURE** a departure intended to be unobserved **2.** *US* CLOTHING same as **sneaker** (*informal*) **3. UNTRUSTWORTHY PERSON** a person regarded as cunning and deceitful (*insult*) ■ *adj* **STEALTHILY DONE** done stealthily or furtively ○ *a sneak peek at the gifts* [Late 16C. Origin ?]

USAGE sneaked or **snuck**? The formerly regional and/or nonstandard past tense and past participle ***snuck*** has sneaked into mainstream English during the past 20 years. It is used in print by some of the United States' best writers, especially in informal, often humorous contexts, and in fictional dialogue. It is used even in formal contexts in Canada.

sneak up on *vt* **1.** to approach stealthily, with the intention of surprising or frightening somebody or something **2.** to arrive more quickly than expected ○ *The weekend sneaked up on me.*

sneak·box /sneék bòks/ *n* a flat-bottomed boat with low sides and usually camouflaged, used by hunters of duck and other waterfowl

sneak·er /sneékər/ *n* a shoe with a rubber sole and, usually, a cloth upper (*often used in the plural*)

sneak·ing /sneéking/ *adj* **1. HIDDEN FROM OTHERS** unknown to or hidden from others **2. SLIGHT** slight but persistent ○ *a sneaking suspicion* **3. DECEPTIVE** deceptive or given to cunning and deception —**sneak·ing·ly** *adv*

sneak pre·view *n* a public screening of a movie prior to its general release, in order to test public reaction to it

sneak thief *n* a thief who surreptitiously steals unguarded or unsecured articles when the opportunity arises

sneak·y /sneékee/ **(-i·er, -i·est)** *adj* done, doing something, or in the habit of behaving in an underhanded and unfair way —**sneak·i·ly** *adv* —**sneak·i·ness** *n*

sneer /sneer/ *n* **EXPRESSION OF SCORN** a facial expression of scorn or hostility in which the upper lip may be raised ■ *v* **(sneered, sneer·ing, sneers) 1.** *vi* **FEEL OR SHOW SCORN** to feel or show scorn, contempt, or hostility, either in speech or facial expression **2.** *vt* **UTTER SOMETHING WITH SCORN** to say something with scorn or contempt [14C. Origin ?] —**sneer·er** *n* —**sneer·ing** *adj* —**sneer·ing·ly** *adv*

sneeze /sneez/ *vi* **(sneezed, sneez·ing, sneez·es)** to suddenly, forcefully, and involuntarily expel air through the nose and mouth because of irritation of the nasal passages ■ *n* an act or sound of sneezing [15C. Alteration of obsolete *fnese* < Old English *fneosan*, an imitation of the sound of breathing] —**sneez·er** *n* —**sneez·y** *adj*

sneeze·guard /sneéz gaàrd/ *n US* a plastic or glass cover hanging over a food display such as a salad bar or a buffet to protect it from contamination

sneeze·weed /sneéz weèd/ *n* a perennial wild plant. Flowers: yellow to dark red, resembling daisies. Native to: North America. Genus: *Helenium*.

sneeze·wort /sneéz wùrt, -wàwrt/ *n* a plant with silvery leaves that when powdered induce sneezing. Flowers: small, white, resembling daisies. Native to: Europe, Asia. Latin name: *Achillea ptarmica*.

snell /snel/ *n* a short piece of gut or nylon used to connect a fishhook or lure to a longer line [Mid-19C. Origin ?]

Snel·len chart /snéllən-/ *n* a chart for vision testing on which are printed rows of letters and numbers in decreasing size from top to bottom [Mid-19C. After Herman *Snellen* (1834–1908), Dutch ophthalmologist]

Snell's law /snélz-/ *n* the law stating that for a light ray passing between two media the ratio of the sines of the angle of incidence and the angle of refraction is a constant [Late 19C. After Willebrord Van Roijen *Snell* (1591–1626), Dutch astronomer and mathematician]

SNG *abbr* INDUST synthetic (or substitute) natural gas

snick /snik/ *n* **1. SNIP** a small cut or notch **2. CLICK** a small clicking noise ■ *v* **(snicked, snick·ing, snicks) 1.** *vt* **SNIP SOMETHING** to cut something slightly **2.** *vi* **MAKE CLICK** to make a small clicking noise [Late 17C. Probably < *snick* in obsolete *snick or snee* "to cut or thrust with a knife in a fight" < alteration of Dutch *steken* "thrust" + dialect variant of *snij(d)en* "cut"]

snick·er /sníkər/, **snig·ger** /sníggər/ *v* **(-ered, -er·ing, -ers; -gered, -ger·ing, -gers) 1.** *vi* **LAUGH DISRESPECTFULLY** to laugh disrespectfully in a covert way **2.** *vt* **SAY SOMETHING WITH DERISION** to speak derisively or with disrespectful laughter of somebody or something ■ *n* **DISRESPECTFUL LAUGH** a disrespectful laugh or its sound [Late 17C. Origin ?]

snick·er·doo·dle /sníkər doōd'l/ *n* a traditional cinnamon-flavored cookie

snide /snīd/ **(snid·er, snid·est)** *adj* derisively sarcastic [Mid-19C. Origin ?] —**snide·ly** *adv*

sniff /snif/ *v* **(sniffed, sniff·ing, sniffs) 1.** *vti* **BREATHE IN THROUGH NOSE** to breathe in through the nose quickly, briefly, and audibly, e.g., in smelling something or to prevent mucus from dripping, or smell something by breathing in quickly **2.** *vt* **SUSPECT SOMETHING** to have a suspicion of something, especially something bad ○ *sniff trouble* ■ *n* **1. BRIEF INHALATION** an instance or sound of sniffing **2. SUSPICION** a hint or suspicion, especially of something bad [14C. An imitation of the sound]

sniff at *vt* to show contempt or disdain for somebody or something

sniff out *vt* to discover something, especially something bad, by investigation (*informal*)

sniff·er /sníffər/ *n* **1. SOMEBODY WHO SNIFFS** somebody who sniffs, especially who takes drugs by inhaling them **2. DEVICE MONITORING DATA TRANSMISSION** a device or program that monitors and analyzes computer network traffic, detecting bottlenecks and problems **3. PROGRAM TO CAPTURE NETWORK DATA** a program on a computer system designed legitimately or illegitimately to capture data being transmitted on a network, often used by hackers to appropriate passwords and user names

snif·fle /sníff'l/ *vi* **(-fled, -fling, -fles) 1. INHALE MUCUS** to inhale through the nose to prevent mucus from dripping out of it **2. WEEP QUIETLY** to sniff repeatedly while gently weeping ■ *n* **1. ACT OF SNIFFLING** an instance or sound of sniffling ■ **snif·fles** *npl* **SLIGHT COLD** a slight cold that causes sniffling (*informal*) [Mid-17C. An imitation of the sound] —**snif·fler** *n*

sniff·y /sníffee/ **(-i·er, -i·est)** *adj* (*informal*) **1.** behaving in a haughty, disdainful way **2.** tending to sniff a lot, e.g., because of a cold —**sniff·i·ly** *adv* —**sniff·i·ness** *n*

snif·ter /sníftər/ *n* **1.** a stemmed glass with a bowl that tapers upward, typically used for brandy **2.** a small amount of drink, especially of alcohol (*informal*) [Mid-18C. An imitation of the sound of sniffing or snuffling]

snig /snig/ **(snigged, snig·ging, snigs)** *vt Can* to drag something heavy, especially a log, by means of ropes or chains [Late 18C. Origin ?]

snig·ger *vti, n* same as **snicker**

snig·ging track /snígging-/, **snig·ging trail** *n Can* a road through a forest to a logging area, along which logs are transported

snig·gle /snígg'l/ *vti* **(-gled, -gling, -gles)** to fish for or catch eels by putting a baited hook into crevices where they hide ■ *n* a baited hook used for catching eels [Mid-17C. < *snig* "young eel," origin ?] —**snig·gler** *n*

snip /snip/ *vti* **(snipped, snip·ping, snips) CUT SOMETHING WITH SMALL STROKES** to cut something with scissors or shears, especially using small strokes ■ *n* **1. A CUT** a short quick cut, made with scissors **2. SMALL PIECE** a small piece of something that has been snipped off **3. ACT OR SOUND OF SNIPPING** the act or sound of using scissors to snip something **4. IMPERTINENT PERSON** somebody regarded as behaving in ways inappropriate to his or her age or class (*informal insult*) ■ *interj* **SOUND OF SNIPPING** used to represent the sound that scissors make [Mid-16C. < Dutch or Low German *snippen*, an imitation of the sound]

snipe /snīp/ *n* (*plural* **snipes** or *same*) **1. WADING BIRD** a wading bird with a long straight beak. Native to: marshes and riverbanks of the northern hemisphere. Genus: *Gallinago*. **2. SHOT FIRED FROM CONCEALMENT** a shot fired from a concealed place ■ *vi* **(sniped, snip·ing, snipes) SHOOT FROM CONCEALED PLACE** to shoot at people from a concealed position [14C. Probably < Old Norse *snípa*]

snipe·fish /snīp fish/ (*plural same* or **-fish·es**) *n* a fish with a long snout and a spine extending from its dorsal fin to its tail. Native to: tropical and temperate waters. Family: Macrorhamphosidae.

snip·er /snīpər/ *n* **1.** somebody who shoots people from a concealed position **2.** a member of the armed forces who is trained to shoot enemy soldiers from a concealed position

snip·pet /sníppət/ *n* a small piece of something such as information or music [Mid-17C. < SNIP]

snip·pet·y /sníppətee/ *adj US* same as **snippy**

snip·ping *n* same as **snip** *n* (sense 2)

snip·py /sníppee/ **(-pi·er, -pi·est)** *adj* behaving in a curt and irritable way (*informal*) —**snip·pi·ly** *adv* —**snip·pi·ness** *n*

snips /snips/ *n* shears used for cutting sheet metal (*takes a singular or plural verb*)

snit /snit/ *n* a state of mild irritation or bad temper [Mid-20C. Origin ?]

snitch /snich/ (*slang*) *v* **(snitched, snitch·ing, snitch·es) 1.** *vi* **INFORM ON SOMEBODY** to tell somebody in authority about another person's wrongdoing ○ *Friends don't snitch on each other.* **2.** *vt* **PILFER SOMETHING** to steal something in a sneaky way, especially something of little value ■ *n* **INFORMER** somebody who informs on others [Late 17C. Origin ?] —**snitch·er** *n*

sniv·el /snívv'l/ *vi* (**-eled** or **-elled, -el·ing** or **-el·ling, -els**) **1. SNIFF** to sniff repeatedly **2. WHINE** to behave in a whining, tearful, or self-pitying way **3. SNIFFLE** to have a runny nose ■ *n* **SNIVELING** an act of sniveling [Assumed Old English *snyflan* < Germanic] —**sniv·el·er** *n*— **sniv·el·ing** *n, adj*—**sniv·el·y** *adj*

snob /snob/ *n* **1.** an admirer and cultivator of people with high social status who disdains those considered inferior **2.** somebody who disdains people considered to have inferior knowledge or tastes [Late 18C. Origin ?]—**snob·ber·y** *n*—**snob·bism** *n*—**snob·by** *adj*

ORIGIN ***Snob*** originally meant "shoemaker" (a sense that survives in places). Cambridge University students of the late 18th century adopted it as a slang term for a "townsman, somebody not a member of the university," and it seems to have been this usage that formed the basis in the 1830s for the emergence of a new general sense "member of the lower classes." The modern sense "somebody who admires and cultivates social superiors" received a considerable boost when Thackeray used it in his *Book of Snobs* (1848). As for the origins of the word itself, the suggestion that it comes from *s.nob.*, short for Latin *sine nobilitate* "without nobility," is ingenious but ignores the word's early history.

snob ap·peal *n* qualities intended to appeal to a sense of snobbery in people and make them want to be part of or have something

snob·bish /snóbbish/ *adj* displaying an offensively superior condescending manner —**snob·bish·ly** *adv*—**snob·bish·ness** *n*

SNOBOL /snṓ bàwl/ *n* a high-level computer programming language designed for dealing with strings of symbols [Mid-20C. < letters in *string-oriented symbolic language*, after COBOL]

snoek /snook/ (*plural* **snoeks** or *same*) *n* a long predatory fish of the mackerel family. Native to: Australia, New Zealand, southern Africa. Latin name: *Thyrsites atun*. [Late 18C. Via Afrikaans < Middle Dutch *snoec* "pike"]

snol·ly·gos·ter /snóllee gòstər/ *n US* somebody, especially a politician, whose actions are motivated by self-interest rather than by high principles (*slang*) [Mid-19C. Origin ?]

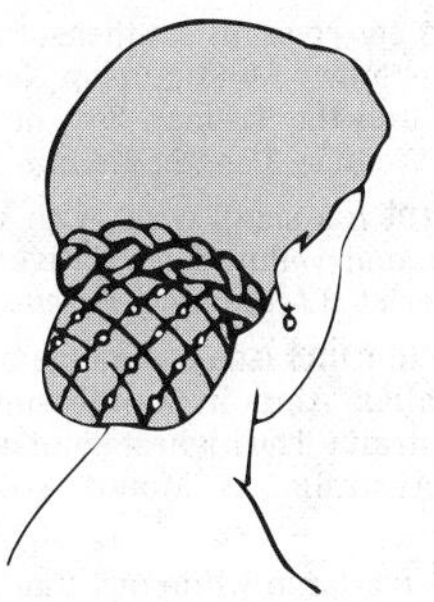

snood

snood /snood/ *n* **1. DECORATIVE HAIR NET** a net that holds a woman's hair at the back of her head **2. RIBBON WORN BY UNMARRIED SCOTTISH WOMEN** in the 17th and 18th centuries, a hairband or ribbon worn by unmarried women in Scotland ■ *vt* (**snood·ed, snood·ing, snoods**) **HOLD HAIR IN SNOOD** to fasten the hair with a snood [Old English *snōd*, < Indo-European, "spin, sew"]

snook[1] /snook, snŏŏk/ (*plural same* or **snooks**) *n* a large bony fish that lives in warm seas and rivers. Latin name: *Centropomus undecimalis*. [Late 17C. < Dutch *snoek* "pike," later form of Middle Dutch *snoec*]

snook[2] /snook, snŏŏk/ *n* a gesture made as a sign of contempt, by putting the thumb to the nose with the fingers outstretched [Late 18C. Origin ?]

snook·er /snŏŏkər/ *n* **1. GAME LIKE POOL** a pool game in which a white ball struck with a cue is used to hit fifteen red balls and six balls of different colors into any of six pockets **2. POSITION IN SNOOKER** a position in snooker in which a player is forced to play an indirect shot because another ball is between the cue ball and the target ball ■ *vt* (**-ered, -er·ing, -ers**) **1. TRICK SOMEBODY** to deceive somebody through trickery (*informal*) ○ *snookered by a fast-talking salesman* **2. PUT SOMEBODY AT DISADVANTAGE IN SNOOKER** to put a snooker player in the position of being forced to play an indirect shot because another ball is between the cue ball and the target ball [Late 19C. Origin ?]

ORIGIN The most widely canvassed theory of the origins of the word ***snooker*** is that it is an adaptation of late 19th-century British army slang *snooker* "new recruit." The game was invented, as a diversion perhaps from the monotony of billiards, by British army officers serving in India in the 1870s, and the story goes that the term ***snooker*** was applied to it by Colonel Sir Neville Chamberlain (1856–1944), at that time a subaltern stationed in Jubbulpore, in allusion to the inept play of one of his brother officers.

snoop /snoop/ (*informal*) *vi* (**snooped, snoop·ing, snoops**) **PRY** to pry into other people's business or affairs, especially surreptitiously ■ *n* **1. SOMEBODY WHO SNOOPS** somebody who pries into other people's lives **2. SECRET INVESTIGATION** a surreptitious investigation of somebody's private life or property [Mid-19C. < Dutch *snoepen* "eat on the sly"] —**snoop·er** *n*

snoop·er·scope /snóopər skōp/ *n* a device that converts infrared radiation into a visual image and is used for seeing in the dark

snoop·y /snóopee/ (**-i·er, -i·est**) *adj* tending to pry into the affairs of others

snoot[1] /snoot/ *n* a nose or snout (*informal*) [Mid-19C. Variant of SNOUT]

snoot[2] /snoot/ (**snoot·ed, snoot·ing, snoots**) *vt US* to treat somebody haughtily (*informal*) [Early 20C. Back-formation < SNOOTY]

snoot·y /snóotee/ (**-i·er, -i·est**) *adj* (*informal*) **1.** having or showing a haughty condescending manner, especially to those considered socially inferior **2.** catering to people regarded as having high social status ○ *a snooty country club* [Early 20C. < SNOOT[2]] —**snoot·i·ly** *adv*—**snoot·i·ness** *n*

snooze /snooz/ (*informal*) *vi* (**snoozed, snooz·ing, snooz·es**) to have a short sleep ■ *n* a short sleep [Late 18C. Origin ?] —**snooz·er** *n*

snore /snawr/ *vi* (**snored, snor·ing, snores**) to breathe noisily while asleep because of vibrations of the soft palate ■ *n* a snorting or whistling sound made while sleeping [14C. Origin ?] —**snor·er** *n*

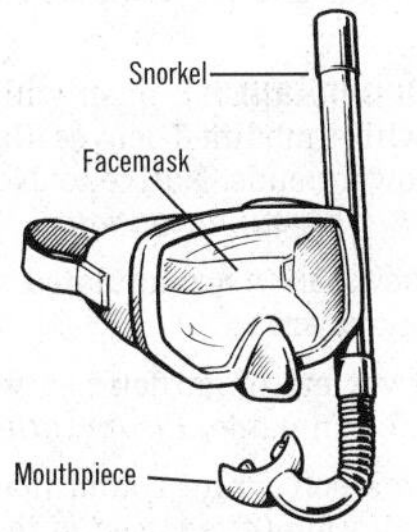

snorkel

snor·kel /snáwrk'l/ *n* **1. BREATHING APPARATUS** a curved tube that projects above the water and enables somebody to breathe while swimming face-down near the surface **2. VENTILATOR ON SUBMARINE** a shaft on a diesel-powered submarine for ventilation and for engine intake and exhaust, which enables the submarine to stay submerged near the surface for long periods **3. DEVICE ON TANK** a device on a tank or other vehicle that functions like the snorkel on a submarine and enables the vehicle to go through shallow water ■ *vi* (**-keled, -kel·ing, -kels**) **SWIM WITH SNORKEL** to swim underwater breathing air through a snorkel [Mid-20C. < German dialect *Schnorchel* "nose"]— **snor·kel·er** *n*

snor·kel·ing /snáwrk'ling/ *n* the activity or pastime of swimming with a snorkel

snort /snawrt/ *v* (**snort·ed, snort·ing, snorts**) **1.** *vi* **FORCE AIR THROUGH NOSE** to make a harsh sound by forcing air through the nostrils **2.** *vi* **SHOW CONTEMPT** to express a feeling, especially of contempt or impatience, by snorting **3.** *vti* DRUGS **INHALE DRUG** to inhale a powdered drug through the nostrils (*slang*) ■ *n* **1. HARSH SOUND** an instance or sound of snorting **2. GULP OF ALCOHOL** a short drink, especially of alcohol, taken all at once (*informal*) **3.** DRUGS **INHALATION OF DRUG** an act of snorting a drug (*slang*) **4.** NAVY same as **snorkel** *n* (sense 2) (*slang*) [14C. Probably variant of SNORE] —**snort·er** *n*— **snort·ing** *n, adj*

snot /snot/ *n* **1.** an offensive term for mucus produced in the nose (*slang*) **2.** an offensive term for somebody whose behavior is regarded as arrogant or condescending (*slang insult*) [Old English *gesnot* < Germanic]

snot-nosed *adj* an offensive term meaning regarded as being young and precocious but not to be taken seriously (*slang*)

snot·ty /snóttee/ (**-ti·er, -ti·est**) *adj* (*slang*) **1.** an offensive term meaning wet or dirty with nasal mucus **2.** an offensive term meaning behaving in an arrogant and condescending manner **3.** an offensive term describing actions that are regarded as mean or rude —**snot·ti·ly** *adv* —**snot·ti·ness** *n*

snout /snowt/ *n* **1. ANIMAL'S NOSE** the projecting part of a vertebrate's head, consisting of the nose and mouth, especially that of a mammal such as a pig **2. PROJECTING PART OF INSECT'S HEAD** the projecting part of the head of an insect or other invertebrate such as a weevil **3. PROJECTION** something that sticks out, e.g., the muzzle of a gun **4.** same as **nose** (*slang*) **5.** GEOG **STEEP END OF GLACIER** the leading face of a glacier, usually heavily loaded with rock debris [13C. < Middle High German, Middle Dutch *snūt(e)* < Germanic]— **snout·ed** *adj*

snout bee·tle *n* INSECTS same as **weevil** (sense 1) [< the shape of its head]

snow /snō/ *n* **1. ICE CRYSTAL FLAKES** water vapor in the atmosphere that has frozen into ice crystals and falls to the ground in the form of flakes **2. SNOW ON GROUND** a layer of fallen snow **3. SUBSTANCE RESEMBLING SNOW** a substance that resembles snow in color or texture **4.** ELEC **WHITE SPECKS ON TELEVISION SCREEN** random patterns of small white specks on a television or radar screen caused by electrical interference **5. WHIPPED DESSERT** a dessert made of whipped egg whites, sugar, and fruit **6.** METEOROL **FALL OF SNOW** an amount of snow that falls at one time ○ *had a heavy snow last night* **7.** DRUGS **NARCOTIC DRUG** cocaine or heroin in the form of a white powder (*slang*) ■ *v* (**snowed, snow·ing, snows**) **1.** *vi* **TO FALL AS SNOW** to fall from the sky as snow ○ *It's snowing!* **2.** *vt* **COVER SOMETHING WITH SNOW** to cover, close in, or block something with a fall of snow ○ *We were snowed in for two days.* **3.** *vti* **FALL LIKE SNOW** to fall or scatter like snow, or make something fall in this way **4.** *vt* **PERSUADE SOMEBODY WITH GLIB TALK** to overwhelm or deceive somebody especially with flattery or charm (*slang*) ○ *She snowed us into buying worthless stock.* [Old English *snāw* < Indo-European]

snow under *vt US* to defeat an opposing team soundly ◇ **be snowed under (with something)** to be overwhelmed with something, especially work

Snow /snō/, **C. P., Baron Snow of Leicester** (1905–80) British novelist and critic. His 11-novel series *Strangers and Brothers* examines English life in the mid-20th century. Full name **Snow, Charles Percy**

> "The official world, the corridors of power."
> [C.P. Snow, *Homecomings*; 1956]

snow·ball /snṓ bàwl/ *n* **1. BALL OF SNOW** a ball of compacted snow that is thrown, especially by children **2.** *US* **FROZEN SNACK** a frozen snack made from crushed ice and colored, flavored syrup ■ *vti* (**-balled, -ball·ing, -balls**) **1. INCREASE RAPIDLY** to increase rapidly or at an accelerating rate, or to cause something to increase in this way ○ *The scandal snowballed to include reports of other illegal activities.* **2. THROW SNOWBALLS** to throw snowballs at each other or at somebody else ◇ **not have a snowball's chance (in hell)** to have no chance at all (*informal*)

Snow·belt /snṓ bèlt/, **Snow Belt** *n* the northern regions of the United States, especially the Midwest and Northeast, which have a large amount of snow in winter

snow·ber·ry /snṓ bèrree/ (*plural* **-ries**) *n* an ornamental bush with white berries. Flowers: pink. Native to: North America, naturalized in Great Britain. Genus: *Symphoricarpos.*

snow·bik·ing /snṓ bĭking/ *n* the sport of riding mountain bikes with studded tires over snow-covered slopes or trails

snow·bird /snṓ bùrd/ *n* **1.** somebody who spends the winter in a place that has a warmer climate (*informal*) **2.** any bird that is seen chiefly in winter, e.g., a snow bunting or a fieldfare

snow·blad·ing /snṓ blàyding/ *n* SKIING same as **skiboarding**

snow-blind, snow-blind·ed *adj* affected by snow blindness

snow blind·ness *n* a condition of temporary blindness caused by the bright sunlight and intense radiation reflected from snow or ice, which causes swelling of parts of the eyeball and severe pain

snow·blink /snṓ blìngk/ *n* a white glow in the sky, especially in polar regions, caused by the reflection of light from distant snowfields

snow·blow·er /snṓ blō ər/ *n* a machine that clears snow from roads by scooping it into a fast-rotating spiral blade and ejecting it to one side

snow·board /snṓ bàwrd/ *n* a board with bindings for the feet that somebody stands on to slide down snow slopes ■ *vi* (**-board·ed, -board·ing, -boards**) to slide down snow slopes using a snowboard —**snow·board·er** *n* —**snow·board·ing** *n*

snow·bound /snṓ bòwnd/ *adj* prevented from moving or leaving a place by a heavy fall of snow

snow bunt·ing *n* a white finch with dark markings that nests on tundra and winters in coastal regions. Latin name: *Plectrophenax nivalis.*

snow·bush /snṓ bŏosh/ *n US* a spiny bush. Flowers: small, white. Native to: California, Oregon. Latin name: *Ceanothus cordulatus.*

snow·cap /snṓ kàp/ *n* a covering of snow on a mountain peak —**snow·capped** *adj*

snow cone *n N Am, Carib* a snack consisting of crushed flavored ice served in a paper cone

Snow·don, Mount /snṓd'n/ mountain in Gwynedd, northwestern Wales. It is the highest peak in Wales. Height: 3,560 ft./1,085 m.

Snow·do·ni·a Na·tion·al Park /snō dṓnee ə-/ national park incorporating Mount Snowdon, in northwestern Wales, established in 1951. Area: 840 sq. mi./2,171 sq. km.

snow·drift /snṓ drìft/ *n* a bank of snow piled up by the wind

snow·drop /snṓ dròp/ *n* an early spring-flowering plant that grows from a bulb. Flowers: small, white, drooping. Native to: Europe, Asia. Latin name: *Galanthus nivalis.*

snow·fall /snṓ fàwl/ *n* **1.** a period during which snow falls or an instance of snow falling **2.** the amount of snow that falls in a location over a period of time ○ *What is the average snowfall for the area?*

snow fence *n* a portable flexible fence made of upright slats or heavy plastic mesh, designed to stop snow from drifting onto roads or ski runs

snow·field /snṓ fèeld/ *n* a large area permanently covered in snow

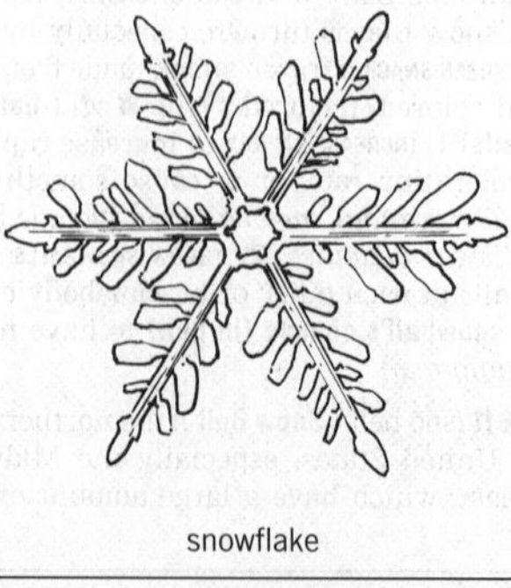

snowflake

snow·flake /snṓ flàyk/ *n* **1.** an individual mass of ice crystals that falls with others as snow **2.** a garden plant grown from a bulb. Flowers: white, drooping. Genus: *Leucojum.* **3.** BIRDS same as **snow bunting**

snow goose *n* a goose with white feathers and black wing tips. Native to: Arctic regions, migrating to coastal areas of North America. Latin name: *Anser caerulescens.*

snow-in-sum·mer *n* a perennial plant with wooly stems and notched silvery green leaves. Flowers: white. Native to: Europe. Latin name: *Cerastium tomentosum.*

snow job *n* an attempt to mislead or persuade somebody by insincere talk or flattery (*slang*)

snow leop·ard *n* a large cat with a thick pale gray or brown coat marked with dark splotches. Native to: mountainous regions of Central Asia. Latin name: *Panthera uncia.*

snow line *n* **1.** the line of altitude above which there is permanent snow **2.** the line of latitude marking the edge of a perennial snow field or polar region

snow·mak·ing /snṓw màyking/ *n* the science or process or making artificial snow, e.g., at a ski area

snow·man /snṓ màn/ (*plural* **-men** /-mèn/) *n* **1.** a roughly human figure made by piling up and shaping snow **2.** an ornament resembling a snowman, especially one suggesting a man

snow·melt /snṓ mèlt/ *n* **1.** runoff produced when snow melts **2.** the season when snow melts

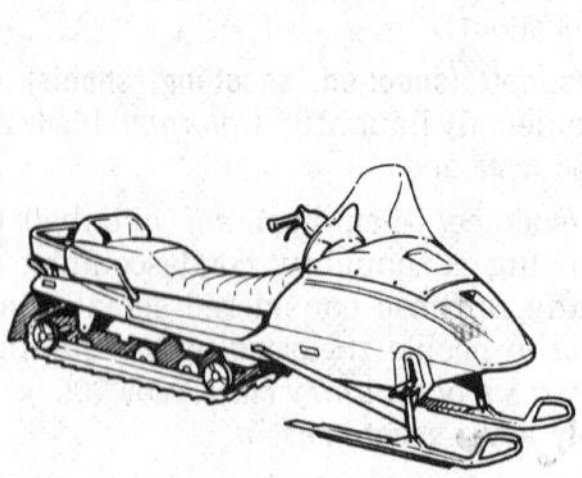

snowmobile

snow·mo·bile /snṓmə bèel, -mō-/ *n* a small motorized vehicle with runners and a continuous track, used for traveling over snow —**snow·mo·bil·er** *n* —**snow·mo·bil·ing** *n*

snow-on-the-moun·tain *n* a bush with white-edged leaves and white modified leaves (**bracts**) at the base of the flower petals. Native to: North America. Latin name: *Euphorbia marginata.*

snow·pack /snṓw pàk/ *n* accumulated snow, usually in a mountainous area

snow pea *n* a variety of garden pea with an edible thin flat pod. Latin name: *Pisum sativum.*

snow pel·let *n* a soft white round mass of ice that falls as precipitation (*often used in the plural*)

snow·per·son /snṓ pùrss'n/ (*plural* **-peo·ple** /-pèep'l/ or **-per·sons**) *n* a snowman or snowwoman

snow plant *n* a plant with a fleshy reddish stalk that often flowers before the snow has melted. Flowers: scarlet. Native to: mountains of western North America. Latin name: *Sarcodes sanguinea.*

snow·plough *n, vi* UK spelling of **snowplow**

snow·plow /snṓ plòw/ *n* **1.** VEHICLE FOR CLEARING SNOW a vehicle or an implement that can be fixed to a vehicle, used for clearing snow from roads or paths **2.** CONTROL TECHNIQUE IN SKIING a technique used in skiing in which the points of the skis are brought together to make a V-shape, enabling the skier to turn or stop ■ *vi* (**-plowed, -plow·ing, -plows**) SKI IN SNOWPLOW POSITION to use the snowplow position to turn or stop in skiing

snow scoot·er *n* **1.** a vehicle used on snow for fun, consisting usually of a single flat runner like a ski with a seat and a steering mechanism mounted on it **2.** a small motorized vehicle on runners for traveling over snow —**snow scoot·ing** *n*

snow·shed /snṓ shèd/ *n* a shelter over an open section of a railroad track, especially on a mountainside, to prevent it from getting covered in snow

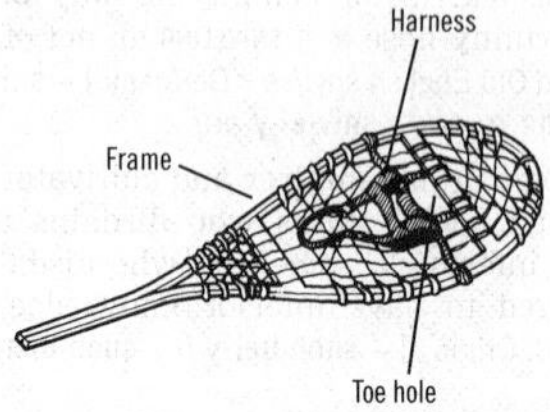

snowshoe

snow·shoe /snṓ shŏo/ *n* a metal or wood framework with interwoven straps that is attached to a boot allowing the wearer to walk on snow without sinking ■ *vi* (**-shoed, -shoe·ing, -shoes**) to walk on snow wearing snowshoes —**snow·sho·er** *n*

snow·shoe hare, snow·shoe rabbit *n* a hare with a white winter coat that turns brown in summer and large, heavily furred hind feet that allow it to move quickly in snow. Native to: North America. Latin name: *Lepus americanus.*

snow·storm /snṓ stàwrm/ *n* a storm with heavy snow

snow·suit /snṓ sŏot/ *n* an insulated, often water-resistant garment of one or two pieces worn by children in cold snowy weather

snow throw·er *n* VEHICLES same as **snowblower**

snow tire *n* a tire with a deep tread pattern or studs to provide extra traction for a vehicle driving in snowy conditions

snow-white *adj* as white as fresh snow —**snow white** *n*

snow·wom·an /snṓ wŏommən/ (*plural* **-wom·en** /-wìmin/) *n* **1.** a roughly human figure made by piling up and shaping snow and with features suggesting a woman **2.** an ornament resembling a snowwoman

snow·y /snṓ ee/ *adj* **1.** resembling snow, especially in color or purity ○ *a snowy beard* **2.** characterized by the presence of snow ○ *a snowy day* —**snow·i·ly** *adv* —**snow·i·ness** *n*

Snow·y /snṓ ee/ river in southeastern Australia. It rises in the Snowy Mountains in New South Wales and flows into the Tasman Sea, near the town of Orbost in Victoria. Length: 270 mi./430 km.

snow·y e·gret *n* a small egret with white feathers, black legs, and yellow feet. Native to: North and South America. Latin name: *Egretta thula.*

Snow·y Moun·tains /snṓ ee-/ range of peaks within the Australian Alps, in southeastern New South Wales, Australia. The highest point, and the highest peak in Australia, is Mount Kosciuszko, 7,310 ft./2,228 m.

snow·y owl *n* a large white owl that builds its nest on the ground and feeds mainly on lemmings. Native to: Arctic. Latin name: *Nyctea scandiaca.*

snow·y plov·er *n* a small shorebird with white underparts, found on sandy coasts, sand flats, and alkali ponds. Native to: United States, Mexico. Latin name: *Charadrius alexandrinus.*

SNP /snip/ *abbr* BIOTECH single nucleotide polymorphism

snub /snub/ *vt* (**snubbed, snub·bing, snubs**) **1.** TREAT SOMEBODY RUDELY to treat somebody with deliberate coldness or contempt **2.** BRING SOMETHING TO STOP to stop a line from paying out or something attached to a line from getting away by wrapping the line around something **3.** *US* STUB SOMETHING OUT to extinguish something by stubbing it out ■ *n* HUMILIATING ACTION a remark or act intended to humiliate or insult somebody ■ *adj* SMALL short and flat or turned up at the end ○ *a snub nose* [14C. < Old Norse *snubba*] —**snub·ber** *n*

snub·by /snúbbee/ (**-bi·er, -bi·est**) *adj* **1.** tending to treat people with a lack of regard, e.g., by ignoring or insulting them **2.** same as **snub-nosed**

snub-nosed *adj* **1.** having a very short barrel or a blunt end ○ *snub-nosed pliers* **2.** having a nose that is short and flat or turned up

snuck past participle, past tense of **sneak**

snuff[1] /snuf/ *vt* (**snuffed, snuff·ing, snuffs**) **1. EXTINGUISH FLAME** to extinguish a flame, e.g., that of a burning candle **2. TRIM WICK OF CANDLE** to remove the burned end from the wick of a candle **3. DESTROY SOMETHING** to put an end to somebody or something (*informal*) ○ *snuff out enthusiasm* ○ *made a diving catch that snuffed a sixth-inning rally* ■ *n* **SOOTY WICK** the sooty, charred end of a candle wick [14C. Origin ?]

snuff[2] /snuf/ *n* **1. POWDERED TOBACCO** tobacco in the form of powder, taken by sniffing it up the nostrils **2. AMOUNT OF SNUFF** a portion of snuff ■ *vi* (**snuffed, snuff·ing, snuffs**) **TAKE SNUFF** to inhale snuff [Late 17C. < Dutch *snuf*, shortening of *snuftabak* "sniffing tobacco"]

snuff[3] /snuf/ *v* (**snuffed, snuff·ing, snuffs**) **1.** *vt* **INHALE SOMETHING** to inhale something through the nose **2.** *vti* **SNIFF** to sniff noisily, or to examine something by sniffing it ○ *The hounds snuffed the ground searching for the trail.* ■ *n* **SNIFFING SOUND** an instance or sound of snuffing [Early 16C. < Dutch *snuffen* "snuffle" < Germanic, "of the nose"]

snuff·box /snúf bòks/ *n* a small ornamental box for powdered tobacco

snuff-col·ored *adj* of a dark yellowish brown color

snuff·er /snúffər/ *n* a device used to extinguish a candle, consisting of a long handle with a cone shape at one end

snuff·ers /snúffərz/ *n* an instrument resembling a pair of scissors, used for trimming wicks or extinguishing candles or oil lamps (*takes a singular or plural verb*)

snuff film *n* MOVIES same as **snuff movie**

snuf·fle /snúff'l/ *v* (**-fled, -fling, -fles**) **1.** *vi* **BREATHE NOISILY** to breathe noisily through a partially blocked nose **2.** *vti* **SPEAK NASALLY** to speak or say something in a nasal or whining way **3.** *vi* **SNIFF** to make repeated sniffing sounds ■ *n* **SOUND OF SNUFFLING** an instance or sound of snuffling [Late 16C. Probably < Low German, Dutch *snuffelen*, ultimately an imitation of the sound] —**snuf·fler** *n* —**snuf·fly** *adj*

snuff mov·ie *n* a pornographic movie or video that allegedly ends with the murder of one of the participants in a sex act (*slang*)

snuff·y /snúffee/ (**-i·er, -i·est**) *adj* **1. IRRITABLE** in a bad temper and easily annoyed **2. LIKE SNUFF** like snuff in color or smell **3. COVERED WITH SNUFF** soiled or marked with snuff —**snuff·i·ness** *n*

snug /snug/ *adj* (**snug·ger, snug·gest**) **1. COZY** warm and comfortable **2. SMALL BUT COMFORTABLE** small in size but offering a comfortable well-arranged space ○ *a snug cottage* **3. SHELTERED** protected from the weather ○ *The fishing boats were snug in the harbor.* **4. CLOSE-FITTING** fitting comfortably close or too close ○ *The sweater was perhaps a little too snug.* **5. SEAWORTHY** seaworthy because of being well-built **6. CONCEALED** offering a safe and private hiding place **7. FINANCIALLY SECURE** allowing one to live comfortably and securely, without having to worry about money ■ *n* **1.** *UK* **SMALL ROOM IN PUB** a small room or enclosed area in a pub allowing a small number of people to sit in private **2. PEG FOR HOLDING BOLT** a small peg used to hold the head of a bolt in place while a nut is tightened onto the end ■ *v* (**snugged, snug·ging, snugs**) **1.** *vi* **SNUGGLE** to lie closely together or curl up in a cozy way ○ *snugged with a book near the fire* **2.** *vt* **MAKE SOMEBODY SNUG** to make somebody comfortable and warm **3.** *vti* **SECURE BOAT** to make a boat secure to weather a storm [Late 16C. Probably < N Germanic or Low Dutch] —**snug·ly** *adv*

snug·ger·y /snúggəree/ (*plural* **-ies**) *n UK* **1.** a place that is warm and comfortable **2.** same as **snug** *n* (sense 1)

snug·gle /snúgg'l/ (**-gled, -gling, -gles**) *v* **1.** *vi* to get into a comfortable, cozy position, especially close to another person **2.** *vt* to draw close to somebody or something to offer or receive comfort and affection ○ *snuggled in front of the fireplace* [Late 17C. < SNUG]

Sny·der /snídər/, **Gary** (*b.* 1930) US writer. His poetry, translations, and essays show the influence of his interests in ecology, Zen Buddhism, and Native American culture, and include the Pulitzer Prize-winning verse collection *Turtle Island* (1975).

> "Americans would rather live by a Chamber-of-Commerce Creationism...satisfied with a divinely presented Shopping Mall. The integrity and character of our own ancestors is dismissed with 'I couldn't live like that' by people who barely know how to live *at all.*"
> [Gary Snyder, "Ancient Forests of the Far West," *The Practice of the Wild*; 1990]

so[1] /sō/ CORE MEANING: a conjunction indicating the reason for an action or situation, or its result ○ *Let's go upstairs and talk, so we can have a little privacy.* ○ *Keep your password secret so that others cannot access your account.* ○ *I had the flu, so I couldn't attend the meeting.*

1. *conj* **IN ORDER THAT** introduces the reason for doing what has just been mentioned ○ *The poles are joined together so as to enclose an area of about twenty feet in diameter.* ○ *He held her tight so that she wouldn't fall.* **2.** *conj* **INTRODUCES RESULT** introduces the result of the situation that has just been mentioned ○ *Everything is done on a shoestring, so their prices are very low.* **3.** *conj* **INDICATES SIMILARITY** indicates that two events or situations are alike in some way ○ *Just as my circumstances have changed, so too have my goals in life.* **4.** *adv* **INDICATES IDENTITY** indicates that what is true of one person or thing is also true of another person or thing (*followed by auxiliary or modal, or by the main verb "do," "have," or "be"*) ○ *If you can keep a secret, so can I.* **5.** *adv* **AS IT IS** indicates that something is the way it has been described ○ *Nebraska has the potential to be very important, and will soon be so, both politically and commercially.* **6.** *adv* **REFERS BACK** refers back to something that has just been mentioned ○ *Lunch may be purchased on the island, for those who desire to do so.* **7.** *adv* **TO SUCH EXTENT** emphasizes the degree of something by mentioning its result ○ *He is so busy working at Nathan's, he doesn't have time to take classes.* **8.** *adv* **EMPHASIZES QUALITY** adds emphasis to the meaning of an adverb or adjective ○ *I was so scared.* ○ *He acts so stubbornly sometimes.* **9.** *conj* **THEREFORE OR IN CONSEQUENCE** introduces an event in a sequence ○ *It's not working out so we'll have to go back to the beginning and start again.* ○ *She said she would like to see me again so I gave her my phone number.* **10.** *conj* **INVITES COMMENT** introduces a new topic, or a question or comment about something ○ *So what are we going to do about it?* ○ *So I see you've changed your mind.* **11.** *adv* **INDICATES POSITION OR DIMENSIONS** indicates the position or dimensions of something, using actions or gestures ○ *Hold onto the boat like so, and hoist yourself up.* **12.** *adv* **INDEED** used to contradict a negative statement (*nonstandard*) ○ *"You never explained what to do." "I did so!"* **13.** *adv* **INTRODUCES COMMAND** used to introduce commands (*informal*) ○ *So stop it already!* [Old English *swā* < Indo-European] ◇ **and so on** *or* **forth** used at the end of a list to indicate that there are other things that could be mentioned ○ *These systems are traditionally used in industries such as insurance, banking, universities, and so on.* ○ *Remove any additional hardware from the system (mouse, network card, fax board, modem, and so forth.)* ◇ **so be it** expresses agreement or resignation ○ *I wish you'd think again, but never mind – so be it!* ◇ **so much, so many** a limited or unspecified degree or amount ○ *The government can only do so much.* ○ *I can only take so many insults.* ◇ **so much for** (*informal*) **1.** used to indicate that there is nothing more that can be said or done about something ○ *So much for the morning. I still had the afternoon to get through.* **2.** used to indicate that something has not been successful or helpful ○ *So much for that brilliant plan!* ◇ **so that** in order that ◇ **so there** used to express defiance, triumph, or finality ◇ **so what?** used to ask rather rudely why something is important, implying that it is not ○ *You amass all these facts, but the question is, "so what?"*

SPELLCHECK See ***sew***.

so[2] /sō/ *n* MUSIC another spelling of **sol**[1]

so[3] *abbr* Somalia (*used in Internet addresses*) See table at **domain name**

SO *abbr* **1.** significant other **2.** COMM standing order **3.** BASEBALL strike-out

S.O. *abbr* **1.** FIN seller's option **2.** BASEBALL strike-out

soak /sōk/ *v* (**soaked, soak·ing, soaks**) **1.** *vti* **STEEP IN LIQUID** to immerse something in liquid for a period of time, or be immersed in liquid **2.** *vt* **MAKE SOMEBODY OR SOMETHING WET** to make something or somebody completely wet (*often passive*) ○ *We got soaked in the rain on the way home.* **3.** *vti* **ABSORB** to draw something such as moisture in through the pores or other small holes ○ *Use a paper towel to soak up the spill.* **4.** *vti* **PERMEATE SOMETHING** to penetrate something by saturating it and passing into pores or small holes ○ *The water quickly soaked through her shoes.* **5.** *vti* **REMOVE STAIN BY SOAKING** to remove something, especially a mark or a stain from an item of clothing, by leaving it in liquid for a time **6.** *vt* **OVERCHARGE SOMEBODY** to charge or tax somebody an excessive amount (*slang*) **7.** *vti* **GET DRUNK** to drink too much alcohol, or make somebody drunk (*informal*) ■ *n* **1. ACT OF SOAKING** an act or instance of immersing something in liquid ○ *had a long, leisurely soak in the bathtub* **2. SOAKING LIQUID** a solution or liquid in which to soak something **3.** same as **drunkard** (*slang*) [Old English *socian*, form of *sūcan* (see SUCK)] —**soak·er** *n*

soak·ing /sṓking/ *n* **1. INSTANCE OF OVERPAYING** an instance of being overcharged for something (*informal*) **2. DRENCHING** an instance of being made very wet (*informal*) **3. STEEPING** an act or the process of steeping something in liquid ■ *adj* **VERY WET** very wet, especially because of being rained on (*informal*)

SYNONYMS See ***wet***.

so-and-so (*plural* **so-and-sos**) *n* **1.** somebody or something not named or specified (*informal*) **2.** somebody regarded as annoying or disagreeable (*informal insult*)

Soane /sōn/, **Sir John** (1753–1837) British architect. He was an exponent of the neoclassical style, seen in his churches, private houses, and public buildings, most notably the Bank of England, London, England (1792–1833).

soap /sōp/ *n* **1. CLEANSING AGENT** a solid, liquid, or powdered preparation made by reacting potassium or sodium hydroxide with animal or vegetable oils. Use: cleaning. **2.** same as **soap opera** (*informal*) **3. METALLIC SALT COMBINED WITH FATTY ACID** a metallic salt of a fatty acid, often made with calcium, copper, aluminum, or lithium. Use: bases for waterproofing agents, ointments, greases. ■ *v* (**soaped, soap·ing, soaps**) **1.** *vt* **PUT SOAP ON SOMETHING OR SOMEBODY** to put soap on something or somebody, especially in the process of washing **2.** *vti* **CAJOLE** to flatter somebody, especially with the intention of persuading or soothing (*slang*) [Old English *sāpe* < Germanic]

soap·bark /sṓp baàrk/ *n* **1.** a bark containing saponin. Use: formerly, soap substitute. **2.** an evergreen tree that yields soapbark. Native to: South America. Latin name: *Quillaja saponaria*.

soap·ber·ry /sṓp bèrree/ (*plural* **-ries**) *n* **1.** a pulpy fruit that is rich in saponins. Use: soap substitute. **2.** a tree or bush that bears soapberries. Native to: tropical America. Genus: *Sapindus*.

soap·box /sṓp bòks/ *n* **1. PLATFORM FOR SPEAKING** something used as a platform for making an impromptu speech **2. BOX FOR SOAP** a box in which soap is packed ■ *vi* (**-boxed, -box·ing, -box·es**) *US* **SPEAK UNOFFICIALLY** to make an unofficial speech in public (*informal*)

soap bub·ble *n* **1.** a bubble formed with soapy water **2.** something that is beautiful but that does not last

soap op·e·ra *n* **1.** a serial on television or radio that deals with the lives of a group of characters, especially in a melodramatic or sentimental way **2.** a series of events that resembles the events of a soap opera in melodrama or sentimentality [Because originally often sponsored by soap manufacturers]

soap plant *n US* a plant with bulbs or other parts used as soap. Genus: *Chlorogalum*.

soap pow·der *n* a detergent in powdered form used in washing machines

AKG London

soapstone: Nigerian carving (12th to 15th centuries)

soap·stone /sṓp stṑn/ *n* a dark gray or green soft soapy compact variety of talc. Use: decorative carving.

soap·suds /sṓp sùdz/ *npl* same as **suds** *npl* (sense 1) —**soap·suds·y** *adj*

soap·wort /sṓp wùrt, -wàwrt/ *n Can, UK* a plant with roots and leaves that yield saponin. Flowers: pink and white. Native to: Europe. Latin name: *Saponaria officinalis.* US term **bouncing Bet**

soap·y /sṓpee/ (**-i·er, -i·est**) *adj* **1. WITH SOAP** full of or covered with soap **2. LIKE SOAP** having the look or feel of soap ○ *a soapy texture* **3. INSINCERE** given to excessive insincere flattery (*slang*) —**soap·i·ness** *adv*

soar /sawr/ *vi* (**soared, soar·ing, soars**) **1. INCREASE RAPIDLY** to increase rapidly in number, volume, size, or amount ○ *soaring prices* **2. FLY** to fly or rise high in the air **3. GLIDE HIGH** to glide on rising currents of air **4. BECOME MORE INTENSE** to rise to a higher, more intense, or exalted level ○ *Hopes for peace soared at the end of the day's talks.* ■ *n* **ACT OF SOARING** the act of soaring, or the height or range reached by soaring [14C. < Old French *essorer* < Latin *ex-* "out" + *aura* "air"] —**soar·er** *n*

SPELLCHECK soar or **sore**? Do not confuse the spelling of ***soar*** and ***sore***, which sound similar. ***Soar*** is chiefly used as a verb, meaning "increase rapidly" or "fly or rise high in the air": *The plane soared into the clouds. Prices are soaring.* ***Sore*** is an adjective meaning "painful" (as in *a sore finger*) or a noun meaning "a painful skin infection or wound" (as in *open sores on his arms and legs*).

Soa·res /swaár esh/, **Mário** (*b.* 1924) prime minister (1976–78, 1983–85) and president (1986–96) of Portugal. He was instrumental in the restoration of democratic government there. Full name **Soares, Mário Alberto Nobre Lopes**

so·a·ve /sō aá vày/ *n* a dry white blended wine from northeastern Italy [Mid-20C. After a village in N Italy]

So·ay /sṓ ay, sóy/ *n* a small dark brown horned sheep, belonging to an ancient breed originating in Soay, Outer Hebrides

sob /sob/ *v* (**sobbed, sob·bing, sobs**) **1.** *vi* **GASP WHILE CRYING** to make gasping sounds while crying **2.** *vt* **SPEAK WHILE SOBBING** to say something while sobbing **3. sob your·self** *vr* **BECOME BY SOBBING** to get into a particular state by sobbing ○ *sobbed herself to sleep* ■ *n* **SOUND OF SOBBING** an act or sound of sobbing ○ *stifled a sob* [12C. Probably < Low Dutch] —**sob·bing·ly** *adv*

so·ba /sṓbə/ *n* a Japanese dish of buckwheat noodles [Late 19C. < Japanese]

so·ber /sṓbər/ *adj* **1. NOT INTOXICATED** not under the influence of drugs or alcohol **2. TENDING NOT TO DRINK** not in the habit of drinking much alcohol or using drugs **3. SERIOUS** serious and thoughtful in demeanor or quality ○ *a sober face* **4. DULL** lacking vitality or brightness in appearance ○ *He always dresses in sober colors.* **5. NOT FANCIFUL OR SPECULATIVE** based on facts and rational thinking rather than on speculation ○ *a sober assessment of the situation* ■ *vti* (**-bered, -ber·ing, -bers**) **1.** same as **sober up 2. BECOME OR MAKE SOMEBODY SERIOUS** to become more serious or thoughtful, or make somebody become so ○ *His expression sobered.* [14C. Via French < Latin *sobrius*] —**so·ber·ly** *adv* —**so·ber·ness** *n*

sober up *vti* make somebody sober after being drunk, or become sober

so·ber·ing /sṓbəring/ *adj* making somebody give serious thought to important things ○ *a sobering experience* ○ *had a sobering effect* —**so·ber·ing·ly** *adv*

so·ber·sides /sṓbər sìdz/ *n* somebody who is solemn and serious —**so·ber·sid·ed** *adj*

so·bre·me·sa /sòbray máysə/ *n Hispanic* the time after a meal during which participants sit around the table drinking and talking [< Spanish < *sobre* "on top of" + *mesa* "table"]

so·bri·e·ty /sə brī́ ətee, sō-/ *n* **1. ABSTINENCE** abstinence from or moderation in the use of alcohol or drugs **2. SERIOUSNESS** the quality of being serious and thoughtful **3. DULLNESS** a lack of vitality or brightness [15C. Directly or via French < Latin *sobrietas* < *sobrius* "sober"]

so·bri·quet /sṓbri kày, -kèt, sṑbri káy, -két/, **sou·bri·quet** /soóbri-, sōo bri-/ *n* an unofficial name or nickname, especially a humorous one [Mid-17C. < French, "a tap under the chin"]

sob sis·ter *n* (*informal*) **1.** a journalist who writes or edits sentimental stories or answers problems sent in by readers **2.** *US* an ineffective helper of others

sob sto·ry *n* a story told to gain somebody's sympathy or pity, especially when offered as an excuse (*informal*)

so·ca /sṓkə/ *n* a style of Caribbean music that combines calypso and soul and has a fast beat [Late 20C. < SOUL + CALYPSO]

soc·age /sókij, sṓkij/, **soc·cage** *n* a feudal system of holding land in which the tenant either paid rent or performed a fixed service, usually agricultural and nonmilitary in nature [14C. < Anglo-Norman < *soc* variant of *soke* "right of jurisdiction"] —**soc·ag·er** *n*

So·Cal /sṓ kàl/ *adj* relating to the southern part of California or to the people living there and their culture (*informal*) —**SoCal** *n*

so-called *adj* **1.** popularly known as, but not necessarily by the speaker or writer ○ *the so-called information superhighway* **2.** incorrectly known as ○ *a so-called art expert*

USAGE Quotation marks should not be used around expressions immediately following words like ***so-called*** and *self-styled*: *He is a so-called generalissimo of capitalism* [not *a so-called "generalissimo of capitalism"*].

soc·cage *n* HIST another spelling of **socage**

soc·cer /sókər/ *n* a game in which two teams of 11 players try to score by kicking or butting a round ball into the net goals on either end of a rectangular field [Late 19C. < *Assoc.*, abbreviation of ASSOCIATION (in ASSOCIATION FOOTBALL) + *-er*, suffix added to shortened forms of words]

soc·cer mom *n* a mother who devotes herself to her children's leisure activities, e.g., driving them to and from sports activities

~~soceity~~ incorrect spelling of **society**

so·cia·ble /sṓshəb'l/ *adj* **1. GREGARIOUS** inclined to seek out the company of other people **2. FRIENDLY** friendly and pleasant to other people **3. OFFERING OPPORTUNITY FOR SOCIAL INTERACTION** allowing people to mix in an informal way ○ *a sociable occasion* [Mid-16C. Directly or via French < Latin *sociabilis* < *socius* "companion"] —**so·cia·bil·i·ty** /sṓshə bíllətee/ *n* —**so·cia·ble·ness** *n* —**so·cia·bly** *adv*

USAGE sociable or **social**? ***Social*** is a neutral word that classifies a person or thing as being concerned in some way with society or its organization. A *social club* is a place provided for people to enjoy themselves, and a *social worker* is involved in providing a service for the welfare of a person or community. ***Sociable***, by contrast, refers to a person's capacity to deal with other people in social contexts, so a *sociable worker* is a worker who enjoys the company of colleagues.

so·cial /sṓshəl/ *adj* **1. RELATING TO SOCIETY** relating to human society and how it is organized **2. RELATING TO INTERACTION OF PEOPLE** relating to the way in which people in groups behave and interact ○ *the social sciences* **3. LIVING IN A COMMUNITY** living or preferring to live as part of a community or colony rather than alone ○ *social insects such as ants* **4. OFFERING OPPORTUNITY FOR INTERACTION** allowing people to meet and interact with others in a friendly way ○ *a social club* **5. RELATING TO HUMAN WELFARE** relating to human welfare and the organized welfare services that a community provides ○ *social services* **6. OF RANK IN SOCIETY** relating to or considered appropriate to a rank in society, especially the upper classes **7. SOCIABLE** tending to seek out the company of others (*informal*) ○ *a very social person* **8. GROWING IN CLUMPS** describes plants that grow in clumps or masses ■ *n* **INFORMAL GET-TOGETHER** an informal gathering or party, usually of a particular group of people who meet regularly [Mid-17C. Via French < Latin *socialis* < *socius* "companion"] —**so·cial·ly** *adv*

USAGE See ***sociable***.

PRONUNCIATION The word ***social***, as in *Social Security*, is correctly pronounced /sṓshəl/. The now widely used pronunciation /sṓsəl/, in which the "sh" sound becomes "s," is regarded as incorrect, even though it can be associated with some regional US speech patterns.

so·cial an·thro·pol·o·gy *n UK* same as **cultural anthropology** —**so·cial an·thro·pol·o·gist** *n*

so·cial as·sis·tance *n Can* same as **social security**

social capital *n* the educational, social, and cultural advantages that somebody from the upper middle classes is believed to possess

so·cial climb·er *n* somebody who tries to rise in status by associating with people of a higher social class (*disapproving*) —**so·cial climb·ing** *n*

so·cial cog·ni·tion *n US* thought processes involved in understanding and dealing with other people

so·cial con·tract, so·cial com·pact *n* an agreement among individual people in a society or between the people and their government that outlines the rights and duties of each party. It derives from the ideas of Hobbes, Locke, and Rousseau and involves people giving up freedoms in return for benefits such as state protection.

So·cial Cred·it *n* a Canadian conservative political party founded in 1935 —**So·cial Cred·it·er** *n*

so·cial Dar·win·ism *n* a discredited social theory stating that the political and economic advantages in a developed society are derived from the biological advantages of its collective membership —**so·cial Dar·win·ist** *n*

so·cial de·moc·ra·cy, So·cial De·moc·ra·cy *n* the political belief that a change from capitalism to socialism can be achieved gradually and democratically —**so·cial dem·o·crat** *n* —**so·cial dem·o·crat·ic** *adj*

so·cial dis·ease *n* **1.** a sexually transmitted disease (*informal; used euphemistically*) **2.** *US* a disease that is brought about or affected by the socioeconomic conditions in which people live, e.g., tuberculosis

so·cial drink·er *n* somebody who only consumes alcoholic beverages in the company of other people and in moderation

so·cial en·gi·neer·ing *n* the use of policies that are based on the findings of social science to deal with social problems

so·cial in·sur·ance *n* state insurance that uses compulsory contributions to pay for benefits for unemployed and retired people

so·cial in·sur·ance num·ber *n Can* a unique reference number assigned to a person for the purposes of taxation, employment insurance, and pensions

so·cial·ism /sṓshə lìzəm/, **So·cial·ism** *n* **1. POLITICAL SYSTEM OF COMMUNAL OWNERSHIP** a political theory or system in which the means of production and distribution are controlled by the people and operated according to equity and fairness rather than market principles **2. MOVEMENT BASED ON SOCIALISM** a political movement based on principles of socialism, typically advocating an end to private property and to the exploitation of workers **3. STAGE BETWEEN CAPITALISM AND COMMUNISM** in Marxist theory, the stage after the proletarian revolution when a society is changing from capitalism to communism, marked by pay distributed according to work done rather than need

so·cial·ist /sṓshəlist/, **So·cial·ist** *n* **BELIEVER IN SOCIALISM** somebody who believes in or supports socialism or a socialist party ■ *adj* **1. ADVOCATING SOCIALISM** relating to, based on, or advocating socialism **2.** RELATING TO SOCIALISTS relating to socialists or a socialist party —**so·cial·is·tic** /sṓshə lístik/ *adj* —**so·cial·is·ti·cal·ly** *adv*

So·cial·ist La·bor Par·ty *n* a Marxist political party in the United States

so·cial·ist re·al·ism *n* an artistic doctrine officially sanctioned in many Communist countries, especially during the 1930s–50s, that proposed the idea that art and literature should serve to promote and glorify the ideals of a socialist state

so·cial·ite /sṓshə līt/ *n* somebody who is well known in fashionable society

so·ci·al·i·ty /sṓshee állətee/ (*plural* **-ties**) *n* **1.** the quality of being social, or an instance of it **2.** the tendency to form social groups or live in a community

so·cial·ize /sṓshə līz/ (**-ized, -iz·ing, -iz·es**) *v* **1.** *vi* TAKE PART IN SOCIAL ACTIVITIES to take part in social activities, or behave in a friendly way to others ○ *a group of friends who like to socialize after work* **2.** *vt* TRAIN SOMEBODY TO BE SOCIAL to give somebody the skills required for functioning successfully in society or in a particular society ○ *socialize a child* **3.** *vt* MAKE SOMETHING PUBLICLY OWNED to place something under public ownership or control —**so·cial·i·za·tion** /sṓshəli záysh'n/ *n* —**so·cial·iz·er** *n*

so·cial·ized med·i·cine *n US* a system of national health care that provides medical care to all and is regulated and subsidized by the government

so·cial·ly re·spon·si·ble in·ves·tor *n* a person, company, or other organization with a policy of ethical investment

so·cial-mind·ed *adj US* concerned with the conditions of human society and the welfare of others

so·cial mo·bil·i·ty *n* the possibility for people in a society to change their class or social status within their lifetimes

so·cial psy·chol·o·gy *n* the branch of psychology that deals with how groups behave and how individual members are affected by the group to which they belong —**so·cial psy·chol·o·gist** *n*

so·cial re·al·ism *n* the use of realistic portrayals of life in art or literature to make a social or political point

so·cial sci·ence *n* **1.** the study of people in society and how they relate to one another and to the group to which they belong **2.** a discipline that studies a specific area of human society, e.g., sociology, psychology, economics, political science, history, or anthropology —**so·cial sci·en·tist** *n*

so·cial sec·re·tar·y *n* somebody whose job is to arrange social activities and handle correspondence for a person or organization

so·cial se·cu·ri·ty *n* **1.** *also* **So·cial Se·cu·ri·ty** a government program that provides economic security to people who are retired, unemployed, or unable to work. The US Social Security program was established in 1935 and its funds come from employers and employees. **2.** money paid to somebody by a government through a social security program

So·cial Se·cu·ri·ty num·ber *n* in the United States, a unique reference number assigned to each person within the Social Security system. It remains the same throughout the person's life.

so·cial ser·vice *n* a service provided by a government agency for the welfare of a person or community. Such services include housing, child protection, free school lunches, and health care. (*often used in the plural*)

so·cial ser·vic·es *n* a government agency that provides social services to individuals or a community (*takes a singular or plural verb*)

so·cial stud·ies *n* an academic subject devoted to the study of society and including geography, economics, and history (*takes a singular or plural verb*)

so·cial wel·fare *n* the social services provided by a state or by a private organization

so·cial work *n* the profession or work of providing people in need with social services —**so·cial work·er** *n*

so·ci·e·ty /sə sī ətee/ (*plural* **-ties**) *n* **1.** RELATIONSHIPS AMONG GROUPS the sum of social relationships among groups of humans or animals **2.** STRUCTURED COMMUNITY OF PEOPLE a structured community of people bound together by similar traditions, institutions, or nationality **3.** CUSTOMS OF A COMMUNITY the customs of a community and the way it is organized, e.g., its class structure ○ *the role of women in society* **4.** SUBSET OF COMMUNITY a particular section of a community that is distinguished by particular qualities ○ *In those days, the subject was never mentioned in polite society.* **5.** PROMINENT PEOPLE the prominent or fashionable people in a community, or their social life **6.** COMPANIONSHIP the state of being with other people ○ *seek the society of coworkers* **7.** GROUP SHARING INTERESTS an organized group of people who share an interest, aim, or profession [Mid-16C. Via French < Latin *societas* "companionship" < *socius* "companion"] —**so·ci·e·tal** *adj*

So·ci·e·ty of Friends *n* the Christian denomination consisting of the Quakers

So·ci·e·ty of Je·sus *n* the Roman Catholic religious order of the Jesuits

So·cin·i·an /sō sínnee ən/ *n* a follower of Laelius and Faustus Socinus, Italian theologians who preached belief in God, but rejected other traditional Christian doctrines such as the Trinity and the divinity of Christ ■ *adj* relating to the Socinians and their beliefs [Mid-17C. < modern Latin *Socinianus* < *Socinus*] —**So·cin·i·an·ism** *n*

socio- *prefix* society, social ○ *sociopath* ○ *sociopolitical* [Via French < Latin, < *socius* "companion"]

so·ci·o·bi·ol·o·gy /sṑssee ō bī óllәjee, sṑshee-/ *n* the study of the social behavior of animals and humans and how this is related to genetics and the survival of species —**so·ci·o·bi·o·log·i·cal** /sṑssee ō bī ə lójjik'l, sṑshee ō-/ *adj*

so·ci·o·cul·tur·al /sṑssee-kúlchərəl, sṑshee-/ *adj* relating to or involving cultural and social factors —**so·ci·o·cul·tur·al·ly** *adv*

so·ci·o·ec·o·nom·ic /sṑssee ō ѐkə nómmik, sṑshee-, -ѐekə nómmik/ *adj* relating to or involving economic and social factors —**so·ci·o·ec·o·nom·i·cal·ly** *adv*

sociol. *abbr* sociology

so·ci·o·lin·guis·tics /sṑssee ō ling gwístiks, sṑshee-/ *n* the study of the relationships between language and social and cultural factors (*takes a singular verb*) —**so·ci·o·lin·guist** /sṑssee ō líng gwist, sṑshee-/ *n* —**so·ci·o·lin·guis·tic** *adj*

so·ci·ol·o·gy /sṑssee óllәjee, sṑshee-/ *n* **1.** the study of the origin, development, and structure of human societies and the behavior of individual people and groups in society **2.** the study of a particular social institution and the part it plays in society [Mid-19C. < French *sociologie* < Latin *socius* "companion"] —**so·ci·o·log·ic** /sṑssee ə lójjik, sṑshee-/ *adj* —**so·ci·o·log·i·cal** /sṑssee ə lójjik'l, sṑshee-/ *adj* —**so·ci·o·log·i·cal·ly** *adv* —**so·ci·ol·o·gist** *n*

so·ci·om·e·try /sṑssee ómmətree, sṑshee-/ *n* the statistical study of behavior and relationships within social groups, especially expressed in terms of preferences —**so·ci·o·met·ric** /sṑssee ō méttrik, sṑshee-/ *adj* —**so·ci·om·e·trist** *n*

so·ci·o·path /sṑssee ō pàth, sṑshee-/ *n* PSYCHIAT same as **psychopath** (sense 1) (*technical*) [Mid-20C. After PSYCHOPATH] —**so·ci·o·path·ic** /sṑssee ō páthik, sṑshee-/ *adj* —**so·ci·op·a·thy** /sṑssee óppəthee, sṑshee-/ *n*

so·ci·o·po·lit·i·cal /sṑssee ō pə líttik'l, sṑshee-/ *adj* relating to or involving both social and political factors

so·ci·o·psy·cho·log·i·cal /sṑssee ō sīkə lójjik'l, sṑshee-/ *adj* **1.** relating to or involving social psychology **2.** relating to or involving both social and psychological factors

sock[1] /sok/ *n* **1.** (*plural* **socks** or **sox** *informal* /soks/) a soft, usually knitted covering for the foot and ankle that may reach as high as the knee. It is usually worn inside a shoe. **2.** METEOROL same as **windsock** [Old English *socc* "light shoe, slipper," via Germanic < Latin *soccus* < Greek *sukkhos* "(kind of) shoe"]

sock away *vt* to save money for the future (*informal*) [< the practice of storing savings in a sock]

sock in *vt* to close an airport to air traffic temporarily because of poor visibility (*informal; usually passive*)

sock[2] /sok/ (*informal*) *vti* (**socked, sock·ing, socks**) to hit somebody or something hard, usually with the fist ■ *n* a hard hit or blow, usually with the fist [Late 17C. Origin ?] ◇ **sock it to somebody** to subject somebody to a physical or verbal attack (*informal*)

sock·dol·a·ger /sok dóllәjәr/, **sock·dol·o·ger** *n US* (*dated informal*) **1.** a decisive blow or argument **2.** something outstanding or remarkable [Mid-19C. Probably fanciful < SOCK[2]]

sock·et /sókət/ *n* **1.** SHAPED HOLE FOR CONNECTION a hole or recess in something specially shaped to receive a specific object or part, e.g., the hole that receives a light bulb or one that receives a plug on an electrical device **2.** *UK* ELEC same as **outlet** (sense 5) **3.** ANAT HOLLOW IN BODY a bony hollow in the body into which another part fits ■ *vt* (**-et·ed, -et·ing, -ets**) **1.** PUT IN SOCKET to insert something into a socket **2.** FIT SOMETHING WITH SOCKET to provide something with a socket [13C. < Anglo-Norman *soket* "small plowshare" < Old French *sok* "plowshare"]

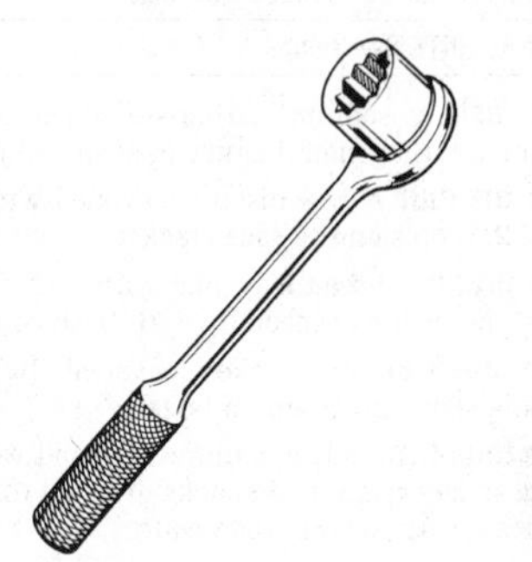

socket wrench

sock·et wrench *n* a long-handled wrench with interchangeable heads that fit over nuts and bolts of various sizes and a ratchet that makes tightening nuts and bolts easier

sock·eye /sók ī/ (*plural* **-eyes** or *same*), **sock·eye salm·on** *n* a food fish of the salmon family that has red flesh. Native to: Pacific waters. Latin name: *Oncorhynchus nerka*. [Late 19C. Alteration of Salish *sukai* "fish of fishes"]

sock·o /sókō/ *adj US* producing a strong impression (*informal*) [Early 20C. < SOCK[2]]

so·cle /sṓk'l/ *n* a base that sticks out from under the bottom of a wall, or the lowest part of the base of a column or pedestal [Early 18C. Via French < Latin *socculus* "small light shoe" < *soccus* (see SOCK[1])]

Soc·ra·tes /sókrə tèez/ (469–399 B.C.) Greek philosopher. His philosophy has survived through the writings of his pupils, especially Plato. He employed what became known as the "Socratic method" to question conventional assumptions about morality, justice, and other social concepts. Charged with atheism and corrupting youth, he was condemned to death.

> "The unexamined life is not worth living."
> [Socrates. Quoted in *Apology*, Plato; 4th century B.C.]

So·crat·ic /sə kráttik/ *adj* relating to Socrates, his philosophy, or his method of arriving at the truth ■ *n* a student or follower of Socrates —**So·crat·i·cal·ly** *adv* —**So·crat·i·cism** *n* —**So·crat·ist** /sókrətist/ *n*

So·crat·ic i·ro·ny *n* ignorance feigned in order to elicit explanations from somebody whose own ignorance can then be exposed through subsequent clever questioning

So·crat·ic meth·od *n* a means developed by Socrates of arriving at the truth by continually questioning, obtaining answers, and criticizing the answers

So·cred /sṓ krèd/ *n Can* a member or supporter of a Social Credit movement or political party [Mid-20C. Contraction of SOCIAL CREDIT] —**So·cred** *adj*

sod[1] /sod/ *n* **1.** TURF a surface section or strip of earth with growing grass and roots **2.** GROUND ground or soil (*literary*) ■ *vt* (**sod·ded, sod·ding, sods**) COVER WITH TURF to cover ground with sods [15C. < Middle Dutch or Low German *sode* "turf"]

sod[2] /sód/ *UK n* **1.** ANY PERSON used, often humorously or affectionately, to refer to a person (*slang; sometimes* *offensive*) ○ *lucky sod* **2.** **OFFENSIVE TERM** an offensive term for somebody regarded as thoughtless, annoying, or objectionable (*slang insult*) ■ *vt* **OFFENSIVE TERM** an offensive term used to express anger with somebody or about something or defiance of somebody or something (*slang*) [Early 19C. Shortening of SODOMITE]

so·da /sṓdə/ *n* **1.** *US* **SOFT DRINK** a flavored and carbonated drink, served cold **2.** BEVERAGES same as **soda water** (sense 1) **3.** **ICE CREAM IN FLAVORED CARBONATED WATER** a refreshment made with flavored carbonated water and ice cream, usually served in a tall glass **4.** **SODIUM** sodium that is chemically combined with other elements **5.** CHEM same as **sodium bicarbonate** **6.** CHEM same as **sodium carbonate** (sense 1) **7.** CHEM same as **sodium hydroxide** **8.** CARDS **CARD THAT STARTS FARO** the card from the top of the pack that is turned face up in the dealing box at the start of the card game faro [15C. Via Italian, "saltwort" (from which sodium carbonate is obtained) < Arabic *suwwād*]

REGIONAL NOTE See *tonic*.

so·da ash *n* sodium carbonate when sold commercially. Use: manufacture of soap and paper.

so·da bis·cuit *n* **1.** a biscuit leavened with baking soda **2.** FOOD same as **soda cracker**

so·da bread *n* bread leavened with soda instead of yeast, associated especially with Irish cooking

so·da crack·er *n* a cracker leavened slightly with baking soda and cream of tartar

so·da foun·tain *n* **1.** a counter or stand where beverages, ice cream, and snacks are sold (*dated*) **2.** a device for dispensing soda water

so·da jerk *n* a server of food and beverages at a soda fountain (*dated slang*)

so·da lime *n* a mixture of sodium hydroxide and calcium hydroxide. Use: moisture and carbon dioxide absorbent.

so·da·list /sṓdəlist/ *n* a member of a sodality

so·da·lite /sṓdə lìt/ *n* a blue, grayish, or yellow translucent aluminosilicate mineral containing sodium and chlorine. Source: alkaline igneous rocks.

so·dal·i·ty /sō dállətee/ (*plural* **-ties**) *n* **1.** a Roman Catholic lay society that is run as a charity or a religious fellowship **2.** an association or fellowship [Early 17C. Directly or via French < Latin *sodalitas* "fellowship" < *sodalis* "fellow, companion"]

so·da ni·ter *n* MINERALS same as **Chile saltpeter**

so·da pop *n US* a flavored and carbonated drink, served cold (*informal*)

so·da si·phon *n UK* same as **siphon bottle**

so·da-straw *adj* offering only a very narrow field of view or means of interpreting events (*slang*) [Late 20C.]

so·da wa·ter *n* **1.** a carbonated water drunk alone or used as a mixer in alcoholic drinks **2.** a weak solution of water, baking soda, and acid, taken to aid digestion

sod·bus·ter /sód bùstər/ *n* **1.** AGRIC same as **farmer 2.** a plow used to break the sod **3.** *Can* a prairie homesteader, especially one raising crops (*informal*)

sod·den /sódd'n/ *adj* **1.** **THOROUGHLY WET** extremely wet and heavy with retained moisture **2.** **DRUNK** having dulled senses as a result of excessive drinking ■ *vti* (**-dened, -den·ing, -dens**) **MAKE OR BECOME SODDEN** to make somebody or something sodden, or become sodden [13C. Obsolete past participle of SEETHE] —**sod·den·ly** *adv*—**sod·den·ness** *n*

SYNONYMS See *wet*.

so·di·um /sṓdee əm/ *n* a soft silver white metallic element that reacts readily with other substances and is essential to the body's fluid balance. Source: common salt, calcium chloride. Use: catalyst, tracer, in chemical processes. Symbol **Na**. See table at **element** [Early 19C. < SODA; from its being isolated from caustic soda]

so·di·um ben·zo·ate *n* a white crystalline powder. Use: food preservative, antiseptic, manufacture of pharmaceuticals. Formula: $C_7H_5O_2Na$.

so·di·um bi·car·bon·ate *n* a white, crystalline, slightly alkaline salt. Use: leavening agent, antacid, in effervescent drinks, fire extinguishers. Formula: $NaHCO_3$.

so·di·um car·bon·ate *n* **1.** a white crystalline salt of carbonic acid. Use: water softener, manufacture of glass, ceramics, cleansing agents, paper. Formula: Na_2CO_3. **2.** CHEM same as **washing soda**

so·di·um chlo·rate *n* a colorless crystalline salt. Use: weed killer, bleaching agent, manufacture of explosives. Formula: $NaClO_3$.

so·di·um chlo·ride *n* a colorless crystalline compound. Source: sea water, halite deposits. Use: preservative, food seasoning. Formula: NaCl.

so·di·um cit·rate *n* a white crystalline salt. Use: photography, buffering agent in foods, anticoagulant in stored blood. Formula: $Na_3C_6H_5O_7$.

so·di·um cy·a·nide *n* a poisonous white salt. Use: fumigant, gold and silver mining, manufacture of steel and dyes. Formula: NaCN.

so·di·um cy·cla·mate *n* CHEM same as **cyclamate**

so·di·um di·chro·mate *n* a red or orange crystalline salt. Use: leather tanning, manufacture of dyes and inks, oxidizing agent, corrosion inhibitor. Formula: $Na_2Cr_2O_7$.

so·di·um fluor·ide *n* a poisonous colorless crystalline salt. Use: pesticide, in metallurgical processes, trace amounts for water fluoridation and tooth decay prevention. Formula: NaF.

so·di·um fluor·o·ac·e·tate *n* a white poisonous powder. Use: killing rats and mice. Formula: $C_2H_2FNaO_2$.

so·di·um glu·ta·mate *n* CHEM same as **monosodium glutamate**

so·di·um hy·drox·ide *n* a brittle white alkaline solid. Use: manufacture of paper, rayon, soap, chemicals, pharmaceuticals. Formula: NaOH.

so·di·um hy·po·chlo·rite *n* a green crystalline unstable salt, usually kept in solution. Use: bleach, disinfectant, water purifier. Formula: NaOCl.

so·di·um hy·po·sul·fite *n* CHEM same as **sodium thiosulfate**

so·di·um ni·trate *n* a white crystalline salt. Use: curing of meats, rocket propellant, fertilizer, manufacture of explosives, pottery, glass enamels. Formula: $NaNO_3$.

so·di·um per·ox·ide *n* a yellowish odorless powder. Use: bleaching agent, antiseptic, disinfectant. Formula: Na_2O_2.

so·di·um phos·phate *n* a sodium salt of phosphoric acid. Use: medical preparations, cleaning agents.

so·di·um pro·pi·o·nate *n* a colorless crystalline powder. Use: spoilage retardant in packaged foods. Formula: $C_3H_5NaO_2$.

so·di·um pump *n* the exchange of sodium ions for potassium ions across a cell membrane

so·di·um sil·i·cate *n* a compound of sodium and silicate, often in solution. Use: preservatives, textile processing, cement.

so·di·um sul·fate *n* a bitter white salt. Use: manufacture of glass, wood pulp, rayon, dyes, detergents, ceramic glazes, cathartics. Formula: Na_2SO_4.

so·di·um thi·o·sul·fate *n* a white crystalline salt. Use: photographic fixer, bleach. Formula: $Na_2S_2O_3$.

so·di·um-va·por lamp *n* an electric lamp containing neon gas and sodium vapor through which a current runs to produce an orange-yellow light used for street lighting

Sod·om /sóddəm/ *n* **1.** in the Bible, a city full of moral corruption and evil that was destroyed along with Gomorrah by God **2.** a place that is regarded as corrupt

sod·om·ite /sóddə mìt/ *n* an offensive term for somebody who practices anal intercourse [14C. Via French and late Latin < Greek *Sodomitēs* "inhabitant of Sodom" < *Sodoma* "Sodom"] —**sod·o·mit·ic** /sòddə míttik/ *adj*

sod·om·ize /sóddə mìz/ (**-ized, -iz·ing, -iz·es**) *vt* an offensive term meaning to have anal intercourse with somebody

sod·om·y /sóddəmee/ *n* **1.** an offensive term for anal intercourse **2.** an offensive term for sexual intercourse with an animal [13C. Directly or via French < medieval Latin *sodomia* < ecclesiastical Latin *peccatum Sodomiticum* "sin of Sodom"]

Sod's Law *n UK* same as **Murphy's Law** (*informal*) [Late 20C. < SOD²]

so·ev·er /sō évvər/ *adv* in any way or to any degree possible

so·fa /sṓfə/ *n* a long upholstered seat that has a back and arms and is made to seat more than one person [Early 17C. Via French < Arabic *ṣuffa* "long bench"]

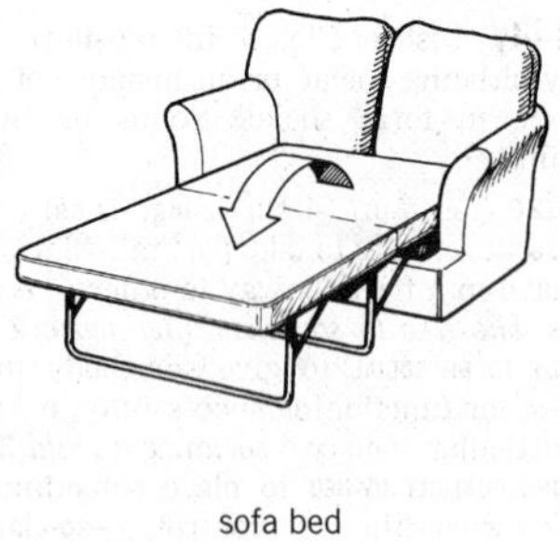

sofa bed

so·fa bed *n* a sofa that can be temporarily converted into a bed as required, e.g., by unfolding its seat

so·far /sṓ faar/ *n* a way of locating survivors at sea by measuring the time it takes sound waves to reach three shore locations from an explosion set off underwater by the survivors [Mid-20C. Acronym < *sound fixing and ranging*]

sof·fit /sóffət/ *n* the underside of a structural component of a building, e.g., the underside of a roof overhang or the inner curve of an arch [Early 17C. Via French *soffite* or Italian *soffitto* < Latin *suffixus* "fastened underneath" (see SUFFIX)]

So·fi·a /sṓfee ə, səfée ə/ capital city of Bulgaria, situated in the Sofia basin, about 40 mi./64 km from the Yugoslavian border. Population: 1,096,389 (2001).

S. of Sol. *abbr* BIBLE Song of Solomon

soft /sawft, soft/ *adj* **1.** **MALLEABLE** easily shaped, bent, or cut **2.** **YIELDING** giving way to externally applied pressure or weight ○ *a soft cushion* **3.** **SMOOTH-TEXTURED** having a texture that is smooth to the touch ○ *soft fur* **4.** **WITH SMOOTH OUTLINE** having no sharp or jagged edges ○ *furniture designed with soft lines* **5.** **QUIET-SOUNDING** quiet and soothing in sound **6.** **EASY ON EYES** lacking glare or intensity of light or color **7.** **MILD** not blowing strongly or falling heavily ○ *a soft rain* **8.** **AFFECTIONATE** conveying love and tenderness **9.** **EMOTIONAL** easily moved to tender emotions **10.** **COWARDLY** lacking determination or strength of character **11.** **LENIENT** lenient in treatment or punishment, often too lenient **12.** **UNDEMANDING** requiring little effort or attention (*informal*) ○ *a soft job* **13.** **NOT WELL TONED** out of good physical condition **14.** **INCAPABLE OF ENDURING HARDSHIP** unable or unwilling to put up with hardship or privation, especially from having lived a life of ease **15.** **LACKING GOOD SENSE** lacking intelligence or sound judgment (*informal*) **16.** **LACKING SIGNIFICANCE** dealing with other than serious issues or facts ○ *soft news* **17.** **NOT EASILY VERIFIABLE** relating to, dealing with, or based on data that is not easily proved or disproved using scientific method **18.** **NOT COERCIVE** based on negotiation, flexibility, and good will rather than on coercion ○ *a soft sell* **19.** same as **soft-core** **20.** **VULNERABLE** unprotected against violent attack **21.** MIL **UNARMORED** describes military vehicles and sites with little or no protection against military attack **22.** FIN **RELATING TO PAPER MONEY** relating to currency or a monetary system that is not backed by gold and is therefore not easily convertible to a foreign currency **23.** COMM **DECLINING ECONOMICALLY** exhibiting a downward trend, e.g., in price, demand, or economic activity **24.** PHON **SIBILANT OR FRICATIVE** describes the consonant sounds "c" and "g" when pronounced as a fricative, as in "dance" and "age," instead of as a stop, as in "cat" and "get" **25.** PHON **PALATALIZED** describes a consonant that is palatalized in a Slavic language **26.** PHYS **LOW-ENERGY** describes radiation that has low energy and lacks penetrating ability ■ *adv* **SOFTLY** in a quiet, tender, or lenient way ■ *n* **SOMETHING SOFT** a soft thing or part of something

[Old English *sōfte* (earlier *sēfte*) < Germanic] —**soft·ly** *adv* —**soft·ness** *n* ◇ **be soft on somebody** to be romantically attracted to somebody

soft·back /sáwft bàk, sóft-/ *n, adj* PUBL same as **paperback** *n, adj*

soft·ball /sáwft bàwl, sóft-/ *n* **1.** baseball played with a larger softer ball on a smaller field, between two teams of ten people **2.** the ball used to play softball

soft-boiled *adj* **1.** describes an egg that is boiled so that the yolk is soft, but the white is firm **2.** having or showing a sympathetic or sentimental nature

soft·bound /sáwft bòwnd, sóft-/ *adj US* PUBL same as **paperback**

soft chan·cre *n* MED same as **chancroid** (sense 2)

soft coal *n* INDUST same as **bituminous coal**

soft-coat·ed wheat·en ter·ri·er *n* a terrier with a soft wavy pale-golden coat and a docked tail, belonging to a medium-sized breed that originated in Ireland

soft cop·y *n* data stored on a computer disk, as distinct from data that is printed on paper

soft-core *adj* sexually suggestive or provocative without being explicit

soft·cov·er /sáwft kùvvər, sóft-/ *n, adj* PUBL same as **paperback** *n, adj*

soft drink *n* a nonalcoholic and usually carbonated beverage, usually served chilled

soft drug *n* an illegal drug that is thought by some to be less addictive and harmful than the narcotic drugs heroin and cocaine

soft·en /sáwfən, sóffən/ (**-ened, -en·ing, -ens**) *vti* **1.** MAKE OR BECOME LESS HARD to become soft or softer, or make something soft or softer **2.** BE KINDER to become gentler or less harsh, or make something gentler or less harsh **3.** WEAR SOMEBODY DOWN to make somebody's resolve less firm, or become less firmly resolved **4.** HARASS ENEMY to weaken an enemy's resistance or morale by continuous bombardment, or be weakened in this way **5.** REDUCE SOMETHING to decline, e.g., in price, demand, or economic activity, or make something do this

soft·en·er /sáwfənər, sóff-/ *n* a substance added to something such as water or laundry to make it softer

soft fo·cus *n* a deliberate slight blurring of a photograph or a filmed image, giving it a hazy appearance, in order to achieve a special effect such as romance or nostalgia (*hyphenated before a noun*)

soft gam·ma re·peat·er *n* ASTRON same as **magnetar**

soft goods *npl* textiles and the items such as clothing and bedding that are made from them

soft hail *n* METEOROL same as **graupel**

soft-heart·ed *adj* showing sympathy, kindness, or generosity —**soft-heart·ed·ly** *adv* —**soft-heart·ed·ness** *n*

soft·ie *n* another spelling of **softy**

soft-kill *adj US* intended to disable, not kill, an enemy

soft land·ing *n* a landing of a spacecraft, especially on the moon, without enough impact to cause damage

soft mon·ey *n* political funds raised from unions, corporations, and wealthy donors outside the restrictions of the Bipartisan Campaign Reform Act of 2002, which can be used to fund political parties at state rather than federal level

soft pal·ate *n* the fleshy rear portion of the roof of the mouth, extending from the hard palate at the front and tapering to the hanging uvula at the rear. It elevates to close off the nasal passages when swallowing, sucking, and pronouncing some sounds.

soft ped·al *n* a pedal on a piano that reduces the usual volume. It shifts the hammers so that they do not strike all the strings of each note or so that they strike the strings with less force.

soft-ped·al *vti* **1.** to reduce the volume of music played on a piano by operating the soft pedal **2.** to try to make something seem less important, noticeable, or objectionable (*informal*)

soft rock *n* rock music that tends to be slower and more melodic than hard rock, often influenced by folk or country and western music

soft rot *n* a bacterial or fungal plant disease that causes plant parts, especially fruits and vegetables, to decay into a pulpy mass

soft sell *n* a method of selling or advertising goods and services that uses subtlety and persuasion, rather than aggressive insistence (*informal*; *hyphenated before a noun*)

soft-shell *adj* used to describe an animal that lives in water and has a soft or thin and brittle shell, sometimes as a result of having recently molted

soft-shelled tur·tle *n* a freshwater turtle with sharp claws, a pointed snout, and a soft flat shell covered with leathery skin. Family: Trionychidae.

soft-shoe *n* tap dancing for which soft-soled shoes without metal taps are worn (*often used before a noun*)

soft shoul·der *n* a soft strip of ground alongside a road

soft soap *n* **1.** flattery used for the purpose of persuading or distracting somebody (*informal*) **2.** a liquid or semiliquid soap, usually made with potassium hydroxide

soft-soap *vt* to use flattery to persuade or distract somebody (*informal*)

soft-spo·ken *adj* speaking or said with a quiet gentle voice

soft spot *n* a place, position, or area in which something is weak or vulnerable ◇ **have a soft spot for somebody** *or* **something** to have especially tender feelings or affection for somebody or something

soft top *n UK* same as **ragtop**

soft touch *n* somebody who can be easily persuaded to do something such as give a loan or handout

soft·ware /sáwft wér, sóft-/ *n* programs and applications that can be run on a computer system, e.g., word processing or database packages (*often used before a noun*)

soft·ware en·gi·neer·ing *n* the application of mathematics and technology to the design, implementation, and testing of computer programs to optimize their production and support

soft·ware pi·ra·cy *n* the illegal duplication of copyrighted software or the installation of copyrighted software on more computers than authorized under terms of the software license agreement

soft wa·ter *n* naturally occurring or treated water in which soap lathers easily because of low levels of calcium and magnesium salts

soft wheat *n* wheat with soft kernels and weak gluten that is relatively low in protein. Use: cakes, cookies, pastries, livestock feed.

soft·wood /sáwft wòŏd, sóft-/ *n* **1.** the open-grained wood of a pine, cedar, or other coniferous tree. Many softwoods are, in fact, hard and durable. **2.** a tree that yields softwood, e.g., a pine or cedar

soft·y /sáwftee, sóftee/ (*plural* **-ies**), **soft·ie** *n* somebody regarded as weak, timid, or sentimental (*informal*)

Sog·di·an /sógdee ən/ *n* **1.** a member of a people who lived in Central Asia **2.** the extinct Iranian language of the Sogdian people [Mid-16C. Via Latin < Greek *Sogdianos* < Old Persian *Suguda*] —**Sog·di·an** *adj*

sog·gy /sóggee, sáwgee/ (**-gi·er, -gi·est**) *adj* **1.** THOROUGHLY WET soaked through with moisture **2.** WITH TOO MUCH LIQUID unpleasantly wet and heavy in texture **3.** UNINTERESTING lacking animation or vitality [Early 18C. < obsolete *sog* "area of marshy ground"] —**sog·gi·ly** *adv* —**sog·gi·ness** *n*

Sog·ne Fjord /sóngnə-/ inlet of the North Sea in southwestern Norway. Length: 125 mi./200 km.

soh /sō/ *n UK* MUSIC same as **sol**[1]

So·ho /sṓhō/ *n* **1.** *also* **So·Ho** an area of the lower west side of Manhattan well known for its art studios and galleries **2.** an area of central London well known for its theaters, restaurants, and clubs [In sense 1 < SOUTH + *Houston Street*]

soi-di·sant /swaàdee zaàN, -zaán/ *adj* self-styled or so-called [< French, "saying yourself"]

soi·gné /swaa nyáy, swaà nyay/, **soi·gnée** *adj* **1.** neat and elegant in dress and appearance **2.** designed or furnished in an elegant style [Early 19C. < French, past participle of *soigner* "care for" < Germanic]

soil[1] /soyl/ *n* **1.** TOP LAYER OF LAND the top layer of most of the Earth's land surface, consisting of the unconsolidated products of rock erosion and organic decay, along with bacteria and fungi (*often used before a noun*) **2.** TYPE OF EARTH earth or ground of a particular kind ○ *sandy soil* **3.** COUNTRY a country or state (*literary*) ○ *their native soil* **4.** FARMING agricultural life and work (*literary*) **5.** NURTURING MEDIUM a medium in which growth and development takes place (*literary*) [13C. Via Anglo-Norman, "piece of land" < Latin *solium* "seat," by association with *solum* "ground, soil"]

soil[2] /soyl/ *vt* (**soiled, soil·ing, soils**) **1.** MAKE DIRTY to make somebody or something dirty or stained **2.** BRING DISHONOR ON SOMEBODY to damage somebody's reputation, character, or good name ■ *n* **1.** DIRT dirt or dirtiness ○ *remove soil from linens* **2.** MORAL CORRUPTION immoral behavior or lack of moral standards (*literary*) [13C. < Old French *soill(i)er* "to soil, wallow"]

SYNONYMS See *dirty*.

soil[3] /soyl/ *n* excrement or sewage [15C. < Old French *souille* "muddy place" < *soill(i)er* "to soil, wallow"]

soil bank *n* land retired from crop production and planted with soil-building plants under a program that provides subsidies for the retired land

soiled /soyld/ *adj* stained or marked, especially during normal use

SYNONYMS See *dirty*.

soil·ure /sóylyər/ *n* the soiling or staining of something (*literary*) [14C. < Old French *soilleure* < *soillier* "to soil, wallow"]

soi·ree /swaa ráy/, **soi·rée** *n* a party or gathering held in the evening, especially in somebody's home [Late 18C. < *French*, < *soir* "evening" < Latin *sero* "at a late hour" < *serus* "late"]

soix·ante-neuf /swaàs aaN nő́f/ *n* same as **sixty-nine** (*slang offensive*) [< French, "sixty-nine"; from the position of the couple]

so·journ /sṓ jùrn/ (*literary*) *n* a short stay at a place ■ *vi* (**-journed, -journ·ing, -journs**) to stay at a place for a time [13C. < Anglo-Norman *sujurn*, Old French *sojorn* < Old French *sojourner* "spend the day" < Latin *sub-* "under" + late Latin *diurnum* "day"] —**so·journ·er** *n*

So·ko·to /sṓkə tṓ/ capital city of Sokoto State, northwestern Nigeria, situated about 300 mi./483 km northwest of Abuja. Population: 199,900 (1995).

sol[1] /sōl/ *n* a syllable that represents the fifth note in a scale when singing solfeggio. In fixed solfeggio it represents the note G. [14C. < medieval Latin, shortening of Latin *solve* "purge!, release!", word sung to this note in a medieval hymn]

sol[2] /sawl, sōl/ *n* a liquid colloidal solution [Late 19C. Shortening of SOLUTION]

sol[3] /sol/ *n* a copper or silver coin formerly used in France, worth 12 deniers [Late 16C. < obsolete French, shortening of Latin *solidus* (see SOLDIER)]

sol[4] /sōl/ (*plural* **sol·es** /sṓlays/) *n* the main unit of currency in Peru. See table at **currency** [< Spanish, literally "sun" < Latin]

Sol /sol/ *n* **1.** the personification of the Sun (*literary*) **2.** in Roman mythology, the god of the Sun. Greek equivalent **Helios** [14C. < Latin, "sun"]

so·la[1] /sṓlə/ *adj* used as a stage direction to indicate that a girl or woman character appears alone on stage [stage Mid-18C. <. Latin, form of *solus* "alone"]

so·la[2] GEOG plural of **solum**

sol·ace /sólləss/ *n* **1.** RELIEF FROM EMOTIONAL DISTRESS comfort at a time of sadness, grief, or disappointment **2.** SOURCE OF COMFORT somebody or something that provides comfort at a time of sadness, grief, or disappointment ■ *vt* (**-aced, -ac·ing, -ac·es**) PROVIDE SOMEBODY WITH COMFORT to comfort somebody at a time of sadness, grief, or disappointment [13C. Via French < Latin *solatium* < *solari* "to comfort"] —**sol·ac·er** *n*

so·lan /sṓlən/, **so·lan goose** *n* a bird of the gannet family having a white body, yellowish head, and black wingtips. Native to: North Atlantic. Latin name: *Morus bassanus.* [15C. Probably < Old Norse *súla* "gannet" + *and-* "duck"]

sol·a·na·ceous /sòllə náyshəss/ *adj* relating to or belonging to the nightshade family of plants, a family that includes the potato, tomato, and tobacco [Early 19C. < modern Latin *Solanaceae* < Latin *solanum* (see SOLANUM)]

so·la·nine /sṓlə nèen/ *n* a bitter poisonous alkaloid found in several plants of the nightshade family. Use: formerly to treat epilepsy, bronchitis, asthma. Formula: $C_{45}H_{73}NO_{15}$.

so·la·num /sə láanəm/ (*plural* **-nums** or *same*) *n* a plant of the nightshade family, e.g., the potato or eggplant. Genus: *Solanum.* [Late 16C. Via modern Latin < Latin < *sol* "sun"]

so·lar /sṓlər/ *adj* **1. FROM SUN** relating to or originating from the Sun **2. OPERATING USING ENERGY FROM SUN** using the Sun's radiation as a source of energy **3. MEASURED BY SUN'S POSITION** measured with reference to the Earth's movement in relation to the Sun [15C. < Latin *solaris* < *sol* "sun"]

so·lar a·pex *n* the point in space toward which the Sun appears to be moving, located in the constellation Hercules

so·lar bat·ter·y *n* an arrangement of several solar cells for converting solar radiation into electricity

so·lar cell *n* an electric cell that converts solar radiation directly into electricity. Solar cells are mounted on solar panels used on satellites and spacecraft.

so·lar con·stant *n* the average amount of solar radiation received at the outer atmosphere at the Earth's mean distance from the Sun, equal to 0.140 watt per square centimeter

so·lar cy·cle *n* a cycle in the Sun's activity lasting on average 11 years, during which changes in the Sun's internal magnetic field occur. Sunspot activity is greatest in the middle of the cycle.

so·lar day *n* the time taken for the Earth to make a complete revolution on its axis, measured with respect to the Sun

so·lar e·clipse *n* an eclipse in which the Moon blocks all or part of the Sun's light from reaching the Earth's surface, because it passes directly between the Earth and the Sun

so·lar en·er·gy *n* **1.** energy radiated from the Sun in the form of heat and light, used by green plants for photosynthesis and harnessed as solar power **2.** energy obtained from radiation emitted by the Sun

so·lar flare *n* a brief sudden eruption of high-energy hydrogen gas from the surface of the Sun, associated with sunspots. It causes interruptions of communication systems on Earth.

so·lar fur·nace *n* a furnace equipped with a series of concave mirrors that are motorized to follow the Sun and focus its radiation to obtain and maintain extremely high temperatures

so·lar gain *n* the amount of heat produced in a building by solar radiation, e.g., through windows or transparent walls

so·lar heat·ing *n* the use of radiation emitted by the Sun to heat water or air that is passed through heat-absorbing panels

so·lar·i·a LEISURE plural of **solarium**

so·lar·im·e·ter /sṑlə rímmətər/ *n* an instrument used to measure solar radiation

so·lar·i·um /sə lérree əm, sō-/ (*plural* **-i·a** /-ee ə/ or **-i·ums**) *n* a room built for the purpose of enjoying sunlight, usually with large windows or glass walls, especially a room in a hospital or other health care establishment [Mid-19C. < Latin, "sundial, terrace" < *sol* "sun"]

so·lar·ize /sṓlə rīz/ (**-ized, -iz·ing, -iz·es**) *vt* **1.** to affect or damage something with solar radiation **2.** to overexpose photographic materials to light for deliberate effect, usually in order to exaggerate highlights —**so·lar·i·za·tion** /sṑləri záysh'n/ *n*

so·lar month *n* one-twelfth of a solar year, equal to 30 days, 10 hours, 29 minutes, 3.8 seconds

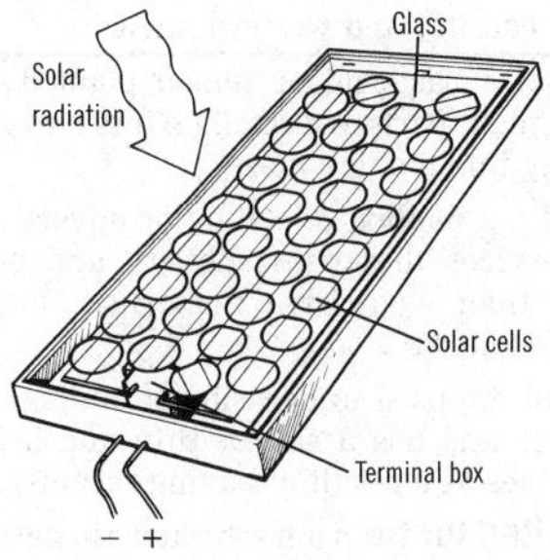

solar panel

so·lar pan·el *n* a large panel containing solar cells or heat-absorbing plates that convert the Sun's radiation into energy for use, e.g., in heating buildings and powering satellites and spacecraft

so·lar plex·us *n* **1.** a mass of nerve cells in the upper abdomen behind the stomach, kidneys, and other internal organs **2.** a point on the upper abdomen just below where the ribs separate. A sharp blow to this region can cause loss of consciousness. [< its radial network of nerves]

so·lar sys·tem *n* the Sun and all the planets, satellites, asteroids, meteors, and comets that are subject to its gravitational pull

so·lar wind /-wínd/ *n* the flow of high-speed ionized particles from the Sun's surface into interplanetary space

so·lar year *n* the time taken for the Earth to move around the Sun, equal to 365 days, 5 hours, 48 minutes, 45.51 seconds

so·la·tion /sō láysh'n/ *n* the process of changing from a gel to a liquid [Early 20C. < SOL[2]]

so·la·ti·um /sə láyshee əm/ (*plural* **-ti·a** /-shee ə/) *n* damages awarded for emotional suffering, as opposed to financial loss or physical injury or suffering [Early 19C. < Latin (see SOLACE)]

sold past participle, past tense of **sell**

sol·der /sóddər/ *n* **1. ALLOY FOR JOINING METAL** an alloy with a low melting point, usually a mixture of tin and lead, used to solder electrical components to a circuit board or to join metal objects together **2. SOMETHING THAT UNITES** something that forms a bond or union ■ *vti* (**-dered, -der·ing, -ders**) **1. JOIN THINGS WITH SOLDER** to work with solder, or join things using solder **2. UNITE TO FORM WHOLE** to come together in unity, or establish a bond of unity between people or things [14C. < French *soudure* < *souder* "fasten together" < Latin *solidare* < *solidus* "solid"] —**sol·der·er** *n*

sol·der·ing i·ron /sóddəring-/ *n* a tool with a point that is heated for melting and applying solder

sol·di COINS plural of **soldo**

~~**soldiar**~~ incorrect spelling of **soldier**

sol·dier /sṓljər/ *n* **1. SOMEBODY SERVING IN ARMY** somebody who serves in a military organization **2. ARMY MEMBER BELOW OFFICER RANK** a member of an army, of a rank below commissioned officer **3. DEDICATED WORKER** somebody who works with dedication for a cause **4. SKILLED WARRIOR** a skilled and experienced fighter or military strategist **5. ANT THAT PROTECTS COLONY** a sterile member of an ant or termite colony with a large head and powerful jaws. Its role is to defend the colony. ■ *vi* (**-diered, -dier·ing, -diers**) **1. SERVE IN ARMY** to serve as a soldier in an army **2. PRETEND TO WORK** to give the appearance of working while really idling [13C. < Old French, "somebody having pay" < *soulde* "(soldier's) pay" < Latin *solidus (nummus)* "Roman gold coin," literally "solid (coin)"] —**sol·dier·ly** *adj*

CULTURAL NOTE ***The Good Soldier,*** a novel (1915) by Ford Madox Ford. Considered Ford's masterpiece, it describes an American couple's tragic involvement with an English army captain (the good soldier of the title) and his domineering wife. A powerful study of the conflict between sexuality and contemporary moral values, it is admired in particular for its innovative and intricate narrative structure.

soldier on *vi* to persevere despite difficulties or setbacks

sol·dier of for·tune *n* somebody who joins or serves in an army for profit or adventure

sol·diers' home *n US* an institution funded by the government for the care of war veterans

sol·dier·y /sṓljəree/ *n* **1.** soldiers as a group **2.** the profession or skill of a soldier

sol·do /sáwldō/ (*plural* **-di** /-dee/) *n* a copper coin used in the former Italian states until the 19th century, worth one-twentieth of a lira [Late 16C. Via Italian < Latin *solidus (nummus)* "Roman gold coin," literally "solid (coin)"]

Sol·dot·na /sol dótnə/ city in southern Alaska, on the Kenai Peninsula, southwest of Anchorage. Population: 3,947 (2002 estimate).

sold-out *adj* describes an entertainment venue or performance for which all available tickets have been sold

sole[1] /sōl/ *n* **1. BOTTOM OF FOOT** the underside of the foot from the toes to the heel **2. BOTTOM OF SHOE** the underside of a shoe, boot, or other piece of footwear, sometimes excluding the heel **3. BOTTOM SURFACE OF GOLF CLUB** the underside of the head of a golf club ■ *vt* (**soled, sol·ing, soles**) **1. PUT SOLE ON SHOE** to put a sole on a shoe, boot, or other piece of footwear **2. PLACE GOLF CLUB ON GROUND** to put the sole of a golf club on the ground in preparation for a stroke [14C. Via French < Latin *solea* "sandal" < *solum* "foot"]

SPELLCHECK sole or **soul**? Do not confuse the spelling of ***sole*** and ***soul,*** which sound similar. There are several words spelled ***sole***: one means "the underside of the foot or of a shoe," and can also be used as a verb meaning "put a sole on a shoe"; another is a noun denoting a fish; a third is an adjective meaning "only" or "exclusive" (as in *the sole reason, sole responsibility*). ***Soul*** is a noun meaning "a person's nonphysical aspect or spirit," "spiritual depth," or simply "a person," as in *heart and soul, a novel that lacks soul, not a soul to be seen.* ***Soul*** is also used in such compounds as *soul-destroying, soul mate, soul music,* and *soul-searching.*

sole[2] /sōl/ *adj* **1. ONLY** only one ○ *the sole reason* **2. EXCLUSIVE** belonging to one person or group ○ *has sole responsibility for the department* **3. UNFETTERED** free from the interference of others **4.** LAW **UNMARRIED** having no husband or wife [13C. Via French < Latin *sola,* form of *solus*] —**sole·ness** *n*

SPELLCHECK See ***sole***[1].

sole[3] /sōl/ (*plural* **soles** or *same*) *n* **1.** a brownish ocean fish with a small mouth and both eyes on the upper side of its flat body. It is valued as a food fish. Family: Soleidae. **2.** the flesh of a sole or a similar fish, as food [14C. Via French < Provençal *sola* < Latin *solea* "sandal" (see SOLE[1])]

SPELLCHECK See ***sole***[1].

sol·e·cism /sóllə sizzəm, sṓlə-/ *n* **1. GRAMMATICAL MISTAKE** a mistake in grammar or syntax **2. ERROR** something incorrect, inappropriate, or inconsistent **3. BREACH OF GOOD MANNERS** an action that breaks the rules of etiquette or good manners [Mid-16C. Directly or via French < Latin *soloecismus* < Greek *soloikismos* < *soloikos* "speaking incorrectly," literally "of Soloi" (in ancient Cilicia, E Turkey), whose colonial Attic dialect was considered barbarous] —**sol·e·cist** *n* —**sol·e·cis·ti·cal** /sòllə sístik'l, sṑlə-/ *adj* —**sol·e·cis·ti·cal·ly** *adv*

sole·ly /sṓl lee/ *adv* **1.** for nothing other than ○ *sold the company solely for commercial reasons* **2.** to the exclusion of all else or others ○ *He is solely to blame.*

~~**solemly**~~ incorrect spelling of **solemnly**

sol·emn /sólləm/ *adj* **1. EARNEST** having or showing sincerity and gravity **2. HUMORLESS** having or showing no joy or humor **3. FORMAL** characterized by ceremony or formality **4. RELIGIOUS** observed with sacred or religious ceremony **5. AWE-INSPIRING** inspiring wonder or reverence [14C. Via French < Latin *sol(l)emnis* "customary, religious," < *sollus* "whole, entire" + an unknown element] —**sol·emn·ly** *adv* —**sol·emn·ness** *n*

so·lem·ni·fy /sə lémnə fī/ (**-fied, -fy·ing, -fies**) *vt* to make something solemn or serious

so·lem·ni·ty /sə lémnətee/ (*plural* **-ties**) *n* **1. SOLEMN QUALITY** the solemn nature or quality of something **2. SOLEMN CEREMONY** a formal or solemn ceremony held to observe an occasion or event (*often used in the* *plural)* 3. LAW **LEGAL FORMALITY** a formality that must be complied with before a contract or agreement can become effective

sol·em·nize /sólləm nīz/ (**-nized, -niz·ing, -niz·es**) *v* 1. *vt* **CELEBRATE WITH CEREMONY** to observe an event or occasion with ceremony or formality 2. *vt* **PERFORM A MARRIAGE CEREMONY** to celebrate a marriage with a religious ceremony 3. *vt* **MAKE DIGNIFIED** to bring dignity or formality to something 4. *vi* **SPEAK SOLEMNLY** to speak or reflect with great seriousness —**sol·em·ni·za·tion** /sòlləmni záysh'n/ *n*

so·le·no·don /sō léenə dòn, -lénnə-/ *n* a rare nocturnal insect-eating mammal with a long snout and a long scaly tail. Native to: Caribbean. Family: Solenodontidae. [Mid-19C. < modern Latin, literally "pipe tooth" < Greek *sōlēn* "pipe, channel"]

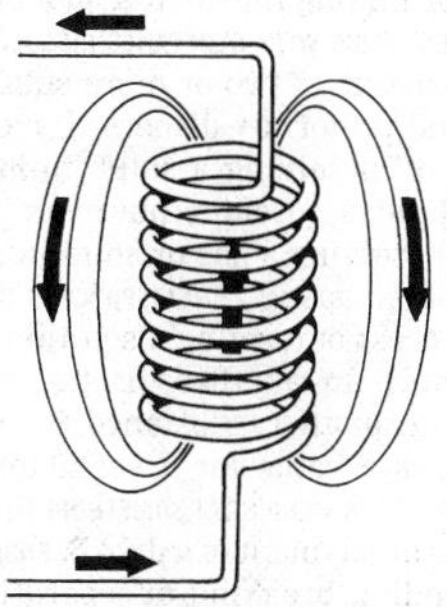

solenoid

so·le·noid /sōlə nòyd/ *n* a device consisting of a cylindrical coil of wire surrounding a movable iron core that moves along the length of the coil when an electric current is passed through it. Solenoids are used as switches and relays, e.g., in a motor vehicle to complete the circuit between the battery and starter motor. [Early 19C. < French *solénoïde* "pipe-shaped" < Greek *sōlēn* "pipe, channel"] —**so·le·noi·dal** /sōlə nóyd'l/ *adj* —**so·le·noi·dal·ly** *adv*

So·lent /sōlənt/ arm of the English Channel separating the Isle of Wight from mainland England. Length: 15 mi./24 km.

sole·plate /sōl plàyt/ *n* 1. the underside of an iron for pressing clothes 2. the plate that supports the bases of the studs used in framing a wall

sole pro·pri·e·tor *n* an individual who is the sole owner of a business that is neither a partnership nor a company —**sole pro·pri·e·tor·ship** *n*

sole trad·er *n UK* same as **sole proprietor**

so·le·us /sōlee əss/ (*plural* **-le·i** /-lee ī/) *n* a broad flat muscle in the calf of the leg that helps to flex the ankle and depress the sole of the foot [Late 17C. < modern Latin < Latin *solea* "sandal" (see SOLE[1])]

sol-fa /sōl fàa/ *n* MUSIC same as **tonic sol-fa** ■ *vti* (**sol-faed, sol-fa·ing, sol-fas**) to sing a tune using the sol-fa syllables

sol·fa·ta·ra /sòlfə taàrə/ *n* a vent in a volcano through which sulfur-rich gases and steam escape, leaving bright yellow sulfur deposits [Late 18C. < Italian, "sulfurous volcano" < *solfo* "sulfur" < Latin *sulfur*] —**sol·fa·ta·ric** *adj*

sol·fège *n* MUSIC same as **solfeggio** [Early 20C. Via French < Italian *solfeggio* (see SOLFEGGIO)]

sol·feg·gio /sol féjj ō, sōl-/ (*plural* **-gi** /-jee/ or **-gios**) *n* an exercise in singing using the sol-fa syllables [Late 18C. < Italian < *sol-fa* "sol-fa"]

sol·fe·ri·no /sòlfə réenō/ *adj* of a purplish red color [Mid-19C. After *Solferino*, Italian town near which a battle was fought just before the dye was discovered] —**sol·fe·ri·no** *n*

so·li ARTS plural of **solo**

so·lic·it /sə líssit/ (**-it·ed, -it·ing, -its**) *v* 1. *vti* **PLEAD FOR SOMETHING** to try to get something by making insistent requests or pleas 2. *vt* **ASK SOMEBODY FOR SOMETHING** to plead with or petition a person or group for something 3. *vti* **OFFER SEX FOR MONEY** to offer to participate in sexual activities with somebody in return for money 4. *vt* **GET SOMEBODY TO DO SOMETHING WRONG** to attempt to draw somebody into participating in illegal or immoral acts [15C. Via French < Latin *sollicitare* "disturb" < *sollicitus* "completely moved" < *sollus* "whole" + *citus*, past participle of *ciere* "move"] —**so·lic·i·ta·tion** /sə lìssə táysh'n/ *n*

so·lic·i·tor /sə líssətər/ *n* 1. **TOP LEGAL OFFICER** the chief officer for legal matters in a city, town, or county, or in a government department 2. **SOMEBODY WHO SOLICITS CONTRIBUTIONS** somebody who solicits something, especially financial contributions 3. *UK* **LAWYER** a lawyer who gives legal advice, draws up legal documents, and does preparatory work for barristers. A solicitor who holds an advocacy qualification may also represent clients in court. —**so·lic·i·tor·ship** *n*

so·lic·i·tor gen·er·al (*plural* **so·lic·i·tors gen·er·al**) *n* 1. a law officer appointed to assist the attorney general, and whose primary responsibility is to present the government's case to the Supreme Court 2. a high-ranking law officer equivalent to a state attorney general

So·lic·i·tor Gen·er·al (*plural* **So·lic·i·tors Gen·er·al**) *n Can* a member of a federal or provincial cabinet responsible for law enforcement, prisons, and some forms of licensing

so·lic·i·tous /sə líssətəss/ *adj* 1. **CONCERNED** expressing an attitude of concern and consideration 2. **READY AND WILLING** full of eagerness to do something 3. **METICULOUS** paying very careful attention to details [Mid-16C. < Latin *sollicitus* (see SOLICIT)] —**so·lic·i·tous·ly** *adv* —**so·lic·i·tous·ness** *n*

so·lic·i·tude /sə líssə tòod/ *n* 1. concern and consideration shown for somebody or something 2. a cause of concern or uneasiness (*often used in the plural*)

sol·id /sólləd/ *adj* 1. **NOT SOFT OR YIELDING** consisting of compact unyielding material 2. **NOT HOLLOW** having no open interior spaces 3. **UNADULTERATED OR UNMIXED** made of the same material throughout 4. **OF STRONG AND SECURE CONSTRUCTION** built out of strong substantial material and not likely to break or collapse 5. **UNINTERRUPTED** continuing without breaks or openings ○ *It took a solid two hours to crack the code.* 6. **NOURISHING** providing ample nourishment 7. **UNANIMOUS** in complete agreement ○ *Support for the amendment was solid.* 8. **RELIABLE** able to be relied or depended upon 9. **FINANCIALLY SECURE** in sound financial condition 10. MATH **THREE-DIMENSIONAL** having the three dimensions of length, breadth, and depth, or relating to geometric figures that have three dimensions 11. CHEM **RETAINING ITS SHAPE** of a shape that resists change, unlike a liquid or gas 12. LANGUAGE **AS SINGLE WORD** written as one word without a space or hyphen 13. PRINTING **WITHOUT SPACES** without spaces between lines of type in printing ■ *n* 1. **SOLID THING** something that is solid 2. MATH **SOLID FIGURE** a three-dimensional geometric figure or object 3. CHEM **SUBSTANCE THAT RETAINS SHAPE** a substance that resists change in shape, unlike a liquid or gas [14C. Directly or via French < Latin *solidus* "firm, whole"] —**so·lid·i·ty** /sə líddətee/ *n* —**sol·id·ly** *adv* —**sol·id·ness** *n*

sol·id an·gle *n* a three-dimensional angle formed at the vertex of a cone or the intersection of three planes

sol·i·dar·i·ty /sòllə dárrətee/ *n* harmony of interests and responsibilities among individuals in a group, especially as manifested in unanimous support and collective action for something [Mid-19C. < French *solidarité* < *solidaire* < *solide* "solid"]

Sol·i·dar·i·ty /sòllə dárrətee/ *n* a federation of trade unions in Poland, founded in 1980. Under the leadership of Lech Walesa, it challenged the Soviet-backed government of the day. [Late 20C. Translation of Polish *Solidarność*]

sol·id ge·om·e·try *n* the branch of geometry that deals with three-dimensional figures

sol·i·di PRINTING, COINS plural of **solidus**

so·lid·i·fy /sə líddə fī/ (**-fied, -fy·ing, -fies**) *vti* 1. to become compact or firm, or make something compact or firm 2. to become strong and united, or make something strong and united —**so·lid·i·fi·a·ble** *adj* —**so·lid·i·fi·ca·tion** /sə lìddəfi káysh'n/ *n* —**so·lid·i·fi·er** *n*

sol·id of rev·o·lu·tion *n* a three-dimensional mathematical figure formed by rotating a plane figure around an axis in its plane

sol·id smoke *n* a silica-based porous solid (**aerogel**) that is extremely light because it is 99.8% air

sol·id so·lu·tion *n* a crystalline substance in which different kinds of atoms or molecules share the same structure, e.g., an alloy

sol·id-state *adj* 1. working by means of the flow of electric current through solid material, as in semiconductors and transistors. The term is usually used to distinguish modern electronic equipment from earlier devices that made use of vacuum tubes or heated filaments. 2. relating to the electronic characteristics of solids, especially at the atomic or molecular level

sol·i·dus /sólləd əss/ (*plural* **-di** /-dī/) *n* 1. *Can, UK* a line sloping from right to left, used to separate items of information in dates, in fractions, and in presenting alternatives, as in "and/or" (*technical*) US term **virgule** 2. a gold coin used in the Roman Empire from the 4th century B.C. It remained in use in Europe until the 12th century A.D. [14C. < Latin *solidus (nummus)* (see SOLDIER)]

so·li·fluc·tion /sōlə flúksh'n/ *n* the slow movement of soil downhill as a result of water saturation after rainfall or the melting of ice [Early 20C. < Latin *solum* "ground" + *fluct-*, past participle of *fluere* "flow"]

So·li·hull /sōlee húl, sóllee hùl/ city in the Midlands, near Birmingham, central England. Population: 203,922 (1996).

so·lil·o·quize /sə líllə kwīz/ (**-quized, -quiz·ing, -quiz·es**) *vi* to speak a soliloquy in the course of a play —**so·lil·o·quist** *n* —**so·lil·o·quiz·er** *n*

so·lil·o·quy /sə lílləkwee/ (*plural* **-quies**) *n* 1. the act of speaking while alone, especially when used as a theatrical device that allows a character's thoughts and ideas to be conveyed to the audience 2. a section of a play or other drama in which a soliloquy is spoken [14C. < late Latin *soliloquium* "a speaking alone" < Latin *solus* "alone" + *loqui* "speak"]

So·ling·en /zṓlingən/ city in North Rhine-Westphalia State, west central Germany. Population: 165,973 (1997).

sol·ip·sism /sólləp sìzzəm, sṓləp-/ *n* the belief that the only thing somebody can be sure of is that he or she exists, and that true knowledge of anything else is impossible [Late 19C. < Latin *solus* "alone" + *ipse* "self"] —**sol·ip·sist** *n* —**sol·ip·sis·tic** /sòlləp sístik, sōləp-/ *adj* —**sol·ip·sis·ti·cal·ly** *adv*

sol·i·taire /sóllə tèr/ *n* 1. CARDS **CARD GAME FOR ONE** a card game played by one person, the object of which is to form sequences of cards, using up all the cards from several piles dealt face down 2. JEWELRY **SINGLE GEMSTONE** a gem, especially a diamond, that is set alone in a ring 3. BIRDS **SONGBIRD** a songbird of the thrush family. Native to: North and Central America, Caribbean. Genus: *Myadestes*. [14C. Via French, "recluse" < Latin *solitarius* (see SOLITARY)]

sol·i·tar·y /sóllə tèrree/ *adj* 1. **DONE ALONE** done without the company of other people 2. **SHUNNING COMPANY** preferring to be or live alone 3. **SECLUDED** in a remote location, apart from others 4. **SINGLE** existing as the only one of its kind ○ *a solitary boat on the sea* 5. ZOOL **NOT LIVING IN SOCIAL GROUPS** describes animals that live alone or in pairs rather than in colonies or social groups 6. BOT **GROWING SINGLY** describes flowers that grow singly rather than as a cluster ■ *n* (*plural* **-ies**) 1. **RECLUSE** somebody who lives alone or prefers to be alone 2. CRIME same as **solitary confinement** [14C. < Latin *solitarius* < *solus* "alone"] —**sol·i·tar·i·ly** *adv* —**sol·i·tar·i·ness** *n*

sol·i·tar·y con·fine·ment *n* confinement of a prisoner in an area or cell isolated from other prisoners, used as a punishment or for protection

sol·i·tude /sóllə tòod/ *n* 1. **STATE OF BEING ALONE** the state of being alone, separated from other people, whether considered as a welcome freedom from disturbance or as an unhappy loneliness 2. **REMOTENESS** a quality of quiet remoteness or seclusion in places from which human activity is generally absent 3. **LONELY PLACE** a remote or uninhabited place (*literary*) [14C. Directly or via French < Latin *solitudo* < *solus* "alone"] —**sol·i·tu·di·nous** /sòllə tòod'nəss/ *adj*

CULTURAL NOTE ***One Hundred Years of Solitude***, a novel (1967) by Colombian writer Gabriel García Márquez. It recounts a hundred years in the lives of the Buendía family, founders of the town of Macondo in Colombia, a story that mirrors the history of the nation. Marquez's skillful use of fantasy and myth to convey the depth of his characters' experiences makes this a key work in the magic realism school of literature.

sol·i·tud·i·nar·i·an /sòllə toodə nérree ən/ *n* somebody who lives or prefers to be alone (*literary*)

sol·ler·et /sòllə rét/ *n* a shoe made of steel plates riveted together, forming part of a suit of armor [14C. Via the diminutive of Old French *soller* "shoe" < late Latin *subtel* "hollow of the foot" < *sub* "under" + *talus* "ankle"]

sol·mi·za·tion /sòlmə záysh'n/ *n* the assigning of separate syllables to different musical pitches for singing or training the ear, as in solfeggio [Mid-18C. French *solmisation* < *solmiser* "sing sol-fa"]

soln. *abbr* CHEM, MATH solution

so·lo /sṓlō/ *n* (*plural* **-los** or **-li** /-lee/) **1. MUSICAL PIECE PERFORMED BY ONE PERSON** a piece of music performed by one musician or singer, or a passage for a single player or singer within a longer piece for two or more, a choir, or an orchestra **2. PERFORMANCE BY ONE ARTIST** a performance by a single artist such as a musician, singer, or dancer with or without accompaniment **3. ACT DONE BY SINGLE PERSON** an action or feat carried out by one person alone, e.g., a flight in an aircraft or a climb up a mountain **4.** CARDS **CARD GAME FOR INDIVIDUAL PLAYERS** a card game in which players play on their own, not in pairs or teams, especially solo whist ■ *adj* **1. FOR SINGLE PERFORMER** intended for or executed by somebody performing singly, not as one of a group **2. DONE BY ONE PERSON** carried out by one person unaccompanied by anyone else ■ *adv* **ALONE** unaccompanied by anyone, or not performing or doing something as one of a group ■ *vi* (**-loed, -lo·ing, -los**) **DO SOMETHING WITHOUT ASSISTANCE** to do something alone, without help or accompaniment, especially to fly an aircraft without an instructor or to perform an artistic solo [Late 17C. Via Italian < Latin *solus* "alone"]

so·lo·ist /sṓlō ist/ *n* somebody who performs a solo, especially a musical solo —**so·lo·is·tic** /sṓlō ístik/ *adj*

So·lo man /sṓlō-/ *n* an extinct variety of the human species Homo sapiens that lived 50,000 years ago during the late Pleistocene epoch [Because fossils were discovered near the Solo River, Java]

Sol·o·mon[1] /sólləmən/ *n* somebody wise (*informal*) [After SOLOMON[2]]

Sol·o·mon[2] /sólləmən/ (*fl* 10th century B.C.) king of Israel. The second son of David and Bathsheba, he ruled Israel from 961 to 922 B.C. Famed for his wisdom, he is generally acknowledged as the builder of the Temple in Jerusalem. He is credited with writing the biblical *Song of Solomon* and *Proverbs*.

Solomon Islands

Sol·o·mon Is·lands country comprising over 35 islands and atolls in the southern Pacific Ocean. It became an independent member of the British Commonwealth in 1978. Language: English. Currency: Solomon Islands dollar. Capital: Honiara. Population: 509,190 (2003). Area: 10,639 sq. mi./27,556 sq. km. —**Sol·o·mon Is·land·er** *n*

Sol·o·mon Sea arm of the western South Pacific Ocean, east of New Guinea and west of the Solomon Islands

Sol·o·mon's seal *n* **1.** a six-pointed symbol resembling a star, made up of one triangle laid on top of another facing the other way. Examples are the Star of David that is the symbol of Judaism, and the hexagram that healers of former times believed had the power to cure diseases. **2.** a perennial woodland plant. Native to: northern countries. Flowers: drooping, whitish, in pairs. Latin name: *Polygonatum multiflorum*.

so·lon /sṓlən/ *n* **1.** *US* a member of a law-making body **2.** somebody wise, especially an experienced and wise legislator or politician (*literary*) [Early 17C. After SOLON]

So·lon /sṓlən, sṓ lon/ (638?–559? B.C.) Athenian political leader, legislator, and poet. He introduced wide-ranging legal and political reforms and is considered the founder of Athenian democracy.

so·lon·chak /sṑlən chák, sṓlən chàk/ *n* an intrazonal soil with a grayish crust that develops in semiarid and desert areas and contains large amounts of soluble salts [Early 20C. < Russian, "salt marsh, salt lake" < *sol* "salt"]

so·lo·netz /sṑlə néts, sṓlə nèts/, **so·lo·nets** *n* an intrazonal soil with a blackish crust developed from solonchak soil by leaching of the salts [Early 20C. < Russian, "salt marsh, salt lake" < *sol* "salt"]

so long *interj* used to say goodbye (*informal*)

so·lo stop *n* a stop on an organ with a penetrating tone, used in isolated passages of organ pieces to give the effect of a single instrument playing the melody

sol·stice /sólstiss, sṓl-/ *n* **1.** either of the times when the Sun is farthest from the equator, on or about June 21 or December 21. The summer solstice falls in June in the northern hemisphere but in December in the southern hemisphere, and vice versa for the winter solstice. **2.** either of the two points on the ecliptic when the Sun reaches its northernmost or southernmost point relative to the celestial equator [13C. Via French < Latin *solstitium* < *sol* "Sun" + *stit-*, past participle of *sistere* "stand still"] —**sol·sti·tial** /sol stísh'l, sōl-/ *adj*

Georg Solti

Sol·ti /shṓltee/, **Sir Georg** (1912–97) Hungarian conductor. Associated particularly with the music of late romantic composers, he held important posts in Germany, the United Kingdom, and the United States, where he conducted the Chicago Symphony Orchestra (1969–91).

sol·u·bil·i·ty /sòllyə bíllətee/ (*plural* **-ties**) *n* **1.** the extent to which one substance is able to dissolve in another **2.** a measure of one substance's ability to dissolve in a specific amount of another substance at standard temperature and pressure

sol·u·bi·lize /sóllyəbə līz/ (**-lized, -liz·ing, -liz·es**) *vti* to make a substance soluble or more soluble, or become soluble or more soluble

sol·u·ble /sóllyəb'l/ *adj* **1. DISSOLVING** able to be dissolved in another substance. The level of solubility often varies with temperature. (*often used in combination*) ○ *water-soluble* **2. DESIGNED TO DISSOLVE** designed to be dissolved in water **3. CAPABLE OF BEING SOLVED** able to be solved or answered [14C. Via French < late Latin *solubilis* < *solvere* "loosen, dissolve"] —**sol·u·bly** *adv*

sol·u·ble glass *n* CHEM same as **sodium silicate**

sol·u·ble RNA *n* BIOCHEM same as **transfer RNA**

so·lum /sṓləm/ *n* the upper layer of a soil profile where the formation of new soil takes place and where most plant roots and soil animals are found [Mid-19C. < Latin, "ground, foundation"]

so·lus /sṓləss/ *adj* used as a stage direction to indicate that a character appears alone on stage ○ *Enter Hector solus* [Late 16C. < Latin, "alone"] —**so·lus** *adv*

sol·ute /sól yoot/ *n* a substance dissolved in another substance ■ *adj* dissolved in a solution [15C. < Latin *solut-* (see SOLUTION)]

so·lu·tion /sə lo͞osh'n/ *n* **1. WAY OF RESOLVING DIFFICULTY** a method of successfully dealing with a problem or difficulty **2. ANSWER TO PUZZLE** the answer to a puzzle or question **3. FINDING OF ANSWER** the process of resolving a difficulty or finding the answer to a puzzle or question **4.** CHEM **FLUID WITH SUBSTANCE DISSOLVED IN IT** a substance consisting of two or more substances mixed together and uniformly dispersed, most commonly the result of dissolving a solid, fluid, or gas in a liquid. It is also possible, however, to form a solution by dissolving a gas or solid in a solid or one gas in another gas. **5.** CHEM **PROCESS OF FORMING MIXED FLUID** the process of forming a solution or dissolving one substance in another, or the state of being dissolved in another substance **6.** MATH **VALUE SATISFYING EQUATION** a value for a variable that satisfies an equation **7.** LAW **ENDING OF SOMETHING** the termination of a dispute or payment of a debt **8. ENDING OF SOMETHING** the act of ending, breaking, or separating something (*literary*) ■ *vt* (**-tioned, -tion·ing, -tions**) **SOLVE SOMETHING** to find a solution to something [14C. Via French < Latin *solution-* < *solut-*, past participle of *solvere* "loosen, dissolve"]

so·lu·tion set *n* the set of values for a variable that satisfy an equation

So·lu·tre·an /sə lo͞otree ən/, **So·lu·tri·an** *adj* belonging to a prehistoric culture that existed in Europe between 40,000 B.C. and 12,000 B.C., at the end of the Paleolithic period, in which people worked with leaf-shaped flint blades [Late 19C. < French *solutréen* < *Solutré*, village in E France]

solv·a·ble /sólvəb'l/ *adj* capable of being solved —**solv·a·bil·i·ty** *n*

sol·vate /sól vàyt/ *vti* (**-vat·ed, -vat·ing, -vates**) to enter into solution with a solvent, or cause a solute to dissolve in solution with a solvent ■ *n* a compound consisting of an ion or molecule of solute combined with one or more of solvent [Early 20C. < SOLVENT] —**sol·va·tion** /sol váysh'n/ *n*

Sol·vay proc·ess /sól vay-/ *n* an industrial process for producing sodium carbonate or washing soda from common salt. A solution of salt is saturated with ammonia and carbon dioxide is passed through it, which causes sodium hydrogen carbonate to precipitate. It is then heated to obtain sodium carbonate. [Late 19C. After Ernest *Solvay* (1838–1922), Belgian chemist]

solve /solv, sawlv/ (**solved, solv·ing, solves**) *vt* **1. DEAL WITH PROBLEM SUCCESSFULLY** to find a way of dealing successfully with a problem or difficulty **2. FIND ANSWER TO PUZZLE** to find the answer to a question or puzzle **3.** MATH **FIND ANSWER TO MATH PROBLEM** to work out the solution to an equation or other mathematical problem [15C. < Latin *solvere* "loosen, dissolve"] —**solv·er** *n*

ORIGIN The Latin word *solvere* "to loosen, dissolve," from which ***solve*** is derived, is also the source of the English words *absolute, absolve, dissolve, resolve, soluble*, and *solution*.

sol·vent /sólvənt, sáwl-/ *adj* **1. HAVING ENOUGH MONEY** having enough money to cover expenses and debts **2. DISSOLVING SOMETHING** able to dissolve substances ■ *n* **SUBSTANCE THAT DISSOLVES THINGS** a substance in which other substances are dissolved, often a liquid [Early 17C. Directly or via French < Latin *solvent-*, present participle of *solvere* "loosen, dissolve"] —**sol·ven·cy** *n* —**sol·vent·ly** *adv*

sol·vol·y·sis /sol vólləsiss, sawl-/ *n* a chemical reaction in which a dissolved solute and its solvent combine to form a new compound

Farrar, Straus and Giroux, Inc.

Aleksandr Isayevich Solzhenitsyn

Sol·zhe·ni·tsyn /sòlzhə néetsin, səlzhə nyéetsin/, **Aleksandr** (*b.* 1918) Russian writer. His imprisonment in the former Soviet Union for political dissent (1945–53) inspired early novels such as *One Day in the Life of Ivan Denisovich* (1962). He was expelled after the publication of *The Gulag Archipelago* (1974–78), and lived in exile in the United States for 20 years, returning to Russia after the collapse of the Soviet Union. He won a Nobel Prize in literature (1970). Full name **Solzhenitsyn, Aleksandr Isayevich**

> "How can you expect a man who's warm to understand one who's cold?"
> [Aleksandr Solzhenitsyn, *One Day in the Life of Ivan Denisovich*; 1962]

> "The salvation of mankind lies only in making everything the concern of all."
> [Aleksandr Solzhenitsyn, *Nobel lecture*; 1972]

som /sōm/ (*plural same*) *n* the main unit of currency of Kyrgyzstan. See table at **currency** [Via Kyrgyz < Chuvash, "sum, payment"]

so·ma[1] /sṓmə/ (*plural* **-ma·ta** /-mətə/ or **-mas**) *n* **1.** all the cells and tissues in the body considered collectively, with the exception of germ cells **2.** the body considered separately from the mind or soul [Mid-19C. Via modern Latin < Greek *sōma* "body"]

so·ma[2] /sṓmə/ *n* **1.** an intoxicating drink made from plant juice, mentioned in the Vedas, the most ancient sacred writings of Hinduism **2.** the plant that soma is made from, thought to be ephedra but not identified in the Vedas [Early 19C. < Sanskrit]

So·ma·li /sō maálee, sə-/ (*plural same* or **-lis** or **-li·ans**) *n* **1.** a member of an Islamic African people living mainly in Somalia **2.** the Cushitic national language of Somalia, also spoken in eastern Ethiopia. Native speakers: 5 million. [Early 19C. < Somali] —**So·ma·li** *adj*

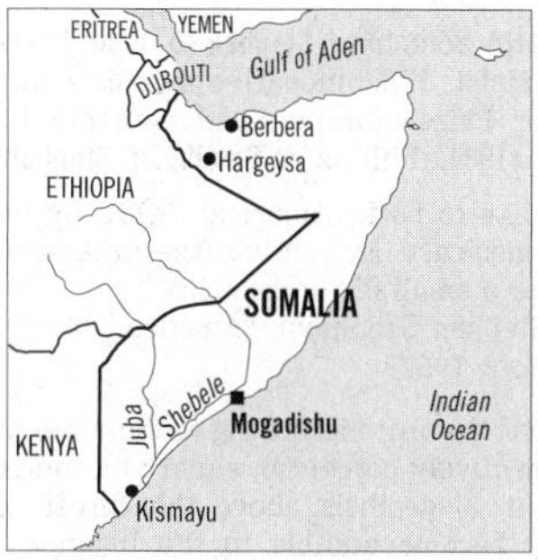

Somalia

So·ma·li·a /sō maálee ə, sə-/ country in eastern Africa. It consists of the former Italian Somaliland and British Somaliland, both of which united to become independent Somalia in 1960. During the civil war that broke out in the early 1990s, the northern part of the country declared independence as the Republic of Somaliland. Language: Somali. Currency: Somali shilling. Capital: Mogadishu. Population: 8,025,190 (2003). Area: 246,200 sq. mi./637,700 sq. km. Official name **Somali Democratic Republic**

So·ma·li·an /sə maályen/ *n* PEOPLES, LANG same as **Somali** —**So·ma·li·an** *adj*

So·ma·li·land /sō maálee lànd, sə-/ **1.** region in northeastern Africa, comprising Somalia, Djibouti, and part of Ethiopia **2.** autonomous region of northern Somalia, consisting of the former British Somaliland, which is seeking independent nation status. Language: Somali. Currency: Somaliland shilling. Capital: Hargeisa. Population: 3,500,000 (2001). Area: 68,000 sq. mi./137,600 sq. km.

So·ma·re /sə maáree/, **Sir Michael** (*b.* 1936) prime minister of Papua New Guinea. The country's first prime minister (1975–80), he was removed from office by a vote of no confidence, served again from 1982–5, with the same result, and as a member of the National Alliance Party was reappointed in 2002.

somat- *prefix* same as **somato-** (*used before vowels*)

so·ma·ta BIOL plural of **soma**[1]

so·mat·ic /sō máttik/ *adj* **1.** AFFECTING BODY AS DISTINCT FROM MIND relating to or affecting the body, especially the body as considered to be separate from the mind **2.** ANAT RELATING TO OUTER WALLS OF BODY relating to the outer walls of the body, not the inner organs **3.** BIOL OF SOMATIC CELL relating to a somatic cell [Late 18C. < Greek *sōmatikós* "bodily" < *sōma* "body"] —**so·mat·i·cal·ly** *adv*

so·mat·ic cell *n* any body cell except a reproductive cell

so·ma·ti·cize /sō máttə sīz/ (**-cized, -ciz·ing, -ciz·es**) *vti* to believe mistakenly that an emotional pain is a physical symptom

so·mat·ic nerv·ous sys·tem *n* the part of the nervous system that serves the sense organs and muscles of the body wall and limbs, and brings about voluntary muscle activity

somato- *prefix* body ○ *somatoplasm* [< Greek *sōmat-*, stem of *sōma*]

so·ma·tol·o·gy /sòmə tólləjee/ *n* **1.** the study of both the physiology and anatomy of the body **2.** the branch of anthropology that studies human development through variation and change in physical characteristics —**so·ma·to·log·ic** /sòmətə lójjik/ *adj* —**so·ma·to·log·i·cal** *adj* —**so·ma·to·log·i·cal·ly** *adv*

so·mat·o·me·din /sō màttə méed'n, sòmətə-/ *n* a hormone produced in the liver that stimulates the growth of bone and muscle [Late 20C. < SOMATO- + INTERMEDIARY]

so·mat·o·plasm /sō máttə plàzzəm, sṓmətə-/ *n* the protoplasm of body cells as distinct from the protoplasm of germ cells —**so·mat·o·plas·tic** /sō màttə plástik, sòmətə-/ *adj*

so·mat·o·pleure /sō máttə ploor, sṓmətə-/ *n* a fold of embryonic tissue in vertebrates formed by the fusion of ectoderm and mesoderm that gives rise to an embryo's inner and outer membranes —**so·mat·o·pleu·ral** /sō màttə ploorəl, sòmətə-/ *adj* —**so·mat·o·pleu·ric** *adj*

so·mat·o·sen·so·ry /sə màttə sénssəree, sòmətə-/ *adj* describes sensory stimuli coming from the skin and internal organs and the perception of these stimuli

so·mat·o·stat·in /sō màttə státt'n, sòmətə-/ *n* a hormone produced in the hypothalamus that inhibits the release of growth hormone [Late 20C. < SOMATO- + Latin *stat-*, past participle of *stare* "stand"]

so·mat·o·tro·pin /sə màttə trṓpin, sòmətə-/, **so·ma·to·tro·phin** /-trṓfin/ *n* BIOL same as **growth hormone** [Mid-20C. < SOMATO- + -TROPIC] —**so·mat·o·tro·pic** *adj*

so·mat·o·type /sə máttə tīp, sṓmətə-/ *n* the type of physical build that somebody has

som·ber /sómbər/ *adj* **1.** DARK AND GLOOMY lacking light or brightness and producing a dull, dark, or melancholy atmosphere **2.** DARK IN COLOR having a color or tone that is dark, dull, or suitable for a serious mood or occasion **3.** SERIOUS AND MELANCHOLY marked by or conveying strict seriousness combined with sadness or a troubled state of mind [Mid-18C. < French *sombre* "gloomy" < assumed Vulgar Latin *subumbrare* "to shadow" < Latin *sub* "under" + *umbra* "shade"] —**som·ber·ly** *adv* —**som·ber·ness** *n*

som·bre *adj* Can, UK spelling of **somber**

som·bre·ro /som bréro/ (*plural* **-ros**) *n* a straw or felt hat with a very wide upturned brim, originally worn by men in Mexico and some other Spanish-speaking countries [Late 16C. < Spanish, "hat" < *sombra* "shade" < assumed Vulgar Latin *subumbrare* (see SOMBER)]

Som·bre·ro /som brérrō/ northernmost islet in the Lesser Antilles. A dependency of Anguilla, it is the site of an important lighthouse protecting the passage between the Atlantic Ocean to the Caribbean Sea. Area: 0.15 sq. mi./0.4 sq. km.

some *stressed* /sum/; *unstressed* /səm/ CORE MEANING: a grammatical word used to indicate an unspecified or unknown quantity of people or things ○ (adj) *There is always some risk in any project.* ○ (pron) *There was plenty of food left over, so I took some.*

1. *adj, pron* A LITTLE used to indicate an unspecified number, quantity, or proportion of a total, generally a fairly small to average or reasonable one ○ *I agree with you to some extent.* ○ *Some of you, I know, will disagree with me.* **2.** *adj* QUITE A FEW used with a slight emphasis to indicate an unspecified but fairly large number or quantity ○ *We have been debating this problem for some months now.* **3.** *adj* PARTICULAR BUT UNSPECIFIED used to indicate an unspecified single person or thing, often in a dismissive way (*informal*) ○ *He was reading some medical book.* **4.** *adj* USED FOR EMPHASIS used to emphasize that somebody or something is impressive or remarkable in some way (*informal*) ○ *That was some performance you put on for us!* **5.** *adv* APPROXIMATELY used to indicate that a number is approximate ○ *for some 30 years* **6.** *adv* TO SMALL EXTENT to a small extent or degree (*informal*) ○ *I do write some, but not as much as I'd like.* **7.** *adv* A GREAT DEAL a great deal, at a considerable rate, or vigorously (*informal*) ○ *I'm going to have to study some to get through this exam.* [Old English *sum* "one, somebody" < Indo-European, "together with"] ◇ **and then some** used to emphasize that more, often considerably more, has been done than was suggested in a previous statement (*informal*)

SPELLCHECK some or **sum**? Do not confuse the spelling of ***some*** and ***sum***, which sound similar. ***Some*** refers to an unspecified amount, number, thing, or person, as in *buy some milk, some ten days ago, undergoing some kind of therapy, Some of them refused to leave.* ***Sum*** refers to a total amount, as in *a sum of money, the sum total of his knowledge*, and is also used as a verb, especially in *sum up* meaning "summarize" (*summed up the story in a couple of sentences*).

-some[1] *suffix* **1.** characterized by a particular quality, condition, or thing ○ *troublesome* ○ *quarrelsome* **2.** a group containing a particular number of members ○ *foursome* [Old English *-sum*]

-some[2] *suffix* **1.** body ○ *cytosome* **2.** chromosome ○ *autosome* [< Greek *sōma* "body"]

some·bod·y /súm bòddee, súmbədee/ *pron* an unspecified or unidentified person ○ *Somebody just rang the doorbell.* ■ *pron, n* (*plural* **-ies**) an important or well-known person ○ *She didn't want mediocre success; she wanted to be somebody.*

some·day /súm dày/ *adv* at some unknown, unspecified, and usually fairly distant time in the future

some·how /súm hòw/ *adv* **1.** in some unspecified or unknown way, often with great effort or difficulty ○ *He somehow managed to scramble back on board.* **2.** for some unknown or inexplicable reason ○ *She somehow forgot to tell anyone where she was going.*

some·one /súm wùn/ *pron* same as **somebody**

some·place /súm plàyss/ *adv* same as **somewhere** (*informal*)

som·er·sault /súmmər sàwlt/, **sum·mer·sault** *n* **1.** ACROBATIC ROLLING OVER OF BODY an acrobatic movement in which the body is rolled over, feet over head, either forward or backward, on the ground or in midair, finally returning to an upright position **2.** REVERSAL OF OPINION OR DECISION a complete change of mind or reversal of policy (*informal*) ■ *vi* (**-sault·ed, -sault·ing, -saults**) PERFORM SOMERSAULT to perform an acrobatic somersault [Early 16C. < Middle French *sombresault*, alteration of *sobresault* < Latin *super* "over, above" + *saltus* "leap"]

Som·er·set /súmmər sèt/ **1.** county in southwestern England that includes Glastonbury, Exmoor, and Cheddar. Taunton is the county town. Population: 498,093 (2001). Area: 1,335 sq. mi./3,458 sq. km. **2.** town in southeastern Massachusetts, on the western bank of the Taunton River, across from Fall River. Population: 18,645 (2002 estimate).

Som·er·set, Edward Seymour, 1st Duke of (1506?–52) Protector of England (1547–50). The brother of Jane Seymour, he became Protector of England during the minority of the future Edward VI. Rivalry with the Duke of Northumberland led to his execution. Known as **Protector Somerset**

Som·er·set Is·land island in Nunavut, Canada, in the Arctic Archipelago, north of the Boothia Peninsula. Area: 9,570 sq. mi./24,786 sq. km.

Som·er·ville /súmmər vìl/ city in eastern Massachusetts, on the Mystic River. It is a northwestern suburb of Boston, and was founded in 1630. Population: 76,922 (2002 estimate).

Som·er·ville, Mary (1780–1872) British scientist. She wrote several major works explaining scientific matters, including *On the Connexion of the Physical Sciences* (1834).

some·thing /súmthing/ *pron* **1.** **UNSPECIFIED THING** an unspecified or unidentified object, phenomenon, action, utterance, or feeling ○ *Don't just stand there; do something!* ○ *I had a feeling that there was something wrong.* ○ *Would you like something to eat?* **2.** **UNSPECIFIED AMOUNT** an unspecified and approximate amount expressed in relation to a specific number or quantity ○ *something over 50* ○ *something between 20 and 30%* **3.** **SUGGESTING RESEMBLANCE** used to suggest that one thing or person resembles another to an extent or has some of the qualities of the other ○ *There's definitely something of the knight errant about him.* **4.** **RATHER** used to qualify a description of a thing or event and tone it down or make it sound more guarded ○ *It was something of a disappointment.* **5.** **IMPRESSIVE PERSON OR THING** an impressive or important person or thing ○ *He's really something!* ■ *adv* **1.** **SOMEWHAT** slightly or to some degree ○ *It sounds something like what she might have said.* **2.** **TO EXTREME DEGREE** used to intensify the effect of an adjective, especially a strong adjective used as an adverb (*informal*) ○ *It hurts something awful.* **3.** **AND A BIT MORE** used to indicate that a number is slightly higher than the one mentioned (*informal*) ○ *She's fifty something.* ◇ **something else** somebody or something really special, remarkable, or extreme (*informal*) ○ *That performance was something else!* ◇ **have something to do with somebody** *or* **something** to be connected with or involve somebody or something

some·time /súm tìm/ *adv* **1.** **AT SOME TIME** at some unspecified or unknown time ○ *They intend to marry sometime soon.* **2.** **FORMERLY** at one time in the past (*formal*) ○ *our speaker today, sometime a professor at Princeton University* **3.** **OCCASIONALLY** occasionally or sporadically (*archaic*) ■ *adj* **1.** **FORMER** referring to somebody who at one time in the past had the job, position, or status in question ○ *a sometime student at this university* **2.** **OCCASIONAL** occasional or sporadic ○ *an author and sometime lecturer*

some·times /súm tìmz/ *adv* **1.** from time to time, not continually or every time ○ *We go to the theater sometimes.* **2.** at one time in the past (*archaic*) [Early 16C. < SOMETIME + -s, possessive (genitive) singular suffix]

some·way /súm wày/ *adv* using some means or method that is not yet known or not indicated ○ *We'll figure it out someway.*

some·what /súm wòt, -hwòt/ *adv* to some extent or degree ○ *The hot night had cooled somewhat.*

some·where /súm wèr, -hwèr/ *adv* **1.** in, to, or at some unspecified place ○ *He lives somewhere in North Dakota.* **2.** used in giving approximate amounts, numbers, or times ○ *somewhere around 300* ○ *somewhere between three and four o'clock* ◇ **get somewhere** to make progress toward achieving something

some·wheres /súm wèrz, -hwèrz/ *adv US regional, Can* same as **somewhere** (*nonstandard*)

USAGE See ***anyways***.

---

so·mite /sṓ mìt/ *n* **1.** one of a series of paired blocks of cells that develop along the back of a vertebrate embryo, giving rise to the vertebral column and most of the skeletal muscles **2.** a body segment, usually one of several, into which the bodies of some animals such as earthworms and crayfish are divided along their length [Mid-19C. < SOMA[1]] —**so·mit·al** /sṓmət'l/ *adj* —**so·mit·ic** /sō míttik/ *adj*

Somme /som, sawm/ river in northern France, flowing from near St. Quentin into the English Channel. The Somme valley was the scene of a major World War I battle in 1916, which resulted in more than one million casualties. Length: 150 mi./241 km.

som·me·lier /sùmm'l yáy/ *n* a wine steward in a restaurant, hotel, or other establishment, who supervises the ordering, storing, and serving of wine [Early 20C. < French, variant of *somm(er)ier* "officer in charge of provisions" < *somme* "burden" < Greek *sāgma* "covering, packsaddle"]

somn- *prefix* same as **somni-** (*used before vowels*)

som·nam·bu·late /som námbyə làyt/ (**-lat·ed, -lat·ing, -lates**) *vi* same as **sleepwalk** (sense 1) (*technical*) —**som·nam·bu·lance** *n* —**som·nam·bu·la·tion** /som nàmbyə láysh'n/ *n* —**som·nam·bu·la·tor** *n*

som·nam·bule /sóm nam byòòl/ *n* a person who walks while sleeping [Mid-19C. < French]

som·nam·bu·lism /som námbyə lìzzəm/ *n* walking while asleep (*technical*) —**som·nam·bu·list** *n* —**som·nam·bu·lis·tic** /som nàmbyə lístik/ *adj*

somni- *prefix* sleep ○ *somnifacient* [< Latin *somnus*]

som·ni·fa·cient /sòmnə fáysh'nt/ *adj* describes a drug designed to induce sleep

som·nif·er·ous /som níffərəss/ *adj* making somebody, or designed to make somebody, feel sleepy —**som·nif·er·ous·ly** *adv*

som·no·lent /sómnələnt/ *adj* **1.** **SLEEPY** feeling sleepy or tending to fall asleep **2.** **LACKING ACTIVITY** quiet and with little or no activity **3.** **SLEEP-INDUCING** making somebody feel sleepy [15C. Via French < Latin *somnōlentus* "sleepy" < *somnus* "sleep"] —**som·no·lence** *n* —**som·no·lent·ly** *adv*

So·mo·za Gar·cí·a /sə mṓzə-/, **Anastasio** (1896–1956) Nicaraguan general and national leader. He was president of Nicaragua (1937–47, 1950–56). After his assassination he was succeeded by his sons, Luis Somoza Debayle (1922–67) and Anastasio Somoza Debayle (1925–80), the latter of whom was overthrown in 1979 by the Sandinista Liberation Front and later assassinated in Paraguay. Full name **Somoza García, Anastasio**

~~somthing~~ incorrect spelling of **something**

son /sun/ *n* **1.** **MALE CHILD** a male child in relation to his parents **2.** **MALE IN FAMILY** a male descendant **3.** **MALE CONNECTED WITH SOMETHING** a man or boy referred to in terms of his connection with a place, a time in history, or a sphere of interest ○ *the achievements of the sons of the Industrial Revolution* **4.** **ANIMAL'S YOUNG** a male offspring of an animal **5.** **TERM OF ADDRESS** an affectionate, or sometimes condescending, way of addressing a boy or man (*informal*) [Old English *sunu* < Indo-European, "give birth"] —**son·less** *adj* —**son·like** *adj*

SPELLCHECK son or **sun**? Do not confuse the spelling of ***son*** and ***sun***, which sound similar. A ***son*** is "a male child in relation to his parents": *They have two daughters and three sons.* The ***sun*** (in astronomical contexts, ***Sun***) is the star that gives us heat and light: *The sun shone all day; observations of the Sun and the stars.* The word ***sun*** is also used as a verb, as in *sunning herself on the patio*, and in phrases such as *everything under the sun*, meaning "things of all kinds."

CULTURAL NOTE *Sons and Lovers*, a novel (1913) by British writer D. H. Lawrence. Lawrence's first major novel, and his most autobiographical work, it centers on a family living in a Nottinghamshire coalmining community. Gertrude Morel is frustrated by life with her less refined and increasingly drunken husband and devotes herself to her children, focusing on her son Paul after the death of his brother William. When Paul falls in love, first with a local girl and subsequently with a married woman, he finds it hard to break the bonds of attachment to his mother.

Son /sun/ *n* a title that Christians give to Jesus Christ, especially when referred to as the second person in the Holy Trinity

so·nant /sṓnənt/ *adj* **1.** **HAVING SOUND** producing or possessing a sound (*formal*) **2.** PHON **VOICED** describes a speech sound made with vibration of the vocal cords **3.** PHON **SYLLABIC** describes a consonant that is capable of forming a syllable on its own, without a vowel ■ *n* PHON **1.** **VOICED SOUND** a sound made with vibration of the vocal cords **2.** **SYLLABIC CONSONANT** a consonant capable of forming a syllable on its own, without a vowel [Mid-19C. < Latin *sonant-*, present participle of *sonare* "sound"] —**so·nance** *n* —**so·nan·tal** /sō nánt'l/ *adj* —**so·nan·tic** /-nántik/ *adj*

so·nar /sṓ naar/ *n* **1.** a system that determines the position of unseen underwater objects by transmitting sound waves and measuring the time it takes for their echo to return after hitting the object **2.** a device that uses sonar [Mid-20C. Acronym < *sound navigation ranging*, after RADAR]

so·na·ta /sə naatə/ *n* **1.** a piece of classical music for a solo instrument or a small ensemble. It consists of several movements, at least one of which is in sonata form. **2.** a piece of baroque keyboard music in a single movement [Late 17C. < Italian < feminine past participle of *sonare* "sound" < Latin *sonare*]

so·na·ta form *n* an important musical form developed in the 18th century consisting of three sections, an exposition, development, and recapitulation, and used especially for the first movement of sonatas, concertos, and symphonies

son·a·ti·na /sònnə teenə/ *n* a short, usually technically undemanding sonata [Early 18C. < Italian, "little sonata" < *sonata* (see SONATA)]

son·dage /sawn daazh/ *n* a deep trench dug in order to study the relative positions of human artifacts in horizontal layers [Mid-20C. < French, "sounding, bore hole" < *sonder* (see SOUND[2])]

sonde /sond/ *n* a collection of instruments that can be lowered down a borehole or carried into the upper atmosphere by balloon or rocket to transmit information relating to the conditions encountered [Early 20C. < French, "plumb line, sound" < *sonder* (see SOUND[2])]

Stephen Sondheim

Sond·heim /sónd hìm/, **Stephen** (*b.* 1930) US composer and lyricist. His innovative musicals include the Pulitzer Prize-winning *Sunday in the Park with George* (1984). Full name **Sondheim, Stephen Joshua**

> "I like to be in America! / O.K. by me in America! / Ev'rything free in America / For a small fee in America!"
> [Stephen Sondheim, "America," *West Side Story*; 1957]

sone /sōn/ *n* a unit measuring the loudness of sound as subjectively perceived, equal to a tone of 1 kilohertz at 40 decibels above the threshold where sounds become audible to the listener [Mid-20C. < Latin *sonus* "sound"]

son et lu·mière /sàwn ay loo myèr/ *n* an outdoor nighttime spectacle that combines dramatic lighting effects with recorded sounds and music, usually staged at the site of a famous and historical building, often telling its history [< French, "sound and light"]

song /sawng, song/ *n* **1.** **SET OF WORDS SUNG** a usually relatively short musical composition consisting of words set to music and the music itself **2.** **ART OF SINGING** the art or practice of singing **3.** **INSTRUMENTAL WORK IN VOCAL STYLE** an instrumental work written in the style of a composition for the voice, or, in popular music, any musical work **4.** ZOOL **ANIMAL CALL** the sounds made by a bird, insect, whale, frog, or other animal to attract a mate or defend territory **5.** LITERAT same as **poetry** (*literary*) **6. POEM** a long poem, especially one that tells a story (*literary*) ○ *the Song of Roland* [Old English *sang* < Indo-European, "sing"] —**song·like** *adj* ◇ **for a song** very cheaply (*informal*)

Song /song/ *n* HIST same as **Sung**

song and dance *n* a long-winded attempt to explain or justify something (*informal*)

song·bird /sáwng bùrd, sóng-/ *n* a bird with a musical call, especially a passerine belonging to the group that includes larks, finches, and thrushes. Suborder: Oscines.

song·book /sáwng bo͝ok, sóng-/ *n* a book containing the words and music for a collection of songs

song cy·cle *n* a set of songs linked by a common subject or underlying musical theme or forming a narrative, often with words by a single poet and music by a classical composer

song·fest /sáwng fèst, sóng-/ *n* US an informal gathering of people for the purpose of singing folk or popular songs together

song·ful /sáwngf'l, sóng-/ *adj* resembling song, especially in having a pleasing melody —**song·ful·ly** *adv* —**song·ful·ness** *n*

Song·hai[1] /sòng gī́, sòng hī́/ (*plural same* or **-hais**), **Song·hay** (*plural same* or **-hays**) *n* **1.** a member of a people living in West Africa, mainly in Mali and Niger. The Songhai established a powerful empire in this area during the 7th century A.D., and they remained the dominant ethnic group until the 16th century. **2.** the Nilo-Saharan language of the Songhai. Native speakers: 2 million. —**Song·hai** *adj*

Song·hai[2] /sòng gī́, sòng hī́/, **Song·hay** state in western Africa during the 15th and 16th centuries. Its capital was Gao, which stood on the Niger River in what is now Mali.

Song of Sol·o·mon *n* a book of the Bible that consists of a set of love poems, forming part of the Protestant scripture. Traditionally attributed to King Solomon, it is now thought to have been written by several later authors. See table at **Bible**

Song of Songs *n* a book of the Bible that corresponds to the Song of Solomon, forming part of the Jewish and Roman Catholic scriptures. See table at **Bible**

song·smith /sáwng smìth, sóng-/ *n* MUSIC same as **songwriter**

song spar·row *n* a brown-and-white finch with a musical call. Native to: North America. Latin name: *Melospiza melodia*.

song·ster /sáwngstər, sóng-/ *n* **1.** a singer, especially a talented one **2.** a bird with a musical call **3.** same as **poet** (sense 1) (*literary*)

song·stress /sáwngstrəss, sóng-/ *n* a female singer, songwriter, or poet (*dated; sometimes offensive*)

song thrush *n* a small songbird with brown upper parts and a white breast speckled with brown. Native to: Europe, Asia. Latin name: *Turdus philomelos*.

song·writ·er /sáwng rītər, sóng-/ *n* a writer of songs —**song·writ·ing** *n*

son·ic /sónnik/ *adj* **1. RELATING TO SOUND OR SOUND WAVES** relating to, using, or producing sound or sound waves **2. AUDIBLE TO HUMAN EAR** able to be heard by the human ear **3. RELATING TO SPEED OF SOUND** relating to or traveling at the speed of sound in air, approximately 760 mi. per hour/1,220 km per hour at sea level [Early 20C. < Latin *sonus* "sound"]

son·ic bar·ri·er *n* PHYS same as **sound barrier**

son·ic boom *n* a noise heard as a loud boom at ground level resulting from the shock waves created by an aircraft flying above the speed of sound

son·ics /sónniks/ *n* the study of sound or, more generally, elastic wave motion (*takes a singular verb*)

son-in-law (*plural* **sons-in-law**) *n* the husband of somebody's daughter

son·net /sónnət/ *n* a short poem with 14 lines, usually ten-syllable rhyming lines, divided into two, three, or four sections. There are many rhyming patterns for sonnets, and they are usually written in iambic pentameter. [Mid-16C. Directly or via French < Italian *sonnetto* < Old Provençal *son* "poem" < Latin *sonus* "sound"]

son·net·eer /sònnə teer/ *n* **1.** a poet who writes sonnets **2.** a writer whose poems are regarded as mediocre (*disapproving*)

son·net se·quence *n* a set of sonnets written by one poet and unified by a single theme or idea

son·ny /súnnee/, **son·ny boy** *n* used as an affectionate, or sometimes condescending, way of addressing a man or boy (*informal*)

so·no·buoy /sónnə bo͞o ee, -bòy, sáwnə bo͞oee, -bòy/ *n* a buoy with equipment for detecting underwater noises and transmitting them by radio [Mid-20C. < Latin *sonus* "sound"]

son of a bitch *n* (*plural* **sons of bitch·es**) **1. TABOO TERM** a highly offensive term for somebody, usually a man, regarded as hateful, despicable, or intensely annoying (*taboo insult*) **2. ANY PERSON** used as a familiar, humorous, and slightly vulgar term for a person, usually a man, who has the named characteristic (*slang; sometimes considered offensive*) ○ *He's a lucky son of a bitch.* ■ *interj* **EXCLAMATION OF ANGER** used as a swearword to express anger or defiance (*slang; sometimes considered offensive*)

son of a gun (*informal*) *n* (*plural* **sons of guns**) a person, especially a man, and usually somebody affectionately or kindly regarded ■ *interj* used to express mild annoyance or surprise

son of God *n* **1.** a being regarded as superhuman or angelic **2.** a believer in the Christian faith

Son of God, Son of Man *n* Jesus Christ, considered by Christians as the Messiah

son·o·gram /sónnə gràm, sṓnə-/ *n* a graphical representation of sound, especially in the three dimensions of frequency, time, and intensity

So·no·ma /sə nṓmə/ town northeast of San Francisco in Sonoma County, northern California. It lies at the heart of an important wine-producing region. Population: 9,354 (2002 estimate).

So·no·ma Val·ley region of western California, northeast of San Francisco. Extending northward from the city of Sonoma, it is famous for its wineries and is a major tourist destination.

So·no·ra /sə náwrə/ state in northwestern Mexico, on the border with the United States. Capital: Hermosillo. Population: 2,216,969 (2000). Area: 69,820 sq. mi./180,833 sq. km.

So·no·ran De·sert /sə nàwrən-/ one of the largest deserts in North America, situated in southwestern Arizona, southern California, and northwestern Mexico. Area: 120,000 sq. mi./310,799 sq. km.

so·nor·i·ty /sə náwrətee/ (*plural* **-ties**) *n* **1.** a sonorous quality **2.** a sound, especially a rich deep sound [Early 16C. Via French < medieval Latin *sonoritas* < Latin *sonorus* (see SONOROUS)]

so·no·rous /sónnərəss, sə náwrəss/ *adj* **1. PRODUCING SOUND** producing or possessing sound **2. RESONANT** sounding with loud, deep, and clear tones **3. HAVING IMPRESSIVE MANNER OF SPEAKING** speaking, spoken, or expressed in a rich, full, and impressive manner [Early 17C. < Latin *sonorus* "noisy, loud" < *sonor* "sound" < *sonare* "make a sound"] —**so·no·rous·ly** *adv* —**so·no·rous·ness** *n*

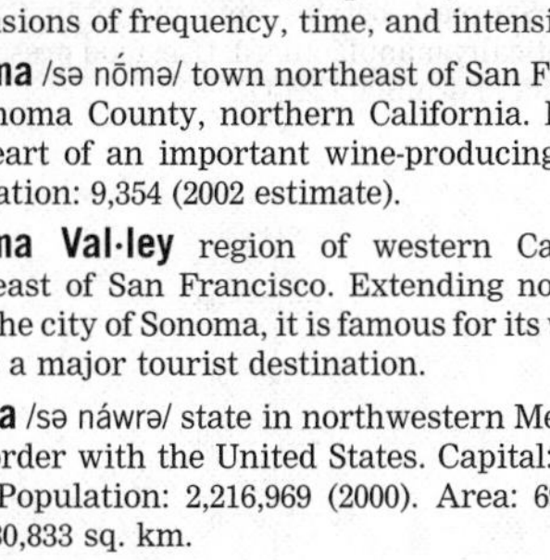
Popperfoto

Susan Sontag

Son·tag /són tàg/, **Susan** (*b.* 1933) US writer. She is best known for her social commentary such as the article *Notes on "Camp"* (1964) and *Illness as Metaphor* (1978). She has also written novels and short stories.

"The camera makes everyone a tourist in other people's reality, and eventually in one's own."
[Susan Sontag, *New York Review of Books*; April 18, 1974]

soon /soon/ *adv* **1. AFTER SHORT TIME** within or after a short time ○ *She soon realized that she had made a mistake.* **2. QUICKLY** quickly or without much delay ○ *How soon will you be ready?* ○ *I'll soon see about that!* **3. EARLY** before a reasonable or the desired length of time has elapsed ○ *Do you really have to go so soon?* ○ *It's a bit soon to be thinking of leaving, isn't it?* **4. WILLINGLY** used when expressing a preference for one alternative over another or an equal willingness to accept either, and often in the comparative form "sooner" ○ *I'd sooner stay in than go out.* ○ *I'd as soon stay in as go out.* [Old English *sōna* < W Germanic] ◇ **as soon as** immediately after ◇ **no sooner...than** immediately after one thing had happened, another took place ◇ **sooner or later** inevitably or certainly at some as yet unspecifiable time

Soon·er State *n* a nickname for Oklahoma

soot /so͝ot, soot/ *n* a black powdery form of carbon produced when coal, wood, or oil is burned, which rises up in fine particles with the flames and smoke ■ *vt* (**soot·ed, soot·ing, soots**) to sprinkle or cover something with soot [Old English *sōt* "something that sits" < Germanic, "sit"]

sooth /sooth/ *n* same as **truth** (sense 1) (*archaic* or *literary*) [Old English *sōþ* "true" < Indo-European, "be"] —**sooth·ly** *adv*

soothe /soo*th*/ (**soothed, sooth·ing, soothes**) *v* **1.** *vt* to make pain or discomfort less severe **2.** *vti* to make somebody less angry, anxious, or upset [Old English *sōþian* "prove to be true, verify" < *sōþ* (see SOOTH)] —**sooth·er** *n* —**sooth·ing** *adj* —**sooth·ing·ly** *adv* —**sooth·ing·ness** *n*

sooth·say·er /so͝oth sày ər/ *n* a predictor of future events —**sooth·say** *vi*

soot·y /so͝ottee/ (**-i·er, -i·est**) *adj* **1.** covered in soot, or lined or blocked with soot **2.** resembling soot in its blackness, dirtiness, or powdery texture

soot·y grouse *n* BIRDS same as **blue grouse**

soot·y mold *n* **1.** a plant disease characterized by a black velvety fungus **2.** a fungus that causes sooty mold. Genus: *Meliola* or *Capnodium*.

sop /sop/ *n* **1. SOMETHING GIVEN TO SATISFY DISCONTENTED PERSON** something offered as a concession or gesture to pacify somebody who is angry or discontented **2. FOOD DIPPED IN LIQUID** a piece of food dipped or soaked in liquid before it is eaten **3. OFFENSIVE TERM** an offensive term that deliberately insults somebody, especially a man, regarded as lacking courage (*dated insult*) ■ *vti* (**sopped, sop·ping, sops**) **MAKE OR BECOME SOAKING WET** to make something thoroughly wet, or become thoroughly wet [Old English *sopp* "bread dipped in liquid" < *sūpan* "swallow, taste" < Germanic, "take liquid"]

sop up *vt* to soak up a liquid with something absorbent

SOP *abbr* standard operating procedure

sop. *abbr* MUSIC soprano

soph. *abbr* US EDUC sophomore

soph·ism /sóf ìzzəm/ *n* an argument or explanation that seems very clever or subtle on the surface but is actually flawed, misleading, or intended to deceive [14C. Via French and Latin < Greek *sophisma* "acquired skill, clever device" < *sophos* "skilled in a craft, clever, wise"]

soph·ist /sóffist/ *n* **1.** *also* **Soph·ist** a member of a school of ancient Greek professional philosophers who were expert in and taught the skills of rhetoric, argument, and debate, but were criticized for specious reasoning. The sophists were active before and during the time of Socrates and Plato, who were their main critics. **2.** a deceptive person who offers clever-sounding but flawed arguments or explanations [Mid-16C. Via Latin *sophista* < Greek *sophistēs* "master of a craft, man clever in practical affairs," also "cheat" < *sophos* "skilled in a craft, clever, wise"]

so·phis·tic /sə fístik/, **so·phis·ti·cal** /-fístik'l/ *adj* **1.** clever-sounding and plausible but based on shallow or dishonest thinking or flawed logic **2.** relating to sophists [Mid-16C. Via Latin *sophisticus* < Greek *sophistikos* < *sophos* "skilled in a craft, clever, wise"] —**so·phis·ti·cal·ly** *adv*

so·phis·ti·cate *v* /sə fístə kàyt/ (**-cat·ed, -cat·ing, -cates**) **1.** *vt* **MAKE SOMEBODY MORE CULTURED OR WORLDLY** to make somebody more cultured or worldly, especially by educating out or destroying his or her naturalness, naiveté, or innocence **2.** *vt* **MAKE SOMETHING MORE COMPLEX** to make something more advanced or complex than before **3.** *vti* PHILOSOPHY **USE SOPHISTRY** to use sophistic arguments, or make reasoning or an argument sophistic **4.** *vt* **CORRUPT SOMETHING** to make something impure, false, or adulterated ■ *n* /sə fístəkət/ **CULTURED OR WORLDLY PERSON** a person with cultivated tastes and refined manners who knows how the world works [14C. < medieval Latin *sophisticat-*, past participle of *sophisticare* "deceive with words, disguise" < Latin *sophisticus* (see SOPHISTIC)] —**so·phis·ti·ca·tor** *n*

so·phis·ti·cat·ed /sə fístə kàytəd/ *adj* **1. KNOWLEDGEABLE AND CULTURED** knowledgeable about the ways of the world, self-confident, and not easily deceived **2. SUITABLE FOR SOPHISTICATED PEOPLE** appealing to or frequented by sophisticated people **3. ADVANCED** complex, advanced, and very up-to-date ○ *a sophisticated computer network* —**so·phis·ti·cat·ed·ly** *adv*

so·phis·ti·ca·tion /sə fìstə káysh'n/ *n* **1. KNOWLEDGEABLENESS AND REFINEMENT** a combination of worldly wisdom, self-confidence, and refinement in a person **2. ADVANCED TECHNICAL DEVELOPMENT** advanced technical development and complexity **3. ACT OF SOPHISTICATING** the process of sophisticating something or somebody

soph·is·try /sóffistree/ (*plural* **-tries**) *n* **1.** a method of argumentation that seems clever but is actually flawed or dishonest **2.** PHILOSOPHY same as **sophism** [14C. Via French < Latin *sophistria* < *sophista* (see SOPHIST)]

~~**sophmore**~~ incorrect spelling of **sophomore**

Soph·o·cles /sóffə kleez/ (496?–406? B.C.) Greek dramatist. The seven tragedies of his 123 plays that survive in complete texts, including *Electra*, *Oedipus Rex*, and *Antigone*, demonstrate the powerful treatment of moral and religious themes that made him one of the greatest dramatists of all time.

> "Wonders are many, and none is more wonderful than man."
> [Sophocles, *Antigone*; after 441 B.C.]

soph·o·more /sóffə màwr, sóf màwr/ *n* **1.** a second-year student in a high school or college **2.** somebody in the second year of a project or program [Late 17C. < obsolete *sophum*, early form of SOPHISM + ER[1], probably altered as if < Greek *sophos* "skilled in a craft, clever, wise" + *mōros* "dull"]

soph·o·mor·ic /sòffə máwrik/ *adj* **1.** showing the naive lack of judgement that accompanies immaturity (*disapproving*) **2.** relating to sophomores at high school or university

-sophy *suffix* wisdom, knowledge, science ○ *theosophy* [< Greek *sophia* < *sophos* "skilled in a craft, clever, wise"]

so·por /sópər/ *n* a very deep sleep or state of unconsciousness [Mid-17C. < Latin, "sleep"]

sop·o·rif·ic /sòppə ríffik, sōpə-/ *adj* **1. MAKING SOMEBODY SLEEPY** causing sleep or drowsiness **2. FEELING SLEEPY** experiencing sleepiness or drowsiness **3. TEDIOUS** dull and boring ■ *n* **SLEEP-INDUCING DRUG** a drug or other substance that induces sleep —**sop·o·rif·i·cal·ly** *adv*

sop·ping /sópping/, **sop·ping wet** *adj* thoroughly wet

SYNONYMS See *wet*.

sop·py /sóppee/ (**-pi·er, -pi·est**) *adj* **1. OVERLY SENTIMENTAL OR AFFECTIONATE** excessively affectionate or sentimental (*informal*) **2. SOAKING** thoroughly wet **3.** *US* **RAINY** characterized by heavy rainfall —**sop·pi·ly** *adv* —**sop·pi·ness** *n*

so·pra·ni·no /sòpprə neenō/ (*plural* **-nos**) *n* a musical instrument, usually a wind instrument, that has a pitch higher than any others in its family [Early 20C. < Italian, "little soprano" < *soprano* (see SOPRANO)]

so·pran·o /sə prànnō, sə praanō/ (*plural* **-os**) *n* **1. WOMAN OR BOY WITH HIGHEST VOICE** a woman, girl, or boy with the highest register of singing voice **2. HIGHEST SINGING VOICE** the highest register of singing voice a woman, girl, or boy can have **3. SINGING PART FOR SOPRANO VOICE** a singing part written for somebody with the highest register of voice **4. MUSICAL INSTRUMENT WITH HIGH PITCH** a musical instrument, especially a wind instrument, with the highest or second-highest pitch of instruments in its family [Early 18C. < Italian < *sopra* "above" < Latin *supra*]

so·pran·o clef *n* a C clef in which middle C is designated by the first line of the staff, formerly used for the soprano vocal line

Sop·with /sóp wìth/, **Sir Thomas** (1888–1989) British aircraft designer and yachtsman. His company produced many of the British aircraft used during World War I, including the Sopwith Camel. Full name **Sopwith, Sir Thomas Octave Murdoch**

SOR, s.o.r. *abbr* COMM sale or return

so·ra /sáwrə/ *n* a small grayish brown bird, which is seldom seen. Native to: bogs and swamps of North America. Latin name: *Porzana carolina*. [Early 18C. Origin ?]

sorb /sawrb/ *n* **1.** TREES same as **service tree 2.** *also* **sorb ap·ple** the berry of the service tree [Early 16C. Via French < Latin *sorbum* "serviceberry"] —**sor·bic** *adj*

Sorb /sawrb/ *n* a member of a Slavic people living mainly in the upper Spree Valley between eastern Germany and southwestern Poland. There are about 150,000 Sorbs, who are descendants of an earlier people known as Wends. [Mid-19C. Via German *Sorbe* < Wendish *serbje* "Serb"]

sorb apple *n* BOT same as **sorb** (sense 2)

sor·bet /sáwrbət, -bày/ *n* a frozen dessert, usually made with fruit syrup and sometimes egg whites, whisked until smooth [Late 16C. Via French *sorbet* and Italian *sorbetto* < Turkish *şerbet* "cool drink" (see SHERBET)]

sor·bic ac·id /sàwrbik-/ *n* a white crystalline solid acid. Source: berries of mountain ash or synthetically manufactured. Use: food preservative, fungicide. Formula: $C_6H_8O_2$.

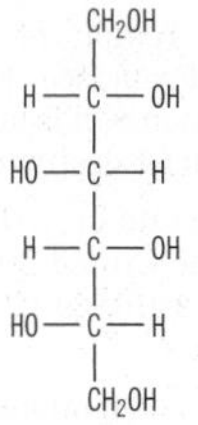

sorbitol

sor·bi·tol /sáwrbə tàwl/ *n* a white crystalline sweet alcohol. Source: berries of mountain ash or synthetically manufactured. Use: sweetener, moisturizer, manufacture of Vitamin C. Formula: $C_6H_{14}O_6$.

Sor·bonne /sawr bón/ *n* a part of the University of Paris, founded in 1253, that contains the faculties of science and literature

sor·bose /sáwr bòss/ *n* a six-carbon sugar that is an isomer of fructose [Late 19C. < SORBITOL]

sor·cer·er /sáwrssərər/ *n* somebody who is believed or claims to have magical powers [Early 16C. < French *sorcier* < Latin *sort-* "lot, fortune"]

sor·cer·ess /sáwrssərəss/ *n* a woman who is believed or claims to have magical powers

sor·cer·y /sáwrssəree/ *n* the supposed use of magic —**sor·cer·ous** *adj*

sor·did /sáwrdəd/ *adj* **1.** demonstrating the worst aspects of human nature such as immorality, selfishness, and greed **2.** dirty and depressing [Late 16C. Via French and Latin *sordidus* < *sordes* "dirt"] —**sor·did·ly** *adv* —**sor·did·ness** *n*

sor·di·no /sawr deenō/ (*plural* **-ni** /-nee/) *n* a device used to muffle or soften the tone of a musical instrument, e.g., a mute for a stringed or brass instrument or a damper on a piano [Late 16C. < Italian < *sordo* "unable to speak or hear" < Latin *surdus*]

sore /sawr/ *adj* (**sor·er, sor·est**) **1. PAINFUL** painful or tender because of an injury, infection, or unaccustomed exercise **2. ANNOYING** causing annoyance or embarrassment ○ *Her dismissal has always been a sore point.* **3. UPSET** angry or irritated, especially because of something said or done by another person in the recent past (*informal*) ○ *He was still sore because I kidded him about his tie.* **4. URGENT** requiring urgent action to provide relief ○ *The survivors of the flood are in sore need of help.* **5. DISTRESSING** causing great worry or distress (*literary*) ○ *The child's illness was a sore trial to her entire family.* ■ *n* **INFECTED SPOT** a painful open skin infection or wound ■ *adv* same as **sorely** (*archaic*) [Old English *sār* < Germanic] —**sore·ness** *n*

SPELLCHECK See *soar*.

sore·head /sáwr hèd/ *n* somebody who is regarded as easily offended or angered (*informal*)

sore·ly /sáwrlee/ *adv* to a great extent or degree ○ *I was sorely tempted to say "I told you so."*

sor·gho *n* AGRIC another spelling of **sorgo**

sorghum

sor·ghum /sáwrgəm/ (*plural* **-ghums** or *same*) *n* **1.** a drought-resistant cereal plant, widely cultivated in tropical and warm areas. Use: food grain, animal feed, hay and fodder. Genus: *Sorghum*. **2.** a syrup made from the juice of some varieties of sorghum [Late 16C. Via modern Latin < Italian *sorgo* (see SORGO)]

sor·go /sáwrgō/, **sor·gho** *n* a variety of sorghum cultivated as a source of syrup [Mid-18C. Via Italian < Vulgar Latin *syricum (granum)* "Syrian (grain)"]

so·ri BOT plural of **sorus**

sor·i·tes /sə rī teez/ (*plural same*) *n* an argument consisting of a series of premises arranged so that the predicate of each premise forms the subject of the next. The conclusion unites the subject of the first premise with the predicate of the last. [Mid-16C. Via Latin < Greek *sōreitēs* < *sōros* "heap"]

So·rop·ti·mist /sə róptimist/ *n* a member of an international organization (**Soroptimist International**) of professional women and businesswomen that promotes public service. It was founded in California in 1921. [Early 20C. Blend of Latin *soror* "sister" + OPTIMIST]

so·ror·ate /sáwrə ràyt/ *n* a custom in some societies in which a widower marries a younger sister of his deceased wife [Early 20C. < Latin *soror* "sister"]

so·ror·i·cide /sə ráwrə sīd/ *n* **1.** the murder of a sister **2.** a killer of his or her sister [Mid-17C. < Latin *soror* "sister"] —**so·ror·i·cid·al** /sə ràwrə sīd'l/ *adj*

so·ror·i·ty /sə ráwrətee, -rórrətee/ (*plural* **-ties**) *n* a social society for women who are students at a college or university, with a name consisting of individually pronounced Greek letters [Mid-16C. < medieval Latin *sororitas* < Latin *soror* "sister"]

sorp·tion /sáwrpsh'n/ *n* the taking in or holding of something, either by absorption or adsorption [Early 20C. Back-formation < ABSORPTION and ADSORPTION]

sor·rel[1] /sáwrəl, sórrəl/ (*plural* **-rels** or *same*) *n* a sharp-tasting plant of the dock family. Use: salad greens, medicines. Genus: *Rumex*. [14C. < Old French *surele* < *sur* "sour"]

sor·rel[2] /sáwrəl, sórrəl/ *adj* **REDDISH BROWN** of a reddish brown color ■ *n* **1. BROWN WITH RED ADDED** a brown color with a red tone **2. REDDISH BROWN ANIMAL** a horse or other animal with a reddish brown coat [15C. < Old French *sorel* < *sor* "yellowish"]

sorrel[3] /sáwrəl, sórrəl/ *n* *Carib* a red, spiced drink traditionally made from the sepals of hibiscus flowers at Christmas time [French *roselle* "*Hibiscus sabdariffa*"]

sor·rel tree *n* TREES same as **sourwood**

Sor·ren·to /sə réntō/ town and resort on the southern shore of the Bay of Naples, in Naples Province, Campania Region, in southern Italy. Population: 16,536 (2001).

sor·row /sórrō, sáwrō/ *n* **1.** GRIEF a feeling of deep sadness caused by a loss or misfortune **2.** SADDENING BURDEN an unfortunate event, experience, or other cause of sorrow ■ *vi* (**-rowed, -row·ing, -rows**) GRIEVE to feel or express deep sadness over something (*literary*) [Old English *sorg* < Germanic, "care"] —**sor·row·er** *n* ◇ **drown your sorrows** to take alcoholic drink in order to try to forget a source of sadness or disappointment (*informal*)

sor·row·ful /sórrōf'l, sáwrōf'l/ *adj* **1.** feeling or expressing sorrow **2.** characterized by or causing sorrow —**sor·row·ful·ly** *adv* —**sor·row·ful·ness** *n*

sor·ry /sórree, sáwree/ *adj* (**-ri·er, -ri·est**) **1.** APOLOGETIC feeling or expressing regret for an action that has upset or inconvenienced somebody, or is likely to do so **2.** SYMPATHETIC feeling or expressing sympathy or empathy, especially because of something that has happened ○ *I felt sorry it had to end that way.* ○ *Don't start feeling sorry for yourself.* **3.** PITIFUL pitifully bad or neglected ○ *a sorry little cottage with an overgrown garden* **4.** VERY BAD pathetically or contemptibly unsatisfactory ○ *a sorry excuse for a car* ■ *interj* **1.** USED AS APOLOGY used as an apology for hurting, interrupting, or inconveniencing somebody ○ *Sorry – I didn't realize that I stepped on your foot.* **2.** ASKING SOMEBODY TO REPEAT SOMETHING used with an interrogative inflection to ask somebody to repeat something (*informal*) ○ *Sorry? What did you just say?* **3.** USED AS CORRECTING REMARK used to introduce a correction in speech ○ *The company employs 10,000 – sorry, 12,000 workers nationwide.* [Old English *sārig* < *sār* (see SORE)] —**sor·ri·ly** *adv* —**sor·ri·ness** *n* ◇ **say you're sorry** to apologize to somebody

sort /sawrt/ *n* **1.** CATEGORY a category of persons or things with shared attributes, to which somebody or something can be assigned ○ *What sort of instrument is that?* **2.** PARTICULAR TYPE a particular type of person (*informal*) ○ *She'll help – she's a good sort.* **3.** SIMILAR THING something similar to a particular thing ○ *It's a sort of play with dancing.* **4.** COMPUT SORTING OF DATA a process of arranging data in a set order **5.** PRINTING LETTER OR SYMBOL a character in a font of type (*often used in the plural*) **6.** MANNER a manner of doing something (*archaic*) ■ *vt* (**sort·ed, sort·ing, sorts**) **1.** CATEGORIZE PEOPLE OR THINGS to place people or things in categories according to shared attributes ○ *clothes sorted into piles* **2.** PUT THINGS IN SEQUENCE to arrange things in a set order, especially automatically, as some computer programs do with data [14C. Via French < Latin *sort-* "lot, fortune"] —**sort·a·ble** *adj*—**sort·er** *n* ◇ **of a sort, of sorts** used to indicate that something is not very good ○ *We had a meal of sorts at the airport.* ◇ **out of sorts 1.** slightly unwell **2.** not in a very good mood ◇ **sort of** ⚠ somewhat (*informal*) ○ *This place is sort of strange.*

USAGE The expression ***sort of*** tends to be overused, even though it is not only vague but also very informal. In formal writing it is best to avoid usages like *He looked sort of unhappy*; the more formal words *somewhat* and *rather* are preferable.

USAGE See ***kind***[2].

SYNONYMS See ***type***.

sort out *vt* **1.** RESOLVE SOMETHING EFFECTIVELY to deal effectively with a problem ○ *I think we've sorted out our difficulties with the printer.* **2.** SEPARATE SOMETHING to separate something from the mixture it exists in, or from another group of things **3.** PUT SOMETHING IN ORDER to organize or disentangle something ○ *It took weeks to sort out the cluttered desk.* **4.** REACH CONCLUSION to think and come to a conclusion about a problem or difficulty

sor·ta·tion /sawr táysh'n/ *n* the process of sorting items into categories or into a set order, especially when done by machine or computer

sor·tie /sáwrtee/ *n* **1.** ATTACK ON ENEMY an attack made by a small military force into enemy territory **2.** AIRCRAFT MISSION a mission flown by a combat aircraft **3.** SHORT TRIP a brief trip away from home, especially to an unfamiliar place (*humorous*) **4.** PEOPLE ON SORTIE the personnel engaged in a military sortie ■ *vi* (**-tied, -tie·ing, -ties**) MIL MAKE SORTIE to make a sortie against an enemy position [Late 17C. < French, past participle of *sortir* "go out"]

sor·ti·lege /sáwrt'lij/ *n* **1.** the supposed foretelling of the future by drawing lots **2.** the supposed practice of magic or sorcery [14C. Via French < Latin *sortilegus* "prophetic, soothsayer" < *sort-* "lot, fortune" + *legere* "read"]

so·rus /sáwrəss/ (*plural* **-ri** /-rī/) *n* **1.** a cluster of spore cases on the underside of some fern fronds **2.** a spore-producing organ in some algae, fungi, and lichens [Mid-19C. Via modern Latin < Greek *sōros* "heap"]

SOS /èss ō éss/ *n* **1.** an international radio signal that ships or aircraft in serious distress can use to call for help. It consists of the letters "SOS" in Morse code (... – – – ...). **2.** a call or signal requesting help [Early 20C. < letters that are clear and easy to transmit; popularly regarded as abbreviation of *save our souls*]

So·sa /sóssə/, **Sammy** (*b.* 1968) Dominican baseball player. He played for the Chicago White Sox (1989–92) and the Chicago Cubs (1992–). In 1998 he hit a record-breaking 66 home runs, but was overtaken at the end of the season by Mark McGwire. Born **Sosa, Samuel Peralta**

so·sa·tie /sə saátee/ *n S Africa* curried or spicy meat grilled on a skewer [Mid-19C. Via Afrikaans < Malay *sesate*]

so-so (*informal*) *adj* neither very good nor very bad ○ *The food was so-so, but the atmosphere was wonderful.* ■ *adv* neither very well nor very badly ○ *feeling so-so*

sos·te·nu·to /sòstə nóotō/ *adv* with notes sustained to or beyond the notated value (*used as a musical direction*) ■ *n* (*plural* **sos·te·nu·tos**) a piece of music, or a section of a piece, played sostenuto [Mid-18C. < Italian, past participle of *sostinere* "sustain" < Latin *sustinere* (see SUSTAIN)] —**sos·te·nu·to** *adj*

sot /sot/ *n* an offensive term for somebody who habitually drinks alcohol to excess (*literary*) [Pre-12C. Via Old French, "fool" < medieval Latin *sottus*]

so·te·ri·ol·o·gy /sō tèeree óllәjee/ *n* the doctrine of salvation, especially the Christian doctrine of salvation through Jesus Christ [Mid-18C. < Greek *sōtēria* "salvation"] —**so·te·ri·o·log·ic** /sō tèeree ə lójjik/ *adj*

So·thic cy·cle /sóthik-, sòthik-/ *n* a cycle of 1460 Sothic years in the ancient Egyptian calendar [Early 19C. < Greek *Sōthis*, the star Sirius, used in calendar calculations]

So·thic year *n* a year of $365\frac{1}{4}$ days in the ancient Egyptian calendar, based on the first appearance of the dog star (**Sirius**) above the horizon [See SOTHIC CYCLE]

So·tho /só tō, sóo tóo/ (*plural same* or **-thos**) *n* **1.** a member of a large group of peoples who live in southern Africa, mainly in Botswana, Lesotho, and South Africa **2.** the group of Bantu languages of the Sotho people. There are three main languages in the group, Sesotho or Southern Sotho, Pedi or Northern Sotho, and Tswana. [Early 20C. < Bantu] —**So·tho** *adj*

So·to ♦ **de Soto, Hernando**

so·tol /só tōl/ *n* **1.** a prickly-leaved desert plant. Flowers: whitish, in dense clusters. Native to: southwestern United States, Mexico. Genus: *Dasylirion*. **2.** *Hispanic* an alcoholic drink made from the sap of the sotol plant [Late 19C. Via American Spanish *sotole* < Nahuatl *tzotolli*]

sot·tish /sóttish/ *adj* **1.** in the habit of drinking far too much alcohol **2.** showing the effects of having drunk too much alcohol

sot·to vo·ce /sòttō vṓchee, -cháy/ *adv* in a soft voice, so as not to be overheard [Mid-18C. < Italian, "under (the) voice"] —**sot·to vo·ce** *adj*

sou /soo/ *n* a French coin no longer in use, worth only a small amount [15C. < French, back-formation < Old French *sous*, plural of *sout* "sou" < Latin *solidus (nummus)* (see SOLDIER)]

sou·brette /soo brét/ *n* **1.** MAIDSERVANT IN COMEDY a pretty, flirtatious woman's role in a comedy, especially one in which she plays a lady's maid involved in romantic intrigues **2.** ACTOR PLAYING SOUBRETTE an actor who often plays soubrettes **3.** DISMISSIVE TERM a dismissive term for a young woman whose behavior is interpreted as flirtatious (*dated*) [Mid-18C. < French, "lady's maid" < Provençal *soubreto* "coy" < Latin *superare* "surpass" < *super* "above"]

sou·bri·quet *n* another spelling of **sobriquet**

~~souce~~ incorrect spelling of **source**

sou·chong /soo cháwng, -chóng/ *n* black China tea [Mid-18C. < Cantonese *síu-chúng* "small kind"]

sou·cou·yant /sóo koo yaán/ *n Carib* somebody, usually a woman, who according to legend sucks people's blood and can shed her skin, change into a ball of fire, and fly around by night. It is said that she must return to her skin before daylight, and that salt and thorn-trees offer protection against her. [Mid-20C. < Caribbean creole]

souf·fle /sóoff'l/ *n* a soft blowing sound inside somebody's chest, heard through a stethoscope and caused by blood flowing through blood vessels [Late 19C. < French, "breath" < *souffler* (see SOUFFLÉ)]

souf·flé /soo fláy/ *n* a baked or chilled dish that has been made light by adding whisked egg whites. Hot soufflés are usually based on a thick milk sauce and are baked, while cold soufflés are made with gelatin and set by chilling. [Early 19C. < French, past participle of *souffler* "blow, puff up" < Latin *sufflare*] —**souf·flé** *adj*

Sou·fri·ere Hills Vol·ca·no /sóofree èr-/ volcano on the island of Montserrat in the Caribbean Sea. It erupted in 1997, leaving large parts of the island uninhabitable. Height: 3,002 ft./915 m.

sough /sow, suf/ (*archaic or literary*) *vi* (**soughed, sough·ing, soughs**) to make a soft rustling, sighing, or murmuring sound, like the wind in trees ■ *n* a sound like that made by a gentle wind through trees [Old English *swōgan* < Germanic]

sought past participle, past tense of **seek**

sought-af·ter *adj* in high demand because scarce ○ *Blue diamonds are among the most sought-after gems.*

souk /sook/, **suq** *n* an open-air market in North Africa or Southwest Asia [Early 19C. < Arabic *sūķ*]

souk·ous /sóo kóoss/ *n* a style of dance music originally from the Democratic Republic of the Congo, combining guitar, drums, and vocals [Late 20C. Probably < Lingala < French *secouer* "to shake"]

soul /sōl/ *n* **1.** NONPHYSICAL ASPECT OF PERSON the complex of human attributes that manifests as consciousness, thought, feeling, and will, regarded as distinct from the physical body **2.** FEELINGS a person's emotional and moral nature, where the most private thoughts and feelings are hidden ○ *Her soul was in turmoil.* **3.** SPIRIT SURVIVING DEATH in some systems of religious belief, the spiritual part of a human being that is believed to continue to exist after the body dies. The soul is sometimes regarded as subject to future reward and punishment, and sometimes as able to take a form that allows it to remain on or return to earth. **4.** SPIRITUAL DEPTH evidence of spiritual or emotional depth and sensitivity, either in a person or in something created by a person ○ *Though technically perfect, the drawing lacked soul.* **5.** ESSENCE the deepest and truest nature of people or a nation, or what gives somebody or something a distinctive character ○ *In my travels I hoped to discover the soul of the Russian people.* **6.** TYPE OF PERSON somebody of a particular type, especially one regarded sympathetically or with familiarity ○ *Poor soul! What will he do now?* **7.** ANYONE anyone at all (*used in negative statements*) ○ *You have to promise not to tell a soul.* **8.** INDIVIDUAL PERSON an individual person, especially when thought of as making up the number of a group (*usually used in the plural*) ○ *a country of some 10 million souls* **9.** PERFECT EXAMPLE a good example, or personification, of a positive quality ○ *The hotel manager was the soul of discretion.* **10.** SOMEBODY ESSENTIAL TO SOMETHING the leader of or the most influential person in a group or movement **11.** AFRICAN AMERICAN SPIRIT a quality regarded as characterizing African American culture, especially as manifested in understanding and in social customs, speech, and music **12.** MUSIC same as **soul music** [Old English *sāwol* < Germanic] ◇ **sell your**

soul to abandon your principles in order to obtain wealth or success

SPELLCHECK See *sole*[1].

Soul /sōl/ *n* in the Christian Science religion, the name for God

soul broth·er *n* a man who is an Afro-Caribbean or African American like the person in question (*dated*)

soul food *n* the traditional foods of African Americans of the South. Typical dishes are yams, chitterlings, black-eyed peas, and collard greens.

soul·ful /sṓlf'l/ *adj* deeply or sincerely emotional —**soul·ful·ly** *adv* —**soul·ful·ness** *n*

soul kiss *n US* same as **French kiss**

soul·less /sṓl ləss/ *adj* **1.** lacking warmth, sensitivity, or feeling ○ *soulless bureaucrats* **2.** lacking anything that might stimulate or engage the feelings —**soul·less·ly** *adv* —**soul·less·ness** *n*

soul mate *n* somebody with whom somebody else naturally shares deep feelings and attitudes

soul mu·sic *n* a style of African American popular music with a strong emotional quality, related to gospel music and rhythm and blues

soul-search·ing *n* a thorough examination of personal thoughts and feelings, especially when faced with a difficult problem

soul sis·ter *n* a woman who is an Afro-Caribbean or African American like the person in question (*dated*)

sound[1] /sownd/ *n* **1.** SOMETHING AUDIBLE something that can be heard ○ *not a sound in the whole house* ○ *the sound of gunfire* **2.** VIBRATIONS SENSED BY EAR vibrations traveling through air, water, or some other medium, especially those within the range of frequencies that can be perceived by the human ear. At sea level and freezing point, the speed of sound through the air is 760 mi./1,220 km per hour. **3.** IMPLICATION an impression of somebody or something formed from limited but significant information, especially information lately received ○ *From the sound of it she's finally found a job she really likes.* **4.** EARSHOT the distance or area within which something can be heard ○ *Our house was within sound of the church bells.* **5.** ELECTRONICS REPRODUCED MUSIC OR SPEECH the music, speech, or other sounds heard through an electronic device such as a television, radio, or loudspeaker, especially with regard to volume or quality ○ *Please turn down the sound.* **6.** BROADCAST RECORDING OF MUSIC OR SPEECH the recording, editing, and replaying of music, speech, or sound effects in the broadcast or entertainment industry **7.** LING BASIC ELEMENT OF SPOKEN LANGUAGE a basic element of speech formed by the vocal tract and interpreted through the ear, or a combination of such sounds **8.** MUSIC TYPE OF MUSIC the distinctive quality that identifies bands or music from a particular place, area, or studio, or belonging to a particular movement or style ■ *v* (**sound·ed, sound·ing, sounds**) **1.** *vi* SEEM to give a particular impression when mentioned or described ○ *The meal sounded awful.* **2.** *vi* INDICATE CONDITION to give a particular impression about a physical or mental condition via speech or writing ○ *He sounded exhausted when I talked to him on the phone.* **3.** *vi* HAVE PARTICULAR QUALITY WHEN HEARD to give a particular impression to a hearer about the quality of the noise or the identity of the source of the noise ○ *That sounds like the mailman.* **4.** *vti* MAKE A NOISE to make a particular noise so as to be heard, or make something produce such a noise ○ *Somewhere down the corridor, an alarm sounded.* **5.** *vt* ANNOUNCE SOMETHING to spread the news of or signal something by making a noise, or produce a similar effect by saying something ○ *She sounded a note of caution about the likely result of the reorganization.* **6.** *vt* PHON ARTICULATE A SOUND to pronounce a letter or sound, especially in a context in which it might be silent ○ *You don't sound the "p" in "psychic."* **7.** *vt* MED TEST BODILY CONDITION BY CAUSING SOUND to observe the sound made by an organ of the body for testing or diagnostic purposes [13C. Via French < Latin *sonus*]

sound off *vi* **1.** to express strong feelings through speech, or complain loudly about something (*informal*) ○ *always sounding off about high property taxes* **2.** to chant or count in turn while marching

sound out *vt* **1.** to find out somebody's opinions about something before committing to a course of action **2.** to try reading a new word by pronouncing it letter by letter or syllable by syllable ○ *Be sure to sound out the new words before you ask for help.*

sound[2] /sownd/ *adj* **1.** SENSIBLE based on good sense and valid reasoning ○ *a sound argument* **2.** NOT DAMAGED without any serious damage or decay **3.** HEALTHY free from injury, disease, or illness **4.** COMPLETELY ACCEPTABLE worthy of approval, especially as agreeing with traditional views or conforming to conventional behavior ○ *morally sound opinions* **5.** DEEP AND PEACEFUL unbroken by waking and untroubled by dreams or discomfort ○ *She had a sound night's sleep.* **6.** COMPLETE including all necessary aspects and details ○ *sound knowledge of the subject* **7.** THOROUGH painful and thorough ○ *a sound spanking* **8.** FIN WITH LITTLE FINANCIAL RISK financially secure and likely to make money **9.** LOGIC VALID WITH TRUE PREMISES having a true conclusion that follows from true premises **10.** LAW LEGALLY VALID valid in law ■ *adv* DEEPLY in a deep and peaceful way ○ *sound asleep* [12C. Shortening of Old English *gesund* < W Germanic] —**sound·ly** *adv* —**sound·ness** *n*

SYNONYMS See *valid*.

sound[3] /sownd/ *v* (**sound·ed, sound·ing, sounds**) **1.** *vti* NAUT MEASURE DEPTH to measure the depth of water using a weighted line or sonar **2.** *vi* ZOOL DIVE DOWN to dive suddenly and swiftly downward (*refers to whales*) **3.** *vt* MED EXAMINE SOMETHING WITH PROBE to use a surgical probe to examine a body cavity or passage such as the bladder or to dilate a constriction ■ *n* MED SURGICAL PROBE a surgical probe used to sound body cavities [14C. Via French *sonder* < Vulgar Latin *subundare* < Latin *sub* "under" + *unda* "wave"] —**sound·er** *n*

sound[4] /sownd/ *n* **1.** GEOG WIDE CHANNEL a broad channel between two large bodies of water, or between an island and the mainland **2.** GEOG OCEAN INLET a long wide arm of the sea **3.** FISH AIR BLADDER the air bladder of a fish [Old English *sund* < Germanic]

sound·a·like /sównd ə lìk/ *n* **1.** a performer whose voice or musical style closely resembles that of a particular well-known performer **2.** a word that sounds similar to another word but has a different spelling

sound bar·ri·er *n* a sudden increase in the force of air opposing an aircraft or other moving body as it approaches the speed of sound, producing a sonic boom

sound bite *n* a short comment intended or suitable for broadcasting in a news program, especially one made by a politician. Their use is often regarded as manipulative.

sound·board /sównd bàwrd/ *n* a thin sheet of wood placed under or above the strings of a musical instrument to increase resonance. On a violin it is the top of the instrument.

sound bow *n* the thick part of a bell, where the clapper strikes

sound·box /sównd bòks/ *n* the hollow chamber in a stringed instrument that increases its resonance

sound card *n* a computer circuit board that allows a personal computer to receive sound in digital form and reproduce it through speakers

sound ef·fect *n* a recording or imitation of a sound used in a movie, radio or television program, play, or other theatrical performance ■ **sound ef·fects** *npl* all the sounds in a movie, broadcast, or theater production other than dialogue and music

sound hole *n* an opening near the center of a hollow stringed instrument that increases resonance

sound·ing[1] /sównding/ *n* **1.** NAUT DEPTH MEASUREMENT a measurement of the depth of water, taken using sonar or a weighted line **2.** METEOROL ATMOSPHERIC MEASUREMENT a measurement of the conditions in the atmosphere at a specific altitude ■ **sound·ings** *npl* **1.** PRELIMINARY INQUIRY INTO OPINION a sampling of the views of a group of people taken before committing to a course of action ○ *taking soundings about the popularity of the council's plans* **2.** NAUT WATER WHERE DEPTH MEASUREMENTS ARE TAKEN a place where the water is shallow enough for a sounding line to be used to determine its depth [14C. < SOUND[2]]

sound·ing[2] /sównding/ *adj* having an impressive or resonant sound (*literary*) [14C. < SOUND[1]] —**sound·ing·ly** *adv*

sound·ing board *n* **1.** a person or group that gives feedback on preliminary ideas before they are considered for further development **2.** MUSIC same as **soundboard** **3.** ACOUSTICS a rooflike structure built above a pulpit or platform to direct the speaker's voice to the audience [< SOUNDING[1]]

sound·ing line *n* a weighted line with measurements marked on it, used for determining the depth of water [< SOUNDING[1]]

sound·ing rock·et *n* a rocket used to make scientific observations within the Earth's atmosphere [< SOUNDING[1]]

sound·less /sówndləss/ *adj* not making any noise —**sound·less·ly** *adv* —**sound·less·ness** *n*

sound mix·er *n* a person or machine that combines or balances sounds for a recording, broadcast, or movie soundtrack

sound·post /sównd pōst/ *n* a small piece of wood inside the body of a stringed instrument that supports the bridge and transmits the vibrations to the back

sound·proof /sównd proòf/ *adj* constructed so that no sound can enter or escape ■ *vt* (**-proofed, -proof·ing, -proofs**) to line or seal a room so that no sound can enter or escape

sound rang·ing *n* a method of locating the source of a sound by measuring the travel time of sound waves to a microphone at a fixed position

sound shift *n* a systematic change over time in the pronunciation of a set of sounds in a language

sound spec·tro·graph *n* an electronic instrument that makes a graphic representation of sound qualities

sound stage *n* a large room or studio, usually soundproof, where movie scenes are shot

sound sys·tem *n* electronic equipment for amplifying sound, used in recording, broadcasting, or live at public gatherings

sound·track /sównd tràk/ *n* **1.** SOUND RECORDING FOR MOVIE the recorded music, dialogue, and sound effects in a movie or video production **2.** STRIP CARRYING MOVIE SOUND a thin strip at the edge of a movie reel or videotape on which sound is recorded **3.** MUSIC FROM MOVIE a commercially released recording of the music that has been used in a movie

sound truck *n US* a truck with loudspeakers attached to the roof, used for broadcasting political messages or sales pitches

sound wave *n* an audible pressure wave caused by a disturbance in water or air and carried forward in a ripple effect

soup /soop/ *n* **1.** LIQUID FOOD a liquid food made by cooking meat, fish, vegetables, or other ingredients in water, milk, or stock **2.** SOMETHING THICK AND SWIRLING something with the consistency or appearance of soup, especially a swirling liquid or dense fog ○ *the primordial soup of hydrogen, oxygen, and other gases* **3.** *US* EXPLOSIVE nitroglycerin or gelignite (*slang*) [Mid-17C. Via French *soupe* < late Latin *suppa* < assumed *suppare* "soak"] ◇ **from soup to nuts** used to emphasize the variety or the wide range of something ◇ **in the soup** in difficulties or trouble (*informal*)

soup up *vt* to make changes to a car, motorcycle, engine, or similar machine in order to make it more powerful (*informal*) [< SOUP "drug injected into a horse to increase its speed"]

soup·çon /soop sáwN, soòp sòn/ *n* a very small amount of something [Mid-18C. Via French, "suspicion" < Latin *suspicion-* (see SUSPICION)]

soup du jour /soòp də joòr/ (*plural* **soups du jour** /*pronunc. same*/) *n* the featured soup of the day on the menu of a restaurant [Mid-20C. < French "soup of the day"]

Sou·pha·nou·vong /soò faa noo vóng/ (1909–95) prince and president of Laos (1975–86). He fought for independence from French rule and helped to found the nationalist Pathet Lao in 1950.

soup kitch·en *n* a place that serves free meals to people of a lower income group

soup·spoon /so͞op spo͞on/ *n* a spoon with a round bowl for eating soup

soup·y /so͞opee/ (**-i·er, -i·est**) *adj* **1.** LIKE SOUP like soup in appearance or consistency **2.** DAMP OR FOGGY unpleasantly damp or foggy (*informal*) **3.** SENTIMENTAL highly sentimental (*informal*)

sour /sowr/ *adj* **1.** SHARP-TASTING having a tart or sharp taste that is acidic though not necessarily unpleasant, like the taste of vinegar, lemons, or unripe apples **2.** BAD THROUGH FERMENTATION unpleasantly rancid in taste or smell because of fermentation ○ *It was so hot that the milk went sour in hours.* **3.** DISSATISFIED characterized by ill temper or feelings of bitterness or dissatisfaction ○ *a sour look* **4.** UNFRIENDLY unpleasant, unfriendly, or ill-disposed, having previously been harmonious, friendly, or approving ○ *After two years the partnership began to turn sour.* **5.** UNPLEASANT causing distaste or discomfort **6.** AGRIC LACKING LIME describes soil that is too acidic because of a lack of lime, and is therefore unfavorable to crops **7.** INDUST SULFUROUS AND ACIDIC describes crude oil or gas that is foul-smelling, toxic, and acidic because of excessive levels of sulfur compounds ■ *vti* (**soured, sour·ing, sours**) **1.** BECOME OR MAKE SOMEBODY DISSATISFIED to become bad-tempered, embittered, or unfriendly, or make somebody become so ○ *A breach of diplomacy soured relations between the two countries.* **2.** BECOME OR MAKE SOMETHING SOUR to become sour in taste, smell, or composition, or make something sour in this way ■ *n* **1.** SHARPNESS sharpness or tartness of taste ○ *added some sugar to tone down the sour* **2.** COCKTAIL WITH LEMON OR LIME a cocktail made with whiskey, lemon or lime juice, and often sugar [Old English *sūr* < Germanic] —**sour·ly** *adv* —**sour·ness** *n*

sour·ball /sówr bàwl/ *n US* a round hard piece of candy with a tart flavor

source /sawrss/ *n* **1.** ORIGIN the place, person, or thing through which something has come into being or from which it has been obtained **2.** PROVIDER OF INFORMATION a person, organization, book, or other text that supplies information or evidence ○ *a reliable source* **3.** ARTS WORK ON WHICH ANOTHER IS BASED a creation that forms the basis of or inspiration for a later work, e.g., a story or work of art **4.** GEOG BEGINNING OF RIVER the spring or fountain from which a river or stream first issues from the ground, or the area around this **5.** ELECTRONICS ELECTRODE SUPPLYING CURRENT in a field effect transistor, the electrode from which the electrical current originates ■ *vt* (**sourced, sourc·ing, sourc·es**) **1.** LOCATE SOMETHING FOR USE to get parts, materials, or information from elsewhere **2.** SPECIFY SOURCES OF SOMETHING WRITTEN to list the people or materials used in researching a written work ○ *The book has been thoroughly sourced.* [14C. < Old French *sourse* < past participle of *sourdre* "rise, spring" < Latin *surgere*]

SYNONYMS See ***origin***.

source book, **source·book** *n* a document or collection of documents that is the main source of information about a subject of study

source code *n* computer code written in a recognized programming language that can be converted into machine code

source lan·guage *n* the language from which a translation is made

sour cher·ry *n* **1.** a sharp-tasting red or blackish fruit used mainly in cooking and preserves **2.** a bush or small tree that produces sour cherries. Native to: Europe, Asia. Latin name: *Prunus cerasus*.

sour cream *n* smooth thick cream that has been soured artificially, used in cooking and baking and as a topping

sour·dine /so͝or deen, soor deen/ *n* **1.** a reed instrument with a soft tone similar to a bassoon. It is no longer in use. **2.** MUSIC same as **sordino** **3.** a stop on an organ that produces a low muted tone [Early 17C. Via French < Italian *sordina*, form of *sordino* (see SORDINO)]

sour·dough /sówr dō/ *n* **1.** FERMENTING DOUGH fermenting dough used as a leavening agent in making bread **2.** SOURDOUGH BREAD bread made with sourdough **3.** *Can, Northwest US* VETERAN PROSPECTOR an experienced prospector, especially in northwestern Canada and Alaska (*informal*)

sour grapes *n* the scornful denial that something is attractive or desirable because it is unobtainable [In allusion to Aesop's fable *The Fox and the Grapes* where the fox disparages some grapes as sour when he cannot reach them]

sour gum *n* a tree with glossy leaves and light wood. Native to: eastern United States. Latin name: *Nyssa sylvatica*.

sour mash *n* **1.** a grain mash that is a mixture of new and old batches, used in distilling some kinds of whiskey **2.** whiskey distilled using sour mash

sour milk *n Southern US* sour milk that has curdled

sour or·ange *n US* same as **bitter orange**

sour·puss /sówr po͝oss/ *n* somebody regarded as gloomy or bad-tempered (*informal*)

sour·sop /sówr sòp/ (*plural* **-sops** or *same*) *n* **1.** a spiny fruit with a tart fibrous pulp **2.** a tree with spicy fragrant leaves that produces soursops. Native to: tropical America. Latin name: *Annona muricata*.

sour·wood /sówr wo͝od/ (*plural* **-woods** or *same*) *n* a tree with thick bark, small white flowers, and sour-tasting leaves. Native to: eastern United States. Latin name: *Oxydendrum arboreum*.

Sou·sa /so͞ozə, -sə/, **John Philip** (1854–1932) US military bandmaster and composer. His rousing patriotic compositions include "The Stars and Stripes Forever" (1897). Known as **the March King**

> "Jazz will endure just as long as people hear it through their feet instead of their brains."
> [Attributed to John Philip Sousa]

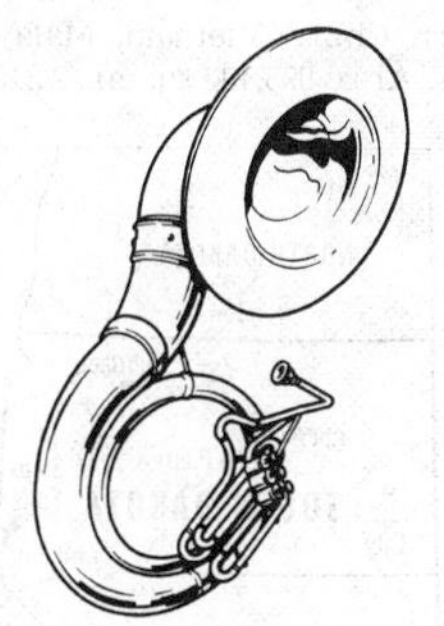

sousaphone

sou·sa·phone /so͞ozə fōn, so͞ossə-/ *n* a large brass instrument with a flaring bell that resembles a tuba. It is used in military marching bands. [Early 20C. After John Philip SOUSA] —**sou·sa·phon·ist** *n*

sous-chef /so͞o-/ *n* a head chef's assistant and deputy [Late 17C.< French, "under chef"]

souse /sowss/ *v* (**soused, sous·ing, sous·es**) **1.** *vti* DRENCH OR SOAK to make something soaking wet, or become soaking wet **2.** *vti* PLUNGE INTO LIQUID to plunge into a liquid, or plunge something into a liquid **3.** *vt* PICKLE SOMETHING to steep something in vinegar or brine in order to preserve it (*often passive*) **4.** *vt* MAKE SOMEBODY INTOXICATED to make somebody extremely intoxicated (*slang; usually passive*) ■ *n* **1.** LIQUID USED IN PICKLING the brine or vinegar used in pickling **2.** PICKLED FOOD pickled food, especially pork trimmings **3.** *also* **souse meat** *Southern US* HEADCHEESE sausage made of edible trimmings from the head and feet, usually pork **4.** *Carib* BROTH MADE WITH PORK a broth made with a pig's snout, feet, and sometimes tail, boiled with vegetables and seasonings **5.** DRUNKARD somebody who is habitually drunk (*slang*) **6.** BINGE a bout of heavy drinking (*dated*) [14C. < Old French *sous*]

REGIONAL NOTE See ***headcheese***.

sous·lik *n* ZOOL another spelling of **suslik**

sou-sou /so͞o so͞o/, **su·su** *n Carib* an arrangement for saving money whereby participants pay a sum each month for a fixed period of time and take turns borrowing the total amount accumulated [Early 20th C. < Yoruba *eesu* or *esusu* "fund where several people pool their money, each paying a fixed sum and each drawing out the total in rotation," probably influenced by French *sou* "coin"]

Sousse /sooss/ city and port in east central Tunisia. Population: 125,000 (1994).

sou·tache /soo tásh/ *n* a narrow ornamental braid in a herringbone pattern, used for trimming garments [Mid-19C. Via French < Hungarian *sujtás*]

sou·tane /soo taán/ *n* a priest's robe or cassock, especially one with buttons down the front [Mid-19C. Via French < Italian *sottana* < *sotto* "below" < Latin *subtus*]

Sout·er /so͞otər/, **David** (*b.* 1939) associate justice of the US Supreme Court. He was appointed an associate justice in 1990 and developed a reputation as a judicial centrist. Full name **Souter, David Hackett**

sou·ter·rain /so͞otə ráyn/ *n* an ancient underground room or passage [Mid-18C. < French, "underground"]

south /sowth/ *n* **1.** DIRECTION TO RIGHT FACING RISING SUN the direction that lies directly to the right of somebody facing the rising sun or that is located toward the bottom of a conventional map of the world **2.** COMPASS POINT OPPOSITE NORTH the compass point that lies directly opposite north **3.** *also* **South** AREA IN SOUTH the part of an area, country, or region that is situated in or toward the south **4.** POSITION EQUIVALENT TO SOUTH the position equivalent to south in any diagram consisting of four points at 90-degree intervals ■ *adj* **1.** *also* **South** IN SOUTH situated in, facing, or coming from the south of a place, region, or country **2.** BLOWING FROM SOUTH describes a wind that blows from the south ■ *adv* TOWARD SOUTH in or toward the south [Old English *sūþ* < Germanic]

South *n* **1.** the region of the United States that includes the states south of the Mason-Dixon Line **2.** the states of the Confederacy during the Civil War

South Africa

South Af·ri·ca country in southern Africa. It became a fully democratic republic in 1994 when it rejoined the British Commonwealth (after withdrawing in 1961). Language: Afrikaans, English, Ndebele, Northern Sotho, Southern Sotho, Swati, Tsonga, Tswana, Venda, Xhosa, Zulu. Currency: rand. Capital: Pretoria. Population: 42,768,678 (2003). Area: 470,693 sq. mi./1,219,090 sq. km. Official name **Republic of South Africa** —**South Af·ri·can** *n, adj*

South Af·ri·can Dutch *n* LANG same as **Cape Dutch** (*not used in South Africa*)

South Af·ri·can Eng·lish *n* a variety of English spoken in South Africa. See panel on next page

South A·mer·i·ca fourth largest continent in the world, lying between the Atlantic and Pacific oceans southeast of North America and stretching from the isthmus of Panama southward to Cape Horn. Population: 317,846,000 (1996). Area: 6,880,000 sq. mi./17,819,100 sq. km. —**South A·mer·i·can** *adj, n*

South A·mer·i·can try·pan·o·so·mi·a·sis *n* same as **Chagas' disease**

South·amp·ton /sow thámptən, sowth hámptən/ city in Hampshire, southern England. It is one of England's principal ports. Population: 217,445 (2001).

South·amp·ton Is·land island in Nunavut, Canada, between Foxe Basin and Hudson Bay. Area: 15,913 sq. mi./41,214 sq. km.

South A·sia region comprising the countries of Bangladesh, Bhutan, India, the Maldives, Nepal, Pakistan, and Sri Lanka

South A·sian Eng·lish *n* a variety of English spoken in South Asia. See panel on next page

WORLD ENGLISH ***South African English*** is the variety of English used in the Republic of South Africa. Since the early 19th century it has been the mother tongue of settlers of British origin and a second language, in varying degrees, of indigenous Afrikaners, Africans, and Asians. Since 1994, the nation has had 11 official languages: English, Afrikaans, Ndebele, Sotho (Northern and Southern), Swati, Tsonga, Tswana, Venda, Xhosa, and Zulu. South African English tends not to pronounce *r* in words such as *art, door,* and *worker,* and, among Africans, generally has full vowels in all syllables (e.g., *seven* is pronounced "seh-ven" not "sev'n"). In the speech of middle-class British South Africans distinctive usages are common: e.g., the vowels in *park* and *trap* are heard by outsiders as "pork" and "trep," and in *fair hair* as "fay hay." A curiosity of the grammar is the affirmative "*no*," as in *How are you? – No, I'm fine,* probably adopted from Afrikaans. With its parent Dutch, this language has provided the bulk of local borrowings: e.g., *Afrikaner* "a white South African of Dutch or Huguenot origin," *apartheid* "former policy of separate racial development," *bakkie* "pickup truck," *braai* "barbecue," *drift* "ford," *kloof* "ravine," the now internationalized *trek* "journey," and *veld,* pronounced /felt/, "open country," with its hybrid extensions *highveld* and *backveld.* Words from African languages include *impala, muti* (medicine), *sangoma* (diviner), and *tshwala* (sorghum beer). Distinctive English words are the now-archaic *bioscope* (movie), *location* (district set aside for a particular group), and *robot* (traffic light).

WORLD ENGLISH ***South Asian English*** is the variety of English that has been used since the 17th century in South Asia. Usage varies greatly from area to area, primarily because of the influence of local languages on pronunciation, grammar, and vocabulary, e.g., Bangla (formerly called Bengali) in Bangladesh and the Indian state of Bengal, Hindi in northern India, Tamil in southern India and Sri Lanka, Urdu in Pakistan and India, and Sinhalese in Sri Lanka. At the same time, however, there is considerable uniformity throughout the region as a consequence of British administrative, legal, and commercial usage, the presence of English-language media schools based on British models, and, more recently, local television.

South Asian English pronounces *r* in words such as *art, door,* and *worker.* It tends to have full vowels in all syllables (e.g., *seven* is pronounced "seh-ven" not "sev'n"), and it is widely considered to have a singsong quality often compared with that of English speakers in Wales. Two widespread grammatical features are, first, questions without word-order inversion, as in *What you would like to buy, please? Where you are coming from? Why you are doing this?* Second is the end-of-sentence use of *only* for emphasis: *He is coming once a week only* for *He only comes once a week.* Widely used in the region are adopted local expressions such as: *gherao* (in industrial actions, surrounding people so that they cannot leave a place; also used as a verb, e.g., *He was gheraoed yesterday*); *wallah* "man," used in compounds like *dhobiwallah* meaning "laundry man"; and the numbers *lakh* "one hundred thousand," e.g., *a lakh of rupees,* and *crore* "ten million" in *They have crores of rupees.* Hybridization of English with indigenous usages is common, as in *policewallah* "policeman," and *goondaism* "behaving like a *goonda* or thug," itself a South Asian word.

South Aus·tra·lia state occupying the central part of southern Australia. Founded in 1834, it was the only Australian colony set up as a free settlement rather than a penal colony. Capital: Adelaide. Population: 1,527,400 (2003). Area: 379,900 sq. mi./984,000 sq. km. —**South Aus·tral·i·an** *n, adj*

South Bend city in northern Indiana, on the Kankakee and St. Joseph rivers, southwest of Elkhart. It is home to the University of Notre Dame. Population: 106,558 (2002 estimate).

south·bound /sówth bòwnd/ *adj* leading, going, or traveling toward the south

South·bridge /sówth brìj/ town in south central Massachusetts, north of the Connecticut border, east of Springfield and southwest of Worcester. Population: 17,398 (2002 estimate).

south by east *n* the direction or compass point midway between south and south-southeast —**south by east** *adj, adv*

south by west *n* the direction or compass point midway between south and south-southwest —**south by west** *adj, adv*

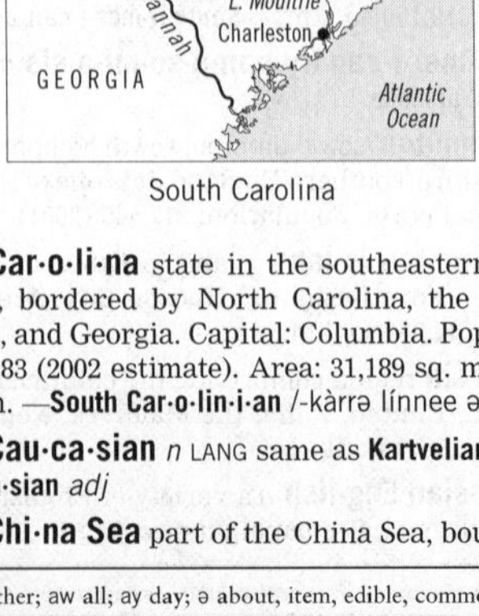

South Carolina

South Car·o·li·na state in the southeastern United States, bordered by North Carolina, the Atlantic Ocean, and Georgia. Capital: Columbia. Population: 4,107,183 (2002 estimate). Area: 31,189 sq. mi./80,779 sq. km. —**South Car·o·lin·i·an** /-kàrrə línnee ən/ *n, adj*

South Cau·ca·sian *n* LANG same as **Kartvelian** —**South Cau·ca·sian** *adj*

South Chi·na Sea part of the China Sea, bounded by southeastern China, Vietnam, Malaysia, and the Philippines. Area: 895,400 sq. mi./2,319,000 sq. km.

South Dakota

South Da·ko·ta state in the north central United States, bordered by North Dakota, Minnesota, Iowa, Nebraska, Wyoming, and Montana. Capital: Pierre. Population: 761,063 (2002 estimate). Area: 77,121 sq. mi./199,742 sq. km. —**South Da·ko·tan** *n, adj*

South·down /sówth dòwn/ *n* a breed of small-to-medium hornless English sheep with short dense wool. Raised for: mutton. [Late 18C. After the SOUTH DOWNS]

South Downs chalk ridge extending along the southern coast of England, through Hampshire and East Sussex

south·east /sowth éest/ *n* **1.** COMPASS POINT BETWEEN SOUTH AND EAST the direction or compass point midway between south and east **2.** *also* **South·east** AREA IN SOUTHEAST the part of an area, region, or country that is situated in or toward the southeast ■ *adj* **1.** *also* **South·east** IN SOUTHEAST situated in, facing, or lying toward the southeast of a region, place, or country **2.** BLOWING FROM SOUTHEAST describes a wind that blows from the southeast ■ *adv* TOWARD SOUTHEAST in or toward the southeast

South·east A·sia /sowth èest-/ region comprising the countries of Brunei, Cambodia, East Timor, Indonesia, Laos, Malaysia, Myanmar, the Philippines, Singapore, Thailand, and Vietnam —**South·east A·sian** *n, adj*

South·east A·sia Trea·ty Or·ga·ni·za·tion *n* a former alliance of countries for economic cooperation and defense against communism in Southeast Asia and the South Pacific, formed in 1954 and disbanded in 1977. Its members were the United States, the United Kingdom, France, Australia, New Zealand, the Philippines, and Thailand.

south·east by east *n* the direction or compass point midway between southeast and east-southeast —**south·east by east** *adj, adv*

south·east by south *n* the direction or compass point midway between southeast and south-southeast —**south·east by south** *adj, adv*

south·east·er /sowth éestər/ *n* a storm or wind that blows from the southeast

south·east·er·ly /sowth éestərlee/ *adj* **1.** IN SOUTHEAST situated in or toward the southeast **2.** BLOWING FROM SOUTHEAST describes a wind that blows from the southeast ■ *n* (*plural* **-lies**) WIND FROM SOUTHEAST a wind that blows from the southeast —**south·east·er·ly** *adv*

south·east·ern /sowth éestərn/ *adj* **1.** IN SOUTHEAST situated in the southeast of a region or country **2.** FACING SOUTHEAST facing the southeast **3.** *also* **South·east·ern** OF SOUTHEAST native to the southeast of a region or country —**south·east·ern·most** *adj*

south·east·ward /sowth éestwərd/ *adj* IN SOUTHEAST toward or in the southeast ■ *n* POINT IN SOUTHEAST a direction toward or a point in the southeast ■ *adv* *also* **south·east·wards** /-wərdz/ TOWARD SOUTHEAST in a southeasterly direction —**south·east·ward·ly** *adv, adj*

South·end-on-Sea /sòwth end-/ city in Essex, eastern England, on the Thames Estuary. Population: 160,257 (2001).

south·er /sówthər/ *n* a strong wind that blows from the south

south·er·ly /sú̱thərlee/ *adj* **1.** IN SOUTH situated in or toward the south **2.** BLOWING FROM SOUTH describes a wind that blows from the south ■ *n* (*plural* **-lies**) WIND FROM SOUTH a wind that blows from the south —**south·er·ly** *adv*

south·ern /sú̱thərn/ *adj* **1.** IN SOUTH situated in the south of a region or country **2.** SOUTH OF EQUATOR lying south of the equator or south of the celestial equator **3.** FACING SOUTH facing the south **4.** *also* **South·ern** OF SOUTH native to the south of a region or country **5.** BLOWING FROM SOUTH describes a wind that blows from the south [Old English *suþerne* < Germanic]

South·ern /sú̱thərn/, **E. M.** (*b.* 1938) British biochemist. He devised various techniques for studying genetic patterns in DNA, including southern blot. Full name **Southern, Edwin Mallor**

South·ern Alps /sú̱thərn-/ mountain range on the South Island, New Zealand. It extends from the far north to the extreme southwest of the island. Its highest peak is Mount Cook, 12,316 ft./3,754 m.

South·ern blot *n* a technique for transferring DNA restriction fragments onto a membrane filter enabling them to be identified with a gene probe [Late 20C. After E. M. SOUTHERN]

South·ern Cross *n* a constellation of the southern hemisphere containing four bright stars forming a cross. The smallest of the 88 constellations, it contains the Coalsack, a dark cloud of dust obscuring the stars beyond it in the Milky Way. See illustration at **constellation**

South·ern Crown *n* ASTRON same as **Corona Australis**

south·ern·er /sú̱thərnər/, **South·ern·er** *n* somebody who comes from the southern part of a country or region

south·ern hem·i·sphere *n* **1.** the half of Earth that is south of the equator **2.** the southern half of an imaginary sphere that contains the universe and is divided horizontally by the celestial equator

South·ern·ism /sú̱thər nìzzəm/ *n* **1.** an expression or pronunciation that is characteristic of the southern United States **2.** an attitude or custom that is characteristic of the South, especially in the United States

south·ern·most /sú̱thərn mòst/ *adj* situated farthest south

South·ern Pai·ute, **South·ern Pi·ute** *n* **1.** a member of a Native North American people who lived in Utah, Nevada, Arizona, and California, and now live in

Utah **2.** the Uto-Aztecan language of the Southern Paiute people —**South·ern Pai·ute** *adj*

South·ern prick·ly ash *n* same as **Hercules' club** (sense 2)

South·ern Rho·de·sia former name for **Zimbabwe**

South·ern So·tho *n* LANG same as **Sesotho**

south·ern·wood /sŭthərn wòod/ (*plural* **-woods** or *same*) *n* an ornamental bush with fragrant gray bitter-tasting leaves. Native to: Europe. Latin name: *Artemisia abrotanum.*

South·ey /sówthee, sŭthee/, **Robert.** (1774–1843) British poet. He was one of the Lake Poets, along with Wordsworth and Coleridge. He became poet laureate in 1813.

> "Now tell us all about the war / And what they fought each other for."
> [Robert Southey, "The Battle of Blenheim"; 1800]

South Geor·gia uninhabited mountainous island in the South Atlantic Ocean, southeast of the Falkland Islands. A dependency of the United Kingdom, it was first visited by Captain James Cook in 1775. Area: 1,387 sq. mi./3,592 sq. km.

South Had·ley /-háddlee/ town in south central Massachusetts, east of the Connecticut River and northeast of Holyoke. It is home to Mount Holyoke College. Population: 17,248 (2002 estimate).

South Hol·land province in the west central Netherlands. Capital: The Hague. Population: 3,397,343 (2000). Area: 1,104 sq. mi./2,860 sq. km.

south·ing /sówthing/ *n* **1.** the distance a point is south of a reference latitude **2.** the distance covered as a ship sails toward the south

South Is·land the larger and more southerly of the two main islands of New Zealand, in the southwestern Pacific Ocean. Population: 931,566 (1996). Area: 58,093 sq. mi./150,460 sq. km.

South Ko·re·a /-kə rée ə, -kō-/ country in East Asia that occupies the southern portion of the Korean Peninsula. Language: Korean. Currency: won. Capital: Seoul. Population: 48,289,037 (2003). Area: 38,328 sq. mi./99,268 sq. km. Official name **Republic of Korea** —**South Ko·re·an** *n, adj*

South·land /sówthlənd/ administrative region of New Zealand, occupying the southernmost tip of the South Island. Capital: Invercargill. Population: 91,002 (2001). Area: 20,514 sq. mi./53,132 sq. km.

south·paw /sówth pàw/ *n* a left-handed person, especially a left-handed baseball pitcher, a left-handed fiddler, or a boxer who leads with the left hand (*informal*) [Late 19C. Originally used of left-handed baseball players, from the pitcher's orientation on the mound (since baseball diamonds are traditionally oriented to the same points of the compass)]

south pole *n* **1.** GEOG another spelling of **South Pole 2.** the south end of the axis of rotation of a planet or other astronomical object **3.** the point where the southern end of the Earth's axis intersects the celestial sphere

South Pole *n* the southern end of the Earth's axis at the latitude of 90° S

South·port /sówth pàwrt/ city in Merseyside, in northwestern England. Population: 90,959 (1991).

South Port·land city in southwestern Maine, on the southern shore of Casco Bay, southeast of Portland. Population: 23,255 (2002 estimate).

South Sas·katch·e·wan river rising in the Rocky Mountains and flowing north into Lake Winnipeg, Canada. Length: 865 mi./1,390 km.

South Sea Bub·ble *n* frenzied speculation in the South Sea Company in early 18th-century Britain. In 1720 the company collapsed, ruining many banks and private investors. The company had taken over much of the national debt in return for sole trading rights in the area.

South Seas *npl* **1.** the southern part of the Pacific Ocean **2.** all the ocean waters south of the equator

South Shields /-shéeldz/ port in Tyne and Wear, northeastern England. Population: 83,704 (1991).

south-south·east *n* the direction or compass point midway between south and southeast ■ *adj, adv* in, from, facing, or toward the south-southeast —**south-south·east·er·ly** *adv*

south-south·west *n* the direction or compass point midway between south and southwest ■ *adj, adv* in, from, facing, or toward the south-southwest —**south-south·west·er·ly** *adv*

South Ta·ra·na·ki Bight /-tàrrə nàkee bīt/ gulf on the southwestern coast of the North Island, New Zealand. It extends from Otakeho in the west to Kakaramea in the east.

South Vi·et·nam former country in Southeast Asia between 1954 and 1976. It occupied the southern part of modern-day Vietnam. —**South Vi·et·nam·ese** *n, adj*

south·ward /sówthwərd/ *adj* IN SOUTH toward or in the south ■ *n* POINT IN SOUTH a direction toward or a point in the south ■ *adv also* **south·wards** /-wərdz/ TOWARD SOUTH in a southerly direction —**south·ward·ly** *adv, adj*

south·west /sowth wést/ *n* **1.** COMPASS POINT BETWEEN SOUTH AND WEST the direction or compass point midway between south and west **2.** *also* **South·west** AREA IN SOUTHWEST the part of an area, region, or country that is situated in or toward the southwest **3. South·west** SW STATES the region of the United States that includes Texas, New Mexico, Arizona, Nevada, and California, and sometimes regarded as extending northward to Utah and Colorado ■ *adj* **1.** *also* **South·west** IN SOUTHWEST situated in, facing, or lying toward the southwest of a region, place, or country **2.** BLOWING FROM SOUTHWEST describes a wind that is blowing from the southwest ■ *adv* TOWARD SOUTHWEST in or toward the southwest

South·west A·sia region comprising Afghanistan and countries in the Arabian Peninsula and bordering the eastern Mediterranean

south·west by south *n* the direction or compass point midway between southwest and south-southwest —**south·west by south** *adj, adv*

south·west by west *n* the direction or compass point midway between southwest and west-southwest —**south·west by west** *adj, adv*

South·west Cape southernmost point in New Zealand, situated at the southern tip of Stewart Island

south·west·er /sowth wéstər, sow-/ *n* **1.** a storm or wind that blows from the southwest **2.** CLOTHING same as **sou'wester** (senses 1–2)

south·west·er·ly /sowth wéstərlee, sow-/ *adj* **1.** IN SOUTHWEST situated in or toward the southwest **2.** BLOWING FROM SOUTHWEST describes a wind that blows from the southwest ■ *n* (*plural* **-lies**) WIND FROM SOUTHWEST a wind that blows from the southwest —**south·west·er·ly** *adv*

south·west·ern /sowth wéstərn/ *adj* **1.** IN SOUTHWEST situated in the southwest of a region or country **2.** FACING SOUTHWEST situated in or facing the southwest **3.** *also* **South·west·ern** OF SOUTHWEST native to the southwest of a region or country —**south·west·ern·most** *adj*

south·west·ward /sowth wéstwərd/ *adj* IN SOUTHWEST toward or in the southwest ■ *n* POINT IN SOUTHWEST a direction toward or a point in the southwest ■ *adv also* **south·west·wards** /-wərds/ TOWARD SOUTHWEST in a southwesterly direction —**south·west·ward·ly** *adv, adj*

South York·shire metropolitan county in northern England. Area: 603 sq. mi./1,562 sq. km.

Sou·van·na Phou·ma /soo vaánaa póomaa/ (1901–84) prince and prime minister of Laos (1951–54, 1956–58, 1960, 1962–75). He negotiated the treaty of independence from French rule (1953). He was deposed in a coup in 1975.

~~**souvenier**~~ incorrect spelling of **souvenir**

sou·ve·nir /soovə néer/ *n* something bought or kept as a reminder of a place or occasion [Late 18C. < French, "memory," use of verb < Latin *subvenire* "come into mind"]

sou·vlak·i·a /soov laákee ə/ *npl* Greek kabobs consisting of pieces of marinated meat, usually lamb, skewered and broiled [Mid-20C. < modern Greek, "small skewers" < *souvla* "skewer"]

sou'west·er /sow wéstər/ *n* **1.** a long waterproof coat, originally made of oilskin, now usually of rubber or plastic, worn during stormy weather at sea **2.** a waterproof hat with a broad brim covering the back of the neck, originally made of oilskin, now usually of rubber or plastic. Sou'westers were originally worn by sailors and fishermen. ■ METEOROL same as **southwester** (sense 1) [Mid-19C. Contraction of SOUTHWESTER]

Sov. *abbr* Soviet

sover·eign /sóvvrən/ *n* **1.** MONARCH the ruler or permanent head of a state, especially a king or queen **2.** OLD BRITISH GOLD COIN a gold coin worth one pound, used in Britain between the early 17th and the early 20th centuries ■ *adj* **1.** INDEPENDENT self-governing and not ruled by any other state ○ *a sovereign state* **2.** WITH COMPLETE POWER having supreme authority or power ○ *The king is the sovereign ruler of the land.* **3.** OUTSTANDING outstanding, e.g., in its excellence or effectiveness ○ *Her voice was her sovereign talent.* [13C. Via Old French *souverein* < Vulgar Latin *superanus* < Latin *super* "above"] —**sov·er·eign·ly** *adv*

sover·eign·tist /sóvvrəntist/ *n Can* a supporter of sovereignty for Quebec

sover·eign·ty /sóvvrəntee/ (*plural* **sov·er·eign·ties**) *n* **1.** TOP AUTHORITY supreme authority, especially over a state **2.** INDEPENDENCE the right to self-government without interference from outside **3.** INDEPENDENT STATE a politically independent state

sov·er·eign·ty as·so·ci·a·tion *n Can* a proposed type of economic and political association between a sovereign Quebec and the rest of Canada

~~**soveriegn**~~ incorrect spelling of **sovereign**

~~**soverign**~~ incorrect spelling of **sovereign**

so·vi·et /sṓvee ət, -ét/ *n* **1.** an elected government council that existed at local, regional, and national levels in the former Soviet Union. The highest was the Supreme Soviet. **2.** a council in the early political organization of the Russian Revolution in 1917 [Early 20C. < Russian *sovet* "council"] —**so·vi·et·ism** *n*

So·vi·et *adj* TYPICAL OF U.S.S.R. relating to the former Soviet Union, or to its people, culture, or political system ■ *n* SOMEBODY FROM U.S.S.R. somebody who came from the former Soviet Union ■ **So·vi·ets** *npl* LEADERS OF THE SOVIET UNION the government of the former Soviet Union, or the leaders of the former Communist bloc

So·vi·et·ol·o·gist /sṓvee ə tólləjist/ *n* a scholar who studies the former Soviet Union, especially its government and political history

So·vi·et Un·ion /sṓvee ət yóonyən/ former federation of Communist states in Eastern Europe and northern and central Asia from 1922 until 1991. Moscow was its capital. Then the largest country in the world, the Soviet Union was the Communist superpower during the Cold War. Official name **Union of Soviet Socialist Republics**

sow[1] /sō/ (**sowed, sown** /sōn/ or **sowed, sow·ing, sows**) *v* **1.** *vti* PLANT SEED to scatter or plant seed on an area of land in order to grow crops **2.** *vt* INTRODUCE IDEA to instill and spread an idea, especially one which is negative or divisive ○ *Increased competition will only sow discord among the members of the company.* **3.** *vt* SPREAD SOMETHING THICKLY to spread something thickly with something (*often passive*) ○ *a sky sown with stars* [Old English *sāwan* < Indo-European] —**sow·a·ble** *adj* —**sow·er** *n*

SPELLCHECK See ***sew***

sow[2] /sow/ *n* **1.** FEMALE HOG an adult female hog **2.** ADULT FEMALE ANIMAL the adult female of several animals such as the bear, mink, badger, guinea pig, and hedgehog **3.** METALL CHANNEL FOR MOLTEN IRON a channel through which molten iron runs into a mold in the process of casting pig iron **4.** METALL HARDENED IRON a mass of iron that has hardened in a channel or mold in the process of casting pig iron [Old English *sugu* < Indo-European]

Sow. *abbr S Asia* Sowbhagyawati

sow·back /sów bàk/ *n* a long ridge of earth left by a glacier [Late 19C. Because supposed to resemble a pig's back]

sow·bel·ly /sów bèllee/ *n* fatty salt pork

REGIONAL NOTE See *fatback*.

Sow·bhag·ya·wa·ti /sə bùggyə wúttee/ *n S Asia* a title used before the name of a married woman whose husband is still alive, roughly equivalent to the English term "Mrs." [< Sanskrit]

sow·bread /sów brèd/ (*plural* **-breads** or *same*) *n* a cyclamen, especially one with a single nodding flower. Native to: southern Europe. Genus: *Cyclamen*. [Mid-16C. Because supposedly eaten by hogs]

sow bug /sów-/ *n* same as **wood louse** [Because it resembles a hog in shape]

So·we·to /sə wáytō, sə wéttō/ township in southern Johannesburg, Gauteng Province, South Africa. Population: 596,632 (1991). [Mid-20C. Acronym for "South Western Townships"]

sown past participle of **sow**[1]

sow this·tle /sów thìss'l/ *n* a prickly-leaved plant. Flowers: yellow. Native to: Europe, Asia. Genus: *Sonchus*. [Origin ?]

sox CLOTHING plural of **sock**[1] (sense 1) (*informal*)

soy /soy/, **soy·a** /sóy ə/ *n* **1.** PLANTS the soybean plant **2.** FOOD same as **soy sauce** ■ *adj* made or derived from soybeans ○ *soy inks* [Late 17C. Via Dutch, Malay, and Japanese < Chinese *jiàngyoú* "soybean oil"]

soy·a bean *n UK* PLANTS, FOOD same as **soybean**

soy·bean /sóy bèen/ *n* **1.** the oil- and protein-rich seed of the soybean plant. Use: soy sauce, soymilk, tofu, textured vegetable protein. **2.** a plant cultivated around the world for its nutritious seeds, for soil improvement, and to provide grazing for animals. Native to: southeastern Asia. Latin name: *Glycine max*.

So·yin·ka /shaw yíngkə/, **Wole** (*b.* 1934) Nigerian writer and political activist. His plays, poems, and novels examine the relationship between traditional and modern African cultures, and include *Poems from Prison* (1969). He won a Nobel Prize in literature (1986). Full name **Soyinka, Akinwande Oluwole**

> "There is only one home to the life of a tortoise; there is only one shell to the soul of man: there is only one world to the spirit of our race. If that world leaves its course and smashes on the boulder of the great void, whose world will give us shelter?"
> [Wole Soyinka, *Death and the King's Horseman*; 1975]

soy·milk /sóy mìlk/ *n* a milk substitute made from soybeans, often with vitamins and sugar added

soy sauce *n* a dark salty liquid made by fermenting soybeans in brine, used to flavor foods

soz·zled /sózz'ld/ *adj* extremely intoxicated (*informal*) [Late 19C. < dialect *sozzle* "splash, mess," probably an imitation of the sound]

SP *abbr* **1.** NAVY shore patrol **2.** ELEC single pole **3.** ARMY specialist **4.** NAVY submarine patrol

sp. *abbr* **1.** special **2.** BIOL species **3.** specific **4.** MED, BIOL specimen **5.** spelling

Sp. *abbr* **1.** Spain **2.** Spaniard **3.** Spanish

s.p. *abbr* without children [Latin *sine prole*]

spa /spaa/ *n* **1.** same as **health spa** **2.** a resort with mineral springs **3.** a tub with a device for aerating or swirling water [Early 17C. After *Spa*, resort town in Belgium, famous for mineral springs]

SpA *abbr* COMM limited company (*used after the name of an Italian company*) [Italian *Società per Azioni*]

space /spayss/ *n* **1.** INTERVAL OF TIME a period or interval of time ○ *In the space of two hours the situation was resolved.* **2.** ENOUGH ROOM room to fit or accommodate something or somebody ○ *There isn't space for the table.* **3.** AREA SET APART an area set apart or available for use ○ *floor space* **4.** REGION BEYOND EARTH'S ATMOSPHERE the region that lies beyond the Earth's atmosphere, and all that it contains ○ *space travel* **5.** REGION BETWEEN ALL ASTRONOMICAL OBJECTS the region, usually of negligible density, between all astronomical objects in the universe **6.** THREE-DIMENSIONAL EXPANSE WHERE MATTER EXISTS the unbounded three-dimensional expanse in which all matter exists **7.** PRINTING BLANK AREA BETWEEN TYPE a blank area between characters, words, or lines of type, or an interval the width of a single character **8.** MUSIC INTERVAL BETWEEN LINES OF MUSICAL STAFF an interval between the lines of the musical staff **9.** COMMUNICATION TIME OR AREA AVAILABLE FOR ADVERTISING broadcast time or an area in a publication available for specific use, e.g., by advertisers **10.** MATH SET OF POINTS GOVERNED BY AXIOMS in mathematics, a collection of points that have geometric properties in that they obey set rules (**axioms**), e.g., a Euclidean space that is governed by Euclidean geometry. Each non-Euclidean geometry, having its own axioms, has its own non-Euclidean space containing a collection of points governed by those axioms. **11.** PRINTING PIECE OF TYPE TO CREATE BLANK a piece of type used to create a blank interval in printing **12.** FREEDOM TO ASSERT IDENTITY the freedom or opportunity to assert a personal identity or fulfill personal needs (*informal*) ○ *I need my own personal space.* **13.** COMMUNICATION INTERVAL IN TELEGRAPHIC TRANSMISSION an interval during the transmission of a telegraphic message when the key is not in contact ■ *v* (**spaced, spac·ing, spac·es**) **1.** *vt* SET THINGS APART to set things some distance apart or arrange them with gaps between **2.** *vi* BECOME DAZED to become distracted, forgetful, or inattentive (*slang*) [13C Via French *espace* < Latin *spatium* "space, distance"]
space out *v* **1.** *vt* same as **space** *v* (sense 1) **2.** *vti* to become distracted, forgetful, or inattentive, or cause somebody to become distracted, forgetful or inattentive (*slang*)

space age, Space Age *n* the era marked by the exploration of space, often considered as beginning in 1957 when the Soviet Union launched Sputnik —**space-age** *adj*

space·band /spáyss bànd/ *n* a device used in printing to provide variable but even spacing between words in a justified line

space bar *n* a horizontal bar at the bottom of a keyboard or typewriter that is pressed to introduce a space

space bi·ol·o·gy *n* BIOL same as **exobiology**

space blan·ket *n* a plastic wrapping with aluminum foil coating that is used to restore body heat in people affected by exposure or exhaustion

space·bridge /spáyss brìj/ *n* a way of communicating internationally by television, using transmissions from orbiting satellites

space ca·det *n* somebody whose behavior is regarded as mildly strange, especially somebody who seems disoriented or out of touch with a situation (*slang*)

space cap·sule *n* a vehicle or cabin designed to support life and used for transporting human beings or animals in outer space or at very high altitudes within the Earth's atmosphere

space charge *n* the net electric charge distributed in a given volume of space

space·craft /spáyss kràft/ (*plural same* or **-crafts**) *n* a vehicle or device designed for travel or use in space

spaced-out /spàyst-/, **spaced** /spayst/ *adj* inattentive, dazed, confused, or lightheaded from or as if from drug use (*slang*)

space·far·ing /spáyss fèrring/ *n* the use of spacecraft for the exploration of outer space —**space·far·ing** *adj*

space·flight /spáyss flìt/ *n* flight beyond the Earth's atmosphere, or an instance of this

space heat·er *n* a small portable appliance used to heat a small area

space·lab /spáyss làb/ *n* a laboratory in space used to carry out scientific experiments

space lat·tice *n* CRYSTALS same as **lattice** *n* (sense 4)

space·less /spáyssləss/ *adj* (*literary*) **1.** with no limits **2.** not occupying any space

space·man /spáyss màn, -mən/ (*plural* **-men** /-mèn, -mən/) *n* **1.** a man who is an astronaut **2.** in science fiction, a traveler to Earth from outer space

space med·i·cine *n* the branch of medicine dealing with the effects of space flight on the human body

Popperfoto
Space Needle

Space Nee·dle *n* a tall tower in downtown Seattle, Washington, with a revolving restaurant and observation deck near the top. It was built for the 1962 World's Fair.

space o·pe·ra *n* a science fiction drama involving space travel and, often, extraterrestrial beings (*informal*)

space·port /spáyss pàwrt/ *n* an installation for launching, testing, landing, and maintaining spacecraft

space probe *n* a satellite or other spacecraft that is designed to explore the solar system and transmit data back to Earth

spac·er /spàyssər/ *n* something inserted between two other things to keep them apart, e.g., a pierced bar threaded on a multistring necklace to prevent the strands from tangling

space·ship /spáyss shìp/ *n* a vehicle designed to transport people or materials through outer space

space shut·tle *n* a reusable spacecraft designed to transport people and cargo between Earth and space, with two solid rocket boosters and an external fuel tank that are jettisoned after takeoff

space sick·ness *n* motion sickness experienced as a result of space flight

space sta·tion *n* a spacecraft or satellite designed to be occupied by a crew for extended periods of time and used as a base for the exploration, observation, and research of space

AKG London
spacesuit: astronaut Buzz Aldrin on the moon

space·suit /spáyss sòot/ *n* a sealed pressurized suit designed to support the wearer's life in space

space-time, space-time con·tin·u·um *n* a four-dimensional system consisting of three spatial coordinates and one for time, in which it is possible to locate events

space-time foam *n* PHYS same as **quantum foam**

space·walk /spáyss wàwk/ *n* an excursion by an astronaut or cosmonaut outside the spacecraft ■ *vi* (**-walked, -walk·ing, -walks**) to go out of a spacecraft in order to perform a task or experiment —**space·walk·er** *n*

space·ward /spáysswərd/ *adj* moving in the direction of outer space ■ *adv also* **space·wards** /-wərdz/ in the direction of outer space

space·wom·an /spáyss wòommən/ (*plural* **-wom·en** /-wìmmin/) *n* **1.** a female astronaut **2.** in science fiction, a female traveler to Earth from outer space

space writ·er *n* a writer paid according to the area of print taken up by what is written

spac·ey *adj* another spelling of **spacy** (*slang*)

Spac·ey /spáyssee/, **Kevin** (*b.* 1964) US actor. He won an Academy Award for best actor for *American Beauty* (1999) and for best supporting actor for *The Usual Suspects* (1995).

spa·cial /spáysh'l/ *adj* another spelling of **spatial**

spac·ing /spáyssing/ *n* **1.** the space between several things, e.g., between words or lines in type, or the way this space is arranged **2.** the act of arranging things in spaces

spa·cious /spáyshəss/ *adj* **1.** containing ample space **2.** expansive and broad in scope —**spa·cious·ly** *adv* —**spa·cious·ness** *n*

Spack·le /spák'l/ *tdmk* a trademark for a compound used in surfacing interior walls

spac·y /spáyssee/ (**-i·er, -i·est**), **spac·ey** *adj* same as **spaced-out** (*slang*)

spade[1] /spayd/ *n* a digging tool with a wide shallow blade flattened where it meets the shaft so it can be pushed into the ground with the foot ■ *vti* (**spad·ed, spad·ing, spades**) to dig, cut, or remove something using a spade [Old English *spadu* < Indo-European] ◇ **call a spade a spade** to say plainly and bluntly what you mean

spade[2] /spayd/ *n* **1.** PLAYING CARD a playing card of the suit of spades. ◊ **spades 2.** BLACK SYMBOL ON PLAYING CARD a black symbol shaped like a stylized spade on a playing card. ◊ **spades 3.** TABOO TERM a highly offensive term for somebody, especially a man, who is of African descent (*taboo*) [Late 16C. < Italian, plural of *spada* "sword" (the sign used on Italian cards) < Latin *spatha* "broadsword" (see SPATULA)] ◇ **in spades** to a very great degree (*informal*)

spade·fish /spáyd fish/ (*plural same* or **-fish·es**) *n* a deep-bodied bony fish. Native to: Atlantic coastal waters. Family: Ephippidae. [Early 18C. < its shape]

spade·foot toad /spàyd foot-/ *n* a burrowing toad found in drier regions of the world, with a hardened edge on its hind feet that is used for excavating deep burrows. Family: Pelobatidae.

spades /spaydz/ *n* one of the four suits used in cards, with a black figure shaped like a stylized spade as its symbol (*takes a singular or plural verb*)

spade·work /spáyd wùrk/ *n* **1.** preliminary work that is often hard drudgery **2.** work done using a spade

spa·di·ces BOT plural of **spadix**

spa·dille /spə díl/ *n* in some card games, e.g., ombre, the highest trump card [Late 17C. Via French < Spanish *espadilla* "small sword" < Latin *spatha* (see SPADE[2])]

spa·dix /spáydiks/ (*plural* **-di·ces** /spáydi seez/) *n* a fleshy or succulent plant spike that bears tiny flowers and is usually enclosed in a leafy sheath (**spathe**) [Mid-18C. Via Latin "palm branch torn off with its fruit" < Greek < *span* "to pull"]

spaetz·le /shpéts'l, shpétslə/ (*plural same* or **-les**), **spätz·le** *n* a hot dish from southern Germany and Alsace consisting of very small noodles or dumplings formed by pressing batter through a colander into boiling water. It is often served with gravy or sauce. [< German dialect, literally "little sparrows"]

~~**spagetti**~~ incorrect spelling of **spaghetti**

spa·ghet·ti /spə géttee/ *n* **1.** STRING-SHAPED PASTA pasta in the shape of long thin strings **2.** COOKED STRING-SHAPED PASTA a dish of long thin strings of boiled pasta, usually served with a sauce **3.** *US* ELEC TUBING FOR COVERING BARE WIRE insulating tubing used to cover bare wire. Can term **sleeving** [Mid-19C. < Italian (plural), diminutive of *spago* "string"]

spa·ghet·ti·ni /spàggə teénee/ *n* pasta that is thinner than spaghetti but thicker than vermicelli [Mid-20C. < Italian, diminutive of *spaghetti* (see SPAGHETTI)]

spa·ghet·ti squash *n* an oval winter squash with a yellow rind whose cooked flesh can be scraped out in long strands that resemble spaghetti

spa·ghet·ti West·ern *n* a low-budget Western made in Europe by an Italian movie company, characterized by extreme and melodramatic violence

Spain

Spain /spayn/ country in southwestern Europe on the Iberian Peninsula, east of Portugal. Language: Spanish. Currency: euro. Capital: Madrid. Population: 40,217,413 (2003). Area: 195,364 sq. mi./505,990 sq. km. Official name **Kingdom of Spain**

spake past tense of **speak** (*archaic*)

spall /spawl/ *n* a small fragment, splinter, or chip of stone or ore ■ *vti* (**spalled, spall·ing, spalls**) to break up into small chips, flakes, or splinters [15C. Origin ?]

spal·la·tion /spaw láysh'n/ *n* **1.** a nuclear reaction in which several particles are emitted from the nucleus of an atom after bombardment with high-energy particles or radiation **2.** the removal of the surface layers of a rock by meteorite impact

spal·peen /spáwl peen/ *n Ireland* **1.** a mischievous and cunning person **2.** an impoverished farm laborer [Late 18C. < Irish *spailpín*]

spam /spam/ *n* ELECTRONIC JUNK MAIL an unsolicited, often commercial, message transmitted through the Internet as a mass mailing to a large number of recipients ■ *vti* (**spammed, spam·ming, spams**) **1.** SEND UNWANTED E-MAIL to send an unsolicited e-mail message, often an advertisement, to many people **2.** POST UNWANTED ELECTRONIC MESSAGES to post a message many times to a newsgroup, or an inappropriate message to multiple newsgroups [Late 20C. Probably from a sketch in the UK television comedy series *Monty Python's Flying Circus* in which all items on a menu contained Spam™] —**spam·mer** *n*

Spam *tdmk* a trademark for canned chopped meat, mainly pork, that is pressed into a loaf

spam kill·er *n* a piece of software that automatically identifies and deals with spam in incoming e-mail

spam·ming /spámming/ *n* the sending of unsolicited electronic messages through the Internet to a large number of recipients

span[1] /span/ *n* **1.** DISTANCE BETWEEN LIMITS the distance or expanse between two extremes or limits **2.** DISTANCE BETWEEN BRIDGE SUPPORTS the extent or space between abutments or supports, e.g., on a bridge or arch, or a portion of the structure that is supported in this way **3.** AVIAT same as **wingspan 4.** PERIOD FOR MAINTENANCE OF COGNITIVE FUNCTION the period of time during which a mental function or act can be maintained ○ *a short attention span* **5.** PERIOD OF TIME a period of time, especially the lifetime of a person **6.** MEASURE OLD MEASUREMENT an old measurement based on the distance from the end of the thumb to the end of the little finger of a spread hand, approximately 9 in./23 cm ■ *vt* (**spanned, span·ning, spans**) **1.** EXTEND OVER OR ACROSS SOMETHING to reach or extend over or across something **2.** MEASURE SOMETHING WITH THE HAND to measure something by or as if by the hand with fingers and thumb fully extended [Old English *spann* < Germanic]

span[2] /span/ *vt* (**spanned, span·ning, spans**) TIE SOMETHING to lash or tie something ■ *n* **1.** STRIP OF ROPE a strip of rope that has been tied down at one end **2.** PAIR OF HORSES DRIVEN TOGETHER a pair of horses or other animals harnessed and driven together [Mid-18C. < Dutch < *spannen*, "harness"]

span[3] /span/ past tense of **spin** (*archaic*)

Span. *abbr* Spanish

spa·na·ko·pi·ta /spaanə kópeetə, -kə péetə/ *n* a traditional Greek dish of spinach and feta cheese baked in phyllo dough [Mid-20C. < modern Greek *spanakopēta* "spinach pie"]

Span·dau /spán dòw/ district of Berlin, Germany, the site of a prison where Nazi war criminals were confined after World War II. Population: 192,895 (1986).

span·dex /spán dèks/ *n* a synthetic stretch fabric or fiber made from polyurethane [Mid-20C. < EXPAND]

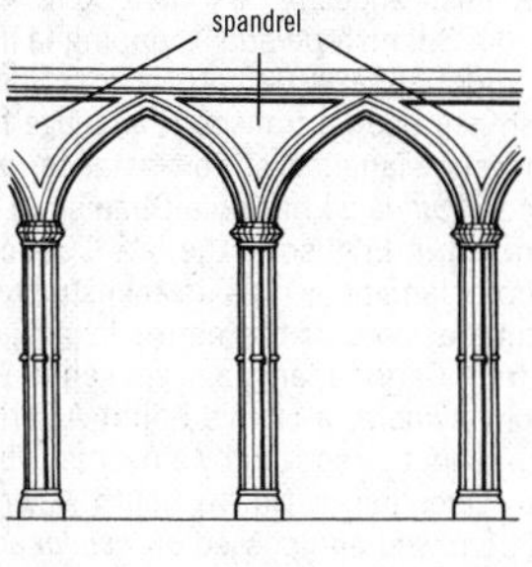

spandrel

span·drel /spándrəl/, **span·dril** *n* **1.** the triangular space between the right or left exterior curve of an arch and the framework of another arch **2.** the area between two arches and a horizontal cornice above them [15C. Origin ?]

spang /spang/ *adv US* completely, squarely, or exactly on target or in the middle of something (*informal*) [Mid-19C. Origin ?]

span·gle /spáng g'l/ *n* **1.** SMALL SHINY DECORATION a small shiny piece of metal or plastic used for decoration on clothing **2.** SMALL SPARKLING OBJECT a small sparkling spot or object ■ *v* (**-gled, -gling, -gles**) **1.** *vt* SPRINKLE SOMETHING WITH SPANGLES to sprinkle or adorn something with spangles **2.** *vi* GLITTER WITH SPANGLES to sparkle or glitter as if adorned with spangles [15C. < obsolete *spang* "glittering ornament" < Dutch *spange* "clasp"] —**span·gly** *adj*

Spang·lish /spáng glish/ *n* a variety of Spanish characterized by many borrowings from English [Mid-20C. Blend of SPANISH + ENGLISH] —**Spang·lish** *adj*

Span·iard /spánnyərd/ *n* somebody who comes from Spain [14C. < Old French *Espaignart* < Latin *Hispania* "Spain"]

spaniel

span·iel /spánnyəl/ *n* a small or medium-sized dog characterized by a long wavy silky coat, usually short legs, and large drooping ears [14C. < Old French *espaigneul* "Spanish" < Latin *Hispania* "Spain"]

Span·ish /spánnish/ *n* LANG ROMANCE LANGUAGE a Romance language that is the official language of Spain and of many Central and South American countries, including Argentina, Bolivia, Chile, Colombia, Costa Rica, Cuba, Mexico, and Peru. It is also spoken widely elsewhere, including in the southwestern United States. Native speakers: 358 million. Other speakers: 59 million. See panel on next page ■ *npl* PEOPLES PEOPLE OF SPAIN the people of Spain ■ *adj* **1.** RELATING TO SPAIN relating to Spain, or its people or culture **2.** LANG OF SPANISH relating to Spanish [13C. < SPAIN]

Span·ish A·mer·i·ca /spànnish-/ part of America that was colonized by the Spanish from the 16th century and where Spanish is still widely spoken. It includes

LANGUAGE HERITAGE *Spanish* Much of English is made up of words from other languages, and Spanish is a very important contributor in this respect, especially in US English. US English has naturalized and adapted not only Spanish words per se, but also words from varieties of Spanish such as American Spanish and Mexican Spanish, and words originating in the languages of Central and South America.

Some well-known and easily recognizable Spanish émigrés to English are direct borrowings: ***corral*** (late 16th century), ***matador*** (late 17th), ***pompano*** (late 18th), ***piñata*** (late 19th), and ***mano a mano*** (late 20th). Other émigrés are less recognizable as Spanish because of alterations that have occurred over time. A prime example is ***mandarin*** (a high-ranking official). It arrived in English in the late 16th century via Spanish *mandarin* from Sanskrit *mantrin-* "counselor." The ***mandarin*** orange took a further detour through French. Other English words whose Spanish ancestry has been somewhat obscured in this manner include ***parade*** (mid-17th century via French from Spanish *parada* "stopping (a horse)"), ***launch*** (the boat, late 17th from Spanish *lancha* "pinnace"), and the informal ***savvy*** (late 18th from Spanish *sabe (usted)?* "you know?").

Spanish has been a transport language for many other words now naturalized into English and coming from other ancestral languages. For instance, ***armadillo, bonanza, fronton,*** and ***salsa*** go back via Spanish to Latin; ***barrio*** and ***acequia*** go back via Spanish to Arabic; and ***guitar*** goes back via Spanish to Greek. And ***contraband,*** which arrived in English in the late 16th century via Spanish *contrabanda* from Italian *contrabbando*, literally "against proclamation," has its ancestral roots in Germanic. A number of English words migrating from Spanish have ultimate roots in the native languages of Central and South America. For example, ***caiman*** came into English from Carib, a language spoken in Venezuela and neighboring countries. Spanish gave us ***alpaca,*** which it got from Aymara, a Native South American language of Bolivia and Peru. From Nahuatl, a Native Central American language spoken by a people living in southern Mexico and in Central America, Spanish gave us ***chili.*** And from Quechua, a Native South American language used by people from the Andes such as the Incas, Spanish borrowed and passed on ***condor*** and ***pampas.***

Moving from international geographic distribution to more locally regional areas, American Spanish—a variety of Spanish spoken in the western hemisphere— gave us ***ranch.*** It arrived in English in the early 19th century as an adaptation of American Spanish *rancho* "group of people who eat together," from French *ranger* "to arrange in position." Other such contributions are ***burrito*** (mid-20th century, from an American Spanish word meaning "small burro," from Spanish *burro*) and ***taco*** (mid-20th, via American Spanish from a Spanish word meaning "wad"). Mexican Spanish — a variety of Spanish spoken in Mexico, the western and southwestern United States, and in many Hispanic communities elsewhere in the nation — has given English ***stampede*** (early 19th century from Mexican Spanish *estampida*, from a Spanish word meaning "uproar"), ***luminaria*** (mid-20th from Mexican Spanish, ultimately from Latin *luminaria*, the plural of *luminarium* "light"), and ***macho*** (early 20th from a Mexican Spanish adjective meaning "masculine," itself via Spanish from Latin *masculus*).

In terms of US dialect distribution, many English words of Spanish origin are still used chiefly in the western and southwestern United States. Some are ***arroyo, mesa, olla,*** and ***ranchero.*** Others, for example, ***quinceañera,*** an elaborate formal party given for a 15-year-old-girl, are used chiefly in Hispanic communities throughout the nation. In the manner of some other languages, Spanish readily combined with English to yield compound words like ***bongo drums, cargo pants, pampas grass, broncobuster, big enchilada, ranch house, ranch dressing,*** and ***tequila sunrise.***

much of Central and South America and some Caribbean islands. —**Span·ish A·mer·i·can** *n, adj*

Span·ish bay·o·net *n* a plant with stiff pointed leaves and a long woody stem. Flowers: white. Native to: America. Genus: *Yucca.* [< its sword-shaped leaves]

Span·ish ce·dar *n* 1. a tree with reddish fragrant wood. Native to: tropical America. Genus: *Cedrela.* 2. the wood of a Spanish cedar. Use: making cigar boxes.

Span·ish chest·nut *n* same as **chestnut** (sense 2)

Span·ish fly *n* 1. a green European blister beetle, source of the stimulant and irritant cantharides. Latin name: *Lytta vesicatoria* or *Cantharis vesicatoria.* 2. a toxic preparation made from the crushed dried bodies of the Spanish fly. Use: formerly, as an aphrodisiac and to treat skin blisters.

Span·ish gui·tar *n* the classical six-stringed form of guitar

Span·ish ham *n* in Hispanic cooking, air-cured ham from hogs fed on sweet acorns

Span·ish In·qui·si·tion *n* an ecclesiastical tribunal of the Roman Catholic Church established in Spain in 1542, and finally suppressed in 1834, under which large numbers of people deemed to be heretics were tortured and executed

Span·ish mack·er·el *n* a large game fish of the tuna family. Native to: Atlantic coast of North and South America. Latin name: *Scomberomorous maculatus.*

Span·ish Main /-máyn/ *n* 1. in the 16th and 17th centuries, a region of Spanish America from the isthmus of Panama to the mouth of the Orinoco river 2. the part of the Caribbean Sea crossed by Spanish ships in colonial times

Span·ish moss *n* a plant of the pineapple family that grows on trees in long drooping matted clusters of grayish green filaments. Native to: southeastern United States, South America. Latin name: *Tillandsia usneoides.*

Span·ish nee·dles (*plural same*) *n* PLANTS same as **beggar's lice** (sense 1) [< its spiny fruit]

Span·ish om·e·let *n* an omelet served with an often spicy sauce of tomato, green pepper, and onion [Because it contains ingredients typical of Spanish cuisine]

Span·ish on·ion *n* an onion with yellow skin and a mild flavor. Latin name: *Allium fistulosum.*

Span·ish pa·pri·ka *n* a spicy but fairly mild food seasoning made from red peppers

Span·ish rice *n* rice cooked with onion, green pepper, tomato, and seasonings

Span·ish Sa·ha·ra former name for **Western Sahara**

Span·ish sau·sage *n* in Hispanic cooking, sausage made from minced pork flavored with paprika and other spices

Span·ish Town second largest city in Jamaica, in the southeast of the island on the Cobre River, near Kingston. It was the capital of the island from 1535 until the 1870s. Population: 92,383 (1991).

spank[1] /spangk/ *vt* (**spanked, spank·ing, spanks**) to strike somebody, usually on the buttocks with the open hand in punishment ■ *n* an open-handed slap on the buttocks [Early 18C. Probably an imitation of the sound]

spank[2] /spangk/ *vi* to move briskly, spiritedly, or smartly [Early 19C. Probably back-formation < SPANKING[2]]

spank·er /spángkər/ *n* 1. the fore-and-aft sail on the mast nearest the stern of a square-rigged ship 2. somebody who spanks somebody else in punishment [Mid-17C. Origin ?]

spank·ing[1] /spángking/ *n* a beating with the flat of the hand on somebody's buttocks, given as punishment [Mid-19C. < SPANK[1]]

spank·ing[2] /spángking/ *adj* 1. EXCEPTIONAL with an unusual quality that makes something exceptional or remarkable of its kind 2. BRISK lively, or moving briskly, especially a breeze ■ *adv* VERY extremely and impressively ○ *a spanking new car* [Mid-17C. Origin ?]

span·ner /spánnər/ *n* 1. a wrench with a hook or pin at one or both ends of the head for engaging corresponding notches or holes on the object to be turned 2. *UK* same as **wrench** *n* (sense 1) [Mid-17C. < German < *spannen* "harness horses or oxen to a vehicle" < Germanic]

span·worm /spán wùrm/ *n US* INSECTS same as **inchworm**

spar[1] /spaar/ *n* 1. POLE SUPPORTING RIGGING a thick strong pole used to support rigging on a ship 2. LATERAL SUPPORT OF PLANE'S WING any of the principal lateral members supporting the wing of an airplane 3. METAL POLE a metal pole that is part of a machine for lifting or moving heavy objects ■ *vt US* PROVIDE WITH SPARS to provide something with spars [14C. Probably < Old French *esparre* or Old Norse *sperra*]

spar[2] /spaar/ *vi* (**sparred, spar·ring, spars**) 1. BOXING ENGAGE IN BOXING to box, especially to fake a blow in order to draw an opponent or create an opening 2. BOXING USE LIGHT BLOWS to engage in a practice or exhibition bout of boxing or martial arts using light blows 3. FIGHT USING FEET AND SPURS to fight using the feet and spurs to strike an opponent (*refers to gamecocks*) 4. ARGUE to engage in argument ■ *n* BOXING 1. PRACTICE BOUT a practice or exhibition bout of boxing 2. PARTICULAR MOTION IN BOXING a motion in boxing for attack or defense [Late 16C. Origin ?]

spar[3] /spaar/ *n* any light-colored lustrous mineral that cleaves easily [Late 16C. < Low German] —**spar·ry** *adj*

SPAR /spaar/, **Spar** *n US* a member of the women's branch of the US Coast Guard during World War II. The unit was disbanded in 1946. [Mid-20C. Acronym < Latin *semper paratus* "always ready," the Coast Guard's motto]

spare /sper/ *vt* (**spared, spar·ing, spares**) 1. REFRAIN FROM HARMING SOMEBODY to refrain from killing, punishing, or harming somebody or something 2. TREAT SOMEBODY LENIENTLY to treat somebody leniently or refrain from treating somebody harshly 3. SAVE SOMEBODY FROM DOING SOMETHING to save or relieve somebody from the effort or trouble of doing something ○ *I went myself to spare her the trouble.* 4. AFFORD SOMETHING to give up or be able to contribute something from one's resources, especially without inconvenience ○ *I can't spare any time to exercise.* 5. WITHHOLD SOMETHING to withhold or avoid something ○ *They spared no expense on the wedding.* 6. USE SOMETHING FRUGALLY to use or dispense something frugally 7. REFRAIN FROM USING SOMETHING to refrain from using something ■ *adj* 1. KEPT IN RESERVE kept in reserve for emergency use 2. SUPERFLUOUS more than what is needed 3. LEAN with a muscular physique and no excess fat 4. SCANTY lacking in quantity or extent ○ *a spare diet* 5. PLAIN lacking embellishment or fullness ○ *spare prose* ■ *n* 1. SOMETHING EXTRA something extra that is kept in reserve 2. AUTOMOT same as **spare tire** 3. KNOCKING DOWN PINS IN TWO TRIES in bowling, an instance of knocking down all the pins in two successive rolls 4. BOWLING SCORE a score made in bowling by using two successive rolls to knock down all ten pins [Old English *sparian* < Germanic] —**spare·ly** *adv* —**spare·ness** *n* ◇ **to spare** more than what is needed

spare·rib /spér rìb/ *n* a rib of pork from which most of the meat has been removed, usually cooked in a barbecue or Chinese sauce [Late 16C. By folk etymology < Low German *ribbesper* "pickled pork ribs roasted on a spit," by association with SPARE]

spare time *n* time not spent working or attending to other day-to-day responsibilities

spare tire *n* 1. an extra tire mounted somewhere on a motor vehicle and carried in case of a flat tire 2. a roll of extra flesh around somebody's waist (*humorous*)

sparge /spaarj/ (**sparged, sparg·ing, sparg·es**) *vt* 1. to scatter, spray, or sprinkle something 2. to introduce air or gas into a liquid to agitate it [Late 16C. Directly or via French < Latin *spargere* "scatter"] —**sparg·er** *n*

spar·id /spárrəd/ (*plural same* or **-ids**) *n* an ocean fish with a compressed body, large head, and sharp teeth. Porgies and breams are sparids. Native to: warm regions. Family: Sparidae. [Late 20C. < modern Latin *Sparidae* < Greek *sparos* "sea bream"]

spar·ing /spérring/ *adj* 1. FRUGAL showing careful restraint in the use of resources 2. SCANTY limited or restricted in quantity 3. MERCIFUL inclined to be lenient or merciful —**spar·ing·ly** *adv*

spark[1] /spaark/ *n* 1. FIERY PARTICLE a small piece of a burning substance thrown off in combustion or produced in friction 2. ELEC ELECTRIC DISCHARGE a quick bright discharge of electricity between two conductors 3. SOMETHING THAT ACTIVATES a factor or device that sets off or acts as a stimulant, inspiration, or catalyst ○ *a spark of interest* 4. SOMETHING CAPABLE OF

DEVELOPMENT a latent trace of something capable of development ○ *had a real spark of genius* ■ *v* (**sparked, spark·ing, sparks**) **1.** *vt* STIMULATE OR INCITE SOMETHING to stimulate or initiate a burst of activity ○ *The issue sparked an emotional debate.* **2.** *vi* EMIT SPARKS to throw off sparks **3.** *vi* ELEC PRODUCE SPARKS to have an electric ignition working properly so that it generates sparks (*refers to internal combustion engines*) [Old English *spærca*. Origin ?]

spark off *vt* to activate or act as a catalyst for something

spark[2] /spaark/ (*archaic*) *n* a vain young man, especially one concerned with fashion and appearance ■ *vti* (**sparked, spark·ing, sparks**) to try to persuade somebody to become romantically or sexually involved [Early 16C. Probably < SPARK[1]]

Dame Muriel Spark

Spark /spaark/, **Dame Muriel** (*b.* 1918) British writer. She is best known for her novels, including *Memento Mori* (1959) and *The Prime of Miss Jean Brodie* (1961). Full name **Spark, Dame Muriel Sarah**

"To me education is a leading out of what is already there in the pupil's soul."
[Dame Muriel Spark, *The Prime of Miss Jean Brodie*; 1961]

spark cham·ber *n* a device for tracking the path of a subatomic particle, consisting of charged plates that cause the particle to ionize the gas present and create sparks

spark coil *n* the induction coil that produces the spark discharge to start combustion in an internal combustion engine

spark e·ro·sion *n* a process for shaping metal, similar to conventional machining but using an electric arc from a moving electrode to remove metal

spark gap *n* a space between two electrodes across which a discharge of electricity occurs, e.g., the gap between electrodes of a spark plug in an internal combustion engine

spark·ing plug /spaárking-/ *n UK* AUTOMOT same as **spark plug** (sense 1)

spar·kle /spaárk'l/ *v* (**-kled, -kling, -kles**) **1.** *vti* GLITTER to give off or reflect light in brilliant glittering flashes, or make something do this **2.** *vi* BE LIVELY OR BRILLIANT to perform brilliantly or be vivacious, witty, or enthusiastic **3.** *vi* EMIT BUBBLES to effervesce (*refers to wine and other drinks*) **4.** *vi* THROW OFF SPARKS to throw off sparks ■ *n* **1.** SHINING PARTICLE a little spark or shining particle **2.** ANIMATION lively or brilliant animation and vivacity **3.** EFFERVESCENCE effervescence in wine and other drinks [12C. < SPARK[1]] —**spark·ly** *adj*

spar·kle·ber·ry /spaárk'l bèrree/ (*plural* **-ries**) *n US* PLANTS same as **farkleberry** [Late 19C. Alteration of FARKLEBERRY]

spar·kler /spaárklər/ *n* **1.** HANDHELD FIREWORK a handheld firework that throws off sparks as it burns **2.** SPARKLING GEM a diamond or other sparkling gem (*informal*) **3.** same as **sparkling wine** (*informal*) **4.** SOMETHING THAT SPARKLES something that reflects or gives off brilliant flashes of light or throws off sparks

spar·kling /spaárkling/ *adj* **1.** REFLECTING GLITTERING LIGHT reflecting or giving off light in brilliant glittering flashes **2.** EFFERVESCENT describes drinks that are effervescent ○ *sparkling water* **3.** VIVACIOUS intelligently vivacious or witty

spar·kling wa·ter *n* water charged with carbon dioxide to make it effervescent

spar·kling wine *n* wine that is made effervescent naturally through a second fermentation in the bottle or artificially through the introduction of carbon dioxide

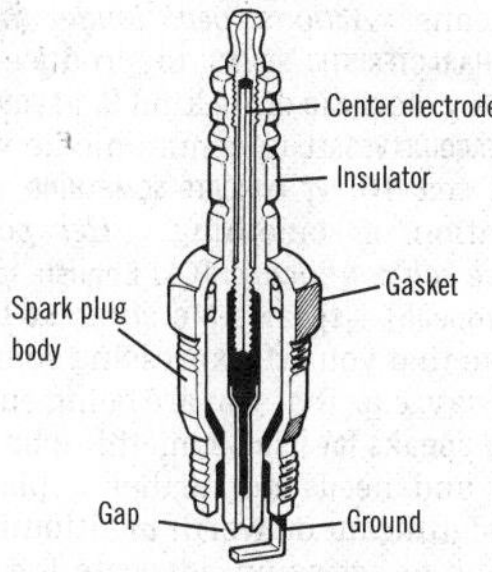

spark plug

spark plug *n* **1.** a device that ignites the fuel mixture in the cylinder in an internal-combustion engine by emitting a spark **2.** an inspirer of enthusiasm for a project or task (*informal*)

sparks /spaarks/ *n* the radio operator on a ship or aircraft (*informal; takes a singular verb*)

spark trans·mit·ter *n* an obsolete form of radio transmitter that used power generated from the discharge of a condenser across a spark gap

spark·y /spaárkee/ (**-i·er, -i·est**) *adj* very lively and enthusiastic

spar·ring part·ner /spaáring paàrtnər/ *n* **1.** somebody who spars with a boxer to help in training **2.** somebody who regularly debates or disputes with somebody else

spar·row /spárrō/ *n* **1.** a small dull-colored songbird with a short sturdy beak for cracking seeds. Family: Passeridae. **2.** a bird of the bunting family that resembles a sparrow. Family: Emberizidae. [Old English *spearwa* < Germanic]

spar·row·grass /spárrō gràss/ *n regional* FOOD same as **asparagus** (sense 1) [Mid-17C. Alteration]

spar·row hawk *n* **1.** a kestrel. Native to: North America. Latin name: *Falco sparverius*. **2.** a small hawk that preys on smaller birds and has short broad wings, a long tail, and a dark gray to blackish back. Native to: Europe, Asia. Latin name: *Accipiter nisus*.

sparse /spaarss/ (**spars·er, spars·est**) *adj* thinly spread, or occurring with many spaces in between [Early 18C. < Latin *sparsus*, past participle of *spargere* "scatter"] —**sparse·ly** *adv* —**sparse·ness** *n* —**spar·si·ty** *n*

Spar·ta /spaártə/ town in the southern Peloponnesus, Greece, the site of an ancient city-state that was an important military power between the 6th and 4th centuries B.C. Population: 14,084 (1991).

Spar·ta·cus /spaártəkəss/ (*d.* 71 B.C.) Roman slave and rebel leader. He led an uprising that defeated several Roman armies before he was killed in battle against the Roman commander Crassus.

spar·tan /spaárt'n/ *adj* marked by stern discipline, frugality, simplicity, or courage ■ *n* a strong and self-disciplined person [Mid-17C. < SPARTAN] —**spar·tan·ly** *adv*

Spar·tan /spaárt'n/ *n* somebody who came from ancient Sparta ■ *adj* relating to the ancient Greek city-state of Sparta, or its people or culture [15C. < SPARTA]

Spar·tan·burg /spaárt'n bùrg/ city in northwestern South Carolina, in the foothills of the Blue Ridge Mountains, northeast of Greenville. Population: 39,068 (2002 estimate).

spar·te·ine /spaártə èen, -ee ìn/ *n* a bitter poisonous alkaloid. Source: Scotch broom. Use: medicines. [Mid-19C. < modern Latin *Spartium*, genus name of broom < Greek *sparton* "esparto"]

spar var·nish *n US* a durable waterproof varnish for use on exterior wooden surfaces

spasm /spázzəm/ *n* **1.** an involuntary sudden muscle contraction **2.** a sudden brief emotion, sensation, or action ○ *a spasm of pain* [14C. Via French and Latin < Greek *spasmos* < *span* "to pull"]

spas·mod·ic /spaz móddik/ *adj* **1.** INTERMITTENT occurring at uneven intervals **2.** EXCITABLE prone to sudden outbursts of emotion **3.** AFFECTED BY SPASMS affected or characterized by spasms **4.** RESEMBLING SPASM resembling a spasm in sudden brief intensity [Late 17C. < modern Latin *spasmodicus* < Greek *spasmōdēs* < *spasmos* (see SPASM)] —**spas·mod·i·cal·ly** *adv*

spas·mo·lyt·ic /spàzmə líttik/ *n, adj* MED, PHARM same as **antispasmodic**

spas·tic /spástik/ *adj* **1.** AFFECTED BY SPASMS relating to or affected by spasms **2.** OFFENSIVE TERM an offensive term meaning lacking physical coordination or the ability to perform competently (*dated*) ■ *n* **1.** OFFENSIVE TERM an offensive term for somebody with a disability that affects physical coordination (*dated*) **2.** OFFENSIVE TERM an offensive term that deliberately insults somebody's coordination or competence (*slang insult*) [Mid-18C. Via Latin < Greek *spastikos* < *span* "to pull"] —**spas·ti·cal·ly** *adv* —**spas·tic·i·ty** /spa stíssətee/ *n*

spas·tic co·lon *n* MED same as **irritable bowel syndrome**

spat[1] /spat/ *n* **1.** PETTY QUARREL a brief quarrel usually concerning petty matters **2.** *US* SOUND OF RAINDROPS FALLING the sound of raindrops falling ■ *vi* (**spat·ted, spat·ting, spats**) **1.** QUARREL PETTILY to quarrel briefly over a petty matter **2.** *US* MAKE SPATTERING SOUND to make the sound of rain falling in large spattering drops [Early 19C. Origin ?]

spat[2] /spat/ past participle, past tense of **spit**[1]

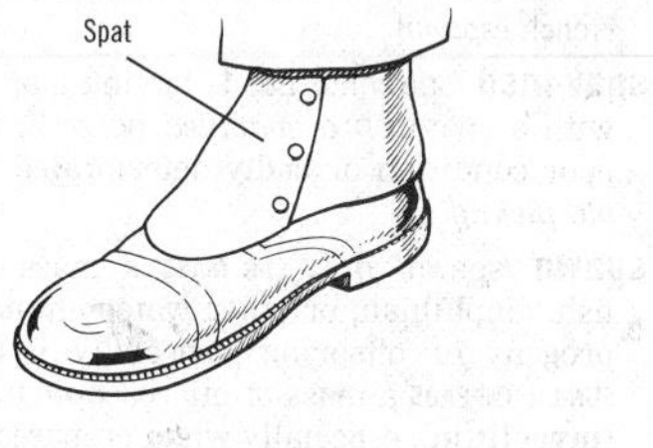

spat

spat[3] /spat/ *n* a short cloth or leather gaiter, popular in the late 19th and early 20th centuries, worn over a shoe to cover the instep and the ankle [Early 19C. Shortening of *spatterdash* "knee-length protective legging"]

spat[4] /spat/ *n* an immature bivalve mollusk, e.g., an oyster [Mid-17C. < Anglo-Norman]

spatch·cock /spách kòk/ *n* SPLIT BIRD FOR COOKING a chicken or other fowl that is split, dressed, and broiled or roasted on a spit ■ *vt* (**-cocked, -cock·ing, -cocks**) **1.** PREPARE FOWL FOR ROASTING to prepare a chicken or other fowl for roasting by splitting it open **2.** INSERT SOMETHING AWKWARDLY to introduce or interpose something into a piece of writing, especially in a forced or inappropriate way [Late 18C. Origin ?]

spate /spayt/ *n* **1.** LARGE QUANTITY a large quantity of something ○ *a spate of rumors* **2.** OUTBURST a sudden strong outburst ○ *a spate of jealousy* **3.** FLOOD a flood, or the state of overflowing ○ *After the heavy rain the river was in spate.* [15C. Origin ?]

spathe /spayth/ *n* a leafy sheath (**bract**) that encloses the cluster of flowers (**spadix**) in some plants such as the arum and sometimes resembles a petal [Late 18C. < Latin *spatha* (see SPATULA)] —**spathed** *adj*

spath·ic /spáthik/ *adj* resembling spar minerals, especially in being easy to split [Late 18C. < German *Spat(h)* "spar"]

spath·u·late /spáttyoolət/ *n UK* BIOL same as **spatulate**

spa·tial /spáysh'l/, **spa·cial** *adj* relating to, occupying, or happening in space [Mid-19C < Latin *spatium* "space, distance"] —**spa·ti·al·i·ty** /spàyshee állətee/ *n* —**spa·tial·ly** *adv*

spa·ti·o·tem·po·ral /spàyshee ō témpərəl, -témprəl/ *adj* **1.** relating to, existing in, or having the qualities of both space and time **2.** relating to a four-dimensional space-time system [Early 20C. < Latin *spatium* "space, distance" + TEMPORAL[1]] —**spa·ti·o·tem·po·ral·ly** *adv*

Spät·le·se /shpáyt làyzə/ *n* the grade of high-quality German table wine above Kabinett, made from late-picked grapes and typically medium sweet [Early 20C. < German, "late vintage"]

spat·ter /spáttər/ *v* (**-tered, -ter·ing, -ters**) **1.** *vti* **THROW OR COME OUT IN DROPS** to expel something in small scattered drops or splashes, or come out in this way **2.** *vt* **SPLASH SOMETHING WITH LIQUID** to splash something with or as if with a liquid, especially if the liquid leaves a mark or residue **3.** *vt* **DEFAME SOMEBODY** to defame or sully somebody's character ■ *n* **1. DROPLET OF SOMETHING SPATTERED** a droplet or splash of something spattered ○ *got a few spatters of paint on the floor* **2. SMALL AMOUNT** a small amount of something ○ *a spatter of applause* **3. ACT OF SPATTERING** an act of spattering or being spattered **4. SPATTERING SOUND** the sound of spattering [Mid-16C. Ultimately < W Germanic]

spat·ter·dock /spáttər dòk/ *n* a North American water lily. Flowers: globe-shaped, yellow. Latin name: *Nuphar advena.*

spat·u·la /spáchələ/ *n* **1.** a flat flexible metal, plastic, or rubber utensil with a handle, used to scoop, lift, spread, or mix **2.** *UK* same as **tongue depressor** [Early 16C. < Latin, "small broadsword," var of *spathula* < *spatha* "broadsword" < Greek *spathē* "broad blade"]

spat·u·late /spáchələt/, **spath·u·late** /spáthyələt, spáthyə layt/ *adj* describes a leaf that is shaped like a spatula, with a narrow tapering base and a broad rounded tip

spätz·le *n* FOOD another spelling of **spaetzle**

spav·in /spávvin/ *n* an ailment of horses involving a swelling or enlargement of the hock joint [15C. < Old French *espavin*]

spav·ined /spávvind/ *adj* **1.** having a spavin or lame with a spavin ○ *a spavined horse* **2.** in extremely poor condition or badly deteriorated ○ *a spavined old pickup*

spawn /spawn/ *n* **1. EGG MASS** a mass of eggs of a fish, amphibian, or other water animal **2. OFFSPRING** progeny or offspring, especially if numerous **3. FUNGAL THREADS** a mass of microscopic fungal threads (**mycelium**), especially when prepared on a growth medium for starting a new culture of the fungus **4. SEED** a seed, germ, or the source of something ■ *v* (**spawned, spawn·ing, spawns**) **1.** *vi* **DEPOSIT EGGS** to produce and deposit eggs **2.** *vi* **PRODUCE YOUNG** to produce offspring in large numbers **3.** *vt* **GIVE RISE TO SOMETHING** to generate or give rise to something ○ *The storm has spawned at least one tornado.* **4.** *vt* **START NEW FUNGUS CULTURE** to start a new culture of a fungus using spawn [15C. < Anglo-Norman *espaundre* "shed roe," variant of Old French *espandre* "shed, spill, pour out" < Latin *expandere* (see EXPAND)] —**spawn·er** *n*

spay /spay/ (**spayed, spay·ing, spays**) *vt* to surgically remove a female animal's ovaries and adjacent parts of the uterus [15C. < Old French *espeer* "cut with a sword" < *espee* "sword" < Latin *spatha* (see SPATULA)]

spaz /spaz/, **spazz** *n* (*plural* **spaz·zes**) an offensive term that deliberately insults somebody's coordination or competence (*slang insult*) ■ *vi* (**spazzed, spaz·zing, spaz·zes**) same as **spaz out** (*slang offensive*) [Mid-20C. Shortening and alteration of SPASTIC]

spaz out *vi* an offensive term meaning to do something clumsily or incompetently (*slang*)

spazz *n, vi* another spelling of **spaz** (*slang offensive*)

SPCA *abbr US* Society for the Prevention of Cruelty to Animals

SPCC *abbr US* Society for the Prevention of Cruelty to Children

SPE *abbr* FIN, ACCT special-purpose entity

~~**speach**~~ incorrect spelling of **speech**

speak /speek/ (**spoke** /spōk/ or **spake** *archaic* /spayk/, **spo·ken** /spṓkən/, **speak·ing, speaks**) *v* **1.** *vti* **TALK** to utter words or articulate sounds with the voice, or communicate something orally ○ *so shocked I could hardly speak* **2.** *vi* **EXPRESS THOUGHTS AND OPINIONS** to communicate thoughts, opinions, or feelings by uttering with the voice ○ *speak your mind* **3.** *vt* **BE ABLE TO USE LANGUAGE** to know and be able to converse in a particular language ○ *learning to speak French* **4.** *vi* **BE ON GOOD TERMS** to be on good and friendly terms with somebody ○ *They're not speaking anymore.* **5.** *vi* **DELIVER SPEECH TO AUDIENCE** to make a speech or deliver an address **6.** *vti* **EXPRESS IN WRITING** to express something or make a statement in writing ○ *Her poetry speaks of the joy of solitude.* **7.** *vti* **COMMUNICATE NONVERBALLY** to communicate something by other than verbal means ○ *Actions speak louder than words.* **8.** *vi* **MAKE CHARACTERISTIC SOUND** to produce or make a sound characteristic of its kind **9.** *vt* **COMMUNICATE WITH ANOTHER SEAGOING VESSEL** to communicate with another vessel at sea **10.** *vt* **INDICATE SOMETHING** to be a sign or indication of something ○ *Her poise spoke of impressive self-confidence.* [Old English *specan, sprecan* < Indo-European] —**speak·a·ble** *adj* ◇ **so to speak** used to indicate that you are expressing something in an unusual way, e.g., that you are being euphemistic ◇ **something speaks for itself** something has an obvious meaning and needs no further explanation ◇ **to speak of** significant or worth mentioning

speak for *vt* to act as an advocate for or speak on behalf of another person or a group

speak out *vi* **1.** to express opinions boldly, freely, and frankly **2.** to talk loudly, or loudly enough to be heard

speak to *vt* to address a particular issue ○ *a program that speaks to the needs of international students*

speak up *vi* **1.** to talk loudly enough to be heard **2.** to express opinions freely and frankly

speak up for *vt* to speak in support or on behalf of somebody or something

-speak /speek/ *suffix* vocabulary or a way of speaking that is characteristic of a particular group or sphere of activity (*disapproving*) ○ *adspeak*

SYNONYMS See *jargon*[1].

---

speak·eas·y /spéek èezee/ (*plural* **-ies**) *n* a place where alcoholic beverages are sold and consumed illegally, especially formerly during Prohibition [Late 19C. < speaking softly so as not to attract attention]

speak·er /spéekər/ *n* **1. SOMEBODY WHO MAKES SPEECH** somebody who makes a speech or gives a lecture **2. SOMEBODY WHO SPEAKS** somebody who speaks, especially somebody able to speak a particular language ○ *Spanish speakers* **3.** *US* **SPOKESPERSON** a representative or spokesperson for a group **4.** BROADCAST same as **loudspeaker**

Speak·er *n* the presiding officer of a legislative body such as the US House of Representatives or the British House of Commons

speak·er·phone /spéekər fòn/ *n* a telephone equipped with a loudspeaker and microphone

speak·ing /spéeking/ *adj* **1. INVOLVING SPEECH** involving speech or speaking **2. ABLE TO USE PARTICULAR LANGUAGE** able to speak a particular language (*usually used in combination*) ○ *French-speaking students* **3. APPARENTLY REAL** resembling a real person or object ○ *the speaking image of her aunt*

speak·ing in tongues *n* the making of utterances that are not recognizable as any known language and have no formal linguistic content

speak·ing tube *n* a pipe through which conversation can be conducted between people in different parts of something such as a ship or building

speak·o /spéekō/ (*plural* **-os**) *n* a mistake caused by the failure of a computer speech-recognition program to recognize a particular word correctly (*slang*)

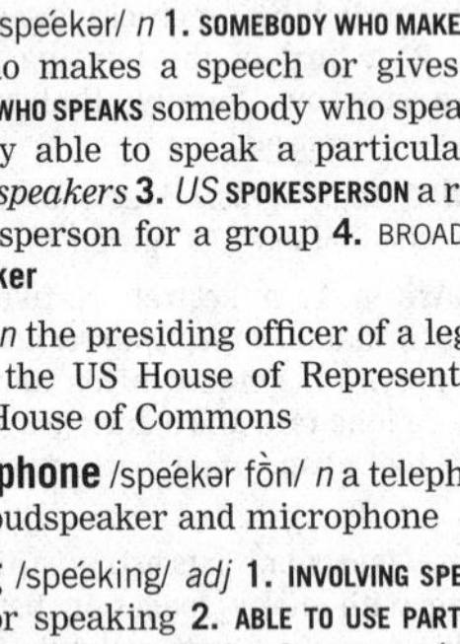

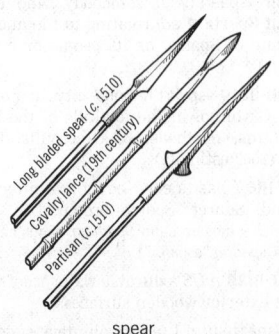

spear

spear[1] /speer/ *n* **1. LONG-HANDLED WEAPON WITH BLADE** a weapon for throwing or thrusting that has a long handle and a blade or head with a sharpened point **2. WEAPON FOR SPEARING FISH** a weapon with a sharp point and barbs used for catching fish by piercing them ■ *v* (**speared, spear·ing, spears**) **1.** *vti* **PIERCE SOMETHING WITH SPEAR** to stab, pierce, or take somebody or something with or as though using a spear **2.** *vt US* **CATCH BALL WITH THRUST OF ARM** to catch a ball with an abrupt thrust of the arm [Old English *spere* < Germanic] —**spear·er** *n* —**spear·man** *n*

spear[2] /speer/ *n* a young blade, shoot, or stalk of a plant such as asparagus or grass ■ *vi* (**speared, spear·ing, spears**) to bear a spear or send one up through the soil [15C. Alteration of SPIRE[1]]

spear car·ri·er *n* **1.** a minor member of the cast in a play or opera **2.** an unimportant or irrelevant contributor to something (*informal*)

spear·fish /spéer fìsh/ *n* (*plural* **same** or **-fish·es**) a large ocean billfish that is related to the marlin and sailfish and has a very long, pointed upper jaw. Genus: *Tetrapturus.* ■ *vi* (**-fished, -fish·ing, -fish·es**) to fish using a spear or spear gun

spear grass *n* PLANTS same as **feather grass**

spear gun *n* a gun designed to shoot a barbed spear underwater, used to catch fish

spear·head /spéer hèd/ *vt* (**-head·ed, -head·ing, -heads**) **ACT AS LEADER OF EVENT** to act as the leader or driving force of an event or undertaking ■ *n* **1. DRIVING FORCE IN EVENT** the leading or driving element or force in an undertaking **2.** MIL **LEADING FORCES IN MILITARY ATTACK** the leading forces in a military attack **3.** ARMS **POINTED HEAD OF SPEAR** the pointed head of a spear

spear·mint /spéer mìnt/ (*plural* **same** or **-mints**) *n* a common mint, the leaves and essential oil of which are used for flavoring. Latin name: *Mentha spicata.* [Mid-16C. < the stem's resemblance to a spear]

spear side *n* a husband's or father's side of a family (*literary*) [< SPEAR[1] as a former symbol of man's domain]

spear·wort /spéer wùrt, -wàwrt/ (*plural* **same** or **-worts**) *n* a buttercup with spear-shaped leaves. Flowers: small, yellow. Native to: Europe, Asia, eastern United States.

spec /spek/ (*informal*) *n* a detailed description of something, especially one that provides somebody with enough information to make that thing (*usually used in the plural*) ■ *vt* (**spec'd** or **specced, spec'·ing** or **spec·cing, specs**) to provide specifications for something [Late 18C. Shortening of SPECIFICATION] ◇ **on spec 1.** without being sure of profit, reward, or success (*informal*) **2.** *UK* with a chance of achieving something but no certainty of it

spec. *abbr* **1.** special **2.** specialist **3.** specification

spe·cial /spésh'l/ *adj* **1. UNUSUAL OR BETTER** distinct, different, unusual, or superior in comparison to others of the same kind ○ *a very special occasion* ○ *received special consideration* **2. HELD IN ESTEEM** regarded with particular esteem or affection ○ *a special friend* **3. RESERVED** unique to or reserved for a specific person or thing ○ *It's my special chair.* **4. MADE FOR SPECIFIC PURPOSE** made or used for a specific purpose or occasion ○ *Firefighters used special breathing equipment.* **5. ARRANGED FOR SPECIFIC PURPOSE** planned for a specific occasion or purpose ○ *made a special visit to the factory* **6. ADDITIONAL** in addition to or more than is usual ○ *a special issue of the newspaper* **7. INVOLVING SPECIAL-NEEDS CHILDREN** designed or intended for educating children who have physical disabilities or learning difficulties ■ *n* **1. SOMETHING RESERVED FOR SPECIFIC PURPOSE** something designed or reserved for a specific purpose or occasion **2. TEMPORARY REDUCTION IN PRICE** a temporary reduction in the price of an item **3. TELEVISION PROGRAM NOT PART OF SCHEDULE** a television program that is not part of a network's regular schedule **4. DISH NOT ON USUAL MENU** a dish that a restaurant or other food outlet offers in addition to the standard menu, or one that is available for a low price [12C. Directly or via French < Latin *specialis* < *species* (see SPECIES)] —**spe·cial·ness** *n* ◇ **on special** being sold at a reduced price

spe·cial act *n* an act passed by a legislative body intended to apply only to a specific individual or situation

Spe·cial Air Ser·vice *n* ARMY full form of **SAS**

spe·cial as·sess·ment *n US* a specific local tax levied on private property to meet the cost of a public improvement that will result in an increase in the value of the property

spe·cial court-mar·tial *n* a court-martial held to try offenses of an intermediate kind and presided over by three officers

spe·cial de·liv·er·y *n* the delivery of mail more quickly than or outside normal delivery times for an extra fee

spe·cial draw·ing rights *n* a method of settling international debts through the International Monetary Fund in order to stabilize exchange rates

spe·cial ed·u·ca·tion *n* teaching modified to serve students with special educational needs

spe·cial ef·fects *npl* extraordinary visual effects in a motion picture or television program achieved by technical means, either optically, digitally, or mechanically

Spe·cial Forc·es *npl* a branch of the US Army trained in guerrilla warfare and counterinsurgency tactics

spe·cial hand·ling *n* the handling of fourth-class and parcel post mail as first-class mail for an additional fee

spe·cial-in·ter·est group, **spe·cial in·ter·est** *n* a group seeking to influence government policy in favor of an interest or issue

spe·cial·ism /spéshə lìzzəm/ *n* **1.** concentration in a field of study **2.** same as **specialty** (sense 1)

spe·cial·ist /spéshəlist/ *n* **1.** SOMEBODY IN PARTICULAR INTEREST somebody who specializes in an occupation, interest, or field of study **2.** TYPE OF PHYSICIAN a medical doctor who practices in a specific field **3.** *US* ENLISTED RANK IN US ARMY an enlisted person in the US Army with special technical skills, of a rank in a series numbered from 4 to 7 between corporal and sergeant first class —**spe·cial·ist** *adj* —**spe·cial·is·tic** /spèshə lístik/ *adj*

spe·ci·al·i·ty /spèshee állətee/ (*plural* **-ties**) *n UK* same as **specialty** (senses 1–2, 4)

spe·cial·i·za·tion /spèshəli záysh'n/ *n* **1.** ACT OF BECOMING SPECIALIZED the act or process of becoming specialized **2.** EDUC same as **specialty** (sense 1) **3.** BIOL ADAPTATION OF ORGANISM the adaptation of an organism or a part of an organism to a specific function or condition in response to environmental conditions **4.** BIOL ADAPTED BODY PART an organism or a part of an organism that has been adapted to a specific function or condition

spe·cial·ize /spéshə lìz/ (**-ized, -iz·ing, -iz·es**) *v* **1.** *vi* DEVOTE TIME TO ACTIVITY to devote time exclusively to an interest, skill, or field of study ○ *She's specializing in pediatrics.* **2.** *vi* CONCENTRATE ON PRODUCT to concentrate on a particular activity, area, or group of products ○ *The store specializes in water sports.* **3.** *vt* ADAPT SOMETHING TO SPECIFIC PURPOSE to adapt something to suit a specific purpose **4.** *vi* BECOME ADAPTED to become adapted to a specific function or condition **5.** *vt* SPECIFY SOMETHING to specify or make specific mention of something

spe·cial ju·ry *n* LAW same as **blue-ribbon jury**

~~**speciall**~~ incorrect spelling of **special**

spe·cial·ly /spésh'lee/ *adv* for a special or particular purpose, person, or occasion ○ *It was intended specially for preschoolers.* ○ *I had it specially made.*

USAGE See *especially.*

spe·cial needs *npl* the requirements, especially in education, that some people have because of physical or mental challenges

Spe·cial O·lym·pics *n* an international athletic competition for athletes who are physically or mentally challenged (*takes a singular or plural verb*)

spe·cial op·er·a·tions, **spe·cial ops** *n* a branch of a military force engaged in covert operations, especially in enemy territory ■ *npl* covert operations undertaken by military personnel, especially in enemy territory

spe·cial plead·ing *n* **1.** pleading in a court trial that introduces new or special matter and that avoids allegations of matter pleaded by the opposite side, instead of direct denial of those allegations **2.** an argument that presents only one aspect of an issue and avoids any unfavorable aspects

spe·cial-pur·pose en·ti·ty *n* a business operation legally created for a special purpose that, if receiving at least 3% of its capital from outside investors, can be omitted from the parent company's financial records

spe·cial rel·a·tiv·i·ty *n* PHYS same as **relativity** (sense 1)

spe·cial school *n* a school catering to students who have special educational needs, e.g., because of physical or mental challenges

spe·cial ses·sion *n* a session of a legislature, court, or council held in addition to and outside of regularly scheduled sessions

spe·cial team *n* a group of football players who are sent onto the field to perform only in specific situations, e.g., during a kickoff or punt

spe·cial the·o·ry of rel·a·tiv·i·ty *n* PHYS same as **relativity** (sense 1)

spe·cial·ty /spésh'ltee/ (*plural* **-ties**) *n* **1.** SOMETHING SOMEBODY SPECIALIZES IN a skill, field of study, interest, or activity in which somebody specializes **2.** MEDICAL SPECIALIZATION an area of medicine in which somebody specializes **3.** SPECIALIZED PRODUCT a product or service that somebody is specialized in producing ○ *Prime rib is the house specialty.* **4.** DISTINCTIVE FEATURE a notable or distinctive characteristic or quality ○ *Evasiveness is a specialty of his.* **5.** LAW LEGAL AGREEMENT a legal agreement made under seal

spe·ci·a·tion /spe̋eshee áysh'n, spe̋essee-/ *n* the evolutionary formation of new biological species, usually by one species that divides into two or more species that are genetically unique [Early 20C. < SPECIES] —**spe·ci·ate** /spe̋eshee àyt, spe̋essee-/ *vi*

spe·cie /spe̋eshee, -ssee/ *n* money in the form of coins [Mid-16C. Shortening of Latin *in specie* "in kind" < *species* (see SPECIES)] ◇ **in specie 1.** in the form of coins **2.** in a similar way or kind **3.** in the form specified

~~**speciel**~~ incorrect spelling of **special**

spe·cies /spe̋e sheez, -seez/ (*plural same*) *n* **1.** BIOL TAXONOMIC GROUP a subdivision of a genus considered as a basic biological classification and containing individuals that resemble one another and may interbreed **2.** BIOL ORGANISMS IN SPECIES the organisms belonging to a species **3.** HUMANKIND human beings or the human race **4.** TYPE OF SOMETHING a kind, sort, or variety of something **5.** CHEM ATOM CATEGORY a category of atomic nucleus, ion, molecule, or atom **6.** LOGIC SUBDIVISION OF GENUS in logic, a collection of objects or individuals that, on the basis of shared features, form a subdivision of a genus **7.** CHR BREAD AND WINE IN COMMUNION the bread and wine used in Christian Communion, or their outward form after consecration [14C. < Latin, "appearance, kind" < *specere* "look at"]

SYNONYMS See *type.*

spe·cies bar·ri·er *n* the ability of cells belonging to members of a species to identify genes alien to the species and prevent them combining with its genome. The species barrier usually prevents members of different species from producing healthy offspring if they mate, and is also thought to prevent the transmission of some diseases between species.

spe·cies·ism /spe̋esheez ìzzəm, spe̋esseez-/ *n* the belief that the human race is superior to other species, and that exploitation of animals for the advantage of humans is justified

specif. *abbr* **1.** specific **2.** specifically

spe·cif·ic /spə síffik/ *adj* **1.** PRECISE precise and detailed, avoiding vagueness ○ *specific instructions* **2.** RELATING TO IDENTIFIED THING acting on or relating to something identified or particularized ○ *The instructions are specific to this task.* **3.** DISTINCTIVE with individual qualities that allow a distinction to be made or make a distinction necessary ○ *discussing these specific problems* **4.** BIOL OF BIOLOGICAL SPECIES relating to a biological species **5.** MED CAUSED BY PARTICULAR INFECTIOUS AGENT describes a disease caused by a particular infectious agent **6.** PHYS DENOTING PHYSICAL PROPERTY used to indicate that a physical property is being expressed with reference to a particular quantity such as mass, volume, or length **7.** COMM LEVIED PER UNIT describes taxes or duties levied on a per-unit basis using number, weight, or volume ■ *n* DETAIL a precise quality or detail (*usually used in the plural*) ○ *didn't go into specifics* [Mid-17C. < late Latin *specificus* "constituting a kind" < Latin *species* (see SPECIES)] —**spe·cif·i·cal·ly** *adv* —**spec·i·fic·i·ty** /spèssə físsətee/ *n*

spe·cif·ic ab·sorp·tion rate *n* MED full form of **SAR**

spec·i·fi·ca·tion /spèssəfi káysh'n/ *n* **1.** DETAILED DESCRIPTION a detailed description, especially one providing information needed to make, build, or produce something (*usually used in the plural*) ○ *a look at the engine specification* **2.** SPECIFYING the specifying of something **3.** LAW INTELLECTUAL PROPERTY DESCRIPTION a detailed description of intellectual property, as required by law

spe·cif·ic charge *n* the ratio of the electric charge of an elementary particle divided by its mass

spe·cif·ic grav·i·ty *n* same as **relative density**

spe·cif·ic heat *n* the amount of heat needed to raise the temperature of one gram of a substance by one degree, usually measured in joules per kilogram per kelvin

spe·cif·ic im·pulse *n* a measure of the fuel efficiency of a rocket, expressed as the number of pounds of thrust produced per pound of propellant used per second

spe·cif·ic lan·guage im·pair·ment *n* an inability to develop the expected language skills in a child without difficulties in hearing or learning, possibly because of an inability to process sound

~~**specificly**~~ incorrect spelling of **specifically**

spe·cif·ic per·form·ance *n* a court order compelling somebody to carry out an obligation, often something stipulated in a contract

spe·cif·ic re·sis·tance *n* ELEC same as **resistivity** (sense 1)

spe·cif·ic vol·ume *n* the volume of a unit mass of a substance, equal to the reciprocal of the density. Symbol ***v***

spec·i·fy /spéssə fì/ (**-fied, -fy·ing, -fies**) *vt* **1.** STATE SOMETHING EXPLICITLY to state or identify something in detail or explicitly ○ *Can you specify a date when the order will be delivered?* **2.** STIPULATE SOMETHING to state something or make it a condition ○ *The rules specify that pets cannot be kept here.* **3.** INCLUDE SOMETHING IN SPECIFICATION to include or state something in a specification ○ *We had specified a 48-speed CD drive.* [13C. Directly or via French *spécifier* < late Latin *specificare* < *specificus* (see SPECIFIC)] —**spec·i·fi·a·ble** /spéssə fì əb'l, spèssə fì əb'l/ *adj* —**spec·i·fi·er** *n*

~~**speciman**~~ incorrect spelling of **specimen**

spec·i·men /spéssəmən/ *n* **1.** REPRESENTATIVE THING something that is representative because it is characteristic of its kind or of a whole, especially something that serves as an example ○ *a specimen of his handwriting* **2.** SAMPLE OF BODY MATERIAL a sample used for testing and diagnosis, e.g., of urine or blood **3.** TYPE OF PERSON somebody who displays particular characteristics (*informal*) ○ *"turning away with disgust from the loathsome specimen of humanity before him"* (Baroness Orczy, *The Scarlet Pimpernel*; 1905) [Early 17C. < Latin < *specere* "look at"]

spe·cious /spe̋eshəss/ *adj* **1.** appearing to be true but really false ○ *a specious claim* **2.** superficially attractive but actually of no real interest or value [14C. < Latin *speciosus* "good-looking" < *species* (see SPECIES)] —**spe·cious·ly** *adv* —**spe·cious·ness** *n*

speck /spek/ *n* **1.** PARTICLE a tiny amount or particle of something ○ *a speck of dust* **2.** SMALL SPOT a very small mark or stain ■ *vt* (**specked, speck·ing, specks**) MARK SOMETHING WITH SPECKS to mark something with specks (*usually passive*) [Old English *specca.* Origin ?]

speck·le /spék'l/ *n* a small spot or mark, often a small irregular patch of contrasting color, e.g., on plumage or an eggshell ■ *vt* (**-led, -ling, -les**) to mark something with speckles (*usually passive*) [15C. < Middle Dutch *spekkel*]

speck·led /spék'ld/ *adj* **1.** with a pattern of many small spots or small irregular patches, often of a contrasting color **2.** with parts that contrast distinctly with each other ○ *a speckled career* ○ *speckled shadows*

speck·led trout *n* FISH same as **brook trout**

speck·le in·ter·fe·rom·e·try *n* a technique for reducing distortions in photographic images of astronomical objects by combining a number of images of very short exposure

specs /speks/ *npl* same as **spectacles** (*see* **spectacle**) (*informal*) [Early 19C. Shortening]

SPECT *abbr* PHYS single photon emission computed tomography

spec·ta·cle /spéktək'l/ *n* **1.** SOMETHING REMARKABLE THAT CAN BE SEEN an object, phenomenon, or event that is witnessed, especially one that is impressive, unusual, or disturbing **2.** LAVISH DISPLAY an impressive performance or display, especially something staged as a form of entertainment **3.** UNPLEASANT CENTER OF ATTENTION somebody or something that attracts attention by being unpleasant or ridiculous ○ *You are making a spectacle of yourself.* ■ **spec·ta·cles** *npl* EYEGLASSES a pair of glass or plastic lenses worn in a frame in front of the eyes to help correct imperfect vision [14C. Via French < Latin *spectaculum* < *spectare* "to watch" < *specere* "look at"]

ORIGIN The Latin word *specere* "to look at" and its stem *spect-*, from which ***spectacle*** is derived, are also the source of English *aspect, circumspect, conspectus, conspicuous, despise, expect, inspect, perspective, prospect, respect, specimen, specter, spectrum,* and *suspect.*

spec·ta·cled /spéktək'ld/ *adj* **1.** wearing spectacles **2.** having markings on the face that encircle the eyes in a way that resembles spectacles

spec·ta·cled bear *n* a rare bear that is black with white markings around the eyes. It is vulnerable to extinction because of habitat loss. Native to: grasslands and forests of the Andes. Latin name: *Tremarcto ornatus.*

spec·tac·u·lar /spek tákyələr/ *adj* **1.** VISUALLY IMPRESSIVE impressive or dramatic to look at or watch **2.** REMARKABLE remarkably large, great, or speedy ■ *n* EXTRAVAGANZA a lavish celebration or artistic production [Late 17C. < SPECTACLE after ORACULAR related to ORACLE and similar pairs] —**spec·tac·u·lar·ly** *adv*

spec·tate /spék tàyt, spèk táyt/ (**-tat·ed, -tat·ing, -tates**) *vi* to watch an activity or event without participating [Early 18C. Back-formation < SPECTATOR]

spec·ta·tor /spék tàytər/ *n* **1.** somebody who watches or observes, especially somebody who watches an activity or event **2.** *US* CLOTHING same as **spectator shoe** [Late 16C. Directly or via French < Latin *spectare* "to watch" (see SPECTACLE)] —**spec·ta·to·ri·al** /spèktə táwree əl/ *adj* —**spec·ta·tor·ship** *n*

spec·ta·tor shoe, **spec·ta·tor** *n* a shoe, especially one for women, in two contrasting colors of leather

spec·ta·tor sport *n* a sport that attracts spectators in large numbers

spec·ter /spéktər/, **spec·tre** *n* **1.** a ghostly presence or apparition **2.** a threat or prospect of something unpleasant ○ *the specter of my performance review* [Early 17C. Directly or via French < Latin *spectrum* "image, apparition" (see SPECTRUM)]

spec·ti·no·my·cin /spèktinō mīss'n/ *n* an antibiotic with a wide range of effectiveness against penicillin-resistant pathogens. Use: treatment of gonorrhea. [Mid-20C. < modern Latin *Streptomyces spectabilis,* bacterium that is its source < Latin *spectabilis,* "visible"]

spec·tra PHYS, PHARM plural of **spectrum**

spec·tral /spéktrəl/ *adj* **1.** relating to specters or in the form of a specter **2.** produced by a spectrum or relating to a spectrum —**spec·tral·i·ty** /spek trállətee/ *n* —**spec·tral·ly** *adv* —**spec·tral·ness** *n*

spec·tral class *n* ASTRON same as **spectral type**

spec·tral line *n* a discrete band of light in a spectrum associated with a specific wavelength and used to identify substances. Characteristic spectral lines are emitted by atoms and molecules and may be used to identify substances.

spec·tral type *n* a classification system for stars based on an analysis of the light they emit. This analysis also gives information on a star's temperature and chemical composition.

spec·tre *n* another spelling of **specter**

spec·trin /spéktrin/ *n* a fibrous protein in the membranes of red blood cells [Mid-20C. < SPECTER, because first isolated from red blood cells lacking hemoglobin, called "ghosts"]

spectro- *prefix* spectrum ○ *spectroscope* [< SPECTRUM]

spec·tro·chem·is·try /spéktrō kèmmistree/ *n* the branch of chemistry that deals with the spectra formed during chemical activity, e.g., the emission spectra of substances burned in an arc or spark —**spec·tro·chem·i·cal** *adj*

spec·tro·gram /spéktrə gràm/ *n* a photograph or representation of a spectrum

spec·tro·graph /spéktrə gràf/ *n* an instrument consisting of a spectrometer and related equipment used to obtain a visual record of a spectrum —**spec·tro·graph·ic** /spèktrə gráffik/ *adj* —**spec·tro·graph·i·cal·ly** *adv* —**spec·trog·ra·phy** /spek tróggrəfee/ *n*

spec·tro·he·li·o·gram /spèktrō heélee ə gràm/ *n* an image of the Sun produced using a narrow wavelength band of the radiation it emits

spec·tro·he·li·o·graph /spèktrō heélee ə gràf/ *n* an instrument used to obtain images of the Sun over a narrow band of wavelengths —**spec·tro·he·li·o·graph·ic** /-heélee ə gráffik/ *adj* —**spec·tro·he·li·og·ra·phy** /-heélee óggrəfee/ *n*

spec·tro·he·li·o·scope /spèktrō heélee ə skōp/ *n* an instrument used for viewing the Sun's spectrum —**spec·tro·he·li·o·scop·ic** /-heélee ə skóppik/ *adj*

spec·trom·e·ter /spek trómmətər/ *n* an instrument used to disperse radiant energy or particles into a spectrum and measure properties such as wavelength, mass, energy, or index of refraction —**spec·tro·met·ric** /spèktrə méttrik/ *adj* —**spec·trom·e·try** *n*

spec·tro·pho·tom·e·ter /spèktrōfə tómmətər/ *n* an instrument used to measure the relative intensities of wavelengths in a spectrum —**spec·tro·pho·to·met·ric** /-fōtə méttrik/ *adj* —**spec·tro·pho·to·met·ri·cal·ly** *adv* —**spec·tro·pho·tom·e·try** *n*

spec·tro·po·lar·im·e·ter /spèktrō pōlə rímmətər/ *n* an instrument used to determine the amount of polarized light reflected from a source such as a distant star or galaxy —**spec·tro·po·lar·i·met·ric** /-pōləri méttrik/ *adj* —**spec·tro·po·lar·i·met·ric·al** *adj* —**spec·tro·po·lar·im·e·try** *n*

spec·tro·scope /spéktrə skōp/ *n* an instrument for dispersing light, usually light in the visible range, into a spectrum in order to measure it —**spec·tro·scop·ic** /spèktrə skóppik/ *adj* —**spec·tro·scop·i·cal·ly** *adv*

spec·tro·scop·ic a·nal·y·sis *n* the use of spectroscopy to determine the chemical composition, energy levels, and molecular structure of substances

spec·tros·co·py /spek tróskəpee/ *n* the study of spectra, especially to determine the chemical composition of substances and the physical properties of molecules, ions, and atoms —**spec·tros·co·pist** *n*

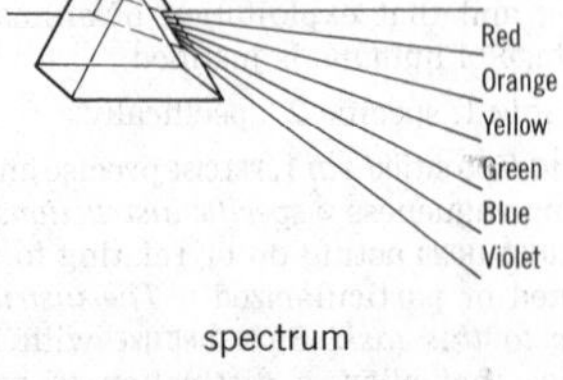

spectrum

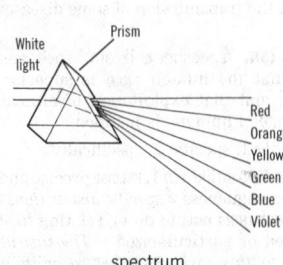

spec·trum /spéktrəm/ (*plural* **-tra** /-trə/ or **-trums**) *n* **1.** DISTRIBUTION OF COLORED LIGHT a continuous distribution of colored light produced when a beam of white light is dispersed into its components, e.g., by a prism **2.** PARTICULAR RADIATION FREQUENCY RANGE a range of radiation frequencies that have a particular property **3.** RECORD OF RADIATION WAVELENGTHS OF SUBSTANCE a visual record of the wavelengths of the radiation or particles emitted by a substance, used as a means of analyzing its physical properties such as energy and mass **4.** RANGE OF VALUES a range of values, especially one with opposite values at its limits ○ *a spectrum of opinions between the two extremes* **5.** PHARM RANGE OF DRUG TARGETS the range of organisms that an antibiotic can kill [Late 19C. < Latin, "image, apparition" < *specere* "look at"]

spec·u·la OPTICS, MED, BIRDS plural of **speculum**

spec·u·lar /spékyələr/ *adj* **1.** relating to mirrors or having the characteristics of a mirror **2.** carried out using a speculum [Late 16C. < Latin *specularis* < *speculum* (see SPECULUM)]

spec·u·late /spékyə làyt/ (**-lat·ed, -lat·ing, -lates**) *v* **1.** *vti* CONJECTURE to form a conjecture on the basis of incomplete facts or information **2.** *vi* CONSIDER POSSIBILITIES to think over possibilities **3.** *vi* MAKE RISKY DEALS FOR PROFIT to engage in financial transactions such as commodity trading that have an element of risk, especially in the short term, with the hope of making a profit **4.** *vi* TAKE RISKS to take risks in an attempt to achieve something or get some benefit [Late 16C. < Latin *speculat-,* past participle of *speculari* "observe, spy out" < *specere* "look at"]

spec·u·la·tion /spèkyə láysh'n/ *n* **1.** OPINION BASED ON INCOMPLETE INFORMATION a conclusion, theory, or opinion based on incomplete facts or information **2.** REASONING BASED ON INCOMPLETE INFORMATION reasoning based on incomplete facts or information ○ *mere speculation* **3.** RISKY TRANSACTION a financial transaction that involves risk, but is potentially profitable ○ *a failed speculation on a dot-com* **4.** MAKING OF RISKY TRANSACTIONS the practice of engaging in financial transactions that are risky, but potentially profitable

spec·u·la·tive /spékyə làytiv, -lətiv/ *adj* **1.** USING INCOMPLETE INFORMATION based on conjecture or incomplete facts or information **2.** FORMING CONCLUSIONS NOT BASED ON FACT given to forming conclusions or opinions that are not based on fact **3.** RISKY BUT POTENTIALLY PROFITABLE risky in nature, but potentially profitable ○ *speculative investments* —**spec·u·la·tive·ly** *adv* —**spec·u·la·tive·ness** *n*

spec·u·la·tor /spékyə làytər/ *n* somebody who speculates, especially financially

spec·u·lum /spékyələm/ (*plural* **-la** /-lə/ or **-lums**) *n* **1.** OPTICS MIRROR a mirror or other reflective surface in an optical instrument such as a telescope **2.** MED MEDICAL INSTRUMENT a medical instrument used to hold open a body passage such as the anus or vagina so that it can be examined **3.** BIRDS COLORED PATCH ON BIRD'S WINGS a patch of color on the wings of ducks and some other birds [Late 16C. < Latin, "mirror" < *specere* "look at"]

spec·u·lum met·al *n* an alloy of copper and tin, sometimes with other metals. It is hard, brittle, white, resistant to corrosion and, because it can be highly polished, is used for metal mirrors.

sped past participle, past tense of **speed**

speech /speech/ *n* **1.** SPEAKING ABILITY the ability to speak (*often used before a noun*) **2.** COMMUNICATION BY SPEAKING the act of communicating by speaking **3.** UTTERANCES things that are said ○ *recordings of human speech* **4.** SPOKEN LANGUAGE spoken language, especially as distinct from the written language ○ *effective communication in both speech and writing* **5.** ADDRESS a talk given to an audience **6.** PARTICULAR WAY OF SPEAKING a particular way of speaking or using language, especially that of a person or group [Old English *spǣc* < *specan* (see SPEAK)]

speech com·mu·ni·ty *n* a group that includes all the speakers of a single language or dialect. They may be widely dispersed geographically.

speech·i·fy /speéchə fī/ (**-fied, -fy·ing, -fies**) *vi* **1.** to talk in a tedious and self-important manner, especially in giving an opinion **2.** to give a speech or speeches —**speech·i·fi·ca·tion** /speéchəfi káysh'n/ *n* —**speech·i·fi·er** *n*

speech·less /speéchləss/ *adj* **1.** TEMPORARILY UNABLE TO SPEAK temporarily unable to speak or unable to think of something to say, e.g., because of surprise or fear **2.** UNABLE TO SPEAK lacking the power of speech **3.**

REMAINING SILENT choosing not to say anything **4.** UNSPOKEN not expressed in words **5.** HARD TO EXPRESS difficult or impossible to put into words —**speech·less·ly** *adv* —**speech·less·ness** *n*

speech·mak·er /speéch màykər/ *n* somebody who makes a speech, especially somebody who frequently makes speeches —**speech·mak·ing** *n*

speech pa·thol·o·gy *n* the study, diagnosis, and treatment of speech disorders, including failure of speech development in children and language disorders resulting from acquired brain dysfunction —**speech pa·thol·o·gist** *n*

speech-read·ing *n* COMMUNICATION same as **lip-reading**

speech rec·og·ni·tion *n* a system of computer input and control in which the computer can recognize spoken words and transform them into digitized commands or text. With such a system, a computer can be activated and controlled by voice commands or take dictation as input to a word processor or a desktop publishing system.

speech syn·the·sis *n* computer-generated audio output that resembles human speech

speech ther·a·py *n* the treatment of disorders that prevent people from speaking clearly —**speech ther·a·pist** *n*

speech·writ·er /speéch rìtər/ *n* somebody who writes speeches for other people, especially professionally

speed /speed/ *n* **1.** RATE OF MOVEMENT OR HAPPENING the rate at which something moves, happens, or functions **2.** RAPIDITY fast movement, progress, or operation **3.** RATE OF MOVEMENT IRRESPECTIVE OF DIRECTION rate of movement irrespective of direction. It is equal either to distance traveled divided by travel time, or to rate of change of distance with respect to time. **4.** DRUGS same as **amphetamine** (*slang*) **5.** MECH ENG GEAR RATIO a gear ratio in a motor, engine, or driving mechanism ○ *a ten-speed bicycle* ○ *operates at three different speeds* **6.** PHOTOGRAPHY PHOTOGRAPHIC FILM'S SENSITIVITY TO LIGHT a measure of the sensitivity of photographic film to light, expressed numerically according to any of various rating systems **7.** SUCCESS success or prosperity (*archaic*) ■ *v* (**sped** /sped/ or **speed·ed, speed·ing, speeds**) **1.** *vti* GO OR MOVE QUICKLY to go or move quickly, or make somebody or something do this **2.** *vi* DRIVE FAST to drive fast, especially in excess of the speed limit **3.** *vi* HAPPEN QUICKLY to pass or happen quickly or more quickly ○ *days speeding by* **4.** *vi* DRUGS USE AMPHETAMINES to be under the influence of amphetamines (*slang*) **5.** *vti* MAKE OR BE PROSPEROUS to prosper, or cause somebody or something to prosper (*archaic*) [Old English *spēd* "success, prosperity" < Indo-European, "prosper"] ◇ **be** *or* **get up to speed 1.** to reach the maximum or desirable rate of movement or progress **2.** to be or become fully informed about the latest developments

speed up *vti* to increase in rate or speed, or make somebody or something do this

speed·ball /speéd bàwl/ *n* **1.** GAME RESEMBLING SOCCER a team game similar to soccer, in which the ball can be passed forward with the hands and caught when in mid-air **2.** ILLEGAL DRUG MIXTURE a combination of illegal drugs such as cocaine and heroin taken by injection (*slang*) **3.** COFFEE WITH ADDED ESPRESSO a cup of regular coffee with an added shot of espresso (*slang*)

speed·boat /speéd bòt/ *n* a motorboat capable of traveling at high speeds

speed brake *n* a flap on an aircraft wing used to decrease speed in flight before landing

speed bump *n* a raised area or ridge on a road surface designed to limit traffic speeds

speed cam·er·a *n* a roadside-mounted camera that automatically photographs a vehicle passing by it at excessive speed. It provides traffic police with concrete evidence of speeding offenses.

speed dat·ing *n* an organized gathering of singles at which the participants meet privately for a few minutes of conversation with a number of potential partners and decide who among those they have met they would like to meet again

speed de·mon *n* somebody who habitually drives too fast in a motor vehicle (*informal*)

speed di·al *n* a function on a telephone that enables numbers to be stored in a memory so that they can be dialed by pressing a single button ○ *I have her number on speed dial.*

speed·er /speédər/ *n* a motorist who violates established speed limits

speed freak *n* somebody who is addicted to amphetamines (*slang*)

speed·ing /speéding/ *n* the offense of driving a vehicle at a speed above the designated speed limit ■ *adj* moving or working quickly

speed lim·it *n* the maximum permitted speed, usually set by law, at which a vehicle may travel on a specific stretch of road

speed mer·chant *n UK* somebody who habitually drives too fast in a motor vehicle (*informal*)

speed of light *n* the constant and universal speed at which all electromagnetic radiation travels through a vacuum, 2.998 ± 10^8 meters per second. Symbol **c**

speed of sound *n* the speed at which sound waves travel through a medium

speed·om·e·ter /spə dómmətər/ *n* an instrument that continuously measures a vehicle's speed and displays it either numerically or by means of a needle on a dial

speed-read /speéd reèd/ *vti* to read something very fast using a learned technique of skimming the text

speed skate *n* an ice skate designed for racing. It has a blade that is much longer than on a standard skate. —**speed skat·er** *n*

speed skat·ing *n* the sport of racing competitively on speed skates. Two skaters race against each other on a wide oval track divided into two lanes.

speed trap *n* a stretch of road kept under hidden surveillance by police officers monitoring vehicle speeds, usually using radar equipment

speed·up /speéd up/ *n* **1.** an increase in rate or speed **2.** *US* a demand for an increase in productivity from a work force without a corresponding pay increase

speed walk·ing *n* TRACK AND FIELD same as **race walking**

speed·way /speéd wày/ *n* **1.** a racetrack for cars or motorcycles **2.** a road on which vehicles are allowed to travel at high speeds

speed·well /speéd wèl/ *n* a perennial plant of the snapdragon family with opposite leaves. Flowers: blue or pinkish, in clusters. Native to: Europe. Genus: *Veronica*. [Late 16C. < SPEED (verb) + WELL[2]]

speed·writ·ing /speéd rìting/ *n* a system of shorthand writing that uses combinations of standard letters, as distinct from other systems that use symbols

speed·y /speédee/ (**-i·er, -i·est**) *adj* **1.** accomplished or achieved quickly **2.** capable of moving very fast —**speed·i·ly** *adv* —**speed·i·ness** *n*

speed zone *n* an area where a different, usually reduced, speed limit is in effect

~~speek~~ incorrect spelling of **speak**

speiss /spīss/ *n* a compound of arsenic or antimony formed during the smelting of ores such as iron, nickel, and copper [Late 18C. < German *Speise* "food, speiss"]

spe·lae·an /spə leé ən/, **spe·le·an** *adj* relating to caves, or found in caves [Mid-19C. Via Latin < Greek *spēlaion* "cave"]

spe·le·ol·o·gy /speelee óllәjee/ *n* **1.** the scientific study or exploration of caves **2.** *UK* LEISURE same as **spelunking** —**spe·le·o·log·i·cal** /speelee ә lójjik'l/ *adj* —**spe·le·ol·o·gist** *n*

spell[1] /spel/ (**spelled, spell·ing, spells**) *v* **1.** *vti* NAME OR WRITE LETTERS OF WORD to name or write in correct order the constituent letters of a word, part of a word, or group of words **2.** *vt* FORM WORD to form a word when arranged in the correct order **3.** *vt* SIGNIFY SOMETHING to be a sign or indication of something ○ *Increased interest rates could spell trouble for some corporate borrowers.* [13C. < Old French *espeller* < Germanic]

spell out *vt* **1.** MAKE SOMETHING COMPLETELY CLEAR to state something clearly, allowing no room for misunderstanding **2.** READ SOMETHING WITH DIFFICULTY to read something with difficulty or very slowly, especially by reading out words one letter at a time **3.** FIGURE SOMETHING OUT to figure something out by careful study or analysis

spell[2] /spel/ *n* **1.** WORDS WITH SUPPOSED MAGICAL POWER a word or series of words believed to have magical power, spoken to invoke the magic **2.** INFLUENCE OF MAGIC WORDS the influence that a spell has over somebody or something **3.** FASCINATION a compelling fascination or attraction ■ *vt* (**spelled, spell·ing, spells**) INFLUENCE SOMEBODY OR SOMETHING USING SPELL to put somebody or something under the influence of a spell [Old English, "talk, speech" < Germanic]

spell[3] /spel/ *n* **1.** SHORT PERIOD a period of indeterminate, but usually short duration (*informal*) ○ *Let's sit a spell.* ○ *achieved great things with the club in his short spell as manager* **2.** PERIOD OF PARTICULAR WEATHER a period of weather of a particular type ○ *a warm spell* **3.** BOUT OF PARTICULAR ILLNESS a period in which somebody has a particular illness or medical condition ○ *a fainting spell* **4.** PERIOD OF WORK a period of work or purposeful activity **5.** TURN ON DUTY somebody's turn to work or perform a duty **6.** SHORT DISTANCE a short unspecified distance (*informal*) ○ *down the road a spell* ■ *vt* (**spelled, spell·ing, spells**) *N Am, Scotland* RELIEVE SOMEBODY to relieve somebody of a task temporarily, especially in order to allow him or her to rest [Late 16C. < variant of obsolete *spele* "take the place of somebody," origin ?]

spell·bind·ing /spél bìnding/ *adj* holding somebody's attention and interest completely [Late 20C. < SPELL[2]] —**spell·bind** *vt* —**spell·bind·er** *n* —**spell·bind·ing·ly** *adv*

spell·bound /spél bòwnd/ *adj* having your attention and interest held completely by somebody or something [Late 18C. < SPELL[2]]

spell·check·er /spél chèkər/ *n* a computer program that compares words in a text with a file of correctly spelled words in order to detect misspellings [Late 20C. < SPELL[1]] —**spell·check** *n, vt*

spell·down /spél dòwn/ *n US* same as **spelling bee**

spell·er /spéllər/ *n* **1.** somebody who spells words, especially in a particular way ○ *an excellent speller* **2.** a book for teaching or improving spelling [15C. < SPELL[1]]

spell·ing /spélling/ *n* **1.** ABILITY TO SPELL the ability to spell words correctly **2.** FORMING OF WORDS BY ORDERING LETTERS the forming of words with letters in a conventionally accepted order (*often used before a noun*) **3.** EXAMPLE OF LETTER ORDER an example of how a word is spelled [15C. < SPELL[1]]

spell·ing bee *n* a competition in which the object is to see who can spell the most words correctly

spell·ing pro·nun·ci·a·tion *n* a variant pronunciation of a word that differs from the standard pronunciation and is influenced by the way a word is spelled

spelt /spelt/ *n* a hardy variety of wheat of inferior quality, sometimes grown in mountainous regions. Latin name: *Triticum spelta*. [Pre-12C. < late Latin *spelta*]

spel·ter /spéltər/ *n* impure zinc, often used as a cheap alternative for bronze in cast decorative items [Mid-17C. Ultimately < W Germanic]

spe·lunk·ing /spə lúngking, spi-/ *n* the sport or pastime of exploring caves [Mid-20C. < Latin *spelunca* "cave" < Greek *spelunx*] —**spe·lunk·er** *n*

Spe·mann /shpáy màn/, **Hans** (1869–1941) German embryologist. He discovered the organizer function in embryonic development and won the Nobel Prize in physiology or medicine (1935).

spen·cer /spénssər/ *n* **1.** a short jacket worn by boys in the late 18th and early 19th centuries **2.** a very short jacket worn by women over a high-waisted gown in the late 18th and early 19th centuries [Late 18C. After George John *Spencer* (1758–1834), second Earl Spencer]

Spen·cer /spénssər/, **Herbert** (1820–1903) British philosopher and social theorist. He applied evolutionary theory to ethics and sociology, and coined the phrase "survival of the fittest." His major work is *A System of Synthetic Philosophy* (1862–93).

"The liberty the citizen enjoys is to be measured not by the governmental machinery he lives under, whether representative or other, but by the paucity of restraints it imposes on him."

[Herbert Spencer, *The Man Versus the State*; 1884]

Barnaby's

Sir Stanley Spencer

Spen·cer, Sir Stanley (1891–1959) British painter. Many of his works, e.g., *The Resurrection, Cookham* (1923–27), place traditional biblical scenes in contemporary settings.

Spen·cer Gulf large coastal inlet in South Australia, flanked by the Eyre and Yorke peninsulas. Length: 200 mi./320 km.

Spen·ce·ri·an /spen seérree ən, -sérree-/ *adj* describes a style of handwriting with perfectly formed letters and ornamentation of capitals [Mid-19C. After Platt Rogers *Spencer* (1800–64), US calligrapher]

spend /spend/ (**spent** /spent/, **spend·ing, spends**) *v* **1.** *vti* PAY MONEY to pay out money in exchange for goods or services **2.** *vt* DEVOTE TIME OR EFFORT to devote time, energy, or thought to something ○ *spent a lot of time thinking about it* **3.** *vt* PASS TIME to pass a particular amount of time in a particular place or way ○ *spend a week in Hawaii* **4.** *vt* USE SOMETHING UP to deplete something totally **5.** *vt* SACRIFICE SOMETHING to sacrifice something, especially for a cause ○ *spent her life working for reform* [Pre-12C. Partly < Latin *expendere* "pay" (see EXPEND); partly < Old French *despendre* "expend" < Latin *dispendere* (see DISPENSE)] —**spend·er** *n*

Spen·der /spéndər/, **Sir Stephen** (1909–95) British poet and editor. He was a prominent member of the left-wing British literary movement in the 1930s, and edited *Encounter* from 1953 to 1967. His works include *Collected Poems, 1928–85* (1986) and *Journals 1939–83* (1986). Full name **Spender, Sir Stephen Harold**

spend·ing mon·ey /spénding-/ *n* cash used or available for personal expenses, especially expenditure on nonessential items

spend·thrift /spénd thrìft/ *n* somebody who spends money recklessly or extravagantly ■ *adj* tending to spend money recklessly or extravagantly [Late 16C. < SPEND + THRIFT in the archaic sense "savings, earnings"]

spend·y /spéndee/ *adj* same as **expensive** (*slang*)

Spen·ser /spénssər/, **Edmund** (1552?–99) English poet. He wrote the epic romance *The Faerie Queene* (published in three parts, 1590–96), a panoramic historical allegory and one of the classics of English Renaissance literature. —**Spen·se·ri·an** /spen seéree ən/ *adj*

> "Upon a great adventure he was bond, / The greatest Gloriana to him gave, / (That greatest Glorious Queene of Faery lond) / To winne him worshippe, and her grace to have, / Which of all earthly thinges he most did crave."
> [Edmund Spenser, *The Faerie Queene*; 1590]

Spen·se·ri·an stan·za *n* a stanza devised by Edmund Spenser that contains eight lines of iambic pentameter and a ninth of iambic hexameter, using the rhyming scheme ababbcbcc. The scheme is used in *The Faerie Queene.*

spent /spent/ past participle, past tense of **spend** ■ *adj* **1.** CONSUMED used or used up ○ *tossed the spent match into the fire* **2.** EXHAUSTED totally depleted of energy or strength ○ *felt totally spent by the end of the day* **3.** FINISHED at an end **4.** FISH EXHAUSTED OF SPAWN OR SPERM describes a female fish that has deposited all its spawn or a male fish that has used up all its sperm

sperm[1] /spurm/ *n* PHYSIOL **1.** same as **spermatozoon 2.** same as **semen** (*informal; not in technical use*) [14C. Via late Latin < Greek *sperma* "seed, semen" < *speirein* "to sow"]

sperm[2] /spurm/ *n* **1.** INDUST same as **spermaceti 2.** INDUST same as **sperm oil 3.** MARINE BIOL same as **sperm whale** [Mid-19C. Shortening]

sper·ma·ce·ti /spùrmə séttee/ *n* a white waxy solid. Source: oil in the head of sperm whales and other cetaceans. Use: formerly, in cosmetics, candles, and ointments. [Late 15C. < medieval Latin, < late Latin *sperma* (see SPERM[1]) + Latin *ceti* "of a whale"]

sper·ma·ry /spúrməree/ (*plural* **-ries**) *n* an organ in which male reproductive cells are developed. The testes are spermaries.

spermat- *prefix* same as **spermato-** (*used before vowels*)

sper·ma·the·ca /spùrmə theékə/ *n* a receptacle for storing sperm in the reproductive tracts of some invertebrates such as insects [Early 19C. < late Latin *sperma* (see SPERM[1])] —**sper·ma·the·cal** *adj*

sper·mat·ic /spur máttik/ *adj* **1.** relating to, carrying, or containing semen **2.** relating to a spermary or to the spermatic cord —**sper·mat·i·cal·ly** *adv*

sper·mat·ic cord *n* a cord by which a testis is suspended in the scrotum. It contains the vas deferens as well as nerves, vessels, and veins.

sper·ma·tid /spúrmətid/ *n* a cell that, with three others, forms from a spermatocyte and develops into a spermatozoon

sper·ma·ti·um /spur máyshee əm, -shəm/ (*plural* **-ti·a** /-shee ə, -shə/) *n* a cell that functions as a male reproductive cell in some algae, fungi, and lichens [Mid-19C. Via modern Latin < Greek *spermation*, diminutive of *sperma* (see SPERM[1])]

spermato- *prefix* **1.** sperm, spermatozoon ○ *spermatogenesis* **2.** seed ○ *spermatophyte* [< Greek *spermat-*, stem of *sperma* (see SPERM[1])]

sper·mat·o·cide /spur máttə sìd/ *n* PHARM same as **spermicide** —**sper·mat·o·cid·al** /spùrmətə sìd'l/ *adj*

sper·mat·o·cyte /spur máttə sìt/ *n* a cell that develops from a spermatogonium. It divides into four spermatids by means of the kind of cell division known as meiosis.

sper·mat·o·gen·e·sis /spùrmətə jénnəssiss/ *n* the formation and development of spermatozoa in the testes —**sper·mat·o·ge·net·ic** /-jə néttik/ *adj*

sper·mat·o·go·ni·um /spùrmətō gṓnee əm/ (*plural* **-ni·a** /-nee ə/) *n* a cell in the male testes that develops and divides to form spermatocytes. These subsequently divide to form spermatids, from which spermatozoa finally develop. —**sper·mat·o·go·ni·al** *adj*

sper·mat·o·phore /spur máttə fàwr/ *n* a capsule or mass that encloses spermatozoa in insects and other lower animals and is transferred to the female during insemination —**sper·ma·toph·o·ral** /spùrmətə fáwrəl/ *adj*

sper·mat·o·phyte /spur máttə fìt, spúrmətə-/ *n* a plant such as an angiosperm or a gymnosperm that produces seeds —**sper·mat·o·phyt·ic** /spur màttə fíttik, spùrmətə-/ *adj*

sper·mat·or·rhe·a /spùrmətə reé ə/ *n* the involuntary emission of semen without orgasm

sper·mat·o·zo·a BIOL plural of **spermatozoon**

sper·mat·o·zo·id /spur màttə zṓ id, spùrmətə-/ *n* a male reproductive cell, resembling a ribbon, produced in algae, ferns, fungi, mosses, and some gymnosperms. It can move by means of flagella. [Mid-19C. < SPERMATOZOON]

sper·mat·o·zo·on /spur màttə zṓ on, spùrmətə-/ (*plural* **-zo·a** /-zṓ ə/) *n* a male reproductive cell (**gamete**) that has an oval head with a nucleus, a short neck, and a tail by which it moves to find and fertilize an ovum —**sper·mat·o·zo·an** *adj*

sperm bank *n* a place that stores semen until it is required for use in artificial insemination

sperm count *n* **1.** the concentration of sperm in a given volume of seminal fluid, taken as an index of male fertility **2.** a test to determine a man's sperm count

spermi- *prefix* same as **spermo-**

sper·mic /spúrmik/ *adj* BIOL same as **spermatic**

sper·mi·cide /spúrmə sìd/ *n* a contraceptive cream or gel used in conjunction with a birth-control device. Use: kills spermatozoa. —**sper·mi·cid·al** /spùrmə sìd'l/ *adj*

sper·mi·o·gen·e·sis /spùrmee ō jénnəssiss/ *n* the stage of spermatogenesis during which a spermatid is transformed into a spermatozoon —**sper·mi·o·ge·net·ic** /-jə néttik/ *adj*

spermo-, spermi- *prefix* seed, sperm [< Greek *sperma* (see SPERM[1])]

sperm oil *n* a pale yellow oil obtained from the head of the sperm whale. Use: formerly, industrial lubricant.

sperm·o·phile /spúrmə fìl/ *n* a ground squirrel that eats grain and is often regarded as a pest. Native to: North America. Genera: *Citellus* or *Spermophilus.* [Early 19C. < modern Latin *spermophilus* "seed lover" < Latin *sperma* (see SPERM[1])]

sperm whale *n* the largest of the toothed whales, whose massive square head has a cavity filled with a mixture of sperm oil and spermaceti [Shortening of *spermaceti whale*]

-spermy *suffix* fertilization ○ *polyspermy* [< Greek *sperma* (see SPERM[1]) + -Y[2]]

Sper·ry /spérree/, **Elmer Ambrose** (1860–1930) US inventor and engineer. He invented the gyroscopic compass (1910) and ship and airplane stabilizers (1913). He held over 400 patents.

Sper·ry, Roger W. (1913–94) US neurobiologist. He shared the Nobel Prize in physiology or medicine (1981) for his split-brain research. Full name **Sperry, Roger Wolcott**

sper·ry·lite /spérree lìt/ *n* a silvery white platinum arsenide mineral. Use: source of platinum. [Early 20C. After Francis L. *Sperry* (d. 1906), Canadian chemist]

spes·sar·tine /spéssər teen/, **spes·sar·tite** /-tìt/ *n* a yellow or reddish brown garnet that contains manganese. Use: gems. [Mid-19C. < French, after *Spessart*, S Germany]

spew /spyoo/ *vti* (**spewed, spew·ing, spews**) **1.** VOMIT SOMETHING to vomit something that has been eaten **2.** POUR OUT FORCEFULLY to flow out forcefully, or force something out in a stream ○ *a volcano spewing ash* **3.** SAY SOMETHING FORCEFULLY to utter something in an angry, forceful, or relentless way ■ *n* VOMIT something ejected from the mouth, especially vomit [Old English *spīwan* < Indo-European "to spit," an imitation of the sound] —**spew·er** *n*

Spey /spay/ river in northern Scotland, flowing from Loch Lochy to the Moray Firth. Length: 107 mi./171 km.

Spe·yer /spí ər, shpí ər/ city in southwestern Germany. At the Diet of Speyer in 1529 the followers of Martin Luther registered a formal protest, which gave rise to the term "Protestant." Population: 45,100 (1989). English name **Spires**

SPF *n* the degree to which a sun cream, lotion, screen, or block provides protection for the skin against the sun. Full form **sun protection factor**

Spgs. *abbr* Springs (*in place names*)

sphag·num /sfágnəm/ *n* moss growing in wet acid temperate regions that decays and becomes compacted to form peat. Genus: *Sphagnum.* [Mid-18C. Via modern Latin < Greek *sphagnos*, type of shrub] —**sphag·nous** *adj*

sphal·er·ite /sfállə rìt/ *n* a yellow or brownish zinc sulfide mineral. Use: source of zinc. [Mid-19C. < Greek *sphaleros* "slippery, uncertain," because the mineral is easily confused with galena]

sphen- *prefix* same as **spheno-** (*used before vowels*)

sphene /sfeen/ *n* a brown black mineral composed of calcium titanium silicate. Source: igneous rocks. [Early 19C. Via French < Greek *sphēn* "wedge"]

spheno- *prefix* wedge-shaped ○ *sphenodon* [< Greek *sphēn* "wedge"]

sphe·no·don /sfeénə dòn/ *n* REPT same as **tuatara** [Late 19C. < modern Latin < Greek *sphēn* "wedge" + *odōn*, variant of *odous* "tooth"]

sphe·noid /sfee nòyd/ *adj* **1.** shaped like a wedge **2.** relating to the sphenoid bone ■ *n* ANAT same as **sphenoid bone**

sphe·noid bone *n* a bone with prominent wings at the base of the cranium. It forms part of the walls and roof of the nasal cavity.

spher- *prefix* same as **sphero-** (*used before vowels*)

sphere /sfeer/ *n* **1.** GLOBE an object similar in shape to a ball **2.** MATH THREE-DIMENSIONAL SURFACE a three-dimensional closed surface consisting of all points that are a given distance from a center **3.** MATH ROUND SOLID FIGURE the solid figure bounded by a sphere, or the volume it encloses **4.** FIELD OF KNOWLEDGE OR ACTIVITY a field of knowledge, interest, or activity **5.** AREA OF INFLUENCE an area of control or influence ○ *took no interest in matters beyond her sphere* **6.** GROUP IN SOCIETY a level or group within a society **7.** ASTRONOMICAL OBJECT an astronomical object such as a planet, moon, or star (*literary*) **8.** ASTRON same as **sky** (*literary*) **9.** REVOLVING CELESTIAL SHELL in early astronomical theory, a revolving concentric transparent shell on which the Sun, Moon, planets, and stars were thought to be fixed as they moved around the Earth ■ *vt* (**sphered, spher·ing, spheres**) **1.** ENCIRCLE SOMETHING to surround, encircle, or enclose something (*literary*) **2.** RAISE SOMETHING ALOFT to place something in the sky or in heaven, among the celestial spheres (*literary*) **3.** FORM SOMETHING INTO BALL to form something into the shape of a ball [13C. Via French < Latin *sphaera* < Greek *sphaira* "ball"] —**spher·al** *adj* —**sphe·ric·i·ty** /sfe ríssətee/ *n*

sphere of in·flu·ence *n* a geographic region or area of activity in which a state, organization, or person is dominant

spher·i·cal /sféerək'l, sférr-/, **spher·ic** /sféerik, sférr-/ *adj* **1.** ROUND shaped like a sphere **2.** OF SPHERES relating to a sphere or to spheres in general **3.** OF ASTRONOMICAL OBJECTS relating to astronomical objects **4.** OF SPHERES OF ANCIENT ASTRONOMY relating to the spheres of ancient astronomy —**spher·i·cal·ly** *adv* —**spher·i·cal·ness** *n*

spher·i·cal ab·er·ra·tion *n* a fault in a lens or curved mirror in which light passing through the edge has a different focal point from light passing through the center, resulting in blurred images

spher·i·cal an·gle *n* an angle formed on a sphere at the point at which any two circles of maximum radius intersect

spher·i·cal co·or·di·nates *npl* a set of coordinates used for locating a point in space, representing its distance from an origin and two angles describing its orientation relative to perpendicular axes extending from that origin

spher·i·cal ge·om·e·try *n* the geometry of figures formed on the surface of a sphere

spher·i·cal pol·y·gon *n* a geometric figure formed on the surface of a sphere, bounded by three or more arcs of great circles

spher·i·cal tri·an·gle *n* a spherical polygon that has three sides

spher·i·cal trig·o·nom·e·try *n* trigonometry dealing with spherical triangles

spher·ics /sféeriks, sférriks/, **sfer·ics** *n* the study of electromagnetic radiation emanating from natural sources in the atmosphere (*takes a singular verb*) [Mid-20C. Shortening of ATMOSPHERICS]

sphero- *prefix* sphere, spherical ○ *spheroplast* [Via Latin < Greek *sphaira* "sphere, ball"]

sphe·roid /sféer oyd, sfé royd/ *n* a three-dimensional object that is shaped like a sphere, but is not perfectly round, e.g., an ellipsoid —**sphe·roi·dal** /sfi róyd'l, sfe-/ *adj* —**sphe·roi·dal·ly** *adv* —**sphe·roi·dic·i·ty** /sfeer oy díssətee, sfè roy-/ *n*

sphe·rom·e·ter /sfə rómmətər/ *n* an instrument used to measure the curvature of a surface

spher·o·plast /sféerō plàst, sférrō-/ *n* a bacterium or yeast cell that has lost part of its cell wall and is as a result spherical in shape and more sensitive to osmosis

spher·ule /sféer ool, sfé rool/ *n* a minute sphere or globule [Mid-17C. < late Latin *spherula* "small sphere" < Latin *sphaera* (see SPHERE)] —**spher·u·lar** *adj*

spher·u·lite /sféeryə lìt, sférryə-/ *n* a spherical mass of radiating crystal fibers. Source: volcanic rocks. —**spher·u·lit·ic** /sfeeryə líttik, sfèrryə-/ *adj*

spher·y /sféeree/ *adj* **1.** having the shape of a sphere **2.** relating to or resembling a planet, star, or other astronomical object (*literary*)

sphinc·ter /sfíngktər/ *n* a circular band of muscle that surrounds an opening or passage in the body, especially the anus, and narrows or closes the opening by contracting [Late 16C. Via Latin < Greek *sphigktēr* < *sphiggein* "bind tight"] —**sphinc·ter·al** *adj*

sphin·ges MYTHOL plural of **sphinx**

sphin·go·sine /sfíng gə sèen, -gəss'n/ *n* a long-chain amino glycol that is part of the lipids found in nerve tissue [Late 19C. < Greek *sphiggos* "of a sphinx" < *sphigg-*, stem of *sphigx* "sphinx"]

sphinx

sphinx /sfingks/ (*plural* **sphinx·es** or **sphin·ges** /sfín jèez/) *n* **1.** COMPOSITE CREATURE IN GREEK MYTHOLOGY in Greek mythology, a winged creature with a lion's body and a woman's head. It strangled all who could not answer its riddle, but killed itself when Oedipus answered correctly. **2.** COMPOSITE CREATURE IN EGYPTIAN MYTHOLOGY in Egyptian mythology, a creature with a lion's body and the head of a man, ram, or bird **3.** STATUE a statue of a sphinx **4.** SOMEBODY MYSTERIOUS somebody regarded as mysterious or inscrutable [Late 16C. Via Latin < Greek *sphigx*]

sphinx·like /sfíngks lìk/ *adj* difficult to understand or find out about

sphinx moth *n* INSECTS same as **hawk moth** [Because its appearance suggests a sphinx]

sphra·gis·tics /sfrə jístiks/ *n* the study of seals and signet rings (*takes a singular verb*) [Mid-19C. Directly or via French < late Greek *sphragistikos* "of seals (for impressing designs)" < Greek *sphragis* "seal"] —**sphra·gis·tic** *adj*

sp ht *abbr* PHYS specific heat

sphygm- *prefix* same as **sphygmo-** (*used before vowels*)

sphyg·mic /sfígmik/ *adj* relating to the pulse of an artery [Early 18C. < Greek *sphugmikos* < *sphugmos* (see SPHYGMO-)]

sphygmo- *prefix* pulse of an artery ○ *sphygmograph* [< Greek *sphugmos* "pulsation" < *sphug-*, stem of *spuzein* "throb"]

sphyg·mo·graph /sfígmə gràf/ *n* an apparatus used to make a graphical record of variations in blood pressure and pulse —**sphyg·mo·graph·ic** /sfigmə gráffik/ *adj* —**sphyg·mog·ra·phy** /sfig móggrəfee/ *n*

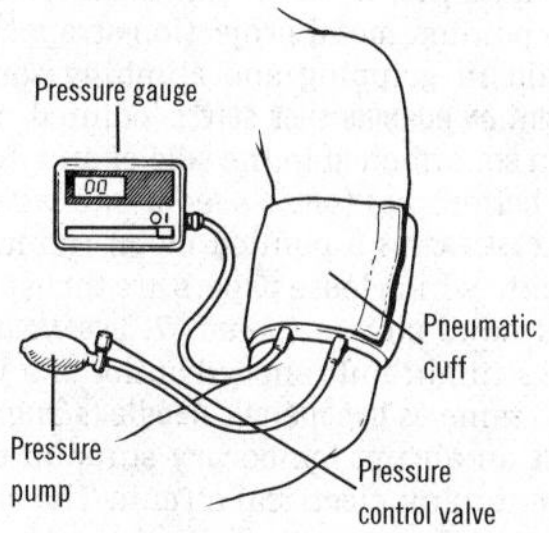

sphygmomanometer

sphyg·mo·ma·nom·e·ter /sfìg mōmə nómmətər/ *n* an instrument used to measure blood pressure in an artery that consists of a pressure gauge, an inflatable cuff placed around the upper arm, and an inflator bulb or pressure pump

spic /spik/ *n* a highly offensive term for a Spanish-speaking person from Mexico, Puerto Rico, or Central or South America (*taboo*) [Early 20C. Shortening and alteration of *spiggoty*, probably < broken English *(no) speaka de (English)* "I don't speak English"]

spi·ca /spíkə/ (*plural* **-cae** /-see/ or **-cas**) *n* a bandage applied to a limb in an overlapping figure-eight pattern to immobilize it [14C. < Latin, "ear of grain"; from its spiraling shape]

spic-and-span *adj* another spelling of **spick-and-span**

spi·cate /spī kàyt/ *adj* growing in the form of a spike, or having flowers that grow in spikes [Mid-17C. < Latin *spicatus*, past participle of *spicare* "provide with sharp points" < *spica* "spike, ear of grain"]

spic·ca·to /spi kaátō/ *n* a technique of playing staccato on stringed instruments, in which the bow is allowed to bounce on the string ■ *adj, adv* played using the technique of allowing the bow to bounce on the string [Early 18C. < Italian, past participle of *spiccare* "pick off, detach"]

spice /spīss/ *n* **1.** AROMATIC PLANT SUBSTANCE USED AS FLAVORING an aromatic plant substance used as a flavoring, e.g., nutmeg or ginger **2.** FLAVORINGS FROM PLANTS food flavorings derived from the nonleafy parts of plants (*often used before a noun*) **3.** EXCITEMENT OR INTEREST a source of excitement or interest **4.** *US* STRONG SMELL a pungent odor or fragrance (*often used before a noun*) **5.** TRACE OF SOMETHING a tiny amount of something ■ *vt* (**spiced, spic·ing, spic·es**) **1.** SEASON SOMETHING WITH SPICE to season food or beverages with spice **2.** MAKE SOMETHING MORE EXCITING to introduce excitement or interest into something ○ *spiced the speech with joking asides* [13C. Via Old French *espice* < late Latin *species* (plural) "goods, wares" < Latin (singular) "appearance, kind"]

spice·ber·ry /spīss bèrree/ (*plural* **-ries**) *n* **1.** a spicy orange, red, or black berry **2.** a tree or bush that produces spiceberries, e.g., the wintergreen

spice·bush /spīss bòosh/ *n* a bush of the laurel family with aromatic leaves. Flowers: yellow, in dense clusters. Native to: North America. Latin name: *Lindera benzoin.*

~~**spicey**~~ incorrect spelling of **spicy**

spick-and-span /spìk-/, **spic-and-span** *adj* **1.** very clean and neat (*not hyphenated after a verb*) **2.** showing no sign of damage or wear and tear [Late 16C. Shortening of *spick-and-span-new* < variant of SPIKE[1] + dialect *span-new* "completely new" < Old Norse *spánnyr* "new chip" < *spán* "chip"]

spick·et /spíkit/ *n regional* same as **spigot** [15C. Alteration of SPIGOT]

REGIONAL NOTE See *spigot.*

spic·u·la BIOL plural of **spiculum**

spic·ule /spíkyool/ *n* **1.** a small hard needle-shaped part, especially one of the calcium- or silicon-containing supporting parts of some invertebrates such as sponges and corals **2.** a slender column of relatively cool high-density gas that rapidly erupts from the solar chromosphere and then falls back. There can be as many as 250,000 spicules rising above the solar surface at any moment. [Late 18C. Anglicized < SPICULUM] —**spic·u·lar** *adj* —**spic·u·late** /spíkyələt, spíkyə làyt/ *adj*

spic·u·lum /spíkyələm/ (*plural* **-la** /-lə/) *n* BIOL same as **spicule** (sense 1) [Mid-18C. < modern Latin, "small spike" < Latin *spica* "spike, ear of grain"]

spic·y /spíssee/ (**-i·er, -i·est**) *adj* **1.** SEASONED WITH SPICE smelling or tasting strongly of spices **2.** INVOLVING IMPROPRIETY arousing interest as a result of involving scandal or sexual impropriety (*informal*) **3.** VIVACIOUS having a very lively personality **4.** BOT PRODUCING SPICES describes plants or plant parts from which spices are obtained —**spic·i·ly** *adv* —**spic·i·ness** *n*

spi·der /spídər/ *n* **1.** EIGHT-LEGGED ANIMAL THAT SPINS WEBS a predatory invertebrate animal with four pairs of legs and two or more abdominal organs (**spinnerets**) used for spinning webs that serve as nests and traps for prey. It is popularly thought to be an insect, although it is an arachnid. Order: Araneae. See illustration on next page **2.** *regional* FRYING PAN a cast-iron frying pan, originally one with legs or feet for cooking on a hearth (*dated*) **3.** *US* TRIVET a trivet for supporting a pan on a hearth **4.** MECH ENG MECHANICAL DEVICE a mechanical device that

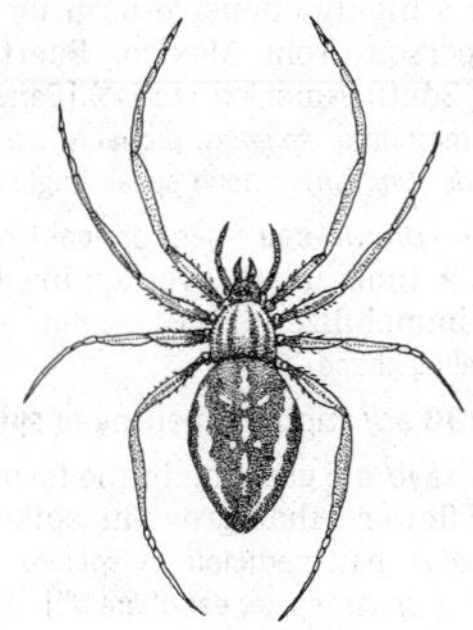

spider

has radiating arms, spokes, or other parts **5.** NAUT **FRAME SECURING REDUNDANT ROPES** a circular frame at the base of a ship's mast, used to secure ropes when sails are not in use **6.** ONLINE **PROGRAM SEARCHING INTERNET FOR INFORMATION** a computer program that searches the Internet for newly accessible information to be added to the index examined by a standard search tool (**search engine**) **7.** CUE GAMES **CUE REST** a multiposition cue rest with wide legs designed to lift the cue tip over an intervening ball **8.** TRANSP same as **spider phaeton** [Old English *spiþra* < *spinnan* (see SPIN)]

REGIONAL NOTE ***Spider*** in the sense "frying pan" is an old-fashioned New England and Southern term that formerly competed with Midland *skillet*. Today, *frying pan* and *fry pan* are usual throughout the United States.

spi·der bee·tle *n* a wingless beetle, many varieties of which are pests to stored food in households and warehouses. Family: Ptinidae.

spi·der crab *n* a sea crab with a small triangular body and long slender legs. Family: Majidae.

spi·der food *n* specific words embedded in a webpage in order to make it more likely to be found by search engines (*slang*) [Late 20C. < *spider* "search engine"]

spi·der·gram /spídər gràm/ *n* a diagram resembling a spider's body and legs, in which information relating to a topic is noted down in boxes joined by radiating lines to a central box containing the topic

spi·der hole *n* (*informal*) **1.** a concealed sniper position, e.g., in a cave or a camouflaged hole dug in the ground **2.** a camouflaged and reinforced hole dug in the ground and used as a hiding place [< the habit of some spiders such as the trapdoor spider of digging concealed holes with hinged lids]

spi·der-hunt·ing wasp *n* a large black or metallic-blue solitary wasp that preys on spiders. Family: Pepsidae.

spi·der lil·y *n* PLANTS same as **crinum**

spi·der mite *n* a tiny web-spinning mite. Some spider mites are garden and crop pests. Family: Tetranychidae.

spi·der mon·key *n* a tree-dwelling monkey with long slender limbs, a long prehensile tail, and a small head. Native to: Central and South America. Genus: *Ateles*.

spi·der phae·ton *n* a high-bodied lightweight fast horse carriage with large wheels

spi·der plant *n* a common houseplant grown for its long narrow variegated leaves and clusters of plantlets. Flowers: white. Latin name: *Chlorophytum variegatum*.

spi·der·web /spídər wèb/ *n* a web that is constructed by a spider to entrap prey, using silk produced from fluid from its abdominal glands

spi·der·wort /spídər wùrt, -wàwrt/ *n* a plant widely grown as a houseplant. Flowers: pink, blue, or violet. Genus: *Tradescantia*. [< the resemblance of the stamens to a spider's legs]

spi·der·y /spídəree/ *adj* **1. THIN AND IRREGULAR** having thin lines or constituent parts that form irregular angles **2. SPIDER-INFESTED** infested with spiders **3. LIKE SPIDER** resembling a spider in shape or movement

Spid·la /spíddlə/, **Vladimir** (*b.* 1951) prime minister of the Czech Republic (2002–). A founder member of the center-left Czech Social Democratic Party and former deputy prime minister, he was elected prime minister in 2002.

spie·gel·ei·sen /speégˈl ìz'n/, **spie·gel** /speégˈl/ *n* pig iron containing high concentrations of manganese and carbon. It is added to steel in the late stages of production to adjust the final composition. [Mid-19C. < German < *Spiegel* "mirror" + *Eisen* "iron"]

spiel /speel, shpeel/ (*informal*) *n* an irritatingly long or predictably glib speech, e.g., a rambling apology or prepared sales patter ■ *vi* (**spieled, spiel·ing, spiels**) to deliver a spiel [Late 19C. < German, "play, game"]

spiel off *vt* to say something very quickly or by rote ○ *spiel off a list of names*

Express Newspapers

Steven Spielberg

Spiel·berg /speél bùrg/, **Steven** (*b.* 1947) US movie director and producer. His movies include *E.T.* (1982), *Jurassic Park* (1993), and the Academy Award-winning *Schindler's List* (1993).

"When I grow up I still want to be a director."
[Steven Spielberg, *Time*; July 15, 1985]

spiff /spif/ (**spiffed, spiff·ing, spiffs**) [Late 19C. Origin ?]

spiff up *vt* to make somebody or something more attractive especially by adding enhancing features (*informal*)

spiff·y /spíffee/ (**-i·er, -i·est**) *adj* stylish or modern and attractive (*informal*) ○ *"a spiffy collection of supercomputers blinking away in a room of their own"* (Kathleen O'Gorman *Detroit Free Press*; 1997) [Mid-19C. Origin ?] —**spiff·i·ly** *adv* —**spiff·i·ness** *n*

spig·ot /spíggət/ *n* **1.** *US* **INDOOR FAUCET** an indoor faucet **2.** *US* **OUTDOOR FAUCET** a faucet situated outdoors **3. TAP FITTED TO CASK** a tap, usually wooden, that is attached to a cask **4. PLUG FOR CASK HOLE** a plug for the vent hole of a cask [14C. Origin ?]

REGIONAL NOTE The word ***spigot*** for an indoor faucet spreads southward and westward out of Pennsylvania, where it yields to the New England term *faucet* in the northernmost counties. To the west, *faucet* and *tap* are usual in the Inland North. In the Upper Midwest and Western states, the form *spicket* reflects Midland and Southern influence.

spike[1] /spīk/ *n* **1. POINTED METAL OR WOODEN PIECE** a sharply pointed piece of metal or wood, especially one of a number along the top of a railing, fence, or wall **2. SHARP POINT** a narrow sharp point **3. LARGE NAIL** a long heavy metal nail **4. METAL PART FOR GRIPPING AND CLIMBING** a sharp pointed metal projection strapped to a boot as an aid in gripping and climbing something **5. METAL POINT ON RUNNING SHOE SOLE** a pointed metal stud, part of a set attached to the sole of an athlete's shoe to give better grip (*often used in the plural*) **6. METAL ROD FOR LOOSE PAPERS** a pointed metal rod mounted on a base onto which loose papers are thrust, especially rejected news stories (*dated*) **7. UNBRANCHED ANTLER OF DEER** the straight unbranched antler of a young deer **8.** DRUGS same as **hypodermic needle** (*slang*) **9. VARIATION IN VOLTAGE** an abrupt temporary surge in the voltage or current in an electrical circuit. The change may be caused by turning off appliances, a lightning strike, or power being restored after an outage. **10. IMAGE OF PEAK AND FALL** a graphic representation of a sharp rise followed by a sharp fall, especially on a graph or as a reading on an instrument **11. SUDDEN BRIEF INCREASE** a sharp and brief rise in something **12. DOWNWARD SMASH OF VOLLEYBALL** a hard smash of a volleyball, hit close to the net and straight down into the opponent's court **13.** FOOTBALL **SIGN OF VICTORY AFTER TOUCHDOWN** in football, a slamming of the ball to the ground in the end zone to signify triumph after a player has scored a touchdown **14.** *US* FISH **MACKEREL** a young mackerel **15.** *UK* **HOSTEL FOR PEOPLE WITHOUT HOMES** a hostel that houses people who have no place to live (*dated slang*) ■ **spikes** *npl* **1. PAIR OF SHOES WITH METAL STUDS** a pair of athletic shoes whose soles are equipped with pointed metal studs to give better traction **2.** CLOTHING **SPIKE HEEL SHOES** a pair of spike heel shoes (*informal*) ■ *v* (**spiked, spik·ing, spikes**) **1.** *vt* **SECRETLY ADD SOMETHING TO DRINK** to put alcohol, a drug, or a poison into somebody's drink surreptitiously (*informal*) **2. FLAVOR PUNCH WITH ALCOHOL** to add alcohol such as wine to punch **3.** *vt* **CAUSE INJURY WITH SPIKES ON SHOE** to injure another player or competitor with the spikes of an athletic shoe **4.** *vi* **RISE ABRUPTLY** to rise sharply and briefly **5.** *vt* MEDIA **DISCARD POTENTIAL NEWS STORY** to reject or decide not to use a news story (*slang*) **6.** *vt* **SMASH VOLLEYBALL DOWNWARD** to leap high close to the net and hit a volleyball straight down into an opponent's court **7.** *vt* **RENDER SOMETHING USELESS** to make something useless or ineffective (*informal*) ○ *spike a rumor* **8.** *vt* **DISABLE CANNON WITH SPIKE** to render a cannon useless by driving a spike into its vent [13C. Ultimately < Indo-European, "sharp point"] —**spiked** *adj* ◇ **hang up your spikes** *US* to retire from a job, especially in a professional sport

spike[2] /spīk/ *n* **1.** an ear of grain such as wheat or barley **2.** a long cluster of flowers attached directly to a stem, with the newest flowers at the tip [14C. < Latin *spica* "ear of grain"]

spike heel *n* a high pointed heel on a woman's shoe, or a shoe with such a heel

spike lav·en·der *n* a mint related to lavender that yields an oil used in paints. Flowers: light purple. Native to: Europe. Latin name: *Lavandula latifolia*.

spike·let /spīklət/ *n* a small flower spike, especially one of the basic units of the flower cluster of a grass or sedge

spike·nard /spīk naard/ (*plural* **-nards** or *same*) *n* **1. HIMALAYAN PLANT** a perennial aromatic plant of the valerian family. Flowers: pinkish purple. Native to: Himalayan range. Latin name: *Nardostachys jatamansi*. **2. ANCIENT FRAGRANT OINTMENT** a fragrant ointment derived from spikenard, used in ancient times **3. PLANT WITH AROMATIC ROOT** a plant of the ginseng family with purplish berries and aromatic roots. Flowers: small, whitish. Native to: North America. Latin name: *Aralia racemosa*. [14C. < medieval Latin *spica nardi* "spike of nard," translation of Greek *nardou stakhus*]

spik·y /spīkee/ (**-i·er, -i·est**) *adj* **1.** having one or more narrow sharp points **2.** easily made angry (*informal*) —**spik·i·ly** *adv* —**spik·i·ness** *n*

spile /spīl/ *n* **1. HEAVY SUPPORTING POST** a heavy timber post driven into the ground as a foundation or support **2. WOODEN PEG** a wooden peg, especially one used as a plug or stopper **3. TREE-TAPPING SPOUT** a tap for drawing sap from the sugar maple tree ■ *vt* (**spiled, spil·ing, spiles**) **1. SUPPORT SOMETHING WITH POST** to provide or support something with a heavy timber post driven into the ground **2. TAP TREE FOR SAP** to draw sap from a tree with a spout or spigot [Early 16C. Via Dutch *spijl* < Middle Dutch or Middle Low German *spile* "splinter, wooden pin"]

spill[1] /spil/ *v* (**spilled** or **spilt** /spilt/, **spill·ing, spills**) **1.** *vti* **FLOW FROM CONTAINER** to flow from a container, or allow something to flow from a container, especially accidentally and usually with resulting loss or waste **2.** *vi* **COME OUT OF CONFINED SPACE** to come out from a building or other confined space in large numbers ○ *The fans spilled out onto the field.* **3.** *vt* **DIVULGE SOMETHING** to reveal or divulge something, often unintentionally (*informal*) ○ *spilled the news* **4.** *vti* **FALL OFF SOMETHING** to fall off something onto the ground or floor, or make somebody fall off something such as a horse, bicycle, or motorbike (*informal*) **5.** *vt* SAILING **LET WIND OUT OF SAIL** to let the wind escape from a sail ■ *n* **1. ACT OF FALLING FROM SOMETHING** a tumble to the ground or floor, especially from a bicycle, motorbike, or horse (*informal*) **2. SOMETHING THAT RUNS OVER** a quantity of something that flows accidentally or unintentionally from a container or confined area, or an instance of this ○ *Workers fought hard to contain the spill.* **3.** GEOG same as **spillway** [Old English *spillan* "kill" < Germanic] —**spill·a·ble** *adj* —**spill·er** *n*

spill over *vi* **1.** to overflow a container or an enclosed area **2.** to spread out from a confined space into a nearby area

spill[2] /spil/ *n* **1.** a splinter or twist of paper used to light something such as a pipe or candle **2.** CONSTR same as **spile** *n* (sense 2) [14C. < Middle Low German *spile*]

spill·age /spíllij/ *n* **1.** the act of spilling something **2.** a quantity of something that has been spilled

Spil·lane /spi láyn/, **Mickey** (*b.* 1918) US writer. His crime fiction is known for its raw energy and violence. Many of his stories feature the detective Mike Hammer. Born **Spillane, Frank Morrison**

spill·o·ver /spíl òvər/ *n* **1.** same as **spillage** (sense 2) **2.** a spread or expansion of something from a confined space into a nearby area **3.** an indirect effect of something

spill·way /spíl wày/ *n* a channel for carrying away excess water, e.g., at a reservoir or dam

spilt past participle, past tense of **spill**[1]

spilth /spilth/ *n US* same as **spillage** [Early 17C. < SPILL[1]]

spim /spim/ *n* unsolicited e-mail that arrives on a personal computer screen in the form of an instant message [Late 20C. Blend of SPAM + *instant message*] —**spim·mer** *n*

spin /spin/ *v* (**spun** /spun/ or **span** *archaic* /span/, **spun, spin·ning, spins**) **1.** *vti* **ROTATE SOMETHING QUICKLY** to turn round and round rapidly, or make something turn round and round rapidly, as if on an axis ○ *He spun a coin.* ○ *dancers spinning around the room* **2.** *vi* **ROTATE FREELY** to revolve or rotate rapidly around an axis ○ *Our wheels spun on the ice.* **3.** *vi* **FACE ABOUT QUICKLY** to turn around rapidly to face in the opposite direction **4.** *vti* **CREATE YARN FROM RAW MATERIALS** to twist raw fibers, e.g., of wool, silk, or cotton, so that they form a continuous yarn or thread **5.** *vti* **MAKE WEB OR COCOON** to make a web or cocoon from filaments extruded from the body **6.** *vti* **GIVE PUBLIC BIASED INFORMATION** to present information in a way meant to influence public opinion ○ *Nobody will give you an unvarnished fact; it has to be spun and interpreted.* **7.** *vti* **ROTATE SOMETHING RAPIDLY IN CHANGED DIRECTION** to strike, throw, or kick something in a way that makes it revolve and change direction when it hits something, or rotate and change direction in this way **8.** *vti* AVIAT **MAKE AIRCRAFT DIVE STEEPLY** to go into a steep spiral dive, or make an aircraft do this **9.** *vt* MUSIC **PLAY RECORDING** to play a piece of recorded music (*informal*) **10.** *vt* **INVENT STORY** to make up an extended story or a series of lies **11.** *vti* **SHAPE PUBLIC OPINION** to cast somebody's remarks or relate a story in such a way as to influence public opinion in a desired way (*slang*) **12.** *vti* **DRY SOMETHING BY ROTATION** to remove water, especially from washed clothes, by rotating them rapidly in a machine **13.** *vi* **BECOME DIZZY** to feel dazed, as if whirling round ○ *My head was spinning.* **14.** *vi* **DRIVE FAST AND WELL** to drive smoothly and speedily **15.** *vi* FISHING **FISH WITH RAPIDLY MOVING BAIT** to fish with a rod, line, and reel, constantly drawing a revolving bait or lure through the water ■ *n* **1.** **ROTATION** a quick rotating movement **2.** **ROTATION CAUSING CHANGED DIRECTION** rotation given to a ball to make it change direction **3.** **INTERPRETIVE POINT OF VIEW** a viewpoint, bias, or interpretation meant to influence public opinion ○ *There's no way the company can put a favorable spin on this disaster.* **4.** **ROTATION WHILE SKATING** a stationary rotation during figure skating **5.** AVIAT **SPIRALING DIVE** a steep spiral dive in an aircraft **6.** **SHORT JOURNEY IN VEHICLE** a brief journey taken for pleasure in a motor vehicle (*informal*) **7.** **DRYING OPERATION IN WASHING MACHINE** the rapid rotation of washed clothes in a washing machine to remove most of the moisture from them **8.** **DIZZY STATE** a state of mental disorientation or dizziness **9.** PHYS **ANGULAR MOMENTUM** the intrinsic angular momentum of an elementary particle or system of such particles independent of its motion **10.** PHYS **QUANTUM PROPERTY OF ANGULAR MOMENTUM** the quantum property or number of an elementary particle that is a measure of its intrinsic angular momentum and magnetic moment [Old English *spinnan* < Indo-European, "to stretch, spin"] ◇ **in a spin** in a state of confusion or panic (*dated*) ◇ **spin your wheels** expend a lot of effort without making progress

spin off *v* **1.** *vti* to derive a new product, material, or service from something that already exists, or be derived in this way **2.** *vt* to divest a company of a subsidiary by distributing the subsidiary's shares to stockholders in the parent corporation

spin out *v* **1.** *vi* **LOSE CONTROL OF VEHICLE** to skid out of control **2.** *vt* **MAKE SUPPLIES LAST** to make something last longer than it ordinarily would, usually by careful management **3.** *vt* **PROLONG SOMETHING** to make an activity last for an unnecessarily long time

spi·na bif·i·da /spīnə bíffidə/ *n* a congenital condition in which part of the spinal cord or meninges protrudes through a cleft in the spinal column, resulting in loss of voluntary movement in the lower body [< modern Latin, "spine split in two"]

spin·ach /spínich/ *n* an annual plant widely cultivated for its edible dark green leaves. Use: eaten cooked as a vegetable or raw in salads. Latin name: *Spinacia oleracea*. [14C. Via Old French *espinache* and Spanish *espinaca* < Arabic *isbānāk* < Persian *aspānāk*]

spi·nal /spīn'l/ *adj* **1.** **OF SPINE** on, in, near, or relating to the spine of a vertebrate animal **2.** **LIKE SPINE** resembling the spine of a vertebrate animal ■ *n* MED **SPINAL ANESTHETIC** an anesthetic used to induce spinal anesthesia (*informal*) —**spi·nal·ly** *adv*

spi·nal an·es·the·sia *n* **1.** anesthesia of the lower half of the body induced by injecting an anesthetic into the fluid surrounding the spinal cord **2.** the loss of sensation in part of the body caused by injury to the spinal column

spi·nal ca·nal *n* a passage that runs through the opening in the middle of each vertebra of the spinal column and contains the spinal cord, the meninges, nerve roots, and blood vessels

spi·nal col·umn *n* the axis of the skeleton of a vertebrate animal, extending from the head and consisting of a series of interconnected vertebrae that enclose and protect the spinal cord

spi·nal cord *n* a thick whitish cord of nerve tissue extending from the bottom of the brain through the spinal column and giving rise to pairs of spinal nerves that supply the body. The spinal cord and brain together form the central nervous system.

spi·nal men·in·gi·tis *n* inflammation of the membranes surrounding the spinal cord that particularly affects young children

spi·nal tap *n* MED same as **lumbar puncture**

spin an·gu·lar mo·men·tum *n* PHYS same as **spin** *n* (sense 9)

spin con·trol *n* the attempt to evoke a desired public response by the presentation of biased or select information (*slang*)

spin cy·cle *n* **1.** a phase in which newly washed laundry is spun rapidly in a washing machine in order to extract most of the water **2.** *US* an instance of, or the degree to which, public opinion is manipulated by efforts to control interpretation of something such as a leader's words (*slang*)

spin·dle /spínd'l/ *n* **1.** **SPECIALLY SHAPED ROD FOR SPINNING THREAD** a handheld rod with a notched end through which strands of natural fibers are drawn, then twisted into thread and wound around the rod **2.** **THREAD-SPINNING ROD ON SPINNING WHEEL** a device similar to the handheld spindle, attached to a spinning wheel **3.** **MECHANICAL THREAD-SPINNING DEVICE** a device on a spinning machine for spinning thread and winding it onto bobbins **4.** **SPINDLE-SHAPED PIECE OF WOOD** a long thin piece of wood that is shaped like a spindle, e.g., a table leg or baluster **5.** **SPINDLE-SHAPED CELL STRUCTURE** a spindle-shaped structure consisting of a network of microtubule fibers along which chromosomes are distributed and drawn apart during meiosis and mitosis **6.** **SPIKE FOR HOLDING PERSONAL PAPERS** an upright spike attached to a base, on which letters or bills are impaled **7.** *regional* INSECTS same as **dragonfly** **8.** MECH ENG **ROTATING ROD FOR DEVICE** a rotating rod on a device such as a lathe, turntable, or door handle **9.** NAUT **WARNING SIGNAL FOR BOATS** a metal rod surmounted by a ball or lantern and attached to a rock or shoal. Use: warning for approaching vessels. ■ *v* (**-dled, -dling, -dles**) **1.** *vt* **IMPALE PAPERS ON SPINDLE** to impale letters or bills on a spindle **2.** *vt* **EQUIP SOMETHING WITH SPINDLE** to provide something with a spindle or spindles **3.** *vi* BOT **GROW TALL AND THIN** to grow a tall slender weak stem [Old English *spinel* < Germanic]

spin·dle cell *n* a narrow, elongated cell characteristic of some cancers

spin·dle tree *n* an evergreen or deciduous tree or bush with small flowers, red fruits, and hard wood. Use: formerly, to make spindles. Genus: *Euonymus*.

spin·dly /spíndlee/ (**-dli·er, -dli·est**), **spin·dling** /spíndling/ *adj* long or tall, thin, and weak-looking

spin doc·tor *n* somebody whose job is to present to the public the policies, actions, or words of a person or organization in their best possible light (*informal*)

spin·dri·er *n* HOUSEHOLD another spelling of **spin-dryer**

spin·drift /spín drìft/ *n* **1.** spray that blows from the surface of the sea **2.** blowing snow or sand [Early 17C. < alteration (probably after SPIN) of obsolete *spoon* "run before a sea" origin ?]

spin-dry *vt* to remove most of the water from washed laundry by spinning it in a washing machine or spin-dryer

spin-dry·er, **spin·dri·er** *n* a machine that forces most of the water out of wet laundry by spinning it rapidly in a perforated drum

spine /spīn/ *n* **1.** ANAT same as **spinal column** **2.** PRINTING **VERTICAL BACK OF BOOK** the back of a book cover to which the pages are attached **3.** ZOOL **HARD SHARP PROJECTION ON ANIMAL'S BODY** a sharp stiff projection on the body of an animal, e.g., the quill of a porcupine or the ray of a fish's fin **4.** BOT **SHARP POINT ON PLANT** a stiff sharp pointed outgrowth on a plant, e.g., on a rose or cactus **5.** GEOG **RIDGE IN MOUNTAINS** a continuous ridge in a range of mountains or hills [14C. Via French < Latin *spina* "thorn"]

spine-chill·er *n* something such as a novel or movie that is meant to frighten people —**spine-chill·ing** *adj* —**spine-chill·ing·ly** *adv*

spi·nel /spə nél/ *n* a hard crystalline, usually red, oxide mineral containing magnesium, aluminum, iron, and sometimes manganese. Use: gems. [Early 16C. Via French < Italian *spinella* < Latin *spina* "thorn"; from its pointed crystals]

spin e·lec·tron·ics *n* PHYS same as **spintronics** —**spin-e·lec·tron·ic** *adj*

spine·less /spīnləss/ *adj* **1.** seriously lacking willpower or strength of character **2.** lacking a spinal column —**spine·less·ly** *adv* —**spine·less·ness** *n*

SYNONYMS See ***cowardly***.

spin·et /spínnit/ *n* **1.** *US* a small upright piano or electronic organ **2.** a small harpsichord, popular in the 18th century, that has the strings set at a slant to the keyboard [Mid-17C. Via French < Italian *spinetta*]

spine-tin·gling *adj* causing nervous fear or excitement —**spine-tin·gling·ly** *adv*

spi·nif·er·ous /spī níffərəss/ *adj* having, producing, or bearing spines or needles [Mid-17C. < Latin *spina* "thorn"]

spi·ni·fex /spīnə fèks/ (*plural* **-fex·es** or *same*) *n* a perennial grass that has sharp pointed leaves and grows in circular mounds in dry inland areas. Native to: Australia. Genera: *Plectrachne* or *Triodia*. [Early 19C. < modern Latin, "thorn-maker" < Latin *spina* "thorn"]

spin·mei·ster /spín mīstər/ *n* POL same as **spin doctor** (*informal*)

spin·na·ker /spínnəkər/ *n* a large triangular sail set at the front of a yacht for running before the wind [Mid-19C. Origin ?]

spin·ner /spínnər/ *n* **1.** **SOMEBODY OR SOMETHING THAT SPINS** a person, object, or device that spins **2.** FISHING **FISHING LURE** a fishing lure that spins in the water when the line is reeled in **3.** AVIAT **COVER FOR AIRCRAFT PROPELLER** a streamlined dome-shaped cap (**fairing**) that fits over the hub of the propeller of an aircraft

spin·ner·et /spìnnə rét, spínnə rèt/ *n* **1.** a tiny tubular structure, usually one of two pairs, that exudes the fluid produced by the abdominal glands of a silk-producing spider **2.** a perforated device for extruding filaments of synthetic fiber

spin·ney /spínnee/ (*plural* **-neys**) *n UK* a small thicket or wood [Late 16C. Via Old French *espinei* "thorny hedge" < Latin *spinetum* < *spina* "thorn"]

spin·ning frame /spínning-/ *n* a machine that draws

out fibers, twists them into yarn or thread, and winds them onto spindles

spin·ning jen·ny *n* a spinning machine invented in the 18th century that had more than one spindle, allowing one person to spin several yarns at once

spin·ning mule *n* TEXTILES same as **mule**[1] (sense 5)

spin·ning top *n* LEISURE same as **top**[2]

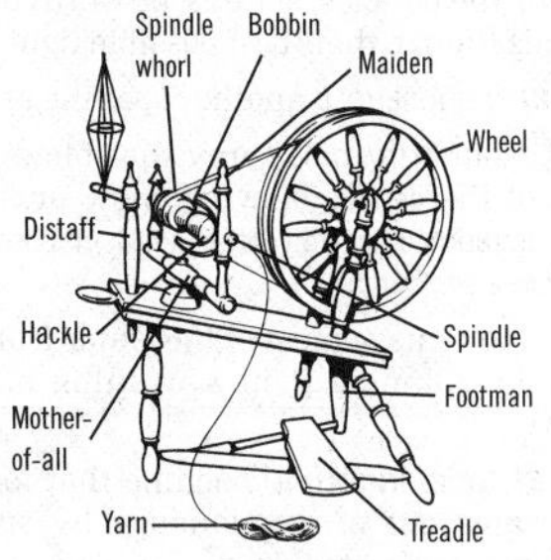

spinning wheel

spin·ning wheel *n* a domestic device for spinning yarn by means of a large wheel driven by hand or a treadle

spi·node /spī́nōd/ *n* MATH same as **cusp** (sense 4) [Mid-19C. Blend of SPINE + NODE]

spin·off /spín àwf, -ôf/ *n* **1. DERIVATIVE OF SOMETHING** a product, material, or service deriving from something that already exists **2. CORPORATE DIVESTITURE** a divestiture by a company of a division or subsidiary by the sale or distribution of shares of stock in a newly created independent company **3. NEWLY CREATED COMPANY** a company created by a spin-off

spin-or·bit coup·ling *n* the interaction between two specific quantum physical properties of a particle

spi·nous /spī́nəss/ *adj* with, covered with, or resembling spines [Mid-17C. < Latin *spinosus* < *spina* "thorn"]

spin·out /spín òwt/ *n* an uncontrolled skid in a motor vehicle

Spi·no·za /spi nṓzə/, **Baruch** (1632–77) Dutch philosopher. Rejecting the Judaism of his cultural background, he developed a philosophy that combined rationalist and pantheistic elements. His major work was *Ethics* (1677).

> "The human mind is part of the infinite intellect of God. Therefore, when we say the human mind perceives this or that, we are saying nothing but that God...has this or that idea."
> [Baruch Spinoza, *Ethics*; 1677]

Spi·no·zism /spə nṓ zìzzəm/ *n* the philosophical system developed by Baruch Spinoza, defining God as a unique impersonal deity with an infinite number of attributes and modes —**Spi·no·zist** *n*

spin sta·bi·li·za·tion *n* a method of steadying the flight of a projectile such as a bullet, shell, or rocket by spinning it around its long axis

spin·ster /spínstər/ *n* **1. OFFENSIVE TERM** an offensive term for a woman who has remained unmarried beyond the usual age (*dated*) **2. SPINNER OF YARN** a woman whose livelihood is spinning yarn (*archaic*) **3.** LAW **UNMARRIED WOMAN IN LEGAL DOCUMENTS** in some legal documents, a woman who has never married [14C. < SPIN] —**spin·ster·hood** *n*

spin·thar·i·scope /spin thárrə skōp/ *n* an instrument used to detect ionizing radiation such as alpha particles that produces flashes of light on a phosphorescent screen [Early 20C. < Greek *spintharis* "spark"]

spin-the-bottle *n* a game in which players take turns spinning a bottle and kiss the person it points to when it stops spinning

spin·to /spíntō/ *adj* describes an operatic voice that is both lyric and dramatic [Mid-20C. < Italian, "pushed"]

spin·tron·ics /spin trónniks/ *n* the study of magnetic and electric fields produced by electron spin (*takes a singular verb*) —**spin·tron·ic** *adj*

spi·nule /spī́ nyoòl/ *n* a tiny spine or thorn —**spi·nu·lose** /spī́nyə lōss/ *adj*

spin·y /spī́nee/ (**-i·er, -i·est**) *adj* **1. WITH SPINES** with or covered with spines **2. THORNY** with thorns or prickles **3. LIKE SPINE** shaped like a spine —**spin·i·ness** *n*

spin·y ant·eat·er *n* ZOOL same as **echidna**

spin·y eel *n* a freshwater fish resembling an eel that has a sensitive elongated snout with tubular nostrils and several sharp spines in front of the dorsal fin. Native to: Africa, Asia. Family: Mastacembelidae.

spin·y-head·ed worm *n* a parasitic unsegmented worm that has a proboscis composed of rows of hooked spines, used for attachment to a vertebrate's intestinal wall. Phylum: Acanthocephala.

spin·y lob·ster *n* a large edible crustacean that is like a lobster but has a spiny shell and lacks enlarged pincers. Family: Palinuridae.

spir·a·cle /spī́rək'l, spírrək'l/ *n* **1.** GEOL **VENT IN LAVA FLOW** a small vent in a lava flow that allows the escape of built-up gases **2.** INSECTS **SMALL APERTURE IN INSECT** a small paired aperture along the side of the thorax or abdomen of an insect or spider through which air enters and leaves **3.** FISH **SMALL GILL SLIT** a small gill slit or opening behind the eye area of some fishes such as skates and rays **4.** MARINE BIOL **BLOWHOLE** a blowhole of a whale, dolphin, or similar ocean mammal (*technical*) [Early 17C. Via French < Latin *spiraculum* < *spirare* "breathe"] —**spi·rac·u·lar** /spə rákyələr, spī-/ *adj*

spi·rae·a *n* PLANTS another spelling of **spirea**

spi·ral /spī́rəl/ *n* **1. CONTINUOUS CIRCLING FLAT CURVE** in mathematics, a flat curve or series of curves that constantly increase or decrease in size in circling around a central point **2.** MATH same as **helix** (sense 2) **3. SOMETHING WITH CURVING CIRCULAR PATTERN** something that has a helical or spiral form **4.** AVIAT **FLIGHT MANEUVER** a maneuver in which an aircraft makes a continuous banking turn as it descends **5.** ECON **ACCELERATING ECONOMIC CHANGE** a continuously accelerating increase or decrease in prices, wages, or interest rates ■ *adj* **1. CONTINUOUSLY CIRCLING WITH FLAT CURVES** with a flat curve or series of curves that constantly increase or decrease in size in circling around a central point **2. HELICAL** like a helix in shape ■ *v* (**-raled** or **-ralled, -ral·ing** or **-ral·ling, -rals**) **1.** *vti* **MOVE SOMETHING IN SPIRAL** to move in a spiral, or make something move in a spiral **2.** *vi* **CHANGE AT INCREASING PACE** to increase or decrease at a continuously accelerating rate ○ *spiraling inflation* **3.** *vti* **SHAPE SOMETHING LIKE SPIRAL** to take on a spiral shape, or make something take on a spiral shape [Mid-16C. < medieval Latin *spiralis* "coiled" < Latin *spira* (see SPIRE[2])] —**spi·ral·ly** *adv* —**spi·roid** *adj*

spi·ral bind·ing *n* a binding in which pages are fastened together with a spiral of wire or plastic that coils through a series of punched holes —**spi·ral-bound** *adj*

spi·ral gal·ax·y *n* a galaxy consisting of an older central nucleus of stars from which extend two spiral arms of gas, dust, and newer stars

spi·ral of Ar·chi·me·des *n* a spiral curve formed by a point moving at constant speed to or from a fixed point and along a line rotating, also at a constant speed, about the point

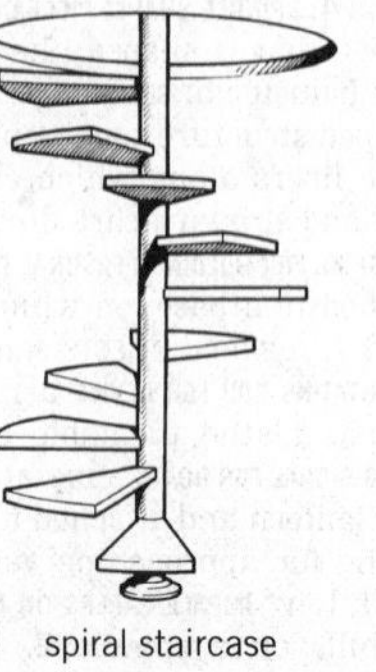
spiral staircase

spi·ral stair·case *n* a staircase that winds around a central axis

spi·rant /spī́rənt/ *n, adj* PHON same as **fricative** [Mid-19C. < Latin *spirant-*, present participle of *spirare* "breathe"]

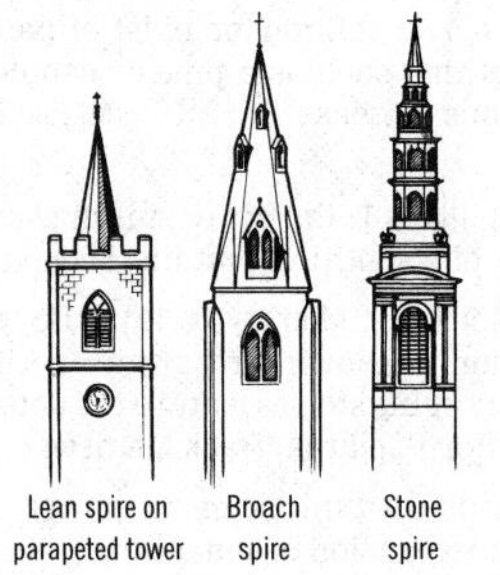

spire

spire[1] /spīr/ *n* **1. NARROW TAPERING STRUCTURE TOPPING SOMETHING** a tall narrow pointed structure on the top of a roof, tower, or steeple **2. POINTED PLANT SHOOT** a slender pointed part of a plant, e.g., a blade of grass or the top of a tree **3. UPWARD-FACING SPIKE** the top part of something narrow and pointed such as a mountain peak ■ *vi* (**spired, spir·ing, spires**) **RISE TO POINT** to rise to a narrow point [Old English *spīr* < Indo-European, "sharp point"]

spire[2] /spīr/ *n* **1.** a spiral or coil **2.** a convolution of a spiral or coil [Late 16C. Via Latin *spira* "coil" < Greek *speira*]

spi·re·a /spī rée ə/, **spi·rae·a** *n* an ornamental flowering bush. Flowers: small white or pink, in dense clusters. Native to: northern hemisphere. Genus: *Spiraea*. [Mid-17C. Via modern Latin < Greek *speiraia* "privet" < *speira* "coil"]

spire·let /spī́rlət/ *n* ARCHIT same as **flèche** (sense 1) [Mid-19C. < SPIRE[1]]

spi·ril·lum /spī ríləm/ (*plural* **-la** /-lə/) *n* a spiral-shaped or curved bacterium with a rigid body, that lives only in the presence of oxygen. Genus: *Spirillum*. [Late 19C. < modern Latin, "little spiral" < Latin *spira* (see SPIRE[2])] —**spi·ril·lar** *adj*

spir·it /spírrət/ *n* **1. LIFE FORCE OF PERSON** the vital force that characterizes a human being as being alive **2. WILL** will or sense of self ○ *He retained an indomitable spirit.* **3. ENTHUSIASM** enthusiasm and energy ○ *Alice responded with spirit.* **4. DISPOSITION** somebody's personality or temperament ○ *She has a generous spirit.* **5. ATTITUDE** a person's attitude or state of mind ○ *in the spirit of compromise* **6. GROUP LOYALTY** the enthusiasm and loyalty that somebody feels through belonging to a group ○ *school spirit* **7. IMPORTANT INFLUENCE** somebody or something that is a divine, inspiring, or animating influence ○ *one of the guiding spirits of the Peace Movement* **8. REAL MEANING** the intention behind something such as a rule or decree, rather than its literal interpretation **9. SHARED OUTLOOK** the prevailing mood or outlook characteristic of a place or time **10. PERSON** somebody who displays a particular quality **11. SOUL** in some beliefs, somebody's soul, especially that of a dead person **12.** PARANORMAL **SUPERNATURAL ENTITY** a supernatural being that does not have a physical body, e.g., a ghost, angel, or demon **13.** BEVERAGES **ALCOHOLIC DRINK** a strong alcoholic liquor made by distillation (*often used in the plural*) ○ *She never drank spirits.* **14.** CHEM **DISTILLED LIQUID** any liquid produced by distillation, especially a distilled solution of ethanol and water (*often used in the plural*) **15.** CHEM **ALCOHOLIC SOLUTION** a solution of an essence or volatile substance in alcohol (*often used in the plural*) ■ **spir·its** *npl* **MOOD** a particular frame of mind or mood ○ *The group was in high spirits, talking and laughing.* ■ *vt* (**-it·ed, -it·ing, -its**) **REMOVE SOMEBODY OR SOMETHING SECRETLY** to take somebody or something away quickly in a secret or mysterious way ○ *spirited him out of the room* [13C. Via Anglo-Norman < Latin *spiritus* "breath" < *spirare* "breathe"] ◇ **in high spirits** elated and happy ◇ **in poor spirits** sad or dejected

ORIGIN The Latin word *spirare* "to breathe," from which **spirit** is derived, is also the source of English *aspire, conspire, expire, inspire, perspire, respire,* and *transpire*.

Spir·it *n* CHR same as **Holy Spirit**

spir·it·ed /spírrətəd/ *adj* **1.** LIVELY lively and vigorous **2.** ANIMATED with great animation **3.** BEHAVING IN SPECIFIC WAY behaving in a way that has a particular feeling, mood, or character (*usually used in combination*) ○ *low-spirited* —**spir·it·ed·ly** *adv* —**spir·it·ed·ness** *n*

spir·it gum *n* a glue made from a solution of gum in ether. Use: especially to stick false hair to an actor's skin.

spir·it·ism /spírrə tìzzəm/ *n* PARANORMAL same as **spiritualism** (sense 1) —**spir·it·ist** *n* —**spir·it·is·tic** /spìrrə tístik/ *adj*

spir·it lamp *n* a lamp that uses alcohol as fuel

spir·it·less /spírrətləss/ *adj* lacking courage or energy —**spir·it·less·ly** *adv* —**spir·it·less·ness** *n*

spir·it lev·el *n UK* same as **level** *adj* (sense 1)

spir·i·to·so /spìrrə tṓssō/ *adv* in a lively and vivacious way, or to be played in this way (*used as a musical direction*) [Early 18C. < Italian, "spirited"] —**spi·ri·to·so** *adj*

spir·its of am·mo·ni·a *n* CHEM same as **sal volatile** (sense 2)

spir·its of harts·horn /-haárts hàwrn/ *npl* ammonium hydroxide (*archaic*) [Because hart's horn was an early source of ammonia]

spir·i·tu·al /spírrichoo əl/ *adj* **1.** OF SOUL relating to the soul or spirit, usually in contrast to material things **2.** OF RELIGION relating to religious or sacred things rather than worldly things **3.** TEMPERAMENTALLY OR INTELLECTUALLY AKIN connected by an affinity of the mind, spirit, or temperament ○ *spiritual mother of the young artist* **4.** REFINED showing great refinement and concern with the higher things in life ■ *n* **1.** FOLK HYMN a religious song, especially one arising from African American culture **2.** THINGS OF SPIRIT matters concerning the spirit ○ *He was deeply concerned with anything to do with the spiritual.* [14C. Via French *spirituel* < Latin *spiritualis* < *spiritus* (see SPIRIT)] —**spir·i·tu·al·ly** *adv* —**spir·i·tu·al·ness** *n*

spir·i·tu·al bou·quet *n* in the Roman Catholic Church, a promise of, or performance of, devotional acts, performed on behalf of another, e.g., in memory of somebody who has died

spir·i·tu·al·ism /spírrichoo ə lìzzəm/ *n* **1.** BELIEF IN COMMUNICATION WITH DEAD PEOPLE the belief that the spirits of dead people can communicate with the living, especially through mediums **2.** PRACTICES OF COMMUNICATING WITH DEAD PEOPLE the practices used among people who believe that communication occurs between the dead and the living **3.** RELIGIOUS BELIEFS EMPHASIZING SPIRITUAL MATTERS a system of belief that emphasizes the spiritual nature of existence **4.** PHILOSOPHY EMPHASIZING SPIRITUAL NATURE OF REALITY the philosophical doctrine that all reality is spiritual, not material **5.** SPIRITUAL STATE the quality or state of being spiritual —**spir·i·tu·al·ist** *n*

spir·i·tu·al·i·ty /spìrrichoo állətee/ (*plural* **-ties**) *n* **1.** the quality or condition of being spiritual **2.** the property or revenue belonging to a church or church official (*often used in the plural*)

spir·i·tu·al·ize /spírrichoo ə lìz/ (**-ized, -iz·ing, -iz·es**) *vt* **1.** to give something a spiritual content **2.** to attribute a spiritual meaning to something —**spir·i·tu·al·i·za·tion** /-ələ záysh'n/ *n*—**spir·i·tu·al·iz·er** *n*

spir·i·tu·al·ty /spìrrichoo àltee/ (*plural* **-ties**) *n* CHR same as **spirituality** (sense 2)

spir·i·tu·el /spìrrichoo él/, **spir·i·tu·elle** *adj* showing a refined and graceful intellect [Late 17C. < French (see SPIRITUAL)]

spir·i·tu·ous /spírrichoo əss/ *adj* containing alcohol or made by distillation (*formal*) —**spir·i·tu·ous·ness** *n*

spir·it var·nish *n* a varnish consisting of a resin dissolved in alcohol

spir·ket·ting /spúrkəting/ *n* a thick planking used to line and reinforce the decks and ports of a wooden ship [Mid-18C. < obsolete *spurket* "space between the deck and side of a ship," origin ?]

spiro-[1] *prefix* breathing, respiration ○ *spirograph* [< Latin *spirare* "breathe"]

spiro-[2] *prefix* **1.** spiral, coil ○ *spirochete* **2.** molecule with two rings having one shared atom ○ *spironolactone* [< Latin *spira* (see SPIRE[2])]

spi·ro·chete /spírə keet/ *n* a coiled rod-shaped bacterium, many of which cause diseases such as syphilis and relapsing fever. Order: Spirochaetales. [Late 19C. < modern Latin *Spirochaeta* < Latin *spira* (see SPIRE[2]) + *chaeta* "hair"]

spi·ro·che·to·sis /spìrə kee tṓssiss/ (*plural* **-ses** /-seez/), **spi·ro·chae·to·sis** (*plural* **-ses**) *n* a disease caused by a spirochete

spi·ro·graph /spírə gràf/ *n* an instrument that makes a record of the depth and rapidity of somebody's breathing [Late 19C. < SPIRO-[1]] —**spi·ro·graph·ic** /spìrə gráffik/ *adj* —**spi·ro·graph·i·cal·ly** *adv* —**spi·rog·ra·phy** /spī róggrəfee/ *n*

spi·ro·gy·ra /spìrə jírə/ *n* a multicellular freshwater green alga. Genus: *Spirogyra*. [Late 19C. < modern Latin < Latin *spira* (see SPIRE[2]) + Greek *guros* "round"]

spi·rom·e·ter /spī rómmətər/ *n* an instrument for measuring the capacity of the lungs [Mid-19C. < SPIRO-[1]] —**spi·ro·met·ric** /spìrə méttrik/ *adj* —**spi·rom·e·try** *n*

spi·ro·no·lac·tone /spìrənō láktōn/ *n* a steroid that acts as a diuretic. Use: treatment of edema, hypertension. Formula: $C_{24}H_{32}O_4S$. [Mid-20C. < *spirolactone* earlier name < SPIRO-[1]]

spi·ru·li·na /spìrrə línə, spìrə-/ *npl* cyanobacteria valued as a rich source of protein, containing vitamins, minerals, essential fatty acids, and antioxidants. Spirulina are grown in tanks and harvested to be made into nutritional supplements. Genus: *Spirulina*. [< modern Latin < Latin *spirula* "small spiral shell" < *spira* (see SPIRE[2])]

spir·y /spíree/ *adj* shaped like a spire (*literary*) [Early 17C. < SPIRE[1]]

spit[1] /spit/ *v* (**spit** or **spat** /spat/, **spit·ting, spits**) **1.** *vi* EJECT SALIVA to expel saliva forcefully from the mouth **2.** *vi* EXPEL SALIVA TO SHOW CONTEMPT to show anger, contempt, or hatred by or as if by expelling saliva **3.** *vt* EXPEL SOMETHING FROM YOUR MOUTH to eject something such as food forcefully from the mouth **4.** *vti* EMIT SOMETHING to sputter and emit something such as sparks or fat **5.** *vi* HISS to make hissing explosive sounds **6.** *vi* RAIN OR SNOW LIGHTLY to rain or snow lightly or in scattered drops or flakes **7.** *vt* UTTER SOMETHING ANGRILY to utter something sharply and angrily ■ *n* **1.** SPITTLE FROM MOUTH saliva, especially when ejected from the mouth **2.** EXPULSION OF SOMETHING FROM MOUTH a forceful ejection of saliva or something else from the mouth [Old English *spittan* < Indo-European] —**spit·ter** *n* ◇ **spit it out** to say something at once, especially something that has been withheld (*informal*; *usually used as a command*)

spit up *vt* to regurgitate or cough up something (*refers to babies*)

spit[2] /spit/ *n* **1.** THIN ROD FOR ROASTING SOMETHING a thin rod on which something is impaled for roasting over a fire **2.** LAND PROJECTING FROM SHORE an elongated point of land or shoal projecting into a body of water ■ *vt* (**spit·ted, spit·ting, spits**) **1.** IMPALE SOMETHING ON SPIT to impale something on a roasting spit **2.** IMPALE SOMEBODY to impale somebody on a long pointed object [Old English *spitu* < Indo-European, "sharp point"]

spit and pol·ish *n* meticulous care in presenting a neat appearance, especially in the armed forces (*informal*)

spit·ball /spít bàwl/ *n* **1.** a tiny wad of paper chewed and moistened with saliva that is thrown as a prank **2.** in baseball, an illegal pitch that is made to curve deceptively because it has been moistened with saliva

spitch·cock /spích kòk/ *n* an eel split and then grilled or fried [Early 17C. Origin ?]

spit curl *n* a spiral curl of dampened hair that is laid flat against the skin of the cheek or forehead [< its being fixed in place with saliva]

spite /spìt/ *n* a malicious, usually small-minded desire to harm or humiliate somebody ■ *vt* (**spit·ed, spit·ing, spites**) to harm, hinder, or humiliate somebody out of small-mindedness [13C. Shortening of DESPITE] ◇ **in spite of** notwithstanding, or without taking account of something

spite·ful /spítfəl/ *adj* full of or showing petty maliciousness —**spite·ful·ly** *adv* —**spite·ful·ness** *n*

spit·fire /spít fìr/ *n* a quick-tempered person

Spit·fire *n* a British fighter plane used by the Royal Air Force during World War II

spit·ting co·bra /spìtting-/ *n US* ZOOL same as **ringhals**

spit·ting dis·tance *n* a short enough distance to seem within reach (*informal*)

spit·ting im·age *n* an exact likeness (*informal*) ○ *the spitting image of his father* [Alteration of *spit and image* < SPIT[1] "exact likeness"]

spit·tle /spítt'l/ *n* **1.** saliva, especially that has been or is about to be expelled from the mouth **2.** something that looks like frothy saliva, especially the secretions from spittlebugs deposited on plants (**cuckoo spit**) [15C. Alteration (after SPIT[1]) of dialect *spattle* < Germanic]

spit·tle·bug /spítt'l bùg/, **spit·tle in·sect** *n* a small jumping plant-sucking insect whose larvae produce cuckoo spit

spit·toon /spi tóon/ *n* a container, formerly common in public places such as bars, into which tobacco chewers spit [Mid-19C. < SPIT[1]]

spitz /spits/ *n* a dog belonging to a breed that has a pointed muzzle, erect pointed ears, and a tightly curled tail [Mid-19C. Shortening of German *Spitzhund* "pointed dog"]

Spitz /spits/, **Mark** (*b.* 1950) US swimmer. He won seven gold medals and set seven world records at the 1972 Olympic Games.

spiv /spiv/ *n UK* an offensive term for a man whose way of dressing is considered ostentatiously stylish and whose integrity is doubted (*slang insult*) [Mid-20C. Origin ?] —**spiv·vy** *adj*

splanch·nic /splángknik/ *adj* relating to the intestines (*technical*) [Late 17C. Via modern Latin *splanchnicus* < Greek *splagkhnikos* < *splagkhna* "entrails"]

splash /splash/ *v* (**splashed, splash·ing, splash·es**) **1.** *vt* SPATTER LIQUID to scatter a liquid in large drops or amounts ○ *She splashed water over the side of the bathtub.* **2.** *vi* BE SPATTERED ABOUT to scatter or fly up in large drops or amounts ○ *The waves splashed against the rocks.* **3.** *vt* SPATTER DROPS OF LIQUID ON SOMETHING to wet or dirty something by spattering it with liquid ○ *She splashed her blouse with the hot tea.* **4.** *vti* MAKE YOUR WAY THROUGH WATER to make your way through water or another liquid, scattering it about ○ *They splashed through the puddles.* **5.** *vt* ADD CONTRASTS TO SOMETHING to apply contrasting color or light to something **6.** *vt* DISPLAY SOMETHING PROMINENTLY to display something such as a news headline, story, or photograph conspicuously (*usually passive*) ○ *The story was splashed across the front page.* ■ *n* **1.** NOISE OR INSTANCE OF WATER SCATTERING a sound or act of splashing **2.** PATCH OF COLOR an area of contrasting color or light, often irregular ○ *The dark forest was dappled with splashes of moonlight.* **3.** TINY AMOUNT OF LIQUID a very small quantity of one liquid added to another (*informal*) ○ *Just a splash of milk in my coffee, please.* **4.** SOMETHING SPLASHED something or an amount that has been splashed **5.** MARK CAUSED BY SCATTERED LIQUID a mark or stain made by something splashing or being splashed ○ *The backs of her legs were covered with splashes.* **6.** PROMINENT DISPLAY a conspicuous display, e.g., a prominent news headline, story, or photograph [Early 18C. Probably alteration of PLASH[1]] ◇ **make a splash** to attract a great deal of attention or publicity

splash down /splásh dòwn/ *vi* to land in the sea after a space flight

splash·back /splásh bak/ *n UK* same as **backsplash**

splash·board /splásh bàwrd/ *n* **1.** a screen for preventing water from splashing into a boat **2.** a protective guard that prevents mud or water from splashing the upper part of a motor vehicle and the people traveling in it

splash·down /splásh down/ *n* the landing of a spacecraft or missile in the sea after a flight

splash·guard /splásh gaàrd/ *n US* a flap attached behind the wheel of a vehicle to prevent mud or water from splashing up onto the vehicle, or onto the vehicles following. Can term **mud flap**

splash·y /spláshee/ (**-i·er, -i·est**) *adj* **1.** ATTRACTING NOTICE attracting a lot of attention (*informal*) **2.** COLORFUL with lots of bright colors **3.** MAKING SPLASHES with great splashing of liquid —**splash·i·ly** *adv* —**splash·i·ness** *n*

splat /splat/ *n* WET SMACKING SOUND a sound made when something soft and wet hits something hard ■ *adv* WITH SMACK with a wet smacking sound ■ *interj* IMITATING IMPACT used to imitate the sound made when something soft and wet hits something hard [Late 19C. An imitation of the sound]

splat·ter /splátter/ *vti* (**-tered, -ter·ing, -ters**) to spatter or splash something, or be spattered or splashed ■ *n* a spatter or splash [Late 18C. Origin ?]

splat·ter·punk /splátter pùngk/ *n* a form of narrative, e.g., a story, movie, or comic strip, that contains a large amount of gory violence (*slang*)

splay /splay/ *vti* (**splayed, splay·ing, splays**) **1.** SPREAD SOMETHING WIDE AND OUTWARD to spread out something such as the fingers or toes, or be spread out **2.** TURN SOMETHING OUT AWKWARDLY to turn something outward in an awkward manner **3.** ARCHIT INCLINE SIDES OF OPENING to give the sides of an opening in a wall an oblique angle, so that the opening is wider on one side than on the other ■ *adj also* **splayed 1.** SPREAD FLAT AND OUTWARD sloping, turning, or spread flatly and outward **2.** TURNED AWKWARDLY OUTWARD turned awkwardly outward ■ *n* ARCHIT INCLINE GIVEN TO SIDES OF OPENING an oblique angle given to the sides of an opening in a wall [14C. Shortening of DISPLAY]

splayed /splayed/ *adj* same as **splay**

splay·foot /spláy fòot/ (*plural* **-feet** /-fèet/) *n* **1.** a foot with fallen arches, often with widely spread toes, or the condition that causes this **2.** a foot that is excessively turned outward, or the condition causing it —**splay·foot·ed** *adj* —**splay·foot·ed·ly** *adv*

spleen /spleen/ *n* **1.** a ductless vascular organ in the left upper abdomen of humans and other vertebrates that helps to destroy old red blood cells, form lymphocytes, and store blood **2.** anger or bad temper [13C. Via Latin *splen* < Greek *splēn*] —**spleen·ful** *adj*

spleen·wort /spleen wùrt, -wàwrt/ (*plural* **-worts** or *same*) *n* an evergreen fern of temperate and tropical regions that has feathery fronds. Genus: *Asplenium*. [Late 16C. < the former belief that it cured illnesses of the spleen]

splen·dent /spléndənt/ *adj* (*literary*) **1.** reflecting light so that it shines **2.** distinguished or illustrious [15C. < Latin *splendent-*, present participle of *splendere* "shine"]

splen·did /spléndəd/ *adj* **1.** MAGNIFICENT impressive because of quality or size **2.** RADIANT reflecting light brilliantly **3.** EXCELLENT excellent or highly enjoyable **4.** ACCLAIMED very well known and acclaimed [Early 17C. < Latin *splendidus* < *splendere* "shine"] —**splen·did·ness** *n*

splen·did·ly /spléndədlee/ *adv* in a fine or admirable way ○ *a splendidly restored old castle*

splen·dif·er·ous /splen díffərəss/ *adj* magnificent and wonderful (*humorous*) [Mid-19C. < SPLENDOR] —**splen·dif·er·ous·ly** *adv* —**splen·dif·er·ous·ness** *n*

splen·dor /spléndər/ *n* **1.** the condition of being magnificent, impressive, or brilliant **2.** something that is magnificent, impressive, or brilliant ○ *the splendors of ancient Greece* [15C. Directly or via French < Latin < *splendere* "shine"] —**splen·dor·ous** *adj*

splen·dour *n* Can, UK spelling of **splendor**

sple·nec·to·my /splə néktəmee/ (*plural* **-mies**) *n* surgical removal of the spleen [Mid-19C. < Greek *splēn* "spleen"]

sple·net·ic /splə néttik/ *adj* **1.** OF SPLEEN relating to the spleen (*dated*) **2.** BAD-TEMPERED extremely bad-tempered or spiteful (*literary*) ■ *n* SOMEBODY BAD-TEMPERED somebody regarded as bad-tempered or spiteful (*literary or dated*) [Mid-16C. < Latin *spleneticus* < *splen* (see SPLEEN)] —**sple·net·i·cal·ly** *adv*

splen·ic /spléenik, splénnik/ *adj* relating to, in, or near the spleen [Early 17C. < Greek *splēn* "spleen"]

sple·ni·us /spléenee əss/ (*plural* **-ni·i** /-nee ī/) *n* either of two muscles on each side of the neck that reach from the base of the skull to the upper back and rotate and extend the head and neck [Mid-18C. Via modern Latin < Greek *splēnion* "bandage, compress"] —**sple·ni·al** *adj*

sple·no·meg·a·ly /spléenō méggəlee, splènnə-/ *n* unusual enlargement of the spleen [Early 20C. < Greek *splēn* "spleen" + *megal-* "great"]

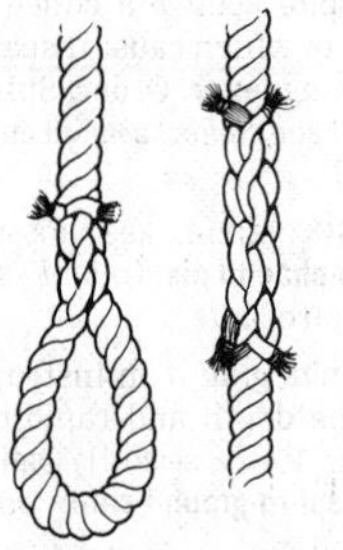

splice

splice /splīss/ *vt* (**spliced, splic·ing, splic·es**) **1.** JOIN ROPES to join two pieces of rope or wire by weaving the strands of each into the other **2.** JOIN ENDS OF FILM OR TAPE to join the ends of two pieces of film or magnetic tape, e.g., in editing **3.** JOIN PIECES OF WOOD to join two pieces of wood by overlapping them and bolting or otherwise attaching them **4.** MARRY TWO PEOPLE to join a couple in marriage (*slang; often passive*) **5.** GENETICS INSERT GENETIC MATERIAL to join together or insert pieces of DNA in order to alter the genetic structure of an organism ■ *n* **1.** CONNECTION a join made by connecting two pieces of something **2.** JUNCTION OF SPLICING the junction where something has been spliced [Early 16C. < Middle Dutch *splissen*] —**splic·er** *n*

spliff /splif/ *n* a marijuana cigarette (*slang*) [Mid-20C. Origin ?]

spline /splīn/ *n* **1.** FLAT KEY FORMED IN SHAFT a flat, relatively narrow key that is integral to a shaft, produced by milling a longitudinal groove **2.** GUIDE FOR DRAWING CURVES a flat flexible strip of something used in drawing curved lines **3.** same as **slat** *n* (sense 1) **4.** CONNECTING STRIP a thin narrow piece of wood, metal, or plastic that fits onto or into the edges of tiles or boards and connects them together [Mid-18C. Origin ?]

splint /splint/ *n* **1.** DEVICE TO IMMOBILIZE BROKEN BONE a strip of rigid material used to keep a broken bone or other injured body part from moving **2.** STRIP OF WOOD USED IN BASKETRY a thin strip of wood used to weave something such as a basket or chair seat **3.** WOOD SLIVER FOR LIGHTING FIRES a sliver of wood used to carry a flame, e.g., to light a fire or a candle **4.** WOODWORK same as **splinter** *n* (sense 1) **5.** MIL, HIST METAL PLATE IN ARMOR any overlapping metal plate or strip used in making a suit of armor **6.** VET ENLARGEMENT OF HORSE'S LEG BONE a condition that occurs in young horses, consisting of painful bony outgrowths in or near the splint bones on the inner sides of the legs ■ *vt* (**splint·ed, splint·ing, splints**) **1.** IMMOBILIZE INJURED PART to immobilize a broken bone or injured body part with a rigid support **2.** STRENGTHEN SOMETHING to give support or added strength to something [13C. < Middle Low German or Middle Dutch *splinte*]

splint bone *n* either of a pair of thin bones on either side of the cannon bone in the lower legs of horses and other hoofed animals

splin·ter /splíntər/ *n* **1.** THIN SHARP FRAGMENT a small thin sharp piece of wood, metal, stone, glass, or other material broken from a larger piece **2.** BOMB FRAGMENT a metal fragment thrown from an exploding bomb or shell **3.** POL same as **splinter group** ■ *vti* (**-tered, -ter·ing, -ters**) **1.** BREAK SOMETHING INTO SHARP FRAGMENTS to break something into thin sharp fragments, or be broken into thin sharp fragments **2.** DIVIDE GROUP to split a larger group into factions or independent groups, or be split in this way [14C. < Middle Dutch] —**splin·ter·y** *adj*

splin·ter group *n* a group formed by individuals who have dissociated themselves from a larger organization, usually because of disagreement

split /split/ *v* (**split, split·ting, splits**) **1.** *vti* DIVIDE SOMETHING LENGTHWISE to divide something lengthwise into two or more parts, or be divided lengthwise into two or more parts, usually by force **2.** *vti* BURST SOMETHING to burst something apart, or rip apart **3.** *vt* AFFECT SOMETHING VIOLENTLY to disturb or disrupt something with a violently jarring presence ○ *shouts splitting the air* **4.** *vti* SEPARATE SOMETHING INTO PARTS to divide a whole into parts, or be separated from the rest or from a whole **5.** *vt* SEPARATE SOMETHING BY ADDING SOMETHING BETWEEN to separate a whole into its components by interposing something **6.** *vti* DIVIDE SOMETHING INTO FACTIONS to make a group divide into factions because of disagreement, or separate from a main group because of disagreement **7.** *vt* DIVIDE SOMETHING INTO SHARES to share something among a group ○ *split the proceeds* **8.** *vt* POL DIVIDE VOTE FOR CANDIDATES to divide a vote between candidates of different parties **9.** *vti* LEAVE PLACE to go away from a place (*slang*) **10.** *vt* WIN HALF OF GAMES to win half the games of a series or one of a double-header **11.** *vt* FIN DIVIDE SHARES OF STOCK to divide shares of stock so that stockholders receive more shares at a proportionately lower value, leaving the total value unchanged ■ *n* **1.** ACT OF BREAKING APART the action of breaking or splitting something **2.** CRACK a crack or break in something, especially one that runs lengthwise **3.** FRAGMENT a piece broken off from the whole **4.** DIVISION THROUGH DISAGREEMENT a breach in a group, caused by a disagreement between members **5.** LAYER OF ANIMAL HIDE a single thickness of animal hide other than the outermost layer **6.** INDUST LEATHER leather made from a single inner layer of animal hide **7.** BOWLING ARRANGEMENT OF STANDING BOWLING PINS in bowling, a batch of remaining pins in which the pins are clustered into two groups with a large gap in between **8.** PORTION a share, especially a share of money (*informal*) **9.** FOOD ICE CREAM DESSERT a dessert of fruit with ice cream and a topping of flavored syrup, nuts, and whipped cream **10.** HANDICRAFT STRIP OF WOOD FOR BASKETRY a strip of flexible wood, usually willow, used for basketry **11.** BEVERAGES HALF-BOTTLE a half-bottle of alcohol or carbonated beverage **12.** *US* BEVERAGES HALF-GLASS a half-glass of an alcoholic beverage **13.** WINE QUARTER-SIZE WINE BOTTLE a wine bottle holding 6 to 6.5 oz/0.1875 liters ■ *adj* **1.** BROKEN broken, divided, or separated into parts **2.** DISUNITED divided because of disagreement **3.** FIN DIVIDED INTO SMALLER STOCK UNITS describes shares of stock that have been divided into smaller units [Late 16C. < Dutch *splitten*]

split up *v* **1.** *vi* END RELATIONSHIP to end a relationship or a marriage **2.** *vti* SEND PEOPLE DIFFERENT WAYS to go off in a different direction, or send individuals off in different directions **3.** *vt* DIVIDE SOMETHING INTO PARTS to divide something into separate parts

Split /split/ chief city and port of Dalmatia, southern Croatia, on the Adriatic Sea. Population: 189,388 (1991).

split board *n* a type of snowboard that comes apart lengthwise to form two separate pieces that can be used as skis

split brain *n* a brain that has the corpus callosum surgically severed or missing from birth, so that the two hemispheres of the brain are not connected

split de·ci·sion *n* in boxing, a win awarded by a majority of judges, rather than by a unanimous decision

split end *n* **1.** in football, a player at the end of an offensive line that lines up some distance outside the rest of the line **2.** the damaged end of a hair that has separated into strands

split in·fin·i·tive *n* an infinitive in which the "to" and the verb are separated by another word, as in the phrase "to seriously think"

USAGE What is wrong with a **split infinitive**? The ***split infinitive*** is a stylistic issue that has been rationalized into a grammatical one. There is no grammatical basis for rejecting split infinitives, since to regard an infinitive with *to* as an inseparable unit has no support in the typical structures of English grammar, which freely separates particles, auxiliary verbs, and other qualifiers from the words to which they belong (e.g., in *I have never been to Paris* the word *never* separates *have* from *been*). The issue is one of style and not of grammar. If splitting an infinitive produces awkwardness, it is better to avoid it, but if the split is natural and supports or clarifies the meaning, there can be no objection to it. The adverb belongs closely with the verb in the infinitive in cases such as *They agreed to flatly forbid such actions* and *They were plotting to secretly copy the files,* but can be moved to a more comfortable position in other cases such as *We expect to further modernize our services* (revise as: *... to modernize our services further*) and *I would like to briefly mention a few points* (revise as: *I would like briefly to …*). It is usually advisable to avoid splitting the infinitive with an adverbial phrase (e.g., *They were trying to in some way improve the situation*). In some cases, however, even an adverbial phrase cannot be separated from its verb: *Prices are likely to more than double* (in which *more than double* is effectively regarded as a set verb phrase). The guiding principle, in sum, is that the split infinitive is acceptable when the rhythm and meaning of the sentence call for it or when its use is that of a set verb phrase. It should be avoided (either by repositioning or by rephrasing) when it seems stilted or awkward, or creates ambiguity, especially in formal writing where its inclusion may draw criticism.

split-lev·el *adj* describes a house or room built on two levels with steps between them —**split-lev·el** *n*

split pea *n* a pea that has been shelled, dried, and split in half, used especially in soup

split per·son·al·i·ty *n* **1.** a tendency toward erratic mood or temperament changes **2.** PSYCHIAT ➧ **multiple personality disorder**

split pin *n* a two-pronged metal pin that holds things together when its prongs are passed through holes on both parts and then bent back

split rail *n US* a fence rail split lengthwise from a log

split-rail fence *n regional* same as **zigzag fence**

REGIONAL NOTE See ***zigzag fence***.

split ring *n* a small steel ring with two spiral turns, often used as a key ring or as a means of fastening two parts together

splits /splits/ *n* a gymnastic action in which the legs are fully extended in opposite directions until the body is sitting on or very close to the floor (*takes a singular or plural verb*) ○ *do the splits*

split screen *n* a movie or television screen frame divided into more than one image

split sec·ond *n* an extremely brief amount of time

split-sec·ond *adj* carried out instantly, or depending on instant skill or judgment

split shift *n* a single work period that is divided into two or more sessions of work, separated by an interval that is longer than a normal rest or meal break

split stitch *n* in embroidery, a back stitch in which each new stitch is made through the center of the previous one

split·ter /splíttər/ *n* an electronic or other device that divides something into parts, e.g., a software device that enables a long file to be divided into sections or a device that splits a telephone signal so that it can carry voice and data transmissions simultaneously

split tick·et *n US* a ballot cast by a voter for candidates of more than one political party

split·ting /splítting/ *adj* causing intense pain ○ *a splitting headache* ■ *n* a Freudian defense mechanism in which somebody separates something unpleasant such as an idea into parts that are each less threatening than the whole

split-up *n* an instance or the act of separating, e.g., the ending of a relationship between two people

splodge /sploj/ *UK n* same as **splotch** ■ *vt* (**splodged, splodg·ing, splodg·es**) same as **splotch** [Early 17C. Origin ?]

splotch /sploch/ *n* a large irregular spot, stain, or discoloration ■ *vt* (**splotched, splotch·ing, splotch·es**) to mark, stain, or discolor something with one or more large spots [Early 17C. Origin ?]

splurge /splurj/ (*informal*) *v* (**splurged, splurg·ing, splurg·es**) **1.** *vi* **INDULGE** to indulge in something extravagant or expensive **2.** *vt* **SPEND MONEY EXTRAVAGANTLY** to spend money in an extravagant or wasteful way ■ *n* **1. BOUT OF EXTRAVAGANCE** a period of indulgence or extravagant spending **2. GRAND DISPLAY** a showy display of something such as wealth [Early 19C. Origin ?]

splut·ter /splúttər/ *v* (**-tered, -ter·ing, -ters**) **1.** *vi* **MAKE SPITTING SOUND** to make a spitting or choking sound **2.** *vti* **SAY SOMETHING INCOHERENTLY** to say something in a choking incoherent manner **3.** *vti* **SPIT SOMETHING OUT** to scatter saliva, liquid, or particles of food from the mouth ■ *n* **1. INCOHERENT SPEECH** a burst of choking incoherent speech **2. CHOKING NOISE** a spitting choking noise [Late 17C. Origin ?] —**splut·ter·er** *n* —**splut·ter·ing** *n, adj*

Dr. Spock

Spock /spok/, **Dr.** (1903–98) US pediatrician and political activist. His book *The Common Sense Book of Baby and Child Care*, first published in 1946, which went through numerous editions and sold tens of millions of copies worldwide, popularized a new, permissive philosophy of parenting. He was a vociferous public opponent of the Vietnam War and of nuclear weapons. Full name **Spock, Benjamin McLane**

spod·u·mene /spójjə meen/ *n* a crystalline mineral that contains lithium and occurs in grayish white, greenish, or lilac forms. Use: source of lithium, gems. [Early 19C. Via French < Greek *spodoumenos* "burned to ashes" < *spodos* "ashes"; from its grayish color]

spoil /spoyl/ *v* (**spoiled** or **spoilt** /spoylt/, **spoil·ing, spoils**) **1.** *vt* **IMPAIR SOMETHING** to damage or ruin something in such a way that a quality such as worth, beauty, or usefulness is diminished **2.** *vt* **HARM SOMEBODY BY OVERINDULGENCE** to harm the character of somebody, especially a child, by repeated overindulgence **3.** *vt* **TREAT SOMEBODY INDULGENTLY** to treat somebody with indulgence out of a desire to please ○ *The hotel staff really spoiled us.* **4.** *vt* **MAKE SOMEBODY CONSIDER SOMETHING UNSATISFACTORY** to make somebody dissatisfied with what is usually offered by greatly exceeding it in quality ○ *All that sun spoils you for vacations in the far North.* **5.** *vi* **BECOME ROTTEN** to become unfit to eat because of decay **6.** *vt* **TAKE PROPERTY FROM SOMEBODY** to take property from somebody by force or violence (*archaic*) ■ *n* **1. WASTE FROM EXCAVATION** waste material removed from an excavation **2. STEALING** the act of plundering (*archaic*) ■ **spoils** *npl* **1. PROPERTY SEIZED BY VICTOR** valuables or property seized by the victor in a conflict **2. SOMETHING GAINED THROUGH EFFORT** something valuable or desirable gained through effort, opportunism, or other means **3.** *US* **REWARDS AND BENEFITS OF WINNING** the rewards and benefits considered by a winning political party to be its due [13C. Via Old French *espoillier* "plunder, despoil" < Latin *spoliare* < *spolium* "booty"] ◇ **be spoiling for** be eager for something, usually a conflict or confrontation ○ *spoiling for a victory after last year's losses*

spoil·age /spóylij/ *n* **1. DECAYING** the process of decaying or becoming damaged, or the condition of being decayed or damaged **2. WASTE** waste arising from decay or damage **3. AMOUNT WASTED** the amount of something wasted because of decay or damage

spoiled /spoyld/ *adj* **1.** severely or irrevocably impaired, e.g., by damage or decay **2.** willful or selfish because of having been overindulged

spoil·er /spóylər/ *n* **1. AIRFOIL FOR CONTROLLING LIFT AND DRAG** a narrow hinged airfoil attached lengthwise to the upper surface of an aircraft wing. It is raised to increase drag and reduce lift during banking and descent. **2. AUTOMOBILE AIR DEFLECTOR** a fixed air deflector on the rear of an automobile, designed to keep it on the ground during high speeds **3. SOMEBODY WHO CAN RUIN ANOTHER'S WIN** a candidate for office, or a competitor in sports, who cannot win but can or does prevent an opponent from doing so **4. SOMEBODY WHO WRECKS SOMETHING** somebody or something that ruins or wrecks something **5. ROBBER** somebody or something that robs or pillages

spoil·sport /spóyl spàwrt/ *n* somebody whose conduct spoils the pleasure of others

spoils sys·tem *n* a practice in which a winning political party gives government jobs and public appointments to its supporters

spoilt past participle, past tense of **spoil**

Spo·kane /spō kán/ **1.** river in the northwestern United States. It rises in Idaho and flows across Washington State into the Columbia River. Length: 120 mi./190 km. **2.** city in eastern Washington, situated on the falls of the Spokane River. It is a commercial and manufacturing center. Population: 196,305 (2002 estimate).

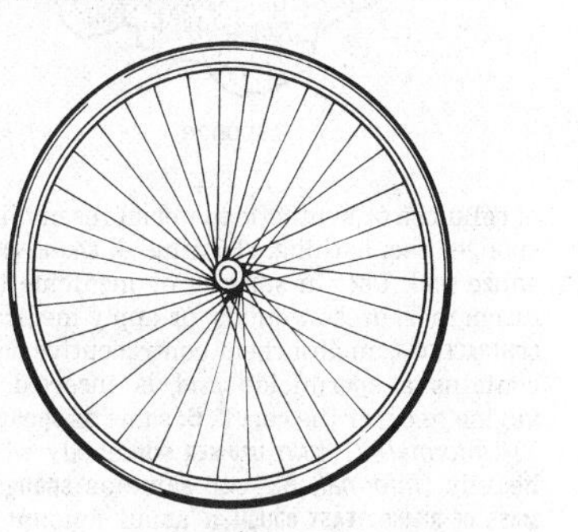
spoke

spoke[1] /spōk/ *n* **1. SUPPORTING ROD FOR WHEEL RIM** a bar or rod that extends from the hub of a wheel to support or brace the rim **2. KNOB ON SHIP'S WHEEL** a knob that sticks out from the rim of a ship's wheel **3. RUNG** a rung of a ladder [Old English *spāca* < Indo-European, "pointed object"] —**spoked** *adj*

spoke[2] past tense of **speak**

spo·ken /spṓkən/ past participle of **speak** ■ *adj* **1.** expressed with the voice ○ *the spoken word* **2.** speaking in a particular way, e.g., with a particular voice quality, accent, command of the language, or attitude (*used in combination*) ○ *well-spoken* ◇ **spoken for 1.** already owned or reserved by somebody **2.** already married, engaged, or romantically committed to somebody (*dated*)

SYNONYMS See ***verbal***.

spokes·man /spṓksmən/ (*plural* **-men** /-mən/) *n* somebody, especially a man, authorized to speak on behalf of another person or other people [Early 16C. < SPOKE[2] after CRAFTSMAN etc.]

spokes·per·son /spṓks pùrss'n/ (*plural* **-peo·ple** /-peep'l/ or **-per·sons**) *n* somebody authorized to speak on behalf of another person or other people [Late 20C. After SPOKESMAN]

spokes·wom·an /spṓks wòomman/ (*plural* **-wom·en** /-wìmmin/) *n* a woman authorized to speak on behalf of another person or other people [Mid-17C. After SPOKESMAN]

spo·li·a·tion /spòlee áysh'n/ *n* **1. PLUNDERING** the seizing of things by force **2. SEIZURE OF SHIPS** the seizure or plundering of neutral ships at sea by a belligerent power in time of war **3. ALTERATION OF DOCUMENT** the alteration or destruction of a document so as to make it invalid or unusable as evidence [15C. < Latin *spoliation-* < *spoliare* (see SPOIL)] —**spo·li·a·tor·y** /spṓlee ə tàwree/ *adj*

spon·da·ic /spon dáy ik/ *adj* relating to spondees or written in spondees [Late 16C. < French *spondaïque* < Greek *spondeios* (see SPONDEE)]

spon·dee /spón dee/ *n* a metrical foot of two long or stressed syllables [14C. Via French < Greek *spondeios* "libational" < *spondē* "libation"; because the spondee was often used in songs accompanying libations]

spon·dy·li·tis /spòndə lítiss/ *n* inflammation of the vertebrae and the attached disks and ligaments [Mid-19C. < Latin *spondylus* "vertebra" < Greek *spondulos*]

sponge /spunj/ *n* **1. OCEAN ANIMAL** a chiefly ocean-dwelling invertebrate animal with a porous fibrous skeleton composed of calcium carbonate, silica, and spongin. Sponges often live in colonies and attach themselves to underwater objects. Phylum: Porifera. See illustration on next page **2. NATURAL MATERIAL USED FOR BATHING** a lightweight porous absorbent piece of the skeleton of some sponges. Use: bathing, cleaning. **3. SYNTHETIC MATERIAL USED FOR BATHING** a piece

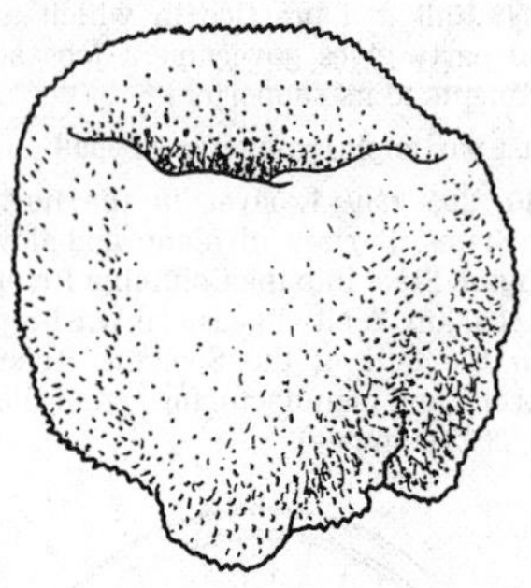

sponge

of cellulose or synthetic material resembling a true sponge. Use: bathing, cleaning. **4.** GAUZE PAD a folded gauze pad. Use: in surgery or medicine to absorb discharges, dress wounds, or apply medications. **5.** CONTRACEPTIVE an absorbent contraceptive device that contains a spermicide and is inserted into the vagina to cover the cervix **6.** same as **sponger** (sense 1) (*informal*) **7.** HEAVY DRINKER somebody who drinks heavily (*informal*) **8.** FOOD same as **sponge cake 9.** MASS OF RISING YEAST DOUGH a small amount of yeast dough that is allowed to rise before being kneaded with the rest of the batch **10.** ACT OF CLEANING the act of rubbing or bathing somebody or something with a wet sponge or cloth **11.** POROUS METAL a porous metal capable of absorbing large quantities of gas, obtained by reduction without melting of a metal compound or by electrolysis ■ *v* **(sponged, spong·ing, spong·es) 1.** *vt* CLEAN SOMEBODY OR SOMETHING to wipe or clean somebody or something with a wet sponge or cloth **2.** *vt* REMOVE SOMETHING to remove or destroy something by rubbing **3.** *vt* ABSORB LIQUID to absorb liquids with a sponge or with the efficiency of a sponge **4.** *vt* GET SOMETHING BY IMPOSING ON GENEROSITY to get something by imposing on the generosity of others **5.** *vi* LIVE OFF OTHERS to live at the expense of others, repeatedly imposing on them and making no effort to live independently (*informal*) **6.** *vi* COLLECT SPONGES to dive for sponges under the sea [Pre-12C. Via Latin *spongia* < Greek *spoggos*] —**spong·er** *n*

sponge bag *n UK* same as **ditty bag** (sense 2)

sponge bath *n* a body cleansing just using a sponge and some water, without immersion, usually performed on somebody confined to bed

sponge cake *n* a light open-textured cake made of flour, eggs, sugar, flavoring, but no shortening

spong·er /spúnjər/ *n* **1.** somebody who lives off others, habitually imposing on their generosity and making no effort to live independently (*informal*) **2.** somebody who dives for sponges, or a ship used for gathering sponges

spon·gi·form /spúnjə fàwrm/ *adj* having an open texture containing many holes, resembling the texture of a sponge [Early 19C. < SPONGE]

spong·i·form en·ceph·a·lop·a·thy *n* a brain disease in humans and animals in which areas of the brain slowly degenerate and take on a spongy appearance

spon·gin /spúnjin/ *n* a protein that forms the skeletal framework of sponges [Mid-19C. < SPONGE]

spon·gi·o·blast /spúnjee ə blàst/ *n* an embryonic cell in the brain and spinal cord that develops into supporting connective tissue (**neuroglia**) [Early 20C. < Latin *spongia* (see SPONGE)] —**spon·gi·o·blas·tic** /spùnjee ə blástik/ *adj*

spong·y /spúnjee/ **(-i·er, -i·est)** *adj* **1.** OPEN-TEXTURED having a light open texture full of holes or cavities **2.** ABSORBENT absorbent and elastic **3.** SOFT AND WET soft and full of water —**spong·i·ness** *n*

spong·y mes·o·phyll, spong·y pa·ren·chy·ma *n* a spongy tissue layer of irregularly shaped chlorophyll-bearing cells interspersed with air spaces, sandwiched between the upper and lower epidermal layers of a leaf

~~**sponser**~~ incorrect spelling of **sponsor**

spon·son /spónss'n/ *n* **1.** NAVY GUN PLATFORM ON SHIP a gun platform sticking out from the side of a ship. A gun can be mounted in such a way that it can fire both fore and aft. **2.** ARMS, HIST GUN TURRET a gun turret mounted on the side of an early tank **3.** CANOEING AIR CHAMBER IN CANOE an air chamber that runs along each side of a canoe to help keep it afloat **4.** AVIAT STABILIZER FOR SEAPLANE an air-filled structure or small wing projecting from the lower hull of a seaplane to stabilize it in water **5.** NAUT SUPPORT FOR PADDLE WHEEL a structural support for a paddle wheel on a ship [Mid-19C. Origin ?]

spon·sor /spónssər/ *n* **1.** SOMEBODY RESPONSIBLE FOR ANOTHER somebody who becomes responsible for somebody else, especially during education, apprenticeship, or probation **2.** BROADCAST RADIO OR TELEVISION ADVERTISER a person or a business that pays for radio or television programming by buying advertising time **3.** CONTRIBUTOR TO FUNDING OF EVENT a person or organization that provides or pledges money to help fund an event, especially an event run by another person or group **4.** CONTRIBUTOR TO CHARITY a person or organization that donates money to a charity on the basis of the performance of a participant in an organized fundraising event **5.** POL LEGISLATOR a legislator who proposes and supports the passage of a bill **6.** SUPPORTER a country, organization, or group that supports or organizes an activity, or vouches for the acceptability of another **7.** CHR SOMEBODY ANSWERING AT CHILD'S BAPTISM somebody who answers on behalf of a child at baptism and becomes responsible for the child's religious upbringing (*formal*) ■ *vt* **(-sored, -sor·ing, -sors)** ACT AS SPONSOR TO SOMEBODY to act as a sponsor to somebody or something [Mid-17C. < late Latin, "baptismal sponsor" < Latin *spons-*, past participle of *spondere* "pledge"] —**spon·so·ri·al** /spon sáwree əl/ *adj* —**spon·sor·ship** *n*

ORIGIN The Latin word *spondere* "to pledge," from which ***sponsor*** is derived, is also the source of English *despond, respond, riposte,* and *spouse.*

SYNONYMS See ***backer.***

spon·ta·ne·i·ty /spòntə née ətee, -náy ətee/ *n* **1.** behavior that is natural and unconstrained and is the result of impulse, not planning **2.** the generating or provoking of activity from within, rather than as a result of external influences

spon·ta·ne·ous /spon táynee əss/ *adj* **1.** ARISING FROM INTERNAL CAUSE resulting from internal or natural processes, with no apparent external influence **2.** ARISING FROM IMPULSE arising from natural impulse or inclination, rather than from planning or in response to suggestions from others **3.** UNRESTRAINED naturally unrestrained or uninhibited **4.** BOT GROWING UNCULTIVATED growing without cultivation [Mid-17C. < late Latin *spontaneus* "of your own accord" < Latin *sponte* in same sense] —**spon·ta·ne·ous·ly** *adv* —**spon·ta·ne·ous·ness** *n*

spon·ta·ne·ous a·bor·tion *n* MED same as **miscarriage** (sense 1)

spon·ta·ne·ous com·bus·tion *n* the ignition of a combustible material such as hay as a result of internal heat generation usually caused by rapid oxidation

spon·ta·ne·ous gen·er·a·tion *n* BIOL same as **abiogenesis**

spon·ta·ne·ous ig·ni·tion *n* PHYS same as **spontaneous combustion**

spon·ta·ne·ous re·cov·er·y *n* in psychology, the return of an extinguished conditioned response without reinforcement

~~**spontanious**~~ incorrect spelling of **spontaneous**

spon·toon /spon tóon/ *n* a short pike used by some infantry officers in the 18th century [Mid-18C. Via French < Italian *spontone* < *punto* "point" < Latin *punctum* (see POINT)]

spoof /spoof/ *n* **1.** HOAX a good-humored hoax **2.** AMUSING SATIRE a light amusing satire **3.** ONLINE FRAUDULENT SPAM E-MAIL a method of sending e-mail using a false name or e-mail address to make it appear that the e-mail came from somebody other than the true sender ■ *v* **(spoofed, spoof·ing, spoofs) 1.** *vt* DECEIVE SOMEBODY to deceive or fool somebody **2.** *vt* SATIRIZE SOMEBODY OR SOMETHING to satirize somebody or something good-naturedly **3.** *vti* ONLINE SEND FRAUDULENT E-MAIL TO SOMEBODY to send e-mail using a false name or e-mail address [Late 19C. Invented name for a game involving hoaxing] —**spoof·er** *n* —**spoof·ing** *n*

spook /spook/ *n* (*informal*) **1.** GHOST a ghost or a ghostly figure **2.** same as **spy** *n* (sense 1) ■ *v* **(spooked, spook·ing, spooks) 1.** *vt* HAUNT SOMEBODY to haunt somebody as a ghost **2.** *vt* STARTLE SOMEBODY to startle or make an animal or person feel uneasy **3.** *vi* BE FRIGHTENED to feel frightened or uneasy [Early 19C. < Dutch]

spook·y /spóokee/ **(-i·er, -i·est)** *adj* **1.** SCARILY SUGGESTIVE OF SUPERNATURAL frightening or unnerving because suggesting the presence of supernatural forces (*informal*) **2.** AMAZING strange or amazing, often in a way that seems supernatural (*informal*) **3.** EASILY FRIGHTENED easily frightened or startled —**spook·i·ly** *adv* —**spook·i·ness** *n*

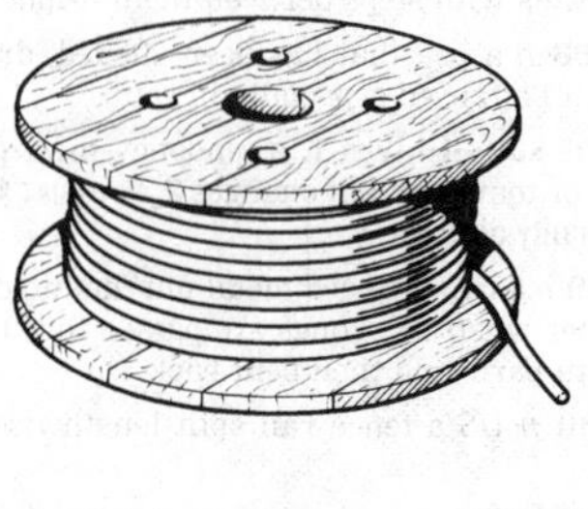

spool

spool[1] /spool/ *n* **1.** CYLINDER ON WHICH SOMETHING IS WOUND a cylinder around which thread, tape, or film is wound. It has a central hole and a rim at each end. **2.** AMOUNT ON SPOOL the amount of something wound on a spool ■ *vti* **(spooled, spool·ing, spools)** WIND SOMETHING ON SPOOL to wind something on a spool or on something similar to a spool such as a reel or bobbin, or be wound in this way [14C. Directly or via French < Middle Dutch *spoele*]

spool[2] /spool/ **(spooled, spool·ing, spools)** *vi* to transfer computer data for printing into a computer's memory store so that it can be printed later without slowing down the computer's operations [Late 20C. < SPOOL[1]; sometimes thought to be an acronym < *simultaneous peripheral operation on line*] —**spool·ing** *n*

spoon /spoon/ *n* **1.** EATING UTENSIL a utensil used for eating or preparing food, consisting of a shallow oval bowl attached to a handle **2.** FISHING SHINY FISHING LURE a bright oval metal fishing lure with a hook attached **3.** GOLF GOLF CLUB a number three wood, used for hitting long high drives from the fairway (*dated*) **4.** DRUGS QUANTITY OF DRUG a quantity of hard drugs, especially a two-gram measure of heroin (*slang*) **5.** CRIME, SOCIOL GANG MEMBER a paroled street gang member who returns to his turf and reengages in gang violence (*slang*) ■ *v* **(spooned, spoon·ing, spoons) 1.** *vt* EAT FOOD USING SPOON to eat, scoop, or carry something with a spoon or with the action of somebody using a spoon **2.** *vt* HOLLOW SOMETHING OUT to dig or scrape a hollow in something, or dig something out to leave a hollow **3.** *vt* GOLF HIT BALL UP in golf, to hit a ball upward with a scooping action, often as a result of an imperfect stroke **4.** *vi* FISHING USE SPOON FISHING LURE to fish with a spoon lure **5.** *vi* BE AMOROUS to indulge in amorous behavior such as kissing and caressing (*informal*) [Old English *spōn* "wood chip" < Indo-European, "flat piece of wood"] —**spoon·ful** *n*

spoonbill

spoon·bill /spóon bìl/ *n* **1.** a wading bird with a long flat beak shaped like a spoon. Native to: tropical regions. Family: Threskiornithidae. **2.** *US* a duck with a broad beak, e.g., a shoveler

spoon bread *n Southern US* a soft moist bread made with cornmeal, eggs, milk, and shortening, baked in a bowl and eaten with a spoon

spoon·er·ism /spóonə rìzzəm/ *n* an accidental transposition of initial consonant sounds or parts of words, especially in an amusing way, e.g., "half-warmed fish" for "half-formed wish" [Early 20C. After Reverend William *Spooner* (1844–1930), British educator]

spoon·ey *adj* another spelling of **spoony** *(dated)*

spoon-feed *vt* **1.** to feed somebody, especially a child or hospital patient, using a spoon **2.** to cater to somebody completely, requiring him or her to make no effort at all

spoon·y /spóonee/, **spoon·ey** (**-i·er, -i·est**) *adj* foolishly sentimental or amorous *(dated)*

spoor /spoor, spawr/ *n* the visible trail of an animal, especially one being hunted for sport ■ *vti* (**spoored, spoor·ing, spoors**) to track an animal by following its trail [Early 19C. Via Afrikaans < Middle Dutch] —**spoor·er** *n*

spor- same as **sporo-** *(used before vowels)*

Spor·a·des /spórrə deéz/ group of Greek islands in the Aegean Sea, north of the island of Euboea

spo·rad·ic /spə ráddik/ *adj* **1.** occurring at intervals that have no apparent pattern **2.** describes a disease that appears in scattered or isolated instances or locations [Late 17C. Via medieval Latin < Greek *sporadikos* < *sporad-* "scattered"] —**spo·rad·i·cal·ly** *adv*

SYNONYMS See ***periodic***.

spo·ran·gi·o·phore /spə ránjee ə fàwr/ *n* a thread (**hypha**) from a fungus or a projection from the cone of a horsetail from which spore-forming sacs develop

spo·ran·gi·um /spə ránjee əm/ (*plural* **-gi·a** /-jee ə/) *n* a hollow spore-producing organ in fungi, ferns, and some other plants [Early 19C. < modern Latin, "spore vessel" < Greek *spora* "sowing, seed" + *aggeion* "small vessel" (see ANGIO-)]

spore /spawr/ *n* **1.** ASEXUAL REPRODUCTIVE STRUCTURE a small, usually one-celled reproductive structure produced by seedless plants, algae, fungi, and some protozoans that is capable of developing into a new individual **2.** DORMANT BACTERIUM a dormant resistant form taken by some bacteria in response to adverse conditions ■ *vi* (**spored, spor·ing, spores**) PRODUCE SPORES to produce or release spores [Mid-19C. Via modern Latin < Greek *spora* "sowing, seed"]

spore case *n* BOT same as **sporangium**

spo·rif·er·ous /spaw ríffərəss/ *adj* producing or releasing spores

sporo- *prefix* spore ○ *sporoplasm* ○ *sporocyte* [< Greek *spora* "sowing, seed"]

spo·ro·carp /spáwrō kaàrp/ *n* **1.** the spore-producing organ in red algae and some fungi and slime molds **2.** the hard round spore-producing organ of some ferns that grow in water

spo·ro·cyst /spáwrō sìst/ *n* **1.** CASE PROTECTING SPOROZOITES a protective case produced by sporozoans in which sporozoites develop **2.** ENCASED SPOROZOITE a sporozoite protected within a case **3.** STRUCTURE PRODUCING SPORES a structure that produces spores, formed by a parasite within its host

spo·ro·cyte /spáwrō sìt/ *n* a cell from which spores are produced

spo·ro·gen·e·sis /spàwrō jénnəssiss/ *n* **1.** the production or formation of spores **2.** reproduction by means of spores —**spo·rog·e·nous** /spaw rójjənəss/ *adj*

spo·rog·o·ny /spə róggənee, spaw-/ *n* the process in sporozoans by which sporozoites are formed from multiple fission of an encysted zygote

spo·ro·phore /spáwrə fàwr/ *n* an organ in fungi that produces spores

spo·ro·phyll /spáwrə fil/, **spo·ro·phyl** *n* a leaf or modified leaf that bears spore-producing organs, e.g., the fertile leaf of a fern or club moss

spo·ro·phyte /spáwrə fìt/ *n* in plants that alternate between sexual and asexual phases, a plant in its asexual spore-producing phase —**spo·ro·phyt·ic** /spàwrə fíttik/ *adj*

spo·ro·plasm /spáwrə plàzzəm/ *n* an infective mass of protoplasm contained inside a spore that is injected into a host cell by various parasitic organisms

spo·ro·pol·len·in /spàwrə póllənin/ *n* a polymer found in the outer layer of pollen and some spores

spo·ro·tri·cho·sis /spàwrə tri kóssiss/ *n* a serious infectious disease caused by a fungus *Sporothrix schenckii* that enters the body from soil or wood via a skin wound. It typically produces skin ulcers and nodules on the lymph nodes. [Early 20C. < modern Latin *Sporotrichum* < *spora* (see SPORE) + Greek *thrix* "hair"]

spo·ro·zo·an /spàwrə zṓ ən/ *n* a parasitic single-celled organism (**protozoan**) that has alternating sexual and asexual generations and reproduces by means of spores. The malaria parasites are sporozoans. Class: Sporozoa. [Late 19C. < modern Latin *Sporozoa* < Greek *spora* "sowing, seed" + *zōion* "animal"] —**spo·ro·zo·an** *adj*

spo·ro·zo·ite /spàwrə zṓ ìt/ *n* a small infectious motile stage in the life of sporozoans produced by sporogony, usually within a host [Late 19C. < modern Latin *Sporozoa* (see SPOROZOAN)]

spor·ran /spáwrən, spórrən/ *n* a leather pouch, sometimes decorated with fur, worn hanging from a belt in front of the kilt in men's traditional Scottish Highland dress [Mid-18C. Via Scottish Gaelic < Middle Irish *sporán*]

sport /spawrt/ *n* **1.** COMPETITIVE PHYSICAL ACTIVITY an individual or group competitive activity involving physical exertion or skill, governed by rules, and sometimes engaged in professionally *(often used in the plural)* **2.** PASTIME an active pastime participated in for pleasure or exercise **3.** SOMEBODY CHEERFUL somebody who remains cheerful when losing or in an unpleasant situation *(informal)* **4.** SOMEBODY WHO PLAYS FAIRLY somebody noted for abiding by the rules in a game or for generally honorable behavior *(informal)* **5.** GOOD COMPANION a good-natured, easy-going, or sociable person *(informal)* **6.** JOKING good-natured joking *(formal)* ○ *a harmless prank done in sport* **7.** DERISION contemptuous mockery *(formal)* **8.** OBJECT OF RIDICULE an object of ridicule or mockery *(formal)* **9.** SOMEBODY OR SOMETHING MANIPULATED BY OTHERS somebody or something manipulated by external forces *(literary)* **10.** GAMBLER a gambler, especially somebody who gambles on sporting events *(informal)* **11.** *US* FORM OF ADDRESS a casual form of address, especially used between men or boys *(informal)* **12.** BIOL MUTATED ORGANISM a plant or animal that deviates markedly from its parent stock or type, usually as a result of mutation, especially mutation of somatic tissue **13.** BIOL UNUSUAL CHARACTER the mutant character of a mutated organism **14.** AMOROUS BEHAVIOR amorous behavior, e.g., kissing or caressing *(archaic)* ■ *v* (**sport·ed, sport·ing, sports**) **1.** *vt* WEAR SOMETHING to wear or display something, usually proudly or with the intention of impressing others *(informal)* **2.** *vi* PLAY HAPPILY to romp and play happily *(formal)* **3.** *vi* ENJOY YOURSELF to enjoy yourself, especially by taking part in outdoor physical activity *(formal)* **4.** *vi* MAKE JOKES to joke or trifle with somebody *(formal)* **5.** *vi* BIOL MUTATE to produce or undergo a mutation [14C. Shortening of DISPORT] —**sport·er** *n* —**sport·ful** *adj* —**sport·ful·ly** *adv* —**sport·ful·ness** *n*

sport climb·ing *n* a sport in which competitors ascend walls, often artificial ones, on difficult routes that have bolts in place

sport·ing /spáwrting/ *adj* **1.** USED IN SPORTS relating to or used in sports activities ○ *sporting dogs* **2.** FAIR in keeping with the principles of fair competition, respect for other competitors, and personal integrity **3.** OF GAMBLING relating to gambling, or taking an interest in gambling **4.** RISKING willing to take a risk —**sport·ing·ly** *adv*

sport·ing chance *n* an even or good chance of succeeding

spor·tive /spáwrtiv/ *adj* **1.** PLAYFUL playful and frolicsome **2.** JOKING done as a joke **3.** FOND OF SPORTS regularly taking part in sports **4.** SEXUALLY ACTIVE frequently indulging in sexual activity, or tending to enjoy it *(archaic)* —**spor·tive·ly** *adv* —**spor·tive·ness** *n*

sports /spawrts/ *adj* **1.** relating to or used in physical or recreational activities ○ *sports equipment* **2.** designed for informal or outdoor wear

sports car *n* a small car with a low center of gravity designed for fast acceleration and for handling at high speeds

sports·cast /spáwrts kàst/ *n* a radio or television broadcast of a sports event or of sports news [Mid-20C. After BROADCAST] —**sports·cast·er** *n*

sports drink *n* a soft drink that is intended to quench thirst faster than water and replenish the sugar and minerals lost from the body during physical exercise

sports grounds *npl* an area of land on which competitive sports events are held

sports jacket *n* **1.** a man's jacket similar in style to a suit jacket but worn on more informal occasions with pants of a different material or color **2.** *US* a collarless jacket fitting closely at the wrists, hem, and collar, usually made of synthetic fabric and worn over sports clothes or for casual dress

sports·man /spáwrtsmən/ (*plural* **-men** /-mən/) *n* **1.** a man who participates in sports **2.** somebody, especially a man, who behaves fairly, observing rules, respecting others, and accepting defeat graciously —**sports·man·like** *adj*

sports·man·ship /spáwrtsmən shìp/ *n* **1.** conduct considered fitting for a sportsperson, including observance of the rules of fair play, respect for others, and graciousness in losing **2.** participation in sports

sports med·i·cine *n* the branch of medicine concerned with preventing and treating injuries resulting from sports

sports·per·son /spáwrts pùrss'n/ (*plural* **-per·sons** or **-peo·ple** /-peèp'l/) *n* **1.** somebody who participates in sports **2.** somebody who behaves fairly, observing rules, respecting others, and accepting defeat graciously

sports sup·ple·ment *n* a dietary supplement used by athletes to enhance performance

sports·wear /spáwrts wèr/ *n* clothes appropriate for casual or informal occasions

sports·wom·an /spáwrts wòommən/ (*plural* **-wom·en** /-wìmmin/) *n* **1.** a woman who participates in sports **2.** a woman who behaves fairly, observing rules, respecting others, and accepting defeat graciously

sports·writ·er /spáwrts rìtər/ *n* somebody who writes about sports, especially for a newspaper or magazine

sport tour·er *n* a four-door motor vehicle with four-wheel drive and a hinged rear door, resembling both a station wagon and an SUV in styling, capable of towing a boat and hauling gear

sport-u·til·i·ty ve·hi·cle, **sport-u·til·i·ty**, **sport ute** *informal* *n* a four-wheel-drive vehicle used for everyday driving, but suitable for rough terrain

sport·y /spáwrtee/ (**-i·er, -i·est**) *adj* **1.** FOR SPORTS designed or appropriate for sports or leisure activities **2.** ENTHUSIASTIC ABOUT SPORTS enthusiastic about sports or outdoor activities and regularly taking part in them **3.** SIMILAR TO SPORTS CAR having features resembling the style or performance of a sports car **4.** *US* SPORTING in keeping with the principles of fair play, generosity, and honor **5.** *US* FLASHY smart, bright, and expensive-looking, sometimes excessively so

spor·u·late /spáwryə làyt/ (**-lat·ed, -lat·ing, -lates**) *vi* to produce spores [Late 19C. < modern Latin *sporula* "small spore" < *spora* (see SPORE)] —**spor·u·la·tion** /spàwryə láysh'n/ *n*

spot /spot/ *n* **1.** SMALL ROUND AREA a small defined area, especially one that is more or less circular, that is different in color, material, or texture from the surrounding area **2.** STAIN a dirty mark or stain **3.** MARK ON SKIN a mark or blemish on the skin, especially a pimple **4.** PLACE a place, point, position, or location ○ *Do you remember the exact spot?* **5.** GEOGRAPHIC LOCATION a geographic location or area ○ *a local spot of pristine beauty* **6.** ANNOUNCEMENT OR ADVERTISEMENT a brief announcement or advertisement inserted between regular radio or television programs **7.** ASPECT OF SOMETHING a particular aspect or part of something larger ○ *a weak spot in her argument* **8.** TIME SLOT OF PERFORMER the appearance of a performer in a variety show, or the scheduled or regular time for that appearance **9. AWKWARD SITUATION** an awkward or difficult situation (*informal*) **10. ENTERTAINMENT LOCALE** a place of entertainment **11. POSITION IN SERIES** a position in a series or sequence **12.** *US* **MONEY** a piece of paper money worth a particular amount (*dated slang; usually used in combination*) ○ *She handed me a ten spot.* **13. SMALL AMOUNT** a small amount, e.g., of liquid to drink or of work to do **14.** ARTS same as **spotlight** *n* (sense 1) **15.** FISH **FOOD FISH OF N AMERICAN ATLANTIC** a small edible ocean fish in the croaker family. It has a small spot near the gill on each side. Native to: Atlantic coast of North America. **16.** CUE GAMES **DOT ON BILLIARD TABLE** a small black dot on the table in snooker or pool that marks where a ball should be placed **17.** CARDS **SYMBOL ON PLAYING CARD** one of the traditional symbols, heart, diamond, spade, or club, on a playing card **18.** *US* CARDS **PLAYING CARD** a playing card from two to ten of any of the four suits ○ *a six spot* **19.** LEISURE **DOT ON GAME PIECE** one of the dots on a domino or dice **20.** ELECTRONICS **ILLUMINATED POINT ON CATHODE-RAY TUBE** the point on the face of a cathode-ray tube at which the phosphor is illuminated by the impact of an electron beam **21. CHARACTER BLEMISH** a blemish on somebody's character or reputation (*archaic*) ■ *adj* **1.** COMM **AVAILABLE IMMEDIATELY** describes goods or currencies that are paid for and delivered immediately after a sale **2.** BROADCAST **ORIGINATING LOCALLY** describes a news report that is broadcast from the place where it happens ■ *v* (**spot·ted, spot·ting, spots**) **1.** *vt* **SEE SOMEBODY OR SOMETHING** to see or detect somebody or something suddenly **2.** *vti* **MAKE OR BECOME STAINED** to mark or dirty something with stains, or become marked or dirtied with stains **3.** *vt* **MARK SOMETHING WITH DOTS** to mark something with dots of a different color **4.** *vt US* **REMOVE STAINS FROM SOMETHING** to remove stains or marks from something **5.** *vt* **BLEMISH SOMEBODY'S CHARACTER** to blemish somebody's character or reputation **6.** *vt US* **POSITION SOMEBODY OR SOMETHING** to position somebody or something in a specific location **7.** *vt US* **DISTRIBUTE AT INTERVALS** to distribute people or things at intervals ○ *spotted the outfielders far into the stadium* **8.** *vti* **ADJUST FIRE** to adjust gunfire for accuracy by observation **9.** *vt US* SPORTS **GIVE SOMEBODY ADVANTAGE** to concede an advantage or point margin to an opponent in a game or contest as a handicap (*informal*) **10.** *vt* **LEND MONEY TO SOMEBODY** to give or lend money to somebody, or pay for something for somebody (*slang*) ○ *Will somebody spot me twenty bucks?* [12C. Origin ?] ◇ **hit the high spots** to focus or touch on the most important points or things (*informal*) ◇ **hit the spot** to be absolutely what is required for total satisfaction, especially in terms of food or drink (*informal*) ◇ **in a spot** in a difficult or embarrassing position (*informal*) ◇ **on the spot 1.** in the exact place where something is happening **2.** immediately **3.** in a difficult situation or under pressure ◇ **put somebody on the spot** to put somebody in a difficult or embarrassing position, especially a position of having to make an instant judgment or decision

spot check *n* a quick random inspection usually made without prior notice —**spot-check** *vt*

spot·less /spóttləss/ *adj* **1.** impeccably clean ○ *a spotless kitchen* **2.** beyond reproach ○ *a spotless reputation* —**spot·less·ly** *adv* —**spot·less·ness** *n*

spot·light /spót līt/ *n* **1. FOCUSED BEAM OF LIGHT** a strong beam of light that can be directed to illuminate a small area, especially one focusing attention on a stage performer **2. LAMP** a lamp that produces a strong narrow beam of light that can be directed at will, e.g., one mounted on a police car **3. FOCUS OF ATTENTION** the focus of public attention ■ *vt* (**-lit** /-lit/ or **-light·ed, -light·ing, -lights**) **1. ILLUMINATE SOMETHING WITH LIGHT BEAM** to direct a beam of light on somebody or something **2. FOCUS ATTENTION ON SOMEBODY OR SOMETHING** to focus public attention on somebody or something

spot mar·ket *n* a market in which commodities, securities, or currencies are traded for immediate payment and delivery

spot price *n* the market price for goods, currencies, or securities at a specific time

spot·ted /spóttəd/ *adj* **1.** patterned with spots **2.** stained or soiled with spots of something

spot·ted cranes·bill *n* PLANTS same as **wild geranium**

spot·ted fe·ver *n* a fever accompanied by skin eruptions, e.g., Rocky Mountain spotted fever, typhus, or epidemic cerebrospinal meningitis

spot·ted sal·a·man·der *n* a common salamander that has an irregular row of yellow or orange spots running down each side of its black back. Native to: eastern North America. Latin name: *Ambystoma maculatum*.

spot·ted sand·pi·per *n* a small bird that has spots on its white breast during the breeding season. Native to: small lakes and streams of North America. Latin name: *Actitis macularia*.

spot·ter /spóttər/ *n* **1. SOMEBODY WATCHING OUT FOR SOMETHING** somebody or something that watches for and locates something (*often used before a noun*) ○ *a spotter plane* **2. SOMEBODY OR SOMETHING LOCATING ENEMY POSITIONS** a person or aircraft that locates and reports enemy positions **3.** *US* **PERSON EMPLOYED TO SPY** somebody employed to spy on fellow employees to check their honesty (*informal*) **4.** *US* BROADCAST, SPORTS **SPORTSCASTER'S ASSISTANT** an assistant to a sportscaster who identifies the players in a game **5.** SPORTS **SPORTS ASSISTANT** somebody whose job is to stand by and guard against injury during a sports practice, e.g., in gymnastics or water-skiing **6. TALENT SCOUT** somebody who looks out for new talent or material **7. SOMEBODY WHO MARKS SOMETHING** somebody who puts marks or dots on something **8.** *US* **SOMEBODY WHO REMOVES SPOTS** somebody who removes spots, especially in dry cleaning

spot·ting *n* MED same as **breakthrough bleeding**

spot·ty /spóttee/ (**-ti·er, -ti·est**) *adj* **1. INCONSISTENT** inconsistent in quality or character **2.** *UK* **PIMPLY** covered in pimples **3. SPOTTED** patterned with spots —**spot·ti·ly** *adv* —**spot·ti·ness** *n*

spot-weld *vt* to join overlapping pieces of metal by making a series of small welds dotted about, instead of making a large continuous weld. Spot-welding is used when the bond is subject to light temporary stresses, but not to structural loads. ■ *n* a joint between overlapping metal parts, formed by making a series of small welds —**spot-weld·er** *n*

spouge /spuj/ *n Carib* Barbadian dance music with a lively beat [Late 20C. Invented word]

spou·sal /spówz'l/ *adj* relating to a husband or wife

spou·sal e·quiv·a·lent *n* somebody who becomes equivalent to a husband or wife, especially for the purposes of tax, pension, or government benefits

spouse /spowss, spowz/ *n* somebody's husband or wife [12C. Via Old French *spous* < Latin *sponsus*, past participle of *spondere* "pledge, betroth"]

spouse e·quiv·a·lent *n* LAW same as **spousal equivalent**

spout /spowt/ *vti* (**spout·ed, spout·ing, spouts**) **1. DISCHARGE JET OF SOMETHING** to discharge a substance forcibly in a jet or stream, or be discharged in this way **2.** ZOOL **DISCHARGE AIR FROM BLOWHOLE** to discharge air and water through a blowhole **3. TALK AT GREAT LENGTH ABOUT SOMETHING** to talk about something tediously and at great length, usually with no regard for the listener's interest ■ *n* **1. TUBE FOR POURING LIQUID** a tube or pipe out of which a liquid is poured **2. CHUTE FOR DISCHARGE OF SOLID SUBSTANCE** a chute through which something solid such as grain is discharged **3. STREAM OF LIQUID** a continuous and forceful stream of liquid **4.** BUILDINGS, METEOROL same as **waterspout 5.** ZOOL **AIR AND WATER FROM BLOWHOLE** a burst of air and water from a whale or other sea animal's blowhole [14C. < Middle Dutch *spouten*]

spout·ing /spówting/ *n Northeast US* the system of gutters and downspouts that carry rainwater from the roof of a building

spp. *abbr* BIOL species (*plural*)

S.P.Q.R., SPQR *abbr* the senate and people of Rome [Latin *Senatus Populusque Romanus*]

sprain /sprayn/ *n* a painful injury to the ligaments of a joint caused by wrenching or overstretching ■ *vt* (**sprained, sprain·ing, sprains**) to injure a joint by a sudden wrenching or overstretching of its ligaments [Early 17C. Origin ?]

sprang past tense of **spring**

sprat /sprat/ *n* **1.** (*plural* **sprats** or *same*) **SMALL EDIBLE FISH** a small fish of the herring family. Native to: northeastern Atlantic Ocean, North Sea. Latin name: *Clupea sprattus*. **2. SMALL HERRING** a small or young herring or similar fish such as an anchovy **3. SPRAT AS FOOD** the flesh of a sprat as food **4. SOMEBODY YOUNG OR UNIMPORTANT** a young, small, or unimportant person (*dated*) [Old English *sprot* < W Germanic]

sprawl /sprawl/ *vi* (**sprawled, sprawl·ing, sprawls**) **1. SIT OR LIE AWKWARDLY** to sit or lie with the arms and legs spread awkwardly in different directions **2. EXTEND IN DISORDERED WAY** to extend over or across something in a disordered, awkward, or ugly way ○ *handwritten notes sprawled across the page* ■ *n* **1. AWKWARD SITTING OR LYING POSITION** a sitting or lying position in which the arms and legs are spread out awkwardly **2. UNCHECKED GROWTH OF URBAN AREA** the scattered, unplanned, and unchecked expansion of a town or city into the surrounding countryside **3. URBANIZED AREAS ON CITY'S EDGE** the urbanized areas on the edge of a town or city that have developed as a result of unplanned and unchecked expansion [Old English *sprēawlian* "move convulsively" < Indo-European, "strew"] —**sprawl·er** *n* —**sprawl·ing** *adj* —**spraw·ly** *adj*

spray[1] /spray/ *n* **1. LIQUID PARTICLES** a moving cloud or mist of water or other liquid particles **2. JET OF LIQUID** a jet of fine particles of liquid from an atomizer or pressurized container **3. CONTAINER FOR RELEASING LIQUID** an atomizer or pressurized container that releases fine particles of a liquid (*often used before a noun*) **4. LIQUID IN PRESSURIZED CONTAINER** a liquid product that is packaged in an atomizer or pressurized container, e.g., a deodorant, paint, or insecticide (*often used before a noun*) ■ *v* (**sprayed, spray·ing, sprays**) **1.** *vt* **DISCHARGE LIQUID FROM PRESSURIZED CONTAINER** to disperse a liquid in the form of fine particles, or apply a liquid in this form to the surface of something **2.** *vt* **PAINT SOMETHING WITH PAINT SPRAY** to paint or mark something using a paint spray ○ *spray the car red* ○ *He sprayed his name on the wall.* **3.** *vi* **URINATE** to put out a stream of urine, e.g., as a cat does when marking its territory [Early 17C. < Middle Dutch *sprayen* "sprinkle"] —**spray·er** *n*

spray[2] /spray/ *n* **1. PLANT SPRIG** a shoot or branch of a plant, with flowers, leaves, or berries on it **2. FLOWER ARRANGEMENT** a decorative arrangement of flowers and foliage **3. DECORATION IMITATING FLOWERS AND FOLIAGE** something decorative made in imitation of a sprig of flowers and foliage, e.g., a brooch [13C. Origin ?]

spray can *n* a small pressurized container used to disperse liquids in a fine mist

spray gun *n* a device that uses pressure to apply atomized paint or other liquids, operated by means of a trigger

spread /spred/ *v* (**spread, spread·ing, spreads**) **1.** *vt* **OPEN SOMETHING TO FULLEST EXTENT** to open or extend something to its fullest area **2.** *vti* **EXTEND WIDELY** to extend over a large area, or cause something to extend over a large area ○ *A vast plain spread out before them.* **3.** *vti* **EXTEND IN TIME** to extend something over a period of time, or be extended over a period **4.** *vti* **EXTEND IN RANGE** to extend over a wider range, or cause something to cover a wider range than before **5.** *vt* **SEPARATE THINGS BY STRETCHING** to separate things by stretching or pulling, so that they become far apart **6.** *vti* **BECOME OR MAKE KNOWN** to become widely known, or make something widely known **7.** *vt* **APPLY COATING TO SOMETHING** to coat something with a layer of a substance, especially one smoothly applied **8.** *vti* **DISPERSE** to disperse something over a wide area, or be dispersed in this way ○ *Let's spread out so we can search over a wider area.* **9.** *vti* **SEND OUT IN ALL DIRECTIONS** to send out something in all directions, or to be sent out in all directions ○ *The lamp spread its light.* **10.** *vt* **DISPLAY SOMETHING IN FULL** to exhibit or display something in its fullest extent **11.** *vt* **DIVIDE SOMETHING UP** to divide, share, or split something up among several people or groups ○ *They decided to spread out the money more evenly among the various departments.* **12.** *vt* **GET TABLE READY FOR MEAL** to prepare a table for a meal **13.** *vt* **PUT FOOD ON TABLE** to lay out food or a meal on a table ■ *n* **1. EXTENSION OF SOMETHING** the extension, diffusion, or distribution of something over an area, range, or time **2. VARIETY** a wide variety of things **3. LIMIT OF EXTENSION** the limit to which something can be extended **4. DISTANCE BETWEEN THINGS** the distance or range between two points or things **5. EXPANSE OF LAND** a large expanse of land **6. RANCH OR FARM** a piece of land and its buildings used for ranching or farming **7. BED OR TABLE COVER** a covering for a bed or table **8.** WIDENING OF BODY a widening of the hips and waist owing to weight gain (*informal*) **9.** FOOD SPREADABLE FOOD a food with a soft texture, designed to be spread on bread or crackers **10.** FOOD MEAL a large meal laid out on a table (*informal*) **11.** MEDIA PAIR OF FACING PAGES two facing pages in a newspaper, magazine, or book, often with material printed across the fold **12.** MEDIA EXTENSIVE STORY OR AD an advertisement or story that occupies two or more columns in a newspaper or magazine **13.** AVIAT PLANE'S WINGSPAN the wingspan of an airplane (*informal*) **14.** FIN DIFFERENCE BETWEEN BID AND OFFER the difference between the asking price and the bid price of a security **15.** *US* FIN COMMODITIES MARKET TRANSACTION a transaction in a commodities market in which an investor takes long and short positions in different commodities or different delivery dates in the same commodity **16.** JEWELRY GEMSTONE SIZE the size of a gemstone when viewed from above, expressed in carats ■ *adj* **1.** EXTENDED extended or stretched out **2.** JEWELRY SHALLOW describes a gemstone that is shallow and flat **3.** PHON SAID WITH LIPS STRAIGHT describes a speech sound that is pronounced with the lips forming a horizontal line [Old English *sprǣdan* < Indo-European, "strew"] —**spread·able** *adj*

spread bet·ting *n* a form of gambling that involves betting on the movement of a stock price in relation to a given range of high and low values. If the stock price moves outside the values on a given day, the bettor wins a multiple of the original stake times the number of points above or below the set range.

spread cit·y *n* a city that has no defined center but is not a suburb of a major city

spread ea·gle *n* **1.** SYMBOLIC IMAGE OF EAGLE the image of an eagle with its wings and legs outstretched, especially when used as an emblem of the United States. The spread eagle appears on the Great Seal of the United States. **2.** SKATING FIGURE in ice skating, a figure performed with the blades touching heel to heel **3.** POSTURE WITH SPREAD LIMBS a way of standing or lying with arms and legs spread apart

spread-ea·gle *v* **1.** *vt* FORCE SOMEBODY INTO SPREAD-OUT POSITION to force somebody to stand or lie with arms and legs spread apart, especially when being arrested or searched **2.** *vi* ADOPT POSITION WITH SPREAD LIMBS to stand or lie with arms and legs spread apart **3.** *vt* STRETCH BODY ACROSS to stand or lie with limbs spread wide across a gap or an object **4.** *vi* PERFORM SKATING FIGURE in ice skating, to perform a spread eagle ■ *adj US* **1.** OVERLY PATRIOTIC boastful or chauvinistically patriotic about the United States (*slang*) **2.** IN SPREAD-OUT POSITION standing or lying with arms and legs spread apart. Can term **spread-eagled**

spread-ea·gled *adj Can, UK* same as **spread-eagle** *adj* (sense 2)

spread·er /spréddər/ *n* **1.** DEVICE FOR DISTRIBUTING SEED OR FERTILIZER a machine used by farmers and gardeners to spread manure, fertilizer, seed, or similar material over the ground (*usually used in combination*) **2.** IMPLEMENT FOR SPREADING an implement used for spreading soft substances, e.g., a spatula, trowel, or broad-bladed knife (*usually used in combination*) **3.** DEVICE FOR SEPARATING THINGS a device used to hold things such as cables or wires apart, e.g., a bar

spread·ing fac·tor /sprédding-/ *n* BIOL same as **hyaluronidase**

spread·sheet /spréd shèet/ *n* **1.** a computer program that displays numerical data in cells in a simulated accountant's worksheet of rows and columns in which hidden formulas can perform calculations on the visible data. Changing the contents of one cell can cause automatic recalculation of other cells. **2.** the display or printout of a spreadsheet, showing the many lines and columns of a ledger

sprech·ge·sang /shprékhgə zàng, shprék-/, **Sprech·ge·sang** *n* a style of singing that incorporates aspects of ordinary nonmusical speech [Early 20C. < German, "speech song"]

sprech·stim·me /shprékh shtìmmə, shprék-/, **Sprech·stim·me** *n* **1.** the voice used to sing sprechgesang **2.** MUSIC same as **sprechgesang** [Early 20C. < German, "speech voice"]

spree /spree/ *n* **1.** a session of extravagant self-indulgent activity, especially of spending or drinking, but also of criminal activity **2.** a fun-filled sociable outing (*dated*) [Late 18C. Origin ?]

sprez·za·tu·ra /sprètsə tóorə/ *n* **1.** unstudied grace in art, music, or literature **2.** elegant unstudied carelessness in attitude and personal behavior [Mid-20C. < Italian]

sprig /sprig/ *n* **1.** SMALL BRANCH a shoot, stem, or twig cut or broken from a plant ○ *garnished with a sprig of parsley* **2.** DECORATION an artistic representation of a sprig that is usually repeated in rows on fabric or wallpaper to produce a decorative pattern **3.** YOUTH a young man (*dated*) **4.** CONSTR SMALL NAIL a small headless tack that tapers to a point ■ *vt* (**sprigged, sprig·ging, sprigs**) **1.** DECORATE SOMETHING WITH SPRIG PATTERN to decorate fabric, wallpaper, or pottery with a pattern of sprigs ○ *a dress of sprigged cotton* **2.** BOT CUT TWIGS FROM PLANT to cut small twigs or branches from a plant **3.** CONSTR NAIL SOMETHING WITH TACKS to nail something using small headless tacks that taper to a point [14C. Origin ?] —**sprig·ger** *n* —**sprig·gy** *adj*

spright·ly /sprítlee/ *adj* (**-li·er, -li·est**) full of life and vigor, especially with a light and springy step ■ *adv* in a lively and vigorous way [Early 16C. < variant of SPRITE] —**spright·li·ness** *n*

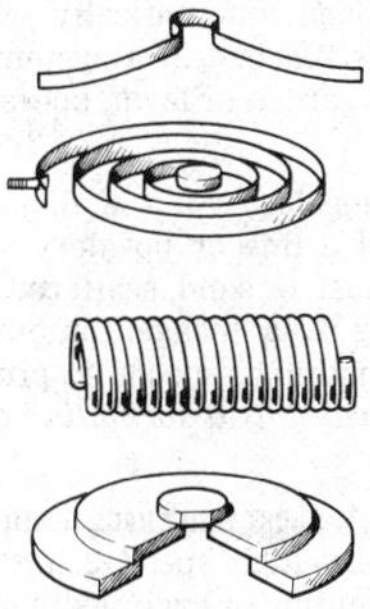

spring

spring /spring/ *v* (**sprang** /sprang/, **sprung** /sprung/, **spring·ing, springs**) **1.** *vi* MOVE SUDDENLY IN SINGLE MOVEMENT to move rapidly upward or forward in a single movement or in a series of rapid movements ○ *He sprang to his feet.* ○ *The lid sprang open.* ○ *She sprang to my defence.* **2.** *vt* LEAP OVER SOMETHING to leap over a barrier **3.** *vi* RAPIDLY RESUME ORIGINAL POSITION to move back rapidly to an original position after being forced in another direction ○ *A branch sprang back and hit me in the face.* **4.** *vi* EMERGE RAPIDLY to appear or come into existence quickly ○ *There are new houses springing up all around the village.* **5.** *vi* COME FROM SOMEBODY'S LIPS to be uttered, especially as a sudden and almost involuntary reaction to something ○ *A cry of rage sprang from his lips.* **6.** *vi* ORIGINATE FROM SOMETHING to originate from a particular source ○ *His behavior seems to spring from an innate sense of insecurity.* **7.** *vi* BE DESCENDED to be descended from a person or family **8.** *vt* MAKE SOMETHING OPERATE to operate a device or trap by releasing a mechanism that was held in check **9.** *vt* FIT SOMETHING WITH SPRINGS to provide something, e.g., a vehicle or piece of furniture with springs (*usually passive*) ○ *a sprung floor* **10.** *vi* JUMP OUT OF PLACE to move suddenly out of place, or come suddenly loose, within a mechanism **11.** *vti* WARP OR SPLIT to crack, split, or warp, or cause wood to do this **12.** *vt* SUDDENLY REVEAL SOMETHING TO SOMEBODY to make something known to somebody, or present somebody with something, unexpectedly or suddenly (*informal*) ○ *You can't just spring a decision like that on me!* **13.** *vt* GET SOMEBODY OUT OF PRISON to release somebody from prison or help somebody escape from prison (*slang*) **14.** *vi* PAY FOR SOMETHING to pay for something, usually on behalf of another person (*slang*) ○ *I'll spring for lunch.* **15.** *vt* HUNTING MOVE ANIMAL FROM COVER to move an animal or bird out into the open during a hunting expedition **16.** *vi* ARCHIT RISE to extend upward from a base, e.g., from the top part of a column ■ *n* **1.** COIL OF METAL a resilient metal coil that will store energy when compressed and will release energy when returning to its original shape. Use: for cushioning, in clockwork. **2.** ABILITY TO REGAIN SHAPE the ability of an object to revert rapidly to its original position after being extended, compressed, or placed under tension ○ *a mattress with a lot of spring left in it* **3.** ONWARD OR UPWARD LEAP a rapid forward or upward movement **4.** SEASON OF YEAR the season between winter and summer during which many plants produce leaves and flowers. It runs from March to May in the northern hemisphere, and September to November in the southern hemisphere. **5.** TIME OF RENEWAL a time of new growth and regeneration **6.** WATER EMERGING FROM UNDERGROUND a source of water that flows out of the ground as a small stream or pool **7.** ORIGIN OF SOMETHING a source from which something, e.g., a character trait, a feeling, or a situation, proceeds or develops (*literary; often used in the plural*) ○ *the springs of her ambition* ■ *adj* **1.** HAPPENING IN SPRINGTIME relating to, occurring in, or appropriate to the season of spring ○ *spring fashions* **2.** GROWN IN SPRINGTIME normally grown or growing in the season of spring ○ *spring flowers* **3.** FULL OF SPRINGS having or containing springs, especially for cushioning or as part of a clockwork mechanism ○ *a spring mattress* **4.** RECOILING acting like a spring in being held back then quickly releasing energy [Old English *springan* < Indo-European, "rapid movement"]

REGIONAL NOTE See *dairy*.

CULTURAL NOTE ***The Rite of Spring***, a ballet (1913) with music by the Russian composer Igor Stravinsky. This one-act work is based on traditional dances performed at pagan festivals in Russia. Its use of dissonance and irregular pulsating rhythms combined with Nijinsky's unorthodox choreography resulted in a famous riot at the first performance in Paris on May 29.

spring beau·ty *n* a spring-flowering succulent herbaceous plant of the purslane family. Flowers: white or pinkish. Native to: eastern North America. Genus: *Claytonia*.

spring·board /spríng bàwrd/ *n* **1.** FLEXIBLE DIVING BOARD a flexible board secured to a base at one end and projecting over the water at the other, used for diving **2.** GYMNASTIC EQUIPMENT a flexible board on which gymnasts bounce in order to gain height for vaulting **3.** EVENT OR FACTOR PROVIDING OPPORTUNITY an event, activity, or plan that provides an opportunity for something or helps to promote future success

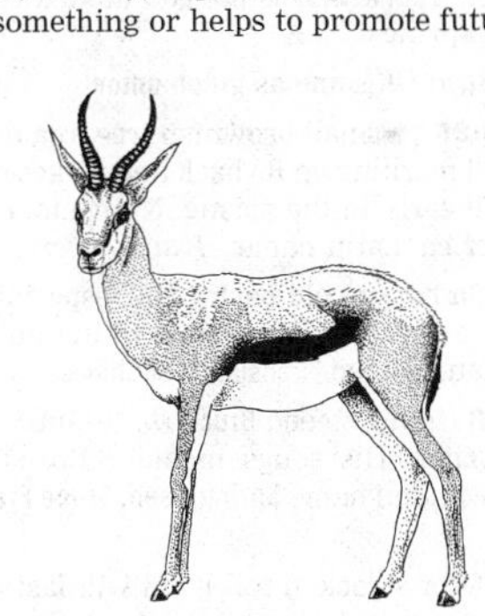
springbok

spring·bok /spríng bòk/ (*plural same* or **-boks**) *n* a small swift gazelle noted for its ability to leap high in the air repeatedly when startled. Native to: semiarid regions of southern Africa. Latin name: *Antidorcas marsupialis*. [Late 18C. < Afrikaans, "leaping he-goat"]

spring break *n* a vacation from school or college in the spring, usually lasting at least a week

spring·buck /spríng bùk/ (*plural same* or **-bucks**) *n* ZOOL same as **springbok**

spring chick·en *n* a chicken less than ten months old [Because formerly available for eating only in spring] ◇ **no spring chicken** no longer young, inexperienced, or agile

spring-clean·ing *n* the thorough cleaning of a house or room, traditionally at the end of the winter

Spring·dale /spríng dàyl/ city in northwestern Arkansas, north of Fayetteville. Population: 50,941 (2002 estimate).

springe /sprinj/ *n* a snare or trap for small animals, consisting of a noose attached to a branch under tension [13C. Ultimately < Germanic]

spring·er /spríngər/ *n* **1.** SOMEBODY OR SOMETHING THAT LEAPS a person or animal that springs or leaps **2.** BREED same as **springer spaniel 3.** ARCHIT **WEDGE-SHAPED STONE** the first wedge-shaped stone (**voussoir**) of an arch resting on the top section of the arch's supporting pillar (**impost**) **4.** AGRIC **COW READY TO GIVE BIRTH** a cow that is on the point of giving birth to a calf

spring·er span·iel *n* a hunting dog with a long wavy coat, short legs, and floppy ears, belonging to either an English or a Welsh breed

spring fe·ver *n* a feeling of restlessness, yearning, lust, or sometimes laziness, believed to be brought on by the coming of spring

Spring·field /spríng fe̅eld/ **1.** capital of Illinois, on the southern bank of the Sangamon River, west of Decatur. President Abraham Lincoln lived in Springfield from 1844 until 1861 and is buried there. Population: 111,834 (2002 estimate). **2.** city in south central Massachusetts, on the Connecticut River, north of the Connecticut border. It is home to the Basketball Hall of Fame. Population: 151,915 (2002 estimate).

Spring·field ri·fle *n* a bolt-action .30-caliber rifle developed at the federal arsenal in Springfield, Massachusetts, used by the US Army in World War I

spring·form pan /spríng fawrm-/ *n* a cake pan with a detachable base that fastens to the rim with a spring or clamp

spring·head /spríng hèd/ *n* **1.** the source of a particular way of thinking **2.** the source of a stream

spring·house /spríng hòwss/ (*plural* **-hous·es** /-hòwzəz/) *n* a storehouse built over a spring, formerly used to keep meat and dairy products fresh and cool

REGIONAL NOTE See *dairy*.

spring·ing /sprínging/ *n* the point at which an arch, vault, or dome rises from its support

spring line *n* a rope by means of which a sailing vessel is made fast to an anchorage, usually one of two

spring-load·ed *adj* describes a mechanism that is fixed in place or controlled by a spring

spring lock *n* a lock that is bolted automatically by means of a spring

spring on·ion *n UK* same as **green onion**

spring peep·er *n* a small brownish tree frog that has an X-shaped marking on its back and makes a shrill peeping call early in the spring. Native to: eastern North America. Latin name: *Hyla crucifer*.

spring roll *n* a hot or cold pastry roll, especially one made with a meat and vegetable filling and fried until crisp and golden [Translation of Chinese *chūn juǎn*]

Spring·steen /spríng ste̅en/, **Bruce** (*b.* 1949) US singer and songwriter. His songs include "Born in the U.S.A." (1984). Full name **Springsteen, Bruce Frederick Joseph**

> "The life of a rock-'n-roll band will last as long as you look down into the audience and can see yourself, and your audience looks up at you and can see themselves."
> [Bruce Springsteen. Quoted in *Springsteen*, Robert Hilburn; 1985]

spring·tail /spríng tàyl/ *n* a primitive wingless insect with a forked abdominal structure that helps it spring through the air. Order: Collembola.

spring tide *n* **1.** a tide that occurs near the times of the new moon and full moon and has a greater than average range **2.** a great rush of emotion (*literary*)

spring·tide /spríng tīd/ *n* same as **springtime** (*literary*)

spring·time /spríng tīm/ *n* **1.** the season of spring, between winter and summer **2.** the earliest, freshest, and most pleasant stage of somebody's life, a relationship, or a period of time (*literary*)

spring·wood /spríng wòod/ *n* young relatively soft wood that develops just beneath the bark of trees in spring

spring·y /springee/ (**-i·er, -i·est**) *adj* **1.** springing back strongly to its original shape after being compressed or extended **2.** tending to make a lot of springing movements (*informal*) —**spring·i·ly** *adv* —**spring·i·ness** *n*

sprin·kle /spríngk'l/ *v* (**-kled, -kling, -kles**) **1.** *vt* **DISTRIBUTE SMALL AMOUNTS OF SOMETHING** to scatter small drops of a liquid, or particles of a fine or powdery substance, e.g., sugar, ashes, or flour, over the surface of something **2.** *vt* **SCATTER OR BE SCATTERED THROUGHOUT THINGS** to scatter things in among other things, at random or as though at random, or be scattered among other things in this way ○ *fields sprinkled with poppies* **3.** *vi* **RAIN VERY SLIGHTLY** to rain very gently in fine drops, usually for a short period **4.** *vt* **GIVE SOMETHING OUT IN SMALL AMOUNTS** to distribute a substance, emotion, or commodity in small amounts ■ *n* **1.** **ACT OF SPRINKLING** the action of scattering small drops of liquid or particles of a fine or powdery substance **2.** same as **sprinkling** (sense 1) **3.** **LIGHT RAIN** a light rain falling in fine or sporadic drops ■ **sprin·kles** *npl* FOOD **SUGAR PARTICLES FOR DECORATING CAKES** small pieces of colored sugar or candy that are scattered over the surface of ice cream, cakes, or cookies as a decoration [14C. Origin ?]

sprin·kler /springklər/ *n* **1.** a device that sends out a moving spray of water, used for watering gardens or for suppressing fires **2.** a plastic or metal nozzle perforated with many small holes that fits onto a watering can or hose

sprin·kler sys·tem *n* **1.** a system for extinguishing fires, designed to release water from overhead nozzles that open automatically when a specific temperature is reached **2.** a system of sprinklers for watering a garden or lawn, operated by a single control

sprin·kling /springkling/ *n* **1.** a small quantity of drops of liquid or of a fine or powdery substance, e.g., sugar, snow, dust, or sand, scattered on or throughout something **2.** a meager amount or a small number of something, especially spread over a wide area ○ *There was only a sprinkling of people in the hall.*

sprint /sprint/ *n* **1.** **SHORT SWIFT RACE** a short race run or cycled at a very high speed **2.** **FAST FINISHING RUN** a burst of fast running or cycling during the last part of a longer race **3.** **BURST OF ACTIVITY** a sudden burst of activity or speed ■ *vi* (**sprint·ed, sprint·ing, sprints**) **GO AT TOP SPEED** to run, swim, or cycle as rapidly as possible [Mid-16C. < Old Norse *spretta* "jump"]

sprint·er /sprintər/ *n* an athlete or cyclist who takes part in a short race run or cycled at a very high speed

sprit /sprit/ *n* a pole that crosses a fore-and-aft sail diagonally [Old English *sprēot* < Germanic]

sprite /sprīt/ *n* **1.** **SUPERNATURAL ELFIN CREATURE** in folklore, a small supernatural being like an elf or a fairy, especially one associated with water **2.** **SOMEBODY LIKE ELF** a small or delicately built person who is likened to an elf or a fairy **3.** **GHOST** in folklore, a ghost or spirit **4.** COMPUT **INDEPENDENT GRAPHIC OBJECT** an independent graphic object that moves freely across a computer screen [14C. Via French < Latin *spiritus* (see SPIRIT)]

sprit·sail /sprít sàyl/; *nautical* /spritsəl/ *n* a sail that is extended by being mounted on a sprit

spritz /sprits/ *vt* (**spritzed, spritz·ing, spritz·es**) to spray a fine jet of liquid through a nozzle ■ *n* a fine spray of liquid squirted through a nozzle [Early 20C. < German *spritzen* "squirt, splash"]

spritz·er /spritsər/ *n* a drink consisting of wine, generally white, diluted with sparkling water [Mid-20C. < German, "splash" < *spritzen* "to squirt, splash"]

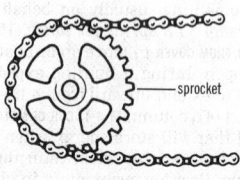

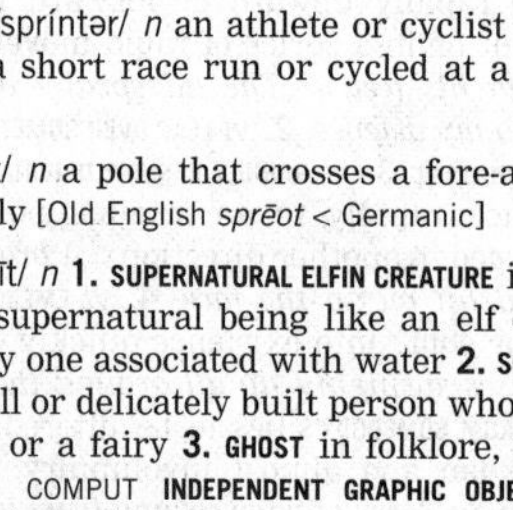

sprocket

sprock·et /spròkət/ *n* **1.** a projecting tooth on a wheel or cylinder that engages with the links of a chain or with perforations in film to make the chain or film move forward **2.** *also* **sprock·et wheel** a wheel with sprockets [Mid-16C. Origin ?]

sprog /sprog/ *n UK* a child or baby (*slang*) [Mid-20C. Origin ?]

sprout /sprowt/ *v* (**sprout·ed, sprout·ing, sprouts**) **1.** *vti* **DEVELOP SHOOTS** to develop buds or shoots **2.** *vi* **GERMINATE** to begin to grow from a seed **3.** *vti* **GROW** to grow from something, or have something growing from or on it ○ *His chin was suddenly sprouting hair.* **4.** *vti* **EMERGE** to emerge and grow rapidly, or cause something to emerge and grow rapidly ○ *New tourist hotels were sprouting up all along the coast.* ■ *n* **1.** **NEW GROWTH ON PLANT** a new growth on a plant, e.g., a bud or shoot **2.** **SOMETHING LIKE SPROUT** somebody or something that grows rapidly **3.** PLANTS, FOOD same as **Brussels sprout** ■ **sprouts** *npl* **EDIBLE SHOOTS OF PLANTS** newly sprouted seeds or beans, eaten especially in sandwiches, salads, and stir-fries [Old English *-sprūtan* < Germanic]

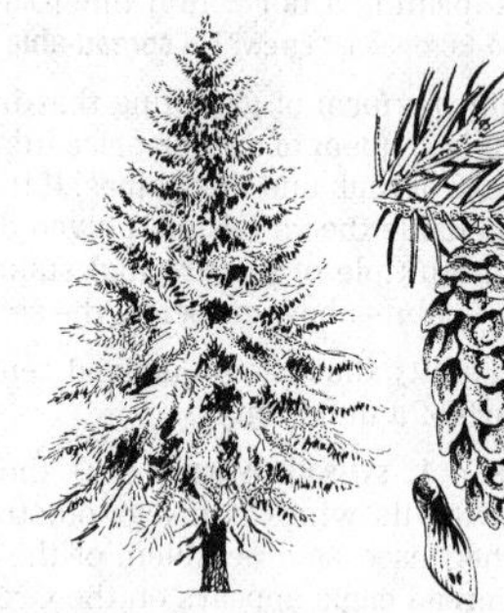

spruce

spruce[1] /sprooss/ (*plural* **spruc·es** or *same*) *n* **1.** an evergreen tree of the pine family with a pyramid shape, short needles, drooping cones, and soft light wood. Genus: *Picea*. **2.** the soft light wood of a spruce tree [Early 17C. Shortening of *Spruce fir* "Prussian fir" < alteration of obsolete *Pruce* "Prussia" < medieval Latin *Prussia*]

spruce[2] /sprooss/ *vti* (**spruced, spruc·ing, spruc·es**) to make a person, usually yourself, or a place cleaner and neater in appearance ○ *sprucing up the city for the celebrations* ■ *adj* having a clean and well-cared-for appearance ○ *a spruce young man* [Late 16C. Origin ?] —**spruce·ly** *adv*

spruce beer *n* a fermented drink whose ingredients include spruce leaves and twigs

spruce grouse *n* a common plump game bird with a black throat and breast. Native to: coniferous forests of North America. Latin name: *Dendragapus canadensis*.

spruce pine *n* a tall pine with soft wood and needles in pairs. Native to: southeastern United States. Latin name: *Pinus glabra*.

sprue[1] /sproo/ *n* a tropical disease of unknown origin involving deficient absorption of nutrients from the intestine and marked by persistent diarrhea, weight loss, and anemia [Late 19C. < Dutch *spruw* "the disease thrush"]

sprue[2] /sproo/ *n* **1.** a vertical channel in a mold, used to pour in molten material **2.** a piece of waste material from molding plastic or metal, especially one of the supporting pieces that connect small parts molded at the same time [Early 19C. Origin ?]

sprung past participle of **spring**

sprung rhythm *n* a system of prosody that uses metrical feet with a varying number of syllables in an effort to evoke the irregular stresses and rhythms of ordinary speech

spry /sprī/ (**spry·er** or **spri·er, spry·est** or **spri·est**) *adj* markedly brisk and active, especially at an advanced age [Mid-18C. Origin ?] —**spry·ly** *adv* —**spry·ness** *n*

spud /spud/ *n* **1.** FOOD same as **potato** (senses 1–2) (*slang*) **2.** GARDENING **GARDEN IMPLEMENT** a spade with a sharp narrow blade, used for cutting through roots and digging up weeds ■ *v* (**spud·ded, spud·ding, spuds**)

1. *vi* START DRILLING OIL WELL to use a large bit to drill the upper part of the bore of a new oil well 2. *vt* GARDENING DIG SOMETHING UP WITH SPUD to use a spud to dig up weeds or cut through roots [15C. Origin ?]

spume /spyoom/ (*literary*) *n* a mass of fine bubbles on the surface of a liquid, especially on the ocean ■ *vi* (**spumed, spum·ing, spumes**) to produce or have a mass of fine bubbles on the surface [14C. Directly or via French < Latin *spuma* "foam"] —**spum·y** *adj*

spu·mo·ni /spoo mṓnee/, **spu·mo·ne** *n* an Italian ice cream composed of differently colored and flavored layers, often containing nuts and candied fruit [Early 20C. < Italian < *spuma* "foam" < Latin]

spun past participle, past tense of **spin**

spun glass *n* 1. INDUST same as **fiberglass** (sense 1) 2. blown glass that has slender, often spiral glass threading or filigree incorporated into it

spunk /spungk/ *n* 1. PLUCKINESS spiritedness or eager willingness (*informal*) 2. TABOO TERM a highly offensive term for semen (*taboo*) 3. TINDER a combustible material, especially soft wood or twigs, that can be used to kindle fires [Mid-16C. Origin ?]

spunk·y /spúngkee/ (**-i·er, -i·est**) *adj* very lively, determined, and courageous (*informal*) —**spunk·i·ly** *adv* —**spunk·i·ness** *n*

spun silk *n* inexpensive fabric or yarn made from short-fibered silk combined with silk waste

spun sug·ar *n US* FOOD same as **cotton candy**

spun yarn *n* rope or cord made from several light yarns twisted or spun together

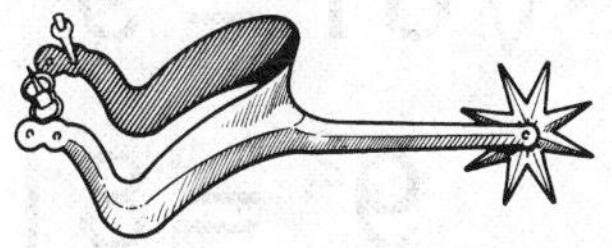

spur

spur /spur/ *n* 1. DEVICE ATTACHED TO RIDER'S HEEL a small spike or spiked wheel attached to the heel of a rider's boot that is nudged into the horse's sides to encourage it to go faster 2. INDUCEMENT something that encourages a person or organization to take action or to make a greater effort, e.g., the hope of a reward or the fear of punishment 3. PROJECTION something that projects outward at an angle from a larger object 4. PROJECTING PLANT PART a tubular extension from a flower part, as, e.g., in larkspur and columbine 5. SHORT BRANCH OR SHOOT a short branch or lateral shoot from a stem or branch of a plant 6. HORNY PROJECTION a sharp horny projection on the legs of some male birds such as domestic roosters above the claws 7. PROJECTING ANIMAL PART a pointed extension or projecting part (**process**) on some animals, e.g., the stiff outgrowth on the legs of some insects and birds 8. SHORT BONY OUTGROWTH a bony outgrowth, usually a normal part of the body but sometimes one that develops such as that on the bottom of the heel after an injury 9. SPIKE ON LEG OF GAMECOCK a sharp metal spike attached to the leg of a gamecock 10. PART OF RAILROAD a short section of railroad track leading off a main line 11. MOUNTAIN RIDGE a ridge that projects outward from a mountain range and descends toward a valley floor 12. ROAD OFF MAJOR ROAD a short side road leading off a main road ■ *v* (**spurred, spur·ring, spurs**) 1. *vt* ENCOURAGE SOMEBODY TO TRY HARDER to stimulate a person or organization to take action or make greater efforts in the hope of a reward or in the fear of punishment ○ *"Public schools are spurred to perform better thanks to new reforms."* (*US News & World Report*; December 1998) 2. *vt* MAKE HORSE GO FASTER to encourage a horse to go faster by nudging spurs into its sides 3. *vt* PUT SPURS ON SOMEBODY OR SOMETHING to equip somebody or something with spurs 4. *vi* RIDE FAST to ride fast, using spurs (*literary*) 5. *vi* GO QUICKLY to go or proceed hastily (*literary*) [Old English *spura* < Indo-European, "to kick"] —**spurred** *adj* ◇ **on the spur of the moment** on impulse and without forethought ◇ **win** *or* **gain your spurs** 1. to gain recognition and respect for the first time 2. in the past, to be given the rank of knight

SYNONYMS See ***motive***.

spurge /spurj/ *n* an herbaceous plant or bush that has flowers without petals and a bitter milky juice. Genus: *Euphorbia*. [14C. < Old French *espurge* < *espurgier* "purge" < Latin *expurgare* (see EXPURGATE)]

spur gear *n* a gear whose teeth are arranged along the rim parallel to its axis of rotation

spurge lau·rel *n* a low-growing evergreen bush with elongated glossy leaves. Flowers: yellow. Native to: Europe, Asia. Latin name: *Daphne laureola*.

spu·ri·ous /spyoóree əs/ *adj* 1. NOT GENUINE different from what it is claimed to be, not authentic, or not valid or well-founded ○ *spurious arguments* 2. BOT RESEMBLING ANOTHER PLANT PART having the outward appearance of another plant part but not its function or origin 3. ILLEGITIMATE born to parents not legally married to each other (*archaic*) [Late 16C. < Latin *spurius* "illegitimate child"] —**spu·ri·ous·ly** *adv* —**spu·ri·ous·ness** *n*

spurn /spurn/ *v* (**spurned, spurn·ing, spurns**) 1. *vti* REJECT SOMEBODY OR SOMETHING WITH DISDAIN to reject a person, offer, gift, or advances with scorn and contempt 2. *vt* THRUST SOMETHING AWAY WITH FOOT to reject something by pushing it away with the foot (*archaic*) ■ *n* (*archaic*) 1. SCORNFUL REJECTION a contemptuous or scornful rejection 2. KICK a kick with the foot [Old English *spurnan* < Indo-European] —**spurn·er** *n*

spur-of-the-mo·ment *adj* happening, made, or done in haste, without reflection or preparation ○ *a spur-of-the-moment purchase*

spur·ry /spúr ee, spúrree/ (*plural* **-ries**), **spur·rey** (*plural* **-reys**) *n* a low-growing plant of the pink family with linear whorled leaves. Flowers: small, white. Native to: Europe. Genus: *Spurgula*. [Late 16C. < Dutch *spurrie*]

spurt /spurt/ *n* 1. JET OF LIQUID OR GAS a sudden stream of liquid or gas, forced out under pressure 2. SUDDEN BURST OF ENERGY a short intense burst of energy, interest, action, or speed ○ *I had a spurt of energy as I was digging.* 3. SUDDEN INCREASE a sudden increase in the amount, development, or speed of something ○ *a fourth-quarter spurt in inflation* ■ *vti* (**spurt·ed, spurt·ing, spurts**) GUSH OUT to gush out in a pressurized stream or jet, or cause a liquid or gas to do this ○ *Blood spurted from the wound.* [Mid-16C. Origin ?]

spur·tle /spúrt'l/ *n Scotland* a short stick, frequently with a decorative end, used for stirring oatmeal [Early 16C. Origin ?]

spur wheel *n* MECH ENG same as **spur gear**

spu·ta MED plural of **sputum**

sput·nik /spútnik, spoŏt-/ *n* one of a series of ten artificial Earth-orbiting satellites launched by the former Soviet Union starting in 1957 [Mid-20C. < Russian, "fellow traveler"]

sput·ter /spúttər/ *v* (**-tered, -ter·ing, -ters**) 1. *vi* MAKE POPPING SOUND to make a popping, spitting sound 2. *vi* SPEAK EXPLOSIVELY to make sounds or pronounce words in an explosive way, especially when angry or excited 3. *vi* SPIT OUT FOOD AND SALIVA to spray out drops of saliva or food particles, especially when talking or laughing while eating 4. *vti* PHYS REMOVE SURFACE ATOMS BY ION BOMBARDMENT to cause, or experience, an effect in which the atoms of a surface are removed through bombardment by ions, e.g., in cathode evaporation in a discharge tube 5. *vt* PHYS USE METAL TO COAT SOMETHING to use metal removed by the process of sputtering to coat something ■ *n* 1. NOISE OF SPUTTERING the noise of a person, fire, candle, or other object sputtering 2. INCOHERENT SPEECH the confused or incoherent speech of somebody who is angry or excited [Late 16C. < Dutch *sputteren* "spray"] —**sput·ter·er** *n*

spu·tum /spyoótəm/ (*plural* **-ta** /-tə/) *n* a substance coughed up from the respiratory tract and usually ejected by mouth, e.g., saliva, phlegm, or mucus [Late 17C. < Latin, "saliva" < *spuere* "to spit"]

spy /spī/ *n* (*plural* **spies**) 1. SOMEBODY EMPLOYED TO OBTAIN SECRET INFORMATION an employee of a government who seeks secret information in or from another country, especially about military matters ○ *a spy ring* 2. EMPLOYEE WHO OBTAINS INFORMATION ABOUT RIVALS an employee of a company who seeks secret information about rival organizations 3. SECRET OBSERVER OF OTHERS a watcher of other people in secret 4. ACT OF SPY an instance of acting as a spy ■ *v* (**spied, spy·ing, spies**) 1. *vi* ACT AS SPY to work, operate, or function as a spy 2. *vi* ENGAGE IN ESPIONAGE to maintain a network of spies and gather intelligence in other clandestine ways 3. *vi* OBSERVE IN SECRET to keep watch secretly or furtively on somebody or something in order to gain information ○ *Have you been spying on us again?* 4. *vi* INVESTIGATE to try to discover information about something or somebody by means of intensive covert investigations ○ *trying to spy into their customers' purchasing habits* 5. *vt* SEE SOMEBODY OR SOMETHING SUDDENLY to catch sight of somebody or something, often by chance ○ *I happened to look out of the window and spied him scuttling across the yard.* 6. *vt* DISCOVER SOMETHING BY OBSERVATION to discover something by close observation [13C. < Old French *espie* < *espier* "to spy" < Germanic]

spy out *vt* 1. to discover something by close and discreet examination ○ *Once he had spied out her weaknesses, he would know how to apply pressure.* 2. to try to gain information about something by close and discreet examination or by secret reconnaissance ○ *sent scouts ahead to spy out the land between the river and the mountains*

spy·glass /spī́ glàss/ *n* a telescope that is small enough to be held in the hand

spy·mas·ter /spī́ màstər/ *n* the leader of espionage and intelligence-gathering activities for a country or organization, especially in fictional spy stories

spy·ware /spī́ wèr/ *n* software surreptitiously installed on a hard disk without the user's knowledge that relays encoded information on his or her identity and Internet use via an Internet connection

sq. *abbr* 1. sequence 2. MIL squadron 3. MEASURE square *adj* (sense 5) [Latin, "the one that follows"]

Sq. *abbr* 1. MIL Squadron 2. square *n* (sense 4) (*used in addresses*)

SQL /èss kyoo él, seékwəl/ *n* a standardized language that approximates the structure of natural English for obtaining information from databases. Full form **structured query language**

squab /skwob/ *n* (*plural* **squabs** or *same*) 1. YOUNG BIRD a young bird just starting to fly, especially a pigeon, sometimes cooked as a delicacy 2. CUSHION a thick cushion used especially as the seat or sometimes as the back of a chair or sofa ■ *adj* (**squab·ber, squab·best**) NEWLY HATCHED newly hatched and not flying yet [Late 17C. Origin ?]

squab·ble /skwóbb'l/ *vi* (**-bled, -bling, -bles**) to have a petty argument over a trivial matter ■ *n* a noisy argument over a petty matter [Early 17C. An imitation of the sound]

squad /skwod/ *n* 1. GROUP OF POLICE OFFICERS a group of police officers, generally assigned to a particular task ○ *the bomb squad* 2. *US* GROUP OF SOLDIERS one of three or four groups of soldiers that make up a platoon 3. SPORTS TEAM an athletic team ○ *the volleyball squad* 4. TEAM OF PEOPLE a small group of people engaged in the same activity ○ *a squad of volunteers* [Mid-17C. Via French *escouade* and Italian *squadra* or Spanish *escuadra* < assumed Vulgar Latin *exquadra* (see SQUARE)]

squad car *n* a police car linked by radio with police headquarters

squad·ron /skwóddrən/ *n* 1. NAVAL UNIT a naval unit containing two or more divisions of a fleet 2. AIR FORCE UNIT a unit of a tactical air force belonging to a group and containing two or more flights 3. CAVALRY UNIT an armored cavalry unit belonging to a regiment and containing two or more troops 4. GROUP an organized group of people, animals, or objects [Mid-16C. < Italian *squadrone* "large squad" < *squadra* (see SQUAD)]

squad room *n US* 1. a room in a police station where officers are briefed 2. a room in a barracks where a number of soldiers are housed

squa·lene /skwáy leen/ *n* a hydrocarbon that is an intermediate in the formation of cholesterol.

Source: human sebum, shark-liver oil. [Early 20C. < modern Latin *Squalus* < Latin, "an ocean fish"]

squal·id /skwólləd/ *adj* **1.** neglected, insanitary and unpleasant **2.** lacking in honesty, dignity, and moral value ○ *a squalid little scandal* [Late 16C. < Latin *squalidus* "filthy, rough" < *squalere* "be filthy" < *squalus* "filthy"] —**squal·id·ly** *adv* —**squal·id·ness** *n*

SYNONYMS See *dirty*.

squall[1] /skwawl/ *n* **1. WINDSTORM** a sudden strong wind, often with heavy rain or snow **2. BRIEF DISTURBANCE** a short but noisy disturbance ■ *vi* (**squalled, squall·ing, squalls**) **BLOW STRONGLY** to blow strongly and suddenly (*refers to winds*) [Late 17C. Origin ?]

squall[2] /skwawl/ *vi* (**squalled, squall·ing, squalls**) to cry or yell hoarsely ■ *n* a noisy cry or yell [Mid-17C. Origin ?] —**squall·er** *n*

squall line *n* a series of small storms that occur along a cold front

squall·y /skwáwlee/ (**-i·er, -i·est**) *adj* **1.** occurring in or characterized by strong gusts, often accompanied by rain or snow **2.** marked by sudden short noisy arguments

squal·or /skwóllər/ *n* **1.** shabbiness and dirtiness resulting from poverty or neglect **2.** a state of moral degradation [Early 17C. < Latin, "dirtiness, roughness" < *squalere* (see SQUALID)]

squa·ma /skwáymə, skwáa-/ (*plural* **-mae** /-mee/) *n* a scale, or a structure resembling a scale, of the type that make up the covering of fish, reptiles, and some mammals [Early 18C. < Latin, "scale"]

squa·mate /skwáy màyt, skwáa-/ *n* a reptile of the order that comprises all lizards and snakes and includes about 6,000 species. Order: Squamata. ■ *adj* having scales, or structures resembling scales, of the type that make up the covering of fish, reptiles, and some mammals —**squa·ma·tion** /skwə máysh'n/ *n*

squa·mi·form /skwáymə fàwrm/ *adj* resembling a scale or scales of the type that make up the covering of fish, reptiles, and some mammals

squa·mo·sal /skway mṓss'l, skwə-/ *n* a thin plate-shaped bone of the vertebrate skull that forms the forward and upper part of the temporal bone in humans [Mid-19C. < Latin *squamosus* (see SQUAMOUS)]

squa·mous /skwáyməss, skwáa-/, **squa·mose** /-mṓss/ *adj* **1. OF SCALES ON BODY** covered with, consisting of, or resembling scales or thin plates of the type that make up the covering of fish, reptiles, and some mammals **2. CONSISTING OF SCALE-SHAPED CELLS** describes a layer of skin (**epithelium**) made up of small scale-shaped cells **3. OF SKULL BONE** relating to the squamosal in the vertebrate skull [15C. < Latin *squamosus* < *squama* "scale"]

squa·mous cell car·ci·no·ma *n* a common type of cancer that usually develops in the epithelial layer of the skin but sometimes in various mucous membranes of the body

squa·mu·lose /skwáymyə lṑss, skwáamyə-/ *adj* having or consisting of tiny scales of the type that make up the covering of fish, reptiles, and some mammals [Mid-19C. < *squamule* "small scale" < Latin *squamula* < *squama* "scale"]

squan·der /skwóndər/ *vt* (**-dered, -der·ing, -ders**) to spend or use something precious in a wasteful and extravagant way ■ *n* extravagant spending [Late 16C. Origin ?] —**squan·der·er** *n*

Squan·to /skwóntō/ (1585?–1622) Wampanoag interpreter. He helped the Pilgrims of Plymouth Colony by interpreting for them and showing them how to fish and grow food in New England.

square /skwer/ *n* **1. EQUILATERAL RECTANGLE** a geometric figure with four right angles and four equal sides **2. RECTANGULAR OBJECT** an object in the shape of a square, or a rectangle that is nearly a square **3. ON GAME BOARD** one of the four-sided areas marked out on the board used to play chess, checkers, or other games **4. OPEN SPACE IN CITY** an open, usually four-sided area in a city or town where two or more streets meet, often containing trees, grass, and benches for recreational use **5. CITY BLOCK** a block of buildings surrounded by four streets **6. RESULT OF MULTIPLICATION** the product resulting from multiplying a number or term by itself ○ *The square of 7 is 49.* **7. DRAWING INSTRUMENT** an "L"- or "T"-shaped instrument made of plastic, wood, or metal, used for drawing or measuring right angles **8. DULL UNFASHIONABLE PERSON** an unfashionable person who is out of touch with current popular culture (*dated slang*) **9.** same as **square meal** (*informal*) ○ *getting his three squares a day* ■ *adj* **1. SHAPED LIKE SQUARE** having the shape of a square, with four more or less equal sides and angles ○ *a square table* **2. FORMING RIGHT ANGLE** intersecting at, having, or making a right angle ○ *square corners* **3. CUBIC** in the shape of a cube ○ *a square block of stone* **4. VAGUELY SQUARE IN SHAPE** roughly square or angular in shape, and looking firm and solid **5. OF MEASUREMENT OF SURFACE AREA** used to describe a measurement of area in which the specified unit refers to the length of each side of a square whose surface area constitutes the measurement ○ *100 square feet* **6. WITH SIDES OF SPECIFIED LENGTH** used to describe a square area with sides of a particular length ○ *a room approximately ten feet square* **7. STRAIGHT OR LEVEL** adjusted or made to be perfectly straight, even, level, or lined up with something else ○ *Make sure the picture is square on the wall.* **8. COMPLETELY FAIR** completely fair, honest, and direct ○ *a square deal* **9. NOT OWING MONEY** with all outstanding debts paid up ○ *She paid me back this morning – we're square now.* **10. BORING AND OLD-FASHIONED** boring, unfashionable, and out of touch with current popular culture (*dated slang*) ■ *v* (**squared, squar·ing, squares**) **1.** *vt* **MAKE SOMETHING SQUARE** to make something into a square or rectangular shape **2.** *vt* **MULTIPLY NUMBER BY ITSELF** to multiply a number or term by itself ○ *Seven squared equals 49.* **3.** *vt* **DIVIDE SOMETHING INTO SQUARES** to divide a surface, sheet of paper, or other object into squares **4.** *vt* **SET SOMETHING STRAIGHT** to move an object, item of clothing, or part of the body so that it is straight or level **5.** *vt* **PUT SOMETHING AT RIGHT ANGLES** to adjust something so that it is at right angles to something else, or test something for this alignment **6.** *vi* **BE AT RIGHT ANGLES** to be at right angles to something else **7.** *vt* **BRING SCORES LEVEL** to level the scores, especially in a ball game **8.** *vt* **SETTLE THINGS FAIRLY** to arrive at a fair and equal agreement with somebody about something, especially about paying off money owed ○ *He squared his accounts and left town.* **9.** *vti* **CONCUR OR MAKE SOMETHING AGREE** to agree with another person, fact, event, or idea, or make two facts, events, or ideas concur ○ *does not square with what we know* **10. square your·self** *vr US* **IMPROVE IMPRESSION** to try to improve a relationship or the impression that somebody has of you ○ *Have you squared yourself with the boss?* **11.** *vt* **GET SOMEBODY TO APPROVE SOMETHING** to obtain somebody's agreement or consent to something, sometimes by offering an inducement (*informal*) ○ *I've squared it with the landlord, it'll be OK to repaint the room.* **12.** *vt* **BRIBE SOMEBODY** to bribe another person (*slang*) ○ *You'll get a good table, I've squared the maitre d'.* ■ *adv* **1. AT RIGHT ANGLES** so as to be even, straight, level, or at right angles to something **2. DIRECTLY** in a direct or forceful way (*informal*) ○ *She drove square into the wall.* **3. HONESTLY** in an honest and straightforward way (*informal*) [13C. < Old French *esquare* < Latin *quadrum* < Latin *quat-* "four"] —**square·ness** *n* —**squar·er** *n* —**squar·ish** *adj* ◇ **on the square 1.** at right angles to something, or constructed with right angles **2.** in an honest and direct manner, or direct and honest **3.** done on equal terms, or being on equal terms with somebody ◇ **out of square 1.** not at right angles to something **2.** not in agreement with each other

square away *vt* **1.** to put things in order or complete some necessary activities, especially in order to get ready for something ○ *I've got my equipment squared away for the trip.* **2.** to square the yards of a square-rigged sailing vessel

square off *vi* to take the proper stance for beginning to fight

square up *v* **1.** *vi* **SETTLE DEBTS** to pay bills, accounts, or other sums of money owed to somebody **2.** *vti* **ARRANGE OR BE ARRANGED SATISFACTORILY** to arrange something in an acceptable or pleasing way, or be arranged in an acceptable or pleasing way **3.** *vi* **FACE SOMETHING UNPLEASANT** to confront something unpleasant or frightening **4.** *vi* **ADOPT AGGRESSIVE POSTURE** to put up fists or adopt a similar posture that shows a readiness to fight

square brack·et *n* PRINTING same as **bracket** *n* (sense 3)

square dance *n* **1.** a country dance featuring dancers in pairs or sets, lively music played on fiddles and other instruments, and a caller who announces the steps **2.** a country dance in which four couples form a square —**square danc·er** *n* —**square danc·ing** *n*

square knot *n US* a symmetrical knot that will not slip after tying, made by passing one end of a rope over and around another first in one direction, then in the opposite direction. Can term **reef knot**

square·ly /skwérlee/ *adv* **1. DIRECTLY** in a direct or forceful way ○ *She met my gaze squarely.* **2. HONESTLY** in an honest and straightforward way **3. AT RIGHT ANGLES** in or into a position that is at right angles to something else

square ma·trix *n* a mathematical matrix that has equal numbers of rows and columns

square meal *n* a filling and nourishing meal

square meas·ure *n* a unit or system of units for measuring an area, e.g., a hectare or an acre

square one *n* the beginning or starting point of an activity or process (*informal*) ○ *The experiment failed, so we're back to square one.*

square pyr·a·mid *n* a solid figure with a base that is a square and four faces that are triangles meeting at a common point

square-rigged *adj* having principal sails that are at right angles to the length of the ship

square-rig·ger *n* a sailing vessel equipped with square-shaped sails

$$\sqrt{81} = 9$$

$$9^2 = 81$$

square root

square root *n* a number or quantity that when multiplied by itself gives a particular number or quantity. For example, 4 or –4 is the square root of 16.

square sail *n* a sail with four sides that is usually suspended horizontally on the mast

square shoot·er *n* a straightforward and honest person (*informal*)

square tim·ber *n Can* logs that have been squared off for export

squar·rose /skwá rṑss, skwáa-/ *adj* with many scales or scabs (*dated*) [Mid-18C. < Latin *squarrosus* "scurfy"]

squash

squash[1] /skwosh/ (*plural same* or **squash·es**) *n* **1.** the fruit of any plant of the gourd family, cooked and eaten as a vegetable **2.** a plant yielding or cultivated for its edible gourds. Genus: *Cucurbita.* [Mid-17C. Shortening of Narraganset *asquutasquash* "green things that may be eaten raw"]

squash[2] /skwosh/ *v* (**squashed, squash·ing, squash·es**) **1.** *vt* **CRUSH SOMETHING WITH PRESSURE** to apply pressure to something so that its volume or size is reduced and it is flattened, crushed, or put out of shape ○ *managed to squash it flat before packing it* **2.** *vti* **ENTER OR PUT SOMETHING INTO SMALL SPACE** to force your way into a confined space, or force something into a confined space ○ *people trying to squash into the elevator* **3.** *vt* **PUT DOWN REBELLION** to suppress a revolt or uprising completely by using force **4.** *vt* **MAKE SOMEBODY FEEL SMALL** to silence somebody with a crushing remark or answer **5.** *vi* **BECOME FLAT** to become flat, often making a squelching sound ■ *n* **1.** RACKET GAMES **BALL GAME IN WALLED COURT** a game for two or four participants played in an enclosed court with long-handled rackets and a small ball that may be hit off any of the walls **2. MANY PEOPLE IN SMALL SPACE** a situation in which a lot of people are crushed into a small space **3. ACTION OR NOISE OF SQUASHING** the action or noise that results when something is being squashed [Mid-16C. < Old French *esquasser* < medieval Latin *quassare* (see QUASH²)] —**squash·er** *n*

squash bug *n* a large black bug that is destructive to plants of the gourd family such as squash and pumpkins. Native to: North America. Latin name: *Anasa tristis.*

squash·y /skwóshee/ (**-i·er, -i·est**) *adj* **1. EASILY SQUASHED** soft and easily squashed **2. OVERRIPE** overripe and full of juice **3. SOFT AND WET** soft and waterlogged **4. LOOKING SQUASHED** having a squashed appearance

squat¹ /skwot/ *vi* (**squat·ted, squat·ting, squats**) **1. CROUCH DOWN** to crouch down with the knees bent and the thighs resting on the calves **2. CROUCH DOWN LOW** to crouch close to the ground like an animal, especially in order to avoid being seen **3. OCCUPY PROPERTY WITHOUT LEGAL CLAIM** to occupy land or buildings without permission of the owner or other rights holder ■ *adj* (**squat·ter, squat·test**) **1. SHORT AND SOLID** short and solidly built **2. IN CROUCHED POSTURE** in a crouched position ■ *n* **1. ACTION OF SQUATTING** the action of crouching down with the knees bent and the thighs resting on the calves **2. SQUATTING POSITION** a crouched posture with knees bent and thighs resting on calves **3. WEIGHTLIFTING EXERCISE** an exercise in weightlifting in which the lifter raises a barbell while rising from a crouching position **4.** *UK* **PROPERTY OCCUPIED BY SQUATTERS** a piece of property that is occupied by squatters **5. HARE'S LAIR** the den of a hare [14C. < Old French *esquatir* "crush" < Latin *coactus*, past participle of *cogere* "force together"] —**squat·ness** *n*

squat² *n* same as **diddlysquat** (*slang*) [Mid-20C. Origin?]

squat·ly /skwóttlee/ *adv* in a solid unyielding manner ○ *The piano stood squatly by the window.*

squat·ter /skwóttər/ *n* **1.** an illegal occupant of land or property, especially somebody who takes over and lives in somebody else's empty house **2.** a person or animal that crouches down

squat·ty /skwóttee/ (**-ti·er, -ti·est**) *adj* **1.** short and thickset **2.** positioned close to the ground

squaw /skwaw/ *n* **1.** an offensive term for a Native North American woman or wife (*dated*) **2.** an offensive term for a woman or wife (*slang*) [Mid-17C. < Narraganset *squaws* "woman" or Massachusett *squa*]

USAGE Because the term ***squaw*** is now generally avoided, traditional names of plants and animals that contain it are also being shunned in favor of more scientific alternatives. For example: the preferred term for *squawfish* is now *Colorado pikeminnow.*

squaw·fish /skwáw fish/ (*plural same* or **-fish·es**) *n* same as **Colorado pikeminnow**

squawk /skwawk/ *v* (**squawked, squawk·ing, squawks**) **1.** *vi* **UTTER HARSH CRY** to utter a loud harsh cry **2.** *vti* **COMPLAIN LOUDLY** to complain or protest about something noisily and annoyingly (*informal*) **3.** *vti* **SAY SOMETHING LOUDLY AND SHRILLY** to say something in a loud harsh voice (*informal*) ■ *n* **1. RAUCOUS CRY** a loud raucous cry **2. NOISY COMPLAINT** a noisy and annoying complaint or protest (*informal*) [Early 19C. An imitation of the sound] —**squawk·er** *n*

squawk box *n* a public-address system or one of its speakers, originally box-shaped (*dated slang*)

squeak /skweek/ *v* (**squeaked, squeak·ing, squeaks**) **1.** *vi* **MAKE HIGH-PITCHED SOUND** to make a short high-pitched sound or cry **2.** *vt* **SAY SOMETHING SHRILLY** to say something in a high-pitched voice **3.** *vi* **BARELY MANAGE SOMETHING** to manage to pass, win, or survive something by the narrowest of margins (*informal*) ○ *squeaked through her final exams* **4.** *vi* **BE INFORMER** to give information or evidence about somebody to the police (*slang disapproving*) ■ *n* **HIGH-PITCHED CRY** a short high-pitched sound or cry [14C. An imitation of the sound]

squeak·er /skwéékər/ *n* **1. SOMEBODY OR SOMETHING THAT SQUEAKS** a person, animal, or device that makes a short high-pitched sound or cry **2. NARROWLY WON VICTORY** a competition, election, race, or other event that is won by a very slight margin (*slang*) **3. SNITCH** somebody who informs on somebody to the police (*slang disapproving*)

squeak·y /skwéékee/ (**-i·er, -i·est**) *adj* **1.** having a tendency to squeak **2.** designed to make a squeaking noise when pressed —**squeak·i·ly** *adv*

squeak·y-clean *adj* **1.** so clean that it squeaks when rubbed ○ *His hair was squeaky-clean.* **2.** appearing to be almost unnaturally free from general human shortcomings (*informal*)

squeal /skweel/ *v* (**squealed, squeal·ing, squeals**) **1.** *vti* **GIVE SHORT HIGH CRY** to say something, speak, or make a sound in a loud high-pitched tone **2.** *vi* **BECOME INFORMER** to give information or evidence against somebody to the police (*slang disapproving*) ■ *n* **1. SHRILL CRY** a short high cry expressing pain, excitement, delight, or other strong emotion **2. LOUD HIGH SOUND** the screaming sound made by tires when a vehicle brakes suddenly [13C. An imitation of the sound] —**squeal·er** *n*

squea·mish /skwéémish/ *adj* **1. EASILY MADE TO FEEL SICK** easily sickened by such sights as blood or physical injuries **2. EASILY OFFENDED** easily shocked by such things as violence, the mention of bodily functions, or strong language **3. FASTIDIOUS** excessively scrupulous about manners or behavior [14C. < Anglo-Norman *escoymous*] —**squea·mish·ly** *adv* —**squea·mish·ness** *n*

squee·gee /skwéé jèe/ *n* **1. IMPLEMENT FOR CLEANING WINDOWS** a T-shaped implement edged with plastic or rubber that is drawn across the surface of windows to remove water after washing **2. IMPLEMENT TO ELIMINATE LIQUID** an implement, usually a rubber roller, that is used in printing and photography to remove excess water or ink ■ *vt* (**-geed, -gee·ing, -gees**) **WIPE WITH SQUEEGEE** to wipe or smooth a surface using a squeegee [Mid-19C. < obsolete *squeege* "press," alteration of SQUEEZE]

squee·gee man *n* a man or youth who enters stopped traffic without invitation, attempting to wash motorists' windshields for money (*slang*)

squeeze /skweez/ *v* (**squeezed, squeez·ing, squeez·es**) **1.** *vt* **PRESS SOMETHING FROM TWO SIDES** to press something hard in the hand or between two other objects, especially in order to reduce its size or alter its shape **2.** *vt* **PRESS SOMEBODY AFFECTIONATELY** to exert slight pressure on part of somebody's body such as the hand, knee, or shoulder, usually as a sign of affection and reassurance **3.** *vti* **APPLY PRESSURE** to exert pressure on something ○ *Come on, squeeze harder!* **4.** *vt* **HUG SOMEBODY** to hold somebody tightly in your arms **5.** *vt* **PUSH PERSON OR OBJECT INTO GAP** to force a person, object, or part of the body into or through a small or narrow space **6.** *vi* **PUSH INTO OR THROUGH SMALL SPACE** to push into or through a small, narrow, or crowded space ○ *I squeezed through a gap in the fence.* **7.** *vt* **FIND TIME FOR SOMEBODY OR SOMETHING** to find time or space for somebody or something in a busy schedule ○ *I could squeeze you in at 9:30.* **8.** *vt* **PRESS FRUIT TO OBTAIN JUICE** to compress a piece of fruit, especially a citrus fruit, in order to extract its juice **9.** *vt* **OBTAIN SOMETHING USING PHYSICAL PRESSURE** to extract something by exerting physical pressure on somebody or something **10.** *vt* **EXTORT MONEY OR FAVORS** to obtain something such as money or favors from somebody by means of psychological pressure or threats **11.** *vt* **REQUIRE MONEY FROM SOMEBODY** to make financial demands on somebody, especially for rent and taxes, that place the person in a difficult situation **12.** *vt* **EXCLUDE SOMEBODY** to put an end to somebody's participation in a field of activity ○ *squeezed them out by means of aggressive marketing* **13.** *vt* **PRODUCE SOMETHING WITH DIFFICULTY** to make an effort to produce something ○ *He managed to squeeze out a timid "thank you."* **14.** *vi* **BARELY MANAGE** to barely succeed in winning, passing, or surviving something ○ *managed to squeeze through the exam with a D* **15.** *vt* BASEBALL **BUNT BALL** in baseball, to bunt the ball attempting to bring in the runner from third base **16.** *vt* CARDS **PLAY CARD** in bridge or whist, to lead a card that may force an opponent to discard a valuable card **17.** *vi* **COLLAPSE** to condense or collapse under pressure **18.** *vt* HANDICRAFT **MAKE IMPRESSION** to make an impression or mold of an object using a soft material such as wax or plaster of Paris ■ *n* **1. PHYSICAL PRESSING** a pressing action ○ *gave the sponge a quick squeeze* **2. SOMETHING PRESSED OUT** an amount pressed out of something ○ *Add a squeeze of lemon.* **3. HUG** a hug or close embrace **4. TOUCH THAT SHOWS AFFECTION** the action of briefly clasping somebody's hand, arm, knee, or other part of the body, usually as a sign of affection or reassurance **5. CROWD OF PEOPLE OR THINGS** a group of people or objects crowded together **6.** BASEBALL same as **squeeze play** (sense 1) **7.** CARDS same as **squeeze play** (sense 2) (*informal*) **8.** HANDICRAFT **IMPRESSION OF OBJECT** an impression or mold of an object made by using a soft material such as wax or plaster of Paris **9.** COMM **FINANCIAL PRESSURE** a financial pressure in the form of reduced profit margins or product shortages **10. OFFENSIVE TERM** an offensive term for a sexual or romantic partner (*slang; sometimes considered offensive*) [Mid-16C. Alteration of obsolete *queise*, origin ?] —**squeez·a·ble** *adj* ◇

put the squeeze on somebody (*slang*) **1.** to exert pressure on somebody by means of force and threats in order to extort money or goods or to obtain some other end such as a confession **2.** to place somebody in a difficult situation, especially financially, or pressure somebody to do something

squeeze off *vt* to fire a bullet from a gun

squeeze·box /skwééz bòks/ *n* a concertina or small accordion (*informal*)

squeeze play *n* **1.** in baseball, a play in which the batter bunts the ball in an attempt to bring in the runner from third base **2.** in bridge or whist, a play in which an opponent is forced to discard a valuable and potentially winning card

squeez·er /skwéézər/ *n* a tool or device for squeezing something, especially a kitchen tool for pressing the juice out of citrus fruits ○ *a lemon squeezer*

squelch /skwelch/ *v* (**squelched, squelch·ing, squelch·es**) **1.** *vt* **PUT END TO SOMETHING** to suppress or put a stop to something ○ *squelched the uprising* **2.** *vt* **SILENCE SOMETHING** to silence something such as a rumor or an unwanted remark (*slang*) **3.** *vi* **MAKE SUCKING SOUND** to move with or make a sucking or gurgling sound like that of somebody walking on muddy ground **4.** *vt* **CRUSH SOMETHING** to crush something by trampling ■ *n* **1. SUCKING SOUND** a sucking or gurgling sound like that of somebody walking on muddy ground **2. CRUSHING RETORT** an ingenious or cutting answer to something somebody has said (*slang*) **3.** ELECTRONICS **ELECTRONIC CIRCUIT** an electronic circuit that automatically reduces the gain of a receiver in response to an input signal that exceeds a predetermined level [Early 17C. An imitation of the sound] —**squelch·er** *n* —**squel·chy** *adj*

sque·teague /skwə téég/ (*plural same* or **-teagues**) *n* a large fish of the croaker family, especially an Atlantic weakfish. Native to: Atlantic Ocean. Genus: *Cynoscion.* [Early 19C. < Algonquian]

squib /skwib/ *n* **1. SHORT JOURNALISTIC PIECE** a short humorous piece that acts as a filler in a newspaper **2. PIECE OF SATIRE** a short satirical piece of writing or speech **3.** AEROSP **DEVICE FOR FIRING ROCKET ENGINE** a small device for firing a rocket engine **4. SMALL FIRECRACKER** a small firecracker **5. DUD FIRECRACKER** a faulty firecracker that burns without exploding **6. SOMEBODY UNIMPORTANT** somebody regarded as insignificant or mean-spirited (*archaic*) ■ *v* (**squibbed, squib·bing, squibs**) **1.** *vt* **SATIRIZE SOMEBODY** to write a satirical piece about somebody **2.** *vi* **SET OFF FIREWORK** to set off a small firecracker **3.** *vt* FOOTBALL **KICK BALL LOW** in football, to kick the ball in such a way that it wobbles as it bounces along the ground [Early 16C. Origin ?]

squib kick *n* in football, a kick of the ball so that it wobbles as it bounces along the ground in order to make it hard to field and return

squid /skwid/ (*plural same* or **squids**) *n* **1.** a ocean cephalopod mollusk that has two long tentacles and eight shorter arms, a long tapered body, two triangular fins, and an internal shell. Order: Teuthoidea. See illustration on next page **2.** a dish of

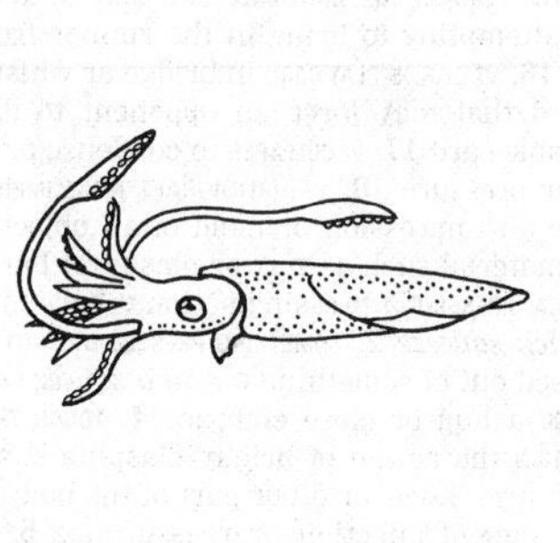

squid

squid that has been prepared and cooked for eating [Late 16C. Origin ?]

squig·gle /skwígg'l/ *n* **1.** WAVY LINE a wavy or curly line or movement **2.** ILLEGIBLE WORD an illegible handwritten word or words ■ *vi* **(-gled, -gling, -gles)** (*informal*) **1.** SQUIRM to twist, squirm, or wriggle **2.** DRAW SQUIGGLES to draw wavy or curly lines [Early 19C. Origin ?] —**squig·gler** *n* —**squig·gly** *adj*

squill /skwil/ *n* **1.** a plant grown from a bulb. Flowers: small, blue, white, pink, or purple, drooping. Native to: Europe, Asia, Africa. Genus: *Scilla* or *Pushkinia*. **2.** PLANTS same as **sea onion 3.** PHARM dried slices of a sea onion's bulb. Use: formerly, expectorant, diuretic. [14C. Via Latin *squilla* "shrimp, squill" < Greek *skilla*]

squil·la /skwíllə/ *n* a burrowing ocean crustacean that has eyes on stalks and large grasping appendages. Genus: *Squilla*. [Early 16C. < Latin, "shrimp" (see SQUILL)]

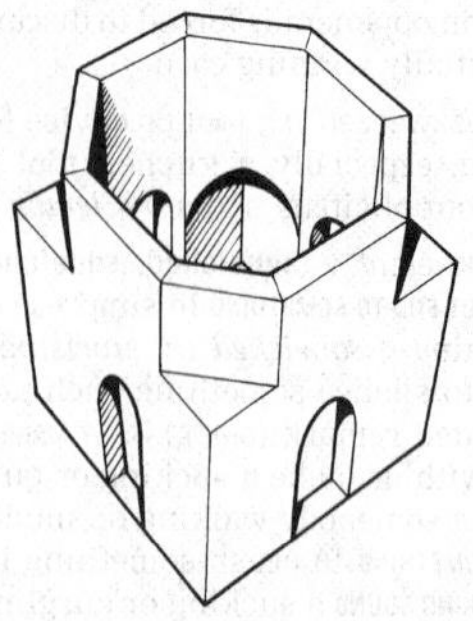

squinch

squinch[1] /skwinch/ *n* an arch, corbeling, or lintel built across the upper inside corner of a square tower to support the weight of a spire or other structure above [Mid-19C. Alteration of dialectal *scunch*, abbreviation of *scuncheon* < Old French *escoinson*, literally "corner out" < *coin* "corner" (see COIN)]

squinch[2] /skwinch/ **(squinched, squinch·ing, squinch·es)** *v* **1.** *vt* to scrunch up the eyes or face **2.** *vi* to crouch so as to take up less space [Early 19C. Probably blend of SQUINT + PINCH]

squin·gy /skwínjee/ **(-gi·er, -gi·est)** *adj Carib* **1.** small and dried-up in appearance **2.** worthless [Late 20C. < Caribbean alteration of SQUINCH[2]]

squint /skwint/ *v* **(squint·ed, squint·ing, squints) 1.** *vi* PARTLY CLOSE EYES to half-close the eyes so as to see better ○ *a photo of them squinting into the camera in bright sunlight* **2.** *vti* HAVE EYES NOT LOOKING IN PARALLEL to have eyes that are not aligned in parallel, or move the eyes so that they are not aligned in parallel **3.** *vi* GLANCE ASIDE to glance or look at something sideways **4.** *vi US* LOOK ASKANCE to regard something with disapproval (*disapproving*) ○ *Congress clearly is squinting at the prospect of increased funding for the program.* ■ *n* **1.** ACTION OF NARROWING EYES the act of narrowing the eyes to try to see better **2.** EYE CONDITION a condition in which the eyes are not aligned in parallel, causing a cross-eyed appearance. Technical name **strabismus 3.** QUICK GLIMPSE a quick look or glance at something, often to the side (*informal*) **4.** ARCHIT same as **hagioscope** ■ *adj* **1.** CROSS-EYED with a squint or a cross-eyed appearance **2.** ASKEW not level or properly aligned (*informal*) [Mid-16C. Shortening of *asquint*, origin ?] —**squint·er** *n* —**squint·y** *adj* ◇ **have** *or* **take a squint at something** to have a look at something (*informal*)

squint-eyed *adj* **1.** WITH SQUINT with one or both eyes looking slightly inward or outward rather than in parallel **2.** LOOKING WITH EYES PARTLY CLOSED looking with the eyes partly closed in order to see better **3.** ASKANCE looking askance or sidelong

squir·ar·chy *n* HIST another spelling of **squirearchy**

squire /skwīr/ *n* **1.** RURAL LANDOWNER a country landowner in England, often the main local landowner **2.** HIST ATTENDANT TO KNIGHT a young apprentice knight who acted as an attendant to a knight in the Middle Ages **3.** MAN WHO ESCORTS WOMAN a man who is escorting a woman or going out with her regularly (*dated*) **4.** TITLE GIVEN TO RURAL DIGNITARY a title of respect given to a magistrate or local dignity, especially in a rural district (*dated*) ■ *vt* **(squired, squir·ing, squires)** ESCORT SOMEBODY to escort or go out with a man or a woman (*dated; often passive*) [13C. Shortened < Old French *esquier, escuier* (see ESQUIRE)]

squire·ar·chy /skwīr aarkee/, **squir·ar·chy** *n* the main rural landowners collectively, especially the social, economic, or political class formed by such landed proprietors [Late 18C. < SQUIRE + HIERARCHY] —**squire·ar·chal** /-aark'l/ *adj* —**squire·ar·chic** /-aarkik/ *adj*

squirm /skwurm/ *vi* **(squirmed, squirm·ing, squirms) 1.** WRIGGLE FROM DISCOMFORT to wriggle the body, especially because of discomfort or in an attempt to break free from being held **2.** FEEL EMOTIONAL DISTRESS to feel very uncomfortable, especially because of shame, embarrassment, or revulsion ○ *a tough question that made the press office squirm* ■ *n* WRIGGLING MOVEMENT a wriggling movement, especially from discomfort or as an attempt to break free from being held [Late 17C. Origin ?] —**squirm·er** *n* —**squirm·y** *adj*

squirrel

squir·rel /skwúr əl/ *n* **1.** SMALL BUSHY-TAILED RODENT a small rodent that has a long bushy tail, lives in trees, and eats nuts and seeds. Family: Sciuridae. **2.** RODENT LIKE SQUIRREL a rodent related to or resembling the true squirrel, e.g., the ground squirrel, flying squirrel, or chipmunk **3.** HOARDER somebody who hoards something (*informal*) ■ *vt* **(-reled, -rel·ing, -rels)** HOARD SOMETHING to hoard or save things ○ *squirreled away some money* [14C. < Anglo-Norman *esquirel*, literally "little squirrel" < Latin *sciurus* < Greek *skiouros* < *skia* "shadow" + *oura* "tail"]

squir·rel cage *n* **1.** ROTATING FRAMEWORK FOR ANIMAL a cage containing a cylindrical wheel that goes around when a small pet rodent runs inside it **2.** DULL TASK a dull repetitive, seemingly purposeless task **3.** MECH ENG WINDING IN INDUCTION MOTORS a rotor of an induction motor consisting of copper bars mounted in slots around the periphery

squir·rel corn *n* a low-growing wild plant with divided leaves and small tubers resembling grains of corn. Flowers: whitish yellow. Native to: eastern United States. Latin name: *Dicentra canadensis*.

squir·rel·fish /skwúr əl fish/ (*plural same* or **-fish·es**) *n* a brightly colored nocturnal fish. Native to: tropical reefs. Family: Holocentridae. [Origin ?]

squir·rel·ly /skwúr əlee/ *adj* **1.** *US* an offensive term meaning very irrational or odd **2.** resembling or characteristic of a squirrel

squir·rel mon·key *n* a small long-tailed monkey that has soft yellowish gray, brown, or reddish fur, a white face, and a black muzzle. Native to: Central and South America. Genus: *Saimiri*.

squirt /skwurt/ *v* **(squirt·ed, squirt·ing, squirts) 1.** *vti* FORCE OR BE FORCED OUT to force something out of a narrow opening in a strong quick stream, or be pushed out in this way ○ *The ketchup squirted all over the table.* ○ *managed to squirt the last of the toothpaste out of the tube* **2.** *vt* SQUIRT LIQUID OVER SOMETHING to hit or cover somebody or something with liquid that is forced out of a narrow opening in a strong quick stream ○ *She squirted me with her water bottle.* ■ *n* **1.** STREAM OF EJECTED LIQUID a small stream of liquid forced out of a narrow opening ○ *a squirt of body lotion* **2.** INSTRUMENT FOR SQUIRTING LIQUID an instrument that is used to dispense liquid in a thin quick stream, e.g., a syringe **3.** OFFENSIVE TERM an offensive term that deliberately insults somebody's young age or small size, especially in response to perceived impudence (*informal insult*) [15C. An imitation of the sound of something being squirted]

squirt gun *n* same as **water pistol**

squirt·ing cu·cum·ber /skwùrting-/ *n* a vine of the gourd family with oblong fruits that burst when ripe, ejecting seeds and juice. Native to: Mediterranean. Latin name: *Ecballium elaterium*.

squish /skwish/ *v* **(squished, squish·ing, squish·es) 1.** *vt* SQUEEZE SOMETHING to squeeze or crush something soft **2.** *vi* MAKE SOFT SPLASHING NOISE to make a sucking or soft splashing sound when subjected to pressure, as when being walked on or squeezed ■ *n* **1.** SOFT SPLASHING NOISE a sucking or soft splashing sound **2.** *US* OFFENSIVE TERM an offensive term for somebody perceived as weak or cowardly (*slang insult*) [Mid-17C. Probably alteration of SQUASH[2]]

squish·y /skwíshee/ **(-i·er, -i·est)** *adj* **1.** SOFT soft and giving under pressure **2.** OVERLY SENTIMENTAL overly sentimental or romantic **3.** WEAK lacking in courage or resolution (*slang*) ○ *a squishy foreign policy*

sr *symbol* MEASURE steradian

Sr *symbol* CHEM ELEM strontium

sr. *abbr* **1.** senior **2.** Suriname (*used in Internet addresses*) See table at **domain name**

Sr. *abbr* **1.** Senhor **2.** *also* **sr.** senior **3.** señor **4.** Signor **5.** Sir **6.** CHR Sister

Sra. *abbr* **1.** Senhora **2.** Señora

srad·dhaa /sraadə/, **shrad·dh** /shraadə/ *n* an annual Hindu ritual, including the offering of food and water to dead ancestors [Late 18C. < Sanskrit *śrāddha* < *śraddhā* "faith, trust"]

SRAM *abbr* COMPUT static random access memory

Sra·nan·ton·go /sraanən tóng gō/, **Sra·nan** /sraanən/ *n* a creole language based on English that is the lingua franca of Suriname [Mid-20C. < Sranantongo, "Suriname tongue"] —**Sra·nan·ton·go** *adj*

Sra·van·a /sraavənə/ *n* in the Hindu calendar, the fifth month of the year, lasting 31 days and falling about the same time as July to August. See table at **calendar**

S-R con·nec·tion *n* in psychology, the relationship between a stimulus and a response

Sreb·re·ni·ca /srèbbrə neétsə/ town in Bosnia-Herzegovina, southeastern Europe, situated between Sarajevo and Tuzla. Declared a Muslim enclave during the Bosnian-Serbian-Croatian War from 1991 to 1995, it was invaded by Serb troops and subsequently placed under international protection. Population: 37,211 (1991).

Sri /sree, shree/, **Shri** /shree/ *n* **1.** *S Asia* a title of respect for a man, equivalent to "Mr." **2.** a title of respect for a Hindu deity or holy man **3.** HINDUISM same as **Lakshmi** [Late 18C. Via Hindi < Sanskrit *śrī* "lord," literally "beauty, wealth, majesty"]

SRI *abbr* FIN socially responsible investor

Sri Lan·ka /shree lángkə/ island country in South Asia, off the tip of southeastern India in the Indian Ocean. It became an independent member of the British Commonwealth in 1948. Language: Sinhalese. Currency: Sri Lankan rupee. Capital: Colombo. Administrative capital: Sri Jayawardenepura. Population: 19,408,635 (2001). Area: 25,332 sq. mi./65,610 sq. km. Official name **Democratic Socialist Republic of Sri Lanka**. Former name **Ceylon** (until 1972). See map on next page —**Sri Lan·kan** *n, adj*

Sri Lanka

Sri·man /sréeman, shréeman/ *n* same as **Sri** (sense 1)

Sri·na·gar /sree núggar, shrínna gaàr/, **Srī·na·ger** capital city of the state of Jammu and Kashmir, northwestern India. Population: 971,357 (2001).

Sri Vi·jay·a /shréevi jàya/, **Shriv·i·jay·a** *n* an Indonesian kingdom centered in Palembang, Sumatra, that dominated the maritime trade of Southeast Asia between the 7th and 14th centuries [Late 19C. < Hindi]

sRNA *abbr* BIOCHEM soluble RNA

SRO *abbr* **1.** TRAVEL single room occupancy **2.** standing room only

Srta. *abbr* **1.** Senhorita **2.** Señorita

SS[1] *abbr* **1.** SOC SCI Social Security **2.** SHIPPING, TRANSP steamship **3.** CHR Sunday school **4.** LAW sworn statement

SS[2] *n* a paramilitary organization founded by Hitler in 1925 as a personal bodyguard. During World War II, the SS was responsible for administering concentration camps. [Early 20C. < German *Schutzstaffel* "defense squadron"]

ss. *abbr* PUBL sections

SS. *abbr* CHR Saints

SSA *abbr US* SOC SCI, GOV Social Security Administration

SSB *abbr* MEDIA, COMMUNICATION single sideband (transmission)

SSE[1] *n* the detection and removal of weapons of mass destruction, suspected weapons of this type, and precursor materials used in building them. Full form **sensitive site exploitation**

SSE[2] *abbr* COMPASS south-southeast

SSG *abbr US* MIL Staff Sergeant

SSgt *abbr* MIL Staff Sergeant

SSI *abbr US* Supplemental Security Income

SSM *abbr* ARMS surface-to-surface missile

SSN *abbr US* GOV Social Security Number

ssp. *abbr* BIOL subspecies

SSR *abbr* HIST Soviet Socialist Republic

SSRI *abbr* MED selective serotonin reuptake inhibitor

SST *abbr* TRANSP supersonic transport

SSW *abbr* COMPASS south-southwest

st *abbr* **1.** ONLINE São Tomé and Príncipe (*used in Internet addresses*) See table at **domain name** **2.** MEASURE short ton

ST *abbr* TIME standard time

st. *abbr* **1.** LITERAT stanza **2.** start **3.** state **4.** LAW statute **5.** PRINTING stet **6.** HANDICRAFT stitch

St.[1] *abbr* **1.** Saint **2.** Strait **3.** Street (*used in addresses*)

St.[2] for saints, see under first name

-st *suffix* same as **-est**[1]

Sta *abbr* GEOG Santa[1]

stab /stab/ *v* (**stabbed, stab·bing, stabs**) **1.** *vt* **THRUST KNIFE INTO SOMEBODY OR SOMETHING** to thrust a knife or other sharp pointed instrument into somebody or something **2.** *vti* **JAB FINGER OR OBJECT** to thrust a finger or an object sharply at something ○ *He stabbed his potato angrily with his fork.* **3.** *vi* **HURT LIKE KNIFE WOUND** to cause a sudden sharp hurting sensation, like that of a knife wound ○ *Pain stabbed at her temples.* ■ *n* **1. ACT OF STABBING SOMEBODY** the action of thrusting a knife or other sharp pointed instrument into somebody (*often used before a noun*) ○ *a stab wound* **2. INJURY FROM STABBING** an injury or wound sustained from a thrust of a knife or other sharp pointed instrument ○ *The stab was deep enough to require stitches.* **3. SUDDEN PAINFUL FEELING** a sudden brief sensation, especially of pain ○ *felt a sudden stab of loss* **4. ATTEMPT** an attempt at something (*informal*) ○ *Each of us made a stab at solving the problem.* **5. SEVERE CRITICISM** a severe criticism of somebody [15C. Origin ?] —**stab·ber** *n* ◇ **a stab in the back** a betrayal, or an act of treachery (*informal*) ◇ **stab somebody in the back** to betray or harm somebody who trusts you

~~**stabalize**~~ incorrect spelling of **stabilize**

Sta·bat Ma·ter /staa bat maatar/ *n* a Latin hymn that was composed in the 13th century and concerns the grief of the Virgin Mary at the crucifixion of Jesus Christ [Mid-19C. < Latin *stabat mater dolorosa* "the mother stood, full of grief," first words of the hymn]

stab·bing /stábbing/ *n* an incident in which somebody is deliberately stabbed with a knife or sharp object ■ *adj* brief, sharp, and sudden, as if from the thrust of a knife ○ *a stabbing pain in the side*

sta·bile *n* /stáy beel/ **SCULPTURE ATTACHED TO SOMETHING** an abstract sculpture made of wire, metal, or other materials and attached to fixed supports ■ *adj* /stáyb'l, stáy bīl/ **1. STABLE** in a fixed position **2.** CHEM **NOT CHANGING CHEMICALLY** not readily undergoing chemical change [Late 18C. < Latin *stabilis* "stable"]

sta·bil·i·ty /sta bíllatee/ *n* **1. STABLE QUALITY** the condition of being stable ○ *policies aimed at creating economic stability* **2. MENTAL FIRMNESS** mental or psychological firmness **3.** MECH ENG **ABILITY TO ADJUST TO LOAD CHANGES** a property of a transmission system that allows changes in load to be met without any reduction in performance **4.** METEOROL **AIR MASS WITHOUT UPWARD MOVEMENT** a condition of no upward movement in an air mass **5.** METEOROL **RESISTANCE TO AIR CURRENTS** a measure of the tendency of an air mass to be influenced by convection currents **6.** ECOL **ABILITY TO MAINTAIN BALANCE** the ability of an ecological community to resist disturbance caused by environmental changes, or the ability to return to its original state after disturbance **7.** AEROSP, NAUT **RESISTANCE TO CHANGED POSITION** the capability of an aircraft, rocket, or ship to maintain a position and to return to it if displaced **8.** CHEM **RESISTANCE TO CHEMICAL CHANGE** a resistance to chemical change **9.** PHYS **MEASURE OF MAINTAINING EQUILIBRIUM** a measure of the difficulty of displacing an object or system from equilibrium

sta·bi·li·za·tion /stàyb'lī záysh'n/ *n* the action of becoming stable or of making something stable

sta·bi·li·za·tion fund *n* a reserve of money that a country uses to maintain its official exchange rate by buying and selling foreign exchange

sta·bi·lize /stáyb'l īz/ (**-lized, -liz·ing, -liz·es**) *v* **1.** *vti* to become stable, or make something stable ○ *The patient's condition has stabilized.* **2.** *vt* to keep something at the same level

sta·bi·liz·er /stáyb'l īzar/ *n* **1. STABILIZING PERSON OR THING** something that or somebody who acts to bring stability **2.** AVIAT **AIRFOIL THAT STABILIZES AIRCRAFT** an airfoil or combination of airfoils, e.g., in the tail assembly of an airplane, that keeps an aircraft or missile aligned with the direction of flight. A vertical stabilizer controls yawing, or side-to-side motion, while a horizontal stabilizer controls pitching, or up-and-down motion. **3.** NAUT **FINS TO CONTROL SHIP'S ROLLING** one or more pairs of submerged fins, often gyroscopically controlled, used to minimize the rolling of a ship in rough waters **4.** CHEM **ADDITIVE THAT MAINTAINS CHEMICAL PROPERTIES** a chemical compound added to another substance to make it resistant to change **5.** ELEC **DEVICE TO PRODUCE CONSTANT VOLTAGE** a device used to maintain a constant voltage from a source of direct current **6.** INDUST **SOMETHING ADDED TO DISPERSE PAINT** a substance added to a fast-drying paint to improve the dispersion of pigment ■ **sta·bi·liz·ers** *npl UK* same as **training wheels**

sta·bi·liz·er bar *n* AUTOMOT same as **roll bar**

sta·ble[1] /stáyb'l/ *adj* **1. NOT CHANGING** steady and not liable to change ○ *Prices have remained stable.* **2. NOT LIKELY TO MOVE** steady or firm and not liable to move **3. NOT EXCITABLE** having a calm and steady temperament, rather than being excitable or given to apparently irrational behavior **4.** CHEM, PHYS **NOT READILY UNDERGOING CHANGE** not subject to changes in chemical or physical properties **5.** PHYS **NOT NATURALLY RADIOACTIVE** incapable of becoming a different isotope or element by radioactive decay [13C. Via Anglo-Norman and Old French < Latin *stabilis*] —**sta·ble·ness** *n* —**sta·bly** *adv*

sta·ble[2] /stáyb'l/ *n* **1. BUILDING FOR HORSES** a building in which horses, and sometimes other large types of livestock, are kept **2. HORSES OWNED BY SOMEBODY** the group of horses, especially racehorses, owned by one person or kept and trained at one establishment **3. PEOPLE WORKING IN STABLE** the people who work in a stable, especially a training establishment for racehorses **4. GROUP UNDER MANAGEMENT** a group of people managed by the same person or organization ○ *a stable of bestselling authors* ■ *vti* (**sta·bled, sta·bling, sta·bles**) **PUT OR LIVE IN STABLE** to keep or put a horse or other large animal in a particular building, or be kept in a particular building ○ *We stabled our horses in the barn.* [13C. Via Old French *estable* < Latin *stabulum*]

sta·ble fly *n* a biting bloodsucking fly resembling a housefly that attacks humans and domestic animals. Latin name: *Stomoxys calcitrans.*

sta·bling /stáybling/ *n* **1.** a stable or stables **2.** accommodation for horses, usually but not always in a stable

~~**stablize**~~ incorrect spelling of **stabilize**

stab stitch *n* a very small straight stitch designed to hold pieces of fabric together without showing as more than a dot on the surface

stab·vest /stáb vèst/ *n* a padded vest of tough material, designed to protect a police officer against attacks with knives or other sharp implements

stacc. *abbr* MUSIC staccato

stac·ca·to /sta kaatō/ *adv* **IN QUICK SEPARATE NOTES** as rapid short detached notes (*used as a musical direction*) ■ *adj* **1. PLAYED SEPARATELY** played as rapid short detached notes **2. QUICK AND CLIPPED** rapid, brief, and clipped in sound ○ *a staccato voice* ■ *n* (*plural* **-tos**) **STACCATO PASSAGE** a staccato passage in music [Early 18C. < Italian, "detached"]

sta·chys /stáykiss/ *n* a plant with spiked whorls of purple, reddish, or white flowers, e.g., lamb's ears or betony. Genus: *Stachys.* [Mid-16C. Via modern Latin < Greek *stakhus* "ear of grain"]

stack /stak/ *n* **1. HEAPED PILE OF THINGS** a pile of things more or less neatly arranged one on top of another ○ *a stack of chairs* **2. LARGE NUMBER** a large number or amount (*informal*) ○ *She has stacks of money.* **3. LARGE PILE OF SOMETHING STORED OUTDOORS** a large pile of hay, straw, or grain, often conical in shape, stored outdoors **4.** ARCHIT **CHIMNEY OR CHIMNEYS** a tall chimney or group of chimneys arranged together **5.** AVIAT **AIRCRAFT WAITING TO LAND** a number of aircraft waiting a turn to land at an airport, circling at different heights **6.** GEOG **ROCKY PILLAR RISING FROM COASTAL WATERS** a steep-sided pillar of rock that has been isolated from nearby cliffs at the shoreline by the erosion of the waves **7.** COMPUT **LIST IN COMPUTER MEMORY** an area in a computer memory where data can be stored temporarily in a list in which the last item entered is the first one removed. A control program uses a stack to save register information and return addresses temporarily so that it can restore the environment on returning from another procedure to which it has jumped. **8.** ARMS **ARRANGEMENT OF FIREARMS** a group of firearms formed in a pyramid, especially three rifles with their muzzles leaning against each other **9.** CONSTR **VERTICAL PIPE** a vertical duct or waste pipe ■ **stacks** *npl* **BOOK STORAGE IN LIBRARY** an area of a library, usually not open to the public, where books are stored on shelves ■ *v* (**stacked, stack·ing, stacks**) **1.** *vti* **PUT OR BE IN ORGANIZED PILE** to put things one on top of another to form a pile, or be arranged in this way **2.** *vt* **PUT THINGS ON SHELF** to arrange objects on a shelf **3.** *vt* **HEAP SOMETHING WITH PILES OF OBJECTS** to load or heap something with large piles of articles or objects ○ *The bins were stacked with bargains.* **4.** *vt* **MANIPULATE SITUATION UNETHICALLY** to arrange something underhandedly to ensure a desired outcome **5.** *vti* AVIAT **FLY, OR KEEP AIRCRAFT, IN STACK** to keep aircraft waiting to land at an airport circling at different heights, or be kept in this position [13C. < Old Norse *stakkr* < Germanic, "stick, pole"] —**stack·a·ble** *adj* —**stack·er** *n* ◇ **be stacked against somebody** to amount to an unfair disadvantage for somebody ◇ **blow your stack** to have a sudden angry outburst (*slang*) ◇ **stack the deck** *or* **cards** (*slang*) **1.** to arrange playing cards in a deck for the purposes of cheating **2.** to arrange something dishonestly or unethically so as to gain an unfair advantage

stack up *v* **1.** *vti* **PUT IN STACK** to put things in a stack, or be put in a stack **2.** *vi* **MEASURE UP** to be measurable against or comparable to something **3.** *vi* **ADD UP** to add up to a total **4.** *vi* **SEEM REASONABLE** to make sense (*usually with negatives*)

stacked /stakt/ *adj* **1. DISHONESTLY ARRANGED** unfairly or dishonestly manipulated or arranged **2. OFFENSIVE TERM** an offensive term meaning having large breasts (*slang*) **3.** AVIAT **DISPOSED AT DIFFERENT HEIGHTS** circling at different heights prior to landing

stacked heel *n* a wide high heel made of different colored layers of wood or material simulating wood

stack·up /sták ùp/ *n US* AVIAT same as **stack** (sense 5)

stac·te /stáktee/ *n* in the Bible, a sweet spice mentioned as being used by the ancient Jews in making incense [14C. Via Latin < Greek *staktē* < *staktos*, past participle of *stazein* "drip, ooze"]

stad·dle /stádd'l/ *n* a supporting base to keep stored hay off the ground (*regional or archaic*) [Old English *staþol* < Indo-European, "to stand"]

stad·hold·er /stád hōldər/, **stadt·hold·er** *n* **1.** the chief magistrate of the Dutch republic between the 16th and 18th centuries **2.** formerly, a governor or viceroy of a province in the Netherlands [Mid-16C. Partial translation of Dutch *stadhouder* "place holder"] —**stad·hold·er·ate** *n* —**stad·hold·er·ship** *n*

sta·di·a[1] plural of **stadium**

sta·di·a[2] /stáydee ə/ *n* a method of measuring distances or differences in elevation using a telescopic instrument calibrated to correspond to distances from the surveyor [Mid-19C. Directly or via Italian < Latin, plural of *stadium* (see STADIUM)]

sta·di·um /stáydee əm/ (*plural* **-di·ums** or **-di·a** /-dee ə/) *n* **1. ARENA WITH TIERED SEATS** a place where people watch sports or other activities, usually a large enclosed flat area surrounded by tiers of seats for spectators **2.** ANCIENT HIST **ANCIENT GREEK RACETRACK** in ancient Greece, a racetrack for footraces that had tiers of seats at each side and one end **3.** MEASURE, ANCIENT HIST **ANCIENT GREEK MEASUREMENT UNIT** in ancient Greece, a unit of linear measure equal to about 607 ft./185 m [14C. Via Latin < Greek *stadion* "racetrack, unit of measure"]

stadt·hold·er *n* HIST, LAW another spelling of **stadholder**

Madame de Staël: portrait (1808–9) by Elisabeth Vigée-Lebrun

Staël /staal/, **Madame de** (1766–1817) French writer. She is credited with disseminating the theories of romanticism in works such as *Germany* (1810). Full name **Staël-Holstein, Baronne Anne Louise Germaine de**. Born **Necker, Anne Louise Germaine**

> "Love is above the laws, above the opinion of men; it is the truth, the flame, the pure element, the primary idea of the moral world."
> [Madame de Staël, *Zulma and Other Tales*; 1813]

staff[1] /staf/ *n* **1. WORKERS** people who are employed by a company or an individual employer **2. BODY WITHIN LARGER GROUP** a particular group of employees within a company, institution, or organization ○ *the teaching staff* **3.** *UK* EDUC same as **faculty** (sense 3) **4. PEOPLE WHO WORK FOR LEADER** a group of people who serve a leader or an executive of a company, organization, or institution **5.** (*plural* **staffs** or **staves** /stayvz/) **LARGE HEAVY STICK** a stick, rod, or pole, e.g., a stick used as a support while walking, or a rod used as a symbol of authority in ceremonies **6.** (*plural* **staffs** or **staves**) same as **flagpole** **7.** *Malaysia, Singapore* HR, EDUC **EMPLOYEE** a member of staff working for a company, organization, or school **8.** MIL **GROUP OF AIDES TO COMMANDER** a group of officers in the armed services who assist a commanding officer or work at headquarters as advisers or planners **9.** (*plural* **staffs** or **staves**) MUSIC **SET OF LINES FOR WRITING MUSIC** a set of five horizontal lines, together with the four spaces between them, on which the notes of music are written **10.** MEASURE **GRADUATED ROD USED FOR MEASURING** a graduated rod used for testing or measuring something, e.g., in surveying ■ *adj* **1. EMPLOYED WITH SALARY** employed full-time, not on a freelance basis **2.** HR **CONCERNED WITH STAFF** for or relating to the staff of a company, institution, or organization ■ *vt* (**staffed, staff·ing, staffs**) **PROVIDE ORGANIZATION WITH WORKERS** to provide a place or organization with employees (*often passive*) [Old English *stæf* "stick, rod" < Indo-European, "to support"]

staff[2] /staf/ *n* a building material of plaster and fibrous material used as a temporary, especially decorative, finish on the outside of a structure [Late 19C. Origin ?]

Staf·fa /stáffə/ uninhabited island in the Inner Hebrides, western Scotland. Its many caverns include Fingal's Cave. Area: 0.2 sq. mi./0.5 sq. km.

staff col·lege *n* a school in which military officers receive leadership training in preparation for higher positions, e.g., as staff officers or commanders

staff·er /stáffər/ *n* a member of the staff of an organization (*informal*) ○ *White House staffers*

staff·ing /stáffing/ *n* the act of providing people to do jobs

staff·man /stáf màn/ (*plural* **-men** /-mèn/) *n UK* same as **rodman**

staff of Aes·cu·la·pi·us /-èskyə láypee əss/ *n* a symbol for the medical profession consisting of a staff with a single snake entwined around it

staff of·fi·cer *n* a military officer who assists a commanding officer or works as a planner or adviser at a headquarters

staff of life *n* bread, or sometimes another food, considered as an essential part of the human diet (*literary*)

Staf·ford·shire /stáffərd shēer, -shər/ county in the Midlands, central England. It includes the Potteries. Stafford is the county town. Population: 806,744 (2001). Area: 1,049 sq. mi./2,716 sq. km.

Staf·ford·shire bull ter·ri·er /-bòol térree ər-/, **Staf·ford·shire ter·ri·er** *n* a bull terrier belonging to a breed with a short broad head and ears that hang down

staff per·son (*plural* **staff peo·ple** or **staff per·sons**) *n* a member of the staff of an educational institution or other organization

staff·room /stáf ròom, -ròom/ *n UK* a room used only by the teachers in a school, e.g., for relaxation between classes

staff ser·geant *n* a noncommissioned officer in the US Army or Marine Corps and in the British Army of a rank above sergeant, and in the US Air Force of a rank above senior airman

stag /stag/ *n* **1. MATURE MALE DEER** an adult male deer, especially a male red deer **2. CASTRATED ADULT ANIMAL** a male animal, e.g., a pig, castrated after it reaches maturity **3.** *US* **SOMEBODY UNACCOMPANIED AT SOCIAL EVENT** somebody who goes to a social function without a partner (*informal*) ■ *adj* **RESTRICTED TO MEN** for men only, and often involving activities that would not be felt appropriate when women are present (*informal*) ■ *adv* **ALONE** without a companion on a social occasion (*informal*) ■ *vi* (**stagged, stag·ging, stags**) *US* **ATTEND EVENT WITHOUT DATE** to attend a social event without a companion (*informal*) [Assumed Old English *stagga* < Indo-European, "pointed"]

stag bee·tle *n* a large beetle the male of which has long extended jaws (**mandibles**) shaped like a stag's antlers. Family: Lucanidae.

stage /stayj/ *n* **1. AREA IN THEATER** the area in a theater where a performance takes place, especially a platform on which actors perform a play **2. DRAMATIC PROFESSION** the profession of acting, drama, or the theater **3. PLATFORM** a raised platform where speeches are made and ceremonies are carried out, e.g., in a hall or auditorium **4. PERIOD OR STEP DURING PROCESS** a step, level, or period in the development or progress of something ○ *The project is still in its early stages.* **5. SETTING IN WHICH SOMETHING HAPPENS** the scene of an event or series of events ○ *The summit marks her first appearance on the world stage.* **6. SIGNIFICANT PHASE** an important phase of cultural, economic, or social development **7. PART OF JOURNEY** a distinct section of a journey, especially one after which a stop is made **8.** AEROSP **DETACHABLE ROCKET UNIT** a separable unit of a rocket or spacecraft that contains fuel and can be jettisoned after the fuel is exhausted **9.** CONSTR **PLATFORM FOR WORKERS** a raised platform, especially a scaffolding for workers during the construction of a building **10.** TRANSP same as **stagecoach** **11.** FOOD INDUST **PLATFORM FOR DRYING FOOD** a platform used to dry fish or meat **12.** RECORDING same as **sound stage** **13.** BIOL **PERIOD OF DEVELOPMENT OF ORGANISM** a distinct period of development in the life of an organism when its form is different from earlier or later periods **14.** MEASURE **ELEVATION OF RIVER SURFACE** a measure of how much the surface of a river or stream rises above a given point **15.** SCI **PLATFORM FOR MOUNTING MICROSCOPIC SPECIMEN** the small platform of an optical microscope on which a specimen is placed for examination **16.** GEOL **PERIOD OF ROCK STRATA** a relatively short geologic distinct period, a subdivision of a series, during which rock strata are deposited **17.** ELEC **UNIT OF ELECTRICAL COMPONENTS** a group of components that form part of an electronic or electrical system ■ *vt* (**staged, stag·ing, stag·es**) **1. ORGANIZE PERFORMANCE FOR PUBLIC** to put on a play, concert, exhibition, or similar event for an audience **2. ORGANIZE EVENT** to organize or carry out something such as an event that will attract attention or publicity **3. SET PLAY IN PLACE OR TIME** to set a play in a particular place or time ○ *staged the drama in the Regency period* **4.** MED **CLASSIFY PHASES OF DISEASE** to classify the progress of a disease [13C. < Old French *estage* < Latin *stat-*, past participle of *stare* "stand"] —**stage·a·bil·i·ty** /stàyjə bíllətee/ *n* —**stage·a·ble** *adj* —**stage·a·bly** *adv* ◇ **by** *or* **in easy stages** in an unhurried undemanding way ◇ **on stage** performing in something, especially as an actor ◇ **set the stage (for something)** to make the preparations or produce the conditions necessary for something to happen or begin ◇ **take center stage** to draw people's or public attention

stage brace *n* a brace used to support upright pieces of scenery in a play

stage busi·ness *n* THEATER same as **business** *n* (sense 8)

stagecoach

stage·coach /stáyj kòch/ *n* a large four-wheeled horse-drawn coach formerly used to carry passengers and mail over a regular route

CULTURAL NOTE ***Stagecoach***, a movie (1939) by John Ford. Considered the first modern Western, it portrays an encounter between a diverse group of stagecoach passengers and an intimidating outlaw, the Ringo Kid (played by John Wayne). Its convincing and intriguing characters, magnificent desert setting, gripping narrative, and exciting climax made it a landmark in US movie-making.

stage·craft /stáyj kràft/ *n* the technique or art of writing, adapting, or putting plays on stage

stage di·rec·tion *n* an instruction for an actor in the script of a play

stage door *n* a door in the back or side of a theater that leads directly backstage and is usually used by performers

stage ef·fect *n* a special visual or auditory effect created on a theatrical stage by lighting, scenery, or sound

stage fright *n* fear or nervousness felt by somebody before going in front of an audience to speak or perform

stage·hand /stáyj hànd/ *n* a manual worker in a theater, e.g., somebody who sets up and removes stage sets

stage left *n* the part of a stage that is to a performer's left when facing the audience

stage-man·age *v* **1.** *vt* to control an organized event, especially in a way that is not public, so that it happens exactly as planned **2.** *vti* to carry out the work of a stage manager, especially on a particular production —**stage-man·age·ment** *n*

stage man·ag·er *n* an assistant of the director of a play who supervises backstage activities

stage name *n* the name a performer or entertainer uses for professional purposes, as opposed to his or her real name

stage right *n* the part of a stage that is to a performer's right when facing the audience

stage-struck *adj* loving the theater and intensely wanting to be part of it, especially as a performer

stage wait *n* an unintentional pause in the action of a play, especially one caused by an actor's missing a cue

stage whis·per *n* **1.** something said on stage that for the purposes of the play is supposed to be a whisper but is intended to be heard by the audience **2.** a loud whisper intended to be overheard

stag·ey *adj* another spelling of **stagy**

stag·fla·tion /stag fláysh'n/ *n* a period of rising prices and unemployment but little growth in consumer demand and business activity [Mid-20C. Blend of STAGNATION + INFLATION] —**stag·fla·tion·ar·y** *adj*

Stagg /stag/, **Amos Alonzo** (1862–1965) US football coach. He coached at the University of Chicago (1892–1932) and College of the Pacific (1933–46), where he continued as an assistant until the age of 98.

stag·ger /stággər/ *v* (**-gered, -ger·ing, -gers**) **1.** *vi* MOVE UNSTEADILY, NEARLY FALLING to move or walk unsteadily, almost but not quite falling over **2.** *vt* MAKE PERSON OR ANIMAL STUMBLE to make a person or animal stumble or nearly fall, especially by a blow **3.** *vt* ASTONISH SOMEBODY to completely astonish or amaze somebody (*often passive*) **4.** *vt* ARRANGE ACTIVITIES FOR SEPARATE TIMES to arrange activities so that they do not overlap **5.** *vt* PUT THINGS INTO ALTERNATING OR ZIGZAG PATTERN to arrange things so that they do not form a straight line, especially in an alternating or zigzag pattern (*often passive*) **6.** *vi* HESITATE to hesitate or falter **7.** *vt* AVIAT ADJUST EDGE OF BIPLANE'S WING to make the leading edge of one wing of a biplane project beyond the leading edge of the other wing ■ *n* **1.** STUMBLE NEARLY RESULTING IN FALL an unsteady movement in which a person or animal almost falls **2.** AVIAT ARRANGEMENT OF BIPLANE WINGS a design in which the leading edge of one wing of a biplane is ahead of that of the other wing [Mid-16C. Alteration of obsolete *stacker* < Old Norse *stakkra* < *staka* "push" < Germanic, "pole"] —**stag·ger·er** *n*

stag·ger·bush /stággər bŏosh/ (*plural* **-bush·es** or *same*) *n* a deciduous bush of the heath family with poisonous leaves. Flowers: white or pink, in clusters. Native to: eastern United States. Latin name: *Lyonia mariana*.

stag·gered /stággərd/ *adj* **1.** shocked or astounded at something **2.** not arranged consecutively or in a straight line

stag·gered hours *npl* an arrangement in a business in which employees arrive and leave at different times but work hours that overlap for part of the time

stag·ger·ing /stággəring/ *adj* with the effect of shocking or astounding people —**stag·ger·ing·ly** *adv*

stag·gers /stággərz/ *n* (*takes a singular or plural verb*) **1.** same as **blind staggers** **2.** a form of vertigo associated with decompression sickness, with symptoms including dizziness, weakness, and confusion

stag·horn /stág hàwrn/ *n* **1.** **stag's horn** a stag's antler, or a piece of this used as material for carved objects **2.** **stag's horn** PLANTS same as **staghorn fern** **3.** **stag's horn** PLANTS same as **staghorn moss** **4.** PLANTS same as **staghorn sumac** ■ *adj* made from a piece of a stag's antlers

stag·horn cor·al *n* a form of stony coral branched like a deer's antlers. Genus: *Acropora*.

stag·horn fern *n* a fern with broad leaves like antlers and smaller clinging leaves, often cultivated as a houseplant. Genus: *Platycerium*.

stag·horn moss *n* a plant with creeping stems like antlers and tiny overlapping leaves. Latin name: *Lycopodium clavatum*.

stag·horn su·mac *n* a bush with downy branches, red fruit, and compound leaves that turn crimson or purple in fall. Flowers: greenish, in clusters. Native to: eastern United States. Latin name: *Rhus typhina*. [< the resemblance of its branches to a deer's antlers in velvet]

stag·hound /stág hòwnd/ *n* a hound like a large foxhound, used, especially formerly, in hunting stags

stag·ing /stáyjing/ *n* **1.** TECHNIQUE OF PRESENTING STAGE PLAY the activity, process, or style of presenting a play on a stage **2.** CONSTR SCAFFOLDING FOR BUILDING a temporary structure of supports and platforms used while people are building or working on something **3.** AEROSP TECHNIQUE FOR INCREASING SPACECRAFT'S VELOCITY a technique to increase the velocity achieved by a spacecraft's launch vehicle by using multiple propulsive stages, each being jettisoned after use

stag·ing ar·e·a *n* **1.** a place where soldiers and military equipment are gathered for final organization, outfitting, and training before deployment on an operation **2.** a place where people stop or assemble before undertaking an activity or task

stag·nant /stágnənt/ *adj* **1.** STILL AND UNMOVING not flowing or moving **2.** FOUL OR STALE stale or impure from lack of motion **3.** NOT DEVELOPING not developing or making progress **4.** INACTIVE not active or lively ○ *a stagnant week on the stock market* [Mid-17C. < Latin *stagnant-*, present participle of *stagnare* (see STAGNATE)] —**stag·nan·cy** *n* —**stag·nant·ly** *adv*

stag·nate /stág nàyt/ (**-nat·ed, -nat·ing, -nates**) *vi* **1.** NOT DEVELOP OR MAKE PROGRESS to fail to develop, progress, or make necessary changes **2.** STOP FLOWING to stop flowing or moving **3.** BECOME FOUL to become stale or impure through not flowing or moving **4.** BECOME INACTIVE to become listless and inactive [Mid-17C. < Latin *stagnat-*, past participle of *stagnare* < *stagnum* "pool, swamp"] —**stag·na·tion** /stag náysh'n/ *n* —**stag·na·to·ry** *adj*

stag night, **stag par·ty** *n UK* same as **bachelor party** (*informal*)

stag's horn *n* PLANTS, ZOOL same as **staghorn**

stag·y /stáyjee/ (**-i·er, -i·est**), **stag·ey** *adj* exaggerated or artificial in manner, as if in a play —**stag·i·ly** *adv* —**stag·i·ness** *n*

staid /stayd/ *adj* sedate and settled in habits or temperament, sometimes to the point of dullness [Mid-16C. Obsolete past participle of STAY[1], literally "fixed, settled"] —**staid·ly** *adv* —**staid·ness** *n*

stain /stayn/ *n* **1.** DISCOLORED PATCH a discolored mark made by something such as blood, wine, or ink **2.** COLOR FINISH a liquid that is applied to something, especially wood, to darken it or change its color without hiding its texture or grain **3.** BIOL DYE USED TO COLOR MICROSCOPIC SPECIMENS a dye used to color tissues and cells to make features more visible under a microscope **4.** INDUST DYE FOR TEXTILES OR LEATHER a dye used in liquid form to color textiles or leather **5.** CHARACTER BLEMISH something that detracts from a somebody's good reputation ■ *v* (**stained, stain·ing, stains**) **1.** *vti* LEAVE MARK ON SOMETHING to make a discolored mark on something, or be liable to cause or suffer discolored marks (*often passive*) **2.** *vt* DYE SOMETHING to dye something a different or deeper color using liquid or pigment that penetrates the surface **3.** *vt* TARNISH SOMETHING to disgrace or detract from something ○ *reprehensible acts that stained his reputation* **4.** *vt* MICROBIOL COLOR ORGANIC SPECIMENS to color organic materials with dyes to make features more visible under a microscope [15C. Partly < Old Norse *steina* "paint"; partly < Old French *desteindre* "discolor" < Latin *tingere* "to dye"] —**stain·a·ble** /stáynəb'l/ *adj* —**stain·er** *n*

stained glass /stàynd-/ *n* glass that has been colored so that it can be used to make a mosaic picture, especially in a window. Stained glass may be made by enameling, burning pigments into the surface, or by fusing metallic oxides with it. (*hyphenated before a noun*)

Staines /staynz/ city in Surrey, southern England. Population: 51,167 (1991).

stain·less /stáynləss/ *adj* **1.** RESISTANT TO RUST resisting rust or corrosion **2.** WITHOUT STAINS not discolored or marked by stains **3.** ENTIRELY REPUTABLE not tarnished by any blemishes of character or reputation ■ *n* METALL same as **stainless steel** —**stain·less·ly** *adv*

stain·less steel *n* a corrosion-resistant steel containing at least 12 percent chromium that has many domestic and industrial uses, e.g., making cutlery, ball bearings, and turbine blades (*hyphenated before a noun*)

stair /ster/ *n* **1.** SINGLE STEP a step in a series of steps leading from one floor or level to another **2.** SERIES OF STEPS a flight of steps leading from one floor or level to another ■ **stairs** *npl* SET OF STEPS a set or several sets of steps leading from one floor or level to another [Old English *stǣger* < Indo-European, "to step"]

SPELLCHECK stair or **stare**? Do not confuse the spelling of ***stair*** and ***stare***, which sound similar. ***Stair*** is a noun denoting a step or series of steps, as in *climb up the stairs to the top floor*, and is also found in related compound words such as *staircase* and *downstairs*. ***Stare*** is a verb or noun referring to a fixed look or facial expression with the eyes wide open (as in *staring at her in astonishment, a vacant stare*) and is also used figuratively: *The solution to the problem was staring us in the face.*

stair·case /stér kàyss/ *n* a set of stairs in a building, usually with banisters or handrails

stair·head /stér hèd/ *n* the landing at the top of a flight of stairs

stair rod *n* a rod laid to hold a carpet in place against the bottom of a riser in a staircase

stair·way /stér wày/ *n* a passageway from one floor or level of a building to another, consisting of stairs or a staircase

stair·well /stér wèl/ *n* the vertical space in a building where stairs are located

stake[1] /stayk/ *n* **1.** THIN POINTED POST IN GROUND a thin wooden or metal post that is driven into the ground to mark or support something **2.** POST TO TIE SOMEBODY TO a wooden post to which somebody was tied and burned in an old form of execution **3.** FORM OF EXECUTION the method of execution in which somebody was tied to a post and burned **4.** POST THAT RETAINS LOAD an independent upright post inserted into sockets of a flat wagon or truck to keep long loads such as logs in place **5.** MORMON CHURCH DISTRICT an administrative district in the Church of Jesus Christ of Latter-Day Saints that consists of wards, each governed by a president and two counselors ■ *v* (**staked, stak·ing, stakes**) **1.** *vt* SUPPORT OR STRENGTHEN SOMETHING WITH STAKE to support or strengthen something using a stake **2.** *vt* TETHER SOMETHING TO STAKE to tie or tether something to a stake **3.** *vi* MARK OR FENCE AREA WITH STAKES to mark out, confine, or fence off an area using stakes driven into the ground around the boundary **4.** *vt* ASSERT SOMETHING to assert something, usually rights, over something such as an area of land [Old English *staca* < Germanic, "stick, pole"] ◇ **(pull) up stakes** to leave and move to another place

stake out *vt* **1.** WATCH PLACE CONTINUOUSLY to watch a place continuously from a hidden vantage point (*informal*) **2.** ESTABLISH BOUNDARIES to establish the boundaries of an area intended to be used or controlled **3.** ESTABLISH

AND CLARIFY POSITION to establish and clarify a personal position in a situation

stake[2] /stayk/ *n* **1.** MONEY RISKED IN GAMBLING an amount of money risked in a bet or game **2.** SHARE OR INTEREST IN SOMETHING a share or interest in something, particularly through money risked in it **3.** PERSONAL INVOLVEMENT personal or emotional interest, concern, or involvement ○ *We had a huge stake in his success.* **4.** MIN EXTRACT same as **grubstake** *n* (sense 1) ■ **stakes** *npl* **1.** DEGREE OF RISK the degree of hazard or danger involved in a situation **2.** PRIZE AVAILABLE the prize, reward, or success available in a gamble or competition **3.** PRIZE MADE UP OF CONTRIBUTIONS the total of bets made by players in a gambling game that is taken by the winner **4.** CARDS AMOUNT OF BETS IN POKER in poker, the cash values assigned to chips, bets, or raises ■ *vt* (**staked, stak·ing, stakes**) **1.** WAGER SOMETHING to bet something, especially money, on something **2.** RISK LOSS OF SOMETHING to risk the loss of something valuable ○ *I'm prepared to stake my reputation on it.* **3.** SUPPLY SOMEBODY WITH NECESSITIES to give or lend somebody something needed or wanted ○ *staked him money to pay the rent for a month* **4.** FIN INVEST IN SOMETHING to put money into something, especially initial capital [Mid-16C. Origin ?] ◇ **at stake** at risk of being lost

stake-and-rid·er fence *n regional* a fence made of split rails each resting on and set at angles to the next, forming a zigzag

stake·hold·er /stáyk hòldər/ *n* **1.** a person or group with a direct interest, involvement, or investment in something, e.g., the employees, stockholders, and customers of a business concern ○ *"...demonstrating how to build powerful stakeholder relationships based on trust..."* (*Marketing Week*; December 1998) **2.** a holder and payer of bets in a gambling game — **stake·hold·ing** *n*

stake·out /stáyk òwt/ *n* (*informal*) **1.** hidden surveillance of somebody or something, especially by the police **2.** the place from which surveillance is carried out, especially by the police

Sta·kha·nov·ite /stə kaánə vìt/ *n* in the former Soviet Union, a worker who received a reward for increasing production ■ *adj* rewarding people who work very hard, especially in the former Soviet Union [Mid-20C. After Aleksei Grigorevich *Stakhanov* (1906–77), Soviet mine worker]

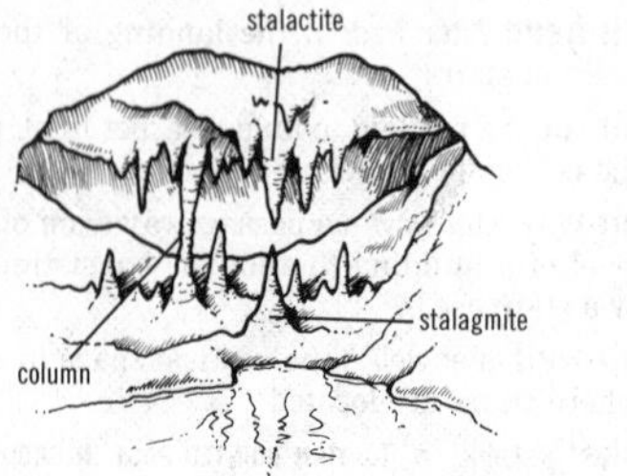

stalactite and stalagmite

sta·lac·tite /stə lák tìt/ *n* a conical hanging pillar in a limestone cave that has gradually built up as a deposit from ground water seeping through the cave's roof [Late 17C. < modern Latin *stalactites* < Greek *stalaktos* "dripping" < *stalak-*, stem of *stalassein* "to drip"] —**stal·ac·tit·ic** /stàllək títtik/ *adj*

sta·lag /staá laag, stá làg/ *n* a German prisoner of war camp in World War II for officers and lower ranks [Mid-20C. < German, contraction of *Stammlager* "main camp"]

sta·lag·mite /stə lág mìt/ *n* a conical pillar in a limestone cave that is gradually built upward from the floor as a deposit from ground water seeping through and dripping from the cave's roof [Late 17C. < modern Latin *stalagmites* < Greek *stalagmos* "something dropped" < *stalak-*, stem of *stalassein* "to drip"] —**stal·ag·mit·ic** /stàlləg míttik/ *adj*

stale[1] /stayl/ *adj* (**stal·er, stal·est**) **1.** KEPT TOO LONG no longer fresh ○ *This bread has gone stale.* **2.** LOW IN OXYGEN stagnant and low in oxygen owing to lack of circulation or ventilation ○ *stale air* **3.** FREQUENTLY HEARD AND BORING heard too often before and no longer interesting or amusing ○ *his stale old jokes* **4.** OUT OF CONDITION ineffective, enervated, or bored because of doing too much of the same thing **5.** LAW LEGALLY EXPIRED having lost legal force through lack of use or elapse of time **6.** BANKING NOT NEGOTIABLE BECAUSE OF DELAY describes financial statements or checks that are not negotiable by a bank because a time limit has expired ■ *vti* (**staled, stal·ing, stales**) LOSE FRESHNESS to become stale, or make something become stale [13C. < Old French *estale* "settled" < *estal* "standing place" < Germanic] —**stale·ly** *adv* —**stale·ness** *n*

stale[2] /stayl/ *vi* (**staled, stal·ing, stales**) VET same as **urinate** (*refers to livestock*) ■ *n* the urine of livestock, especially horses and cattle [14C. Origin ?]

stale·mate /stáyl màyt/ *n* **1.** SITUATION WITH NO POTENTIAL WINNERS in a contest, a situation in which neither side can take any further worthwhile action **2.** CHESS CHESS SITUATION WITH NO WINNER in chess, a situation in which no winner is possible because neither player can move a piece without placing the king in check ■ *vt* (**-mat·ed, -mat·ing, -mates**) PUT SOMEBODY OR SOMETHING INTO STALEMATE to put somebody or something into a situation in which no further worthwhile action is possible (*often passive*) [Mid-18C. < obsolete *stale* (< Anglo-Norman *estale* "fixed position" < Germanic) + MATE[2]]

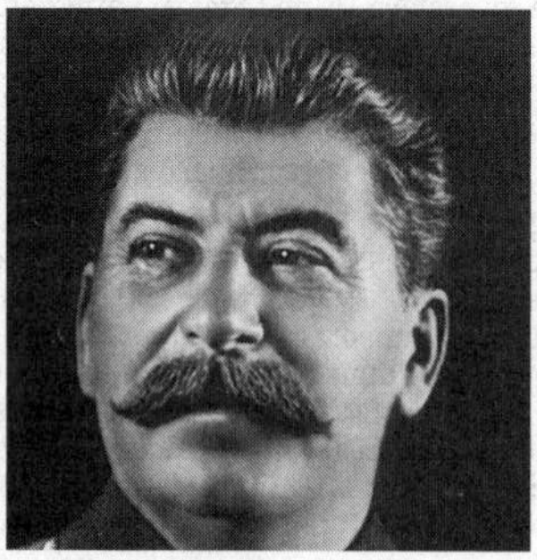

Joseph Stalin

Sta·lin /staálin/, **Joseph** (1879–1953) Georgian-born Soviet leader. He was the general secretary of the Soviet Communist Party (1922–53). He ruled the former Soviet Union as a dictator after 1930, eliminating political opponents in a series of purges and causing nationwide famine with his collectivist agricultural policy. After World War II, he extended Soviet control over most of Eastern Europe. Born **Dzhugashvili, Iosif Vissarionovich**

> "One death is a tragedy; a million deaths a statistic."
> [Attributed to Joseph Stalin]

Sta·lin·grad /staálin gràd/ former name for **Volgograd** (1925–61)

Sta·lin·ism /staálə nìzzəm/ *n* the political principles and economic policies developed by Joseph Stalin from Marxist-Leninist thought, which included centralized autocratic rule and total suppression of dissent —**Sta·lin·ist** *n, adj*

Sta·lin Peak former name for **Ismail Samani Peak**

stalk[1] /stawk/ *n* **1.** PLANT STEM the main stem or axis of a plant that is fleshy rather than woody **2.** SUPPORTIVE PART OF PLANT a supporting part of a plant, e.g., a leaf stem (**petiole**) or flower stalk (**pedicel**) **3.** SLENDER SUPPORTING PART a thin cylindrical part of something that acts as a support, e.g., of a glass **4.** SLENDER STRUCTURAL PART OF ANIMAL a slender supporting structure for an organ or body of an animal [14C. Probably alteration of obsolete *stale* "stile of a ladder, handle" < Old English *stalu* "upright piece"] —**stalked** *adj* —**stalk·less** *adj*

stalk[2] /stawk/ *v* (**stalked, stalk·ing, stalks**) **1.** *vt* FOLLOW SOMEBODY STEALTHILY to follow or try to get close to a person or animal unobtrusively **2.** *vi* WALK STIFFLY AND ANGRILY to walk in a stiff, angry, or proud way **3.** *vt* TROUBLE SOMEBODY STEADILY AND MALEVOLENTLY to assail somebody in a steady and sinister way ○ *villages stalked by the threat of famine* **4.** *vt* LAW HARASS SOMEBODY PERSISTENTLY to harass somebody criminally by persistent, inappropriate, and unwanted attention, e.g., by constantly following, telephoning, e-mailing, or writing to him or her ■ *n* **1.** STEALTHY PURSUIT a stealthy pursuit or hunt of something **2.** STIFF WALK a stiff, angry, or proud walk [Assumed Old English *stealcian* < Germanic, "to steal"] —**stalk·a·ble** *adj* —**stalk·er** *n*

SYNONYMS See ***follow***.

stalk-eyed *adj* used to describe crustaceans and flies that have eyes located on stalks (**pedicels**)

stalk·ing /stáwking/ *n* **1.** the act or process of stealthily following or trying to approach somebody or something **2.** the crime of harassing somebody with persistent, inappropriate, and unwanted attention —**stalk·ing·ly** *adv*

stalk·ing horse *n* **1.** MEANS TO DISGUISE OBJECTIVE something used as a means of disguising a real objective **2.** POL DECEPTIVE CANDIDATE FOR ELECTION a candidate who is in an election only to conceal the potential candidacy of somebody else, to divide the opposition, or to determine how strong the opposition is **3.** HUNTING FAKE HORSE a horse or figure of a horse that is used as cover in the hunting of game

stalk·y /stáwkee/ (**-i·er, -i·est**) *adj* **1.** long or tall and thin like a stalk **2.** with stalks, especially many stalks ○ *stalky background plants in the garden* — **stalk·i·ly** *adv* —**stalk·i·ness** *n*

stall[1] /stawl/ *n* **1.** SMALL AREA SELLING OR DISPENSING GOODS a booth, table, counter, or compartment set up to display goods for sale or information to give out **2.** COMPARTMENT FOR LARGE ANIMAL a compartment in a building where a single large animal lives or is fed or milked **3.** AUTOMOT SITUATION IN WHICH ENGINE HALTS a situation in which an engine stops abruptly because of insufficient fuel, being braked too suddenly, or mechanical failure **4.** SMALL ROOM a very small room, or partitioned area in a room, for a shower or toilet **5.** AVIAT SUDDEN DIVE BY AIRCRAFT a situation in which an aircraft suddenly dives because the airflow is obstructed and lift is lost. The loss of airflow can be caused by insufficient air speed or by an excessive angle of an airfoil when the aircraft is climbing. **6.** CHR SEAT IN CHURCH a pew or enclosed seat in a church **7.** AUTOMOT SPACE FOR PARKING a space marked off for parking a motor vehicle in a garage or parking lot **8.** MED SHEATH FOR FINGER a protective covering for a finger or thumb ■ **stalls** *npl UK* SEATS CLOSEST TO STAGE the seats in a theater or movie house on the ground floor nearest the stage or screen ■ *v* (**stalled, stall·ing, stalls**) **1.** *vti* AUTOMOT STOP OR MAKE ENGINE STOP to stop working suddenly, or make an engine do this **2.** *vti* AVIAT PLUNGE OR CAUSE TO PLUNGE to go into a sudden dive, or cause a sudden dive in an aircraft **3.** *vt* AGRIC PUT LARGE ANIMAL INTO STALL to put a large animal into a compartment where it will live or be fed or milked **4.** *vti* STOP PROGRESSING, OR MAKE SOMETHING STOP to stop making progress, or cause something to stop making progress ○ *stalled the project* ○ *a project that stalled* [Old English *steall* "standing place" < Germanic]

stall[2] /stawl/ *v* (**stalled, stall·ing, stalls**) **1.** *vti* DELAY WITH HESITATION OR EVASION to delay or obstruct somebody, or use delaying tactics **2.** *vi* SPORTS UNDULY PROLONG POSSESSION OF BALL in a football or basketball game, to prolong holding the ball when in the lead so as to use up time and prevent an opponent from scoring ■ *n* DECEPTIVE PRETEXT a pretext or ruse used to delay or deceive somebody [Early 19C. Alteration of obsolete *stale* "decoy, pickpocket's accomplice" < Anglo-Norman *estale* "something set up"]

stall-feed *vt* to keep an animal in a stall while fattening it for slaughter

stall·ing an·gle /stáwling-/ *n* the angle relative to the horizontal at which the flow of air around an airfoil changes abruptly, resulting in significant changes in the lift and drag of an aircraft

stal·lion /stállyən/ *n* **1.** an uncastrated adult male horse, especially one kept for breeding **2.** a man who is regarded as having great sexual prowess (*informal*) [14C. < Anglo-Norman *estaloun*]

Stal·lone /stə lṓn/, **Sylvester** (*b.* 1946) US actor. He is best known for playing heroes in Hollywood action movies, most notably a boxer in the *Rocky* series (1976–90). Full name **Stallone, Michael Sylvester Enzio**

stal·wart /stáwlwərt/ *adj* **1.** DEPENDABLE dependable and loyal **2.** STRONG sturdy and strong ■ *n* HARD-WORKING LOYAL

SUPPORTER a faithful, dependable, and hard-working supporter of somebody or something ○ *phones manned by party stalwarts* [15C. Scottish variant of obsolete *stalworth* < Old English *stǣlwierþe* "good, serviceable," literally "having a worthy foundation" < *staþol* "foundation" (see STADDLE) + *weorþ* (see WORTH)] —**stal·wart·ly** *adv* —**stal·wart·ness** *n*

sta·men /stáymən/ (*plural* **-mens** or **-mi·na** /stáymənə, stámmənə/) *n* the male reproductive organ of a flower, typically consisting of a stalk (**filament**) bearing a pollen-producing anther at its tip [Mid-17C. < Latin, "thread"] —**sta·mi·nal** /stáymən'l, stámmə-/ *adj* —**sta·mi·nif·e·rous** /stàymə níffərəss, stàmmə-/ *adj*

Stam·ford /stámfərd/ city in southwestern Connecticut, founded in 1641. Population: 119,850 (2002 estimate).

stam·i·na /stámmənə/ *n* enduring physical or mental energy and strength that allows somebody to do something for a long time [Early 18C. < Latin, plural of *stamen* "thread"] —**stam·i·nal** *adj*

sta·mi·nate /stáymənət, stámmə-, -nàyt/ *adj* describes plants that have stamens, especially flowers with stamens but without female parts (**carpels**)

stam·i·node /stáymə nōd, stámmə-/, **stam·i·no·di·um** /stàymə nōdee əm, stàmmə-/ (*plural* **-di·a** /-dee ə/) *n* a sterile or vestigial stamen. It forms a conspicuous part of some flowers, e.g., in the iris. [Early 19C. < modern Latin *staminodium* < *stamen* "thread"]

stam·mel /stámm'l/ *n* **1.** a coarse woolen cloth, usually red. Use: in medieval times, undergarments. **2.** a bright red color, like that of stammel cloth [Mid-16C. Alteration of obsolete *stamin*, via French < Latin *stamineus* "consisting of threads" < *stamen* "thread"] —**stam·mel** *adj*

stam·mer /stámmər/ *vti* (**-mered, -mer·ing, -mers**) to speak, or say something, with many quick hesitations and repeated consonants or syllables because of a speech condition or a strong emotion ■ *n* a speech condition that makes somebody speak with involuntary hesitations and repetition of consonants or syllables. Stammering will usually respond to treatment from a speech therapist. [Old English *stamerian* < Germanic, "halt, stutter"] —**stam·mer·er** *n*

stamp /stamp/ *n* **1.** GUMMED PAPER PAYING FOR POSTAGE a small piece of gummed paper that is stuck on an envelope or package to show that postage has been paid **2.** CANCELLATION ACROSS POSTAGE STAMP a mark put across a postage stamp on an envelope or package to show that the stamp has been used **3.** SMALL BLOCK FOR PRINTING DESIGN a small block with a raised design or lettering that can be printed onto paper by inking the block and pressing it to the paper **4.** DESIGN PRINTED ONTO PAPER WITH STAMP a design printed onto paper using a stamp in order to show that a document has been read, canceled, or officially approved **5.** GUMMED PAPER AS OFFICIAL MARK a piece of printed gummed paper affixed to a document as an official sign of something such as approval or validity **6.** CHARACTERISTIC OF SOMETHING a characteristic or distinguishing sign or impression **7.** TYPE OR KIND a class or type of something **8.** WAY OF PAYING FOR SOMETHING a piece of paper that can be purchased as a way of redeeming part or all of the amount charged for goods or a service **9.** ACT OF BANGING DOWN FOOT the action of bringing a foot down forcefully on a surface **10.** INDUST MACHINE FOR CRUSHING ROCKS AND ORE a machine that crushes rocks and ore by a weight being lifted and dropped ■ *v* (**stamped, stamp·ing, stamps**) **1.** *vt* PUT STAMP ON DOCUMENT to press a stamp onto a document leaving a design or lettering on it in order to show that it has been seen, dated, canceled, or officially approved **2.** *vt* MAIL STICK POSTAGE STAMP ON SOMETHING to stick a stamp on an envelope or package **3.** *vti* BANG FOOT DOWN to bring a foot down forcefully on a surface **4.** *vi* WALK FORCEFULLY to walk by taking short forceful steps **5.** *vt* HAVE LASTING EFFECT ON SOMEBODY to have a lasting effect or influence on somebody **6.** *vi UK* SUPPRESS SOMETHING OR SOMEBODY to suppress or eradicate something or somebody ○ *He stamped on any suggestion he should resign.* **7.** *vt* INDUST CRUSH ROCKS to crush or pound rocks and ore [12C. Probably < assumed Old English *stampian* "pound" < Germanic] —**stamp·a·ble** *adj* —**stamped** *adj*

stamp out *vt* **1.** ERADICATE SOMETHING to put an end to something **2.** EXTINGUISH SOMETHING to extinguish something by stamping on it with the feet **3.** CUT SOMETHING OUT USING SHARP TOOL to cut out a shape or object by pressing a sharp-edged machine or tool onto a material

Stamp Act *n* a law passed in the British Parliament in 1765 introducing a tax on legal documents, commercial contracts, licenses, publications, and playing cards in the North American colonies. Because of colonial opposition, the first Stamp Act was repealed in March 1766 but it was later replaced by others.

stamp col·lect·ing *n* the collecting of postage stamps as a hobby or investment —**stamp col·lec·tor** *n*

stam·pede /stam pēed/ *n* **1.** HEADLONG RUSH OF ANIMALS an uncontrolled headlong rush of frightened animals **2.** HEADLONG SURGE OF CROWD an uncontrolled surging rush of a crowd of people **3.** SUDDEN RUSH OF PEOPLE DOING SOMETHING a sudden rush of many people all doing or wanting to do something at the same time ○ *There was a stampede to take advantage of the low prices.* **4.** FESTIVAL INCLUDING RODEO in the western United States and especially in Canada, a celebration, usually held annually, that includes a rodeo along with contests, exhibitions, dancing, and entertainment (*regional*) ■ *v* (**-ped·ed, -ped·ing, -pedes**) **1.** *vti* RUSH FORWARD IN FRIGHTENED SURGE to rush forward in a frightened headlong surge, or make animals or people surge forward **2.** *vt* FORCE SOMEBODY INTO DOING SOMETHING to force somebody to do something before he or she is ready or has properly thought about it [Early 19C. < Mexican Spanish *estampida* < Spanish, "uproar"] —**stam·ped·er** *n*

stamp·er /stámpər/ *n* **1.** SOMEBODY OR SOMETHING THAT STAMPS a person or device used for stamping **2.** MACHINE FOR STAMPING SOMETHING a tool or machine that stamps something, especially ore being pulverized **3.** RECORDING MOLD FOR DISK RECORDINGS a mold from which disk recordings are pressed

stamp·ing ground /stámping-/ *n* a place where somebody is habitually found (*informal*)

stamp mill *n* a machine in which rocks and ore are finely crushed, usually operated by hydraulic power, or a building housing one or more such machines

stan /staan/ *n* a central Asian country, especially one bordering Afghanistan, whose name ends with the suffix "-stan" (*slang*)

stance /stanss/ *n* **1.** ATTITUDE TOWARD SOMETHING an attitude or view that somebody takes about something **2.** WAY OF STANDING the way that a person or an animal stands **3.** POSITION OF WHEELS the position of a vehicle's wheels in relation to its bodywork ○ *The newer model has a wider stance and a taller cab.* **4.** POSITION OF PLAYER the position in which a player holds the body in attempting to hit a ball, e.g., in baseball or golf **5.** CLIMBING PLACE FOR PITCHING AND BELAYING a place where a mountain climber can pitch and belay **6.** *Scotland* TRANSP TRANSPORTATION WAITING PLACE a place where buses or taxis wait for passengers [Mid-16C. Via French, "position" < Italian *stanza* (see STANZA)]

stanch[1] *adj* same as **staunch**[1]

USAGE See *stanch*[2].

stanch[2] /stawnch, staanch, stanch/ (**stanched, stanch·ing, stanch·es**), **staunch** /stáwnch/ (**staunched, staunch·ing, staunch·es**) *v* **1.** *vti* STOP LIQUID FLOW to stop the flow of a liquid, particularly blood, or be stopped from flowing **2.** *vt* STOP WOUND FROM BLEEDING to stop a wound from bleeding or exuding pus **3.** *vt* ASSUAGE SOMETHING to assuage or allay something bad [14C. < Old French *estanchier* < Latin *stant-*, present participle of *stare* (see STATION)] —**stanch·a·ble** *adj* —**stanch·er** *n*

USAGE stanch or **staunch**? There are two words spelled both ***staunch*** and ***stanch***. The adjective ***staunch*** is the most commonly used form in the meaning "loyal" (*a staunch defender of freedom*), though ***stanch*** can also mean the same thing. Conversely, ***stanch*** is much more common as a verb meaning "to stop the flow of liquid," though ***staunch*** can also mean the same thing: *trying to stanch the flow of blood.*

stan·chion /stánchən/ *n* **1.** UPRIGHT SUPPORTING POLE a vertical pole, bar, or beam used to support something **2.** AGRIC FRAME FOR CONFINING COW an upright frame in which the neck of a cow is loosely fitted, usually to confine the cow for milking ■ *vt* (**-chioned, -chion·ing, -chions**) SUPPORT SOMETHING WITH POLE to support something using a vertical pole, bar, or beam [15C. < Old French *estanchon* < *estance* "prop, support"]

stand /stand/ *v* (**stood** /stŏŏd/, **stand·ing, stands**) **1.** *vti* BE OR SET UPRIGHT to be in an upright position, or put something in an upright position ○ *I was standing to the left of him.* ○ *Stand the box in the corner.* **2.** *vi* GET UP ON FEET to get up into an upright position from a sitting or lying position ○ *The newborn foal tried to stand but only collapsed again.* **3.** *vi* BE IN PARTICULAR PLACE to be situated or positioned in a particular place ○ *The castle stands on a headland.* **4.** *vi* BE IN PARTICULAR STATE to be in a particular condition or state ○ *The old place stands in need of a few repairs.* ○ *The document can't be published as it stands.* **5.** *vi* MEASURE IN HEIGHT to be of a particular height when upright ○ *He stood six feet tall.* **6.** *vi* BE AT PARTICULAR POINT to be at a particular point while subject to change or fluctuation ○ *The balance of the account stands at $400.* **7.** *vi* REMAIN MOTIONLESS to remain in a particular place without moving or being used ○ *The car stood outside the office all morning.* **8.** *vi* REMAIN VALID to continue to be in effect or existence ○ *Her world record still stands.* **9.** *vi* STOP to come to a halt ○ *I had to stand and catch my breath.* **10.** *vi* GATHER AND LIE to gather somewhere and not flow away ○ *rainwater standing in pools* **11.** *vt* TOLERATE SOMETHING OR SOMEBODY UNPLEASANT to accept or put up with something or somebody regarded as unpleasant ○ *He can't stand being kept waiting.* **12.** *vt* UNDERGO SOMETHING WITHOUT HARM to resist or bear something without being harmed or damaged ○ *The mechanism is too delicate to stand rough handling.* **13.** *vt* SUBMIT TO SOMETHING to submit or be subjected to something ○ *I am prepared to stand trial.* **14.** *vt* BUY SOMETHING FOR SOMEBODY to pay for something such as a drink for somebody else to have ○ *My uncle offered to stand dinner for all of us.* **15.** *vt* BENEFIT FROM SOMETHING to benefit from something, or be no worse for something ○ *I could stand to lose a few more pounds.* **16.** *vi* POL SEEK ELECTION to enter an election as a candidate ○ *She decided not to stand at the next election.* **17.** *vi* MIL FIGHT RESOLUTELY to fight resolutely or give battle, often after having been in retreat ○ *The general was convinced the enemy would not stand if attacked.* ■ *n* **1.** ACT OF STANDING the act or an example of standing ○ *a long stand in the airport* **2.** ATTITUDE an opinion that somebody has or an attitude that somebody adopts ○ *Management took a tough stand on absenteeism.* **3.** SUPPORTING STRUCTURE a framework or structure on which something is supported ○ *a music stand* **4.** PIECE OF FURNITURE a piece of furniture on which clothes or accessories are hung or supported (*often used in combination*) ○ *an umbrella stand* ○ *a hat stand* **5.** STATIONARY CONDITION a state of having stopped or being stationary ○ *The runaway vehicle came to a stand in a field.* **6.** PLACE WHERE SOMETHING IS SOLD a booth or stall where something is sold or given out (*often used in combination*) ○ *a refreshment stand* **7.** EXHIBITION AREA one of several places in an exhibition where something is displayed **8.** BOT AREA OF GROWING THINGS a group of several plants, especially trees, growing together in one place ○ *a stand of trees* **9.** LAW same as **witness stand** **10.** HALT TO FIGHT a halt made, especially by a force that has been retreating, to give battle ○ *Custer's last stand* **11.** TRANSP PLACE FOR WAITING VEHICLES a place where vehicles, especially taxis, wait to pick up passengers (*usually used in combination*) ○ *a taxi stand* **12.** THEATER STOP FOR PERFORMANCE a halt made to give a performance during a tour by a performer or theatrical company ○ *a three-week stand out of town* ■ **stands** *npl* PLACE FOR SPECTATORS a large seating area for spectators in a sports stadium [Old English *standan* < Indo-European] —**stand·ee** /stan dēe/ *n* ◇ **stand or fall by something** to succeed or fail depending on particular circumstances

USAGE See *sit*.

stand by *v* **1.** *vi* REMAIN READY to wait in a state of readiness to act if required ○ *Stand by for further orders.* **2.** *vi* BE PRESENT WITHOUT ACTION to be present while something is happening but play no part in it ○ *I'm not prepared to stand by and let this go on.* **3.** *vt* SUPPORT SOMEBODY to support or remain faithful to somebody ○ *Her friends all stood by her.* **4.** *vt*

ADHERE TO SOMETHING to continue to assert or believe in something ○ *I stand by what I said yesterday.*
stand down *v* **1.** *vi* **RESIGN** to resign from office or withdraw from a contest **2.** *vi* **END TESTIMONY** to leave a witness stand after having been questioned **3.** *vti* **END DUTY** to end somebody's period of duty, or go off duty, especially military duty **4.** *vti* MIL **GO OFF ALERT** to go off alert, or be taken off alert or out of a combat zone
stand for *vt* **1. MEAN SOMETHING** to mean or represent something else **2. BELIEVE IN SOMETHING** to believe in something strongly and fight for it ○ *To agree with this would go against everything I stand for.* **3.** POL **BECOME CANDIDATE FOR SOMETHING** to enter an election as a candidate for a particular office **4. TOLERATE SOMETHING** to put up with something ○ *She won't stand for any nonsense.* **5.** NAUT **HEAD FOR PLACE** to set a course for a particular destination ○ *The fleet stood for home.*
stand in *vi* to take the place of somebody or something else as a substitute ○ *I'm looking for someone to stand in for me next week.*
stand off *vti* **1.** to keep at a distance from something, or make somebody or something stay at a distance **2.** to sail a vessel away from something such as a shore
stand on *v* **1.** *vt* to insist on something or see it as being important ○ *We don't stand on ceremony in this house.* **2.** *vi* to continue sailing on the same course
stand out *vi* **1. BE CONSPICUOUS** to be conspicuous or prominent **2. STICK OUT** to project or protrude from something **3. REFUSE TO ACCEPT SOMETHING** to refuse to accept or comply with something, especially after others have done so ○ *stood out against the court's decision and appealed it*
stand to *vti* to take up position in readiness for military action, or make somebody do this
stand up *v* **1.** *vti* to rise to an upright position, or make something do this **2.** *vi* to be seen as still valid or right despite being closely examined or criticized ○ *I don't think her testimony will stand up in court.*
stand up for *vt* **1.** to defend the interests of somebody **2.** same as **stand up with**
stand up to *v* **1.** *vt* to resist or refuse to be cowed by somebody ○ *He'll back down if you stand up to him.* **2.** *vi* to undergo something that is potentially damaging without being badly affected ○ *These cars are able to stand up to being driven on rough terrain.*
stand up with *vt* to act as best man or maid of honor for somebody who is getting married

stand-a·lone *adj* able to operate as a self-contained unit independently of a computer network or system

stan·dard /stándərd/ *n* **1. LEVEL OF QUALITY OR EXCELLENCE** the level of quality or excellence attained by somebody or something **2. LEVEL OF QUALITY ACCEPTED AS NORM** a level of quality or excellence that is accepted as the norm or by which actual attainments are judged (*often used in the plural*) **3.** MUSIC **ITEM IN USUAL REPERTOIRE** something, especially a song or other piece of music, that is very popular or is performed as part of the usual repertoire of a performer or performers ○ *played all the old standards* **4.** FIN **COMMODITY AS BASIS OF CURRENCY VALUE** the commodity or commodities on which the value of a currency or monetary system is based **5. AUTHORIZED MODEL OF UNIT OF MEASUREMENT** an authorized model used to define a unit of measurement **6. DISTINCTIVE FLAG** a flag with a distinctive design that is the emblem of, and often a focus of loyalty to, a particular nation, person, or group **7.** MIL **DEVICE USED AS BATTLE RALLYING POINT** a flag or other symbolic device attached to a pole and used as a rallying point for troops in battle **8.** COINS **PROPORTION OF METAL IN COIN** the proportion of gold or silver and of nonprecious metal that a coin is legally required to contain **9.** HERALDRY **LONG TAPERING FLAG** a long tapering flag ending in two points and with heraldic devices on it, used in heraldry as an emblem of a person or group. It was formerly carried on ceremonial occasions by or before the nobleman to whom it belonged. **10.** BOT **PLANT WITH STRAIGHT BARE STEM** a plant, especially a fruit tree or rose, trained in such a way that the leaves and flowers grow at the top of a straight bare stem **11.** HOUSEHOLD **SUPPORTING BASE** a base or support for something such as a large tall vase **12.** BOT **LARGE UPPER PETAL OF PEA** the large upper petal in the flowers of plants of the pea family ■ **stan·dards** *npl* **PRINCIPLES** principles or values that govern a person's behavior ■ *adj* **1. NORMAL** constituting or not differing from the norm **2. WIDELY USED AND RESPECTED** very widely used and generally regarded as authoritative ○ *the standard text in thermodynamics* **3.** GRAM **GRAMMATICALLY CORRECT** regarded as correct or acceptable by the majority of educated speakers of or authorities on a language **4.** BOT **TRAINED TO GROW WITH STRAIGHT STEM** describes plants that are trained in such a way that the leaves and flowers grow at the top of a straight bare stem [12C. Via Anglo-Norman *estaundart* "flag to which troops rally" < Old French *estandart*] —**stan·dard·ly** *adv*

standard atmosphere *n* MEASURE same as **atmosphere** (sense 6)

stan·dard-bear·er *n* **1.** a leader or prominent and inspiring representative of a movement, cause, or party **2.** the bearer of a standard or flag, especially for a military unit

Stan·dard·bred /stándərd brèd/ *n* a horse belonging to a North American breed specially bred for speed and stamina in harness races

stan·dard can·dle *n* MEASURE same as **candela**

stan·dard cell *n* an electric cell that produces a constant known voltage and can be used to calibrate voltage-measuring equipment

stan·dard cost *n* the budgeted expenditure of a regular manufacturing process against which the actual cost is measured

stan·dard de·vi·a·tion *n* a statistical measure of the amount by which a set of values differs from the arithmetical mean, equal to the square root of the mean of the differences' squares

stan·dard e·lec·trode po·ten·tial *n* the voltage developed by an electrode of a particular element placed in a solution of the element's ions, measured against that of hydrogen under standardized conditions

Stan·dard Eng·lish *n* the variety of the English language used by educated speakers and regarded as representing correct usage in grammar, spelling, vocabulary, and punctuation, while taking into account some regional differences

stan·dard er·ror *n* in statistics, the standard deviation of the sample in a frequency distribution divided by the square root of the number of values in the sample. It is a measure of the variability that a constant would be expected to show during sampling.

stan·dard gauge *n* the gauge used for most public railroad systems worldwide, the distance between the rails being 4 ft. $8\frac{1}{2}$ in./143.5 cm

Stan·dard Gen·er·al·ized Mark·up Lan·guage *n* COMPUT full form of **SGML**

stan·dard·ize /stándər dīz/ (**-ized, -iz·ing, -iz·es**) *vt* **1.** to remove variations and irregularities in something and make all types or examples of it the same or bring them into conformity with one another **2.** to assess something or determine its properties by comparing it with a standard —**stan·dard·i·za·tion** /stàndərdi záysh'n/ *n* —**stan·dard·iz·er** *n*
standardize on *vt* to choose something as a standard and remove variations and irregularities

stan·dard·ized test *n* a test, administered according to standardized procedures, that assesses a student's aptitude by comparison with a standard

stan·dard lamp *n UK* same as **floor lamp**

stan·dard of liv·ing *n* the level of material comfort enjoyed by a person, group, or society

stan·dard op·er·at·ing pro·ce·dure *n* a procedure that is usually followed when carrying out an operation or dealing with a situation

stan·dard state *n* the pure form of a chemical substance that is stable at a given pressure and temperature

stan·dard time *n* a system of measuring time in relation to the natural day, usually based on the mean solar time at the central meridian of a particular time zone

stand·by /stánd bī/ *n* **1. PERSON OR THING READILY AVAILABLE** somebody or something that can always be relied on to be available and useful, especially if needed as a substitute or in an emergency **2.** TRAVEL **UNRESERVED TICKET OR PASSENGER WITHOUT RESERVATION** an unreserved ticket or a passenger having no prior reservation on a mode of public transportation such as an aircraft ■ *adj* **1. HELD IN RESERVE** able to be used as a replacement ○ *standby generator* **2.** TRAVEL **UNRESERVED AND SUBJECT TO AVAILABILITY** made available, usually at a lower price, shortly before the departure of a flight when there are seats remaining unsold, or using a ticket made available in this way ■ *adv* TRAVEL **ON STANDBY BASIS** on the basis of having no prior reservation to travel ○ *flew standby from Washington to Amsterdam* [Late 18C] ◇ **on standby** available for use or service if necessary

stand-down, stand·down /stánd dòwn/ *n* a return to normal status after being on alert, or the withdrawal of a military presence

stand-in *n* **1.** somebody or something that acts as a temporary replacement **2.** a replacement for an actor in a movie, e.g., during preparatory or dangerous action —**stand-in** *adj*

stand·ing /stánding/ *n* **1. STATUS AND REPUTATION** somebody's reputation or position, e.g., in society or business ○ *a person of some standing in computer electronics* **2. DURATION** the period over which something has been in existence ○ *a friend of long standing* ■ *adj* **UPRIGHT** performed while standing rather than sitting or moving ○ *received a standing ovation* ■ **stand·ings** *npl* **LISTING OF SCORES** the official record of the relative positions of competitors taking part in an event ■ *adj* **1. PERMANENT** remaining permanently in existence or in force ○ *You have a standing invitation to visit us whenever you wish.* **2. NOT FLOWING** not flowing, or containing water that cannot flow or run away ○ *a pool of standing water* **3.** AGRIC **NOT CUT DOWN** growing where planted, having not been cut down ○ *a standing forest*

USAGE See *sit.*

stand·ing ar·my *n* a permanent professional military force maintained by a country in times of peace as well as war

stand·ing com·mit·tee *n* a committee that remains in existence permanently in order to deal with a particular issue

stand·ing crop *n* the total mass of living things of all kinds or of one specific kind found in an area or ecosystem at a specific time

stand·ing or·der *n* **1.** an order or rule, especially one governing military procedures, that remains in force on all relevant occasions until it is specifically revoked **2.** *UK* an instruction given by an account holder to a bank to pay a specific sum of money at fixed intervals to a person or account

stand·ing rig·ging *n* the wires and ropes holding the masts and spars of a sailing ship or boat that are more or less permanently fixed in place

stand·ing room *n* space where people can only stand, not sit

stand·ing wave *n* a stationary wave characterized by points of zero vibration and points of maximum vibration, occurring when two waves of equal frequency and intensity traveling in opposite directions combine [Because the points of minimum and maximum vibration remain stationary]

Stan·dish /stándish/, **Miles** (1584?–1656) English-born American colonist. He sailed with the Pilgrims in the *Mayflower* to New England, became a leader of the Plymouth Colony, and with John Alden founded the town of Duxbury, Massachusetts.

stand·off /stánd àwf, -ôf/ *n* **1.** a situation in which no result or conclusion can be reached because the two sides in a contest or dispute are equally matched or are equally intransigent **2.** a state of equality, e.g., in a sports contest or an election **3.** RUGBY same as **stand-off half**

stand-off half *n* in rugby, a player who plays behind the forwards and the scrum half, provides a link between them and the three-quarter backs, and often has control of the team's tactics

stand·off in·su·la·tor *n* an insulator that supports an electrical conductor and keeps it at a distance from other conducting elements. The insulators supporting power lines are examples of this.

stand·off·ish /stànd áwfish, -óffish/ *adj* reluctant to show friendship or enter into conversation with other people —**stand·off·ish·ly** *adv* —**stand·off·ish·ness** *n*

stand·off mis·sile *n* a guided missile that can be fired from an aircraft at a sufficient distance from its target to be out of range of enemy defenses

stand oil *n* a thick drying oil used in oil enamel paints, made by heating linseed or another oil to a high temperature [Translation of German *Standöl*; it was formerly prepared by allowing linseed oil to stand]

stand·out /stánd òwt/ *n* somebody or something that is especially prominent or outstanding (*informal*)

stand·pat·ter /stánd pàttər/ *n US* a resister of change, especially in politics

stand·pipe /stánd pìp/ *n* a vertical open-ended pipe attached to a pipeline to act as a pressure regulator, ensuring that the pressure head at that point cannot exceed the length of the pipe

stand·point /stánd pòynt/ *n* a way of considering an event or issue, or one of the contexts in which an event or issue can be considered ○ *From an ecological standpoint, this is an utter disaster.*

stand·still /stánd stìl/ *n* a situation in which all movement or activity ceases and further movement or activity is prevented ○ *Traffic is at a standstill.*

stand·still a·gree·ment *n* an agreement that things should remain as they are, especially one between a creditor country and a debtor country that needs extra time to repay its debt

stand·up /stánd ùp/ *adj* **1. INVOLVING SOLO PERFORMANCE BY COMEDIAN** involving a performance by a comedian standing alone on stage telling jokes or stories to an audience ○ *stand-up comedy* **2. AT WHICH PEOPLE STAND** where or at which people stand, especially to eat or drink ○ *A large standup buffet was laid out for the reception.* **3. STANDING ERECT** standing erect and not folded down **4.** *US* **TRUSTWORTHY** showing the qualities of honesty, loyalty, and dependability (*informal*) ■ *n* **STANDUP COMEDY** comedy in which the performer stands alone on stage telling jokes or stories to an audience

Stan·field /stán feeld/, **Robert Lorne** (1914–2003) Canadian lawyer and politician. He was premier of Nova Scotia (1956–67).

Stan·ford-Bi·net test /stànfərd bi náy-/ *n* an intelligence test commonly given to children [Early 20C. After *Stanford* University, California + Alfred *Binet*, (1857–1911), French psychologist]

stan·hope /stán hòp/ *n* a light open horse-drawn carriage with a single seat and two or four wheels [Early 19C. After Fitzroy H. R. *Stanhope* (1787–1864), British cleric for whom one was first made]

Stan·i·slav·sky /stànni slaáv skee, -slaáf-, stənyi slaáf skyee/, **Stan·i·slav·ski, Konstantin** (1863–1938) Russian actor and theater director. He helped to found the Moscow Arts Theater (1889) and there adopted methods of training actors that greatly influenced theater in the 20th century. Full name **Stanislavsky, Konstantin Sergeyevich Alexeyev** —**Stan·i·slav·ski·an** *adj*

Stan·i·slav·sky meth·od *n* THEATER, ARTS same as **Method**

stank past tense of **stink**

Stan·ley /stánnlee/ capital of the Falkland Islands. Population: 1,232 (1986).

Stan·ley /stánlee/, **Sir H. M.** (1841–1904) British journalist and explorer. On his African expeditions he located David Livingstone at Ujiji on Lake Tanganyika (1871), traced the Lualaba and Congo rivers to the sea (1874–77), and laid the foundations for the establishment of the Congo Free State (1879–84). Full name **Stanley, Sir Henry Morton**. Born **Rowlands, John**

Stan·ley Cup HOCKEY the trophy that is awarded to the National Hockey League team that wins the annual championship

Stan·ley Pool former name for **Malebo Pool**

stann- *prefix* tin ○ *stanniferous*

stan·nic /stánnik/ *adj* relating to or containing tin, especially with a valence of four [Late 18C. < late Latin *stannum* "tin"]

stan·nic sul·fide *n* a yellow or gold-colored solid compound of sulfur and tin. Use: pigment.

stan·nif·er·ous /sta nífərəss/ *adj* containing or yielding tin [Early 19C. < late Latin *stannum* "tin"]

stan·nite /stá nìt/ *n* a gray metallic oxide mineral containing copper, iron, and tin. Use: source of tin. [Mid-19C. < late Latin *stannum* "tin"]

stan·nous /stánnəss/ *adj* relating to or containing tin, especially with a valence of two [Mid-19C. < late Latin *stannum* "tin"]

stan·nous fluor·ide *n* a white crystalline powder with a bitter salty taste. Use: fluoride toothpaste. Formula: SnF_2.

Stan·sted /stán stèd/ third largest airport serving London, England, to the northeast of the city

Stan·thorpe /stán thàwrp/ town in southeastern Queensland, Australia. It is one of the highest towns in the state at 2,660 ft./811 m. Population: 10,515 (2002 estimate).

Stan·ton /stánt'n/, **Edwin McMasters** (1814–69) US lawyer and government official. He was US attorney general (1860–61) and secretary of war (1862–68) under presidents Abraham Lincoln and Andrew Johnson. His expulsion from the cabinet became the cause of Johnson's impeachment.

Stan·ton, Elizabeth Cady (1815–1902) US social reformer. She worked in the abolitionist and temperance movements, and after 1840 devoted herself to the campaign for women's suffrage and civil rights.

> "We hold these truths to be self-evident: that all men and women are created equal."
> [Elizabeth Cady Stanton, "Declaration of Sentiments" *at the First Women's Rights Convention, Seneca Falls, New York, History of Woman Suffrage*; 1881]

stan·za /stánzə/ *n* a number of lines of verse forming a separate unit within a poem. In many poems, each stanza has the same number of lines and the same rhythm and rhyme scheme. [Late 16C. Via Italian < assumed Vulgar Latin *stantia* "a standing, stopping place" < Latin *stare* "to stand"] —**stan·za·ic** /stan záy ik/ *adj*

sta·pe·dec·to·my /stàypi déktəmee/ (*plural* **-mies**) *n* surgical removal of the stapes of the ear. It is performed in treating some forms of hearing loss. [Late 19C. < modern Latin *staped-*, stem of *stapes* (see STAPES)]

sta·pe·des ANAT plural of **stapes**

sta·pe·li·a /stə peélee ə/ (*plural* **-as** or *same*) *n* a plant similar to the cactus, with thick fleshy four-angled stems and no leaves. Flowers: large, mottled, foul-smelling. Native to: Africa. Genus: *Stapelia.* [Late 18C. < modern Latin, after Jan Bode van *Stapel* (d. 1636), Dutch botanist]

sta·pes /stáy peez/ (*plural same* or **-pe·des** /stə peé deez/) *n* a small stirrup-shaped bone in the middle ear of mammals, the innermost of the three small bones that transmit vibration to the inner ear [Mid-17C. < medieval Latin, "stirrup"] —**sta·pe·di·al** /stə peédee əl/ *adj*

staph /staf/ *n* MED same as **staphylococcus** (*informal*) [Early 20C. Shortening]

staph·y·lo·coc·cus /stàffəlō kókəss/ (*plural* **-coc·ci** /-kóksì/) *n* a bacterium that typically occurs in clusters resembling grapes, normally inhabits the skin and mucous membranes, and may cause disease. These bacteria commonly infect the skin, eyes, and urinary tract, and some produce toxins responsible for septicemia and food poisoning. Genus: *Staphylococcus.* [Late 19C. < modern Latin < Greek *staphulē* "bunch of grapes" + *kokkos* "berry"] —**staph·y·lo·coc·cal** *adj*

sta·ple[1] /stáyp'l/ *n* **1. BENT WIRE USED TO FASTEN PAPERS** a small thin piece of metal wire bent into the shape of a flattened U with square corners, used to fasten things together, especially sheets of paper. The staple is driven through the material by a device that also bends its two ends inward and flattens them so that they grip the material firmly. **2. U-SHAPED FASTENER FOR WOOD OR MASONRY** a small U-shaped piece of strong metal wire with two sharp points, usually driven into a surface to hold something such as a bolt or cable in place ■ *vt* (**-pled, -pling, -ples**) **FASTEN SOMETHING WITH STAPLES** to fasten something to something else or in position with staples [Old English *stapol* "post, pillar" < Germanic]

sta·ple[2] /stáyp'l/ *n* **1. BASIC INGREDIENT OF DIET** a food that forms the basis of the diet of the people of a region or of an animal **2. PRINCIPAL OR RECURRING INGREDIENT** a principal or continually recurring ingredient or feature of something ○ *Lurid stories are a staple of tabloid journalism.* **3. MOST IMPORTANT PRODUCT OF TRADE** the commodity or product that is most important to the trade of a country, region, or organization **4.** *US* **RAW MATERIAL** a raw material, especially the principal raw material produced or grown in a region **5.** MANUF **WOOL, COTTON, OR FLAX FIBER** wool, cotton, or flax fiber graded according to its length and fineness ■ *vt* (**-pled, -pling, -ples**) MANUF **GRADE FIBERS** to grade wool, cotton, or flax fiber according to its length and fineness [14C. Via French < Middle Low German, Middle Dutch *stapel* "shop; pillar" < Germanic]

sta·ple gun *n* a powerful device used to drive heavy metal staples into wood or masonry

sta·pler /stáyplər/ *n* a device that fastens paper and other materials together using staples, usually consisting of a flat metal base, a spring-loaded magazine of staples, and a top section

star /staar/ *n* **1. MASS OF GAS IN SPACE** a gaseous mass in space that generates energy by thermonuclear reactions, e.g., the Sun. Stars range in size from that of a planet to one larger than the Earth's orbit. **2. POINT OF LIGHT IN NIGHT SKY** an astronomical object usually visible as a small bright point of light in the night sky **3. STAR SHAPE** a shape representing or based on that of a star as seen in the night sky, usually having five or more triangular points radiating from a center **4. STAR-SHAPED SYMBOL OF MERIT OR RANK** a star-shaped object or symbol used as a sign of merit, quality, or rank **5.** PRINTING, LING same as **asterisk** **6. POPULAR PERFORMER** a very famous, successful, and popular performer, especially in a field of entertainment or in sports **7. MOST IMPORTANT OR PROFICIENT PERSON** an especially proficient or important member of a group **8.** ASTROL **ASTRONOMICAL OBJECT IN RELATION TO FATE** a planet or constellation believed to influence somebody's character or fate on Earth ■ **stars** *npl* ASTROL **DESTINY** somebody's future, especially as supposedly revealed in a horoscope (*informal*) ■ *v* (**starred, star·ring, stars**) **1.** *vt* **HAVE SOMEBODY AS LEADING PERFORMER** to have somebody as the leading performer or as one of the leading performers **2.** *vi* **BE LEADING PERFORMER** to be the leading performer or one of the leading performers in something such as a movie or play ○ *starring in his first major movie* **3.** *vt* PRINTING same as **asterisk** **4.** *vt* **COVER OR DECORATE SOMETHING WITH STARS** to cover or decorate something with stars, or with many brilliant or colorful objects so as to give an effect comparable to that of the stars in the night sky ■ *adj* **OUTSTANDING** very or most important, skillful, or successful ○ *our star player* [Old English *steorra* < Indo-European] ◇ **see stars** to see flashes of light, e.g., after receiving a hard blow to the head

star an·ise *n* **1.** a star-shaped fruit consisting of 6 to 12 woody single-seeded carpels, with an aniseed flavor. Use: in Chinese cooking and medicine, source of oil. **2.** an evergreen tree that yields star anise. Native to: China. Latin name: *Illicium verum.*

star ap·ple *n* **1.** an apple-shaped fruit with a smooth greenish purple skin and a star-shaped arrangement of seeds inside **2.** an evergreen tree that produces star apples. Native to: tropical America. Latin name: *Chrysophyllum cainito.*

Sta·ra Za·go·ra /staárə zə gáwrə/ city in central Bulgaria, situated about 95 mi./153 km west of the Black Sea port of Burgas. Population: 151,218 (1996).

star bill·ing *n* the fact of being advertised as the leading performer in something

star·board /staárbərd/ *n* **RIGHT-HAND SIDE** the direction to the right of somebody facing the front of a ship or aircraft ■ *adj* **ON RIGHT-HAND SIDE** on, toward, or from the right-hand side of somebody facing the front of a ship or aircraft ■ *adv* **TOWARD RIGHT-HAND SIDE** toward starboard or the starboard side of a ship or aircraft ■ *vt* (**-board·ed, -board·ing, -boards**) **TURN TOWARD RIGHT** to turn or move something, especially the helm, toward starboard [Old English *stēorbord* < *stēor* "steering paddle" + *bord* (see BOARD)]

star·burst /staár bùrst/ *n* **1.** a pattern of lines or light rays radiating outward from a center **2.** a strong sudden burst of star formation

star·burst ga·lax·y *n* a galaxy in a stage of intense star production

star·burst mol·e·cule *n* CHEM same as **dendrimer**

star cac·tus *n* a cactus with spines arranged in clusters like stars. Flowers: yellow. Native to: Mexico. Genus: *Astrophytum.*

starch /staarch/ *n* **1.** CARBOHYDRATE SUBSTANCE a natural substance composed of chains of glucose units, made by plants and providing a major energy source for animals. The two main components of starch are amylose and amylopectin. Formula: $(C_6H_{10}O_5)_n$. **2.** STIFFENING SUBSTANCE FOR FABRICS a white powder extracted from potatoes and grain. Use: fabric stiffener. **3.** STARCHY FOODSTUFF a foodstuff that contains a large amount of starch **4.** STIFF AND FORMAL MANNER behavior marked by a stiff manner and formality **5.** COURAGE great courage or energy ■ *vt* (**starched, starch·ing, starch·es**) STIFFEN FABRIC to stiffen fabric with starch [Assumed Old English *stercan* "stiffen" < Germanic, "be rigid"]

star cham·ber *n* a court or tribunal noted for being harsh, arbitrary, and unaccountable in its proceedings

Star Cham·ber *n* a court established by King Henry VII of England to try civil and criminal cases, especially those involving the security of the state, in secret. It was noted for its arbitrary proceedings and was abolished in 1641. [Because the ceiling of the original courtroom was decorated with stars]

starch syr·up *n* a syrup containing dextrose, maltose, and dextrin that is created through the incomplete hydrolysis of glucose

starch·y /staárchee/ (**-i·er, -i·est**) *adj* **1.** containing a large amount of starch, or like starch, especially in consistency **2.** very formal and unbending, and apparently lacking in warmth or a sense of humor —**starch·i·ly** *adv* —**starch·i·ness** *n*

star con·nec·tion *n* an electrical connection in a polyphase system in which the windings have one end connected to a common junction and the other ends connected to separate load points

star-crossed *adj* believed to be destined by fate to be unhappy ○ *a star-crossed political campaign from the outset* [< the belief in the influence of the stars over human lives]

star·dom /staárdəm/ *n* **1.** the status of a star performer in sports or entertainment, and the fame and prestige that go with it **2.** star performers considered as a group

star·dust /staár dùst/ *n* **1.** a dreamy romantic sentimental feeling, or an imaginary substance, usually represented as starry and twinkling, that is supposed to induce this feeling **2.** far distant stars in a cluster or strewn like a cloud of bright dust in the night sky

stare /ster/ *vi* (**stared, star·ing, stares**) **1.** LOOK FIXEDLY to look directly at somebody or something for a long time without moving the eyes away, usually as a result of curiosity or surprise, or to express rudeness or defiance **2.** BE WIDE OPEN WITH SHOCK to look wide open with shock, fear, or amazement (*refers to eyes*) **3.** BE OBVIOUS to be obvious or blatant ○ *The answer was staring at you all the time; you just couldn't see it.* ■ *n* **1.** LONG CONCENTRATED LOOK a long concentrated look at somebody or something, often full of curiosity or hostility **2.** FACIAL EXPRESSION a facial expression in which the eyes are wide open with shock or amazement and looking fixedly at somebody or something [Old English *starian* < Germanic, "be rigid"] —**star·er** *n*

SPELLCHECK See ***stair.***

SYNONYMS See ***gaze.***

stare down *vt* **1.** to look somebody directly in the eyes until he or she is forced to look away **2.** to intimidate somebody or something into backing down ○ *two hostile nations trying to stare each other down*

sta·rets /staár yits/ (*plural* **star·tsy** /staártsee/) *n* a religious teacher or spiritual adviser in the Russian Orthodox Church, especially one who is a monk or holy man [Early 20C. < Russian, "elderly man, elder"]

star fac·et *n* one of the eight small triangular facets that surround the table of a gem cut in the brilliant style

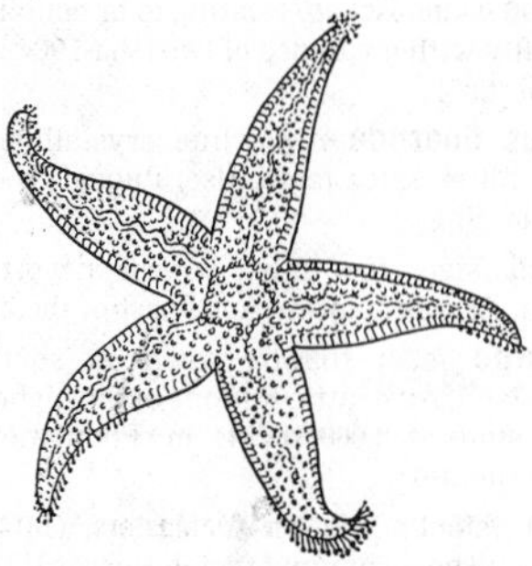

starfish

star·fish /staár fìsh/ (*plural same* or **-fish·es**) *n* an invertebrate ocean animal (**echinoderm**) whose body consists of five or more arms radiating from a central disk. Starfish have a central mouth on the underside and feed on oysters and other mollusks on shores and the seabed. Class: Asteroidea.

star·fish flow·er *n* same as **stapelia**

star·flow·er /staár flòwr/ *n* a plant with star-shaped flowers, e.g., star-of-Bethlehem and some plants of northeastern North America

star fruit *n* FOOD same as **carambola** (sense 2)

star·gaze /staár gàyz/ (**-gazed, -gaz·ing, -gaz·es**) *vi* **1.** to observe the stars at night **2.** to engage in daydreaming

star·gaz·er /staár gàyzər/ *n* **1.** DAYDREAMER somebody given to daydreaming **2.** ASTRONOMER somebody who studies the stars (*informal*) **3.** TROPICAL OCEAN FISH a bottom-dwelling tropical ocean fish that has eyes and mouth on the top of its head. Families: Uranoscopidae or Dactyloscopidae.

star grass *n* a plant of the daffodil family with long leaves that look like grass. Flowers: star-shaped, white or yellow. Native to: tropical and temperate regions. Genus: *Hypoxis.*

star jump *n* an exercise in which a person jumps in the air with legs apart and arms extended out from the shoulder in a comparable direction

stark /staark/ *adj* **1.** FORBIDDINGLY BARE AND PLAIN forbidding in its bareness and lack of any ornament, relieving feature, or pleasant prospect **2.** UNAMBIGUOUS AND HARSH presented in plain, unambiguous, and usually rather harsh terms ○ *confronting stark reality* **3.** COMPLETE having reached the fullest extent or degree of something **4.** WITHOUT CLOTHES completely unclothed and uncovered **5.** RIGID showing or affected by rigor mortis (*archaic*) ■ *adv* UTTERLY to the utmost degree [Old English *stearc* < Germanic, "be rigid"] —**stark·ly** *adv* —**stark·ness** *n*

Hulton-Deutsch Collection/Corbis

Dame Freya Stark

Stark /staark/, **Dame Freya** (1893–1993) British writer. She wrote over 30 travel books describing aspects of Southwest Asian culture, especially life in the deserts. Full name **Stark, Dame Freya Madeline**

stark·ers /staárkərz/ *adj UK* completely unclothed and uncovered (*slang*) [Early 20C. Shortening and alteration of STARK-NAKED]

star key *n* a key or button on, e.g., a telephone or keypad, that is marked with an asterisk symbol

stark-na·ked *adj* completely unclothed and uncovered

star·let /staárlət/ *n* a young woman actor seen as a possible major movie star of the future

star·light /staár lìt/ *n* the light that comes from the stars

star·ling[1] /staárling/ *n* **1.** a common songbird with a stocky body, a strong beak, strong legs, and glossy greenish black feathers covered in white spots, which gathers in large noisy flocks. Native to: Europe. Latin name: *Sturnus vulgaris.* **2.** a songbird with a stocky body, a strong beak and strong legs, which often has glossy greenish or bluish feathers. Native to: Europe, Africa, Asia, Australasia, western Pacific. Family: Sturnidae. [Old English *stærlinc* "little starling" < *stær* "starling" < Germanic]

star·ling[2] /staárling/ *n* a structure made of piles surrounding a pier of a bridge to protect the pier from floating debris [Late 17C. Origin ?]

star·lit /staár lìt/ *adj* lit by light from the stars

star-nosed mole *n* a mole that has a ring of small pink fleshy tentacles surrounding its nose. Native to: North America. Latin name: *Condylura cristata.*

star-of-Beth·le·hem (*plural* **stars-of-Beth·le·hem** or *same*) *n* a perennial plant of the lily family that has long slender leaves. Flowers: white, star-shaped, in clusters on a central stalk. Native to: Europe. Genus: *Ornithogalum.* [Late 16C. < its abundance in Palestine]

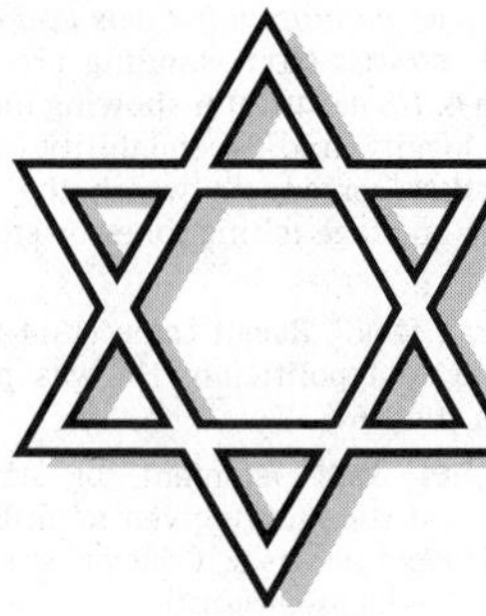

Star of David

Star of Da·vid *n* a symbol of the Jewish faith and of the state of Israel consisting of two equilateral triangles superimposed on each other to form a six-pointed star

Starr /staar/, **Ringo** (*b.* 1940) British musician. He attained fame as the drummer of the Beatles (1962–70). Born **Starkey, Richard**

star ru·by *n* a ruby that reflects light in a star shape when cut with a convex surface

star·ry /staáree/ (**-ri·er, -ri·est**) *adj* **1.** WITH MANY STARS SHINING bright with many shining stars **2.** COVERED WITH STARS covered or decorated with stars **3.** SIMILAR TO STAR relating to stars, or similar in shape or brightness to a star

star·ry-eyed *adj* having a happy and enthusiastic or romantic attitude that is naive and unrealistic

Stars and Bars *n* the first flag of the Confederacy during the Civil War, which had two red stripes and one white, and a circle of white stars representing the seceded states (*takes a singular or plural verb*)

Stars and Stripes *n* the national flag of the United States, which has 13 alternating red and white stripes and one star for each state on a blue field (*takes a singular or plural verb*)

star sap·phire *n* a sapphire that reflects light in a star shape when cut with a convex surface

star shell *n* an artillery shell designed to burst in midair and release a flare or a shower of lights

star·ship /staár shìp/ *n* a spaceship designed to travel between stars or star systems, as yet existing only in science fiction

star sign *n* a sign of the zodiac, especially the sign under which somebody was born

star-span·gled *adj* **1.** covered or decorated with stars **2.** attended by many important people, usually politicians or movie stars ○ *The State Dinner was a star-spangled gathering unequaled in history.*

Star-Span·gled Ban·ner *n* **1.** the national anthem of the United States **2.** the national flag of the United States

star·struck /staár strùk/ *adj* **1.** feeling or showing an awed fascination with stars from the world of entertainment or with becoming such a star **2.** overawed in the presence of somebody famous

star-stud·ded *adj* containing many well-known actors or performers

star sys·tem *n* **1.** a group of astronomical objects that forms a distinct physical entity in space, e.g., a star and its planets or a cluster of stars **2.** the system of deliberately exploiting an individual star performer, both on screen and off, to sell motion pictures

start /staart/ *v* (**start·ed, start·ing, starts**) **1.** *vti* **BEGIN** to begin doing something or begin something **2.** *vti* **BEGIN HAPPENING** to begin happening, or make something begin happening ○ *The movie starts at 7 o'clock.* **3.** *vt* **CREATE SOMETHING** to bring something into being as an entity or operation ○ *start a business* **4.** *vt* **BEGIN WORKING** to commence work on something ○ *start a project* **5.** *vt* **HELP SOMEBODY BEGIN SOMETHING** to help somebody out in beginning an activity such as a journey or career **6.** *vi* **GO FROM PARTICULAR LEVEL** to begin at a particular level ○ *Prices start at fifteen dollars.* **7.** *vti* **PLAY FIRST IN CONTEST** to be in a race or play at the beginning of a game, or select somebody to do this ○ *finally agreed to start the rookie in the next game* **8.** *vi* **BEGIN ARGUING** to begin arguing or making a fuss (*informal*) ○ *Please don't start.* **9.** *vi* **MAKE SUDDEN MOVEMENT** to make a sudden movement out of surprise, pain, fear, or anger **10.** *vti* **MOVE SUDDENLY** to go very quickly from being still to moving, or cause a person or animal to do this **11.** *vt* **CAUSE ANIMAL TO APPEAR** to cause a hunted animal to appear suddenly from its hiding place or den **12.** *vt* **RAISE SOMETHING** to raise or care for something in the early stages of its growth ○ *start some plants in early spring* **13.** *vi* **FLOW VIOLENTLY OUT** to flow violently or suddenly out of something ○ *water starting from the barrel's seams* **14.** *vti* AUTOMOT **BEGIN WORKING, OR MAKE ENGINE BEGIN** to begin working, or make an engine begin to operate **15.** *vti* **COME LOOSE** to come loose from the proper place, or cause something to come loose from its proper place ■ *n* **1. BEGINNING** the first part of something that proceeds through time ○ *We missed the start of the play.* **2. PLACE OR TIME OF START** the place or time at which something starts ○ *The start of the race is scheduled for noon.* **3. QUICK SUDDEN MOVEMENT** a quick sudden movement from being still to moving **4. SUDDEN INVOLUNTARY MOVEMENT** a sudden involuntary movement caused by surprise, pain, fear, or anger **5. INSTANCE OF PARTICIPATING** the fact or an instance of participating in a race or game ○ *winning three out of five starts* **6. POSITION AHEAD OF OTHERS** a position of being ahead of other competitors ○ *get a start on the rest* **7. POSITION AT BEGINNING** a set of circumstances at the beginning of something ○ *He needed a better start in life.* **8. SIGNAL TO BEGIN** the signal to begin something such as a race [12C. Probably < Old English *styrtan* "to jump" < Germanic] ◇ **for a start, for starters** used in an argument to indicate that you are making the first point of many ◇ **to start with** at the beginning

start in *vi* **1.** to begin to do something (*informal*) ○ *Let's start in now so we can get this work done.* **2.** *US* to begin to scold or criticize somebody ○ *Don't start in on me again, I haven't done anything wrong.*

start off *v* **1.** *vi* **SET OFF** to begin moving in a particular direction, or begin a journey ○ *She turned and started off up the hill.* **2.** *vti* **BEGIN** to begin to do something, or cause or help somebody to begin to do something ○ *Let's start off by introducing ourselves.* **3.** *vt* **MAKE SOMEBODY START TALKING OR LAUGHING** to do something that causes somebody else to start doing something such as talking, laughing, crying, or misbehaving (*informal*) ○ *Stop it, or you'll start her off again.*

start on *vt* **1.** to begin to work on or deal with something or somebody, usually something that will take a long time to finish ○ *As soon as I've finished cleaning the kitchen, I'm going to start on the bathroom.* **2.** to begin to scold, criticize, or attack somebody (*informal*) ○ *Look, don't start on me. It's not my fault!*

start out *vi* **1. BEGIN JOURNEY** to set off on a journey ○ *If we start out at about nine, we should be there in time for lunch.* **2. BEGIN** to do something at the beginning of a process ○ *He starts out trying to prove she's guilty and ends up convincing everyone she's innocent.* **3. INTEND** to intend to do something, or have something as an initial intention ○ *I didn't start out to cause a lot of trouble.* **4. BEGIN STAGE OF LIFE** to make a start in something such as adult life or a career ○ *young people who are starting out in journalism*

start up *v* **1.** *vti* **BEGIN TO OPERATE** to begin to operate, or make something begin to operate ○ *start the engine up* **2.** *vti* **OPEN BUSINESS** to begin something such as a business venture ○ *started up her own accounting practice* **3.** *vi* **BEGIN TO MAKE SOUND** to begin to make a sound, especially a characteristic sound, or begin to speak ○ *First a solitary blackbird started up, and soon the whole forest was alive with birdsong.* **4.** *vi* **RISE SUDDENLY** to rise suddenly to a standing or upright position ○ *He started up from his chair at the loud sound and rushed to the window.*

START /staart/ *abbr* INTERNAT REL Strategic Arms Reduction Talks

start·er /staártər/ *n* **1. FIRST COURSE OF MEAL** a first course of a meal, or something suitable to be eaten as a first course of a meal **2.** MECH ENG **STARTING DEVICE FOR ENGINE** a device for starting a machine or engine, especially an electrically operated device that causes the internal-combustion engine in a motor vehicle to fire **3.** SPORTS **SOMEBODY SIGNALING START OF RACE** somebody who gives the signal for a race to start **4.** SPORTS **COMPETITOR WHO STARTS** a horse or competitor who starts in a race **5.** SPORTS **PLAYER AT BEGINNING OF GAME** a player who takes the field for a team at the beginning of a game **6.** BASEBALL **FIRST PITCHER** in baseball, the pitcher who pitches first for a baseball team, either regularly or in a specific game ■ *adj* **USED TO START** used to start something or as an introduction to something for people with little experience of it ○ *a starter set of paints* ◇ **for starters** as the first thing to be done, considered, or dealt with (*informal*)

start·er home *n* a small property suitable for somebody who is buying a home for the first time

start·er kit *n* same as **starter pack**

start·er pack *n* a set containing the materials, equipment, or information required by somebody who wishes to begin a particular activity

start·er's pis·tol *n* SPORTS same as **starting gun**

star this·tle *n* a plant belonging to the daisy family. Flowers: purple, encircled by radiating spines. Native to: Europe, Asia. Genus: *Centaurea.*

start·ing block *n* either of a pair of objects that runners brace their feet against at the start of a sprint race. The blocks are made up of a base that can be firmly placed onto the track and angled supports for the runners' feet.

start·ing gate *n* **1.** a line of stalls into which racehorses are put at the start of a race that have gates at the front that spring open simultaneously when operated by the starter **2.** a physical barrier or electronic beam that automatically starts a timing device when a competitor passes through it, e.g., at the start of a skiing race

start·ing grid *n* a pattern of lines marked on an auto racing track, with numbered starting positions. The cars that record the fastest times in practice or qualifying occupy the front positions.

start·ing gun *n* a gun fired as the signal for a race to start

start·ing line *n* a line marked across a racetrack to show runners where to start

start·ing line-up *n* an official list of the players who will begin a game or the competitors who will begin a race

start·ing point *n* **1.** a basis from which something can start or develop **2.** the place from which you start a journey

start·ing ro·ta·tion *n* the order in which the manager of a baseball or softball team plays the pitchers at the start of games

star·tle /staárt'l/ (**-tled, -tling, -tles**) *vti* to disconcert or frighten a person or animal into making an involuntary movement, or become disconcerted or frightened by a sudden shock [Old English *steartlian* < Germanic] —**star·tler** *n*

star·tling /staártling/ *adj* provoking surprise, fright, wonder, or alarm —**star·tling·ly** *adv*

start page *n* the webpage to which a visitor to a website is automatically taken first, or the page to which a user is automatically taken first whenever he or she goes online

star·tsy CHR plural of **starets**

start-up /staárt ùp/, **start-up** *n* **1.** something that is just beginning operations, e.g., a company **2.** the beginning of an activity such as the construction of a building

star·va·tion /staar váysh'n/ *n* the state of not having enough food, or of losing strength or dying through lack of food

starve /staarv/ (**starved, starv·ing, starves**) *v* **1.** *vti* **WEAKEN OR DIE BECAUSE OF HUNGER** to weaken or die through lack of food, or cause somebody to do this ○ *The besieged city was starved into submission.* **2.** *vi* **BE HUNGRY** to be very hungry (*informal*) ○ *I'm starving! What's for dinner?* **3.** *vt* **DEPRIVE SOMEBODY** to deprive somebody or something of something vitally needed ○ *starved for affection* **4.** *vi* **NEED** to feel deprived of something, or feel a great need or desire for something ○ *starving for a kind word* [Old English *steorfan* "die" < Germanic, "be stiff"] —**starv·er** *n*

starve out *vt* to force an enemy to surrender by making necessary food and supplies inaccessible

starved /staarvd/ *adj* **1.** thin, gaunt, or unhealthy-looking through lack of food **2.** extremely hungry (*informal*)

starve·ling /staárvling/ *n* a very thin and hungry-looking person or animal (*archaic*)

starv·ing /staárving/ *adj* **1.** very weak or dying because of hunger **2.** very hungry (*informal*)

stash /stash/ *n* **1. HIDDEN STORE** a secret store of something such as money or valuables (*informal*) **2. HIDING PLACE** a secret hiding place (*informal*) **3. SECRET STORE OF DRUGS** a store of illegal drugs kept for personal consumption (*slang*) ■ *vt* (**stashed, stash·ing, stash·es**) **1. HIDE SOMETHING** to put something into a secret hidden storage place (*informal*) **2. PUT SOMETHING AWAY** to put something somewhere, e.g., in a convenient place or where it belongs ○ *We'll eat after we've stashed our gear.* [Late 18C. Origin ?]

sta·sis /stáyssiss, stássiss/ *n* **1. MOTIONLESS STATE** a state in which there is neither motion nor development, often resulting from opposing forces balancing each other **2.** MED **STOPPAGE OF FLOW OF BODY FLUIDS** a condition in which body fluids such as blood or the contents of the bowel are prevented from flowing normally through their channels **3.** BIOL **STATE OF NO CHANGE** a state in which there is little or no apparent change in a species of organism over a long period of time. It is most evident in so-called living fossils such as the coelacanth, which have remained unchanged for many millions of years. [Mid-18C. Via modern Latin < Greek, "standing, stoppage"]

stat[1] /stat/ *n* same as **statistic** (senses 1–2) (*informal*) [Mid-20C. Shortening]

stat[2] /stat/ *adv* used in prescriptions to indicate that a drug is to be given immediately ■ *adj* urgent ○ *The doctor received a stat page while on call.* [Late 19C. Shortening of Latin *statim* "immediately"]

-stat *suffix* **1.** a device for stabilizing or regulating ○ *rheostat* **2.** a device for focusing something in a single direction ○ *siderostat* **3.** a substance or device that inhibits the growth or flow of something ○ *fungistat* ○ *hemostat* [Via modern Latin *-stata* < Greek *statos* "standing," *statēs* "maker of something to stand"]

stat·am·pere /stat ámpir/ *n* the unit of electric current in the CGS system formerly in use (*dated*) [Mid-20C. < STATIC]

state /stayt/ *n* **1.** MOSTLY AUTONOMOUS REGION OF FEDERAL COUNTRY an area forming part of a federal country such as the United States or Australia with its own government and legislature and control over most of its own internal affairs **2.** COUNTRY a country or nation with its own sovereign independent government **3.** GOVERNMENT a country's government and those government-controlled institutions that are responsible for its internal administration and its relationships with other countries ○ *state-owned companies* **4.** CONDITION the condition that something or somebody is in ○ *a house in a poor state of repair* **5.** PHYSICAL STAGE a growth or developmental stage of an animal or plant ○ *the larval state* **6.** FORM any form or quantifiable condition in which a physical substance can be, depending on its temperature and other circumstances **7.** CEREMONIOUS STYLE a very formal, dignified, or grand way of doing something in which all the appropriate ceremonies are observed ○ *The senator will lie in state in the Capitol rotunda.* **8.** NERVOUS, UPSET, OR EXCITED CONDITION a very nervous, upset, or excited frame of mind or manner of behaving ○ *He was in a state by the time she finally arrived.* ○ *Don't get into a state worrying about money.* **9.** BAD PHYSICAL CONDITION a very messy or disreputable condition (*informal*) ○ *The house is in such a state that we'll never get it clean.* ■ *adj* **1.** RELATING TO GOVERNMENT involving or relating to the government of a nation or an autonomous federal region within a nation ○ *state security* **2.** HELD OR RUN BY STATE owned, operated, or financed by a nation or an autonomous region within a federalized nation ○ *state schools* **3.** DONE WITH FULL CEREMONY involving many grand rituals and ceremonies, especially those appropriate to a head of state ○ *a state banquet* ■ *vt* (**stat·ed, stat·ing, states**) **1.** EXPRESS SOMETHING IN WORDS to express something in spoken or written words, especially to announce something publicly in a deliberate formal way ○ *I have already stated my position on this issue.* **2.** LAW DECLARE SOMETHING WITH FORCE OF LAW to declare something officially so that it has the force of a law or regulation ○ *It is expressly stated in your contract that you must not work for another employer.* **3.** MUSIC PLAY MUSICAL THEME FOR FIRST TIME to play a musical theme or motif for the first time before it is repeated and developed within a piece of music [12C. Directly or via French < Latin *status* "way of standing, condition" (as in *status rei publicae* "condition of the republic")] ◇ **the state of play** a stage reached in a situation or activity

state at·tor·ney *n* LAW same as **state's attorney**

state bank *n* a bank that receives its charter from, and operates under the laws of, a state of the United States

state cap·i·tal·ism *n* an economic system in which the state controls the use of capital and the means of production

state·craft /stáyt kràft/ *n* the art of governing or managing the affairs of a country well

stat·ed /stáytəd/ *adj* **1.** laid down by an official agreement or in a legal document **2.** announced previously, especially in a public medium

stat·ed case *n* LAW same as **case stated**

State De·part·ment *n* the department of the United States government that deals with foreign affairs and is headed by a cabinet secretary and staffed by career foreign service officers

state·hood /stáyt hòòd/ *n* the status of a state in a federal union, especially in the United States, as opposed to that of a territory or dependency

state·hood·er /stáyt hòòdər/ *n* somebody who advocates full US state status for, e.g., a territory or dependency

state·house /stáyt hòwss/ (*plural* **-hous·es** /-hòwzəz/), **State·house** *n* a building in which a state legislature convenes in any of the US state capitals

state·less /stáytləss/ *adj* not being a citizen of any country and having no nationality

state line *n* the official boundary between two US states

state·ly /stáytlee/ (**-li·er, -li·est**) *adj* **1.** characterized by an impressively weighty and dignified but graceful manner **2.** grand and imposing in appearance — **state·li·ness** *n*

state·ment /stáytmənt/ *n* **1.** EXPRESSION IN WORDS the expression in spoken or written words of something such as a fact, intention, or policy, or an instance of this ○ *a statement of intent* **2.** SOMETHING SAID something that somebody says that is not a question or an exclamation and that expresses an idea or facts in definite terms ○ *We were unable to verify the truth of that statement.* **3.** SPECIALLY PREPARED PUBLIC ANNOUNCEMENT a specially prepared announcement or reply that is made public ○ *Has she made a statement to the press?* **4.** ACCOUNT OF FACTS an account of the facts relating to a crime or case given to the police or in a court of law, usually for use as evidence ○ *The police asked me if I wished to make a statement.* **5.** WORDLESS EXPRESSION OF IDEA an expression of an idea, opinion, or concept made in a nonverbal way ○ *Her art is a powerful statement of her political beliefs.* **6.** BANKING PRINTED RECORD OF BANK ACCOUNT a printed record of all transactions that have taken place over a period of time in a bank account and of the amount of the holder's current credit or debt **7.** FIN CUSTOMER'S ACCOUNT an account issued to a customer showing charges made, payments received, and any balance owing **8.** MUSIC FIRST PRESENTATION OF MUSICAL THEME the first presentation of a theme or idea that is to be developed later in a piece of music **9.** COMPUT COMPUTER INSTRUCTION a computer instruction written in a source language

Sta·ten Is·land /stàtt'n-/ one of the five boroughs of New York. It has a regular ferry service to Manhattan, and the Verrazano-Narrows Bridge connects it to Brooklyn. It is mainly residential. Population: 378,977 (2002 estimate).

state of af·fairs *n* a set of circumstances ○ *This regrettable state of affairs cannot be allowed to continue.*

state of con·cern *n* INTERNAT REL same as **rogue state** (*formal*)

state of the art *n* the most advanced level of knowledge and technology currently achieved in any field at any given time —**state-of-the-art** *adj*

state of war *n* **1.** armed conflict between states or other groups, with or without a formal declaration of war **2.** the situation brought about by a declaration of war, with or without the commencement of actual armed conflict, in which special internationally agreed laws apply

state pris·on *n* a prison run by a state of the United States in which prisoners convicted of serious crimes are held

stat·er[1] /stáytər/, **Stat·er** *n* somebody who comes from a particular state or type of state, especially in the United States (*usually used in combination*) ○ *Bay Staters are from Massachusetts.* [< STATE]

sta·ter[2] /stáytər/ *n* an ancient Greek coin in gold or silver [14C. Via late Latin < Greek *statēr* < base of *histanai* "weigh"]

state·room /stáyt ròòm, -ròòm/ *n* a large and luxuriously furnished private cabin on a ship or a private sleeping compartment on a train

States /stayts/ *npl* GEOG same as **United States** (*informal*)

state's at·tor·ney *n* an attorney who acts as prosecutor in court cases on behalf of a state

state school *n* US **1.** a college or university that is supported primarily by a state's public funds **2.** an institution, usually a prison for delinquent minors, that is controlled and financed by a state government (*informal*)

state se·cret *n* a piece of information, usually considered important to national security, that is supposed to be known only to people whom the state authorizes to know

state's ev·i·dence *n* evidence given for the prosecution in a criminal trial in the United States and other nations, sometimes by one of the accused or by an accomplice to the crime, or the person who agrees to give such evidence ○ *His accomplice turned state's evidence in exchange for a reduced sentence.*

States-Gen·er·al *npl* the legislative body in France before 1789, consisting of representatives of the three estates of the realm

state·side /stáyt sīd/ *adv* in or toward the continental United States ■ *adj* relating to, in, or toward the continental United States

states·man /stáytsmən/ (*plural* **-men** /-mən/) *n* **1.** a senior politician, especially a man, who plays an important role in government or international affairs **2.** a senior politician, especially a man, who is widely respected for integrity and impartial concern for the public good —**states·man·like** *adj* —**states·man·ship** *n*

state so·cial·ism *n* a political and economic system in which the state controls major industries and banks and plans its economic and social welfare programs in order to bring about an egalitarian society —**state so·cial·ist** *n*

states·per·son /stáyts pùrss'n/ (*plural* **-per·sons** or **-peo·ple** /-peep'l/) *n* **1.** a senior politician who plays an important role in government or international affairs **2.** a senior politician who is widely respected for integrity and impartial concern for the public good

states·wom·an /stáyts wòòmmən/ (*plural* **-wom·en** /-wìmmin/) *n* **1.** a senior woman politician who plays an important role in government or international affairs **2.** a senior woman politician who is widely respected for integrity and impartial concern for the public good

state troop·er *n* a member of the highway patrol police of a state

state·wide /stáyt wīd, stàyt wīd/ US *adj* affecting or happening throughout an entire state ○ *a statewide search for the escaped prisoner* ■ *adv* throughout an entire state

stat·ic /státtik/ *adj* **1.** MOTIONLESS not moving or changing, or fixed in position **2.** PHYS OF FORCES NOT CAUSING MOVEMENT relating to forces, weight, or pressures that act without causing movement **3.** PHYS INVOLVING STATICS relating to, involving, or characteristic of statics **4.** ELEC INVOLVING STATIONARY ELECTRIC CHARGES relating to, involving, or characteristic of stationary electric charges **5.** BROADCAST CAUSED BY ELECTRICAL INTERFERENCE relating to or caused by electrical interference in a radio or television broadcast **6.** COMPUT NOT NEEDING TO BE REFRESHED describes a random-access-memory computer chip that retains its contents without having to be refreshed by a central processor ■ *n* **1.** BROADCAST ELECTRICAL INTERFERENCE electrical interference in a radio or television broadcast, causing a random crackling noise or disruption of a picture **2.** ELEC same as **static electricity** **3.** OPPOSITION OR INTERFERENCE criticism, opposition, or unwanted interference by somebody else (*informal*) ○ *getting a lot of static from the boss* [Mid-19C. Via modern Latin < Greek *statikos* "causing to stand" < *statos* "standing"] —**stat·i·cal·ly** *adv*

stat·i·ce /státtəssee/ *n* PLANTS same as **sea lavender** [Mid-18C. < modern Latin < Greek *statikos* "causing to stand" (see STATIC); because it stops the flow of blood]

stat·ic e·lec·tric·i·ty *n* a stationary electric charge that builds up on an insulated object such as a capacitor or a thundercloud

stat·ic line *n* a rope attached to an aircraft and a parachutist's parachute that automatically opens the parachute

stat·ic pres·sure *n* pressure not caused by motion at a point on the surface of an object moving freely in a flowing fluid

stat·ics /státtiks/ *n* a branch of mechanics that deals with forces and systems in equilibrium (*takes a singular verb*)

stat·ic tube *n* a tube used to measure the static pressure present in a moving fluid

stat·in /státtin/ *n* a drug belonging to a group that reduces cholesterol in the blood

sta·tion /stáysh'n/ *n* **1.** STOP ON ROUTE a place along a train or bus route where passengers are picked up or set down, often with amenities such as ticket offices, waiting rooms, refreshments, toilets, and facilities for goods and parcels **2.** LOCAL BRANCH OF ORGANIZATION a local branch or headquarters of an official organization such as the police force, fire department, or ambulance service **3.** SPECIALLY EQUIPPED BUILDING a building or group of buildings that provides a particular function or service ○ *a pumping station* **4.** BROADCASTING BUILDING a place equipped to make and broadcast radio or television programs **5.** BROADCASTING CHANNEL a television or radio channel **6.** USUAL PLACE the place or position where somebody or something is usually to be found or is supposed to be found **7.** POSITION FOR PERFORMING TASK a position where somebody performs a task, e.g., in a factory, or the equipment used in performing a task **8.** RANK the position somebody holds in society or in an organization in terms of rank **9.** SHEEP OR CATTLE FARM a large farm in Australia or New Zealand where sheep or cattle are raised **10.** MIL MILITARY POSTING a place where military personnel are sent to carry out duties **11.** NAUT PLACE ON SHIP FOR CREW MEMBER a place on board a ship where a crew member carries out duties **12.** NAVY PLACE WHERE SHIP IS SENT a place where a naval ship or fleet is sent for a period of duty **13.** CIV ENG SURVEYOR'S REFERENCE POINT a fixed point used by surveyors as a reference **14.** CHR STATION OF CROSS in Christianity, one of the Stations of the Cross **15.** HIST MILITARY OR GOVERNMENT SETTLEMENT IN INDIA a place where military officers or government officials lived in India while it was under British rule **16.** *S Asia* SETTLEMENT a town ○ *He's out of station today.* ■ *vt* (**-tioned, -tion·ing, -tions**) PUT SOMEBODY OR SOMETHING IN PLACE to assign somebody to a particular place, or put something in a particular place (*often passive*) [Mid-16C. Via French < Latin *station-* "standing still" < *stat-*, past participle of *stare* "stand"]

sta·tion·ar·y /stáyshə nèrree/ *adj* **1.** NOT MOVING not moving, especially at a standstill after being in motion **2.** IMMOBILE fixed in position and not able to be moved **3.** UNCHANGING not changing **4.** STAYING IN ONE PLACE showing a tendency to remain in the same place [15C. Directly or via French < medieval Latin *stationarius* "motionless, (in classical Latin) of a military station" < Latin *station-* (see STATION)]

SPELLCHECK stationary or **stationery**? Do not confuse the spelling of ***stationary*** with ***stationery***, which sound similar. The two words are distantly related but have quite different meanings. ***Stationary*** is an adjective meaning "not moving" (normally used of vehicles), whereas ***stationery*** is a noun meaning "paper and other things used for writing," including envelopes, which may help you to remember the "e."

sta·tion·ar·y bi·cy·cle *n* FITNESS same as **exercise bike**

sta·tion·ar·y front *n* a weather condition in which the boundary between a cold air mass and a warm air mass is stationary

sta·tion·ar·y or·bit *n* an orbit around an astronomical object that has the same period as one revolution of the astronomical object. An object in such an orbit appears stationary above the surface.

sta·tion·ar·y point *n UK* MATH same as **critical point** (sense 2)

sta·tion·ar·y wave *n* PHYS same as **standing wave**

sta·tion break *n* a time when a radio or television program is interrupted by an announcement giving the name, and sometimes other details, of the company that is broadcasting the program

sta·tion·er /stáysh'nər/ *n* a person or store that sells stationery

ORIGIN In medieval Latin, a *stationarius* was originally a "trader who kept a permanent stall" (as opposed to an itinerant seller) – the word's source, the Latin stem *station-*, meant literally "standing, keeping still." Such permanent stores were comparatively rare in the Middle Ages. Of those that did exist, the commonest were bookstores, licensed by the universities, and so English adopted the Latin term. It has since come down in the world somewhat to "seller of paper, pens, etc.", a sense first recorded in the mid-17th century, but the earlier application is preserved in the name of the "Stationers' Company," a London livery company to which booksellers and publishers belong.

sta·tion·er·y /stáyshə nèrree/ *n* paper, envelopes, and other things used in writing

SPELLCHECK See ***stationary***.

sta·tion house *n* a building housing a police department or precinct office, or a fire department

sta·tion·mas·ter /stáysh'n màstər/ *n* somebody whose job is to oversee the running of a railroad station

Sta·tions of the Cross *npl* **1.** a series of 14 images around the inside of a Roman Catholic church, each representing a stage in Jesus Christ's road to Calvary **2.** a Roman Catholic devotion in which a prayer is said before each of the Stations of the Cross

sta·tion stop *n* a railroad station at which a particular train stops to set down or pick up passengers ○ *Reading is your next station stop.*

sta·tion-to-sta·tion (*dated*) *adj* charged from the time somebody answers the telephone ■ *adv* by a station-to-station telephone call

sta·tion wag·on *n* an automobile with an extended area behind the rear seats that provides extra seating or carrying capacity, usually with a tailgate [Because originally a covered carriage for transporting passengers to and from train stations]

stat·ism /stáy tìzzəm/ *n* the theory, or its practice, that economic and political power should be controlled by a central government leaving regional government and the individual with relatively little say in political matters —**stat·ist** *n*

sta·tis·tic /stə tístik/ *n* **1.** ELEMENT OF DATA a single element of data from a collection **2.** NUMERICAL VALUE OR FUNCTION a numerical value or function, e.g., a mean or standard deviation, used to describe a sample or population **3.** PIECE OF INFORMATION somebody or something treated as a piece of data or information [Late 19C. Back-formation < STATISTICS] —**sta·tis·ti·cal** *adj* —**sta·tis·ti·cal·ly** *adv*

sta·tis·ti·cal me·chan·ics *n* the branch of physics that analyzes macroscopic systems by applying statistical principles to their microscopic constituents (*takes a singular verb*)

sta·tis·tics /stə tístiks/ *n* a branch of mathematics that deals with the analysis and interpretation of numerical data in terms of samples and populations (*takes a singular verb*) ■ *npl* a collection of numerical data (*takes a plural verb*) ○ *this month's sales statistics* [Late 18C. < German *Statistik* < Latin *status* (see STATE)] —**stat·is·ti·cian** /stàttə stísh'n/ *n*

sta·tive /stáytiv/ *adj* describes a verb that deals with states, e.g., "know" or "own," as opposed to one that deals with actions, e.g., "listen," "talk," or "go" ■ *n* a verb dealing with states not actions [Mid-17C. < Latin *stativus* < *stat-* (see STATION)]

~~**statment**~~ incorrect spelling of **statement**

stato- *prefix* **1.** balance, equilibrium ○ *statoscope* **2.** resting ○ *statoblast* [< Greek *statos* "standing" < Indo-European, "to stand"]

stat·o·blast /státtə blàst/ *n* a chitin-encased body that serves as a means of asexual reproduction for freshwater bryozoans. It can withstand climatic extremes and prolonged dormancy.

stat·o·cyst /státtə sìst/ *n* a fluid-filled organ of balance in some invertebrates such as the lobster. It contains suspended bony granules that, along with sensory cells, help it to determine its position.

stat·o·lith /státtə lìth/ *n* **1.** any tiny bony granule that is suspended in fluid within a statocyst and whose movement is detected by sensory hairs that determine an invertebrate's position **2.** a starch grain or other particle inside plant cells that moves in response to gravity and is thought to influence the way shoots or other organs grow —**stat·o·lith·ic** /stàttə líthik/ *adj*

sta·tor /stáytər/ *n* a stationary part in a machine, e.g., a motor or generator, around which or in which a rotor rotates [Late 19C. < modern Latin, "somebody or something that stands" < Latin *stat-* (see STATION)]

stat·o·scope /státtə skōp/ *n* a sensitive aneroid barometer used to detect small changes in atmospheric pressure, often used in aircraft to determine changes in altitude

stat·u·ar·y /stáchoo èrree/ *n* **1.** STATUES CONSIDERED TOGETHER statues considered collectively **2.** ART OF MAKING STATUES the art and techniques of making statues ■ *adj* ABOUT STATUES relating to, belonging to, typical of, or for statues [Mid-16C. < Latin *statuarius* "of a statue" < *statua* (see STATUE)]

stat·ue /stáchoo/ *n* a three-dimensional image of a human being or animal that is sculpted, modeled, cast, or carved [14C. Via French < Latin *statua* < *statuere* "set up" < *status* (see STATE)]

Barnaby's
Statue of Liberty

Stat·ue of Lib·er·ty *n* a huge statue of a woman holding a torch and a book inscribed "July 4, 1776." It stands in New York Harbor. At 152 ft./46 m high, it is one of the tallest statues in the world. A gift from France to the United States, it was unveiled in 1886.

stat·u·esque /stàchoo ésk/ *adj* like a statue, especially in having classical beauty, elegance, or proportions —**stat·u·esque·ly** *adv*

stat·u·ette /stàchoo ét/ *n* a small, usually portable statue

stat·ure /stáchər/ *n* **1.** the standing height of somebody or something **2.** somebody's standing or level of achievement [13C. Via French < Latin *statura* < *stat-* (see STATION)]

sta·tus /stáytəss, státtəss/ *n* **1.** RANK the relative position or standing of somebody or something in a society or other group **2.** PRESTIGE high rank or standing, especially in a community, work force, or organization **3.** CONDITION a condition that is subject to change ○ *What's the current status of the investigation?* **4.** LAW LEGAL STANDING somebody's standing in terms of the law [Late 18C. < Latin (see STATE)]

sta·tus bar *n* a bar on a computer screen that displays information about an application being used

Sta·tus In·di·an *n Can* a member of an indigenous people whom the federal government recognizes as having special rights and privileges, especially residence on a reservation

sta·tus quo /-kwṓ/ *n* the condition or state of affairs that currently exists [< Latin, "the state in which"]

sta·tus sym·bol *n* a possession that is a sign of wealth or prestige

stat·ute /stáchoot/ *n* **1.** a law established by a legislative body **2.** a permanent established rule or law, especially one involved in the running of a company or other organization [13C. Via French < late Latin *statutum* "something set up" < Latin *statuere* (see STATUE)] —**stat·u·ta·ble** *adj*

stat·ute book *n* a record of the acts that have been passed by a legislature and remain in force

stat·ute law *n* the body of law that has been enacted by a legislature, or a specific law so enacted

stat·ute mile *n* MEASURE same as **mile** (sense 1) [Because it is fixed by law]

stat·ute of lim·i·ta·tions *n* a statute that lays down the time within which legal proceedings must be started

stat·u·to·ry /stáchə tàwree/ *adj* **1.** CONTROLLED BY STATUTE regulated or imposed by statute **2.** OF STATUTE relating to a statute **3.** SUBJECT TO PENALTY covered by a statute, and subject to the penalty laid down by that statute —**stat·u·to·ri·ly** *adv*

stat·u·to·ry dec·la·ra·tion *n* a declaration that somebody makes under oath according to statute

stat·u·to·ry hol·i·day *n* in Canada, a holiday when working hours and official business are limited by law

stat·u·to·ry rape *n* under US law, the offense of having sexual relations with somebody who has not reached the legal age of consent

stat·volt /stat vṓlt/ *n* the unit of electric potential difference in the CGS system formerly in use (*dated*) [Mid-20C. < STATIC]

Stauf·fen·berg /stówfən bùrg, shtówfən bo͝ork/, **Claus Schenk, Count** (1907–44) German army officer. He was the leader of the unsuccessful July Plot (1944) to assassinate Adolf Hitler.

staunch[1] /stawnch/, **stanch** /stawnch, stanch/ *adj* **1.** showing loyalty, dependability, and enthusiasm **2.** solidly built or substantial [15C. < Anglo-Norman *estaunche* < Old French *estanchier* "to stop" (see STANCH[2])] —**staunch·ly** *adv* —**staunch·ness** *n*

USAGE See *stanch*[2].

staunch[2] *vt* same as **stanch**[2]

USAGE See *stanch*[2].

stau·ro·lite /stáwrə lìt/ *n* a reddish brown or black aluminosilicate mineral containing iron and magnesium that often occurs in cross-shaped crystals. Source: metamorphic rocks. Use: gems. [Late 18C. < Greek *stauros* "cross"; because it often forms twin crystals in the shape of a cross] —**stau·ro·lit·ic** /stàwrə líttik/ *adj*

Sta·vang·er /staa vaángər/ city and port in southwestern Norway. Population: 108,437 (2001).

stave /stayv/ *n* **1.** BAND OF WOOD a long thin piece of wood, one of several sealed together to make the hull of a boat or the body of a container such as a barrel **2.** RUNG OR BAR OF WOOD a bar or strip of wood or other material, especially one that forms a rung in a ladder or a crosspiece between the legs of a chair **3.** MUSIC same as **staff**[1] *n* (sense 9) **4.** LITERAT POETRY STANZA a stanza of poetry ■ *v* (**staved** or **stove** /stōv/, **staved, stav·ing, staves**) **1.** *vti* BREAK STAVES to break a barrel, a tub, or a boat's hull by smashing its staves in, or break by having the staves smashed in **2.** *vti* BREAK HOLE IN OBJECT to smash a hole in the side of a boat or a barrel, or be smashed in this way **3.** *vt* BREAK SOMETHING INWARD to strike something such as a door or a rib and make it break inward **4.** *vt* FIT STAVE TO SOMETHING to fit a stave to something such as a chair or a ladder [14C. Back-formation < *staves*, plural of STAFF[1]]

stave off *vt* to avoid or prevent something unpleasant, often only temporarily ○ *staved off hunger with candy*

staves plural of **staff**[1] *n* (senses 5–6), **stave**

staves·a·cre /stáyvz àykər/ *n* **1.** the poisonous seeds of a species of delphinium. Use: in herbal medicine as external parasiticide; formerly, to cause vomiting. **2.** a delphinium with poisonous seeds used in herbal medicine. Flowers: purple. Native to: Europe, Asia. Latin name: *Delphinium staphisagria*. [14C. Alteration of Latin *staphisagria* < Greek *staphis agria* "wild raisin"]

Stav·ro·pol /stav rōp'l/ city in southwestern Russia. It is a center for transportation and heavy industry. Population: 418,112 (1995).

stay[1] /stay/ *v* (**stayed** or **staid, stayed, stay·ing, stays**) **1.** *vi* REMAIN to continue to be in the same place, condition, or state ○ *Stay there and wait for me.* ○ *Try to stay alert.* **2.** *vi* RESIDE FOR SHORT TIME to spend some time or live temporarily in a place ○ *We've stayed at some beautiful hotels.* **3.** *vti* PASS SOME TIME to spend a particular length of time at a place or in doing something ○ *Alicia stayed too long in the sun and got burned.* **4.** *vi* REMAIN IN CONTENTION to keep up with somebody or something, especially by going along with the leader or leaders of a race **5.** *vt* PERSEVERE WITH SOMETHING to continue to do something, especially to support something such as an idea, plan, or project ○ *You should stay the course until the task is completed.* **6.** *vt* UNDERGO SOMETHING to endure, put up with, or survive something, especially something trying, difficult, or unpleasant ○ *The runner had trouble staying the final mile.* **7.** *vi* BE AROUND FOR SOMETHING to be present long enough to take part in something, especially a meal **8.** *vi* LINGER to linger or wait somewhere ○ *Stay a moment.* **9.** *vt* STOP SOMETHING to put a stop to something ○ *They put sandbags across the doorway to try to stay the floodwater.* **10.** *vt* POSTPONE OR HINDER to postpone, hinder, or delay something ○ *stay a trip until the weather improves* **11.** *vt* ALLEVIATE SOMETHING IN SHORT TERM to relieve or ease temporarily something such as hunger, thirst, or other physical need **12.** *vt* RESTRAIN SOMETHING to hold something back or in check **13.** *vt* LAW SUSPEND LEGAL PROCESS TEMPORARILY to suspend a judgment or proceedings temporarily **14.** *vi Scotland* RESIDE to live permanently in a place ○ *Where do you stay?* **15.** *vi* GAMBLING STAKE SAME AMOUNT to stake the same amount of money on a poker hand as the person who last raised the stake ■ *n* **1.** A VISIT a short period of temporarily residing away from home, especially as a visitor or guest ○ *planning a weekend stay with friends in the country* ○ *booked an overnight stay at a small hotel* **2.** CURB OR CHECK something that acts to stop or delay something negative happening **3.** LAW TEMPORARY HALT a temporary halt in legal proceedings, or a period during which a judgment may not be carried out ○ *a stay of execution* [15C. Via Old French *ester* < Latin *stare* "to stand"] ◇ **stay put 1.** to remain in a place or position **2.** to remain combined and mixed together (*refers to mixtures*)

stay on *vi* to remain somewhere after others have left or after the expected time of leaving

stay out *vi* to be away from home, usually for or until a specific time

stay up *vi* to remain awake and not go to bed at the normal time

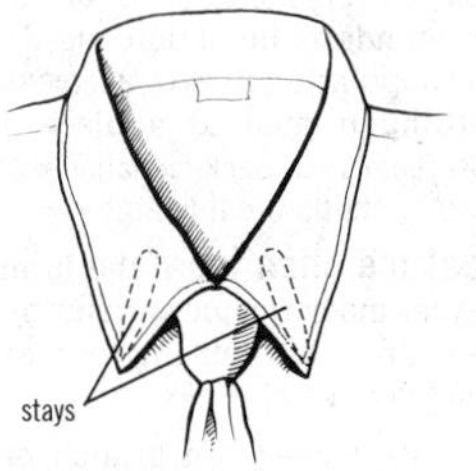

stay (sense 2)

stay[2] /stay/ *n* **1.** A SUPPORT something that gives extra support to something else, e.g., a brace, prop, or buttress **2.** CLOTHING STIFFENER a small bone or piece of metal or plastic used as a stiffener in corsets and girdles and in shirt collars ■ **stays** *npl* STIFFENED CORSET a corset that is stiffened with strips of whalebone, metal, or other material ■ *vt* (**stayed, stay·ing, stays**) **1.** COMFORT SOMEBODY to give somebody comfort or strength (*formal*) **2.** SUPPORT SOMETHING to provide support for something (*archaic*) [Early 16C. < Old French *estaye* < Germanic]

stay[3] /stay/ *n* **1.** NAUT ROPE SUPPORTING MAST a rope or cable used to support a mast **2.** CONSTR STEADYING ROPE a rope used for steadying or guiding something, especially on a chimney or flagpole ■ *vti* (**stayed, stay·ing, stays**) NAUT, SAILING TURN ONTO OTHER TACK to turn onto the other tack, or make a vessel turn onto the other tack [Old English *stæg* < Indo-European, "make stand"]

stay-at-home *adj* **1.** preferring a quiet domestic routine to traveling or to leading a busy social life **2.** relating to or being somebody who stays or works at home ○ *a stay-at-home parent* —**stay-at-home** *n*

stay a·way or·der *n UK* LAW same as **restraining order**

stay·er /stáy ər/ *n* **1.** SOMEBODY WHO STAYS somebody or something that stays **2.** SOMEBODY PERSISTENT somebody with much stamina and persistence **3.** HORSE OR DOG THAT RACES PERSISTENTLY a racehorse or greyhound that has stamina and competes to the end of a race, even under difficult conditions

stay·ing pow·er /stáy ing pòwer/ *n* the ability to keep doing something or keep trying, especially over long periods of time

stay·sail /stáy sàyl/; *nautical* /stáyss'l/ *n* an extra sail hoisted on one of the stays of a sailing vessel

stay stitch·ing *n* an extra line of stitches reinforcing a seam, used to prevent stretching and fraying

stbd. *abbr* NAUT starboard

STD *abbr* MED sexually transmitted disease

std. *abbr* standard

Ste. *abbr* CHR woman saint [French *Sainte*]

stead /sted/ *n* the position or role of somebody or something else [Old English *stede* "place" < Indo-European, "to stand"] ◇ **stand somebody in good stead** to be useful to somebody, especially at a later time

stead·fast /stéd fàst/, **sted·fast** *adj* **1.** firm and unwavering in purpose, loyalty, or resolve **2.** firmly fixed or constant [Pre-12C. < STEAD + FAST[1] "fixed"] —**stead·fast·ly** *adv* —**stead·fast·ness** *n*

stead·y /stéddee/ *adj* (**-i·er, -i·est**) **1.** STABLE fixed, stable, or not easily moved ○ *Can you hold the ladder so that it's steady?* **2.** STAYING SAME showing no tendency to change or fluctuate ○ *Oil prices are steady at the moment.* **3.** CONSTANT OR CONTINUOUS coming in a regular nonstop flow ○ *a steady stream of traffic* **4.** REGULAR OR ORDINARY reliable, but often rather dull or routine ○ *a steady job* **5.** UNRUFFLED not easily upset or excited ○ *It's a job that requires steady nerves.* **6.** STAID OR SERIOUS having a serious and calm attitude or character ○ *Joe was always a steady kind of guy.* **7.** REGULAR OR INDUSTRIOUS regular, habitual, or industrious ○ *a steady worker* ■ *adv* (**-i·er, -i·est**) STEADILY in a steady way ■ *vti* (**-ied, -y·ing, -ies**) BECOME OR MAKE SOMETHING STEADY to become steady, or make something steady ■ *n* (*plural* **-ies**) SOMEBODY DATED REGULARLY somebody with whom a specific person regularly goes on dates (*informal*) ■ *interj* **1.** BE CAREFUL used to tell somebody to be careful or be calm **2.** NAUT KEEP TO PRESENT COURSE used to tell somebody steering a ship or boat to keep to the present course [Mid-13C. < STEAD] —**stead·i·er** *n* —**stead·i·ly** *adv* —**stead·i·ness** *n* ◇ **go steady** to go out together regularly as a couple (*informal*)

stead·y state *n* a condition of stability or equilibrium in a system, e.g., in the energy levels of an atom, in which there is little or no change over time

stead·y-state the·o·ry *n* a theory in astronomy that the universe has always existed at a uniform density that is maintained because new matter is created continuously as the universe expands

steak /stayk/ *n* **1.** CUT OF BEEF a thick slice of beef from a lean part of a cow **2.** PIECE OF MEAT OR FISH a piece of a meat other than beef, e.g., pork, ham, venison, or veal, or of a large fish such as cod, salmon, or tuna **3.** SERVING OF GROUND MEAT ground meat formed into a solid shape, usually a flat roundish shape, and served broiled, fried, or barbecued [15C. < Old Norse *steik* "meat roasted on a spit"]

steak·house /stáyk hòwss/ (*plural* **-hous·es** /-hòwzəz/) *n* a restaurant that specializes in serving beef steaks

steak knife *n* a table knife with a sharp, usually serrated blade, suitable for cutting steak

steak tar·tare /-taar taár/ *n* freshly ground beef that is mixed with raw egg and chopped onions and served uncooked [*Tartare* < French, "Tatar"]

steal /steel/ *v* (**stole** /stōl/, **sto·len** /stṓlən/, **steal·ing, steals**) **1.** *vti* TAKE SOMETHING UNLAWFULLY to take something that belongs to somebody else, illegally or without the owner's permission **2.** *vt* TAKE SOMETHING FURTIVELY to take or get something secretly, surreptitiously, or through trickery ○ *steal a glance* **3.** *vt* DISHONESTLY PRESENT SOMEBODY'S WORK AS YOURS to take something that somebody else has created, especially ideas, theories, or a piece of writing, and present it as your own **4.** *vi* SNEAK to move quietly, especially in the hope of not been seen or caught **5.** *vi* PASS UNNOTICED to pass or move without being noticed (*literary*) ○ *Dawn was stealing over the mountaintops.* **6.** *vt* SUCCEED AT SOMETHING UNEXPECTEDLY to win or succeed at something unexpectedly, luckily, or dishonestly at the expense of another or others (*informal*) **7.** *vti* BASEBALL GAIN BASE WITHOUT HIT in baseball, to gain a base by running without the ball being hit by the batter and in the absence of an error by the fielding team ■ *n* **1.** BARGAIN something that does not cost very much or that costs a lot less than would be expected (*informal*) **2.** BASEBALL STOLEN BASE in baseball, a stolen base **3.** ACT OF STEALING an act of stealing something [Old English *stelan* < Germanic] —**steal·er** *n*

SPELLCHECK steal or **steel**? Do not confuse the spelling of ***steal*** and ***steel***, which sound similar. ***Steal*** is chiefly used as a verb, meaning "take illegally or without permission" or "move quietly," as in *steal a car, steal past the door.* ***Steel*** can be used as a noun, denoting a hard strong metal, an alloy of iron (as in *stainless steel*), or as a verb, meaning particularly "make unfeeling or tough enough": *He steeled himself for the blow.*

SYNONYMS ***steal, pinch, filch, purloin, pilfer, embezzle, misappropriate***

CORE MEANING: to take property unlawfully

steal to take something that belongs to somebody else, illegally or without the owner's permission ○ *Last year, 22,000 cars were stolen in that region.* ○ *a robbery in which more than $20 million was stolen from a Geneva bank* **pinch** (*informal*) to steal something or take something without permission ○ *Who's pinched my pen?* ○ *I had my purse pinched on the subway.* **filch** (*informal*) to steal something opportunistically, usually a small item or something of little value ○ *He filched the wood he needed from his neighbor's yard.* **purloin** (*formal or humorous*) to steal something, especially when the theft breaks another's trust ○ *They pledge to prosecute sales of knock-off drugs, purloined software, pirated videos, and the like.* ○ *The former inspector told how he had once caught a member of his team purloining a top-secret document.* **pilfer** to steal small items of little value, especially habitually ○ *accused the children of pilfering fruit from her orchard* ○ *It is estimated that 25% of food sent as aid to the camps is being pilfered and sold on the black market.* **embezzle** to take for personal use money or property that has been given on trust by others, without their knowledge. ○ *She denies embezzling thousands of dollars while she was company treasurer.* ○ *The former attorney general embezzled public funds and should be extradited to face the charge, US prosecutors argued yesterday.* **misappropriate** to take something, especially money, dishonestly or in order to use it for an improper or illegal purpose ○ *The chief executive insisted that no money had been misappropriated and used for personal expenses.* ○ *The defendant was found guilty of misappropriating public funds.*

stealth /stelth/ *n* **1.** ACTION TO AVOID DETECTION the action of doing something slowly, quietly, and covertly, in order to avoid detection **2.** FURTIVENESS secretive, dishonest, or cunning behavior or actions ■ *adj* **1.** MIL ALMOST UNDETECTABLE BY RADAR used to describe aircraft whose design incorporates technology and materials that minimize the likelihood of detection by enemy radar ○ *a stealth fighter* **2.** SECRET done in a highly secret way so as to be unnoticed (*slang*) ○ *conducted a stealth fundraising campaign* [13C. < assumed Old English *stǣlþ* < Germanic] —**stealth·ful** *adj*

stealth tax *n* a new tax or a tax increase that is introduced largely unnoticed, or an additional charge that is effectively a tax though not officially classed as one

stealth tow·er *n* a wireless telecommunications tower camouflaged so as to be ecologically friendly and aesthetic, e.g., one configured as a pine tree (*informal*)

stealth·y /stélthee/ (**-i·er, -i·est**) *adj* **1.** done quietly, slowly, and cautiously in order to escape notice **2.** secretive, furtive, or cunning —**stealth·i·ly** *adv* —**stealth·i·ness** *n*

SYNONYMS See ***secret.***

steam /steem/ *n* **1.** VAPORIZED WATER the vapor that is formed when water is boiled **2.** MIST OF WATER VAPOR the visible mist that forms when water vapor condenses in the air **3.** VAPOR a visible form of vapor of any kind **4.** POWER stamina, strength, or speed (*informal*) ○ *running out of steam* ■ *adj* **1.** DRIVEN BY STEAM driven or powered by steam ○ *a steam turbine* **2.** USING STEAM using steam to do something ○ *a steam iron* ■ *v* (**steamed, steam·ing, steams**) **1.** *vi* PRODUCE STEAM to produce steam, or be produced as steam **2.** *vti* COOK IN STEAM to cook something in the steam of boiling water, or be cooked in this way **3.** *vi* MOVE BY STEAM to move or be powered by steam **4.** *vi* GENERATE STEAM to generate steam (*refers especially to boilers*) **5.** *vi* GET ANGRY to be or become very angry (*informal*) ○ *Neighbors are steaming about the noisy late-night flights.* **6.** *vi* MOVE FAST to move very quickly and energetically (*informal*) [Old English *stēam* < Germanic] ◇ **get up steam** to gather together enough energy and speed to do something (*informal*)

steam up *vti* to become clouded with condensation, or make something become clouded with condensation

steam bath *n* a steam-filled room or compartment that people go into to relax and refresh themselves through sweating

steam·boat /steém bòt/ *n* a boat with an engine powered by steam

steam chest *n* a compartment in a steam engine from which steam is supplied to the valve of the engine

steam dis·til·la·tion *n* the process of separating or purifying a liquid by passing steam through it

steamed /steemd/ *adj* **1.** cooked by steaming ○ *steamed rice* **2.** very angry or upset (*informal*) ○ *I was steamed when they didn't turn up.*

steam en·gine *n* an engine powered by steam, typically incorporating a flywheel attached to a reciprocating piston that in turn is driven by the expansive action of steam generated in a boiler

steam·er /steémər/ *n* **1.** BOAT POWERED BY STEAM a boat or ship that is powered by a steam engine or engines **2.** PAN FOR STEAMING FOOD a covered pan with a perforated base that fits on top of a saucepan of boiling water so that the food inside is cooked by steam **3.** CONTAINER FOR STEAMING WOOD a container in which wood is treated with steam to make it pliable **4.** FOOD SOFT-SHELL CLAM a soft-shell clam, especially when steamed and eaten

steam·er chair *n* a collapsible adjustable outdoor chair made of wooden slats, usually with a removable cushion and used around a pool, on a patio, or in a garden

steam·er rug *n US* a warm blanket that can be put over the knees and legs for warmth, used especially by passengers sitting on the deck of a ship

steam·er trunk *n* a traveler's trunk, especially one that is shallow enough to fit underneath a bunk on a ship

steam·fit·ter /steém fittər/ *n* somebody whose job is to install and repair pipes and accessories that carry steam

steam-gen·er·at·ing heav·y-wa·ter re·ac·tor *n* a nuclear reactor that uses ordinary water as the coolant and heavy water as the moderator

steam·ing /steéming/ *adj* **1.** EMITTING STEAM emitting steam or filled with steam **2.** VERY ANGRY very angry or upset (*informal*) **3.** VERY HOT extremely hot (*informal*) ○ *We were steaming by the end of the game.*

steam i·ron *n* an electric iron with a chamber for water. As the iron heats up, steam is produced and channeled through holes in the face of the iron to dampen the laundry.

steam jack·et *n* a covering or casing surrounding the cylinders and heads of a steam engine to keep the surfaces hot and dry

steam or·gan *n UK* same as **calliope**

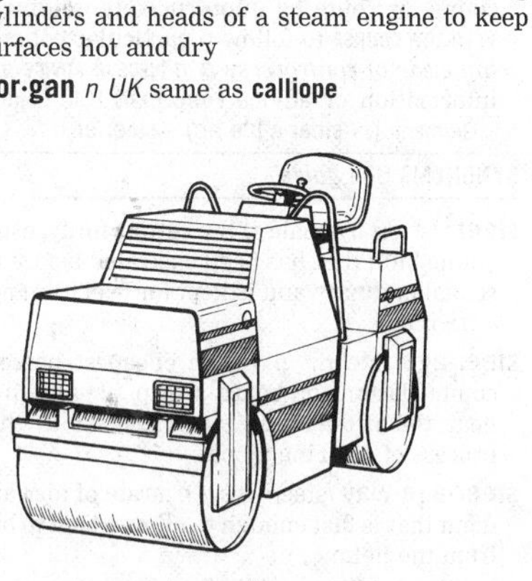

steamroller

steam·rol·ler /steém ròlər/ *n* **1.** VEHICLE FOR FLATTENING ROADS a specialized vehicle, originally steam-powered, with large heavy rollers for wheels, designed to flatten and compress newly laid road surfaces **2.** CRUSHING FORCE somebody or something that is a powerful driving force, often crushing or dismissing anybody or anything that might stand in the way ■ *v* (**-lered, -ler·ing, -lers**) *also* **steam·roll** (**-rolled, -roll·ing, -rolls**) **1.** *vt* FLATTEN ROAD to flatten and compress a newly laid road surface using a steamroller **2.** *vt* RUTHLESSLY CRUSH SOMEBODY OR SOMETHING to crush or dismiss anybody or anything that might stand in the way ○ *steamroller everyone else's ideas* **3.** *vt* ADVANCE SOMETHING to move something forward in an aggressive way that does not tolerate opposition ○ *The legislation was steamrollered through Congress.* **4.** *vi* PROCEED FORCEFULLY to move or proceed with overwhelming force ○ *Product placement in movies has steamrollered ahead.*

steam room *n* a room with a steam bath in it, or a room that can be filled with steam and used as a steam bath

steam·ship /steém shìp/ *n* a ship with an engine powered by steam

steam shov·el *n* a large steam-powered excavating machine, especially an earthmover that has a bucket on a boom fixed to a jib that can be rotated

steam ta·ble *n* a table used for keeping cooked food hot by circulating hot water or steam underneath the food containers

steam·tight /steém tìt/ *adj* designed or sealed so that steam cannot escape

steam tur·bine *n* a turbine that uses the heat energy of steam to generate the power for mechanical rotation

steam·y /steémee/ (**-i·er, -i·est**) *adj* **1.** OVERTLY SEXUAL involving or featuring sexual behavior or sexual passion (*informal*) **2.** HOT AND CLAMMY unbearably or uncomfortably hot and humid **3.** FULL OF STEAM full of, affected by, or like steam —**steam·i·ly** *adv* —**steam·i·ness** *n*

ste·ap·sin /stee áps'n/ *n* a pancreatic lipase that aids the digestion of fats [Late 19C. Blend of Greek *stear* "solid fat, tallow" + PEPSIN]

ste·a·rate /steé ə ràyt, steé ràyt/ *n* a salt or ester of stearic acid [Mid-19C. < Greek *stear* "solid fat, tallow"]

ste·ar·ic /stee árrik, steérik/ *adj* **1.** relating to, containing, or typical of stearin or fat **2.** about, derived from, or containing stearic acid [Mid-19C. < Greek *stear* "solid fat, tallow"]

ste·ar·ic ac·id *n* a colorless odorless waxy crystalline fatty acid. Source: animal tallow, vegetable oils. Use: manufacture of candles, cosmetics, soaps, lubricants, medicines. Formula: $C_{18}H_{36}O_2$.

ste·a·rin /steé ərin, steérin/, **ste·a·rine** /steé ə reèn, steérin/ *n* **1.** a colorless ester of glycerol and stearic acid. Use: manufacture of soap, candles, adhesives. **2.** BIOCHEM same as **stearic acid 3.** a waxy solid mixture of stearic and palmitic acids [Early 19C. < Greek *stear* "solid fat, tallow"]

ste·a·tite /steé ə tìt/ *n* MINERALS same as **soapstone** [Mid-18C. Via Latin < Greek *steatitis (lithos)* "tallow-like (stone)" < *stear* "solid fat, tallow"] —**ste·a·tit·ic** /steé ə títtik/ *adj*

steato- *prefix* fat ○ *steatopygia* [< Greek *steat-*, stem of *stear* "solid fat, tallow"]

ste·at·o·pyg·i·a /stee àttə píjjee ə, -píjee ə/ *n* an accumulation of fat on the buttocks [Early 19C. < STEATO- + Greek *pugē* "buttocks"] —**ste·a·to·py·gous** /steé ətə pígəss/ *adj*

ste·at·or·rhe·a /steé ətə reé ə/ *n* an unusual condition in which an excess of fat is present in stools

ste·at·or·rhoe·a *n* MED UK spelling of **steatorrhea**

steed /steed/ *n* a horse, especially a lively spirited one (*literary*) [Old English *stēda* "stallion" < Germanic]

steel /steel/ *n* **1.** STRONG ALLOY OF IRON AND CARBON a strong alloy of iron containing up to 1.5 percent carbon along with small amounts of other elements such as manganese, chromium, and nickel **2.** SOMETHING MADE OF STEEL something made of steel, e.g., a weapon **3.** KNIFE SHARPENER a steel rod, often with a handle, that knives are drawn back and forward along in order to sharpen them **4.** TOUGHNESS determination, toughness, or great strength of character ■ *adj* STRONG OR HARD like steel, especially in strength or hardness ■ *vt* (**steeled, steel·ing, steels**) **1.** STRENGTHEN SOMEBODY FOR ORDEAL to make somebody unfeeling or tough enough to withstand a setback or trial ○ *steeled myself for the news* **2.** TREAT SOMETHING WITH STEEL to coat, plate, edge, or point something with steel [Old English *stēli* < Indo-European, "stand, be solid"]

SPELLCHECK See ***steal.***

steel band *n* a group of musicians who play steel drums and often specialize in calypsos

steel blue *adj* having cold grayish blue color —**steel blue** *n*

steel drum *n* a Caribbean percussion instrument made by hammering an oil drum into a concave shape with flattened areas that make musical notes when struck

Steele, Mount /steel/ peak in the St. Elias Range, in southwestern Yukon Territory, Canada. Height: 16,644 ft./5,073 m.

Steele /steel/, **Sir Richard** (1672–1729) English playwright and essayist who founded and contributed to the influential journals the *Tatler* (1709–11) and the *Spectator* (1711–12)

steel en·grav·ing *n* **1.** a print made from an engraved steel plate **2.** the art, technique, or process of engraving on a steel plate

steel gray *adj* of a dark bluish gray color —**steel grey** *n*

steel gui·tar *n* a fretless guitar played on a horizontal stand with a pick and a movable metal slide

steel·head /stéel hèd/ (*plural* **-heads** or *same*) *n* an anadromous rainbow trout with a silver coloration, popular for sport fishing. Native to: North Pacific Ocean.

steel pan *n* MUSIC same as **steel drum**

steel-trap *adj US* very quick and keen [< *a mind like a steel trap*]

steel wool *n* thin strands of steel tangled together to form an abrasive mass, used for cleaning and polishing

steel·work /stéel wùrk/ *n* something made from steel, especially a structural framework

steel·work·er /stéel wùrkər/ *n* somebody whose job is making steel in a steelworks

steel·works /stéel wùrks/ *n* a factory where steel is made

steel·y /stéelee/ *adj* **1.** like steel, especially in color or hardness, or in being tough or determined **2.** made of steel (*dated or literary*) —**steel·i·ness** *n*

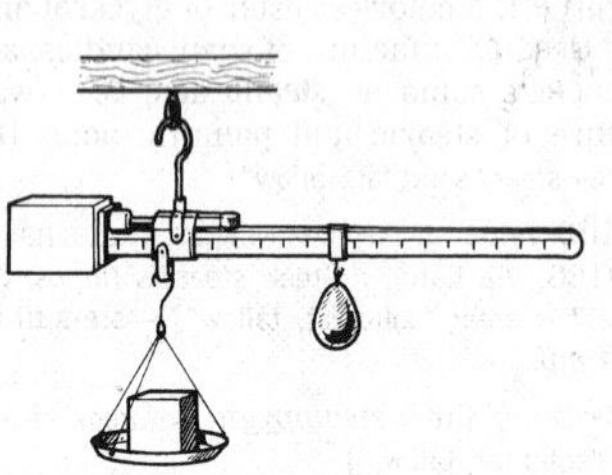

steelyard

steel·yard /stéel yaard/ *n* a portable balance for weighing objects. The object is hung on a hook and a counterweight is moved along a scaled arm to find the weight. [Mid-17C. < STEEL + YARD[1] "rod, spar"]

steen·bok /stéen bòk/ (*plural* **-boks** or *same*), **stein·bok** /stīn-/ *n* a small slender antelope with short straight horns, long legs, and a reddish brown coat. Native to: grasslands of southern Africa. Latin name: *Raphicerus campestris*. [Late 18C. Via Afrikaans < Middle Dutch *steenboc* "stone buck"]

steep[1] /steep/ *adj* **1.** SLOPING SHARPLY sloping very sharply, often to the extent of being almost vertical **2.** RAPID OR HUGE faster or greater than is usual or expected ○ *a steep decline in demand* **3.** EXCESSIVE unreasonably or excessively high, especially in cost (*informal*) **4.** TAXING very ambitious or difficult ■ *n* SOMETHING STEEP something that is steep, e.g., a slope [Old English *stēap* "high" < Germanic, "lofty, deep"] —**steep·ly** *adv* —**steep·ness** *n*

steep[2] /steep/ *v* (**steeped, steep·ing, steeps**) **1.** *vti* IMMERSE IN LIQUID to soak something in a liquid, or be soaked in a liquid, especially for cleaning or softening or in order to extract something **2.** *vt* PERMEATE SOMEBODY OR SOMETHING to permeate somebody or something with a substance or quality, usually over a long period (*usually passive*) ○ *steeped in tradition* ■ *n* **1.** SOAKING an act or the process of steeping something in a liquid **2.** LIQUID FOR SOAKING a liquid that something is or can be steeped in [14C. < assumed Old English *stiepan* < Germanic]

steep·en /stéepən/ (**-ened, -en·ing, -ens**) *vti* to become steep or steeper, or make something become steep or steeper

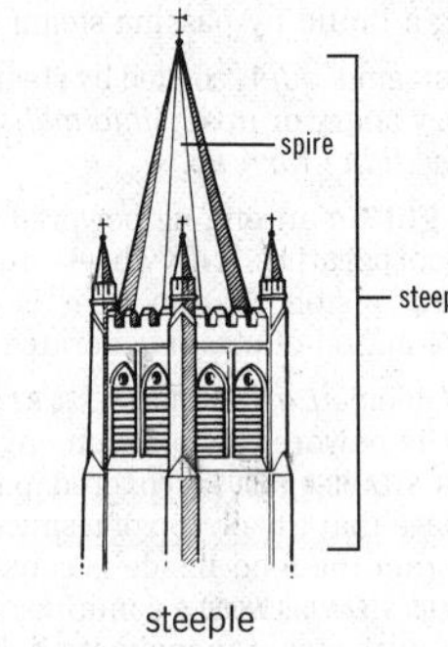

steeple

stee·ple /stéep'l/ *n* **1.** a tower forming part of a Christian church or another building, usually with a spire on top **2.** BUILDINGS same as **spire**[1] *n* (sense 1) [Old English *stēpel* < Germanic, "lofty, deep"] —**stee·pled** *adj*

stee·ple·bush /stéep'l bo͝osh/ *n* TREES same as **hardhack** [Mid-19C. Origin ?]

stee·ple·chase /stéep'l chàyss/ *n* **1.** HORSERACE WITH JUMPS ON TRACK a horserace run over a course that has constructed obstacles, e.g., hedges, ditches, and water jumps, that the horses must jump over **2.** TRACK-AND-FIELD EVENT a track-and-field event in which runners must jump over a water jump as well as hurdles ■ *vi* (**-chased, -chas·ing, -chas·es**) RUN STEEPLECHASE to compete in a steeplechase [Late 18C. Because a church steeple was originally the competitors' goal] —**stee·ple·chas·er** *n*

stee·ple·jack /stéep'l jàk/ *n* somebody who builds or repairs tall structures, especially steeples and chimneys

steer[1] /steer/ *v* (**steered, steer·ing, steers**) **1.** *vti* DIRECT VEHICLE to guide the direction of movement of something such as a motor vehicle or ship using a steering wheel, rudder, or other device **2.** *vi* MANEUVER IN PARTICULAR WAY to go or move in a particular way or direction when being driven or propelled ○ *This car steers to the left.* **3.** *vt* INFLUENCE SOMEBODY IN PARTICULAR DIRECTION to encourage somebody to take a particular course or route by unobtrusively guiding them **4.** *vi* FOLLOW COURSE to follow a particular course ○ *steering clear of controversy* ■ *n* PIECE OF ADVICE a piece of information or advice (*informal*) [Old English *stīeran* < Germanic] —**steer·a·ble** *adj* —**steer·er** *n*

SYNONYMS See ***guide***.

steer[2] /steer/ *n* a male of the cattle family, especially a young bull, that has been castrated before reaching sexual maturity and is kept for beef [Old English *stēor* < Germanic]

steer·age /stéerij/ *n* **1.** the cheapest passenger accommodations on board a ship, usually in the area near the rudder and steering gear **2.** the act or process of steering a boat

steer·age·way /stéerij wày/ *n* a rate of forward movement that is fast enough to allow a boat to be steered from the helm

steer·ing col·umn /stéering-/ *n* the part in a motor vehicle that connects the steering wheel, or the handlebars on a motorcycle, with the steering gear

steer·ing com·mit·tee *n* a group of selected people who decide agendas and topics for discussion, and prioritize urgent business, especially one acting for a legislative body or other assembly

steer·ing gear *n* the mechanism in a vehicle or ship that allows it to be steered

steer·ing wheel *n* **1.** a wheel in a vehicle or ship that is connected by way of the steering column to the steering gear and is turned to change direction **2.** in computer games, a wheel used to control movement

steers·man /stéerzmən/ (*plural* **-men** /-mən/) *n* somebody, especially a man, who steers a boat or ship [Old English *stēoresman* "man for steering" < form of *stēor* "steering" < Germanic]

steers·per·son /stéerz pùrss'n/ *n* somebody who steers a boat or ship

steers·wom·an /stéerz wo͝omən/ (*plural* **-wom·en** /-wimmin/) *n* a woman who steers a boat or ship

steeve[1] /steev/ *n* a spar with a pulley block at one end that is used for stowing cargo on a boat or ship ■ *vt* (**steeved, steev·ing, steeves**) to stow cargo in the hold of a boat or ship and make it secure [Mid-19C. Origin ?]

steeve[2] /steev/ *vti* (**steeved, steev·ing, steeves**) to incline upward, or make a bowsprit incline upward ■ *n* the angle at which a bowsprit inclines upward from the horizontal [Mid-17C. Origin ?]

Stef·fens /stéffənz/, **Lincoln** (1866–1936) US journalist. The author of articles exposing business and political corruption, he was a leader of the so-called muckraking school of journalism. Full name **Steffens, Joseph Lincoln**

> "Liberty is the right of any person to stand up anywhere and say anything whatsoever that everybody thinks."
> [Lincoln Steffens, *Autobiography*; 1931]

steg a·nal·y·sis *n* the process of searching through computer files to find slight deviations in expected patterns that may reveal the presence of hidden messages [Late 20C. *Steg* < STEGANOGRAPHY]

steg·a·nog·ra·phy /stèggə nógrəffee/ *n* **1.** the production and placing in computer files of secret messages so small as to be detectable only by special software **2.** the art of secret writing [16C. < modern Latin *steganographia* < Greek *steganos* "covered"]

Steg·ner /stégnər/, **Wallace** (1909–93) US writer. He wrote fiction and nonfiction, both often set in the American West, and won a Pulitzer Prize for *Angle of Repose* (1972). Full name **Stegner, Wallace Earle**

steg·o·saur /stéggə sàwr/, **steg·o·sau·rus** /stèggə sáwrəss/ *n* a plant-eating dinosaur that lived in the Jurassic and Early Cretaceous periods and had tough bony dorsal plates and spikes. Genus: *Stegosauria*. [Early 20C. < modern Latin *Stegosaurus* < Greek *stegos* "plate" + *sauros* "lizard"]

Steich·en /stīkən/, **Edward** (1879–1973) Luxembourg-born US photographer. His works did much to establish photography as an art form. He headed the photography department of New York City's Museum of Modern Art (1947–62). Full name **Steichen, Edward Jean**

stein /stīn/ *n* **1.** a large beer mug, especially a German earthenware or pewter one, often with a hinged lid **2.** the amount of beer or other liquid that a stein holds [Mid-19C. < German, shortening of *Steinkrug* "stoneware mug"]

Gertrude Stein: photographed by Man Ray (1930)

Stein /stīn/, **Gertrude** (1874–1946) US writer. Her works, experimental in language and style, include *Three Lives* (1909), *The Autobiography of Alice B. Toklas* (1933), and *Four Saints in Three Acts* (1934), an opera with music by Virgil Thomson.

> "Remarks are not literature."
> [Gertrude Stein, *The Autobiography of Alice B. Toklas*; 1933]

> "You are all a lost generation."
> [Gertrude Stein, *on the young men who served in World War I*]

Viking Press
John Steinbeck

Stein·beck /stīn bèk/, **John** (1902–68) US writer. His novels, notable for their social realism, include *Of Mice and Men* (1937) and *The Grapes of Wrath* (1939). He won a Nobel Prize in literature (1962). Full name **Steinbeck, John Ernst**. See Cultural note at **grape, mice**

> "And where a number of men gathered together, the fear went from the faces, and anger took its place. And the women sighed with relief, for they knew it was all right—the break had not come; and the break would never come as long as fear could turn to wrath."
> [John Steinbeck, *The Grapes of Wrath*; 1939]

stein·bok *n* ZOOL same as **steenbok**

Rick Baid
Gloria Steinem

Stein·em /stīnəm/, **Gloria** (*b.* 1934) US feminist. A leading member of the women's movement, she was one of the founders of *Ms.* magazine (1972).

> "We are becoming the men we wanted to marry."
> [Gloria Steinem, *Ms.*; July/August 1982]

Stein·er /stīnər, shtīnər/, **Rudolf** (1861–1925) Austrian philosopher. He founded the Anthroposophical Society (1912) to promote his intellectually based spirituality. The Waldorf School movement is based on his work.

> "The man of the present day would far rather believe that disease is connected only with immediate causes for the fundamental tendency in the modern view of life is always to seek what is more convenient."
> [Rudolf Steiner, *The Manifestations of Karma*; 1925]

ste·la /steélə/ (*plural* **-lae** /-lee/) *n* ARCHAEOL same as **stele** (sense 1) [Late 18C. Via Latin < Greek *stēlē* "standing stone"]

ste·le /steel, steélee/ (*plural* **-lae** /-lèe/) *n* **1.** an ancient stone slab or pillar, usually engraved, inscribed, or painted, and set upright **2.** the cylindrical core of the stem and roots of a plant that contains the sap-conducting vascular tissues and varying amounts of packing tissue **(pith)** [Early 19C. < Greek *stēlē* "standing stone"] —**ste·lar** *adj*

Stel·la /stéllə/, **Frank** (*b.* 1936) US artist. His abstract geometric forms are often painted on irregularly shaped canvases. Full name **Stella, Frank Philip**

stel·lar /stéllər/ *adj* **1.** INVOLVING STARS relating to, consisting of, or like a star or stars **2.** EXCEPTIONAL exceptionally good ○ *got stellar grades* **3.** INVOLVING FAMOUS PEOPLE full of famous people, especially those in the movie or entertainment industries [Mid-17C. < late Latin *stellaris* < Latin *stella* "star"]

stel·lar nurs·er·y *n* a region within a nebula where intense new star formation takes place

stel·lar wind *n* a stream of ionized particles ejected from the surface of a star

stel·late /stéllət, sté làyt/, **stel·lat·ed** /stéllətəd, sté làytəd/ *adj* **1.** having a central part with smaller parts radiating out from it, like a starfish, some flower heads, and some crystal formations **2.** shaped like a star [Mid-17C. < Latin *stella* "star"]

Stel·ler's jay /stèllərz-/ *n* a gregarious bird with a black high-crested head and blue and black feathers. Native to: western North America. Latin name: *Cyanocitta stelleri*. [After Georg Wilhelm *Steller* (1709–46), German naturalist and explorer]

stem[1] /stem/ *n* **1.** MAIN AXIS OF PLANT the main stalk of a plant that bears buds and shoots **2.** SECONDARY PLANT BRANCH a secondary stalk of a plant, bearing a leaf, bud, or flower **3.** NARROW CONNECTING PART a long slim part of an object, e.g., the part that connects the base of a wine glass to its bowl, or the hollow tube on a smoker's pipe **4.** CYLINDRICAL WATCH PART a short rod, usually with an expanded crown at the end of it, that is used in winding a watch **5.** GENEALOGICAL LINE the major line of descent in a family tree **6.** GRAM BASE OF WORD the base of a word, to which affixes are added **7.** PHARM same as **INN stem** **8.** PRINTING VERTICAL LETTER PART an upright stroke, especially the main one, in a letter or character **9.** MUSIC VERTICAL PART OF MUSIC NOTE the vertical part that extends from the head of a written musical note **10.** NAUT UPRIGHT BOW TIMBER the main upright timber at the bow of a ship ■ *v* (**stemmed, stem·ming, stems**) **1.** *vi* ORIGINATE to derive, originate, or be caused by something ○ *This behavior stems from some trauma in his childhood.* **2.** *vt* REMOVE STEM OF SOMETHING to take off the stem or part of the stem from something, especially a flower, fruit, or vegetable **3.** *vt* NAUT ADVANCE AGAINST TIDE OR WIND to make headway sailing against a tide or wind [Old English *stefn* < Indo-European, "to stand"] —**stem·less** *adj* —**stemmed** *adj* ◇ **from stem to stern** through the whole of a place, especially a ship

stem[2] /stem/ *v* (**stemmed, stem·ming, stems**) **1.** *vt* PREVENT SOMETHING FROM FLOWING to hinder, obstruct, or stop something from flowing, especially by creating a dam or plug **2.** *vt* STOP SOMETHING UP to plug something such as a blast or drill hole by packing it **3.** *vti* SKIING TURN SKI IN to turn the tip of a ski or skis inward in order to turn or slow down ■ *n* SKIING TURNING IN OF SKI an act or the technique of turning the tip of a ski or skis inward in order to turn or slow down [13C. < Old Norse *stemma* < Germanic, "halt, stammer"]

STEM *abbr* EDUC science, technology, engineering, mathematics

stem cell *n* an undifferentiated cell that can give rise to other cells of the same type indefinitely or from which specialized cells such as blood cells develop

stem chris·tie *n* a skiing turn performed by stemming one ski and then bringing the other parallel to it during the turn [< STEM[2]]

stem gin·ger *n* round portions of the underground stem of a ginger plant, cooked until tender and preserved in syrup

stem·ma /stémmə/ (*plural* **-ma·ta** /-mətə/) *n* **1.** FAMILY TREE a diagram of the genealogy of a person or a family **2.** LITERAT DIAGRAM OF TEXTS OF LITERARY WORK a diagram like a family tree that shows the relationships between different texts of a literary work **3.** ZOOL EYE OF ARTHROPOD a simple eye or facet of a compound eye of some arthropods [Mid-17C. Via Latin < Greek *stemma* "garland"; from the ancient Roman practice of placing garlands on images of their ancestors]

stem·son /stémssən/ *n* a timber attached to the stem and keelson in the bow of a wooden ship [Mid-18C. < STEM[1] after KEELSON]

stem turn *n* SKIING same as **stem**[2] [< STEM[2]]

stem·ware /stém wèr/ *n* glasses, goblets, and other glass vessels that have stems

stench /stench/ *n* a very strong unpleasant smell, especially a lingering smell associated with death or decay [Old English *stenc* "odor" < Germanic]

SYNONYMS See *smell*.

stench trap *n* a device used in a sewer to prevent foul-smelling gases from rising, especially one that has a water seal

stencil

sten·cil /sténss'l/ *n* **1.** PLATE WITH CUTOUT DESIGN a thin sheet of material with a shape cut out of it through which paint or ink is applied to mark the shape on another surface **2.** PATTERN the design, lettering, or other characters marked using a stencil ■ *vt* (**-ciled** or **-cilled, -cil·ing** or **-cil·ling, -cils**) **1.** MAKE PATTERN USING STENCIL to apply a design, lettering, or other characters to a surface using a stencil **2.** DECORATE SOMETHING USING STENCIL to decorate or mark a surface such as a wall or paper using a stencil [Early 18C. < Old French *estenceler* "decorate with bright colors" < Latin *scintilla* "spark"] —**sten·cil·er** *n*

Stend·hal /sten daál/ (1783–1842) French novelist and one of the first realists in 19th-century literature. His best-known works are *Le Rouge et le noir* (*The Red and the Black*) (1830) and *La Chartreuse de Parma* (*The Charterhouse of Parma*) (1839). Pseudonym of **Beyle, Marie-Henri**

> "A novel is a mirror which passes over a highway. Sometimes it reflects to your eyes the blue of the skies, at others the churned-up mud of the road."
> [Stendhal, *The Red and the Black*; 1830]

Sten·gel /sténg gəl/, **Casey** (1890?–1975) US baseball player and manager. One of baseball's most successful managers, he led the New York Yankees to ten pennants and seven World Series (1948–60) and subsequently managed the New York Mets (1962–65). He was legendary for his combination of outspokenness and malapropisms, which came to be called "Stengelese." Known as **the Professor, the Old Professor**. Full name **Stengel, Charles Dillon**

> "Managing is getting paid for home runs someone else hits."
> [Casey Stengel, recalled on his death; September 29, 1975]

> "There are three things you can do in a baseball game. You can win, or you can lose, or it can rain."
> [Casey Stengel. Quoted in *Norton Book of Sports*, George Plimpton; 1992]

Sten gun /stén-/ *n* a light, cheaply manufactured submachine gun formerly used by the British Army, especially in World War II [Acronym < R. V. V. *Shepherd* + H. J. *Turpin*, its designers + *Enfield* in Greater London, England]

sten·o /sténnō/ (*plural* **-os**) *n* (*informal*) **1.** OCCUPATIONS same as **stenographer** **2.** *US* same as **stenography** (sense 1) [Early 20C. Shortening]

steno- *prefix* narrow, small ○ *stenothermal* [< Greek *stenos*]

sten·o·bath·ic /stènnə báthik/ *adj* able to live only within a narrow range of depth of water [Early 20C. < STENO- + Greek *bathos* "depth"] —**sten·o·bath** /sténnə bàth/ *n*

sten·o·graph /sténnə gràf/ *n* **1.** SHORTHAND TYPEWRITER a machine like a small typewriter with keys for shorthand characters **2.** SHORTHAND CHARACTER a character in a system of shorthand writing ■ *vt*

(**-graphed, -graph·ing, -graphs**) WRITE OR TYPE SOMETHING IN SHORTHAND to record something in shorthand by writing or using a stenograph

ste·nog·ra·pher /stə nóggrəfər/ *n* **1.** somebody who uses a stenograph **2.** somebody who is skilled at or whose job involves writing shorthand and typing up reports and letters from shorthand copy

ste·nog·ra·phy /stə nóggrəfee/ (*plural* **-phies**) *n* **1.** the act, process, or skill of recording something in shorthand by writing or by using a stenograph **2.** something that has been recorded in written shorthand or by using a stenograph —**sten·o·graph·ic** /stènnə gráffik/ *adj* —**sten·o·graph·i·cal·ly** *adv*

sten·o·ha·line /stènnō háy līn, -há līn/ *adj* unable to tolerate wide variations in salinity of water [Mid-20C. < STENO- + Greek *hal-* "salt"]

ste·no·sis /stə nṓssiss/ *n* a constriction or narrowing of a duct, passage, or opening in the body [Late 19C. < modern Latin < Greek *stenos* "narrow"] —**ste·nosed** /stə nṓzd, -nṓst/ *adj* —**ste·not·ic** /stə nóttik/ *adj*

sten·o·ther·mal /stènnə thúrm'l/ *adj* able to live only within a narrow temperature range

sten·o·type /sténnə tīp/ *n* a machine whose keyboard is used to record speech by means of phonetic shorthand

sten·o·typ·y /sténnə tīpee/ *n* a form of phonetic shorthand that uses combinations of letters to represent sounds and short words —**sten·o·typ·ic** /stènnə típpik/ *adj* —**sten·o·typ·ist** *n*

stent /stent/ *n* an open tubular structure of stainless steel or plastic that is inserted into an artery or another bodily tube to keep it from becoming blocked by disease [Mid-20C. After Charles T. *Stent* (1807–85), British dentist]

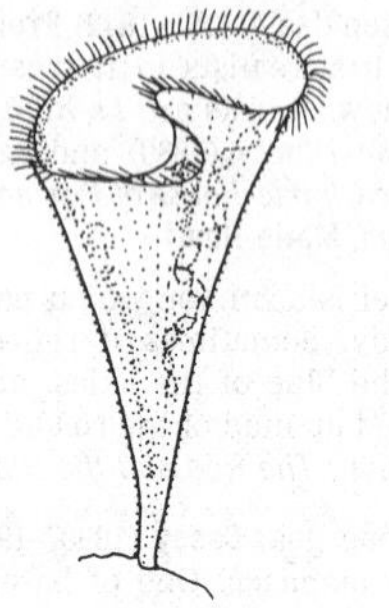

stentor (sense 2)

sten·tor /stén tàwr/ *n* **1.** somebody with a loud powerful voice **2.** a trumpet-shaped protozoan with a mouth at the broad end. Genus: *Stentor*. [Early 17C. After *Stentor*, strong-voiced Greek herald in the Trojan war]

sten·to·ri·an /sten táwree ən/ *adj* loud, powerful, or declamatory in tone

step /step/ *n* **1.** SHORT MOVEMENT WITH FOOT a short movement made by raising one foot and lowering it ahead of the other foot **2.** DISTANCE OF STEP the distance traveled in taking a step **3.** SOUND OF FOOTFALL the sound made by putting the foot down **4.** FOOTPRINT the footprint made by putting the foot down on a surface ○ *saw her steps in the snow* **5.** WAY OF WALKING a particular manner of walking **6.** SHORT WAY a very short distance ○ *a few steps away* **7.** RAISED SURFACE a raised surface for the foot, especially in a series going up or down **8.** STAGE IN PROGRESS a stage in a progression toward some goal or target ○ *a step toward lifting the embargo* **9.** DEGREE OR GRADE a degree, rank, or grade, especially on a scale ○ *took the issue one step further* **10.** MUSIC DEGREE OF MUSICAL SCALE a degree of a musical staff or scale **11.** MUSIC MUSICAL INTERVAL the interval between two degrees of a musical scale **12.** DANCE DANCE MOVE a movement of the feet and body that forms part of a dance **13.** same as **step aerobics** (*informal*) ○ *a step class* ■ **steps** *npl* **1.** STAIRS a flight of stairs **2.** PATH MADE BY SOMEBODY ELSE a route, path, or course set by somebody else ○ *She followed in her mother's steps and became an architect.* ■ *v* (**stepped, step·ping, steps**) **1.** *vti* MOVE FOOT to move a foot on top of something or in a particular direction ○ *Please step aside.* **2.** *vi* WALK FEW STEPS to walk a short distance or to a specific place ○ *Would you step into my office?* **3.** *vi* DANCE MOVE IN REGULAR RHYTHM to move at a measured pace, e.g., in a dance **4.** *vi* EASILY WALK INTO SITUATION to come into a new situation with ease or with little preparation ○ *Within a week of graduating she stepped into a fantastic job.* **5.** *vt* ARRANGE SOMETHING IN STEPS to arrange or organize something in steps **6.** *vt* MAKE STEPS IN SOMETHING to provide or furnish something with steps **7.** *vt* MEASURE SOMETHING BY STEPS to measure something by walking or pacing its length **8.** *vt* NAUT FASTEN MAST to place a ship's mast in its step ■ *n* NAUT MAST SUPPORT the block in which the heel of the mast of a sailing vessel is fixed (*informal*) [Old English *stæpe* < Germanic, "to tread"] —**stepped** *adj* —**step·per** *n* ◇ **be in** *or* **out of step 1.** to agree or disagree with somebody or something in your attitudes or opinions **2.** to move in unison with or at a different pace and rhythm from other people ◇ **step by step** gradually ◇ **step on it** to hurry (*slang*) ◇ **take steps** to take action ◇ **watch your step 1.** to be careful and cautious **2.** to tread carefully

SPELLCHECK step or **steppe**? Do not confuse the spelling of ***step*** and ***steppe***, which sound similar. ***Step*** relates to a short movement of the foot, either as a noun or a verb (*took her first steps at nine months, Don't trip over the step, stepped inside*). ***Steppe*** is a noun denoting "an extensive, usually treeless plain" (*the steppes of Central Asia*).

step aside *vi* to resign, retire, or withdraw from a position, especially so that somebody else can fill it

step down *v* **1.** *vi* WITHDRAW FROM POSITION to resign, retire, or withdraw from a position **2.** *vt* DECREASE IN STAGES to lower or decrease something in stages, or become lower in stages **3.** *vt* REDUCE VOLTAGE to reduce voltage using a transformer

step in *vi* to intervene or become involved in something

step on *vt* to treat somebody with arrogant disregard or active unkindness ○ *She's constantly stepping on other people's feelings.*

step out *vi* **1.** LEAVE BRIEFLY to leave a place for a brief period **2.** WALK WITH LONG STRIDES to walk fast, with longer strides than usual **3.** DATE SOMEBODY to go on a date or to a social gathering with somebody (*informal*) **4.** *US* WITHDRAW FROM ACTIVITY to withdraw from some activity (*informal*) **5.** *US* TO BE UNFAITHFUL to be unfaithful to a spouse or partner (*informal*)

step up *v* **1.** *vt* RAISE SOMETHING IN STAGES to raise or increase something in stages **2.** *vt* RAISE VOLTAGE to raise voltage using a transformer **3.** *vi* COME FORWARD to come forward, e.g., to stand for an office or position or to take responsibility for something

step- *prefix* related because of remarriage, not by blood ○ *stepson* ○ *stepmother* [Old English *stēop-* < Germanic]

step aer·o·bics *n* an exercise program done to music that involves performing different movements with the arms and legs while stepping onto and off a small portable platform (*takes a singular or plural verb*)

step·broth·er /stép brùthər/ *n* a boy or man who has brothers or sisters through the remarriage of a parent to somebody who has children

step change *n* a change that makes a significant difference in the size or value of something or the way in which something is done ■ *vt* to change something in a significant way

step·child /stép chīld/ (*plural* **-chil·dren** /-chìldrən/) *n* the son or daughter of a stepparent

step dance *n* a dance in which feet and leg movements are important, often performed with the dancer remaining in one spot

step·daugh·ter /stép dàwtər/ *n* the daughter of somebody's spouse by a previous marriage

step-down *adj* **1.** decreasing in quantity, size, or status, especially in stages **2.** serving to lower voltage —**step-down** *n*

step·fam·i·ly /stép fàmməlee/ (*plural* **-lies**) *n* a family in which there is a stepparent

step·fa·ther /stép faàthər/ *n* a man who has married somebody's mother after the death of or divorce from the person's father

step func·tion *n* a mathematical function, e.g., a waveform, that remains constant in value over a given interval but changes abruptly in value from one interval to the next

steph·a·no·tis /stèffə nṓtiss/ (*plural* **-tis·es** or *same*) *n* an ornamental vine or bush with leathery leaves. Flowers: fragrant, white, waxy. Genus: *Stephanotis*. [Mid-19C. < Greek *stephanōtis* "fit for a crown" < *stephanos* "crown, wreath" < *stephein* "to crown"]

Ste·phen /steévən/ (1090?–1154) king of England. He seized the throne on the death of Henry I (1135), but was engaged in civil war throughout his reign with supporters of Matilda, Henry's daughter.

Ste·phen I /steév'n/, **St.** (975?–1038) king of Hungary. He founded the Hungarian state and established Christianity in Hungary. He is the country's patron saint.

Ste·phen, St. (*d.* A.D. 36) Christian martyr. Condemned to death on a charge of blasphemy, he was the first Christian martyr. Known as **the Protomartyr**

Ste·phens /steévənz/, **Alexander** (1812–83) US politician. He was vice president of the Confederacy (1861–65) and served in the US House of Representatives (1843–59 and 1873–82).

Ste·phens /steév'nz/, **Frederick George** (1828–1907) British artist and art critic. A member of the Pre-Raphaelite Brotherhood, he abandoned painting for writing in the 1850s.

Ste·phen·son /steévənssən/, **George** (1781–1848) British railroad engineer. He built the Liverpool & Manchester Railway (opened 1830) and the *Rocket*, the steam locomotive that established the viability of the railroad as a means of passenger transportation.

Ste·phen·son /steévənss'n/, **Robert** (1803–59) British civil engineer and politician. The son of George Stephenson, he was noted as a builder of bridges in the United Kingdom, Egypt, and Canada.

step-in *adj* describes a garment without fastenings that is put on by stepping into it ■ **step-ins** *npl* a step-in article of clothing, especially panties with wide legs worn by women in the 1920s and 1930s (*dated*)

step·lad·der /stép làddər/ *n* a folding ladder that has flat broad steps and a hinged supporting frame

step ma·chine *n* a type of exercise machine with two large pedals that are depressed alternately to imitate the action of stepping

step·moth·er /stép mùthər/ *n* a woman who has married somebody's father after the death of or divorce from the person's mother

step·par·ent /stép pèrrənt/ *n* a stepfather or stepmother —**step·par·ent·ing** *n*

steppe /step/ *n* an extensive, usually treeless plain, often dry and grass-covered [Late 17C. Via German < Russian *step*]

SPELLCHECK See ***step***.

Steppes /steps/ *npl* the vast grassy plains of Russia and Ukraine

step·ping stone /stépping-/, **step·ping·stone** *n* **1.** a stage or step that helps achieve a goal **2.** one of a series of stones on which somebody is able to step, e.g., to cross shallow water

step·sis·ter /stép sìstər/ *n* a girl or woman who has brothers or sisters through the remarriage of a parent to somebody who has children

step·son /stép sùn/ *n* the son of somebody's spouse by a previous marriage

step stool *n* a stool with hinged steps that can be folded

step turn *n* a turn in which a skier lifts one ski in a desired direction, brings it down, and then aligns the other ski with it

step-up *adj* **1.** increasing in quantity, size, or status, usually in stages **2.** serving to raise voltage —**stepped-up** *adj* —**step-up** *n*

step·wife /stép wīf/ (*plural* **-wives** /-wīvz/) *n* a man's ex-wife and the mother of his children, or his current wife and the stepmother of his children [Late 20C. < STEP- + *ex-wife*]

step·wise /stép wīz/ *adj* **1.** arranged in or resembling steps **2.** *US* in music, moving from one adjacent tone to another in intervals of a second —**step·wise** *adv*

step·wives plural of **stepwife**

-ster *suffix* **1.** associated with, doing, or making a particular thing ○ *gangster* ○ *punster* **2.** having a particular characteristic ○ *youngster* [Old English *-estre*, feminine suffix < Germanic]

ste·ra·di·an /stə ráydee ən/ *n* the basic International System unit of measurement of a solid angle in a sphere. One steradian is the solid angle made at the center of a sphere by an area on the surface of the sphere equal to the square of the sphere's radius. Symbol **sr** [Late 19C. < STEREO- + RADIAN]

ster·co·ra·ceous /stùrkə ráyshəss/ *adj* consisting of or resembling dung or feces [Mid-18C. < Latin *stercor-* "dung"]

stere /steer/ *n* a cubic meter, equal to 35.32 cubic ft. [Late 18C. Via French *stère* < Greek *stereos* (see STEREO-)]

stere- *prefix* same as **stereo-** (*used before vowels*)

ster·e·o /stérree ō, steer-/ (*plural* **-os**) *n* **1. DEVICE PRODUCING STEREOPHONIC SOUND** an audio system or device that reproduces stereophonic sound **2. STEREOPHONIC REPRODUCTION** stereophonic sound reproduction **3. STEREOSCOPIC PHOTOGRAPHY** photography using stereoscopy **4.** PRINTING same as **stereotype** *n* (sense 2) [Late 19C. Shortening]

stereo- *prefix* **1.** three-dimensional ○ *stereology* **2.** solid ○ *stereotaxis* [< Greek *stereos* "solid" < Indo-European, "stiff"]

ster·e·o·bate /stérree ō bàyt, steeree-/ *n* **1.** a masonry platform that supports a building **2.** ARCHIT same as **stylobate** [Mid-19C. < Latin *stereobates* < Greek *stereos* "solid" + *-batēs* "walker"]

ster·e·o·chem·is·try /stèrree ō kémmistree, steeree-/ *n* the study of the spatial distribution of atoms in a compound and its effects on the compound's properties —**ster·e·o·chem·i·cal** *adj*

ster·e·o·chrome /stérree ə krōm, steeree-/ *n* a wall painting that uses water glass as a medium or preservative [Mid-19C. < German *Stereochrom* < Greek *stereos* "solid" + *khroma* "color"] —**ster·e·o·chro·my** *n*

ster·e·o·gram /stérree ə gràm, steeree-/ *n* **1.** PHOTOGRAPHY same as **stereograph 2.** a diagram or picture that shows objects as though in relief

ster·e·o·graph /stérree ə gràf, steeree-/ *n* a picture with two superimposed images or two almost identical pictures placed side by side which, when viewed through special glasses or a stereoscope, produce a three-dimensional image

ster·e·og·ra·phy /stèrree óggrəfee, steeree-/ *n* **1.** the technique or art of depicting a three-dimensional object on a flat surface **2.** the study and construction of defined geometric objects —**ster·e·o·graph·ic** /stèrree ə gráffik, steeree-/ *adj* —**ster·e·o·graph·i·cal·ly** *adv*

ster·e·o·i·so·mer /stèrree ō íssəmər, steeree-/ *n* one of a group of molecules that have identical atoms connected in the same order but in different spatial arrangements

ster·e·o·i·som·er·ism /stèrree ō ī sómmə rìzzəm, steeree-/ *n* isomerism in which the atoms in molecules are connected in the same order but in different spatial arrangements —**ster·e·o·i·so·mer·ic** /stèree ō īssə mérrik, steeree-/ *adj*

ster·e·ol·o·gy /stèrree óllajee, steeree-/ *n* the study of the properties of three-dimensional structures and objects based on two-dimensional views of them —**ster·e·o·log·i·cal** /stèrree ə lójjik'l, steeree-/ *adj*

ster·e·om·e·try /stèrree ómmətree, steeree-/ *n* the measurement of volume —**ste·re·o·met·ric** /stèrree ə méttrik, steeree-/ *adj*

ster·e·o·mi·cro·scope /stèrree ō mīkrə skōp, steeree-/ *n* a microscope with two optically separate eyepieces to make viewed objects look three-dimensional —**ster·e·o·mi·cros·co·py** /-mī króskəpee/ *n*

ster·e·o·phon·ic /stèrree ə fónnik, steeree-/ *adj* using an audio system based on two or more soundtracks to make recorded sound seem more natural when reproduced —**ster·e·o·phon·i·cal·ly** *adv* —**ster·e·oph·on·y** /stèrree óffənee, steeree-/ *n*

ster·e·op·sis /stèrree ópsiss, steeree-/ *n* three-dimensional vision

ster·e·op·ti·con /stèrree ópti kòn, steeree-/ *n* a slide projector able to allow one image to gradually replace another [Mid-19C. < modern Latin < Greek *stereos* "solid" + *optikos* "optic"]

ster·e·o·scope /stérree ə skōp, steeree-/ *n* a device resembling a pair of binoculars in which two-dimensional pictures of a scene taken at slightly different angles are viewed concurrently, one with each eye, creating the illusion of three dimensions

ster·e·o·scop·ic /stèrree ə skóppik, steeree-/ *adj* **1.** involving, producing, or resembling the effects of seeing something as three-dimensional **2.** produced by or relating to a stereoscope —**ster·e·o·scop·i·cal·ly** *adv*

ster·e·os·co·py /stèrree óskəpee, steeree-/ *n* the visual perception of objects as being three-dimensional

ster·e·o·se·lec·tive /stèrree ō si léktiv, steeree-/ *adj* describes a chemical reaction in which one stereoisomer is affected more rapidly than another —**ster·e·o·se·lec·tive·ly** *adv*

ste·re·o·spe·cif·ic /stèrree ō spə síffik, steeree-/ *adj* relating to a process in which atoms are in a fixed spatial position —**ste·re·o·spe·cif·i·cal·ly** *adv* —**ste·re·o·spec·i·fic·i·ty** /stèrree ō spèssə físsətee, steeree-/ *n*

ster·e·o·tax·is /stèrree ō táksiss, steeree-/ *n* **1.** the movement of an entire organism in response to contact with a solid object **2.** neurological surgery involving the insertion of delicate instruments that are guided to the relevant area by the use of three-dimensional scanning techniques —**ster·e·o·tac·tic** *adj* —**ster·e·o·tac·ti·cal·ly** *adv* —**ster·e·o·tax·ic** *adj* —**ster·e·o·tax·i·cal·ly** *adv*

ster·e·ot·ro·pism /stèrree óttrə pìzzəm, steeree-/ *n* BOT same as **thigmotropism** —**ster·e·o·trop·ic** /stèrree ə tróppik, steeree-/ *adj*

ster·e·o·type /stérree ə tīp, steeree-/ *n* **1. OVERSIMPLIFIED CONCEPTION** an oversimplified standardized image of a person or group **2.** PRINTING **METAL PRINTING PLATE** a metal printing plate cast from a mold in another material such as papier-mâché **3.** PSYCHOL same as **stereotypy** (sense 1) ■ *vt* (**-typed, -typ·ing, -types**) **1. REDUCE SOMEBODY TO OVERSIMPLIFIED CATEGORY** to categorize individuals or groups according to an oversimplified standardized image or idea **2.** PRINTING **PRINT SOMETHING USING STEREOTYPE** to cast or print something using a stereotype [Late 18C. < French *stéréotype* "solid-block printing"] —**ster·e·o·typ·er** *n* —**ster·e·o·typ·i·cal** /stèrree ə típpik'l, steeree-/ *adj* —**ster·e·o·typ·i·cal·ly** *adv* —**ster·e·o·typ·ist** *n*

ster·e·o·ty·py /stérree ə tīpee, steeree-/ *n* **1.** a pattern of persistent, fixed, and repeated speech or movement that is apparently meaningless and is characteristic of some mental conditions **2.** the process of casting or printing stereotypes

ster·ic /stérrik, steer-/ *adj* related to the way atoms are spatially arranged [Late 19C. < STEREO-] —**ster·i·cal·ly** *adv*

ste·rig·ma /stə rígmə/ (*plural* **-ma·ta** /-mətə/ or **-mas**) *n* a tiny stalk that bears a spore or spores in a fungus [Mid-19C. Via modern Latin < Greek, "support" < *sterizein* "to support"]

ster·ile /stérrəl, -īl/ *adj* **1.** MED **FREE FROM INFECTIVE ORGANISMS** free from living bacteria and other microorganisms **2.** BIOL **INFERTILE** incapable of becoming pregnant or of inducing pregnancy **3.** ECOL **BARREN** incapable of supporting vegetation **4.** BIOL **NOT PRODUCING SEEDS** not producing seeds, fruit, or spores **5. DULL AND UNCREATIVE** unstimulating, uncreative, and lacking in ideas that will lead to any useful outcome [15C. Via French < Latin *sterilis*] —**ster·il·ant** /stérrələnt/ *n* —**ster·ile·ly** *adv* —**ste·ril·i·ty** /stə rílləte e/ *n*

ster·il·ize /stérrə līz/ (**-ized, -iz·ing, -iz·es**) *vt* **1.** to kill all living microorganisms in something in order to make it incapable of causing infection **2.** to stop a person or animal from reproducing, e.g., by surgical removal or alteration of reproductive organs —**ster·il·i·za·tion** /stèrrəli záysh'n/ *n* —**ster·il·iz·er** *n*

~~**sterio**~~ incorrect spelling of **stereo**

ster·let /stúrlət/ (*plural* **-lets** or *same*) *n* a small sturgeon that is commercially used for caviar production. Native to: Black and Caspian seas. Latin name: *Acipenser ruthenus*. [Late 16C. < Russian *sterlyad* < Germanic]

ster·ling /stúrling/ *n* **1.** METALL same as **sterling silver** **2. BRITISH CURRENCY** the currency in pounds and pence used in the United Kingdom ■ *adj* **1. OF STERLING SILVER** made of sterling silver **2. ADMIRABLE** admirable or valuable ○ *a sterling record of social responsibility* [13C. Probably diminutive of STAR]

ster·ling ar·e·a *n* the group of countries that use UK currency or that link the value of their own currency to that of sterling

ster·ling sil·ver *n* **1.** an alloy containing at least 92.5% silver with the remainder usually copper **2.** objects made of sterling silver

stern[1] /sturn/ *adj* **1.** rigid, strict, and uncompromising **2.** grim, austere, or forbidding in appearance [Old English *styrne* < Indo-European, "stiff"] —**stern·ly** *adv* —**stern·ness** *n*

stern[2] /sturn/ *n* **1. REAR OF SHIP** the rear part of a ship or boat **2. BACK PART** the rear part of something ■ *adj* **IN REAR** located at or resembling the stern [13C. Probably < Old Norse *stjórn* "rudder" < Germanic]

Stern /sturn/, **Isaac** (1920–2001) Russian-born US violinist. He achieved international acclaim and recorded many of the works in the classical repertoire.

Stern, Otto (1888–1969) German-born US physicist. He won the Nobel Prize in physics (1943) for his research into the magnetic properties of atoms.

ster·na ANAT plural of **sternum**

Stern·berg ➧ **von Sternberg, Josef**

Sterne /sturn/, **Laurence** (1713–68) Irish novelist. His comic masterpiece, *The Life and Opinions of Tristram Shandy* (1759–67), anticipated many of the techniques of the modern novel. See Cultural note at **sentimental**

> "Digressions, incontestably, are the sunshine; they are the life, the soul of reading; take them out of this book for instance, you might as well take the book along with them."
> [Laurence Sterne, *The Life and Opinions of Tristram Shandy*, 1759–67]

ster·nite /stúr nīt/ *n* a shield or cover on the underside of a segment of an insect [Mid-19C. < STERNUM]

Ster·no /stúrnō/ *tdmk* a trademark for canned liquid cooking fuel

sterno- *prefix* the sternum ○ *sternocostal* [< Greek *sternon* "breastbone"]

ster·no·cla·vic·u·lar /stùrnō klə víkyələr/ *adj* relating to or connecting the sternum and clavicle

ster·no·cos·tal /stùrnō kóst'l/ *adj* situated between or relating to the sternum and ribs [Late 18C. < STERNO- + Latin *costa* "rib"]

stern·post /stérn pōst/ *n* the main upright timber in the stern of a vessel

stern·sheets /stúrn sheets/ *npl* the space at the rear of an open boat that is behind the rowers' bench [Mid-17C. < STERN[2] + SHEET[2] "forward or after section of a boat"]

stern·son /stúrnssən/ *n* a reinforcing timber at the joint of a sternpost and keelson at the stern of a wooden vessel [Mid-19C. < STERN[2] after KEELSON]

ster·num /stúrnəm/ (*plural* **-nums** or **-na** /-nə/) *n* **1.** same as **breastbone** (*technical*) **2.** the chitinous ventral plate covering the abdomen of an arthropod [Mid-17C. Via modern Latin < Greek *sternon* "breastbone"] —**ster·nal** *adj*

ster·nu·ta·tion /stùrnyə táysh'n/ *n* the act or an instance of sneezing (*formal*) [Mid-16C. < Latin *sternutation-* < *sternutat-*, past participle of *sternutare* "keep sneezing" < *sternuere* "to sneeze"]

ster·nu·ta·to·ry /stur nyóotə tàwree/ *adj* causing or resulting in sneezing ■ *n* (*plural* **-ries**) a substance that causes sneezing [Early 17C. < late Latin *sternutatorius* < Latin *sternutat-* (see STERNUTATION)]

stern·ward /stúrnwərd/ *adj* located in or moving toward the stern of a boat or ship ■ *adv also* **stern·wards** /-wərdz/ in the direction of a ship's or boat's stern

stern·way /stúrn wày/ *n* the backward movement of a ship or boat

stern-wheel·er *n* a boat propelled by a large paddle wheel at the rear, especially a riverboat

ster·oid /stéer òyd, sté ròyd/ *n* any of a large group of natural or synthetic fatty substances containing four carbon rings, including the sex hormones [Mid-20C. < STEROL + -OID] —**ste·roid·al** /steer óyd'l, ste róyd'l/ *adj*

ster·ol /stéer àwl, sté ràwl/ *n* a steroid alcohol such as cholesterol that is present in animal and plant lipids [Early 20C. Shortening of CHOLESTEROL]

-sterone *suffix* steroid hormone ○ *androsterone* [< STEROL + -ONE]

ster·tor /stúrtər/ *n* noisy or laborious snoring, heard when somebody is deeply unconscious or when there are obstructed air passages [Early 19C. < modern Latin < Latin *stertere* "to snore"] —**ster·to·rous** *adj* —**ster·to·rous·ly** *adv*

stet /stet/ *vti* (**stet·ted, stet·ting, stets**) to restore, or direct somebody to restore, something that has previously been deleted from a printed or written text ■ *n* a word or mark indicating that previously deleted printed or written matter should be restored [Mid-18C. < Latin, "let it stand"]

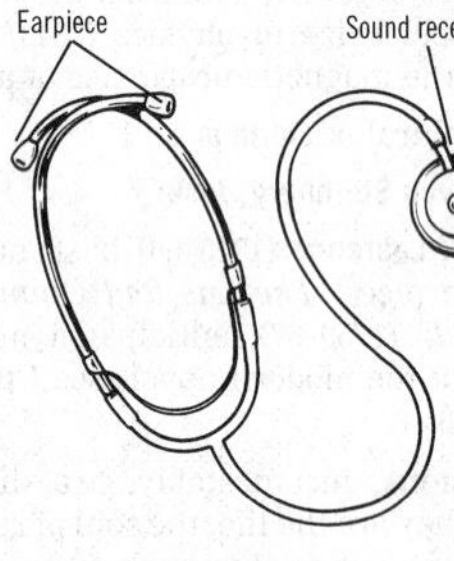

stethoscope

steth·o·scope /stéthə skòp/ *n* a medical instrument used for listening to breathing, heartbeats, and other sounds made by the body [Early 19C. < Greek *stēthos* "chest"] —**steth·o·scop·ic** /stèthə sköppik/ *adj*

Stet·son /stétsən/ *tdmk* a trademark for hats with wide brims and high crowns

Stet·tin /shte téen/ German name for **Szczecin**

Steu·ben /stóobən, styóobən/, **Friedrich Wilhelm Ludolf Gerhard Augustin von, Baron von** (1730–94) Prussian-born American revolutionary soldier. As inspector-general of the Continental Army, he was responsible for improving its training, organization, and discipline.

ste·ve·dore /stéevə dàwr/ *n* somebody whose job is to load and unload ships ■ *vti* (**-dored, -dor·ing, -dores**) to work as a dockworker, loading and unloading ships, or unload a particular ship [Late 18C. < Spanish *estibador*, Portuguese *estivador* < *estibar* "stow a cargo" < Latin *stipare* "press together"]

ste·ve·dore's knot *n* a knot that forms a lump to prevent a line from passing through a hole

Ste·vens /stéev'nz/, **John** (1749–1838) US inventor and engineer. He pioneered steam power, patenting a steam propulsion system (1791) and building the world's first oceangoing steamboat (1808).

Ste·vens, John Paul (*b.* 1920) associate justice of the US Supreme Court. Known as a moderate, he was appointed an associate justice in 1975.

Ste·vens, Nettie Maria (1861–1912) US biologist and geneticist. She was one of the first scientists to prove that chromosomes determine the sex of an organism.

Ste·vens, Thaddeus (1792–1868) US politician. He twice served in the US House of Representatives (1849–53 and 1859–68), opposed slavery, and led the move to impeach President Andrew Johnson.

Ste·vens, Wallace (1879–1955) US poet. His poems have a strongly philosophical bent. He won a Pulitzer Prize for his *Collected Poems* (1954).

> "I do not know which to prefer, / The beauty of inflections / Or the beauty of innuendoes, / The blackbird whistling / Or just after."
> [Wallace Stevens, "Thirteen Ways of Looking at a Blackbird," *Harmonium*; 1923]

Ste·vens-John·son syn·drome *n* a severe inflammation of the skin and mucous membranes, often after a respiratory infection or as an allergic reaction to drugs [Mid-20C. After Albert Mason *Stevens* (1884–1945) and Frank Chambliss *Johnson* (1894–1934), US pediatricians]

Ste·ven·son /stéevənss'n/, **Adlai** (1900–65) US politician and diplomat. He helped found the United Nations in 1945 and was a popular Democratic governor of Illinois (1949–53) before losing two presidential elections to Dwight D. Eisenhower (1952, 1956).

> "My definition of a free society is a society where it is safe to be unpopular."
> [Adlai Stevenson, *Speech, Detroit*; October 7, 1952]

> "Those who corrupt the public mind are just as evil as those who steal from the public purse."
> [Adlai Stevenson, *Speech, Albuquerque, NM*; September 12, 1952]

Ste·ven·son, Adlai E. (1835–1914) vice president of the United States (1893–97). A Democrat, he served in the US House of Representatives (1875–77, 1879–81) and as Grover Cleveland's vice president. Full name **Stevenson, Adlai Ewing**

> "No administration can conduct a sound foreign policy when the future sits in judgment on the past and officials are held accountable as dupes, fools, or traitors for anything that goes wrong."
> [Adlai E. Stevenson, *Call to Greatness*; 1954]

Ste·ven·son, Robert Louis (1850–94) Scottish writer. He lived in Europe, the United States, and, after 1889, in Samoa. Among his many books of travel, autobiography, and verse, he is best remembered for classic adventure tales such as *Treasure Island* (1883) and *Kidnapped* (1886). Full name **Stevenson, Robert Louis Balfour**. See Cultural note at **treasure**

> "Old and young, we are all on our last cruise."
> [Robert Louis Stevenson, "Crabbed Age and Youth," *Virginibus Puerisque*; 1881]

stew[1] /stoo/ *n* **1. SIMMERED DISH** a dish of meat, fish, or vegetables, or a combination of them, that is cooked by slow simmering **2. MIXTURE** a widely assorted mixture **3. BROTHEL** a house of prostitution (*archaic*) ■ *v* (**stewed, stew·ing, stews**) **1.** *vti* **COOK BY SIMMERING** to cook something by long slow simmering, or be cooked in this way **2.** *vi* **BE UPSET** to be deeply troubled or agitated **3.** *vi* **BE VERY HOT** to swelter or become uncomfortably hot [14C. < Old French *estuve* "steam bath"] ◇ **in a stew** agitated, anxious, or in a difficult situation (*informal*)

stew[2] /stoo/ *n US* AVIAT same as **flight attendant** (*dated slang*) [Late 20C. Shortening of STEWARDESS]

stew·ard /stóo ərd/ *n* **1. PLANE OR SHIP ATTENDANT** somebody who attends to passengers on an aircraft or ship, or manages provisions and dining aboard a ship **2. PROPERTY MANAGER** somebody who manages somebody else's property, finances, or household **3. HOTEL OR CLUB MANAGER** somebody who manages arrangements concerning meals or lodging at a hotel, club, college, or other establishment **4. OFFICIAL AT PUBLIC EVENT** a marshal or official at a large public event **5.** POL same as **shop steward** ■ *v* (**-ard·ed, -ard·ing, -ards**) **1.** *vti* **ACT AS STEWARD** to act as a steward for a person or event **2.** *vt* **GUIDE OR DIRECT SOMETHING** to guide or direct something such as a project to completion ○ *successfully stewarded the fundraising campaign to completion on time* ○ *stewarded the bill through Congress to the President* [Old English *stigweard* < *stig* "house, hall" + *weard* "keeper" (see WARD)] —**stew·ard·ship** *n*

stew·ard·ess /stóo ərdəss/ *n* a female flight attendant on a passenger airplane (*dated*)

Jimmy Stewart

Stew·art /stóo ərt/, **Jimmy** (1908–97) US movie actor. He was an appealing drawling presence in dozens of movies, and was most closely identified with his roles in *Mr. Smith Goes to Washington* (1939) and *It's a Wonderful Life* (1946). Full name **Stewart, James Maitland**

Stew·art /stóo ərt, styóo-/, **Potter** (1915–85) associate justice of the US Supreme Court (1958–81)

> "...I know it when I see it."
> [Potter Stewart, *defining* pornography, *in a concurring opinion in a 6–3 Supreme Court ruling that overturned a ban on pornographic movies*; June 22, 1964]

Stew·art Is·land island in New Zealand, south of the South Island. Population: 387 (2001). Area: 670 sq. mi./1,735 sq. km.

stewed /stood/ *adj* **1.** cooked by slow simmering **2.** very intoxicated (*slang*)

stg. *abbr* MONEY sterling

stge. *abbr* storage

Sth. *abbr* COMPASS South

STI *abbr* MED sexually transmitted infection

stib·ine /stí been, -in/ *n* a highly toxic foul-smelling gas, or a derivative of one, produced by the action of hydrochloric acid on an antimony and zinc alloy. Use: fumigant. Formula: SbH_3. [Mid-19C. < Greek *stibi* "antimony" + -INE]

stib·nite /stíb nīt/ *n* a soft grayish antimony sulfide mineral. Use: source of antimony. [Mid-19C. < STIBINE]

stich /stik/ *n* a line of poetry [Early 18C. < Greek *stikhos* "row, rank, line of verse"]

stich·o·myth·i·a /stìkə míthee ə/ *n* in ancient Greek drama, a form of dramatic dialogue in which characters speak single lines alternately [Mid-19C. < Greek *stikhomuthia* "speaking in lines"] —**stich·o·myth·ic** *adj*

stick[1] /stik/ *n* **1. THIN BRANCH** a thin branch or shoot cut or broken from a tree **2. PIECE OF WOOD USED FOR FUEL** a piece of wood used as fuel or as construction material **3. SPECIALLY SHAPED PIECE OF WOOD** a long often cylindrical piece of wood or other material used for a particular purpose ○ *a hockey stick* **4. ROD** a rod, wand, or baton **5. WALKING CANE OR CUDGEL** a cane, club, or cudgel **6. SHORT THIN THING** a short slender part or piece ○ *a stick of celery* **7. SOMETHING USED TO SECURE COMPLIANCE** something used to intimidate or coerce somebody into compliant behavior ○ *tempted them with the carrot but subtly threatened them with the stick* **8. SHIP'S MAST** a mast or spar on a ship **9. FURNITURE** a piece of furniture (*informal*) ○ *We need a few sticks to furnish the apartment.* **10.** ARMS **BOMBS FALLING ON TARGET AT INTERVALS** a group of bombs that are arranged to fall on a target at regular intervals **11.** AVIAT **PARACHUTISTS JUMPING TOGETHER** a group of parachutists all jumping at the same time **12.** AUTOMOT **CAR WITH STICK SHIFT** a car with a manual transmission (*informal*) **13.** *US* **OFFENSIVE TERM** an offensive term for somebody who is regarded as dull, unduly formal, or stuffy (*informal*) **14.** *US* DRUGS **CANNABIS CIGARETTE** a marijuana cigarette (*dated slang*) ■ **sticks** *npl* **REMOTE PLACE** a rural or remote place or district, especially one that is regarded as unsophisticated or unfashionable (*informal*) ○ *living out in the sticks* ■ *vt* (**sticked, stick·ing, sticks**) GARDENING **SUPPORT PLANT WITH STICK** to support a plant with a stake or stick [Old English *sticca* "peg" < Indo-European, "to stick, stab"]

stick[2] /stik/ *v* (**stuck** /stuk/, **stick·ing, sticks**) **1.** *vti* **FASTEN SOMETHING WITH ADHESIVE** to fasten or fix something by means of an adhesive, or remain fastened or fixed in this way **2.** *vt* **FASTEN SOMETHING WITH POINTED OBJECT** to fasten something in position by thrusting a pointed object such as a pin or nail through it **3.** *vti* **PENETRATE SOMETHING** to pierce, stab, or puncture something, or be pierced, stabbed, or punctured **4.** *vti* **PROTRUDE** to protrude, or make something protrude ○ *She stuck her head out of the car window.* **5.** *vt* **PUT SOMETHING SOMEWHERE** to place or put something in a location or position (*informal*) ○ *Stick it on the shelf.* **6.** *vti* **BE UNABLE TO MOVE** to be at a standstill or unable to move or proceed, or make something do this ○ *be stuck in traffic* **7.** *vt* **PUZZLE SOMEBODY** to bewilder or perplex somebody (*usually passive*) ○ *stuck for an answer* **8.** *vi* **STAY IN MIND** to remain in somebody's mind ○ *He told me all the facts but they didn't stick.* **9.** *vi US* ONLINE **RETURN TO WEBSITE** to return often to a particular site on the World Wide Web (*informal*) **10.** *vt* **IMPOSE SOMETHING ON SOMEBODY** to impose something unpleasant on or take advantage of somebody (*usually passive*) ○ *was always stuck with the boring jobs* **11.** *vt* **KILL ANIMAL** to kill an animal by stabbing ○ *stick a pig* ■ *n* **1. ABILITY TO ADHERE** the adhesive quality of something such as glue or tape **2.** EXTREME SPORTS, SURFING **BOARD** a skateboard, snowboard, or surfboard (*slang*) [Old English *stician* < Indo-European] ◇ **stick in your craw** *or* **throat** to go against your sense of what is right and make you feel angry or resentful (*informal*) ◇ **stick it to somebody** to exploit somebody or treat somebody unfairly (*informal*) ◇ **stick it out** to persist with something to the end, even when doing so is difficult ◇ **stuck on somebody** infatuated with somebody (*informal*)

stick around *vi* to linger or wait for somebody or something (*informal*)

stick at *vt* to persist at something ○ *stick at a job until it's done*

stick by *vt* to remain loyal to somebody or something ○ *I'll stick by you no matter what.*

stick out *v* **1.** *vti* to protrude, or make something protrude **2.** *vt* to endure something disagreeable ○ *stick out a long wait*

stick to *v* **1.** *vti* **ADHERE TO SOMETHING** to adhere to something, or make something adhere to something else **2.** *vt* **BE LOYAL TO ANOTHER** to be loyal or close to somebody or something **3.** *vt* **PERSIST WITH SOMETHING** to persist faithfully or stubbornly with something **4.** *vt* **REMAIN FOCUSED ON SOMETHING** to keep to and remain focused on something such as a topic without digression ○ *stick to the point*

stick together *vi* to stay close physically or to remain unified ○ *stuck together through thick and thin*

stick up *v* **1.** *vti* to protrude or point upward, or make something do this **2.** *vt US* to carry out an armed robbery on somebody (*informal*)

stick up for *vt* to defend a belief or a person

stick with *vt* **1.** to persist with something in spite of difficulties or opposition **2.** to remain loyal or faithful to somebody or something

stick·ball /stík bàwl/ *n US* a game using baseball rules and played with a rubber ball and a broomstick or other stick

stick broom *n regional* a push broom that is strong enough to use outdoors

REGIONAL NOTE See ***yard broom***.

stick·er /stíkər/ *n* **1.** an adhesive label, poster, or paper **2.** something that sticks, especially a barbed part of a plant

stick·er price *n* same as **list price**

stick-fight·ing *n Carib* a highly stylized form of fighting in which two chanting combatants attempt to score points by striking each other with sticks

stick fig·ure *n* a simple or crude drawing of a person or animal with single lines for the torso, arms, and legs, and a circle for the head

stick·han·dle /stík hànd'l/ (**-dled, -dling, -dles**) *vt* in ice hockey and lacrosse, to control and maneuver a ball or puck using a stick —**stick·han·dler** *n* —**stick·han·dling** *n*

stick·ie /stíkee/ *n US* a self-sticking slip of paper sold in pads

stick·i·ness /stíkeenəss/ *n* **1.** the condition or fact of being sticky **2.** the extent to which a website attracts, and especially retains, visitors

stick·ing point *n* an issue, detail, or item likely to cause difficulty or prevent progress from being made, e.g., in a negotiation

stick insect

stick in·sect *n* a long brown or green insect that resembles a twig. Family: Phasmidae.

stick-in-the-mud *n* an offensive term for somebody who is regarded as resisting new ideas or practices (*informal*)

stick·le·back /stík'l bàk/ (*plural* **-backs** or *same*) *n* a small spiny-backed fish found in both salt and fresh water that has distinctive nest-building and courtship behavior. Family: Gasterosteidae. [15C. < Old English *sticel* "thorn, sting" < Germanic]

stick·ler /stíklər/ *n* **1.** somebody who insists that every detail must be correct **2.** a puzzling or perplexing problem [Mid-16C. < *stickle*, alteration of obsolete *stightle* "keep trying to control things" < Old English *stihtian* "arrange, settle"]

stick-on *adj* designed to be attached to something by means of an adhesive that has already been applied to one surface of the object to be stuck on ○ *stick-on labels*

stick pin *n* an ornamental pin with a long shaft and a decoration or design at one end

stick·seed /stík seed/ *n* a plant with prickly seeds that can stick to clothing. Native to: Europe, Asia, North America. Genus: *Lappula*.

stick shift *n* **1. MANUAL TRANSMISSION** a manually operated transmission in a motor vehicle **2. GEARSHIFT** a gearshift that operates a manual transmission **3. MANUAL VEHICLE** a motor vehicle with a manual transmission

stick tack·le *n* in field hockey, an illegal challenge when a player hits another player's stick instead of the ball

stick·tight /stík tìt/ *n* a plant with barbed fruits that can stick to clothing or fur

stick-to-it-ive·ness /stik to͞o itivnəss/ *n* tenacious, dogged perseverance

stick·um /stíkəm/ *n* a glue or other adhesive substance (*informal*)

stick·up /stík ùp/, **stick-up** *n* an armed robbery (*informal*)

stick·weed /stík weed/ (*plural* **-weeds** or *same*) *n* a plant with clinging seeds, especially ragweed. Native to: North America.

stick·y /stíkee/ (**-i·er, -i·est**) *adj* **1. COVERED IN SOMETHING GLUEY** covered in something gluey or viscous **2. ADHESIVE** having adhesive qualities **3. HUMID AND HOT** uncomfortably warm and humid ○ *sticky weather* **4. DIFFICULT** difficult, unpleasant, or involving problems (*informal*) ○ *a sticky situation* **5.** ONLINE **ATTRACTING VISITORS** describes an Internet site that attracts, and especially retains, visitors (*informal*) —**stick·i·ly** *adv*

stick·y-fin·gered *adj* having a tendency to steal things (*informal*)

stick·y tape *n* plastic tape coated with adhesive on one side, usually sold in the form of a reel, used mainly for attaching pieces of paper together, e.g., when wrapping a package

stick·y wick·et *n* an awkward or difficult situation (*informal*)

Stieg·litz /steeglits/, **Alfred** (1864–1946) US photographer. A promoter of photography as an art form, he was known for portraiture and wrote extensively on photographic technique. He was the husband of Georgia O'Keeffe.

stiff /stif/ *adj* **1. RIGID** rigid, inflexible, or hard to move **2. NOT SUPPLE** painful and not supple ○ *stiff muscles* **3. SEVERE** very harsh or severe ○ *a stiff punishment* **4. TAXING** difficult or demanding ○ *stiff competition* **5. FORCEFUL** having force or power ○ *a stiff breeze* **6. STRONG** strong or potent to the taste or in effect on the body ○ *a stiff drink of black coffee* **7. RESOLUTE** showing determination and resolve ○ *stiff resistance* **8. TOO HIGH** higher than is justified or usual ○ *stiff prices* **9. FORMAL** rigidly formal or distant in manner ○ *a stiff manner* **10.** NAUT **NOT LIKELY TO CAPSIZE** describes a ship or boat that is relatively stable in the water **11. INTOXICATED** having had too much alcohol to drink (*slang*) ■ *adv* **1. TOTALLY** totally or utterly ○ *bored stiff* ○ *scared stiff* **2. IN STIFF WAY** in a stiff way or manner ■ *n* **1.** *US* **PERSON** a person, especially somebody of a particular type (*slang*) ○ *a lucky stiff* **2.** *US* **OFFENSIVE TERM** an offensive term for somebody regarded as unpleasant or excessively formal (*slang insult*) **3.** *US* **OFFENSIVE TERM** an offensive term for a customer who leaves insufficient tips (*slang insult*) **4. CORPSE** a dead body (*slang*) **5. FLOP** something that is an utter failure (*slang*) ■ *vt* (**stiffed, stiff·ing, stiffs**) (*slang*) **1. CHEAT SOMEBODY OF MONEY** cheat somebody out of money owed **2. NOT PAY SOMEBODY** to fail to pay somebody an amount due or expected ○ *He stiffed me on the tip.* [Old English *stīf* < Indo-European, "to compress, pack"] —**stiff·ish** *adj* —**stiff·ly** *adv* —**stiff·ness** *n*

stiff-arm *adj US* SPORTS same as **straight-arm**

stiff·en /stíffən/ (**-ened, -en·ing, -ens**) *vti* **1.** to become rigid or inflexible, or make something do this **2.** to make something stronger or more effective, or become stronger or more effective ○ *Lawmakers decided to stiffen the penalties for noncompliance with the new statute.* —**stiff·en·er** *n*

stif·fie *n* another spelling of **stiffy** (*offensive slang*)

stiff-necked *adj* extremely obstinate and arrogant

stif·fy /stíffee/ (*plural* **-fies**), **stif·fie** *n* an offensive term for an erect penis (*slang*)

sti·fle[1] /stīf'l/ (**-fled, -fling, -fles**) *v* **1.** *vti* **SUFFOCATE** to impair somebody's breathing, or find it hard to breathe **2.** *vt* **CHECK OR REPRESS SOMETHING** to curb, repress, or prevent the development of something ○ *stifled the spreading discontent* **3.** *vt* **REPRESS PHYSICAL ACT** to cut off a physical act such as a yawn or laugh before it develops [14C. Probably alteration (after Old Norse *stífla* "stop up") of Old French *estouffer* "smother"] —**sti·fler** *n*

sti·fle[2] /stīf'l/ *n* the joint in the hind leg of a four-legged animal that corresponds to the human knee [14C. Origin ?]

sti·fling /stīfling/ *adj* **1.** uncomfortably hot and stuffy **2.** repressive in not allowing full expression —**sti·fling·ly** *adv*

stig·ma /stígmə/ *n* **1. SIGN OF SOCIAL UNACCEPTABILITY** the shame or disgrace attached to something regarded as socially unacceptable **2.** BOT **PLANT PART** the part of a flower's female reproductive organ (**carpel**) that receives the male pollen grains. It is generally located at the tip of a slender stalk-shaped projection (**style**). **3.** (*plural* **stig·ma·ta** /stig maatə, stígmətə/) MED **MARK ON SKIN** a mark on the skin indicating a medical condition **4.** INSECTS **SPOT ON BUTTERFLIES** a colored mark or spot, often resembling an eye, found on some protozoans and invertebrates, especially butterflies and other lepidopterans [Late 16C. Via Latin < Greek, "mark on the skin" < *stig-*, stem of *stizein* "to prick"]

stig·mas·ter·ol /stig mástə ràwl/ *n* a sterol found in plants. Use: manufacture of progesterone. [Early 20C. < shortening of *Physostigma* + STEROL]

stig·ma·ta /stig maatə, stígmətə/ *npl* marks on the hands and feet resembling the wounds from Jesus Christ's crucifixion ■ MED plural of **stigma** (sense 3) [Mid-17C. < Greek, plural of *stigma* (see STIGMA)]

stig·mat·ic /stig máttik/ *adj* **1.** socially unacceptable (*formal*) **2.** OPTICS same as **anastigmatic** ■ *n* CHR somebody affected with stigmata [Late 16C. < Latin *stigmat-* < Greek *stigmat-*, stem of *stigma* (see STIGMA)]

stig·ma·tism[1] /stígmə tìzzəm/ *n* **1.** the properties of an anastigmatic lens **2.** the condition in which the eye focuses properly [Mid-19C. Back-formation < ASTIGMATISM]

stig·ma·tism[2] /stígmə tìzzəm/ *n* the condition of having stigmata [< STIGMATA]

stig·ma·tist /stígmətist/ *n* CHR same as **stigmatic**

stig·ma·tize /stígmə tìz/ (**-tized, -tiz·ing, -tiz·es**) *v* **1.** *vt* to label somebody or something as socially unacceptable **2.** *vti* to mark somebody with stigmata, or be marked with stigmata —**stig·ma·ti·za·tion** /stìgməti záysh'n/ *n* —**stig·ma·tiz·er** *n*

stilb /stilb/ *n* a unit of luminescence equal to 1 candela per square centimeter [Mid-20C. < French < Greek *stilbein* "to glitter"]

stil·bene /stíl been/ *n* a crystalline solid. Use: manufacture of dyes. Formula: $C_{14}H_{12}$. [Mid-19C. < Greek *stilbein* "to glitter"]

stil·bes·trol /stil béstràwl/ *n* CHEM same as **diethylstilbestrol** [Mid-20C. < STILBENE + ESTRUS]

stil·bite /stíl bìt/ *n* a white or yellow zeolite mineral containing calcium and sodium [Early 19C. < Greek *stilbein* "to glitter"; from its lustrous crystals]

stile[1] /stìl/ *n* **1.** a step or rung designed to make it easier to climb over a fence or wall **2.** same as **turnstile** [Old English *stigel* < Indo-European, "to step, climb"]

SPELLCHECK stile or **style**? Do not confuse the spelling of ***stile*** and ***style***, which sound similar. ***Stile*** is a noun denoting a means of climbing over a fence or wall, or a noun denoting a vertical piece in a door or frame; it is also found in the compound word *turnstile*. ***Style*** is a noun or verb referring to the way something is done, designed, written, etc., as in *different styles of architecture, have your hair styled.*

stile[2] /stìl/ *n* a vertical piece in a door, frame, or panel [Late 17C. Probably via Dutch *stijl* "prop, doorpost" < Latin *stilus* "column, post" (see STYLUS)]

SPELLCHECK See ***stile***[1]

sti·let /stílət/ *n* **1.** a wire inserted in a catheter to give it rigidity **2.** a fine wire used as a probe in surgery [Late 17C. Via French < Italian *stiletto* (see STILETTO)]

sti·let·to /sti léttō/ *n* (*plural* **-tos** or **-toes**) **1.** ARMS **SMALL DAGGER** a small dagger with a narrow tapering blade **2.** HANDICRAFT **POINTED TOOL** a pointed tool for making holes in fabric or leather **3.** CLOTHING same as **stiletto heel** ■ *vt* (**-toed, -to·ing, -tos**) **STAB SOMEBODY WITH STILETTO** to stab somebody using a stiletto [Early 17C. < Italian, "small dagger" < *stilo* "dagger" < Latin *stilus* (see STYLUS)]

sti·let·to heel *n* a high pointed heel on a woman's shoe, or a shoe with such a heel

still[1] /stil/ *adj* **1. NOT MOVING** motionless and undisturbed **2.** BEVERAGES **NOT CARBONATED** describes a drink that is not sparkling or bubbly **3. QUIET** subdued, gentle, or quiet **4.** PHOTOGRAPHY **TAKING STATIC PHOTOGRAPHS** designed for, or relating to the process of, taking photographs as opposed to making movies ■ *adv* **SILENTLY OR WITHOUT MOTION** without sound or movement ■ *n* **1. PEACE** silence or peace (*literary*) ○ *the still of the night* **2.** MOVIES **SCENE FROM MOTION PICTURE** a photographic print, either made from a single frame of a motion-picture film or shot independently with a still camera during production ■ *v* (**stilled, still·ing, stills**) **1.** *vti* **MAKE SOMEBODY CALM** to cause somebody to become quiet, calm, soundless, or immobile, or become quiet, calm, soundless, or immobile **2.** *vt* **RELIEVE EMOTION** to allay or relieve an emotion such as fear or doubt ○ *stilled our fears* [Old English *stille* < Indo-European, "stay put"] —**still·ness** *n*

still[2] /stil/ *adv* **1. EXISTING NOW** used to indicate that a situation that used to exist has continued and exists now ○ *The original is still my favorite.* ○ *I still believe it's a mistake.* ○ *It was still light.* **2. EVEN AT THIS TIME** used to emphasize that something is the case even up to the point mentioned ○ *Her birthday is still a month away.* ○ *He may still be around.* ○ *Still to come...* **3. EVEN MORE** used to emphasize that there is even more of a quality or quantity (*often used with a comparative*) ○ *Profits next year will be larger still.* ○ *The market for flour is equal to almost any in the West, and it will be still better.* **4. NEVERTHELESS** used to emphasize that something remains the case in spite of the situation mentioned ○ *It's not very good. Still, it's better than nothing.* [13C. < STILL[1]] ◇ **still and all** nonetheless or notwithstanding (*informal*)

USAGE See *yet*.

still[3] /stil/ *n* **1.** an apparatus for distilling liquids, especially alcohol **2.** BEVERAGES same as **distillery** [Mid-16C. Shortening of DISTILL]

Still /stil/, **Clyfford** (1904–80) US painter. He painted vast abstract expressionist works with dominant jagged areas of intense color.

still a·larm *n US* an alarm given by telephone in which the warning signal is not heard in the place where it is set off

still·birth /stíl bùrth/ *n* the birth of a dead fetus after the 28th week of pregnancy

still·born /stíl bàwrn/ *adj* **1.** dead at birth **2.** useless or ineffectual from the start [Mid-16C. < STILL[1] in the obsolete sense "dead"]

~~stilleto~~ incorrect spelling of stiletto

still frame *n* a single frame from a motion-picture or television program displayed as a photograph

still hunt *n* a hunt in which game is stalked or ambushed

still life: *Still life with Dessert and Bouquet* (1632) by Georg Flegel

still life (*plural* **still lifes**) *n* **1.** a representation of inanimate objects such as fruit, flowers, or food, often in a domestic setting, in paintings, pictures, or photographs (*hyphenated before a noun*) ○ *a still-life class* **2.** the style or genre of still life in paintings, pictures, or photographs

Still's dis·ease /stílz-/ *n* chronic arthritis that develops in children under the age of 16 [Early 20C. After Sir George *Still* (1868–1941), British physician]

stilt /stilt/ *n* **1. POLE FOR WALKING** either of two poles with footrests high off the ground on which somebody balances and walks **2.** CONSTR **SUPPORTING POST** a tall post or column that supports a structure above land or water **3.** BIRDS **LONG-LEGGED WADING BIRD** a black and white shorebird with a straight beak and extremely long red legs that lives near ponds and marshes. Genera: *Himantopus* or *Cladorhynchus*. ■ *vt* (**stilt·ed, stilt·ing, stilts**) **RAISE SOMETHING ON STILTS** to place or raise something up on stilts [14C. Probably < Low German < Indo-European, "to set up"]

stilt·ed /stíltəd/ *adj* **1. NOT FLUENT** lacking fluency so as to be halting or unnatural in flow **2. FORMAL** pompous or unduly formal **3.** CONSTR **RESTING ON VERTICAL PIECES OF STONE** describes an arch that is joined to the top part of the pillar, column, or wall (**impost**) supporting it by vertical pieces of stone —**stilt·ed·ly** *adv* —**stilt·ed·ness** *n*

Stil·ton /stíltən/ *n* either of two strong-flavored British white cheeses made from whole milk, one veined with blue mold, the other plain [Mid-18C. After a village in E England]

Stil·well /stil wèl, stíllwəl/, **Joseph** (1883–1946) US army general. He commanded US forces in China, Burma, and India during World War II. Full name **Stilwell, Joseph Warren**. Known as **Vinegar Joe**

Stim·son /stímssən/, **Henry** (1867–1950) US politician and government official. He was US secretary of state (1929–33) and secretary of war (1940–45). Full name **Stimson, Henry Lewis**

stim·u·lant /stímmyələnt/ *n* **1. SOURCE OF STIMULUS** something that provides a stimulus, incentive, or quickening **2.** PHARM **AGENT PRODUCING INCREASE IN FUNCTIONAL ACTIVITY** a drug or other agent that produces a temporary increase in the functional activity of a body organ or part ■ *adj* **INCREASING ACTIVITY** increasing physical activity or acting as a stimulus or incentive

stim·u·late /stímmyə làyt/ (**-lat·ed, -lat·ing, -lates**) *v* **1.** *vt* **ENCOURAGE SOMETHING** to encourage something such as an activity or a process so that it will begin, increase, or develop ○ *stimulate discussion* **2.** *vt* **MAKE SOMEBODY INTERESTED** to cause somebody to become interested in or excited about something **3.** *vt* PHYSIOL **CAUSE BODY PART TO RESPOND** to cause physical activity in something such as a nerve or an organ **4.** *vti* PHYSIOL **MAKE SOMEBODY MORE ALERT** to cause somebody to become more alert or active, as by the use of caffeine or a drug [Early 16C. < Latin *stimulat-*, past participle of *stimulare* "to goad" < *stimulus* "goad, stake"] —**stim·u·la·ble** *adj* —**stim·u·lat·ing** *adj* —**stim·u·lat·ing·ly** *adv* —**stim·u·la·tion** /stìmmyə láysh'n/ *n* —**stim·u·la·tive** *adj* —**stim·u·la·tor** *n* —**stim·u·la·to·ry** *adj*

stim·u·lus /stímmyələss/ (*plural* **-li** /-lì/) *n* **1. INCENTIVE** something that encourages an activity or a process to begin, increase, or develop **2. SOMETHING AROUSING INTEREST** an agent or factor that provokes interest, enthusiasm, or excitement **3.** PHYSIOL **CAUSE OF PHYSICAL RESPONSE** something that causes a physical response in an organism, e.g., a drug or an electrical impulse [Late 17C. < Latin, "goad, stake"]

sting /sting/ *v* (**stung** /stung/, **sting·ing, stings**) **1.** *vti* **INJECT SOMEBODY WITH TOXIN** to prick somebody's skin and inject a small quantity of a poisonous or irritant substance, causing a sharp pain that is often followed by itchiness and swelling **2.** *vti* **FEEL OR CAUSE SHARP PAIN** to feel a sharp pain, usually only for a short period of time, or make somebody do this ○ *His eyes were stinging from the onions.* **3.** *vt* **UPSET SOMEBODY** to make somebody feel upset, hurt, or annoyed ○ *I was stung by her harsh criticisms.* **4.** *vt* **GOAD SOMEBODY** to urge somebody on, usually with criticism ○ *words that stung them into action* ■ *n* **1. WOUND CAUSED BY STING** a skin wound that may hurt, swell up, and itch, caused by an insect, plant, or animal piercing the skin and injecting a small quantity of a poisonous or irritant substance **2.** *UK* ZOOL same as **stinger**[1] (sense 2) **3. SHARP PAIN** a short sharp pain, e.g., that caused by the application of an antiseptic to a fresh wound **4. HURTFUL QUALITY** the hurtful nature of something such as criticism **5. POWER TO UPSET** the power to inflict mental or emotional discomfort ○ *threats that have lost their sting* **6.** BOT same as **stinging hair** **7.** CRIME, POLICE **UNDERCOVER OPERATION** a complex undercover operation to catch criminals (*slang; often used before a noun*) **8. ORCHESTRATED SWINDLE** an underhanded scheme, especially a carefully planned and orchestrated swindle (*slang*) [Old English *stingan* < Germanic] —**sting·ing·ly** *adv*

sting·a·ree /stíngə rèe, stìngə rée/ (*plural* **-rees** or *same*) *n* FISH another spelling of **stingray**

sting·er[1] /stíngər/ *n* **1. SOMETHING STINGING** something that stings, especially a hurtful or critical comment **2. POISON-INJECTING ORGAN** the sharp organ through which an insect or other animal injects poison to immobilize its prey or for defense **3. SHARP BLOW** a sharp blow or slap that causes a smarting pain (*informal*) **4.** *US* CRIME, POLICE **UNDERCOVER OFFICER** a law enforcement officer who is taking part in an undercover operation (*informal*) [Mid-16C. < STING]

sting·er[2] /stíngər/ *n* **1.** a cocktail consisting of crème de menthe and brandy **2.** *UK* a whiskey and soda with crushed ice [Early 20C. Alteration of *stengah* < Malay *satĕngah* "half"]

Sting·er *tdmk* a device used by police that is covered in spikes and can be thrown across a road to puncture an automobile's tires

sting·ing hair *tdmk n* a glandular plant hair that releases an irritant chemical when touched, e.g., on a stinging nettle

sting·ing net·tle /stínging-/ *n* PLANTS same as **nettle** *n* (sense 1)

sting·ray /sting rày/ (*plural* **-rays** or *same*) *n* a ray with a flexible tail shaped like a whip that has poisonous spines on it. Native to: shallow warm waters. Family: Dasyatidae. See illustration on next page

stin·gy /stínjee/ (**-gi·er, -gi·est**) *adj* **1.** not generous in giving or spending money **2.** ungenerously small or

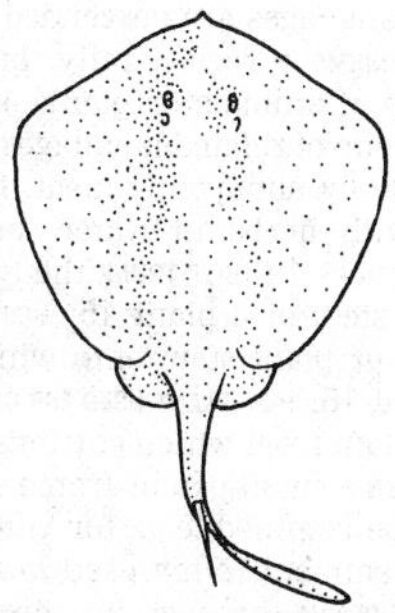
stingray

inadequate ○ *a stingy tip* [Mid-17C. Origin ?] —**stin·gi·ly** *adv* —**stin·gi·ness** *n*

stink /stingk/ *vi* (**stank** /stangk/ or **stunk** /stungk/, **stunk, stink·ing, stinks**) **1. SMELL HORRIBLE** to have a very strong and unpleasant smell **2. BE WORTHLESS** to be very bad or worthless (*informal*) ○ *This poetry stinks.* **3. BE CORRUPT** to be despicably corrupt or dishonest (*informal*) ○ *The whole voting process stinks.* **4. HAVE UNDESIRABLE QUALITY** to have a large amount of an undesirable quality (*informal*) ○ *a career that stinks of nepotism* ■ *n* **1. FOUL SMELL** a strong and unpleasant smell **2. SCANDAL** a scandal, fuss, or trouble (*informal*) ○ *"even if there was a stink, he had plenty good friends in San Francisco"* (Robert Louis Stevenson, *The Wrecker*; 1896) [Old English *stincan* "to smell" < W Germanic] —**stink·i·ly** *adv* —**stink·y** *adj* ◇ **make** *or* **raise a stink** to cause trouble, especially by protesting (*slang*)

SYNONYMS See *smell*.

stink out *vt UK* same as **stink up**
stink up *vt* to give something a very strong and unpleasant smell ○ *The smell of rotting potatoes stank the whole place up.*

stink·a·roo *n* another spelling of **stinkeroo** (*slang offensive*)

stink bomb *n* a practical joker's toy in the form of a small glass or plastic capsule that, when smashed, emits a horrible smell

stink·bug /stíngk bùg/ *n* an insect that emits foul-smelling secretions. It typically has a flattish body, and is often camouflaged to blend with its surroundings. Family: Pentatomidae.

stink·er /stíngkər/ *n* **1. SOMETHING UNPLEASANT** something that is very difficult or unpleasant (*informal*) ○ *That last exam was a real stinker.* **2. OFFENSIVE TERM** an offensive term for somebody regarded as obnoxious or hateful (*slang insult*) **3. SPITTING SEABIRD** a seabird that feeds on offal and carrion and spits a foul-smelling oil at aggressors, e.g., a fulmar or petrel (*informal*) **4.** *US* **SOMETHING SHODDY** something of very poor quality (*slang*)

stink·er·oo /stìngkə róo, stíngkə ròo/ (*plural* **-oos**), **stink·a·roo** (*plural* **-roos**) *n US* an offensive term for somebody regarded as irritating, loathsome, or otherwise unpleasant (*slang*) [Mid-20C. < STINK + fanciful suffix *-eroo* "something large or remarkable"]

stink·horn /stíngk hàwrn/ *n* a fungus with a thick white stalk and a thimble-shaped foul-smelling cap containing spores. The smell attracts flies, which disperse the spores. Order: Phallales.

stink·ing /stíngking/ *adj* **1. SMELLY** having or giving off a very strong and unpleasant smell **2. EXTREMELY BAD** unpleasant or contemptible as an action or behavior (*informal*) ○ *"This was, of course, a stinking lie."* (Richard Kadrey, *Metrophage*; 1995) **3. INTOXICATED** very intoxicated with alcohol (*slang*) ■ *adv* **USED FOR EMPHASIS** used to emphasize the contemptible extent of something (*informal*) ○ *stinking rich* —**stink·ing·ly** *adv* —**stink·ing·ness** *n*

stink·ing ash *n* a deciduous tree with fragrant greenish white flowers and fruits that are used in brewing. Native to: eastern North America. Latin name: *Ptelea trifoliata*.

stink·ing cham·o·mile *n* a weed with foul-smelling leaves. Flowers: resembling a daisy. Native to: Europe. Latin name: *Anthemis cotula*.

stink·o /stíngkō/ *adj* **1.** very intoxicated with alcohol (*slang*) **2.** *US* of the poorest quality (*informal*) ○ *a stinko bowl of stew*

stink·pot /stíngk pòt/ *n* **1. SOMETHING WITH HORRIBLE SMELL** something that has a very strong and unpleasant smell (*slang*) **2. OFFENSIVE TERM** an offensive term for somebody considered very unpleasant or unpopular (*slang insult*) **3.** REPT **SMALL TURTLE** a small species of musk turtle that emits a foul-smelling secretion from its cloacal glands. Native to: ponds and sluggish streams of the United States. Latin name: *Sternotherus odoratus*. **4.** ARMS **STINKING WEAPON** in former times, a military weapon consisting of an earthenware pot that released a suffocating vapor when thrown into an enemy position or onto an enemy ship

stink·stone /stíngk stṑn/ *n* rock, especially limestone, that gives off a highly unpleasant odor when rubbed or struck [Early 20C. Translation of German *Stinkstein*]

stink·weed /stíngk wēēd/ (*plural* **-weeds** or *same*) *n* **1.** PLANTS same as **wall rocket** **2.** a plant with unpleasant-smelling flowers or foliage, e.g., mayweed or pennycress

stink·wood /stíngk wŏŏd/ (*plural* **-woods** or *same*) *n* **1.** a hard durable unpleasant-smelling wood. Use: furniture-making. **2.** a tree with unpleasant-smelling wood, especially a South African deciduous tree with hard wood [Mid-18C. Translation of Dutch *stinkhout*]

stint[1] /stint/ *v* (**stint·ed, stint·ing, stints**) **1.** *vi* **BE MISERLY** to be ungenerous in offering, providing, or giving something ○ *For a really good mousse, don't stint on the chocolate.* **2.** *vt* **DENY SOMEBODY SOMETHING** to deny somebody something out of miserliness, or deny yourself something, usually in an act of sacrifice ○ *"your mother and me economizing and stinting ourselves to give you a University education"* (Thomas Hardy, *Tess of the d'Urbervilles*; 1891) **3.** *vi* **UNDERGO STOPPAGE OR HALT** to stop or halt (*archaic*) ■ *n* **1. ALLOTTED TIME** a fixed period of time spent on a task or job ○ *do a two-year stint as an apprentice* **2. LIMITATION** limitation or restriction, especially in time or amount ○ *"I gave him time and thought without stint"* (Willa Cather, *The Professor's House*; 1925) **3. STOPPAGE** a pause or stoppage (*archaic*) [Old English *styntan* "to blunt" < Germanic; later reinforced by related Old Norse *stytta* "shorten"] —**stint·er** *n*

stint[2] /stint/ (*plural* **stints** or *same*) *n* BIRDS same as **sandpiper** [15C. Origin ?]

stipe /stīp/ *n* **1.** the stalk of a mushroom or fern **2.** ZOOL same as **stipes** (senses 1–2) [Late 18C. Via French < Latin *stipes* "post, log"]

sti·pel /stīp'l/ *n* a structure shaped like a tiny leaf or scale located at the base of a leaflet of a compound leaf [Early 19C. Via French < modern Latin *stipella* "small stipule" < Latin *stipula* "straw, stalk"] —**sti·pel·late** /stī péllət, sti péllət, stīpə làyt/ *adj*

sti·pend /stī pènd, -pənd/ *n* a fixed amount of money paid at regular intervals as a salary or to cover living expenses [15C. Directly or via French < Latin *stipendium* "soldier's pay" < *stips* "payment" + *pendere* "weigh out"]

SYNONYMS See *wage*.

sti·pes /stī pēēz/ (*plural* **stip·i·tes** /stíppi tēēz/) *n* **1.** the second or bottom mouthpart of some insects and crustaceans **2.** the eyestalk of a crayfish or crab **3.** BOT same as **stipe** (sense 1) [Mid-18C. Via modern Latin < Latin, "post, log"] —**sti·pi·form** /stīpə fàwrm/ *adj*

stip·i·tate /stíppi tàyt/ *adj* having or supported by a stipe [Late 18C. < modern Latin *stipitatus* < Latin *stipit-*, stem of *stipes* "post, log"]

stip·i·tes ZOOL, BOT plural of **stipes**

stip·ple /stípp'l/ *vt* (**-pled, -pling, -ples**) **1.** ART **PAINT SOMETHING BY DABBING** to paint, draw, or engrave something using dots or short dabbing strokes **2.** ART **APPLY PAINT WITH DABBING STROKES** to apply paint or another substance in dots or short dabbing strokes **3. MAKE SURFACE MATERIAL APPEAR GRAINY** to give something such as wet paint or plaster a rough grainy texture with dabbing strokes **4. DAPPLE SURFACE WITH DOTS** to mark something with dots or speckles (*literary*; *usually passive*) ○ *its lime-green clapboard stippled with sunlight* ■ *n* **1.** ART **ARTISTIC TECHNIQUE** the technique of painting, drawing, or engraving using dots or short dabbing strokes **2.** CONSTR **DABBED FINISH** a rough grainy finish in wet paint or plaster, produced by means of dabbing strokes [Mid-18C. < Dutch *stippelen* "keep pricking" < *stip* "point, dot"] —**stip·pler** *n* —**stip·pling** *n*

stip·u·late[1] /stíppyə làyt/ (**-lat·ed, -lat·ing, -lates**) *v* **1.** *vt* **SPECIFY SOMETHING** to specify something such as a condition when making an agreement or an offer ○ *The contract stipulates which expenses will be covered.* **2.** *vti* **DEMAND SOMETHING** to make a specific demand for something, usually as a condition in an agreement ○ *stipulate a price* **3.** *vt* **MAKE FORMAL PROMISE** to promise something formally or legally **4.** *vi* LAW **AGREE** to agree, in terms of the conduct of a legal proceeding ○ *We will stipulate to our receipt of all pertinent discovery documents, Your Honor.* **5.** *vt* LAW **ADMIT FACT** to confess, admit, or agree to a fact rather than require the opposition to prove that fact ○ *Will the defendant stipulate her presence at the scene of the crime?* [Early 17C. < Latin *stipulat-*, past participle of *stipulari* "demand, bargain"] —**stip·u·la·ble** *adj* —**stip·u·la·tion** /stìppyə láysh'n/ *n* —**stip·u·la·tor** *n* —**stip·u·la·to·ry** *adj*

stip·u·late[2] /stíppyələt/ *adj* describes a stem or stalk that has a pair of growths resembling leaves (**stipules**) at the base [Late 18C. < STIPULE]

stip·ule /stíppyool/ *n* either of a pair of small growths at the base of a leaf stalk or stem that resemble leaves [Late 18C. Directly or via French < Latin *stipula* "straw, stalk"] —**stip·u·lar** /stíppyələr/ *adj*

stir[1] /stur/ *v* (**stirred, stir·ring, stirs**) **1.** *vt* **MIX INGREDIENTS** to move a liquid around with a spoon, stick, or other implement in order to mix or cool the contents ○ *Slowly stir the cream into the soup.* **2.** *vi* **BE ABLE TO BE STIRRED** to be of a consistency that allows a spoon or other implement to be moved around **3.** *vti* **MOVE GENTLY** to move gently, or make something do this **4.** *vi* **LEAVE PLACE** to move or leave, especially from a favorite or usual place ○ *The guards were told not to stir from their posts.* **5.** *vi* **MOVE AFTER RESTING** to get up and move about, especially after a rest ○ *anyone stirring at this early hour* **6.** *vt* **MAKE SOMEBODY OUT** to rouse somebody into action **7.** *vt* **STIMULATE IMAGINATION** to stimulate something such as somebody's imagination or memory (*formal*) **8.** *vi* **BE FELT** to begin to be experienced as an emotion (*formal*) ○ *Deep-seated bitterness stirred within him.* **9.** *vti* **MAKE SOMEBODY EMOTIONAL** to arouse a strong emotional reaction in somebody ○ *music that never fails to stir me* **10.** *vi* **HAPPEN** to happen or be current (*informal*) ○ *What's stirring this week on Capitol Hill?* ■ *n* **1. ACT OF STIRRING** an act or instance of stirring a liquid **2. COMMOTION** a lively reaction, usually either excitement or controversy **3. SLIGHT MOVEMENT** a gentle movement [Old English *styrian* "agitate" < Indo-European, "to whirl"] —**stir·ra·ble** *adj* —**stir·rer** *n*

stir up *vt* **1.** to cause trouble or a confrontation deliberately **2.** to cause something such as dust to rise and swirl around

stir[2] /stur/ *n* CRIME same as **prison** (*dated slang*) [Mid-19C. Origin ?]

stir-cra·zy *adj* mentally unsettled as a result of spending a long time in a confined space such as a prison cell (*informal or humorous*) [< STIR[2]]

stir-fry *vt* to fry small pieces of food rapidly in a small amount of oil over high heat, stirring continuously. This method is used extensively in Chinese cooking. ■ *n* a dish of food prepared by stir-frying

Stir·ling /stúrling/ city in central Scotland, on the Forth River. Population: 78,833 (2001).

Stir·ling en·gine *n* an external-combustion engine in which heat generated on the outside of the cylinders causes either air or an inert gas within the cylinders to expand and drive the pistons [Mid-19C. After Rev. Robert *Stirling* (1790–1878), Scottish cleric and engineer]

Stir·ling's for·mu·la *n* a mathematical formula used to calculate the approximate value of the factorial of a very large number [Mid-20C. After James *Stirling* (1692–1770), Scottish mathematician]

stirps /sturps/ (*plural* **stir·pes** /stúr pēēz/) *n* **1. ANCESTRAL STOCK** a line of descendants from a common ancestor **2.** *US* LAW **ANCESTOR** an ancestor from whom a particular family is descended **3. PLANT VARIETY** a plant variety in which the characteristics are fixed through cultivation [Late 17C. < Latin, "stem, lineage"]

stir·ring /stúr ing/ *adj* **1. CAUSING EMOTIONAL REACTION** causing an emotional or excited reaction **2. LIVELY** full of energy and vitality ○ *a stirring rendition of a Chopin mazurka* ■ *n* **1. MOVEMENT** a slight movement **2. AROUSING OF FEELING** the awakening of something, especially an emotion or memory (*formal*) —**stir·ring·ly** *adv*

stir·rup /stúr əp/ *n* **1. RIDER'S FOOT SUPPORT** a flat-bottomed metal ring hanging from a strap on each side of a horse's saddle to provide support for a rider's foot **2. SUPPORTING STRAP** a loop or strap that supports a foot or passes under a foot, e.g., the straps supporting a woman's feet in childbirth **3.** NAUT **SHIP'S ROPE** one of a set of ropes hanging from a sail-supporting spar (**yard**) on a ship. Loops at the bottom allow another rope for standing on to be threaded through. [Old English *stīgrāp* "rope for getting up" < *stīgan* "go up" + *rāp* (see ROPE)]

stir·rup bone *n* ANAT same as **stapes** [< its shape]

stir·rup cup *n* a farewell drink of alcohol, originally one shared with a departing horseback rider

stir·rup i·ron *n* the metal ring of a riding stirrup

stir·rup leath·er *n* a leather strap that attaches a stirrup to the saddle

stir·rup pants *npl* women's stretch pants with straps attached that pass under the feet

stir·rup pump *n* a portable hand-operated pump, held on the ground with the feet, that draws water from a bucket and sprays it out. It is used to fight small fires. [< the shape of the foot-piece used to hold the pump in place]

stish·ov·ite /stíshə vīt/ *n* a rare crystalline form of quartz. Source: meteor craters. [Mid-20C. After Sergey Mikhailovich *Stishov* (b.1937), Russian mineralogist]

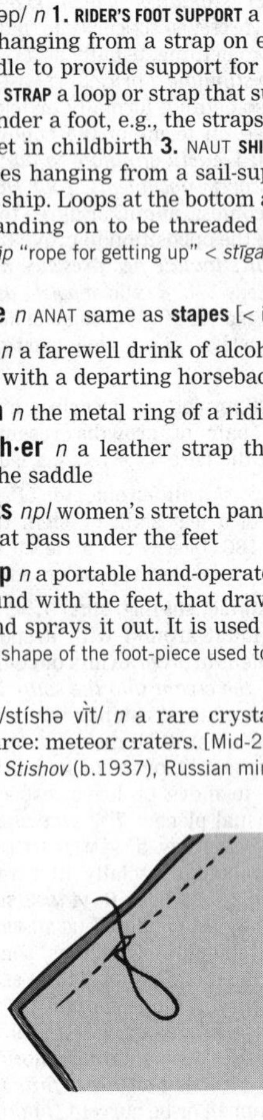

Running stitch

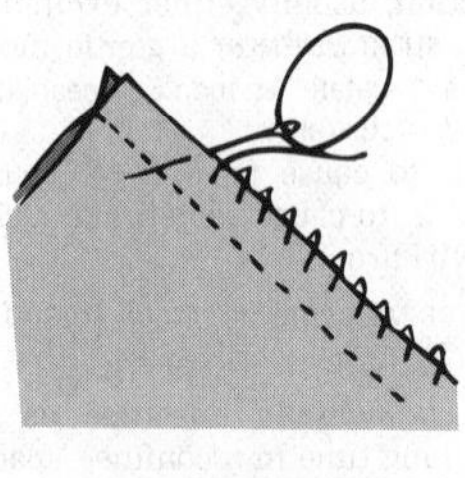

Overcast stitch

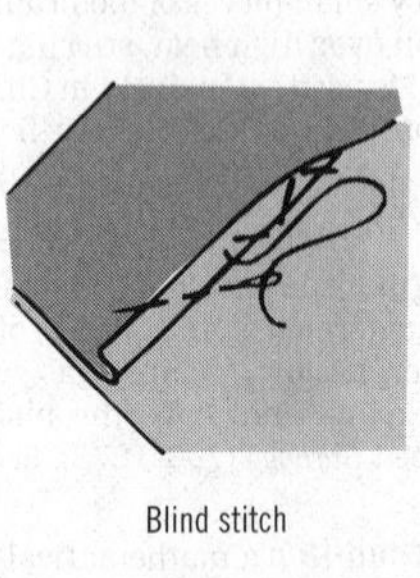

Blind stitch

stitch

stitch /stich/ *n* **1. LENGTH OF THREAD IN MATERIAL** a short length of thread that has been passed through one or more pieces of material, either for decoration or to join pieces together **2. SURGICAL THREAD** a single loop of surgical thread used to close up a wound **3. LOOP OF WOOL** a single loop of wool or similar material, passed around a knitting needle or a crochet hook **4. STYLE OF NEEDLEWORK** a style of sewing or knitting ○ *lock stitch* **5. ACHING PAIN** a cramp in the side of the abdomen caused e.g., by exercising or laughing **6. GARMENT** a piece of clothing (*informal*) ○ *didn't have a stitch on* **7.** AGRIC **RIDGE BETWEEN FURROWS** the ridge between two adjacent furrows in a field ■ *vt* (**stitched, stitch·ing, stitch·es**) **1. SEW SOMETHING** to join, finish, or decorate something with stitches **2. CLOSE WOUND** to close a wound with one or more stitches **3. BIND PAGES** to bind the pages of a book, pamphlet, or other publication with thread or staples [Old English *stice* "prick" < Indo-European, "jab"] —**stitch·er** *n* ◇ **a stitch in time saves nine** dealing promptly with a minor problem will prevent it from developing into a more complicated or larger-scale problem ◇ **in stitches** laughing a great deal

stitch up *vt* **1. SEW SOMETHING TOGETHER** to sew fabric or an article, or repair something by sewing it **2. CLOSE WOUND** to close a wound with stitches (*informal*) **3. ARRANGE DEAL** to complete negotiations or arrange a deal satisfactorily (*informal*) **4.** *UK* **MAKE SOMEBODY APPEAR GUILTY** to deliberately make somebody innocent appear to be guilty of something (*informal*) ○ *He claimed the police had stitched him up.*

stitch·er·y /stíchəree/ *n* needlework, especially when it is functional rather than decorative

stitch-up *n UK* a deliberate attempt to achieve an unfair outcome (*informal*) ○ *Everyone felt her appointment to the board had been a stitch-up.*

stitch·wort /stích wùrt, -wàwrt/ (*plural* **-worts** or *same*) *n* a perennial creeping wild plant of the chickweed family. Flowers: small, white, star-shaped. Genus: *Stellaria.* [< its former use to cure sharp pains in the side]

stk. *abbr* COMM stock

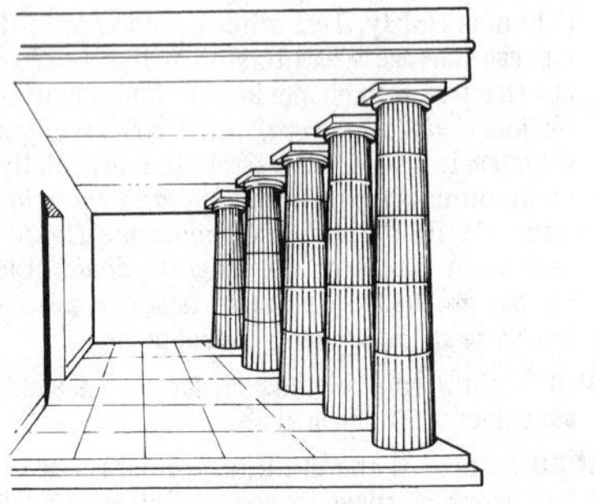

stoa

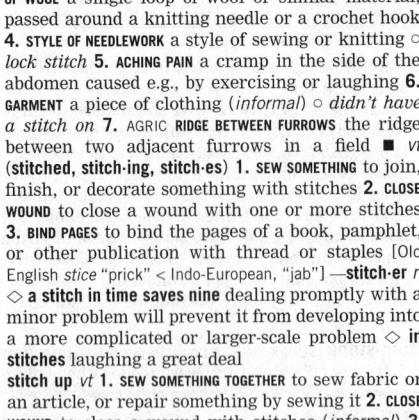

sto·a /stṓ ə/ (*plural* **sto·as** or **sto·ae** /stṓ ee/) *n* in ancient Greece, a covered walkway, usually with a row of columns on one side and a wall on the other [Early 17C. < Greek]

stoat /stōt/ (*plural* **stoats** or *same*) *n* an ermine, especially in its brown summer coat [15C. Origin ?]

stob /stob/ *n Southern US, UK regional* a stake or stump [14C. Probably variant of STUB]

sto·chas·tic /stə kástik/ *adj* **1.** STATS **RANDOM** involving or showing random behavior **2.** STATS **INVOLVING PROBABILITY** involving or subject to probabilistic behavior **3. INVOLVING GUESSWORK** involving guesswork or conjecture (*formal*) [Mid-20C. < Greek *stokhastikos* < *stokhos* "target, aim," literally "pointed stake"] —**sto·chas·ti·cal·ly** *adv*

stock /stok/ *n* **1. SUPPLY OF GOODS AVAILABLE FOR SALE** a supply of goods for sale, kept on the premises by a store or business **2. RESERVE OF SOMETHING** a supply held in reserve for future use **3. AVAILABLE AMOUNT OF SOMETHING** the amount of something such as a natural resource or a service available ○ *an alarming fall in North Atlantic fish stocks* **4.** FIN **TOTAL SHARES ISSUED** the total number of shares issued by a company or sector **5.** FIN **INVESTOR'S CAPITAL SHARE** the share of capital held by an individual investor (*often used in the plural*) **6.** *UK* FIN same as **capital stock** **7. SOMEBODY'S REPUTATION** somebody's standing or reputation ○ *Her stock is high in terms of public opinion because of her aid work.* **8.** AGRIC same as **livestock** **9. ANCESTRAL DESCENT** ancestry, usually with reference to race, ethnic group, region, or profession **10. ORIGINAL VARIETY** the original variety from which other similar plants, animals, or languages are descended **11.** BIOL **GROUP OF RELATED ORGANISMS** a race, family, breed, or other related group of animals or plants **12.** LING **RELATED LANGUAGES** a group of related languages **13.** FOOD **BROTH** a liquid made by simmering meat, fish, bones, or vegetables with herbs in water, used in soups, stews, and sauces **14.** BOT **TRUNK** the trunk of a tree, or the main stem of a plant **15.** BOT **PLANT RECEIVING GRAFT** a plant or plant stem onto which a shoot or bud is grafted **16.** BOT **PLANT USED FOR CUTTINGS** a plant or part of a plant from which cuttings are taken **17.** AGRIC **ANIMAL PEN** a small pen or frame where a single animal can be confined, e.g., for veterinary examination or treatment (*often used in the plural*) **18.** ARMS **PART OF FIREARM** the part of a firearm to which the barrel and firing mechanism are attached. It is held in the hand or rested against the shoulder. **19.** ARMS **PART OF GUN CARRIAGE** the long beam on a field artillery carriage that extends behind it. When placed on the ground, it becomes the piece's third point of contact, along with the two wheels. **20.** AGRIC, HIST **PART OF PLOW** the frame of a horse-drawn plow **21. HANDLE OF SOMETHING** the handle of something such as a fishing rod, whip, or carpentry tool **22. WOODEN BLOCK** a block of wood, especially the block from which a bell is hung **23. SUPPORTING PART** an upright supporting part **24.** NAUT **ANCHOR PART** the crosspiece on some types of anchors **25. RAW MATERIAL** the basic material from which something is manufactured **26.** MOVIES **UNEXPOSED FILM** movie film that has not yet been exposed **27.** METALL **PIECE OF METAL** a piece of cut metal ready to be processed, especially by forging **28.** (*plural* **stocks** or *same*) PLANTS **FLOWERING PLANT** a widely grown ornamental plant. Flowers: fragrant, brightly colored, in clusters. Native to: Europe, southern Asia. Genus: *Matthiola.* **29.** RIDING **RIDING NECKCLOTH** a white neckcloth now worn only as part of formal riding dress **30.** CHR **CLERICAL SHIRT FRONT** a broad piece of cloth worn on the chest below a clerical collar by members of the clergy in some denominations of the Christian Church **31.** LEISURE **UNDISTRIBUTED CARDS OR COUNTERS** a pile of cards or counters not dealt out at the start of a game, but picked up during it **32.** *US* THEATER **SYSTEM OF PRESENTING PLAYS** a system by which a permanent theater company presents a set of works during a season, usually in its own theater. Can term **repertory** **33.** THEATER **REPERTOIRE OF PLAYS** a theater company's repertoire of plays **34.** *US* THEATER same as **stock company** (sense 2) **35.** *UK* **HUB** the hub of a wheel **36.** GEOL **ROCK MASS** a roughly circular mass of exposed igneous rock **37.** RAIL same as **rolling stock** (sense 1) ■ *adj* **UNORIGINAL** typical or familiar and lacking originality ○ *When pushed for an answer, he gave the stock response.* ■ *v* (**stocked, stock·ing, stocks**) **1.** *vt* **HAVE PRODUCT IN STOCK** to have an item available for sale **2.** *vt* **FILL SOMETHING WITH GOODS FOR SALE** to fill something with a supply of goods for sale ○ *stocked the supermarket shelves with their new product* **3.** *vt* **FILL SOMETHING WITH SUPPLY FOR FUTURE** to fill something with a plentiful supply of something for future use ○ *We've stocked the freezer with ice cream for the children.* **4.** *vt* **SUPPLY FARM WITH ANIMALS** to supply a farm with livestock **5.** *vi* BOT **SPROUT ANEW** to sprout new shoots **6.** *vt* **PUNISH SOMEBODY IN STOCKS** formerly, to punish somebody by putting him or her in the stocks [Old English *stocc* "tree trunk" < Germanic] —**stock·er** *n* ◇ **take stock 1.** to think carefully about something so that you can form an opinion about it **2.** COMM to make an inventory of the stock, especially at the end of a season in a store or business

stock up *vi* to collect a large supply of something for future use ○ *stock up on canned goods*

stock·ade /sto káyd/ *n* **1. DEFENSIVE BARRIER** a tall fence or enclosure made of wooden posts driven into the ground side by side to keep out enemies or intruders **2. AREA INSIDE BARRIER** an area surrounded by a stockade **3.** MIL **MILITARY PRISON** a prison on a military base, especially an army or air force base ■ *vt* (**-ad·ed, -ad·ing, -ades**) **SURROUND AREA WITH STOCKADE** to enclose an area with a stockade [Early 17C. Via obsolete French *estocade* < Spanish *estacada* < *estaca* "stake" < Germanic]

stock·breed·er /stók breedər/ *n* somebody who breeds and rears livestock —**stock·breed·ing** *n*

stock·bro·ker /stók brōkər/ *n* somebody who buys and sells stocks, shares, and other securities for clients —**stock·bro·ker·age** *n* —**stock·brok·ing** *n*

stock·bro·ker belt *n UK* an affluent residential area outside a city inhabited by middle-class professional people who commute to the city to work

stock car *n* **1.** a standard passenger car that has been modified for professional racing **2.** a railroad car used for transporting livestock

stock cer·tif·i·cate *n* a certificate specifying the number of shares owned by a person or a company in a corporation's stock

stock com·pa·ny *n* **1.** a company that has its capital divided into shares that are freely tradable **2.** a permanent theater company that puts on a repertoire of plays, usually in its own theater

stock cu·be *n UK* same as **bouillon cube**

stock ex·change *n* **1.** FIN same as **stock market** (sense 1) **2.** a building in which a stock exchange is situated

stock farm *n* a farm on which animals such as cattle, sheep, and hogs are bred and raised

stock·fish /stók fìsh/ (*plural same* or **-fish·es**) *n* a fish, usually cod or haddock, that has been cured by being split and air-dried without the addition of salt [13C. Translation of Low German and Middle Dutch *stokvisch* < *stok* "stick, tree trunk" + *visch* "fish"]

Stock·haus·en /shtók hòwz'n, stók-/, **Karlheinz** (*b.* 1928) German composer. A major figure in the musical avant-garde from the late 1950s, he incorporates serialism, random elements, and electronic sound in his work.

> "Music is mathematics, the mathematics of listening, mathematics for the ears."
> [Karlheinz Stockhausen. Quoted in "In the Service of Music: The Quest for Perfection," *Conversations with Stockhausen*, Mya Tannenbaum; 1987]

stock·hold·er /stók hōldər/ *n* somebody who owns one or more shares of a company's stock —**stock·hold·ing** *n*

Stock·holm /stók hōm/ capital city of Sweden, on the eastern coast of the country. Population: 754,948 (2002).

Stock·holm syn·drome *n* a condition experienced by some people who have been held as hostages for an extended time in which they begin to identify with and feel sympathetic toward their captors [Late 20C. Because a hostage taken during a bank robbery in Stockholm exhibited this]

stock·i·nette /stòkə nét, stókə nèt/, **stock·i·net** *n* a stretchy knitted fabric. Use: bandages, dishcloths. [Late 18C. Probably alteration of *stocking net*]

stock·i·nette stitch *n US* a pattern in knitting that alternates rows of plain and purl stitches. Can term **stocking stitch**

stock·ing /stóking/ *n* **1.** either of a pair of tightly fitting leg coverings for women, made of silk, nylon, or wool (*often used in the plural*) **2.** CLOTHING same as **sock**[1] (sense 1) (*dated or formal*) **3.** same as **Christmas stocking** (*informal*) **4.** ZOOL a differently colored part of the lower leg of an animal, especially a horse [Late 16C. < STOCK in the obsolete sense "stocking"] —**stock·inged** *adj*

ORIGIN The use of ***stocking*** to mean a leg covering may have arisen from the blackly humorous comparison of the stocks in which people's legs were restrained as punishment with "leggings, hose." Until comparatively recently ***stocking*** was a unisex term (as it still is in the expression "in your stockinged feet"); the restriction to women's hose is a 20th-century development.

stock·ing cap *n* a tightly fitting cone-shaped knitted cap with a tapering tail that often has a tassel on the end

stock·ing fil·ler *n UK* same as **stocking stuffer**

stock·ing mask *n* a nylon stocking pulled over the head to disguise the features, usually worn by somebody committing a crime

stock·ing stitch *n Can, UK* same as **stockinette stitch**

stock·ing stuff·er *n* a small, usually inexpensive Christmas gift, especially one put into a Christmas stocking

stock-in-trade *n* **1.** a resource that somebody needs and regularly makes use of, especially at work ○ *Courtesy and composure are the receptionist's stock-in-trade.* **2.** the goods and equipment that need to be kept on the premises for a business or store to operate normally

stock·job·ber /stók jòbbər/ *n* **1.** *US* a stockbroker, especially an unscrupulous dealer trading in worthless securities (*dated*) **2.** *UK* formerly, a dealer on the London stock exchange who dealt only with brokers, not with members of the public —**stock·job·ber·y** *n* —**stock·job·bing** *n*

stock·keep·ing /stók kèeping/ *n* regulation of its inventory by a retailer or other trader

stock·keep·ing u·nit *n* BUSINESS, COMPUT full form of **SKU**

stock·man /stókmən, -màn/ (*plural* **-men** /-mən, -mèn/) *n* **1.** MAN BREEDING FARM ANIMALS a man who owns or breeds farm animals, especially cattle **2.** MAN TENDING LIVESTOCK a man who takes care of the livestock on a farm or ranch **3.** COMM MAN WORKING IN WAREHOUSE a man who works in a warehouse or stockroom

stock mar·ket *n* **1.** FINANCIAL MARKET an organized market where brokers meet to buy and sell stocks and shares **2.** FINANCIAL TRADING the activity of buying and selling stocks and shares, or the global market for stocks and shares (*hyphenated before a noun*) **3.** AGRIC PLACE WHERE ANIMALS ARE AUCTIONED a building with an arena in which farm animals are auctioned

stock op·tion *n* a right to buy or sell stock at a fixed price, especially one granted by a corporation to an employee as a form of compensation or reward for performance

stock·per·son /stók pùrss'n/ (*plural* **-per·sons** or **-peo·ple** /-pèep'l/) *n* **1.** BREEDER OF FARM ANIMALS somebody who owns or breeds farm animals, especially cattle **2.** SOMEBODY TENDING LIVESTOCK somebody who takes care of the livestock on a farm or ranch **3.** COMM WORKER IN WAREHOUSE somebody who works in a warehouse or stockroom

stock·pile /stók pìl/ *vti* (**-piled, -pil·ing, -piles**) to collect and store large amounts of things such as equipment or weapons for future use ■ *n* a large supply of something such as food or weapons, often accumulated in anticipation of future difficulties —**stock·pil·er** *n*

SYNONYMS See ***collect***[1].

Stock·port /stók pàwrt/ city in Cheshire, northwestern England. Population: 291,100 (2000).

stock·pot /stók pòt/ *n* a large pot for cooking soups and stock

stock·room /stók ròom, -ròom/ *n* a room where merchandise or supplies are stored in a store, office, or factory

stocks /stoks/ *n* (*takes a singular or plural verb*) **1.** in former times, a wooden frame in which an offender was secured by the hands and feet or by the head and hands and left in public to be ridiculed or abused **2.** a frame that supports a boat or ship while it is being built [14C. Plural of STOCK, in the sense "post, tree trunk"]

stock sad·dle *n* a large and heavy saddle for a horse with a raised pommel, originally used on ranches in the western and southwestern United States

stock-still *adv* absolutely motionless

stock·tak·ing /stók tàyking/ *n* **1.** the process of evaluating a situation, especially a personal situation **2.** *UK* same as **inventory** *n* (sense 2)

Stock·ton /stóktən/ city and inland port in central California, on the San Joaquin River, south of Sacramento. Population: 262,835 (2002 estimate).

Stock·ton, Frank (1834–1902) US writer. His whimsical short stories include "The Lady or the Tiger?" (1882). Born **Stockton, Francis Richard**

Stock·ton, Richard Nathaniel (1730–81) American patriot. A New Jersey delegate to the Continental Congress (1775–78), he was a signatory of the Declaration of Independence (1776).

Stock·ton-on-Tees /stóktən on tèez/ port in County Durham, northeastern England. Population: 83,576 (1991).

stock·wom·an /stók wòommən/ (*plural* **-wom·en** /-wìmmin/) *n* **1.** WOMAN BREEDING FARM ANIMALS a woman who owns or breeds farm animals, especially cattle **2.** WOMAN TENDING LIVESTOCK a woman who takes care of the livestock on a farm or ranch **3.** COMM WOMAN WORKING IN WAREHOUSE a woman who works in a warehouse or stockroom

stock·y /stókee/ (**-i·er, -i·est**) *adj* **1.** short and broad with a strong-looking physique **2.** somewhat overweight —**stock·i·ly** *adv* —**stock·i·ness** *n*

stock·yard /stók yàard/ *n* a large enclosed yard with pens or covered stables where livestock is kept before being sold, slaughtered, or shipped

stodg·y /stójjee/ (**-i·er, -i·est**) *adj* **1.** UNIMAGINATIVE lacking originality, flair, or imagination (*informal*) ○ *another stack of stodgy poems* **2.** FORMAL OR POMPOUS boringly or laughably conventional, formal, or pompous (*informal*) ○ *one of his stodgy dinner parties* **3.** FILLING heavy and filling to eat and usually fairly tasteless (*informal*) **4.** HEAVY AND PLODDING heavy, bulky, and plodding —**stodg·i·ly** *adv* —**stodg·i·ness** *n*

stoep /stoop/ *n S Africa* a porch or veranda [Late 18C. Via Afrikaans < Dutch]

sto·gy /stṓgee/ (*plural* **-gies**), **sto·gie**, **sto·gey** (*plural* **-geys**) *n* **1.** a long slim inexpensive cigar **2.** *US* a heavy boot or shoe that is crudely made [Mid-19C. Shortening of *Conestoga*, probably because used by drivers of Conestoga wagons]

sto·ic /stṓ ik/ *n* somebody who is unemotional, especially somebody who shows patience and endurance during adversity ■ *adj also* **sto·i·cal** /stṓ ik'l/ showing admirable patience and endurance in the face of adversity without complaining or getting upset [Late 16C. < STOIC] —**sto·i·cal·ly** *adv*

SYNONYMS See ***impassive***.

Sto·ic /stṓ ik/ *n* a member of an ancient Greek school of philosophy that asserted that happiness can only be achieved by accepting life's ups and downs as the products of unalterable destiny. The school was founded around 308 B.C. by Zeno. [14C. < Latin *Stoicus* < Greek *stoa* "porch," referring to the Painted Porch in Athens, where Zeno taught] —**Sto·ic** *adj*

sto·i·cal *adj* same as **stoic**

stoi·chi·ol·o·gy /stòykee óllәjee/ *n* the study of the elements or principles of any discipline, especially the chemical principles underlying cell and tissue physiology [Mid-19C. < Greek *stoikheion* "element," after German *Stöchiologie*] —**stoi·chi·o·log·i·cal** /stòykee ə lójjik'l/ *adj*

stoi·chi·om·e·try /stòykee ómmətree/ *n* **1.** the branch of chemistry concerned with measuring the proportions of elements that combine during chemical reactions **2.** a measure of the relative proportions of the elements that take part in a chemical reaction [Mid-19C. < Greek *stoikheion* "element," after German *Stöchiometrie*] —**stoi·chi·o·met·ric** /stòykee ō méttrik/ *adj* —**stoi·chi·o·met·ri·cal·ly** *adv*

sto·i·cism /stṓ i sìzzəm/ *n* emotional indifference, especially admirable patience and endurance shown in the face of adversity

Sto·i·cism /stṓ i sìzzəm/ *n* the beliefs of the ancient Greek school of Stoic philosophy

stoke /stōk/ (**stoked, stok·ing, stokes**) *v* **1.** *vti* ADD FUEL to add fuel to a fire and stir it up to make it burn more intensely **2.** *vti* TEND BOILER to be responsible for adding fuel to and tending a boiler or furnace **3.** *vt* MAKE EXTREMELY ENTHUSIASTIC to make somebody feel extremely eager, enthusiastic, and excited about doing something (*slang*) ○ *I was stoked to be competing.* [Mid-17C. Back-formation < STOKER]

stoke up *v* **1.** *vt* ADD FUEL TO FIRE to add fuel to a fire or a furnace and stir it up so that it burns more intensely **2.** *vt* INTENSIFY EMOTION to cause an emotion such as anger or fear to be felt more strongly **3.** *vi* EAT IN BULK to eat food in large quantities, because or as if more food may not be had (*informal*)

stoked /stōkt/ *adj* in an excited or euphoric state, especially from having taken drugs (*slang*)

stoke·hold /stṓk hōld/ *n* the boiler room of a steamship

stoke·hole /stṓk hōl/ *n* **1.** the opening through which fuel is added to a boiler or furnace **2.** NAUT same as **stokehold** [Mid-17C. Translation of Dutch *stookgat*]

Stoke-on-Trent /stŏk on trént/ city in Staffordshire, central England. It is a major pottery manufacturing center. Population: 249,000 (2000).

stok·er /stṓkər/ *n* **1.** somebody whose job it is to add fuel to and tend a furnace or boiler, e.g., on a steamship **2.** *US* a mechanical device for adding fuel to a furnace [Mid-17C. < Dutch < Middle Dutch *stoken* "poke with a stick"]

Sto·ker /stṓkər/, **Bram** (1847–1912) Irish writer. He is best known for the classic vampire story *Dracula* (1897). Full name **Stoker, Abraham**

Stokes-Ad·ams syn·drome /stŏks áddəms-/ *n* episodes of temporary dizziness or fainting caused by disruption or extreme slowing of the heartbeat and consequent brief stoppage of blood flow [Early 20C. After William *Stokes* (1804–75) and Robert *Adams* (1791–1875), Irish physicians]

Stok·ow·ski /stə káwfskee, -ków-/, **Leopold** (1882–1977) British-born US conductor. He brought the Philadelphia Orchestra international recognition as its principal conductor (1912–38). Full name **Stokowski, Leopold Antoni Stanisław Boleslawowicz**

STOL /stawl, stol/ *n* **1.** a flying system that gives an aircraft the ability to take off and land on a very short runway. Full form **short takeoff and landing 2.** an aircraft fitted with the STOL system

stole[1] /stōl/ past tense of **steal**

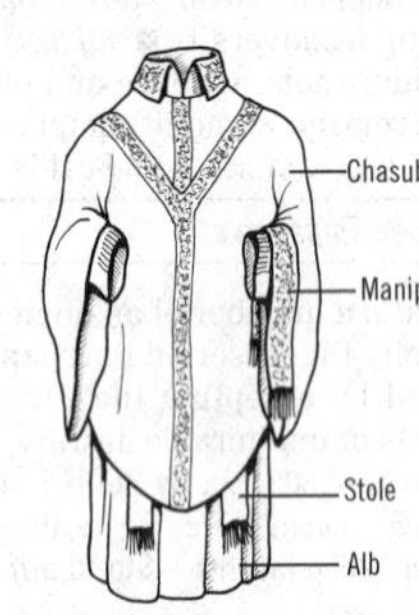

stole (sense 2)

stole[2] /stōl/ *n* **1.** WOMAN'S SCARF a woman's scarf or shawl, often made of fur or worn as part of evening wear **2.** ECCLESIASTICAL SCARF a long, narrow, and usually embroidered scarf made of silk or linen, worn by various members of the clergy **3.** ROMAN ROBE a draped robe worn by women of high standing in ancient Rome [Pre-12C. Via Latin < Greek *stolē* "robe, equipment"]

sto·len past participle of **steal**

stol·id /stóllɪd/ *adj* solemn, unemotional, and not easily excited or upset [Late 16C. Directly or via French < Latin *stolidus* "dense, stupid"] —**sto·lid·i·ty** /stə líddətee/ *n* —**stol·id·ly** *adv* —**stol·id·ness** *n*

SYNONYMS See *impassive*.

stol·len /stṓlən, shtṓlən/ (*plural same* or **-lens**) *n* a rich sweet German fruit bread made with nuts, raisins, and other dried fruits. It is traditionally served at Christmas. [Early 20C. < German < Old High German *stollo* "post, support"]

sto·lon /stṓ lòn, stṓlən/ *n* **1.** a long stem or shoot that arises from the central rosette of a plant and droops to the ground. It may form new plants where it touches the soil. **2.** a budding of the body wall in simple organisms, especially an extension of some colonial organisms such as hydroids that anchors the colony to a rock or other substrate [Early 17C. < Latin *stolon-*] —**sto·lon·ate** /-àyt/ *adj* —**sto·lon·if·er·ous** /stṓlə níffərəss/ *adj*

sto·ma /stṓmə/ (*plural* **-ma·ta** /-mətə/) *n* **1.** BOT PLANT PORE a tiny pore in the outer layer (**epidermis**) of a plant leaf or stem that controls the passing of water vapor and other gases into and out of the plant **2.** ZOOL MOUTH OR SIMILAR STRUCTURE a mouth, or an opening that acts as or is shaped like a mouth **3.** SURG SURGICAL OPENING an artificial opening made in an organ of the body, especially an opening in the colon or ileum made via the abdomen [Late 17C. Via modern Latin < Greek, "mouth"] —**sto·mal** *adj* —**sto·ma·tal** *adj* —**sto·ma·tous** *adj*

stom·ach /stúmmək/ *n* **1.** VERTEBRATES' DIGESTIVE ORGAN an organ resembling a sac in which food is mixed and partially digested. It forms part of the digestive tract of vertebrates and is situated between the esophagus and the small intestine. **2.** ABDOMEN the abdomen of a vertebrate (*not used technically*) **3.** COMPARTMENT OF ANIMAL'S STOMACH a digestive chamber in the four-part stomach of ruminant animals (*not used technically*) **4.** INVERTEBRATES' DIGESTIVE ORGAN a digestive organ in some invertebrate animals in which food is mixed, stored, and partially digested **5.** SEAT OF UNPLEASANT FEELINGS the part of the body in which disgust, nausea, and fear are experienced ○ *The very idea makes me sick to my stomach.* **6.** RESISTANCE TO UNPLEASANTNESS the ability to withstand disgust, nausea, or fear ○ *This is not a job for someone with a weak stomach.* **7.** WILLINGNESS TO DO SOMETHING an appetite or willingness to do something or tolerate something ○ *no stomach for a fight* ■ *vt* (**-ached, -ach·ing, -achs**) TOLERATE SOMETHING to put up with something ○ *I find their gloating hard to stomach.* [14C. Via French and Latin < Greek *stomakhos* "throat, gullet" < *stoma* "mouth"]

stom·ach·ache /stúmmək àyk/ *n* a pain in the abdominal region, caused by a minor condition such as indigestion or an infection

stom·ach-churn·ing *adj* producing feelings of disgust, nausea, or fear

stom·ach crunch *n* an exercise in which you lie flat on your back with your legs bent and then raise the upper part of your body a few inches off the ground without using your hands

stom·ach·er /stúmməkər/ *n* a stiff panel of material, often decorated with embroidery or jewels, worn over the chest and abdomen by women in the 17th and 18th centuries, and earlier by both sexes

sto·mach·ic /stə mákik/ *adj also* **sto·mach·i·cal** /-mákik'l/ associated with the stomach —**sto·mach·i·cal·ly** *adv*

stom·ach pump *n* the equipment, consisting of a tube, funnel, and bucket, used to flush out the stomach contents of somebody who has swallowed a dangerous substance such as a poison (*informal*)

stom·ach tooth *n* either of the first canine teeth in the lower jaw of humans, whose appearance is popularly believed to be hastened by stomach upsets in infants

stom·ach-turn·ing *adj* producing feelings of disgust or nausea

sto·ma·ta plural of **stoma**

sto·ma·ti·tis /stṓmə tī́tiss/ *n* inflammation of the mucous tissue lining the mouth [Mid-19C. < Greek *stomat-*, stem of *stoma* "mouth"] —**sto·ma·tit·ic** /-títtik/ *adj*

sto·ma·tol·o·gy /stṓmə tólləjee/ *n* the branch of medicine or dentistry that is concerned with the study of the mouth and diseases of the mouth [Late 19C. < Greek *stomat-*, stem of *stoma* "mouth"] —**sto·ma·to·log·ic** /stṓmətə lójjik/ *adj* —**sto·ma·to·log·i·cal** *adj* —**sto·ma·tol·o·gist** *n*

sto·mat·o·pod /stṓmətə pòd, stō máttə-/ *n* a shellfish with abdominal gills and a second pair of claws, e.g., the squilla. Order: Stomatopoda. [Late 19C. < Greek *stomat-*, stem of *stoma* "mouth"]

-stome *suffix* mouth, stoma ○ *peristome* [< Greek *stoma* "mouth"] —**-stomous** *suffix*

sto·mo·de·um /stṓmə dée əm/ (*plural* **-de·a** /-dée ə/), **sto·mo·dae·um** (*plural* **-dae·a**) *n* a depression in the surface of an early embryo that develops into the mouth [Late 19C. < modern Latin < Greek *stoma* "mouth" + *hodaios* "on the way, becoming" < *hodos* "way, road"] —**sto·mo·de·al** *adj*

stomp /stomp/ *v* (**stomped, stomp·ing, stomps**) **1.** *vti* WALK WITH HEAVY STEPS to tread heavily and noisily, or bring your feet down heavily and noisily, often in anger **2.** *vt* TREAD HEAVILY ON SOMETHING to bring a foot down heavily on something or somebody with the intention of causing damage or injury (*informal*) ■ *n* **1.** JAZZ DANCE a jazz dance with stamping foot movements **2.** JAZZ MUSIC jazz music accompanying the stomp [Early 19C. Variant of STAMP] —**stomp·er** *n* —**stomp·ing·ly** *adv*

stomp·ing ground *n* same as **stamping ground** (*informal*)

-stomy *suffix* a surgical operation that creates an artificial opening ○ *gastrostomy* [< Greek *stoma* "mouth"]

stone /stōn/ *n* **1.** HARD NONMETALLIC MATERIAL the hard solid nonmetallic substance that rocks are made of. Use: building material. **2.** ROCK FRAGMENT a small piece of rock of any shape **3.** SHAPED ROCK FRAGMENT a piece of rock that has been shaped for a particular purpose, e.g., a gravestone (*often used in combination*) **4.** SMALL HARD MASS a small hard mass, e.g., a hailstone (*usually used in combination*) **5.** same as **gemstone 6.** BOT HARD MASS INSIDE FRUIT the hard central part of some fruits e.g., cherries, plums, olives, and peaches, that contains the seed **7.** (*plural same* or **stones**) *UK* MEASURE UNIT OF WEIGHT in the United Kingdom, a unit of weight equivalent to 14 lb./6.35 kg. It is used especially for expressing somebody's weight. ○ *He's trying to get down to 12 stone.* **8.** MED MINERAL MASS INSIDE ORGAN a small hard mass of mineral material formed in an organ such as the kidney or gall bladder. Technical name **calculus** (sense 3) **9.** COLORS LIGHT GRAY OR BEIGE a dull light gray or beige color **10.** SPORTS CURLING BLOCK the shaped and polished mass of granite or iron that is slid along the ice in the game of curling **11.** PRINTING PRINTER'S TABLE a very smooth flat table used for arranging printing type (*dated*) **12.** TESTICLE a testicle (*archaic slang or Carib*) ■ *adj* **1.** OF STONE OR STONEWARE made of stone or stoneware **2.** COLORS OF THE COLOR STONE light gray to beige in color ■ *adv* **1.** EMPHASIZING QUALITY LIKE STONE used to emphasize the degree of a quality associated with stone, e.g., coldness, stillness, or lifelessness **2.** USED FOR EMPHASIS used to emphasize the degree of a quality (*slang*) ○ *stone fine* ○ *stone tired* ■ *vt* (**stoned, ston·ing, stones**) **1.** THROW STONES AT SOMEBODY to throw stones at somebody or something, especially as a form of punishment, execution, or vandalism **2.** REMOVE STONE FROM FRUIT to remove the hard central part from a piece of fruit such as a plum **3.** *US* RUB SOMETHING WITH STONE to polish or sharpen something on a stone or with a stone [Old English *stān* < Indo-European] —**stone·less** *adj* —**stone·like** *adj* ◇ **be carved** *or* **set** *or* **cast in (tablets of) stone** to be so firmly established as to make changes impossible or unthinkable ◇ **cast** *or* **throw the first stone** to be the first person to quarrel with, accuse, or criticize somebody else ◇ **leave no stone unturned** to be very thorough in making a search or in carrying out a task

Stone /stōn/, **Edward Durell** (1902–78) US architect. His most prestigious commission was the Kennedy Center for the Performing Arts in Washington, D.C. (1964–71).

Stone, Harlan Fiske (1872–1946) chief justice of the US Supreme Court (1941–46)

Stone, Lucy (1818–93) US feminist and abolitionist. She organized the first US Woman's Rights Convention (1850) and founded the *Women's Journal* (1870).

> "We want rights. The flour merchant, the house builder, and the postman charge us no less on account of our sex; but when we endeavor to earn money to pay all these, then, indeed, we find the difference."
>
> [Lucy Stone, *Speech,* "Disappointment Is the Lot of Women"; October 17–18, 1855]

Stone, Oliver (*b.* 1946) US movie director. His movies deal with contemporary social and political issues, often controversially. He won Academy Awards for best director for *Platoon* (1986) and *Born on the Fourth of July* (1989).

Stone, Thomas (1743–87) American patriot. A Maryland delegate to the Continental Congress (1775–78), he was a signatory of the Declaration of Independence (1776).

Stone Age *n* the earliest period of human history, in which tools and weapons were made of stone rather than metal. It is divided into the Paleolithic, Mesolithic, and Neolithic periods. It extends from around 2.5 million years ago to around 2400 B.C.

Stone-Age /stṓn àyj/ *adj* **1.** dating from the Stone Age, the earliest period of human history **2.** *also* **stone-age** hopelessly behind the times

stone bass /-bàss/ *n* a large dark brown and yellow fish of the perch family. Native to: Atlantic, Mediterranean. Latin name: *Polyprion americanus.* [Because it inhabits rocky ledges and wrecks]

stone-blind *adj* an offensive term meaning completely unable to see —**stone-blind·ness** *n*

stone boat *n Midwest* same as **mudboat**

REGIONAL NOTE See *mudboat.*

stone-broke *adj US* having no money at all (*informal*) Can term **stony-broke**

stone·cat /stṓn kàt/ (*plural* **-cats** or *same*) *n* a slender yellowish brown catfish that inhabits the beds of streams, rivers, and lakes, typically under stones. Native to: North America. Latin name: *Noturus flavus.*

stone cell *n* a short squat plant cell that performs a strengthening function. It occurs in large numbers in fruits such as the quince and the pear.

stone·chat /stṓn chàt/ (*plural* **-chats** or *same*) *n* a small songbird, the male of which has a black head, brown back, chestnut breast, and white rump. Native to: grassy regions, dry plains of Europe, Asia and Africa. Latin name: *Saxicola torquata.* [Late 18C. Because its call suggests the sound of colliding stones]

stone-cold *adj* completely cold, especially too cold to be palatable ■ *adv* completely and utterly (*informal*) ○ *stone-cold sober*

stone crab *n* a large crab that lays several million eggs and can be a serious pest to oyster beds. Native to: coast of southern United States. Latin name: *Menippe mercenaria.*

stone·crop /stṓn kròp/ (*plural* **-crops** or *same*) *n* **1.** an annual or perennial flowering plant with fleshy leaves. Native to: northern temperate regions. Genus: *Sedum.* **2.** a plant related or similar to the stonecrop [Pre-12C. STONE (because the plant grows on rocks) + CROP in the obsolete sense "flower cluster, ear of grain"]

stone cur·lew *n* a brownish, wading bird with a large head and eyes and thick knee joints, that is active at night. Native to: open dry stony regions worldwide. Family: Burhinidae.

stone·cut·ter /stṓn kùttər/ *n* **1.** somebody who cuts and carves stone **2.** a machine that is used to cut stone and concrete, especially a hand-held power tool with a circular blade —**stone·cut·ting** *n*

stoned /stōnd/ *adj* **1.** relaxed, excited, or euphoric from taking illegal drugs, especially marijuana (*slang*) **2.** very intoxicated (*informal*)

stone-dead *adj* definitely or completely lifeless

stone-deaf *adj* an offensive term meaning completely unable to hear

stone-faced *adj* same as **stony-faced**

stone·fish /stṓn fìsh/ (*plural* **-fish·es** or *same*) *n* a tropical ocean fish whose mottled and knobby body serves as camouflage in its rocky habitat. Genus: *Synanceja.*

stone·fly /stṓn flī/ (*plural* **-flies** or *same*) *n* an insect that, in its wingless juvenile stage, lives among stones in rivers and streams. The adults have long antennae and usually two pairs of wings. Both larvae and adults are used as fishing bait. Order: Plecoptera.

stone fruit *n* BOT same as **drupe**

stone·ground /stṓn grównd/ *adj* ground in the traditional way with millstones rather than with metal rollers

stone·heart·ed /stṓn haártəd/ *adj* same as **stony-hearted**

Barnaby's

Stonehenge

Stone·henge /stṓn hénj/ prehistoric monument on Salisbury Plain, southern England, consisting of two concentric circles of large standing stones. It was built between 2800 and 1500 B.C. and is thought to have been an astronomical calendar or a temple to the Sun.

stone lil·y *n* a fossil of a sea lily

stone mar·ten *n* **1.** a marten that has dark brown fur with a lighter throat and undersides. Native to: woods of Europe and Asia. Latin name: *Martes foina.* **2.** the fur of the stone marten [Because it inhabits rocky inlets and crevices]

stone·ma·son /stṓn màyss'n/ *n* somebody who makes and repairs stone structures or shapes and prepares stone used as a building material —**stone·ma·son·ry** *n*

stone mint *n* an aromatic plant of the mint family found in dry woodlands and grasslands. Flowers: small, tubular, purplish or white, in clusters. Use: formerly, remedy for snakebite and fever. Native to: eastern North America. Latin name: *Cunila origanoides.* [Because it grows in rocky places]

Stone Moun·tain /stṓn-/ massive granite outcropping near Atlanta, northern Georgia, United States. A monumental memorial to the Confederacy is carved on its northern face. Height: 1,686 ft./514 m.

stone pine *n* a pine tree with an umbrella-shaped crown that is cultivated for its seeds. Native to: Mediterranean. Latin name: *Pinus pinea.*

ston·er /stṓnər/ *n* a regular smoker of marijuana (*slang*)

stone·roll·er /stṓn rōlər/ (*plural* **-ers** or *same*) *n* a small brown freshwater minnow, the male of which turns orange and digs nests in stream beds during the breeding season. Latin name: *Campostoma anomalum.* [Late 19C. Because it moves stones as it feeds]

stone's throw *n* a very short distance

stone·wall /stṓn wàwl/ (**-walled, -wall·ing, -walls**) *v* **1.** *vti* to create obstructions or refuse to cooperate, especially by avoiding answering questions or providing desired information **2.** *vi UK* to create obstructions or employ delaying tactics, especially in order to hinder parliamentary business —**stone·wall·er** *n*

stone·ware /stṓn wèr/ *n* dense opaque nonporous pottery that is fired at a very high temperature

stone·washed /stṓn wòsht, -wàwsht/ *adj* washed with small pumice pebbles to give a worn faded look

stone·work /stṓn wùrk/ *n* **1.** the parts of a building or other structure that are made of stone **2.** the process of building with stone —**stone·work·er** *n*

stone·wort /stṓn wùrt, -wàwrt/ (*plural same* or **-worts**) *n* a green alga that grows in fresh or slightly salty water and resembles a plant, having structures resembling leaves arranged on a long structure resembling a stem and jointed branches, often encrusted with lime. Family: Characeae.

ston·y /stṓnee/ (**-i·er, -i·est**), **ston·ey** *adj* **1.** COVERED WITH STONES covered with or having a great many stones **2.** OF OR LIKE STONE made of stone or similar to stone in appearance, texture, or color **3.** EMOTIONLESS expressing no emotion, especially no friendliness or pity ○ *a stony silence* —**ston·i·ly** *adv* —**ston·i·ness** *n*

ston·y-broke *adj Can, UK* same as **stone-broke** (*informal*)

ston·y cor·al *n* a coral with a robust external calcium-based skeleton that forms reefs and islands. Order: Scleractinia or Madreporaria.

ston·y-faced *adj* showing not the slightest emotion, especially no sign of friendliness

ston·y-heart·ed *adj* having or showing no compassion or kindness —**ston·y-heart·ed·ness** *n*

ston·y-iron me·te·or·ite *n* a meteorite consisting of metal and stony material

ston·y me·te·or·ite *n* a meteorite that is composed mainly of rock-forming silicate minerals, especially olivine, plagioclase, and pyroxene

stood past participle, past tense of **stand**

USAGE See *sit.*

stooge /stooj/ *n* **1.** COMIC LOSER a comic actor, usually part of a double act, who acts as the butt of most of the jokes **2.** SOMEBODY EXPLOITED somebody who is exploited by others, especially somebody used by criminals in committing their crimes (*slang insult*) **3.** *US* POLICE same as **stool pigeon** (sense 1) (*slang*) **4.** HUNTING same as **stool pigeon** (sense 3) (*slang*) ■ *vi* (**stooged, stoog·ing, stoog·es**) BE TAKEN ADVANTAGE OF to be taken advantage of by another (*informal*) [Early 20C. Origin ?]

stook /stŏŏk, stook/ *UK* AGRIC *n* same as **shock**[2] ■ *vt* (**stooked, stook·ing, stooks**) same as **shock**[2] [14C. Origin ?]

stool /stool/ *n* **1.** SIMPLE SEAT a simple seat with three or four legs and no back or armrests **2.** EXCREMENT a piece of excrement **3.** TOILET a toilet or toilet seat (*slang*) **4.** BOT PLANT BASE the base of a plant, from which shoots or suckers sprout **5.** BOT CLUMP OF SHOOTS a clump of shoots or suckers sprouting from the base of a plant **6.** *US* HUNTING HUNTER'S DECOY a real or artificial bird used by hunters as a decoy **7.** *W Africa* CHIEF'S THRONE the throne of a tribal chief ■ *vi* (**stooled, stool·ing, stools**) **1.** SPROUT SHOOTS to sprout shoots or suckers from a stool **2.** *US* EVACUATE BOWELS to evacuate the bowels **3.** HUNTING BE DECOY OR HUNT WITH DECOY to be a decoy for a hunter of wildfowl, or to hunt wildfowl using decoys **4.** *US* POLICE BE STOOL PIGEON to provide information to law enforcement agencies about criminals (*slang*) [Old English *stōl* "chair" < Indo-European, "to stand"]

stool·ie /stóolee/ *n* POLICE same as **stool pigeon** (sense 1) (*informal*) [Early 20C. Shortening]

stool pi·geon *n* **1.** POLICE INFORMER somebody who informs on criminals or their activities to the police (*slang*) **2.** DECOY CRIMINAL a criminal working as a decoy for a gang of criminals, with the job of distracting attention from their activities (*slang*) **3.** HUNTING HUNTER'S DECOY PIGEON a pigeon, or a dummy of a pigeon, used by a hunter as a decoy [Because hunters' decoys were originally tied to a wooden platform]

stoop[1] /stoop/ *v* (**stooped, stoop·ing, stoops**) **1.** *vti* BEND BODY to bend the top half of the body forward and downward **2.** *vi* WALK OR STAND BENT OVER to walk or stand with the head and shoulders bent forward and downward **3.** *vi* DO SOMETHING UNETHICAL to act in an unethical or self-degrading way ○ *I never imagined you would stoop so low.* **4.** *vi* CONDESCEND to do something reluctantly and with the attitude of somebody who considers such action unworthy ○ *"He could not stoop to love; No lady in the land had power His frozen heart to move."* (Sir Walter Scott, *Waverley*; 1814) **5.** *vi* SWOOP DOWN to swoop down with wings folded, e.g., when attacking prey (*refers to birds*) ■ *n* **1.** BENT POSTURE a posture in which the head and shoulders are bent forward and downward **2.** BIRD'S DOWNWARD SWOOP the downward swoop of a bird of prey [Old English *stūpian* < Germanic] —**stoop·er** *n* —**stoop·ing** *adj* —**stoop·ing·ly** *adv*

stoop[2] /stoop/ *n* a small porch at the entrance to a house [Mid-18C. < Dutch *stoep*]

stoop[3] /stoop/ *n* CHR another spelling of **stoup**

stoop·ball /stóop bàwl/ *n* a game based on baseball in which a player throws a ball against a stoop or wall, with the number of bounces representing the number of bases reached [Mid-20C. < STOOP[2]]

stop /stop/ *v* (**stopped, stop·ping, stops**) **1.** *vti* DISCONTINUE SOMETHING to cease doing something, or make somebody cease doing something ○ *She's trying to stop smoking.* **2.** *vti* CEASE MOVING to come to a standstill,

or bring something to a standstill ○ *Stop the car!* **3.** *vti* **END** to come to an end, or bring something to an end ○ *The rain has stopped.* **4.** *vt* **PREVENT SOMETHING FROM HAPPENING** to cause something not to happen or not to be done ○ *We couldn't stop the roof from caving in.* **5.** *vt* **PREVENT SOMEBODY FROM DOING SOMETHING** to cause somebody not to do or not to be able to do a particular thing ○ *a way of stopping the children from climbing the fence* **6.** *vi* **PAUSE** to pause in order to do something before continuing ○ *I urge you to stop and think before deciding.* **7.** *vi* **INTERRUPT TRIP** to interrupt a trip in order to make a brief visit somewhere ○ *Stop at the post office on the way into town.* **8.** *vti UK* **STAY BRIEFLY** to stay for a short time (*informal*) ○ *The children's friends like to stop the night.* **9.** *vt* **FILL HOLE** to fill or block a hole ○ *We need to stop the cracks in the wall.* **10.** *vt* **BLOCK SOMETHING** to block or plug something such as a pipe or a wound so that nothing can pass through it ○ *Grease has stopped the drain.* **11.** *vt* BANKING **INTERDICT CHECK** to prevent the honoring of a check by an instruction to the bank on which it was to have been drawn **12.** *vt* MUSIC **PRESS MUSICAL STRING** to press a string on a musical instrument in order to produce a note **13.** *vt* MUSIC **COVER HOLE ON INSTRUMENT** to use a finger to close a hole on a wind instrument in order to produce a note **14.** *vt* MUSIC **PUT HAND INSIDE FRENCH HORN** to alter the tone and pitch of a French horn by putting a hand inside the bell **15.** *vt* BOXING **KNOCK SOMEBODY OUT** to defeat an opponent in boxing by a knockout **16.** *vti* CARDS **BLOCK BRIDGE SUIT** to block the winning of a suit in bridge **17.** *vt* **BE HIT BY SOMETHING** to be hit by something, usually a punch or a bullet (*informal*) **18.** *vt* **DEFEAT SOMEBODY OR SOMETHING** to defeat an opponent or competitor (*informal*) ○ *Nothing's going to stop us now.* ■ *n* **1. STANDSTILL** a complete end or lack of movement **2. BREAK IN TRIP** a short break in a trip, e.g., to rest or to visit somebody **3. PLACE VISITED ON WAY** a place visited while on a trip **4. PAUSE MADE ON ROUTE** a place where a bus or a train regularly pauses on its route ○ *Is this your stop?* **5. BLOCKAGE** a blockage or obstruction **6. PLUG THAT BLOCKS** something that is used to block the flow or passage of something, e.g., a plug or a stopper **7. DEVICE PREVENTING MOVEMENT** a device or control that prevents movement (*often used in combination*) ○ *a doorstop* **8.** FIN **ORDER INTERDICTING CHECK** an order to a bank not to honor a check ○ *I had to put a stop on the lost check.* **9.** MUSIC **STOPPING ON MUSICAL INSTRUMENT** an act of stopping a string or a hole on a musical instrument **10.** MUSIC **SUBSET OF ORGAN PIPES** a subset of organ pipes or harpsichord strings with a common tone color that can be played in isolation by silencing the remaining pipes or strings **11.** MUSIC **ORGAN CONTROL** a knob or lever on an organ or harpsichord that isolates a subset of pipes or strings **12.** PHOTOGRAPHY **CAMERA'S APERTURE SETTING** one of the graded settings for the size of the aperture of a camera lens **13.** PHOTOGRAPHY same as **diaphragm** (sense 3) **14.** NAUT **SHORT ROPE** a short length of line used to tie up something such as a sail **15.** PHON **SPEECH SOUND** a consonant sound made by closing the passage of air through the mouth and then suddenly opening it again **16.** ZOOL **PART OF ANIMAL'S FACE** the area between the nose and the forehead of a cat or a dog **17.** FENCING **FENCING COUNTERTHRUST** a swift counterthrust made at the time of a fencing opponent's thrust that seeks to make contact first **18.** ARCHIT **CARVING** a carving that finishes the end of a molding [Old English *-stoppian* "block up," via W Germanic < late Latin *stuppare* "to stuff" < Latin *stuppa* "plug, stopper" < Greek *stuppē*] —**stop·pa·ble** *adj*
◇ **pull out all the stops** to make every possible effort in order to accomplish something ◇ **put a stop to something** to bring something to an end, usually quickly and permanently

stop by *vti* **1.** to interrupt a trip in order to make a brief visit somewhere ○ *Can you stop by the supermarket on your way home?* **2.** to visit a person or place briefly ○ *Stop by any time!*

stop down *vti* to make the aperture of a camera lens smaller

stop off *vi* to interrupt a trip briefly in order to do something or see somebody ○ *We stopped off at the supermarket on the way home.*

stop bath *n* an acid solution in which a negative or print is immersed in order to halt the developing process

stop bit *n* in serial communications, a bit that signals the end of a transmission unit

stop·cock /stóp kòk/ *n* a valve or faucet used to turn on, turn off, or regulate the flow of a fluid in a pipe

stop co·don *n* a sequence of three chemical units (**base pairs**) linking complementary strands of DNA or RNA that indicates the end of a protein synthesis. The three stop codons are thymine-adenine-guanine, thymine-adenine-adenine, and thymine-guanine-adenine.

stope /stōp/ *n* an excavation that resembles steps, used especially in the mining of ore ■ *vti* (**stoped, stop·ing, stopes**) to make stopes in a mine, or extract ore in this way [Mid-18C. Origin ?]

~~stoped~~ incorrect spelling of **stopped**

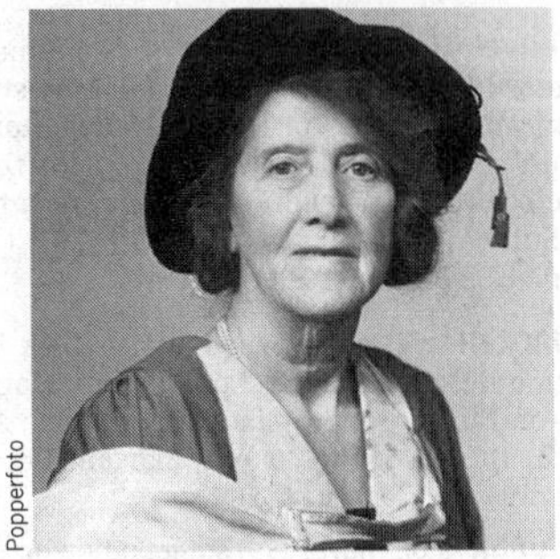

Popperfoto

Marie Stopes

Stopes /stōps/, **Marie** (1880–1958) Scottish pioneer advocate of birth control and writer. She wrote prolifically promoting scientific methodology of birth control, and established the first birth control clinic in Britain (1921). Full name **Stopes, Marie Charlotte Carmichael**

> "An impersonal and scientific knowledge of the structure of our bodies is the surest safeguard against prurient curiosity and lascivious gloating."
> [Marie Stopes, *Married Love*; 1918]

stop·gap /stóp gàp/ *n* something used as a temporary substitute for something that is needed ■ *adj* used as a temporary substitute for something that is needed ○ *a stopgap spending bill*

stop·light /stóp lìt/ *n* **1.** ROADS same as **traffic light 2.** AUTOMOT same as **brake light**

stop-off *n* TRAVEL same as **stopover**

stop or·der *n* an order to a stockbroker to buy or sell a stock when it has risen or fallen to a fixed price

stop·o·ver /stóp òvər/ *n* **1.** a usually brief halt on a journey **2.** a place where somebody makes a brief halt on a trip

stop·page /stóppij/ *n* **1.** the act of stopping the movement of something **2.** a situation in which something has been stopped or blocked ○ *a work stoppage*

Popperfoto

Sir Tom Stoppard

Stop·pard /stóppərd, stóp aard/, **Sir Tom** (*b.* 1937) Czech-born British dramatist. He had instant success with *Rosencrantz and Guildenstern are Dead* (1966). Later plays include *Arcadia* (1993). Born **Straussler, Tom**

> "Life is a gamble, at terrible odds—if it was a bet, you wouldn't take it."
> [Sir Tom Stoppard, *Rosencrantz and Guildenstern Are Dead*; 1966]

stop pay·ment *n* an order by a person or organization to a bank telling it that a check is not to be paid

stop·per /stóppər/ *n* **1. CORK OR PLUG** something that is put into an opening in order to close it **2. SOMEBODY OR SOMETHING THAT STOPS SOMETHING** somebody or something that brings something to a stop **3.** CARDS **CARD THAT PREVENTS TAKING OF SUIT** a card held by somebody that will prevent opponents from taking all the tricks in that suit during a hand of bridge **4.** BASEBALL **ACE RELIEF PITCHER** the most effective relief pitcher who is brought on to win important games (*informal*) ■ *vt* (**-pered, -per·ing, -pers**) **CLOSE SOMETHING WITH STOPPER** to close or secure something with a stopper

stop·ple /stópp'l/ *n* same as **stopper** *n* (sense 1) [15C. < STOP] —**stop·ple** *vt*

stopwatch

stop·watch /stópp wòch/ *n* a special watch that can be started and stopped instantly and is used to measure the amount of time somebody or something takes, e.g., a runner in a race

stor·age /stáwrij/ *n* **1. STORING OR BEING STORED** the act of storing something, or the condition of being stored **2. SPACE FOR STORING** space in which to store things, especially the amount of such space **3.** COMPUT **MEDIUM FOR STORING DATA** any device or medium used for deposit, retention, and retrieval of computer data, especially a hard disk or floppy disk **4.** FIN **PRICE FOR STORING** the price charged for storing something **5.** ELEC **RECHARGING OF BATTERY** the recharging of a battery

stor·age bat·ter·y *n* a rechargeable battery consisting of one or more cells for producing electrical energy from stored chemical energy

stor·age cell *n* ELECTRONICS same as **secondary cell**

stor·age dump *n* a printout of all the data held in system storage in a computer

sto·rax /stáw ràks/ *n* **1. TREE WITH DROOPING WHITE FLOWERS** a deciduous or evergreen tree or bush, some species of which are grown as ornamentals. Flowers: white, drooping in long clusters. Native to: tropical or subtropical regions. Genus: *Styrax.* **2. FRAGRANT GUM RESIN** a vanilla-scented gum resin obtained from the tree species, *Styrax officinale* **3. FRAGRANT BALSAM** a fragrant liquid balsam obtained from the bark of the Asian liquidambar tree species, *Liquidambar orientalis* [14C. Via Latin < Greek, variant of *sturax*]

store /stawr/ *v* (**stored, stor·ing, stores**) **1.** *vt* **PUT SOMETHING AWAY** to put something away for use in the future **2.** *vt* **PUT SOMETHING INTO SAFEKEEPING** to put or hold something somewhere for safekeeping, e.g., in a warehouse **3.** *vi* **SURVIVE STORAGE** to survive or stay fresh while being kept in storage ○ *Apples will store well in a cool humid building.* **4.** *vt* **STOCK SOMETHING WITH ITEMS** to fill or provide something with other things **5.** *vt* COMPUT **HOLD DATA** to enter or save data or programs into a computer memory ■ *n* **1. PLACE SELLING GOODS** a place where merchandise is offered for retail sale to customers **2. QUANTITY SAVED FOR FUTURE USE** a quantity or collection put away for future use ○ *a store of grain in a silo* **3. PLACE WHERE GOODS ARE KEPT** a place where merchandise is kept in quantity, e.g., a warehouse **4. GREAT QUANTITY** a great quantity or large collection ○ *a rich store of memories* ○ *a weapon store* ■ **stores** *npl* **SUPPLIES** items or materials needed for something such as a business, expedition, or vessel ■ *adj US* **COMMERCIALLY BOUGHT** purchased from a retail store ○ *store bread* [13C. Via Old French *estorer* "build, supply" < Latin *instaurare*] —**stor·a·ble** *adj* ◇ **in store 1.** about to happen in the future ○ *She has a surprise in store for you.* **2.** in a large amount ○ *He has come back* *with money in store.* ◇ **mind the store** to be in charge of running something, usually in the temporary absence of the person who is normally in charge (*informal*) ◇ **set** *or* **lay** *or* **put great store by something** to consider something to be important, valuable, or worthwhile

store-bought *adj* bought already made from a retail store rather than being homemade

store build·er *n* a computer program used to create a virtual storefront for a retailer

store·front /stáwr frùnt/ *n* **1.** ENTRANCE SIDE OF STORE the side of a store that faces the street or parking lot and includes the main entrance, usually having one or more large windows that display the store's goods **2.** ROOM OR BUILDING WITH STOREFRONT a room, suite of rooms, or building that has a storefront **3.** VIRTUAL STORE ON WEB a virtual store on the World Wide Web providing product information, ordering capability, and provision for secure transfer of payment ■ *adj* **1.** LOCATED ON STOREFRONT located on or near the side of the store where the main entrance is **2.** BASED IN STOREFRONT working or based in a storefront rather than in a more professional or expensive location ○ *a storefront clinic*

store·house /stáwr hòwss/ (*plural* **-hous·es** /-hòwzəz/) *n* **1.** a place where things are stored **2.** an abundant source, collection, or supply ○ *She's a storehouse of information on local history.*

store·keep·er /stáwr keepər/ *n* **1.** somebody who runs a retail store or shop, usually the owner of a small store **2.** a manager of the supplies or stores of a military unit, ship, or organization

store·room /stáwr ro͞om, -ro͝om/ *n* a room or enclosed space where things are stored

store·wide /stáwr wīd/ *adj* applying to or involving all of a department store or other retail store or its merchandise

sto·rey *n* BUILDINGS Can, UK spelling of **story**[2]

sto·reyed *adj* BUILDINGS Can, UK spelling of **storied**[2]

sto·ried[1] /stáwreed/ *adj* **1.** decorated with images of scenes from history or legend **2.** interesting, famous, or celebrated in stories and books (*literary*) ○ *the storied outlaw Robin Hood* [14C. < STORY[1]]

sto·ried[2] /stáwreed/ *adj* having stories, usually of a particular number (*often used in combination*) ○ *a multistoried shopping mall* [Early 17C. < STORY[2]]

stork

stork /stawrk/ (*plural* **storks** *or same*) *n* a large wading bird that has a long legs, a long neck, a long straight beak, and often black and white feathers. Family: Ciconiidae. [Old English *storc* < Indo-European, "stiff"]

storks·bill /stáwrks bìl/ (*plural* **-bills** *or same*) *n* a plant of the geranium family with lobed leaves and fruits with a beak-shaped tip. Flowers: pink or purple, in clusters. Genus: *Erodium.*

storm /stawrm/ *n* **1.** VIOLENT WEATHER a disturbance in the air above the Earth, with strong winds and usually also with rain, snow, sleet, or hail and sometimes lightning and thunder **2.** HEAVY RAIN OR SNOW a heavy fall of rain, snow, or sleet, often occurring with strong winds **3.** METEOROL STRONG WIND a wind of between 64 mi./103 km and 72 mi./116 km per hour, classified as force 11 on the Beaufort scale **4.** RAIN OF OBJECTS a heavy bombardment of solid objects **5.** OUTBURST OF FEELING a sudden strong outpouring of feeling in reaction to something, e.g., of protest or laughter ○ *a storm of anger* **6.** *US* BUILDINGS same as **storm window** (*informal; often used in the plural*) **7.** MIL SUDDEN STRONG ATTACK a sudden strong attack on a defended place or position ■ *v* (**stormed, storm·ing, storms**) **1.** *vti* ATTACK VIOLENTLY to attack or capture a place, especially a well-defended one, suddenly and with great force ○ *stormed the barricades* **2.** *vti* BE ANGRY OR SAY SOMETHING ANGRILY to be violently and noisily angry, or say something in this way **3.** *vi* RUSH WITH VIOLENCE OR ANGER to go somewhere in a rush, violently or angrily ○ *stormed out of the room in a huff* **4.** *vi* METEOROL BLOW WITH OR WITHOUT PRECIPITATION to blow strongly, drop large amounts of rain, snow, or sleet, or do both together [Old English < Indo-European, "to whirl"] ◇ **a storm in a teacup** *UK* a fuss over something trivial ◇ **take somebody** *or* **something by storm 1.** to capture a place or overwhelm a body of enemies suddenly and with great force **2.** to make a great and immediate impression on somebody or something ◇ **up a storm** *US* with great energy and enthusiasm or skill (*informal*) ○ *danced up a storm at the party*

storm beach *n* an accumulation of coarse sand and stones that is built up by storm action on a shore above the high-water mark

storm belt *n* a region on the surface of the Earth where there are frequent storms

storm·bound /stáwrm bòwnd/ *adj* unable to leave, go out, or get in touch with anyone because of a strong storm

storm cel·lar *n* a shelter underground used as a refuge during a windstorm

storm cen·ter *n* **1.** the central region of a cyclonic storm, with a low barometric pressure and relatively calm conditions **2.** a focus of trouble or disturbance

storm cloud *n* **1.** a large dark cloud that is a sign of approaching heavy rain or a storm **2.** a sign that violence, especially war, is soon to break out

storm col·lar *n* a thick high collar on a jacket or coat

storm door *n* a door added outside the main door of a house to provide additional protection against extreme weather

storm drain *n UK* same as **storm sewer**

storm glass *n UK* same as **weatherglass** (sense 2)

storm·ing /stáwrming/ *n* the act of suddenly and violently attacking or capturing a place

storm pet·rel *n* a small seabird with black or brown feathers and a white rump. Native to: northern Atlantic, Mediterranean. Family: Hydrobatidae. [Because the bird's appearance was thought to forebode a storm]

storm·proof /stáwrm pro͞of/ *adj* able to withstand the wind, rain, or other elements of a storm, or providing protection from them

storm sew·er *n* a large drain built to carry away excess water from a road during heavy rain

storm surge *n* a rise in sea level above the usual tide level as a hurricane or other intense storm moves over water, causing flooding when the storm comes ashore

storm-tossed *adj* subjected to or disturbed by storms

storm troop·er *n* **1.** MEMBER OF NAZI MILITIA a member of the S.A., a private militia of the Nazi Party that used tactics of violence and brutality **2.** SOLDIER OF ATTACK FORCE a member of a military shock force specially trained to carry out attacks **3.** *US* SOMEBODY LIKE NAZI STORM TROOPER a cruel, brutal, and ruthless person [< *storm troop*, translation of German *Sturmabteilung*]

storm warn·ing *n* an announcement on radio or television to alert people that a storm is imminent

storm win·dow *n* a window added outside an ordinary house window to provide additional protection against extremes of weather

storm·y /stáwrmee/ (**-i·er, -i·est**) *adj* **1.** affected by or experiencing a storm or frequent storms **2.** dominated by or subject to strong emotions or disturbances —**storm·i·ly** *adv* —**storm·i·ness** *n*

storm·y pet·rel *n* **1.** BIRDS same as **storm petrel** **2.** somebody who causes or brings trouble

Storn·o·way /stáwrnə wày/ *n Can* the name of the house that is the official residence of the leader of the political opposition in Canada

sto·ry[1] /stáwree/ *n* (*plural* **-ries**) **1.** FACTUAL OR FICTIONAL NARRATIVE a factual or fictional account of an event or series of events **2.** SHORT FICTIONAL PROSE PIECE a work of prose fiction that is shorter than a novel **3.** PLOT OF FICTION OR DRAMA the plot of a novel, play, motion picture, or other fictional narrative work **4.** ACCOUNT OF FACTS what somebody says has happened ○ *changed her story several times* **5.** FALSEHOOD something that one person tells another that is not true (*informal*) ○ *Don't give me any stories.* ○ *You're telling stories again.* **6.** MEDIA NEWS REPORT a report in the news of something that has happened **7.** MEDIA SUBJECT FOR REPORT a subject or material for a news report **8.** LITERAT LEGEND OR ROMANCE traditional tales and legends, or the literature based on such tales ■ *vt* (**-ried, -ry·ing, -ries**) DECORATE WITH LEGENDARY SCENES to decorate something with images of scenes from history or legend [13C. Via Anglo-Norman *estorie* < Latin *historia* (see HISTORY)] ◇ **a likely story** something that is probably untrue (*informal ironic*) ◇ **the same old story** what always happens or is said (*disapproving*) ◇ **to make** *or* **cut a long story short** to say something in a brief rather than a longer and more detailed way

sto·ry[2] /stáwree/ (*plural* **-ries**) *n* **1.** a floor or level in a building **2.** a set of rooms, or space, on a particular floor of a building [14C. Shortening of Anglo-Latin *historia* < Latin (see HISTORY)]

Sto·ry /stáwree/, **Joseph** (1779–1845) associate justice of the US Supreme Court (1811–45). He was known for his antislavery opinions and wrote many legal works.

sto·ry·board /stáwree bàwrd/ *n* a set of sketches, arranged in sequence on panels, outlining the scenes that will make up something to be filmed, e.g., a motion picture, television show, or advertisement

sto·ry·book /stáwree bo͝ok/ *n* a book of stories for children ■ *adj* characteristic of or like something found in children's stories rather than the real world

sto·ry line *n* ARTS same as **story**[1] *n* (sense 3)

sto·ry·tell·er /stáwree tèllər/ *n* **1.** a teller or writer of stories **2.** somebody who tells lies (*informal*) —**sto·ry·tell·ing** *n*

stoss /stoss, stawss, shtōss/ *adj* describes a mountain, hill, or slope that faces the direction of an oncoming glacier [Late 19C. < German, "a thrust, push"]

sto·tin /sto teén/ *n* a subunit of Slovenian currency. See table at **currency** [< Slovene, "hundredth"]

sto·tin·ka /stō tíngkə/ (*plural* **-ki** /-kee/) *n* a subunit of Bulgarian currency. See table at **currency** [Late 19C. < Bulgarian, "hundredth"]

Stough·ton /stówt'n/ town in eastern Massachusetts, south of Boston and northwest of Brockton. Population: 27,227 (2002 estimate).

stoup /stoop/, **stoop** *n* a basin for holy water in a church [14C. < Old Norse *staup* "drinking vessel"]

stout /stowt/ *adj* **1.** THICKSET OR HEAVY thicker and heavier in body than an average person of the same height **2.** COURAGEOUS AND DETERMINED possessing or showing courage and determination **3.** STRONG strong and substantial ○ *stout footwear* **4.** STRONG IN STRUCTURE strong and substantial in structure ■ *n* **1.** BEVERAGES DARK STRONG BEER a strong, very dark, almost black beer made from roasted malted barley **2.** *US* CLOTHING SIZE OF GARMENT FOR LARGE PERSON a size of clothing that fits somebody who is heavier than average, or a garment in such a size **3.** *US* STOUT PERSON a person who is thicker-waisted and heavier than average [13C. < Anglo-Norman < Germanic] —**stout·ish** *adj* —**stout·ly** *adv* —**stout·ness** *n*

stout·en /stówt'n/ (**-ened, -en·ing, -ens**) *vti* to become stout or stouter, or make somebody or something stout or stouter

stout·heart·ed /stòwt haártəd/ *adj* having or showing courage and resolution —**stout·heart·ed·ly** *adv* —**stout·heart·ed·ness** *n*

stove[1] /stōv/ *n* **1.** APPLIANCE FOR COOKING OR HEATING an appliance that uses electricity, gas, or solid fuel to produce heat for cooking or for heating **2.** HEAT-PRODUCING CHAMBER OR DEVICE a chamber or device that is used to heat or dry something, e.g., a kiln ■ *vt* (**stoved, stov·ing, stoves**) INDUST **HEAT SOMETHING IN STOVE** to treat something by heating it in a stove in order to coat it with a surface such as enamel [15C. Probably < Middle Dutch or Middle Low German, "heated room"]

stove[2] /stōv/ past participle, past tense of **stave**

stove·pipe /stṓv pīp/ *n* **1.** a pipe used as a chimney for a fuel-burning stove, usually made of sheet steel formed into a tube **2.** CLOTHING same as **stovepipe hat**

stove·pipe hat *n* a tall tube-shaped silk hat for a man

stove·pi·ping /stṓv pīping/ *n* a rigidly vertical management style that discourages lateral lines of responsibility and hinders communication among individual groups within a corporate or government structure [Early 21C. < the vertical arrangement of a stovepipe]

sto·ver /stṓvər/ *n US* leaves and stalks of corn that are left in a field after harvesting and are dried for use as fodder [Mid-17C. < Anglo-Norman *estover*, variant of Old French *estoveir* "be necessary" < Latin *est opus* "it is necessary"]

stow /stō/ (**stowed, stow·ing, stows**) *vt* **1. PUT SOMETHING AWAY NEATLY** to pack something or put something away, especially when the result is neat and orderly **2. FILL SOMETHING WITH TIGHTLY PACKED THINGS** to fill something with other things, especially things packed tightly ○ *to stow a boat's hold with cargo* **3. STORE SOMETHING FOR LATER USE** to store something for use in the future **4. HOLD SOMETHING** to be capable of containing something **5. STOP SOMETHING** to stop doing something (*slang*) ○ *Stow this silly chatter.* **6. LODGE SOMEBODY TEMPORARILY** to find a room or a place for somebody to stay, often for only a short time [14C. < Old English *stōw* "place" < Germanic, "to stand"]
stow away *vi* to hide on a ship or aircraft in the hope of being taken somewhere without having to pay

stow·age /stṓ ij/ *n* **1. STOWING OF THINGS** the loading, packing, or storing of something, or a way of doing this **2. SITUATION OR ARRANGEMENT OF THINGS PACKED** the condition of being stowed, or the arrangement of things stowed **3. THINGS STOWED** something that is stowed somewhere or is to be stowed **4. PLACE OR SPACE FOR STOWING** a place, container, or space for stowing things **5. FEE FOR STOWING** a fee or fees for stowing something

stow·a·way /stṓ ə wày/ *n* somebody who hides on a ship or aircraft in the hope of being taken somewhere without paying

Stowe /stō/, **Emily Howard** (1831–1903) Canadian doctor. She was the first Canadian woman to practice medicine in Canada. She founded Woman's Medical College in Toronto (1883). Born **Jennings, Emily**

Library of Congress
Harriet Beecher Stowe

Stowe, Harriet Beecher (1811–96) US writer and abolitionist. She is best known for her antislavery novel *Uncle Tom's Cabin* (1852). Born **Beecher, Harriet Elizabeth**. See Cultural note at **cabin**

"The bitterest tears shed over graves are for words left unsaid and deeds left undone."
[Harriet Beecher Stowe, *Little Foxes*; 1865]

STP *abbr* PHYS standard temperature and pressure

STR *abbr* BROADCAST synchronous transmitter receiver

str. *abbr* **1.** TRANSP steamer **2.** *also* **Str.** GEOG strait **3.** MUSIC stringed **4.** MUSIC strings **5.** stroke **6.** LITERAT strophe

stra·bis·mus /strə bízməss/ *n* OPHTHALMOL same as **squint** (*technical*) [Late 17C. Via modern Latin < Greek *strabismos* < *strabizein* "to squint" < *strabos* "squinting"] —**stra·bis·mal** *adj* —**stra·bis·mic** *adj* —**stra·bis·mi·cal** *adj*

Stra·chey /stráychee/, **Lytton** (1880–1932) British writer. A member of the Bloomsbury Group, he wrote *Eminent Victorians* (1918) and other biographies known for illuminating the personality of their subjects. Full name **Strachey, Giles Lytton**

Strad /strad/ *n* a Stradivarius violin (*informal*) [Late 19C. Shortening]

strad·dle /strádd'l/ *v* (**-dled, -dling, -dles**) **1.** *vt* **SIT OR STAND ASTRIDE SOMETHING** to sit or stand so that one leg is on one side and the other leg is on the other side of something or somebody **2.** *vt* **EXTEND TO OTHER SIDE OF SOMETHING** to extend across something or be divided by something and have parts on both sides of it ○ *The city straddles the river.* **3.** *vt* **APPLY TO MORE THAN ONE THING** to exist in, belong to, or apply to more than one situation or category ○ *The rule of the dynasty straddled the end of one century and the beginning of the next.* **4.** *vt* **SPREAD LEGS APART** to spread your legs apart, usually so that they are on both sides of something **5.** *vi* **SIT OR WALK WITH LEGS APART** to sit, stand, or walk with your legs spread apart or on each side of something **6.** *vti US* **FAVOR BOTH SIDES** to appear to favor both sides of an issue, or resist committing to one side or the other **7.** *vt* MIL **FIRE SHELLS FOR RANGE** to fire a salvo of artillery shells at a target so that some fall in front of it and some behind it, in order to find the correct range ■ *n* **1. POSITION ASTRIDE OR ACROSS SOMETHING** a position in which somebody or something is astride or on both sides of something **2. ACT OF STRADDLING** an act of putting one leg on each side of something **3.** *US* **NONCOMMITTAL POSITION** a position on an issue that seems to favor both sides or resists committing to one side or the other **4.** FIN **STOCK TRANSACTION** the simultaneous holding of options to buy and sell a commodity or security at a set price during a specific period of time, ensuring a profit whether the values rises or falls [Mid-16C. Probably variant of obsolete *striddle* "keep striding" < earlier form of STRIDE] —**strad·dler** *n*

Stra·di·va·ri /stràddə vérree, -vaáree/, **Antonio** (1644–1737) Italian violin maker. The instruments that he produced, including violas and cellos, are among the most highly prized in the world.

Strad·i·var·i·us /stràddə vérree əss/ *n* a violin or other stringed instrument that was made by the Italian violin maker Antonio Stradivari or his sons [Mid-19C. Latinized form of STRADIVARI]

strafe /strayf/ *vt* (**strafed, straf·ing, strafes**) to attack a position or troops on the ground with machine-gun or cannon fire from a low-flying aircraft ■ *n* a machine-gun or cannon attack by low-flying aircraft on a ground target [Early 20C. < German *strafen* "punish"] —**straf·er** *n*

strag·gle /strágg'l/ *vi* (**-gled, -gling, -gles**) **1. STRAY FROM GROUP** to lag behind, wander away from, or become separated from a group ○ *rounding up steers that had straggled from the main herd* **2. COME OR GO WITHOUT A PATTERN** to move, come, or go in an irregular or disorganized way, usually in ones or twos ○ *People were still straggling in half an hour after the meeting had started.* **3. BECOME SCATTERED** to be or become spread out irregularly over a wide area ○ *primitive shanties straggling over the dunes* **4. GROW MESSILY** to grow or hang in a messy or irregular way, often in separate disorderly strands or wisps ○ *The roses had been allowed to straggle across the path.* ○ *A few gray wisps straggled from underneath his cap.* ■ *n* **STRAGGLED GROUP OR ARRANGEMENT** a disorganized, scattered, or messy group or arrangement [15C. Origin ?] —**strag·gling** *adj* —**strag·gly** *adj*

strag·gler /strágg'lər/ *n* somebody or something that straggles, especially a person or animal that lags behind or becomes separated from a group ○ *fell behind to wait for the stragglers*

straight /strayt/ *adj* **1. NOT CURVED** extending or proceeding in one single direction, without bends, curves, irregularities, or deviations **2. LEVEL** level, even, or properly positioned ○ *Your tie isn't straight.* **3. ACCURATE** accurate or correct ○ *You can rely on her for the straight figures.* **4. CANDID** making no attempt to deceive or to soften the truth ○ *give a straight answer* ○ *Are you being straight with me?* **5. HONEST** honest, fair, and upright ○ *straight dealings* **6. NEAT** in a neat and orderly state with things properly arranged or cleared away ○ *Make sure the room's straight before the guests arrive.* **7. CONSISTENT** not straying from agreed or published principles or policies ○ *the straight party line* **8. CONSECUTIVE** following one after another, without interruption ○ *The team celebrated its tenth straight win.* **9. NOT DILUTED** not diluted or mixed with any other drink ○ *straight whiskey* **10. NOT FUNNY** not intended to be funny or unconventional ○ *playing both straight and comic roles* **11. WITH UNBENT ARM** delivered with the arm unbent ○ *a straight left to the body* **12.** *US* **NOT DISCOUNTED** not sold at a reduced price regardless of how many are bought **13.** same as **heterosexual** (*informal*) **14. CONVENTIONAL** unremarkable or conventional in outlook, style, or way of life (*informal*) ○ *gave up being a rock musician and got a straight job* **15. NOT USING DRUGS** not using or addicted to drugs (*slang*) ■ *adv* **1. WITHOUT BENDING** without bending, curving, or diverging from a course **2. IMMEDIATELY** without delay or detour ○ *She went straight home.* **3. IN LEVEL POSITION** in a level, even, or proper position ○ *Put your hat on straight.* **4. CLEARLY** clearly and correctly or logically ○ *I can't think straight with all this noise going on.* **5. CANDIDLY** without any attempt to deceive or soften the truth ○ *Give it to me straight.* **6. INTO NEAT CONDITION** in or into a neat and orderly condition ○ *We'll have to put the place straight after the party.* **7. WITH NO INTERRUPTION** one after another, without interruption ○ *three nights straight* **8. WITHOUT BEING DILUTED** without being diluted or mixed with any other drink **9. WITHOUT BEING FUNNY** without trying to be funny or unconventional ○ *She decided to play the role straight.* ■ *n* **1. SOMETHING STRAIGHT** something that is straight, e.g., a line **2. FIVE CARDS IN SEQUENCE** in poker, a hand in which the cards form a continuous sequence but are not all of the same suit **3.** *Can, UK* SPORTS same as **straightaway** *n* (sense 1) **4.** ROADS same as **straightaway** *n* (sense 2) **5.** same as **heterosexual** (*informal*) **6. CONVENTIONAL PERSON** somebody who has a conventional outlook, style, or way of life (*informal*) **7.** *US* **CIGARETTE WITHOUT FILTER** a cigarette with no filter [14C. Old past participle of STRETCH] —**straight·ish** *adj* —**straight·ly** *adv* —**straight·ness** *n* ◇ **go straight** to give up being a criminal and start living within the law (*informal*) ◇ **put** *or* **set somebody straight** to make somebody understand the reality of a situation

USAGE straight or **strait**? Do not confuse ***straight*** with ***strait***, which has the same pronunciation and similar spelling but is unrelated in origin. ***Straight*** is an adjective meaning "not curved," as in *a straight line*; ***strait*** is a noun denoting a narrow body of water or a difficult situation, as in *dire straits*. ***Strait*** was formerly used as an adjective meaning "narrow, confined" or "strict," but these senses survive only in derived or combined forms such as *straitened*, *straitjacket*, and *strait-laced*. *Straitened*, meaning "restricted," is used chiefly in the phrase *straitened circumstances* and should not be confused with *straightened*, meaning "made straight." *Straitjacket* and *strait-laced* have the alternate spellings *straightjacket* and *straight-laced*.

straight-a·head *adj US* showing little variation from what is usual or typical ○ *straight-ahead Italian opera*

straight and nar·row *n* the orthodox and law-abiding way to live life (*informal*)

straight an·gle *n* an angle of 180°

straight-arm *vt* **1. PUSH OPPONENT AWAY WITH OUTSTRETCHED ARM** in football, to push an opponent away with the arm stretched fully out and the hand upturned and stiff **2.** *US* **WARD OFF OR TURN ASIDE** to ward somebody off or turn somebody aside with or as if with an outstretched arm ■ *n US* **ACT OF STRAIGHT-ARMING SOMEBODY** an act or instance of straight-arming somebody

straight ar·row *n* somebody who is honest and upright (*informal*) —**straight-ar·row** *adj*

straight·a·way /stráyt ə wày/ *adv* **AT ONCE** immediately and without hesitation ■ *n* **1.** *US* **STRAIGHT TRACK** a part of a racetrack that does not bend **2. STRAIGHT ROAD** a straight stretch of highway ■ *adj US* **WITHOUT CURVES** following a straight course, without any turns or curves

straight chain *n* an open chain of atoms in a molecule that has no side branches

straight·edge /stráyt ėj/ *n* a rigid strip of wood, metal, or plastic used to draw a straight line or to check for straightness

straight·en /stráyt'n/ (**-ened, -en·ing, -ens**) *vti* to make something straight, or become straight —**straight·en·er** *n*

straighten out *vti* **1.** to make something straight, or become straight ○ *The road straightens out after this next bend.* **2.** to make something clear or satisfactory, or become clear or satisfactory ○ *I want to straighten things out between us.*

straighten up *v* **1.** *vti* to stand up straight, or make somebody stand up straight **2.** *vt* to make something neat and orderly

straight·er /stráytər/ *n W Africa* somebody who repairs the bodies of vehicles damaged in accidents, especially by beating out dents

straight face *n* a serious expression on somebody's face that does not betray the fact that he or she really wants to laugh —**straight-faced** *adj* —**straight-faced·ly** /stràyt fáystlee, -fáyssədlee/ *adv*

straight flush *n* in poker, a hand in which all the cards are of the same suit and form a continuous sequence

straight·for·ward /stràyt fáwrwərd/ *adj* **1.** EASY not difficult to understand or carry out **2.** FRANK truthful and to the point **3.** STRAIGHT OR DIRECT following a straight or direct path ■ *adv also* **straight·for·wards** /-wərdz/ IN STRAIGHTFORWARD WAY in a straightforward way or direction —**straight·for·ward·ly** *adv* —**straight·for·ward·ness** *n*

SYNONYMS See *easy.*

straight·jack·et *n, vt* another spelling of **straitjacket**

straight-line *adj* **1.** *US* HAPPENING IN STRAIGHT LINE in, happening along, or measured along a straight line ○ *straight-line motion* ○ *a straight-line extrapolation of growth* **2.** *US* MECH ENG LAID OUT IN A STRAIGHT LINE having components that are arranged in a straight line **3.** MOVING IN STRAIGHT LINE designed to move or transmit motion in a straight line **4.** ALLOCATED AT A FIXED RATE prorated over a given term in equal amounts payable or deductible at specified intervals ○ *straight-line depreciation*

straight man *n* a comedian whose role is to say or do things that allow another comedian to deliver a punch line or make witty or humorous comments in response

straight off *adv* right away or at once (*informal*)

straight-out *adj* (*informal*) **1.** showing directness or bluntness ○ *a straight-out refusal* **2.** *US* complete and unmitigated ○ *a straight-out jerk*

straight pok·er *n* poker in which each player is dealt five cards and no more cards can be drawn

straight ra·zor *n* a razor with a single straight blade that is hinged to a slotted handle into which the blade can be folded when not in use

straight shoot·er *n* somebody who is honest, frank, and ethical (*informal*)

straight stitch *n* a simple stitch that forms a straight line on the surface of a fabric

straight-talk·ing *adj* direct and straightforward in dealing with others

straight tick·et *n US* a ballot cast for all the candidates of the same political party

straight-to-vid·e·o *adj* released only in video format rather than shown in movie theaters

straight up *adv US* served as a cocktail without any ice

straight·way /stráyt wày/ *adv US* **1.** at once and without delay **2.** by a direct route

strain[1] /strayn/ *v* (**strained, strain·ing, strains**) **1.** *vi* MAKE EXTREME EFFORT to have to make an unusually great or even painful physical or mental effort in order to do something ○ *The office strained to complete the work on time.* ○ *strained to hear the speaker* **2.** *vi* PULL VIOLENTLY to pull at or push against something, especially an obstacle or restraint, with great force or violence ○ *straining at the leash* **3.** *vt* MAKE GREAT DEMANDS ON SOMETHING to make something seem barely adequate to meet the demands placed on it ○ *a story that strains credulity* ○ *Taking on more debt would strain our resources to the limit.* **4.** *vti* MAKE SOMETHING LESS CORDIAL to make a relationship less friendly or more difficult, or become less friendly or more difficult ○ *The recent crisis has strained relations between the two countries.* **5.** *vt* INJURE SOMETHING to damage a part of the body through using it too hard or too much **6.** *vti* PULL OR STRETCH TIGHT to pull or stretch something until it is tight, or be pulled or stretched until tight **7.** *vti* PASS SOMETHING THROUGH STRAINER to pass something, or be passed, through a mesh or filter to remove solids or larger particles ○ *Strain the stock and return it to the pan.* **8.** *vt* REMOVE SOMETHING USING STRAINER to separate part of something from the rest using a strainer **9.** *vt* HUG SOMEBODY to hold somebody closely and tightly (*literary*) **10.** *vt* PHYS DEFORM STRUCTURE to deform a body or material by applying an external force to it ■ *n* **1.** STRESS intense demand on body, mind, or resources that can only be met with great effort ○ *under considerable strain* ○ *It's the strain of living with him day after day that's wearing me out.* **2.** DEMAND THAT CAUSES STRESS something that places great demands on somebody or something, or makes something seem barely adequate ○ *unexpected expenses that are a strain on our budget* **3.** GREAT EXERTION a great or extremely taxing exertion or effort ○ *It was a real strain to lift it but we managed it.* **4.** PHYSICAL INJURY an injury to a part of the body caused by excessive use or by a twisting or stretching of muscles or tendons beyond their normal range **5.** ACT OF FILTERING an act of passing something through a strainer **6.** PULLING FORCE a pulling or stretching force exerted on something ○ *the strain on the rope* **7.** PHYS DEFORMATION OF STRUCTURE the deformation of a body or material caused by applying an external force to it [14C. Via Old French *estreindre* "draw tight" < Latin *stringere* "draw tight, bind"]

strain[2] /strayn/ *n* **1.** LINE OF ANCESTRY a line of ancestry or a group of descendants from a common ancestor **2.** SUBGROUP OF ORGANISM a subgroup of a species of organism distinguished by specific characteristics, sometimes developed by breeders for those characteristics **3.** INHERITED QUALITY OR TRAIT an inherited tendency, character, or trait **4.** TRACE a trace of a particular and often unexpected quality or tone ○ *glimpsed a strain of impatience* **5.** CHARACTER OR MOOD the style, character, mood, or theme of something **6.** MUSIC MUSICAL THEME a musical theme or melody **7.** ELOQUENT LANGUAGE OR WORDS language that is eloquent, passionate, poetic, or otherwise heightened [Old English *strēon* "offspring," originally "gain" < Indo-European, "to spread flat"]

strained /straynd/ *adj* **1.** TENSE characterized by tension and covert hostility ○ *relations already strained by trade disputes* **2.** NOT NATURAL not natural or spontaneous but done with effort ○ *a strained smile* **3.** PASSED THROUGH STRAINER having been passed through a strainer to separate out solids or large particles

strain·er /stráynər/ *n* **1.** a device, usually incorporating a mesh or other filter, for separating solids from liquids or small particles from large **2.** *US* a device that is used to tighten or stretch something

strain gauge *n* **1.** a device that measures pressure or stress, using the change of electrical resistance in a wire that is subjected to the same stress as the object being measured **2.** *US* ENG same as **extensometer**

strain·ing beam, strain·ing piece *n* a horizontal beam that connects the tops of two vertical posts (**queen posts**) in a roof truss

strait /strayt/ *n* (*often used in the plural*) **1.** CHANNEL JOINING LARGE BODIES OF WATER a narrow body of water that joins two larger bodies of water **2.** DIFFICULT SITUATION a situation that is difficult or involves hardship ○ *The collapse of the stock market put many brokers in serious financial straits.* ■ *adj* (*archaic*) **1.** NARROW OR CONFINED narrow or with very little room **2.** STRICT OR RIGID very strict or severe [14C. Via Old French *estreit* < Latin *strictus* "narrow," past participle of *stringere* "draw tight, bind"] —**strait·ly** *adv* —**strait·ness** *n*

USAGE See *straight.*

strait·ened /stráyt'nd/ *adj* made very difficult, restricted, or narrow ○ *had lost all their money and were living in straitened circumstances*

USAGE See *straight.*

strait·jack·et /stráyt jàkət/, **straight·jack·et** *n* **1.** CONFINING JACKET-SHAPED GARMENT a jacket-shaped garment with long sleeves that can be tied together, used to restrict the arm movements of somebody who is thought to be dangerous **2.** THING THAT RESTRICTS something that limits somebody's freedom of action or initiative ○ *a bureaucratic straitjacket of regulations* ■ *vt* (**-et·ed, -et·ing, -ets**) **1.** PUT STRAITJACKET ON SOMEBODY to put somebody into a straitjacket to restrict arm movements **2.** RESTRICT SOMEBODY to limit somebody's freedom of action or initiative

USAGE See *straight.*

strait-laced, straight-laced *adj* **1.** prudish, or very strict in morals **2.** *US* tightly laced, or tightly laced into a garment —**strait-lac·ed·ly** /stràyt láyssədlee, -láystlee/ *adv* —**strait-lac·ed·ness** /-láyssədnəss/ *n*

USAGE See *straight.*

strake /strayk/ *n* a continuous band of wooden planks or metal plates along the hull of a boat or ship [15C. < assumed Old English *straca* < Germanic, "rigid"]

stra·mo·ni·um /strə mṓnee əm/ *n* a preparation of dried leaves and flowers of the jimsonweed containing alkaloids. Use: formerly, as a medicine. [Mid-17C. < modern Latin]

strand[1] /strand/ *n* LAND AT WATER'S EDGE a strip of land along the edge of a body of water ■ *v* (**strand·ed, strand·ing, strands**) **1.** *vti* RUN SOMETHING AGROUND to leave or run a ship or sea animal aground, or be left or driven aground **2.** *vt* LEAVE SOMEBODY IN DIFFICULTY to put or leave somebody in a difficult or helpless position (*often passive*) ○ *stranded without any means of getting home* **3.** *vt* BASEBALL LEAVE SOMEBODY ON BASE in baseball, to leave a base runner on a base at the end of an inning [Old English, origin ?] —**strand·ed** *adj*

strand[2] /strand/ *n* **1.** SINGLE FILAMENT a single fiber, wire, or thread, especially one of several braided or twisted together to form something such as a rope or cable **2.** LENGTH OF ROPE a length of something such as rope or cotton, made from braided or twisted filaments **3.** HUMAN HAIR OR HAIRS a human hair, or a tress of hair **4.** LENGTH OF TISSUE RESEMBLING THREAD a length of animal, plant, or mineral fiber or tissue that resembles a thread **5.** STRING OF BEADS a length of strung pearls or beads, especially when twisted like a rope **6.** ELEMENT OF WHOLE an element that with others makes up a larger complex whole ■ *vt* (**strand·ed, strand·ing, strands**) MAKE SOMETHING BY INTERWEAVING to make something such as a rope or cable by braiding or twisting together fibers or filaments ○ *to strand a rope* [15C. Origin ?]

strand·ed cot·ton /strándəd-/ *n* an embroidery cotton made up of six strands of thread loosely twisted together

strand·line /stránd lìn/ *n* a shoreline, especially an earlier shoreline above the present one

strange /straynj/ *adj* (**strang·er, strang·est**) **1.** UNEXPECTED OR EXTRAORDINARY not expected, usual, or ordinary ○ *That's a strange time to hold a wedding.* **2.** UNFAMILIAR not known or experienced previously ○ *There seemed to be a lot of strange faces in the audience.* **3.** HARD TO EXPLAIN difficult to explain or understand ○ *It's strange that they never thought to mention this before.* **4.** UNACCUSTOMED not yet used to or familiar with something ○ *strange to these new surroundings* **5.** ILL AT EASE uncomfortable, embarrassed, or slightly sick ○ *I've been feeling a little strange since I took the medicine.* **6.** EXOTIC from a different place or environment, or of a different kind **7.** RESERVED reserved or distant in manner **8.** PHYS SHOWING QUANTUM CHARACTERISTIC OF STRANGENESS showing or having the quantum characteristic of strangeness ■ *adv* IN UNUSUAL WAY in a strange way (*nonstandard*) [13C. Via Old French *estrange* < Latin *extraneus* "foreign" < *extra*, form of *exter* "outside"]

strange·ly /stráynjlee/ *adv* **1.** in an unusual or puzzling way ○ *You've been strangely quiet this evening.* **2.** used to indicate that the speaker finds something odd or puzzling ○ *Strangely, they seemed to have no firm plan of action.*

strange·ness /stráynjnəss/ *n* **1.** the condition or quality of being strange **2.** a quantum characteristic of some elementary particles that is conserved in strong and electromagnetic, but not weak, interactions and has a value (**strangeness number**) of zero for most particles

strange·ness num·ber *n* the value of the quantum characteristic of strangeness, equal to the hypercharge minus the baryon number

strange par·ti·cle *n* an elementary particle having a strangeness number other than zero [Because such particles' long lifetimes were hard to explain]

strange quark *n* a quark that has an electric charge equal to $-\frac{1}{3}$ that of the electron and a strangeness number of –1

strang·er /stráynjər/ *n* **1.** UNFAMILIAR PERSON somebody whom somebody else does not know **2.** NEWCOMER somebody who is new to a place **3.** OUTSIDER somebody who does not belong to a specific organization or group **4.** VISITOR OR GUEST somebody who does not live in a specific house or community but is a visitor or guest **5.** PERSON UNACCUSTOMED TO SOMETHING somebody who is not familiar or acquainted with a particular thing ○ *Being a stranger to hard physical work, he found the job exhausting.* **6.** ALIENATED PERSON somebody who has become distanced or alienated from somebody or something ○ *She is a stranger to her former colleagues.* **7.** PERSON NOT PRIVY TO TRANSACTION somebody who is neither privy nor party to a transaction [14C. < Old French *estrangier* < *estrange* "foreign" (see STRANGE)]

CULTURAL NOTE ***The Stranger***, a novel by French writer Albert Camus (1942). This classic existentialist work is also known as *The Outsider.* Set in Algiers, it recounts how a young man's extreme sense of alienation leads him to commit murder. During his trial, however, the absurdities of the judicial process compel him to acknowledge the value of human life.

strang·er crime, **strang·er-on-strang·er crime** *n* crimes of violence in which the perpetrator is somebody whom the victim does not know

stran·gle /stráng g'l/ (**-gled, -gling, -gles**) *v* **1.** *vti* KILL OR DIE BY CHOKING to kill a person or an animal by squeezing the throat and cutting off oxygen to the lungs, or die in this way **2.** *vi* CHOKE to choke or suffocate **3.** *vti* SUPPRESS UTTERANCE to suppress the utterance of a sound, or be suppressed ○ *strangled a sob* **4.** *vti* STIFLE OR BE STIFLED IN DEVELOPMENT to hinder or stop the growth or development of something, or be hindered or stopped ○ *Businesses say the high interest rates are strangling the economy.* [13C. Via Old French *estrangler* < Latin *strangulare* (see STRANGULATE)] —**stran·gler** *n*

stran·gle·hold /stráng g'l hōld/ *n* **1.** power over something or somebody that is complete and prevents any movement or change **2.** in wrestling, an illegal hold that chokes an opponent

stran·gler fig *n* a fig that germinates in the crown of another tree, which it envelops with aerial roots and eventually kills. Native to: Caribbean, Florida.

stran·gles /stráng g'lz/ *n* an infectious disease of horses in which they experience inflammation and abscesses of the mucous membranes of the respiratory tract, causing strangling. It is caused by the bacterium *Streptococcus equi.* (*takes a singular verb*)

stran·gu·late /stráng gyə làyt/ (**-lat·ed, -lat·ing, -lates**) *v* **1.** *vt* to strangle a person or animal **2.** *vti* to constrict an organ or duct of the body, or become constricted, so as to stop the flow of a fluid [Mid-17C. Via Latin *strangulare* < Greek *straggalan* < *straggalē* "halter, cord"] —**stran·gu·la·tion** /stràng gyə láysh'n/ *n*

stran·gu·ry /stráng gyəree/ *n* painful and slow urination caused by spasms that make urine come out drop by drop [14C. Via Latin < Greek *straggouria* < *stragx* "drop" + *ouron* "urine"]

strap /strap/ *n* **1.** FLEXIBLE STRIP USED FOR BINDING a narrow flexible strip of a material such as leather, plastic, or metal, used to bind or secure something **2.** LOOP OF MATERIAL USED AS HANDLE a loop of flexible material by which something such as a bag can be carried **3.** STRIP OF MATERIAL HOLDING UP GARMENT a thin strip of material that forms part of a garment and passes over the shoulder **4.** LOOP TO HOLD ON TO a hanging loop of material in a bus or train for standing passengers to hold onto for support **5.** STROP a strop for sharpening a straight razor **6.** LEATHER STRIP FOR FLOGGING a long narrow strip of leather used for flogging or beating ■ *vt* (**strapped, strap·ping, straps**) **1.** SECURE SOMETHING WITH STRAP to secure or bind somebody or something with a strap ○ *strapped his son into the back seat* **2.** *UK* MED same as **tape** *v* (sense 3) **3.** BEAT SOMEBODY WITH STRAP to beat or flog somebody with a strap **4.** SHARPEN RAZOR to sharpen a straight razor on a strop [Early 17C. Originally a Scottish dialect form of STROP]

strap up *vt UK* MED same as **tape** *v* (sense 4)

strap·hang·er /stráp hàngər/ *n* (*informal*) **1.** a passenger who stands while riding a bus or train and holds onto a strap that is suspended from the roof **2.** *US* a rider or commuter on a bus, subway, or another form of public transportation

strap hinge *n* a hinge with a flap fastened to the exposed surface of a door, lid, or gate

strap·less /strápləss/ *adj* without shoulder straps or covering ■ *n* a woman's garment that does not have shoulder straps or covering

strap·pa·do /strə páydō, -paàdō/ (*plural* **-does**) *n* **1.** a form of torture in which somebody is hoisted by a rope around the wrists, which are bound behind the back, and then dropped and jerked to a stop before reaching the ground **2.** a device used in strappado [Mid-16C. Alteration of French *(e)strapade* < Italian *strappata* < *strappare*, origin ?]

strapped /strapt/ *adj* in need of money (*informal*) ○ *strapped for cash*

strap·per /strápper/ *n* somebody who is big and powerfully built (*informal*)

strap·ping /strápping/ *adj* ROBUST tall and powerfully built (*informal*) ■ *n* **1.** STRAPS straps in general, or a set of straps **2.** MATERIAL FOR STRAPS material for making straps or for use as straps

strap·py /stráppee/ (**-pi·er, -pi·est**) *adj* with straps, especially when they are an important part of the look or design of something (*informal*) ○ *strappy sandals*

strap work *n* decorative work in the form of crossing or interlaced bands on the outside of a building, especially in Tudor architecture

Stras·berg /stráss bùrg/, **Lee** (1901–82) Austro-Hungarian-born US actor and teacher. Following the theories of Stanislavsky, he developed and taught the influential Method Acting technique. Born **Strassberg, Israel**

Stras·bourg /stráz bùrg/ capital city of Bas-Rhin Department, Alsace Region, northeastern France. It is the site of the headquarters of the European Parliament and the Council of Europe. Population: 264,115 (1999).

strass /strass/ *n* same as **paste**[1] *n* (sense 5) [Early 19C. < German, after Joseph *Strasser*, 18C German jeweler]

Strass·man /stráss màn/, **Fritz** (1902–80) German chemist. With physical chemist Otto Hahn he was responsible for the discovery of nuclear fission (1938).

stra·ta plural of **stratum**

strat·a·gem /stráttəjəm/ *n* **1.** CLEVER SCHEME a clever ruse or scheme that is designed to deceive others or achieve a goal **2.** RUSE FOR DECEIVING ENEMY a military tactic or maneuver that is designed to deceive an enemy **3.** USE OF CLEVER SCHEMES the use of stratagems, or skill in using stratagems [15C. Via French < Greek *stratēgēma* < *stratēgos* "general" (see STRATEGY)]

~~stratagy~~ incorrect spelling of **strategy**

stra·te·gic /strə teéjik/, **stra·te·gi·cal** /-ik'l/ *adj* **1.** TYPICAL OF STRATEGY relating to, involving, or typical of strategy or a strategy ○ *strategic planning* **2.** DONE FOR REASONS OF STRATEGY necessary to a strategy, or done because a strategy requires it ○ *a strategic retreat* **3.** DISPLAYING SOUND STRATEGY displaying a sound strategy or plan of action ○ *showing strategic timing in selling a stock short* **4.** MIL DESTROYING ENEMY'S FIGHTING CAPACITY done with the intention of destroying an enemy's military capability ○ *strategic bombing* **5.** MIL NECESSARY FOR FIGHTING WAR necessary for fighting a war, or essential to the military forces fighting a war ○ *strategic metals* ○ *strategic air bases*

stra·te·gi·cal·ly /strə teéjikəlee/ *adv* **1.** as part of, or in a way useful to, a strategy **2.** in a clever or useful way

Stra·te·gic De·fense In·i·tia·tive *n* a planned US system of defense against nuclear attack in which incoming missiles would be destroyed by laser weapons mounted in satellites or by antimissile missiles

strategic hamlet *n* during the Vietnam War, a fortified South Vietnamese village designed to protect its inhabitants from attacks launched by the Viet Cong or the North Vietnamese army

stra·te·gic plan·ning *n* the planning of all the activities of a business to ensure competitive advantage and profitability

stra·te·gics /strə teéjiks/ *n* the science or art of military strategy (*takes a singular verb*)

strat·e·gist /stráttəjist/ *n* somebody who develops and executes strategy

strat·e·gize /stráttə jīz/ (**-gized, -giz·ing, -giz·es**) *vi* to plan or decide on a strategy

strat·e·gy /stráttəjee/ (*plural* **-gies**) *n* **1.** PLANNING IN ANY FIELD a carefully devised plan of action to achieve a goal, or the art of developing or carrying out such a plan ○ *business strategy* **2.** MIL PLANNING OF WAR the science or art of planning and conducting a war or a military campaign **3.** BIOL ADAPTATION IMPORTANT TO EVOLUTIONARY SUCCESS in evolutionary theory, a behavior, structure, or other adaptation that improves viability [Early 19C. Via French *stratégie* < Greek *stratēgia* "generalship" < *stratēgos* "general" < *stratos* "army" + *agein* "to lead"]

stra·te·gy game *n* a computer game, e.g., a war game, in which a player makes overall decisions rather than assuming the role of a specific character

Strat·ford /strátfərd/ **1.** city on the Avon River in southeastern Ontario, Canada. It is home to the annual Stratford Festival, founded in 1953 to present Shakespeare's plays and other arts events. Population: 29,676 (2001). **2.** town in southwestern Connecticut on Long Island Sound. It is a residential suburb of Bridgeport and a manufacturing center. Population: 50,171 (2002 estimate).

Strat·ford-up·on-A·von /-áyvən/ city in Warwickshire, west central England. It was the birthplace of William Shakespeare. Population: 111,484 (2001).

stra·ti METEOROL plural of **stratus**

strati- *prefix* stratum, layer ○ *stratigraphy* [< STRATUM]

stra·tic·u·late /strə tíkyələt/ *adj* describes a rock formation that is made up of thin layers [Late 19C. < STRATUM, after PARTICULATE] —**stra·tic·u·la·tion** /strə tìkyə láysh'n/ *n*

strat·i·fi·ca·tion /stràttəfə káysh'n/ *n* **1.** the process of stratifying something, or the state of being stratified **2.** a layer, caste, class, or group into which something is stratified [Early 17C. < French < *stratifier* (see STRATIFY)] —**strat·i·fi·ca·tion·al** *adj*

strat·i·fi·ca·tion·al gram·mar *n* a form of grammar in which language is analyzed in terms of layers linked to one another by rules

strat·i·fied charge en·gine /stràttifīd chárj enjin/ *n* an internal-combustion engine with two layers of fuel density within the cylinder. A rich mixture is adjacent to the spark plug whose combustion assists in the ignition of a lean mixture in the remainder of the cylinder.

strat·i·form /stráttə fawrm/ *adj* **1.** COMPOSED OF LAYERS composed of layers, or with a layered appearance or arrangement **2.** FORMED AS LAYER forming or formed as a layer **3.** METEOROL LIKE STRATUS CLOUD like or having the form of a stratus cloud [Mid-19C. < STRATUM, STRATUS]

strat·i·fy /stráttə fī/ (**-fied, -fy·ing, -fies**) *v* **1.** *vti* FORM INTO LAYERS to form something into a layer or layers, or become formed into a layer or layers **2.** *vti* SOC SCI FORM INTO STATUS GROUPS to form castes, classes, or other groups based on status, or be formed into such groups **3.** *vt* AGRIC STORE SEEDS IN CHILLED MOIST ENVIRONMENT to store seeds in chilled moist sand, peat moss, or other material to preserve them [Mid-17C. < French *stratifier* < modern Latin *stratum* (see STRATUM)]

strat·i·graph·ic /străttə gráffik/, **strat·i·graph·i·cal**

/-gráffik'l/ *adj* relating to stratigraphy —**strat·i·graph·i·cal·ly** *adv*

stra·tig·ra·phy /strə tíggrəfee/ (*plural* **-phies**) *n* **1.** STUDY OF ROCK STRATA the study of the origin, composition, and development of rock strata **2.** DISPOSITION OF ROCK STRATA the way in which rock strata are arranged, and the chronology of their formation **3.** ARCHAEOL VERTICAL SECTION THROUGH GROUND a section cut vertically through the Earth showing its different layers and allowing artefacts to be dated according to the layers in which they are found [Mid-19C. < STRATUM] —**stra·tig·ra·pher** *n* —**stra·ti·graph·ist** *n*

stra·to·cu·mu·lus /stràytō kyóomyələss, stràttō-/ (*plural* **-li** /-lī/) *n* a cloud formation in a low-lying extensive layer with large dark round or rolling masses [Late 19C. < STRATUS]

strat·o·pause /stráttə pàwz/ *n* the boundary layer between the stratosphere and the mesosphere, at about 30 mi./50 km above the Earth's surface [Mid-20C. < STRATOSPHERE, after TROPOPAUSE]

strat·o·sphere /stráttə sfeer/ *n* **1.** the region of the Earth's atmosphere between the troposphere and mesosphere, from 6 mi./10 km to 30 mi./50 km above the Earth's surface. It has no clouds and is marked by gradual temperature increase. **2.** a very high or the highest level or position ○ *The failure of the harvest is likely to send food prices into the stratosphere.* [Early 20C. < STRATUM]

strat·o·spher·ic /stràttə sféerik, -sférrik/ *adj* **1.** relating or belonging to the stratosphere **2.** very or excessively high —**strat·o·spher·i·cal·ly** *adv*

strat·o·vol·ca·no /stràytō vol káynō, stràttō-/ (*plural* **-noes** or **-nos**) *n* a volcano consisting of layers of lava alternating with ash or cinder [Mid-20C. < STRATUM]

stra·tum /stráytəm, stráttəm/ (*plural* **-ta** /-tə/ or **-tums**) *n* **1.** LEVEL WITHIN SYSTEM a layer or level within an ordered system ○ *the various strata of meaning within the text* **2.** LAYER OF SOCIETY a social class or level of society consisting of people of similar cultural, economic, or educational status **3.** GEOL same as **bed** *n* (sense 12) **4.** LAYER OF ATMOSPHERE OR SEA a layer of the atmosphere or the sea, regarded as lying between horizontal planes **5.** LAYER OF CELLS a layer of living cells [Late 16C. Via modern Latin < Latin, "something thrown down" < past participle of *sternere* "lay or throw down"] —**stra·tal** *adj*

USAGE The plural of ***stratum*** is *strata*, reflecting the word's Latin history. A variant plural *stratums* exists but is relatively infrequent. People sometimes use the false plurals *stratas* and (after Latin) *stratae*, which treat *strata* as a singular, but these are incorrect: *all strata* [not *stratas* or *stratae*] *of society.*

stra·tus /stráytəss, stráttəss/ (*plural* **-ti** /-tī/) *n* a low-lying flat gray cloud formation [Early 19C. < modern Latin < Latin, past participle of *sternere* "lay or throw down"]

Strauss /strowss, shtrowss/, **Johann** (1804–49) Austrian conductor and composer. His compositions include many waltzes and marches. Known as **Johann Strauss the Elder**

Strauss, Johann (1825–99) Austrian composer. The son of Johann Strauss the Elder, he wrote operettas including *Die Fledermaus* (1874) and waltzes and other dance pieces including *The Blue Danube* (1867). Known as **Johann Strauss the Younger**

Strauss, Richard (1864–1949) German conductor and composer. His late romantic symphonic poems and operas such as *Der Rosenkavalier* (1911) develop the ideas of Richard Wagner and are characterized by rich harmonization.

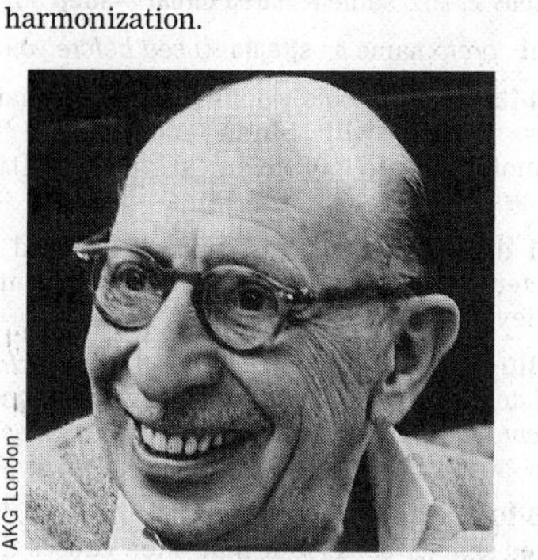
AKG London

Igor Stravinsky

Stra·vin·sky /strə vínskee/, **Igor** (1882–1971) Russian-born US composer. A major figure in 20th-century music, he experimented widely with musical styles and forms and wrote the music for Sergei Diaghilev's ballets *The Firebird* (1910), *Petrushka* (1911), and *The Rite of Spring* (1913). Full name **Stravinsky, Igor Fyodorovich**

> "Too many pieces of music finish too long after the end."
> [Attributed to Igor Stravinsky]

straw /straw/ *n* **1.** STALKS OF THRESHED CEREAL CROPS the stalks of threshed cereal crops such as wheat or barley. Use: bedding and food for animals, weaving into objects such as baskets, thatching. **2.** THIN TUBE FOR DRINKING a long thin tube used for sucking up a drink **3.** DRIED GRASS STALK a single dried stalk of a cereal crop or grass **4.** ITEM MADE OF STRAW something made of straw, e.g., a hat or basket **5.** SOMETHING WORTHLESS anything of little or no importance or value **6.** COLOR a pale brownish yellow color ■ *adj* **1.** *US* WORTHLESS worthless or of little value **2.** *US* ACTING AS FRONT relating to or acting as a straw man **3.** OF STRAW COLOR of the brownish yellow color of straw [Old English *strēaw* < Indo-European, "spread"] —**straw·y** *adj* ◇ **a straw in the wind** a relatively minor incident or thing that gives some indication of what is likely to happen ◇ **clutch** *or* **grasp at straws** to be willing to try anything that may help in a desperate situation ◇ **draw the short straw** to be chosen from a group of people to do a difficult or unpleasant task

strawberry

straw·ber·ry /stráw bèrree/ (*plural* **-ries**) *n* **1.** a small sweet red fruit containing many achenes resembling seeds **2.** a plant that spreads by means of rooting stems and bears strawberries. Genus: *Fragaria.*

straw·ber·ry blond *adj* describes hair that is very pale in color with a reddish or pinkish tinge ■ *n* somebody with strawberry blond hair

straw·ber·ry bush *n* a bush or small tree with tiny flowers and scarlet pods and seeds. Native to: eastern North America. Latin name: *Euonymus americanus.*

straw·ber·ry mark *n* a raised red birthmark, often found on the scalp or face, containing small blood vessels

straw·ber·ry roan *n* a horse that has a coat of reddish hairs mixed with white

straw·ber·ry shrub *n* TREES same as **Carolina allspice**

straw·ber·ry to·ma·to *n* **1.** a round yellow edible fruit produced by a tropical plant and often used in preserves and pickles **2.** a hairy tropical plant of the nightshade family bearing edible yellow fruit. Genus: *Physalis.*

straw·ber·ry tree *n* an evergreen tree of the heath family with berries resembling strawberries. Flowers: white or pink. Native to: southern Europe. Latin name: *Arbutus unedo.*

straw·board /stráw bàwrd/ *n* a coarse cardboard made of straw pulp and used in making packaging materials and book covers

straw boss *n* a worker who also supervises a small work crew, acting as an assistant to the foreman (*informal*) [< US farms, where the second-in-command was formerly responsible for straw coming out of the thresher]

straw col·or *n* COLORS same as **straw** *n* (sense 6) —**straw-col·ored** *adj*

straw·flow·er /stráw flòwr/ *n* a plant with flower heads that remain colorful when dried. Native to: Australia. Latin name: *Helichrysum bracteatum.*

straw-hat *adj US* describes a theater that operates only in the summer [< the relatively rustic beginnings of these theaters]

straw man *n* **1.** FRONT FOR SOMEBODY somebody who acts as a front for somebody else's questionable or illegal activities **2.** UNIMPORTANT ISSUE OR PERSON an issue or person of little significance, put forward to be easily defeated **3.** FIGURE MADE OF STRAW a straw figure made to resemble a human being

straw mush·room *n* a small brown or pale-colored edible mushroom used in Chinese cooking. It has a delicate flavor and a slightly gelatinous texture. Latin name: *Volvariella volvacea.*

straw poll *n* an unofficial poll or vote used to discover the likely result of an election or the trend of opinion regarding an issue

Straw·son /stráwss'n/, **P. F.** (*b.* 1919) British philosopher associated with the analytic and linguistic philosophy movement. His early work explores the relationships between logic and ordinary language, while his later work is a metaphysical exploration of the structure of human thought and language. Full name **Strawson, Peter Frederick**

straw vote *n* same as **straw poll**

straw wine *n* a sweet wine made from grapes that have been partially dried in the sun, especially on a bed of straw

straw·worm /stráw wùrm/ *n* INSECTS same as **caddis worm** [Because it infests stalks of grain]

stray /stray/ *vi* (**strayed, stray·ing, strays**) **1.** WANDER OFF to leave the correct course or wander away from the correct place ○ *The sheep strayed onto the road through the broken fence.* **2.** BECOME SEPARATED FROM GROUP to move away from or become separated from a flock or group **3.** MOVE CASUALLY to move or turn in a casual or abstracted or unconsciously compulsive way toward something ○ *Her eyes strayed again to the window.* **4.** DIGRESS FROM SUBJECT to digress from the main subject, or become diverted from the main or appropriate object of attention ○ *stray from the point* **5.** DEPART FROM ACCEPTED STANDARDS to depart from traditional or accepted standards of behavior **6.** MEANDER to take an indirect course **7.** WANDER ABOUT AIMLESSLY to roam or wander without a particular purpose or destination (*literary*) ○ *stray through the woods* ■ *adj* **1.** LOST OR HOMELESS homeless, lost, or wandering ○ *a stray dog* **2.** SCATTERED OR SEPARATED scattered, separated, or happening accidentally or randomly ○ *stray shots* ■ *n* **1.** SOMEBODY LOST somebody, especially a child, who is lost **2.** HOMELESS ANIMAL a lost or homeless domestic animal ■ **strays** *npl* ELECTRONICS ELECTRICAL INTERFERENCE electrical interference in a radio or television broadcast, causing disruption of a signal [13C. Shortening of Old French *estraier*] —**stray·er** *n*

streak /streek/ *n* **1.** THIN STRIPE OF CONTRASTING COLOR a long thin stripe or band that is a different color from its background or surroundings **2.** SHORT PERIOD OR UNBROKEN RUN a short period or unbroken run, especially of good or bad luck ○ *The team is finally having a winning streak.* **3.** CONTRASTING CHARACTERISTIC a characteristic of somebody or something, especially one that is only occasionally evident or that contrasts with other characteristics ○ *a happy-go-lucky streak* **4.** LAYER OF SOMETHING a layer or strip of something **5.** METEOROL LIGHTNING a flash of lightning **6.** MINERALS MARK OF MINERAL POWDER the characteristically colored mark that a mineral makes when scratched on unglazed porcelain **7.** BOT VIRAL PLANT DISEASE a viral disease of plants such as potatoes or tomatoes that produces discolored markings on stems and leaves **8.** MICROBIOL LINEAR GROWTH OF BACTERIA a linear growth of bacteria on the surface of a culture medium, produced by drawing a contaminated needle across the medium ■ *v* (**streaked, streak·ing, streaks**) **1.** *vt* MARK SOMETHING WITH STREAKS to mark or cover something with streaks **2.** *vt* LIGHTEN HAIR to lighten strands or sections of hair with a bleach or dye **3.** *vi* BECOME STREAKED to become streaked or form streaks **4.** *vi* DASH OR RUSH to move at great speed **5.** *vi* RUN NAKED IN PUBLIC to run quickly through a public place with no clothes on, usually as a joke or publicity stunt (*informal*) [Old English *strica* < Germanic, "touch lightly"] —**streaked** *adj* —**streak·ing** *n*

streak·er /streékər/ *n* somebody who runs quickly through a public place with no clothes on, usually as a joke or publicity stunt (*informal*)

streak of lean *n regional* same as **salt pork**

REGIONAL NOTE See *fatback.*

streak·y /streékee/ (**-i·er, -i·est**) *adj* **1. MARKED WITH STREAKS** covered or marked with streaks ○ *I cleaned the windows twice but they still looked streaky.* **2. OCCURRING AS STREAKS** occurring in the form of streaks in something else **3. INCONSISTENT** variable and uneven in quality ○ *Her work's a bit streaky.* —**streak·i·ly** *adv* —**streak·i·ness** *n*

stream /streem/ *n* **1. SMALL RIVER** a narrow and shallow river **2. CONSTANT FLOW** a constant flow of liquid or gas **3. AIR OR WATER CURRENT** a current of air or water **4. CONTINUOUS SERIES** a continuous series or flow of people, things, or events **5. QUICK OR UNBROKEN FLOW** a quick or uninterrupted burst, flow, or succession ○ *a stream of questions* **6. PREVAILING ATTITUDE** a general or prevailing attitude, drift, or trend **7. BEAM OF LIGHT** a steady ray or beam of light **8.** *UK* EDUC **GROUP OF PUPILS OF SIMILAR ABILITY** a group or level in which students of similar ability are placed and taught together ■ *v* (**streamed, stream·ing, streams**) **1.** *vi* **FLOW IN LARGE QUANTITIES** to flow, or appear to flow, continuously or quickly and in large quantities ○ *Blood was streaming from the wound.* ○ *Sunlight streamed through the open window.* **2.** *vi* **MOVE IN SAME DIRECTION** to move continuously in large numbers in the same direction **3.** *vti* **PRODUCE FLOW OF LIQUID** to emit or produce liquid in a continuous flow ○ *His eyes streamed tears.* **4.** *vti* **FLOAT FREELY** to float or trail freely in air, wind, or water, or cause something to do this ○ *an advertising banner streaming behind the airplane* **5.** *vti UK* EDUC **PUT PUPILS IN ABILITY GROUPS** to place students in groups according to their ability **6.** *vt* ONLINE **BROADCAST SOMETHING ON INTERNET** to broadcast something via the Internet [Old English *strēam* < Indo-European, "to flow"]

stream·bed /streém bèd/ *n* a channel through which a stream flows or used to flow

stream·er /streémər/ *n* **1. NARROW FLAG** a long narrow flag or banner **2. DECORATIVE PAPER STRIP** a long narrow strip of colored paper or other material that is used for decoration **3.** ASTRON **LUMINOUS STREAK IN SKY** any one of the luminous streaks that make up the aurora borealis and the aurora australis **4.** MEDIA **HEADLINE RUNNING ACROSS FULL PAGE** a large headline that extends the entire width of a newspaper page

stream·ing /streéming/ *n* **1.** *Can, UK* same as **tracking** (sense 4) **2.** BIOL same as **cyclosis 3.** ONLINE the playing of sound or video over the Internet in real time

stream·let /streémlət/ *n* a small stream

stream·line /streém lìn/ *vt* (**-lined, -lin·ing, -lines**) **1. MAKE SOMETHING MORE EFFICIENT** to make something such as a business, organization, or manufacturing process more efficient, especially by simplifying or modernizing it **2. DESIGN OR BUILD WITH SMOOTH SHAPE** to design or build something with a smooth shape so that it moves with minimum resistance through air or water ■ *n* **1. CONTOUR DESIGNED TO MINIMIZE RESISTANCE** a contour of a body, e.g., of a car, boat, or airplane, designed to minimize resistance when moving through air or water **2.** PHYS **LINE IN FLUID** a line in a fluid indicating the direction of the velocity of a particle —**stream·lined** *adj* —**stream·lin·ing** *n*

stream·line flow *n* a flow of fluid in which the particles follow continuous paths and the fluid velocity at a recorded point either remains constant or varies regularly with time

stream of con·scious·ness *n* **1.** a literary style that presents a character's continuous random flow of thoughts as they arise (*hyphenated before a noun*) **2.** the continuous uninterrupted flow of thoughts and feelings through somebody's mind

~~strech~~ incorrect spelling of **stretch**

Streep /streep/, **Meryl** (*b.* 1949) US actor. She won Academy Awards for *Kramer vs. Kramer* (1979) and *Sophie's Choice* (1982). Born **Streep, Mary Louise**

street /street/ *n* **1. PUBLIC ROAD IN TOWN** a public road, especially in a town or city, usually lined with buildings **2. BUILDINGS ON STREET** the buildings that line a street **3. PART OF ROAD BETWEEN SIDEWALKS** the part of a road that lies between the sidewalks and is used by vehicles **4. PEOPLE LOCATED ON STREET** the people who work or live on a street **5. URBAN MILIEU** the modern urban environment as a public arena ○ *The word on the street is that Micky knows who did it and is out to get him.* **6. PARTICULAR ENVIRONMENT** the social context or world of a particular group of people ○ *the view of the Republican street* **7. REPRESENTATIVE GROUP OF PEOPLE** ordinary people considered collectively as representatives of the majority opinion of a particular group ■ *adj* **RELATED TO MODERN URBAN SOCIETY** widely found or used in a modern urban environment or fashionable in modern urban culture, especially among young people or the underworld ○ *Street language has worked its way into the mainstream language.* [Old English *strǣt*, via W Germanic < late Latin *strata* "paved road" < Latin *sternere* "pave, throw down"] ◇ **on the street** having no place to live ◇ **on the streets** working as a prostitute ◇ **right up somebody's street** exactly suitable or appropriate for somebody ◇ **streets ahead (of somebody** *or* **something)** *UK* much better in some way than somebody or something ◇ **the man** *or* **person** *or* **woman in the street** the average man or person or woman

street Ar·ab, **street ar·ab** *n* an offensive term for a child who has run away from home and lives on the streets (*archaic*) [< the perception of Arabs as nomadic]

street·car /streét kaàr/ *n* a public passenger vehicle that runs through city streets on metal rails built into the road surface ○ *a streetcar line*

street cred·i·bil·i·ty *n* popularity and acceptance among fashionable urban people, especially the young —**street-cred·i·ble** *adj*

street crime *n* criminal activity occurring in a public place, usually in an urban area, including theft of personal property, drug dealing, and gang violence

street door *n* the door of a house or other building that opens onto the street

street fight·er *n* **1.** somebody whose fighting skills were learned on the streets rather than through formal training as a boxer **2.** somebody who is tough, cunning, and aggressive (*informal*)

street·light /streét lìt/, **street·lamp** /-làmp/ *n* one of a series of lights that illuminates a road or street at night

street name *n* an informal or colloquial name given to an illegal drug by those who sell or use it ○ *"Smack" has long been used as a street name for heroin.*

street·scape /streét skàyp/ *n* an artistic portrayal of a street and its activities, especially a busy city street

street-smart *adj* same as **streetwise**

street smarts *npl* the ability to survive in a hostile or dangerous urban environment

street the·a·ter *n* dramatic entertainment usually performed outdoors, e.g., in a park or shopping mall

street val·ue *n* the price that something illegal would be worth if sold to a customer

street vi·rus *n* the natural virulent strain of a virus as distinguished from a less virulent strain of the same organism that has been grown or treated in a laboratory

street·walk·er /streét wàwkər/ *n* a prostitute who solicits in the streets (*informal*) —**street·walk·ing** *n*

street·wise /streét wìz/ *adj* shrewd and experienced enough to be able to survive in the often difficult and dangerous environment of a modern city (*informal*)

Streis·and /strì sand/, **Barbra** (*b.* 1942) US singer, actor, and movie director. The star of musicals, comedies, and dramas, she won an Academy Award for her acting debut in *Funny Girl* (1968). Born **Streisand, Barbara Joan**

> "What does it mean when people applaud?...The lack of applause – that I can respond to."
> [Barbra Streisand, *Life*, May 22, 1964]

strelitzia

stre·lit·zi·a /strə lítsee ə/ (*plural* **-as** or *same*) *n* a widely cultivated perennial plant. Flowers: showy, often unusual or irregular in shape. Native to: southern Africa. Genus: *Strelitzia.* [Late 18C. After Charlotte of Mecklenburg-*Strelitz* (1744–1818), queen of George III of Great Britain and Ireland]

strength /strength/ *n* **1. PHYSICAL POWER** the physical power to carry out demanding tasks ○ *It took all our strength to lift the heavy table.* **2. EMOTIONAL TOUGHNESS** the necessary qualities required to deal with stressful or painful situations ○ *She showed great strength throughout the trial.* **3. SOURCE OF SUPPORT** a source of strength or support **4. RESISTANCE** the ability to withstand force, pressure, or stress ○ *tensile strength* **5. DEFENSIVE ABILITY** the ability to resist attack **6. ASSET OR QUALITY** a valuable or useful ability, asset, or quality ○ *One of the strengths of this system is its adaptability.* **7. DEGREE OF INTENSITY** the degree of intensity, e.g., of color, light, smell, or sound **8. FORCE OR EFFECTIVENESS** force, effectiveness, or intensity, e.g., of beliefs, feelings, or expression ○ *It's difficult to recall the strength of purpose which once gripped me.* **9. PERSUASIVE POWER** power to convince or persuade, e.g., by argument or suggestion ○ *the strength of her argument* **10. POTENCY** the potency of something such as an alcoholic drink or a drug **11. NUMBER OF PEOPLE NEEDED** the number of people required to make something such as an army, team, or work force complete and enable it to function effectively ○ *at half strength* **12.** FIN **MAINTENANCE OF PRICES** the tendency of prices to be stable or rise [Old English *strengþu* < Germanic, "strong"] ◇ **go from strength to strength** to go on from one success or achievement to another and get progressively better ◇ **in strength** in large numbers ◇ **on the strength of something** on the basis of something

strength·en /stréngthən/ (**-ened, -en·ing, -ens**) *vti* to make something stronger or more powerful, or increase in strength or power —**strength·en·er** *n*

~~strenous~~ incorrect spelling of **strenuous**

~~strenth~~ incorrect spelling of **strength**

stren·u·ous /strénnyoo əss/ *adj* **1.** requiring physical effort, energy, stamina, or strength ○ *strenuous exercise* **2.** active, energetic, or determined ○ *strenuous efforts* [Early 17C. < Latin *strenuus* "brisk, active"] —**stren·u·os·i·ty** /strènnyoo óssətee/ *n* —**stren·u·ous·ly** *adv* —**stren·u·ous·ness** *n*

SYNONYMS See *hard.*

strep /strep/ *n* (*informal*) **1.** MICROBIOL same as **streptococcus 2.** MED same as **strep throat** —**strep** *adj*

strept- *prefix* same as **strepto-** (*used before vowels*)

strep·ta·vid·in /strèptə víddin/ *n* a protein that interacts strongly with biotin and is used in immunologic and biochemical assays [Mid-20C. < STREPT- + AVIDIN]

strep throat *n* an acute sore throat caused by the bacterium *Streptococcus pyogenes* and accompanied by fever and inflammation

strepto- *prefix* **1.** streptococcus ○ *streptokinase* **2.** twisted chain ○ *streptococcus* **3.** streptomyces ○ *streptothricin* [< Greek *streptos* "twisted" < *strephein* "to turn, twist"]

strep·to·ba·cil·lus /strèptō bə sílləss/ (*plural* **-li** /-lì/) *n* a rod-shaped bacterium that often causes diseases such as rat-bite fever. Individual cells join to form structures resembling chains. Genus: *Streptobacillus.*

strep·to·car·pus /strèptə kaárpəss/ (*plural* **-pus·es**) *n* a plant that often has only one large leaf. Flowers: brightly colored, tubular. Native to: subtropical regions. Genus: *Streptocarpus.* [Early 19C. < modern Latin < Greek *streptos* "twisted" + *karpos* "fruit"; because its fruit is spirally twisted]

strep·to·coc·cus /strèptə kókəss/ (*plural* **-coc·ci** /-kók sī, -kó kī/) *n* a spherical bacterium that often causes diseases such as scarlet fever or pneumonia. The bacteria link together in pairs or chains. Genus: *Streptococcus.* [Late 19C. < modern Latin < Greek *streptos* "twisted" + *coccus* "berry"] —**strep·to·coc·cal** *adj* —**strep·to·coc·cic** /strèptə kóksik, -kókik/ *adj*

strep·to·dor·nase /strèptə dáwr nàyss, -nàyz/ *n* an enzyme derived from streptococci that can liquefy pus [Mid-20C. < STREPTOCOCCUS + contraction of *deoxyribonuclease*]

strep·to·kin·ase /strèptō kí nàyss, -kī-, -nàyz/ *n* an enzyme produced by streptococci. Use: dissolving blood clots. [Mid-20C. < streptococcal]

strep·to·ly·sin /strèptə líssən/ *n* a substance that breaks down red blood cells and is produced by streptococci

strep·to·my·ces /strèptə mī seez/ (*plural same*) *n* an aerobic soil bacterium. Some streptomyces produce antibiotics. Genus: *Streptomyces.* [Mid-20C. < modern Latin < Greek *strepto-* "twisted" + *mukēs* "fungus"; because it forms twisted chains and resembles mold]

strep·to·my·cin /strèptə mīssən/ *n* an antibiotic produced from the soil bacterium *Streptomyces griseus.* Use: treatment of bacterial infections such as tuberculosis.

stress /stress/ *n* **1.** STRAIN FELT BY SOMEBODY mental, emotional, or physical strain caused, e.g., by anxiety or overwork. It may cause such symptoms as raised blood pressure or depression. **2.** CAUSE OF STRAIN something that causes stress **3.** SPECIAL IMPORTANCE special emphasis, importance, or significance attached to something **4.** EMPHASIS ON SYLLABLE the emphasis placed on a sound or syllable by pronouncing it more loudly or forcefully than those surrounding it in the same word or phrase **5.** EMPHASIS IN POETRY the emphasis placed on a syllable or word as part of the rhythm of a poem or line of poetry **6.** ACCENT IN MUSIC the emphasis placed on a note as part of the rhythm of a piece of music, or a mark representing this **7.** PHYS FORCE DEFORMING BODY a force or system of forces exerted on a body and resulting in deformation or strain ■ *vt* (**stressed, stress·ing, stress·es**) **1.** EMPHASIZE SOMETHING to place emphasis on or attach importance to something **2.** PRONOUNCE SOMETHING FORCEFULLY to pronounce a word or syllable more loudly or forcefully than those surrounding it **3.** SUBJECT SOMEBODY OR SOMETHING TO STRAIN to cause somebody or something to experience mental, emotional, or physical stress [14C. Partly shortening of DISTRESS; partly < Old French *estresse* "narrowness" < Latin *strictus* "compressed"] —**stressed** *adj* —**stres·sor** *n*

SYNONYMS See *worry.*

stress out *vti* to affect somebody with emotional, mental, or physical stress, or be so affected (*informal*)

STRESS /stress/ *abbr* COMPUT structural engineering system solver

stressed out *adj* unable to relax or function properly as the result of experiencing emotional or mental stress (*informal; hyphenated when used before a noun*)

stress frac·ture *n* a small fracture of a bone caused by repeated physical strain, sometimes experienced, e.g., by gymnasts, long-distance runners, or marching soldiers

stress·ful /strésfəl/ *adj* causing or involving mental or physical stress —**stress·ful·ly** *adv* —**stress·ful·ness** *n*

stress man·age·ment *n* physical and psychological techniques designed to enable people to cope with strain and anxiety

stress mark *n* a mark placed before, on, or after a syllable that is to be stressed when the word containing it is pronounced

stress pup·py *n* somebody who complains a lot about being stressed but actually seems to enjoy it (*informal*)

stretch /strech/ *v* (**stretched, stretch·ing, stretch·es**) **1.** *vti* EXTEND BY FORCE to lengthen, widen, or extend something, or become lengthened, widened, or extended, especially by force **2.** *vi* EXPAND AND REGAIN ORIGINAL SHAPE to be capable of expanding and returning to the original shape afterward **3.** *vti* EXTEND EXCESSIVELY to extend something excessively so that the shape is permanently altered, or be extended in this way ○ *The sleeves of this sweater have stretched.* **4.** *vti* EXTEND TO FULL LENGTH to straighten or extend the body or part of it, especially the limbs, to full length ○ *She woke up, yawned, and stretched.* ○ *The cat lay stretched out by the fire.* ○ *stretched his arms* **5.** *vt* STRAIN BODY PART to strain a part of the body such as a muscle **6.** *vti* TAUTEN to make something taut or tight, or become taut or tight **7.** *vt* SUSPEND SOMETHING BETWEEN TWO POINTS to suspend something, or make something reach, between two points **8.** *vi* EXTEND IN SPACE to spread out or extend over an area or in a particular direction **9.** *vti* EXTEND OVER TIME to last or continue over a period of time, or prolong something **10.** *vt* MAKE SMALL AMOUNT GO FURTHER to make limited supplies or resources go further than usual, planned, or expected **11.** *vi* BE ENOUGH to be sufficient to allow something ○ *Will the budget stretch to hiring a temporary assistant?* **12.** *vt* EXCEED LIMIT OR BREAK RULE to exceed a limit or break a rule that would usually prohibit something **13.** *vt* PUSH SOMETHING TO LIMIT to strain or push something to the limit ○ *You're stretching my patience.* **14.** *vt* PUSH SOMEBODY TO LIMIT OF ABILITY to cause somebody to make full use of his or her abilities or intellect, e.g., with challenging or demanding work **15.** *vt* EXAGGERATE SOMETHING to make something sound better or worse than it really is, especially in order to make it seem more impressive (*informal*) ○ *To call his house a mansion is stretching it a bit.* **16.** *vt* KNOCK SOMEBODY DOWN to knock somebody down with a blow (*informal*) ■ *n* **1.** STRETCHING EXERCISE the straightening and extending of a part of the body, e.g., as an exercise **2.** EXPANSE a large expanse of something, especially land or water **3.** PERIOD OF TIME an uninterrupted period of time **4.** CRIME PRISON TERM a term of imprisonment (*slang*) **5.** ELASTICITY the ability to expand and return to the original shape afterward **6.** DIFFICULT CHALLENGE something that is difficult to achieve (*informal*) **7.** SPORTS STRAIGHT PART OF RACETRACK the straight part of a racetrack, especially the final section approaching the finishing line **8.** FINAL STAGE the final stage of an event, task, process, or period of time, especially one that has been difficult or challenging **9.** BASEBALL POSITION BY PITCHER the position taken by a pitcher in order to hold a runner close to a base ○ *He had so many base runners that he was pitching from the stretch all day.* **10.** AUTOMOT LONG PASSENGER CAR a limousine that has an extended body (*informal*) ○ *hired a stretch for the prom* ■ *adj* **1.** ELASTIC made of or being a material that has great elasticity ○ *wore stretch pants for skiing* **2.** EXTENDED TO PROVIDE EXTRA SPACE extended or enlarged in order to provide extra space, e.g., for additional seating ○ *a stretch limousine* [Old English *streccan*, probably < Germanic, "rigid"] —**stretch·a·bil·i·ty** /strèchə bíllətee/ *n* —**stretch·a·ble** *adj* ◇ **at a stretch 1.** continuously ○ *worked five hours at a stretch* **2.** with great difficulty or effort ○ *could get there by six at a stretch* ◇ **at full stretch** using all the energy or resources available

stretch·er /stréchər/ *n* **1.** MED DEVICE FOR CARRYING SOMEBODY LYING DOWN a device consisting of a sheet of material such as canvas stretched over a frame, used to carry somebody in a lying position who is sick, injured, or dead **2.** ART FRAME FOR ARTIST'S CANVAS a wooden frame over which a canvas for an oil painting is stretched **3.** FURNITURE BAR BRACING FURNITURE LEGS a bar that joins and braces the legs of a chair, table, or other piece of furniture **4.** CONSTR STRONG BEAM USED AS BRACE a strong, usually horizontal beam or bar that is used as a brace in the framework of a structure **5.** CONSTR STONE WITH LONG EDGE FACING OUT a brick or stone laid in a wall so that its longer edge forms part of the face of the wall **6.** EXAGGERATED STORY an exaggerated story, or a lie based partly on the truth (*slang*)

stretch·er-bear·er *n* somebody who helps carry a stretcher, especially a soldier given the task in wartime

stretch knit *n* knitted fabric that can stretch and return to its original shape afterward (*hyphenated before a noun*)

stretch mark *n* a mark left on the skin of the abdomen, breasts, buttocks, or thighs after pregnancy or weight loss (*often used in the plural*)

stretch-out *n US* **1.** INDUST EXTENDING TIME TO MEET PRODUCTION QUOTA changing a production schedule so that the same amount of goods can be produced over a longer period of time **2.** INDUST ADDITIONAL WORK WITHOUT ADDITIONAL PAY an industrial practice in which workers are required to do more work with little or no additional compensation **3.** FIN LENGTHENING OF TIME FOR DEBT REPAYMENT a restructuring of a debt payment schedule so that the debt can be paid back over a longer period of time

stretch·y /stréchee/ (**-i·er, -i·est**) *adj* capable of being stretched, usually returning to its original shape afterward, or tending to stretch —**stretch·i·ness** *n*

stret·to /stréttō/ (*plural* **-tos** or **-ti** /-tee/) *n* **1.** in a fugue or similar musical work, the successive statements of the theme very close together in time **2.** the speeding up of a piece of music at a climactic moment [Mid-18C. Via Italian, "narrow, tight" < Latin *strictus* (see STRICT)]

streu·sel /stróoz'l, stròyz'l/ *n* a crumbly topping for cakes and quick breads made of sugar, flour, butter, cinnamon, and often chopped nuts [Early 20C. < German < *streuen* "sprinkle"]

strew /stroo/ (**strewed, strewn** /stroon/ or **strewed, strew·ing, strews**) *v* (*often passive*) **1.** *vt* to scatter something, especially carelessly or untidily ○ *Clothes were strewn all over the floor.* **2.** *vti* to cover an area with loosely or carelessly scattered objects or material ○ *The retreating army strewed the area with landmines.* ○ *a rock-strewn path* [Old English *strewian* < Indo-European] —**strew·er** *n*

stri·a /strí ə/ (*plural* **-ae** /-ee/) *n* **1.** a thin narrow groove or channel in the surface of something, e.g., a decorative feature on a column **2.** ANAT a stripe, streak, or narrow band, e.g., a band of nerve fibers or stretch marks seen in pregnancy (**striae gravidarum**) **3.** GEOL same as **striation** (sense 3) [Mid-16C. < Latin, "furrow, channel"]

stri·ate /strí àyt/ *vt* (**-at·ed, -at·ing, -ates**) to mark something with parallel grooves, ridges, stripes, or narrow bands ■ *adj* ANAT same as **striated** [Late 17C. < Latin *striat-*, past participle of *striare* < *stria* "furrow, channel"]

stri·at·ed /strí àytəd/ *adj* marked with parallel grooves, ridges, stripes, or narrow bands

stri·at·ed mus·cle *n* a muscle or muscle tissue that shows light and dark bands within the muscle fibers

stri·a·tion /strī áysh'n/ *n* **1.** STRIPY PATTERN a patterning or marking with parallel grooves or narrow bands **2.** ANAT BANDING OR BAND WITHIN MUSCLE FIBER the striped pattern of striated muscle, or any of the light and dark bands that make up this effect **3.** GEOL NARROW MARK a narrow groove or scratch on an exposed rock face, caused by abrasion by hard rock fragments embedded in a moving glacier

strick·en /stríkən/ past participle of **strike** *v* (senses 6, 25) ■ *adj* **1.** DEEPLY OR BADLY AFFECTED deeply or very badly affected by something such as grief, misfortune, or trouble (*often used in combination*) ○ *grief-stricken* **2.** AFFECTED BY ILLNESS experiencing severe physical symptoms caused by illness or injury **3.** HIT BY MISSILE injured, struck, or wounded, e.g., by a missile —**strick·en·ly** *adv*

strick·le /strík'l/ *n* **1.** MANUF BOARD FOR LEVELING OFF EXCESS MATERIAL a board used to level off excess grain or other material in a container or measuring device **2.** SHAPING TOOL a tool used to shape the surface of a mold ■ *vt* (**-led, -ling, -les**) MANUF USE STRICKLE ON SOMETHING to level or shape something with a strickle [Old English *stricel* < Germanic]

~~strickly~~ incorrect spelling of **strictly**

strict /strikt/ *adj* **1.** SEVERE IN MAINTAINING DISCIPLINE severe in maintaining discipline, or rigorous in ensuring that rules are obeyed **2.** ENFORCED RIGOROUSLY needing to be closely obeyed ○ *strict guidelines for admission* **3.** PRECISE exact, precise, or narrowly interpreted ○ *a strict interpretation of the statute* **4.** FAITHFUL closely observing rules, principles, or practices ○ *strict* *party loyalty* **5.** ABSOLUTE complete, utter, or absolute **6.** BOT GROWING UPRIGHT growing upward at or very close to the vertical [15C. < Latin *strictus*, past participle of *stringere* "draw tight"] —**strict·ly** *adv* —**strict·ness** *n*

ORIGIN The Latin word *stringere* "to draw tight," from which **strict** is derived, is also the source of English *constrain, constrict, distress, district, prestige, restrain, restrict, strain*[1], *stress,* and *stringent.*

stric·ture /stríkchər/ *n* **1.** LIMIT OR RESTRICTION a limit or restriction, especially one that seems unfair or too harsh (*formal*) **2.** SEVERE CRITICISM a severe criticism or strongly critical remark (*formal*) **3.** MED CONSTRICTION OF BODY PASSAGE a constriction or narrowing of a body passage [14C. < Latin *strictura* < *strictus* (see STRICT)] —**stric·tured** *adj*

stride /strīd/ *v* (**strode** /strōd/, **strid·den** /strídd'n/, **strid·ing, strides**) **1.** *vi* WALK WITH LONG STEPS to walk with long regular steps, often briskly or energetically **2.** *vti* TAKE LONG STEP OVER SOMETHING to cross or step over something with a long step **3.** *vti* STRADDLE SOMETHING to sit or stand astride something (*archaic or literary*) ■ *n* **1.** LONG STEP a long step, especially one taken briskly or energetically **2.** DISTANCE COVERED BY LONG STEP the distance covered when somebody or something takes a long step **3.** ADVANCE TOWARD IMPROVING SOMETHING an advance or step toward improving or developing something **4.** WAY OF WALKING a way of walking or running in long regular steps, often taken briskly or energetically **5.** ZOOL COORDINATED FORWARD MOVEMENT BY ANIMAL an act of forward motion by a four-legged animal consisting of a coordinated cycle of movements that brings the legs back to their original positions **6.** MUSIC same as **stride piano** [Old English *strīdan* "straddle," probably < Germanic] —**strid·er** *n* ◇ **hit** *or* **reach your stride** *US* to become familiar with and at ease with something so that you can do it easily and well ◇ **take something in (your) stride** to accept something without being unduly upset or worried about it

stri·dent /strīd'nt/ *adj* **1.** harsh, loud, grating, or shrill ○ *strident tones of voice* **2.** loudly, strongly, or urgently expressed ○ *strident opposition* [Mid-17C. < Latin *strident-*, present participle of *stridere* "creak"] —**stri·dence** *n* —**stri·den·cy** *n* —**stri·dent·ly** *adv*

stride pi·an·o *n* a style of jazz piano-playing in which the right hand plays the melody while the left hand alternates between playing a single note and a related chord [< STRIDE "straddle"; from the movements of the left hand]

stri·dor /strīdər/ *n* **1.** a harsh, grating, or creaking noise **2.** a harsh high-pitched wheezing sound made when breathing in or out, caused by obstruction of the air passages [Mid-17C. < Latin < *stridere* "to creak"]

strid·u·late /stríjjə làyt/ (**-lat·ed, -lat·ing, -lates**) *vi* to make a chirping or grating sound by rubbing parts of the body together, as male crickets and grasshoppers do [Mid-19C. < French *striduler* < Latin *stridere* "to creak"] —**strid·u·lant** *adj* —**strid·u·la·tion** /strìjjə láysh'n/ *n* —**strid·u·la·tor** *n* —**strid·u·la·to·ry** *adj* —**strid·u·lous** *adj*

strife /strīf/ *n* bitter and sometimes violent conflict, struggle, or rivalry [12C. < Old French *estrif*] —**strife·less** *adj*

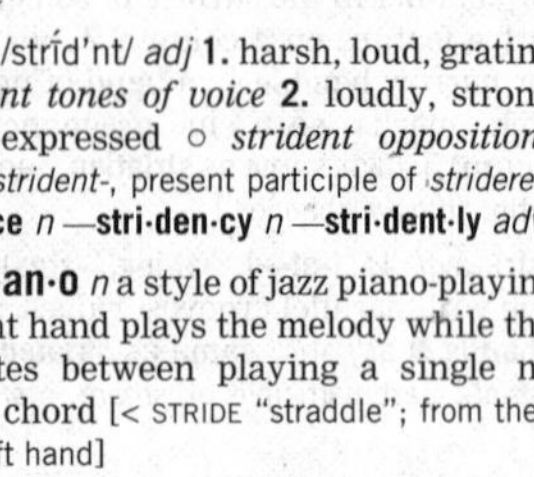

strigil

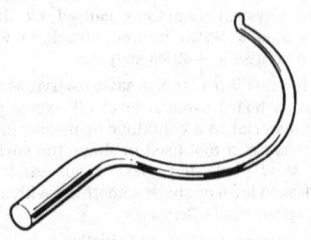

strig·il /stríjjəl/ *n* in ancient Greece and Rome, an instrument with a curved blade used to scrape dirt and sweat from the skin after bathing or exercising [Late 16C. < Latin *strigilis*]

stri·gose /strī gōss/ *adj* **1.** covered with fine scales or short bristles **2.** with thin, closely spaced grooves or ridges [Late 18C. < modern Latin *strigosus* < Latin *striga* "row, strip"]

strike /strīk/ *v* (**struck** /struk/, **strik·ing, strikes**) **1.** *vti* HIT SOMEBODY OR SOMETHING to hit somebody or something with a hand, tool, weapon, or other object ○ *She was struck on the arm by a piece of falling masonry.* **2.** *vti* DELIVER BLOW to deliver or inflict something such as a blow or punch **3.** *vti* COLLIDE WITH SOMEBODY OR SOMETHING to crash into, knock hard against, or collide with somebody or something ○ *The car swerved and struck a tree.* **4.** *vti* MIL ATTACK SOMEBODY OR SOMETHING to make a military attack on somebody or something ○ *The enemy struck under cover of darkness.* **5.** *vti* STOP WORKING AS PROTEST to stop working as a collective form of protest against an employer, often to achieve a specific aim ○ *were striking for a pay increase* ○ *struck the auto plant* **6.** (*past participle* **strick·en** /stríkən/ or **struck**) *vti* AFFECT SOMEBODY SUDDENLY to affect somebody suddenly or unexpectedly ○ *The illness can strike at any age.* ○ *was stricken with a heart attack* **7.** *vti* FIND OR DISCOVER SOMETHING to come across, find, or discover something, especially suddenly or unexpectedly **8.** *vti* PENETRATE SOMETHING to penetrate or seem to go right through something ○ *The pain struck deep into my shoulder blade.* **9.** *vt* KNOCK SOMETHING AWAY to remove something with a blow ○ *She struck the wasp from the window screen.* **10.** *vti* PRODUCE FIRE to produce fire by friction, or be produced by friction **11.** *vt* PRODUCE MUSICAL SOUND to produce a musical note by pressing a key or keys or by touching a string or strings **12.** *vti* LIGHT MATCH to cause a match to light by friction, or be lit by friction ○ *The matches won't strike if they get damp.* **13.** *vt* PRESS KEY TO OPERATE SOMETHING to press a key on something such as a computer keyboard or musical instrument **14.** *vti* INDICATE TIME BY MAKING SOUND to indicate the time by making a sound such as chiming (*refers to clocks*) **15.** *vt* MAKE SOMETHING BY STAMPING to make or form something such as a coin by stamping or punching **16.** *vti* SHINE ON SOMETHING to fall or shine on something ○ *Moonbeams struck the placid water on the lake.* **17.** *vt* BE NOTICED BY SOMEBODY to catch somebody's attention, or be noticed by somebody or something **18.** *vt* BE PERCEIVED BY SOMEBODY to be perceived by or become audible to somebody **19.** *vt* MAKE PARTICULAR IMPRESSION ON SOMEBODY to have a particular effect on or make a particular impression on somebody **20.** *vt* ENTER SOMEBODY'S MIND to enter somebody's mind or occur to somebody, especially suddenly **21.** *vt* AFFECT WITH EMOTION to affect somebody or cause somebody to be affected with an emotion in a deep, painful, or sudden way **22.** *vti* DAMAGE SOMETHING OR SOMEBODY to hit and damage or injure something or somebody **23.** *vi* BITE OR STING SUDDENLY to deliver a sudden fast bite or sting, typically resulting in injury to the one bitten or stung ○ *Suddenly the snake struck.* **24.** *vti* HAPPEN SUDDENLY to happen to somebody or something suddenly or unexpectedly ○ *Disaster struck when the volcano suddenly erupted.* **25.** (*past participle* **strick·en** or **struck**) *vt* CROSS OUT to cancel, delete, or cross something out ○ *The judge ordered that the preceding remark be stricken from the record.* **26.** *vt* AGREE TO TERMS to agree on the terms of something ○ *struck a deal* **27.** *vt* REACH AGREEMENT to achieve something such as a balance or compromise by careful consideration or calculation **28.** *vt* ADOPT POSE to adopt or assume something such as a pose or attitude **29.** *vti* TAKE BAIT to take or attempt to take a bait (*refers to fish*) ○ *The fish are striking today.* **30.** *vti* BOT GROW ROOTS to send out and establish roots **31.** *vt* DISMANTLE SOMETHING to dismantle something such as a tent or stage set **32.** *vt* LOWER SOMETHING IN RESPECT OR SURRENDER to lower something such as a flag or sail, especially as a sign of respect or surrender **33.** *vt* SAILING LOWER MAST to lower a ship's mast **34.** *vt* SHIPPING LOWER THINGS INTO SHIP'S HOLD to lower something such as cargo into the hold of a ship **35.** *vi US* NAVY ATTEMPT TECHNICAL RATING IN US NAVY to work hard in order to achieve a technical rating in the US Navy **36.** *vt* MANUF same as **strickle** ■ *n* **1.** HIT OR BLOW a blow delivered with a hand, tool, weapon, or other object **2.** SOUND OF HIT a sound produced by striking somebody or something **3.** WORK STOPPAGE a work stoppage by employees as a protest against an employer, often to achieve a specific aim **4.** REFUSAL TO DO SOMETHING AS PROTEST a refusal to carry out a regular action or activity such as eating or paying rent as a form of protest ○ *a hunger strike* **5.** MIL MILITARY ATTACK a military attack, especially one using aircraft **6.** SUCCESS IN FINDING SOMETHING a success in finding or discovering something, especially a valuable mineral source such as gold or oil **7.** BOWLING KNOCKING DOWN OF ALL BOWLING PINS the knocking down of all the pins with the first ball in a session of bowling **8.** BASEBALL MISSED PITCH a pitch in baseball that is swung at and missed or is in the strike zone and not hit **9.** COINS COINS STRUCK AT SAME TIME the number of coins or medals struck at one time **10.** GEOL DIRECTION OF GEOLOGIC FORMATION the compass direction of a horizontal line on a sloping rock surface, used to define geologic features such as bedding or faults **11.** MANUF same as **strickle** *n* (sense 1) **12.** VET ANIMAL DISEASE CAUSED BY FLIES an animal disease caused by an infestation of flies or fly eggs in open wounds or moist areas of the skin **13.** FISHING PULL ON FISHING LINE BY FISH a pull on a fishing line indicating that a fish has taken the bait **14.** BOT SENDING OUT OF PLANT ROOTS the establishment of roots by a plant cutting or seedling [Old English *strīcan* < Germanic, "touch lightly"] ◇ **on strike 1.** not working as a form of protest against an employer, often to achieve a specific aim **2.** refusing to undertake usual tasks as a form of protest ◇ **strike it rich** to be extremely lucky or successful, particularly in money matters (*informal*)

strike down *vt* **1.** CAUSE SOMEBODY TO FALL to hit and cause somebody or something to fall **2.** CAUSE SOMEBODY TO BECOME VERY ILL to affect somebody or cause somebody to become seriously ill, especially suddenly **3.** KILL SOMEBODY to cause somebody to die, especially suddenly or unexpectedly **4.** *US* CAUSE SOMETHING TO BECOME INVALID to cause something to be no longer in effect or valid ○ *a lower court ruling that was struck down upon appeal*

strike off *vt* **1.** to cancel or remove something from a list, record, or register by crossing it out ○ *An officer struck off the names of the passengers as they boarded the cruise ship.* **2.** to print a copy, document, or publication

strike on *vt* to think of something, especially suddenly or by chance

strike out *v* **1.** *vi* FAIL to be unsuccessful (*informal*) ○ *I tried three times to get that job, but struck out completely.* **2.** *vti* BASEBALL HAVE THREE STRIKES to put a batter out with three strikes, or be made out with three strikes **3.** *vi* SET OUT ENERGETICALLY to set out energetically, especially for a particular destination or in a particular direction ○ *We struck out at sunrise, determined to get there by nightfall.* **4.** *vi* ATTACK SOMEBODY OR SOMETHING to make an attack on somebody or something, either physically or verbally **5.** *vt* DRAW LINE THROUGH SOMETHING to draw a line through written or printed matter in order to cancel or delete it **6.** *vi* BEGIN SOMETHING to begin doing something, especially independently

strike up *v* **1.** *vti* to begin playing or singing something ○ *struck up the band and played a waltz* **2.** *vt* to begin something, or cause something to begin ○ *struck up a friendship*

strike upon *vt* same as **strike on**

strike·bound /strík bòwnd/ *adj* closed or unable to operate because people have stopped working as a form of protest

strike·break·er /strík bràykər/ *n* **1.** a worker who continues on the job while other employees are on strike **2.** somebody hired to do the work of somebody who is on strike

strike·break·ing /strík bràyking/ *n* **1.** the act of working for an employer while other employees are on strike **2.** action intended to break up a workers' strike

strike fault *n* a geologic fault with a horizontal line (**strike**) parallel to the rock strata

strike-out *n* in baseball, an out made by a batter charged with three strikes

strike·o·ver /strík ōvər/ *n* **1.** the typing of one character over another already typed without erasing the first one **2.** a character or word that has been typed over by something else

strike pay *n* money paid by a labor union to members who are on strike

strike price *n Can, UK* same as **striking price**

strik·er /strī́kər/ *n* **1. SOMEBODY ON STRIKE** somebody who has joined others in ceasing work in protest against working conditions or to compel an employer to accept their demands **2.** SOCCER **ATTACKING FOOTBALL PLAYER** an attacking player in a soccer team whose main role is to score goals **3. DEVICE THAT STRIKES TO TELL TIME** a device that strikes to tell the time, e.g., a hammer in a clock or a clapper in a bell **4.** ARMS **MECHANISM THAT DRIVES FIRING PIN** the mechanical part of a firearm that drives the firing pin forward **5.** *US* NAVY **SAILOR WORKING TO GET TECHNICAL RATING** somebody enlisted in the US Navy who is working hard toward a technical rating

strike-slip fault *n* a geologic fault that moves in a direction parallel to its strike

strike zone *n* in baseball, the area above home plate, between the batter's armpits and knees, through which the ball must travel in order to be called a strike

strik·ing /strī́king/ *adj* **1. CONSPICUOUS** conspicuous, marked, or noticeable **2. ATTRACTIVE OR IMPRESSIVE** attracting attention, especially in an impressive or unusual way **3.** HR **ON STRIKE** not working as a collective form of protest against an employer, often to achieve a specific aim —**strik·ing·ly** *adv* —**strik·ing·ness** *n*

strik·ing dis·tance *n* sufficient closeness to reach or achieve something ○ *within striking distance of the camp*

strik·ing price *n US* the price at which the holder of stock options or warrants has the right to buy or sell. Can term **strike price**

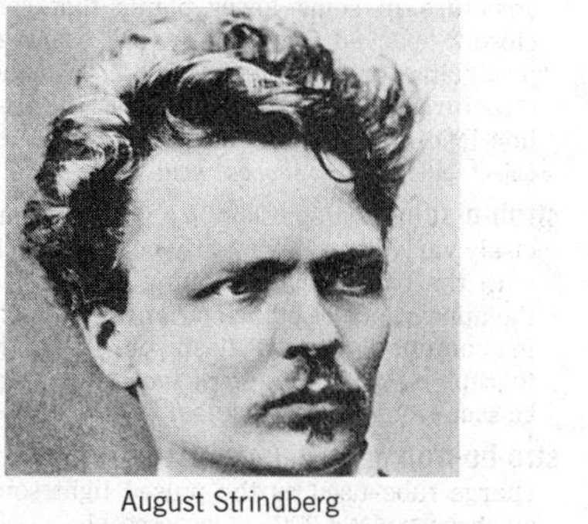

August Strindberg

Strind·berg /strínd bùrg, strín-/, **August** (1849–1912) Swedish dramatist. Often considered the greatest figure in Swedish literature, he greatly influenced European and US dramatists with his naturalistic novels and plays, notably *Miss Julie* (1888). Full name **Strindberg, Johan August** —**Strind·berg·i·an** /strind búrgee ən, strin-/ *adj*

> "I loathe people who keep dogs. They are cowards who haven't got the guts to bite people themselves."
> [August Strindberg, *A Madman's Diary*, 1895]

Strine /strīn/, **strine** *n* Australian English, especially a humorous representation in writing of Australian pronunciation, e.g., "Emma Chisit" for "How much is it?" (*humorous*) [Mid-20C. Representing supposed Australian pronunciation of AUSTRALIAN]

string /string/ *n* **1. THIN CORD** a thin cord or twine, usually made of twisted fibers, used for fastening, hanging, or tying **2. SOMETHING LIKE STRING** something that resembles string in form or texture **3. SUCCESSION OF ITEMS** a series of similar or connected acts, events, or things **4. LINE OF THINGS** a series of things forming or arranged in a line, usually one behind the other **5. GROUP OF ASSOCIATED THINGS** a group of similar things belonging to, managed by, or connected with a single person or a set of people **6. SEQUENCE OF SIMILAR ELEMENTS** a sequence of items of the same nature, e.g., letters, numbers, symbols, binary digits, sounds, or words **7. OBJECTS THREADED TOGETHER** a set of objects connected with a single thread **8.** MUSIC **CORD STRETCHED ACROSS MUSICAL INSTRUMENT** a cord made of nylon, wire, or gut that is stretched across a musical instrument and plucked, bowed, or otherwise vibrated to produce sound **9.** RACKET GAMES **TIGHT CORD ACROSS SPORTS RACKET** a thin cord that is tightly stretched across the face of a sports racket and interwoven with others to form a mesh **10.** ARCHERY **CORD ACROSS ARCHER'S BOW** in archery, the cord stretched between the ends of a bow **11.** BOT, FOOD **PLANT FIBER** a tough chewy fiber in a fruit or vegetable **12.** BUILDINGS same as **stringboard 13.** DESIGN same as **stringcourse 14. SOMEBODY CHOSEN AND RANKED ON ABILITY** a person or group of people chosen, especially for a sports team, and ranked on the basis of ability (*usually used in combination*) ○ *a second-string quarterback* ○ *played first string in the last quarter of the game* **15.** CUE GAMES **BILLIARDS HIT DETERMINING PLAYING ORDER** in billiards, an act of hitting the cue ball toward the head cushion (**lag**) to determine who will play first **16.** CUE GAMES same as **balkline** (sense 1) **17.** LAWN BOWLS **TEN FRAMES OF BOWLING** a game of bowling consisting of ten frames **18.** PHYS, ASTRON **HYPOTHETICAL ONE-DIMENSIONAL ENTITY** a hypothetical one-dimensional entity that vibrates as it moves through space and is held to be a fundamental component of matter **19.** *Southwest US* AGRIC **HERD OF HORSES** the herd of saddle horses from which ranch hands select their mounts **20.** ZOOL **TENDON** a tendon or ligament of an animal (*archaic*) ■ **strings** *npl* MUSIC **1. MUSICIANS PLAYING STRINGED INSTRUMENTS** the section of an orchestra consisting of musicians who play instruments with strings **2. STRINGED INSTRUMENTS OF ORCHESTRA** all the instruments of an orchestra or other musical ensemble that have strings, considered as a group ■ *v* (**strung** /strung/, **string·ing, strings**) **1.** *vt* **PUT THINGS ON STRING** to thread things onto a string **2.** *vt* **HANG SOMETHING BETWEEN POINTS** to hang or stretch something between two points **3.** *vt* **ARRANGE SOMETHING IN LINE** to arrange or extend something in a line or series **4.** *vt* **PROVIDE SOMETHING WITH STRINGS** to provide something such as a sports racket or musical instrument with a string or strings **5.** *vt* **FASTEN SOMETHING WITH STRING** to bind, fasten, hang, or tie something with a string or strings **6.** *vt* COOK **REMOVE FIBERS FROM FOOD** to remove the stringy fibers from fruit or vegetables before cooking or eating **7.** *vi* **BECOME STRINGY** to form strings, or become stringy **8.** *vti* CUE GAMES **DETERMINE BILLIARDS PLAYING ORDER** in billiards, to hit the cue ball toward the head cushion (**lag**) to determine who will play first ■ *adj* **MADE OF STRING** made of a mesh of string or similar material [Old English *streng* < Germanic, "stiff"] —**stringed** *adj* —**string·less** *adj* ◇ **have somebody on a string** to be able to control somebody easily ◇ **pull strings** to use influence to try to gain an advantage ◇ **pull the strings** to be in control, although not obviously so ◇ **with no strings (attached)** without any conditions or restrictions being made

string along *v* (*informal*) **1.** *vt* **DECEIVE SOMEBODY OVER LONG TIME** to deceive or fool somebody over an extended period of time, especially by keeping him or her in a state of false hope **2.** *vi* **GO WITH SOMEBODY** to accompany or stay with somebody, often in a casual manner ○ *She wanted to string along with us when we went to the shops.* **3.** *vi* **AGREE WITH SOMEBODY** to agree or go along with somebody or somebody's idea or suggestion

string up *vt* **1.** to suspend somebody or something on a string or strings **2.** to kill somebody by hanging (*informal*)

string band *n* a group of musicians who play folk or country music on stringed instruments

string bass /-báyss/ *n* MUSIC same as **double bass**

string bean *n* **1. BEAN POD** a slim green bean pod cooked as a vegetable **2.** PLANTS **CULTIVATED BEAN PLANT** a small bushy or tall climbing bean plant that produces string beans. Latin name: *Phaseolus vulgaris.* **3. TALL AND THIN PERSON** somebody who is tall and thin (*informal*)

string·board /stríng bàwrd/ *n* a board that covers the ends of the steps on a staircase [Because the board "strings" the steps together]

string·course /stríng kàwrss/ *n* a decorative feature on a building in the form of a horizontal band or molding

stringed in·stru·ment *n* a musical instrument in which bowing or plucking causes the vibration of a string or strings tightly stretched across a soundboard, e.g., a violin or guitar

strin·gen·do /strin jéndō/ *adv* at an accelerating tempo (*used as a musical direction*) [Mid-19C. < Italian, present participle of *stringere* "press, squeeze" < Latin, "draw tight, bind"] —**strin·gen·do** *adj*

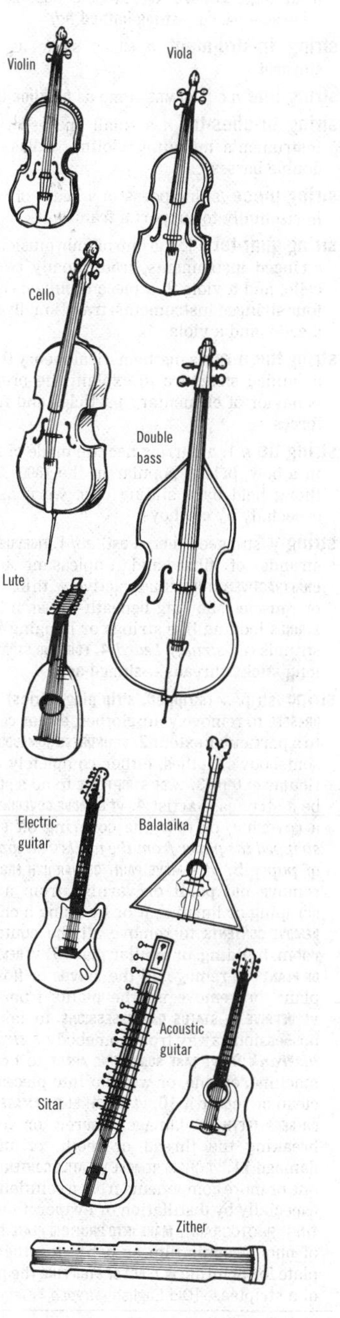

stringed instruments

strin·gent /strínjənt/ *adj* strictly controlled or enforced [Early 17C. < Latin *stringent-*, present participle of *stringere* "draw tight, bind"] —**strin·gen·cy** *n* —**strin·gent·ly** *adv*

string·er /stríngər/ *n* **1.** MEDIA **FREELANCE OR PART-TIME JOURNALIST** a journalist, often covering a specific geographic area, who works on a freelance or part-time basis for a newspaper, network, or news agency **2.** CONSTR **HORIZONTAL TIMBER** a heavy horizontal timber used for structural purposes **3.** BUILDINGS same as **stringboard 4.** AEROSP, NAUT **AUXILIARY MEMBER OF WING** a light auxiliary part parallel with the main structural members of a wing or fuselage, used mainly for bracing and stabilizing **5.** SPORTS **PLAYER OF PARTICULAR ABILITY** a member of a team who is ranked according to excellence or skill (*usually used in combination*) **6.** GEOL **NARROW MINERAL VEIN** a narrow or discontinuous linear vein of ore mineral

string·halt /stríng hàwlt/ *n* a condition of horses marked by sudden lifting of and lameness in the hind legs, caused by muscle spasms [Early 16C. < STRING + HALT²] —**string·halt·ed** *adj*

string in·stru·ment *n* MUSIC same as **stringed instrument**

string line *n* CUE GAMES same as **balkline** (sense 1)

string or·ches·tra *n* a small orchestra of stringed instruments including violins, violas, cellos, and double basses

string·piece /stríng pēess/ *n* a beam of wood placed horizontally to support a framework

string quar·tet *n* **1.** a group of four musicians playing stringed instruments, traditionally two violins, a cello, and a viola **2.** a piece of music composed for four stringed instruments, traditionally two violins, a cello, and a viola

string the·o·ry *n* a mathematical theory that provides a unified structure to explain the properties and behavior of elementary particles and fundamental forces

string tie *n* **1.** a narrow necktie made of ribbon, tied in a bow, briefly popular in the 1890s **2.** a narrow thong held by a sliding clip, worn as a necktie, especially by cowboys

string·y /stríngee/ (**-i·er, -i·est**) *adj* **1. FIBROUS** containing strands of fiber and unpleasant to chew **2. UNATTRACTIVELY THIN** unattractively thin, with bones or muscles showing beneath the skin **3. RESEMBLING STRINGS** looking like strings or hanging in long thin strands ○ *a stringy beard* **4. FORMING STRANDS** forming long sticky threads —**string·i·ness** *n*

strip¹ /strip/ *v* (**stripped, strip·ping, strips**) **1.** *vi* **GET UNDRESSED** to remove your clothes, either completely or to a particular extent **2.** *vt* **UNDRESS SOMEBODY** to remove somebody's clothes, either completely or to a particular extent **3.** *vi* **DO STRIPTEASE** to do a striptease, or be a striptease artist **4.** *vt* **REMOVE COVERING** to take off a covering, or take the covering off something ○ *stripped the paper from the walls* ○ *stripped the walls of paper* **5.** *vt* **REMOVE PAINT OR VARNISH FROM SURFACE** to remove old paint or varnish from a surface by scraping or burning it or by using a chemical **6.** *vt* **REMOVE CONTENTS** to remove all the contents from a room, building, or similar place **7.** *vt* **REMOVE ALL LEAVES OR PLANTS** to remove all the leaves or flowers from a plant, or remove all the plants from an area **8.** *vt* **DEPRIVE OF STATUS OR POSSESSIONS** to take status or possessions away from somebody ○ *stripped him of his rank* **9.** *vt* **TAKE SOMETHING APART** to break down a machine, engine, or weapon into pieces in order to clean or repair it **10.** *vti* MECH ENG **DAMAGE SCREW THREAD OR GEAR TEETH** to damage a screw or gearwheel by breaking the thread or teeth, or undergo this damage **11.** *vt* CHEM **REMOVE VOLATILE CONTENT** to separate one or more components from a solution or mixture, especially by distillation or evaporation **12.** *vt* PRINTING, PHOTOGRAPHY **MAKE INTO PRINTING PLATE** to put pieces of photographic film or paper together to make a plate for printing ■ *n* **ACT OF STRIPPING** the performance of a striptease [Old English *-strȳpan* < Germanic]

USAGE stripping or **striping**? The present participle of ***strip*** is ***stripping***, as in *stripping paint.* The present participle of ***stripe*** is ***striping***, as in *busy striping the football field with yardage lines.*

strip² /strip/ *n* **1. LONG FLAT PIECE** a long flat narrow piece of something **2.** AVIAT same as **airstrip 3.** PUBL same as **comic strip 4.** COMM **ROAD LINED WITH BUSINESSES** a road lined with stores, shopping centers, restaurants, and other businesses **5.** *UK* SPORTS **SPORTS CLOTHES** the uniform worn by a specific sports team such as a soccer team ■ *vt* (**stripped, strip·ping, strips**) **DIVIDE INTO STRIPS** to cut, tear, or divide something into strips [15C. Probably < Low German *strippe* "strap, thong"]

strip³ /strip/ (**stripped, strip·ping, strips**) *vt* to remove the last remaining milk from the udder of a cow or goat by hand after machine-milking [Early 17C. Origin ?]

strip club *n* a club or bar where people can watch striptease acts [< STRIP¹]

strip crop·ping *n* the growing of different crops in an arrangement of lines or bands to prevent soil erosion [< STRIP²]

stripe¹ /strīp/ *n* **1. LONG NARROW BAND** a long narrow band of a different color, composition, or texture from the surrounding surface or background **2. PATTERN** a pattern of stripes **3.** TEXTILES **FABRIC** a fabric with a pattern of stripes **4.** MIL **INDICATION OF RANK** a narrow band or V-shaped piece of fabric, sewn onto a uniform as a symbol of rank **5.** *US* **TYPE OF PERSON** a recognizable type of person with a specific character or set of opinions ○ *This is a tyrant of a very different stripe.* ○*"...portals of all stripes face a challenging future..."* (*Washington Post*; November 1998) ■ *vt* (**striped, strip·ing, stripes**) **MARK SOMETHING WITH STRIPES** to put a pattern of stripes on something [15C. Probably < Middle Dutch or Middle Low German *strīpe*] —**strip·y** *adj*

USAGE See *strip*¹.

stripe² /strīp/ *n* a blow from a whip, lash, cane, or belt [15C. Probably < Low German or Dutch]

striped /strīpt/ *adj* patterned or marked with stripes [15C. < STRIPE¹]

striped bass /-báss/ *n* a large game fish with black stripes that travels up rivers to breed. Native to: US coastal waters. Latin name: *Morone saxatilus.*

striped ma·ple *n* a maple that has green bark marked with white stripes. Native to: northeastern United States, southeastern Canada. Latin name: *Acer pennsylvanicum.*

striped mar·lin *n* a large game and food fish with dark blue vertical stripes on the sides. Native to: Pacific. Latin name: *Makaira audax.*

striped mus·cle *n* ANAT same as **striated muscle**

striped skunk *n* a common skunk that has a white cap on its head and white stripes down each side of the spine. Native to: North America. Latin name: *Mephitis mephitis.*

strip·er /strīpər/ *n* **1.** a member of the armed forces or of a flight or ship's crew whose stripes on the uniform indicate rank or length of service (*slang; usually used in combination*) ○ *a three-striper* **2.** FISH same as **striped bass** [Early 20C. < STRIPE¹]

strip-graz·ing *n* a system in which cattle or other livestock are periodically allocated a fresh strip of pasture to graze by the moving of an electrified fence across the field [< STRIP²]

strip joint *n* same as **strip club** (*informal*) [< STRIP¹]

strip·light /stríp līt/ *n* a row of shaded lamps used to light a theater stage [Early 20C. < STRIP²]

strip·ling /strípling/ *n* a boy in his early teenage years, who has not yet grown to his full size [14C. Probably < STRIP²]

strip mall *n* a long building facing a road, divided into separate stores and businesses with parking spaces in front [< STRIP²]

strip mine *n* a mine where mineral seams near the surface of the ground are exposed by stripping away soil and land [< STRIP²] —**strip min·ing** *n*

strip par·ty *n* a party for a group of women at which a male stripper performs

stripped-down *adj* deprived of all but the most essential or simple features [< STRIP¹]

strip·per¹ /stríppər/ *n* **1. STRIPTEASE ARTIST** a performer of striptease acts **2. PAINT OR WALLPAPER REMOVER** a tool or substance used for removing paint, varnish, wallpaper, or other substances from a surface **3. SOMEBODY WHO STRIPS SOMETHING** somebody whose job is to strip something [Late 16C. < STRIP¹]

strip·per² /stríppər/, **strip·per well** *n US* a small oil or gas well with limited production capacity [Mid 20C. < STRIP³]

strip pok·er *n* a variety of the card game poker in which, at each round, players who lose have to remove an item of their clothing [< STRIP¹]

strip·py /stríppee/ *n* patchwork in which broad strips of fabric are pieced together in vertical bands, then quilted ■ *adj* consisting of strips [Early 19C. < STRIP²]

strip-search *vti* to compel somebody to undress completely while searching for concealed drugs, weapons, or contraband [< STRIP¹] —**strip search** *n*

strip steak *n US* a boneless steak from the upper part of the loin [< STRIP²; from its long narrow shape]

strip·tease /stríp tēez, strìp tēez/ *n* an entertainment in which the performer slowly undresses in an erotic way, usually with music as an accompaniment [Mid-20C. < STRIP¹] —**strip·teas·er** *n*

strive /strīv/ (**strove** /strōv/ or **strived, striv·en** /strívvən/ or **strived, striv·ing, strives**) *vi* **1. TRY HARD** to try hard to achieve or get something **2. OPPOSE** to fight in opposition to something **3. COMPETE** to compete resolutely against somebody or something [12C. < Old French *estriver* "contend" < *estrif* "strife"] —**striv·er** *n*

SYNONYMS See *try.*

strobe /strōb/ *n* **1.** ELECTRONICS same as **strobe light 2.** ELECTRONICS same as **stroboscope 3.** an electronic pulse of short duration used to examine the characteristics of a periodic waveform **4.** the process of viewing vibrations or rotational motion with a stroboscope [Mid-20C. Shortening of STROBOSCOPE]

strobe light *n* a high-intensity flashing beam of light produced by charging a capacitor to a very high voltage then discharging it as a high-intensity flash of light in a tube

stro·bi·la /strə bīlə/ (*plural* **-lae** /-lee/) *n* **1.** the segmented body of a tapeworm, usually excluding the head (**scolex**) and neck **2.** a chain of buds that are attached to the body of some jellyfish and that later develop into individual offspring [Mid-19C. Via modern Latin < Greek *strobilē* "twisted plug of lint," form of *strobilos* (see STROBILUS)]

stro·bi·la·tion /stròbbə láysh'n/ *n* the process of dividing into segments to form reproductive structures such as the buds produced by jellyfish

stro·bi·lus /strŏbələss/ (*plural* **-li** /-lī/) *n* **1.** the cone of a coniferous plant, or a similar cone-shaped structure in some lower plants that consists of closely packed fertile leaves bearing spore-producing organs (*technical*) **2.** a cone-shaped structure in flowering plants, e.g., the fruit of the hop [Mid-18C. Via late Latin < Greek *strobilos* "twisted object, pine cone" < *strobos* "whirling"]

strob·o·scope /strṓbə skṓp/ *n* a flashing lamp of precisely variable periodicity that can be synchronized with the frequency of moving machinery to give the appearance of being stationary. It is often used in conjunction with flash or stop-action photography. [Mid-19C. < Greek *strobos* "whirling"] —**stro·bo·scop·ic** /strṑbə skóppik/ *adj*

stro·bo·tron /strṓbə tròn/ *n* the triggered gas-discharge tube used as the pulsed light source in a stroboscope [Mid-20C. < STROBOSCOPE]

strode past tense of **stride**

Stroess·ner /stréssnər/, **Alfredo** (*b.* 1912) Paraguayan soldier and dictator. As commander-in-chief of armed forces, he overthrew President Federico Chavez in 1954 and held office until he was overthrown in 1989.

stro·ga·noff /strṓgə nàwf, -nòf/, **Stro·ga·noff** *adj* cooked in a wine sauce with sour cream ■ *n* FOOD same as **beef stroganoff** [Mid-20C. < French, after Count Pavel Aleksandrovich *Stroganov* (1772–1817), Russian diplomat]

Stro·heim ♦ **von Stroheim, Erich**

stroke /strōk/ *n* **1. STOPPAGE OF BLOOD FLOW TO BRAIN** a sudden blockage or rupture of a blood vessel in the brain resulting in, e.g., loss of consciousness, partial loss of movement, or loss of speech. Technical name **cerebrovascular accident 2. SUDDEN OCCURRENCE** a sudden instance or occurrence of something that has a strong or unexpected effect ○ *a stroke of luck* **3. HITTING OF BALL** in racket games or golf, the hitting of a ball or the way in which this is done **4.** SWIMMING **SINGLE MOVEMENT IN SWIMMING** a single complete movement of the arms and legs when swimming **5.** SWIMMING **SWIMMING STYLE** a style of swimming, using the arms and legs in a specific way ○ *a difficult swimming stroke* **6.** ENG **MOVEMENT OF PISTON** a single movement, up or down, of a piston in an engine, or the distance that a piston travels in a single movement **7.** ART **BRUSH OR PEN LINE** a single line or mark made with a brush or pen ○ *a brush stroke* **8.** ART **SINGLE MOVEMENT OF BRUSH OR PEN** a single movement of a brush or pen to make a line or mark **9. VERBAL ENCOURAGEMENT** a usually positive comment or statement, e.g., a compliment made by one person to another ○ *I need all the positive strokes I can get right now.* **10. STRIKING OF CLOCK** a single sound made by a clock that is striking ○ *at the stroke of seven* **11. HIT** a hit or blow made by the hand, a cane, or a tool **12.** CARESSING MOVEMENT a gentle caressing movement of the hand over fur, hair, or skin **13.** SINGLE MOVEMENT IN SERIES a single movement forming part of a series of movements, e.g., the beat of a wing or the swing of a pendulum ○ *a wing stroke* **14.** ROWING SINGLE PULL in rowing, a single movement of the oars through the water **15.** ROWING ROWING STYLE a particular rowing style **16.** ROWING ROWER WHO KEEPS TIME a rower in a racing boat who sets the pace for the crew **17.** *UK* PRINTING same as **slash** *n* (sense 5) **18.** ADDITIONAL FEATURE a small additional feature that has an effect on the style or nature of something ○ *a stroke of sarcasm* **19.** PSYCHOL ELEMENT OF SOCIAL RECOGNITION in transactional analysis, a unit of social recognition between two or more people that, in its simplest form, can be a one-word greeting such as "hello" ■ *v* (**stroked, strok·ing, strokes**) **1.** *vt* CARESS SOMETHING to move the hand gently over something as if caressing it ○ *stroked the cat gently* **2.** *vt* HIT BALL SMOOTHLY in various sports, to hit or kick a ball smoothly **3.** *vt* COMPLIMENT SOMEBODY to behave in an encouraging or solicitous way toward somebody as a way of persuading or eliciting cooperation **4.** *vi* ROWING MOVE OARS to row at a particular speed or rate of the oars **5.** *vt* ROWING SET ROWING PACE to be the rower who sets the pace for the crew **6.** *vt* PUSH SOMETHING GENTLY to push something somewhere gently with a light movement of the hand **7.** *vt* CROSS SOMETHING OUT to draw a line through something ■ *adj US* PORNOGRAPHIC relating to or of the nature of pornography (*slang*) [Old English *strācian* < Indo-European, "rub, press"] ◇ **different strokes for different folks** used to emphasize that people are all individuals and that what suits one will not necessarily suit another (*dated slang*)

stroke play *n Can, UK* in golf, a way of scoring in which the total number of strokes taken for the round is counted rather than the number of holes won. US term **medal play**

stroll /strōl/ *v* (**strolled, stroll·ing, strolls**) **1.** *vti* WALK UNHURRIEDLY to walk along somewhere in a slow unhurried way, especially for enjoyment **2.** *vi* PERFORM EFFORTLESSLY to do, obtain, or achieve something in a casual effortless way ○ *strolled through the exam* ■ *n* LEISURELY WALK a slow leisurely walk for pleasure ○ *went for a stroll in the park* [Early 17C. Probably < German *strollen* "wander," variant of *strolchen* < *Strolch* "vagabond, fortune teller"]

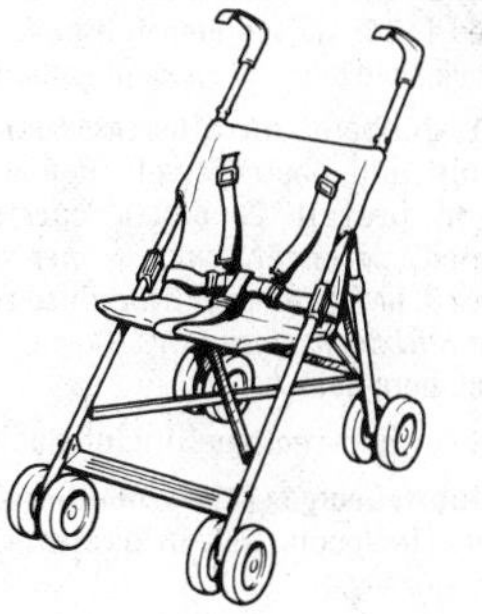

stroller

stroll·er /strṓlər/ *n* **1.** a light chair with wheels in which a young child can be pushed around **2.** somebody who is walking in a slow leisurely way for pleasure

stroll·ing /strṓling/ *adj* going from place to place to earn a living, especially by entertaining ○ *strolling minstrels*

stro·ma /strṓmə/ (*plural* **-ma·ta** /-mətə/) *n* **1.** the connective tissue that provides the framework of an organ or other anatomical structure rather than carrying out its functions **2.** the fluid-filled interior of a chloroplast containing enzymes and other components required for photosynthesis, including the light-trapping components [Mid-19C. Via modern and late Latin < Greek *strōma* "bed, cushion"] —**stro·mat·ic** /strō máttik/ *adj*

stro·mat·o·lite /strō mátt'l ìt/ *n* a very old fossil formed in sedimentary rock by sea cyanobacteria and consisting of a rounded or columnar calcium-containing mass of many layers [Mid-20C. < late Latin *stromat-*, stem of *stroma* (see STROMA)] —**stro·mat·o·lit·ic** /strō màtt'l íttik/ *adj*

Strom·bo·li /strómbəlee, strom bṓlee/ volcanic island in the Italian Lipari Islands in the Tyrrhenian Sea, north of Sicily. Area: 5 sq. mi./13 sq. km.

Stro·min·ger /strómminjər/, **Andrew** (*b.* 1955) US physicist. His work has been influential in merging the study of black holes with that of string theory.

strong /strawng/ *adj* **1.** PHYSICALLY POWERFUL having the physical strength needed to exert considerable force, e.g., in lifting, pulling, or pushing something **2.** USING FORCE using great physical force **3.** ROBUST AND STURDY sturdy, well made, and not easily damaged or broken **4.** EMOTIONALLY RESILIENT having the necessary emotional qualities to deal with stress, grief, loss, risk, and other difficulties **5.** HEALTHY AND WELL being in good health, especially after an illness ○ *feeling stronger every day* **6.** THRIVING thriving, developing well, and likely to continue so ○ *a strong economy* **7.** LIKELY TO SUCCEED very likely to succeed, win, or come to be something ○ *a strong candidate for the job.* **8.** CONVINCING supported by facts or good evidence and likely to be correct or effective ○ *a strong argument* **9.** KNOWLEDGEABLE very skillful or knowledgeable in a particular subject or area ○ *Physics was never one of my strongest subjects!* **10.** EXERTING INFLUENCE influential or authoritative by virtue of having or holding power **11.** EFFECTIVE having a powerful effect ○ *strong painkillers* **12.** FELT POWERFULLY felt or expressed with a powerful effect ○ *She has strong views on the subject.* **13.** DISTINCTIVE bold, clearly defined, and prominent ○ *strong features* **14.** EXTREME unusually severe of its kind ○ *Strong measures were taken to prevent a riot.* **15.** INTENSE IN IMPRESSION having an intense, powerful, or vivid effect on the senses ○ *a strong smell of garlic* **16.** EASY TO DETECT easy to detect or receive ○ *The signal will be stronger as you get closer.* **17.** CONCENTRATED containing a lot of the main ingredient and not diluted or watery ○ *strong black coffee* **18.** ALCOHOLIC containing much alcohol **19.** FAST MOVING flowing or blowing at high speed ○ *a strong current* **20.** CHEM FULLY IONIZED producing ions freely in solution **21.** MIL WELL DEFENDED well defended and difficult to capture ○ *a strong fortress* **22.** OF PARTICULAR NUMBER having a particular number of members ○ *a force 50,000 strong* **23.** OPTICS WITH HIGH MAGNIFICATION having a powerful magnifying or corrective ability ○ *a strong lens* **24.** COMM WITH HIGH PRICES characterized by high or rising prices ○ *a strong currency* **25.** GRAM WITH CHANGED VOWEL describes an irregular verb that changes the vowel in the stem in its different forms, e.g., "ring," which has the forms "rang" and "rung" [Old English *strang* < Germanic] —**strong·ly** *adv* ◇ **come on strong** (*slang*) **1.** to behave or express something aggressively **2.** to begin to have a vivid or powerful effect ◇ **going strong** thriving and doing well

strong-arm (*informal*) *adj* using or involving coercion or physical force ○ *ready to use strong-arm tactics* ■ *vt* to use coercion against somebody to induce cooperation

strong·box /stráwng bòks/ *n* a secure metal box or safe where money or valuables can be kept

strong breeze *n* a wind of between 25 and 31 mi./40 and 50 km per hour, classified as force six on the Beaufort scale

strong force *n* PHYS same as **strong interaction**

strong gale *n* a wind of between 47 and 54 mi./76 and 87 km per hour, classified as force nine on the Beaufort scale

strong·hold /stráwng hṑld/ *n* **1.** a place that is fortified or that can easily be defended **2.** a place where a particular group, activity, or set of opinions is concentrated

strong in·ter·ac·tion *n* a fundamental force between elementary particles that is responsible for binding protons and neutrons together in an atomic nucleus and other interactions between elementary particles (**hadrons**). Mediated by gluons, the interaction is the most powerful force known and is responsible for the particle creation that occurs when high-energy particles collide.

strong lan·guage *n* language that expresses something in a forceful way, especially with abusive words or swearing

strong·man /stráwng màn/ (*plural* **-men** /-mèn/) *n* **1.** a powerful, typically dictatorial, leader who rules by force **2.** a man who performs feats of strength, e.g., at a carnival or circus

strong-mind·ed *adj* **1.** determined and persevering in the face of difficulty **2.** confident, intelligent, and independent in thought —**strong-mind·ed·ly** *adv* —**strong-mind·ed·ness** *n*

strong point *n* an area for which somebody has a talent ○ *Tact was never his strong point.*

strong·point /stráwng pòynt/ *n* a fortified place that can be defended

strong·room /stráwng ro͞om, -ro͝om/ *n* a reinforced room designed to withstand fire or theft and used for the storage of valuables

strong side *n* in football, the side of the offensive formation with more players and the tight end

strong suit *n* **1.** same as **strong point 2.** in various card games, the suit in which a player or team holds the most cards or the most face cards

strong-willed *adj* determined to prevail in the face of difficulty or opposition

strong·wom·an /stróng wo͝omən/ (*plural* **-wom·en** /-wìmmin/) *n* a woman who performs feats of strength, e.g., at a carnival or circus, or who competes in weightlifting competitions

stron·gyle /strón jìl/, **stron·gyl** *n* a parasitic nematode worm related to the hookworms that infests the intestinal tract of mammals. Superfamily: Strongyloidea. [Mid-19C. < modern Latin *Strongylus* < Greek *stroggulos* "round, compact"]

stron·gy·loi·di·a·sis /strònjə loy dī́ əssiss/ *n* intestinal infestation in mammals by strongyles, producing various severe and sometimes fatal intestinal disorders, especially in individuals with weakened immune systems [Mid-20C. < modern Latin *Strongyloidea*, superfamily name < *Strongylus* (see STRONGYLE)]

stron·gy·lo·sis /strònjə lṓssiss/ *n* an illness, usually of horses, caused by infection with strongyles

stron·tia /strónshee ə, -tee ə/ *n* CHEM same as **strontium monoxide** [Early 19C. Back-formation < STRONTIAN]

stron·ti·an /strónshee ən, strόntee-/ *n* **1.** MINERALS same as **strontianite 2.** CHEM same as **strontium monoxide 3.** CHEM same as **strontium** [Late 18C. After *Strontian*, W Scotland]

stron·ti·an·ite /strónshee ə nìt, stróntee-/ *n* a variously colored strontium carbonate mineral. Use: source of strontium.

stron·ti·um /strónshee əm, -tee-/ *n* a soft yellow or silvery white metallic element of the alkaline-earth group, found only in combination with other substances. Source: strontianite, celestite. Use: fireworks, flares, alloys. Symbol **Sr.** See table at **element** [Early 19C. < STRONTIA]

stron·ti·um 90 /stròntee əm nī́ntee/ *n* a radioactive isotope of strontium with a mass number of 90, present in nuclear fallout and assimilated like calcium in bone formation

stron·ti·um mon·ox·ide *n* a white insoluble solid resembling quicklime. Use: purification of sugar. Formula: SrO.

stron·ti·um u·nit *n* a unit of measurement of the amount of strontium 90 in an organic substance such as soil or bone, in relation to the concentration of calcium in the same substance

Stroop ef·fect /stro͞op-/ *n* difficulty in identifying the colors in which names of colors are written. For example, if the word "red" is printed in green ink, people are likely to say "red" when asked the color of the printed word. [Mid-20C. After John Ridley *Stroop* 1897–1973, US psychologist]

strop /strop/ *n* **1.** LEATHER STRAP FOR SHARPENING a leather strap used for sharpening a straight razor **2.** STRAP FOR CARGO a strap of leather or rope used for lifting cargo ■ *vt* (**stropped, strop·ping, strops**) SHARPEN RAZOR to sharpen a straight razor on a strop [14C. < Low German and Dutch, via W Germanic < Latin *stroppus* < Greek *strophos* "twisted cord"]

stro·phe /strṓfee/ *n* **1.** the first type of metrical form in a poem that alternates two contrasting metrical forms **2.** the first of two movements made by the chorus in a classical Greek drama, or the part of an ode sung during this [Early 17C. < Greek *strophē* "turning"] —**stro·phic** /stróffik, strṓfik/ *adj*

stro·phoid /strṓ fòyd/ *n* a plane curve symmetrical to the x-axis, generated by a point whose distance from the y-axis along a straight line is equal to the y-intercept [Late 19C. < Greek *strophos* "twisted cord"]

strop·py /stróppee/ (-pi·er, -pi·est) *adj UK* bad-tempered and uncooperative (*informal*) [Mid-20C. Origin ?]

stroud /strowd/ *n* a rough woolen fabric. Use: originally by British traders in trade with Native North Americans. [Late 17C. Origin ?]

strove past tense of **strive**

struck /struk/ past participle, past tense of **strike** ■ *adj US* closed temporarily or working at reduced output because of a labor dispute

struck ju·ry *n* a jury reduced to the proper number when lawyers for the two sides have eliminated names from a list of candidates

struck meas·ure *n* a quantity of something such as grain measured by leveling the substance with the top of a container

struc·tur·al /strúkchərəl/ *adj* 1. RELATING TO STRUCTURE relating to the way parts are put together or how they work together ○ *made some structural repairs* ○ *a structural reorganization of the company* 2. USED IN CONSTRUCTION suitable for use in construction ○ *structural fiberglass* 3. RESULTING FROM STRUCTURE relating to or resulting from the organization or functioning of a political or economic system ○ *gloomy predictions based on lack of structural change in the stock market* 4. BASIC TO STRUCTURE constituting an important or essential part of a structure 5. CHEM CAUSED BY ATOMIC ARRANGEMENT relating to or caused by the arrangement of atoms in a molecule 6. GEOG OF ROCK STRUCTURE relating to or caused by movement of the Earth's surface —**struc·tur·al·ly** *adv*

struc·tur·al for·mu·la *n* an expanded chemical formula representing the arrangement of atoms and bonds within a molecule

struc·tur·al gene *n* a gene that codes for a protein required for the cell's own use

struc·tur·al·ism /strúkchərə lìzzəm/ *n* 1. SOC SCI a method of sociological analysis based on the notion of human society as a network of interrelations whose patterns and significance can be analyzed 2. PSYCHOL same as **structural psychology** 3. LING same as **structural linguistics** —**struc·tur·al·ist** *n, adj*

struc·tur·al·ize /strúkchərə lìz/ (-ized, -iz·ing, -iz·es) *vt* to arrange or organize something so that it has a structure

struc·tur·al lin·guis·tics *n* a branch of linguistics that emphasizes the significance of the interrelations between the elements that constitute a linguistic system (*takes a singular verb*) —**struc·tur·al lin·guist** *n*

struc·tur·al psy·chol·o·gy *n* a school of psychology of the early part of the 20th century that sought to organize the components of subjective experience in a hierarchy from simplest to most complex —**struc·tur·al psy·chol·o·gist** *n*

struc·tur·al steel *n* strong steel shaped for use in construction

struc·ture /strúkchər/ *n* 1. SOMETHING BUILT OR ERECTED a building, bridge, framework, or other object that has been put together from many different parts 2. SYSTEM OF PARTS a system or organization made up of interrelated parts functioning as a whole 3. WAY THAT PARTS LINK OR FUNCTION the way in which the different parts of something link or work together, or the fact of being linked together ○ *the structure of local government* ○ *The essay is interesting, but it lacks structure.* 4. BIOL PART OF ORGANISM a part of a body or organism identifiable by its shape and other properties, e.g., tissue or an organ 5. CHEM ARRANGEMENT OF ATOMS the arrangement of atoms in a molecule 6. GEOL COMPONENT PARTS OF ROCKS the physical disposition of a rock mass or its mineral components ■ *vt* (-tured, -tur·ing, -tures) GIVE STRUCTURE TO SOMETHING to organize or arrange something into a whole [15C. Directly or via French < Latin *structura* < *struct-*, past participle of *struere* "build"]

ORIGIN The Latin word *struere* "to build," from which ***structure*** is derived, is also the source of the English words *construct, construe, destroy, instruct,* and *obstruct.*

struc·tured /strúkchərd/ *adj* 1. planned, organized, and controlled 2. with a definite shape, form, or pattern ○ *For business wear, suits need a more structured look.*

struc·tured pro·gram·ming *n* a style of computer programming in which a program consists of a hierarchy of simple subroutines

struc·tured que·ry lan·guage *n* COMPUT full form of **SQL**

struc·tur·i·zer /strúkchər ìzər/ *n* a hair conditioner designed to strengthen and restructure the hair shaft

stru·del /strood'l/ *n* a pastry made with very thin pastry rolled and baked with a filling, usually of chopped apples, raisins, and sugar [Late 19C. < German]

strug·gle /strúgg'l/ *vi* (-gled, -gling, -gles) 1. TRY TO OVERCOME PROBLEM to make a great effort to deal with a challenge, problem, or difficulty ○ *He was struggling with his math homework.* 2. MAKE GREAT PHYSICAL EFFORT to make a great physical effort to achieve or obtain something ○ *A rescue party struggled to reach the stranded climbers.* 3. FIGHT BY WRESTLING to fight with somebody by grappling and wrestling 4. WRITHE TO ESCAPE to move and wriggle forcefully in an attempt to escape 5. MOVE WITH DIFFICULTY to move with great effort ○ *so weak I just managed to struggle out of bed* ■ *n* 1. GREAT EFFORT TO OVERCOME DIFFICULTIES a great effort made over a period of time to overcome difficulties or achieve something 2. FIGHT a prolonged fight or conflict 3. HARD TASK a strenuous physical or mental effort, or something requiring this [14C. Origin ?] —**strug·gler** *n*

strug·gle for ex·is·tence *n* the ongoing effort to survive and reproduce in an environment of competing organisms

strum /strum/ *v* (**strummed, strum·ming, strums**) 1. *vti* PLAY INSTRUMENT BY BRUSHING STRINGS to play a guitar or other stringed instrument by brushing the strings with the fingers or a pick 2. *vt* PLAY TUNE to play a tune by strumming an instrument ■ *n* SOUND OF STRUMMING the sound of somebody strumming an instrument [Late 18C. An imitation of the sound] —**strum·mer** *n*

stru·ma /stroomə/ (*plural* **-mae** /-mee/ or **-mas**) *n* 1. BOT a swelling at the base of a moss capsule 2. MED same as **goiter** 3. MED same as **scrofula** (*archaic*) [Mid-16C. Via modern Latin < Latin, "scrofulous tumor"] —**stru·mat·ic** /stroo máttik/ *adj* —**stru·mose** *adj* —**stru·mous** *adj*

strum·pet /strúmpət/ *n* an offensive term for a prostitute or a woman regarded as too sexually active (*archaic*) [14C. Origin ?]

strung /strung/ past participle, past tense of **string** ■ *adj US* very tired, tense, and overwrought

strung out *adj* 1. DRUGGED under the influence of a drug, especially a narcotic drug (*slang*) 2. WEAKENED debilitated by long-term drug use (*slang*) 3. OVERWROUGHT tired, tense, or overwrought (*informal*)

strut /strut/ *v* (**strut·ted, strut·ting, struts**) 1. *vi* WALK IN ARROGANT WAY to walk in a stiff or proud way that suggests arrogance or pomposity 2. *vt* SHOW OFF to show something off to other people in an ostentatious way 3. *vt* PROP SOMETHING WITH PLANKS to support a structure with planks or boards ■ *n* 1. SUPPORTING MEMBER a long rigid plank, board, or other structural member used as a support in building 2. STRUTTING WALK a stiff proud way of walking [Old English *strūtian* "protrude stiffly" < Indo-European, "stiff"]

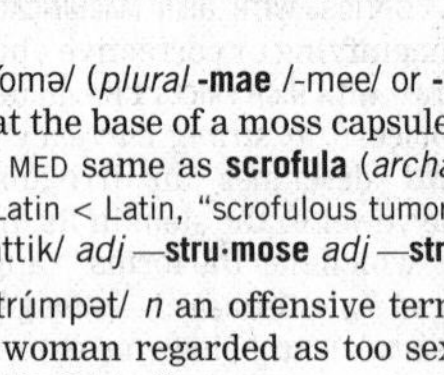

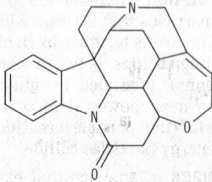

strychnine

strych·nine /strík nìn, -neen/ *n* a bitter white poisonous alkaloid obtained from nux vomica and related plants. Use: rodenticide, nervous system stimulant. Formula: $C_{21}H_{22}N_2O_2$. [Early 19C. < French < modern Latin *Strychnos* < Latin *strychnon* "nightshade" < Greek *strukhnos*] —**strych·nic** /stríknik/ *adj*

Strze·leck·i Range /strez lékee-/ range of hills in southern Victoria, Australia. Highest peak: 1,640 ft./500 m.

STS *abbr* GENETICS sequence tagged site

Stu·art /stoo ərt/, **Charles Edward** (1720–88) grandson of James II of England and claimant to the British throne. The son of James Francis Edward Stuart, he led the Jacobite uprising in Scotland in 1745 and after its failure lived in exile in Europe. Known as **Bonnie Prince Charlie, the Young Pretender**

Stu·art, Gilbert (1755–1828) US artist. Of the many portraits he painted, the best known are of George Washington. Full name **Stuart, Gilbert Charles**

Stu·art /stoo ərt, styoo ərt/, **James Ewell Brown** (1833–64) US Confederate general. His reconnaissance missions played an important part in several Confederate victories and made him a popular hero. Known as **Jeb Stuart**

Stu·art, James Francis Edward (1688–1766) son of James II of England and claimant to the British throne. He was supported in his claim to the British throne by France and by the Jacobites in their unsuccessful rising in Scotland (1715). After 1719 he lived in Rome. Known as **the Old Pretender**

stub /stub/ *n* 1. SHORT REMAINING PART a short part of something that is left after the main part has been removed or used 2. SMALL SECTION OF TICKET OR CHECK a small detachable section of a ticket, check, or voucher, retained as a record of a transaction 3. STUMP OF TREE OR PLANT the stump of a tree or plant 4. SMALL PROJECTION a small projection from a surface ■ *vt* (**stubbed, stub·bing, stubs**) 1. BANG TOE to bang a toe against something accidentally 2. GARDENING DIG SOMETHING UP BY ROOTS to dig up a plant or tree by the roots 3. AGRIC CLEAR LAND OF STUMPS to clear land of tree stumps [Old English *stubb* "tree stump" < Germanic]

stub out *vt* to put out a cigarette or cigar by pushing the burning end against something

stub·ble /stúbb'l/ *n* 1. the short spiky growth of beard on a man's face when he has not shaved 2. short stalks left in the ground after a grain crop has been harvested [13C. Via Old French *estuble* < Latin *stupula* "straw, stalk," alteration of *stipula*] —**stub·bly** *adj*

stub·born /stúbbərn/ *adj* 1. UNREASONABLY DETERMINED unreasonably and obstructively determined to persevere or prevail 2. DOGGED carried out in a determined, persistent way ○ *met with stubborn resistance* 3. HARD TO REMOVE difficult to remove or deal with ○ *a stubborn stain* [14C. Origin ?] —**stub·born·ly** *adv* —**stub·born·ness** *n*

~~**stubborness**~~ incorrect spelling of **stubbornness**

Stubbs /stubz/, **George** (1724–1806) British painter and engraver. He specialized in painting animals, particularly horses.

stub·by /stúbbee/ *adj* 1. SHORT AND STOCKY short and stocky in build 2. SHORT AND THICK short and thick, broad, or blunt ○ *stubby fingers* 3. WITH MANY STUBS with projecting stubs or short bristles

stub nail *n* a short thick nail

stuc·co /stúkō/ *n* 1. WALL PLASTER plaster used for surfacing interior or exterior walls, often used in association with classical moldings 2. DECORATIVE PLASTER WORK decorative work molded from stucco ■ *vt* (**-coed, -co·ing, -coes** or **-cos**) COVER WALL WITH STUCCO to apply a coating of stucco to a wall [Late 16C. < Italian < Germanic] —**stuc·co·er** *n*

stuck /stuk/ past participle, past tense of **stick**[2] ■ *adj* 1. JAMMED OR CAUGHT jammed, caught, or held in an immovable position ○ *The drawer was stuck fast.* 2. UNABLE TO FIND SOLUTION not able to find a solution or way out of a situation 3. PIERCED pierced by a sharp object

stuck-up *adj* snobbish and conceited (*informal*)

stud[1] /stud/ *n* 1. BREEDING STALLION a male animal, especially a stallion, used for breeding 2. SEXUALLY ACTIVE MAN a man considered to be sexually active or good at sex (*informal*) 3. CARDS same as **stud poker** 4.

ESTABLISHMENT WITH STALLIONS a stable or farm where male animals, especially stallions, are kept for breeding **5. GROUP OF STALLIONS** a group of male animals, especially stallions, used for breeding [Old English *stōd* "standing place" < Germanic] ◇ **at stud** available for breeding with female animals, especially mares

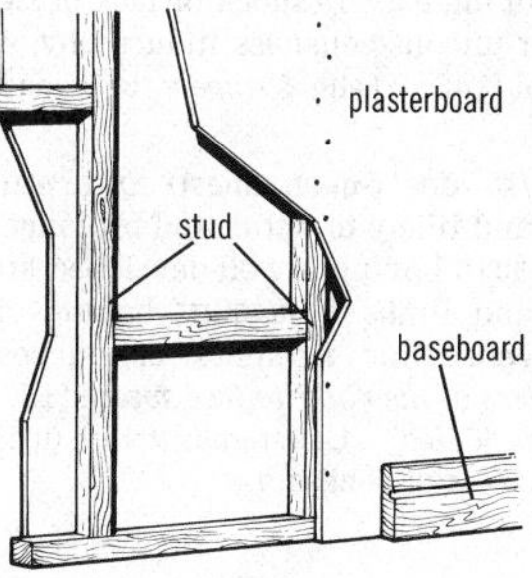

stud (sense 5)

stud² /stud/ *n* **1.** CLOTHING **FASTENER FOR SHIRT** a fastener for dress shirts or collars consisting of a small disk attached to a short rod **2.** AUTOMOT **PROJECTION ON TIRE** a small metal point embedded in the surface of a tire for better traction on snow and ice **3. METAL KNOB** a small metal knob, rivet, or nail head that protrudes slightly from a surface, especially for decorative effect **4.** JEWELRY **EARRING** an earring for pierced ears that has a simple rounded head or is set with a single gemstone **5.** CONSTR **VERTICAL SUPPORT** a vertical length of lumber to which material such as lath or plasterboard is attached in constructing a wall **6. HEADLESS BOLT** a headless bolt that is smooth in the center and threaded at each end **7.** ENG **PROTRUSION ON MACHINE** a projecting pin on a machine that serves as a support ■ *vt* (**stud·ded, stud·ding, studs**) **1. SUPPLY SOMETHING WITH STUDS** to fit or decorate something with studs ○ *a studded leather jacket* **2. OCCUR THROUGHOUT SOMETHING** to be present or visible throughout something ○ *a star-studded cast* [Old English *studu* < W Germanic] ◇ **studded with** scattered or dotted with something

stud·book /stúd bŏŏk/ *n* a book containing a record of the parentage of purebred animals, especially horses or dogs

stud·ding·sail /stúnss'l, stúdding sàyl/ *n* an additional sail on an extra yard and boom at either side of a square sail, for use in light winds [Mid-16C. Origin ?]

stu·dent /stŏŏd'nt/ *n* **1. PERSON STUDYING** somebody who studies at a school, college, or university **2. KNOWLEDGEABLE OR INTERESTED PERSON** somebody who has studied or takes much interest in a particular subject ○ *a student of human foibles* ■ *adj* **IN TRAINING FOR JOB** studying as part of the training for a job or profession ○ *student pilots* [15C. Alteration of Old French *estudiant* < Latin *student-*, present participle of *studere* "be diligent"]

stu·dent bod·y *n* the students of a school collectively

stu·dent coun·cil *n* an elected group of students with consultative powers in school administration, especially in a high school

stu·dent gov·ern·ment *n* a representative assembly of college or university students with consultative powers

stu·dent lamp *n* a desk lamp with a flexible stalk allowing the light to be moved into different positions

stu·dent loan *n* a loan taken by a student to pay for educational expenses, usually at a favorable rate of interest that is subsidized by the government

stu·dent·ship /stŏŏd'nt shìp/ *n UK* EDUC same as **scholarship** (sense 1)

Stu·dent's t-test *n* STATS same as **t-test** [After *Student*, pen name of W. S. Gosset (1876–1937), British statistician]

stu·dents' un·ion *n UK* same as **student union**

stu·dent teach·er *n* a student enrolled in a teacher preparation program who is doing practice teaching under supervision

stu·dent un·ion *n* a building or area at a college or university used primarily for the social or recreational activities of students, with food and beverage services

stud·horse /stúd hàwrss/ *n* a stallion used for breeding

stud·ied /stúddeed/ *adj* thought about or planned in advance rather than being spontaneous ○ *an air of studied nonchalance*

stud·ies /stúddeez/ *n* a particular subject of study, especially an educational course or academic specialization (*takes a singular or plural verb*) ○ *Women's studies is very popular.*

~~**studing**~~ incorrect spelling of **studying**

stu·di·o /stŏŏdee ō/ *n* **1. RECORDING PRODUCTION ROOM** a room or building equipped for making movies, television or radio productions, or musical recordings **2. SMALL APARTMENT** a one-room apartment **3.** MOVIES **MOVIE COMPANY** a commercial movie production company **4. ARTIST'S WORKPLACE** a place where an artist, photographer, or musician works **5.** DANCE **DANCE SCHOOL** a place where dance is taught or can be practiced ■ **stu·di·os** *npl* MOVIES **MOVIE PRODUCTION BUILDINGS** all the buildings connected with a movie production company, used for shooting and producing movies [Early 19C. Via Italian < Latin *studium* (see STUDY)]

stu·di·o a·part·ment *n* BUILDINGS same as **studio** (sense 2)

stu·di·o couch *n* a usually backless sofa that can be converted into a double bed by sliding out a frame from underneath

stu·di·o flat *n UK* same as **studio** (sense 2)

stu·di·o sys·tem *n* the process by which major Hollywood studios made a large number of movies economically and simultaneously from the silent era into the 1950s, using contract actors and controlling every aspect of production

stu·di·ous /stŏŏdee əss/ *adj* **1.** having a thoughtful nature and a tendency to study **2.** careful and painstaking, with considerable attention to detail ○ *a studious investigation* [14C. < Latin *studiosus* < *studium* (see STUDY)] —**stu·di·ous·ly** *adv* —**stu·di·ous·ness** *n*

stud·ly /stúdlee/ (**-li·er, -li·est**) *adj* (*slang*) **1.** describes a man who is considered sexually attractive **2.** impressive or exceptionally good ○ *a player with a studly scoring record*

stud·muf·fin /stúd mùffin/ *n US* a man regarded as being physically attractive (*slang*)

stud pok·er *n* poker in which all but the first card are dealt face up, allowing players to see one another's hands [Mid-19C. Probably shortening of *studhorse poker*, origin ?]

stud·y /stúddee/ *v* (**-ied, -y·ing, -ies**) **1.** *vti* **LEARN ABOUT SOMETHING** to learn about a subject by reading and researching **2.** *vti* **TAKE EDUCATIONAL COURSE** to take a course at a college or university **3.** *vt* **INVESTIGATE SOMETHING** to discover facts about something by doing research or experiments ○ *a team of researchers studying the effects of sleep deprivation* **4.** *vt* **LOOK AT AND CONSIDER SOMETHING** to look at or read something and think about it carefully ○ *He studied the map, frowning.* **5.** *vt* THEATER **LEARN LINES** to learn the lines spoken by a character in a play ■ *n* (*plural* **-ies**) **1. PROCESS OF LEARNING** the process of learning about a subject by reading, thought, intuition, or research ○ *devoted the afternoons to study* **2. INVESTIGATION** an investigation or research project designed to discover facts about something **3. REPORT ON RESEARCH** a work such as a report, thesis, or book that is the result of research or an investigation ○ *published a new study of women in the workplace* **4. ROOM FOR STUDYING** a room used for work that involves reading, thinking, or writing **5.** ARTS **PREPARATORY WORK OF ART** a small drawing or sculpture done as preparation for a larger work **6.** MUSIC **INSTRUMENTAL WORK** an instrumental work intended for teaching or practice **7.** THEATER **SOMEBODY LEARNING SOMETHING** somebody who is learning something, especially a role in a play, described in relation to how fast he or she learns ○ *She's a quick study.* [12C. < Old French *estudier* (verb), *estudie* (noun) < Latin *studium* "zeal, care" < *studere* "be diligent"] ◇ **in a brown study** *UK* deep in thought (*dated*)

stud·y hall *n* **1.** *US* a period during the school day assigned for study rather than classroom instruction **2.** a schoolroom used for independent study rather than instruction

stud·y leave *n* leave of absence from a course of study, granted for the purposes of carrying out additional research

stuff /stuf/ *vt* (**stuffed, stuff·ing, stuffs**) **1. FILL SOMETHING** to fill something by pushing things into it ○ *What are you stuffing the cushions with?* **2. PUSH THINGS INTO CONTAINER** to push things into a container, often hurriedly or forcefully **3. PUT SOMETHING SOMEWHERE HURRIEDLY** to put something somewhere in a quick careless way ○ *stuffed it under the pillow, out of sight* **4. EAT TOO MUCH** to eat, or feed somebody, a lot of food **5. FILL FOOD WITH STUFFING** to put stuffing or filling into food such as pasta, meat, or vegetables **6. PRESERVE DEAD ANIMAL** to fill a dead animal's skin with material to make it look lifelike and suitable for display **7.** POL **SUBMIT INVALID VOTES** to put invalid ballots into a ballot box to rig an election **8. OFFENSIVE TERM** an offensive term meaning to have sex with a woman (*taboo*) **9.** INDUST **TREAT LEATHER** to treat leather with chemicals that preserve and soften it ■ *n* **1. THINGS** material things generally, especially when unidentified, worthless, or unwanted ○ *What's all this stuff doing in my office?* **2. WORDS OR ACTION** action, speech, or writing ○ *all that stuff in the news about changing weather patterns* ○ *I really like her stuff.* **3. POSSESSIONS** personal possessions ○ *stopped by to collect her stuff* **4. PERSONAL QUALITIES** personal qualities ○ *She's got the stuff heroes are made of.* **5. SPECIALTY** something that somebody does uniquely or very well ○ *She knows her stuff.* **6. FOOLISH WORDS OR ACTION** foolish or blameworthy action, speech, or writing ○ *stuff and nonsense* **7.** *US* SPORTS **SPIN** spin given to a ball ○ *Ryan really had his stuff yesterday.* **8. DRUGS** a drug, especially heroin (*informal*) **9.** same as **money** (sense 1) (*slang*) **10. WOOLEN FABRIC** woolen fabric, especially as distinguished from fabric made from other natural fibers (*dated*) [14C. < Old French *estoffer* "equip" < Germanic] —**stuff·er** *n* ◇ **be made of sterner stuff** to be less easily discouraged, frightened, or upset ◇ **do your stuff** to do what is required or expected ◇ **get stuffed** an offensive phrase expressing disagreement or impatience (*slang*) ◇ **strut your stuff** to do something impressively, suggesting talent for it or thorough preparation (*slang*) ◇ **stuff it** an offensive phrase used to dismiss something angrily or carelessly (*slang*) ◇ **that's the stuff** used to indicate satisfaction with what has been done or given (*dated*)

CULTURAL NOTE ***The Right Stuff***, a book (1979) by Tom Wolfe. This imaginative account of the early years of the US space program contrasts the media's manipulation of the story and the public's hunger for heroes with the real-life experiences of the astronauts. It was made into a movie by Philip Kaufman in 1983. Subsequent to the novel, *right stuff* entered the general language, meaning "the complex of courage, self-worth, technical know-how, emotional stability, and dependability needed for a person to accomplish great things in any profession or field."

stuffed /stuft/ *adj* **1.** completely full, especially after eating too much (*informal*) **2.** filled with stuffing or some other filling

stuffed shirt *n* a pompous, formal, or self-important person (*informal*)

stuff·ing /stúffing/ *n* **1.** a mixture of well-flavored or highly seasoned ingredients used to stuff meat or vegetables **2.** feathers, fabric, or artificial fiber used as filling for cushions or pillows ◇ **knock the stuffing out of somebody** (*informal*) **1.** to beat or defeat somebody severely **2.** to have a sudden weakening effect on somebody

stuff·ing box *n* an enclosure containing compressed packing that is used to prevent leakage around a moving part such as a piston rod

stuff·y /stúffee/ (**-i·er, -i·est**) *adj* **1. AIRLESS** without any fresh air, and often too warm **2. STRAIT-LACED** very old-fashioned, strict, or conventional **3. BLOCKED WITH MUCUS** blocked with mucus, making breathing difficult ○ *a stuffy nose* —**stuff·i·ly** *adv* —**stuff·i·ness** *n*

stull /stul, stŏŏl/ *n* a supporting timber in a mine or mineshaft [Late 18C. Origin ?]

stul·ti·fy /stúltə fì/ (**-fied, -fy·ing, -fies**) *vt* **1. DIMINISH INTEREST** to dull somebody's interest by being repetitive, tedious, and boring **2. MAKE SOMEBODY SEEM STUPID** to cause somebody or something to seem unintelligent or silly **3.** RENDER SOMETHING USELESS to render something useless or ineffectual **4.** LAW PROVE SOMEBODY INCAPABLE OF LEGAL RESPONSIBILITY to show or allege somebody to be not legally responsible because of a psychiatric disorder or instability [Mid-18C. < late Latin *stultificare* "make foolish" < Latin *stultus* "foolish," literally "immovable"] —**stul·ti·fi·ca·tion** /stùltəfi káysh'n/ *n* —**stul·ti·fi·er** *n*

stum /stum/ *n* WINE same as **must**² ■ *vt* (**stummed, stumming, stums**) to ferment wine by adding stum to it while it is in a cask or vat [Mid-17C. < Dutch *stom* "dumb"]

stum·ble /stúmb'l/ *vi* (**-bled, -bling, -bles**) **1.** TRIP OVER to trip when walking or running **2.** WALK UNSTEADILY to walk unsteadily, as if intoxicated **3.** SPEAK OR ACT HESITATINGLY to speak or act in a halting, confused, or blundering way ○ *spoke the verse without stumbling* **4.** MAKE SLIGHT ERROR make a minor mistake **5.** MAKE DISCOVERY BY CHANCE to find or come across something by chance ○ *I stumbled across the note while I was cleaning the closet.* ■ *n* **1.** MISTAKE a mistake or hesitation **2.** ACT OF TRIPPING an instance of tripping over something [14C. Probably < variant of Old Norse *stumra* "walk unsteadily" < Germanic] —**stum·bler** *n* —**stum·bling·ly** *adv*

SYNONYMS See *hesitate*.

stum·ble·bum /stúmb'l bùm/ *n* US **1.** an offensive term for somebody who appears to do things in a blundering unskillful way (*slang insult*) **2.** a losing prizefighter

stum·bling block *n* something that stands in the way of achieving a goal or of understanding something [Early 16C. Translation of Greek *proskomma* "something you stumble against"]

stump /stump/ *n* **1.** BASE OF TREE the base of a tree trunk and its roots after the tree has fallen or been cut down **2.** REMAINING SMALL PART the part of something such as a limb that is left after the main part has been removed **3.** ART CYLINDRICAL DRAWING TOOL in drawing, a short pointed piece of rolled paper, cork, rubber, or leather, used to shade and soften lines **4.** HEAVY FOOTSTEP the sound of a heavy footstep ■ **stumps** *npl* LEGS somebody's legs (*slang*) ■ *v* (**stumped, stump·ing, stumps**) **1.** *vt* BAFFLE SOMEBODY to baffle somebody by presenting a problem that seems impossible to solve **2.** *vi* US POL CAMPAIGN to campaign for elective office (*informal*) **3.** *vi* WALK HEAVILY to walk heavily and often angrily **4.** *vt* CUT TREE TO STUMP to cut down a tree, leaving a stump **5.** *vt* REMOVE STUMPS to clear an area of land of tree stumps **6.** *vt regional* STUB TOE to stub a toe against something accidentally [13C. < Middle Low German < Germanic] —**stump·er** *n* ◇ **on the stump** engaged in making political speeches to win office (*informal*)

stump·age /stúmpij/ *n* US standing timber, or the amount of money it would bring if cut

stump·work /stúmp wùrk/ *n* raised embroidery with small decorative stitches made over pieces of padding [Early 20C. Because the designs are raised on stumps of wood]

stump·y /stúmpee/ (**-i·er, -i·est**) *adj* short, thick, and unattractive —**stump·i·ness** *n*

stun /stun/ (**stunned, stun·ning, stuns**) *vt* **1.** SHOCK SOMEBODY to shock, upset, or amaze somebody ○ *a tragedy that stunned the nation* **2.** MAKE SOMEBODY UNCONSCIOUS to make a person or animal unconscious for a short time with a blow or drug **3.** OVERWHELM SENSE to overwhelm one of the senses, e.g., with loud noise or very bright light [14C. Via Anglo-Norman *estuner* < assumed Vulgar Latin *extonare* < Latin *tonare* "to thunder"]

stun belt *n* an electric belt that can deliver a sudden shock, used by law enforcement officers as a means of controlling potentially violent or unruly prisoners, especially while in transit

stung past participle, past tense of **sting**

stun gre·nade *n* a nonlethal grenade that creates a loud bang and a bright flash when it explodes and is intended to temporarily disorient people

stun gun *n* a gun used for stunning animals or people for a short while without causing injury

stunk past participle, past tense of **stink**

stun·ner /stúnnər/ *n* **1.** an impressive or beautiful person or thing (*informal*) **2.** same as **stun gun**

stun·ning /stúnning/ *adj* strikingly impressive or attractive in appearance ○ *They looked stunning at the reception.* —**stun·ning·ly** *adv*

stun·sail /stúnss'l/ *n* SAILING same as **studdingsail** [Mid-18C. Contraction]

stunt¹ /stunt/ *n* **1.** DANGEROUS FEAT something dangerous that is done as a challenge or to entertain people **2.** SOMETHING UNDERHANDED DONE FOR ATTENTION something underhanded, silly, or unusual that is done to gain unfair advantage or to attract attention ○ *a publicity stunt* ■ *vi* (**stunt·ed, stunt·ing, stunts**) **1.** FOOTBALL SHIFT DEFENSIVE LINEMEN in football, to shift the positions of defensive linemen to improve their chances of avoiding offensive linemen's blocks **2.** PERFORM STUNTS to perform dangerous feats as a challenge or to entertain people [Late 19C. Origin ?]

stunt² /stunt/ *vt* (**stunt·ed, stunt·ing, stunts**) RESTRICT GROWTH to restrict the growth of something so that it does not develop to its normal size ■ *n* **1.** SOMETHING NOT FULLY DEVELOPED something that has not grown to its normal size because its growth has been restricted **2.** BOT PLANT DISEASE a plant disease that inhibits growth [Old English, "unintelligent, dull" < Germanic]

stunt dou·ble *n* somebody who replaces a movie actor in scenes involving potentially dangerous action sequences

stunt·man /stúnt màn/ (*plural* **-men** /-mèn/) *n* a man whose job is to take the place of a movie actor in a scene involving danger or requiring acrobatic skill

stunt·per·son /stúnt pùrss'n/ (*plural* **-peo·ple** /-peèp'l/ or **-per·sons**) *n* somebody whose job is to take the place of a movie actor in a scene involving danger or requiring acrobatic skill

stunt·wom·an /stúnt wòommən/ (*plural* **-wom·en** /-wìmmin/) *n* a woman whose job is to take the place of a movie actor in a scene involving danger or requiring acrobatic skill

stu·pa /stóopə/ *n* a Buddhist shrine, temple, or pagoda that houses a relic or marks the location of an auspicious event [Late 19C. < Sanskrit *stūpah*]

stupe¹ /stoop/ *n* a hot, damp, and sometimes medicated compress used in former times [14C. Via Latin *stuppa* "tow" < Greek *stuppē*; from the use of tow in making compresses]

stupe² /stoop/ *n* an offensive term for somebody regarded as unintelligent (*slang insult*) [Mid-18C. Shortening of STUPID]

stu·pe·fa·cient /stoopə fáysh'nt/ *adj* causing stupor ■ *n* a drug or other agent that causes stupor [Mid-17C. < Latin *stupefacient-*, present participle of *stupefacere* (see STUPEFY)]

stu·pe·fac·tion /stoopə fáksh'n/ *n* **1.** great amazement or astonishment **2.** the inability to think clearly because of boredom, tiredness, or amazement [15C. Via French < medieval Latin *stupefaction-* < Latin *stupefacere* (see STUPEFY)]

stu·pe·fy /stóopə fī/ (**-fied, -fy·ing, -fies**) *vt* **1.** to amaze or astonish somebody **2.** to make somebody unable to think clearly because of boredom, tiredness, or amazement [15C. Via French *stupéfier* < Latin *stupefacere* < *stupere* "be stunned" + *facere* "make"] —**stu·pe·fi·er** *n* —**stu·pe·fy·ing·ly** *adv*

stu·pen·dous /stoo péndəss/ *adj* impressively large, excellent, or great in extent or degree ○ *a stupendous achievement* [Mid-17C. < Latin *stupendus*, gerundive of *stupere* "be stunned"] —**stu·pen·dous·ly** *adv* —**stu·pen·dous·ness** *n*

stu·pid /stóopəd/ *adj* **1.** REGARDED AS UNINTELLIGENT regarded as showing a lack of intelligence, perception, or common sense ○ *a stupid mistake* **2.** SILLY irritatingly silly or time-wasting ○ *had us playing stupid games* **3.** ADDS EMPHASIS used to express anger, annoyance, or frustration (*informal*) ○ *I can't get the stupid thing to work!* **4.** DAZED in a dazed state, e.g., from shock, fatigue, or the effects of drugs or alcohol ○ *almost stupid with tiredness* [Mid-16C. < Latin *stupidus* < *stupere* "be stunned"]

stu·pid·i·ty /stoo píddətee/ *n* **1.** lack of intelligence, perception, or common sense **2.** extremely rash or thoughtless behavior

stu·pid·ly /stóopədlee/ *adv* **1.** in a way that demonstrates lack of intelligence, perception, or common sense ○ *I had stupidly forgotten to note down the date I mailed it.* **2.** in a way that suggests diminished ability to perceive or reason ○ *He gazed stupidly after her.*

~~**stupify**~~ incorrect spelling of **stupefy**

stu·por /stóopər/ *n* **1.** an acute lack of mental alertness brought on, e.g., by shock or lack of sleep **2.** a state of near-unconsciousness induced by, e.g., drugs or alcohol [14C. < Latin < *stupere* "be stunned"] —**stu·por·ous** *adj*

stur·dy /stúrdee/ (**-di·er, -di·est**) *adj* **1.** WELL MADE solidly made and likely to withstand prolonged use **2.** WITH STRONG BUILD having a well-developed strong-looking body and limbs **3.** RESOLUTE having or displaying decisiveness or firmness of purpose ○ *sturdy defenders of the right to free speech* [13C. < Old French *estourdir* "dazed" < Latin *turdus* "thrush (the bird)"] —**stur·di·ly** *adv* —**stur·di·ness** *n*

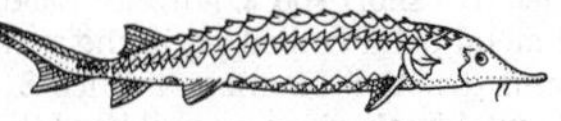

sturgeon

stur·geon /stúrjən/ (*plural* **-geons** or *same*) *n* **1.** a large bottom-feeding fish with a long snout and tough bony-plated skin. Native to: northern rivers, coastal waters. Family: Acipenseridae. **2.** the flesh of a sturgeon as food [13C. < Old French *esturgeon* < Germanic]

Sturm und Drang /shtòorm òond draáng/ *n* **1.** a movement in late 18th-century German literature whose works typically portray the tortured emotions of a central character who violently rejects society **2.** a state of extreme emotional upheaval (*literary*) ○ *movies that explore his own personal Sturm und Drang* [Late 18C. < German, "storm and stress"]

Sturt /sturt/, **Charles** (1795–1869) British explorer and administrator. He explored the river system of southeastern Australia (1829–30) and attempted to reach the center of the continent (1844–46).

stut·ter /stúttər/ *v* (**-tered, -ter·ing, -ters**) **1.** *vti* SPEAK WITH STAMMER to say something haltingly, repeating sounds frequently when attempting to pronounce them, either from nervousness or as the result of a speech disorder ○ *managed to stutter an apology* **2.** *vi* SPUTTER to make repeated short noises ○ *The motor stuttered briefly and then died again.* ■ *n* **1.** STAMMERING AS SPEECH DISORDER a speech disorder that makes somebody repeat speech sounds that he or she finds difficult to pronounce ○ *has a slight stutter* **2.** BURST OF SPUTTERING a burst of repeated short noises [Early 16C. Alteration of obsolete *stut* < Germanic] —**stut·ter·er** *n* —**stut·ter·ing** *adj* —**stut·ter·ing·ly** *adv*

Stutt·gart /stòot gaàrt/ capital of Baden-Württemberg State, in southwestern Germany. Population: 588,482 (1997).

Stuy·ve·sant /stívissənt/, **Peter** (1610?–72) Dutch colonial administrator. He was the last Dutch governor of New Netherland in present-day New York (1647–64), which he was forced to surrender to English troops.

STV *abbr* subscription television

sty¹ /stī/ *n* (*plural* **sties**) same as **pigpen** (sense 1) ■ *vt* (**stied, sty·ing, sties**) to put or keep a pig in a pigpen [Old English *stī-*, probably form of *stig* "house, hall"]

sty² /stī/ (*plural* **sties**), **stye** *n* a temporary swelling on an eyelid at the base of an eyelash [Early 17C. Shortening of obsolete *styany* < *styan* (< Old English *stīgan* "ascend" < Germanic) + EYE; probably taken as "sty on eye"]

Styg·i·an /stíjjee ən/ *adj* **1.** PITCH-BLACK unremittingly dark and frightening, as hell is imagined to be (*literary*) **2.** OF STYX relating to the Styx, the river in

Greek mythology that the souls of the dead were ferried across into Hades **3. BINDING** eternally binding, as were promises sworn on the banks of the river Styx in Greek mythology (*literary*) [Mid-16C. < Latin *Stygius* < Greek *Stugios* < *Stux* "the Styx"]

styl- *prefix* same as **stylo-** (*used before vowels*)

sty·lar /stílər/ *adj* relating to or using a stylus

style /stīl/ *n* **1. DISTINCTIVE FORM** a distinctive and identifiable form in an artistic medium such as music, architecture, or literature ○ *a facade in the neoclassical style* ○ *a different style of jazz* **2. WAY OF DOING SOMETHING** a way of doing something, especially a way regarded as expressing a particular attitude or typifying a particular period (*often used in combination*) ○ *a hands-on management style* ○ *old-style politics* ○ *Confrontation just isn't his style.* **3. WAY OF WRITING OR PERFORMING** the way in which something is written or performed, as distinct from its content **4. FLAIR** impressive flair in the way something is done, especially a quality that suggests a self-confident willingness to exhibit skill or good taste ○ *furnished with impeccable style* **5. FASHION** the prevailing or customary fashion ○ *a look that has gone out of style* **6. CUT OF HAIR OR CLOTHING** a way in which clothes or hair are cut or shaped ○ *dressed in all the latest styles* ○ *That style really suits you.* **7. LUXURIOUSNESS** elegance or lavishness ○ *dining in style* **8.** PUBL **PUBLISHING CONVENTIONS** a set of conventions for presenting published material, e.g., punctuation and typography **9. SUNDIAL POINTER** the pointer on a sundial **10.** BOT **FLOWER PART** an extension of a flower's ovary, shaped like a stalk, that supports the stigma **11.** ZOOL same as **stylet** (sense 2) **12.** ARTS, HIST same as **stylus** (sense 3) **13. TITLE** a name or title, especially one that is official or legally correct (*formal*) ■ *vt* (**styled, styl·ing, styles**) **1. SHAPE SOMETHING** to give something a particular shape or design ○ *hair styled in the most up-to-date fashion* **2. CAUSE SOMETHING TO CONFORM** to bring something into conformity with a style **3. NAME SOMEBODY** to give somebody or something a name or title (*formal*) [13C. Via French < Latin *stilus* "stake, pointed writing instrument, style"] —**styl·er** *n* ◇ **cramp somebody's style** to restrict what somebody is able to do or would like to do, often by limiting the person's capacity to impress others (*informal*)

SPELLCHECK See ***stile***[1].

-style /stīl/ *suffix* with the characteristics of or in the manner of ○ *colonial-style buildings* ○ *moving slowly and stealthily panther-style*

style·book /stīl bo͝ok/ *n* a publisher's guide for presenting material, used by writers and editors

sty·let /stílət/ *n* **1.** MED **WIRE PREVENTING BLOCKAGE IN NEEDLE** a fine wire inserted into a catheter or hollow needle to prevent it from becoming blocked when not in use **2.** ZOOL **PART SHAPED LIKE BRISTLE** a thin long organ or appendage shaped like a bristle, e.g., any of the mouthparts of some insects **3. LONG POINTED INSTRUMENT** any long thin pointed instrument (*formal*) [Late 17C. Via French < Italian *stiletto* (see STILETTO)]

sty·li plural of **stylus**

styli- *prefix* same as **stylo-**

styl·ing /stíling/ *n* **1.** the act or an instance of shaping or arranging somebody's hair (*often used before a noun*) ○ *styling mousse* **2.** an instance of creating something, especially something artistic, in a particular or idiosyncratic way (*informal*) ○ *the zany comedy stylings of the country's favorite stand-up*

styl·ish /stílish/ *adj* **1.** having confident good taste and appreciation of what is fashionable **2.** having or showing impressive skill or accomplishment ○ *the most stylish player in the team* —**styl·ish·ly** *adv* —**styl·ish·ness** *n*

styl·ist /stílist/ *n* **1.** HAIR **HAIRDRESSER** a hairdresser, especially a senior hairdresser in a salon **2.** ARTS, LITERAT **ACCOMPLISHED ARTIST** somebody whose creative work shows a distinctive and accomplished style **3.** COMM **DESIGNER** a designer who is consulted on matters of style, especially somebody responsible for creating a distinctive visual image for a product or company

sty·lis·tic /stī lístik/ *adj* relating to matters of style, especially in literature and the arts ○ *stylistic brilliance compromised by a thinness of content* —**sty·lis·ti·cal·ly** *adv*

sty·lis·tics /stī lístiks/ *n* the branch of linguistics that deals with determining which features of written or spoken language characterize specific groups or contexts, especially literary genres or works (*takes a singular verb*)

sty·lite /stí līt/ *n* a Christian ascetic in ancient times who lived alone on top of a tall pillar [Mid-17C. < late Greek *stulitēs* < Greek *stulos* "pillar"] —**sty·lit·ic** /stī líttik/ *adj*

styl·ize /stí līz/ (**-ized, -iz·ing, -iz·es**) *vt* to design something in a particular artistic style —**styl·i·za·tion** /stīli záysh'n/ *n* —**styl·ized** *adj* —**styl·iz·er** *n*

stylo-, **styli-** *prefix* style, column ○ *stylograph* [< Latin *stylus* (see STYLUS)]

sty·lo·bate /stílə bàyt/ *n* a continuous raised platform of masonry supporting a row of columns [Mid-16C. Via Latin *stylobata* < Greek *stulobatēs* "column step"]

sty·lo·graph /stílə gràf/ *n* a fountain pen that has a thin hollow tube as its writing point instead of the traditional nib

sty·log·ra·phy /stī lóggrəfee/ *n* the art of drawing or engraving using a stylus —**sty·lo·graph·ic** /stìlə gráffik/ *adj* —**sty·lo·graph·i·cal·ly** *adv*

sty·loid /stí lòyd/ *adj* describes a bony protuberance (**process**) that is long and thin

sty·lo·lite /stílə līt/ *n* a join between two layers of limestone that in cross section looks like a row of interlocking pegs —**sty·lo·lit·ic** /stìlə líttik/ *adj*

stylus (sense 3)

sty·lus /stíləss/ (*plural* **-li** /-lī/) *n* **1.** RECORDING **PHONOGRAPH NEEDLE** the jewel-tipped needle of a phonograph that rests in the grooves of a record as it revolves and transmits vibrations to the cartridge **2.** ELECTRONICS **MACHINE TRACING PEN** the tracing pen on an electronic device such as a seismograph or polygraph that converts an electrical signal into a written record **3.** ART, HIST **ENGRAVING TOOL** a pointed instrument used for engraving, especially one used in ancient times for writing on clay or wax tablets **4.** COMPUT **DEVICE FOR TOUCHING SCREEN** a pointed device for use on a computer screen that responds to pressure [Early 18C. Alteration of Latin *stilus* "stake, pointed writing instrument"]

sty·mie /stímee/, **sty·my** *vt* (**-mied, -mie·ing, -mies; -mied, -my·ing, -mies**) **1. HINDER PROGRESS OF SOMEBODY OR SOMETHING** to prevent somebody or something from making further progress **2.** GOLF **BLOCK OPPONENT'S LINE** to obstruct the line between a golf opponent's ball and the hole (*dated*) ■ *n* (*plural* **-mies**) **1. PROBLEM SITUATION** a situation in which obstacles hinder progress **2.** GOLF **OBSTRUCTION OF OPPONENT'S BALL** a situation in which one golfer's ball blocks another's (*dated*) [Mid-19C. Origin ?]

styp·sis /stípsiss/ *n* the use of a styptic substance, or its effect [Late 19C. Via late Latin < Greek *stupsis* < *stuphein* "to contract"]

styp·tic /stíptik/ *adj* slowing down the rate of bleeding or stopping bleeding altogether, whether by causing the blood vessels to contract or by accelerating clotting ■ *n* a styptic drug, cream, or lotion [14C. Via late Latin < Greek *stuptikos* < *stuphein* "to contract"]

styp·tic pen·cil *n* an astringent substance in solid form in a small cylindrical container that is applied to stop bleeding from small cuts, e.g., after shaving

sty·rax /stí ràks/ *n* TREES same as **storax** (sense 1) [Mid-16C. Via Latin < Greek *sturax*]

sty·rene /stí reen/ *n* a colorless flammable liquid hydrocarbon. Use: manufacture of synthetic rubber, plastic. Formula: C_8H_8. [Late 19C. < Latin *styrax* (see STYRAX)]

Sty·ro·foam /stírə fōm/ *tdmk* a trademark for a light plastic material used to make disposable items, insulation, and packing materials

Popperfoto

William Styron

Sty·ron /stírən/, **William** (*b.* 1925) US writer. His novel *The Confessions of Nat Turner* (1967) won a Pulitzer Prize. His other works include *Sophie's Choice* (1979). Full name **Styron, William Clark, Jr.**

> "Depression is a wimp of a word for a howling tempest in the brain."
> [William Styron, *Darkness Visible*; 1990]

STYS *abbr* speak to you soon (*used in e-mails or text messages*)

Styx /stiks/ *n* in Greek mythology, the river across which the souls of the dead were ferried into the underworld [14C. Via Latin < Greek *Stux*]

Suá·rez Gon·zá·lez /swaárəz gən zaáləss/, **Adolfo** (*b.* 1932) prime minister of Spain (1976–81). He guided the country toward democracy after the death of General Franco.

suave /swaav/ (**suav·er, suav·est**) *adj* **1.** polite and charming, especially in a way that seems affected or insincere **2.** well groomed and pleasingly dressed (*dated*) [Early 16C. Directly or via French < Latin *suavis* "sweet, agreeable" < Indo-European] —**suave·ly** *adv* —**suave·ness** *n* —**suav·i·ty** *n*

sub /sub/ *n* **1. SUBSTITUTE** a substitute, especially a substitute player in a game (*informal*) **2.** NAVY same as **submarine** *n* (sense 1) **3. SANDWICH** a sandwich made with a long roll **4. SUBTITLE** a subtitle to a document or printed matter (*informal*) ■ *v* (**subbed, sub·bing, subs**) (*informal*) **1.** *vi* **REPLACE SOMEBODY** to take the place of somebody temporarily, usually in a work situation **2.** *vti* **SUBCONTRACT** to subcontract work, or work as a subcontractor **3.** *vt* **SUBTITLE SOMETHING** to add subtitles to something [Late 17C. Shortening]

sub- *prefix* **1.** under, below, beneath ○ *subcutaneous* ○ *subfloor* **2.** subordinate, secondary ○ *subparagraph* **3.** less than completely ○ *subliterate* **4.** subdivision ○ *subkingdom* ○ *subcontinent* **5.** bordering on ○ *subequatorial* **6.** smaller or younger than ○ *subcompact* ○ *subteen* **7.** nearly, partly, somewhat ○ *subfossil* **8.** containing less than the normal amount of an element ○ *suboxide* [< Latin *sub* "under"]

sub·ab·dom·i·nal *adj*
sub·a·cute *adj*
sub·a·cute·ly *adv*
sub·a·gen·cy *n*
sub·ar·id *adj*
sub·as·sem·bly *n*
sub·av·er·age *adj*
sub·base·ment *n*
sub·block *n*
sub·branch *n*
sub·caste *n*
sub·cat·e·go·ry *n*
sub·chap·ter *n*
sub·chief *n*
sub·clan *n*
sub·clas·si·fi·ca·tion *n*
sub·clas·si·fy *vt*
sub·clause *n*
sub·col·lec·tion *n*
sub·col·o·ny *n*
sub·com·man·der *n*
sub·com·mis·sion *n*
sub·com·mis·sion·er *n*
sub·con·fer·ence *n*
sub·coun·cil *n*
sub·cra·ni·al *adj*
sub·dean *n*
sub·de·part·ment *n*
sub·des·ert *n*
sub·di·a·lect *n*
sub·di·rec·tor *n*
sub·dis·ci·pline *n*
sub·dis·trib·u·tor *n*
sub·dis·trict *n*
sub·en·try *n*
sub·file *n*
sub·freez·ing *adj*
sub·gen·re *n*
sub·gla·cial *adj*
sub·gla·cial·ly *adv*
sub·hu·mid *adj*
sub·in·dex *n*
sub·in·dus·try *n*
sub·le·thal *adj*

sub·le·thal·ly *adv*
sub·lev·el *n*
sub·li·brar·i·an *n*
sub·lit·er·ate *adj*
sub·lot *n*
sub·mas·ter *n*
sub·mem·ber *n*
sub·me·tal·lic *adj*
sub·min·i·mal *adj*
sub·min·i·mum *adj*
sub·mo·lec·u·lar *adj*
sub·o·ce·an·ic *adj*
sub·of·fi·cer *n*
sub·op·ti·mal *adj*
sub·or·ga·ni·za·tion *n*
sub·par *adj*
sub·par·a·graph *n*
sub·part *n*
sub·per·i·os·te·al *adj*
sub·phy·lar *adj*
sub·phy·lum *n*
sub·pop·u·la·tion *n*
sub·prin·ci·pal *n*
sub·prod·uct *n*
sub·pro·fes·sion·al *adj*
sub·pro·gram *n*
sub·re·gion *n*
sub·re·gion·al *adj*
sub·sam·ple *n*
sub·scale *n*
sub·sci·ence *n*
sub·sect *n*
sub·sec·tor *n*
sub·seg·ment *n*
sub·sense *n*
sub·se·ries *n*
sub·skill *n*
sub·spe·cial·ist *n*
sub·spe·cial·i·za·tion *n*
sub·spe·cial·ize *vi*
sub·spe·cial·ty *n*
sub·style *n*
sub·sur·face *adj, n*
sub·sys·tem *n*
sub·teen *n*
sub·tem·per·ate *adj*
sub·theme *n*
sub·thresh·old *adj*
sub·top·ic *n*
sub·tor·rid *adj*
sub·tribe *n*
sub·type *n*
sub·typ·i·cal *adj*
sub·va·ri·e·ty *n*

sub·ac·id /sub ássid/ *adj* **1.** mildly unkind or critical in tone (*literary*) **2.** moderately sour in flavor (*archaic*) —**sub·a·cid·i·ty** /sùbbə síddətee/ *n* —**sub·ac·id·ly** *adv*

sub·a·cute scle·ros·ing pan·en·ceph·a·li·tis /súbbə kyoot sklə rṑzing pàn en sèffə lítiss/ *n* a severe, usually fatal, inflammatory disease of the brain, chiefly affecting children and linked to infection from measles

sub·ad·ar /sóobə daár/, **sub·ah·dar** *n* in the former British Indian army, the chief Indian officer in a company of Indian soldiers [Late 17C. < Urdu, Persian *ṣūbahdār* < *ṣūbah* "Mughal province" + Persian *-dār* "holder"]

sub·aer·i·al /sub érree əl/ *adj* formed or situated on or just below the surface of the soil ○ *a plant with subaerial roots*

sub·ah·dar *n* MIL another spelling of **subadar**

sub·al·pine /sub ál pìn/ *adj* relating to or growing naturally on the lower slopes of mountains, especially the areas below the tree line

sub·al·tern /su báwltərn, súbb'l tùrn/ *n* **1.** MIL JUNIOR OFFICER an officer in the British Army of a rank below captain, especially a second lieutenant **2.** SUBORDINATE PERSON a person holding a subordinate or inferior position **3.** LOGIC IMPLIED PROPOSITION a proposition that is implied by a universal proposition ■ *adj* **1.** SUBORDINATE in a subordinate or inferior position **2.** LOGIC IMPLIED in logic, implied as a proposition by a universal proposition [Late 16C. < late Latin *subalternus* < Latin *alternus* "one after another" (see ALTERNATE)]

sub·al·ter·nate /sub áwltərnət/ *adj* **1.** describes a leaf whose leaflets are arranged in semistaggered rows, neither fully alternate nor fully opposite **2.** in a subordinate or inferior position —**sub·al·ter·na·tion** /sub àwltər náysh'n/ *n*

sub·ant·arc·tic /sùb an taárktik/ *adj* relating to the area between the Antarctic Circle and the South Pole

sub·a·pi·cal /sùb áppik'l/ *adj* below or near an apex —**sub·ap·ic·al·ly** *adv*

sub·ap·os·tol·ic /sùb apə stóllik/ *adj* belonging to the period in the history of the Christian Church that immediately followed the time of the Apostles

sub·aq·ua /sùb aákwə/ *adj* relating to or providing facilities for underwater sports such as scuba diving [Mid-20C. < SUB- + Latin *aqua* "water"]

sub·a·quat·ic /sùbbə kwáttik, -kwóttik/ *adj* **1.** existing or able to exist partly in water and partly on land **2.** relating or belonging to underwater regions

sub·a·que·ous /sub áykwee əss, -ák-/ *adj* living, found, or formed under water

sub·a·rach·noid /sùbbə rák nòyd/ *adj* situated beneath the middle of the three membranes (**arachnoids**) that cover the brain and spinal cord

sub·arc·tic /sub aárktik/ *adj* **1.** relating to the area bordering the Arctic Circle to the south **2.** similar to the regions that border the Arctic Circle, e.g., in landscape or weather conditions

sub·a·tom·ic /sùbbə tómmik/ *adj* **1.** occurring as part of an atom, or smaller than an atom ○ *a subatomic particle* **2.** on a scale smaller than the atom, or involving phenomena at this level

sub·au·di·tion /sùb aw dísh'n/ *n* **1.** the act of understanding a word or thought that is implied but not actually expressed in speech or writing **2.** a word, idea, or thought understood by a hearer or reader that is implied but not expressed [Mid-17C. < late Latin *subaudition-* < Latin *audire* "hear"]

sub·ax·il·lar·y /sub áksə lèrree/ *adj* **1.** located beneath the armpit **2.** growing beneath the axil in plants

sub·base /súb bàyss/ *n* **1.** a deep layer of large stones that forms the lowest level of a roadbed or of the foundation of a building **2.** the lowest section of any base or foundation, e.g., the bottom part of a pedestal

sub·bi·tu·mi·nous /sùb bi tóomənəss, -tyóomə-/ *adj* describes a type of soft coal that has an intermediate carbon content

sub·cal·i·ber /sub kállibər/ *adj* describes ammunition whose caliber is smaller than that of the gun from which it is fired. Smaller ammunition is often used for practice because it is cheaper.

sub·car·ti·lag·i·nous /sùb kaart'l ájjənəss/ *adj* **1.** lying beneath cartilage or a body part composed of cartilage **2.** made up partly of cartilage

sub·ce·les·tial /sùb sə léschəl/ *adj* belonging to the earth, not to the heavens or the stars (*literary*)

sub·cel·lu·lar /sub séllyələr/ *adj* **1.** existing inside a cell, or relating to the component parts of cells **2.** on a scale smaller than a cell, or involving phenomena at this level

sub·chas·er /súb chàyssər/ *n* same as **submarine chaser** (*informal*)

sub·class /súb klàss/ *n* **1.** a smaller group among several into which a main class is divided **2.** BIOL a subdivision of a class in the classification of plants and animals **3.** MATH same as **subset**

sub·cla·vi·an /sub kláyvee ən/ *adj* located under the collarbone (**clavicle**) [Mid-17C. < modern Latin *subclavius* < Latin *clavis* "key"]

sub·clin·i·cal /sub klínnik'l/ *adj* describes an early stage or mild form of a medical condition, no symptoms of which are detectable —**sub·clin·i·cal·ly** *adv*

sub·com·mit·tee /súbkə mìttee/ *n* a committee set up by and consisting of members of an existing committee to deal with a specific issue

sub·com·pact /sub kóm pàkt/ *n* a small car, usually the smallest and lightest model in a manufacturer's range

sub·con·scious /sub kónshəss/ *adj* present in the mind without awareness of it ■ *n* mental activity not directly perceived by the consciousness, from which memories, feelings, or thoughts can influence behavior without realization of it —**sub·con·scious·ly** *adv* —**sub·con·scious·ness** *n*

sub·con·ti·nent /sub kónt'nənt/ *n* **1.** a large area that is an identifiably separate part of a continent **2.** *also* **Sub·con·ti·nent** the area encompassing the countries of India, Pakistan, and Bangladesh regarded as a distinct part of South Asia —**sub·con·ti·nen·tal** /sùb kont'n ént'l/ *adj, n*

sub·con·tract /sub kón tràkt, súb kòn trakt/ *n* SECONDARY CONTRACT a secondary contract in which the person or company originally hired in turn hires somebody else to do all or part of the work ■ *v* (**-tract·ed, -tract·ing, -tracts**) **1.** *vt* GIVE WORK UNDER SUBCONTRACT to pass on work to a second person or company under the terms of a subcontract **2.** *vi* TAKE ON WORK FROM CONTRACTOR to work on contract with a person or company who is a contractor to somebody else —**sub·con·trac·tor** *n*

sub·con·trar·y /sub kóntrəree/ *adj* describes logical propositions that are related to each other in such a way that both cannot be false at the same time, although both may be true ■ *n* (*plural* **-ies**) a subcontrary logical proposition [Early 17C. < late Latin *subcontrarius*, translation of Greek *hupenantios* "contrary"]

sub·cor·tex /sub káwr tèks/ (*plural* **-ti·ces** /-tə seèz/) *n* the parts of the brain that lie immediately beneath the cerebral cortex —**sub·cor·ti·cal** *adj*

sub·cul·ture /súb kùlchər/ *n* **1.** an identifiably separate social group within a larger culture, especially one regarded as existing outside mainstream society **2.** a bacterial culture that is grown from another culture —**sub·cul·tur·al** /sùb kúlchərəl/ *adj*

sub·cu·ta·ne·ous /sùbkyə táynee əss/ *adj* located, living, or made beneath the skin —**sub·cu·ta·ne·ous·ly** *adv*

sub·dea·con /sub deékən/ *n* **1.** a member of the Roman Catholic clergy who acts as a deacon's assistant, e.g., by preparing the vessels that are to be used in celebrating Mass **2.** a cleric ranking just above a lector in an Eastern Church

sub·di·ac·o·nate /sùb dī ákənət/ *n* the position or term of office of a subdeacon —**sub·di·ac·o·nal** *adj*

sub·di·rec·to·ry /sùbdi réktəree, sùb dī-/ (*plural* **-ries**) *n* a directory created within another directory on a magnetic storage device such as a hard disk

sub·di·vide /sùbdi víd/ (**-vid·ed, -vid·ing, -vides**) *v* **1.** *vt* to divide a section, or all the sections, of something into sections that are smaller still **2.** *vi* to be divided, or be able to be divided, into sections that are smaller still —**sub·di·vid·er** *n*

sub·di·vi·sion /sùbdi vízh'n, súbdi vìzh'n/ *n* **1.** SUBDIVIDING OF SOMETHING the dividing of a divided part into units that are smaller still **2.** SUBSIDIARY SECTION a section of something that is itself a division of a larger thing **3.** DEVELOPMENT SITE an area of land divided up into building lots —**sub·di·vi·sion·al** /sùbdi vízh'nəl/ *adj*

sub·do·main name /sùbdə máyn-, -dō-/, **sub·do·main** *n* **1.** a second level of Internet domain names created by the administrator of the domain **2.** a subdivision of the two-letter country domain names into two- or three-letter organizational subdomains, e.g., "ac.uk" for United Kingdom academic sites and "com.au" for Australian commercial sites.

sub·dom·i·nant /sub dómminənt/ *n* **1.** the fourth note in a major or minor musical scale **2.** a musical key, chord, or harmony based on a subdominant

sub·duct /səb dúkt/ (**-duct·ed, -duct·ing, -ducts**) *vi* to be carried under the edge of an adjoining continental or oceanic plate, causing tensions in the Earth's crust that can produce earthquakes or volcanic eruptions [Late 16C. < Latin *subduct-*, past participle of *subducere* "draw up" (see SUBDUE)] —**sub·duc·tion** *n*

sub·due /səb dóo/ (**-dued, -du·ing, -dues**) *vt* **1.** BRING SOMEBODY UNDER FORCIBLE CONTROL to bring a person or group of people under control using force **2.** SOFTEN SOMETHING to soften something, or make something less intense ○ *idealism subdued by experience* **3.** REPRESS EMOTIONS to repress or control feelings ○ *worked hard to subdue her irritation* [14C. Via Old French *souduire* "seduce" < Latin *subducere* "draw up" < *ducere* "to lead"] —**sub·du·a·ble** *adj* —**sub·du·er** *n*

sub·dued /səb dóod/ *adj* **1.** NOT HARSH not bright, loud, or intense, or made less bright, loud, or intense ○ *subdued lighting* **2.** LOW-SPIRITED sad or in low spirits **3.** QUIET quiet and restrained ○ *speaking in subdued tones*

sub·dur·al /sùb dóorəl/ *adj* beneath the dura mater that covers the brain and spinal cord

sub·ed·i·tor /sub éddətər/ *n* **1.** *UK* an assistant editor helping to prepare material for publication **2.** *UK* same as **copyreader**

sub·e·qua·to·ri·al /sùb ekwə táwree əl, -skwə-/ *adj* relating to or situated in the regions that lie just north and south of the equator

su·ber·in /sóobərən/ *n* a waxy waterproof substance found in the cell walls of many plants, especially cork [Early 19C. < French *subérine* < Latin *suber* "cork"]

su·ber·ize /sóobə rīz/ (**-ized, -iz·ing, -iz·es**) *vt* to deposit suberin in plant cell walls during their conversion to cork tissue [Late 19C. < Latin *suber* "cork"]

sub·fam·i·ly /súb fàmməlee/ (*plural* **-lies**) *n* **1.** a subdivision of a family in the classification of plants and animals **2.** a smaller group of related languages within a language family

sub·field /súb fèeld/ *n* a mathematical field that is a subset of another field

sub·floor /súb flàwr/ *n* an underlying layer of rough or unfinished material supporting a finished floor

sub·floor·ing /súb flàwring/ *n* a subfloor, or the material used to make a subfloor

sub·fos·sil /súb fòss'l/ *adj* partially fossilized ■ *n* a partially fossilized organism

sub·ge·nus /súb jeenəss/ (*plural* **-gen·e·ra** /-jènnərə/) *n* a category in the classification of plants and animals that is larger than a species but smaller than a genus

sub·grade /súb gràyd/ *n* the bed of ground on which the foundations of a road, railroad, or building are laid

sub·group /súb gròop/ *n* **1.** a smaller group distinguished in some way from the larger group of which it is a part **2.** a mathematical group whose members are also members of a larger group

sub·gum /súb gùm/ *n* a Chinese dish with a base of mixed vegetables [Mid-20C. < Chinese (Cantonese) *shâp kám* "mixed brocade"]

sub·head /súb hèd/, **sub·head·ing** /súb hèdding/ *n* a heading or title subordinate to the main one

sub·hu·man /sub hyóomən, -yóomən/ *adj* **1.** relating to or displaying behavior that is distastefully inferior in sophistication, moral standards, or intelligence to what is regarded as usual for human beings ○ *a subhuman thug* **2.** at the level of biological development that is considered just below humans

sub·i·ma·go /súbbi máygō, -maágō/ (*plural* **-ma·goes** or **-mag·i·nes** /-máygə neez/) *n* a mayfly or related insect in a metamorphic stage in which functional wings are present but not all adult features have developed fully

sub·in·feu·da·tion /sùb infyoo dáysh'n/ *n* **1.** in the feudal system, the leasing of a portion of the land held by a feudal lord's servant (**vassal**) to somebody else who became the servant's servant in turn **2.** a portion of land granted to a feudal servant under the terms of subinfeudation —**sub·in·feu·date** /-fyoo dàyt/ *vt*

sub·ir·ri·gate /sub írri gàyt/ (**-gat·ed, -gat·ing, -gates**) *vt* to irrigate land from below the surface of the ground, e.g., with porous pipes laid underground —**sub·ir·ri·ga·tion** /sùb iri gáysh'n/ *n*

su·bi·to /sóobitō/ *adv* suddenly or abruptly (*used as a musical direction*) [Early 18C. < Italian < Latin *subire* "come over"]

subj. *abbr* **1.** GRAM subject **2.** subjective **3.** GRAM subjunctive

sub·ja·cent /sub jáyss'nt/ *adj* (*formal*) **1.** lying under or just below something **2.** next to something and at a lower level than it ○*"in the damper tracts of subjacent country and along the river-courses"* (Thomas Hardy, *Jude the Obscure*; 1895) [Late 16C. < Latin *subjacent-*, present participle of *subjacere* "lie under" < *jacere* "lie"] —**sub·ja·cen·cy** *n* —**sub·ja·cent·ly** *adv*

sub·ject *n* /súb jèkt/ **1.** TOPIC something that is being discussed, examined, or otherwise dealt with ○ *the subject of our conversation* ○ *On the subject of staff changes, I have some news.* **2.** COURSE OF STUDY a branch of learning that forms a course of study (*often used in the plural*) **3.** SOMEBODY TREATED OR ACTED UPON somebody who receives treatment or is the focus of an activity ○ *not an appropriate subject for hypnosis* **4.** PERSON RULED BY ANOTHER somebody who is ruled by a king, queen, or other authority **5.** ARTS, LITERAT THING REPRESENTED BY ARTIST somebody or something that an artist, writer, or photographer represents in a piece of work ○ *the subject of her latest biography* **6.** GRAM GRAMMATICAL PERFORMER OF ACTION the part of a sentence or utterance, usually a noun, noun phrase, or equivalent, that the rest of the sentence asserts something about and that agrees with the verb. The subject typically performs the action expressed by the verb. "She" and "The dog" are the subjects of "She gave me the book" and "The dog was found asleep" respectively. **7.** MUSIC MUSICAL THEME the principal theme or melodic phrase that is developed in a musical composition ■ *adj* /súb jèkt/ **1.** PRONE TO likely to be affected by something ○ *areas subject to flooding* ○ *a child subject to mood swings* **2.** RULED under the control of somebody or something such as a ruler or a law, and obliged to obey ○ *a subject nation* ○ *not subject to the laws that apply in this country* ■ *adv* **sub·ject to** DEPENDING depending on somebody or something ○ *The plans have been drawn up, subject to your final approval.* ■ *vt* /səb jékt/ (**-ject·ed, -ject·ing, -jects**) **1.** GIVE SOMEBODY UNPLEASANT EXPERIENCE to cause somebody to undergo something unpleasant ○ *recruits subjected to rigorous physical training* **2.** SUBMIT SOMETHING TO TREATMENT to make something undergo a particular kind of treatment ○ *proposals subjected to detailed scrutiny* **3.** OVERPOWER SOMEBODY to bring a person or group under the power or influence of another person or group ○ *a nation subjected to rule from overseas* [14C. Via French < Latin *subjectus* < *subicere* "place under" < *jacere* "lie"]

SYNONYMS ***subject, topic, matter, issue, subject matter, theme, burden***

CORE MEANING: what is under discussion

subject something that is being discussed, examined, or otherwise dealt with ○ *I didn't bring up the subject of money with my cousin.* ○ *Restoration of the wreck will be the subject of an exhibition at the Maritime Museum this year.* **topic** something dealt with in a text or in discussion ○ *The paper identified four major topics for consideration.* ○ *the current topic of conversation* **matter** something that is being considered or needs to be dealt with ○ *Readers may have their own views on this matter.* ○ *It may help to hold short family meetings to discuss matters like holidays.* **issue** something for discussion or of general concern ○ *I want to talk to you on the issue of late delivery.* ○ *These are sensitive issues and need to be handled carefully.* **subject matter** the material dealt with in a book, movie, discussion, or other medium ○ *Most of the documentation aids are graphic representations of the subject matter.* ○ *a photographer whose subject matter is the narrow streets of lower Manhattan* **theme** the subject of a discourse, discussion, piece of writing, or artistic composition ○ *Death and the passing of time are the principal themes of this book.* **burden** (*literary*) the main or recurring theme in a book, piece of music, speech, or argument ○ *The main burden of the report's criticisms focus on lack of communication.* ○ *Tantalizing unfulfillment is part of the play's emotional burden.*

sub·jec·tion /səb jéksh'n/ *n* **1.** the bringing of a person or people under the control of another, usually by force **2.** the subjecting of somebody to something

sub·jec·tive /səb jéktiv/ *adj* **1.** NOT IMPARTIAL based on somebody's opinions or feelings rather than on facts or evidence ○ *Of course, that's only my subjective impression.* **2.** PHILOSOPHY EXISTING BY PERCEPTION existing only in the mind and not independently of it **3.** MED OBSERVED ONLY BY PATIENT describes a medical condition that is perceived to exist only by the patient and is not recognizable to anyone else **4.** GRAM RELATING TO SUBJECT OF VERB relating to or forming the subject of a verb —**sub·jec·tive·ly** *adv* —**sub·jec·tive·ness** *n*

sub·jec·tive i·de·al·ism *n* a philosophical theory arguing that the external world only exists because it is perceived to exist, and does not have existence of its own

sub·jec·tiv·ism /səb jéktə vizzəm/ *n* **1.** EMPHASIS ON PERSONAL INTERPRETATION emphasis on personal feelings or responses as opposed to external facts or evidence **2.** PHILOSOPHY THEORY OF VALIDITY OF KNOWLEDGE a theory stating that people can only have knowledge of what they experience directly **3.** PHILOSOPHY THEORY OF VALIDITY OF MORAL STANDARDS a theory stating that the only valid moral standard is the one imposed by somebody's own conscience, and therefore that society's moral codes are invalid —**sub·jec·tiv·ist** *adj* —**sub·jec·tiv·is·tic** /səb jèktə vístik/ *adj* —**sub·jec·tiv·is·ti·cal·ly** *adv*

sub·jec·tiv·i·ty /sùb jek tívvətee/ *n* **1.** interpretation based on personal opinions or feelings rather than on external facts or evidence **2.** concentration on personal, individual responses in artistic expression

sub·ject line *n* a line in an e-mail that indicates the subject of the message

sub·ject mat·ter *n* the matter dealt with in a book, movie, discussion, or other medium ○ *contains subject matter unsuitable for children*

SYNONYMS See ***subject.***

sub·join /sub jóyn/ (**-joined, -join·ing, -joins**) *vt* to add something at the end of what has already been written or said (*formal*)

sub ju·di·ce /sub jóodəssee, -yóodə kày/ *adj* currently under consideration by a judge or a court of law and therefore not to be commented upon publicly [Early 17C. < Latin, "under a judge"]

sub·ju·gate /súbjə gàyt/ (**-gat·ed, -gat·ing, -gates**) *vt* to bring somebody, especially a people or nation, under the control of another, e.g., by military conquest [15C. < Latin *subjugat-*, past participle of *subjugare* < *jugum* "yoke"] —**sub·ju·ga·ble** *adj* —**sub·ju·ga·tion** /sùbjə gáysh'n/ *n* —**sub·ju·ga·tor** *n*

sub·junc·tive /səb júngktiv/ *n* **1.** GRAMMATICAL MOOD a grammatical mood that expresses doubts, wishes, and possibilities **2.** SUBJUNCTIVE VERB a verb or form in the subjunctive ■ *adj* RELATING TO SUBJUNCTIVE in or relating to the subjunctive [Mid-16C. < late Latin *subjunctivus* < past participle of Latin *subjungere* "subordinate" < *jungere* "to join"] —**sub·junc·tive·ly** *adv*

USAGE The subjunctive mood in English is distinguishable from the regular form of verbs (called the *indicative* mood) only in the third person present singular, which omits the final *-s* (as in *make* rather than *makes*), and in the forms *be* and *were* of the verb *to be.* A typical use of the subjunctive is in clauses introduced by *that* expressing a wish or suggestion: *I suggested that she drop by for a drink before the concert. They demanded that he answer their questions.* The form *were* is used in clauses introduced by *if, as if, as though,* or *supposing,* as in: *If you were to go, you might regret it. It's not as though he were an expert. Suppose I were to meet you outside the theater.* The subjunctive also occurs in fixed expressions such as *as it were, be that as it may, come what may,* and *far be it from me.*

sub·king·dom /súb kìngdəm/ *n* a category in the classification of plants and animals that is smaller than a kingdom and larger than a phylum

sub·lease *n* /súb leess/ an arrangement to rent a property from somebody who is already renting it from somebody else ■ *vt* /sub léess/ (**-leased, -leas·ing, -leas·es**) same as **sublet** —**sub·les·see** /sùb le sée/ *n* —**sub·les·sor** /sub lé sàwr/ *n*

sub·let /sub lét/ *vti* (**-let, -let·ting, -lets**) to rent a property to or as a subsidiary tenant ■ *n* a property, especially an apartment, that is rented from somebody who is renting it from somebody else

sub·li·mate /súbblə màyt/ *v* (**-mat·ed, -mat·ing, -mates**) **1.** *vt* PSYCHOL to channel impulses or energies regarded as unacceptable, especially sexual desires, toward an activity that is more socially acceptable, often a creative activity **2.** *vti* CHEM same as **sublime** *v* (senses 1–2) ■ *n* CHEM a chemical substance formed as a result of sublimation [15C. < Latin *sublimat-*, past participle of *sublimare* "elevate" < *sublimis* "elevated"]

sub·li·ma·tion /sùbblə máysh'n/ *n* **1.** the channeling of impulses or energies regarded as unacceptable, especially sexual desires, toward activities regarded as more socially acceptable, often creative activities **2.** a process in which a substance is converted directly from a solid to a gas or from a gas to a solid without an intermediate liquid phase

sub·lime /sə blím/ *adj* (**-lim·er, -lim·est**) **1.** BEAUTIFUL so awe-inspiringly beautiful as to seem almost heavenly ○ *the composer at his most sublime* **2.** MORALLY WORTHY of the highest moral or spiritual value **3.** COMPLETE complete or utter ○ *in sublime ignorance* **4.** EXCELLENT excellent or particularly impressive (*informal*) ○ *a sublime pasta creation* ■ *n* SOMETHING SUBLIME something that is sublime ○ *going from the sublime to the ridiculous* ■ *v* (**-limed, -lim·ing, -limes**) **1.** *vti* CHEM CONVERT SOLID SUBSTANCE TO GAS to convert a substance directly from a solid to a gas or from a gas to a solid without an intermediate liquid phase, or undergo this process **2.** *vti* CHEM CONVERT THEN RECONVERT to convert a solid directly into a gas and then back to a solid again without an intermediate liquid phase, or undergo this process **3.** *vt* MAKE SOMETHING PURE to make something such as an emotion finer or purer [14C. < Latin *sublimis* "elevated"] —**sub·lime·ly** *adv* —**sub·lime·ness** *n* —**sub·lim·i·ty** /sə blímmətee/ *n*

Sub·lime Porte /sə blīm páwrt/ *n* HIST same as **Porte** [Early 17C. < French, "High Gate," translation of Turkish *Babiâli*, referring to the palace gate where justice was administered]

sub·lim·i·nal /sub límmin'l/ *adj* entering, existing in, or affecting the mind without conscious awareness ○ *subliminal messages* [Late 19C. < SUB- + Latin *limin-* "threshhold"] —**sub·lim·i·nal·ly** *adv*

sub·lim·i·nal ad·ver·tis·ing *n* advertising in the form of images flashed onto the screen during a movie or television show that are too brief to be noticed but long enough to be registered subconsciously

sub·lin·gual /sub líng gwəl/ *adj* **1.** situated under the tongue **2.** describes medicines that are administered by being placed under the tongue to dissolve —**sub·lin·gual·ly** *adv*

sub·lit·er·a·ture /sub líttrəchər, -líttrə choŏr/ *n US* popular literature, e.g., crime novels and romances

sub·lit·to·ral /sub líttərəl/ *adj* relating to, living near, or located in the shallow water near a shoreline ■ *n* the area of a sea that lies between the shore and the continental shelf

sub·lu·na·ry /sub lo͞onəree/ *adj* **1.** relating to or found in the area of space that lies between the Moon and the Earth **2.** belonging to the material world rather than to the spiritual or intellectual world (*archaic or literary*)

sub·lux·a·tion /sùb luk sáysh'n/ *n* a partial dislocation of bones that leaves them misaligned but still in some contact with each other

sub·ma·chine gun /sùbmə sheén-/ *n* a lightweight portable machine gun fired from the hip or the shoulder. It can fire either in single rounds or continuous bursts.

sub·man·dib·u·lar /sùb man díbbyələr/ *adj* relating to or located under the lower jaw

sub·mar·gin·al /sub maárjin'l/ *adj* falling below a necessary minimum, especially the minimum conditions necessary for profitability —**sub·mar·gin·al·ly** *adv*

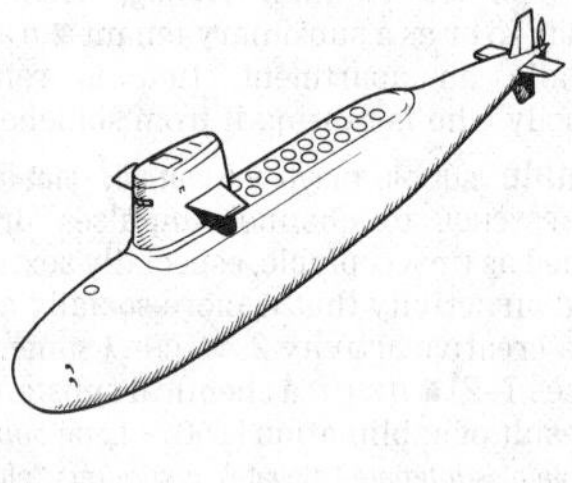

submarine

sub·ma·rine /súbmə reén/ *n* **1.** UNDERWATER BOAT a boat built to operate and travel for long periods under water **2.** LONG SANDWICH a sandwich made with a long roll cut horizontally ■ *adj* UNDERWATER taking place or growing under water, especially in the sea ○ *submarine research* —**sub·ma·rin·er** /sùb mə reénər, -márrənər/ *n*

sub·ma·rine chas·er *n* a small maneuverable ship designed for pursuing and attacking submarines (*informal*)

sub·max·il·lar·y /sub máksə lèrree/ *adj* ANAT same as **submandibular**

sub·me·di·ant /sub meédee ənt/ *n* **1.** the sixth note in a major or minor musical scale **2.** a musical key, chord, or harmony based on a submediant

sub·merge /səb múrj/ (**-merged, -mer·ging, -mer·ges**) *v* **1.** *vt* PLUNGE SOMETHING IN LIQUID to put something into water or some other liquid so that all of it is under the surface **2.** *vi* GO UNDER WATER to go under the surface of water or another liquid **3.** *vt* SUPPRESS SOMETHING to keep something such as feelings or a secret hidden from others [Early 17C. < Latin *submergere* "dip under" < *mergere* "dip"] —**sub·merged** *adj* —**sub·mer·gence** *n*

sub·merse /səb múrss/ (**-mersed, -mers·ing, -mers·es**) *vt* same as **submerge** (sense 1) [Early 18C. < Latin *submers-*, past participle of *submergere* (see SUBMERGE)] —**sub·mer·sion** /səb múrsh'n, -zh'n/ *n*

sub·mers·i·ble /səb múrssəb'l/ *adj* **1.** FOR UNDERWATER USE designed for use underwater **2.** NOT DAMAGED UNDER WATER capable of being put under water without being damaged ■ *n* UNDERWATER BOAT an underwater vessel, especially a small craft designed for use at deep levels

sub·mi·cro·scop·ic /sùb mīkrə skóppik/ *adj* too small to be seen with an optical microscope —**sub·mi·cro·scop·i·cal·ly** *adv*

sub·min·i·a·ture /sub mínnee əchər, -mínnee ə choŏr, -mínnichər/ *adj* **1.** SMALLER THAN MINIATURE smaller in size than miniature **2.** SMALLER THAN COMPACT CAMERA describes a camera substantially smaller than a compact camera, using film smaller than the 35mm miniature format ■ *n* VERY SMALL CAMERA a subminiature camera

sub·min·i·a·tur·ize /sub mínnee əchə rīz, -mínnichə rīz/ (**-ized, -iz·ing, -iz·es**) *vt* to manufacture something that is very small in scale —**sub·min·i·a·tur·i·za·tion** /sub mìnnee əchəri záysh'n, sub mìnnəchəri záysh'n/ *n*

sub·mis·sion /səb mísh'n/ *n* **1.** YIELDING, OR READINESS TO YIELD a willingness to yield or surrender to somebody, or the act of doing so ○ *demanded nothing less than total submission to his authority* **2.** IDEA SUBMITTED something put forward for consideration or approval, e.g., a suggestion, proposal, or plan **3.** ACT OF SUBMITTING SOMETHING the act of submitting or handing in something such as a proposal to be considered or written work to be judged **4.** LAW AGREEMENT TO ARBITRATE an agreement between parties in a dispute to have a contested matter arbitrated **5.** WRESTLING WITHDRAWAL FROM WRESTLING BOUT an acknowledgment by a wrestler that he or she cannot continue a bout because of pain

sub·mis·sive /səb míssiv/ *adj* giving in or tending to give in to the demands or authority of others —**sub·mis·sive·ly** *adv* —**sub·mis·sive·ness** *n*

sub·mit /səb mít/ (**-mit·ted, -mit·ting, -mits**) *v* **1.** *vt* PROPOSE OR HAND IN SOMETHING to hand something in or put something forward for consideration, approval, or judgment ○ *Applications must be submitted in triplicate.* **2.** *vi* YIELD to accept somebody else's authority or will, especially reluctantly or under pressure **3.** *vi* AGREE to agree to undergo something ○ *had to submit to intensive questioning* **4.** *vi* DEFER to defer to another's knowledge, judgment, or experience **5.** *vt* ARGUE POINT to state or argue that something is the case (*formal*) [14C. < Latin *submittere* "send under" < *mittere* "send"] —**sub·mit·ta·ble** *adj* —**sub·mit·tal** *n* —**sub·mit·ter** *n*

SYNONYMS See *yield*.

sub·mon·tane /sùb món tàyn/ *adj* **1.** relating to or found in the foothills or on the lower slopes of a mountain **2.** passing under or through a mountain —**sub·mon·tane·ly** *adv*

sub·mu·co·sa /sùb myoo kṓzə/ *n* a layer of loosely meshed microscopic fibers and associated cells occurring beneath a mucous membrane, e.g., in the small intestine [Late 19C. < modern Latin < *mucosa* (see MUCOSA)]

sub·mul·ti·ple /sub múltip'l/ *n* a number that can be divided into another an exact number of times and leave no remainder. For example, 7 is a submultiple of 35. ■ *adj* able to be divided into another number an exact number of times without leaving a remainder [Late 17C. < late Latin *submultiplus* < *multiplus* (see MULTIPLE)]

sub·nor·mal /sub náwrm'l/ *adj* lower or less than normal or average —**sub·nor·mal·i·ty** /sùb nawr mállətee/ *n* —**sub·nor·mal·ly** *adv*

sub·note·book /sub nṓt boŏk/ *n* a portable personal computer that is smaller and lighter than a notebook

sub·or·bi·tal /sub áwrbət'l/ *adj* **1.** relating to the region below the eye socket (**orbit**) **2.** not designed to make a complete orbit of Earth or another astronomical object

sub·or·der /súb àwrdər/ *n* a taxonomic category that is a subdivision of an order and usually contains several similar families

sub·or·di·nar·y /sə báwrd'n èrree/ (*plural* **-ies**) *n* in heraldry, a small shape or design, e.g., a lozenge, that can appear on a coat of arms and is smaller than the most prominent shape (**ordinary**)

sub·or·din·ate *adj* /sə báwrd'nət/ **1.** OF LESSER RANK lower than somebody in rank or status **2.** OF LESS IMPORTANCE secondary in importance **3.** GRAM MODIFYING acting as a modifying noun, adjective, or adverb within a sentence ■ *n* /sə báwrd'nət/ SOMEBODY IN JUNIOR POSITION somebody who is lower in rank or status than another ■ *vt* /sə báwrd'n àyt/ (**-at·ed, -at·ing, -ates**) **1.** MAKE SOMETHING SECONDARY to treat something as less important and allow something else to dominate or take priority ○ *had increasingly subordinated her research to the demands of her busy work schedule* **2.** PLACE SOMEBODY IN LOWER RANK to give somebody or regard somebody as having a lower rank or status than another [15C. < medieval Latin *subordinatus*, past participle of *subordinare* "place below" < Latin *ordinare* (see ORDAIN)] —**sub·or·di·nate·ly** *adv* —**sub·or·di·nate·ness** *n* —**sub·or·di·na·tion** /sə bàwrd'n áysh'n/ *n*

sub·or·di·nate clause *n* a clause that cannot stand alone as a separate sentence since its meaning depends on the meaning of the main clause and simply gives additional information. In the sentence "We had to run because we were late," the clause "because we were late" is the subordinate clause and "We had to run" is the main clause.

sub·or·di·nate con·junc·tion, **sub·or·di·nat·ing con·junc·tion** /sə bàwrd'n ayting-/, **sub·or·di·na·tor** /sə báwrd'n àytər/ *n* a conjunction that introduces a subordinate clause. It may be either one word such as "although," "because," or "since," or a group of words such as "in order that" or "as long as."

sub·orn /sə báwrn/ (**-orned, -orn·ing, -orns**) *vt* to persuade somebody to commit a crime or other wrongdoing, e.g., to bribe another party to tell lies in court [Early 16C. < Latin *subornare* "equip secretly" < *ornare* "equip"] —**sub·or·na·tion** /sùb awr náysh'n/ *n* —**sub·or·na·tive** *adj* —**sub·orn·er** *n*

sub·os·cine /sub ó sīn/ *adj* relating to, typical of, or belonging to the large subgroup of passerine birds that are not songbirds and are mainly found in America. ◊ **oscine**

sub·ox·ide /sub ók sīd/ *n* an oxide containing less oxygen than the normal oxide formed by a specific element

sub·pe·na *n*, *vt US* LAW another spelling of **subpoena**

sub·plot /súb plòt/ *n* **1.** a second and less prominent story within a book, play, or movie **2.** a division of a plot of land, used especially for crop husbandry experiments

sub·poe·na /sə peénə/, **sub·pe·na** *n* a written legal order summoning a witness or requiring evidence to be submitted to a court or similar deliberative body ■ *vt* (**-naed, -na·ing, -nas**) to summon a witness with a written legal order, or require something to be submitted in evidence to a court or other deliberative body [15C. < Latin *sub poena* "under penalty," first words of the writ] —**sub·poe·naed** *adj*

sub·po·lar /sub pṓlər/ *adj* **1.** being near the Arctic or the Antarctic polar region **2.** relating to, belonging to, or found in the areas that border the Arctic and Antarctic

sub·ring /súb rìng/ *n* in mathematics, a ring that is a subset of a larger ring

sub·ro·gate /súbbrə gàyt/ (**-gat·ed, -gat·ing, -gates**) *vt* to substitute one person for another, especially in transferring a right or claim [15C. < Latin *subrogat-*, past participle of *subrogare* "ask for in place of" < *rogare* "ask, beg"]

sub·ro·ga·tion /sùbbrə gáysh'n/ *n* the substitution of one claim for another, especially the transfer of the right to receive payment of a debt to somebody other than the original creditor

sub ro·sa /sub rṓzə/ *adv* in a secret or private way [Mid-17C. < Latin, "under the rose" (as an emblem of confidentiality hung above council tables)]

sub·rou·tine /súb roo tēen/ *n* a sequence of programming statements that performs a single task and can be used repeatedly

subs. *abbr US* subscription

sub-Sa·har·an *adj* relating to the area of Africa south of the Sahara desert

sub·scribe /səb skrīb/ (**-scribed, -scrib·ing, -scribes**) *v* **1.** *vi* MAKE ADVANCE PAYMENT to agree to pay for and receive or use something over a fixed period of time, e.g., a periodical, series of books, or set of tickets to musical or dramatic performances **2.** *vti* PROMISE TO GIVE MONEY REGULARLY to pledge to make regular donations to something, especially a charity **3.** *vti* GUARANTEE TO INVEST IN SOMETHING to promise to pay for something when it will occur, e.g., the financing of a new business or a new issue of stock **4.** *vi* SUPPORT VIEW to support or believe in a theory or view ○ *those who subscribe to progressive ideals* **5.** *vi* ONLINE PUT NAME ON MAILING LIST to add your name and e-mail address to a mailing list in order to receive messages from a website automatically, usually without charge **6.** *vt* LAW SIGN NAME ON LEGAL DOCUMENT to sign a legal document to indicate agreement or approval of its terms (*formal*) [15C. < Latin *subscribere* "write underneath" < *scribere* "write"] —**sub·scrib·er** *n*

sub·script /súb skrìpt/ *n* a character that is printed on a level lower than the rest of the characters on the line, e.g., the "2" in the chemical formula "H_2O" ■ *adj* printed on a lower level than other characters in a line of type [Early 18C. < Latin *subscript-*, past participle of *subscribere* (see SUBSCRIBE)]

sub·scrip·tion /səb skrípsh'n/ *n* **1.** ADVANCE PAYMENT FOR SOMETHING an agreement to pay for and receive or use something over a fixed period of time, e.g., a periodical, series of books, or set of tickets to musical or dramatic performances ○ *a movie channel subscription* **2.** PLEDGE TO PAY FOR SOMETHING a promise to pay for something when it will occur, e.g., the financing of a new business or a new issue of stock **3.** LAW SIGNING OF DOCUMENT OR SIGNATURE the process of signing a legal document as an indication of approval of its terms, or an approving signature on a document (*formal*) **4.** TOTAL AGREEMENT a full agreement with or approval of something (*literary*) **5.** *UK* MEMBERSHIP FEE a fee paid for membership in a club or society [15C. < Latin *subscription-* < past participle of *subscribere* (see SUBSCRIBE)]

sub·scrip·tion li·brar·y *n* a library that lends books in return for a regular fee

sub·sec·tion /súb sèkshən/ *n* any of the smaller parts into which a section may be divided, e.g., in a legal or official document

sub·sel·li·um /səb séllee əm/ (*plural* **-li·a** /-lee ə/) *n* CHR, FURNITURE same as **misericord** [Early 18C. < Latin, "low seat" < *sella* "seat"]

sub·se·quence[1] /súbsəkwənss/ *n* something that happens after something else, or the occurrence of something after something else [15C. < SUBSEQUENT]

sub·se·quence[2] /súb sēekwənss/ *n* a sequence within another mathematical sequence [Early 20C. < SUB- + SEQUENCE]

sub·se·quent /súbsəkwənt/ *adj* later in time or order than something else [15C. Directly or via French < Latin *subsequent-*, present participle of *subsequi* "follow closely" < *sequi* "follow"]

sub·se·quent·ly /súbsəkwəntlee/ *adv* at a later time, and often as a consequence

sub·sere /súb sēer/ *n* a secondary development of a natural plant and animal community after destruction by fire, flood, or human action [Early 20C. < SUB- + SERE[2]]

sub·serve /səb súrv/ (**-served, -serv·ing, -serves**) *vt* to help to further, promote, or bring something about [Early 17C. < Latin *subservire* "serve under" < *servire* (see SERVE)]

sub·ser·vi·ent /səb súrvee ənt/ *adj* **1.** TOO EAGER TO OBEY too submissive or eager to follow the wishes or orders of others **2.** OF LESSER IMPORTANCE in a position of secondary importance **3.** INSTRUMENTAL IN SOMETHING helping to achieve something or bring something about [Mid-17C. < Latin *subservient-*, present participle of *subservire* "serve under" < *servire* (see SERVE)] —**sub·ser·vi·ence** *n* —**sub·ser·vi·ent·ly** *adv*

sub·set /súb sèt/ *n* a mathematical set whose elements are contained in another set

sub·shell /súb shèl/ *n* an orbital within an electron energy level (**shell**)

sub·shrub /súb shrùb/ *n* a low-growing plant with woody stems and main branches and nonwoody tips that die back each year [Mid-19C. Translation of modern Latin *suffrutex* < Latin *frutex* "shrub"] —**sub·shrub·by** *adj*

sub·side /səb sīd/ (**-sid·ed, -sid·ing, -sides**) *vi* **1.** DIMINISH IN INTENSITY to become less active or intense **2.** DROP TO LOWER LEVEL to sink to a low or lower level **3.** SINK TO BOTTOM to sink to the bottom of a liquid **4.** GRADUALLY SIT OR LIE DOWN to sink into a sitting or lying position, e.g., out of exhaustion (*formal*) [Mid-17C. < Latin *subsidere* "settle down" < *sidere* "settle"]

sub·si·dence /səb sīd'nss, súbsədənss/ *n* **1.** the sinking down of land resulting from natural shifts or human activity, frequently causing structural damage to buildings **2.** the waning or lessening of something

sub·sid·i·ar·i·ty /səb sìddee árrətee/ *n* **1.** the principle that political power should be exercised by the smallest or least central unit of government **2.** the fact or quality of being subsidiary [Mid-20C. Translation of German *Subsidiarität*]

sub·sid·i·ar·y /səb síddee èrree/ *adj* **1.** OF LESSER IMPORTANCE having secondary importance, or occupying a subordinate position **2.** IN SUPPORTING ROLE serving to aid, supplement, or support something **3.** *US* AS SUBSIDY in the form of a subsidy ■ *n* (*plural* **-a·ries**) **1.** SOMEBODY OR SOMETHING AUXILIARY somebody or something that occupies a secondary or subordinate position **2.** PART OF LARGER COMPANY a company controlled or owned by a larger one [Mid-16C. < Latin *subsidiarius* < *subsidium* (see SUBSIDY)] —**sub·sid·i·ar·i·ly** *adv*

sub·sid·i·ar·y coin *n* a coin that has a lower denomination than that of a standard unit of currency

sub·si·dize /súbssə dīz/ (**-dized, -diz·ing, -diz·es**) *vt* **1.** to contribute money to somebody or something, especially to give a government grant to a private company, organization, or charity to help it to continue to function **2.** to reduce the cost of something by providing a subsidy —**sub·si·diz·a·ble** *adj* —**sub·si·di·za·tion** /sùbssədi záysh'n/ *n* —**sub·si·diz·er** *n*

sub·si·dy /súbssədee/ (*plural* **-dies**) *n* **1.** a grant or gift of money from a government to a private company, organization, or charity to help it to function **2.** a monetary gift or contribution to somebody or something, especially to pay expenses [14C. Via Anglo-Norman < Latin *subsidium* "reserve troops" < *sedere* "sit"]

sub·sist /səb síst/ (**-sist·ed, -sist·ing, -sists**) *v* **1.** *vi* MANAGE TO LIVE to remain alive or viable, especially with the help of something **2.** *vt* MAINTAIN SOMEBODY OR SOMETHING to support or maintain somebody or something by providing something that is needed, e.g., by supplying troops with food or businesses with capital (*formal*) **3.** *vi* BE ATTRIBUTABLE TO SOMETHING to have a particular thing as its reason or origin (*formal*) **4.** *vi* BE INHERENT to reside in or consist of a particular thing (*formal*) **5.** *vi* PHILOSOPHY, MATH EXIST IN ABSTRACT to have a timeless conceptual existence (*refers to numbers or mathematical sets*) [Mid-16C. Directly or via French < Latin *subsistere* "stand up to" < *sistere* (see ASSIST)] —**sub·sis·tent** *adj* —**sub·sist·er** *n*

sub·sis·tence /səb sístənss/ *n* **1.** CONDITION OF MANAGING TO STAY ALIVE the condition of being or managing to stay alive, especially when there is barely enough food or money for survival **2.** CONTINUING TO EXIST the condition of continuing to exist **3.** MATH, PHILOSOPHY QUALITY OF ABSTRACT EXISTENCE the quality that something possesses of existing independently, timelessly, or by virtue of its essence

sub·sis·tence al·low·ance *n* **1.** a sum of money given to an employee to cover special expenses incurred in the performance of his or her work **2.** an advance paid to a new employee or soldier to help to meet living costs until wages begin to be paid

sub·sis·tence crop *n* a crop grown by a farmer principally to feed his or her family, with little or nothing left over to sell

sub·sis·tence farm·ing *n* farming that generates only enough produce to feed the farmer's family, with little or nothing left over to sell —**sub·sis·tence farm·er** *n*

sub·sis·tence lev·el *n* a standard of living that provides barely enough food and money on which to survive

sub·sis·tence wage *n* a wage so low that it is barely enough to live on

sub·so·cial /sub sṓsh'l/ *adj* describes insects that associate with others but without any fixed or organized social structure —**sub·so·cial·ly** *adv*

sub·soil /súb sòyl/ *n* the compacted soil beneath the topsoil ■ *vt* (**-soiled, -soil·ing, -soils**) to turn, break, or stir the compacted soil beneath the topsoil

sub·soil·er /súb sòylər/ *n* **1.** a farm implement consisting of a frame with long sturdy vertical tines. It is drawn through the soil to break up compacted subsoil in order to improve drainage and aeration. **2.** an operator of a subsoiler

sub·so·lar /sub sṓlər/ *adj* **1.** located directly below the Sun on the Earth's surface when the Sun is at its highest point **2.** located in the equatorial region that lies between the tropics of Cancer and Capricorn

sub·song /súb sàwng, -sòng/ *n* an unstructured song of a bird that is quieter and lower-pitched than full song and is often performed by young adult birds

sub·son·ic /sub sónnik/ *adj* **1.** slower than 760 mph/1,220 kph, the speed at which sound travels in air **2.** flying at speeds slower than the speed of sound, especially not designed to fly above the speed of sound —**sub·son·i·cal·ly** *adv*

sub·spe·cies /súb spēesheez, -seez/ (*plural same*) *n* a category used to classify plants and animals whose populations are distinct, e.g., in distribution, appearance, or feeding habits, but can still interbreed —**sub·spe·cif·ic** /sùb spə síffik/ *adj* —**sub·spe·cif·i·cal·ly** *adv*

sub·stage /súb stàyj/ *n* a component assembly in a microscope that contains the condenser, mirror, or other accessories and is located below the stage

sub·stance /súbstənss/ *n* **1.** MATERIAL a kind of matter or material **2.** TANGIBLE PHYSICAL MATTER physical reality that can be touched and felt **3.** PRACTICAL VALUE real or practical value or importance ○ *There was nothing of substance in the document.* **4.** MATERIAL WEALTH wealth in the form of money and possessions **5.** GIST OF MEANING the actual or essential meaning of something said or written ○ *the substance of their argument* **6.** PHILOSOPHY ESSENCE the unchanging essence of something **7.** PHILOSOPHY SOMETHING SPECIFIC something that is individual and caused [13C. Via French < Latin *substantia* "essence" (translation of Greek *hupostasis*) < *substare*, literally "stand under" < *stare* "to stand"]

sub·stance a·buse *n* the excessive consumption or misuse of a substance for the sake of its nontherapeutic effects on the mind or body, especially drugs or alcohol

sub·stance P *n* a peptide found in body tissues, especially nervous tissue, that is involved in the transmission of pain and in inflammation

~~substancial~~ incorrect spelling of **substantial**

sub·stan·dard /sub stándərd/ *adj* below the expected or required standard of quality

sub·stan·tial /səb stánsh'l/ *adj* **1.** CONSIDERABLE considerable in amount, extent, value, or importance **2.** STURDY solidly built **3.** FILLING providing a lot of nourishment **4.** RICH wealthy and prosperous **5.** REAL AND TANGIBLE actual and real in a palpable way **6.** PHILOSOPHY OF SUBSTANCE consisting of or involving substance ■ *n* IMPORTANT PART an important or essential part [14C. Directly or via French < ecclesiastical Latin *substantialis* "having substance" (translation of Greek *hupostatikos*) < *substare* (see SUBSTANCE)] —**sub·stan·ti·al·i·ty** /səb stànshee állətee/ *n* —**sub·stan·tial·ness** *n*

sub·stan·tial·ism /səb stánsh'l ìzzəm/ *n* the philosophical doctrine that beings or entities of substantial reality underlie all phenomena —**sub·stan·tial·ist** *n*

sub·stan·tial·ize /səb stánsh'l ɪ̄z/ (**-ized, -iz·ing, -iz·es**) *vti* to make something that is imaginary, theoretical, or spiritual become palpable, or become palpable

sub·stan·tial·ly /səb stánsh'lee/ *adv* **1.** in an extensive, substantial, or ample way **2.** in essence

sub·stan·ti·ate /səb stánshee àyt/ (**-at·ed, -at·ing, -ates**) *vt* **1.** to confirm that something is true or valid **2.** to give something an actual physical existence [Mid-17C. < medieval Latin *substantiat-*, past participle of *substantiare* "give substance to" < Latin *substantia* (see SUBSTANCE)] —**sub·stan·ti·a·ble** *adj* —**sub·stan·ti·a·tion** /səb stànshee áysh'n/ *n* —**sub·stan·ti·a·tive** *adj* —**sub·stan·ti·a·tor** *n*

sub·stan·tive *adj* /súbstəntiv/ **1. WITH PRACTICAL IMPORTANCE** having practical importance, value, or effect ○ *a substantive agreement* **2. SUBSTANTIAL** substantial in amount or quantity ○ *a substantive meal* **3. ESSENTIAL** relating to the substance of something **4. INDEPENDENT** continuing independently **5.** GRAM **USED LIKE NOUN** relating to or used like a noun **6.** GRAM **EXPRESSING EXISTENCE** expressing existence, as with the verb "to be" **7.** LAW **RELATING TO LEGAL PRINCIPLES** relating to the essential principles that a court applies in its work, not to the rules of procedure and practice **8.** INDUST **DIRECTLY ATTACHING AS DYE COLOR** attaching as a color directly to a material being dyed without the use of a fixing substance **9.** MIL **PERMANENT** describes a rank or appointment that is permanent ■ *n* /súbstəntiv, səb stántiv/ GRAM **NOUN** a noun, or a word or group of words used like a noun [15C. Directly or via French < late Latin *substantivus* < Latin *substantia* (see SUBSTANCE)] —**sub·stan·ti·val** /sùbstən tɪ̄v'l/ *adj* —**sub·stan·tive·ly** *adv*

sub·stan·tive right *n* a basic human right that is regarded as existing naturally and indispensably, e.g., the right to life or liberty

sub·stan·ti·vize /səb stántə vɪ̄z/ (**-vized, -viz·ing, -viz·es**) *vt* to make a word or words function like a noun —**sub·stan·ti·vi·za·tion** /səb stàntəvi záysh'n/ *n*

sub·sta·tion /súb stàysh'n/ *n* **1.** a branch of a main electrical power station where electrical current is converted, redistributed, or modified in strength **2.** an office, building, or installation that is a branch of something larger, especially a branch of a post office

sub·stit·u·ent /səb stíchoo ənt/ *n* an atom or group of atoms that replaces another atom or group in a molecule [Late 19C. < Latin *substituent-*, present participle of *substituere* "set up under" (see SUBSTITUTE)]

sub·sti·tute /súbstə to͞ot/ *v* (**-tut·ed, -tut·ing, -tutes**) **1.** *vti* **REPLACE SOMEBODY OR SOMETHING** to put somebody or something in place of another, or take the place of another (*often passive*) **2.** *vt* CHEM **REPLACE ATOM OR ATOMS** to replace an atom or group of atoms in a molecule with another atom or group **3.** *vt* MATH **REPLACE MATHEMATICAL ELEMENT** to replace one mathematical element with another of equal value ■ *n* **1. REPLACEMENT** somebody or something that takes the place of another ○ *Herb teas can be a pleasant substitute for coffee or tea.* **2.** SPORTS **REPLACEMENT PLAYER** a team member in a game who is ready to replace another on the field **3.** GRAM **GRAMMATICALLY REPLACEABLE WORD** a word that can take the place of another grammatically, e.g., "did" for "yelled" in the sentence "I yelled and he did, too" [15C. < Latin *substitutus*, past participle of *substituere* "set up under" < *statuere* (see STATUE)] —**sub·sti·tut·a·ble** *adj* —**sub·sti·tu·ter** *n*

USAGE See *replace*.

sub·sti·tute teach·er *n* a teacher who temporarily takes the place of another

sub·sti·tu·tion /sùbstə to͞osh'n/ *n* **1. ACT OF REPLACING** the replacement of somebody or something with another, especially one team member with another on the field **2. SOMEBODY OR SOMETHING THAT REPLACES** somebody or something that replaces another, especially one team member who replaces another on the field **3.** MATH **REPLACEMENT OF MATHEMATICAL ELEMENT** the replacement of one mathematical element with another of equal value **4.** LOGIC **REPLACEMENT OF LOGICAL EXPRESSION** the replacement of one logical expression with another, or a replaced logical expression —**sub·sti·tu·tion·al** *adj* —**sub·sti·tu·tion·al·ly** *adv*

sub·sti·tu·tive /súbstə to͞otiv/ *adj* acting or usable as a substitute [Early 17C. Partly < SUBSTITUTE, partly < Latin *substitutivus* < past participle of *substituere* (see SUBSTITUTE)] —**sub·sti·tu·tive·ly** *adv* —**sub·sti·tu·tiv·i·ty** /sùbstətoo tívvətee/ *n*

sub·strate /súb stràyt/ *n* **1.** CHEM a substance that is acted upon in a biochemical reaction **2.** ELECTRONICS a single crystal of a semiconductor used as the basis for an integrated circuit or transistor **3.** BIOL same as **substratum** (sense 6) **4.** BIOL same as **medium** *n* (sense 10) [Early 19C. Anglicization of SUBSTRATUM]

sub·strat·o·sphere /sub stráttə sfeer/ *n* the lowest layer of the Earth's atmosphere, at a height of about 12 mi./20 km above the Earth

sub·stra·tum /súb stràytəm, -stràttəm/ (*plural* **-ta** /-tə/) *n* **1. UNDERLYING BASE** an underlying base, layer, or element **2.** AGRIC same as **subsoil 3.** GEOL same as **bedrock** (sense 2) **4.** PHOTOGRAPHY **BASE FOR EMULSION** a layer of a substance placed on a photographic film or plate as a foundation for an emulsion **5.** LING **SET OF RETAINED INDIGENOUS LINGUISTIC FEATURES** a set of linguistic features retained from the speech of an indigenous culture, especially one that influences the language of a colonizer **6.** BIOL **NONLIVING FOUNDATION FOR GROWING ORGANISM** the nonliving material or base on which an organism lives or grows **7.** PHILOSOPHY **ESSENCE** the essential substance of something [Mid-17C. < modern Latin < form of past participle of Latin *substernere* "spread underneath" < *sternere* "lay or throw down"] —**sub·stra·tal** *adj* —**sub·stra·tive** *adj*

sub·struc·ture /súb strùkchər/ *n* **1.** the foundation of an erected structure **2.** any underlying structure that supports or gives strength to something —**sub·struc·tur·al** /sub strúkchərəl/ *adj*

sub·sume /səb so͞om/ (**-sumed, -sum·ing, -sumes**) *vt* **1.** to include or incorporate something into a larger order, category, or classification **2.** to show that a rule applies to something [Mid-16C. < medieval Latin *subsumere* "take up so as to include" < Latin *sumere* "take"] —**sub·sum·a·ble** *adj*

sub·sump·tion /səb súmpshən/ *n* **1.** the act of subsuming something, or the fact of being subsumed **2.** something that is subsumed [Mid-17C. < medieval Latin *subsumption-* < past participle of *subsumere* (see SUBSUME)] —**sub·sump·tive** *adj*

sub·tan·gent /súb tànjənt/ *n* the part of the x-axis in a two-dimensional coordinate system that is included by the ordinate of a specific point on a curve and the tangent at that point

sub·ten·ant /sub ténnənt/ *n* a renter of a property from a tenant who in turn rents it from the owner —**sub·ten·an·cy** *n*

sub·tend /səb ténd/ (**-tend·ed, -tend·ing, -tends**) *vt* **1.** to be opposite and delimit the extent of an angle or side of a geometric figure **2.** to lie underneath something so as to surround or enclose it [Late 16C. < Latin *subtendere* "stretch underneath" < *tendere* "stretch, extend"]

sub·ter·fuge /súbtər fyo͞oj/ *n* a plan, action, or device designed to hide a real objective, or the process of hiding a real objective [Late 16C. Directly or via French < late Latin *subterfugium* < Latin *subterfugere* "flee secretly" < *fugere* "flee"]

sub·ter·mi·nal /sub túrmən'l/ *adj* positioned very near the end of something

sub·ter·ra·ne·an /sùbtə ráynee ən/, **sub·ter·ra·ne·ous** /-nee əss/ *adj* **1.** existing or situated below ground level **2.** existing or carried on in secret [Early 17C. < Latin *subterraneus* "underground" < *terra* "earth, land"] —**sub·ter·ra·ne·an·ly** *adv*

sub·text /súb tèkst/ *n* an underlying meaning or message —**sub·tex·tu·al** /sub tékschoo əl/ *adj*

sub·ti·dal /sub tɪ̄d'l/ *adj* continuously submerged in the area of a tidal estuary system

sub·til·i·sin /sub tílləssin/ *n* a protein-digesting enzyme produced by bacteria. Use: detergents. [Mid-20C. < Latin *subtilis* (see SUBTLE) in modern Latin sense "subtle"]

sub·til·ize /sútt'l ɪ̄z, súbtə lɪ̄z/ (**-ized, -iz·ing, -iz·es**) *v* **1.** *vti* to make or use subtle distinctions in discussing something **2.** *vt* to make something increasingly refined —**sub·til·i·za·tion** /sùtt'li záysh'n, sùbtəli-/ *n* —**sub·til·iz·er** *n*

sub·ti·tle /súb tɪ̄t'l/ *n* **1. CAPTION FOR FOREIGN-LANGUAGE MOVIE** a printed translation of the dialogue in a foreign-language movie, usually appearing at the bottom of the screen **2. CAPTION IN SILENT MOVIE** a caption for the action or dialogue of a silent movie, appearing at intervals as a full-screen panel **3. LESSER TITLE** a second and subsidiary title for something such as a book ■ *vt* (**-tled, -tling, -tles**) **1. PROVIDE SUBTITLES FOR SOMETHING** to provide subtitles for a movie **2. GIVE SUBTITLE TO BOOK** to give a subtitle to something such as a book —**sub·tit·u·lar** /sub tíchələr/ *adj*

sub·tle /sútt'l/ *adj* **1. SLIGHT** slight and not obvious **2. PLEASANTLY UNDERSTATED** pleasantly delicate and understated **3. ABLE TO MAKE REFINED JUDGMENTS** intelligent, experienced, or sensitive enough to make refined judgments and distinctions **4. INGENIOUS** cleverly indirect and ingenious [14C. Via Old French *sutil* < Latin *subtilis* "fine, thin" < *sub tela* "beneath the weaving"] —**sub·tle·ness** *n* —**sub·tly** *adv*

sub·tle·ty /sútt'ltee/ (*plural* **-ties**) *n* **1.** the quality or state of being subtle **2.** a distinction that is difficult to make but is important (*often used in the plural*)

~~subtley~~ incorrect spelling of **subtly**

sub·to·tal /súb tōt'l/ *n* a sum of part of a set of figures ■ *vt* (**-taled, -tal·ing, -tals**) to calculate the total of part of a set of figures

sub·tract /səb trákt/ (**-tract·ed, -tract·ing, -tracts**) *v* **1.** *vti* to perform the arithmetical calculation of deducting one number or quantity from another **2.** *vt* to withdraw or take away something from a larger unit [Mid-16C. < Latin *subtract-*, past participle of *subtrahere* "pull away" < *trahere* "pull"] —**sub·tract·er** *n*

sub·trac·tion /səb tráksh'n/ *n* **1.** MATH **DEDUCTION OF NUMBER** the act or process of deducting one number or quantity from another. Symbol – **2. REMOVAL FROM SOMETHING LARGER** a withdrawal or deduction of something from a larger whole **3.** LAW **WITHDRAWAL OF BENEFIT** the withdrawal or withholding of a benefit

sub·trac·tive /səb tráktiv/ *adj* **1.** MATH **ABLE TO SUBTRACT** having the power to subtract one number or quantity from another **2.** MATH **INDICATING SUBTRACTION** indicating or needing subtraction **3.** PHYS **REMAINING AFTER ABSORPTION BY TINTED FILTERS** describes the color that remains after all other components of the visible spectrum have been absorbed by tinted filters

sub·tra·hend /súbtrə hènd/ *n* a number that is to be deducted from another number [Late 17C. < Latin *subtrahendus*, literally "be subtracted," form of *subtrahere* "pull away" < *trahere* "pull"]

sub·trop·i·cal /sub tróppik'l/ *adj* relating to or found in areas between tropical and temperate regions, and experiencing tropical conditions at some times of the year or nearly tropical conditions all year round

sub·trop·ics /sub tróppiks/ *npl* the area of the Earth adjacent to the tropics

su·bu·late /súbbyə làyt, -lət/ *adj* describes a plant part that is long and thin and tapers to a point [Mid-18C. < modern Latin *subulatus* < Latin *subula* "awl"]

sub·um·brel·la /súb um brèllə/ *n* the inwardly curving underside of a jellyfish

sub·u·nit /súb yo͞onit/ *n* **1.** a unit that forms part of a larger unit **2.** a part of a large molecule or complex that can be dissociated from the whole without rupture of covalent chemical bonds

sub·u·nit vac·cine *n* a vaccine that creates a bodily immunity to a virus or bacterium from whose DNA the vaccine is made

sub·urb /sú bùrb/ *n* a district, especially a residential one, on the edge of a city or large town [14C. Directly or via French < Latin *suburbium* "near a city" < *urbs* "city"]

sub·ur·ban /sə búrbən/ *adj* **1.** relating to, belonging to, or located in a suburb **2.** resembling a suburb or its residents

sub·ur·ban·ite /sə búrbə nɪ̄t/ *n* somebody who lives in the suburbs

sub·ur·ban·ize /sə búrbə nɪ̄z/ (**-ized, -iz·ing, -iz·es**) *vt* to give something the appearance or character of a suburb —**sub·ur·ban·i·za·tion** /sə bùrbəni záysh'n/ *n*

sub·ur·bi·a /sə búrbee ə/ *n* suburbs collectively, or the people who live in them

sub·ven·tion /səb vénshən/ *n* (*formal*) **1.** a sum of money given by an official body such as a government, especially to an institution of learning, study, or research **2.** the giving of help or support, especially financial [15C. Via French < late Latin *subvention-* < Latin *subvenire* "come to somebody's help" < *venire* "come"] —**sub·ven·tion·ar·y** *adj*

sub·ver·sion /səb vúrzh'n, -vúrsh'n/ *n* **1.** an action, plan, or activity intended to undermine or overthrow a government or other institution **2.** the destruction or ruining of something [14C. Directly or via French < late Latin *subversion-* < Latin *subvers-*, past participle of *subvertere* (see SUBVERT)]

sub·ver·sive /səb vúrssiv/ *adj* intended or likely to undermine or overthrow a government or other institution ■ *n* somebody involved in activities intended to undermine or overthrow a government or other institution [Mid-17C. < medieval Latin *subversivus* < Latin *subvers-* (see SUBVERSION)] —**sub·ver·sive·ly** *adv* —**sub·ver·sive·ness** *n*

sub·vert /səb vúrt/ (**-vert·ed, -vert·ing, -verts**) *vt* to undermine or overthrow a government or other institution [14C. Directly or via French < Latin *subvertere* "turn from below" < *vertere* "to turn"] —**sub·vert·er** *n*

sub·vi·rus /sub vīrəss/ *n* an infective agent that is structurally more primitive than a virus, e.g., a prion —**sub·vi·ral** *adj*

sub·vo·cal /sub vṓk'l/ *adj* mouthed or mentally pictured but not sounded out loud —**sub·vo·cal·ly** *adv*

sub·vo·cal·ize /sub vṓk'l ìz/ (**-ized, -iz·ing, -iz·es**) *vti* to mouth words or other speech sounds without saying them out loud —**sub·vo·cal·i·za·tion** /sub vṓk'li záysh'n/ *n*

sub·way /súb wày/ *n* **1.** *N Am, Scotland* an underground railroad, especially one powered by electricity **2.** *UK* a passage under a road or railroad for pedestrians to get to the other side

sub·ze·ro /sùb zeérō/ *adj* being below zero degrees in temperature

suc·cah *n* JUDAISM another spelling of **sukkah**

~~**succede**~~ incorrect spelling of **succeed**

suc·ceed /sək seéd/ (**-ceed·ed, -ceed·ing, -ceeds**) *v* **1.** *vi* **ACHIEVE INTENTION** to manage to do what is planned or attempted ○ *We succeeded in persuading them to change their decision.* **2.** *vi* **GAIN FAME, WEALTH, OR POWER** to realize a goal, especially to gain fame, wealth, or power **3.** *vi* **MAKE SIGNIFICANT PROGRESS** to do well in an activity, making admirable progress or recording impressive achievements ○ *She was one of the first women to succeed in the sciences.* **4.** *vi* **PROSPER** to thrive or prosper **5.** *vti* **BE NEXT AFTER SOMEBODY** to follow somebody occupying a post or position ○ *Mary succeeded him as president over a year ago.* ○ *will succeed to the title* **6.** *vt* **FOLLOW SOMETHING IN TIME** to come after something in time (*often passive*) **7.** *vi* **BE INHERITED BY SOMEBODY** to pass to somebody as an inheritance (*formal*) [14C. Directly or via French < Latin *succedere* "go after" < *cedere* "give way"] —**suc·ceed·a·ble** *adj* —**suc·ceed·er** *n*

suc·cen·tor /sək séntər/ *n* a deputy to a precentor at a church or cathedral [Mid-17C. < late Latin < Latin *succinere* "sing to" < *canere* "sing"] —**suc·cen·tor·ship** *n*

suc·cès de scan·dale /sük sày də skaaN dáal/ (*plural same*) *n* something that is successful because it is controversial, e.g., a book, movie, or play, or the success that is gained as a result of controversy [< French, "success of scandal"]

suc·cès d'es·time /sük sày de steém/ (*plural same*) *n* a book, movie, or play that is successful with critics but not with the public, or the success that is gained through critical acclaim [< French, "success of esteem"]

suc·cès fou /sük sày fóo/ (*plural* **suc·cès fous** /*pronunc. same*/) *n* an overwhelming success [< French, "mad success"]

~~**succesful**~~ incorrect spelling of **successful**

~~**succesive**~~ incorrect spelling of **successive**

suc·cess /sək séss/ *n* **1. ACHIEVEMENT OF INTENTION** the achievement of something planned or attempted **2. ATTAINMENT OF FAME, WEALTH, OR POWER** impressive achievement, especially the attainment of fame, wealth, or power **3. SOMETHING THAT TURNS OUT WELL** something that turns out as planned or intended **4. SOMEBODY SUCCESSFUL** somebody who is wealthy, famous, or powerful because of a record of achievement [Mid-16C. < Latin *successus* < past participle of *succedere* (see SUCCEED)]

suc·cess·ful /sək séssf'l/ *adj* **1. TURNING OUT WELL** having the intended result **2. POPULAR** popular and making a lot of money ○ *a successful play* **3. WITH RECORD OF SIGNIFICANT ACHIEVEMENTS** having achieved or gained much, especially wealth, fame, or power —**suc·cess·ful·ly** *adv* —**suc·cess·ful·ness** *n*

suc·ces·sion /sək sésh'n/ *n* **1. SERIES IN TIME** a sequence of people or things coming one after the other in time ○ *rented a succession of dingy apartments around town* ○ *a succession of blows* **2. FOLLOWING** the following of one thing after another ○ *three wins in succession* **3. TAKING UP OF TITLE OR POSITION** the assumption of a position or title, the right to take up a position or title, or the order in which a position or title is taken up **4.** ECOL **DEVELOPMENT OF PLANT AND ANIMAL COMMUNITY** the series of changes that create a full-fledged plant and animal community, e.g., from the colonization of bare rock to the establishment of a forest [14C. Directly or via French < Latin *succession-* < past participle of *succedere* (see SUCCEED)] —**suc·ces·sion·al** *adj* —**suc·ces·sion·al·ly** *adv*

suc·ces·sion crop *n* a crop that follows another crop as a successive planting, or a crop of a variety with a different rate of growth

suc·ces·sive /sək séssiv/ *adj* following in an uninterrupted sequence [15C. < medieval Latin *successivus* < Latin *success-*, past participle of *succedere* (see SUCCEED)] —**suc·ces·sive·ly** *adv* —**suc·ces·sive·ness** *n*

suc·ces·sor /sək séssər/ *n* somebody or something that follows another and takes up the same position [13C. < Latin < *success-*, past participle of *succedere* (see SUCCEED)] —**suc·ces·so·ral** *adj*

suc·cess sto·ry *n* somebody or something that is very successful

suc·ci ZOOL plural of **succus**

suc·ci·nate /súksə nàyt/ *n* an ester of succinic acid [Late 18C. < SUCCINIC ACID]

suc·cinct /sək síngkt/ *adj* expressed with brevity and clarity, with no wasted words [15C. Directly or via French < Latin *succinctus*, past participle of *succingere* "encompass from below" < *cingere* "gird"] —**suc·cinct·ly** *adv* —**suc·cinct·ness** *n*

suc·cin·ic ac·id /sək sìnnik-/ *n* a colorless odorless acid. Source: amber, plant and animal tissues, artificially synthesized. Use: manufacture of lacquers, perfumes, pharmaceuticals. Formula: $C_4H_6O_4$. [< Latin *succinum* "amber" < *succus* "juice, moisture, sap"]

suc·cin·yl·cho·line /sùksən'l kṓ leèn, sùksənil-/ *n* an intravenous drug. Use: muscle relaxant during surgery. [Mid-20C. < SUCCINIC ACID]

suc·cor /súkər/ (*literary*) *n* **1. HELP FOR SOMEBODY OR SOMETHING** help or relief for somebody or something in a difficult or unpleasant situation **2. SOMEBODY OR SOMETHING GIVING HELP** somebody or something that provides help or relief ■ *vt* (**-cored, -cor·ing, -cors**) **GIVE HELP TO SOMEBODY OR SOMETHING** to provide help or relief to somebody or something in a difficult or unpleasant situation [13C. Via Old French *sucurs* < medieval Latin *succursus* < Latin *succurrere* "run under" < *currere* "run"] —**suc·cor·er** *n*

suc·co·ry /súkəree/ *n* PLANTS same as **chicory** (sense 2) [Mid-16C. Alteration of obsolete French *cicorée* (see CHICORY) after Middle Low German *suckerie*, Middle Dutch *sūkerie*]

suc·co·tash /súkə tàsh/ *n* kernels of corn and lima beans cooked together, often with tomatoes [Mid-18C. < Narraganset *msiquatash* "boiled corn and beans"]

Suc·coth *n* JUDAISM another spelling of **Sukkoth**

suc·cour /súkər/ *n, vt* Can, UK spelling of **succor**

suc·cu·bus /súkyəbəss/ (*plural* **-bi** /-bī/ or **-bus·es**) *n* in medieval times, a woman demon that was believed to have sexual intercourse with men while they were asleep [14C. < medieval Latin, alteration of late Latin *succuba* "somebody who lies under another" < Latin *cubare* "lie down"]

suc·cu·lent /súkyələnt/ *adj* **1. JUICY AND TASTY** juicy and pleasant to the taste **2. WITH FLESHY WATER-STORING PARTS** describes plants that have thick fleshy leaves and stems that can store water **3. INTERESTING** exciting and interesting (*informal*) ■ *n* **SUCCULENT PLANT** a plant with thick fleshy leaves and stems that can store water, e.g., a cactus or aloe [Early 17C. Directly or via French < Latin *succulentus* < *succus* "juice, moisture, sap"] —**suc·cu·lence** *n* —**suc·cu·lent·ly** *adv*

suc·cumb /sə kúm/ (**-cumbed, -cumb·ing, -cumbs**) *vi* **1.** to be unable to resist or oppose something **2.** to die from an illness or injury [15C. Directly or via French < Latin *succumbere* "lie under" < *cumbere* "lie"]

SYNONYMS See ***yield***.

suc·cus /súkəss/ (*plural* **-ci** /-kī/) *n* a fluid, especially a secretion, of plant or animal origin [Late 18C. < Latin, "juice, moisture, sap"]

suc·cuss /sə kúss/ (**-cussed, -cus·sing, -cuss·es**) *vt* to shake a patient in order to detect the presence of air or fluid in a body cavity, especially the space between the lungs and the chest wall [Mid-19C. < Latin *succuss-* "shaken," past participle of *succutere* < *sub* "away" + *quatere*, "shake"] —**suc·cus·sion** *n*

~~**suceed**~~ incorrect spelling of **succeed**

~~**sucessful**~~ incorrect spelling of **successful**

~~**sucessive**~~ incorrect spelling of **successive**

such /such/ *adj* **1. OF PARTICULAR KIND** of the kind mentioned or understood from the context ○ *I've never heard such nonsense.* **2. SO MUCH** to so great an extent or degree ○ *Don't be such a fool.* ■ *adv* **VERY** extremely or to a great degree ○ *I had never seen such gorgeous flowers.* ■ *pron* **THIS** this, or something of this kind ○ *Such was his fate.* [Old English *swilc* < Germanic, "so formed"] ◇ **such as** used for giving an example ○ *desert plants such as cacti* ◇ **such ... as** used for making comparisons ○ *It wasn't such a good holiday as we thought it would be.* ◇ **such as it is** being what it is and no more

USAGE such ... as or **such ... that**? *We are such stuff as dreams are made on* (Shakespeare, *The Tempest*, Act 4, scene 1, modernized spelling). In sentences of this type ***such*** is followed by *as* and not by a relative pronoun *that, who*, etc.: *The federal government has only such powers as* [not *that*] *are given to it by the states.* However, the construction *such ... that ...* indicates the consequence of a stated circumstance: *The flooding has caused such hardship that the region will need a great deal of government aid.*

such and such *adj* not specified or named ■ *pron* something that is not specified or named

such·like /súch lìk/ *pron* others of the same kind as those just mentioned (*informal*) ■ *adj* similar to the kind just mentioned

such·ness /súchnəss/ *n* an essential quality or condition

Su·chow ▸ **Suzhou**

suck /suk/ *v* (**sucked, suck·ing, sucks**) **1.** *vti* **DRAW LIQUID OUT WITH MOUTH** to draw the liquid out of something with the mouth ○ *The baby sucked on her bottle.* **2.** *vti* **MAKE PULLING MOUTH MOVEMENTS ON SOMETHING** to hold something in the mouth and make movements with the tongue and lips as if drawing liquid out of it ○ *sucked his thumb* **3.** *vti* **MAKE SOMETHING DISSOLVE IN MOUTH** to consume something by making it slowly dissolve in the mouth, rolling the tongue around it ○ *sucking cough drops for a sore throat* **4.** *vt* **EXTRACT SOMETHING** to draw something out of a container (*often passive*) ○ *Fuel is sucked into the cylinder.* **5.** *vt* **PULL SOMETHING IRRESISTIBLY** to pull or draw something somewhere with a powerful or irresistible force ○ *The swirling currents suck swimmers under.* **6.** *vi* **BE VERY BAD** to be very bad or inferior (*slang*) ○ *The movie really sucked, so we walked out.* ■ *n* **ACT OF SUCKING SOMETHING** an act of sucking something [Old English *sūcan* < Indo-European, "take liquid"]

suck back *vt* to drink something in gulps

suck in *v* **1.** *vti* **BREATHE IN** to breathe in sharply, or breathe something in sharply **2.** *vt* INVOLVE SOMEBODY IN SOMETHING to make somebody become more and more involved in something in a way that he or she is unable to prevent **3.** *vt* DECEIVE SOMEBODY to trick or deceive somebody (*slang*)

suck off *vt* an offensive term meaning to perform fellatio on a man (*slang*)

suck up *vt* to try to please or win the favor of somebody important by being extremely flattering or helpful (*informal*)

suck·er /súkər/ *n* **1.** SOMEBODY EASILY FOOLED an easily fooled or tricked person (*informal*) **2.** SOMEBODY WHO GIVES IN EASILY somebody who has little resistance to and is easily influenced by something (*informal*) ○ *He's a real sucker for flattery.* **3.** *UK* same as **suction cup 4.** *US* PERSON OR THING used to refer, usually with emphasis or some degree of irritation, to any person or thing somebody happens to be dealing with (*slang*) ○ *Let's see if we can get this sucker to work.* **5.** same as **lollipop** (*informal*) **6.** MARINE BIOL ORGAN THAT CLINGS BY SUCTION a muscular organ, found on the tentacles of octopuses and similar sea animals, used to cling to or hold things such as prey **7.** ZOOL ORGAN FOR SUCKING IN FOOD the mouth of an animal such as the leech or lamprey that is adapted for sucking in food **8.** BOT SHOOT GROWING FROM ROOT a shoot that grows from the underground root or stem of a plant and is often able to produce its own roots and grow into a new plant **9.** ZOOL ANIMAL LIVING ON MOTHER'S MILK a young animal that is still taking milk from its mother, e.g., a young pig or whale **10.** MECH ENG SUCTION PUMP PISTON the piston or piston valve of a suction pump **11.** MECH ENG SUCTION PIPE a pipe through which a liquid is drawn by means of suction **12.** FISH FRESH-WATER FISH a bony bottom-feeding freshwater fish with a downward-facing sucking mouth without teeth. Native to: North America. Family: Catostomidae. ■ *v* (**-ered, -er·ing, -ers**) **1.** *vt* TRICK SOMEBODY to take advantage of somebody's ignorance, innocence, or foolishness to trick him or her (*informal*) ○ *got suckered into the deal* **2.** *vi* BOT PRODUCE SUCKERS to produce or form suckers on a root or stem (*refers to plants*) **3.** *vt* BOT REMOVE SUCKERS to remove the suckers from a plant

suck·er bite *n regional* same as **monkey bite** [Because the marks are thought to resemble those left by the suckers of an octopus]

REGIONAL NOTE See ***monkey bite***.

suck·er·fish /súkər fish/ (*plural same* or **-fish·es**) *n* FISH same as **remora**

suck·er punch *n* a blow delivered when somebody is not expecting it

suck·er-punch *vt* to hit somebody with a sucker punch

suck·ing /súking/ *adj* still feeding on its mother's milk and not yet weaned ○ *sucking pig*

suck·ing louse *n* a wingless primitive parasitic insect with mouthparts specially adapted for sucking body fluids, e.g., the head louse and pubic louse that infest human beings. Suborder: Siphunculata.

suck·le /súk'l/ (**-led, -ling, -les**) *v* **1.** *vti* to take milk from a mother's breast, teat, or udder, or allow a young child or animal to do this **2.** *vt* to nourish somebody or something (*literary*) [14C. Probably back-formation < SUCKLING]

suck·ling /súkling/ *n* a human baby or young animal that is still feeding on its mother's milk, e.g., a calf or pig [13C. < SUCK]

su·cra·lose /sŏŏkrə lōz/ *n* an artificial noncaloric sweetener created from sugar by replacing three hydroxyl groups with three chlorine atoms

su·crase /sŏŏ krayss, -krayz/ *n* BIOCHEM same as **invertase** [Early 20C. < SUCROSE + -ASE]

su·cre /sŏŏ kray/ *n* formerly, the main unit of currency in Ecuador [Late 19C. After Antonio José de SUCRE]

Su·cre /sŏŏ kray/ judicial capital of Bolivia, located in the center of the country, southeast of La Paz. Population: 178,426 (1998).

Su·cre, Antonio José de (1795–1830) Venezuelan-born South American soldier, nationalist leader, and president of Bolivia (1826–28). After helping to liberate Ecuador, Peru, and Bolivia from Spanish rule, he became Bolivia's first president.

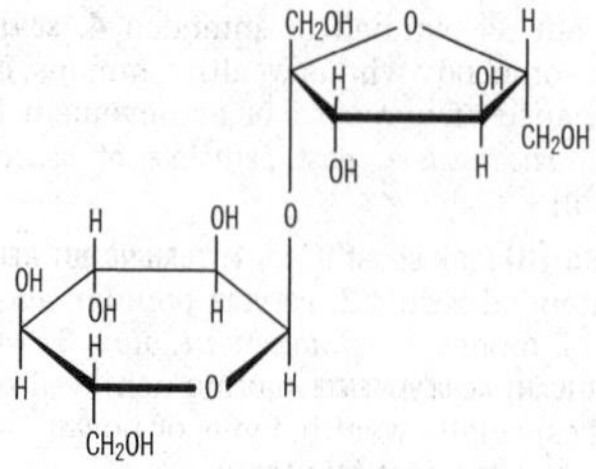

sucrose

su·crose /sŏŏ krŏss, -krōz/ *n* a disaccharide found naturally in many plants. Use: production of sugar. Formula: $C_{12}H_{22}O_{11}$. [Mid-19C. < French *sucre* "sugar"]

suc·tion /súksh'n/ *n* **1.** the physical force created by a difference in pressure such as that caused by sucking a liquid through a straw **2.** the act or process of sucking [Early 17C. < late Latin *suction-* < past participle of *sugere* "suck"]

suc·tion cap *n* same as **suction cup**

suc·tion cup *n* a round, slightly cupped piece of plastic or rubber that when pressed onto a flat surface sticks to it by suction

suc·tion pump *n* a pump that works by means of the suction created when a piston is moved up and down inside a cylinder

suc·tion stop *n* PHON same as **click** *n* (sense 4) (*technical*)

suc·to·ri·al /suk táwree əl/ *adj* **1.** specially adapted for sucking or for clinging on by suction **2.** having one or more suckers for feeding or for clinging on to something [Mid-19C. < modern Latin *suctorius* < past participle of Latin *sugere* "suck"]

Sudan

Su·dan /soo dán/ **1.** largest country in Africa, in the northeast of the continent, south of Egypt. Language: Arabic. Currency: dinar. Capital: Khartoum. Population: 38,114,160 (2003). Area: 967,490 sq. mi./2,505,800 sq. km. Official name **Republic of the Sudan 2.** region of savanna and dry grassland in West Africa, between the Sahara and the tropical forest belt —**Su·da·nese** /sŏŏd'n éez, -éess/ *n, adj*

Su·dan·ic /soo dánnik/ *n* GROUP OF LANGUAGES SPOKEN IN SUDAN a group of Chari-Nile languages spoken in Sudan ■ *adj* **1.** OF SUDANIC relating to Sudanic **2.** OF SUDAN relating to Sudan, or to its people or culture

su·da·to·ri·um /sŏŏdə táwree əm/ (*plural* **-ri·a** /-ree ə/) *n* a room, especially in an ancient Roman bathhouse, in which people are made to sweat by hot air or steam [Mid-18C. < Latin < form of *sudatorius* "for sweating" < *sudare* "to sweat"]

Sud·bur·y /súdbəree, -bree/ city in east central Ontario, Canada, north of Georgian Bay. Population: 103,879 (2001).

sudd /sud/ *n* a floating mass of reeds and weeds that obstructs some tropical rivers, especially the White Nile [Late 19C. < Arabic, "obstruction" < *sadda* "obstruct"]

sud·den /súdd'n/ *adj* done or happening quickly or unexpectedly [13C. Via Anglo-Norman *sudein* < Latin *subitaneus* < *subire* "go secretly" < *ire* "go"] —**sud·den·ly** *adv* —**sud·den·ness** *n* ◇ **all of a sudden** in a sudden and unexpected way

sud·den death *n* the continuation of play in a tied sports contest until one team or player scores, that team or player being declared the winner

sud·den in·fant death syn·drome *n* MED same as **crib death** (*technical*)

sud·den oak death *n* a serious disease caused by the fungus *Phytophthora ramorum* that affects many tree species. It has led to the death of various species of oak in California and Oregon, although European species appear to be less at risk.

su·dor·if·er·ous /sŏŏdə rífərəss/ *adj* producing sweat [Late 16C. < late Latin *sudorifer* "sudorific" < Latin *sudor* "sweat"]

su·dor·if·ic /sŏŏdə ríffik/ *adj* causing the production of sweat ■ *n* a drug or other agent that causes sweating [Early 17C. < modern Latin *sudorificus* < late Latin *sudorifer* (see SUDORIFEROUS)]

Su·dra /sŏŏdrə/, **Shu·dra** /shŏŏdrə/ *n* **1.** the lowest of the four Hindu castes, the members of which were segregated as ritually unclean by the other castes because they performed tasks that were regarded as polluting. There is a wide range of subgroups within the Sudra caste, some being landowners. **2.** a member of the Sudra caste [Mid-17C. < Sanskrit *śūdra*]

suds /sudz/ *npl* (*takes a plural verb*) **1.** BUBBLES a froth of bubbles on the surface of soapy water **2.** SOAPY WATER water with soap or detergent dissolved in it ○ *rinsed the glass in the suds* ■ *n* same as **beer** (sense 1) (*slang; takes a singular verb*) ■ *v* (**sudsed, sud·sing, sud·ses**) **1.** *vt* WASH SOMETHING to rinse or wash something in soapy water **2.** *vi* CREATE FOAM to form suds [Mid-16C. Probably < Middle Dutch *sudse* "marsh, bog"] —**suds·y** *adj*

sue /soo/ (**sued, su·ing, sues**) *v* **1.** *vti* to take legal action against somebody to obtain something, usually compensation for a wrong **2.** *vi* to make a humble, earnest, or begging request for something (*formal*) ○ *sued for peace after the long siege* [12C. Via Anglo-Norman *suer* "follow" < Latin *sequi*] —**su·a·ble** *adj* —**su·er** *n*

suede /swayd/ *n* **1.** LEATHER WITH VELVETY SURFACE leather with the flesh side turned outward and rubbed up to make a velvety nap **2.** FABRIC LIKE SUEDE a woven fabric that looks like suede ■ *vti* (**sued·ed, sued·ing, suedes**) GIVE SOMETHING VELVETY NAP to give leather or fabric a velvety nap [Mid-17C. < French *gants de Suède* "gloves of Sweden"] —**sued·ed** *adj*

sue·dette /sway dét/ *n* a synthetic fabric with the appearance and texture of suede. Use: clothing, upholstery.

su·et /sŏŏ ət/ *n* a hard white fat found on the kidneys and loins of sheep and cattle. Use: cooking, tallow. [14C. Probably < Anglo-Norman, literally "small suet" < *sue, seu* "tallow, suet" < Latin *sebum*]

Sue·to·ni·us /swee tōnee əss/, **Gaius Tranquillus** (69?–140) Roman biographer and historian. His works include biographies of 12 Roman emperors.

Su·ez /sŏŏ əz/ port in northeastern Egypt, at the head of the Gulf of Suez and at the southern end of the Suez Canal. Population: 417,000 (1998).

Su·ez Ca·nal canal in northeastern Egypt, connecting the Mediterranean and the Red Sea. It was opened in 1869. Length: 121 mi./195 km.

suf·fer /súffər/ (**-fered, -fer·ing, -fers**) *v* **1.** *vti* FEEL PAIN to feel pain or great discomfort in body or mind **2.** *vti* UNDERGO SOMETHING UNPLEASANT to experience or undergo something unpleasant or undesirable **3.** *vti* ENDURE SOMETHING to put up with something painful or unpleasant ○ *She may be rich and famous now, but she certainly suffered for her art when she was younger.* ○ *I do not suffer fools gladly.* **4.** *vi* HAVE ILLNESS to have a disease or a physical or psychological condition ○ *suffers from asthma* **5.** *vi* HAVE A WEAKNESS to have a bad quality, weakness, or flaw ○ *He suffers from an inflated ego.* **6.** *vi* APPEAR TO BE LESS GOOD to become or appear to be less good ○ *suffers in comparison* **7.** *vi* BE ADVERSELY AFFECTED to be adversely affected by something ○ *The business suffered when the partnership ended.* **8.** *vt* ALLOW SOMETHING to allow something to happen or to be done (*archaic or literary*) ○ *Suffer the little children to come unto me.* [12C. Via Anglo-Norman *suffrir* < Latin *sufferre* "carry up from underneath, sustain" < *ferre* "carry"] —**suf·fer·a·ble** *adj* —**suf·fer·er** *n*

~~**sufferage**~~ incorrect spelling of **suffrage**

suf·fer·ance /súffərənss/ *n* **1. TOLERANCE OF SOMETHING PROHIBITED** tacit permission for or tolerance of something, because no action is taken to prevent it **2. ENDURANCE OF DIFFICULTY OR PAIN** the capacity to withstand difficulty or pain **3. PATIENT ENDURANCE** the fact of enduring hardship patiently (*archaic*) ◇ **on sufferance** as a result of permission or consent given reluctantly and liable to be withdrawn

suf·fer·ing /súffəring/ *n* **1.** physical or psychological pain and distress **2.** an experience that is painful or distressing

suf·fice /sə físs/ (**-ficed, -fic·ing, -fic·es**) *vti* to be enough for somebody or something [14C. < Old French *suffic-* < Latin *sufficere* "make up to" < *facere* "make"]

~~**sufficiant**~~ incorrect spelling of **sufficient**

suf·fi·cien·cy /sə físh'nssee/ (*plural* **-cies**) *n* **1.** an amount of something that is enough for somebody or something **2.** the fact or state of being enough

suf·fi·cient /sə físh'nt/ *adj* as much as is needed [14C. Directly or via French < Latin *sufficient-*, present participle of *sufficere* (see SUFFICE)] —**suf·fi·cient·ly** *adv*

suf·fi·cient rea·son *n* the philosophical principle that nothing happens by chance and that an explanation must be available for everything

suf·fix *n* /súffiks/ a letter or group of letters added at the end of a word or word part to form another word, e.g., "-ly" in "quickly" or "-ing" in "talking" ■ *vt* /súffiks, sə fíks/ (**-fixed, -fix·ing, -fix·es**) to add something as a suffix [Early 17C. < modern Latin *suffixum* < form of Latin *suffixus*, past participle of *suffigere* "fasten underneath" < *figere* "fix"] —**suf·fix·al** /súffiks'l, sə fíks'l/ *adj* —**suf·fix·a·tion** /sùffik sáysh'n/ *n*

suf·fo·cate /súffə kàyt/ (**-cat·ed, -cat·ing, -cates**) *vti* **1. DIE FROM LACK OF AIR** to die from lack of air, or kill somebody by stopping him or her from breathing **2. STOP BREATHING** to deprive somebody of air or prevent somebody from breathing, or be unable to breathe **3. FEEL, OR MAKE SOMEBODY, TOO WARM** to feel uncomfortable through excessive heat and lack of fresh air, or make somebody feel uncomfortable in this way **4. PREVENT SOMEBODY OR SOMETHING FROM DEVELOPING** to confine and restrict somebody or something with adverse effects, or be or feel confined and restricted in development or self-expression [15C. < Latin *suffocat-*, past participle of *suffocare* "narrow up" < *fauc-* "throat, narrow entrance"] —**suf·fo·cat·ing** *adj* —**suf·fo·cat·ing·ly** *adv* —**suf·fo·ca·tion** /sùffə káysh'n/ *n*

Suf·folk[1] /súffək/ county in eastern England. It is largely agricultural. Ipswich is the county town. Population: 668,553 (2001). Area: 1,467 sq. mi./3,800 sq. km. ■ city in southeastern Virginia, burned by the British in 1779 and occupied by Union troops in 1862. Population: 69,966 (2002 estimate).

Suf·folk[2] /súffək/ *n* a large black-faced hornless sheep belonging to a breed that originated in England and is kept for meat [Mid-19C. After SUFFOLK[1]]

Suf·folk punch *n* a powerful horse with short legs and a chestnut brown coat, belonging to a breed that originated in England and is used for pulling loads such as plows or carts [< dialect *punch* "stocky draught horse," shortening of PUNCHINELLO]

suf·fra·gan /súffrəgən/ *n* **1.** a Christian bishop appointed to assist the main bishop in a diocese **2.** the Christian bishop of a diocese who is an assistant to the archbishop of the province to which the diocese belongs [14C. Via French < medieval Latin *suffraganeus* "assisting" < Latin *suffragium* "support, a vote"] —**suf·fra·gan** *adj*

suf·frage /súffrij/ *n* **1. RIGHT TO VOTE** the right to vote in public elections **2. ACT OF VOTING** a vote or the act of voting (*archaic*) **3.** RELIG **SHORT PRAYER** a short prayer on behalf of somebody, especially a prayer said as part of a Christian litany [14C. Directly or via French < Latin *suffragium* "support, a vote"]

suf·fra·gette /sùffrə jét/ *n* a woman campaigning for the right of women to vote in elections, especially one who took part in militant protests in the United Kingdom in the early 20th century

suf·fra·gist /súffrəjist/ *n* a supporter of the extension of the right to vote to a particular group, especially to women, or to all people above a particular age —**suf·fra·gism** *n*

suf·fuse /sə fyóoz/ (**-fused, -fus·ing, -fus·es**) *vt* to spread over or through something (*usually passive*) ○ *A blush suffused his face with color.* [Late 16C. < Latin *suffus-*, past participle of *suffundere* "pour from below" < *fundere* "pour"] —**suf·fu·sion** *n* —**suf·fu·sive** /sə fyóossiv, -ziv/ *adj*

Su·fi /sóofee/ (*plural* **-fis**) *n* a Muslim mystic [Mid-17C. < Arabic *ṣūfī* "woolen"; because of their woolen garments] —**Su·fi** *adj* —**Su·fic** *adj* —**Su·fism** *n*

~~**suficient**~~ incorrect spelling of **sufficient**

sug·ar /shóoggər/ *n* **1. SWEET-TASTING SUBSTANCE** a sweet-tasting substance, usually in the form of tiny hard white or brown grains. Source: sugar cane, sugar beet. Use: sweetener for food, drinks. **2. PORTION OF SUGAR** a spoonful, lump, cube, or other portion of sugar ○ *likes his coffee black with two sugars* **3. SWEET CARBOHYDRATE** a simple carbohydrate that is sweet-tasting, crystalline, and soluble in water **4. TERM OF ENDEARMENT** used as a term of endearment (*informal*) **5. STRONG DRUG** a strong drug, e.g., heroin or LSD (*dated slang*) ■ *v* (**-ared, -ar·ing, -ars**) **1.** *vt* **ADD SUGAR TO SOMETHING** to add sugar to food or a drink **2.** *vi* **MAKE SUGAR** to make sugar or form sugar crystals **3.** *vi* **MAKE MAPLE SYRUP** to boil maple sap to make maple syrup and maple sugar **4.** *vt* **TRY TO MAKE SOMETHING MORE AGREEABLE** to try to make something more appealing or flattering, or to make something unpleasant seem less so [13C. Via French and medieval Latin < Arabic *sukkar* < Sanskrit *śarkarā* "grit, ground sugar"] —**sug·ared** *adj* —**sug·ar·less** *adj*

sugar off *vi* to boil maple sap to make maple syrup and maple sugar

sug·ar ap·ple *n* TREES same as **sweetsop**

sug·ar beet *n* a variety of beet with a large whitish conical root that is an important commercial source of sugar. Latin name: *Beta vulgaris.*

sug·ar·ber·ry /shóoggər bèrree/ (*plural* **-ries**) *n* PLANTS same as **hackberry**

sug·ar·bird /shóoggər bùrd/ *n* a nectar-eating bird with dull brownish feathers, a long curved beak, and a very long tail. Native to: Africa. Genus: *Promerops.*

sug·ar bush *n* a wood or group of trees consisting mainly of sugar maples

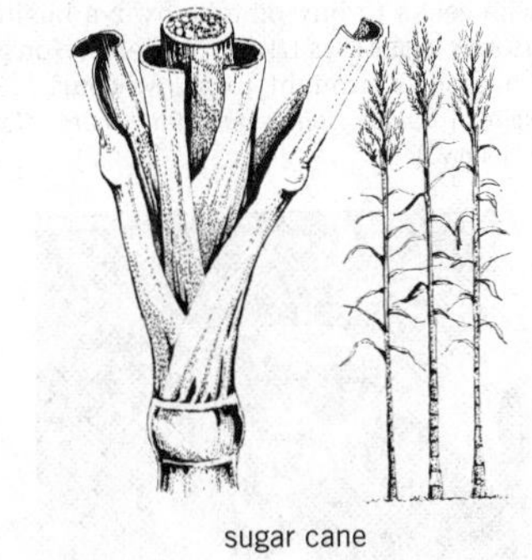

sugar cane

sug·ar cane *n* a tall tough-stemmed species of grass grown in warm regions throughout the world as a source of sugar, which is obtained from its sweet sap. Latin name: *Saccharum officinarum.* (*hyphenated when used before a noun*)

sug·ar·coat /shóoggər kòt/ (**-coat·ed, -coat·ing, -coats**) *vt* **1.** to make something unpleasant seem less so **2.** to enclose something in a hard sugar shell, or coat something with sugar

sug·ar corn *n US* PLANTS same as **sweet corn**

sug·ar-cured *adj* cured in a mixture of sugar, salt, and a nitrate or nitrite ○ *sugar-cured bacon*

sug·ar dad·dy *n* a rich man who gives money and gifts to a younger partner in a relationship (*informal*)

sug·ar gum *n* a small eucalyptus tree with smooth bark, barrel-shaped fruit, and sweet-tasting leaves. Latin name: *Eucalyptus cladocalyx.*

sug·ar·house /shóoggər hòwss/ (*plural* **-houses** /-hòwzəz/) *n US* a refinery where sugar is processed, especially one in which maple sap is boiled to produce maple syrup and maple sugar

sug·ar loaf *n* **1.** a solid cone-shaped mass of refined sugar **2.** something that has a conical shape like a cone of sugar, e.g., a hill

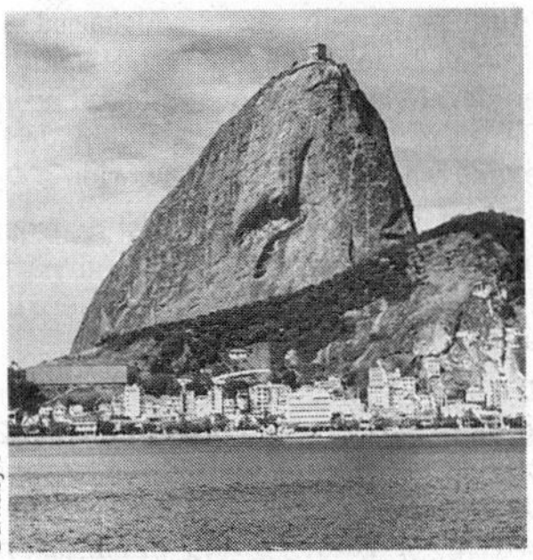

Barnaby's

Sugarloaf Mountain

Sug·ar·loaf Moun·tain /shóoggər lōf-/ peak on the edge of Rio de Janeiro, Brazil, that provides a panoramic view of the city. Height: 1,296 ft./395 m.

sug·ar ma·ple *n* a maple tree from whose sweet sap maple sugar and maple syrup are made. Native to: North America. Latin name: *Acer saccharum.*

sug·ar of lead *n* INDUST same as **lead acetate**

sug·ar pine *n* a tall pine tree that exudes a sugary resin and is also valued for timber. Native to: western North American coast. Latin name: *Pinus lambertiana.*

sug·ar·plum /shóoggər plùm/ *n* a small round candy made of boiled and flavored sugar

sug·ar shack *n* AGRIC same as **sugarhouse**

sug·ar snap, sug·ar snap pea *n* a variety of garden pea with an edible thin flat pod. Latin name: *Pisum sativum.*

sug·ar·y /shóoggəree/ *adj* **1. CONTAINING SUGAR** containing a great deal of sugar **2. LIKE SUGAR** looking or tasting like sugar **3. EXAGGERATEDLY PLEASANT** exaggeratedly and often insincerely pleasant or amiable **4. SENTIMENTAL** cloyingly sentimental —**sug·ar·i·ness** *n*

sug·gest /səg jést, sə jést/ (**-gest·ed, -gest·ing, -gests**) *vt* **1. REFER SOMEBODY OR SOMETHING FOR CONSIDERATION** to propose somebody or something as a possible choice, plan, or course of action for somebody else to consider ○ *He couldn't do the job himself but he suggested that John might.* ○ *Feel free to suggest something else.* **2. REMIND SOMEBODY OF SOMETHING** to remind somebody of something or make somebody think of something ○ *The sound of the flute is meant to suggest the rippling of a brook.* **3. IMPLY SOMETHING** to imply or hint at something ○ *I'm not suggesting the deal is off, but we may need to renegotiate.* **4. INDICATE SOMETHING AS LIKELY** to indicate that something is likely ○ *Declining catches suggest the area is overfished.* [Early 16C. Back-formation < SUGGESTION] —**sug·gest·er** *n*

SYNONYMS See ***recommend.***

sug·gest·i·ble /səg jéstəb'l, sə jést-/ *adj* **1.** easily influenced by other people **2.** capable of being suggested —**sug·gest·i·bil·i·ty** /səg jèstə bíllətee, sə jèstə-/ *n*

sug·ges·tion /səg jéschən, sə jés-/ *n* **1. IDEA OR PROPOSAL** an idea or proposal put forward for consideration **2. SLIGHT TRACE** a slight trace, indication, or hint of something ○ *There is no suggestion of bias in her recommendation.* **3. ACT OF SUGGESTING** the act or process of suggesting something ○ *I'm open to suggestion on different approaches.* **4. ABILITY TO CONJURE UP ASSOCIATIONS** the ability of words or images to conjure up ideas or feelings, the process by which they do this, or an idea or image conjured up by something **5. PUTTING IDEAS INTO SOMEBODY'S MIND** the deliberate introduction into somebody's mind of an opinion, belief, or instruction, e.g., through hypnosis or advertising, so that it is accepted or acted on as that person's own idea ○ *The power of suggestion is used in TV commercials to make us want a product.* [14C. Directly or via French < Latin *suggestion-* < *suggerere* "bring up" < *gerere* "bring"]

sug·ges·tive /səg jéstiv, sə jést-/ *adj* **1.** able to conjure up ideas or images in the mind, or able to start a train of thought **2.** implying or hinting at something rude or improper, especially something of a sexual nature —**sug·ges·tive·ly** *adv* —**sug·ges·tive·ness** *n*

Su·har·to /sə haártō, sŏŏ-/, **Mohamed** (*b.* 1921) president of Indonesia (1967–98). His authoritarian regime developed a petroleum-based economy. He was forced to resign as the economy declined and his regime was accused of corruption.

Sui /sway/ *n* a Chinese dynasty lasting from A.D. 581 to A.D. 618 that succeeded the Han dynasty, united all of northern China, and reconquered southern China

su·i·cid·al /sŏŏ i sīd'l/ *adj* **1.** WANTING TO COMMIT SUICIDE intending or wishing to commit suicide **2.** RELATING TO SUICIDE produced by or involving a wish to commit suicide **3.** EXTREMELY DANGEROUS likely to lead to death, destruction, or ruin, or very much against somebody's own best interests —**su·i·cid·al·ly** *adv*

su·i·cide /sŏŏ i sīd/ *n* **1.** KILLING YOURSELF the act of deliberately killing yourself **2.** SOMEBODY WHO COMMITS SUICIDE somebody who intentionally kills himself or herself **3.** DOING SOMETHING AGAINST OWN BEST INTERESTS the act of doing something that seems contrary to your own best interests and seems likely to lead to a disaster such as financial ruin or loss of position or reputation ○ *Adopting a policy like that would be political suicide.* [Mid-17C. < modern Latin *suicidium* "killing of yourself," *suicida* "somebody who kills himself or herself," both < Latin *sui* "of yourself"]

su·i·cide bomb·er *n* a person who deliberately allows himself or herself to be killed in the process of attempting to destroy something or kill somebody —**su·i·cide bomb·ing** *n*

su·i·cide pact *n* an agreement between two or more people that they will kill themselves at the same time

su·i·cid·er /sŏŏ i sīdər/ *n* POL same as **suicide bomber** (*informal*)

su·i·cide ter·ror·ist *n* an attacker, e.g., a person wearing concealed explosives, who intends to die while destroying a target [Early 21C.] —**su·i·cide ter·ror·ism** *n*

su·i·cide watch *n* the regular checking by prison guards of the cells of prisoners who are thought likely to commit suicide

su·i ge·ne·ris /sŏŏ ī jénnəriss, sŏŏ ee-/ *adj* unique or occupying a class of its own [< Latin, "of its own kind"]

sui ju·ris /sŏŏ ī jŏŏriss, sŏŏ ee yŏŏriss/ *adj* competent to assume legal responsibility for his or her own affairs [< Latin, "of its own right"]

su·int /sŏŏ int, swint/ *n* the grease found in sheep's wool, formed from dried perspiration [Late 18C. < French < *suer* "to sweat" < Latin *sudare*]

suit /soot/ *n* **1.** CLOTHES MADE OF SAME MATERIAL a set of clothes made from the same material, consisting of a jacket and pants or a skirt, sometimes together with a vest **2.** CLOTHES FOR PARTICULAR PURPOSE a piece of clothing or set of clothes worn for a particular purpose (*often used in combination*) ○ *a diving suit* **3.** CARDS SET OF PLAYING CARDS one of the four different sets of 13 playing cards in a pack **4.** LAW LEGAL PROCEEDINGS a case brought to a law court **5.** PETITION a petition, especially to somebody in authority (*formal*) **6.** BUSINESS EXECUTIVE a business executive, especially when seen as an anonymous bureaucrat (*slang*) ○ *The hotel was full of suits.* **7.** SET OF THINGS a set of things, especially sails or tools **8.** WOOING OF WOMAN a man's wooing of a woman and attempts to persuade her to marry him (*archaic*) ■ *v* (**suit·ed, suit·ing, suits**) **1.** *vti* BE RIGHT to be appropriate to or the right thing for somebody or something ○ *Choose casual clothes to suit the informal mood.* **2.** *vt* BE SATISFYING TO SOMEBODY to be something that a person likes or enjoys ○ *We could meet for lunch if that suits you.* **3.** *vti* BE CONVENIENT TO SOMEBODY to be convenient or acceptable to somebody **4.** *vt* LOOK GOOD ON SOMEBODY to look good on somebody or go well with something ○ *The color suits you.* **5.** *vt* MAKE SOMETHING SUITABLE to adapt something in order to meet requirements or circumstances **6. suit your·self** *vr* PLEASE YOURSELF to do what you prefer [13C. < Anglo-Norman *siute* < assumed Vulgar Latin *sequere* "follow," alteration of Latin *sequi*] ◇ **be somebody's strong suit** to be something at which somebody is particularly good ◇ **follow suit 1.** to do the same as somebody else has done **2.** to play a card of the same suit as the previous player

suit up *vi* to put on a uniform or a special costume in preparation for an activity, especially a sports event

suit·a·ble /sŏŏtəb'l/ *adj* of the right type or quality for a particular purpose or occasion —**suit·a·bil·i·ty** /sŏŏtə bíllətee/ *n* —**suit·a·ble·ness** *n*

suit·a·bly /sŏŏtəblee/ *adv* **1.** in a way that is right for a particular purpose or occasion ○ *arrived suitably dressed in a light linen jacket* **2.** to an appropriate or the expected extent ○ *The children were suitably impressed.*

suit·case /sŏŏt kàyss/ *n* a rectangular case used for carrying clothes and other belongings during travel

suite /sweet/ *n* **1.** SET OF ROOMS a set of rooms, e.g., in a hotel **2.** SET OF MATCHING FURNITURE a set of matching furniture for a room, e.g., a bed, end tables, and a dresser for a bedroom **3.** COMPUT INTEGRATED SOFTWARE PACKAGE a collection of integrated application programs functioning as a single program, each of which can incorporate data from the others, eliminating the need for re-entry or transfer of data **4.** MUSIC SET OF INSTRUMENTAL WORKS PERFORMED TOGETHER a set of instrumental pieces, especially dances, intended to be performed together **5.** PEOPLE WITH VIP a group of followers, servants, or advisers accompanying somebody important [Late 17C. Via French < assumed Vulgar Latin *sequere* (see SUIT)]

SPELLCHECK suite or **sweet**? Do not confuse the spelling of ***suite*** and ***sweet***, which sound similar. A ***suite*** is a set of rooms, furniture, computer programs, or musical works, as in *the presidential suite, a three-piece suite, Tchaikovsky's Nutcracker Suite.* ***Sweet*** refers to the presence of sugar or the absence of salt or bitterness (*sweet drinks*), and also has approving meanings such as "pleasant" or "kind" (*sweet music, a sweet person*); as a noun it denotes "an item of sweet food."

---

suit·ing /sŏŏting/ *n* material for making suits

suit·or /sŏŏtər/ *n* **1.** MAN WOOING WOMAN a man who is trying to persuade a woman to marry him (*formal*) **2.** BUSINESS SOMEBODY SEEKING TO TAKE OVER BUSINESS somebody who seeks to buy or take over a business **3.** LAW SOMEBODY WHO BRINGS LAWSUIT somebody on whose behalf a case is brought to a law court [13C. Via Anglo-Norman *seutor, suitour* < Latin *secutor* "follower" < *sequi* "follow"]

Sukarno

Popperfoto

Su·kar·no /soo kaárnō/ (1901–70) president of Indonesia (1945–67). He led the fight for Indonesia's independence from the Netherlands and became the country's first president.

Su·kar·no·pu·tri /soo kaárnə pŏŏtree/, **Megawati** (*b.* 1947) Indonesian president. After ten years as a member of parliament for the Indonesian Democratic Party, she formed the Indonesian Democratic Party of Struggle in 1996. She was elected vice president in 1999 and president in 2001.

su·ki·ya·ki /sŏŏkee yaákee/ *n* a Japanese dish consisting of thin slices of meat, vegetables, and noodles, cooked quickly in a sweet soy sauce [Early 20C. < Japanese, literally "slice-grill"]

suk·kah /sŏŏkə, -kaá/, **suc·cah** *n* a temporary light shelter with a roof of branches built in Jewish homes, yards, or temples for the festival of Sukkoth [Late 19C. < Hebrew *sukkāh* "hut"]

Suk·koth /sŏŏ kōt, -kōth, -kōss, -kəss/, **Suc·coth, Suk·kot** *n* an eight-day Jewish autumn harvest festival. Date: from the eve of the 15th of Tishri. [Late 19C. < Hebrew *sukkōṯ*, plural of *sukkāh* "hut"]

Su·la·we·si /sŏŏlə wáyssee/ island in Indonesia, in the Malay Archipelago east of Borneo. Population: 13,732,500 (1995). Area: 72,989 sq. mi./189,040 sq. km.

Su·lay·man I another spelling of **Suleiman I**

sul·cate /súl kàyt/ *adj* marked with lengthwise parallel grooves ○ *a sulcate shell/stem* [Mid-18C. < Latin *sulcatus*, past participle of *sulcare* "furrow" < *sulcus* "furrow, trench"] —**sul·ca·tion** /sul káysh'n/ *n*

sul·cus /súlkəss/ (*plural* **-ci** /-kī/) *n* a shallow groove or depression, especially any of those separating the convolutions of the surface of the brain [Mid-17C. < Latin, "furrow, trench"]

Su·lei·man I (the Mag·ni·fi·cent) /sŏŏ lay maán, sŏŏlə-/, **Su·lay·man I** (1494–1566) Ottoman sultan. He ruled from 1520 to 1566, extending the Ottoman Empire throughout the Balkans, Southwest Asia, and North Africa, and encouraging artistic and scientific endeavors.

sulf- *prefix* sulfur ○ *sulfite* [< SULFUR]

sulfa- *prefix* drug synthesized from sulfonamide ○ *sulfadimidine*

sul·fa·di·a·zine /sùlfə dī ə zeén, -dī əzin/ *n* a sulfa drug. Use: treatment of bacterial infections, especially in weakened patients. Formula: $C_{10}H_{10}N_4O_2S$. [Mid-20C. < *sulfa-* (see SULFA DRUG)]

sul·fa·di·mi·dine /sùlfə dímmə deén/ *n* PHARM same as **sulfamethazine** [Mid-20C. < SULF- + DI-[1] + *pyrimidine*]

sul·fa drug /súlfə-/ *n* a bacteriostatic drug synthesized from sulfonamide. Use: treatment of bacterial infections, but now rarely used because of its toxicity and the resistance of bacteria to it. [< shortening of SULFANILAMIDE]

sul·fa·meth·a·zine /sùlfə méthə zeén/ *n* a sulfonamide. Use: treatment of bacterial infections. Formula: $C_{12}H_{14}N_4O_2S$. [Mid-20C. < *sulfa-* (see SULFA DRUG)]

sul·fa·nil·a·mide /sùlfə níllə mīd/ *n* the first sulfa drug. Use: formerly, treatment of bacterial infections. Formula: $C_6H_8N_2O_2S$. [Mid-20C. < SULF- + ANILINE]

sul·fa·tase /súlfə tàyss, -tàyz/ *n* an enzyme that accelerates the decomposition of sulfuric esters

sul·fate /súl fàyt/ *n* SULFURIC ACID SALT OR ESTER a salt or ester of sulfuric acid ■ *v* (**-fat·ed, -fat·ing, -fates**) **1.** *vti* MAKE LAYER OF LEAD SULFATE to make a layer of lead sulfate form on the plates of a battery, or become covered with lead sulfate **2.** *vt* TREAT SOMETHING WITH SULFUR to treat something with sulfur, sulfuric acid, or a sulfate **3.** *vt* CONVERT SOMETHING TO SULFATE to convert something to a sulfate —**sul·fa·tion** /sul fáysh'n/ *n*

sul·fide /súl fīd/ *n* a compound in which sulfur is typically combined with one or more electropositive elements or groups

sul·fite /súl fīt/ *n* a salt or ester of sulfurous acid —**sul·fit·ic** /sul fíttik/ *adj*

sulfon- *prefix* sulfonic ○ *sulfonyl* [< SULFONE]

sul·fon·a·mide /sul fónnə mīd/ *n* one of a group of compounds responsible for the antibacterial action of sulfa drugs, which work by depriving bacteria of the ability to synthesize folic acid [Late 19C. < SULFONE]

sul·fo·nate /súlfə nàyt/ *n* a salt or ester of sulfonic acid ■ *vt* to treat an organic substance with sulfuric acid [Late 19C. < SULFONIC] —**sul·fo·na·tion** /sùlfə náysh'n/ *n*

sul·fone /súl fōn/ *n* a compound containing the sulfonyl group in which sulfur is attached to two carbon atoms [Late 19C. < German *Sulfon* < *Sulfur* "sulfur"]

sul·fon·ic /sul fónnik/ *adj* relating to, containing, or derived from the acid group SO_2OH [Late 19C. < German *Sulfon* (see SULFONE)]

sul·fon·ic ac·id *n* a strong organic acid. Use: manufacture of dyes, drugs.

sul·fo·ni·um /sul fónee əm/ *n* an ion or radical containing sulfur with a valence of three [Late 19C. < SULFUR]

sul·fon·meth·ane /sùl fōn mé thàyn/ *n* a colorless, crystalline, potentially addictive hypnotic drug. Formula: $C_7H_{16}O_4S_2$.

sul·fo·nyl /súlfə nìl/ *n* the bivalent chemical group SO_2 [Early 20C. < SULFONIC]

sul·fo·nyl·ur·e·a /sùlfənil yoŏree ə/ *n* a drug belonging to a group of drugs taken orally that lower blood sugar. Use: treatment of diabetes.

sul·fur /súlfər/, **sul·phur** *n* a nonmetallic yellow element that occurs alone in nature or combined in sulfide and sulfate minerals. Use: manufacture of sulfuric acid, matches, fungicides, and gunpowder. Symbol **S**. See table at **element** [14C. Via Anglo-Norman < Latin *sulfur, sulphur*] —**sul·fur·y** *adj*

sul·fu·rate /súlfə ràyt, súlfyə-/ (**-rat·ed, -rat·ing, -rates**) *vt* to treat or combine something with sulfur —**sul·fu·ra·tion** /sùlfə ráysh'n, sùlfyə-/ *n*

sul·fur bac·te·ri·um *n* a bacterium that is capable of metabolizing sulfur or inorganic sulfur compounds. Genus: *Thiobacillus*.

sul·fur di·ox·ide *n* a colorless pungent toxic gas and air pollutant formed by burning sulfur or fuels containing sulfur. Use: food preservative, fumigant, bleaching agent, manufacture of sulfuric acid.

sul·fur·e·ous /sul fyoŏree əss/ *adj* CHEM same as **sulfurous** —**sul·fur·e·ous·ly** *adv* —**sul·fure·ous·ness** *n*

sul·fu·ric /sul fyoŏrik/ *adj* relating to or containing sulfur, especially with a valence of six

sul·fu·ric ac·id *n* a strong colorless oily corrosive acid. Use: batteries, manufacture of fertilizers, explosives, detergents, dyes, chemicals. Formula: H_2SO_4.

sul·fur·ize /súlfə rìz, súlfyə-/ (**-ized, -iz·ing, -iz·es**) *vt* to treat or combine something with sulfur or a sulfur compound —**sul·fur·i·za·tion** /sùlfəri záysh'n, sùlfyəri-/ *n*

sul·fur·ous /súlfərəss, súlfyə-/ *adj* **1. CONTAINING SULFUR** relating to or containing sulfur, especially with a valence of four **2. SIMILAR TO BURNING SULFUR** with the color or acrid smell of burning sulfur **3. RELATING TO HELL** relating to hell or hellfire (*literary*) **4. FIERY** expressing strong feelings of anger, either physically or in words (*literary*) [15C. < Latin *sulphurosus*, or < SULFUR] —**sul·fur·ous·ly** *adv* —**sul·fur·ous·ness** *n*

sul·fur·ous ac·id *n* a weak colorless acid made by dissolving sulfur dioxide in water. Use: disinfectant, food preservative, bleaching agent. Formula: H_2SO_3.

sul·fur pearl *n* a very large bacterium, typically between 0.1 and 0.3 mm in size but sometimes larger, found in sediments off the coast of western Namibia. It uses nitrates as its source of oxygen in oxidizing and breaking down sulfur compounds. Latin name: *Thiomargarita namibiensis*.

sul·fur spring *n* a spring with significant amounts of sulfur compounds in the water

sul·fur tri·ox·ide *n* a toxic, irritating liquid occurring in three forms with different melting points. Use: chemical synthesis.

sul·fur·yl /súlfə rìl, súlfyə-/ *n* CHEM same as **sulfonyl**

sulk /sulk/ *vi* (**sulked, sulk·ing, sulks**) **BE ANGRILY SILENT** to refuse to talk to or associate with others as a show of resentment for a real or imagined grievance ■ *n* **1. BAD-TEMPERED SILENCE** a period, state, or show of resentfulness and refusal to communicate **2. SOMEBODY WHO SULKS** somebody who sulks [Late 18C. Back-formation < SULKY] —**sulk·er** *n*

sulk·y /súlkee/ *adj* (**-i·er, -i·est**) in a bad mood and refusing to communicate because of resentment for a real or imagined grievance ■ *n* (*plural* **-ies**) a light open two-wheeled vehicle for one person, pulled by one horse [Mid-18C. Origin ?] —**sulk·i·ly** *adv* —**sulk·i·ness** *n*

Sul·la /súllə/, **Lucius Cornelius** (138–78 B.C.) Roman general. He successfully led the aristocratic party during the civil war of 88–86 B.C. and then became dictator of Rome (82–79 B.C.).

sul·lage /súllij/ *n* **1.** sewage or any other form of waste or refuse **2.** solid material deposited by flowing water, e.g., by a river [Mid-16C. Origin ?]

sul·len /súllən/ *adj* **1. HOSTILELY SILENT** showing bad temper or hostility by a refusal to talk, behave sociably, or cooperate cheerfully **2. CLOUDY AND DULL** dull and gray because of clouds, fog, or haze (*literary*) ○ *sullen prairie skies* **3. SLOW-MOVING** moving slowly (*literary*) ○ *a sullen stream* [14C. < Anglo-Norman *sulein* "alone" < *sol* "sole, single" < Latin *solus*] —**sul·len·ly** *adv* —**sul·len·ness** *n*

Sul·li·van /súlləvən/, **Sir Arthur** (1842–1900) British composer. He is best known for his 14 popular comic operas to librettos by Sir William S. Gilbert, including *H.M.S. Pinafore* (1878), *The Pirates of Penzance* (1879), and *The Mikado* (1885). Full name **Sullivan, Sir Arthur Seymour**

Sul·li·van, Harry Stack (1892–1949) US psychiatrist. He developed the influential theory that personality and psychiatric disorders are formed by the interaction of personal and social forces.

Sul·li·van, John L. (1858–1918) US boxer. He was the last bare-knuckled heavyweight champion of the world (1882–92). Full name **Sullivan, John Lawrence**

Sul·li·van, Louis (1856–1924) US architect. His tall steel-framed buildings, built mostly in Chicago, were the world's first skyscrapers. Full name **Sullivan, Louis Henri**

sul·ly /súllee/ (**-lied, -ly·ing, -lies**) *vt* **1.** to spoil or detract from something, especially somebody's reputation, that has previously been pure and honorable, or become spoiled or tarnished ○ *a reputation sullied by scandal* **2.** to make something dirty [Late 16C. Origin ?] —**sul·lied** *adj*

Sul·ly /súllee/, **Thomas** (1783–1872) British-born US artist. He is known for his colorful romantic portraits, including several of US presidents.

sul·phur *n* CHEM ELEM another spelling of **sulfur**

Sul·phur /súlfər/ city in southwestern Louisiana, northeast of Port Arthur, Texas, and northwest of Lake Charles. Population: 20,042 (2002 estimate).

sul·phur but·ter·fly *n* a butterfly that has yellow or orange wings with black markings. Genus: *Colias*.

Sul·ston /súlstən/, **Sir John** (*b.* 1942) British biochemist. As director of the Sanger Centre near Cambridge, UK (1992–2000), he played a pivotal role in the International Human Genome Project. He shared the 2002 Nobel Prize in physiology or medicine with Sydney Brenner and Robert Horvitz.

sul·tan /súltən/ *n* **1.** the sovereign ruler of an Islamic country, especially formerly the head of the Ottoman Empire **2.** a man who is powerful in some sphere of activity, especially one who behaves in a domineering or tyrannical fashion (*literary*) [Mid-16C. Directly or via French < medieval Latin *sultanus* < Arabic *sulṭān* "ruler, power" < Aramaic *salīṭā* "rule"] —**sul·tan·ic** /sul tánnik/ *adj*

sul·tan·a /sul tánnə/ *n* **1.** a wife, mother, sister, daughter, or mistress of a sultan **2.** a small dried seedless white grape [Late 16C. < Italian, feminine of *sultano* "sultan" < Arabic *sulṭān* (see SULTAN)]

sul·tan·ate /súltənət, súltə nàyt/ *n* **1. COUNTRY RULED BY SULTAN** a country ruled by a sultan **2. RANK OF SULTAN** the rank or position of sultan **3. SULTAN'S REIGN** the period of a sultan's reign

sul·try /súltree/ *adj* **1.** oppressively hot and damp **2.** giving a suggestion of underlying passion and sensuality [Late 16C. < obsolete *sulter* "swelter." Origin ?] —**sul·tri·ly** *adv* —**sul·tri·ness** *n*

Su·lu Sea /soŏloo-/ arm of the Pacific Ocean west of the Philippines and northeast of Borneo

Sulz·ber·ger /súlz bùrgər/, **Arthur Hays** (1891–1968) US newspaper publisher. Married to the daughter of Adolph S. Ochs, publisher of the *New York Times*, he worked his way through the management ranks to become publisher upon Ochs' death (1935) and served in this position until 1961.

> "We tell the public which way the cat is jumping. The public will take care of the cat."
>
> [Arthur H. Sulzberger, *Time*, May 8, 1950]

sum[1] /sum/ *n* **1. MONEY** an amount of money **2. TOTAL** the total amount resulting when two or more numbers or quantities are added together **3. ARITHMETICAL CALCULATION** a mathematical problem involving adding, subtracting, multiplying, or dividing numbers, especially one given to students to solve **4. COMBINED TOTAL** the combined total amount or quantity of something **5.** MATH **LIMIT OF SUM OF SERIES** the limit, as n increases indefinitely, of the sum of the first n terms of an infinite series **6. GIST** the essential point of something that somebody has said or written (*literary*) ■ *vt* (**summed, sum·ming, sums**) **ADD UP AMOUNTS** to add together two or more amounts to find their total (*formal*) [13C. Via French < Latin *summa* "sum, substance" < form of *summus* "highest"] —**sum·ma·bil·i·ty** /sùmmə bíllətee/ *n* —**sum·ma·ble** *adj* ◇ **in sum** in short or as a summary

SPELLCHECK See *some*.

ORIGIN The semantic development of ***sum*** from "highest" to "sum total" resulted from the Roman practice of counting columns of figures from the bottom upward, the total being written at the top.

sum up *vti* **1. SUMMARIZE SOMETHING** to present the main points or substance of something concisely **2. REVIEW EVIDENCE FOR JURY** to summarize the main points of a court case for a jury (*refers to a judge*) **3. BRIEFLY DESCRIBE SOMEBODY OR SOMETHING** to describe or evaluate somebody or something concisely

sum[2] /soom/, **som** *n* the main unit of currency in Uzbekistan. See table at **currency** [Late 20C. Via Uzbek *sŭm* < Chuvash *sum, som* "payment"]

su·mac /soŏ màk, shoŏ-/, **su·mach** *n* **1.** a tree or bush of the cashew family with red hairy fruit, and feathery leaves. Flowers: green, in clusters. Genus: *Rhus*. **2.** the ground dried leaves of one species of sumac. Use: tanning, dyeing. [14C. Directly or via French < medieval Latin *sumac(h)* < Arabic *summāḳ*]

~~**sumary**~~ incorrect spelling of **summary**

Su·ma·tra /soŏ maàtrə/ island in western Indonesia, separated from the Malay Peninsula by the Strait of Malacca. It is the westernmost of the Sunda Islands. Population: 40,830,400 (1995). Area: 182,860 sq. mi./473,605 sq. km. —**Su·ma·tran** *n, adj*

Su·mer /soŏmər/ ancient country of southern Mesopotamia, in present-day Iraq. Archaeological discoveries reveal the area to have been first settled in the 5th millennium B.C. It became prosperous and powerful from about 3000 B.C., and fell into decline from about 1760 B.C., when it was absorbed into Babylonia and Assyria.

Su·me·ri·an /soŏ meéree ən, -mérree-/ *n* **1.** a member of an ancient people that built the civilization of Sumer **2.** the language of ancient Sumer, unrelated to any other known language. Sumerian is the oldest language preserved in writing, its cuneiform tablets dating from about 3000 B.C. —**Su·me·ri·an** *adj*

sum·ma /súmmə, soŏmmə/ (*plural* **-mae** /-mì, -mee/) *n* a summary of what is known of a subject, especially a medieval treatise on theology, philosophy, canon law, or alchemy [15C. < Latin (see SUM[1])]

sum·ma cum lau·de /soŏmmə koŏm lów dày, sùmmə kum láwdee/ *adv, adj US* with the highest level of academic honors at graduation [< Latin, "with highest praise"]

sum·mae plural of **summa**

sum·mand /sú mànd, sə mánd/ *n* a number or quantity in a sum [Mid-19C. < medieval Latin *summandus* "for adding," form of *summare* (see SUMMATION)]

sum·mar·i·ly /sə mérrəlee/ *adv* immediately and without discussion or attention to formalities

sum·ma·rize /súmmə rìz/ (**-rized, -riz·ing, -riz·es**) *vti* to give a shortened version of something that has been said or written, stating its main points —**sum·ma·ri·za·tion** /sùmməri záysh'n/ *n* —**sum·ma·riz·er** *n*

sum·ma·ry /súmməree/ *n* (*plural* **-ries**) **SHORT VERSION CONTAINING GIST OF SOMETHING** a shortened version of something that has been said or written, containing only the main points ■ *adj* **1. IMMEDIATE** done immediately and with little discussion or attention to formalities ○ *a summary execution* **2. GIVING ONLY MAIN POINTS** shortened and giving only the main points of something **3.** LAW **RELATING TO LOWER COURTS** relating to, dealt with, or given by lower courts operating without the formality of full proceedings [15C. < Latin *summarium* < *summa* (see SUM[1])] —**sum·ma·ri·ness** *n*

sum·ma·tion /su máysh'n/ *n* **1.** *US* LAW **FINAL ARGUMENT IN COURT** the final summing-up of an argument in a court of law **2. SUMMARY OF SOMETHING SAID** a summary of something that has been said or written **3. TOTAL** a total amount or aggregate **4. ADDITION** the process of adding something up to find a total [Mid-18C. < modern Latin *summation-* < medieval Latin *summare* "add" < Latin *summa* (see SUM[1])] —**sum·ma·tive** /súmmətiv/ *adj*

sum·mer[1] /súmmər/ *n* **1. WARMEST SEASON** the warmest season of the year, falling between spring and autumn. It runs from June to August in the northern hemisphere, and December to February in the southern hemisphere. **2. WARM WEATHER** the warm weather associated with the summer season **3. PERIOD OF GREAT HAPPINESS** a period of greatest happiness, success, or fulfillment in the life of somebody or something **4. YEAR** a year, especially of somebody's age (*literary*) ○ *a man of 70 summers* ■ *v* (**-mered, -mer·ing, -mers**) **1.** *vi* **SPEND SUMMER** to spend the summer ○ *They summer at the lake.* **2.** *vt* **PASTURE ANIMALS FOR SUMMER** to keep cattle or other animals on a designated pasture during the summer [Old English *sumor, sumer* < Germanic] —**sum·mer·y** *adj*

sum·mer[2] /súmmər/ *n* **1.** a principal horizontal beam in a building used to support floor joists **2.** a stone that lies atop a pier, column, or wall and supports one or more arches **3.** ARCHIT same as **lintel** [13C. Via Anglo-Norman *sumer,* Old French *som(i)er* "main beam" < late Latin *sagmarius* "packhorse" < *sagma* "packsaddle" < Greek]

sum·mer camp *n* a place, usually residential, offering outdoor recreational activities and skill development for children during the summer

sum·mer cy·press *n* a bushy annual plant with narrow light green leaves that turn red in fall. It spreads rapidly as a weed and is toxic to grazing animals. Native to: Europe and western Asia, naturalized elsewhere. Latin name: *Bassia scoparia.*

sum·mer·house /súmmər hòwss/ (*plural* **-hous·es** /-hòwzəz/) *n* **1. sum·mer house** *US* a house, e.g., in the mountains or by the shore, used during summer vacations **2.** a small building or structure in a garden or park to give seating and shade during the summer

sum·mer·sault *n, vi* GYMNASTICS another spelling of **somersault**

sum·mer sa·vor·y *n* PLANTS same as **savory[1]**

sum·mer school *n* a course of study held during the summer vacation, usually an extra course for high school or college students, especially for those with fewer than the standard number of credits for their standing

sum·mer squash *n* a squash eaten as a vegetable shortly after picking in the summer. Latin name: *Cucurbita pepo melopepo.*

sum·mer stock *n US* productions of plays and musicals by stock companies in the summer

sum·mer·time /súmmər tìm/ *n* the season of summer

sum·mer·tree /súmmər trèe/ *n* ARCHIT same as **summer[2]** (sense 1)

sum·mer·wood /súmmər wŏŏd/ *n* wood produced late in a tree's annual growth cycle, which is harder and less porous than early-season growth (**springwood**)

sum·mit /súmmit/ *n* **1. TOP-LEVEL DIPLOMATIC CONFERENCE** a meeting between heads of government or other high-ranking officials to discuss a matter of great importance **2. HIGHEST POINT** the highest point or top of something, especially a mountain **3. POINT OF GREATEST SUCCESS OR INTENSITY** the point or time at which something is at its most successful or intense ■ *vti* (**-mit·ed, -mit·ing, -mits**) CLIMBING **REACH TOP OF MOUNTAIN** to climb to the summit of a mountain or peak [14C. < Old French *som(m)ete, sumet* "small top" < *som, sum* "top" < Latin *summum,* neuter of *summus* "highest"]

sum·mit con·fer·ence *n* POL same as **summit** *n* (sense 1)

sum·mit·eer /sùmmi téer/ *n* a participant in a summit conference

sum·mit·ry /súmmitree/ *n US* the practice of holding, or deciding matters of international importance through, summit conferences

sum·mon /súmmən/ (**-moned, -mon·ing, -mons**) *v* **1.** *vt* **CALL SOMEBODY INTO COURT** to order somebody to appear in court by serving a summons **2.** *vt* **SEND FOR SOMEBODY** to send or be a signal for somebody to come ○ *We were summoned to his presence.* **3.** *vt* **CONVENE GROUP** to call together a formal or official body ○ *They summoned a meeting to debate the issue.* **4.** *vt* **CALL UPON SOMEBODY** to request or require somebody to do something ○ *She summoned him to help her.* **5.** *vi* **MANAGE TO GET SOMETHING** to gather the resources, especially courage or strength, to cope with or do something ○ *trying to summon up the courage to tell him the news* [13C. Via French < Latin *summonere* "remind secretly" < *sub-* "under" + *monere* "warn"]

sum·mons /súmmənz/ *n* **1. COURT ORDER TO DEFENDANT** a written order to somebody to appear in court to answer a complaint **2. COURT ORDER TO WITNESS** a written order to a witness or juror to appear in court **3. ORDER BY AUTHORITY TO APPEAR** an authoritative demand to appear in a specific place at a specific time ■ *vt* (**-monsed, -mons·ing, -mons·es**) **SERVE SOMEBODY WITH SUMMONS** to serve somebody with a summons to appear in court [13C. < Old French *somonse,* past participle of *somondre* < Latin *summonere* (see SUMMON)]

Sum·ner /súmnər/, **Charles** (1811–74) US politician. A US senator (1851–74) from Massachusetts, he was a passionate abolitionist.

Barnaby's

sumo

su·mo /sŏŏmō/ *n* traditional Japanese wrestling in which each contestant tries to force the other outside a circle or force him to touch the ground other than with the soles of his feet [Late 19C. < Japanese *sumō*]

sump /sump/ *n* **1. RESERVOIR FOR LIQUID** a low area into which a liquid drains, e.g., a pit or reservoir **2.** same as **cesspool** (sense 1) **3.** *UK* AUTOMOT same as **oil pan** **4.** MIN EXTRACT **DRAINAGE RESERVOIR IN MINE** an area at the bottom of a mineshaft into which water drains and is then pumped away **5.** MIN EXTRACT **ADVANCE EXCAVATION** an excavation ahead of the main excavation of a mineshaft or tunnel [15C. < Middle Dutch *somp,* Middle Low German *sump*]

sump pump *n* a pump used to remove liquid from a sump, especially water that has accumulated in a basement

sump·ter /súmptər/ *n* a packhorse, mule, or other pack animal (*archaic*) [Late 16C. < Old French *sommetier* "packhorse driver" < late Latin *sagmarius* (see SUMMER[2])]

~~**sumptious**~~ incorrect spelling of **sumptuous**

sump·tu·ar·y /súmpchoo èrree/ *adj* **1.** relating to or controlling personal spending **2.** intended to regulate personal behavior on moral or religious grounds [Early 17C. < Latin *sumptuarius* < *sumptus* "expense" (see SUMPTUOUS)]

sump·tu·ous /súmpchoo əss/ *adj* **1.** magnificent or grand in appearance **2.** entailing great expense [15C. Via French < Latin *sumptuosus* < *sumptus* "expense" < past participle of *sumere* "spend" < *emere* "take"] —**sump·tu·ous·ly** *adv* —**sump·tu·ous·ness** *n*

Sum·ter /súmtər/ city in east central South Carolina, southwest of Florence and east of Columbia. Population: 39,382 (2002 estimate).

sum to·tal *n* **1.** a combined total of separate components ○ *The sum total of his belongings is the clothes on his back.* **2.** a numerical amount obtained by adding sums

sum-up *n* a concise presentation of the main points or substance of something

sun /sun/ *n* **1.** ASTRON **STAR** a star or bright astronomical object, especially one around which planets orbit **2.** ASTRON **SUN'S RADIATION** the light or heat emitted by the Sun **3. SOMEBODY LIKE SUN** somebody or something thought to resemble the Sun in radiance, glory, or warmth, or in being the center of a society (*literary*) **4. DAY OR YEAR** a day or year (*literary*) ○ *a woman of many suns* ■ *v* (**sunned, sun·ning, suns**) **1. sun yourself** *vr* **WARM OR TAN YOURSELF IN SUNLIGHT** to expose your body to the sun's rays for warmth or for a suntan ○ *The cat lay sunning herself on the lawn.* **2.** *vt* **WARM OR DRY SOMETHING IN SUNLIGHT** to expose something to the sun's rays for warmth or drying [Old English *sunne* < Indo-European] ◇ **everything under the sun** things of all kinds ◇ **take the sun** to go out in the sunshine, especially with the aim of gaining some benefit to your health or well-being ◇ **under the sun** in the whole world

---

SPELLCHECK See *son.*

Sun *n* the star at the center of our solar system around which Earth and the eight other planets orbit

Sun. *abbr* CALENDAR Sunday

sun·baked /sún bàykt/ *adj* **1.** hard and dry from prolonged exposure to the sun **2.** baked by a process of exposure to the sun

sun·bath /sún bàth/ *n* an act or period of exposing the body to the sun or a sun lamp, especially in order to get a tan

sun·bathe /sún bày*th*/ (**-bathed, -bath·ing, -bathes**) *vi* to expose the body to sun or a sun lamp, especially in order to get a tan —**sun·bathe** *n* —**sun·bath·er** *n*

sun·beam /sún bèem/ *n* a ray of light emitted by the Sun

sun bear *n* a small bear with sleek black fur, a light-colored muzzle, and a yellowish breast marking. Native to: forests of Southeast Asia. Latin name: *Helarctos malayanus.*

sun·bed /sún bèd/ *n UK* same as **tanning bed**

Sun·belt /sún bèlt/, **Sun Belt** *n US* the southern and southwestern states of the United States, having a warm sunny climate

sun·bird /sún bùrd/ *n* **1.** a small brightly colored songbird with a long thin curved beak, which feeds on insects and nectar. Native to: South and Southeast Asia, Africa, Australia. Family: Nectariniidae. **2.** a person from the northern United States, usually a retiree, who spends the winter months in the Sunbelt (*informal*)

sun·bit·tern *n* a solitary water bird with mottled brownish feathers and a chestnut marking like a sunburst when its wings are spread. Native to: Central and South America. Latin name: *Eurypyga helius.*

sun·block /sún blòk/ *n* a substance applied to the skin as a cream or lotion to give complete protection from the sun's ultraviolet rays

sun·bon·net /sún bònnət/ *n* a bonnet with a wide brim and a flap at the back, worn by babies and, formerly, by women to protect the face and neck from the sun

sun·bow /sún bō/ *n* a spectrum of colors similar to a rainbow produced by sunlight refracting through spray, mist, or water vapor, e.g., above a waterfall [After RAINBOW]

sun·burn /sún bùrn/ *n* inflammation and sometimes blistering of the skin caused by overexposure to ultraviolet radiation from the sun ■ *vti* (**-burned** or

-burnt /-bùrnt/, **-burn·ing**, **-burns**) to be affected by sunburn, or cause the skin to be affected by sunburn

sun·burned /sún bùrnd/, **sun·burnt** /-bùrnt/ *adj* affected by sunburn

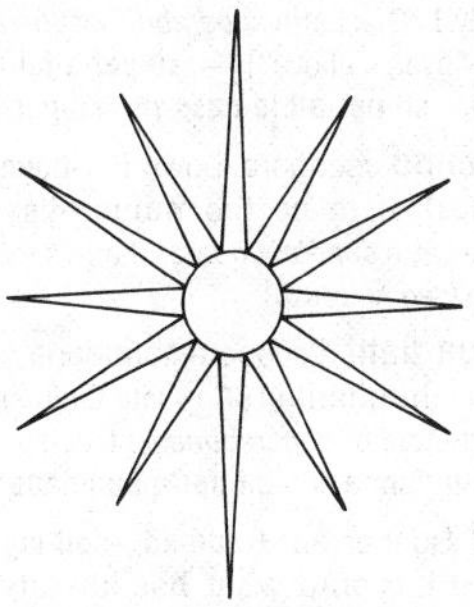

sunburst (sense 2)

sun·burst /sún bùrst/ *n* **1. SUDDEN BURST OF SUNSHINE** a sudden appearance of the sun from behind clouds **2. SUN-SHAPED DESIGN** a design meant to resemble the sun, consisting of a series of rays extending outward from a central circle **3. SUN-SHAPED BROOCH** a brooch or other ornament designed as a sunburst

sun·choke /sún chōk/ *n US* PLANTS, FOOD same as **Jerusalem artichoke** [Late 20C. < SUNFLOWER + ARTICHOKE]

sun·dae /sún dày/ *n* an ice-cream dessert served with toppings such as whipped cream, fruit, nuts, and flavored syrup [Late 19C. Alteration of SUNDAY]

Sun·da Is·lands /súndə-, sŏŏndə-/ island group of the Malay Archipelago between the South China Sea and the Indian Ocean. It consists of two groups, the Greater Sunda Islands, which include Sumatra, Java and Borneo, and the Lesser Sunda Islands, which include Bali and Timor.

sun dance *n* an important ceremonial dance of Native North American peoples living on prairies, held annually in honor of the Sun

Sun·da·nese /sùndə néez, -néess/ (*plural same*) *n* **1.** PEOPLES a member of a people living in the western part of Java, most of whom are Muslims **2.** LANG the Austronesian language of the Sundanese people. Native speakers: 27,000,000. [Late 19C. < Sundanese *Sunda*, western part of Java] —**Sun·da·nese** *adj*

Sun·day /sún dày, -dee/ *n* **1. 1ST DAY OF WEEK** the day of the week after Saturday and before Monday **2. CHRISTIAN SABBATH DAY** in Christian tradition, the day set aside for the Sabbath ■ *adj* **1. OF SUNDAY** relating to or occurring on a Sunday **2. FOR SPECIAL OCCASIONS** worn or used for special occasions **3. ONLY AT WEEKENDS OR AS HOBBY** engaging in an activity only at weekends or as a hobby, and therefore lacking experience, efficiency, or professional skill ○ *These Sunday drivers are a menace on the roads.* [Old English *sunnandæg* "day of the sun," translation of Latin *dies solis*]

Sun·day-go-to-meet·ing *adj* suitable for attending a church service (*informal*)

Sun·day punch *n US* **1.** a boxer's most powerful punch, especially a knockout blow **2.** an action that comes as a devastating blow to an opponent or rival

Sun·days /sún dàyz, -deez/ *adv* every Sunday

Sun·day school *n* a school or class offering children religious education or activities on Sundays

sun deck *n* **1.** an open upper deck on a passenger ship **2.** *UK* same as **deck** *n* (sense 4)

sun·der /súndər/ (**-dered, -der·ing, -ders**) *vti* to separate something into parts, especially by force, or be separated in this way (*literary*) [Old English *sundrian* < *sundor* "apart" < Indo-European] —**sun·der·er** *n*

Sun·der·land /súndərlənd/ city and port in Tyne and Wear, northeastern England. Population: 294,261 (1996).

sun·dew /sún dōō/ *n* a plant that produces a rosette of hairy sticky leaves that are used to trap and digest insects. Native to: Australia, New Zealand. Family: Droseraceae. [Translation of Latin *ros solis*; because the drops of juice the plant secretes resemble dew]

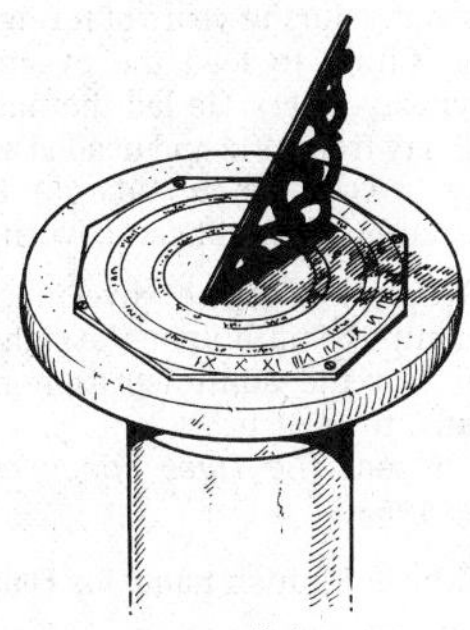

sundial

sun·di·al /sún dī əl/ *n* an instrument that shows the time of day by the position of a sun-generated shadow cast by a fixed arm (**gnomon**) onto a graduated plate or surface

sun disk *n* an ancient Egyptian Sun god symbol, consisting of a disk with wings and two serpents

sun·dog /sún dàwg, -dòg/ *n* **1.** ASTRON same as **parhelion** **2.** a small spectrum of light occasionally visible in the sky at the same altitude as the Sun, either to the left or right of the Sun, and sometimes on both sides simultaneously

sun·down /sún dòwn/ *n* the time when the Sun sets

sun·down·er /sún dòwnər/ *n UK, S Africa* an alcoholic drink taken early in the evening, around sunset (*informal*)

sun·drenched /sún drèncht/ *adj* describes a place that enjoys a large amount of hot sunshine

sun·dress /sún drèss/ *n* a light sleeveless summer dress with a low bodice that exposes the shoulders, back, and arms to the sun

sun-dried *adj* dried out naturally by the sun, not by applying artificial heat

sun·dries /súndreez/ *npl* small miscellaneous items, often of too little value to be mentioned individually

sun·drops /sún dròps/ (*plural same*) *n* PLANTS same as **evening primrose**

sun·dry /súndree/ *adj* assorted, but considered as a single category or group, usually for the sake of convenience ○ *and other sundry items* [Old English *syndrig* "separate, distinct" < W Germanic] ◇ **all and sundry** everyone without exception (*takes a plural verb*)

Sunds·vall /sŏŏndz vaàl/ city and port on the Gulf of Bothnia, Sweden, situated about 250 mi./400 km north of Stockholm. Population: 94,328 (1998).

sun·fish /sún fìsh/ (*plural same* or **-fish·es**) *n* **1.** a small to medium-sized spiny-finned freshwater fish, often with iridescent colors. Native to: North America. Family: Centrarchidae. **2.** *Can, UK* same as **ocean sunfish**

sun·flow·er /sún flòwr/ *n* **1.** a tall annual plant grown commercially for its edible seeds and the oil extracted from them. Flowers: large heads of yellow petals with a dark center. Latin name: *Helianthus annuus*. **2.** a plant related to the sunflower. Genus: *Helianthus*. [Mid-16C. Translation of modern Latin *flos solis* and Greek *helianthos*]

sun·flow·er oil *n* oil extracted from sunflower seeds, used in cooking and salad dressings

Sun·flow·er State *n* a nickname for Kansas

sung past participle of **sing**

Sung /sŏŏng/, **Song** *n* a Chinese imperial dynasty that lasted from A.D. 960–1279, under which science, philosophy, and the arts thrived [Late 17C. < Chinese *Song*]

sun·gaz·er /sún gàyzər/ *n* a lizard that grows to about 14 in./35.6 cm long and is known for its habit of basking in the sun. Native to: southern Africa. Latin name: *Cordylus giganteus*.

sun·glass /sún glàss/ *n* a convex lens used to focus the sun's rays so as to produce heat, especially in order to start a fire ■ **sun·glass·es** *npl* eyeglasses with tinted or darkened lenses to protect the eyes from sunlight or its glare

sun·glow /sún glō/ *n* a pale pink or yellow glow seen in the sky just before sunrise or just after sunset

sun god, **sun-god** *n* **1.** the Sun worshiped as a god **2.** a god that personifies or is seen as controlling the Sun

sun-grebe *n* a diving bird of the finfoot family that lives along rivers and lakes. Native to: South America. Family: Heliornithidae.

sun·hat /sún hàt/ *n* a hat with a broad brim, designed to cover the head and shade the face and neck from the sun

sunk /sungk/ past participle, past tense of **sink** ■ *adj* without hope of success (*informal*)

USAGE See *sink*.

sunk·en /súngkən/ *adj* **1. SUBMERGED** submerged beneath the surface of something ○ *a sunken galleon* **2. HOLLOW-LOOKING** appearing hollow or concave ○ *sunken cheeks* **3. SUNK LOWER** having settled to a lower level **4. AT LOWER ELEVATION** set at a lower level than something adjoining [Old past participle of SINK]

USAGE See *sink*.

sunk fence *n* a ditch containing a fence or wall that separates lands without spoiling the appearance of the landscape

sun·lamp /sún làmp/ *n* **1.** a lamp that emits ultraviolet light, used to get a suntan or for therapeutic purposes **2.** a lamp with parabolic mirrors that are directed to focus light, used in cinema photography

sun·less /súnnləss/ *adj* **1.** deprived of or lacking sunlight **2.** lacking joy or happiness

sun·light /sún līt/ *n* light emitted by the Sun —**sun·lit** /sún lìt/ *adj*

sun lounge *n UK* same as **sunroom**

sunn /sun/ *n* **1.** a strong light plant fiber. Use: rope, sacks. **2.** a thin-branched tropical plant whose inner bark yields sunn. Native to: Asia, Australia. Latin name: *Crotalaria juncea*. [Late 18C. Via Hindi < Sanskrit *śāṇa-* "made of hemp"]

Sun·na /sŏŏnnə, súnnə/, **Sun·nah** *n* one of the basic sources of Islamic law, based on Muhammad's words and deeds as recorded in the Hadith. The Sunna complements and often explains the Koran. [Early 18C. < Arabic, "rule, custom"]

Sun·ni /sŏŏnnee/ (*plural same* or **-nis**) *n* **1.** the largest branch of Islam, which believes in the traditions of the Sunna and accepts the first four caliphs as rightful successors to Muhammad **2.** a member of the Sunni branch of Islam [Late 16C. < Arabic, "lawful" < *sunna* "rule, custom"]

Sun·nite /sŏŏ nīt, sú-/ *n* ISLAM same as **Sunni** (sense 2)

sun·ny /súnnee/ (**-ni·er, -ni·est**) *adj* **1. FULL OF SUNSHINE** characterized by a lot of sunshine ○ *sunny weather* ○ *a beautiful sunny day* **2. FULL OF SUNLIGHT** bright with or exposed to sunlight ○ *a bright, sunny room* **3. CHEERFUL** characterized by or showing happiness or cheerfulness —**sun·ni·ly** *adv* —**sun·ni·ness** *n*

sun·ny-side up *adj* describes a fried egg that is not turned over in cooking and so has a visible yellow yolk uppermost

Sun·ny·vale /súnnee vàyl/ city near San Jose at the southern end of San Francisco Bay in northern California. Situated at the heart of Silicon Valley, it is an important center for the manufacture of high-tech equipment. Population: 129,687 (2002 estimate).

sun par·lor *n US* BUILDINGS same as **sunroom**

sun pro·tec·tion fac·tor *n* HEALTH full form of **SPF**

sun·quake /sún kwàyk/ *n* a violent seismic event on the Sun caused by solar flares

sun·rise /sún rīz/ *n* **1. COMING UP OF SUN** the rising of the sun above the eastern horizon each morning **2. GLOW FROM RISING SUN** an atmospheric glow and coloring near the horizon as the Sun rises **3. TIME SUN RISES** the time at which the Sun rises above the horizon in the morning

Sun·rise Cer·e·mo·ny *n* a rite of passage into adulthood for Apache girls, a day-long event involving dancing and praying. The ceremony re-enacts a creation tale about the White Painted Woman who is supposed to have survived a great flood in an abalone shell.

sun·roof /sún ro͝of/ *n* a small panel in the roof of a car that can be raised or slid back to let in air and light

sun·room /sún ro͝om, -ro͞om/ *n* a room with large windows designed to receive the maximum sunlight

sun·screen /sún skreen/ *n* a substance applied to the skin as a cream, lotion, or oil to protect it from burning without preventing tanning

sun·set /sún sèt/ *n* **1.** GOING DOWN OF SUN the setting of the Sun below the western horizon in the evening **2.** GLOW FROM SETTING SUN an atmospheric glow and coloring near the horizon as the Sun sets **3.** TIME SUN SETS the time at which the Sun sets below the horizon in the evening **4.** LAST PART the period during which somebody or something is declining, coming to an end, or approaching death

CULTURAL NOTE ***Sunset Boulevard,*** a movie (1950) by Billy Wilder. Wilder uses the story of the relationship between an out-of-favor screenwriter and a faded and eccentric silent-movie star to create one of the cinema's most savage satires on the cynicism and ruthlessness of the Hollywood system. The performances, camerawork, and direction all reinforce the powerful atmosphere of corruption and decay.

sun·shade /sún shàyd/ *n* something under which somebody is protected from the sun, e.g., an awning or parasol

sun·shine /sún shīn/ *n* **1.** DIRECT SUNLIGHT direct rays of the sun, producing heat and light ○ *a ray of sunshine* **2.** SUNNY PLACE a place where the sun's rays are falling ○ *Let's sit in the sunshine.* **3.** SOURCE OF GOOD FEELINGS somebody or something that produces joy, happiness, or other good feelings ○ *bringing a little bit of sunshine into people's lives* ■ *adj* GIVING ACCESS TO PUBLIC describes a law or legislation requiring that meetings and records of some governmental bodies be open to the public ○ *The sunshine laws allow me to read the minutes of the meeting.* —**sun·shin·y** *adj*

Sun·shine Coast /sùn shīn-/ region in southeastern Queensland, Australia, consisting of the 28 mi./45 km stretch of coastline between Noosa Heads and Caloundra. It is a popular tourist destination.

sun·shine law *n* a law that prohibits closed meetings of public bodies ○ *The sunshine law enabled us to read the minutes of the zoning board's meetings.*

Sun·shine State *n* a nickname for Florida

sun·spot /sún spòt/ *n* any of the relatively cool dark patches that appear in cycles on the Sun's surface and possess a powerful magnetic field

sun·stone /sún stōn/ *n* MINERALS same as **aventurine** (sense 2) [Translation of Latin *gemma solis*]

sun·stroke /sún strōk/ *n* a condition caused by prolonged and excessive exposure to the sun and characterized by feverishness, faintness, convulsions, and coma. It results when the temperature becomes too extreme to be handled by the body's heat-regulating mechanism. Technical name **insolation**

sun·suit /sún so͞ot/ *n* a child's one-piece garment usually consisting of shorts and a bib top with shoulder straps, worn in hot weather

sun·tan /sún tàn/ *n* HEALTH same as **tan**[1] *n* (sense 1) —**sun·tanned** *adj*

sun·trap /sún tràp/ *n UK* a sheltered area with bright sunlight and little or no wind

sun·up /sún ùp/ *n US* METEOROL same as **sunrise** (sense 3)

Sun Val·ley /sùn-/ city in central Idaho, in the Sawtooth Mountains, east of Boise. Population: 1,447 (2001).

sun·ward /súnnwərd/ *adj* turned toward or in the direction of the Sun ■ *adv also* **sun·wards** /-wərdz/ in the direction of the sun

sun·ya·ta /sho͞onyə taa/ *n* a tenet of Mahayana Buddhism stating that all things ultimately are "empty," being neither existent nor nonexistent [Early 20C. < Sanskrit *śūnyatā* "emptiness"]

Sun Yat-sen /so͝on yàt sén/ (1866–1925) Chinese revolutionary leader. He developed his democratic political philosophy during years of foreign travel and returned to China to lead the overthrow of the Manchu dynasty (1911). He led the nationalist Kuomintang Party from 1912 and headed an opposition government in Guangzhou (1917–25), but failed to establish a national republican government.

> "The foundation of the government of a nation must be built upon the rights of the people, but the administration must be entrusted to experts."
> [Sun Yat-sen, *The Three Principles of the People*; 1953]

Suo·mi /swáwmee/ Finnish name for **Finland**

sup[1] /sup/ *vti* (**supped, sup·ping, sups**) **1.** SIP LIQUID to drink small amounts of liquid at one time **2.** EAT SOMETHING BY SPOONFUL to eat with a spoon something that is swallowed directly such as soup or oatmeal ■ *n* SIP OF LIQUID a small amount or mouthful of liquid [Old English *sūpan* < Germanic]

sup[2] /sup/ (**supped, sup·ping, sups**) *vi* to eat your evening meal [14C. < Old French *souper* < *soupe* (see SOUP)] —**sup** *n*

sup. *abbr* **1.** superior **2.** GRAM superlative **3.** GRAM supine **4.** supplement **5.** supplementary **6.** supply **7.** supra

su·pa·ri /soo paaree/ *n S Asia* broken areca palm nuts, which are chewed with betel leaves, especially after meals, as a digestive aid [Mid-17C. < Hindi *supārī*]

Sup. Ct. *abbr US* **1.** Superior Court **2.** Supreme Court

Supdt. *abbr* PUBLIC ADMIN Superintendent

su·per /so͞opər/ *adj* **1.** EXCELLENT having outstanding or excellent qualities (*informal*) ○ *a super idea* **2.** VERY GREAT exceptionally large or powerful (*informal*) **3.** EXCESSIVE greater than what is normal ■ *adv* ESPECIALLY to or in a high or extreme degree (*informal*) ○ *Everyone has been super helpful.* ■ *n* **1.** BUILDING SUPERINTENDENT a superintendent, especially of an apartment building (*informal*) **2.** same as **supervisor** (*informal*) **3.** *US* SOMETHING BIGGER OR BETTER something superior in grade or quality or larger in size **4.** THEATER same as **supernumerary** (*informal*) **5.** HIGH-OCTANE GASOLINE high-octane gasoline **6.** AGRIC TOP OF BEEHIVE WITH HONEY a removable upper part of a beehive in which the bees store honey **7.** HANDICRAFT OPEN-WEAVE FABRIC FOR BINDINGS a starched cotton gauze fabric. Use: reinforcement for the bindings of books. ■ *interj* GREAT! used to express enthusiasm, approval, or agreement (*informal*) [Mid-19C. < SUPER-, or shortening of various words beginning with SUPER-]

super. *abbr* **1.** superfine **2.** superior

super- *prefix* **1.** something larger, stronger, or faster than others of its kind ○ *superstore* **2.** over, above, on ○ *supernatant* ○ *superstructure* **3.** exceeding the usual limits ○ *superheat* **4.** a more inclusive group or category ○ *superclass* **5.** in addition to, over and above ○ *superfetation* **6.** greater in size, quality, number, or degree, superior ○ *superhuman* [< Latin *super* "over, above" < Indo-European]

su·per·a·chiev·er *n*
su·per·a·gent *n*
su·per·ath·lete *n*
su·per·bright *adj*
su·per·car *n*
su·per·cau·tious *adj*
su·per·chic *adj*
su·per·civ·i·lized *adj*
su·per·clean *adj*
su·per·com·fort·a·ble *adj*
su·per·com·pet·i·tive *adj*
su·per·con·fi·dent *adj*
su·per·con·ser·va·tive *adj*
su·per·con·ven·ient *adj*
su·per·de·luxe *adj*
su·per·ef·fec·tive *adj*
su·per·ef·fi·cient *adj*
su·per·ex·pen·sive *adj*
su·per·fast *adj*
su·per·high *adj*
su·per·hot *adj*
su·per·in·tel·lec·tu·al *adj*
su·per·in·tel·li·gent *adj*
su·per·large *adj*
su·per·light *adj*
su·per·lux·ur·i·ous *adj*
su·per·mod·ern *adj*
su·per·nor·mal *adj*
su·per·nor·mal·i·ty *n*
su·per·nor·mal·ly *adv*
su·per·pa·tri·ot·ic *adj*
su·per·play·er *n*
su·per·po·lite *adj*
su·per·pow·er·ful *adj*
su·per·qual·i·ty *adj*
su·per·rich *adj, n*
su·per·ro·man·tic *adj*
su·per·safe *adj*
su·per·sale *n*
su·per·sharp *adj*
su·per·size *adj*
su·per·sized *adj*
su·per·sleuth *n*
su·per·slick *adj*
su·per·smart *adj*
su·per·smooth *adj*
su·per·soft *adj*
su·per·so·phis·ti·cat·ed *adj*
su·per·spe·cial *adj*
su·per·spy *n*
su·per·strength *adj*
su·per·strong *adj*
su·per·sweet *adj*
su·per·thick *adj*
su·per·thin *adj*
su·per·tight *adj*
su·per·wide *adj*

su·per·a·ble /so͞opərəb'l/ *adj* capable of being overcome [Early 17C. < Latin *superabilis* < *superare* "overcome" < *super* "over, above"] —**su·per·a·bil·i·ty** /so͞opərə bílləteе/ *n* —**su·per·a·ble·ness** *n* —**su·per·a·bly** *adv*

su·per·a·bound /so͞opərə bównd/ (**-bound·ed, -bound·ing, -bounds**) *vi* to be too numerous or abundant [14C. < late Latin *superabundare* < Latin *super* "over, above" + *abundare* (see ABOUND)]

su·per·a·bun·dant /so͞opərə búndənt/ *adj* too numerous or abundant [15C. < late Latin *superabundant-*, present participle of *superabundare* (see SUPERABOUND)] —**su·per·a·bun·dance** *n* —**su·per·a·bun·dant·ly** *adv*

su·per·add /so͞opər ád/ (**-add·ed, -add·ing, -adds**) *vt* to add something onto what has already been added [15C. < Latin *superaddere* < *super* "over, above" *addere* (see ADD)] —**su·per·ad·di·tion** /-dísh'n/ *n* —**su·per·ad·di·tion·al** *adj*

su·per·a·gen·cy /so͞opər àyjənssee/ (*plural* **-cies**) *n* a large government agency made up of or controlling other agencies

su·per·al·loy /so͞opər á lòy/ *n* a heat-resistant alloy with superior mechanical properties, often one with aerospace applications

su·per·an·nu·ate /so͞opər ánnyoo àyt/ (**-at·ed, -at·ing, -ates**) *v* **1.** *vti* to become retired with a pension, or retire somebody with a pension **2.** *vt* to reject something or cause something to be rejected because of obsolescence [Mid-17C. Back-formation < SUPERANNUATED] —**su·per·an·nu·a·tion** /-anyoo áysh'n/ *n*

su·per·an·nu·at·ed /so͞opər ánnyoo àytəd/ *adj* **1.** RETIRED having been retired with a pension **2.** WORN OUT used so much as to be able to offer no more useful service **3.** OUT-OF-DATE no longer in fashion [Mid-17C. < medieval Latin *superannuatus* "more than a year old" < Latin *super* "over, above" + *annus* "year"]

su·perb /soo púrb, sə-/ *adj* **1.** EXCELLENT of the highest quality **2.** GRAND impressive in size or appearance **3.** SUMPTUOUS rich and sumptuous in appearance or detail [Mid-16C. Via French < Latin *superbus* "proud, superior" < *super* "over, above"] —**su·perb·ly** *adv* —**su·perb·ness** *n*

Su·per Bowl a service mark for the championship game of the National Football League, played each year between the champions of the National Football Conference and the American Football Conference

su·per·bug /so͞opər bùg/ *n* a bacterium that has become resistant to the antibiotics normally used to treat it

su·per·cal·en·der /so͞opər kàlləndər/ *n* a machine with an extra large number of rollers to give a glossy finish to paper ■ *vt* (**-dered, -der·ing, -ders**) to produce a glossy finish on paper using a supercalender

su·per·car·go /so͞opər kaargō/ (*plural* **-gos**) *n* an officer who is in charge of the cargo and commercial matters aboard a merchant ship [Late 17C. < alteration of Spanish *sobrecargo* < *sobre-* "over" + *cargo* (see CARGO)]

su·per·cav·i·ta·tion /so͞opər kavə táysh'n/ *n* the formation of a large bubble around a fast-moving underwater object such as a submarine or torpedo that greatly reduces the viscous drag of the water —**su·per·cav·i·tat·ing** /-kávvi tàyting/ *adj* —**su·per·cav·i·ty** *n*

~~**supercede**~~ incorrect spelling of **supersede**

su·per·cen·te·na·ri·an /so͞opər sent'n érree ən/ *n* a person who is at least 100 years old

su·per·cen·ter /so͞opər sèntər/ *n US* a supermarket with other departments such as a pharmacy, banking center, or clothing department (*often used with retail trade names*)

su·per·charge /so͞opər chaarj/ (**-charged, -charg·ing, -charg·es**) *vt* **1.** to charge something such as the atmosphere or a remark with excessive emotion or energy **2.** to increase the power of an internal-combustion engine by means of a supercharger

su·per·charg·er /sòopər chaàrjər/ *n* a device that supplies air to an internal-combustion engine at a pressure greater than the ambient atmospheric pressure in order to increase its power

su·per·cil·i·ar·y /sòopər síllee èrree/ *adj* **1.** relating to or located in the region of the eyebrow **2.** describes markings above an animal's eye [Mid-18C. < Latin *supercilium* "eyebrow" (see SUPERCILIOUS)]

su·per·cil·i·ous /sòopər síllee əss/ *adj* full of contempt and arrogance [Early 16C. < Latin *superciliosus* < *supercilium* "eyebrow" < *super* "above" + *cilium* "eyelid"]

su·per·class /sòopər klàss/ *n* a taxonomic category of related organisms of a rank above class

su·per·clus·ter /sòopər klùstər/ *n* an association of clusters of galaxies

su·per·col·lid·er /sòopər kə lĭdər/ *n* a very large high-energy particle accelerator

su·per·com·put·er /sòopər kəm pyòotər/ *n* a computer with the very highest processing speeds, used for solving complex problems and creating simulations

su·per·con·duc·tiv·i·ty /sòopər kòndək tívvətee/ *n* the ability of some metals, alloys, and ceramics to conduct electric current with negligible internal resistance at temperatures near absolute zero and, in some cases, at higher temperatures —**su·per·con·duct·ing** /-kən dúkting/ *adj* —**su·per·con·duc·tion** /-dúksh'n/ *n* —**su·per·con·duc·tive** /-dúktiv/ *adj* —**su·per·con·duc·tor** /-dúktər/ *n*

su·per·con·ti·nent /sòopər kònt'nənt/ *n* one of the large continental masses believed to have broken into several parts that drifted apart to form the present continents. These land masses included Pangea, Gondwanaland, and Laurasia.

su·per·cool /sòopər kòol/ *vti* (**-cooled, -cool·ing, -cools**) to cool a liquid below its freezing point without changing it to a solid, or be cooled in this way ■ *adj* extremely fashionable in attitude or image (*informal*)

su·per·crip /sòopər krìp/ *n US* a physically challenged person who is very fit and takes part in strenuous sports (*informal; sometimes offensive*) [Late 20C. < SUPER- + shortening of CRIPPLE]

su·per·crit·i·cal /sòopər kríttik'l/ *adj* **1. HIGHLY CRITICAL** highly critical of something, e.g., a person's work **2.** PHYS **SELF-SUSTAINING AS NUCLEAR REACTION** describes a nuclear chain reaction that sustains itself explosively because a single transformation produces more than one other transformation **3.** PHYS **ABOVE CRITICAL TEMPERATURE AND PRESSURE** describes a fluid at temperatures and pressures higher than those at which the liquid and gaseous states of the given substance would have the same density

su·per·dup·er /sòopər dòopər/ *adj* exceptionally good, large, or efficient (*slang; often used ironically*) [Doubling of SUPER]

su·per·e·go /sòopər éegō, sòopər èegō/ (*plural* **-gos**) *n* according to Freudian theory, the part of the mind that acts as a conscience to the ego, developing moral standards and rules through contact with parents and society [Early 20C. Translation of German *Über-Ich*]

su·per·el·e·va·tion /sòopər elə váysh'n/ *n* the distance in height between the inside and outside edges of the bed of a banked road or track

su·per·er·o·gate /sòopər érrə gàyt/ (**-ga·ted, -ga·ting, -gates**) *vi* to do or perform something beyond what is required or expected (*archaic*) [Late 16C. < late Latin *supererogare* (see SUPEREROGATION)] —**su·per·er·o·ga·tor** *n*

su·per·er·o·ga·tion /sòopər erə gáysh'n/ *n* the performance of work beyond what is required or expected [Early 16C. < late Latin *supererogation-* < *supererogare* "pay over and above" < Latin *super* "over, above" + *erogare* "spend" < *rogare* "ask, beg"]

su·per·e·rog·a·to·ry /sòopərə róggə tàwree/ *adj* **1.** performed to an extent beyond what is required or expected **2.** beyond what is sufficient or necessary, and not wanted —**su·per·er·o·ga·to·ri·ly** *adv*

su·per·fam·i·ly /sòopər fàmməlee/ (*plural* **-lies**) *n* a taxonomic category of related organisms of a rank above family

su·per·fec·ta /sòopər féktə/ *n US* a bet, especially in horseracing, in which the bettor, in order to win, must pick the first four finishers in the correct sequence [Late 20C. < SUPER + PERFECTA]

su·per·fe·cun·da·tion /sòopər fekən dáysh'n/ *n* **1.** the fertilization of two or more ova at different times during one menstrual cycle by sperm from the same or different males **2.** the fertilization of an unusually large number of ova at the same time

su·per·fe·ta·tion /sòopər fee táysh'n/ *n* the fertilization of a second ovum after the start of pregnancy, resulting in the presence of two fetuses at different stages of development in the same uterus. It is a regular occurrence in some animal species. [Early 17C. Directly or via French < modern Latin *superfetation-* < *superfetare* "conceive a second time" < Latin *super* "over, above" + *foetus* "offspring"]

su·per·fi·cial /sòopər físh'l/ *adj* **1. NOT PROFOUND** concerned with or understanding only the obvious ○ *a superficial knowledge of the subject* **2. RELATING TO SURFACE** relating to, affecting, or located on or near the surface of something ○ *a superficial wound* **3. WITHOUT DEPTH OF CHARACTER** shallow in character or attitude ○ *I find her quite superficial.* **4. CURSORY** swift and not thorough ○ *after a superficial examination of the injury* **5. ONLY APPARENTLY SO** only seeming to be real or the case ○ *The picture bears a superficial resemblance, nothing more.* **6. INSIGNIFICANT** having little significance or substance ○ *superficial changes to the policy* [14C. < Latin *superficies* < *super* "over, above" + *facies* "appearance, form, face"] —**su·per·fi·ci·al·i·ty** /-fishee állətee/ *n* —**su·per·fi·cial·ly** *adv*

su·per·fi·cies /sòopər físheez/ (*plural same*) *n* **1.** the outer surface or area of something **2.** the outward appearance or form of something [Mid-16C. < Latin (see SUPERFICIAL)]

su·per·fine /sòopər fĭn, sòopər fĭn/ *adj* **1. FINEST IN TEXTURE** of extremely fine grain or texture **2. FINEST IN QUALITY** of the highest quality or grade **3. AFFECTEDLY REFINED** excessively refined in manner —**su·per·fine·ness** *n*

su·per·flu·id /sòopər flòo id/ *n* a fluid characterized by the absence of viscosity at temperatures near absolute zero. The only known example is liquid helium. ■ *adj* relating to or exhibiting the properties of a superfluid —**su·per·flu·id·i·ty** /sòopər floo íddətee/ *n*

su·per·flu·i·ty /sòopər flòo ətee/ (*plural* **-ties**) *n* **1.** something beyond what is necessary **2.** an excessive or overabundant supply of something

su·per·flu·ous /sə púrfloo əss/ *adj* **1.** in excess of what is needed ○ *a lot of superfluous detail* **2.** not essential ○ *superfluous to the discussion* [14C. Directly or via French < Latin *superfluus* < *superfluere* "overflow" < *super* "over, above" + *fluere* "to flow"] —**su·per·flu·ous·ly** *adv* —**su·per·flu·ous·ness** *n*

su·per·gal·ax·y /sòopər gálləksee/ (*plural* **-ies**) *n* ASTRON same as **supercluster**

su·per·gene /sòopər jeen/ *n* a group of genes that lie close together on a chromosome, function as a unit, and are rarely separated

su·per·germ /sòopər jùrm/ *n* MICROBIOL same as **superbug**

su·per·gi·ant /sòopər jĭ ənt/ *n* an extremely large brilliant star with a luminosity thousands of times greater than that of the Sun. The stars Rigel and Betelgeuse are supergiants.

su·per·glue /sòopər glòo/ *n* a fast-acting glue that forms a strong bond by polymerization

su·per·graph·ics /sòopər gràffiks/ *n* simple brightly colored graphic designs of very large proportions (*takes a singular or plural verb*)

su·per·grav·i·ty /sòopər gràvvətee/ *n* a theory in physics that encompasses all known fundamental interactions and uses hypothetical particles (**gravitons**) to carry the gravitational force. It has largely been supplanted by superstring theory.

su·per·group /sòopər gròop/ *n* a rock music group whose performers are already famous from having performed individually or in other groups

su·per·heat /sòopər heèt/ *vt* (**-heat·ed, -heat·ing, -heats**) **1. HEAT LIQUID WITHOUT VAPORIZATION** to heat a liquid above its pressure-related boiling point without causing it to vaporize **2. HEAT VAPOR TO SATURATION** to heat a vapor not in contact with its liquid to the point at which a lowering of temperature or increase in pressure will not change it to a liquid **3. MAKE SOMETHING VERY HOT** to heat something to an extremely high temperature ■ *n* **HEAT FOR SUPERHEATING** the heat used to superheat a vapor —**su·per·heat·er** *n*

su·per·heav·y /sòopər hévvee/ *adj* describes a chemical element having more than 110 protons in the nucleus, and, according to theoretical studies, likely to have special stability

su·per·heav·y·weight /sòopər hévvee wàyt/ *n* **1. WEIGHT CATEGORY IN AMATEUR BOXING** in amateur boxing, a weight category for competitors who weigh more than 201 lb./91 kg **2. BOXER COMPETING AT SUPERHEAVYWEIGHT** an amateur boxer who competes at superheavyweight level **3. SOMEBODY IN HEAVIEST WEIGHT DIVISION** a sportsperson, especially a wrestler or weightlifter, who competes in the heaviest weight division —**su·per·heav·y·weight** *adj*

su·per·he·lix /sòopər heèliks/ (*plural* **-hel·i·ces** /-hèlli seèz, -heèli-/) *n* a form of DNA in which the helical molecule is coiled in on itself

su·per·he·ro /sòopər heèrō/ (*plural* **-roes**) *n* a fictional character, e.g., from a cartoon, who has superhuman powers and uses them to fight crime or evil

su·per·het·er·o·dyne /sòopər héttərə dĭn/ *adj* relating to a method of receiving radio signals in which the incoming signal is mixed with a frequency generated by the receiver. The resulting intermediate frequency is amplified and then decoded. ■ *n* a radio receiver that operates using the superheterodyne method of receiving signals [Early 20C. < SUPERSONIC]

su·per·high fre·quen·cy /sòopər hĭ-/ *n* a radio frequency between 3,000 and 30,000 megahertz

su·per·high·way /sòopər hĭ wày/ *n* **1.** a highway or expressway designed for high-speed traffic, with several lanes in each direction **2.** ONLINE same as **information superhighway**

su·per·hu·man /sòopər hyòomən, -yòomən/ *adj* **1.** beyond ordinary human capability ○ *made a superhuman effort to move the boulder* **2.** having higher or greater powers than those usually possessed by a human being ○ *a superhuman being* [Early 17C. < late Latin *superhumanus* < Latin *super* "over, above" + *humanus* "human"] —**su·per·hu·man·i·ty** /-hyoo mánnətee, -yoo-/ *n* —**su·per·hu·man·ly** *adv*

su·per·im·pose /sòopərim pṓz/ (**-posed, -pos·ing, -pos·es**) *vt* **1.** to place something such as a transparent image on or over something else, often with the result that both things appear simultaneously, although one may partially obscure the other **2.** to add a feature or element without incorporating it ○ *superimpose one culture on another* —**su·per·im·po·si·tion** /-impə zísh'n/ *n*

su·per·in·cum·bent /sòopərin kúmbənt/ *adj* lying or resting on or above something [Mid-17C. < Latin *superincumbent-*, present participle of *superincumbere* "lie on top of" < *super* "over, above" + *incumbere* (see INCUMBENT)] —**su·per·in·cum·bençe** *n* —**su·per·in·cum·ben·cy** *n* —**su·per·in·cum·bent·ly** *adv*

su·per·in·duce /sòopərin dòoss/ (**-duced, -duc·ing, -duc·es**) *vt* to introduce somebody or something additional [Mid-16C. < Latin *superinducere* "bring in upon" < *super* "over, above" + *inducere* (see INDUCE)] —**su·per·in·duc·tion** /-dúksh'n/ *n*

su·per·in·fec·tion /sòopərin féksh'n/ *n* an infection that develops during drug treatment for another infection, caused by a different microorganism that is resistant to the treatment used for the first infection —**su·per·in·fect** *vt*

su·per·in·tend /sòopərin ténd/ (**-tend·ed, -tend·ing, -tends**) *vt* to be responsible for and supervise something such as a project or job [Early 17C. Back-formation < SUPERINTENDENT]

~~superintendant~~ incorrect spelling of **superintendent**

su·per·in·ten·dent /sòopərin téndənt/ *n* **1. SOMEBODY IN CHARGE** an administrator or manager of something such as an office or school system **2. JANITOR** somebody in charge of the maintenance of a building **3. HIGH-RANKING POLICE OFFICER** in the United Kingdom and

Canada, a police officer of a rank above inspector, and in the United States a police officer of high rank, especially the head of a police department ■ *adj* **IN CHARGE** acting in an administrative or supervisory capacity [Mid-16C. < ecclesiastical Latin *superintendent-*, present participle of *superintendere* "oversee" < Latin *super* "over, above" + *intendere* (see INTEND); translation of Greek *episkopos* "overseer"] —**su·per·in·ten·dence** *n* —**su·per·in·ten·den·cy** *n*

su·pe·ri·or /sə peéree ər/ *adj* **1. HIGHER IN QUALITY** above average or better than another in quality or grade **2. BETTER THAN OTHERS** surpassing others in something such as intellect, achievement, or ability **3. HIGHER IN RANK** higher in rank, position, or authority than another **4. IN HIGHER LOCATION** upper, or situated higher up **5. CONDESCENDING** adopting or showing an attitude of condescension toward others ○ *He gave a superior smile.* **6. LARGER** greater in number or amount ○ *a quantity superior to our needs* **7. UNCONCERNED** above being affected or influenced by something ○ *She considered herself superior to such taunts.* **8.** ANAT **NEARER HEAD** nearer the head than another body part **9.** BOT **ABOVE OTHER FLOWER PARTS** describes an ovary of a flower whose stamens, petals, and sepals arise either beside or below it **10.** PRINTING same as **superscript** ■ *n* **1. SOMEBODY OR SOMETHING HIGHER OR BETTER** somebody or something higher in rank, position, authority, or quality than another ○ *Don't argue with your superiors.* **2.** PRINTING same as **superscript** **3.** RELIG **SOMEBODY IN CHARGE OF RELIGIOUS ORDER** the head of a religious order or institution [14C. Via French < Latin, "higher" < *superus* "above" < *super*] —**su·pe·ri·or·i·ty** /sə peéree áwrətee/ *n* —**su·pe·ri·or·ly** *adv*

Su·pe·ri·or, Lake /sə peéree ər/ lake in North America. The northernmost and westernmost of the Great Lakes, it is also the world's largest freshwater lake. Area: 31,700 sq. mi./82,100 sq. km. Depth: 1,333 ft./406 m. Length: 350 mi./560 km.

su·pe·ri·or con·junc·tion *n* the position of an astronomical object in which it is opposite Earth on the far side of the Sun

su·pe·ri·or court *n* in some states of the United States, a court that is higher than an inferior court, but lower than an appellate court

su·pe·ri·or·i·ty com·plex *n* an exaggerated sense of being better than other people

su·pe·ri·or plan·et *n* a planet whose distance from the Sun is greater than that of Earth. The superior planets are Mars, Jupiter, Saturn, Uranus, Neptune, and Pluto.

su·per·ja·cent /sòopər jáyss'nt/ *adj* lying on or above something [Late 16C. < Latin *superjacent-*, present participle of *superjacere* "lie above" < *super* "over, above" < *jacere* "lie"]

su·per·jet /sòopər jèt/ *n* a large supersonic jet plane

su·per·la·tive /soo púrlətiv/ *adj* **1. EXCELLENT** of the highest quality or degree **2.** GRAM **HIGHEST IN DEGREE OF COMPARISON** expressing the highest degree of grammatical comparison of an adjective or adverb ○ *The superlative form of an adjective or adverb typically has the ending "-est."* ■ *n* **1.** GRAM **GRAMMATICAL FORM** the grammatical form of an adjective or adverb that expresses the highest degree of comparison ○ *Put "tiny" into the superlative and you get "tiniest."* **2.** GRAM **SUPERLATIVE ADJECTIVE OR ADVERB** a superlative form of an adjective or adverb ○ *the difference between a comparative and a superlative* **3. SOMEBODY OR SOMETHING EXCELLENT** somebody or something of the highest quality **4. EXAGGERATED PRAISE** an exaggerated description or way of referring to somebody or something, usually expressing admiration ○ *heaping superlatives on their performance* [14C. Via French < Latin *superlativus* < past participle of *superferre* "carry above" < *super* "over, above" + *ferre* "carry"] —**su·per·la·tive·ly** *adv* —**su·per·la·tive·ness** *n*

su·per·lin·er /sòopər lìnər/ *n* a large luxurious ocean-going passenger ship

su·per·load /sòopər lòd/ *n US* a vehicle load that exceeds the permitted weight or dimensions and requires a special permit to be transported over streets and highways

su·per·lu·na·ry /sòopər lòonəree/, **su·per·lu·nar** /-lòonər/ *adj* **1.** located beyond the Moon **2.** belonging to a supposed higher world or celestial plane [Early 17C. After SUBLUNARY]

su·per·man /sòopər màn/ (*plural* **-men** /-mèn/) *n* **1.** a man possessing exceptional or superhuman strength, abilities, or powers **2.** in the philosophy of Nietzsche, an ideal man who, through creativity and integrity, is able to transcend good and evil and is the goal of human evolution [Early 20C. Translation of German *Übermensch*]

CULTURAL NOTE ***Superman***, a comic strip created by US writer Jerry Siegal and drawn by US artist Joseph Shuster that first appeared in 1938. The alter ego of "mild-mannered reporter" Clark Kent is Superman, an almost invincible, crime-fighting superhero in a red cape, who was originally sent to Earth as a child from the doomed planet Krypton. The story has been made into radio shows, musicals, television series, and feature movies.

su·per·mar·ket /sòopər maarkət/ *n* a large self-service retail store selling food and household goods

su·per·mas·sive black hole /sòopər màssiv-/ *n* an extremely large black hole with a mass ranging from a few million to more than several billion solar masses that is believed to be at the center of many large galaxies

sup·er·max /sòopər màks/ *n US* describes a prison that is protected or made secure by the most extensive and elaborate security arrangements that are available or in current use

su·per·mod·el /sòopər mòdd'l/ *n* a fashion model who is extremely well paid and in very high demand by fashion designers and photographers

su·per·mom /sòopər mòm/ *n* a woman who cares for a home and family, is involved in children's and community activities, and often also may be employed full-time (*informal*)

su·per·nal /soo púrn'l/ *adj* (*literary*) **1.** coming from or located in the sky **2.** suited to or characteristic of the sky [15C. Via French < Latin *supernus* "heavenly" < *super* "over, above"] —**su·per·nal·ly** *adv*

su·per·na·tant /sòopər náyt'nt/ *n* the usually clear liquid left above a precipitate or sediment [Mid-17C. < Latin *supernatant-*, present participle of *supernatare* "float above" < *super* "over, above" + *natare* (see NATATORY)]

su·per·nat·u·ral /sòopər náchərəl/ *adj* **1. NOT OF NATURAL WORLD** relating to or attributed to phenomena that cannot be explained by natural laws **2. RELATING TO DEITY** relating to or attributed to a deity **3. MAGICAL** relating to or attributed to magic or the occult ■ *n* **1. SUPERNATURAL THINGS** supernatural beings or phenomena **2. WORLD OF SUPERNATURAL THINGS** the realm of supernatural beings or phenomena —**su·per·nat·u·ral·ly** *adv* —**su·per·nat·u·ral·ness** *n*

su·per·nat·u·ral·ism /sòopər náchərə lìzzəm/ *n* **1.** the quality or condition of being supernatural **2.** the belief that supernatural or divine beings and phenomena intervene in human events —**su·per·nat·u·ral·ist** *n, adj* —**su·per·nat·u·ral·is·tic** /-nàchərə lístik/ *adj*

su·per·no·va /sòopər nṓvə/ (*plural* **-vae** /-vee/ or **-vas**) *n* a catastrophic explosion of a large star in the latter stages of stellar evolution, with a resulting short-lived luminosity from 10 to 100 million times that of the Sun

su·per·nu·mer·ar·y /sòopər nóomə rèrree/ *adj* **1. EXTRA** exceeding the usual number **2.** HR **SUBSTITUTING** employed as a substitute or extra worker ■ *n* (*plural* **-ies**) **1. SOMEBODY OR SOMETHING EXTRA** somebody or something in addition to the usual number **2.** THEATER **ACTOR WITH WALK-ON PART** an actor who appears on stage, but has no lines to speak **3.** HR **SUBSTITUTE EMPLOYEE** somebody employed as a substitute or extra worker [Early 17C. < late Latin *supernumerarius* < Latin *super* "over, above" + *numerus* "number"]

su·per·or·der /sòopər àwrdər/ *n* a taxonomic category of related organisms of a rank above order

su·per·or·di·nate /sòopər áwrd'nət/ *n* **1.** a word whose meaning encompasses the meaning of another more specific word. "Animal" is a superordinate of "cat." **2.** somebody or something of superior rank, status, or class [Early 17C. < SUPER- + SUBORDINATE] —**su·per·or·di·nate** *adj*

su·per·or·gan·ism /sòopər áwrgə nìzzəm/ *n* a group of organisms functioning as a social unit, e.g., an insect colony

su·per·o·vu·la·tion /sòopər ovyə láysh'n/ *n* increased frequency of ovulation or production of a large number of ova at one time. It is often caused by the administration of gonadotropin hormones, which are prescribed to induce ovulation in infertility. —**su·per·o·vu·late** /-óvvyə làyt/ *vi*

su·per·per·son /sòopər pùrss'n/ (*plural* **-peo·ple** /-peép'l/ or **-per·sons**) *n* **1.** somebody who succeeds in combining several roles with apparent ease **2.** an imaginary or fictional person with superhuman powers

su·per·phos·phate /sòopər fóss fàyt/ *n* a commercially produced fertilizer prepared by treating phosphate mineral deposits with acid, either sulfuric acid, phosphoric acid, or a mixture of the two

su·per·plas·tic /sòopər plástik/ *adj* describes alloys that are capable of being easily shaped and molded at high temperatures without fracturing —**su·per·plas·tic·i·ty** /-pla stíssətee/ *n*

su·per·pose /sòopər pṓz/ (**-posed, -pos·ing, -pos·es**) *vt* **1.** to place or lay one object on top of or above another **2.** to move one geometric figure so that it coincides exactly with another [Early 19C. Probably < French *superposer*, back-formation < *superposition* "superposing" < Latin *superponere* "place over" < *super-* "over, above" + *ponere* "to place"] —**su·per·pos·a·ble** *adj* —**su·per·posed** *adj* —**su·per·po·si·tion** /-pə zísh'n/ *n*

su·per·pow·er /sòopər pòwr/ *n* **1.** an extremely powerful nation with greater political, economic, or military power than most other nations **2.** extremely high electrical or mechanical power —**su·per·pow·ered** *adj*

su·per·sat·u·rat·ed /sòopər sáchə ràytəd/ *adj* **1.** used to describe a chemical solution containing a greater amount of solute than usually possible at a specific temperature and pressure, often as a result of cooling **2.** used to describe a vapor containing more gaseous material than usually possible at a specific temperature and pressure —**su·per·sat·u·ra·tion** /-sachə ráysh'n/ *n*

su·per·sav·er /sòopər sàyvər/ *n* an airline ticket that is cheaper than the usual price and must usually be bought a specific amount of time before the date of travel

su·per·scribe /sòopər skrìb/ (**-scribed, -scrib·ing, -scribes**) *vt* to write or print something such as a name or address above, outside, or on the surface of something else

su·per·script /sòopər skrìpt/ *n* a letter, character, or symbol that is written above, or above and to the right or left of, another character ■ *adj* written or printed as a superscript

su·per·scrip·tion /sòopər skrípsh'n/ *n* **1.** something that is written, printed, or engraved above, outside, or on the surface of something else **2.** the act of writing or printing something above, outside, or on the surface of something else

su·per·sede /sòopər seéd/ (**-sed·ed, -sed·ing, -sedes**) *vt* **1.** to take the place or position of something that is less efficient, less modern, or less appropriate, or cause something to do this **2.** to succeed somebody or something in a role, office, or function (*formal*) [15C. Via French < Latin *supersedere* "be superior to" < *super* "over, above" + *sedere* "sit"] —**su·per·sed·a·ble** *adj* —**su·per·sed·ence** *n* —**su·per·sed·er** *n*

USAGE Note that ***supersede*** is correctly spelled *-sede* and not *-cede*.

su·per·sen·si·ble /sòopər sénssəb'l/ *adj* above or beyond the perception of the senses —**su·per·sen·si·bly** *adv*

su·per·sen·si·tive /sòopər sénssətiv/ *adj* MED same as **hypersensitive** —**su·per·sen·si·tive·ly** *adv* —**su·per·sen·si·tiv·i·ty** /-sènssə tívvətee/ *n*

su·per·sen·so·ry /sòopər sénssəree/ *adj* same as **supersensible**

su·per·serv·er /sòopər sùrvər/ *n* an extremely powerful computer that controls a network or networks of other computers

su·per·set /sóopər sèt/ *n* in mathematics, a set that contains one or more other sets

su·per·son·ic /sòopər sónnik/ *adj* relating to, produced by, or capable of reaching a speed that is faster than the speed at which sound travels through the air [Early 20C. < SUPER- + Latin *sonus* "sound"] —**su·per·son·i·cal·ly** *adv*

su·per·son·ics /sòopər sónniks/ *n* the science or study of supersonic motion or phenomena (*takes a singular verb*)

su·per·son·ic trans·port *n* a transport aircraft that travels at supersonic speed

su·per·star /sóopər staar/ *n* an extremely famous or successful person, especially in sports or entertainment —**su·per·star·dom** *n*

su·per·state /sóopər stàyt/ *n* a powerful country with a very large geographic area and population, especially one created by the union or federation of a number of nations or states

su·per·sta·tion /sóopər stàysh'n/ *n* a television channel broadcast nationally or internationally through satellite and cable

sup·er·sti·tial /sòopər stísh'l/ *n* an animated advertisement that pops up on a viewer's screen between page views on the Internet [Late 20C. < SUPER- + INTERSTITIAL]

su·per·sti·tion /sòopər stísh'n/ *n* **1.** an irrational, but usually deep-seated belief in the magical effects of a specific action or ritual, especially in the likelihood that good or bad luck will result from performing it **2.** irrational and often quasi-religious belief in and reverence for the magical effects of some actions and rituals or the magical powers of some objects [15C. Via French < Latin *superstition-* < *superstes* "standing over (in awe)" < *super* "over, above" + *stare* "to stand"]

su·per·sti·tious /sòopər stíshəss/ *adj* **1.** convinced that performing or not performing specific actions brings good or bad luck, that some events or phenomena are omens, and, generally, fearfully believing in a supernatural dimension to events **2.** based on a false or irrational belief in, or fear of, the supernatural

su·per·store /sóopər stàwr/ *n* **1.** a very large supermarket or store offering a wider and more varied range of consumer goods than other stores of the same type **2.** a retail chain or single store that specializes in a range of related products offered at discount prices ○ *a computer superstore*

su·per·stra·tum /sóopər stràytəm, -stràttəm/ (*plural* **-ta** /-stràytə, -stràttə/) *n* **1.** a layer, especially of rock or sedimentation, on top of another one **2.** the language of an invading or colonizing population in relation to the language of an indigenous population that it changes or influences

su·per·string /sóopər strìng/ *n* a hypothetical one-dimensional entity **(string)** of extremely short length, held to be a fundamental component of matter in some theories of elementary particles involving supersymmetry

su·per·struc·ture /sóopər strùkchər/ *n* **1. UPPER PART OF SHIP** the part of a ship above the main deck **2. VISIBLE PART OF BUILDING** the part of a building above its foundations **3. PART DEVELOPED ON BASE** a physical or intellectual structure built on or developed from a fundamental form, base, or concept **4.** POL **INSTITUTIONS ASSOCIATED WITH PARTICULAR ECONOMY** in Marxist theory, the complex of social, legal, and political institutions that are an extension and reflection of the type of economy operating in a particular society —**su·per·struc·tur·al** /sòopər strúkchərəl/ *adj*

su·per·sym·me·try /sòopər símmətree/ *n* a theory in physics proposing a type of symmetry that would apply to all elementary particles

su·per·tank·er /sóopər tàngkər/ *n* a very large tanker ship, usually with a capacity of 300,000 tons/275,000 tonnes or more

su·per·tax /sóopər tàks/ *n* ECON same as **surtax** *n* (sense 2)

su·per·ti·tle /sóopər tìt'l/ *n US* a translation of words being spoken or sung in a foreign language during the performance of a play or opera, projected on a screen above the stage. Can term **surtitle** [Late 20C. After SUBTITLE]

su·per·ton·ic /sòopər tònnik/ *n* the note one step above the tonic in a major or minor scale, or the harmony built upon this note

Su·per Tues·day *n* a Tuesday in a presidential election year on which many states hold primary elections, the results of which provide the basis for choosing the parties' presidential candidates

su·per·vene /sòopər veen/ (**-vened, -ven·ing, -venes**) *vi* (*formal*) **1.** to follow or come about unexpectedly, usually interrupting or changing what is going on **2.** to follow immediately after something [Mid-17C. < Latin *supervenire* < *super* "over, above" + *venire* "come"] —**su·per·ven·tion** /-vénsh'n/ *n*

su·per·ven·ient /sòopər veenee ənt/ *adj* existing only as a result of the presence or combination of other characteristics or qualities [Late 16C. < Latin *supervenient-*, present participle of *supervenire* (see SUPERVENE)] —**su·per·ven·ience** *n*

su·per·vise /sóopər vìz/ (**-vised, -vis·ing, -vis·es**) *vti* **1.** to watch over an activity or task being carried out by somebody and ensure that it is performed correctly **2.** to be in charge of a group of people engaged in an activity or task and keep order or ensure that they perform it correctly [Late 16C. < medieval Latin *supervis-*, past participle of *supervidere* "oversee" < Latin *super* "over, above" + *videre* "see"] —**su·per·vis·ion** /sòopər vízh'n/ *n*

~~**superviser**~~ incorrect spelling of **supervisor**

su·per·vi·sor /sóopər vìzər/ *n* **1. BOSS** somebody whose job is to oversee and guide the work or activities of a group of other people **2.** EDUC **MAIN TEACHER OF SUBJECT** a teacher or other school official who oversees the teaching and teachers of a single subject area **3.** PUBLIC ADMIN **ELECTED OFFICIAL** an elected official in various local authorities such as townships and counties **4.** *UK* EDUC **TUTOR FOR GRADUATE** in some British universities, a teacher assigned to supervise the work of an individual student, especially research done by a graduate student —**su·per·vi·sor·ship** *n* —**su·per·vi·so·ry** /sòopər vìzəree, sóopər vìzəree/ *adj*

USAGE ***Supervisor*** is the only correct spelling of this word. It is sometimes misspelled with an *-er* ending, on the model of many other English words, notably *adviser* (which has a variant spelling in *-or*).

su·per·weed /sóopər weed/ *n* an indestructible or ineradicable weed that could hypothetically evolve as a hybrid of ordinary weeds and genetically modified plants

su·per·wom·an /sóopər wòomən/ (*plural* **-wom·en** /-wìmmin/) *n* **1.** a woman who succeeds in combining several roles such as worker, wife, mother, and homemaker with apparent ease **2.** an imaginary or fictional woman with superhuman powers

su·pi·nate /sóopə nàyt/ (**-nat·ed, -nat·ing, -nates**) *v* **1.** *vti* **TURN PALM UPWARD** to turn the hand so that the palm faces upward, or be turned in this way **2.** *vti* **TURN SOLE UPWARD** to turn the foot so that the sole is facing upward, or be turned in this way **3.** *vi* **LIE FACING UPWARD** to turn the face upward or lie in a supine position with the face upward [Mid-19C. < Latin *supinat-*, past participle of *supinare* "turn backward" < *supinus* "lying on the back"] —**su·pi·na·tion** /sòopə náysh'n/ *n*

su·pi·na·tor /sóopə nàytər/ *n* a muscle, especially in the forearm, that supinates a hand or foot

su·pine /sóo pìn/ *adj* **1. LYING ON BACK** lying on the back and with the face upward **2. PALM UPWARD** having the palm of the hand facing upward or away from the body **3. FAILING TO ACT** utterly passive or inactive, especially in a situation where a vigorous reaction is called for ■ *n* GRAM **TYPE OF LATIN NOUN** a Latin noun formed from a past participle stem and having only accusative and ablative inflections [15C. < Latin *supinus* "lying on the back"]

~~**supose**~~ incorrect spelling of **suppose**

sup·per /súppər/ *n* **1. EVENING MEAL** a light meal eaten in the evening **2. MAIN EVENING MEAL** the main meal of the day when taken in the evening **3. SOCIAL EVENT** an evening social event that includes a meal [13C. < Old French *soper* "eat supper" < *soupe* "sop, broth" (see SOUP)]

◇ **sing for your supper** to work or do something in exchange for your food and board, or for something that you want

CULTURAL NOTE ***The Last Supper***, a painting (1495–97) by Italian artist Leonardo da Vinci. Painted directly onto a wall in the monastery of Santa Maria delle Grazie in Milan, it depicts the moment when Jesus Christ declares that one of his companions will betray him. It is noted for its magnificent composition and powerful depiction of the outrage of the disciples, the serenity of Jesus Christ, and the guilt of Judas.

sup·per club *n* **1.** *US* a restaurant serving fancy evening meals and sometimes featuring entertainment **2.** a group of people who get together periodically to dine in restaurants

sup·per·time /súppər tìm/ *n* the time at which supper is served or eaten

sup·plant /sə plánt/ (**-plant·ed, -plant·ing, -plants**) *vt* **1.** to take the place or position of somebody by force or intrigue **2.** to take the place of something, especially something much used, inferior, outmoded, or irrelevant [13C. Directly or via French < Latin *supplantare* "trip up, overthrow" < *sub-* "up from beneath" + *planta* "sole of the foot"] —**sup·plan·ta·tion** /sù plan táysh'n/ *n* —**sup·plant·er** *n*

sup·ple /súpp'l/ (**-pler, -plest**) *adj* **1. FLEXIBLE** flexible and elastic **2. MOVING EASILY** capable of bending, stretching, and moving with ease, fluidity, and grace **3. ADAPTABLE** adaptable and responsive in grappling with problems or dealing with new challenges **4. COMPLIANT** excessively compliant and willing to agree (*literary*) [13C. Via French < Latin *supplex* "submissive," literally "bending under" < *-plex* "fold"] —**sup·ple·ly** *adv* —**sup·ple·ness** *n*

sup·ple·jack /súpp'l jàk/ (*plural* **-jacks** or *same*) *n* **1.** a woody vine with bluish fruits. Flowers: tiny, white. Native to: southeastern United States. Latin name: *Berchemia scandens*. **2.** a tropical vine whose wood is used for making walking sticks. Native to: Central and South America. Latin name: *Paullinia curvassica*.

sup·ple·ment *n* /súppləmənt/ **1. ADDITION** an addition to something to increase its size or make up for a deficiency ○ *a useful supplement to the family income* **2.** PUBL **PUBLICATION** a publication that amplifies or corrects one already published **3.** PUBL **PERIODICAL PART** an additional section included in or sold with a magazine or newspaper, especially an additional section that appears regularly **4.** PHARM **FOOD** a substance with a specific nutritional value taken to make up for a real or supposed deficiency in diet **5.** COMM **EXTRA CHARGE** a charge payable in addition to the basic charge for a special service or under set conditions **6.** MATH **ANGLE OR ARC** an angle or arc that, when added to another, makes 180° or a semicircle ■ *vt* /súpplə mènt/ (**-ment·ed, -ment·ing, -ments**) **1. MAKE ADDITION TO SOMETHING** to increase, extend, or improve something by adding something to it ○ *supplemented their diet with vitamins* **2. BE ADDITIONAL PART OF SOMETHING** to be a supplement to something ○ *Her remarks supplemented the report.* [14C. < Latin *supplementum* < *supplere* "fill out, complete" (see SUPPLY)] —**sup·ple·men·tal** /sùpplə mént'l/ *adj* —**sup·ple·men·tal·ly** *adv* —**sup·ple·men·ta·tion** /sùpplə men táysh'n/ *n* —**sup·ple·ment·er** *n*

sup·ple·men·ta·ry /sùpplə méntəree/ *adj* **1. ADDITIONAL** additional to an existing one or to the usual number or amount **2. COMPLETING** making up for something that is lacking ■ *n* (*plural* **-ries**) **SOMETHING ADDITIONAL** an additional thing, person, or question —**sup·ple·men·tar·i·ly** /sùpplə men térrəlee/ *adv*

sup·ple·men·ta·ry an·gle *n* an angle that when added to another angle makes up 180°

sup·ple·tion /sə pleesh'n/ *n* the use of an unrelated word to fill the gap when some inflected or derived forms of a word are missing, as "was" forms the past tense of "to be" [14C. Via French < medieval Latin *suppletion-* < past participle of Latin *supplere* (see SUPPLY)] —**sup·ple·tive** /sə pleetiv, súpplətiv/ *adj*

sup·pli·ant /súpplee ənt/ *adj* expressing a humble and sincere appeal to somebody who has the power to grant a request (*formal*) ■ *n* same as **supplicant** [15C. < French, present participle of *supplier* "supplicate" < Latin *supplicare* "bend under" < *supplex* (see SUPPLE)] —**sup·pli·ance** *n* —**sup·pli·ant·ly** *adv*

sup·pli·cant /súpplәkәnt/ *n* somebody who makes a humble and sincere appeal to a person with the power to grant the request (*formal*) ■ *adj* same as **suppliant** [Late 16C. < Latin *supplicant-*, present participle of *supplicare* (see SUPPLIANT)] —**sup·pli·ca·to·ry** *adj*

sup·pli·ca·tion /sùpplә káysh'n/ *n* (*formal*) **1.** a humble and sincere appeal to somebody who has the power to grant a request **2.** the addressing of humble and sincere appeals to somebody with the power to grant them —**sup·pli·cate** /súpplә kàyt/ *vti*

~~**suppliment**~~ incorrect spelling of **supplement**

sup·ply /sә plī́/ *vt* (**-plied, -ply·ing, -plies**) **1. PROVIDE** to give, sell, or make available something that is wanted or needed by somebody or something ○ *supplied equipment for the expedition* **2. SATISFY NEED** to satisfy a need or requirement (*formal*) **3. MAKE UP FOR LACK** to make up for a deficiency, loss, or lack **4. SERVE AS SUBSTITUTE IN INSTITUTION** to act as a substitute in a place such as a church (*formal*) ■ *n* (*plural* **-plies**) **1. AVAILABLE AMOUNT** an amount or quantity of something available for use ○ *a plentiful supply of food and drink* **2. PROVISION** the act or business of giving, selling, or making available something that is wanted or needed by somebody or something, or the system that does this ○ *the supply of electric power to villages in the mountains* **3.** ECON **QUANTITY AVAILABLE IN MARKET** the quantity of a good or service available in a market at a specific time **4. SUBSTITUTE** a replacement for somebody, especially for a preacher (*formal*) ■ **sup·plies** *npl* **NEEDED THINGS** the things, especially food and equipment, that a group of people need to survive and operate, or that are needed to carry out a task or activity ○ *Our supplies were running very low.* [14C. Via Old French *supplier* "meet a deficiency" < Latin *supplere* "fill up" < *plere* "fill"] —**sup·pli·a·ble** *adj*—**sup·pli·er** *n* ◇ **in short supply** present or available only in small or insufficient quantities

sup·ply and de·mand *n* the relationship between the availability of a good or service and the need or desire for it among consumers

sup·ply-side ec·o·nom·ics *n* economic policies that promote conditions favoring the producers of goods and services (*takes a singular or plural verb*)

sup·ply teach·er *n UK* same as **substitute teacher**

sup·port /sә páwrt/ *vt* (**-port·ed, -port·ing, -ports**) **1. KEEP SOMETHING OR SOMEBODY STABLE** to keep something or somebody upright or in place, or prevent something or somebody from falling ○ *Those pillars support the roof.* **2. BEAR WEIGHT** to be strong enough to hold a particular object or weight in place without breaking or giving way ○ *Are you sure the ice is thick enough to support our weight?* **3. SUSTAIN SOMEBODY FINANCIALLY** to provide somebody with money and the other necessities of life over a period of time ○ *She succeeds in supporting her family on what she earns.* **4. GIVE ACTIVE HELP AND ENCOURAGEMENT** to give active help, encouragement, or money to somebody or something ○ *We support the charity through voluntary work.* **5. BE IN FAVOR OF SOMETHING** to be in favor of something, e.g., a cause, policy, or organization, and wish to see it succeed ○ *Do you support the committee's policy on membership fees?* **6. BE PRESENT AND GIVE ENCOURAGEMENT** to give encouragement to somebody or something by being present at an event ○ *Why not come along on Saturday and support the school team?* **7. GIVE ASSISTANCE OR COMFORT** to give assistance or comfort to somebody in difficulty or distress ○ *He supported me throughout the crisis.* **8. CORROBORATE STORY** to give something greater credibility by being consistent with it or providing further evidence for it ○ *There is further evidence that supports the defendant's claim.* **9. ENABLE SOMETHING TO LIVE** to provide sufficient food and water or the appropriate conditions or facilities to enable people or animals to live or allow something to function ○ *A better irrigation system would enable the area to support a larger population.* **10. PROVIDE ASSISTANCE WITH COMPUTER SYSTEM** to provide technical advice and assistance to the users of a product, especially a computing system or package **11.** COMPUT **PERMIT USE OF SOFTWARE OR DEVICES** to be designed to allow something, e.g., a specific type of software, computer device, or programming language, to operate with it ○ *This card cannot support parallel and serial ports.* **12.** ARTS **PLAY SMALL ROLE ALONGSIDE SOMEBODY** to play a subsidiary role alongside an actor with a leading part in a play or movie **13. TOLERATE SOMETHING** to put up with something unpleasant (*formal*) ○ *The Court will not support such behavior.* ■ *n* **1. SOMETHING THAT SUPPORTS** a means of holding something upright or in place, or of preventing it from falling ○ *If you remove those supports the plank will fall down.* **2. REINFORCEMENT TO HOLD THINGS IN PLACE** physical force or reinforcement used to hold things steady or in place ○ *Stakes give the plant extra support.* **3. ACTIVE ASSISTANCE OR ENCOURAGEMENT** active assistance and encouragement to, or an approving and encouraging attitude toward, somebody or something ○ *Support for the cause continues to rise.* **4. HELP IN CRISIS** practical help or sympathy and encouragement received from others, e.g., friends, family, or charitable organizations, especially during times of crisis and change ○ *Without the support of my family, I would not have survived the ordeal.* **5. SUPPORTIVE PERSON OR THING** somebody who or something that provides help, money, encouragement, or comfort **6. GROUP OF SUPPORTERS** the supporters of an organization such as a political party, or of an individual person, considered as a group ○ *His support is drawn mainly from the rural areas.* **7. TECHNICAL ASSISTANCE** technical assistance and advice offered by the manufacturer or supplier of something, especially a computer device or program, to the user **8.** ARTS **SUPPORTING BANDS OR ENTERTAINERS** the other band or bands, or the other entertainers, appearing in a program along with the main attraction [14C. Via French < Latin *supportare* "bear up" < *portare* "carry"] —**sup·port·a·bil·i·ty** /sә pàwrtә bíllәtee/ *n* —**sup·port·a·ble** *adj*—**sup·port·a·bly** *adv* ◇ **in support of** in order to support somebody or something

sup·port ar·e·a *n* an area with a supply of military material and personnel standing ready for use

sup·port·er /sә páwrtәr/ *n* **1. SOMEBODY WHO SUPPORTS SOMETHING** somebody who supports somebody or something, such as a cause, idea, course of action, or political party ○ *greeted by a crowd of supporters* **2.** CLOTHING **SUPPORTING GARMENT** a garment that supports or protects a part of the body, especially one used by male athletes to protect the genitals **3. STANDING FIGURE** either of a pair of standing figures on either side of a shield in a coat of arms

sup·port group *n* a group of people with a problem or concern in common who meet regularly to discuss it and support one another

sup·port hose *npl* elasticized stockings that support the veins in the lower legs, used by people with varicose veins or bad circulation

sup·port·ing /sә páwrting/ *adj* **1.** accompanying and assisting, but secondary to, the main action or the main participants in something ○ *a supporting role in the contract negotiations* **2.** appearing in the same movie, play, or program as the main star or attraction ○ *supporting acts*

sup·por·tive /sә páwrtiv/ *adj* giving support, especially moral or emotional support —**sup·por·tive·ness** *n*

sup·port lev·el *n* the price at which a security whose price has been falling begins to attract investors again because of its intrinsic worth

sup·port stock·ings *npl UK* same as **support hose**

sup·port sys·tem *n* the group of family, friends, colleagues, or professionals available to help a person or organization when required

sup·pose /sә pṓz/ (**-posed, -pos·ing, -pos·es**) *v* **1.** *vti* **BELIEVE TO BE TRUE** to believe or imagine something to be the case ○ *I suppose you haven't heard the news.* **2.** *vi* **IMAGINE AS POSSIBLE** to consider or imagine something to be a possibility ○ *Suppose that he doesn't know about your plan.* **3.** *vt* **MAKE SOMETHING A PRECONDITION** to require something as a precondition ○ *Your plan supposes that there are enough presents to go around.* **4.** *vt* **INDICATING TENTATIVENESS** used to indicate real or polite hesitancy when making a statement, suggestion, or request ○ *Well, I suppose I'd better be going.* ○ *I don't suppose you could lend me the $50, could you?* **5.** *vti* **USED TO SHOW RELUCTANT AGREEMENT** used when agreeing to do something, or agreeing that something is the case, to show that you do so reluctantly, uncertainly, or noncommittally ○ *"You know it's the right thing to do, don't you?" – "I suppose so."* ○ *All right, I suppose I can just about manage it.* [14C. < French *supposer*, alteration of Latin *supponere* (see SUPPOSITION) after French *poser* "to place"] —**sup·pos·a·ble** *adj* —**sup·pos·er** *n* ◇ **be supposed to do something 1.** to be expected to do something as the result of a previous agreement or arrangement, or an obligation ○ *You were supposed to wait for me here.* **2.** to be expected to do something as the result of an action or set of conditions ○ *The light's supposed to come on when the tank is empty.* ◇ **be not supposed to do something** to be not allowed or not expected to do something ○ *You weren't supposed to tell anyone that!* ○ *Surely it's not supposed to make a noise like that.*

sup·posed /sә pṓzd, -pṓzәd/ *adj* accepted, at least by some, as correct, real, or having a quality, but on slender or uncertain evidence ○ *Frankly, I'm very dubious about this supposed brilliant idea of his.*

sup·pos·ed·ly /sә pṓzәdlee/ *adv* as some people believe, or as people were led to believe ○ *He was supposedly going to pick us up after work.* ○ *a supposedly instant remedy*

sup·pos·ing /sә pṓzing/ *conj* imagining or assuming something to be the case ○ *Supposing she comes, will you let her in?*

sup·po·si·tion /sùppә zísh'n/ *n* **1.** something that it is suggested might be true, or that is accepted as true on the basis of some evidence but without proof ○ *That seems a reasonable supposition on the basis of his previous behavior.* **2.** the mental act of supposing something to be the case, or ideas that result from supposing, especially as opposed to ideas based on firm evidence ○ *All this is mere supposition.* [Late 16C. Directly or via French < Latin *supposition-* < *supposit-*, past participle of *supponere* "place under" < *ponere* "to place"] —**sup·po·si·tion·al** *adj* —**sup·po·si·tion·al·ly** *adv*

sup·po·si·tious /sùppә zíshәss/ *adj* based on supposition rather than firm evidence or proof (*formal*)

sup·pos·i·ti·tious /sә pòzzә tíshәss/ *adj* substituted for something else in order to deceive (*formal*) [Early 17C. < Latin *supposititius* < *supposit-* (see SUPPOSITION)] —**sup·pos·i·ti·tious·ly** *adv*

sup·pos·i·tive /sә pózzәtiv/ *adj* expressing or relating to supposition, or introducing a clause expressing a supposition ■ *n* a conjunction that introduces a clause expressing a supposition, e.g., "if," "provided that," or "supposing"

sup·pos·i·to·ry /sә pózzә tàwree/ (*plural* **-ries**) *n* a medicated mass that melts at body temperature, designed to be inserted into the rectum, vagina, or urethra [14C. < medieval Latin *suppositorium* < Latin *supposit-* (see SUPPOSITION)]

sup·press /sә préss/ (**-pressed, -press·ing, -press·es**) *vt* **1. CAUSE TO STOP** to put an end to something, especially something perceived as a threat, by the use of force or a prohibition ○ *suppressed all complaints with a gag order* **2. PREVENT SOMETHING** to prevent something from happening, operating, or becoming apparent, or restrain something and limit its effects ○ *Some slimming drugs are designed to suppress appetite.* ○ *Her voice shook with suppressed anger.* **3. STOP SPREAD OR PUBLICATION** to prevent information or evidence from becoming known, or written material from being published ○ *The report was suppressed for political reasons.* **4.** PSYCHOL **RESIST SOMETHING CONSCIOUSLY** to resist thoughts or feelings consciously as they arise, and try to banish them from the mind **5.** ELECTRONICS **DIMINISH OSCILLATION** to reduce unwanted noise or oscillation in a circuit or unwanted frequencies in a signal **6.** BIOL **REDUCE BODILY FUNCTION** to cause the reduction or cessation of a normal bodily function such as menstruation or growth, or undergo such a reduction or cessation **7.** GENETICS **INHIBIT GENE EFFECT** to cancel or reverse the effects of a gene [14C. < Latin *suppress-*, past participle of *supprimere* "push down" < *premere* "press"] —**sup·pres·ser** *n* —**sup·press·i·bil·i·ty** /sә prèssә bíllәtee/ *n* —**sup·press·i·ble** *adj*

sup·pres·sant /sә préss'nt/ *n* a substance, medication, or activity that restrains or limits the effects of something (*often used in combination*) ○ *an appetite suppressant*

sup·pres·sion /sə présh'n/ *n* **1. FORCEFUL PREVENTION** conscious and forceful action to put an end to something, destroy it, or prevent it from becoming known **2. STATE OF CONSTRAINT** the state of being forcefully restrained or held back **3.** PSYCHOL **AVOIDANCE OF THOUGHTS AND FEELINGS** conscious avoidance or inhibition of memories, desires, or thoughts **4.** ELECTRONICS **DIMINISHING OF OSCILLATION** reduction of unwanted noise or oscillation in a circuit or of unwanted frequencies in a signal **5.** BIOL **DEVELOPMENTAL FAILURE** the failure of an organ, tissue, or part to develop **6.** PHYSIOL **CESSATION OF BODY FUNCTION** the reduction or stoppage of a normal bodily function such as secretion or excretion **7.** MED **REMOVAL OF SYMPTOMS** the lessening or abolition of a symptom or the outward signs of a disease **8.** GENETICS **REVERSAL OF MUTATION** the cancellation or reversal of the effect of a gene, especially of one genetic mutation by another

sup·pres·sive /sə préssiv/ *adj* having the effect of suppressing something —**sup·pres·sive·ly** *adv*

sup·pres·sor /sə préssər/ *n* **1.** a gene that prevents the expression of another gene **2.** a device that reduces unwanted interference or current in a circuit

sup·pres·sor T cell, sup·pres·sor cell *n* a T cell that diminishes or suppresses the immune response to an antigen of B cells and other T cells

sup·pu·rate /súppyə ràyt/ (**-rat·ed, -rat·ing, -rates**) *vi* to produce or discharge pus as a result of an injury or infection [Mid-16C. < Latin *suppurat-*, past participle of *suppurare* < *pus* "pus"] —**sup·pu·ra·tion** /sùppyə ráysh'n/ *n* —**sup·pu·ra·tive** *adj*

su·pra /sóoprə/ *adv* used in formal writing to refer the reader back to something at an earlier point in the same text (*formal*) [Early 16C. < Latin, "above, beyond"]

supra- *prefix* **1.** over, on top of ○ *suprarenal* **2.** transcending ○ *supranational* [< Latin *supra* "above, beyond"]

su·pra·chi·as·mat·ic nu·cle·us /sóoprə kī əz màttik-/ *n* an area in the front part of the hypothalamus, on the underside of the brain, responsible for maintaining the circadian rhythm

su·pra·lap·sar·i·an /sóoprə lap sáiree ən/ *n* in Christianity, somebody who believes that prior to the general fall of humanity God preordained the salvation of some souls [Mid-17C. < SUPRA- + Latin *lapsus* "sin, falling" (see LAPSE)] —**su·pra·lap·sar·i·an·ism** *n*

su·pra·lim·i·nal /sóoprə límmən'l/ *adj* at or above the threshold of consciousness —**sup·ra·lim·i·nal·ly** *adv*

su·pra·mo·lec·u·lar /sóoprə mə lékyələr/ *adj* **1.** more complex in form than a molecule **2.** composed of more than one molecule

su·pra·na·tion·al /sóoprə náshən'l, -náshnəl/ *adj* not limited by the concerns or boundaries of a single nation —**su·pra·na·tion·al·ism** *n* —**su·pra·na·tion·al·ly** *adv*

su·pra·or·bi·tal /sóoprə áwrbət'l/ *adj* located above the bony socket (**orbit**) of the eye

su·pra·re·nal /sóoprə réen'l/ *adj* located above the kidneys

su·pra·seg·men·tal /sóoprə seg mént'l/ *adj* in phonetics, connected with features of speech such as pitch and stress that accompany rather than constitute phonemes —**su·pra·seg·men·tal·ly** *adv*

su·prem·a·cist /sə prémməssist, soo-/ *n* somebody who believes that a group is innately superior to others and therefore is entitled to dominate them (*usually used in combination*)

su·prem·a·cy /sə prémməssee, soo-/ *n* a position of superiority or authority over all others [Mid-16C. < SUPREME, after PRIMACY]

su·prem·a·tism /sə prémmə tìzzəm, soo-/ *n* a school of cubist painting from early 20th-century Russia [Mid-20C. < Russian *suprematizm* < French *suprématie* "supremacy"] —**su·prem·a·tist** *n*

su·preme /sə préem, soo-/ *adj* **1. ABOVE ALL OTHERS** greater than or superior to any other, especially above all others in power, authority, rank, status, or skill ○ *holding supreme authority* ○ *In women's long-distance running, she still reigns supreme.* **2. HIGHEST IN DEGREE** of the greatest or most admirable kind ○ *a supreme example of the architect's skill* **3. ULTIMATE** greater than any that have gone before, or the greatest possible ○ *the supreme sacrifice* **4. IN HIGHEST DEGREE** in the highest degree or of the most unmitigated kind ○ *viewed them with supreme contempt* [15C. < Latin *supremus* "uppermost" < *superus* "upper" < *super* "over, above"] —**su·preme·ly** *adv*

su·prême /sə prém, soo-/ *adj* served with a suprême sauce ○ *chicken suprême* [Early 19C. < French, "supreme"]

Su·preme Be·ing *n* RELIG same as **God**

su·preme com·man·der *n* a military commander in charge of all allied forces in a theater of war or in a coalition such as NATO

Su·preme Court *n* **1. HIGHEST COURT** the highest federal court, consisting of nine justices appointed by the President with the advice and consent of Congress and making decisions solely on constitutional matters **2. HIGHEST STATE COURT** the highest appellate court in many states of the United States **3. HIGHEST COURT IN COUNTRY** the highest court in a country, or in a state or territory of a federation

su·prême sauce *n* a rich sauce made of chicken or veal stock with added cream and egg yolks

Su·preme So·vi·et *n* the two-chamber national legislature of the former Soviet Union, or a similar legislature in any one of the former Soviet republics

~~**supress**~~ incorrect spelling of **suppress**

~~**suprise**~~ incorrect spelling of **surprise**

supt., Supt. *abbr* superintendent

supvr. *abbr* supervisor

suq *n* COMM another spelling of **souk**

Su·qua·mish /sə kwáamish, skwáamish/ (*plural* **-mish·es** or *same*) *n* **1.** a member of a Native North American people who live along the Puget Sound in Washington State **2.** the Salish language of the Suquamish people [Mid-19C. < Salish] —**Su·qua·mish** *adj*

Sur. *abbr* Suriname

sur- *prefix* **1.** over, above, on top of ○ *surprint* **2.** additional, extra ○ *surcharge* [Via French < Latin *super* "over, above"]

su·ra /sóorə/ *n* a chapter of the Koran [Early 17C. < Arabic *sūra*]

Su·ra·ba·ya /sóorə bī́ ə/ city on northeastern Java Island, Indonesia. Population: 2,351,303 (1997).

su·rah /sóorə/ *n* a twilled silk or rayon fabric. Use: women's clothing. [Late 19C. Anglicization of French *surat* "Surat," port in W India]

su·ral /sóorəl/ *adj* relating to the calf of the leg (*technical*) [Early 17C. < Latin *sura* "calf of the leg"]

Su·rat /sòo rát, sóorət/ city, port, and administrative headquarters of Surat District, Gujarat State, western India. Population: 2,811,466 (2001).

sur·base /súr bàyss/ *n* an architectural molding at the top of a base such as a pedestal or baseboard —**sur·base·ment** /sur báyssmənt/ *n*

sur·based /sur báyst/ *adj* describes an arch with a rise of less than half its span [Mid-18C. < French *surbaissé* "flattened" < *baisser* "to lower" < medieval Latin *bassus* "low"]

sur·cease /sər séess, súr sèess/ *vti* (**-ceased, -ceas·ing, -ceas·es**) to cease, or bring something to an end (*formal*) ■ *n* a cessation, especially a temporary one (*literary*) [15C. < Anglo-Norman *surseser* "refrain" < Latin *supersedere* (see SUPERSEDE); influenced by CEASE]

sur·charge /súr chaàrj/ *v* (**-charged, -charg·ing, -charg·es**) **1.** *vti* **CHARGE EXTRA** to add an additional charge to the amount somebody has to pay **2.** *vti* **OVERCHARGE** to charge somebody too much for something **3.** *vt* **MAKE SOMEBODY RESPONSIBLE FOR REPAYMENT** to make somebody repay from personal funds any losses stemming from negligent or intentional mismanagement of a fiduciary responsibility **4.** *vt* **RAISE STAMP VALUE** to overprint an existing postage stamp so as to increase its face value **5.** *vt* **OVERBURDEN SOMEBODY OR SOMETHING** to place too great a load on somebody or in or on something, e.g., a ship (*literary*) ■ *n* **1. EXTRA CHARGE** an excess or extra charge **2. MARK ON STAMP** a mark on a postage stamp increasing its face value [15C. < Old French *surcharger* < *charger* "to charge" (see CHARGE)] —**sur·charg·er** *n*

sur·cin·gle /súr sing g'l/ *n* a broad band fastened around the body of a horse to hold a rug or pack in place [14C. < Old French *surcengle*, literally "belt over" < *cengle* "belt, girdle" < Latin *cingulum* (see CINGULUM)]

surcoat

sur·coat /súr kōt/ *n* **1.** a short tunic worn over armor in medieval times **2.** a short sleeveless garment worn as part of the ceremonial costume of an order of knighthood [14C. < Old French *surcote* "overcoat" < *cote* "coat"]

surd /surd/ *n* **1.** in mathematics, an irrational root or irrational number, or an expression containing one or the other **2.** a consonant pronounced without vibration of the vocal cords [Mid-16C. < Latin *surdus* "unable to hear or speak"]

sure /shoor/ *adj* (**sur·er, sur·est**) **1. DEFINITELY TRUE** unquestionably true or real and not in doubt ○ *One thing is sure, we'll never make the same mistake again!* **2. FIRMLY BELIEVING** believing strongly and for a good reason, or knowing for a fact, that something is true or the case ○ *Are you sure that she understood you?* **3. BOUND TO OCCUR** inevitably going to do something or to happen, or confidently expected to be going to do something or to happen ○ *He's sure to notice that something's missing.* **4. CERTAIN TO OBTAIN SOMETHING** definitely able to or definitely going to obtain or achieve something ○ *Many people book early in order to be sure of the best seats.* **5. VERY CONFIDENT** very confident about something, especially personal beliefs or abilities ○ *It was her self-confidence that made her so sure of her answer.* **6. ALWAYS EFFECTIVE** effective, accurate, and reliable at all times ○ *His aggressive manner is a sure sign that he is frightened.* **7. FIRM AND SECURE** firm, secure, and steady ○ *The fad had gained a sure hold on every teenager.* **8. UNERRING** showing both confidence and competence ○ *a sure grasp of the complexities of the situation* **9. DEPENDABLE** able to be safely relied on ○ *a sure friend in times of trouble* ■ *adv* (*informal*) **1.** US **UNDOUBTEDLY** used to give emphasis to something that somebody is saying and to indicate that somebody does not expect anyone to disagree with it ○ *This sure tastes good.* **2. YES** used to indicate emphatic or enthusiastic assent ○ *I asked him if he'd like to come and he said, "Sure!"* [14C. Via French < Latin *securus* (see SECURE)] —**sure·ness** *n* ◇ **be sure and do** *or* **to do something** used to tell somebody to remember to do something ○ *Be sure and introduce us.* ◇ **for sure 1.** without a doubt, or inevitably (*informal*) ○ *He seems ideal for the job, he'll get it for sure.* **2.** definitely and precisely ○ *He couldn't say for sure what time he'd be home* ◇ **make sure (that) 1.** to check that something is the case, or that something has been done as instructed or requested ○ *We have to assess our market to try to make sure our products are competitive.* **2.** to take the necessary action to have something done or make something happen ○ *Could you make sure that he's in bed before ten?* ◇ **sure enough** as was expected ○ *He had a reputation for punctuality, and, sure enough, as the clock struck eight, he appeared.* ◇ **sure of yourself** extremely confident ◇ **to be sure** used when admitting or agreeing that something is true, even though it may not agree with most of what you are saying ○ *He's* *charming, to be sure, but I still don't trust his motives.*

USAGE The use of *sure* as an adverbial intensifier, as in the sentence *We sure are glad to see you!* is characteristic of informal US usage; its use in formal writing is inappropriate.

sure-fire *adj* always successful or effective (*informal*)

sure-foot·ed *adj* **1.** skilled and confident in moving or climbing, and so unlikely to stumble or fall **2.** confident and competent, and so unlikely to err —**sure-foot·ed·ly** *adv* —**sure-foot·ed·ness** *n*

sure·ly /shŏorlee/ *adv* **1.** USED TO INVITE RESPONSE used as a means of getting somebody to confirm, deny, agree, or disagree with something being said, by adding in an element of challenging self-assurance or considerable hesitancy ○ *Surely you've met before.* **2.** WITHOUT FAIL definitely or unavoidably ○ *slowly but surely* **3.** WITHOUT DOUBT without a doubt or without fail ○ *Did he get his message across? He surely did.* **4.** *Southern US* **YES** used to show ready agreement

sure thing (*informal*) *n* something that can be relied on to happen or to be successful ■ *adv* used to express assent, agreement, or willingness to do something

sur·e·ty /shŏorətee/ (*plural* **-ties**) *n* **1.** somebody who pledges that another's obligations will be met in case of default **2.** the condition or quality of being sure (*formal*) [14C. Via Old French *surete* < Latin *securitas* < *securus* (see SECURE)] —**sur·e·ty·ship** *n*

surf: a surfer rides a wave at La Jolla Beach, California

surf /surf/ *n* FOAMY WAVES the lines of foamy waves that break on a seashore or reef ○ *play in the surf* ■ *v* (**surfed, surf·ing, surfs**) **1.** *vi* USE SURFBOARD to ride waves on a surfboard **2.** *vt* RIDE WAVES IN PARTICULAR AREA to go surfing in a particular place ○ *Have you surfed Waikiki?* **3.** *vti* ONLINE SEARCH MEDIUM FOR ENTERTAINMENT to go on the Internet or watch television for recreation, education, or entertainment, frequently changing the site or channel [Late 17C. Origin ?] —**surf·a·ble** *adj* —**surf·er** *n* —**surf·ing** *n* —**surf·y** *adj* ◇ **surf's up** *US* used to indicate that it is time to start doing something (*slang*)

sur·face /súrfəss/ *n* (*plural* **-fac·es**) **1.** OUTER PART the outermost or uppermost part of a thing, the one that is usually presented to the outside world, and can be seen and touched **2.** UPPER PART OF EARTH, SEA, WATER the part of the Earth, the sea, or any water that meets the atmosphere **3.** SOLID FLAT AREA a solid flat area, e.g., a countertop or the top of a piece of furniture, especially an area on which it is suitable to work **4.** THIN APPLIED OUTER LAYER a relatively thin outer layer or coating applied to something, usually to give it a smooth finish ○ *a nonstick surface* **5.** SUPERFICIAL PART the easily visible or apparent parts or aspects of something or somebody, or those that somebody or something chooses to display to the world, especially when contrasted with the actual reality of the person or thing ○ *This surface of cool composure concealed a passionate heart.* **6.** MATH TWO-DIMENSIONAL EXTENT a flat or curved continuous area definable in two dimensions ○ *the surface of a sphere* ■ *adj* **1.** USED ON SURFACE occurring or used on, or relating to, the surface of something ○ *surface lubricants* **2.** APPARENT apparent, but not real, deep-seated, or well-founded, or put on for effect or to deceive and not natural or deeply felt ○ *surface affection* ○ *The plan has surface appeal.* **3.** ON LAND OR SEA operating or transported over land or sea but not in the air ○ *surface transport* **4.** NOT SUBMARINE operating on the surface of the water, as opposed to being submersible ○ *surface ships* ■ *v* (**-faced, -fac·ing, -fac·es**) **1.** *vi* COME TO TOP to come to or appear at the surface, especially of water ○ *She surfaced after a dive of 20 minutes.* **2.** *vi* APPEAR to reappear after being hidden or out of reach for a time ○ *She surfaced in Berlin after the war.* **3.** *vi* BECOME KNOWN to become apparent or known ○ *The information surfaced during a routine investigation.* **4.** *vt* GIVE SURFACE TO SOMETHING to provide something with a surface, especially with a smooth outer layer ○ *surfacing the road* **5.** *vt* TREAT SURFACE to treat the surface of something, especially in order to smooth or perfect it **6.** *vi* WORK NEAR TOP to mine at or near the Earth's surface [Early 17C. < French < *sur-* "upon" + *face* (see FACE), after Latin *superficies*] —**sur·fac·er** *n* ◇ **on the surface** to outward appearances or when examined superficially ○ *appears cool and collected on the surface* ◇ **scratch the surface** to deal with only a very small or relatively unimportant part of something

sur·face-ac·tive *adj* having the property of reducing the surface tension of a liquid so that the liquid spreads out, rather than collecting in droplets

sur·face lift *n* a ski lift that carries skiers uphill while they are standing on their skis

sur·face mail *n* mail that is transported by sea or land, as opposed to by air

sur·face noise *n* noise produced as a phonograph stylus travels over a revolving record, caused by friction, dust, scratches, or static electricity on the record

sur·face run-off *n* the flow of water over the surface of the ground occurring when rainfall is not absorbed into the soil or evaporated

sur·face struc·ture *n* in some types of grammar, a representation of the sequence of syntactic elements that constitute an actual phrase or sentence

sur·face ten·sion *n* the property of liquids that gives their surfaces a slightly elastic quality and enables them to form into separate drops. It is caused by the interaction of molecules at or near the surface that tend to cohere and contract the surface into the smallest possible area. Symbol γ, σ

sur·face-to-air *adj* launched from a ship or from the ground against a target in the air ○ *surface-to-air missiles*

sur·face-to-sur·face *adj* launched from a ship or from the ground against another ship or a target on the ground ○ *a surface-to-surface missile*

sur·fac·tant /sur fáktənt/ *n* **1.** an agent that reduces the surface tension of liquids so that the liquid spreads out, rather than collecting in droplets, e.g., a detergent or a drug **2.** a surface-active lipoprotein substance secreted naturally in the lungs, lack of which causes respiratory problems especially in premature babies [Mid-20C. < SURFACE + ACTIVE]

surf and turf *n* a meal, menu, or dish including both seafood and meat, especially steak and lobster

sur·fa·ri /sur faaree/ (*plural* **-ris**) *n* a vacation or trip specially organized for surfers [Mid-20C. Alteration of SAFARI after SURF]

surf·bird /súrf bùrd/ *n* a winter shorebird with dark spotted feathers and a black tail with a white base. Native to: Pacific coasts of North and South America. Latin name: *Aphriza virgata*. [< its being found among wave-washed rocks along the shoreline]

surf·board /súrf bàwrd/ *n* a long narrow board, with a rounded or pointed front end, on which a surfer stands while riding waves —**surf·board·er** *n* —**surf·board·ing** *n*

surf·boat /súrf bōt/ *n* a light sturdy boat, often with a raised prow and stern and buoyancy chambers, suitable for use in high surf

surf·cast·ing /súrf kàsting/ *n* a method of fishing in which a baited line is tossed into the surf from the shore or a boat —**surf·cast·er** *n*

surf clam *n* a large edible clam inhabiting the surf of coastal waters. Family: Mactridae.

surf duck *n* BIRDS same as **surf scoter**

sur·feit /súrfət/ *n* **1.** EXCESSIVE NUMBER an excessive number or quantity of something, especially so much of it that people become sickened, repelled, or bored by it **2.** OVERINDULGENCE overindulgence, or a bout of overindulgence, in something, especially food or drink **3.** DISGUST OR REVULSION disgust or revulsion resulting from overindulgence (*literary*) ■ *vt* (**-feit·ed, -feit·ing, -feits**) GIVE SOMEBODY SURFEIT to give somebody a surfeit of something [13C. < Old French, past participle of *surfaire* "overdo" < *faire* "do" (see AFFAIR)] —**sur·feit·er** *n*

Surf·ers Par·a·dise /sùrfərz párrə dīss/ coastal town in southeastern Queensland, Australia. It is a major tourist resort, and the center of the Gold Coast region. Population: 4,141 (1991).

surf fish *n* FISH same as **surfperch**

sur·fi·cial /sur físh'l/ *adj* relating to or occurring on a surface, especially the surface of the Earth [Late 19C. Blend of SURFACE + SUPERFICIAL]

surf·perch /súrf pùrch/ (*plural* **-perch·es** or *same*) *n* a bony fish resembling a perch. Native to: North American Pacific coasts. Family: Embiotocidae.

surf sco·ter *n* a large ocean duck, the male of which is mostly black with white patches on its head. Native to: North America. Latin name: *Melanitta perspicillata*.

surg. *abbr* **1.** surgeon **2.** surgery **3.** surgical

surge /surj/ *vi* (**surged, surg·ing, surg·es**) **1.** MOVE LIKE WAVES to move in or like a wave, rising up and subsiding and sweeping forward or back ○ *The boat surged in the rising swell.* **2.** MAKE CONCERTED RUSH to move in a body, especially to make a sudden concerted rush in a particular direction ○ *The crowd surged toward the exit.* **3.** INCREASE SUDDENLY to increase strongly and suddenly **4.** NAUT SLIP WHILE BEING TURNED to slip while being turned on a capstan or windlass (*refers to ropes and cables*) ■ *n* **1.** LARGE MOTION a powerful rising and falling, or forward rushing movement, like that of the sea **2.** BURST OF FEELING a sudden, intense experience of an emotion, especially one that seems to rush through somebody like a wave ○ *a surge of anger* **3.** SUDDEN INCREASE a sudden increase in something, often one that is relatively short-lived ○ *a surge in demand* **4.** POWER INCREASE a sudden and temporary increase in electrical current or voltage **5.** ASTRON ENERGETIC SOLAR PROMINENCE an energetic solar prominence lasting for several minutes, which accompanies a solar flare **6.** NAUT SLIP OF ROPE a sudden slipping or slackening of a rope or cable on a boat or ship [Early 16C. < French *surgir* "rise up," *sourge-*, stem of *sourdre* "spring up," both < Latin *surgere* "rise up from below"] —**surg·er** *n*

sur·geon /súrjən/ *n* **1.** a doctor specializing in operations that involve gaining access to the patient's body, e.g., by making incisions into it, in order to correct faults, repair injuries, or treat diseases **2.** a medical officer in the armed services or on board a ship [14C. Via Anglo-Norman < Old French *cirurgien* < *cirurgie* (see SURGERY)]

sur·geon·fish /súrjən fish/ (*plural same* or **-fish·es**) *n* a tropical fish that is often brightly colored and has spines at the base of its tail that it uses to inflict wounds. Family: Acanthuridae. [< an imagined resemblance of its spines to a surgeon's needle]

sur·geon gen·er·al (*plural* **sur·geons gen·er·al**) *n* **1.** the chief medical officer in many branches of the military service **2.** the cabinet-level chief public health officer of the United States, or the chief public health officer of some individual states

sur·geon's knot *n* a surgical knot of a type that can be relied on to remain tight

surge pro·tec·tor *n* an electrical device designed to protect a computer against the harmful effects of power surges and spikes and sudden outages

sur·ger·y /súrjəree/ (*plural* **-ies**) *n* **1.** MEDICAL PROCEDURES INVOLVING OPERATIONS medical treatment that involves operations on or manipulations of the patient's body and, usually, cutting the body open to perform these **2.** BRANCH OF MEDICINE the branch of medicine that deals with diseases and conditions treated by operation or manipulation, or the range of diseases treated in this way **3.** SURGEON'S ART OR ACTIVITY the art or activity of performing surgery **4.** OPERATING ROOM a hospital or clinic room where surgery is performed **5.** *UK* DOCTOR'S OFFICE a doctor's, dentist's, or veterinarian's office [14C. Via Old French *cirurgerie* < Greek *kheirourgia* "working with the hands" < *kheir* "hand" + *ergon* "work"]

sur·gi·cal /súrjik'l/ *adj* **1.** OF SURGERY relating to or accomplished by surgery ○ *surgical removal of warts* **2.** RESULTING FROM SURGERY as a result of of surgery ○ *surgical scar* **3.** PRECISE like surgery in requiring or being characterized by great skill or great precision ○ *surgical strikes* [Late 18C. Alteration (after SURGEON) of French *cirurgical* < *cirurgien* "surgeon" < *cirurgie* (see SURGERY)] —**sur·gi·cal·ly** *adv*

Su·ri·ba·chi, Mount /sŏŏrə baáchee/ *n* hill on Iwo Jima, site of the raising of the US flag by US Marines during World War II on February 23, 1945

su·ri·cate /sŏŏrə kàyt/ *n* ZOOL same as **meerkat** [Late 18C. Via French < obsolete Dutch *surikat*]

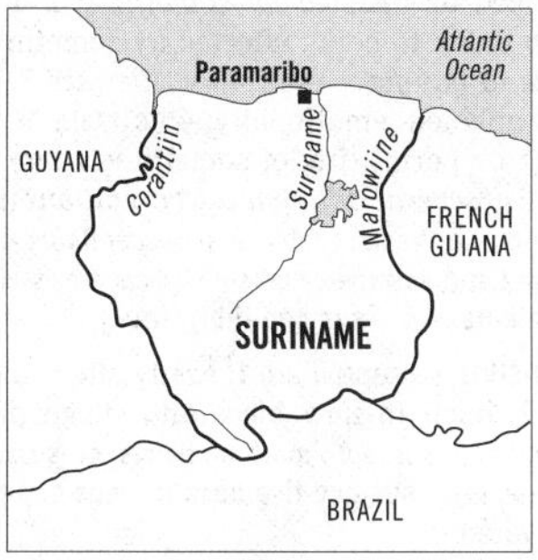

Suriname

Su·ri·na·me /sŏŏri naámə, sŏŏrə nàm/ country in northeastern South America, north of Brazil, on the Atlantic Ocean. Language: Dutch. Currency: Suriname guilder. Capital: Paramaribo. Population: 435,449 (2003). Area: 63,037 sq. mi./163,265 sq. km. Official name **Republic of Suriname**. Former name **Dutch Guiana** (until 1948) —**Su·ri·na·mese** /sŏŏrə na meéz, -meéss/ *n, adj*

Su·ri·na·me toad *n* AMPHIB same as **pipa**[1]

sur·jec·tion /sur jéksh'n/ *n* a mathematical function for which each element of a set is the image of at least one element of another set [Mid-20C. < SUR-, after INJECTION] —**sur·jec·tive** *adj*

sur·ly /súrlee/ (**-li·er, -li·est**) *adj* bad-tempered, unfriendly, rude, and somewhat threatening ○ *a person with a surly manner* [Late 16C. Alteration of obsolete *sirly* "lordly, imperious" < SIR] —**sur·li·ness** *n*

sur·mise /sur mī́z/ *vti* (**-mised, -mis·ing, -mis·es**) to conclude that something is the case on the basis of only limited evidence or intuitive feeling ■ *n* a conclusion drawn on only limited evidence or intuitive feeling [Early 16C. < Anglo-Norman *surmis*, past participle of *surmettre* "accuse," literally "put over" < Latin *mittere* "send"] —**sur·mis·a·ble** *adj* —**sur·mis·er** *n*

sur·mount /sur mównt/ (**-mount·ed, -mount·ing, -mounts**) *vt* **1.** OVERCOME DIFFICULTY to deal with a difficulty successfully **2.** GET TO TOP OF SOMETHING to get over the top of a physical obstacle (*formal*) **3.** BE PLACED ATOP SOMETHING to be positioned on top of something or rise above it (*formal*) ○ *the statues surmounting the parapet* **4.** PUT SOMETHING ATOP SOMETHING ELSE to place something on top of or above something (*formal*) ○ *surmount the parapet with a row of statues* [14C. < French *surmonter* "climb over" < *monter* "mount" (see MOUNT[1])] —**sur·mount·a·bil·i·ty** /sur mòwntə bílləte e/ *n* —**sur·mount·a·ble** *adj* —**sur·mount·er** *n*

sur·mul·let /sur múllət/ (*plural* **-lets** or *same*) *n* US FISH same as **goatfish** [Late 17C. < French *surmulet* < Old French *sor* "red, brown" + *mulet* (see MULLET)]

sur·name /súr nàym/ *n* **1.** SOMEBODY'S FAMILY NAME the name that identifies somebody as belonging to a particular family and that he or she has in common with other members of that family **2.** DESCRIPTIVE ADDITION TO NAME a descriptive addition to somebody's name e.g., "the Great" in "Catherine the Great" (*archaic*) ■ *vt* (**-named, -nam·ing, -names**) GIVE SOMEBODY SURNAME to give or transmit a surname to somebody (*usually passive*) [14C. Translation of Old French *surnom*, literally "name above" < *nom* "name"] —**sur·nam·er** *n*

~~**suround**~~ incorrect spelling of **surround**

sur·pass /sur páss/ (**-passed, -pass·ing, -pass·es**) *vt* **1.** EXCEED EXPECTATIONS to go beyond what was expected or hoped for, usually by being bigger, better, or greater **2.** DO BETTER THAN SOMEBODY OR SOMETHING to be bigger, greater, better, or worse than somebody or something else **3.** BE BEYOND SOMEBODY'S ABILITY to be beyond somebody's ability to deal with or understand (*formal*) [Mid-16C. < French *surpasser* "transgress," literally "pass beyond" < *passer* (see PASS)] —**sur·pass·a·ble** *adj*

sur·pass·ing /sur pássing/ *adj* of a quality far superior to others (*literary*) ○ *a view of surpassing beauty* —**sur·pass·ing·ly** *adv*

sur·plice /súrpləss/ *n* a white ecclesiastical outer garment like a smock, with wide, often flared sleeves, and varying in length [13C. Via Anglo-Norman *surpliz* < medieval Latin *superpellicium* "(vestment worn) over a fur garment" < *pellicium* "fur coat"]

sur·plus /súrpləss/ *n* **1.** EXCESS AMOUNT an amount remaining after the original purpose has been served or the original requirement met **2.** EXCESS MONEY an amount of money remaining after all liabilities have been met ○ *The government is predicting a trade surplus this year.* **3.** ACCT EXTRA WORTH the amount by which the net worth of a company's assets exceeds the value of its owned stock ■ *adj* ADDITIONAL TO REQUIREMENTS not required to meet existing needs, or left over after these have been met ○ *surplus clothing* ○ *be surplus to requirements* [14C. Via Anglo-Norman < medieval Latin *superplus*, literally "more beyond" < Latin *plus* "more"]

sur·plus·age /súrpləssij/ *n* **1.** LAW IRRELEVANT MATTER an irrelevant matter introduced into legal proceedings **2.** VERBIAGE redundant words or arguments (*formal*) **3.** SURPLUS an excess of something (*formal*)

sur·plus val·ue *n* in Marxist economic theory, the difference between the price of a product produced by labor and the value of labor itself in terms of the wages paid to workers

sur·print /súr prìnt/ PRINTING *vt* (**-print·ed, -print·ing, -prints**) same as **overprint** ■ *n* same as **overprint** *n* (sense 1)

sur·prise /sər prī́z/ *vt* (**-prised, -pris·ing, -pris·es**) **1.** MAKE SOMEBODY AMAZED to cause somebody to feel sudden wonder or amazement, especially at something unexpected (*often passive*) ○ *I'm surprised that nobody's thought of this before.* ○ *It doesn't really surprise me that nobody accepted the offer.* **2.** CATCH SOMEBODY OR SOMETHING UNAWARE to attack, come upon, or catch somebody or something unexpectedly ○ *I surprised a huge raccoon going through the garbage last night.* **3.** GIVE SOMEBODY SOMETHING UNEXPECTEDLY to make an unexpected gift to somebody ○ *surprised me with flowers* **4.** TRICK SOMEBODY INTO DOING SOMETHING to cause somebody to do something, especially to admit something, unexpected by trickery or deceit ○ *Her boss surprised her into admitting she left work early every day.* ■ *n* **1.** AMAZEMENT a feeling of shock, wonder, or bewilderment produced by an unexpected event ○ *Imagine my surprise when she told me she was already married.* **2.** SOMETHING UNEXPECTED something that produces a feeling of surprise, especially an unexpected event or gift (*often used before a noun*) ○ *He told me he had a surprise for me, but I haven't seen it yet.* ○ *a surprise visit* **3.** ABILITY TO CAUSE SURPRISE the fact of happening unexpectedly or the ability to take somebody unawares ○ *We don't want to lose the element of surprise.* [15C. < French, past participle of *surprendre* "overtake" < *sur-* "over" + Latin *prehendere* "seize"] —**sur·prised** *adj* —**sur·pris·er** *n* —**sur·pris·ing** *adj* —**sur·pris·ing·ly** *adv* ◇ **surprise, surprise!** (*informal*) **1.** used when making a surprise announcement or presenting something that is supposed to be a surprise **2.** used ironically to suggest that something is anything but unexpected ○ *Well, surprise, surprise, the weather forecasters got it wrong again.* ◇ **take somebody by surprise** to happen unexpectedly to somebody ○ *Their arrival took everybody by surprise.*

~~**surprize**~~ incorrect spelling of **surprise**

surr. *abbr* surrender

sur·ra /sŏŏrə, súrrə/ *n* a tropical disease similar to sleeping sickness that affects camels and horses, and occasionally cattle and dogs. It is caused by a protozoan but transmitted by biting flies. [Late 19C. < Marathi *sūra* "air breathed through the nostrils"]

sur·re·al /sə reé əl/ *adj* weirdly unfamiliar, distorted, or disturbing, like the experiences in a dream or the objects or experiences depicted in surrealism ■ *n* the bizarre or unreal qualities associated with surrealism [Mid-20C. Back-formation < SURREALISM] —**sur·re·al·ly** *adv*

sur·re·al·ism /sə reé ə lìzzəm/ *n* **1.** an early 20th-century movement in art and literature that tried to represent the subconscious mind by creating fantastic imagery and juxtaposing ideas that seem to contradict each other **2.** surreal art or literature [Early 20C. < French *surréalisme* "beyond realism"] —**sur·re·al·ist** *n, adj* —**sur·re·al·is·tic** /sə reè ə lístik/ *adj* —**sur·re·al·is·ti·cal·ly** *adv*

sur·re·but·tal /sùrri bútt'l/ *n* in a civil court action, an act of giving evidence to support the third reply (**surrebutter**) of the person bringing the action (**plaintiff**)

sur·re·but·ter /sùrri búttər/ *n* in a civil court action, the third reply of the person bringing the action (**plaintiff**), in response to the defendant's third statement (**rebutter**) [Late 16C. < REBUTTER, after SURREJOINDER]

sur·re·join·der /sùrri jóyndər/ *n* in a civil court action, the second reply of the person bringing the action (**plaintiff**), in response to the defendant's second statement (**rejoinder**)

sur·ren·der /sə réndər/ *v* (**-dered, -der·ing, -ders**) **1.** *vi* DECLARE YOURSELF DEFEATED to declare to an opponent that he or she has won so that fighting or conflict can cease **2.** *vt* GIVE UP POSSESSION OF SOMETHING to relinquish possession or control of something because compelled to do so, as a result of a defeat, or on the orders of a higher authority ○ *surrender territory* ○ *surrender your passport* **3.** *vt* GIVE SOMETHING OUT OF COURTESY to give a seat, position, or office to somebody as a courtesy or as a gesture of goodwill **4.** **sur·ren·der your·self** *vr* GIVE SELF UP TO SOMETHING to yield to a strong emotion, influence, or temptation **5.** *vt* LAW ABANDON RIGHTS TO SOMETHING to give up or abandon rights to something, especially to give up a lease before it has expired ■ *n* **1.** GIVING UP FIGHT an act of declaring defeat at the hands of an opponent ○ *The French demanded an unconditional surrender.* **2.** GIVING UP CONTROL an act of relinquishing control or possession to somebody or something **3.** DELIVERY INTO LEGAL CUSTODY the delivery of a prisoner or fugitive into legal custody **4.** LAW ABANDONMENT OF LEGAL RIGHTS the abandonment of legal rights, especially the giving up of a lease or an insurance policy before it has expired **5.** GIVING SELF UP TO AUTHORITIES an act of willing submission to authorities [15C. < Anglo-Norman, "give over" < *render* "give (back)," variant of Old French *rendre* (see RENDER)]

SYNONYMS See ***yield***.

sur·ren·der val·ue *n* the amount of money that somebody would receive on terminating a life insurance policy

sur·rep·ti·tious /sùr əp tíshəss/ *adj* done in a concealed or underhand way to escape notice, especially disapproval [15C. < Latin *surreptitius* < *surripere* "seize secretly," literally "seize from beneath" < *rapere* "seize"] —**sur·rep·ti·tious·ly** *adv* —**sur·rep·ti·tious·ness** *n*

SYNONYMS See ***secret***.

sur·rey /súr ee/ (*plural* **-reys**) *n* a late 19th-century horse-drawn four-wheeled carriage with two or four seats, used for short pleasure trips [Late 19C. After SURREY]

Sur·rey /súr ee/ county in southern England. The administrative center is Kingston-upon-Thames.

Population: 1,059,015 (2001). Area: 648 sq. mi./1,677 sq. km.

sur·ro·gate *adj* /súr əgət/ **SUBSTITUTING FOR SOMEBODY OR SOMETHING** taking the place of somebody or something else ■ *n* /súr əgət/ **1. SOMEBODY AS SUBSTITUTE** somebody who acts as a replacement for somebody else **2. WOMAN WHO GIVES BIRTH FOR ANOTHER** a woman who bears a child for a couple, with the intention of handing it over at birth. She is usually either artificially inseminated with the man's sperm or implanted with a fertilized egg from the woman. **3.** LAW **ESTATE-SETTLING JUDGE** a judge in some states who probates wills and settles estates **4.** PSYCHOL **SUBSTITUTE AUTHORITY FIGURE** a respected person who replaces a lost or nonexistent parent in somebody's unconscious, e.g., a teacher or older sibling ■ *vt* /súr ə gàyt/ (**-gat·ed, -gat·ing, -gates**) **APPOINT AS STAND-IN** to put somebody in somebody else's place [Mid-16C. < Latin *surrogatus*, past participle of *surrogare* "ask for in place of" < *rogare* "ask, beg"] —**sur·ro·ga·cy** *n*

sur·round /sə równd/ *vt* (**-round·ed, -round·ing, -rounds**) **1. ENCLOSE SOMETHING** to occupy the space all around something **2. CLOSE OFF MEANS OF ESCAPE** to encircle something completely, especially an enemy's military position **3. BE AROUND SOMEBODY** to associate closely with somebody ■ *n* **1. AREA AROUND** an area, border, or frame around a thing or place **2. SURROUNDINGS** the immediate environment of something or somebody (*often pl*) **3.** *US* HUNTING **METHOD OF HUNTING** a method of hunting in which animals are driven into a place from which they cannot escape [Early 17C. Via Old French *suronder* "overflow" < late Latin *superundare* < Latin *unda* "wave"]

sur·round·ings /sə równdingz/ *npl* the immediate environment of somebody or something, including events, circumstances, scenery, conditions, people, and objects

sur·round sound *n* a system of recording and reproducing sound that uses three or more channels and speakers in order to create the effect of the listener being surrounded by sound sources

sur·sum cor·da /sùrssəm káwrdə, sòorsəm-/ *n* **1.** in the Roman Catholic Church, a short sentence (**versicle**) spoken by a priest during Mass, just before the preface **2.** a cry or exhortation, especially of hope (*literary*) [< late Latin, "(lift) up (your) hearts," the versicle's opening words]

sur·tax /súr tàks/ *n* **1. ANOTHER TAX** a tax that is charged in addition to other taxes **2. HIGHER TAX** a higher level or levels of tax imposed on individuals and corporations when income or profits exceed a specific amount ■ *vt* (**-taxed, -tax·ing, -tax·es**) **CHARGE SOMEBODY SURTAX** to charge somebody with an additional or higher tax [Late 19C. < French *surtaxe* "over tax" < *taxe* "tax" < *taxer* (see TAX)]

sur·ti·tle /súr tìt'l/ *n Can, UK* same as **supertitle**

~~surveilance~~ incorrect spelling of **surveillance**

sur·veil·lance /sər váylənss/ *n* continual observation of a person or group, especially one suspected of doing something illegal [Early 19C. < French < *surveiller* "watch over" < *veiller* "keep watch" < Latin *vigilare* (see VIGILANT)] —**sur·veil·lant** *adj, n*

sur·vey *vt* /sər váy/ (**-veyed, -vey·ing, -veys**) **1. CONSIDER SOMETHING GENERALLY** to look at or consider something in a general or very broad way **2. LOOK AT SOMETHING CAREFULLY** to look at or consider somebody or something closely, especially in order to form an opinion **3. PLOT MAP OF SOMEWHERE** to make a detailed map of an area of land, including its boundaries, area, and elevation, using geometry and trigonometry to measure angles and distances **4. QUESTION PEOPLE IN POLL** to do a statistical study of a sample population by asking questions about age, income, opinions, buying preferences, and other aspects of people's lives **5.** *UK* **INSPECT BUILDING** to inspect a building in order to determine its structural soundness or assess its value ■ *n* /súr vày/ (*plural* **-veys**) **1. GENERAL VIEW** an examination of a subject or situation from a very broad and general perspective **2. CRITICAL INSPECTION** a very detailed, critical examination of something such as a situation or event **3. ACT OF MEASURING LAND** an act of taking detailed measurements of an area of land **4. GROUP DOING SURVEY** a team of surveyors working together **5. REPORT ON LAND MEASUREMENT** a report that shows the results of a survey **6. AREA SURVEYED** an area of land that is being or has been surveyed **7. ANALYSIS OF POLL SAMPLE** a statistical analysis of answers to a poll of a sample of a population, e.g., to determine opinions, preferences, or knowledge [15C. Via Anglo-Norman *surveier* < medieval Latin *supervidere* "oversee" < Latin *videre* "see"] —**sur·vey·a·ble** *adj*

~~surveyer~~ incorrect spelling of **surveyor**

sur·vey·or /sər váy ər/ *n* somebody whose occupation is taking accurate measurements of land areas in order to determine boundaries, elevations, and dimensions

sur·vey·or's chain *n* MEASURE same as **chain** (sense 9)

sur·vey·or's lev·el *n* an instrument with a telescope and a level attached, mounted on a tripod and rotating around the vertical axis, used for measuring elevations of land

sur·vey·or's meas·ure *n* a system of measurement that uses the surveyor's chain, 22 yd./about 20 m, as its base unit

sur·viv·al /sər vív'l/ *n* **1.** the fact of remaining alive or in existence, especially after facing life-threatening danger, or of continuing in a present position or office ○ *The doctor said she had a fifty-fifty chance of survival.* ○ *fighting for her political survival* **2.** a custom, idea, or belief that remains when other similar things have been lost or forgotten

sur·vi·val·ist /sər vívəlist/ *n* somebody who seeks to survive an impending disaster by hoarding weapons and food, often going off to live alone or with a like-minded group —**sur·viv·al·ism** *n*

sur·viv·al suit *n* a close-fitting waterproof suit made of insulating and often buoyant material that covers the whole body so that the wearer can survive long periods in cold water

sur·vive /sər vív/ (**-vived, -viv·ing, -vives**) *v* **1.** *vi* **NOT DIE OR DISAPPEAR** to remain alive or in existence or able to live or function, especially succeed in staying alive when faced with a life-threatening danger ○ *He was shot three times at close range and survived.* ○ *A fragment of the manuscript still survives.* ○ *How can you survive on $70 a week?* **2.** *vt* **LIVE THROUGH SOMETHING** to come through a life-threatening experience or a period of difficulty and remain alive, in existence, or in a previous position or life ○ *She survived three assassination attempts.* ○ *The government narrowly survived a vote of no confidence.* **3.** *vt* **LIVE LONGER THAN SOMEBODY** to remain alive after the death of a particular person ○ *He survived his wife by only three months.* [15C. Via Anglo-Norman *survivre* < Latin *supervivere* "live beyond" < *vivere* "to live"] —**sur·viv·a·bil·i·ty** /sər vívə bíllətee/ *n* —**sur·viv·a·ble** *adj*

~~surviver~~ incorrect spelling of **survivor**

sur·vi·vor /sər vívər/ *n* **1. SOMEBODY WHO SURVIVES** somebody who remains alive despite being exposed to life-threatening danger ○ *There were no survivors from the plane crash.* **2. SOMEBODY WITH GREAT POWERS OF ENDURANCE** somebody who shows a great will to live or a great determination to overcome difficulties and carry on **3.** LAW **INHERITOR** the one of two or more people having joint interests in property who lives longer than the other or others and is, therefore, entitled to the entire property **4.** PSYCHOL **SOMEBODY OVERCOMING TRAUMATIC EXPERIENCE** somebody who has been psychologically damaged by a trauma such as rape or an addiction and seeks to overcome its effects

Su·sann /soo zán/, **Jacqueline** (1926–74) US writer. Her first novel, *Valley of the Dolls* (1968), was a best-seller.

Popperfoto

Jacqueline Susann

Su·san·na /soo zánnə/ *n* in the Apocrypha, a woman of Babylon who was saved by the prophet Daniel after being falsely accused of adultery

~~susceptable~~ incorrect spelling of **susceptible**

sus·cep·ti·bil·i·ty /sə sèptə bíllətee/ *n* **1. LIKELIHOOD OF BEING AFFECTED** the likelihood of being affected, or a tendency to be affected, by a specific thing ○ *susceptibility to colds* **2. SENSITIVITY** the tendency to be affected by strong feelings and emotions **3.** PHYS same as **magnetic susceptibility** ■ **sus·cep·ti·bil·i·ties** *npl* **FEELINGS** somebody's feelings, especially those of somebody who easily becomes upset

sus·cep·ti·ble /sə séptəb'l/ *adj* **1. EASILY AFFECTED** easily influenced or affected by something **2. LIKELY TO BE AFFECTED** liable to being affected by something ○ *susceptible to hay fever and other allergies* **3. EMOTIONAL** easily affected emotionally **4. CAPABLE OF SOMETHING** capable or permitting of something (*formal*) ○ *susceptible of several different interpretations* [Early 17C. Directly or via French< late Latin *susceptibilis* < past participle of Latin *suscipere* "take up" < *capere* "take"] —**sus·cep·ti·ble·ness** *n* —**sus·cep·ti·bly** *adv*

sus·cep·tive /sə séptiv/ *adj* **1.** easily affected by something **2.** open to new ideas and suggestions [Mid-15C. < Latin *suscept-*, past participle of *suscipere* (see SUSCEPTIBLE)] —**sus·cep·tive·ness** *n* —**sus·cep·tiv·i·ty** /sə sèp tívvətee/ *n*

su·shi /sóoshee, sóo-/ *n* small cakes of cold boiled rice, shaped by hand or wrapped in seaweed and topped with pieces of raw or cooked fish, vegetables, or egg [Late 19C. < Japanese]

Su·si·an /sóozee ən/ *n* LANG same as **Elamite** (sense 2) [Mid-16C. < Latin *Susianus* < Greek *Sousa* "Susa," city in present-day W Iran, where Elamite was spoken] —**Su·si·an** *adj*

Su·sit·na /soo sítnə/ river in Alaska, flowing from the Alaska Range into the Pacific Ocean at Cook Inlet. Length: 313 mi./504 km.

sus·lik /sússlik/ (*plural* **-liks** or *same*), **sous·lik** /sóosslik/ *n* a ground squirrel with large eyes and small ears that lives in dry open areas. Native to: Europe, Asia. Latin name: *Citellus citellus*. [Late 18C. < Russian]

~~suspecious~~ incorrect spelling of **suspicious**

sus·pect *v* /sə spékt/ (**-pect·ed, -pect·ing, -pects**) **1.** *vt* **BELIEVE SOMEBODY IS GUILTY** to believe that somebody may have committed a crime or wrongdoing without having any proof ○ *How can they suspect him of murder?* **2.** *vt* **DOUBT SOMETHING** to doubt the truth or validity of something ○ *We suspect her reasons for wanting to be friends with us.* **3.** *vt* **BELIEVE SOMETHING TO BE SO** to think that something is probable or likely ○ *I rather suspect that we haven't heard the last of this business.* **4.** *vti* **HAVE SUSPICIONS** to be suspicious, or be suspicious about something ■ *n* /súss pèkt/ **SOMEBODY WHO MIGHT BE GUILTY** somebody who is suspected of a wrongdoing ■ *adj* /súss pèkt/ **1. SUSPICIOUS** thought or likely to be false or untrustworthy ○ *All his claims about the wealth of his family are rather suspect.* **2. LIKELY TO CONTAIN SOMETHING ILLEGAL** looking likely to contain something dangerous or illegal ○ *inspected the suspect luggage* [14C. < Latin *suspect-*, past participle of *suspicere* "look up at" < *specere* "look at"] ◇ **the usual suspects** people, businesses, or organizations frequently mentioned in the context of a particular activity (*informal*)

USAGE suspect or **suspicious**? These two adjectives have overlapping meanings and are sometimes confused. ***Suspicious***, the more frequent and versatile of the two, may describe a person who suspects or somebody or something that causes suspicion: *Her behavior made us suspicious. There were a couple of suspicious characters standing outside the bank. Her behavior was suspicious.* ***Suspect*** is used chiefly of things that cause doubt, suspicion, or distrust because they seem likely to be false, illegal, or dangerous: *His claims sounded suspect. The police confiscated a suspect package. The remains of a suspect tuna sandwich were sent away for analysis.*

~~suspence~~ incorrect spelling of **suspense**

sus·pend /sə spénd/ (**-pend·ed, -pend·ing, -pends**) *v* **1.** *vt* **HANG SOMETHING FROM ABOVE** to hang something from above, especially so that it can swing freely **2.** *vt* **STOP SOMETHING FOR PERIOD** to stop something or make something ineffective, usually for a short time **3.** *vt* **BAR SOMEBODY FOR PERIOD** to bar somebody from a privilege, a position, or an organization, usually when under suspicion of wrongdoing **4.** *vt* **POSTPONE SOMETHING** to delay or defer action on a decision or a judgment until more of the facts are known **5.** *vt* CHEM **DISPERSE SOMETHING IN LIQUID** to cause particles to be dispersed in a liquid or gas **6.** *vt* MUSIC **SUSTAIN NOTE** to hold a note until the next note or chord is sounded, so that they are heard together **7.** *vi* FIN **STOP MAKING PAYMENTS** to cease payment on something, especially because of an inability to meet financial obligations [13C. Directly or via French < Latin *suspendere* "hang up" < *pendere* "hang"] —**sus·pend·i·bil·i·ty** /sə spèndə bíllətee/ *n* —**sus·pend·i·ble** *adj* ◇ **be suspended** to hang over or above something as vapor or particles, or be dispersed through something as particles

sus·pend·ed an·i·ma·tion *n* **1.** the stopping or slowing of the vital functions of an organism for some period of time, especially by freezing **2.** a state, often caused by asphyxia, in which an organism loses consciousness and stops breathing so that it appears to be dead

sus·pend·ed sen·tence *n* a sentence imposed on somebody found guilty of a crime that need not be served as long as the individual commits no other crime during the term of the sentence

sus·pend·er /sə spéndər/ *n* **1.** a strap, usually made of elastic, worn over the shoulder and with a clip at either end to attach to pants so that they do not fall down (*usually used in the plural*) **2.** ARCHIT something that allows something else to hang, e.g., one of the cables on a suspension bridge **3.** *UK* CLOTHING same as **garter** (sense 2)

sus·pend·er belt *n UK* same as **garter belt**

sus·pense /sə spénss/ *n* **1. UNCERTAINTY** the state or condition of being unsure or in doubt about something **2. ENJOYABLE TENSION** a feeling of tense excitement about how something such as a mystery novel or movie will end **3. ANXIETY** a state of anxiety or intense worry about something [15C. Via Anglo-Norman < Latin *suspensus*, past participle of *suspendere* (see SUSPEND)] —**sus·pense·ful** *adj*

sus·pense ac·count *n* a financial account in which entries are made temporarily, until it is determined where they belong

sus·pen·sion /sə spénsh'n/ *n* **1. TEMPORARY STOP** an interruption of something for a period of time **2. TEMPORARY REMOVAL** the temporary removal of somebody from a team, position, school, or organization, especially as punishment **3.** LAW **POSTPONEMENT OF SENTENCE** a delay in the carrying out of a sentence or the making of a decision or judgment **4.** TRANSP **SYSTEM REDUCING VIBRATION OF VEHICLE** a system of springs and shock absorbers on a wheeled vehicle that reduces the impact of bumps and uneven running surfaces on the occupants and gives the wheels better contact **5.** FIN **END TO REPAYING DEBTS** an end to the repayment of financial obligations because of a lack of money **6.** CHEM **DISPERSION OF PARTICLES** a dispersion of fine solid particles in a liquid or gas, removable by filtration **7.** MUSIC **TECHNIQUE FOR CREATING DISSONANCE** a technique in which a note of the first chord is held into the second chord, the dissonance created being resolved by moving a step lower in the third chord

sus·pen·sion bridge *n* a bridge with a roadway that is suspended from cables anchored by towers at either end and often supported by structures at regular intervals

sus·pen·sion point *n US* each of a series of dots, usually three, used in printed and written material to indicate an omission from text being reproduced or an incomplete phrase (*often used in the plural*)

sus·pen·sive /sə spénssiv/ *adj* **1. STOPPING SOMETHING** causing or tending to cause something to stop or be deferred **2. CAUSING TENSION** causing, arousing, or relating to a feeling of doubt or anxious excitement **3. UNDECIDED ABOUT SOMETHING** inclined to delay making a decision or judgment —**sus·pen·sive·ly** *adv* —**sus·pen·sive·ness** *n*

sus·pen·soid /sə spén sòyd/ *n* a solution of very fine solid particles dispersed throughout a liquid [Early 20C. < SUSPENSION]

sus·pen·so·ry /sə spénssəree/ *n* (*plural* **-ries**) **1.** ANAT **LIGAMENT OR MUSCLE** a ligament or muscle from which a structure or part is suspended **2.** MED **BANDAGE OR SLING** something that holds part of the body in position while it heals, e.g., a bandage or a sling ■ *adj* **1. TEMPORARILY STOPPING SOMETHING** temporarily interrupting or delaying the completion of something **2.** ANAT **SUPPORTING** providing support for an organ or body part

sus·pen·so·ry lig·a·ment *n* a ligament that provides support for an organ or another body part, especially a fibrous membrane that holds the lens of the eye in place

sus·pi·cion /sə spísh'n/ *n* **1. FEELING OF SOMETHING WRONG** an unsubstantiated belief that something is the case, especially a belief that something wrong has happened or that somebody may have committed a crime ○ *a sneaking suspicion that she was the one who ate the last cookie* **2. MISTRUST OR DOUBTS** a feeling of mistrust or doubt, especially because something wrong has happened and has not been explained ○ *an atmosphere of suspicion* **3. CONDITION OF BEING SUSPECTED** the condition of being suspected of something, especially wrongdoing ○ *under suspicion* **4. SMALL AMOUNT** a tiny amount of something such as a color or flavor ○ *just a suspicion of garlic* [13C. Via French < Latin *suspicion-* < *suspicere* (see SUSPECT)] —**sus·pi·cion·al** *adj*

sus·pi·cious /sə spíshəss/ *adj* **1. AROUSING SUSPICION** creating or liable to create suspicion ○ *under suspicious circumstances* **2. TENDING TO SUSPECT** inclined or tending to believe that something is wrong ○ *a suspicious nature* **3. SUGGESTING DOUBT** showing or indicating suspicion ○ *a suspicious look* —**sus·pi·cious·ly** *adv* —**sus·pi·cious·ness** *n*

USAGE See ***suspect***.

sus·pire /sə spír/ (**-pired, -pir·ing, -pires**) *vi* (*dated literary*) **1.** to draw in breath **2.** to give a sigh [15C. < Latin *suspirare* "breathe up" < *spirare* "breathe"] —**sus·pi·ra·tion** /sùspə ráysh'n/ *n*

Sus·que·han·na[1] /sùskwə hánnə/ *n* PEOPLES same as **Susquehannock**

Sus·que·han·na[2] /sùskwə hánnə/ river that rises in central New York, flowing across Pennsylvania before emptying into the Chesapeake Bay in Maryland. Length: 447 mi./719 km.

Sus·que·han·nock /sùskwə hánnək/ (*plural same* or **-nocks**), **Sus·que·han·na** /-hánnə/ (*plural same* or **-nas**) *n* a member of an extinct Native North American people who lived along the Susquehanna River in New York, Pennsylvania, and Maryland [Early 17C. < Algonquian]

suss /sus/ (**sussed, suss·ing, suss·es**) *vt UK* to discover or understand something such as somebody's motives, a situation, or how to use something (*informal*) ○ *I think I've finally got this camera sussed.* [Mid-20C. Shortening of SUSPECT]

Sus·sex /sússiks/ former county of southeastern England

Sus·sex Drive, 24 Sus·sex Drive *n Can* the address of the official residence of the Prime Minister of Canada

Sus·sex span·iel *n* a dog with long ears and a golden silky coat, belonging to a breed of short-legged spaniel [Mid-19C. After SUSSEX]

Suss·kind /súss kìnd/, **Leonard** (*b.* 1940) US physicist. He pioneered the extension of string theory to the problem represented by black holes.

sus·tain /sə stáyn/ *vt* (**-tained, -tain·ing, -tains**) **1. NOURISH SOMEBODY** to provide somebody with nourishment or the necessities of life **2. SUPPORT SOMETHING FROM BELOW** to keep something in position by holding it from below ○ *The floor will not sustain the weight of a grand piano.* **3. PROVIDE SOMEBODY WITH MORAL SUPPORT** to keep somebody going with emotional or moral support **4. WITHSTAND SOMETHING** to manage to withstand something and continue in spite of it **5. BE AFFECTED BY SOMETHING** to experience a setback, injury, damage, loss, or defeat ○ *sustained several broken bones* **6. MAINTAIN SOMETHING** to make something continue to exist ○ *sustaining the audience's interest* **7. KEEP PRETENSE GOING** to maintain a pretense successfully **8. CONFIRM SOMETHING** to confirm that something is true or valid ○ *sustained the lower court's ruling* **9.** LAW **VALIDATE SOMETHING** to decide that a statement or objection is valid or justified ■ *n* MUSIC **PROLONGED MUSICAL NOTE** a musical note that is prolonged [13C. < Anglo-Norman *sustein-*, stem of *sustenir* < Latin *sustinere* "hold up" < *tenere* "hold"] —**sus·tain·ment** *n*

sus·tain·a·ble /sə stáynəb'l/ *adj* **1.** able to be maintained **2.** exploiting natural resources without destroying the ecological balance of an area ○ *sustainable agriculture* —**sus·tain·a·bil·i·ty** /sə stàynə bíllətee/ *n* —**sus·tain·a·bly** *adv*

sus·tain·a·ble de·vel·op·ment *n* economic development maintained within acceptable levels of global resource depletion and environmental pollution

sus·tained yield /sə stàynd-/ *n* **1.** the ongoing supply of a natural resource such as timber by scheduled harvesting **2.** the amount of a natural resource such as timber obtained by scheduled harvesting

sus·tain·ing ped·al /sə stáyning-/ *n* the right pedal of a piano, used to keep the dampers off the strings so that they can vibrate freely

sus·tain·ing pro·gram *n US* a radio or television program that does not have commercials because the station or network on which it is broadcast supports it

sus·te·nance /sústənənss/ *n* **1. NOURISHMENT** something, especially food, that supports life ○ *There isn't much sustenance in a small chocolate bar.* **2. LIVELIHOOD** a means of supporting somebody financially **3. CONDITION OF BEING PROVIDED FOR** the condition of being provided with the necessities of life ○ *"I have hardly a penny in the world – I am staying with my aunt for my bare sustenance."* (Thomas Hardy, *Far from the Madding Crowd*; 1874) [13C. < Anglo-Norman *sustenaunce* < *sustenir* (see SUSTAIN)]

sus·ten·tac·u·lar /sùstən tákyələr/ *adj* describes cells or fibers whose only function is to serve as a support [Late 19C. < modern Latin *sustentaculum* "support" < Latin *sustentare* (see SUSTENTATION)]

sus·ten·ta·tion /sùstən táysh'n/ *n* (*formal*) **1.** something that supports or sustains something else **2.** a means of support [14C. Via French < Latin *sustentare* "keep holding up" < *sustinere* (see SUSTAIN)] —**sus·ten·ta·tive** /sústən tàytiv, sə sténtətiv/ *adj*

su·su *n* FIN another spelling of **sou-sou**

Su·su /soō soō/ (*plural same* or **-sus**) *n* **1.** a member of a people who live in West Africa, mainly in Guinea and Sierra Leone **2.** the Mande language of the Susu people. Native speakers: 700,000. [Late 18C. < Susu] —**Su·su** *adj*

su·sur·rate /soōssə ràyt/ (**-rat·ed, -rat·ing, -rates**) *vi* to whisper or rustle softly [Early 17C. Back-formation < *susurration* < Latin *susurrare* < *susurrus* "whisper," an imitation of the sound] —**su·sur·rant** *adj* —**su·sur·ra·tion** /soōssə ráysh'n/ *n*

su·sur·rus /sə súrrəss/ *n* a whispering or murmuring sound (*literary*) [15C. < Latin (see SUSURRATE)]

Suth·er·land /sú*th*ərlənd/, **Donald** (*b.* 1934) Canadian-born US actor. His many movies include *M*A*S*H* (1970) and *Ordinary People* (1980).

Suth·er·land, Dame Joan (*b.* 1926) Australian operatic soprano. In a career stretching from 1947 to 1990, she became an opera singer of international renown, noted especially for her coloratura roles in Italian opera. See illustration on next page

Su·ther·land Falls falls on the South Island, New Zealand. It is one of the highest in the world. Height: 1,904 ft./580 m.

Dame Joan Sutherland: performing in *Lucia di Lammermoor*

~~**sutle**~~ incorrect spelling of **subtle**

Sut·lej /súttlij/ river in South Asia, flowing through Tibet, India, and Pakistan. Length: 901 mi./1,450 km.

sut·ler /súttlər/ *n* somebody who follows an army and sells goods to the soldiers (*archaic*) [Late 16C. < obsolete Dutch *soeteler* < *soetelen* "befoul, do menial work"] —**sut·ler·ship** *n*

su·tra /sóotrə/ *n* **1.** a short aphoristic summary of the teachings of Hinduism, created to be memorized and later incorporated into Hindu literature **2.** *also* **sut·ta** /sóottə/ a classic religious text of Buddhism, especially one regarded as a discourse of the Buddha [Early 19C. < Sanskrit *sūtram* "aphorism," literally "thread"]

sut·tee /sə tée, sú tee/, **sa·ti** *n* **1.** in South Asia, the now illegal practice of a Hindu widow throwing herself on her husband's funeral pyre **2.** a Hindu widow who throws herself on her husband's funeral pyre [Late 18C. < Sanskrit *satī* "good woman," feminine present participle of *as-* "be"] —**sut·tee·ism** *n*

Sut·ter /súttər/, **John Augustus** (1803–80) German-born US pioneer. He founded a colony in Mexican California (1839), and an employee discovered gold there (1848), initiating the Gold Rush. Sutter lost everything and spent the rest of his life vainly seeking compensation for his discovery.

su·ture /sóochər/ *n* **1.** MATERIAL FOR SURGICAL STITCHING a piece of material used to close a wound or connect tissues, e.g., catgut, thread, or wire **2.** SURGICAL SEAM the line formed where a wound has been closed or tissues have been joined **3.** SEAM a seam or line at which two edges have been joined **4.** ANAT IMMOVABLE JOINT a joint, especially in the skull, in which the bones are tightly bound together by fibrous connective tissue so as to prevent movement between them **5.** ZOOL LINE AT POINT OF JUNCTURE a distinguishable line at the junction of adjacent structures, e.g., between the chambers of a mollusk shell or between the exoskeletal plates of an insect **6.** BOT LINE ON SEED POD OR FRUIT a line along which a seed pod or fruit will split to release its seeds ■ *vt* (**-tured, -tur·ing, -tures**) SURG CLOSE WOUND to close a wound by joining the edges [15C. < Latin *sutura* < *sut-*, past participle of *suere* "sew"] —**su·tur·al** *adj* —**su·tur·al·ly** *adv*

SUV *abbr* sport-utility vehicle

Su·va /sóovə/ capital and largest city of Fiji. Situated on the southeastern coast of Viti Levu Island, it is Fiji's main seaport. Population: 77,366 (2000).

~~**survivor**~~ incorrect spelling of **survivor**

Su·wan·nee /sə wónnee/ river in the southeastern United States. It rises in southern Georgia and flows 190 mi./306 km through Florida into the Gulf of Mexico.

sux·a·me·tho·ni·um /súksə me thónee əm/ *n UK* same as **succinylcholine** [Mid-20C. Alteration and contraction of *succinylmethylammonium* < *succinyl* < SUCCINIC ACID]

su·ze·rain /sóozərən, syóozə ràyn/ *n* a ruler or nation that controls a dependent nation's international affairs but allows it to control its internal affairs [Early 19C. < Old French *suserain*] —**su·ze·rain·ty** *n*

Su·zhou /sóo jṓ/, **Suchow** /-chów/, **Xuzhou** /-jṓ/ city on the Grand Canal in southern Jiangsu Province, eastern China. It is an important transportation and industrial center. Population: 897,757 (1991).

Suz·man /sóozmən, sóozmən/, **Helen** (*b.* 1917) South African politician. As a member of the South African parliament and cofounder (1959) of the Progressive Party, she campaigned against apartheid and assisted the transition to majority rule in South Africa.

Su·zu·ki /soo zóokee/, **Harunobu** (1725?–70) Japanese artist. He is noted for his color prints and woodcuts, many of which were used to illustrate books.

sv *abbr* **1.** El Salvador (*used in Internet addresses*) See table at **domain name** **2.** under the word or term

Sv *symbol* MEASURE sievert

SV *abbr* **1.** RELIG Holy Virgin **2.** NAUT sailing vessel **3.** RELIG Your Holiness [Sense 1 Latin *Sancta Virgo*; sense 3 Latin *Sanctitas Vestra*]

s.v. *abbr* under the word or term [Latin *sub voce*]

SV40 *n* a virus that causes cancer in monkeys and is widely used in genetic and medical research [< abbreviation of *simian virus*]

Sval·bard /svál baard/ Norwegian archipelago in the Arctic Ocean. Population: 3,309 (1991). Area: 23,957 sq. mi./62,049 sq. km.

svc. *abbr* service

svelte /svelt, sfelt/ *adj* graceful and slender in figure or contour [Early 19C. Via French < Italian *svelto* "stretched," past participle of *svellere* "pluck out" < Latin *vellere* "pull"]

Sven·ga·li /sven gaálee, sfen-/ *n* somebody who controls and manipulates somebody else, usually for evil purposes [Early 20C. After a villainous hypnotist in the novel *Trilby* (1894), by George du Maurier]

Sver·drup Is·lands /sférdrəp-/ island group in Nunavut, Canada, within the Queen Elizabeth Islands, comprising Axel Heiberg, Ellef Ringnes, and Amund Ringnes

SVGA *n* a modified specification for video display controllers used in personal computers. Full form **super video graphics array**

SW *abbr* **1.** MEDIA short wave **2.** COMPASS southwest **3.** COMPASS southwestern

Sw. *abbr* **1.** Sweden **2.** LANG Swedish

swab /swob/ *n* **1.** SMALL STICK WITH COTTON a small stick, wire, or plastic wand with cotton attached to one or both ends, often used to clean wounds, apply medicine, or obtain a specimen of something **2.** MOP a mop used to clean decks or floors **3.** SOMEBODY WHO MOPS somebody who uses a mop to clean, especially on a ship **4.** *US* SAILOR a sailor (*slang*) **5.** SOMEBODY WORTHLESS somebody regarded as uncouth or worthless (*archaic slang*) **6.** SURG SOFT MATERIAL FOR MOPPING UP BLOOD a small piece of gauze, cotton, or other soft material, used to mop up blood during surgery **7.** MED SPECIMEN a specimen of mucus or another secretion obtained by using a swab **8.** PIECE OF MATERIAL FOR CLEANING GUN a small piece of absorbent material that is used to clean the bore of a firearm ■ *vt* (**swabbed, swab·bing, swabs**) **1.** MOP SOMETHING to clean something such as a floor or deck with a mop **2.** CLEAN SOMETHING UP to clean up something such as a spill **3.** MED CLEAN WOUND WITH SWAB to clean out or apply medicine to a wound with a soft piece of material [Mid-17C. Back-formation < obsolete *swabber* "deck mop" < obsolete Dutch *zwabben* "to mop"]

swab·bie /swóbbee/ *n US* same as **swab** *n* (sense 4) (*slang*)

swad·dle /swódd'l/ (**-dled, -dling, -dles**) *vt* **1.** WRAP SOMEBODY IN SOMETHING to wrap or bandage somebody or something with something **2.** WRAP BABY UP TIGHTLY to wrap a baby tightly in soft material **3.** SMOTHER SOMEBODY OR SOMETHING to restrain somebody or something with a complete wrapping [15C. < form of SWATHE[1]]

swad·dling clothes /swóddling-/ *npl* long strips of linen or another soft material, used in some cultures to wrap babies in order to keep them still and calm

Swa·de·shi /swaa dáyshee, -déshee/ *S Asia adj* describes goods produced within the country of India ■ *n* the practice of favoring domestic products and refusing to buy imported goods as part of the struggle for independence in India [Early 20C. Via Hindi *svadeśī* < Sanskrit *svadeśaḥ* "your own country"]

swag /swag/ *n* **1.** CURTAIN an ornamental drapery or curtain that hangs in a curve between two points **2.** FESTOON an ornamental draping of fruit or flowers **3.** LOOT stolen property (*slang*) **4.** LURCHING MOVEMENT a lurching or swaying movement ■ *vi* (**swagged, swag·ging, swags**) MOVE WITH LURCH to move with a lurching or swaying movement [Early 16C. Probably < N Germanic]

swage /swayj/ *n* **1.** a tool or die used to shape cold metal by hammering or applying pressure **2.** ENG same as **swage block** ■ *vt* (**swaged, swag·ing, swag·es**) to bend or shape metal with a swage [14C. < Old French *souage* "decorative molding"] —**swag·er** *n*

swage block *n* a metal block with holes or grooves used to shape cold metal

swag·ger /swággər/ *vi* (**-gered, -ger·ing, -gers**) **1.** STRUT AROUND to walk in an arrogant or proud way **2.** BRAG to talk boastfully about personal accomplishments ■ *n* ARROGANT WALK an arrogant or proud way of walking or behaving [Early 16C. Probably < SWAG] —**swag·ger·er** *n* —**swag·ger·ing·ly** *adv*

swag·ger stick *n* a short stick often carried by an army officer

Swa·hi·li /swaa heélee, swə-/ (*plural same* or **-lis**) *n* **1.** a member of a people who live mainly along the eastern coasts and islands of eastern and southern Africa **2.** LANG same as **Kiswahili** [Early 19C. Via Kiswahili < Arabic *sawāḥilīy* "of the coasts" < *sāḥil* "coast"] —**Swa·hi·li** *adj*

swain /swayn/ *n* (*archaic or literary*) **1.** a young man who lives in the country **2.** a man who is somebody's admirer or lover [Late 16C. < Old Norse *sveinn* "boy, servant" < Germanic, "your own"]

SWAK /swak/ *abbr* sealed with a kiss

swale /swayl/ *n* **1.** a depression between slopes that provides for drainage **2.** *US* a low area of land, especially one that is moist or marshy [Early 16C. Origin ?]

swal·low[1] /swóllō/ *v* (**-lowed, -low·ing, -lows**) **1.** *vti* PASS FOOD DOWN THROAT to take in food or liquid through the mouth and pass it down the throat into the stomach **2.** *vi* GULP to perform the act of swallowing, usually as an emotional response to something ○ *swallowing hard to hold back the tears* **3.** *vt* DESTROY SOMETHING to engulf or destroy something **4.** *vt* SUPPRESS FEELINGS to refrain from expressing thoughts or feelings ○ *Swallow your pride and apologize.* **5.** *vt* BELIEVE SOMETHING to accept something as true without questioning it (*informal*) ○ *They'll never swallow anything so far-fetched.* **6.** *vt* ENDURE SOMETHING to put up with something unpleasant without saying or doing anything to stop it **7.** *vt* RETRACT REMARK to withdraw a statement or remark as false or unjustified ■ *n* **1.** ACT OF PASSING SOMETHING DOWN THROAT the act of taking something in through the mouth and down the throat **2.** AMOUNT PASSED DOWN THROAT an amount taken into the mouth and passed down the throat [Old English *swelgan* < Indo-European]

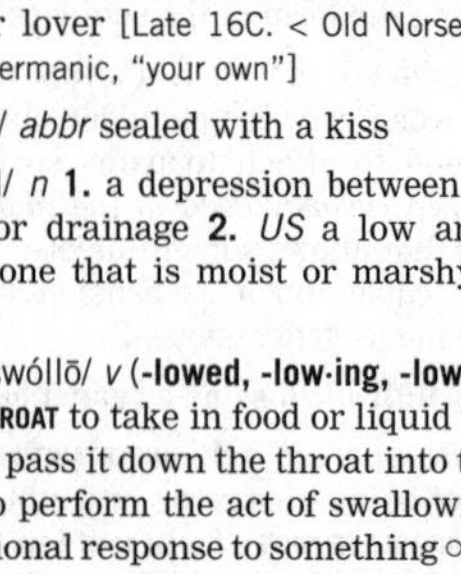
swallow

swal·low[2] /swóllō/ *n* a small graceful songbird with long pointed wings, a notched or forked tail and rapid flight that migrates annually. Family: Hirundinidae. [Old English *swealwe* < Germanic]

swal·low dive *n UK* same as **swan dive** [< SWALLOW[2]]

swal·low·tail /swóllō tàyl/ (*plural* **-tails** or *same*) *n* **1.** a colorful butterfly distinguished by the small tails that extend from the ends of its hind wings. Family: Papilionidae. **2.** the tail of a swallow or similar bird —**swal·low-tailed** *adj*

swal·low-tailed coat *n* a man's evening tailcoat with a split rounded tail

swal·low·wort /swóllō wùrt, -wàwrt/ *n* PLANTS same as **celandine** (sense 1)

swam past tense of **swim**

swa·mi /swáamee/ *n* a title of respect for a Hindu saint or religious teacher [Late 18C. Via Hindi < Sanskrit *svāmin-* "being your own master"]

swamp /swomp/ *n* **WETLAND** an area of land, usually fairly large, that is always wet and is overgrown with various shrubs and trees ■ *v* (**swamped, swamp·ing, swamps**) **1.** *vt* **OVERBURDEN SOMEBODY** to overwhelm somebody by being too much or too many to cope with (*usually passive*) **2.** *vt* **INUNDATE AREA** to submerge an area in water **3.** *vti* NAUT **SINK BOAT** to cause a boat to fill with water and sink, or become full of water and sink [Early 17C. Origin ?] —**swamp·y** *adj*

swamp boat *n* a flat-bottomed boat powered by an airplane propeller, used to travel in swamps and over shallow water

swamp bug·gy *n US* a light vehicle used to travel in areas with swamps and shallow lakes

swamp cy·press *n* TREES same as **bald cypress**

swamp·er /swómpər/ *n* **1.** *US* **SWAMP DWELLER OR WORKER** somebody who lives or works in a swamp, especially in the South **2.** *US* **SOMEBODY WHO CLEARS SWAMP** somebody who clears a swamp of trees and undergrowth or who clears a path through a forest so that logs can be moved **3. TRUCK DRIVER'S ASSISTANT** an assistant to a truck driver **4.** *US* **HELPER IN RESTAURANT** somebody who helps in a restaurant

swamp fe·ver *n* **1.** *US* a disease that is liable to be contracted by people in swampy areas, e.g., malaria or leptospirosis **2.** equine infectious anemia (*dated*)

swamp·land /swómp lànd/ *n* an area of land that is always moist or that contains swamps

swamp pink *n* a wild rare orchid that grows in wet places. Native to: northeastern United States. Flowers: rose-colored, marked with purple. Genus: *Arethusa.*

swan

swan /swon/ *n* a large graceful water bird with webbed feet, a long slender neck, and usually white feathers. Family: Anatidae. ■ *vi* (**swanned, swan·ning, swans**) *UK* to wander around in a relaxed way, especially one regarded as irresponsible or selfish (*informal*) [Old English, "singer" < Indo-European, "make a sound"] —**swan·like** *adj*

CULTURAL NOTE ***Swan Lake***, a ballet (1876) by Russian composer Peter Ilyich Tchaikovsky. Tchaikovsky's first ballet is the romantic tale of Prince Siegfried, who falls in love with Odette, one of a group of swans he has seen metamorphose into beautiful maidens. When he realizes he has been tricked into declaring his love for another swan-maiden, Siegfried rushes to Odette and the two drown themselves in the Lake of Tears.

Swan /swon/ river in southwestern Western Australia, flowing through the city of Perth. Length: 240 mi./386 km.

swan dive *n* a dive performed with the back arched, the legs held together straight, and the arms outstretched

swank /swangk/ *adj* **1. GRAND** extremely elegant or fashionable (*informal*) **2.** *US* **VERY SHOWY** extremely pretentious and ornate ■ *n* **ELEGANCE** the quality of being very chic or smart in style or appearance ■ *vi* (**swanked, swank·ing, swanks**) **SHOW OFF** to behave or swagger in an arrogant, conceited, or pretentious way [Early 19C. Origin ?]

swank·y /swángkee/ *adj* very stylish and expensive (*informal*) —**swank·i·ly** *adv* —**swank·i·ness** *n*

swan·ner·y /swónnəree/ (*plural* **-ies**) *n* a place where mute swans gather and breed together

swan·ny /swónnee/ *interj Southern US* used to express pleasant surprise (*informal*) [Mid-19C. Probably < English dialect pronunciation of *(I) shall warrant ye*]

swans·down /swónz dòwn/, **swan's-down** *n* **1.** the soft down feathers of a swan **2.** a soft woolen fabric. Use: baby clothes. **3.** TEXTILES same as **flannelette**

Swan·sea /swónzee/ city and port in southern Wales, at the mouth of the Tawe River. Population: 223,301 (2001). Welsh name **Abertawe**

swan·skin /swón skin/ *n* a cotton or woolen fabric that is very soft to the touch

swan song *n* **1.** a final appearance, performance, or work, as a farewell to a career or profession **2.** a song of legendary beauty said to be sung only once by a swan during its lifetime, when it is dying

swap /swop/, **swop** *vti* (**swapped, swap·ping, swaps; swopped, swop·ping, swops**) **TRADE SOMETHING** to trade or exchange somebody or something for somebody or something else (*informal*) ○ *Let's swap seats so I can sit next to Louise* ■ *n* **1. EXCHANGE** a trade or exchange (*informal*) **2. SOMEBODY OR SOMETHING EXCHANGED** somebody or something that is traded or exchanged for somebody or something else (*informal*) **3.** FIN **CONTRACT** a contract in which the parties exchange liabilities on outstanding debts, either as a means of managing debt or in the business of trading [14C. Probably an imitation of the sound of hands striking together (to seal an agreement)] —**swap·pa·ble** *adj*

swap con·tract *n* a contract that involves a reciprocal exchange of some kind, especially one in which the contracting parties agree to exchange cash flows

swap meet *n* **1.** a flea market where new, used, and sometimes rare or specialty items are sold **2.** a gathering that people, especially hobbyists, attend for the purpose of exchanging things

swap·tion /swópsh'n/ *n* an option on a contract giving the holder the right to enter into a swap [Late 20C. Contraction of *swap option*]

sward /swawrd/ *n* an area of turf or grass ■ *vti* (**sward·ed, sward·ing, swards**) to cover something with turf or grass, or become covered with turf or grass [Old English *sweard* "hairy skin, rind" < Germanic]

swarf /swawrf/ *n* **1.** the fine metallic shavings removed by grinding or cutting tools **2.** debris, especially from disintegrating satellites, that is in orbit around Earth (*informal*) [Mid-16C. Origin ?]

swarm[1] /swawrm/ *n* **1. GROUP OF INSECTS** a large group of insects, especially bees or gnats, in flight **2. LARGE MASS** a large crowd or group of people or animals moving in a confused or disorderly way ■ *v* (**swarmed, swarm·ing, swarms**) **1.** *vi* **FORM FLYING GROUP** to form a flying group, especially in order to found a new colony ○ *Do bees swarm often?* **2.** *vi* **MOVE IN MASS** to move or gather in a large crowd ○ *people swarmed all over the road* **3.** *vi* **BE OVERRUN** to be overrun with a large mass or group ○ *swarming with people* **4.** *vt* **CAUSE SOMETHING TO SWARM** to cause something to swarm, or produce a swarm [Old English *swearm* < Germanic, an imitation of the sound of buzzing]

swarm[2] /swawrm/ (**swarmed, swarm·ing, swarms**) *vi* to climb up somewhere using the arms and legs [Mid-16C. Origin ?]

swarm cell, swarm spore *n* BIOL same as **zoospore**

swart /swawrt/ *adj* same as **swarthy** (*archaic or literary*) [Old English *sweart* < Indo-European, "dirty, black"]

swarth·y /swáwrthee/ (**-i·er, -i·est**) *adj* having a dark and often weather-beaten complexion [Late 16C. Alteration of obsolete *swarty* < SWART] —**swar·thi·ly** *adv* —**swar·thi·ness** *n*

swash /swosh, swawsh/ *n* **1. CHANNEL** a narrow channel through which tides flow **2. SANDBAR** a sandbar that is washed over by waves **3. SPLASH** the motion or sound of the motion of water splashing or washing over something **4.** same as **swashbuckler** (sense 1) ■ *v* (**swashed, swash·ing, swash·es**) **1.** *vi* **WASH OVER** to strike or move with a splashing sound **2.** *vt* **SPLASH SOMETHING** to throw a liquid at or on something, especially with a splashing sound **3.** *vi* **STRUT** to move in a swaggering, pretentious way (*dated*) [Early 16C. Probably an imitation of the sound of splashing liquid or of a blow]

swash·buck·ler /swósh bùklər, swáwsh-/ *n* **1.** a bold and swaggering swordsman or adventurer **2.** a play, novel, or movie about a swordsman or adventurer [Mid-16C. < SWASH + BUCKLER, from the sound of swords striking shields] —**swash·buck·ling** *adj*

swash let·ter *n* an ornate italic letter with elaborate flourishes and tails [Origin ?]

swas·ti·ka /swóstikə/ *n* **1.** a Nazi and fascist symbol formed by a Greek cross with the four ends of the arms bent in a clockwise direction **2.** an ancient religious symbol formed by a Greek cross, usually with the four ends of the arms bent at right angles in a clockwise or counterclockwise direction [Late 19C. < Sanskrit *svastikaḥ* "good-luck sign" < *svasti* "good luck"]

swat /swot/, **swot** *vti* (**swat·ted, swat·ting, swats; swot·ted, swot·ting, swots**) **STRIKE OR SLAP SOMETHING** to strike or slap somebody or something sharply ■ *n* **1. SHARP BLOW** a sharp blow or slap **2.** *US* **ATTEMPT** a try at doing something [Early 17C. Alteration of SQUAT[1] in the obsolete sense "crush, flatten"]

SWAT /swot/ *n US* a police unit that is trained in the use of military weapons and tactics. Full form **Special Weapons and Tactics**

swatch /swoch/ *n* a piece cut from a material such as fabric or carpeting, used as a sample [Early 16C. Origin ?]

swath /swoth/, **swathe** /swayth/ *n* **1. WIDTH CUT** the width cut by a single passage of a scythe or mowing machine **2. PATH CUT** the path through a crop made during a single passage of a scythe or mowing machine **3. AMOUNT CUT** the amount of grass or grain left in the path made by a single passage of a scythe or mowing machine [Old English *swæþ* "track" < Germanic] ◇ **cut a swath through something** to destroy or use up a large part of something

swathe[1] /swayth/ *vt* (**swathed, swath·ing, swathes**) **1. WRAP SOMEBODY OR SOMETHING COMPLETELY** to wrap somebody or something completely with bandages or a similar covering **2. ENVELOP SOMEBODY OR SOMETHING** to envelop, cover, or hide somebody or something ■ *n* **WRAPPING** a bandage, wrapping, or other binding [Old English *swaþian* "wrap up," origin ?]

swathe[2] /swayth/ *n* same as **swath**

swat·ter /swóttər/, **swot·ter** *n* **1.** a flat meshed flexible piece of metal or plastic attached to a long handle, used to kill insects, especially flies **2.** a baseball player who frequently makes extra-base hits, especially home runs

sway /sway/ *v* (**swayed, sway·ing, sways**) **1.** *vti* **SWING** to swing back and forth, or cause something to do this **2.** *vi* **LEAN OVER REPEATEDLY** to lean or bend to one side or in different directions in turn **3.** *vti* **WAVER BETWEEN OPINIONS** to go back and forth between two or more opinions, or make somebody do this **4.** *vt* **INFLUENCE SOMEBODY** to persuade or influence somebody to believe or do something (*usually passive*) ○ *Don't let yourself be swayed.* **5.** *vi* **MOVE GRACEFULLY** to move back and forth in a graceful way **6.** *vi* **STAGGER** to move from side to side in a clumsy and unsteady way **7.** *vt* NAUT **HOIST SOMETHING** to hoist a yard, mast, or other spar (*technical*) ■ *n* **1. SWINGING MOTION** the act of swinging back and forth **2. CONTROL OVER SOMEBODY** rule or control over a person, group, or area [13C. Probably < N Germanic] —**sway·a·ble** *adj* —**sway·er** *n* ◇ **hold**

sway to have control or influence over a person or place

sway·back /swáy bàk/ *n* an extreme inward or downward curving of the spine in horses and human beings

sway bar *n US* AUTOMOT same as **antiroll bar**

Swa·zi /swaázee/ (*plural same* or **-zis**) *n* **1.** a member of an African people who live in Swaziland and parts of eastern South Africa **2.** the Bantu language of the Swazi people, an official language of Swaziland. Native speakers: 2 million. [Late 19C. Alteration of Nguni *Mswati*, former Swazi king] —**Swa·zi** *adj*

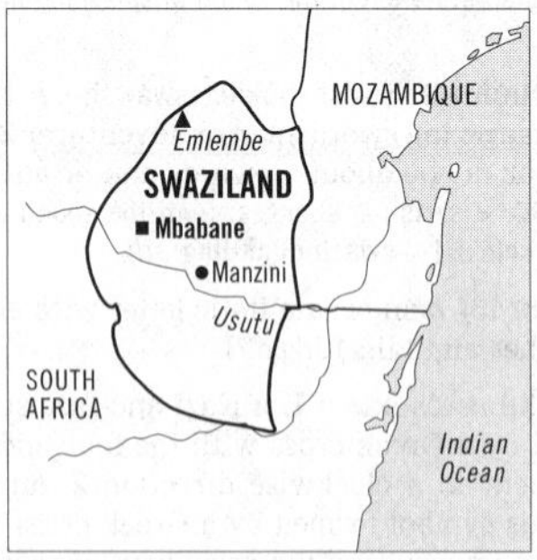

Swaziland

Swa·zi·land /swaázee lànd/ landlocked country in southern Africa. It became an independent member of the British Commonwealth in 1968. Language: Swazi, English. Currency: lilangeni. Capital: Mbabane. Population: 1,161,219 (2003). Area: 6,704 sq. mi./17,363 sq. km. Official name **Kingdom of Swaziland**

swbd, **swbd.** *abbr* switchboard

SWbS *abbr* COMPASS southwest by south

SWbW *abbr* COMPASS southwest by west

swear /swer/ (**swore** /swawr/, **sworn** /swawrn/, **swear·ing**, **swears**) *v* **1.** *vti* **AFFIRM TRUTH OF SOMETHING** to declare solemnly or forcefully that what is said is true, sometimes calling somebody or something thought to be sacred as a witness ○ *She swore on her mother's grave that she had done as she had been asked.* **2.** *vti* **SOLEMNLY PROMISE SOMETHING** to promise something very solemnly ○ *He swore that he would serve humanity.* **3.** *vi* **USE OFFENSIVE WORD OR WORDS** to use blasphemous or obscene language, usually as an expression of strong feelings or with the intention of giving offense **4.** *vti* **TAKE OATH** to make a formal promise in a court of law or when taking up an official position **5.** *vti* **DECLARE SOMETHING ON OATH** to make a solemn statement under oath, especially in a court of law, or make somebody do this **6.** *vt* **MAKE SOMEBODY MAKE PROMISE** to cause somebody to make a solemn promise to do something ○ *We were sworn to secrecy.* [Old English *swerian* < Indo-European] —**swear·er** *n*

swear by *vt* **1.** to have great faith or complete confidence in the effectiveness of something or the ability of somebody for a designated purpose or task **2.** to use the name of somebody or something thought to be sacred in order to reinforce a solemn declaration or promise

swear in *vt* to cause somebody to make a formal promise in a court of law or when taking up an official position

swear off *vt* to make a solemn promise to give something up, especially a bad habit

swear out *vt* to issue a warrant for arrest by making a charge or accusation under a formal oath

swear·word /swér wùrd/ *n* a word or phrase that is considered unacceptable in polite language, especially one that is blasphemous or obscene, used to express strong feelings or give offense

sweat /swet/ *n* **1. MOISTURE ON SKIN** the clear salty liquid that passes to the surface of the skin when somebody is hot or as a result of strenuous activity, fear, anxiety, or illness **2. STATE OF HAVING SWEAT ON SKIN** the production or secretion of sweat, e.g., during strenuous activity or illness, or a state of fear or anxiety that causes this **3. HARD OR BORING WORK** hard, unpleasant, or tedious work **4.** SCI **LIQUID EXUDED TO SURFACE** drops of liquid that ooze through and collect on the surface of something, e.g., sap on a tree **5.** PHYS **MOISTURE CONDENSED ON SURFACE** drops of liquid that appear on the surface of something, usually by condensation of water vapor from the surrounding warmer air **6.** HORSERACING **RUN BEFORE RACE** a run that a horse has before a race, as exercise ■ **sweats** *npl US* CLOTHING **TWO-PIECE SPORTS OUTFIT** a sweatshirt and sweatpants made of matching fabric and worn together for sport or casual activities (*informal*) ■ *v* (**sweat·ed, sweat·ing, sweats**) **1.** *vti* **PERSPIRE** to produce a clear salty liquid on the surface of the skin as a result of being hot or as a result of strenuous activity, fear, anxiety, or illness **2.** *vt* **MAKE SOMEBODY SWEAT** to make somebody sweat, e.g., as a medical treatment **3.** *vt* **WET OR MARK SOMETHING WITH SWEAT** to make something damp or stained with sweat **4.** *vti* **COOK SOMETHING IN OWN JUICES** to cook something in a pan in its own juices with a small amount of fat or oil until tender, or be cooked in this way **5.** *vt* **HEAT SOLDER UNTIL IT MELTS** to heat solder until it melts and runs between surfaces to bond them **6.** *vi* **WORK HARD** to work very hard or overwork (*informal*) **7.** *vt* **OVERWORK OR UNDERPAY EMPLOYEES** to make somebody work very hard, often in poor conditions or for low wages (*informal*) **8.** *vt* **EXTORT INFORMATION FROM SOMEBODY** to force somebody to give up information, especially by relentless interrogation or physical violence (*informal*) **9.** *vi* **BE UNDER STRESS** to be very anxious, impatient, or afraid (*informal*) ○ *He left them sweating in the corridor while he made up his mind.* **10.** *vi* **SUFFER FOR WRONGDOING** to suffer physically or mentally, especially as a punishment (*informal*) **11.** *vti* SCI **EXUDE LIQUID AT SURFACE** to produce or form as liquid beads by oozing through the surface of something and collecting there **12.** *vti* SCI **FORM OR APPEAR AS MOISTURE** to form as moisture on a surface, usually by condensation of water vapor from the surrounding warmer air, or produce moisture in this way **13.** *vti* AGRIC **REMOVE MOISTURE FROM SOMETHING** to remove moisture from something, or have moisture removed, e.g., when fermenting fruits or tobacco or when curing animal hides [Old English *swǣt* < Indo-European] —**sweat·less** *adj* ◇ **no sweat 1.** used to say that something can be done with ease and without foreseeable problems (*slang*) ○ *We'll get it there on time. No sweat.* **2.** not requiring effort or difficulty ○ *the no sweat way to learn a language*

sweat off *vt* to get rid of excess weight by sweating, e.g., in a sauna or through strenuous activity

sweat out *vt* **1. GET RID OF ILLNESS BY SWEATING** to relieve the symptoms of an illness by maintaining a raised body temperature, and hence cause profuse sweating **2. ENDURE SOMETHING TO END** to carry on doing something difficult or put up with something unpleasant until it is over (*informal*) **3.** *US* **WAIT FOR SOMETHING ANXIOUSLY** to wait for something in a state of anxiety (*slang*)

sweat·band /swét bànd/ *n* **1.** a strip of terry cloth worn around the head or wrists to stop sweat running into the eyes or onto the hands while playing sports **2.** a strip of fabric or leather sewn inside a hat to protect it from damage by sweat

sweat·box /swét bòks/ *n* **1. DEVICE FOR REMOVING WATER FROM HIDES** a device in which hides or some fruits are placed to remove water **2. CONFINED PLACE** a very small room, especially a narrow cell where a prisoner is confined for punishment (*informal*) **3. PLACE WHERE SOMEBODY SWEATS** a place where somebody is made to sweat through heat or fear (*informal*)

sweat·ed /swéttəd/ *adj* **1.** made to work very hard in poor conditions for low wages **2.** performed or produced by employees who are made to work very hard in poor conditions for low wages

sweat eq·ui·ty *n* **1.** equity in property earned by virtue of carrying out manual work to improve the property or make it habitable **2.** manual labor contributed in restoring a property with a view to gaining some equity in it

sweat·er /swéttər/ *n* **1.** a warm knitted piece of clothing, usually with long sleeves, worn on the upper part of the body **2.** somebody who sweats in a particular way

sweat gland *n* a small tube-shaped gland in the skin of most parts of the body from which sweat is released

sweat lodge *n* a hut, cavern, or building heated by steam from water poured over hot rocks and used, especially by Native Americans, for therapeutic or ritual sweating

sweat·pants /swét pànts/ *npl* long pants made of a soft knitted fabric, often with elastic at the waist and ankles, worn casually or for exercising

sweat·shirt /swét shùrt/ *n* a long-sleeved pullover or zipped jacket made of soft knitted fabric, worn casually or for sport

sweat·shop /swét shòp/ *n* a small factory or other establishment where employees are made to work very hard in poor conditions for low wages

sweat suit *n* a sweatshirt and sweatpants made of matching fabric and worn together for sport or casual activities

sweat·y /swéttee/ (**-i·er, -i·est**) *adj* **1. DAMP WITH SWEAT** damp with or smelling of sweat **2. CAUSING SWEAT** making somebody sweat **3.** SCI **WITH MOISTURE ON SURFACE** having drops of exuded or condensed liquid on the surface —**sweat·i·ly** *adv* —**sweat·i·ness** *n*

Swed. *abbr* Sweden

swede /sweed/ *n UK* same as **rutabaga** [Early 19C. < SWEDE; from its introduction (into Scotland) from Sweden]

Swede /sweed/ *n* somebody who comes from Sweden [Early 17C. < Middle Low German or Middle Dutch *Swēde*, probably < Old Norse *Svíar* (plural) "Swedes" + *þjóð* "people"]

Sweden

Swe·den /sweéd'n/ country in Scandinavia, in northwestern Europe. Language: Swedish. Currency: krona. Capital: Stockholm. Population: 8,878,085 (2003). Area: 173,732 sq. mi./449,964 sq. km. Official name **Kingdom of Sweden**

Swe·den·borg /sweéd'n bàwrg/, **Emanuel** (1688–1772) Swedish scientist and theologian. His theology, deriving from his mystical experiences, was the basis of a religious movement. Born **Swedberg, Emanuel** —**Swe·den·bor·gi·an** /sweéd'n báwrjee ən, -gee ən/ *n, adj*

Swed·ish /sweédish/ *n* **OFFICIAL LANGUAGE OF SWEDEN** the official language of Sweden and an official language of Finland, belonging to the North Germanic branch of the Indo-European family of languages. Native speakers: 8.5 million. ■ *adj* **1. OF SWEDEN** relating to Sweden, or its people or culture **2. OF SWEDISH** relating to the Swedish language [Early 17C. <SWEDEN or SWEDE]

LANGUAGE HERITAGE See *Scandinavian.*

Swed·ish mas·sage *n* a system of massage employing both active and passive exercising of the muscles and joints

Swed·ish mile *n* a unit of measure used in Sweden equal to 6.2 mi./10 km

sween·y /sweénee/, **sween·ey** *n* atrophy of the shoulder muscles of horses resulting from harness pressure on nerves going to these muscles [Early 19C. Origin ?]

sweep /sweep/ *v* (**swept** /swept/, **sweep·ing**, **sweeps**) **1.** *vti* **CLEAN PLACE WITH BRUSH** to remove something such as dust, dirt, debris, or snow from the floor or ground with a brush, broom, or similar implement **2.** *vt* **MOVE SOMETHING WITH HORIZONTAL STROKE** to move something with a long smooth stroke or a quick brushing stroke ○ *I swept the papers off the desk.* **3.** *vti* **BRUSH AGAINST GROUND** to brush against a horizontal surface such as the floor or the ground **4.** *vi* **MOVE WITH SPEED AND FORCE** to move quickly, smoothly, and forcefully, often in a large body or group ○ *The crowd swept across the bridge.* **5.** *vi* **MOVE WITH DIGNITY** to move quickly and smoothly with a proud, majestic, or self-important air ○ *swept angrily out of the room* **6.** *vti* **MOVE ACROSS PLACE** to move quickly and forcefully across an area ○ *the gales that are sweeping the country* **7.** *vti* **SPREAD THROUGH PLACE** to pass or spread quickly through a place ○ *The news swept through the city.* **8.** *vt* **CARRY SOMEBODY OR SOMETHING ALONG** to carry somebody or something quickly and forcefully in the same direction ○ *swept along by the current* **9.** *vt* **STRONGLY INFLUENCE SOMEBODY** to strongly influence or overwhelm somebody (*often passive*) ○ *We were swept along by their enthusiasm.* **10.** *vti* **WIN SOMETHING OVERWHELMINGLY** to win something easily and overwhelmingly, or win all the games in a series or set of games for a championship ○ *watched them sweep to victory* **11.** *vi* **STRETCH OUT IN ARC** to extend in a long smooth graceful curve or a wide circle ○ *plains sweeping down to the coast* **12.** *vti* **EXTEND OVER WIDE AREA** to be directed over a wide range or the entire area of something ○ *Her eyes swept around the room.* **13.** *vti* **SEARCH PLACE FOR SOMETHING** to search a place for something, e.g., an area of water for mines or a room for hidden recording devices **14.** *vt* **CLEAR CHIMNEY** to remove soot from the inside of a chimney with a long-handled brush ■ *n* **1. BOUT OF CLEANING WITH BRUSH** a cleaning of something with a brush, broom, or similar implement **2. BRUSHING STROKE** a quick brushing stroke **3. LONG SMOOTH MOVEMENT** a long smooth curved movement ○ *with a sweep of her arm* **4. LONG SMOOTH CURVE** a long smooth graceful curve ○ *the sweep of the coastline* **5. WIDE EXPANSE** a wide expanse or extent ○ *the sweep of the horizon* **6. CURVED RANGE** the range over which something is directed, usually a wide arc or circle ○ *stay out of the sweep of the searchlights* **7. BROAD RANGE** the broad range or comprehensive nature of something ○ *the sweep of history* **8. SEARCH** a thorough search of a place ○ *a sweep of the neighborhood* **9. OVERWHELMING VICTORY** an overwhelming or absolute victory ○ *their sweep to power* **10. WINDMILL SAIL** a sail of a windmill **11. POLE FOR LIFTING BUCKET IN WELL** a long pole used as a lever to raise or lower a bucket in a well **12.** OCCUPATIONS same as **chimney sweep** **13.** BOATING **OAR FOR PROPELLING BOAT** a long oar that is used to propel small boats or sometimes act as a rudder **14.** ELECTRONICS **ELECTRON BEAM MOTION IN CATHODE-RAY TUBE** the steady movement of the electron beam across the fluorescent surface of a cathode ray tube. The motion may be straight, as with television screens, or circular, as with radar screens. ■ **sweeps** *npl* **TELEVISION RATINGS IN PARTICULAR PERIOD** a periodic survey of television ratings that is used to determine advertising rates, or the period when these ratings are done [13C. Probably < past tense of Old English *swāpan* "sweep" < Germanic, "to swing"] —**sweep·y** *adj* ◇ **make a clean sweep (of somebody** *or* **something) 1.** to have a complete change by getting rid of everyone or everything unwanted or unnecessary **2.** to win every competition, race, or contest in a series of competitions, races, or contests

sweep away, sweep aside *vt* to remove, dismiss, or destroy something quickly, forcefully, and completely

sweep up *vti* to remove dust, dirt, or debris from the floor or ground with a brush, broom, or similar implement

sweep·back /sweép bàk/ *n* an aircraft wing that slants backward toward the tail assembly, forming an acute angle with the fuselage

sweep·er /sweépər/ *n* **1. SOMEBODY WHO SWEEPS** somebody whose job involves sweeping something, usually floors or roads **2. SOMETHING THAT SWEEPS** a device or machine, usually fitted with brushes, that sweeps something such as a floor or a road **3.** SPORTS **ROVING DEFENSIVE PLAYER** in soccer and some other team sports, a defensive player who is not assigned to cover an attacking player, but plays across the field in the space between other defenders and the goalkeeper **4.** *S Asia* **INDIAN HOUSE CLEANER** a woman or girl who is employed to clean somebody's house

sweep·ing /sweéping/ *adj* **1. ON LARGE SCALE** wide-ranging and comprehensive, usually affecting a large number of people or things ○ *sweeping reforms* **2. TOO GENERAL** failing to take specific exceptions or details into consideration ○ *a sweeping condemnation of modern youth* **3. OVERWHELMING** complete, overwhelming, or decisive ○ *a sweeping victory* **4. WITH BROAD EXTENT** covering a large area, usually a wide arc or circle ○ *included in her sweeping glance* ■ *n* **ACT OF USING BRUSH** the action of somebody who sweeps with a brush or broom ■ **sweep·ings** *npl* **THINGS SWEPT UP** dirt and refuse swept up —**sweep·ing·ly** *adv* —**sweep·ing·ness** *n*

sweeps /sweeps/ *US npl* a periodic survey of television ratings that is used to determine advertising rates, or the period when these ratings are done (*takes a plural verb*) ■ *n* same as **sweepstakes** (*informal; takes a singular or plural verb*)

sweep·stakes /sweép stàyks/ (*plural same*) *n* **1.** a lottery in which the payout is determined by the amount paid in and the winner determined by the outcome of a horse race **2.** the prize offered or won in a sweepstakes

sweet /sweet/ *adj* **1. TASTING OR SMELLING OF SUGAR** tasting or smelling of sugar or a similar substance **2. CONTAINING OR RETAINING SUGAR** containing a relatively large amount of sugar, or retaining some natural sugars ○ *sweet cider* **3. NOT BITTER, SALT, OR SOUR** associated with the basic taste sensation that is not bitter, salt, or sour **4. FRESH** not stale, rancid, or soured ○ *sweet water* **5. NOT SALTY** not salty or saline ○ *sweet butter* **6. PLEASING TO SENSES** pleasing to any of the senses ○ *the sweet strains of the violin* **7. SATISFYING** desirable, gratifying, or satisfying ○ *Revenge turned out not to be sweet after all.* **8. KIND** kind, thoughtful, or generous ○ *He's so sweet: he never forgets my birthday.* **9. VERY PLEASING TO LOOK AT** having an appearance that is charming or endearing ○ *a sweet little cottage by the lake* **10. EXCELLENT** excellent or extremely good (*slang*) **11. RESPECTED** dear, respected, or beloved (*archaic*) ○ *Indeed, my sweet lord.* **12.** AGRIC **NOT ACIDIC** describes land that contains no acid or corrosive substances **13.** INDUST **CONTAINING LITTLE OR NO SULFUR** describes gasoline or oil that contains little or no sulfur ○ *rising costs of sweet crude* **14.** *Carib* **PLEASURABLE** pleasing and delightful ■ *adv* **PLEASANTLY** in a pleasant manner ○ *sing sweet* ■ *n* **1. SWEET FOOD** an item of sweet food **2. SENSATION OF SWEETNESS** a sweet taste or smell ○ *had to take the bitter with the sweet* **3. SOMETHING PLEASANT** a pleasant thing or experience (*literary*) ○ *squander the sweets of life* **4. DEAR** used as a term of endearment ○ *Come to me, my sweet.* **5.** *UK* same as **candy** *n* (sense 2) **6.** *US* FOOD same as **sweet potato** (*informal*) **7.** *UK* **DESSERT** a course or dish of sweet food served at or near the end of a meal **8.** INDUST **SULFUR-FREE NATURAL GAS OR OIL** a natural gas or crude oil that is essentially free from acidic or odorous sulfur compounds [Old English *swēte* < Indo-European] —**sweet·ish** *adj*—**sweet·ly** *adv*—**sweet·ness** *n* ◇ **be sweet on somebody** to be in love with somebody (*dated informal*)

SPELLCHECK See *suite*.

sweet a·ca·cia *n* same as **huisache**

sweet a·lys·sum *n* a widely-cultivated annual plant. Native to: Europe. Flowers: low-growing, fragrant white, pink, purple, in clusters. Latin name: *Lobularia maritima.*

sweet-and-sour *adj* cooked in or served with a sauce that has sugar and vinegar among the ingredients

sweet bas·il *n* PLANTS same as **basil**

sweet bay *n* **1.** a magnolia bush or tree with yellow-green leaves and red fruit. Flowers: fragrant, white. Native to: eastern United States. Latin name: *Magnolia virginia.* **2.** TREES same as **bay**[4] (sense 1)

sweet birch *n* **1.** a hard dark wood **2.** a birch with smooth blackish brown bark and aromatic stems that yield methyl salicylate. Native to: eastern United States. Latin name: *Betula lenta.*

sweet·bread /sweét brèd/ *n* the pancreas or thymus of a calf, lamb, or other young animal soaked, fried, and eaten as food

sweet·bri·ar /sweét brìr/ (*plural* **-ars** or *same*), **sweet·bri·er** (*plural* **-ers** or *same*) *n* a rose that has a long stem with prickles and fragrant leaves. Flowers: rosy pink or white, single. Native to: Europe, Asia. Latin name: *Rosa rubiginosa.*

sweet cher·ry *n* **1.** a sweet firm-fleshed cherry **2.** a cultivated variety of cherry tree

sweet cic·e·ly /-síss'lee/ (*plural same*) *n* **1.** a plant with aromatic fleshy roots. Flowers: small, white, in clusters. Native to: America, Asia. Genus: *Osmorhiza.* **2.** a perennial plant with aromatic compound leaves. Flowers: small, white, in umbels. Native to: Europe. Latin name: *Myrrhis odorata.*

sweet ci·der *n US* BEVERAGES same as **cider** (sense 1)

sweet clo·ver *n* PLANTS same as **melilot**

sweet corn *n* **1.** the sweet yellow kernels of some varieties of corn, cooked and eaten as a vegetable **2.** a variety of corn with yellow kernels that contain a high concentration of sugar. Latin name: *Zea mays rugosa.*

sweet·en /sweét'n/ (**-ened, -en·ing, -ens**) *v* **1.** *vti* **INCREASE IN SWEETNESS** to make something taste sweet or sweeter by adding sugar or another natural or artificial substance, or become sweet or sweeter in flavor **2.** *vt* **IMPROVE TASTE OR SMELL OF SOMETHING** to make something taste or smell more pleasant **3.** *vt* **MAKE SOMETHING MORE DESIRABLE** to make something more attractive, agreeable, or acceptable ○ *sweeten the offer* **4.** *vt* **SOFTEN SOMEBODY** to make somebody kinder, gentler, friendlier, or calmer ○ *might sweeten his temper* **5.** *vt* **PERSUADE SOMEBODY** to persuade somebody by flattery, cajolery, or bribery to accept or agree to something **6.** *vti* INDUST **IMPROVE PROPERTIES OF SOMETHING** to improve a product such as petroleum by making it less corrosive and foul-smelling, or by making its color more acceptable, or be improved in this way. Petroleum products are sweetened during refining by the removal of sulfides or the conversion of them into disulfides. **7.** *vt US* AGRIC, GARDENING **LESSEN ACIDITY OF** to make something less acidic by adding a chemical preparation to it ○ *He spread some lime in the garden to sweeten the soil.* **8.** *vt US* FIN **INCREASE VALUE OF COLLATERAL** to add securities to collateral so that its value is increased **9.** *vt* CARDS **INCREASE VALUE OF POT** in poker, to add stakes to a pot remaining from a previous deal (*informal*)

sweet·en·er /sweét'nər/ *n* **1.** a natural or artificial substance that is added to food or drink to make it sweet or sweeter, especially a synthetic substance used in place of sugar **2.** something given as a bribe, incentive, or means of persuading somebody to accept or agree to something (*informal*)

sweet·en·ing /sweét'ning/ *n* **1.** a substance that makes food or drink sweet or sweeter, especially an artificial additive **2.** the act of making something sweet or sweeter

sweet-eye *n Carib* a loving or flirtatious wink

sweet fern *n* a bush with aromatic leaves similar to those of a fern. Flowers: small, brownish, in heads. Native to: eastern North America. Latin name: *Comptonia peregrina.*

sweet flag *n* a perennial marsh plant with narrow sword-shaped leaves and an aromatic rootstock. Flowers: tiny, greenish. Latin name: *Acorus calamus.*

sweet gale *n* a bush of the bayberry family that grows in marshy regions and has aromatic lance-shaped leaves. Native to: Europe, Asia, North America. Latin name: *Myrica gale.*

sweet gum *n* **1.** an amber aromatic tree resin **2.** a tree of the witch hazel family that has lobed leaves, hard wood, and round prickly fruit clusters, and is the source of an amber aromatic resin. Native to: North America. Latin name: *Liquidambar styraciflua.*

sweet·heart /sweét haàrt/ *n* **1. AFFECTIONATE TERM OF ADDRESS** used as a term of endearment, usually to a lover or child **2. KIND PERSON** a kind or obliging person ○ *Be a sweetheart and make me a cup of coffee.* **3. BOYFRIEND OR GIRLFRIEND** a boyfriend, girlfriend, or lover (*dated*) **4. SOMETHING CHERISHED** something cherished for its fine qualities and often considered one of a kind

sweet·heart a·gree·ment *n* an arrangement arrived at secretly to benefit some at the expense of the rest, especially an industrial agreement between union and management representatives that is not in the workers' best interest [< the privileged treatment of one party]

sweet·heart neck·line *n* on women's clothing, a low-cut neckline with two curves over the bust, making the bodice look heart-shaped

sweet·ie /swēetee/ *n* (*informal*) **1.** used as a term of endearment **2.** a likable or lovable person or animal

sweet·ie pie *n* somebody who is lovable or likable (*informal*)

sweet·ing /swēeting/ *n* an eating apple with sweet flesh

sweet mar·jo·ram *n* an herb with aromatic leaves used as a seasoning in cookery and salads. Flowers: small, purple. Native to: Mediterranean. Latin name: *Origanum majorana.*

sweet·meat /swēet mèet/ *n* a superior type of candy or confectionery served at the end of a meal or with tea (*archaic*)

sweet·ness and light *n* pleasantness and friendliness or peace and harmony, especially in contrast to normal behavior or circumstances ○ *He has a vile temper, but when he gets his way, he's all sweetness and light.*

sweet noth·ings *npl* romantic words or phrases

sweet oil *n* a mild-flavored oil, e.g., sweet almond oil or grapeseed oil

sweet pea *n* a widely cultivated climbing plant of the legume family. Flowers: sweet-scented, butterfly-shaped. Native to: Italy. Latin name: *Lathyrus odoratus.*

sweet pep·per *n* **1.** a bell-shaped red, green, or orange fruit eaten raw or cooked as a vegetable **2.** a plant that produces sweet peppers. Latin name: *Capsicum frutescens grossum.*

sweet po·ta·to *n* **1.** a fleshy orange root cooked and eaten as a vegetable **2.** a vine that produces sweet potatoes. Flowers: funnel-shaped, purplish. Native to: tropical America. Latin name: *Ipomoea batatas.* **3.** *US* same as **ocarina** (*informal*)

sweet·shop /swēet shòp/ *n UK* same as **candy store**

sweet-smell·ing *adj* having a pleasant smell

sweet·sop /swēet sòp/ (*plural* **-sops** or *same*) *n* **1.** a fruit with a hard green rind and a sweet edible pulp **2.** an evergreen bush that produces sweetsops. Native to: tropical America. Latin name: *Annona squamosa.* [< the sweet pulp of its fruit]

sweet sor·ghum *n* PLANTS same as **sorgo**

sweet spot *n* **1.** the most effective place to hit the ball on a racket, bat, club, or other piece of sports equipment **2.** the price for a product at which the most profit is achieved [< SWEET "desirable"]

sweet sul·tan (*plural* **sweet sul·tans** or *same*) *n* a bush with large varicolored flowers. Native to: eastern Mediterranean region. Latin name: *Centaurea moschata.*

sweet talk *n* flattering or pleasing words used to persuade somebody (*informal*)

sweet-talk *vti* to use flattering or pleasing words in order to persuade somebody to do something (*informal*)

sweet tooth *n* a fondness for sweet food

sweet wil·liam /-wíllyəm/ (*plural* **sweet wil·liams** or *same*) *n* a plant widely grown in gardens. Flowers: white, pink, red, or purple, with banded or mottled patterns, in flat clusters. Native to: Europe, Asia. Latin name: *Dianthus barbatus.*

sweet wood·ruff *n* PLANTS same as **woodruff**

swell /swel/ *v* (**swelled, swelled** or **swol·len** /swṓlən/, **swell·ing, swells**) **1.** *vti* **INCREASE IN SIZE** to become, or make something, larger, fuller, or rounder, or expand in size or shape, usually as a result of pressure from within ○ *the wind swelled the sails* **2.** *vi* MED **BECOME LARGER THAN NORMAL** to increase in size temporarily, typically as a result of injury, infection, or other medical condition ○ *My ankles had swelled in the heat.* **3.** *vti* **INCREASE IN QUANTITY** to increase something in number or amount, usually by adding to it, or increase in this way ○ *new members to swell the ranks of the choir* **4.** *vti* **INCREASE IN DEGREE** to make something stronger or more intense, or become stronger or more intense ○ *could feel indignation swelling inside her* **5.** *vti* MUSIC **INCREASE AND DECREASE IN LOUDNESS** in music, to grow gradually louder and softer in turn, or gradually increase and decrease volume in this way **6.** *vti* **FILL WITH EMOTION** to be filled with a strong feeling or emotion, or cause somebody's heart or soul to be filled with a strong feeling or emotion ○ *His heart swelled with pride.* **7.** *vi* **UNDULATE ON SURFACE** to rise and fall on the surface of something in long large waves ■ *n* **1. UNDULATION OF SEA SURFACE** the rising and falling movement of a large area of the sea as a long wave travels through it without breaking ○ *forecasting rough seas, a heavy swell, and strong winds* **2. ROUND SHAPE** the full, round shape of something **3. BULGE** a bulge or protuberance **4. INCREASING OF SIZE** an increase in size, fullness, or roundness **5. INCREASING OF NUMBER** an increase in number, amount, or degree **6. PROCESS OF SWELLING** the process or an instance of swelling **7. GENTLE SLOPE** a low hill or gentle slope **8.** MUSIC **CRESCENDO THEN DECRESCENDO** a gradual increase in the loudness of music followed by a gradual decrease, or the sign indicating this **9.** MUSIC same as **swell box** **10. FASHIONABLE PERSON** a fashionably and expensively dressed person (*dated informal*) **11. SOMEBODY OF HIGH STATUS** a very important person, especially in society or politics (*dated informal*) ■ *adj* **1. GOOD** very good (*dated*) ○ *did a swell job* **2. GRAND** grand, stylish, or fashionable (*informal dated*) [Old English *swellan* < Germanic]

swell box *n* a device on an organ, usually an enclosed box with pipes, that permits crescendo and decrescendo, a characteristic otherwise lacking on this instrument

swelled head /swéld-/ *n* a feeling of exaggerated self-importance, usually stimulated by personal success or by praise received from others

swell·fish /swél fish/ (*plural same* or **-fish·es**) *n* a puffer fish [< its ability to inflate by swallowing air]

swell·head /swél hèd/ *n US* somebody regarded as conceited and arrogant (*informal*) —**swell·head·ed** *adj* —**swell·head·ed·ness** *n*

swell·ing /swélling/ *n* **1.** an increase in size of part of the body, typically as a result of injury, infection, or other medical condition ○ *The swelling should go down in a couple of days.* **2.** a bulge or protuberance caused by swelling

swel·ter /swéltər/ *vi* (**-tered, -ter·ing, -ters**) **BE OPPRESSED BY HEAT** to feel uncomfortably hot ○ *We had been sweltering in a hot car all afternoon.* ■ *n* **1. UNPLEASANT HEAT** excessive or oppressive heat **2. SENSATION OF HOTNESS** an uncomfortable feeling produced by extreme heat [15C. < Old English *sweltan* "die" < Germanic, "to burn"]

swel·ter·ing /swéltəring/ *adj* **1.** oppressively hot **2.** feeling uncomfortably hot —**swel·ter·ing·ly** *adv*

swept past participle, past tense of **sweep**

swept·back /swépt bàk, swèpt bák/ *adj* describes a wing that is angled backward toward the aircraft's tail

swept·wing /swépt wìng/ *adj* describes an aircraft or missile that has sweptback wings

swerve /swurv/ *vti* (**swerved, swerv·ing, swerves**) to make a sudden change in direction, often to avoid a collision, or make something change direction suddenly ○ *had to swerve the car to avoid a pedestrian* ■ *n* a sudden change in direction [Old English *sweorfan* "file, scour, turn aside" < Indo-European, "to turn"]

swev·en /swévvən/ *n* a dream or a vision experienced in sleep (*archaic or literary*) [Old English *swef(e)n* < Indo-European, "to sleep"]

Sweyn I /swayn/ (960?–1014) king of Denmark. He first invaded England in 994, and by 1014 established his rule sufficiently for his son Canute II to become king (1016–35). Known as **Sweyn Forkbeard**

swid·den /swídd'n/ *n* a place temporarily cleared for agriculture by cutting back and burning off previous growth [Late 18C. Variant of obsolete *swithen* "burn" < Old Norse *sviðna* "be singed"]

swift

swift /swift/ *adj* **1. HAPPENING FAST** happening or done very quickly or suddenly ○ *issued a swift denial* **2. ACTING FAST** acting very quickly or promptly ○ *They were swift to respond.* **3. MOVING FAST** moving or able to move very quickly ■ *adv* **QUICKLY** very quickly ○ *a swift-flowing river* ■ *n* **1.** (*plural same* or **swifts**) BIRDS **SMALL BIRD RESEMBLING SWALLOW** a small dark bird with long narrow wings, related to the hummingbirds and resembling a swallow. Family: Apodidae. **2.** REPT **SMALL FAST LIZARD** a small fast-running lizard. Native to: North America. Genera: *Sceloporus* or *Uta.* **3.** TEXTILES **REEL ON MACHINE** the reel on which yarn is placed while it is wound off [Old English, "quick, moving along a course" < Germanic, "swing, bend"] —**swift·ly** *adv* —**swift·ness** *n*

Swift /swift/, **Jonathan** (1667–1745) Anglo-Irish author and cleric. The dean of St. Patrick's, Dublin, he was the leading satirist of his age. He wrote *A Tale of a Tub* (1704) and *Gulliver's Travels* (1726). See Cultural note at **travel**. Known as **Dean Swift** —**Swift·i·an** *adj*

> "He had been eight years upon a project for extracting sunbeams out of cucumbers, which were to be put into vials hermetically sealed, and let out to warm the air in raw inclement summers."
> [Jonathan Swift, "A Voyage to Laputa," *Gulliver's Travels*; 1726]

> "We have just enough religion to make us hate, but not enough to make us love one another."
> [Jonathan Swift, *Thoughts on Various Subjects*; 1711]

> "There is nothing in this world constant, but inconstancy."
> [Jonathan Swift, *A Critical Essay upon the Faculties of the Mind*; 1709]

Swift Cur·rent /swìft kúr ənt, -kúrrənt/ town and railroad hub in southwestern Saskatchewan, Canada, 152 mi./245 km west of Regina. Population: 14,821 (2001).

swift fox *n* a small fox with large ears. Native to: western North America. Latin name: *Vulpes velox.*

swift·let /swíftlət/ *n* a small cave-dwelling swift whose nest is used in making birds' nest soup. Native to: South Asia. Genus: *Collocalia.*

swig /swig/ (*informal*) *vti* (**swigged, swig·ging, swigs**) to drink something in large gulps ■ *n* a large gulp of drink [Mid-16C. Origin ?] —**swig·ger** *n*

swill /swil/ *v* (**swilled, swill·ing, swills**) **1.** *vti* **DRINK LOT OF SOMETHING** to drink large amounts of something (*disapproving*) **2.** *vti* **MOVE LIQUID AROUND IN SOMETHING** to make liquid move around or over something, or move in this way ○ *He swilled the water around in the bucket.* **3.** *vt* **WASH SOMETHING WITH WATER** to wash or rinse something by flooding or filling it with water **4.** *vt* AGRIC **FEED ANIMALS WITH WATERY FEED** to feed animals, especially hogs, with a watery feed typically containing kitchen waste or food byproducts ■ *n* **1.**

AGRIC **ANIMAL FEED** a watery feed for livestock, especially hogs, typically containing kitchen waste or food byproducts **2. KITCHEN WASTE** kitchen waste or general refuse **3. LARGE DRINK** a large drink or mouthful of drink **4. INFERIOR FOOD OR DRINK** inferior or unpleasant food or drink **5. SLOPPY LIQUID MIXTURE** a sloppy liquid mixture or mess **6. NONSENSE** talk or writing that is utter nonsense (*informal*) [Old English *swillan* < Indo-European] —**swill·er** *n*

swim /swim/ *v* (**swam** /swam/, **swum** /swum/, **swim·ming, swims**) **1.** *vi* **MOVE THROUGH WATER** to move or propel yourself unsupported through water using natural means of propulsion such as legs, tails, or fins **2.** *vt* **TRAVEL DISTANCE BY SWIMMING** to cross a particular stretch of water or travel a particular distance by swimming **3.** *vt* **COMPETE IN SWIMMING RACE** to take part as a competitor in a swimming race, especially one of a particular length **4.** *vt* **SWIM WITH PARTICULAR STROKE** to swim using a particular stroke **5.** *vi* **BE DIZZY** to be dizzy or confused ○ *The noise made my head swim.* **6.** *vi* **SEEM TO MOVE OR SPIN** to appear to move, whirl, or sway ○ *words swimming on the page* **7.** *vi* **FLOAT ON SURFACE** to float on the surface of a liquid ○ *oil swimming on the water* **8.** *vi* **BE COVERED IN LIQUID** to be surrounded or covered with a large quantity of liquid ○ *meat swimming in gravy* **9.** *vi* **HAVE PLENTY** to have a large amount of something ○ *not exactly swimming in offers* ■ *n* **1. SPELL OF SWIMMING** a period of time spent swimming, usually for pleasure or exercise (*often used before a noun*) ○ *went for her morning swim* ○ *a swim club* **2. SMOOTH MOVEMENT** a smooth gliding movement **3. DIZZINESS** dizziness or confusion ○ *with my head in a swim* **4.** FISHING **PLACE WITH MANY FISH** a place where fish are found in abundance [Old English *swimman* < Germanic] —**swim·ma·ble** *adj* —**swim·mer** *n* ◇ **be in the swim** to be involved with the latest fashions or trends

swim blad·der *n* ZOOL same as **air bladder** (sense 1)

~~**swiming**~~ incorrect spelling of **swimming**

swim·mer·et /swìmmə rét, swímmə rèt/ *n* an abdominal appendage of shrimp, lobsters, and some other crustaceans that is adapted for swimming and, in females, for carrying eggs

swim·mer's itch *n* an inflammation of the skin caused by the larvae of some schistosomes that penetrate the skin and cause itching

swim·ming /swímming/ *n* the action or activity of making progress unsupported through water using the arms and legs, whether for pleasure, exercise, or sport

swim·ming·ly /swímminglee/ *adv* very smoothly, easily, and successfully ○ *The whole evening went swimmingly.*

swim·ming pool *n* a water-filled structure in which people can swim, usually set into the ground outdoors or the floor indoors, or a building that houses such a structure

swim·ming trunks *npl* a piece of clothing worn by men and boys for swimming

swim·suit /swím so͞ot/ *n* a piece of clothing worn for swimming

swim·wear /swím wèr/ *n* clothing worn for swimming or with swimsuits

swin·dle /swínd'l/ *vt* (**-dled, -dling, -dles**) to obtain something from somebody, especially money, by deception or fraud ○ *I've been swindled!* ■ *n* a transaction in which one person or organization obtains something from another by deception or fraud [Late 18C. Back-formation < *swindler* < German *Schwindler* "cheat" < *schwindeln* "be dizzy" < Old High German *swintan* "vanish"] —**swin·dler** *n*

swine /swīn/ (*plural same*) *n* **1.** a hog, boar, or similar animal **2.** an offensive term that deliberately insults somebody's manners or principles (*insult*) [Old English *swīn* < Indo-European] —**swin·ish** *adj*

swine fe·ver *n* a very infectious and often fatal viral disease of pigs marked by fever, weakness, lesions, loss of appetite, and diarrhea

swine·herd /swīn hùrd/ *n* somebody who tends hogs (*archaic or literary*)

swine·pox /swīn pòks/ *n* an infectious viral disease of hogs marked by lesions of the skin

swing /swing/ *v* (**swung** /swung/, **swing·ing, swings**) **1.** *vti* **MOVE TO AND FRO** to move freely from side to side or backward and forward, usually hanging from a fixed point, or make something move in this way **2.** *vti* **PIVOT OR ROTATE** to move or turn in a circle or an arc, usually pivoting around a fixed point, or make something move or turn in this way ○ *The door swung open.* **3.** *vti* **SUSPEND OR HANG SOMETHING** to fix something so that it can swing, or be fixed in this way **4.** *vti* **MOVE IN CURVE** to move in a smooth curve, or make something move in this way ○ *The limousine swung into the driveway.* **5.** *vi* **WALK WITH SWAYING MOTION** to walk with a swaying motion in a relaxed or easy manner **6.** *vti* **STRIKE WITH SWEEPING BLOW** to hit or attempt to hit somebody or something with a sweeping blow or stroke ○ *swung wildly at the ball* **7.** *vti* **RIDE ON SWINGING SEAT** to move backward and forward on a swinging seat, or make somebody move in such a way by pushing the person or the seat **8.** *vti* **FLUCTUATE OR VACILLATE** to change from one feeling or condition to another, sometimes quickly or suddenly, or make something or somebody change in this way ○ *Their mood swung between elation and gloom.* **9.** *vt* **ARRANGE OR MANIPULATE SOMETHING** to achieve a desired change or result by using influence, persuasion, or other means (*informal*) ○ *swing a deal* **10.** *vi* **BE HANGED FOR SOMETHING** to be hanged as punishment for something (*informal*) **11.** *vi* **SWAP SEXUAL PARTNERS** to have a number of sexual partners, especially by exchanging them within a group (*slang*) **12.** *vi* **BE LIVELY** to be lively or animated (*slang*) ○ *The party was really swinging by the time we arrived.* **13.** *vi* **BE MODERN AND FASHIONABLE** to be interested in and involved in modern or fashionable trends (*slang*) **14.** *vti* MUSIC **PLAY JAZZ** to play a passage or musical work in big-band jazz music, or be played in this way ■ *n* **1. HANGING SEAT** a seat hung from a frame or branch for somebody to sit on and move backward and forward, especially one on which children play **2. SWINGING MOVEMENT** the process of swinging, or a swinging movement ○ *the swing of the pendulum* **3. RANGE OF MOVEMENT** the curve or distance covered by something as it swings **4. SWEEPING STROKE OR BLOW** a sweeping stroke, blow, or punch ○ *took a swing at the ball* **5. WAY OF SWINGING** the manner of movement used to swing a bat or club or bowl a ball ○ *practicing her golf swing* **6. SHIFT OR FLUCTUATION** a sudden or significant change, especially in the way people think or act ○ *frequent mood swings* **7. UP-AND-DOWN CYCLIC CHANGES** the up-and-down cycles of something such as business profits, economic growth, or stock prices **8. STEADY PROGRESSION** a steady progression or advance across territory, or through a process, activity, or phase ○ *took a swing through the Midwest* **9.** *US* **A CIRCULAR TOUR** a tour or course that finishes where it began, e.g., as part of a political campaign **10.** MUSIC **STYLE OF JAZZ MUSIC** jazz music of the 1930s and 1940s, suitable for dancing and generally played by big bands **11.** DANCE **LIVELY DANCE STYLE** lively dancing for couples involving syncopated steps, spins, and jumps, with one partner often swinging and lifting the other off the ground [Old English *swingan* "flog, rush" < Germanic, "violent circulatory movement"] —**swing·y** *adj* ◇ **get into the swing of things** to get into the established rhythm or routine ◇ **in full swing** in vigorous progress

swing around *vi* **1.** to turn around quickly or suddenly **2.** to change direction quickly or suddenly

swing by *vti* to visit a person or place briefly on the way to another location (*informal*)

swing bridge *n* a low movable bridge that pivots horizontally on a pier in midstream and is swung parallel to the stream to allow ships to pass

swing-by *n* a deliberate change in the course of an interplanetary vehicle caused by moving through the gravitational field of an astronomical object, especially that of a planet

swing door *n UK* same as **swinging door**

swinge /swinj/ (**swinged, swinge·ing, swing·es**) *vt* to punish somebody severely, especially by beating or flogging (*literary*) [Old English *swengan* < Germanic]

swinge·ing /swínjing/ *adj UK* causing great harm or hardship ○ *swingeing cuts in spending*

swing·er /swíngər/ *n* **1.** somebody who or something that swings ○ *caught on the chin by a left-handed swinger* **2.** somebody who lives an unconventional and hedonistic life, especially somebody who exchanges sexual partners with others (*slang*)

swing·ing /swínging/ *adj* **1. LIVELY** lively and animated ○ *a swinging party* **2. FASHIONABLE** spirited and fashionable (*dated*) **3. OFTEN CHANGING SEXUAL PARTNERS** frequently changing or exchanging sexual partners (*slang*)

swing·ing door *n* a door that can be opened by pushing from either side, especially one that swings shut automatically

swin·gle /swíng g'l/ *n* a wooden instrument like a knife or paddle used to beat hemp or flax and scrape woody portions out of the material ■ *vt* (**-gled, -gling, -gles**) to beat and scrape hemp or flax with a swingle [15C. < Middle Dutch *swinghel*]

swin·gle·tree /swíng g'l trèe/ *n Can, UK* same as **whiffletree**

swing·man /swíngmən/ (*plural* **-men** /-mən/) *n US* a player who is able to play in two different positions, especially a basketball player who can play both forward and guard [Mid-20C. < the player's shifting positions]

swing shift *n* **1.** a period of work beginning in the afternoon and ending at night. It overlaps between the day shift and the night shift. **2.** a group of employees working on a swing shift

swing vot·er *n* somebody who does not consistently vote for the same political party in elections

swing-wing *adj* describes an aircraft whose wings are constructed to allow them to move backward and forward relative to the fuselage during flight. The rearward configuration improves streamlining at high speeds, while the forward configuration improves lifting qualities during takeoff and landing. ■ *n* an airplane with variable-sweep wings

swipe /swīp/ *v* (**swiped, swip·ing, swipes**) **1.** *vt* **STEAL SOMETHING** to steal something, often with a snatching movement (*informal*) **2.** *vti* **HIT SOMEBODY OR SOMETHING HARD** to strike or attempt to strike somebody or something with a forceful swinging or sweeping blow **3.** *vti* **PUT CARD THROUGH MACHINE** to pass a plastic card on which data has been stored magnetically through an electronic reading device, e.g., to gain access to a building or to initiate a banking transaction, or to be read successfully by such a device ○ *I can't get the card to swipe.* ■ *n* **1. SWINGING BLOW** a forceful swinging or sweeping blow ○ *took a swipe at me but missed* **2. CRITICAL ATTACK** a critical remark or attack (*informal*) **3. PIVOTED POLE** a long pole used as a lever to raise or lower a bucket in a well [Early 19C. Probably variant of SWEEP] —**swip·er** *n*

swipe card *n* a plastic card on which data has been stored magnetically that is read and decoded by an electronic device that the card is passed through

swirl /swurl/ *v* (**swirled, swirl·ing, swirls**) **1.** *vti* **TURN WITH CIRCULAR MOTION** to turn around and around with a twisting or spiraling movement, or make something move in this way ○ *caught up in a swirling throng of dancers and musicians* **2.** *vi* **BE DIZZY** to be dizzy or confused ■ *n* **1. CIRCULAR MOTION** a turning, twisting, spiraling movement, or something that moves in this way **2. SPIRAL** a curl, twist, or spiral ○ *a carpet with black swirls on a red background* **3. CONFUSION** dizziness or confusion [15C. Origin ?] —**swirl·y** *adj*

swish /swish/ *v* (**swished, swish·ing, swish·es**) **1.** *vi* **MAKE, OR MOVE WITH, WHISTLING SOUND** to make the soft smooth whistling or rustling sound of something moving quickly through the air, or move with such a sound **2.** *vt* **MOVE SOMETHING WITH WHISTLING SOUND** to cause something to make or move with a swishing sound ○ *swishing a sword* **3.** *vt* **CUT WITH SWIFT SHARP BLOW** to cut or strike something or somebody with a swift sharp swishing blow **4.** *vt* BASKETBALL **SINK BASKETBALL** to throw a basketball through the hoop in such a way that it makes a quiet swishing sound and does not hit the rim ○ *swished a pair of free throws* ■ *n* **1. SWISHING SOUND** a soft smooth whistling or rustling sound ○ *heard the swish of her skirt* **2. SWISHING MOVEMENT** a movement that makes a swishing sound

○ *the angry swish of its tail* **3.** BASKETBALL **BASKETBALL SHOT** in basketball, a shot that goes through the hoop with a quiet swishing sound and does not hit the rim **4. STICK** a rod used to beat or flog a person or animal **5. SHARP BLOW** a sharp blow to a person or animal made with a rod **6.** *US* **OFFENSIVE TERM** an offensive term for a gay man that deliberately insults his manner or behavior as being more characteristic of a woman (*slang insult*) ■ *adj* **1. ELEGANT** elegant and fashionable (*informal*) ○ *a swish restaurant* **2.** *US* **OFFENSIVE TERM** an offensive term meaning gay and stereotypically effeminate (*insult*) [Mid-18C. Probably an imitation of the sound made when moving through or brushing against something] —**swish·y** *adj*

Swiss /swiss/ *n* (*plural same*) **1. SOMEBODY FROM SWITZERLAND** somebody who comes from Switzerland **2. DIALECT SPOKEN IN SWITZERLAND** any dialect of German, French, or Italian spoken in Switzerland ■ *adj* **OF SWITZERLAND** relating to Switzerland, or to its peoples or cultures [Early 16C. < French *Suisse* < Middle High German *Swīz* "Switzerland"]

Swiss ball *n* FITNESS same as **exercise ball**

Swiss chard *n* a variety of beet whose large edible leaves and stems are similar to spinach and are cooked and eaten as a vegetable. Latin name: *Beta vulgaris cicla*.

Swiss Guard *n* a group of Swiss-born soldiers employed to protect the pope at the Vatican, or a member of this group

swiss mus·lin *n* a fine cotton fabric, often with a raised pattern. Use: clothes, curtains.

swiss roll, Swiss roll *n UK* same as **jelly roll**

Swiss steak, swiss steak *n US* a piece of meat, usually a cut of beef such as round steak, braised with vegetables

switch /swich/ *n* **1. BUTTON OR LEVER CONTROLLING ELECTRICAL CIRCUIT** a mechanical or electronic device that opens, closes, or changes the connections in an electrical circuit, e.g., one used to turn a light or machine on or off **2. SUDDEN CHANGE** a quick or sudden change **3. SUBSTITUTION** an exchange or substitution **4. THIN ROD OR CANE** a thin flexible stick, especially one used for punishment **5. BEATING** a blow or beating with a switch or other thin object **6. OPERATION OF SWITCH** the act or process of operating a switch **7.** HAIR **PONYTAIL HAIRPIECE** a hairpiece in the form of a false ponytail **8.** ZOOL **TIP OF ANIMAL'S TAIL** a tuft of hair at the end of the tail of a cow or other animal **9.** CARDS **CARD GAME** a card game in which the suit can be changed during play **10.** RAIL **DEVICE FOR SHIFTING TRAINS BETWEEN TRACKS** a device enabling trains to transfer from one track to another, usually including movable rails **11.** RAIL **RAILROAD SIDING** a railroad siding onto which trains can be detoured **12.** TELECOM **ROUTING DEVICE USED IN TELEPHONE EXCHANGES** a device used in a telephone exchange to route transmissions between network nodes **13.** COMPUT **TECHNIQUE FOR CONTROLLING PROGRAM'S LOGIC** in computing, a programmed technique for indicating which alternative path to take at a decision point in a program's logic ■ *v* (**switched, switch·ing, switch·es**) **1.** *vti* **CHANGE, SHIFT, OR TRANSFER** to change from one time, activity, or situation to another, often quickly or suddenly, or cause somebody or something to make such a change ○ *The dancing class has been switched from Friday afternoon to Saturday morning.* **2.** *vti* **MAKE EXCHANGE OR SUBSTITUTION** to exchange two similar or related things, or put one in the place of the other, sometimes secretly or surreptitiously **3.** *vti* ELEC **CHANGE ELECTRICAL FUNCTION** to make an electrical device do something different by operating a switch to cause current to stop or start flowing or change its path ○ *He switched the radio to a different station.* **4.** *vti US* RAIL **MOVE TRAIN BETWEEN TRACKS** to move a locomotive or train from one track to another **5.** *vti* **FLICK OR SWING TO AND FRO** to move quickly from side to side or backward and forward, or make something move in this way ○ *The cat switched her tail in annoyance.* **6.** *vt* **BEAT SOMEBODY WITH SWITCH** to beat somebody with a switch, especially as a punishment ■ *adj* **WITH FEET REVERSED** in skateboarding and similar sports, used to describe a stance in which the foot that the rider usually puts nearer the front is nearer the back (*slang*) [Late 16C. Probably < Middle Dutch *swijch* "twig"] —**switch·a·ble** *adj* —**switch·er** *n*

switch off *vti* **1. TURN OFF EQUIPMENT** to turn off a piece of electrical equipment, or be turned off **2. STOP PAYING ATTENTION** to stop paying attention, lose interest, or stop thinking about something, or make somebody do this (*informal*) **3. TAKE TURNS** to do something one after the other in turns, or occur alternately (*informal*) ○ *We switch off working Saturdays.*

switch on *v* **1.** *vti* to turn on a piece of electrical equipment, or be turned on **2.** *vt* to suddenly and automatically produce something such as a smile, charm, or tears for effect and without sincerity

switch·back /swích bàk/ *n* **1. TWISTY ROAD WITH MANY HILLS** a road or track with many steep uphill and downhill slopes and sharp bends **2. SHARP BEND ON STEEP SLOPE** a sharp bend on a road or track going steeply uphill or downhill **3.** *UK* LEISURE same as **roller coaster** (sense 1) ■ *vi* (**-backed, -back·ing, -backs**) **BEND SHARPLY** to form or move in sharp turns in alternating directions while going uphill or downhill ○ *The trail climbs and then switchbacks to the summit.*

switch·blade /swích blàyd/, **switch·blade knife** *n* a pocketknife with a blade that springs out of the handle automatically when a button is pressed

switch·board /swích bàwrd/ *n* **1.** a manually operated device for interconnecting telephone lines and routing telephone calls, usually within a telephone exchange or in a workplace, hotel, or other large building **2.** one or more insulating panels containing the electrical devices and instruments such as switches, circuit breakers, fuses, and meters required to operate electrical equipment

switch·er·oo /swìchə ro͞o/ (*plural* **-oos** *informal*) *n* a sudden unexpected change, reversal, or switching of something (*slang*) [Mid-20C. Fancifully < SWITCH]

switch·gear /swích geer/ *n* a device used solely to open and close electric circuits, especially one used to control a high-current application, e.g., a power and transforming station or an electric motor

switch·grass /swích gràss/ *n* a panic grass used for forage and hay. Native to: western North America. Latin name: *Panicum virgatum*. [Mid-19C. Alteration of QUITCH GRASS after SWITCH]

switch-hit·ter *n* **1.** in baseball, a batter who hits both left-handed and right-handed with equal skill **2.** an offensive term for somebody who is bisexual (*slang*) [<switching the batting arm] —**switch-hit** *vi*

switch·man /swíchmən/ (*plural* **-men** /-mən/) *n* somebody, especially a man, who switches trains to the proper tracks at a rail junction

switch·per·son /swích pùrss'n/ (*plural* **-per·sons** or **-peo·ple** /-peep'l/) *n* somebody who switches trains to the proper tracks at a rail junction

switch·yard /swích yaàrd/ *n* a railroad yard or terminal in which railroad cars are moved between tracks and trains are assembled and disassembled

swith·er /swíthər/ (**-ered, -er·ing, -ers**) *vi Scotland* to hesitate or be indecisive [Early 16C. Origin ?]

Switz. *abbr* Switzerland

Swit·zer /swítsər/ *n* a member of the Swiss Guard [Mid-16C. < Middle High German *Swītzer* < *Swīz* "Switzerland"]

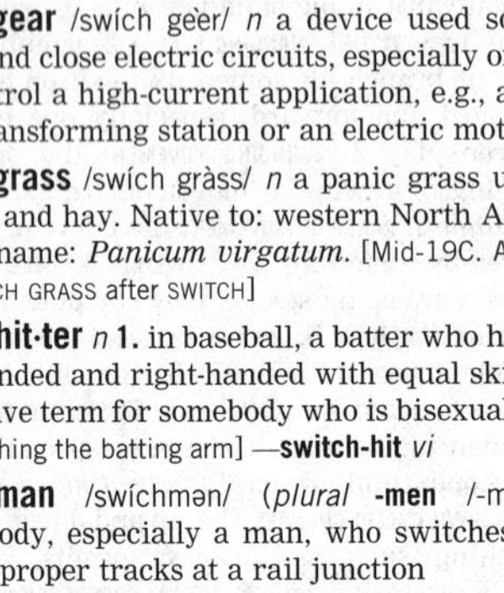

Switzerland

Swit·zer·land /swítsər lànd/ country in west central Europe. It has been neutral since 1515. Language: German, French, Italian, Romansch. Currency: Swiss Franc. Capital: Bern. Population: 7,318,638 (2003). Area: 15,940 sq. mi./41,285 sq. km. Official name **Swiss Confederation**

swive /swīv/ (**swived, swiv·ing, swives**) *vti* to have sexual intercourse with somebody (*archaic*) [Old English *swīfan* "to sweep" < Germanic]

swiv·el /swívv'l/ *v* (**-eled, -el·ing, -els**) **1.** *vti* **PIVOT OR ROTATE** to turn freely or horizontally in a circle, or make something turn in this way **2.** *vt* **PROVIDE SOMETHING WITH PIVOTING JOINT** to fit, attach, or support something with a joint that allows complete freedom of movement ■ *n* **1. DEVICE ALLOWING PART TO TURN** a joint or fastening that allows a mechanical part attached to it to turn freely **2. SUPPORT ALLOWING SOMETHING TO PIVOT** a pivoting support that allows something such as a gun, chair, or camera to turn from side to side or up and down, sometimes in a full circle **3.** ARMS **PIVOTING GUN** a gun that can be turned from side to side horizontally because of the pivoting mount supporting it [14C. < Old English *swīfan* "sweep"]

swiv·el chair *n* a chair, generally an office chair, mounted on a central support with a device that enables it to turn horizontally in a circle

swiv·el-hipped *adj* moving with loosely swinging hips, usually in an exaggerated manner

swiv·et /swívvət/ *n US* a flustered or agitated state (*informal*) [Late 19C. Origin ?]

swiz·zle /swízz'l/ *n US* an iced cocktail, usually containing rum, that is stirred to make it frothy or to frost the glass ■ *vt* (**-zled, -zling, -zles**) to stir a drink with a swizzle stick to mix the ingredients, make it frothy, or reduce its effervescence [Early 19C. Origin ?]

swiz·zle stick *n* a small thin plastic rod used for stirring a drink to mix the ingredients, make it frothy, or reduce its effervescence

swol·len past participle of **swell**

swoon /swoon/ *vi* (**swooned, swoon·ing, swoons**) **1. FEEL FAINT WITH JOY** to be overwhelmed by happiness, excitement, adoration, or infatuation **2. FALL IN FAINT** to experience a sudden and usually brief loss of consciousness ■ *n* **1. RAPTURE** a condition of overwhelming happiness, excitement, or infatuation **2. LOSS OF CONSCIOUSNESS** a sudden and usually brief loss of consciousness [13C. Shortening of *aswoon* < Old English *geswōgen* "in a swoon," past participle of assumed *swōgan* "suffocate." Origin ?] —**swoon·y** *adj*

swoop /swoop/ *v* (**swooped, swoop·ing, swoops**) **1.** *vi* **MAKE SWEEPING DESCENT** to descend quickly and suddenly with a sweeping movement, usually from the air **2.** *vi* **POUNCE** to make a sudden swift attack or raid on something or somebody ○ *Police swooped down on dozens of apartments.* **3.** *vt* **SEIZE SOMETHING QUICKLY OR SUDDENLY** to seize or snatch something in a sudden swift movement ○ *shoppers swooping up bargains* ■ *n* **1. SUDDEN DESCENT** a sudden sweeping descent **2. SUDDEN ATTACK** a sudden swift attack or raid [Mid-16C. Probably variant of SWEEP] ◇ **at** *or* **in one fell swoop** in a single action

swoosh /swoosh, swo͝osh/ *v* (**swooshed, swoosh·ing, swoosh·es**) **1.** *vti* **MAKE OR MOVE WITH RUSHING SOUND** to make or move with the rushing or swirling sound of fast-moving water, or make something move with such a sound ○ *skiers swooshing through the snow* **2.** *vi* **GUSH** to flow freely with a swirling motion ■ *n* **SWOOSHING SOUND** a swooshing sound or movement [Mid-19C. An imitation of the sound]

swop *vti, n* another spelling of **swap**

sword /sawrd/ *n* **1.** a handheld weapon with a long blade that is sharp on one or both edges and sometimes slightly curved. See illustration on next page **2.** the use of force, violence, or military power ○ *The pen is mightier than the sword.* [Old English *sweord* < Germanic] ◇ **cross swords (with somebody)** to argue or come into conflict with somebody ◇ **put somebody to the sword** to kill somebody violently, especially in war (*literary*)

sword and sor·cer·y *adj* set in a fantasy place or time with a technology that has not advanced beyond bladed weapons and in which magic is important (*informal*)

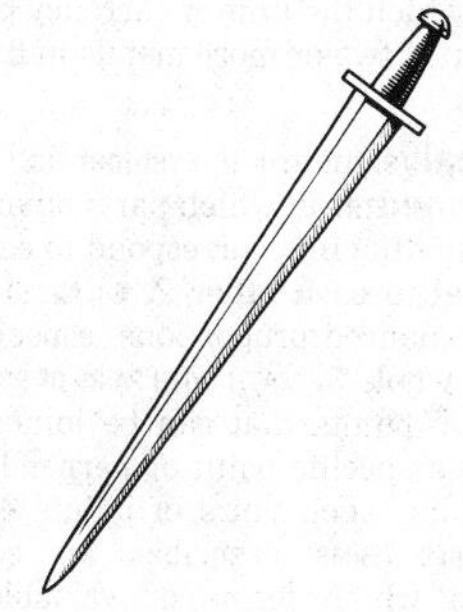

sword

sword bay·o·net *n* a bayonet with a very long blade

sword·bear·er /sáwrd bèrrər/ *n* an official who carries a sword that is a symbol of somebody's authority, e.g., a sovereign's sword

sword·bill /sáwrd bìl/ *n* a hummingbird with a beak longer than its body. Native to: South America. Latin name: *Ensifera ensifera.*

sword cane *n US* a hollow cane or walking stick whose handle is also the handle of a narrow sword hidden inside the cane. Can term **swordstick**

sword dance *n* a dance in which swords are used, especially a Scottish Highland dance in which somebody dances over swords crossed on the floor

sword fern *n* a fern with long fronds shaped like swords, e.g., the variety from which the Boston fern was developed. Latin name: *Nephrolepis exaltata.*

swordfish

sword·fish /sáwrd fìsh/ (*plural same* or **-fish·es**) *n* **1.** a large ocean fish with an upper jaw that extends into a long point. Latin name: *Xiphias gladius.* **2.** the flesh of a swordfish as food

sword grass *n* a grass with leaves that have very sharp edges

sword knot *n* a decorative ribbon or tassel on the hilt of a sword

sword lil·y *n* PLANTS same as **gladiolus** (sense 1) [< its sword-shaped leaves]

Sword of Dam·o·cles *n* something that threatens to bring imminent disaster [See DAMOCLES]

sword·play /sáwrd plày/ *n* fighting with a sword, especially when done with skill

swords·man /sáwrdzmən/ (*plural* **-men** /-mən/) *n* somebody, especially a man, who fights with a sword —**swords·man·ship** *n*

swords·per·son /sáwrdz pùrss'n/ (*plural* **-peo·ple** /-pèep'l/ or **-per·sons**) *n* somebody who fights with a sword

sword·stick /sáwrd stìk/ *n Can, UK* same as **sword cane**

sword-swal·low·er *n* a performer who passes or creates an illusion of passing a sword down his or her throat to its hilt

swords·wom·an /sáwrdz wòommən/ (*plural* **-wom·en** /-wìmmin/) *n* a woman who fights with a sword

sword·tail /sáwrd tàyl/ *n* a small brightly colored freshwater fish with a long sword-shaped tail, popular as an aquarium fish. Native to: Central America. Latin name: *Xiphophorus helleri.*

swore past tense of **swear**

sworn /swawrn/ past participle of **swear** ■ *adj* **1.** made under oath ○ *a sworn statement* **2.** determined to maintain a particular situation ○ *sworn enemies*

swot *vti, n* another spelling of **swat**

SWOT a·nal·y·sis /swót-/ *n* an examination of the strengths, weaknesses, opportunities, and threats connected with an organization, used as a way of evaluating its likelihood of success or developing strategy [Acronym < *strengths, weaknesses, opportunities, threats*]

swot·ter *n* another spelling of **swatter**

SWPA *abbr* Southwestern Pacific Area

swum past participle of **swim**

swung past participle, past tense of **swing**

swung dash *n* a character (~) used in printing to represent all or part of a word previously spelled out

sy *abbr* Syria (*used in Internet addresses*) See table at **domain name**

syb·a·rite /síbbə rìt/ *n* somebody devoted to luxury and the gratification of sensual desires [< SYBARITE; because Sybaris had a reputation for luxury and indulgence] —**syb·a·rit·ic** /sìbbə ríttik/ *adj*

Syb·a·rite /síbbə rìt/ *n* somebody who was born in or was a citizen of Sybaris, an ancient Greek city in southern Italy [Mid-16C. Via Latin *Sybarita* < Greek *Subaris* "Sybaris," ancient Greek city in S Italy] —**Syb·a·rit·ic** /sìbbə ríttik/ *adj*

syc·a·mine /síkə mìn, -min/ *n* a tree mentioned in the Bible and thought to be the black mulberry [Early 16C. < Greek *sukaminon* < Hebrew *šiḳmāh*]

sycamore

syc·a·more /síkə màwr/ (*plural* **-mores** or *same*) *n* **1.** TYPE OF MAPLE TREE a tree of the maple family, naturalized in northern Europe and North America, with five-lobed leaves and two-winged fruits. Native to: central and southern Europe, Asia. Latin name: *Acer pseudoplatanus.* **2.** *US* LARGE SPREADING PLANE TREE a large spreading plane tree with lobed leaves, round spiked fruit clusters, and flaking bark. Native to: central and eastern North America. Latin name: *Platanus occidentalis.* **3.** FIG TREE a fig tree with edible fruit. Native to: Africa, Southwest Asia. Latin name: *Ficus sycomorus.* [14C. Via Old French *sicamor* < Greek *sukomoros* "fig-mulberry"]

syce /sīss/, **saice, sice** *n* formerly in India, a groom, stable hand, or other attendant [Mid-17C. Via Persian, Urdu *sā'is* < Arabic < *sūs* "tend a horse"]

~~**sycho**~~ incorrect spelling of **psycho**

sy·co·ni·um /sī kṓnee əm/ (*plural* **-ni·a** /-nee ə/) *n* a fleshy fruit in which numerous seeds are borne inside the enlarged hollow tip of the flower stalk, e.g., a fig [Mid-19C. < modern Latin < Greek *sukon* "fig"]

syc·o·phant /síkəfənt, -fànt, sīkə-/ *n* a servile or obsequious person who flatters somebody powerful for personal gain [Mid-16C. Via Latin *sycophanta* < Greek *sukophantēs* "informer" < *sukon* "fig, obscene gesture" + *-phantes* "shower" (< *phanein* "to show")] —**syc·o·phan·cy** *n* —**syc·o·phan·tic** /sìkə fántik, sīkə-/ *adj* —**syc·o·phan·ti·cal·ly** *adv*

sy·co·sis /sī kṓssiss/ *n* inflammation of hair follicles, especially of the beard, caused by bacterial infection and marked by pustules and encrustations [Late 16C. Via modern Latin < Greek *sukōsis* < *sukon* "fig"]

Syd·en·ham's cho·re·a /sídd'nəmz-, síd'n hàmz-/ *n* a neurological disease of children and pregnant women, sometimes following rheumatic fever, in which those affected experience involuntary jerking movements of the body [Late 19C. After Thomas *Sydenham* (1624–89), English physician]

Syd·ney /sídnee/ capital of New South Wales, southeastern Australia. Population: 3,986,700 (1998).

AKG London

Sydney Opera House

Syd·ney Op·er·a House *n* an arts center in Sydney Harbor, Australia, that was designed by Jörn Utzon and completed in 1973. Its unusual sail-shaped towers make it Australia's best-known building.

sy·e·nite /sī ə nìt/ *n* a light-colored coarse-grained igneous rock consisting mainly of feldspar [Late 18C. < Latin *syenites (lapis)* "(stone of) Syene" (Aswan, Egypt)] —**sy·e·nit·ic** /sī ə níttik/ *adj*

~~**sylable**~~ incorrect spelling of **syllable**

~~**sylabus**~~ incorrect spelling of **syllabus**

syl·la·bar·y /síllə bèrree/ (*plural* **-ies**) *n* a list or set of written characters in which each character represents a single syllable e.g., the Japanese kana

syl·la·bi EDUC, LAW plural of **syllabus**

syl·lab·ic /si lábbik/ *adj* **1.** INVOLVING SYLLABLES relating to, involving, or typical of a syllable or syllables **2.** MARKED BY CLEAR ENUNCIATION clearly enunciated with every syllable distinct **3.** BEING SYLLABLE WITHOUT VOWEL describes a consonant that acts as a syllable without a vowel, as does the "l" in "bottle" **4.** BASED ON NUMBER OF SYLLABLES describes verse in which the rhythm is set by the number of syllables rather than accents, stresses, or vowel strengths ■ *n* SYLLABIC CONSONANT OR SOUND a syllabic consonant, character, or sound

syl·lab·i·fy /si lábbə fì/ (**-fied, -fy·ing, -fies**), **syl·lab·i·cate** /-kàyt/ (**-cat·ed, -cat·ing, -cates**) *vt* to break a word down into syllables in speech or writing [Early 20C. Back-formation < *syllabification* < Latin *syllaba* (see SYLLABLE)] —**syl·lab·i·ca·tion** /-làbbə káysh'n/ *n* —**syl·lab·i·fi·ca·tion** /-làbbəfi káysh'n/ *n*

syl·la·bism /síllə bìzzəm/ *n* **1.** the use of characters that stand for individual syllables in writing **2.** the breaking down of words into syllables, in speech or writing

syl·la·ble /sílləb'l/ *n* **1.** UNIT OF SPOKEN LANGUAGE a unit of spoken language that consists of one or more vowel sounds alone, a syllabic consonant alone, or any of these with one or more consonant sounds **2.** LETTERS CORRESPONDING TO SPOKEN SYLLABLE one or more letters in a word that roughly correspond to a syllable of spoken language **3.** MENTION the slightest bit of something that is spoken or written (*usually used in negative statements*) ○ *Don't breathe a syllable of this – it's a secret.* ■ *vt* (**-bled, -bling, -bles**) PRONOUNCE SOMETHING CLEARLY to pronounce something in distinct or separate syllables [14C. < Anglo-Norman *sillable*, alteration of Old French *sillabe*, via Latin *syllaba* < Greek *sullabē* < *sullambanein* "bring together" < *lambanein* "take"]

syl·la·bub /síllə bùb/, **sil·la·bub** *n* **1.** a light soft cold dessert made from cream whipped with brandy, wine or sherry, lemon juice, and a little sugar **2.** a drink made of sweetened milk or cream curdled with wine or cider [Mid-16C. Origin ?]

syl·la·bus /sílləbəss/ (*plural* **-bi** /-bì/ or **-bus·es**) *n* **1.** a summary or list of the main topics of a course of study, text, or lecture **2.** *US* a short note that precedes the report of a decided legal case and summarizes the ruling [Mid-17C. < modern Latin, originally misprint of Latin *sittybas* "indexes" < Greek *sittuba* "index, label"]

Syl·la·bus, **Syl·la·bus of Er·rors** *n* a list of religious doctrines condemned by the Roman Catholic Church as erroneous

syl·lep·sis /si lépsiss/ (*plural* **-lep·ses** /-lép seez/) *n* **1.** the use of a word that relates to, qualifies, or governs two or more other words but agrees in number, gender, or case with only one of them. "Neither Fred nor I want to" is an example of syllepsis, where "want" agrees with "I" but not "Fred." **2.** the use of a word that relates to, qualifies, or governs two or more other words but has a different meaning in relation to each, as in the example "He picked up his hat and a taxi" [Late 16C. Via late Latin < Greek *sullēpsis* "a taking together" < *sullambanein* (see SYLLABLE)]

syl·lo·gism /síllə jìzzəm/ *n* **1. LOGICAL ARGUMENT INVOLVING THREE PROPOSITIONS** a formal deductive argument made up of a major premise, a minor premise, and a conclusion. An example is, "All birds have feathers, penguins are birds, therefore penguins have feathers." **2. DEDUCTIVE REASONING** reasoning from the general to the specific **3. EXAMPLE OF DEDUCTION** an example of deductive reasoning **4. SPECIOUS ARGUMENT** a subtle piece of reasoning, or one that seems true but is actually false or deceptive [14C. Via Latin < Greek *sullogismos* < *sullogizesthai* "infer" < *logos* "reason"]

syl·lo·gis·tic /sìllə jístik/ *adj* relating to, using, or typical of syllogisms [Mid-17C. Via Latin < Greek *sullogistikos* < *sullogizesthai* (see SYLLOGISM)] —**syl·lo·gis·ti·cal·ly** *adv*

syl·lo·gize /síllə jìz/ (**-gized, -giz·ing, -giz·es**) *vti* to reason or infer something by means of syllogisms [15C. Via late Latin *syllogizare* < Greek *sullogizesthai* (see SYLLOGISM)] —**syl·lo·giz·er** *n*

sylph /silf/ *n* **1.** a woman or girl who is slight and graceful **2.** an elemental soulless female being imagined to inhabit the air [Mid-17C. < modern Latin *sylpha*] —**sylph·ic** *adj*

sylph·like /sílf lìk/ *adj* having a slight and graceful figure

syl·van /sílvən/, **sil·van** *adj* **1. OF FOREST** relating to, typical of, or found in a forest (*literary*) **2. WOODED** covered in or full of trees (*literary*) **3. RURAL** characteristic of the countryside, especially in an idyllic way ■ *n* **INHABITANT OF FOREST** a person, animal, or spirit that lives in a forest

syl·van·ite /sílvə nìt/ *n* a mixed telluride mineral containing gold and silver, occurring in long striated crystals [Late 18C. After TRANSYLVANIA]

Syl·va·nus *n* MYTHOL another spelling of **Silvanus**

syl·vat·ic /sil váttik/ *adj* **1.** affecting wild animals ○ *sylvatic plague* **2.** same as **sylvan** *adj* (senses 1–2)

syl·vi·cul·ture *n* AGRIC another spelling of **silviculture**

syl·vite /síl vìt/, **syl·vine** /-veen, -vin/ *n* a colorless transparent potassium chloride mineral. Use: source of potassium. [Mid-19C. < modern Latin *(sal digestivus) Sylvii* "(digestive salt) of Sylvius" (François de la Boë Sylvius (1614–72), Flemish chemist)]

sym. *abbr* **1.** symbol **2.** CHEM symmetrical **3.** MUSIC symphony **4.** MED symptom

sym- *prefix* another spelling of **syn-** (*used before b, m, and p*)

sym·bi·o·gen·e·sis /sìm bì ō jénnəssiss/ *n* a hypothetical evolutionary process in which mitochondria and chloroplasts developed from symbiotic organisms within the cell

sym·bi·ont /símbee ònt, -bì-/ *n* an animal or plant living in close and often mutually beneficial association with another of a different species [Late 19C. < SYM- + Greek *bioun* "to live" < *bios* "life"] —**sym·bi·on·tic** /sìmbee óntik, -bì-/ *adj*

sym·bi·o·sis /sìm bì óssiss, -bee-/ (*plural* **-o·ses** /-ó seez/) *n* **1.** a close association of animals or plants of different species that is often, but not always, of mutual benefit **2.** a cooperative, mutually beneficial relationship between two people or groups [Early 17C. Via modern Latin and Greek *sumbiōsis* "a living together" < *bios* "life"] —**sym·bi·ot·ic** /sìm bì óttik, sìmbee-/ *adj* —**sym·bi·ot·i·cal** *adj* —**sym·bi·ot·i·cal·ly** *adv*

sym·bi·ote /sím bì òt/ *n* an organism, person, or thing that exists in or depends on a symbiotic relationship with something or somebody else [Late 19C. Back-formation < *symbiotic*]

~~**symble**~~ incorrect spelling of **symbol**

sym·bol /símb'l/ *n* **1. SOMETHING THAT REPRESENTS SOMETHING ELSE** something that stands for or represents something else, especially an object representing an abstraction **2. SIGN WITH SPECIFIC MEANING** a written or printed sign or character that represents something in a specific context, e.g., an operation or quantity in mathematics or music **3.** PSYCHOANAL **OBJECT REPRESENTING SOMETHING REPRESSED IN UNCONSCIOUS** an object or act that represents an impulse or wish in the unconscious mind that has been repressed [15C. Via Latin < Greek *sumbolon* "mark" < *sumballein* "compare" < *ballein* "throw"]

SPELLCHECK See *cymbal*.

sym·bol·ic /sim bóllik/, **sym·bol·i·cal** /-ik'l/ *adj* **1. REPRESENTING SOMETHING ELSE** acting as a symbol ○ *white doves symbolic of peace* **2. INVOLVING USE OF SYMBOLS** characterized by or involving the use of symbols or symbolism ○ *symbolic poetry* **3. OF SYMBOLS** relating to or typical of symbols —**sym·bol·i·cal·ly** *adv*

sym·bol·ic lan·guage *n* **1.** an artificially constructed language with many symbols, used for precise formulations, e.g., in symbolic logic or mathematics **2.** a computer programming language that expresses memory addresses and operation codes in symbols recognizable to the programmer rather than in machine language

sym·bol·ic log·ic *n* the branch of formal logic that studies the meaning and relationships of statements through precise mathematical methods and a standardized system of symbols and rules of inference

sym·bol·ism /símbə lìzzəm/ *n* **1. USE OF SYMBOLS** the use of symbols to invest things with a representative meaning or to represent something abstract by something concrete **2. SYSTEM OF SYMBOLS** a set or system of symbols **3. SYMBOLIC MEANING** symbolic meaning or quality **4.** ARTS **ARTISTIC USE OF SYMBOLS** the artistic method of revealing ideas or truths through the use of symbols **5.** *also* **Sym·bol·ism** ARTS **19C LITERARY AND ARTISTIC MOVEMENT** a 19th-century literary and artistic movement that sought to evoke, rather than describe, ideas or feelings through the use of symbolic images **6.** CHR **BELIEF IN SYMBOLIC NATURE OF COMMUNION** in Christianity, the belief that the bread and wine used in the Communion are symbols and not literally the flesh and blood of Jesus Christ

sym·bol·ist /símbəlist/ *n* **1. SOMEBODY USING SYMBOLS** somebody who uses symbols or symbolism **2. SOMEBODY SKILLED AT INTERPRETING SYMBOLS** somebody skilled in the study or interpretation of symbols **3.** *also* **Sym·bol·ist** ARTS **SOMEBODY INVOLVED IN 19C ARTISTIC SYMBOLISM** a writer or artist involved in or associated with the 19th-century movement of symbolism **4.** CHR **SOMEBODY BELIEVING COMMUNION USES SYMBOLS** in Christianity, a believer that the bread and wine used in the Communion are symbols and not literally the flesh and blood of Jesus Christ ■ *adj* **1. OF OR USING SYMBOLS** relating to, involving, or using symbols **2.** *also* **Sym·bol·ist** ARTS **ASSOCIATED WITH 19C ARTISTIC SYMBOLISM** involved in, associated with, or typical of the 19th-century movement of symbolism —**sym·bol·is·tic** /sìmbə lístik/ *adj*

sym·bol·ize /símbə lìz/ (**-ized, -iz·ing, -iz·es**) *v* **1.** *vt* **BE SYMBOL OF SOMETHING** to serve as a symbol of something **2.** *vt* **REPRESENT SOMETHING** to represent something by means of a symbol **3.** *vi* **USE SYMBOLS** to use symbols or symbolism —**sym·bol·i·za·tion** /sìmbəli záysh'n/ *n*

sym·bol·o·gy /sim bólləjee/ *n* **1.** the study or interpretation of symbols **2.** the use of symbols to represent things

~~**symetrical**~~ incorrect spelling of **symmetrical**

~~**symetry**~~ incorrect spelling of **symmetry**

sym·met·al·lism /sim mètt'l ìzzəm/ *n* a system of coinage in which the unit of currency consists of a combination of two or more metals in fixed relative proportions

sym·met·ri·cal /si méttrik'l/, **sym·met·ric** /-méttrik/ *adj* **1. EXHIBITING SYMMETRY** in which parts on either side of a central dividing line correspond to each other or are identical to each other **2. BALANCED** relating to or having balanced proportions, especially in two halves of a whole **3.** MATH **WITH PAIRS OF POINTS** used to describe two points that can be joined by a line bisected by a specific point or perpendicular, or a shape that has such pairs of points **4.** MATH **WITH INTERCHANGEABLE TERMS** describes an equation or function in which terms or variables may be interchanged without altering its value or form **5.** CHEM **WITH SYMMETRICAL MOLECULAR STRUCTURE** with atoms or groups that display symmetry about a plane in a chemical structure **6.** ANAT **ON OPPOSITE SIDES** describes body parts that have the same function but are situated on opposite sides, either of the same organ or the same body —**sym·met·ri·cal·ly** *adv*

sym·met·ric ma·trix *n* a square matrix that is identical to the matrix formed by transposing its rows and columns

sym·me·trize /símmə trìz/ (**-trized, -triz·ing, -triz·es**) *vt* to give symmetry to something

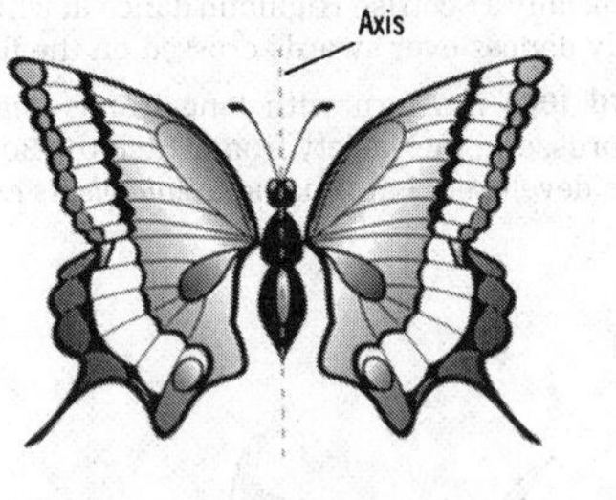

symmetry

sym·me·try /símmətree/ (*plural* **-tries**) *n* **1. PROPERTY OF SAMENESS** the property of being the same or corresponding on both sides of a central dividing line **2. BALANCED PROPORTIONS** harmony or beauty of form that results from balanced proportions **3.** MATH **EXACT CORRESPONDENCE IN POSITION** a correspondence in the position of pairs of points of a geometric object that are equally positioned about a point, line, or plane that bisects the object **4.** PHYS **STATE OF INVARIANCE** a state of invariance shown by some phenomena when changes of orientation, charge, or parity are made [Mid-16C. Via Latin < Greek *summetria* "similar measure" < *metron* "measure"]

sym·pa·thec·to·my /sìmpə théktəmee/ (*plural* **-mies**) *n* formerly, the surgical interruption of a pathway in the sympathetic nervous system by cutting out a nerve segment [Early 20C. < SYMPATHETIC + -ECTOMY]

sym·pa·thet·ic /sìmpə théttik/ *adj* **1. FEELING OR SHOWING SYMPATHY** showing, having, or resulting from shared feelings, pity, or compassion **2. APPROVING** showing favor, agreement, or approval ○ *was sympathetic to their request* **3. PROVOKING SYMPATHY** provoking sympathy, interest, or compassion ○ *a sympathetic character in a novel* **4. SUITED** agreeably suited to somebody's tastes or mood ○ *a sympathetic environment* **5.** ACOUSTICS **PRODUCED BY OTHER SOUNDS** describes vibrations such as musical tones that are produced in something as a result of similar vibrations at the same frequency from something else **6.** ANAT **OF SYMPATHETIC NERVOUS SYSTEM** relating or belonging to the sympathetic nervous system or to one of its components [Mid-17C. < SYMPATHY after PATHETIC] —**sym·pa·thet·i·cal·ly** *adv*

sym·pa·thet·ic mag·ic *n* magic based on the belief that somebody or something can be supernaturally affected by something done to an object representing the person or thing

sym·pa·thet·ic nerv·ous sys·tem *n* the part of the autonomic nervous system that is active during stress or danger and is involved in regulating pulse and blood pressure, dilating pupils, and changing muscle tone

sym·pa·thet·ic string *n* a string on a musical instrument that vibrates by itself when other strings are bowed or plucked

sym·pa·thize /símpə thīz/ (**-thized, -thiz·ing, -thiz·es**) *vi* **1.** to share the feelings of somebody else or show pity or compassion for another ○ *I can sympathize; the same thing happened to me.* **2.** to share the ideas or ideals of another person or group —**sym·pa·thiz·er** *n*

sym·pa·tho·lyt·ic /sìmpəthō líttik/ *adj* describes a drug that opposes or blocks the effects of the sympathetic nervous system ■ *n* a drug or agent that acts against the sympathetic nervous system [Mid-20C. < SYMPATHETIC + -LYTE]

sym·pa·tho·mi·met·ic /sìmpəthō mi méttik/ *adj* describes a drug that stimulates the sympathetic nervous system or produces physiological effects similar to it ■ *n* a drug or agent that stimulates the sympathetic nervous system [Early 20C. < SYMPATHETIC]

sym·pa·thy /símpəthee/ (*plural* **-thies**) *n* **1.** CAPACITY TO SHARE FEELINGS the ability to enter into, understand, or share somebody else's feelings **2.** FEELINGS CAUSED BY SYMPATHY the feelings of somebody who enters into or shares another's feelings **3.** SORROW FOR ANOTHER'S PAIN the feeling or expression of pity or sorrow for the pain or distress of somebody else ○ *We extended our sympathies to the widow.* **4.** INCLINATION TO FEEL ALIKE the inclination to think or feel the same as somebody else **5.** AGREEMENT agreement or harmony with something or somebody else ○ *a plan in sympathy with our wishes* **6.** ALLEGIANCE OR LOYALTY allegiance or loyalty to a group or cause (*often used in the plural*) ○ *nationalist sympathies* [Late 16C. Via Latin *sympathia* < Greek *sumpatheia* < *sumpathēs* "feeling with" < *pathos* "feeling"]

sym·pa·thy strike *n* a strike by workers demonstrating their support for another group of strikers rather than against their own employer

sym·pa·thy vote *n* a vote that people give to somebody for whom they feel pity or affection

sym·pat·ric /sim páttrik/ *adj* describes species that occupy roughly the same area of land but do not interbreed [Early 20C. < Greek *patra* "fatherland" < *patēr* "father"] —**sym·pat·ri·cal·ly** *adv* —**sym·pat·ry** /símpətree/ *n*

sym·phon·ic /sim fónnik/ *adj* **1.** relating to, involving, or typical of a musical symphony, or resembling one in form or content **2.** harmonious in sound, color, or composition —**sym·phon·ic·al·ly** *adv*

sym·phon·ic po·em *n* an extended piece of music for a symphony orchestra that is based on a literary, artistic, or ideological theme such as a folktale or landscape

sym·pho·nist /símfənist/ *n* a composer of symphonies or symphonic works

sym·pho·ny /símfənee/ (*plural* **-nies**) *n* **1.** COMPLEX MUSICAL COMPOSITION a major work for an orchestra, including wind, string, and percussion instruments, usually composed in four movements, at least one of which is in sonata form **2.** MUSIC same as **symphony orchestra** **3.** CONCERT BY SYMPHONY ORCHESTRA a concert performed by a symphony orchestra **4.** HARMONIOUS COMPOSITION OR ARRANGEMENT something that is harmoniously composed ○ *The painting was a symphony of blues, greens, and yellows.* **5.** HARMONY OF SOUNDS OR COLORS harmony or agreement of sounds or colors (*archaic*) [13C. Via Latin *symphonia* "sound of instruments, harmony" < Greek *sumphōnia*, literally "sounding together" < *phōnē* "sound"]

sym·pho·ny or·ches·tra *n* a large orchestra that includes wind, string, and percussion instruments and plays symphonies and other works scored for these instruments

sym·phy·sis /símfəssiss/ (*plural* **-phy·ses** /-fə seez/) *n* **1.** ANAT GROWING TOGETHER OF BONES OR PARTS the natural merging of two or more separate bones or parts of the body **2.** ANAT JOINT WITH LITTLE MOVEMENT a joint in which the bones are connected by tough cartilage (**fibrocartilage**) and there is very little movement between them, e.g., between adjacent vertebrae in the spinal column **3.** MED BONE CONDITION a condition in which two or more separate bones or parts of the body have merged **4.** BOT FUSION OF PLANT PARTS a fusion of two similar organs or parts of a plant **5.** ANAT, BOT LINE MARKING SYMPHYSIS a point or line where a symphysis occurs [Late 16C. Via modern Latin < Greek *sumphusis* "growing together" < *phusis* "growth"] —**sym·phy·se·al** /sim fízzee əl/ *adj*

sym·po·di·um /sim pṓdee əm/ (*plural* **-di·a** /-dee ə/) *n* a main plant stem that develops from a series of lateral branches, often in a zigzag pattern, e.g., the stem of a grapevine [Mid-19C. < modern Latin < Greek *pod-* "foot"] —**sym·po·di·al** *adj*

sym·po·si·a plural of **symposium**

sym·po·si·arch /sim pṓzee aark/ *n* a supervisor of a symposium [Early 17C. < Greek *sumposiarkhos* < *sumposion* (see SYMPOSIUM)]

sym·po·si·ast /sim pṓzee àst/ *n* a participant in a symposium [Mid-17C. < Greek *sumposiazein* "drink together" < *sumposion* (see SYMPOSIUM)]

sym·po·si·um /sim pṓzee əm/ (*plural* **-si·ums** or **-si·a** /-zee ə/) *n* **1.** FORMAL MEETING FOR DISCUSSION OF SUBJECT a formal meeting held for the discussion of a subject, during which individual speakers may make presentations **2.** PUBL PUBLISHED COLLECTION OF OPINIONS a published collection of opinions or writings on a subject, often in a periodical **3.** ANCIENT HIST DRINKING PARTY IN ANCIENT GREECE a drinking party in ancient Greece, usually with music and philosophical conversation [Late 16C. Via Latin < Greek *sumposion* "drinking party" < *sumpotēs* "drinker with another" < *potēs* "drinker"] —**sym·po·si·ac** *adj*

symp·tom /símptəm/ *n* **1.** an indication of a disease or other disorder, especially one experienced by the patient, e.g., pain, dizziness, or itching, as opposed to one observed by the doctor (**sign**) ○ *A sore throat and fever were the symptoms of the virus they all had.* **2.** a sign or indication of the existence of something, especially something undesirable ○ *early symptoms of a recession* [Mid-16C. Via late Latin *symptoma* < Greek *sumptōma* "occurrence" < *sumpiptein* "fall together" < *piptein* "fall"] —**symp·tom·less** *adj*

symp·to·mat·ic /sìmptə máttik/ *adj* **1.** CHARACTERISTIC typical or indicative of something, especially something undesirable ○ *symptomatic of the breakdown in communication between children and parents* **2.** MED INDICATING ILLNESS indicating or typical of a particular illness **3.** MED OF SYMPTOMS relating to, affecting, or based on a symptom or symptoms of bodily disorder ○ *Only symptomatic relief is available for the common cold.* [Late 17C. < late Latin *symptomaticus* < *symptoma* (see SYMPTOM)] —**symp·to·mat·i·cal·ly** *adv*

symp·to·ma·tol·o·gy /sìmptəmə tólləjee/ (*plural* **-gies**) *n* **1.** the study of the relationships between symptoms and diseases **2.** the set of symptoms that are associated with a disease or that affect a patient [Late 18C. < Greek *sumptōmat-*, stem of *sumptōma* (see SYMPTOM)]

symp·tom·ize /símptə mīz/ (**-ized, -iz·ing, -iz·es**) *vt* to be an indication of the existence of something

syn- *prefix* together, together with, united ○ *syncarpous* [< Greek *sun* "together"]

syn·aer·e·sis *n* CHEM, LING, PHON another spelling of **syneresis**

syn·aes·the·sia *n* PSYCHOL, LITERAT another spelling of **synesthesia**

syn·a·gogue /sínnə gòg/ *n* **1.** the place of worship and communal center of a Jewish congregation **2.** a body of followers of Judaism who worship together [12C. Via French and late Latin *synagoga* < Greek *sunagōgē* "assembly" < *sunagein* "bring together" < *agein* "to lead"] —**syn·a·gog·al** /sìnnə gógg'l/ *adj* —**syn·a·gog·i·cal** /sìnnə gójjik'l/ *adj*

syn·a·le·pha /sìnnə leéfə/, **syn·a·loe·pha** *n* the blending of two adjacent vowels into one, e.g., when a word ending in a vowel is immediately followed by a word beginning with a vowel [Mid-16C. Via late Latin < Greek *sunaloiphē* < *sunaleiphein* "smear together" < *aleiphein* "to smear"]

syn·apse /sí nàps, sə náps/ *n* a junction between two nerve cells, where the club-shaped tip of a nerve fiber almost touches another cell in order to transmit signals ■ *vi* (**-apsed, -aps·ing, -aps·es**) to form a synapse between nerve cells [Late 19C. Anglicization of SYNAPSIS]

syn·ap·sis /sə nápsiss/ (*plural* **-ap·ses** /-áp seez/) *n* the pairing of homologous chromosomes from each parent during the initial phase (**prophase**) of cell division [Mid-17C. Via modern Latin < Greek *sunapsis* "connection" < *haptein* "join"]

syn·ap·tic /sə náptik/ *adj* **1.** relating to or involving a junction between nerve cells **2.** relating to, involving, or typical of synapsis [Late 19C. < SYNAPSIS or SYNAPSE after Greek *sunaptikos* "connective"]

syn·ap·tol·o·gy /sìn ap tólləjee/ *n* the study of junctions between nerve cells (**synapses**) and synaptic connections in the nervous system

syn·ar·thro·sis /sìn aar thrṓssiss/ (*plural* **-thro·ses** /-thrō seez/) *n* a rigid joint formed by the union of two bones and connected by fibrous tissue —**syn·ar·thro·di·al** /-thrṓdee əl/ *adj* —**syn·ar·thro·di·al·ly** *adv*

sync /singk/, **synch** (*informal*) *n* **1.** SYNCHRONIZATION the relationship between things that are happening or working at the same time, especially the correspondence of sound and image in a film **2.** HARMONY harmony or agreement ■ *vti* (**synced, sync·ing, syncs; synched, synch·ing, synchs**) SYNCHRONIZE to synchronize something, or be synchronized [Early 20C. Shortening]

SPELLCHECK See *sink*.

syn·car·pous /sin kaárpəss/ *adj* describes the female reproductive parts (**gynoecium**) of a flower in which the carpels are fused —**syn·car·py** /sín kaarpee/ *n*

syn·cat·e·gor·e·mat·ic /sìn ka tə gàwrə máttik/ *adj* describes an expression that has meaning only in conjunction with another expression [Early 19C. Via medieval Latin *syncategorematicus* < Greek *sugkatēgorēmatikos* "predicating jointly" < *katēgorein* "to predicate"]

synch *n, vti* same as **sync**

syn·chon·dro·sis /sìng kon drṓssiss/ (*plural* **-dro·ses** /-drō seez/) *n* **1.** a joint in which there is slight movement between bones that are held together by cartilage, e.g., between the ribs and the breastbone **2.** a joint in which the cartilage linking two bones in childhood is replaced by bone as development progresses [Late 16C. Via modern Latin < late Greek *sugkhondrōsis* < *khondros* "cartilage"]

syn·chro /síngkrō/ (*plural* **-chros**) *n* ELEC ENG same as **selsyn** [Mid-20C. Shortening of *synchronizing*]

synchro- *prefix* synchronous, synchronized ○ *synchroscope* [< SYNCHRONOUS]

syn·chro·cy·clo·tron /sìngkrō sī́klə tròn/ *n* a particle accelerator that compensates for increases in the relativistic mass of accelerated particles and so achieves greater energies by using the synchronizing effects of a frequency-modulated electric field

syn·chro·flash /síngkrō flàsh/ *n* a mechanism in a camera that opens the shutter at the moment when the light from the flashbulb or electronic flash is brightest

syn·chro·mesh /síngkrō mèsh/ *n* a gear system in which the speeds of the driving and driven parts are synchronized before they engage so that gear changes are made smoother —**syn·chro·mesh** *adj*

syn·chro·nal /síngkrən'l/ *adj* happening at the same time [Mid-17C. < late Latin *synchronus* (see SYNCHRONOUS)]

syn·chron·ic /sin krónnik/ *adj* relating to something, especially a language, as it exists at a point in time and not historically [Mid-19C. < late Latin *synchronus* (see SYNCHRONOUS)] —**syn·chron·i·cal·ly** *adv*

syn·chro·nic·i·ty /sìngkrə nissətee/ *n* **1.** same as **synchronism** (sense 1) **2.** the coincidence of events that seem related, but are not obviously caused one by the other. The term was first used in this sense in the work of the psychologist Carl Jung.

syn·chro·nism /síngkrə nìzzəm/ *n* **1.** the simultaneous occurrence of two or more things **2.** an arrangement in chronological order showing historical events that happened or people who were alive around the same time [Late 16C. < Greek *sugkhronismos* < *sugkhronos* (see SYNCHRONOUS)] —**syn·chro·nis·tic** /sìngkrə nístik/ *adj* —**syn·chro·nis·ti·cal·ly** *adv*

syn·chro·nize /síngkrə nīz/ (**-nized, -niz·ing, -niz·es**) *v* **1.** *vt* MAKE THINGS WORK AT SAME TIME to make something work at the same time or the same rate as something else **2.** *vt* SET WATCHES TO SAME TIME to set timepieces to indicate the same time as each other **3.** *vi* GO TOGETHER to go or work together or in unison **4.** *vi* HAPPEN TOGETHER to happen at the same time **5.** *vt* MOVIES ALIGN SOUND AND IMAGE OF MOVIE to make the soundtrack of a movie match up with the action **6.** *vt* COMPUT UPDATE PARALLEL COMPUTER FILES to copy a file from one computer system or electronic device to another in order to maintain the information on both at the same level, e.g., to keep an address book on a desktop computer current with one on a PDA [Early 17C. < SYNCHRONISM] —**syn·chro·ni·za·tion** /sìngkrəni záysh'n/ *n*

syn·chro·nized sleep /sìngkrə nīzd-/ *n* BIOL same as **slow-wave sleep**

syn·chro·nized swim·ming *n* a sport in which swimmers perform coordinated movements in time to music in the manner of a dance

syn·chron·o·scope /síngkrənə skōp/ *n* MECH ENG, ELEC ENG same as **synchroscope**

syn·chro·nous /síngkrənəss/ *adj* **1.** OCCURRING SIMULTANEOUSLY happening at the same time **2.** WORKING AT SAME RATE working or moving at the same rate **3.** PHYS WITH SAME PERIOD AND PHASE having the same period and phase of oscillation or cyclic movement [Mid-17C. Via late Latin *synchronus* < Greek *sugkhronos* < *khronos* "time"] —**syn·chro·nous·ly** *adv* —**syn·chro·nous·ness** *n*

syn·chro·nous mo·tor *n* an electric motor that operates at a speed directly proportional to the frequency of the applied voltage source

syn·chro·nous op·er·a·tion *n* an event that occurs regularly or predictably when triggered by the completion of another process, e.g., the production of a receipt by an ATM for a completed transaction

syn·chro·nous or·bit *n* an orbit that keeps time with the rotation of the orbited object, so that the orbiting body is always directly over the same point on the surface of the orbited body

syn·chro·ny /síngkrənee/ (*plural* **-nies**) *n* occurrence at the same time or movement at the same rate, or an example of this phenomenon

syn·chro·scope /síngkrə skōp/ *n* **1.** an instrument that is used to find whether or not two things such as moving machine parts are moving in phase with one another **2.** an instrument used to indicate the difference in frequency between two alternating current supplies

syn·chro·tron /síngkrə tròn/ *n* a particle accelerator in which charged particles traveling at near the speed of light are guided around a doughnut-shaped tube by powerful magnets, producing synchrotron radiation

syn·chro·tron ra·di·a·tion *n* short wave radiation, from infrared to conventional X-rays, produced in a synchrotron. Use: analysis of the structure of proteins, viruses, inorganic materials such as metals.

syn·cline /sín klīn/ *n* a fold in a rock formation that is shaped like a basin or trough and contains younger rocks in its core —**syn·cli·nal** /sin klīn'l/ *adj*

syn·co·pate /síngkə pàyt/ (**-pat·ed, -pat·ing, -pates**) *vt* **1.** to modify a musical rhythm by shifting the accent to a weak beat of the bar **2.** to shorten a word by the loss of one or more sounds or letters from the middle —**syn·co·pa·tor** *n*

syn·co·pa·tion /sìngkə páysh'n/ *n* **1.** a rhythmic technique in music in which the accent is shifted to a weak beat of the bar **2.** PHON same as **syncope** (sense 2)

syn·co·pe /síngkəpee/ *n* **1.** the action of fainting, or a fainting fit (*technical*) **2.** the shortening of a word by the loss of sounds or letters from its middle [Mid-16C. Via late Latin < Greek *sugkopē* < *sugkoptein* "cut short" < *koptein* "to cut"] —**syn·co·pal** *adj* —**syn·cop·ic** /sing kóppik/ *adj*

syn·cre·tism /síngkrə tìzzəm/ *n* **1.** the combination of different systems of philosophical or religious belief or practice **2.** the use of a single inflectional form of a word to cover functions previously covered by two separate forms, e.g., "spun" in English, now used for both the past tense and the past participle although the past tense used to be "span" [Early 17C. Via modern Latin *syncretismus* < Greek *sugkrētismos* "union" < *sugkrētizein* "unite (against a common enemy)"] —**syn·cret·ic** /sing kréttik/ *adj* —**syn·cre·tist** *n* —**syn·cre·tis·tic** /sìngkrə tístik/ *adj*

syn·cre·tize /síngkrə tīz/ (**-tized, -tiz·ing, -tiz·es**) *vti* to combine aspects of different systems of philosophical or religious belief or practice [Late 17C. < Greek *sugkrētizein* "unite (against a common enemy)"] —**syn·cre·ti·za·tion** /sìngkrəti záysh'n/ *n*

~~**syncronous**~~ incorrect spelling of **synchronous**

syn·cy·ti·um /sin síshəm, -shee əm/ (*plural* **-ti·a** /-shə, -shee ə/) *n* a mass of cytoplasm within a cell membrane that contains multiple nuclei and is often the result of cellular fusion, e.g., in some slime molds [Late 19C. < SYN- + Greek *kutos* "hollow vessel"] —**syn·cy·ti·al** /sin síshee əl/ *adj*

synd. *abbr* syndicate

syn·dac·tyl /sin dákt'l/ *adj* having two or more fingers or toes joined together. This may be a natural condition, as in some animals, or congenital, as in people with webbed toes. —**syn·dac·tyl** *n* —**syn·dac·tyl·ism** *n* —**syn·dac·ty·ly** *n*

syn·de·sis /síndəsiss/ *n* the use in grammar of constructions in which clauses are joined by conjunctions [Early 20C. < German < Greek *desis* "binding" < *dein* "bind"]

syn·des·mo·sis /sìndəss mṓssiss/ (*plural* **-mo·ses** /-mṓ seez/) *n* an immovable joint in which the bones are held firmly by fibrous tissue, but are not very close together, e.g., at the lower ends of the tibia and fibula [Late 16C. < Greek *sundesmos* "ligament" < *sundein* (see SYNDETIC)] —**syn·des·mot·ic** /-móttik/ *adj*

syn·det·ic /sin déttik/ *adj* describes a grammatical construction in which two clauses are joined by a conjunction [Early 17C. < Greek *sundetikos* < *sundein* "bind together" < *dein* "bind"] —**syn·det·i·cal·ly** *adv*

syn·det·on /síndə tòn, síndətən/ *n* a grammatical construction in which two clauses are joined by a conjunction [Mid-20C. Back-formation < ASYNDETON, POLYSYNDETON]

syn·dic /síndik/ *n* **1.** somebody appointed to represent an organization such as a corporation or a university in business transactions **2.** a government official, especially a civil magistrate, in some European countries [Early 17C. Via French, "delegate" < late Latin *syndicus* < Greek *sundikos* "defendant's advocate" < *dikē* "judgment"] —**syn·di·cal** *adj* —**syn·dic·ship** *n*

syn·di·cal·ism /síndikə lìzzəm/ *n* **1.** a revolutionary political doctrine that advocates the seizure of the means of production by workers organized in trade unions **2.** a system of government by which workers organized in trade unions control the means of production [Early 20C. < French *syndicalisme* < *syndic* (see SYNDIC)] —**syn·di·cal** *adj* —**syn·di·cal·ist** *adj, n* —**syn·di·cal·is·tic** /sìndikə lístik/ *adj*

syn·di·cate *n* /síndəkət/ **1.** GROUP OF BUSINESSES an association of businesses jointly contributing capital to a major project **2.** BUSINESS THAT SELLS NEWS MATERIALS a business or agency that sells news stories or photographs to the media **3.** GROUP OF NEWSPAPERS UNDER SAME OWNER a group of newspapers that have the same owner **4.** GROUP OF PEOPLE a group of people who combine to carry out a business, enterprise, or some other common purpose **5.** CRIME ASSOCIATION OF GANGSTERS an association of gangsters that controls an area of organized crime **6.** POL COUNCIL OF SYNDICS a council or body of syndics **7.** POL JURISDICTION OF GOVERNMENT OFFICIAL the office or jurisdiction of a government official, especially a civil magistrate, in some European countries ■ *v* /síndə kàyt/ (**-cat·ed, -cat·ing, -cates**) **1.** *vt* SELL SOMETHING FOR MULTIPLE PUBLICATION to sell something such as an article or a comic strip for publication in a number of newspapers or magazines simultaneously **2.** *vt* US SELL TV PROGRAMS TO INDEPENDENT STATIONS to sell television or radio programs directly to independent stations **3.** *vt* CONTROL SOMETHING AS SYNDICATE to control or manage something as a syndicate **4.** *vi* COME TOGETHER AS SYNDICATE to come together to form a syndicate [Early 17C. Via French < medieval Latin *syndicatus* < late Latin *syndicus* (see SYNDIC)] —**syn·di·ca·tion** /sìndi káysh'n/ *n*

syn·drome /sín drōm/ *n* **1.** a group of signs and symptoms that together are characteristic or indicative of a specific disease or other disorder **2.** a group of things or events that form a recognizable pattern, especially of something undesirable [Mid-16C. Via modern Latin < Greek *sundromē* "running together" < *dramein* "run"]

syne /sīn/ *adv Scotland* since then [14C. Contraction of obsolete *sithen* < Old English *siððan* (see SINCE)]

syn·ec·do·che /si nékdəkee/ *n* a figure of speech in which the word for part of something is used to mean the whole, e.g., "sail" for "boat," or vice versa [14C. Via Latin < Greek *sunekdokhē* < *sunekdekhesthai* "take on a share of" < *ekdekhesthai* "take"] —**syn·ec·doch·ic** /sìn ek dókik, sìnnək-/ *adj* —**syn·ec·doch·i·cal** *adj* —**syn·ec·doch·i·cal·ly** *adv*

syn·e·cious /si néeshəss/, **syn·oe·cious** *adj* having male and female organs on the same flower or other structure [Mid-19C. < SYN- + Greek *oikos* "house"]

syn·e·col·o·gy /sìnni kólləjee/ *n* the branch of ecology that deals with the structure and development of entire ecological communities and the interrelationships of the plants and animals within them —**syn·e·co·log·ic** /sìnnikə lójjik/ *adj* —**syn·e·co·log·i·cal** *adj* —**syn·e·co·log·i·cal·ly** *adv*

sy·nec·tics /si néktiks/ *n* an approach to solving problems based on the creative thinking of a group of people from different areas of experience and knowledge (*takes a singular verb*) [Mid-20C. Via late Latin *synecticus* "producing an effect immediately" < Greek *sunektikos* < *ekhein* "to hold"]

syn·er·e·sis /si nérrəssiss, -néerəssiss/, **syn·aer·e·sis** *n* **1.** LIQUID SEPARATION IN GEL the process by which a liquid is separated from a gel owing to further coagulation **2.** MERGING OF VOWELS INTO DIPHTHONG the merging of two vowels into a diphthong **3.** MERGING OF VOWELS INTO ONE SYLLABLE the merging of two vowels into one syllable without making it into a diphthong [Late 16C. Via late Latin < Greek *sunairesis* "contraction" < *hairein* "take"]

syn·er·gism /sínnər jìzzəm/ *n* **1.** BUSINESS, MED same as **synergy** **2.** in Christian theology, the doctrine that the human will and the Holy Spirit work together to bring about spiritual regeneration or salvation [Mid-18C. < SYNERGY] —**syn·er·gis·tic** /sìnnər jístik/ *adj* —**syn·er·gis·ti·cal·ly** *adv*

syn·er·gist /sínnərjist/ *n* something that works in combination with something else to increase its effect, e.g., a drug that increases the effect of another drug

syn·er·gy /sínnərjee/ (*plural* **-gies**) *n* **1.** the working together of two or more people, organizations, or things, especially when the result is greater than the sum of their individual effects or capabilities **2.** the phenomenon in which the combined action of two things such as drugs or muscles is greater than the sum of their effects individually. In the case of drugs, the result may be dangerous to the patient. [Mid-17C. Via Latin < Greek *sunergia* < *sunergein* "work together" < *ergos* "work"] —**syn·er·get·ic** /sìnnər jéttik/ *adj* —**syn·er·get·i·cal·ly** *adv* —**syn·er·gic** /si núrjik/ *adj*

syn·e·sis /sínnəssiss/ *n* grammatical agreement according to meaning rather than strict syntax, e.g., the use of a plural pronoun with a singular antecedent., as in "If anyone is looking for me, tell them I'll be back soon," with "them" being used instead of "him" or "her" to refer back to "anyone." [Late 19C. Via modern Latin < Greek *sunesis* "union" < *sunienai* "bring together" < *hienai* "send"]

syn·es·the·sia /sìnnəss théezhə/, **syn·aes·the·sia** *n* **1.** PHYSIOL SENSATION FELT ELSEWHERE IN BODY the feeling of sensation in one part of the body when another part is stimulated **2.** PSYCHOL STIMULATION OF ONE SENSE ALONGSIDE ANOTHER the evocation of one kind of sense impression when another sense is stimulated, e.g., the sensation of color when a sound is heard **3.** LITERAT **RHETORICAL DEVICE** in literature, the description of one kind of sense perception using words that describe another kind of sense perception, as in the phrase "shining metallic words" (*literary*) [Late 19C. < modern Latin < *syn-* (< Greek *sun* "together") + stem of Greek *aisthēsis* "sensation," after ANESTHESIA] —**syn·es·thet·ic** /-théttik/ *adj*

syn·fu·el /sín fyoo͝ əl/ *n* a liquid fuel synthesized from a nonpetroleum source such as coal, oil shale, or waste plastics. Use: a substitute for a petroleum product. [Late 20C. < SYNTHETIC]

syn·ga·my /síng gəmee/ *n* sexual reproduction through the fusion of gametes [Early 20C. < SYN- + Greek *gamos* "marriage"] —**syn·gam·ic** /sing gámmik/ *adj* —**syn·ga·mous** *adj*

AKG London

J. M. Synge: portrait by John B. Yeats

Synge /sing/, **J. M.** (1871–1909) Irish dramatist. A dominant figure of the Irish Renaissance, he wrote the controversial masterpiece, *The Playboy of the Western World* (1907). Full name **Synge, John Millington**. See Cultural note at **playboy**

"In a good play every speech should be as fully flavored as a nut or apple, and such speeches cannot be written by anyone who works among people who have shut their lips on poetry."
[J. M. Synge, *The Playboy of the Western World*; 1907]

syn·ge·ne·ic /sìnjə née ik/ *adj* having an identical or closely similar genetic makeup, especially one that will allow the transplantation of tissue without provoking an immune response [Mid-20C. < Greek *sungeneia* "kinship" < *genos* "kind, type"] —**syn·ge·ne·i·cal·ly** *adv*

syn·gen·e·sis /sin jénnəssiss/ *n* reproduction involving fusion of male and female genetic material —**syn·ge·net·ic** /sìnjə néttik/ *adj*

syn·kar·y·on /sin kárree on/ *n* a cell nucleus formed through the fusion of male and female nuclei [Early 20C. < SYN- + Greek *karuon* "seed"] —**syn·kar·y·on·ic** /sin kàrree ónnik/ *adj*

syn·ki·ne·sis /sìngkə néessiss/, **syn·ki·ne·sia** /-néezhə/ *n* the performing of an unintended movement when making a voluntary one —**syn·ki·net·ic** /sìngkə néttik/ *adj*

syn·od /sínnəd/ *n* **1.** a special council of church members that holds regular meetings to discuss religious issues **2.** an assembly or council held for the discussion of issues (*formal*) [14C. Via late Latin < Greek *sunodos* "meeting" < *hodos* "way"] —**syn·od·al** /sínnəd'l, si nódd'l/ *adj*

syn·od·ic /si nóddik/, **syn·od·i·cal** /-ik'l/ *adj* **1.** relating to the alignment of astronomical objects, or the interval between occasions when the same astronomical objects are aligned **2.** relating to or having the character of a church synod —**syn·od·i·cal·ly** *adv*

syn·od·ic month *n* ASTRON same as **lunar month** (sense 1)

syn·oe·cious *adj* BOT another spelling of **synecious**

~~**synonim**~~ incorrect spelling of **synonym**

~~**synonomous**~~ incorrect spelling of **synonymous**

syn·o·nym /sínnə nìm/ *n* **1. WORD MEANING SAME AS ANOTHER** a word that means the same, or almost the same, as another word in the same language, either in all of its uses or in a specific context. Examples of synonyms in this sense are "environment" and "surroundings" and the verbs "tear" and "rip." **2. ALTERNATIVE NAME** a word or expression that is used as another name for something in some styles of speaking or writing or to emphasize a specific aspect or association. Examples include "Gotham" and "New York." **3.** BIOL **REJECTED DUPLICATE TAXONOMIC NAME** a duplicate taxonomic name that has been rejected or replaced [15C. < Latin *synonymum* < Greek *sunōnumos* "synonymous" < *onuma* "name"] —**syn·o·nym·ic** /sìnnə nímmik/ *adj* —**syn·o·nym·i·ty** /sìnnə nímmətee/ *n*

syn·on·y·mize /si nónnə mīz/ (**-mized, -miz·ing, -miz·es**) *vt* to provide an analysis or listing of the synonyms of a word or expression

syn·on·y·mous /si nónnəməss/ *adj* **1.** meaning the same, or almost the same, as another word in the same language, or being an alternative name for somebody or something **2.** having an implication similar to the idea expressed by another word ○ *Andy Warhol is synonymous with pop art.* —**syn·on·y·mous·ly** *adv* —**syn·on·y·mous·ness** *n*

syn·on·y·my /si nónnəmee/ (*plural* **-mies**) *n* **1. EQUIVALENCE OF MEANING** the state or quality of being synonymous **2. STUDY OF SYNONYMS** the study, classification, and distinguishing of synonyms **3. ANNOTATED LIST OF SYNONYMS** a list or book of synonyms, with emphasis on the discrimination of meanings **4.** BIOL **LIST OF TAXONOMIC NAMES** a record of scientific names, often chronological, that have been applied to a taxonomic group

syn·op·sis /si nópsiss/ (*plural* **-op·ses** /-óp seez/) *n* **1.** a condensed version of a text, e.g., a summary of the plot of a book, play, movie, or television show **2.** a concise outline or survey of a subject [Early 17C. Via late Latin < Greek *sunopsis* "general view" < *opsis* "view"]

syn·op·size /si nóp sīz/ (**-sized, -siz·ing, -siz·es**) *vt* to summarize or make a synopsis of something

syn·op·tic /si nóptik/ *adj* **1.** constituting a general view of the whole of a subject **2.** METEOROL relating to or showing simultaneous weather conditions over a large area ■ *adj, n* BIBLE another spelling of **Synoptic** [Early 17C. Via modern Latin < Greek *sunoptikos* < *sunopsis* (see SYNOPSIS)] —**syn·op·ti·cal** *adj* —**syn·op·ti·cal·ly** *adv*

Syn·op·tic /si nóptik/ *adj* describes the gospels of Matthew, Mark, and Luke that tell the story of Jesus Christ's life and ministry from a similar point of view and are similar in structure ■ *n* **1.** one of the Synoptic gospels of Matthew, Mark, or Luke **2.** BIBLE same as **synoptist**

syn·op·tist /si nóptist/ *n* an author of one of the Synoptic gospels

syn·os·to·sis /sìn oss tóssiss/ (*plural* **-to·ses** /-tō seez/) *n* the formation of a single bone from the fusion of two adjacent bones —**syn·os·tot·ic** /-tóttik/ *adj*

syn·o·vi·a /sī nōvee ə/ *n* PHYSIOL same as **synovial fluid** [Mid-17C. < modern Latin *sinovia*] —**syn·o·vi·al** *adj*

syn·o·vi·al flu·id *n* a clear viscous fluid that lubricates the linings of joints and the sheaths of tendons

sy·no·vi·tis /sīnō vītəss/ *n* inflammation of the synovial membrane of a joint —**syn·o·vit·ic** /-víttik/ *adj*

syn·sep·al·ous /sin sépp'ləss/ *adj* BOT same as **gamosepalous** [Mid-19C. < SYNTHETIC + SEPAL]

syn·tac·tic /sin táktik/, **syn·tac·ti·cal** /-ik'l/ *adj* **1.** relating to the rules or patterns of syntax **2.** correctly formed according to the rules or accepted structures of syntax [Early 19C. Via Latin < Greek *suntaktikos* < *suntassein* (see SYNTAX)] —**syn·tac·ti·cal·ly** *adv*

syn·tag·ma /sin tágmə/ (*plural* **-ma·ta** /-mətə/ or **-mas**), **syn·tagm** /sín tàm/ *n* a linguistic unit made up of sets of phonemes, words, or phrases that are arranged sequentially [Mid-17C. Via late Latin < Greek *suntagma* < *suntassein* (see SYNTAX)]

syn·tag·mat·ic /sìn tag máttik/, **syn·tag·mic** /sin tágmik/ *adj* relating to syntactic units, or to the function and behavior of a word or phrase within a syntactic unit

syn·tax /sín tàks/ *n* **1. ORGANIZATION OF WORDS IN SENTENCES** the ordering of and relationship between the words and other structural elements in phrases and sentences. The syntax may be of a whole language, a single phrase or sentence, or of an individual speaker. **2. BRANCH OF GRAMMAR** the branch of grammar that studies syntax **3. RULES OF SYNTAX** an exposition of or set of rules for producing grammatical structures according to the syntax of a language **4. RULES GOVERNING PROGRAM STRUCTURE** the rules governing which statements and combinations of statements in a programming language will be acceptable to a compiler for that language **5. RULES FOR DERIVING LOGICAL FORMULAS** the part of logic that gives the rules that define which combinations of expressions in the logical system yield well-formed formulas **6. RULE-BASED ARRANGEMENT** the arrangement of any group of elements in a systematic or rule-based manner [Late 16C. Directly or via French < late Latin < Greek *suntaxis* < *suntassein* "put in order" < *tassein* "arrange"]

syn·tax·in /sin ták sìn/ *n* a cell protein responsible for propelling neurotransmitter chemicals from one neuron to the next

syn·te·ny /síntənee/ *n* the occurrence of two or more genes on the same chromosome, whether or not they are linked —**syn·ten·ic** /sin ténnik/ *adj*

synth /sinth/ *n* MUSIC same as **synthesizer** (*informal*) [Late 20C. Shortening]

syn·the·sis /sínthəssiss/ (*plural* **-the·ses** /-thə seez/) *n* **1. RESULT OF COMBINATION** a new unified whole resulting from the combination of different ideas, influences, or objects **2. COMBINING OF VARIOUS COMPONENTS INTO WHOLE** the process of combining different ideas, influences, or objects into a new whole **3.** CHEM **FORMATION OF CHEMICAL COMPOUNDS** the formation of compounds through one or more chemical reactions involving simpler substances **4.** MUSIC **PRODUCING OF SOUND WITH SYNTHESIZER** the production of music or speech using an electronic synthesizer **5.** LING **USE OF INFLECTIONS** the expression of syntactic relationships by means of inflections rather than word order or prepositions and other function words **6.** PHILOSOPHY **IDEA RESOLVING CONTRADICTIONS** in Hegelian philosophy, the new idea that resolves the conflict between the initial proposition (**thesis**) and its negation (**antithesis**) **7.** PHILOSOPHY **DEDUCTIVE REASONING** the process of deductive reasoning from first principles to a conclusion [15C. Via Latin, "collection" < Greek *sunthesis* < *suntithenai* "put together" < *tithenai* "put"] —**syn·the·sist** *n*

syn·the·sis gas *n* a mixture of carbon monoxide and hydrogen derived from the breakdown of carbon- and hydrogen-containing materials. Use: manufacture of ammonia, other chemicals.

syn·the·size /sínthə sīz/ (**-sized, -siz·ing, -siz·es**) *v* **1.** *vti* **COMBINE VARIOUS COMPONENTS INTO NEW WHOLE** to combine different ideas, influences, or objects into a new whole, or be combined in this way **2.** *vt* **PRODUCE SUBSTANCE BY CHEMICAL PROCESS** to produce a substance or material by chemical or biological synthesis **3.** *vt* **PRODUCE MUSIC ELECTRONICALLY** to produce music using an electronic synthesizer —**syn·the·si·za·tion** /sìnthəssi záysh'n/ *n*

syn·the·siz·er /sínthə sīzər/ *n* **1. ELECTRONIC MUSICAL INSTRUMENT** a device that generates and modifies sounds electronically, especially a musical instrument **2. MANUFACTURER OF SYNTHETIC SUBSTANCES** somebody or something involved in the synthesis of substances or materials **3. SOMEBODY WHO COMBINES COMPONENTS** somebody who combines ideas, influences, or objects into a new whole

syn·thes·pi·an /sin théspee ən/ *n* a digital image of a person created by a precise full-body scan and used by animators to produce animated characters or films [Late 20C. Blend of SYNTHETIC + THESPIAN]

syn·thet·ic /sin théttik/ *adj* **1. MADE BY CHEMICAL PROCESS** made artificially by chemical synthesis, especially so as to resemble a natural product **2. INSINCERE** not genuine, especially expressed but not genuinely felt ○ *synthetic expressions of sympathy* **3.** PHILOSOPHY **WITH TRUTH DEPENDING ON FACTS** describes a proposition whose truth or falsity is a matter of facts and not merely a matter of the meaning of the words in the sentence **4.** LING **USING INFLECTIONS TO EXPRESS SYNTAX**

describes a language that expresses syntactic relationships by means of inflections rather than word order or prepositions and other function words ■ *n* **1. CHEMICALLY PRODUCED SUBSTANCE OR MATERIAL** a substance or material produced by chemical processes and not occurring naturally **2. ARTIFICIAL FIBER** a synthetic textile fiber, or an item of clothing made of this (*usually used in the plural*) [Late 17C. Via French or modern Latin < Greek *sunthetikos* "component" < *sunthetos* "combined" < *suntithenai* (see SYNTHESIS)] —**syn·thet·i·cal** *adj* —**syn·thet·i·cal·ly** *adv*

syn·thet·ic res·in *n* a resin produced by polymerization of simple molecules, and not obtained directly from plant substances

syn·thet·ic rub·ber *n* a compound synthesized from unsaturated hydrocarbons that resembles rubber

syn·ton·ic /sin tónnik/ *adj* **1.** describes somebody who is emotionally attuned to his or her environment **2.** in ego psychology, used to describe behavior that does not conflict with somebody's basic attitudes and beliefs and, therefore, is not anxiety-provoking (*used in combination*) ○ *ego-syntonic* [Late 19C. < Greek *suntonos* "attuned" < *suntenein* "draw tight"] —**syn·ton·i·cal·ly** *adv*

syn·type /sín tīp/ *n* a member of a set of specimens that have equal status as the basis for the description of a new species

sy·pher /sífər/ (**-phered, -pher·ing, -phers**) *vt* to join planks with chamfered edges so as to form a flush surface [Mid-19C. Variant of CIPHER]

syph·i·lis /síffəliss/ *n* a serious sexually transmitted disease caused by the spirally twisted bacterium *Treponema pallidum* that affects many body organs and parts, including the genitals, brain, skin, and nervous tissue [Early 18C. < modern Latin, after the person allegedly first affected (according to Girolamo Fracastoro (1483–1553), Veronese physician)] —**syph·i·loid** *adj*

syph·i·lit·ic /sìffə líttik/ *adj* relating to, caused by, or affected by syphilis ■ *n* an offensive term for somebody who has syphilis [Late 18C. < modern Latin *syphiliticus* < *syphilis* (see SYPHILIS)] —**syph·i·lit·i·cal·ly** *adv*

syph·i·lo·ma /sìffə lṓmə/ (*plural* **-ma·ta** /-mətə/ or **-mas**) *n* MED same as **gumma**

sy·phon *n, vt* another spelling of **siphon**

Syr·a·cuse /sírrə kyo͝oss/ **1.** capital city and port of Syracuse Province, Sicily, situated about 35 mi./56 km south of Catania. Population: 126,721 (1999). **2.** city in New York beside Onondaga Lake, west of Utica, and east of Rochester. Population: 145,164 (2002 estimate).

syr·ah /sírrə/ *n* **1.** a typically strong full-bodied red wine made from a variety of black grape grown mainly in France and the United States **2.** a black grape variety. Use: to make syrah wine. [Early 19C. Alteration of SHIRAZ]

Syria

Sy·ria /sírree ə/ country in Southwest Asia, bordered by Turkey, Iraq, Jordan, Israel, Lebanon, and the Mediterranean Sea. Capital: Damascus. Population: 17,585,540 (2003). Area: 71,498 sq. mi./185,180 sq. km. Official name **Syrian Arab Republic** —**Syr·i·an** *n, adj*

Syr·i·ac /sírree àk/ *n* a form of Aramaic used between the 3rd and 13th centuries that survives in some Eastern Orthodox churches —**Syr·i·ac** *adj*

sy·rin·ga /si ríng gə/ *n* **1.** TREES same as **mock orange** (sense 1) **2.** a lilac flower or bush. Genus: *Syringa.* [Mid-17C. < modern Latin < Greek *surigx* "panpipes"]

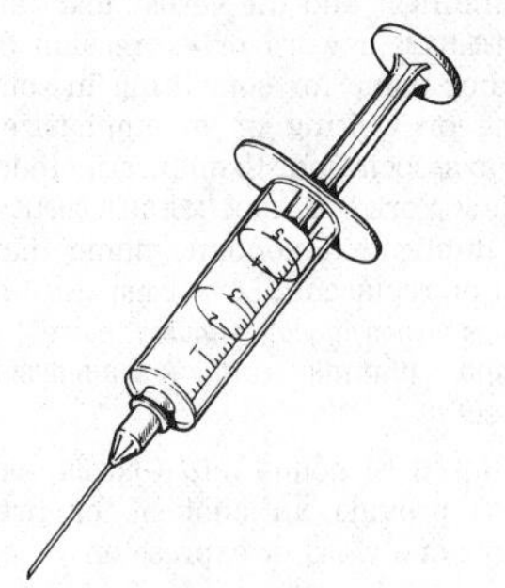

syringe

sy·ringe /si rínj/ *n* **1. INSTRUMENT FOR WITHDRAWING AND EJECTING FLUIDS** an instrument consisting of a piston in a small tube, used in conjunction with a hollow needle or tube for the withdrawal and injection of fluids and for cleaning wounds **2. DEVICE FOR PUMPING AND SPRAYING LIQUIDS** a device similar to a medical syringe that is used for spraying or extracting fluids by means of pressure or suction ■ *vt* (**-ringed, -ring·ing, -rin·ges**) **USE SYRINGE ON SOMETHING** to clean, spray, or inject something using a syringe [15C. Via medieval Latin *syringa* < Greek *surigx* "panpipes"]

sy·rin·ges plural of **syrinx**

sy·rin·go·my·e·li·a /si rìng gō mī éelee ə/ *n* a chronic progressive disease of the spinal cord in which tubular fluid-filled cavities form in the nerve tissue, causing sensory disturbances and, eventually, loss of voluntary movement [Late 19C. < SYRINGE + MYEL-] —**sy·rin·go·my·el·ic** *adj*

syr·inx /sírringks/ (*plural* **syr·inx·es** or **sy·rin·ges** /sə ríng geez, sə rín jeez/) *n* **1.** MUSIC **PANPIPES** a set of panpipes **2.** BIRDS **VOCAL ORGAN OF BIRD** the vocal organ of a bird, usually situated near the junction between the trachea and bronchi **3.** ANCIENT HIST **CORRIDOR IN EGYPTIAN TOMB** a narrow corridor or gallery in an ancient Egyptian tomb **4.** MED **CAVITY IN SPINAL CORD** any of the tubular fluid-filled cavities formed in the nerve tissue of the spinal cord in cases of syringomyelia [Early 17C. Via Latin < Greek *surinx* "panpipes"] —**sy·rin·ge·al** /sə ríng gee əl, sə rínjee əl/ *adj*

syr·phid /súrfid/, **syr·phus fly** /súrfəss-/ *n* a dipteran fly that hovers and darts, feeds on nectar and pollen, and has coloration mimicking that of a bee or wasp. Family: Syrphidae. [Late 19C. < modern Latin *Syrphidae* < *Syrphus* < Greek *surphos* "gnat"] —**syr·phid** *adj*

Syr·tis Ma·jor /sùrtiss máyjər/ highly conspicuous wedge-shaped dark area on the surface of Mars in the equatorial region, first observed in 1659

syr·up /sírrəp/, **sir·up** *n* **1. SWEET LIQUID** a liquid made of sugar dissolved in water by heating, widely used in candy making. Syrups vary in density and strength, and can be boiled down to form caramel. **2. FLAVORED SWEET LIQUID** a flavored thick sweet liquid **3.** PHARM **PHARMACEUTICAL LIQUID** a thick sweet liquid used to convey oral medicines **4.** same as **maple syrup 5.** same as **corn syrup** [14C. Directly or via French < medieval Latin *siropus* < Arabic *šarāb* "drink"]

syr·up·y /sírrəpee/ (**-i·er, -i·est**) *adj* **1.** resembling syrup in taste, quality, or consistency **2.** excessively sentimental in a cloying fashion

SYS *abbr* see you soon (*used in e-mails or text messages*)

sys·op /síss op/ *n* a system operator, usually one who runs a bulletin board (*informal*) [Late 20C. Contraction]

syst. *abbr* system

sys·tal·tic /si stáltik/ *adj* describes an organ such as the heart that undergoes alternating rhythmic contraction and dilation [Late 17C. Via late Latin < Greek *sustaltikos* < *sustellein* (see SYSTOLE)]

sys·tem /sístəm/ *n* **1. COMPLEX WHOLE FORMED FROM RELATED PARTS** a combination of related parts organized into a complex whole ○ *a social system* **2. SET OF PRINCIPLES** a scheme of ideas or principles by which something is organized ○ *the democratic system* ○ *the metric system* **3. WAY OF PROCEEDING** a method or set of procedures for achieving something ○ *I have worked out a system for identifying likely failures.* **4. ORDERLINESS** the use or result of careful planning and organization ○ *There doesn't seem to be any system in his working methods.* **5. ESTABLISHED SOCIAL ORGANIZATION** the established social order, especially when regarded as oppressive ○ *You can't beat the system.* **6. WHOLE BODY** the human or animal body as a unit ○ *foods that are not good for the system* **7. GROUP OF RELATED BODY PARTS** a set of organs or structures in the body that have a common function ○ *the nervous system* **8.** COMPUT **SET OF COMPUTER COMPONENTS** an assembly of computer hardware, software, and peripherals functioning together ○ *The system's down again.* **9.** ENG **ASSEMBLY OF COMPONENTS** an assembly of mechanical or electronic components that function together as a unit **10.** TRANSP **TRANSPORT NETWORK** a physical network of roads, railways, and other routes for travel, transport, or communication **11.** ASTRON **GROUP OF ASTRONOMICAL OBJECTS** a group of astronomical objects or other gravitationally linked objects **12.** MINERALS **MINERAL CLASSIFICATION** a division used in the classification of minerals according to their crystal structures **13.** GEOL **CLASSIFICATION OF ROCKS ACCORDING TO DATE** a division of rocks larger than a series but smaller than a stage, used to distinguish formations of a specific era or period **14.** SCI **ASSEMBLY OF SUBSTANCES IN EQUILIBRIUM** an assembly of substances in chemical or physical equilibrium **15.** MUSIC **GROUP OF MUSICAL STAVES** a number of musical staves that are grouped together by a line or brace in a score and are played simultaneously [Early 17C. Directly or via French < late Latin *systema* < Greek *sustēma* < *sunistanai* "combine" < *histanai* "set up"] —**sys·tem·less** *adj* ◇ **all systems go** used to indicate that everything is functioning and an operation or activity can start (*informal*)

sys·tem·at·ic /sìstə máttik/, **sys·tem·at·i·cal** /-ik'l/ *adj* **1. DONE METHODICALLY** carried out in a methodical and organized manner **2. WELL ORGANIZED** habitually using a method or system for organization **3. METHODICAL** deliberate and regular in a methodical manner **4. BASED ON SYSTEM** constituting, based on, or resembling a system **5.** BIOL **RELATING TO TAXONOMIC CLASSIFICATION** in accordance with a system of taxonomic classification (**systematics**) [Mid-17C. Via late Latin < Greek *sustēmatikos* < *sustēma* (see SYSTEM)] —**sys·tem·at·i·cal·ly** *adv*

sys·tem·at·ic de·sen·si·ti·za·tion *n* a therapy for phobias and other anxiety disorders in which patients are gradually given longer and longer exposures to the object of their fears

sys·tem·at·ics /sìstə máttiks/ *n* the study of systems and classification, especially the science of classifying organisms (*takes a singular verb*)

sys·tem·a·tism /sístəmə tìzzəm/ *n* the practice of classifying information in a systematic manner

sys·tem·a·tist /sístəmətist/ *n* **1. SOMEBODY CONSTRUCTING SYSTEMS** somebody who constructs a system or systems **2.** BIOL **SOMEBODY CLASSIFYING ORGANISMS** somebody who classifies organisms according to a taxonomic system **3. SOMEBODY ADHERING TO SYSTEM** somebody who conforms to a system or method

sys·tem·a·tize /sístəmə tīz/ (**-tized, -tiz·ing, -tiz·es**) *vti* to arrange something according to a system, or be arranged according to a system [Mid-18C. < Greek *sustēmat-*, stem of *sustēma* (see SYSTEM)] —**sys·tem·a·ti·za·tion** /sìstəməti záysh'n/ *n* —**sys·tem·a·tiz·er** *n*

sys·tem·ic /si stémmik/ *adj* **1. OF SYSTEM** relating to or affecting a system as a whole **2.** PHYSIOL **AFFECTING WHOLE BODY** affecting the whole body, as distinct from having a local effect ○ *a systemic infection* **3.** BOT **AFFECTING WHOLE PLANT** describes an herbicide or other chemical that works by spreading through all the tissues of a plant instead of just staying on the surface ■ *n* AGRIC **SYSTEMIC CHEMICAL** a systemic herbicide, pesticide, or other chemical —**sys·tem·i·cal·ly** *adv*

sys·tem·ic cir·cu·la·tion *n* the main part of the blood circulation, as distinct from the pulmonary circulation

sys·tem·ize /sístə mīz/ (**-ized, -iz·ing, -iz·es**) *vt* same as

systematize —**sys·tem·i·za·tion** /sìstəmi záysh'n/ *n* —**sys·tem·iz·er** *n*

sys·tem op·er·a·tor *n* somebody who manages an online bulletin board or maintains a computer network

sys·tems a·nal·y·sis *n* the determination of the data-processing requirements of a company, project, procedure, or task, and the designing of computer systems to fulfill them —**sys·tems an·a·lyst** *n*

sys·tems en·gi·neer·ing *n* the design and implementation of production systems that require the integration of diverse and complex tasks, e.g., automobile assembly lines —**sys·tems en·gi·neer** *n*

sys·tem soft·ware *n* the operating system and utility programs used to operate and maintain a computer system and provide resources for application programs such as word processors and spreadsheets

sys·to·le /sístəlee/ *n* the contraction of the heart, during which blood is pumped into the arteries [Mid-16C. Via late Latin < Greek *sustolē* < *sustellein* "contract" < *stellein* "put"] —**sys·tol·ic** /si stóllik/ *adj*

syz·y·gy /sízzəjee/ (*plural* **-gies**) *n* **1.** CONJUNCTION OF THREE ASTRONOMICAL OBJECTS the straight-line conjunction or opposition of three astronomical objects such as the Sun, Earth, and Moon **2.** PAIR OF CONNECTED THINGS a pair of related things that are either similar or opposite (*formal*) **3.** LITERAT UNIT OF TWO METRICAL FEET in classical verse, a metrical unit of two feet [Early 17C. Via late Latin < Greek *suzugia* < *suzugos* "paired" < *zugon* "yoke"] —**syz·y·get·ic** /sìzzə jéttik/ *adj* —**syz·y·get·i·cal·ly** *adv* —**sy·zyg·i·al** /si zíjjee əl/ *adj*

SZ *abbr* Swaziland (*used in Internet addresses*) See table at **domain name**

Szcze·cin /shché cheen/ capital city and port of Szczecin Province, northwestern Poland. Population: 419,000 (1997). German name **Stettin**

Sze·chuan, **Sze·chwan** another spelling of **Sichuan**

Sze·ged /sé gèd/ city and river port in southeastern Hungary. Population: 159,133 (1999).

Szell /sel, zel/, **George** (1897–1970) Hungarian-born US conductor. As the musical director of the Cleveland Orchestra from 1946 to 1970, he established the orchestra as one of the finest in the world.

Szi·lard /zíllərd, zə laard/, **Leo** (1898–1964) Hungarian-born US biophysicist. He worked on uranium fission and contributed to the development of the atomic bomb, but later advocated only peaceful uses of atomic energy.

> "We turned the switch, saw the flashes, watched for ten minutes, then switched everything off and went home. That night I knew the world was headed for sorrow."
> [Attributed to Leo Szilard]

t[1] /tee/ (*plural* **t's**), **T** (*plural* **T's** or **Ts**) *n* **1.** the 20th letter of the English alphabet, representing a consonant sound **2.** a written representation of the letter "t" ◇ **to a T** exactly

t[2] *symbol* **1.** PHYS time **2.** MEASURE troy

T[1] (*plural* **T's** or **Ts**) *n* something shaped like a letter "T"

T[2] *symbol* **1.** PHYS absolute temperature **2.** PHYS kinetic energy **3.** PHYS period **4.** PHYS surface tension **5.** MEASURE temperature **6.** PHYS tesla **7.** CHEM ELEM tritium

T[3] *abbr* **1.** TELECOM telephone (number) (*used to contrast with E (e-mail address) and F (fax number)*) **2.** MATH tera-

t. *abbr* **1.** MEASURE tare **2.** MEASURE teaspoon **3.** MEASURE teaspoonful **4.** MUSIC tempo **5.** MUSIC tenor **6.** GRAM tense **7.** MEASURE ton *or* tons **8.** GRAM transitive

T. *abbr* **1.** MEASURE tablespoon **2.** tablespoonful **3.** Tuesday

T1 *n* a high-capacity telephone line suitable for high-speed digital access to the Internet, handling 24 voice or data channels simultaneously. ◊ **T3**

T3 *n* a high-capacity telephone line handling 672 voice or data channels simultaneously and capable of transferring data at speeds great enough to provide full-screen full-motion video. ◊ **T1**

T4 slip /tee fáwr-/ *n Can* a form that states the wages paid to and taxes withheld from an employee [*T4* < the official designation of the form]

Ta *symbol* CHEM ELEM tantalum

TA *abbr* **1.** teaching assistant **2.** transactional analysis **3.** TRANSP Transit Authority

tab[1] /tab/ *n* **1.** FLAP FOR HOLDING a small strip, loop, or other attachment to something, used for lifting, moving, hanging, opening, or closing **2.** TAG OR LABEL a small piece of paper, cloth, or plastic attached to something and containing information about the object **3.** CLOTHING FLAP ON GARMENT a small strip or square of fabric attached to a garment for decoration **4.** BEVERAGES same as **pull-tab** **5.** RESTAURANT CHECK the check for a meal or drinks in a restaurant or bar (*informal*) **6.** AEROSP AUXILIARY AIRFOIL a small auxiliary airfoil on a control surface such as an aileron or rudder, used as a stabilizer ■ *vt* (**tabbed, tab·bing, tabs**) PUT TAB ON SOMETHING to attach a tab to something [Early 17C. Origin ?] ◇ **keep tabs on somebody** *or* **something** to watch somebody *or* something closely (*informal*) ◇ **pick up the tab** to pay the bill (*informal*)

tab[2] /tab/ *n* a key on a computer keyboard, or a device or key on a typewriter, that advances the next character to a predetermined position, used to align lines or columns ■ *vt* (**tabbed, tab·bing, tabs**) to move the cursor on a computer screen from one place in a document to another using the tab key [Early 20C. Shortening of TABULATOR]

tab[3] /tab/ *n* a tablet or piece of paper containing a drug, especially one that is illegal (*informal*) [Mid-20C. Shortening of TABLET]

tab[4] /tab/ *n* THEATER same as **tableau curtain** [Early 20C. Shortening]

TAB /tab/ *abbr* MED typhoid-paratyphoid A-paratyphoid B (vaccine)

tab. *abbr* table

ta·ban·ca /tə bángkə/ *n Carib* a painful feeling of unrequited love [Late 19C. Probably < Carib]

tabard (sense 3)

tab·ard /tábbərd/ *n* **1.** SLEEVELESS OVERGARMENT a sleeveless tunic with slits at the sides, worn by women and girls, especially catering staff **2.** HERALD'S COAT an official coat worn by a herald, bearing the sovereign's coat of arms **3.** HIST KNIGHT'S JACKET a sleeveless or short-sleeved garment worn by a knight over his armor [13C. < Old French *tabart*]

tab·a·ret /tábbə rèt/ *n* a hard-wearing fabric with alternate satin and watered-silk stripes. Use: upholstery. [Late 18C. Probably < TABBY]

Ta·bas·co[1] /tə báskō/ *tdmk* a trademark for a hot-tasting sauce made from peppers, vinegar, and spices

Ta·bas·co[2] /tə báskō/ state in south central Mexico, on the southern shores of the Gulf of Mexico. Capital: Villahermosa. Population: 1,891,829 (2000). Area: 9,490 sq. mi./24,578 sq. km.

tab·bou·leh /tə bo͝olee/, **ta·boo·li** *n* a Southwest Asian salad made with bulgur wheat and finely chopped tomatoes, mint, and parsley [Mid-20C. < Arabic *tabbūla*]

tab·by /tábbee/ *n* (*plural* **-bies**) **1.** STRIPED CAT a brown or gray cat with a striped or mottled coat **2.** PET FEMALE CAT a domestic cat, especially a female one **3.** OFFENSIVE TERM an offensive term for a woman who is considered to be gossipy, spiteful, and interfering (*literary insult*) **4.** TEXTILES SILK WITH STRIPED PATTERN watered silk or taffeta with a striped or wavy pattern **5.** TEXTILES PLAIN FABRIC a plain-woven fabric ■ *adj* **1.** HAVING STRIPED COAT describes a cat that has a brown or gray coat with a striped or mottled pattern **2.** STRIPED OR BRINDLED having a striped or wavy pattern **3.** TEXTILES RESEMBLING TABBY resembling or made of tabby [Late 16C. Via French *tabis* < Arabic *'attābī*, after *al-'Attābiyya*, quarter of Baghdad, Iraq]

ORIGIN It was the stripes on the fabric called ***tabby*** that led to the application of the word to striped or mottled cats. The usage is first recorded in the 1660s.

tab·er·na·cle /tábbər nàk'l/ *n* **1.** *also* **Tab·er·na·cle** BIBLE TENT FOR CARRYING ARK OF COVENANT in the Bible, a portable tent used as a sanctuary for the Ark of the Covenant by the Israelites during the Exodus **2.** *also* **Tab·er·na·cle** JUDAISM JEWISH TEMPLE the Jewish Temple, regarded as representing the presence of God **3.** JUDAISM same as **sukkah** **4.** RELIG EVANGELICAL PLACE OF WORSHIP a place of worship, especially in some evangelical Christian denominations **5.** CHR CONTAINER FOR HOLY BREAD AND WINE a box or case in which the consecrated bread and wine of Communion are kept **6.** ARCHIT NICHE FOR ICON a canopied recess or niche for an icon **7.** NAUT SOCKET FOR MAST a support for the foot of a ship's mast **8.** HUMAN BODY the human body considered as a place temporarily housing the soul or principle of life (*literary*) [13C. Directly or via French < Latin *tabernaculum* "tent" < *taberna* "hut"] —**tab·er·nac·u·lar** /tàbbər nákyələr/ *adj*

Tab·er·na·cles /tábbər nàk'lz/ *n* JUDAISM, CALENDAR same as **Sukkoth**

ta·bes /táybeez/ (*plural same*) *n* **1.** progressive wasting of the body, usually as a result of a chronic disease **2.** MED same as **tabes dorsalis** [Late 16C. < Latin, "wasting away"] —**ta·bet·ic** /tə béttik/ *adj*

ta·bes dor·sa·lis /-dawr sáyliss/ *n* a disorder of the nervous system characteristic of late-stage syphilis and marked by degeneration of nerve fibers, wasting, pain, and inability to move the leg muscles. Tabes dorsalis is now rare because syphilis can be effectively treated at a much earlier stage. [< late Latin, "dorsal tabes"]

tab key *n* a key on a computer keyboard that advances the next character to a predetermined position

tab·la /ta͞ablə, túbblə/ *n* a South Asian musical instrument consisting of a pair of small drums played with the hands [Mid-19C. Via Persian and Hindi < Arabic *ṭabl* "drum"]

tab·la·ture /tábblə cho͝or, -chər/ *n* **1.** a musical notation in which the notes themselves are not represented, but rather the hand positions required to play them. It is used especially in early lute and modern popular guitar music. **2.** a tablet or other flat surface that has been engraved or painted [Late 16C. Via French < Italian *tavolatura* < *tavolare* "set to music" < *tavola* "table"]

ta·ble /táyb'l/ *n* **1.** ITEM OF FURNITURE WITH FLAT TOP a piece of furniture with a flat top and one or more legs, used for placing things on or doing things at **2.** PLACE FOR EATING MEALS WHILE SEATED a table at which people sit to eat meals **3.** FLAT SURFACE FOR SPECIFIC PURPOSE a raised flat surface with a nondomestic or office use, e.g., one at which a surgeon operates or one on which a piece of machinery rests **4.** FOOD SERVED the food provided in a household or restaurant in terms of its quality or quantity **5.** PEOPLE SITTING AT TABLE a group of people sitting at a table, especially for a meal ○ *The whole table erupted in laughter.* **6.** ARRANGEMENT OF INFORMATION IN COLUMNS an arrangement of information or data into columns and rows or a condensed list **7.** GEOG same as **tableland** **8.** ARCHIT BAND OR PANEL ON WALL a band of masonry or a rectangular panel on a wall, either raised or depressed and with ornamentation or inscriptions **9.** FLAT SURFACE OF GEM the upper horizontal surface of a cut gem **10.** SLAB FOR INSCRIPTION a slab of wood, stone, or metal for inscription **11.** BOARD GAMES PART OF BACKGAMMON BOARD either one of the two hinged halves of a backgammon board **12.** MUSIC FRONT PART OF STRINGED INSTRUMENT the part of the body of a stringed instrument that acts as a sounding board **13.** ANAT PLATE OF BONE a flat layer of bone, especially either one of the inner or outer surfaces of the skull that are separated by a more spongy bone (**diploë**) **14.** AREA ON PALM an area on the palm defined by four lines, regarded as significant in palmistry ■ **ta·bles** *npl* ANCIENT HIST **ANCIENT TABLETS INSCRIBED WITH LAWS** tablets on which some ancient Greek, Roman, and Hebrew laws were inscribed, or the laws themselves ■ *vt* (**-bled, -bling, -bles**) **1. POSTPONE DISCUSSION OF SOMETHING** to postpone discussion of a bill or motion until a later time **2. ENTER INFORMATION INTO TABLE** to enter information in a tabular form **3. PUT SOMETHING ON TABLE** to place or lay something on a table **4.** *Can, UK* **PROPOSE SOMETHING** to put forward a bill, motion, or proposal for discussion at a meeting [Pre-12C. Directly or via French < Latin *tabula* "board, slab"] —**table·ful** *n* ◇ **drink somebody under the table** to continue drinking until after other people present are completely intoxicated ◇ **on the table 1.** put forward for discussion at a meeting **2.** postponed for discussion at a later time ◇ **turn the tables (on somebody)** to reverse a situation and gain the advantage from somebody who had previously held it ◇ **under the table** secretly and often illegally, in the form of a bribe ○ *He paid under the table for his rent-stabilized apartment.*

tab·leau /tá blō, ta blṓ/ (*plural* **-leaux** /-lṓz/ or **-leaus**) *n* **1.** a vivid and wide-ranging description or display **2.** a visually dramatic scene or situation that suddenly arises **3.** THEATER same as **tableau vivant** [Late 17C. Via French < Old French *tablel* "small table" < *table* (see TABLE)]

tab·leau cur·tain *n* either of a pair of stage curtains that are drawn to each side and upward by a cord

tab·leau vi·vant /tábblō vee vaáN, ta blṓ-/ (*plural* **tab·leaux vi·vants** /*pronunc. same*/) *n* a representation of a scene by a group in appropriate costume posing silent and motionless [< French, "living picture"]

Ta·ble Bay /táyb'l-/ inlet of the Atlantic Ocean, overlooked by Table Mountain, southwestern South Africa. Length: 12 mi./19 km.

ta·ble·cloth /táyb'l klàwth, -klòth/ *n* a cloth for covering a table, especially before it is set for a meal

ta·ble danc·ing *n* a type of erotic dancing or striptease performed on a tabletop in front of a customer or small group of customers

ta·ble d'hôte /taáb'l dṓt, taáblə-/ *n* a restaurant meal or menu offering a series of courses at a fixed price [Early 17C. < French, "host's table"]

ta·ble foot·ball *n UK* same as **foosball**

ta·ble-hop *vi* to circulate among tables in a restaurant or nightclub in a sociable way (*informal*) —**ta·ble-hop·per** *n*

ta·ble knife *n* a knife used at table with a fork for cutting food, especially the food of a main course

ta·ble·land /táyb'l lànd/ *n* an extensive elevated region of flat land

ta·ble lin·en *n* linens used in setting a table, especially tablecloths and napkins

ta·ble man·ners *npl* actions and behavior considered to be polite or socially correct when eating a meal with other people

ta·ble·mate /táyb'l màyt/ *n US* somebody sitting at the same table as another, especially for a meal

Ta·ble Moun·tain flat-topped mountain overlooking Cape Town, southwestern South Africa. Height: 3,563 ft./1,086 m.

ta·ble·spoon /táyb'l spoon/ *n* **1. SERVING SPOON** a large serving spoon a size larger than a dessertspoon **2.** *also* **ta·ble·spoon·ful** /táyb'l spoon fool/ **MEASURE BASED ON CAPACITY OF TABLESPOON** a unit of capacity used in recipes, equal to half a fluid ounce/15 ml or three teaspoons **3.** *also* **ta·ble·spoon·ful AMOUNT HELD BY TABLESPOON** the amount of food or liquid that a tablespoon can hold

tab·let /tábblət/ *n* **1. PILL** a small solid pill containing a measured medicinal dose, usually intended to be taken orally **2. SMALL FLAT CAKE OF SOMETHING** a measured amount of something compressed and packaged for ease of use **3. INSCRIBED STONE OR WOODEN SLAB** a slab of stone, wood, or metal used for inscription or engraving **4. SHEETS OF PAPER FASTENED TOGETHER** a number of sheets of paper for writing or drawing, fastened together along one edge **5. SHEET OF MATERIAL TO WRITE ON** a thin stiff sheet of wood, slate, or ivory on which somebody writes **6.** ARCHIT same as **table** (sense 8) **7. PERSONAL COMPUTER** a small thin portable personal computer that relies on a pen instead of a keyboard to input information [14C. < Old French, "little table" < *table* (see TABLE)]

ta·ble talk *n* **1.** informal conversation on subjects considered suitable during a meal **2.** in bridge, the discussion of bidding and strategy across the table with a partner, which is not permitted by the rules

ta·ble ten·nis *n* a game that resembles tennis and is played with small paddles and a light hollow ball on a table divided by a net

ta·ble·top /táyb'l tòp/ *n* the flat upper surface of a table ■ *adj* designed for use on a tabletop or similar surface

ta·ble·ware /táyb'l wèr/ *n* dishes, plates, glasses, flatware, and other articles used at meals

ta·ble wine *n* an unfortified wine for drinking with meals

tab·loid /táb lòyd/ *n* **1.** *also* **tab·loid news·pa·per SMALL NEWSPAPER WITH SHORT ARTICLES** a small-format popular newspaper with a simple style, many photographs, and sometimes an emphasis on sensational stories **2. CONDENSED PIECE OF WRITING** a piece of writing, especially a news story, in a condensed form ■ *adj* **SENSATIONALIST** relating to or characteristic of tabloid newspapers, especially in having a popular sensationalist style [Late 19C. < proprietary name for tablets of condensed medicine]

ORIGIN ***Tabloid*** was registered as a proprietary name for a brand of tablet in 1884 by Burroughs, Wellcome, and Company. It was the underlying notion of "compression" or "condensation" that led to its application to newspapers of small page size and "condensed" versions of news stories that emerged at the beginning of the 20th century.

---

tab·loid TV *n* a television program that combines gossip, scandal, and news about media celebrities in the style associated with tabloid journalism (*informal*)

ta·boo /tə bóo/, **ta·bu** *adj* **1. SOCIALLY OR CULTURALLY PROHIBITED** forbidden to be used, mentioned, or approached because of social or cultural rather than legal prohibitions **2. UNACCEPTABLE** not acceptable or healthful (*humorous*) ○ *Sweets and fats are strictly taboo.* **3.** RELIG **SACRED AND PROHIBITED** set apart as sacred and at the same time forbidden to be used ■ *n* (*plural* **-boos;** *plural* **-bus**) **1. PROHIBITION** a prohibition or rejection of some types of behavior or language because they are considered socially unacceptable **2. FORBIDDEN BEHAVIOR** a subject or behavior that is forbidden or disapproved of because it is considered socially unacceptable **3.** RELIG **PROHIBITION ON GROUNDS OF BEING SACRED** the practice, especially in some Polynesian societies, of regarding some things, people, or types of behavior as sacred and therefore forbidden to be used, made contact with, or engaged in ■ *vt* (**-booed, -boo·ing, -boos; -bued, -bu·ing, -bus**) **1. FORBID OR DISCOURAGE SOMETHING** to prohibit or disapprove of some types of behavior or language because they are considered socially unacceptable **2.** RELIG **PROHIBIT SOMETHING BECAUSE SACRED** to regard some things, people, or types of behavior as sacred and therefore forbidden to be used, made contact with, or engaged in [Late 18C. < Polynesian *tabu*]

ta·boo·li *n* FOOD another spelling of **tabbouleh**

ta·bor /táybər/, **ta·bour** *n* a small drum played with one hand while the other hand plays a pipe. Tabors were used especially in the Middle Ages. [13C. < Old French *tabour*] —**ta·bor·er** *n*

Ta·bor, Mount /táybər/ peak in northern Israel, east of Nazareth. In the Bible, it is the site of the transfiguration of Jesus Christ. Height: 1,929 ft./588 m.

Ta·bo·ra /ta báwrə/ capital city of Tabora Region, west-central Tanzania, situated about 220 mi./354 km northwest of Dodoma. Population: 960,000 (1995).

tab·o·ret /tàbbə rét, -ráy/, **tab·ou·ret** *n* **1.** a low solid seat without arms or a back **2.** HANDICRAFT same as **tambour** *n* (sense 1) **3.** a small tabor or tambourine [Mid-17C. < French, "small tabor"]

ta·bour *n* MUSIC another spelling of **tabor**

Ta·briz /taa bréez/ city in northwestern Iran, capital of East Azerbaijan Province. Tabriz has been severely damaged over the centuries by earthquakes. Population: 1,191,043 (1996).

ta·bu *adj, n, vt* CULTL ANTHROP, RELIG another spelling of **taboo**

tab·u·lar /tábbyələr/ *adj* **1. ARRANGED IN TABLE** arranged in a table or in columns and rows **2. HAVING FLAT SURFACE** having a flat surface that resembles a table **3.** CRYSTALS **BROAD AND FLAT** describes crystals that are broad and flat **4.** GEOL **SPLITTING INTO THIN PLATES** describes rock that is made up of and splits readily into thin horizontal plates **5.** MATH **COMPUTED USING TABLE** calculated with or making use of a table, e.g., of logarithms [Mid-17C. < Latin *tabularis* < *tabula* "board, slab"] —**tab·u·lar·ly** *adv*

tab·u·la ra·sa /tàbbyələ raássə, -raázə/ (*plural* **tab·u·lae ra·sae** /tàbbyəlee raássee, -raázee/) *n* **1.** the mind at birth, regarded as having no innate conceptions **2.** an opportunity to make a clean break or a fresh start [Mid-16C. < Latin, "scraped table"]

tab·u·lar·ize /tábbyələ rìz/ (**-ized, -iz·ing, -iz·es**) *vt* same as **tabulate** *v* (sense 1) —**tab·u·lar·i·za·tion** /tàbbyələri záysh'n/ *n*

tab·u·late *vt* /tábbyə làyt/ (**-lat·ed, -lat·ing, -lates**) **1. ARRANGE INFORMATION IN TABLE** to arrange information systematically in a table or in columns and rows **2. MAKE SOMETHING FLAT** to give a flat top or upper surface to something (*usually passive*) ■ *adj* /tábbyələt, -làyt/ **FLAT** with a flat surface that resembles a table [Late 16C. < late Latin *tabulatus* < Latin *tabula* "board, slab"] —**tab·u·la·ble** *adj* —**tab·u·la·tion** /tàbbyə láysh'n/ *n*

tab·u·la·tor /tábbyə làytər/ *n* **1.** a person or device that tabulates information **2.** COMPUT same as **tab**[2]

ta·bun /taá boon/ *n* an organic phosphorus compound. Use: lethal chemical weapon. Formula: $C_5H_{11}N_2O_2P$. [Mid-20C. < German]

TAC *abbr* MIL Tactical Air Command

tac·a·ma·hac /tákəmə hàk/, **tac·ma·hack** /tákmə-/ *n* **1.** a resinous tree gum. Use: ointments, incense. **2.** a tree that yields tacamahac resin, especially the balsam poplar [Late 16C. Via obsolete Spanish *tacamahaca* < Nahuatl *tecomahiyac*]

Tac·an /tá kàn/ *n* an aircraft navigation system using UHF signals emitted from a transmitting station to determine distance and bearing [Mid-20C. Acronym < TACTICAL + AIR + NAVIGATION]

ta·cet /tássət, táyssət, taá kèt/ *n* a musical direction instructing a musician not to play or sing a passage or phrase [Early 18C. < Latin, "(it) is silent" < *tacere* "be silent"]

tach /tak/ *n* same as **tachometer** (*informal*) [Mid-20C. Shortening]

Ta·ché /taa sháy/, **Sir Etienne-Paschal** (1795–1865) Canadian politician. A local and federal office holder, he chaired the conference (1864) that paved the way for the unification of Canada.

tach·e·om·e·try /tàkee ómmətree/ *n* CONSTR same as **tachymetry** —**tach·e·o·met·ric** /tàkee ə méttrik/ *adj* —**tach·e·o·met·ri·cal·ly** *adv*

tach·i·na fly /tákənə-/ *n* a bristly fly whose larvae live as parasites on other insects. They are sometimes used to control harmful insect species. Family: Tachinidae. [< modern Latin *Tachina* < Greek *takhinos* "swift"]

tach·i·nid /tákənid/ *n* INSECTS same as **tachina fly** ■ *adj* relating to the family of insects that the tachina fly belongs to [Late 19C. < modern Latin *Tachinidae* < *Tachina* (see TACHINA FLY)]

tach·ism /tá shìzzəm/, **tach·isme** *n* action painting in which random blotches of color are used as a method of instinctive expression [Mid-20C. < French *tachisme* < *tache* "spot"] —**tach·ist** *n, adj*

ta·chis·to·scope /tə kístə skōp/ *n* an instrument for displaying visual images very briefly, used to test perception and memory [Late 19C. < Greek *takhistos* "swiftest" < *takhus* "swift"] —**ta·chis·to·scop·ic** /tə kìstə skóppik/ *adj* —**ta·chis·to·scop·i·cal·ly** *adv*

tach·o·gram /tákə gràm/ *n* a record in graph form produced by a tachograph

tach·o·graph /tákə gràf/ *n* an instrument that produces a record of the use and readings of a tachometer, especially one in a commercial vehicle or bus recording speeds and distances traveled. In effect, a tachograph records the hours worked by a driver. [Early 20C. < Greek *takhos* "speed"]

ta·chom·e·ter /ta kómmətər/ *n* a device used to determine speed of rotation, typically of a vehicle's crankshaft, usually measured in revolutions per minute [Early 19C. < Greek *takhos* "speed"] —**tach·o·met·ric** /tàkə méttrik/ *adj* —**tach·o·met·ri·cal·ly** *adv* —**ta·chom·e·try** *n*

tachy- *prefix* accelerated, rapid ○ *tachygraphy* [< Greek *takhus* "swift"]

tach·y·ar·rhyth·mi·a /tàkee ə ríthmee ə/ *n* a medical condition in which the heartbeat is fast and irregular

tach·y·car·di·a /tàkee kaárdee ə/ *n* an excessively rapid heartbeat, typically regarded as a heart rate exceeding 100 beats per minute in a resting adult [Late 19C. < TACHY- + Greek *kardia* "heart"] —**tach·y·car·di·ac** *adj* —**tach·y·card·ic** *adj*

ta·chyg·ra·phy /ta kíggrəfee/ *n* **1.** the shorthand system used by the ancient Greeks and Romans **2.** the abbreviated cursive writing used in medieval times for Latin and Greek —**ta·chyg·ra·pher** *n* —**tach·y·graph·ic** /tàki gráffik/ *adj* —**tach·y·graph·i·cal·ly** *adv*

tach·y·lite /tákə līt/, **tach·y·lyte** *n* black volcanic glass formed by the chilling of basaltic magma [Mid-19C. < German *Tachylyt* < Greek *takhu-* "quickly," from its rapid decomposition in acids, + *lutos* "soluble"] —**tach·y·lit·ic** /tàkə líttik/ *adj*

ta·chym·e·try /ta kímmətree/ *n* the measurement of distances, elevations, and directions at speed using a type of theodolite —**ta·chym·e·ter** *n* —**tach·y·met·ric** /tàki méttrik/ *adj* —**tach·y·met·ri·cal·ly** *adv*

tach·y·on /tákee òn/ *n* a hypothetical elementary particle that always travels faster than the speed of light

tach·yp·ne·a /tàkip neé ə, tàki-/ *n* unusually fast breathing, generally considered to be over 20 breaths per minute in a resting adult [Late 19C. < TACHY- + Greek *pnoiē* "breathing" < *pnein* "breathe"]

tach·yp·noe·a *n* MED UK spelling of **tachypnea**

tac·it /tássit/ *adj* understood or implied without being stated openly [Early 17C. < Latin *tacitus*, past participle of *tacere* "be silent"] —**tac·it·ly** *adv* —**tac·it·ness** *n*

tac·i·turn /tássi tùrn/ *adj* habitually uncommunicative or reserved in speech and manner [Late 18C. Via French *taciturne* < Latin *taciturnus* < *tacitus* (see TACIT)] —**tac·i·tur·ni·ty** /tàssi túrnətee/ *n* —**tac·i·turn·ly** *adv*

SYNONYMS See ***silent***.

Tac·i·tus /tássitəss/ (A.D. 55?–117?) Roman historian. The author of histories of the Roman Empire, he also held various government posts and was famed as an orator. Full name **Tacitus, Gaius Cornelius**

> "It is part of human nature to hate the man you have hurt."
> [Tacitus, *De Vita Iulii Agricola (Agricola)*; 98?]

tack[1] /tak/ *n* **1.** COMM same as **thumbtack 2. SMALL NAIL** a small sharp nail with a broad head **3. COURSE OF ACTION** a course of action or method of approach intended to achieve something, especially one adopted after another has failed **4.** SAILING **CHANGE IN DIRECTION OF SAILING** a change in the direction of movement of a sailboat made in order to maximize the benefit from the wind **5.** SAILING **PART OF ZIGZAG SAILING COURSE** a stage or series of stages in the zigzag movement of a sailboat that is changing direction in order to maximize the benefit from the wind **6.** SAILING **DIRECTION OF SAILING** the direction of movement of a sailboat in relation to the side from which the wind is blowing, effected by the position of its sails **7.** SAILING **ROPE HOLDING DOWN SAIL** a rope holding down the corner of some sails, or the corner that is held down **8.** HANDICRAFT **TEMPORARY STITCH** a long loose temporary stitch, often used to align seams in preparation for final sewing **9. SLIGHT STICKINESS** slight stickiness, e.g., of glue or paint that has not yet dried ■ *v* (**tacked, tack·ing, tacks**) **1.** *vt* **ATTACH SOMETHING WITH THUMBTACK** to attach something light to a board or wall with a thumbtack **2.** *vt* CONSTR **FASTEN SOMETHING WITH TACKS** to attach something with small sharp broad-headed nails **3.** *vi* **CHANGE APPROACH** to take a different course of action or use a different method **4.** *vt* **PUT THINGS TOGETHER ARBITRARILY** to bring different things together to form an arbitrary or illusory whole **5.** *vti* SAILING **CHANGE DIRECTION OF SAILING BOAT** to change the direction or course of a sailboat or ship, or steer a sailboat or ship on alternate tacks, or be sailed or steered in this way **6.** *vt UK* HANDICRAFT same as **baste**[2] [14C. < Old N French *taque* "fastening" < Germanic]

tack on *vt* to add something to something else either as a supplement or an afterthought

tack[2] /tak/ *n* saddles, bridles, and other parts of a horse's harness [Late 18C. Shortening of TACKLE]

tack[3] /tak/ *n* goods that are tasteless and vulgar or cheap and shoddy (*informal*) [Late 20C. Back-formation < TACKY[2]]

tack[4] /tak/ *n* foodstuff, especially of the poor quality fed to a ship's crew in the days of sailing ships (*slang*) [Late 16C. Origin ?]

tack·board /ták bàwrd/ *n US* same as **bulletin board** (sense 1) (*informal*)

tack·le /ták'l/ *n* **1. ATTEMPT TO STOP OPPONENT'S PROGRESS** in football, field hockey, and some other games, a physical challenge against an opposing player who has the ball, puck, or other object of possession. A tackle is made by seizing and forcing the opponent to the ground in football, by using the foot in soccer, and with the stick in field hockey. **2. SPECIALIZED EQUIPMENT** the equipment used for a specialized activity such as fishing, angling or rock climbing **3.** MECH ENG **ROPES AND PULLEYS** equipment consisting of ropes and pulleys used for lifting heavy weights through increased mechanical advantage **4.** SAILING **SHIP'S RIGGING** the gear and rigging of a sailboat **5.** FOOTBALL **LINEMAN NEXT TO END** in football, a lineman positioned between a guard and an end, or the position of such a player ■ *vt* (**-led, -ling, -les**) **1. UNDERTAKE PROJECT** to undertake or deal with something that requires effort **2. CONFRONT SOMEBODY** to open a conversation or discussion on a difficult issue with somebody who would prefer to avoid it ○ *Have you tackled them about paying for it?* **3.** SPORTS **MAKE TACKLE ON SOMEBODY** in football, field hockey, and some other games, to make a physical challenge on an opposing player **4. HARNESS ANIMAL** to put a harness on an animal, especially a horse [13C. Probably < Low German *takel* "ship's rigging" < *taken* "seize"] —**tack·ler** *n*

tack weld·ing *n* the welding of two metals by individual welds at isolated points

tack·y[1] /tákee/ (**-i·er, -i·est**) *adj* slightly sticky to the touch [Late 18C. < TACK[1]] —**tack·i·ly** *adv* —**tack·i·ness** *n*

tack·y[2] /tákee/ (**-i·er, -i·est**) *adj* (*informal*) **1.** perceived as vulgar, lacking in taste, or no longer fashionable **2.** appearing to be cheaply made or in need of repair [Early 19C. Origin ?] —**tack·i·ly** *adv* —**tack·i·ness** *n*

Tac·lo·ban /táklō bàn/ port and city on Leyte Island in central Philippines. During World War II, US forces landed on beaches south of the city at the start of a campaign to liberate the Philippines. Population: 137,200 (1990).

tac·ma·hack *n* TREES another spelling of **tacamahac**

ta·co /taákō/ (*plural* **-cos**) *n* a crisp fried corn tortilla usually filled with meat, lettuce or cabbage, tomatoes, cheese, and hot sauce [Mid-20C. Via American Spanish < Spanish, "wad"]

Ta·co·ma /tə kṓmə/ city in western Washington State, a deep-water port on Commencement Bay, an arm of Puget Sound. Population: 197,553 (2002 estimate).

tac·o·nite /tákə nīt/ *n* a banded iron formation consisting of layers of the iron oxides magnetite and hematite that may be extracted from pulverized rock using a magnet [Early 20C. After *Taconic*, mountain range in New York State]

tact /takt/ *n* **1.** skill in situations in which other people's feelings have to be considered **2.** an intuitive sense of what is right or appropriate [Early 17C. Via French < Latin *tactus* "(sense of) touch" < *tangere* "to touch"]

tact·ful /táktfəl/ *adj* having or showing concern about upsetting or offending people —**tact·ful·ly** *adv* —**tact·ful·ness** *n*

tac·tic /táktik/ *n* a method used or a course of action followed in order to achieve an immediate or short-term goal [Mid-17C. Via modern Latin < Greek *taktikos* "of arrangement" < *taktos* "arranged" < *tassein* "arrange"]

tac·ti·cal /táktik'l/ *adj* **1. OF TACTICS** relating to or involving tactics **2. AS MEANS TO END** done or made for the purpose of trying to achieve an immediate or short-term goal **3. SHOWING SKILLFUL PLANNING** showing skillful planning in order to accomplish something **4.** MIL **WITH LIMITED MILITARY OBJECTIVE** used to support limited military operations ○ *tactical forces* **5.** MIL **FOR SHORT DISTANCE** designed to be used over a short distance ○ *tactical weapons* **6.** MIL **SUPPORTING OTHER MILITARY OBJECTIVE** undertaken or for use in support of other military and naval operations ○ *tactical bombing* —**tac·ti·cal·ly** *adv*

tac·tics /táktiks/ *n* the science of organizing and maneuvering forces in battle to achieve a limited or immediate goal (*takes a singular verb*) ■ *npl* the art of finding and implementing means to achieve immediate or short-term goals (*takes a plural verb*) —**tac·ti·cian** /tak tísh'n/ *n*

tac·tile /tákt'l, ták tīl/ *adj* **1. OF TOUCH** relating to or used for the sense of touch **2. TANGIBLE** capable of being perceived by the sense of touch **3. PLEASANT TO TOUCH** pleasing or interesting to the sense of touch **4. HABITUALLY TOUCHING PEOPLE** inclined to touch people a lot, e.g., while talking to them **5.** ARTS **APPARENTLY THREE-DIMENSIONAL** giving an illusion of physical solidity and tangibility [Early 17C. Directly or via French < Latin *tactilis* < *tactus* (see TACT)] —**tac·tile·ly** *adv* —**tac·til·i·ty** /tak tíllətee/ *n*

tac·tile cor·pus·cle, **tac·tile bud** *n* a tiny egg-shaped touch receptor that responds to light pressure and is found in the skin of the palms, lips, soles, and other hairless sensitive areas

tact·less /táktləss/ *adj* not concerned about upsetting or offending people, or showing a lack of such concern —**tact·less·ly** *adv* —**tact·less·ness** *n*

tac·tu·al /tákchoo əl/ *adj* relating to the sense of touch, or imparting the sensation of contact [Mid-17C. < Latin *tactus* (see TACT)] —**tac·tu·al·ly** *adv*

tad /tad/ *n* (*informal*) **1.** a very slight amount or degree of something **2.** a small child, especially a boy [Late 19C. Origin ?] ◇ **a tad** somewhat

ta·djah /taa jaá/ *n Carib* ISLAM same as **tazia** [Late 20C. Variant]

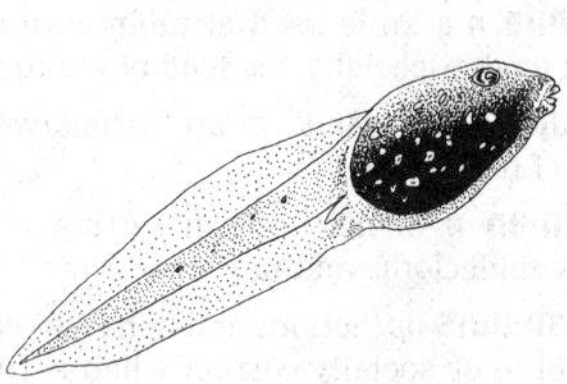

tadpole

tad·pole /tád pōl/ *n* the larva of a frog, toad, or salamander that has a limbless rounded body, gills, and a tail [15C. < earlier forms of TOAD + POLL]

Ta·dzhik, etc. *n, adj* PEOPLES, LANG another spelling of **Tajik, etc.**

Tae Bo /tī bṓ/ *n* a fitness regime based on exercising to music and performing movements that derive from martial arts such as tae kwon do [Late 20C. < TAE KWON DO + BOXING]

Tae·gu /tī goŏ/ city in southern South Korea, capital of North Kyongsang Province. It is an important industrial, agricultural, and commercial center. Population: 2,449,139 (1995).

Tae·jon /tī jáun, -jón/ city in central South Korea, capital of South Ch'ungch'ong Province. It is a major road and rail junction, industrial and agricultural center. Population: 1,049,578 (1990).

tae kwon do /tī kwon dṓ/ *n* a Korean martial art resembling karate but also employing a wide range of kicking moves [Mid-20C. < Korean, "art of hand and foot fighting"]

tael /tayl/ *n* **1.** a varying unit of weight used in East Asia, usually around 1.75 oz/38 g **2.** a silver coin that was a unit of currency in China between 1889 and 1912, equivalent to a tael of silver [Late 16C. Via Portuguese < Malay *tahil*, unit of weight]

tae·ni·a /téenee ə/ (*plural* **-ni·ae** /-nee èe/ or **-ni·as**), **te·ni·a** (*plural* **-ni·ae** or **-ni·as**) *n* **1.** ANAT **PART SHAPED LIKE RIBBON** a body part that resembles a ribbon, especially muscle or nervous tissue **2.** ARCHIT **HORIZONTAL BAND IN DORIC ARCHITECTURE** in the Doric order of ancient Greek architecture, a narrow band (**fillet**) between the main beam (**architrave**) across the top of the columns and the frieze above **3.** ZOOL **PARASITIC TAPEWORM** a large parasitic tapeworm. Genus: *Taenia*. **4.** CLOTHING **NARROW HEADBAND** a fillet or headband worn in ancient Greece [Mid-16C. Via Latin < Greek *tainia* "band"]

tae·ni·a·cide /téenee ə sìd/, **te·ni·a·cide** *n* a substance for killing tapeworms

tae·ni·a·fuge /téenee ə fyoòj/, **te·ni·a·fuge** *n* a drug or other agent that expels tapeworms from the body

tae·ni·a·sis /tee nî əssis/, **te·ni·a·sis** *n* infestation with adult tapeworms, usually following the eating of raw or undercooked meat containing tapeworm larvae

taf·fe·ta /táffətə/ *n* a stiff lustrous silk or a silky fabric with a slight rib. Use: women's clothes. [14C. Via medieval Latin or Old French *taffetas* < Persian *tāftah* < *tāftan* "to shine"]

taff·rail /táf ràyl/ *n* **1.** the rail around the stern of a ship **2.** the upper flat and often carved part of a ship's stern [Early 19C. < Dutch *taffereel* "small table" < *tafel* "table"]

taf·fy /táffee/ *n* **1.** a chewy candy made of sugar or molasses boiled down and pulled until glossy and light in color **2.** flattery of an insincere kind (*dated informal*) [Early 19C. Probably dialect form of TOFFEE]

Taft /taft/, **Helen Herron** (1861–1943) US first lady (1909–13). She was responsible for the planting of thousands of cherry trees in Washington, D.C.

Taft, Robert A. (1889–1953) US politician. A conservative Republican senator from Ohio (1938–53), he led the opposition to the Democratic administrations of Franklin D. Roosevelt and Harry S. Truman. He was cosponsor of the Taft-Hartley Act (1947), which tightened restrictions on labor unions. Full name **Taft, Robert Alphonso**. Known as **Mr. Republican**

Bettmann/Corbis
William Howard Taft

Taft, William Howard (1857–1930) 27th president of the United States. A Republican, he was president from 1909 to 1913 and chief justice of the US Supreme Court from 1921 to 1930. See table at **president**

> "Well, I have one consolation. No candidate was ever elected ex-president by such a large majority!"
> [Attributed to William Howard Taft, referring to his disastrous defeat by Woodrow Wilson in the 1912 presidential election.]

tag[1] /tag/ *n* **1.** **LABEL** a small piece of cloth, paper, plastic, or other material attached to something as a label or means of identification **2.** **TIP AT END OF SHOELACE** a plastic or metal tip attached to the end of a shoelace or cord to prevent it from fraying **3.** **SMALL LOOSE OR RAGGED PIECE** a small piece of a material hanging loosely or raggedly from the main piece **4.** COMPUT **CLASSIFYING LABEL FOR DATA** a label that describes a piece of data, e.g., to facilitate later retrieval or text formatting **5.** CRIME **ELECTRONIC DEVICE WORN BY OFFENDER** an electronic device worn, usually on the ankle or wrist, by a convicted offender serving a sentence in the community to allow his or her movements to be monitored **6.** ZOOL **TIP OF ANIMAL'S TAIL** the tip of an animal's tail, especially if in a contrasting color with the rest of the tail **7.** AGRIC, ZOOL **MATTED LOCK OF WOOL** a dirty matted lock of wool or hair in an animal's fleece or coat **8.** FISHING **ATTACHMENT TO ARTIFICIAL FLY** a piece of usually brightly colored material tied around the shank of the hook in the body of an artificial fly **9.** LITERAT **WELL-KNOWN QUOTATION** a well-known or hackneyed quotation, often in Latin, usually intended to add dignity or weight to a speech or piece of writing **10.** LANGUAGE **EPITHET** a descriptive word or phrase used, especially frequently, about somebody or something **11.** LITERAT **ENDING FOR PIECE OF WRITING** something ending or added to a piece of writing, e.g., a refrain, the cue line ending an actor's speech, or a final speech addressed to the audience **12.** LING same as **tag question** **13.** AUTOMOT same as **license plate** **14.** **GRAFFITI ARTIST'S SIGNATURE** a signature or identifying symbol used by a graffiti artist ■ *v* (**tagged, tag·ging, tags**) **1.** *vt* **LABEL SOMETHING WITH TAG** to attach a tag to something or label something with a tag **2.** *vt* **ADD SOMETHING AT END** to add an additional piece or section to the end of something, especially a piece of writing ○ *tagged on a couple of extra lines at the end* **3.** *vt* **ATTACH EPITHET TO SOMEBODY** to give somebody a nickname, or assign a verbal label to somebody **4.** *vt* CRIME **ATTACH ELECTRONIC TAG TO OFFENDER** to make an offender wear an electronic tag **5.** *vt US* LAW **TICKET CAR** to attach a ticket to a vehicle to notify the driver that a violation has been committed **6.** *vt US* LAW **CHARGE SOMEBODY WITH CRIME** to charge somebody with a crime (*often passive*) ○ *He was tagged for theft.* **7.** *vt* **ATTACH RHYMES TO TEXT** to put unrhymed verse or prose into rhyme **8.** *vt* AGRIC **REMOVE TAGS FROM ANIMAL** to remove tags from the fleece or coat of an animal **9.** *vti* **FOLLOW CLOSELY** to follow closely behind somebody [15C. Origin ?]

tag along *vi* to accompany or follow somebody, often when your presence is unwanted

tag[2] /tag/ *n* **1.** LEISURE **CHILDREN'S CHASING AND TOUCHING GAME** a children's game in which one player is chosen to chase the others and try to touch one of them. Anyone touched becomes "it" and is then the player who does the chasing. **2.** BASEBALL **INSTANCE OF PUTTING RUNNER OUT** in baseball, an instance of getting a runner out by touching him or her with the ball before he or she reaches the base **3.** WRESTLING same as **tag wrestling** **4.** WRESTLING **INSTANCE OF SWITCHING PLACES IN WRESTLING** in wrestling, an instance of touching a partner's hand in order to switch places ■ *vt* (**tagged, tag·ging, tags**) **1.** **CATCH PLAYER IN GAME OF TAG** in the children's game of tag, to touch a player making that player "it" **2.** BASEBALL **TOUCH RUNNER WITH BALL** in baseball, to get a runner out by touching him or her with the ball before he or she reaches the base **3.** WRESTLING **TOUCH PARTNER'S HAND IN WRESTLING** in tag wrestling, to touch the hand of a partner in order to switch places [Mid-18C. Origin ?]

tag up *vi* in baseball, to touch a base before running to the next one after a fly ball is caught

Ta·ga·log /tə gaàləg, -gaà lòg/ (*plural same* or **-logs**) *n* **1.** a member of a people who originally lived in the Manila area of the Philippines **2.** the Austronesian language of the Tagalog people, the basis of Filipino. Native speakers: 17 million. [Early 19C. < Tagalog *tagá* "native" + *ilog* "river"] —**Ta·ga·log** *adj*

tag·a·long /tággə làwng/ *n* somebody or something that persistently follows another, especially somebody whose attentions are unwelcome

tag day *n* a day when people collect money for charity and give donors a tag to wear

tag end *n* **1.** the very last or last remaining part of something **2.** a loose or detached piece of something

tagged im·age file for·mat /tagd-/ *n* COMPUT full form of **TIFF**

tag·ger /tággər/ *n* a graffiti artist who spray-paints his or her name or symbol on a public structure (*slang*)

tag·gers /tággərz/ *npl* iron or steel in thin sheets coated with tin [Mid-19C. Perhaps because used to make shoelace tags]

ta·gine /tə zhéen/ *n* **1.** a cooking pot with a high cone-shaped earthenware lid and a cast-iron or earthenware base, used especially for stews in Moroccan cuisine and requiring little liquid **2.** a Moroccan stew cooked very slowly in a tagine and consisting usually of meat or poultry combined with fruit [< Arabic *tajin*]

ta·gli·a·tel·le /taàlyə téllee/ *n* pasta in the form of long narrow ribbons [Late 19C. < Italian < *tagliare* "cut into strips"]

tag line *n US* **1.** the final line of a joke, story, or drama, delivering a humorous or dramatic point **2.** a phrase repeatedly used in connection with a person, organization, or product, especially in publicity

tag·ma /tágmə/ (*plural* **-ma·ta** /-mətə/) *n* a distinct functional region of the body of an arthropod, e.g., a thorax [Early 20C. < Greek, "something arranged" < *tag-*, stem of *tassein* "arrange"]

tag·meme /tág mèem/ *n* any one of the various positions in the structure of a sentence into which a word or phrase of a specific grammatical type can fit [Mid-20C < Greek *tagma* (see TAGMA)] —**tag·mem·ic** /tag méemik/ *adj*

tag·mem·ics /tag méemiks/ *n* a grammatical analysis of language based on the way in which the different elements that make up a sentence are arranged within it (*takes a singular verb*)

Popperfoto
Rabindranath Tagore

Ta·gore /tə gáwr/, **Rabindranath** (1861–1941) Indian writer. A prolific writer of poetry, plays, short stories, and novels, he revolutionized Bengali poetry by using colloquial language and new verse forms, and translated his own works into English. He was awarded the Nobel Prize in literature (1913).

tag ques·tion *n* a short clause added on to a statement to turn it into a question, e.g., "don't you?" or "isn't it?", or a statement with a question clause attached. The main function of a tag question is to cue a response from the listener or obtain his or her agreement to the original statement.

tag team *n* a team of two or more wrestlers, only one of whom may wrestle at a time. Wrestlers can change places only after touching hands.

tag·uan /taà gwaàn/ *n* a large nocturnal flying squirrel that leaps from tree to tree with the help of skin flaps that stretch between its limbs. Native to: Southeast Asia. Latin name: *Petaurista petaurista*. [Early 19C. Probably < local name in the Philippines]

Ta·gus /táygəss/ the longest river of the Iberian Peninsula, in southwestern Europe. It enters the Atlantic Ocean at Lisbon, Portugal. Length: 626 mi./1,007 km. Portuguese name **Tejo**. Spanish name **Tajo**

tag wres·tling *n* a form of wrestling in which wrestlers compete in teams of two or more, taking turns to enter the ring, a touch of hands being required for a changeover

ta·hi·ni /tə héenee/, **ta·hi·na** /-nə/ *n* an oily paste made from crushed sesame seeds. Use: seasoning. [Mid-20C. < Arabic *ṭaḥīnā* < *ṭaḥana* "grind"]

Ta·hi·ti /tə héetee/ island of French Polynesia, the largest of the Society Islands, in the southern Pacific

Ocean. Population: 115,820 (1998). Area: 400 sq. mi./1,000 sq. km. —**Ta·hi·tian** /tə héesh'n/ *n, adj*

Ta·hoe, Lake /taáhō/ lake in the western United States, situated on the border of Nevada and California. Area: 192 sq. mi./497 sq. km.

tahr /taar/ *n* a cud-chewing animal similar to a goat, with a shaggy coat and curved horns. Native to: mountains in South Asia. Genus: *Hemitragus*. [Mid-19C. < Nepalese *thār*]

tah·sil /taa seél/ *n* in parts of South Asia, an administrative district [Mid-19C. Via Urdu and Persian < *taḥṣīl* "revenue" < Arabic *ḥaṣala* "collect"]

tah·sil·dar /taá seél daar/ *n* in parts of South Asia, a government official in charge of collecting taxes and other revenues in a tahsil [Late 18C. Via Urdu *taḥṣīldār* < Persian, "revenue-holder" < *taḥṣīl* (see TAHSIL)]

Tai /tī/ *n* a group of tonal languages spoken in Southeast Asia, including Thai and Lao. Tai is sometimes considered to be related to the Sino-Tibetan language family. [Late 17C. Variant of THAI] —**Tai** *adj*

tai chi /tī cheé/, **Tai Chi, T'ai Chi, tai chi chuan** /-chee chwaán/, **Tai Chi Chuan, T'ai Chi Ch'uan** *n* a Chinese form of physical exercise characterized by a series of very slow and deliberate balletic body movements [Mid 18C. < Chinese, literally "extreme limit"]

tai·ga /tīgə/ *n* the subarctic coniferous forests located south of the tundra in North America, northern Europe, and Asia [Late 19C. < Russian]

tail /tayl/ *n* **1.** REAR PART OF ANIMAL'S BODY the flexible rear part, or a movable extension to the rear part, of a vertebrate animal's body that begins above the anus and often contains the terminal vertebrae **2.** LAST PART the rear, last, or lowest part of something ○ *the tail of the procession* **3.** AVIAT REAR OF AIRCRAFT the rear part of an aircraft together with horizontal and vertical stabilizing surfaces attached to it **4.** ARMS REAR OF MISSILE the rear part of a missile or bomb, including structures for controlling the angle of the trajectory **5.** COINS REVERSE OF COIN the reverse side of a coin **6.** ASTRON STREAM OF GAS FROM COMET the luminous stream of gas and dust particles driven by the solar wind from a comet as it approaches and then recedes from the Sun **7.** PEOPLE IN LINE a line of people or things **8.** HAIR LONG PIECE OF HAIR a long lock or braid of hair **9.** PRINTING BOTTOM OF PAGE the bottom of a printed page, or the margin between the bottom of the page and the lowest line of type **10.** CLOTHING LONG PART OF SHIRT the part of a shirt that hangs below the waist and is typically tucked into pants **11.** CLOTHING LONG PART OF FORMAL COAT either of two long panels at the back of a man's formal coat **12.** SOMEBODY FOLLOWING ANOTHER a secret follower or observer of somebody (*informal*) ○ *The police put a round-the-clock tail on the suspect.* **13.** TRAIL somebody's trail, especially when being followed or pursued (*informal*) **14.** HIST same as **horsetail** (sense 2) **15.** BOTTOM the buttocks (*informal*) **16.** TABOO TERM a highly offensive term meaning a woman's genitals (*taboo*) **17.** TABOO TERM a highly offensive term meaning sexual intercourse with a woman (*taboo*) **18.** TABOO TERM a highly offensive term meaning a woman perceived as a potential partner for sexual intercourse (*taboo*) ■ **tails** *npl* **1.** CLOTHING MAN'S FORMAL COAT a formal, usually black coat for a man, cut short at the front and with two long panels at the back **2.** CLOTHING MAN'S EVENING CLOTHES full evening clothes for a man **3.** TAIL OF COIN the reverse side of a coin turned up after a toss ■ *v* (**tailed, tail·ing, tails**) **1.** *vt* FOLLOW SOMEBODY SECRETLY to follow somebody secretly in order to keep watch on him or her (*informal*) ○ *Someone must have tailed you back to the house.* **2.** *vi* FOLLOW to follow behind somebody or something ○ *She strode out purposefully, leaving the rest of the party to tail along behind.* **3.** *vi* FORM LINE to form a long line when moving, especially a long spread-out line **4.** *vt* VET REMOVE TAIL OF ANIMAL to remove or cut short the tail of an animal **5.** *vt* REMOVE STALK FROM FRUIT to remove the stalk from something such as a piece of fruit **6.** *vt* JOIN THINGS END TO END to join two or more things end to end **7.** *vti* CONSTR BUILD, OR BE BUILT, INTO WALL to build one end of something such as a joist, beam, or brick, into a wall, or be fixed into a wall at one end **8.** *vi* NAUT LIE WITH STERN IN PARTICULAR DIRECTION to lie with the stern pointing in a particular direction when moored (*refers to a boat*) [Old English *tægel* < Germanic] —**tail·less** *adj* —**tail·less·ness** *n* ◇ **the tail that wags the dog** used for indicating that a situation is ridiculous because something of less importance is in control of something more important (*informal*) ◇ **turn tail** to turn and walk or run away, especially in a cowardly way ◇ **with your tail between your legs** in an abject ashamed manner (*informal*)

SPELLCHECK tail or **tale**? Do not confuse the spelling of ***tail*** and ***tale***, which sound similar. ***Tail*** can be used as a noun, meaning "the rear part of something, e.g., an animal, aircraft, or comet," or as a verb meaning "to follow behind": *The dog wagged its tail. She was being tailed by a private detective.* ***Tale*** is only used as a noun, meaning "a narrative" and also "an untrue report," as in *traditional folk tales, telling tales out of school.*

SYNONYMS See ***follow***.

tail off *vi* to grow less, smaller, or fainter, usually gradually

tail·back /táyl bàk/ *n* in football, the offensive back positioned farthest behind the line of scrimmage

tail beam *n* CONSTR same as **tailpiece** (sense 4)

tail·bone /táyl bōn/ *n* ANAT same as **coccyx**

tail·coat /táyl kōt/ *n* a formal, usually black coat for a man, cut short at the front and with two long tails at the back

tail end *n* **1.** the last or hindmost part of something **2.** the buttocks (*informal*)

tail·en·der /tayl éndər/ *n* somebody or something that comes at or toward the end of something (*informal*)

tail fan *n* a fan-shaped structure at the rear end of some crustaceans such as the lobster

tail·fin /táyl fìn/ *n* the fin attached to the tail of a fish

tail·gate /táyl gàyt/ *n* **1.** GATE AT BACK OF VEHICLE a gate at the back of a truck or utility vehicle that can be laid flat or dropped down during loading or unloading **2.** GATE IN WATERWAY a gate controlling the flow of water at the lower end of a lock in a waterway ■ *v* (**-gat·ed, -gat·ing, -gates**) **1.** *vti* DRIVE CLOSE BEHIND to drive very close behind another vehicle **2.** *vi* HAVE TAILGATE PARTY to have a tailgate party —**tail·gat·er** *n*

tail·gate par·ty *n* a social gathering before a sports event held in a parking lot outside the stadium. Spectators park close together and use their vehicles and the adjoining space for picnicking, barbecuing, and other activities.

tail grab *n* in snowboarding, a move in which the back of the board is maneuvered upward and grabbed with the hand

tail·ing /táyling/ *n* the end of something such as a beam that is built into a wall during construction ■ **tail·ings** *npl* the waste left after ore has been extracted from rock

tail lamp *n* AUTOMOT same as **taillight**

taille /tī, tayl/ *n* a tax levied by the French monarch on his subjects before the French Revolution [Mid-16C. < French, "tax," literally "a cut"]

Taille·ferre /tīə fér/, **Germaine** (1892–1983) French composer. She was a member of the Paris-based group of composers known as "Les Six" and later experimented with polytonality and unusual combinations of voices and instruments, including *Concerto des Vaines Paroles* (*Concerto of Empty Words*) (1958).

tail·light /táyl lìt/ *n* a red light, usually one of two, mounted at the rear of a vehicle

tai·lor /táylər/ *n* CLOTHES MAKER somebody who makes or repairs clothes ■ *v* (**-lored, -lor·ing, -lors**) **1.** *vti* MAKE CLOTHES to make clothes to meet a particular need or for a particular person **2.** *vt* ADAPT SOMETHING to adapt something to make it suitable for a particular purpose **3.** *vi* WORK AS TAILOR to work as a tailor making or repairing clothes [13C. Via Anglo-Norman *taillour*, Old French, *tailleur* "cutter" < *taillier* "to cut" < late Latin *taliare* < Latin *talea* "twig, cutting"]

tai·lor·bird /táylər bùrd/ *n* a bird of the warbler family that makes a nest by sewing leaves together with plant fibers. Native to: tropical Asia. Genus: *Orthotomus*.

tai·lored /táylərd/ *adj* **1.** MADE TO FIT NEATLY describes clothes marked by a neat fit with trim lines and a clean and formal or severe look **2.** MADE FOR PARTICULAR PURPOSE made or adapted for a particular purpose **3.** MADE BY TAILOR made individually by a tailor

tai·lor-made *adj* **1.** IDEAL FOR SOMEBODY OR SOMETHING perfectly suited to somebody or for a purpose **2.** MADE BY TAILOR made by a tailor rather than in a factory ■ *n* SOMETHING MADE BY TAILOR a garment made by a tailor

tai·lor's chalk *n* chalk used by tailors to mark out the positions of cuts or alterations on material

tail·piece /táyl peèss/ *n* **1.** END something that forms an end or is added at the end of something **2.** PRINTING DECORATION AT BOTTOM OF PAGE a decoration at the bottom of a page, e.g., at the end of a chapter **3.** MUSIC PART OF STRINGED INSTRUMENT a piece of wood or metal at the lower end of a stringed instrument such as a violin, to which the strings are attached **4.** BEAM EMBEDDED IN WALL a beam that has one end embedded in a wall

tail·pipe /táyl pìp/ *n* a pipe through which exhaust gases are expelled from an internal-combustion engine, e.g., in a motor vehicle or aircraft

tail·plane /táyl plàyn/ *n* the horizontal part of the tail of an aircraft, designed to give stability

tail·race /táyl ràyss/ *n* **1.** a channel that carries away water that has passed through a mill wheel or turbine **2.** a channel that carries away mine tailings in water

tail rotor *n* a small rotor on the tail of a helicopter that prevents the helicopter from spinning in the direction opposite to the rotation of the main rotor

tail·skid /táyl skìd/ *n* **1.** a support or runner on the underside of the tail of an aircraft **2.** a skidding of the rear wheels of a motor vehicle

tail·spin /táyl spìn/ *n* **1.** a state of great confusion or distress (*informal*) **2.** a rapid and uncontrolled spiral descent of an aircraft

tail·stock /táyl stòk/ *n* a movable part of a lathe that supports the free end of the workpiece and allows it to rotate freely

tail·wind /táyl wìnd/ *n* a wind that is blowing in the direction in which a ship or aircraft is traveling in. A tailwind adds to an aircraft's effective speed.

Tai·nan /tī naán/ city in southwestern Taiwan. It is Taiwan's oldest city and former capital. Population: 721,832 (1999).

Taine /ten/, **Hippolyte** (1828–93) French historian and philosopher. An exponent of positivism, he advocated the use of scientific methods in the analysis of literature, history, and human nature. Full name **Taine, Hippolyte Adolphe**

Tai·no /tīnō/ (*plural same* or **-nos**) *n* **1.** a member of an extinct Native Central American people who lived on the Caribbean islands of the Greater Antilles and the Bahamas **2.** the Arawak language of the Taino people [Mid-19C. < Taino] —**Tai·no** *adj*

taint /taynt/ *vt* (**taint·ed, taint·ing, taints**) **1.** POLLUTE SOMETHING to pollute or contaminate something with something undesirable or dangerous **2.** CORRUPT SOMEBODY MORALLY to corrupt somebody morally, or detract from somebody's reputation by associating him or her with something reprehensible **3.** FLAVOR SOMETHING to unintentionally give a scent or flavor of one thing to another **4.** SPOIL SOMETHING to make something such as fruit or vegetables rotten ○ *The peaches are tainted.* ■ *n* **1.** IMPERFECTION DETRACTING FROM QUALITY an imperfection that detracts from the quality of somebody or something ○ *a taint on her reputation* **2.** SOMETHING THAT POLLUTES something that detracts from the purity or cleanliness of something [Late 16C. Partly < Anglo-Norman *teint* "colored, dyed" < Latin *tingere* "moisten, dye," partly < Old French *ataint* "convicted," past participle of *ateindre* (see ATTAIN)] —**taint·less** *adj*

'tain't /taynt/ *contr* it ain't (*nonstandard*)

tai·pan[1] /tī pàn/ *n* a foreigner in charge of a business or trading operation in China or Hong Kong, especially a powerful business tycoon [Mid-19C. < Chinese (Cantonese) *daaihbāan*]

tai·pan[2] /tī pàn/ *n* a large rare and highly venomous snake, brown in color with a lighter brown belly, that can grow to 11 ft./3.3 m in length. Native to:

northern Australia. Latin name: *Oxyuranus scutellatus.* [Mid-20C. < Aboriginal]

Tai·pei /tī páy, -báy/, **T'ai·pei** government seat of Taiwan. The largest city on the island, it is regarded by the Taiwanese government as its temporary capital. Population: 2,646,474 (2000).

Tai·ping /tī píng/ *n* a supporter of or participant in a rebellion against the Manchu dynasty in China between 1850 and 1864 [Mid-19C. < Chinese *tài píng* "great peace"]

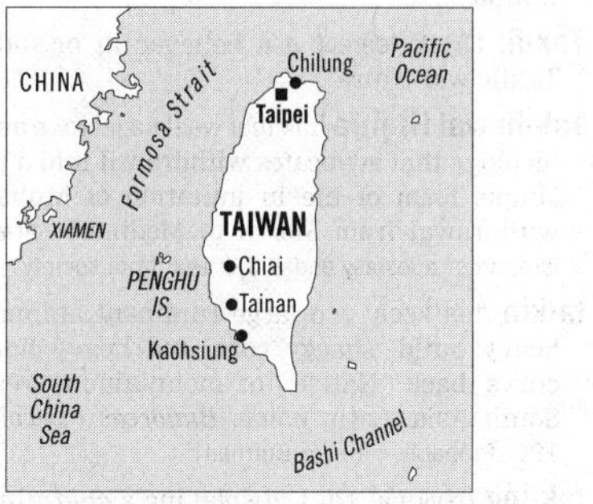

Taiwan

Tai·wan /tī wa̋an/ country occupying the island of Taiwan and neighboring small islands, administered separately since 1949 by a Chinese Nationalist government after its retreat from mainland China. It is claimed as a province by the People's Republic of China. Language: Chinese. Currency: New Taiwan dollar. Administrative capital: Taipei. Population: 22,603,000 (2003). Area: 13,900 sq. mi./36,000 sq. km. —**Tai·wan·ese** /tī waa née̋z/ *n, adj*

Tai·yu·an /tī ywa̋an, tī yoo a̋an/ capital city of Shanxi Province in northern China, southwest of Beijing. Population: 2,100,000 (1995).

taj /taaj/ *n* a tall brimless conical cap, often richly decorated, worn by Muslims as a mark of distinction [Late 19C. Via Arabic < Persian *tāj* "crown"]

ta·ji·ah /ta jée ə/ *n Carib* another spelling of **tadjah**

Ta·jik /taa jík/ (*plural* **-jiks** or *same*), **Ta·dzhik** (*plural* **-dzhiks** or *same*) *n* **1.** somebody who comes from Tajikistan **2.** the official Iranian language of Tajikistan. Native speakers: 4.5 million. [Early 19C. < Persian] —**Ta·jik** *adj*

Ta·jik·i /taa jíkee/, **Tad·zhik·i** *n* LANG same as **Tajik** (sense 2) ■ *adj* relating to the Tajik people or their language or culture

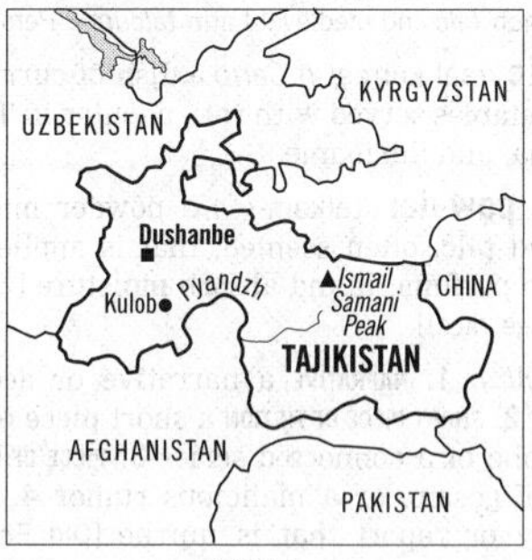

Tajikistan

Ta·jik·i·stan /taa jíki stàn, -staàn/, **Ta·dzhik·i·stan** country in southeastern Central Asia, bordered by Kyrgyzstan, Uzbekistan, China, and Afghanistan. It was part of the Soviet Union until 1991. Language: Tajik. Currency: Tajik ruble. Capital: Dushanbe. Population: 6,863,752 (2003). Area: 55,250 sq. mi./143,100 sq. km. Official name **Republic of Tajikistan**

Taj Ma·hal /taaj mə ha̋al/ *n* a white marble mausoleum in Agra, northern India, completed in 1643 in memory of Mumtaz Mahal, the wife of Mughal emperor Shah Jahan. It is considered the greatest example of Mughal architecture.

Ta·jo /tákhō/ ➧ **Tagus**

Taj Mahal

ta·ka /ta̋akə/ *n* the main unit of Bangladeshi currency. See table at **currency** [Late 20C. Via Bangla *ṭākā* < Sanskrit *ṭaṅkaḥ* "stamped coin"]

Ta·kak·kaw Falls /tákə kaw-/ falls, located in Yoho National Park, British Columbia. Once considered as Canada's highest waterfall, in the 1980s it was determined that the main drop was only 833 ft./254 m, making it shorter overall than Della Falls, also in British Columbia. Height: 1,223 ft./373 m.

take /tayk/ *v* (**took** /to͝ok/, **tak·en** /táykən/, **tak·ing, takes**) **1.** *vt* CARRY SOMETHING to carry or transport something or somebody from one place to another ○ *We'll need to take plenty of warm clothing.* **2.** *vt* REMOVE SOMETHING to remove or steal something belonging to somebody else ○ *I wish you wouldn't take things without asking.* **3.** *vt* WIN SOMETHING to capture or gain possession of a place, area, or object, or win something in a contest or competition ○ *took the town after a long siege* ○ *took first prize in the competition* **4.** *vt* GET A HOLD OF SOMEBODY to get a hold of something or somebody using a hand, or receive something into your hand ○ *She took him by the arm and steered him out of the room.* **5.** *vt* SELECT SOMETHING OR SOMEBODY to choose an individual object or person from a number available ○ *Here, take a chocolate.* **6.** *vt* GET INTO OR ONTO SOMETHING to place yourself in something, or start to occupy something ○ *Please take a seat.* **7.** *vt* CLAIM OR ASSUME SOMETHING to obtain something, especially credit, glory, or blame, or accept or maintain that this is deserved ○ *He doesn't mind taking the credit for the party's recent successes.* **8.** *vt* REGULARLY RECEIVE SOMETHING to buy, consume, or perform something as a regular habit ○ *We take the Sunday paper.* ○ *I've stopped taking lunch breaks.* **9.** *vt* LEAD SOMEBODY SOMEWHERE to enable somebody to go toward a particular place or in a particular direction, or go along something that leads to a particular place ○ *Will this road take us to the beach?* ○ *Take the first road on the left.* **10.** *vt* AGREE TO PERFORM SOMETHING to agree to perform or assume the duties associated with something ○ *I decided to take the job.* **11.** *vt* ACCEPT SOMETHING to accept something as valid, true, or satisfactory ○ *The machine refused to take my card.* **12.** *vt* BEAR SOMETHING to endure, deal with, accept, or put up with something, especially when it is unpleasant or unavoidable ○ *She cannot take criticism.* **13.** *vt* REACT TO SOMETHING to behave, feel, or act in response to being told or finding out about something ○ *I don't know how they will take the news.* **14.** *vt* HAVE STRENGTH TO HOLD SOMETHING UP to be capable of supporting something physically, without collapsing or breaking ○ *Will the shelf take the weight of all those books?* **15.** *vt* TRAVEL BY MEANS OF SOMETHING to use a particular means of transport to make a journey ○ *Let's take a taxi.* **16.** *vt* HAVE ROOM FOR SOMETHING to be capable of containing a particular amount or quantity of something ○ *The tank takes 20 gallons.* **17.** *vt* WRITE SOMETHING to record something in a written form ○ *Do you mind if I take notes?* **18.** *vt* PHOTOGRAPHY CAPTURE SOMETHING ON CAMERA to use a camera to make a photograph ○ *Let's take a few photos to record the event.* **19.** *vt* EDUC STUDY SOMETHING to study something on a formal basis ○ *I took physics in my senior year.* **20.** *vt* START TO DO SOMETHING to start to perform or occupy something ○ *The new treasurer takes office next month.* **21.** *vt* DO SOMETHING to carry something out ○ *I'll take action on this immediately.* **22.** *vt* TRAVEL OVER OR AROUND SOMETHING to travel over or around something, especially in a vehicle or on a motorcycle or horse and in a particular way ○ *He took the bend too fast.* **23.** *vt* DERIVE FROM SOMETHING OR SOMEBODY to copy or derive something from a particular text or author (*often passive*) ○ *That quote is taken from Shakespeare.* **24.** *vt* CONSIDER SOMETHING to use somebody or something as an example or as a subject for consideration or discussion ○ *Let's take your last point first.* **25.** *vt* REQUIRE PARTICULAR LENGTH OF TIME to need a particular amount of time to be completed or performed ○ *The trip usually takes about three hours.* **26.** *vt* NEED SOMETHING IN ORDER TO FUNCTION to need a particular thing in order to operate ○ *This cassette recorder takes four batteries.* **27.** *vt* REQUIRE SOMETHING FOR SUCCESS to require something, especially a particular quality or characteristic, for something to be achieved ○ *It took a lot of courage to admit that you were wrong.* **28.** *vt* EXPERIENCE EMOTION OR HAVE VIEW to experience a particular emotion, have a particular reaction, or adopt a particular opinion with regard to something ○ *They looked so pathetic that I took pity on them.* **29.** *vt* INTERPRET SOMETHING IN PARTICULAR WAY to interpret, recognize, or understand something, especially somebody's words or actions, in a particular way ○ *I took her silence as a rejection.* **30.** *vt* ASSUME SOMETHING to make an assumption, usually a mistaken one, about somebody's identity or about the nature of a thing or a situation ○ *I took you for her sister.* **31.** *vt* CONSUME SOMETHING to swallow or receive something into the body or system ○ *He refuses to take his medicine.* **32.** *vt* EXPOSE BODY TO ELEMENTS to go or sit out in the sun, or expose the body to other elements ○ *She was lying on the beach, taking the sun.* **33.** *vi* WORK OR BE SUCCESSFUL to work or have an effect in the intended way ○ *The flu shot didn't take.* **34.** *vi* BOT START TO GROW to start to grow by producing roots ○ *The plant has taken nicely.* **35.** *vt* MEASURE SOMETHING to measure something in an accurate way using a special instrument or procedure ○ *His temperature was normal when I took it this morning.* **36.** *vi* BECOME ILL to become noticeably or suddenly unwell or more unwell ○ *The whole family took sick.* **37.** *vt* MATH SUBTRACT NUMBER to subtract a number or quantity from something ○ *Take 19 from 36 and you get 17.* **38.** *vt* ASSUME CHARGE OF SOMETHING to assume control of something as somebody who holds authority or has the attention of others ○ *She took the chair at the meeting.* **39.** *vt* HAVE SEX WITH SOMEBODY to penetrate somebody in an act of sexual intercourse, especially perfunctorily or without the person's consent **40.** *vti* FISHING BITE to bite the hook or fly at the end of an angler's line or the bait containing the hook (*refers to fish*) ○ *The fish just weren't taking that morning.* **41.** *vt* CHEAT SOMEBODY to cheat or swindle somebody, especially out of a particular amount of money (*informal*) ■ *n* **1.** MOVIES CAMERA SHOT a single uninterrupted recording of a piece of the action in a film by a camera. There may be several takes of a particular shot, but only one is eventually used. ○ *This is the 15th take of this scene.* **2.** COMM MONEY OBTAINED IN BUSINESS TRANSACTIONS the amount of money received from customers or clients during a fixed period of time ○ *What was the take last week?* **3.** MUSIC SINGLE UNINTERRUPTED SOUND RECORDING a single uninterrupted session in which a work or section of a work is recorded by audio recording equipment **4.** FISHING GRABBING OF BAIT the action of a fish in picking up or grabbing a bait or lure **5.** IMPRESSION a personal impression or opinion of something (*informal*) ○ *What's your take on his presentation?* [Pre-12C. < Old Norse *taka*] —**tak·a·ble** *adj* —**tak·er** *n* ◇ **be taken with somebody** *or* **something** to find somebody or something pleasing or attractive ◇ **on the take** taking or willing to take bribes (*informal*) ◇ **take it 1.** to be able to tolerate a situation, usually one involving hardship, punishment, or criticism **2.** to assume that something is true ○ *I take it that you want some breakfast.* ◇ **take it or leave it 1.** used to indicate that somebody can either accept or refuse something, but cannot alter the conditions **2.** to have no strong feelings about an idea or activity one way or the other ○ *Jogging is okay, I can take it or leave it.*

take after *vt* **1.** to look or behave like somebody else, especially within the same family **2.** to begin to pursue somebody ○ *The dog took after the rabbit.*

take apart *vt* **1.** DISMANTLE SOMETHING to reduce something whole to its individual parts or pieces **2.** BEAT SOMEBODY SEVERELY to give somebody a severe beating or inflict a heavy defeat on somebody (*informal*) **3.** CRITICIZE SOMEBODY OR SOMETHING to criticize somebody or something in a severe and detailed way (*informal*)

take away *vt* **1.** to remove or take somebody or something elsewhere **2.** to subtract a number or quantity

take back *vt* **1.** WITHDRAW SOMETHING to withdraw something said or written **2.** REGAIN POSSESSION OF SOMETHING to gain possession of something previously held but lost or given up **3.** COMM RETURN SOMETHING BOUGHT AS UNACCEPTABLE to return unwanted or unsatisfactory goods to the place where they were bought for a refund or exchange **4.** COMM ACCEPT GOODS BACK to accept goods returned as unwanted or unsatisfactory and offer a refund or exchange **5.** REACCEPT SOMEBODY to accept somebody back into a relationship or home **6.** REMIND SOMEBODY OF PAST to remind somebody of an earlier time

take down *vt* **1.** LOWER SOMETHING IN POSITION to move something from a higher position to a lower one **2.** WRITE SOMETHING DOWN to make a note of something in writing ○ *take down the names and addresses of the witnesses* **3.** DISMANTLE SOMETHING to dismantle or demolish something **4.** HUMILIATE SOMEBODY to make somebody less arrogant or powerful ○ *That public criticism sure took him down a peg or two!* **5.** WRESTLING FORCE OPPONENT TO FALL to force an opponent to the mat during a wrestling match

take for *vt* to think of somebody or something as being of a particular description, often mistakenly ○ *Do you take me for a fool?*

take in *vt* **1.** UNDERSTAND SOMETHING to understand and remember something ○ *Children can't be expected to take in so much new information in one lesson.* **2.** ACCEPT SOMETHING AS REAL to accept something as real or true ○ *The news was such a shock that we still haven't taken it in.* **3.** INCLUDE SOMETHING to include something within the scope of something such as a list or plan ○ *The study takes in the whole postwar period.* **4.** DECEIVE SOMEBODY to deceive somebody by presenting a false appearance ○ *We were all taken in by her plausible manner.* **5.** ACCEPT SOMEBODY AS PAYING GUEST to accept people as paying guests into a home **6.** GIVE SOMEBODY SHELTER to give somebody shelter in your home **7.** GO TO SEE ENTERTAINMENT to go and see some kind of entertainment or sport ○ *take in a movie* **8.** WORK ON SOMETHING AT HOME to do paid work on something at home ○ *takes in ironing twice a week* **9.** HANDICRAFT MAKE GARMENT NARROWER to alter a garment to make it narrower **10.** *US* BRING SOMEBODY TO POLICE STATION to bring somebody as a prisoner or witness to a police station

take off *v* **1.** *vt* HAVE BREAK FROM WORK to spend a particular amount of time not working ○ *I took a day off for the wedding.* **2.** *vt* REMOVE GARMENT to remove something you are wearing **3.** *vt US* RELEASE SOMETHING to remove the restraining effect of something ○ *Take the brake off.* **4.** *vt* STOP SOMETHING OPERATING to end the operation of something ○ *took off regular boats to the island* **5.** *vt* MATH DEDUCT AMOUNT to deduct an amount from a price or sum **6.** *vi* AVIAT BEGIN FLYING to leave the ground and begin flying **7.** *vi* SPORTS JUMP to leave the ground at the beginning of a jump ○ *took off from the diving board* **8.** *vi* DEPART to leave, especially in a hurry or on short notice (*informal*) **9.** *vi* SUCCEED to begin suddenly to be very successful or popular (*informal*)

SYNONYMS See *imitate*.

take on *v* **1.** *vt* HIRE SOMEBODY to hire additional people to do work **2.** *vt* UNDERTAKE TASK to begin doing something, or accept responsibility for something ○ *I can't take on any more projects at the moment.* **3.** *vt* ADOPT SOMETHING to acquire or display a different character ○ *Her voice took on a kindlier tone.* **4.** *vt* OPPOSE SOMEBODY OR SOMETHING to oppose somebody or something in a competition or fight ○ *took on the city council* **5.** *vt* TRANSP TAKE SOMETHING ON BOARD to have people or things loaded on board a vessel or vehicle **6.** *vi* BE UPSET to show extreme feelings, especially grief (*dated informal*) **7.** *vti Carib* WORRY ABOUT SOMETHING to pay attention to or worry about somebody or something (*slang*)

take out *v* **1.** *vt* REMOVE SOMETHING to remove or extract something from another substance **2.** *vt* OBTAIN SOMETHING OFFICIALLY to obtain something such as a permit, mortgage, or insurance by applying for it **3.** *vt* BRING SOMETHING INTO OPEN to bring something into the open from a place where it was contained or concealed **4.** *vt* HAVE SOMEBODY AS COMPANION to take somebody as a companion or guest to a social event or function **5.** *vt* DIRECT ANGER AT SUBSTITUTE to express or relieve a strong feeling such as anger or frustration by directing it against somebody or something that is not the actual cause of it ○ *Don't take it out on me because you didn't get the job.* **6.** *vt* DESTROY SOMETHING to destroy, kill, or neutralize somebody or something (*slang*) ○ *took out enemy artillery* **7.** *vi US* BEGIN JOURNEY to start out on a journey ○ *took out for the frontier*

take over *vti* **1.** to obtain or assume control of something, or gain control of something from somebody else ○ *taken over by a larger company* **2.** to begin to do something or operate something in place of somebody else ○ *She takes over when I finish my shift.*

take to *vt* **1.** FORM LIKING FOR SOMEBODY to develop a liking for somebody or something, especially quickly **2.** START DOING OR USING SOMETHING to start doing or using something as a habit, especially for help or consolation ○ *I've taken to checking that all the windows are locked before I leave the house.* **3.** ADAPT YOURSELF to adapt yourself to something, or become comfortable with something new ○ *quickly took to the new procedure* **4.** GO TO PLACE to go to a place, especially for safety ○ *The slightest cough or sneeze would make him take to his bed.* ○ *took to their cars and fled*

take up *vt* **1.** LIFT SOMETHING OR SOMEBODY to lift or raise something or somebody **2.** BEGIN DOING SOMETHING REGULARLY to begin doing something regularly either as an occupation or a hobby **3.** BEGIN DOING SOMETHING AGAIN to begin doing something again after a break ○ *take up where you left off* **4.** USE SOMETHING WASTEFULLY to make use of or occupy something, especially in a wasteful or unwelcome way ○ *I don't want to take up too much of your time.* ○ *took up the whole of the back seat* **5.** ACCEPT OFFER to accept something offered ○ *took up his offer to stay for another year* **6.** ABSORB SOMETHING to absorb a liquid **7.** HANDICRAFT SHORTEN GARMENT to raise the hem of a garment such as a skirt to make the garment shorter **8.** *US* PAY OFF DEBT to pay off a debt such as a mortgage

take up on *vt* to accept somebody's offer or wager ○ *I'll take you up on that sometime.*

take up with *vt* **1.** to raise a matter for discussion with somebody **2.** to begin associating with a particular person or people

take·a·way[1] /táyk ə wày/, **take-a·way** *n* a football play in which the defensive team gains control of the ball from the offensive team by recovering a fumble or intercepting a pass

take·a·way[2] /táyk ə wày/ *UK adj* FOOD same as **takeout** ■ *n* same as **takeout**

take·down /táyk dòwn/ *n* **1.** *US* INSTANCE OF HUMILIATION an instance of making somebody less arrogant or powerful **2.** ARMS EASILY DISASSEMBLED FIREARM a firearm designed to be disassembled easily and quickly **3.** WRESTLING, MARTIAL ARTS WRESTLING MOVE FORCING OPPONENT TO GROUND a move in wrestling or martial arts that forces an opponent to the ground ■ *adj* EASILY DISASSEMBLED describes a weapon that can be disassembled quickly

take-home pay *n* the amount of pay left to an employee after all deductions such as those for tax have been made

tak·en past participle of **take**

take-no-pris·on·ers *adj* persistent in an assertive way

take·off /táyk àwf, -òf/ *n* **1.** AVIAT BEGINNING OF FLIGHT the process of leaving the ground and beginning to fly **2.** SPORTS BEGINNING OF JUMP the act or point of leaving the ground at the beginning of a jump **3.** POINT OF RAPID GROWTH a point at which substantial success or economic expansion is achieved and the prospect of further success or growth seems assured **4.** IMITATION an imitation of somebody or something, especially for comic effect (*informal*)

take·out /táyk òwt/ *adj* **1.** FOR EATING ELSEWHERE bought ready-made and taken away to be eaten elsewhere ○ *selling takeout food* **2.** SELLING TAKEOUT FOOD selling ready-made food for eating elsewhere ■ *n* **1.** FOOD PREPARED FOOD BOUGHT FOR EATING ELSEWHERE a meal bought ready-made for eating elsewhere **2.** PLACE SELLING FOOD FOR EATING ELSEWHERE a restaurant or store that sells ready-made food for eating elsewhere

take·o·ver /táyk òvər/ *n* **1.** an assumption of control of a corporation achieved by buying a majority of its shares ○ *The conglomerate's takeover of the small manufacturer stunned investors.* **2.** the seizure of control of a country or organization by using force

take-up *n* **1.** the degree to which something made available is accepted or used by people **2.** a part of a mechanism onto which something such as tape is wound

Tak·fir·i /tak féeree/ *n* a believer in or follower of Takfir wal Hijira

Tak·fir wal Hi·ji·ra /tak féer waal hə jéerə/ *n* an Islamic ideology that advocates withdrawal into a pure and simple form of life in imitation of Muhammad's withdrawal from Mecca to Medina [< Arabic "declaration of apostasy and withdrawal from society"]

ta·kin /taá keén/ *n* a large ruminant animal with a heavy build, shaggy coat, and heavy horns that curve back. Native to: mountainous regions of South Asia. Latin name: *Budorcas taxicolor*. [Mid-19C. Probably < Tibeto-Burman]

tak·ing /táyking/ *adj* **1.** displaying a charming or fascinating appeal **2.** infectious (*informal*)

tak·ings /táykingz/ *npl* money received through sales by a business (*informal*)

ta·ki·ta·ki /taákee taákee/ *n* LANG same as **Sranantongo** [Alteration of TALK] —**ta·ki·ta·ki** *adj*

Ta·ko·ma Park /tə kṓmə-/ city in central Maryland, a northeastern suburb of Washington, D.C. Population: 17,687 (2002 estimate).

ta·la /taálə/ (*plural same* or **-las**) *n* the main unit of Samoan currency. See table at **currency** [Mid-20C. < Polynesian]

tal·a·poin /tállə pòyn, -pwàn/ *n* **1.** a small olive-green guenon monkey. Native to: swampy forests in western equatorial Africa. Latin name: *Cercopithecus talapoin* or *Miopithecus talapoin*. **2.** in Myanmar and Thailand, a Buddhist monk [Late 16C. Via French and Portuguese < Mon *tala pói* "lord of merit"]

ta·lar·i·a /tə lérree ə/ *npl* in Greek mythology, winged sandals worn by characters especially by Hermes [Late 16C. < Latin, plural of *talaris* "of the ankles" < *talus* "ankle"]

talc /talk/ *n* **1.** same as **talcum powder 2.** a soft mineral consisting of hydrated magnesium silicate. Source: igneous and metamorphic rocks. Use: talcum powder. ■ *vt* (**talcked** or **talced, talck·ing** or **talc·ing, talcs**) to put talcum powder on something [Late 16C. Via French *talc* and medieval Latin *talcum* < Persian *ṭalk*]

tal·ca·rie /taál kùrree/ *n Carib* a dish of curried meat or vegetables served with roti, popular in Trinidad, Guyana, and Suriname

tal·cum pow·der /tálkəm-/ *n* a powder made from purified talc, often scented, that is applied to the skin to perfume it and absorb moisture [< medieval Latin (see TALC)]

tale /tayl/ *n* **1.** NARRATIVE a narrative or account of events **2.** SHORT PIECE OF FICTION a short piece of fiction, often one of a connected series **3.** PIECE OF GOSSIP an item of gossip, or a malicious rumor **4.** FALSEHOOD a story or report that is untrue [Old English *talu* < Germanic]

SPELLCHECK See *tail*.

CULTURAL NOTE ***The Canterbury Tales***, a collection of stories (1387–1400) by English writer Geoffrey Chaucer. The tales, mainly in verse, are told by a group of pilgrims traveling to the shrine of St. Thomas à Becket in Canterbury, England. They range from the bawdy "Miller's Tale" to reworks of traditional stories, e.g., the "Nun's Priest's Tale" about Chanticleer the cock. The Prologue sets the scene for the journey and contains colorful descriptions of the pilgrims themselves.

Tal·e·ban *npl* ISLAM another spelling of **Taliban**

tale·bear·er /táyl bérrər/ *n* somebody who informs against other people or spreads malicious rumors —**tale·bear·ing** *n*

tal·ent /tállənt/ *n* **1.** NATURAL ABILITY an unusual natural ability to do something well, especially in artistic areas that can be developed by training **2.** SOMEBODY WITH EXCEPTIONAL ABILITY a person or people with an exceptional ability **3.** *UK* POSSIBLE ROMANTIC PARTNERS people considered collectively as possible romantic or sexual partners (*slang*) **4.** MEASURE ANCIENT UNIT an ancient unit of weight and money [14C. Via Old French, "mental inclination" < Latin *talentum* "balance, sum of money" < Greek *talanton*] —**tal·ent·less** *adj*

SYNONYMS ***talent, gift, aptitude, flair, bent, knack, genius***
CORE MEANING: the natural ability to do something well
talent a natural ability to do something well that can be developed by training ○ *a persuasive speaker with a natural talent for diplomacy* ○ *Our company has a great wealth of underutilized talent.* **gift** a natural ability, especially an artistic ability, or a social skill ○ *Hannah had inherited a gift for music.* ○ *He had the rare gift of speaking only when something needed to be said.* **aptitude** a natural tendency to do something well, especially one that can be further developed ○ *He showed little aptitude for business.* ○ *Depending on the aptitude of the students, anything from two to ten topics may be appropriate.* **flair** a natural ability to do something well, especially creative or artistic ability ○ *a new writer-director of visual invention and cinematic flair* **bent** a strong natural inclination or liking for something ○ *The books feature two friends with a bent for detecting crime.* ○ *Technical schools were for students who had a practical bent.* **knack** a particular skill, especially one that might be innate or intuitive and therefore difficult to teach ○ *a knack with children* ○ *an obvious knack for sales* **genius** exceptional intellectual or creative ability ○ *Rachmaninoff's unequaled genius for lyrical melody* ○ *He was a man of considerable genius who is not given enough credit for his contribution to science.*

tal·ent con·test *n* ARTS same as **talent show**

tal·ent·ed /tálləntəd/ *adj* showing an exceptional natural ability to do something

tal·ent scout *n* somebody whose job is to search for people who have exceptional abilities in some field such as entertainment or sports and recruit them for professional work

tal·ent show *n* a public performance made up of acts by amateur entertainers who compete for a prize and are sometimes given professional opportunities

ta·ler *n* COINS another spelling of **thaler**

tales /taylz, táy leez/ (*plural* **ta·les** /táy leez/) *n* **1.** a writ used to summon people to court to fill vacancies on a jury **2.** a group of people summoned to court to fill vacancies on a jury (*takes a plural verb*) [15C. < Latin *tales de circumstantibus* "such of the bystanders," phrase in the writ]

tales·man /táylzmən, táy leezmən/ (*plural* **-men** /-mən/) *n* somebody selected from a group to fill a vacant seat in a jury

tale·tell·er /táyl tèllər/ *n* **1.** a teller of stories **2.** somebody who informs against other people or spreads malicious rumors —**tale·tell·ing** *n*

ta·li ANAT plural of **talus**[1]

Tal·i·ban /táali baan/, **Tal·e·ban** *npl* a strict Islamic group that ruled Afghanistan from 1996 until 2001 [Late 20C. Via Pashto < Persian, "students"]

tal·i·on /tállee ən/ *n* a punishment that has the same nature as the crime, e.g., the death penalty for murder [15C. Via Anglo-Norman < Latin *talion-*]

tal·i·pes /tállə peez/ *n* MED same as **clubfoot** (*technical*) [Mid-19C. < modern Latin < Latin *talus* "ankle" + *pes* "foot"]

tal·i·pot /tállə pòt/ *n* a tall palm tree with very large fan-shaped leaves and a massive inflorescence. Native to: Southeast Asia. Latin name: *Corypha umbraculifera.* [Late 17C. Via Malayalam < Sanskrit *tālīpatra* < *tālī* "fan palm" + *patra* "leaf"]

tal·is·man /tállissmən, tálliz-/ *n* **1.** an object believed to give magical powers to somebody who carries or wears it, e.g., a stone or jewel **2.** something believed to have magical properties [Mid-17C. Via French or Spanish < Greek *telesma* "something consecrated" < *telein* "complete, consecrate" < *telos* "result"] —**tal·is·man·ic** /tàlliss mánnik, tàlliz-/ *adj*

talk /tawk/ *v* (**talked, talk·ing, talks**) **1.** *vti* EXPRESS SOMETHING BY SPEAKING to speak, or express something using speech ○ *talk nonsense* **2.** *vi* HAVE CONVERSATION ABOUT SOMETHING to address spoken words to somebody, or have a conversation with somebody ○ *talked for an hour* **3.** *vt* DISCUSS SUBJECT to discuss a particular subject ○ *talk business* **4.** *vi* COMMUNICATE to communicate in a way other than by speaking ○ *talk in sign language* **5.** *vti* SPEAK PARTICULAR LANGUAGE to use, or be able to use, a particular language to communicate with people ○ *talks Italian* **6.** *vi* REVEAL INFORMATION to reveal information, especially when being pressured to do so ○ *They interrogated her for hours but she wouldn't talk.* **7.** *vi* GOSSIP to discuss the affairs of others, or spread rumors ○ *People are starting to talk.* **8.** *vi* MAKE SOUNDS LIKE SPEECH to imitate the sounds of speech ○ *The baby is beginning to talk.* **9.** *vi* LECTURE to give a speech or lecture on a subject **10.** *vi* BE FRIENDLY WITH SOMEBODY to be on sufficiently friendly terms with somebody to be able to have a conversation ○ *They're not talking right now.* **11.** *vi* BE PERSUASIVE to have the power to influence or persuade people (*informal*) ○ *Money talks!* **12.** *vt* USED TO CALL ATTENTION used to direct somebody's attention to a particular aspect of something under discussion (*informal*) ○ *We're talking several weeks' work here.* ■ *n* **1.** CONVERSATION a conversation or exchange of ideas or information between two or more people **2.** THINGS SAID the things said by somebody or by a group of people in conversation ○ *The talk after dinner was mostly about politics.* **3.** SPEECH MADE TO AUDIENCE a speech or lecture, given before an audience **4.** GOSSIP ABOUT OTHERS idle or malicious conversation about the affairs of others **5.** EMPTY SPEECH speech about something without any intention of taking action ○ *He's all talk.* **6.** THING TALKED ABOUT a subject of discussion or gossip among a group of people ○ *the talk of the town* **7.** WAY OF SPEAKING a particular way of speaking ○ *baby talk* ■ **talks** *npl* NEGOTIATIONS formal discussions among parties to bring about a resolution to a problem ■ *adj* BROADCAST BROADCASTING TALK involving mainly interviews, discussions, and telephone calls from viewers or listeners ○ *talk radio* [13C. Ultimately < Germanic] —**talk·er** *n* ◇ **talk about** used to emphasize a comment or statement (*informal*) ○ *Talk about a dream job!* ◇ **walk the talk** to act on what you profess to believe in or value

talk at *vt* to speak to somebody without showing any interest in listening to the person's reply

talk back *vi* to make an impudent reply

talk down *vt* **1.** PREVENT SOMEBODY FROM SPEAKING to prevent somebody from speaking by saying something loudly and ignoring attempts to interrupt **2.** PERSUADE SOMEBODY TO LOWER PRICE to persuade a seller to lower the price of something **3.** TELL SOMEBODY HOW TO LAND AIRCRAFT to give radio guidance to somebody on how to land an aircraft **4.** MAKE SOMETHING SEEM LESS IMPRESSIVE to discuss something in a way that makes it seem less important or successful than it is

talk down to *vt* to speak to somebody in a superior or condescending way

talk into *vt* to persuade somebody to do something by talking to him or her ○ *We talked her into staying for dinner.*

talk out *vt* **1.** to settle a difference of opinion through discussion **2.** *UK* to prevent the passage of a piece of legislation, especially a bill in parliament, by prolonging the discussion of it until it is too late to vote on it

talk out of *vt* **1.** to dissuade somebody from doing something by talking to him or her ○ *talked him out of buying a car* **2.** to use words to convince somebody to give you something

talk over *vt* **1.** to discuss something at length or thoroughly **2.** to persuade somebody to agree with an opinion or point of view ○ *talked them over to our side*

talk up *vt* to praise something in the hope of making it popular or successful

talk·a·thon /táwkə thòn/ *n* a long period of discussion

talk·a·tive /táwkətiv/ *adj* tending to talk readily and at length —**talk·a·tive·ness** *n*

SYNONYMS ***talkative, chatty, gossipy, garrulous, loquacious***
CORE MEANING: talking a lot
talkative tending to talk readily and at length ○ *The normally talkative champion refused to be drawn on his prospects for the tournament.* **chatty** talking freely about unimportant things in a friendly way ○ *My niece was her usual chatty self, talking about her hamster.* **gossipy** talking with relish about other people and their lives, often unkindly or maliciously ○ *articles ranging from the informative to the gossipy* ○ *a gossipy neighbor* **garrulous** excessively or pointlessly talkative ○ *a garrulous pest with a thousand stories to tell to anyone who would listen* **loquacious** tending to talk a great deal ○ *Never loquacious, she was for the moment totally lost for words.* ○ *Her loquacious elder brother was talking enthusiastically about the new venture.*

talk·back /táwk bàk/ *n* a system of communication in a broadcasting studio that enables the staff to speak to each other without the speech being broadcast

talk·board /táwk bàwrd/ *n* an online discussion group on a specific topic, sometimes involving experts who will answer questions

talk·ie /táwkee/ *n* an early movie with a soundtrack (*dated*) [Early 20C. Shortening of *talking picture*, after MOVIE]

talk·ing book /tàwking-/ *n* a book that has been recorded onto an audio cassette, originally intended for people who cannot see well enough to read

talk·ing head *n* somebody who talks at length into a camera in a television broadcast, usually shown only from the shoulders up, e.g., a newscaster (*informal*)

talk·ing point *n* **1.** INTERESTING ITEM FOR DISCUSSION a topic, or aspect of something, that provokes a lot of discussion **2.** SOMETHING SUPPORTING ARGUMENT something that supports an argument, e.g., a particularly convincing point **3.** PUBLICITY POINT a claim made about a product in publicity material that is considered particularly interesting or persuasive to potential customers

talk·ing-to *n* a scolding given to somebody, especially by somebody in authority (*informal*)

talk ra·di·o *n* a broadcast format involving interviews, discussions, and telephone call-ins

talk show *n* **1.** a television or radio program in which ordinary people discuss aspects of their lives or current social issues **2.** a television or radio program made up mainly of interviews with guests, especially famous people

talk·y /táwkee/ (**-i·er, -i·est**) *adj* **1.** containing too much dialogue and not enough action ○ *a talky and dull movie* **2.** tending to talk a great deal

tall /tawl/ *adj* **1.** VERY HIGH reaching or having grown to a considerable or above average height ○ *tall trees* **2.** OF PARTICULAR HEIGHT having reached a particular height ○ *five feet tall* **3.** LARGE substantial, demanding, or difficult to deal with ○ *a tall order* **4.** INCREDIBLE exaggerating the events of something beyond the bounds of probability, especially in a boastful way ○ *a tall story* ■ *adv* PROUDLY in a proud or courageous way ○ *There are times when you must stand tall and defend your beliefs.* [Old English *getæl* "quick, ready" < Germanic, "to count"] —**tall·ish** *adj* —**tall·ness** *n*

Tal·la·de·ga /tàllə deégə, -dáygə/ city in eastern Alabama, west of Talladega National Forest and east of Birmingham. Population: 15,026 (2002 estimate).

tal·lage /tállij/ *n* **1.** ROYAL TAX a tax levied by the Norman and Angevin kings of England on royal lands and towns **2.** TAX LEVIED BY LORD in feudal times, a tax levied by a lord on his vassals or tenants ■ *vt* (**-laged, -lag·ing, -lag·es**) LEVY TAX ON SOMEBODY OR SOMETHING to levy a tax, especially a tallage, on somebody or something [13C. < Old French *taillage* < *taillier* "to cut"]

Tal·la·has·see /tàllə hássee/ capital of Florida, situated in the northern part of the state. Population: 155,171 (2002 estimate).

tall·boy /táwl bòy/ *n* **1.** *UK* FURNITURE same as **highboy 2.** a tall can of beer that holds 16 oz/.48 liter (*informal*)

Tall·chief /táwl cheef/, **Maria** (*b.* 1925) US ballerina. She was the prima ballerina with the New York City Ballet (1948–65) and was inducted into the

National Women's Hall of Fame (1996). Born **Betty Marie Tallchief**

Tal·ley·rand /tállee rànd/, **Charles Maurice de** (1754–1838) French politician and diplomat. His long career spanned the French Revolution and the Napoleonic period. As foreign minister, he represented France at the Congress of Vienna (1814–15). Full name **Talleyrand-Périgord, Charles Maurice de**

"Mistrust first impulses; they are nearly always good."
[Attributed to Charles Maurice de Talleyrand]

Tal·linn /tállin, taálin/ capital of Estonia, on the Bay of Tallinn, an inlet of the Gulf of Finland, opposite Helsinki, Finland. Population: 408,329 (2000).

tal·lis *n* JUDAISM same as **tallith**

Tal·lis /tálləss/, **Thomas** (1510?–85) English composer. He was a major composer of religious choral works.

tal·lith /taálith, taa léet/ (*plural* **tal·lith·im** /taálə théem/ or **tal·liths**), **tal·lis** /taáliss/ (*plural* **tal·lis·im** /taálə séem/) *n* a four-cornered fringed prayer shawl of white material with a black, blue, or purple stripe, traditionally worn by Jewish men, especially at morning prayers [Early 17C. < Rabbinic Hebrew *ṭallīt* < biblical Hebrew *ṭillel* "to cover"]

tall oil *n* an oily liquid produced as a byproduct of a chemical process in the manufacture of wood pulp. Use: making soaps, emulsions. [Early 20C. Partial translation of German *Tallöl* < Swedish *tallolja* < *tall* "pine" + *olja* "oil"]

tal·low /tállō/ *n* **1. FATTY SUBSTANCE** a hard fatty substance extracted from the fat of sheep and cattle. Use: candles, soap. **2. SUBSTANCE MADE FROM VEGETABLE MATTER** a substance similar to tallow, made from vegetable matter ■ *vt* (**-lowed, -low·ing, -lows**) **COVER SOMETHING WITH TALLOW** to cover or grease something with tallow [13C. < Low German] —**tal·low·y** *adj*

tall ship *n* a sailing ship with at least two masts, usually square-rigged

tal·ly /tállee/ *v* (**-lied, -ly·ing, -lies**) **1.** *vti* **AGREE** to agree, correspond, or come to the same amount, or cause two or more things to do this **2.** *vt* **COUNT SOMETHING** to count or reckon items **3.** *vt* **REGISTER SOMETHING IN ACCOUNT** to register something in an account of items **4.** *vti* **KEEP SCORE** to keep a record of a score or account **5.** *vti* SPORTS, LEISURE **MAKE SCORE** to gain a point, run, goal, or other score in a contest **6.** *vt* **PUT LABEL OR TAG ON SOMETHING** to put an identifying label or tag on something ■ *n* (*plural* **-lies**) **1. RECORD OF ITEMS** a record or account of items such as things bought or points scored ○ *keep a tally* **2.** SPORTS, LEISURE **SINGLE SCORE** a single score in a contest, e.g., a run or a touchdown **3. IDENTIFYING LABEL OR MARK** something that identifies something, e.g., a label or mark **4. COUNTERPART** something that corresponds to or is the counterpart of something else **5. MARK REPRESENTING NUMBER** a mark or marks representing a number, especially a set of four short vertical lines crossed by a diagonal fifth line used for numbering things in fives [15C. Via Anglo-Norman < Latin *talea* "twig, cutting"] —**tal·li·er** *n*

ORIGIN The Latin word *talea* "twig, cutting," from which ***tally*** is derived, is also the source of English *detail, entail, retail,* and *tailor.*

tal·ly·ho /tállee hṓ/ *interj* **EXCLAMATION THAT FOX HAS BEEN SIGHTED** used by a participant in a fox hunt to let others know that a fox has been sighted ■ *n* (*plural* **-hos**) **1. FOX HUNTER'S CRY** a cry by a participant in a fox hunt to let others know that a fox has been sighted **2.** TRANSP same as **four-in-hand** (sense 1) ■ *vi* (**-hoed, -ho·ing, -hos**) **SHOUT "TALLYHO"** to give a shout of "tallyho" [Late 18C. Probably alteration of French *taïaut*]

Tal·mud /taál mòod, tálməd/ *n* the collection of ancient Jewish writings that forms the basis of Jewish religious law, consisting of the early scriptural interpretations (**Mishnah**) and the later commentaries on them (**Gemara**) [Mid-16C. < postbiblical Hebrew *talmūd* "instruction" < Hebrew *lāmad* "learn"] —**Tal·mu·dic** /taal móodik, tal-/ *adj* —**Tal·mu·di·cal** *adj* —**Tal·mud·ist** *n*

tal·on /tállən/ *n* **1. HOOKED CLAW** a hooked claw, especially of a bird of prey **2. SOMETHING LIKE CLAW** something that looks like a claw, e.g., a curled human finger **3. PART OF LOCK** the part of a lock that the key presses when turned and that causes the bolt to slide out **4.** ARCHIT same as **ogee** (sense 2) **5.** CARDS **UNDEALT CARDS** in some card games, e.g., solitaire, the remainder of the deck of cards after a deal [14C. Via French < assumed Vulgar Latin *talon-* "heel, spur" < Latin *talus* "ankle"] —**tal·oned** *adj*

ta·luk /taa lóok/ (*plural* **-lu·ka** /-lóokə/) *n S Asia* **1.** a subdivision of a district in South Asia **2.** a piece of hereditary land in South Asia [Late 18C. < Urdu, Persian *ta'alluḳ* "estate" < Arabic *ta'allaḳa* "be attached"]

ta·lus[1] /táyləss/ (*plural* **-li** /-lī/) *n* the bone in the ankle that connects with the lower leg bones to form the ankle joint [Late 16C. < Latin, "ankle"]

ta·lus[2] /táyləss/ (*plural* **-lus·es**) *n* **1. AREA OF RUBBLE** a sloping area of rock rubble **2. ROCK RUBBLE** rock rubble, e.g., at the base of a cliff **3.** MIL **BASE OF FORTIFICATION** the sloping base of a fortification [Mid-17C. Origin ?]

tal·weg *n* GEOG another spelling of **thalweg**

tam /tam/ *n* CLOTHING same as **tam-o'-shanter** (*informal*) [Late 19C. Shortening]

ta·ma·le /tə maálee/ *n* a Mexican dish made by mixing fried chopped meat with peppers and seasonings, rolling the mixture in cornmeal dough, wrapping it in corn husks, and then steaming it [Late 17C. Back-formation < American Spanish *tamales*, plural of *tamal* < Nahuatl *tamalli*]

ta·man·du·a /tə mándoo ə/, **ta·man·du** /-doo/ *n* a small tree-living toothless anteater with a long prehensile tail. Native to: Central and South America. Latin name: *Tamandua tetradactyla* or *Tamandua mexicana.* [Early 17C. Via Portuguese < Tupi *tamanduá* "ant hunter"]

tam·a·rack /támmə ràk/ *n* **1.** the dense wood of a North American larch **2.** a deciduous larch with bluish green needles and oval cones. Native to: North America. Latin name: *Larix laricina.* [Early 19C. < Canadian French *tamarac* < Algonquian]

tam·a·rau /tàmmə rów/ (*plural* **-raus**), **tam·a·rao** (*plural* **-raos**) *n* a small rare buffalo. Native to: swamps of Mindoro Island, Philippines. Latin name: *Bubalus mindorensis.* [Late 19C. < Tagalog]

ta·ma·ri /tə maáree/ *n* a rich Japanese soy sauce [Late 20C. < Japanese]

ta·ma·ril·lo /tàmmə ríllō/ (*plural* **-los**) *n US* **1.** a fruit that resembles a plum **2.** a tree or bush that is cultivated for its tamarillos. Native to: Peruvian Andes. Latin name: *Cyphomandra betacea.* ► Can term **tree tomato** [Mid-20C. Alteration of TOMATILLO]

tam·a·rin /támmərin/ *n* a small monkey that has a long tail and is highly vocal. Native to: South America. Genus: *Saguinus.* [Late 18C. Via French < Galibi]

tam·a·rind /támmərind/ *n* **1.** FOOD **FRUIT** a pod containing many seeds within an acid-tasting pulp. Use: preserves, drinks, medicines. **2.** INDUST **WOOD** a very hard reddish wood **3.** TREES **TROPICAL TREE** a tropical evergreen tree that produces tamarinds and yields tamarind wood. Flowers: yellow with red streaks. Latin name: *Tamarindus indica.* [Mid-16C. Via Old French < Arabic *tamr hindī* "Indian date"]

tam·a·risk /támmərisk/ *n* a tree or bush with leaves resembling scales. Flowers: white to pink, in terminal spikes. Native to: Europe, Asia, Africa. Genus: *Tamarix.* [14C. < late Latin *tamariscus*, variant of Latin *tamarix*]

Ta·ma·tave /taámaa taáv/ former name for **Toamasina**

Ta·mau·li·pas /taà mow léepəss/ state in northeastern Mexico. Capital: Ciudad Victoria. Population: 2,747,114 (2000). Area: 30,476 sq. mi./78,932 sq. km.

Ta·ma·yo /taa maá yṓ/, **Rufino** (1899–1991) Mexican artist. His abstract paintings are influenced by folk themes, pre-Columbian art, and European styles such as cubism and fauvism.

tam·bac *n* METALL same as **tombac**

tam·ba·la /taàm baálə/ (*plural same* or **-las**) *n* a subunit of Malawian currency. See table at **currency** [Late 20C. < Chewa, "rooster"]

Tam·bo /támbō/, **Oliver** (1917–93) South African political leader. He was leader of the African National Congress (1967–91) and a prominent opponent of apartheid in South Africa. He was in exile from 1960 to 1990.

"The need for us to take up arms will never transform us into prisoners of the idea of violence."
[Oliver Tambo, *Independent on Sunday (London)*; April 25, 1993]

tam·bo·ra /tam báwrə/ *n Hispanic* a Mexican variation on the waltzes that German farmers brought to central Mexico in the 19th century [< American Spanish, "double-headed drum" < Spanish *tambor* "drum"]

tam·bour /tám bòor/ *n* **1.** HANDICRAFT **EMBROIDERY FRAME** a round frame on which material is stretched while it is being embroidered **2.** HANDICRAFT **EMBROIDERY** embroidery done on a tambour **3.** FURNITURE **FLEXIBLE ROLLING TOP OF DESK** a flexible rolling top of a desk or sliding front of a cabinet, made of thin strips of wood attached to canvas **4.** MUSIC, MIL **DRUM** a drum, especially a snare drum **5.** ARCHIT **CIRCULAR WALL** a circular wall, especially one supporting a dome ■ *vti* (**-boured, -bour·ing, -bours**) HANDICRAFT **EMBROIDER DESIGN USING FRAME** to embroider something using a round frame [15C. Via French < Persian *tabīra* "drum"]

tam·bou·ra /tam bóorə/, **tan·pu·ra** /tan póorə/ *n* a stringed instrument resembling a lute without frets, used in South Asian and Balkan music to produce a harmonic drone [Late 16C. Via Arabic and Persian < Persian *dunbara* "lamb's tail"]

tam·bou·rin /támbərin/ *n* **1. DANCE** an 18th-century Provençal dance in a two-beat rhythm, usually accompanied by a drum **2. MUSIC** the music for a tambourin **3. DRUM** a small Provençal drum [Late 18C. < French, "small drum" < *tambour* (see TAMBOUR)]

tam·bou·rine /tàmbə réen/ *n* a shallow single-headed drum with jingling metallic disks in its frame, held in one hand and played by shaking it or striking it with the free hand [Late 16C. < French, "small drum" < *tambour* (see TAMBOUR)] —**tam·bou·rin·ist** *n*

tam·bu-bam·bu band /tàmboo bámboo-/ *n Carib* a small band of musicians using bamboo sticks as instruments and parading through the streets during carnival, especially in Trinidad

Tam·bur·laine ▸ **Tamerlane**

tame /taym/ *adj* (**tam·er, tam·est**) **1. NO LONGER WILD** changed from a wild or uncultivated state to one suitable for domestic use or life **2. FRIENDLY TOWARD PEOPLE** describes an animal or bird unafraid of human contact **3. DOCILE** habitually inclined to submit to the wishes of others **4. BLAND** lacking in the qualities that make something interesting, e.g., imagination, adventurousness, or inspiration ○ *a tame rendition of the anthem* **5. SLOW-MOVING** describes a river or part of a river with very little current ■ *vt* (**tamed, tam·ing, tames**) **1. DOMESTICATE SOMETHING** to make a wild animal or uncultivated land suitable for domestic life or use **2. SUBDUE SOMEBODY** to remove the wildness, spirit, or energy from somebody or something **3. MODERATE SOMETHING** to make something much less harsh or extreme **4. BRING SOMETHING UNDER HUMAN CONTROL** to bring a natural force under human control ○ *a series of dams to tame the raging river* [Old English *tam* < Indo-European, "constrain"] —**tam·a·ble** *adj* —**tame·ly** *adv* —**tame·ness** *n* —**tam·er** *n*

Tam·er·lane /támmər làyn/, **Tam·bur·laine** /támbər-/ (1336–1405) Turkic ruler and conqueror. His conquests established an empire that extended from India to the Mediterranean Sea. He died while trying to invade China, and was buried in his capital, Samarkand. Born **Timur**

"It is better to be at the right place with 10 men than absent with 10,000."
[Attributed to Tamerlane]

Tam·il /támm'l/ (*plural* **-ils** or *same*) *n* **1.** a member of a Dravidian people who live in southern India and northern Sri Lanka **2.** the Dravidian language of the Tamil people. Native speakers: 50 million. [Mid-18C. < Tamil *Tamil*] —**Tam·il** *adj*

LANGUAGE HERITAGE See ***Dravidian.***

Tam·il Na·du /tàmmil naa dóo/ state in southern India. Capital: Chennai. Population: 62,110,839 (2001). Area: 50,216 sq. mi./130,058 sq. km.

tam·is /támmee/ (*plural* **-is** /támmis/) *n* COOK same as **tammy**[2] [Early 17C. Via French < medieval Latin *tamisium* < Germanic]

Tam·ma·ny Hall /támmanee-/ *n* a political organization formed as a fraternal society in New York in 1789 but mainly known for political corruption in the early 20th century [Mid-19C. After *Tamanend* (1653?–1750), Delaware leader said to have welcomed William Penn (1682)]

Tam·muz /taá mo͞oz, taa mo͞oz/ *n* in the Jewish calendar, the fourth month of the religious year, lasting 29 days and falling about the same time as June to July. See table at **calendar** [Mid-16C. Via Hebrew *Tammūz* < Babylonian *Du'uzu*, a deity]

tam·my[1] /támmee/ (*plural* **-mies**) *n* CLOTHING same as **tam-o'-shanter** (*informal*) [Late 19C. < TAM]

tam·my[2] /támmee/ *n* (*plural* **-mies**) *also* **tam·my cloth** a fine strainer made of woolen cloth ■ *vt* (**-mied, -my·ing, -mies**) to strain something such as a sauce using a tammy [Mid-18C. Probably < French *tamis*]

tam-o'-shan·ter /támmə shántər/ *n* a brimless Scottish wool hat, usually with a bobble at the center of the crown [Mid-19C. < *Tam O' Shanter*, eponymous hero of a poem by Robert BURNS]

ta·mox·i·fen /tə móksə fen/ *n* a drug that inhibits the actions of estrogen. Use: treatment of breast cancer, some types of infertility. Formula: $C_{26}H_{29}NO$. [Late 20C. Shortening of *metamoxifen* < META- + AMINE + OXY- + PHENYL]

tamp /tamp/ *vt* (**tamped, tamp·ing, tamps**) **1. PACK SOMETHING DOWN** to pack or push something down, especially by tapping it repeatedly **2. FILL DRILL HOLE WITH SUBSTANCE** to pack a substance such as sand or dirt into a drill hole above an explosive ■ *n* **TAMPING DEVICE** a device for pushing tobacco down into the bowl of a pipe [Early 19C. Origin ?]

Tam·pa /támpə/ seaport in west central Florida, on Tampa Bay, an arm of the Gulf of Mexico. Population: 315,140 (2002 estimate).

tam·per[1] /támpər/ (**-pered, -per·ing, -pers**) *vi* **1.** to interfere with something in a way that damages it or has harmful results **2.** to try to corrupt or influence somebody or affect the outcome of something ○ *tampering with the jury* [Mid-16C. Probably variant of TEMPER] —**tam·per·er** *n*

tam·per[2] /támpər/ *n* **1.** ARMS the casing around the core of a nuclear weapon that reflects neutrons back into the core, slowing the expansion of the nuclear reaction and increasing the weapon's power **2.** somebody or something that packs something down with repeated blows **3.** *UK* same as **tamp** [Mid-19C. < TAMP]

Tam·pe·re /támpərə, -pe ray/ city in southwestern Finland, situated about 105 mi./169 km northwest of Helsinki. Population: 193,174 (2000).

tam·per·proof /támpər pro͞of/ *adj* designed to be difficult to tamper with

Tam·pi·co /tam péekō/ seaport in eastern Mexico, situated on the Pánuco River close to the Gulf of Mexico. Population: 295,442 (2000).

tam·pi·on /támpee ən/, **tom·pi·on** /tómpee-/ *n* a plug or cover for the muzzle of a gun to keep out moisture and dust when it is not in use [15C. < French *tampon* (see TAMPON)]

tam·pon /tám pòn/ *n* **1. PLUG OF MATERIAL USED DURING MENSTRUATION** a cylindrical plug of soft material inserted in the vagina during menstruation to absorb blood **2. PAD TO CONTROL BLEEDING** a pad of cotton or other absorbent fabric that is used for plugging wounds or for controlling blood flow in body cavities, especially during surgery ■ *vt* (**-poned, -pon·ing, -pons**) **CONTROL BLOOD FLOW** to use a tampon to plug a wound or to control blood flow in a body cavity, especially during surgery [Mid-19C. < French, "plug, bung," variant of *tapon* "piece of cloth to stop a hole" < assumed Frankish *tappo* "stopper"]

tam·pon·ade /tàmpə náyd/ *n* the insertion of a tampon during surgery to check bleeding

tam-tam /túm tùm, tám tàm/ *n* **1.** a large gong **2.** MUSIC another spelling of **tom-tom** [Mid-19C. Origin ?]

tan[1] /tan/ *n* **1. SUNTAN** the brownish color that the skin takes on after being exposed to ultraviolet light, especially from the Sun or a sunlamp **2. LIGHT BROWN COLOR** a light brown orange-tinged color **3.** MANUF same as **tanbark** (sense 1) **4.** CHEM same as **tannin** ■ *v* (**tanned, tan·ning, tans**) **1.** *vti* **GET OR GIVE SOMEBODY SUNTAN** to give somebody's skin a brownish color, or take on such a color **2.** *vt* **CONVERT HIDE TO LEATHER** to convert an animal skin or hide into leather by treating it with something such as tannin **3.** *vt* **BEAT SOMEBODY** to give a beating to somebody (*informal*) ■ *adj* (**tan·ner, tan·nest**) **1. OF LIGHT BROWN COLOR** of a light brown orange-tinged color **2. SUN-BRONZED** bronzed by the sun or some other source of ultraviolet light **3.** MANUF **OF PROCESS OF TANNING HIDES** relating to or used in the process of tanning animal skins and hides [Pre-12C. < medieval Latin *tannare* "tan, dye a tawny color" < *tannum* "tanbark"] —**tan·na·ble** *adj* —**tan·nish** *adj*

tan[2] /tan/ *abbr* MATH tangent

Tan /tann/, **Amy** (*b.* 1952) US writer. She came to prominence with her first novel, *The Joy Luck Club* (1989), which deals with the relationships between Chinese-born women and their US-born daughters.

tan·a /taánə/ *n* **1.** a small lemur with a gray-brown back, whitish underparts, and a dark stripe that runs along the back and encircles each eye. Native to: Madagascar. Latin name: *Phaner furcifer*. **2.** a mainly ground-dwelling tree shrew with a brownish coat that has a black stripe along the back. Native to: Borneo, Sumatra. Genus: *Lyongale*. [Early 19C. Via modern Latin < Malay *tūpai tāna* "ground squirrel"]

Ta·na, Lake /taánə/ largest lake in Ethiopia, in the north central Ethiopian highlands. Area: 832 sq. mi./2,156 sq. km.

Ta·na·ba·ta /taá naa baá taa/ *n* in Japan, an annual festival during which people write down their wishes and hang them with other decorations on branches of bamboo. Date: July 7. [Early 20C. < Japanese]

Tan·ach /taa naákh/, **Tan·akh** *n* the sacred book of Judaism consisting of the Torah, Prophets, and Hagiographa [Mid-20C. < Hebrew *tĕnak*, acronym < *tōrāh* "law" + *nĕbī'īm* "prophets" + *kĕtūbīm* "Hagiographa"]

tan·a·ger /tánnəjər/ *n* a songbird that is usually fairly small and brightly colored in bold patterns and has a conical beak. Native to: North and South America, Caribbean. Family: Thraupidae. [Early 17C. < modern Latin *Tanagra* < Tupi *tangará*]

Tan·akh *n* JUDAISM another spelling of **Tanach**

Ta·na·mi Des·ert /tə naámi-/ desert in central Australia that extends eastward from Tennant Creek in the Northern Territory into Western Australia. Area: 71,200 sq. mi./184,500 sq. km.

Ta·nan·a·rive /taa naánə reév/ former name for **Antananarivo**

tan·bark /tán baárk/ *n* **1. TREE BARK USED AS TANNIN** the bark of some trees, especially oak and hemlock, used as a source of tannin **2. BARK FOR GROUND COVERAGE** tree bark with the tannin removed, used as a ground covering, especially in circus arenas, racetracks, and other places where animals are kept **3. CIRCUS RING** the part of a circus arena that is covered with tanbark **4.** TREES same as **tan oak**

Tan·cred /tángkrid/ (1078–1112) Norman soldier and regent of Antioch (1104–12). He distinguished himself as a military leader at the battles of Nicaea and Dorylaeum (1097) in the First Crusade. He also took part in the capture of Jerusalem (1099).

tan·dem /tándəm/ *n* **1.** *Can, UK* CYCLING same as **tandem bicycle 2. HORSE-DRAWN CARRIAGE** a two-wheeled carriage drawn by two horses harnessed one behind the other **3. HORSE TEAM HARNESSED IN SINGLE FILE** a team of two horses harnessed one behind the other **4. ARRANGEMENT IN SINGLE FILE** a setup in which two things are arranged one behind the other **5. VEHICLE WITH AXLES CLOSE TOGETHER** a vehicle with two axles close together ■ *adv* **ONE BEHIND ANOTHER** with one behind the other ○ *We'll ride tandem.* ■ *adj* **OF TWO TOGETHER** describes sports activities undertaken by two people together, usually positioned one behind the other, especially when one person is a novice ○ *tandem parachute jumping* [Late 18C. < Latin, "at length" (< *tam* "so" + demonstrative suffix *-dem*), humorously interpreted as "in a straight line"] ◇ **in tandem 1.** in partnership or cooperation **2.** with one behind the other

tan·dem bi·cy·cle *n US* a bicycle that has two seats and two sets of handlebars and pedals, one behind the other, so that it can be ridden by two people at the same time. Can term **tandem**

tan·door /tan do͝or/ *n* a clay oven used especially in the cuisine of northern South Asia for cooking food quickly at high temperature [Mid-19C. Via Urdu *tandūr*, Persian *tanūr* < Arabic *tannūr* "oven, furnace"]

tan·door·i /tan do͝oree/ *adj* baked or cooked in a tandoor, usually after being marinated in a mixture of yogurt and spices ■ *n* (*plural* **-is**) a dish or meal of tandoori food (*informal*) [Mid-20C. < Persian and Urdu < Urdu *tandūr*, Persian *tanūr* (see TANDOOR)]

Tan·dy /tándee/, **Jessica** (1909–94) British-born US actor. She acted in the first production of *A Streetcar Named Desire* (1947) and won an Academy Award for *Driving Miss Daisy* (1989).

Ta·ney /táwnee/, **Roger** (1777–1864) chief justice of the US Supreme Court (1836–64). He is best known for his controversial decision in the Dred Scott case (1857), which asserted the legitimacy of slavery. Full name **Taney, Roger Brooke**

tang[1] /tang/ *n* **1. STRONG TASTE** a distinctively sharp strong taste **2. PUNGENT SMELL** a smell that has a sharp biting quality **3. SUGGESTION** a slight hint or flavor of a particular thing ○ *a cake with a tang of lemon* **4. SHARP END GOING INTO HANDLE** the sharp part at one end of a chisel, knife blade, or other similar tool that secures it to the handle or shaft ■ *vt* (**tanged, tang·ing, tangs**) **1. SUPPLY SOMETHING WITH TANG** to put a tang on something such as a knife or chisel **2. GIVE TANG TO SOMETHING** to mark something with a sharp distinctive smell or taste ○ *mountain breezes tanged with the scent of pine* [14C. < N Germanic] —**tang·y** *adj*

tang[2] /tang/ *n* a loud, often harsh, ringing noise [Early 17C. An imitation of the sound] —**tang** *vti*

Tang /taang/, **T'ang** *n* a wealthy Chinese dynasty that lasted from A.D. 618 to A.D. 907 and was renowned for its encouragement and patronage of the arts, especially poetry and ceramics, and the development of printing [Mid-17C. < Chinese *táng*] —**Tang** *adj*

tan·ga /tang gaá/ *n* an undergarment or the lower part of a bikini made of two small triangles of fabric fastened with ties [Early 20C. Via Portuguese, "triangular loincloth" < Bantu]

Tan·ga /táng gə, taáng-/ city in northeastern Tanzania, on the Indian Ocean. Population: 187,634 (1988).

~~**tangable**~~ incorrect spelling of **tangible**

Tan·gan·yi·ka /tàng gən yeékə/ former country in East Africa, constituting the mainland part of what is now Tanzania —**Tan·gan·yi·kan** *n, adj*

Tan·gan·yi·ka, Lake /taáng gən yeékə/ lake in east central Africa, with shorelines in Burundi, Tanzania, Zambia, and the Democratic Republic of the Congo. Area: 12,700 sq. mi./32,900 sq. km. Length: 420 mi./680 km.

Tan·ge Ken·zo /taáng gay kénzō/ (*b.* 1913) Japanese architect. He is often considered Japan's greatest modern architect. His works include the Peace Center at Hiroshima (1949).

tan·ge·lo /tánjə lō/ (*plural* **-los**) *n* **1.** a citrus fruit with smooth easily peeled skin and sharp-tasting orange flesh **2.** a hybrid between a tangerine tree and a grapefruit tree that produces tangelos [Early 20C. Blend of TANGERINE + POMELO]

tan·gent /tánjənt/ *n* **1. LINE OR SURFACE THAT TOUCHES ANOTHER** a line, curve, or surface that touches another curve or surface but does not cross or intersect it **2. TRIGONOMETRIC FUNCTION** for a given angle in a right-angled triangle, a trigonometric function equal to the length of the side opposite the angle divided by the length of the adjacent side. See illustration on next page **3. PART OF SURVEY LINE** the part of a survey line that is straight **4. DIGRESSION** a change of topic that is not relevant to the subject currently under consideration **5.** MUSIC **PART OF CLAVICHORD** a part of the clavichord that resembles a small hammer and strikes the strings ■ *adj* **1.** MATH same as **tangential**

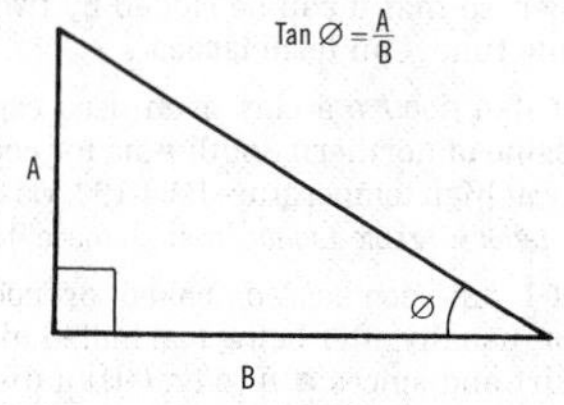

tangent (sense 2)

(sense 2) **2. TOUCHING AT ONE POINT** touching only at a single point **3. TOUCHING BUT NOT CROSSING** in contact, but not crossing or intersecting **4. AWAY FROM POINT** not relevant to the subject currently under consideration [Late 16C. < Latin *tangent-*, present participle of *tangere* "touch"] —**tan·gen·cy** *n* ◇ **go off at** *or* **on a tangent** to change quickly and suddenly to a different subject or line of thought

---

ORIGIN The Latin word *tangere* "to touch," from which ***tangent*** is derived, is also the source of English *attain, contact, intact, tact, tangible,* and *tax,* and possibly also of *taste.*

---

tan·gent gal·va·nom·e·ter *n* a device with a compass needle suspended horizontally in a vertical coil through which a direct current is passed, causing deflection of the needle proportional to the size of the current. It can be used to calculate the strength of the Earth's magnetic field.

tan·gen·tial /tan jénshəl/ *adj* **1.** with only slight relevance to the current subject **2.** relating to or involving a tangent —**tan·gen·tial·ly** *adv*

tan·ger·ine /tánjə reén, tánjə reén/ *n* **1. CITRUS FRUIT** a citrus fruit with easily peeled orange skin and sweet flesh **2. CITRUS TREE** a citrus tree, widely cultivated in tropical and warm regions, that produces tangerines. Native to: Southeast Asia. Latin name: *Citrus reticulata.* **3. BRIGHT ORANGE COLOR** a bright orange color like that of a tangerine [Mid-19C. < *Tangerine* "of or from Tangier," probably after Spanish *Tangerino*] —**tan·ger·ine** *adj*

tan·gi·ble /tánjəb'l/ *adj* **1. ABLE TO BE TOUCHED** able to be touched or perceived through the sense of touch ○ *a tangible coldness* **2. ACTUAL** capable of being understood and evaluated, and therefore regarded as real ○ *There is no tangible evidence to support this claim.* **3. ABLE TO BE REALIZED** capable of being given a physical existence ○ *tangible financial benefits* ■ *n* **SOMETHING TANGIBLE** something that has a physical form, especially a financial asset (*often used in the plural*) [Late 16C. Directly or via French < late Latin *tangibilis* "that may be touched" < Latin *tangere* "to touch"] —**tan·gi·bil·i·ty** /tánjə bíllətee/ *n* —**tan·gi·bly** *adv*

Tan·gier /tan jeér/ port city in northern Morocco. Population: 526,215 (1994).

tan·gle[1] /táng g'l/ *v* (**-gled, -gling, -gles**) **1.** *vti* **BECOME TWISTED** to become twisted together into a jumbled mass, or make something become twisted into a jumbled mass **2.** *vt* **CATCH AND HOLD SOMETHING** to catch and entwine somebody or something in something that is difficult to get out of, e.g., a net or trap ○ *I got my jacket tangled in the branches.* **3.** *vt* **TRAP SOMEBODY IN DIFFICULT SITUATION** to trap somebody in a complicated, awkward, or dangerous situation ○ *tangled in a web of controversy* **4.** *vi* **COME INTO CONFLICT** to become involved in a confrontation or disagreement with somebody, especially somebody powerful or important (*informal*) ○ *Don't tangle with those people.* ■ *n* **1. JUMBLED MASS** a mass of fibers, lines, or other things twisted together **2. DIFFICULTY** a complicated and confused situation or problem **3. STATE OF MENTAL UPSET** a state of mental or emotional confusion or upset **4. ARGUMENT** a confrontation or disagreement with somebody (*informal*) [14C. Origin ?] —**tan·gle·ment** *n* —**tan·gler** *n* —**tan·gly** *adj*

tan·gle[2] /táng g'l/, **tan·gle weed** *n* a large brown seaweed that grows on shores at or below the level of low tide [Mid-16C. Probably via Norwegian *tångel* < Old Norse *þongull* < *þang* "bladder wrack"]

Popperfoto
tango

tan·go /táng gō/ *Hispanic n* (*plural* **tan·gos**) **1. DANCE OF LATIN AMERICAN ORIGIN** a stylized Latin American ballroom dance in 2/4 time in which the steps are marked by glides and sudden pauses **2. MUSIC** the music for a tango ■ *vi* (**tan·goed, tan·go·ing, tan·gos**) **DANCE TANGO** to dance a tango [Late 19C. < Argentine Spanish] —**tan·go·ist** *n*

Tan·go *n* a code word for the letter "T," used in international radio communications

tan·gram /tán gràm/ *n* a puzzle of Chinese origin that involves putting together seven pieces, usually a square, a parallelogram, and five triangles, to form different shapes [Mid-19C. Origin ?]

Tang·shan /taáng shaán/ city in Hebei Province, northern China, southeast of Beijing. Population: 1,540,000 (1995).

Tan·guy /taang geé, taN-/, **Yves** (1900–55) French-born US artist. He is known for his surrealist paintings of organic forms in dream landscapes.

Tang Yin /taáng yín/ (1470–1523) Chinese painter and poet. One of the most important Ming dynasty artists, he is known for his paintings of landscapes and elegant women.

Ta·ni /taánee/, **Buncho** (1763–1840) Japanese artist. A noted book illustrator, he was responsible for introducing Western style to Japanese painting.

tan·i·er *n Carib* PLANTS another spelling of **tannia**

Tan·i·za·ki Jun·i·chi·ro /taáni zaákee jóoni cheérō/ (1886–1965) Japanese writer. His novels present the conflict between modern Western-influenced realities and traditional values.

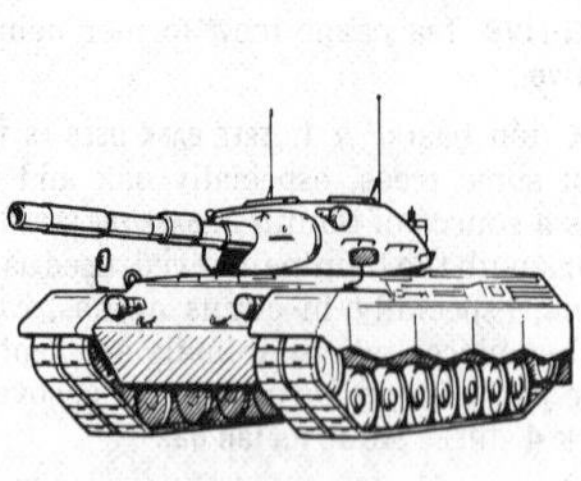
tank (sense 6)

tank /tangk/ *n* **1. LARGE CONTAINER** a large container for storing liquids or gases **2. AMOUNT HELD BY TANK** the amount of liquid or gas that a tank holds ○ *bought a tank of gas* **3. CONTAINER FOR FISH** a sturdy container with rectangular glass sides, used for keeping live fish or reptiles in **4. POND OR RESERVOIR** a fairly small body of water, especially one used for water storage **5. JAIL** prison, or a prison cell (*informal*) **6. MIL ARMORED VEHICLE** a large armored combat vehicle with treads, a rotating turret, and a heavy gun **7.** CLOTHING same as **tank top** **8.** PHOTOGRAPHY **CONTAINER FOR DEVELOPING FILM** a lightproof container for developing film, designed so that processing chemicals can be poured in and out without light entering **9.** PHOTOGRAPHY **TRAY FOR PROCESSING SHEETS OF FILM** a large tray or container for processing a number of sheets of film together ■ *v* (**tanked, tank·ing, tanks**) **1.** *vt* **PUT SOMETHING IN TANK** to put or keep something in a tank **2.** *vti* **STOP TRYING TO WIN COMPETITION** to make no effort to win, especially in a sports competition (*informal*) ○ *He tanked in the second set.* **3.** *vti US* **FAIL** to suffer a serious defeat or failure (*slang*) ○ *The movie tanked at the box office.* **4.** *vi* **DROP SHARPLY IN PRICE** to drop sharply in price to the point of bottoming out (*slang*) ○ *Tech stocks tanked.* [Early 17C. < Gujarati *tākū*, Marathi *ṭākē* "pond, cistern"] —**tank·ful** *n*

tank up *v* **1.** *vti* to fill the fuel tank of a motor vehicle (*informal*) **2.** *vi* to drink enough alcohol to become drunk (*slang*)

tan·ka[1] /taáng kaá/ (*plural* **-kas** or *same*) *n* **1.** a five-line Japanese verse form in which the first and third lines have five syllables each and the other lines have seven syllables each **2.** a poem with a tanka verse structure [Late 19C. < Japanese < *tan* "short" + *ka* "song"]

tan·ka[2] /tángkə/ *n* a Tibetan Buddhist painting in a form that can be rolled up, displayed, or carried as a banner [Early 20C. < Tibetan *t'áṅka* "image, painting"]

tank·age /tángkij/ *n* **1. TANK CAPACITY** the amount that can be held by a tank or tanks **2. STORAGE IN TANK** the storage of something in a tank, or the cost of this **3.** AGRIC **FERTILIZER** a byproduct of the slaughter of livestock consisting of carcass trimmings cooked to reduce moisture and drained of surplus fat. Use: feed supplement, fertilizer.

tank·ard /tángkərd/ *n* **1.** a large mug with a handle and sometimes a hinged lid, made of glass, pewter, or silver plate, typically used for drinking beer **2.** the amount of liquid that a tankard holds [14C. Origin ?]

tank car *n* a railroad car that has a large tank for transporting liquids, semiliquids, or gases in bulk

tank de·stroy·er *n* an armored military vehicle or aircraft mounted with antitank guns and designed to destroy tanks

tanked /tangkt/, **tanked-up** *adj* extremely drunk (*slang*)

tank en·gine, tank lo·co·mo·tive *n* a steam engine that carries its water supply in tanks at the sides of the boiler instead of carrying it in a tender

tank·er /tángkər/ *n* a ship, truck, or airplane designed to carry large quantities of liquid or gas

tank farm *n* a site with several large storage tanks, especially ones containing oil

tank farm·ing *n* AGRIC same as **hydroponics**

tan·ki·ni /tang keénee/ *n* a woman's swimsuit with a bikini bottom and a brief tank top [Late 20C. Blend of TANK TOP + BIKINI]

tank lo·co·mo·tive *n* RAIL same as **tank engine**

tank suit *n* a one-piece swimsuit with a scoop neck and wide shoulder straps [< *swimming tank*]

tank top *n* a sleeveless garment with a scoop- or V-neck [Probably because it resembles a garment worn by the crews of armored tanks]

tank town *n* a small town [Because trains stopped at such towns only to take on water]

tank trap *n* something designed to stop or slow the movement of military tanks, e.g., a concrete block

tank wag·on *n UK* same as **tank car**

tan·nage /tánnij/ *n* **1.** the tanning of animal hides or skins **2.** an animal skin or hide that has been tanned

tan·nate /tá nàyt/ *n* a salt or ester of tannic acid [Early 19C. < TANNIC]

tan·ner /tánnər/ *n* somebody who tans animal skins [Pre-12C. Both < TAN[1] and via Old French *tanere* < medieval Latin *tannator*]

tan·ner·y /tánnəree/ (*plural* **-ies**) *n* a building or factory where animal skins and hides are tanned

tan·ni·a /tánnee ə/, **tan·i·er** /tánnee ər/ *n Carib* a plant with large, arrow-shaped dark green leaves, grown for its long, thin tubers, which must be cooked before eating. Native to: tropical South America, Caribbean. Latin name: *Xanthosoma sagittifolium.*

tan·nic /tánnik/ *adj* relating to, containing, or derived from tannin [Mid-19C. < French *tannique* < *tanin* (see TANNIN)]

tan·nic ac·id *n* CHEM same as **tannin**

tan·nin /tánnin/ *n* a brownish or yellowish compound found in plants. Use: tanning, dyes, astringents. [Early 19C. < French *tanin* < *tan* "tanbark" < medieval Latin *tannum*]

tan·ning /tánning/ *n* **1. BROWNING OF SKIN** the browning of skin when it is exposed to the sun or some other ultraviolet light source **2. CONVERSION OF ANIMAL SKIN INTO LEATHER** the conversion of animal skins and hides into leather **3. SOUND BEATING** a sound beating or whipping

tan·ning bed *n* an apparatus resembling a bed with a special canopy that emits rays of ultraviolet light so that the person lying on it develops a tan

tan oak *n* a large evergreen hardwood tree of the beech family whose bark is used for tanning. Native to: California, Oregon. Latin name: *Lithocarpus densiflorus*.

Ta·no·an /taánō ən/ *n* a group of Native North American languages spoken mainly in New Mexico and Arizona. Native speakers: 3,000. [Late 19C < Spanish *Tano* "Tewa"] —**Ta·no·an** *adj*

tan·pur·a *n* MUSIC same as **tamboura**

tan·rec *n* ZOOL same as **tenrec**

tan·sy /tánzee/ (*plural* **-sies**) *n* **1.** an aromatic perennial plant of the daisy family with leaves divided into toothed leaflets. Flowers: yellow, in flat-topped clusters. Use: formerly, in cooking and medicine. Native to: Europe, Asia. Latin name: *Tanacetum vulgare*. **2.** a plant similar to the tansy, e.g., ragwort [13C. Origin ?]

Tan·ta /taántə/ city in northeastern Egypt, in the Nile delta, capital of Gharbiyah Governorate. Population: 380,000 (1992).

tan·tal·ic /tan tállik/ *adj* relating to or containing tantalum, especially with a valence of five

tan·ta·lite /tánt'l īt/ *n* a reddish black mixed oxide mineral containing tantalum, iron, and manganese. Source: granites, pegmatites. Use: source of tantalum.

tan·ta·lize /tánt'l īz/ (**-lized, -liz·ing, -liz·es**) *vt* to tease or torment somebody by letting the person see, but not have, something that is desirable [Late 16C. < Latin *Tantalus* "Tantalus"] —**tan·ta·li·za·tion** /tànt'li záysh'n/ *n* —**tan·ta·liz·er** *n*

tan·ta·liz·ing /tánt'l īzing/ *adj* **1.** tempting but unavailable or unattainable **2.** causing feelings of excitement, pleasure, or anticipation ○ *tantalizing glimpses of tropical landscapes* —**tan·ta·liz·ing·ly** *adv*

tan·ta·lum /tánt'ləm/ *n* a dense blue-gray metallic element. Use: electronic components, alloys, in plates and pins for orthopedic surgery. Symbol **Ta**. See table at **element** [Early 19C. Via modern Latin < Latin *Tantalus* "Tantalus," because of its inability to absorb acid even when it is immersed in it]

tan·ta·lus /tánt'ləss/ *n* a lockable stand or case for decanters of alcoholic drinks, especially spirits [Late 19C. < TANTALUS]

Tan·ta·lus /tánt'ləss/ *n* in Greek mythology, a king who was condemned to stand in water under a fruit tree. Whenever he tried to drink or eat, the water or fruit receded beyond his reach. [Mid-18C. Via Latin < Greek]

tan·ta·mount /tántə mòwnt/ *adj* equivalent to a particular thing in effect, outcome, or value, especially something unpleasant ○ *an answer that was tantamount to a refusal* [Mid-17C. < Anglo-French *tant amunter* "amount to as much" < Old French *tant* "as much" + *amonter* "to amount"]

tan·ta·ra /tan tárrə, -taárə, tántərə/ *n* **1.** a fanfare or blast on a horn, especially when used to announce something important **2.** a sound that resembles a tantara [Mid-16C. An imitation of the sound]

tant·ie /tántee/, **Tant·ie** *n Carib* **1.** an aunt **2.** an older woman [Late 19C. < French Creole, blend of French *tante* + AUNTIE]

tan·tiv·y /tan tívvee/ *n* (*plural* **-ies**) **1. HUNTER'S SHOUT** a hunting cry, especially one given by a hunter riding a horse at full gallop **2. FAST MOVEMENT** a fast ride, especially on a horse going at full gallop ■ *adj* **SPEEDY** moving very fast, especially when on a horse going at full gallop ■ *interj* **USED AS A HUNTING CRY** used as a hunting cry, especially by a hunter riding a horse at full gallop [Mid-17C. Probably an imitation of the sound of galloping horses, influenced by TANTARA] —**tan·tiv·y** *adv*

Tan·tra /túntrə, tántrə/ *n* the sacred books of Tantrism. They were written between the 7th and 17th centuries A.D. and mostly consist of a dialogue between Shiva and his wife Shakti. [Late 18C. < Sanskrit, "loom, warp, groundwork, system, doctrine"]

Tan·trism /tún trìzzəm, tán-/ *n* a movement in Hinduism and Buddhism, especially a variety based on yoga and intended to release energy through sexual intercourse in which the orgasm is withheld or delayed —**Tan·tric** *adj* —**Tan·trist** *n*

tan·trum /tántrəm/ *n* an outburst of anger, especially a childish display of rage or bad temper [Early 18C. Origin ?]

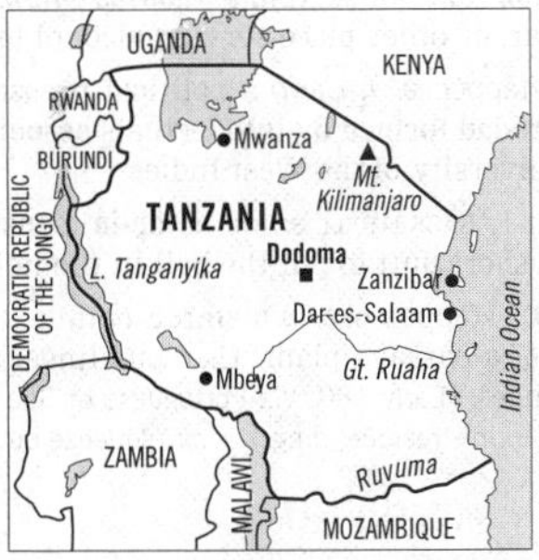

Tanzania

Tan·za·ni·a /tànzə neé ə/ country in East Africa, including the islands of Zanzibar and Pemba. It became an independent member of the British Commonwealth, as Tanganyika, in 1961. It changed its name to Tanzania after the union with Zanzibar in 1964. Language: Kiswahili, English. Currency: Tanzanian shilling. Capital: Dodoma. Population: 35,922,454 (2003). Area: 364,900 sq. mi./945,100 sq. km. Official name **United Republic of Tanzania** —**Tan·za·ni·an** *n, adj*

Tao /tow, dow/ *n* **1. ULTIMATE REALITY** in Taoist philosophy, the ultimate reality in which all things are located or happen **2.** *also* **tao UNIVERSAL ENERGY** in Taoist philosophy, the universal energy that makes and maintains everything that exists **3. RELATIONSHIP BETWEEN INDIVIDUAL AND UNIVERSE** in Taoist philosophy, the order and wisdom of individual life, and the way that this harmonizes with the universe as a whole [Mid-18C. < Chinese *dào* "way, path, right way (of life), reason"]

Taoi·seach /teéshək/ *n* the prime minister of the Republic of Ireland [Mid-20C. < Irish, "chief, leader"]

Tao·ism /tów ìzzəm, dów-/ *n* **1.** a Chinese philosophy that advocates a simple life and a policy of noninterference with the natural course of things. It was founded in the 6th century B.C. by the mystic and philosopher Lao-tzu. **2.** a popular Chinese religion that seeks harmony and long life through the philosophy of Taoism combined with pantheism and magical practices —**Tao·ist** *n, adj* —**Tao·is·tic** /tow ístik, dow-/ *adj*

Ta·or·mi·na /tòw ər meénə/ resort town in Messina Province, eastern Sicily, situated about 28 mi./45 km north of Catania. Population: 10,120 (1996).

Taos /towz, dowz/ (*plural same*) *n* a member of a Native North American people of the Pueblo group living to the northeast of of Santa Fe, New Mexico

Tao Te Ching /tòw tə chíng, dòw də jíng/ *n* the most important Taoist text, a collection of 81 poems by the mystic and philosopher Lao-tzu, the founder of Taoism [< Chinese, "the Book of the Way"]

tap[1] /tap/ *v* (**tapped, tap·ping, taps**) **1.** *vti* **HIT SOMETHING LIGHTLY** to hit something or somebody lightly, especially more than once **2.** *vt* **HIT OBJECT AGAINST SOMETHING ELSE** to hit an object lightly against something else **3.** *vt* **MAKE SOUND** to produce something such as a noise or rhythm by tapping **4.** *vi* **MOVE MAKING LIGHT SOUNDS** to move making a series of light noises **5.** *vi* **DO TAP DANCE** to perform a tap dance **6.** *vt* **REINFORCE SHOE** to attach a small piece of leather or metal to the toe or heel of a shoe to cover worn parts or to protect against wear **7.** *vt US* **GIVE POSITION TO SOMEBODY** to select and appoint somebody for a particular role or office (*usually passive*) ○ *tapped her as the publicity chair* ○ *"The coal industry was tapped to lead the way for reform"* (*US News & World Report*; December 1998) ■ *n* **1. LIGHT BLOW** a light blow, especially one that produces a noise **2. SOUND OF BLOW** the sound made by a light blow **3. METAL PART ON TAP-DANCING SHOE** a metal tip attached to the toe or heel of a tap-dancing shoe so that it can produce sounds **4. TAP-DANCING** the performing of tap dancing (*informal*) **5. REINFORCEMENT FOR SHOE** a small piece of leather or metal attached to the toe or heel of a shoe to cover a worn part or to protect against wear **6.** PHON **TOUCH OF TONGUE TO MOUTH TOP** the production of a speech sound made when any flexible speech organ hits any hard part of the mouth, e.g., when the tongue is brought into contact with the hard palate [12C. Origin ?] —**tap·pa·ble** *adj*

tap[2] /tap/ *n* **1. BARREL PLUG** a stopper in a cask or barrel, used to seal in the contents and also to allow liquid to be drawn off at a controlled rate **2. BEER FROM CASK** liquid, especially beer, that has been drawn from a tap in a cask or barrel and is regarded as having particular qualities because of this **3.** TELECOM **LISTENING DEVICE** a device put into a telephone or other telecommunication equipment in order to secretly listen to or record other people's conversations **4.** SURG **SURGICAL FLUID EXTRACTION** a surgical procedure that involves drawing off a body fluid using a hollow needle or tube **5. TOOL FOR SCREW THREADS** a tool used to make an internal screw thread **6.** ELEC **TEMPORARY CONNECTION IN CIRCUIT** a point in a circuit where a temporary connection may be made **7.** FIN **SECURITY ON MARKET AT PREDETERMINED PRICE** a government security made available gradually on the stock market when its price reaches a predetermined level **8.** *UK* CONSTR same as **faucet** ■ *v* (**tapped, tap·ping, taps**) **1.** *vt* TELECOM **PLACE LISTENING DEVICE ON PHONE LINE** to fit a device into a telephone or other telecommunication equipment in order to secretly listen to or record other people's conversations **2.** *vt* **ATTACH TAP** to attach a tap to something in order to draw off or control the flow of liquid **3.** *vt* **DRAW LIQUID FROM BARREL** to draw off liquid such as wine or beer from a barrel by means of a tap **4.** *vt* SURG **DRAW FLUID FROM BODY** to surgically draw off fluid from a part of the body **5.** *vt* FORESTRY **OBTAIN SAP** to cut into a tree in order to draw off sap or resin **6.** *vt* ELEC ENG **GET INTO POWER SUPPLY** to connect to a power supply and divert energy from it, usually illegally **7.** *vti* **PUT RESOURCE TO USE** to make use of a resource or supply of something (*informal*) ○ *tapped into our capital* **8.** *vt* **BORROW MONEY** to borrow a sum of money from somebody (*informal*) ○ *She tapped me for 20 bucks.* **9.** *vt* MECH ENG **MAKE INTERNAL SCREW THREAD** to cut an internal screw thread into something [Old English *tæppa* (noun), *tæppian* (verb) < Germanic] —**tap·pa·ble** *adj* ◇ **on tap 1.** available for immediate use (*informal*) **2.** available to be drawn from a container (*informal*) **3.**

REGIONAL NOTE See ***spigot***.

tap[3] /tap/ *n Southwest US* a leather stirrup cover [Shortening of TAPADERA]

ta·pa /taápə, táppə/ *n* **1.** the inner bark of the paper mulberry tree **2.** a strong fabric made from tapa [Early 19C. < Polynesian]

ta·pa·de·ra /tapə dáirə/ *n Hispanic* a leather stirrup cover [Mid-19C. < Spanish, "cover, lid, stopper" < *tapar* "stop up, cover"]

ta·pas /taá paass/ *npl* small snacks that are often served as an appetizer along with alcoholic drinks, originally in Spain [Mid-20C. Plural of Spanish *tapa* "cover, lid"]

tap dance *n* **1.** a step dance performed by somebody wearing shoes with metal tips to make a rhythmic sound **2.** behavior designed to avoid making a commitment or final decision (*informal*) —**tap danc·er** *n* —**tap-danc·ing** *n*

tap-dance *v* **1.** *vi* to perform a dance or dances wearing shoes with metal tips at the toes and heels to make a rhythmic sound **2.** *vti* COMMUNICATION to engage in intricate evasion or hesitation in an effort to avoid making a commitment or a definitive statement (*informal*) —**tap-danc·ing** *n*

tape /tayp/ *n* **1. VIDEO OR AUDIO CASSETTE** a cassette used for audio or video recording or playback ○ *Put the* *tape in the player.* **2. STRIP OF STICKY MATERIAL** a long strip of plastic or cloth with adhesive on one or both sides, usually on a roll **3. LONG NARROW STRIP OF MATERIAL** a long narrow strip of material such as paper, fabric, or plastic used to secure or tie something **4. FINISH LINE MARKER** a long strip of material that marks the finish line in a race **5. MAGNETIC TAPE** magnetic tape used in cassettes and some computers **6.** same as **tape measure 7.** RECORDING same as **tape recording** ■ *v* **(taped, tap·ing, tapes) 1.** *vti* **RECORD SOMETHING** to record something, especially music or a television program, on magnetic tape **2.** *vt* **FIX SOMETHING** to secure, fasten, or strengthen something using tape **3.** *vt* MED **BANDAGE TIGHTLY** to tie a bandage tightly around an injured body part **4.** *vt* **MEASURE SOMETHING** to measure something using a tape measure [Old English *tæppe* "narrow strip of cloth," origin ?]

tape up *vt* MED same as **tape** *v* (sense 3)

tape deck *n* a piece of electrical equipment that plays and records tapes, especially audio cassettes

tape grass *n* a perennial grass that grows largely submerged in fresh water, forming tufts of long narrow leaves. Flowers: inconspicuous, pinkish white. Latin name: *Vallisneria spiralis.*

tape·line /táyp lìn/ *n* MEASURE same as **tape measure**

tape ma·chine *n UK* same as **ticker** (sense 1)

tape meas·ure *n* a long roll or strip of fabric, plastic, paper, or thin metal that is marked off in inches or centimeters for measuring the length of something

ta·pe·nade /taàpə naàd/ *n* a paste made from puréed black olives, capers, and anchovies [< French, < Provençal *tapeno* "caper"]

ta·per /táypər/ *vti* **(-pered, -per·ing, -pers) 1. GET OR MAKE NARROWER** to become narrower at one end, especially gradually, or make something do this **2. REDUCE GRADUALLY** to become smaller in size or amount, or less important, especially gradually, or make something do this ○ *Sales of the first album are beginning to taper off.* ■ *n* **1. SLIM CANDLE** a slim candle that is narrower at the top than at the bottom **2. STRIP FOR TRANSFERRING FLAME** a strip of wood or waxed paper used for taking a flame to light something else **3. NARROWING OF SHAPE** a gradual narrowing in the shape of something ○ *a spire with a pronounced taper* **4. DIM LIGHT** a faint source of light, e.g., from a small candle [Pre-12C. Alteration of Latin *papyrus* "papyrus," whose pith was used for candle wicks] —**ta·per·ing** *adj* —**ta·per·ing·ly** *adv*

tape re·cord·er *n* a machine that can record and play cassette or reel-to-reel tapes, especially one with its own speaker —**tape-re·cord** *vt*

tape re·cord·ing *n* a recording made on magnetic tape, especially an audio recording

tap·es·try /táppəstree/ (*plural* **-tries**) *n* **1. FABRIC WITH WOVEN DESIGN** a heavy piece of fabric with a woven pattern or picture. Use: wall hanging, upholstery. **2. EMBROIDERY RESEMBLING TAPESTRY** embroidery stitched on canvas to resemble tapestry **3. SOMETHING VARIED AND INTRICATE** something that is considered to be rich, varied, or intricately interwoven ○ *the rich tapestry of life* [14C. < French *tapisserie* < *tapis* "carpet" < Greek *tapēt-*]

CULTURAL NOTE ***The Bayeux Tapestry,*** a large embroidery (1092) found at Bayeux in northern France. A remarkable work of art and an important historical document, it consists of a band of linen measuring 231 ft./70 m by 20 in./50 cm, embroidered with vivid scenes that depict the Norman conquest of England. Its existence was first recorded in 1476 at Bayeux, where it was used to decorate the nave of the cathedral.

tap·es·try moth *n* a moth whose caterpillars eat fabrics made from wool and other natural fibers. The adults are brown with white-tipped forewings and prefer damp conditions. Latin name: *Trichophaga tapetzella.*

ta·pe·tum /tə peétəm/ (*plural* **-ta** /-tə/) *n* **1.** a specialized membrane or layer of cells **2.** a layer of cells in the wall of the eye of nocturnal and deep-sea animals that reflects light back onto the retina, enhancing visual sensitivity in dim light. Light reflected by this layer is responsible for the shining eyes of cats seen when they are illuminated at night. [Early 18C. < late Latin < Latin *tapete* < Greek *tapēt-*] —**ta·pe·tal** *adj*

tape·worm /táyp wùrm/ *n* a flatworm with a long ribbon-shaped segmented body that exists in many varieties and lives mainly as a parasite in the gut of vertebrate animals. Infestation is common among domestic animals, and humans can also become infested, especially by eating undercooked meat containing tapeworm larvae. Class: Cestoda. Technical name **cestode**

tap·hole /táp hòl/ *n* a hole at the bottom of a furnace for drawing off molten metal or slag

ta·phon·o·my /tə fónnəmee/ *n* the scientific study of fossilization [Mid-20C. < Greek *taphos* "grave"] —**taph·o·nom·ic** /tàffə nómmik/ *adj* —**ta·phon·o·mist** *n*

tap·house /táp hòwss/ (*plural* **-houses** /-hòwzəz/) *n* an inn, bar, or other place serving alcohol (*archaic*)

tap·i·a /táppee ə/ *n Carib* a political pressure group in Trinidad formed by intellectuals associated with the University of the West Indies

tap-in *n* **1.** BASKETBALL same as **tip-in** (sense 1) **2.** in golf, a short putt to put the ball in the hole

tap·i·o·ca /tàppee ṓkə/ *n* a starch obtained from the roots of a cassava plant. Use: puddings, thickener for sauces. [Early 18C. Via Portuguese or Spanish < Tupi *tipioca* < *tipi* "residue, dregs" + *ok* "squeeze out"]

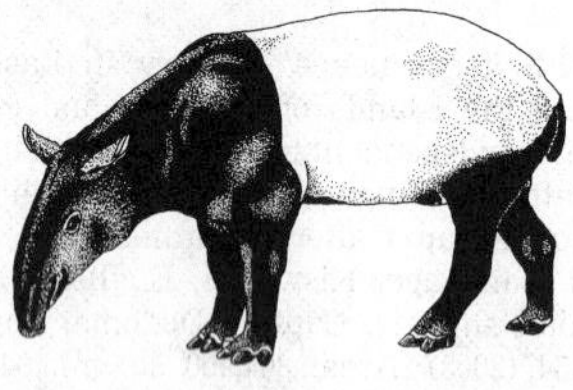

tapir

ta·pir /táypər, tə peér/ (*plural* **-pirs** or *same*) *n* a nocturnal hoofed forest-dwelling mammal that has short limbs and a fleshy snout and feeds on fruit and vegetation. Native to: Central and South America, Southeast Asia. Family: Tapiridae. [Late 18C. Via Portuguese or Spanish < Tupi *tapira*]

tap-off *n* BASKETBALL same as **tip-off**[2]

Tap·pan /táppən/, **Arthur** (1786–1865) US philanthropist. He cofounded the American Anti-Slavery Society (1833) and the American and Foreign Anti-Slavery Society (1840).

Tap·pan, Lewis (1788–1873) US philanthropist. The brother of Arthur Tappan, he founded the first US credit-rating service (1841) and shared his brother's abolitionist commitment and activities.

Tap·pan Zee /táppən zeé/ widening of the Hudson River near Tarrytown in southeastern New York. It is about 10 mi./16 km long and up to 3 mi./5 km wide.

tap·per[1] /táppər/ *n* somebody or something that draws off or controls the flow of a liquid (*often used in combination*) ○ *a rubber-tapper* [Early 19C. < TAP[1]]

tap·per[2] /táppər/ *n* **1.** somebody or something that hits something or somebody lightly, especially more than once, or that makes a tapping sound **2.** same as **tapster** (*archaic*) [Pre-12C. < TAP[2]]

tap·pet /táppit/ *n* a lever, arm, or other machine part that transfers motion from a cam to a part such as a valve or push rod [Mid-18C. < TAP[1]]

tap·ping /tápping/ *n UK* same as **tap**[2] *n* (sense 6)

tap·room /táp rŏŏm, -rōōm/ *n* a barroom in a place such as a hotel

tap·root /táp rŏŏt/ *n* a long tapering root that extends downward below the stem of some plants and has fine lateral roots. It often serves as a food storage organ, e.g., in the carrot. [Early 17C. < TAP[2]]

taps /taps/ *n* (*takes a singular or plural verb*) **1.** a bugle call or other signal given at the end of the day, especially in a military camp, as an order that lights should be put out **2.** a bugle call or other signal given at a funeral or memorial service, especially a military one [Early 19C. < TAP[1], or alteration of *taptoo,* variant of TATTOO[2]]

tap·ster /tápstər/ *n* somebody who serves drinks in a bar (*archaic*) [Old English *tæpestre,* originally feminine of TAPPER[2]]

tap wa·ter *n* water that comes out of the faucet

ta·que·ri·a /taàkə reé ə/ *n Hispanic* an establishment that prepares and sells Mexican food [Late 20C. < Mexican Spanish *taquería* < *taco* (see TACO)]

tar[1] /taar/ *n* **1. THICK BLACK LIQUID** a thick black liquid obtained through the destructive distillation of an organic substance such as wood or coal **2. TOBACCO SMOKE RESIDUE** the particulate residue from tobacco smoke ■ *vt* **(tarred, tar·ring, tars) COVER SOMETHING WITH TAR** to coat or cover something, especially a road surface, with tar [Old English *teoru* < Indo-European] —**tar·ry** *adj* ◇ **be tarred with the same brush** to have or display the same faults, bad habits, or unpleasant characteristics ◇ **tar and feather somebody** to smear tar over somebody and cover the tar with feathers as a form of punishment

tar[2] /taar/ *n* SAILING same as **sailor** (sense 1) (*archaic informal*) [Late 17C. Origin ?]

Tar·a, Hill of /taàrə/ hill in County Meath, Ireland, northwest of Dublin. It was the seat of the Irish kings until about A.D. 560. Height: 507 ft./155 m.

tar·a·did·dle *n* another spelling of **tarradiddle** (*informal*)

ta·ra·ma·sa·la·ta /taà raa maa sə laàtə/ *n* a creamy pink or beige paste made from smoked fish roe. It is usually served in the form of a pâté or dip as an appetizer or snack. [Early 20C. < modern Greek < *taramas* "preserved roe" (< Turkish *tarama* "preparation of soft roe or red caviar") + *salata* "salad"]

Ta·ra·na·ki /tàrrə nákee/ administrative region of New Zealand, located in the southwestern part of the North Island and including the city of New Plymouth. Population: 102,858 (2001). Area: 4,880 sq. mi./12,640 sq. km.

Ta·ra·na·ki, Mount /tàrrə nákee/ dormant volcano near the western coast of the North Island, New Zealand. Height: 8,261 ft./2,518 m.

tar·an·tass /taàrən taàss/ *n* a large Russian horse-drawn carriage with four wheels and no springs [Mid-19C. < Russian *tarantas*]

tar·an·tel·la /tàrrən téllə/ *n* **1.** a whirling dance from southern Italy in 6/8 time **2.** the music for a tarantella [Late 18C. < Italian < TARANTO]

Popperfoto

Quentin Tarantino

Ta·ran·ti·no /tàrrən teénō/, **Quentin** (*b.* 1963) US movie director and screenwriter. His first movie, *Reservoir Dogs* (1992), followed by *Pulp Fiction* (1994), established him as an important but controversial moviemaker. Full name **Tarantino, Quentin Jerome**

> "To me, violence is a totally aesthetic subject. Saying you don't like violence in movies is like saying you don't like dance sequences in movies. I do like dance sequences in movies, but if I didn't, it doesn't mean I should stop dance sequences being made."
> [Quentin Tarantino, *True Romance;* 1995]

tar·an·tism /tárrən tìzzəm/ *n* a nervous condition characterized by uncontrollable body movements, common in southern Italy between the 15th and 17th centuries and formerly believed to be caused by the bite of the tarantula [Mid-17C. < Italian *tarantismo* < TARANTO]

Ta·ran·to /taárən tō/ city, port, and administrative center of Taranto Province, Apulia Region, southern Italy. Population: 202,033 (2001).

tarantula

ta·ran·tu·la /tə ránchələ/ (*plural* **-las** or **-lae** /-lee/) *n* **1.** a large spider that has a hairy body and legs and feeds on invertebrates, toads, small reptiles, and young birds. Native to: tropical and subtropical America. Family: Theraphosidae. **2.** a wolf spider formerly believed to cause tarantism with its bite. Native to: Europe. Latin name: *Lycosa tarentula.* [Mid-16C. Via medieval Latin < Italian *tarantola* < TARANTO]

Ta·ra·ru·a Range /tàrrə róo ə-/ mountain range in the southern part of the North Island, New Zealand, north of Wellington. Its highest point is Mitre Peak, 5,154 ft./1,571 m.

Ta·ra·wa /tə raáwə, tárrə waá/ atoll in the west central Pacific Ocean and capital of Kiribati. It was retaken in World War II by US Marines from the Japanese in November 1943. Population: 28,802 (1990). Area: 9 sq. mi./23 sq. km.

tar·ax·a·cum /taa ráksəkəm/ *n* **1.** an herbal remedy extracted from dandelion roots or leaves. Use: mild laxative, liver tonic, diuretic. **2.** a plant such as the dandelion that produces flower heads made up of numerous florets and with seeds attached to whitish hairs. Genus: *Taraxacum.* [Early 18C. Via medieval Latin *altaraxacon* < Arabic, Persian *ṭarakšakūn* "dandelion, wild endive" < Persian *talk* "bitter" + *čakūk* "purslane"]

tar ba·by *n* a very troublesome situation, especially one that is difficult or impossible to get out of (*dated*) [Early 20C. < the Uncle Remus story *Brer Rabbit and the Tar Baby* by J. C. Harris]

Tar·bell /taárb'l/, **Ida** (1857–1944) US journalist. One of the "muckrakers," she is known for *The History of the Standard Oil Company* (1904). Full name **Ida Minerva Tarbell**

tar·boosh /taar bóosh/, **tar·bush** *n* a brimless, usually red, felt hat, similar to a fez, that has a silk tassel and is worn by Muslim men by itself or with a turban [Early 18C. Via Egyptian Arabic *ṭarbūš* < Ottoman Turkish *terpōş*, Turkish *tarbuş* < Persian *sarpūš* < *sar* "head" + *pūš* "cover"]

tar cam·phor *n* INDUST same as **naphthalene**

tar·di·grade /taárdi gràyd/ *n* **TINY WATER ANIMAL** a tiny invertebrate water animal with a short body and four pairs of stubby legs. Phylum: Tardigrada. ■ *adj* **1. RELATING TO TARDIGRADES** relating to or belonging to the tardigrades **2. SLUGGISH** sluggish or slow moving [Early 17C. Directly or via French < Latin *tardigradus* "walking slowly" < *tardus* "slow"]

tar·dive dys·ki·ne·sia /taárdiv-/ *n* a condition marked by involuntary movements of the tongue and facial muscles, especially after prolonged treatment with phenothiazine tranquilizers or similar drugs [< French *tardif* (see TARDY)]

tar·dy /taárdee/ *adj* (**-di·er, -di·est**) **1. LATE** later than the expected or usual time **2. SLUGGISH** slow to move or react (*archaic or literary*) ■ *n* (*plural* **-dies**) **INSTANCE OF LATENESS** an instance of being late, especially for school or work, that is noted down as a misdemeanor ○ *Just one more tardy and you'll be staying after school.* [Mid-16C. < French *tardif* < Latin *tardus* "slow, sluggish"] —**tar·di·ly** *adv* —**tar·di·ness** *n*

tare[1] /ter/ *n* **1. VETCH PLANT** a trailing or scrambling vetch plant that has compound leaves with paired leaflets and tendrils. Flowers: bluish or purplish, in spikes. Native to: Europe, North Africa. Genus: *Vicia.* **2. VETCH SEED** the seed of a tare or vetch **3. PROBLEMATIC WEED** in the Bible, a weed found growing among crops, usually considered to be darnel [13C. Origin ?]

SPELLCHECK tare or **tear**? Do not confuse the spelling of ***tare*** and ***tear***, which sound similar. There are two words spelled ***tare***, one denoting a type of plant, the other the weight of a container, packaging, or vehicle: both are rarely encountered in general usage. The word ***tear***, meaning "to pull apart or rip" and "to move or act quickly," or as a noun "a hole or split," is much more common: *Tear it in half. There's a tear in this sheet. They were tearing down the road to catch the bus.*

tare[2] /ter/ *n* **1. WEIGHT OF PACKAGING** the weight of a container or of the packaging used to wrap goods **2. ALLOWANCE FOR WEIGHT OF PACKAGING** an allowance for the packaging around goods, deducted from the total weight and not included in transportation costs **3. UNLADEN WEIGHT OF VEHICLE** the weight of a motor vehicle without fuel, cargo, passengers, or equipment **4. CONTAINER OF KNOWN WEIGHT** a container of known weight that is used as a counterbalance when calculating the net weight of a cargo ■ *vt* (**tared, taring, tares**) **WEIGH PACKAGING** to weigh packaging in order to calculate the amount of tare to be deducted from a cargo [15C. Via French, "waste in goods, deficiency" < Arabic *ṭarḥ* "that which is deducted" < *ṭaraḥa* "reject, subtract"]

SPELLCHECK See ***tare***[1].

targe /taarj/ *n* a round shield, especially one used by Scottish Highlanders (*archaic*) [Pre-12C. Probably < Old Norse *targa* "shield"; reinforced by Old French *targe* "light shield"]

tar·get /taárgət/ *n* **1. OBJECT AIMED AT IN SHOOTING** a round object or surface marked with concentric circles that is aimed at in archery, rifle shooting, and similar sports **2. SOMEBODY OR SOMETHING AIMED AT** an area, surface, object, or person aimed at ○ *The bird's bright plumage makes it an easy target.* **3. GOAL** a goal or objective toward which effort is directed ○ *Our target is to raise $20,000 for cancer research.* **4. SOMEBODY OR SOMETHING ON RECEIVING END** somebody or something that is the focus or object of the behavior or actions of others ○ *the target of her anger* **5.** CIV ENG **MARKER FOR TAKING LEVELS** a sliding weight on a surveyor's leveling rod that is used to help determine proper levels **6.** PHYS **SOMETHING HIT BY PARTICLE ACCELERATOR BEAM** a substance that is hit by a beam of electrons or other elementary particles or ions from a particle accelerator in order to start a nuclear reaction **7.** PHYS **SURFACE HIT BY ELECTRONS** a surface or electrode, often luminescent, that is hit by an electron beam to produce an output signal, e.g., in an X-ray tube or a television camera tube **8. SMALL SHIELD** a small round shield (*archaic*) ■ *vt* (**-get·ed, -get·ing, -gets**) **1. MAKE SOMEBODY OR SOMETHING TARGET** to make a person or thing the focus or object of something ○ *a program that targets the 18–34 age group* **2. AIM SOMETHING** to aim something at or direct something toward a person, group, or thing ○ *The missiles were targeted on the enemy capital.* [13C. < TARGE]

tar·get·cast /taárgət kàst/ (**-cast** or **-cast·ed, -cast·ing, -casts**) *vi* to broadcast a website only to a group of people who are known to be potentially interested, and not to everyone on the Internet [Late 20C. Blend of TARGET + BROADCAST]

tar·get date *n* the date by which it is expected that something such as a project or piece of work will be completed

tar·get lan·guage *n* **1. TRANSLATION LANGUAGE** the language into which a text is to be translated **2. LANGUAGE BEING LEARNED** a foreign language that is being learned **3.** COMPUT **COMPUTER COMPILATION LANGUAGE** the machine-readable instructions in which a computer program written in a high-level language is to be compiled

tar·get man *n* in soccer, a forward whose role is to receive high passes and crosses, especially in front of the goal

tar·get of op·por·tu·ni·ty *n* a military target that is visible or detectable and within range, although no attack on it has been planned or requested

Tar·gum /taár gŏom, -gōom/ *n* a translation of part of the Bible in Aramaic [Late 16C. Via Hebrew < Aramaic *targūm* "interpretation" < *targēm* "interpret"] —**Tar·gu·mic** /taar gōomik/ *adj* —**Tar·gu·mist** /taar gōomist/ *n*

Tar Heel /taár hèel/, **Tar·heel** *n* US somebody who comes from North Carolina [Mid-19C. Origin ?]

Tar Heel State *n* a nickname for North Carolina

tar·iff /tárrif/ *n* **1. DUTY LEVIED ON GOODS** a duty levied by a government on imported or exported goods **2. LIST OF LEVIES** a list or system of import or export tariffs **3. LIST OF COSTS** a list of fees, fares, or other prices charged by a business ■ *vt* (**-iffed, -iff·ing, -iffs**) **SET COST OF SOMETHING** to fix a tariff or price on something [Late 16C. Via Italian *tariffa* < Arabic *ta'rīf* "notification, inventory of fees to be paid" < *'arrafa* "notify"]

Tar·king·ton /taárkingtən/, **Booth** (1869–1946) US writer. His novels include the Pulitzer Prize-winning *The Magnificent Ambersons* (1918). Full name **Tarkington, Newton Booth**

> "There are two things that will be believed of any man whatsoever, and one of them is that he has taken to drink."
> [Booth Tarkington, *Penrod*; 1914]

Tar·kov·sky /taar káwfskee/, **Andrei** (1932–86) Russian movie director. He is noted for his highly personal and symbolic movies such as *Solaris* (1972).

> "The goal of all art is...to explain to people the reason for their appearance on this planet; or, if not to explain, at least to pose the question."
> [Andrei Tarkovsky, *Sculpting in Time: Reflections on the Cinema*; 1989]

tar·la·tan /taárlət'n/ *n* an open-weave transparent highly starched cotton muslin. Use: stiffener for collars and other parts of clothes. [Early 18C. < French *tarlatane*]

tar·mac /taár màk/ US *n* **ROAD SURFACING MATERIAL** a material used for surfacing roads ■ *vt* (**-macked, -macked, -mack·ing, -macks**) **1. COVER WITH TARMAC** to cover the surface of a road with tarmac **2. PARK** to park an airplane on a surfaced area at an airport or air base [Early 20C. Originally a trademark]

tar·mac·a·dam /taár mə káddəm/ *n* a mixture of broken stone and tar used for surfacing roads

tarn /taarn/ *n* a small mountain lake, especially one formed by the action of glaciers [14C. < N Germanic]

tar·nish /taárnish/ *vti* (**-nished, -nish·ing, -nish·es**) **1. MAKE OR BECOME DULL AND DISCOLORED** to lose shine and become dull because of oxidation or rust, or make something do this **2. DAMAGE SOMEBODY'S REPUTATION** to damage somebody's reputation or good name, or become damaged ■ *n* **1. DISCOLORATION** the dullness or discoloration of metal affected by oxidation or rust **2. FILM OF DISCOLORATION ON METAL** the film of discoloration that forms on metal **3. SULLIED CONDITION** the damaged condition of somebody's reputation or good name [15C. < French *terniss-*, stem of *ternir* "make dull"] —**tar·nish·a·ble** *adj*

ta·ro /taárō, tárrō/ (*plural* **-ros**) *n* a perennial plant cultivated in tropical regions for its edible starchy tubers and also widely grown as an ornamental plant. Native to: Southeast Asia. Latin name: *Colocasia esculenta.* [Mid-18C. < Polynesian]

tar·ok /tárrək/ *n* a card game developed in medieval times that uses a pack of cards consisting of 56 cards equivalent to modern cards, plus 22 tarot cards [Early 17C. < Italian *tarocchi* (see TAROT)]

tar·ot /tárrō, tə rṓ/ *n* **1.** a system of fortune-telling using a special pack of 78 cards consisting of 4 suits of 14 cards together with 22 picture cards **2.** *also* **tar·ot card** a card used in tarot ▶ See illustration on next page [Late 19C. < French < Italian *tarocchi* plural of *tarocco*]

tarot

tarp /taarp/ *n* INDUST same as **tarpaulin** (*informal*) [Early 20C. Shortening]

tar·pan /taar pán/ *n* a small gray-brown horse with a short thick neck, erect mane, and a stripe along the back. It is now extinct. Native to: southern Russia, Poland. [Mid-19C. < Turkic]

tar·pa·per /taár pàypər/ *n* a heavy paper coated with tar. Use: waterproofing in building.

tar·pau·lin /taar páwlin, taárpəlin/ *n* **1.** a heavy waterproof material, especially treated canvas, used as a covering and to protect things from moisture **2.** a sheet of tarpaulin [Early 17C. Probably < TAR[1] + PALL[2] + -ING[2]]

Tar·pei·an Rock /taar peé ən-/ *n* a rock on the Capitoline Hill in ancient Rome, from which traitors were hurled to their deaths [Early 17C. After *Tarpeia*, legendary betrayer of the Roman citadel to the Sabines, reputedly buried at the foot of the rock]

tar pit *n* an area where tar or asphalt naturally accumulates, trapping animals and preserving their bones

tar·pon /taárpən/ (*plural same* or **-pons**) *n* an ocean fish with a streamlined body and thick silvery scales. Native to: tropical and subtropical waters. Genus: *Megalops*. [Late 17C. Probably < Dutch *tarpoen*]

Tar·quin·i·us Su·per·bus /taar kwìnnee əss soo púrbəss/, **Lucius** (*fl* 6th century B.C.) king of Rome. According to tradition, he was the last of the Etruscan kings of Rome (534–510 B.C.), and was dethroned after his son raped Lucretia, a Roman matron.

tar·ra·did·dle /tàrrə dídd'l/, **tar·a·did·dle** *n* (*informal*) **1.** nonsense or idle talk **2.** a small lie [Late 18C. Probably suggesting unintelligible speech]

tarragon

tar·ra·gon /tárrə gòn, -gən/ *n* a perennial herb with narrow aromatic leaves. Use: flavoring food. Native to: temperate regions of Asia. Latin name: *Artemisia dracunculus*. [Mid-16C. < medieval Latin *tragonia*, *tarchon*]

Tar·ra·go·na /tàrrə gṓnə/ city, port, and administrative center of Tarragona Province, northeastern Spain. It has extensive Roman remains. Population: 117,184 (2002).

~~**tarrif**~~ incorrect spelling of **tariff**

tar·ry /tárree/ (**-ried, -ry·ing, -ries**) *vi* **1.** REMAIN to stay temporarily at a place **2.** LINGER to delay a departure or arrival, especially in an idle way **3.** WAIT to wait in expectation of somebody or something [13C. Origin ?] —**tar·ri·er** *n*

Tar·ry·town /tárree tòwn/ village on the Hudson River in southeastern New York. The writer Washington Irving was a longtime resident, and the village is part of the Sleepy Hollow country where many of his short stories are set. Population: 11,447 (2002 estimate).

tar·sal /taárss'l/ *adj* **1.** OF TARSUS relating to the group of bones forming the ankle joint (**tarsus**) **2.** OF PART OF EYELID relating to the small section of connective tissue (**tarsus**) along the edge of the eyelid ■ *n* BONE OF ANKLE any of the group of bones forming the ankle joint (**tarsus**) [Early 19C. < TARSUS]

tar·si·er /taárssee ər, taárssee ày/ *n* a small nocturnal animal with large eyes and delicate grasping fingers and toes ending in pads that lives in trees. Native to: Philippines, Indonesia, and neighboring islands. Genus: *Tarsius*. [Late 18C. < French < *tarse* "tarsus"; from its long tarsal bones]

tar·so·met·a·tar·sus /taárssō metə taárssəss/ (*plural* **-tar·si** /-sī, -seè/) *n* the bone in the lower leg of birds that connects to the toes [Mid-19C. < TARSUS]

tar·sus /taárssəss/ (*plural* **tar·si** /-sī, -seè/) *n* **1.** ANKLE BONES the group of bones that forms the ankle joint in vertebrates, located between the inner bone of the lower leg (**tibia**) and the main skeleton of the foot (**metatarsus**) **2.** PART OF EYELID the small section of connective tissue along the edge of the eyelid **3.** BIRDS same as **tarsometatarsus 4.** PART OF ARTHROPOD LEG the part of the leg of an arthropod that is farthest from the tibia [Late 17C. Via modern Latin < Greek *tarsos* "eyelid, flat part of the foot"]

Tar·sus /taárssəss/ city in southern Turkey, near the Mediterranean Sea. During Roman rule in the 1st century B.C. it was one of the most prominent cities of Asia Minor. Population: 246,206 (1997).

tart[1] /taart/ *adj* **1.** having a sharp and sour, but usually pleasant, flavor **2.** sharp, cutting, or critical [14C. < Old English *teart* "painful, severe," origin ?] —**tart·ly** *adv* —**tart·ness** *n*

tart[2] /taart/ *n* a pie that has no top crust and is usually filled with something sweet such as fruit or custard [14C. < Old French *tarte*]

tart[3] /taart/ *n* an offensive term for a woman prostitute or a woman regarded as sexually provocative (*slang*) [Mid-19C. Probably shortening of SWEETHEART]

tar·tan[1] /taárt'n/ *n* **1.** SCOTTISH WOOL FABRIC a Scottish wool or worsted fabric woven in a wide range of checked or plaid patterns, many of which are associated with specific Scottish clans. The association between clans and tartan has no historical basis and arose in the 19th century. **2.** PATTERN OF TARTAN a pattern of tartan, officially registered and associated with a specific clan, regiment, or other organization **3.** TARTAN GARMENT a piece of clothing made of tartan **4.** TRADITIONAL HIGHLAND DRESS the traditional dress of the Scottish Highlands ○ *wearing the tartan with pride* [15C. Origin ?]

tar·tan[2] /taárt'n/ *n* a Mediterranean sailing ship with a single mast and a lateen sail [Early 17C. Via French *tartane* < Old Provençal *tartana* "buzzard"]

tar·tar /taártər/ *n* **1.** a hard deposit of mostly organic material that forms on teeth at the gum line and contributes to dental decay if not regularly removed **2.** a substance consisting mostly of potassium bitartrate that is deposited in wine casks during fermentation [14C. Via medieval Latin *tartarum* < medieval Greek *tartaron*] —**tar·tar·ous** *adj*

Tar·tar /taártər/ *n* **1.** PEOPLES, LANG same as **Tatar 2.** *also* **tar·tar** somebody regarded as fearsome or ferocious (*sometimes offensive*) [14C. Directly or via French *Tartare* < medieval Latin *Tartarus* < Turkish] —**Tar·tar** *adj* —**Tar·tar·ian** /taar térree ən/ *adj* —**Tar·tar·ic** /-tárrik/ *adj*

tar·tare sauce *n* FOOD another spelling of **tartar sauce**

tar·tar·ic ac·id /taar tàrrik-/ *n* a white crystalline organic acid. Source: wine vat tartar. Use: foods, beverages, photographic processes. Formula: $(CHOH)_2(COOH)_2$.

tar·tar sauce, **tar·tare sauce** *n* a mayonnaise mixed with capers and chopped pickles that is served as an accompaniment to fish [< French *Tartare* (see TARTAR)]

tar·tar steak *n* FOOD same as **steak tartare**

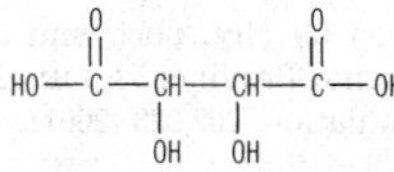

tartaric acid

Tar·ta·rus /taártərəss/ *n* **1.** in Greek mythology, the lowest part of the underworld, where the worst evildoers were imprisoned **2.** in Greek mythology, Hades or the underworld in general [Mid-16C. Via Latin < Greek *Tartaros*]

Tar·ta·ry /taártəree/ historical region of eastern Europe and Central Asia. In the Middle Ages, Tartary was the area from western Russia to the Sea of Japan. Later, the Crimea was called European Tartary and Turkistan was called Asian Tartary.

tart·let /taártlət/ *n* a small tart, usually for one person [15C. < French *tartelette*, diminutive of *tarte* "pie, tart"]

tar·trate /taár tràyt/ *n* a salt or ester of tartaric acid [Late 18C. < French < *tartre* "tartar"]

tar·trat·ed /taár tràytəd/ *adj* in the form of a tartrate

Tartt /taart/, **Donna** (*b.* 1963) US writer. Her novels include *The Secret History* (1992) and *The Little Friend* (2002).

Tar·tu /taártoo/ city in eastern Estonia, on the Emajogi River. Population: 101,901 (1997).

Tar·tuffe /taar to͝of, -tóof/, **Tar·tufe** *n* a religious hypocrite [After the main character in Molière's play *Tartuffe* (1664)] —**Tar·tuf·fi·an** *adj*

tart·y /taártee/ (**-i·er, -i·est**) *adj* an offensive term that describes a woman's appearance as vulgar or gaudy (*slang*)

tar·weed /taár weèd/ *n* a strong-smelling resinous plant. Flowers: yellow, like daisies. Native to: western North America, Chile. Genus: *Madia*.

TAS *abbr* **1.** TELECOM telephone answering system **2.** AEROSP true air speed

Tas. *abbr* Tasmania

Ta·ser /táyzər/ *tdmk* a trademark for a type of nonlethal weapon that transmits electrical pulses to contract muscle tissue in order to incapacitate somebody

Tash·kent /tash ként, taásh-/ capital city of Uzbekistan, situated in the eastern part of the country. Population: 2,142,700 (1999).

task /task/ *n* **1.** JOB ASSIGNED TO SOMEBODY a piece of work that somebody is given to do, usually short in duration or with a deadline **2.** ASSIGNMENT a piece of work or an assignment, especially one that is important or difficult ■ *vt* (**tasked, task·ing, tasks**) **1.** ASSIGN WORK TO SOMEBODY to assign a task to somebody ○ *tasked me with writing the letter* **2.** BURDEN SOMEBODY to burden somebody excessively with work or duties [13C. Via Old N French *tasque* "duty, tax" < medieval Latin *tasca* < Latin *taxare* (see TAX)] ◇ **take somebody to task** to scold or criticize somebody

SYNONYMS See ***job***.

task·bar /tásk baàr/ *n* a bar at the bottom of a computer screen displaying buttons that show, among other things, which programs are currently running

task force *n* **1.** a formation of military units put together on a temporary basis to accomplish a specific mission **2.** a group of people and resources temporarily brought together for a specific purpose

task·mas·ter /tásk màstər/ *n* **1.** somebody who assigns and supervises work, especially in a demanding way **2.** a responsibility or discipline that is very demanding or requires a lot of hard work

task·mis·tress /tásk mìstrəss/ *n* a woman who assigns and supervises work, especially in a demanding way

task·work /tásk wùrk/ *n* unpleasant, demanding, or difficult work

Tas·man /tázmən/ administrative region of New Zealand, occupying the northwestern corner of the South Island. Population: 41,352 (2001). Area: 5,613 sq. mi./14,538 sq. km.

Tas·man /tázmən, taáss maàn/, **Abel** (1603?–59) Dutch navigator. Between 1632 and 1655 he made several expeditions to the Indian and Pacific oceans, reaching Tasmania and New Zealand (1642). Tasmania is named for him. Full name **Tasman, Abel Janszoon**

Tas·ma·ni·a /taz máynee ə/ **1.** island in the Tasman Sea, separated from the southeastern coast of Australia by the Bass Strait. Area: 26,380 sq. mi./68,330 sq. km. **2.** state in southeastern Australia, occupying the island of Tasmania. First settled by the British in 1803, it became a separate colony in 1825. Capital: Hobart. Population: 477,100 (2003). Former name **Van Diemen's Land** (1642–1856) —**Tas·ma·ni·an** *n, adj*

Tasmanian devil

Tas·ma·ni·an dev·il *n* a burrowing carnivorous marsupial characterized by a black coat with white markings and large powerful jaws. Native to: formerly, all Australia, but now confined to remote regions of Tasmania. Latin name: *Sarcophilus harrisii.*

Tas·ma·ni·an wolf *n* ZOOL same as **thylacine**

Tas·man Sea /tázmən-/ region of the South Pacific Ocean lying between Australia and New Zealand

Tass /tass/ *n* the official news agency of the former Soviet Union [Early 20C. < Russian, acronym < *Telegrafnoe agentsvo Sovetskogo Soyuza* "Telegraphic Agency of the Soviet Union"]

tasse /tass/ *n* ARMS same as **tasset** [Mid-16C. Origin ?]

tas·sel /táss'l/ *n* **1.** DECORATION MADE OF BUNCHED LOOSE THREADS a bunch of loose parallel threads that are tied together at one end and used as a decoration, e.g., on curtains, cushions, or clothes **2.** AGRIC TUFT AT END OF CORN something resembling a tassel, especially the tuft of male flowers at the top of the main stem of a corn plant ■ *v* (**-seled** or **-selled, -sel·ing** or **-sel·ling, -sels**) **1.** *vt* DECORATE SOMETHING WITH TASSELS to decorate something such as a curtain, cushion, or item of clothing with tassels **2.** *vt* REMOVE TASSEL FROM CORN to remove the tassel from an ear of corn **3.** *vi* AGRIC PRODUCE TUFT ON CORN to produce a tuft of stamens at the end of a flower cluster, especially as seen on an ear of corn [14C. < Old French, "clasp"] —**tas·sel·ly** *adj*

tas·set /tássət/ *n* any of a set of overlapping metal plates attached to and hanging below an armored breastplate in a suit of armor to protect the lower part of the trunk and the thighs [Mid-19C. < French *tassette* < *tasse* "pouch"]

tas·sie /tássee/ *n N England, Scotland* a small cup, glass, or goblet (*archaic*) [Early 18C. < *tass*, via French *tasse* < Arabic *ṭasa* "cup" < Persian *tašt* "bowl"]

taste /tayst/ *n* **1.** SMALL QUANTITY SAMPLED a small quantity of something eaten, drunk, or sampled to assess its effect on the sensory receptors on the surface of the tongue or in the mouth ○ *Can I have a taste of that?* **2.** EXPERIENCE OF SOMETHING a brief sample or experience of something, especially for the first time ○ *a taste of freedom* **3.** LIKING FOR SOMETHING a tendency to like or enjoy something ○ *She has developed a taste for modern art.* **4.** ABILITY TO JUDGE AESTHETICALLY the faculty of making discerning judgments in aesthetic matters ○ *He has good taste.* **5.** SENSE OF SOCIALLY ACCEPTABLE a sense of what is proper or acceptable socially ○ *The remark was in poor taste.* **6.** PHYSIOL SENSE THAT IDENTIFIES FLAVORS the sense that perceives the distinctive qualities of something such as a food by means of the sensory organs in the tongue (**taste buds**) **7.** PHYSIOL SENSATION STIMULATED IN TASTE BUDS the sensation stimulated in the taste buds when food, drink, or other substances are in contact with them. Sweetness, saltiness, bitterness, and sourness are considered the four basic taste sensations, and all flavors combine these in various ways with the sense of smell. ○ *has a salty taste* **8.** PHYSIOL ASSESSMENT OF TASTE OF SOMETHING an act of putting a small amount of something in the mouth in order to try it or test its flavor ■ *vt* (**tast·ed, tast·ing, tastes**) **1.** HAVE PARTICULAR FLAVOR to have a particular effect on the taste buds ○ *This tastes horrible.* **2.** PHYSIOL DISCERN FLAVOR OF SOMETHING to discern the flavor of a substance by means of the taste buds **3.** TEST SOMETHING FOR FLAVOR to put a small amount of food or drink into the mouth in order to try it or to test its flavor ○ *Taste this for salt.* **4.** EXPERIENCE SOMETHING to experience something, especially for the first time or only briefly ○ *He had tasted success.* [13C. < Old French *taster* "to touch"] —**tast·a·ble** *adj*

taste bud *n* a sensory receptor on the surface of the tongue or in the mouth that sends signals to the brain when stimulated by specific chemicals, producing the sense of taste. Taste buds are classified according to the type of substance they respond to: sweet, salty, bitter, or sour.

taste·ful /táystf'l/ *adj* **1.** having or showing good aesthetic taste **2.** having a pleasant flavor —**taste·ful·ly** *adv* —**taste·ful·ness** *n*

taste·less /táystləss/ *adj* **1.** having little or no flavor **2.** showing a lack of taste or judgment in aesthetic or social matters —**taste·less·ly** *adv* —**taste·less·ness** *n*

taste·mak·er /táyst màykər/ *n* somebody who influences decisions about what is tasteful or stylish, e.g., in fashion or the arts

tast·er /táystər/ *n* **1.** JUDGE OF FOOD OR DRINK QUALITY a specialist who tastes food or drink to judge its quality **2.** DEVICE USED FOR TASTING a device or container used for tasting, e.g., a small cup for tasting wine **3.** SOMEBODY TESTING FOR POISON somebody engaged to test an important person's food or drink by sampling it first in case it contains poison

tast·y /táystee/ (**-i·er, -i·est**) *adj* **1.** having a pleasant or full flavor **2.** *US* in good taste —**tast·i·ly** *adv* —**tast·i·ness** *n*

tat /tat/ (**tat·ted, tat·ting, tats**) *vti* to work at tatting, or produce an item by tatting [Late 19C. Back-formation < TATTING]

TAT *abbr* thematic apperception test

ta-ta *interj UK* used as a childish or familiar way of saying goodbye (*informal*) [Early 19C. Origin ?]

ta·ta·mi /tə taámee, taa-/ (*plural same* or **-mis**) *n* a straw mat, used especially in Japanese homes as a floor covering [Early 17C. < Japanese]

Ta·tar /taátər/ *n* **1.** MEMBER OF HISTORICAL CENTRAL ASIAN PEOPLE a member of a people who came from east central Asia and founded an empire stretching into Serbia, Russia, and Ukraine. The Tatars joined with the Mongols, and their combined empire flourished until the 16th century, when they were defeated by the Russians and the Ottoman Turks. **2.** DESCENDANT OF TATARS a descendant of the Tatars. Most now live in an area of European Russia between the Volga River and the Ural Mountains, with communities in Crimea and Siberia. **3.** TATAR LANGUAGE the Turkic language of the Tatars. Native speakers: 6 million. [Early 17C. < Turkish] —**Ta·tar** *adj* —**Ta·tar·i·an** /taa térree ən/ *adj* —**Ta·tar·ic** /taa tárrik/ *adj*

Ta·tar·stan /taàtər stán/ autonomous republic in the plains of the Volga River, central Russia. Capital: Kazan. Population: 3,743,600 (1994). Area: 26,255 sq. mi./68,000 sq. km.

Tate /tayt/, **Allen** (1899–1979) US writer. His poems include "Ode to the Confederate Dead" (1926). Full name **Tate, John Orley Allen**

> "Row after row with strict impunity / The headstones yield their names to the element, / The wind whirrs without recollection."
> [Allen Tate, "Ode to the Confederate Dead," *Collected Poems 1921–76*; 1978]

ta·ter /táytər/ *n regional* FOOD same as **potato** [Mid-18C. Alteration]

Ta·ti /taá teé/, **Jacques** (1908–82) French actor and movie director. He is noted for his wryly humorous movies, in several of which he played the lovably bumbling character Monsieur Hulot. Born **Tatischeff, Jacques**

ta·tie /táytee/ *n regional, UK* FOOD same as **potato** [Late 18C. Alteration]

Tat·lin /táttlin/, **Vladimir** (1885–1953) Russian sculptor and painter. His abstract sculptures made from different industrial materials led to the foundation of constructivism.

~~**tatoo**~~ incorrect spelling of **tattoo**

Ta·tra Moun·tains /taátrə-, táttrə-/ highest range of the Carpathian Mountains of central Europe, extending along the border between Poland and Slovakia. The highest peak is Gerlachovka, 8,711 ft./2,655 m.

tat·ter /táttər/ *n* **1.** RAGGED PIECE OF CLOTH a torn or ragged piece of cloth **2.** RUINED STATE a ruined or damaged state (*usually used in the plural*) ○ *The policy was in tatters.* ■ *vti* (**-tered, -ter·ing, -ters**) BECOME OR MAKE RAGGED to become ragged or torn, or make something do this [15C. < Old Norse *totrar* (plural) "rags"]

tat·ter·de·mal·ion /tàttərdə máylyən, -máylee ən/ *adj* raggedly dressed and unkempt ■ *n* somebody wearing ragged clothes [Early 17C. < TATTERED + ?]

tat·tered /táttərd/ *adj* **1.** RAGGED ragged or torn to shreds **2.** DRESSED IN RAGS dressed in ragged clothes **3.** SHABBY shabby and rundown

tat·ter·sall /táttər sàwl, táttərss'l/ *n* **1.** a pattern of squares or checks formed by dark lines on a light or brightly colored background **2.** cloth with a tattersall pattern [Late 19C. After *Tattersall's* horse market, London, England, from the traditional design of horse blankets]

tat·tie /táttee/ *n Scotland* FOOD same as **potato** (*informal*) [Late 18C. Alteration]

tat·tie-bo·gle /táttee bŏg'l/ *n Scotland* AGRIC same as **scarecrow** (*informal*)

tat·ting /tátting/ *n* **1.** a form of lace made with a shuttle **2.** the process or craft of making tatting [Mid-19C. Origin ?] —**tat·ter** *n*

tat·tle /tátt'l/ *v* (**-tled, -tling, -tles**) **1.** *vi* GOSSIP to gossip about the personal secrets or plans of others **2.** *vti* DISCLOSE SECRET to disclose somebody's personal or private information **3.** *vi* TALK IDLY to talk or chatter idly ■ *n* **1.** SOMEBODY WHO GOSSIPS a gossip or informer **2.** IDLE GOSSIP idle talk, chatter, or gossip [15C. Probably < Middle Flemish *tatelen*, an imitation of the sound]

tat·tler /táttlər/ *n* **1.** somebody who gossips, reveals secrets, or talks idly **2.** a long-legged shorebird related to the sandpipers and noted for its long migrations. Genus: *Heteroscelus.*

tat·tle·tale /tátt'l tàyl/ *n* same as **telltale** *n* (sense 5) (*often used by or to children*) ■ *adj* same as **telltale**

tat·too[1] /ta toó, tə-/ *n* (*plural* **-toos**) a permanent picture, design, or other marking made on the skin by pricking it and staining it with an indelible dye ■ *vt* (**-tooed, -too·ing, -toos**) to mark the skin with a tattoo, or form a tattoo on the skin [Mid-18C. < Polynesian] —**tat·too·er** *n* —**tat·too·ist** *n*

tat·too[2] /ta toó, tə-/ *n* (*plural* **-toos**) **1.** MIL EVENING MILITARY DISPLAY FOR ENTERTAINMENT a military display, often with a variety of items, performed as an entertainment, usually in the evening **2.** CALL TO RETURN TO QUARTERS a bugle or drum call that tells soldiers to return to their quarters in the evening **3.** REGULAR BEATING ON SURFACE a steady rhythmic beating made on a surface such as a drum ○ *the tattoo of rain on a flat roof* ■ *vti* (**-tooed, -too·ing, -toos**) BEAT SOMETHING WITH STEADY

RHYTHM to beat a steady rhythm, or beat with a steady rhythm on something such as a drum [Mid-17C. < Dutch *taptoe* "shut the tap (of the beer barrel)," a signal at closing time in taverns]

tat·ty /táttee/ (**-ti·er, -ti·est**) *adj* shabby, run-down, or in poor condition [Mid-20C. < *tat* "rag"] —**tat·ti·ly** *adv* —**tat·ti·ness** *n*

Ta·tum /táytəm/, **Edward** (1909–75) US geneticist. His work with George W. Beadle on genetic mutations earned them the Nobel Prize in physiology or medicine (1958). Full name **Tatum, Edward Lawrie**

tau /tow, taw/ *n* **1.** the 19th letter of the Greek alphabet, represented in the English alphabet as "t." See table at **alphabet** **2.** BIOCHEM same as **tau protein** [14C. < Greek]

Taube /tawb, towb/, **Henry** (*b.* 1915) Canadian-born US inorganic chemist. His study of electron transfer reactions won him a Nobel Prize (1983).

tau cross *n* a cross shaped like a T

taught past participle, past tense of **teach**

tau neu·tri·no *n* a subatomic particle of the lepton family with no electric charge and a mass less than 69 times that of an electron, created during the decay of a tauon

taunt[1] /tawnt/ *vt* (**taunt·ed, taunt·ing, taunts**) **1.** PROVOKE OR RIDICULE SOMEBODY to provoke, ridicule, or tease somebody in a hurtful or mocking way **2.** TANTALIZE SOMEBODY to tantalize somebody, e.g., by refusing to disclose a secret ■ *n* HURTFUL REMARK a remark intended to provoke, ridicule, or tease somebody in a hurtful or mocking way [Early 16C. < French *tant (pour tant)* "so much (for so much)" < Latin *tantus* "so great"] —**taunt·er** *n* —**taunt·ing** *adj* —**taunt·ing·ly** *adv*

taunt[2] /tawnt/ *adj* describes a ship's mast that is taller than average [Early 17C. Origin ?]

Taun·ton /táwntən/ city in southeastern Massachusetts, on the Taunton River, southeast of Attleboro and north of Fall River. Population: 56,647 (2002 estimate).

Tau·nus /táwnəss, tównəss/ mountain range in west central Germany, extending northeastward from the eastern bank of the Rhine River. Highest peak: 2,887 ft./880 m.

tau·on /táw òn/ *n* an unusually massive subatomic particle of the lepton family with the same charge as an electron, but nearly 3,500 times its mass [Late 20C. < TAU]

taupe /tōp/ *n* a dark brownish gray color [Early 20C. Via French < Latin *talpa* "mole"] —**taupe** *adj*

tau pro·tein *n* a protein that maintains the stability of the microtubules that serve as a transport system within brain cells, but also implicated in the formation of masses of fibrous protein in the brains of people with Alzheimer's disease

Tau·ri ZODIAC plural of **Taurus** (sense 3)

tau·rine[1] /táw rīn/ *adj* relating to or resembling a bull [Early 17C. < Latin *taurinus* < *taurus* "bull"]

tau·rine[2] /táw reen, táwrin/ *n* a crystalline derivative of cysteine found in bile and nerve tissue [Mid-19C. < TAUROCHOLIC ACID]

tau·ro·chol·ic ac·id /tàwrə kòllik-/ *n* a bile acid present as a sodium salt in humans that breaks down to produce taurine [Mid-19C. < Greek *tauros* "bull" + *kholē* "bile"]

tau·rom·ach·y /taw rómməkee/ *n* the activity or skill of bullfighting

Tau·rus /táwrəss/ *n* **1.** CONSTELLATION IN NORTHERN HEMISPHERE a zodiacal constellation of the northern hemisphere located between Aries and Gemini and containing the bright star Aldebaran, the Pleiades and Hyades, and the Crab Nebula. See illustration at **constellation** **2.** ZODIAC SIGN OF ZODIAC the second sign of the zodiac, represented by a bull and lasting from approximately April 20 to May 20. Taurus is classified as an earth sign, and its ruling planet is Venus. **3.** (*plural* **Tau·rus·es** or **Tau·ri**) ZODIAC SOMEBODY BORN UNDER TAURUS somebody whose birthday falls between April 20 and May 20 [14C. < Latin *taurus* "bull"] —**Tau·re·an** *n* —**Tau·rus** *adj*

Tau·rus Moun·tains /tàwrəss-/ mountain range in southern Turkey, parallel to the Mediterranean coast. Its highest peak is Aladag, 12,251 ft./3,734 m.

Taus·sig /tówssig/, **Helen** (1898–1986) US pediatrician. She studied and treated blue babies and played a major role in exposing the dangers of thalidomide to the developing fetus. Born **Helen Brooke**

taut /tawt/ *adj* **1.** STRETCHED TIGHTLY pulled or stretched tightly **2.** PHYSIOL FIRM AND FLEXED flexed and working, as opposed to being in a relaxed state ○ *taut muscles* **3.** STRESSED stressed, tense, or anxious **4.** CONCISE concise and efficient in the use of language or reasoning ○ *taut prose* **5.** NAUT KEPT IN GOOD ORDER trim, tidy, and well-run ○ *runs a taut ship* [13C. Origin ?] —**taut·ly** *adv* —**taut·ness** *n*

taut- *prefix* same as **tauto-** (*used before vowels*)

taut·en /táwt'n/ (**-ened, -en·ing, -ens**) *vti* to become tightly stretched, or stretch something such as a rope tight

tauto- *prefix* the same, identical ○ *tautomer* [< Greek *tauto* "the same thing" < *to* "the" + *auto* "same"]

tau·tog /táw tàwg, taw táwg/ *n* a large dark-colored edible fish of the wrasse family. Native to: Atlantic coast of North America. Latin name: *Tautoga onitis*. [Mid-17C. < Narraganset *tautauog*]

tau·tol·o·gy /taw tóllәjee/ (*plural* **-gies**) *n* **1.** LINGUISTIC REDUNDANCY the redundant repetition of a meaning in a sentence, using different words **2.** INSTANCE OF LINGUISTIC REDUNDANCY an instance of redundant repetition of a meaning in a sentence, using different words **3.** LOGIC LOGICAL TRUE PROPOSITION a proposition or statement that, in itself, is logically true —**tau·to·log·i·cal** /tàwtə lójjik'l/ *adj* —**tau·to·log·i·cal·ly** *adv*

tau·to·mer /táwtəmər/ *n* a compound exhibiting tautomerism [Early 20C. < TAUTO- + ISOMER]

tau·tom·er·ism /taw tómmə rìzzəm/ *n* the property permitting some compounds to exist as a mixture of two isomers that are interconvertible and thus in equilibrium —**tau·to·mer·ic** /tàwtə mérrik/ *adj*

tau·to·nym /táwtə nìm/ *n* a species name in which the epithet for the species is the same as that of the genus, e.g., the name of the filarial worm *Loa loa*. This kind of name is used for animal, but not plant species. —**tau·to·nym·ic** /tàwtə nímmik/ *adj* —**tau·ton·y·my** /taw tónnəmee/ *n*

tav /taaf, taav, tawf, tawv/, **taw** *n* the 23rd and final letter of the Hebrew alphabet, represented in the English alphabet as "t." See table at **alphabet** [Mid-17C. < Hebrew *tāw*]

Ta·vel /taa vél/ *n* a dry rosé wine from southeastern France [Late 19C. After *Tavel*, France]

Tav·en·er /távvənər/, **John** (*b.* 1944) British composer. He is particularly noted for his choral works, which are often based on religious or spiritual themes. Full name **Tavener, John Kenneth**

tav·ern /távvərn/ *n* a café, bar, or inn [13C. Via French *taverne* < Latin *taberna* "hut, inn"]

ta·ver·na /tə vúrnə, taa vérnə/ *n* **1.** a small restaurant or café in Greece or run by Greeks **2.** a guesthouse in Greece that has a bar [Early 20C. Via modern Greek < Latin *taberna* "hut, inn"]

Tav·ern·er /távvərnər/, **John** (1490?–1545) English composer. His complex and elaborate church music is transitional between the late medieval and the Renaissance styles.

taw[1] /taw/ (**tawed, taw·ing, taws**) *vt* to whiten animal skins by applying alum or other mineral salts [Old English *tawian* < Germanic, "make"] —**taw·er** *n*

taw[2] /taw/ *n* **1.** MARBLE USED TO HIT OTHERS a fancy marble that is shot at others **2.** LINE FROM WHICH PLAYER SHOOTS MARBLES in a game of marbles, the line from which a player must shoot **3.** GAME PLAYED WITH MARBLES a game of marbles in which the object is to shoot as many marbles as possible out of a circular area where they have been placed [Early 18C. Origin ?]

taw[3] *n* another spelling of **tav**

ta·wa /taáwə/ *n* a tall forest tree of the laurel family with purple fruit. Native to: New Zealand. Latin name: *Beilschmiedia tawa*. [Mid-19C. < Maori]

taw·dry /táwdree/ *adj* (**-dri·er, -dri·est**) **1.** GAUDY AND OF POOR QUALITY gaudy, cheap in appearance, and of inferior quality **2.** MEAN-SPIRITED mean-spirited and lacking in human decency ■ *n* CHEAP GAUDY FINERY finery that is gaudy, cheap in appearance, and of inferior quality [Early 17C. Shortening of *tawdry lace*, alteration of *St. Audrey's lace*] —**taw·dri·ly** *adv* —**taw·dri·ness** *n*

ORIGIN Anna, Anglo-Saxon king of East Anglia, had a daughter called Etheldreda, who became queen of Northumbria. She had an inordinate fondness in her youth for fine lace neckerchiefs, and when she later developed a fatal tumor of the neck, she regarded it as divine retribution for her former extravagance. After her death in 679 she was canonized and made patron saint of Ely in eastern England. In the Middle Ages fairs were held in her memory, known as "St. Audrey's fairs" (Audrey is a conflated form of Etheldreda), at which lace neckerchiefs were sold. These were often made from cheap gaudy material, and by the 17th century the eroded form ***tawdry*** was being used generally for "cheap and gaudy."

taw·ny /táwnee/ (**-ni·er, -ni·est**) *adj* **1.** of an orangey brown color tinged with gold **2.** describes port wine that has matured for at least ten years in the barrel before bottling and is therefore paler than ruby port [14C. Via Anglo-Norman *tauné* < Old French *tané* < *tan* "tanbark"] —**taw·ni·ness** *n*

taw·ny owl *n* a common round-headed owl with brown or gray feathers, black eyes, tawny markings, and a hooting call. Native to: woods forests from Europe to China. Latin name: *Strix aluco*.

tawse /tawz/, **taws** *Scotland n* a leather strap split at the end, formerly used to punish schoolchildren with a blow to the palm of the hand ■ *vti* (**tawsed, taws·ing, taws·es**) to hit a pupil on the hand with a tawse [Early 16C. Plural of *taw* "lash, whip" < TAW[1]]

tax /taks/ *n* **1.** STRAIN a strain or heavy demand **2.** MONEY PAID TO GOVERNMENT an amount of money levied by a government on its citizens and used to run the government, the country, a state, a county, or a municipality **3.** CHARGE PAID BY MEMBERS an amount charged to members of a club or organization to be used for expenses ■ *vt* (**taxed, tax·ing, tax·es**) **1.** CHARGE TAX ON SOMETHING to charge a tax on something such as a company's or person's income **2.** MAKE DEMANDS ON SOMEBODY OR SOMETHING to strain or make heavy demands on somebody or something ○ *You're starting to tax my patience.* **3.** ACCUSE OR CHARGE SOMEBODY to accuse or charge somebody with an offence ○ *She was taxed for failure to appear in court.* **4.** LAW DETERMINE COSTS OF LITIGATION to determine the costs of litigation and the total amount of costs payable at the end of a trial (*dated*) [13C. Via French < Latin *taxare* "censure, assess" < *tangere* "to touch"] —**tax·a·ble** *adj*, *n* —**tax·er** *n* —**tax·less** *adj*

tax- *prefix* same as **taxo-** (*used before vowels*)

ta·xa ZOOL plural of **taxon**

tax·a·tion /tak sáysh'n/ *n* **1.** SYSTEM OF LEVYING TAXES the system whereby taxes are levied on some types of income, earnings, or purchases **2.** MONEY COLLECTED IN TAXES the amount of money raised by collecting taxes **3.** TAX ON SOMETHING an amount levied as a tax on something —**tax·a·tion·al** *adj*

tax a·void·ance *n* the practice of paying as little tax as possible by claiming all allowable deductions from income

tax break *n* same as **tax relief** (*informal*)

tax-de·duct·i·ble *adj* used to describe an expenditure that can be deducted from taxable income to lower the amount of tax owed by a person or business

tax-de·ferred *adj* not taxable until a later time, often after retirement

tax·eme /ták seem/ *n* a small linguistic feature, e.g., selection, order, or phonetic modification [Mid-20C. < TAXIS] —**tax·e·mic** /tak seémik/ *adj*

tax e·va·sion *n* an illegal activity in which a taxpayer seeks to hide taxable income or claim unauthorized tax deductions

tax-ex·empt *adj* legally exempt from taxation

tax-free *adj* not subject to taxation

tax ha·ven *n* a country with favorable tax rates

tax hol·i·day *n* a period during which a company is exempt from state taxation, e.g., when just starting out in business

tax·i /táksee/ *n* (*plural* **-is** or **-ies**) CAR TAKING PAYING PASSENGERS a car, usually with a taximeter, whose driver is paid to transport passengers, typically for short distances ■ *vti* (**-ied, -i·ing** or **-y·ing, -is** or **-ies**) **1.** TRANSPORT SOMEBODY OR BE TRANSPORTED to transport somebody or something, or be transported, especially in a car (*informal*) ○ *taxi the children to school* **2.** AVIAT MOVE AIRCRAFT ON GROUND to make an aircraft move under its own power on the ground, usually before takeoff or after landing, or move on the ground in this way **3.** TRANSP TAKE OR BE TAKEN IN TAXI to transport somebody or something in a taxi, or be transported in a taxi [Early 20C. Shortening of *taximeter cab*]

taxi- *prefix* same as **taxo-**

tax·i·cab /táksi kàb/ *n* VEHICLES same as **taxi** [Early 20C. Contraction of *taximeter cab*]

tax·i·der·my /táksi dùrmee/ *n* the art or skill of preparing, stuffing, and presenting dead animal skins so that they appear lifelike [Early 19C. < Greek *taxis* "arrangement" (see TAXIS)] —**tax·i·der·mal** /tàksi dúrm'l/ *adj* —**tax·i·der·mist** *n*

tax·i·me·ter /táksee meetər/ *n* a device installed in a taxi that automatically calculates and displays the fare, which is usually based on time, distance traveled, or a combination of both [Late 19C. < French *taximètre* < *taxe* "charge, tariff"]

tax·i·met·rics /tàksə méttriks/ *n* BIOL same as **numerical taxonomy** (*takes a singular verb*)

tax in·cen·tive *n* an incentive in the form of a reduction of, or an exemption from, the tax to which somebody would normally be liable

tax·ing /táksing/ *adj* placing numerous or severe demands on somebody —**tax·ing·ly** *adv*

tax in·spec·tor *n UK* an official whose job is to assess the amount of tax that is payable by a person or organization and ensure the tax is paid

tax·i·plane /táksee plàyn/ *n US* an aircraft that is available for hire

tax·i rank *n UK* same as **taxi stand**

tax·is /táksiss/ *n* **1.** movement of a cell or microorganism toward or away from the source of a stimulus **2.** the manipulating of a displaced body part to return it to its normal position, e.g., in a case of hernia [Late 16C. < Greek, "order, arrangement" < *tassein* "arrange"]

-taxis *suffix* **1.** movement in response to a stimulus ○ *hydrotaxis* **2.** arrangement, order of parts ○ *phyllotaxis* [< Greek *taxis* (see TAXIS)]

tax·i squad *n* in professional football, a group of players who practice with the team but are not allowed to play in official games [Mid-20C. < the use by a football team owner of his reserve players as taxi drivers]

tax·i stand *n* an area reserved for parked taxicabs awaiting customers

tax·i·way /táksee wày/ *n* a path used by aircraft when taxiing to and from a runway or other ground facility

tax loss *n* a transaction that results in a reduced tax liability, even though it may not be associated with an actual cash loss, e.g., the loss associated with depreciation expenses

tax man (*plural* **tax men**) *n* **1.** the taxing authority of a region or nation (*informal*) **2.** somebody who collects taxes

taxo-, **taxi-** *prefix* order, arrangement ○ *taxonomy* [< Greek *taxis* (see TAXIS)]

Tax·ol /ták sàwl/ *tdmk* a trademark for paclitaxel, a drug used in the treatment of cancer

tax·on /ták sòn/ (*plural* **ta·xa** /-sə/ or **tax·ons**) *n* a group to which organisms are assigned according to the principles of taxonomy, including species, genus, family, order, class, and phylum [Early 20C. Back-formation < TAXONOMY]

tax·on·o·my /tak sónnəmee/ (*plural* **-mies**) *n* **1.** GROUPING OF ORGANISMS the science of classifying plants, animals, and microorganisms into increasingly broader categories based on shared features. Traditionally, organisms were grouped by physical resemblances, but in recent times other criteria such as genetic matching have also been used. **2.** PRINCIPLES OF CLASSIFICATION the practice or principles of classification **3.** STUDY OF CLASSIFICATION the study of the rules and practice of classifying living organisms [Early 19C. < French *taxonomie* < Greek *taxis* (see TAXIS)] —**tax·o·nom·ic** /tàksə nómmik/ *adj* —**tax·o·nom·i·cal·ly** *adv* —**tax·on·o·mist** *n*

tax·pay·er /táks pày ər/ *n* somebody who pays taxes, especially income tax —**tax·pay·ing** *adj*

tax rate *n* the percentage of income paid in income taxes

tax re·lief *n* tax savings in the form of allowable deductions, e.g., pension contributions, capital gains losses, and business losses

tax re·turn *n* the set of government forms on which earnings and expenses are recorded in order to calculate the tax liability of a person or business

tax shel·ter *n* an investment activity that tends to reduce income tax liability —**tax-shel·tered** *adj*

-taxy *suffix* order, arrangement ○ *epitaxy* [< Greek *-taxia* < *tag-*, stem of *tassein* "arrange"]

tax year *n* a period of twelve months over which income or profits are calculated for purposes of taxation

Tay /tay/ the longest river in Scotland, flowing eastward through Loch Tay and emptying into the North Sea through the Firth of Tay. Length: 120 mi./190 km.

Tay, Firth of /tay/ estuary of the Tay River on the eastern coast of Scotland, an inlet of the North Sea. It is spanned by the Tay Bridge.

tay·ber·ry /táy bèrree/ (*plural* **-ries**) *n* **1.** a sweet dark red berry that is a cross between a blackberry and a raspberry **2.** a bush that bears tayberries, produced by crossing a blackberry with a raspberry [Late 20C. After the TAY River]

Elizabeth Taylor

Tay·lor /táylər/, **Elizabeth** (*b.* 1932) British-born US movie actor. She became a star while still a child, in *National Velvet* (1944) and won Academy Awards for *Butterfield 8* (1960) and *Who's Afraid of Virginia Woolf?* (1966). She has continued to be in the public eye as a celebrity and an activist on behalf of AIDS patients. Full name **Taylor, Dame Elizabeth Rosemond**

"Success is a great deodorant."
[Elizabeth Taylor, *ABC TV*; April 6, 1977]

Tay·lor, Frederick Winslow (1856–1915) US industrial engineer. He contributed to industrial efficiency by applying "scientific management," based upon time-and-motion studies.

Tay·lor, George (1716–81) Irish-born American patriot. He was a signatory of the Declaration of Independence (1776) as Pennsylvania delegate to the Continental Congress (1776–77).

Tay·lor, Joseph, Jr. (*b.* 1941) US physicist. He shared the Nobel Prize in physics with Russell A. Hulse (1993) for researching binary pulsars. Full name **Joseph Hooton Taylor, Jr.**

Tay·lor, Maxwell D. (1901–87) US general. A hero of World War II and the Korean War, he chaired the US Joint Chiefs of Staff (1962–64) and was involved in the US escalation of the war in Vietnam. Full name **Taylor, Maxwell Davenport**

Tay·lor, Paul (*b.* 1930) US dancer and choreographer who performed with the Martha Graham Company before forming his own company (1955). His best-known works are *Three Epitaphs* (1956) and *Aureole* (1962).

Library of Congress

Zachary Taylor

Tay·lor, Zachary (1784–1850) US military leader and 12th president of the United States. He was a hero of the Mexican War (1846–47) prior to becoming president (1849–50). Known as **Old Rough and Ready**. See table at **president**

Tay·lor ser·ies *n* a basic theorem of calculus relating an approximation of the value of a continuous function at a point to the successive derivatives of the function evaluated at the point [Early 19C. After Brook *Taylor* (1685–1731), English mathematician]

Tay·myr·i·a /tay mīree ə/ autonomous region in north central Siberia, Russia. Capital: Dudinka. Population: 47,300. Area: 332,859 sq. mi./862,100 sq. km.

tay·ra /tīrə/ *n* an agile weasel similar to the marten, with a brown coat and a buff patch on the throat. Native to: South America. Latin name: *Eira barbara*. [Mid-19C. Via Portuguese or Spanish *taira* < Tupi]

Tay-Sachs dis·ease /tày sáks-/ *n* a genetic disease that principally affects Jews of eastern European ancestry, marked by accumulation of lipids in the brain and nerves and resulting in loss of sight and brain functions [Early 20C. After Warren *Tay* (1843–1927), British ophthalmologist, and Bernard *Sachs* (1858–1944), US neurologist]

ta·zi·a /ta zée ə/ *n* a large, decorated, paper and bamboo model of the tomb of either of the martyred grandsons of the prophet Muhammad, paraded during the festival of Muharram [Early 19C. < Arabic *ta'ziya* "mourning, consolation"]

taz·za /táatsə/ *n* an ornamental vessel that has a shallow bowl, usually mounted on a pedestal [Early 19C. Via Italian < Arabic *ṭasa* (see TASSIE)]

Tb *symbol* CHEM ELEM terbium

TB *abbr* **1.** NAVY torpedo boat **2.** *also* **t.b.** ACCT trial balance **3.** *also* **T.B.** MED tuberculosis

TBA, tba *abbr* to be announced

T-ball *n* a form of baseball played by children in which the ball is not pitched, but is rested on a tee in front of the batter

T-bar *n* **1.** a ski tow for two people, shaped like an inverted "T," in which skiers rest against a horizontal bar on each side of a central shaft **2.** a metal bar that is T-shaped in cross section

TBC *abbr* ONLINE to be continued

TBD *abbr* **1.** to be determined **2.** to be discussed

Tbi·li·si /təbə léessee/ capital of the Republic of Georgia, in the east central part of the country, on the Kura River. Population: 1,310,000 (1999).

T-bill *n* FIN same as **Treasury bill**

T-bone steak *n* a large thick steak containing a T-shaped bone

tbs., tbsp. *abbr* MEASURE tablespoon

tc *abbr* ONLINE Turks and Caicos Islands (*used in Internet addresses*) See table at **domain name**

Tc *symbol* CHEM ELEM technetium

TC *abbr* AUTOMOT twin carburetors

TCDD *n* an extremely toxic byproduct of herbicide manufacture. Formula: $C_{12}H_4O_2Cl_4$. Full form **tetrachlorodibenzodioxin**

T cell *n* a white blood cell (**lymphocyte**) that matures in the thymus and is essential for various aspects of immunity, especially in combating viral infections and cancers [< abbreviation of *thymus-derived*]

AKG London

Peter Ilyich Tchaikovsky

Tchai·kov·sky /chī káwfskee/, **Peter Ilyich** (1840–93) Russian composer. He was a major composer of the romantic era, writing works including symphonies, piano concertos, and ballet scores such as *Swan Lake* (1876).

tchotch·ke /chóchkə, -keè/ *n* a trinket or piece of bric-a-brac [Mid-20C. < Yiddish *tshatshke*]

T-com·merce *n* business conducted by means of interactive television

TCP/IP *n* a protocol used for transmitting data between computers and as the basis for standard protocols on the Internet. Full form **transmission control protocol/Internet protocol**

TD *abbr* **1.** ARMS tank destroyer **2.** FOOTBALL touchdown **3.** *also* **T.D.** GOV Treasury Department

TDD *abbr* telecommunications device for the deaf

TDM *abbr* time-division multiplexing

TDY *abbr* MIL temporary duty

te /tee/ *n* MUSIC UK spelling of **ti**[1] [Mid-19C. Alteration of si[1]]

Te *symbol* CHEM ELEM tellurium

tea (sense 5)

tea /tee/ *n* **1.** DRIED LEAVES OF ASIAN PLANT the dried leaves of an Asian plant, often shredded, used to make a drink by adding boiling water **2.** TEA DRINK a drink made with tea, served either hot or iced **3.** DRINK MADE BY INFUSION a drink made by the infusion of plant leaves or flowers ○ *drank some herbal tea* **4.** DRIED LEAVES OR FLOWERS FOR INFUSION dried plant leaves or flowers, e.g., from herbs, used as the basis of a tea drink ○ *bought a packet of herbal tea* **5.** ASIAN EVERGREEN BUSH an evergreen bush with toothed leathery leaves that are dried to make tea. Flowers: fragrant, cup-shaped. Native to: Asia. Latin name: *Camellia sinensis.* **6.** AFTERNOON MEAL a light meal taken in the afternoon, usually consisting of cake, sandwiches, and tea or other nonalcoholic drinks, or an afternoon social event at which this meal is eaten **7.** *UK* EVENING MEAL a meal eaten early in the evening **8.** BREAKFAST in Guyana, the first meal of the day **9.** DRUGS same as **marijuana** (*dated slang*) [Mid-17C. Probably via Dutch *tee* and Malay *teh* < Chinese (Amoy dialect) *te*]

SPELLCHECK tea or **tee**? Do not confuse the spelling of ***tea*** and ***tee***, which sound similar. ***Tea*** is a hot drink, a plant used to make it, or a light meal at which it is drunk, as in *a cup of tea, tea leaves, a tea party.* ***Tee*** can refer to a peg used in golf or to a T-shirt; the golf word ***tee*** is also used as a verb, as in *teed off at the 18th hole.*

tea bag *n* a small bag made of permeable paper or cloth containing tea leaves that is placed in boiling water to make one serving of tea

tea ball *n* a small perforated metal ball for holding tea leaves that is placed in boiling water to make tea

tea·ber·ry /teè bèrree/ (*plural* **-ries**) *n* PLANTS **1.** same as **wintergreen** (sense 1) **2.** same as **withe rod** [Late 18C. Because the leaves can be used as a substitute for tea]

tea cad·dy *n* a small container, usually with a tight-fitting lid, for holding tea leaves

tea·cake /teè kàyk/ *n US* a plain cookie, cake, or biscuit served with tea

tea cart *n* HOUSEHOLD same as **tea wagon**

tea cer·e·mo·ny *n* a Japanese ritual in which tea is prepared, served, and drunk in a prescribed manner

teach /teech/ (**taught** /tawt/, **teach·ing, teach·es**) *v* **1.** *vt* IMPART KNOWLEDGE TO SOMEBODY to impart knowledge or skill to somebody by instruction or example ○ *taught me how to drive* **2.** *vti* GIVE LESSONS IN SUBJECT to give lessons in or provide information about a subject ○ *taught Spanish to them* **3.** *vti* GIVE LESSONS TO SOMEBODY to give lessons to a person or animal ○ *teaches the students on Wednesdays* **4.** *vt* MAKE SOMEBODY UNDERSTAND SOMETHING to bring understanding of something to somebody, especially through an experience ○ *The experience taught me a lesson I'll never forget.* **5.** *vti* TEACH REGULARLY to be a teacher in an institution ○ *teaches college* **6.** *vt* ADVOCATE SOMETHING to advocate or preach something ○ *a philosophy that teaches nonviolence* [Old English *tǣcan* < Indo-European, "to show"] —**teach·a·ble** *adj*

SYNONYMS ***teach, educate, train, instruct, coach, tutor, school, drill***

CORE MEANING: to impart knowledge or skill in something

teach to impart knowledge or skill to somebody by instruction or example ○ *He taught math at the school for 21 years.* ○ *He taught me a great deal about crosswords, and I taught him how to swim.* **educate** to give knowledge to or develop the abilities of somebody by teaching, in school and elsewhere ○ *dispute over the best way of educating children according to their needs* ○ *The police stress that they want to educate bad drivers as much as prosecute them.* **train** to teach the skills necessary for a task or job by means of instruction, observation, and practice ○ *It is important for professionals to be trained to work with volunteers.* ○ *We hired new staff and trained them in skills ranging from bookkeeping to business administration.* **instruct** to teach somebody a subject, methodology, or skill ○ *a manual instructing users how to run the computer software* ○ *We got a professional to instruct us in scuba-diving.* **coach** to give somebody private instruction in a particular subject, prepare somebody for an examination, or teach sporting, artistic, or life skills ○ *On Saturdays I used to coach the local softball team.* ○ *When he's not playing himself, he spends his time coaching promising young players.* **tutor** to give somebody individual tuition in a subject or skill ○ *A blues guitarist of considerable talent, he has been tutoring my son for years.* **school** to train somebody in a skill or area of expertise in a thorough and detailed way ○ *She was schooled in classical drawing in Rome.* ○ *Even before college, he was being schooled to take over the family business.* **drill** to make somebody repeat a sequence of exercises or procedures over and over again in order to learn it ○ *The most common intonation patterns should be drilled early in the course.* ○ *The recruits were drilled endlessly on the parade ground.*

teach·er /teéchər/ *n* **1.** somebody who teaches, especially as a profession **2.** an occurrence, idea, or object from which something may be learned ○ *Experience is a great teacher.* —**teach·er·ly** *adj*

teach·er bird *n* BIRDS same as **ovenbird** (sense 1) [An imitation of its call]

teach·ers col·lege, teach·ers' col·lege *n* a college for the training of teachers

teach·er's pet *n* **1.** a student who is especially favored by a teacher and consequently resented by other students (*insult*) **2.** a special favorite of somebody in authority

teach-in *n* an extended period of speeches, lectures, and discussions, usually held at a college or university as part of a political or social protest

teach·ing /teéching/ *n* **1.** TEACHER'S PROFESSION the profession or practice of being a teacher **2.** SOMETHING TAUGHT something that is taught, e.g., a point of doctrine (*often used in the plural*) ■ *adj* **1.** FOR TEACHING used for or in teaching **2.** THAT TEACHES being a person or establishment that teaches

teach·ing as·sis·tant *n* a graduate student in a college or university who teaches, especially undergraduates, in return for tuition and usually a small stipend —**teach·ing as·sis·tant·ship** *n*

teach·ing hos·pi·tal *n* a hospital that provides supervised practical training for medical students, student nurses, or other healthcare professionals, often in conjunction with a medical school

teach·ing prac·tice *n UK* same as **practice teaching**

tea co·zy *n* a soft padded cover for keeping a teapot warm

tea·cup /teè kùp/ *n* **1.** a small-to-medium-sized cup, usually used with a saucer, especially for serving tea **2.** *also* **tea·cup·ful** /teè kup fo͝ol/ the amount a teacup holds

tea dance *n* an afternoon social event at which people dance with partners and tea may be served

tea gar·den *n* **1.** a garden or outdoor restaurant where tea and light refreshments are served to the public **2.** a plantation where tea is grown

tea gown *n* a loose, usually waistless, dress of light thin fabric trimmed with lace, worn by women in the late 19th century for afternoon social occasions at which men would not be present

tea·house /teè hòwss/ (*plural* **-hous·es** /-hòwzəz/) *n* especially in China or Japan, a restaurant that serves tea and light refreshments

teak /teek/ *n* **1.** INDUST DURABLE WOOD the durable red-brown wood of a South and Southeast Asian tree. Use: furniture, shipbuilding. **2.** TREES TALL ASIAN TREE a tall tree valued for its timber. Native to: South Asia, Myanmar, Malay Archipelago. Latin name: *Tectona grandis.* **3.** INDUST, TREES WOOD OR TREE LIKE TEAK a wood or tree similar to true teak **4.** COLORS YELLOWISH BROWN a yellowish brown color [Late 17C. Via Portuguese < Tamil or Malayalam *tēkku*] —**teak** *adj*

tea·ket·tle /teè kètt'l/ *n* a kettle used for boiling water

teak·wood /teèk wo͝od/ *n* INDUST same as **teak** (sense 1)

teal /teel/ (*plural same* or **teals**) *n* **1.** a greenish blue color **2.** a small freshwater surface-feeding duck with bright iridescent blue or green patches on the wings. Genus: *Anas.* [13C. Origin ?] —**teal** *adj*

tea leaf *n* **1.** a dried leaf or shredded part of the dried leaf of the tea plant, used to make tea **2.** a tea leaf, or part of a leaf, after it has been infused (*often used in the plural*)

team /teem/ *n* **1.** SIDE IN SPORTS COMPETITION a group of people forming one side in a sports competition **2.** COOPERATIVELY FUNCTIONING GROUP a number of people organized to function cooperatively as a group **3.** ANIMALS WORKED TOGETHER two or more animals worked together, especially to pull a vehicle or agricultural equipment **4.** TEAM OF ANIMALS WITH VEHICLE a team of animals and the vehicle harnessed to them **5.** ANIMALS PERFORMING TOGETHER a group of animals that perform or are shown together **6.** GROUPING OF ANIMALS a grouping of animals, e.g., a flock, brood, or herd ■ *v* (**teamed, team·ing, teams**) **1.** *vti* FORM INTO TEAM to form a team, or put people or animals together to form a team ○ *teamed together to organize the parade* **2.** *vti* PUT SOMETHING WITH COMPLEMENTARY OBJECT to combine something with another object, particularly one that matches or complements it **3.** *vt* TRANSPORT SOMETHING BY TEAM to transport something using a team of animals **4.** *vi* DRIVE TEAM to drive a team of farm animals or a truck [Old English *tēam* < Indo-European, "to lead"]

SPELLCHECK team or **teem**? Do not confuse the spelling of ***team*** and ***teem***, which sound similar. ***Team*** can be used as a noun or verb, referring to a group of people or animals who work together, as in *a team of designers, a team of oxen, teaming up with a former rival.* Both words spelled ***teem*** are only used as verbs, one meaning "have an extremely large number in a place," the other "rain very hard" and "pour out": *The river teemed with fish. It's teeming down outside.*

team build·ing *n* activities designed to encourage people to work cooperatively

team·mate /teém mày̆t/ *n* a member of the same team as somebody else

tea mon·ey *n Hong Kong* money offered to somebody as a bribe or in return for services provided (*informal*)

team play·er *n* a member of a group who cooperates with other people and who subordinates personal interests in order to achieve a common goal

team spir·it *n* an enthusiastic attitude toward working productively with a team or work group

team·ster /teémstər/ *n* **1.** a driver of a truck that is used commercially for hauling loads **2.** a driver of a team of animals used for hauling

Team·ster *n* a member of the Teamsters Union

Team·sters Un·ion *n* a labor union, the International Brotherhood of Teamsters, Chauffeurs, Warehousemen, and Helpers of America, whose members are mainly truck drivers

team teach·ing *n* an instructional program involving two or more subjects that are taught in a coordinated way by specialist teachers

team·work /teém wùrk/ *n* **1.** a cooperative effort by a group or team **2.** work produced by a group or team

tea par·ty *n* an afternoon social event at which tea is served

tea·pot /teé pòt/ *n* a covered container with a spout and handle, used for making and serving tea

tea·poy /teé pòy/ *n* **1.** a small three-legged ornamental table or stand **2.** a small table used to hold a tea caddy and tea service [Early 19C. By folk etymology (after TEA) < Hindi *tipāī*, alteration of Persian *si-pāya* "three-footed"]

tear[1] /ter/ *v* (**tore** /tawr/, **torn** /tawrn/, **tear·ing, tears**) **1.** *vti* PULL OR COME APART to pull something such as paper or cloth into pieces, or come apart or rip ○ *She tore open the package.* **2.** *vt* MAKE HOLE IN SOMETHING to make a hole or opening in something such as a garment, leaving jagged edges ○ *tore her skirt on a nail* **3.** *vt* CUT SOMETHING UNEVENLY to cut something, especially flesh, leaving jagged edges **4.** *vt* SPRAIN BODY PART to injure a muscle or ligament so that some of the tissue is pulled apart and separated **5.** *vt* SEPARATE SOMETHING BY FORCE to remove or separate something using force **6.** *vti* CAUSE MENTAL PAIN to cause somebody extreme distress or emotional conflict ○ *The memory tore at his heart.* **7.** *vt* DISRUPT SOMETHING to divide or fragment something ○ *an organization that was torn by internal conflict* **8.** *vi* MOVE OR ACT QUICKLY OR CARELESSLY to move or act with great or careless speed (*informal*) ○ *tearing down the road* ■ *n* **1.** RESULT OF TEARING a hole or split caused by tearing **2.** TEARING OF SOMETHING an act of tearing something **3.** HURRY a hurry or rush **4.** SPREE an unrestrained activity or indulgence (*informal*) [Old English *teran* < Indo-European, "to split"] —**tear·a·ble** *adj* —**tear·er** *n*

SPELLCHECK See ***tare***[1].

SYNONYMS ***tear, rend, rip, split***

CORE MEANING: to pull or come apart by force

tear to pull something such as paper or cloth into pieces, or come apart ○ *He tore the paper into little strips.* ○ *She was always climbing trees and tearing her clothes.* **rend** to pull something apart violently, or be pulled apart violently ○ *Something exploded with a sound of rending wood and metal and shattering glass.* **rip** to roughly tear something apart or off, or become torn in this way ○ *She ripped open the envelope.* ○ *You can't wear those flimsy clothes skateboarding – if you fall off, you'll rip them to shreds.* **split** to divide something with a single movement, usually by force and into two parts ○ *found him splitting wood to start a fire* ○ *Split the cake in half horizontally and sandwich it together with frosting.*

tear apart *vt* **1.** DESTROY SOMETHING to destroy something by shattering it into pieces **2.** FRAGMENT GROUP OF PEOPLE to cause division, separation, or conflict in a group or organization ○ *War tore the family apart.* **3.** DISTRESS SOMEBODY to cause somebody extreme distress or emotional conflict ○ *the strain of separation was tearing us apart* **4.** SEARCH SOMETHING to search a place thoroughly, often causing disruptions and mess ○ *The police tore the house apart looking for evidence.*

tear away *vt* to force or reluctantly persuade yourself or somebody else to leave a place or object ○ *tore herself away from the festivities*

tear down *vt* to demolish, destroy, or dismantle something such as a building

tear into *vt* to attack somebody or something vigorously, either physically or verbally

tear off *vt* **1.** to remove a covering quickly and carelessly ○ *He tore off his shirt.* **2.** to produce something quickly and carelessly

tear up *vt* to tear something into small pieces, e.g., in order to destroy it

tear[2] /teer/ *n* **1.** DROP OF FLUID FROM EYE a single drop of salty fluid secreted by the lacrimal gland of the eye **2.** DROP OF LIQUID a drop of liquid or hardened fluid, especially one with a round base and narrower top ○ *tears of rain running down the window* ■ **tears** *npl* **1.** EXCESS OF LIQUID IN EYES a greater than usual amount of liquid produced by the eye or eyes, often accompanying intense emotions, or caused by irritation of the eye **2.** CRYING weeping accompanied by intense emotion **3.** LIQUID BATHING EYE the salty liquid secreted by the lacrimal gland that moistens and protects the surface of the eye and its surrounding tissue ■ *vi* (**teared, tear·ing, tears**) PRODUCE TEARS to produce tears, especially in excessive amounts ○ *My eyes tear a lot during the allergy season.* [Old English *tēar* < Indo-European] —**tear·less** *adj*

SPELLCHECK tear or **tier**? Do not confuse the spelling of ***tear*** and ***tier***, which sound similar. A ***tear*** is a drop of fluid secreted by the eye, as in *burst into tears*. A ***tier*** is a row or layer one above the other or a level of a hierarchy, as in *a two-tier system of taxation.*

tear·down /tér dòwn/ *n* **1.** a building that is scheduled to be demolished, either because it is in poor condition or in order to build a new structure on its site **2.** the process or an instance of tearing something down

tear·drop /teér dròp/ *n* **1.** PHYSIOL same as **tear**[2] (sense 1) **2.** something shaped like a teardrop

tear duct /teér-/ *n* a passage that conveys tears, especially the duct that drains tears from the inner corner of the eye into the nasal cavity

tear·ful /teérf'l/ *adj* **1.** crying, about to cry, or feeling like crying, usually because of an emotion such as great sadness **2.** sad enough to cause weeping ○ *a tearful occasion* —**tear·ful·ly** *adv* —**tear·ful·ness** *n*

tear gas /teér-/ *n* a chemical agent, delivered by a grenade or other means, that incapacitates somebody by irritating the eyes —**tear-gas** *vt*

tear·ing /térring/ *adj* violent or frenzied ○ *in a tearing hurry*

tear·jerk·er /teér jùrkər/ *n* a story or artistic work that is excessively sentimental (*informal*) —**tear-jerk·ing** *adj*

tear-off /tér-/ *adj* produced in a block of paper in sheet form, or perforated, so that individual pieces can be removed easily

tea·room /teé ròom, -ròom/ *n* a restaurant or café serving tea and other beverages, as well as light refreshments (*often used in the plural*)

tea rose *n* a cultivated bushy or climbing rose. Flowers: large, tea-scented, pale pink or yellow. Native to: China. Latin name: *Rosa odorata.*

tear sheet /tér-/ *n* a single page taken from a magazine or other periodical, often used to prove to an advertiser that an advertisement has been published

tear·stain /teér stàyn/ *n* a mark or track left by tears —**tear-stained** *adj*

tear·y /teéree/ (**-i·er, -i·est**) *adj* **1.** WET WITH TEARS wet with or full of tears **2.** ABOUT TO CRY seeming to be about to cry **3.** CAUSING WEEPING causing or sad enough to cause weeping **4.** LIKE TEARS resembling tears —**tear·i·ly** *adv* —**tear·i·ness** *n*

tear·y-eyed *adj* **1.** with tears in the eyes, especially caused by emotion **2.** characterized by weeping, especially when caused by sadness

tease /teez/ *v* (**teased, teas·ing, teas·es**) **1.** *vti* MAKE FUN OF SOMEBODY to make fun of somebody, either playfully or maliciously **2.** *vti* DELIBERATELY ANNOY SOMEBODY to deliberately annoy or irritate a person or an animal **3.** *vt* PERSUADE SOMEBODY BY COAXING to urge somebody, especially to do something, by continual coaxing **4.** *vt* AROUSE FEELING WITHOUT GIVING SATISFACTION to arouse hope, curiosity, or especially physical desire in somebody with no intention of giving satisfaction **5.** *vt* HAIR MAKE HAIR LOOK THICKER to comb the hair with quick short movements toward the roots so that it stands up away from the head **6.** *vt* TEXTILES PULL FIBERS APART to pull fibers apart by combing or carding **7.** *vt* TEXTILES RAISE NAP BY COMBING to raise the nap on cloth by combing it with a wire brush **8.** *vt* BIOL SEPARATE TISSUE to separate the parts of a tissue specimen gently with a needle in preparation for examination under a microscope ■ *n* **1.** SOMEBODY WHO TEASES PLAYFULLY somebody who has a tendency to make fun of or annoy others **2.** SOMEBODY WHO TEASES SEXUALLY somebody who teases somebody else sexually **3.** PROVOCATIVE OPENING REMARK an opening remark or action intended to stimulate curiosity or interest **4.** ACT OF TEASING an act of teasing somebody or something [Old English *tǣsan* < W Germanic] —**teas·ing** *adj* —**teas·ing·ly** *adv*

tease out *vt* **1.** to gradually separate things that are tangled up, or gradually separate something from an object with which it is entangled **2.** to gradually extract something such as the truth or information

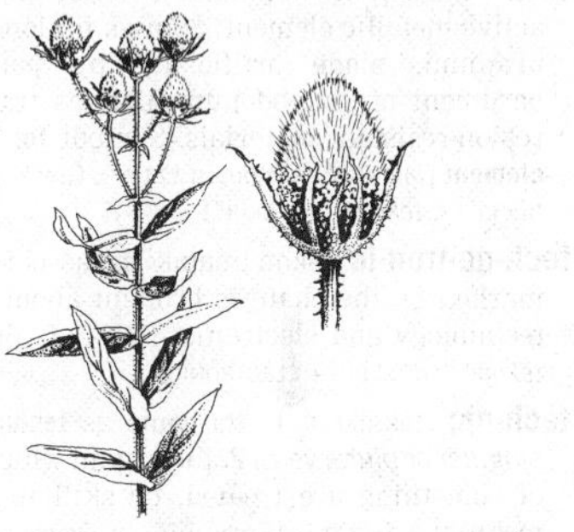

teasel

tea·sel /teéz'l/, **tea·zel, tea·zle** *n* **1.** PRICKLY PLANT a prickly plant with flowers covered with hooked leaves (**bracts**). Native to: Europe, Asia. Genus: *Dipsacus.* **2.** TEASEL FLOWER HEADS the flower heads of the teasel. Use: formerly, to raise fabric nap in the textile industry. **3.** IMPLEMENT USED TO RAISE NAP an industrial implement or device used to raise the nap on fabric [Old English *tǣsel* < W Germanic]

teas·er /teézər/ *n* **1.** same as **tease** *n* (sense 1) **2.** TRICKY PROBLEM a tricky or difficult problem or question **3.** MARKETING ADVERTISEMENT OFFERING GIFT an advertisement offering something free such as a bonus or gift **4.** MEDIA PREVIEW OF SHOW, BOOK, OR MOVIE a preview intended to arouse curiosity and interest in a forthcoming broadcast or publication (*informal*) **5.** INDUST IMPLEMENT FOR TEASING WOOL an implement or device for teasing fibers, especially wool

tea ser·vice, tea set *n* a set of matching articles used for serving tea, e.g., cups, saucers, and a teapot

tea·shop /teé shòp/ *n* COMM same as **tearoom**

tea·spoon /teé spoon/ *n* **1.** SMALL SPOON a small spoon, used especially for stirring tea and other beverages and for eating desserts **2.** *also* **tea·spoon·ful** /teé spoon fòol/ AMOUNT TEASPOON HOLDS the amount of a liquid or solid held by a teaspoon **3.** *also* **tea·spoon·ful** ONE-THIRD OF TABLESPOON a standard household measure equal to one-third of a tablespoon or 5 ml

teat /teet, tit/ *n* **1.** a protuberance on the breast or udder of a female mammal through which milk is excreted for the nourishment of young **2.** *UK* same as **nipple** (sense 2) [12C. < Old French *tete* < Germanic] —**teat·ed** *adj*

tea ta·ble *n* a small table at which tea is served

tea·time /tée tìm/ *n* **1.** the usual time at which tea is served, typically mid- or late afternoon **2.** *UK* the time at which the evening meal is served

tea tow·el *n UK* same as **dishtowel**

tea tray *n* a tray intended for carrying a tea service

tea tree *n* a tree or bush from whose leaves an antiseptic oil (**tea tree oil**) is obtained. Use: in cosmetics, lotions. Native to: Australia, New Zealand. Genus: *Leptospermum*.

tea trol·ley *n Can, UK* same as **tea wagon**

tea wag·on *n* a small household cart from which tea can be served

tea·zel, **tea·zle** *n* PLANTS, INDUST another spelling of **teasel**

Te·bet *n* JUDAISM, CALENDAR another spelling of **Tevet**

tech /tek/ (*informal*) *n* **1.** OCCUPATIONS same as **technician 2.** SCI same as **technology 3.** a technical college or institute ○ *Cal Tech* **4.** THEATER same as **technical rehearsal** ■ *adj* SCI technical or technological ○ *left behind by tech advances* [Early 20C. Shortening]

tech. *abbr* **1.** technical **2.** technician **3.** technology

tech cit·y *n* a town or city where a large number of people are employed in advanced technology industries, especially those connected with computing and electronic engineering

teched *adj US* another spelling of **tetched**

tech·ie /tékee/, **tek·kie** *n* somebody who is interested in, adept at, or a student of a technology, especially one based on computing or electronics (*informal*) [Mid-20C. < TECHNICAL]

tech·ne·ti·um /tek neéshee əm/ *n* a silvery gray radioactive metallic element. Source: fission products of uranium, made artificially by particle bombardment of molybdenum. Use: as tracer, in corrosion-resistant materials. Symbol **Tc**. See table at **element** [Mid-20C. < modern Latin < Greek *tekhnētos* "artificial" < *tekhnē* "art, skill"]

tech·ne·tron·ic /tèknə trónnik/ *adj* associated with or marked by the changes brought about by modern technology and electronics [Mid-20C. Blend of Greek *tekhnē* "art, skill" + ELECTRONIC]

tech·nic /téknik/ *n* **1.** SCI same as **technics** (*takes a singular or plural verb*) **2.** the way in which the basics of something are treated, or skill in handling a technique (*dated*) [Early 17C. < Greek *tekhnikos* (see TECHNICAL)]

tech·ni·cal /téknik'l/ *adj* **1.** RELATING TO INDUSTRY OR APPLIED SCIENCE relating to or specializing in industrial techniques or subjects or applied science **2.** MECHANICAL relating to the operation of a machine, system, or technique ○ *The Internet connection is down because of a technical fault.* **3.** BELONGING TO SPECIALIZED AREA belonging to or involving a specialized subject, field, or profession ○ *a technical glossary* **4.** STRICTLY INTERPRETED according with a strict interpretation of rules or words **5.** SKILLED IN PRACTICAL SUBJECTS skilled in practical or scientific subjects **6.** EXHIBITING TECHNIQUE exhibiting or deriving from technique or the use of technique ○ *a high level of technical expertise* **7.** FIN ANALYZING PRICES AND MARKET INDICATORS describes a type of security analysis based on past prices and volume levels as well as other market indicators **8.** CLOTHING HIGH-TECH describes outdoor clothing that has been made using state-of-the-art materials and techniques ○ *Our technical fleece jacket has advanced dual construction.* ■ *n* **1.** BASKETBALL same as **technical foul 2.** ARMED PICKUP TRUCK a civilian pickup truck equipped with, e.g., a machine gun, rocket-propelled grenade launcher, or antitank gun, used by irregulars or militia in counterinsurgency operations [Early 17C. < Greek *tekhnikos* "of art or skill" < *tekhnē* "art, skill"] —**tech·ni·cal·ly** *adv*

tech·ni·cal draw·ing *n* a precise scale drawing of something, usually professionally prepared for architectural, engineering, or industrial purposes, showing dimensions or quantities

tech·ni·cal foul *n* in basketball, a foul against a player or coach for unsporting behavior or language rather than for physical contact with an opponent

tech·ni·cal·i·ty /tèkni kállətee/ (*plural* **-ties**) *n* **1.** POINT UNDERSTOOD ONLY BY SPECIALISTS a piece of information that is understood by or relevant only to a specialist, e.g., a detail or a term **2.** TRIVIAL POINT FROM STRICTLY APPLYING RULES a minor point arising from a rigorous interpretation of laws or rules ○ *a legal technicality* **3.** QUALITY OF BEING TECHNICAL the quality or condition of being technical

tech·ni·cal knock·out *n* in boxing, a decision that ends a match because one of the participants is too badly injured to continue fighting

tech·ni·cal re·hears·al *n* a rehearsal of a play or other theatrical presentation for the purpose of making sure that lights, sound, and any other technical effects are cued correctly and in working order

tech·ni·cal ser·geant *n* a noncommissioned officer in the US Air Force of a rank above staff sergeant

tech·ni·cal sup·port *n* a repair or advice service offered to customers by some computer hardware and software manufacturers, usually by telephone, fax, or e-mail

tech·ni·cian /tek nísh'n/ *n* **1.** SPECIALIST IN INDUSTRIAL TECHNIQUES somebody who is skilled in industrial techniques or the practical application of a science **2.** LABORATORY EMPLOYEE somebody employed to do practical work in a laboratory **3.** SOMEBODY HIGHLY SKILLED somebody who has mastered an artistic, athletic, or other specialized skill at a high level ○ *She's a superb technician who plays with lightning speed.*

Tech·ni·col·or /tékni kùllər/ *tdmk* a trademark for an early color process for making movies that used three-color separation negatives and a dye transfer process with three matrices made from the negatives

tech·nics /tékniks/ *n* the science or rules of a field of knowledge, especially a technical one (*takes a singular or plural verb*)

tech·ni·kon *n S Africa* a technical college or technical university

~~**technique**~~ incorrect spelling of **technique**

tech·nique /tek néek/ *n* **1.** PROCEDURE OR SKILL REQUIRED the procedure, skill, or art used in a specific task **2.** TREATMENT OF BASICS the way in which the basics of something such as an artistic work or a sport are treated **3.** SKILL POSSESSED skill or expertise in doing a specific thing ○ *a pianist with superb technique* **4.** SPECIAL ABILITY a special ability or knack [Early 19C. < French < Greek *tekhnikos* (see TECHNICAL)]

tech·no /téknō/ *n* electronic dance music characterized by its quick tempo and use of digitally synthesized instruments [Late 20C. Shortening of TECHNOLOGY]

techno- *prefix* technology, technological ○ *technophobia* [Shortening]

tech·no·bab·ble /téknō bàbb'l/ *n* language in which technical terms are overused

tech·noc·ra·cy /tek nókrəssee/ (*plural* **-cies**) *n* **1.** a social system in which scientists, engineers, and technicians have high social standing and political power **2.** a philosophy that advocates the enlistment of a bureaucracy of highly trained engineers, scientists, or technicians to run the government and society

tech·no·crat /téknə kràt/ *n* **1.** a bureaucrat who is intensively trained in engineering, economics, or a form of technology **2.** a proponent of government by technicians —**tech·no·crat·ic** /tèknə kráttik/ *adj*

tech·no·freak /téknō freek/ *n* a technical expert in, or obsessive enthusiast of, information systems (*informal*)

technol. *abbr* SCI technology

tech·nol·o·gize /tek nóllə jìz/ (**-gized, -giz·ing, -giz·es**) *vti* to modify or modernize something by introducing technology, or be modified or modernized by the introduction of technology

tech·nol·o·gy /tek nólləjee/ (*plural* **-gies**) *n* **1.** APPLICATION OF TOOLS AND METHODS the study, development, and application of devices, machines, and techniques for manufacturing and productive processes ○ *recent developments in seismographic technology* **2.** METHOD OF APPLYING TECHNICAL KNOWLEDGE a method or methodology that applies technical knowledge or tools ○ *a new technology for accelerating incubation* ○*"...Maryland-based firm uses database and Internet technology to track a company's consumption of printed goods..."* (*Forbes Global Business and Finance*; November 1998) **3.** MACHINES AND SYSTEMS machines, equipment, and systems considered as a unit ○ *the latest laser technology* **4.** CULTL ANTHROP SUM OF PRACTICAL KNOWLEDGE the sum of a society's or culture's practical knowledge, especially with reference to its material culture [Early 17C. < Greek *tekhnologia* "systematic treatment" < *tekhnē* "art, skill"] —**tech·no·log·ic** /tèknə lójjik/ *adj*—**tech·no·log·i·cal** *adj*—**tech·no·log·i·cal·ly** *adv*—**tech·nol·o·gist** *n*

tech·no·phile /téknə fìl/ *n* a lover of new technology or computerization

tech·no·phobe /téknə fōb/ *n* somebody who dislikes new technology or computerization

tech·no·pho·bi·a /téknə fōbee ə/ *n* fear of or resistance to new technology or computerization

tech·no·struc·ture /téknō strùkchər/ *n* a network of controlling technocrats in an organization or society

tech·no·thril·ler /téknō thrìllər/ *n* a suspenseful book or movie in which the plot turns on seemingly plausible technological wonders

tech·y *adj* another spelling of **tetchy**

~~**tecnical**~~ incorrect spelling of **technical**

~~**tecnique**~~ incorrect spelling of **technique**

tec·ta ANAT plural of **tectum**

tec·ton·ic /tek tónnik/ *adj* **1.** relating to the forces that produce movement and deformation of the Earth's crust **2.** relating to construction and architecture [Mid-17C. Via late Latin < Greek *tektonikos* < *tekton* "builder, carpenter"] —**tec·ton·i·cal·ly** *adv*

tec·ton·ic plate *n* a segment of the Earth's crust that moves relative to other segments and is characterized by volcanic and seismic activity around its margins

tec·ton·ics /tek tónniks/ *n* (*takes a singular verb*) **1.** the study of the mechanisms and results of large-scale movement of the Earth's crust, e.g., that producing mountain ranges and extensive fault systems **2.** the science or practice of building construction

tec·trix /téktriks/ (*plural* **-tri·ces** /-tri séez/) *n* BIRDS same as **covert** *n* (sense 3) [Late 19C. < modern Latin < Latin *tect-*, past participle of *tegere* "to cover"] —**tec·tri·cial** /tek trísh'l/ *adj*

tec·tum /téktəm/ (*plural* **-ta** /-tə/) *n* a part in the body that forms a covering or is arranged like a roof, especially the back upper section of the midbrain [Early 20C. < Latin, "roof" < *tegere* "to cover"] —**tec·tal** *adj*

Te·cum·seh /tə kúmssə/ (1768?–1813) Shawnee leader. He attempted to form an alliance of Native North American peoples to fight against US expansion into the Midwest. He was killed in battle fighting on the British side in the War of 1812 (1812–14).

> "Where today are the Pequot? Where are the Narraganset, the Mohican, the Pocanet, and other powerful tribes of our people? They have vanished before the avarice and oppression of the white man, as snow before the summer sun."
> [Tecumseh. Quoted in *Bury My Heart at Wounded Knee*, Dee Brown; 1970]

ted /ted/ (**ted·ded, ted·ding, teds**) *vt* to spread or shake up mown grass in order to dry it when making hay [15C. < Old Norse *teðja* "spread (manure)"]

ted·der /téddər/ *n* a machine or person that spreads or shakes up mown grass so that it can dry during hay making

ted·dy[1] /téddee/ (*plural* **-dies**) *n* same as **teddy bear** [Early 20C. See TEDDY BEAR]

ted·dy[2] /téddee/ (*plural* **-dies**) *n* a woman's one-piece undergarment serving as both bra and panties [Early 20C. Origin ?]

ted·dy bear *n* a furry stuffed toy in the shape of a stylized bear cub [Early 20C. After Theodore ("*Teddy*") ROOSEVELT]

ORIGIN President Theodore Roosevelt was fond of bear-hunting. His nickname, "Teddy," was used in a humorous poem in the *New York Times* about the adventures of two bears. Their names (Teddy B and Teddy G) were then appropriated to two bears in the Bronx Zoo whose popularity caused toy manufacturers to market toy bears as ***teddy bears***.

ted·dy boy, Ted·dy boy *n* a young man in the United Kingdom in the 1950s and early 1960s who followed the fashion of dressing in Edwardian style with tight narrow trousers, pointed shoes, and long sideburns [Mid-20C. Nickname for *Edward*, alluding to EDWARD VII]

Te De·um /tay dáy əm, tee dée əm/ *n* **1.** an ancient Christian hymn praising God that is sung or recited at matins in the Roman Catholic Church or at morning prayers in the Church of England **2.** a Christian service of thanksgiving that uses the Te Deum [Pre-12C. < Latin *Te Deum laudamus* "Thee God, we praise," the first words of the hymn]

te·di·ous /téedee əss/ *adj* boring because of being long, monotonous, or repetitive [15C. Directly or via French < late Latin *taediosus* < Latin *taedium* (see TEDIUM)] —**te·di·ous·ly** *adv* —**te·di·ous·ness** *n*

SYNONYMS See ***boring***[1].

te·di·um /téedee əm/ *n* the quality of being boring, monotonous, too long, or repetitive [Mid-17C. < Latin *taedium* "weariness, disgust" < *taedere* "be wearisome"]

tee[1] /tee/ *n* **1.** T the letter T **2.** CLOTHING same as **T-shirt** (*informal*) **3.** T-SHAPED THING something with the shape or form of a capital "T," e.g., two pipes joined to form this shape **4.** SPORTS **TARGET** a mark aimed at in curling, quoits, and some other games [15C. Representing the pronunciation of the name of the letter]

SPELLCHECK See ***tea***.

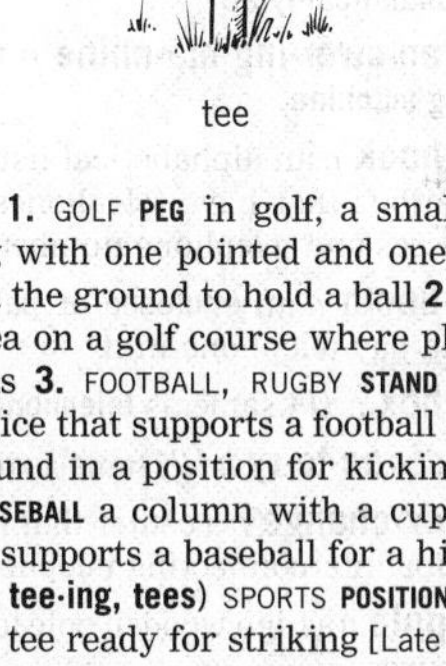

tee

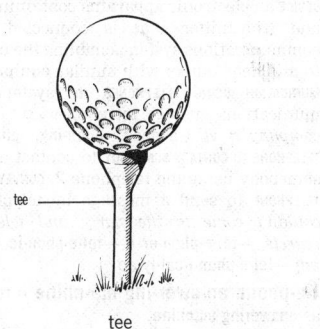

tee[2] /tee/ *n* **1.** GOLF **PEG** in golf, a small wooden or plastic peg with one pointed and one cupped end, inserted in the ground to hold a ball **2.** GOLF **STARTING AREA** an area on a golf course where play for a new hole begins **3.** FOOTBALL, RUGBY **STAND FOR FOOTBALL** a plastic device that supports a football or rugby ball on the ground in a position for kicking **4.** BASEBALL **STAND FOR BASEBALL** a column with a cupped top on a stand that supports a baseball for a hitter in T-ball ■ *vti* (**teed, tee·ing, tees**) SPORTS **POSITION BALL** to place a ball on a tee ready for striking [Late 17C. Origin ?]

SPELLCHECK See ***tea***.

tee off *vi* **1.** to hit the ball from a tee at the start of a hole of golf **2.** to start a new activity (*informal*)

tee[3] /tee/ (**teed, tee·ing, tees**) [Probably alteration of PEE]

tee off *vt* to make somebody angry or annoyed (*informal*)

tee-ball *n* BASEBALL same as **T-ball**

teed off *adj* angry, especially because of something that somebody has done (*informal*) [Probably alteration of *peed (pissed) off*]

tee-hee /tee hée/, **te-hee** *interj* used to indicate brief, especially mocking or gloating, laughter [14C. An imitation of the sound] —**tee-hee** *vi*

teem[1] /teem/ (**teemed, teem·ing, teems**) *vi* to have an extremely large number of people, animals, or things in a place ○ *streets teeming with shoppers* [Old English *tēman* < Germanic]

SPELLCHECK See ***team***.

teem[2] /teem/ (**teemed, teem·ing, teems**) *v* **1.** *vi* to rain very hard **2.** *vt* to pour out or empty something [14C. < Old Norse *tœma* "to empty" < *tómr* "empty"]

SPELLCHECK See ***team***.

teen /teen/ (*informal*) *adj* same as **teenage** ■ *n* same as **teenager** [Early 19C. Shortening]

teen·age /téen àyj/, **teen-age, teen·aged** /-àyjd/, **teen-aged** *adj* **1.** aged between 13 and 19 ○ *teenage girls* **2.** relating to teenagers ○ *teenage styles* [Early 20C. < THIRTEEN, FOURTEEN, etc]

teen·ag·er /téen àyjər/ *n* a young person between the ages of 13 and 19

SYNONYMS See ***youth***.

teens /teenz/ *npl* **1.** the years in somebody's life between the ages of 13 and 19, or the years between 13 and 19 in a century **2.** the numbers ending in "-teen" [Late 16C. < THIRTEEN, FOURTEEN, etc]

teen·sy /téenssee/ (**-si·er, -si·est**) *adj* same as **teeny** (*informal*) [Late 19C. Probably < TEENY]

teen·sy-ween·sy /-wéenssee/ *adj* same as **teeny-weeny** (*informal*) [After TEENY-WEENY]

teenth /teenth/ *n* DRUGS same as **sixteenth** (sense 2) (*slang*) [Shortening]

tee·ny /téenee/ (**-ni·er, -ni·est**) *adj* very small (*informal*) [Early 19C. Alteration of TINY, after WEENY]

teen·y·bop·per /téenee bòppər/ *n* a young teenager, usually a young girl, who follows the latest fads in fashion and music [Mid-20C. < TEENAGER or TEENS, influenced by TEENY]

tee·ny-wee·ny *adj* very small (*informal*)

tee·pee *n* CULTL ANTHROP another spelling of **tepee**

Tees /teez/ river in northeastern England, flowing into the North Sea at Teesmouth. Length: 80 mi./128 km.

tee shirt *n* CLOTHING same as **T-shirt**

tee·ter /téetər/ (**-tered, -ter·ing, -ters**) *vi* **1.** TOTTER to walk or move unsteadily and as if about to fall ○ *teetering along in her high heels* **2.** BE IN PRECARIOUS POSITION to be in a precarious position in which things could imminently go badly wrong ○ *an economy teetering on the verge of recession* **3.** VACILLATE to vacillate or fluctuate between different attitudes or positions ○ *teetered between wanting to go and not wanting to go* **4.** same as **seesaw** *v* (senses 2–3) ○ *teetered between wanting to go and not wanting to go* [Mid-19C. Variant of dialect *titter* < Germanic]

tee·ter·board /téetər bàwrd/ *n* **1.** an acrobat's device consisting of a board on a fulcrum used to propel somebody standing on the low end into the air when another person jumps onto the high end **2.** *Northeast US* same as **seesaw** *n* (sense 1)

tee·ter-tot·ter *n* LEISURE same as **seesaw** *n* (sense 1)

teeth ANAT plural of **tooth**

teethe /teeth/ (**teethed, teeth·ing, teethes**) *vi* to grow milk teeth [15C. < TEETH]

teeth·er /téethər/ *n* an object such as a teething ring on which a baby can bite while teething

teeth·ing ring *n* a ring of hard rubber or plastic on which a baby can bite when teething

teeth·ridge /téeth rìj/ *n* ANAT same as **alveolar ridge**

tee·to·tal /tée tṓt'l/ *adj* **1.** completely abstaining from alcoholic beverages **2.** complete and absolute [Mid-19C. < initial letter of TOTAL + TOTAL] —**tee·to·tal·er** *n* —**tee·to·tal·ism** *n*

tee·to·tum /tee tṓtəm/ *n* a top spun with the fingers, formerly used in a game of chance [Early 18C. < Latin *totum* "all" + its initial letter "T," inscribed on one side of the toy]

teff /tef/, **tef** *n* an annual grass cultivated for its seed, that is used as a grain. Native to: North Africa. Latin name: *Eragrostis tef*. [Late 18C. < Amharic *ṭēf*]

te·fil·lin /tə fíllin/ *npl* small leather boxes containing Hebrew texts ritually worn by Orthodox Jewish men [Early 17C. < Aramaic *tĕpillīn* "prayers"]

TEFL /téff'l/ *abbr* teaching of English as a foreign language

Tef·lon /téf lòn/ *tdmk* a trademark for polytetrafluoroethylene, a plastic with nonstick properties that is used as a coating, e.g., for cookware

teg /teg/ *n US* a doe that is in the second year of life [Early 16C. Origin ?]

teg·men /tégmən/ (*plural* **-mi·na** /-mənə/), **teg·men·tum** /teg méntəm/ (*plural* **-ta** /-tə/) *n* **1.** BOT **INNER LAYER IN SEED** the inner layer of a seed's coat **2.** INSECTS **INSECT FOREWING** the forewing of a primitive insect such as the cockroach **3.** BIOL **COVERING PART** a covering part in a plant or animal [Early 19C. < Latin < *tegere* "to cover"] —**teg·men·tal** *adj* —**teg·mi·nal** *adj*

te·gu /tə gṓo/ (*plural* **-gus** or *same*) *n* a fast-running lizard that grows up to 4 ft./120 cm long. Native to: Central and South America. Genus: *Tupinambis*. [Mid-20C. Shortening of *teguexin* < Nahuatl *tecoixin* "lizard"]

Te·gu·ci·gal·pa /te gòossee gálpə/ capital of Honduras, in the south central part of the country. Population: 1,037,600 (2000).

teg·u·lar /téggyələr/, **teg·u·lat·ed** /téggyə làytəd/ *adj* relating to or resembling tiles [Early 19C. < Latin *tegula* "tile" < *tegere* "to cover"]

teg·u·ment /téggyəmənt/ *n* the protective outer covering of an organism [15C. < Latin *tegumentum* "covering" < *tegere* "to cover"] —**teg·u·men·tal** /tèggyə mént'l/ *adj* —**teg·u·men·ta·ry** /tèggyə méntəree, -méntree/ *adj*

te-hee *interj, vi* another spelling of **tee-hee**

Teh·ran /te ráan, -rán/, **Teh·rān** capital of Iran, in the northern part of the country. Population: 11,689,000 (2002).

Tei·de, Pico de ♦ Pico de Teide

te ig·i·tur /tay íggi tòor, -íjji tòor/ *n* the first prayer of the Roman Catholic Mass, beginning "te igitur clementissime Pater," which translates as "thee, therefore, most merciful Father" [Early 19C. < Latin, "thee, therefore," its opening words]

teig·lach /táygləkh, tíglәkh/ *n* a Jewish or German confection made from spiced dough shaped into small balls and simmered in honey, nuts, and spices (*takes a singular or plural verb*) [Early 20C. < Yiddish *teyglekh* < *teyg* "dough" < Old High German *teic*]

tei·id /tée id/ *adj* belonging to a reptile family of large carnivorous lizards with forked tongues, native to Central and South America [Mid-20C. < modern Latin *Teiidae* < Portuguese *teiu* "lizard" < Tupi *tejú*]

Teil·hard de Char·din /tay yáar də shaar dáN/, **Pierre** (1881–1955) French priest, paleontologist, and theologian. He was one of the discoverers of Peking man, and in his major work, *The Phenomenon of Man* (1955), he argued that scientific evolutionary theory is compatible with Christian doctrine.

"From an evolutionary point of view, man has stopped moving, if he ever did move."
[Pierre Teilhard de Chardin, *The Phenomenon of Man*; 1955]

Te·jo /táy zhō/ ♦ **Tagus**

Te Ka·na·wa /tə káanəwə, tay-/, **Dame Kiri** (*b.* 1944) New Zealand opera singer. She made her debut as a soprano at Covent Garden in 1970 and went on to perform at major opera houses worldwide. Full name **Te Kanawa, Dame Kiri Janette**

tek·kie *n* COMPUT another spelling of **techie** (*informal*)

tek·tite /ték tìt/ *n* a small dark-colored glassy object, possibly resulting from meteoric impact, found in groups at various locations throughout the world [Early 20C. < Greek *tēktos* "molten" < *tēkein* "melt"]

tel. *abbr* TELECOM **1.** telegram **2.** telegraph **3.** telegraphic **4.** telephone

te·la /téelə/ (*plural* **-lae** /-lee/) *n* a delicate part or tissue in the body with a fine or intricate pattern like a web [Early 20C. < Latin, "web"]

tel·aes·the·sia *n* PARAPSYCHOL another spelling of **telesthesia**

tel·a·mon /téllə mòn, téllәmәn/ (*plural* **-mo·nes** /tèllə mō neez/) *n* ARCHIT same as **atlas** (sense 3) [Early 17C. < Greek, after *Telamon*, Greek mythical hero]

tel·an·gi·ec·ta·sia /te lànjee ek táyzhə/, **tel·an·gi·ec·ta·sis** /-ek táyssiss/ *n* permanent dilation of the capillaries and small blood vessels, especially in the face and thighs, producing dark red blotches [Mid-19C. < Greek *telos* "end" + *aggeion* "vessel" + *ektasis* "extension"] —**tel·an·gi·ec·tat·ic** /-táttik/ *adj*

Tel A·viv-Ya·fo /tèl ə veev yaáfō/, **Tel A·viv-Jaf·fa** /-jáffə/ city in west central Israel, on the Mediterranean Sea. It comprises the historic Arab town of Jaffa and modern Tel Aviv. Population: 348,100 (1999).

tel·co /télkō/ (*plural* **-cos**) *n* a telecommunications company (*informal*) ○ *"Those on the front lines of networking, such as telcos, Internet service providers..."* (*Forbes Global Business and Finance*; November 1998) [Late 20C. Shortening]

tel·co ho·tel *n* ONLINE same as **Internet hotel**

tele- *prefix* **1.** distant, operating at a distance ○ *telecommute* **2.** television ○ *telegenic* **3.** telegraph, telephone ○ *telebanking* [< Greek *tēle* "far away"]

tel·e·bank·ing /téllə bàngking/ *n* a system of transacting business with a bank by telephone

tel·e·bridge /téllə brìj/ *n* a telephone system that enables three or more people to be connected simultaneously ○ *"Group classes are limited to 15 participants and are held on a telebridge."* (*The Washington Post*; July 1998)

tel·e·cam·er·a /téllə kàmmərə, -kàmmrə/ *n* a television camera

tel·e·cast /téllə kàst/ *n* a television broadcast ■ *vti* (**-cast** or **-cast·ed, -cast·ing, -casts**) to broadcast a program on television —**tel·e·cast·er** *n*

tel·e·com /téllə kòm/ *n* same as **telecommunication** (*informal*) [Mid-20C. Shortening]

tel·e·com·mu·ni·ca·tion /tèllə kə myoōni káysh'n/ *n* the transmission of encoded sound, pictures, or data over significant distances, using radio signals or electrical or optical lines

tel·e·com·mu·ni·ca·tions /tèllə kə myoōni káysh'nz/ *n* the science and technology of transmitting information electronically by wires or radio signals with integrated encoding and decoding equipment (*takes a singular or plural verb*) ■ *npl* information transmission over communications lines (*takes a plural verb*)

tel·e·com·mute /tèllə kə myoōt/ (**-mut·ed, -mut·ing, -mutes**) *vi* to work from home on a computer linked to the workplace via modem —**tel·e·com·mut·er** /tèlli kə myoōtər/ *n* —**tel·e·com·mut·ing** *n*

tel·e·com·put·ing /tèllə kəm pyoōting/ *n* the act of sending information to or receiving information from another computer via modem or local area network

tel·e·coms /téllə kòmz/ *n* same as **telecommunications** (*informal*; *takes a singular or plural verb*) [Contraction]

tel·e·con·fer·enc·ing /tèllə kónfərənssing, -kónfrənssing/ *n* a system of videoconferencing that uses a restricted band of frequencies and allows participants to be connected by telephone lines —**tel·e·con·fer·ence** *n, vi*

tel·e·course /télli kàwrss/ *n* a course of televised lectures offered by an educational institution

tel·e·den·si·ty /tèllə dénssətee/ *n* a measure of telephone availability, expressed as the number of main lines per 100 inhabitants in a country

tel·e·dra·ma /téllə draàmə, -dràmmə/ *n* a drama filmed to be broadcast on television

tel·e·du /téllə doō/ (*plural* **-dus** or *same*) *n* a carnivorous animal of the weasel family with a dark coat and a white stripe down its back. Native to: Southeast Asia. Latin name: *Mydaus javanensis*. [Early 19C. < Javanese]

tel·e·film /téllə film/ *n* a movie made for television

teleg. *abbr* TELECOM **1.** telegram **2.** telegraph **3.** telegraphic **4.** telegraphy

tel·e·ga /tə léggə/ *n* a simple four-wheeled Russian cart [Mid-16C. < Russian]

tel·e·gen·ic /tèllə jénnik/ *adj* pleasant and attractive when viewed on television [Mid-20C. After PHOTOGENIC] —**tel·e·gen·i·cal·ly** *adv*

tel·e·gram /téllə gràm/ *n* a message sent by telegraph [Mid-19C. After TELEGRAPH]

tel·e·graph /téllə gràf/ *n* **1.** LONG-DISTANCE COMMUNICATION THROUGH WIRES a method of long-distance communication by coded electric impulses transmitted through wires **2.** TELECOM same as **telegram** ■ *v* (**-graphed, -graph·ing, -graphs**) **1.** *vti* SEND SOMETHING BY WIRE to send a message to somebody by telegraph **2.** *vt* INDICATE SOMETHING INDIRECTLY to communicate a thought or feeling indirectly or without words ○ *had telegraphed her annoyance with a frown* **3.** *vt* SHOW INTENTION to give advance notice of intentions, especially unwittingly, to an audience or opponent ○ *telegraphed the decision in last week's press conference* [Early 18C. < French *télégraphe* "something that writes far" < *graphe* (see -GRAPH)] —**te·leg·ra·pher** /tə léggrəfər/ *n* —**te·leg·ra·phist** /tə léggrəfist/ *n*

tel·e·graph·ese /tèllə gra feéz, -feéss/ *n* language reduced to its essential elements without regard to elegance or grammar, as typically found in telegrams

tel·e·graph·ic /tèllə gráffik/ *adj* **1.** concise or elliptical in spoken or written expression **2.** relating to telegraphy or telegrams —**tel·e·graph·i·cal·ly** *adv*

tel·e·graph plant *n* a pod-bearing bush with small leaflets that jerk spasmodically in hot sunshine. Native to: tropical Asia. Latin name: *Desmodium gyrans*.

tel·e·graph pole *n UK* same as **telephone pole**

te·leg·ra·phy /tə léggrəfee/ *n* the system, study, or operation of telegraph communications

Tel·e·gu *n, adj* LANG, PEOPLES another spelling of **Telugu**

tel·e·im·mer·sion /tèllə i múrsh'n, -zh'n/ *n* an enhanced teleconferencing technology that uses banks of video cameras linked to computers to enable users in remote locations to collaborate as if they were in the same room

tel·e·ki·ne·sis /tèllə ki neéssis, -kī-/ *n* the supposed psychic power to move or change the shape of inanimate objects without the use of physical force —**tel·e·ki·net·ic** /-néttik/ *adj* —**tel·e·ki·net·i·cal·ly** *adv*

Te·lem·a·chus /tə lémmәkəss/ *n* in Greek mythology, the son of Odysseus, who waited with his mother, Penelope, for his father's return after the Trojan War

Te·le·mann /táylə maàn/, **Georg Philipp** (1681–1767) German composer. A prolific composer, he bridged the baroque and early classical periods in works that include 40 operas and numerous orchestral suites and chamber pieces.

tel·e·mark /téllə maàrk/ *n* a turn in cross-country skiing accomplished by putting the outside ski forward and turning it slowly inward [Early 20C. After *Telemark*, region in Norway] —**tel·e·mark** *vi*

tel·e·mar·ket·ing /tèllə maàrkəting/ *n* selling or promoting goods and services by telephone —**tel·e·mar·ket·er** *n*

tel·e·mat·ics /tèllə máttiks/ *n* the study of the processes involved in the long-distance transmission of computer data (*takes a singular verb*) [Late 20C. Blend of TELECOMMUNICATION + INFORMATICS] —**tel·e·mat·ic** *adj*

tel·e·med·i·cine /téllə mèddəssin/ *n* the use of video links, e-mail, telephone, or another telecommunications system to transmit medical information, e.g., in consultations between a doctor and patient or in supervision of medical staff

te·le·men·tor·ing /tèllə méntəring/ *n* the practice of conducting a mentoring relationship remotely, usually by e-mail

tel·e·me·ter /téllə meétər, tə lémmətər/ *n* **1.** REMOTE MEASURING DEVICE a device used to record information about a remote object or event and transmit it to an observer **2.** DEVICE FOR MEASURING DISTANCES DIRECTLY a device used for measuring distances directly that does not use rods or chains across the distance to be measured ■ *vt* (**-tered, -ter·ing, -ters**) TRANSMIT DATA to collect and transmit data about a remote object, especially using a satellite —**tel·e·met·ric** /tèllə méttrik/ *adj* —**tel·e·met·ri·cal·ly** *adv* —**te·lem·e·try** /tə lémmətree/ *n*

Te·le·mun·do /tèllə moōndō/ *n* a Mexican television network

tel·en·ceph·a·lon /tèllən séffələn, -séffə lòn/ *n* the part of the brain that is farthest forward, consisting of the cerebral hemispheres —**tel·en·ce·phal·ic** /-ensə fállik/ *adj*

te·le·o·log·i·cal /tèllee ə lójjik'l, teélee-/, **te·le·o·log·ic** /-lójjik/ *adj* relating to the study of ultimate causes in nature or of actions in relation to their ends or utility —**te·le·o·log·i·cal·ly** *adv*

tel·e·o·log·i·cal ar·gu·ment *n* an argument for God's existence from the presence of order, interpreted as design, in the universe

tel·e·ol·o·gy /tèllee óllәjee, teélee-/ *n* **1.** STUDY OF CAUSES the study of ultimate causes in nature **2.** APPROACH TO ETHICS an approach to ethics that studies actions in relation to their ends or utility **3.** GOAL-DIRECTED ACTIVITY an activity that tends toward the achievement of a goal [Mid-18C. < modern Latin *teleologia* "science of ends" < Greek *telos* "end"] —**tele·ol·o·gism** *n* —**tel·e·ol·o·gist** *n*

tel·e·ost /téllee òst/, **tel·e·os·te·an** /tèllee óstee ən, teélee-/ *n* a bony fish with rayed fins in a suborder that includes most living species, numbering around 20,000, but excluding sturgeons, gars, sharks, rays, and related fish. Subclass: Teleostei. [Mid-19C. < Greek *telos* "end" + *osteon* "bone"]

tel·e·path /téllə pàth/ *n* somebody who claims to communicate by telepathy

tel·e·pa·thize /tə léppə thīz/ (**-thized, -thiz·ing, -thiz·es**) *vi* to claim or be believed to communicate by telepathy

te·lep·a·thy /tə léppəthee/ *n* supposed communication directly from one person's mind to another's without speech, writing, or other signs or symbols —**tel·e·path·ic** /tèllə páthik/ *adj* —**tel·e·path·i·cal·ly** *adv*

tel·e·phone /téllə fōn/ *n* **1.** ELECTRONIC COMMUNICATIONS DEVICE an electronic apparatus containing a receiver and transmitter that is connected to a telecommunications system, enabling the user to speak to and hear others with similar equipment **2.** COMMUNICATION USING TELEPHONES a system of communications using telephones ○ *a telephone company* ■ *vti* (**-phoned, -phon·ing, -phones**) **1.** USE TELEPHONE TO CONTACT SOMEBODY to contact and speak to somebody using the telephone **2.** CONVEY SOMETHING BY TELEPHONE to send a message by telephone ○ *Bob couldn't come to the party and telephoned his regrets.* —**tel·e·phon·er** *n* —**tel·e·phon·ic** /tèllə fónnik/ *adj* —**tel·e·phon·i·cal·ly** *adv*

tel·e·phone an·swer·ing ma·chine *n* TELECOM same as **answering machine**

tel·e·phone book *n* an alphabetical listing of people or organizations that have telephones, along with their addresses and telephone numbers

tel·e·phone booth *n* an enclosed or partly enclosed space with a pay telephone in it

tel·e·phone box *n UK* same as **telephone booth**

tel·e·phone di·rec·to·ry *n UK* same as **telephone book**

tel·e·phone ex·change *n* a center that houses equipment used for interconnecting telephone lines

tel·e·phone pole *n* a high wooden pole for supporting telephone wires

tel·e·phone tag *n* a situation in which two people repeatedly return each other's telephone calls and leave recorded messages without succeeding in speaking directly to each other (*informal*)

te·leph·o·ny /tə léffənee/ *n* the science, technology, or system of communication by telephone

tel·e·pho·to /téllə fōtō/ *adj* producing a large image of a distant object ■ *n* (*plural* **-tos**) **1.** PHOTOGRAPHY same as **telephoto lens 2.** a photograph taken using a telephoto lens

tel·e·pho·tog·ra·phy /tèllə fə tóggrəfee/ *n* the photographing of distant objects with the use of special lenses or electronic equipment —**tel·e·pho·to·graph·ic** /tèllə fōtə gráffik/ *adj*

tel·e·pho·to lens *n* a camera lens that integrates a telescope

tel·e·play /télla plày/ *n* a treatment or script for a play written for presentation on television

tel·e·port /télla pàwrt/ (**-port·ed, -port·ing, -ports**) *v* **1.** *vt* to move an object supposedly by means of telekinesis **2.** *vi* in science fiction and fantasy, to move instantly from one place to another by futuristic, paranormal, or magical means [Mid-20C. < TELE- + Latin *portare* "carry"] —**tel·e·por·ta·tion** /tèlla pawr táysh'n/ *n*

tel·e·pres·ence /télla prèzz'nss/ *n* the virtual presence of somebody whose actions are transmitted by electronic signals to a physically remote site, e.g. in telesurgery

tel·e·print·er /télla prìntar/ *n Can, UK* TELECOM a piece of equipment for telegraphic communication that uses a device like a typewriter for data input and output. US term **teletypewriter**

tel·e·proc·ess·ing /tèlla pró sèssing/ *n* the use of computer terminals in different locations, connected to a main computer, to process data

Tel·e·PrompT·er /télla pròmptar/ *tdmk* a trademark for a device showing text for somebody speaking on television to read

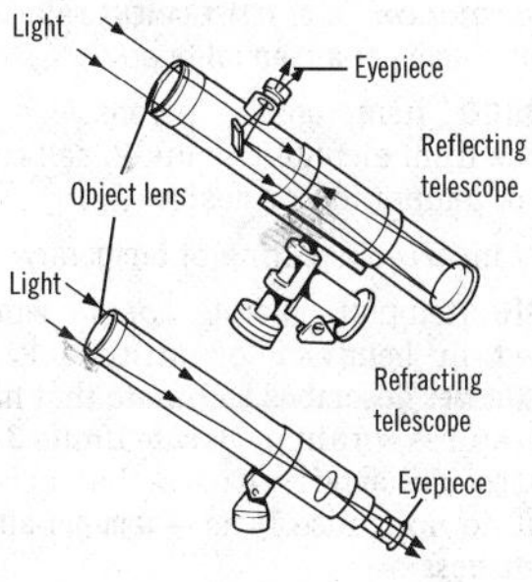

telescope

tel·e·scope /télla skōp/ *n* **1.** DEVICE FOR LOOKING AT DISTANT OBJECTS a device for making distant objects appear nearer and larger by means of compound lenses or concave mirrors **2.** ASTRON same as **radio telescope** ■ *v* (**-scoped, -scop·ing, -scopes**) **1.** *vi* COLLAPSE NEATLY INSIDE ONE ANOTHER to slide neatly one inside another like the sections of a telescope **2.** *vt* CONDENSE SOMETHING to make something shorter in time or length ○ *telescoped his adventure into a one-hour talk* [Mid-17C. < Italian *telescopio* or modern Latin *telescopium*, both literally "looking far" < Greek *skopein* "look"]

tel·e·scop·ic /tèlla skóppik/ *adj* **1.** ENLARGING having the ability to make something distant seem nearer or larger ○ *a telescopic lens* **2.** ABLE TO SEE FAR able to see great distances ○ *telescopic vision* **3.** OF TELESCOPES relating to or visible only by using a telescope **4.** COLLAPSIBLE consisting of parts that slide one inside another ○ *a tripod with telescopic legs* —**tel·e·scop·i·cal·ly** *adv*

tel·e·scop·ic sight *n* a telescope mounted on a rifle and used for sighting, especially on distant targets

Tel·e·sco·pi·um /tèlla skópee am/ *n* a constellation of the southern hemisphere [Early 19C. < modern Latin (see TELESCOPE)]

te·les·co·py /ta léskapee/ *n* the science and technology of making and using telescopes

tel·e·ser·vic·es /tèlla súrvissaz/ *npl* products and services that combine the retail use of the telephone and computers

tel·e·shop·ping /télla shòpping/ *n* the practice or activity of ordering goods advertised on television by phone or computer

tel·e·ster·e·o·scope /tèlla stérree a skōp, -stéeree-/ *n* a binocular telescope or telescopic stereoscope adapted to provide a three-dimensional view of distant objects or landscapes

tel·es·the·sia /tèllass théezha/, **tel·aes·the·sia** *n* the supposed perception of phenomena or events considered beyond the range of normal senses [Late 19C. < TELE- + Greek *aisthēsis* "perception"] —**tel·es·thet·ic** /-théttik/ *adj*

te·le·stich /ta léstik, télla stìk/ *n* an acrostic or poem in which the last letters in each line spell a word [Mid-17C. < Greek *telos* "end" + *stikhos* "row, line of verse"]

Te·les·to /ta léstō/ *n* a very small natural satellite of Saturn, discovered in 1980. It is irregular in shape with a maximum dimension of 19 mi./30 km, and occupies an intermediate orbit.

tel·e·sur·ger·y /télla sùrjaree/ *n* surgery carried out by a surgeon who is not physically present at the site of the operation, using specialized electronic communications and robots

tel·e·text /télla tèkst/ *n* a system of broadcasting news and other information in written form that can be viewed on specially equipped television sets, superimposed on, or in place of, the picture

tel·e·the·a·ter /télla theè atar/ *n* a viewing area where horseraces are broadcast live on video screens, e.g., in an off-track betting parlor

tel·e·thon /télla thòn/ *n* a lengthy television broadcast that combines entertainment with appeals to donate to a charity [Mid-20C. Blend of TELE- + MARATHON]

tel·e·tran·scrip·tion /tèlla tran skrípsh'n/ *n* the transcription of a television program by the use of videotape

tel·e·type·writ·er /tèlla tīp rītar/ *n US* a telegraphic communication device similar to a typewriter used for data input and output. Can term **teleprinter**

te·leu·to·spore /ta lóota spàwr/ *n* BIOL same as **teliospore** [Late 19C. < Greek *teleutē* "completion" < *telos* "end"] —**te·leu·to·spor·ic** /ta lóota spáwrik/ *adj*

tel·e·van·ge·list /tèlla vánjalist/ *n* a Christian evangelist who broadcasts on television [Late 20C. Blend of TELEVISION + EVANGELIST] —**tel·e·van·gel·ism** *n*

tel·e·vise /télla vīz/ (**-vised, -vis·ing, -vis·es**) *vt* to broadcast something on television [Early 20C. Back-formation < TELEVISION]

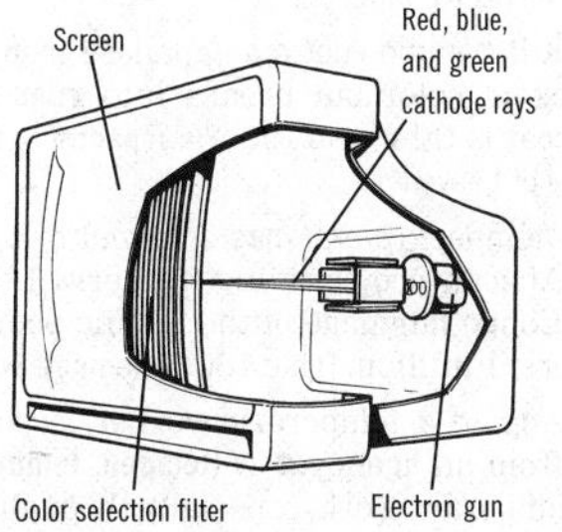

television

tel·e·vi·sion /télla vìzh'n/ *n* **1.** *also* **tel·e·vi·sion set** DEVICE FOR RECEIVING IMAGES AND SOUNDS an electronic device for receiving and reproducing the images and sounds of a combined audio and video signal **2.** BROADCAST CONTENT the image, sound, or content of a combined audio and video broadcast ○ *spent the evening watching television* **3.** BROADCASTING INDUSTRY the industry concerned with the making and broadcasting of programs combining images and sounds ○ *works in television* **4.** VIDEO BROADCASTING SYSTEM a system of capturing images and sounds, broadcasting them via a combined electronic audio and video signal, and reproducing them to be viewed and listened to —**tel·e·vi·sion·al** *adj* —**tel·e·vi·sion·al·ly** *adv* —**tel·e·vi·sion·a·ry** *adj* —**tel·e·vi·sual** /tèlla vízhoo al/ *adj*

tel·e·vi·sion tube *n* MEDIA same as **tube** *n* (sense 6)

tel·e·work·ing /télla wùrking/ *n* HR working by telecommuting —**tel·e·work·er** *n*

tel·ex /té lèks/ *n* **1.** COMMUNICATIONS SYSTEM a communications system using teletypewriters that communicate via telephone lines **2.** MESSAGE a message sent or received by telex ■ *vti* (**-exed, -ex·ing, -ex·es**) SEND SOMETHING BY TELEX to send a message to somebody by telex [Mid-20C. Blend of TELEPRINTER + EXCHANGE]

tel·fer, etc. TRANSP another spelling of **telpher, etc.**

Tel·ford /télfard/ industrial city in Shropshire, west central England. Population: 115,000 (1991).

te·li·a FUNGI plural of **telium**

tel·ic /téllik, téelik/ *adj* directed toward a definite end or purpose [Mid-19C. < Greek *telikos* "final" < *telos* "end"]

te·li·o·spore /téelee a spàwr/ *n* a resting spore that develops in rust and smut fungi in the fall and germinates in the spring [Early 20C. < TELIUM] —**te·le·o·spor·ic** /téelee a spáwrik/ *adj*

te·li·um /téelee am/ (*plural* **-li·a** /-lee a/) *n* the spore case of a rust or smut fungus that bears teliospores [Early 20C. < Greek *telos* "end"] —**te·li·al** *adj*

tell /tel/ *v* (**told** /tōld/, **tell·ing, tells**) **1.** *vt* RELATE EVENTS OR FACTS to give an account in speech or writing of events or facts ○ *tell a story* **2.** *vt* EXPRESS SOMETHING to express a particular thing in speech ○ *tell a lie* **3.** *vt* INFORM SOMEBODY to inform somebody of something ○ *Who told you?* ○ *Jim told us the news.* **4.** *vti* EXPRESS SOMETHING IN WORDS TO SOMEBODY to express thoughts or feelings to somebody in words **5.** *vt* ORDER SOMEBODY to command or order somebody to do something **6.** *vt* DISTINGUISH ONE FROM OTHER to distinguish two or more people or things ○ *couldn't tell one from the other* **7.** *vt* DISCERN SOMETHING to ascertain or perceive something ○ *couldn't tell whether she was pleased or not* **8.** *vt* REVEAL FUTURE to purport to reveal future events ○ *tell your fortune* **9.** *vi* REVEAL SECRET to reveal secret or damaging information, especially to an authority ○ *Don't worry – I won't tell.* **10.** *vt* COUNT THINGS to count things such as votes cast or beads as part of a prayer ○ *tell a rosary* ■ *n* REVEALING ACTION an action that unconsciously reveals secret information [Old English *tellan* < Germanic, "put in order"] —**tell·a·ble** *adj*
◇ **all told** altogether, or when everything else is taken into consideration ◇ **tell it like it is** to give a frank and accurate account of something (*informal*)
◇ **tell me about it!** (*informal*) **1.** used to indicate heartfelt agreement **2.** used wryly to indicate to a speaker that you too have had a similar experience to the one being described, usually a negative experience ◇ **there's no telling** it is impossible to ascertain or predict a particular thing ○ *There's no telling how fast the disease will spread.* ◇ **you're telling me!** used to indicate agreement with an observation (*informal*)

tell against *vt* to play a part in determining a negative outcome for somebody ○ *His extreme nervousness told against him in the interview.*

tell apart *vt* to distinguish two or more similar people or things

tell off *vt* to scold or rebuke somebody, especially in anger (*informal*)

tell on *vt* **1.** to report damaging or incriminating information about somebody to an authority **2.** to have an adverse effect on somebody or something

Tell, William *n* ➧ **William Tell**

tell-all *adj* not withholding any information, even what may be considered secret, private, or unsuitable ■ *n* a book or other writing, especially biographical or autobiographical, that withholds no information about its subject

tel·ler /tèllar/ *n* **1.** BANK EMPLOYEE an employee in a bank or savings institution who receives and pays out money **2.** COUNTER OF VOTES somebody who counts votes in an election or legislature **3.** SOMEBODY WHO TELLS somebody who tells something ○ *a teller of tales*

Tel·ler /téllar/, **Edward** (1908–2003) Hungarian-born US physicist. He helped construct the first atomic bomb (1945) and was the principal architect of the hydrogen bomb, first tested in 1952.

> "The main purpose of science is simplicity and as we understand more things, everything is becoming simpler."
> [Edward Teller, *Conversations on the Dark Secrets of Physics*; 1991]

tel·lin /téllin/ (*plural* **-lins** or *same*) *n* a bivalve sea mollusk that lives in intertidal sand. Genus: *Tellina.* [Early 18C. Via Latin < Greek *tellinē* "type of shellfish"]

tell·ing /télling/ *adj* **1.** very effective or expressive ○ *a telling indictment* **2.** revealing information inadvertently or indirectly ○ *a telling glance* —**tell·ing·ly** *adv*

tell·tale /tél tàyl/ *adj* CLEARLY SHOWING SOMETHING clearly showing or indicating something that is secret or hidden ○ *telltale signs* ■ *n* **1.** MONITORING DEVICE a device or signal intended to monitor a machine or system **2.** RAIL SIGN OF HAZARD vertical strips suspended above a railroad track to warn of an imminent low bridge or tunnel **3.** SAILING WIND STRIPS strips of ribbon hung aloft on a sailboat to show apparent wind direction **4.** RACKET GAMES METAL STRIP a horizontal metal strip across the front wall of a squash or racquetball court, above which the ball must be bounced **5.** SOMEBODY WHO TELLS SECRETS a person, especially a child, who tells others about another person's secrets or bad behavior

tel·lu·rate /téllyə ràyt/ *n* a salt or ester of telluric acid [Early 19C. < TELLURIUM]

tel·lu·ri·an /tə lŏŏree ən, te-/ *adj* relating to Earth or life on Earth ■ *n* in science fiction, an inhabitant of Earth [Mid-19C. < Latin *tellus* "earth"]

tel·lu·ric[1] /tə lŏŏrik, te-/ *adj* **1.** originating or coming from Earth or its atmosphere **2.** GEOG same as **tellurian** [Mid-19C. < Latin *tellus* "earth"]

tel·lu·ric[2] /tə lŏŏrik, te-/ *adj* relating to or containing tellurium, especially in a high valence [Early 19C. < TELLURIUM]

tel·lu·ric ac·id *n* a white crystalline inorganic acid. Use: chemical reagent. Formula: H_6TeO_6. [< TELLURIC[2]]

tel·lu·ride /téllyə rīd/ *n* a binary compound of tellurium with an electropositive element or group [Mid-19C. < TELLURIUM]

tel·lu·ri·on /tə lŏŏree ən, te-/ *n* a model that shows how day and night and the seasons result from the Earth's orbit and its tilted axis in relation to the Sun [Mid-19C. < Latin *tellus* "earth"]

tel·lu·ri·um /tə lŏŏree əm, te-/ *n* a semimetallic element that occurs naturally, both in a native state and in mineral ores. Source: refining of copper and lead. Use: alloys, various manufacturing processes. Symbol **Te**. See table at **element** [Early 19C. < Latin *tellus* "earth," after URANIUM]

tel·lur·ize /téllyə rīz/ (**-ized, -iz·ing, -iz·es**) *vt* to cause something to combine with tellurium

tel·lu·rom·e·ter /tèllyə rómmətər/ *n* a device that measures distances using the time that microwaves or radio waves take to be transmitted across the distance to be measured [Mid-20C. < Latin *tellus* "earth"]

tel·lu·rous /téllyərəss, tə lŏŏrəss, te-/ *adj* relating to or containing tellurium, especially in a low valence [Mid-19C. < TELLURIUM, after FERROUS]

Tel·lus /télləss/ *n* in Roman mythology, the goddess of the Earth and of fertility [< Latin, "earth"]

tel·ly /téllee/ (*plural* **-lies**) *n* **1.** *UK* MEDIA same as **television** (*informal*) **2.** SKIING same as **telemark** [Mid-20C. Shortening]

Tel·net /tél nèt/ *n also* **TELNET** a terminal emulation program that allows computer users to connect interactively to a server and access remote sites, e.g., on the Internet ■ *vti* (**-net·ted, -net·ting, -nets**) to access a remote computer [Late 20C. < TELE- + NETWORK]

telo- *prefix* end, terminal ○ *telophase* [< Greek *telos* "end"]

tel·o·cen·tric /teèlə séntrik, tèllə-/ *adj* describes a chromosome whose centromere is located at or near one end

tel·o·lec·i·thal /teèlə léssithəl, tèllə-/ *adj* describes reptile, shark, or bird eggs in which the yolk is concentrated at one end [Late 19C. < TELO- + Greek *lekithos* "egg yolk"]

tel·o·me·rase /téllәmə ràyss, -ràyz/ *n* an enzyme found in cancers that, by re-forming the telomeres at the ends of chromosomes, prevents the shortening that usually limits the number of replications and thus allows cancer growth

tel·o·mere /téllə meèr, teèlə-/ *n* a region of DNA at the end of a chromosome that protects the start of the genetic coding sequence against shortening during successive replications

tel·o·phase /téllə fàyz, teèlə-/ *n* the final stage of cell division, in which daughter cell nuclei form around chromosomes at opposite ends of the dividing mother cell —**tel·o·phas·ic** /tèllə fáyzik, teèlə-/ *adj*

tel·pher /télfər/, **tel·fer** *n* a car or other carrying unit suspended from a cable in a telpherage ■ *vt* (**-phered, -pher·ing, -phers; -fered, -fer·ing, -fers**) to transport somebody or something in a container suspended from cables [Late 19C. Contraction < TELE- + -PHORE] —**tel·pher·ic** *adj*

tel·pher·age /télfərij/, **tel·fer·age** *n* a transportation system in which passengers or goods are carried in containers suspended from cables

tel·son /télss'n/ *n* the terminal segment of an arthropod or arachnid body, e.g., the stinger of a scorpion [Mid-19C. < Greek, "limit"] —**tel·son·ic** /tel sónnik/ *adj*

Tel·star /tél staàr/ *n* a communications satellite used for transmitting television programs and telephone messages. Two of these were launched by the United States in 1962 and 1963. [Mid-20C. < TELE- + STAR]

Tel·u·gu /téllə gŏŏ/ (*plural same* or **-gus**), **Tel·e·gu** *n* **1.** a Dravidian language of central and southeastern India, especially the state of Andhra Pradesh. Native speakers: over 10 million. **2.** a member of a Telugu-speaking people [Late 18C. < Kannada and Tamil] —**Te·lu·gu** *adj*

LANGUAGE HERITAGE See ***Dravidian***.

Te·ma /teèmə/ city in southeastern Ghana, on the Gulf of Guinea, near Accra. Population: 180,600 (1990 estimate).

te·maz·e·pam /tə mázzə pàm/ *n* a benzodiazepine drug used for the short-term treatment of insomnia [Late 20C. < *tem-*, origin ? + OXAZEPAM]

tem·blor /témblər, -blàwr/ *n* an earthquake or tremor [Late 19C. < American Spanish, "trembling" < Vulgar Latin *tremulare* "tremble"]

tem·er·ar·i·ous /tèmmə rérree əss/ *adj* showing a reckless confidence that may be offensive (*literary*) [Mid-16C. < Latin *temerarius* < *temere* "rashly, blindly"]

te·mer·i·ty /tə mérrətee/ *n* reckless confidence that might be offensive [15C. < Latin *temeritas* "rashness" < *temere* "rashly, blindly"]

tem·mok·u /témmō kŏŏ/ *n* a Japanese iron glaze that is black in color but breaks into rust where the glaze coat is thin [Late 19C. Via Japanese < Chinese *tiān mù* "eye of heaven"]

Tem·ne /témnee/ (*plural* **-nes** or *same*) *n* **1.** a member of an African people living in Sierra Leone **2.** the Niger-Congo language of the Temne people. Native speakers: 1 million. [Late 18C. < Temne] —**Tem·ne** *adj*

temp /temp/ *n* a temporary worker, especially one hired from an agency ■ *vi* (**temped, temp·ing, temps**) to do temporary work, especially through an agency ○ *Terry's temping with a bank.* [Early 20C. Shortening of TEMPORARY]

temp. *abbr* **1.** temperance **2.** METEOROL, MICROBIOL temperate **3.** METEOROL temperature **4.** BIOCHEM, ENG, COMPUT template **5.** ANAT temporal **6.** OCCUPATIONS temporary

tem·pe *n* FOOD another spelling of **tempeh**

Tem·pe /témpee/ city in central Arizona, on the Salt River. Population: 159,508 (2002 estimate).

tem·peh /tém pày/, **tem·pe** *n* fermented soy beans, popular as a health food and in some Asian cuisines [Mid-20C. < Indonesian *tempe*]

tem·per /témpər/ *n* **1.** TENDENCY TO ANGER a tendency to get angry easily and suddenly ○ *has quite a temper* **2.** ANGRY STATE a state of anger or annoyance ○ *got himself into a terrible temper* **3.** EMOTIONAL CONDITION an emotional condition or predisposition of a particular kind ○ *an even temper* **4.** CALM STATE a state of calm and balance ○ *lost his temper* **5.** METALL HARDNESS OF METAL the degree of hardness of a metal **6.** ADDITIVE something added to improve the consistency or strength of something ■ *vt* (**-pered, -per·ing, -pers**) **1.** SOFTEN SOMETHING to make something less harsh or unacceptable, especially by adding something to it ○ *temper criticism with kindness* **2.** MAKE SOMEBODY STRONGER to make somebody stronger through exposure to hardship ○ *tempered by combat duty* **3.** STRENGTHEN MATERIAL to improve the consistency of something, e.g., glass, by heating it or by adding something to it **4.** HARDEN METAL to harden metal by heating it to very high temperatures and then cooling it ○ *temper steel* **5.** MUSIC TUNE EARLY KEYBOARD INSTRUMENT to tune a baroque keyboard instrument so that consistent harmonic intervals are achieved throughout its range [Pre-12C. < Latin *temperare* "mix, restrain yourself" < *tempus* "time"] —**tem·per·a·bil·i·ty** /tèmpərə bíllətee, tèmprə-/ *n* —**tem·per·a·ble** *adj* —**tem·per·er** *n*

tem·per·a /témpərə/ *n* **1.** PAINTING TECHNIQUE a technique of painting with colors made from powdered pigments mixed with water and egg yolk, size, or casein **2.** *US* PAINT the mix of pigments, water and other substances used in tempera **3.** TEMPERA PAINTING a painting done in tempera [Mid-19C. < Italian < Latin *temperare* (see TEMPER)]

tem·per·a·ment /témprəmənt, témpərə-/ *n* **1.** QUALITY OF MIND a prevailing or dominant quality of mind that characterizes somebody **2.** MOODINESS excessive moodiness, irritability, or sensitivity **3.** HIST MEDIEVAL PHYSIOLOGICAL CLASSIFICATION in medieval physiology, the quality of mind resulting from various proportions of the four cardinal humors in somebody **4.** MUSIC NOTE INTERVAL SETTING the subtle relationship of the pitches of notes of keyboard instruments and the consequences this has for harmony

tem·per·a·men·tal /tèmprə mént'l, tèmpərə-/ *adj* **1.** EASILY UPSET easily upset or irritated **2.** UNPREDICTABLE unpredictable and erratic in behavior ○ *a temperamental car* **3.** OF TEMPERAMENT relating to temperament —**tem·per·a·men·tal·ly** *adv*

tem·per·ance /témprənss, -pərənss/ *n* **1.** total abstinence from alcoholic drink **2.** self-restraint in the face of temptation or desire

~~temperary~~ incorrect spelling of **temporary**

tem·per·ate /témprət, -pərət/ *adj* **1.** MILD mild or restrained in behavior or attitude **2.** METEOROL WITHOUT EXTREMES describes a climate that has a range of temperatures within moderate limits **3.** MICROBIOL NOT SPREADING describes viruses that exist in host cells, but do not cause lysis —**tem·per·ate·ly** *adv* —**tem·per·ate·ness** *n*

Tem·per·ate Zone *n* the parts of Earth that lie between the tropics and the polar circles and generally have hot summers, cold winters, and intermediate falls and springs

tem·per·a·ture /témpərə chŏŏr, -chər, témprə-/ *n* **1.** DEGREE OF HEAT the degree of heat as an inherent quality of objects expressed as hotness or coldness relative to something else **2.** RELATIVE DEGREE OF HEAT the heat of something measured on a scale such as the Fahrenheit or Celsius scale. Symbol **T, t** **3.** BODY HEAT the degree of heat in a living organism **4.** FEVER human body heat in excess of 98.6° F/37.0° C ○ *running a temperature* **5.** DEGREE OF EXCITEMENT the level of excitement or tension in a situation ○ *When the opposition filed in, the temperature in the room went up.* [15C. Directly or via French < Latin *temperatura* < *temperare* (see TEMPER)]

tem·per·a·ture gra·di·ent *n* the rate of change in air temperature over distance, especially elevation

tem·per·a·ture-hu·mid·i·ty in·dex *n* a measure of ambient humidity relative to heat as it affects human comfort

tem·per·a·ture in·ver·sion *n* METEOROL same as **inversion** (sense 3)

tem·pered /témpərd/ *adj* **1.** WITH PARTICULAR TEMPER having a temper or temperament of a particular type (*usually used in combination*) ○ *even-tempered* **2.** WELL PROPORTIONED having components combined in a balanced and suitable proportion **3.** METALL HARDENED hardened through a tempering process ○ *tempered steel* ○ *tempered glass* **4.** MUSIC TUNED TO TEMPERAMENT describes a keyboard instrument tuned to a particular temperament, especially equal temperament

~~temperment~~ incorrect spelling of **temperament**

tem·per tan·trum *n* an outburst of anger, especially a childish display of rage or bad temper

~~temperture~~ incorrect spelling of **temperature**

tem·pest /témpəst/ *n* **1.** a severe commotion or disturbance, especially an emotional upheaval **2.** a severe storm with very high winds and often rain, hail, or snow (*literary*) [13C. Via French < Latin *tempestas* < *tempus* "time"]

CULTURAL NOTE ***The Tempest***, a play (1611) by English dramatist William Shakespeare. An elaborate blend of comedy, drama, and fantasy, it is set on an enchanted island where Prospero, rightful duke of Milan, has lived since being usurped by his brother Antonio. Using his magical powers, Prospero conjures up a storm that forces Antonio and his companions onto the island, paving the way for an ingenious reconciliation. The word *sea-change*, meaning a change caused by the sea and, figuratively, a major transformation, comes from Act I, Scene ii of this play: "Nothing of him that doth fade,/ But doth suffer a sea-change/ Into something rich and strange.".

tem·pes·tu·ous /tem péschoo əss/ *adj* **1.** frequently turbulent and giving rise to many emotions ○ *a tempestuous relationship* **2.** having or affected by frequent or violent storms ○ *tempestuous seas* —**tem·pes·tu·ous·ly** *adv* —**tem·pes·tu·ous·ness** *n*

tem·pi MUSIC plural of **tempo**

Tem·plar /témplər/ *n* HIST same as **Knight Templar** [13C. < the place in Jerusalem (*Temple of Solomon*) where the medieval order had its headquarters]

tem·plate /témplət/ *n* **1. MASTER** something that serves as a master or pattern from which other similar things can be made **2.** ENG **PATTERN** a mechanical pattern or mold with one or more shapes used to guide the manufacture or drawing of objects with a similar shape **3.** CONSTR **SHORT BEAM** a short beam of metal, wood, or stone, used to distribute weight or pressure in a structure **4.** BIOCHEM **MASTER MOLECULE** a molecule that provides a pattern for the synthesis of other molecules in biochemical reactions **5.** COMPUT **MASTER FILE** a computer file that is used as a master for creating others similar to it [Late 17C. Alteration of TEMPLET, after PLATE]

tem·ple[1] /témp'l/ *n* **1. BUILDING FOR WORSHIP** a building used as a place of worship **2.** JUDAISM same as **synagogue** **3. MORMON CHURCH** a place of worship for the Church of Jesus Christ of Latter-Day Saints where sacred ordinances such as marriage are executed **4. MEETING PLACE** a building where a fraternal order holds meetings and rites **5. SPECIAL PLACE** an institution or building considered as a guardian of, or reservation for, a particular activity ○ *a temple of learning* **6. HOLY DWELLING** a place where something holy or divine is thought to dwell, e.g., the body of a holy person [Pre-12C. < Latin *templum* "sacred place, place for worship"]

tem·ple[2] /témp'l/ *n* **1.** the part of each side of the head between the eye and the ear **2.** either of the stem-shaped pieces on a pair of glasses that are connected to the frame and rest on the ears [14C. Via Old French < Latin *tempora*, plural of *tempus* "temple, time"]

tem·ple[3] /témp'l/ *n* the part of a loom that keeps the cloth being woven stretched to the proper width [15C. < French]

Tem·ple *n* **1.** either of two successive temples in Jerusalem. The First Temple, built by Solomon in 957 B.C., was destroyed by Nebuchadnezzar II in 586 B.C. The Second Temple was destroyed by the Romans in A.D. 70. **2.** either of two groups of buildings in Paris and London built on sites that once belonged to the Knights Templar. The London site is now the home of two of the Inns of Court. [< TEMPLE[1]]

Tem·ple /témp'l/, **Shirley ➧ Black, Shirley Temple**

tem·plet /témplət/ *n* same as **template** (*archaic*) [< TEMPLE[3]]

tem·ple tree *n* US same as **frangipani** (sense 1) [Because commonly planted on graves]

tem·po /témpō/ (*plural* **-pi** /-pee/ or **-pos**) *n* **1.** the speed at which a musical composition or passage is performed **2.** the pace or rate of something ○ *the tempo of urban life* [Mid-17C. Via Italian < Latin *tempus* "time"]

tem·po·la·bile /tèmpō láy bīl, -b'l/ *adj* changing at an uneven rate [Mid-20C. < Latin *tempus* "time" + *labilis* < *labi* "to slip"]

tem·po·ral[1] /témpərəl, -prəl/ *adj* **1. RELATING TO TIME** relating to measured time **2. BRIEF** lasting only a short time **3.** RELIG **OF THIS WORLD** relating to life in the world, not to spiritual life **4.** CHR **RELATING TO LAITY** relating to the laity, not to the clergy in the Christian Church **5.** GRAM **RELATING TO TENSES** relating to grammatical tenses or the expression of time in a language [14C. Directly or via French < Latin *temporalis* < *tempus* "time"] —**tem·po·ral·ly** *adv*

tem·po·ral[2] /témpərəl, -prəl/ *adj* relating to or located in the region of the temples on the head [Late 16C. < late Latin *temporalis* < Latin *tempus* "temple, time"]

tem·po·ral bone *n* either of a pair of bones that form part of the sides and base of the skull and contain the middle and inner ears [< TEMPORAL[2]]

tem·po·ral·i·ty /tèmpə rállətee/ *n* the quality or state of being connected with time or the world ■ **tem·po·ral·i·ties** *npl* the secular property and assets of a church [14C. < late Latin *temporalitas* < Latin *temporalis* (see TEMPORAL[1])]

tem·por·al·ize /témpərə līz, témprə-/ (**-ized, -iz·ing, -iz·es**) *vt* to make something temporal or secular

tem·po·ral lobe *n* either of two lobes of the brain, located on the side of each cerebral hemisphere, that contain the auditory centers responsible for hearing [< TEMPORAL[2]]

tem·po·rar·y /témpə rèrree/ *adj* **1. HAVING LIMITED DURATION** lasting or designed to last for a limited time **2. NOT NEEDED FOR LONG** describes computer files and folders that hold information that is not needed for long and may be deleted automatically ■ *n* (*plural* **-ies**) **WORKER HIRED FOR LIMITED TIME** a paid worker in an office or other workplace hired for a limited time only [Mid-16C. < Latin *temporarius* < *tempus* "time"] —**tem·po·rar·i·ly** /tèmpə rérrəlee/ *adv* —**tem·po·rar·i·ness** *n*

SYNONYMS ***temporary, fleeting, passing, transitory, ephemeral, evanescent, short-lived***

CORE MEANING: lasting only a short time

temporary lasting or designed to last for a limited time ○ *The acid caused only temporary injury to the man's eyes.* ○ *In some organizations, temporary jobs offer a step on the way to regular employment.* **fleeting** passing or fading quickly ○ *a fleeting moment of happiness* ○ *Most reviewers predicted the book would enjoy only fleeting success.* **passing** superficial and not long-lasting ○ *This man had no feelings for her other than a passing fancy.* ○ *Who is to say that the views of popular personalities are of anything more than passing interest?* **transitory** not permanent or lasting, but existing only for a short time ○ *transitory peace and stability* ○ *the transitory nature of stardom* **ephemeral** lasting for a short time and leaving no permanent trace ○ *Fashions are ephemeral; new ones regularly drive out the old.* **evanescent** (*literary*) disappearing after a short time and soon forgotten ○ *a shimmering evanescent bubble* ○ *a shifting, changing, fluid evanescent reality* **short-lived** lasting or living for only a short period of time ○ *a short-lived mood disorder which is likely to resolve rapidly without treatment* ○ *The actor has recently been tempted out of his short-lived retirement.* ○ *a short-lived perennial plant*

tem·po·rar·y re·strain·ing or·der *n* LAW same as **restraining order** (sense 2)

tem·po·rize /témpə rīz/ (**-rized, -riz·ing, -riz·es**) *vi* to use delaying tactics to gain time, especially in order to avoid coming to a decision or committing yourself —**tem·po·riz·er** *n*

tem·po·ro·man·dib·u·lar joint /tèmpərō man dìbbyələr-/ *n* either of the joints connecting the lower part of the jaw (**mandible**) with the temporal bone on each side of the head. Both joints act together when the jaw is moved. [< TEMPORAL[2]]

tem·po·ro·man·dib·u·lar joint syn·drome *n* DENT full form of **TMJ syndrome**

~~temprature~~ incorrect spelling of **temperature**

tempt /tempt/ (**tempt·ed, tempt·ing, tempts**) *vt* **1. INCITE DESIRE IN SOMEBODY** to cause desire or craving to arise in somebody ○ *I was tempted by that chocolate cake!* **2. INCITE SOMEBODY TO TRANSGRESSION** to persuade or attempt to persuade somebody to do something considered wrong **3. BE INVITING TO SOMEBODY** to be inviting or attractive to somebody ○ *The sightseeing tour tempted us.* **4. RISK SOMETHING** to risk the possible destructive powers of something ○ *tempt fate* [13C. Via Old French *tempter* < Latin *temptare* "feel, try, test"] —**tempt·a·ble** *adj*

temp·ta·tion /temp táysh'n/ *n* **1. DESIRE FOR SOMETHING BAD** a desire or craving for something, especially something considered wrong ○ *yield to temptation* **2. INCITEMENT OF DESIRE** the incitement of desire or craving in somebody **3. CAUSE OF DESIRE** somebody or something that tempts somebody ○ *too many temptations for me here*

tempt·er *n* somebody who tempts somebody else to do something considered wrong

Tempt·er *n* CHR same as **Satan**

tempt·ing /témpting/ *adj* causing desire or craving to arise in somebody ○ *a tempting offer* —**tempt·ing·ly** *adv* —**tempt·ing·ness** *n*

temp·tress /témptriss/ *n* an offensive term for a woman that deliberately insults her sexuality and public behavior (*dated*)

tem·pu·ra /tem pŏŏrə/ *n* a Japanese dish of vegetables or seafood coated in light batter and deep-fried [Mid-20C. < Japanese]

tem·pus fu·git /tèmpŏŏss fyŏŏjit/ time flies [Latin]

ten /ten/ *n* **1. 10** the number 10 **2. SOMETHING WITH VALUE OF 10** something in a numbered series, e.g., a playing card, with a value of ten ○ *the ten of clubs* ○ *to play the ten* **3. GROUP OF TEN** a group of ten people or objects **4. TEN DOLLARS** a ten-dollar bill [Old English *tēn(e), tīen(e)* < Indo-European] ◇ **hang ten** to ride a surfboard with your toes hanging over the front of the board ◇ **ten to one** with overwhelming odds in favor of a particular thing happening or being true (*informal*) ○ *She said it was an accident, but ten to one she's lying.*

ten·a·ble /ténnəb'l/ *adj* **1. WITH REASONABLE SUPPORTING ARGUMENTS** justified in a fair or rational way and able to be defended because there is sufficient evidence or reason **2. ABLE TO BE OCCUPIED** capable of being occupied or held, usually by a particular person or for a particular period of time (*formal*) **3.** MIL **CAPABLE OF BEING DEFENDED IN BATTLE** able to be held successfully against an enemy attack [Late 16C. < French *tenir* "to hold"] —**ten·a·bil·i·ty** /tènnə bíllətee/ *n* —**ten·a·ble·ness** *n* —**ten·a·bly** *adv*

ten·ace /té nàyss, ténnəss/ *n* a combination of two high cards in the same suit that do not form a sequence, e.g., a jack and a king [Mid-17C. Via French < Spanish *tenaza* "pincers, tongs"]

te·na·cious /tə náyshəss/ *adj* **1. DETERMINED OR STUBBORN** tending to stick firmly to any decision, plan, or opinion without changing or doubting it **2. TIGHTLY HELD** difficult to loosen, shake off, or pull away from ○ *his tenacious grip* **3. PERSISTENT** persisting for a long time and difficult to change, destroy, or get rid of ○ *a tenacious head cold* **4. ABLE TO REMEMBER MANY THINGS** capable of absorbing and retaining a large store of information and of recalling details accurately **5. STICKY OR CLINGING** sticking or clinging to something else, especially a surface ○ *tenacious burrs* **6.** ENG **NOT EASILY DISCONNECTED** holding together tightly or fused solidly [Early 17C. < Latin *tenac-* "holding fast" < *tenere* "to hold"] —**te·na·cious·ly** *adv* —**te·na·cious·ness** *n* —**te·nac·i·ty** /tə nássətee/ *n*

te·nac·u·lum /tə nákyələm/ (*plural* **-la** /-lə/ or **-lums**) *n* a long-handled instrument with a slender sharp hook, used especially in surgery to grasp and hold arteries or other body parts [Late 17C. < Latin, "holder" < *tenere* "to hold"]

ten·an·cy /ténnənssee/ (*plural* **-cies**) *n* **1. OCCUPATION OF PROPERTY FOR RENT** exclusive possession, for a fixed period, of property or land owned by somebody else, in return for an agreed rent. This is usually under the terms of a lease or a similar legal entitlement or agreement. **2. TIME OF SOMEBODY'S TENANCY** a period of time when a piece of property such as a house or farm is legally occupied and used by somebody paying an agreed rent **3. PLACE LIVED IN BY TENANT** a piece of property that somebody is entitled to use or occupy on condition that an agreed rent is paid to the owner [15C. < TENANT]

ten·ant /ténnənt/ *n* **1. RENTER OF PROPERTY** somebody who rents a building, house, apartment, plot of land, or piece of property for a fixed period of time. This arrangement is usually under the terms of a lease or a similar legal entitlement or agreement. **2.** OCCUPIER OF PLACE somebody living in or on a property ■ *vti* (**-ant·ed, -ant·ing, -ants**) PAY RENT TO OCCUPY PROPERTY to live in or on somebody else's property as a tenant [14C. < Anglo-Norman *tenaunt*, Old French *tenant* < *tenir* "to hold" < Latin *tenere* "hold, keep"] —**ten·ant·a·ble** *adj*—**ten·ant·ed** *adj* —**ten·ant·less** *adj*

ORIGIN The Latin word *tenere* "to hold, keep," from which ***tenant*** is derived, is also the source of English *abstain, contain, continent*[1], *continue, countenance, detain, maintain, obtain, retain, sustain, tenacious, tenement, tenet, tennis, tenon, tenor*, and *tenure*.

ten·ant far·mer *n* a farmer who rents a farm, plot, or agricultural land, and pays the owner in cash or with produce

ten·ant·ry /ténnəntree/ *n* **1.** all tenants or tenant farmers, especially all those renting property from a particular landowner (*formal*) **2.** same as **tenancy** (sense 1) (*dated*)

ten-cent store *n US* COMM same as **five-and-dime**

tench /tench/ (*plural same* or **tench·es**) *n* a freshwater game fish related to the carp, with a heavy greenish body, small scales, and a barbel on each side of its mouth. Native to: Europe, western Asia. Latin name: *Tinca tinca*. [14C. Via Old French *tenche* < late Latin *tinca*]

Ten Com·mand·ments *npl* according to the Bible, the ten laws given by God to Moses. They summarize human obligations to each other and to God.

tend[1] /tend/ (**tend·ed, tend·ing, tends**) *vi* **1.** to be generally inclined or likely to react or behave in a particular way, or be in the habit of doing something **2.** to make a gentle steady movement in a particular direction [14C. Via Old French *tendre* "move toward" < Latin *tendere* "stretch, extend"]

ORIGIN The Latin word *tendere* "to stretch, extend," from which ***tend*** is derived, is also the source of English *attend, contend, détente, distend, extend, intend, ostensible, portend, pretend, tendency, tender*[1], *tense*[1], and *tent*[1].

tend[2] /tend/ (**tend·ed, tend·ing, tends**) *v* **1.** *vt* TAKE CARE OF SOMEBODY to do or provide the things that a person, animal, or plant needs for health, comfort, and welfare **2.** *vt* BE IN CHARGE OF SOMETHING to manage something, especially something that needs constant supervision ○ *tend bar* **3.** *vi* GIVE ATTENTION TO SOMEBODY OR SOMETHING to give your attention to a particular person or task [12C. Shortening of ATTEND] —**ten·dance** *n*

~~**tendancy**~~ incorrect spelling of **tendency**

ten·den·cious *adj* another spelling of **tendentious**

ten·den·cy /téndənssee/ (*plural* **-cies**) *n* **1.** a way in which somebody or something typically behaves or happens, or is likely to react, behave, or happen **2.** a gradual, but steady progress, development, or shift of opinion in a particular direction ○ *a tendency toward greater assertiveness* [Early 17C. < medieval Latin *tendentia* < Latin *tendere* "tend, be inclined to"]

ten·den·tious /ten dénshəss/, **ten·den·cious** *adj* written or spoken with personal bias in order to promote a cause or support a viewpoint [Early 20C. < TENDENCY] —**ten·den·tious·ly** *adv* —**ten·den·tious·ness** *n*

ten·der[1] /téndər/ *adj* **1.** PHYSICALLY PAINFUL hurting or unusually sensitive when touched or pressed **2.** WITH GENTLE FEELING showing care, gentleness, and feeling **3.** KIND AND SYMPATHETIC sensitive and caring toward others and often feeling emotions intensely ○ *a tender disposition* **4.** PLEASANTLY SOFT FOR EATING soft enough for the teeth to go through easily without much chewing ○ *a tender juicy steak* **5.** YOUNG AND DEFENSELESS vulnerably young, weak, and inexperienced ○ *at a tender age* **6.** FRAGILE so delicate, soft, or weak as to be hurt, crushed, or broken easily ○ *tender flower petals* **7.** BOT, AGRIC NEEDING PROTECTION FROM HARSH WEATHER easily damaged or killed by unsuitable weather or conditions, especially frost and cold ○ *a tender plant* [13C. Via French *tendre* < Latin *tener* "delicate, tender"] —**ten·der·ly** *adv* —**ten·der·ness** *n*

CULTURAL NOTE ***Tender is the Night***, a novel (1934) by F. Scott Fitzgerald. Set on the French Riviera in the 1930s, it focuses on a group of glamorous US expatriates. Psychologist Richard Diver's attempts to nurse his wife and former patient, Nicole, and his involvement with a visiting woman actor, lead to his mental collapse. A powerful depiction of human frailty, it is also admired for the elegance of its prose.

ten·der[2] /téndər/ *v* (**-dered, -der·ing, -ders**) **1.** *vt* OFFER SOMETHING FORMALLY IN WRITING to present something formal or official, in the form of a document ○ *tender a resignation* **2.** *vi* COMM OFFER TO SUPPLY SOMETHING to offer to undertake a job or supply goods ○ *tender for a contract* **3.** *vt* LAW OFFER SUM IN SETTLEMENT to offer to pay money or goods as a way of settling a debt or claim ■ *n* **1.** COMM FORMAL OFFER TO UNDERTAKE JOB a formal offer to undertake a job or supply goods ○ *Their tender was accepted because it was the lowest.* **2.** same as **money** ○ *legal tender* **3.** COMM ACT OF TENDERING the act of tendering for a contract **4.** LAW OFFER MADE TO SETTLE SOMETHING a formal offer to settle legal proceedings on payment of an amount of damages [Mid-16C. Via Old French *tendre* < Latin *tendere* "hold out, stretch"] —**ten·der·a·ble** *adj* —**ten·der·er** *n*

tend·er[3] /téndər/ *n* **1.** SMALL BOAT FERRYING TO LARGE BOAT a small boat used to go to and from a larger one such as a yacht **2.** RAIL VEHICLE CARRYING SUPPLIES FOR STEAM ENGINE the permanently coupled rear part of a large steam locomotive, used for carrying its coal and water **3.** SOMEBODY WHO TENDS somebody who tends something or somebody [15C. Shortening of *attender* (< ATTEND), or < TEND[2]]

ten·der·foot /téndər fòot/ (*plural* **-feet** /-fèet/ or **-foots**) *n* **1.** BEGINNER AT SOMETHING somebody just starting to do or try something, with little or no previous experience of it (*informal*) **2.** SOMEBODY UNUSED TO TOUGH OUTDOOR LIFE a new arrival at a place where the work and conditions are rough, e.g., on a ranch or mine **3.** LOWEST RANK IN SCOUTS a member of the lowest rank of a Boy or Girl Scout troop (*dated*)

ten·der·heart·ed /tèndər haártəd/ *adj* quick to feel or show compassion and sympathy for other people —**ten·der·heart·ed·ly** *adv* —**ten·der·heart·ed·ness** *n*

ten·der·ize /téndə rīz/ (**-ized, -iz·ing, -iz·es**) *vt* to make meat tender by beating it, soaking it in a marinade, or sprinkling it with a special substance (**tenderizer**) that breaks down its fibers —**ten·der·i·za·tion** /tèndəri záysh'n/ *n*

ten·der·iz·er /téndə rīzər/ *n* **1.** a commercial preparation containing enzymes that break down fibrous tissue in meat **2.** a wooden or metal mallet used to pound meat. It has a short handle and a fairly broad head with a hammering surface covered in shallow bumps.

ten·der·loin /téndər lòyn/ *n* **1.** a prime cut of lean tender beef, pork or lamb taken from the curve of the ribs at the backbone **2.** a part of a city where prostitution, vice, and extortion are common (*informal*)

ten·di·ni·tis /tèndə nītiss/, **ten·do·ni·tis** *n* inflammation of a tendon usually occurring after excessive use, as in a sports injury [Early 20C. < modern Latin *tendin-*, stem of *tendo* "tendon"]

ten·don /téndən/ *n* an inelastic cord or band of tough white fibrous connective tissue that attaches a muscle to a bone or other part [Mid-16C. Directly and via French < medieval Latin *tendon-*, stem of *tendo*, translation of Greek *tenōn* "sinew" < *teinein* "stretch"] —**ten·di·nous** *adj*

ten·don ham·mer *n* MED same as **plexor**

ten·do·ni·tis *n* MED another spelling of **tendinitis**

ten·dril /téndril/ *n* **1.** a modified stem, leaf, or other part of a climbing plant, usually in the form of a thread, that coils around and attaches the plant to supporting objects **2.** a slim, wispy, curling, or winding piece of something, especially hair (*literary*) [Mid-16C. < Middle French *tendrillon* "little shoot, little cartilage" < *tendron* "shoot, cartilage" < Old French *tendre* (see TENDER[1])]

Ten·e·brae /ténnə bràY, -bree/ *n* in the Roman Catholic Church, the office of matins and lauds for the last three days of Holy Week (*takes a singular or plural verb*) [Mid-17C. < Latin, "darkness," because candles are extinguished during the service in memory of the darkness at the Crucifixion]

te·neb·ri·o·nid /tə nébbree ə nìd, tènnə brī ə nìd/ (*plural* **-nids** or *same*) *n* INSECTS same as **darkling beetle** [Early 20C. < modern Latin]

te·neb·ri·ous *adj* same as **tenebrous**

ten·e·brism /ténnə brìzzəm/, **Ten·e·brism** *n* a style of painting, popular in 17th-century Naples and Spain and largely associated with Caravaggio, that uses large areas of shadow and dark colors, sometimes with a shaft of light [Mid-20C. < Italian *tenebroso* "dark"] —**tene·brist** *n*

ten·e·brous /ténnəbrəss/, **te·neb·ri·ous** /tə nébbree əss/ *adj* dark, murky, or obscured by shadows (*literary*) [15C. < Old French *tenebrus* < Latin *tenebrae* "darkness"] —**ten·e·bros·i·ty** /tènnə bróssətee/ *n* —**ten·e·brous·ness** *n*

ten·e·ment /ténnəmənt/ *n* **1.** a large residential building in a city, usually of three or more stories and with only basic amenities, where a large number of people live in self-contained rented apartments **2.** a piece of property, e.g., land or houses, held by one person but owned by another [14C. Via Old French, "tenure" < medieval Latin *tenementum* < Latin *tenere* "to hold"]

~~**tenent**~~ incorrect spelling of **tenant**

Ten·er·ife /tènnə rée fay, -réef/, **Ten·er·iffe** largest of the Canary Islands, in Santa Cruz de Tenerife Province, Spain. Population: 701,034 (2001). Area: 785 sq. mi./2,034 sq. km.

te·nes·mus /tə nézməss/ *n* an urgent, painful, and unsuccessful attempt to defecate or urinate [Early 16C. Via medieval Latin < Greek *tēnesmos* < *teinein* "stretch, strain"]

~~**Tenessee**~~ incorrect spelling of **Tennessee**

ten·et /ténnət/ *n* an established fundamental belief, especially one relating to religion or politics ○ *a basic tenet of Christianity* [Late 16C. < Latin, "he or she holds," form of *tenere* "to hold"]

ten·fold /tén fòld/ *adj* **1.** TIMES TEN multiplied by ten **2.** WITH TEN PARTS made up of ten parts ■ *adv* TEN TIMES OVER to ten times the amount or number, or multiplied by or up to that amount or number

ten-four, 10–4 *interj* used to express affirmation or confirmation [< police code "message received"]

ten-gal·lon hat *n* a cowboy hat with a high round uncreased crown and a wide brim

ten·ge /tén gày/ (*plural same*) *n* the main unit of Kazakh currency. See table at **currency** [Late 20C. < Kazakh]

te·ni·a, etc. another spelling of **taenia. etc.**

Tenn. *abbr* Tennessee

Ten·nent /ténnənt/, **Gilbert** (1703–64) Irish-born American cleric. His fiery preaching helped to create the religious revival known as the "Great Awakening" in the North American Middle Colonies in the 1730s.

Ten·nent, William (1673–1745) Irish-born American cleric. Many of the students at his "Log College" in Pennsylvania, including his son Gilbert, became important figures in the Great Awakening of the 1730s.

ten·ner /ténnər/ *n* a ten-dollar bill (*informal*)

~~**Tennesee**~~ incorrect spelling of **Tennessee**

Ten·nes·see /tènnə sée/ **1.** state in the eastern central

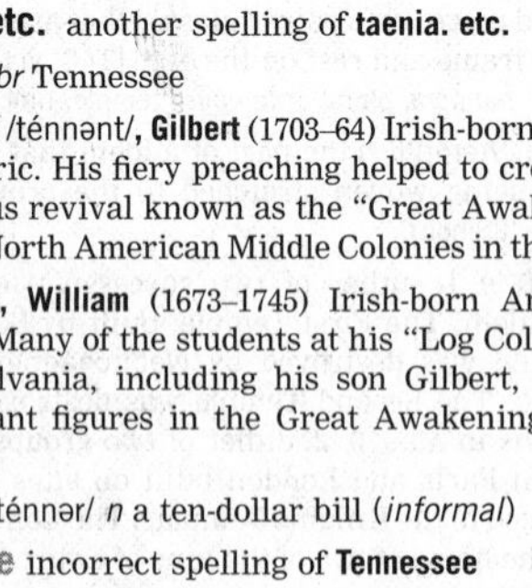

Tennessee

United States, bordered by Kentucky, Virginia, North Carolina, Georgia, Alabama, Mississippi, Arkansas, and Missouri. Capital: Nashville. Population: 5,797,289 (2002 estimate). Area: 42,146 sq. mi./109,158 sq. km. **2.** river of the southeastern United States, formed by the confluence of the Holston and French Broad rivers and flowing into the Ohio River. Length: 652 mi./1,050 km. See illustration on previous page —**Ten·nes·se·an** *n, adj*

Ten·nes·see Walk·ing Horse, **Ten·nes·see Walk·er** *n* a saddle horse with a characteristic fast easy gait, belonging to a breed developed in Tennessee from Standardbred and Morgan stock

Ten·niel /ténnyəl/, **Sir John** (1820–1914) British illustrator. He contributed more than 2,300 cartoons to the British satirical magazine *Punch* from 1850 to 1901. His illustrations for *Alice's Adventures in Wonderland* (1865) and *Through the Looking-Glass* (1872) fixed the images of Lewis Carroll's characters for generations of children.

ten·nis /ténniss/ *n* a game played on a rectangular court by two players or two pairs of players, who use rackets to hit a ball back and forth over a net stretched across a marked-out court [14C. Probably < Old French *tenez* "hold!", form of *tenir* "to hold, receive"]

ten·nis ball *n* a white or yellow fuzzy cloth-covered hollow rubber ball about 3 in./7.5 cm in diameter, used in tennis. In lawn tennis the ball is pressurized, and in paddle tennis it is punctured.

ten·nis brace·let *n US* a slim chain-style bracelet made with small diamonds or other precious stones

ten·nis el·bow *n* a painful inflammation of the tendon in the outer elbow region caused by excessive and repetitive strain from overuse, e.g., as a result of playing tennis or similar sports. It may be treated with rest, massage, or steroid drugs.

ten·nis shoe *n* CLOTHING same as **sneaker**

ten·nis skirt *n* a short skirt, traditionally white, worn by some women tennis players

Ten·ny·son /ténniss'n/, **Alfred, 1st Baron Tennyson of Freshwater and Aldworth** (1809–92) British poet. His many works include *The Lady of Shalott* (1832), *In Memoriam* (1850), and *The Charge of the Light Brigade* (1854). He was poet laureate (1850–92). Known as **Alfred, Lord Tennyson** —**Ten·ny·so·ni·an** /tènni sṓnee ən/ *n, adj*

> "For words, like Nature, half reveal / And half conceal the Soul within."
> [Alfred Tennyson, *In Memoriam*; 1850]

> "'Forward the Light Brigade!' / Was there a man dismay'd? / Not tho' the soldier knew / Some one had blunder'd: / Their's not to make reply, / Their's not to reason why, / Their's but to do and die: / Into the valley of Death / Rode the six hundred."
> [Alfred Tennyson, "The Charge of the Light Brigade," *Maud and Other Poems*; 1855]

Te·noch·ti·tlán /te nṓch tee tla̓an/ ancient capital of the Aztecs, in Lake Texcoco, now modern Mexico City. It was founded in 1325 and destroyed by the Spanish in 1521.

ten·on /ténnən/ *n* **PROJECTION ON WOOD FOR MAKING JOINT** a projection on one piece of wood that fits into a matching recess (a mortise) on another piece so as to make a joint ■ *vt* (**-oned, -on·ing, -ons**) **1. MAKE TENON ON WOOD** to make a tenon on a piece of wood **2. JOIN PIECES OF WOOD USING TENON** to join two pieces of wood using a tenon [Early 17C. < Old French, < *tenir* "to hold"] —**ten·on·er** *n*

ten·on saw *n* a small thin saw with a strong back, used especially for cutting tenons

ten·or /ténnər/ *n* **1. HIGH MALE VOICE** the highest natural male singing voice, or a man whose voice is in this register **2. UPPER RANGE INSTRUMENT** an instrument with a range similar to a tenor voice (*often used before a noun*) ○ *a tenor saxophone* **3. WAY SOMETHING IS PROGRESSING** the direction in which something is steadily moving (*formal*) **4. GENERAL NATURE OF SOMETHING** the overall nature, pattern, or meaning of something, especially a written or spoken statement (*formal*) ○ *The general tenor of the reply was positive.* **5.** LAW **EXACT WORDS OF DEED** the exact wording of a document **6.** LAW **EXACT COPY** an exact copy or transcript of a document [13C. Via Anglo-Norman, Old French < Latin, "continuous course" < *tenere* "to hold"]

ten·or clef *n* a C clef in which middle C is represented by the second highest line on the staff, used in music for the cello, bassoon, and tenor trombone. It was formerly used to notate the tenor voice.

ten·or drum *n* a medium-size drum without snares

ten·or·ite /ténnə rìt/ *n* a black copper oxide mineral [Mid-19C. After Michele *Tenore* (1781–1861), president of the Naples Academy of Sciences in Italy]

ten·o·syn·o·vi·tis /tènnō sīnə vítiss, -sinə-/ *n* inflammation of a tendon sheath, usually in the wrist, with swelling and audible creaking on movement. It often results from repetitive movements as in typing or some sports. [Late 19C. < modern Latin < Greek *tenōn* "tendon"]

te·not·o·my /tə nóttəmee/ (*plural* **-mies**) *n* the surgical cutting of a tendon

ten·pen·ny nail /tèn pènnee-/ *n US* a nail 3 in./7.6 cm long (*dated*)

ten·pin /tén pìn/ *n* any of the ten pins used in bowling

ten·pin bowl·ing, **ten·pins** /tén pìnz/ *n Can, UK* an indoor game in which players try to knock down ten pins at the far end of a special bowling alley by rolling a heavy ball at them. US term **bowling**

ten·pound·er /tèn pówndər/ *n US* FISH same as **ladyfish** (sense 1)

ten·rec /tén rèk/ (*plural* **-recs** or *same*), **tan·rec** /tán rèk/ *n* a small to medium-sized insect-eating mammal with a long pointed snout. Native to: Madagascar, Comoros. Family: Tenrecidae. [Late 18C. Via French *tanrec* < Malagasy *tàndraka, tràndraka*]

TENS /tenz/ *n* a method of treating chronic pain by applying electrodes to the skin and passing small electric currents through sensory nerves and the spinal cord, thus suppressing the transmission of pain signals. Full form **transcutaneous electrical nerve stimulation**

tense[1] /tenss/ *adj* (**tens·er, tens·est**) **1. WORRIED AND NERVOUS** affected by anxious feelings or mental strain, so that it is impossible to behave in a natural relaxed way **2. RESTRAINED AND UNNATURAL** causing feelings of anxiety, nervousness, and uncertainty, so that natural relaxed talk or behavior is impossible ○ *a tense wait* **3. TIGHT AND STIFF** stretched or held tight and stiff ○ *tense muscles* **4.** PHON **PRONOUNCED WITH TAUT MUSCLES** describes a speech sound that is pronounced with muscular effort, is relatively long in duration, and is accurate in articulation ■ *vti* (**tensed, tens·ing, tens·es**) **BECOME OR MAKE TENSE** to become tense, or make something such as a muscle or part of the body become tense [Late 17C. < Latin *tensus* "stretched," past participle of *tendere* "stretch"] —**tense·ly** *adv* —**tense·ness** *n*

tense up *vti* same as **tense**[1] *v*

tense[2] /tenss/ *n* one of the sets of forms of a verb that express the different times at which action takes place relative to the speaker or writer, e.g., the present, past, or future ○ *in the future tense* [14C. Via Old French *tens* "time" < Latin *tempus*] —**tense·less** *adj*

USAGE Strictly speaking, the English language has only two *tenses*, the present (*go, eat, die*) and the past (*went, ate, died*). All other expressions of time are formed by combining auxiliary verbs with the present participle, past participle, or infinitive, as in the progressive or continuous aspect (*I was going*), the perfect or perfective aspect (*They have eaten*), and the future (*He will die*). They are, however, commonly referred to as tenses.

ten·sile /ténss'l, tén sìl/ *adj* **1.** relating to or involving tension **2.** capable of being stretched or pulled out of shape [Early 17C. < medieval Latin *tensilis* < Latin *tendere* "stretch"] —**ten·sile·ly** *adv* —**ten·sile·ness** *n* —**ten·sil·i·ty** /ten síllətee/ *n*

ten·sile strength *n* the maximum stretching force that a material such as wire can withstand before breaking

ten·sim·e·ter /ten símmətər/ *n* an instrument used to measure differences in vapor pressure [Early 20C. < TENSION]

ten·si·om·e·ter /tènssee ómmətər/ *n* **1. INSTRUMENT FOR MEASURING TENSILE STRENGTH** an instrument used to measure tensile strength **2. INSTRUMENT FOR MEASURING SURFACE TENSION** an instrument used to measure the surface tension of liquids **3.** GEOL **INSTRUMENT FOR MEASURING SOIL MOISTURE** an instrument used to measure the moisture content of soils [Early 20C. < TENSION]

ten·sion /ténshən/ *n* **1. ANXIOUS FEELINGS** mental worry or emotional strain that makes natural relaxed behavior impossible **2. UNEASY FEELING IN RELATIONSHIP** a state of wariness, mistrust, controlled hostility, or fear of hostility felt by countries, groups, or people in their dealings with one another (*often used in the plural*) **3. TAUTNESS** the degree to which something such as a wire, string, thread, or muscle is stretched **4.** LITERAT **BUILDUP OF SUSPENSE** the buildup of suspense in a fictional work, leading to the denouement **5.** LITERAT **SENSE OF CONFLICT** the way that opposing characters clash or interact in an interesting way with each other in a literary work **6.** HANDICRAFT **DEVICE CONTROLLING TIGHTNESS OF THREAD** a device on a sewing machine or a loom that regulates how tight the thread is **7.** PHYS **PULLING FORCE** a force that pulls or stretches something **8.** PHYS **STRESS FROM TENSION** the stress resulting from a force of tension, or a measure of it **9.** ELEC **VOLTAGE** voltage or electromotive force (*often used in combination*) ○ *high-tension wires* [Mid-16C. Directly or via French < Latin *tension-* "stretching" < *tendere* "stretch"] —**ten·sion·al** *adj*

ten·si·ty /ténssətee/ *n* the state or quality of being tense

ten·sive /ténssiv/ *adj* relating to or causing tension [Early 18C. < French *tensif* < Latin *tendere* "stretch"]

ten·som·e·ter *n* PHYS same as **tensiometer** (senses 1–2)

ten·sor /ténssər, tén sàwr/ *n* **1.** a muscle that tenses or stretches a part of the body **2.** a generalization of a vector that is a mathematical entity specified with respect to a given coordinate system and able to undergo transformation to other coordinate systems [Early 18C. < modern Latin < Latin *tendere* "stretch"] —**ten·so·ri·al** /ten sáwree əl/ *adj*

ten-speed *adj* with ten different gears controlling the speed ■ *n* a ten-speed bicycle

ten-strike *n* **1.** BOWLING same as **strike** *n* (sense 7) **2.** *US* a great achievement, result, or action (*informal*)

tent[1] /tent/ *n* **1. COLLAPSIBLE SHELTER** a collapsible movable shelter consisting of a tough fabric or plastic cover held up by poles and kept in place by ropes and pegs **2. OBJECT LIKE TENT** something that looks like a tent, is constructed in a similar way, or serves a similar purpose ○ *an oxygen tent* ■ *v* (**tent·ed, tent·ing, tents**) **1.** *vt* **COVER SOMETHING AS TENT DOES** to form a raised nonrigid cover over something ○ *Tent the roast with aluminum foil.* **2.** *vi* **CAMP** to live or camp in a tent **3.** *vt* **SUPPLY TENT FOR SOMEBODY** to accommodate a person or group of people in tents, or provide somebody or something with tents [13C. Via Old French *tente* < Latin *tenta* "tent" < *tendere* "stretch"]

tent[2] /tent/ *n* a cone-shaped expandable plug of soft material such as gauze used to keep a wound or orifice open ■ *vt* (**tent·ed, tent·ing, tents**) to open or expand a wound or orifice with a tent [14C. < French *tente* < *tenter* < Latin *temptare* "feel, try"]

ten·ta·cle /téntək'l/ *n* **1. LONG FLEXIBLE ORGAN** a long flexible organ around the mouth or on the head of some animals, especially invertebrates such as squid, used in holding, grasping, feeling, or moving **2. HAIR ON PLANT LEAF** a sticky glandular hairy projection from the leaf of an insect-eating plant such as the sundew, whose secretions trap and digest prey **3. SOMETHING FAR-REACHING** something that gradually insinuates its influence or control (*literary; usually used in the plural*) [Mid-18C. < modern Latin *tentaculum* < Latin *temptare* "feel, try"] —**ten·ta·cled** *adj* —**ten·tac·u·lar** /ten tákyələr/ *adj*

tent·age /téntij/ *n* tents in general or considered as a group

ten·ta·tive /téntətiv/ *adj* **1.** said or done in a slow, hesitant, and careful way that reveals a lack of confidence **2.** likely to have changes before becoming final and complete ○ *a tentative draft of the document* [Late 16C. < medieval Latin *tentativus* < Latin *tentare*, variant of *temptare* "feel, try"] —**ten·ta·tive·ly** *adv* —**ten·ta·tive·ness** *n*

tent cat·er·pil·lar *n* a destructive caterpillar that builds large tent-shaped communal webs in the branches of trees. Genus: *Malacosoma.*

tent dress *n* a wide full dress that hangs loose from the shoulders

tent·ed /téntəd/ *adj* **1.** WITH TENT SHAPE constructed or shaped like a tent **2.** CAMPED IN TENTS staying in tents, or supplied with tents as shelter **3.** WITH TENTS covered in tents (*literary*)

ten·ter /téntər/ *n* a frame on which cloth is held taut during various phases of its manufacture, especially while it dries ■ *vt* (**-tered, -ter·ing, -ters**) to stretch cloth on a tenter [13C. < medieval Latin *tentorium* < Latin *tendere* "stretch"]

ten·ter·hook /téntər hoŏk/ *n* one of the hooks used to hold cloth taut on a frame during manufacture, especially while it dries ◇ **be on tenterhooks** to be anxious or in great suspense

tenth /tenth/ *n* **1.** ONE OF TEN PARTS OF SOMETHING one of ten equal parts of something **2.** ORDINAL NUMBER CORRESPONDING TO 10 the ordinal number assigned to item number 10 in a series **3.** MUSIC **MUSICAL INTERVAL** a musical interval equal to an octave plus a third [Old English *teogoþa, tēoþa* < Germanic; later < TEN] —**tenth** *adj, adv*

tent stitch *n* a short parallel diagonal stitch used to fill in an area in needlepoint or embroidery

ten·u·is /ténnyoo iss/ (*plural* **-u·es** /-yoo èez/) *n* a voiceless stop consonant in classical Greek grammar [Mid-17C. < Latin, "thin, fine," translation of Greek *psilon* "bare, smooth"]

ten·u·ous /ténnyoo əss/ *adj* **1.** WEAK AND UNCONVINCING not based on anything significant or substantial, and therefore unlikely to stand up to rigorous examination ○ *That's an extremely tenuous argument.* **2.** EXTREMELY DELICATE AND FINE thin and fine, and therefore easily broken (*literary*) **3.** SCI **DILUTED** thin or diluted in consistency [Late 16C. < Latin *tenuis* "thin, fine"] —**te·nu·i·ty** /te noó ətee/ *n* —**ten·u·ous·ly** *adv* —**ten·u·ous·ness** *n*

ten·ure /ténnyər/ *n* **1.** APPOINTMENT OR PERIOD OF APPOINTMENT the occupation of an official position, or the length of time that an official position is occupied (*formal*) ○ *during her tenure as president* **2.** EDUC, HR **PERMANENT STATUS** the position of having a formal secure appointment until retirement, especially at an institution of higher learning after working there on a temporary or provisional basis **3.** PROPERTY **RIGHTS** the rights of a tenant to hold property, or the holding of property as a tenant [15C. < Old French, "tenure, estate" < Latin *tenere* "to hold"] —**ten·ured** *adj*

ten·ure-track *adj* guaranteed consideration for tenure in the US and Canadian system of academic employment ○ *offered a tenure-track position at the university*

te·nu·to /tay noótō, tə-/ *adv, adj* indicating that a musical note should be held for its full value (*used as a musical direction*) [Mid-18C. < Italian, past participle of *tenere* "to hold" < Latin]

Ten·zing Nor·gay /tènzing náwr gay/, **Ten·zing Nor·kay** /-náwr kay/ (1914?–86) Nepalese mountaineer. He and Sir Edmund Hillary were the first to reach the summit of Mount Everest (1953).

Ten·zin Gyat·so /tènzin gyát sō/ (*b.* 1935) 14th Dalai Lama (1940–). After a Tibetan rebellion against Chinese rule, he fled into exile (1959). He led the nonviolent opposition to continued Chinese rule in Tibet, for which he received the Nobel Peace Prize (1989).

te·o·cal·li /tèe ə kállee, tày ə kaálee/ (*plural* **-lis**) *n* a temple in ancient Mexico or Central America, or the pyramidal mound on which one was built [Early 17C. Via American Spanish < Nahuatl *teokalli* "deity's house"]

te·o·sin·te /tày ō síntee, tèe ə-/ *n* a tall annual grass grown for forage, related to, and perhaps the ancestor of, corn. Native to: Mexico, Central America. Latin name: *Zea mexicana.* [Late 19C. Via French *téosinté* < Nahuatl *teocintli*]

Te·o·ti·hua·cán /tày ō tèewə kaán/ ancient city in central Mexico, northeast of Mexico City, now an archaeological site that contains the remains of the earliest city in the western hemisphere (c. 300 B.C. – A.D. c. 700)

te·pa /teépə/ *n* a soluble crystalline compound. Use: insect sterilization, cancer treatment, textile fireproofing. Formula: $C_6H_{12}N_3OP$. [Mid-20C. Acronym < TRI- + ETHYLENE + PHOSPH- + AMIDE]

te·pal /teép'l, tépp'l/ *n* any of the parts that form the outer whorl (**perianth**) of flowers such as the tulip, in which there is no differentiation into petals and sepals [Mid-19C. < French, blend of *sépale* "sepal" + *pétale* "petal"]

tep·a·ry bean /téppəree-/ *n* an annual twining bean grown for its round edible seeds. Native to: southwestern United States, Mexico. Latin name: *Phaseolus acutifolius latifolius.* [Early 20C. Origin ?]

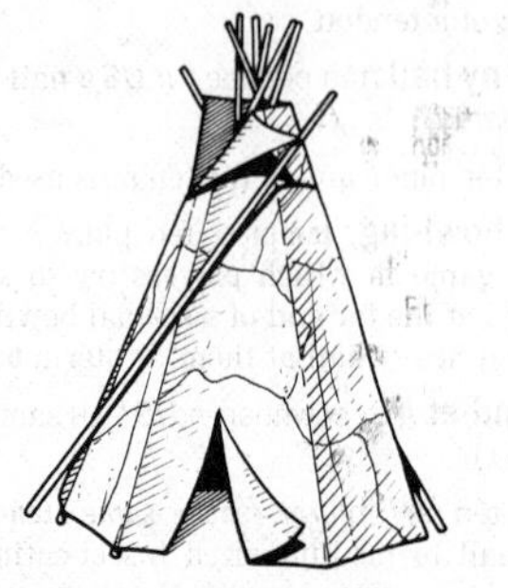

tepee

te·pee /teé pee/, **tee·pee**, **ti·pi** (*plural* **-pis**) *n* a conical tent built around several long branches or wooden poles that meet and cross at the top. A tepee is traditionally made of animal hide and used as a dwelling by Plains Indians and some other Native North American peoples. [Mid-18C. < Dakota *típi* "dwelling" < *tí* "dwell"]

teph·ra /téffrə/ *n* solid material ejected explosively from a volcano, e.g., ash, dust, and boulders [Mid-20C. < Greek, "ashes"]

tep·id /téppid/ *adj* **1.** slightly warm ○ *tepid water* **2.** showing little enthusiasm or warmth ○ *tepid applause* [14C. < Latin *tepidus* < *tepere* "be warm"] —**te·pid·i·ty** /tə píddətee/ *n* —**tep·id·ly** *adv* —**tep·id·ness** *n*

TEPP /tep/ *n* a crystalline compound (**organophosphate**). Use: insecticide, stimulant for nervous system. Formula: $C_8H_{20}O_7P_2$. Full form **tetraethyl pyrophosphate**

te·qui·la /tə keélə/ *n* a strong Mexican liquor made by redistilling the fermented juice of the agave plant (**mescal**). It is drunk neat or used as a base for cocktails. [Mid-19C. < Mexican Spanish, after *Tequila*, town in central Mexico]

te·qui·la sun·rise *n* a cocktail consisting of tequila combined with orange juice and grenadine

ter. *abbr* **1.** GEOG, BUILDINGS terrace **2.** ARMY, ZOOL territorial **3.** GEOG, ZOOL, POL territory

Ter. *abbr* Terrace (*used in addresses*)

ter- *prefix* three, threefold ○ *terpolymer* [< Latin *ter* "three times" < Indo-European, "three"]

tera- *prefix* **1.** one trillion (10^{12}). Symbol **T** **2.** in the binary system, a trillion (2^{40}) ○ *terabyte* [< Greek *teras* "monster"]

ter·a·byte /térrə bìt/ *n* **1.** a unit of computer data or storage space equivalent to 1,024 gigabytes **2.** COMPUT one trillion bytes

ter·a·flop /térrə flòp/ *n* one trillion floating-point operations per second, a measure of computer speed [Late 20C. < TERA- + acronym < *floating-point operations per second*]

ter·a·hertz /térrə hùrts/ (*plural same*) *n* a unit of frequency equal to one trillion hertz

te·rai /tə rí/ *n* a wide-brimmed felt hat with a double crown, once widely worn in the subtropics [Late 19C. After TERAI]

Te·rai /tə rí/ area of marshy land in the foothills of the Himalaya range in northern India and southern Nepal

terai hat *n* CLOTHING same as **terai**

ter·aph /térrəf/ (*plural* **-a·phim** /-ə fìm/) *n* an image or idol worshiped by ancient Semitic peoples [14C.Originally plural, via late Latin and Greek < Hebrew *tĕrāpīm*]

terato- *prefix* **1.** malformed ○ *teratogen* **2.** tumor ○ *teratoma* [< Greek *terat-*, stem of *teras* "monster"]

ter·a·to·car·ci·no·ma /tèrrətō kaarss'n ṓmə/ (*plural* **-mas** or **-ma·ta** /-ṓmətə/) *n* a malignant teratoma, most often occurring in the testes

te·rat·o·gen /tə ráttəjən, térrətəjən/ *n* an agent that interrupts or alters the normal development of a fetus, with results that are evident at birth, e.g., a chemical, virus, or ionizing radiation —**ter·a·to·gen·e·sis** /tèrrətə jénnəssiss/ *n* —**ter·a·to·gen·ic** /tèrrətə jénnik/ *adj*

ter·a·toid /térrə tòyd/ *adj* affected by a visible condition caused by the interruption or alteration of normal development

ter·a·tol·o·gy /tèrrə tóllәjee/ *n* the scientific study of visible conditions caused by the interruption or alteration of normal development —**ter·a·to·log·ic** /tèrrətə lójjik/ *adj* —**ter·a·tol·o·gist** *n*

ter·a·to·ma /tèrrə tṓmə/ *n* a tumor composed of various tissues such as bone, hair, and teeth not normally found together at the site of origin and probably derived from embryonic remnants. They most often occur in the ovary, where they are benign, and in the testis, where they are malignant. —**ter·a·to·ma·tous** *adj*

ter·bi·um /túrbee əm/ *n* a silvery gray metallic element of the rare-earth group. Source: monazite, bastnaesite. Use: lasers, X-rays, television tubes. Symbol **Tb**. See table at **element** [Mid-19C. After *Ytterby*, village in Sweden] —**ter·bic** *adj*

terce /turss/ *n* in the Roman Catholic Church, the third of the seven separate hours (**canonical hours**) that are set aside for prayer each day [14C. < Old French, variant of *tierce* (see TIERCE)]

Ter·cei·ra /tər sáyrə, -sírə/ second largest island in the Azores archipelago, in the North Atlantic Ocean. Population: 59,248 (1991). Area: 153 sq. mi./397 sq. km.

ter·cel /túrss'l/ (*plural* **-cels** or *same*), **tier·cel** /teérss'l/ *n* a male falcon or hawk used in falconry [14C. < Old French *terçuel* < Latin *tertius* "third"]

ter·cen·ten·a·ry /tùrss'n ténnəree, tùr séntə'n èrree/, **ter·cen·ten·ni·al** /-ténnee əl/ *n* (*plural* **-ries;** *plural* **-als**) a year, or an exact day, 300 years after an event, usually one of special historic significance ■ *adj* coinciding with the 300th anniversary of an event, and often celebrating or commemorating this [Mid-19C. < Latin *ter* "three times"]

ter·cet /túrssət/ *n* a group of three lines of verse that rhyme with each other or with another group of three [Late 16C. Via French < Italian *terzetto* < Latin *tertius* "third"]

ter·e·binth /térrə bìnth/ (*plural* **-binths** or *same*) *n* a tree of the cashew family that yields turpentine. Native to: Mediterranean. Latin name: *Pistacia terebinthus.* [14C. Directly or via French < Latin *terebinthus* < Greek *terebinthos*]

ter·e·bin·thine /tèrrə bínthin, -bín thìn/ *adj* **1.** relating to the terebinth tree **2.** resembling or consisting of turpentine [Early 16C. < Latin *terebinthinus* < *terebinthus* (see TEREBINTH)]

te·re·do /tə reédō, -ráy-/ (*plural* **-dos** or *same*) *n* MARINE BIOL same as **shipworm** [14C. Via Latin < Greek *terēdōn* < *teirein* "rub hard, wear away, bore"]

Ter·ence /térrənss/ (185–159 B.C.) Roman playwright. His six surviving comedies, based on Greek originals, are forerunners of the modern comedy of manners. Full name **Publius Terentius Afer**

> "The quarrels of lovers are the renewal of love."
>
> [Terence, *Heauton Timoroumenos*; 2nd century B.C.]

Te·re·sa (of Á·vi·la) /tə reéssə əv aávilə, -ràyssə-/, **St.** (1515–82) Spanish nun. Famous for the mystical visions she experienced, she was also the founder of the order of the Discalced Carmelites (1562). Born **Cepeda y Ahumada, Teresa de**

> "Untilled soil, however fertile it may be, will bear thistles and thorns; and so it is with man's mind."
> [Teresa (of Ávila), "Maxims for Her Nuns"; 1566?]

Express Newspapers

Mother Teresa

Te·re·sa (of Cal·cut·ta) /tə reéssə-/, **Mother** (1910–97) Albanian-born nun. After 1948 she devoted her life to helping the poor and the sick of Kolkata (formerly Calcutta). She founded the Missionaries of Charity (1950) and opened a shelter for dying people (1952). She won the Nobel Peace Prize (1979). Born **Bojaxhiu, Agnes Gonxha**

> "The poor are our brothers and sisters...people in the world who need love, who need care, who have to be wanted."
> [Mother Teresa (of Calcutta), "Saints Among Us," *Time*; December 29, 1975]

> "The biggest disease today is not leprosy or tuberculosis, but rather the feeling of being unwanted, uncared for and deserted by everybody."
> [Mother Teresa (of Calcutta), *Observer (London)*; October 3, 1971]

Te·resh·ko·va /tè resh kṓvə/, **Valentina** (*b.* 1937) Soviet cosmonaut. She was the first woman to fly in space (June 16–19, 1963).

~~**terestrial**~~ incorrect spelling of **terrestrial**

te·rete /tə reét/ *adj* describes a plant part that is smooth, cylindrical, and tapering, e.g., a grass stem [Early 17C. < Latin *teret-* "rounded"]

ter·ga ZOOL plural of **tergum**

ter·giv·er·sate /tər jívvər sàyt, túrjivər-, tùrji vúr-/ (**-sat·ed, -sat·ing, -sates**) *vi* (*formal*) **1.** to make deliberately unclear, ambiguous, or contradictory statements **2.** to change sides or loyalties [Mid-17C. < Latin *tergiversat-*, past participle of *tergiversare* "turn your back" < *tergum* "back" + *vertere* "turn"] —**ter·gi·ver·sant** /tùrji vúrss'nt, tər jívvərss'nt/ *n* —**ter·gi·ver·sa·tor** *n* —**ter·gi·ver·sa·tor·y** /tùrji vúrssə tàwree, tər jívvərssə-/ *adj*

ter·gum /túrgəm/ (*plural* **-ga** /-gə/) *n* a thick plate covering the dorsal surface of a body segment of an arthropod, or the movable segments of a barnacle's shell [Early 19C. < Latin, "back"] —**ter·gal** *adj*

ter·i·ya·ki /tèrree yaákee/ *n* a Japanese dish consisting of broiled shellfish or meat brushed with a marinade of soy sauce, sugar, and rice wine [Mid-20C. < Japanese, "glaze grill"]

term /turm/ *n* **1.** NAME OR WORD FOR SOMETHING a word or combination of words, especially one used to mean something very specific or one used in a specialized area of knowledge or work ○ *The correct legal term is "easement."* **2.** PERIOD OF TIME SOMETHING LASTS the length of time that something lasts, with a fixed beginning and end, often a period during which a person holds an appointment or office or serves time in a correctional institution (*formal*) ○ *during her term of office* **3.** LAW, POL PERIOD OF TIME BODY CONTINUES MEETING a length of time over which a political or legal body such as a legislature or court of law regularly assembles and carries out its formal duties **4.** EDUC DIVISION OF ACADEMIC YEAR one of the sections of the academic year during which students attend a school, college, or university and receive regular instruction **5.** DEADLINE FOR PAYMENT a specific time, especially for making a payment **6.** MED EXPECTED TIME FOR BIRTH OF CHILD the time at the end of a woman's pregnancy when the baby is expected to be born ○ *a pregnancy that came to term* **7.** LOGIC SUBJECT OR PREDICATE OF PROPOSITION in traditional Aristotelian logic, the subject or the predicate of a categorical proposition **8.** LOGIC NAME OR INDIVIDUAL VARIABLE in modern logic, a name or individual variable **9.** MATH MATHEMATICAL EXPRESSION a mathematical expression that forms part of a fraction or proportion, is part of a series, or is associated with another by a plus or minus sign **10.** SCULPTURE SCULPTURED PILLAR a sculptured pillar, especially one with a bust without arms or an animal portrait on top of a square post **11.** LAW ESTATE OF LIMITED DURATION an estate limited to a prescribed period ■ **terms** *npl* **1.** WAY PEOPLE GET ALONG TOGETHER the treatment given by one person, nation, or power to another, or the opinions or attitudes they have or express toward each other ○ *on good terms with the neighbors* **2.** PARTS THAT MAKE UP AGREEMENT the requirements laid down formally in an agreement or contract, or proposed by one side when negotiating an agreement ○ *the terms of the lease* **3.** LANGUAGE the words that somebody uses, or specifically chooses to use, when speaking or writing ○ *defended his position in robust terms* ■ *vt* (**termed, term·ing, terms**) USE PARTICULAR WORD FOR SOMETHING to describe or refer to something using a particular name or expression ○ *His followers were termed "Roundheads."* [13C. Via French *terme* "limit of time or space" < Latin *terminus* "end, boundary, limit"] ◇ **come to terms (with something)** to reach a state of acceptance or of agreement about something ◇ **in no uncertain terms** very forcefully, unambiguously, and bluntly ○ *I told him in no uncertain terms what I thought of his suggestion.* ◇ **in terms of something** in relation to something ◇ **not be on speaking terms (with somebody)** to have had a quarrel or disagreement with somebody, so that neither one will speak to the other

term. *abbr* **1.** TRANSP, COMPUT terminal **2.** termination

ter·ma·gant /túrməgənt/ *n* an offensive term that deliberately insults a woman's temperament, suggesting a propensity for arguing, criticizing, and quarreling [13C. Via Old French *Tervagant*, overbearing non-Christian deity in medieval mystery plays < Italian *Trivigante*] —**ter·ma·gan·cy** *n*

term as·sur·ance *n UK* INSUR same as **term insurance**

-termer *suffix* somebody who serves a term as a political appointee or in prison ○ *a second-termer*

ter·mi·na·ble /túrmənəb'l/ *adj* able to be terminated (*formal*) ○ *The contract is terminable at any time.* [15C. < obsolete *termine* "terminate," via French < Latin *terminare* (see TERMINATE)] —**ter·mi·na·bil·i·ty** /tùrmənə bíllətee/ *n* —**ter·mi·na·bly** *adv*

ter·mi·nal /túrmən'l/ *adj* **1.** CAUSING DEATH inevitably, but often gradually, leading to the death of the patient affected ○ *a terminal illness* **2.** DYING affected by a fatal illness or condition that is approaching its final stages ○ *a terminal cancer patient* **3.** RELATING TO DYING PATIENTS for or concerned with patients with terminal conditions ○ *terminal care* **4.** AT VERY END forming or found at the extreme point or limit of something, or relating to the very end of something **5.** *US* ENDING SERIES constituting the end of a series of things ○ *the terminal performance of the "Mostly Mozart" concerts* **6.** *US* INSUR, LAW OF FIXED DURATION lasting for a given period or term (*formal*) ○ *terminal mortgage payments* **7.** BOT AT END OF STEM positioned at the tip or end of a stem, stalk, or branch ■ *n* **1.** TRANSP STATION AT END OF TRANSPORTATION ROUTE a building or complex containing facilities needed by transportation operators and passengers at either end of a travel or shipping route by air, rail, road, or sea **2.** TRANSP same as **terminus** (sense 1) **3.** COMPUT DEVICE LINKED TO COMPUTER a remote input or output device linked to a computer, or a combination of such devices, e.g., a keyboard and video display **4.** END PART a section or point that forms the end of something **5.** ELEC ELECTRICAL CONDUCTOR a conductor attached at the point where electricity enters or leaves a circuit, e.g., on a battery ○ *a battery terminal* **6.** ARCHIT ORNAMENTAL CARVING an ornamental carving or figure at the end of a larger structure [15C. < Latin *terminalis* < *terminus* "end, boundary, limit"]

SYNONYMS See *deadly.*

ter·mi·nal·ly /túrmənəlee/ *adv* **1.** in a way that leads inevitably but often gradually to the death of the patient affected ○ *terminally ill* **2.** at the tip or end section

ter·mi·nal mo·raine *n* a ridge of rock, gravel, and soil across a valley at the end of a glacier or ice field

ter·mi·nal serv·er *n* a hardware device that links a large number of terminals such as personal computers, printers, and modems to a local or wide area network through a single network connection

ter·mi·nal ve·loc·i·ty *n* the constant speed that a falling object reaches when the downward gravitational force equals the frictional resistance of the medium through which it is falling, usually air

ter·mi·nate /túrmə nàyt/ (**-nat·ed, -nat·ing, -nates**) *v* **1.** *vti* FINISH to come to an end, or bring something to an end ○ *terminate a broadcast* **2.** *vt* FIRE SOMEBODY to discontinue somebody's or a group's employment ○ *He was terminated after 20 years in the job.* **3.** *vt* MURDER SOMEBODY to murder or assassinate somebody (*slang*) [Late 16C. < Latin *terminat-*, past participle of *terminare* < *terminus* "end, boundary, limit"] —**ter·mi·na·tive** *adj* —**ter·mi·na·tor·y** /túrmənə tàwree/ *adj*

ter·mi·nat·ing dec·i·mal *n* a decimal fraction with a finite number of digits

ter·mi·na·tion /tùrmə náysh'n/ *n* **1.** ENDING OF SOMETHING the process of bringing something to an end or of being brought to an end, or an instance of this (*formal*) **2.** TIP OR EDGE something that forms the end or final limit of something (*formal*) **3.** FINAL OUTCOME something that happens or is produced as a result of something else (*formal*) **4.** MED ABORTION an induced abortion (*technical*) **5.** LING WORD ENDING a word ending, e.g., a suffix or an inflection [14C. Directly or via French < Latin *termination-* < *terminat-* (see TERMINATE)] —**ter·mi·na·tion·al** *adj*

ter·mi·na·tion shock *n* the continually shifting boundary of the solar system and the start of interstellar space, where the solar wind abruptly slows down, 8 billion–9.5 billion miles from the Sun

ter·mi·na·tor /túrmə nàytər/ *n* **1.** SOMEBODY OR SOMETHING THAT TERMINATES SOMETHING somebody or something that puts an end to something (*formal*) **2.** KILLER a killer, especially a hired killer (*slang*) **3.** ASTRON LINE BETWEEN LIGHT AND DARK the boundary between the part of a moon or planet that is illuminated and the part that is dark

ter·min·a·tor gene *n* a gene inserted into genetically modified plants that makes them unable to produce seed after one season

ter·mi·ni plural of **terminus**

ter·mi·nol·o·gy /tùrmə nóllәjee/ (*plural* **-gies**) *n* **1.** the expressions and words, or a set of expressions and words, used by people involved in a specialized activity or field of work **2.** the systematic study of names and terms [Early 19C. < German *Terminologie* < medieval Latin *terminus* "term"] —**ter·mi·no·log·i·cal** /tùrminə lójjik'l/ *adj* —**ter·mi·no·log·i·cal·ly** *adv* —**ter·mi·nol·o·gist** *n*

SYNONYMS See *jargon*[1].

term in·sur·ance *n* life insurance that pays a sum of money only if the person who is covered dies within a specific period of time

ter·mi·nus /túrmənəss/ (*plural* **-ni** /-nī/ or **-nus·es**) *n* **1.** a town, city, or location at the end or beginning of a fixed transport route such as a railroad or bus route **2.** a point where something stops or reaches its end **3.** SCULPTURE same as **term** (sense 10) [Mid-16C. < Latin, "end, boundary, limit"]

ter·mi·nus ad quem /-ad kwém/ *n* the objective or finishing point of something [< Latin, "end to which"]

ter·mi·nus a quo /-aa kwṓ/ *n* the starting point of something [< Latin, "end from which"]

termitarium: Queensland, Australia

ter·mi·tar·i·um /tùrmə térree əm/ (*plural* **-i·a** /-ee ə/) *n* a nest, sometimes extremely large, made by a group of termites

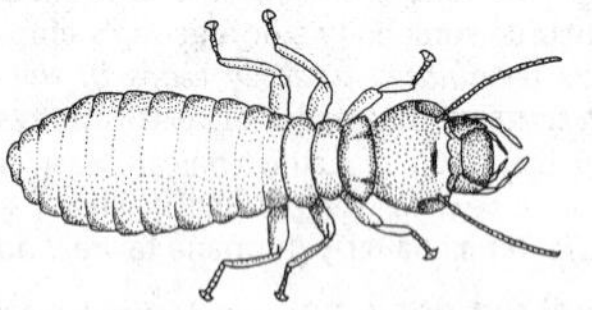

termite

ter·mite /túr mīt/ *n* a light-colored social insect that forms large colonies. Many species live in warm or tropical regions, feed on wood, and are highly destructive to trees and wooden structures. Order: Isoptera. [Late 18C. < Latin *termit-* "woodworm"] —**ter·mit·ic** /tər míttik/ *adj*

term·less /túrmləss/ *adj* **1.** having no end or limit (*literary*) **2.** not depending on any terms and conditions (*formal*)

term of art *n* **1.** a word or phrase with a special meaning, used in a specific field of knowledge **2.** the preferred word or phrase for something

term pa·per *n* a long essay required of a student during an academic term

tern[1] /turn/ (*plural* **terns** or *same*) *n* a seabird, typically white with a black head, related to gulls but with a slenderer body and wings, a pointed beak, and a forked tail. Family: Sternidae. [Late 17C. < N Germanic]

tern[2] /turn/ *n* **1.** a set of three things, especially three numbers that together form a winning combination in a lottery or other gambling game **2.** a schooner with three masts [14C. < French *terne* < Latin *terni* (see TERNARY)]

ter·na·ry /túrnəree/ *adj* **1.** THREEFOLD consisting of three things or parts, or arranged in groups of three (*formal*) ○ *ternary form* **2.** MATH WITH BASE OF 3 describes the number system, or a number belonging to it, that has 3 as its base ○ *a ternary logarithm* **3.** MATH WITH THREE VARIABLES involving or having three variables **4.** METALL WITH THREE COMPONENTS describes an alloy that consists of three components **5.** CHEM WITH THREE ATOMS OR MOLECULES describes chemical compounds consisting of three active elements, e.g., three atoms, molecules, or radicals [15C. < Latin *ternarius* < *terni* "three at a time" < *ter* "three times"]

ter·na·ry sys·tem, ter·na·ry num·ber sys·tem *n* the number system that uses 3 as a basis for counting or ordering, numbers being expressed as sequences of the digits 0, 1, and 2

ter·nate /túr nàyt, túrnət/ *adj* describes a compound leaf that is divided into three more or less equal parts [Mid-18C. < modern Latin *ternatus* < medieval Latin *ternare* "make threefold" < Latin *terni* (see TERNARY)] —**ter·nate·ly** *adv*

terne /turn/ *n* **1.** an alloy of lead and tin with antimony. Use: coating. **2.** METALL same as **terneplate** [Mid-19C. Probably < French, "dull, tarnished"]

terne·plate /túrn plàyt/ *n* a steel or iron plate coated with terne

Ter·ni /túrnee/ capital of Terni Province, Umbria Region, central Italy. Population: 105,018 (2001).

ter·pene /túr peen/ *n* an aromatic hydrocarbon obtained from plant oils [Late 19C. < German *Terpentin* "turpentine"] —**ter·pe·nic** /tur péenik/ *adj*

ter·pin·e·ol /tur pínnee àwl/ *n* a derivative of pine oil that has a distinctive lilac smell. Use: perfumery. [Late 19C. < *terpin*, an organic compound < TERPENE]

ter·pol·y·mer /tur póllәmәr/ *n* a polymer consisting of three monomers

Terp·sich·o·re /turp síkəree/ *n* in Greek mythology, the Muse of choral songs and dance, one of the nine Muses believed to inspire and nurture the arts [< Greek *Terpsikhorē*, literally "delighting in dance" < *terpein* "to delight" + *khoros* "dance"]

terp·si·cho·re·an /tùrpsikə rée ən, tùrpsi káwree ən/ (*formal or humorous*) *adj also* **terp·si·cho·re·al** relating to or resembling dance ■ *n* a dancer

terr. *abbr* **1.** terrace **2.** territorial **3.** territory

Terr. *abbr* Terrace (*used in addresses*)

ter·ra /térrə/ (*plural* **-rae** /térree/) *n* a light-colored highland or mountainous area of the Moon or of a planet [Early 17C. Directly or via Italian < Latin, "earth, land"]

ter·ra al·ba /tèrrə álbə/ *n* a white substance used in the making of paints and paper, e.g., kaolin or gypsum [< Latin, "white earth"]

ter·race /térrəss/ *n* **1.** PORCH OR WALKWAY WITH PILLARS a promenade or portico, usually with columns or a balustrade along the side or sides **2.** STRIP OF AGRICULTURAL LAND ON HILLSIDE a flat, fairly narrow, level strip of ground, bounded by a vertical or steep slope and constructed on a hillside so that the land can be cultivated **3.** FLAT AREA BESIDE BUILDING a paved or grassy area immediately outside and on a level with a building, used for sitting or eating outdoors **4.** BUILDINGS BALCONY a level outdoor surface that extends from one of the upper floors of an apartment or house **5.** ROW OF IDENTICAL HOUSES JOINED TOGETHER a long row of houses built together in the same style, separated only by shared dividing side walls **6.** BUILDINGS SET ON RAISED GROUND a row of houses facing down from a raised position on or along the top of a piece of sloping ground, or built on a raised bank of ground **7.** ROOFTOP PATIO a flat roof used as living space **8.** GEOG AREA OF NATURAL GROUND ALONG COAST a flat raised strip of beach or ground that has been formed naturally along the coast, beside a river or lake, or along the side of a valley by erosion or the changing sea level **9.** CIV ENG CONSTRUCTED BANK OF GROUND a raised bank of ground, artificially constructed **10.** *US* URBAN PLAN STREET SET ON HILL a street constructed along a piece of raised or sloping ground ■ *vt* (**-raced, -rac·ing, -rac·es**) AGRIC FORM TERRACE ON LAND to convert land into a terrace or terraces [Early 16C. < Old French, "rubble, platform" < Latin *terra* "earth, land"]

ter·raced house /tèrrəst-/, **ter·race house** *n UK* same as **row house**

ter·rac·ing /térrəssing/ *n* **1.** a series of level, fairly narrow strips of ground constructed on a hillside that would otherwise be too steep for cultivation **2.** the act or process of creating a terrace or terraces

ter·ra cot·ta /tèrrə kóttə/ *n* **1.** REDDISH BROWN POTTERY CLAY unglazed reddish brown hard-baked clay, often used to make pottery objects **2.** SOMETHING MADE OF TERRA COTTA a work of art or craft modeled in terra cotta, or terra cotta items generally **3.** BROWNISH RED COLOR a reddish brown color, like that of terra cotta [Early 18C. < Italian, "baked earth"] —**ter·ra cot·ta** *adj*

ter·rae ASTRON plural of **terra**

ter·ra fir·ma /tèrrə fúrmə/ *n* solid ground, in contrast to water or air [< Latin, "firm land"]

ter·rain /tə ráyn/ (*plural* **-rains** or *same*) *n* **1.** ground or a piece of land seen in terms of its surface features or general physical character, especially for crossing it or using it for military purposes ○ *surveyed the local terrain* **2.** GEOL same as **terrane** ○ *mountainous terrain* [Early 18C. Via French < Latin *terrenum* "land, ground" < *terrenus* "of the earth" < *terra* "earth, land"]

ter·ra in·cog·ni·ta /tèrrə in kog néetə, -in kógnitə/ (*plural* **ter·rae in·cog·ni·tae** /tèrree in kog néetee, -in kógnitee/) *n* **1.** a country or region that is unknown or has not been explored **2.** a subject or area of knowledge that has not been explored and about which nothing is known [< Latin, "unknown land"]

ter·rane /tə ráyn, té ràyn/ *n* a section of the Earth's crust that is defined by clear fault boundaries, with stratigraphic and structural properties that distinguish it from adjacent rocks [Early 18C. Via French < Latin *terrenus* (see TERRAIN)]

Ter·ra No·va Na·tion·al Park /tèrrə nṓvə-/ national park and wildlife preserve on eastern Newfoundland Island, Canada. Area: 154 sq. mi./400 sq. km.

ter·ra nul·li·us /-nə lée əss, -nóollee əss/ *n* in Australia, the idea and legal concept that when the first Europeans arrived in Australia the land was owned by no one and therefore open to settlement. It has been judged not to be legally valid. [< Latin, "land belonging to no one"]

ter·ra·pin /térrəpin/ (*plural* **-pins** or *same*) *n* **1.** a moderate-sized turtle. Native to: brackish water in eastern North America. Latin name: *Malaclemys terrapin*. **2.** a turtle with four webbed feet, a shell like that of a tortoise, and a retractable head. Terrapins are usually smaller than tortoises, live in fresh water and on land, and are carnivorous. Family: Emydidae. **3.** *regional* REPT same as **tortoise** (sense 1) [Early 17C. Alteration of Virginia Algonquian *torope*]

REGIONAL NOTE Terrapin in the sense "tortoise" is a common term throughout the Middle Atlantic and Southern states. A variant is *dry-land terrapin*.

ter·ra·que·ous /te ráykwee əss, te rák-/ *adj* consisting of areas of water and areas of dry land [Mid-17C. < Latin *terra* "earth, land" + AQUEOUS]

ter·rar·i·um /tə rérree əm/ (*plural* **-i·ums** or **-i·a** /-ee ə/) *n* **1.** an enclosure that is used for keeping or observing small land animals or reptiles such as lizards in a simulated natural environment **2.** a sealed glass container used for growing ornamental plants that require a high level of humidity [Late 19C. < modern Latin < Latin *terra* "earth, land," after AQUARIUM]

ter·raz·zo /tə rázzō, te raátsō/ *n* mosaic that is made by laying marble or stone chips in mortar and grinding them to a polished level surface. Use: floor or wall coverings. [Early 20C. < Italian, "terrace"]

Ter·re Haute /tèrrə hṓt/ city in western Indiana, on the eastern bank of the Wabash River, northwest of Bloomington and southwest of Indianapolis. Population: 58,642 (2002 estimate).

ter·rene /te réen, tə-/ *adj* **1.** worldly or earthly as opposed to heavenly or spiritual (*archaic or literary*) **2.** consisting of or like earth [14C. Via Anglo-Norman < Latin *terrenus* (see TERRAIN)] —**ter·rene·ly** *adv*

ter·re·plein /térrə plàyn/ *n* a raised embankment or platform behind a parapet where heavy guns are positioned [Late 16C. Via French < Italian *terrapieno* < *terrapienare* "fill with earth" < *terra* "earth" + *pieno* "full"]

~~terrestial~~ incorrect spelling of **terrestrial**

ter·res·tri·al /tə réstree əl/ *adj* **1.** RELATING TO EARTH relating to Earth rather than other planets **2.** BELONGING TO LAND belonging to the land rather than the sea or air **3.** LIVING OR GROWING ON LAND living or growing on land rather than in the sea or the air **4.** BROADCAST BY LAND-BASED TRANSMITTER broadcast by a land-based transmitter rather than by satellite ○ *a terrestrial TV channel* **5.** WORLDLY OR MUNDANE worldly or mundane as opposed to heavenly ■ *n* DWELLER ON PLANET EARTH especially in science fiction, a person or animal who lives on Earth [14C. < Latin *terrestris* < *terra* "earth, land"] —**ter·res·tri·al·ly** *adv* —**ter·res·tri·al·ness** *n*

ter·res·tri·al guid·ance *n* a missile or rocket guidance system in which the missile is programmed with precise details of its flight path, enabling it to follow a predetermined route. Data provided include gravitational field, magnetic field, and atmospheric pressure.

ter·res·tri·al link *n* a telecommunications connection that runs on or below the ground

ter·res·tri·al plan·et *n* any of the four planets that are nearest the Sun and are similar in density and composition. The terrestrial planets are Mars, Venus, Mercury, and Earth.

ter·res·tri·al ra·di·a·tion *n* electromagnetic radiation in the form of heat emitted by the Earth as it cools down at night, especially when the air is dry and there are no clouds

ter·res·tri·al tel·e·scope *n* a telescope used for viewing objects on Earth rather than in space. It has an objective and a four-lens eyepiece that give an upright image.

ter·ret /térrət/ *n* **1.** either of two metal rings attached to the driving harness of a horse, through which the reins are passed to prevent them from slipping around the horse's flanks **2.** a metal ring on a dog's collar to which a leash can be attached [Late 15C. < Old French *toret* "little ring" < *tour* (see TOUR)]

terre verte /tèr vúrt/ *n* a grayish green pigment of powdered glauconite. Use: in paints. [< French, "green earth"]

ter·ri·ble /térrəb'l/ *adj* **1.** EXTREME very serious or severe ○ *a terrible cold* **2.** VERY UNPLEASANT very unpleasant or harrowing ○ *The past few days have been a terrible time.* **3.** EXTREMELY LOW IN QUALITY of a very low standard or quality ○ *My cooking isn't that great, but it's not terrible.* **4.** ILL OR UNHAPPY unwell, or extremely unhappy ○ *You look terrible. Are you ill?* **5.** TROUBLING causing considerable fear or anxiety ○ *a terrible shock* ○ *a terrible sight* **6.** FORMIDABLE causing awe or dread ○ *a terrible responsibility* [14C. Via French < Latin *terribilis* < *terrere* "frighten"] —**ter·ri·ble·ness** *n*

ter·ri·bly /térrəblee/ *adv* **1.** to an extreme degree ○ *I'm terribly pleased that you can come.* **2.** in a way that is extremely difficult or painful ○ *affected terribly by the news*

ter·ric·o·lous /te ríkələss, tə-/ *adj* living in or on the soil [Mid-19C. < Latin *terricola* "earth-dweller" < *terra* "earth, land"]

terrier

ter·ri·er /térree ər/ *n* a small lively dog belonging to any of the breeds originally developed to hunt animals living in underground burrows, but now common as pets. Examples include the Airedale, cairn, fox, Scottish, and West Highland terriers, and the schnauzer. [15C. < Old French *(chien) terrier* "terrier (dog)" < Latin *terra* "earth"]

ter·ri·fic /tə ríffik/ *adj* **1.** VERY GREAT very great in size, force, or degree ○ *terrific speed* **2.** VERY GOOD exceptionally good in a way that inspires enthusiasm (*informal*) **3.** VERY FRIGHTENING inspiring a sense of terror [Mid-17C. < Latin *terrificus* "frightening" < *terrere* "frighten"]

ter·rif·i·cal·ly /tə ríffikəlee/ *adv* to a very high degree or very great extent

~~terrificly~~ incorrect spelling of **terrifically**

ter·ri·fy /térrə fī/ (**-fied, -fy·ing, -fies**) *vt* **1.** to make somebody feel very frightened or alarmed **2.** to coerce somebody to do something by using threats ○ *terrified into naming the members* [Late 16C. < Latin *terrificare* < *terrificus* (see TERRIFIC)] —**ter·ri·fi·er** *n* —**ter·ri·fy·ing** *adj* —**ter·ri·fy·ing·ly** *adv*

ter·rig·e·nous /te ríjjənəss, tə-/ *adj* relating to a sediment derived from land erosion that may be formed or deposited on the land or found underwater in shallow ocean areas [Late 17C. < Latin *terrigenus* "earth-born" < *terra* "earth, land"]

ter·rine /te réen, tə-/ *n* **1.** a coarse pâté or similar cold food cooked and sometimes served in a small dish with a tight-fitting lid **2.** a dish used for cooking terrines **3.** HOUSEHOLD same as **tureen** [Early 18C. < French, form of Old French *terrin* "earthen" < Latin *terra* "earth"]

ter·ri·to·ri·al /tèrrə táwree əl/ *adj* **1.** RELATING TO OWNED LAND relating to land or water owned or claimed by an entity, especially a government **2.** ZOOL ASSERTING OWNERSHIP OF AREA having a tendency to appropriate an area or territory and to protect that area or territory against intruders of the same species, particularly other males **3.** RELATING TO RESERVE ARMY relating to a reserve army that has been trained for use in emergencies —**ter·ri·to·ri·al·ly** *adv*

Ter·ri·to·ri·al *n* a member of a reserve army that has been trained for use in emergencies

ter·ri·to·ri·al court *n* a court in an administrative territory of the United States that has local and federal jurisdiction

ter·ri·to·ri·al·ism /tèrrə táwree ə lìzzəm/ *n* **1.** a social system in which the landowners hold or control most of the positions of power and authority **2.** a system of civil government in which the citizens of a territory are penalized unless they adopt the same religion as their civil ruler. Historically it is associated particularly with the Lutheran Church in Germany. —**ter·ri·to·ri·al·ist** *n*

ter·ri·to·ri·al·i·ty /tèrrə tawree állətee/ *n* **1.** the ranking of a region as a territory **2.** a pattern of animal behavior marked by the establishment, demarcation, and defense of an area that can support the growth and activity of an animal or group of animals

ter·ri·to·ri·al·ize /tèrrə táwree ə līz/ (**-ized, -iz·ing, -iz·es**) *vt* **1.** to organize something on a territorial basis **2.** to enlarge a country by adding more territory or territories to it —**ter·ri·to·ri·al·i·za·tion** /tèrrə tàwree əli záysh'n/ *n*

ter·ri·to·ri·al wa·ters *npl* the area of sea around a country's coast recognized as being under that country's jurisdiction

ter·ri·to·ry /térrə tàwree/ (*plural* **-ries**) *n* **1.** LAND land, or an area of land **2.** GOVERNED GEOGRAPHIC AREA a geographic area that is owned and controlled by a government or country **3.** *also* **Ter·ri·to·ry** AREA OF COUNTRY WITH SEPARATE GOVERNMENT an area of a country or empire such as the United States, Canada, or Australia that is not a state or province but has a separate organized government **4.** FIELD OF INQUIRY a field of knowledge, investigation, or experience **5.** ZOOL AREA THAT ANIMAL CONSIDERS ITS OWN an area that an animal considers as its own and that it defends against intruders of the same species **6.** COMM DISTRICT THAT AGENT COVERS the district that an agent, especially a sales representative, is responsible for **7.** SPORTS AREA DEFENDED BY TEAM the area of a playing field defended by a team [14C. < Latin *territorium* < *terra* "earth, land"] ◇ **come** *or* **go with the territory** to be an inseparable part of or accompaniment to something else (*informal*)

ter·ror /térrər/ *n* **1.** INTENSE FEAR intense or overwhelming fear **2.** TERRORISM violence or the threat of violence carried out for political purposes **3.** SOMETHING CAUSING FEAR something that causes intense fear, e.g., an event or situation ○ *a rabid dog that became the terror of the neighborhood* **4.** ANNOYING PERSON an annoying, difficult, or unpleasant person, particularly a naughty child (*informal*) [14C. Via French < Latin < *terrere* "frighten"]

Ter·ror *n* HIST same as **Reign of Terror**

ter·ror·ism /térrə rìzzəm/ *n* violence or the threat of violence, especially bombing, kidnapping, and assassination, carried out for political purposes

ter·ror·ist /térrərist/ *n* somebody who uses violence, especially bombing, kidnapping, and assassination, to intimidate others, often for political purposes —**ter·ror·is·tic** /tèrrə rístik/ *adj*

ter·ror·ize /térrə rīz/ (**-ized, -iz·ing, -iz·es**) *vt* **1.** to intimidate or coerce somebody with violence or the threat of violence **2.** to fill somebody with feelings of intense fear over a period of time —**ter·ror·i·za·tion** /tèrrəri záysh'n/ *n* —**ter·ror·iz·er** *n*

ter·ror-strick·en, ter·ror-struck *adj* filled with a feeling of intense fear

ter·ry /térree/ (*plural* **-ries**) *n* **1.** a fabric that has uncut loops of thread on both sides. Use: towels, bath mats, bathrobes. **2.** an uncut loop of thread in the pile of a fabric that consists of such loops [Late 18C. Origin ?]

Ter·ry /térree/, **Dame Ellen** (1847–1928) British actor. A noted Shakespearean actor, she maintained a stage partnership with Sir Henry Irving that lasted 24 years. Full name **Terry, Dame Ellen Alicia**

> "What is a diary as a rule? A document useful to the person who keeps it, dull to the contemporary who reads it, invaluable to the student, centuries afterwards, who treasures it!"
> [Dame Ellen Terry, *The Story of My Life*; 1908]

ter·ry cloth *n* TEXTILES same as **terry** (sense 1)

ter·ry tow·el·ing *n UK* same as **terry** (sense 1)

terse /turss/ (**ters·er, ters·est**) *adj* **1.** brief and unfriendly, often conveying annoyance ○ *a terse exchange between the two delegates* **2.** concise and economically phrased [Early 17C. < Latin *tersus* "wiped off, clean," past participle of *tergere* "wipe"] —**terse·ly** *adv* —**terse·ness** *n*

ter·tial /túrsh'l/ *adj, n* BIRDS same as **tertiary** *adj* (sense 2) [Mid-19C. < Latin *tertius* "third"]

ter·tian /túrsh'n/ *adj* describes a fever, especially a malarial fever, with symptoms that appear every other day ■ *n* a tertian fever or set of symptoms [14C. < Latin *(febris) tertiana* "(fever) of the third (day)" < *tertius* "third"]

ter·ti·ar·y /túrshee èrree, -sharee/ *adj* **1.** THIRD third in degree, order, place, or importance (*formal*) **2.** BIRDS DESCRIBES BIRD'S INNERMOST FLIGHT FEATHERS describes the few flight feathers nearest a bird's body on the rear edge of a wing, making up the third row of feathers **3.** CHEM FORMED BY REPLACEMENT OF ATOMS relating to or derived by the replacement of three atoms or groups, especially the replacement of the three hydrogen atoms in ammonia with alkyl groups to form amines **4.** CHEM OF THREE BONDED CARBONS relating to or containing a carbon atom that has direct bonds to three other carbon atoms ■ *n* (*plural* **-ies**) **1.** BIRDS BIRD'S INNERMOST FLIGHT FEATHER a feather on the innermost rear edge of a bird's wing **2.** CHR MEMBER OF LAY GROUP in the Roman Catholic Church, a member of a group of the laity associated with a religious order [Mid-16C. < Latin *tertiarius* "of the third part or rank" < *tertius* "third"]

Ter·ti·ar·y *n* the period of geologic time, 65 million to 1.6 million years ago, during which mammals became dominant and modern plants evolved. See table at **geologic time** —**Ter·ti·ar·y** *adj*

ter·ti·ar·y care *n* care or treatment provided by an institution specializing in a particular branch of medicine

ter·ti·ar·y col·or *n* a color made by mixing two secondary colors together or by mixing a primary color with the secondary color closest to it

ter·ti·ar·y in·dus·try *n* the field of industry that provides services such as transportation or finance rather than manufacturing or extracting raw materials

ter·ti·ar·y syph·i·lis *n* the final stage of syphilis in which the disease spreads throughout the body, affecting the brain, spinal cord, heart, skin, bones, and joints

ter·ti·um quid /túrshəm-, tùrshee əm-/ *n* an unknown or indefinite thing or factor that is related to but cannot be classified as belonging to either of two other areas or categories [< late Latin, "some third thing"]

Ter·tul·lian /tər túllyən/ (160?–225?) Roman theologian. He was the first important theological writer in Latin, and his often impassioned works greatly influenced his successors.

> "The blood of the martyrs is the seed of the Church."
> [Tertullian, *Apologeticus*; 197?]

ter·va·lent /tur váylənt/ *adj* CHEM, BIOCHEM same as **trivalent** —**ter·va·len·cy** *n*

ter·za ri·ma /tèrtsə réemə/ (*plural* **ter·ze rime** /tèrt say rée may/) *n* a rhyming verse form of Italian origin consisting of three-line, 11-syllable verses (**tercets**), with the middle line of one verse rhyming with the first and third lines of the next [< Italian, "third rhyme"]

ter·zet·to /turt séttō/ (*plural* **-tos** or **-ti** /-tee/) *n* a musical trio for instruments or voices [Early 18C. < Italian (see TERCET)]

TESL /téss'l/ *abbr* teaching of English as a second language

tes·la /tésslə/ *n* the derived unit of magnetic flux density in the SI system, equal to a flux of one weber in an area of one square meter. Symbol **T** [Late 19C. After Nikola TESLA]

Tes·la /tésslə/, **Nikola** (1856–1943) Croatian-born US electrical engineer. A pioneer of alternating-current systems, he is also credited with many inventions including high-frequency generators (1890) and the tesla coil (1891).

tes·la coil *n* a transformer that has an air, rather than iron, core and is used to produce high voltages at high frequencies, e.g., the flyback transformer in a CRT monitor, or ignition coil in an automobile [After Nikola TESLA]

TESOL /té sàwl, tée sàwl/ *abbr* EDUC **1.** Teachers of English to Speakers of Other Languages **2.** teaching of English to speakers of other languages

tes·sel·late /téssə làyt/ (**-lat·ed, -lat·ing, -lates**) *v* **1.** *vt* to construct, pave, or decorate something with small pieces of stone or glass to give a mosaic effect **2.** *vi* to fit together without leaving any spaces (*refers to geometric shapes*) [Late 18C. < Latin *tessellatus* "made of small square stones" < *tessera* (see TESSERA)] —**tes·sel·la·tion** /tèssə láysh'n/ *n*

tes·ser·a /téssərə/ (*plural* **-ser·ae** /-sə rée/) *n* **1.** a small square of stone, tile, or glass used to make a mosaic **2.** a piece of bone or wood that was used in ancient Greece and Rome as a die, tally, or ticket [Mid-17C. Via Latin < Greek *tesseres*, variant of *tessares* "four"; from the sides of a square] —**tes·ser·al** *adj*

tes·ser·act /téssə ràkt/ *n* the four-dimensional extension of a cube [Late 19C. < Greek *tesseres* (see TESSERA) + *aktis* "ray"]

tes·si·tu·ra /tèssi tóorə/ (*plural* **-ras** or **-re** /-tóor ày/) *n* the pitch range that predominates in a piece of music [Late 19C. Via Italian < Latin *textura* "web, structure, weaving" (see TEXTURE)]

test[1] /test/ *n* **1.** EXAMINATION a series of questions, problems, or practical tasks to gauge somebody's knowledge, ability, or experience **2.** BASIS FOR EVALUATION a basis for evaluating or judging something or somebody **3.** TRIAL RUN-THROUGH OF PROCESS a trial run-through of a process or on equipment to find out if it works **4.** DIFFICULT SITUATION an often difficult situation or event that will provide information about somebody or something **5.** EXAMINATION OF PART OF BODY an examination of part of the body or of a body fluid or specimen in order to find something out, e.g., whether it is functioning properly or is infected ○ *a pregnancy test* ○ *an eye test* **6.** PROCEDURE TO DETECT PRESENCE OF SOMETHING a procedure to ascertain the presence of or the properties of a substance ○ *a test for nitrates in drinking water* **7.** CHEM REACTIVE SUBSTANCE a substance or a reagent that reacts in a specific way to show the presence of a substance **8.** RESULT OF PROCEDURE a result of a procedure to ascertain the presence of a substance ○ *Your test hasn't come back yet.* ■ *v* (**test·ed, test·ing, tests**) **1.** *vt* TRY SOMETHING OUT to try something out, e.g., by touching, operating, or experiencing it, in order to find out what it is like, how well it works, or what it feels like **2.** *vt* EVALUATE SOMETHING to use something on a trial basis in order to evaluate it **3.** *vt* ASK SOMEBODY QUESTIONS to ask somebody questions or make somebody do a practical activity in order to gauge knowledge, skill, or experience **4.** *vt* CARRY OUT MEDICAL TEST to carry out a test on part of the body or on a bodily specimen **5.** *vti* EXAMINE SOMETHING TO DETECT PRESENCE to examine something in order to ascertain the presence of or the properties of a substance ○ *tested the water for bacteria* **6.** *vi* ACHIEVE PARTICULAR TEST RESULT to achieve a particular result on a test ○ *She tested positive for rubella immunity.* **7.** *vi* US EDUC ACHIEVE ACADEMIC RATING to achieve a rating in academic examination ○ *tested poorly in math skills* **8.** *vt* MAKE DEMANDS ON SOMEBODY to make considerable demands on somebody, particularly somebody's skills or abilities [14C. Via Old French, "pot" < Latin *testum* "earthenware pot"] —**test·a·bil·i·ty** /tèstə bíllətee/ *n* —**test·a·ble** *adj*

test[2] /test/ *n* the hard outer covering or shell of some invertebrates, e.g., mollusks and crustaceans [Mid-16C. < Latin *testa* "tile, shell"]

test. *abbr* **1.** LAW testator **2.** LAW testatrix **3.** BIBLE testimony

Test. *abbr* BIBLE Testament

tes·ta /téstə/ (*plural* **-tae** /-tee/) *n* the protective covering of a seed from a flowering plant [Late 18C. < Latin "tile, shell"]

tes·ta·ceous /te stáyshəss/ *adj* **1.** made of shell, or having a shell or other hard covering **2.** of a reddish brown color like a brick (*technical*)

tes·tae BOT plural of **testa**

tes·ta·ment /téstəmənt/ *n* **1.** PROOF something that shows that something else exists or is true ○ *His remarkable recovery is a testament to the doctor's skill.* **2.** FORMAL STATEMENT OF BELIEFS a formal statement or speech outlining beliefs (*formal*) **3.** LAW same as **will**[2] *n* (sense 6) (*archaic*) ○ *last will and testament* **4.** JUD-CHR COVENANT BETWEEN GOD AND HUMANKIND in Judaism and Christianity, a covenant made between God and humankind (*formal*) [13C. < Latin *testamentum* "legal will" < *testis* "witness"] —**tes·ta·men·tal** /tèstə mént'l/ *adj*

ORIGIN The Latin word *testis* "witness," from which ***testament*** is derived, is also the source of English *attest, contest, detest, intestate, protest, testicle, testify,* and *testimony.*

Tes·ta·ment *n* **1.** either of the two major divisions of the Christian Bible, known as the Old Testament and the New Testament **2.** a printed copy of the New Testament

tes·ta·men·tar·y /tèstə méntəree, -méntree/ *adj* **1.** bequeathed or set out in a will **2.** relating to a legal will (*formal*)

tes·tate /tés tàyt, téstət/ *adj* having made a legally valid will ■ *n* somebody who has made a legally valid will [15C. < Latin *testatus*, past participle of *testari* "bear witness, make your will" < *testis* "witness"] —**tes·ta·cy** /téstəssee/ *n*

tes·ta·tor /tés tàytər, te stáytər/ *n* somebody, especially a man, who has made a legally valid will [14C. Via Anglo-Norman < Latin < *testari* (see TESTATE)]

tes·ta·trix /tés tày triks, te stáy triks/ (*plural* **-tri·ces** /te stáytrə sèez, tèstə trī́-/) *n* a woman who has made a legally valid will [Late 16C. < late Latin, feminine of Latin *testator* (see TESTATOR)]

test ban *n* an agreement between nations to suspend testing of some or all nuclear weapons [< TEST[1]]

test bed *n* a facility designed and equipped to test engines and machinery under circumstances as close to actual operating conditions as possible [< TEST[1]]

test card *n* UK same as **test pattern** [< TEST[1]]

test case *n* **1.** GROUND-BREAKING LEGAL CASE an important legal case that establishes a precedent referred to in future cases **2.** US LAW CASE INTENDED TO TEST CONSTITUTIONALITY a case brought with the intention of challenging the constitutionality of a statute **3.** TELLING EVENT an event that provides an opportunity to prove or disprove a hypothesis [< TEST[1]]

test·cross /tést kràwss/ *n* **1.** GENETIC CROSS TECHNIQUE a procedure used especially in plant breeding whereby a plant's genetic constitution is inferred by examining the progeny resulting from crossing it with another individual of known genetic makeup **2.** RESULT OF TESTCROSS a plant produced by a testcross ■ *vt* (**-crossed, -cross·ing, -cross·es**) SUBJECT ORGANISM TO TESTCROSS to subject a plant to a testcross to infer its genetic constitution [Mid-20C. < TEST[1]]

test drive *n* a short drive in a car or other motor vehicle in order to see what it is like, usually with a view to buying it [< TEST[1]] —**test-drive** *vt*

test·er[1] /téstər/ *n* **1.** SOMEBODY WHO TESTS PRODUCTS somebody whose job it is to try out new products **2.** SAMPLE OF PRODUCT a sample of a product, especially a cosmetic **3.** EQUIPMENT TO CHECK PROPER FUNCTIONING a piece of equipment that tests if a machine or device is working properly **4.** SMALL FOOD THERMOMETER a small thermometer inserted into something that is cooking to determine if it is done **5.** SOMEBODY WHO CONDUCTS TESTS somebody who administers or carries out tests ○ *a water tester* [14C. < TEST[1]]

tes·ter[2] /téstər/ *n* a canopy, especially one over a four-poster bed or a pulpit [14C. < medieval Latin *testerium* < Latin *testa* "tile, shell, (in late Latin) head"]

tes·tes ANAT plural of **testis**

tes·ti·cle /téstik'l/ *n* the male gonad or sperm-producing gland (**testis**) usually with its surrounding membranes, particularly in humans or other higher vertebrates [15C. < Latin *testiculus* "small testis" < *testis* (see TESTIS)] —**tes·tic·u·lar** /te stíkyələr/ *adj*

tes·ti·fy /téstə fī/ (**-fied, -fy·ing, -fies**) *vi* **1.** MAKE DECLARATION UNDER OATH IN COURT to declare something that can be taken as evidence under oath in a court of law **2.** AFFIRM SOMETHING FROM EXPERIENCE to make a factual statement based on personal experience, or declare something to be true from personal experience **3.** PROVE OR DEMONSTRATE to be clear evidence of something (*formal*) **4.** CHR TALK ABOUT EXPERIENCE AS CHRISTIAN to talk to an audience or group of listeners about personal experience as a Christian [14C. < Latin *testificari* "make yourself a witness" < *testis* "witness"] —**tes·ti·fi·ca·tion** /tèstəfi káysh'n/ *n* —**tes·ti·fi·er** *n*

tes·ti·mo·ni·al /tèstə mṓnee əl/ *n* **1.** RECOMMENDATION a favorable report on the qualities and virtues of somebody or something **2.** TRIBUTE something given, held, or done in order to honor or thank somebody **3.** STATEMENT BACKING UP CLAIM a statement backing up a claim or supporting a fact ■ *adj* OF TESTIMONY OR TESTIMONIAL relating to or consisting of testimony or a testimonial

tes·ti·mo·ny /téstə mṑnee/ (*plural* **-nies**) *n* **1.** EVIDENCE GIVEN IN COURT evidence that a witness gives to a court of law. It may take the form of a written or oral statement detailing what the witness has seen or knows about a case. **2.** PROOF something that supports a fact or a claim ○ *This win is testimony to the tactical skill of the coach.* **3.** BIBLE TEN COMMANDMENTS the Ten Commandments inscribed on two stone tablets, or the Ark of the Covenant in which the tablets were stored **4.** CHR PUBLIC AVOWAL a public profession of Christian faith or religious experience [14C. < Latin *testimonium* < *testis* "witness"]

test·ing /télsting/ *adj* subjecting somebody or something to challenging difficulties ○ *A testing time lies ahead for the new administration.*

tes·tis /téstiss/ (*plural* **tes·tes** /té steez/) *n* either of the paired male reproductive glands, roundish in shape, that produce sperm and male sex hormones, and hang in a small sac (**scrotum**) [Early 18C. < Latin, "witness," because it "bears witness" to a man's virility]

test mar·ket·ing *n* the use of a sample of a larger market to try out a marketing strategy or product [< TEST[1]]

tes·tos·ter·one /te stóstə rṑn/ *n* a male steroid hormone produced in the testicles and responsible for the development of secondary sex characteristics. Use: produced synthetically for treatment of androgen deficiency. Formula: $C_{19}H_{28}O_2$. [Mid-20C. < TESTIS + *-sterone* (blend of STEROL + KETONE)]

test pa·per *n* a small piece of paper soaked in reagent such as litmus that is used to show the presence of or properties of a substance [< TEST[1]]

test pat·tern *n* a geometric pattern transmitted by a television broadcaster to help viewers to tune in their television sets and obtain optimum reception [<TEST[1]]

test pi·lot *n* a pilot who flies new aircraft in order to assess their performance [<TEST[1]]

test-screen·ing *n* a screening of a provisional version of a movie to test audience reaction [<TEST[1]]

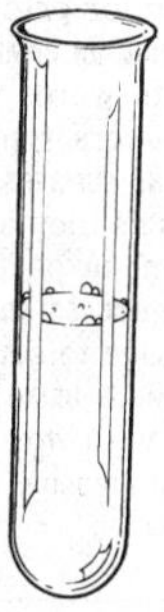

test tube

test tube *n* a small glass tube-shaped container that is closed and rounded at one end and open at the other, used to mix, heat, and store chemicals in laboratories. See illustration on next page [<TEST[1]]

test-tube *adj* made in a test tube or by other artificial means, rather than occurring or arising naturally

test-tube ba·by *n* a baby that has been conceived by fertilizing a woman's egg in a laboratory (**in vitro fertilization**) and then inserting it in her womb to develop normally for the remainder of the pregnancy (*informal*)

tes·tu·di·nal /te sto͝od'nəl/, **tes·tu·di·nar·y** /-èrree/ *adj* resembling a tortoise or the shell of a tortoise

tes·tu·do /te sto͝odō/ (*plural* **-din·es** /-sto͝od'n ēez/) *n* a movable shelter against missiles from above, used by the ancient Roman army in siege warfare. It was either a single structure that could be carried or was made by soldiers holding their shields above their heads to form a protective roof. [14C. < Latin, "tortoise's shell, shelter" < *testa* "tile, shell"]

tes·ty /téstee/ (**-ti·er, -ti·est**) *adj* impatient and easily upset or annoyed [14C. < Anglo-Norman *testif* < Latin *testa* "tile, shell, (in late Latin) head"] —**tes·ti·ly** *adv* —**tes·ti·ness** *n*

Tet /tet/ *n* in Vietnam, and in Vietnamese communities, a festival held over three days to mark the lunar New Year [Late 19C. < Vietnamese]

te·tan·ic /te tánnik/ *adj* **1.** relating to tetanus or to the sustained contraction of the muscles that is characteristic of tetanus **2.** capable of producing muscle spasms such as those seen in tetanus [Early 18C. Via Latin < Greek *tetanikos* < *tetanos* (see TETANUS)] —**te·tan·i·cal·ly** *adv*

tet·a·nize /tétt'n īz/ (**-nized, -niz·ing, -niz·es**) *vt* to cause tetanic spasms in a muscle —**tet·a·ni·za·tion** /tètt'ni záysh'n/ *n*

tet·a·nus /tétt'nəss/ *n* **1.** an acute infectious disease, usually contracted through a penetrating wound, that causes severe muscular spasms and contractions, especially around the neck and jaw. The spasms are caused by a toxin released by the bacterium *Clostridium tetani.* **2.** sustained muscle contraction, e.g., induced by electrical stimulation [14C. Via Latin < Greek *tetanos* "muscular spasm" < *teinein* "stretch"] —**tet·a·nal** *adj* —**tet·a·noid** *adj*

tet·a·ny /tétt'nee/ *n* repeated prolonged contraction of muscles, especially of the face and limbs, caused by low blood calcium arising from, e.g., an underactive parathyroid gland or vitamin D deficiency [Late 19C. Via French, "intermittent tetanus" < Latin *tetanus* (see TETANUS)]

tetched /techt/, **teched** *adj US* unable to function in a logical or reasonable way (*informal*) [Mid-20C. Alteration of TOUCHED]

tetch·y /téchee/ (**-i·er, -i·est**), **tech·y** *adj* oversensitive and easily upset or annoyed (*informal*) [Late 16C. Probably < *tache* "blemish, defect" < French] —**tetch·i·ly** *adv* —**tetch·i·ness** *n*

tête-à-tête /tàytə táyt/ *n* **1. INTIMATE CONVERSATION FOR TWO** a private conversation between two people **2. TYPE OF SOFA** a two-seater sofa shaped like an S, allowing those seated to face each other ■ *adv* **INTIMATELY** in private with only two people present [< French, "head-to-head"]

tête-bêche /tàyt bésh/ *adj* describes a pair of stamps, one of which is printed right side up and the other upside down [< French, "(sleeping) head to foot"]

teth /tayt, tayth, tet, teth/ *n* the ninth letter of the Hebrew alphabet, represented in the English alphabet as "t." See table at **alphabet** [Early 19C. < Hebrew]

teth·er /té*th*ər/ *n* a rope or chain attached to an animal and attached to something at the other end, restricting the animal's movement ■ *vt* (**-ered, -er·ing, -ers**) to tie something, especially an animal, with a rope or chain in order to restrict its movement [14C. < Old Norse *tjóðr* < Germanic, "fasten"] ◇ **at the end of your tether** having reached the limit of your patience, strength, or endurance

teth·er·ball /té*th*ər bàwl/ *n* a game for two players who use their hands to hit in opposite directions a ball that is on a length of rope attached to the top of a pole. The object of the game is to wind the rope completely around the pole.

Te·thys /téethiss/ *n* **1. TITAN** in Greek mythology, a Titan who was the wife of Oceanus and the mother of thousands of sea and river gods and nymphs **2. MOON OF SATURN** a large natural satellite of Saturn, discovered in 1684. It has a diameter of 651 mi./1,050 km and is Saturn's ninth most distant satellite, orbiting at a distance of 182,900 mi./295,000 km. **3. ANCIENT SEA** an ancient sea that is thought to have separated Laurasia and Gondwanaland, surviving vestigially today as the Mediterranean [Late 19C. Via Latin < Greek *Tēthus*]

Tet·ley /téttlee/, **Glen** (*b.* 1926) US dancer and choreographer. He danced with internationally known companies including those of Robert Joffrey, Martha Graham, and the American Ballet Theatre, and became associated with the National Ballet of Canada in 1986. His choreography includes *Tagore* (1989).

Te·ton[1] /tée tòn, tée't'n/ (*plural same* or **-tons**), **Te·ton Da·ko·ta** *n* **1.** a member of a group of Native North American peoples who lived in western parts of the Great Plains, and now live mainly in North and South Dakota. Included in this group are the Oglala, Hunkpapa, and Miniconjou peoples. **2.** the Siouan language of the Teton people. Native speakers: 6,000. [Early 19C. < Dakota *thíthuwa* "dwellers on the prairie"] —**Te·ton** *adj*

Te·ton[2] /tée tòn/ range of the Rocky Mountains in northwestern Wyoming and southwestern Idaho. The highest peak is Grand Teton, 13,770 ft./4,197 m.

Te·ton Da·ko·ta *n, adj* PEOPLES, LANG same as **Teton**[1]

Té·touan /te twaán/, **Te·tuán** city in northern Morocco on the Mediterranean Sea, near Tangier. Population: 367,349 (1994).

tetr- *prefix* same as **tetra-** (*used before vowels*)

tet·ra /téttrə/ (*plural* **-ras** or *same*) *n* a brightly-colored freshwater fish that lives in tropical regions and is kept as an aquarium fish. Family: Characidae. [Mid-20C. Shortening of modern Latin *Tetragonopterus* < late Latin *tetragonum* (see TETRAGON) + Greek *pteron* "wing"]

tetra- *prefix* four ○ *tetrastich* [< Greek < Indo-European]

tet·ra·ba·sic /tèttrə báyssik/ *adj* describes an acid that contains four atoms of replaceable hydrogen in a molecule —**tet·ra·ba·sic·i·ty** /tèttrə bay sissátee/ *n*

tet·ra·brach /téttrə bràk/ *n* a word consisting of four short syllables in Latin or classical Greek literature [Early 20C. < Greek *tetrabrakhus* "four short" < *brakhus* "short"]

tet·ra·caine /téttrə kàyn/ *n* a crystalline compound chemically related to procaine. Use: local anesthetic. Formula: $C_{15}H_{24}N_2O_2$.

tet·ra·chlo·ride /tèttrə kláw rīd/ *n* a compound that has four chlorine atoms in each molecule

tet·ra·chlo·ro·me·thane /tèttrə klawrə mé thàyn/ *n* CHEM same as **carbon tetrachloride**

tet·ra·chord /téttrə kàwrd/ *n* a group of four musical notes, the first and last of which form a perfect fourth, used principally in ancient Greek music —**tet·ra·chor·dal** /tèttrə káwrd'l/ *adj*

te·trac·id /te trássid/ *n* **1.** a base that can react with four molecules of a monobasic acid to form a salt **2.** an alcohol with four OH groups per molecule

tet·ra·cy·clic /tèttrə sīklik/ *adj* describes a compound whose molecular structure contains four rings

tet·ra·cy·cline /tèttrə sī kleen/ *n* a broad-spectrum antibiotic. Source: bacteria of the genus *Streptomyces*, synthesized from chlortetracycline. Use: treatment of acne, general infections. Formula: $C_{22}H_{24}N_2O_8$. [Mid-20C. < TETRACYCLIC]

tet·rad /té tràd/ *n* **1. SERIES OF FOUR** a group or series of four things or people **2.** GENETICS **GROUP OF FOUR CHROMOSOMES** a group of four chromosomes in a diploid cell that is about to undergo the cell division (**meiosis**) that produces sex cells **3.** BIOL **GROUP OF FOUR CELLS** a group of four cells produced by the division (**meiosis**) of a single parent cell, e.g., as it occurs in the formation of pollen and spores **4.** CHEM **ATOM WITH VALENCE OF FOUR** an atom or chemical group with a valence of four [Mid-17C. < Greek *tetrad-*, stem of *tetras* "four"]

tet·ra·dac·tyl·ous /tèttrə dáktələss/ *adj* with four toes or fingers

te·trad·y·mite /te tráddə mīt/ *n* a gray metallic sulfide mineral containing tellurium and bismuth. Use: source of tellurium. [Mid-19C. < German *Tetradymit* < Greek *tetradumos* "fourfold"; from the double twin crystals in which it is usually found]

tet·ra·eth·yl lead /tèttrə èth'l léd/ *n* a colorless, extremely poisonous, oily liquid. Use: gasoline antiknock agent now often restricted or banned because it produces air pollution and poisons catalytic converters. Formula: $Pb(C_2H_5)_4$.

tet·ra·gon /téttrə gòn/ *n* a two-dimensional geometric figure formed of four sides and four angles [Early 17C. < late Latin *tetragonum* < Greek *tetragōnos* "four-angled" < *gōnos* "angled"] —**te·trag·o·nal** /te trággən'l/ *adj*

tet·ra·gram /téttrə gràm/ *n* a word that has four letters

Tet·ra·gram·ma·ton /tèttrə grámmə tòn/ *n* a four-letter Hebrew name for God revealed to Moses, usually written YHVH or YHWH (Exodus 3:13–14). Orthodox Jews regard this name as too sacred to be pronounced. [14C. < Greek, neuter of *tetragrammatos* "having four letters" < *gramma* "letter"]

tet·ra·he·dra MATH plural of **tetrahedron**

tet·ra·he·drite /tèttrə hée drīt/ *n* a gray to black metallic sulfide mineral containing copper, iron, and antimony. Use: source of copper and other metals. [Mid-19C. Directly < TETRAHEDRON or < Greek *tetraedron*]

tet·ra·he·dron /tèttrə héedrən/ (*plural* **-drons** or **-dra** /-drə/) *n* a three-dimensional geometric figure formed of four faces [Late 16C. < Greek *tetraedron*, neuter of *tetraedros* "four-sided" < *hedra* "face"] —**tet·ra·he·dral** *adj* —**tet·ra·he·dral·ly** *adv*

tet·ra·hy·dro·can·nab·i·nol /tèttrə hī drō kə nábbə nàwl/ *n* CHEM full form of **THC**

tet·ra·hy·drox·y /tèttrə hī dróksee/ *adj* describes a molecule that has four hydroxyl groups

te·tral·o·gy /te trálləjee, -trólləjee/ (*plural* **-gies**) *n* a series of four related literary, dramatic, artistic, or musical works [Mid-17C. < Greek *tetralogia* "four dramas" < *-logia* "discourse"]

tet·ra·mer /téttrəmər/ *n* a polymer that is formed from four identical monomers —**tet·ra·mer·ic** /tèttrə mérrik/ *adj*

te·tram·er·ous /te trámmərəss/ *adj* with four parts, or with parts arranged in multiples of four —**te·tram·er·ism** *n*

te·tram·e·ter /te trámmətər/ *n* **1. VERSE LINE WITH FOUR FEET** a line of verse that has four metrical feet **2. LINE WITH FOUR PAIRS OF FEET** in classical poetry, a line of verse made up of four pairs of feet **3. VERSE IN TETRAMETER** poetry that is written in tetrameters [Early 17C. Via late Latin < Greek *tetrametron*, form of *tetrametros* "having four measures" < *metron* "measure"]

tet·ra·ploid /téttrə plòyd/ *adj* possessing four matched sets of chromosomes in the cell nucleus ■ *n* a tetraploid cell, nucleus, or organism —**tet·ra·ploi·dy** *n*

tet·ra·pod /téttrə pòd/ *n* **1.** a vertebrate animal that has four limbs or legs **2.** a device comprising four arms projecting from a central point at 120° to each other, making a tripod with the fourth arm projecting vertically upward [Early 19C. Via modern Latin *tetrapodus* < Greek *tetrapod-* "four-footed" < *pous* "foot"]

tet·ra·po·dy /te tráppədee/ (*plural* **-dies**) *n* a line of verse consisting of four feet —**tet·ra·po·dic** /tèttrə póddik/ *adj*

te·trap·ter·ous /te tráptərəss/ *adj* describes insects that have four wings

tet·rarch /té traárk/ *n* **1.** RULER OF QUARTER OF COUNTRY the ruler of a quarter of a country or province **2.** JOINT RULER one of four joint rulers **3.** SUBORDINATE PRINCE a ruler of a subordinate principality, especially in the eastern provinces of the Roman Empire **4.** PHALANX COMMANDER the commander of a subdivision of a Macedonian phalanx in ancient Greece [Pre-12C. Via late Latin *tetrarcha* < Greek *tetrarkhēs* "four ruling" < *arkhēs* "ruler"] —**te·trar·chic** /te traárkik/ *adj*

tet·rar·chy /té traárkee/ (*plural* **-chies**), **tet·rar·chate** /-kayt, té traárkət/ *n* **1.** government by four rulers **2.** the rule or domain of one of four joint rulers

tet·ra·spore /téttrə spawr/ *n* an asexual spore that occurs after reproductive cell division (**meiosis**), usually in groups of four, in red algae —**tet·ra·spor·ic** /tèttrə spáwrik/ *adj*

tet·ra·stich /téttrə stìk/ *n* a poem, verse, or strophe that has four lines [Late 16C. Via Latin *tetrastichon* < Greek *tetrastikhos* "containing four rows" < *stikhos* "row, line of verse"] —**tet·ra·stich·ic** /tèttrə stíkik/ *adj*

tet·ra·syl·la·ble /tèttrə síllәb'l/ *n* a word with four syllables —**tet·ra·syl·lab·ic** /tèttrə si lábbik/ *adj*

tet·ra·tom·ic /tèttrə tómmik/ *adj* **1.** with four atoms per molecule **2.** with four replaceable atoms or radicals

tet·ra·va·lent /tèttrə váylənt/ *adj* with a valence of four —**tet·ra·va·lence** *n*

tet·raz·zi·ni /tèttrə zeénee/, **Tet·raz·zi·ni** *adj US* made with noodles, mushrooms, and almonds in a cream sauce, topped with Parmesan cheese and oven-browned [Mid-20C. After Luisa *Tetrazzini* (1874–1940), Italian opera singer]

tet·ri /téttree/ (*plural same*) *n* a subunit of Georgian currency. See table at **currency** [Late 20C. < Georgian]

tet·rode /té trōd/ *n* a four-element electron tube containing an anode, a cathode, a control grid, and an additional electrode or screen grid

tet·ro·do·tox·in /tèttrədō tóksin/ *n* a potent neurotoxin found in puffers

te·trox·ide /te trók sīd/, **te·trox·id** /te tróksid/ *n* a compound that has four oxygen atoms per molecule [Mid-19C. < TETRA-]

tet·ryl /téttril/ *n* a yellow crystalline compound. Use: explosives detonator. Formula: $C_7H_5N_5O_8$.

Te·tuán another spelling of **Tétouan**

Teut. *abbr* Teutonic

Teu·to·burg For·est /tóytə bùrg-/, **Teu·to·bur·ger Wald** /tóytə burgər váwld/ ridge of wooded hills in northwestern Germany, scene of a major Roman defeat by Germans in A.D. 9

Teu·ton /toót'n/ *n* **1.** a member of an ancient Germanic people who originally came from Jutland and invaded Gaul in the 2nd century B.C. They were wiped out by the Romans in 102 B.C. **2.** somebody from a German-speaking culture, especially from Germany, Switzerland, or Austria [Early 18C. < Latin *Teutoni* or *Teutones* (plural) "the Teutons"]

Teu·ton·ic /too tónnik/ *adj* **1.** describes attributes stereotypically associated with German-speaking cultures or people **2.** relating to the ancient Teuton people, or their culture —**Teu·ton·i·cal·ly** *adv*

Teu·ton·ic Knights, **Teu·ton·ic Or·der** *n* a German religious and military order that was founded as a charitable order in Palestine in 1190 during the Third Crusade but became a military organization operating in Eastern Europe. In the 13th century it conquered Prussia, where it introduced Christianity through killing many of the native inhabitants and colonizing it with Germans.

Teu·ton·ism /toót'n ìzzəm/ *n* **1.** a German characteristic, custom, or idiom **2.** German society or civilization —**Teu·ton·ist** *n*

Teu·ton·ize /toót'n īz/ (**-ized, -iz·ing, -iz·es**) *vti* to become German, or make something German —**Teu·ton·i·za·tion** /toót'ni záysh'n/ *n*

Te·vet /táy vàyss, te vét/, **Te·bet** *n* in the Jewish calendar, the tenth month of the religious year, lasting 29 days and falling about the same time as December to January. See table at **calendar**

Te·wa /táywə/ (*plural* **-was** or *same*) *n* **1.** a member of a group of Pueblo peoples who live in northern New Mexico **2.** the Tanoan language of the Tewa people. Native speakers: under 3,000. [Mid-19C. < Tewa *téwa* "moccasins"] —**Te·wa** *adj*

Tewkes·bur·y /tóoks bèrree, -bəree, tyóoks-/ market town in Gloucestershire, west central England, with a medieval abbey church. Population: 76,405 (2001).

Tewks·bur·y /tóoksbəree/ town in northeastern Massachusetts, northeast of Billerica and southeast of Lowell. Population: 29,355 (2002 estimate).

Tex. *abbr* **1.** Texan **2.** Texas

Tex·ar·kan·a /tèks aar kánnə, tèksər-/ two cities forming one single community on either side of the Texas-Arkansas border, one in southwestern Arkansas, the other in northeastern Texas. Population: 63,473 (2002 estimate).

Texas

Tex·as /téksəss/ state in the southwestern United States, bordered by Oklahoma, Arkansas, Louisiana, the Gulf of Mexico, Mexico, and New Mexico. Capital: Austin. Population: 21,779,893 (2002 estimate). Area: 267,277 sq. mi./692,244 sq. km. —**Tex·an** *n, adj*

Tex·as blue·bon·net *n* PLANTS same as **bluebonnet** (sense 1)

Tex·as fe·ver *n* an infectious disease of cattle that is characterized by high fever, anemia, and severe weight loss, is caused by a protozoan, and is transmitted by tick bites. The discovery in 1893 that ticks transmitted this disease was the first demonstration that arthropods could act as disease vectors.

Tex·as leagu·er *n* in baseball, a fly ball that drops between infielders and outfielders, resulting in a base hit [< *Texas League*, minor league in baseball]

Tex·as Rang·er *n* a member of the Texas state police

Tex·as tow·er *n US* an offshore radar tower that is built on a base that resembles an offshore oil platform [Mid-20C. < its resemblance to a Texan oil rig]

Tex-Mex /téks mèks/ *adj Hispanic* showing a blend of Texan and Mexican cultures or cuisines [< shortening]

text /tekst/ *n* **1.** MAIN BODY OF BOOK the main body of a book or other printed material, as distinct from the introduction, index, illustrations, and headings **2.** WRITTEN MATERIAL words that have been written down, typed, or printed **3.** WRITTEN VERSION OF SOMETHING a written, typed, or printed version of something such as a speech or a statement ○ *the full text of the President's speech* **4.** COMMUNICATION same as **text message** **5.** EDITION one among the extant forms or versions of a written work ○ *compared various texts to arrive at this reading* **6.** ORIGINAL WORDING the original wording of a piece of writing, especially the Bible, as opposed to a translation, summary, or revision **7.** BIBLE PASSAGE a short passage from the Bible that is read aloud and on which a sermon is based **8.** EDUC BOOK FOR STUDY a book or piece of writing that is used for academic study or discussion **9.** EDUC same as **textbook** **10.** PRINTING TYPEFACE a style of type that is suitable for printing running text **11.** COMPUT WORDS APPEARING ON COMPUTER SCREEN computer data that represents words, numbers, and other typographical characters, typically stored in ASCII format **12.** LETTERS AND NUMBERS ON PHONE SCREEN alphanumeric characters as they appear on the viewing screen of a cell phone or pager (*often used before a noun*) ○ *a text message* ■ *vt* SEND TEXT MESSAGE TO SOMEBODY to send a text message to somebody on his or her cell phone ■ *adj* COMPUT USING WORDS associated with or designed for use with words in written form ○ *a text file* [14C. Via Old French < Latin *textus* "woven material, literary composition" < past participle of *texere* "weave"]

ORIGIN The Latin word *texere* "to weave," from which *text* is derived, is also the source of the English words *context, pretext, texture,* and *tissue.*

text·book /tékst bòók/ *n* a book that treats a subject comprehensively and is used by students as a basis for study ■ *adj* typical overall and in detail, and thus a suitable example for study ○ *a textbook case of superpower aggression*

text box *n* a box within a computer dialog box in which characters such as text, dates, or numbers can be typed and edited

text chat *n* a real-time communication between Internet users in which messages are typed via a keyboard

text e·di·tion *n* **1.** the printed version of something that is published in some other form such as a CD-ROM or on the Internet **2.** *US* an edition of a book designed for use in education

text ed·i·tor *n* a computer program that permits the creation and editing of stored text

text file *n* a computer file consisting of alphanumeric characters exclusive of transmission characters

tex·tile /ték stīl/ *n* **1.** cloth or fabric that is woven, knitted, or otherwise manufactured **2.** raw material that is used for making fabrics, e.g., fiber or yarn [Early 17C. < Latin *textilis* < past participle of *texere* "weave"]

text in·dex *n* an index of some or all of the words in something such as a computer file or database field, used to aid searching and retrieval

text mes·sage *n* a message sent in textual form, especially one designed to appear on the viewing screen of a cellular phone or pager —**text mes·sag·ing** *n*

text proc·ess·ing *n* the use of a computer to create, store, edit, and print or display text

tex·tu·al /tékschoo əl/ *adj* **1.** relating to the way a book or piece of writing is written **2.** consisting of words or text [14C. < medieval Latin *textualis* < Latin *textus* (see TEXT)] —**tex·tu·al·ly** *adv*

tex·tu·al crit·i·cism *n* **1.** the study of a group of manuscripts, especially of the Bible or works of literature, in order to determine which is the original or most authentic one **2.** the critical study of a work of literature involving a detailed analysis of the way in which it was written, e.g., its context, use of language, and principal themes —**tex·tu·al crit·ic** *n*

tex·tu·al·ism /tékschoo ə lìzzəm/ *n* **1.** unswerving adherence to a text, especially a text from the Bible **2.** detailed and critical analysis of a text —**tex·tu·al·ist** *n*

tex·tu·ar·y /tékschoo èrree/ *adj* same as **textual** (*formal*) [Early 17C. < medieval Latin *textuarius* < Latin *textus* (see TEXT)]

tex·ture /tékschər/ *n* **1.** FEEL OF SURFACE the feel and appearance of a surface, especially how rough or smooth it is **2.** STRUCTURE OF SOMETHING the structure of a substance or material such as soil or food, especially how it feels when touched or chewed **3.** ROUGH QUALITY the rough quality of a surface or fabric ○ *a fabric that has a lot of texture* **4.** DISTINCTIVE CHARACTER the typical and distinctive character of something complex ○ *The book captures the texture of 1950s provincial England.* **5.** WAY ARTIST DEPICTS SURFACE the way in which an artist depicts the quality or appearance of a surface **6.** EFFECT OF DIFFERENT COMPONENTS OF MUSIC the effect of the different components of a piece of music such as melody, harmony, rhythm, or the use of different instruments **7.** COMPUT **DETAIL OF GRAPHICS** in computer graphics, surface detail added to images ■ *vt* (**-tured, -tur·ing, -tures**) **GIVE ROUGH FEEL TO SURFACE** to give a surface a rough and grainy feel [15C. Via French < Latin *textura* "a weaving" < past participle of *texere* "weave"] —**tex·tur·al** *adj* —**tex·tur·al·ly** *adv* —**tex·tured** *adj*

tex·tured veg·e·ta·ble pro·tein *n* full form of **TVP**

tex·tur·ing /tékschəring/ *n* in computer graphics, the adding of surface detail to an image

T-for·ma·tion *n* in football, an offensive formation in which the center, quarterback, and fullback are in a straight line with the halfbacks on either side of and sometimes slightly behind the fullback, roughly forming a T

tg *abbr* Togo (*used in Internet addresses*) See table at **domain name**

TG *abbr* LING transformational grammar

TGAL *abbr* ONLINE think globally, act locally

TGIF, T.G.I.F. *abbr* Thank God it's Friday *or* Thank goodness it's Friday (*informal*)

TGV *n* in France and some other countries, a very high-speed train [< French, abbreviation of *train (à) grande vitesse* "high-speed train"]

th *abbr* Thailand (*used in Internet addresses*) See table at **domain name**

Th *symbol* CHEM ELEM thorium

Th. *abbr* **1.** BIBLE Thessalonians **2.** CALENDAR Thursday

-th *suffix* **1.** in a series or sequence ○ *tenth* ○ *fortieth* **2.** another spelling of **-eth**[1]

Thack·er·ay /thákə rày/, **William Makepeace** (1811–63) British novelist. Serialization of his novel *Vanity Fair* (1847–48) established him as a major literary figure. He is remembered for his humorous and moralizing portraits of middle- and upper-class life in Britain.

> "If a man's character is to be abused, say what you will, there's nobody like a relation to do the business."
> [William Makepeace Thackeray, *Vanity Fair*; 1847–48]

Thad·dae·us /tháddee əss, thə dée əss/ *n* one of the 12 apostles of Jesus Christ. He is traditionally identified with St. Jude (Mark 3:16–19, Matthew 10:2–4).

Thai /tī/ (*plural* **Thais** or *same*) *n* **1.** somebody who comes from Thailand **2.** the official language of Thailand, belonging to the Tai group of languages. Native speakers: 25 million. [Early 19C. < Thai, "free"] —**Thai** *adj*

Thailand

Thai·land /tī lànd, -lənd/ country in Southeast Asia bordered by Myanmar, Laos, Cambodia, the Gulf of Thailand, Malaysia, and the Andaman Sea. Language: Thai. Currency: baht. Capital: Bangkok. Population: 64,265,276 (2003). Area: 198,115 sq. mi./513,115 sq. km. Official name **Kingdom of Thailand.** Former name **Siam** (until 1939)

Thai·land, Gulf of /tī lànd, -lənd/ wide inlet of the South China Sea separating Vietnam, Cambodia, and eastern Thailand from the Malay Peninsula. Length: 500 mi./800 km.

thal·a·mus /thálləməss/ (*plural* **-mi** /-mī/) *n* **1.** either of a pair of egg-shaped masses of gray matter lying beneath each cerebral hemisphere in the brain that relay sensory information to the cerebral cortex. They are concerned with awareness of all the main senses except for smell. **2.** BOT same as **receptacle** (sense 2) [Late 17C. Via Latin, "inner chamber" < Greek *thalamos*] —**tha·lam·ic** /thə lámmik/ *adj* —**tha·lam·i·cal·ly** *adv*

Tha·las·sa /thə lássə/ *n* a small inner natural satellite of Neptune, discovered in 1989 by the space probe Voyager 2. It is approximately 50 mi./80 km in diameter.

thal·as·se·mi·a /thàllə séemee ə/ *n* a hereditary form of anemia, particularly prevalent around the Mediterranean, that is caused by a dysfunction in the synthesis of the red blood pigment hemoglobin [Mid-20C. < Greek *thalassa* "sea" (from its discovery in Mediterranean countries) + *haima* "blood"] —**thal·as·se·mic** *adj*

tha·las·sic /thə lássik/ *adj* **1.** living in or growing in the sea **2.** relating to a sea or ocean, especially a smaller inland sea [Mid-19C. < French *thalassique* < Greek *thalassa* "sea"]

thal·as·soc·ra·cy /thàllə sókrəssee/ (*plural* **-cies**), **tha·lat·toc·ra·cy** /-tókrəssee/ *n* naval or commercial supremacy over a large area of sea or ocean [Mid-19C. < Greek *thalassokratia* "authority over the sea" < *thalassa* "sea"] —**tha·las·so·crat** /thə lássə kràt/ *n*

tha·las·so·ther·a·py /thàllәssō thérrəpee/ *n* a therapeutic treatment that involves bathing in sea water [Late 19C. < Greek *thalassa* "sea"]

tha·lat·toc·ra·cy *n* POL same as **thalassocracy**

tha·ler /taálər/ (*plural same* or **-lers**), **ta·ler** *n* a former silver coin used in Austria, Germany, and Switzerland [Late 18C. < archaic German (now *Taler*)]

Tha·les (of Mi·le·tus) /thày leez-/ (625?–546? B.C.) Greek philosopher. He is traditionally regarded as the founder of Greek philosophy.

Tha·li·a /thə lī ə, tháylee ə, tháylyə/ *n* **1.** in Greek mythology, the Muse of comedy, one of the nine Muses believed to inspire and nurture the arts **2.** in Greek mythology, one of the three Graces who lived on Mount Olympus and tended the goddess Aphrodite

tha·lid·o·mide /thə líddə mīd/ *n* a synthetic drug found to cause physical malformations in fetuses when taken by pregnant women. Use: formerly, sedative and hypnotic. [Mid-20C. < *thal* (extracted from PHTHALIC ACID) + *ido* (extracted from *imido-* < IMIDE) + *mide* (extracted from IMIDE)]

thal·li BIOL plural of **thallus**

thal·lic /thállik/ *adj* relating to or containing thallium, especially with a valence of three

thal·li·um /thállee əm/ *n* a soft highly toxic white metallic element. Source: lead and zinc smelting. Use: manufacture of low-melting glass, photocells, infrared detectors. Symbol **Tl**. See table at **element** [Mid-19C. < Greek *thallos* "green shoot" (because its spectrum is marked by a green band)]

thal·lo·phyte /thállə fīt/ *n* a plant that has no stem, roots, or leaves, e.g., algae, lichens, and fungi [Mid-19C. < modern Latin *Thallophyta* < Greek *thallos* "green shoot" + *phuton* "plant"] —**thal·lo·phyt·ic** /thàllə fíttik/ *adj*

thal·lous /thálləss/ *adj* relating to or containing thallium, especially with a valence of one

thal·lus /thálləss/ (*plural* **-li** /-lī/ or **-lus·es**) *n* the body of an organism such as an alga or liverwort that is not differentiated into leaves, stems, and roots [Early 19C. < Greek *thallos* "green shoot" < *thallein* "to bloom"] —**thal·loid** /thá lòyd/ *adj*

thal·weg /taál vèg/, **tal·weg** *n* a line connecting the lowest points of successive cross sections through a river channel or valley [Mid-19C. < German < obsolete *Thal* "valley" (now *Tal*) + *Weg* "path"]

Thames /temz/ **1.** river in southeastern Ontario, Canada. It rises near Woodstock, flows through London, and empties into Lake St. Clair near Chatham. Length: 160 mi./260 km. **2.** major river of southern England. It flows through London before emptying into the North Sea. Length: 210 mi./338 km. **3.** tidal estuary formed by the confluence of the Shetucket and Yantic rivers in southeastern Connecticut and flowing southward into Long Island Sound. The Yale-Harvard boat race has taken place there since 1878. Length: 210 mi./338 km.

than *stressed* /than/; *unstressed* /thən/ CORE MEANING: used after a comparative adjective or adverb in order to introduce the second element of a comparison ○ (prep) *paying more than $490 a year in fees* ○ (prep) *The hole was no deeper than 12 ft.* ○ (conj) *The risk may be higher than the figures indicate.*

1. *conj* **STATING PREFERENCE** used to introduce a rejected alternative in a contrast between two alternatives, in order to state a preference ○ *more a state of mind than a physical condition* **2.** *conj US* **WHEN** used especially after inverted constructions to say when something happened ○ *Barely had she opened the door than the phone started to ring.* **3.** *prep* **COMPARED TO** in contrast with or in preference to (*informal*) ○ *I'm older than him.* [Old English *þanne, þonne, þænne, þan* < Germanic]

USAGE ***Than*** (a conjunction and a preposition) and ***then*** (an adverb and an adjective) are used differently and have different meanings even though they may sound similar when pronounced. Do not use ***than*** when ***then*** is called for, as in: *If the meal is ready, then* [not *than*] *you should sit at the table. She was the then-president* [not *than-president*] *of the society.* Conversely, do not use ***then*** when ***than*** is called for, as in: *The hole was no deeper than* [not *then*] *12 feet.*

USAGE than he or **than him**? Because ***than*** is a preposition as well as a conjunction, either construction is possible, as is the fuller form *than he is.* The form *than him* is common in conversation and other spoken contexts (*We're older than him*) but is still frowned upon in formal writing where *We're older than he is* is preferred.

than·a·tol·o·gy /thànnə tólləjee/ *n* the study of the medical, psychological, and sociological aspects of death and the ways in which people deal with it [Mid-19C. < Greek *thanatos* "death"] —**than·a·to·log·i·cal** /thànnət'l ójjik'l/ *adj* —**than·a·tol·o·gist** *n*

Than·a·tos /thánnə tàwss/ *n* **1.** in Greek mythology, the personification of death and the son of Nyx, goddess of the night. Roman equivalent **Mors 2.** the universal death instinct theorized by Sigmund Freud [Mid-20C. < Greek, "death"]

thane /thayn/ *n* **1.** an Anglo-Saxon nobleman of low rank who held lands in return for military service to a lord **2.** a baron in feudal Scotland, or a hereditary tenant of the Scottish crown [Old English *þegn* < Germanic, "boy, man"] —**than·age** *n* —**thane·ship** *n*

Than·et, Isle of /thánnit/ coastal region in Kent, southeastern England. It was formerly an island.

thank /thangk/ (**thanked, thank·ing, thanks**) *vt* **1.** to express feelings of gratitude to somebody or be grateful to somebody ○ *We'd like to thank you for a wonderful evening.* ○ *Thank goodness you got here in time.* **2.** to blame somebody or hold somebody responsible for something ○ *You have only yourself to thank for this situation.* [Old English *þancian* < Indo-European] ◇ **I'll thank you to** *or* **not to** used in an ironic or angry way to ask somebody to do *or* not do something ○ *I'll thank you not to mention that again.*

thank·ful /thángkfəl/ *adj* **1.** feeling or expressing gratitude ○ *We must be thankful for small mercies.* **2.** glad or relieved about something —**thank·ful·ness** *n*

thank·ful·ly /thángkfəlee/ *adv* **1.** used to express approval or relief about a situation (*informal*) ○ *Thankfully, it didn't rain until the game was over.* **2.** with feelings or expressions of gratitude ○ *They thankfully accepted her offer of a room for the night.*

USAGE ***Thankfully*** is used in two ways: as a conventional adverb of manner (*They received the good news thankfully*), and as a sentence adverb (*Thankfully, the news was good*). Some people dislike the second use, although the objection is not as strong as that to *hopefully* used in a corresponding way.

thank·less /thángkləss/ *adj* **1.** not likely to be appreciated or rewarded ○ *a thankless task* **2.** not showing or feeling gratitude —**thank·less·ly** *adv* —**thank·less·ness** *n*

thanks /thangks/ *interj* **USED TO EXPRESS GRATITUDE** used to express gratitude to somebody ○ *Goodbye, and* *thanks!* ■ *npl* **1.** EXPRESSION OF GRATITUDE an expression of gratitude for something ○ *Many thanks for your help yesterday.* **2.** GRATITUDE FOR SOMETHING gratitude or appreciation for something ◇ **no thanks to somebody** *or* **something** despite somebody or something or without somebody's assistance ◇ **thanks a lot** used to express great gratitude (*informal; sometimes used ironically*) ○ *Thanks a lot for coming over.* ○ *You took my glass? Thanks a lot!* ◇ **thanks to somebody** *or* **something** because of somebody or something

thanks·giv·ing /thàngks gívving, thángks gìvving/ *n* **1.** PRAYER OF THANKS a prayer that offers thanks to God **2.** GIVING OF THANKS an expression or an act of giving thanks **3.** PUBLIC ACKNOWLEDGMENT OF DIVINE GOODNESS a public acknowledgment or celebration of divine goodness

Thanks·giv·ing Day, **Thanks·giv·ing** *n* **1.** a legal holiday marking the feast given in thanks for the harvest by the Pilgrim colonists in 1621. Date: fourth Thursday in November. **2.** *Can* in Canada, a legal holiday observed as a day of giving thanks for the harvest and other good things received. Date: second Monday in October.

thank you *interj* used to express gratitude to somebody

thank-you *n* an expression of gratitude to somebody ○ *a big thank-you to all our readers* ■ *adj* expressing gratitude to somebody for something ○ *Send a thank-you note promptly.*

Thant /thaant, thant/, **U** (1909–74) Burmese politician. Following a series of senior government posts, he became secretary-general of the United Nations (1961–71).

thar /t͟haar/ *adv regional* same as **there** (*nonstandard*)

Thar Des·ert /taar-/ desert in northwestern India, in the state of Rajasthan, extending across the border into Pakistan. Area: 100,000 sq. mi./260,000 sq. km.

Tharp /thaarp/, **Twyla** (*b.* 1941) US dancer and choreographer. Her individual dance style combines ballet, tap, and jazz.

"The notion of doing something impossibly new usually turns out to be an illusion."
[Twyla Tharp, *Independent (London)*; December 8, 1995]

Thar·sis /thaarssiss/ *n* an extensive shallow bulge on the surface of Mars in the northern hemisphere about 1200 mi./2000 km across and 5 mi./8 km high, supporting several volcanoes

Thá·sos /táss awss/ island in northeastern Greece, in the Aegean Sea, about 5 mi./8 km from the mainland. Population: 13,111 (1981). Area: 378 sq. mi./979 sq. km.

that *stressed* /t͟hat/; *unstressed* /t͟hət/ CORE MEANING: a grammatical word used to indicate somebody or something that has already been mentioned or identified, or something that is understood by both the speaker and hearer ○ (adj) *Do you remember that discussion we had?* ○ (adj) *Later that week I saw her again.* ○ (pron) *Is that why you're here?* ○ (pron) *Don't touch that!*

1. *adj, pron* INDICATING FAMILIAR PERSON OR THING used to refer to somebody or something not described, but familiar to the speaker and hearer and not requiring identification ○ (adj) *Did you read that e-mail I sent?* ○ (adj) *that woman we met yesterday* ○ (pron) *That was a great year.* **2.** *adj, pron* INDICATING DISTANCE FROM SPEAKER indicating somebody or something a distance away from you, or further away from another, referred to as "this" ○ (adj) *You see that girl over there?* ○ (adj) *That bag looks more spacious than this one.* ○ (pron) *What's that you're doing?* ○ (pron) *That looks much nicer than this.* **3.** *adj* INDICATING TYPE used to characterize a particular type, person, or thing ○ *I really want a sleep that goes on forever.* **4.** ⚠ *pron* IDENTIFYING SOMEBODY OR SOMETHING used to introduce a clause giving more information to identify the person or thing mentioned ○ *the committee that deals with such matters* ○ *Take the road that forks to the left.* ○ *on the day that he left* **5.** *conj* EXPRESSING COMMENT OR FACT used to introduce a noun clause expressing a comment on a situation or a supposed or real fact ○ *It was clear that she wanted to see the concert.* ○ *The report stated that sales were improving.* **6.** *conj* EXPRESSING RESULT used to introduce a clause expressing result or effect ○ *It made such a noise that we had to cover our ears.* **7.** *conj* EXPRESSING CAUSE used to introduce a clause expressing the cause of a feeling ○ *I feel hurt that you should think such a thing.* ○ *He's sorry that he told her now.* **8.** *conj* EXPRESSING PURPOSE used to introduce a clause expressing purpose (*literary*) ○ *We continue to give, that others may receive and live.* **9.** *conj* EXPRESSING DESIRE OR AMAZEMENT used after an understood but unspoken statement such as "I wish" or "If only" to introduce a clause expressing desire, amazement, or indignation (*literary*) ○ *Oh that I had never set eyes on her!* ○ *That you could think such a thing!* **10.** *adv* TO SPECIFIC DEGREE used to specify the extent of something ○ *I came that close to hitting the car in front.* **11.** *adv* SO VERY used before adjectives to emphasize the quality they are describing (*informal*) ○ *I didn't think she'd be that upset.* [Old English *þæt* < Indo-European] ◇ **that is** in other words, or to be specific ○ *You need a further qualification, that is, a Ph.D.* ◇ **that's that 1.** used to say that something is finished or dealt with **2.** used to say that something has been settled and there will be no more discussion on it

---

USAGE that or who? For centuries ***that*** has been used to refer to people as well as things: *the person who* or *that arrived.* Sometimes ***that*** can be clumsy: *He's the one that did it.* But it is not incorrect, and is occasionally the most appropriate choice of relative pronoun: *anything or anyone that can help* is more elegant than *anything that or anyone who can help.*

USAGE that or which? The relative pronoun ***that*** introduces a restrictive clause, i.e., a clause that is essential for identifying the noun it follows: *Any aircraft that has a leaking engine is not airworthy.* It is not preceded by a comma. The relative pronoun ***which*** introduces a nonrestrictive clause, i.e., one providing additional information about the noun it follows and not essential for its identification: *The second house on the block, which was built in 1980, has ten rooms.* ***Which*** is preceded by a comma, and also followed by one if it does not end the sentence: *He gave me a taste of it, which I enjoyed. The largest house, which stands on the corner, is up for sale.* A ***which*** clause refers only to an inanimate noun or a complete sentence: *I arrived late, which annoyed them.*

USAGE that not that there: Avoid using *there* in formal writing as an adjectival intensifier of a noun preceded by ***that***: *That* [not *That there*] *house is for sale.*

---

that·a·way /t͟hátta wày/ *adv US regional, Can* in that direction, or over there (*humorous or regional*) ○ *The masked man went thataway, Sheriff.* [Mid-19C. Alteration of *that way*]

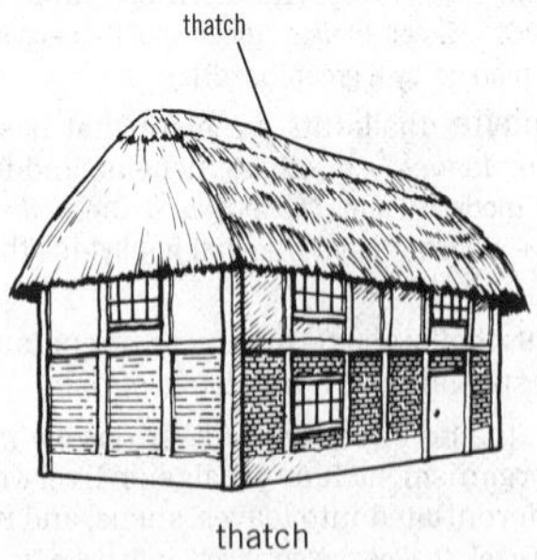

thatch

thatch /thach/ *n* **1.** PLANT MATERIAL USED FOR ROOF a plant material used as roofing on a house, e.g., straw or rushes **2.** ROOF a roof made of thatch **3.** HAIR ON SOMEBODY'S HEAD the hair on somebody's head, especially when it is thick ○ *The child had an unmistakable thatch of red hair.* **4.** GARDENING LAYER OF DEAD MATERIAL IN GRASS a matted layer of dead plant material that builds up next to the soil at the base of lawn grasses ■ *vti* (**thatched, thatch·ing, thatch·es**) ROOF BUILDING WITH THATCH to put a roof of thatch on a building, or work at doing this [Old English *þeccan.* < Indo-European "to cover"] —**thatched** *adj*—**thatch·er** *n*

Thatch·er /tháchər/, **Margaret, Baroness Thatcher of Kesteven** (*b.* 1925) British prime minister (1979–90). The leader of the Conservative Party from 1975, and the first woman prime minister of Great Britain, she pursued policies of privatization and economic deregulation. Born **Roberts, Margaret Hilda**. See table at **prime minister**

Margaret Thatcher

"We must find ways to starve the terrorist and the hijacker of the oxygen of publicity on which they depend."
[Margaret Thatcher, *Speech to the American Bar Association, London*; July 15, 1985]

"Remember, George: this is no time to go wobbly."
[Margaret Thatcher, *to President George H.W. Bush during the Persian Gulf War*, March 8, 1991, quoted in *The New Yorker*; December 7, 1992]

thatch·ing /tháching/ *n* **1.** the craft or process of constructing or repairing thatched roofs **2.** INDUST same as **thatch** *n* (sense 1)

thaumato- *prefix* miracle ○ *thaumatology* [< Greek *thaumat-*, stem of *thauma* "marvel, wonder"]

thau·ma·tol·o·gy /thàwmə tólləjee/ *n* the study or description of miracles

thau·ma·trope /tháwmə trōp/ *n* a card with different pictures on either side so that when the card is rapidly twirled, the images appear to combine [Early 19C. < Greek *thauma* "wonder" + *tropos* "turning"] —**thau·ma·trop·i·cal** /thàwmə tróppik'l/ *adj*

thau·ma·turge /tháwmə tùrj/, **thau·ma·tur·gist** /tháwmə tùrjist/ *n* a performer of magic or supposed miracles [Early 18C. Via medieval Latin < Greek *thaumatourgos* < *thauma* "wonder" + *-ergos* "working"]

thau·ma·tur·gy /tháwmə tùrjee/ *n* the performance of miracles or magic —**thau·ma·tur·gic** /thàwmə túrjik/ *adj*

thaw /thaw/ *v* (**thawed, thaw·ing, thaws**) **1.** *vti* MELT to melt, or make something melt **2.** *vti* DEFROST to defrost frozen food, or become defrosted ○ *Leave the cake out to thaw.* **3.** *vi* BECOME LESS COLD to become less cold or numb through exposure to heat ○ *Come thaw out by the fire.* **4.** *vi* BE WARM ENOUGH TO MELT ICE to be warm enough for snow and ice to melt **5.** *vi* BECOME LESS HOSTILE to become less hostile, tense, or aloof ○ *The atmosphere thawed.* ■ *n* **1.** PROCESS OF THAWING the action or process of thawing **2.** LESSENING OF HOSTILITY a lessening of hostility, tension, or aloofness **3.** WARMER WEATHER a period of weather warm enough to melt snow and ice [Old English *þawian* < Germanic]

Thay·er /tháy ər, ther/, **Sylvanus** (1785–1872) US soldier and educator. As the long-term superintendent (1817–33) of the US Military Academy at West Point, he is credited with transforming it into a fully effective institution. Known as **Father of West Point**

Th.B. *abbr* EDUC, RELIG Bachelor of Theology [Latin *Theologiae Baccalaureus*]

THC *n* the main active chemical in cannabis. Full form **tetrahydrocannabinol**

Th.D. *abbr* EDUC, RELIG Doctor of Theology [Latin *Theologiae Doctor*]

the *stressed/emphatic* /t͟hee/; *unstressed; before a vowel* /t͟hee/; *unstressed; before a consonant* /t͟hə/ CORE MEANING: an adjective, the definite article, used before a noun denoting somebody or something that has already been mentioned or identified, or something that is understood by both the speaker

and hearer, as distinct from "a" or "an" ○ *The movie ended with the hero riding off into the desert.* ○ *The food was excellent but the service was poor.*
1. *adj* **INDICATING ONE AS DISTINCT FROM ANOTHER** used to refer to one in particular of a number of things or people, identified as distinct from all others by the use of a modifier ○ *Put them in the small bag.* ○ *the door on the left* ○ *the girl who answered the phone* ○ *the right to vote* ○ *the points made earlier* **2. INDICATING GENERIC CLASS** used to refer to a person or thing considered generically or universally ○ *Exercise is good for the heart.* ○ *She played the violin.* ○ *The dog is a loyal pet.* **3. INDICATING SHARED EXPERIENCE** used to refer to objects and concepts associated with the shared experience of a culture, society, or community ○ *go to the hospital* ○ *thinking about the future* ○ *lying in the sun* **4. ALL PEOPLE OF PARTICULAR TYPE** used before adjectives to refer generically to people of a particular type or class ○ *new measures to help the unemployed* ○ *They say the good always die young.* **5. TITLES AND NAMES** used before titles and some names such as place names ○ *the king of Spain* ○ *the Times newspaper* ○ *the president of the United States* **6. QUALIFYING NAMES AND TITLES** used in names and titles before adjectives and nouns that distinguish somebody from others of the same name or title ○ *Ivan the Terrible* ○ *Henry the Fifth* **7. INDICATING PARTS OF BODY** used instead of a possessive such as "my" or "your" to refer to a part of somebody's body ○ *patted him on the head* ○ *took her by the hand* **8. INDICATING MOST FAMOUS OR IMPORTANT** the best, only, or most outstanding ○ *It's the place to be.* **9. EXPRESSING RATES AND RATIOS** used to indicate how many units apply to each or every thing measured ○ *available at $60 the ton* **10. INDICATING FAMILY RELATIONSHIP** used instead of a possessive such as "your" or "my" to refer to somebody having a particular family relationship (*informal*) ○ *Give my regards to the family.* ○ *How's the wife?* **11. PERIOD OF TIME** used to refer to a period of time, especially a decade or an era ○ *living in the sixties* **12.** *adv, adj* **TO THAT EXTENT** used adverbially to emphasize that somebody or something is true to a particular extent (*used before comparatives*) ○ *She looks the better for her holiday.* ○ *the worse for wear* **13.** *adv* **BY HOW MUCH OR BY THAT MUCH** used adverbially to indicate how one amount or quality changes in relation to another (*used before each of two comparative adjectives or adverbs*) ○ *the cheaper the better* ○ *The more you exercise, the fitter you'll feel.* [Old English *þe*, earlier *se* < Indo-European]

the- *prefix* same as **theo-** (*used before vowels*)

The·a·no /thee áanō/ (*fl* 5th century B.C.) Greek philosopher and mathematician. She and her two daughters carried on the Pythagorean School after the death of her husband Pythagoras. She wrote treatises on mathematics, physics, medicine, and child psychology and is credited with writing the treatise on the "Golden Mean."

the·an·thro·pism /thee ánthrə pìzzəm/ *n* **1.** the assigning of human characteristics to a god or gods **2.** the Christian doctrine that the human and the divine are united in Jesus Christ [Early 19C. < Greek *theanthrōpos* "god-man" < *theos* "god" + *anthrōpos* "man"] —**the·an·throp·ic** /thée ən thróppik/ *adj* —**the·an·thro·pist** *n*

the·ar·chy /thée aàrkee/ (*plural* **-chies**) *n* **1. RULE BY GOD** rule by God, by a god, or by priests **2. COMMUNITY UNDER DIVINE RULE** a community that is ruled by God, by a god, or by priests **3. HIERARCHY OF GODS** a hierarchy or system of gods [Mid-17C. < Greek *thearkhia* < *theos* "god"] —**the·arch·ic** *adj*

theat. *abbr* ARTS **1.** theater **2.** theatrical

the·a·ter /thée ətər/, **the·a·tre** *n* **1. PLACE FOR PLAYS** a building, room, or other setting where plays or other dramatic presentations are performed **2. PLACE WHERE MOVIES ARE SHOWN** a building, room, or other setting where movies are shown **3. ROOM WITH TIERS OF SEATS** a room with rising tiers of seats, used for lectures, demonstrations, or assemblies **4. PLAYS** plays or other dramatic literature **5. DRAMA AS ART OR PROFESSION** dramatic performance as an art, profession, or way of life ○ *She decided to make the theater her life.* **6. DRAMATIC QUALITY** dramatic or theatrical quality or effectiveness ○ *As a public speaker he has a great sense of theater.* **7. PLACE OF SIGNIFICANT EVENTS** the place or realm where significant actions or events take place ○ *the political theater* **8.** MED same as **operating room** (*informal*) **9.** *US* GEOG **LAND THAT RISES IN STEPS** a natural land formation that rises by steps or gradations ■ *adj* **FOR USE IN THEATER OF OPERATIONS** relating to or for use in a military theater of operations [14C. Via Old French and Latin < Greek *theatron* < *theasthai* "to watch"]

the·a·ter·go·ing /thée ətər gṑ ing/ *n* the practice of going to the theater, especially regularly ■ *adj* attending the theater, especially regularly ○ *The theatergoing public is being shortchanged by plays of this standard.* —**the·a·ter·go·er** *n*

the·a·ter-in-the-round (*plural* **the·a·ters-in-the-round**) *n* **1.** a theater in which the stage is in the center with the seats surrounding on all sides **2.** drama or the style of drama written for performance in a theater-in-the-round

the·a·ter of cru·el·ty *n* a form of surrealist drama emphasizing that human beings live in a threatening world with precarious moral values

the·a·ter of op·er·a·tions *n* an area where fighting takes place during a war

The·a·ter of the Ab·surd *n* a form of drama that represents the absurdity of human life in a meaningless universe by deliberately unrealistic means and by ignoring or distorting conventions of plot and characterization

the·a·ter of war *n* a large area of land, sea, and air in which warfare may take place

the·a·tre *n* ARTS another spelling of **theater**

the·at·ri·cal /thee áttrik'l/ *adj* **1. RELATING TO THEATER** relating to or characteristic of the theater or dramatic performance **2. MARKED BY ARTIFICIAL EMOTION** full of exaggerated or false emotion ■ *n* **ACTOR** a professional actor ■ **the·at·ri·cals, the·at·rics** *npl* **1. PERFORMANCES IN THEATER** the performance of plays **2. EXAGGERATED EMOTIONAL DISPLAY** dramatic behavior —**the·at·ri·cal·ism** *n* —**the·at·ri·cal·i·ty** /thee àttri kálləteе/ *n* —**the·at·ri·cal·ly** *adv* —**the·at·ri·cal·ness** *n*

the·ba·ine /théebə èen, thi báy in/ *n* a poisonous alkaloid that causes convulsions similar to those caused by strychnine. Source: opium. Use: formerly, as medicine. Formula: $C_{19}H_{21}NO_3$. [Mid-19C. < Greek *Thēbai* "Thebes"; because Upper Egypt was an important source of opium]

the·be /tébbé/ (*plural same*) *n* a subunit of Botswanan currency. See table at **currency** [Late 20C. < Setswana, "shield"]

The·be /thée bee/ *n* a small natural satellite of Jupiter, discovered in 1980. With a diameter of 60 mi./100 km, it is Jupiter's fourth most distant satellite, orbiting at a distance of 138,000 mi./222,000 km. [Mid-18C. Via Latin, a nymph < Greek]

Thebes /theebz/ **1.** city of ancient Greece, in Boeotia, northwest of present-day Athens. A celebrated city in Greek myth, it was the most important city in Boeotia from the beginning of the 6th century B.C. and was destroyed by Alexander the Great in 335 B.C. **2.** capital city of ancient Egypt, situated on both sides of the Nile River, south of present-day Cairo. It first appeared in Egyptian records in the middle of the 3rd millennium B.C., and served as the capital of Egypt until 1085 B.C. It is across the Nile from the Valley of the Kings, the site of the tombs of the pharaohs. —**The·ban** *n, adj*

the·ca /théekə/ (*plural* **-cae** /thée sèe, -kèe/) *n* an enclosing organ, capsule, or sheath, e.g., the spore case of a moss or the horny covering of the pupa of an insect [Early 17C. Via Latin < Greek *thēkē* "case"] —**the·cal** *adj* —**the·cate** /thée kàyt/ *adj*

the·co·dont /théekə dònt/ *adj* **WITH TEETH IN SOCKETS** describes animals whose teeth are set in sockets ■ *n* **1. EXTINCT PREHISTORIC REPTILE** an extinct reptile that lived in the Triassic period, had teeth set in sockets, and was the ancestor of the dinosaur. Order: Thecodontia. **2. THECODONT REPTILE** a reptile with teeth set in sockets [Mid-19C. < Latin *theca* (see THECA)]

thé dan·sant /tày daaN saáN/ (*plural* **thés dan·sants** /*pronunc. same*/) *n* same as **tea dance** [< French, "dancing tea"]

thee /thee/ *pron* a form of "thou" used as the object of a verb or preposition to mean "you" (*archaic regional*) [Old English *þē*, objective form of *þū* (see THOU²)]

theft /theft/ *n* the act or crime of stealing somebody else's property [Old English *þēoft* < Germanic]

~~theif~~ incorrect spelling of **thief**

the·ine /thée èen, -in/ *n* caffeine, particularly as found in tea [Mid-19C < modern Latin *Thea*, former genus name of the tea plant < Dutch *t(h)ee* (see TEA)]

their /ther/ *adj* **1.** belonging to or relating to a specific group of people or things ○ *They have sold their house and moved to Arizona.* **2.** ⚠ belonging to him or her (*informal*) ○ *Everyone should make their own way home.* [12C. < Old Norse *þeirra* "theirs"]

USAGE their, there, or **they're**? Do not confuse these three words, as they have different meanings and spellings, and they function differently. ***Their*** is a pronominal adjective: *Their* [not *They're* or *There*] *decisions have been made.* ***There*** can be an adverb or a pronoun, e.g., *Look over there* [not *their* or *they're*] *quickly. There* [not *They're* or *Their*] *are several unanswered questions.* ***They're*** is a contraction of "they are," as in *They're* [not *There* or *Their*] *sitting in the front row.*

USAGE See ***they***.

---

theirs /therz/ *pron* **1.** belonging to a specific group of people or things ○ *Theirs was the biggest house in the town.* **2.** belonging to an individual person (*informal*) ○ *I have spare copies of the agenda if anyone has forgotten theirs.*

the·ism /thée ìzzəm/ *n* **1.** belief that one God created and rules humans and the world, not necessarily accompanied by belief in divine revelation such as through the Bible **2.** belief in the existence of a god or gods [Late 17C. < Greek *theos* "god"] —**the·ist** *n* —**the·is·tic** /thee ístik/ *adj* —**the·is·ti·cal** *adj* —**the·is·ti·cal·ly** *adv*

them /them/; *unstressed* /thəm/ *pron* **1. OBJECTIVE FORM OF "THEY"** used to refer to a group of people or things other than the speaker or people addressed ○ *I'll put them in a box for you.* **2.** ⚠ **HIM OR HER** used instead of "him" or "her" to refer to a person without specifying gender (*informal*) ○ *If anyone is looking for me, tell them I'll be back soon.* **3. THOSE** a dialect form of "those" (*regional or nonstandard*) ○ *Give me one of them oranges.* **4.** *regional* **THEMSELVES** used instead of "themselves" when the object of a verb refers to the same people or things as the subject of the verb (*nonstandard*) ○ *They got them a new car.* [12C. < Old Norse *þeim*]

USAGE See ***they***.

---

the·mat·ic /thə máttik/ *adj* **1. RELATING TO THEME** relating to or being a theme **2.** LING **RELATING TO WORD STEM** relating to the stem of a word **3.** LING **LAST BEFORE INFLECTION** describes the last part of a word stem before the inflectional ending ○ *a thematic vowel* [Late 17C. < Greek *thematikos* < *thema* "proposition"] —**the·mat·i·cal·ly** *adv*

the·mat·ic ap·per·cep·tion test *n* a test for exploring aspects of personality in which somebody is shown pictures of people in various situations and asked to describe what is happening. The presumption is that emotions, prejudices, and other psychological states of the subject will be projected onto the figures in the pictures.

theme /theem/ *n* **1. SUBJECT OF DISCUSSION OR COMPOSITION** the subject of a discourse, discussion, piece of writing, or artistic composition **2. DISTINCT AND UNIFYING IDEA** a distinct, recurring, and unifying quality or idea ○ *Efficiency will be the theme of this organization.* **3. REPEATED MELODY** a melody that is repeated, often with variations, throughout a piece of music ○ *one of the themes of the concerto* **4. MUSIC IN FILM** a song or tune that is played at the beginning or end of, or during, a movie or television program and is identified with it ○ *the theme from "The Magnificent Seven"* **5. ESSAY OR WRITTEN EXERCISE** a short essay or written exercise for a student **6.** GRAM same as **stem**¹ *n* (sense 6) ■ *adj* **WITH DISTINCT SUBJECT** with one distinct and recurring subject, principle, or idea ○ *We ate at a Wild West theme restaurant.* ■ *vt* (**themed, them·ing, themes**) **GIVE SOMETHING DISTINCT CHARACTER** to give something a single distinct character or subject ○ *The local bar has been themed as an*

Irish pub. [13C. Via Old French and Latin < Greek *thema* "proposition"]

USAGE Like some other verbs formed from nouns that have undergone "functional shift," ***theme*** has not gained wide acceptance (it is associated with the jargon of commerce and popular culture). It is best, therefore, to avoid sentences like these: *She worked hard to theme her valedictory speech. The party was themed as a Renaissance ball.* Acceptable alternatives are: *She worked hard to develop the theme of her valedictory speech. The party theme was a Renaissance ball.* Similarly, it is advisable to avoid using the adjective *themed* alone or in combination with other words, as in *a baroque-themed concert,* where *a concert with a baroque theme* is the safer choice.

SYNONYMS See ***subject.***

theme park *n* an amusement park in which all of the entertainments and facilities are designed around a specific subject or idea

theme par·ty (*plural* **theme par·ties**) *n* a party at which a particular subject or idea, e.g., Hollywood movies or the 1960s, determines the way the guests dress and what food, decorations, or games are provided

theme song *n* a tune or song that is associated with a particular performer or one that is played in every episode of a television or radio series

The·mis·to·cles /thə místə kleez/ (527?–460? B.C.) Greek general and political leader. He built up the Athenian navy and led it to victory over the Persians at the battle of Salamis (480 B.C.), laying the foundations for Athenian domination of Greece.

> "Athens holds sway over all Greece; I dominate Athens; my wife dominates me; our newborn son dominates her."
> [Attributed to Themistocles]

~~**themometer**~~ incorrect spelling of **thermometer**

them·self /thəm sélf/ *pron* ⚠ used as a reflexive pronoun to refer to somebody whose sex is not indicated (*nonstandard*)

USAGE ***Themself*** is a reflexive pronoun that is sometimes used informally in speech instead of *himself or herself* when the sex of the person is not known or not relevant: *Any member of the party would try to distance themself from this policy.* Its use, however, is not acceptable in standard English and should be avoided.

them·selves /thəm sélvz, them-/ *pron* **1. REFLEXIVE OF "THEY" OR "THEM"** used to refer to a group of people or things when the object of a verb is the same as the subject ○ *They all made themselves at home.* **2. THEIR NORMAL SELVES** their real or normal selves (*usually used in negative statements*) ○ *They haven't been themselves since the accident.* **3. EMPHASIZING** used to emphasize the people or things being referred to ○ *They themselves would rather have gone to a movie.* **4. HIMSELF OR HERSELF** used to refer to an individual person without using "himself" or "herself" (*informal*) ○ *Everyone needs to take care of themselves.*

then /then/ CORE MEANING: an adverb used to indicate a particular time in the past or future ○ *We were much happier then.* ○ *Until then, he'll be staying with me.*

1. *adv* **INDICATING SPECIFIC TIME** indicates a specific time in the past or future ○ *Life was easier then.* **2.** *adv* **AFTER THAT** after that or subsequently in time, order, or position ○ *Fry the onions and garlic, then the vegetables.* ○ *We went for a walk, then came home.* **3.** *adv* **THEREFORE** that being the case, or in that case ○ *Then why don't you go back?* **4.** *adv* **IN ADDITION** in addition to something else, or besides what has been mentioned ○ *I have to pay the money, then a penalty on top of that!* **5.** *adj* **BEING AT THAT TIME** being at that time, or existing or belonging to the time mentioned ○ *the then governor* [Old English *þænne* < Indo-European] ◇ **(but) then again** used to introduce a contrasting and additional fact that has to be taken into account ○ *It was a brave thing to do, but then again I would have expected no less of her.* ◇ **then and there** immediately and in that very place ○ *Did you expect me to hand over the money then and there?*

USAGE See ***than.***

the·nar /thée naar/ *n* **1. PALM OF HAND** the palm of the hand (*technical*) **2. BASE OF THUMB** the fleshy area at the base of the thumb ■ *adj* **IN PALM OR BALL OF THUMB** relating to or in the palm of the hand or the fleshy area at the base of the thumb [Mid-17C. < Greek, "palm of the hand"]

Thé·nard /tay naar/, **Louis Jacques, Baron** (1777–1857) French chemist. He discovered hydrogen peroxide and potassium peroxide, as well as a pigment used to color porcelain and known as "Thénard's blue." He wrote a once-standard treatise on chemistry.

thence /thenss/ *adv* (*formal or literary*) **1. FROM THERE** from that place ○ *We went by boat to Rotterdam and thence to Amsterdam.* **2. THEREFORE** from that fact, or therefore **3. THEREAFTER** from that time, or thereafter [13C. < obsolete *thenne* < W Germanic]

thence·forth /thenss fáwrth/ *adv* from that time on

thence·for·ward /-wərdz/, **thence·for·wards** *adv* from that place or time on or forward

theo- *prefix* god ○ *theocentric* [< Greek *theos* < Indo-European, "to shine, sky, heaven"]

the·o·bro·mine /thée ō brṓ meen/ *n* a white alkaloid powder that has effects similar to caffeine. Source: cacao beans. Use: diuretic, vasodilator, treatment of cardiovascular disorders. Formula: $C_7H_8N_4O_2$. [Mid-19C. < modern Latin *Theobroma*, genus name of the cacao tree, literally "food of the gods" < Greek *brōma* "food"]

the·o·cen·tric /thée ō séntrik/ *adj* with God, a god, or gods as the focal point —**the·o·cen·tri·cism** *n* —**the·o·cen·tric·i·ty** /-sen tríssətee/ *n* —**the·o·cen·trism** *n*

the·oc·ra·cy /thee ókrəssee/ (*plural* **-cies**) *n* **1.** government by a god or by priests **2.** a community governed by a god or priests [Early 17C. < Greek *theokratia* "rule of the gods"] —**the·o·crat** /thée ə kràt/ *n* —**the·o·crat·ic** /thée ə kráttik/ *adj* —**the·o·crat·i·cal** *adj* —**the·o·crat·i·cal·ly** *adv*

The·oc·ri·tus /thee ókrətəss/ (310?–250? B.C.) Greek poet. His graceful lyrics were the foundation of European pastoral poetry.

the·od·i·cy /thee óddissee/ (*plural* **-cies**) *n* argument in defense of God's goodness despite the existence of evil [Late 18C. Anglicization of French *Théodicée*, title of a book by Gottfried LEIBNIZ, literally "justice of the gods" < Greek *dikē* "justice"] —**the·od·i·ce·an** /thee òddi sée ən/ *adj*

the·o·di·ver·si·ty /thée ō di vúrssətee, -dīvúrssətee/ *n* the phenomenon of the appearance, in the late 20th and early 21st centuries, of many different new religious denominations, beliefs, and movements

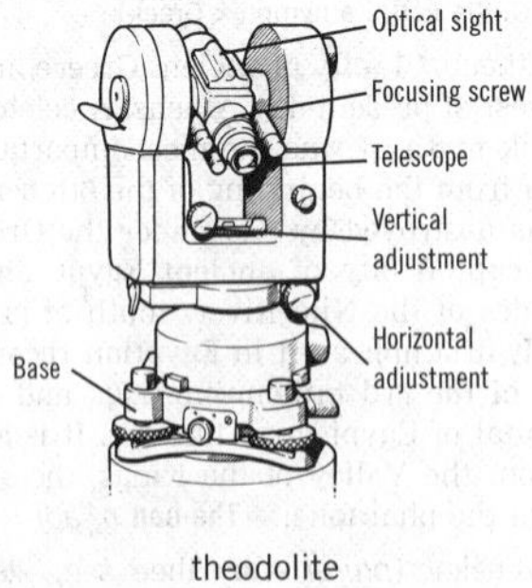

theodolite

the·od·o·lite /thee óddə līt/ *n* an optical instrument consisting of a rotating telescopic sight, used by a surveyor to measure horizontal and vertical angles [Late 16C. < modern Latin *theodelitus*] —**the·od·o·lit·ic** /thee òddə líttik/ *adj*

The·o·do·ra /thée ə dáwrə/ (A.D. 508?–548) Byzantine empress. She was the wife of Justinian I, with whom she shared power (527–48). She acted to save the throne during the Nika riots (532).

The·o·do·rak·is /thée ə daw raákiss/, **Mikis** (*b.* 1925) Greek composer. His wide-ranging output includes music for the movie *Zorba the Greek* (1965).

The·o·dore Roo·se·velt Na·tion·al Park /thée ə dawr-/ national park in western North Dakota, established in 1978 near the Little Missouri River. Area: 110 sq. mi./285 sq. km.

The·o·dor·ic /thee óddə rìk/ (A.D. 454?–526) king of the Ostrogoths. King from 474, he invaded Italy in 488 and founded the Ostrogothic kingdom there in 493 after conquering the country, making Ravenna the capital and bringing a period of peace. Known as **Theodoric the Great**

The·o·do·sius I /thée ə dṓshəss, -dṓshee əss/ (A.D. 346?–395) Roman emperor. As emperor of both the Eastern (379–95) and Western (392–95) Roman empires, he was the last ruler to unite the empire. He was a champion of Orthodox Christianity. Known as **Theodosius the Great**

the·og·o·ny /thee óggənee/ (*plural* **-nies**) *n* the origin and descent of the gods, or an account of this [Early 17C. < Greek *theogonia* "birth of the gods"] —**the·o·gon·ic** /thée ə gónnik/ *adj* —**the·og·o·nist** *n*

theol. *abbr* RELIG **1.** theologian **2.** theological **3.** theology

the·o·lo·gi·an /thée ə lṓjən/ *n* an expert in, or student of, theology

the·o·log·i·cal /thée ə lójjik'l/, **the·o·log·ic** /-lójjik/ *adj* relating to, using, engaged in, or typical of theology —**the·o·log·i·cal·ly** *adv*

the·o·log·i·cal vir·tues *npl* faith, hope, and charity, the three spiritual graces that, according to Christian theology, are given directly by God

the·ol·o·gize /thee óllə jīz/ (**-gized, -giz·ing, -giz·es**) *v* **1.** *vt* to give a theological or religious significance to something **2.** *vi* to theorize, speculate, or discourse on religious topics —**the·ol·o·giz·er** *n*

the·ol·o·gy /thee óllәjee/ (*plural* **-gies**) *n* **1. STUDY OF RELIGION** the study of religion, especially the Christian faith and God's relation to the world **2. RELIGIOUS THEORY** a religious theory, school of thought, or system of belief **3. COURSE OF RELIGIOUS TRAINING** a course of specialized religious training, especially one intended to lead students to a vocation in the Christian Church [14C. Via French and Latin < Greek *theologia* "study of divine things"] —**the·ol·o·gist** *n*

the·o·mor·phic /thée ə máwrfik/ *adj* in the form or likeness of a deity [Late 19C. < Greek *theomorphos* "of divine form"] —**the·o·mor·phism** *n*

the·on·o·my /thee ónnəmee/ *n* the state of being governed by God, a god, or priests —**the·on·o·mous** *adj*

the·oph·a·ny /thee óffənee/ (*plural* **-nies**) *n* the appearance of a god in a visible form to a human being [Mid-17C. Via medieval Latin < Greek *theophaneia* "appearance of the gods"] —**the·o·phan·ic** /thée ə fánnik/ *adj*

The·oph·i·lus /thee óffələss/ *n* a crater on the Moon northwest of Mare Nectaris. It is approximately 60 mi./100 km in diameter and has a central mountain 7200 ft./2200 m in height.

The·o·phras·tus /thée ə frástəss/ (372?–287 B.C.) Greek philosopher. Succeeding Aristotle as head of the Lyceum in Athens, he is remembered for an influential treatise on botany and his *Characters*, sketches of personality types.

the·oph·yl·line /thee óffəlin, thée ō fí leen/ *n* a white crystalline alkaloid. Source: tea leaves or synthetically made. Use: vasodilator, diuretic, treatment of bronchial asthma. Formula: $C_7H_8N_4O_2.H_2O$. [Late 19C. < modern Latin *Thea* (see THEINE) + PHYLLO-]

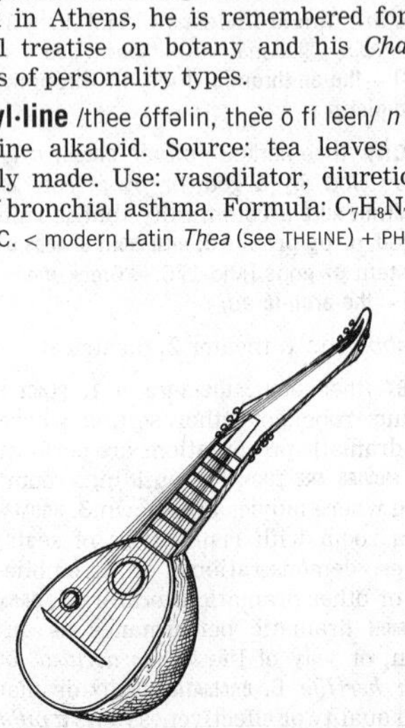

theorbo

the·or·bo /thee áwrbō/ *n* a stringed instrument from the 17th century similar to the lute except larger and with an extra set of bass strings longer than the main set. See illustration on previous page [Early 17C. Via Italian *tiorba* < Turkish *torba* "bag"] —**the·or·bist** *n*

the·o·rem /theé ərəm, theérəm/ *n* **1.** a proposition or formula in mathematics or logic that is provable from a set of axioms and basic assumptions **2.** an idea that is accepted or proposed as true [Mid-16C. Via late Latin < Greek *theōrēma* "speculation" < *theōrein* "look at" < *theōros* "spectator"] —**the·o·re·mat·ic** /theé ərə máttik, theérə máttik/ *adj* —**the·o·re·mat·i·cal·ly** *adv*

the·o·ret·i·cal /theé ə réttik'l/, **the·o·ret·ic** /-réttik/ *adj* **1.** BASED ON THEORY about, involving, or based on theory **2.** DEALING WITH THEORY dealing with theory or speculation rather than practical applications **3.** SPECULATIVE inclined to or skilled in speculative contemplation or theorizing **4.** HYPOTHETICAL existing only in theory [Early 17C. < late Latin *theoreticus* < Greek *theoretikos* < *theōrētos* "observable" < *theorein* "look at"] —**the·o·ret·i·cal·ly** *adv*

the·o·re·ti·cian /theé ərə tísh'n, theérə-/ *n* somebody who is skilled in considering theories, or is learned in the theoretical aspect of a subject

the·o·ret·ics /theé ə réttiks/ *n* the theoretical or speculative aspect of a subject (*takes a singular verb*)

the·o·rist /theé ərist, theérist/ *n* somebody who holds or expounds a theory

the·o·rize /theé ə rīz, theér īz/ (**-rized, -riz·ing, -riz·es**) *v* **1.** *vi* to speculate or form a theory about something **2.** *vt* to conceive of something in a theoretical way ○ *Research scientists were able to theorize the existence of the particle before it was actually discovered.* —**the·o·ri·za·tion** /theé əri záysh'n, theéri-/ *n* —**the·o·riz·er** *n*

the·o·ry /theé əree, theéree/ (*plural* **-ries**) *n* **1.** RULES AND TECHNIQUES the body of rules, ideas, principles, and techniques that applies to a subject, especially when seen as distinct from actual practice ○ *economic theories* ○ *Many coaches have a good grasp of the theory of football but can't motivate players.* **2.** SPECULATION abstract thought or contemplation **3.** IDEA FORMED BY SPECULATION an idea of or belief about something arrived at through speculation or conjecture ○ *She believed in the theory that you catch more flies with honey than with vinegar.* **4.** HYPOTHETICAL CIRCUMSTANCES a set of circumstances or principles that is hypothetical ○ *That's the theory, but it may not work out in practice.* **5.** SCIENTIFIC PRINCIPLE TO EXPLAIN PHENOMENA a set of facts, propositions, or principles analyzed in their relation to one another and used, especially in science, to explain phenomena [Late 16C. Via late Latin < Greek *theōria* "contemplation, theory" < *theōros* "spectator"] ◇ **in theory** under hypothetical or ideal circumstances but perhaps not in reality

the·o·ry of games *n* MATH same as **game theory**

the·o·ry of mind *n US* the way somebody conceives of mental activity in others, including how children conceptualize mental activity in others and how they attribute intention to and predict the behavior of others

~~**theorys**~~ incorrect spelling of **theories**

theos. *abbr* RELIG **1.** theosophical **2.** theosophy

the·os·o·phy /thee óssəfee/ (*plural* **-phies**) *n* any religious philosophy based on intuitive insight into the nature of God [Mid-17C. Via medieval Latin < late Greek *theosophia* "knowledge of the gods"] —**the·o·soph·ic** /theé ə sóffik/ *adj* —**the·o·soph·i·cal** *adj* —**the·o·soph·i·cal·ly** *adv* —**the·os·o·phism** *n* —**the·os·o·phist** *n*

The·os·o·phy /thee óssəfee/ *n* the teachings of the Theosophical Society, a religious movement founded in New York in 1875, incorporating chiefly Buddhist and Brahmanic theories such as reincarnation and karma —**The·o·soph·i·cal** /theé ə sóffik'l/ *adj* —**The·o·so·phist** *n*

The·ra /theérə/ island and tourist center in the Cyclades group, Greece, north of Crete. Destroyed by a volcanic eruption in 1500 B.C., it is sometimes claimed as the origin of the Atlantis legend. Population: 10,000 (1994). Area: 29 sq. mi./76 sq. km.

therap. *abbr* MED **1.** therapeutic **2.** therapeutics

ther·a·peu·tic /thèrrə pyóotik/ *adj* **1.** relating to, involving, or used in the treatment of disease or disorders **2.** working or done to maintain somebody's health [Mid-16C. < French *therapeutique* or late Latin *therapeutica* < Greek *therapeutēs* "somebody who treats" < *therapeuein* (see THERAPY)] —**ther·a·peu·ti·cal·ly** *adv*

ther·a·peu·tic clon·ing *n* the use of cloning to produce new body tissues from stem cells, for use in the treatment of disease or injury. ◊ **reproductive cloning**

ther·a·peu·tic in·dex *n* the ratio of the dose of a drug that causes cell damage to the dose typically needed to effect a cure. Use: indicates relative drug safety.

ther·a·peu·tics /thèrrə pyóotiks/ *n* the branch of medicine that deals with methods of treatment and healing, especially the use of drugs to treat diseases (*takes a singular verb*)

ther·a·pist /thérrəpist/ *n* **1.** somebody trained to treat disease, disorders, or injuries, especially somebody who uses methods other than drugs and surgery **2.** a psychoanalyst or a professional from another school of psychotherapy who is trained to treat mental and emotional problems with psychological methods

the·rap·sid /thə rápsid/ *n* an extinct reptile of an order that lived during the Permian and Triassic periods. Many therapsids are thought to be ancestors of the mammals. Order: Therapsida. [Early 20C. < modern Latin *Therapsida* < Greek *thēr* "wild animal" + *hapsis* "vault"]

ther·a·py /thérrəpee/ (*plural* **-pies**) *n* **1.** treatment of physical, mental, or behavioral problems that is meant to cure or rehabilitate somebody (*often used in combination*) ○ *radiation therapy* **2.** psychoanalysis or techniques from another school of psychotherapy, intended to treat mental and emotional problems with psychological methods [Mid-19C. Via modern Latin < Greek *therapeia* < *therapeuein* "treat medically" < *theraps* "attendant"]

Ther·a·va·da /thèrrə vaádə/ *n* the doctrines of the Hinayana Buddhists [Late 19C. < Pali, "doctrine of the elders"]

there /th̲er/; *unstressed* /th̲ər/ CORE MEANING: an adverb used to indicate a place, either one that has already been mentioned or is understood, or one indicated by pointing or looking ○ *I don't know how to get there by car.* ○ *May I sit there?*

1. *adv* IN OR TO THAT PLACE used to indicate position in or motion towards a place relatively distant from the speaker **2.** *adv* AT THAT POINT used to refer to a point reached in an activity or process ○ *I suggest we pause there and have coffee.* ○ *And there we end our news bulletin.* **3.** *adv* ON THAT MATTER on that matter, or with respect to that ○ *I can't agree with you there.* **4.** *adv* AT SUCCESSFUL POINT used to indicate that something has reached a final or successful point or stage ○ *We're not the best yet, but we're getting there.* **5.** *adv* USED TO IDENTIFY used to identify somebody or something emphatically ○ *They ran into that house there.* **6.** *pron* INTRODUCING SENTENCE used to introduce a sentence stating that something exists, develops, or can be seen ○ *There's a stain on this sweater.* ○ *There remain several important issues to be discussed.* **7.** *interj* USED TO EXPRESS FEELINGS used to express strong feelings such as anger, satisfaction, relief, finality, or reassurance ○ *There! I told you she would make it.* [Old English *þær* < Indo-European] ◇ **be there for somebody** to be ready to give your support, sympathy, or friendship to somebody ◇ **not all there** not fully conscious, rational, or aware of something ◇ **there and then** immediately and in that very place ◇ **there, there** used to console, soothe, or comfort somebody ○ *There, there. Don't cry.* ◇ **there you are 1.** used when giving somebody something **2.** used to express triumph at having been seen to be right **3.** used to express resignation or sorrow at something that has happened ◇ **don't even go there** used to indicate that a topic is considered too unpleasant for further discussion (*informal humorous*)

USAGE When the pronoun ***there*** opens a sentence with a subsequent linking verb like *be, appear,* or *seem,* the verb must agree with the grammatical subject coming *after* the verb: *There is* [not *are*] *a beach nearby. There are* [not *is*] *beaches and motels nearby. There appear* [not *appears*] *to be mistakes in your essay. There appears* [not *appear*] *to be a mistake in your essay. There's* stands for "there is." It should be used only with a singular grammatical subject, as in: *There's a lot still to be done. There's a car in the garage.* It is nonstandard English to say: *There's three cars in the garage. There's a lot of children in the hall.* An easy way to ensure the correct agreement between the verb and the subject is to reorder the words in your sentences mentally without ***there***: *Three cars are in the garage. A lot of children are in the hall.* By contrast, you would never say *Three cars is in the garage. A lot of children is in the hall.* With compound grammatical subjects, ***there*** used with a singular linking verb is acceptable only when the compound subject is regarded not as two separate entities but as a single compound noun. Thus it is acceptable to say: *There is/There's food and drink for everybody.* Stylistically, *There is/are* sentences tend to be flat and lacking in emphasis, so it is wise to avoid using them frequently.

USAGE See *their.*

there·a·bouts /th̲èrrə bówts/, **there·a·bout** /-bówt/ *adv* near that place, amount, number, or time ○ *We're expecting twenty guests or thereabouts.*

there·af·ter /th̲er áftər/ *adv* after that time or from that time on ○ *She graduated from college and shortly thereafter found a good job.*

there·at /th̲er át/ *adv* (*formal or literary*) **1.** at that time or place **2.** because of that

there·by /th̲er bī/ *adv* **1.** by means of or because of that ○ *Interest rates may fall, thereby discouraging investment.* **2.** in connection with or with reference to that ○ *Thereby hangs a tale.*

~~**therefor**~~ incorrect spelling of **therefore**

there·fore /th̲ér fàwr/ *adv* **1.** and so, or because of that ○ *This statement is true; therefore that statement must be false.* **2.** accordingly, or to that purpose ○ *We were forbidden to attend and therefore stayed at home.*

USAGE ***Therefore*** and ***thus*** are both fairly formal words that introduce a statement that is a consequence of the previous statement. They should not be used as empty connectors when what follows them does not derive from what precedes them: *Your grade on the test was 20%; therefore, you have failed.* It is tautologous to use *so therefore*: just ***therefore*** is sufficient. Punctuation around ***therefore*** requires some care. There is no comma between clauses where ***therefore*** is in the second clause, but instead a semicolon or a new sentence: *I had forgotten my key; therefore, I could not open the door. She left the library at 4 o'clock. She was therefore not there when the murder took place.*

there·from /th̲er frúm, -fróm/ *adv* from that place or thing (*archaic or formal*)

there·in /th̲er ín/ *adv* in that matter, respect, or detail ○ *Therein lies the problem.*

there·in·af·ter /th̲èr in áftər/ *adv* from then on in something, especially a legal document (*formal*)

ther·e·min /thérrəmin/ *n* an early electronic musical instrument producing a tremulous sound whose pitch and volume is controlled by the distance between two antennae and the player's hands [Early 20C. After Leo *Theremin* (1896–1993), Russian engineer]

there·of /th̲er úv, -óv/ *adv* (*formal*) **1.** of or about that ○ *a levy of $50 per annum or part thereof* **2.** from that as a reason or cause

there·on /th̲er ón/ *adv* **1.** on the place or surface just mentioned (*formal*) ○ *a metal plate with an inscription thereon* **2.** regarding the point just mentioned (*archaic*) ○ *income and capital expense, including tax thereon*

The·re·sa of Li·sieux /tə reéssə əv lee zyő/ (1873–97) French nun. She is the author of *The Story of a Soul* (1898), in which she described the "little way," the simple path to Christianity. With Joan of Arc, she is a patron saint of France.

there·to /th̲er tóo/ *adv* to that thing just mentioned (*formal*)

there·to·fore /th̲èrtə fáwr/ *adv* before or up to that time (*formal*)

there·un·der /thər úndər/ *adv* below that, or after that, especially in a legal document (*formal*)

there·up·on /thèrrə pón/ *adv* **1.** at that point in time ○ *She was found to have leaked information to a rival firm, and he thereupon insisted on her dismissal.* **2.** upon or concerning that point (*formal*)

there·with /thər wíth, -wíth/, **there·with·al** /-with áwl, -with-/ *adv* **1.** with that, or as well as that (*formal*) **2.** at that point, or immediately

~~therfore~~ incorrect spelling of **therefore**

the·ri·an·throp·ic /thèeree ən thróppik, -an-/ *adj* describes an imaginary being such as a centaur that is partly human and partly animal [Late 19C. < Greek *thērion* "small wild animal" + *anthrōpos* "human being"] —**the·ri·an·throp·ism** /thèeree ánthrə pìzzəm/ *n*

the·ri·o·mor·phic /thèeree ə máwrfik/ *adj* in the form of an animal, or thought of as being in animal form [Late 19C. < Greek *thērion* "small wild animal"]

ther·i·zin·o·saur /thèrrə zínnə sàwr/ *n* an herbivorous dinosaur that walked relatively upright and had a long neck, long arms and claws, and a short tail [Mid-20C. < modern Latin *Therizinosaurus*, literally "scythe lizard," from the shape of its claws]

therm /thurm/ *n* a unit of heat equal to 100,000 British thermal units or 1.055 x 10^8 joules [Late 19C. < Greek *thermē* "heat"]

therm. *abbr* PHYS thermometer

therm- *prefix* same as **thermo-** (*used before vowels*)

ther·mae /thúrmee/ *npl* hot springs or baths, especially the public baths of ancient Rome [Mid-16C. Via Latin < Greek *thermai* < *thermē* "heat"]

ther·mal /thúrm'l/ *adj* **1.** PHYS **INVOLVING HEAT** relating to, affected by, or producing heat ○ *thermal energy* **2.** **HOT OR WARM** hot or warm, especially because of the presence of hot springs ○ *thermal baths* **3.** MANUF **USING HEAT FOR PRODUCTION** using heat to produce something **4.** CLOTHING **INTENDED FOR BODY WARMTH** designed to retain body heat ○ *thermal underwear* ■ *n* METEOROL **AIR COLUMN** a current of warm air rising through cooler surrounding air ○ *watching hawks ride thermals* ■ **ther·mals** *npl UK* **THERMAL CLOTHING** thermal clothing, especially underwear (*informal*) [Mid-18C. < French < Greek *thermē* "heat"] —**ther·mal·ly** *adv*

ther·mal bar·ri·er *n* the problematic heating effect caused by air friction on an aircraft flying at high speed

ther·mal con·duc·tiv·i·ty *n* the rate at which heat flows through a material between points at different temperatures, measured in watts per meter per degree. Symbol **λ, κ**

ther·mal crack·ing *n* the breaking down of a hydrocarbon using heat

ther·mal ef·fi·cien·cy *n* the work done by a heat engine divided by the thermal energy required to operate it

ther·mal im·ag·ing *n* the use of a device that detects the different levels of infrared energy given off by areas of different temperatures and displays these as a pattern on a screen

ther·mal·ize /thúrm'l ìz/ (**-ized, -iz·ing, -iz·es**) *vt* to slow neutrons in a nuclear reactor to give them thermal energy and so produce fission —**ther·mal·i·za·tion** /thùrm'li záysh'n/ *n*

ther·mal neu·tron *n* PHYS same as **slow neutron**

ther·mal noise *n* noise in an electronic circuit such as an amplifier caused by electrons in conducting elements that are agitated by the absorption of heat

ther·mal pol·lu·tion *n* the discharge of water or other liquid that is hot enough to harm wildlife into a natural body of water

ther·mal print·er *n* an output device that produces visible characters by moving heated wires over specially treated heat-sensitive paper

ther·mes·the·sia /thùrmə stéezhə/ *n* sensitivity to heat and cold, or to changes in temperature [Late 19C. < modern Latin < Greek *thermē* "heat" + *aisthēsis* "perception"]

ther·mic /thúrmik/ *adj* PHYS same as **thermal** *adj* (sense 1) [Mid-19C. < Greek *thermē* "heat"] —**ther·mi·cal·ly** *adv*

-thermic *suffix* relating to heat ○ *exothermic* [< Greek *thermē* "heat"]

therm·i·on /thúr mì ən/ *n* a positive ion or electron given off by a very hot material such as a hot cathode —**therm·i·on·ic** /thùrmee ónnik/ *adj*

therm·i·on·ic cur·rent *n* an electric current generated by the flow of electrons leaving a heated cathode and flowing to other electrodes

therm·i·on·ic e·mis·sion *n* the emission of electrons or ions from a solid or liquid as a result of its thermal energy

therm·i·on·ics /thùrmee ónniks/ *n* the branch of electronics that deals with the emission of electrons from hot bodies (*takes a singular verb*)

therm·i·on·ic tube *n US* an electronic component that consists of an evacuated glass tube containing a heated cathode that emits electrons, an anode that collects the electrons, and other electrodes. Can term **thermionic valve**

therm·i·on·ic valve *n Can, UK* same as **thermionic tube**

therm·is·tor /thúr mìstər/ *n* a semiconductor device with a resistance that is very sensitive to temperature, resistance decreasing as the temperature increases [Mid-20C. Contraction of *thermal resistor*]

ther·mite proc·ess /thúr mìt-/ *n* INDUST same as **aluminothermy**

thermo- *prefix* **1.** heat ○ *thermochemistry* **2.** thermoelectricity ○ *thermocouple* [< Greek *thermē* "heat"]

ther·mo·bar·ic /thùrmō báa rik, -bárrik/ *adj* describes a bomb that disperses a cloud of explosive material that then ignites, creating a pressure wave

ther·mo·ba·rom·e·ter /thùrmō bə rómmətər/ *n* an instrument that measures both air temperature and pressure

ther·mo·cau·ter·y /thùrmō káwtəree/ *n* the use of a heated instrument such as a hot wire to destroy tissue, especially in cauterizing wounds

ther·mo·chem·is·try /thùrmō kémmistree/ *n* the branch of chemistry that deals with the relationship between chemical action and heat —**ther·mo·chem·i·cal** /thùrmō kémmik'l/ *adj* —**ther·mo·chem·i·cal·ly** *adv* —**ther·mo·chem·ist** *n*

ther·mo·cline /thúrmō klìn/ *n* a layer of water, e.g., in a lake, where there is an abrupt change in temperature that separates the warmer surface water from the colder deep water

ther·mo·cou·ple /thúrmō kùpp'l/ *n* a device for measuring temperature in which two wires of different metals are joined. The potential difference between the wires is a measure of the temperature of something they touch.

ther·mo·dur·ic /thùrmō dóorik/ *adj* describes a microorganism that is capable of surviving high temperatures or pasteurization [Early 20C. < THERMO- + Latin *durare* "endure"]

ther·mo·dy·nam·ic /thùrmō dì námmik/, **ther·mo·dy·nam·i·cal** /-námmik'l/ *adj* **1.** relating to or involving thermodynamics **2.** obeying or affected by the laws of thermodynamics —**ther·mo·dy·nam·i·cal·ly** *adv*

ther·mo·dy·nam·ics /thùrmō dì námmiks/ *n* the branch of physics that deals with the conversions from one to another of various forms of energy and how these affect temperature, pressure, volume, mechanical action, and work (*takes a singular verb*) ■ *npl* thermodynamic processes or phenomena (*takes a plural verb*) —**ther·mo·dy·nam·i·cist** *n*

ther·mo·e·lec·tric /thùrmō i léktrik/, **ther·mo·e·lec·tri·cal** /-lék trik'l/ *adj* involving a direct relationship between temperature of materials and the production of electricity —**ther·mo·e·lec·tri·cal·ly** *adv*

ther·mo·e·lec·tric·i·ty /thùrmō i lek tríssətee/ *n* electricity produced by maintaining a temperature difference at the point where two different materials come into contact, e.g., in a thermocouple

ther·mo·e·lec·tron /thùrmō i lék tròn/ *n* an electron emitted by a material that is at high temperature

ther·mo·form /thúrmə fàwrm/ (**-formed, -form·ing, -forms**) *vt* to shape plastic using heat and pressure —**ther·mo·form·a·ble** /thùrmə fáwrməb'l/ *adj*

ther·mo·gen·e·sis /thùrmō jénnəsiss/ *n* the production of heat in a person's or animal's body by physiological processes, especially metabolic processes —**ther·mo·ge·net·ic** /-jə néttik/ *adj*

ther·mo·gram /thúrmə gràm/ *n* **1.** an image or record of the heat radiating from the body, made by thermography **2.** a record of temperatures made by a thermograph

ther·mo·graph /thúrmə gràf/ *n* **1.** an instrument that continuously records temperature readings **2.** a device that shows patterns of heat radiated from a person's or an animal's body, used in diagnostic thermography

ther·mog·ra·phy /thər móggrəfee/ *n* **1.** the recording of a visual image of the heat that bodies emit as infrared radiation. The technique is used to diagnose disease and tumors, especially breast tumors. **2.** the process of producing a raised image on a printed surface by using heat to fuse a resinous powder and wet ink to the surface —**ther·mog·ra·pher** *n* —**ther·mo·graph·ic** /thùrmə gráffik/ *adj* —**ther·mo·graph·i·cal·ly** *adv*

ther·mo·junc·tion /thùrmō júngkshən/ *n* a point at which two dissimilar metals of differing temperatures come into contact, producing a thermoelectric current

ther·mo·la·bile /thùrmō láyb'l, -láy bìl/ *adj* describes substances such as some enzymes that are easily destroyed or altered by heat

ther·mo·lu·mi·nes·cence /thùrmō loomi néss'nss/ *n* phosphorescence released by some previously irradiated substances when they are heated. The process is used by geologists and archaeologists to date rocks and pottery. —**ther·mo·lu·mi·nes·cent** *adj*

ther·mol·y·sis /thər mólləsiss/ *n* **1.** loss of body heat, e.g., by sweating **2.** the breaking down of a substance by heat —**ther·mo·lyt·ic** /thùrmə líttik/ *adj*

ther·mo·mag·net·ic /thùrmō mag néttik/ *adj* relating to the relationship between heat and magnetism, and especially the effects of heat upon the magnetic properties of a substance

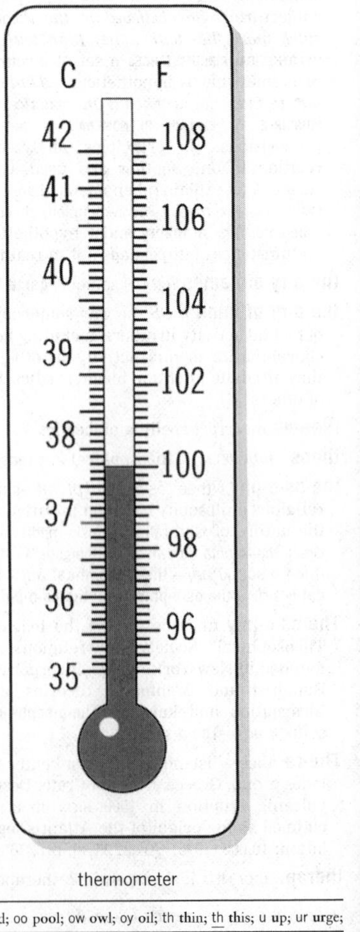

thermometer

ther·mom·e·ter /thər mómmətər/ *n* an instrument for measuring temperature, e.g., an instrument with a graduated glass tube and a bulb containing mercury or alcohol that rises in the tube when the temperature increases. See illustration on previous page [Mid-17C. < French *thermomètre* < Greek *thermos* "warm" < *thermē* "heat" + *-mètre* (see -METER)]

ther·mom·e·try /thər mómmətree/ *n* temperature measurement and the branch of physics concerned with measuring temperature —**ther·mo·met·ric** /thùrmō méttrik/ *adj* —**ther·mo·met·ri·cal** *adj* —**ther·mo·met·ri·cal·ly** *adv*

ther·mo·nas·ty /thúrmə nàstee/ *n* the movement of plant parts in response to a change in temperature, e.g., the opening of flowers

ther·mo·nu·cle·ar /thùrmō nóoklee ər/ *adj* relating to or making use of nuclear fusion ○ *thermonuclear energy* ○ *thermonuclear war*

ther·mo·nu·cle·ar re·ac·tion *n* a reaction in which nuclei of light atoms fuse together producing large amounts of energy. This type of reaction occurs at very high temperatures, e.g., those inside the Sun.

ther·mo·pe·ri·od·ism /thùrmō péeree ə dìzzəm/, **ther·mo·pe·ri·o·dic·i·ty** /-peeree ə dìssətee/ *n* the response of a plant to cycles of temperature such as the regular cycles of day and night —**ther·mo·pe·ri·od·ic** /thùrmō peeree óddik/ *adj*

ther·mo·phile /thúrmə fīl/ *n* an organism that thrives in a warm environment, e.g., a bacterium —**ther·mo·phile** *adj* —**ther·mo·phil·ic** /thùrmə fíllik/ *adj* —**ther·mo·phil·ous** /thər móffələss/ *adj*

ther·moph·y·lous /thər móffələss/ *adj* bearing leaves only in the warmer part of the year

ther·mo·pile /thúrmə pīl/ *n* a set of thermocouples, either joined in series for increased voltage or in parallel for increased current, used to measure radiant energy or to convert radiant energy into electric current

ther·mo·plas·tic /thùrmō plástik/ *n* a substance that becomes soft and pliable when heated, without a change in its intrinsic properties. Polystyrene and polyethylene are thermoplastics. —**ther·mo·plas·tic** *adj* —**ther·mo·plas·tic·i·ty** /thùrmō pla stíssətee/ *n*

Ther·mop·y·lae /thər móppəlee/ pass in ancient Greece, northwest of Athens, that controlled entry to central Greece. It was the site of the battle of 480 B.C. fought by Leonidas I and thousands of his troops, all of whom were killed by the Persian army, led by Xerxes I.

ther·mo·re·cep·tor /thùrmō ri séptər/ *n* a sensory receptor, usually a nerve ending in the skin, that is stimulated by heat or cold

ther·mo·reg·u·la·tion /thùrmō regyə láysh'n/ *n* the maintenance of a steady body temperature regardless of changes in the environment —**ther·mo·reg·u·late** /thùrmō réggyə làyt/ *vi* —**ther·mo·reg·u·la·tor** *n*

ther·mo·rem·a·nent /thùrmō rémmənənt/ *adj* relating to or being the permanent magnetism that something such as molten rock acquires from the Earth's magnetic field as it cools and hardens

Ther·mos /thúrməss/ *tdmk* a trademark for an insulated or vacuum container used to hold a liquid and maintain it at a constant temperature

ther·mo·scope /thúrmə skōp/ *n* an instrument that measures changes in temperature by their effects on a substance, e.g., the change in volume of a gas —**ther·mo·scop·ic** /thùrmə skóppik/ *adj* —**ther·mo·scop·i·cal** *adj* —**ther·mo·scop·i·cal·ly** *adv*

ther·mo·set·ting /thúrmō sètting/ *adj* describes a plastic that sets permanently when heated

ther·mo·sphere /thúrmə sfeer/ *n* the region of the atmosphere above the mesosphere in which temperature steadily increases with height, beginning at about 53 mi./85 km above the Earth's surface

ther·mo·sta·ble /thùrmō stáyb'l/ *adj* describes substances such as some toxins that are able to withstand heat without being destroyed or altered —**ther·mo·sta·bil·i·ty** /thùrmō stə bíllətee/ *n*

ther·mo·stat /thúrmə stàt/ *n* **1.** a device that regulates temperature by means of a temperature sensor such as a bimetallic strip. Thermostats are used in vehicle engines and domestic heating systems. **2.** a device that activates a mechanism or system such as a fire alarm or a sprinkler system in response to a change in temperature —**ther·mo·stat·ic** /thùrmə státtik/ *adj* —**ther·mo·stat·i·cal·ly** *adv*

ther·mo·tax·is /thùrmə táksiss/ *n* movement of a living organism toward or away from a heat source —**ther·mo·tac·tic** /thùrmə táktik/ *adj* —**ther·mo·tax·ic** /-táksik/ *adj*

ther·mo·ther·a·py /thùrmō thérrəpee/ (*plural* **-pies**) *n* the use of heat to alleviate pain and stiffness, especially in joints and muscles, and to increase circulation, or a procedure involving this

ther·mot·ro·pism /thər móttrə pìzzəm/ *n* the movement of a plant part toward or away from a source of heat —**ther·mo·trop·ic** /thùrmə tróppik, -trṓpik/ *adj*

-thermy *suffix* heat ○ *diathermy* [< modern Latin *-thermia* < Greek *thermē* "heat"]

the·ro·pod /théerə pòd/ *n* a carnivorous dinosaur with strong hind legs and short front limbs, e.g., a tyrannosaur or megalosaur. Suborder: Theropoda. [Early 20C. < modern Latin *Theropoda* < Greek *thēr* "wild animal" + *pod-* "foot"] —**the·rop·o·dan** /thi róppədən/ *adj*

The·roux /thə ro͞o/, **Paul** (*b.* 1941) US writer. He is known for his travel books such as *The Great Railway Bazaar* (1975) and his novels such as *The Mosquito Coast* (1981). Full name **Theroux, Paul Edward**

> "Travel is a vanishing act, a solitary trip down a pinched line of geography to oblivion."
> [Paul Theroux, *The Old Patagonian Express: By Train Through the Americas*; 1979]

~~**thesarus**~~ incorrect spelling of **thesaurus**

the·sau·rus /thə sáwrəss/ (*plural* **-ri** /-rī/ or **-rus·es**) *n* **1.** BOOK OF WORD GROUPS a book that lists words related to each other in meaning, usually giving synonyms and antonyms **2.** BOOK OF SUBJECT-RELATED VOCABULARY a dictionary of words relating to a specific subject **3.** TREASURY a place in which valuable things are stored [Early 19C. Via Latin, "treasury" < Greek *thēsauros* "storehouse"]

these /theez/ *pron, adj* the form of "this" used before a plural noun or with a multiple referent ○ (pron) *These are the people I was telling you about.* ○ (adj) *These delays, along with the paperwork, can be costly for banks.* [Old English *þæs, þās*, plural of *þes* (see THIS)]

theses plural of **thesis**

The·se·us /théessee əss, théess yo͞oss/ *n* in Greek mythology, a hero who performed many brave deeds, including slaying the Minotaur, defeating the Amazons, and descending into Hades to rescue Persephone

the·sis /théessiss/ (*plural* **the·ses** /théé séez/) *n* **1.** PROPOSITION a proposition advanced as an argument **2.** ESSAY SUBJECT a subject for an essay **3.** LENGTHY ACADEMIC PAPER a dissertation based on original research, especially as work toward an academic degree **4.** STATEMENT an unproved statement, especially one serving as a premise in an argument **5.** MUSIC DOWNBEAT the downbeat of a bar of music **6.** LITERAT STRESSED SYLLABLE a long syllable, on which the stress naturally falls, in classical Greek and Latin poetry **7.** LITERAT UNSTRESSED SYLLABLE a short unstressed syllable in modern accentual poetry **8.** PHILOSOPHY FIRST STAGE OF DIALECTIC the first of three stages in Hegelian dialectic [14C. Via Latin < Greek, "proposition, stressed beat"]

thes·pi·an /théspee ən/ *n* somebody who acts on the stage ■ *adj* relating to the theater or the profession of acting (*literary*) [Early 19C. < *Thespis*, Greek poet (6C B.C.), regarded as the father of Greek tragedy]

Thess. *abbr* BIBLE Thessalonians

Thes·sa·lo·ni·an /thèssə lónee ən/ *n* somebody who came from the ancient Greek city of Thessaloníki [Early 16C. < Latin *Thessalonica*, Greek *Thessalonikē* "Thessaloníki"] —**Thes·sa·lo·ni·an** *adj*

Thes·sa·lo·ni·ans /thèssə lṓnee ənz/ *n* either of two books of the Bible that were originally letters addressed to the Christians of Thessalonica (modern Thessaloníki) and are traditionally attributed to St. Paul. (*takes a singular verb*) See table at **Bible**

Thes·sa·lo·ní·ki /thè saa law neékee/ capital city of the department of Thessaloníki, northeastern Greece. Population: 383,967 (1991).

Thes·sa·ly /théssəlee/ region in north central Greece, consisting mainly of a broad plain. Area: 5,382 sq. mi./13,940 sq. km. —**Thes·sa·li·an** /thə sáylee ən/ *n, adj*

the·ta /tháytə, théetə/ *n* the eighth letter of the Greek alphabet, represented in the English alphabet as "th." See table at **alphabet** [Early 17C. Via Greek < Phoenician]

the·ta rhythm, the·ta wave *n* a pattern of brain waves with a frequency between 4 and 7 Hz seen on an electroencephalogram. The pattern is normal in children under the age of 12 but in adults may be a sign of stress or mental disorder.

thet·ic /théttik/, **thet·i·cal** /théttik'l/ *adj* in classical poetry, relating to or having stress [Late 17C. < Greek *thetikos* < *thetos* "placed, stressed" < *tithenai* "to place"] —**thet·i·cal·ly** *adv*

the·ur·gy /theé ərjee/ *n* **1.** RELIG SUPERNATURAL OR DIVINE INTERVENTION the supposed intervention of supernatural or divine powers in human affairs **2.** RELIG PERSUADING SUPERNATURAL TO INTERVENE the art of trying to secure intervention of supernatural or divine powers in human affairs **3.** PARANORMAL MAGIC PERFORMED FOR GOOD magic with the alleged help of benevolent spirits, as practiced by neo-Platonists [Mid-16C. Via late Latin < Greek *theourgia* "ritual, mystery" < *theos* "god" + *ergon* "work"] —**the·ur·gic** /thee úrjik/ *adj* —**the·ur·gi·cal·ly** *adv* —**the·ur·gist** *n*

thew /thyoo/ *n* muscle or muscular strength (*archaic; often used in the plural*) [Old English *þēaw* "custom, habit" < Indo-European, "to watch"] —**thew·y** *adj*

they /thay/ *pron* **1.** PEOPLE OR THINGS ALREADY MENTIONED the people or things already mentioned or identified, or understood by both the speaker and hearer **2.** PEOPLE IN GENERAL used to refer to people in general when making statements about the things people do, think, or say ○ *As people and businesses move to the suburbs, bank branches follow, so they say.* **3.** ⚠ HE OR SHE used instead of "he" or "she" to refer to a person without specifying gender (*informal*) ○ *A friend phoned the other day and they told me what you had said.* [12C. < Old Norse *þeir*]

USAGE Because English does not have a gender-neutral third person singular pronoun that can be used to refer to people, ***they***, together with the associated words *their* and *them*, is often used in this role and is a revival of an older use that was once well established in English. In more formal contexts, and when the individuality of the subject is significant, it is necessary to use *he or she, his or her*, or *him or her*, but these phrases are too cumbersome to provide a solution in informal conversational usage, e.g., *Everyone taking the test should do the best they can. If anyone asks who I am, tell them that I'm his sister.* A way of avoiding the need to use *he or she* in writing can be to use a plural: *Students taking the test should do the best they can.*

they'd /thayd/ *contr* **1.** they had **2.** they would

they'll /thayl/ *contr* **1.** they shall **2.** they will

they're /ther/ *contr* they are

USAGE See ***their***.

they've /thayv/ *contr* they have

THI *abbr* PHYS temperature-humidity index

thi- *prefix* same as **thio-** (*used before vowels*)

thi·a·ben·da·zole /thī ə béndə zōl/, **ti·a·ben·da·zole** /tī-/ *n* a white compound. Use: treatment of parasitic worm infestations, fungal infections. Formula: $C_{10}H_7N_3S$. [Mid-20C. Contraction of THIAZOLE + BENZENE + IMIDAZOLE]

thi·a·mine /thī ə meèn, -əmin/, **thi·a·min** /-əmin/ *n* a B vitamin that plays a role in carbohydrate metabolism. Source: grains, meat, yeasts.

thi·a·zide /thī ə zīd, -əzid/ *n* a compound belonging to a group of compounds that inhibit the reabsorption of sodium and increase the release of calcium by the kidneys, promoting greater water excretion. Use: diuretic, treatment of high blood pressure. [Mid-20C. < *thiadiazine* chemical compound (< THIO- + AZINE) + OXIDE]

thi·a·zine /thī̍ ə zeèn/ *n* an organic compound containing a ring composed of four carbon atoms, a sulfur atom, and a nitrogen atom. Use: dyes, tranquilizers.

thi·a·zole /thī̍ ə zōl/, **thi·a·zol** /thī̍ ə zàwl/ *n* **1.** a volatile colorless liquid with a sharp odor. Use: dyes, fungicides. Formula: C_3H_3NS. **2.** a compound derived from thiazole. Use: dyes, fungicides, chemical-reaction accelerators.

thick /thik/ *adj* **1. DEEP OR BROAD** of relatively large extent from surface to surface or side to side ○ *a thick carpet* ○ *The child wrote her name in thick capital letters.* **2. LARGE IN DIAMETER** having a large diameter ○ *a thick cable* **3. IN DEPTH OR BREADTH** having a particular depth or breadth ○ *a wall two feet thick* **4. FILLED** densely covered or filled ○ *The air was thick with mosquitoes.* **5. HARD TO SEE THROUGH** permitting little or no light to enter ○ *a thick mist* **6. NOT CLEAR** not articulating words clearly ○ *a voice thick with emotion* **7. PRONOUNCED** readily noticeable or distinct ○ *I found her thick southern accent charming.* **8. DENSE** composed of many densely packed objects ○ *a thick forest* ○ *thick hair* **9. FRIENDLY** allied in a close relationship (*informal*) ○ *They seem very thick with each other.* **10. VISCOUS** having a liquid consistency that is not free-flowing ○ *thick paint* **11. OF HEAVY FABRIC** made of thick material ○ *thick socks* **12. OFFENSIVE TERM** an offensive term meaning regarded as lacking the ability to learn and understand quickly (*informal insult*) ■ *adv* **MAKING DEEP LAYER** in a way that produces something deep, broad, or dense ○ *Spread the jam on thick.* ■ *n* **1. MOST ACTIVE PART** the most intense, crowded, or busiest part of something ○ *in the thick of the battle* **2. DENSEST PART** the part of something with the greatest depth, density, or breadth ○ *in the thick of the jungle* [Old English *þicce* < Germanic] —**thick·ly** *adv* ◇ **thick and fast** in large numbers and with great frequency ◇ **through thick and thin** no matter what might happen

thick·en /thíkən/ (**-ened, -en·ing, -ens**) *v* **1.** *vti* to become thick or thicker, or make something thick or thicker **2.** *vi* to become more complicated or puzzling ○ *The plot thickens.* —**thick·en·er** *n* —**thick·en·ing** *n*

thick·et /thíkit/ *n* a dense or tangled growth of small trees or bushes

thick·film tech·nol·o·gy /thìk film-/ *n* a method of fabricating electronic circuitry in which a glaze is printed onto a glass or ceramic support, then wiring and components such as microchips are added

thick·head /thík hèd/ *n* an offensive term that deliberately insults somebody's intelligence (*slang insult*) —**thick·head·ed** *adj* —**thick·head·ed·ness** *n*

thick-knee *n* a large long-legged shorebird with distinctive enlarged knee joints. Native to: mainly semidesert regions. Family: Burhinidae.

thick·ness /thíknəss/ *n* **1. THICK QUALITY** the quality or state of being thick **2. DIMENSION** the dimension between two surfaces of an object, especially the shortest dimension as opposed to the width or the length **3. SINGLE LAYER** an individual layer **4. THICK PART** a part of something that is thick

thick·o /thíkō/ (*plural* **-os**) *n UK* an offensive term that deliberately insults somebody's intelligence (*slang insult*)

thick·set /thík sèt/ *adj* **1.** having a stocky physique **2.** growing closely together ○ *a thickset bed of peonies*

thick-skinned *adj* **1.** not easily offended by criticism or insults **2.** insensitive to other people's feelings or circumstances

thick-wit·ted *adj* an offensive term meaning regarded as unintelligent (*insult*) —**thick-wit·ted·ly** *adv* —**thick-wit·ted·ness** *n*

thief /theef/ (*plural* **thieves** /theevz/) *n* somebody who steals something, especially one who intends to escape notice [Old English *þēof* < Germanic]

~~**thier**~~ incorrect spelling of **their**

thieve /theev/ (**thieved, thiev·ing, thieves**) *vti* to steal something, or steal things [Old English *þēofian* < *þēof* (see THIEF)] —**thiev·er·y** *n*

thiev·ish /theévish/ *adj* **1.** relating to or characteristic of thieves **2.** given to stealing things [15C. < *thieves*, plural of THIEF] —**thiev·ish·ly** *adv* —**thiev·ish·ness** *n*

thigh /thī/ *n* **1.** the top of the leg between the knee and the hip **2.** the part of an animal's leg that corresponds to a human thigh [Old English *þēoh* < Indo-European, "to swell"]

thigh·bone /thī̍ bōn/ *n* ANAT same as **femur** (sense 1)

thig·mo·tax·is /thìgmə táksiss/ *n* same as **stereotaxis** [Early 20C. < Greek *thigma* "touch"] —**thig·mo·tac·tic** *adj* —**thig·mo·tac·ti·cal·ly** *adv*

thig·mot·ro·pism /thig móttrə pìzzəm/ *n* a directional growth movement (**tropism**) of a plant part, especially a tendril, in response to physical contact with a surface [Early 20C. < Greek *thigma* "touch"] —**thig·mo·trop·ic** /thìgmə tróppik, -trṓpik/ *adj*

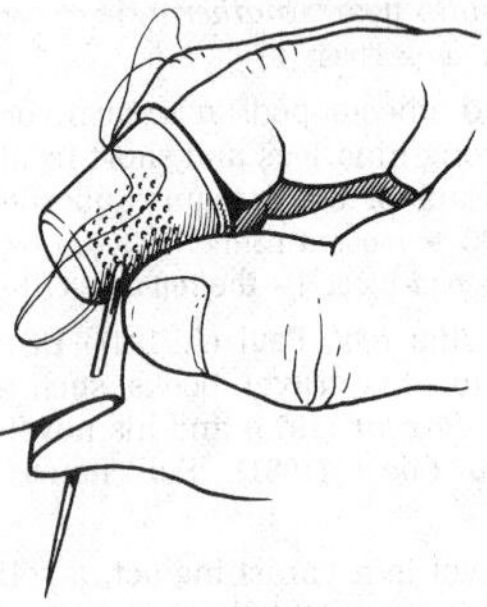

thimble

thim·ble /thímb'l/ *n* **1.** HANDICRAFT **COVER FOR FINGER WHEN SEWING** a small protective cap for a finger, used to push a needle through fabric **2.** NAUT **RING PROTECTING LOOP FROM WEAR** a metal ring, concave on the outside, that fits into a loop in a rope or an eye in a sail **3.** MECH ENG **METAL SLEEVE** a small metal tube or sleeve used in machinery [Old English *þȳmel* "leather thumb protector" < *þūma* (see THUMB)]

thim·ble·ber·ry /thímb'l bèrree/ (*plural* **-ries**) *n* **1.** a red or dark-purple thimble-shaped raspberry **2.** a bush that produces thimbleberries. Native to: North America. Latin name: *Rubus parviflorus, ubus occidentalis, Rubus odoratus.*

thim·ble·ful /thímb'l fòol/ *n* a very small amount of liquid

thim·ble·rig /thímb'l rìg/ *n* **1. GUESSING GAME USING TRICKERY** a trick in which a participant guesses which of three cups covers an object after somebody has moved them about, using sleight of hand to change the object's location **2.** *US* **SOMEBODY MOVING CUP** somebody moving the cup in thimblerig ■ *vt* (**-rigged, -rig·ging, -rigs**) **SWINDLE SOMEBODY** to cheat or swindle somebody —**thim·ble·rig·ger** *n*

thim·ble·weed /thímb'l weèd/ *n* a plant of the buttercup family with a thimble-shaped fruiting head. Flowers: white. Native to: North America. Latin name: *Anemone virginiana* or *Anemone cylindrica.*

Thim·bu ➧ **Thimphu**

thi·mer·o·sal /thī mérrə sàl/ *n* a cream-colored mercury compound. Use: local antiseptic. Formula: $C_9H_9HgNaO_2S$. [Mid-20C. Probably contraction of THIO- + MERCURY + SALICYLATE]

Thim·phu /thímfoo/, **Thim·bu** /-boo/ capital city of Bhutan, situated in the western part of the country at an altitude of 7,770 ft./2,368 m. Population: 22,000 (1999).

thin /thin/ *adj* (**thin·ner, thin·nest**) **1. SHALLOW OR NARROW** of relatively small extent from surface to surface or side to side ○ *A thin layer of snow covered the path.* ○ *Draw a thin line.* **2. OF SMALL DIAMETER** having a small diameter ○ *thin wire* **3. SLIM** having very little body fat **4. SPARSE** composed of few things widely spaced ○ *thin hair* ○ *a thin forest* **5. WATERY** with a free-flowing consistency similar to that of water ○ *a thin soup* ○ *thin paint* **6. LIGHTWEIGHT** made of light or flimsy material ○ *a thin summer dress* ○ *thin cotton socks* **7. EASY TO SEE THROUGH** permitting light to enter or pass through ○ *thin mist* **8. QUIET IN NOISE VOLUME** lacking volume or resonance ○ *a thin sound* **9. UNCONVINCING** lacking credibility or adequacy ○ *a thin excuse* **10.** *US* **WEAK** lacking intensity or color **11.** PHOTOGRAPHY **LACKING CONTRAST** of a photographic negative, lacking density or contrast ■ *adv* **IN THIN MANNER** in a way that produces something shallow, narrow, or sparse ○ *Spread the paint thin.* ■ *vti* (**thinned, thin·ning, thins**) **MAKE OR BECOME THINNER** to reduce something in thickness or number, or become reduced in thickness or number ○ *You can thin the paint before you use it.* ○ *The crowd started to thin out in the evening.* [Old English *þynne* < Indo-European, "stretch"] —**thin·ly** *adv* —**thin·ness** *n*

SYNONYMS ***thin, lean, slender, slim, emaciated, scraggy, scrawny, skinny***

CORE MEANING: without much flesh, the opposite of fat

thin having very little body fat ○ *I was surprised at how thin her face had become.* **lean** having no excess body fat and looking muscular and fit ○ *a tall lean runner* **slender** gracefully and attractively thin ○ *A tall, slender model walked down the fashion-show runway.* **slim** slender and well-proportioned ○ *Tall and slim, the ballerina's body had the tautness of an athlete's.* **emaciated** extremely thin, especially because of starvation or illness ○ *Aid officials in the war zone reported seeing seriously undernourished, even emaciated people.* **scraggy** or **scrawny** thin and bony ○ *a scraggy neck* ○ *A scraggy old cat lives in the barn.* **skinny** thin, especially in an unappealing or unhealthy way ○ *I think my arms and legs are too skinny.* ○ *A new-born chimpanzee looks like a skinny little thing compared with a human baby.*

thine /thīn/ *pron, adj* belonging to or associated with you, when "you" is singular (*archaic; used before a vowel*) ○ (pron) *Thine is the womb where our riches have birth.* ○ (adj) *Know thine enemy.* [Old English *þīn*, possessive form of *þū* (see THOU[2])]

thin·film tech·nol·o·gy /thìn film-/ *n* a method of fabricating electronic circuitry in which a thin layer of semiconductor is applied to a glass or ceramic support, then wiring and passive components such as resistors are added

thing /thing/ *n* **1. OBJECT** an inanimate object ○ *What's that thing over there?* **2. UNSPECIFIED ITEM** an unnamed or unspecified object ○ *I need a few things in town.* **3. OCCURRENCE** something that occurs, or something that is done ○ *The fire was a terrible thing.* **4. WORD OR THOUGHT** a thought or an utterance ○ *Don't say another thing!* **5. DETAIL** a piece of information ○ *You forgot one important thing.* **6. SOMETHING AIMED AT** the objective of an action ○ *The thing is to win.* **7. MATTER OF CONCERN** a matter of responsibility or concern ○ *I have several things to do.* **8. DEED TO BE DONE** an act or deed done or to be done ○ *She promises to do great things.* **9. LIVING BEING** a person or animal, often spoken of affectionately ○ *The poor thing was soaked to the bone.* **10. GARMENT** an article of clothing ○ *This old thing?* **11. SOMETHING THAT CAN BE POSSESSED** an object or right that can be possessed or owned **12. PREFERRED ACTIVITY** a favorite activity or special interest (*informal*) ○ *Golf's not really my thing.* **13. FASHION** the current fashion (*informal*) ○ *When we were young, we considered it the latest thing.* **14. STRONG LIKE OR DISLIKE** a particularly strong feeling of attraction or repulsion (*informal*) ○ *He's got a thing about spiders.* **15. IDEAL** something that is needed or desirable (*informal*) ○ *Iced tea would be just the thing.* ■ **things** *npl* **1. BELONGINGS** personal items owned or carried ○ *You can leave your things in my room.* **2. APPARATUS** equipment for a particular activity ○ *a drawer for all my writing things* **3. AFFAIRS** general matters or circumstances ○ *How are things today?* [Old English *þing* "assembly" < Germanic, "time"] ◇ **all** *or* **other things being equal** in a situation in which there is little difference between two or more people or things ○ *Other things being equal, I would choose the cheaper vacation.* ◇ **be on to a good thing** to know something advantageous, or know about something that will give you an advantage ◇ **first things first** do not try to do things in the wrong order, omitting an important basic step ◇ **it comes to the same thing** it has the same result ◇ **make a (big) thing of something** to exaggerate the importance of something and make a fuss about it

ORIGIN The long-lost ancestral meaning of ***thing*** is "time" (the related Gothic *theihs*, for example, meant "time"). Its prehistoric Germanic precursor evolved semantically via "appointed time" to "judicial or legislative assembly." This was the meaning it originally had in English, and it survives in other Germanic languages (the Icelandic parliament is known as the *Althing*, literally "general assembly"). In English, however, the word moved on through "subject for discussion in such an assembly" to "subject in general, affair, matter" and finally "entity, object."

thing·a·ma·bob /thíngəmə bòb/, **thing·um·a·bob** *n* same as **thingamajig** [Mid-18C. Alteration of *thingumbob* < obsolete *thingum* (see THINGUMMY)]

thing·a·ma·jig /thíngəmə jìg/, **thing·um·a·jig** *n* a word used when the proper word for something is not known or does not come to mind [Early 19C. < obsolete *thingum* (see THINGUMMY)]

thing-in-it·self (*plural* **things-in-them·selves**) *n* an object that exists even though we have no experience or perception of it [Translation of German *Ding an sich*]

thing·ness /thíngnəss/ *n* status as a material thing, as distinct from something that is abstract

thing·um·a·bob *n* another spelling of **thingamabob**

thing·um·a·jig *n* another spelling of **thingamajig**

thing·um·my /thíngəmee/ (*plural* **-mies**) *n* same as **thingamajig** [Late 18C. Alteration of obsolete *thingum* < THING]

thing·y /thíngee/ (*plural* **-ies**) *n* same as **thingamajig**

think /thingk/ *v* (**thought** /thawt/ or **thunk** *nonstandard* /thungk/, **think·ing, thinks**) **1.** *vti* **FORM THOUGHTS** to use the mind to consider ideas and make judgments ○ *Think carefully before you start writing.* **2.** *vt* **HAVE SOMETHING AS OPINION** to believe something, or have something as an opinion ○ *I don't think it will rain today.* ○ *She seems to think she's a good dancer.* **3.** *vti* **COMPREHEND SOMETHING** to imagine or understand something or the possibility of something ○ *I can't think of letting you leave so soon.* **4.** *vti* **HAVE IN MIND** to bring something to mind ○ *I can't think what the date is today.* ○ *I hadn't thought about him for months.* **5.** *vt* **CONCENTRATE ON SOMETHING** to focus the attention on something ○ *He thinks golf day and night.* **6.** *vi* **HAVE REGARD FOR SOMEBODY** to regard somebody with care or concern ○ *You need to think of your family.* **7.** *vt* **VIEW SOMEBODY OR SOMETHING AS SOMETHING** to regard somebody or something in a particular way ○ *Don't think me unkind.* **8.** *vti* **INTEND** to have something as a plan ○ *She thought she'd go out after dinner.* **9.** *vt* **FORESEE SOMETHING** to anticipate something happening ○ *I didn't think he'd actually do it.* ○ *I didn't think you'd be early* **10.** *vt* **BE HEEDFUL OF SOMETHING** to be attentive or considerate enough to do something ○ *Didn't you think to ask about her mother?* **11.** *vi* **CHOOSE SOMETHING** to make a mental choice ○ *Think of a card and I'll try to guess what it is.* **12.** *vt* **INFLUENCE OUTCOME WITH MIND** to bring something to a particular condition using the mind ○ *Try to think the pain away.* ■ *n* **SPELL OF THINKING** an act of thinking, or a period of time spent thinking (*informal*) ○ *She sat down to have a think.* [Old English *þencan* < Indo-European] —**think·a·ble** *adj* ◇ **have got another think coming** used to say that somebody is mistaken (*informal*) ○ *If he thinks I'm going to help him he's got another think coming.* ◇ **not think much of somebody** *or* **something** to regard somebody or something as not being very good ◇ **that's what you think!** used to say that somebody is quite wrong in a belief, assumption, or expectation (*informal*) ○ *"It shouldn't take too long." "That's what you think!"* ◇ **think better of something** to change your mind and decide not to do something ○ *She was about to speak her mind, but then thought better of it.* ◇ **think nothing of something** to regard something as not being unusual ○ *She thinks nothing of working all night to finish a project.* ◇ **think twice** to consider something very carefully ○ *You should think twice about lending them so much money.*

think out *vt* to consider something carefully, taking account of possible problems or consequences ○ *He hadn't really thought the policy out properly.*

think over *vt* to reflect on something ○ *Maybe you'd like to think it over before you sign.*

think through *vt* to consider or reflect on something carefully, especially in order to reach a decision ○ *I needed some time to think it through.*

think up *vt* to invent or devise something ○ *I've thought up an easy way to do it.*

think·er /thíngkər/ *n* **1.** somebody known for being intellectually creative and authoritative, especially in a particular field of study ○ *a leading political thinker* **2.** somebody who thinks deeply about things

CULTURAL NOTE ***The Thinker***, a sculpture (1880) by French artist Auguste Rodin. Originally part of a larger work called *The Gates of Hell*, the bronze figure of a naked man hunched in concentration represents Dante pondering his great poem, the *Divine Comedy*. Much reproduced, the statue has become a modern icon.

think·ing /thíngking/ *adj* **RATIONAL** capable of using the mind to reason or reflect ○ *the thinking person's choice* ■ *n* **1. FORMING OF THOUGHTS** use of the mind to form thoughts ○ *There's a lot of thinking to do before we make that decision.* **2. JUDGMENT** opinions or conclusions arrived at ○ *What's your thinking on the political situation?*

think·ing cap ◇ **put your thinking cap on** to think carefully about something, especially to find a solution to a problem

think piece *n* an article giving somebody's analysis or opinion of a situation or event, written to provoke thought

think tank *n* a committee of experts that undertakes research or gives advice, especially to a government

thin·ner /thínnər/ *n* a liquid such as turpentine that is used to dilute paint or varnish

thin-skinned *adj* **1.** easily offended by criticism or insults **2.** covered in a thin peel or rind

thio- *prefix* containing sulfur ○ *thiophene* [< Greek *theion* "sulfur"]

thi·o·car·ba·mide /thì ō kaárbə mīd/ *n* CHEM same as **thiourea**

thi·o·cy·a·nate /thì ō sí ə nàyt/ *n* a salt or ester of thiocyanic acid

thi·o·cy·an·ic ac·id /thì ō sī ànnik-/ *n* an unstable colorless liquid. Use: salts or esters in insecticides. Formula: HSCN.

thi·ol /thí àwl/ *n* an organic compound similar to an alcohol but in which the oxygen atom has been replaced by a sulfur atom. Thiols are liquids with penetrating unpleasant smells.

thi·o·mer·sal /thì ō múrss'l/ *n UK* same as **thimerosal** [Mid-20C. < THIO- + MERCURY + SALICYLATE]

thi·on·ic /thī ónnik/ *adj* relating to or containing sulfur [Late 19C. < Greek *theion* "sulfur"]

thi·o·nyl /thí ə nìl/ *n* containing the chemical group SO [Mid-19C. < Greek *theion* "sulfur"]

thi·o·pen·tal so·di·um /thì ə pent'l-/ *n* a fast-acting barbiturate. Use: general anesthetic, hypnotic.

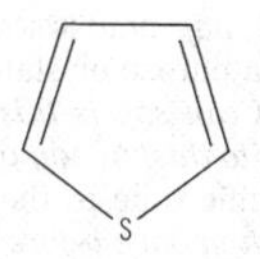

thiophen

thi·o·phen /thí əfən, -ə fèn/, **thi·o·phene** /-ə feèn/ *n* a colorless liquid with a faint odor of benzene. Use: solvent, manufacture of dyes, resins, pharmaceuticals. Formula: C_4H_4S. [Late 19C. < THIO- + PHENO-]

thi·o·rid·a·zine /thì ə ríddə zeèn/ *n* a synthetic compound that is a white or yellow powder. Use: tranquilizer for psychotic patients.

thi·o·sul·fate /thì ō súl fàyt/ *n* a salt or ester of thiosulfuric acid

thi·o·sul·fu·ric ac·id /thì ō sul fyoórik-/ *n* an unstable acid known only in the form of salts or esters or in solution. Formula: $H_2S_2O_3$.

thi·o·te·pa /theè ō teèpə/ *n* a crystalline compound of tepa that contains sulfur. Use: treatment of malignant tumors.

thi·o·ur·a·cil /thì ō yoórə sìl/ *n* a compound belonging to a group of bitter-tasting white crystalline compounds. Use: treatment of hyperthyroidism.

thi·o·u·re·a /thì ō yoóree ə/ *n* a soluble crystalline substance. Use: manufacture of resins, photographic processes. Formula: $CS(NH_2)_2$.

third /thurd/ *n* **1. ONE OF THREE PARTS** one of three equal parts into which something is or may be divided **2. ORDINAL NUMBER CORRESPONDING TO 3** item number three in a series **3. ONE AFTER SECOND IN IMPORTANCE** somebody or something ranking next after second in authority or precedence **4.** AUTOMOT **VEHICLE GEAR** in a motor vehicle, the forward gear between second and fourth **5.** BASEBALL same as **third base** **6.** MUSIC **MUSICAL INTERVAL** in a standard musical scale, the interval between one note and another that lies two notes above or below it. In the scale of C major, C and E form a third. **7.** MUSIC **MUSICAL NOTE THIRD AWAY** in a standard musical scale, a note that is a third away from another note **8.** MUSIC **COMBINED HARMONIC** a harmonic of a combination of two tones a third apart **9.** *UK* EDUC **UNIVERSITY DEGREE** the lowest class of honors degree awarded by a British university **10.** BALLET same as **third position** [Old English *þirdda, þridda* < Indo-European, "three"] —**third** *adj, adv*

CULTURAL NOTE ***The Third Man***, a movie (1949) by British director Sir Carol Reed. Set in Vienna immediately after World War II, this stylish and gripping film noir recounts US writer Holly Martins' attempts to discover the truth behind the mysterious death of his old friend Harry Lime. It is made particularly memorable by its dramatic war-ravaged setting, innovative lighting and editing, and haunting zither theme.

third base *n* **1.** in baseball, the base to the batter's left that is the third of four bases on the diamond and that must be touched safely to score a run **2.** in baseball, the position played by the fielder playing nearest to third base —**third base·man** *n*

third class *n* **1. THIRD IN CLASSIFICATION SYSTEM** the next below second in grade or category **2.** TRAVEL **CHEAPEST ACCOMMODATION** the least expensive and least luxurious accommodation on a ship or train **3.** MAIL **MAIL CLASS** a class of mail in the United States and Canada for unsealed printed matter —**third-class** *adj, adv*

third de·gree *n* intensive interrogation, especially when accompanied by rough physical treatment (*informal*) ○ *The interrogators gave the suspects the third degree.* [< the interrogation required to reach the "third degree," the highest rank in Freemasonry]

SYNONYMS See ***question***.

third-de·gree burn *n* a burn of the most serious kind, in which the skin and the tissues beneath it are severely damaged

third di·men·sion *n* **1.** the added dimension of depth that distinguishes a solid object from one that is two-dimensional or planar **2.** a quality that makes something more vivid —**third-di·men·sion·al** *adj*

third es·tate *n* the third social class, traditionally the commons, in a society divided into estates

third eye·lid *n* ZOOL same as **nictitating membrane**

third force *n* a group that mediates between two opposing political groups or parties

third·hand /thurd hánd/ *adj, adv* **1.** used by, or after having been used by, two previous owners **2.** from or through two intermediate sources

third·ly /thúrdlee/ *adv* used to introduce the third point in an argument or discussion

third mar·ket *n* over-the-counter trading of securities listed on a stock exchange

third par·ty *n* **1.** somebody who is involved in a legal matter but not as a principal party ○ *The signatures need to be witnessed by a third party.* **2.** a major political party that operates in opposition to the two parties usually operating in a state or nation with a two-party system

third per·son *n* **1.** VERB OR PRONOUN FORM the form of a verb or a pronoun used to refer to somebody or something being spoken about **2.** SET OF GRAMMATICAL FORMS the grammatical set containing the forms indicating the third person **3.** WRITING IN THIRD PERSON a style of writing using forms that are in the third-person, more objective than writing in the first person ○ *Write your account in the third person.*

third-per·son *adj* **1.** describes verbs or pronouns that designate somebody spoken about. In English, the third-person singular subject pronouns are "he," "she," "it," and "one," and the third-person plural subject pronoun is "they." **2.** displaying the character that a player of a computer game represents on screen from an external viewpoint, rather than through the character's eyes ○ *a third-person action game*

third po·si·tion *n* in ballet, a position in which the feet are turned outward with the heel of the front foot touching the instep of the back foot

third rail *n* **1.** a rail from which some electrically powered trains pick up current **2.** an issue or situation that is highly charged, fraught with controversy, or dangerous to deal with ○ *tax hikes as a third rail in US politics*

third-rate *adj* of a low or the lowest quality

third read·ing *n* the third presentation of a bill to a legislative assembly. In the UK Parliament, it is to discuss a committee's report. In the US Congress, it is the final presentation before a vote.

Third Reich *n* the Nazi regime in Germany between 1933 and 1945

Third Re·pub·lic *n* the French system of government set up after Napoleon III's reign. It lasted until 1940.

third-stream *n* music that draws from both classical music and jazz [Mid-20C. After MAINSTREAM] —**third-stream** *adj*

Third Way *n UK* a centralist political direction or ideology that is neither Socialist nor Conservative, but combines aspects of free-market capitalism with egalitarian social aims

Third World, third world *n* the developing nations of Africa, Asia, and Latin America, generally less economically advanced than the industrialized nations but with varied economies. Originally the Third World was contrasted with the First World, the capitalist industrial nations, and the Second World, the industrialized Communist nations. [Translation of French *tiers monde*] —**Third World·er** *n*

thirst /thurst/ *n* **1.** NEED FOR LIQUID a desire or need to drink a liquid, or the feeling of dryness in the mouth and throat caused by a need for a liquid **2.** STRONG CRAVING a strong desire for something ○ *a thirst for knowledge* ■ *vi* (**thirst·ed, thirst·ing, thirsts**) **1.** EXPERIENCE THIRST to feel a thirst for a liquid **2.** EXPERIENCE DESIRE to desire something strongly ○ *thirsted for news of home* [Old English *þurst* < Indo-European, "be dry"] —**thirst·er** *n*

thirst snake *n* a small nonvenomous snake with long needle-shaped teeth. Native to: Southeast Asia, tropical America. Genus: *Dipsas.*

thirst·y /thúrstee/ (**-i·er, -i·est**) *adj* **1.** NEEDING LIQUID feeling the need to drink a liquid ○ *Gardening on a hot morning always makes me thirsty.* **2.** LACKING WATER having insufficient water, especially in the form of irrigation ○ *The land was thirsty for rain.* **3.** DESIRING having a strong desire or craving ○ *thirsty for companionship* **4.** CAUSING THIRST causing the need to drink a liquid (*informal*) ○ *thirsty work* —**thirst·i·ly** *adv* —**thirst·i·ness** *n*

thir·teen /thur te͞en/ *n* **1.** 13 the number 13 **2.** SOMETHING WITH VALUE OF 13 something in a numbered series with a value of 13 **3.** GROUP OF 13 a group of 13 objects or people [Old English *prēotīne* < *prēo* "three" + *-tīne* "ten"]

Thir·teen Col·o·nies /thùr teen kólləneez/ *npl* the thirteen British colonies in North America that became the founding states of the United States (1776). They are New Hampshire, Massachusetts, Rhode Island, Connecticut, New York, New Jersey, Pennsylvania, Delaware, Maryland, Virginia, North Carolina, South Carolina, and Georgia.

thir·teenth /thur te͞enth/ *n* **1.** ONE OF 13 PARTS one of 13 equal parts into which something is or may be divided **2.** ORDINAL NUMBER CORRESPONDING TO 13 item number 13 in a series **3.** MUSICAL NOTE the note an octave and a sixth above the principal note in a musical scale —**thir·teenth** *adj, adv*

thir·ti·eth /thúrtee əth/ *n* **1.** one of 30 equal parts into which something is or may be divided **2.** item number 30 in a series —**thir·ti·eth** *adj, adv*

thir·ty /thúrtee/ *n* (*plural* **-ties**) **1.** 30 the number 30 **2.** GROUP OF 30 a group of 30 objects or people **3.** SCORE IN TENNIS in a game of tennis, the score awarded to a player with a score of 15 on winning a further point ■ **thir·ties** *npl* **1.** NUMBERS 30 TO 39 the numbers 30 to 39, particularly as a range of temperature ○ *in the low thirties* **2.** YEARS FROM 30 TO 39 the years from 30 to 39 in a century **3.** PERIOD FROM AGE 30 TO 39 the period of somebody's life from the age of 30 to 39 [Old English *prītig* < Germanic, "twice three"] —**thir·ty** *adj, pron*

thir·ty-eight *n US* a handgun with a .38 caliber.

thir·ty-sec·ond note *n* a musical note with the time value of one thirty-second of a whole note. It is written as a filled note-head with a stem and three tails.

thir·ty·some·thing /thúrtee sùmthing/ *n* somebody who is between 30 and 40 years old (*informal; usually used in the plural*) —**thir·ty·some·thing** *adj*

thir·ty-thir·ty *n US* a rifle that fires a .30 caliber cartridge with a 30-grain powder charge, usually written .30–.30.

thir·ty-two·mo /thùrtee to͞o mṑ/ (*plural* **thir·ty-two·mos**) *n* a size of book page traditionally created by folding a single sheet of standard-sized printing paper 5 times, giving 32 leaves or 64 pages [Late 18C. Pronunciation of the printers' abbreviation *32mo*]

Thir·ty Years War *n* a war in Europe between 1618 and 1648, which developed into a struggle for dominance between various powers, notably France, Spain, Sweden, and the Holy Roman Empire. It began as a war between the Catholic Holy Roman Emperor and some of his Protestant German states.

Thi·ru·van·an·thap·u·ram /thèeroo vùnnən thúppoo rum/ port and capital city of Kerala State, southern India. Population: 523,723 (1991).. Former name **Trivandrum**

this /*th*iss/ CORE MEANING: a grammatical word used to indicate somebody or something already mentioned or identified or something understood by both the speaker and hearer ○ (adj) *This book is brilliant.* ○ (adj) *This holiday – how much is it going to cost?* ○ (pron) *Is this why you've been so happy lately?* ○ (pron) *I first encountered this while traveling abroad.*

1. *adj, pron* CLOSE BY used to indicate somebody or something present or close by, especially as distinct from somebody or something further away, referred to as "that" ○ (adj) *I much prefer this painting to that one.* ○ (pron) *What's this?* **2.** *adj, pron* PREVIOUSLY MENTIONED used to indicate somebody or something just mentioned **3.** *adj, pron* INDICATING WORDS TO FOLLOW used to indicate a phrase or statement about to be said ○ (adj) *All I can say is this one word – no.* ○ (pron) *Hey, listen to this!* **4.** *adj, pron* STATED TIME used to refer to a specific time in the past or present ○ (pron) *I expected him back before this.* ○ (adj) *At this particular moment she felt she'd never experience such happiness again.* **5.** *adj* NOT PREVIOUSLY MENTIONED used to indicate somebody or something not previously mentioned, especially when telling a story to give a sense of immediacy (*informal*) ○ *Then this woman came running up to me, shouting at the top of her voice.* **6.** *adv* TO THIS DEGREE used to emphasize the degree of a feeling or quality ○ *I was this close to quitting.* [Old English *þis, þes* < Indo-European] ◇ **this and that** miscellaneous unimportant things

---

USAGE In formal writing, ***this*** should not be used as an intensifier modifying a noun, where the definite article *the* or the indefinite articles *a/an* are the appropriate choices. Usages like these are informal: *When I reached work I had this uncomfortable thought that I had not locked the door. You've just got to call this person I know in the main office to straighten out your scheduling problem. Suddenly this woman selling cosmetics appeared at my door.* The more acceptable wording is *the uncomfortable thought; a person I know in the main office; a woman selling cosmetics.*

---

this·a·way /*th*íssə wày/ *adv regional* this way (*humorous*)

This·be *n* MYTHOL ➧ **Pyramus and Thisbe**

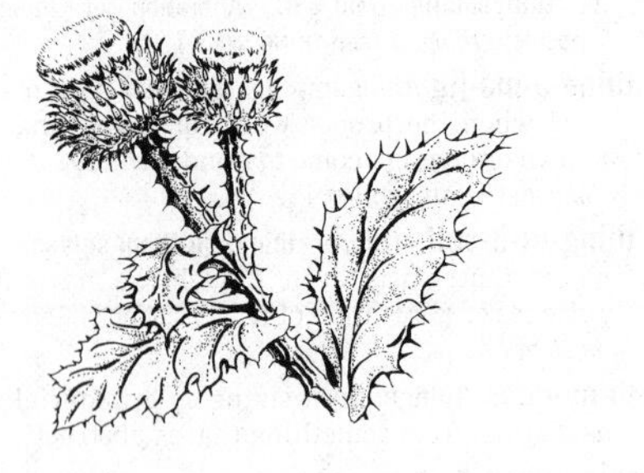

thistle

this·tle /thíss'l/ *n* **1.** a plant with prickly stems and leaves. Flowers: dense, rounded, usually purple, flower heads surrounded by thorny bracts. Genera: *Carduus* or *Cirsium* or *Onopordum.* **2.** a prickly plant similar to a thistle [Old English *þistel* < Germanic]

this·tle bird *n regional* BIRDS same as **goldfinch** [Because it feeds on thistle seeds]

this·tle but·ter·fly *n* INSECTS same as **painted lady** [Because its larvae live on thistles]

this·tle·down /thíss'l dòwn/ *n* **1.** the fluffy mass of hairs attached to the seeds of the mature flower head of a thistle **2.** a material or substance that is fine and silky and so resembles thistledown, e.g., a baby's hair or a delicate fabric

thist·ly /thíss'lee/ (**-li·er, -li·est**) *adj* **1.** full or consisting of thistles **2.** difficult to deal with ○ *thistly problems in economics*

thith·er /*th*í*th*ər/ *adv* to or in the direction of that place (*archaic or formal*) ○*"I will set thee on thy way to Benares, if thou goest thither, and tell thee what must be known by us."* (Rudyard Kipling, *Kim*; 1901) [Old English *þider*, alteration (after *hider* "hither") of *þæder* "that place" < Germanic]

thith·er·to /*th*ì*th*ər to͞o, *th*í*th*ər to͞o/ *adv* until that time (*archaic formal*) [15C. After HITHERTO]

thith·er·ward /*th*í*th*ərwərd/ *adv* same as **thither** (*archaic formal*)

thix·o·trop·ic /thìksə tróppik, -trṓpik/ *adj* becoming fluid when shaken or stirred and returning to a gel state when allowed to stand [Early 20C. < Greek *thixis* "touch"] —**thix·o·trope** /thíksə trṑp/ *n* —**thix·ot·ro·py** /thik sóttrəpee/ *n*

Th.M. *abbr US* EDUC, RELIG Master of Theology [Latin *Theologiae Magister*]

THNQ *abbr* ONLINE thank you (*used in e-mails or text messages*)

tho /*th*ō/ *adv, conj* same as **though** (*informal*) [Representing the pronunciation]

~~thoght~~ incorrect spelling of **thought**

thole[1] /thōl/ *n* ROWING same as **tholepin** [Old English *þol* < Indo-European, "stick out"]

thole[2] /thōl/ *vt N England, Scotland* to experience or bear something such as pain or grief patiently or uncomplainingly [Old English *þolian* < Indo-European, "support, lift up"]

thole·pin /thṓl pìn/ *n* a small upright wooden peg in the gunwale of a boat, usually provided in pairs to support an oar and act as a pivot when the oar is used

tho·los /thṓ làwss/ (*plural* **-loi** /-lòy/) *n* an ancient Greek circular domed building, especially a Mycenaean dry-stone tomb [Mid-17C. < Greek]

Thom·as /tómməss/ *n*, **St.** (*fl* A.D. 1st century) one of the 12 apostles of Jesus Christ. His reluctance to recognize Jesus Christ's resurrection until he had seen and touched his wounds gave rise to the phrase "doubting Thomas" (John 14:1–7, John 20:19–29).

Thom·as, Clarence (*b.* 1948) associate justice of the US Supreme Court. A prominent African American conservative, he became an associate justice in 1991.

Dylan Thomas

Thom·as, Dylan (1914–53) Welsh poet. His best known work includes the poem "Fern Hill" and the radio play *Under Milk Wood* (1954).

> "It is spring, moonless night in the small town, starless and bible-black, the cobblestreets silent and the hunched, courters'-and-rabbits' wood limping invisible down to the sloeblack, slow, black, crowblack, fishingboat-bobbing sea."
> [Dylan Thomas, *Under Milk Wood*; 1954]

Tho·mism /tṓ mìzzəm/ *n* the philosophical and theological doctrines of Thomas Aquinas, which formed the basis of medieval scholasticism [Early 18C. After St. *Thomas* AQUINAS] —**Tho·mist** *n, adj* —**Tho·mis·tic** /tō místik/ *adj*

Thomp·son /tómps'n/ **1.** main tributary of the Fraser River in southern British Columbia, Canada. Length: 304 mi./489 km. **2.** town in central Manitoba, Canada, on the Burntwood River. Population: 13,256 (2001).

Thomp·son, Benjamin, Count Rumford (1753–1814) US-born British physicist and politician. He is best known for his research into the nature of heat and friction.

Thomp·son, Daley (*b.* 1958) British athlete. In the decathlon he was Olympic gold medalist (1980 and 1984) and world champion (1983). Born **Thompson, Francis Morgan**

> "In my sport you have to peak ten times."
> [Daley Thompson, *Sunday Times (London)*; October 11, 1981]

Thomp·son, David (1770–1857) British-born Canadian explorer. He was the first to map comprehensively Canada's western territories.

Thomp·son, Dorothy (1894–1961) US journalist. Her radio broadcasts and syndicated column *On the Record* (1936–41) alerted US citizens to the coming dangers posed by the Nazis in Germany. She also published many books and was one of the most widely read women in the United States.

Thomp·son, Hunter S. (*b.* 1939) US journalist. An iconoclastic commentator of American culture, his *Fear and Loathing in Las Vegas* (1972) exemplifies the style of writing dubbed "New Journalism." Full name **Thompson, Hunter Stockton**

> "Mainline gambling is a very heavy business—and Las Vegas makes Reno seem like your friendly neighborhood grocery store. For a loser Vegas is the meanest town on earth."
> [Hunter S. Thompson, *Fear and Loathing in Las Vegas*; 1972]

Thomp·son, Sir John Sparrow David (1845–94) prime minister of Canada (1892–94). A lawyer and Conservative politician, he helped negotiate several international treaties.

Thomp·son sub·ma·chine gun /tómsən-/ *n* a relatively lightweight submachine gun introduced in 1915. It was intended as an infantry weapon. [Early 20C. After the US manufacturing company]

Thom·son /tómss'n/, **Charles Edward Poulett, 1st Baron of Sydenham** (1799–1841) British colonial administrator. He was governor-general of Canada (1839–41) and worked to unite Upper and Lower Canada (1840).

Thom·son, Virgil (1896–1989) US composer and critic. His symphonies, ballets, and musical "portraits" draw on US folk tunes, and include the Pulitzer Prize-winning score for the documentary movie *Louisiana Story* (1948). Full name **Thomson, Virgil Garnett**

Thom·son ef·fect /tómss'n-/ *n* the phenomenon of temperature differences within a conductor or semiconductor causing an electric potential gradient [Late 19C. After William *Thomson* (1st Baron KELVIN)]

Thomson's gazelle

Thom·son's ga·zelle *n* a small gazelle that has a broad black stripe on its side. Native to: grasslands and dry woodlands of Africa. Latin name: *Gazella thomsoni*. [Late 19C. After Joseph *Thomson*, Scottish explorer (1858–94)]

-thon *suffix* same as **-athon** (*used after a vowel*) ○ *talkathon* [< MARATHON]

thong /thawng, thong/ *n* **1.** LONG THIN PIECE OF LEATHER a thin strip of something, especially leather, used for fastening or supporting things **2.** BRAIDED WHIP a whip made of braided leather, cord, or some other material **3.** LIGHT SANDAL a light sandal held on by strips of material that join the sole of the sandal at either side of the foot and between the first and second toes **4.** BIKINI OR UNDERWEAR BOTTOM a narrow piece of cloth or leather that goes between the legs and is attached to a band around the hips, worn as a bikini bottom or as underwear [Old English *þwong* < Germanic]

Thor /thawr/ *n* in Norse mythology, the god of thunder and eldest son of Odin. Thursday is named for him.

tho·ra·cen·te·sis /thàwrə sen teéssiss/ (*plural* **-te·ses** /-teé seez/) *n* a surgical procedure in which a needle is inserted through the chest wall in order to withdraw fluid, blood, or air [Mid-19C. < THORACO- + Greek *kentēsis* "pricking" < *kentein* "to prick"]

tho·ra·ces ANAT, ZOOL plural of **thorax**

tho·rac·ic /thə rássik/ *adj* involving or located in the chest —**tho·rac·i·cal·ly** *adv*

tho·rac·ic duct *n* the main duct of the lymphatic system, which drains lymph from smaller lymph vessels in the trunk and returns it to the bloodstream by emptying into a major vein. In human beings, it ascends in front of the spinal column and discharges into the left subclavian vein at the base of the neck.

thoraco- *prefix* chest, thorax ○ *thoracolumbar* [< Greek *thōrak-*, stem of *thōrax*]

tho·ra·co·lum·bar /thàwrəkō lúmbər/ *adj* describes the thoracic and lumbar areas of the body

tho·ra·cot·o·my /thàwrə kóttəmee/ (*plural* **-mies**) *n* a surgical incision made in the chest wall

tho·rax /tháw ràks/ (*plural* **tho·rax·es** or **tho·ra·ces** /thə ráy seèz, tháwrə-/) *n* **1.** UPPER PART OF TORSO the part of the human body between the neck and abdomen, enclosed by the ribs and containing the heart and lungs **2.** UPPER PART OF ANIMAL'S BODY the area corresponding to the human thorax in other vertebrates **3.** PART BETWEEN HEAD AND ABDOMEN the middle division of the body of an insect, crustacean, or arachnid [14C. Via Latin < Greek *thōrax* "chest, breastplate"]

Tho·ra·zine /tháwrə zeèn/ *tdmk* a trademark for chlorpromazine

Tho·reau /thə rṓ, tháw rō/, **Henry David** (1817–62) US essayist and philosopher. He was a leading transcendentalist and libertarian. His works include the essay "Civil Disobedience" (1849) and *Walden* (1854), in which he describes a life lived simply and close to nature. Born **David Henry Thoreau**

> "The mass of men lead lives of quiet desperation."
> [Henry David Thoreau, *Walden, or Life in the Woods*; 1854]

tho·ri·a /tháwree ə/ *n* CHEM same as **thorium dioxide** [Mid-19C. < THORIUM, after MAGNESIA]

tho·ri·an·ite /tháwree ə nīt/ *n* a rare black radioactive mineral that is an oxide of thorium mixed with rare-earth metals. Use: source of thorium and uranium. [Early 20C. < THORIA + -ITE[1]]

tho·rite /tháw rīt/ *n* a rare brown, black, or yellow radioactive thorium silicate mineral. Use: source of thorium. [Mid-19C. < THOR]

tho·ri·um /tháwree əm/ *n* a soft silvery white radioactive metallic element. Source: thorite, thorianite. Use: alloys, source of nuclear energy. Symbol **Th**. See table at **element** [Mid-19C. < THOR] —**tho·ric** *adj*

tho·ri·um di·ox·ide *n* an insoluble white powder. Use: catalyst, manufacture of gas mantles, refractories, ceramics, optical glass. Formula: ThO_2.

tho·ri·um se·ries *n* one of the natural radioactive decay series that shows how the unstable isotope thorium-232 changes by stages into the stable isotope lead-208

thorn /thawrn/ *n* **1.** SHARP POINT ON PLANT STEM a sharply pointed woody growth projecting from the stem of some trees, bushes, and woody plants **2.** PLANT WITH THORNS a tree, bush, or woody plant that has thorns **3.** WOOD OF TREE WITH THORNS the wood of a tree or bush with thorns **4.** RUNIC LETTER a runic letter used to represent both of the "th" sounds, as in "this" and "thick," in Old English and Middle English. It also represents the voiceless "th" sound, as in "thick," in Old Norse and Icelandic and was formerly used as a phonetic symbol. [Old English *þorn* < Germanic] —**thorned** *adj* —**thorn·less** *adj* —**thorn·like** *adj* ◇ **be a thorn in (somebody's) flesh** *or* **side** to be a source of constant irritation to somebody

thorn ap·ple *n* **1.** the fruit of a hawthorn **2.** *UK* same as **jimsonweed**

thorn·back /tháwrn bàk/ (*plural* **-backs** or *same*) *n* a ray with one to three rows of large hooked spines on its back. Latin name: *Raja clavata* or *Platyrhinoidis triseriatis*.

thorn·bill /tháwrn bìl/ (*plural* **-bills** or *same*) *n* **1.** a small songbird with a short sharp beak. Native to: Australia. Family: Acanthizidae. **2.** a hummingbird with a beak that resembles a thorn. Native to: South America. Genera: *Ramphomicron* or *Chalcostigma*.

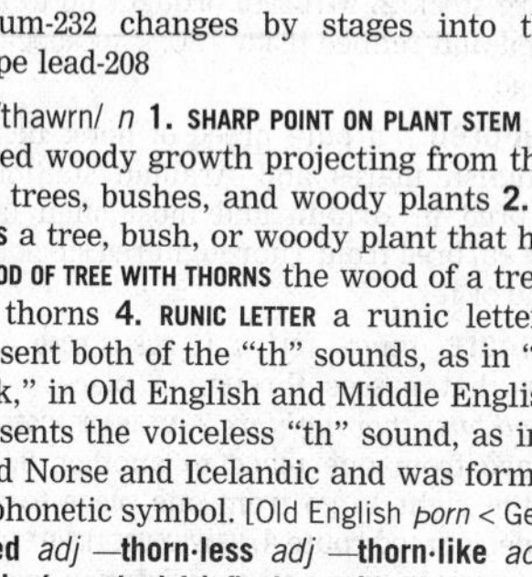

Dame Sybil Thorndike

Thorn·dike /tháwrn dīk/, **Dame Sybil** (1882–1976) British actor. A member of the Old Vic Theater, London, she played the title role in George Bernard Shaw's *St. Joan* more than 2,000 times after he wrote the part for her in 1924. Full name **Thorndike, Dame Agnes Sybil**

Thorn·hill /tháwrn hìl/, **Sir James** (1675–1734) British painter. His work, in the baroque style and executed chiefly for royal and noble patrons, includes decorations for the cupola of St. Paul's Cathedral, London, England.

Thorn·ton /tháwrnt'n/, **Matthew** (1714–1803) American patriot. He was a signatory of the Declaration of Independence (1776) as a delegate from New Hampshire.

thorn·y /tháwrnee/ (**-i·er, -i·est**) *adj* **1.** complicated and difficult to resolve **2.** covered in or full of thorns —**thorn·i·ly** *adv* —**thorn·i·ness** *n*

tho·ron /tháw ròn/ *n* a radioactive isotope of radon with a half-life of 55 seconds, formed by the radioactive decay of thorium [Early 20C. < THORIUM, after RADON]

thor·ough /thúrrō/ *adj* **1.** EXTREMELY CAREFUL extremely careful to include everything that is needed ○ *She's very thorough in her research methods.* **2.** DONE FULLY complete in every detail and carried out with care ○ *The doctor gave me a thorough examination.* **3.** ABSOLUTE being so to the fullest extent or in the truest sense of the word ○ *a thorough bore* [Old English *þuruh* "from end to end," variant of *þurh* (see THROUGH)] —**thor·ough·ly** *adv* —**thor·ough·ness** *n*

SYNONYMS See *careful.*

thor·ough·bass /thúrrō bàyss, thúrrə-/ *n* MUSIC same as **continuo** [Mid-17C. < THOROUGH "all the way through"]

thor·ough·bred /thúrrə brèd/ *n* **1.** PUREBRED ANIMAL a purebred animal, especially a horse **2.** WELL-BRED PERSON somebody who has been brought up to be refined and well-mannered ■ *adj* **1.** PUREBRED bred from pure stock **2.** WELL-BRED brought up to be well-mannered and refined [Early 18C. < THOROUGH "all the way through"]

Thor·ough·bred *n* a pure breed of horse descended from English mares and Arabian stallions, originally bred in Britain and most often used for racing ■ *adj* bred from Thoroughbred stock or characteristic of it

thor·ough·fare /thúrrə fèr/ *n* **1.** PUBLIC ROAD a public highway that passes through a place ○ *a truck blocking a busy thoroughfare* **2.** MEANS OF ACCESS a way or passage from one place to another **3.** RIGHT OF PASSAGE the right to go from one place to another along a designated route **4.** HEAVILY USED ROUTE a stretch of road or water, or a pathway between two places, that is used by many people [14C. < THOROUGH "from end to end" + obsolete *fare* "way, journey"]

thor·ough·go·ing /thùrrō gō ing, thùrrə-/ *adj* **1.** carried out in an extremely careful and thorough way ○ *not very thoroughgoing when it comes to housework* **2.** being so to the fullest extent or in the truest sense of the word ○ *a thoroughgoing pragmatist* [Early 19C. < THOROUGH "all the way through"]

thor·ough·paced /thùrrō páyst, thùrrə-/ *adj* describes a horse that is thoroughly trained so as to be able to perform all paces well

thor·ough·pin /thúrrō pin, thúrrə-/ *n* inflammation and swelling above the hock joint on both sides of a horse's leg, affecting the flexor tendon and causing lameness [Late 18C. < THOROUGH "all the way through"; from the appearance of the swelling, like a pin passing through the tendon]

thor·ough·wort /thúrrō wùrt, -wàwrt/ (*plural* **-worts** or *same*) *n US* PLANTS same as **boneset** [Late 16C. < THOROUGH "through," because the plant's stem appears to grow through its leaves]

thorp /thawrp/, **thorpe** *n* a small village (*archaic; often used in place names*) [Old English *þorp* < Germanic]

Thorpe /thawrp/, **Ian** (*b.* 1982) Australian swimmer. One of the outstanding freestyle swimmers in the history of the sport, by the age of 20 he had broken 15 world records and won three Olympic gold medals and eight World Championship titles. Full name **Thorpe, Ian James**. Known as **Thorpedo**

Thorpe, Jim (1888–1953) US athlete. One of the outstanding athletes of the 20th century, he won Olympic gold medals for the pentathlon and decathlon (1912) and played professional baseball (1913–19) and football (1917–29). Full name **Thorpe, James Francis**. Born **Wa-tho-huck**

those /thōz/ *pron, adj* the form of "that" used before a plural noun or with a multiple referent ○ *Those are the ones I prefer.* ○ *Do you remember those outings to the seaside?* [Old English *þās* (see THESE)]

Thoth /thōth, tōt/, **Thot** *n* in Egyptian mythology, the god of the moon, associated with writing and wisdom. He is usually depicted as a man with the head of an ibis, or as a baboon. ◊ **Hermes Trismegistus**

thou[1] /thow/ (*plural* **thous** or *same*) *n* a thousand, especially when referring to money (*slang*) [Mid-19C. Shortening of THOUSAND]

thou[2] /thow/ *pron* **1.** refers to you, the person being addressed or written to (*archaic or regional; used in familiar address to one person*) **2.** *also* **Thou** used to address God, e.g., in prayers and hymns [Old English *þū* < Indo-European]

thoub *n* a white robe worn by Muslim clerics

though /thō/ *conj* **1.** ALTHOUGH in spite of the fact that ○ *Though she served as president of the student government in her senior year, she was attracted to journalism rather than politics.* ○ *He didn't receive any special treatment, even though he is a close friend of the chairman.* **2.** AND YET used to introduce added information that restricts the applicability of a previous statement ○ *The weather has improved a lot, though it still doesn't feel like spring.* ■ *adv* **1.** DESPITE BEING used as a link between words, phrases, or clauses, that usually makes one of them function as an admission that partially contradicts the other ○ *Progress, though steady, has been very slow.* ○ *Small though it is, the device produces enormous quantities of heat.* **2.** HOWEVER used in or following a statement that restricts the applicability of the statement that preceded it ○ *So they got married. That, though, was not the end of the story.* [Old English *þeah* < Indo-European; partly < Old Norse *þó*]

USAGE See *although.*

thought[1] *n* **1.** THINKING the activity or process of thinking ○ *deep in thought* **2.** IDEA PRODUCED BY MENTAL ACTIVITY an idea, plan, conception, or opinion produced by mental activity ○ *The thought had crossed my mind.* **3.** SET OF IDEAS the intellectual, scientific, and philosophical ideas associated with a particular place, time, or group ○ *medieval religious thought* **4.** REASONING POWER the ability to think and reason ○ *felt incapable of rational thought* **5.** CONSIDERATION the process or an instance of considering somebody or something ○ *I didn't give it another thought.* **6.** INTENTION an intention of doing something ○ *I had no thought of offending anybody.* **7.** EXPECTATION an expectation or hope that something will happen ○ *entertained no thoughts of failure* **8.** SMALL AMOUNT a small amount on a comparative scale ○ *Could you be a thought quieter, please?* **9.** COMPASSIONATE CONSIDERATION a feeling of respect, affection, or consideration for somebody or something ○ *no thought for other people* [Old English *þōht* < Germanic] ◇ **perish the thought!** used to indicate, often humorously, that something is too terrible to be thought of

thought[2] /thawt/ past participle, past tense of **think**

thought·ful /tháwtfəl/ *adj* **1.** CONSIDERATE treating people in a kind and considerate way, especially by anticipating their wants or needs **2.** PENSIVE appearing to be deep in thought **3.** CAREFULLY THOUGHT OUT showing the application of careful thought —**thought·ful·ly** *adv* —**thought·ful·ness** *n*

thought·less /tháwtləss/ *adj* **1.** INCONSIDERATE showing a lack of consideration for other people or for consequences **2.** DONE WITHOUT THOUGHT showing a lack of planning or forethought **3.** UNABLE TO THINK not having or using the faculty of thought —**thought·less·ly** *adv* —**thought·less·ness** *n*

thought-out *adj* showing evidence of careful planning (*usually used in combination*)

thought-pro·vok·ing *adj* interesting and causing somebody to engage in careful thought

~~thourough~~ incorrect spelling of **thorough**

thou·sand /thówz'nd/ *n* (*plural same* or **-sands**) **1.** 1,000 the number 1,000 **2.** FOURTH DIGIT TO LEFT OF DECIMAL the fourth digit to the left of the decimal point in the decimal number system **3.** LARGE NUMBER a very large number or amount (*informal*) ○ *must have told him a thousand times* ■ **thou·sands** *npl* VERY MANY a very large but unspecified number ○ *sold thousands of copies* [Old English *þūsend* < Germanic, "swollen hundred"< Indo-European, "to swell"]

Thou·sand Is·land dress·ing *n* a salmon-pink salad dressing containing mayonnaise, tomato sauce, chopped gherkins, onions, and spices

Thou·sand Is·lands /thòwz'nd-/ group of more than 1,000 small islands in southeastern Ontario and northern New York State, in the St. Lawrence River.

thou·sandth /thówz'nth/ *n* one of a thousand equal parts of something

~~thousend~~ incorrect spelling of **thousand**

thp, **t.hp.** *abbr* MEASURE thrust horsepower

Thrace /thrayss/ region in southeastern Europe, forming part of present-day Greece, Bulgaria, and Turkey. Area: 3,312 sq. mi./8,578 sq. km. —**Thra·cian** *adj, n*

Thra·co-Phryg·i·an /thràykō fríjjee ən/ *n* a branch of the Indo-European family of languages of which all members except for Armenian are now extinct [Early 20C. < *Thracian*] —**Thra·co-Phryg·i·an** *adj*

thrall /thrawl/ *n* (*literary*) **1.** DOMINATION a condition of being controlled by a more powerful person or force ○ *Millions are now in thrall to the factitious excitements of reality television.* **2.** SOMEBODY WHOSE LIFE IS CONTROLLED somebody whose life is completely controlled by a more powerful person or a moral or intellectual force **3.** SOMEBODY CONTROLLED BY SOMETHING somebody who is controlled by a particular physical or mental need ○ *a thrall to alcohol* [Pre-12C. < Old Norse *þræll* < Germanic, "run"] —**thrall·dom** *n*

thrash /thrash/ *v* (**thrashed, thrash·ing, thrash·es**) **1.** *vt* DEFEAT OPPONENT DECISIVELY to defeat a person or team decisively, especially in a sports competition ○ *The home team was thrashed in the playoffs.* **2.** *vt* BEAT PERSON OR ANIMAL to beat a person or animal violently **3.** *vti* TOSS ABOUT to toss or move the body and limbs about in an uncontrolled or restless way ○ *thrashed around unable to sleep* **4.** *vi* PADDLE WITH LEGS to move the legs up and down in the water while performing a swimming stroke **5.** *vti* AGRIC same as **thresh** *v* (sense 1) **6.** *vti* SAIL BOAT INTO TIDE OR WIND to sail a boat against the direction of the tide or wind ■ *n* **1.** BEATING a blow or beating with a whip or stick **2.** SOCIAL PARTY a party or celebration (*dated informal*) **3.** MUSIC same as **thrash metal** [Late 16C. Variant of THRESH]

SYNONYMS See *defeat.*

thrash out *vt Can, UK* to discuss and develop all the possibilities of a situation in order to reach a decision about it. US term **hash out**

thrash·er /thráshər/ *n* **1.** a long-tailed brownish bird with a down-curving beak and a speckled breast. Native to: North America. Family: Mimidae. **2.** FISH, AGRIC same as **thresher** (senses 1, 3)

thrash·ing /thráshing/ *n* **1.** a violent physical beating **2.** a decisive defeat in a sports competition

thrash met·al *n* a very fast, often discordant type of heavy metal music, strongly influenced by punk

thread /thred/ *n* **1.** FINE TWISTED CORD fine cord made of two or more twisted fibers. Use: sewing, weaving. **2.** PIECE OF THREAD a length of thread **3.** RIDGE ON SCREW the continuous helical ridge on a screw or pipe **4.** VERY THIN STRIP a fine strand of solid material, trickle of liquid, or wisp of gas **5.** FILAMENT OF SPIDER'S WEB one of the filaments of a spider's web **6.** SOMETHING CONNECTING ELEMENTS a continuous unifying element running through a story, argument, discussion, or series of events **7.** DISCUSSION ON INTERNET a series of messages in an Internet discussion group (**forum**), commenting on or replying to a previous message **8.** HUMAN LIFE the course of human life, believed by the ancient Greeks to be spun, measured out, and cut by the Fates **9.** MIN EXTRACT VEIN OF ORE a thin seam of ore or coal ■ **threads** *npl* CLOTHING same as **clothes** (*slang*) ■ *v* (**thread·ed, thread·ing, threads**) **1.** *vt* PASS SOMETHING THROUGH HOLE to pass something such as thread, photographic film, magnetic tape, or ribbon through a hole or gap in something else **2.** *vt* STRING

BEADS ON THREAD to string beads or pearls on a thread or wire 3. *vti* GO CAREFULLY to move along carefully, following a winding route ○ *We threaded our way through the crowded streets.* 4. *vt* INTERSPERSE THINGS to distribute something at intervals in something else ○ *hair threaded with gray* 5. *vt* MECH ENG PRODUCE SCREW THREAD to produce a thread on a screw or bolt, or within a material into which a bolt or screw may be inserted 6. *vi* COOK FORM THREAD to form a fine thread when dropped from a spoon (*refers to sugar syrup*) [Old English *þrǣd* "twisted cord" < Indo-European, "to turn, twist"] —**thread·like** *adj* ◇ **lose the thread (of something)** to cease to follow or understand the connection between the parts of a story or argument

thread·bare /thréd bèr/ *adj* 1. WORN AWAY TO REVEAL THREADS so heavily used that the soft part of the fabric has been worn away to reveal the threads beneath 2. OVERUSED SO NO LONGER CONVINCING having been used so often as to be no longer convincing ○ *the same old threadbare excuses* 3. MEAGER not large, varied, or substantial enough to be satisfactory ○ *eked out a threadbare existence* 4. SHABBILY DRESSED wearing worn-out shabby clothes —**thread·bare·ness** *n*

thread·er /thréddər/ *n* a device for threading a needle, consisting of a loop of extremely fine wire attached to a flat metal disk that is held between the thumb and forefinger

thread·fin /thréd fìn/ (*plural* **-fins** or *same*) *n* a sea fish with long rays resembling threads on the lower parts of its pectoral fin. Native to: tropical waters. Family: Polynemidae.

thread vein *n* a very slender vein, especially one that is visible through the skin

thread·worm /thréd wùrm/ *n* a long nematode worm, e.g., a pinworm

thread·y /thréddee/ (**-i·er, -i·est**) *adj* 1. MED ONLY JUST PERCEPTIBLE describes a weak and barely perceptible pulse 2. SOUNDING WEAK sounding thin and lacking in power and tone ○ *thready voice* 3. LIKE THREAD resembling thread 4. HAVING MANY THREADS consisting of or containing many threads, especially loose or visible ones 5. COOK FORMING THREADS thick and sticky enough to form threads when dropped from a spoon —**thread·i·ness** *n*

threat /thret/ *n* 1. DECLARATION OF INTENT TO CAUSE HARM the expression of an intention to cause harm or pain ○ *The terrorists might carry out their threat to kill the hostages.* 2. SIGN OF SOMETHING BAD an indication that something unpleasant or dangerous is going to happen ○ *a threat of severe thunderstorms* 3. SOMEBODY OR SOMETHING LIKELY TO CAUSE HARM a person, animal, or thing likely to cause harm or pain ○ *The dog is no threat.* [Old English *þrēat* "crowd, menace" < Indo-European, "press in"]

threat·en /thrétt'n/ (**-ened, -en·ing, -ens**) *v* 1. *vti* EXPRESS HOSTILE INTENTION TOWARD SOMEBODY to express an intention to do something that will cause harm, trouble, or inconvenience to somebody else unless that person does what is demanded ○ *They threatened us with legal action.* ○ *She threatened to tell my wife.* 2. *vt* EXPRESS THREAT TO SOMEBODY to express or indicate an intention to harm or kill somebody ○ *He threatened me with a knife.* 3. *vti* BE THREAT TO SOMETHING to be a source of actual or potential harm to something ○ *an injury that could threaten his career* 4. *vti* SIGNIFY SOMETHING BAD HAPPENING to signify that something bad is going to happen, especially that bad weather is going to arrive ○ *Dark clouds threatened rain.* 5. *vi* SUGGEST UNWELCOME CONSEQUENCES to seem likely to result in something unpleasant ○ *The dispute threatened to escalate into all-out war.* [Old English *þrēatnian* "press in on" < *þrēat* (see THREAT)] —**threat·en·er** *n*

threat·ened /thrétt'nd/ *adj* describes an organism or species that is in danger of becoming extinct

threat·en·ing /thrétt'ning/ *adj* 1. EXPRESSING THREAT expressing an intention to cause somebody deliberate harm or pain ○ *a threatening gesture* 2. SUGGESTING SEVERE WEATHER likely to bring rain or severe weather ○ *a threatening sky* 3. MAKING SOMEBODY FEEL ANXIOUS OR FEARFUL causing somebody to feel anxious, fearful, and unconfident —**threat·en·ing·ly** *adv*

threat ma·trix *n* a daily list and assessment of credible threats to US interests and assets domestically and internationally, prepared for the President of the United States and other very high-level government officials by the CIA

Thred·bo /thrédbō/ ski resort in the Australian Alps, New South Wales, Australia. Population: 2,065 (1991).

three /three/ *n* 1. 3 the number 3 2. SOMETHING WITH VALUE OF 3 something in a numbered series, e.g., a playing card, with a value of 3 ○ *the three of clubs* ○ *to throw a three* 3. GROUP OF THREE a group of three objects or people [Old English *þrī*, *þrēotīne* < Indo-European]

three-bag·ger *n* BASEBALL same as **triple** (*slang*)

three-base hit *n* same as **triple**

three-card mon·te *n* a game in which three cards are dealt face up and then turned face down and moved around. The bettor must then guess the position of a particular card.

three-col·or *adj* using, produced by, or relating to a color printing process in which the print is produced by superimposing separate plates for the colors yellow, magenta, and cyan

three-D, 3-D *n* a three-dimensional effect ■ *adj* MATH, ARTS same as **three-dimensional** (senses 1–2) (*informal*)

three-D ac·cel·er·a·tor *n* computer hardware that improves three-D graphics presentation

three-deck·er *n* 1. SOMETHING WITH THREE LEVELS a vehicle, building, or other construction with three levels or floors 2. SHIP WITH THREE DECKS a warship with three decks set with guns, or any ship with three decks 3. SANDWICH WITH THREE SLICES OF BREAD a sandwich consisting of two layers of filling between three slices of bread

three-di·men·sion·al *adj* 1. WITH THREE DIMENSIONS possessing or appearing to possess the dimensions of height, width, and depth 2. APPEARING TO HAVE DEPTH creating the illusion of depth behind a flat surface 3. BELIEVABLE represented with sufficient complexity to be convincing

three-field sys·tem *n* a system of crop rotation that was in operation in western Europe by the 9th century. One-third of land was left fallow, one-third planted in spring grains, and one-third in the season's crops such as barley and vegetables.

three·fold /three fōld/ *adj* 1. CONSISTING OF THREE made up of three parts 2. THREE TIMES AS MANY OR MUCH being or having three times as many or as much ■ *adv* BY THREE TIMES by three times as many or as much

three-four time *n* a time signature in which there are three beats to the measure and each beat is a quarter note. A waltz is in three-four time.

3G *n* a wireless communications technology designed to provide high-speed mobile access to the Internet, entertainment, information, and intranets (*often used before a noun*) Full form **Third Generation**

three-gait·ed *adj US* describes a horse that is able to perform the standard three paces, the walk, the trot, and the canter

Three Kings *n* BIBLE same as **Magi**

Three Kings Is·lands /three kingz-/ group of uninhabited islands 31 mi./50 km northwest of the North Island, New Zealand. The islands are a wildlife refuge. Area: 3 sq. mi./8 sq. km.

three-leg·ged race *n* a race in which pairs of runners compete with their adjacent legs bound together

Three Mile Is·land /three mīl-/ island in the Susquehanna River, near Harrisburg, southeastern Pennsylvania. An accidental release of radioactivity at the nuclear plant on the island in 1979 led to stricter regulation of the US nuclear industry.

three-mile lim·it *n* the outer limit of a country's territorial waters, three nautical miles from shore

three·pence /thréppənss, thrúppənss/, **thrup·pence** /thrúppənss/ *n* 1. a former British coin worth three old pennies 2. a sum of three pennies, especially old pence (*dated; takes a singular verb*)

three·pen·ny /thréppənee, thrúppənee/, **thrup·pen·ny** /thrúppənee/ *adj* (*dated*) 1. worth or costing three pennies, especially old pence 2. worth or costing very little

three-phase *adj* 1. consisting of three separate phases 2. describes an electrical system or circuit of three alternating voltages that have the same frequency but are separated by one third of a cycle

three-piece *adj* consisting of three matching or coordinated pieces ■ *n* a suit consisting of matching trousers or skirt, vest or blouse, and jacket

three-ply *adj* 1. WITH THREE LAYERS consisting of three layers or laminations 2. WITH THREE STRANDS made up of three twisted strands ■ *n* THREE-PLY KNITTING YARN knitting yarn made up of three twisted strands

three-point land·ing *n* an aircraft landing in which the two main wheels of the landing gear and the nose or tail wheel touch the ground at the same time

three-quar·ter *adj* 1. BEING THREE-FOURTHS OF SOMETHING being three-fourths of something measurable or countable, e.g., length, an area, or a time interval ○ *a three-quarter moon* 2. BEING THREE QUARTERS OF FULL LENGTH being three quarters of the full or usual length ○ *a three-quarter coat* 3. ARTS WITH FACE TURNED TO SIDE describes a portrait that shows the subject's face turned slightly to one side

three-quar·ter bind·ing *n* bookbinding in which the spine and most of the sides of a book are covered in the same material

three-quar·ter length *adj* 1. describes a sleeve that ends somewhere between the elbow and the wrist 2. describes a coat that ends somewhere between the hips and the knees

three-ring cir·cus *n* 1. a circus in which performances take place simultaneously in three separate rings 2. a situation full of activity and confusion (*informal*)

three Rs /three àarz/, **3 Rs** *npl* the skills of reading, writing, and arithmetic, considered as the basis of elementary education [Presumed to have originated with a toast proposed by Sir William Curtis (1752–1829), illiterate Lord Mayor of London]

three·score /three skáwr/ *adj, n* same as **sixty** (*archaic*) ○ *threescore years and ten*

three·some /threessəm/ *n* 1. GROUP OF THREE a group of three people 2. SEXUAL EXPERIENCE a sexual experience involving three people 3. ACTIVITY FOR THREE a game or activity for three people 4. TYPE OF GOLF GAME a golf game involving three players, one playing one ball and the other two taking alternate shots to play another ball

three-spine stick·le·back, three-spined stick·le·back *n* a small stickleback of temperate fresh and salt water that has three dorsal spines. Latin name: *Gasterosteus aculeatus*.

three-square *adj* shaped like an equilateral triangle when viewed in cross section

three strikes, three strikes and you're out *n* a law that mandates long prison sentences for criminals with three felony convictions

three-toed sloth *n* a slow tree-dwelling mammal that has three long-clawed toes on each forefoot. Genus: *Bradypus*.

three-toed wood·peck·er *n* a woodpecker with three toes on each foot. Native to: North America. Latin name: *Picoides tridactylus* or *Picoides arcticus*.

three-way *adj* 1. involving three participating people or things 2. providing routes to three different places from one point ○ *a three-way junction*

three-wheel·er *n* a vehicle with three wheels, e.g., a small car or a tricycle

Three Wise Men *n* BIBLE same as **Magi**

threm·ma·tol·o·gy /thrèmmə tóllәjee/ *n* the science of breeding domesticated plants and animals [Late 19C. < Greek *thremmat-* "nursling"]

thren·o·dy /thrénnədee/ (*plural* **-dies**), **thre·node** /three nōd, thré nōd/ *n* a song, poem, or speech of lament for the dead [Mid-17C. < Greek *thrēnōidia* < *thrēnos* "lament" + *ōidē* "song"] —**thre·no·di·al** /thrə nṓdee əl/ *adj* —**thre·nod·ic** /thrə nóddik/ *adj* —**thren·o·dist** *n*

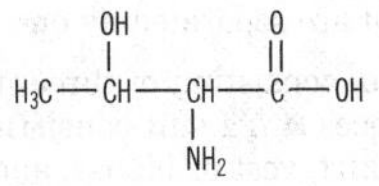

threonine

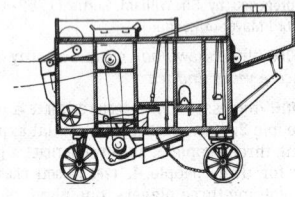

thre·o·nine /thrée ə neen, -ənin/ *n* an amino acid that is a component of proteins and an essential nutrient in the diets of humans and animals. Formula: $C_4H_9NO_3$. [Mid-20C. < *threose*, kind of sugar + -INE]

thresh /thresh/ *v* (**threshed, thresh·ing, thresh·es**) **1.** *vti* SEPARATE SEEDS FROM PLANT to use a machine, flail, or other implement to separate the seeds of a harvested plant from the straw and chaff, husks, or other residue **2.** *vt* same as **thrash** *v* (sense 2) **3.** *vt* EXAMINE EXHAUSTIVELY to examine something such as an issue or a proposal, exhaustively **4.** *vti* same as **thrash** *v* (sense 3) ■ *n* THRESHING an act of threshing a harvested crop [Old English *þerscan* < Indo-European, "to rub"]

thresh·er /thréshər/ *n* **1.** a harvester of a crop with a machine, flail, or other implement **2.** AGRIC same as **threshing machine 3.** *also* **thresh·er shark** a large, widely distributed shark that has a curved elongated upper lobe on the tail with which it agitates or threshes the water. Family: Alopiidae.

~~**threshhold**~~ incorrect spelling of **threshold**

threshing machine

thresh·ing ma·chine *n* a static power-driven agricultural machine formerly used to beat or rub harvested plants in order to separate the seeds from the rest of the plant

thresh·old /thré shōld/ *n* **1.** STARTING POINT the point at which something begins or changes ○ *on the threshold of maturity* **2.** LEVEL AT WHICH EFFECT STARTS the level that must be reached for a psychological or physiological effect to begin or be noticeable ○ *the threshold of consciousness* ○ *her pain threshold* **3.** WOOD OR STONE BELOW DOOR a piece of stone or hardwood that forms the bottom of a doorway **4.** ENTRANCE a doorway or entrance [Old English *þerscold* < Germanic]

threw past tense of **throw**

thrice /thrīss/ *adv* **1.** THREE TIMES three times over (*archaic or literary*) **2.** THREEFOLD by three times as many or as much (*archaic or literary*) **3.** GREATLY to a high degree (*archaic*) [12C. Alteration of *thries* < Old English *þriga* "three times" < *þrī* (see THREE)]

thrift /thrift/ *n* **1.** PRUDENT USE OF MONEY AND GOODS the sensible and cautious management of money and goods in order to waste as little as possible and obtain maximum value **2.** *US* BANKING SAVINGS AND LOAN ASSOCIATION a savings and loan association or savings bank **3.** PLANT WITH PINK OR WHITE FLOWERS a perennial evergreen plant of the plumbago family. Flowers: dense, round, pink or white. Genus: *Armeria*. **4.** ZOOL STRONG GROWTH vigorous and healthy growth of living things such as plants (*formal*) [13C. < Old Norse *þrift* "prosperity" < *þrífask* (see THRIVE)]

thrift in·sti·tu·tion *n US* BANKING same as **thrift** (sense 2)

thrift·less /thríftləss/ *adj* **1.** showing carelessness and wastefulness in the handling of money and other resources **2.** having little value or usefulness (*archaic*) —**thrift·less·ly** *adv* —**thrift·less·ness** *n*

thrift shop *n* a store that sells used goods, particularly clothing, usually to benefit charity

thrift·y /thríftee/ (**-i·er, -i·est**) *adj* **1.** CAREFUL WITH MONEY AND RESOURCES managing money and resources in a cautious and sensible way so as to waste as little as possible **2.** PROSPEROUS prosperous and thriving (*archaic*) **3.** *US* GROWING WELL growing healthily and vigorously —**thrift·i·ly** *adv* —**thrift·i·ness** *n*

thrill /thril/ *vti* (**thrilled, thrill·ing, thrills**) **1.** BE OR MAKE SOMEBODY VERY EXCITED to feel intense excitement, or make somebody experience intense excitement ○ *The children were thrilled by the amusement park.* **2.** BE PLEASURABLE to feel great pleasure, or make somebody feel great pleasure ○ *It thrilled me to see my old friends.* **3.** VIBRATE OR CAUSE TO VIBRATE to vibrate, or make something or somebody quiver or vibrate ■ *n* **1.** CAUSE OF GREAT EXCITEMENT a source or cause of intense excitement, and often pleasure **2.** FEELING OF EXCITEMENT a feeling of intense excitement, which may be experienced as a quivering or trembling sensation **3.** MED TREMOR ASSOCIATED WITH HEART-VALVE DEFECTS a slight vibration of the chest wall often associated with some types of heart-valve conditions [Old English *þȳrlian* "go through" < *þȳrel* "hole" < *þruh* "through"]

thrill·er /thríllər/ *n* **1.** a book, play, or movie that has an exciting plot involving crime, mystery, or espionage **2.** somebody or something that thrills people

thrill·ing /thrílling/ *adj* **1.** causing intense excitement **2.** characterized by trembling or vibrating —**thrill·ing·ly** *adv*

thrips /thrips/ (*plural same*) *n* a tiny sucking insect with four long thin wings fringed with hairs. It feeds on the sap of plants. Order: Thysanoptera. [Late 18C. Via Latin < Greek, "woodworm"]

thrive /thrīv/ (**thrived** or **throve** /thrōv/, **thrived** or **thriv·en** /thrívvən/, **thriv·ing, thrives**) *vi* **1.** to grow vigorously and healthily **2.** to be successful and often profitable [13C. < Old Norse *þrífask* "grasp for yourself" < *þrífa* "seize"] —**thriv·er** *n*

thrive on *vt* to enjoy and be stimulated by something generally considered difficult or undesirable

thro' /throo/, **thro** *prep, adv* same as **through** (*informal or literary*) [15C. Variant]

throat /thrōt/ *n* **1.** DIGESTIVE AND BREATHING PASSAGE the part of the airway and digestive tract between the mouth and both the esophagus and the windpipe **2.** FRONT OF NECK the front part of the neck of an animal or human being **3.** NARROW PART a narrow part or passage that resembles a human's or animal's throat in shape or function **4.** OPENING OF TUBULAR ORGAN OF FLOWER the opening of a tubular organ of a flower, e.g., of a corolla ■ *vt* (**throat·ed, throat·ing, throats**) *US* UTTER SOMETHING IN DEEP TONES to speak or sing something in a deep or hoarse voice [Old English *þrote* < Germanic] —**throat·ed** /thrṓtəd/ *adj* ◇ **be at each other's throats** to be constantly quarreling or fighting ◇ **jump down somebody's throat** to speak angrily and impatiently to somebody ◇ **ram** *or* **force something down somebody's throat** to make repeated and emphatic attempts to get somebody to listen to or accept a view or belief

throat-clear·ing *adj* being an overly long, often verbose and repetitive preliminary to something else ○*"In his first chapter, a throat-clearing introduction that goes on for eighty-nine pages, he tells in outline what he will tell at great length in the chapters that lie ahead."* (Daniel Quammen *Harper's Magazine*; June 2003)

throat·latch /thrṓt làch/ *n* the strap that passes under a horse's jaw to hold its bridle in place

throat mi·cro·phone, **throat mike** *informal n* a microphone that is placed in contact with the throat to pick up the vibrations produced by speech

throat·y /thrṓtee/ (**-i·er, -i·est**) *adj* **1.** sounding deep and husky **2.** deep or rough in tone, as though having been produced in the throat —**throat·i·ly** *adv* —**throat·i·ness** *n*

throb /throb/ *vi* (**throbbed, throb·bing, throbs**) **1.** BEAT RAPIDLY AND FORCEFULLY to beat or pulsate in a rapid forceful way ○ *My head is throbbing.* **2.** BEAT REGULARLY to have a regular rhythmic beat ■ *n* **1.** SINGLE BEAT a single beat or pulsation **2.** REGULAR BEAT a regular beat or pulsation [14C. Probably an imitation of pulsating] —**throb·bing** *adj* —**throb·bing·ly** *adv*

throe /thrō/ *n* PANG a spasm of pain ■ **throes** *npl* **1.** EFFECTS OF PANGS the effects of severe physical pain **2.** EFFECTS OF UPHEAVAL the effects of an upheaval or struggle [12C. Origin ?] ◇ **in the throes of something** in the process of doing something, usually something difficult or unpleasant

thromb- *prefix* same as **thrombo-** (*used before vowels*)

throm·bi MED plural of **thrombus**

throm·bin /thrómbin/ *n* an enzyme in blood that causes clotting by catalyzing the conversion of fibrinogen to fibrin [Late 19C. < THROMBO-]

thrombo- *prefix* blood clot ○ *thromboplastic* [< Greek *thrombos* "clot"]

throm·bo·cyte /thrómbə sīt/ *n* BIOL same as **platelet** —**throm·bo·cyt·ic** /thròmbə síttik/ *adj*

throm·bo·cy·to·pe·ni·a /thròmbə sītə péenee ə/ *n* the state of having fewer than the normal number of blood platelets per unit volume of blood, often associated with hemorrhaging [Early 20C. < THROMBOCYTE] —**throm·bo·cy·to·pe·nic** *adj*

throm·bo·em·bo·lism /thròmbō émbə lìzzəm/ *n* the blockage of a blood vessel by a blood clot (**thrombus**) that has broken away from its site of origin —**throm·bo·em·bol·ic** /thròmbō em bóllik/ *adj* —**throm·bo·em·bo·lit·ic** /thròmbō embə líttik/ *adj*

throm·bo·ki·nase /thrómbō kī nàyss, -nàyz/ *n* BIOCHEM same as **thromboplastin**

throm·bol·y·sis /throm bólləssiss/ *n* the breaking down of a blood clot by infusion of an enzyme into the blood —**throm·bo·lyt·ic** /thròmbə líttik/ *adj*

throm·bo·phle·bi·tis /thròmbō flə bītiss/ *n* inflammation of a vein with the formation of a blood clot

throm·bo·plas·tic /thròmbō plástik/ *adj* causing or increasing blood-clot formation —**throm·bo·plas·ti·cal·ly** *adv*

throm·bo·plas·tin /thròmbō plástin/ *n* a blood-clotting factor in blood platelets that converts prothrombin to thrombin

throm·bose /thróm bōz/ (**-bosed, -bos·ing, -bos·es**) *vti* to affect something such as a coronary artery with thrombosis, or be affected by thrombosis

throm·bo·sis /throm bṓssiss/ (*plural* **-bo·ses** /-bō seez/) *n* the formation or presence of one or more blood clots that may partially or completely block an artery or vein [Early 18C. < modern Latin < Greek *thrombos* "clot"] —**throm·bot·ic** /throm bóttik/ *adj*

throm·box·ane /throm bók sàyn/ *n* a substance in platelets that causes blood clotting and constriction of blood vessels

throm·bus /thrómbəss/ (*plural* **-bi** /-bī/) *n* a blood clot that forms in a blood vessel and remains at the site of formation [Late 17C. Via modern Latin < Greek *thrombos* "clot"]

throne /thrōn/ *n* **1.** CHAIR OF MONARCH OR BISHOP an ornate chair, often raised on a platform and covered by a canopy, occupied by a monarch or bishop on ceremonial occasions **2.** PERSON ON THRONE somebody who has the status to occupy a throne **3.** POWER OF ROYAL PERSON the power, rank, and privileges of a monarch **4.** ANGEL OF SEVENTH-HIGHEST ORDER an angel of the seventh of the nine orders of angels in the traditional Christian hierarchy ■ *v* (**throned, thron·ing, thrones**) **1.** *vti* PUT SOMEBODY ON THRONE to place somebody on a throne, or be placed on a throne **2.** *vi* SIT ON THRONE to be seated on a throne [12C. Via Old French *trone* < Greek *thronos*] —**throne·less** *adj*

Throne Speech *n Can* a speech written by the Canadian government outlining its proposed measures for the legislative session, read at the opening of Parliament by the sovereign, the Governor General, or the Lieutenant Governor

throng /thrawng/ *n* CROWD a large crowd of people or objects ■ *v* (**thronged, throng·ing, throngs**) 1. *vt* CROWD INTO PLACE to crowd into or fill a place 2. *vi* MOVE IN CROWD to move or gather in a throng 3. *vt* CROWD AROUND SOMEBODY to surround and push against somebody [Old English *geþrang* < Germanic, "to press, crowd"]

thros·tle /thróss'l/ *n* 1. a thrush, especially a song thrush (*literary*) 2. a machine formerly used for the continuous spinning of cotton or wool fibers [Old English *þrostle* < Indo-European]

throt·tle /thrótt'l/ *n* 1. VALVE CONTROLLING FLUID FLOW a valve used to control the flow of a fluid, especially the amount of fuel and air entering the cylinders of an internal-combustion engine 2. CONTROL FOR THROTTLE a pedal or lever for controlling a throttle valve ■ *v* (**-tled, -tling, -tles**) 1. *vt* KILL PERSON OR ANIMAL BY CHOKING to kill or injure a person or animal by squeezing the throat 2. *vt* SILENCE OR SUPPRESS SOMEBODY OR SOMETHING to prevent somebody or something from expressing an opinion freely or from engaging in an activity 3. *vt* STOP SOMETHING FROM PROGRESSING to prevent something from continuing or developing ○ *policies that throttle foreign investment* 4. *vti* REGULATE FUEL FLOW USING THROTTLE to regulate the amount of fuel entering an engine using a throttle 5. *vti* REGULATE ENGINE SPEED to regulate the speed of an engine by using a throttle [14C. < THROAT] —**throt·tler** *n*

throt·tle·hold /thrótt'l hōld/ *n US* WRESTLING same as **stranglehold**

through /throo/ CORE MEANING: a grammatical word used to indicate movement from one side or end of something to or past the other side or end
1. *prep, adv* PASSING ACROSS passing from one side or end of something to the other ○ *bored a hole through the wall* ○ *trying to find a way through* 2. *prep, adv* TRAVELING ACROSS traveling across or to various places in a town, country, or area ○ *He spent the summer traveling through Europe.* ○ *We're not stopping long; we're just passing through.* 3. *prep, adv* AMONG in the midst of, or having things or people all around or on either side of ○ *She wandered through the crowds milling around outside the cathedral.* ○ *I'd like to browse through and see if there are any articles that interest me.* 4. *prep, adv* PAST BARRIER past the limitations or difficulties of something such as a barrier or a problem ○ *the problems involved in wading through acres of bureaucracy* ○ *The road has been narrowed to prevent larger vehicles getting through.* 5. *prep, adv* FROM BEGINNING TO END from the beginning until the end or conclusion of ○ *Martin and Johanson's works will be on view through June.* ○ *I can't come I'm afraid; I'm working through.* 6. *prep, adv* TO CONCLUSION to completion, to a usually successful conclusion, or so as to have finished with something ○ *She sailed through the exam.* ○ *They had to twist a few arms to get the proposal through.* ○ *The champion, as expected, is through to the second round.* 7. *prep* VIA by way or means of ○ *I'll send you a copy through the mail.* 8. *prep* OVER EXTENT OF happening or existing over the entire extent of or affecting all of ○ *A flu of epidemic proportions swept through the town.* 9. *prep* BECAUSE OF as a result of ○ *Through his mishandling of our affairs, we'll be lucky to have any credit at all this year.* 10. *prep* UP TO AND INCLUDING up to and including that time ○ *Museum hours are 2–4 p.m. Tuesdays through Fridays.* 11. *adv* THOROUGHLY completely and in every part ○ *Your clothes are wet through.* 12. *adv* ABLE TO SPEAK ON PHONE so as to establish a telephone connection with somebody ○ *We've been trying to get through all morning but the lines are busy.* ○ *You're through to Ms. Spriggs.* 13. *adj* GOING DIRECTLY going directly without stopping or requiring a change ○ *The through train leaves on the hour.* 14. *adj* PASSING THROUGH SOMETHING proceeding or extending from one side or end of something to the other or through something and beyond it ○ *a through room* ○ *through traffic* [Old English *þurh* < Indo-European, "pass through"] ◇ **be through with somebody** (*informal*) 1. to want to have nothing else to do with somebody 2. to have finished doing something, often something unpleasant, to somebody ○ *When I'm through with him, he really will have a headache!* ◇ **be through with something** to have finished with something (*informal*) ◇ **through and through** completely

through-com·posed *adj* describes a song with different music for each verse, especially without pauses between the verses, or an opera that is not clearly divided into arias and recitatives

through·out /throo ówt/ *prep, adv* 1. through or during the whole of ○ *Societies throughout history believed they had reached the frontiers of human accomplishment.* ○ *Throughout, they maintained their dignity.* 2. happening or existing in all parts of ○ *The group is seeking experts of any age throughout the area.* ○ *The house is carpeted throughout.*

through·put /throo pòot/ *n* the amount of something such as data or raw material that is processed over a given period [After INPUT and OUTPUT]

through·way /throo wày/, **thru·way** *n* ROADS same as **expressway**

throve past tense of **thrive**

throw /thrō/ *vt* (**threw** /throo/, **thrown** /thrōn/, **throw·ing, throws**) 1. SEND SOMETHING FROM HAND to propel something through the air by swinging the arm and releasing the object from the hand ○ *throw a rock through a window* 2. SEND FORTH SOMETHING INTO AIR to propel something through or into the air by a mechanical means, or to emit or radiate something ○ *Is the fireplace throwing any heat yet?* 3. DROP SOMETHING CARELESSLY to put or drop something somewhere without paying attention to where it is left ○ *throws magazines all over the place* 4. FORCE SOMEBODY OR SOMETHING SOMEWHERE to put somebody or something forcefully into a particular position or in a particular direction ○ *He was thrown out.* 5. PUT SOMEBODY OR SOMETHING IN DIFFERENT CIRCUMSTANCES to bring somebody or something suddenly or unexpectedly into a particular state, especially an undesirable one ○ *thrown out of a job* ○ *thrown into confusion* 6. HURL SOMEBODY TO GROUND to make a movement that causes somebody, e.g., an opponent in wrestling or judo or a horseback rider to fall to the ground 7. DISCONCERT SOMEBODY to take somebody by surprise to the extent that he or she does not know how to react ○ *His unexpected arrival threw me.* 8. PROJECT LIGHT to send out light to illuminate a place, or create a shadow by blocking light 9. CAST DOUBT OR SUSPICION to cause doubt or suspicion in people's minds by saying or doing something 10. DIRECT EYES to direct a look or glance quickly or suddenly ○ *She threw me a warning look.* 11. HAVE EXTREME REACTION to react with a sudden outburst of strong emotion, e.g., anger or ill-temper ○ *throw a tantrum* 12. MOVE OPERATING SWITCH OR LEVER to move something, usually a switch or lever, to make a machine or system operate or to connect up a system 13. BUILD SOMETHING HASTILY to build or erect something hastily ○ *The enemy threw a bridge across the moat.* 14. MAKE OBJECT ON POTTER'S WHEEL to produce a ceramic object by turning clay on a potter's wheel 15. TURN MATERIAL ON LATHE to turn wood or metal on a lathe 16. MAKE MATERIAL INTO YARN to make silk or filaments into thread by twisting or spinning 17. DELIVER PUNCH to deliver a punch or blow with a movement of the arm 18. HOST PARTY to organize and be the host at a party 19. LOSE SOMETHING INTENTIONALLY to lose a fight, race, or contest deliberately, e.g., by not trying or by committing a foul 20. PROJECT VOICE to project a vocal sound so that it seems to be coming from elsewhere 21. LEISURE ROLL DICE to tip or roll dice onto a flat surface to obtain a score, or score a particular number in this way 22. GIVE BIRTH TO YOUNG to give birth to young (*refers especially to cows*) 23. *Malaysia, Singapore* same as **throw away** (sense 1) ○ *Once you get your new card you can throw the old one.* ■ *n* 1. ACT OF THROWING an act of throwing something such as a ball or missile, or dice in a game 2. DISTANCE THROWN the distance that something is thrown or can be thrown 3. SPORTS WAY OF THROWING an act of being thrown, or a way of throwing an opponent, in wrestling or judo 4. LEISURE SCORE THROWN the score obtained by throwing something such as dice or darts in a game 5. EACH each item or attempt (*informal*) ○ *I didn't buy any; they were ten dollars a throw.* 6. HOUSEHOLD COVER FOR FURNITURE a loose cover used to protect furniture 7. MECH ENG MOVEMENT OF MACHINE PART the maximum movement in a single direction of a machine part driven by a crank, cam, or eccentric 8. PHYS DEFLECTION OF MEASURING INSTRUMENT the distance moved by the tip of the needle of a measuring instrument 9. GEOL VERTICAL DISPLACEMENT ALONG GEOLOGIC FAULT the vertical displacement up or down produced by movement along a geologic fault [Old English *þrāwan* "twist, hurl" < Indo-European, "to twist"] —**throw·er** *n* ◇ **throw yourself into something** to start doing something with great energy and commitment

SYNONYMS ***throw, chuck, fling, hurl, toss, cast***

CORE MEANING: to send something through the air

throw to propel something through the air by swinging the arm and releasing the object from the hand ○ *Fred applauded and threw his hat into the air.* ○ *Police sprayed tear gas when about 500 protesters threw rocks at a passenger train.* **chuck** (*informal*) to throw something, especially in a careless or casual way ○ *He chucked the forms in the wastebasket.* **fling** to throw something or somebody carelessly or forcefully ○ *She flung herself face down on the bed.* ○ *Seb flung aside his pitchfork and climbed down from the loft.* **hurl** to throw something with great force ○ *Rebels fired gunshots and hurled grenades at the police station.* ○ *The elephant seized the boy with its trunk and hurled him to the ground.* **toss** to throw something small or light in a casual or careless way ○ *One of the children tossed a ball high in the air.* ○ *David sat back in his armchair, tossing aside his magazine.* **cast** to throw something to a particular place or into a particular thing, or to throw a fishing line or net ○ *He was cast overboard like so much ballast.*

throw away *vt* 1. DISCARD SOMETHING to get rid of something no longer wanted 2. WASTE SOMETHING to fail to take advantage of an opportunity to do something 3. SAY SOMETHING IN OFFHAND MANNER to say a line in a play in a way that makes it seem unimportant, even though it may be crucial to the plot 4. PUT CARD DOWN in a card game, to discard a card

throw in *vt* 1. to contribute a comment to a conversation or discussion 2. to add something as an extra, especially another item at no extra cost when selling something

throw off *vt* 1. STYMIE PURSUER to make a pursuer lose something such as a scent or a trail 2. MAKE SOMEBODY FLUSTERED to confuse or unsettle somebody by doing something unexpected 3. GIVE OFF SOMETHING to emit a substance into the air 4. FREE YOURSELF FROM SOMETHING to get rid of something troublesome or oppressive 5. TAKE CLOTHES OFF HASTILY to remove an item of clothing in a hurried or careless way 6. SAY SOMETHING IN OFFHAND WAY to say or write something in a casual manner

throw on *vt* to put an item of clothing on in a hurried or careless way

throw out *vt* 1. DISCARD SOMETHING to get rid of something no longer wanted, especially something that has been kept for a while 2. EJECT SOMEBODY to eject somebody forcibly from a place 3. DISMISS SOMEBODY to expel somebody from membership of an organization 4. SUGGEST SOMETHING to make a suggestion, proposal, or hint, especially in an informal way 5. PUT BASEBALL PLAYER OUT in baseball, to throw the ball to a teammate who puts the runner out 6. GIVE OFF SOMETHING to emit a substance into the air 7. REJECT LAWSUIT to reject a lawsuit so that the defendant does not have to stand trial 8. DISCONCERT SOMEBODY to confuse or unsettle somebody by doing something unexpected

throw over *vt* to end a romantic or sexual relationship with somebody (*informal*)

throw together *vt* (*informal*) 1. to make something in a hurry or carelessly 2. to cause people to meet and become acquainted with each other in a casual or unplanned way

throw up *v* 1. *vt* BUILD SOMETHING HASTILY to erect a building or structure quickly 2. *vti* VOMIT to vomit the contents of the stomach (*informal*) 3. *vt* ABANDON SOMETHING to give something up, especially something important or valuable (*informal*)

throw·a·way /thrṓ ə wày/ *adj* 1. DISPOSABLE designed to be thrown away after use 2. WASTEFUL tending to discard things too readily ○ *a throwaway society* 3. OFFHAND said or written in an apparently offhand manner 4. ABANDONED BY PARENTS OR GUARDIANS having been thrown out by parents or guardians and living on the streets ■ *n* 1. SOMETHING TO BE DISCARDED an object designed to be thrown away after use 2. ADVERTISING LEAFLET OR HANDBILL an advertising leaflet or handbill that is discarded after being read 3. ABANDONED CHILD

OR YOUNG PERSON a child or young person thrown out by parents or guardians and living on the streets

throw·back /thrṓ bàk/ *n* **1. ORGANISM REVERTING TO EARLIER TYPE** an organism with the characteristics of an earlier type **2. REVERSION TO EARLIER TYPE** reversion to an earlier ancestral type **3. ANIMAL OR PERSON RESEMBLING ANCESTOR** an animal or person bearing a striking resemblance to an ancestor **4. ANACHRONISTIC THING** something contemporary that seems to belong to the past

throw-in *n* **1. RETURN OF SOCCER BALL TO PLAY** an act of returning a soccer ball to play from the sideline by propelling it from behind the head with both hands **2. RETURN OF BALL FROM OUTFIELD** an act of returning a baseball after it has been hit to the outfield **3. RETURN OF BASKETBALL TO PLAY** an act of returning a basketball to play by passing it onto the court **4.** CARDS **STRATAGEM AT BRIDGE** a surrender of a trick at bridge to an opponent who must then make a lead that will cost one or more tricks

throw·ing stick /thrṓ ing-/ *n* a device used in many traditional societies for launching a spear or dart

thrown past participle of **throw**

throw pil·low *n* a small decorative pillow placed on a couch or an armchair

throw rug *n* HOUSEHOLD same as **scatter rug**

throw·ster /thrṓstər/ *n* somebody who twists filaments into thread

throw weight *n* the total weight of a missile's payload, including the warhead and guidance system but not the rocket

thru /throo/ *prep, adv, adj* same as **through** (*informal*)

thrum[1] /thrum/ *v* (**thrummed, thrum·ming, thrums**) **1.** *vti* **STRUM** to strum on a stringed instrument **2.** *vi* **TAP STEADILY** to drum on something, especially with the fingers **3.** *vti* **SAY OR SPEAK MONOTONOUSLY** to say something or talk monotonously ■ *n* **MONOTONOUS BEAT** a low monotonous beating sound [Late 16C. An imitation of the sound] —**thrum·mer** *n*

thrum[2] /thrum/ *n* **1. THREAD END LEFT ON LOOM** an unwoven end or row of ends from warp threads that are left on a loom after the web has been cut off **2. FRINGE** a short fringe or thread end ■ **thrums** *npl* **YARN PIECES ADDED TO CANVAS** short pieces of yarn inserted in canvas in order to create a rough surface and prevent chafing or leaks ■ *vt* (**thrummed, thrum·ming, thrums**) **1. ADD FRINGES TO SOMETHING** to put fringes on something **2. INSERT YARN PIECES IN CANVAS** to insert pieces of yarn in canvas in order to create a rough surface and prevent chafing or leaks [Old English *þrum* < Indo-European]

~~**thruogh**~~ incorrect spelling of **through**

thrup·pence *npl* MONEY same as **threepence**

thrup·pen·ny *adj* MONEY same as **threepenny**

thrush

thrush[1] /thrush/ (*plural* **thrush·es** or *same*) *n* **1.** a small to medium-sized songbird with a slender beak, usually a speckled breast, and an often melodious song. It belongs to the family that includes the robin, wood thrush, and hermit thrush. Family: Turdidae. **2.** a bird that resembles a thrush, e.g., a North American waterthrush [Old English *þrysce* < W Germanic]

thrush[2] /thrush/ *n* **1. FUNGAL DISEASE OF MOUTH** a fungal infection of the mouth characterized by white patches **2. FUNGAL INFECTION OF VAGINA** a fungal infection of the vagina characterized by a white discharge and itching **3. DISEASE OF HORSE'S HOOF** infection of the fleshy part of a horse's foot (**frog**), causing softening of the horn and a foul-smelling discharge [Mid-17C. Origin ?]

thrust /thrust/ *v* (**thrust, thrust·ing, thrusts**) **1.** *vt* **PUSH SOMEBODY OR SOMETHING FORCEFULLY** to push somebody or something with a single movement of considerable force ○ *He thrust his hands into his pockets.* **2.** *vt* **FORCE SOMEBODY INTO SOMETHING** to force somebody to accept or deal with something ○ *He was thrust into the limelight.* **3.** *vti* **STRETCH OR EXTEND** to stretch or extend something, or be stretched or extended, with a dramatic or forceful effect ○ *towers thrusting skyward* **4.** *vti* **ATTACK BY STABBING** to attack somebody with a piercing or stabbing movement with a weapon **5.** *vti* **FORCE WAY** to move with a determined or forceful pushing motion ○ *We thrust our way through the crowd to the bar.* **6.** *vt* **INSERT SOMETHING** to add or insert material, usually inappropriately, into a context ■ *n* **1. GIST OR AIM OF SOMETHING** the chief meaning, direction, or purpose of something ○ *the thrust of her argument* **2. FORCEFUL PUSH** a forceful push or shove **3. FORWARD MOVEMENT** a forward movement or impetus **4. STABBING ACTION** a piercing or stabbing action **5. MILITARY ATTACK** a military assault or offensive **6.** AEROSP **REACTIVE FORCE OF EXPELLED GASES** the reactive force of expelled gases such as those generated by a rocket ship or jet engine **7.** ENG **FORCE OF PROPELLER** a propulsive force produced by a rotating propeller, e.g., on a ship or aircraft **8.** GEOL **FORCE IN EARTH'S CRUST** a force in the Earth's crust that results in recumbent folding of rock strata **9.** GEOL same as **thrust fault** **10.** CIV ENG **FORCE EXERTED BY STRUCTURE** the continuous force exerted sideways or downward by one structure on another, e.g., by an arch on an abutment or a rafter against a wall [12C. < Old Norse *þrýsta*] —**thrust·ful** *adj*

thrust bear·ing *n* a bearing designed to withstand axial loading and to prevent movement along the axis of a loaded shaft

thrust·er /thrústər/ *n* **1. ROCKET THAT CONTROLS ALTITUDE** a rocket on a spacecraft or high-altitude aircraft that controls an altitude or flight path **2. MANEUVERING DEVICE ON OIL-DRILLING VESSEL** a jet or propeller on an oil-drilling ship or offshore rig, used to maneuver it into position **3. SURFBOARD OR SAILBOARD WITH EXTRA FIN** a surfboard or sailboard equipped with one or more extra fins designed to give it greater speed or maneuverability

thrust fault *n* an inclined fault in which rocks on the lower side of the slope are displaced downward

thrust stage *n* a stage surrounded on three sides by the audience

thru·way *n* ROADS another spelling of **throughway**

Thu, Thu. *abbr US* CALENDAR Thursday

Thu·cyd·i·des /thoo síddi dèez/ (460?–400? B.C.) Athenian historian. A major figure in the development of historical writing, he is known for his *History of the Peloponnesian War*, a conflict in which he himself had fought.

> "War, which robs people of the easy supply of their daily wants, is a violent schoolmaster matching most men's tempers to their condition."
> [Thucydides, *History of the Peloponnesian War*; 431–413 B.C.]

> "Happiness depends on being free, and freedom depends on being courageous."
> [Thucydides, *History of the Peloponnesian War*; 431–413 B.C.]

thud /thud/ *n* **1. DULL HEAVY SOUND** a loud dull sound made by a heavy object impacting with a surface **2. DULL HEAVY BLOW** a blow that makes a dull heavy sound ■ *vi* (**thud·ded, thud·ding, thuds**) **MAKE THUD** to make a dull heavy sound [Early 16C. Probably < Old English *þyddan* "thrust"]

thug /thug/ *n* **1.** somebody, especially a criminal, who is brutal and violent **2.** *also* **Thug** a member of a former secret organization of robbers in India, worshipers of the goddess Kali, who strangled their victims [Early 19C. < Hindi *ṭhag* "swindler, cheat, robber" < Sanskrit *sthagayati* "covers, conceals"] —**thug·ger·y** *n* — **thug·gish** *adj*

thug·gee /thúggee/ *n* the method of robbery and murder by strangulation, characteristic of the former thugs of India [Mid-19C. < Hindi *ṭhagī* < *ṭhag* (see THUG)]

thu·ja /thóojə, -yə/ (*plural* **-jas** or *same*), **thu·ya** /thóoyə/ (*plural* **-yas** or *same*) *n* TREES same as **arborvitae** [Mid-18C. Via modern Latin *Thuja* < medieval Latin *thuia* "cedar" < Greek]

thu·li·um /thóolee əm/ *n* a very rare soft bright silvery gray metallic element of the lanthanide series. Source: monazite, bastnaesite. Use: X-ray source. Symbol **Tm**. See table at **element** [Late 19C. After *Thule*, most northerly region to the ancients; because first found in Norway]

thumb /thum/ *n* **1. THICKEST DIGIT ON HUMAN HAND** the thickest digit of the human hand, located next to the forefinger. It can be moved to face and touch the other fingers so that objects can be grasped. **2. ANIMAL'S DIGIT RESEMBLING HUMAN THUMB** a short thick digit in some animals, e.g., in many primates, that is adapted for grasping and corresponds to the human thumb **3. SECTION OF GLOVE FOR THUMB** the part of a glove or mitten that covers the thumb **4.** ARCHIT same as **ovolo** ■ *v* (**thumbed, thumb·ing, thumbs**) **1.** *vti* **HITCH RIDE** to obtain or try to obtain a ride by signaling with the thumb to passing drivers **2.** *vt* **MAKE SOMETHING DIRTY BY USE** to soil or cause wear on something, especially a book, by repeated handling (*often passive*) ○ *a well-thumbed book* **3.** *vti* **FLIP THROUGH PRINTED MATTER** to glance through the pages of a book or magazine [Old English *þūma* < Indo-European] —**thumb·less** *adj* ◇ **all thumbs** extremely awkward or clumsy ◇ **stick out like a sore thumb** to be completely obvious, or conspicuously out of place ◇ **twiddle your thumbs** to be idle or unoccupied, especially involuntarily ◇ **under somebody's thumb** under the influence and control of somebody

Thumb /thum/, **"General" Tom** (1838–83) US entertainer. Three feet four inches tall, he starred in various exhibitions and circuses (1842–82). Born **Stratton, Charles Sherwood**

thumb·hole /thúm hṑl/ *n* **1.** a hole in something such as a bowling ball into which a thumb can be inserted in order to provide a grip **2.** a hole in a wind instrument that is covered and uncovered by the thumb to produce notes

thumb in·dex *n* a series of labeled indentations cut into the pages of a book down the edge opposite the binding to allow a particular section to be located quickly —**thumb-in·dex** *vt*

thumb knot *n* same as **overhand knot**

thumb·nail /thúm nàyl/ *n* **1. NAIL OF THUMB** the hard growing plate of keratin on the surface of the tip of the thumb **2.** COMPUT **MINIATURE GRAPHIC IMAGE** a small version of a larger graphic image displayed on a computer monitor so as to save space ■ *adj* **CONCISE** covering the salient points concisely ○ *a thumbnail sketch*

thumb·nut /thúm nùt/ *n* CONSTR same as **wing nut**

thumb pi·an·o *n* a box-shaped African musical instrument with a row of tuned metal or wooden strips that vibrate when plucked by the thumb

thumb·print /thúm prìnt/ *n* an impression of the fleshy pad near the tip of the thumb, often used to identify people

thumb·screw /thúm skròo/ *n* **1.** an instrument of torture used to crush the thumbs **2.** a screw with a flat head to be turned with the thumb and forefinger

thumbs down *n* an indication of disapproval or rejection (*informal*)

thumb·stall /thúm stàwl/ *n* a sheath of rubber, leather, or fabric used to protect the thumb, e.g., by covering a dressing on an injured thumb

thumbs up *n* an indication of approval or acceptance (*informal*)

thumb·tack /thúm tàk/ *n* a short pin with a large flat head used for attaching papers or cards to a board by pressing into the board with the thumb ■ *vt* (**-tacked, -tack·ing, -tacks**) to affix papers or cards with one or more thumbtacks

Thum·mim /thúmmim/ *n* JUDAISM ➧ **Urim and Thummim** [Mid-16C. < Hebrew *tummīm*, plural of *tōm* "completeness"]

thump /thump/ *v* (**thumped, thump·ing, thumps**) **1.** *vi* PALPITATE OR POUND to beat very fast or loudly because of fear or excitement (*refers to the heart*) **2.** *vi* MAKE DULL HEAVY SOUND to make the loud dull sound that a heavy object makes when it impacts with a surface **3.** *vti* STRIKE HEAVILY to strike somebody or something heavily with the fist or an object **4.** *vt* DEFEAT SOMEBODY CONVINCINGLY to inflict a humiliating defeat upon somebody (*informal; often passive*) ○ *Our team was thumped 9–0.* ■ *n* **1.** DULL HEAVY SOUND the loud dull sound made by a heavy object impacting with a surface ○ *I heard a loud thump from next door.* **2.** HEAVY BLOW a heavy blow struck with the fist or an object [Mid-16C. An imitation of the sound] —**thump·er** *n*

thump·ing /thúmping/ (*informal*) *adj* huge, resounding, or impressive ○ *won by a thumping majority* ■ *adv* extremely or exceptionally ○ *a thumping good read* —**thump·ing·ly** *adv*

Thun /toon/ town in the canton of Bern, central Switzerland. Population: 39,854 (1998).

thun·ber·gia /thùn búrjə, -jee ə/ *n* a widely cultivated ornamental plant of the acanthus family with opposite pairs of simple leaves. Flowers: five-lobed, tubular. Native to: Africa, South Asia. Genus: *Thunbergia*. [Late 18C. < modern Latin *Thunbergia*, after C. P. *Thunberg* (1743–1822), Swedish botanist]

thun·der /thúndər/ *n* **1.** LOUD NOISE FOLLOWING LIGHTNING a loud rumbling noise caused by the rapid expansion of air suddenly heated by lightning **2.** NOISE RESEMBLING THUNDER a loud deep rumbling noise resembling thunder **3.** THREATENING OR VEHEMENT UTTERANCE a manifestation of somebody's anger in an explosion of strong words ■ *v* (**-dered, -der·ing, -ders**) **1.** *vi* MAKE LOUD NOISE FOLLOWING LIGHTNING to make a loud rumbling noise caused by the rapid expansion of air suddenly heated by lightning **2.** *vi* RUMBLE LOUDLY LIKE THUNDER to make a loud deep rumbling noise resembling thunder **3.** *vti* SHOUT VEHEMENTLY to shout something loudly and angrily [Old English *þunor* (noun), *þunrian* (verb) < Indo-European] ◇ **steal somebody's thunder** to prevent somebody from receiving acclaim for doing something by doing it or something similar first

thun·der·a·tion /thùndə ráysh'n/ *n US* used as an expression of annoyance or surprise (*humorous*)

Thun·der Bay /thúndər-/ city in northwestern Ontario, Canada, on Thunder Bay, an arm of Lake Superior. Population: 103,215 (2001).

The Purcell team/Corbis

thunderbird: totem pole, Stanley Park, Vancouver, Canada

thun·der·bird /thúndər bùrd/ *n* in Native North American mythology, a bird that produces thunder

thun·der·bolt /thúndər bōlt/ *n* **1.** FLASH OF LIGHTNING WITH THUNDER a flash of lightning accompanied by a crash of thunder **2.** STARTLING OCCURRENCE a sudden shocking action, occurrence, pronouncement, or piece of news **3.** MYTHOLOGICAL WEAPON WIELDED BY GODS in mythology, a destructive missile hurled to Earth by a god in a flash of lightning **4.** FORMIDABLE PERSON OR THING somebody or something that resembles a thunderbolt in energy or destructive power

thun·der·clap /thúndər klàp/ *n* **1.** CRASH OF THUNDER a loud crashing noise produced by thunder **2.** STARTLING OCCURRENCE a sudden shocking occurrence or piece of news **3.** NOISE RESEMBLING THUNDER a sudden loud sound resembling thunder

thun·der·cloud /thúndər klòwd/ *n* a large dark cumulonimbus cloud that produces thunder and lightning

thun·der·head /thúndər hèd/ *n* the upper rounded mass of a cumulonimbus cloud associated with the development of a thunderstorm

thun·der·ing /thúndəring/ *UK* (*dated informal*) *adj* very great ■ *adv* extremely or exceptionally —**thun·der·ing·ly** *adv*

thun·der·ous /thúndərəss, -drəss/ *adj* **1.** resembling thunder in its loudness ○ *thunderous applause* **2.** angry and threatening —**thun·der·ous·ly** *adv*

thun·der run *n* formerly, either of two inclined wooden troughs down which iron balls were rolled offstage to simulate thunder as a theatrical sound effect

thun·der sheet *n* a large sheet of metal shaken to simulate thunder as a theatrical sound effect

thun·der·show·er /thúndər shòw ər/ *n* a shower of rain during a thunderstorm

thun·der·stone /thúndər stōn/ *n* a naturally occurring long tapering piece of rock, formerly believed to be a thunderbolt

thun·der·storm /thúndər stàwrm/ *n* a storm with thunder, lightning, heavy rain, and sometimes hail

thun·der·struck /thúndər strùk/ *adj* so surprised, incredulous, or startled as to be in a state of shock

thun·der·y /thúndəree/ *adj* **1.** causing or indicating the onset of thunder or a thunderstorm **2.** resembling thunder in sound

thunk[1] /thungk/ (*informal*) *n* same as **thud** *n* (sense 1) ■ *vi* to make a thudding sound [Mid-20C. An imitation of the sound]

thunk[2] /thungk/ past participle, past tense of **think** (*nonstandard*)

Thur. *abbr* CALENDAR Thursday

Thur·ber /thúrbər/, **James** (1894–1961) US writer and cartoonist. He is known for his humorous and poignant portrayals of the frustrations and absurd situations of modern life. Full name **Thurber, James Grover**

> "Then, with that faint fleeting smile playing about his lips, he faced the firing squad; erect and motionless, proud and disdainful, Walter Mitty, the undefeated, inscrutable to the last."
> [James Thurber, "The Secret Life of Walter Mitty," *My World—And Welcome to It*; 1942]

thu·ri·ble /thóorəb'l/ *n* RELIG same as **censer** [15C. Directly or via French < Latin *t(h)uribulum* < Greek *thuos* "sacrifice, incense"]

thu·ri·fer /thóorəfər/ *n* somebody who carries the censer in religious ceremonies [Mid-19C. < late Latin < Greek *thuos* "sacrifice, incense"]

Thur·mond /thúrmənd/, **Strom** (1902–2003) US politician. He was first elected to the Senate in 1954 as a Democrat but switched to the Republican Party (1964). In 1996 he became the oldest person ever to serve in Congress, and in 1997 he became the longest-serving US senator.

Thurs. *abbr* CALENDAR Thursday

Thurs·day /thúrz dày, -dee/ *n* the fourth day of the traditional working week, coming after Wednesday and before Friday [Old English *þu(n)resdæg* "day of thunder," translation of late Latin *Jovis dies* "day of Jupiter (the god of thunder)"]

Thurs·day Is·land /thúrz day-/ island in the Torres Strait, off the northeastern coast of Australia. Area: 1.4 sq. mi./3.6 sq. km.

Thurs·days /thúrz dàyz, -deez/ *adv* every Thursday

thus /thuss/ *adv* (*formal*) **1.** as a result ○ *He did no work at all, and thus was fired.* **2.** in this way ○ *Touch your left knee with your right elbow thus.* [Old English *þus*, origin ?] ◇ **thus far** up to this point ○ *The evidence thus far suggested that he was innocent.*

USAGE ***thus*** **not** ***thusly***: The form ***thusly***, meaning "in this way," is regarded as humorous, so in formal contexts ***thus*** is the appropriate choice: *The sentence reads thus* [not *thusly*]. *The guests were seated thus* [not *thusly*] *in the State Dining Room.*

USAGE See ***therefore***.

thus·ly /thússlee/ *adv US* same as **thus** (sense 2) (*humorous*)

USAGE See ***thus***.

Thut·mo·se III /thoot mṓssə/ (*d.* 1450 B.C.) Egyptian pharaoh. He became pharaoh in 1504 B.C. Through military conquest, he extended the Egyptian empire eastward as far as the Euphrates River, and with the vast wealth of his eastern territories erected great temples and other imperial buildings in Egypt.

thu·ya *n* TREES another spelling of **thuja**

thwack /thwak/ *vt* (**thwacked, thwack·ing, thwacks**) to strike somebody or something with a flat object such as the flat of the hand ■ *n* a sharp smacking blow with a flat object [Early 16C. An imitation of the sound] —**thwack·er** *n*

thwart /thwawrt/ *v* (**thwart·ed, thwart·ing, thwarts**) **1.** *vt* FRUSTRATE SOMETHING to prevent somebody or somebody's plan from being successful **2.** *vti* PLACE OR BE PLACED ACROSS to place one thing across another, or be placed across something (*archaic*) ■ *adj* EXTENDING ACROSS situated or extending across something ■ *n* CROSSWISE SEAT IN BOAT a crosswise seat or transverse member on a rowboat, canoe, or similar small boat ■ *prep, adv* same as **athwart** (*archaic*) [13C. < Old Norse *þvert*] —**thwart·ed·ly** /thwáwrtədlee/ *adv* —**thwart·er** *n*

THX *abbr* ONLINE thanks (*used in e-mails or text messages*)

thy /thī/ *adj* belonging or relating to you, the second person singular possessive corresponding to "thou" (*archaic*) [12C. Shortening of THINE]

Thy·es·tes /thī ésteez/ *n* in Greek mythology, the brother of Atreus and king of Mycenae. After usurping the throne from his brother, he was tricked into eating the flesh of his own sons. —**Thy·es·te·an** *adj*

thy·la·cine /thī́lə sīn, -ləssin/ *n* a large carnivorous marsupial that resembles a dog and has brownish fur and black stripes across the back. It was once widespread throughout Australia but is now thought to be extinct. Native to: Tasmania. Latin name: *Thylacinus cynocephalus*. [Mid-19C. < modern Latin *Thylacinus* < Greek *thulakos* "pouch"]

thyme

thyme /tīm, thīm/ *n* a small low-growing bush with small aromatic leaves. Use: cooking, source of thymol. Genus: *Thymus*. [15C. Via Old French *thym* < Greek *thumon* < *thuein* "burn, sacrifice"; from its use as incense] —**thym·y** *adj*

SPELLCHECK Do not confuse the spelling of ***thyme*** and ***time***, which sound similar. ***Thyme*** is a bush whose leaves are used in cooking. ***Time*** is a dimension, or the minute or hour as indicated by a clock, and can also be used as a verb: *space and time, asked the time, timed at one hour two minutes.*

thy·mec·to·my /thī méktəmee/ (*plural* **-mies**) *n* surgical removal of the thymus gland [Early 20C. < THYMUS]

thy·mi ANAT plural of **thymus**

-thymia *suffix* condition or state of mind ○ *cyclothymia* [Via modern Latin < Greek *thumos* "mind"]

thy·mic[1] /thīmik/ *adj* relating to the thymus [Mid-17C. < THYMUS]

thy·mic[2] /tīmik, thīmik/ *adj* relating to thyme [Mid-19C. < THYME]

thy·mi·dine /thīmə dēen/ *n* a nucleoside in DNA, consisting of thymine linked to deoxyribose [Early 20C. < THYMINE + -IDINE]

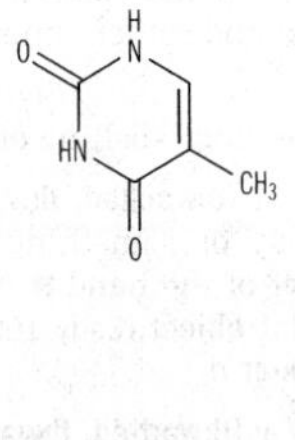

thymine

thy·mine /thī mēen, thīmin/ *n* one of the four nitrogenous bases in DNA in which it pairs with adenine. Formula: $C_5H_6N_2O_2$. Symbol **T** [Late 19C. < THYMIC[1]]

thy·mo·cyte /thīmə sīt/ *n* a small white blood cell **(lymphocyte)** occurring in the thymus that is a precursor of a T-cell

thy·mol /thī màwl/ *n* a colorless crystalline phenol with an aromatic odor. Source: thyme oil, synthetically made. Use: fungicide, preservative, vermifuge, perfumes. Formula: $C_{10}H_{14}O$. [Mid-19C. < Greek *thumon* (see THYME)]

thy·mo·ma /thī mṓmə/ (*plural* **-mas** or **-ma·ta** /-mətə/) *n* a tumor of the thymus [Early 20C. < Greek *thumos* (see THYMUS)]

thy·mo·sin /thīməssin/ *n* a hormone that influences the development and differentiation of T-cells in the thymus [Mid-20C. < Greek *thumos* (see THYMUS)]

thy·mus /thīməss/ (*plural* **-mus·es** or **-mi** /-mī/), **thy·mus gland** *n* an organ, located at the base of the neck, that is involved in development of cells of the immune system, particularly T cells. It is prominent in the young but shrinks after puberty. [Late 16C. Via modern Latin < Greek *thumos* "warty growth resembling a bunch of thyme" < *thumon* (see THYME)]

thy·ra·tron /thīrə tròn/ *n* a gas-filled hot-cathode tube that acts as an electronic switch or relay in which a signal applied to the control grid initiates anode current but does not limit it [Early 20C. < Greek *thura* "door"]

thy·ris·tor /thī rístər/ *n* a semiconductor device that has two stable switches used for conductive and nonconductive modes [Mid-20C. Blend of THYRATRON + TRANSISTOR]

thyro- *prefix* thyroid ○ *thyrotropin* [< THYROID]

thy·ro·cal·ci·to·nin /thìrō kàlssə tṓnin/ *n* BIOCHEM same as **calcitonin**

thy·roid /thī ròyd/ *n* **1.** ANAT same as **thyroid gland 2.** ANAT same as **thyroid cartilage 3.** PHARM **MEDICINE OBTAINED FROM ANIMAL THYROID GLAND** a preparation obtained from the thyroid gland of an animal. Use: treating conditions of the thyroid gland. ■ *adj also* **thy·roi·dal** /thī róyd'l/ **1. OF THYROID GLAND** relating to, situated in, or secreted by the thyroid gland **2. OF THYROID CARTILAGE** relating to the thyroid cartilage [Early 18C. < obsolete French *thyroide* < Greek *thura* "door"; from the oblong shape of the cartilage in front of the throat]

thy·roid car·ti·lage *n* the largest cartilage of the larynx, forming the projection called the Adam's apple

thy·roid·ec·to·my /thì roy déktəmee/ (*plural* **-mies**) *n* surgical removal of the thyroid gland or part of it

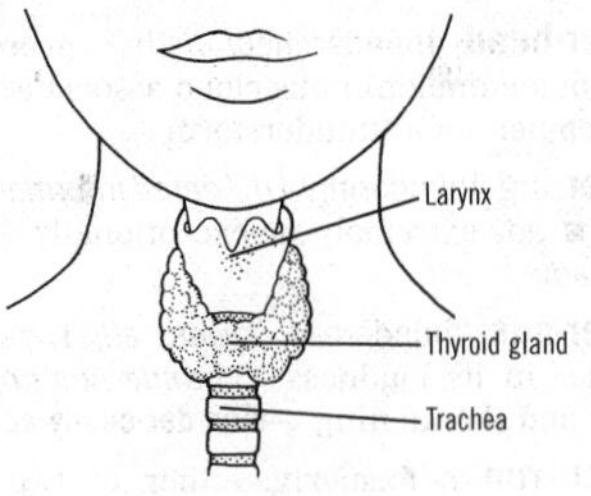

thyroid gland

thy·roid gland *n* an endocrine gland located in the neck of human beings and other vertebrate animals that secretes the hormones responsible for controlling metabolism and growth. Excessive action of the thyroid gland can cause Graves' disease, while underactivity can cause myxedema.

thy·roid hor·mone *n* either of the two hormones, thyroxine and triiodothyronine, that are secreted by the thyroid gland and regulate body metabolism and growth

thy·roid·i·tis /thì roy dītiss/ *n* inflammation of the thyroid gland. This may be acute, as a result of bacterial infection, or chronic, as a result of an autoimmune response in which lymphocytes invade the gland.

thy·roid-stim·u·lat·ing hor·mone *n* BIOCHEM same as **thyrotropin**

thy·ro·tox·i·co·sis /thìrō toksə kṓssiss/ *n* MED same as **hyperthyroidism** (sense 1)

thy·ro·tro·pin /thìrə trṓpin/, **thy·ro·tro·phin** /-trṓfin/ *n* a hormone that is secreted by the anterior lobe of the pituitary gland and stimulates release of hormones by the thyroid gland [Mid-20C. < THYRO- + -TROPIC + -IN]

thy·ro·tro·pin-re·leas·ing hor·mone *n* a peptide hormone that is produced by the hypothalamus and controls the release of thyrotropin by the pituitary gland

thy·rox·ine /thī rók sēen/, **thy·rox·in** /-róksin/ *n* the principal hormone secreted by the thyroid gland, which stimulates metabolism and is essential for normal growth and development. A synthetic form is used to treat hypothyroidism. [Early 20C. < THYRO- + OXY- + INDOLE (from a misunderstanding of its chemical structure), altered after -INE]

thyrse /thurss/ *n* a flower head that consists of numerous branching clusters of individual flowers arising from a single main stem, e.g., in lilacs [Early 17C. Via French < Latin *thyrsus* "stalk of plant"] —**thyr·soid** *adj*

thyr·sus /thúrssəss/ (*plural* **thyr·si** /thúrssī/) *n* **1.** in Greek mythology and art, a staff tipped with a pine cone, carried by the Greek god Dionysus and his followers **2.** BOT same as **thyrse** [Late 16C. Via Latin < Greek *thursos* "stalk of a plant, staff carried by Dionysus"]

thy·sa·nu·ran /thìssə nóorən/ *n* INSECTS same as **bristletail** [Mid-19C. < modern Latin *Thysanura* < Greek *thusanos* "tassel, fringe" + *oura* "tail"] —**thy·sa·nu·rous** *adj*

thy·self /thī sélf/ *pron* (*archaic*) **1.** the form of "thy" used to refer to the same person who is being addressed and is the subject of the verb **2.** used to emphasize that the person being addressed is also being referred to [Pre-12C. Originally < THEE + SELF (adjective), but interpreted as being < THY + SELF (noun)]

THz *abbr* PHYS, MEASURE terahertz

ti[1] /tee/ *n US* a syllable that represents the seventh note in a scale when singing solfeggio. In fixed solfeggio it represents the note B. [Mid-19C. Alteration of SI[1]]

ti[2] /tee/ (*plural* **tis**) *n* a woody plant with leaves that yield a useful fiber and roots that are used as food or in beverages. Native to: Polynesia, Australia. Genus: *Cordyline*. [Mid-19C. < Tahitian and Maori]

Ti *symbol* CHEM ELEM titanium

TIA *abbr* **1.** ONLINE thanks in advance (*used in e-mails or text messages*) **2.** MED transient ischemic attack

ti·a·ben·da·zole PHARM same as **thiabendazole**

Tian·an·men Square /tyàan àan mèn-/ *n* a large square in central Beijing, China, that is a traditional site for festivals, rallies, and demonstrations. In 1989, it was the scene of a prodemocracy demonstration led by students in which hundreds were killed when troops were ordered to clear the square.

Tian·jin /tyèn jín/ municipality in northeastern China, near Beijing. It is a major industrial center and port. Population: 9,420,000 (1995).

Tian Shan ♦ **Tien Shan**

tiara

ti·ar·a /tee áarə, -érrə/ *n* **1. WOMAN'S JEWELED CORONET** a small jeweled semicircular headdress worn by a woman on formal occasions **2. POPE'S CROWN** a headdress consisting of three coronets with an orb and a cross on top, worn by the pope or carried before him on ceremonial occasions **3. PERSIAN KING'S CROWN** a high headdress worn by an ancient Persian king [Mid-16C. Directly and via Italian < Latin < Greek *tiara(s)*] —**ti·ar·aed** *adj*

Ti·ber /tībər/ river of central Italy. Rising in the Apennines, it flows through Rome and empties into the Tyrrhenian Sea. Length: 252 mi./406 km.

Ti·be·ri·us /tī bēeree əss/ (42 B.C.–A.D. 37) Roman emperor. His reign (A.D. 14–37) was marked by revolts and conspiracies. Full name **Tiberius Julius Caesar Augustus**

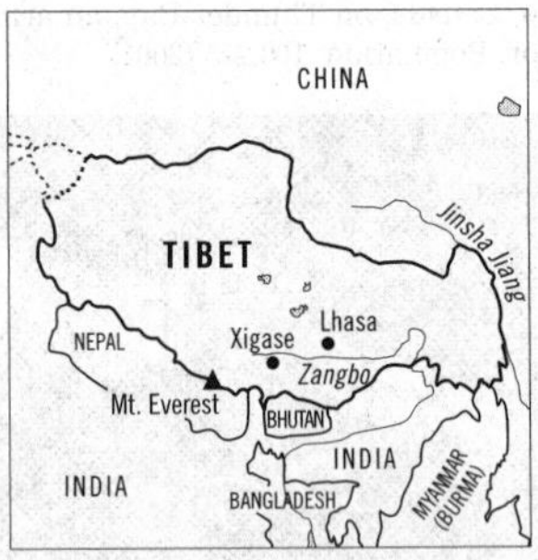

Tibet

Ti·bet /tə bét/ former independent state in and to the north of the Himalayan range, since 1965 a province-level administrative region of China. With an average elevation of more than 12,000 ft./4,000 m, it is the highest region in the world. Capital: Lhasa. Population: 2,620,000 (2000). Area: 471,800 sq. mi./1,222,000 sq. km. Official name **Tibet Autonomous Region**

Ti·bet·an /tə bétt'n/ *n* **1.** somebody who comes from Tibet **2.** the Tibeto-Burman language of Tibet, spoken also in neighboring parts of China, Nepal, and India. Native speakers: 6 million. —**Ti·bet·an** *adj*

Ti·bet·an Bud·dhism *n* BUDDHISM same as **Lamaism**

Ti·bet·o-Bur·man /tə bèttō búrmən/ *n* a branch of the Sino-Tibetan family of languages that includes Tibetan, Burmese, and many other languages of South and Southeast Asia —**Ti·bet·o-Bur·man** *adj*

tib·i·a /tíbbee ə/ (*plural* **-i·ae** /-ee ēe/ or **-i·as**) *n* **1. INNER BONE OF LOWER LEG** the inner and larger of the two bones in the lower leg, extending from the knee to the ankle bone alongside the fibula **2.** BONE IN ANIMAL'S LEG a bone in the lower leg of vertebrates corresponding to the human tibia **3.** PART OF INSECT'S LEG the fourth segment of an insect's leg, between the femur and the tarsus **4.** PART OF BIRD'S LEG the lower, often feathered segment of a bird's leg **5.** MUSIC ANCIENT WIND INSTRUMENT an ancient flute, originally made from an animal's tibia [Late 17C. < Latin, "shinbone, pipe"] —**tib·i·al** *adj*

tib·i·o·fib·u·lar /tìbbee ō fíbbyələr/ *adj* relating to the tibia and fibula, the bones of the lower leg

tib·i·o·tar·sus /tìbbee ō taárssəss/ (*plural* **-tar·si** /-sī/) *n* the main bone of a bird's lower leg, formed by a fusion of the tibia and some of the bones of the tarsus

tic /tik/ *n* **1.** a sudden involuntary spasmodic muscular contraction, especially of facial, neck, or shoulder muscles, which may become more pronounced when somebody is stressed **2.** a distinctive behavioral trait or quirk [Early 19C. Via French < Italian *ticchio*]

tic dou·lou·reux /tìk doolə roó, -rő/ *n* MED same as **trigeminal neuralgia** [< French, "painful tic"]

tich *n UK* another spelling of **titch** (*informal*)

Ti·ci·no /ti cheénō/ river in western Europe, a tributary of the Po River. Length: 154 mi./248 km.

tick[1] /tik/ *n* **1.** RECURRING CLICK a slight quiet recurring clicking sound, especially one made by a clock or watch **2.** DEGREE ON SCALE an increment on a scale, especially the smallest amount by which a security may rise or fall in a stock or bond market **3.** *UK* MOMENT a very short time (*informal*) ○ *I'll be back in a tick.* **4.** *UK* same as **check** *n* (sense 8) ■ *v* (**ticked, tick·ing, ticks**) **1.** *vi* MAKE RECURRING CLICKING SOUND to make a slight quiet recurring clicking sound **2.** *vi* FUNCTION PROPERLY to function well or in the right way (*informal*) **3.** *vi* REGISTER TAXI FARE BY CLICKING to make a clicking sound while registering the progressive increase of a taxi fare **4.** *vt UK* same as **check** *v* (sense 7) [13C. Origin ?] ◇ **what makes somebody tick** what causes somebody to behave and think in a particular way (*informal*)

tick away, tick by *vi* to pass or elapse at a steady pace (*refers to time*)

tick off *vt* **1.** to make somebody angry (*informal*) **2.** *UK* same as **check off**

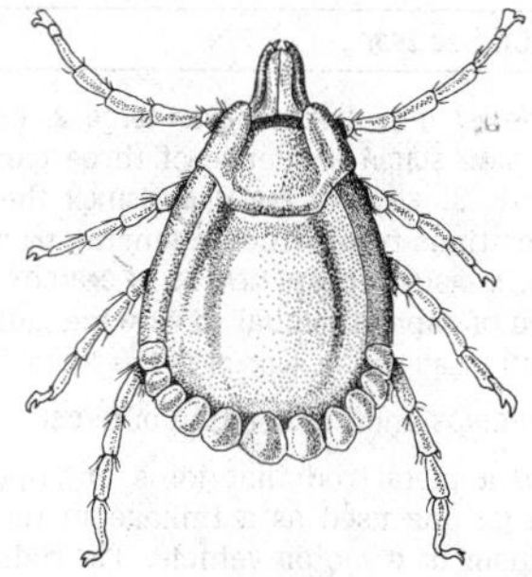

tick

tick[2] /tik/ *n* **1.** a small wingless bloodsucking insect that lives on the skin of humans and warm-blooded animals and may transmit diseases. Families: Argasidae or Ioxidae. **2.** a parasitic fly that lives on the skin of sheep, cattle, horses, and other animals [Old English *ticia* < Germanic]

tick[3] /tik/ *n* the cloth case or covering that is filled with cotton, feathers, or other materials to form a pillow or mattress [15C. Via Middle Dutch *tēke* < Greek *thēkē* "cover, case"]

tick[4] /tik/ *n UK* a system of credit for customers, especially an informal system (*dated informal*) ○ *bought it on tick* [Mid-17C. Shortening of TICKET "note of goods received on credit"]

tick·bird /tík bùrd/ *n* a bird that feeds on ticks, e.g., an oxpecker

tick-borne *adj* describes a disease in which the causative microorganism is transmitted by the bite of a tick, e.g., Lyme disease or many forms of encephalitis

tick·er /tíkər/ *n* **1.** FIN MACHINE DISPLAYING STOCK PRICES an electronic device that displays the prices of securities, formerly a telegraphic receiving instrument that automatically printed stock quotations on ticker tape **2.** HEART somebody's heart (*slang*) **3.** WATCH a small portable timepiece (*dated informal*)

tick·er tape *n* formerly, a continuous paper ribbon on which a ticker automatically printed stock quotations

tick·er-tape ma·chine *n US* FIN same as **ticker** (sense 1)

tick·er-tape pa·rade *n* a parade honoring a visiting celebrity who is showered with shredded paper or confetti, formerly ticker tape, from buildings while being driven through the streets

tick·et /tíkit/ *n* **1.** PASS FOR ENTERTAINMENT a printed piece of cardboard or paper showing that the holder is entitled to admission to a place of public entertainment or a sports facility **2.** TRAVEL PASS a printed piece of cardboard or paper showing that the holder is entitled to be traveling on a means of transport **3.** NOTIFICATION OF TRAFFIC OFFENSE a printed notice that a traffic or parking offense has been committed and a fine must be paid **4.** LABEL OR TAG a small piece of card attached to an article, showing the price or other details **5.** POL GROUP OF CANDIDATES RUNNING TOGETHER a list of candidates put forward by one party or group in an election **6.** PRECISELY WHAT IS NEEDED the right, just, desired, or appropriate thing (*informal*) ○ *A month in Europe would be just the ticket.* **7.** TRANSP QUALIFICATION OF PILOT OR SHIP'S OFFICER a certificate of qualification as a ship's captain or an aircraft pilot ■ *vt* (**-et·ed, -et·ing, -ets**) **1.** GIVE PARKING TICKET TO SOMEBODY to issue a motor vehicle or its driver a ticket for a traffic or parking violation **2.** ATTACH TICKET TO ARTICLE to attach a ticket to an item, showing the price or other details **3.** ISSUE PASS TO SOMETHING to issue a ticket for admission to something **4.** CATEGORIZE SOMEBODY OR SOMETHING to assign somebody to a particular category, or designate something for a particular purpose [Early 16C. < obsolete French *étiquet* "ticket, label" < Old French *estiquier* "to stick"; from the idea of sticking on a label]

tick·et scal·per *n* somebody who buys tickets for a theatrical or sporting event and resells them at a profit

tick·et tout *n UK* same as **ticket scalper**

tick·et·y-boo /tìkətee boó/ *adj Can, UK* perfectly fine (*dated informal*)

tick·ey /tíkee/ (*plural* **-eys**) *n* a small silver threepenny coin in use in South Africa between 1806 and 1961 [Late 19C. Origin ?]

tick fe·ver *n* an acute infectious disease transmitted by the bite of a tick, e.g., Rocky Mountain spotted fever or Texas fever

tick·ing /tíking/ *n* a strong cotton fabric, often twilled. Use: mattress and pillow covers. [Mid-17C. < TICK[3]]

tick·le[1] /tík'l/ *v* (**-led, -ling, -les**) **1.** *vt* MAKE SOMEBODY LAUGH AND TWITCH to touch, prod, stroke, or caress lightly a sensitive part of somebody's body, usually so as to produce involuntary laughter and wriggling **2.** *vti* CAUSE ITCHINESS to cause an itchy or scratchy feeling by lightly touching a sensitive part of the body ○ *This feather boa tickles.* **3.** *vi* FEEL ITCHY to experience an itchy or scratchy feeling ○ *My foot tickles.* **4.** *vt* PLEASE OR AMUSE SOMEBODY to make somebody pleased, or appeal to somebody's sense of humor (*often passive*) ■ *n* **1.** TOUCH THAT MAKES SOMEBODY LAUGH a light touch, prod, stroke, or caress applied to a sensitive part of somebody's body, usually so as to produce involuntary laughter and wriggling **2.** ITCHY FEELING an itchy or scratchy feeling caused when a sensitive part of the body is touched lightly by something, especially material **3.** SENSATION LIKE TICKLING an itchy or scratchy sensation similar to that of being tickled by material ○ *have a tickle in my throat* [14C. Probably < TICK[1] "touch lightly"] ◇ **tickled pink** *or* **silly** *or* **to death** extremely pleased (*informal*) ◇ **tickle somebody's fancy** to please or entertain somebody (*informal*)

tick·le[2] /tík'l/ *n Can* a narrow strait or entrance to a harbor, especially in Newfoundland (*often used in place names*) [Late 18C. Origin ?]

tick·ler /tíklər/ *n* **1.** *US* COMM same as **tickler file 2.** *US* a single-entry journal in which obligations are entered chronologically **3.** ELEC ENG same as **tickler coil**

tick·ler coil *n* a small coil connected in series with a radio vacuum tube's plate circuit and inductively coupled to a coil located in a grid circuit to provide regenerative feedback

tick·ler file *n US* a file consisting of reminders of matters that must be dealt with

tick·lish /tíklish/ *adj* **1.** SENSITIVE TO TICKLING sensitive to being tickled **2.** PROBLEMATIC requiring careful or delicate handling because of its risk or difficulty **3.** TOUCHY easily irritated, angered, or upset —**tick·lish·ly** *adv* —**tick·lish·ness** *n*

tick·ly /tíklee/ (**-li·er, -li·est**) *adj* producing a tickling or itching sensation on the surface of the skin

tick·seed /tík seed/ *n* an annual or perennial plant with opposite-lobed leaves, sometimes grown as an ornamental. Flowers: resembling daisies. Native to: North America. Genus: *Coreopsis.* [Because their seeds resemble the insects]

tick·tack /tík tàk/, **tic·tac** *n* **1.** a clicking or tapping sound **2.** *US* a device operated from a distance to make a tapping sound on a window or door as a practical joke [Mid-16C. An imitation of the sound]

tick-tack-toe, tic-tac-toe *n* a game played by two players who alternately mark squares in a grid with O's or X's, the winner being the first to get three marks in a row [Probably an imitation of the sound of an earlier game in which players brought pencils down on slates with their eyes closed]

tick·tock /tík tòk/ *n* the clicking sound made by a clock or watch ■ *vi* (**-tocked, -tock·ing, -tocks**) to make a quiet recurring clicking sound (*refers to clocks or watches*) [Mid-19C. An imitation of the sound]

tick tre·foil *n* a plant with trifoliate leaves and jointed seed pods that break into segments and cling to fur or clothing. Use: forage. Native to: tropics, subtropics. Genus: *Desmodium.* [Because the joints of the pods stick to things as ticks cling to the fur of animals]

tick·y-tack·y /tíkee tàkee/, **tick·y-tack** /tíki tàk/ (*informal*) *adj* dull, unimaginative, and often of uniform quality or design ■ *n* dull, unimaginative, or inferior materials, or something made from them [Reduplication of TACKY[2] "shoddy"]

Ti·con·de·ro·ga /tī kondə rṓgə/ village in northeastern New York, on the La Chute River. It is the site of Fort Ticonderoga, an important strategic fortification in the French and Indian War (1754–63) and the American Revolution (1775–83). Population: 5,149 (1990).

tic·tac *n* another spelling of **ticktack**

tic-tac-toe *n* LEISURE another spelling of **tick-tack-toe**

t.i.d. *abbr* PHARM three times a day (*used in doctors' prescriptions*) [Latin *ter in die*]

tid·al /tíd'l/ *adj* **1.** OF TIDES relating to or affected by tides **2.** DEPENDENT ON TIDE having a time of departure dependent on the phase of a tide ○ *a tidal ferry* **3.** DEFINED BY TIDE LEVEL changing in character or accessibility according to the level of the tide ○ *a tidal island* **4.** FLUCTUATING not constant but fluctuating between periods of intense activity and periods of little activity —**tid·al·ly** *adv*

tid·al air *n* the volume of air that passes in and out of the body during normal breathing

tid·al ba·sin *n* an artificial basin cut in rock that fills up at high tide

tid·al pow·er, tid·al en·er·gy *n* the generation of electricity using the force created by the rise and fall of ocean tides

tid·al vol·ume *n* PHYSIOL same as **tidal air**

tid·al wave *n* **1.** an enormous and destructive ocean wave caused by extremely strong winds, seaquakes, or earthquakes **2.** a powerful widespread expression or surge of something ○ *a tidal wave of public emotion*

tid·bit /tíd bìt/ *n* **1.** a small, usually bite-sized piece of delicious food **2.** a small piece of interesting information or gossip [Mid-17C. Origin ?]

tid·dly·wink /tíddlee wìngk/, **tid·dle·dy·wink** /tídd'ldee-/ *n* a plastic disk used in the game of tiddlywinks [Mid-19C. Origin ?]

tid·dly·winks /tíddlee wìngks/, **tid·dle·dy·winks** /tídd'ldee-/ *n* a game in which players try to flip plastic disks into a cup by pressing them on the side with a larger disk

tide /tīd/ *n* **1.** RISE AND FALL OF OCEAN the cyclic rise and fall of the ocean or another body of water produced by the attraction of the Moon and Sun, occurring about every twelve hours **2.** INFLOW OR OUTFLOW OF WATER the ebb or flow of water at a specific place resulting from the cyclic rise and fall of the ocean **3.** GEOG same as **flood tide** (sense 1) **4.** GENERAL TREND something that rises and falls, especially a tendency or trend ○ *the tide of public opinion* **5.** PERIOD OF TIME a period of time or a season (*archaic; usually used in combination*) ○ *Yuletide* **6.** PHYS GRAVITATIONAL STRESS ON SOMETHING a stress caused by gravitational attraction, e.g., in the atmosphere or on an astronomical object ■ *v* (**tid·ed, tid·ing, tides**) **1.** *vti* CARRY ALONG ON TIDE to carry somebody or something along on the tide, or be carried along in this way **2.** *vi* EBB AND FLOW to ebb and flow like the tide [Old English *tīd* "time" < Indo-European, "to divide"] —**tide·less** *adj* ◇ **swim against the tide** to have an opinion or take a stance that is different from or opposite to that taken by most others ◇ **swim with the tide** to follow the opinions and attitudes of other people ◇ **turn the tide** to reverse the way things happen

SPELLCHECK Do not confuse the spelling of ***tide*** and ***tied***, which sound similar. ***Tide*** refers to the rise and fall of the ocean, or a general trend: *waiting for the tide to come in, the tide of events.* This word is also used as a verb, in related senses and also with *over* to mean "help somebody through a difficult time, especially with a loan or gift of money": *gave me $100 to tide me over.* ***Tied*** is the past tense and participle of *tie* "fasten things together," and is also used as an adjective referring to something loaned on specific conditions.

tide over *vt* to help somebody through a difficult time, especially with a loan or gift of money

tide gauge *n* a gauge used to measure the level of tidal movement

tide·land /tīd lànd, -lənd/ *n* **1.** land that is covered by water at high tide **2.** land submerged beneath territorial waters (*often used in the plural*)

tide·line /tīd līn/ *n* a line made on a shore by the highest point of a tide

tide·mark /tīd maark/ *n* **1.** MARK LEFT BY TIDE a mark made by the highest or lowest point of a tide **2.** MARKER INDICATING LEVELS OF TIDES a marker indicating the highest or lowest point of a tide **3.** POINT MARKING RISE OR FALL a point that somebody or something has reached, risen above, or fallen below

tide race *n* a fast tidal current

tide-rip *n* GEOG same as **rip current**

tide ta·ble *n* a table showing the expected times and levels of tides at a specific place

tide·wa·ter /tīd wàwtər/ *n* **1.** WATER AFFECTED BY TIDES water whose movement or level is affected by tides **2.** WATER COVERING LAND AT HIGH TIDE water at high tide covering land that is dry at low tide **3.** *US* SEACOAST a coastal region, especially that of eastern Virginia

Tide·wa·ter /tīd wàwtər/ *n* an English dialect spoken in eastern Virginia

tide·way /tīd wày/ *n* **1.** a channel in which a tide runs **2.** a current in a tidal channel

tid·ings /tīdingz/ *npl* news or information (*literary*) ○ *I bring you glad tidings.* [Old English *tīdung*, alteration of Old Norse *tīðendi* "events"]

ti·dy /tīdee/ *adj* (**-di·er, -di·est**) **1.** NEAT IN APPEARANCE having a neat orderly appearance **2.** METHODICAL tending to perform tasks in a systematic way **3.** CONSIDERABLE considerable and significant (*informal*) ○ *cost a tidy sum* **4.** *US* SATISFACTORY adequate or satisfactory, especially when circumstances are taken into account (*informal*) ○ *negotiated a tidy severance package* ■ *vti* (**-died, -dy·ing, -dies**) MAKE SOMETHING OR SOMEBODY TIDY to make somebody or something neat and orderly ○ *We need to tidy the place up before they arrive.* ■ *n* (*plural* **-dies**) **1.** *UK* ACT OF MAKING SOMETHING TIDY an act of making something neat and orderly (*informal*) **2.** *US* HOUSEHOLD same as **antimacassar** **3.** BOX FOR HOLDING SMALL OBJECTS a box for holding small objects that would otherwise be messily unsorted ○ *a desk tidy* [13C. < TIDE "time"] —**ti·di·ly** *adv* —**ti·di·ness** *n*

tidy-up *n UK* same as **tidy** *n* (sense 1) (*informal*)

ti·dy·tips /tīdee tìps/ (*plural same*) *n* an annual plant cultivated as an ornamental. Flowers: white-tipped, like daisies. Native to: western United States. Latin name: *Layia platyglossa.*

tie /tī/ *v* (**tied, ty·ing, ties**) **1.** *vt* FASTEN SOMETHING WITH ROPE to fasten things together with a rope, string, or cord **2.** *vt* FASTEN SOMETHING BY KNOTTING to fasten something with a knot or bow **3.** *vi* SPORTS, LEISURE HAVE EQUAL SCORE to achieve the same score or place as somebody else in a game, race, or competition **4.** *vt* MAKE KNOT to make a knot or bow with rope, string, or cord **5.** *vt* CONNECT THINGS to make a connection or link between people or things **6.** *vt* RESTRICT to restrict somebody to particular conditions **7.** *vt* MUSIC SUSTAIN MUSICAL NOTE to hold a musical note from one bar to the next, thereby extending its value **8.** *vt* MUSIC CONNECT NOTES WITH CURVED LINE in musical notation, to connect two notes with a curved line ■ *n* **1.** STRIP OF FABRIC WORN AROUND NECK a long thin piece of fabric worn around the neck, under a shirt collar, and tied at the front so that the ends hang down **2.** CONNECTION something that links or unites people or things **3.** SOMETHING FOR ATTACHING a long thin piece of material such as rope or wire used to fasten or close something else ○ *Where are the ties for the garbage bags?* **4.** SPORTS, LEISURE EQUAL OUTCOME an equal score or result in a game, race, or competition **5.** RAIL WOODEN BEAM SUPPORTING RAIL a wooden beam laid across a railroad track to support the rails **6.** CONSTR STRENGTHENING BEAM a connecting, strengthening, or supporting beam or rod **7.** RESTRICTION something that restricts or confines somebody or something **8.** MUSIC CURVED LINE INDICATING EXTENSION OF NOTES a curved line shown above or below two musical notes of the same pitch, indicating that they are to be sounded without a break for their combined duration **9.** CIV ENG SURVEYING MEASUREMENT either of two measurements on a survey line used to fix the position of a reference point ■ *adj* MADE EQUAL having an equal outcome [Old English *tīgan* < Germanic, "pull"] ◇ **tie one on** to get drunk (*informal*)

USAGE See ***tide***.

tie down *vt* to prevent somebody from acting freely and make the person confirm something ○ *tied him down to a completion date in January*

tie in *v* **1.** *vi* TALLY to be consistent with something **2.** *vi* COMPLEMENT to complement or be closely associated with something ○ *This book has been brought out to tie in with the film.* **3.** *vti* CONNECT to fit something in with something else, or fit in with something ○ *I hope to tie in a visit to my sister with my business trip.*

tie up *v* **1.** *vt* BIND SOMETHING to fasten or bind something using rope or string **2.** *vti* NAUT DOCK BOAT, OR BE DOCKED to moor a boat or ship by securing lines, or be moored in this way **3.** *vt* OCCUPY SOMEBODY OR SOMETHING to keep somebody or something busy ○ *I'm going to be tied up all afternoon in meetings.* **4.** *vt* COMPLETE SOMETHING to complete the work needed for something **5.** *vti* STOP to bring something to a halt, or come to a halt **6.** *vt* FIN INVEST MONEY WITH RESTRICTIONS to invest money in such a way that it cannot be used for other purposes ○ *money tied up in a certificate of deposit* **7.** *vt* LAW PLACE RESTRICTIONS ON PROPERTY to place legal restrictions on the selling or alienation of property

tie·back /tī bàk/ *n* a length of cord or fabric used to hold a curtain to one side

tie beam *n* a beam that pulls together a structure and stops it spreading outward, e.g., the bottom horizontal member of a roof truss

tie·break·er /tī bràykər/, **tie·break** /-bràyk/ *n* a means of deciding the winner of a game or competition when there is a tie —**tie·break·ing** *adj*

tie clip, **tie clasp** *n* an ornamental clip that holds a necktie in place

tied /tīd/ *adj* loaned on condition of being spent only on goods or services supplied by the lender

SPELLCHECK See ***tide***.

tie-dye *vt* to dye designs on cloth by tightly tying portions of it with waxed thread so that the dye only affects the exposed areas ■ *n* a piece of fabric whose designs are made by tie-dyeing (*informal*) —**tie-dye·ing** *n*

tie-in *n* **1.** LINK a link or relationship with something **2.** JOINT PROMOTION OF PRODUCTS an arrangement by which related products are sold, promoted, or marketed together, e.g., a book or toy along with a movie **3.** RELATED PRODUCT a product that is sold, promoted, or marketed in close connection with another **4.** SALE REQUIRING DUAL PURCHASES a sale in which items are advertised or sold with the stipulation that they must be purchased together, or a product sold in this way

~~**tieing**~~ incorrect spelling of **tying**

tie line *n* a telephone line that connects two private exchanges

tie·man·nite /teémə nīt/ *n* a dark gray mineral compound of mercury and selenium [Mid-19C. < After J. C. W. F. *Tiemann* (1848–99), German scientist]

Tien Shan /tyèn shaán/, **Tian Shan** /tyàn-/ mountain range in Central Asia, stretching about 1,500 mi./2,400 km from Kyrgyzstan in the west through northwestern China to Mongolia in the east. The highest point is Victory Peak, 24,406 ft./7,439 m.

tie·pin /tī pìn/ *n UK* same as **tie tack**

Ti·e·po·lo /tee éppə lō, tyéppō lō/, **Giovanni Battista** (1696–1770) Italian artist. He is famous for his murals of religious or mythological scenes that were painted for Venetian rococo interiors.

tier /teer/ *n* **1.** ROW OF SEATS IN RISING SERIES a row placed one above and behind another row, e.g., a set of seats in a theater **2.** LAYER a layer or level placed one above the other in a series (*often used in combination*) ○ *a three-tier cake* **3.** LEVEL IN HIERARCHY a hierarchical level in an organization (*often used in combination*) ■ *vt* (**tiered, tier·ing, tiers**) ARRANGE THINGS IN RISING ROWS to arrange things in rows rising one above the other [15C. < French *tire* "rank, sequence, order" < *tirer* "draw out, elongate"] —**tiered** *adj*

SPELLCHECK See ***tear***[2].

tierce /teerss/ *n* **1.** CHR same as **terce** **2.** CARDS THREE CARDS OF SAME SUIT a sequence of three cards of the same suit **3.** FENCING PARRYING POSITION the third of eight positions from which a fencing parry can be made **4.** MEASURE FORMER MEASURE OF CAPACITY a former measure of capacity equal to 42 wine gallons [15C. Via French < Latin *tertia*, form of *tertius* "third"]

tier·cel *n* BIRDS another spelling of **tercel**

tie rod *n* a metal rod that joins or supports two parts, e.g., one used as a linkage in the steering mechanism of a motor vehicle. Tie rods are also used to keep trusses and arches from spreading.

Ti·er·ra del Fue·go /tee èrrə del fwáygō/ archipelago off the southern tip of South America. Separated from the mainland by the Strait of Magellan, and bordered by the Atlantic, the Antarctic, and the Pacific oceans, the islands belong partly to Argentina and partly to Chile.

tie tack, **tie tac** *n* an ornamental pin used to fasten a necktie to the front of a shirt

tie-up *n* **1.** DELAY a temporary delay or obstruction, e.g., in the flow of traffic **2.** CONNECTION something that connects one thing with another **3.** *US* DOCKING PLACE a mooring place for a boat or ship

tif *abbr* a file extension for a TIFF file. Full form **tagged image file format**

tiff /tif/ *n* **1.** QUARREL a minor quarrel **2.** ILL HUMOR a brief period of bad temper ■ *vi* (**tiffed, tiff·ing, tiffs**) ARGUE to have a minor quarrel with somebody [Early 18C. Probably suggesting the sound of escaping gas]

TIFF /tif/ *n* a format for a computer file that contains bit-mapped graphics. Full form **tagged image file format**

tif·fa·ny /tíffənee/ *n* a fine gauzy fabric [Early 17C. Via Old French *tifanie* < Greek *theophaneia* "vision of God"]

Tif·fa·ny /tíffənee/, **Charles Lewis** (1812–1902) US jeweler and retailer. He introduced the British standard of sterling silver in the United States and founded Tiffany and Company (1853).

Tif·fa·ny, Louis Comfort (1848–1933) US glassmaker and interior designer. He is known for the stained glass, vases, and lamps produced by his Tiffany Studios. He patented the iridescent glass used in his flowing art nouveau pieces.

TIFF file, TIF file *n* a graphic file in a format often used for storing bit-mapped images

tif·fin /tíffin/ *n S Asia* **1.** a light midday meal or snack **2.** FOOD same as **tiffin carrier** [Early 19C. Variant of *tiffing* < obsolete *tiff* "to drink," origin ?]

tif·fin car·ri·er *n S Asia* a carrier consisting of several metal containers stacked one on top of another, used to carry prepared food

tiger

ti·ger /tígər/ (*plural* **-gers** or *same*) *n* **1.** a carnivorous cat, the largest member of the cat family, that has a tawny coat and black stripes. Native to: Asia. Latin name: *Panthera tigris.* **2.** a fierce, brave, or forceful person [13C. Via Old French *tigre* < Greek *tigris*]

ti·ger bee·tle *n* a fast-running predatory beetle with strong sharp jaws for digging and brightly colored patterned wing covers. Native to: warm regions. Family: Cicindelidae. [< its predatory habits]

ti·ger cat *n* **1.** a small striped or spotted cat, e.g., a margay, serval, or ocelot **2.** a domestic cat with blotched or striped markings resembling those of a tiger

ti·ger·eye /tígər ī/ *n* MINERALS same as **tiger's-eye**

ti·ger lil·y *n* **1.** an Asian lily. Flowers: red or orange with dark purple or brown spots. Latin name: *Lilium lancifolium* or *Lilium tigrinium.* **2.** any lily that resembles the Asian tiger lily [< its coloring]

ti·ger moth *n* a moth that has bold black and yellow or orange markings, especially on its wings. Family: Arctiidae.

ti·ger sal·a·man·der *n* a large black salamander with yellow or green stripes. Native to: North America. Latin name: *Ambystoma tigrinum.* [< its stripes]

ti·ger's-eye *n* a striped yellow-brown rock composed of bands of quartz and crocidolite. Use: gems.

ti·ger shark *n* a large striped or spotted shark with a voracious and indiscriminate appetite. Native to: tropics. Latin name: *Galeocerdo cuvieri.*

ti·ger swal·low·tail *n* a large butterfly with a deeply forked tail and yellow wings with black stripes. Native to: North America. Latin name: *Palilio glaucus* or *Palilio rutilus.*

tight /tīt/ *adj* **1.** SNUG fitting the body very closely ○ *a tight sweater* **2.** TAUT stretched so that there is no slack ○ *pulled the rope tight* **3.** FIXED firmly secured or held ○ *a tight knot* **4.** SEALED sealed against gas or liquid leaks ○ *An air lock must have a tight seal.* **5.** STRICT strictly controlled or administered ○ *Security was tight for the conference.* **6.** CRAMPED lacking sufficient space to move freely ○ *It's going to be tight in the back seat.* **7.** HAVING NO EXTRA TIME allowing no time beyond what is needed to do something ○ *a tight schedule* **8.** HAVING NO EXTRA MONEY allowing no money beyond what is required ○ *working to a tight budget* **9.** MISERLY excessively frugal with money ○ *He's too tight to lend you the money.* **10.** HARD TO GET OUT OF difficult or dangerous to handle ○ *We're in a tight fix now.* **11.** WITH CLOSE RIVALS characterized by well-matched competitors or teams ○ *a tight race* **12.** DRUNK intoxicated with alcohol (*slang*) **13.** WELL DONE arranged or performed with style and precision ○ *a tight performance by the whole team* **14.** SUCCINCT characterized by clear concise expression ○ *tight prose* **15.** *US* INTIMATE having a very close relationship with somebody (*informal*) ○ *He's tight with his boss.* **16.** HARD TO GET characterized by conditions in which demand exceeds supply, often with concomitant rising prices ○ *a tight economy* ■ *adv* FIRMLY in a firm, close, snug, or secure way ○ *hold on tight* [14C. Alteration of obsolete *thight* "dense, thick" < Old Norse *þéttr* "watertight, dense"] —**tight·ly** *adv* —**tight·ness** *n* ◇ **in a tight spot** *or* **corner** in a difficult or dangerous situation ◇ **sleep tight** used to wish somebody a sound night's sleep

tight·en /tít'n/ (**-ened, -en·ing, -ens**) *vti* to become tight or tighter, or cause something to become tight or tighter —**tight·en·er** *n*

tight end *n* in football, a player who lines up near to the tackle

tight·fist·ed /tīt fístəd/ *adj* disinclined to spend money —**tight·fist·ed·ly** *adv* —**tight·fist·ed·ness** *n*

tight·fit·ting /tīt fítting/ *adj* **1.** fitting closely to the body ○ *tightfitting jeans* **2.** fitting closely on to a container so that its contents are not exposed to the air ○ *a tightfitting lid*

tight·knit /tīt nít/ *adj* **1.** closely united by love, friendship, or common interests ○ *a tightknit community* **2.** arranged or functioning as a well-structured whole

tight-lipped *adj* **1.** unwilling to communicate ○ *He is remaining tight-lipped in the face of intense press speculation.* **2.** having the lips firmly closed, e.g., in anger or pain

tight·rope /tīt rōp/ *n* a rope or wire stretched taut and suspended above the ground, on which somebody walks or performs a balancing act ◇ **walk a tightrope** to have to deal cautiously with a precarious situation, often one involving a choice or compromise

tights /tīts/ *npl* **1.** a one-piece close-fitting garment made of opaque colored material, covering the body from the waist to the feet and worn by women and girls for warmth and casual wear **2.** a one-piece close-fitting garment covering the body from the neck or waist to the feet, worn especially by men and women dancers and acrobats **3.** *UK* same as **pantyhose**

tight·wad /tīt wòd/ *n* somebody who dislikes spending money (*insult*)

Tig·lath-pi·le·ser I /tìg lath pī léezər/ (*fl* 11th century B.C.) Assyrian king (1115–1076 B.C.). He expanded his kingdom by conquering Babylonia and recovering Armenia from invaders.

tig·lic ac·id /tìgglik-/ *n* a viscous poisonous colorless liquid. Source: croton oil. Use: pharmaceutical preparations, manufacture of perfumes. Formula: $C_5H_8O_2$. [< modern Latin *(Croton) tiglium,* scientific name of the tree from whose seeds croton oil is obtained]

ti·glon /tíglən/, **ti·gon** /tígən/ *n* the offspring of a male tiger and a female lion [Mid-20C. Blend of TIGER + LION]

TIGR /tígər/ *n UK* a bond linked to US treasury bonds, profits from which are subject to UK tax when the bond is cashed or redeemed. Full form **Treasury Investment Growth Receipts**

Ti·gray /tée gray/, **Ti·gre** region in northeastern Ethiopia, bordering Eritrea. Capital: Mekele. Population: 3,136,267 (1994). Area: 25,400 sq. mi./65,786 sq. km.

ti·gress /tígrəss/ *n* **1.** a female tiger **2.** a fierce, brave, or passionate woman [Late 16C. < TIGER after French *tigresse* "tigress"]

Ti·gri·nya /tə greényə/ *n* a Semitic language of northern Ethiopia. Native speakers: 4 million. [Mid-19C. < Tigrinya] —**Ti·gri·nya** *adj*

Tig·ris /tígriss/ river in Southwest Asia. It rises in southeastern Turkey, flows through Iraq, and joins the Euphrates to form the Shatt Al-Arab, which empties into the Persian Gulf. Length: 1,180 mi./1,900 km.

Ti·jua·na /ti wáanə, -hwáanə/ city in northwestern Mexico, just south of the United States border. It is an industrial and tourist center. Population: 1,210,820 (2000).

tike *n* another spelling of **tyke**

ti·ki /téekee/ *n* **1.** a small carved human fetal figure, especially in greenstone, representing an ancestor and worn as an amulet by some Maori and Polynesian peoples **2.** a stone or wooden representation of a Polynesian god [Late 18C. < Maori, "image"]

tik·ka /tíkə/ *adj* a South Asian dish of skewered meat that is marinated and then roasted in an oven [Mid-20C. < Punjabi *ṭikkā*]

til /til/ *n* FOOD same as **sesame** (sense 1) [Mid-19C. < Sanskrit *tila*]

'til *conj, prep* another spelling of **till**[1]

ti·lak /tíllək/ *n* a decorative or symbolic mark worn by Hindus on the forehead [Late 19C. < Sanskrit *tilaka*]

ti·la·pi·a /tə láapee ə, -láypee-/ (*plural* **-as** or *same*) *n* a freshwater fish of the cichlid family, introduced and cultivated worldwide. Native to: tropical Africa. Genus: *Tilapia.* [Mid-19C. < modern Latin]

Til·burg /tíl bùrg/ industrial city in North Brabant Province, southern Netherlands. Population: 193,238 (2000).

til·de /tíldə/ *n* in some languages, a mark (~) placed over a letter to show that the pronunciation is nasalized, e.g., over "a" or "o" in Portuguese, or palatalized, e.g., over "n" in Spanish [Mid-19C. Via Spanish < Latin *titulus* "heading"]

Til·den /tíldən/, **Bill** (1893–1953) US tennis player. He won many singles and doubles titles, including seven in the US Open and three at Wimbledon. Full name **Tilden II, William Tatem**

Til·den, Samuel Jones (1814–86) US politician. He was governor of New York (1874–77). He ran for US president and won the popular vote but lost in the electoral college to Rutherford B. Hayes (1876).

tile /tīl/ *n* **1.** COVERING FOR FLOORS, ROOFS, OR WALLS a thin flat or curved piece of baked, sometimes glazed, clay or synthetic material used to cover roofs, floors, and walls, or for decoration **2.** SHORT PIPE IN DRAIN a short pipe of baked clay, concrete, or plastic used in making a drain **3.** HOLLOW BLOCK a hollow block of baked clay, concrete, or gypsum used as a building material for walls or floors **4.** TILES COLLECTIVELY tiles considered collectively **5.** LEISURE PLAYING PIECE a rectangular playing piece in various games such as mahjongg ■ *v* (**tiled, til·ing, tiles**) **1.** *vt* LAY TILES ON SOMETHING to cover a surface with tiles **2.** *vt* FIT WITH DRAINAGE TILES to put drainage tiles in something **3.** *vti* COMPUT ARRANGE WINDOWS ON COMPUTER SCREEN to arrange the windows on a computer screen side by side so that all are visible [Pre-12C. < Latin *tegula*] —**til·er** *n*

tile·fish /tīl fìsh/ (*plural same* or **-fish·es**) *n* a long blue deep-water fish with yellow spots on its upper body. Native to: Atlantic coast of North America. Latin name: *Lopholatilus chamaeleonticeps.*

til·ing /tīling/ *n* **1.** LAID TILES tiles that have been laid **2.** LAYING OF TILES the laying of tiles on a roof, wall, or floor **3.** TILES tiles collectively

till[1] /til/, **'till, 'til** *conj, prep* same as **until** [Old English *til* "up to a particular point" < Germanic, "aim, goal"; sometimes taken as shortening of UNTIL]

USAGE till or **until**? Both words have the same meaning and function (conjunction and preposition), and are largely interchangeable. ***Till*** is more likely to be heard in speech: *Just wait till we get home!* ***Until*** is more usual at the beginning of a sentence: *Until we actually get on the train we won't know our destination.* The spellings *'til* and *'till* reflect the commonly held belief that ***till*** is a shortened form of ***until***, but ***till*** is in fact the older form.

till[2] /til/ *n* **1.** a box, drawer, or tray in which money is kept, e.g., in a cash register **2.** available cash [15C. Origin ?]

till[3] /til/ (**tilled, till·ing, tills**) *vt* to prepare land for the growing of crops by plowing or harrowing [Old

English *tilian* "cultivate, strive to obtain something" < Germanic, "aim, purpose"] —**till·a·ble** *adj* —**till·er** *n*

till[4] /til/ *n* sediment of various particle sizes deposited by the direct action of ice [Late 17C. Origin ?]

till·age /tíllij/ *n* **1.** the plowing or harrowing of land in preparation for growing crops **2.** land that has been tilled [15C. < TILL[3]]

til·land·si·a /ti lándzee ə/ *n* an epiphytic plant of the pineapple family, e.g., Spanish moss. Native to: tropical or subtropical America. Genus: *Tillandsia.* [Mid-18C. < modern Latin, after Elias *Tillands* (1640–93), Swedish botanist]

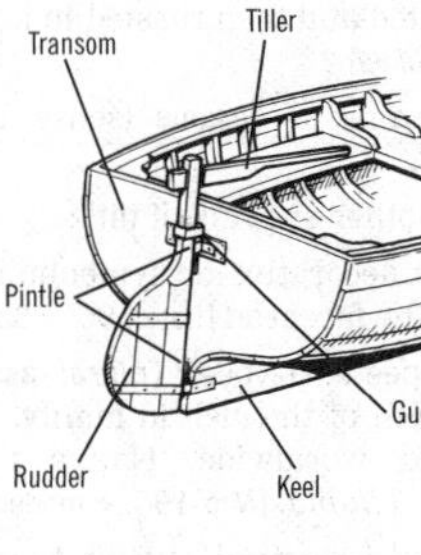

tiller

til·ler[1] /tíllər/ *n* the means by which a small boat is steered, consisting of a handle attached to the rudder [14C. < Anglo-Norman *telier* "weaver's beam" < Latin *tela* "web"]

til·ler[2] /tíllər/ *n* a person or machine that plows or cultivates the soil [Pre-12C. < TILL[3]]

til·ler[3] /tíllər/ *n* a shoot growing from the base of a stem, especially the stem of a grass [Mid-17C. Probably < Old English *telgor* "extended" < *telga* "branch"]

Til·ley /tíllee/, **Sir Samuel Leonard** (1818–96) Canadian politician. He was a provincial and federal official who advocated confederation and the development of Canadian railroads.

Til·lich /tíllik, tíllikh/, **Paul** (1886–1965) German-born US philosopher and theologian. He emigrated to the United States in 1933. His scholarly and popular books sought to reconcile existential philosophy and contemporary secular culture with Christian faith, and included *The Courage to Be* (1952) and *Systematic Theology* (1951–63). Full name **Tillich, Paul Johannes**

> "Religion is the state of being grasped by an ultimate concern... which itself contains the answer to the question of the meaning of our life."
> [Paul Tillich, *Christianity and the Encounter of the World Religions*; 1961]

tilt[1] /tilt/ *v* (**tilt·ed, tilt·ing, tilts**) **1.** *vti* SLOPE to slant, or cause something to slant ○ *She tilted her head as she listened.* **2.** *vi* HAVE AS PREFERENCE to tend toward favoring a particular opinion, course of action, or side in a dispute ○ *a political party that tilted toward peace not war* **3.** *vi* CRITICIZE to make a spoken or written attack on somebody or something **4.** *vi* STRUGGLE to combat or struggle against somebody or something **5.** *vti* HIST CHARGE WITH LANCE to attack an opponent using a lance **6.** *vi* HIST JOUST WITH SOMEBODY to take part in a joust against somebody **7.** *vi* HIST POINT LANCE to hold a lance ready for combat in a joust **8.** *vt* ENG USE TILT HAMMER ON SOMETHING to work on something using a tilt hammer ■ *n* **1.** ACT OF TILTING an act of tilting or of causing something to tilt **2.** INCLINED SURFACE a slanted surface or position ○ *His hat was at a rakish tilt.* **3.** CRITICISM a spoken or written attack on somebody or something **4.** *US* PREFERENCE a tendency to favor a particular opinion, course of action, or side in a dispute **5.** HIST ACTIVITY OF JOUST a jousting contest **6.** HIST LANCE THRUST a thrust made with a lance in a jousting contest **7.** ENG same as **tilt hammer** [14C. Probably < assumed Old English *tyltan* "fall over" < Germanic, "unsteady"] —**tilt·er** *n* ◇ **(at) full tilt** at full speed

tilt[2] /tilt/ *n* a canvas cover or canopy used to cover an otherwise open boat, booth, or trailer of a truck [15C. < Old English *teld* < W Germanic]

tilth /tilth/ *n* **1.** TILLING OF LAND the plowing of land in preparation for growing crops **2.** TILLED LAND land under cultivation **3.** CONDITION OF LAND the condition of a piece of tilled land, in terms of its cultivation history and suitability for crops **4.** DEGREE OF FINENESS OF SOIL the degree of fineness of soil particles in the topmost soil layer [Old English *tilþ(e)* < *tilian* (see TILL[3])]

tilt ham·mer *n* a heavy drop hammer used to forge metal, pivoted by a lever [< TILT[1]]

tilt·yard /tilt yaard/ *n* a place, usually enclosed, where a jousting contest was held [Early 16C. < TILT[1]]

Tim. *abbr* BIBLE Timothy

Ti·ma·ru /tímmə ro͞o/ city on the east central coast of the South Island, New Zealand. Population: 26,745 (2001).

tim·bal /tímb'l/, **tym·bal** *n* same as **kettledrum** (*archaic*) [Late 17C. < French *timbale*, alteration (after *cymbale* "cymbal") of obsolete *tamballe* < (influenced by *tambour* "drum") Spanish *atabal* < Arabic *aṭ -ṭabl* "the drum"]

tim·bale /tímb'l, tim baal/ *n* **1.** FOOD DISH MADE IN MOLD a dish consisting of a mixture of ingredients, often set with eggs, made in a mold and served hot or cold **2.** HOUSEHOLD COOKING MOLD a small deep or tall mold in which a timbale is cooked ■ **tim·bales** *npl* MUSIC LATIN AMERICAN DRUMS a pair of cylindrical drums, commonly played in Latin American dance music [Early 19C. < French (see TIMBAL)]

tim·ber /tímbər/ *n* **1.** GROWING TREES standing trees or their wood, especially when suitable for sawing into building materials **2.** WOODED LAND land covered with trees **3.** same as **lumber**[1] *n* (sense 1) **4.** CONSTR LARGE WOODEN BUILDING SUPPORT a large piece of wood, usually squared, used in a building, e.g., as a beam **5.** SHIPPING PART OF SHIP'S FRAMEWORK a large piece of wood used in the framework of a wooden ship **6.** SOMEBODY AS SUITABLE MATERIAL FOR POSITION somebody with the right qualities for a position ○ *She's definitely congressional timber.* ■ *adj* MADE OF TIMBERS constructed of timbers ■ *interj* WARNING OF FALLING TREE used by a lumberjack to warn others that a tree has been cut and is about to fall ■ *vt* (**-bered, -ber·ing, -bers**) PROVIDE WITH TIMBERS to build, cover, or support something with timbers [Old English, "a building" < Indo-European, "build"]

tim·bered /tímbərd/ *adj* **1.** made of timber, or having exposed timbers (*often used in combination*) ○ *a half-timbered house* **2.** covered with growing trees

tim·ber·head /tímbər hèd/ *n* the top of a timber of a ship that projects above the deck and is used as a tall post (**bollard**) for securing the ship to a wharf or dock

tim·ber hitch *n* a knot used to tie a rope around a spar or log that is to be hoisted or hauled

tim·ber·ing /tímbəring/ *n* timber, or objects made of timber

tim·ber·land /tímbər lànd/ *n* an area of wooded land, especially one with trees that have commercial value as lumber

tim·ber·line /tímbər līn/ *n* the altitude or latitude above which trees will not grow

tim·ber rat·tle·snake *n* a poisonous rattlesnake that is yellowish brown with wide dark bands and feeds on small mammals. Native to: eastern United States. Latin name: *Crotalus horridus.*

tim·ber wolf *n* ZOOL same as **gray wolf**

tim·ber·work /tímbər wùrk/ *n* something constructed of timbers, or the timber parts of something

tim·ber·yard /tímbər yaard/ *n UK* same as **lumberyard**

tim·bre /támbər, taaNbrə/ *n* **1.** the quality of a speech sound that comes from its tone rather than its pitch or volume **2.** the quality or color of tone of an instrument or voice [Mid-19C. Via French, originally "drum, bell hit with a hammer" < Greek *tumpanon* "drum"]

tim·brel /tímbrəl/ *n* in the Bible, a tambourine or small hand drum [Early 16C. Origin ?]

Tim·buk·tu[1] /tìm buk to͞o/ *n* a place that is far away or extremely remote (*informal*) [Mid-19C. After TIMBUKTU[2]]

Tim·buk·tu[2] /tìm buk to͞o/ ➧ **Tombouctou**

time /tīm/ *n* **1.** SYSTEM OF DISTINGUISHING EVENTS a dimension that enables two identical events occurring at the same point in space to be distinguished, measured by the interval between the events. Symbol ***t*** **2.** PERIOD WITH LIMITS a limited period during which an action, process, or condition exists or takes place ○ *elapsed time* **3.** *also* **Time** METHOD OF MEASURING INTERVALS a system for measuring intervals of time ○ *sidereal time* ○ *Central Daylight Time* **4.** MINUTE OR HOUR the minute, hour, or similar measurement as indicated by a clock ○ *What time is it?* **5.** TIME AS CAUSATIVE FORCE time conceived as a force capable of acting on people and objects ○ *time's ravages* **6.** MOMENT SOMETHING OCCURS a moment or period at which something takes place ○ *at the time of her 90th birthday* **7.** SUITABLE MOMENT a moment or period chosen as appropriate for something to be done or to take place ○ *The times for the games will be announced.* **8.** UNALLOCATED PERIOD a period that is not allocated for a specific purpose ○ *I had time on my hands.* **9.** PERIOD NEEDED a period required, allocated, or taken to complete an activity ○ *How much time?* **10.** PERIOD WITH PARTICULAR QUALITY a period, activity, or occasion that has a particular quality or characteristic (*often used in the plural*) ○ *They've been through some rough times.* ○ *We had an interesting time there.* **11.** APPOINTED MOMENT a designated or customary moment or period at which something is done or takes place ○ *It's time to get up.* **12.** *UK* CLOSING TIME the time at which a pub or bar is legally required to close **13.** INTERVAL a limited but unspecified period ○ *We stayed for a time.* **14.** HISTORICAL PERIOD a period in history, often characterized by a particular event or person (*often used in the plural*) ○ *in Shakespeare's time* ○ *ancient times* **15.** THE HERE AND NOW the present as distinguished from the past or future (*often used in the plural*) ○ *technology that is ahead of the times* **16.** GEOL GEOLOGIC DIVISION a chronological division of geologic history **17.** ANTICIPATED MOMENT a moment in which an important event such as a birth or death is expected to happen ○ *He knew his time had come.* **18.** SOMEBODY'S LIFETIME a period during which somebody is alive, especially the most active or productive period in somebody's life ○ *She'd been a well-known athlete in her time.* ○ *We didn't worry about such trifles in my time.* **19.** APPRENTICESHIP PERIOD a period during which somebody is an apprentice ○ *had served his time* **20.** CRIME PRISON TERM a term in prison (*informal*) ○ *serve time for robbery* **21.** MIL MILITARY SERVICE a term of military service **22.** SEASON a period during which particular climatic conditions prevail ○ *the rainy times of the year* **23.** INSTANCE a separate occasion of a recurring event ○ *I told you three times.* **24.** MUSIC TEMPO OF MUSIC the relative speed at which a musical composition is played **25.** MUSIC MUSICAL BEAT the number of beats per measure of a musical composition **26.** PERIOD WORKED the period during a day or week that somebody works ○ *working half time* **27.** PAY RATE a rate of pay ○ *paid double time* **28.** SPORTS PLAYING PERIOD a period of play in a game **29.** SPORTS same as **timeout** *n* (sense 1) ■ *v* (**timed, tim·ing, times**) **1.** *vt* MEASURE HOW LONG SOMETHING TAKES to measure or record the duration, speed, or rate of something **2.** *vt* SCHEDULE SOMETHING to plan the moment or occasion for something, especially in order to achieve the best result or effect ○ *time an entrance* **3.** *vt* SET TIME OF SOMETHING to regulate or set the time of something such as a clock or a train's schedule **4.** *vi* STAY IN RHYTHM to keep time to a rhythmic or musical beat [Old English *tīma* "period of time" < Germanic, "extend"] ◇ **all in good time** no sooner than is appropriate ◇ **all the time** continuously ◇ **at one time 1.** at a time in the past **2.** simultaneously ◇ **at the same time 1.** simultaneously **2.** nevertheless ◇ **at times** sometimes ◇ **behind the times** out of touch with modern fashions, methods, or attitudes ◇ **bide your time** to wait patiently for the right opportunity ◇ **for old times' sake** in fond memory of the past ○ *We had lunch at the café we used to frequent, for old times' sake.* ◇ **for the time being** for a short period of time starting from now ◇ **from time to time** occasionally ◇ **have no time for somebody** *or* **something** to regard somebody or something with dislike or contempt ◇ **have the time of your life** to have a very enjoyable experience ◇ **in good time 1.** early enough ○ *got there in good time so we could find a parking space* **2.**

quickly ◇ **in (less than) no time** in a very short period of time ◇ **in time 1.** early enough ○ *We were in time for the concert.* **2.** after some time has passed ○ *He'll understand in time that you were trying to help him.* **3.** in the correct rhythm ○ *clapping in time to the music* ◇ **in your own time** at a speed or pace that feels natural and comfortable ◇ **keep time 1.** to show the time accurately **2.** to do something in the correct rhythm, or in the same rhythm as somebody or something else ◇ **live on borrowed time** to enjoy an unexpected extension of life ◇ **make time with somebody** *N Am, N England* to pursue somebody as a sexual partner (*informal*) ◇ **mark time 1.** to continue marching in rhythm without moving forward **2.** to do something that makes no contribution toward achieving a goal or ambition while awaiting an opportunity to make progress ◇ **on time** at the scheduled time ◇ **once upon a time** used at the beginning of fairy tales and children's stories to indicate that something happened a long time ago or in an imaginary world ◇ **on your own time** not during working hours ◇ **pass the time of day (with somebody)** to engage in casual conversation with somebody ◇ **play for time** to delay action or a decision in the hope that conditions will be more favorable later on ◇ **take time out (from)** to take a short break from work or another activity ○ *took time out from her studies to travel for a year* ◇ **take your time 1.** to take whatever time is necessary **2.** to do something unacceptably slowly ◇ **time after time, time and (time) again** repeatedly ◇ **time out of mind** for an extremely long time ◇ **time was** there was a time in the past ◇ **time will tell** it is impossible to know or judge something until some time in the future ○ *Time will tell whether I have made the right decision.*

SPELLCHECK see *thyme*

CULTURAL NOTE ***A Brief History of Time***, a book (1988) by British physicist Stephen Hawking. This best-selling text aims to describe fundamental concepts in physics in terms that the general reader can understand. It covers a wide range of subjects, from the origin of the universe to the nature of time itself, and explains the theories put forward by other scientists such as Galileo, Newton, and Einstein.

time out *vti* to fail to respond after a predetermined interval, and thus cause a suspension of activity or a call for intervention from a user, or to cause this to happen to somebody (*refers to computers or peripheral devices*) ○*"...a dialog box suggested that the server had timed me out." (Internet Magazine*; November 1998)

time and a half *n* a rate of pay equal to one and a half times the normal rate, usually paid for overtime work

time and mo·tion stud·y *n* an analysis of the working practices of, e.g., a person, department, or factory, done with the idea of finding ways to increase efficiency

time bomb *n* **1.** ARMS **BOMB EXPLODING AT FIXED TIME** a bomb with a timing mechanism that allows it to explode at a set time **2. FUTURE DANGER** something that is not dangerous or harmful at the moment but is likely to become so **3.** COMPUT **TIME-TRIGGERED COMPUTER VIRUS** a computer virus either existing independently or included in a larger program that is triggered by date or by the length of time a computer application is used

time cap·sule *n* a container of articles representative of the present, placed in a building's foundation or buried for a future generation to find and learn about the period it represents

time·card /tīm kaàrd/ *n* a card that an employee has stamped by a time clock when starting and finishing work

time clock *n* a clock with a mechanism for stamping employees' timecards when they start and finish work

time-con·sum·ing *adj* taking up or wasting a great deal of time

time de·pos·it *n* a bank deposit from which a withdrawal can be made only after a set period of time or after giving notice

time di·la·tion, time dil·a·ta·tion *n* the principle that time elapsed is relative to motion, such that time passes more slowly for a system in motion than for one at rest relative to an outside observer. Further, as predicted by Einstein's special theory of relativity, time passes increasingly slowly as the motion relative to the observer approaches the speed of light.

timed-re·lease, time-re·lease *adj* formulated to release an active ingredient gradually to prolong its effect

time ex·po·sure *n* **1.** the exposure of photographic film for an unusually long time to achieve a desired effect **2.** a photograph taken by time exposure

time frame *n* a period of time during which something takes place or is planned to take place ○ *What's the time frame for the project?*

time fuse *n* a fuse that can be set to trigger an explosion at a specific time

time-hon·ored *adj* respected or continued because of having been the custom for a long time

time im·me·mo·ri·al *n* **1.** time so distant in the past as to be beyond memory or record **2.** the time prior to a date fixed as the start of the keeping of official legal records, before which no claims or rights are valid

time·keep·er /tīm keèpər/ *n* **1. SOMEBODY RECORDING TIME ELAPSED** a recorder of the time elapsed during a sports event **2. SOMEBODY RECORDING TIME WORKED** a recorder of time worked by employees **3.** *UK* **SOMEBODY CONSIDERED IN TERMS OF PUNCTUALITY** an employee considered in terms of his or her punctuality ○ *She's a hard worker and a good timekeeper.* **4. WATCH OR CLOCK** an instrument for recording or showing the time, e.g., a watch or clock —**time·keep·ing** *n*

time lag *n* an amount of time that passes between two connected events

time-lapse pho·tog·ra·phy *n* a method of filming a slow process such as the opening of a flower by taking a series of single exposures, then showing them at higher speed to simulate continuous action

time·less /tīmləss/ *adj* **1.** remaining invariable throughout time ○ *fiction that has a timeless appeal* **2.** having no beginning or end —**time·less·ly** *adv* —**time·less·ness** *n*

time lim·it *n* a period of time within which something must be done or is effective

time line *n* a linear representation of significant events in a subject area such as the history of art, shown in chronological order

time loan *n* a loan that has to be repaid by or on a given date

time lock *n* a lock on a device such as a safe or bank vault with a timing mechanism that allows it to open only at set times

time·ly /tīmlee/ (**-li·er, -li·est**) *adj* happening or done at the right time or an appropriate time ○ *a timely intervention* —**time·li·ness** *n* —**time·ly** *adv*

time ma·chine *n* a fictional or hypothetical machine that can be used to travel backward or forward in time

time note *n US* a legal document that specifies a date for repayment, e.g., a promissory note

time-off *n* time that somebody spends away from work, study, or other usual duties

Time of Trou·bles *n* the period of Russian history between the death of Tsar Ivan IV (1584), when the boyars attempted to regain control of Russia, and the selection of Michael Romanov as tsar in 1613

time·ous /tīməss/ *adj Scotland* happening or done in good time —**time·ous·ly** *adv*

time out *n* **1.** a short break or rest from work or other activities ○ *took time out from her studies to travel for a year* **2.** a brief solitary period of rest and quiet, often imposed upon an overly excited or hyperactive child

time·out /tīm òwt/ *n* **1.** SPORTS **TIME DURING WHICH GAME STOPS** in some games, a break taken to allow players to rest, receive medical treatment, confer, or be substituted **2.** COMPUT **LACK OF COMPUTER RESPONSE** an interruption in the operation of a computer when a device such as a printer or disk drive does not respond to a command in a predetermined amount of time. A timeout usually results in a message to the user giving the option of retrying or canceling the command. ■ *interj* **REQUEST FOR BREAK** used to ask for or suggest a break in a game or an activity

time-out room *n* a room, e.g., in a school or daycare center, in which an overly excited or hyperactive child is sent for a rest period in order to calm down

time·piece /tīm peèss/ *n* an instrument for recording or showing the time, especially one that does not strike or chime, e.g., a watch or clock

tim·er /tīmər/ *n* **1. TIME-SETTING DEVICE** a device that can be preset to start or stop something at a given time or that sounds after a set period of time **2. TIME-RECORDING DEVICE** a device for recording, showing, or measuring time, e.g., a stopwatch **3. SOMEBODY TRACKING TIME** somebody who measures or records elapsed time **4.** AUTOMOT **DEVICE CONTROLLING IGNITION** a device in an internal-combustion engine that controls the timing of the spark in the cylinders

time-re·lease *adj* PHARM same as **timed-release**

times /tīmz/ *prep* used to indicate that a number is to be multiplied by another ○ *Three times two is six.*

time·sav·ing /tīm sàyving/ *adj* designed to reduce the length of time taken to do something —**time·sav·er** *n*

time·scale /tīm skàyl/ *n* **1.** a period of time scheduled for something to be completed **2.** a measurement of time relative to the time in which a typical event occurs, e.g., in geologic or cosmic time

time se·ries *n* a sequence of data gathered at uniformly spaced intervals of time

time-served *adj UK* having completed an apprenticeship and therefore fully competent to work as a tradesperson

time·serv·er /tīm sùrvər/, **time-server** *n* somebody whose opinions and behavior change to suit the times and circumstances without regard for principle —**time·serv·ing** *n, adj*

time·share /tīm shèr/ *n* **1.** TRAVEL same as **time-sharing** (sense 1) **2.** a property, usually an apartment in a resort area, that is jointly owned by people who use it at different times

time-shar·ing *n* **1.** the joint ownership of a property such as an apartment in a resort area, in which each owner may occupy the property for part of the year **2.** a technique for the concurrent use of a computer by many people working at remote terminals, each apparently operating as the only user of the computer's resources. The apparent simultaneous use is possible because the computer's processing speed is extremely fast in comparison with a person's typing speed at a keyboard. —**time-share** *vti*

time sheet *n* a sheet or card on which the hours worked by an employee are recorded

time sig·na·ture *n* a sign used in music to show meter, represented by a fraction in which the upper figure shows beats per measure and the lower figure shows each beat's time value

times sign *n* MATH same as **multiplication sign**

times ta·ble *n* MATH same as **multiplication table** (*informal; often used in combination*)

time-stamp *n* a part of the financial order-routing process in which the time of day is stamped on an order when it is received on the trading floor and when it is completed

time stud·y *n* INDUST same as **time and motion study**

time·ta·ble /tīm tàyb'l/ *n UK* same as **schedule** *n* (sense 3)

time-test·ed *adj* proven to be effective over a long period

time tri·al *n* a race in which competitors compete individually for the fastest time

time warp *n* a hypothetical distortion in the continuum of space-time, popular in science fiction, allowing time to stand still or people to travel from one time to another

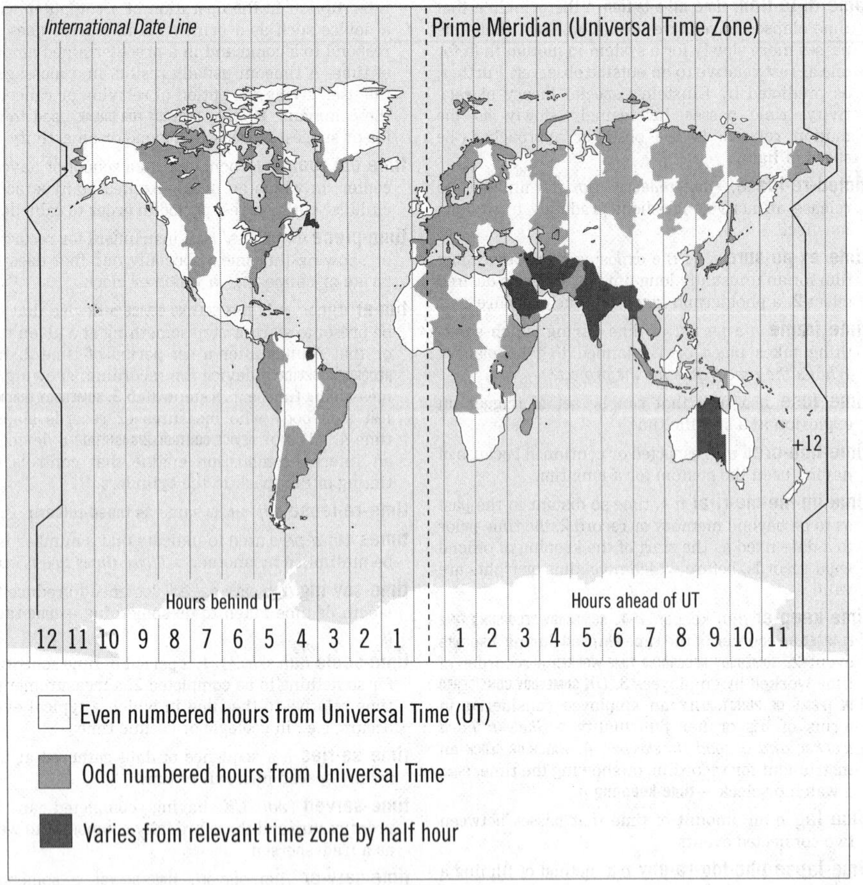

time zone

time·work /tīm wùrk/ *n* work paid according to the time it takes, especially by the hour or the day —**time·work·er** *n*

time·worn /tīm wàwrn/ *adj* **1.** showing the effects of having been used for a long period of time **2.** having lost effectiveness through overuse ○ *a timeworn phrase*

time zone *n* any of the 24 longitudinal areas into which the world is divided and within which the same standard time is used

tim·id /tímmid/ *adj* demonstrating a lack of courage or self-assurance [Mid-16C. Directly or via French < Latin *timidus* "fearful" < *timere* "to fear"] —**ti·mid·i·ty** /ti míddətee/ *n* —**tim·id·ly** *adv*

tim·ing /tīming/ *n* **1.** JUDGMENT OF WHEN TO ACT the ability to choose or the choice of the best moment to do or say something, e.g., in performing music or comedy or in sports ○ *a comedian with an immaculate sense of timing* ○ *split-second timing* **2.** RECORDING OF TIME the measurement and recording of the time taken to do something **3.** AUTOMOT ADJUSTMENT OF VALVES OF ENGINE the adjustment of the sequence and relative position of the valves and crankshaft of an automobile engine such that maximum output power is achieved

tim·ing gear *n* the drive in an internal-combustion engine between the crankshaft and the camshaft [Because it causes the valves to open and close at the right time]

Ti·mi·şoa·ra /tèemee shwaárə/ capital city of Timiş County, western Romania. Population: 332,277 (1997).

Tim·mins /tímminz/ mining town in eastern Ontario, Canada. Population: 31,148 (2001).

ti·moc·ra·cy /ti mókrəssee/ (*plural* **-cies**) *n* **1.** government in which the possession of property is a qualification for holding office **2.** a form of government in which honor is the guiding principle [15C. Via French and medieval Latin < Greek *timokratia* < *timē* "honor, value"] —**ti·mo·crat·ic** /tìmmə kráttik/ *adj*

Ti·mor /tée mawr, tee máwr/ island in the Malay Archipelago. It is the largest and easternmost of the Lesser Sunda Islands, bordered on the north by the Savu and Banda seas and on the south by the Timor Sea. Population: 3,900,000 (1990). Area: 11,900 sq. mi./30,820 sq. km.

Ti·mor-Les·te /tèe mawr léstay/ independent nation on the eastern half of the island of Timor in Southeast Asia. Its annexation by Indonesia in 1975 led to protracted internal conflict, and though a plebiscite for independence in 1999 met with Indonesian military intervention, it gained full independence in 2002. Capital: Dili. Population: 997,853 (2003). Area: 5,743 sq. mi./14,874 sq. km. Former name **East Timor**

tim·or·ous /tímmərəss/ *adj* showing fear or hesitancy [15C. Via French < medieval Latin *timorosus* < Latin *timere* "to fear"] —**tim·or·ous·ly** *adv* —**tim·or·ous·ness** *n*

Ti·mor Sea /tèe mawr-/ arm of the Indian Ocean separating the island of Timor from northern Australia. Area: 174,000 sq. mi./450,000 sq. km.

tim·o·thy /tímməthee/ *n* a perennial grass with a cylindrical flower spike, widely cultivated for hay and pasture. Native to: temperate regions. Latin name: *Phleum pratense*. [Mid-18C. After *Timothy* Hanson, American farmer who introduced the grass to the Carolinas around 1720]

Tim·o·thy /tímməthee/ *n* either of two books of the Bible, originally letters addressed to St. Timothy and traditionally attributed to St. Paul. They are concerned with the organization of Christian doctrine and codes of Christian behavior. See table at **Bible**

Timothy, St. /tímməthee/ in the Bible, an early Christian missionary, and friend and disciple of St. Paul.

tim·o·thy grass *n* PLANTS same as **timothy**

tim·pa·ni /tímpənee/, **tym·pa·ni** *n* a set of two or more kettledrums, usually played as part of an orchestra (*takes a singular or plural verb*) [Late 19C. < Italian, plural of *timpano* "kettledrum" < Greek *tumpanon* "drum"] —**tim·pa·nist** *n*

tin /tin/ *n* **1.** METALLIC ELEMENT a silvery, easily shaped metallic element. Source: oxide ore. Use: alloys such as solder, bronze, and pewter, protective coating for steel. Symbol **Sn**. See table at **element 2.** *UK* FOOD INDUST same as **can**[2] *n* (sense 1) **3.** SHEET-METAL CONTAINER a container with a lid, made of thin sheet metal and often decorated **4.** *UK* AMOUNT IN TIN the amount that a tin holds ○ *ate a tin of beans* **5.** CORRUGATED IRON corrugated or galvanized iron ■ *adj* **1.** MADE OF TIN made from thin sheet metal coated with tin **2.** MADE OF CORRUGATED IRON made of corrugated or galvanized iron ■ *vt* (**tinned, tin·ning, tins**) **1.** *UK* FOOD INDUST same as **can**[2] *v* (sense 1) **2.** COAT SOMETHING WITH TIN to coat or plate something with tin [Old English < Germanic]

tinamou

tin·a·mou /tínnə moo/ (*plural* **-mous** or *same*) *n* a short round-bodied ground-dwelling bird. Native to: grassy and jungle areas of Central and South America. Family: Tinamidae. [Late 18C. Via French < Carib *tinamu*]

Tin·ber·gen /tín bùrgən, -bèrkhən/, **Jan** (1903–94) Dutch economist. He was a pioneer of econometrics and an economic adviser to the League of Nations Secretariat (1936–38). He shared the first Nobel Prize in economics (1969).

tin·cal /tíngk'l/ *n* a sodium borate mineral formed by the weathering of borax [Mid-17C. Probably via Portuguese < Persian, Urdu *tinkār* < Sanskrit *taṅkana*]

tin can *n* **1.** a container made of tin or aluminum, especially one used for food **2.** *US* a naval destroyer (*informal*)

tinct /tingkt/ *n* same as **tint** *n* (sense 1) (*archaic*) ■ *vti* (**tinct·ed, tinct·ing, tincts**) same as **tint** *v* (*archaic*) ■ *adj* tinted or colored (*literary*) [15C. < Latin *tinctus* (see TINT)]

tinct. *abbr* PHARM tincture

tinc·ture /tíngkchər/ *n* **1.** ALCOHOL SOLUTION a solution of a plant extract or chemical in alcohol ○ *tincture of iodine* **2.** TINGE OR COLOR a tint or slight coloration **3.** TINY AMOUNT OF SOMETHING a hint or small amount of something **4.** HERALDRY HERALDIC COLOR a color, metal, or fur used in heraldry ■ *vt* (**-tured, -tur·ing, -tures**) **1.** ADD TINT TO SOMETHING to give something a hint of color **2.** IMBUE SOMETHING to suffuse something with a quality or property ○ *praise tinctured with criticism* [14C. < Latin *tinctura* "dyeing" < *tinctus* (see TINT)]

tin·der /tíndər/ *n* material that is easily combustible and can be used for lighting a fire, e.g., dry sticks [Old English *tynder* < Germanic, "ignite, kindle"]

tin·der·box /tíndər bòks/ *n* **1.** a person, place, or situation that is likely to become violent **2.** a metal box containing tinder, often fitted with a flint and steel, formerly used for lighting fires

tine /tīn/ *n* **1.** a thin pointed projection of a utensil or implement such as a fork or pitchfork **2.** a pointed branch of a deer's antler [Old English *tind* < Germanic] —**tined** *adj*

tin·e·a /tínnee ə/ *n* an infection of the skin caused by fungi living as parasites on the outer layer of the skin, nails, or hair [14C. < Latin, "gnawing worm, moth"] —**tin·e·al** *adj*

tin·e·a bar·bae /-baárbee/ *n* MED same as **barber's itch** (*technical*) [< Latin, "tinea of the beard"]

tin·e·a cru·ris /-króoriss/ *n* same as **jock itch** (*technical*) [< Latin, "tinea of the leg"]

tin·e·a ped·is /-péddiss/ *n* MED same as **athlete's foot** (*technical*) [< Latin, "tinea of the foot"]

tin ear *n* an inability to perceive differences in musical sounds or subtleties in speech (*informal*)

tin·e·id /tínnee id/ *n* a very small moth found worldwide whose larvae either eat fabrics of animal origin or are scavengers. Family: Tineidae. [Mid-19C. < modern Latin *Tineidae* (plural) < Latin *tinea* "moth"]

tin·foil /tín fòyl/ *n* **1.** aluminum in a very thin sheet. Use: food wrap. **2.** tin, or an alloy of tin and lead, in a very thin sheet

ting /ting/ *n* a light high-pitched ringing sound, like that of a small bell ■ *vti* (**tinged, ting·ing, tings**) to produce a light high-pitched ringing sound, or cause something to produce such a sound [Early 17C. An imitation of the sound]

ting-a-ling /tíngə lìng/ *n* a tinkling sound resembling that made by a small bell [An imitation of the sound]

tinge /tinj/ *n* **1.** SLIGHT ADDED COLOR a slight amount of a color added to something **2.** SLIGHT ADDED ELEMENT a slight amount of something such as an emotion or a flavor ○ *with a tinge of regret in her voice* ■ *vt* (**tinged, tinge·ing** or **ting·ing, ting·es**) **1.** ADD COLOR TO SOMETHING to add a slight amount of color to something **2.** MIX IN ELEMENT OF SOMETHING to mix a slight amount of something with something else (*often passive*) ○ *celebrations tinged with sadness* [15C. < Latin *tingere* "soak, dye"]

tin·gle /tíng g'l/ *vti* (**-gled, -gling, -gles**) to feel a sensation of stinging, pricking, or vibration, e.g., from cold or a slight electric shock, or cause somebody to feel this ○ *The frost made our faces tingle.* ■ *n* a sensation of stinging, pricking, or vibration [14C. Variant of TINKLE] —**tin·gler** *n* —**tin·gling·ly** *adv* —**tin·gly** *adj*

tin god *n* somebody, often in a position of minor authority, who is regarded as behaving in a self-important overbearing way

tin hat *n* a steel helmet (*informal*)

tin·horn /tín hàwrn/ *n* somebody relatively insignificant who pretends to be wealthy, influential, or important, especially a gambler (*informal*) [Late 19C. < the horn-shaped metal can used to shake the dice in chuck-a-luck]

tin·horn dic·ta·tor *n* a dictatorial head of a state who is regarded as insignificant in terms of global politics (*informal*)

tin·ker /tíngkər/ *n* **1.** UNSKILLFUL WORKER a clumsy or unskillful worker, especially at repair work **2.** SOMEBODY GOOD AT MANY TASKS somebody able to do many different kinds of work successfully **3.** ACT OF FIDDLING WITH SOMETHING an act of fiddling with something in an attempt to repair it **4.** TRAVELING POT MENDER in former times, somebody who traveled from place to place mending metal household items such as pots and pans **5.** FISH YOUNG MACKEREL a mackerel that is not fully grown **6.** *UK* NAUGHTY CHILD a mischievous or badly-behaved child (*informal*) ■ *vi* (**-kered, -ker·ing, -kers**) **1.** FIDDLE WITH SOMETHING to fiddle with something in an attempt to repair it ○ *had been tinkering with the car all morning* **2.** HANDLE SOMETHING UNSKILLFULLY to handle something clumsily or unskillfully **3.** BE TRAVELING POT MENDER in former times, to work as a traveling pot mender [13C. Origin ?] —**tin·ker·er** *n*

tin·ker's damn, tin·ker's dam *n* the slightest possible amount of care, heed, or value (*informal; used in negative statements*) ○ *This car isn't worth a tinker's damn.* [Probably < the reputation of tinkers for cursing]

tin·kle /tíngk'l/ *v* (**-kled, -kling, -kles**) **1.** *vti* JINGLE LIGHTLY to make light metallic ringing sounds, or cause something to make light metallic ringing sounds **2.** *vi* same as **urinate** (*informal*) ■ *n* **1.** JINGLING SOUND a series of light metallic ringing sounds **2.** URINATION an act of urinating (*informal*) **3.** *UK* TELEPHONE CALL a call on the telephone (*informal*) [14C. < obsolete *tink* "make a faint metallic sound," origin ?] —**tin·kly** *adj*

Tin·ley Park /tínnlee-/ town in northeastern Illinois, northeast of Joliet. It is a southwestern suburb of Chicago. Population: 52,142 (2002 estimate).

tin liz·zie /-lízzee/ *n* a cheap, old, or dilapidated car (*informal*) [< *Tin Lizzie*, nickname for the Model T Ford automobile]

tinned /tind/ *adj UK* same as **canned** (sense 1)

tin·ner /tínnər/ *n* **1.** a worker in a tin mine **2.** INDUST same as **tinsmith**

tin·ni·tus /ti nítiss, tínnitəss/ *n* a continual noise in the ear, e.g., a ringing or roaring, usually caused by damage to the hair cells of the inner ear [Mid-19C. < Latin < *tinnire* "to ring, tinkle," an imitation of the sound]

tin·ny /tínnee/ (**-ni·er, -ni·est**) *adj* **1.** HAVING THIN METALLIC SOUND lacking a full resonant sound ○ *banging out tunes on a tinny old piano* **2.** CONSISTING OF TIN yielding, containing, or having the characteristics of tin **3.** TASTING OF METAL having a metallic taste **4.** INFERIOR IN QUALITY cheaply or shoddily made —**tin·ni·ly** *adv* —**tin·ni·ness** *n*

tin-o·pen·er *n UK* same as **can opener**

Tin Pan Al·ley *n* (*dated*) **1.** a city district in which the business of composing and publishing popular music is carried on **2.** popular music composers and publishers considered collectively [*Tin pan* "tinny piano," from the cheap pianos associated with music publishers' offices]

tin plate *n* steel or iron in thin sheets coated with tin

tin-pot *adj* inferior in quality or importance (*informal*)

tin·sel /tínssəl/ *n* **1.** GLITTERING MATERIAL a thin strip of glittering metal foil, paper, or plastic, used for decoration **2.** SOMETHING SHOWY something worthless that appears glamorous ■ *vt* (**-seled** or **-selled, -sel·ing** or **-sel·ling, -sels**) **1.** PUT TINSEL ON SOMETHING to decorate something with tinsel or other glittering material **2.** MAKE SOMETHING SHOWY to give something a gaudy flashy quality ■ *adj* **1.** MADE OF TINSEL made of or decorated with tinsel **2.** GAUDY appearing glamorous but in fact worthless [15C. < French *étincelé* "sparkling" (especially with metallic thread), later form of Old French *estincele* "spark" < Latin *scintilla*] —**tin·sel·ly** *adj*

Tin·sel·town /tínssəl tòwn/ *n* Hollywood and the US movie industry regarded as a place of insubstantial glamour (*informal disapproving*)

tin·smith /tín smìth/ *n* a maker or repairer of objects made of tin or other easily worked metals

tin snips *npl* shears used for cutting sheet metal

tin·stone /tín stōn/ *n* MINERALS same as **cassiterite**

tint /tint/ *n* **1.** PALE SHADE a shade of a color, especially a pale one **2.** COLOR WITH WHITE ADDED a color mixed with white to give low saturation and high lightness **3.** TRACE OF COLOR a slight amount of a color **4.** HAIR DYE a dye for the hair **5.** SMALL ADDITION a barely noticeable addition of something **6.** PRINTING BACKGROUND COLOR a pale color printed as a background onto which another color is printed **7.** ART SHADING IN ENGRAVING a shading effect in engraving, produced by a series of parallel lines ■ *vti* (**tint·ed, tint·ing, tints**) GIVE TINT TO SOMETHING to color or shade something with a tint, or acquire a tint [Early 18C. Variant of TINCT < Latin *tinctus*, past participle of *tingere* "soak, dye"] —**tint·er** *n*

Tin·tag·el /tin tájjəl/ coastal town in Cornwall, southwestern England, said to be the birthplace of the legendary King Arthur. Population: 1,800 (1998 estimate).

tin·tin·nab·u·la plural of **tintinnabulum**

tin·tin·nab·u·la·tion /tìntə nabyə láysh'n/ *n* the ringing of bells [Mid-19C. < Latin *tintinnabulum* (see TINTINNABULUM)] —**tin·tin·nab·u·lar** /tìntə nábbyələr/ *adj*

tin·tin·nab·u·lum /tìntə nábbyələm/ (*plural* **-la** /-lə/) *n* a small bell with a high clear ring [Late 16C. < Latin, "bell" < *tintinnare* "ring repeatedly" < *tinnire* "to ring," an imitation of the sound]

Tin·to·ret·to /tìntə réttō/ (1518?–94) Italian painter. Based in Venice, he painted large murals in the mannerist style, using free brush strokes and dramatic foreshortened perspectives. Born **Robusti, Jacopo**

> "Grant me paradise in this world; I'm not so sure I'll reach it in the next."
> [Attributed to Tintoretto]

tin·type /tín tīp/ *n* PHOTOGRAPHY same as **ferrotype**

tin·ware /tín wèr/ *n* objects made of tin plate, especially utensils

tin whis·tle *n* MUSIC same as **penny whistle**

tin·work /tín wùrk/ *n* things made of tin

tin·works /tín wùrks/ (*plural same*) *n* a place where tin is smelted and rolled

ti·ny /tīnee/ *adj* (**-ni·er, -ni·est**) extremely small ■ *n* (*plural* **-nies**) a very young child (*informal*) [Late 16C. < obsolete *tine* "very small," origin ?] —**ti·ni·ly** *adv* —**ti·ni·ness** *n*

-tion *suffix* action or process, or the result of an action or process ○ *pollution* [Directly or via French < Latin *-tion-*]

tip[1] /tip/ *n* **1.** POINTED END the end of an object, especially a narrow or pointed end ○ *a pencil with a sharp tip* **2.** PART ON END a piece attached to the end of something else ■ *vt* (**tipped, tip·ping, tips**) **1.** PROVIDE END FOR SOMETHING to provide something with an end, or form the end of something **2.** COVER END OF SOMETHING to cover or decorate the end of something ○ *shoes with steel-tipped toes* **3.** TAKE END OFF SOMETHING to remove the end from something [15C. Probably < Old Norse *typpi* < Germanic, "upper extremity"] ◇ **on the tip of somebody's tongue 1.** nearly, but not quite, brought to mind **2.** on the verge of being said but remaining unsaid ◇ **the tip of the iceberg** the small visible or obvious part of a largely unseen problem or difficulty

tip[2] /tip/ *v* (**tipped, tip·ping, tips**) **1.** *vti* TILT SOMETHING to cause something to move from a level or upright position, or be moved in this way ○ *sitting with his chair tipped back* **2.** *vti* KNOCK SOMETHING OVER to turn something on its side or upside down, or become turned on the side or upside down ○ *High winds caused the truck to tip over on its side.* **3.** *vt* POUR SOMETHING OUT to remove a container's contents by moving it from a level or upright position ○ *tipped the gravel onto the path* **4.** *vti UK* DUMP GARBAGE to dispose of refuse **5.** *vt* TAKE OFF YOUR HAT to touch or lift a hat as a greeting ■ *n* **1.** ACT OF TIPPING an act of tipping something **2.** TILT an incline from vertical or horizontal **3.** *UK* GARBAGE DUMP a place to dump refuse [14C. Origin ?] —**tip·pa·ble** *adj*

tip[3] /tip/ *n* **1.** GRATUITY a gift of money for a service, especially as an amount above what is owed **2.** WARNING OR INFORMATION an item of advance or confidential information that may give the person who receives it an advantage **3.** HELPFUL HINT a useful suggestion or idea for doing something ○ *cooking tips* ■ *vti* (**tipped, tip·ping, tips**) **1.** GIVE GRATUITY to give somebody a gift of money in return for a service, especially in addition to what is owed **2.** INFORM SOMEBODY to give somebody advance, inside, or confidential information [Early 17C. Origin ?] —**tip·per** *n*
tip off *vt* to give somebody a warning or some useful advance information ○ *The police had been tipped off about the girl's whereabouts.*

tip[4] /tip/ *n* **1.** LIGHT HIT a light glancing blow **2.** BASEBALL DEFLECTED BASEBALL a baseball struck so that it glances off the bat ■ *v* (**tipped, tip·ping, tips**) **1.** *vt* HIT SOMEBODY OR SOMETHING LIGHTLY to strike somebody or something with a light glancing blow **2.** *vt* BASEBALL DEFLECT BASEBALL WITH BAT to strike a baseball so that it glances off the bat **3.** *vi Southern US* TIPTOE ALONG to walk quietly on tiptoe [15C. Origin ?]

tip-and-run *adj UK* striking quickly then withdrawing immediately

tip·cart /típ kaàrt/ *n* a cart whose load is emptied by tilting its body [Late 19C. < TIP[2]]

ti·pi *n* CULTL ANTHROP another spelling of **tepee**

~~tipical~~ incorrect spelling of **typical**

tip-in *n* **1.** in basketball, a goal scored by lightly pushing a rebound into the basket with the fingertips **2.** in hockey, a goal scored at very close range by giving a short stroke with the stick [< TIP[4]]

tip-off[1] *n* (*informal*) **1.** a piece of advance information, or a warning given in an effort to help **2.** a sign or indication of something, or that something is likely to happen [< TIP[3]]

tip-off[2] *n* in basketball, the start of a period of play in which two players try to tap a jump ball to one of their teammates [< TIP[4]]

Tip·per·ar·y /tìppə rérree/ former county in Munster Province, southern Republic of Ireland, now divided into the counties of Tipperary North Riding and Tipperary South Riding. Population: 133,535 (2002). Area: 1,643 sq. mi./4,225 sq. km.

tip·pet /típpit/ *n* **1.** STOLE WITH HANGING ENDS a stole or cape, often made of fur, with long ends that hang down the front **2.** STOLE OF ANGLICAN CLERGY a long stole worn around the shoulders and over the robes of Anglican clergy during services **3.** HANGING END OF GARMENT a long hanging end worn attached to a sleeve, hood, or cape, worn in medieval times and up to the 16th century **4.** BIRDS same as **ruff**[1] (sense 2) **5.** FISHING PART TO WHICH FLY IS TIED in angling, the thin end section of a leader to which a fly is tied [14C. Probably < TIP[1]]

Tip·pett /típpit/, **Sir Michael** (1905–98) British composer. He is noted for the mystical quality of many of his orchestral, instrumental, and vocal works. Full name **Tippett, Sir Michael Kemp**

tip·ping point *n* **1.** a defining moment in a series of events at which time a series of consequential, often momentous and irreversible reactions occur **2.** the stage during an epidemic when the agent, especially a virus, begins to increase very rapidly in a population

tip·ple[1] /típp'l/ *v* (**-pled, -pling, -ples**) **1.** *vi* DRINK ALCOHOL HABITUALLY to drink alcoholic liquor habitually or excessively **2.** *vti* DRINK ALCOHOL REPEATEDLY to drink alcoholic liquor repeatedly a little at a time ■ *n* ALCOHOLIC DRINK a type or drink of alcoholic liquor (*informal*) [Mid-16C. Probably back-formation < *tippler* "ale seller" < N Germanic]

tip·ple[2] /típp'l/ *n* MIN EXTRACT **1.** DEVICE FOR UNLOADING ORE CARS a device for tipping coal or ore cars to unload them **2.** PLACE FOR UNLOADING ORE a place where ore or coal cars are unloaded **3.** PLACE FOR SCREENING COAL a place where coal is screened and loaded into trucks or railroad cars [Mid-19C. < TIP[2]]

tip·pler[1] /típplər/ *n* a habitual drinker of alcoholic beverages [Late 16C. < TIPPLE[1]]

tip·pler[2] /típplər/ *n* a domestic pigeon of a breed kept for show [Mid-19C. < TIPPLE[2], because it often turns over backward in flight]

tip·py /típpee/ (**-pi·er, -pi·est**) *adj* not stable and likely to tilt or tip over

tip·staff /típ stàf/ (*plural* **-staves** /-stàyvz/ or **-staffs**) *n* **1.** in former times, a metal-tipped staff carried as a sign of official authority **2.** in former times, a court official who carried a staff, e.g., a bailiff or constable [Mid-16C. Contraction of *tipped staff* < TIP[1]]

tip·ster /típstər/ *n* somebody who provides or sells information to horserace betters or financial speculators [Mid-19C. < TIP[3]]

tip·sy /típsee/ (**-si·er, -si·est**) *adj* **1.** slightly drunk **2.** inclined to tilt or tip [Late 16C. < TIP[2]] —**tip·si·ly** *adv* —**tip·si·ness** *n*

tip·toe /típ tō/ *vi* (**-toed, -toe·ing, -toes**) **1.** WALK WITH HEELS RAISED to walk on the toes and the balls of the feet with the heels off the ground **2.** MOVE CAUTIOUSLY to move or proceed quietly or cautiously ■ *n* POSITION WITH HEELS RAISED a standing position in which the heels are raised off the ground and the weight is on the front part of the feet, with the body often also stretched up to gain extra height ○ *walking on tiptoe* ■ *adj* **1.** WALKING ON TOES walking or standing on the toes or balls of the feet **2.** CAUTIOUS proceeding with caution or stealth ■ *adv* ON TIPS OF TOES on the toes or the balls of the feet [14C. < TIP[1]]

tip·top /típ tòp/ (*informal*) *adj* OF TOP QUALITY of the highest quality or rank ■ *adv* WELL exceptionally well ■ *n* **1.** SUMMIT the highest point **2.** HIGHEST QUALITY the highest degree of quality or excellence [Early 18C. Doubling of TOP[1], after TIP[1]]

tip-up *adj* designed to tilt upward or fold up [< TIP[2]]

ti·rade /tī ràyd, tī ráyd/ *n* a long angry speech, usually of criticism or denunciation [Early 19C. < French, "volley" < *tirer* "to draw" < assumed Vulgar Latin *tirare*]

ti·ra·mi·su /teèrə meè sōō, -mi sōō/ *n* an Italian dessert made with layers of sponge cake soaked in espresso coffee, Marsala, mascarpone cheese, and chocolate [Late 20C. < Italian *tira mi sù* "pick me up"]

Ti·ra·na /ti raánə/ capital city of Albania, in the central part of the country, situated 17 mi./27 km from the Adriatic coast. Population: 343,078 (2001).

tire[1] /tīr/ (**tired, tir·ing, tires**) *vti* **1.** to make somebody feel in need of rest or sleep, or grow weaker and less energetic and feel a need for rest or sleep **2.** to lose interest in and become bored and impatient with somebody or something, or cause somebody to do this [Old English *tyrian*, origin ?]

tire[2] /tīr/ *n* a woman's head covering or ornament (*archaic*) [14C. Shortening of ATTIRE]

tire[3] /tīr/ *n* **1.** RUBBER EDGING FOR WHEEL a hollow band of rubber, often reinforced with fibers of other material, fitted around the outer edge of a vehicle's wheel and filled with compressed air **2.** SOLID RUBBER EDGING a solid band of rubber fitted to a wheel's edge, e.g., on baby carriages and children's bicycles **3.** METAL EDGING a band of metal fitted for reinforcement to the rims of wheels on various vehicles, e.g., handcarts and railroad cars

tired /tīrd/ *adj* **1.** NEEDING REST in need of rest or sleep, or weakened and made less active by exertion **2.** NO LONGER INTERESTED having lost patience or interest ○ *grew tired of hearing the same complaints* **3.** OVERUSED no longer new or fresh because of overuse ○ *a tired old slogan* [15C. < TIRE[1]] —**tired·ly** *adv* —**tired·ness** *n*

tired out *adj* thoroughly tired

Ti·ree /tī reé/ island of the Inner Hebrides, western Scotland. Population: 950 (1991). Area: 29 sq. mi./76 sq. km.

tire·less /tírləss/ *adj* never slackening or stopping, and apparently immune to tiredness or fatigue [Late 16C. < TIRE[1]] —**tire·less·ly** *adv* —**tire·less·ness** *n*

Ti·re·si·as /tī reéssee əss/ *n* in Greek mythology, a blind seer from Thebes who often delivered prophecies to Oedipus

tire·some /tírssəm/ *adj* causing weariness, annoyance, or boredom [Early 16C. < TIRE[1]] —**tire·some·ly** *adv* —**tire·some·ness** *n*

Tîr·gu Mu·reș /tùrgoo moór esh/ capital city of Mureș County in central Romania. Population: 165,534 (1997).

tir·ing /tíring/ *adj* causing somebody to feel tired, usually because requiring great physical or mental exertion [Late 16C. < TIRE[1]]

Tír na n-Óg /teér na nòg/ *n* in Irish legend, a land of eternal youth [Late 19C. < Irish, "land of the young"]

ti·ro *n* another spelling of **tyro**

Ti·rol /tə rṓl, tī-/, **Ty·rol** province in western Austria, lying within the Alps. Capital: Innsbruck. Population: 663,603 (1998). Area: 4,883 sq. mi./12,647 sq. km. —**Ti·ro·le·an** /tìrrə leé ən/ *n, adj* —**Tir·o·lese** /tìrrə leéz, -leéss/ *n, adj*

Ti·ros /tī ròss/ (*plural same*) *n* a satellite with infrared and television equipment for transmitting weather data to Earth [Late 20C. Acronym < *television infrared observational satellite*]

Tir·so de Mo·li·na /teérssō day mō leé naa/ (1571?–1648) Spanish playwright and theologian. He is the author of several hundred plays, including the comedy *The Trickster of Seville* (1630), which has the first literary presentation of Don Juan. Pseudonym of **Téllez, Gabriel**

Tir·than·ka·ra /teer thúngkərə/ *n* a traditional holy man of Jainism, belonging to a group believed to have attained personal immortality through enlightenment, and by their teaching to have made a path for others to follow [Mid-19C. < Sanskrit *tīrthaṁkaraḥ* "ford maker" < *tīrtham* "ford, passage" + *kṛ-* "make"]

Ti·ruch·chi·rap·pal·li /tìrrəchə raápəlee/ city in Tiruchchirappalli District, Tamil Nadu State, southern India. Population: 387,223 (1991). Former name **Trichinopoly**

Ti·ru·nel·ve·li /tìrrōō nélvəlee/ city in Tirunelveli District, Tamil Nadu State, southern India. Population: 431,603 (2001).

Tir·yns /tírrinz/ ancient city in Argolis Department in the Peloponnesus, southern Greece, situated between Naplion and Mycenae

'tis /tiz/ *contr* it is (*archaic or literary*)

ti·sane /ti zán/, **ptis·an** *n* an infusion of leaves or flowers used as a beverage, e.g., an herbal tea [14C. Via French < Greek *ptisanē* "barley water"]

Tish·a b'Av /tìshə baáv/ *n* in Judaism, a fast on the ninth day of the month of Av to commemorate the destruction of the First and Second Temples [< Hebrew *tišāh bēāb* "ninth of Av"]

Tish·ri /tíshree/ (*plural* **-ris**) *n* in the Jewish calendar, the seventh month of the religious year, lasting 30 days and falling about the same time as September to October. See table at **calendar** [Mid-17C. < Hebrew *tišrī*]

Ti·siph·o·ne /ti síffənee/ *n* in Greek mythology, one of the three Furies. The others were Alecto and Megaera.

tis·sue /tíshoo/ *n* **1.** PIECE OF ABSORBENT PAPER a piece of soft absorbent paper that can be used as a handkerchief or a towel **2.** INDUST same as **tissue paper 3.** BIOL GROUP OF CELLS IN ORGANISM organic body material in animals and plants made up of large numbers of cells that are similar in form and function and their related intercellular substances. The four basic types of tissue are nerve, muscle, epidermal, and connective. **4.** INTRICATE SERIES an intricate interrelated series of things ○ *a tissue of lies* **5.** TEXTILES GAUZY FABRIC a thin, finely woven fabric with a gauzy texture [14C. < Old French *tissu* < past participle of *tistre* "weave" < Latin *texere*]

tis·sue cul·ture *n* **1.** the growth of tissue outside an organism in a nutrient medium, or the techniques involved in this process **2.** the tissue grown in a culture medium

tis·sue pa·per *n* a thin soft paper. Use: wrapping and protecting delicate items.

tis·sue plas·min·o·gen ac·ti·va·tor *n* an anticlotting enzyme that is produced naturally in blood vessel linings and is genetically engineered for use in treating heart attacks, dissolving blood clots, and preventing heart muscle damage

tis·sue type *n* the chemical characteristics of the body tissue of an organism that determine whether or not the tissue is immunologically compatible with the tissue of another organism —**tis·sue type** *vti*

Ti·sza /tíss aw/ major tributary of the Danube River in eastern Europe. Length: 600 mi./970 km.

tit[1] /tit/ *n* **1.** same as **teat 2.** an offensive term for a woman's breast (*slang*) [Old English *titt* < Germanic]

tit: great tit

tit[2] /tit/ *n* a small active songbird with a short beak and strong feet, e.g., a tufted titmouse or a great tit. Native to: northern hemisphere, Africa. Family: Paridae. [Early 18C. Shortening of TITMOUSE]

Tit. *abbr* BIBLE Titus

ti·tan /tít'n/ *n* somebody whose power, achievement, intellect, or physical size is extraordinarily impressive [Early 19C. < TITAN]

Ti·tan /tít'n/ *n* **1.** in Greek mythology, one of the twelve children of Uranus and Gaia, supreme rulers of the universe until they were overthrown by Zeus **2.** a large natural satellite of Saturn [15C. Via Latin < Greek]

ti·tan·ate /tít'n àyt/ *n* a compound that is a salt or an ester of titanic acid

Ti·ta·ni·a /tī táynee ə, ti-/ *n* **1.** in medieval folklore, the wife of Oberon and queen of the fairies **2.** the largest moon of the planet Uranus, the fourth most distant satellite observable from the Earth, orbiting at a distance of 262,000 mi./436,000 km with a diameter of 947 mi./1578 km. Although it was one of the first two satellites of Uranus to be discovered in 1787, Oberon being the other, Titania is officially designated as Uranus III.

ti·tan·ic[1] /tī tánnik/ *adj* **1.** having extraordinary physical strength or size **2.** of extraordinary power, scope, or impressiveness [Mid-19C. < TITANIC] —**ti·tan·i·cal·ly** *adv*

ti·tan·ic[2] /tī tánnik/ *adj* relating to or containing titanium, especially with a valence of four [Early 19C. < TITANIUM]

Ti·tan·ic /tī tánnik/ *adj* relating to or like a mythological Titan [Mid-17C. < Greek *titanikos* < *Titanes*, plural of *Titan* "Titan"]

ti·tan·ic ac·id *n* an acid that is the hydrated form of titanium dioxide. Use: for fixing dyes. Formula: H_2TiO_3.

ti·tan·ic ox·ide *n* CHEM same as **titanium dioxide**

ti·tan·if·er·ous /tīt'n íffərəss/ *adj* yielding or containing titanium [Early 19C. < TITANIUM]

Ti·tan·ism /tīt'n ìzzəm/ *n* a spirit of defiance of authority, conventional society, and the established order

ti·tan·ite /tīt'n īt/ *n* MINERALS same as **sphene** [Mid-19C. < TITANIUM]

ti·ta·ni·um /tī táynee əm/ *n* a strong, lightweight, corrosion-resistant silvery metallic element. Source: rutile, ilmenite. Use: manufacture of alloys for aerospace industry. Symbol **Ti**. See table at **element** [Late 18C. < TITAN (sense 2), after URANIUM]

ti·ta·ni·um di·ox·ide *n* a white crystalline compound. Source: rutile, ilmenite, other minerals. Use: pigment for durable paints and plastics. Formula: TiO_2.

ti·ta·ni·um white *n* **1.** CHEM same as **titanium dioxide** **2.** a brilliant white paint pigment consisting primarily of titanium dioxide

ti·tan·o·saur /tī tánnə sàwr, tīt'nə-/ *n* a huge herbivorous sauropod dinosaur of the Cretaceous and Jurassic periods, found especially in South America. Genus: *Titanosaurus*. [Late 19C. < modern Latin *Titanosaurus* < Greek *Titan* "Titan" + *sauros* "lizard"]

ti·tan·o·there /tī tánnə thèer, tīt'nə-/ *n* a large mammal similar to a rhinoceros that lived in North America during the Tertiary Period [Mid-20C. < modern Latin *Titanotherium* < Greek *Titan* "Titan" + *therion* "wild beast"]

ti·tan·ous /tīt'nəss/ *adj* relating to or containing titanium with a valence of three [Mid-19C. < TITANIUM]

tit·bit /tít bìt/ *n UK* same as **tidbit**

titch /tich/ *n UK* a very small person (*informal*) [Mid-20C. < Little *Tich*, stage name of British comedian Harry Relph (1868–1928), who was very small]

ORIGIN Harry Relph got his nickname *Little Tich*, from his supposed resemblance to the so-called Tichborne claimant. This was the title given to Arthur Orton, who, in an English cause célèbre of the 1860s, returned from Australia claiming to be Roger Tichborne, the heir to an English baronetcy who had supposedly been lost at sea.

ti·ter /tītər/ *n* **1.** the concentration of a substance in solution as determined by titration **2.** the concentration of an antibody in serum [Mid-19C. < French *titre* "qualification, quality (of gold or silver alloy)," variant of *title* (see TITLE)]

tit for tat *n* the repayment a wrong or injury suffered by inflicting equivalent harm on the doer (*hyphenated when used before a noun*) ○ *tit-for-tat strikes* [Mid-16C. Origin ?]

tithe /tīth/ *n* **1.** SOMEBODY'S FINANCIAL SUPPORT FOR CHURCH one tenth of somebody's income or produce paid voluntarily or as a tax for the support of a church or its clergy **2.** OBLIGATION OF SUPPORTING CHURCH FINANCIALLY the obligation to pay a tithe to a church or its clergy **3.** ASSESSMENT OR CONTRIBUTION a voluntary contribution or tax payment, especially when it constitutes one tenth of somebody's income **4.** SMALL PART OF SOMETHING one tenth or a small part of something ■ *v* (**tithed, tith·ing, tithes**) **1.** *vti* PAY ONE TENTH OF INCOME to contribute or pay one tenth of your income or produce, especially to support a church **2.** *vt* COLLECT TENTH OF INCOME OF SOMEBODY to assess or collect the payment of one tenth of the income of somebody [Old English *tēoþa* "tenth, tithe"] —**tith·a·ble** *adj* —**tith·er** *n*

tith·ing /tīthing/ *n* **1.** the assessing or paying of tithes **2.** one tenth part of something [Old English *tēoþung* < TITHE]

ti·ti[1] /tee tèe, tèe tèe/ (*plural* **-tis**) *n* a tree-dwelling monkey with a round face, thick soft fur, and a long tail. Native to: tropical South America. Genus: *Callicebus*. [Mid-18C. Via Spanish *tití* < Aymara]

ti·ti[2] /tī tī, tèe tèe/ (*plural* **-tis**) *n* **1.** an evergreen bush or small tree with glossy leathery leaves. Flowers: fragrant, white or pinkish. Native to: southeastern United States. Latin name: *Cliftonia monophylla*. **2.** a small evergreen tree or bush with leathery leaves and yellow fruit. Native to: southeastern United States, Central and South America. Latin name: *Cyrilla racemiflora*. [Early 19C. Origin ?]

ti·tian /tísh'n/, **Ti·tian** *adj* of a gold-tinged auburn color ○ *titian hair* [Late 19C. After TITIAN, who used the color frequently]

AKG London

Titian: self-portrait (1555)

Ti·tian /tísh'ən/ (1485?–1576) Italian painter. The foremost Venetian painter of the Renaissance, he painted portraits and religious and mythological scenes that are noted for their rich coloration. Born **Vecellio, Tiziano**

> "It is not bright colors but good drawing that makes figures beautiful."
> [Titian. Quoted in *Marvels of the Painter's Art*, Carlo Ridolfi; 1648]

Ti·ti·ca·ca, Lake /titti kaákə/ lake in east central South America, extending from southeastern Peru to western Bolivia. It is the largest lake on the continent and the highest navigable lake in the world, about 12,500 ft./3,810 m above sea level. Area: 3,200 sq. mi./8,300 sq. km.

tit·il·late /títt'l àyt/ (**-lat·ed, -lat·ing, -lates**) *v* **1.** *vti* to excite or stimulate somebody pleasurably, usually in a mildly sexual way **2.** *vt* to cause a tingling sensation in somebody by touching him or her lightly [Early 17C. < Latin *titillare* "tickle"] —**tit·il·lat·ing** *adj* —**tit·il·lat·ing·ly** *adv* —**tit·il·la·tion** /tìtt'l áysh'n/ *n* —**tit·il·la·tive** *adj*

USAGE titillate or **titivate**? These two unrelated verbs look and sound similar and are sometimes confused. To ***titillate*** is to excite or stimulate somebody, usually in a mildly sexual way, whereas to ***titivate*** is to improve the appearance: *She was accused of titillating her readers with details of the actor's private life. He was titivating himself in front of the mirror.*

tit·i·vate /títti vàyt/ (**-vat·ed, -vat·ing, -vates**), **tit·ti·vate** *vti* to improve the appearance of somebody or something by neatening or adding decoration [Early 19C. Alteration of *tidivate*, origin ?] —**tit·i·va·tion** /tìtti váysh'n/ *n* —**tit·i·va·tor** *n*

USAGE See *titillate*.

tit·lark /tít laàrk/ *n* BIRDS same as **pipit** [Mid-17C. < TIT[2] + LARK[1]]

ti·tle /tīt'l/ *n* **1.** NAME a name that identifies a book, movie, play, painting, musical composition, or other literary or artistic work **2.** DESCRIPTIVE HEADING a descriptive heading for something such as a book chapter, a magazine article, or a speech **3.** PUBL same as **title page** **4.** PUBLISHED OR RECORDED WORK a work published or recorded by a company ○ *this spring's new titles* **5.** DESIGNATION ADDED TO NAME a word added to and usually preceding somebody's name to indicate his or her rank, social status, or profession, or as a courtesy, e.g., "Mr.", "Ms.", "Dr.", or "Lord" **6.** NAME DESCRIBING POSITION a name that describes somebody's job or position in a company or organization ○ *a job title* **7.** CHAMPIONSHIP the status of champion in a sport or competition ○ *a title fight* **8.** LAW RIGHT TO POSSESS PROPERTY a legal right to possess and dispose of property **9.** LAW EVIDENCE OF PROPERTY RIGHTS the evidence of legal right to property **10.** LAW DOCUMENT a document giving the legal right to property **11.** LAW RIGHT OR PROOF OF RIGHT a legitimate right, or something providing proof or justification for a claim **12.** LAW CLAIM BASED ON RIGHT a claim based on a legitimate right **13.** LAW DIVISION a division of a law, statute, or law book **14.** LAW LAW HEADING a heading for a lawsuit or legal action, or one that names a document or statute **15.** CHR REQUIREMENT OF ORDINATION a source of income or office in the church required of a candidate by the Church of England before ordination **16.** CHR ROMAN CATHOLIC CHURCH IN ROME a Roman Catholic church in or near Rome that has a bishop or cardinal as its nominal head ■ **ti·tles** *npl* MOVIES, MEDIA CREDITS OR SUBTITLES ON SCREEN the written presentation on the screen of credits, narration, or subtitles in a movie or television program ■ *vt* (**-tled, -tling, -tles**) **1.** NAME SOMEBODY OR SOMETHING to give a name or title to somebody or something **2.** CALL SOMEBODY BY TITLE to call somebody by a particular title [Pre-12C. Via French < Latin *titulus* "inscription"] —**ti·tled** *adj*

ti·tle bar *n* a horizontal bar at the top of a computer screen that usually shows the names of the program and file that is currently in use

ti·tle deed *n* a deed or document that is evidence of somebody's legal right to property

ti·tle·hold·er /tīt'l hòldər/ *n* **1.** somebody who holds a sports championship title **2.** somebody who holds a legal title to property —**ti·tle·hold·ing** *n*

ti·tle page *n* a page at the beginning of a book that gives its title and the name of the author and publisher

ti·tle role *n* the role in a play or movie that gives the work its name

ti·tle track *n* the song or piece of music whose name is used as the title of a particular recording

ti·tlist /tīt'list/ *n* SPORTS same as **titleholder** (sense 1)

tit·man /títmən/ (*plural* **-men** /-mən/) *n Northeast US* **1.** the runt of a litter, especially of hogs **2.** an offensive term for a person regarded as short in stature [Early 19C. < obsolete *tit* "something small, runt," origin ?]

tit·mouse /tít mòwss/ (*plural* **-mice** /-mīss/) *n* BIRDS same as **tit**[2] [14C. Alteration (influenced by *mouse*) of *titmose* < obsolete *tit* "something small, runt" + *mose* "titmouse" (< Old English *māse*)]

AKG London

Tito

Ti·to /teètō/ (1892–1980) Yugoslav patriot and president of Yugoslavia (1942–77). After leading partisan forces against the Germans in World War II, he established a Communist state independent of the Soviet Union. Known as **Marshal Tito**. Born **Broz, Josip**

> "I am the only Yugoslav."
> [Attributed to Tito]

Ti·to·ism /teètō ìzzəm/ *n* the form of Communism associated with Tito and practiced by him in Yugoslavia, especially involving the pursuit of national interests independent of the then Soviet Union and its satellites —**Ti·to·ist** *n, adj*

ti·trant /tī́trənt/ *n* a reagent that is added in titration, e.g., a solution of known concentration [Mid-20C. < TITRATE]

ti·trate /tī́ tràyt/ (**-trat·ed, -trat·ing, -trates**) *vt* to measure the concentration of a solution by titration [Late 19C. < French *titrer* < *titre* (see TITER)] —**ti·trat·a·ble** *adj*

ti·tra·tion /tī tráysh'n/ *n* a method of calculating the concentration of a dissolved substance in a known volume of test solution by adding measured quantities of a reagent of known concentration until a reaction occurs

ti·tre *n* CHEM, BIOCHEM Can, UK spelling of **titer**

ti·tri·met·ric /tītrə méttrik/ *adj* using or calculated by titration [Late 19C. < TITRATION] —**ti·tri·met·ri·cal·ly** *adv*

tit·ter /títtər/ *vi* (**-tered, -ter·ing, -ters**) to laugh quietly or giggle in a self-conscious or nervous way ■ *n* a quiet self-conscious or nervous laugh or giggle [Early 17C. An imitation of the sound] —**tit·ter·er** *n* —**tit·ter·ing** *n* —**tit·ter·ing·ly** *adv*

tit·ti·vate *vti* another spelling of **titivate**

tit·tle /títt'l/ *n* **1.** a tiny bit of something **2.** a small mark used in printing and writing, e.g., an accent, punctuation mark, or diacritical mark [14C. < medieval Latin *titulus* "small superscript mark" < Latin, "title"]

tit·tle-tat·tle *n* idle gossip ■ *vi* (**tit·tle-tat·tled, tit·tle-tat·tling, tit·tle-tat·tles**) to gossip idly [Early 16C. Doubling of TATTLE] —**tit·tle-tat·tler** *n*

tit·tup /títtəp/ *vi* (**-tuped** or **-tupped, -tup·ing** or **-tup·ping, -tups**) to move in a lively prancing way ■ *n* a sometimes exaggerated lively prancing movement [Late 17C. Origin ?]

tit·ty (*plural* **-ties**) *n* a woman's breast (*slang; often considered offensive*)

tit·u·ba·tion /tìchə báysh'n/ *n* an unsteady or stumbling gait or a head tremor, often caused by a disorder of the cerebellum [Mid-17C. < Latin *titubare* "stagger"]

tit·u·lar /tíchələr/ *adj* **1.** IN NAME ONLY having a particular title, rank, or position, but not possessing the power or exercising the functions usually associated with it **2.** WITH TITLE OF RANK holding a title of rank **3.** FROM TITLE derived from or figuring in the title of a work such as a book or movie **4.** CHR FROM INACTIVE SEE bearing the title of a see or monastery that is no longer active ■ *n* **1.** SOMEBODY WITH TITLE OF RANK somebody who holds a title of rank **2.** HOLDER OF NOMINAL TITLE somebody who holds a title in name only [Late 16C. < Latin *titulus* "title"] —**tit·u·lar·ly** *adv* —**tit·u·lar·y** *n*

Ti·tus /tī́təss/ *n* **1.** in the Bible, an early Christian leader and a disciple of St. Paul. **2.** a book of the Bible, originally a letter addressed to Titus and traditionally attributed to St. Paul. It contains advice on the organization of the Christian Church. See table at **Bible**

Ti·tus /tī́təss/ (A.D. 39–81) Roman general and emperor. He captured and destroyed Jerusalem in A.D. 70. As emperor (79–81) he was noted for his leniency and generosity, and he also completed the Colosseum in Rome. Full name **Titus Flavius Sabinus Vespasianus**

Tiv /tiv/ (*plural* **Tivs** or *same*) *n* **1.** a member of a people living in West Africa, mainly in southern Nigeria and neighboring Cameroon **2.** the Benue-Congo language of the Tiv people. Native speakers: 1.5 million. [Mid-20C. < Bantu] —**Tiv** *adj*

Ti·Vo /tée vō/ *tdmk* a trademark for a type of digital video recorder that automatically records selected television programs each time they are broadcast and stores them on a hard disk

Ti·vo·li /tívvəlee/ city in central Italy, near Rome, location of the Renaissance-period Tivoli Gardens and the ruined villa of the emperor Hadrian. Population: 49,342 (2001).

Ti·wa /téewə/ (*plural* **-was** or *same*) *n* **1.** a member of a group of Pueblo peoples who lived in New Mexico and who now live mainly in Texas and northern New Mexico **2.** the Tanoan language of the Tiwa people. Native speakers: 5,000. [Early 18C. < Tiwa] —**Ti·wa** *adj*

Tiz·ard /tíz aard/, **Dame Cath** (*b.* 1931) governor-general of New Zealand (1990–96). After an extensive career in local government, she became mayor of Auckland in 1983 and the first woman to hold the post of governor-general. Full name **Tizard, Dame Catherine Anne**

tiz·zy /tízzee/ *n* a nervous agitated or confused state (*informal*) [Mid-20C. Origin ?]

tj *abbr* ONLINE Tajikistan (*used in Internet addresses*) See table at **domain name**

T-joint (*plural* **T-joints** or **tee-joints**) *n* a joint in wood or other material forming the letter T

tk. *abbr* TRANSP truck

TKO *abbr* BOXING technical knockout

tkt. *abbr* ticket

Tl *symbol* CHEM ELEM thallium

t.l. *abbr* INSUR total loss

TLA *abbr* three-letter acronym

Tlax·ca·la /tlaaks káalə, -kállə/ **1.** state in east central Mexico. Capital: Tlaxcala. Population: 962,646 (2000). Area: 1,559 sq. mi./4,037 sq. km. **2.** capital city of Tlaxcala State in east central Mexico. It is the site of the Church of San Francisco, the oldest church in North America (1521). Population: 77,000 (2002).

TLC *abbr* tender loving care (*informal*)

Tlem·cen /tlem sén/ city in northwestern Algeria. Population: 126,882 (1987).

Tlin·git /tlíng git, tlíngit/ (*plural* **-gits** or *same*) *n* **1.** a member of a group of Native North American peoples who lived on coastal southeastern Alaska and who now live mainly there and in British Columbia **2.** the Na-Dene language of the Tlingit people. Native speakers: 2,000. [Mid-19C. < Tlingit, "person"] —**Tlin·git** *adj*

t.l.o. *abbr* INSUR total loss only

T lym·pho·cyte *n* BIOL same as **T cell**

tm *abbr* ONLINE Turkmenistan (*used in Internet addresses*) See table at **domain name**

Tm *symbol* CHEM ELEM thulium

TM *abbr* **1.** LAW trademark **2.** ONLINE trust me (*used in e-mails or text messages*)

T.M. *abbr* HINDUISM transcendental meditation

T-man *n* a special investigator of the Department of the Treasury (*informal*)

tme·sis /tméessiss, méessiss, tə méessiss/ *n* the separation of the parts of a word by inserting a word or words between them [Mid-16C. < Greek *tmēsis* "cutting" < *temnein* "cut"]

TMJ syn·drome *n* a painful condition involving the temporomandibular joint and the muscles used for chewing, sometimes causing clicking sounds and restricted jaw movement. It is usually associated with a faulty dental bite. Full form **temporomandibular joint syndrome**

TMT *abbr* technology, media, and telecommunications

tn *abbr* ONLINE Tunisia (*used in Internet addresses*) See table at **domain name**

TN *abbr* Tennessee

tng. *abbr* training

tnpk., **Tnpk.** *abbr* ROADS turnpike

TNT *n* a yellow flammable crystalline compound. Use: explosive. Formula: $C_7H_5N_3O_6$. Full form **trinitrotoluene**

TNX *abbr* ONLINE thanks (*used in e-mails or text messages*)

to[1] *stressed* /too/; *unstressed* /tŏŏ, tə/ CORE MEANING: a preposition or adverb indicating the direction, destination, or position of somebody or something ○ *I met him on his way to school.* ○ *She climbed all the way to the top.* ○ *You'll see a supermarket to your left.*

1. *prep* INDICATES DIRECTION indicates the direction or destination of somebody or something ○ *He was on his way to the party.* **2.** *prep* INDICATES POSITION indicates the position of somebody or something ○ *To the right of the door is a bulletin board.* **3.** *prep* FORMS INFINITIVE used before the base form of a verb to make the infinitive of that verb ○ *I want to leave now.* **4.** *prep* INDICATES PURPOSE used with the base form of a verb to indicate the intention or purpose of an action ○ *The news agency is used to distribute information.* **5.** *prep* INDICATES RECIPIENT indicates the recipient of something (*used with a noun phrase to form the indirect object*) ○ *Give it to me.* ○ *mail sent to another user on the same computer* **6.** *prep* INDICATES DIRECTION OF FEELING OR ACTION indicates who or what a particular feeling or action is directed toward ○ *I was very grateful to her for everything she did for me.* **7.** *prep* INDICATES ATTACHMENT indicates that two things are joined together ○ *Each triangle consists of three square faces joined to one another along two edges.* **8.** *prep* UNTIL indicates that something goes on until a point in time or until it reaches a fixed amount ○ *He closes the store on Mondays and opens from Tuesday to Saturday.* **9.** *prep* INDICATES RANGE indicates a range of things or topics ○ *Medical studies have explored everything from pollution to pesticides to genetics to parental occupations to electromagnetic fields.* **10.** *prep* INDICATES RESULT OF CHANGE indicates what somebody or something is changing into or becoming ○ *Their excitement soon turned to gloom when they saw what the climb entailed.* **11.** *prep* INDICATES SIMULTANEITY indicates that two things are happening at the same time, especially that a particular sound or music accompanies another action ○ *I woke up to the sound of the telephone ringing.* **12.** *prep* INDICATES EQUALITY indicates equality, e.g., of two weights, amounts, or measurements ○ *There are 12 inches to the foot.* **13.** *prep* AS COMPARED WITH indicates comparison between two things such as scores in a game ○ *The score was 5 to 3 in favor of our team.* **14.** *prep* BEFORE HOUR indicates the number of minutes before the hour ○ *It was five to seven before they arrived home.* **15.** *prep* same as **at**[1] (*regional*) ○ *He's over to the doctor's.* **16.** *adv* SHUT OR ALMOST SHUT indicates that a door is shut, or covering the opening but not completely or firmly shut ○ *He pulled the door to after him.* **17.** *adv* CONSCIOUS AGAIN into a state of lucidity and consciousness ○ *came to in the recovery room* ○ *brought the patient to* **18.** *adv* NAUT INTO WIND into the direction from which the wind is blowing ○ *turned the yacht to* [Old English *tō*. < Germanic]

SPELLCHECK to, too, or **two?** Do not confuse the spelling of ***to, too,*** and ***two***, which sound similar. ***To*** has a wide variety of uses, especially as a preposition indicating, among other things, direction or destination (as in *flying to New York*), position (as in *standing to the right*), a recipient (as in *give it to me*), and range (as in *from A to B*); it also indicates the infinitive of a verb (as in *to go*). ***Too*** means "in addition" or "more than is desirable": *Are you leaving too? It's too cold to go swimming.* ***Two*** is the number 2, as in *two boys and four girls.*

to[2] *abbr* ONLINE Tonga (*used in Internet addresses*) See table at **domain name**

TO, T/O *abbr* SPORTS turnover

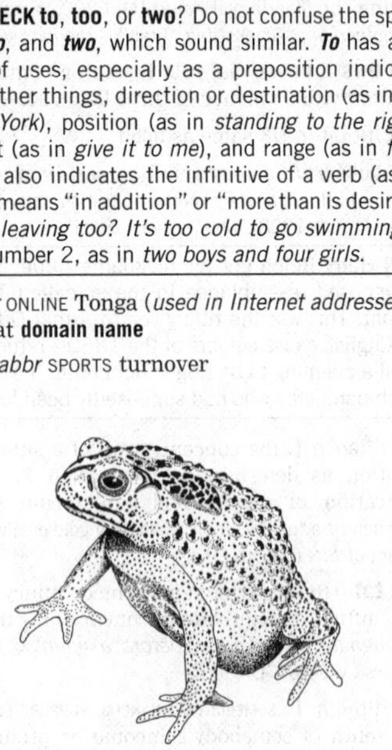

toad

toad /tōd/ *n* **1.** AMPHIBIAN SIMILAR TO FROG a small squat tailless amphibian distributed nearly worldwide. It is similar to a frog, but has dry warty skin and, except for breeding in water, lives mostly on land. Family: Bufonidae. **2.** AMPHIBIAN RESEMBLING TOAD an amphibian similar to a toad but belonging to a different taxonomic family, e.g., the horned toad **3.** OFFENSIVE TERM an offensive term for somebody considered loathsome or disgusting [Old English *tādige*, origin ?] —**toad·ish** *adj*

toad·fish /tṓd fish/ (*plural same* or **-fish·es**) *n* a scaleless spiny bottom-feeding fish with a broad flattened head and wide mouth. Native to: tropical and temperate seas. Family: Batrachoididae.

toad·flax /tṓd flàks/ (*plural* **-flax·es** or *same*) *n* **1.** a narrow-leaved plant widespread in North America. Flowers: spurred, two-lipped, orange-and-yellow, similar to snapdragon's. Native to: Europe. Latin name: *Linaria vulgaris.* **2.** a plant related to the common toadflax and similar to it. Flowers: lilac-colored. Genus: *Linaria.*

toad·stone /tṓd stṑn/ *n* a stone or similar object believed to have formed in the head or body of a toad, formerly worn around the neck as a charm against evil and disease

toad·stool /tṓd sto͞ol/ *n* a poisonous umbrella-shaped fungus with a spore-producing round flat cap on a stalk [14C. Because it resembles a small stool and grows where toads are found]

toad stran·gler *n regional* a heavy downpour

REGIONAL NOTE See *trashmover.*

toad·y /tṓdee/ *n* (*plural* **-ies**) a self-serving person who behaves in a servile sycophantic manner, fawning on and flattering people with power or influence ■ *vi* (**-ied, -y·ing, -ies**) to behave in a servile sycophantic manner, fawning on and flattering people with power or influence in order to achieve an advantage [Early 19C. Shortening of *toadeater* "toady"] —**toad·y·ish** *adj* —**toad·y·ism** *n*

Toa·ma·si·na /twaàmə seénə/ city and major port on the Indian Ocean, in eastern Madagascar, situated about 130 mi./209 km northeast of Antananarivo. Population: 127,441 (1993). Former name **Tamatave**

to and fro *adv* **1.** backward and forward **2.** here and there in movement —**to-and-fro** *adj, n* —**to·ing and fro·ing** *n*

toast /tōst/ *n* **1. BREAD BROWNED WITH HEAT** sliced bread that has been browned on both sides with heat, in a toaster, under a grill, or in front of an open fire **2. CALL TO HONOR SOMEBODY OR SOMETHING** a call to a gathering to honor somebody or something by raising glasses and drinking **3. RAISING OF GLASSES TO HONOR SOMEBODY** an act of raising a glass and drinking in honor of somebody or something **4. SOMEBODY OR SOMETHING HONORED** somebody or something honored by a toast **5. SOMEBODY ADMIRED** somebody who is the object of much attention or admiration ○ *the toast of Hollywood* ■ *v* (**toast·ed, toast·ing, toasts**) **1.** *vti* **HEAT AND BROWN BREAD** to heat and brown bread or other food in a toaster, on a grill, or in front of an open fire, or become browned in this way **2.** *vt* **WARM BODY** to warm the body or a part of the body near a source of heat **3.** *vti* **DRINK IN HONOR OF SOMEBODY** to drink or propose a drink in honor of somebody or something [14C. Via Old French *toster* "roast" < Latin *tost-*, past participle of *torrere* "scorch"] ◇ **be toast** (*slang*) **1.** to be in serious trouble ○ *Do that again and you're toast!* **2.** to be in a nonfunctioning state (*refers to a computer*)

toast·er /tṓstər/ *n* a small electrical appliance for making toast that works by exposing the bread to heated electrical coils

toast·er ov·en *n* an electric device that is portable and can work both as a toaster and as a small oven

toast·mas·ter /tṓst màstər/ *n* somebody who proposes toasts and introduces speakers at a banquet or reception

toast·mis·tress /tṓst mìstrəss/ *n* a woman who proposes toasts and introduces speakers at a banquet or reception

toast rack *n* a stand that holds slices of toast on end and separate from each other

toast·y /tṓstee/ (**-i·er, -i·est**) *adj* pleasantly warm

Tob. *abbr* BIBLE Tobit

to·bac·co /tə bákō/ (*plural* **-cos** or *same*) *n* **1. DRIED LEAVES PROCESSED FOR SMOKING** the dried leaves of a plant of the nightshade family, processed primarily for smoking in cigarettes, cigars, and pipes **2. PLANT WHOSE LEAVES ARE SMOKED** a plant of the nightshade family, cultivated for its large leaves that are dried and processed primarily for smoking. Native to: tropical America. Genus: *Nicotiana.* **3. PRODUCT MADE FROM TOBACCO LEAVES** any product made from tobacco leaves, e.g., cigarettes **4. HABIT OF USING TOBACCO** the habit of using tobacco products **5. CROP OF TOBACCO** a crop of tobacco referred to collectively [Late 16C. < Spanish *tabaco*]

to·bac·co bud·worm *n* a destructive rust-colored moth caterpillar that feeds on the leaves and buds of tobacco plants. Latin name: *Heliothis virescens.*

to·bac·co horn·worm *n* the larva of a large hawk moth that feeds on the leaves of tobacco plants. Native to: North America, Caribbean. Latin name: *Manduca sexta.*

to·bac·co mo·sa·ic *n* a viral disease that affects tobacco and nightshade and is caused by the tobacco mosaic virus

to·bac·co mo·sa·ic vi·rus *n* a retrovirus that causes mosaic disease in tobacco and other plants belonging to the nightshade family

to·bac·co moth *n* a drab gray scavenger moth that infests tobacco and is a pest in tobacco storage facilities. Latin name: *Ephestia elutella.*

to·bac·co·nist /tə bákənist/ *n* a person or shop that specializes in selling tobacco products and supplies such as cigarettes, tobacco, and pipes [Mid-17C. < TOBACCO + -IST]

to·bac·co road *n US* a shabby poverty-stricken rural community [Mid-20C. < the title of a novel by Erskine CALDWELL]

to·bac·co worm *n US* INSECTS same as **tobacco hornworm**

~~**tobaco**~~ incorrect spelling of **tobacco**

To·ba·go /tə báygō/ island in the Caribbean, part of Trinidad and Tobago. Population: 50,282 (1990). Area: 120 sq. mi./300 sq. km.

To·ba So·jo /tōbaa sṓjō/ (1053–1140) Japanese artist and Buddhist high priest. He is noted for his Buddhist icons and humorous paintings.

To·bey /tṓbee/, **Mark** (1890–1976) US artist. He is noted for the "white writing" calligraphic technique used in his abstract paintings.

To·bin /tṓbin/, **James** (1918–2002) US economist. As a professor at Harvard (1947–50) and Yale (1959–88), he examined the effect of national economic policies on consumer investment and spending. He was awarded the 1981 Nobel Prize in economics.

To·bit /tṓbit/ *n* **1.** in the Bible, a pious Israelite living in Nineveh at the end of the 8th century B.C. **2.** a book of the Roman Catholic Bible and the Protestant Apocrypha that contains the story of Tobit. See table at **Bible**

to·bog·gan /tə bóggən/ *n* **LONG NARROW SLED** a long narrow sled without runners, made of strips of wood running lengthwise and curled up at the front, used for coasting downhill on snow ■ *vi* (**-ganed, -gan·ing, -gans**) **1. RIDE TOBOGGAN** to ride on a toboggan **2.** *US* **FALL RAPIDLY** to fall or decline rapidly (*informal*) [Early 19C. Via Canadian French *tabagane* < Mi'kmaq *topāgan* "sled"] —**to·bog·gan·er** *n* —**to·bog·gan·ist** *n*

To·bruk /tə bro͝ok/ city and port in northeastern Libya, on the Mediterranean Sea. British forces were besieged there during World War II. Population: 94,006 (1984).

to·by jug /tṓbee/, **to·by** (*plural* **-bies**), **To·by** *n* a beer mug or jug in the shape of a rotund man wearing a three-cornered hat [Mid-19C. < *Toby* (nickname for *Tobias*), common 19C name for a man or boy]

toc·ca·ta /tə kaátə/ (*plural* **-tas**) *n* a composition for a keyboard instrument written in a free style that includes full chords and elaborate runs and is intended to show off the player's technique [Early 18C. < Italian < feminine past participle of *toccare* "touch" < assumed Vulgar Latin]

To·char·i·an /tō kérree ən/, **To·khar·i·an** *n* **1.** a member of a Central Asian people who lived in the Tarim Basin in western China before being defeated by the Uigurs during the 9th century A.D. They are believed to have spread into China from Eastern Europe. **2.** the extinct language of the Tocharian people. It forms a separate branch of the Indo-European family and shows close resemblances to some western branches of the family. [Early 20C. < Latin *Tochari* < Greek *Tokharoi* "the Tocharians"] —**To·char·i·an** *adj*

to·coph·er·ol /tō kóffə ràwl/ *n* one of a group of fat-soluble compounds that make up vitamin E, present in vegetable oils and leafy greens [Mid-20C. < Greek *tokos* "childbirth" + *pherein* "to bear"]

Tocque·ville /tṓk vìl/, **Alexis de** (1805–59) French historian and political writer. After visiting the United States, he wrote the influential *Democracy in America* (1835–40), his most famous work. Full name **de Tocqueville, Alexis Charles Henri Maurice Clérel**

> "What is understood by republican government in the United States is the slow and quiet action of society upon itself."
> [Alexis de Tocqueville, *Democracy in America*; 1835–40]

> "If I were asked...to what the singular prosperity and growing strength of that people [the Americans] ought mainly to be attributed, I should reply: To the superiority of their women."
> [Alexis de Tocqueville, *Democracy in America*; 1835–40]

toc·sin /tóksin/ *n* **1. ALARM** an alarm sounded by means of a bell **2. BELL** a bell that sounds an alarm **3. WARNING** a warning signal [Late 16C. Via French < Old Provençal *tocasenh* < *tocar* "to strike" (< assumed Vulgar Latin *toccare*) + *senh* "bell" (< Latin *signum* "signal")]

to·day /tə dáy/ *adv* **1. ON THIS DAY** on or during this day, as distinct from yesterday or tomorrow ○ *She is working today.* **2. IN PRESENT TIME** during the present time or age ○ *Children today have far more sophisticated toys than we ever had.* ■ *n* **1. THIS DAY** this day, as distinct from yesterday or tomorrow **2. PRESENT AGE** the present time or age ○ *the fashions of today* ■ *adj* **MODERN** modern or of the present day ○ *a today look* [Old English *tō dæge* "(this) day"]

Todd /tod/, **Alexander R., Baron Todd of Trumpington** (1907–97) British chemist. For his work on vitamins B_1 and E, he was awarded the Nobel Prize in chemistry (1957). He was the first chancellor of the University of Strathclyde, Scotland. Full name **Todd, Alexander Robertus**

tod·dle /tódd'l/ *vi* (**-dled, -dling, -dles**) **1. TAKE SHORT UNSTEADY STEPS** to walk with short unsteady steps, as a child does when learning to walk **2. WALK UNHURRIEDLY** to walk at a leisurely pace (*informal*) ■ *n* **1. UNSTEADY STEPS** a gait with short unsteady steps **2. UNHURRIED WALK** a leisurely walk (*informal*) [Late 16C. Origin ?]

tod·dler /tóddlər/ *n* **1.** a young child who is learning to walk **2.** any standard size of clothing for children between the ages of one and three

tod·dy /tóddee/ (*plural* **-dies**) *n* **1.** a drink made with alcoholic liquor, hot water, sugar, and sometimes spices **2.** the sweet sap of a variety of Asian palm tree used as a beverage, either fresh or fermented [Late 18C. Via Hindi *tāṛī* "palm sap" < Sanskrit *tālah* "palm," probably < Dravidian]

todg·er /tójjər/ *n* a man's penis (*slang; often considered offensive*) [Mid-20C. Origin ?]

to-do /tə do͞o/ (*plural* **to-dos**) *n* a fuss, especially an angry complaint or protest (*informal*)

to·dy /tṓdee/ (*plural* **-dies**) *n* a small bird with a short tail, a bright green back, red throat, and a long straight beak. Native to: Caribbean. Family: Todidae. [Late 18C. Probably via French *todier* < Latin *todus*, a small bird]

toe /tō/ *n* **1. DIGIT OF HUMAN FOOT** one of the digits of the human foot, equivalent to the fingers and thumb of the hand **2. DIGIT OF VERTEBRATE'S FOOT** a part corresponding to the human toe in other vertebrates **3. FRONT PART OF HOOF** the forepart of an animal's hoof **4. FRONT PART OF SHOE OR SOCK** the part of a shoe, boot, sock, or stocking that covers the toes and the front part of the foot **5. PART RESEMBLING TOES** a part that resembles the front part of a foot in form or position ○ *the toe of Italy* **6.** GOLF **END OF GOLF CLUB HEAD** the end of the head of a golf club **7.** MECH ENG **LOWER END OF SHAFT** the lower end of a vertical shaft that turns in a bearing **8.** GEOG **BASE OF EMBANKMENT** the base of an embankment, cliff, wall, or dam ■ *v* (**toed, toe·ing, toes**) **1.** *vt* **TOUCH SOMETHING WITH TOES** to touch, kick, reach, or mark something with the toes or the front part of the foot **2.** *vi* **STAND WITH TOES POINTED** to stand or move with the toes pointed in a particular direction **3.** *vt* GOLF **STRIKE GOLF BALL** to strike a golf ball with the front part of the head of the club **4.** *vt* CONSTR **DRIVE NAIL AT ANGLE** to drive in a nail or spike at an angle **5.** *vt* CONSTR **FASTEN SOMETHING WITH ANGLED NAIL** to fasten something with a nail or spike driven in at an angle [Old English *tā* < Indo-European, "to point"] —**toed** *adj* ◇ **on your toes** alert and ready for action ◇ **step on somebody's toes** to offend or upset somebody by interfering with something considered to be that person's own responsibility ◇ **turn up your toes** to die (*informal*)

toe·a /tóy ə/ (*plural same* or **-as**) *n* a subunit of Papua New Guinean currency. See table at **currency** [Late 20C. < Motu, "conical shell," used as currency]

toe and heel *n* a technique used by race drivers for operating the brake and accelerator simultaneously with the right foot, using the heel for one pedal and the toe for the other

toe·cap /tṓ kàp/ *n* a metal or leather covering reinforcing the toe of a shoe or boot

toe dance *n* a dance performed on tiptoe ■ *vi* to perform a toe dance —**toe danc·er** *n*

TOEFL /tṓf'l/ *tdmk* a trademark for a standardized English language test taken by speakers of other languages who are applying to colleges in the United States. Full form **Test of English as a Foreign Language**

toe·hold /tṓ hṑld/ *n* **1. SMALL ADVANTAGE** a small advantage or gain that can be used to get a larger one later **2. SMALL RECESS IN ROCK FOR FOOT** a small recess or ledge in a rock giving support for the toes **3. HOLD ON FOOT** a wrestling hold in which one competitor holds the foot and twists the leg of the other

toe-in *n* the alignment of a motor vehicle's front wheels so that the front edges are slightly closer together than the rear edges to improve its steering capabilities and reduce tire wear

toe loop *n* a jump in which an ice skater, skating backward, takes off from one skate, makes one rotation in the air, and lands on the outer edge of the same skate

toe·nail /tṓ nàyl/ *n* **1. NAIL ON TOE** the nail of a toe **2. NAIL DRIVEN IN AT ANGLE** a nail driven in at an angle, e.g., to join intersecting structural parts ■ *vt* (**-nailed, -nail·ing, -nails**) **JOIN SOMETHING WITH ANGLED NAILS** to join parts of a structure with nails driven in at an angle

toe ring *n* a ring worn on the toe, particularly a silver ring worn by married Hindu women

toe shoe *n* a woman ballet dancer's slipper made of satin, tied with ribbons, and having a stiff blocked toe, worn for performing or practicing on points

toe-to-toe *adj* involving two people, groups, or organizations in direct opposition to each other ■ *adv* in direct opposition to each other

toff /tof/ *n UK* a rich or upper-class person, especially somebody who is elegantly dressed (*informal*) [Mid-19C. Probably variant of *tuft*, golden plume worn by titled students at Oxford and Cambridge]

tof·fee /táwfee, tóffee/ *n* a candy that can be soft and chewy or hard and brittle, made by boiling brown sugar or molasses with butter and sometimes flavorings or nuts [Early 19C. Variant of TAFFY]

tof·fee ap·ple *n UK* same as **candy apple**

to·fu /tṓ fo͞o/ *n* a soft food with no distinctive flavor made from coagulated soybean extract pressed into a cake [Late 18C. Via Japanese < Chinese *dòufǔ* "fermented beans"]

tog /tog/ (*informal*) *npl* **togs** clothes of any kind ○ *golf togs* ■ *vti* (**togged, tog·ging, togs**) to dress up, or dress somebody up, usually in smart clothing [Late 18C. Shortening of obsolete slang *togeman* < obsolete French *togue* "cloak" < Latin *toga* (see "toga")]

to·ga /tṓgə/ *n* **1.** an outer garment worn by the citizens of ancient Rome, consisting of a semicircular piece of cloth draped around the body **2.** a robe of office [Early 17C. < Latin] —**to·gaed** *adj*

to·ga prae·tex·ta /tṑgə pri tékstə/ (*plural* **to·gae prae·tex·tae** /tṑgee pri tékstee/) *n* a toga with a purple border worn in ancient Rome by some magistrates and priests, and by boys before the age of puberty [< Latin, "bordered toga"]

to·ga vi·ri·lis /tṑgə və réeliss/ (*plural* **to·gae vi·ri·les** /tṑjee və rée lèez, tṑgee-/) *n* a white toga worn in ancient Rome by men and by boys from the age of 14 or 15 as a sign of manhood and citizenship [< Latin, "men's toga"]

to·geth·er /tə gé*th*ər/ CORE MEANING: an adverb indicating that people are with one another, or that something is done with another person or other people, or by joint effort ○ *My brother and I always walked to school together.*

1. *adv* **WITH OTHERS** in company with others in a group or in a place ○ *We only come together on family occasions.* **2.** *adv* **INTERACTING WITH ONE ANOTHER** interacting, communicating, or in a relationship with one another ○ *They get on well together.* **3.** *adv* **BY JOINT EFFORT** cooperating with one another or by joint or combined effort ○ *Let's work together on this one.* **4.** *adv* **INTO CONTACT** indicates that two or more things are put into contact with one another, or unite to form a single whole ○ *The garment had been sewn together roughly.* **5.** *adv* **COLLECTIVELY** considered collectively or as a whole ○ *Taken together, these developments add up to a significant change in policy.* **6.** *adv* **IN INTEGRATED COHERENT STRUCTURE** in or into a unified structure or a coherent integrated whole ○ *If you understand how something is put together, you will use it better.* **7.** *adv* **INTO ORDERLY CONDITION OR STATE** into an orderly condition or a stable and effective emotional state (*informal*) ○ *"I'm just trying to get my life together," he said quietly.* **8.** *adv* **IN AGREEMENT** in or into agreement or harmony ○ *They can't seem to get together on anything.* **9.** *adv* **SIMULTANEOUSLY** at the same time ○ *They both answered together.* **10.** *adv* **UNINTERRUPTEDLY** without interruption ○ *It has been raining four days together.* **11.** *adv* **IN COUPLE** indicates that two people are married, having a sexual relationship, or form an established and recognized couple (*informal*) ○ *got back together again after a trial separation* **12.** *adj* **STABLE AND SELF-CONFIDENT** emotionally stable, self-confident, and well-organized (*informal*) ○ *She's a very together person.* [Old English *tōgædere* < *to* "to" + Germanic, "joined together"] ◇ **together with** as well as or in addition to

USAGE When *together with* forms an addition to the grammatical subject of a verb, the verb agrees with the grammatical subject. In the following sentence the grammatical subject is *remark*: *This remark, together with earlier comments of the same kind, was not well received.*

to·geth·er·ness /tə gé*th*ərnəss/ *n* a feeling of closeness to others

tog·ger·y /tóggəree/ *n* (*informal*) **1.** clothes **2.** *US* a place to buy clothes, e.g., a clothing or specialty shop [Early 19C. < TOG]

tog·gle /tógg'l/ *n* **1. FASTENER ON CLOTHES** a small peg sewn on clothes or on a bag, inserted crosswise into a loop or buttonhole and used as a fastener **2. PEG INSERTED IN LOOP** a peg or rod that is inserted crosswise into a loop at the end of a rope, chain, or strap to hold or fasten something **3.** COMPUT **KEY FOR SWITCHING BETWEEN OPERATIONS** a key or command that switches back and forth between computer operations each time it is used **4.** NAUT **PIN INSERTED INTO KNOT** a pin inserted into a nautical knot to keep it from coming undone **5.** ENG **SOMETHING WITH TOGGLE JOINT** a toggle joint or a device with a toggle joint ■ *v* (**-gled, -gling, -gles**) **1.** *vti* COMPUT **SWITCH BETWEEN OPERATIONS WITH ONE KEY** to switch back and forth between two computer operations using the same key or command **2.** *vt* **SUPPLY OR FASTEN SOMETHING WITH TOGGLES** to supply or fasten something with a toggle or toggles [Late 18C. Origin ?] —**tog·gler** *n*

tog·gle bolt *n* a threaded bolt that has a nut with spring-loaded hinged wings attached and is used especially for securing things to hollow walls. When the bolt is inserted into a hole in the wall, the wings spread open inside, pressing back against the wall's inner surface and allowing the bolt to be tightened.

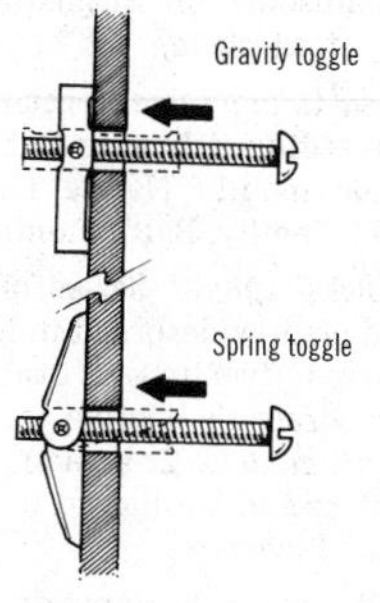

toggle bolt

tog·gle iron, tog·gle har·poon *n* a whaling harpoon with a pivoting barb that keeps the whale from freeing itself

tog·gle joint *n* a device with two arms hinged together so that pressure applied at the pivot point to straighten the device exerts force along the two arms

tog·gle switch *n* **1.** a small spring-loaded mechanical switch that opens and closes an electric circuit by manual operation **2.** COMPUT same as **toggle** *n* (sense 3)

To·gliat·ti /tōl yaátee/ industrial city on the Volga River in southern European Russia. Population: 855,365 (1995).

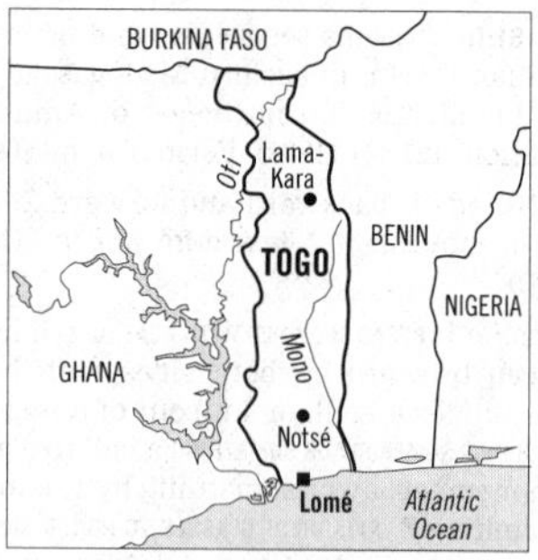

Togo

To·go /tṓgō/ country in West Africa, bordered by Burkina Faso, Benin, the Gulf of Guinea, and Ghana. Language: French. Currency: franc. Capital: Lomé. Population: 5,429,299 (2003). Area: 21,925 sq. mi./56,785 sq. km. Official name **Togolese Republic** —**To·go·lese** /tṑgə lēez, -lēess/ *n, adj*

To·go·land /tṓgō lànd/ former German protectorate in western Africa, divided between British and French administration in 1922. British Togoland was incorporated into Ghana (1956) and French Togoland became independent as Togo (1960).

Tog·rul Beg /tògril bég/ (993?–1063) Turkish Seljuk leader. The founder of the Seljuk dynasty, he conquered most of Iran and Iraq, gaining control of Baghdad in 1055.

togue /tōg/ (*plural same* or **togues**) *n US* FISH same as **lake trout** [Late 19C. Via Canadian French < Mi'kmaq *atoğwa:su*]

to·he·ro·a /tṑ ə rṓ ə/ (*plural same* or **-as**) *n* **1.** a large edible mollusk with a hinged shell. Native to: New Zealand coasts. Latin name: *Amphidesma ventricosum*. **2.** a greenish soup made from the toheroa [Late 19C. < Maori]

To·ho·no O'O·dham /tō hṓnō ṓ ə daàm/ (*plural same* or **To·ho·no O'O·dhams**) *n* PEOPLES, LANG same as **Papago** [Late 20C. < Papago, "desert people"] —**To·ho·no O'O·dham** *adj*

toil[1] /toyl/ *n* **HARD WORK** hard exhausting work or effort ■ *vi* (**toiled, toil·ing, toils**) **1. WORK HARD** to work long and hard **2. PROGRESS SLOWLY** to progress slowly and with difficulty [13C. < Anglo-Norman *toiler* "drag around" < Latin *tudicula* "machine for bruising olives" < *tudes* "hammer"] —**toil·er** *n*

SYNONYMS See *work*.

toil[2] /toyl/ *n* a net, snare, or other thing that entraps or entangles (*archaic or literary; often used in the plural*) [Early 16C. Via Old French *toile* "cloth, web" < Latin *tela*]

toile /twaal/ *n* **1.** a sheer cotton or linen fabric **2.** a prototype of a designer garment made up in a cheap fabric so that alterations can be made [Late 18C. Via French < Latin *tela* "web"]

toile de Jouy /-də zhwée/ *n* a fabric with a white or light-colored background and a floral or pastoral print, usually in one color only. Use: curtains, upholstery. [Mid-18C. < French, after *Jouy*-en-Josas, town near Paris, France]

toi·let /tóylət/ *n* **1.** FIXTURE FOR DISPOSING OF BODY WASTE a bowl-shaped fixture with a waste drain and a flushing device connected to a water supply, used for defecating and urinating **2.** ROOM WITH TOILET a room with a toilet and usually a sink **3.** *US* OUTDOOR TOILET an outdoor room or building with facilities for defecation and urination **4.** WASHING AND DRESSING the process of attending to your personal appearance and making it presentable, e.g., by washing, dressing, shaving, and fixing your hair (*formal*) **5.** MED CLEANSING ASSOCIATED WITH SURGICAL PROCEDURE a cleansing of part of the body after a medical or surgical procedure, often in preparation for applying dressings or bandages [Late 17C. < French *toilette* "bag for clothing" < Old French *teile* "cloth" < Latin *tela* "web"]

toi·let pa·per *n* a usually soft absorbent paper, especially in a roll, used for cleaning the body after defecating or urinating

toi·let roll *n* a length of toilet paper wound around a cardboard cylinder, or the cardboard cylinder on which the paper is wound

toi·let·ry /tóylətree/ (*plural* **-ries**) *n* a product used in washing or caring for the appearance, e.g., shampoo, deodorant, or soap (*usually used in the plural*)

toi·lette /twaa lét/ *n* the process of attending to your personal appearance and making it presentable [Mid-16C. < French (see TOILET)]

toi·let tis·sue *n* INDUST same as **toilet paper**

toi·let train·ing *n* the process of teaching a young child to control bladder and bowel movements and to use the toilet

toi·let wa·ter *n* a lightly perfumed liquid used to freshen or scent the skin

toil·some /tóylssəm/ *adj* requiring long hard work (*literary*) —**toil·some·ly** *adv* —**toil·some·ness** *n*

toil·worn /tóyl wàwrn/ *adj* worn, damaged, or exhausted by hard work

To·jo Hi·de·ki /tṓjō hée dekee/ (1884–1948) Japanese general and prime minister (1941–44). As minister of war (1940–44) and then premier, he led Japan into World War II, resigning after Allied victories in the Pacific. He was tried and hanged for war crimes.

To·kaj /tō káy, to-, -kī́/ town in northeastern Hungary. It lies at the heart of a wine-producing region. Population: 5,000 (1989).

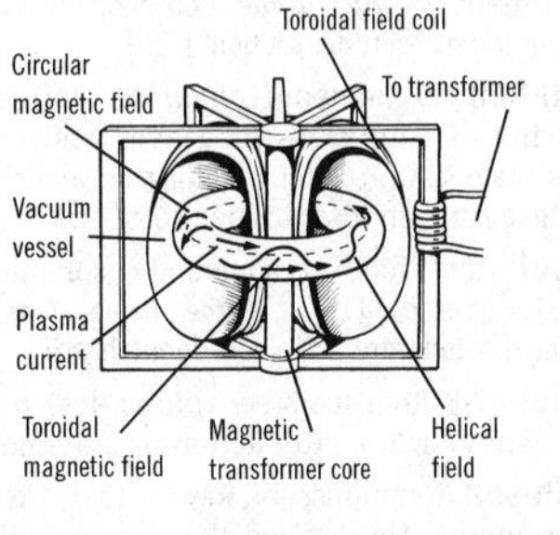

tokamak

to·ka·mak /tókə màk/ *n* an experimental doughnut-shaped nuclear reactor for producing fusion using an electric current and a magnetic field to heat and contain a gaseous plasma [Mid-20C. < Russian, contraction of *toroidal'naya kamera s aksial'nym magnitnym polem* "toroidal chamber with axial magnetic field"]

to·kay /tō káy/ *n* a small lizard that has a retractile claw at the tip of each digit. Native to: South and Southeast Asia. Latin name: *Gekko gecko*. [Mid-18C. Via Malay dialect *toke'* < Javanese *tekèk*]

To·kay /tō káy, to-, -kī́/ *n* **1.** a sweet wine made from a white grape grown in the area around Tokaj, northeastern Hungary **2.** a large sweet white grape variety. Use: to make Tokay. [Early 18C. After TOKAJ (Tokay)]

toke /tōk/ (*slang*) *n* a puff on a cigarette or pipe containing marijuana ■ *vti* (**toked, tok·ing, tokes**) to puff on a cigarette or pipe containing marijuana [Mid-20C. Origin ?]

to·ken /tṓkən/ *n* **1.** SOMETHING REPRESENTING SOMETHING ELSE something that represents, expresses, or is a symbol of something else ○ *Please accept this gift as a token of our appreciation.* **2.** DISK USED LIKE MONEY a disk of metal or plastic used instead of money, e.g., in slot machines **3.** KEEPSAKE an object kept in memory of somebody or something **4.** LING INSTANCE OF EXPRESSION an instance of a word or expression **5.** LING CONCRETE EXAMPLE a written or spoken expression considered as a concrete example ■ *adj* EXISTING AS GESTURE ONLY made, given, or existing merely because expected or required, not because sincere or serving a real purpose ○ *the token student on the committee* [Old English *tācen* < Indo-European "to point, show"]

to·ken·ism /tṓkə nìzzəm/ *n* the practice of making only a symbolic effort at something, especially in order to meet the minimum requirements of the law —**to·ken·is·tic** /tṑkə nístik/ *adj*

To·khar·i·an *n, adj* PEOPLES, LANG another spelling of **Tocharian**

to·ko·no·ma /tṑkə nṓmə/ *n* an alcove in the living room of a Japanese house where a decoration such as flowers or an ornament is displayed [Early 18C. < Japanese]

To·ko·ro·a /tṑkō rṓ ə/ town in the northwestern part of the North Island, New Zealand, that services the paper and timber mills at nearby Kinleith. Population: 14,427 (2001).

Tok Pis·in /tòk píssin/ *n* a creole, originating as a pidgin based on English, that is widely spoken in Papua New Guinea. Native speakers: 2 million. [Mid-20C. < Pidgin English, "talk pidgin"] —**Tok Pis·in** *adj*

To·ky·o /tṓkee ō/ capital city of Japan, located on Tokyo Bay on the eastern coast of Honshu Island. Population: 8,025,538 (2002).

to·la /tṓlə/ *n* a South Asian unit of weight equal to 180 grains troy weight or 11.7 grams [Early 17C. Via Hindi *tolā* < Sanskrit *tulā* "weight"]

to·lar /tṓ laar/ *n* the main unit of Slovenian currency. See table at **currency** [Via Slovene < German *Taler* "thaler"]

tol·booth /tṓl bōōth/ *n Scotland* a town hall or a prison, or a building that performed both functions (*archaic*) [Variant of TOLLBOOTH]

told past participle, past tense of **tell**

tole[1] /tōl/ *n* lacquered or enameled metal used to make decorative objects, usually brightly painted or gilded or both, or objects made of this kind of decorated metal [Mid-20C. Via French *tôle* "sheet iron" < Latin *tabula* "board"]

tole[2] *vt* HUNTING, FISHING another spelling of **toll**[2] *v* (sense 3)

To·le·do[1] /tə léedō/ (*plural* **-dos**) *n* a sword or sword blade of highly tempered steel, made in Toledo, Spain

To·le·do[2] /tə léedō/ **1.** city and major river port in northwestern Ohio, located close to Lake Erie. Population: 309,106 (2002 estimate). **2.** historic city in central Spain, the administrative center of Toledo Province. Population: 70,893 (2002).

To·le·do, Alejandro (*b.* 1946) president of Peru (2001–). A center-left economist who worked for the World Bank before returning to Peru to enter politics, he is the country's first elected president with Native South American roots.

tol·er·a·ble /tóllərəb'l/ *adj* **1.** not too unpleasant or severe to put up with **2.** moderately good, but not outstanding —**tol·er·a·bil·i·ty** /tòllərə bíllətee/ *n* —**tol·er·a·ble·ness** *n* —**tol·er·a·bly** *adv*

tol·er·ance /tóllərənss/ *n* **1.** ACCEPTANCE OF DIFFERENT VIEWS the acceptance of the differing views of other people, e.g., in religious or political matters, and fairness toward the people who hold these different views **2.** TOLERATING OF SOMEBODY OR SOMETHING the act of putting up with somebody or something irritating or otherwise unpleasant **3.** ABILITY TO ENDURE HARDSHIP the ability to put up with harsh or difficult conditions **4.** MED ABILITY TO REMAIN UNAFFECTED the loss of or reduction in the usual response to a drug or other agent as a result of use or exposure over a prolonged period **5.** ENG ALLOWANCE MADE FOR DEVIATION an allowance made for something to deviate in size from a standard, or the limit within which it is allowed to deviate **6.** BIOL ABILITY TO WITHSTAND EXTREMES the ability of an organism to survive in extreme conditions

tol·er·ant /tóllərənt/ *adj* **1.** ACCEPTING DIFFERENT VIEWS accepting the differing views of other people, e.g., in religious or political matters, and treating the people who hold these different views fairly **2.** WITHSTANDING HARSH TREATMENT able to put up with harsh conditions or treatment **3.** MED NOT AFFECTED BY DRUG no longer responding to a drug that has been taken over a prolonged period, or suffering no ill effects from exposure to a harmful substance —**tol·er·ant·ly** *adv*

tol·er·ate /tóllə ràyt/ (**-at·ed, -at·ing, -ates**) *vt* **1.** PERMIT SOMETHING to be willing to allow something to happen or exist **2.** ENDURE SOMETHING to withstand the unpleasant effects of something **3.** ACCEPT EXISTENCE OF DIFFERENT VIEWS to recognize other people's right to have different beliefs or practices without attempting to suppress them **4.** MED BE UNAFFECTED BY DRUG to fail to respond to a drug because the body has built up a resistance to it, or suffer no ill effects from being exposed to a harmful substance [Early 16C. < Latin *tolerat-*, past participle of *tolerare* "bear, endure"] —**tol·er·a·tive** *adj* —**tol·er·a·tor** *n*

tol·er·a·tion /tòllə ráysh'n/ *n* **1.** official acceptance by a government of religious beliefs and practices that are different from those it upholds **2.** the act of tolerating something

tol·i·dine /tóllə deen/ *n* an isomeric derivative of toluene. Use: manufacture of dyes. Formula: $C_{14}H_{16}N_2$. [Late 19C. < TOLYL + *benzidine*]

Tol·kien /tṓl keen, tól-/, **J. R. R.** (1892–1973) South African-born British scholar and writer. A philologist at Oxford University, he wrote *The Hobbit* (1937) and its three-part sequel *The Lord of the Rings* (1954–55). Full name **Tolkien, John Ronald Reuel**

toll[1] /tōl/ *n* **1.** FEE FOR USING ROAD a fee charged for a privilege, usually crossing a bridge or using a road **2.** DAMAGE SUSTAINED the damage done by an accident or disaster in terms of, e.g., people killed, property destroyed, or financial loss ○ *The toll on the environment was significant.* **3.** FIN FEE FOR SERVICES a fee charged for services such as transportation **4.** ROADS same as **tollbooth** (*often used in the plural*) **5.** TELECOM CHARGE FOR TELEPHONE CALL a charge for a long-distance telephone call ■ *vti* (**tolled, toll·ing, tolls**) ROADS CHARGE TOLL ON ROAD to charge a toll for the use of a road or bridge [Pre-12C. Via medieval Latin *toloneum* < Greek *telōnion* "toll house" < *telos* "tax"]

toll[2] /tōl/ *v* (**tolled, toll·ing, tolls**) **1.** *vti* RING SLOWLY AND REPEATEDLY to ring a bell, repeatedly and with long pauses between each ring, especially to announce a death, or be rung in this way ○ *"never send to know for whom the bell tolls; it tolls for thee"* (John Donne, *Devotions*; 1624) **2.** *vt* ANNOUNCE SOMETHING WITH BELL to announce something or call somebody with the repeated slow ringing of a bell ○ *bells tolling the death of the king* **3.** *also* **tole** (**toled, tol·ing, toles**) *vt* LURE FISH OR GAME to lure fish or game into being caught ■ *n* ACT OR SOUND OF BELL TOLLING the act of ringing a bell slowly and repeatedly, or the sound so made [15C. Probably < Old English *-tyllan* "pull"] —**toll·er** *n*

toll·booth /tṓl bōōth/ *n* a booth on a road or bridge where tolls for use of the road or bridge are collected

toll bridge *n* a bridge where a toll is charged for crossing

toll call *n* a long-distance telephone call charged at a higher rate than a local call

Tol·lens re·a·gent /tóllənz-/ *n* a solution of silver nitrate, ammonia, and sodium bicarbonate. Use: testing for aldehydes. [After Bernhard *Tollens* (1841–1918), German chemist]

toll-free *adj* describes a telephone call that is not charged at a higher rate than a local call —**toll-free** *adv*

toll·gate /tōl gàyt/ *n* a gate barring the way on a road or bridge where a toll must be paid to proceed

toll·house /tōl hòwss/ (*plural* **-hous·es** /-hòwzəz/) *n* a shelter or kiosk for a toll collector at a tollgate

Toll House *tdmk US* a trademark for a cookie made with flour, brown sugar, chocolate chips, and often chopped nuts

Leo Tolstoy

Tol·stoy /táwl stòy/, **Leo** (1828–1910) Russian writer. He wrote the epic novels *War and Peace* (1865–69) and *Anna Karenina* (1875–77). A profound social thinker and moralist, he was excommunicated from the Russian Orthodox Church for his radical views on Church authority. Full name **Tolstoy, Count Leo Nikolayevich**. See Cultural note at **war**

> "There are no conditions of life to which a man cannot get accustomed, especially if he sees them accepted by *everyone* about him."
> [Leo Tolstoy, *Anna Karenina*; 1875–77]

Tol·tec /tōl tèk, tól-/ (*plural* **Toltec** or **Toltecs**) *n* a member of a Native Central American people who formerly lived in central Mexico and were succeeded by the Aztecs. They dominated the area between the 10th and the 12th centuries A.D., when they were defeated by the Chichimecs, and their lands were later taken over by the Aztecs. [Late 18C. Via Spanish *tolteca* < Nahuatl *toltecatl* "somebody from Tula," ancient Toltec city] —**Tol·tec** *adj*

to·lu /tə lóo, tō-/ *n* an aromatic resin. Source: South American tree. Use: perfumes, cough medicines. [Late 17C. < Spanish *tolú*, after the town of Santiago de *Tolú* in Colombia, from which it was exported]

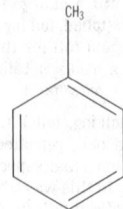

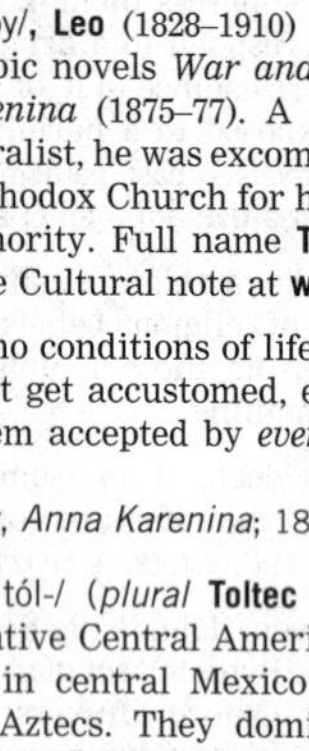

toluene

tol·u·ene /tóllyoo èen/ *n* a colorless liquid aromatic hydrocarbon resembling benzene, but less flammable. Use: solvent, high-octane fuel, organic synthesis. Formula: C_7H_8. [Late 19C. < TOLU]

to·lu·i·dine /tə lóo i dèen/ *n* a derivative of toluene occurring in three forms. Use: manufacture of dyes. Formula: C_7H_9N.

tol·u·ol /tóllyoo àwl/ *n* CHEM same as **toluene**

tol·yl /tó lìl/ *n* a chemical group derived from toluene. Formula: C_7H_7.

tom /tom/ *n* the male of various animals, especially the domestic cat or the turkey [14C. < the name *Tom* (short for *Thomas*)]

Tom /tom/ *n US* same as **Uncle Tom** (*taboo offensive*) [Mid-20C. Shortening]

Tom, Dick, and Har·ry /-hárree/ *n* anyone at all

tomahawk

tom·a·hawk /tómmə hàwk/ *n* a small ax, formerly used as a weapon by some Native North American peoples ■ *vt* (**-hawked, -hawk·ing, -hawks**) to attack or kill somebody with a tomahawk [Early 17C. < Virginia Algonquian *tamahaac*]

to·mal·ley /tə mállee, tó màllee/ *n* a soft green part of the insides of a cooked lobster, often called the liver, but technically an organ called the hepatopancreas, eaten as a delicacy [Mid-17C. Via French *taumalin* < Carib *taumali*]

to·man /tə máan/ *n* **1.** an Iranian coin worth ten rials **2.** a gold coin and former unit of Persian currency [Mid-16C. Via Persian *tūmān* < W Tocharian *tmān*]

Tom and Jer·ry *n US* a hot drink containing rum, brandy, nutmeg, and egg, to which milk is sometimes added [After Corinthian *Tom* and *Jerry* Hawthorne, two characters in the novel *Life in London* (1821) by Pierce Egan]

to·ma·til·lo /tōmə tée yō/ (*plural* **-los**) *n Hispanic* **1.** a purplish sticky edible fruit that grows on a Mexican ground cherry **2.** the ground cherry plant that bears tomatillos. Latin name: *Physalis ixocarpa.* [Early 20C. < Spanish, "small tomato" < *tomate* (see TOMATO)]

tomato

to·ma·to /tə máytō, -máatō/ (*plural* **-toes**) *n* **1.** RED FRUIT a round fruit with bright-red skin and pulpy seedy flesh, eaten cooked or raw as a vegetable **2.** TOMATO PLANT a climbing plant that produces tomatoes and is grown throughout the world, in northern regions usually in greenhouses. Native to: South America. Genus: *Lycopersicon.* **3.** OFFENSIVE TERM an offensive term for a woman who is considered sexually desirable (*dated slang*) [Early 17C. Alteration of Spanish *tomate* < Nahuatl *tomatl*]

PRONUNCIATION ***Tomato*** can be pronounced two ways, and both are correct: /tə máytō, tə máatō/.

to·ma·to fruit·worm *n* the larva of a moth that is destructive to corn, cotton, tomatoes, and other crops. Native to: United States. Latin name: *Heliothis zea.*

to·ma·to horn·worm *n* the larva of a North American hawk moth that feeds on the leaves of tomato plants. Latin name: *Manduca quinquemaculata.*

to·ma·to sphinx *n* the adult form of a tomato hornworm

tomb /toom/ *n* **1.** GRAVE a grave or other place for burying a dead person **2.** BURIAL CHAMBER a cave or chamber used for burying a dead person **3.** MONUMENT a monument to a dead person, often built over the place where he or she is buried **4.** same as **death** (*literary*) ○ *go to the tomb unrepentant* **5.** HARDENED ENCLOSURE a hardened enclosure for a closed nuclear reactor, designed to contain radioactive emissions [12C. Via French *tombe* < Greek *tumbos* "mound, tomb"]

Tom·ba /tóm baa/, **Alberto** (*b.* 1966) Italian skier. In 1988 he won the first of many medals, including Olympic gold medals and World Cups in slalom and giant slalom events.

tom·bac /tóm bàk/, **tam·bac** /tám-/ *n* an alloy of copper and zinc, often with tin and arsenic, originally used in some Southeast Asian countries to make gongs and bells and now used worldwide to make inexpensive jewelry [Early 17C. Via French < Malay *tembaga* "copper, brass"]

tom·bo·lo /tómbəlō/ (*plural* **-los**) *n* a narrow strip of sand or shingle that links one island to another or to the mainland [Late 19C. Via Italian, "sand dune" < Latin *tumulus* (see TUMULUS)]

Tom·bouc·tou /tòN book tóo/, **Tim·buk·tu** /tìm buk-/ city in central Mali, on the southern edge of the Sahara Desert. Population: 36,000 (1998).

tom·boy /tóm bòy/ *n* a girl who dresses or behaves in a way regarded as boyish, especially a girl who enjoys rough boisterous play [Mid-16C. < the name *Tom* (short for *Thomas*)] —**tom·boy·ish** *adj* —**tom·boy·ish·ness** *n*

tomb·stone /tóom stōn/ *n* an ornamental stone on or at the site of a grave, often with the dead person's name and dates of birth and death engraved on it

Tomb·stone /tóom stōn/ city in southeastern Arizona. Its history as a lawless mining town has made it a popular tourist center. Population: 1,537 (2002 estimate).

tom·cat /tóm kàt/ *n* **1.** MALE CAT a male domestic cat **2.** OFFENSIVE TERM an offensive term for a man who seeks many sexual partners or has casual sex with many partners (*slang*) ■ *vi* (**-cat·ted, -cat·ting, -cats**) OFFENSIVE TERM an offensive term meaning to seek many sexual partners or have casual sex with many partners (*slang; refers to men*)

tom·cod /tóm kòd/ *n* either of two small sea fishes of the cod family. Native to: North American Atlantic and northern Pacific waters. Latin name: *Microgradus tomcod* or *Microgradus proximus.*

Tom Col·lins *n* an alcoholic cocktail consisting of gin, lemon or lime juice, soda water, and sugar [Late 19C. Origin ?]

tome /tōm/ *n* **1.** a book, especially a large heavy book on a serious subject (*formal or humorous*) **2.** a single volume of a book made up of several volumes [Early 16C. Via French < Greek *tomos* "section, volume"]

-tome *suffix* **1.** segment, part ○ *myotome* **2.** cutting instrument ○ *microtome* [Via modern Latin *-tomus* < Greek *tomos* "cutting, section"]

to·men·tum /tə méntəm/ (*plural* **-ta** /-tə/) *n* a downy covering of tiny hairs on leaves and other plant parts [Late 17C. < Latin, "stuffing for a cushion"] —**to·men·tose** /tə mén tōss, tō men tōss/ *adj*

tom·fool /tòm fóol/ *n* somebody considered very foolish (*dated*) [14C. < the name *Tom* (short for *Thomas*)] —**tom·fool** *adj* —**tom·fool·ish** *adj*

tom·fool·er·y /tom fóoləree/ (*plural* **-ies**) *n* (*dated*) **1.** silly behavior **2.** a silly action or statement

Tom·lin·son /tómmlinssən/, **Ray** (*b.* 1941) US computer programmer. He devised the first e-mail program and sent the first e-mail (1971).

~~**tommorrow**~~ incorrect spelling of **tomorrow**

Tom·my /tómmee/ (*plural* **-mies**), **Tom·my At·kins** /-átkinz/ *n UK* a private in the British army (*dated*

slang) [Late 19C. < *Thomas Atkins*, name used on sample forms in the British army]

tom·my bar *n* a rod used to provide leverage in turning a box wrench [< the name *Tommy* (short for *Thomas*)]

Tom·my gun *n* a handheld machine gun, especially a Thompson submachine gun (*informal*)

tom·my·rot /tómmee ròt/ *n* complete nonsense (*dated informal*) [Late 19C. < the name *Tommy* (short for *Thomas*), used for somebody considered foolish]

tom·my·to /tómmee tṑ/ (*plural* **-toes**) *n Southern US* same as **cherry tomato**

REGIONAL NOTE ***Tommyto*** is a common term in the middle Interior South, from the western Carolinas to Arkansas. It occurs in diminishing numbers in every section of the Gulf States except Lower Texas, where it is absent.

to·mo·gram /tṓmə gràm/ *n* an image, especially one of the body, made using tomography [Mid-20C. < TOMOGRAPHY]

to·mog·ra·phy /tə móggrəfee/ *n* the technique of using ultrasound, gamma rays, or X-rays to produce a focused image of the structures across a specific depth within the body, while blurring details at other depths [Mid-20C. < Greek *tomos* "cutting, section"] —**to·mo·graph·ic** /tṑmə gráffik/ *adj*

to·mor·row /tə máwrō/ *n* **1. NEXT DAY** the day after today **2. FUTURE** a future time, or the future in general ○ *the leaders of tomorrow* ■ *adv* **1. ON NEXT DAY** on the day after today **2. IN FUTURE** in the future, or at some time in the future [Old English *tō morgenne* "in the morning"] ◇ **like** *or* **as if there was** *or* **were no tomorrow** used to emphasize the degree of speed, intensity, or carelessness with which somebody is doing something (*informal*) ○ *He was spending money like there was no tomorrow.*

tom·pi·on *n* MIL same as **tampion**

Tomp·kins /tómkinz/, **Daniel D.** (1774–1825) vice president of the United States (1817–25). He was governor of New York (1807–13) before becoming James Monroe's vice president.

toms /tomz/ *npl* MUSIC same as **tom-tom** [Early 20C. Shortening]

Tomsk /tomsk/ city in southern Siberian Russia, on the Tom River. Population: 605,216 (1995).

Tom Thumb *n* in English folklore, a character who was no taller than his father's thumb

tom·tit /tóm tìt/ *n* a small, active bird, especially a tit (*informal*) [Early 18C. < name *Tom* (short for *Thomas*)]

tom-tom /tóm tòm/, **tam-tam** /tám tàm/ *n* **1. DRUM HIT WITH HANDS** a drum hit with the hands, especially a drum with a long narrow shell and a small head, first used as a signaling instrument **2. DEEP-SIDED DRUM IN MODERN DRUM KIT** a deep-sided drum that forms part of a modern drum kit, deeper in tone than a snare drum but not as deep as a bass drum **3. SOUND OF BEATING DRUM** the sound of a drum being repeatedly beaten, especially slowly and monotonously [Late 17C. < Telugu *ṭamaṭama* or Hindi *ṭam ṭam*, an imitation of the drum's sound]

-tomy *suffix* cutting, incision ○ *lobotomy* [Via modern Latin < Greek *-tomia* < *tomos* "cutting, section"]

ton[1] /tun/ *n* **1. US UNIT OF WEIGHT** in the United States, a customary unit of weight, equal to 2,000 lb./907 kg **2. UK UNIT OF WEIGHT** in the United Kingdom, an imperial unit of weight, equal to 2,240 lb./1,016 kg **3.** MEASURE same as **metric ton 4.** MEASURE same as **displacement ton 5. UNIT MEASURING SHIP'S INTERNAL CAPACITY** a unit used to measure the capacity of the inside of a ship, equal to 100 cu. ft./28.3 cu. m **6.** MEASURE same as **freight ton 7. LARGE AMOUNT OR NUMBER** a very large amount of something or a very large number of people or things (*informal; often used in the plural*) ○ *tons of things to do* [13C. Variant of TUN] ◇ **like a ton of bricks** with great severity, force, or authority (*informal*) ○ *If you're late she'll come down on you like a ton of bricks.*

ton[2] /toN/ *n* **1.** the current trend in fashion **2.** the group of people who like to stay at the cutting edge of fashion [Mid-18C. < French, "tone"]

ton·al /tṓn'l/ *adj* **1.** relating to tone or tonality **2.** relating to music written in a harmonic system in which there is a key —**ton·al·ly** *adv*

to·nal·i·ty /tō nállətee/ *n* **1. QUALITY OF TONE** the quality of tone, especially that of an instrument or voice **2.** MUSIC same as **key**[1] *n* (sense 4) **3.** MUSIC **SYSTEM OF MUSICAL TONES** the relationship between the notes and chords of a passage or work that tends to establish a central note or harmony as its focal point **4. ARRANGEMENT OF COLORS** the scheme connecting the color tones in a work of art such as a painting

Ton·bridge /tún brìj/ town in Kent, southeastern England. Population: 31,600 (2001).

ton·do /tóndō/ (*plural* **-dos**) *n* a circular painting or relief carving [Late 19C. < Italian, shortening of *rotondo* "round" < Latin *rotundus* (see ROTUND)]

tone /tōn/ *n* **1. DISTINCTIVE KIND OF SOUND** a sound with a distinctive quality ○ *The first bell has a clearer tone.* **2. WAY OF SPEAKING** the way somebody says something as an indicator of what that person is feeling or thinking ○ *a defiant tone in her voice* **3. GENERAL QUALITY** the general quality or character of something as an indicator of the attitude or view of the person who produced it ○ *the optimistic tone of the report* **4. MACHINE SOUND** a sound, especially one produced by a machine **5. PREVAILING CHARACTER** the characteristic style that something has, particularly in relation to elegance or standing ○ *Neon signs lower the tone of the place.* **6. SHADE OF COLOR** a shade of a color ○ *a green with a more vibrant tone* **7.** ARTS **COMBINATION OF COLOR AND SHADING** the overall blend of color and light and shade in a painting or photograph **8.** PHYSIOL **FIRMNESS OF MUSCLES** the natural firmness of muscles, or of the body generally, when not being flexed **9.** PHON **INTONATION** the way a syllable of a word is spoken in terms of pitch ○ *the rising tone signifying a question* **10.** MUSIC **TIMBRE** the quality of a sound that makes it distinctive, e.g., in a voice or musical instrument **11.** MUSIC **PLAINSONG** a melody used in singing plainsong, e.g., in psalms **12.** MUSIC same as **note** (sense 7) ■ *v* (**toned, ton·ing, tones**) **1.** *vi* **BLEND IN WITH SOMETHING** to be similar to something else, especially in color or brightness, and fit well with it **2.** *vti* PHOTOGRAPHY **CHANGE COLOR OF PHOTOGRAPH** in photography, to develop a monochrome silver negative into a color image by means of a chemical solution, or be developed in this way **3.** *vt* PHON **SAY SOMETHING WITH PARTICULAR PITCH** to say a syllable or word with a particular pitch **4.** PHYSIOL **STRENGTHEN MUSCLES** to make muscles firmer and stronger [13C. Via French *ton* < Greek *tonos* "tension, tone"]

tone down *vt* **1.** to make something less extreme, usually in order to make it less offensive or controversial **2.** to make something less loud, bright, or intense

tone up *vt* to make muscles, or the body in general, firmer and stronger

Tone /tōn/, **Wolfe** (1763–98) Irish revolutionary. He was the founder of the Society of United Irishmen in 1791. His efforts on behalf of Irish nationalism resulted in a death sentence. Full name **Tone, Theobald Wolfe**

tone arm *n* a record player's pivoting or sliding arm with a stylus on its end

tone clus·ter *n* a group of adjacent notes played together and forming a chord, usually resulting in a dissonant sound

tone col·or *n* MUSIC same as **timbre** (sense 2)

tone con·trol *n* a control on a radio, record player, or other piece of audio equipment that adjusts the tone it produces, accentuating the higher or lower sound frequencies

tone-deaf *adj* unable to hear the differences between musical notes —**tone-deaf·ness** *n*

tone lan·guage *n* a language in which the meaning of a fixed sequence of sounds depends on the pitch in which it is pronounced, different tones identifying different words. Tone languages include the Bantu languages of Africa and Chinese.

tone·less /tṓnləss/ *adj* **1.** lacking expression in speech **2.** lacking brightness or vitality —**tone·less·ly** *adv*—**tone·less·ness** *n*

ton·eme /tṓ nèem/ *n* a phoneme in a tone language in which the distinctive feature is a tone [Early 20C. After PHONEME] —**to·ne·mic** /tō néemik/ *adj*

tone po·em *n* MUSIC same as **symphonic poem**

ton·er /tṓnər/ *n* **1. SKIN COSMETIC** a lotion or light astringent used to improve the look or feel of the skin, especially of the face **2. INK** ink in powder or liquid form for a photocopier or computer printer **3. PHOTOGRAPHIC CHEMICAL** a chemical solution used in photograph development

tone row, tone se·ries *n* a sequence of notes that is the basis of a piece of serial music, especially a series of 12 notes

to·net·ic /tō néttik/ *adj* relating to a language in which changes in pitch distinguish meaning [Early 20C. After PHONETIC] —**to·net·i·cal·ly** *adv*

tong[1] /tong/ (**tonged, tong·ing, tongs**) *vt* **1.** to lift or move something with tongs **2.** to curl the hair with curling tongs [Mid-19C. < TONGS]

tong[2] /tong/ *n* a Chinese secret society thought to be involved in criminal activity [Late 19C. < Chinese (Cantonese) *t'ŏng* "hall, meeting place"]

ton·ga /tóng gə/ *n* in South Asia, a light horse-drawn carriage available for hire [Late 19C. < Hindi *tāgā*]

Ton·ga[1] /tóng gə/ (*plural* **-gas** or *same*) *n* **1.** a member of a people living in south central Africa, mainly in southwestern Zambia and northwestern Zimbabwe **2.** the Bantu language of the Tonga people. Native speakers: 990,000. [Mid-19C. < Tonga] —**Ton·ga** *adj*

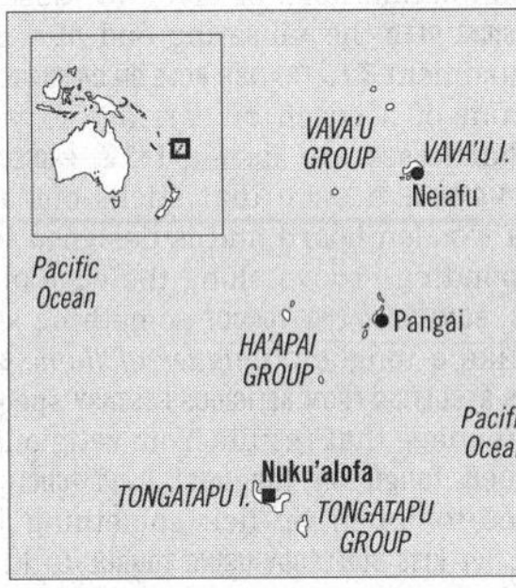

Tonga

Ton·ga[2] /tóng gə, tóngə/ independent island nation consisting of more than 150 islands in the southern Pacific Ocean. It became an independent member of the British Commonwealth in 1970. Language: English, Tongan. Currency: pa'anga. Capital: Nukualofa. Population: 108,141 (2003). Area: 290 sq. mi./750 sq. km. Official name **Kingdom of Tonga**

Ton·gan /tóng gən/ *n* **1.** somebody who comes from Tonga **2.** the Polynesian language of Tonga. Native speakers: 123,000. [Mid-19C. < TONGA[2]] —**Ton·gan** *adj*

Ton·ga·ri·ro, Mount /tòng gə reérō, tòngə-/ active volcano in New Zealand, in the central part of the North Island. It last erupted in 1926. Height: 6,458 ft./1,968 m.

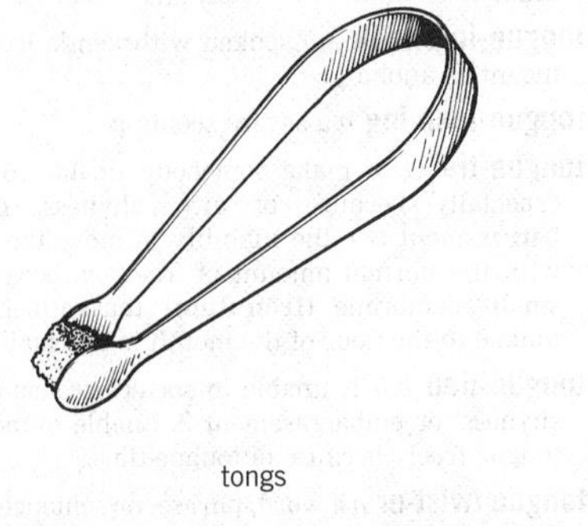

tongs

tongs /tongz/ *npl* a utensil for handling things that consists of two hinged or sprung arms that press together in a pinching movement around the object to be lifted [Old English *tang* < Indo-European, "to bite"]

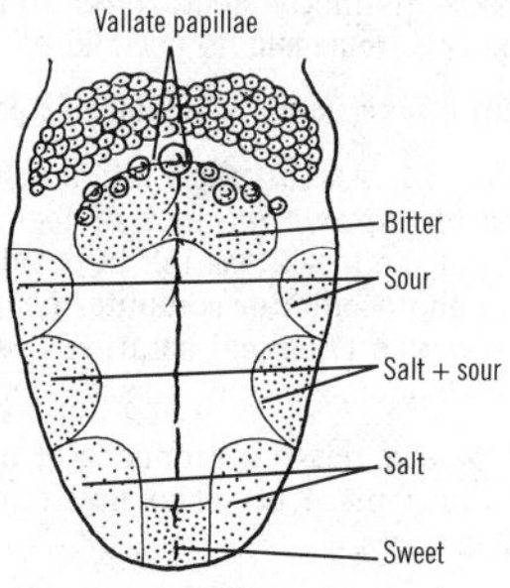

tongue: taste-sensitive areas of the human tongue

tongue /tung/ *n* **1.** FLESHY ORGAN INSIDE MOUTH the movable fleshy organ attached to the bottom of the inside of the mouth of humans and most animals, used for tasting, licking, swallowing, and, in humans, speech. Technical name **glossa** (sense 1) **2.** ANIMAL'S TONGUE AS FOOD the tongue of an animal, especially a cow, used as food **3.** LANGUAGE a language or dialect **4.** WAY OF SPEAKING somebody's manner of speaking ○ *She can have a sharp tongue when she's annoyed.* **5.** ABILITY TO SPEAK the power of speech ○ *She was so overwhelmed her tongue deserted her.* **6.** FLAP IN SHOE the middle flap in the opening of a shoe or boot **7.** PIN IN BUCKLE the pivoting pin in a buckle **8.** CLAPPER IN BELL the small swinging hammer inside a bell that hits against the inside of the bell to make the sound **9.** GEOG STRIP OF LAND a narrow strip of land sticking out into an ocean, lake, or river **10.** MUSIC VIBRATING END OF MUSICAL REED the vibrating end of a reed in a wind instrument **11.** TRANSP POLE ON CARRIAGE the pole at the front of a coach or carriage to which the horses' harnesses are fastened **12.** PROJECTING STRIP FITTING INTO GROOVE a strip that sticks out along the edge of a wooden board and is designed to fit into a corresponding groove along the edge of another board **13.** SOMETHING LIKE TONGUE something shaped or moving like a tongue ○ *tongues of flame* ■ **tongues** *npl* SPEECH RESULTING FROM RELIGIOUS ECSTASY speech in no known language that results from religious ecstasy ■ *v* (**tongued, tongu·ing, tongues**) **1.** *vt* TOUCH SOMETHING WITH TONGUE to touch or lick something with the tongue **2.** *vt* KISS SOMEBODY USING TONGUE to kiss somebody with the lips open and the tongue touching the inside of the other person's mouth (*informal*) **3.** *vti* MUSIC USE TONGUE TO ARTICULATE INSTRUMENT'S NOTES to use the tongue to block the flow of air on a wind or brass instrument, thereby separating one note from another **4.** *vt* CUT TONGUE ALONG EDGE OF BOARD to cut a tongue along the edge of a wooden board in order to make one half of a tongue-and-groove joint [Old English *tunge* < Indo-European] —**tongued** *adj* —**tongue·less** *adj* ◇ **hold your tongue** to keep silent

SYNONYMS See *language.*

tongue-and-groove joint *n* a joint made between two wooden boards consisting of a projecting strip or tongue along the edge of one board and a groove along the edge of the other

tongue de·pres·sor *n* a wide flat plastic or wooden stick that a doctor uses to hold down the tongue in order to examine the mouth and throat

tongue-in-cheek *adj* spoken with gentle irony and meant as a joke

tongue-lash·ing *n* a severe scolding

tongue-tie *vt* to make somebody unable to speak, especially because of awe, shyness, or embarrassment ■ *n* the inability to move the tongue with the normal amount of freedom, because the small membrane (**frenulum**) that attaches the tongue to the floor of the mouth is unusually short

tongue-tied *adj* **1.** unable to speak because of awe, shyness, or embarrassment **2.** unable to move the tongue freely because of tongue-tie

tongue twist·er *n* a word, phrase, or sentence that is difficult to say because of its unusual sequence of sounds, especially an invented sentence such as "She sells seashells by the seashore"

tongue worm *n* a tongue-shaped parasite with a hooked mouth that infests the lungs or nostrils of mammals, reptiles, and birds. Phylum: Arthropoda.

ton·ic /tónnik/ *n* **1.** BEVERAGES same as **tonic water** **2.** *regional* SOFT DRINK a flavored and carbonated drink, served cold **3.** SOMETHING THAT LIFTS SPIRITS something that lifts the spirits or makes somebody feel better generally **4.** MEDICINE PRODUCING SENSE OF WELL-BEING a medicine that purports to make patients feel stronger, more energetic, and generally healthier **5.** MUSIC FIRST NOTE OF SCALE the first note of a musical scale and the harmony built on this note **6.** PHON STRESSED SYLLABLE the syllable that has the main stress in a word ■ *adj* **1.** LIFTING SPIRITS lifting the spirits and creating a feeling of general well-being **2.** BOOSTING ENERGY designed or serving to boost energy and generally create a feeling of strength and health **3.** PHYSIOL RELATING TO MUSCLE TONE relating to or affecting muscular tone or contraction **4.** MUSIC RELATING TO FIRST MUSICAL NOTE relating to or based on the first note of a musical scale **5.** PHON OF STRESSED SYLLABLE relating to or forming the main stressed syllable in a word **6.** LING same as **tonetic** [Mid-17C. Via French *tonique* < Greek *tonikos* "of stretching" < *tonos* "tension, tone"] —**ton·i·cal·ly** *adv*

REGIONAL NOTE Tonic in the sense "soft drink" is an old Boston word that extended northward, westward, and southward into New England according to the Boston truck routes. Other regional synonyms include *pop* (Inland North and West), *soda* (Northeast), and *cold drink* (Lower South).

ton·ic ac·cent *n* **1.** a musical accent produced by higher pitch, not by stress **2.** a stress on a syllable created through a change in pitch

to·nic·i·ty /tō níssətee/ *n* **1.** the state or quality of being tonic **2.** the state or quality of muscles that are slightly contracted or ready to contract

ton·ic sol-fa *n* a system of using syllables to denote degrees of a musical scale, in which the syllables are movable depending on the key of the piece

ton·ic wa·ter *n* a carbonated drink with a bitter taste, originally and still sometimes containing quinine, drunk on its own as a soft drink or used as an ingredient in cocktails [Because it was originally drunk to stimulate the appetite or digestion]

to·night /tə nít/ *adv* on or during the night or evening of the present day ■ *n* the night or evening of the present day [Old English *tō niht* "at night"]

ton·ka bean /tóngkə-/ *n* **1.** a fragrant black almond-shaped seed. Use: perfume, scenting tobacco, and snuff. **2.** a leguminous tree that produces tonka beans. Native to: tropical America. Latin name: *Dipteryx odorata.*

Ton·kin, Gulf of /tón kìn, tóng-/ arm of the South China Sea, on the coast of northeastern Vietnam and southeastern China

Ton·le Sap /tòn lay sáp/ largest lake in Southeast Asia, in western Cambodia, linked to the Mekong River by the Tonle Sap River. A shallow lake, it swells from 1,000 sq. mi./2,600 sq. km in the dry season to 4,020 sq. mi./10,400 sq. km in the monsoon season.

ton·nage /túnnij/ *n* **1.** WEIGHT IN TONS weight measured in imperial or metric tons **2.** SHIP'S SIZE the size of a ship measured in tons or cubic feet or meters of seawater displaced **3.** SHIP'S CAPACITY the capacity of a ship measured in cubic feet or meters **4.** WEIGHT OF SHIP'S CARGO the weight of a ship's cargo, measured in tons **5.** DUTY CHARGED ON SHIP'S CARGO the duty charged at a rate per ton on a ship's cargo **6.** SIZE OF FLEET OF SHIPS the size of a fleet of ships such as a merchant company's fleet or a nation's warships, calculated as the combined weights or carrying capacities of all ships [15C. < TON[1]]

tonne /tun/ *n* MEASURE same as **metric ton** [Late 19C. Via French < medieval Latin *tunna*]

ton·neau /tə nṓ, tónnō/ (*plural* **-neaus**) *n* the back-seat compartment of an open-top vintage car [Late 18C. < French, "barrel" (because of its shape) < *tonne* (see TONNE)]

ton·neau cov·er *n* a detachable protective cover for the open bed of a pickup truck or the passenger compartment of a convertible car whose top is down

to·nom·e·ter /tō nómmətər/ *n* **1.** an instrument, often one fitted with a range of tuning forks, that measures the exact pitch of a sound **2.** an instrument that measures pressure in a part of the body, e.g., the blood vessels, or the eyeball as a test for glaucoma [Early 18C. < Greek *tonos* "tension, tone"] —**to·no·met·ric** /tṓnə méttrik/ *adj* —**to·nom·e·try** *n*

to·no·plast /tṓnə plàst/ *n* the semipermeable membrane separating a fluid-filled internal cavity (**vacuole**) from the surrounding cytoplasm inside a plant cell [Late 19C. < Greek *tonos* "tension, tone"]

tons /tunz/ *adv* to a great degree or extent ○ *The weather's tons better today.* [Early 20C. Plural of TON[1]]

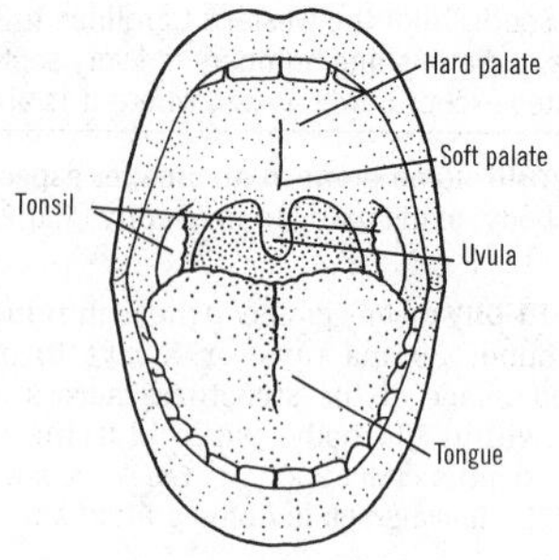

tonsil

ton·sil /tónssəl/ *n* **1.** either of two small oval masses of tissue, one on either side of the back of the mouth, that are important for the body's immune system **2.** a lump of tissue shaped like a tonsil of the mouth, e.g., either of two small lumps in the brain (**tonsils of the cerebellum**) [Late 16C. < Latin *tonsillae* "tonsils"] —**ton·sil·lar** *adj*

~~**tonsilitis**~~ incorrect spelling of **tonsillitis**

ton·sil·lec·to·my /tònssə léktəmee/ (*plural* **-mies**) *n* a surgical procedure to remove the tonsils of the mouth

ton·sil·li·tis /tònssə lítiss/ *n* inflammation of the tonsils of the mouth, caused either by bacteria or a virus, which makes the throat very sore and can lead to fever and earache —**ton·sil·lit·ic** /-líttik/ *adj*

ton·so·ri·al /ton sáwree əl/ *adj* relating to barbers or their work (*formal or humorous*) [Early 19C. < Latin *tonsorius* < *tonsor* "barber" < *tondere* "to clip"]

ton·sure /tónshər/ *n* **1.** PARTIALLY SHAVED HEAD a shaved patch on the crown of the head of a priest or monk in some religious orders **2.** SHAVING OF HEAD the shaving of the head, especially to make a shaved patch on the crown of a priest or monk's head ■ *vt* (**-sured, -sur·ing, -sures**) PARTIALLY SHAVE HEAD to shave the crown of the head [14C. Directly or via French < Latin *tonsura* < *tondere* "to clip"]

ton·tine /tón teen, ton téen/ *n* an investment or insurance plan in which contributors pay equal amounts into a common fund and receive equal dividends and benefits from it, with the final surviving contributor receiving everything [Mid-18C. < French, after Lorenzo *Tonti* (1630–95), Neapolitan banker]

ton·to /tóntō/ *adj* an offensive term meaning psychiatrically disordered (*insult*) [Late 20C. < Spanish]

to·nus /tṓnəss/ *n* the normal state of a healthy muscle when resting in a state of slight contraction [Late 19C. Via Latin < Greek *tonos* "tension, tone"]

ton·y /tṓnee/ *adj* having an aristocratic, expensive, or stylish presentation (*informal*) [Late 19C. < TONE]

To·ny /tṓnee/ (*plural* **-nys**) *n* in the United States, an award made annually for achievement in the theater [Mid-20C. < *Tony,* nickname of Antoinette Perry (1888–1946), US actor and producer]

too /too/ *adv* **1.** AS WELL used to indicate that a person, thing, or aspect of a situation applies in addition to the one just mentioned ○ *You can come too.* **2.** MORE THAN IS DESIRABLE more of an amount or degree of something than is desirable, necessary, or fitting ○ *too flamboyant for my taste* **3.** EXTREMELY used to emphasize a quality ○ *You're too kind.* **4.** VERY used to modify the force of a negative statement in order to sound polite or cautious ○ *didn't look too happy*

5. **INDEED** used to emphasize the force of a statement or command ○ *You did too!* [Old English *tō* (see TO[1]), in the sense "in addition, furthermore"]

SPELLCHECK See ***to***[1].

too·dle-oo /to͝od'l o͞o/ *interj* same as **goodbye** (*dated informal or humorous*) [Early 20C. Origin ?]

took past tense of **take**

tool /tool/ *n* **1. DEVICE FOR DOING WORK** an object designed to do a specific kind of work such as cutting or chopping by directing manually applied force or by means of a motor **2. MEANS TO END** something used as a means of achieving something **3. SOMETHING USED FOR JOB** something used in the course of somebody's everyday work ○ *Words are the poet's tool.* **4. SOMEBODY MANIPULATED BY ANOTHER** somebody who is easily manipulated, especially to carry out unpleasant or dishonest tasks that somebody else is unwilling to do **5.** MECH ENG same as **machine tool 6.** MECH ENG **CUTTING PART OF MACHINE** the cutting or shaping part of a power-driven device, e.g., the blade on a lathe **7.** HANDICRAFT **BOOKBINDER'S IMPLEMENT** an implement that a bookbinder uses to press a design into leather, cloth, or paper **8.** HANDICRAFT **STAMPED DESIGN ON BOOK** a design pressed into a book cover with a metal tool **9. OFFENSIVE TERM** an offensive term for a penis (*slang*) ■ *v* (**tooled, tool·ing, tools**) **1.** *vt* HANDICRAFT **WORK SOMETHING USING HAND TOOLS** to cut, shape, or form something, especially to press a design into the cover of a book, using hand tools **2.** *vt* INDUST **GIVE SOMEBODY OR SOMETHING TOOLS** to equip somebody or something with tools **3.** *vti* AUTOMOT **DRIVE CAR** to drive a car, especially at high speeds (*slang*) ○ *tooling along at a cool 65* [Old English *tōl* < Germanic, "to manufacture"] —**tool·er** *n*

tool up *vti* **1.** to provide a factory or an industry with the equipment needed for manufacturing ○ *tooled up for producing the new models* **2.** to provide a person, company, or organization with the resources or equipment needed to do something ○ *tooled up for the new inventory system*

tool·bar /to͝ol baar/ *n* a row of icons on a computer screen that are clicked on to perform frequently used functions

tool·ing /to͝oling/ *n* **1. DECORATIVE WORK DONE WITH HAND TOOLS** decorative work done with hand tools, especially the carving of stone or the pressing or stamping of designs onto leather ○ *gold tooling* **2. PROVISION OF INDUSTRIAL MACHINERY** the process of providing a factory or an industry with the equipment needed for manufacturing **3. PROCESS OF WORKING WITH TOOL** the process of working with a hand tool or a machine tool

tool·kit /to͝ol kìt/ *n* **1.** a set of tools, especially for a specific type of work, kept in a special box or bag **2.** a collection of information, resources, and advice for a specific subject area or activity ○ *a best-practice toolkit for housing officials*

tool·mak·er /to͝ol màykər/ *n* somebody who makes or repairs precision tools, especially the cutting or shaping parts of industrial machines —**tool·mak·ing** *n*

tool push·er *n* somebody who supervises drilling operations on a drill rig (*informal*)

tool·room /to͝ol ro͝om, -ro͞om/ *n* a room in a machine shop where tools are stored, maintained, or made

tool·shed /to͝ol shèd/ *n* a small outbuilding where tools are kept, especially one in a yard used for storing gardening tools

tool steel *n* a hard steel used to make the cutting or shaping parts of hand tools and power tools

toon[1] /toon/ *n* **1.** a fragrant hard reddish mahogany. Use: furniture, joinery. **2.** a tree of the mahogany family that bears red flowers and yields toon. Native to: Australia, tropical Asia. Latin name: *Cedrela toona*. [Early 19C. Via Hindi *tūn* < Sanskrit *tunnah*]

toon[2] /toon/ *n* **1.** MOVIES same as **cartoon** (sense 1) **2.** a character in a cartoon [Mid-20C. Shortening of CARTOON]

too·nie /to͞onee/ *n Can* a coin worth two Canadian dollars [Blend of TWO + LOONIE]

toot[1] /toot/ *n* **SOUND OF HORN** a high-pitched hooting sound such as that made by a vehicle's horn or a trumpet or flute ■ *v* (**toot·ed, toot·ing, toots**) **1.** *vti* **MAKE SHORT HOOTING SOUND** to make a short high-pitched hooting sound, or cause something such as a vehicle's horn, a trumpet, or a flute to do this **2.** *vi* **OFFENSIVE TERM** an offensive term meaning to pass gas noisily (*slang*) [Early 16C. An imitation of the sound] —**toot·er** *n*

toot[2] /toot/ (*slang*) *n* **1. DRINKING BOUT** a bout of heavy drinking **2. INHALED ILLEGAL SUBSTANCE** a quantity of an illegal drug, especially cocaine, taken by inhaling through the nose ■ *vti* (**toot·ed, toot·ing, toots**) *US* **INHALE ILLEGAL SUBSTANCE** to inhale an illegal drug, especially cocaine, through the nose [Late 17C. Origin ?]

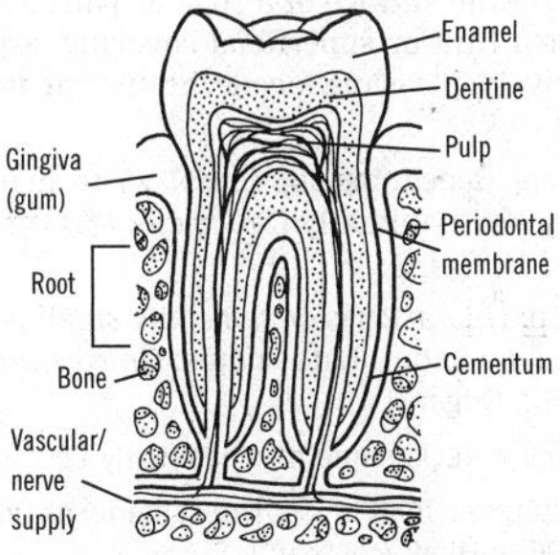

tooth: cross section of a human tooth

tooth /tooth/ *n* (*plural* **teeth** /teeth/) **1. WHITISH BONY OBJECT IN MOUTH** a hard whitish bony object inside a human or vertebrate animal's mouth, used for biting and chewing food **2. INVERTEBRATE PART RESEMBLING TOOTH** a sharp part on an invertebrate made of horny, calcareous, or chitinous material and functioning like or resembling a vertebrate tooth **3. INDENTATION** an object with the shape or function of a tooth, e.g., one of the jagged indentations along the edge of a saw or leaf **4. PART STICKING OUT ON GEAR WHEEL** a part that sticks out from the edge of a gear wheel or sprocket, designed to interlock with a similar part on another wheel **5. SURFACE ROUGHNESS ALLOWING SUBSTANCE TO ADHERE** the roughness of a surface, especially that of paper, that allows paints, glues, and other substances to stick to it **6. TASTE FOR SOMETHING** a liking for the taste of something ○ *a sweet tooth* **7. SOMETHING DESTRUCTIVE** something that has the power to destroy (*usually used in the plural*) ○ *the teeth of the gale* ■ **teeth** *npl* **EFFECTIVE POWER** the power or ability to accomplish something ○ *Sanctions without teeth won't do any good.* ■ *v* (**toothed, tooth·ing, tooths**) **1.** *vt* **PUT TEETH ON SOMETHING** to give something teeth, especially to cut teeth into a saw blade or around the edge of a gear wheel or sprocket **2.** *vi* **FIT TOGETHER WITH INTERLOCKING TEETH** to interlock by means of teeth that fit one set inside the other [Old English *tōþ* < Indo-European] —**toothed** *adj* ◇ **armed to the teeth (with something)** extremely well armed or equipped with something (*informal*) ◇ **cut your teeth (on something)** to learn how to do something and gain experience from it ◇ **get your teeth into something** to start doing something that will be challenging and satisfying ◇ **in the teeth of** against opposition or contradiction from ◇ **kiss teeth** to suck air in noisily through the teeth in order to express displeasure or disagreement (*slang; used in Black English*) ◇ **like pulling teeth** extremely difficult, often because of a lack of cooperation (*informal*) ◇ **set somebody's teeth on edge** to annoy or irritate somebody ◇ **show** *or* **bare your teeth** to indicate that you have power and intend to use it ◇ **tooth and nail** very aggressively, or with every available means

tooth·ache /to͞oth àyk/ *n* a pain in or around a tooth, especially because the tooth is decaying

tooth·ache tree *n* a tree with prickly branches whose fragrant bark was formerly chewed to cure toothache. Native to: North America. Latin name: *Zanthoxylum americanum* or *Zanthoxylum clava-herculis*.

tooth·brush /to͞oth brùsh/ *n* a small brush for cleaning the teeth, with a long handle and a comparatively small head —**tooth·brush·ing** *n*

toothed whale *n* a smallish whale that has teeth and feeds on fish and mollusks. Suborder: Odontoceti.

tooth fair·y *n* in children's folklore, a fairy who takes away the baby tooth that a child leaves under the pillow and replaces it with a coin or small gift

tooth·less /to͞othləss/ *adj* **1.** lacking teeth, especially because the teeth have decayed and fallen out **2.** lacking power, authority, or a forceful manner

tooth·less whale *n* a whale without teeth, but with thin horny plates hanging from the upper jaw through which it filters plankton

tooth·paste /to͞oth pàyst/ *n* a paste brushed onto the teeth to clean them and protect them from decay

tooth·pick /to͞oth pìk/ *n* a thin pointed stick of wood or plastic used to remove pieces of food from between the teeth

tooth pow·der *n* a powder that is mixed to a lather with a damp toothbrush and used to clean the teeth and protect them from decay

tooth shell *n* **1.** a marine invertebrate animal with a tapering shell. Class: Scaphopoda. **2.** the tapering shell of a marine invertebrate animal

tooth·some /to͞othssəm/ *adj* **1.** having a pleasing smell, taste, or appearance **2.** attractive, especially sexually (*dated informal; sometimes offensive*) —**tooth·some·ly** *adv* —**tooth·some·ness** *n*

tooth·wort /to͞oth wùrt, -wàwrt/ (*plural* **-worts** *or same*) *n* **1.** a flowering plant with scaly rhizomes. Flowers: showy, pink or purple. Native to: North America. Latin name: *Cardamine bulbifera*. **2.** a leafless plant that grows on tree roots and has horizontal underground stems (**rhizomes**) covered with scales resembling teeth. Flowers: pinkish. Native to: Europe. Latin name: *Lathraea squamaria*.

tooth·y /to͞othee/ (**-i·er, -i·est**) *adj* having or showing a lot of teeth, large teeth, or protruding teeth —**tooth·i·ly** *adv* —**tooth·i·ness** *n*

too·tle /to͞ot'l/ (*informal*) *v* (**-tled, -tling, -tles**) **1.** *vi* **DRIVE SLOWLY** to proceed slowly or aimlessly, especially in a car **2.** *vti* **MAKE HOOTING SOUND** to make repeated gentle tooting sounds, or cause something to do this ■ *n* **REPEATED SOUND** a gentle repeated tooting sound [Early 19C. < TOOT[1]]

too-too *adj* exaggeratedly and artificially refined or elegant (*informal humorous*)

toots /to͝ots/ *n* an affectionate or patronizing way of addressing somebody, especially a woman (*dated informal; sometimes offensive*) [Mid-20C. Origin ?]

toot·sie /to͝otsee/ *n* **1.** same as **toots** (*dated informal; sometimes offensive*) **2.** another spelling of **tootsy** (sense 1) (*slang*) **3.** same as **prostitute** *n* (sense 1) (*slang*) [Mid-20C. Origin ?]

toot·sy /to͝otsee/ (*plural* **-sies**), **toot·sie** *n* **1.** a foot or toe (*slang*) **2.** *US* same as **toots** (*dated informal; sometimes offensive*) [Mid-19C. Alteration of FOOTSIE]

top[1] /top/ *n* **1. HIGHEST PART** the highest part or point of something (*often used in combination*) ○ *snow on the mountain tops* **2. UPPER SURFACE** the upper side or surface of something ○ *dust on the top of the cupboard* **3. LID OR COVER** the part covering and sealing the open upper side of an object, or an opening on the upper side (*often used in combination*) ○ *bottle tops* **4. GARMENT COVERING UPPER BODY** a piece of clothing, especially women's clothing, covering the upper body **5. MOST IMPORTANT POSITION OR PERSON** the most important position or most senior rank, or the person occupying it ○ *at the top of her profession* **6. BEST PART** the best part or section of something ○ *They only take the top of the group.* **7. MOST EXCELLENT LEVEL** the level of highest excellence ○ *not at the top of his game* **8. MOST INTENSE LEVEL** the level of greatest intensity, power, or force ○ *at the top of her voice* **9. BEGINNING OR EARLIEST PART** the beginning or the first or earliest section of something ○ *the top of the news* **10. CROWN OF HEAD** the crown of the head ○ *from top to toe* **11. PART OF PLANT ABOVE GROUND** the part of a plant that is above the ground ○ *carrot tops* **12. CAR ROOF** the roof of a car, especially a convertible **13.** *UK* AUTOMOT same as **high gear** (sense 1) (*informal*) **14.** BASEBALL **FIRST HALF OF BASEBALL INNING** the first half of an inning in a baseball game **15.** SPORTS same as **topspin 16.** SPORTS **STROKE HITTING BALL ABOVE CENTER** a stroke that puts topspin on a ball by hitting the ball above its center **17.** CARDS **PLAYER'S BEST CARD OR CARDS** the best card or group of cards in a player's hand **18.** NAUT **PLATFORM ON MAST** a platform around the head of a lower mast on a sailing ship, used to stand on or to support rigging **19.** ACOUSTICS **HIGH-FREQUENCY PART OF SOUND** the high-frequency element of a sound **20.** CHEM **VOLATILE PART OF SOLUTION** the fraction of a volatile solution that is collected first during distillation ■ *adj* **1. UPPERMOST OR HIGHEST** situated at the top, or higher than all others ○ *the top shirt on the pile* **2. LEADING OR MOST SUCCESSFUL** most important, senior, successful, or respected ○ *a convention of top academics* **3. OF BEST QUALITY** of the finest quality available ○ *one of the city's top hotels* **4. MAXIMUM** highest in level or degree ○ *at top speed* **5.** *UK* **EXCELLENT** used to indicate approval (*informal*) ○ *He's a top bloke.* ■ *vt* **(topped, top·ping, tops) 1. EXCEED OR BETTER SOMETHING** to do better than something, or be greater than something ○ *profits topping $500 million* **2. OUTRANK ALL OTHERS IN SOMETHING** to be at the head of something such as a list or hierarchy ○ *They've topped the music charts for the fifth week in a row.* **3. ADD TOPPING TO SOMETHING** to put a topping on something (*often passive*) ○ *topped with a layer of melted cheese* **4. CUT TOP OFF SOMETHING** to cut the top off something, especially a vegetable prior to cooking ○ *First top the carrots.* **5. REACH APEX OF SOMETHING** to reach or go over the top of something such as a mountain **6.** SPORTS **PUT TOPSPIN ON BALL** to hit a ball above its center, putting topspin on it **7.** GOLF **HIT GOLF BALL ABOVE CENTER** to hit a golf ball too far above its center, so that it runs along the ground instead of rising into the air **8.** CHEM **DISTILL VOLATILE PART OF SOLUTION** to distill the most volatile part of a solution [Old English *topp* < Germanic, "tuft, crest"] ◇ **blow your top** to lose your temper and fly into a rage (*informal*) ◇ **off the top of your head** without thinking deeply, checking, or planning something

top off *vt* to add an impressive or significant finishing touch to something

top out *vt* to add the final story or other structural feature to a building under construction, usually as part of an official ceremony

top[2] /top/ *n* a toy that spins around on a rounded or pointed base, traditionally a conical wooden toy that is set spinning by pulling a string wrapped around it [Pre-12C. Origin ?]

top- *prefix* same as **topo-** (*used before vowels*)

to·paz /tṓ pàz/ *n* **1. TRANSPARENT BROWN GEMSTONE** a usually brown, transparent precious stone. Source: pegmatite. Use: gems. **2. YELLOWISH GEMSTONE** a yellowish gemstone, especially yellow sapphire or a yellow variety of quartz **3. HUMMINGBIRD WITH YELLOWISH THROAT** a vividly colored hummingbird with a yellowish throat. Native to: South American rain forest. Latin name: *Topaza pella.* **4. YELLOWISH BROWN COLOR** a light yellowish brown color [13C. Via Old French *topace* < Greek *topazos*] —**to·paz** *adj*

to·paz·o·lite /tō pázzə lī̀t/ *n* a yellowish green variety of garnet. Use: gems.

top ba·nan·a *n* (*slang*) **1.** the main person in a group **2.** the leading comedian in a comedy show, especially a vaudeville show

top bil·ling *n* **1.** a performer's status as the star attraction in a show with his or her name appearing first in any list of performers or promotional material **2.** the position of greatest prominence in something

top boot *n* a knee-length boot with a band of differently colored leather around the top

top brass *n* the highest-ranking officers or officials (*informal*)

top-class *adj* belonging to or characteristic of the highest category of something ○ *a top-class tennis player*

top·coat /tóp kṓt/ *n* **1.** a lightweight coat for outdoor wear **2.** a finishing coat of paint, applied over an undercoat

top dead-cen·ter *n* the position of a piston in an engine or pump when it is at the top of its stroke

top dog *n* the most important or powerful person, often somebody who has beaten all other competitors (*informal*)

top dol·lar *n* a very high price (*informal*)

top-down *adj* **1.** having all control in the hands of the people at the most senior levels **2.** starting at the most general level and working toward details or specifics

top-draw·er *n* **1.** the highest level of excellence, or the people at this level **2.** the upper class or highest class in society —**top-draw·er** *adj*

top-dress *vt* to spread a thin layer of something on the ground, especially fertilizer on the surface of soil, a growing crop, or a lawn

top dress·ing *n* **1. SURFACE FERTILIZER** a fertilizer spread thinly on the surface of soil, a growing crop, or a lawn **2. LOOSE GRAVEL AS ROAD SURFACE** loose gravel spread thinly on the surface of a road or path **3. SUPERFICIAL COVERING** a thin or superficial covering, especially a deceptively pleasant facade hiding an unpleasant reality

tope[1] /tōp/ **(toped, top·ing, topes)** *vti* to drink liquor heavily and habitually (*archaic or literary*) [Mid-17C. Origin ?]

tope[2] /tōp/ (*plural* **topes** or *same*) *n* a small gray shark with a long snout. Latin name: *Galeorhinus galeus.* [Late 17C. Origin ?]

tope[3] /tōp/ *n* RELIG same as **stupa** [Early 19C. < Hindi *top*]

to·pee /tṓpee/, **to·pi** *n* CLOTHING same as **pith helmet** [Mid-19C. < Hindi *ṭopī* "hat"]

To·pe·ka /tə peékə/ capital of Kansas, in the northeastern part of the state, on the Kansas River, east of Manhattan and west of Kansas City. Population: 122,103 (2002 estimate).

top·er /tṓpər/ *n* somebody who drinks alcohol heavily and habitually

top-flight /tóp flī̀t/ *adj* of the highest quality or status

top·gal·lant /top gállənt, tóp gàl-/; *nautical use* /tə gállənt/ *n* **1.** *also* **top·gal·lant mast** a ship's mast that is taller than a topmast or is an extension of a topmast **2.** *also* **top·gal·lant sail** a sail set on a topgallant mast

top gear *n UK* same as **high gear** (sense 1)

top gun *n* somebody who is the best in his or her field (*informal*)

CULTURAL NOTE ***Top Gun***, a movie (1986) by English director Tony Scott. A drama about US Navy fighter pilots in training, it centers on two outstanding pilots in the class competing for the much coveted title of "Top Gun." An encounter with enemy aircraft provides them with an opportunity to prove their worth. The movie is memorable for its spectacular, high-speed dogfights. The term "top gun" promptly moved into the general language.

---

top-ham·per *n* the uppermost sails, spars, and other equipment on a sailing ship, especially when regarded as weight to be minimized or monitored because of the destabilizing effect it can have

top hat *n* a man's tall cylindrical hat with a flat top and a narrow brim. It is usually black, is often made of silk, and is worn as part of formal dress.

top-heav·y *adj* **1.** unbalanced or unstable owing to excessive weight at the top **2.** having too many executives or managers in proportion to the number of staff at junior levels —**top-heav·i·ness** *n*

To·phet /tṓfət, tṓ fèt/, **To·pheth** *n* according to the Bible, a place of torment and punishment where the wicked are sent after death [14C. < Hebrew *Tōppeṯ*, area near Jerusalem]

to·phi MED plural of **tophus**

to·phus /tṓfəss/ (*plural* **-phi** /-fī̀/) *n* a hard deposit of crystalline uric acid and its salts in cartilage, joints, or skin. It is a characteristic of gout. [Mid-16C. < Latin, "tufa"] —**to·pha·ceous** /tə fáyshəss/ *adj*

to·pi[1] /tṓpee/ (*plural* **-pis** or *same*) *n* an antelope that has curved horns, a long muzzle, and bluish black and yellow markings. It is said to be the fastest of all the antelopes. Native to: Africa. Latin name: *Damaliscus lunatus.* [Late 19C. Origin ?]

to·pi[2] /tṓpee/ *n* CLOTHING same as **pith helmet**

to·pi·ar·y /tṓpee èrree/ (*plural* **-ies**) *n* **1. SHAPED BUSH** a bush, hedge, or tree trimmed into a decorative shape **2. ART OF SHAPING BUSHES** the art of trimming bushes, hedges, and trees into decorative shapes **3. TOPIARY GARDEN** a garden in which topiaries feature prominently [Late 16C. Via French < Latin *topiarius* < Greek *topos* "place"] —**to·pi·ar·ist** *n*

topi

top·ic /tóppik/ *n* **1.** something dealt with in a text or in discussion **2.** a class of arguments used as a source of proofs in formal reasoning [15C. < *Topics*, title of Aristotle's treatise on rhetorical commonplaces < Latin *Topica* < Greek *topos* "place"]

SYNONYMS See ***subject***.

---

top·i·cal /tóppik'l/ *adj* **1. OF CURRENT INTEREST** relating to something that is of interest or importance at the moment **2. OF TOPICS** relating to topics or in the form of topics ○ *a topical index* **3. LOCAL** relating to or situated in a specific place or part **4.** MED **APPLIED EXTERNALLY** describes drugs or medications that are applied directly to the surface of the part of the body being treated —**top·i·cal·ly** *adv*

top·i·cal·i·ty /tòppi kállətee/ *n* relevance to something that is of interest or importance at the moment

top·ic sen·tence *n* a sentence that states the main idea of a paragraph or larger section of writing, usually placed at or near the beginning

top·knot /tóp nòt/ *n* **1.** a decorative arrangement of hair, or of hairbands or bows, worn on top of the head **2.** a small tuft of feathers on the head of some birds such as some types of quails

top·less /tópləss/ *adj* **1. WITH NOTHING COVERING BREASTS** wearing no covering over the breasts or upper torso **2. LETTING WOMEN SHOW BREASTS IN PUBLIC** describes a place such as a beach where women expose their breasts in public ○ *a topless beach* **3. WITH NO TOP PART** describes a piece of clothing that has no part covering the upper torso ○ *a topless bathing suit* **4. MISSING TOP** lacking or missing a top —**top·less·ness** *n*

top-lev·el *adj* **1.** involving the most senior or influential people ○ *top-level negotiations* **2.** at the highest level of influence or authority ○ *a top-level executive*

top-lev·el do·main *n* the part of an Internet address that identifies an Internet domain, e.g., .edu (education), .com (commercial), or a two-letter country code

top·loft·y /tóp lòftee/ **(-i·er, -i·est)** *adj US* haughty, pretentious, or condescending (*informal*) —**top·loft·i·ly** *adv*

top·mast /tóp màst/ *n* a mast that is taller than the lowest mast and is usually the tallest mast on a ship whose sails run fore-and-aft. It is the next tallest after the topgallant mast on a square-rigged ship.

top·min·now /tóp mìnnō/ (*plural* **-nows** or *same*) *n* a small freshwater fish that swims near the surface in warmer waters and has an upturned mouth for catching prey. Guppies and mollies are topminnows. Families: Cyprinodontidae or Poeciliidae or Goodeidae.

top·most /tóp mṓst/ *adj* highest or uppermost

top·notch /tóp nòch/ *adj* meeting the highest standards of excellence or quality (*informal*) —**top·notch·er** *n*

topo- *prefix* place, region ○ *topotype* [< Greek *topos* "place"]

top of mind *adj US* first among the things a person thinks about (*informal*) ○ *how to keep food safety top of mind among your employees*

top-of-the-range *adj* being the best, most expensive, and most sophisticated available (*not hyphenated after a verb*) ○ *bought the top-of-the-range model*

to·pog·ra·phy /tə póggrəfee/ *n* **1.** MAPPING OF SURFACE FEATURES the study and mapping of the features on the surface of land, including natural features such as mountains and rivers and constructed features such as highways and railroads **2.** AREA'S FEATURES the features on the surface of an area of land **3.** DESCRIPTION OF STRUCTURE a study or detailed description of the various features of an object or entity and the relationships between them —**to·pog·ra·pher** *n* —**top·o·graph·ic** /tòppə gráffik/ *adj* —**top·o·graph·i·cal** *adj* —**top·o·graph·i·cal·ly** *adv*

to·poi LITERAT plural of **topos**

to·pol·o·gy /tə póllajee/ *n* **1.** STUDY OF GEOMETRIC PROPERTIES the study of the properties of geometric figures that are independent of size or shape and are not changed by stretching, bending, knotting, or twisting **2.** FAMILY OF SUBSETS the family of all open subsets of a mathematical set, including the set itself and the empty set, which is closed under set union and finite intersection **3.** ANATOMY OF BODY PART the anatomy of a part of the body **4.** STUDY LINKING TOPOGRAPHY AND TIME the study of changes in topography that occur over time and, especially, of how such changes taking place in an area affect the history of that area **5.** RELATIONSHIPS BETWEEN LINKED ELEMENTS the relationships between parts linked together in a system such as a computer network (*formal*) —**top·o·log·ic** /tòppə lójjik/ *adj* —**top·o·log·i·cal** *adj* —**top·o·log·i·cal·ly** *adv* —**to·pol·o·gist** *n*

top·o·nym /tóppə nìm/ *n* **1.** a name, e.g., a personal name, that is derived from the name of a place **2.** a name given to a place (*formal*) [Late 19C. < TOPO- after SYNONYM]

to·pon·y·my /tə pónnəmee/ *n* the study of the place names of a region or language —**top·o·nym·ic** /tòppə nímmik/ *adj*

to·pos /tṓ pòss, -pòss/ (*plural* **-poi** /-pòy/) *n* a traditional theme, especially one developed in literature or rhetoric [Mid-20C. < Greek, "place, rhetorical commonplace"]

top·o·type /tóppə tìp/ *n* a biological specimen taken from its typical habitat

-topped *suffix* having a top of a particular kind ○ *flat-topped*

top·per /tóppər/ *n* **1.** CLOTHING same as **top hat** (*informal*) **2.** CLOTHING WOMAN'S COAT a woman's short, loose-fitting coat or jacket **3.** SOMEBODY OR SOMETHING DEALING WITH TOPS a person or machine that removes or adds tops **4.** CROWNING COMMENT a remark or joke that improves on or triumphs over a preceding one (*informal*)

top·ping /tópping/ *n* something put on top of food, especially a sauce or garnish

top·ple /tópp'l/ (**-pled, -pling, -ples**) *v* **1.** *vti* FALL OR MAKE SOMETHING FALL OVER to fall forward or tip over, or make something do this **2.** *vi* TOTTER to lean or sway precariously, as if about to fall over **3.** *vt* OVERTHROW SOMEBODY OR SOMETHING to overthrow somebody or something from a position of authority [Mid-16C. < TOP[1]]

top-qual·i·ty *adj* of the highest quality (*not hyphenated after a verb*) ○ *top-quality meat*

top quark *n* a quark with an electric charge of +2/3 and zero strangeness and charm

top-rank·ing *adj* of a senior rank or the highest rank

top-rat·ed *adj* considered highest in quality or rank ○ *the city's ten top-rated restaurants*

top round *n* a lean boneless cut of beef from the outer thigh

tops /tops/ (*informal*) *adj* ranked highest in quality, degree, or esteem ○ *She's tops in her field.* ■ *adv* at the most ○ *Offer him five hundred, tops.*

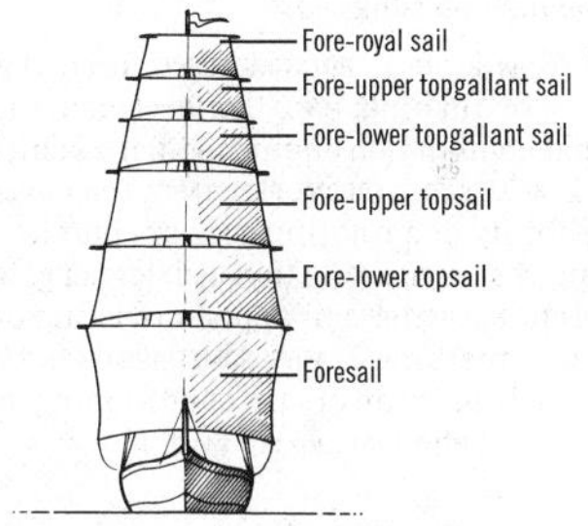

topsail: topsails on a square-rigged ship

top·sail /tóps'l, -sàyl/ *n* a sail set above the lowermost sail on a mast on a square-rigged sailing ship, or above the gaff on a fore-and-aft-rigged ship

top-se·cret *adj* requiring complete secrecy or containing information that must be kept completely secret, especially because its disclosure would endanger national security

top secret/codeword *n* the highest possible security clearance in the US government and armed forces

top ser·geant *n US* a first sergeant in the US Army

top·side /tóp sìd/ *n* **1.** UPPER SIDE the uppermost side of something **2.** UPPER HULL the part of a ship's hull that sits above the water **3.** *US* HIGHEST RANK the highest office or position **4.** *UK* same as **top round** ■ *adj* **1.** ON TOPSIDE OF SHIP relating to or situated on the topside of a ship **2.** *US* HIGH IN RANK of the highest position or rank ■ *adv also* **top·sides** *US* NAUT TO SHIP'S DECK up on or to the deck of a ship

top·soil /tóp sòyl/ *n* TOP LAYER OF SOIL the upper fertile layer of soil, from which plant roots take nutrients ■ *vt* (**-soiled, -soil·ing, -soils**) **1.** SPREAD LAND WITH TOPSOIL to spread topsoil onto farming or gardening land to improve fertility **2.** REMOVE TOPSOIL FROM LAND to remove the top layer of soil from farming or gardening land

top·spin /tóp spìn/ *n* forward spin given to a ball by hitting it on its upper half, making it arc more sharply in the air or bounce higher on impact

top·stitch /tóp stìch/ *n* a row of stitching on the outer or upper side of a garment, near the seam ■ *vt* (**-stitched, -stitch·ing, -stitch·es**) to sew a topstitch on a garment —**top·stitch·ing** *n*

top·sy-tur·vy /tòpsee túrvee/ *adj, adv* **1.** UPSIDE DOWN with the bottom at the top and the top at the bottom **2.** IN OR INTO CONFUSION in or into a confused or chaotic state, especially one in which the natural order or arrangement of things is inverted ■ *n* DISORDER OR CONFUSION a state of complete disorder or confusion [Early 16C. Origin ?] —**top·sy-tur·vi·ly** *adv* —**top·sy-tur·vi·ness** *n*

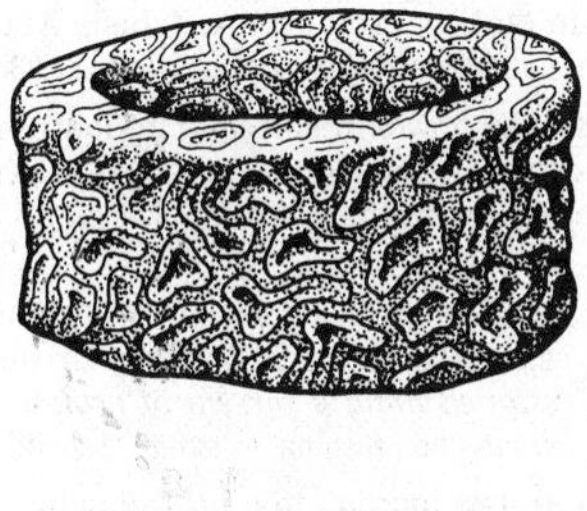

toque

toque /tōk/ *n* **1.** BRIMLESS HAT a close-fitting brimless hat worn by women **2.** CHEF'S HAT a tall white hat worn by chefs **3.** HAT WORN IN PAST a velvet hat with a narrow brim and pouched crown, popular in the 16th century with men and women **4.** *Can* CLOTHING another spelling of **tuque** [Early 16C. < French]

tor /tawr/ *n* a rocky peak of a hill or mountain, specifically one exposed by the weathering of surrounding rock (*often used in place names*) [Old English *torr*, origin ?]

To·rah /táwrə/ *n* **1.** the Jewish Pentateuch, or a parchment scroll on which the Pentateuch is written for use in services in synagogues **2.** the collective body of Jewish teaching embodied in the Hebrew Bible and the Talmud [Late 16C. < Hebrew *tôrāh* "law"]

tor·bern·ite /táwrbər nìt/ *n* a green mineral containing uranium and copper. Use: source of uranium. [Mid-19C. After *Torbern* Olof Bergman (1735–84), Swedish chemist]

torc *n* JEWELRY another spelling of **torque**[2]

torch /tawrch/ *n* **1.** BURNING STICK a stick of wood dipped in wax or with one end wrapped in combustible material, set on fire and carried, especially in former times, as a source of light **2.** *UK* same as **flashlight** (sense 1) **3.** DEVICE EMITTING FLAME a portable device that emits an extremely hot flame, e.g., one used in welding or for stripping paint **4.** SOURCE OF ENLIGHTENMENT a source of guidance or enlightenment (*literary*) ■ *vt* (**torched, torch·ing, torch·es**) SET SOMETHING ON FIRE to set fire to something, especially as an act of arson or terrorism (*slang*) [13C. Via French *torche* < Latin *torques* "torque" < *torquere* "to twist"] —**torch·er** *n* ◇ **carry a torch for somebody** to be in love with somebody, especially when this feeling is secret or unrequited (*informal*)

torch·bear·er /táwrch bérrər/ *n* **1.** somebody who carries a torch, usually in a procession or ceremony **2.** somebody who provides leadership or inspiration

tor·chère /tawr shér/ *n* a tall decorated stand for holding a candle or candelabrum [Early 20C. < French < *torche* (see TORCH)]

tor·chier /tawr cheér/, **tor·chiere** *n* a tall floor lamp that gives indirect upward lighting [Early 20C. Variant of TORCHÈRE]

torch·light /táwrch lìt/ *n* **1.** the light from a torch **2.** same as **torch** *n* (sense 1)

tor·chon lace /táwr shòn-/ *n* lace made from coarse linen or cotton, with a simple open pattern

torch song *n* a popular sentimental song about unrequited love [< the torch as a symbol of unrequited love] —**torch sing·er** *n*

torch·wood /táwrch wòod/ *n* **1.** a resinous wood once used to make torches **2.** a tree yielding torchwood. Native to: Florida, Caribbean. Genus: *Amyris*.

torch·y /táwrchee/ (**-i·er, -i·est**) *adj* typical or reminiscent of a torch song (*informal*)

tore[1] /tawr/ past tense of **tear**[1]

tore[2] /tawr/ *n* ARCHIT same as **torus** (sense 2) [Mid-17C. Via French < Latin *torus* "bulge"]

tor·e·a·dor /táwree ə dàwr/ *n* a bullfighter, especially one on horseback [Early 17C. < Spanish < *torear* "fight bulls" < *toro* "bull" (see TORERO)]

to·re·ro /tə rérrō/ (*plural* **-ros**) *n* a bullfighter, especially one on foot [Early 18C. < Spanish < *toro* "bull" < Latin *taurus*]

to·reu·tics /tə róotiks/ *n* the art of making detailed reliefs in metal using the techniques of embossing and engraving (*takes a singular verb*) [Mid-19C. < Greek *toreutikos* < *toreus* "boring tool"] —**to·reu·tic** *adj*

to·ri plural of **torus**

tor·ic /táwrik/ *adj* ring- or doughnut-shaped like a torus, or relating to tori

tor·ic lens *n* an eyeglass lens used to correct the vision of somebody with astigmatism. It is curved in such a way as to have a different focal length along each axis.

to·ri·i /táwree eè/ (*plural same*) *n* a gateway to a Japanese Shinto temple that has two posts and two crosspieces [Early 18C. < Japanese, "bird's perch"]

tor·ment *vt* /tawr mént/ (**-ment·ed, -ment·ing, -ments**) **1.** INFLICT PAIN ON SOMEBODY OR SOMETHING to inflict torture, pain, or anguish on a person or animal **2.** TEASE SOMEBODY to tease a person or animal persistently ■ *n* /táwr mènt/ **1.** TORTURE severe mental anguish or physical pain **2.** CAUSE OF ANGUISH a source of severe mental anguish or physical pain **3.** CAUSE OF ANNOYANCE a source of annoyance or anxiety [13C. Via Old French < Latin *tormentum* "catapult, torment" < *torquere* "to twist"] —**tor·ment·ed·ly** *adv* —**tor·ment·ing·ly** *adv*

tor·ment·er *n* another spelling of **tormentor**

tor·men·til /táwrmən tìl/ (*plural* **-tils** *or same*) *n* a downy plant with an astringent root. Flowers: yellow. Use: medicine, tanning, dyeing. Latin name: *Potentilla erecta*. [14C. < French *tormentille* < Latin *tormentum* (see TORMENT)]

tor·men·tor /tawr méntər/, **tor·ment·er** *n* **1.** CAUSE OF TORMENT a cause of mental anguish, physical pain, annoyance, or anxiety **2.** THEATER CURTAIN MASKING STAGE WINGS a curtain or screen at each side of a theater stage that hides the wings from the audience **3.** MOVIES ECHO-REDUCING DEVICE IN FILMING a panel of sound-absorbent material used to eliminate echo on a movie set [13C. < Anglo-Norman *tormentour*, Old French *tormenteor* < Latin *tormentum* (see TORMENT)]

torn /tawrn/ past participle of **tear**[1] ■ *adj* reluctant or unable to make a choice ○ *torn between her children and her career*

tor·na·do /tawr náydō/ (*plural* **-dos** or **-does**) *n* **1.** COLUMN OF SWIRLING WIND an extremely destructive funnel-shaped rotating column of air that passes in a narrow path over land **2.** AFRICAN WINDSTORM a short-lived but severe windstorm, especially one that occurs on the West African coast **3.** FRANTIC PERSON OR STATE a state of frenzied activity or intense emotion, or somebody in such a state (*informal*) [Mid-16C. Probably alteration of Spanish *tronada* "thunderstorm" < Latin *tonare* "to thunder"] —**tor·nad·ic** /-náydik, -náddik/ *adj*

~~**tornament**~~ incorrect spelling of **tournament**

torn·il·lo /tawr neé yō, -neélō/ (*plural* **-los**) *n Hispanic* PLANTS same as **screw bean** [Mid-19C. Via American Spanish < Spanish, "screw" < Latin *tornus* "lathe" < Greek *tornos*]

to·roid /táwr òyd/ *n* MATH same as **torus** (sense 1) —**to·roid·al** /tə róyd'l/ *adj*

To·ron·to /tə róntō/ capital city of Ontario Province, Canada, located on the northwestern shore of Lake Ontario. Population: 4,366,508 (2001). —**To·ron·to·ni·an** /tə ròn tōnee ən, tàwrən-/ *n, adj*

to·rose /táw rōss/, **to·rous** /táwrəss/ *adj* cylindrical and knotted or bulging [Mid-18C. < Latin *torosus* "brawny" < *torus* "bulge"] —**to·ros·i·ty** /taw róssətee/ *n*

tor·pe·do /tawr peédō/ *n* (*plural* **-does**) **1.** SELF-PROPELLED UNDERWATER WEAPON a cylindrical self-propelled missile that is launched from an aircraft, ship, or submarine and travels underwater to hit its target **2.** UNDERWATER MINE an underwater explosive mine (*dated*) **3.** *US* FIREWORK a small gravel-filled firework that explodes when thrown against a hard surface **4.** *US* RAIL RAILROAD DANGER SIGNAL an explosive placed on a railroad track that is detonated by a train running over it and serves as a warning of danger ahead **5.** *US* INDUST EXPLOSIVE FOR OIL WELLS an explosive device used to release the oil from an oil well **6.** *US* FOOD same as **submarine** *n* (sense 2) **7.** FISH same as **electric ray** **8.** *US* CRIME PROFESSIONAL KILLER a hired thug or assassin (*slang*) **9.** SPORTS TYPE OF HOCKEY a fast-paced style of ice hockey played without the red line limiting long passes, using two aggressive forecheckers, two mid-ice forwards, and a single defenseman **10.** SPORTS HOCKEY PLAYER a forechecker in torpedo ice hockey ■ *vt* (**-doed, -do·ing, -does**) **1.** HIT SHIP WITH TORPEDO to hit or destroy a ship with a torpedo **2.** DESTROY SOMETHING to spoil, thwart, or destroy something completely (*informal*) ○ *threatened to torpedo the agreement* [Early 16C. < Latin, "numbness" < *torpere* "be stiff"]

tor·pe·do boat *n* a small light fast boat used to launch torpedoes

tor·pe·do bomb·er *n* an aircraft that carries and launches torpedoes

tor·pe·do tube *n* a tube from which torpedoes are fired from submarines or ships

tor·pid /táwrpid/ *adj* **1.** SLUGGISH lacking physical or mental energy **2.** ZOOL DORMANT describes an animal in a dormant state **3.** MED NUMB describes a part of the body that has lost the ability to move or feel [Early 17C. < Latin *torpidus* < *torpere* "be stiff"] —**tor·pid·i·ty** /tawr píddətee/ *n* —**tor·pid·ly** *adv*

tor·por /táwrpər/ *n* **1.** LACK OF ENERGY lack of mental or physical energy **2.** ZOOL DORMANCY the dormant state of an animal **3.** MED NUMBNESS absence of the ability to move or feel [13C. < Latin < *torpere* "be stiff"] —**tor·por·if·ic** /tàwrpə ríffik/ *adj*

torque[1] /tawrk/ *n* **1.** ROTATING FORCE force that causes twisting or turning, e.g., the force generated by an internal-combustion engine to turn a vehicle's drive shaft **2.** ABILITY TO OVERCOME RESISTANCE the measurement of the ability of a rotating gear or shaft to overcome turning resistance ■ *vt* (**torqued, torquing, torques**) **1.** TWIST OR TURN SOMETHING to apply a twisting or turning force to something **2.** TURN SOMETHING UP to turn something such as heat or air conditioning up (*slang*) [Late 19C. < Latin *torquere* "to twist"]

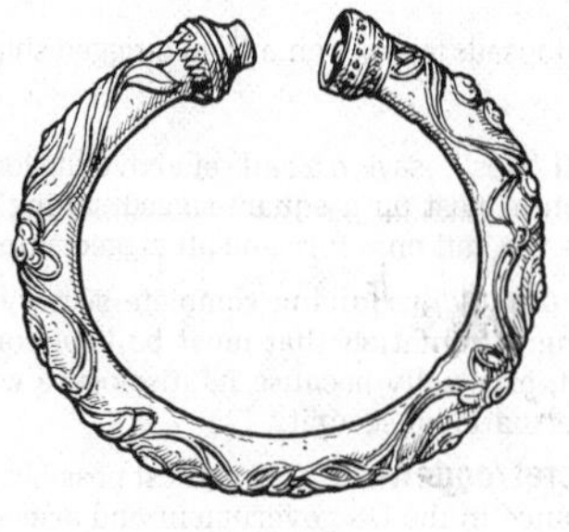

torque

torque[2] /tawrk/, **torc** *n* a metal collar or armband worn by the ancient Gauls and Britons [Mid-19C. Via French < Latin *torques* (see TORCH)]

torque con·vert·er *n* a hydraulic coupling designed to change the mechanical advantage or torque speed between an input and an output shaft

Tor·que·ma·da /tàwrkə maádə/, **Tomás de** (1420–98) Spanish monk. As grand inquisitor for Spain (1487–98), he was notorious for his cruelty. He was largely responsible for the expulsion of the Jews from Spain (1492).

torques /tawrks/ (*plural same*) *n* a ring of color, hair, or feathers around the neck of an animal [Mid-16C. < Latin (see TORCH)]

torque span·ner *n UK* same as **torque wrench**

torque wrench *n* a wrench with a gauge attached for regulating the amount of torque applied to a bolt

torr /tawr/ (*plural same*) *n* a unit of pressure equal to about 133.3 pascals or one millimeter of mercury supported in a column [Mid-20C. After Evangelista TORRICELLI]

Tor·re del Gre·co /tàw ray del grékō/ coastal city near Naples, southern Italy, at the base of Mount Vesuvius. Population: 90,607 (2001).

tor·re·fy /táwrə fī/ (**-fied, -fy·ing, -fies**) *vt* to subject something, especially an ore or chemical, to intense heat for the purpose of removing excess water [Early 17C. < French *torréfier* < Latin *torrere* "scorch"] —**tor·re·fac·tion** /tàwrə fáksh'n/ *n*

Tor·re·mo·li·nos /tàw ray mə leénōss/ major seaside resort in Málaga Province, Andalusia Autonomous Region, southern Spain. Population: 37,235 (1998).

Tor·rens, Lake /táwrənz/ salt lake in South Australia. The second largest lake in Australia, it is often dry at times of low rainfall. Area: 2,200 sq. mi./5,800 sq. km.

tor·rent /táwrənt/ *n* **1.** a fast and powerful rush of liquid, especially water **2.** a violent or tumultuous flow ○ *resigned amid a torrent of protest* [Late 16C. < Latin *torrent-* "hot, rushing" < *torrere* "scorch"]

tor·ren·tial /taw rénshəl, tə-/ *adj* **1.** flowing or falling fast and in great quantities ○ *torrential rain* **2.** intense or abundant ○ *torrential outpouring of emotion* —**tor·ren·tial·ly** *adv*

Tor·re·on /tàwree ṓn/ city in Coahuila State, northern Mexico, on the Nazas River, main city of the agricultural Laguna District. Population: 529,512 (2000).

Tor·res Strait /táwrəss-/ area of sea lying between the northern tip of Cape York, Australia, and the southern coast of Papua New Guinea

Tor·ri·cel·li /tàwrə chéllee/, **Evangelista** (1608–47) Italian mathematician and physicist. He invented the barometer and defined atmospheric pressure. A unit of pressure, the torr, is named for him.

tor·rid /táwrid/ *adj* **1.** FULL OF PASSION full of passion, especially sexual passion **2.** SCORCHING HOT describes weather that is hot and dry enough to scorch land **3.** SCORCHED describes land that has been scorched by extremely hot and dry weather **4.** RAPID rapidly moving ○ *predicted a slowing of the economy from its torrid pace* [Late 16C. Directly or via French < Latin *torridus* < *torrere* "scorch"] —**tor·rid·i·ty** /taw ríddətee/ *n* —**tor·rid·ly** *adv* —**tor·rid·ness** *n*

Tor·rid Zone *n* the region of the Earth that lies between the tropics of Cancer and Capricorn

Tor·ri·jos Her·re·ra /taw reéhōss er ré raa/, **Omar** (1929–81) Panamanian general and national leader. He headed a dictatorship (1968–81) that promoted the interests of less-privileged classes.

tor·sade /tawr saád, -sáyd/ *n* a decorative twist of beads, cord, or fabric [Late 19C. < French < Latin *tors-* (see TORSION)]

Tórs·havn /táwrss hòwn/ administrative headquarters of the Faeroe Islands. It is situated on the island of Streymoy. Population: 14,000 (1990).

tor·si plural of **torso**

tor·si·bil·i·ty /tàwrssə bíllətee/ *n* the ability to undergo or resist twisting [Mid-19C. < TORSION]

tor·sion /táwrsh'n/ *n* **1.** SHAPE CAUSED BY TWISTING the distortion caused by applying torque in opposite directions to each end of an object **2.** MECHANICAL STRESS the stress placed on an object that has been twisted **3.** TWISTING the twisting of something, or a twisted state [15C. Directly or via French < late Latin *torsion-* < Latin *tors-*, past participle of *torquere* "twist"] —**tor·sion·al** *adj* —**tor·sion·al·ly** *adv*

tor·sion bal·ance *n* an instrument that measures small electric or magnetic forces by the degree of twist they produce in a filament

tor·sion bar *n* a metal bar that acts as a spring when subjected to torsion, e.g., in a motor vehicle's suspension system

torsk /tawrsk/ (*plural* **torsks** or *same*) *n UK* same as **cusk** (sense 1) [Early 18C. Via Norwegian < Old Norse *þorskr*]

tor·so /táwrssō/ (*plural* **-sos** or **-si** /-see/) *n* **1.** UPPER BODY the upper part of the human body, not including the head and arms **2.** SCULPTURE a sculpture of a torso, or a broken statue of a human figure with the head, arms, and legs missing **3.** SOMETHING WITH PARTS MISSING something that has parts missing, because it has been mutilated or has not been completed (*literary*) [Late 18C. Via Italian, "trunk of a statue" < Latin *thyrsus* (see THYRSUS)]

tort /tawrt/ *n* in civil law, a wrongful act for which damages can be sought by the injured party [14C. Via Old French < medieval Latin *tortum* < Latin *torquere* "to twist"]

torte /tawrt/ *n* a very rich cake consisting of layers sandwiched together with a cream filling [Mid-18C. Via German < Italian *torta* "cake" < late Latin, type of bread]

Tor·te·lier /tàwrtə lyáy, tawr téll yay/, **Paul** (1914–90) French cellist. He had an international career as a solo performer and was also a skilled teacher.

tor·tel·li·ni /tàwrtə leénee/ *npl* small filled pasta that is shaped into rings, boiled, and served in a soup or sauce [Mid-20C. < Italian, plural of *tortellino* "little cake" < *torta* (see TORTE)]

tor·ti·col·lis /tàwrtə kólliss/ *n* a twisting of the neck to one side, resulting in the head being tilted. It can be temporary, caused by muscle spasm, or a permanent result of a structural condition such as a short neck muscle. [Early 19C. < modern Latin < Latin *tortus* "twisted" + *collum* "neck"] —**tor·ti·col·lar** *adj*

tor·til·la /tawr teé yə/ *n* a thin flat Mexican bread, cooked on a hot griddle and eaten folded, with a filling [Late 17C. < Spanish < *torta* "cake" < late Latin, type of bread]

tor·til·la chip *n* a thin crunchy chip made of corn meal, often served with dips such as salsa and guacamole

tor·til·lon /tàwrtee ón, -yóN/ *n* ART same as **stump**

(sense 3) [Late 19C. < French < *tortiller* "to twist" < Latin *torquere*]

tor·tious /táwrshəss/ *adj* involving or constituting a tort in civil law —**tor·tious·ly** *adv*

tortoise

tor·toise /táwrtəss/ *n* **1.** a slow-moving land-dwelling reptile with a large dome-shaped shell into which it can retract its head and limbs. Family: Testudinidae. **2.** MIL, ANCIENT HIST same as **testudo** **3.** somebody who moves very slowly [15C. Alteration of obsolete *tortuce* < medieval Latin *tortuca*]

tor·toise bee·tle *n* a brightly colored beetle that has a flat rounded body and whose larvae eat leaves. Subfamily: Cassidinae.

tor·toise·shell /táwrtəss shèl/, **tor·toise shell** *n* **1.** OUTER PART OF TURTLE SHELL the hard mottled outer layer of the shell of a hawksbill turtle. Use: combs, ornaments, jewelry. **2.** SYNTHETIC TORTOISESHELL a synthetic substance made to resemble tortoiseshell **3.** TYPE OF CAT a domestic cat with black, cream, and brownish markings **4.** ORANGE-BROWN BUTTERFLY a butterfly that has jagged orange-brown wings with black markings. Family: Nymphalidae. **5.** REPT same as **hawksbill** ■ *adj also* **tor·toise-shell** MOTTLED YELLOW AND BROWN with mottled yellow and brown markings

Tor·to·la /tawr tṓlə/ largest of the British Virgin Islands in the eastern Caribbean Sea. Capital: Road Town. Population: 10,556 (1996). Area: 21 sq. mi./54 sq. km.

tor·to·ni /tawr tṓnee/ *n* rich Italian ice cream often flavored with sherry or rum and chopped cherries or almonds [Early 20C. Probably after an Italian café-owner of 18C Paris]

tor·tri·cid /táwrtrəssid/ *n* a small moth whose larvae live in coiled leaves and are often destructive to plants. Family: Tortricidae. [Late 19C. < modern Latin *Tortrix*, genus name < Latin *tortus* "twisted"]

Tor·tu·ga Is·land /tawr tōōgə-/ island off northern Haiti, in the Caribbean. Population: 22,880 (1982). Area: 69 sq. mi./180 sq. km.

tor·tu·os·i·ty /tàwrchoo óssətee/ (*plural* **-ties**) *n* **1.** the state of being twisted or crooked **2.** a twist or turn

tor·tu·ous /táwrchoo əss/ *adj* **1.** TWISTING AND WINDING with many turns or bends **2.** INTRICATE extremely complex or intricate **3.** DEVIOUS devious or deceitful [14C. Via Anglo-Norman < Latin *tortuosus* < *torquere* "to twist"] —**tor·tu·ous·ly** *adv* —**tor·tu·ous·ness** *n*

USAGE tortuous or **torturous**? Even though both words come ultimately from the same Latin word, meaning "to twist," their meanings diverge in English. A mountain pass is ***tortuous*** ("with many turns or bends"), and by figurative extension, a legal argument can be ***tortuous*** ("complex or intricate") as well. A severe illness, and by figurative extension a decision, may be ***torturous*** ("causing anguish").

tor·ture /táwrchər/ *vt* (**-tured, -tur·ing, -tures**) **1.** INFLICT PAIN ON SOMEBODY to inflict extreme pain or physical punishment on somebody **2.** CAUSE SOMEBODY ANGUISH to cause somebody mental or physical anguish ○ *This headache is torturing me.* **3.** DISTORT SOMETHING to twist or distort something into an unnatural form ■ *n* **1.** INFLICTING OF PAIN infliction of severe physical pain on somebody, e.g., as punishment or to persuade somebody to confess or recant something **2.** METHODS OF INFLICTING PAIN the methods used to inflict physical pain on people **3.** ANGUISH mental or physical anguish [Mid-16C. Directly or via French < late Latin *tortura* < Latin *tortus* "twisted" < *torquere* "to twist"] —**tor·tur·er** *n* —**tor·tur·ing·ly** *adv*

tor·ture lite *n* strong, non-life-threatening coercion of a prisoner, especially in terrorist or combat situations, used by interrogators in order to obtain vital information (*informal*) [Late 20C.]

tor·tur·ous /táwrchərəss/ *adj* **1.** inflicting or designed to inflict severe physical pain, e.g., as punishment **2.** causing great physical or mental anguish [15C. < Anglo-Norman < Old French *torture* (see TORTURE)] —**tor·tur·ous·ly** *adv*

USAGE See ***tortuous.***

tor·u·la /táwryələ, táwrələ/ (*plural* **-lae** /-lee̱, -lī/ or **-las**) *n* **1.** *also* **tor·u·la yeast** an edible yeast that is cultivated for use as a medicine and food additive. Latin name: *Candida utilis.* **2.** a yeast fungus that does not have sexual spores. Many of them grow on dead vegetation and fermented sugars. Genus: *Torula.* [Mid-19C. < modern Latin < Latin *torus* "bulge"]

to·rus /táwrəss/ (*plural* **-ri** /-rī/) *n* **1.** MATH RING-SHAPED SURFACE a doughnut-shaped geometric surface generated by rotating a circle about a line in the same plane as the circle but not intersecting it **2.** ARCHIT MOLDING a large convex molding, especially at the base of a classical column **3.** ANAT RIDGED BODY PART a body part in the shape of a rounded ridge or bulge, e.g., the bony ridge below an eyebrow **4.** BOT FLOWER PART the receptacle of a flower [Mid-16C. < Latin, "bulge"]

To·ry /táwree/ (*plural* **-ries**) *n* **1.** HIST AMERICAN SUPPORTER OF BRITAIN a resident of the American colonies who supported Britain during the American Revolution **2.** BRITISH CONSERVATIVE in Britain, a member of the Conservative Party **3.** CANADIAN CONSERVATIVE in Canada, a member of the Progressive Conservative Party **4.** HIST ENGLISH ROYALIST a member of an English political party, active from the late 17th century until the 1830s, that supported the social order represented by the monarchy and the Church of England **5.** *also* **to·ry** SUPPORTER OF CONSERVATIVE PRINCIPLES somebody who holds politically conservative views **6.** HIST 17C IRISH OUTLAW in 17th-century Ireland, any of the Irish people who became outlaws harrying the English settlers who had displaced and dispossessed them [Mid-17C. Via Irish *tóraidhe* "highwayman" < Old Irish *tóir* "to chase"] —**To·ry** *adj* —**To·ry·ism** *n*

ORIGIN In English, ***Tory*** originally denoted an Irish guerrilla, one of a group of Irishmen who in the 1640s were thrown off their property by the British and took to a life of harrying and plundering the British occupiers. In the 1670s, it was applied as a term of abuse to Irish Catholic royalists, and then more generally to supporters of the Catholic James II, and after 1689 it came to be used for the members of the British political party that had at first opposed the removal of James and his replacement with the Protestants William and Mary.

Tos·ca·ni·ni /tòskə neénee/, **Arturo** (1867–1957) Italian-born conductor. He was conductor at La Scala opera house, Milan, and the Metropolitan Opera, New York, and also conducted the NBC Symphony Orchestra (1937–57).

> "Can't you read? The score demands *con amore*, and what are you doing? You are playing it like married men!"
> [Attributed to Arturo Toscanini]

toss /tawss, toss/ *v* (**tossed, toss·ing, toss·es**) **1.** *vt* LIGHTLY THROW SOMETHING to throw something small or light in a casual or careless way ○ *tossed the letter on the table* **2.** *vt* THROW SOMEBODY OR SOMETHING OUT to get rid of somebody or something (*informal*) ○ *tossed them out of her office* ○ *Just toss it; we don't need it.* **3.** *vti* THROW, OR BE THROWN, REPEATEDLY to be thrown repeatedly up and down or to and fro, or throw something in this way ○ *tossed by the waves* **4.** *vti* THROW COIN to throw a coin upward, usually spinning it with the thumb on the way, the side it falls on being a way of deciding between two options **5.** *vt* MIX SOMETHING to mix something, especially a salad with its dressing, by lifting and turning its parts rather than by stirring **6.** *vt* RIDING THROW RIDER to throw the rider off a horse's back **7.** *vt* THROW SOMEBODY OR SOMETHING UPWARD to hurl somebody or something upward with apparent ease **8.** *vt* JERK HEAD UPWARD to jerk the head upward, e.g., in a gesture of anger or impatience **9.** *vi* MOVE RESTLESSLY to move about restlessly, especially while sleeping ■ *n* **1.** THROWING an act of throwing somebody or something **2.** DECIDING THROW OF COIN an act of spinning a coin in the air in order to decide between two options **3.** HEAD JERK an abrupt jerk of the head [Early 16C. Origin ?]

SYNONYMS See ***throw.***

toss off *vt* **1.** to do something quickly and easily **2.** *also* **toss down** to drink something quickly, often in one gulp

toss·pot /táwss pòt, tóss-/ *n* a drunken person (*archaic or literary*)

toss·up /táwss ùp, tóss-/ *n* **1.** a throw of a coin into the air that decides, by which side it falls on, between two options **2.** an even risk or chance

tos·ta·da /tō staádə/, **tos·ta·do** /tō staádō/ *n* a crisply fried Mexican-style tortilla, usually served with several meat and vegetable toppings, grated cheese, and hot sauce [Mid-20C. < Spanish < past participle of *tostar* "toast"]

tot[1] /tot/ *n* **1.** a small child (*informal*) **2.** a small amount of something, especially liquor [Early 18C. Origin ?]

tot[2] /tot/ (**tot·ted, tot·ting, tots**) [Mid-18C. Shortening of TOTAL, or < Latin *tot* "this number, so many"]

tot up *vt* to add several amounts together to arrive at a total

to·tal /tṓt'l/ *n* SUM the sum of several amounts added or considered together ■ *adj* **1.** OVERALL with everything added or considered together ○ *the total price* **2.** USED FOR EMPHASIS used to emphasize how good, bad, or complete something is ○ *a total success* ■ *vt* (**-taled, -tal·ing, -tals**) **1.** ADD THINGS TOGETHER to add several amounts together to arrive at a total **2.** AMOUNT TO TOTAL to amount to a particular total when added or considered together ○ *The numbers totaled in the hundreds.* **3.** KILL SOMEBODY OR DESTROY SOMETHING to kill, destroy, wreck, or demolish somebody or something (*slang*) ○ *totaled the car* [14C. Via French < medieval Latin *totalis* < Latin *totus* "entire"]

to·tal e·clipse *n* an eclipse in which the entire surface of an astronomical object such as the Sun or the Moon is obscured

to·tal heat *n* PHYS same as **enthalpy**

to·tal in·ter·nal re·flec·tion *n* the complete reflection of a light ray at the boundary of the medium in which it is traveling, when the angle of incidence exceeds the critical angle

to·tal·i·tar·i·an /tō tàllə térree ən/ *adj* relating to or operating a centralized government system in which a single party without opposition rules over political, economic, social, and cultural life [Early 20C. < TOTALITY after AUTHORITARIAN] —**to·tal·i·tar·i·an** *n* —**to·tal·i·tar·i·an·ism** *n*

to·tal·i·ty /tō tállətee/ (*plural* **-ties**) *n* **1.** COMPLETENESS the state of being complete or total **2.** TOTAL AMOUNT the sum or total amount of something **3.** ASTRON FULLNESS OF ECLIPSE the stage of an eclipse at which light is completely obscured

to·tal·i·za·tor /tṓt'li zàytər/ *n* a machine that records and calculates totals, especially one that records bets, odds, and totals, and calculates winnings in the pari-mutuel betting system [Late 19C. After French *totalisateur*]

to·tal·ize /tṓt'l ìz/ (**-ized, -iz·ing, -iz·es**) *vt* to add several amounts to make a total —**to·tal·i·za·tion** /tṓt'li záysh'n/ *n*

to·tal·iz·er /tṓt'l ìzər/ (*plural* **-iz·ers** or **-is·ers**) *n* GAMBLING same as **totalizator**

to·tal·ly /tṓt'lee/ *adv* **1.** in a complete or utter way **2.** used to emphasize how good, bad, or complete something is (*informal*) ○ *I totally hate this!*

to·tal re·call *n* the ability to remember accurately in every detail

to·tal re·flec·tion *n* PHYS same as **total internal reflection**

to·ta·quine /tṓtə kween/ *n* a mixture of quinine and other alkaloids from cinchona bark. Use: treatment of malaria. [Mid-20C. < modern Latin *totaquina* < Latin *totus* "whole" + Spanish *quina* "cinchona bark"]

tote[1] /tōt/ *vt* (**tot·ed, tot·ing, totes**) (*informal*) **1.** CARRY SOMETHING to carry or haul something, especially something heavy **2.** HAVE SOMETHING ON YOUR PERSON to carry something, especially a gun, on your person ■ *n* **1.** HEAVY LOAD a heavy load that is hauled or carried **2.** SOFT BAG a large soft bag with handles [Late 17C. Origin ?] —**tot·er** *n*

REGIONAL NOTE ***Tote*** in the sense "to carry something" is a general-currency term throughout the Southern states. Probably of West African origin, the form extends across the South Midland region as well, including similar Western forms in the Rocky Mountain states.

tote[2] /tōt/ *n UK* a system of betting on horse races using an electronic machine that totals all bets, deducts management charges and taxes, and determines the final odds and payouts (*informal*) [Late 19C. Shortening of TOTALIZATOR]

tote[3] /tōt/ (**tot·ed, tot·ing, totes**) *vt* to add things up (*informal*) [Late 19C. Shortening of TOTAL]

tote bag *n* CLOTHING same as **tote**[1] *n* (sense 2)

tote board *n US* a large electronically operated board displaying statistics such as betting odds or voting results

to·tem /tṓtəm/ *n* **1.** IMPORTANT TRIBAL OBJECT an object, animal, plant, or other natural phenomenon revered as a symbol of a clan or society, and often used in rituals among some peoples **2.** CARVING a carving or other representation of a totem **3.** SYMBOLIC THING something regarded as a symbol, especially something treated with the kind of respect normally reserved for religious icons [Mid-18C. < Ojibwa *nindoodem* "my totem"] —**to·tem·ic** /tō témmik/ *adj*

to·tem·ism /tṓtə mìzzəm/ *n* **1.** the use of totems as symbols of kinship **2.** the organizing of societies into groups whose members share a common totem —**to·tem·ist** *n* —**to·tem·is·tic** /tṓtə místik/ *adj*

totem pole

to·tem pole *n* **1.** among some Native North American peoples, a tall wooden pole carved with totems that symbolize family and historical relationships **2.** a hierarchy, e.g., in a company or organization (*informal*)

toth·er /túthər/, **t'oth·er** *adj, pron* the or that other (*informal*) [14C. Contraction of *the other*]

to·ti·pal·mate /tṓti pál màyt/ *adj* describes birds such as pelicans and cormorants that have all four toes webbed [Late 19C. < Latin *totus* "whole"] —**to·ti·pal·ma·tion** /tṓti pal máysh'n/ *n*

to·tip·o·tent /tō típpətənt/ *adj* describes a cell that is capable of generating new tissue, organs, or individuals, e.g., a fertilized ovum [Early 20C. < Latin *totus* "whole"] —**to·tip·o·ten·cy** *n*

tot lot *n* a playground for young children (*informal*)

tot·ter /tóttər/ *vi* (**-tered, -ter·ing, -ters**) **1.** WALK UNSTEADILY to move or walk unsteadily **2.** WOBBLE to sway or wobble as if about to fall **3.** BE UNSTABLE to be unstable or on the point of collapse ○ *an economic system tottering on the brink of collapse* ■ *n* WOBBLING GAIT a wavering or wobbling gait [13C. Origin ?] —**tot·ter·er** *n* —**tot·ter·ing·ly** *adv* —**tot·ter·y** *adj*

toucan

tou·can /to͞o kàn/ (*plural* **-cans** or *same*) *n* a fruit-eating bird with bright feathers and a very large curved beak. Native to: tropical Central and South America. Family: Ramphastidae. [Mid-16C. Via French < Portuguese *tucano* < Tupi *tucan*]

touch /tuch/ *v* (**touched, touch·ing, touch·es**) **1.** *vti* PUT BODY IN CONTACT WITH SOMETHING to put a part of the body, especially the fingertips, in contact with something so as to feel it **2.** *vti* BE OR PUT SOMETHING IN CONTACT to be in physical contact with an object, or bring something into physical contact with an object ○ *so that the ends are just touching* **3.** *vt* PRESS SOMETHING LIGHTLY to apply the slightest pressure to something ○ *You only have to touch the brake.* **4.** *vt* INTERFERE WITH SOMETHING to interfere with or disturb something by handling it ○ *told the kids not to touch anything on my desk* **5.** *vt* HAVE EFFECT ON SOMEBODY OR SOMETHING to have an effect or influence on somebody or something ○ *events that touched all our lives* **6.** *vt* AFFECT SOMEBODY EMOTIONALLY to affect somebody emotionally, usually arousing gratitude, affection, pity, or compassion ○ *Your concern for my welfare touches me greatly.* **7.** *vt* CONSUME SOMETHING to consume something, especially food or drink, or otherwise make use of something ○ *You've hardly touched your meal.* **8.** *vt* HAVE DEALINGS WITH SOMETHING to have dealings or become involved with something ○ *Don't touch that issue; it's very controversial.* **9.** *vt* MATCH SOMEBODY OR SOMETHING to come close to somebody or something in level of excellence ○ *Others may have more technique, but nobody can touch her style.* **10.** *vt* APPROACH LEVEL to approach or reach a level ○ *profits touching 2 billion* **11.** *vt* APPROACH SOMEBODY FOR MONEY to ask somebody for a loan or gift of money (*slang*) ■ *n* **1.** CONTACT MADE a coming into contact with a part of the body ○ *felt the touch of her hand on my face* **2.** LIGHT STROKE a light pushing or pressing stroke **3.** FEELING SENSE the sense by which the texture, shape, and other qualities of objects are felt through contact with parts of the body, especially the fingertips ○ *the sense of touch* **4.** FELT QUALITIES the quality or combination of qualities experienced through the sensation of touch **5.** SMALL AMOUNT a small but noticeable amount ○ *a touch of malice in her voice* **6.** DETAIL a detail that adds to or completes something **7.** DISTINCTIVE STYLE a distinctive style or general facility in doing something ○ *a sure touch* **8.** ATTACK OF ILLNESS a mild attack of an illness or disease ○ *a touch of bronchitis* **9.** COMMUNICATION the fact of getting into communication, or the state of being in communication ○ *I completely lost touch with my brother.* ○ *Keep in touch.* ○ *I'll get in touch with them if I find anything out.* **10.** ACQUIESCING PERSON somebody considered in terms of his or her willingness to do, allow, or give something, usually money (*slang*) ○ *He's always been a soft touch.* **11.** REQUEST FOR MONEY an act of asking for money, or a sum of money given (*slang*) **12.** AREA OUT OF PLAY in some team sports, the area beyond the touchlines in which the ball is out of play **13.** FENCING FENCING SCORE in competitive fencing, a scoring hit delivered to a specific part of an opponent's body [13C. Via Old French *to(u)chier* < assumed Vulgar Latin *toccare* "to strike"] —**touch·a·ble** *adj* —**touch·a·ble·ness** *n* —**touch·er** *n* ◇ **a touch** somewhat ◇ **be touch and go** to be highly uncertain or precarious

touch down *vi* to land in an aircraft or spacecraft

touch off *vt* **1.** to make something explode, especially by touching it with a flame or smoldering match **2.** to make something begin, especially something that is difficult to control ○ *touched off a bitter disagreement between them*

touch on, touch up·on *vt* **1.** to write or talk about something briefly during the course of a discussion ○ *The report only touches on the financial implications.* **2.** to come close to a particular quality, state, or condition ○ *a sympathetic attitude touching on pity*

touch up *vt* **1.** to make slight improvements to something, e.g., with paint ○ *touched up the photograph* **2.** to make changes to something, especially a photograph, so that it is no longer an accurate representation (*disapproving*)

touch-and-go *adj* highly uncertain or unpredictable (*not hyphenated after a verb*) ○ *a touch-and-go situation*

touch·back /túch bàk/ *n* in football, a play in which the defense recovers and downs a ball that has been kicked or passed into its end zone

touch·down /túch dòwn/ *n* **1.** LANDING a landing made by an aircraft or spacecraft, or the precise moment when it lands **2.** SCORING PLAY in football, a scoring of six points achieved by being in possession of the ball behind an opponent's goal line ■ *adj* OFFERING PHONE AND COMPUTER ACCESS offering computer and telephone connections and Internet access to visitors and business travelers ○ *touchdown center* ○ *touchdown facilities*

tou·ché /too sháy/ *interj* **1.** a word used to acknowledge that somebody has made an especially witty, penetrating, or cogent remark, usually in retaliation **2.** in fencing, a word used to acknowledge that an opponent has made a scoring hit [Early 20C. < French, past participle of *toucher* "touch" < Old French *touchier* (see TOUCH)]

touched /tucht/ *adj* **1.** affected emotionally, especially with gratitude, affection, pity, or compassion **2.** slightly marked or modified by something ○ *blond hair touched with gray*

touch foot·ball *n* an informal noncompetitive version of football in which touching replaces tackling

touch·hole /túch hṑl/ *n* the opening in the breech of an early cannon or gun where a flame or smoldering material was applied to set off the gunpowder

touch·ing /túching/ *adj* causing feelings of warmth, sympathy, and tenderness ■ *prep* concerning or relating to something —**touch·ing·ly** *adv* —**touch·ing·ness** *n*

SYNONYMS See ***moving***.

touch·line /túch lìn/ *n* especially in soccer, either of the lines that mark the side boundaries of a playing area

touch·mark /túch maàrk/ *n* a mark stamped on something made of pewter that identifies the maker

touch-me-not *n* PLANTS **1.** *UK* same as **jewelweed 2.** *US* same as **sensitive plant**

touch pad *n* **1.** an electronic device on which somebody can choose options by touching the display, e.g., an input device in a computer system or a control panel on a microwave oven **2.** a small flat stationary surface on a laptop computer which a user touches to move the cursor

touch screen *n* an input device that allows a user to choose options and commands on a computer by touching the screen

touch·stone /túch stṑn/ *n* **1.** a standard by which something is judged **2.** a hard black stone formerly used to test the purity of gold and silver according to the color of the streak left when the metal was rubbed against it

touch sys·tem *n* a method of typing in which the typist finds the keys with his or her fingers without looking at the keyboard

touch-tone, touch·tone /túch tṑn/ *adj* describes a type of telephone with keys that produce tones when pressed, each of which is decoded as a number at the telephone exchange

touch-type *vi* to type without having to look at the keyboard —**touch-typ·ist** *n*

touch·up /túch ùp/ *n* **1.** a slight improvement to something such as makeup or paintwork **2.** an alteration, especially one made to cover up or repair a flaw

touch·wood /túch wòod/ *n* dry decayed wood that can be used as tinder

touch·y /túchee/ (**-i·er, -i·est**) *adj* **1. EASILY UPSET** liable to become or make somebody angry or upset ○ *a touchy subject* **2. TRICKY** needing care or tact to prevent an undesirable outcome **3. FLAMMABLE** easily catching fire **4. SENSITIVE TO TOUCH** very sensitive to being touched —**touch·i·ly** *adv* —**touch·i·ness** *n*

touch·y-feel·y /-féelee/ *adj* (*informal disapproving*) **1.** physically and emotionally demonstrative to an extent that makes some people feel uncomfortable **2.** encouraging open expression of emotions to an extent that makes some people feel uncomfortable

tough /tuf/ *adj* **1. DIFFICULT** physically or mentally challenging ○ *That's a tough question.* ○ *It's a tough climb to the peak.* **2. VERY STRONG** physically or mentally strong and possessing great endurance ○ *Is he tough enough to make the climb?* **3. RESOLUTE** having or showing firm resolve ○ *She's a tough person to negotiate with.* **4. DURABLE** able to withstand much use, strain, or wear without breaking, tearing, or other damage ○ *boots made of tough leather* **5. HARD TO CHEW OR CUT** not easily chewed or cut ○ *This steak is pretty tough.* **6. THREATENING** characterized by antisocial behavior, crime, and social deprivation ○ *a tough neighborhood* **7. SEVERE** involving or inflicting severe punishment or strict rules ○ *the police policy of being tough on drink-driving* **8. UNFORTUNATE** not fair or reasonable (*informal*) ○ *It was a tough choice to be offered.* **9.** *US* **GREAT** perceived as being the best or most wonderful (*slang dated*) ○ *an album with some tough sounds* ■ *n* **THUG** an aggressive or antisocial person ■ *adv* **AGGRESSIVELY** in an aggressive way that is intended to be perceived as strength and fearlessness (*informal*) ○ *acting tough* ■ *interj* **BAD LUCK!** used to say that something is unfortunate but cannot be helped and is of no concern to the speaker [Old English *tōh* < Germanic] —**tough·ly** *adv* ◇ **tough it out** to be strong and resilient during a time of difficulty (*informal*)

SYNONYMS See ***hard.***

tough·en /túff'n/ (**-ened, -en·ing, -ens**) *vti* **1. MAKE OR BECOME MORE SEVERE** to become stricter or more severe, or make somebody or something so **2. MAKE OR BECOME STRONGER** to become more resolute, hardier, or physically or emotionally stronger, or make somebody so **3. MAKE OR BECOME TOUGHER** to become less easy to cut or chew or less liable to wear or damage, or make something so —**tough·en·er** *n*

tough·ie /túffee/ *n* (*informal*) **1.** something that is difficult to deal with **2.** a tough person, especially a child, regarded with some affection or amusement because he or she is rather self-assertive and resilient

tough love *n* a caring but strict attitude adopted toward a friend or loved one with a problem, as distinct from an attitude of indulgence

tough-mind·ed *adj* able to face hardship and misfortunes in a realistic, determined, and unsentimental way —**tough-mind·ed·ly** *adv* —**tough-mind·ed·ness** *n*

tough·ness /túfnəss/ *n* **1.** the fact or quality of being tough **2.** the resistance of a metal to breaking under repeated twisting and bending forces, measured in kilojoules

Tou·lon /too láwN/ city, port, and naval base in southeastern France, on the Mediterranean Sea. Population: 160,639 (1999).

Tou·louse /too lóoz/ capital city of Haute-Garonne Department, Languedoc-Roussillon Region, southern France. Population: 390,350 (1999).

Tou·louse-Lau·trec /too lòoz lō trék/, **Henri de** (1864–1901) French artist. He is noted especially for his portraits, paintings of Paris nightlife, and posters advertising Parisian artists. Full name **de Toulouse-Lautrec, Henri Marie Raymond**

tou·pee /too páy/ *n* a wig or partial wig worn to cover a bald area [Early 18C. Alteration of French *toupet* "tuft of hair" < Germanic, "topknot"]

AKG London

Henri de Toulouse-Lautrec

tour /toor/ *n* **1. PLEASURE TRIP** a trip visiting several places, usually taken for pleasure **2. PERFORMING TRIP** a long series of performances in different places, e.g., by a rock band or a theater company ○ *The band are on tour at the moment.* **3. TEAM TRIP** a series of games or tournaments played by the same sports team in different locations **4. BRIEF TRIP TO SEE SOMETHING** a short trip or visit for the purpose of viewing or inspecting something **5. PERIOD OF DUTY** a period of military duty, especially in a specific place or for a fixed length of time ■ *vti* (**toured, tour·ing, tours**) **MAKE TOUR** to take part in a tour [14C. Via Old French < Latin *tornus* "lathe"]

tou·ra·co /tóorə kō/ (*plural* **-cos**), **tu·ra·co** *n* a bird with brightly colored feathers and a long tail, which is a weak flyer and hops from branch to branch. Native to: Africa. Family: Musophagidae. [Mid-18C. Via French < a W African language]

tour de force /tòor də fáwrss/ (*plural* **tours de force** /*pronunc. same*/) *n* something done with supreme skill or brilliance [Early 19C. < French, "feat of strength"]

tour·er /tóorər/ *n* *US* CARS same as **touring car**

Tou·rette syn·drome /tōō rét-/, **Tou·rette's syn·drome** /tōō réts-/ *n* a condition in which somebody experiences multiple tics and twitches and utters involuntary vocal grunts and obscene speech [Late 19C. After Gilles de la *Tourette* (1857–1904), French neurologist]

tour·ing car *n* a convertible car, popular in the 1920s, designed for long-distance leisure driving

tour·ing com·pa·ny *n* a theater company that takes part in performing tours rather than performing solely in one venue

tour·ism /tóor ìzzəm/ *n* **1. TRAVEL FOR PLEASURE** the activity of traveling for pleasure **2. TRAVEL BUSINESS** the business of arranging travel and travel services for people **3. TRAVEL TO OBTAIN SERVICE** travel to benefit from a service or activity that is unavailable at home (*usually used in combination*) ○ *health tourism*

tour·ist /tóorist/ *n* **1.** a traveler who visits places away from home for pleasure **2.** TRAVEL same as **tourist class** —**tour·is·tic** /toor ístik/ *adj* —**tour·ist·y** *adj*

tour·ist class *n* the least expensive class of accommodation on an aircraft or ship

tour·ist·ed /tóoristəd/ *adj* visited by a large number of tourists

tour·ist trap *n* a place that is popular with tourists but where, as a result, the prices of goods and services are higher than average

tour·ist·y /tóoristee/ *adj* unpleasantly full of tourists (*informal disapproving*)

tour·ma·line /tóormәlin, -leèn/ *n* a hard, variously colored crystalline borosilicate mineral. Use: electronics, optics, gems. [Mid-18C. < Sinhalese *toramalli* "cornelian"] —**tour·ma·lin·ic** /tòormə línnik/ *adj*

Tour·nai /toor náy/ city in Hainault Province, southwestern Belgium. Population: 67,611 (1999).

tour·na·ment /tóornəmənt, túrnəmənt/ *n* **1.** a sports event made up of a series of games, rounds, or contests **2.** a sporting contest popular in the Middle Ages in which knights took part in jousting or combat, generally with blunted weapons [12C. < Old French *torneiement* "act of jousting" < *torneier* (see TOURNEY)]

tour·ne·dos /tóornə dō/ (*plural same*) *n* a small round cut of fillet steak [Late 19C. < French < *tourner* "to turn" + *dos* "back"]

~~**tournement**~~ incorrect spelling of **tournament**

tour·ney /túrnee/ *n* (*plural* **-neys**) **1.** *US* same as **tournament** (sense 1) **2.** HIST same as **tournament** (sense 2) ■ *vi* (**-neyed, -ney·ing, -neys**) to take part in a medieval tournament [13C. Via Old French *torneier* "to joust, tilt" < Latin *tornare* "to turn"] —**tour·ney·er** *n*

tour·ni·quet /túrnikət/ *n* a tight encircling band applied around an arm or leg in an emergency to stop severe arterial bleeding that cannot be controlled in any other way [Late 17C. < French]

tour of du·ty *n* MIL same as **tour** *n* (sense 5)

Tours /toor, toorz/ capital city of Indre-et-Loire Department, Centre Region, west central France. Population: 132,820 (1999).

tour·ti·ère /tòortee ér/ *n* *Can* **1.** a meat pie, usually of seasoned ground pork, traditionally eaten at Christmas by French Canadians **2.** a baking tin used for making pies or tarts [Mid-20C. < French < *tourte* "pie"]

tou·sle /tówz'l/ *vt* (**-sled, -sling, -sles**) to make hair or fur tangled or ruffled ■ *n* a tangled mass, especially of hair or fur [15C. < obsolete and dialect *touse* "pull, handle roughly" < Germanic] —**tou·sled** *adj*

Tous·saint L'Ou·ver·ture /too sàN loo ver chóor, -tűr/, **François Dominique** (1743–1803) Haitian general and independence leader. Born into slavery, he was active in the movement that led to its abolition in Haiti (1791). The effective ruler of Haiti from 1797, he was captured by the French in 1802. Born **Toussaint, François Dominique**

> "In overthrowing me, you have cut down in San Domingo only the trunk of the tree of liberty. It will spring up again by the roots for they are numerous and deep."
> [François Dominique Toussaint L'Ouverture, *The Black Jacobins*, C. L. R. James; 1938]

tout /towt/ *v* (**tout·ed, tout·ing, touts**) **1.** *vt* **PRAISE SOMEBODY OR SOMETHING** to praise or recommend somebody or something enthusiastically (*usually passive*) ○ *was touted as the next champion* **2.** *vi* **ATTRACT CUSTOMERS** to try to attract customers or support, especially in an aggressive or persistent way ○ *street traders touting for business* **3.** *vt* **TRY TO SELL SOMETHING** to advertise or offer something for sale ○ *tout merchandise on the Internet* **4.** *vi* **SPY ON RACEHORSES** to spy on racehorses in training to get information to sell to bettors **5.** *vti* **SELL INFORMATION ABOUT RACEHORSES** to sell information about racehorses to bettors ■ *n* **1. SOMEBODY WHO SELLS INFORMATION ABOUT RACEHORSES** somebody who obtains information about racehorses and sells it to bettors **2. AGGRESSIVE SELLER** an aggressive salesperson [14C. Ultimately < Germanic, "poke out, project"] —**tout·er** *n*

tout en·sem·ble /tòot aan sáamb'l/ *n* the total appearance or effect of something [Early 18C. < French, "all together"]

to·va·rish /tə vaárich, -rish/, **to·va·rich, to·va·risch** *n* a friend or comrade, often used as a term of address, especially in the former Soviet Union [Early 20C. < Russian *tovarishch*]

tow[1] /tō/ *vt* (**towed, tow·ing, tows**) **PULL SOMETHING** to pull something such as a barge or a broken-down car along by a rope or chain attached to it ■ *n* **1. ACT OF PULLING SOMETHING ALONG** the act of pulling something along by a rope or chain attached to it **2. STATE OF BEING PULLED ALONG** the state of being towed by a rope or chain **3. ROPE OR CHAIN** a rope or chain used for towing something **4. SOMETHING THAT TOWS** something that tows something else [Old English *togian* < Indo-European, "to lead"] —**tow·a·ble** *adj* ◇ **have** *or* **take somebody in tow 1.** to have somebody following or accompanying you **2.** *US* to act as a protector or guide for somebody

SYNONYMS See ***pull.***

tow[2] /tō/ *n* fibers of flax, hemp, or jute, or of a synthetic material such as rayon [Old English *tow-* < Germanic]

tow·age /tṓ ij/ *n* **1.** the act or process of towing somebody or something, or the state of being towed **2.** a charge made for towing something

to·ward /tawrd, tə wáwrd/, **to·wards** /tawrdz, tə wáwrdz/ *prep* **1. IN PARTICULAR DIRECTION** used to indicate that somebody or something is moving or facing in the direction of somebody or something else ○ *They headed off toward town.* **2. SHORTLY BEFORE** shortly before a particular time ○ *toward midnight* **3. WITH SPECIFIC AUDIENCE INTENDED** with a particular target group in mind ○ *remarks slanted toward those sitting in the front row* **4. REGARDING** concerning or with regard to ○ *his attitude toward her* **5. CONTRIBUTING TO** as a contribution to or means of achieving something ○ *a grant toward the cost of refurbishment* [Old English *tōweardes*]

USAGE toward or **towards**? In US English, ***toward*** is the usual form but in British English ***towards*** is more common. The same principle applies to *afterward/afterwards* and to some other adverbs of direction that end in *-ward*, for example, *backward/backwards* and *outward/outwards. Upward*, as in *moved upward*, and *upwards*, as in *increases upwards of 10%*, are also standard. Note that related adjectives of direction always end in *-ward*, not *-wards*, as in *a backward glance* or *an upward trend*. The adverb *forwards* is a seldom used variant of *forward* in US English, and the *-wards* spelling of it is never used as a standard US English adjective.

tow-a·way zone *n* an area where parking is restricted or forbidden and from which parked vehicles may be towed away

tow·bar /tṓ baar/ *n* a rigid metal bar or frame attached to the back of a vehicle and used for towing other vehicles [Mid-20C. < TOW[1]]

tow·boat /tṓ bōt/ *n* **1.** same as **tugboat 2.** *US* a powerful boat with a broad bow, designed for pushing barges on rivers or canals [Early 19C. < TOW[2]]

tow-col·ored *adj* having a pale yellow color like hemp or flax [< TOW[2]]

tow·el /tów əl/ *n* a usually rectangular piece of absorbent cloth or paper, used to dry the body or objects such as dishes ■ *vti* (**-eled** or **-elled, -el·ing** or **-el·ling, -els**) to use a towel to dry somebody or something [13C. < Old French *toaille* < Germanic, "to wash"] ◇ **throw in the towel** to admit or accept defeat when something is proving difficult

tow·el·ette /tòw ə lét/ *n* a small moistened piece of paper or cloth used for cleaning the hands and face

tow·el·ing /tów əling/, **tow·el·ling** *n* a soft absorbent, usually looped cotton fabric. Use: towels, bathrobes.

tow·er[1] /tów ər/ *n* **1. TALL BUILDING** a tall structure, sometimes the upper part or a tall part of a building or structure and sometimes a separate building **2. FORTRESS** a building designed to withstand attack **3. CD SHELF** a tall wooden, plastic, or metal case in which to store CDs or videos **4. COMPUTER CASE** a tall slim case for the CPU and drives of a computer ■ *vi* (**-ered, -er·ing, -ers**) **1. BE TALL** to be very high or tall, or much higher or taller than somebody or something else **2. BE SUPERIOR** to be considerably superior to somebody or something [12C. Via Latin *turris* < Greek] ◇ **a tower of strength** somebody who is reliable and supportive (*informal*)

tow·er[2] /tṓ ər/ *n* somebody or something that tows something such as a vehicle by a rope or chain [Early 17C. < TOW[1]]

Tow·er Bridge *n* a bridge across the Thames River in London, England, that has a tower at each end and a roadway that can be raised to allow large ships through. It was opened in 1894.

tow·er·ing /tów əring/ *adj* **1. HIGH OR TALL** rising very high or standing very tall **2. OUTSTANDING** of the highest quality or importance **3. INTENSE** characterized by extreme or intense emotion or pain ○ *a towering rage* —**tow·er·ing·ly** *adv*

Tow·er of Ba·bel /-báyb'l, -bább'l/ *n* in the Bible, a tower that people started to build too tall, causing God to show his anger by making them speak different languages, which led to the collapse of the project and ultimately to the scattering of people across the world

Tow·er of London *n* a fortress beside the Thames River in London, England, that now displays the British Crown jewels. Building began in 1078.

tow·head /tṓ hèd/ *n* **1. SOMEBODY WITH BLOND HAIR** somebody with pale yellow hair **2. HEAD OF BLOND HAIR** a head that is covered with pale yellow hair **3. LOW ISLAND** a low alluvial island in a river, especially one with a stand of trees [Late 19C. < TOW[2]] —**tow·head·ed** *adj*

tow·hee /tṓ hee, tō hée/ *n* a large long-tailed sparrow that usually feeds on the ground. Native to: North America. Genera: *Pipilo* or *Chlorura*. [Mid-18C. An imitation of the bird's call]

tow·line /tṓ līn/ *n* TRANSP same as **towrope** [Early 18C. < TOW[1]]

town /town/ *n* **1. LARGE AREA OF BUILDINGS** a densely populated area with many buildings, larger than a village and smaller than a city **2. URBAN AREA** a large urban area, either a town, a city, or a borough **3.** POL **UNIT OF LOCAL GOVERNMENT** in parts of the United States and Canada, a unit of local government that is smaller than a county or city **4. LOCAL TOWN** the nearest large town or city, or the town or city in which somebody lives ○ *moving into town* **5. CENTER OF SETTLED AREA** the center of a town or city **6. POPULATION OF SETTLED AREA** the people who live in a town ○ *The whole town's talking about it.* **7. NONACADEMIC POPULATION** the permanent residents of a town that has a university, as opposed to the staff and students of the university ○ *town and gown* **8.** ZOOL **PRAIRIE DOG BURROWS** a group of prairie dog burrows [Old English *tūn* "yard, buildings within an enclosure" < Germanic] —**town·ish** *adj* ◇ **go to town (on somebody or something)** to deal with somebody or something with great enthusiasm or thoroughness (*informal*) ◇ **on the town** spending time enjoying the entertainment available in a town or city, especially if a lot of money is spent (*informal*) ◇ **paint the town red** to go out and celebrate, especially by spending a lot of money on entertainment (*informal*)

CULTURAL NOTE *Our Town*, a play (1938) by Thornton Wilder. This beloved US play depicts daily life in the archetypal small town of Grover's Corners, New Hampshire. On a bare stage, the folksy Stage Manager both directs and comments on the homely activities of Editor Webb, Dr. Gibbs, and their families and friends as they cook, play baseball, and sing in the choir, ache, hope, love, and die. It is an affectionate retelling of an enduring American myth as well as a tribute to the dignity and meaning in unsung lives.

town-and-gown *adj* relating to a town that contains a large population of students in higher education

town clerk *n* a public official responsible for such things as keeping the records of a town and issuing licenses

town coun·cil *n* the people elected or appointed to govern a town

town cri·er *n* **1.** *US* somebody who publicizes information about other people's lives (*informal*) **2.** somebody employed by a town, especially in former times, to make public announcements in the streets

town hall *n* a building that houses the offices of the local administration and often has a public hall that can be used for meetings

town·house /tówn hòwss/ (*plural* **-hous·es** /-hòwzəz/), **town house** *n* **1. FASHIONABLE ROW HOUSE** a two- or three-story house, semidetached or in a row of similar houses and with limited yard space, usually in a fashionable neighborhood **2. HOUSE IN TOWN** a house in a town or city, especially one that belongs to somebody who also has a house in the country **3.** *UK* **OLD TERRACED HOUSE** an old terraced house with three or more stories in a town or city

town·ie /tównee/, **town·y** (*plural* **-ies**) *n* **1.** somebody who lives permanently in a town (*informal*) **2.** a nonacademic resident of a town that has a large proportion of its population studying or teaching at a university in the town

town man·ag·er *n US* an official in charge of the administrative activities of a town

town meet·ing *n* **1. MEETING OF INHABITANTS** a public meeting involving all of the inhabitants of a town **2.** *US* **MEETING OF VOTERS** a public meeting involving all of the voters of a town, with the authority to make legislative decisions **3.** *US* **TELEVISED GATHERING** a television program centering on an issue of national interest, in which people from a town or region ask questions of debaters or speakers ○ *a televised national town meeting on the role of the military in global peacekeeping*

town plan·ning *n UK* same as **urban planning**

town·scape /tówn skàyp/ *n* **1.** a view of a town **2.** a painting or photograph of an urban scene

towns·folk /tównz fōk/ *npl* same as **townspeople**

town·ship /tówn shìp/ *n* **1. SUBDIVISION OF COUNTY** a subdivision of a county, often serving as a unit of local government **2.** *US* **AREA GOVERNED BY TOWN MEETING** in some parts of the United States, an area governed by a town meeting **3. 36 SQUARE MILES** an area of surveyed public land equal to 36 sections or 36 square miles **4. URBAN SETTLEMENT FOR BLACK PEOPLE** in South Africa during the apartheid era, an urban settlement planned for people classed as Black or of mixed ethnic origin, usually with inferior facilities and services

towns·man /tównzmən/ (*plural* **-men** /-mən/) *n* **1.** a man who lives in a town **2.** a man who lives in the same town as somebody else

towns·peo·ple /tównz peep'l/ *npl* the people who live in a town

Towns·ville /tównzvil/ city on the eastern coast of Queensland, Australia. It is a commercial and industrial center. Population: 93,911 (2002 estimate).

towns·wom·an /tównz wŏŏmmən/ (*plural* **-wom·en** /-wìmmin/) *n* **1.** a woman who lives in a town **2.** a woman who lives in the same town as somebody else

town·y *n* another spelling of **townie**

tow·path /tṓ pàth/ (*plural* **-paths** /-pàthz, -pàths/) *n* a path beside a canal or river for people or animals to walk along, especially as they pulled a barge or boat [Late 18C. < TOW[1]]

tow·rope /tṓ rōp/ *n* a rope used to tow something such as a boat or a broken-down car [Mid-18C. < TOW[1]]

tow sack *n Southern US* same as **gunnysack** [< TOW[2], because used for carrying tow]

REGIONAL NOTE *Tow sack* is an Interior Southern term that extends from Virginia in a southerly and westerly direction. Rare in the lower Southeast from the Carolinas to Lower Mississippi, the term may be strongest in the Lower Mississippi Valley, with considerable evidence of usage in Texas and beyond.

tow truck *n US* same as **wrecker** (sense 2)

tox. *abbr* SCI toxicology

tox- *prefix* same as **toxi-** (*used before vowels*)

tox·al·bu·min /toks álbyəmin/ *n* a toxic albumin found in some plants and snake venom

tox·a·phene /tóksə feen/ *n* a waxy amber-colored poisonous compound that smells of pine and is used as an insecticide. Formula: $C_{10}H_{10}Cl_8$. [Mid-20C. < TOXI- + shortening of *chlorinated camphene*]

tox·e·mi·a /tok seemee ə/ *n* a condition produced by the presence of bacterial toxins in the blood, usually with tissue or organ damage, fever, and severe intestinal upset [Mid-19C. < TOX- + Greek *haima* "blood"] —**tox·e·mic** *adj*

toxi- *prefix* poison, poisonous ○ *toxigenic* [< TOXIC]

tox·ic /tóksik/ *adj* **1. INVOLVING SOMETHING POISONOUS** relating to or containing a poison or toxin **2. DEADLY** causing serious harm or death ■ *n* **POISONOUS SUBSTANCE** a poison or toxin [Mid-17C. Via medieval Latin *toxicus* "poisoned" < Greek *toxikos* "of the bow" (Greek *toxikon pharmakon* meant "poison for smearing arrows")] —**tox·i·cal·ly** *adv*

tox·i·cant /tóksikənt/ *n* a toxic substance, especially one used as a pesticide

tox·ic·i·ty /tok síssətee/ (*plural* **-ties**) *n* **1.** the degree to which something is poisonous **2.** the state of being poisonous to somebody or something

toxico- *prefix* poison ○ *toxicogenic* [< Greek *toxikos* (see TOXIC)]

tox·i·co·gen·ic /tòksikō jénnik/ *adj* BIOL, MED same as **toxigenic**

tox·i·col·o·gy /tòksi kólləjee/ *n* the scientific study of poisons, their effects, and their antidotes —**tox·i·co·log·ic** /tòksikə lójjik/ *adj* —**tox·i·co·log·i·cal** *adj* —**tox·i·co·log·i·cal·ly** *adv* —**tox·i·col·o·gist** *n*

tox·i·co·sis /tòksi kṓssiss/ (*plural* **-co·ses** /-kṓ seez/) *n* the harmful effects of a poison, including any disease caused by toxins

tox·ic shock syn·drome *n* an acute, potentially fatal circulatory failure, commonly associated with the use of vaginal tampons, which can create conditions promoting the growth of a toxin-producing staphylococcal bacterium

tox·i·gen·ic /tòksə jénnik/ *adj* **1.** producing poisonous substances **2.** caused or produced by a toxin —**tox·i·ge·nic·i·ty** /tòksəjə níssətee/ *n*

tox·i·ge·nom·ics /tòksi jee nómmiks/ *n* the study of the way known and suspected toxicants act at the genetic level (*takes a singular verb*)

tox·in /tóksin/ *n* **1.** a poison produced by a living organism **2.** a substance that accumulates in the body and causes it harm ○ *drinking plenty of water to eliminate toxins* [Late 19C. < TOXIC]

tox·in-an·ti·tox·in *n* a mixture containing a toxin and slightly less of its antitoxin. Use: formerly, vaccines.

tox·o·ca·ri·a·sis /tòksō kə rī́ əssiss/ *n* an infestation of the larvae of a roundworm arising in human beings from worm eggs picked up from contaminated soil or domestic pets [Mid-20C. < alteration of TOXI- + Greek *kara* "head"]

tox·oid /tók sòyd/ *n* a preparation of an inactive toxin that can stimulate antibody production in the toxin. Use: vaccines. [Early 20C. < shortening of TOXIN]

tox·oph·i·lite /tòk sóffə lī̀t/ *n* an archer or archery enthusiast (*humorous*) [Late 18C. < *Toxophilus*, "lover of the bow," title of a work (1545) by Roger Ascham] —**tox·oph·i·ly** *n*

tox·o·plas·ma /tòksə plázmə/ *n* a microscopic protozoan organism that lives as a parasite in the organs of vertebrates, especially birds and mammals, and can cause disease. Genus: *Toxoplasma*. [Early 20C. < alteration of TOXI-] —**tox·o·plas·mic** *adj*

tox·o·plas·mo·sis /tòksō plaz mṓssiss/ (*plural* **-mo·ses** /-mṓ seez/) *n* a disease of mammals caused by a toxoplasma transmitted to humans via undercooked meat or through contact with infectious animals, especially cats

toy /toy/ *n* **1.** THING TO PLAY WITH something meant to be played with, especially by children **2.** REPLICA a replica of a real object, used for playing with or as an ornament **3.** SOMETHING ENJOYABLE TO USE a belonging that gives the owner pleasure to use ○ *He showed us his latest toy, a new DVD player.* **4.** MINIATURE BREED an animal, especially a dog, that is a miniature version of another animal (*used before nouns*) ○ *a toy poodle* **5.** SOMETHING UNIMPORTANT something of little value or importance **6.** *US* SOMEBODY WHOSE EMOTIONS ARE PLAYED WITH somebody whose feelings and emotions are treated as unimportant (*informal*) **7.** *Southern US* SHOOTER MARBLE a marble used as a shooter ■ *adj* EASILY DISMISSED regarded as irrelevant or of inferior quality (*informal*) [14C. Origin ?] —**toy·er** *n*

toy with *vt* **1.** PLAY WITH SOMETHING to play or fiddle with something, especially because of a lack of real interest in it or preoccupation with something else **2.** THINK ABOUT SOMETHING to consider doing something **3.** TREAT SOMEBODY OR SOMETHING CRUELLY to behave in a cruelly insincere or offhand way toward somebody or something **4.** TREAT SOMEBODY INSINCERELY to treat somebody in an insincere or flirtatious way, merely for amusement

TOY *abbr* ONLINE thinking of you (*used in e-mails or text messages*)

toy boy *n* an offensive term for a young man who is the lover of an older person

toyi-toyi /tóy toy/ *n S Africa* a dance with high steps performed by protesters, accompanied by singing and chanting of slogans [Late 20C. < an African language]

Toyn·bee /tóyn bee/, **Arnold** (1889–1975) British historian. His masterwork, the 12-volume *Study of History* (1934–61), treated history as a succession of civilizations rather than of nations. Full name **Toynbee, Arnold Joseph**

> "Civilization is a movement, not a condition; it is a voyage, not a harbor."
> [Arnold Toynbee, *Reader's Digest*; October 1958]

toy·on /tóy òn/ *n* an evergreen bush with red berries. Flowers: white. Native to: California. Latin name: *Heteromeles arbutifolia*. [Mid-19C. < Mexican Spanish *tollón*]

To·yo·to·mi Hi·de·yo·shi /tōyō tōmee hì de yṓshee/ (1536–98) Japanese general. He united Japan in 1590 and coordinated two unsuccessful invasions of Korea (1592 and 1597).

tp[1], **Tp** *abbr* **1.** *US* toilet paper (*slang*) **2.** township **3.** MIL troop

tp[2] *abbr* ONLINE Timor-Leste (*used in Internet addresses*) See table at **domain name**

TP *abbr* BASEBALL triple play

t.p. *abbr* PUBL title page

TPA *abbr* BIOL tissue plasminogen activator

tpk, **Tpk**, **Tpke** *abbr* TRANSP turnpike

TPN *abbr* BIOCHEM triphosphopyridine nucleotide

Tpr *abbr* POL Trooper

TQM *abbr* BUSINESS total quality management

tr *abbr* ONLINE Turkey (*used in Internet addresses*) See table at **domain name**

TR *abbr* TELECOM transmit-receive

tr. *abbr* **1.** GRAM transitive **2.** LANG, BUSINESS translator **3.** PRINTING transpose **4.** PRINTING transposition **5.** FIN treasurer **6.** MUSIC trill **7.** MIL troop **8.** FIN trust **9.** FIN trustee

tra·be·at·ed /tráybee àytəd/, **tra·be·ate** /tráybee àyt, tráybee ət/ *adj* built using horizontal beams instead of arches [Mid-16C. < Latin *trab-* "beam"] —**tra·be·a·tion** /tràybee áysh'n/ *n*

tra·bec·u·la /trə békyələ/ (*plural* **-lae** /-lee/ or **-las**) *n* **1.** ANAT ROD-SHAPED SUPPORT IN ORGAN a rod-shaped body part that forms an internal support of an organ and divides it into separate chambers **2.** ANAT BAR OF BONY TISSUE a thin bar of bony tissue in spongy bone that, with others, forms a mesh whose interconnecting spaces contain bone marrow **3.** BOT ROD-SHAPED CELL a rod-shaped cell or structure that bridges a cavity, e.g., between cells [Mid-19C. < Latin, "small beam" < *trab-* "beam"] —**tra·bec·u·lar** *adj* —**tra·bec·u·late** *adj*

trace[1] /trayss/ *n* **1.** REMAINING SIGN a sign that remains to show the former presence of somebody or something that is no longer there **2.** TINY QUANTITY a tiny amount of something **3.** BARELY DETECTABLE AMOUNT an amount of something that is detectable, but too small to be quantified **4.** FOOTPRINT a footprint or physical sign of the passage of a person or animal **5.** PATH a path or track left by people or animals regularly passing **6.** LINE MARKING SOMETHING a line made by a recording instrument, e.g., one drawn by a seismograph or one formed on the screen of a cathode ray tube, or the record made in this way **7.** DRAWING a drawing, especially one made using tracing paper **8.** ATTEMPT TO FIND SOMEBODY OR SOMETHING an attempt to find or follow somebody or something **9.** PSYCHOL same as **engram** **10.** MATH INTERSECTION the point of intersection of a line or plane with the surface of a coordinate plane **11.** MATH SUM OF DIAGONAL ENTRIES the sum of the diagonal entries of a square matrix **12.** METEOROL AMOUNT OF PRECIPITATION an amount of precipitation that is too small to be recorded by instruments, or the record of such an amount ■ *v* (**traced, trac·ing, trac·es**) **1.** *vt* FIND SOMEBODY OR SOMETHING to find out where somebody or something is or who or what somebody or something was **2.** *vti* FOLLOW OR BE FOLLOWED to follow or show the course or series of developments of something, or be able to be followed back in time or to a source **3.** *vti* COPY SOMETHING to copy writing, a design, or drawing by putting translucent paper on top of it and drawing the visible outlines on this paper **4.** *vt* DRAW SOMETHING CAREFULLY to draw or write something with great care **5.** *vt* DESCRIBE SOMETHING IN OUTLINE to give an outline or brief description of something **6.** *vt* ARCHIT PUT TRACERY ON SOMETHING to decorate something with tracery **7.** *vi* CARRY OUT SEARCH to search through something [13C. Via Old French *tracier* "make your way" < Latin *trahere* "to pull"] —**trace·a·bil·i·ty** /tràyssə bíllətee/ *n* —**trace·a·ble** *adj* —**trace·a·ble·ness** *n* —**trace·a·bly** *adv* —**trace·less** *adj* —**trace·less·ly** *adv*

ORIGIN See ***trace***[2].

trace[2] /trayss/ *n* **1.** either of the two straps or chains connected to a horse's harness by means of which it pulls something such as a cart (*often used in the plural*) **2.** a hinged bar that enables motion to be transferred from one part of a machine to another [14C. < Old French *trais*, plural of *trait* "strap for harnessing" < Latin *tractus* "drawing" < *trahere* "to pull"] ◇ **kick over the traces** to reject restrictions and controls and do something unconventional (*informal*)

ORIGIN The Latin word *tractus* "drawing," from which ***trace*** is derived, passed into Old French as *trait* "pulling, draft," hence "harness strap." English *trait* derives from this. The French plural *trais* was borrowed into English in the 14th century as ***trace*** "harness strap." It also formed the basis of a Vulgar Latin verb that evolved into Old French *tracier*, from which English in the 14th century got the verb ***trace***. A noun ***trace*** was also derived from *tracier*, and this too was acquired by English as ***trace***, in the 13th century. At first it denoted a "path" or "track"; the modern sense "remaining sign" did not develop until the 17th century.

trace el·e·ment *n* **1.** ELEMENT PRESENT IN TINY AMOUNT a chemical element present in minute, but detectable amounts in something such as a metal or ore **2.** ELEMENT ESSENTIAL FOR HEALTH an element that is required in minute amounts for normal growth and development and the functioning of vital enzyme systems, e.g., zinc, iodine, or manganese **3.** MINUSCULE AMOUNT a very tiny amount ○ *only a trace element of truth to that statement*

trace fos·sil *n* a feature in sedimentary rocks that resulted from the activity of an animal, e.g., a worm cast or footprint

trac·er /tráyssər/ *n* **1.** ARMS same as **tracer bullet** **2.** AMMUNITION ACTING AS TRACER BULLETS ammunition that has been treated to act as tracer bullets ○ *a gun loaded with tracer* **3.** MED, BIOL same as **tracer element** **4.** INVESTIGATION OR INVESTIGATOR an investigation into the whereabouts of something missing such as an item of mail or a cargo shipment, or somebody who carries out such an investigation **5.** MAKER OF TRACINGS somebody or something that makes tracings **6.** TRACKING DEVICE a device that gives out a signal that can be tracked and followed when attached to a vehicle or person

trac·er bul·let *n* a bullet that has been treated with chemicals to make it leave a glowing or smoky trail as it flies

trac·er el·e·ment *n* a radioactive element used in experiments so that its movements can be monitored

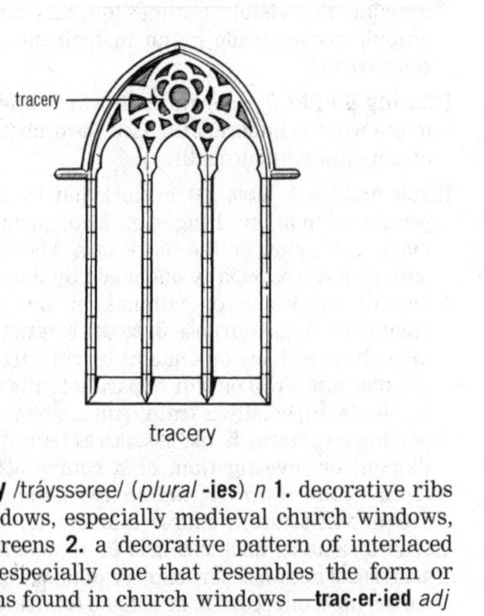

tracery

trac·er·y /tráyssəree/ (*plural* **-ies**) *n* **1.** decorative ribs in windows, especially medieval church windows, and screens **2.** a decorative pattern of interlaced lines, especially one that resembles the form or patterns found in church windows —**trac·er·ied** *adj*

tra·che·a /tráykee ə/ (*plural* **-che·ae** /-kee ee/ or **-che·as**) *n* **1.** ANAT same as **windpipe** (*technical*) **2.** ZOOL a tube in insects and related air-breathing invertebrate animals through which air is drawn into the body by the pumping action of the abdominal muscles **3.** BOT a tubular part of water-conducting plant tissue that provides mechanical support and transport of water and nutrients [14C. < medieval Latin < Greek *(artēria) trakheia* "rough (artery)"] —**tra·che·al** *adj* —**tra·che·ate** /-ət, -àyt/ *adj*

tra·che·id /tráykee id/ *n* a cell in the trachea of conifers and other gymnosperm plants, with bands of lignin thickening the cell walls and adding structural support [Late 19C. < German *Tracheïde* "something belonging to the trachea"] —**tra·che·i·dal** /tray kée id'l, tray kéed'l/ *adj*

tra·che·i·tis /tràykee ítiss/ *n* inflammation of the trachea

tracheo- *prefix* trachea ○ *tracheostomy*

tra·che·o·bron·chi·al /tràykee ō bróngkee əl/ *adj* relating to or located in both the trachea and the bronchi

tra·che·o·e·soph·a·ge·al /tràykee ō i sòffə jée əl/ *adj* relating to or located in both the trachea and the esophagus

tra·che·ole /tráykee ōl/ *n* a fine channel that branches off from an insect's trachea and carries oxygen to its tissues [Early 20C. < TRACHEA]

tra·che·o·phyte /tráykee ō fīt/ *n* a plant that has a system of vascular tissues for conducting water and nutrients through it [Mid-20C. < TRACHEA + Greek *phuton* "plant"]

tra·che·os·co·py /tràykee óskəpee/ (*plural* **-pies**) *n* an examination of the inside of the trachea, e.g., using a laryngoscope —**tra·che·o·scop·ic** /tràykee ə skóppik/ *adj*

tra·che·os·to·my /tràykee óstəmee/ (*plural* **-mies**) *n* **1.** a hole cut in the trachea, e.g., to ensure the airway is unblocked or to suck out secretions **2.** an operation to cut a hole in the trachea

tra·che·ot·o·my /tràykee óttəmee/ (*plural* **-mies**) *n* the making of an incision through the neck into the trachea to assist breathing when the upper airways are blocked

tra·cho·ma /trə kṓmə/ *n* a contagious bacterial eye disease in which scar tissue forms inside the eyelid, eventually causing it to curve inward and the eyelashes to scrape the eye and cause infection [Late 17C. < Greek *trakhōma* "roughness"] —**tra·cho·ma·tous** *adj*

tra·chyte /trá kīt, tráy-/ *n* a fine-grained volcanic rock, characterized by the presence of alkaline feldspar minerals [Early 19C. < Greek *trakhus* "rough" + -ITE[1]] —**tra·chy·toid** /trákə tòyd, tráyki-/ *adj*

tra·chyt·ic /trə kíttik/ *adj* describes igneous rocks in which the crystals are arranged in parallel and show the flow of the molten lava from which they were formed

trac·ing /tráyssing/ *n* **1.** a copy of something made by putting a sheet of translucent paper on top of it and drawing the visible outlines on this paper **2.** a graphic record made by an instrument such as a seismograph

trac·ing pa·per *n* paper through which it is possible to see what is underneath, used for drawing a copy of something underneath

track /trak/ *n* **1.** MARK LEFT a mark left by a moving person, animal, or thing, e.g., a footprint, an animal's paw print, or the mark of a wheel **2.** PATH a path or road, especially one made by the continual passing of people or animals or one specially created for some purpose **3.** COURSE OF TRAVEL the path taken by somebody or something while traveling **4.** RAIL STRUCTURE a rail or pair of parallel rails on which a vehicle, especially a train, runs, along with supporting structures **5.** LINE OF ACTION OR THOUGHT a line of thought or investigation, or a course of action ○ *realized our research was on the wrong track* **6.** SPORTS RACE COURSE a course laid out for racing **7.** SPORTS same as **track and field 8.** RECORDING SEPARATE RECORDING OF MUSIC a separate piece of music or song on a disc, tape, or record **9.** RECORDING PATH FOR RECORDING a separate section of a magnetic tape where the input of a single channel is recorded **10.** RECORDING RECORDED INPUT a recording on separate tracks of a magnetic tape that are combined to give a final version, e.g., of a piece of recorded music or a film **11.** RECORDING same as **soundtrack** (sense 1) **12.** COMPUT SECTION OF COMPUTER DISK a path on the surface of a storage medium such as a diskette or CD-ROM on which information is recorded and from which recorded information is read. The path is a series of concentric rings on floppy disks and hard files and a spiral on video disks and CD-ROMs. **13.** MOVIES same as **tracking shot 14.** AUTOMOT TREADS OF TANK OR BULLDOZER a continuous loop of rubber or metal plates driven by wheels, giving great traction over soft or rough ground, used especially on bulldozers and heavy military vehicles such as tanks **15.** *US* EDUC COURSE OF STUDY a course of study tailored to the relative abilities or needs of a student **16.** BUSINESS CAREER PATH the course or projected course of a career **17.** MANUF MOVING ASSEMBLY LINE a moving belt carrying things along a factory assembly line **18.** HOUSEHOLD SUPPORTING RAIL a usually grooved rail along which something moves such as a lighting fixture or the supporting hooks of a curtain **19.** PHYS PATH OF PARTICLE the path taken by a particle of ionizing radiation in a cloud chamber, bubble chamber, or photographic emulsion **20.** ENG DISTANCE BETWEEN WHEELS the distance between a pair of wheels, e.g., between the front wheels of a motor vehicle ■ **tracks** *npl* DRUGS NEEDLE MARKS marks or scars on the body of a drug user caused by frequent injections (*slang*) ■ *v* (**tracked, track·ing, tracks**) **1.** *vti* FOLLOW TRAIL to follow a trail made by somebody or something, or try to find somebody or something by following a trail left behind **2.** *vti* FOLLOW PATH to follow a path through a place **3.** *vt* MAKE TRACKS WITH MUD ON SOMETHING to carry something, especially mud, on the shoes or feet and leave it on the surface walked on ○ *tracking mud into the house* **4.** *vt* ELEC ENG FOLLOW FLIGHT PATH OF SOMETHING to follow the flight path of a vehicle such as a spacecraft using electronic equipment or radar **5.** *vt* FOLLOW PROGRESS OF SOMETHING to follow the progress or development of something **6.** *vti* MOVIES FILM MOVING OBJECT to follow and film a moving person or object with a mobile camera **7.** *vi* ENG ALIGN to be in alignment or the correct distance apart (*refers to wheels of motor vehicles*) **8.** *vi* RECORDING FOLLOW GROOVE ON RECORD to follow the groove on a phonograph record **9.** *vt US* RAIL SUPPLY SOMETHING WITH TRACKS to supply something, especially a railroad line, with tracks **10.** *vt US* EDUC ASSIGN SOMEBODY TO TRACK to assign a student to an educational track **11.** *vi US* TRAVEL to travel, especially on a long or laborious journey (*informal*) [15C. < French *trac* "footprint, mark"] —**track·a·bil·i·ty** /tràkə bíllətee/ *n* —**track·a·ble** *adj* ◇ **cover your tracks** to remove all signs of having been somewhere or done something (*informal*) ◇ **in your tracks** (*informal*) **1.** suddenly and immediately, just where somebody or something is or in the middle of what somebody or something is doing **2.** as somebody or something is going along ◇ **keep track (of)** to follow, pay attention to, or keep a check on the position or progress of somebody or something ◇ **lose track (of)** to fail to follow or pay attention, or fail to keep an adequate check on the position or progress of somebody or something ◇ **make tracks** to leave, especially hastily (*informal*) ◇ **off the beaten track** away from the places people usually visit and often difficult to find or get to (*informal*) ○ *The cottage is lovely, but it's off the beaten track.* ◇ **off track** not on the correct or desired path or schedule ◇ **on track** on the correct or desired path or schedule

track down *vt* to find a person, animal, or object by searching or following a trail

track·age /trákij/ *n US* **1.** RAILROAD TRACKS railroad tracks collectively **2.** RIGHT TO USE TRACKS the right of one railroad company to use tracks belonging to another company **3.** CHARGE FOR USING TRACKS a fee charged by one railroad company to another for use of its tracks

track and field *n* athletic sports carried out on a running track and an adjacent field, e.g., hurdling or javelin throwing —**track-and-field** *adj*

track·ball /trák bàwl/ *n* a computer pointing device consisting of a freely rotating ball in a socket with sensors that translate its rotation into movements of an on-screen cursor

tracked /trakt/ *adj* moving on tracks, as a military tank or bulldozer does, or along a fixed track, as a dockside crane does

tracked ve·hi·cle *n* a vehicle that is propelled by tracks instead of wheels, e.g., a military tank or a bulldozer

track·er /trákər/ *n* somebody who follows a trail made by another person or an animal, especially in order to guide police, soldiers, or hunters

track e·vent *n* a sports competition that takes place on a running track

track·ing /tráking/ *n* **1.** FOLLOWING OF TRAIL the act or process of following the trail of a person or animal **2.** FUNCTION OF FINDING BEST PICTURE a function on a video player that adjusts the quality of the picture **3.** LEAKING OF CURRENT the leaking of current between two insulated points, e.g., as a result of dampness or dirt **4.** *US* GROUPING OF STUDENTS the grouping of students according to their abilities or needs. Can term **streaming**

track·ing poll *n* an opinion poll in which the same people are asked questions periodically to give an indication of changes in opinion

track·ing shot *n* a camera shot filmed from a moving dolly, following the movement of somebody or something

track·ing sta·tion *n* a place from which the movement of something such as a launched missile or a space vehicle can be followed using radar or radio signals

track·less /trákləss/ *adj* **1.** LACKING PATHS containing no trails or paths and therefore extremely isolated **2.** LEAVING NO TRAIL leaving no track or trail **3.** RUNNING WITHOUT RAILS not needing rails on which to run

track light *n* an electric light that can be moved and repositioned anywhere along the length of an electrified track mounted on a wall or ceiling —**track light·ing** *n*

track·man /trákmən/ (*plural* **-men** /-mən/) *n US* **1.** somebody whose job is to lay and maintain rails **2.** a man who competes in track events

track meet *n* an athletic competition in which teams from several places participate in track events

track rec·ord *n* **1.** a record of the past performance of a person, organization, or thing (*informal*) **2.** a record set at a specific sports arena, as opposed to a national or international record

track shoe *n* either of a pair of lightweight spiked running shoes

track·side /trák sīd/ *n* the area immediately beside a running track or racetrack

track·suit /trák sòot/ *n* a loose-fitting long-sleeved top and matching pants in knitted nylon or cotton, worn by athletes over their sports clothes and by other people as casual wear

track·walk·er /trák wàwkər/ *n* somebody employed to inspect railroad track

track·wom·an /trák wòommən/ (*plural* **-wom·en** /-wìmmin/) *n US* a woman who competes in track events

tract[1] /trakt/ *n* **1.** AREA OF LAND OR WATER an unmeasured expanse of land or water, or a measured area, especially of land **2.** GROUP OF ORGANS a system of organs or body parts that work together to provide for the passage of something such as food or bodily waste products **3.** BUNDLE OF NERVES a group of nerve fibers that forms a pathway from one part of the brain or spinal cord to another [15C. < Latin *tractus* "a drawing out, duration" < *trahere* "to pull"]

tract[2] /trakt/ *n* an anthem sung in some Roman Catholic masses [14C. Via medieval Latin *tractus* < Latin (see TRACT[1])]

tract[3] /trakt/ *n* a pamphlet that sets out a position or an analysis, especially one dealing with a political or religious issue [Pre-12C. < Latin *tractatus* < *tractare* "to handle" < *trahere* "to pull"]

trac·ta·ble /tráktəb'l/ *adj* **1.** very easy to control or persuade **2.** very easy to bend or work with [15C. < Latin *tractabilis* < *tractare* (see TRACT[3])] —**trac·ta·bil·i·ty** /tràktə bíllətee/ *n* —**trac·ta·bly** *adv*

Trac·tar·i·an·ism /trak térree ən ìzzəm/ *n* CHR same as **Oxford Movement** [Mid-19C. < the tracts distributed] —**Trac·tar·i·an** *n, adj*

trac·tate /trák tàyt/ *n* a treatise or short essay (*formal*) [15C. < Latin *tractatus* (see TRACT[3])]

tract house *n* any of many similar houses built on a tract of land —**tract hous·ing** *n*

trac·tile /trákt'l/ *adj* able to be stretched into another shape without breaking [Mid-19C. < Latin *tract-*, past participle of *trahere* "to pull"] —**trac·til·i·ty** /trak tíllətee/ *n*

trac·tion /tráksh'n/ *n* **1. APPLICATION OF WEIGHTS** the application of a pulling force for medical purposes, e.g., to reduce a fracture, maintain bone alignment, relieve pain, or prevent spinal injury **2. FRICTION ALLOWING MOVEMENT** the adhesive friction between a moving object and the surface on which it is moving, e.g., between a tire and the ground, without which the object cannot move **3.** ENG **PULLING** the act or process of pulling something, especially by means of a motor, or the fact or state of being pulled along **4.** AUTOMOT **WAY TO MOVE VEHICLES** a means of moving vehicles **5. WAY TO ACHIEVE PROGRESS** a means by which or the degree to which progress can be made ○ *could not get any traction in trying to push through the legislation* [Early 17C. Directly or via French < medieval Latin *traction-* < Latin *tract-*, past participle of *trahere* "to pull"] —**trac·tion·al** *adj*

tractor

trac·tor /tráktər/ *n* **1. FARM VEHICLE** a motor vehicle used for pulling heavy loads, especially on farms, where its large rear wheels enable it to move in fields **2. FRONT PART OF A HEAVY TRUCK** a large vehicle, the front section of a truck used to haul heavy loads, with a driving cab, engine, and coupling for trailers **3. AIRCRAFT WITH PROPELLER IN FRONT** an aircraft that has its propeller in front of the engine so that it exerts a pull through the air instead of a pushing force **4. PROPELLER** a propeller at the front of an aircraft engine **5.** COMPUT same as **tractor feed** [Late 18C. < Latin *tract-* (see TRACTION)]

ORIGIN The Latin word *trahere* "to pull, draw," from which ***tractor*** is derived, is also the source of English *abstract, attract, contract, detract, distract, extract, retract, retreat, subtract, train, treat, treatise,* and *treaty.*

trac·tor feed *n* a mechanism for feeding paper into a printer, using toothed wheels to mesh with the perforations in continuous paper

trac·tor-trail·er *n* a truck for pulling heavy loads, consisting of a tractor attached to a trailer or semi-trailer

Spencer Tracy

Tra·cy /tráyssee/, **Spencer** (1900–67) US actor. He won Academy Awards for his movies *Captains Courageous* (1937) and *Boys Town* (1938).

"There were times my pants were so thin I could sit on a dime and tell if it was heads or tails."
[Attributed to Spencer Tracy]

trad. *abbr* traditional

trade /trayd/ *n* **1. BUYING AND SELLING** the activity of buying and selling, or sometimes bartering, goods ○ *a suspension of trade between the two countries* **2. AREA OF BUSINESS OR INDUSTRY** a specific area of business or industry ○ *the book trade* **3. OCCUPATION** a skilled occupation, usually one requiring manual labor ○ *learn a trade* **4. PEOPLE IN BUSINESS** the people who work in a specific area of business or industry ○ *You'll never convince the trade that this tax is fair.* **5. WORK IN COMMERCE** work in commerce as opposed to a profession ○ *graduates going into trade* **6. CUSTOMERS** customers or business generated by customers ○ *losing trade to their competitors* **7. COMMERCIAL CUSTOMERS** customers in business and industry, as opposed to the general public, who purchase products related to their business or industry ○ *This counter is for the trade only.* **8. EXCHANGE** an exchange of somebody or something for another ○ *If neither of you likes your room, why don't you do a trade?* **9.** METEOROL same as **trade wind** ○ *the southern trades* **10.** PUBL **BUSINESS PUBLICATION** a publication meant for people in a specific line of business ○ *advertising in all the trades* **11.** *US* **DEAL** a deal or transaction ■ *v* (**trad·ed, trad·ing, trades**) **1.** *vi* **BUY AND SELL GOODS** to take part in buying and selling goods for trade **2.** *vt* **DEAL IN SOMETHING** to buy and sell a particular commodity **3.** *vi US* **SHOP OR BUY REGULARLY FROM BUSINESS** to shop or buy something regularly at a particular place of business **4.** *vt* **EXCHANGE SOMETHING** to give and receive something alternately with somebody else ○ *trading punches* **5.** *vti* **MAKE EXCHANGE** to make an exchange, or exchange somebody or something for another ○ *Each had something the other wanted and they were happy to trade.* [14C. < Middle Low German, "track"] —**trad·a·ble** *adj*—**trade·less** *adj*

trade down *vi* to sell something large or expensive and buy something smaller or less expensive in its place

trade in *vt* to give an old or used item, especially a car, in part payment for a new one

trade on *vt* to take advantage of a personal quality or situation, often unfairly or excessively

trade up *vi* to sell something small or inexpensive and buy something larger and more expensive in its place

trade ac·cep·tance *n* a bill of exchange for the amount of a purchase drawn by the seller on the buyer, signed by the buyer, and often specifying the place and date of payment

trade a·gree·ment *n* a treaty between two or more countries to regulate trade between them

trade as·so·ci·a·tion *n* an organization formed to represent the collective interests of a number of businesses in the same trade

trade book *n* a standard edition of a book, meant for sale to the general public, as opposed to a deluxe or book-club edition

trade cy·cle *n UK* same as **business cycle**

trade def·i·cit *n* the difference, measured in monetary value, between a nation's imports and its exports when the imports exceed the exports

trade dis·count *n* a reduction in the standard price of something, offered by one business to another, e.g., by a manufacturer to a retailer, especially within the same trade

trad·ed op·tion *n* a stock option that is marketable

trade e·di·tion *n* PUBL same as **trade book**

trade fair *n* an occasion when manufacturers and producers can exhibit their products and talk to potential customers

~~**tradegy**~~ incorrect spelling of **tragedy**

trade-in *n* **1.** a used item that is used as part payment for something new, e.g., a used car **2.** a transaction in which an old or used item serves as part payment for something new

trade jour·nal *n* a periodical devoted to news and features relating to a specific trade or profession

trade lan·guage *n* a language used between native speakers of different languages to allow them to communicate so that they can trade with each other

trade-last *n US* an exchange in which somebody repeats an overheard compliment to the complimented person if that person will first offer an overheard compliment about the other (*informal*)

trade·mark /tráyd maàrk/ *n* **1. COMPANY SYMBOL** a name or symbol used to show that a product is made by a specific company and legally registered so that no other manufacturer can use it **2. DISTINCTIVE CHARACTERISTIC** a distinctive characteristic associated with a person or group of people ○ *Quick exits are her trademark.* ■ *vt* (**-marked, -mark·ing, -marks**) **1. REGISTER SOMETHING AS TRADEMARK** to register a name or symbol as a trademark **2. LABEL PRODUCT WITH TRADEMARK** to place a trademark on a product

trade name *n* **1. PRODUCT NAME** a name given by a manufacturer to a product or service **2. NAME USED IN TRADE** a name for something that is usually known or used only by people working in the trade **3. COMPANY NAME** a name under which a company or business operates

trade·off /tráyd àwf, -òf/, **trade-off** *n* a situation in which somebody is prepared to compromise by giving up all or part of one thing in exchange for another ○ *a tradeoff between quality and price*

trade pa·per·back *n* a paperback edition of a book that is superior in production quality to a mass-market paperback edition and is similar to a hardback in size

trade plates *npl UK* same as **dealer plates**

trad·er /tráydər/ *n* **1.** somebody who buys and sells retail goods **2.** somebody who deals in stocks and securities, especially somebody who tries to profit by making frequent deals, each netting a small profit **3.** SHIPPING same as **merchant ship**

trade ref·er·ence *n* a person or company that furnishes a report concerning somebody's credit standing in response to an inquiry by somebody else in the same trade, especially a supplier

trade route *n* a route used by merchant ships or trading vehicles

Tra·des·cant /tráddə skànt/, **John** (1570–1638?) English naturalist. The head gardener to Charles I, he introduced many foreign plants into England and opened an early public museum.

trad·es·can·tia /tràddə skánshə, -skánshee ə/ (*plural* **-tias** or *same*) *n* a plant grown for its striped leaves and blue, white, or pink flowers. Native to: Americas. Genus: *Tradescantia.* [Early 18C. < modern Latin, after John TRADESCANT or his son]

trade school *n* a school that gives instruction in a specific trade or offers general vocational courses

trade se·cret *n* **1.** a secret formula or technique that is used to make a product, known only to the company that manufactures it **2.** a secret (*informal*) ○ *Which shampoo do you use – or is it a trade secret?*

trade show *n* COMM same as **trade fair**

trades·man /tráydzmən/ (*plural* **-men** /-mən/) *n* **1.** a man who works in a skilled trade, especially one related to the construction industry such as plumbing or carpentry **2.** a man involved in retail trade, especially a storekeeper (*dated*)

trades·per·son /tráydz pùrss'n/ (*plural* **-per·sons** or **-peo·ple** /-peèp'l/) *n* **1.** a skilled worker, especially in a trade related to the construction industry such as plumbing or carpentry **2.** a retail dealer, especially a store owner (*dated*)

trades un·ion *n UK* POL same as **labor union**

trades·wom·an /tráydz wòommən/ (*plural* **-wom·en** /-wìmmin/) *n* a woman who works in a skilled trade, especially one related to the construction industry such as plumbing or carpentry

trade un·ion *n UK* same as **labor union** —**trade un·ion·ism** *n* —**trade ùn·ion·ist** *n*

trade-weight·ed in·dex *n* an index reflecting the level of trade between particular nations, e.g., one indicating the value of the dollar in relation to other currencies

trade wind *n* a prevailing tropical wind that blows toward the equator from the northeast in the northern hemisphere or from the southeast in the southern hemisphere. The trade winds are major components of the global weather system. [< *blow trade* "blow in a constant direction"]

tradgedy incorrect spelling of **tragedy**

trad·ing card /tráyding-/ *n* a card with a picture or information on it that is one of a set designed to be collected

trad·ing post *n* **1.** especially in former times, a store in a remote area, where local products can be bartered for supplies **2.** a location where a specific security is traded on the floor of a stock exchange

trad·ing stamp *n* a stamp that can be exchanged for goods, given by a store to customers each time they spend a fixed amount of money

tra·di·tion /trə dísh'n/ *n* **1.** CUSTOM OR BELIEF a long-established action or pattern of behavior in a community or group of people, often one that has been handed down from generation to generation **2.** BODY OF CUSTOMS a body of long-established customs and beliefs viewed as a set of precedents **3.** HANDING DOWN OF CUSTOMS the handing down of patterns of behavior, practices, and beliefs that are valued by a culture **4.** CHR **ACCEPTED UNWRITTEN CHRISTIAN DOCTRINES** the body of Christian doctrines that are accepted as the teachings of Jesus Christ and the apostles without written evidence **5.** ISLAM **TEACHINGS SUPPLEMENTING KORAN** the body of Islamic beliefs and customs that are not written in the Koran, e.g., the words of Muhammad **6.** LAW **TRANSFER OF OWNERSHIP** especially in Roman and Scots law, the formal transfer of ownership of movable property [14C. Via French < Latin *tradition-* < *tradere* "hand over, betray" < *trans-* "across, over" + *dare* "give"] —**tra·di·tion·less** *adj*

SYNONYMS See ***habit.***

tra·di·tion·al /trə díshən'l, -díshnəl/ *adj* **1.** relating to or based on tradition **2.** describes older styles of jazz, usually played by small ensembles featuring clarinet, trumpet, trombone, and rhythm sections. Traditional jazz flourished in New Orleans, Chicago, and Kansas City in the early 20th century. —**tra·di·tion·al·i·ty** /trə dìsh'n állətee/ *n* —**tra·di·tion·al·ize** *vt* —**tra·di·tion·al·ly** *adv*

tra·di·tion·al·ism /trə díshən'l ìzzəm, -díshnə lìzzəm/ *n* **1.** a deep respect for tradition, especially for cultural or religious practices **2.** the idea that all knowledge comes from divine revelation and is passed on by tradition —**tra·di·tion·al·ist** *n* —**tra·di·tion·al·is·tic** /trə dìshən'l ístik, -dìshnə lístik/ *adj*

trad·i·tor /trádditər/ (*plural* **trad·i·to·res** /tràddi táwreez/) *n* an early Christian who betrayed other Christians during the Roman persecutions [14C. < Latin (see TRAITOR)]

tra·duce /trə dóoss/ (**-duced, -duc·ing, -duc·es**) *vt* to say very critical or disparaging things about somebody or something [Late 16C. < Latin *traducere* "convert, transfer, scorn, disgrace" < *trans-* "across, over" + *ducere* "to lead"] —**tra·duce·ment** *n* —**tra·duc·er** *n* —**tra·duc·i·ble** *adj*

tra·du·cian·ism /trə dóosh'n ìzzəm/ *n* the belief that a child inherits a soul as well as its bodily characteristics from its parents [Mid-18C. < late Latin *traducianus* "believer in traducianism" < *tradux* "inheritance, transmission" < *traducere* (see TRADUCE)] —**tra·du·cian** *n, adj* —**tra·du·cian·ist** *n, adj* —**tra·du·cian·is·tic** /trə dòosh'n ístik/ *adj*

Tra·fal·gar, Cape /trə fálgər/ cape in southwestern Spain between Cádiz and the Strait of Gibraltar

traf·fic /tráffik/ *n* **1.** MOVEMENT OF VEHICLES the movement of vehicles on a road or in an area **2.** SEA OR AIR TRANSPORT the movement of ships, trains, or aircraft between two places, or the volume of passengers or goods transported by sea, rail, or air **3.** BUSINESS OF TRANSPORTATION the business of transporting goods or people **4.** TRADE illegal trade in goods such as drugs or weapons **5.** COMMUNICATION **FLOW OF COMMUNICATIONS** the volume or flow of messages carried by a communications system **6.** NEGOTIATIONS dealings or negotiations between people ■ *v* (**-ficked, -fick·ing, -fics**) **1.** *vi* TRADE ILLEGALLY to engage in illegal trading **2.** *vi* HAVE DEALINGS to have dealings with somebody or something ○ *suspected him of trafficking with arms dealers* **3.** *vt* TRADE SOMETHING to trade or exchange anything ○ *We spent the afternoon trafficking gossip.* [Early 16C. Via obsolete French *trafique* < Old Italian *traffico* < *trafficare* "carry on trade"]

traf·fic cir·cle *n* a road junction consisting of a circular island around which traffic can flow continuously

traf·fic cone *n* a marker in the shape of a cone, usually made of orange plastic, used to separate lines of traffic during road repairs or to prevent vehicles from entering an area

traf·fic cop *n* a police officer who directs the flow of traffic, especially at an intersection (*informal*)

traf·fic court *n* a court that deals with people who have committed traffic violations

traf·fic en·gi·neer·ing *n* the design and planning of roads and walkways, considering such factors as pedestrian and vehicular capacity and means for controlling traffic

traf·fic is·land *n* a raised area in the center of a street built to separate lanes of traffic and allow pedestrians to wait safely until they can cross

traf·fic jam *n* a line of traffic that cannot move or moves very slowly or spasmodically because of overcrowding or an obstruction

traf·fick·er *n* somebody who traffics in something, especially illegal goods such as drugs or weapons

traf·fick·ing in per·sons *n* the illegal practice of procuring human beings for unpaid work in physically abusive settings and locations from which they are not allowed to leave

traf·fic light *n* a signal that uses red, green, and amber lights to control traffic, especially at an intersection

traf·fic pat·tern *n* the pattern of routes to which an aircraft is restricted when approaching or circling an airport

traf·fic sig·nal *n* ROADS same as **traffic light**

traf·fic war·den *n UK* a uniformed public official who enforces parking restrictions on the highway and may also direct traffic

trag·a·canth /trággə kànth, trájjə-/ *n* **1.** a reddish or white gum extracted from a plant grown in Asia. Use: pills, adhesives, textile printing, stabilizer, thickener for sauces. **2.** a plant from which tragacanth is obtained, especially a spiny Asian plant with white, yellow, or purple flowers. Genus: *Astragalus.* [Late 16C. Via French < Greek *tragakantha* "goat's thorn" < *tragos* "goat" + *akantha* "thorn"]

tra·ge·di·an /trə jéedee ən/ *n* **1.** an actor who plays tragic roles **2.** a playwright who specializes in tragedies

tra·ge·di·enne /trə jèedee én/ *n* a female actor who plays tragic roles (*dated*) [Mid-19C. < French < *tragédie* (see TRAGEDY)]

trag·e·dy /trájjədee/ (*plural* **-dies**) *n* **1.** VERY SAD EVENT an event in life that evokes feelings of sorrow or grief **2.** DISASTROUS EVENT a disastrous circumstance or event, e.g., serious illness, financial ruin, or fatality **3.** TRAGIC PLAY a serious play with a tragic theme, often involving a heroic struggle and the downfall of the main character **4.** TRAGIC PIECE OF LITERATURE a literary work that deals with a tragic theme **5.** TRAGEDIES AS GENRE the genre of plays or other literary works that deal with tragic themes [14C. Via French *tragédie* < Greek *tragōidia* "goat's song" < *tragos* "goat" + *aeidein* "sing"]

tra·gi ANAT plural of **tragus**

trag·ic /trájjik/, **trag·i·cal** /-ik'l/ *adj* **1.** provoking deep sadness, distress, or grief ○ *a tragic accident* **2.** relating to tragedies as a dramatic genre ○ *a tragic hero* [Mid-16C. Via Latin < Greek *tragikos* "of tragedy" < *tragos* "goat"] —**trag·i·cal·ly** *adv*

trag·ic flaw *n* a character flaw that causes the downfall of the protagonist in a tragedy

trag·ic i·ro·ny *n* the revealing to an audience of a tragic event or consequence that remains unknown to the character concerned. It is a kind of dramatic irony.

trag·i·com·e·dy /tràjji kómmədee/ (*plural* **-dies**) *n* **1.** WORK COMBINING TRAGEDY AND COMEDY a play or other literary work that combines aspects of tragedy and comedy **2.** TRAGICOMIC PLAYS AS GENRE tragicomic plays or literary works considered as a genre **3.** EVENT MIXING TRAGEDY AND COMEDY an event or situation that has both tragic and comical aspects [Late 16C. Via French *tragicomédie* < late Latin *tragicomoedia* < *tragicus* (see TRAGIC) + *comoedia* (see COMEDY)] —**trag·i·com·ic** *adj* —**trag·i·com·i·cal** *adj* —**trag·i·com·i·cal·ly** *adv*

tragopan

trag·o·pan /trággə pàn/ *n* a brightly colored pheasant, the male of which has a bright blue bare throat and fleshy appendages on its head that look like horns. Native to: Asia. Latin name: *Tragopan temminckii.* [Early 17C. Via Latin < Greek, type of hornbill < *tragos* "goat" + *pan* "Pan"]

tra·gus /tráygəss/ (*plural* **-gi** /-gī, -jī/) *n* **1.** the pointed flap of cartilage that lies above the earlobe and partly covers the entrance to the ear passage **2.** a hair growing just inside the opening of the ear passage [Late 17C. Via modern Latin < Greek *tragos* "goat, hairy part of the ear"] —**tra·gal** *adj*

trail /trayl/ *v* (**trailed, trail·ing, trails**) **1.** *vt* FOLLOW SOMEBODY SECRETLY to follow a person or animal either by staying close but out of sight or by looking for signs of movement left behind such as footprints or scent **2.** *vti* FALL BEHIND IN SPORTS COMPETITION to be losing or behind in a race, match, or competition **3.** *vi* LAG to walk slowly, usually from tiredness or boredom **4.** *vti* DRAG SOMETHING, OR BE DRAGGED to be pulled or dragged along, or pull or drag something along **5.** *vi* DRAPE to hang, grow, or float loosely ○ *Her curly hair trailed along her shoulders and down her back.* **6.** *vt* TOW SOMETHING to tow something such as a trailer behind a vehicle **7.** *vt* CERAMICS **DECORATE SOMETHING BY DRIZZLING LIQUID CLAY** to decorate ceramics with liquid clay (**slip**) that is drizzled or sprayed on **8.** *vt* ARMS **CARRY WEAPON IN LOW POSITION** to carry a weapon horizontally or with the butt near to the ground **9.** *vti* MAKE TRACK to make a track through a place ■ *n* **1.** ROUTE THROUGH COUNTRYSIDE a route through the countryside that links paths and points of interest ○ *a nature trail* **2.** MARKS WHERE SOMEBODY OR SOMETHING MOVED a sequence of marks left by somebody or something moving along a surface **3.** PATH a path or track, especially one that has been beaten through a wild area **4.** SCENT FOLLOWED a scent or track that is followed in a hunt **5.** ARMS **BOTTOM OF GUN CARRIAGE** the part of a gun carriage that rests on the ground [14C. Via Old French *trailler* "to tow" < Latin *tragula* "dragnet, sledge," probably < *trahere* "to pull"]

SPELLCHECK trail or **trial**? Do not confuse the spelling of ***trail*** and ***trial***. ***Trail*** can be used as a verb, meaning "follow secretly," "fall behind," or "drag" (as in *The police trailed him to a motel. They trailed the opponents by two points. Your coat is trailing on the ground.*), or as a noun, denoting a path or a track that is followed (as in *a nature trail, a trail of footprints*). ***Trial*** is chiefly used as a noun, referring to a legal process, a test, or a painful experience, as in *trial by jury, a trial of a new drug, trials and tribulations.*

SYNONYMS See ***follow.***

trail away, trail off *vi* to become quieter or fainter in sound and gradually fade away

trail bike *n* a lightweight motorcycle for use on rough terrain

trail·blaz·er /tráyl blàyzər/, **trail·break·er** /-bràykər/ *n* **1.** a pioneer or innovator **2.** somebody who makes a new path through a wilderness —**trail·blaz·ing** *adj, n*

trail·er /tráylər/ *n* **1.** TOWED VEHICLE a vehicle that is towed by another vehicle, e.g., a small open cart or a platform used for transporting a boat **2.** PART OF TRUCK a large van that is pulled by a truck or tractor, used especially for hauling freight **3.** TRANSP same as **mobile home 4.** TEMPORARY HOME OR OFFICE a trailer equipped with facilities for use as a residence or office that is usually left temporarily on a site, e.g., in a campground **5.** MOVIES, MEDIA ADVERTISEMENT FOR MOVIE an advertisement for a movie consisting of extracts from it, shown on television or in a movie theater **6.** PHOTOGRAPHY END OF REEL OF FILM a blank piece of film at the end of a reel **7.** SOMEBODY OR SOMETHING THAT TRAILS somebody or something that trails, especially somebody who lags behind others **8.** BOT PLANT a trailing plant ■ *v* (**-ered, -er·ing, -ers**) **1.** *vt* MOVE SOMETHING BY TRAILER to transport something using a trailer **2.** *vi US* LIVE IN TRAILER to live or travel in a trailer **3.** *vi* GO IN TRAILER to be capable of being transported by trailer

trail·er park *n* a site where people can park and live in trailers or mobile homes

trail·er sail·er *n* a boat that is small enough to be transported on a trailer

trail·head /tráyl hèd/ *n* the start of a trail for walkers, sometimes with an information kiosk

trail·ing ar·bu·tus /-aar byoótəss/ *n* a trailing evergreen bush with leathery leaves. Flowers: fragrant, pink-and-white, in clusters. Native to: eastern North America. Latin name: *Epigaea repens*.

trail·ing edge *n* **1.** the rear edge of a wing, airfoil, or propeller blade **2.** the part of a pulsed signal during which its amplitude decreases

trail mix *n* a snack containing nuts, dried fruit, and seeds [< its use by walkers]

trail rope *n* **1.** a rope that hangs from a balloon or airship and is used for mooring or as a brake **2.** a long rope attached to the trail of a gun carriage

trail·side /tráyl sīd/ *adj* situated beside or relating to the area beside a trail

train /trayn/ *n* **1.** LINKED RAILROAD CARS a number of railroad cars pulled by a locomotive (*often used before a noun*) **2.** TRAILING PART OF GOWN a long part at the back of a gown or robe that trails on the ground **3.** LONG MOVING LINE a long moving line of people or animals **4.** ENTOURAGE a retinue or group of followers **5.** MIL ARMY FOLLOWERS the people and military vehicles supporting or supplying an army unit **6.** SEQUENCE OF EVENTS a series or sequence of events, actions, or things ○ *interrupting her train of thought* **7.** MECH ENG MECHANICAL SERIES a series of connected wheels or other mechanical parts **8.** ARMS LINE OF GUNPOWDER a line of gunpowder or other combustible material **9.** SOMETHING DRAGGED BEHIND something that is pulled or dragged along or that follows something else ■ *v* (**trained, train·ing, trains**) **1.** *vti* LEARN OR TEACH SKILLS to learn the skills necessary to do a job, or teach somebody such skills, especially through practical experience **2.** *vt* DOMESTICATE ANIMAL to teach an animal to behave in ways acceptable to people, especially by repetition or practice **3.** *vti* PREPARE FOR SPORTING COMPETITION to prepare for a sporting competition, or prepare somebody for a sporting competition, usually with a planned program of appropriate physical exercises **4.** *vt* MAKE PLANT GROW AS WANTED to make a plant, bush, or tree grow in a particular way, e.g., by pruning or tying it **5.** *vt* SHAPE HAIR TO ENCOURAGE PARTICULAR GROWTH to comb or otherwise arrange hair to encourage it to grow in a particular direction **6.** *vt* AIM SOMETHING to aim something such as a weapon or camera at somebody or something ○ *trained her binoculars on the nest* **7.** *vt* MAKE SOMETHING BETTER to improve something, especially the mind, with discipline **8.** *vi* TRAVEL BY TRAIN to make a journey by train (*informal*) [Mid-15C. < Old French *traïn* "something that drags or trails behind" < *traïner* "draw, pull"]

SYNONYMS See ***teach.***

train·band /tráyn bànd/ *n* a company of trained civilian militia operating in England and North America between the 16th and the 18th centuries [Mid-17C. Contraction of *trained band*]

train·bear·er /tráyn bèrrər/ *n* an attendant who holds up the train of somebody walking in a procession or other ceremony

train·ee /tray neé/ *n* somebody who is being trained to do a job (*often used after or before a noun*) ○ *a hairdresser trainee* —**train·ee·ship** *n*

train·er /tráynər/ *n* **1.** somebody who trains animals or people, especially racehorses or athletes **2.** an apparatus or device used in training, especially a simulation cockpit in which pilots train **3.** *UK* same as **athletic shoe**

train·ing /tráyning/ *n* **1.** the process of teaching or learning a skill or job (*often used before a noun*) ○ *a training program* **2.** the process of improving physical fitness by exercise and diet

train·ing school *n* **1.** *US* a vocational or technical school **2.** a residential correctional facility where juvenile offenders are taught a trade

train·ing ta·ble *n US* a table in a dining hall, e.g., in a college dormitory, at which athletes in training eat special meals that are part of their regimen

train·ing wheels *npl* **1.** a pair of small wheels fitted to the back wheel of a bicycle to help balance it while somebody is learning to ride **2.** things provided to help beginners use something (*informal*) ○ *The PC comes with training wheels for new users.*

train·load /tráyn lṑd/ *n* the number of people or the amount of cargo that a train can carry ○ *a trainload of tourists*

train·man /tráynmən/ (*plural* **-men** /-mən/) *n* a man who is a member of a train crew, especially a brakeman, who works to assist the conductor

train oil *n* oil from the blubber of a whale or other ocean animal. Use: the manufacture of soap and margarine, as a lubricant, in dressing leather. [< Low German *trān* or Middle Dutch *traen* "train oil"]

train·per·son /tráyn pùrss'n/ (*plural* **-per·sons** or **-peo·ple** /-peép'l/) *n* member of a train crew, especially a brakeman, who works to assist the conductor

train·spot·ter /tráyn spòttər/ *n UK* **1.** somebody whose hobby is collecting the numbers of railroad locomotives **2.** somebody who is considered boring because of his or her staid outlook, narrow interests, or unfashionable appearance (*slang insult*)

train·spot·ting /tráyn spòtting/ *n UK* **1.** a hobby that consists of collecting the numbers of railroad locomotives **2.** the search for a vein that is prominent enough to inject drugs into (*slang*)

traipse /trayps/ (**traipsed, traips·ing, traips·es**) *vi* to walk around casually or without a specific destination ○ *Don't come traipsing in here late again.* [Late 16C. Origin ?]

trait /trayt/ *n* **1.** INDIVIDUAL CHARACTERISTIC a characteristic or quality that distinguishes somebody **2.** INHERITED CHARACTERISTIC a quality or characteristic that is genetically determined **3.** INDICATION a hint or trace of something (*literary*) [Late 16C. Via French, "act of pulling or drawing, line drawn, feature" < Latin *tractus* < *trahere* "to pull"]

trai·tor /tráytər/ *n* somebody who is disloyal or treacherous [13C. Via French < Latin *traditor* "betrayer" < *tradere* (see TRADITION)] —**trai·tor·ous** *adj*

Tra·jan /tráyjən/ (A.D. 53?–117) Roman emperor. Becoming emperor in A.D. 97, he conducted several military campaigns, notably that in Dacia (modern Romania), commemorated by the carvings on a column in Rome. Full name **Marcus Ulpius Trajanus**

> "Anyone who denies that he is a Christian and actually proves this by worshiping our gods is pardoned on repentance, no matter how suspect his past may have been."
> [Trajan. Quoted in *Letters, Trajan with Pliny, The Early Christians*, E. Arnold; 1970]

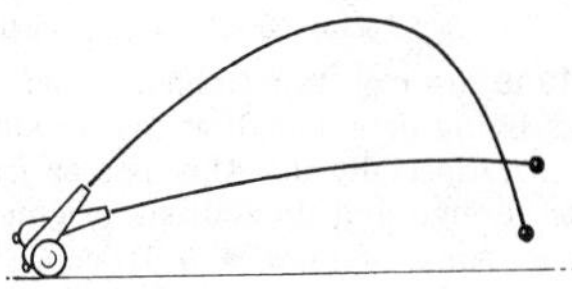

trajectory

tra·jec·to·ry /trə jéktəree/ (*plural* **-ries**) *n* **1.** PATH OF FLYING OBJECT the path that a projectile makes through space under the action of given forces such as thrust, wind, and gravity **2.** CURVE INTERSECTING AT CONSTANT ANGLE a curve or surface that intersects all of a family of curves or surfaces at a constant angle **3.** PATH OF PROCESS OR EVENT the way in which a process or event develops over a period of time [Late 17C. < medieval Latin *trajectorius* "relating to throwing across" < Latin *trajicere* "throw across, pass through" < *trans-* "across, over" + *jacere* "to throw"]

Traj·kov·ski /trī káwfskee/, **Boris** (1956–2004) president of the Former Yugoslav Republic of Macedonia (1999–2004). Representing the center-right Internal Macedonian Revolutionary Organization (VMRO), he was deputy minister of foreign affairs during the Kosovo crisis (1999) and became president later that year.

Tra·lee /trə leé/ town and administrative center of County Kerry, in the southwestern Republic of Ireland. Population: 20,375 (2002).

tram[1] /tram/ *n* **1.** same as **cable car 2.** *UK* same as **streetcar 3.** a small vehicle on rails used to carry coal and other materials in a coal mine [Early 16C. Origin ?]

tram[2] /tram/ (**trammed, tram·ming, trams**) *vt* to adjust or align mechanical parts accurately [Late 19C. < *tram-staff* "straight edge used to adjust a millstone spindle" < *tram* "instrument for drawing ellipses," shortening of TRAMMEL]

tram[3] /tram/ *n* heavy silk thread. Use: horizontal weave in velvet or silk. [Late 17C. Via French *trame* < Latin *trama* "woof of a web"]

~~**tramatic**~~ incorrect spelling of **traumatic**

tram·line /trám līn/ *UK n* a streetcar line ■ **tram·lines** *npl* a pair of parallel lines at either side of a tennis court delimiting the singles and doubles courts (*informal*)

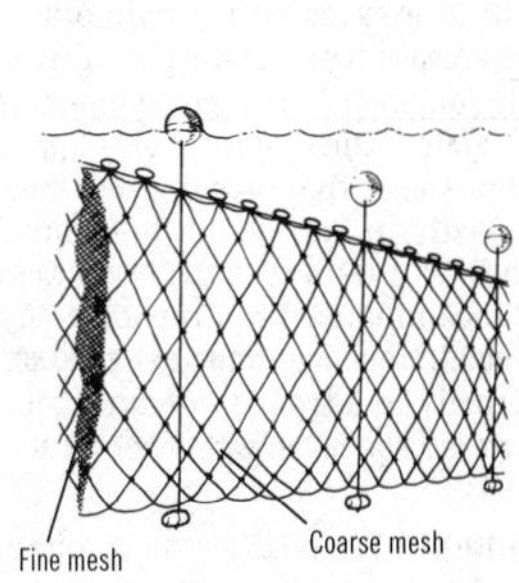

trammel (sense 2)

tram·mel /trámm'l/ *n* **1.** LIMITATION TO FREEDOM something that limits a person's freedom **2.** FISHING NET a fishing net consisting of a fine net between two layers of coarse mesh **3.** *US* SHACKLE a shackle used to teach a horse to amble **4.** DRAWING INSTRUMENT an instrument used to draw ellipses **5.** FIREPLACE HOOK a hook in a fireplace on which a kettle or pot can be hung and raised or lowered ■ *vt* (**-meled, -mel·ing, -mels**) **1.** CONFINE SOMEBODY to restrain somebody or something **2.** ENSNARE SOMETHING to catch or entangle somebody or something **3.** MECH ENG same as **tram**[2] [14C. Via Old French *tramail* < late Latin *tremaculum* < Latin *tres* "three" + *macula* "mesh"]

tra·mon·ta·na /traà mawn taánə/ *n* a cold dry wind that blows down from mountains, especially a north wind that blows into Italy from the Alps [Late 18C. Via Italian, "north wind" < Latin *transmontanus* "beyond the mountains" < *trans-* "across, over" + *mont-* "mountain"]

tra·mon·tane /trə món tàyn, trámmən-/ *adj* **1. BEYOND MOUNTAINS** living or situated on the far side of the mountains, especially the Alps as seen from Italy **2. FOREIGN** foreign and uncivilized, originally from an Italian point of view ■ *n* **1.** METEOROL same as **tramontana** **2. FOREIGNER** somebody from beyond mountains, especially from beyond the Alps as seen from Italy [Late 16C. Via Italian *tramontano* < Latin *transmontanus* (see TRANSMONTANE)]

tramp /tramp/ *n* **1. VAGRANT** a homeless person who travels on foot, often begging for a living **2. SOUND OF FEET** the sound of heavy footsteps or horses' hooves **3.** *UK* **LONG JOURNEY ON FOOT** a long and tiring journey on foot **4. HEAVY STEP** a heavy step or tread **5. OFFENSIVE TERM** an offensive term that deliberately insults a woman who is considered sexually promiscuous or who works as a prostitute **6. METAL PLATE ON BOOT** a metal plate that protects the sole of a boot when the wearer is digging **7. PART OF SPADE** the part of a spade on which the digger's foot presses ■ *v* (**tramped, tramp·ing, tramps**) **1.** *vi* **TREAD HEAVILY** to tread heavily or noisily **2.** *vi* **WALK** to walk, especially a long way **3.** *vt* **COVER DISTANCE ON FOOT** to traverse an area, especially wearily, or cover a distance in a steady weary way **4.** *vt* **CRUSH SOMETHING UNDERFOOT** to crush something by treading on it **5.** *vi* **LIVE AS VAGRANT** to live or wander aimlessly as a vagrant [14C. < Middle Low German *trampen* "to stamp"] —**tramp·er** *n* —**tramp·ing** *n* —**tramp·ish** *adj*

tram·ple /trámp'l/ (**-pled, -pling, -ples**) *vti* **1.** to tread heavily, or tread heavily on something or somebody so as to cause damage or injury **2.** to behave in an insulting contemptuous way, or treat somebody in an insulting contemptuous way [14C. < TRAMP] —**tram·pler** *n*

tram·po·line /trámpə leén/ *n* a strong sheet, usually of canvas, that is stretched tightly on a horizontal frame to which it is connected by springs. It is used for jumping and acrobatics. [Late 18C. < Italian *trampolino* "springboard" < *trampoli* "stilts"] —**tram·po·line** *vi* —**tram·po·lin·er** *n* —**tram·po·lin·ist** *n*

tramp steam·er *n* a merchant ship that carries cargo but does not follow a fixed route

tram·road /trám rōd/ *n* a small railroad used for moving freight, especially in a quarry

tram·way /trám wày/ *n* **1.** *US* a cable or the cables for a cable car **2.** TRANSP same as **tramroad**

trance /transs/ *n* **1. DAZED STATE** a state in which somebody is dazed or stunned or in some other way unaware of the environment and unable to respond to stimuli **2. HYPNOTIC STATE** a hypnotic or cataleptic state **3. RAPTUROUS STATE** a state of rapture or exaltation in which somebody loses consciousness **4. SPIRITUAL MEDIUM'S STATE** the state of apparent semi-unconsciousness that a spiritual medium enters into, allegedly in an attempt to communicate with the dead **5.** MUSIC **HYPNOTIC ELECTRONIC DANCE MUSIC** electronic dance music with a repetitive hypnotic beat ■ *vt* (**tranced, tranc·ing, tranc·es**) **ENTRANCE SOMEBODY** to put somebody in a trance (*literary*) [14C. < Old French *transe* < *transir* "be numb with fear" < Latin *transire* (see TRANSIENT)]

trance chan·nel·ing *n US* PSYCHOL same as **channeling**

tranche /traansh/ *n* a portion of an investment issue or loan [Mid-20C. < French, "slice" < Old French *trenchier* "to cut"]

tran·quil /trángkwəl, tránkwəl/ *adj* **1.** free of any disturbance or commotion ○ *a tranquil morning* **2.** free from or showing no signs of anxiety or agitation [Mid-15C. Via French < Latin *tranquillus*] —**tran·quil·ly** *adv* —**tran·quil·ness** *n*

tran·quil·ize /trángkwə lìz, tránkwə-/ (**-ized, -iz·ing, -iz·es**), **tran·quil·lize** *v* **1.** *vt* **MAKE SOMEBODY CALM WITH MEDICINE** to use medication to induce calmness in a person or animal **2.** *vi* **BECOME CALM** to become calm or calmer **3.** *vi* **HAVE CALMING EFFECT** to have a calming effect —**tran·quil·i·za·tion** /tràngkwəli záysh'n, trànkwəli-/ *n*

tran·quil·iz·er /trángkwə lìzər, tránkwə-/, **tran·quil·liz·er** *n* **1.** a medication that reduces anxiety and tension without affecting mental clarity. Use: treatment of anxiety, neuroses, psychoses. **2.** anything that renders a person or animal calm

tran·quil·li·ty /trang kwíllətee, tran-/, **tran·quil·i·ty** *n* a state of peace and calm [14C. Via French < Latin *tranquillitas* "quietness" < *tranquillus* "tranquil"]

tran·quil·lize *vti* another spelling of **tranquilize**

tran·quil·liz·er *n* another spelling of **tranquilizer**

trans. *abbr* **1.** BUSINESS transaction **2.** LAW transferred **3.** GRAM transitive **4.** LANGUAGE translated **5.** LANGUAGE translation **6.** TRANSP transportation **7.** MATH transpose **8.** MATH transverse

trans- *prefix* **1.** across, on the other side of, beyond ○ *transcontinental* ○ *transfinite* **2.** through ○ *transdermal* **3.** indicating change, transfer, or conversion ○ *transliterate* [< Latin *trans* "across, over, through"]

trans·act /tran zákt, -sákt/ (**-act·ed, -act·ing, -acts**) *vti* to conduct or carry out something such as business [Late 16C. Back-formation < TRANSACTION] —**trans·ac·tor** *n*

trans·ac·tin·ide /tran záktə nìd, -sáktə-/ *n* an element with an atomic number greater than 103 (*often used before a noun*)

trans·ac·tion /tran zákshən, -sákshən/ *n* **1. INSTANCE OF DOING BUSINESS** an instance of doing business of some kind, e.g., a purchase made in a shop or a withdrawal of funds from a bank account **2. ACT OF NEGOTIATING** the act of negotiating something or carrying out a business deal **3. INTERACTION** a communication or activity between two or more people that influences and affects all of them (*formal*) **4.** COMPUT **ADDITION TO DATABASE** an action that adds, removes, or changes data in a database or other computer program ■ **trans·ac·tions** *npl* **PROCEEDINGS** the published records of a learned society [Mid-15C. Via French < late Latin *transactiion-* < Latin *transigere* "drive through, accomplish" < *agere* "drive, do"] —**trans·ac·tion·al** *adj* —**trans·ac·tion·al·ly** *adv*

trans·ac·tion·al a·nal·y·sis *n* a form of psychotherapy that emphasizes the interactions within and between people and classifies these interactions as "adult," "parent," or "child"

trans·ac·tion·al im·mu·ni·ty *n* immunity from prosecution granted to a witness in any offense to which his or her testimony relates

trans·ac·ti·va·tion /tranz àkti váysh'n, transs-/ *n* the process whereby an infecting virus activates another virus's genes that are already integrated into the chromosome of the host bacterium, inducing the host cell to replicate the initial virus

trans·al·pine /tranz ál pìn, transs-/ *adj* **1. BEYOND ALPS** relating to or found in the area beyond the Alps, especially as seen from Italy **2. CROSSING ALPS** relating to or engaged in crossing the Alps ■ *n* **SOMEBODY FROM BEYOND ALPS** somebody who comes from beyond the Alps, especially as seen from Italy [Late 16C. < Latin *transalpinus* < *Alpes* "the Alps"]

trans·am·i·nase /tranz ámmi nàyss, -nàyz, transs-/ *n* an enzyme that catalyzes the transfer of an amino group in the process of transamination

trans·am·i·na·tion /tranz àmmi náysh'n, transs-/ *n* the formation of one amino acid from another

trans·at·lan·tic /trànzət lántik, trànsət-/ *adj* **1.** relating to or engaged in crossing the Atlantic **2.** situated on or coming from the other side of the Atlantic

trans·ax·le /tranz áks'l, transs-/ *n* a combined front axle and transmission in a motor vehicle with front-wheel drive [Mid-20C. < TRANSMISSION + AXLE]

trans·bor·der /trànz báwrdər, trànss-/ *adj* crossing national borders, especially electronically

trans·bound·a·ry /tranz bówndree, transs-/ *adj* crossing or existing across national boundaries

Trans·cau·ca·sia /trànss kaw káy<u>zh</u>ə, -káyzee ə/ region in southeastern Europe, south of the Caucasus Mountains, between the Black and Caspian seas, forming the southern part of Caucasia. It consists of the republics of Georgia, Armenia, and Azerbaijan. Area: 71,853 sq. mi./186,100 sq. km. —**Trans·cau·ca·sian** *adj*

trans·ceiv·er /transs seévər, tran-/ *n* **1.** a radio transmitter and receiver combined in a single, often portable unit **2.** a device that can receive and transmit data, e.g., a modem [Mid-20C. Blend of TRANSMITTER + RECEIVER]

tran·scend /tran sénd/ (**-scend·ed, -scend·ing, -scends**) *vt* **1. GO BEYOND LIMIT** to go beyond a limit or range, e.g., of thought or belief **2. SURPASS SOMETHING** to go beyond something in quality or achievement **3. BE INDEPENDENT OF WORLD** to exist above and apart from the material world [14C. Via French < Latin *transcendere* "climb over or beyond" < *scandere* "climb, mount"]

tran·scen·dent /tran séndənt/ *adj* **1. BETTER** superior in quality or achievement **2.** PHILOSOPHY **BEYOND LIMITS OF EXPERIENCE** in Kant's philosophical system, exceeding the limits of experience and therefore unknowable except hypothetically **3.** PHILOSOPHY **BEYOND CATEGORIES** above or outside all known categories **4.** RELIG **INDEPENDENT OF WORLD** existing outside the material universe and so not limited by it —**tran·scen·dence** *n* —**tran·scen·dent** *n* —**tran·scen·dent·ly** *adv*

tran·scen·den·tal /tràn sen dént'l/ *adj* **1.** PHILOSOPHY **NOT EXPERIENCED BUT KNOWABLE** independent of human experience of phenomena but within the range of knowledge **2. MYSTICAL** relating to mystical or supernatural experience and therefore beyond the material world **3.** same as **transcendent** (sense 1) **4.** MATH **NOT ALGEBRAIC** describes a number or function that is not algebraic and is not the root of an algebraic equation ■ *n* MATH **NUMBER IMPOSSIBLE TO EXPRESS AS INTEGER** a number that cannot be expressed as an integer, e.g., a nonrepeating decimal such as pi [Early 17C. < late Latin *transcendentalis* "transcending the bounds of all categories" < *transcendere* (see TRANSCEND)] —**tran·scen·den·tal·ly** *adv*

tran·scen·den·tal·ism /tràn sen dént'l ìzzəm/ *n* **1.** PHILOSOPHY **EMPHASIZING REASONING** a system of philosophy, especially that of Kant, that regards the processes of reasoning as the key to knowledge of reality **2.** PHILOSOPHY **EMPHASIZING DIVINE** a system of philosophy that emphasizes intuition as a means of knowing a spiritual reality and believes that divinity pervades nature and humanity. It is especially associated with Ralph Waldo Emerson and other New England writers. **3. TRANSCENDENTAL THOUGHT** transcendental thought or language **4. TRANSCENDENTAL NATURE** the state or quality of being transcendental —**tran·scen·den·tal·ist** *n, adj*

tran·scen·den·tal med·i·ta·tion *n* a form of meditation in which a mantra is repeated silently. It is based on Hindu traditions.

trans·con·ti·nen·tal /trànss kontə nént'l/ *adj* **1. ACROSS CONTINENT** extending across a continent **2. BEYOND CONTINENT** situated on or coming from the other side of a continent ■ *n* **TRAIN CROSSING CONTINENT** a train or railroad that crosses a continent —**trans·con·ti·nen·tal·ly** *adv*

tran·scribe /tran skrìb/ (**-scribed, -scrib·ing, -scribes**) *vt* **1. COPY SOMETHING** to write out an exact copy of something **2. EXPAND SOMETHING IN WRITING** to write something out in full from notes or shorthand **3. TRANSLATE SOMETHING** to translate or transliterate something **4.** PHON **WRITE SOUNDS PHONETICALLY** to write speech sounds phonetically **5.** MUSIC **REARRANGE MUSIC** to arrange a piece of music for a different instrument, voice, or combination **6.** BROADCAST **RECORD SOMETHING FOR LATER BROADCASTING** to record something so that it can be broadcast at a later time **7.** BROADCAST **BROADCAST SOMETHING TRANSCRIBED** to broadcast something that has been transcribed earlier **8.** COMPUT **TRANSFER SOMETHING TO OTHER STORAGE FORMAT** to transfer information from one way of storing it on computer to another, or from a computer to an external storage device **9.** GENETICS **CONVERT CODE FOR TRANSMISSION TO RNA** to convert the genetic code carried by DNA into an equivalent form carried by a molecule of messenger RNA **10.** GENETICS **CONVERT GENETIC CODE INTO DNA MOLECULE** to convert the genetic code carried by the RNA of a retrovirus into a molecule of DNA [Mid-16C. < Latin *transcribere* "copy, convey" < *scribere* "write"] —**tran·scrib·a·ble** *adj* —**tran·scrib·er** *n*

tran·script /trán skrìpt/ *n* **1. WRITTEN RECORD** a written record of something, e.g., a copy of the script of a broadcast program or a record of court proceedings

2. STUDENT'S ACADEMIC HISTORY an official document showing the educational work of a student in a school or college **3.** COPY any copy or record **4.** GENETICS RNA WITH TRANSCRIBED CODE a molecule of messenger RNA that carries coded genetic information converted from the genetic code held by the DNA during the process of transcription in living cells **5.** GENETICS DNA CARRYING CODED RETROVIRUS the DNA that carries the coded information of a retrovirus, converted from the genetic code held by the virus's RNA during transcription following the infection of a living cell [Mid-15C. < Latin *transcriptum* < past participle of *transcribere* (see TRANSCRIBE)]

tran·scrip·tase /tran skríp tàyss, -tàyz/ *n* an enzyme that catalyzes the synthesis of messenger RNA from a DNA template during transcription

tran·scrip·tion /tran skrípshən/ *n* **1.** TRANSCRIBING the act or process of transcribing something **2.** TRANSCRIPT something that has been transcribed **3.** PHON PHONETIC REPRESENTATION a phonetic representation of speech using special symbols **4.** GENETICS TRANSFER OF GENETIC CODE the first step in carrying out genetic instructions in living cells, in which the genetic code is transferred from DNA to molecules of messenger RNA, which subsequently direct protein manufacture **5.** GENETICS TRANSFER OF GENETIC INFORMATION the first step in the replication of a retrovirus following its infection of a living cell, in which its genetic code is transferred from RNA to a molecule of DNA —**tran·scrip·tion·al** *adj*

tran·scrip·tive /tran skríptiv/ *adj* used for transcribing or in the form of a transcript —**tran·scrip·tive·ly** *adv*

tran·scrip·tome /tran skríp tòm/ *n* the full complement of unique sequenced RNA molecules with coded genetic information **(transcripts)** that an individual produces

tran·scrip·tom·ics /trànskrip tómmiks/ *n* the scientific classification and analysis of RNA molecules with coded genetic information **(transcripts)** and their formation, structure, and function in an individual (*takes a singular verb*) —**tran·scrip·tom·ic** *adj*

trans·cul·tur·al /transs kúlchərəl/ *adj* extending across cultures or involving more than one culture

trans·cul·tu·ra·tion /trànss kúlchə ráysh'n/ *n* the change in a culture brought about by the diffusion within it of aspects from other cultures

trans·cur·rent /transs kúr ənt, -kúrrənt/ *adj* running across something, especially perpendicular to an expected direction or flow [Early 17C. < Latin *transcurrent-*, present participle of *transcurrere* "run across, traverse" < *currere* "to run"]

trans·cu·ta·ne·ous /trànss kyoo táynee əss/ *adj* MED same as **transdermal**

trans·cu·ta·ne·ous e·lec·tri·cal nerve stim·u·la·tion *n* MED full form of **TENS**

trans·der·mal /tranz dúrm'l, transs-/ *adj* describes something, especially a drug, that is introduced into the body through the skin

trans·der·mal patch *n* a medicated patch applied to the skin. Use: controlled release of medicine into the body.

trans·duce /tranz dóoss, transs-/ (**-duced, -duc·ing, -duc·es**) *vt* **1.** to change one type of energy into another type **2.** to effect the transfer of genetic material from one bacterium to another using a bacteriophage [Mid-20C. Back-formation < TRANSDUCER]

trans·duc·er /tranz dóossər, transs-/ *n* **1.** a device that transforms one type of energy into another, e.g., a microphone, a photoelectric cell, or an automobile horn **2.** a biological entity that converts energy in one form to another, e.g., the rods and cones of the eye or the hair cells of the ear [Early 20C. < Latin *transducere* "lead across, transfer" (see TRADUCE)]

trans·duc·tion /tranz dúksh'n, transs-/ *n* **1.** the transfer of genetic material from one bacterium to another using a bacteriophage **2.** the conversion of stimuli detected in receptor cells to electrical impulses that are then transported by the nervous system, as occurs when the ear converts sound waves into nerve impulses —**trans·duc·tion·al** *adj*

tran·sect /tran sékt/ *vt* (**-sect·ed, -sect·ing, -sects**) to divide something by running or cutting across it ■ *n* a strip of ground along which ecological measurements, e.g., of the number of organisms, are made at regular intervals [Mid-17C. < TRANS- + INTERSECT] —**tran·sec·tion** *n*

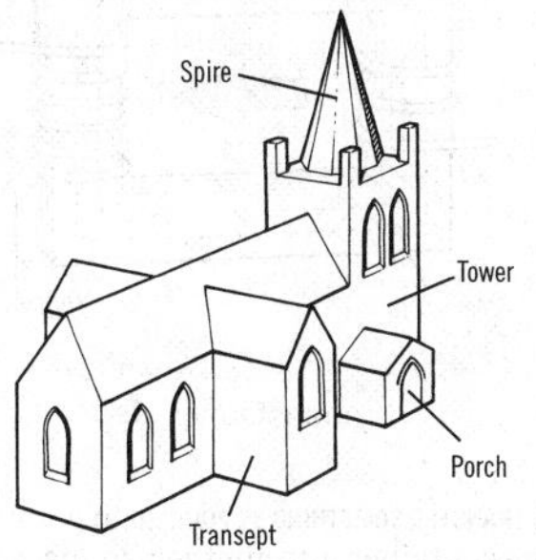

transept

tran·sept /trán sèpt/ *n* **1.** a portion of a cross-shaped church that runs at right angles to the long central part **(nave) 2.** either of the two arms of a transept [Mid-16C. < modern Latin *transeptum* < Latin *trans-* "across" + *saeptum* "enclosure, wall, fence"] —**tran·sep·tal** /tran sépt'l/ *adj*

tran·se·unt /tránssee ənt/, **tran·sient** /tránshənt, tránzhənt, tránzee ənt/ *adj* producing effects outside the mind

transf. *abbr* transferred

trans-fat·ty ac·id /trànss fáttee-/, **trans-fat** /tránss fàt/ *n* an unsaturated fat formed during the hydrogenation of vegetable oils to produce margarine. Trans-fatty acids are viewed as a health risk because they raise cholesterol levels.

trans·fec·tion /transs fékshən/ *n* the infection of a cell with viral DNA leading to production of the virus in the cell [Mid-20C. < TRANS- + INFECTION] —**trans·fect** *vt*

trans·fer *v* /transs fúr, tránss fùr/ (**-ferred, -fer·ring, -fers**) **1.** *vti* MOVE FROM ONE PLACE TO ANOTHER to move from one place to another, or cause somebody or something to do so **2.** *vti* PASS FROM ONE PERSON TO ANOTHER to pass from one person, group, or organization to another, or cause something to be passed from one person, group, or organization to another **3.** *vti* START WORKING ELSEWHERE to employ somebody at a different job or in a different place while working for the same company, or begin employment in such circumstances ○ *transfer to the Chicago branch* **4.** *vti* CHANGE VEHICLES to change from one vehicle or method of transportation to another, or cause somebody to do this **5.** *vti* CHANGE SCHOOLS OR SUBJECTS to move from one school or university to another, or change from one course to another **6.** *vt* LAW CHANGE OWNERSHIP OF SOMETHING to pass ownership rights in something to somebody else ○ *transfer a deed* **7.** *vt* PUT IMAGE ON ANOTHER SURFACE to copy a design or image from a piece of paper onto a different material ■ *n* /tránss fùr/ **1.** CHANGE OF PLACE the conveying of somebody or something from one place or position to another **2.** TICKET ALLOWING PASSENGER TO TRANSFER a ticket that allows a passenger to change from one vehicle to another on a journey, or the place where this is done **3.** SOMEBODY TRANSFERRED somebody who is transferred, e.g., a student **4.** LAW CONVEYANCE the passing of rights or property from one person to another, or a document that conveys rights or property between people **5.** DESIGN APPLIED TO SURFACE an image on a piece of film or paper that is specially designed to be lifted off by heat or pressure and applied permanently to the surface of a material **6.** FIN RECORDING OF SALE the recording of a change of ownership of shares or bonds in the books of the issuer [14C. < Latin *transferre* "carry across" < *ferre* "carry"] —**trans·fer·al** /transs fúr əl/ *n* —**trans·fer·ee** /trànsfə rée/ *n*

trans·fer·a·ble /transs fúr əb'l/, **trans·fer·ra·ble** *adj* able to be transferred, especially to somebody else's ownership —**trans·fer·a·bil·i·ty** /transs fùr ə bíllətee, trànsfərə-/ *n*

trans·fer·a·ble skill *n* a skill that is not limited to a particular academic discipline, area of knowledge, job, or task and is useful in any work situation, e.g., communication or organizational skills

trans·fer·ase /tránsfə ràyss, -ràyz/ *n* any enzyme that catalyzes the transfer of a chemical group from one molecule to another

trans·fer char·ac·ter·is·tic *n* a graphical illustration of the relationship between the input and output of an electronic system

~~**transfered**~~ incorrect spelling of **transferred**

trans·fer·ence /tránsfərənss, transs fúr ənss/ *n* **1.** ACT OF TRANSFERRING the transferring of something from one place or person to another **2.** PROCESS OF BEING TRANSFERRED the change from one person or place to another that happens when something is transferred **3.** PSYCHOL REDIRECTION OF FEELING in psychoanalysis or other psychotherapy, the process in which somebody unconsciously redirects feelings about something onto a new object, often the analyst or therapist —**trans·fer·en·tial** /trànsfə rénsh'l/ *adj*

trans·fer fac·tor *n* a polypeptide that is produced by white blood cells and can transfer immunity from one cell to another or from one person to another

trans·fer·or /trànsfə ráwr/, **trans·fer·rer** /transs fúr ər/ *n* somebody who transfers a title, right, or property to somebody else

trans·fer pay·ment *n* an item of personal income that comes from the state or a financial institution and is not investment income or payment for goods or services

trans·fer·ra·ble *adj* another spelling of **transferable**

trans·fer·rer *n* LAW another spelling of **transferor**

trans·fer·rin /transs férrin/ *n* a serum protein that transports iron to bone marrow for the production of red blood cells [Mid-20C. < TRANS- + Latin *ferrum* "iron"]

trans·fer RNA *n* RNA that attaches amino acids to protein chains being made at ribosomes

trans·fig·u·ra·tion /transs fíggyə ráysh'n/ *n* **1.** a dramatic change in appearance, especially one that reveals great beauty, spirituality, or magnificence **2.** the transfiguring of somebody or something

Trans·fig·u·ra·tion /transs fíggyə ráysh'n/ *n* **1.** in Christianity, the sudden appearance of radiant light emanating from Jesus Christ, recorded in the Bible as happening on a mountaintop in front of three of his disciples **2.** a Christian festival marking the Transfiguration of Jesus Christ. Date: August 6 or, in the Eastern Orthodox Church, August 19.

trans·fig·ure /transs fíggyər/ (**-ured, -ur·ing, -ures**) *vt* to transform the appearance of somebody or something, revealing great beauty, spirituality, or magnificence [14C. < Latin *transfigurare* "change the shape of" < *figura* "shape" (see FIGURE)] —**trans·fig·ure·ment** *n*

trans·fi·nite /transs fí nìt/ *adj* describes a mathematical entity such as a number, group, or quantity that extends beyond infinity [Early 20C. < German *transfinit* < Latin *trans-* "across, over" + *finitus* "finite, limited"]

trans·fi·nite num·ber *n* a system of cardinal and ordinal numbers, used in the comparison of infinite sets, to which several types of infinity can be assigned concurrently

trans·fix /transs fíks/ (**-fixed, -fix·ing, -fix·es**) *vt* **1.** MAKE SOMEBODY IMMOBILE WITH SHOCK to shock or terrify somebody so much as to induce a momentary inability to move **2.** PIERCE THROUGH SOMEBODY to pierce somebody or something through with a weapon or other sharp object **3.** MED CUT COMPLETELY THROUGH LIMB to cut through a part of the body completely, e.g., when amputating a limb [Late 16C. Directly or via Old French *transfixer* < Latin *transfix-*, past participle of *transfigere* "pierce, run through" < *figere* "to fix"] —**trans·fix·ion** *n*

trans·form *v* /transs fáwrm/ (**-formed, -form·ing, -forms**) **1.** *vt* CHANGE SOMETHING DRAMATICALLY to change somebody or something completely, especially improving their appearance or usefulness **2.** *vi* UNDERGO TOTAL CHANGE to change completely for the better **3.** *vt* PHYS CONVERT SOMETHING TO DIFFERENT ENERGY to convert one form of energy to another **4.** *vt* ELEC ENG CHANGE ELECTRICAL CURRENT BY TRANSFORMER to increase or decrease current or voltage by means of a transformer **5.** *vt* MATH **CHANGE MATHEMATICAL EXPRESSION BY OPERATOR** to change the form of a mathematical expression in keeping with a mathematical rule, especially by the substitution of variables or the change of coordinates **6.** *vt* LING **CHANGE CONSTRUCTION BY LINGUISTIC TRANSFORMATION** to apply transformational rules to a linguistic construction ■ *n* /tránss fawrm/ **1.** LING same as **transformation** (sense 9) **2. RESULT OF MATHEMATICAL TRANSFORMATION** a process or rule by which one mathematical entity such as a line or expression can be derived from another [14C. Directly or via French *transformer* < Latin *transformare* "form across" < *formare* < *forma* "mold, shape"] —**trans·form·a·ble** *adj* —**trans·form·a·tive** *adj*

SYNONYMS See *change.*

trans·for·ma·tion /trànsfər máysh'n/ *n* **1. COMPLETE CHANGE** a complete change, usually into something with an improved appearance or usefulness **2. TRANSFORMING** the act or process of transforming somebody or something **3.** MATH **SUBSTITUTION OF VARIABLES** the mathematical conversion of an expression, equation, or function into another equivalent entity, e.g., by the substitution of one set of variables with another **4.** GENETICS **GENETIC CHANGE** a permanent change in the genetic makeup of a cell when it acquires foreign DNA **5.** BIOL **CELL MODIFICATION** the conversion of a normal cell into a malignant cell brought about by the action of a carcinogen or virus **6.** MATH **CHANGE IN POSITION OF AXIS** a change in the position or direction of the axes of a mathematical coordinate system without changing their relative angles **7.** PHYS **CHANGE IN ATOMIC NUCLEUS** the change of one type of atom to another, resulting from a nuclear reaction **8.** LING **STAGE IN GRAMMATICAL CONVERSION** in transformational grammar, the process of converting one linguistic construction or structure to another, following the rules that convert deep structure to surface structure **9.** LING **STAGE IN GRAMMATICAL CONVERSION** in transformational grammar, a construction or structure generated by using the rules that convert deep structure into surface structure **10.** THEATER **SUDDEN SET CHANGE** a sudden changing of a stage set that takes place in sight of the audience —**trans·for·ma·tion·al** *adj* —**trans·for·ma·tion·al·ly** *adv*

USAGE transformation, transmigration, or **transmutation?** ***Transformation*** means "a complete change, usually into something with an improved appearance or usefulness" (*a transformation of the dingy attic into a sunny loft*). ***Transmutation*** is "a change, or the process of changing, from one form, substance, nature, or state into another" (*the transmutation of society from industrial to postindustrial; the transmutation of base metals into gold by alchemy*). It is rather close in meaning to ***transformation***. The two senses of ***transmigration*** are not shared by ***transformation*** and ***transmutation***: "movement from one place to another" (*a huge transmigration of geese from Canada to Florida*), and "the supposed passage of a decedent's soul into another body" (*transmigration of the soul*). Problems occur when people use ***transmigration*** when either ***transformation*** or ***transmutation*** is the correct choice: *an obvious transformation/transmutation* [not *transmigration*] *in attitude from liberal to conservative.*

trans·for·ma·tion·al gram·mar *n* grammar that is based on the theory that language has a deep structure and that there are rules that transform the deep structure into the surface structure. It uses transformational rules to describe a language.

trans·for·ma·tion·al rule *n* **1.** in transformational grammar, a rule that generates one stage from another in the conversion of deep structure into surface structure **2.** in logic, a rule for deriving theorems from axioms

trans·form·er /transs fáwrmər/ *n* **1.** a device that transfers electrical energy from one alternating circuit to another with a change in voltage, current, phase, or impedance **2.** somebody or something that effects a transformation

trans·fuse /transs fyo͞oz/ (**-fused, -fus·ing, -fus·es**) *vt* **1.** MED **GIVE BLOOD TO SOMEBODY** to administer blood obtained from one person into the bloodstream of another person **2.** MED **PUT FLUID INTO SOMEBODY'S BLOODSTREAM** to administer a fluid such as saline or plasma into somebody's bloodstream to replace lost

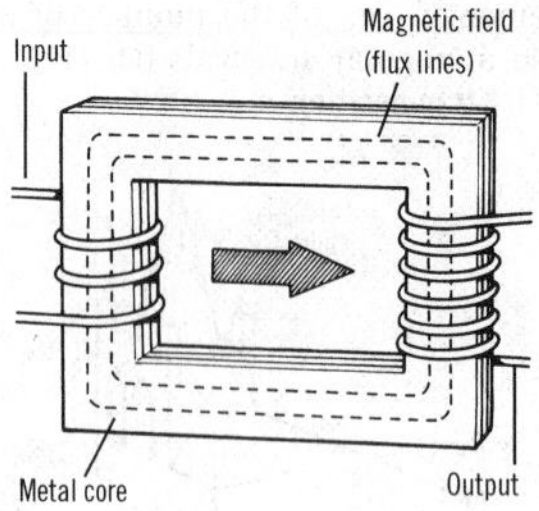

transformer

fluid **3. TRANSFER SOMETHING BY POURING** to pour something from one container into another (*formal or technical*) **4. SPREAD THROUGHOUT SOMETHING** to spread throughout something and affect every part of it [Early 15C. < Latin *transfus-*, past participle of *transfundere* "decant, transfer" < *fundere* "pour"] —**trans·fus·a·ble** *adj* —**trans·fus·er** *n* —**trans·fu·sive** *adj*

trans·fu·sion /transs fyo͞ozh'n/ *n* **1.** the transfer of whole blood, blood components, or bone marrow from a healthy donor into the bloodstream of somebody who has lost blood or who has a blood disorder **2.** the act or process of transfusing something

trans·gen·der /transs jéndər, tranz-/, **trans·gen·dered** /-jéndərd/ *adj* relating to transsexuals or transvestites —**trans·gen·der** *n*

trans·gene /tránss jeen, tránz-/ *n* a gene transferred from one organism to another

trans·gen·ic /transs jénnik, tranz-/ *adj* **1.** describes an animal or plant that contains genes from a different species, transferred using the techniques of genetic modification **2.** describes the technique of transferring genetic material from one organism into the DNA of another —**trans·gen·i·cal·ly** *adv* —**trans·gen·e·sis** /tranz jénnəsiss/ *n*

trans·gress /tranz gréss/ (**-gressed, -gress·ing, -gress·es**) *v* **1.** *vt* **BREAK LAW** to break a law, rule, or moral code ○ *transgress the law* **2.** *vi* **DO WRONG** to commit a crime or do wrong by disobeying a law, command, or moral code ○ *He transgressed against the organization's code of conduct.* **3.** *vt* **OVERSTEP PROPER LIMIT** to go beyond a limit, usually in a blameworthy way ○ *She'd transgressed the bounds of civil behavior.* [15C. Directly or via French *transgresser* < Latin *transgress-*, past participle of *transgredi* "step across, go over" < *gradi* "to step, go"] —**trans·gres·sive** *adj* —**trans·gres·sive·ly** *adv* —**trans·gres·sor** *n*

trans·gres·sion /tranz grésh'n/ *n* **1. ACTION VIOLATING LAW OR CODE** a crime or any act that violates a law, command, or moral code **2. COMMISSION OF WRONGS** the committing of acts that violate a law, command, or moral code **3. OVERSTEPPING LIMIT** an act or the process of overstepping a limit

trans·gres·sive fic·tion *n* a literary genre characterized by graphic exploration of taboo topics, to which the work of writers such as the Marquis de Sade and William Burroughs belongs. It is based on the belief that knowledge is to be found at the very edge of human experience.

tran·ship *vti* TRANSP another spelling of **transship**

trans·hu·mance /transs hyo͞omənss/ *n* the practice of moving livestock between different grazing lands according to season, especially up to mountain pastures in summer and back down into the valleys in winter [Early 20C. < French < *transhumer* "go across ground" < Latin *humus* "ground"] —**trans·hu·mant** *adj*

tran·sient /tránshənt, tránzhənt, tránzee ənt/ *adj* **1. SHORT IN DURATION** lasting for only a short time and quickly coming to an end, disappearing, or changing ○ *a transient emotion* ○ *transient sunlight on an otherwise cloudy day* **2. NOT PERMANENTLY SETTLED IN PLACE** staying in a place for only a short period of time ○ *transient workers* **3.** PHILOSOPHY same as **transeunt** ■ *n* **1. SOMEBODY STAYING BRIEFLY** somebody who stays in a place only briefly, e.g., a migrant laborer or hotel guest **2.** ELEC ENG **BRIEF DISTURBANCE IN ELECTRICAL CIRCUIT** an oscillation or brief disturbance in a system, e.g., a sudden pulse of current or voltage in an electrical circuit [Late 16C. Alteration of Latin *transiens* (stem *transeunt-*), present participle of *transire* "pass away, go across" < *ire* "go"] —**tran·sience** *n* —**tran·sien·cy** *n* —**tran·sient·ly** *adv*

tran·sient i·sche·mic at·tack *n* MED same as **ministroke** (*technical*)

trans·il·lu·mi·nate /trànzi lo͞omə nàyt/ (**-nat·ed, -nat·ing, -nates**) *vt* to shine a bright light through a body organ or cavity to detect disease or other anomaly —**trans·il·lu·mi·na·tion** /trànzi lo͞omə náysh'n/ *n* —**trans·il·lu·mi·na·tor** *n*

tran·sis·tor /tran zístər/ *n* **1.** a small low-powered solid-state electronic device consisting of a semiconductor and at least three electrodes, used as an amplifier and rectifier and frequently incorporated into integrated circuit chips **2.** HOUSEHOLD same as **transistor radio** [Mid-20C. Blend of TRANSFER + RESISTOR]

tran·sis·tor·ize /tran zístə rīz/ (**-ized, -iz·ing, -iz·es**) *vt* to equip a device or circuit with transistors

tran·sis·tor ra·di·o *n* a small portable radio that uses transistors in its circuits

tran·sit /tránzit/ *n* **1. ACT OF TRAVEL ACROSS SOMETHING** the act of traveling or being transported through or across an area, over a distance, or from one place to another ○ *a transit permit* **2.** TRANSP **PUBLIC TRANSPORTATION** the transportation of passengers by means of a local public transportation system ○ *traveled by rapid transit* **3. PUBLIC TRANSPORT SYSTEM** a local public transportation system ○ *city transit* **4.** ASTRON **MOVEMENT OF PLANET ACROSS SUN** the movement of Venus or Mercury across the face of the Sun, or of a moon or its shadow across the face of a planet, as seen from Earth **5.** ASTRON **PASSAGE OF STAR ACROSS MERIDIAN** the apparent movement of a star or planet across the meridian from which it is being observed, caused by the Earth's rotation **6.** ASTROL **CROSSING OF ZODIAC BY PLANET** the passing of a planet across a specific point on the zodiac **7. TRANSITION** a transition or passing, e.g., from life to a supposed spiritual existence after death **8.** CIV ENG **SURVEYING INSTRUMENT** a surveying instrument surmounted by a telescope that can be rotated completely around its horizontal axis, used for measuring vertical and horizontal angles ■ *v* (**-sit·ed, -sit·ing, -sits**) **1.** *vti* **PASS THROUGH SOMETHING** to pass through, over, or across something ○ *They transited the area on foot.* **2.** *vti* ASTRON **MAKE ASTRONOMICAL TRANSIT** to make a transit across the face of the Sun or a planet, or across a meridian **3.** *vt* CIV ENG **REVERSE DIRECTION OF SURVEYING TELESCOPE** to rotate the telescope of a surveying instrument horizontally through 180°, thus reversing its direction [15C. < Latin *transitus* "passage" < *transire* "go across" < *ire* "go"] —**tran·sit·a·ble** *adj* ◇ **in transit** in the process of traveling or being transported from one place to another

tran·sit cir·cle *n* an astronomical telescope that moves in a north-south plane so that it can be used to determine the exact time at which a star, planet, or other astronomical object passes directly overhead

tran·sit in·stru·ment *n* a telescopic instrument that can move only in the plane of a meridian, used to determine the exact time at which a star, planet, or other astronomical object crosses that meridian

tran·si·tion /tran zísh'n/ *n* **1. PROCESS OF CHANGE** a process or period in which something undergoes a change and passes from one state, stage, form, or activity to another **2.** MUSIC **MUSICAL PASSAGE** a passage connecting two sections of a musical composition **3.** MUSIC **CHANGE OF KEY** a progression from one key to another in a piece of music **4.** GRAM **LINKING WORD OR PHRASE** a word, phrase, or passage that links one subject or idea to another in speech or writing **5.** PHYS, CHEM **CHANGE BETWEEN PHASES** a change between phases such as solid to liquid or liquid to gas **6.** ARCHIT **STYLE BETWEEN ROMANESQUE AND GOTHIC** a style of architecture in many buildings dating from the 12th century in western Europe, in which the Romanesque and Gothic styles are combined **7.** PHYS **CHANGE IN ATOMIC NUCLEUS** a change in the energy level or state of an atomic nucleus in which a single quantum of electromagnetic radiation is either lost or gained ■ *vti* (**-tioned, -tion·ing, -tions**) **CAUSE TO CHANGE** to undergo a change of status or condition, or cause somebody or something to undergo a change (*informal*) ○ *"We must transition Social Security from a pay-as-you-go fund to a true pension fund."* (*Speech by H. Ross Perot, Asbury Park Press* 1996) [15C. < Latin *transition-* < *transire* (see TRANSIT)] —**tran·si·tion·al** *adj*

tran·si·tion el·e·ment, tran·si·tion met·al *n* a metallic element such as copper or gold that has an incomplete penultimate electron shell and variable valences, and typically forms colored compounds

tran·si·tion point *n* PHYS same as **transition temperature**

tran·si·tion tem·per·a·ture *n* the temperature at which a substance loses or gains a specific property, especially superconductivity

tran·si·tive /tránzitiv/ *adj* **1.** GRAM needing or usually taking a direct object ○ *a transitive verb* **2.** LOGIC describes a given relation between terms such that if it exists between "a" and "b" and between "b" and "c," then it also exists between "a" and "c." Typical transitive relationships include "is greater than," "is equal to," and "is similar to." —**tran·si·tive·ly** *adv* —**tran·si·tive·ness** *n* —**tran·si·tiv·i·ty** /trànzi tívvətee/ *n*

tran·sit lounge *n* a waiting room at an international airport used mainly by passengers transferring from one flight to another without presenting themselves to customs or immigration officials

tran·si·to·ry /tránzə tàwree/ *adj* not permanent or lasting, but existing only for a short time ○ *a transitory infatuation* —**tran·si·to·ri·ly** /trànzə táwrəlee/ *adv* —**tran·si·to·ri·ness** *n*

SYNONYMS See ***temporary.***

tran·sit pas·sen·ger *n* a passenger at an airport who is there simply to change flights and is therefore not required to go through customs or immigration formalities

tran·sit the·od·o·lite *n UK* same as **transit** *n* (sense 8)

Trans·kei /trànss kī/ former homeland in South Africa, now part of Eastern Cape Province

transl. *abbr* **1.** translated **2.** translation **3.** translator

trans·late /transs láyt, tranz-/ (**-lat·ed, -lat·ing, -lates**) *v* **1.** *vti* **TURN WORDS INTO DIFFERENT LANGUAGE** to reproduce a written or spoken text in a different language while retaining the original meaning ○ *Can you translate that phrase?* **2.** *vi* **BE CAPABLE OF BEING TRANSLATED** to be capable of being translated, or have an equivalent in another language ○ *The idiom doesn't translate well.* **3.** *vt* **CONVERT CODE** to convert computer data to a different form according to an algorithm ○ *translate the program into machine code* **4.** *vt* **SAY SOMETHING IN UNDERSTANDABLE TERMS** to say or explain something in terms that are easier to understand ○ *The attendant muttered something vague, which, when translated, meant "We don't know what happened to your car."* **5.** *vt* **INTERPRET MEANING** to explain the meaning of something not expressed in words, e.g., an action, gesture, or look ○ *I translated his silence as approval.* **6.** *vti* **CHANGE FORM OF SOMETHING** to change something from one form or effect into another, or be changed from one form or effect into another ○ *"Microchips controlled by software now translate the flick of a pilot's wrist into the movement of a wing flap."* (*Discover Magazine*; May 1996) **7.** *vt* **MOVE SOMEBODY OR SOMETHING** to move or carry somebody or something from one place to another, usually with a complete change of condition or scene ○ *She was translated from her small country home to a high-rise city apartment.* **8.** *vt* CHR **TRANSFER CLERGY** to transfer a member of the clergy to another office, especially a bishop to another see **9.** *vt* CHR **MOVE REMAINS OF SAINT** to move the remains or relics of a saint from one place to another **10.** *vt* RELIG **CONVEY SOMEBODY TO HEAVEN** to convey somebody to heaven, especially in a way that is believed not to involve death **11.** *vt* GENETICS **DECIPHER GENETIC INSTRUCTIONS FOR MAKING PROTEIN** to decipher the genetic message carried by a molecule of messenger RNA and assemble the amino acids of a protein chain according to the instructions **12.** *vt* PHYS **MOVE BODY SIDEWAYS IN STRAIGHT LINE** to move a body sideways through space in a direct straight line without rotation [14C. < Latin *translatus*, used as past participle of *transferre* "carry across" < *ferre* "carry"] —**trans·lat·a·bil·i·ty** /trans làytə bílləteе, tranz-/ *n* —**trans·lat·a·ble** *adj*

trans·la·tion /transs láysh'n, tranz-/ *n* **1. VERSION IN ANOTHER LANGUAGE** a word, phrase, or text in another language that has a meaning equivalent to that of the original **2. EXPRESSING OF SOMETHING IN DIFFERENT LANGUAGE** the rendering of something written or spoken in one language in words of a different language ○ *It loses a little in translation.* **3. CHANGE OR TRANSFERENCE** a change in form or state, or transference to a different place, office, or sphere **4.** GENETICS **PROCESS DETERMINING AMINO ACID SEQUENCE** the process by which information in messenger RNA directs the sequence of amino acids assembled by a ribosome during protein synthesis **5.** PHYS **MOTION IN STRAIGHT LINE** the movement of a body in a straight line so that every point on the body follows a parallel path and no rotation takes place —**trans·la·tion·al** *adj*

trans·la·tor /transs láytər, tranz-/ *n* **1.** LANGUAGE **SOMEBODY WHO TRANSLATES** somebody or something that translates, in writing or speech, from one language into another **2.** BROADCAST **TRANSMITTER THAT ALTERS SIGNAL FREQUENCY** a radio transmitter that receives a signal on one frequency and retransmits it on another **3.** COMPUT **COMPUTER CONVERSION PROGRAM** a computer program that converts other programs from one computer language into another —**trans·la·to·ri·al** /trànslə táwree əl, trànzlə-/ *adj*

trans·lit·er·ate /transs líttə ràyt, tranz-/ (**-at·ed, -at·ing, -ates**) *vt* to represent letters or words written in one alphabet using the corresponding letters of another [Mid-19C. < TRANS- + Latin *littera* "letter of the alphabet"] —**trans·lit·er·a·tion** /trans líttə ráysh'n, tranz-/ *n* —**trans·lit·er·a·tor** *n*

trans·lo·cate /transs lṓ kàyt, tranz-/ (**-cat·ed, -cat·ing, -cates**) *vt* to move somebody or something from one place or position to another

trans·lo·ca·tion /transs lō káysh'n, tranz-/ *n* **1. MOVEMENT FROM ONE PLACE TO ANOTHER** movement, or the act of moving something or somebody, from one place or position to another **2.** BOT **MOVEMENT OF FOOD IN PLANTS** the movement of soluble materials within a plant. Common examples are the movement of food materials from the leaves to storage organs, and the movement of dissolved minerals upward from the roots. **3.** GENETICS **TRANSFER OF PART OF CHROMOSOME** the transfer of part of a chromosome to a new position on the same or on a different chromosome with resultant rearrangement of the genes

trans·lu·cent /transs lo͞os'nt, tranz-/ *adj* **1.** allowing light to pass through, but only diffusely, so that objects on the other side cannot be clearly distinguished ○ *a translucent membrane* **2.** having a glowing appearance, as if light were coming through ○ *translucent skin* [15C. < Latin *translucent-*, present participle of *translucere* "shine through" < *lucere* "shine" (see LUCID)] —**trans·lu·cence** *n* —**trans·lu·cen·cy** *n* —**trans·lu·cent·ly** *adv*

trans·lu·nar /transs lo͞onər, tranz-/, **trans·lu·nar·y** /-lo͞onəree/ *adj* situated or coming from beyond the Moon or its orbit around the Earth

trans·ma·rine /trànzmə re͞en/ *adj* **1.** involving crossing a sea or ocean **2.** situated or coming from across a sea or ocean [Late 16C. < Latin *transmarinus* < *marinus* (see MARINE)]

trans·mi·grate /tranz mī gràyt/ (**-grat·ed, -grat·ing, -grates**) *vi* **1.** to move from one place or country to another **2.** according to some religions, to pass into another body at or after death (*refers to the soul*) [15C. < Latin *transmigrat-*, past participle of *transmigrare* < *migrare* "migrate"] —**trans·mi·grant** *adj, n* —**trans·mi·gra·tive** /tranz mīgrətiv/ *adj* —**trans·mi·gra·tor** *n* —**trans·mi·gra·to·ry** /tranz mīgrə tàwree/ *adj*

trans·mi·gra·tion /trànz mī gráysh'n/ *n* **1.** movement by a person or group from one place or country to another **2.** according to some religions, the supposed passage of the dead person's soul into another body at or after death [13C. Directly or via French < late Latin *transmigration-* < Latin *transmigrare* (see TRANSMIGRATE)] —**trans·mi·gra·tion·al** *adj*

USAGE See ***transformation.***

trans·mis·si·ble /tranz míssəb'l/ *adj* able to be transmitted —**trans·mis·si·bil·i·ty** /tranz mìssə bílləti/ *n*

trans·mis·si·ble spong·i·form en·ceph·a·lop·a·thy *n* VET full form of **TSE**

trans·mis·sion /tranz mísh'n/ *n* **1. ACT OF TRANSMITTING** the act or process of transmitting something, especially radio signals, radio or television broadcasts, data, or a disease **2. SOMETHING TRANSMITTED** something transmitted, e.g., a radio signal **3.** BROADCAST **RADIO OR TV BROADCAST** a radio or television broadcast **4.** AUTOMOT **MECHANISM TRANSFERRING POWER TO WHEELS** the mechanical system, including gears and shafts, by which power is transmitted from the engine of a motor vehicle to the drive wheels **5.** AUTOMOT **SET OF GEARS** a set of gears and the protective casing that covers this in a vehicle or engine **6.** PHYS **ABILITY TO LET RADIATION THROUGH** the ability of a material to let incoming radiation pass completely through it [Early 17C. Directly or via French < Latin *transmission-* < *mission-* "a letting go, release" (see MISSION)] —**trans·mis·sive** /tranz míssiv/ *adj* —**trans·mis·sive·ly** *adv* —**trans·mis·sive·ness** *n*

trans·mis·sion line *n* a conductor that carries electricity or other electromagnetic waves, usually over long distances, e.g., a coaxial cable

trans·mit /tranz mít/ (**-mit·ted, -mit·ting, -mits**) *v* **1.** *vt* **SEND SOMETHING** to send something, pass something on, or cause something to spread, from one person, thing, or place to another ○ *The disease is transmitted by droplet infection.* **2.** *vt* **COMMUNICATE INFORMATION** to communicate a message, information, or news ○ *Data was quickly transmitted.* **3.** *vti* TELECOM, MEDIA **SEND SIGNAL** to send a signal by radio waves, satellite, or wire **4.** *vti* BROADCAST **BROADCAST PROGRAM** to broadcast a radio or television program **5.** *vt* PHYS **MAKE RADIATION PASS THROUGH SOMETHING** to make heat, sound, light, or other radiation pass or spread through space or a medium **6.** *vt* PHYS **ALLOW RADIATION THROUGH** to allow heat, sound, or light or other radiation to pass through **7.** *vt* MECH ENG **TRANSFER POWER** to transfer power, force, or movement from one part of a mechanism to another [14C. < Latin *transmittere* "send across" < *mittere* "send"] —**trans·mit·ta·ble** *adj* —**trans·mit·tal** *n*

trans·mit·tance /tranz mítt'nss/ *n* **1.** the act or process of transmitting something **2.** the ability of a material to let incoming radiation pass completely through it, measured as the ratio of incident radiation to transmitted radiation

trans·mit·ter /tranz míttər/ *n* **1. AGENT OR MEANS OF TRANSMISSION** somebody or something that transmits something **2.** BROADCAST **PART OF BROADCASTING EQUIPMENT** a piece of broadcasting equipment that generates a radio-frequency wave, modulates it so that it carries a meaningful signal, and sends it out from an antenna **3.** TELECOM **TELEPHONE PART** the part of a telephone that converts sound waves to electrical impulses

trans·mog·ri·fy /tranz móggrə fī/ (**-fied, -fy·ing, -fies**) *vt* to change the appearance or form of something, especially in a grotesque or bizarre way (*formal*) [Mid-17C. Origin ?] —**trans·mog·ri·fi·ca·tion** /-mòggrəfi káysh'n/ *n*

trans·mon·tane /tranz món tàyn/ *adj* GEOG same as **tramontane** ■ *n* PEOPLES same as **tramontane** *n* (sense 2) [15C. < Latin *transmontanus* < *montanus* "of mountains" < *mont-* "mountain"]

trans·mun·dane /tranz mún dàyn/ *adj* belonging not to this material world and its concerns, but extending beyond them (*literary*)

trans·mu·ta·tion /trànzmyoo táysh'n/ *n* **1. CHANGE** a change, or the process of changing, from one form, substance, nature, or state to another **2.** PHYS **CHANGE OF ONE ELEMENT INTO ANOTHER** the transformation of the atom of one chemical element into the atom of another by disintegration or nuclear bombardment **3.** HIST **CONVERSION TO GOLD** the supposed conversion of base metals into gold or silver by alchemy —**trans·mu·ta·tion·al** *adj*

USAGE See ***transformation.***

trans·mute /tranz myo͞ot/ (**-mut·ed, -mut·ing, -mutes**) *vti*

1. CHANGE to change something from one form, nature, substance, or state to another, or be changed in this way 2. PHYS CHANGE FROM ONE ELEMENT TO ANOTHER to change one chemical element into another through disintegration or nuclear bombardment, or be changed in this way 3. HIST CONVERT BASE METAL TO GOLD in alchemy, to convert a base metal into gold or silver, or be converted in this way [14C. < Latin *transmutare* "change thoroughly" < *mutare* "to change"] —**trans·mut·a·bil·i·ty** /-myootə bíllətee/ *n* —**trans·mut·a·ble** *adj* —**trans·mut·a·bly** *adv* —**trans·mut·a·tive** /-ətiv/ *adj* —**trans·mut·er** *n*

SYNONYMS See ***change***.

trans·na·tion·al /tranz náshən'l, -náshnəl/ *adj* not confined to a single nation or state, but including, extending over, or operating within more than one ■ *n* a company or organization that does business or owns corporations in more than one nation —**trans·na·tion·al·ly** *adv*

trans·o·ce·an·ic /tranz ōshee ánnik/ *adj* **1.** involving crossing an ocean **2.** situated or coming from across an ocean

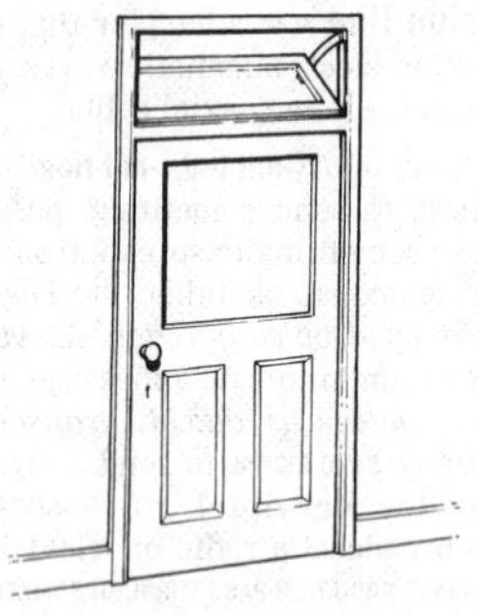

transom

tran·som /tránssəm/ *n* **1.** STRUCTURAL BEAM ABOVE WINDOW a horizontal beam or stone above a window that supports the structure above **2.** CROSSPIECE ABOVE DOOR a crosspiece over a door or between the top of a door and a window above **3.** CROSSBAR THAT DIVIDES WINDOW a crossbar of wood or stone that divides a window horizontally **4.** BUILDINGS WINDOW ABOVE DOOR a small rectangular window over a door **5.** BEAM FOR STRENGTHENING STERN a transverse beam for strengthening the stern of a ship **6.** PLANKING AT SHIP'S STERN the planking forming a flat surface across the stern of a ship **7.** HORIZONTAL BEAM OF CROSS OR GALLOWS the horizontal beam of a cross or gallows [14C. Probably alteration of Latin *transtrum* "crossbeam"]

tran·son·ic /tran sónnik/ *adj* relating to speeds close to the speed of sound or conditions encountered when traveling at those speeds [Mid-20C. < TRANS- + SONIC after SUPERSONIC and ULTRASONIC]

tran·son·ic bar·ri·er *n* AEROSP same as **sound barrier** (*technical*)

transp. *abbr* **1.** transport **2.** transportation

trans·pa·cif·ic /trànspə síffik/ *adj* **1.** involving crossing the Pacific Ocean **2.** situated or coming from across the Pacific Ocean

trans·pa·dane /tránspə dàyn, transs páy dàyn/ *adj* situated on or coming from the northern side of the Po River in northern Italy [Early 17C. < Latin *transpadanus* < *padanus* "of the Padus (River Po)"]

trans·par·en·cy /transs párrənssee/ (*plural* **-cies**) *n* **1.** the quality or state of being transparent **2.** a positive photographic image on a transparent material, especially film or a slide, that can be viewed when light is shone through it. Transparencies are generally viewed using a projector, a light table, or a handheld viewer. [Late 16C. < medieval Latin *transparentia* < *transparent-* (see TRANSPARENT)]

trans·par·ent /transs párrənt/ *adj* **1.** EASILY SEEN THROUGH allowing light to pass through with little or no interruption or distortion so that objects on the other side can be clearly seen ○ *transparent plastic* **2.** FINE ENOUGH TO SEE THROUGH thin or fine enough in texture to see through ○ *transparent fabric* **3.** OBVIOUS AND EASY TO RECOGNIZE clearly recognizable as what he, she, or it really is ○ *a transparent motive* **4.** FRANK completely open and frank ○ *She was grateful for the transparent honesty of the reply.* ○ *They were completely transparent about their motives.* **5.** PHYS LETTING RADIATION THROUGH allowing electromagnetic radiation of specific wavelengths to pass through [15C. Directly or via French < medieval Latin *transparent-*, present participle of *transparere* "shine through" < Latin *parere* "appear"] —**trans·par·ent·ly** *adv*

trans·par·ent con·text *n* in logic, an expression in which the truth-value is not changed when any term is replaced by another with the same reference

trans·pierce /transs peérss/ (**-pierced, -pierc·ing, -pierc·es**) *vt* to pierce through something (*archaic*)

tran·spire /tran spír/ (**-spired, -spir·ing, -spires**) *v* **1.** *vt* COME TO LIGHT to become known or be disclosed ○ *It later transpired that they had been furious at what had happened.* **2.** ⚠ *vi* HAPPEN to take place ○ *What transpired after they left remains a secret.* **3.** *vti* PHYSIOL GIVE OFF VAPOR THROUGH SKIN to give off water vapor through the pores of the skin **4.** *vti* BOT LOSE WATER VAPOR to lose water vapor from a plant's surface, especially through minute surface pores (**stomata**) [15C. Directly or via French *transpirer* < medieval Latin *transpirare* "breathe through" < Latin *spirare* "breathe"] —**tran·spir·a·ble** *adj* —**tran·spi·ra·tion** /trànspə ráysh'n/ *n* —**tran·spi·ra·to·ry** *adj*

USAGE The use of ***transpire*** to mean "happen," as in the sentence *Tell me what transpired at the meeting*, is sometimes criticized, although it has been in common use for several centuries and conveys something of the sense inherent in its uncontroversial meaning "become known or be disclosed": *It transpired that the President had known about the plan all along.*

trans·plant *v* /transs plánt/ (**-plant·ed, -plant·ing, -plants**) **1.** *vt* GARDENING RELOCATE PLANT to remove a plant from the place where it is growing and replant it somewhere else **2.** *vi* GARDENING BE CAPABLE OF BEING MOVED to be capable of being transplanted ○ *Poppies do not transplant well.* **3.** *vt* MOVE SOMEBODY TO ANOTHER PLACE to move somebody or something to another place or position **4.** *vt* SURG TRANSFER BODY ORGAN to transfer an organ or tissue from one body to another or from one place in somebody's body to another ■ *n* /tránss plànt/ **1.** SURG SURGICAL PROCEDURE a surgical operation or procedure to transplant an organ or tissue **2.** SURG TRANSPLANTED ORGAN OR TISSUE an organ or tissue that has been transplanted **3.** GARDENING TRANSPLANTED PLANT a plant that has been transplanted **4.** RESIDENT FROM ELSEWHERE somebody who has moved from one place and become a permanent resident in another (*informal*) [15C. Directly or via French *transplanter* < late Latin *transplantare* "plant across" < *plantare* "to plant"] —**trans·plant·a·ble** *adj* —**trans·plan·ta·tion** /trànss plan táysh'n/ *n* —**trans·plant·er** *n*

trans·po·lar /trans pṓlər/ *adj* crossing or extending across either of the polar regions

tran·spond·er /tran spóndər/, **tran·spon·dor** *n* **1.** a radio or radar transceiver that automatically transmits a signal of its own when it receives a predetermined signal from elsewhere, used especially for locating and identifying objects **2.** a receiving and transmitting device in a communication or broadcast satellite that relays the signals it receives back to Earth [Mid-20C. < TRANSMIT + RESPOND]

trans·pon·tine /transs pón tīn/ *adj* located on or coming from the other side of a bridge [Mid-19C. < TRANS- + Latin *pont-*, stem of *pons* "bridge"]

trans·port *vt* /transs páwrt/ (**-port·ed, -port·ing, -ports**) **1.** TRANSP CARRY SOMEBODY OR SOMETHING to carry somebody or something from one place to another, usually in a vehicle **2.** MAKE SOMEBODY IMAGINE BEING ELSEWHERE to take somebody on a mental or imaginative journey to another place or time ○ *The sounds of the game transported him back to his youth.* **3.** AFFECT SOMEBODY WITH STRONG EMOTION to put somebody in a state of intense or uncontrollable emotion, especially joy ○ *She was transported with joy.* **4.** HIST SEND SOMEBODY TO PENAL COLONY to exile somebody to a penal colony ■ *n* /tránss pàwrt/ **1.** *UK* TRANSP same as **transportation** (senses 1–2) **2.** MIL, SHIPPING CRAFT CARRYING PEOPLE OR FREIGHT a ship or aircraft for carrying passengers, especially military personnel, or freight **3.** EXPERIENCE OR DISPLAY OF INTENSE EMOTION an experience or display of intense and uncontrollable emotion, especially joy (*often used in the plural*) ○ *in transports of delight* **4.** HIST SOMEBODY SENT TO PENAL COLONY somebody exiled to a penal colony [14C. Directly or via French *transporter* < Latin *transportare* "carry across" < *portare* "carry"] —**trans·port·a·bil·i·ty** /transs pàwrtə bíllətee/ *n* —**trans·port·a·ble** *adj* —**trans·por·tive** *adj*

trans·por·ta·tion /trànspər táysh'n/ *n* **1.** TRANSP CONVEYANCE OF SOMEBODY OR SOMETHING the act or business of carrying somebody or something from one place to another, usually in a vehicle **2.** TRANSP MEANS OF TRAVELING a means of traveling or of carrying somebody or something from one place to another **3.** *US* FARE OR CHARGE the fare paid or charge made for traveling in a bus, train, or other public vehicle **4.** HIST PENAL EXILE exile to a penal colony

trans·port café *n UK* same as **truck stop**

trans·port·er /transs páwrtər/ *n* **1.** somebody or something that transports something **2.** a large vehicle used to carry heavy loads, often other vehicles

trans·port·er bridge *n* a bridge consisting of a high overarching framework from which a moving platform is suspended on cables. The platform goes back and forth, carrying vehicles across a body of water.

trans·pose /transs pṓz/ *v* (**-posed, -pos·ing, -pos·es**) **1.** *vt* REVERSE ORDER OF THINGS to make two things change places or reverse their usual order, e.g., two letters in a word **2.** *vt* MOVE SOMETHING TO DIFFERENT POSITION to move something to a different position, especially in a sequence ○ *transposed that section to the end of the essay* **3.** *vt* CHANGE SETTING OF SOMETHING to take something such as a story, incident, or play out of its original setting or time and relocate it in another ○ *transposing the action from Shakespeare's time to the present* **4.** *vti* MUSIC CHANGE MUSIC TO DIFFERENT KEY to rewrite or play a musical composition in a key or at a pitch other than the one in which it was originally written or in which it is usually performed **5.** *vt* MATH MOVE TERM IN EQUATION to transfer a term from one side of an equation to the other, reversing its sign ■ *n* MATH TYPE OF MATRIX a matrix created by interchanging the rows and columns of a previously given matrix [14C. < French *transposer*, alteration (by association with *poser* "to place") of Latin *transponere* < *ponere* "to place"] —**trans·pos·a·bil·i·ty** /-pṓzə bíllətee/ *n* —**trans·pos·a·ble** *adj* —**trans·pos·al** *n* —**trans·pos·er** *n* —**trans·pos·i·tive** /-póssətiv/ *adj*

trans·pos·ing in·stru·ment /trans pṓzing-/ *n* a musical instrument whose part is written in a different key from the notes it produces when it plays, e.g., a horn or clarinet

trans·po·si·tion /trànspə zísh'n/ *n* **1.** REVERSAL OF ORDER a reversal or alteration of the positions or order in which things stand **2.** ACT OF RECASTING the placing of something in a different setting, or the recasting of something in a different language, style, or medium **3.** MUSIC ACT OF CHANGING KEY the rewriting or playing of a piece of music in a key or at a pitch other than the original or usual one **4.** MATH TRANSFER OF TERM IN EQUATION the transfer of a term from one side of an equation to another and the reversal of its sign **5.** GENETICS DNA TRANSFER a transfer of a DNA segment to a new position on the same or another chromosome —**trans·po·si·tion·al** *adj*

trans·po·son /transs pṓ zòn/ *n* a segment of DNA that can move to a new position on the same or another chromosome, often modifying the action of neighboring genes [Late 20C. < TRANSPOSITION]

trans·put·er /transs pyóotər/ *n* a powerful microchip with the functions of a microprocessor that has its own memory and the capability of parallel processing [Late 20C. Blend of TRANSISTOR + COMPUTER]

trans·sex·u·al /transs sékshoo əl/ *n* **1.** somebody who has undergone treatment to change his or her anatomical sex **2.** somebody who identifies himself or herself as a member of the opposite sex —**trans·sex·u·al** *adj* —**trans·sex·u·al·ism** *n*

trans·ship /transs shíp/ (**-shipped, -ship·ping, -ships**), **tran·ship** /tran shíp/ *vti* to transfer goods from one means of transportation to another, or be transferred in this way —**trans·ship·ment** *n*

tran·sub·stan·ti·ate /trànssəb stánshee àyt/ (**-at·ed,**

-at·ing, -ates) *v* **1.** *vi* in Roman Catholic and Eastern Orthodox doctrine, to undergo a change in substance, from bread and wine to the body and blood of Jesus Christ during Communion **2.** *vti* to change from one substance into another, or change something from one substance into another (*formal*) [15C. < medieval Latin *transubstantiat-*, past participle of *transubstantiare* "change the substance of thoroughly" < Latin *substantia* (see SUBSTANCE)] —**tran·sub·stan·tial** *adj* —**tran·sub·stan·tial·ly** *adv*

tran·sub·stan·ti·a·tion /trànssəb stanshee áysh'n/ *n* **1.** the Roman Catholic and Eastern Orthodox doctrine that the bread and wine of Communion become, in substance, but not appearance, the body and blood of Jesus Christ at consecration **2.** the process by which one substance changes into another (*formal*)

tran·su·date /tránssoo dàyt, tran sóo dàyt/ *n* a fluid that passes through the pores or interstices of a membrane

tran·sude /tran sóod/ **(-sud·ed, -sud·ing, -sudes)** *vi* to pass through the pores or interstices of a membrane (*refers to a fluid such as sweat*) [Early 17C. < French *transsuder* "sweat through" < Latin *sudare* "to sweat"] —**tran·su·da·tion** /trànssoo dáysh'n/ *n* —**tran·su·da·to·ry** *adj*

trans·u·ran·ic /trànzyə ránnik/, **trans·u·ra·ni·an** /-ráynee ən/, **trans·u·ra·ni·um** /-ráynee əm/ *adj* having a higher atomic number than uranium

Trans·vaal /tránz vaàl/ independent Afrikaner-dominated territory in South Africa that became a province in the Union of South Africa in 1910. In 1994 the region was divided into the three provinces that are now Gauteng, Limpopo, and Mpumalanga.

trans·val·ue /tranz vállyoo, transs-/ **(-ued, -u·ing, -ues)** *vt* to reevaluate something using a different standard, especially one that differs from conventional or accepted standards and results in a very different assessment of the worth of something —**trans·val·u·a·tion** /tranz vàllyoo áysh'n, transs-/ *n* —**trans·val·u·er** *n*

trans·ver·sal /tranz vúrsəl/ *n* a line that intersects two or more other lines ■ *adj* same as **transverse** —**trans·ver·sal·ly** *adv*

trans·verse /tranz vúrss, tránz vùrss/ *adj* **1.** CROSSWISE lying or extending crosswise or at right angles to something **2.** MATH PASSING THROUGH HYPERBOLA FOCI passing through the foci of a hyperbola ■ *n* CROSSWISE THING something that lies or extends crosswise or at right angles to something [14C. < Latin *transversus*, past participle of *transvertere* "turn across" < *vertere* "to turn"] —**trans·verse·ly** *adv* —**trans·verse·ness** *n*

trans·verse co·lon *n* the part of the colon that passes from right to left across the upper abdominal cavity just beneath the liver and stomach

trans·verse flute *n* a flute with the mouth hole on top of the barrel near one end. The player blows across the hole while holding the flute in a sideways horizontal position. The modern flute used to be known as the transverse flute in order to distinguish it from an end-blown flute such as a recorder.

trans·verse proc·ess *n* either of the two bony projections on the sides of a vertebra

trans·verse wave *n* a wave that makes the medium through which it travels vibrate in a direction at right angles to the direction of its travel

trans·ves·tite /tranz véss tìt/ *n* somebody who adopts the dress and often the behavior of the opposite sex [Early 20C. < German *Transvestit* "cross-dresser" < Latin *vestire* "clothe, dress" (see VEST)] —**trans·ves·tism** *n* —**trans·ves·ti·tism** *n*

Tran·syl·va·nia /trànssil váynyə/ historic region in eastern Europe that now forms the central and northwestern parts of Romania. Area: 24,000 sq. mi./62,000 sq. km. —**Tran·syl·va·ni·an** *adj*

Tran·syl·va·ni·an Alps /trànssil vaynyən-/ mountain range in the Carpathian Mountains, running east to west through south central Romania

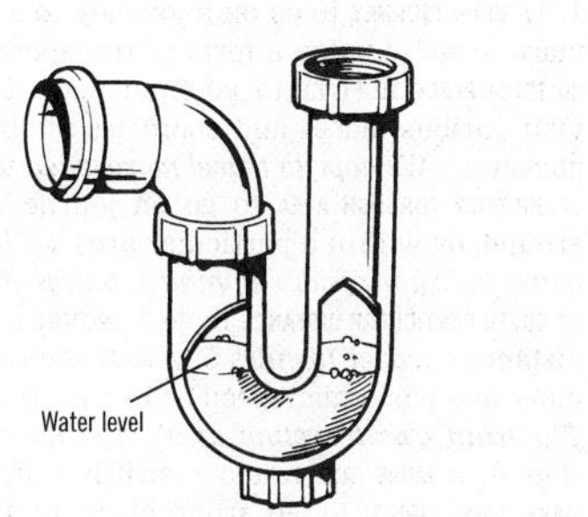

trap (sense 6)

trap[1] /trap/ *n* **1.** SOMETHING DESIGNED TO CATCH ANIMALS a device designed to catch an animal and kill it or prevent it from escaping, e.g., a concealed pit or a mechanical device that springs shut **2.** PLAN TO TRICK SOMEBODY an ambush, scheme, or trick intended to catch somebody unaware and put the person at a disadvantage or in somebody else's power **3.** CONFINING SITUATION a situation from which it is difficult to escape and in which somebody feels confined, restricted, or in somebody else's power ○ *wanted to avoid the trap of being typecast in the same roles* **4.** BUILDINGS same as **trapdoor** **5.** ANAT same as **mouth** *n* (sense 1) (*informal*) ○ *If the media ask questions, keep your trap shut.* **6.** CONSTR SECTION OF DRAINPIPE BLOCKING GAS a curved section of a drainpipe that holds a quantity of water to act as a barrier to prevent sewer gas from rising up the pipe **7.** CONSTR DEVICE PREVENTING PASSAGE OF GAS a device designed to prevent gas, vapor, or other substances passing through or escaping from something **8.** SPORTS DEVICE USED IN TRAPSHOOTING a device that throws clay pigeons into the air for trapshooting **9.** GOLF GOLFING HAZARD a hazard, especially a bunker, on a golf course **10.** SPORTS STARTING STALL FOR GREYHOUND one of the set of stalls from which greyhounds are released at the start of a race **11.** VEHICLES CARRIAGE a light horse-drawn carriage with two wheels ■ **traps** *npl* **1.** *US* MOTOR SPORTS LENGTH OF RACETRACK a measured stretch of track over which electronic timers register the speeds of racing vehicles, especially in drag racing **2.** MUSIC PERCUSSION INSTRUMENTS a set of percussion instruments, especially the drum set used in a dance orchestra or jazz band (*informal*) ■ *v* **(trapped, trap·ping, traps) 1.** *vt* CATCH SOMETHING IN TRAP to catch an animal in a trap so that it is killed or unable to escape **2.** *vi* SET TRAPS FOR ANIMALS to set traps for animals, or make a living by catching animals in traps **3.** *vt* HOLD SOMETHING IN TIGHT GRIP to catch or hold something in a tight grip or narrow space so that it cannot be moved or is painfully squeezed ○ *I trapped my finger in the door.* **4.** *vt* PLACE SOMEBODY IN CONFINING SITUATION to put somebody in a situation from which it is difficult or impossible to escape ○ *They were trapped inside the burning building.* ○ *felt trapped in a dead-end job* **5.** *vt* TAKE SOMEBODY BY SURPRISE to put somebody at a disadvantage by means of an ambush, surprise, clever plan, or trick ○ *She was trapped into admitting the truth.* **6.** *vt* SOCCER CONTROL BALL to bring a moving ball quickly under control using a part of the body **7.** *vt* CRIME CATCH OFFENDER to identify or catch an offender by means of a speed trap or a security device **8.** *vt* PREVENT AIR FROM ESCAPING to prevent air, gas, heat, or a fluid from escaping **9.** *vt* CONSTR EQUIP DRAINPIPE WITH TRAP to put a trap into a drainpipe [Old English *træppe* (in *coltetræppe*, plant name), *treppe* "trap, snare" < Germanic]

trap[2] /trap/ *n UK* same as **traprock** [Late 18C. < Swedish *trapp* < *trappa* "stair" (from the rock's appearance)]

trap[3] /trap/ *n* RIDING same as **trappings** (*dated informal*) ■ *vt* **(trapped, trap·ping, traps)** to provide somebody or something with trappings or adornments ○ *They were all trapped out in the gaudiest of clothes.* [14C. Alteration of French *drap* "cloth" < late Latin *drappus*]

Tra·pa·ni /traa paànee/ seaport and capital city of Trapani Province, northwestern Sicily. Population: 69,688 (1997).

trap·door /tráp dàwr/ *n* a hatch covering a horizontal or sloping opening in a floor, ceiling, or roof [14C. < TRAP[1]]

trap·door spi·der *n* a spider that constructs a tubular silk-lined burrow with a hinged lid like a trapdoor. Native to: warm regions. Family: Ctenizidae.

tra·peze /trə peéz/ *n* a horizontal bar attached to the ends of two ropes hanging parallel to each other, used for gymnastics or for acrobatics, especially in a circus [Mid-19C. Via French *trapèze* < late Latin *trapezium* (see TRAPEZIUM)]

tra·pe·zi·a MATH, ANAT plural of **trapezium**

tra·pe·zi·form /trə peézə fàwrm/ *adj* shaped like a trapezium

tra·pe·zi·i ANAT plural of **trapezius**

tra·pe·zi·um /trə peézee əm/ (*plural* **-zi·ums** or **-zi·a** /-zee ə/) *n* **1.** MATH a quadrilateral that has no parallel sides **2.** *UK* MATH same as **trapezoid** (sense 1) **3.** ANAT a small bone in the wrist at the base of the thumb [Late 16C. Via late Latin < Greek *trapezion* "small table" < *trapeza* "table" < *peza* "foot"] —**tra·pe·zi·al** *adj*

tra·pe·zi·us /trə peézee əss/ (*plural* **-zi·us·es** or **-zi·i** /-zee ì/) *n* either of the two large flat triangular muscles that run from the back of the neck and cover each shoulder. They help to move the shoulder blades and draw the head backward. [Early 18C. < modern Latin < late Latin *trapezium* (see TRAPEZIUM)]

tra·pe·zo·he·dron /trə peézō heé drən/ (*plural* **-drons** or **-dra** /-drə/) *n* a crystal with faces that are all trapezoids in shape [Early 19C. < TRAPEZIUM] —**tra·pe·zo·he·dral** *adj*

trap·e·zoid /tráppə zòyd/ *n* **1.** MATH a quadrilateral that has two parallel sides **2.** *UK* MATH same as **trapezium** (sense 1) **3.** ANAT a small bone in the wrist near the metatarsal bone that connects with the index finger —**tra·pe·zoid·al** /tràppə zóyd'l/ *adj*

trap·per /tráppər/ *n* somebody who makes a living by trapping animals for their fur or hides [Mid-18C. < TRAP[1]]

trap·pings /tráppingz/ *npl* **1.** the dress, accessories, insignia, and other outward signs associated with an office, position, or status ○ *the trappings of power* **2.** an ornamental or ceremonial rig for a horse, including a decorated harness, saddle, and cloth covering [14C. < TRAP[3]]

Trap·pist /tráppist/ *n* a member of the main reformed branch of the Cistercian order of Christian monks, established in 1664 at La Trappe monastery in Normandy and noted for its vow of silence [Early 19C. < French *trappiste* < *La Trappe*]

trap·rock /tráp ròk/ *n* a dark, fine-grained igneous rock used in road construction, e.g., basalt [Early 19C. < TRAP[2]]

trap·shoot·ing /tráp shòoting/ *n* the sport of shooting at clay pigeons thrown by a trap [Late 19C. < TRAP[1]] —**trap·shoot** *n* —**trap·shoot·er** *n*

tra·pun·to /trə póontō/ *n* quilting in which only the design, which is outlined with parallel lines of stitches, is padded to give it a raised look [Early 20C. < Italian, past participle of *trapungere* "embroider" < Latin *pungere* "to prick"]

trash /trash/ *n* **1.** DISCARDED MATERIAL discarded, unwanted, or worthless material or objects **2.** NONSENSE something spoken or written that is regarded as meaningless, absurd, or very inaccurate **3.** POOR QUALITY LITERATURE OR ART literature or art considered worthless or offensive ○ *How can you read such trash?* **4.** OFFENSIVE TERM an offensive term that deliberately insults somebody's social position or morals (*insult*) **5.** AGRIC TRIMMINGS FROM PLANTS twigs, branches, or leaves that have fallen or been trimmed from trees and plants **6.** INDUST SUGAR CANE REFUSE the dry refuse of sugar cane after it has been crushed for the juice, often used as fuel ■ *vt* **(trashed, trash·ing, trash·es) 1.** DESTROY SOMETHING to destroy, severely damage, or vandalize something deliberately (*informal*) ○ *"The storm trashed bridges in Honduras and Central America."* (*US News & World Report*; December 1998) **2.** DISCARD SOMETHING to throw away or discard something (*informal*) **3.** CRITICIZE SOMEBODY SAVAGELY to criticize somebody or something savagely, or condemn somebody or something as worthless (*informal*) **4.** AGRIC REMOVE TWIGS AND BRANCHES to remove twigs, branches, or leaves from plants **5.** INDUST STRIP LEAVES FROM SUGAR CANE to strip the outer leaves from sugar cane [14C. Probably < N Germanic] ◇ **talk trash** to try to intimidate somebody, especially a rival or an opponent in a sporting contest, by being boastful or insulting (*slang*)

trash can *n* same as **garbage can** (*informal*)

trash fish *n US* 1. FISH same as **rough fish** 2. a fish that is not marketable as human food but is used in animal feeds, fertilizers, and paints 3. a fish formerly thought of as unfit for human consumption, but now valued for its quality, e.g., skate or monkfish

trash·man /trásh màn/ (*plural* **-men** /-mèn/) *n US* same as **garbageman**

trash·mov·er /trásh mo͞ovər/ *n Southern US* a storm whose violent winds or heavy rains spread debris

REGIONAL NOTE ***Trashmover*** is common in folk speech across the rural South with other descriptive terms such as *chunk floater, frog strangle, gullywasher, lighter(d)-knot floater, pourdown,* and *toad strangler.*

trash·y /tráshee/ (**-i·er, -i·est**) *adj* of very little worth or merit ○ *a trashy novel* —**trash·i·ly** *adv* —**trash·i·ness** *n*

Tra·si·me·no, Lake /tràzzə méenō/, **Tra·si·mene, Lake** /tràzzə meén/ lake in central Italy, and the largest lake in the Italian peninsula. Area: 49 sq. mi./128 sq. km.

trat·to·ri·a /traàtə reé ə/ (*plural* **-ri·as** or **-ri·e** /-reé ày/) *n* an Italian restaurant, especially one that is simple in style [Early 19C. < Italian < *trattore* "restaurateur" < Latin *tractare* "drag, manage" < *trahere* "pull"]

trau·ma /trówmə, tráwmə/ (*plural* **-mas** or **-ma·ta** /-mətə/) *n* 1. an extremely distressing experience that causes severe emotional shock and may have long-lasting psychological effects 2. a physical injury or wound to the body [Late 17C. < Greek, "wound"]

trau·ma cen·ter *n* a hospital or a department in a hospital that is specially equipped and staffed to treat patients who have sustained complex, life-threatening injuries such as multiple gunshot wounds or severe internal injuries

trau·ma·ta PSYCHOL, MED plural of **trauma**

trau·mat·ic /trow máttik, traw-/ *adj* 1. **EXTREMELY DISTRESSING** extremely distressing, frightening, or shocking, and sometimes having long-term psychological effects 2. PSYCHOL **RELATING TO TRAUMA** relating to or caused by psychological trauma 3. MED **RELATING TO INJURIES** relating to physical injuries or wounds to the body [Mid-17C. Via late Latin < Greek *traumatikos* < *traumat-*, stem of *trauma* "wound"] —**trau·mat·i·cal·ly** *adv*

trau·ma·tism /trówmə tìzzəm, tráwmə-/ *n* the condition resulting from a physical injury or wound or from an emotional shock [Mid-19C. < Greek *traumat-* (see TRAUMATIC)]

trau·ma·tize /trówmə tīz, tráwmə-/ (**-tized, -tiz·ing, -tiz·es**) *vt* 1. to cause somebody to experience severe emotional shock or distress, often resulting in long-lasting psychological damage 2. to cause physical injury to somebody or something [Early 20C. < Greek *traumat-* (see TRAUMATIC)] —**trau·ma·ti·za·tion** /tròwməti záysh'n, tràwməti-/ *n*

trau·ma·tol·o·gy /tròwmə tólləjee, tràwmə-/ *n* the branch of medicine that deals with serious injuries and wounds and their long-term consequences [Late 19C. < Greek *traumat-* (see TRAUMATIC)] —**trau·ma·tol·o·gist** *n*

tra·vail /trə váyl, trá vàyl/ *n* 1. **HARD WORK** work, especially work that involves hard physical effort over a long period 2. MED same as **labor** *n* (sense 6) (*archaic*) ■ *vi* (**-vailed, -vail·ing, -vails**) 1. **WORK HARD** to work long and hard (*literary*) 2. **BE IN LABOR** to undergo the labor of childbirth (*archaic*) [13C. < French, "pain," *travailler* "to toil" < assumed Vulgar Latin *tripalium* "instrument of torture" < Latin *tripalis* "having three stakes" < *palus* "stake"]

trave /trayv/ *n* 1. BUILDINGS same as **crossbeam** 2. BUILDINGS a section of a building formed by crossbeams, e.g., in a ceiling 3. RIDING a frame to restrain a difficult horse while it is being shod [14C. Via Old French, "beam" < Latin *trab-*]

trav·el /trávv'l/ *v* (**-eled** or **-elled, -el·ing** or **-el·ling, -els**) 1. *vi* **GO ON JOURNEY** to go on a journey to a particular place, usually using a form of transportation 2. *vi* **GO FROM PLACE TO PLACE** to go from place to place or visit various places and countries for business or pleasure ○ *We hope to travel more when we retire.* 3. *vt* **JOURNEY THROUGH AREA** to go on journeys through, around, or within a particular area ○ *They liked to travel the countryside stopping at places of interest.* 4. *vt* **COVER PARTICULAR DISTANCE** to go or cover a particular distance ○ *travel 10 miles* 5. *vi* **GO AT PARTICULAR SPEED** to move at a particular speed or in a particular way ○ *The train was traveling at 90 mph when it had to stop.* 6. *vi* **MOVE FAST** to move swiftly (*informal*) 7. *vi* **MAKE SALES TRIPS** to go from place to place as a salesperson or as part of a business ○ *After five years traveling, she wanted an office job.* 8. *vi* **REACT TO BEING TRANSPORTED** to be in a particular condition as a result of being transported ○ *Snakes do not travel well.* 9. *vi* **BE TRANSMITTED** to be transmitted or communicated ○ *News traveled fast.* 10. *vi* **SCAN DURING FILMING** to scan an object or scene in the process of observing or filming it 11. *vi* MECH ENG **MOVE IN FIXED PATH** to move in a fixed path while operating (*refers to a machine part*) 12. *vi US* **ASSOCIATE WITH PARTICULAR GROUP** to associate with a particular person or group ○ *They've been traveling with a new crowd.* 13. *vi* BASKETBALL **TAKE ILLEGAL NUMBER OF STEPS** in basketball, to take more steps while holding the ball than the rules allow ■ *n* 1. **ACTIVITY OF TRAVELING** the activity of going on journeys, usually using a form of transportation, or visiting different places ○ *air travel* 2. MECH ENG **TOTAL DISTANCE MECHANICAL PART MOVES** the total distance that a mechanical part such as a piston inside a cylinder moves 3. *US* **AMOUNT OF TRAFFIC** the amount of traffic at a given place along a route ■ **trav·els** *npl* 1. **SERIES OF JOURNEYS** a series of journeys undertaken by a person or group ○ *She's off on her travels again.* 2. LITERAT **ACCOUNT OF SOMEBODY'S JOURNEYS** an account of the journeys undertaken by a person or group ■ *adj* **FOR TRAVELER** intended for, accompanying, or used by a traveler ○ *a travel iron* [14C. Variant of TRAVAIL] —**trav·el·a·ble** *adj*

CULTURAL NOTE ***Gulliver's Travels***, a satire (1726) by Irish writer Jonathan Swift. It is a four-part account of the adventures of a castaway, ship's surgeon Lemuel Gulliver. First washed ashore in Lilliput, peopled by tiny inhabitants, he subsequently finds himself in Brobdingnag, the kingdom of giants. The third part of the novel deals with his time on the flying island of Laputa and the neighboring continent, occupied by scientists and philosophers, while the final part takes him to the land of the Houyhnhms, where horses rule with benevolent reason over the brutish human Yahoos. Through the characters and situations encountered by Gulliver in his travels Swift takes every opportunity to satirize the people and practices of his time with varying degrees of humor and bitterness.

trav·el a·gen·cy, **trav·el bu·reau** *n* a business that arranges transportation, accommodations, and tours for travelers —**trav·el a·gent** *n*

trav·el·card /trávv'l kaàrd/ *n UK* a ticket entitling the user to an unlimited number of trips on a public transportation system within a designated area and over a fixed period of time

trav·eled /trávv'ld/, **trav·elled** *adj* 1. having been on many journeys, or having a lot of experience as a traveler 2. used by many travelers ○ *Keep to the traveled roads.*

trav·el·er /trávv'lər/, **trav·el·ler** *n* 1. **SOMEBODY ON JOURNEY** somebody who journeys to a specific place or who uses a specific form of transportation 2. **SOMEBODY WHO HAS TRAVELED** somebody who has traveled or travels extensively ○ *an experienced traveler* 3. MECH ENG **MOVING PART** a part of a mechanism that is designed to move in a fixed path 4. NAUT **RING ON ROPE** a metal ring that moves freely on a rope, spar, or rod 5. NAUT **ROPE** a rope, spar, or rod on which a metal ring moves 6. PEOPLES same as **Irish Traveller**

trav·el·er's check *n* an internationally accepted check for a sum in a specific currency that can be exchanged elsewhere for local currency or for goods and is usually guaranteed against loss or theft

trav·e·ler's joy *n* a wild climbing plant that has feathery white seed heads. Native to: Europe. Latin name: *Clematis vitalba*.

trav·e·ler's tale *n* a fantastic, unlikely, or obviously untrue account of something, as given by a traveler to people who do not travel

trav·el·ing /trávv'ling/, **trav·el·ling** *adj* 1. **OF JOURNEYS** related to journeys or the activity of making journeys ○ *traveling expenses* 2. **GOING TO DIFFERENT PLACES** moving from place to place regularly ○ *a traveling exhibition* 3. same as **travel** ■ *n* 1. **EXTENDED TOURIST TRIP** the activity of visiting a number of places or countries as a tourist for an extended period of time, especially as a student or young person ○ *to go travelling for six months* 2. **BASKETBALL RULE VIOLATION** in basketball, a violation of the rules that occurs when the player with the ball takes too many steps without dribbling

trav·el·ing sales·man *n* a salesman whose work consists of traveling around calling on potential customers within a territory

trav·el·ing sales·per·son *n* a salesperson whose work consists of traveling around calling on potential customers within a territory

trav·el·ing sales·wo·man *n* a saleswoman whose work consists of traveling around calling on potential customers within a territory

trav·el·ing wave *n* a wave that continuously carries energy away from its source

trav·el in·sur·ance *n* insurance to cover the eventualities of a period of travel away from home such as flight delay, loss of baggage, theft of money or belongings, or medical costs

trav·elled *adj* another spelling of **traveled**

trav·el·ler *n* another spelling of **traveler**

trav·el·ling *adj* another spelling of **traveling**

trav·e·logue /trávvə lòg/, **trav·e·log** *n* a film, video, or piece of writing, or a lecture accompanied by pictures, video or film, about travel, especially to interesting or remote places, or about one person's travels

trav·el sick·ness *n UK* same as **motion sickness** —**trav·el-sick** *adj*

Trav·ers, Mount /trávvərz/ mountain in the north of the South Island, New Zealand, situated in the northern part of the Southern Alps. Height: 7,671 ft./2,338 m.

tra·verse *v* /trə vúrss/ (**-versed, -vers·ing, -vers·es**) 1. *vt* **MOVE ACROSS AREA** to travel or move across, over, or through an area or a place ○ *traverse the countryside* 2. *vti* **GO BACK AND FORTH ACROSS SOMETHING** to move backward and forward across something ○ *Volunteers traversed the field looking for clues.* 3. *vt* **REACH ACROSS SOMETHING** to extend or reach across something ○ *the bridge traversing the river* 4. *vti* CLIMBING **MOVE AT ANGLE ACROSS SOMETHING** to move at an angle across a rock face while ascending or descending it 5. *vti* SKIING **ZIGZAG DOWN SLOPE** to ski in diagonal runs following a zigzag course down a slope 6. *vti* **SWIVEL GUN** to swivel something, especially a gun, from side to side on a pivot, or be swiveled in this way 7. *vi* FENCING **SLIDE BLADE TOWARD OPPONENT'S HILT** in fencing, to slide the blade of a sword toward an opponent's hilt while at the same time applying pressure to his or her blade 8. *vt* **THWART SOMEBODY OR SOMETHING** to thwart or obstruct somebody or something (*literary*) 9. *vt* LAW **DENY ALLEGATIONS** to deny the opposing party's allegations as set out in the pleading in a lawsuit, formally and, usually, in their entirety 10. *vt* LAW **JOIN ISSUE** to join issue with somebody on an indictment ■ *n* /trávvərss, trə vúrss/ 1. **MOVEMENT ACROSS AREA** a movement or journey across, over, or through something 2. **ROUTE TAKEN** a route or way across, over, or through something 3. CLIMBING **MOVEMENT ACROSS ROCK FACE** a horizontal or oblique movement across a rock face in climbing 4. SKIING **ZIGZAG SKIING RUN** a diagonal zigzag skiing run down a ski slope 5. CONSTR **CROSSBEAM** something that is set across a gap or lies crosswise, e.g., a structural member of a building 6. BUILDINGS **GALLERY** a gallery or loft that crosses from side to side inside a building 7. BUILDINGS **BARRIER WITHIN BUILDING** a railing, curtain, screen, or partition forming a barrier within a building 8. MIL **BARRIER ACROSS TRENCH** a defensive barrier of earth across a trench 9. **OBSTRUCTION**

something that thwarts or obstructs somebody or something (*literary*) **10.** MATH same as **transversal 11.** **ZIGZAG COURSE OF VESSEL** the zigzag course of a sailing vessel in contrary winds **12.** MECH ENG **LATERAL MOVEMENT OF MACHINE PART** the horizontal movement of a machine part such as a lathe or grinding tool as it moves across the work piece **13.** LAW **DENIAL OF ALLEGATIONS** a formal denial of the opposing party's allegations as set out in their pleading in a lawsuit **14.** CIV ENG **SURVEY USING INTERSECTING STRAIGHT LINES** a survey made using a series of intersecting straight lines of known length whose angles of intersection are measured for recording on a map or in a table of data ■ *adj* /trávvərss, trə vúrss/ **CROSSWISE** lying across something [14C. Via French *traverser* < late Latin *tra(ns)versare* < Latin *transversus*, past participle of *transvertere* "turn across" < *vertere* "to turn"] —**tra·vers·a·ble** *adj* —**tra·vers·al** *n* —**tra·vers·er** *n*

tra·verse rod /trávvərss-/ *n US* a rod with a mechanism that allows attached curtains or draperies to be opened and closed with a pull cord

trav·er·tine /trávvər teen/, **trav·er·tin** /-tin/ *n* a hard white or light-colored limestone precipitated in hot springs and caves. Use: facing material in building. [Late 18C. Via Italian *travertino* < Latin *(lapis) tiburtinus* "(stone) of Tibur (Tivoli)"]

trav·es·ty /trávvəstee/ *n* (*plural* **-ties**) **1. FALSE REPRESENTATION** a distorted or debased version of something ○ *It was a kangaroo court, a travesty of justice.* **2.** ARTS **GROTESQUE IMITATION** a literary or artistic work, usually meant as a parody, that ridicules something serious by imitating it in a grotesque or distorted manner ■ *vt* (**-tied, -ty·ing, -ties**) **MAKE TRAVESTY OF SOMETHING** to imitate or ridicule something in a grotesque or distorted manner [Mid-17C. < French *travesti* "dressed in disguise" < *travestir* "disguise, ridicule" < Italian *travestire* < Latin *trans-* "across" + *vestire* "clothe, dress" (see VEST)]

Trav·is /trávviss/, **William Barret** (1809–36) US soldier. He commanded Texan forces against Santa Anna's Mexican army at the Alamo and was killed when it was taken (1836).

tra·vois /trə vóy, trá vòy/ (*plural* **tra·vois** /trə vóyz, trá vòyz/ or **tra·vois·es**) *n* a sled made of two poles connected by a frame and pulled by an animal, formerly used by Native North Americans of the Great Plains [Mid-19C. < Canadian French variant of French *travail* < Latin *trabs* "beam"]

Tra·vol·ta /trə vṓltə/, **John** (*b.* 1954) US actor. His movies include *Saturday Night Fever* (1977), *Grease* (1978), and *Pulp Fiction* (1994).

trawl /trawl/ *n* FISHERIES **1.** same as **trawl net 2.** same as **trawl line** ■ *vti* (**trawled, trawl·ing, trawls**) **1. SEARCH THROUGH LARGE AMOUNT OF INFORMATION** to search for something through a large amount of information or many possibilities **2.** FISHERIES **FISH WITH TRAWL** to use or put out a trawl net or trawl line to catch fish [Mid-16C. < Middle Dutch *traghelen* "drag" < *traghel* "trawl net" < Latin *tragula* < *trahere* "pull"]

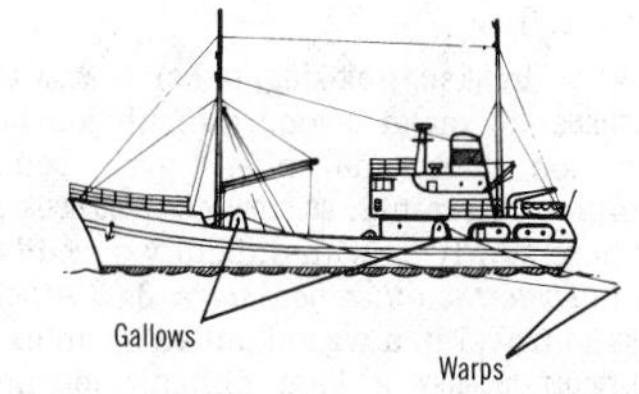

trawler

trawl·er /tráwlər/ *n* **1.** a boat that is used in trawling for fish **2.** somebody who fishes by trawling —**trawl·er·man** *n*

trawl line *n* a long fishing line suspended between buoys that has several shorter lines with baited hooks attached

trawl net *n* a large net that is dragged along the sea bottom behind a commercial fishing boat

tray /tray/ *n* **1. FLAT CARRIER FOR SMALL OBJECTS** a flat piece of plastic, wood, or metal with a raised edge, used for carrying or displaying light objects **2. TRAY AND THINGS IT CARRIES** a tray and the objects on it **3. CONTAINER IN WHICH TO ORGANIZE THINGS** a shallow container, sometimes part of a desk drawer or cabinet, in which to keep items such as stationery or jewelry [Old English *trīg* < Indo-European]

tray ta·ble *n* **1.** a small table that folds down from the back of the seat in front of you in a plane or train **2.** a tray with folding legs, used especially for eating meals in bed

treach·er·ous /tréchərəss/ *adj* **1.** betraying or ready to betray somebody's trust, confidence, or faith **2.** involving hidden dangers or hazards ○ *treacherous seas* [14C. < Old French *trecheros* "deceitfulness" < *trechier* "cheat, trick"] —**treach·er·ous·ly** *adv* —**treach·er·ous·ness** *n*

treach·er·y /tréchəree/ (*plural* **-ies**) *n* **1.** betrayal or deceit **2.** an act or instance of betrayal or deceit [12C. < Old French *trecherie* < *trechier* "cheat, trick"]

trea·cle /treék'l/ *n* **1.** something cloying or excessively sentimental **2.** a preparation used in the past as an antidote to poison **3.** *UK* FOOD same as **molasses** (sense 1) [14C. Via Old French *triacle*, Latin *theriaca* < Greek *thēriakē (antidotos)* "(antidote to) poisonous animals" < *thērion* "wild or poisonous animal" < *thēr* "wild animal"]

ORIGIN ***Treacle*** retained its original meaning of "antidote" when it came into English, but it later gradually broadened out into "medicine," and the practice of disguising the unpleasant taste of medicine with sugar syrup led in the 17th century to its application to "molasses."

trea·cly /treéklee/ *adj* cloying or excessively sentimental —**trea·cli·ness** *n*

tread /tred/ *v* (**trod** /trod/ or **tread·ed, trod·den** /tródd'n/ or **trod, tread·ing, treads**) **1.** *vi* **TRAMPLE ON SOMETHING** to step or put a foot on something, especially so as to crush or damage it **2.** *vti* **WALK OR STEP ON SOMETHING** to take a step or steps, or walk or step on, across, or along something **3.** *vt* **FORM PATH** to form something such as a path by trampling or walking **4.** *vi* **ACT IN PARTICULAR WAY** to proceed or behave in a particular way ○ *You'll have to tread carefully at the next meeting.* **5.** *vi* **CRUSH SOMEBODY OR SOMETHING** to repress or treat somebody or something harshly **6.** *vt* **DO DANCE STEPS** to perform the steps of a dance (*dated*) ■ *n* **1. WAY OF TREADING** a way or sound of walking or stepping ○ *heard the heavy tread of marching feet* **2. ACT OF TREADING** an act of walking or of trampling something **3.** BUILDINGS **HORIZONTAL PART OF STEP** the horizontal part of a step in a staircase **4.** MEASURE **WIDTH OF STEP** the width of the horizontal part of a step, measured from front to back **5.** AUTOMOT **OUTER SURFACE OF TIRE** the part of the surface of a tire or wheel that comes in contact with a road or rail **6.** AUTOMOT **DEPTH OF GROOVES ON TIRE SURFACE** the depth of grooves on the surface of a tire **7.** CLOTHING **PART OF SHOE SOLE TOUCHING GROUND** the part of the sole of a shoe that touches the ground [Old English *tredan* < Germanic] —**tread·er** *n* —**tread·less** *adj*

tread·le /trédd'l/ *n* a lever pushed repeatedly by the foot to provide drive for a machine such as a sewing machine or potter's wheel ■ *vti* (**-led, -ling, -les**) to operate a treadle, or operate a machine by using a treadle [Old English *tredel* "step, stair" < *tredan* (see TREAD)] —**tread·ler** *n*

tread·mill /tréd mìl/ *n* **1. NEVER-ENDING ROUTINE** a monotonous and seemingly endless task, job, or routine **2. EXERCISE MACHINE** a machine with an endless belt on which somebody can walk, jog, or run, used for exercise and stress testing **3. CYLINDER PROVIDING POWER** a continuous belt or series of steps kept moving by people or animals walking on it that is used to provide power to a machine, e.g., to grind grain or raise water from a well

tread sep·ar·a·tion *n* the separation of a tire tread from the rest of the tire on a moving motor vehicle, often a cause of catastrophic accidents when high speed is a factor

treas. *abbr* **1.** treasurer **2.** treasury

trea·son /treéz'n/ *n* **1. BETRAYAL OF COUNTRY** a violation of the allegiance owed by somebody to his or her own country, e.g., by aiding an enemy **2. TREACHERY** betrayal or disloyalty **3. ACT OF BETRAYAL** an act of betrayal or disloyalty [12C. Via Anglo-Norman *treisoun* "treacherous handing over, betrayal" < Latin *tradition-* (see TRADITION)]

trea·son·a·ble /treéz'nəb'l/, **trea·son·ous** /treéz'nəss/ *adj* punishable as treason —**trea·son·a·bly** *adv*

trea·sure /trézhər/ *n* **1. JEWELS AND PRECIOUS OBJECTS** wealth, especially in the form of jewels and precious objects, often accumulated or hoarded **2. SOMETHING VALUABLE** something of great value or worth **3. SOMEBODY HIGHLY VALUED** a highly valued or much loved person ○ *an actor considered one of our national treasures* ■ *vt* (**-ured, -ur·ing, -ures**) **1. REGARD SOMEBODY OR SOMETHING AS VALUABLE** to prize somebody or something as being of great value or worth ○ *treasured the memory of that day* **2. ACCUMULATE AND STORE SOMETHING VALUABLE** to accumulate and store something regarded as valuable [12C. Via French *trésor* < Latin *thesaurus* < Greek *thēsauros* "treasure"] —**treas·ur·a·ble** *adj*

CULTURAL NOTE ***Treasure Island***, a novel (1883) by Scottish writer Robert Louis Stevenson. This classic romance recounts young Jim Hawkins's adventures with a treacherous band of pirates searching for lost treasure on a distant island. The book's most memorable character is one-legged pirate Long John Silver, who carries a pet parrot given to shrieking "Pieces of eight!".

treas·ure house *n* **1.** a place or collection in which many valuable things are located **2.** a building in which treasure is kept

treas·ure hunt *n* a game in which competitors follow a series of clues that lead to a hidden prize

trea·sur·er /trézhərər/ *n* somebody who manages the finances of a government, organization, or corporation, usually the chief financial officer —**treas·ur·er·ship** *n*

Treas·ure State *n* a nickname for Montana

treas·ure-trove *n* **1.** silver or gold coins or bullion found buried and for which there is no known owner **2.** something discovered that is valuable or the source of something valuable ○ *The new store is a treasure-trove of antiques.* [Mid-16C. < Anglo-Norman *tresor trove* < Old French *tresor* "treasure" + *trove*, past participle of *trover* "find"]

treas·ur·y /trézhəree/ (*plural* **-ies**) *n* **1. STORE OF MONEY** the funds or revenues of a government, organization, or corporation, or the place in which they are deposited and disbursed **2. PLACE FOR THINGS OF VALUE** a place in which treasure or other valuable items are stored and preserved **3. COLLECTION OF VALUABLE THINGS** a source or collection of valuable things such as literary or artistic works [13C. < Old French *tresorie* < *tresor* (see TREASURE)]

Treas·ur·y *n* **1.** in many countries, the government department in charge of collecting and managing public revenue **2.** a security issued by the US Treasury

Treas·ur·y bill *n* a short-term obligation issued by the US government, sold at a discount from its face value and redeemed at its face value upon maturity

Treas·ur·y bond *n* an interest-bearing debt security issued by the US government, with an initial life of between ten and thirty years

Treas·ur·y note *n* an intermediate-term, interest-paying debt instrument issued by the US government, with an initial life of between one and ten years

treat /treet/ *v* (**treat·ed, treat·ing, treats**) **1.** *vt* **REGARD SOMEBODY IN PARTICULAR WAY** to behave toward or think of somebody or something in a particular way ○ *They treated us like family.* **2.** *vt* **GIVE MEDICAL AID TO SOMEBODY** to give medical aid to somebody, or apply medical techniques to a disease or symptom in order to provide a cure **3.** *vt* **SUBJECT SOMETHING TO PROCESS OR AGENT** to subject something to a physical, chemical, or biological process or agent such as a chemical reaction or the application of a coating **4.** *vt* **PAY FOR SOMEBODY** to pay for food, drink, entertainment, or gifts for somebody ○ *I'll treat you to lunch at the hotel.* **5.** *vt* **PROVIDE SOMEBODY WITH SOMETHING**

PLEASURABLE to give somebody or yourself something enjoyable ○ *They treated their mother to breakfast in bed.* **6.** *vt* **DEAL WITH SOMETHING IN PARTICULAR WAY** to present or handle a subject, especially in art or literature, in a particular way ○ *treats a delicate subject with great sensitivity* **7.** *vi* **DISCUSS TOPIC** to discuss or deal with a topic in writing or speech ○ *a play that treats of greed and revenge* **8.** *vi* **NEGOTIATE TERMS** to negotiate, especially in order to reach a settlement (*formal*) ○ *refusing to treat with the enemy* ■ *n* **1. ENTERTAINMENT PAID FOR BY SOMEBODY ELSE** something that is given to somebody and paid for by somebody else, e.g., food, entertainment, or a gift **2. ACT OF PAYING FOR SOMEBODY** an act of paying for something such as food, entertainment, or a gift, for somebody **3. SOMETHING ENJOYABLE** something enjoyable, especially when a surprise ○ *It's a treat to see a smile on his face again.* [13C. Via Old French *traitier* "bargain with, negotiate" < Latin *tractare* "handle" < *trahere* "pull"] —**treat·a·ble** *adj* —**treat·er** *n*

trea·tise /tréetiss/ *n* a formal written work that deals with a subject systematically and usually extensively [14C. < Anglo-Norman *tretiz* < Old French *traitier* (see TREAT)]

treat·ment /tréetmənt/ *n* **1. PROVISION OF MEDICAL CARE** the application of medical care to cure disease, heal injuries, or ease symptoms **2. MEDICAL REMEDY** a remedy, procedure, or technique for curing or alleviating a disease, injury, or condition ○ *a new treatment for asthma* **3. WAY OF HANDLING SOMEBODY OR SOMETHING** the particular way in which somebody or something is dealt with or handled ○ *had pretty rough treatment* **4. TREATING OF SOMETHING WITH AGENT** an act of subjecting something to a physical, chemical, or biological process or agent **5. USUAL ACTIONS TAKEN** the usual way of dealing with a person or situation (*informal*) ○ *As guests of the government we got the full VIP treatment.* **6.** MOVIES **SCHEMATIC VERSION OF MOVIE** a schematic version of a movie script, generally without dialogue and individual shots, indicating how the story is to be dealt with in a screenplay **7.** ARTS **PRESENTATION OF SUBJECT** the way of presenting or handling a subject, especially in art or literature

trea·ty /tréetee/ (*plural* **-ties**) *n* **1.** a formal contract or agreement negotiated between countries or other political entities **2.** an agreement or contract between two or more parties [14C. Via Old French *traité* "assembly, agreement, treaty" < Latin *tractatus* < *tractare* (see TREAT)]

trea·ty In·di·an *n Can* PEOPLES, POL same as **Status Indian**

trea·ty port *n* formerly, a port where foreign trade was allowed by a treaty, especially in China, Japan, and Korea

trea·ty rights *npl Can* the rights allocated by the Canadian federal government to some groups of aboriginal people by treaty

Treb·bi·a·no /trèbbee aánō/ *n* **1.** a white wine mainly from Italy and France **2.** a white grape variety. Use: to make Trebbiano and other blended wines. [Late 19C. < Italian, after *Trebbia*, river in north central Italy]

treb·le /trébb'l/ *adj* **1. TRIPLE** three times as many or as much **2. HIGH-PITCHED** high-pitched or shrill **3. OF HIGHEST MUSICAL RANGE** relating to or intended for a boy or girl soprano voice or a high-pitched instrument ■ *n* **1. HIGH-PITCHED SOUND** a high-pitched or shrill sound **2. SOMETHING TRIPLED** something three times as many or as much **3.** MUSIC **HIGH-PITCHED INSTRUMENT OR VOICE** a treble voice, singer, instrument, or part **4.** RECORDING **AUDIO FREQUENCY RANGE** the higher audio frequencies electronically reproduced by a radio, recording, or sound system **5.** RECORDING **CONTROL FOR HIGH-FREQUENCY AUDIO RESPONSE** a control for increasing or decreasing the high-frequency response on a radio or audio amplifier ■ *vti* (**-led, -ling, -les**) **TRIPLE SOMETHING** to become three times as many or as much, or make something become three times as many or as much ○ *Output has trebled over the past year.* [13C. Via French < Latin *triplus* "triple"] —**treb·le·ness** *n* —**treb·ly** *adv*

treb·le clef *n* a clef that puts G above middle C on the second line of the staff, used for soprano and alto voices, high-pitched instruments, and the right hand of keyboard instruments

Tre·blin·ka /tre blíngkə/ site of two Nazi concentration camps in eastern Poland, situated about 60 mi./97 km northeast of Warsaw

treb·u·chet /trèbbyə shét/, **treb·uc·ket** /trèbbyə két/ *n* a medieval siege engine with a sling attached to a wooden arm for hurling large stones [14C. < French *trébuchet* < *trébucher* "overturn"]

tre·cen·to /tray chéntō/ *n* the 14th century, used especially in referring to Italian art and literature [Mid-19C. < Italian, shortening of *mil trecento* "one thousand three hundred"] —**tre·cen·tist** *n*

~~**trecherous**~~ incorrect spelling of **treacherous**

tree /tree/ *n* **1. LARGE PERENNIAL WOODY PLANT** a woody perennial plant that grows to a height of several feet and typically has a single erect main stem with side branches **2. PLANT RESEMBLING TREE** a large bush or nonwoody plant that resembles a tree, e.g., a palm tree or tree fern **3. SOMETHING WITH BRANCHES LIKE TREE** something that has branches or pegs on which to hang things ○ *a hat tree* **4. DIAGRAM OF HIERARCHICAL STRUCTURE** a diagram of a hierarchical structure that shows the relationships between components as branches **5.** CONSTR **WOODEN SUPPORT** a wooden beam, bar, or post that supports or is part of a structure **6.** COMPUT **HIERARCHICAL DATA STRUCTURE** a hierarchical data structure in which each element contains data and may be linked by branches to two or more other elements. Every element has only a single predecessor, except for the first, which is called the root and has no predecessor. **7.** CRYSTALS **CRYSTALLINE GROWTH** a branching growth of crystals, particularly of a metal **8.** CRIME same as **gallows** (*archaic*) **9.** CHR **CROSS JESUS CHRIST DIED ON** in Christianity, the cross on which Jesus Christ was crucified (*archaic*) ■ *vt* (**treed, tree·ing, trees**) **1. FORCE SOMEBODY UP TREE** to chase an animal or person up a tree, or force an animal or person to climb a tree **2. PUT SOMEBODY IN DIFFICULT SITUATION** to force somebody into a position of difficulty or disadvantage (*informal*) **3. STRETCH FOOTWEAR ON SHOETREE** to stretch or shape a shoe or boot on a shoetree [Old English *trēo(w)* < Indo-European, "oak tree"] —**tree·less** *adj* —**tree·less·ness** *n* ◇ **be barking up the wrong tree** to be mistaken, especially as regards the best way to achieve something ◇ **out of your tree** behaving irrationally (*slang*) ◇ **up a tree** in a position of difficulty or disadvantage (*informal*)

tree di·a·gram *n* INFO SCI same as **tree** *n* (sense 4)

tree farm *n* an area where trees are grown commercially for their wood products

tree fern *n* a fern that grows to the height of a tree and has a crown of fronds. Native to: tropics. Family: Cyatheaceae or Marattiaceae.

tree frog *n* a small frog that has long digits with adhesive disks that allow it to climb trees. Native to: America, South Asia, Australia. Family: Hylidae.

tree heath *n* TREES same as **briar**[1] (sense 2)

tree·hop·per /trée hòppər/ *n* a small tree-dwelling insect that feeds on the sap of trees. Many species have grotesque projections on their backs. Family: Membracidae.

tree house *n* a platform, often with a roof and walls, built among the branches of a tree, especially for children to play in

tree·hug·ger /trée hùggər/ *n* somebody who is regarded as excessively devoted to environmental protection (*informal*)

tree line *n* **1.** the edge of a wood or forest **2.** *UK* ECOL same as **timberline**

tree mal·low *n* a tall woody wild or cultivated plant. Flowers: reddish purple. Native to: rocky coastal areas in Europe and North Africa. Latin name: *Lavatera arborea*.

tre·en /trée ən, treen/ *n* tableware and other household utensils made of wood ■ *adj* made of wood (*archaic*) [Old English *trēowen* "made of wood" < TREE]

tree·nail /trée nàyl, trénn'l, trúnn'l/, **tre·nail** /trée nàyl, trénn'l/, **trun·nel** /trúnn'l/ *n* a large cylindrical peg made of dry wood that expands to give a tight fit when it is wet and is used to fasten timbers together, e.g., in ships

tree-of-heav·en (*plural* **trees-of-heav·en**) *n* a quick-growing deciduous tree that is tolerant of pollution and is often planted in urban areas. Native to: China. Latin name: *Ailanthus altissima* or *Ailanthus glandulosa*.

tree of knowl·edge *n* in the Bible, the tree that grew in the Garden of Eden and produced the fruit that was forbidden to Adam and Eve (Genesis 2:9, 3)

tree of life *n* in the Bible, the tree that grew in the Garden of Eden and produced a fruit that gave eternal life to anybody who ate it (Genesis 3:22–24)

tree ring *n* BOT same as **growth ring**

tree shrew *n* a small insect-eating animal resembling a squirrel with a long snout. Native to: forests of Southeast Asia. Family: Tupaiidae.

tree-sit *n* an extended period of time spent by a protester in a handmade tree house in an effort to prevent tree-felling, e.g., by logging companies

tree spar·row *n* **1.** a large sparrow with a chestnut cap and a gray breast with a single dark chest spot. Native to: North America. Latin name: *Spizella arborea*. **2.** a small sparrow that differs from a house sparrow in having a black spot near its ear and a chestnut crown. Native to: Europe, South Asia. Latin name: *Passer montanus*.

tree spik·ing *n* the act of hammering long nails into trees as a form of environmental protest, so as to make it dangerous to cut down the trees using a chain saw

tree sur·geon *n* somebody trained in pruning trees or treating diseased or damaged trees, e.g., by cutting off branches or filling cavities —**tree sur·ger·y** *n*

tree toad *n* AMPHIB same as **tree frog**

tree to·ma·to *n Can, UK* same as **tamarillo**

tree·top /trée tòp/ *n* the highest branches of a tree

tree·ware /trée wèr/ *n* books and other material printed on paper made from wood pulp

tref /trayf/, **treif** *adj* not kosher and hence forbidden to Jews under dietary laws [Mid-19C. < Hebrew *ṭĕrēpāh* "flesh from an animal that has been torn" < *ṭārap* "tear, rend"]

tre·foil /trée fòyl, tré-/ *n* **1. THREE-LOBED SHAPE OR OBJECT** an object or design with three lobes or connected parts, e.g., an emblem used in heraldry **2.** PLANTS **PLANT WITH THREE-LOBED LEAVES** a plant of the pea family that has three-lobed leaves, especially clover **3.** BOT **THREE-LOBED LEAF OR PART** a leaf or other plant part with three lobes **4.** ARCHIT **ORNAMENT IN SHAPE OF CLOVER LEAF** an architectural ornament or form resembling a clover leaf [14C. Via Anglo-Norman *trifoil* < Latin *trifolium* "with three leaves" < *folium* "leaf"]

tre·ha·la /tri haálə/ *n* an edible sugary substance that comes from the pupal case of an Asian beetle [Mid-19C. Via Turkish *tigale* < Persian *tīgāl*]

tre·ha·lase /tri haá làyss, -làyz/ *n* an enzyme that catalyzes the breakdown of trehalose

tre·ha·lose /tri haá lōss, -lōz/ *n* a disaccharide found in yeast, lichen, bacteria, and insects

treil·lage /tray aázh, tráylij/ *n* a trellis or piece of latticework [Late 17C. < French < *treille* < Latin *trichila* "bower, arbor"]

trek /trek/ *vi* (**trekked, trek·king, treks**) **1. MAKE LONG DIFFICULT JOURNEY** to make a long difficult journey, especially on foot and often over rough or mountainous terrain **2. GO SLOWLY OR LABORIOUSLY** to go somewhere slowly or with difficulty ○ *I had to trek across town to the other bookstore.* **3.** *S Africa* **GO BY OX WAGON** to travel in a wagon pulled by an ox ■ *n* **1. LONG DIFFICULT JOURNEY** a long difficult journey, especially on foot and often over rough or mountainous terrain **2.** *S Africa* **STAGE OF JOURNEY** a journey or stage of a journey, especially a migration by ox wagon [Mid-19C. Via Afrikaans < Dutch *trekken* "draw, pull, travel"] —**trek·ker** *n*

CULTURAL NOTE ***Star Trek***, a television series created in 1966 by US writer and producer Gene Roddenberry (1921–91). The adventures of the Starship Enterprise, a 23rd-century spacecraft on a mission "to boldly go where no man has gone before," initially ran for 79 episodes. The popularity of the series later gave rise to numerous movie spinoffs, the follow-up television series

Star Trek: The Next Generation, *Star Trek: Deep Space Nine*, *Star Trek: Voyager*, and *Enterprise*, and a worldwide network of dedicated fans known as Trekkies.

Trek·kie /trékee/ *n* a fan of the science-fiction television series *Star Trek* (*informal*)

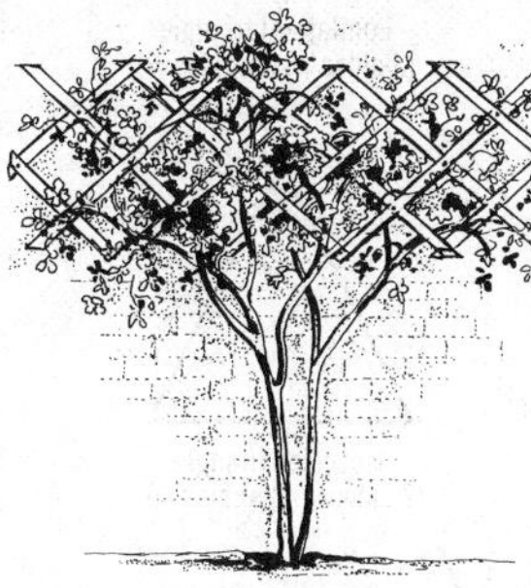

trellis

trel·lis /trélliss/ *n* **1.** LATTICE FOR SUPPORTING PLANT a lattice of wood, metal, or plastic used to support plants, usually fixed to a wall **2.** LATTICEWORK STRUCTURE a structure made of latticework, especially an arch ■ *vt* (**-lised, -lis·ing, -lis·es**) **1.** TRAIN PLANT ON LATTICE to support or train a plant such as a vine on a trellis **2.** MAKE SOMETHING INTO TRELLIS to interweave pieces of wood, metal, or plastic to make a trellis [14C. Via Old French *trelis* < Latin *trilix* "three threads" < *licium* "thread of a warp"]

trel·lis·work /trélliss wùrk/ *n* latticework, usually for supporting plants

trem·a·tode /trémmə tōd/ *n* a flatworm that lives as a parasite in the liver, gut, lungs, or blood vessels of vertebrates, attaching itself by suckers or hooks and sometimes causing serious disease. Class: Trematoda. [Mid-19C. Via modern Latin *Trematoda* < Greek *trēmatōdēs* "perforated" (because many have perforated skins) < *trēma* "hole, orifice"]

trem·ble /trémb'l/ *vi* (**-bled, -bling, -bles**) **1.** SHAKE SLIGHTLY BUT UNCONTROLLABLY to shake with slight movements, continuously and uncontrollably, e.g., from fear, cold, or anger **2.** VIBRATE to shake or vibrate as a result of an external force ○ *We felt the house tremble as the train passed.* **3.** BE AFRAID to be afraid or anxious about something ■ *n* QUIVERING a shaking, vibration, or quivering [14C. Via Old French *trembler* < medieval Latin *tremulare* "shake" < Latin *tremulus* "shaking" < *tremere* "shake"] —**trem·bling** *adj* —**trem·bling·ly** *adv* —**trem·bly** *adj*

trem·bles /trémb'lz/ *n* poisoning in sheep and cattle that have fed on white snakeroot or some other poisonous plants. Affected animals tremble and become weak. (*takes a singular verb*)

tre·men·dous /trə méndəss/ *adj* **1.** extremely large, powerful, or great ○ *There was a tremendous clap of thunder.* **2.** extremely good, successful, or impressive ○ *a tremendous improvement* [Mid-17C. < Latin *tremendus* "fearful" < *tremere* "shake"] —**tre·men·dous·ly** *adv* —**tre·men·dous·ness** *n*

trem·o·lite /trémmə līt/ *n* a white, gray, or pale green hydrated silicate mineral containing calcium, magnesium, and some iron. Source: metamorphic rocks. Use: substitute for asbestos. [Late 18C. After *Tremola*, valley in Switzerland]

trem·o·lo /trémmə lō/ (*plural* **-los**) *n* **1.** the rapid repetition of a tone or the rapid alternation between two tones in singing or playing a musical instrument, which produces a quavering effect **2.** a device in an organ for producing tremolo [Mid-18C. Via Italian < Latin *tremulus* (see TREMBLE)]

trem·or /trémmər/ *n* **1.** SHUDDER a quiver or shudder, e.g., from fear, illness, or nervousness **2.** SUDDEN SENSATION a sudden and usually brief feeling of excitement, nervousness, or anticipation **3.** WAVERING SOUND OR LIGHT a fluctuation in a sound or light **4.** SEISMOL MINOR EARTHQUAKE a quivering or vibration caused by slippage of the Earth's crust at a fault, especially before or after a major earthquake **5.** MED TREMBLING a slight shaking or trembling movement of a part of the body [14C. Directly or via French < Latin, "trembling, terror" < *tremere* "shake"] —**trem·or·ous** *adj*

trem·u·lant /trémmyələnt/ *adj* shaking or trembling [15C. < Latin *tremulus* (see TREMBLE)]

trem·u·lous /trémmyələss/ *adj* **1.** shaking, trembling, or quavering, e.g., from fear or nervousness ○ *in a tremulous voice* **2.** showing fear or nervousness about something [Early 17C. < Latin *tremulus* (see TREMBLE)] —**trem·u·lous·ly** *adv* —**trem·u·lous·ness** *n*

tre·nail *n* CONSTR same as **treenail**

trench /trench/ *n* **1.** DITCH WITH STEEP SIDES a long deep hole dug in the ground, usually with steep or vertical sides **2.** MIL PROTECTION AGAINST ENEMY FIRE a long excavation, often with the excavated earth banked up in front, used as a defense against enemy fire ○ *warfare conducted in the trenches* **3.** OCEANOG VALLEY ON OCEAN FLOOR a long narrow valley on an ocean or sea floor ■ *v* (**trenched, trench·ing, trench·es**) **1.** *vti* DIG TRENCH IN SOMETHING to dig a long deep hole in or through something **2.** *vt* PUT SOMETHING IN TRENCH to place something such as a pipe in a trench **3.** *vt* MIL FORTIFY SOMETHING WITH TRENCHES to fortify a position with trenches as a defense against enemy fire [14C. < Old French *trenche* "ditch, cutting, slice" < *trenchier* "to cut" < Latin *truncare* "cut (off)" < *truncus* "tree trunk"]

trench·ant /trénchənt/ *adj* **1.** direct, incisive, and deliberately hurtful ○ *trenchant criticism* **2.** effective and relevant in the pursuit or achievement of a goal ○ *trenchant opinions* [14C. < Old French, "cutting" < *trenchier* (see TRENCH)] —**trench·an·cy** *n* —**trench·ant·ly** *adv*

Tren·chard /trénch aàrd, trénchərd/, **Hugh Montague, 1st Viscount** (1873–1956) British air force commander. In World War I he played a central role in the formation of the RAF (1918) and became its first marshal.

trench coat *n* a belted double-breasted raincoat, originally modeled on a military coat of World War I

trench·er[1] /trénchər/ *n* formerly, a wooden platter used to serve or cut food (*archaic*) [14C. < Anglo-Norman *trenchour*, Old French *trenchoir* < *trenchier* (see TRENCH)]

trench·er[2] /trénchər/ *n* somebody or something that digs trenches, especially a machine that cuts a furrow or ditch in which to lay cables or pipes [Early 17C. < TRENCH]

trench·er·man /trénchərmən/ (*plural* **-men** /-mən/) *n* a hearty eater

trench fe·ver *n* a contagious illness whose symptoms include fever, headaches, and muscle aches, common among soldiers fighting in trenches in World War I and caused by the bacterium *Rochalimaea quintana*

trench foot *n* a painful condition of the feet caused by prolonged exposure of the feet to cold and wet. It results in loss of sensation, tissue damage, and sometimes gangrene.

trench mor·tar *n* a small cannon capable of firing shells at high trajectories over short distances, often used in trench warfare

trench mouth *n* MED same as **Vincent's angina**

trench war·fare *n* **1.** a form of warfare in which armies conduct attacks on each other from opposing positions in fortified trenches **2.** a long-standing and bitter conflict in which opposing parties continually attack each other

trend /trend/ *n* **1.** TENDENCY a general tendency, movement, or direction ○ *a report documenting recent social trends* **2.** PREVAILING STYLE a current fashion or mode ○ *the latest trends in designer kitchens* ■ *vi* (**trend·ed, trend·ing, trends**) TEND OR MOVE IN PARTICULAR WAY to show a tendency or movement toward something or in a particular direction ○ *public opinion trending toward reunification* [Old English *trendan* "revolve, turn, turn in a particular direction" < Germanic, "roundness"]

trend·oid /trénd òyd/ *n* somebody who slavishly follows the latest trends or fashions (*informal*) —**trend·oid** *adj*

trend·set·ter /trénd sèttər/ *n* somebody or something that starts or popularizes a new trend or fashion —**trend·set·ting** *adj*

trend·y /tréndee/ (*informal*) *adj* (**-i·er, -i·est**) **1.** CURRENTLY FASHIONABLE relating to or exemplifying the latest fashion ○ *a trendy restaurant* **2.** FOLLOWING LATEST FASHION deliberately reflecting or adopting fashionable, often faddish, ideas or tastes ■ *n* (*plural* **-ies**) SOMEBODY FOLLOWING LATEST FASHION somebody who follows the latest trends or fashions, often slavishly —**trend·i·ly** *adv* —**trend·i·ness** *n*

Trent /trent/ third longest river in England. It rises at Biddulph Moor, Staffordshire, and flows into the North Sea via the Humber estuary. Length: 170 mi./270 km.

trente et qua·rante /traaNt ay ka raaNt/ *n* GAMBLING same as **rouge et noir** [Late 17C. < French, "thirty and forty" (winning and losing numbers)]

Tren·ton /trént'n/ capital city of New Jersey, in the west central part of the state, 28 mi./45 km northeast of Philadelphia. Population: 85,650 (2002 estimate).

tre·pan[1] /trə pán/ *n* **1.** SURG EARLY SURGICAL INSTRUMENT an early form of trephine, used especially to cut a hole in the skull **2.** MECH ENG TOOL FOR CUTTING DISK OR CYLINDER a machine tool used to remove a circular disk from a metal sheet or a shallow cylindrical core from a metal ingot or block. The hole is made by removing a concentric ring of material as opposed to disintegrating the material originally within the hole, as with drilling and boring. **3.** MIN EXTRACT ROCK-BORING TOOL a tool for boring holes in rock ■ *vt* (**-panned, -pan·ning, -pans**) **1.** SURG REMOVE CIRCLE OF BONE formerly, to remove a circular section from a bone, especially the skull, with a trepan **2.** MECH ENG CUT SOMETHING OUT to cut a disk or cylindrical core from something using a trepan **3.** MIN EXTRACT BORE HOLE IN ROCK to bore a hole in rock using a trepan [14C. Via medieval Latin *trepanum* "rotary saw" < Greek *trupanon* "borer" < *trupan* "pierce" < *trupē* "hole"] —**trep·a·na·tion** /trèppə náysh'n/ *n* —**tre·pan·ner** *n*

tre·pan[2] /trə pán/, **tra·pan** (*archaic*) *vt* (**-panned, -pan·ning, -pans**) to trap or ensnare somebody or something ■ *n* somebody or something that entraps or ensnares others [Mid-17C. Probably alteration of TRAP[1]]

tre·pang /trə páng/ *n* a large sea cucumber that is eaten in soups, especially in China and Indonesia. Native to: South Pacific, Indian Ocean. Genera: *Holothuria* or *Actinopyga*. [Late 18C. < Malay *teripang*]

tre·phine /tri fīn, tree fīn/ *n* a cylindrical sharp or sawtooth-edged surgical instrument, used especially to cut a hole in the skull. It is also used in corneal grafting to remove an opaque disk from a cornea so that it can be replaced with a clear disk. ■ *vt* (**-phined, -phin·ing, -phines**) to remove a circular section from a bone, especially the skull, or from corneal tissue with a trephine [Early 17C. < Latin *tres fines* "three ends," partly after TREPAN[1]] —**treph·i·na·tion** /trèffə náysh'n/ *n*

trep·i·da·tion /trèppi dáysh'n/ *n* **1.** fear or uneasiness about the future or a future event **2.** an involuntary trembling (*archaic*) [15C. < Latin *trepidation-* < *trepidare* "startle, be agitated"]

trep·o·ne·ma /trèppə néemə/ (*plural* **-ma·ta** /-mətə/ or **-mas**), **trep·o·neme** /tréppə neem/ *n* a spirochete bacterium that lives as a parasite in warm-blooded animals. One species causes syphilis in humans. Genus: *Treponema*. [Early 20C. < modern Latin < Greek *trepein* "turn" + *nēma* "thread"] —**trep·o·ne·mal** *adj*

tres·pass /tréspəss, -pàss/ *vi* (**-passed, -pass·ing, -pass·es**) **1.** ENCROACH ON SOMEBODY to intrude on somebody's privacy or time **2.** BREAK MORAL OR SOCIAL LAW to commit a sin or break a social law (*archaic*) **3.** LAW ENTER SOMEBODY ELSE'S LAND UNLAWFULLY to go onto somebody else's land or enter somebody else's property without permission **4.** LAW CAUSE INJURY to cause injury to the person, property, or rights of another ■ *n* **1.** ENCROACHMENT an intrusion into somebody's privacy or time **2.** SIN a sin or act of wrongdoing (*archaic*) **3.** LAW UNLAWFUL ENTRY ONTO SOMEBODY ELSE'S LAND the act or an instance of going onto somebody else's land or entering somebody else's property without permission [14C. < Old French *trespas* "transgression" < *trespasser* "pass beyond or across" < medieval Latin *transpassare*] —**tres·pass·er** *n*

tress /tress/ *n* a lock of long hair, especially a woman's hair ■ **tress·es** *npl* somebody's hair, especially a woman's long hair [13C. < Old French *tresse*]

tres·tle /tréss'l/ *n* **1.** SUPPORTING FRAMEWORK a supporting framework consisting of a horizontal beam held up by a pair of splayed legs at each end **2.** **TOWER FOR SUPPORTING BRIDGE** a tower with sloping sides braced by horizontal crosspieces that supports a bridge, made of timber, steel, or reinforced concrete **3.** **BRIDGE SUPPORTED BY TOWERS** a bridge consisting of multiple short spans supported by towers with sloping sides braced by horizontal crosspieces [14C. < Old French *trestel* "small beam" < Latin *transtrum* "beam, crossbar"]

trestle table

tres·tle ta·ble *n* a table whose top is supported on trestles

tres·tle·tree /tréss'l treè/ *n* either of the two horizontal beams fixed to a masthead to support the crosstrees

tres·tle·work /tréss'l wùrk/ *n* a system of supporting trestles, e.g., one that supports a bridge

tret·i·noin /trétti nòyn/ *n* a drug related chemically to vitamin A. Use: topical treatment of acne and other skin disorders. [Late 20C. < TRANS- + *retinoic (acid)* (< RETINO-)]

tre·val·ly /trə vállee/ (*plural* **-lies**) *n* an ocean fish with a slender body and sharply forked tail. Native to: Australia. Family: Carangidae. [Late 19C. Alteration of CAVALLA]

Tre·vi·no /trə veénō/, **Lee** (*b.* 1939) US golfer. He won 27 Professional Golfers' Association titles, including six major tournaments. Full name **Trevino, Lee Buck**

Tre·vi·so /tre veézō/ capital city of Treviso Province, Veneto Region, northeastern Italy. Population: 80,144 (2001).

Trev·i·thick /trévvə thìk/, **Richard** (1771–1833) British engineer and inventor. His steam locomotives, using the high-pressure steam engines that he developed, were the first to carry passengers or freight on a regular basis.

trews /trooz/ *npl* close-fitting pants, usually made of plaid cloth, worn by some Scottish army regiments [Mid-16C. < Irish *triús* or Gaelic *triubhas* "close-fitting shorts"]

trey /tray/ (*plural* **treys**) *n* a card, or the face of a die or domino, with three pips [14C. Via Old French *trei(s)* < Latin *tres* "three"]

TRH *abbr* BIOCHEM thyrotropin-releasing hormone

tri- *prefix* three, third ○ *trilateral* [< Latin and Greek < Indo-European]

tri·a·ble /trī́ əb'l/ *adj* **1.** subject to or fit for trial in a court of law **2.** able to be tried or tested [15C. < Anglo-Norman < Old French *trier* (see TRY)] —**tri·a·ble·ness** *n*

tri·ac·id /trī ássid/ *adj* **1.** describes a base capable of reacting with three hydrogen atoms or three molecules of a monobasic acid **2.** describes an acid or a salt containing three replaceable hydrogen atoms

tri·ad /trī́ àd, -əd/ *n* **1.** **SET OF 3** a group of three people or things **2.** MUSIC **MUSICAL CHORD** a musical chord consisting of three notes, especially a chord made up of a tonic, a third, and a fifth **3.** CHEM **ATOM WITH VALENCE OF 3** an atom or chemical group with a valence of three **4.** MIL **US STRATEGIC MISSILE FORCE** a US strategic missile force made up of bombers, land-based ballistic missiles, and submarine-launched ballistic missiles **5.** LITERAT **WELSH LITERARY FORM** a form of composition in ancient Welsh literature in which subjects or statements are arranged in groups of three [Mid-16C. Via French *triade* or late Latin *triad-* < Greek *triad-* "three"] —**tri·ad·ic** /trī áddik/ *adj*

tri·age /tree áazh, treè áazh/ *n* the process of prioritizing sick or injured people for treatment according to the seriousness of the condition or injury [Early 18C. < French < *trier* (see TRY)]

tri·al /trī́ əl, trīl/ *n* **1.** **FORMAL LEGAL PROCESS** a formal examination of the facts and law in a civil or criminal action before a court of law in order to determine an issue **2.** **USE OF COURT TRIAL** the use of a court trial to determine an issue or somebody's guilt or innocence ○ *standing trial for fraud* **3.** **TEST** a test or experiment to determine the quality, safety, performance, usefulness, or public acceptance of something ○ *a drug currently undergoing clinical trials* **4.** **PAINFUL EXPERIENCE** an instance of trouble or hardship, especially one that tests somebody's ability to endure **5.** **SOMEBODY OR SOMETHING TROUBLESOME** somebody or something that causes trouble or annoyance to somebody else ○ *He's such a trial!* **6.** **PRELIMINARY COMPETITION** a sports competition or preliminary test to select candidates for a later competition **7.** **EFFORT** an earnest attempt to do something (*formal*) ○ *a trial to circle the globe in a hot-air balloon* ■ *adj* **1.** **EXPERIMENTAL** done as a test or experiment ○ *a trial separation* **2.** LAW **OF COURT TRIAL** relating to or used in a court trial ○ *a trial judge* [Mid-15C. < Anglo-Norman *triallum* < Old French *trier* (see TRY)]

SPELLCHECK See *trail*

CULTURAL NOTE ***The Trial***, a novel (1925) by Austrian (Czech) writer Franz Kafka. It is the story of Josef K, a young bank clerk who is abruptly arrested for an unspecified misdemeanor. After a long, unsuccessful attempt to discover the nature of his crime, Josef is executed. This enigmatic work is seen as a disturbing allegory of the human condition.

---

tri·al and er·ror *n* a method of finding a satisfactory solution or means of doing something by experimenting with alternatives and eliminating failures

tri·al bal·ance *n* a statement used to check that the debits and credits in a double-entry bookkeeping ledger are equal

tri·al bal·loon *n* a tentative suggestion, proposal, or plan put forward to test opinion or reaction

tri·al by fire *n* a thorough test of somebody's abilities or character under pressure

tri·al court *n* a court in which a case is first decided, as opposed to a court of appeals

tri·al law·yer *n* a lawyer who practices in a trial court as opposed to a court of appeals

tri·a·logue /trī́ ə lòg/, **tri·a·log** *n* discussion involving three people or groups [Mid-16C. Blend of TRI- + DIALOGUE]

tri·al run *n* a test of something new or untried, especially to assess its performance

tri·am·cin·o·lone /trī am sínnə lōn/ *n* a synthetic corticosteroid drug. Use: treatment of skin, oral, and joint inflammations. Formula: $C_{21}H_{27}FO_6$. [Mid-20C. < TRI- + *amyl* + *cinene* + *prednisolone*]

tri·an·gle /trī́ àng g'l/ *n* **1.** **3-SIDED FIGURE** a two-dimensional geometric figure formed of three sides and three angles. The triangle is a fundamental figure of plane geometry, since it is the polygon with the fewest sides and any other polygon can be subdivided into triangles. **2.** **OBJECT WITH 3 SIDES** something shaped like a triangle **3.** **DRAFTING INSTRUMENT FOR RULING LINES** any thin flat three-sided instrument used as a drawing and drafting guide to rule straight lines at specific angles or for determining the angle of ruled lines. Typically the instruments have angles of 90°, 45°, 60°, and 30°. **4.** **3-PERSON RELATIONSHIP** an emotional or sexual relationship involving three people **5.** MUSIC **PERCUSSION INSTRUMENT** a metal bar bent into the shape of a triangle with one angle open, used as a percussion instrument [14C. Directly or via French < Latin *triangulum* < *triangulus* "three-cornered"]

tri·an·gu·lar /trī áng gyələr/ *adj* **1.** **OF TRIANGLE** relating to or in the shape of a triangle **2.** **WITH TRIANGULAR BASE** having a base in the shape of a triangle **3.** **HAVING 3 PARTS** consisting of or involving three people or parts [14C. < late Latin *triangularis* < Latin *triangulum* (see TRIANGLE)] —**tri·an·gu·lar·i·ty** /trī àng gyə lárrətee/ *n* —**tri·an·gu·lar·ly** *adv*

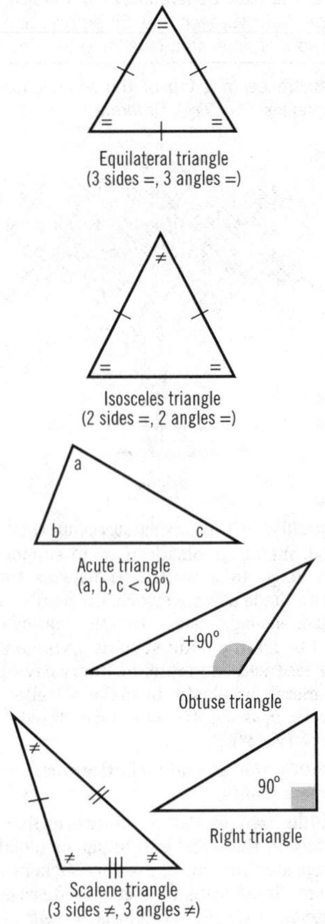

triangle

tri·an·gu·late *vt* /trī áng gyə làyt/ (**-lat·ed, -lat·ing, -lates**) **1.** **MEASURE SOMETHING USING TRIGONOMETRIC RELATIONSHIPS** to measure something using the trigonometric relationships between pairs of sides and angles of triangles **2.** **SURVEY OR MAP SOMETHING BY TRIANGULATION** to survey or map an area by the process of triangulation **3.** **SPLIT SOMETHING INTO TRIANGLES** to divide a surface into triangles **4.** **MAKE SOMETHING TRIANGULAR** to make something into the shape of a triangle ■ *adj* /trī áng gyələt, -làyt/ **MADE UP OF TRIANGLES** shaped like a triangle or made up of triangles [15C. < Latin *triangulum* (see TRIANGLE)] —**tri·an·gu·late·ly** *adv*

tri·an·gu·la·tion /trī àng gyə láysh'n/ *n* **1.** **METHOD FOR DETERMINING LOCATION TRIGONOMETRICALLY** a navigation technique that uses the trigonometric properties of triangles to determine a location or course by means of compass bearings from two points a known distance apart. Space-age global positioning systems enable people to triangulate their location relative to the known positions of Earth-orbiting satellites. **2.** **DIVIDING OF SURVEY AREA INTO TRIANGLES** the division of a large area into adjacent triangles for survey purposes using trigonometric relationships to calculate the dimensions of an area bounded by each triangle. One side (**baseline**) and the angles to the third point of each adjacent triangle are measured, and the lengths of the other sides can be calculated from these measurements. **3.** **SYSTEM OF TRIANGLES** the system of triangles laid out in triangulation

Tri·an·gu·lum /trī áng gyələm/ *n* a small constellation of the northern hemisphere. See illustration at **constellation**

Tri·an·gu·lum Aus·tra·le /-aw stráylee/ *n* a small constellation of the southern hemisphere. See illustration at **constellation**

tri·ar·chy /trī́ àarkee/ (*plural* **-chies**) *n* **1.** a system in which a country is ruled by three leaders **2.** a country ruled by three leaders [Early 17C. < Greek *triarkhia* "triumvirate," or < TRI- + -ARCH]

Tri·as·sic /trī ássik/ *n* the period of geologic time, 248 million to 206 million years ago, during which reptiles flourished and dinosaurs and evergreen forests first appeared. See table at **geologic time** [Mid-19C. < German *Trias* < Latin, "three, triad" < Greek] —**Tri·as·sic** *adj*

tri·ath·lon /trī áthlən, -lòn/ *n* an athletic competition in which the contestants compete in three different events and are awarded points for each to find the best all-around athlete. The events are usually swimming, cycling, and running. [Late 20C. < TRI- + Greek *athlon* "contest"] —**tri·ath·lete** *n*

tri·a·tom·ic /trī ə tómmik/ *adj* containing three atoms in each molecule —**tri·a·tom·i·cal·ly** *adv*

tri·ax·i·al /trī áksee əl/ *adj* having or involving three axes —**tri·ax·i·al·i·ty** /trī àksee állətee/ *n*

tri·a·zine /trī ə zeèn, trī á-/ *n* an organic compound with a six-membered ring containing three carbon and three nitrogen atoms. Formula: $C_3H_3N_3$.

tri·a·zole /trī ə zōl, trī á zōl/ *n* **1.** an organic compound with a five-membered ring containing two carbon and three nitrogen atoms. Formula: $C_2H_3N_3$. **2.** a derivative of triazole. Use: photocopying.

trib·ade /tríbbəd/ *n* a lesbian, especially one who takes part in tribadism [Early 17C. Via French or Latin < Greek *tribas* < *tribein* "rub"]

trib·a·dism /tríbbə dìzzəm/ *n* a lesbian practice in which one partner rubs her genitals against the other's

tri·bal en·roll·ment of·fi·cer *n* a member of a Native American people whose duty is to review ancestral documentation to determine if a candidate for entry into the tribe is ancestrally qualified for membership

trib·al·ism /trīb'l ìzzəm/ *n* **1.** the customs, beliefs, and social organization of a tribe or social group **2.** loyalty to a tribe or social group —**trib·al·ist** *n, adj* —**trib·al·is·tic** /trīb'l ístik/ *adj*

tri·ba·sic /trī báyssik/ *adj* **1.** describes an acid containing three replaceable hydrogen atoms and capable of reacting with three hydroxyl ions per molecule **2.** describes a compound that contains three univalent metal atoms or groups in each molecule

tribe /trīb/ *n* **1.** SOCIAL DIVISION OF PEOPLE a society or division of a society whose members have ancestry, customs, beliefs, and leadership in common **2.** FAMILY a large family (*informal*) **3.** GROUP WITH SOMETHING IN COMMON a group of people who have something in common such as an occupation, social background, or political viewpoint ○ *rebelled against the whole tribe of earnest policy makers* **4.** BIOL TAXONOMIC DIVISION a division in the scientific classification of animals and plants, between a subfamily and a genus **5.** ANCIENT HIST ANCIENT ROMAN SOCIAL GROUP one of the three groups, Latins, Sabines, and Etruscans, into which ancient Roman society was divided [13C. Via Old French *tribu* < Latin *tribus* "one of three ethnic divisions of the Roman people" < *tri-* "three"] —**trib·al** *adj* —**trib·al·ly** *adv*

Tri·be·ca /trī beèkə/, **Tri·Be·Ca** area of lower Manhattan known for its 19th-century cast-iron buildings, originally built as commercial premises and in the late 20th century renovated into artists' lofts, homes, and stores

tribes·man /trībzmən/ (*plural* **-men** /-mən/) *n* a man who is a member of a tribe

tribes·peo·ple /trībz peèp'l/ *npl* people who are members of a tribe

tribes·wom·an /trībz wòommən/ (*plural* **-wom·en** /-wìmmin/) *n* a woman who is a member of a tribe

tribo- *prefix* friction ○ *triboelectricity* [< Greek *tribos* "rubbing" < *tribein* "rub"]

tri·bo·e·lec·tric·i·ty /trībō i lek tríssitee, -eè lek-, trìbbō-/ *n* an electric charge generated by friction, e.g., by rubbing materials together —**tri·bo·e·lec·tric** /trībō i léktrik, trìbbō-/ *adj*

tri·bol·o·gy /trī bólləjee, tri-/ *n* the science and technology of interacting surfaces in relative motion, including the study of friction, lubrication, and wear —**tri·bo·log·i·cal** /trībə lójjik'l, tribbə-/ *adj* —**tri·bol·o·gist** *n*

tri·bo·lu·mi·nes·cence /trībō lòomi néss'nss, trìbbō-/ *n* luminescence caused by friction —**tri·bo·lu·mi·nes·cent** *adj*

tri·bo·ma·te·ri·al /trībō mə teèree əl/ *n* a material based on carbon used to control friction and minimize surface wear

tri·brach /trī bràk/ *n* a metrical foot of three short syllables [Late 16C. Via Latin *tribrachys* < Greek *tribrakhus* < *tri-* "three" + *brakhus* "short"] —**tri·brach·ic** /trī brákik/ *adj*

tri·bro·mo·eth·a·nol /trī brōmō éthə nàwl/ *n* a white crystalline organic compound. Use: general anesthetic. Formula: CBr_3CH_2OH.

trib·u·la·tion /trìbbyə láysh'n/ *n* **1.** great difficulty, affliction, or distress **2.** something that causes great difficulty, affliction, or distress, e.g., an ordeal ○ *the trials and tribulations of the struggling author* [13C. Via French < ecclesiastical Latin *tribulation-* < Latin *tribulare* "afflict, press" < *tribulum* "threshing tool" < *terere* "rub"]

tri·bu·nal /trī byòon'l, tri-/ *n* **1.** LAW COURT a court of justice **2.** JUDGING BODY a body that is appointed to make a judgment or inquiry ○ *an industrial tribunal* **3.** RAISED SEAT a bench or seat on a platform where a judge or magistrate sits [15C. Directly or via Old French < Latin *tribunal* "platform for magistrates" < *tribunus* (see TRIBUNE[1])]

trib·u·nate /tríbbyə nàyt, tri byòonət/ *n* the office, rank, or authority of a tribune in ancient Rome [Mid-16C. < Latin *tribunatus* < *tribunus* (see TRIBUNE[1])]

trib·une[1] /tríb byòon, tri byòon/ *n* **1.** a representative of the common people in the ancient Roman republic, elected annually **2.** a person or institution that defends the rights of the people [14C. Via French < Latin *tribunus* "magistrate" < *tribus* (see TRIBE)] —**trib·u·nar·y** *adj* —**trib·une·ship** *n*

trib·une[2] /tríb byòon, tri byòon/ *n* **1.** PLATFORM a raised platform for a speaker **2.** BISHOP'S THRONE OR SITE OF IT a bishop's throne, or an apse of a Christian basilica containing the throne **3.** CHURCH GALLERY a gallery in a Christian church [Mid-18C. Via French < Italian *tribuna* "raised platform," alteration of Latin *tribunal* < *tribunus* (see TRIBUNE[1])]

trib·u·tar·y /tríbbyə tèrree/ *n* (*plural* **-ies**) **1.** STREAM FEEDING LARGER BODY OF WATER a stream, river, or glacier that joins a larger stream, river, or glacier, or a lake **2.** HIST PAYER OF TRIBUTE formerly, a person or nation that paid a monetary tribute to another ■ *adj* **1.** JOINING LARGER BODY OF WATER flowing into a larger stream, river, or glacier, or into a lake **2.** PAYING TRIBUTE paying tribute in money, goods or praise **3.** HIST PAID AS TRIBUTE paid or owed as a tribute [14C. < Latin *tributarius* "liable to tax or tribute" < *tributum* (see TRIBUTE)]

trib·ute /tríbbyoot/ *n* **1.** EXPRESSION OF GRATITUDE OR PRAISE something said or given to show gratitude, praise, or admiration **2.** EVIDENCE OF GOOD something that is indicative of a value, benefit, or good quality in somebody or something ○ *His success is a tribute to his determination.* **3.** EXTORTED MONEY payment exacted or extorted for protection **4.** HIST PAYMENT BY ONE RULER TO ANOTHER a payment made by one ruler or state to another as a sign of submission **5.** HIST PAYMENT TO FEUDAL LORD in medieval society, a payment made by a vassal to a lord, or an obligation for such payment [14C. Directly or via French < Latin *tributum* < *tribuere* "give out among the tribes" < *tribus* (see TRIBE)]

trib·ute band, **trib·ute group** *n* a musical group that imitates or performs material made popular by a famous predecessor

tri·car·box·yl·ic ac·id cy·cle /trī kaarbok sìllik-/ *n* BIOCHEM same as **Krebs cycle**

trice[1] /trīss/ *n* a very short period of time [15C. < TRICE[2]]

trice[2] /trīss/ (**triced, tric·ing, tric·es**) *vt* to haul up or fasten something, especially with a rope [14C. < Middle Dutch *trīsen* "pull" < *trīse* "pulley"]

tri·cen·ten·a·ry /trī sen ténnaree, trī sént'n èrree/, **tri·cen·ten·ni·al** /trī sen téénnee əl, trīss'n-/ *adj, n* TIME same as **tercentenary**

tri·ceps /trī sèps/ (*plural* **-ceps·es** or *same*) *n* a muscle that has three points of anchorage, especially the large muscle running along the back of the upper arm that straightens the elbow [Late 16C. < Latin, "three-headed" < *caput* "head"]

tri·cer·a·tops /trī sérrə tòps/ (*plural same* or **-tops·es**) *n* a plant-eating dinosaur of the Cretaceous Period, somewhat similar in appearance to a rhinoceros, with a bony crest on the back of its neck and three horns. Genus: *Triceratops.* [Late 19C. < modern Latin < Greek *trikeratos* "three-horned" + *ōps* "face"]

trich- *prefix* same as **tricho-** (*used before vowels*)

tri·chi·a·sis /tri kī əssiss/ *n* the inward growth of hair around a body opening, especially inward growth of the eyelashes, causing irritation of the eyeball [Mid-17C. Via late Latin < Greek *trikhiasis* < *trikhian* "be hairy"]

tri·chi·na /tri kīnə/ (*plural* **-nae** /-nee/ or **-nas**) *n* a small slender nematode worm that infests the intestines of meat-eating mammals and whose larvae form cysts in skeletal muscle. Infection may derive from undercooked meat. Symptoms include diarrhea, nausea, and fever. Latin name: *Trichinella spiralis.* [Mid-19C. < modern Latin < Greek *trikhinos* "hairy" < *thrix* "hair"] —**tri·chi·nal** *adj* —**trich·i·nous** /tríkənəss/ *adj*

trich·i·nize /tríkə nīz/ (**-nized, -niz·ing, -niz·es**) *vt* to infest a person, animal, or meat with trichinae (*often passive*) [Mid-19C. < TRICHINA] —**trich·i·nized** *adj* —**trich·i·ni·za·tion** /trìkəni záysh'n/ *n*

Trich·i·no·po·ly /trìnch inóppəlee/ former name for **Tiruchchirappalli**

trich·i·no·sis /trìkə nōssiss/ *n* a disease caused by infestation with trichinae and marked by fever, muscle pain, and diarrhea, often resulting from eating undercooked pork infected with the larvae

trich·ite /trí kīt/ *n* a dark needle-shaped crystal found in volcanic rock —**tri·chit·ic** /tri kíttik/ *adj*

tri·chlor·eth·yl·ene *n* CHEM same as **trichloroethylene**

tri·chlor·fon /trī kláwr fòn/, **tri·chlor·phon** *n* a crystalline organic compound. Use: insecticide. Formula: $C_4H_8Cl_3O_4P$. [Mid-20C. < TRI- + CHLORO- + *-fon*, shortening of *phosphonate*]

tri·chlo·ride /trī kláw rīd/, **tri·chlo·rid** /-kláwrid/ *n* a compound with three chloride atoms per molecule

tri·chlo·ro·a·ce·tic ac·id /trī klòwrō ə seètik-/ *n* a corrosive toxic acid. Use: astringent, antiseptic, herbicide. Formula: $C_2Cl_3HO_2$.

tri·chlo·ro·e·thane /trī klàwrō é thàyn/ *n* a volatile colorless nonflammable liquid. Use: industrial solvent. Formula: $C_2H_3Cl_3$.

tri·chlo·ro·eth·yl·ene /trī klàwrō éth'l eèn/, **tri·chlor·eth·yl·ene** /trī klawr éth'l-/ *n* a volatile colorless nonflammable liquid. Use: solvent, degreaser, anesthetic. Formula: C_2HCl_3.

tri·chlor·phon *n* CHEM another spelling of **trichlorfon**

tricho- *prefix* hair, filament, thread ○ *trichology* [< Greek *trikh-*, stem of *thrix* "hair"]

trich·o·cyst /tríkə sìst/ *n* a stinging or grasping organ resembling a thread that protrudes and can be ejected from a minute cavity on the surface of some protozoans, especially ciliates —**trich·o·cys·tic** /trìkə sístik/ *adj*

trich·o·gyne /tríkə jīn, -gīn/ *n* a projection resembling a hair on the female sex organ of some fungi, lichens, and algae that attracts and receives the male sex cell prior to fertilization —**tri·cho·gyn·i·al** /trìkə jínee əl, -gínee əl/ *adj* —**tri·cho·gyn·ic** /trìkə jínik, -gínik/ *adj*

trich·oid /trí kòyd/ *adj* resembling hair

tri·chol·o·gy /tri kólləjee/ *n* the study and treatment of hair and its diseases —**tri·cho·log·i·cal** /trìkə lójjik'l/ *adj* —**tri·chol·o·gist** *n*

trich·ome /trí kōm, trī-/ *n* **1.** an outgrowth of a plant's outer cell layer (**epidermis**). Trichomes have various shapes and functions, and include root hairs. **2.** a filamentous chain of cells of bacteria or cyanobacteria [Late 19C. < Greek *trikhōma* "growth of hair" < *thrix* "hair"] —**tri·chom·ic** /tri kómmik, trī-/ *adj*

trich·o·mo·nad /tríkə mō nàd/ *n* a flagellated protozoan that lives as a parasite in the digestive and reproductive tracts of humans and animals. Genus:

Trichomonas. —**trich·o·mo·nad·al** /-mə nádd'l/ *adj* —**trich·o·mon·al** *adj*

trich·o·mo·ni·a·sis /trìkəmə nī́ əssiss/ *n* **1.** a sexually transmitted infection, especially of the vagina, marked by persistent discharge and intense itching. It is caused by a protozoan parasite, *Trichomonas vaginalis.* **2.** an infection of animals caused by parasitic protozoans (**trichomonads**). In cattle, this condition can lead to spontaneous abortion or sterility. [Early 20C. < TRICHOMONAD]

tri·chop·ter·an /trī kóptərən/ *n* INSECTS same as **caddis fly** [Mid-19C. < modern Latin *Trichoptera* < Greek *trikh-* (see TRICHO-) + *ptera,* plural of *pteron* "wing"]

tri·chot·o·my /trī kóttəmee/ (*plural* **-mies**) *n* **1.** the division of something into three categories, classes, elements, or parts (*formal*) **2.** in some beliefs, the division of human nature into body, soul, and spirit [Early 17C. < modern Latin *trichotomia* < Greek *trikha* "in three parts"] —**trich·o·tom·ic** /trìkə tómmik/ *adj* —**tri·chot·o·mous** *adj* —**tri·chot·o·mous·ly** *adv*

tri·chro·ism /trī́ krō ìzzəm/ *n* the property possessed by some crystals of showing three different colors when viewed along each of their three axes [Mid-19C. < Greek *trikhroos* "three-colored"] —**tri·chro·ic** /trī krṓ ik/ *adj*

tri·chro·mat /trī́ krō màt/ *n* somebody who has standard color vision and is able to perceive red, green, and blue [Early 20C. Back-formation < TRICHROMATIC]

tri·chro·mat·ic /trī̀ krō máttik/, **tri·chrome** /trī́ krōm/, **tri·chro·mic** /trī krṓmik/ *adj* **1.** 3-COLOR relating to, involving, or using three colors **2.** COMBINING PRIMARY COLORS involving the combination of the three primary colors to produce the other colors **3.** RELATING TO STANDARD COLOR VISION relating to standard color vision, which is able to perceive red, green, and blue —**tri·chro·ma·tism** /trī krṓmə tìzzəm/ *n*

trich·u·ri·a·sis /trìkyə rī́ əssiss/ *n* intestinal infection with nematodes of the genus *Trichuris.* It usually produces no symptoms but may cause diarrhea and bleeding in severely infected children. [Early 20C. < modern Latin *Trichuris* < Greek *trikh* "hair" + *oura* "tail"]

trick /trik/ *n* **1.** CUNNING DECEPTION a cunning action or plan that is intended to cheat or deceive **2.** PRANK a prank, joke, or mischievous action or plan ○ *played a trick on his sister* **3.** SPECIAL SKILL a special, effective, or ingenious knack, skill, or technique ○ *taught me the tricks of the trade* **4.** SKILLFUL ACT DESIGNED TO AMUSE a skillful act or feat designed to amuse or entertain ○ *taught the dog to do tricks* **5.** ACT OF MAGIC an act of magic or illusion, especially one involving sleight of hand, designed to puzzle or entertain ○ *a conjuring trick* **6.** DECEPTIVE EFFECT OF LIGHT an illusion, especially one caused by the light **7.** PECULIAR HABIT a peculiar characteristic, habit, mannerism, or way of behaving ○ *He has this trick of scratching his ear when he's being evasive.* **8.** UNFORESEEN EVENT a strange event or development that was not anticipated or seems unfair or sad ○ *a cruel trick of fate* **9.** CARDS FROM EACH PLAYER IN ROUND the cards played by all the players participating in one round of a card game and won by an individual player **10.** PERIOD OF DUTY a period of duty, e.g., at the helm of a ship **11.** PROSTITUTE'S CUSTOMER a customer of a prostitute (*slang*) **12.** SEX WITH SOMEBODY FOR MONEY an individual engagement between a prostitute and a client (*slang*) **13.** *US* PRISON TERM a period of imprisonment (*slang*) ■ *vti* (**tricked, trick·ing, tricks**) CHEAT to cheat or deceive somebody ○ *Hundreds of readers were tricked into sending them money.* ■ *adj* **1.** OF TRICKS involving or intended to be used for tricks or trickery ○ *trick photography* **2.** PERFORMING TRICKS skilled at doing tricks **3.** MADE AS IMITATION FOR JOKE made as an imitation of something so that it can be used to play a joke on somebody **4.** MED OCCASIONALLY SYMPTOMATIC displaying symptoms of injury from time to time (*informal*) ○ *a trick ankle* [15C. < Old N French *trique*] —**trick·er** *n* ◇ **do** *or* **turn the trick** to be effective and do what is needed (*informal*) ◇ **how's tricks?** used as a greeting (*dated informal*) ◇ **never** *or* **not miss a trick** to notice everything that is happening, or any opportunity that is advantageous (*informal*) ◇ **show somebody a trick or two** to demonstrate more skill than somebody else ◇ **up to one's (old) tricks** acting in a characteristically idiosyncratic manner in a way that is disapproved of (*informal*)

trick out, trick up *vt* **1.** to decorate or dress somebody or something up, especially in a fancy or garish way **2.** to modify something such as a vehicle or piece of electronic equipment and add a large number of additional features to it

trick·er·y /tríkəree/ (*plural* **-ies**) *n* a trick or prank, especially a trick intended to cheat or deceive, or the use of such tricks

trick·le /trík'l/ *v* (**-led, -ling, -les**) **1.** *vti* FLOW SLOWLY IN THIN STREAM to flow slowly in a thin stream or in drops, or cause something to do this ○ *sweat trickled down his face* **2.** *vi* MOVE SLOWLY OR GRADUALLY to move, come, or go slowly or gradually ○ *The crowd trickled slowly away and the park emptied.* ■ *n* **1.** SLOW THIN FLOW a slow thin flow, movement, or stream ○ *a trickle of blood* **2.** ACT OF FLOWING IN THIN STREAM an act of flowing or of causing a liquid to flow in a slow thin stream [14C. Origin ?]

trick·le charg·er *n* a small low-current device used to recharge batteries slowly and maintain them in a fully charged state —**trick·le charge** *n*

trick·le-down the·o·ry *n* the economic theory that financial and other benefits received by big businesses gradually spread to benefit the rest of society

trick or treat *n* a Halloween custom in which children call at neighbors' houses and threaten to play a trick unless they are given a treat such as candy ■ *interj* used as a greeting by children when they call on a house in order to ask for candy on Halloween —**trick-or-treat** *vi*

trick·ster /tríkstər/ *n* somebody who deceives, swindles, or plays tricks

trick·sy /tríksee/ *adj* **1.** mischievous, playful, or inclined to play tricks **2.** intricate, complicated, or overelaborate —**trick·si·ness** *n*

trick·y /tríkee/ (**-i·er, -i·est**) *adj* **1.** difficult to do or deal with and requiring skill, caution, or tact ○ *a tricky maneuver* ○ *a tricky situation* **2.** likely to cheat or outwit somebody —**trick·i·ly** *adv* —**trick·i·ness** *n*

tri·clad /trī́ klàd/ *n* a flatworm with an intestine that is divided into three sections. Order: Tricladida. [Late 19C. Shortening of modern Latin *Tricladida* < Greek *tri-* "three" + *klados* "branch"]

tri·clin·ic /trī klínnik/ *adj* describes a crystal that has three unequal axes, none of which is perpendicular to another

tri·clin·i·um /trī klínnee əm/ (*plural* **-clin·i·a** /-klínnee ə/) *n* **1.** a couch arranged around three sides of a table and used by ancient Romans to recline on at meals **2.** an ancient Roman dining room, especially one containing a triclinium [Mid-17C. Via Latin < Greek *triklinion* < *triklinos* "room with three couches" < *klinē* "couch"]

tri·col·or /trī́ kùllər/ *n* **1.** 3-COLORED FLAG a flag with three colors **2.** *also* **Tri·col·or** FRENCH NATIONAL FLAG the French national flag, consisting of three equal vertical bands of blue, white, and red **3.** 3-COLORED DOG a black, tan, and white dog ■ *adj also* **tri·col·ored** /-kùllərd/ **1.** 3-COLORED with, involving, or using three colors **2.** WITH 3-COLORED COAT having a coat of black, tan, and white

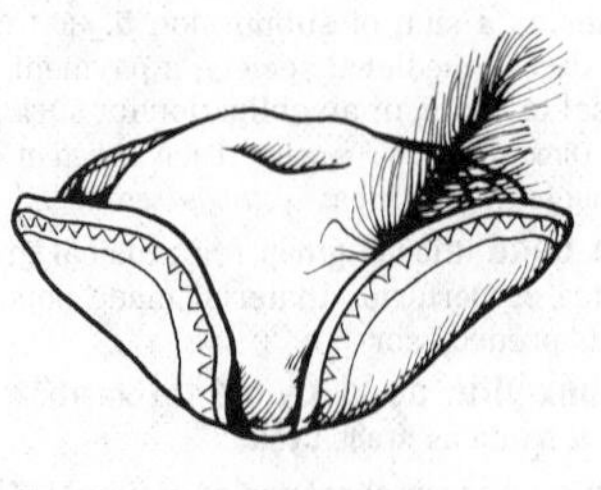
tricorn

tri·corn /trī́ kàwrn/, **tri·corne** *n* **1.** HAT WITH 3-POINTED BRIM a hat with its brim turned up on three sides, making three points, worn by men in the 18th century **2.** MYTHICAL ANIMAL an imaginary animal with three horns ■ *adj* 3-HORNED having three horns or corners [Mid-18C. Directly or via French *tricorne* < Latin *tricornis* "three-horned" < *cornu* "horn"]

tri·cor·nered /trī́ kàwrnərd/ *adj* having three corners

tri·cot /treékō/ *n* **1.** a plain close-knit fabric of natural or artificial fiber. Use: underwear. **2.** a soft ribbed fabric of wool or a wool and cotton blend. Use: dresses. [Late 18C. < French *tricoter* "to knit" < Germanic]

tric·o·tine /trìkə teén, treékə-/ *n* a strong woolen fabric woven with a double twill

tri·cus·pid /trī kúspid/ *adj also* **tri·cus·pi·dal** /-pid'l/ *or* **tri·cus·pi·date** /-pi dàyt/ **1.** 3-POINTED having three cusps or points **2.** OF TRICUSPID VALVE OR TOOTH relating to a tricuspid valve or tooth ■ *n* SOMETHING WITH THREE POINTS something that has three cusps, e.g., a tooth or leaf

tri·cus·pid valve *n* a heart valve consisting of three flaps that prevents blood from flowing back into the right atrium when the right ventricle contracts

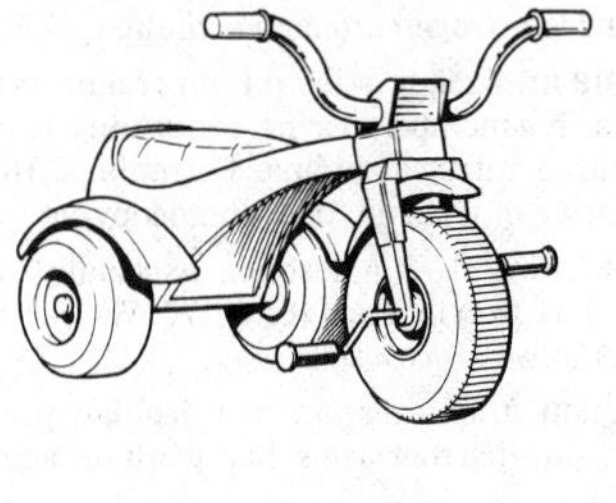
tricycle

tri·cy·cle /trī́ssik'l/ *n* a pedal-driven vehicle with two wheels at the back and one at the front, ridden now especially by young children ■ *vi* (**-cled, -cling, -cles**) to ride a tricycle —**tri·cy·clist** *n*

tri·cy·clic /trī sī́klik/ *adj* having a molecular structure containing three rings ■ *n* PHARM same as **tricyclic antidepressant drug**

tri·cy·clic an·ti·de·pres·sant drug *n* a drug belonging to a group of drugs that have a chemical structure based on three linked carbon rings. Use: treatment of depression.

tri·dac·tyl /trī dákt'l/, **tri·dac·ty·lous** /-dáktələss/ *adj* having three claws, fingers, or toes on each limb

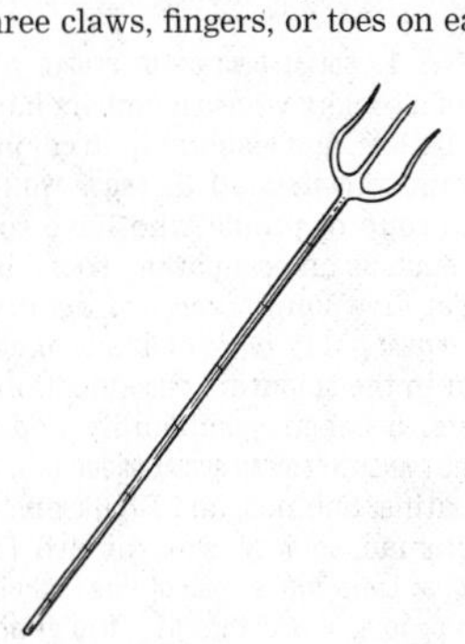
trident

tri·dent /trī́d'nt/ *n* **1.** 3-PRONGED SPEAR an instrument, spear, or weapon with three prongs **2.** MYTHOL 3-PRONGED SPEAR OF POSEIDON OR NEPTUNE in classical mythology, the three-pronged spear carried by the Greek sea god, Poseidon, or his Roman equivalent, Neptune ■ *adj* 3-PRONGED having three prongs, points, or teeth [15C. < Latin *trident-,* stem of *tridens* < *dens* "tooth"]

Tri·dent *n* a US-manufactured ballistic missile system fired from nuclear submarines and in service with the US Navy and the British Royal Navy

tri·den·tal /trī dént'l/, **tri·den·tate** /-dén tàyt/ *adj* with three points, prongs, or teeth

Tri·den·tine /trī dén tīn, -teen/ *adj* relating to the Council of Trent or its decrees, in which the traditional doctrines of Roman Catholicism were reasserted and the Counter Reformation was begun ■ *n* a Roman Catholic who adheres to doctrines laid down by the Council of Trent, especially in opposition to the reforms of the Second Vatican Council [Mid-16C. < medieval Latin *Tridentinus* < Latin *Tridentum* "Trent"]

tri·di·men·sion·al /trī di ménshən'l, -dī-/ *adj* having three dimensions —**tri·di·men·sion·al·i·ty** /trī di mènshə nállətee, -dī-/ *n* —**tri·di·men·sion·al·ly** *adv*

tried /trīd/ past participle, past tense of **try** ■ *adj* (*often used in combination*) **1.** proved through experience or testing to be good, effective, or reliable **2.** subjected to considerable strain, stress, or worry ○ *the sorely tried teacher of a class of noisy students*

tried and true *adj* proved through experience or extensive testing to be good, effective, or reliable ○ *a tried and true method of instruction*

tri·ene /trī een/ *n* a chemical compound that has three double bonds

tri·en·ni·a plural of **triennium**

tri·en·ni·al /trī énnee əl/ *adj* **1. HAPPENING EVERY 3 YEARS** taking place once every three years **2. LASTING 3 YEARS** lasting for a period of three years ■ *n* **1. 3RD ANNIVERSARY** a third anniversary of an event **2. TRIENNIAL EVENT** an event that takes place every three years **3. 3-YEAR PERIOD** a period of three years [Mid-16C. < Latin *triennis* < *triennium* (see TRIENNIUM)] —**tri·en·ni·al·ly** *adv*

tri·en·ni·um /trī énnee əm/ (*plural* **-ni·ums** or **-ni·a** /-nee ə/) *n* a period of three years [Mid-19C. < Latin < *annus* "year"]

tri·er /trī ər/ *n* **1. SOMEBODY WHO TRIES** somebody or something that tries, e.g., a tester of new things **2. TOOL FOR TESTING MATERIALS** a tool or implement designed and used for testing materials, particularly food products, during manufacture **3.** *UK* **SOMEBODY WHO PERSEVERES** somebody who perseveres in doing something despite limited ability or lack of success

Trier /treer/ city in Rhineland-Palatinate State, southwestern Germany. It lies in the center of a wine-growing region. Population: 99,602 (1997).

tri·er·arch /trī ə raàrk/ *n* **1.** the captain of an ancient Greek trireme **2.** in ancient Greece, a citizen commissioned to outfit a trireme for the use of a city-state [Mid-17C. Directly or via Latin < Greek *triērarkhos* "trireme commander"]

tri·er·ar·chy /trī ə raàrkee/ (*plural* **-chies**) *n* **1. SYSTEM FOR SUPPORTING ANCIENT GREEK NAVY** in ancient Greece, the system that required citizens to subsidize triremes **2. OFFICE OF TRIERARCH** the authority, office, or position of a trierarch **3. TRIERARCHS** trierarchs as a group [Mid-19C. < Greek *triērarkhia* < *triērarkhos* "trireme commander"]

Tri·este /tree ést/ seaport and capital city of Friuli-Venezia Region, northeastern Italy. Population: 211,184 (2001).

Tri·este, Gulf of inlet of the northern Adriatic Sea, bordered by Italy, Slovenia, and Croatia

tri·fec·ta /trī féktə/ *n* **1.** a bet, especially on a horserace, that involves selecting the competitors that will come in the first three places in the correct order **2.** a series or set of three things, factors, or influences [Late 20C. Blend of TRI- + PERFECTA]

tri·fid /trī fid/ *adj* describes a tail or organ that is deeply divided into three parts [Mid-18C. < Latin *trifidus* "having three clefts" < *findere* "to split"]

tri·fle /trīf'l/ *n* **1. SOMETHING TRIVIAL** something that has little or no importance, significance, or value ○ *dismissed the complaint as a mere trifle* **2. SMALL QUANTITY** a small amount of something ○ *What he'd earned seemed a trifle beside his mountain of debts.* **3. COLD DESSERT** a cold dessert typically consisting of sponge cake soaked in sherry or fruit juice, spread with jam, jelly, or fruit, and topped with custard, whipped cream, or both **4.** METALL **MEDIUM-HARD PEWTER** pewter of medium hardness ■ **tri·fles** *npl* **PEWTER UTENSILS** objects or utensils made of trifle [13C. < Old French *trufle*, variant of *truffe* "deception"] —**tri·fler** *n* ◇ **a trifle** slightly or somewhat (*formal or humorous*)

trifle with *vt* to treat or take advantage of somebody or something thoughtlessly ○ *had trifled with her affections*

tri·fling /trīfling/ *adj* **1.** insignificant, trivial, or of little value **2.** concerned with matters of little importance ○ *"He is not a trifling, silly young man"* (Jane Austen, *Emma*; 1816) —**tri·fling·ly** *adv*

tri·fo·cal /trī fōk'l/ *adj* describes a lens that has three different sections, each with a different focal point ■ **tri·fo·cals** *npl* eyeglasses with trifocal lenses whose three sections correct separately for near, medium, and distant vision

tri·fold /trī fōld/ *adj* consisting of three parts

tri·fo·li·ate /trī fōlee ət/, **tri·fo·li·at·ed** /-lee àytəd/ *adj* **1.** having three leaves or three parts resembling leaves **2.** same as **trifoliolate**

tri·fo·li·o·late /trī fōlee ələt, -ə làyt/ *adj* **1.** describes a compound leaf consisting of three leaflets that arise from the same point, e.g., a clover leaf **2.** describes a plant having trifoliolate leaves [Early 19C. < TRI- + medieval Latin *foliolum*, diminutive of Latin *folium* "leaf"]

tri·fo·ri·um /trī fáwree əm/ (*plural* **-ri·a** /-ree ə/) *n* a story in a church between the nave arches and the clerestory [13C. < Anglo-Latin] —**tri·fo·ri·al** *adj*

tri·form /trī fàwrm/, **tri·formed** /-fàwrmd/ *adj* having or consisting of three different forms or parts

tri·fur·cate *adj* /trī fúrkət, trī fúr kàyt, trīfər-/ *also* **tri·fur·cat·ed** /-kàytəd/ divided into three branches or forks ■ *vi* /trī fúr kàyt, trīfər kàyt/ (**-cat·ed** /trī fúr kàytəd, trīfər-/, **-cat·ing**, **-cates**) to divide into three branches or forks [Early 18C. < Latin *trifurcus* < *furca* "fork"] —**tri·fur·ca·tion** /trī fur káysh'n/ *n*

trig[1] /trig/ *n* trigonometry, especially as a school subject (*informal*) [Mid-19C. Shortening]

trig[2] /trig/ *regional n* **CHOCK** a brake or supporting block used to stop something from rolling ■ *vt* (**trigged, trig·ging, trigs**) **1. HOLD SOMETHING IN POSITION WITH BLOCK** to stop something from moving with a block or wedge **2. PROP OR SUPPORT SOMETHING** to prop or support something, e.g., with a wedge [Late 16C. Origin ?]

trig. *abbr* MATH **1.** trigonometric **2.** trigonometry

tri·gem·i·nal /trī jémmin'l/ *adj* relating to or involving a trigeminal nerve ■ *n* ANAT same as **trigeminal nerve** [Mid-19C. < modern Latin *trigeminus* "three twins" < Latin *geminus* "twin"]

tri·gem·i·nal nerve *n* either of the fifth pair of cranial nerves that provide the jaw, face, and nasal cavity with motor and sensory functions

tri·gem·i·nal neu·ral·gia *n* a condition involving recurring sudden sharp pain in the face along the branches of a trigeminal nerve

trig·ger /tríggər/ *n* **1. SMALL LEVER THAT FIRES GUN** a small lever that is pressed with a finger to fire a gun **2. LEVER THAT OPERATES MECHANISM** a small lever or device that is pressed or squeezed to operate a mechanism, e.g., by releasing a spring **3. STIMULUS FOR SOMETHING** a stimulus that sets off an action, process, or series of events **4.** ENG **SIGNAL FOR STARTING OPERATION** an automatic or manual pulse or signal for an operation to start ■ *vt* (**-gered, -ger·ing, -gers**) **1. MAKE SOMETHING HAPPEN** to set something off, bring something about, or make something happen ○ *memories triggered by the sight of old photos* **2. FIRE WEAPON BY PULLING TRIGGER** to fire a weapon or initiate an explosion by operating a trigger **3.** ENG **SET SOMETHING IN MOTION** to initiate electrical or mechanical activity that will allow a device to function for a time under its own control [Early 17C. < Dutch *trekker* < *trekken* "pull"]

trig·ger fin·ger *n* **1.** the finger used to pull the trigger on a gun, usually the right-hand forefinger **2.** a disorder, caused by inflammation of the fibrous sheath around a tendon, in which one or more fingers are locked in a bent position and click if forcibly straightened

trig·ger·fish /tríggər fish/ (*plural same* or **-fish·es**) *n* an ocean fish with a thin body and a dorsal fin spine that locks in an erect position as a protection against predators. Native to: tropical coral reefs. Family: Balistidae.

trig·ger-hap·py *adj* (*informal*) **1.** likely or overeager to shoot a firearm without considering the consequences **2.** liable to act in a rash or violent way without considering the consequences

trig·ger·man /tríggər màn/ (*plural* **-men** /-mèn/) *n US* (*informal*) **1.** somebody who shoots somebody else, usually as part of a gang committing a crime **2.** a bodyguard, especially one working for a gangster

tri·glyc·er·ide /trī glíssə rīd/ *n* an ester formed from a molecule of glycerol and three molecules of fatty acids, considered to have adverse effects on human health when consumed in excessive amounts. Source: animal and plant fats and oils.

tri·glyph /trī glif/ *n* in classical architecture, a block carved with three vertical grooves that separates the square panels (**metopes**) in a Doric frieze [Mid-16C. Via Latin < Greek *trigluphos* < *gluphē* "carving"] —**tri·glyph·ic** /trī glíffik/ *adj*

tri·gon /trī gòn/ *n* **1.** a triangular harp or lyre of ancient Greece and Rome **2.** ASTROL same as **triplicity** (sense 3) [Mid-16C. Via Latin *trigonum* < Greek *trigōnon* "triangle" < *gōnia* "angle"]

trigon. *abbr* MATH **1.** trigonometric **2.** trigonometry

trig·o·nal /tríggən'l/ *adj* **1.** in the shape of a triangle **2.** describes a crystal that has three axes of equal length, none of which is perpendicular to another —**trig·o·nal·ly** *adv*

trig·o·no·met·ric /trìggənə méttrik/ *adj* relating to or used in trigonometry —**trig·o·no·met·ri·cal** *adj* —**trig·o·no·met·ri·cal·ly** *adv*

trig·o·no·met·ric func·tion *n* a function of an angle or arc expressed as a ratio of the two sides of a right triangle containing the angle. The trigonometric functions are sine, cosine, tangent, cotangent, secant, and cosecant.

trig·o·nom·e·try /triggə nómmətree/ *n* a branch of mathematics dealing with properties of triangles and their applications, e.g., in surveying [Early 17C. < modern Latin *trigonometria* < Greek *trigonos* "three-cornered" < *trigōnon* (see TRIGON)]

trig·o·nous /tríggənəss/ *adj* describes a stem or other plant part that is triangular in cross section

trig point *n UK* a land surveyor's reference point on high ground, usually marked by a stone pillar set into the ground [Mid-19C. Shortening of *trigonometric point*]

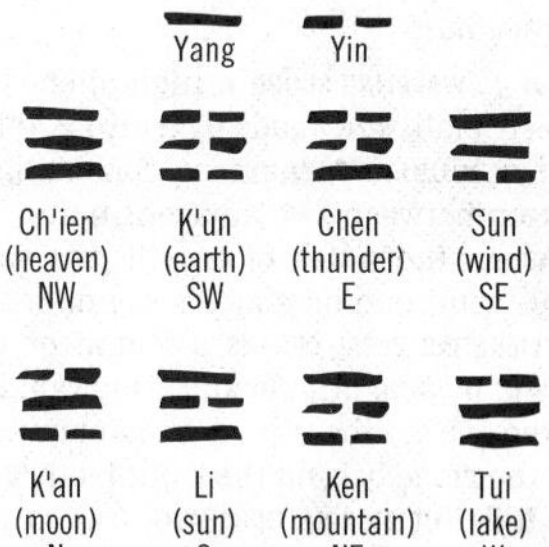

I Ching trigrams

tri·gram /trī gràm/ *n* **1.** a group of three alphabetical letters **2.** each of eight combinations of three solid or broken lines that are joined in pairs to form hexagrams of the I Ching —**tri·gram·mat·ic** /trī grə máttik/ *adj* —**tri·gram·mat·i·cal·ly** *adv*

tri·graph /trī gràf/ *n* a group of three successive letters, especially one representing a single sound such as "igh" in "might" —**tri·graph·ic** /trī gráffik/ *adj* —**tri·graph·i·cal·ly** *adv*

tri·he·dron /trī heédrən/ (*plural* **-drons** or **-dra** /-drə/) *n* a three-dimensional geometric figure formed by the intersection of three planes —**tri·he·dral** *adj*

tri·i·o·do·thy·ro·nine /trì ī ōdō thīrə neen/ *n* an iodine-containing hormone produced by the thyroid gland

tri·jet /trī jèt/ *n* an airplane propelled by three jet engines

trike /trīk/ *n* CYCLING same as **tricycle** (*informal*) [Late 19C. Shortening and alteration]

tri·lat·er·al /trì láttərəl, -láttrəl/ *adj* **1. TRIPARTITE** involving three countries or parties **2. 3-SIDED** describes a geometric figure that has three sides ■ *n* **3-SIDED FIGURE** a geometric figure with three sides —**tri·lat·er·al·ly** *adv*

tri·lat·er·al·ism /trì láttərə lìzzəm, -láttrə-/ *n* three-sided relations or discussions between nations, areas, or groups —**tri·lat·er·al·ist** *n*

tril·by /trílbee/ (*plural* **-bies**) *n* a soft felt hat with a deep crease in the crown and a narrow brim [Late 19C. After *Trilby*, novel by George Du Maurier]

ORIGIN In George Du Maurier's novel, Trilby is an artist's model who falls under the spell of the hypnotist Svengali. In the stage version of the book, the character Trilby wore a soft felt hat with an indented top, and the style soon became fashionable. The novel also dwells on the erotic qualities of Trilby's feet, and for a while in the early 20th century *trilbies* was a slang term for "feet."

tri·lin·e·ar /trī línnee ər/ *adj* consisting of, contained by, or involving three lines

tri·lin·gual /trī líng gwəl/ *adj* **1.** able to speak or use three languages, especially fluently **2.** expressed in or involving three languages —**tri·lin·gual** *n* —**tri·lin·gual·ism** *n* —**tri·lin·gual·ly** *adv*

tri·lit·er·al /trī líttərəl/ *adj* **1.** having three alphabetical letters **2.** having three consonants —**tri·lit·er·al** *n*

AKG London

trilithon

tri·lith·on /trī lí thòn, trī́li thòn/, **tri·lith** /trī́ lìth/ *n* a prehistoric structure consisting of two large vertical stones supporting a horizontal stone laid on top of them [Mid-18C. < Greek < *lithos* "stone"] —**tri·lith·ic** /trī líthik/ *adj*

trill /tril/ *n* **1.** WARBLING SOUND a high-pitched warbling sound, especially one made by a bird **2.** MUSIC MELODIC ORNAMENT a musical ornament consisting of rapid alternation between two adjacent notes. The interval between the notes of a trill can vary but is usually a semitone or major second. **3.** PHON SOUND MADE BY VIBRATING VOCAL ORGANS a sound or consonant made by two vocal organs vibrating rapidly against each other, e.g., the tip of the tongue vibrating against the ridge behind the front teeth ■ *vti* (**trilled, trill·ing, trills**) UTTER SOMETHING WITH TRILL to play, sing, pronounce, or utter something with a trill or a sound resembling a trill [Mid-17C. < Italian *trillare*]

tril·lion /tríllyən/ (*plural same* or **-lions**) *n* **1.** 1 FOLLOWED BY 12 ZEROS the number equal to 10^{12}, written as 1 followed by 12 zeros **2.** *UK* 1 FOLLOWED BY 18 ZEROS the number equal to 10^{18}, written as 1 followed by 18 zeros (*dated*) **3.** LARGE NUMBER OF SOMETHING an exceptionally large but unspecified number or amount of something (*informal; often used in the plural*) ○ *had trillions of fans wanting to meet her* [Late 17C. < French, after *million*] —**tril·lion** *adj*

tril·lionth /tríllyənth/ *n* one of a trillion equal parts of something —**tril·lionth** *adj, adv*

tril·li·um /tríllee əm/ *n* a plant with a cluster of three leaves at the top of the stem. Flowers: single, large, white, pink, or purple, three-petaled. Native to: North America, South Asia. [Mid-19C. < modern Latin]

tri·lo·bate /trī lṓ bàyt/, **tri·lo·bat·ed** /trī lṓ bàytəd/, **tri·lobed** /trī́ lòbd/ *adj* describes a leaf that has three lobes

tri·lo·bite /trī́lə bìt/ *n* an extinct Paleozoic ocean arthropod with a flat oval body and a dorsal exoskeleton divided into three vertical sections. Class: Trilobita. [Mid-19C. < modern Latin *Trilobites* < Greek *lobos* "lobe"] —**tri·lo·bit·ic** /trìlə bíttik/ *adj*

tri·loc·u·lar /trī lókyələr/ *adj* having or consisting of three cavities, cells, or chambers [Mid-19C. < TRI- + Latin *loculus* "little place" < *locus* "place"]

tril·o·gy /trílləjee/ (*plural* **-gies**) *n* **1.** a group or series of three related works, especially of literature or music **2.** a set of three related things [Mid-17C. < Greek *trilogia* < *logos* "word"]

trim /trim/ *v* (**trimmed, trim·ming, trims**) **1.** *vt* MAKE SOMETHING TIDY BY CUTTING to make something neat by clipping, cutting, or pruning **2.** *vt* CUT SOMETHING TO REQUIRED SIZE to reduce something by cutting it to the required shape or size ○ *trimmed the manuscript to 40,000 words.* **3.** *vt* REMOVE EXCESS BY CUTTING to reduce or remove an excess, by cutting ○ *We had to trim the budget.* **4.** *vt* DECORATE SOMETHING to decorate or embellish something ○ *He trimmed the hat with fur.* **5.** *vt* MOVIES EDIT FILM to cut pieces from a film during editing **6.** *vti* SAILING CHANGE ARRANGEMENT OF SAILS to change the position or arrangement of the sails in order to maximize the benefit of the wind **7.** *vt* SHIPPING CHANGE DISTRIBUTION OF CARGO to improve, alter, or maintain a vessel's balance by changing the way the ballast or cargo is distributed **8.** *vi* NAUT BE BALANCED IN WATER to be or become well balanced in the water (*refers to a vessel*) **9.** *vt* AVIAT MAKE ADJUSTMENTS TO IMPROVE AIRCRAFT STABILITY to improve the stability of an aircraft, especially by adjustment of the controls during flight **10.** *vti* ALTER OPINION TO SUIT CIRCUMSTANCES to alter opinions or behavior to suit the circumstances in order to gain acceptance or personal advantage **11.** *vi* ADOPT NEUTRAL POSITION to adopt a neutral position in a dispute between two parties **12.** *vt* BEAT SOMEBODY THOROUGHLY to beat or overwhelm somebody completely (*informal*) ○ *got trimmed regularly at tennis by her partner* **13.** *vt* SCOLD SOMEBODY to reprimand or scold somebody (*informal*) **14.** *vt* CHEAT SOMEBODY to cheat or deceive somebody (*informal*) ■ *adj* (**trim·mer, trim·mest**) **1.** FIT healthy, slim, or in good physical condition ○ *had a trim figure* **2.** NEAT neat, compact, or in good order ■ *n* **1.** ACT OF CUTTING an act or instance of cutting something in order to make it neater ○ *gave the hedge a trim* **2.** HAIRCUT a haircut that neatens rather than changes a hairstyle **3.** SOMETHING USED AS DECORATION something used for decoration, e.g., contrasting material attached to a piece of clothing **4.** AUTOMOT DECORATIVE PARTS OF VEHICLE the accessories and decorative parts added to the interior or exterior of a vehicle **5.** CONSTR DECORATIVE ADDITIONS TO BUILDING the nonstructural decorative additions to a building, especially moldings around doorways, windows, and walls **6.** *US* COMM WINDOW DRESSING the goods, props, and other items placed in a store window **7.** SOMETHING TRIMMED OFF a piece of something removed by trimming **8.** MOVIES FILM CUT DURING EDITING a piece of film eliminated from a shot during editing **9.** AVIAT ADJUSTMENT OF AIRCRAFT FOR STABILITY adjustment of the controls of an aircraft to give stability **10.** AVIAT FLIGHT POSITION the position of an aircraft in flight relative to the horizon **11.** NAUT APPEARANCE OF VESSEL the way a vessel appears when it is fitted out and prepared for sailing **12.** SAILING RELATION BETWEEN SAIL AND DIRECTION the relation between the plane of a sail and the direction in which the vessel is pointing **13.** NAUT POSITION OF VESSEL the position of a ship or boat, especially with reference to the horizontal and to the difference between the depth in water at the front and back of the vessel **14.** NAUT BUOYANCY the relative buoyancy of a submarine [Old English *trymman* "strengthen." < Indo-European, "be solid"] —**trim** *adv* —**trim·ly** *adv* —**trim·ness** *n*

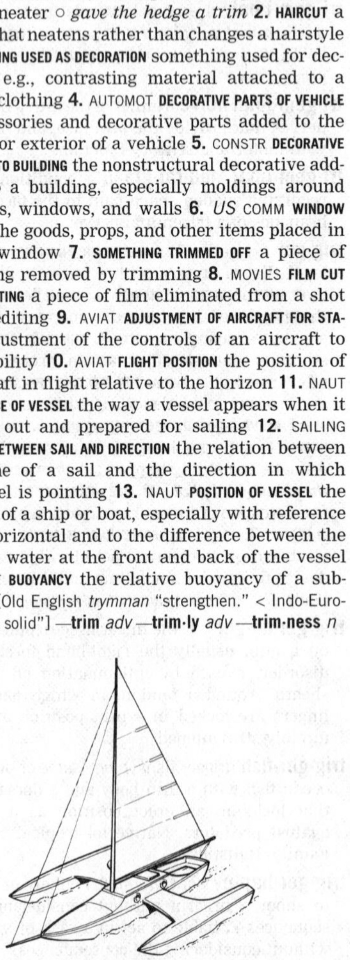

trimaran

tri·ma·ran /trī́mə ràn/ *n* a sailboat with three hulls arranged side by side [Mid-20C. Blend of TRI- + CATAMARAN]

tri·mer /trī́mər/ *n* a polymer formed by combining three identical molecules —**tri·mer·ic** /trī mérrik/ *adj*

trim·er·ous /trímmərəss/ *adj* **1.** having or consisting of three similar parts or segments **2.** describes a flower with parts arranged in groups of three [Early 19C. < Greek *trimerēs* < *meros* "part"]

tri·mes·ter /trī méstər/ *n* **1.** a period of three months, especially one of the three three-month periods into which human pregnancy is divided for medical purposes **2.** each of the three terms into which the academic year is divided by some US colleges, schools, and universities [Early 19C. Via French *trimestre* < Latin *trimestris* "of three months" < *mensis* "month"] —**tri·mes·tral** *adj* —**tri·mes·tri·al** *adj*

trim·e·ter /trímmətər/ *n* a line of verse consisting of three metrical feet

tri·meth·a·di·one /trì methə dī́ ṑn/ *n* a white crystalline bitter-tasting compound with an odor similar to camphor. Use: epileptic anticonvulsant. Formula: $C_6H_9NO_3$. [Contraction of TRI- + METHYL + DI-[1] + -ONE]

tri·meth·o·prim /trī méthə prìm/ *n* a synthetic drug that kills bacteria. Use: treatment of malaria. Formula: $C_{14}H_{18}N_4O_3$. [Mid-20C. Contraction of TRI- + METHYL + OXY- + PYRIMIDINE]

tri·met·ric /trī méttrik/, **tri·met·ri·cal** /-méttrik'l/ *adj* **1.** consisting of one or more trimeters **2.** CRYSTALS same as **orthorhombic**

tri·met·ro·gon /trī méttrə gòn/ *n* a technique in which three aerial photographs are taken at the same time, one vertical and two at oblique angles, in order to obtain more topographical detail [Mid-20C. < TRI- + *Metrogon*, commercial lens]

trim·mer /trímmər/ *n* **1.** SOMEBODY OR SOMETHING THAT TRIMS somebody or something that trims, e.g., a machine for trimming hedges, lawns, or timber **2.** SOMEBODY ALTERING OPINION ACCORDING TO CIRCUMSTANCES somebody who changes his or her opinions or behavior to suit the circumstances in order to gain acceptance or personal advantage **3.** ELECTRONICS VARIABLE CAPACITOR a small variable capacitor used, usually in parallel with a larger capacitor, to adjust overall capacitance **4.** CONSTR CROSSWISE JOIST a joist that runs crosswise with the ends of lengthwise joists fitted into it **5.** SHIPPING SOMEBODY WHO STOWS CARGO somebody who stows cargo on a ship to ensure stability

trim·ming /trímming/ *n* **1.** SOMETHING ATTACHED AS DECORATION a piece of material used as a decoration on clothing or furnishings, e.g., a strip of lace, fur, or braid along the edge of a piece of clothing **2.** ACT OF SOMETHING THAT TRIMS the act of somebody or something that trims **3.** BEATING a thorough defeat or thrashing (*informal*) ■ **trim·mings** *npl* **1.** COOK FOOD ACCOMPANYING MAIN DISH the items of food traditionally served as accompaniments to a main dish **2.** EXTRAS things added to something as accessories or extras **3.** PIECES CUT OFF DURING TRIMMING the parts or pieces cut off when something is trimmed

trim·ming tab *n* AEROSP same as **trim tab**

tri·mo·lec·u·lar /trìmə lékyələr/ *adj* relating to or consisting of three molecules

tri·month·ly /trī múnthlee/ *adj* occurring or done every three months —**tri·month·ly** *adv*

tri·morph /trī́ màwrf/ *n* **1.** a substance, especially a mineral, that occurs in three distinct crystalline forms **2.** one of the crystalline forms in which a trimorph exists

tri·mor·phism /trī máwr fìzzəm/ *n* **1.** the adoption of three successive forms during a life cycle, e.g., the forms of larva, pupa, and adult in some insects **2.** the property of existing in three different crystalline forms [Mid-19C. < Greek *trimorphos* < *morphē* "form"] —**tri·mor·phic** *adj* —**tri·mor·phi·cal·ly** *adv* —**tri·mor·phous** *adj*

tri·mo·tor /trī́ mōtər/ *n* a vehicle, typically an airplane, with three engines

trim tab *n* an auxiliary flight control surface that enables a pilot to make adjustments during flight to correct any unbalanced condition

Tri·mur·ti /tri mo͝ortee/ *n* the Hindu gods Brahma, Vishnu, and Shiva, the creator, preserver, and destroyer respectively, who represent the three forms of the supreme being [Mid-19C. < Sanskrit < *mūrti* "form"]

tri·na·ry /trīnəree/ *adj* **1.** consisting of three parts **2.** progressing in threes

Trin·co·ma·lee /trìnkōmə leé/ town and port in northeastern Sri Lanka. Population: 44,313 (1981).

trine /trīn/ *adj* **1.** **TRIPLE** consisting of three parts **2.** ASTROL **120° APART AS SEEN FROM EARTH** in astrology, used to describe two astronomical objects separated by an angle of 120° as seen from the Earth ■ *n* **1.** **GROUP OF 3** a group of three, or something consisting of three parts **2.** ASTROL **ASPECT OF 120° BETWEEN TWO PLANETS** in astrology, an aspect of 120° between two astronomical objects as seen from the Earth [14C. Via French < Latin *trinus*, singular of *trini* "in threes"] —**tri·nal** *adj*

Trin·i·dad /trínni dàd/ island in the Caribbean, part of Trinidad and Tobago. Population: 1,065,245 (1998). Area: 1,864 sq. mi./4,828 sq. km. —**Trin·i·dad·i·an** /trìnni dáddee ən/ *n, adj*

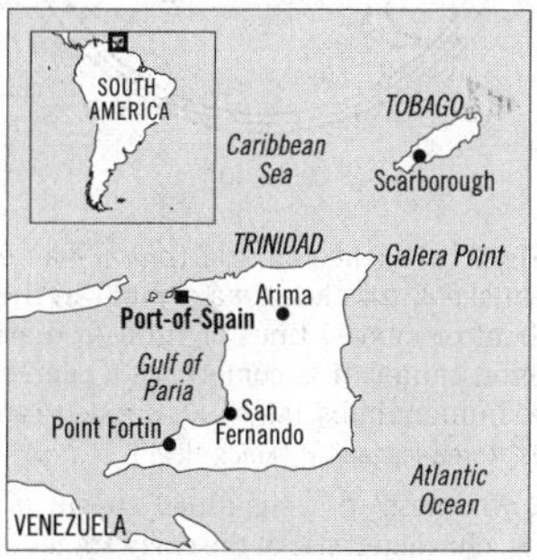

Trinidad and Tobago

Trin·i·dad and To·ba·go /-tə báy gō/ country comprising the two southernmost of the Caribbean Islands, situated off the northeastern coast of Venezuela. It became an independent member of the British Commonwealth in 1962. Language: English. Currency: Trinidad and Tobago dollar. Capital: Port-of-Spain. Population: 1,104,209 (2003). Area: 1,980 sq. mi./5,128 sq. km. Official name **Republic of Trinidad and Tobago**

Tri·nil man /treénil man/ *n* ANTHROP same as **Java man** [Early 20C. After village in Java]

Trin·i·tar·i·an /trìnni térree ən/ *n* somebody who believes in the Christian doctrine of the Trinity —**Trin·i·tar·i·an** *adj* —**Trin·i·tar·i·an·ism** *n*

tri·ni·tro·ben·zene /trī nītrō bén zeèn/ *n* a yellow crystalline compound. Use: explosives. Formula: $C_6H_3(N_3O_2)_3$.

tri·ni·tro·tol·u·ene /trì nìtrō tóllyoo eèn/, **tri·ni·tro·tol·u·ol** /-tóllyoo àwl/ *n* CHEM full form of **TNT**

trin·i·ty /trínnətee/ (*plural* **-ties**) *n* **1.** a group of three **2.** the condition of existing as three persons or things [13C. Via French < Latin *trinitas* < *trinus* "threefold" (see TRINE)]

Trin·i·ty *n* **1.** in Christianity, God seen in three ways as the Father, the Son Jesus Christ, and the Holy Spirit **2.** CHR same as **Trinity Sunday**

Trin·i·ty Sun·day *n* the Sunday that is eight weeks after Easter, when Christians celebrate the doctrine of the Trinity

trin·ket /tríngkit/ *n* **1.** a small object of little value, e.g., an ornament or piece of jewelry **2.** something trivial or unimportant [Mid-16C. Origin ?]

tri·no·mi·al /trī nōmee əl/ *adj* **1.** MATH **HAVING 3 MATHEMATICAL EXPRESSIONS** consisting of three mathematical terms or expressions **2.** BIOL **HAVING 3 NAMES** relating to or consisting of three taxonomic names, denoting the genus, species, and subspecies or variety of an organism ■ *n* MATH **POLYNOMIAL WITH 3 TERMS** a polynomial made up of three terms linked by plus or minus signs [Late 17C. Blend of TRI- + BINOMIAL] —**tri·no·mi·al·ly** *adv*

tri·nu·cle·o·tide /trī nóoklee ə tīd/ *n* a chemical compound consisting of three linked mononucleotides

tri·o /treé ō/ (*plural* **-os**) *n* **1.** **GROUP OF 3** a group or set of three **2.** MUSIC **GROUP OF 3 MUSICIANS** a group of three musicians who perform together **3.** MUSIC **MUSIC FOR 3 MUSICIANS** a piece of music composed for a group of three musicians **4.** MUSIC **MIDDLE SECTION OF MUSICAL PIECE** the middle section of a minuet, march, or other piece of music, composed in a contrasting style and originally written for three instruments **5.** CARDS **SET OF 3 CARDS** a set of three equal-ranking cards, e.g., in piquet [Early 18C. < Italian < *tri-* after *duo* "duet"]

tri·ode /trī ōd/ *n* an electron tube that has an anode, a cathode, and a grid that controls electron flow between the two

tri·ol /trī àwl/ *n* a chemical compound that has three hydroxyl groups

tri·o·let /treé ələt, trī-, treè ə láy/ *n* a poem consisting of eight lines with a rhyme scheme of abaaabab in which the first, fourth, and seventh lines are the same, as are the second and eighth lines [Mid-17C. < French, "small trio"]

tri·ose /trī òss/ *n* a simple sugar containing three carbon atoms

tri·ox·ide /trī ók sīd/ *n* an oxide containing three oxygen atoms per molecule

trip /trip/ *n* **1.** **JOURNEY** a journey of relatively short duration, especially to a place and back again **2.** **FALL CAUSED BY CATCHING FOOT** a fall or stumble caused by catching the foot on something **3.** **ACTION THAT CAUSES FALL** an action that causes somebody to fall or stumble **4.** **LIGHT STEP** a light or nimble skip, step, or tread **5.** **ERROR** a blunder, error, or mistake **6.** ELEC ENG **SOMETHING ACTING AS SWITCH** a catch or switch that activates a mechanism **7.** DRUGS **DRUG-INDUCED HALLUCINATION** the experience produced by taking a hallucinogenic drug (*slang*) **8.** **STIMULATING EXPERIENCE** an intense, emotional, or stimulating experience (*slang*) ○ *a nostalgia trip* **9.** **BRIEF INTENSE INTEREST** an obsessive and often short-lived interest in something (*slang*) **10.** *US* **UNUSUAL OR AMUSING THING** something that somebody enjoys or takes pleasure in, e.g., an experience, event, or person (*slang*) ○ *Living abroad may not be your trip.* ■ *v* (**tripped, trip·ping, trips**) **1.** *vti* **STUMBLE, OR CAUSE SOMEBODY TO STUMBLE** to stumble or fall as a result of catching the foot on something, or cause somebody to stumble or fall in this way ○ *She tripped her opponent deliberately.* ○ *I tripped and fell.* **2.** *vi* **MOVE WITH RAPID LIGHT STEPS** to move, run, walk, or dance with rapid light steps ○ *went tripping off down the road* **3.** *vt* TECH **CAUSE DEVICE TO OPERATE** to operate, or cause a device or system to operate **4.** *vi* **GO ON JOURNEY** to go on a journey, tour, or excursion **5.** *vi* DRUGS **EXPERIENCE DRUG EFFECTS** to experience the effects of a hallucinogenic drug (*slang*) **6.** *vt* NAUT **FREE ANCHOR** to free an anchor from the sea bed so that it hangs loose on the end of its rope or chain **7.** *vt* NAUT **TIP UP YARD** to tilt or tip up a yard or mast so that it can be lowered **8.** *vt* NAUT **RAISE UPPER MAST** to raise one of the upper masts of a sailing ship to remove the bar (**fid**) that supports it so that it can be lowered [14C. < Old French *tripper* < Germanic]

trip up *vti* **1.** to make a mistake, or cause somebody to make a mistake ○ *You're just trying to trip me up with all your questions.* **2.** same as **trip** *v* (sense 1)

tri·pal·mi·tin /trī pálmitin/ *n* CHEM same as **palmitin**

tri·par·tite /trī paár tīt/ *adj* **1.** **INVOLVING 3 PARTIES** involving, made between, or ratified by three parties, groups, or nations ○ *a tripartite agreement* **2.** **IN 3 PARTS** divided into or made up of three parts **3.** BOT **WITH 3 LOBES** describes a leaf that has three deeply divided lobes —**tri·par·tite·ly** *adv*

tri·par·ti·tion /trī paar tísh'n/ *n* a division of something into three parts or among three parties

tripe /trīp/ *n* **1.** the stomach lining of a ruminant such as a cow or sheep, used as food **2.** something absurd, untrue, or worthless (*informal*) [14C. < Old French]

trip ham·mer, trip·ham·mer /tríp hàmmər/ *n* a power hammer with a massive head raised by a cam

tri·phen·yl·meth·ane /trī feén'l méth àyn, -fènn'l-/ *n* a colorless crystalline hydrocarbon. Use: manufacture of dyes. Formula: $CH(C_6H_5)_3$.

tri·phib·i·an /trī fíbbee ən/ *n* **1.** a craft that can operate on water, on land, and in the air **2.** a competitor in a triathlon ■ *adj* same as **triphibious** [Mid-20C. Blend of TRI- + AMPHIBIAN]

tri·phib·i·ous /trī fíbbee əss/ *adj* operating or occurring in the water, on the land, and in the air [Mid-20C. Blend of TRI- + AMPHIBIOUS]

tri·phos·phate /trī fóss fàyt/ *n* a salt or ester with three phosphate groups

tri·phos·pho·py·ri·dine nu·cle·o·tide /trī fòsfō pìrrə deen-/ *n* BIOCHEM same as **NADP**

triph·thong /tríf thòng, tríp-/ *n* **1.** a vowel sound composed of three vowels forming a single syllable **2.** LING same as **trigraph** [Mid-16C. Via French *triphtongue* < medieval Greek *triphthongos* < Greek *phthongos* "sound"] —**triph·thon·gal** /trif thóng g'l, trip-/ *adj*

tri·pin·nate /trī pínnət/ *adj* describes a leaf in which the main stalk bears opposite pairs of leaflets that themselves have a similar arrangement of secondary leaflets that are also similarly subdivided —**tri·pin·nate·ly** *adv*

tripl. *abbr* triplicate

tri·plane /trī plàyn/ *n* an airplane with three main wings positioned above one another

tri·ple /trípp'l/ *adj* **1.** **HAVING 3 PARTS** consisting of three parts, members, or units **2.** **3 TIMES AS MUCH** three times as great, as much, or as many **3.** **DONE 3 TIMES** done or occurring three times **4.** LITERAT **WITH 3 SIMILAR SYLLABLES** having three similar or corresponding syllables in a verse **5.** MUSIC **WITH 3 BEATS** having three musical beats in a measure ○ *music in triple time* ■ *v* (**-pled, -pling, -ples**) **1.** *vti* **MULTIPLY SOMETHING, OR BE MULTIPLIED, THREEFOLD** to become three times as great, as much, or as many, or cause something to become three times as great, as much, or as many **2.** *vi* BASEBALL **MAKE HIT IN BASEBALL** in baseball, to make a hit that allows the batter to reach third base **3.** *vt* BASEBALL **ADVANCE BASE RUNNER** in baseball, to advance a runner by hitting a triple ■ *n* **1.** **SOMETHING 3 TIMES GREATER** a number or amount that is three times greater than another or than usual **2.** BEVERAGES **TREBLE MEASURE** a measure, usually of an alcoholic beverage, containing three times the amount of a single measure **3.** **SET OF 3** a group, series, or set of three things **4.** BASEBALL **HIT WITH THREE BASES** in baseball, a hit that allows a batter to reach third base **5.** *US* HORSERACING same as **trifecta** [14C. Via French or directly < Latin *triplus* < Greek *triplous*]

tri·ple 0 /-ō/, **000** *n* in Australia, the telephone number used to call for police, fire, or ambulance emergency services

tri·ple bond *n* a chemical bond composed of three covalent bonds between two atoms

tri·ple bot·tom line *n* environmental sustainability and social responsibility used as criteria when judging the overall performance of a company, in addition to purely financial considerations

Tri·ple Crown *n* **1.** in horseracing, victory in the Belmont Stakes, Kentucky Derby, and Preakness Stakes in the same season **2.** the accomplishment of leading a baseball league in batting average, runs batted in, and home runs in a single season

tri·ple-deck·er *n* something with three levels or layers, e.g., a building or sandwich

tri·ple-head·er *n* a program of sports contests, e.g., in baseball, in which three games follow one after the other

tri·ple jump *n* a track-and-field event in which contestants perform a short run and three consecutive jumps, landing first on one foot, then the opposite foot, and finally both feet, in continuous motion —**tri·ple jump·er** *n*

tri·ple play *n* a play in baseball in which three outs are made

tri·ple point *n* the temperature and pressure at which the solid, liquid, and gaseous phases of a substance exist in equilibrium

tri·ple rhyme *n* a rhyme in which three syllables rhyme with another three, e.g., "snobbery" and "robbery"

tri·ple sec *n* a sweet colorless liqueur that is orange-flavored

trip·let /tríppl**ə**t/ *n* **1.** ONE OF 3 OFFSPRING each of three children or animals that are delivered by the same mother during one birth **2.** GROUP OF 3 three things that are connected or related to each other in some way **3.** MUSIC GROUP OF 3 NOTES a group of three notes played in the time usually taken by two notes of the same value **4.** LITERAT VERSE OF 3 LINES a poetic stanza of three lines, usually with a single rhyme and sometimes sharing the same metrical pattern **5.** CHEM CHEMICAL UNIT WITH 2 UNPAIRED ELECTRONS an atom, molecule, or radical with two unpaired electrons **6.** PHYS GROUP OF 3 ELEMENTARY PARTICLES a group of three elementary particles with similar characteristics that differ only in their charge **7.** GENETICS same as **codon** [Mid-17C. < TRIPLE, after *doublet*]

tri·ple·tail /trípp'l tàyl/ *n* a large bony ocean fish whose long dorsal, anal, and caudal fins together resemble a three-lobed tail. Native to: mainly tropical waters. Latin name: *Lobotes surinamensis.*

tri·ple-team *vti US* to use three members of a sports team to guard only one opponent, e.g., in basketball or football —**tri·ple team** *n*

tri·ple time *n* a musical meter or time signature with three beats to the bar ○ *a waltz in triple time*

tri·ple-tongu·ing *n* production of a rapid series of notes on a wind or brass instrument by alternating tongue movements to repeat a pattern of three articulated sounds —**tri·ple-tongue** *vi*

tri·ple witch·ing hour *n* a time when stock options, stock index futures, and options on such futures all mature at once. Triple witching hours occur quarterly and are usually marked by highly volatile trading.

tri·plex /trí plèks, trī́-/ *n* a building divided into three apartments on three separate floors, or a single apartment that occupies three floors [Early 17C. < Latin, "threefold"]

trip·li·cate *n* /trípplikət/ SOMETHING WITH 3 IDENTICAL PARTS something that has three identical parts to it or that exists in three identical copies ○ *in triplicate* ■ *adj* /trípplikət/ THREEFOLD triple or tripled ■ *v* /trípplì kàyt/ (**-cat·ed, -cat·ing, -cates**) **1.** *vt* MAKE 3 COPIES OF SOMETHING to make three identical copies of something **2.** *vti* MULTIPLY SOMETHING BY 3 to multiply by three, or cause something to be multiplied by three [15C. < Latin *triplicat-*, past participle of *triplicare* "triple" < *triplex* "threefold"] —**trip·li·ca·tion** /trìppli káysh'n/ *n*

tri·plic·i·ty /tri plíssətee, trī-/ (*plural* **-ties**) *n* **1.** EXISTENCE OF 3 IDENTICAL COPIES the condition of existing in three identical copies **2.** GROUP OF 3 a group or combination of three **3.** ASTROL ZODIACAL DIVISION one of the four groups that the zodiac is traditionally divided into, each separated from the other by 120° and consisting of three astrological signs [14C. < late Latin *triplicitas* < Latin *triplex* "threefold"]

trip·lo·blas·tic /trìpplō blástik/ *adj* used to describe a multicellular animal that has three primary germ layers (**ectoderm; endoderm; mesoderm**) during embryonic development [Late 19C. < Greek *triploos* "threefold" + *-blastos* "bud"]

trip·loid /trí plòyd/ *adj* possessing three representatives of each chromosome ■ *n* a triploid cell, nucleus, or organism —**trip·loi·dy** *n*

trip·ly /trípplee/ *adv* threefold or in a triple number, measure, or degree

tripod

tri·pod /trí pòd/ *n* **1.** a frame or stand with three legs that are usually collapsible, used for supporting something such as a camera, compass, theodolite, or other piece of equipment **2.** a piece of furniture with three legs, e.g., a pot, cauldron, stool, or table [Early 17C. < Latin *tripod-*, stem of *tripus* < Greek *tripous* "three-footed" < *pous* "foot"] —**trip·o·dal** /tríppəd'l, trī́ pòdd'l/ *adj*

trip·o·li /tríppəlee/ *n* a light porous siliceous sedimentary rock containing schist or shells of diatoms and used in powdered form for polishing [Early 17C. < French after TRIPOLI]

Trip·o·li /tríppəlee/ **1.** capital city of Libya, situated on the Mediterranean Sea, in the northwestern part of the country. Population: 1,773,000 (1999). **2.** city in northwestern Lebanon, on the Mediterranean Sea. Population: 160,000 (1998).

Trip·o·li·ta·ni·a /tri pòlli táynee ə, trìppəli-/ ancient region surrounding Tripoli in northwestern Libya. Founded as a Phoenician colony in the 7th century B.C., it was captured by the Turks in the 16th century, and occupied by Italy between 1912 and 1941. —**Trip·o·li·ta·ni·an** *n, adj*

trip·per /tríppər/ *n* **1.** *US* somebody who takes a hallucinogenic drug such as LSD (*slang*) **2.** *UK* somebody who takes a trip or outing, especially one for pleasure (*informal*)

trip·pet /tríppət/ *n* a mechanism that strikes another part at regular intervals or is struck by it [15C. < TRIP]

trip·ping·ly /tríppinglee/ *adv* in a manner that is nimble, lively, or fluent

trip·py /tríppee/ (**-pi·er, -pi·est**) *adj* accompanied by or producing distorted visual or sound effects similar to those associated with psychedelic drugs, especially LSD (*slang*)

trip switch *n* an electric switch designed to interrupt a circuit, or the power to a machine, quickly

trip·tane /tríp tàyn/ *n* a colorless flammable liquid alkane. Use: antiknock compound in aviation fuel. Formula: C_7H_{17}. [Mid-20C. Contraction of *trimethylbutane*]

trip·tych /tríptik/ *n* **1.** a painting or carving consisting of three panels, often made as an altarpiece hinged together so that, when the smaller outer panels are folded, the middle part is entirely covered **2.** in ancient times, a set of three writing tablets hinged or tied together [Mid-18C. < Greek *triptukhos* "threefold" < *ptux* "fold"]

Trip·u·ra /tríppoorə/ state in northeastern India. Capital: Agartala. Population: 23,191,168 (2001). Area: 4,050 sq. mi./10,486 sq. km.

trip·wire /tríp wīr/ *n* **1.** WIRE THAT ACTIVATES EQUIPMENT a wire that activates a device such as a trap, alarm, or camera when it is pulled or disturbed **2.** HIDDEN WIRE FOR TRIPPING PEOPLE a concealed length of wire or rope stretched across the ground for an enemy or intruder to trip over **3.** *US* SOMETHING SMALL THAT ACTS AS TRIGGER a small military operation that could give rise to a larger military operation

tri·que·tral bone /trī kweetrəl-, -kwèttrəl-/, **tri·que·tral** *n* a pyramid-shaped bone in the wrist that connects with the inner bone of the forearm (**ulna**) on the side of the little finger [Mid-17C. < Latin *triquetrus* "three-cornered"]

tri·que·trous /trī kweetrəss, -kwét-/ *adj* triangular, especially in cross section [Mid-17C. < Latin *triquetrus* "three-cornered"]

tri·ra·di·ate /trī ráydee ət/ *adj* having three rays or radiating branches —**tri·ra·di·ate·ly** *adv*

Tri·rat·na /tree rátnə, -rútnə/ *n* the three principal components of Buddhism, namely the Buddha or teacher, the teaching, and the priesthood [< Sanskrit, "three jewels" < *ratna* "jewel"]

tri·reme /trī́ reem/ *n* a galley, originally used by the ancient Greeks as a warship and later adopted by the Romans, that had three rows of oars on each side, arranged one above the other [Early 17C. Directly or via French *trirème* < Latin *triremis* "having three banks of oars" < *remus* "oar"]

tri·sac·cha·ride /trī sákə rìd/ *n* a sugar that has three linked monosaccharide units

tri·sect /trī́ sèkt, trī sékt/ (**-sect·ed, -sect·ing, -sects**) *vt* to divide something into three parts, especially equal parts —**tri·sec·tion** /trī sékshən/ *n* —**tri·sec·tor** *n*

tri·shaw /trī́ shàw/ *n* TRANSP same as **rickshaw** (sense 2)

tris·kai·dek·a·pho·bi·a /trìs kī dèkə fṓbee ə/ *n* an irrational or obsessive fear of the number 13 [Early 20C. < Greek *triskaideka* "thirteen"] —**tris·kai·dek·a·phobe** /trìss kī dékə fōb/ *n* —**tris·kai·dek·a·pho·bic** *adj*

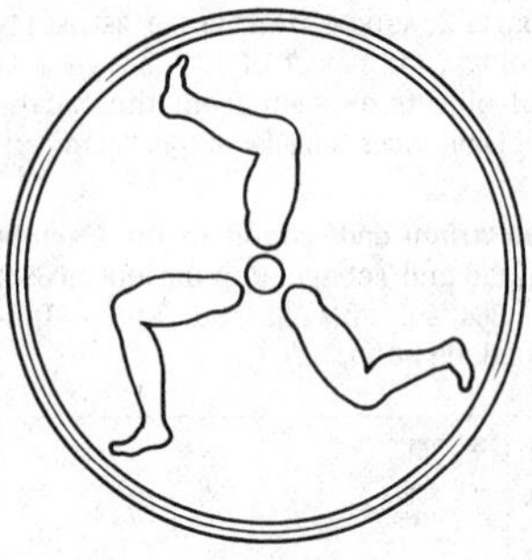

triskelion

tri·skel·i·on /trī skéllee ən, tri-/ (*plural* **-i·a** /-ee ə/), **tri·skele** /trī́ skeel, tríss keel/ *n* a symbol in the form of three bent or curved lines or limbs radiating from a common center. It is sometimes a representation of three human limbs. [Mid-19C. < modern Latin < Greek *triskelēs* "three-legged" < *skelos* "leg"]

tris·mus /trízməss/ *n* a sustained spasm of the jaw muscles, characteristic of the early stages of tetanus [Late 17C. Via modern Latin < Greek *trismos* "grinding"] —**tris·mic** *adj*

tris·oc·ta·he·dron /tri sòktə heedrən/ (*plural* **-drons** or **-dra** /-drə/) *n* a solid with 24 identical triangular faces, each triplet of which rests on a face of an underlying octahedron [Mid-19C. < Greek *tris* "thrice"] —**tris·oc·ta·he·dral** *adj*

tri·so·di·um /trī sṓdee əm/ *adj* containing three sodium atoms in a molecule

tri·so·my /trī sṓmee, trī sṓmee/ *n* the genetic condition of having one or more sets of three chromosomes instead of the usual pairs —**tri·so·mic** /trī sómmik/ *adj*

Tris·tan and I·seult /trìstən ənd i soolt, tri stàn-/, **Tris·tram and I·sol·de** /trìstrəm ənd i sṓldə, -zṓldə/ *npl* in medieval legend, a pair of lovers. Tristan was a knight who fell in love with Iseult, his uncle's bride, after drinking a love potion.

Tris·tan da Cun·ha /trìstən də koonə/ group of volcanic islands in the South Atlantic Ocean, part of the British dependency of St. Helena. Population: 313 (1988). Area: 78 sq. mi./202 sq. km.

tri·state /trī́ stàyt/ *adj US* relating to or involving three adjacent states of the United States

tri·ste·a·rin /trī stee ərin, -steerin/ *n* CHEM same as **stearin** (sense 1)

tris·tich /trístik/ *n* a poem, stanza, refrain, or other division of poetry that consists of three lines [Early 19C. After DISTICH] —**tris·tich·ic** /tri stíkik, trī-/ *adj*

tri·stim·u·lus val·ues /trī stímmyələss-/ *npl* the three values representing the amounts of red, green, and blue light that in combination match a specific color

Tris·tram and I·sol·de *npl* ➧ **Tristan and Iseult**

tri·sul·fide /trī súl fīd/ *n* a sulfide that has three sulfur molecules per atom

tri·syl·la·ble /trī síllәb'l/ *n* a word of three syllables, e.g., "enormous" —**tri·syl·lab·ic** /trìssi lábbik/ *adj* —**tri·syl·lab·i·cal·ly** *adv*

tri·tan·o·pi·a /trìt'n ṓpee ə/ *n* a rare condition in which perception of blue and green becomes confused as a result of the absence of blue-sensitive pigment in the cone cells of the retina [Early 20C. < Greek *tritos* "third" + *anōpia* "blindness"]

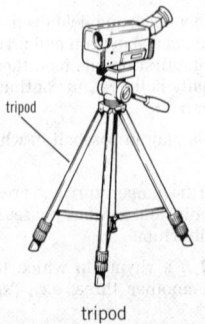

trite /trīt/ (**trit·er, trit·est**) *adj* overused and consequently lacking in interest or originality [Mid-16C. < Latin *tritus*, past participle of *terere* "wear out"] —**trite·ly** *adv* —**trite·ness** *n*

tri·the·ism /trī́thee ìzzəm/ *n* belief in three gods, especially the belief or doctrine that the Christian Trinity of Father, Son, and Holy Spirit consists of three distinct divinities —**tri·the·ist** *n* —**tri·the·is·tic** /trī thee ístik/ *adj*

tri·ti·ate /tríttee àyt, tríshee-/ (**-at·ed, -at·ing, -ates**) *vt* to replace normal hydrogen atoms, or chemically combine something, with tritium —**tri·ti·a·tion** /tríttee áysh'n, trìshee-/ *n*

trit·i·ca·le /trìttə káylee/ *n* a high-protein high-yielding cereal plant that is a hybrid of wheat and rye [Mid-20C. Blend of modern Latin *Triticum* "wheat" + *Secale* "rye"]

trit·i·um /tríttee əm/ *n* a radioactive isotope of hydrogen occurring naturally in trace amounts and having atomic mass 3 and a half-life of 12.3 years. Although rare in nature, it can be produced artificially and is used in tracers and hydrogen bombs. Symbol **T** [Mid-20C. < modern Latin < Greek *tritos* "third"]

tri·ton[1] /trī́t'n/ *n* a large gastropod ocean mollusk with a heavy multicolored spiral shell. Native to: tropical oceans. Family: Cymatiidae. [Late 18C. Via modern Latin < Latin *Triton* "the god Triton"]

tri·ton[2] /trī́ tòn/ *n* the nucleus of a tritium atom, consisting of one proton and two neutrons [Mid-20C. < TRITIUM]

Tri·ton /trī́t'n/ *n* **1.** in Greek mythology, a god of the sea, represented as having the tail of a fish and the upper body of a man **2.** the largest moon of the planet Neptune, about 1,680 mi./2,700 km in diameter, and revolving in a direction counter to that of the planet [Late 16C. Via Latin < Greek *Tritōn*. In sense 2 < its dependence on the planet Neptune, like the god Triton's dependence on the sea god Neptune]

tri·tone /trī́ tòn/ *n* a dissonant musical interval composed of three whole tones

trit·u·rate *vt* /trícha ràyt/ (**-rat·ed, -rat·ing, -rates**) to grind or rub a substance into a fine powder ■ *n* /tríchərət/ a finely ground powder, especially a drug [Mid-18C. < late Latin *triturat-*, past participle of *triturare* "thresh" < Latin *terere* "rub"] —**trit·u·ra·ble** *adj* —**trit·u·ra·tor** *n*

trit·u·ra·tion /trìchə ráysh'n/ *n* **1. GRINDING OF SOMETHING INTO POWDER** the process of grinding or rubbing a substance into a fine powder **2. BEING FINE POWDER** the condition of having been ground or rubbed into a fine powder **3.** PHARM **POWDERED DRUG MIXTURE** a mixture of powdered drugs prepared pharmaceutically **4.** DENT **MIXING OF AMALGAM** the mixing of an amalgam, usually of silver and mercury, for use in filling cavities in teeth

tri·umph /trī́ əmf/ *n* **1. SUCCESS** an act or occasion of winning, being victorious, or overcoming something **2. JOY ABOUT SUCCESS** the happiness, pride, or feeling of elation that comes from winning, being victorious, or overcoming something **3. OUTSTANDING SUCCESS** something that is notable for its exceptional quality or for being a great achievement ○ *The reviews hailed the new production as a triumph.* **4. ROMAN VICTORY PARADE** in ancient Rome, a procession through the streets of Rome to the Capitoline Hill to mark a general's victory over a foreign army ■ *vi* (**-umphed, -umph·ing, -umphs**) **1. WIN OR ACHIEVE SUCCESS** to be successful, especially against an adversary or against difficult odds ○ *triumphed over life's setbacks* **2. BECOME EXULTANT** to experience the happiness, pride, or feeling of elation that comes from winning or overcoming something [14C. Via French < Latin *triumphus*]

tri·um·phal /trī úmf'l/ *adj* celebrating or commemorating a victory, usually a military one ○ *a triumphal procession* —**tri·umph·al·ism** *n*

USAGE triumphal or **triumphant**? ***Triumphal*** is a neutral word that classifies something as simply commemorating a victory, usually a military one: *The band will play a triumphal march.* ***Triumphant*** describes the feelings following a success, or something outstandingly successful: *The winning team returned home triumphant. She told us of her win with a triumphant look on her face. He made a triumphant comeback.*

tri·um·phal arch *n* a monument, usually in the form of an ornamental free-standing arch spanning a street, built to commemorate something, especially an outstanding military victory

tri·um·phant /trī úmfənt/ *adj* **1.** displaying or feeling great pride in having achieved a victory **2.** outstandingly successful or impressive ○ *made a triumphant reappearance in the role he made famous* —**tri·um·phant·ly** *adv*

USAGE See ***triumphal***.

tri·um·vir /trī úmvər/ (*plural* **-virs** or **-vi·ri** /-və rī/) *n* **1.** each of the three people who made up a triumvirate, especially in ancient Rome **2.** somebody who shares power with two other people (*formal*) [Late 16C. < Latin, back-formation < *triumviri* "board of three men" < *trium virum* "of three men"] —**tri·um·vi·ral** *adj*

tri·um·vi·rate /trī úmvərət, -úmvə ràyt/ *n* **1. ROMAN COMMITTEE OF 3 RULERS** a group of three men who together were responsible for public administration or civil authority in the government system of ancient Rome **2. GROUP OF 3 SHARING AUTHORITY** a group of three people who jointly share some responsibility, authority, or power **3. POSITION OF SHARING POWER** the position of being one of three who exercise power or authority **4. TERM OF OFFICE OF SHARED POWER** the duration of the term of office for somebody who shares power or authority with two others **5. RULE BY GROUP OF 3** government or rule by a group of three [Late 16C. < Latin *triumviratus* < *triumviri* (see TRIUMVIR)]

tri·une /trī́ yo͞on/, **Tri·une** *adj* consisting of or being three in one, e.g., in the Christian Trinity ■ *n* a group consisting of three members, especially the Christian Trinity [Early 17C. < TRI- + Latin *unus* "one"]

tri·u·ni·ty /trī yo͞onətee/ (*plural* **-ties**) *n* a group of three

tri·va·lent /trī váylənt/ *adj* **1. WITH VALENCE OF 3** having a chemical valence of three **2. WITH 3 VALENCES** with three chemical valences **3.** BIOCHEM **FORMED BY 3 CHROMOSOMES** formed by three closely associated chromosomes during the first stage of reproductive cell division (**meiosis**) —**tri·va·lence** *n*

Tri·van·drum /tri vándrəm/ former name for **Thiruvananthapuram**

triv·et /trívvit/ *n* **1.** a stand or support, usually metal with three legs, for hot pans and dishes **2.** a device, usually metal with three legs, that fits over the grate of a fire to support a pan or kettle [15C. Probably alteration of Latin *triped-*, stem of *tripes* "three-footed" < *pes* "foot"]

triv·i·a[1] /trívvee ə/ *n* a collection of insignificant or obscure items, details, or information (*takes a singular or plural verb*) [Early 20C. Latinized back-formation < TRIVIAL]

triv·i·a[2] /trívvi ə/ HIST, EDUC plural of **trivium**

triv·i·al /trívvee əl/ *adj* **1. HAVING LITTLE VALUE** lacking in seriousness, importance, or value **2. COMMONPLACE** lacking any qualities that are unique or interesting **3. CONCERNED WITH TRIVIA** relating to or concerned with trivia **4.** MATH **WITH ZERO VALUES** describes the simplest possible case mathematically, especially with all mathematical variables equal to zero [15C. < Latin *trivialis* "relating to the trivium division of subjects," hence "commonplace" (because the trivium was considered to incorporate the less important subjects) < *trivium* (see TRIVIUM)] —**triv·i·al·ly** *adv*

ORIGIN Medieval teachers and scholars recognized seven liberal arts: the lower three, grammar, logic, and rhetoric, were known as the *trivium*, and the upper four, arithmetic, astronomy, geometry, and music, were known as the *quadrivium*. The notion of "less important subjects" led in the 16th century to the use of the derived adjective ***trivial*** for "commonplace, of little importance."

triv·i·al·i·ty /trìvvee állətee/ (*plural* **-ties**), **triv·i·al·ism** /trívvee ə lìzzəm/ *n* **1.** the condition or quality of having little importance or seriousness **2.** something that is considered to lack importance or seriousness

triv·i·al·ize /trívvee ə līz/ (**-ized, -iz·ing, -iz·es**) *vt* to treat something as, or make it appear, less serious, important, or valuable than it really is —**triv·i·al·i·za·tion** /trìvvee əli záysh'n/ *n*

triv·i·al name *n* a common or popular name for a substance that does not describe its exact chemical composition

triv·i·um /trívvee əm/ (*plural* **-i·a** /-ee ə/) *n* grammar, logic, and rhetoric, three of the seven liberal arts that formed the basis of medieval university study, traditionally considered to be less important than the other four [Early 19C. Via medieval Latin < Latin, "place where three roads cross"]

tri·week·ly /trī wéeklee/ *adj* **1. APPEARING OR DONE EVERY 3 WEEKS** occurring, published, or performed once every three weeks **2. DONE 3 TIMES WEEKLY** occurring, published, or performed three times each week ■ *adv* **1. EVERY 3 WEEKS** once every three weeks **2. 3 TIMES WEEK** three times each week ■ *n* (*plural* **-lies**) **1. 3-WEEKLY PUBLICATION** a publication that comes out every three weeks **2. PUBLICATION 3 TIMES PER WEEK** a publication that comes out three times each week

-trix *suffix* **1.** a woman who performs a particular function ○ *dominatrix* **2.** a geometric element that performs a particular function ○ *directrix* [< Latin, feminine form of *-tor*]

tRNA *abbr* BIOCHEM transfer RNA

TRO *abbr* LAW temporary restraining order

Tro·bri·and Is·lands /trṓ bree ànd-, -aand-/ island group of Papua New Guinea in the Solomon Sea, east of New Guinea. Area: 170 sq. mi./440 sq. km.

tro·car /trṓ kaar/ *n* a sharply pointed steel rod sheathed with a tight-fitting cylindrical tube (**cannula**), used together to drain or extract fluid from a body cavity. The whole instrument is inserted then the trocar is removed, leaving the cannula in place. [Early 18C. < French *trocart* < *carre*, "side of an instrument" < Latin *quadrum* "square"]

tro·cha·ic /trō káy ik/ LITERAT *adj* relating to, belonging to, or consisting of trochees ■ *n* **1.** same as **trochee** **2.** a poem, or part of a poem, written in trochees —**tro·cha·ic·al·ly** *adv*

tro·chan·ter /trō kántər/ *n* **1.** either of two rough knobs on the upper thigh bone (**femur**), where the muscles between the thigh and pelvis are attached in humans and other vertebrates **2.** the second segment from the base of an insect's leg [Early 17C. Via French < Greek *trokhantēr* "ball on which the hip bone turns in its socket" < *trekhein* "run"]

tro·chee /trṓkee/ *n* a metrical foot of one stressed syllable followed by an unstressed syllable, e.g., the word "human" [Late 16C. Via Latin *trochaeus* < Greek *trokhaios* "running" < *trekhein* "run"]

troch·le·a /tróklee ə/ *n* an anatomical part or structure with a grooved surface that resembles a pulley, especially the surface of a bone over which a tendon passes [Late 17C. Via Latin < Greek *trokhileia* "pulley"]

troch·le·ar /tróklee ər/ *adj* relating to, situated near, or resembling a trochlea or trochlear nerve

troch·le·ar nerve *n* either of the fourth pair of cranial nerves serving the muscle that is used to rotate the eyeball outward and downward

tro·choid /trṓ kòyd/ *n* MATH **CURVE FORMED BY POINT ON RADIUS** a curve formed by a point on the radius of a circle, or on the extended radius, as the circle rolls along a straight line ■ *adj also* **tro·choi·dal** /trō kóyd'l/ **1.** MATH **ROTATING ABOUT CENTRAL AXIS** rotating, showing rotation, or able to rotate about a central axis **2.** ANAT **RESEMBLING PIVOT** resembling or functioning in the body like a pivot or pulley [Early 18C. < Greek *trokhoeidēs* "wheel-like" < *trokhos* "wheel" < *trekhein* "run"] —**tro·choi·dal·ly** /trō kóyd'lee/ *adv*

troch·o·phore /trókə fàwr/, **troch·o·sphere** /-sfeer/ *n* a free-swimming ciliated larval form of invertebrates such as mollusks and rotifers [Late 19C. < Greek *trokhos* "wheel"]

trod past participle, past tense of **tread**

trod·den past participle of **tread**

trof·fer /tróffər/ *n* *US* an inverted recess in a ceiling that acts as a support and reflector for a fluorescent light [Mid-20C. Blend of TROUGH + COFFER]

trog·lo·dyte /tróggla dìt/ *n* **1.** somebody living in a cave, especially somebody who belonged to a prehistoric cave-dwelling community **2.** a solitary person who lives alone, especially somebody who is antisocial or unconventional [Late 15C. Via Latin *Troglodyta* < Greek *Trōglodutai* "ones who enter a hole," alteration of *Trōgodutai*, an Ethiopian people] —**trog·lo·dyt·ic** /tròggla díttik/ *adj*

tro·gon /trṓ gòn/ *n* a tree-dwelling bird with a short hooked beak, a long tail, and brightly colored feathers. Native to: tropics, subtropics. Family: Trogonidae. [Late 18C. < modern Latin < Greek *trōgein* "gnaw," because the bird chews its nest hole out of rotten wood or termites' nests]

troi·ka /tróyka/ *n* **1.** a carriage of Russian origin drawn by three horses harnessed abreast of each other **2.** a team of three horses harnessed abreast of each other **3.** POL same as **triumvirate** (sense 2) [Mid-19C. < Russian < *troe* "group of three"]

troi·lite /tróy lìt, trṓ a lìt/ *n* a variety of iron sulfide found in some meteorites [Mid-19C. After Domenico *Troili*, 18C Italian scientist]

Troi·lus /tróylass/ *n* in Greek mythology, the son of the Trojan king Priam. He was killed during the Trojan War by the Greek warrior Achilles. In medieval legend he is depicted as the betrayed lover of Cressida.

Trois-Ri·vières /trwaà reev yér/ city on the St. Lawrence River between Quebec City and Montreal, in southern Quebec Province, Canada. Population: 117,758 (2001).

Tro·jan /trṓjan/ *n* **1.** somebody who came from ancient Troy **2.** somebody who is determined, strong, or courageous **3.** *also* **tro·jan** COMPUT same as **Trojan horse** (sense 3) —**Tro·jan** *adj*

Tro·jan horse *n* **1.** HOLLOW HORSE CONCEALING GREEKS in Greek mythology, a hollow wooden horse that hid Greek soldiers, left at the gates of Troy. The Trojans were convinced it was a gift to Athena and dragged it inside. **2.** CONCEALED STRATAGEM somebody or something that is meant to disrupt, undermine, subvert, or destroy an enemy or rival, especially somebody or something that operates while concealed within an organization **3.** COMPUT DESTRUCTIVE COMPUTER PROGRAM a computer program containing a hidden function that causes damage to other programs while appearing to perform a valid function

Tro·jan War *n* the ten-year siege of Troy by the Greeks to recover Helen, the abducted wife of King Menelaus

troll[1] /trōl/ *v* (**trolled, troll·ing, trolls**) **1.** *vti* DRAG BAITED LINE THROUGH WATER to fish by dragging a baited line through water, or from the back of a boat moving slowly **2.** *vti* TROLL IN ONE AREA to troll a particular area, or for a particular type of fish **3.** *vt* LOOK FOR SOMETHING to attempt to find something (*informal*) ○ *trolled through the job ads* **4.** *vi* UK AMBLE ALONG to walk casually **5.** *vti* WANDER AROUND SEARCHING FOR SOMEBODY to wander around a particular area or place, especially in search of a sexual partner (*slang*) **6.** *vti US, Scotland* ROLL OR CAUSE SOMETHING TO ROLL to roll or rotate, or cause something to roll or rotate **7.** *vi* ONLINE FOOL INTERNET USER INTO RESPONDING to lure other Internet users into sending responses to carefully designed incorrect statements (*slang*) **8.** *vti* SING LOUDLY OR ENTHUSIASTICALLY to sing something loudly and with vigor, or be sung loudly and with vigor, especially in a round, refrain, or chorus (*dated*) ■ *n* **1.** LURE USED IN FISHING a lure or bait used for trolling **2.** ACTIVITY OF DRAGGING BAITED FISHING LINE the act or process of fishing by trolling **3.** SEARCH MADE an attempt to find something (*informal*) **4.** ONLINE FALSE STATEMENT USED AS INTERNET LURE a carefully designed incorrect statement designed to lure other Internet users into sending responses (*slang*) [14C. Origin ?] —**troll·er** *n* — **troll·ing** *n*

troll[2] /trōl/ *n* in Scandinavian legend, a supernatural being depicted as either a dwarf or giant and living in caves or under bridges [Early 17C. Via Swedish or Norwegian < Old Norse, "demon"]

trol·ley /tróllee/ *n* (*plural* **-leys**) **1.** TRANSP same as **trolley bus 2.** ELEC DEVICE COLLECTING POWER FROM OVERHEAD WIRE a device carried at the end of a pole that collects current from an overhead electric wire in order to power a vehicle **3.** FOOD WHEELED TABLE a small wheeled table used for serving or moving food and drinks **4.** *Can, UK* WHEELED CART PUSHED BY HAND a wheeled cart that is pushed by hand and used for transporting things, especially luggage at an airport or railroad station or goods in a supermarket. US term **cart 5.** VEHICLES WAGON ON RAILS FOR MOVING THINGS a small open cart that runs on rails and carries materials, especially goods in a factory or coal or other minerals in a mine or quarry **6.** INDUST SUSPENDED TRUCK a small cart or basket suspended from an overhead rail and used, especially in factories and mines, for transporting loads **7.** *UK* MED same as **gurney** ■ *vti* (**-leyed, -ley·ing, -leys**) MOVE BY TROLLEY to travel by or transport something using a wheeled cart on a track or a vehicle powered by electrical current from overhead wires [Early 19C. Probably < TROLL[1] "roll"]

trol·ley bus *n* an electric bus that takes its power from overhead wires by means of a trolley on a pole

trol·ley car *n* TRANSP same as **streetcar**

trol·lop /tróllap/ *n* **1.** an offensive term that deliberately insults a woman who is a prostitute or who is reputed to be sexually promiscuous (*dated insult*) **2.** an offensive term that deliberately insults a girl or woman regarded as slovenly or as having untidy habits (*insult*) [Early 17C. Origin ?] —**trol·lop·y** *adj*

Trol·lope /tróllap/, **Anthony** (1815–82) British novelist. He is best known for two sequences of novels, the Barsetshire novels (1855–67), which have a clerical setting, and the political Palliser novels (1865–80). —**Trol·lop·i·an** /tra lóppee an/ *adj*

> "Love is like any other luxury. You have no right to it unless you can afford it."
> [Anthony Trollope, *The Way We Live Now*; 1875]

trom·bic·u·li·a·sis /trom bìkya lí assiss/, **trom·bi·di·a·sis** /tròmba dí assiss/ *n* infestation with mite larvae (**chiggers**) that often causes severe rickettsial disease or viral disease [Early 20C. < modern Latin *Trombicula*, genus of mites]

trom·bone /trom bṓn, tram-, tróm bōn/ *n* **1.** a brass wind instrument of varying size with a U-shaped slide that is moved to produce different pitches **2.** somebody who plays a trombone [Early 18C. Directly or via French < Italian, "big trumpet" < *tromba* "trumpet" < Germanic] —**trom·bon·ist** /trom bṓnist/ *n*

trom·mel /trómm'l/ *n* a rotating sieve for sizing or screening crushed rock or ore [Late 19C. < German *Trommel* "drum"]

tromp /tromp/ (**tromped, tromp·ing, tromps**) *v* **1.** *vt* same as **tramp** *v* (sense 4) **2.** *vt* DEFEAT OR BEAT SOMEBODY to defeat somebody completely or beat somebody physically **3.** *vi* WALK HEAVILY to tramp or walk with a heavy tread **4.** *vi* STAMP ON SOMETHING to stamp or apply heavy pressure with the feet [Late 19C. Alteration of TRAMP]

trompe l'oeil: fresco (1561?) by Paolo Veronese at the Villa Barbaro, Maser, Italy

trompe l'oeil /tràwmp lóy/ (*plural* **trompe l'oeils** /*pronunc. same*/) *n* **1.** a technique used in realistic paintings to trick the eye, especially through the use of perspective to create an illusion of three-dimensionality **2.** a painting or other artistic object that uses trompe l'oeil [Late 19C. < French, "deceives the eye"]

Trom·sø /trómssō/ city and fishing port in northern Norway, located on the offshore island of Tromsøy. Population: 57,485 (1998).

-tron *suffix* **1.** a device for manipulating atoms or subatomic particles, accelerator ○ *cyclotron* **2.** a vacuum tube ○ *klystron* [< ELECTRON]

tro·na /trṓna/ *n* a grayish white or yellowish hydrated sodium carbonate mineral. Source: salt deposits. [Late 18C. < Swedish]

Trond·heim /trón hàym/ city and port in central Norway. It is situated on Trondheim Fjord, which opens into the Norwegian Sea. Population: 150,117 (2001).

troop /troop/ *n* **1.** BIG GROUP a large group of similar people, animals, or things **2.** MIL MILITARY UNIT a unit of soldiers that forms a subdivision of a cavalry or armored cavalry squadron (*often used before a noun*) ○ *troop movements in the area* **3.** YOUTH ORG SCOUTING UNIT a unit of Girl Scouts or Boy Scouts under an adult leader, usually subdivided into several patrols **4.** ZOOL COLLECTIVE NAME FOR SOME ANIMALS a collective name for some animals, especially monkeys and kangaroos ■ **troops** *npl* **1.** MIL MILITARY GROUP a body of soldiers ○ *Order was restored by flooding the area with troops.* **2.** LARGE NUMBER OF PEOPLE OR THINGS a large number of people or things ■ *vi* (**trooped, troop·ing, troops**) **1.** GO AS LARGE ORDERLY GROUP to move or gather together as a large orderly group **2.** GO AS IF MARCHING to walk somewhere in a deliberate or heavy-footed way, as if marching ○ *After breakfast the family trooped off to the nearby mall.* [Mid-16C. < French *troupe*]

USAGE troop or **troupe**? Both these words can be used as nouns denoting a group of people. ***Troop*** is more general, being applied to any large group, and specifically to a military unit. ***Troupe*** is applied only to a group of actors, circus people, or other entertainers. The verb meaning "to move or gather together as a large orderly group" is spelled ***troop***, not ***troupe***: *The reporters trooped in to speak to the President.*

troop car·ri·er *n* a ship, aircraft, or armored vehicle used for transporting large numbers of military personnel

troop·er /troópar/ *n* **1.** MEMBER OF CAVALRY UNIT a member of a cavalry unit **2.** CAVALRY HORSE a horse in a cavalry unit **3.** *US* MOUNTED POLICE OFFICER a member of a mounted police unit **4.** same as **state trooper**

troop·ship /troóp shìp/ *n* a ship, sometimes one originally in the merchant fleet, used for transporting military personnel

troost·ite /troó stìt/ *n* a grayish or reddish manganese-containing form of the mineral willemite [Mid-19C. After Gerard *Troost* (1776–1850), US geologist]

trop. *abbr* GEOG **1.** tropic **2.** tropical

trop- *prefix* same as **tropo-** (*used before vowels*)

trope /trōp/ *n* **1.** a word, phrase, expression, or image that is used in a figurative way, usually for rhetorical effect **2.** in the medieval Christian church, a phrase or text interpolated into the service of the Mass [Mid-16C. Via Latin *tropus* < Greek *tropos* "turn"]

troph- *prefix* same as **tropho-** (*used before vowels*)

troph·ic /tróffik, trṓfik/ *adj* relating to the nutritive value of food [Late 19C. < Greek *trophikos* < *trophē* (see TROPHO-)] —**troph·i·cal·ly** *adv*

-trophic[1] *suffix* needing or pertaining to a particular kind of food or nutrition ○ *autotrophic* [< Greek *trophē* (see TROPHO-)]

-trophic[2] *suffix* same as **-tropic**

troph·ic cascade *n* in a food web, the cascading effect that a change in the size of one population in the web has on the populations below it

troph·ic lev·el *n* a stage in a food chain that reflects the number of times energy has been transferred through feeding, e.g., when plants are eaten by animals that are in turn eaten by predators. Plants and plant-eating animals occupy the first two levels, followed by carnivores, usually to a maximum of six levels.

tropho- *prefix* nutrition, feeding ○ *trophoblast* [< Greek *trophē* "food, nutrition" < *trephein* "nourish"]

tro·pho·blast /trṓfə blàst, tróffə-/ *n* a thin outer layer **(ectoderm)** that encloses the embryo of mammals, attaches the fertilized ovum to the wall of the womb, and absorbs nutrients —**tro·pho·blas·tic** /trṓfə blástik, tròffə-/ *adj*

tro·pho·derm /trṓfə dùrm, tróffə-/ *n* a trophoblast and its underlying layer **(mesoderm)**

tro·pho·zo·ite /trṓfə zṓ ìt, tròffə-/ *n* the active or feeding form of a protozoan, especially a parasite, as opposed to the resting or reproductive form

tro·phy /trṓfee/ *n* (*plural* **-phies**) **1. TOKEN OF VICTORY** a cup, shield, plaque, medal, or other award given in acknowledgment of a victory, success, or some other achievement, especially in a sporting contest **2. HUNTING OR WAR SOUVENIR** a memento that symbolizes victory or success, e.g., the head of an animal killed during a hunting expedition or something taken from an enemy killed in battle **3. MEMENTO OF SUCCESS** something that symbolizes a personal victory or achievement **4.** ANCIENT HIST **GREEK OR ROMAN VICTORY MEMORIAL** in ancient Greece or Rome, a victory memorial in a public place or near a battlefield, originally a display of enemy weapons **5.** ANCIENT HIST **GREEK OR ROMAN BATTLE COMMEMORATION** a representation of a Greek or Roman battle trophy, e.g., on a commemorative medal, plaque, or monument **6.** ARCHIT **DECORATIVE CARVING OF WEAPONS** a decorative casting or carving showing weapons or armor on a square or circular base ■ *adj* **ENHANCING SOMEBODY'S STATUS** describes a romantic or sexual partner apparently chosen by somebody purely to impress others and enhance his or her status ○ *a trophy wife* ○ *a trophy kitchen* [Early 16C. Via French *trophée* < Latin *tropaeum* "monument to victory" < Greek *tropaion* < *tropē* "a turning"]

-trophy *suffix* **1.** nutrition, food ○ *dystrophy* **2.** growth ○ *hypertrophy* [< Greek *-trophia* < *trophē* (see TROPHO-)]

trop·ic[1] /tróppik/ *n* **1. LINE OF LATITUDE** a line of latitude on the Earth's globe either 23° 26' north of the equator **(tropic of Cancer)** or 23° 26' south **(tropic of Capricorn) 2.** ASTRON **CIRCLE ON CELESTIAL SPHERE** either of two circles on the celestial sphere that have the same latitudes and mark the limits of the apparent north-and-south movement of the Sun. The tropics lie in the same planes as the tropic of Cancer and the tropic of Capricorn. ■ **trop·ics, Trop·ics** *npl* **AREA BETWEEN TROPICS** the area between or near the tropic of Cancer and the tropic of Capricorn [Early 16C. Via Old French *tropique* < Latin *tropicus* < Greek *tropē* "turn"; from the ancient belief that the sun "turned back" at the tropics of Cancer and Capricorn] —**trop·ic** *adj*

CULTURAL NOTE ***Tropic of Cancer***, a novel (1934) by Henry Miller. It is an autobiographical account of a struggling US writer's sojourn in 1930s Paris. Its focus on the protagonist's erotic encounters gained it notoriety and led to it being banned in both the United States and Britain until the 1960s, but its openness was an inspiration for many contemporary writers.

tro·pic[2] /trṓ pik/ *adj* relating to or showing tropism [Early 20C. < Greek *tropē* "turn"]

-tropic, -trophic *suffix* **1.** turning, changing, or reacting in a particular way ○ *dexiotropic* **2.** attracted to, having an affinity for, or moving toward a particular thing ○ *neurotropic* **3.** acting on something in a particular way ○ *vagotropic* [< Greek *tropē* "turn" (see TROPIC[1])]

trop·i·cal /tróppik'l/ *adj* **1.** relating to or characteristic of the tropics **2.** very hot and often combined with a high degree of humidity —**trop·i·cal·i·ty** /tròppi kállətee/ *n* —**trop·i·cal·ly** *adv*

trop·i·cal cy·clone *n* a cyclone that develops over tropical oceans and has winds up to hurricane force

trop·i·cal fish *n* a fish, usually small and brightly colored, that occurs naturally in tropical waters but is often kept in aquariums because of its attractive appearance

trop·i·cal·ize /tróppikə lìz/ (**-ized, -iz·ing, -iz·es**) *vt* to make or adapt something so that it becomes tropical in character or appearance or can be used under tropical conditions —**trop·i·cal·i·za·tion** /tròppikəli záysh'n/ *n*

trop·i·cal storm *n* a severe storm that develops offshore over tropical seas with less than hurricane force winds but with the ability to develop into a hurricane

trop·i·cal year *n* TIME same as **solar year**

trop·ic·bird /tróppik bùrd/ *n* a seabird with long slender tail feathers, small legs, and white feathers with black markings. Native to: tropics. Family: Phaethontidae.

trop·ic of Can·cer *n* a line of latitude that is 23° 26' north of the equator [< the constellation that its celestial projection intersects]

trop·ic of Cap·ri·corn *n* a line of latitude that is 23° 26' south of the equator [< the constellation that its celestial projection intersects]

tro·pine /trṓ peen, trṓpin/, **tro·pin** /trṓpin/ *n* a colorless crystalline alkaloid formed by heating atropine with barium hydroxide. Formula: $C_8H_{15}NO$. [Mid-19C. Shortening of ATROPINE]

tro·pism /trṓ pìzzəm/ *n* the involuntary response of an organism or one of its parts toward or away from a stimulus such as heat or light [Late 19C. < Greek *tropos* "turning" < *trepein* "turn"] —**tro·pis·tic** /trō pístik/ *adj* —**tro·pis·ti·cal·ly** *adv*

tropo- *prefix* **1.** turning, change ○ *tropopause* **2.** tropism ○ *tropotactic* [< Greek *tropē*]

tro·pol·o·gy /trō póllәjee/ (*plural* **-gies**) *n* **1.** LANGUAGE **USE OF FIGURATIVE LANGUAGE** the use of figurative language in speaking or writing **2.** LITERAT **TREATISE ON FIGURATIVE LANGUAGE** a piece of discursive writing on the use of figurative language **3.** CHR **METHOD OF INTERPRETING BIBLE** a method of interpreting the moral teaching of the Bible through its use of figurative language [Early 16C. < TROPE] —**tro·po·log·ic** /trōpə lójjik, tròppə-/ *adj* —**tro·po·log·i·cal·ly** *adv*

tro·po·my·o·sin /trōpə mī́ əssin, tròppə-/ *n* a protein in muscle that interacts with other proteins to regulate contraction

tro·po·nin /trṓpənin, tróppənin/ *n* a protein complex that plays a role in muscle contraction [Mid-20C. Contraction < TROPOMYOSIN + -IN]

tro·po·pause /trṓpə pàwz, tróppə-/ *n* the transitional region of the atmosphere between the troposphere and stratosphere, 10 mi./16 km above the equator and 6 mi./9 km above polar regions [Early 20C. Blend of TROPOSPHERE + PAUSE]

tro·po·sphere /trṓpə sfeer, tróppə-/ *n* the lowest and most dense layer of the atmosphere, extending 6 to 12 mi./10 to 20 km, in which temperature decreases with rising altitude and most weather occurs —**tro·po·spher·ic** /trṑpə sféerik, trṑppə-, -sférrik/ *adj*

tro·po·tax·is /trṑpə táksiss, tròppə-/ *n* the movement of an organism toward or away from a stimulus as a result of comparing sensory input received from paired receptors on both sides of the body —**tro·po·tac·tic** *adj* —**tro·po·tac·ti·cal·ly** *adv*

-tropous *suffix* turning or growing in a particular way ○ *orthotropous* [< Greek *tropos* "turning, changing" < *trepein* "turn"]

trop·po /tróppō/ *adv* too much (*used in musical directions*) [< Italian]

-tropy *suffix* the condition of taking a particular molecular form ○ *allotropy* [< Greek *-tropia* < *tropos* (see -TROPOUS)]

trot /trot/ *v* (**trot·ted, trot·ting, trots**) **1.** *vti* RIDING **MOVE AT PACE SLOWER THAN CANTERING** to move at a rate that is faster than walking but slower than cantering, and in which diagonal pairs of feet are off the ground alternately, or cause a four-legged animal such as a horse to move in this way **2.** *vi* **MOVE AT JOGGING PACE** to move at a jogging pace that is faster than walking but not as fast as running ○ *The team trotted onto the field.* ■ *n* **1. PACE FASTER THAN WALK** the forward movement of a four-legged animal, especially a horse, in which it trots **2.** RIDING **TROTTING PACE** a ride on a horse in which it trots **3. JOGGING PACE** a jogging pace that is faster than a walk but slower than a run **4.** HORSERACING **TROTTERS' RACE** a race for horses who run in harness **5.** FISHING same as **trotline 6.** *US* EDUC same as **pony** *n* (sense 6) (*informal*) ■ **trots** *npl* MED **DIARRHEA** a prolonged bout of diarrhea (*informal; used with "the"*) [13C. < Old French *troter* < Germanic] ◇ **on the trot 1.** *UK* one after the other in succession **2.** *Can, UK* busy, especially doing something that involves walking about a lot

trot out *vt* to bring something out or display something repeatedly, especially in the expectation of gaining admiration or approval (*informal*) ○ *He trots out the same old excuses every time he's late.*

troth /troth/ *n* a solemn pledge, especially the promise to remain faithful exchanged by a bride and groom or an engaged couple (*formal*) [13C. Variant of TRUTH]

trot·line /trót lìn/ *n* a long fishing line with shorter baited lines attached, used in streams or near the shore [Mid-19C. Origin ?]

Leon Trotsky

Trot·sky /trótskee/, **Leon** (1879–1940) Russian revolutionary leader. With Lenin he played a major part in the Bolshevik Revolution of 1917 in Russia. He is credited with creating and directing the Red Army, but failed to take power on Lenin's death and was murdered in exile by one of Stalin's agents. Born **Bronstein, Lev Davidovich**

> "Insurrection is an art, and like all arts it has its laws."
> [Leon Trotsky, *History of the Russian Revolution*; 1933]

Trots·ky·ism /trótskee ìzzəm/ *n* an interpretation of socialism advanced by Leon Trotsky, asserting that fully developed Marxist principles and practices would culminate in a world revolution by the proletariat —**Trots·ky·ist** *n, adj* —**Trots·ky·ite** *n, adj*

trot·ter /tróttər/ *n* **1.** the foot of an animal, especially that of a pig or sheep, when used as food **2.** somebody or something that trots, especially a horse that has been specially trained to trot in harness

trou·ba·dour /trṓobə dàwr, -dòor/ *n* **1. MEDIEVAL POET OR SINGER** a writer or singer of lyric verses about courtly love, especially in parts of Europe between the 11th and 13th centuries **2. LOVE POET OR SINGER** a writer or singer of love poems or songs **3.** *US* **SINGER** a singer who performs while strolling, especially in a restaurant [Early 18C. Via French < Old Provençal *trobador* < *trobar* "compose"]

trou·ble /trúbb'l/ *n* **1. CONDITION OF DISTRESS** a condition of distress, anxiety, or danger ○ *When the bills started to come in, we realized we were in serious trouble.* **2. SOMEBODY OR SOMETHING UPSETTING** a source or cause of worry, distress, or concern ○ *This car has been nothing but trouble.* **3. SOURCE OF DIFFICULTY** something that is extremely difficult or presents a problem ○ *I'm sorry I'm late – I had trouble getting the car to start.* **4. REAL OR APPARENT WEAKNESS** an actual or perceived failing or drawback ○ *Your trouble is that you give up too easily.* **5.** MED **MEDICAL PROBLEMS** an illness or physical condition involving a particular body part that is not functioning as it should ○ *on sick leave with back trouble* **6. EFFORT** the effort or exertion involved in doing something ○ *I hope you like your CD – I went to a lot of trouble to find it.* **7. DISORDER OR UNREST** disorder or unruly behavior in a public place ○ *crowd trouble* **8. MALFUNCTIONING** a condition in which something mechanical or electronic is not functioning or operating as it should ○ *My car has engine trouble.* ■ *v* (**-bled, -bling, -bles**) **1.** *vt* **WORRY OR UPSET SOMEBODY** to cause worry, distress, or concern to somebody or something ○ *I'm troubled by the fact that she hasn't been in touch.* **2.** *vt*

PHYSICALLY AFFECT SOMEBODY to cause pain or discomfort to somebody or something ○ *My arthritis troubles me from time to time.* **3.** *vt* IMPOSE ON SOMEBODY to put somebody to the inconvenience of doing something ○ *Could I trouble you to open the window?* **4.** *vti* MAKE EFFORT to make an effort to do something or take pains in doing it ○ *He hadn't troubled to check the figures.* **5.** *vt* MAKE SOMETHING ROUGH to agitate or disturb something, especially the surface of water (*often passive*) [13C. Via Old French *troubler* < late Latin *turbidare* < Latin *turbidus* "confused, muddy"] —**trou·bler** *n* —**trou·bling** *adj* —**trou·bling·ly** *adv* ◇ **in trouble 1.** discovered in wrongdoing and liable to be punished **2.** pregnant and unmarried (*dated informal; used euphemistically*)

SYNONYMS See ***bother.***

trou·bled /trúbb'ld/ *adj* **1.** ANXIOUS OR UPSET experiencing worry or distress **2.** MARKED BY PROBLEMS characterized by difficulties or adversity ○ *The bill has had a troubled passage through the Senate.* **3.** LACKING INNER CALM experiencing or prone to emotional conflict or psychological difficulties

trou·ble·mak·er /trúbb'l màykər/ *n* somebody who constantly causes problems —**trou·ble·mak·ing** *n, adj*

Trou·bles /trúbb'lz/ *npl* the political and civil unrest in Northern Ireland during the period from 1919 to 1923 and after 1969

trou·ble·shoot /trúbb'l shòot/ (**-shot** /-shòt/, **-shoot·ing, -shoots**) *vti* to operate as somebody who finds and eliminates problems

trou·ble·shoot·ing /trúbb'l shòoting/ *n* **1.** the act or process of identifying and eliminating problems or faults, especially in electronic or computer equipment **2.** the act or process of mediating in political, industrial, or diplomatic disagreements —**trou·ble·shoot·er** *n*

trou·ble·some /trúbb'lssəm/ *adj* **1.** causing difficulties or taking a great deal of time ○ *Fixing the bug in the computer program proved more troublesome than I thought.* **2.** producing annoyance, discomfort, or anxiety, especially in a recurrent way ○ *a troublesome knee injury* —**trou·ble·some·ly** *adv* —**trou·ble·some·ness** *n*

trou·ble spot *n* **1.** a place where trouble occurs, especially a place that is notorious for disruption to civil order or a lack of political control **2.** a location where a fault, flaw, or problem occurs

trou·blous /trúbbləss/ *adj* (*archaic or literary*) **1.** fraught with difficulty or many problems **2.** full of uneasiness or anxiety —**trou·blous·ly** *adv* —**trou·blous·ness** *n*

trough /trawf, trof/ *n* **1.** CONTAINER FOR ANIMAL FOOD OR WATER a long low narrow open container that holds feed or water for animals **2.** INDUST INDUSTRIAL CONTAINER a long low narrow open container used in industry, e.g., in washing, kneading, or mixing substances **3.** CHANNEL FOR LIQUID a narrow channel, gully, or gutter in which liquid passes, especially one under the eaves of a roof for catching rainwater **4.** METEOROL AREA OF LOW PRESSURE an elongated area of low atmospheric pressure that may be associated with a front **5.** GEOG SUNKEN AREA a long hollow area in the surface of the ground or the sea bed, or between waves **6.** LOW POINT a low or negative point, especially a temporary one **7.** ECON LOWEST POINT OF ECONOMIC CYCLE the lowest point or period of an economic cycle **8.** PHYS LOW PART OF WAVE OR SIGNAL the low or negative half of the amplitude in the cycle of a periodic wave or alternating signal [Old English *trog* < Indo-European, "wood, tree"]

trounce /trownss/ (**trounced, trounc·ing, trounc·es**) *vt* **1.** to defeat an opponent or team convincingly **2.** to beat somebody or something severely (*dated*) [Mid-16C. Origin ?]

SYNONYMS See ***defeat.***

troupe /troop/ *n* a group of actors, circus people, or other entertainers, especially one that travels around ■ *vi* (**trouped, troup·ing, troupes**) to travel as or perform in a troupe of actors or entertainers [Early 19C. < French]

USAGE See *troop.*

troup·er /tròopər/ *n* **1.** MEMBER OF TROUPE somebody who is a member of a group of traveling entertainers **2.** SOMEBODY RELIABLE AND DEDICATED somebody who is conscientious, dependable, and selfless **3.** VETERAN THEATRICAL PERFORMER somebody who has been involved in the theater for many years, especially an actor or entertainer

trou·pi·al /tròopee əl/ *n* a large songbird of the blackbird family with bright black and orange feathers. Native to: South America. Latin name: *Icterus icterus.* [Early 19C. < French *troupiale*, alteration (influenced by *troupe* "flock") of American Spanish *turpial*]

trou·ser /trówzər/ *adj* belonging to, concerning, suitable for, or part of trousers ○ *a trouser pocket* ■ *vt* (**-sered, -ser·ing, -sers**) *UK* to obtain or appropriate money or valuables (*slang; used disapprovingly*) ○ *Contestants battle to trouser huge cash prizes.* [Mid-19C. Back-formation < TROUSERS] —**trou·sered** *adj*

trou·sers /trówzərz/ *npl UK* same as **pants** (sense 1) [Early 17C. < Gaelic *triubhas*]

trou·ser suit *n UK* same as **pantsuit**

trous·seau /tròo sō, troo sṓ/ (*plural* **-seaus** or **-seaux** /-sōz, -sṓz/) *n* a bride's clothes and linen, especially items such as nightgowns, underwear, blankets, and sheets, that she has collected during the period of her engagement [Early 19C. < French, "little bundle" < *trousser* "truss"]

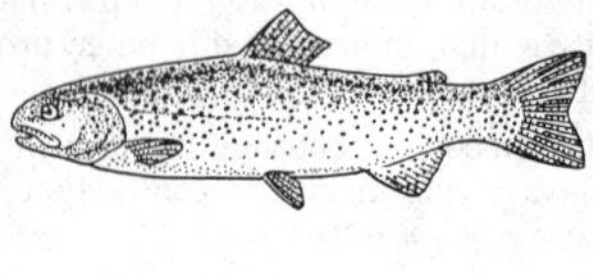

trout

trout /trowt/ (*plural* **trouts** or *same*) *n* **1.** FRESHWATER FISH SIMILAR TO SALMON a freshwater fish that is typically smaller than the related salmon and has a speckled body, small scales, and soft fins. Genus: *Salmo.* **2.** GAME FISH OF SALMON FAMILY a game fish of the salmon family, e.g., the sea trout. Genus: *Salvelinus.* **3.** FISH UNRELATED TO TROUT a fish similar to but unrelated to the trout, e.g., the troutperch [Pre-12C. < late Latin *tructa*]

trout lil·y *n US* PLANTS same as **dogtooth violet** [Probably < its speckled leaves]

trout·perch /trówt pùrch/ (*plural same*) *n* a small freshwater fish with a spotted body, an adipose fin, and rough scales. Native to: North America. Family: Percopsidae.

trou·vaille /troo vī́/ *n* something interesting, amusing, or beneficial discovered by chance ○ *The anecdote was one of her many literary trouvailles.* [Mid-19C. < French, "a find"]

trou·vère /troo vér/ *n* a poet-musician of northern France during the 12th and 13th centuries who wrote poems and songs of courtly love, as well as narrative and satirical works [Late 18C. Via French < Old French *trovere* < *trover* "compose" (see TROVER)]

trove /trōv/ *n* **1.** a collection of discovered valuable items **2.** a discovery of great importance or monetary value [Late 19C. Shortening of TREASURE-TROVE]

tro·ver /trṓvər/ *n* a common law action to recover goods that have been wrongly appropriated by somebody else (*archaic*) [Late 16C. < Anglo-Norman < Old French "to find"]

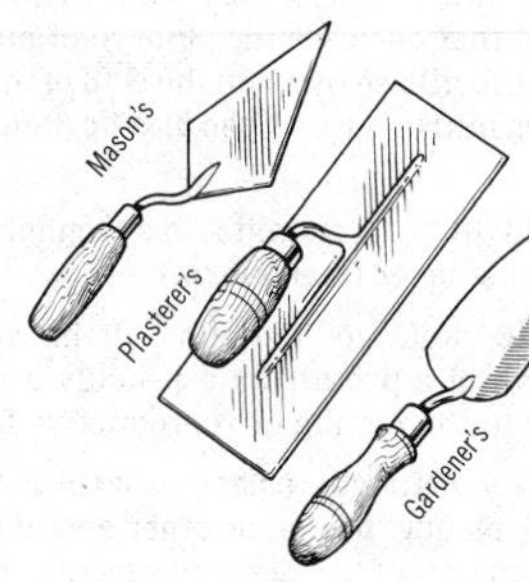

trowel

trow·el /trów əl/ *n* **1.** FLAT-BLADED HAND TOOL a small hand tool with a short handle and a flat, usually pointed blade used for spreading, shaping, and smoothing plaster, cement, or mortar **2.** GARDENER'S SHORT-HANDLED TOOL a hand tool with a short handle and a curved tapering blade, used for making holes to put plants and seedlings in and for other light digging work ■ *vt* (**trow·eled** or **trow·elled, trow·el·ing** or **trow·el·ling, trow·els**) WORK MATERIAL WITH TROWEL to dig, spread, or level something such as earth or mortar using a trowel [14C. Via Old French *troele* < late Latin *truella* "dipper" < Latin *trua* "ladle"] —**trow·el·er** *n* ◇ **lay it on with a trowel** to exaggerate, especially in order to flatter somebody (*informal*)

troy /troy/ *adj* measured in or using the troy weight system [14C. Probably < TROYES, which had a fair at which this weight was used]

Troy /troy/ **1.** city of ancient Greece on the Aegean seacoast, in present-day Turkey. Site of the ten-year Trojan War described in the epic poems of Homer, the city, also called Ilium, was thought to be purely legendary until ruins were discovered by the archaeologist Heinrich Schliemann in 1870. It is now believed to have been founded during the Bronze Age in 3000 B.C. **2.** city in eastern New York northeast of Albany. Population: 48,818 (2002 estimate).

Troyes /trwaa/ capital of Aube Department, in Champagne, northeastern France. Population: 60,958 (1999).

troy weight *n* a system of weights used for precious metals and gemstones, based on a 12-ounce pound, a 20-pennyweight ounce, and a 24-grain pennyweight

trp *abbr* troop

trs. *abbr* PRINTING transpose

tru·ant /tròo ənt/ *n* SOMEBODY ABSENT FROM SCHOOL somebody who is absent without permission or good reason, especially from school ■ *adj* ABSENT absent without permission ■ *vi* (**-ant·ed, -ant·ing, -ants**) BE ABSENT to be absent without permission, especially from school [14C. < Old French, "beggar, vagabond," of Celtic origin] —**tru·an·cy** *n*

truce /trooss/ *n* **1.** CESSATION IN FIGHTING a cessation of military hostilities that both sides agree to hold to, usually for a fixed period ○ *Both sides called a truce.* **2.** AGREEMENT TO STOP FIGHTING an agreement to suspend military hostilities **3.** AGREED BREAK IN ARGUING an agreed break in a dispute or feud, or the agreement to stop arguing [14C. Variant of earlier *trewes*, the plural of *trewe* "treaty, pledge" < Old English *trēow* (see TRUE)]

Tru·cial States /tròosh'l-/ former name for **United Arab Emirates** (until 1971)

truck[1] /truk/ *n* **1.** AUTOMOT LARGE COMMERCIAL FREIGHT TRANSPORT VEHICLE a large vehicle for transporting goods by road **2.** AUTOMOT same as **pickup truck 3.** CART PUSHED BY HAND a cart or barrow with two or more wheels that is pushed by hand and is used for moving heavy objects **4.** *UK* RAIL RAILROAD CAR FOR FREIGHT an open railroad car that carries freight **5.** TRAIN WHEEL UNIT a swiveling frame that the wheels and springs are mounted on at either end of a railroad car **6.** EXTREME SPORTS SKATEBOARD WHEEL UNIT either of a pair of swiveling wheel units on a skateboard **7.** NAUT ROPE GUIDE ON SHIP'S MAST a guide for a ship's ropes, in the form of a disk with holes, fitted horizontally to the top of the mast ■ *v* (**trucked, truck·ing, trucks**)

1. *vti* **TAKE THINGS BY TRUCK** to transport, or transport something, by truck **2.** *vi* **DRIVE TRUCK** to drive a truck, especially as a job (*informal*) **3.** *vi* **STROLL ALONG** to walk or move along at an easy, relaxed pace (*slang*) [Early 17C. Origin ?] ◇ **keep on trucking** to carry on with work or life in a cheerful and relaxed way, in spite of problems (*informal*)

truck^{2} /truk/ *n* **1. DEALINGS** dealings or involvement (*informal*) ○ *We'll have no truck with that kind of behavior.* **2. MARKET PRODUCE** vegetables and fruit grown for market **3. GOODS** traded goods of any kind **4. TRADE** the buying, selling, or bartering of goods **5. STUFF** miscellaneous items (*dated informal*) ○*"Now I wanted thirty dollars' worth of artist truck, for I was always sketching in the woods."* (Robert Louis Stevenson, *The Wrecker*; 1896) **6. PAYMENT IN KIND** payment in goods rather than with money ■ *vti* **(trucked, truck·ing, trucks) 1. EXCHANGE SOMETHING** to exchange or barter something, or take part in the business of bartering **2. BE INVOLVED WITH SOMEBODY** to have dealings with somebody, especially secret or dishonest dealings [12C. < Old French dialect *troquer* "to barter"]

truck·age /trúkij/ *n US* **1.** the carrying of freight by truck **2.** a charge made for transporting goods by truck

truck bomb *n* a truck filled with explosives or chemicals that is crashed into a target or detonated beside it, used as a terrorist weapon

truck·er^{1} /trúkər/ *n* **1.** somebody who drives a truck, especially somebody whose job is transporting goods by truck over long distances **2.** somebody who owns or manages a truck transportation company [Mid-19C. < TRUCK^{1}]

truck·er^{2} /trúkər/ *n* **1.** AGRIC same as **truck farmer 2.** somebody who barters [Mid-16C. < TRUCK^{2}]

truck farm *n* a farm producing vegetables for sale commercially —**truck farm·ing** *n*

truck farm·er *n* a farmer who produces fruit and vegetables for commercial sale

truck·ing /trúking/ *n* the carrying of freight on roads in trucks

truck·le /trúk'l/ (**-led, -ling, -les**) *vi* to behave in a weak or servile way [Early 17C. Shortening of TRUCKLE BED, from the use of such beds by servants] —**truck·ler** *n*

truck·le bed *n UK* same as **trundle bed** [< *truckle* "small wheel," via Anglo-Norman < Greek *trokhileia* "system of pulleys" < *trokhos* "wheel"]

truck·load /trúk lōd/ *n* the quantity carried by a truck, or a quantity large enough to fill a truck

truck stop *n* a roadside station that sells fuel for trucks and has a restaurant for truck drivers

truc·u·lent /trúkyələnt/ *adj* aggressively or sullenly refusing to accept something or do what is asked [Mid-16C. < Latin *truculentus* < *trux* "fierce"] —**truc·u·lence** *n* —**truc·u·lent·ly** *adv*

Tru·deau /troo dṓ/, **Garry B.** (*b.* 1948) US cartoonist. His long-running political comic strip *Doonesbury*, first syndicated in 1970 and awarded a Pulitzer Prize in 1974, frequently provokes controversy with its sharp satire.

> "Satire picks a one-sided fight, and the more its intended target reacts, the more the practitioner gains the advantage."
> [Garry B. Trudeau, *Wall Street Journal*; January 20, 1993]

Tru·deau, Pierre (1919–2000) prime minister of Canada (1968–79 and 1980–84). A Liberal prime minister, he negotiated the Constitution Act (1982) that granted Canada complete independence from the British parliament. Full name **Trudeau, Pierre Elliott**. See table at **prime minister**

> "Canada is a country whose main exports are hockey players and cold fronts. Our main imports are baseball players and acid rain."
> [Pierre Trudeau. Quoted in *Sportswit*, Lee Green; 1984]

> "Living next to you is in some ways like sleeping with an elephant. No matter how friendly and even-tempered the beast, one is affected by every twitch and grunt."
> [Pierre Trudeau, *Speech to the National Press Club, Washington, D.C.*; March 25, 1969]

trudge /truj/ *vti* (**trudged, trudg·ing, trudg·es**) to walk, or walk a particular path or distance, with slow heavy weary steps ■ *n* a long and exhausting walk [Mid-16C. Origin ?] —**trudg·er** *n*

true /troo/ *adj* (**tru·er, tru·est**) **1. REAL OR CORRECT** conforming with reality or fact **2. GENUINE** genuine, not pretended, insincere, or artificial **3. PERSONALLY FAITHFUL** showing loyalty to another person ○ *a true friend* **4. COMMITTED** faithful to a cause, purpose, or religious belief ○ *a true believer* **5. CONFORMING TO STANDARD OR MEASURE** conforming to a standard, measure, or pattern ○ *a true fit* **6. RIGHTFUL** conforming to the way things should be by right ○ *returned to the true owners* **7.** MUSIC **IN TUNE** perfectly in tune ○ *The orchestra maintained true pitch throughout.* **8. CONFORMING TO INCLUSION CRITERIA** meeting the criteria for inclusion in a particular category, in contrast to being given the same name because of superficial resemblance to members of that category ○ *A shooting star is not a true star.* **9.** GEOG **IN RELATION TO EARTH'S POLES** measured in relation to geographic points on the Earth's surface, rather than to points of magnetic attraction ○ *true north* **10.** PHYS **NOT RELATIVE** not relative as a value and corrected for all error factors ■ *adv* **1. IN REAL OR FACTUAL CORRESPONDENCE** in a way that corresponds with reality or fact ○ *His explanations just didn't ring true.* **2. ACCURATELY** so as to arrive at the precise position aimed for ○ *The arrow flew straight and true.* **3. HONESTLY** in a frank and open way that seeks to hide nothing ○ *Tell me true.* **4. CERTAINLY** used to admit the validity or accuracy of a statement, often in a discussion or when considering the advantages and disadvantages of something ○ *True, it does rain a lot here.* **5.** AGRIC **WITHOUT LOSS OF ANCESTRAL FEATURES** without variation from the ancestral form, or producing offspring with the same hereditary characteristics ○ *breed true* ■ *vt* (**trued, tru·ing** or **true·ing, trues**) **ADJUST POSITION OF SOMETHING** to adjust something to make it straight or level or put it in any other required position ■ *n* **1. ALIGNMENT** a correct position, especially a position in relation to the horizontal or vertical ○ *out of true* **2. REALITY** the absolute truth [Old English *trēowe* "trustworthy" < Indo-European, "be solid"] —**true·ness** *n* ◇ **come true** to happen as hoped or expected ◇ **true to life** conforming accurately with reality

true bill *n US* a legal document requesting a criminal trial (**bill of indictment**), formally endorsed by a grand jury and certifying that somebody can be brought to trial

true-blue *adj* completely loyal or faithful ○ *a true-blue pal*

true·born /troó bàwrn/ *adj* having one's true social position or nationality beyond doubt, because it was established at birth ○ *a trueborn French aristocrat*

true bug *n* INSECTS same as **bug** *n* (sense 1)

true-false test *n US* a test in which statements are given that must be marked as either true or false

true-life *adj* presenting matters, especially human relationships, as they are or have been in reality ○ *a true-life adventure story*

true·love /troó lùv/ *n* somebody who is deeply loved by another

true lov·ers' knot, true·love knot *n* a complicated bowknot that is difficult to untie, symbolizing lovers' faithfulness

~~truely~~ incorrect spelling of **truly**

true·pen·ny /troó pènnee/ (*plural* **-nies**) *n US* an honest, loyal, or trustworthy person (*dated*) [< the name given to a coin of genuine metal]

true rib *n* a rib that is attached to the breastbone (**sternum**) by cartilage. The seven uppermost ribs in the human body are true ribs.

true seal *n* MARINE BIOL same as **earless seal**

AKG London

François Truffaut

Truf·faut /troo fṓ/, **François** (1932–84) French movie director and critic. His first movie, the semi-autobiographical *The 400 Blows* (1959), was one of the first movies of the French new wave movement. Other movies include *Shoot the Piano Player* (1960) and *Jules et Jim* (1961).

> "An actor is never so great as when he reminds you of an animal—falling like a cat, lying like a dog, moving like a fox."
> [François Truffaut, *The New Yorker*; February 20, 1960]

truf·fle /trúff'l/ *n* **1.** an underground fungus whose fleshy edible fruiting body is highly valued as a delicacy. Pigs and dogs are often used to sniff out truffles. Genus: *Tuber*. **2.** a rich ball-shaped chocolate with a center of soft chocolate [Late 16C. Alteration of French *trufe*, via Provençal *trufa* < Latin *tuber* "swelling"]

tru·ism /troó ìzzəm/ *n* a statement that is so obviously true and so often repeated that people find it trite or meaningless —**tru·is·tic** /troo ístik/ *adj*

Tru·ji·llo /troo heé yō/ city in a coastal desert region of northwestern Peru, founded in 1534. It is situated next to the remains of an important pre-Incan city. Population: 627,553 (1995).

Tru·ji·llo /troo heé yō/, **Rafael Leonidas** (1891–1961) Dominican soldier and national leader. Elected president in 1930, he remained the army generalissimo and dictator of the Dominican Republic until his assassination by the army. Full name **Trujillo Molina, Rafael Leonidas**

~~truley~~ incorrect spelling of **truly**

trull /trul/ *n* same as **prostitute** *n* (sense 1) (*archaic*) [Early 16C. < Middle High German *trulle*]

tru·ly /troólee/ *adv* **1. SINCERELY** honestly, without affectation or pretense ○ *feel truly sorry* **2. USED FOR EMPHASIS** used to emphasize the extent or degree of something ○ *a truly remarkable achievement* **3. COMPLETELY** to the fullest extent or in the fullest degree ○ *Only she can truly appreciate how happy I feel.* **4. USED TO SIGN LETTER** used alone or with "yours" as a way to sign a letter ◇ **yours truly** used to refer to yourself (*humorous*) ○ *Doubtless they're expecting yours truly to pick them up at the airport.*

Tru·man /troómən/, **Bess** (1885–1982) US first lady. She married Harry S. Truman, a childhood sweetheart, in 1919, and during his presidency (1945–53) was one of his most trusted advisers. Born **Wallace, Elizabeth Virginia**

Tru·man, Harry S. (1884–1972) 33rd President of the United States (1945–53). A Democrat, he became President on the death of Franklin D. Roosevelt and continued to pursue his predecessor's welfare policies. In foreign policy, he acted to contain Communism overseas, especially in the Korean War (1950–53). See table at **president**. See illustration on next page

> "A politician is a man who understands government, and it takes a politician to run a government. A statesman is a politician who's been dead 10 or 15 years."
> [Harry S. Truman, *New York World Telegram and Sun*; April 12, 1958]

Harry S. Truman

"If you can't stand the heat, get out of the kitchen."
[Attributed to Harry S. Truman, *Time*; April 28, 1953]

Trum·bull /trúmb'l/, **John** (1750–1831) US lawyer and poet. A Connecticut judge and one of the "Hartford Wits," he wrote the comic epic *M'Fingal* (1775–82), satirizing British Loyalists during the American Revolution.

"No man e'er felt the halter draw, / With good opinion of the law."
[John Trumbull, *M'Fingal*; 1775–82]

Trum·bull, Jonathan (1710–85) American political leader. He served as Connecticut's colonial governor (1769–84) and was a leader in the American Revolution.

tru·meau /troo mṓ/ (*plural* **-meaux** /-mṓz/) *n* a pillar or a section of wall that separates two doors or two sections of a door [Late 19C. < French, "calf of the leg"]

trump[1] /trump/ *n* **1. CARD FROM HIGHEST SUIT** in card games, a card from a suit declared to be higher in value than any other suit, or the suit itself **2. KEY RESOURCE** a highly valuable resource or advantage, especially one held in reserve for future use **3. FINE PERSON** an admirable or reliable person (*informal*) ■ *vt* (**trumped, trump·ing, trumps**) **1. DEFEAT SOMEBODY BY PLAYING TRUMP** in card games, to beat an opponent or an opponent's card by playing a trump **2. OUTDO SOMEBODY** to defeat or outdo a competitor by bringing a valuable resource or advantage into play [Early 16C. Alteration of TRIUMPH]

trump up *vt* to invent false accusations or false evidence in order to incriminate somebody wrongly

trump[2] /trump/ *n* a trumpet, or the sound of a trumpet (*archaic*) [13C. < Old French *trompe* (see TRUMPET)]

trump card *n* CARDS same as **trump**[1] *n* (senses 1–2) ◇ **play your trump card** to make use of a highly valuable resource or advantage that has been held in reserve

trumped-up *adj* false and deliberately invented, usually in order to incriminate somebody wrongly ○ *trumped-up charges*

trump·er·y /trúmpəree/ (*plural* **-ies**) *n* (*archaic or literary*) **1.** something worthless or useless, often something showy that seems appealing at first glance **2.** empty or ridiculous talk [15C. < French *tromperie* "trickery" < *tromper* "deceive"]

trum·pet /trúmpət/ *n* **1. BRASS INSTRUMENT** a brass musical instrument, either straight or coiled, with three valves and a flared bell. It has a brilliant tone and a middle to high register. **2. SOMETHING SHAPED LIKE TRUMPET** something shaped like the flared bell of a trumpet **3. SOUND OF OR LIKE TRUMPET** a loud high sound made by a trumpet, or a sound such as the call of an elephant **4. PLAYER OF TRUMPET** a player of a trumpet **5.** MED same as **ear trumpet 6. ORGAN STOP** a solo organ stop that imitates the sound of a trumpet ■ *v* (**-pet·ed, -pet·ing, -pets**) **1.** *vti* **ANNOUNCE SOMETHING** to announce something loudly, proudly, or with great ceremony **2.** *vt* **SPEAK IN PRAISE OF SOMETHING** to speak of somebody or something with ostentatious admiration or pride **3.** *vi* **MAKE ELEPHANT'S CALL** to make an elephant's characteristically high-pitched, penetrating call **4.** *vt* **EXPRESS SOMETHING BY TRUMPETING** to convey something with a trumpeting call ○ *The elephant trumpeted a warning.* [14C. < Old French *trompette* "small horn" < *trompe* "horn" < Germanic, probably an imitation of the sound of a horn]

trum·pet creep·er *n* a woody deciduous vine with compound leaves. Flowers: large, red, trumpet-shaped. Native to: North America. Latin name: *Campsis radicans.*

trum·pet·er /trúmpətər/ *n* **1. TRUMPET PLAYER** a musician who plays the trumpet **2. TROPICAL BIRD WITH LOUD CALL** a medium-sized bird that rarely flies and has long legs, a short bill, dark glossy plumage, and a loud call. Native to: tropical South America. Family: Psophidae. **3. PIGEON** a domestic pigeon with a long ruff, heavily feathered feet, and a loud call

trum·pet flow·er *n* **1.** a plant with trumpet-shaped flowers, e.g., the trumpet creeper **2.** the flower of a trumpet flower

trum·pet hon·ey·suck·le *n* a climbing plant with scarlet or orange trumpet-shaped flowers. Native to: North America. Latin name: *Lonicera sempervirens.*

trum·pet vine *n* PLANTS same as **trumpet creeper**

trumps /trumps/ *n* in card games, the suit that is chosen at the outset to be the highest in value (*takes a singular or plural verb*) ○ *Diamonds are trumps.* ◇ **turn up trumps** to prove unexpectedly to be a valuable asset, especially one that plays a decisive role in the success of something

trun·cate /trúng kàyt/ *vt* (**-ca·ted, -cat·ing, -cates**) **1. SHORTEN SOMETHING BY REMOVING PART** to shorten something by cutting off or removing a part **2.** MATH **SHORTEN DECIMAL NUMBER** to restrict the precision of a decimal number by limiting the digits to the right of the decimal point without rounding ■ *adj* **1.** MATH, CRYSTALS, LITERAT same as **truncated** (senses 2–4) **2.** BOT **NOT POINTED** describes a leaf that has a blunt end, so that it looks as if a part has been cut off [15C. < Latin *truncat-*, past participle of *truncare* "cut short, mutilate" < *truncus* "something cut off"] —**trun·cate·ly** *adv* —**trun·ca·tion** /trung káysh'n/ *n*

trun·ca·ted /trúng kàytəd/ *adj* **1. WITH END REMOVED** shortened by having a part cut off or removed **2.** MATH **WITH END REPLACED BY PLANE** describes a geometric figure that has the apex or an end removed and replaced with a plane section, often parallel to the base **3.** CRYSTALS **HAVING INCOMPLETE CORNERS** describes a crystal that lacks the fully formed corners or faces that would be present in a simple form of the crystal **4.** LITERAT **WITH ONE SYLLABLE FEWER** describes a line of poetry that has one syllable fewer in one of its feet than in others in the line

trun·cheon /trúnchən/ *n* **1. POLICE OFFICER'S STICK** a short heavy stick carried by a police officer **2. SYMBOLIC STICK** a baton carried as a symbol of rank or authority **3. SPEAR SHAFT** the shaft of a spear ■ *vt* (**-cheoned, -cheon·ing, -cheons**) **HIT SOMEBODY WITH TRUNCHEON** to hit somebody or something with a truncheon [13C. Via Old N French *tronchon* < Latin *truncus* "something cut off"]

trun·dle /trúnd'l/ *vti* (**-dled, -dling, -dles**) **MOVE HEAVILY ON WHEELS** to move slowly and heavily, especially on wheels or rollers, or move something in this way ■ *n* **1. WHEEL** a small wheel or roller by which something is moved along **2. ROLLING MOVEMENT** a slow heavy movement, especially a rolling movement **3. CART WITH WHEELS** a trolley or cart with small wheels **4.** *US* HOUSEHOLD same as **trundle bed** [Mid-16C. Variant of *trendle* "wheel" < Old English *trendel* "circle" < Germanic]

trun·dle bed *n* a low bed on casters that can be stowed away under another bed

trunk /trungk/ *n* **1. MAIN STEM OF TREE** the main stem of a tree, excluding branches and roots **2.** AUTOMOT **AUTOMOBILE'S STORAGE COMPARTMENT** an enclosed storage compartment in an automobile, usually at the rear **3. LARGE TRAVELING CASE** a large strong traveling case or box with a hinged lid that is bigger, more rigid, and less portable than a suitcase **4. UPPER BODY** the main part of the body of a human being or an animal, excluding the head, neck, and limbs **5. ELEPHANT'S PROBOSCIS** the long muscular proboscis of an elephant, used for grasping, feeding, and drinking **6. MAIN PART** the main part of something that has branches or subsidiary parts leading off it, e.g., a transportation network or an electrical or communications network **7.** ANAT **STEM OF BLOOD VESSEL** the main stem of a blood vessel or nerve, with branches leading off it **8.** NAUT **PART OF CABIN ABOVE DECK** the part of a boat's cabin that sits above the deck **9.** BUILDINGS **DUCT** a duct in a building, e.g., a ventilation duct or a duct carrying electrical wires **10.** ARCHIT **PART OF COLUMN** the shaft of an architectural column, excluding the base and the capital ■ **trunks** *npl* CLOTHING **MEN'S SWIMWEAR** men's shorts worn for sports, especially swimming [15C. Via French *tronc* "tree trunk, alms box" < Latin *truncus* "something cut off"]

trunk·fish /trúngk fish/ (*plural* **-fish·es** or *same*) *n* a brightly colored tropical fish that has a body covered in bony plates. Family: Ostraciidae.

trunk hose *n* short puffed-out breeches worn by men in the late 16th and early 17th centuries. They extended from the waist to the upper or mid thigh.

trunk·ing /trúngking/ *n* a casing used to anchor, conceal, and protect cables and small pipes

trun·nel *n* CONSTR same as **treenail**

trun·nion /trúnnyən/ *n* either of a pair of pivots, especially the cylindrical knobs on the side of a cannon's barrel that allow it to pivot on the gun carriage [Early 17C. < French *trognon* "fruit core, tree stump"] —**trun·nioned** *adj*

Tru·ro /tro͝orō/ town on Cobequid Bay in central Nova Scotia, Canada. Population: 21,442 (2001).

truss /truss/ *vt* (**trussed, truss·ing, truss·es**) **1. BIND SOMEBODY OR SOMETHING** to tie somebody or something up tightly **2.** COOK **TIE SOMETHING FOR COOKING** to prepare meat for roasting by tying it into a neat shape. Birds such as chickens and turkeys are trussed to keep wings and legs close to the body. **3.** CIV ENG **SUPPORT SOMETHING WITH LOAD-BEARING MEMBERS** to support or strengthen a roof, bridge, or other elevated structure with a network of beams and bars **4.** MED **SUPPORT HERNIA** to support a hernia with a specially designed device ■ *n* **1.** MED **SUPPORT FOR HERNIA** a device designed to apply pressure to a hernia to stop it from enlarging or protruding **2.** BOT **FRUIT CLUSTER** a cluster of flowers or fruit on a single branching stem, e.g., on a tomato plant **3.** NAUT **MAST FITTING** a metal fitting used to attach a ship's beam (**yard**) to a mast **4. BUNDLE** a bundle, especially a bundle of hay of varying weight [12C. < Old French *trousse* < *trousser* "to truss"] —**truss·er** *n*

truss bridge *n* a bridge whose supporting structure consists of a network of beams in a series of triangular sections

truss·ing /trússing/ *n* a framework of beams arranged in triangular sections and supporting a roof, bridge, or other structure, or the beams themselves

trust /trust/ *n* **1. RELIANCE** confidence in and reliance on good qualities, especially fairness, truth, honor, or ability **2. POSITION OF OBLIGATION** the position of somebody who is expected by others to behave responsibly or honorably ○ *breached the public trust* **3. HOPE FOR FUTURE** hopeful reliance on what will happen in the future **4. CARE** responsibility for taking good care of somebody or something ○ *We put our children in the trust of a good daycare center.* **5.** *US* **RESPONSIBILITY THAT SOMEBODY HAS** something entrusted to somebody to be responsible for ○ *accepted his responsibilities as a sacred trust* **6.** LAW **HOLDING OF ANOTHER'S PROPERTY** the legal holding and managing of money or property belonging to somebody else, e.g., that of a minor **7.** LAW **ARRANGEMENT TO MANAGE ANOTHER'S PROPERTY** a legal arrangement by which one person (**trustee**) holds and manages money or property belonging to somebody else **8.** COMM **CREDIT** credit given to somebody on purchases made ○ *Let me have it on trust.* **9.** *US* COMM **CARTEL** a combination of corporations with the purpose of reducing competition and controlling prices ■ *v* (**trust·ed, trust·ing, trusts**) **1.** *vti* **RELY ON SOMEBODY OR SOMETHING** to place confidence in somebody or in somebody's good qualities, especially fairness, truth, honor, or ability **2.** *vt* **CONFIDENTLY ALLOW SOMEBODY TO DO SOMETHING** to allow somebody to do something, having confidence that the person will behave responsibly or properly ○ *I trust you to do the right thing.* **3.** *vt* **PLACE SOMETHING IN SOMEBODY'S CARE** to place somebody or something in the care of another person ○ *You could certainly* *trust him with such an important job.* **4.** *vt* **SUPPOSE SOMETHING** to hope or suppose something ○ *I trust you had a good vacation.* **5.** *vt Carib* **GIVE CREDIT TO SOMEBODY** to give somebody credit on a purchase ○ *wouldn't even trust me a carton of milk* [12C. < Old Norse *traust* "confidence," *treysta* "to trust"] —**trust·a·bil·i·ty** /trùstə bíllətee/ *n* —**trust·a·ble** *adj* —**trust·er** *n*

trust·bust·er /trúst bùstər/ *n* a government official who carries out investigations into commercial cartels and works to break them up —**trust·bust·ing** *n*

trust com·pa·ny *n* a bank or other commercial organization that sets up and operates trusts for private individuals and businesses

trus·tee /tru steé/ *n* **1.** LAW **MANAGER OF ANOTHER'S PROPERTY** somebody who is given the legal authority to manage money or property on behalf of somebody else **2.** FIN **FINANCE MANAGER** a member of a group of people responsible for managing the financial affairs of an institution or organization **3.** POL **COUNTRY SUPERVISING TRUST TERRITORY** a country responsible for administering a trust territory ■ *vti* (**-teed, -tee·ing, -tees**) *US* **ENTRUST SOMETHING TO TRUSTEE** to entrust something to a trustee, or act as a trustee

trus·tee·ship /tru steé shìp/ *n* **1.** the status or responsibilities of a trustee, or the period of time for which a trustee holds office **2.** the administration of a country that is not self-governing by a foreign country under terms laid down by the United Nations

trust·ful /trústfəl/ *adj* same as **trusting** —**trust·ful·ly** *adv* —**trust·ful·ness** *n*

trust fund *n* an investment fund managed on behalf of somebody, particularly a minor, by one or more people given legal authority to do so

trust·ing /trústing/ *adj* willing or tending to trust people —**trust·ing·ly** *adv* —**trust·ing·ness** *n*

trust ter·ri·to·ry *n* a country that does not have its own government, but is run by a foreign country under terms laid down by the United Nations

trust·wor·thy /trúst wùrthee/ *adj* deserving trust, or able to be trusted —**trust·wor·thi·ly** *adv* —**trust·wor·thi·ness** *n*

trust·y /trústee/ *adj* (**-i·er, -i·est**) **RELIABLE** able to be relied on ■ *n* (*plural* **-ies**) **1. TRUSTED PERSON** somebody who is trusted **2. TRUSTED PRISONER** a prisoner regarded by the prison authorities as trustworthy and given special privileges —**trust·i·ly** *adv* —**trust·i·ness** *n*

truth /trooth/ *n* **1. SOMETHING FACTUAL** the thing that corresponds to fact or reality ○ *If you tell the truth, you have nothing to fear.* ○ *spoke the truth* **2. TRUE QUALITY** correspondence to fact or reality **3. TRUE STATEMENT** a statement that corresponds to fact or reality ○ *His story was a mixture of truths and untruths* **4. OBVIOUS FACT** something that is so clearly true that it hardly needs to be stated **5. SOMETHING GENERALLY BELIEVED** a statement that is generally believed to be true ○ *a religious truth* **6. HONESTY** honesty and sincerity ○ *I can say in all truth that I never knew about his crimes.* **7. CONFORMITY** adherence to a standard or law **8. LOYALTY** faithfulness to a person or a cause (*dated*) **9.** *UK* **ACCURACY** accuracy of alignment, setting, position, or shape (*dated*) [Old English *trēowth* "faithfulness" < *trēow* (see TRUE)]

Truth *n* in Christian Science, God

Truth /trooth/, **Sojourner** (1797?–1883) US abolitionist. Freed from slavery, she campaigned for the rights of African Americans and women. Born **Van Wagener, Isabella**

> "If de fust woman God ever made was strong enough to turn the world upside down, all 'lone, dese togedder ought to be able to turn it back and get it right side up again, and now dey is asking to do it, de men better let em."
>
> [Sojourner Truth, *Speech at Women's Rights Convention, Akron, Ohio, Narrative of Sojourner Truth*; 1878]

truth-con·di·tion *n* the condition that must apply if a given philosophical proposition is to be true

truth drug *n UK* same as **truth serum**

truth·ful /tro͞othfəl/ *adj* **1.** telling the truth or tending to tell the truth **2.** corresponding to fact or reality —**truth·ful·ness** *n*

truth·ful·ly /tro͞othfəlee/ *adv* in a way that corresponds to fact or reality or expresses the truth

USAGE See *sentence adverb.*

truth se·rum *n* a sedative such as thiopental sodium that is supposed to make the person taking it tell the truth by either reducing inhibitions or causing hypnosis

truth set *n* a set of all the values that make a given mathematical or logic statement true when substituted in the statement

truth ta·ble *n* **1.** a table used to work out the truth or falsity of a compound statement in logic **2.** in electronics and computing, a table used to indicate the value of the output signal from a logic circuit or device for every possible input

truth-val·ue *n* in logic, the truth or falsity of a proposition or of a compound statement consisting of two or more propositions

try /trī/ *v* (**tried, try·ing, tries**) **1.** *vti* **ATTEMPT SOMETHING** to make an attempt or effort to do something **2.** *vt* **TEST SOMETHING FOR PURPOSE OF ASSESSMENT** to test, sample, or experiment with something in order to assess its usefulness, worth, or quality ○ *You get to try the software at home.* **3.** *vt* **VEX SOMEBODY** to subject somebody or something to great strain ○ *The long wait tried her patience.* **4.** *vt* LAW **SUBJECT SOMEBODY TO LEGAL TRIAL** to carry out the trial in court of somebody accused of a crime or offense **5.** *vt* LAW **CONDUCT CASE IN COURT** to conduct a legal case in court ○ *asked when the case would be tried* **6.** *vt* FOOD same as **render** *v* (sense 9) ■ *n* (*plural* **tries**) **1. ATTEMPT MADE** an attempt or effort made to do something ○ *a good try* **2. SCORE IN RUGBY** in rugby, a score achieved by touching the ball on the ground behind the line of the opposing team's posts (**goal line**). Five points are scored for a try in rugby union, and three points in rugby league. [13C. Via Old French *trier* "sift out" < assumed Vulgar Latin *triare*]

SYNONYMS *try, attempt, endeavor, strive*

CORE MEANING: to make an effort to do something

try to make an attempt or an effort to do something ○ *I tried for years to live with my husband, but it was just impossible.* ○ *I will try to get the report to you by Tuesday.* **attempt** to make an effort to do something, especially without much expectation of success ○ *There are various theories which attempt to explain the phenomenon of dreaming.* ○ *The police became involved after some of the cult's members attempted suicide.* **endeavor** to make a serious and sincere effort to do something ○ *the school at which Dot vainly endeavored to teach French* ○ *In his writings, he has endeavored to define patriotism.* **strive** to try hard to achieve or get something ○ *At this hotel we are constantly striving to improve the level of guest services.* ○ *Competing firms must strive to satisfy their customers or they will not prosper.*

try on *vt* to put on an item of clothing in order to test its fit or suitability

try out *vi* **1.** to undergo a competitive test of suitability, especially for a place on a sports team or for a part as an actor ○ *plans to try out for the play* **2.** same as **try** *v* (sense 1)

~~**tryed**~~ incorrect spelling of **tried**

try·ing /trī ing/ *adj* placing great strain on somebody's patience, composure, or good nature, and often physically exhausting as a result —**try·ing·ly** *adv*

try·out /trī òwt/ *n* **1.** a trial to test somebody's suitability, especially to play on a sports team or play a role as an actor **2.** a performance of a play staged prior to its official opening ○ *changes made to the script following the out-of-town tryout*

try·pan blue /trìppən-, trí pàn-/ *n* a blue dye used to distinguish live cells from dead cells. Only dead cells turn blue in the presence of trypan blue. [Shortening of TRYPANOSOME]

try·pan·o·some /tri pánnə sōm, trìppənə-/ *n* a simple microscopic organism (**protozoan**) that lives as a parasite in the blood of some vertebrates, including human beings. It is transmitted by insect bites and causes serious diseases. Genus: *Trypanosoma.* [Early 20C. < modern Latin < Greek *trupanon* "borer" + *sōma* "body"] —**try·pan·o·so·mal** /tri pànnə sṓm'l, trìppənə-/ *adj*

try·pan·o·so·mi·a·sis /tri pànnə sō mī́ əssiss, trìppənə sō-/ *n* a disease caused by infestation with a microscopic organism that lives as a parasite in the blood, especially sleeping sickness

tryp·sin /trípsin/ *n* a pancreatic enzyme that digests proteins [Late 19C. Probably < Greek *tripsis* "rubbing," because first obtained by rubbing a pancreas with glycerin] —**tryp·tic** *adj*

tryp·sin·o·gen /trip sínnəjən/ *n* an inactive substance secreted in the juices of the pancreas and converted into trypsin in the duodenum

tryp·ta·mine /tríptə meén/ *n* an amine formed by the decomposition of tryptophan [Early 20C. < TRYPTOPHAN + -AMINE]

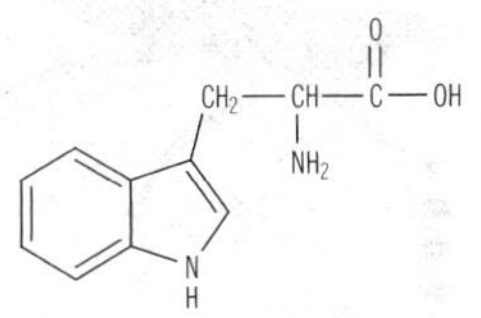

tryptophan

tryp·to·phan /tríptə fàn/ *n* an essential amino acid found in proteins such as casein and fibrin. Formula: $C_{11}H_{12}O_2N_2$. [Late 19C. < *tryptic* "of trypsin" + -PHANE]

try·sail /trī́ss'l, trī́ sàyl/ *n* a strong sail used in stormy weather that is either square or triangular and is set to run parallel to the length of the ship (**fore-and-aft**) [Mid-18C. < *a-try* "hove to"]

try square *n* a woodworking tool used to test and mark out right angles, consisting of a rectangular handle with a thin flat rectangular metal blade fitted perpendicular to it

tryst /trist/ *n* **1. ARRANGEMENT TO MEET** an arrangement to meet, especially one made privately or secretly by lovers **2. SECRET MEETING** a secret meeting, or place of meeting, especially between lovers ■ *vi* (**tryst·ed, tryst·ing, trysts**) **MEET OR ARRANGE TO MEET** to arrange or attend a meeting with somebody, especially secretly with a lover [14C. < Old French *triste* "place to lie in wait" < Germanic] —**tryst·er** *n*

TS, ts *abbr* **1.** MEASURE tensile strength **2.** transsexual

TSA *abbr* TRANSP Transportation Safety Administration [Early 21C.]

tsad·dik *n* JUDAISM another spelling of **tzaddik**

tsa·de *n* another spelling of **sadhe**

tsar /zaar, tsaar/, **czar, tzar** *n* **1. RUSSIAN EMPEROR** an emperor of Russia, before 1917 **2. TYRANT** a tyrant or autocrat **3. SOMEBODY IN AUTHORITY** somebody given authority, especially for dealing with a particular issue or problem (*informal*) ◊ **drug czar** [Mid-16C. Via Russian *tsar'*, Old Slavonic *tsĕsarĭ*, and Gothic *kaisar* < Latin *Caesar* (see CAESAR)] —**czar·dom** *n*

tsar·e·vitch /záarə vìch, tsáarə-/, **czar·e·vitch** *n* the son of a Russian emperor, especially the eldest son [Early 18C. < Russian *tsarevich* < *tsar'* (see TSAR)]

tsa·rev·na /zaa révnə, tsaa-/, **cza·rev·na** *n* **1.** the wife of a tsarevitch **2.** the daughter of a tsar [Late 19C. < Russian < *tsar'* (see TSAR)]

tsa·ri·na /zaa reénə, tsaa-/, **cza·ri·na** *n* **1.** an empress of Russia, before 1917 **2.** the wife or widow of a tsar [Early 18C. < Italian or Spanish *zarina*, feminine of *zar* < Russian *tsar'* (see TSAR)]

tsar·ism /záa rìzzəm/, **czar·ism**, **tzar·ism** *n* **1.** government by an emperor who has absolute power **2.** absolute rule of any kind, especially the cruel abuse of absolute power by a despot —**tsar·ist** *adj, n*

tsats·ke /tsáatskə, cháachkə/ *n US* another spelling of **chachka**

Tsa·vo Na·tion·al Park /saa vō-/ national park and game reserve in Kenya, established in 1948. Area: 7,990 sq. mi./20,700 sq. km.

TSE *n* a disease of a group that causes spongy degeneration of the brain and can be transmitted from one species to another, e.g. BSE. Full form **transmissible spongiform encephalopathy**

Tse·li·no·grad /tsə léenə gràd/ former name for **Astana** (1960–91)

tses·se·be /tse sáybee/ *n S Africa* ZOOL same as **sassaby** [Mid19C. < Setswana *tsessébi*]

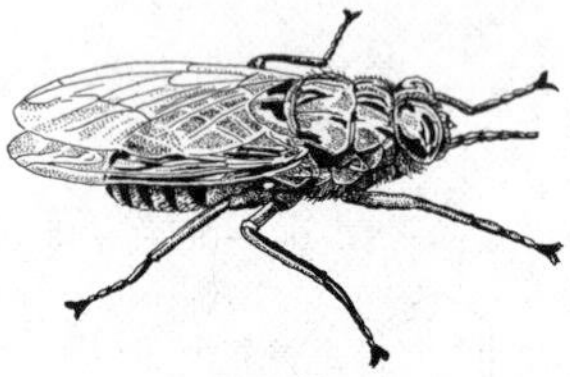

tsetse fly

tset·se fly /tsétsee-, sétsee-/, **tzet·ze fly** *n* a two-winged biting fly that feeds on the blood of humans and animals and is responsible for transmitting several diseases, including sleeping sickness. Native to: central Africa. Genus: *Glossina.* [Mid-19C. Via Afrikaans < Setswana]

T.Sgt. *abbr* MIL Technical Sergeant

TSH *abbr* BIOCHEM thyroid-stimulating hormone

T-shirt *n* **1.** a collarless usually short-sleeved knit shirt without fastenings usually made of cotton and worn for leisure and sports. T-shirts are often printed with designs and slogans. **2.** a man's short-sleeved undershirt [Early 20C. < its T-shape when spread out]

Tshom·be /cháwm bày/, **Moise** (1919–69) prime minister of the Democratic Republic of the Congo (1964–65). He was president of the secessionist state of Katanga (1960–63), was forced into exile when the secession was crushed, and was recalled to the premiership the following year. Full name **Tshombe, Moise Kapenda**

tshwa·la /chwáalə/ *n S Africa* a thick home-brewed beer made from sorghum millet, corn, or other grain that is a traditional drink in South Africa [< Zulu *utshwala*]

tsim·mes *n* FOOD another spelling of **tzimmes**

Tsim·shi·an /chímshee ən, tsímshee ən/ (*plural same* or **-ans**) *n* **1.** a member of a Native North American people who live in coastal southeastern Alaska and British Columbia **2.** the language of the Tsimshian people. Native speakers: 1,500. [Mid-19C. < Tsimshian *čamsián* "inside the Skeena River"] —**Tsim·shi·an** *adj*

tsi·tses *n* JUDAISM another spelling of **tzitzith**

tsk tsk /tìsk tísk/ *interj* used in writing to represent a sucking or clicking sound made to express disappointment, disgust, or sympathy [Mid-20C. An imitation of the sound] —**tsk-tsk** *vti*

Tson·ga /tsáwng gə/ (*plural same* or **-gas**) *n* **1.** a member of a people who live in southern Africa, mainly in Mozambique, Swaziland, and South Africa **2.** the Bantu language of the Tsonga people. Native speakers: 4 million. [Early 20C. < Bantu] —**Tson·ga** *adj*

tsp. *abbr* MEASURE teaspoon

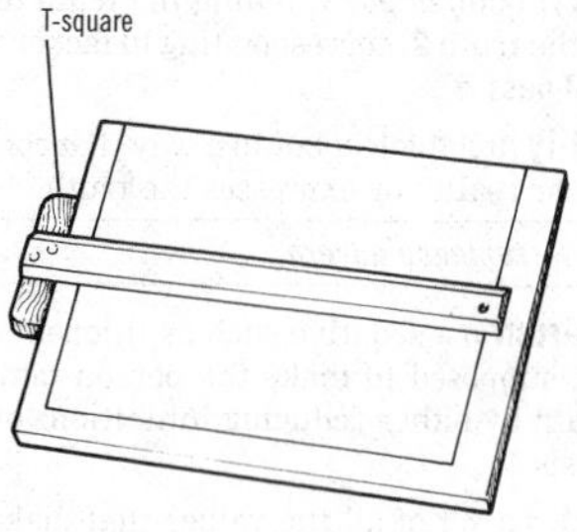

T-square

T-square, **T square** *n* a drawing-board ruler consisting of a rectangular handle with a straight-sided wooden or plastic blade attached perpendicular to it, to form a T shape. The handle sits against the edge of the board.

TSS *abbr* MED toxic shock syndrome

tsu·na·mi /tsoo náamee, soo-/ (*plural* **-mis**) *n* a large destructive ocean wave caused by an underwater earthquake or another movement of the Earth's surface [Late 19C. < Japanese, "harbor wave"] —**tsu·na·mic** *adj*

tsu·ris /tsóoriss, tsúr iss, sóoriss, súr iss/, **tzu·ris** *n* problems or difficulties (*informal; takes a singular verb*) [Early 20C. Via Yiddish *tsores* "troubles" < Hebrew *ṣārāh* "trouble"]

Tsu·shi·ma /tsoo shéemə, tsóo shee maa/ island group in the Korea Strait, southwestern Japan. Population: 48,875 (1985). Area: 270 sq. mi./700 sq. km.

tsut·su·ga·mu·shi dis·ease /tsòotsəgə móoshee-, sóotsə-/ *n* MED same as **scrub typhus** [Early 20C. < Japanese, "disease tick"]

Tsve·ta·e·va /tsvi taa yəvə/, **Marina** (1892–1941) Russian poet. Many of her poems explore issues of female sexuality and were written while she was living in exile from 1922. She returned to the Soviet Union in 1938 but committed suicide after her husband was executed and her daughter arrested. Full name **Tsvetaeva, Marina Ivanovna**

> "I won't be seduced by the thought of / my native language, its milky call. / How can it matter in what tongue I / am misunderstood by whoever I meet?"
> [Marina Tsvetaeva, "Homesickness"; 1934]

Tswa·na /tswáanə, swáanə/ (*plural same* or **-nas**) *n* **1.** a member of a people living in southern Africa, mainly in Botswana, where they form the largest ethnic group **2.** LANG same as **Setswana** [Mid-20C. < Bantu] —**Tswa·na** *adj*

tt *abbr* ONLINE Trinidad and Tobago (*used in Internet addresses*) See table at **domain name**

TT *abbr* **1.** teetotal **2.** BANKING telegraphic transfer **3.** teletypewriter **4.** transit time **5.** LAW trust territory **6.** AGRIC tuberculin-tested

t-test *n* a test of whether a sample of observations comes from a larger sample with a standard distribution of statistical properties

TTL[1] *n* a method of constructing electronic logic circuits. Full form **transistor transistor logic**

TTL[2] *abbr* PHOTOGRAPHY through-the-lens

TTL4N *abbr* ONLINE that's the lot for now (*used in e-mails or text messages*)

T-top *n* an automobile roof with a T-shaped frame and removable panels

TTY *abbr* teletypewriter

Tu. *abbr* CALENDAR Tuesday

T.U. *abbr* **1.** POL trade union **2.** TELECOM transmission unit

tuan /twaan/ *n* in Malay-speaking countries, a respectful form of address for a man [Early 18C. < Malay]

Tua·reg /twáa règ/ (*plural same* or **-regs**) *n* a member of a nomadic people who live in northwestern Africa, mainly in the Sahara and Sahel regions [Early 19C. < Berber] —**Tua·reg** *adj*

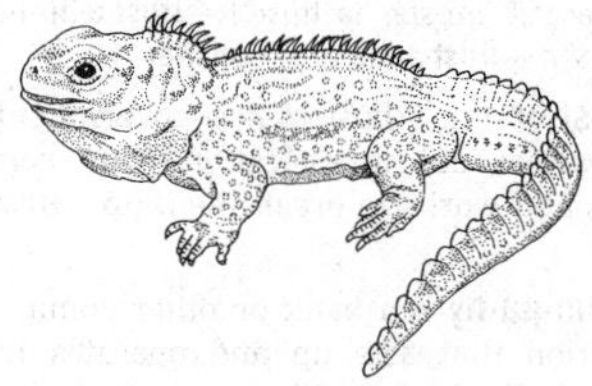

tuatara

tu·a·ta·ra /tòo ə táarə/ *n* a large spiny greenish gray reptile resembling an iguana. Native to: islands off New Zealand. Latin name: *Sphenodon punctatum.* [Late 19C. < Maori, "with spines on its back"]

tub /tub/ *n* **1.** LOW OPEN CONTAINER a low, open, often round container of any size that is used for purposes such as storage and washing **2.** ROUND CONTAINER FOR LIQUIDS a small, often round, plastic or cardboard container for liquid, semiliquid, or soft substances such as ice cream or margarine **3.** AMOUNT HELD BY TUB the contents of a tub **4.** HOUSEHOLD same as **bathtub 5.** BATH an instance of bathing in a bathtub (*informal*) ○ *You'll feel better after a tub and a hot meal.* **6.** POOR QUALITY BOAT a slow unreliable boat (*informal*) **7.** MIN EXTRACT MINE VEHICLE an open-top vehicle on rails used to transport coal and other excavated minerals in a mine ■ *v* (**tubbed, tub·bing, tubs**) **1.** *vt* STORE SOMETHING IN TUB to store or package something in a tub **2.** *vti* BATHE to wash, or wash something or yourself, in a bathtub (*informal*) [14C. < Middle Low German or Middle Dutch]

tu·ba /tóobə/ *n* a low-pitched brass musical instrument held vertically with the bell pointing upward and the mouthpiece set horizontally. It has three to five valves. [Mid-19C. Via French or Italian < Latin, "large war trumpet"]

tu·bal /tóob'l/ *adj* **1.** relating to or in the form of a tube or tubes **2.** relating to or developing in a fallopian tube

tu·bal li·ga·tion *n* a sterilization technique in which a woman's fallopian tubes are tied to prevent ova entering the uterus. It is usually performed using endoscopic surgery.

tu·bate /tóo bàyt/ *adj* tubular in shape

tub·by /túbbee/ (**-bi·er, -bi·est**) *adj* **1.** OVERWEIGHT carrying more body weight than is desirable or advisable (*informal; sometimes considered offensive*) **2.** TUB-SHAPED like a tub in shape **3.** MUSIC LACKING RESONANCE describes a violin or other string instrument that lacks resonance —**tub·bi·ness** *n*

tube /toob, tyoob/ *n* **1.** CYLINDER FOR TRANSPORTING OR STORING LIQUIDS a long hollow cylinder used to transport or store liquids **2.** COLLAPSIBLE CONTAINER WITH CAP a collapsible, generally cylindrical container sealed at one end and closed with a cap at the other. It is used for packaging semiliquid substances such as toothpaste. **3.** ANAT CYLINDRICAL BODY ORGAN a hollow cylindrical organ that transports liquids or gases around the body **4.** ANAT same as **fallopian tube** (*informal; usually used in the plural*) **5.** RAIL UNDERGROUND RAILWAY the underground railway system in London (*informal*) **6.** RAIL UNDERGROUND TRAIN a train on an underground railway system (*informal*) **7.** CYCLING same as **inner tube 8.** ELECTRONICS same as **cathode-ray tube 9.** MEDIA same as **television** (sense 1) **10.** BOT CHANNEL IN PLANT a narrow enclosed channel in a plant, e.g., the organ in a germinating pollen grain that conveys the male gametes to the ovule **11.** BOT FLOWER PART a roughly cylindrical fusion of the petals of a flower such as a daffodil **12.** ELECTRONICS same as **vacuum tube** (*informal*) **13.** MUSIC BODY OF WIND INSTRUMENT the hollow cylinder that forms the main body of a wind instrument, through which the player's breath passes **14.** SURFING PART OF WAVE the tunnel formed when a large rolling wave prepares to break

■ *vt* **(tubed, tub·ing, tubes) 1. FIT SOMETHING WITH TUBE** to supply or fit something with a tube **2. ENCLOSE SOMETHING IN TUBE** to put something in a tube [Early 17C. Via French < Latin *tubus*]

tu·bec·to·my /too béktəmee/ (*plural* **-mies**) *n* the surgical removal of a fallopian tube (*informal*)

tube foot *n* an outgrowth of the body wall of sea invertebrates of the sea urchin family **(echinoderms)**, used for feeding, moving around, or performing other functions depending on the species

tube·less tire /to͞obləss-/ *n* a pneumatic tire that does not require an inner tube because the casing and wheel rim form an airtight seal

tube pan *n* a round cooking pan with a hollow cylinder or cone in the middle, used for baking or molding foods in a ring shape

tu·ber /to͞obər/ *n* **1.** a fleshy swollen part of a root such as a dahlia root or of an underground stem such as a potato that stores food over winter and produces new growth in spring. A stem tuber has buds, popularly called eyes, unlike a root tuber. **2.** a small raised area or swelling on the body [Mid-17C. < Latin, "swelling"]

tu·ber·cle /to͞obərk'l/ *n* **1.** a small raised area on a plant or animal part **2.** a small rounded swelling on the skin or on a mucous membrane, caused by a disease, especially a nodule in the lungs that is the characteristic symptom of tuberculosis [Late 16C. < Latin *tuberculum* "small swelling" < *tuber* "swelling"]

tu·ber·cle ba·cil·lus *n* a rod-shaped bacterium that causes tuberculosis. Latin name: *Mycobacterium tuberculosis.*

tu·ber·cu·lar /tə búrkyələr, too-/ *adj* **1. OF TUBERCULOSIS** relating to, characteristic of, or affected by tuberculosis **2. CAUSED BY TUBERCLE BACILLUS** caused by the tubercle bacillus ○ *tubercular meningitis* **3. NODULE-SHAPED** taking the form of a small rounded swelling or nodule [Late 18C. < Latin *tuberculum* (see TUBERCLE)]

tu·ber·cu·late /tə búrkyələt, too-/ *adj* covered with small rounded swellings or nodules **(tubercles)** [Late 18C. < Latin *tuberculum* (see TUBERCLE)] —**tu·ber·cu·late·ly** *adv* —**tu·ber·cu·la·tion** /tə bùrkyə láysh'n, too-/ *n*

tu·ber·cu·lin /tə búrkyəlin, too-/ *n* a sterile liquid obtained from cultures of the tubercle bacillus and used in a scratch test to establish whether somebody has or has had tuberculosis [Late 19C. < Latin *tuberculum* (see TUBERCLE)]

tu·ber·cu·lo·sis /tə bùrkyə lṓssiss, too-/ *n* an infectious disease that causes small rounded swellings **(tubercles)** to form on mucous membranes, especially a disease **(pulmonary tuberculosis)** that affects the lungs [Mid-19C. < Latin *tuberculum* (see TUBERCLE)] —**tu·ber·cu·loid** /tə búrkyə lòyd, too-/ *adj*

tu·ber·cu·lous /tə búrkyələss, too búrkyələss/ *adj* MED same as **tubercular**

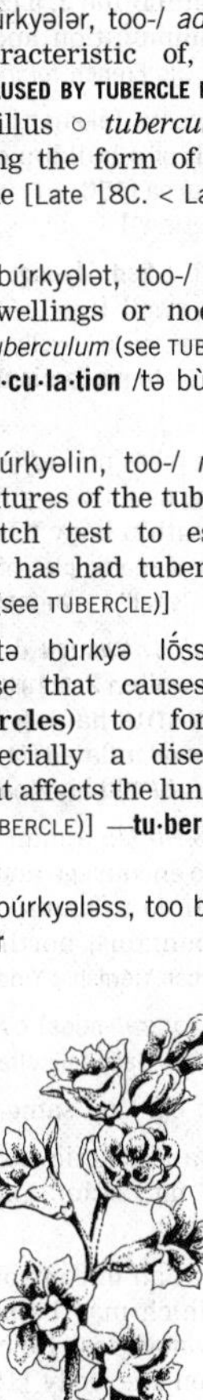

tuberose

tube·rose[1] /to͞ob rōz, to͞obə rōz/ *n* a perennial agave with blade-shaped leaves. Flowers: fragrant, white, in spikes. Native to: Mexico. Latin name: *Polianthes tuberosa.* [Mid-17C. < modern Latin *tuberosa* < Latin *tuberosus* < *tuber* "swelling"]

tu·ber·ose[2] /to͞obə ròss/ *adj* BOT, MED same as **tuberous**

tu·ber·os·i·ty /to͞obə róssətee/ (*plural* **-ties**) *n* a rounded protuberance, especially at a point on a bone where muscles or ligaments are attached

tu·ber·ous /to͞obərəss/ *adj* **1.** relating to tubers or in the form of tubers **2.** producing or covered with knobby growths [Mid-17C. < Latin *tuberosus* (see TUBEROSE[1])]

tube steak *n* same as **hot dog** *n* (sense 1), **frankfurter** (*slang*)

tube top *n* a short strapless stretchy top for women

tube worm *n* a worm that builds itself a tube-shaped shelter that sticks out of the soil

tu·bi·fex /to͞obə fèks/ *n* a thin reddish freshwater worm that builds a tube-shaped shelter in the sand of riverbeds and is used as food for aquarium fish. Genus: *Tubifex.* [Mid-20C. < modern Latin < Latin *tubus* "tube" + *-fex* "maker"]

tub·ing /to͞obing/ *n* **1.** a system or series of tubes **2.** the hollow cylindrical material that tubes are made of **3.** HANDICRAFT same as **piping** *n* (sense 2)

Tü·bing·en /to͞obingən/ university city in Baden-Württemberg State, southwestern Germany. Population: 82,260 (1997).

Tub·man /túbmən/, **Harriet** (1830–1913) US abolitionist. Escaping from slavery in about 1849, she helped other slaves escape to freedom along the clandestine route known as the Underground Railroad.

> "Dere's *two* things I've got a *right* to, and dese are, Death or Liberty—one or tother I mean to have."
> [Harriet Tubman. Quoted in *Scenes in the Life of Harriet Tubman*, Sarah Bradford; 1869]

tu·bo·cu·ra·rine /to͞obō ko͞o raárin, -reén/ *n* **1.** a toxic alkaloid that is the active constituent of curare. Use: muscle relaxant. **2.** the hydrochloride salt of tubocurarine [Late 19C. < TUBE (because shipped in bamboo tubes) + CURARE]

tu·bo·plas·ty /to͞obō plàstee/ (*plural* **-ties**) *n* the surgical repair of one or both fallopian tubes, especially when these have been cut and tied for contraceptive reasons

tub-thump *vi* to speak out in favor of somebody or something in a passionate or aggressive way (*informal*) —**tub-thump·er** *n* —**tub-thump·ing** *adj*

tu·bu·lar /to͞obyələr/ *adj* **1.** shaped like a tube **2.** having a tube or tubes [Late 17C. < Latin *tubulus* (see TUBULE)]

tu·bu·lar bells *npl* a set of tuned metal tubes, usually arranged in a scale and hung from a frame, that are struck with a mallet

tu·bu·late /to͞obyələt, -làyt/ *adj* same as **tubular** [Mid-18C. < Latin *tubulatus* < *tubulus* (see TUBULE)]

tu·bule /to͞o byo͞ol/ *n* a very small tubular part in a plant or animal [Late 17C. < Latin *tubulus* "small tube" < *tubus* "tube"]

tu·bu·lin /to͞obyəlin/ *n* a globular protein found in microscopic filamentous tubes **(microtubules)** in cells

tu·bu·lous /to͞obyələss/ *adj* same as **tubular**

Tu·ca·na /too káynə, -kaánə/ *n* a small faint constellation of the southern hemisphere containing much of the smaller Magellanic Cloud. See illustration at **constellation**

Tuch·man /túk mən/, **Barbara** (1912–89) US historian. She wrote two Pulitzer Prize-winning books, *The Guns of August* (1962), also titled *August 1914*, and *Stilwell and the American Experience in China, 1911–45* (1970). Born **Barbara Wertheim**

tu·chun /too cho͞on, doo jo͞on/ *n* formerly, the military leader of a Chinese province [Early 20C. < Chinese *dūjūn* < *dū* "govern" + *jūn* "military"]

tuck[1] /tuk/ *v* **(tucked, tuck·ing, tucks) 1.** *vt* **FOLD SOMETHING INTO POSITION** to push, fold, or bend something such as a flap of material into a particular place or position **2.** *vti* **DRAW SOMETHING TOGETHER** to pull or draw something together, or be pulled or drawn together **3.** *vt* HANDICRAFT **SEW FOLD** to sew a fold into fabric, e.g., to reduce its length or for decoration **4.** *vt* SURG **TIGHTEN SKIN WITH SURGERY** to perform a surgical operation to remove loose or wrinkled skin, usually for cosmetic reasons ■ *n* **1. TUCKED PART** a part that is tucked safely or neatly into position **2.** HANDICRAFT **PLEAT** a fold sewn into a piece of fabric, e.g., to reduce its length or for decoration **3.** SURG **SURGICAL REMOVAL OF LOOSE SKIN** a surgical operation to remove loose or wrinkled skin, especially for cosmetic reasons **4.** SPORTS **BODY POSITION** a compact body position, adopted in sports such as diving, with the knees drawn up to the chest, the hands around the shins, and the chin held on the chest **5.** NAUT **PART OF SHIP'S STERN** the part of a ship's hull where the side planks or plates join the spar or spars forming the stern [15C. Probably < Middle Dutch *tucken* "draw up"]

tuck away *vt* **1.** to put something in a safe or secluded place **2.** to eat large quantities of food heartily or hungrily (*informal*)

tuck in *v* **1.** *vt* to make somebody, especially a child, comfortable in bed by tucking the bedclothes snugly around the body **2.** *also* **tuck into** *vi* to eat hungrily (*informal*)

tuck up *vt UK* same as **tuck in** (sense 1)

tuck[2] /tuk/ *n* a beating of a drum or a blast on a trumpet as a flourish [15C. Via Old N French *toquer* "to strike" < assumed Vulgar Latin *toccare*]

tuck·a·hoe /túkə hō/ *n* **1.** a plant of the arum family with arrow-shaped leaves and edible roots. Use: formerly, as food by Native North Americans. **2.** a large edible fungus that grows underground on the roots of trees. Native to: southern United States. Latin name: *Poria cocos.* [Early 17C. < Virginia Algonquian *tockawhoughe*]

tuck·er[1] /túkər/ *n* **1.** HANDICRAFT an attachment for a sewing machine, used to sew tucks **2.** CLOTHING a detachable lace or linen cover for the neck and chest, formerly worn by women under a low-cut dress [13C. < TUCK[1]]

tuck·er[2] /túkər/ **(-ered, -er·ing, -ers)** *vt* to tire a person or animal out completely (*informal*) [Mid-19C. Origin ?]

tucker out *vt* same as **tucker[2]**

tuck·et /túkit/ *n* a fanfare played on a trumpet (*archaic*) [Late 16C. < TUCK[2]]

tuck-point *vt US* to finish a wall by sealing the facing joints between the bricks or stones with a thin line of putty or very fine lime-based mortar

tu·co·tu·co /to͞okō to͞okō/ (*plural* **-cos**) *n* a rodent that digs complex systems of burrows. Native to: South America. Latin name: *Ctenomys talarum.* [Mid-19C. An imitation of its call]

Tuc·son /to͞o sòn/ city in southern Arizona, on the Santa Cruz River. Population: 503,151 (2002 estimate).

Tu·cu·mán /to͞okoo maan, to͞okoo maán/ province in northern Argentina. Its capital is San Miguel de Tucumán. Population: 1,265,322 (1999). Area: 8,697 sq. mi./22,524 sq. km.

'tude /tood/ *n* an arrogant or assertive manner or stance assumed as a challenge or for effect (*slang*) [Late 20C. Shortening of ATTITUDE]

-tude *suffix* state, condition, or quality ○ *decrepitude* [Via French < Latin *-tudo*]

Tu·dor /to͞odər/ *adj* **1. OF ENGLISH ROYAL FAMILY OR REIGN** relating to or belonging to the English royal family that ruled between 1485 and 1603, or to this period of English history. The period is spanned by the reigns of Kings Henry VII, Henry VIII, and Edward VI, and Queens Mary I and Elizabeth I. **2. RELATING TO TUDOR ARCHITECTURAL STYLE** relating to or being a style of architecture popular throughout the Tudor period characterized by timber frameworks, visible from the outside, filled in with plaster or brick ■ *n* **MEMBER OF TUDOR FAMILY** a member of the Tudor royal family [Mid-18C. Named after the Welsh squire Owen *Tudor* (d.1461), father of Henry VII]

Tue., Tues. *abbr* CALENDAR Tuesday

Tues·day /to͞oz dày, -dee/ *n* the second day of the traditional working week, coming after Monday and before Wednesday [Old English *Tīwesdæg* "Tiu's day" < *Tīw*, Germanic god of war (translation of Latin *Martis dies* "Mars' day")]

Tues·days /to͞oz dàyz, -deez/ *adv* every Tuesday

tu·fa /to͞ofə/ *n* a porous rock formed from deposited calcium carbonate and found near mineral springs. Use: as medium on which to grow alpine plants. [Late 18C. Via obsolete Italian < late Latin *tofus* "porous rock"] —**tu·fa·ceous** /too fáyshəss/ *adj*

tuff /tuf/ *n* a rock made up of very small volcanic fragments compacted together [Mid-16C. Via French < Latin *tofus*] —**tuff·a·ceous** /tu fáyshəss/ *adj*

tuf·fet /túffət/ *n* **1.** a small mound or clump of grass **2.** a low seat or stool [Mid-16C. Alteration of TUFT]

tuft /tuft/ *n* **1. BUNCH OF FIBERS OR GRASS** a small bunch of hair, grass, feathers, or fibers held or growing together at the base **2. CLUMP OF PLANTS** a small clump of plants or trees **3. BUNCH OF THREADS DRAWN THROUGH UPHOLSTERY** a group of threads drawn through fabric and tied to secure it to material beneath ■ *v* (**tuft·ed, tuft·ing, tufts**) **1.** *vti* **FORM INTO TUFTS** to grow in tufts, or form something into tufts **2.** *vt* HANDICRAFT **SEW TUFTS IN SOMETHING** to sew tufts in fabric, either for decoration or to secure one surface to another [14C. Alteration of Old French *toffe*] —**tuft·ed** *adj* —**tuft·y** *adj*

tuft·ed tit·mouse *n* a common small songbird that is gray with a white breast and has a crest on its head. Native to: eastern North America. Latin name: *Parus bicolor*.

Tu Fu /do͞o fo͞o/ (712–770) Chinese poet. He is often considered to be the greatest of all Chinese poets.

tug /tug/ *v* (**tugged, tug·ging, tugs**) **1.** *vti* **PULL SHARPLY AT SOMEBODY OR SOMETHING** to pull at or drag somebody or something with a sharp forceful movement **2.** *vt* **TOW SHIP** to tow a ship with a tugboat **3.** *vi* **MAKE LABORIOUS EFFORT** to work hard or struggle to do something ■ *n* **1. SHARP PULL** a sharp forceful pull ○ *gave it a tug* **2. STRUGGLE OR CONTEST** a struggle or strenuous contest between opposing forces or people **3.** *Can, UK* same as **tugboat 4. VEHICLE THAT PULLS ANOTHER** a land, sea, air, or space vehicle that is used to pull another **5. CHAIN OR STRAP FOR PULLING** a chain, rope, or strap that is used for pulling or hauling something [13C. Ultimately < Indo-European, "pull"] —**tug·ger** *n*

SYNONYMS See ***pull***.

tug·boat /túg bòt/ *n US* a small powerful boat used to tow ships and barges. Can term **tug**

Tu·ge·la /too gáylə/ river in eastern South Africa, flowing into the Indian Ocean. Length: 312 mi./502 km.

Tu·ge·la Falls /too gáylə-/ series of waterfalls on the Tugela River, KwaZulu-Natal Province, South Africa. Height: 3,110 ft./948 m.

tug of war *n* **1.** an athletic contest in which two teams pull at opposite ends of a rope, the winner being the one who drags the other across a fixed line **2.** a struggle between two evenly matched people, groups, or influences

tu·grik /to͞ogrik/ (*plural same* or **-griks**) *n* the main unit of Mongolian currency. See table at **currency** [Mid-20C. < Mongolian *dughurik* "round thing"]

Tug·well /túggwəl/, **Rexford** (1891–1979) US economist and political scientist. He joined Franklin D. Roosevelt's "Brain Trust" (1932), headed the Resettlement Commission (1935–36), and was governor of Puerto Rico (1941–46). Full name **Tugwell, Rexford Guy**

tu·i /to͞o ee/ (*plural* **-is**) *n* a bird with iridescent dark blue-green feathers, white tufts at the throat, and white spots on the wings. Native to: New Zealand. Latin name: *Prosthemadera novaeseelandiae*. [Mid-19C. < Maori]

tu·i·tion /too ísh'n/ *n* **1.** a sum charged for instruction at a school or university **2.** instruction, especially when given individually or in a small group [15C. Via French < Latin *tuition-* "support" < *tueri* "protect"] —**tu·i·tion·al** *adj*

tuk-tuk /to͝ok to͝ok/ *n* in Thailand, a motor vehicle with three wheels, used as a taxi [Mid-20C. An imitation of the vehicle's sound]

tu·la·re·mi·a /to͞olə réemee ə/ *n* an acute infectious disease of rabbits and rodents caused by the bacterium *Francisella tularensis* that can be spread to other animals and humans by insect bites, contact, or water. Symptoms include enlarged lymph nodes, headaches, muscular pain, and weight loss. [Early 20C. < *Francisella tularensis*, the causative bacterium (after *Tulare* County, California)] —**tu·la·re·mic** *adj*

tu·le /to͞olee/ *n* (*plural* **-les** or *same*) *Southwest US* **BULRUSH OF SW N AMERICA** a bulrush. Native to: marshland of southwestern North America. Latin name: *Scirpus californicus* or *Scirpus acutus*. ■ *npl* **1. tu·les** *regional* **SWAMPY LAND** in northern California, land that is swampy or marshy **2.** *Hispanic* **OUT-OF-THE-WAY PLACE** a place regarded as remote or desolate [Mid-19C. Via American Spanish < Nahuatl *tullin*] ◇ **to be in deep tules** *Hispanic* to be in trouble with the law

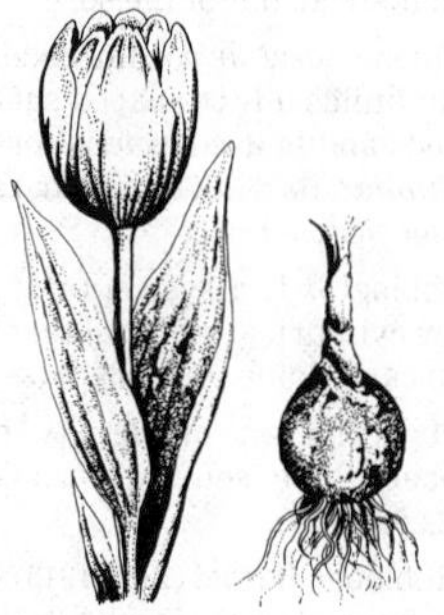

tulip

tu·lip /to͞olip/ *n* **1.** a spring-flowering plant that grows from a bulb and has lance-shaped leaves. Flowers: large, usually single, cup-shaped, variously colored. Native to: western Asia. Genus: *Tulipa*. **2.** the flower or bulb of a tulip plant [Late 16C. Via French *tulipe* < Turkish *tülbend* (see TURBAN); from the shape of the expanded flower]

tu·lip tree, **tu·lip pop·lar** *n* a deciduous tree of the magnolia family with large greenish yellow tulip-shaped flowers and soft light wood. Native to: North America, China. Latin name: *Liriodendron tulipifera* or *Liriodendron chinense*.

tu·lip·wood /to͞olip wo͝od/ *n* the light soft wood of the tulip tree, or the striped wood of similar trees, used in making woodenware or in cabinetmaking

tulle /tool/ *n* a thin netted, often stiffened, silk, nylon, or rayon fabric. Use: ballet costumes, evening dresses, veils. [Early 19C. After the French city *Tulle*]

tul·li·bee /túllə bèe/ (*plural* **-bees** or *same*) *n* a freshwater fish. Native to: Great Lakes, Canada. Latin name: *Coregonus artedii*. [Late 18C. Via Canadian French *toulibi* < Ojibwa *too-nie-bie*]

Tul·sa /túlssə/ city in northeastern Oklahoma, on the Arkansas River, northeast of Oklahoma City. Population: 391,908 (2002 estimate).

tum·ble /túmb'l/ *v* (**-bled, -bling, -bles**) **1.** *vti* **FALL OR MAKE FALL OVER** to fall suddenly and awkwardly, especially rolling over and over, or make somebody or something do this **2.** *vi* **MOVE HASTILY** to move heedlessly or hastily ○ *The puppies tumbled from the room.* **3.** *vi* **ROLL AROUND** to roll around, especially in play **4.** *vi* **DROP STEEPLY** to decrease quickly and by a significant amount ○ *Prices have tumbled on the stock market.* **5.** *vi* **CASCADE OVER SOMETHING** to flow, fall, or spill out over something **6.** *vi* **REALIZE TRUTH** to realize the full significance of something, or see through a deceit (*informal*) ○ *She finally tumbled to it.* **7.** *vti* **TOPPLE FROM POWER** to experience a defeat or fall from power, or cause somebody to experience a defeat or fall from power **8.** *vi* **COME ACROSS BY CHANCE** to come across or stumble on something accidentally **9.** *vi* GYMNASTICS **LEAP OR ROLL** to perform athletic or gymnastic leaps, rolls, or somersaults **10.** *vt* **ROTATE IN TUMBLER** to roll or spin something in a drum or tumbler ■ *n* **1. BAD FALL** an awkward or sudden fall ○ *He had a nasty tumble.* **2. DISORDERLY HEAP** a disorderly or disorganized heap or arrangement **3.** GYMNASTICS **ATHLETIC MOVEMENT** an athletic or gymnastic leap, roll, or somersault [13C. < obsolete Low German *tummelen*]

tum·ble·down /túmb'l dòwn/ *adj* ruined or dilapidated and falling down

tum·ble-dry *vt* to dry wet laundry in the heated rotating drum of a clothes dryer

tum·ble dry·er *n* a machine that dries wet laundry by revolving it through heated air in the rotating metal drum of a dryer

tum·ble·home /túmb'l hòm/ *n* the inward upward slope of a ship's topsides

tum·bler /túmblər/ *n* **1. DRINKING GLASS** a drinking glass with a thick flat bottom and no stem or handle **2. ROUND-BOTTOMED GLASS** formerly, a drinking glass that had a rounded or pointed bottom and so could not be put down until it was empty **3. AMOUNT IN TUMBLER** the amount of liquid that a tumbler holds **4. ACROBAT** somebody who performs athletic or gymnastic leaps, rolls, or somersaults **5. PIGEON THAT DOES SOMERSAULTS IN FLIGHT** a domestic pigeon that can perform backward somersaults in flight **6. PART OF LOCK** the part of a lock that must be engaged by a key in order to move the bolt **7. MACHINE PART** a part of a machine that moves or engages a gear **8. PART OF GUNLOCK** a lever in a gunlock that forces the hammer forward when a trigger is pressed **9.** *Can, UK* same as **tumbling barrel 10. ROCKING TOY** a toy that is weighted so that it rocks when touched

tum·ble·weed /túmb'l wèed/ (*plural* **-weeds** or *same*) *n* a densely branched plant such as the Russian thistle that grows in dry regions and in late summer withers and breaks from its roots to be blown about by the wind

tum·bling /túmbling/ *n* the art, practice, or act of performing leaps, rolls, and somersaults

tum·bling bar·rel, **tum·bling box** *n US* a rotating drum for mixing, polishing, drying, or reducing something inside. Can term **tumbler**

tum·brel /túmbrəl/, **tum·bril** *n* **1.** a cart used during the French Revolution to carry condemned prisoners to be executed by guillotine **2.** a covered cart formerly used to carry ammunition and equipment for the artillery [14C. < Old French *tumberel* < *tomber* "fall"]

tu·me·fac·tion /to͞omə fákshən/ *n* **1.** the swelling of tissue as a result of a buildup of fluid within it **2.** a swollen part or area [15C. < French *tuméfaction* < Latin *tumefacere* (see TUMEFY)]

tu·me·fy /to͞omə fī/ (**-fied, -fy·ing, -fies**) *vti* to swell, or cause tissue to swell [Late 16C. Via French *tuméfier* < Latin *tumefacere* "make swollen" < *tumere* "swell" + *facere* "make"] —**tu·me·fa·cient** /to͞omə fáysh'nt, tyo͞omə-/ *adj*

tu·mes·cent /too méss'nt/ *adj* swollen or showing signs of swelling, usually as a result of a buildup of blood or water within body tissues [Mid-19C. < Latin *tumescent-*, present participle of *tumescere* "become swollen" < *tumere* "swell"] —**tu·mes·cence** *n*

tu·mid /to͞omid/ *adj* **1. SWOLLEN** describes a body part or organ that is swollen **2. BULGING** bulging or sticking out **3. POMPOUS IN STYLE** having language or a style that is bombastic or inflated [Mid-16C. < Latin *tumidus* < *tumere* "swell"] —**tu·mid·i·ty** /too míddətee/ *n*

tumm·ler /túmmlər/ *n US* a man employed as a comedian and host to encourage audience participation, especially one hired to amuse guests at resorts in the Catskill Mountains, north of New York City [Mid-20C. < American Yiddish < Yiddish *tumlen* "to bustle"]

tum·my /túmmee/ (*plural* **-mies**) *n* ANAT same as **stomach** (*informal*) [Mid-19C. Baby-talk alteration of STOMACH]

tum·my but·ton *n UK* ANAT same as **navel** (*informal*)

tum·my tuck *n* a cosmetic surgical operation to remove excess fat, skin, and tissue from the abdomen (*informal*)

tu·mor /to͞omər/ *n* **1.** an uncontrolled growth or mass of body cells, which may be malignant or benign and has no physiological function **2.** an unusual swelling in or on the body [15C. < Latin, < *tumere* "swell"] —**tu·mor·al** *adj*

tu·mor·i·gen·ic /to͞omərə jénnik/ *adj* describes a drug or other agent that may initiate or promote the growth of tumors —**tu·mor·i·gen·e·sis** *n* —**tu·mor·i·ge·nic·i·ty** /to͞omərə jə níssətee/ *n*

tu·mor ne·cro·sis fac·tor *n* a protein that can cause the destruction of tumors. The gene encoding this factor has been used in gene therapy trials for cancer.

tu·mour *n* MED Can, UK spelling of **tumor**

tump /tump/ (**tumped, tump·ing, tumps**) *vti Southern US* to knock something over, or tip over, especially accidentally [Late 19C. Origin ?]

tump·line /túmp lìn/ *n* a band or strap strung across the forehead or chest to support a backpack [Late 18C. < Algonquian *mattump*]

tu·mu·lar /tóomyələr/ *adj* resembling or in the form of a mound or tumulus

tu·mu·li ARCHAEOL plural of **tumulus**

tu·mu·lose /tóomyə lòss/, **tu·mu·lous** /-ləss/ *adj* **1.** having many mounds or small hills **2.** forming or resembling a mound —**tu·mu·los·i·ty** /tòomyə lóssətee/ *n*

tu·mult /tóo mùlt/ *n* **1.** a violent or noisy commotion **2.** a psychological or emotional upheaval or agitation [14C. Directly or via French *tumulte* < Latin *tumultus* "commotion" < *tumere* "swell"]

tu·mul·tu·ar·y /too múlchoo èrre, tyoo-/ *adj* marked by tumult or turbulence

tu·mul·tu·ous /too múlchoo əss, tə-/ *adj* **1.** noisy and unrestrained in a way that shows excitement or great happiness **2.** involving great excitement, confusion, and emotional agitation —**tu·mul·tu·ous·ly** *adv* —**tu·mul·tu·ous·ness** *n*

tu·mu·lus /tóomyələss/ (*plural* **-li** /-lì/) *n* ARCHAEOL same as **barrow**[2] [15C. < Latin, "mound" < *tumere* "swell"]

tun /tun/ *n* **1.** a large cask for beer or wine **2.** a measure of liquid volume, especially one for wine equal to 252 gallons/955 liters [Pre-12C. < medieval Latin *tunna* "cask"]

Tun. *abbr* **1.** Tunisia **2.** Tunisian

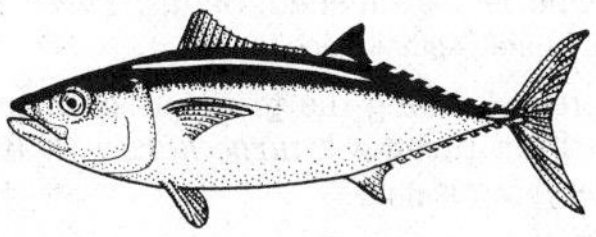

tuna

tu·na[1] /tóonə/ (*plural same* or **-nas**) *n* **1.** a large, fast-swimming, widely distributed ocean fish with a tapering body, large forked tail, and pointed head. Native to: warm and temperate waters. Genus: *Thunnus.* **2.** the firm meaty flesh of the tuna, used as food [Late 19C. < American Spanish]

tu·na[2] /tóonə/ *n* **1.** a cactus that has colored flowers and sweet edible fruit. Latin name: *Opuntia tuna.* **2.** the edible fruit of a tuna cactus [Mid-16C. Via Spanish < Taino]

tu·na fish *n* FOOD same as **tuna**[1] (sense 2)

tun·dish /túndish/ *n* **1.** a trough at the top of a mold into which molten metal is poured **2.** *N Ireland* same as **funnel** *n* (sense 1)

tun·dra /túndrə/ *n* the level or nearly level treeless plain between the ice cap and the timber line of North America, Europe, and Asia that has permanently frozen subsoil [Late 16C. Via Russian < Saami *tundar*]

tune /toon/ *n* **1.** SIMPLE MELODY a series of musical notes that make a simple melody **2.** SONG a melodious song or short piece of music ■ *vt* (**tuned, tun·ing, tunes**) **1.** ADJUST INSTRUMENT FOR PITCH to adjust a musical instrument so that it plays at the correct pitch **2.** ADJUST ENGINE to adjust an engine or machine to make it run better **3.** ADJUST STATION OR CHANNEL to adjust a radio or television set to a station or channel (*usually passive*) **4. tune your·self** ADAPT TO SOMETHING to bring yourself, somebody, or something into harmony or accord with something else **5.** ADJUST ELECTRONIC INSTRUMENT to adjust an electronic device or instrument to the required frequency [14C. Alteration of TONE] —**tun·a·ble** *adj* —**tune·a·ble** *adj* ◇ **call the tune** to be in charge ◇ **change your tune** to change your attitude or opinion ◇ **in tune 1.** played or sung at the appropriate pitch **2.** in accord or agreement with somebody or something **3.** adjusted to the correct frequency or musical pitch ◇ **out of tune 1.** played or sung at the wrong pitch **2.** out of harmony or in disagreement with somebody or something **3.** not adjusted to the correct frequency or musical pitch ◇ **to the tune of something** to the stated exact or approximate amount

tune in *v* **1.** *vti* to adjust a radio or television to receive a signal, program, or channel **2.** *vi* to be attentive or receptive to somebody or something

tune out *v* **1.** *vt* to adjust a radio or television set to eliminate the reception of something undesired such as interference **2.** *vti* to ignore or be unreceptive to somebody or something ○ *"The country was tuning out all things when suddenly there was focus on scandal."* (*US News & World Report*; December 1998)

tune up *vti* **1.** to adjust one or more musical instruments to an accurate or common pitch **2.** to test and improve something as a preparation, e.g., for a competition or meeting

tune·ful /tóonf'l/ *adj* having a pleasant melody —**tune·ful·ly** *adv* —**tune·ful·ness** *n*

tune·less /tóonləss/ *adj* unmusical, lacking a tune, or not producing a tune —**tune·less·ly** *adv* —**tune·less·ness** *n*

tun·er /tóonər/ *n* **1.** a device used for selecting a desired signal from a mixture of signals, e.g., in a radio or television set containing one or more resonant circuits **2.** somebody who tunes musical instruments, especially pianos

tune·smith /tóon smìth/ *n US* a composer of popular songs or music (*informal*)

tune-up *n* **1.** a set of adjustments made to an engine to make it run better **2.** a preliminary trial or warm-up, e.g., a minor sporting event held before a major one

tung oil /túng-/ *n* a quick-drying yellow oil extracted from the seeds of the tung tree, used in paints and varnishes to speed up drying, and also as a waterproofing agent [< Chinese *tóng* "tung tree"]

tung-oil tree *n* TREES same as **tung tree**

tung·state /túng stàyt/ *n* a salt or ester of tungstic acid. Source: tungsten ore.

tung·sten /túngstən/ *n* a hard lustrous gray metallic element with a very high melting point. Source: wolframite, scheelite. Use: high-temperature alloys, lamp filaments, high-speed cutting tools. Symbol **W**. See table at **element** [Late 18C. < Swedish, "heavy stone"]

tung·sten car·bide *n* a fine, very hard, gray crystalline powder made by heating tungsten and carbon together. Use: manufacture of dies, cutting and abrasion tools, durable machine parts.

tung·sten lamp *n* an incandescent electric lamp with a filament made of tungsten

tung·sten steel *n* a hard heat-resistant steel containing between 1% and 20% tungsten, used in tools and high-temperature engineering equipment

tung·stic /túngstik/ *adj* relating to or containing tungsten, especially with a valence of six

tung·stic ac·id *n* a weak acid of tungsten. Use: manufacture of textiles, plastics. Formula: H_2WO_4.

tung·stite /túng stìt/ *n* a rare yellow-green tungsten oxide mineral. Source: tungsten ores.

tung·stous /túngstəss/ *adj* relating to or containing tungsten, especially with a valence of two

tung tree *n* a tree whose large round fruit contains hard seeds that yield tung oil. Native to: East Asia. Genus: *Aleurites.* [See TUNG OIL]

Tun·gus /tóong góoz, tung góoz/ (*plural same* or **-gus·es**) *n* PEOPLES, LANG same as **Evenki** [Early 17C. < Yakut] —**Tun·gus** *adj*

Tun·gus·ic /tóong góozik, tung-/ *n* a group of Altaic languages spoken in northern parts of the People's Republic of China and Asia of the former Soviet Union. Native speakers: 50,000. —**Tun·gus·ic** *adj*

tu·nic /tóonik/ *n* **1.** LOOSE GARMENT a loose wide-necked garment that extends to the hip or knee and is usually worn with a belt or gathered at the waist **2.** GARMENT WORN IN PAST a knee-length garment with sleeves, a round neck, and a loose body worn by men in ancient Rome, or a similar garment worn during the Middle Ages **3.** *UK* CLOTHING, MIL POLICE OR MILITARY JACKET a close-fitting high-collared jacket worn as part of a police or military uniform **4.** SPORTS DRESS a short belted dress worn by women when playing some sports **5.** ANAT FIBROUS MEMBRANE a layer of tissue that covers or lines a body part or organ, especially tubular parts such as the blood vessels **6.** BOT PAPERY COVERING ON BULB a dry, often brown and papery covering around a bulb or corm such as of an onion **7.** RELIG same as **tunicle** [Pre-12C. Directly or via French *tunique* < Latin *tunica*]

tu·ni·ca /tóonikə/ (*plural* **-cae** /-kèe, -sèe/) *n UK* ANAT same as **tunic** (sense 5) [Late 17C. < Latin, "tunic"]

tu·ni·cate /tóonikət, -kàyt/ *n* MARINE BIOL OCEAN ANIMAL a sac-shaped ocean chordate animal that has a tough leathery or rubbery outer coat, e.g., a sea squirt or ascidian. Subphylum: Urochordata. ■ *adj* **1.** MARINE BIOL RELATING TO TUNICATES relating to or classified as a tunicate **2.** *also* **tu·ni·cat·ed** /-kàytəd/ BOT WITH DRY PAPERY COVERING describes a bulb or corm that has a dry, often brown and papery covering **3.** *also* **tu·ni·cat·ed** ANAT WITH COVERING OF TISSUE describes an organ or body part that is covered or lined with a layer of tissue [Mid-18C. < Latin *tunicatus* "covered with a tunic" < *tunica* "tunic"]

tu·ni·cle /tóonik'l/ *n* in Christian worship, a short vestment worn over the alb by a subdeacon at a Mass, or under the dalmatic by a bishop or cardinal at other ceremonies [14C. Directly or via Old French < Latin *tunicula* "small tunic" < *tunica* "tunic"]

tun·ing /tóoning/ *n* **1.** ADJUSTMENT OF INSTRUMENT adjustments made to a musical instrument to make it produce the required pitches **2.** SET OF PITCHES the standard range of pitches to which a musical instrument is tuned **3.** MUSICAL INTONATION the degree to which musical instruments or the voices of a choir are adjusted to a norm

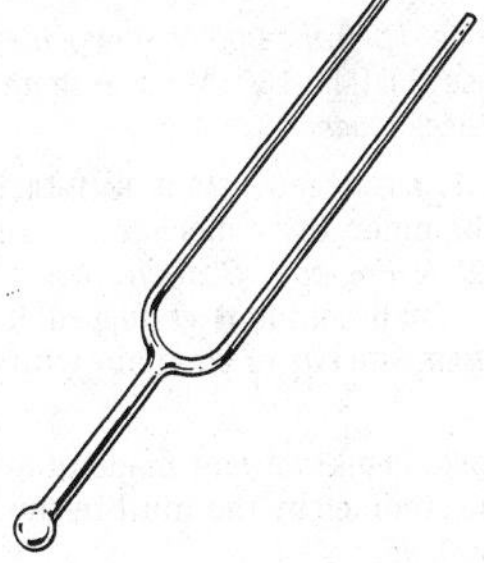

tuning fork

tun·ing fork *n* an instrument with a stem and two prongs that produces a constant pitch when struck, used to tune musical instruments and in acoustics

Tu·nis /tóoniss/ capital of Tunisia, on a shallow lake near the Gulf of Tunis. Population: 1,897,000 (2000).

Tu·nis, Gulf of /tyóoniss/ arm of the Mediterranean Sea in northeastern Tunisia

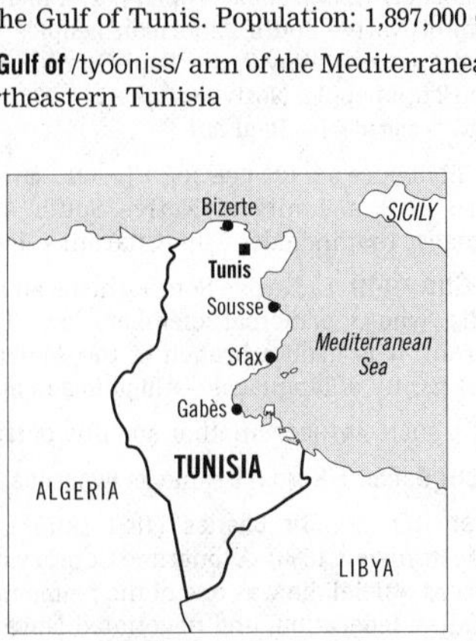

Tunisia

Tu·ni·sia /too néezhə/ country in North Africa, bordered by the Mediterranean Sea, Libya, and Algeria. Language: Arabic. Currency: Tunisian dinar. Capital: Tunis. Population: 9,924,742 (2003). Area: 63,482 sq. mi./164,418 sq. km. Official name **Republic of Tunisia**. See map on previous page —**Tu·ni·sian** *n, adj*

tun·nel /túnn'l/ *n* **1.** PASSAGEWAY UNDER OBSTRUCTION a long passage that allows pedestrians or vehicles to proceed under or through an obstruction such as a river, mountain, or congested area **2.** ANIMAL'S UNDERGROUND PASSAGE an underground passage or system of passages dug by a burrowing animal **3.** PART OF MINE a corridor or working area in a mine **4.** PASSAGE a passage, channel, or route through or under something ■ *v* (**-neled** or **-nelled, -nel·ing** or **-nel·ling, -nels**) **1.** *vti* MAKE TUNNEL to make, burrow, or excavate a tunnel under or through something **2.** *vt* MAKE SOMETHING LIKE TUNNEL to produce or dig something that resembles or is shaped like a tunnel [15C. < Old French *tonel* "small barrel" < medieval Latin *tunna* "cask"] —**tun·nel·er** *n*

tun·nel dis·ease *n* MED same as **ancylostomiasis** [Because caused by tunnel worms]

tun·nel ef·fect *n* a quantum mechanical effect in which elementary particles can pass through barriers that would be impossible under the laws of classical mechanics by apparently disappearing and reappearing on the other side, as through a tunnel

tun·nel·ing /túnn'ling/ *n* **1.** the digging, excavation, or construction of a tunnel **2.** in quantum mechanics, the phenomenon of elementary particles passing through barriers by apparently disappearing and reappearing on the other side, as through a tunnel

tun·nel vault *n* ARCHIT same as **barrel vault**

tun·nel vi·sion *n* **1.** a condition in which peripheral vision is lost or severely limited, so that only objects directly in line with the eyes can be seen **2.** a very limited viewpoint or conception of things

Tun·ney /túnnee/, **Gene** (1898–1978) US boxer. He was the world heavyweight boxing champion (1926–28). Born **Tunney, James Joseph**

tun·ny /túnnee/ (*plural same* or **-nies**) *n* FISH same as **tuna**[1] (sense 1) [Mid-16C. Via French *thon* and Latin *thunnus* < Greek *thunnos*]

tup /tup/ *n* **1.** MECH ENG HEAD OF HAMMER the head of a power hammer or a mechanism resembling a hammer **2.** *N England, Scotland* AGRIC RAM a male sheep used for breeding ■ *vt* (**tupped, tup·ping, tups**) *UK* AGRIC MATE WITH EWE to copulate with a ewe [14C. Origin ?]

tu·pek /tóopik/, **tu·pik** *n* a tent made of animal skins, used in the summer by the Inuit in the Arctic [Mid-19C. < Inuit *tupiq*]

tu·pe·lo /tóopə lō/ (*plural* **-los**) *n* **1.** the soft pale wood of a deciduous tree **2.** a deciduous tree that grows in swamps and on river banks and yields tupelo. Native to: North America, Asia. Genus: *Nyssa*. [Mid-18C. < Creek *'topilwa* "swamp tree"]

Tu·pi /tóopee/ (*plural same* or **-pis**) *n* **1.** a member of a group of Native South American peoples who live in the Amazon valley **2.** the Tupi-Guarani language of the Tupi people. Native speakers: 3,000. [Mid-19C. < Tupi, "comrade"] —**Tu·pi** *adj*

Tu·pi·an /tóopee ən, too pée ən/ *n* **1.** LANG same as **Tupi** (sense 2) **2.** a family of Native South American languages that includes Tupi-Guarani —**Tu·pi·an** *adj*

Tu·pi-Gua·ra·ni *n* a Native South American language family whose principal members are Tupi and Guarani. It is itself a branch of the Andean-Equatorial family of languages. —**Tu·pi-Gua·ra·ni** *adj*

tu·pik *n* CULTL ANTHROP another spelling of **tupek**

tup·pence, etc. *UK* MONEY same as **twopence, etc.**

Tup·per /túppər/, **Sir Charles** (1821–1915) Canadian prime minister (1896). A longtime Conservative government official, he was one of the prime movers of Canadian federation, and negotiated Nova Scotia's entry into the Dominion of Canada (1867).

LANGUAGE HERITAGE ***Tupi-Guarani*** Much of English is made up of words from other languages, and the ***Tupi-Guarani*** group of South American languages is a small but significant contributor in this respect. Names of unfamiliar animals and birds reached English relatively soon after Europeans discovered the New World (usually via Portuguese, Spanish, or sometimes French): the ***agouti*** and the ***toucan*** in the mid-16th century, the ***capybara***, ***eyra***, ***jaguar***, and ***tanager*** in the early 17th, followed later by, for example, ***cougar***, ***jabiru***, ***piranha***, and ***tapir***. Foodstuffs were adopted: ***manioc*** (mid-16th century), ***cashew*** (late 16th), ***cayenne pepper***, and ***tapioca***, for example. Valuable products and their sources became known and used, for instance, ***ipecac*** (a plant from whose dried roots an emetic is made, early 17th century), ***jacaranda*** (a tree with a valuable wood), and ***jaborandi*** (a bush whose dried leaves yield the drug pilocarpine). Tupi also gave us (via Portuguese) the sound of the ***maraca*** (early 17th century).

tuque /took/, **toque** /tōk/ *n Can* a cylindrical stocking cap of double-thickness wool or synthetic yarn [Late 19C. Via Canadian French < French *toque* "toque"]

tu quo·que /too kwṓkwee, -kwō kwày/ *interj* used when accused of an offense to accuse the accuser of the same offense [Late 17C. < Latin, "you too"]

Tur. *abbr* **1.** Turkey **2.** Turkish

tu·ra·co *n* BIRDS another spelling of **touraco**

Tu·ra·ni·an /tŏŏ ráynee ən, tə-/ *n* **1.** URAL-ALTAIC SPEAKER a member of any of the peoples who speak a Ural-Altaic language **2.** OLD LANGUAGE GROUPING a formerly accepted grouping of Asian languages roughly corresponding to the Altaic family with others added (*dated*) ■ *adj* RELATING TO ANCIENT TURKISTAN relating to ancient Turkistan, or to its people or culture [Late 18C. < Persian *Turān* "Turkistan"]

tur·ban /túrbən/ *n* **1.** a man's headdress that consists of a long piece of fabric wrapped around the head or around a small cap, completely covering the hair, worn especially by some Sikhs and Muslims **2.** a woman's hat that is similar in shape to a man's turban [Mid-16C. Via obsolete French *turbant*, Italian *turbante* < Turkish *tülbend* < Persian *dulband*] —**tur·baned** *adj*

tur·ba·ry /túrbəree/ *n* an area of land where turf or peat may be cut or dug [14C. < Anglo-Norman *turberie* < French *tourbe* "turf" < Germanic]

tur·bel·lar·i·an /tùrbə lérree ən/ *n* a free-living flatworm that inhabits wet soil, freshwater, and ocean environments, e.g., a planarian. Class: Turbellaria. [Late 19C. < modern Latin *Turbellaria* < Latin *turbella* "small commotion"] —**tur·bel·lar·i·an** *adj*

tur·bid /túrbid/ *adj* **1.** MUDDY opaque and muddy as when particles and sediment are stirred up **2.** FOGGY dense and cloudy or dark **3.** CONFUSED confused and muddled ○ *turbid thought processes* [Early 17C. < Latin *turbidus* "troubled" < *turba* "disorder"] —**tur·bid·i·ty** /tur bíddətee/ *n* —**tur·bid·ly** *adv*

USAGE turbid or **turgid**? The two words are unrelated in form but can both describe water in their literal meanings (either "opaque and muddy" in the case of ***turbid*** or "swollen and overflowing" in the case of ***turgid***), and can both describe literary styles in their figurative meanings. ***Turgid*** is the more common and means "pompous and overcomplicated" (as in *turgid prose*), whereas ***turbid*** means "confused and muddled" (as in *turbid reasoning*).

tur·bi·dim·e·ter /tùrbi dímmətər/ *n* an instrument that determines the amount of material in suspension in a liquid or gas by measuring the decrease in light transmittance through the fluid —**tur·bi·di·met·ric** /tùrbidi méttrik/ *adj* —**tur·bi·dim·e·try** *n*

tur·bi·dite /túrbi dìt/ *n* a sedimentary deposit laid down by a turbidity current, e.g., on the ocean floor at the bottom of the continental shelf

tur·bid·i·ty cur·rent *n* a rapidly moving current containing dispersed sediments, sometimes started off by seismic shocks or slumping

tur·bi·nate /túrbinət, -nàyt/, **tur·bi·nal** /-n'l/ *adj* **1.** SPIRAL IN SHAPE having a shape like a spiral or scroll **2.** ANAT SHAPED LIKE SCROLL describes any of the three scroll-shaped bones found on the walls of the nasal passages of mammals **3.** ZOOL SHAPED LIKE INVERTED CONE describes a mollusk shell that spirals and is shaped like an inverted cone ■ *n* **1.** ANAT TURBINATE BONE a turbinate bone in the nasal passage of mammals **2.** ZOOL MOLLUSK SHELL a turbinate mollusk shell [Mid-17C. < Latin *turbinatus* < Latin *turbin-* "spiral, spinning top"] —**tur·bi·na·tion** /tùrbi náysh'n/ *n*

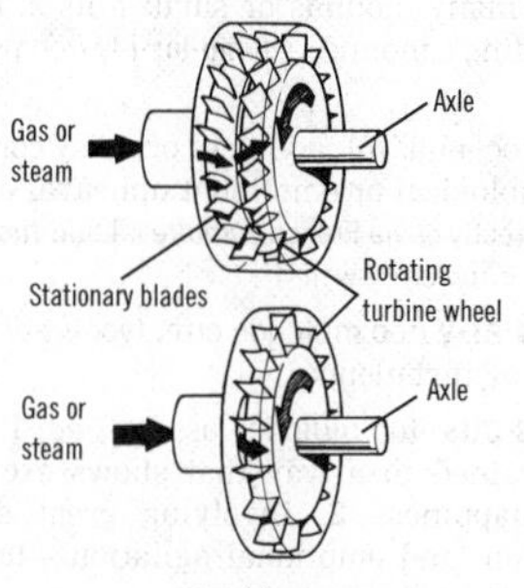

turbine

tur·bine /túr bìn, -bin/ *n* a machine in which a moving fluid such as steam acts on the blades of a rotor to produce rotational motion that can be transformed to electrical or mechanical power [Mid-19C. Via French < Latin *turbin-* "spiral, spinning top"]

tur·bit /túrbit/ *n* a domestic pigeon of a breed with a ruffed neck and breast [Late 17C. Origin ?]

tur·bo[1] /túrbō/ (*plural* **-bos**) *n* ENG **1.** same as **turbine 2.** same as **turbocharger**

tur·bo[2] /túrbō/ (*plural* **-bos**) *n* a gastropod mollusk that has a whorled spiral shell. Genus: *Turbo*. [Mid-17C. < Latin, "spiral, spinning top"]

turbo- *prefix* **1.** using the principle of a turbine, or driven by a turbine ○ *turbocharger* **2.** turbojet ○ *turboprop* [< TURBINE]

tur·bo·charge /túrbō chaarj/ (**-charged, -charg·ing, -charg·es**) *vt* **1.** to equip an engine with a turbocharger, usually to increase its power **2.** to increase the power, speed, or performance of something (*informal*) ○ *resources to turbocharge your career* —**tur·bo·charged** *adj*

tur·bo·charg·er /túrbō chaarjər/ *n* a specialized turbine driven by the exhaust gases of an engine that supplies air under pressure to the engine for combustion [Mid-20C. Contraction of TURBO-SUPERCHARGER]

tur·bo·fan /túrbō fàn/ *n Can, UK* AEROSP **1.** a jet engine in which fans driven by a turbine force air into the exhaust gases, thereby increasing the propelling thrust of the engine **2.** a jet aircraft that has turbofan engines ▶ US term **fanjet**

tur·bo·gen·er·a·tor /tùrbō jénnə ràytər/ *n* a machine used to generate electricity in which steam from coal, oil, or gas is used to drive the turbine

tur·bo·jet /túrbō jèt/ *n* **1.** a jet engine with a gas turbine that uses exhaust gases to provide the propulsive thrust for an aircraft **2.** an aircraft powered by turbojet

tur·bo·prop /túrbō pròp/ *n* **1.** a turbojet engine that powers a propeller **2.** an aircraft whose propellers are driven by a gas turbine

tur·bo·ram·jet /tùrbō rám jèt/ *n* **1.** a turbojet engine in which forward motion is achieved by compression of the fuel **2.** an aircraft powered by a turboramjet

tur·bo·su·per·charg·er /tùrbō sóopər chaarjər/ *n* ENG same as **turbocharger**

tur·bot /túrbət/ (*plural same* or **-bots**) *n* **1.** EUROPEAN FLATFISH a flatfish that is almost circular with bony tubercles on its body and both eyes on the left side. Native to: Europe. Latin name: *Scophthalmus maximus*. **2.** TURBOT AS FOOD the flesh of a turbot as food **3.** FLATFISH a flatfish in the same family as the European turbot, e.g., the spotted turbot of the Pacific. Family: Pleuronectidae. [13C. Via Old French < Old Swedish *törnbut* "thorn-flatfish"; from the bony tubercles on its back]

tur·bu·lence /túrbyələnss/, **tur·bu·len·cy** /-lənssee/ *n* **1.** UNREST a state of confusion characterized by unpredictability and uncontrolled change **2.** METEOROL INSTABILITY IN ATMOSPHERE an instability in the atmosphere that disrupts the flow of the wind, causing gusty, unpredictable air currents **3.** PHYS EDDIES eddies or secondary motion within a moving fluid

tur·bu·lent /túrbyələnt/ *adj* **1.** MOVING VIOLENTLY full of violent motion and agitation ○ *turbulent rapids* **2.** CHAOTIC AND RESTLESS marked by disturbances, changes, and unrest ○ *a turbulent year in politics* **3.** METEOROL ATMOSPHERICALLY UNSTABLE atmospherically unstable, with variations in wind speed and direction [15C. < Latin *turbulentus* < *turba* "disorder"] —**tur·bu·lent·ly** *adv*

tur·bu·lent flow *n* a form of fluid flow in which particles of the fluid move with irregular local velocities and pressures

Tur·co·man *n, adj* PEOPLES, LANG same as **Turkmen**

turd /turd/ *n* **1.** a highly offensive term for a piece of excrement or dung (*taboo*) **2.** a highly offensive term for somebody who is seen as contemptible (*taboo insult*) [Old English *tord* < Indo-European]

tu·reen /tə reén, tŏŏ-/ *n* a wide deep bowl with a lid that is used especially to serve soups, stews, and casseroles [Mid-18C. Alteration of TERRINE]

turf /turf/ *n* (*plural* **turfs** or **turves** /turvz/) **1.** DENSE LAYER OF GRASS a dense thick even cover of grass and roots in the top layer of soil **2.** ARTIFICIAL GRASS artificial grass such as that used on surfaces for playing sport **3.** PIECE OF SOIL WITH GRASS a piece of soil with grass growing in it **4.** PEAT FOR FUEL peat when sold for fuel **5.** AREA OF EXPERTISE an area in which somebody has authority or expertise (*informal*) ○ *industry lobbyists protecting their own turf* **6.** TERRITORY a territory or geographic area (*informal*) **7.** GANG TERRITORY an area or territory that a gang claims as exclusively its own (*informal*) **8.** HORSERACING horseracing as a sport or industry **9.** HORSERACING TRACK a track where horses are raced ■ *vt* (**turfed, turf·ing, turfs**) **1.** COVER SOMETHING WITH TURF to cover an area with pieces of turf **2.** KILL to kill somebody (*slang*) [Old English, < Indo-European] —**turf·y** *adj*

turf out *vt UK* to eject somebody from a place or organization (*informal*)

Ivan Turgenev

Tur·ge·nev /toor gáynyəf/, **Ivan** (1818–83) Russian writer. His best known works include the play *A Month in the Country* (1850) and the novel *Fathers and Sons* (1862). Full name **Turgenev, Ivan Sergeyevich**. See Cultural note at **father**

> "Nature is not a temple, but a workshop, and man's the workman in it."
> [Ivan Turgenev, *Fathers and Sons*; 1862]

tur·ges·cent /tur jéss'nt/ *adj* **1.** swollen or becoming swollen, usually as a result of an accumulation of blood or other fluids **2.** acting pompously, or feeling very self-important [Early 18C. < Latin *turgescent*, present participle of *turgescere* "begin to swell" < *turgere* "swell"] —**tur·ges·cence** *n*

tur·gid /túrjid/ *adj* **1.** POMPOUS AND OVERCOMPLICATED pompous, boring, and overcomplicated ○ *a turgid speech* **2.** OVERFLOWING swollen and overflowing **3.** MED DISTENDED swollen or distended by a buildup of fluid [Early 17C. < Latin *turgidus* < *turgere* "swell"] —**tur·gid·i·ty** /tur jíddətee/ *n* —**tur·gid·ly** *adv*

USAGE See *turbid*.

tur·gor /túrgər/ *n* the normal rigid state of plant cells, caused by outward pressure of the water content of each cell on its membrane [Late 19C. < late Latin < Latin *turgere* "swell"]

Tu·rin /toor rín/ capital of Turin Province, Piedmont Region, northwestern Italy. Population: 865,263 (2001).

Tur·ing /tyŏŏring/, **Alan** (1912–54) British mathematician. He was a major figure in the theoretical development of the computer. During World War II, he worked as a British government cryptographer and helped to break the code of the German Enigma machine. Full name **Turing, Alan Mathison**

Tur·ing ma·chine *n* a mathematical model of a hypothetical computer that can modify its instructions and read from, write on, or erase a potentially infinite tape. It was instrumental in the evolution of computer theory.

Tu·ring test *n* a test in artificial intelligence in which a human interrogator attempts to determine whether an unseen entity is human or a computer

tu·ri·on /tŏŏree òn/ *n* **1.** a bud that breaks off from an water plant and lies submerged and dormant until the following spring, when it produces a new plantlet that floats to the surface **2.** a shoot from an underground root or stem, e.g., in asparagus [Early 18C. Via French < Latin *turion-* "young sprig"]

Turk /turk/ *n* **1.** SOMEBODY FROM TURKEY somebody who comes from Turkey **2.** MEMBER OF TURKISH ETHNIC GROUP a member of the Turkish-speaking ethnic group in Turkey, or, formerly, in the Ottoman Empire **3.** TURKIC SPEAKER a member of a people speaking a Turkic language **4.** OFFENSIVE TERM an offensive term for a Muslim (*archaic*) [14C. Via French *Turc*, medieval Latin *Turcus* < Turkish *Türk*]

Turk. *abbr* **1.** Turkey **2.** Turkish

Tur·ka·na, Lake /tur kaánə/ lake in northwestern Kenya, bordering Ethiopia at its northern end. Area: 2,700 sq. mi./7,100 sq. km. Former name **Rudolf, Lake**

Turk·e·stan ➧ **Turkistan**

turkey

tur·key /túrkee/ (*plural* **-keys**) *n* **1.** LARGE N AMERICAN BIRD a large bird with a bare wattled head and neck and brownish feathers. Raised for: meat. Native to: North America. Latin name: *Meleagris gallopavo.* **2.** TURKEY MEAT the meat of the turkey used for food **3.** LARGE CENTRAL AMERICAN BIRD a large bird similar to the North American turkey. Native to: Central America. Latin name: *Agriocharis ocellata.* **4.** FAILURE something that fails or flops, especially a bad play or movie (*slang*) **5.** *US* OFFENSIVE TERM an offensive term that deliberately insults somebody regarded as unintelligent, incompetent, or socially inept (*slang*) **6.** THREE CONSECUTIVE BOWLING STRIKES in bowling, three strikes in a row (*informal*) [Mid-16C. < the N American bird's resemblance to the guinea fowl, imported through Turkish territory] ◇ **talk turkey** to talk honestly and bluntly (*informal*)

Turkey

Tur·key /túrkee/ country in southeastern Europe and Southwest Asia, bordered by Greece, the Black Sea, Georgia, Armenia, Iran, Iraq, Syria, the Mediterranean Sea, the Aegean Sea, and Bulgaria. Language: Turkish. Currency: Turkish lira. Capital: Ankara. Population: 68,109,469 (2003). Area: 300,948 sq. mi./779,452 sq. km. Official name **Republic of Turkey**

tur·key buz·zard *n* BIRDS same as **turkey vulture**

Tur·key car·pet *n* a handwoven woolen carpet with rich colors and a deep pile

tur·key cock *n* **1.** a male turkey, especially when fully grown **2.** a person regarded as arrogant or conceited (*insult*)

Tur·key red *adj* of the vibrant red color produced using alizarin as a dye [Late 18C. < fabrics made in the Ottoman Empire] —**Tur·key red** *n*

tur·key shoot *n US* **1.** a shooting contest in which rifles are fired at moving targets **2.** something that is easily accomplished (*slang*)

tur·key trot *n* a round dance to ragtime music in which dancers walk springily and make movements with their upper body

tur·key vul·ture *n* a blackish brown vulture with a bare wrinkled red head and neck. Native to: Americas. Latin name: *Cathartes aura.*

Turk·ic /túrkik/ *n* a subgroup of the Altaic family of languages spoken in western and central Asia, including Turkish, Azeri, Kazakh, Kyrgyz, Tatar, Uigur, and Uzbek ■ *adj* relating to Turkic languages, to the region where they are spoken, or to the peoples who speak them

Turk·ish /túrkish/ *adj* **1.** OF TURKEY relating to Turkey, or to its people or culture **2.** OF LANGUAGE OF TURKEY relating to the language of Turkey ■ *n* OFFICIAL LANGUAGE OF TURKEY the Turkic language that is the official language of Turkey, also spoken in Cyprus and several European countries. Native speakers: 50 million. See panel on next page

Turk·ish bath *n* **1.** STEAM BATH a bath in which the bather sweats freely in hot air or steam, followed by a shower and often a massage **2.** ESTABLISHMENT OFFERING TURKISH BATH a commercial establishment where somebody can have a Turkish bath **3.** HOT PLACE a place that is very hot

Turk·ish cof·fee *n* a strong coffee, usually sweetened, made by simmering finely ground coffee and serving the liquid with the grounds

Turk·ish de·light *n* a candy made with flavored gelatin, cut into cubes and dusted with powdered sugar

Turk·ish to·bac·co *n* an aromatic dark tobacco grown in southeastern Europe and Turkey

Turk·ish tow·el *n* a large coarse-fibered cotton towel

Turk·i·stan /túrki stàn, -staán/, **Turk·e·stan** mountainous region of central Asia that stretches from the Caspian Sea to the Gobi Desert. It is divided into three sections, Russian or Western Turkistan, which includes Kazakhstan, Kyrgyzstan, and Uzbekistan, Chinese or Eastern Turkistan, made up of the Xinjiang Uygor Autonomous Region of China, and Afghan Turkistan, consisting of the northeastern part of Afghanistan.

Turk·men /túrkmən/ (*plural same* or **-mens**), **Tur·ko·man**

LANGUAGE HERITAGE ***Turkish*** Much of English is made up of words from other languages, and some are from ***Turkish.*** Though relatively few purely Turkish words have moved directly into English, many words have migrated through Turkish on their way into the language, especially from Arabic and Persian, or have set out from Turkish and found their way by a more circuitous route. A typical example would be Turkish *ordu*, "camp, army," which is represented in English as both ***horde*** and ***Urdu***. The former arrived in the mid-16th century, either directly or via French and German from Polish *horda*, which is from the Turkish word. ***Urdu*** came later, in the late 18th century, via Persian and Urdu *(zabān i) urdū* "(language of the) camp," from the same Turkish *ordū* "camp." Turkish *tülbend*, "turban," represents a significant stage in the development of both ***turban*** and ***tulip***, as it is the source of the words from which ***turban*** was borrowed in the mid-16th century (French *turbant* and Italian *turbante*), and also of the French *tulipe*, from which ***tulip*** was adopted later in the same century, though the Turkish itself goes back further to Persian *dulband*.

Turkish naturally played a part in the migration of words relating to Eastern culture or society: for example, ***bazaar***, immediately from Italian in the late 16th century, but with the Italian via Turkish from Persian *bazaar* "market"; ***divan***, adopted at much the same time via French or Italian from Turkish *dīvān*, itself from Persian; ***fez***, early 19th century via French from Turkish *fes*; ***harem***, mid-17th century, via Turkish from Arabic *ḥaram* "prohibited (place), women's quarters"; ***minaret***, late 17th century from French from Turkish *mināri* from Arabic *manāra* "lighthouse, minaret"; ***yashmak***, mid-19th century directly from Turkish *yaşmak*. Some of the most familiar migrants from Turkish relate to food and drink: ***baklava*** in the mid-17th century; ***bulgur*** wheat, a relatively newcomer, mid-20th century via Turkish from Persian *bulgūr* "bruised grain"; ***caviar***, mid-16th century via French and Italian from Turkish *havyar* (from Persian dialect *khāvyār*); ***coffee***, late 16th century via Turkish *kahve* from Arabic (the Turkish word is also the source, through French, of ***café***); ***meze***, "assortment of snacks or light dishes," early 20th century from Turkish, from Persian *maza* "taste, relish"; ***pilaf***, early 17th century from Turkish *pilâv*, "cooked rice"; ***sherbet***, early 17th century via Turkish *şerbet* and Persian *šerbet* from Arabic *šarbat* "drink" (the Turkish is also the source, through French and Italian, of ***sorbet***); and ***yogurt***, early 17th century. Some other words, all from the early 17th century, whose Turkish origins may be less apparent are ***jackal***, via Turkish from Persian *šagāl*, ***kiosk***, via French from Turkish *kōşk* "villa" from Persian *kūšk* "villa, palace," and ***theorbo***, "stringed instrument like a large lute," via Italian *tiorba* from Turkish *torba* "bag."

/túrkəmən/ (*plural* **-mans**), **Tur·co·man** *n* **1.** a member of an originally nomadic Turkic-speaking people who now live mainly in Turkmenistan and Afghanistan **2.** the Turkic official language of Turkmenistan. Native speakers: 4 million. [Early 20C. Via Persian *turkmān* < Turkish *türkmen*] —**Turk·men** *adj*

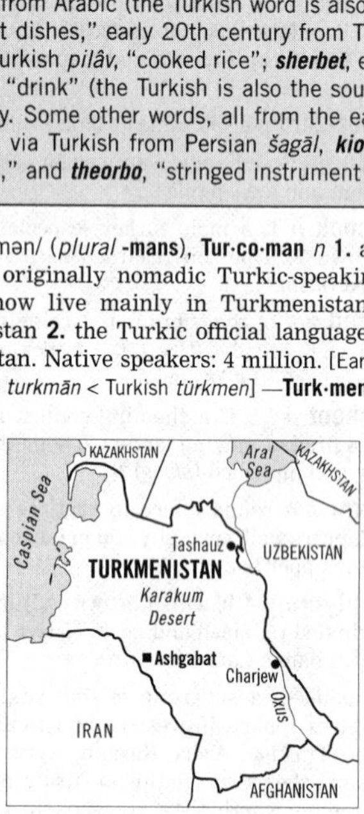

Turkmenistan

Turk·men·i·stan /tùrk meni stán, -staán/ country in southwestern Central Asia, bordered by Kazakhstan, Uzbekistan, Afghanistan, Iran, and the Caspian Sea. Language: Turkmen. Currency: manat. Capital: Ashgabat. Population: 4,775,544 (2003). Area: 188,500 sq. mi./488,100 sq. km. Official name **Republic of Turkmenistan**

Tur·ko·man *n, adj* PEOPLES, LANG same as **Turkmen**

Turks and Cai·cos Is·lands /tùrks ənd káykəss-/ British dependency consisting of two island groups in the northern Caribbean, southeast of the Bahamas and north of Hispaniola. Capital: Cockburn Town. Population: 18,122 (2001). Area: 166 sq. mi./430 sq. km.

Turk's-cap lil·y *n* either of two lilies that have bright nodding flowers with petals that bend sharply backward. Latin name: *Lilium martagon* or *Lilium superbum*.

Turk's-head *n* a knot shaped like a turban, made by weaving a smaller rope around a larger rope or spar

tur·mer·ic /túrmərik/ *n* **1.** a yellow spice made from the dried rhizomes of an Asian plant. Use: cooking, yellow dye. **2.** a tropical Asian plant of the ginger family with yellow flowers and rhizomes that are dried to produce turmeric. Latin name: *Curcuma longa*. [Mid-16C. < French *terre-mérite* "worthy earth"]

tur·mer·ic pa·per *n* a strip of test paper impregnated with turmeric. Use: turns brown in the presence of alkalis and red-brown in the presence of boric acid.

tur·moil /túr mòyl/ *n* **1.** a state of great confusion, commotion, or disturbance **2.** a disruptive event that causes confusion, commotion, or disturbance ○ *a leader untroubled by the nation's turmoils* [Early 16C. Origin ?]

turn /turn/ *v* (**turned, turn·ing, turns**) **1.** *vti* MOVE TO FACE DIFFERENT DIRECTION to move to face in a different direction or toward a particular location, or move something so that it does this ○ *She turned to see what was happening.* ○ *turning his eyes skyward* **2.** *vti* MOVE AROUND AXIS to move around an axis or point in a particular direction, or move something in this way ○ *Turn the handle to the left.* **3.** *vt* USE CONTROL TO OPERATE SOMETHING to control something such as a machine or an appliance or some aspect of its performance by moving a knob, switch, or slider to a different setting ○ *Turn the heat to high.* **4.** *vti* CHANGE DIRECTION OF VEHICLE to go in a different direction when moving or traveling, or make a vehicle change direction ○ *Turn left at the crossroads.* **5.** *vt* GO AROUND SOMETHING to change direction and go around something ○ *to turn a corner* **6.** *vi* FOLLOW DIFFERENT COURSE to change direction and follow a different course ○ *The path turns uphill.* **7.** *vti* MOVE PAGE OVER to move a page so that the other side, or another page, can be read or looked at ○ *turned the pages* **8.** *vti* CHANGE to change or be transformed into somebody or something different, or change or transform somebody or something into somebody or something different ○ *turned into a butterfly* **9.** *vti* CHANGE COLOR to change color, or cause something to change color **10.** *vti* ALTER FOCUS OF SOMETHING to direct the focus of something toward something else, or be focused on something ○ *Her thoughts turned to the past.* **11.** *vi* START DOING SOMETHING DIFFERENT to start doing something new or different, especially as a way of solving a problem or improving a situation **12.** *vi* CONSULT SOMEBODY to seek or appeal for help from somebody ○ *He turned to his mother for advice.* **13.** *vi* CHANGE IN WEATHER to change to become a different temperature or type of weather ○ *It's turned cold again.* **14.** *vti* MAKE SOMEBODY FEEL SLIGHTLY SICK to be sufficiently unpleasant or upsetting to make somebody feel nauseated, or respond with feelings of nausea ○ *violence that turned my stomach* **15.** *vt* GYMNASTICS PERFORM CARTWHEEL to rotate the body to perform a physical action such as a cartwheel or somersault **16.** *vt* TWIST ANKLE to injure the ankle or wrist by twisting or spraining it ○ *She turned her ankle getting off the bus.* **17.** *vt* SEARCH SOMETHING EXTENSIVELY to search a place extremely thoroughly ○ *They turned the house upside down looking for the ticket.* **18.** *vt* PASS TIME OR AGE to pass a particular age, time, or speed ○ *She's just turned sixty.* **19.** *vi* BECOME SOUR to become sour (*refers to milk*) **20.** *vt* PUT SOMETHING INTO CONDITION OR PLACE to cause or allow somebody or something to be in a particular condition or place ○ *The sight turned my blood cold.* ○ *He opened the gate and turned the horses loose.* **21.** *vi* START TO EBB OR FLOW to reach high tide and start to ebb, or reach low tide and start to rise ○ *The tide has turned.* **22.** *vt* WOODWORK, METALL SHAPE SOMETHING ON LATHE to shape or cut something on a lathe **23.** *vt* FORM SOMETHING INTO ROUND SHAPE to shape clay or a pot into a rounded form with the hands or with tools **24.** *vt* EARN MONEY to earn or achieve a monetary gain ○ *The business should turn a profit in this financial year.* **25.** *vti* CHANGE ALLEGIANCE to cause a change in somebody's allegiance, or undergo a change of allegiance ○ *a diplomat who turned spy* **26.** *vi* CONVERT to convert to a religion **27.** *vt* SAY OR WRITE SOMETHING WELL to give a distinctive or pleasing form to something said or written **28.** *vt* GARDENING, AGRIC DIG UP LOWER LEVELS OF SOIL to dig soil so as to bring lower layers up to the surface **29.** *vt* MIL PASS AROUND ENEMY to pass around an enemy in order to attack from the flank or rear ■ *n* **1.** OPPORTUNITY a time when somebody gets an opportunity to do something or somebody is asked to do something, especially when this is rotated among other people ○ *It's your turn to clean up.* **2.** CHANGE OF DIRECTION a change of direction in something such as a road or the plot of a book ○ *Slow down for the turn in the road ahead.* **3.** JUNCTION a fork or corner at which a road or path divides ○ *the third turn on the left* **4.** MOVEMENT OF ROTATION a full or partial rotation ○ *Give the screw a few more turns.* **5.** WINDING a winding of something such as wire around something else **6.** PARTICULAR INCLINATION a particular inclination or tendency ○ *an academic turn of mind* **7.** SUDDEN SCARE a sudden shock or scare ○ *It gave me quite a turn.* **8.** SPELL OF ILLNESS a short period of feeling unwell or faint ○ *She had a nasty turn, but she's OK now.* **9.** END OF TIME PERIOD the point at which one period of time ends and another begins ○ *at the turn of the century* **10.** GOOD OR BAD DEED a deed that helps or harms another person ○ *a good turn* **11.** SHORT OUTING a short walk, excursion, or dance (*dated*) ○ *They took a turn around the park.* **12.** MUSIC MELODIC EMBELLISHMENT a melodic embellishment that is played around a given note, using one note above and one note below the principal note **13.** THEATER INDIVIDUAL THEATRICAL PERFORMANCE a short theatrical solo performance, e.g., in a cabaret **14.** FIN STOCK MARKET TRANSACTION a stock market transaction that includes both a sale and a purchase **15.** MIL ADVANCE PASSING AROUND ENEMY a military advance that passes around an enemy in order to attack from the flank or rear **16.** *Southern US* QUANTITY OF GRAIN the quantity of grain transported to a mill in one delivery **17.** *Can, Southern US* QUANTITY OF FIREWOOD the amount of firewood carried into a house at one time [Pre-12C. < Latin *tornare* "turn on a lathe" < *tornus* "lathe" < Greek *tornos*] —**turn·able** *adj* ◇ **at every turn** everywhere, or at every significant moment ◇ **a turn of phrase** a particular way of expressing yourself ◇ **a turn of speed** the ability to move fast for a short period or the act of doing so ◇ **by turns** one after the other, alternately ◇ **in turn** in a regular order, one after the other ◇ **on the turn** **1.** on the point of going sour **2.** on the point of changing **3.** at high or low tide and just about to ebb or return ◇ **out of turn** **1.** not in a regular or correct order **2.** in an inappropriate way, or at an inappropriate time ◇ **to a turn** perfectly ○ *meat cooked to a turn* ◇ **turn of phrase** a particular way of expressing yourself

REGIONAL NOTE ***Turn*** as in *turn of corn* (the amount of grain carried to the mill at one time) and *turn of wood* (the amount of firewood carried into the house) is a Southern term that once competed with *grist of corn* in the North and *jag of corn* in Pennsylvania and the North Midland region. In the Eastern states, Northern and Midland *armful of wood* contrasts with Southern *turn of wood*.

turn against *vt* to stop approving or being friendly and show definite disapproval or unfriendliness instead, or make somebody change his or her attitude in this way

turn around *v* **1.** *vti* TURN SOMETHING TO FACE OTHER WAY to alter the position of the body or an object so that it faces the opposite direction, or move to face the opposite direction **2.** *vt* IMPROVE SOMETHING SIGNIFICANTLY to cause a significant improvement in something, especially in the profits made by a company or organization ○ *moves to turn the debt around* **3.** *vt*

COMPLETE ALL NECESSARY PROCEDURES to carry out all the necessary procedures between receiving an order or task and shipping the order or completing the task ○ *How long will it take you to turn this work around?* **4.** *vt* **PREPARE VEHICLE BETWEEN TRIPS** to prepare an aircraft for its next flight or a ship for its next sailing

turn away *v* **1.** *vti* **TURN TO FACE SOMEWHERE ELSE** to change position so as to face away from somebody or something, or move somebody or something so as to face in another direction **2.** *vt* **REFUSE ADMISSION TO SOMEBODY** to send somebody away, refusing to see, entertain, or accommodate him or her **3.** *vt* **REFUSE TO ACCEPT SOMETHING** to refuse to listen to somebody or to what somebody wants to say or offer **4.** *vi* **GIVE SOMETHING UP** to reject something as unworthy or undesirable ○ *to turn away from a life of sin*

turn back *v* **1.** *vti* **STOP GOING FORWARD AND RETURN** to stop and return in the direction you have come from, or stop people or vehicles and make them return in the direction they have come from **2.** *vti* **REVERSE** to reverse, or cause something to reverse or go back **3.** *vt* **FOLD SOMETHING BACK** to fold something over and down ○ *turned back the top sheet on the bed*

turn down *vt* **1.** **REJECT SOMETHING** to reject or refuse something such as an offer or application **2.** **REDUCE VOLUME OR INTENSITY** to make something less powerful, bright, loud, or hot, especially by moving a knob, switch, or slider **3.** **FOLD SOMETHING DOWNWARD** to fold something or the top part of something toward the bottom, so that a double layer is formed

turn in *v* **1.** *vt* **RETURN SOMETHING AFTER USE** to give something back to its owner or to whoever is responsible for it ○ *Turn in your key at the desk before leaving.* **2.** *vt* **SUBMIT SOMETHING** to hand in or send in something such as work assigned in school **3.** *vt* **TAKE SOMEBODY TO POLICE** to hand over somebody or something to the police or other authorities **4.** *vt* **PRODUCE RESULT** to achieve a particular outcome ○ *turned in a creditable performance* **5.** *vti* **FOLD INWARD** to arrange something so that it bends or points inward, or be arranged in this way **6.** *vi* **GO TO BED** to go to bed at the end of the day (*informal*)

turn into *v* **1.** *vti* to change or develop into a different form ○ *The caterpillar will turn into a butterfly.* **2.** *vt* to start traveling on a new route, or enter a new place by changing direction ○ *turned into the driveway*

turn off *v* **1.** *vt* **STOP SOMETHING OPERATING** to make a machine or appliance stop working, or something stop flowing, by operating a control **2.** *vt* **SET SOMETHING TO OFF POSITION** to move a device such as a button, knob, or lever so that a machine stops working or something stops flowing **3.** *vti* **GO IN NEW DIRECTION** to split off from a road or path and head a different way, or take a road or path that goes in a new direction **4.** *vti* **DIMINISH ENTHUSIASM** to diminish or destroy somebody's interest or excitement, or stop being interested or excited (*informal*) **5.** *vt* **PREVENT AROUSAL** to prevent or stop somebody from becoming sexually interested or aroused (*informal*)

turn on *v* **1.** *vt* **START SOMETHING OPERATING** to make a machine or appliance operate, or make something start flowing, by operating a control **2.** *vt* **SET SOMETHING TO ON POSITION** to move a device such as a button, knob, or lever so that a machine starts working or something starts flowing **3.** *vt* **ADOPT CALCULATED BEHAVIOR** to display a particular behavior or emotion in a way that people find calculated, irritating, or insincere ○ *He'll really turn on the charm if he thinks he's losing the sale.* **4.** *vt* **REACT AGGRESSIVELY TO SOMEBODY** to react aggressively or violently to somebody **5.** *vt* **MAKE SOMEBODY EXCITED** to interest or excite somebody greatly (*informal*) **6.** *vt* **AROUSE SOMEBODY** to make somebody feel sexually excited (*informal*) **7.** *vti* **TAKE ILLEGAL DRUGS** to take drugs, especially a hallucinogenic drug, or cause somebody to take a hallucinogen or similar drug (*informal*)

turn out *v* **1.** *vt* **SWITCH LIGHT OFF** to make an electric light go out by operating its power switch **2.** *vi* **COME TO EVENT** to come to a place, especially for a special event or public occasion ○ *Hardly anybody turned out for the reunion.* **3.** *vt* **MAKE SOMEBODY LEAVE** to force somebody to leave a room, building, or residence **4.** *vi* **HAPPEN IN PARTICULAR WAY** to happen or result in a particular way, often in a way that was not expected ○ *turned out to be a nice day* **5.** *vt* **MAKE SOMETHING** to create or produce something, especially in a consistent way or by mass production ○ *turning out 400 cars a week* **6.** *vt* **DRESS SOMEBODY UP** to clothe yourself or somebody else in a particular way (*often passive*) **7.** *vti* MIL **SIGNAL GROUP TO ASSEMBLE** to call an organized group of people, usually soldiers, to assemble for duty or for a military parade **8.** *vt* **EMPTY CONTENTS** to take out the contents of a pocket or bag, usually to check or reorganize what is there **9.** *vti* **FOLD OUTWARD** to be arranged so as to bend or point outward, or arrange something in this way

turn over *v* **1.** *vti* **TURN SOMETHING OTHER WAY UP** to alter the position of the body or of an object, bringing the underside uppermost, or move so that the underside is uppermost **2.** *vt* **THINK ABOUT SOMETHING** to give something slow and careful thought, considering different aspects or possibilities **3.** *vt* **GIVE SOMETHING TO SOMEBODY ELSE** to hand something over to the police or other authorities, especially when required to do so **4.** *vt* **DELEGATE SOMETHING** to give the responsibility for something to somebody else ○ *turned over some tasks to her assistant* **5.** *vt* **PUT SOMEBODY UNDER SOMEBODY'S RESPONSIBILITY** to transfer the responsibility for somebody to another person or authority ○ *The principal turned him over to his parents.* **6.** *vt* *UK* **ROB PLACE** to break into a building or premises and steal anything thought to be valuable (*slang; often used in the passive*) **7.** *vti* **START ENGINE, OR BE STARTED** to start an engine or motor, or be started ○ *couldn't get the engine to turn over* **8.** *vt* FIN **HAVE SALES AMOUNTING TO SOMETHING** to have sales or other business transactions totaling a particular amount ○ *The firm turns over several million a month.* **9.** *vti* COMM **SELL AND RESTOCK GOODS** to sell and restock all items for sale, or be sold and restocked ○ *The produce usually turns over in 10 days.*

turn to *vi* to set to work, especially vigorously

turn up *v* **1.** *vt* **INCREASE SOMETHING** to make something louder, brighter, hotter, or more powerful, especially by operating its control **2.** *vti* **UNFOLD UPWARD** to unfold something so that it stands up instead of lying in a flat double layer, or be capable of unfolding in this way **3.** *vt* **SHORTEN GARMENT** to fold and sew the bottom edge of a garment or piece of fabric, so as to shorten it **4.** *vi* **BE FOUND** to reappear or be rediscovered after being lost or in an unknown place, often in a surprising or unexpected way ○ *It'll turn up sooner or later.* **5.** *vt* **FIND SOMETHING BY SEARCHING** to uncover something that was hidden or previously unknown by investigating, hunting, or digging ○ *He didn't expect to turn up such an interesting story.* **6.** *vi* **ARRIVE** to come or appear somewhere, especially in a casual or unplanned way ○ *She just turned up yesterday.* **7.** *vi* **HAPPEN** to take place luckily or unexpectedly to settle matters or put things right ○ *They manage to get along… something always seems to turn up.*

turn·a·bout /túrnə bòwt/ *n* **1.** the act of turning to face in the opposite direction **2.** a shift from one situation, opinion, policy, or attitude to another that is the complete opposite

turn·a·round /túrnə ròwnd/ *n* **1.** **PLACE FOR TURNING AUTOMOBILE AROUND** a circular or curved driveway or section of road where vehicles can turn around **2.** COMM same as **turnabout** **3.** **BIG IMPROVEMENT** a dramatic improvement in a bad or unsatisfactory situation **4.** **TIME TAKEN TO DO ENTIRE JOB** the time it takes to carry out all the necessary procedures between receiving an order or task and the shipment of the order or completion of the task **5.** **PREPARATION OF VEHICLE BETWEEN TRIPS** the process of unloading and reloading, refueling, and checking an aircraft, ship, or vehicle between journeys **6.** TRANSP **TIME SPENT ON VEHICLE'S TURNAROUND** the time taken on the process of unloading and reloading, refueling, and checking an aircraft, ship, or vehicle between journeys

turn-based *adj* describes a computer game in which the action stops while a player makes his or her move, as opposed to continuing in real time ○ *You can choose from turn-based or real-time combat and toggle between the two.*

turn·buck·le /túrn bùk'l/ *n* a device to tighten or loosen rope or wire, consisting of a tube through which the rope or wire is threaded and held so that the tension can be adjusted

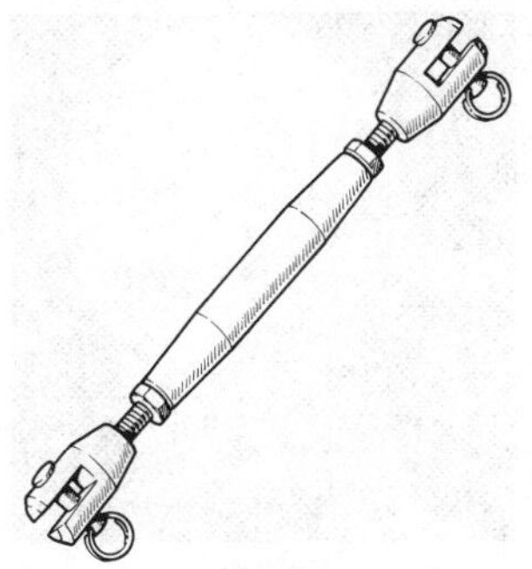

turnbuckle

turn·coat /túrn kṓt/ *n* somebody who abandons or betrays a group or cause and joins its opponents

turn·down /túrn dòwn/ *n* **1.** *US* **REJECTION** a rejection of something such as an offer or application **2.** **SOMEBODY REJECTED** somebody who has been turned down or rejected for something ○ *a credit card turndown* **3.** **SOMETHING FOLDED DOWN** something that is folded down or over from the top **4.** ECON same as **downturn** ■ *adj* **FOLDED DOWN** folded down or over from the top

turned-on *adj* (*slang*) **1.** **SEXUALLY EXCITED** sexually aroused or excited **2.** **HIP** aware of or involved in the most modern trends in culture and fashion **3.** **HIGH ON DRUGS** under the influence of a drug such as cannabis or LSD, or familiar with its effects as a result of having taken it

turn·er /túrnər/ *n* **1.** somebody whose job involves operating a lathe **2.** somebody or something that turns or that is used for turning something else, e.g., a device for turning food while it is cooking ○ *a pancake turner*

Tur·ner /túrnər/, **J. M. W.** (1775–1851) British painter and watercolorist. His powerful landscape and seascape paintings used color to explore the effects of light, and influenced the French impressionists. His works include *Hannibal and his Army Crossing the Alps* (1812) and *Rain, Steam, and Speed* (1844). Full name **Turner, Joseph Mallord William**

> "My business is to paint not what I know, but what I see."
> [Attributed to J. M. W. Turner]

Tur·ner, John Napier (*b.* 1929) Canadian prime minister (1984). He was a Liberal member of the Canadian parliament (1962–75) and leader of the Liberal Party (1984–90). See table at **prime minister**

Tur·ner, Lana (1920–95) US actor. She is known for her roles in such Hollywood movies as *The Postman Always Rings Twice* (1946) and *The Bad and the Beautiful* (1952). Born **Turner, Julia Jean Mildred Frances**

Tur·ner, Nat (1800–31) US slave leader. He led a brief rebellion (1831) of enslaved African Americans that ended in bloodshed. He fled, but after six weeks was captured and hanged.

> "I had a vision—and I saw white spirits and Black spirits engaged in battle, and the sun was darkened—the thunder rolled in the Heavens, and blood flowed in streams—and I heard a voice saying, 'Such is your luck, such you are called to see; and let it come rough or smooth, you must surely bear it.'"
> [Nat Turner, *The Confessions of Nat Turner, the leader of the late insurrection in Southampton, Va.*; 1831]

Tur·ner, Ted (*b.* 1938) US business executive and philanthropist. He built his broadcasting system into an international media empire. Full name **Turner, Robert Edward III**. See illustration on next page

Tur·ner's syn·drome *n* a genetic disorder affecting women in which only one X chromosome per cell is present, instead of two, resulting in underdeveloped ovaries and underdevelopment of the womb,

Ted Turner

vagina, and breasts [Mid-20C. After Henry Hubert *Turner* (1892–1970), US physician]

turn·er·y /túrnəree/ (*plural* **-ies**) *n* **1.** the technique, art, or skill of forming and contouring using a lathe **2.** a room or building where lathes are used

turn·ing /túrning/ *n* **1.** PROCESS OF MAKING TURN the act or process of executing a turn **2.** DEVIATION a deviation from a straight or planned course **3.** *UK* ROADS same as **turn** *n* (sense 3) **4.** HANDICRAFT FABRIC THAT FORMS HEM the amount of fabric that will be turned back to form a hem at the edge of a piece of sewing **5.** MANUF same as **turnery** (sense 1) ■ **turn·ings** *npl* MANUF WASTE MATERIAL FROM LATHE the waste material produced when something is turned on a lathe

turn·ing cir·cle *n UK* same as **turning radius**

turn·ing point *n* **1.** a time or incident that marks the beginning of a completely new, and usually better, stage in somebody's life or in the development of something **2.** a minimum or maximum point on a plane curve

turn·ing ra·di·us *n* the smallest circle in which a vehicle can complete a 360° turn

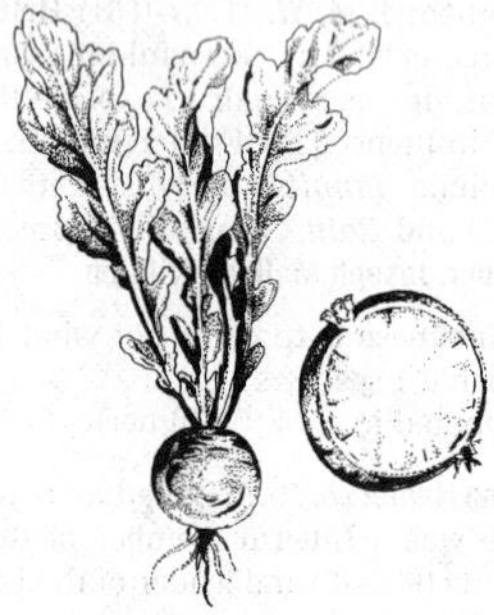

turnip

tur·nip /túrnip/ *n* **1.** a white rounded fleshy root that is cooked and eaten as a vegetable **2.** a plant that produces turnips. Latin name: *Brassica rapa.* [Mid-16C. < *tur-* (origin ?) + Old English *nǣp* "turnip" (< Latin *napus*)]

turn·key /túrn kèe/ *adj* complete and ready to use upon delivery or installation ○ *specified a turnkey system* ■ *n* (*plural* **-keys**) a keeper of keys, especially in a jail (*archaic*)

turn·off /túrn àwf, -òf/ *n* **1.** ROAD BRANCHING OFF MAIN ROAD a road that branches off a main road, especially a highway exit **2.** ACT OF TURNING OFF the act or process of turning off ○ *The truck was too long to make the turnoff.* **3.** SOMETHING DISGUSTING OR OFF-PUTTING somebody or something that causes a complete loss of interest, enthusiasm, or sexual arousal (*informal*)

turn-on *n* somebody or something that causes sexual arousal (*informal*)

turn·out /túrn òwt/ *n* **1.** ATTENDANCE the number of people who attend or take part in an event ○ *expecting a huge turnout for the homecoming game* **2.** POL NUMBER OF VOTERS the number or proportion of voters who register their vote in an election **3.** BUSINESS AMOUNT OF WORK PRODUCED the total quantity or amount produced, e.g., by a particular company or manufacturing process **4.** *US* ROADS WIDENED PART OF STREET a section where a narrow roadway is broader, allowing vehicles to pass each other, pull over, or park **5.** CLOTHING OUTFIT the clothes or equipment somebody is wearing ○ *a smart turnout* **6.** BALLET OUTWARD ROTATION OF DANCER'S LEGS the outward rotating movement from the hip sockets of a classical ballet dancer's legs

turn·o·ver /túrn ṑvər/ *n* **1.** FOOD FILLED PASTRY a filled pastry made by folding a square or circle of pastry in half over a filling to form a semicircle or triangle **2.** HR CHANGE IN EMPLOYEES the number of employees in an organization who leave and are replaced over a given period ○ *job dissatisfaction that results in high turnover* **3.** ACCT AMOUNT OF BUSINESS the amount of business transacted over a given period of time, especially when expressed as gross revenue **4.** COMM THROUGHPUT OF INVENTORY the rate at which business inventory is sold and replaced **5.** FIN NUMBER OF SHARES SOLD the number of shares sold on a stock exchange within a particular period of time **6.** SPORTS LOSS OF POSSESSION in basketball and football, a loss of possession of the ball resulting from error or violation of rules **7.** ACT OF TURNING OVER an act or process of turning something over ○ *a turnover in leadership* ■ *adj* ABLE TO BE FOLDED OVER designed to be turned or folded over

turn·pike /túrn pīk/ *n* **1.** TOLL ROAD a toll expressway or highway, usually a major long-distance one **2.** ROAD BARRIER a gate formerly used to bar the way onto a section of road or a bridge until a toll had been paid **3.** ROAD WITH TURNPIKE in former times, a road that travelers were allowed to use only after paying a toll at the turnpike [14C. < TURN + PIKE[3]]

turn·sole /túrn sṑl/ *n* **1.** a purple dye obtained from a Mediterranean plant **2.** an annual plant that yields turnsole. Native to: Mediterranean. Latin name: *Chrozophora tinctoria.* [14C. Via Old French *tournesole* < Old Italian *tornasole* < *tornare* "turn" + *sol* "sun"]

turn·stile /túrn stīl/ *n* a mechanical barrier designed to let people pass through a narrow opening one at a time between revolving bars

turn·stone /túrn stṑn/ *n* a shorebird with mottled black or tortoiseshell markings. Native to: Arctic coast, migrating southward. Genus: *Arenaria.* [Late 17C. Because it turns over stones to find food]

turn·ta·ble /túrn tàyb'l/ *n* **1.** PHONOGRAPH DECK a phonograph deck, especially without the amplifier and speakers, and as distinct from a separate tape player, CD player, or tuner **2.** REVOLVING PLATFORM ON PHONOGRAPH the flat round revolving plate on which the record rests on a phonograph **3.** ROTATING PLATFORM a rotating platform for turning around a vehicle such as a railroad locomotive so that it is facing another direction

turn·ta·ble lad·der *n UK* same as **aerial ladder**

turn·up *n* **1.** *US* SOMETHING TURNING UP something that turns up or appears unexpectedly **2.** *UK* FOLD AT BOTTOM OF TROUSER LEG something that is designed to be turned or folded up, e.g., a cuff at the bottom of a pants leg **3.** *US* ECON same as **upturn** ■ *adj* FOR TURNING UP designed to be folded or turned up

tur·pen·tine /túrpən tīn/ *n* **1.** OIL USED AS SOLVENT a colorless, flammable, strong-smelling essential oil. Use: paint solvent, in medicine. **2.** SUBSTANCE FROM PINE TREES a viscous substance obtained from coniferous trees. Use: manufacture of paint solvent. **3.** STICKY SUBSTANCE FROM TEREBINTH TREE a brownish yellow sticky mixture of essential oil and resin that comes from the terebinth tree ■ *vt* (**-tined, -tin·ing, -tines**) **1.** TREAT SOMETHING WITH TURPENTINE to treat or thin something with turpentine **2.** EXTRACT TURPENTINE FROM SOMETHING to extract turpentine from trees [14C. Via Old French *terbentine* "terebinth resin" < Greek *terebinthos* "terebinth tree"]

tur·pen·tine tree *n* a tree that yields turpentine, e.g., the terebinth

tur·pi·tude /túrpə tòod/ *n* extreme immorality or wickedness (*formal*) [15C. Directly or via French < Latin *turpitudo* < *turpis* "repulsive"]

turps /turps/ *n* same as **turpentine** *n* (sense 1) (*informal*) [Early 19C. Shortening]

tur·quoise /túr kwòyz, -kòyz/ *n* **1.** a greenish blue semiprecious stone that is a form of aluminum copper phosphate. Source: igneous rocks. Use: gems. **2.** a bright greenish blue color [15C. < Old French *(pierre) turqueise* "Turkish (stone)"; because first found in Turkestan] —**tur·quoise** *adj*

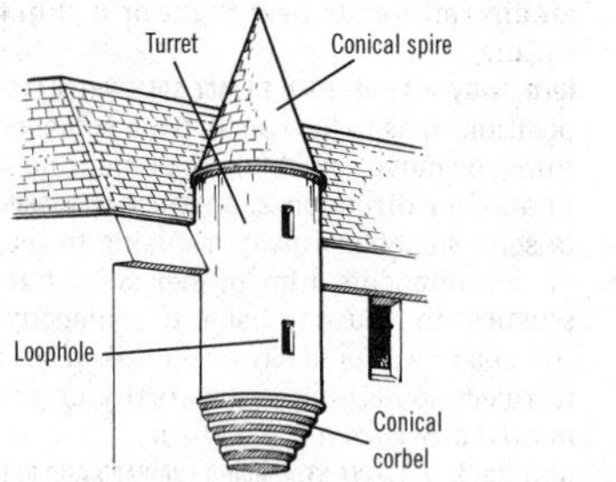

turret (sense 2)

tur·ret /túrrət/ *n* **1.** ARMS DOME CONTAINING GUN a rotating armored structure on a ship or tank, or a dome projecting from the fuselage of an aircraft, containing one or more guns and a gun crew **2.** SMALL TOWER a small rounded tower that projects from a wall or corner of a large building such as a castle **3.** MECH ENG PART OF LATHE a device on a lathe that holds a range of tools [14C. < Old French *tourete* "small tower" < *tour* "tower" < Latin *turris*]

tur·ret·ed /túrrətəd/ *adj* **1.** constructed or designed to include turrets **2.** shaped like a long pointed spiral

tur·ret lathe *n* a lathe for long work pieces, using a large number of tools carried on the revolving tool holder or turret

turtle

tur·tle[1] /túrt'l/ *n* **1.** *US* a water- or land-dwelling reptile with a body protected by a bony shell, e.g., a tortoise or terrapin **2.** *UK* same as **sea turtle** **3.** the flesh of an edible type of turtle used as food [Mid-16C. Origin ?] ◇ **turn turtle** to turn upside down

tur·tle[2] /túrt'l/ *n* same as **turtledove** (*archaic*) [Pre-12C. < Latin *turtur*, an imitation of its call]

tur·tle·back /túrt'l bàk/ *n* an arched cover for protecting the deck of a ship in heavy seas

tur·tle·dove /túrt'l dùv/ *n* **1.** a slender dove with black-and-chestnut upper parts, a pink breast, and a black-and-white neck, noted for its purring call. Native to: Europe, migrating to Africa. Latin name: *Streptopelia turtur.* **2.** *US* BIRDS same as **mourning dove** [13C. < TURTLE[2]]

tur·tle·head /túrt'l hèd/ (*plural* **-heads** or *same*) *n* a perennial plant found near running water. Flowers: white, purplish, greenish, or yellowish. Native to: eastern North America. Genus: *Chelone.* [Mid-19C. < the shape of its flowers]

tur·tle·neck /túrt'l nèk/ *n* **1.** a tight-fitting collar on a garment such as a sweater, reaching high up the neck and then folded down **2.** a sweater or other garment that has a turtleneck **3.** *UK* CLOTHING same as **mock turtle** (sense 1)

turves plural of **turf**

Tus·ca·loo·sa /tùskə lóossə/ city in western Alabama on the Black Warrior River, southwest of Birmingham. Population: 79,149 (2002 estimate).

Tus·can /túskən/ *adj* **1.** OF TUSCANY relating to the Italian region of Tuscany, or its people or culture **2.** OF

STYLE OF ARCHITECTURE relating to a classical order of architecture characterized by plain bases and capitals and unfluted columns ■ *n* **1. SOMEBODY FROM TUSCANY** somebody who comes from Tuscany **2. STANDARD ITALIAN** the standard and literary form of Italian, principally based on the dialect of Florence [14C. Via Old French *tuscan*, Italian *toscano* < Latin *Tuscanus* < *Tuscus* "Etruscan"]

Tus·ca·ny /túskənee/ region in northern Italy, a centre of culture during the Renaissance period. Capital: Florence. Population: 3,536,392 (2000). Area: 8,878 sq. mi./22,993 sq. km.

Tus·ca·ro·ra /tùskə ráwrə/ (*plural same* or **-ras**) *n* a member of an Iroquois people who lived in North Carolina and who now live mainly in New York State and Ontario. In 1722 the Tuscarora joined the Iroquois Confederacy, which then became known as the Six Nations. [Mid-17C. < Iroquois, "hemp gatherer"]

tu·sche /tŏŏshə/ *n* a thick black liquid that is used as a drawing medium in lithography and as a protective coating (**resist**) in silk-screen printing and etching [Late 19C. < German, a back-formation < *tuschen* "draw in ink," via French *toucher* < Old French *touchier* (see TOUCH)]

tush[1] /tŏŏsh/ *n* somebody's buttocks (*slang*) [Mid-20C. Alteration of Yiddish *tokhes*]

tush[2] /tush/ *interj* an expression of mild disapproval or disdain (*archaic*) [Mid-16C. Natural exclamation]

tush·y /tŏŏshee/ (*plural* **-ies**), **tush·ie** *n* same as **tush**[1] (*slang*)

tusk /tusk/ *n* **1. ENLARGED TOOTH** an enlarged pointed front tooth that projects from the mouth in animals such as the elephant, walrus, and wild boar and is often used for fighting **2. TENON JOINT** in joinery, a form of tenon that has a short projecting part to make it stronger ■ *vti* (**tusked, tusk·ing, tusks**) **JAB TUSK INTO SOMEBODY OR SOMETHING** to use a tusk or tusks to attack, dig at, or stab somebody or something [Old English *tūsc*, *tux* < Indo-European, "tooth"] —**tusked** *adj*

Tus·ke·gee /tu skéegee/ city in eastern Alabama, east of Montgomery and west of Phenix City. It is home to Tuskegee University. Population: 11,836 (2002 estimate).

tusk·er /túskər/ *n* a wild boar, elephant, or other animal with large tusks (*informal*)

tusk shell *n* MARINE BIOL same as **tooth shell**

tus·sah /tússə/ (*plural* **-sahs** or *same*) *n* **1. SILK FABRIC** a coarse brownish or yellowish silk fabric with an attractive uneven surface, woven from the silk of the silkworm of an Asian moth **2. SILK THREAD** the silk thread produced by the silkworm of an Asian moth **3. SILKWORM** the silkworm of an Asian moth, from which a coarse silk is obtained. Latin name: *Antheraea paphia*. [Late 16C. < Hindi *tasar*, probably < Sanskrit *tasara* "shuttle"]

Tus·saud /tū sṓ, too-, tə sáwd/, **Madame** (1760–1850) Swiss wax-modeler. She made death masks in Paris of victims of the French Revolution, which she exhibited in Great Britain, and founded Madame Tussaud's Exhibition in London (1835). Born **Grosholtz, Marie**

tus·sis /tússiss/ *n* a cough or coughing (*technical*) [< Latin] —**tus·sal** *adj* —**tus·sive** *adj*

tus·sle /túss'l/ *vi* (**-sled, -sling, -sles**) to have a vigorous physical or verbal struggle with somebody ■ *n* a vigorous physical or verbal struggle [15C. Probably < N English dialect *touse* "pull about"]

tus·sock /tússək/ *n* a small thick clump of growing vegetation, usually coarse grass or sedge [Mid-16C. Origin ?] —**tus·sock·y** *adj*

tus·sock grass *n* a grass that grows in clumps

tus·sock moth *n* a moth whose caterpillars are covered in tufts of brightly colored hair. Some are pests of crops and shade trees. Family: Lymantriidae.

tus·sore /tú sàwr/ (*plural* **-sores** or *same*) *n UK* **1.** TEXTILES same as **tussah** (senses 1–2) **2.** INSECTS same as **tussah** (sense 3) [Late 19C. Alteration of TUSSAH]

tut /tut/, **tut-tut** *interj* a clicking sound made with the tongue, or a spoken imitation of this sound, used as an expression of annoyance or disapproval, sometimes ironically ■ *vi* (**tut·ted, tut·ting, tuts; tut-tut·ted, tut-tut·ting, tut-tuts**) to make a clicking sound with the tongue to express annoyance or dissatisfaction [Early 16C. Natural exclamation]

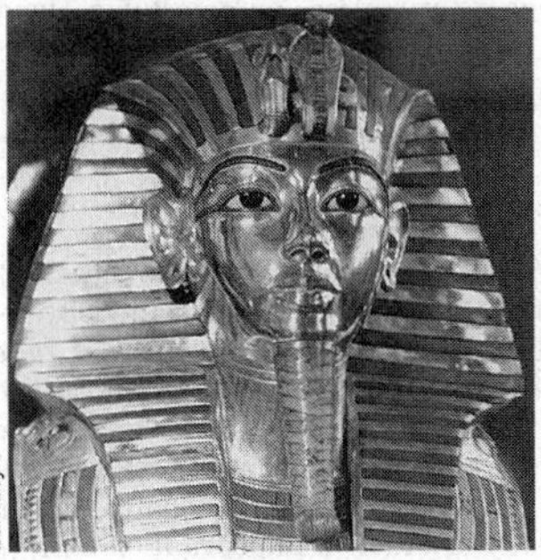

Barnaby's

Tutankhamen

Tu·tan·kha·men /tŏŏt'n kaámən/, **Tu·tan·kha·mun** /-kaa mŏŏn/ (1343–1325 B.C.) Egyptian pharaoh. His sumptuously decorated tomb was discovered almost intact in 1922.

tu·tee /too tée/ *n* the student of a tutor [Early 20C. < TUTOR + -EE]

tu·te·lage /tŏŏt'lij/ *n* **1. TEACHING** instruction and guidance provided by somebody such as a tutor ○ *Under her tutelage, he became a first-rate sailor.* **2. SUPERVISION BY TUTOR** the condition of being supervised or protected by a tutor or guardian **3. CONDITION OF BEING TUTOR** the condition of being a tutor or guardian [Early 17C. < Latin *tutela* "guardianship" < *tut-*, past participle of *tueri* "watch over"]

tu·te·lar·y /tŏŏt'l èrree/, **tu·te·lar** /tŏŏt'lər/ *adj* (*formal* or *literary*) **1. ACTING AS PROTECTOR** acting in the role of a protector or guardian ○ *tutelary saints* **2. OF GUARDIAN** relating to or belonging to a guardian ■ *n* (*plural* **-ies**; *plural* **-lars**) **GUARDING PRESENCE** a tutelary being or person, especially a saint or deity (*literary*) [Early 17C. < Latin *tutelarius* < *tutela* (see TUTELAGE)]

tu·tor /tŏŏtər/ *n* **1. TEACHER** a teacher who instructs an individual student or a small group of students, especially one teaching students in need of remedial work **2.** *US* **LOW-RANKING US UNIVERSITY TEACHER** in some US universities, a teacher of a rank below instructor **3. BRITISH UNIVERSITY TEACHER** in British universities, an academic who is responsible for teaching and advising an allocated group of students ■ *v* (**-tored, -tor·ing, -tors**) **1.** *vti* **ACT AS TUTOR** to give somebody individual tuition in a subject or skill **2.** *vi US* **RECEIVE PRIVATE LESSONS** to study under a tutor [14C. Via Anglo-Norman < Latin, "guardian" < *tut-* (see TUTELAGE)] —**tu·tor·age** *n* —**tu·tor·ship** *n*

SYNONYMS See ***teach***.

tu·to·ri·al /too táwree əl/ *n* **1. LESSON FROM BOOK** a chapter of a book or manual, or a section of a computer program, designed to provide instruction or training using exercises and assignments **2. LESSON WITH TUTOR** a teaching session spent individually or in a small group under the direction of a tutor ■ *adj* **RELATING TO TUTOR** relating to or belonging to a tutor, or to the role and responsibilities of a tutor

Tut·si /tŏŏtsee/ (*plural same* or **-sis**) *n* a member of an African people living in Rwanda and Burundi [Mid-20C. < Bantu] —**Tut·si** *adj*

tut·ti /tŏŏtee/ *n* the part of a musical composition in which all the performers take part, as opposed to a solo section [Early 18C. Via Italian < Latin *totus* "entire"]

tut·ti-frut·ti /tŏŏtee frŏŏtee/ (*plural* **tut·ti-frut·tis**) *n* an ice cream, dessert, or type of candy containing a variety of chopped, usually dried or candied fruit [Mid-19C. < Italian, "all fruits"]

tut-tut *interj, vi* same as **tut**

tu·tu /tŏŏtoo/ *n* a ballet dancer's skirt that is very short and made of layers of stiffened net so that it stands out from the body [Early 20C. < French, baby-talk alteration of *cucu* < *cul* "buttocks" < Latin *culus*]

Express Newspapers

Desmond Tutu

Tu·tu /tŏŏtoo/, **Desmond** (*b.* 1931) South African archbishop and political activist. A leader of the anti-apartheid movement, he was the first Black bishop of Johannesburg (1984) and archbishop of Cape Town (1986–96). He was awarded the Nobel Peace Prize (1984). Full name **Tutu, Desmond Mpilo**

> "If we are to say that religion cannot be concerned with politics then we are really saying that there is a substantial part of human life in which God's writ does not run. If it is not God's, then whose is it? Who is in charge if not the God and Father of our Lord Jesus Christ?"
> [Desmond Tutu. Quoted in *The Words of Desmond Tutu*, Naomi Tutu (ed.); 1989]

tu·tul·bay /too tŏŏl bày/ *adj Carib* utterly confused or bewildered, especially by love (*slang*) [Late 20C. Via French Creole< French *tout troublé* "completely upset"]

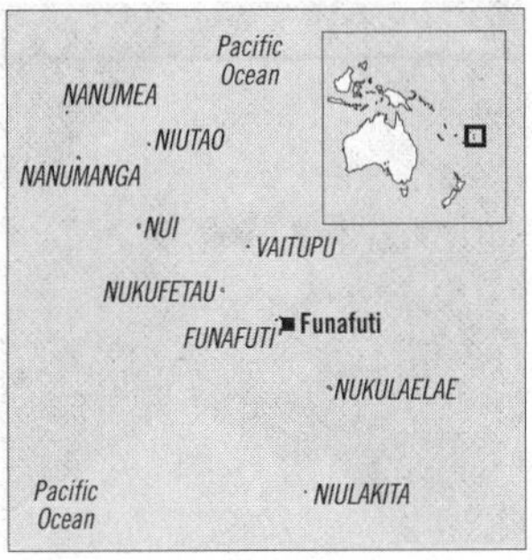

Tuvalu

Tu·va·lu /too vaáloo, tŏŏvə lŏŏ/ country consisting of coral islands in the western Pacific Ocean. Fiji and Samoa, each about 650 mi./1,050 km away, are the islands' nearest neighbors. It became an independent member of the British Commonwealth in 1978. Language: English, Tuvaluan. Currency: Australian dollar. Capital: Funafuti. Population: 11,305 (2003). Area: 10 sq. mi./26 sq. km. Former name **Ellice Islands** (until 1975) —**Tu·val·u·an** /too vaáloo ən, tŏŏvə lŏŏ ən/ *n, adj*

tux /tuks/ *n* CLOTHING same as **tuxedo** (*informal*) [Early 20C. Shortening]

tux·e·do /tuk séedō/ (*plural* **-dos** or **-does**) *n* **1.** a formal set of clothing for a man including an elegantly styled, usually black jacket and matching trousers, usually with a band of silk down each leg, dress shirt, bow tie, and cummerbund **2.** an elegantly styled, usually black jacket worn by men to formal social occasions, especially as part of an outfit for evening wear [Late 19C. After *Tuxedo* Park, town in New York]

tu·yère /too yér, twee-/, **twyer** /twīr/ *n* an opening in the refractory lining and shell of a furnace through which air is forced in order to promote combustion [Late 18C. < French < *tuyau* "pipe"]

Tuz·la /tŏŏzlə/ city in northeastern Bosnia and Herzegovina. Before the Bosnian-Croatian-Serbian War Tuzla was a major road and rail junction and mining center, during the war it became a Bosnian government stronghold and a major United Nations-run refugee center. Population: 121,717 (1991).

tv *abbr* ONLINE Tuvalu (*used in Internet addresses*) See table at **domain name**

TV[1] *n* same as **television** (*informal*) [Mid-20C. Abbreviation]

TV[2] *n* same as **transvestite** (*informal*) [Mid-20C. Abbreviation]

TV din·ner *n* a precooked frozen or chilled meal that can be reheated in the oven or microwave and eaten straight from the tray or dish

Tver /tver/ city in western Russia, at the confluence of the Volga and Tvertsa rivers. Population: 479,610 (1995). Former name **Kalinin** (1933–90)

TV mov·ie *n* a movie that is made to be shown on television and is not usually released in theaters

TVP *n* a high-protein product made from processed soybeans that are formed into chunks or ground and flavored to taste like meat. Full form **textured vegetable protein**

tw *abbr* ONLINE Taiwan (*used in Internet addresses*) See table at **domain name**

T-W *abbr* three-wheeler (motorcycle)

twa /twaa/ *n Scotland* same as **two** (*nonstandard*) [Variant]

twad·dle /twódd'l/ *n* nonsensical or pretentious speech or writing (*informal*) ■ *vi* (**-dled, -dling, -dles**) to speak or write twaddle (*dated informal*) [Late 18C. Origin ?] —**twad·dler** *n*

twain /twayn/ *npl* two people or things (*archaic or literary*) ○ *"Oh, East is East, and West is West, and never the twain shall meet."* (Rudyard Kipling, *The Ballad of East and West*) [Old English *twēgen* < Germanic, "two"]

Library of Congress

Mark Twain

Twain /twayn/, **Mark** (1835–1910) US writer. He wrote humorous travel books and the classic stories *The Adventures of Tom Sawyer* (1876) and *The Adventures of Huckleberry Finn* (1884). Born **Clemens, Samuel Langhorne**. See Cultural note at **adventure**

> "That's always the way; it don't make no difference whether you do right or wrong, a person's conscience ain't got no sense, and it just goes for him *anyway*."
> [Mark Twain, *The Adventures of Huckleberry Finn*; 1884]

> "All say, 'How hard it is that we have to die'—a strange complaint to come from the mouths of people who have had to live."
> [Mark Twain, *Pudd'nhead Wilson*; 1894]

> "Man is the Only Animal that Blushes, Or has to."
> [Mark Twain, *Following the Equator*; 1897]

twang /twang/ *n* **1.** NASAL SOUND a nasal quality of voice associated with various accents ○ *a Texas twang* **2.** SOUND OF TIGHT STRING VIBRATING the sharp resonating noise made when something such as a tight string on an instrument is plucked or released ■ *vti* (**twanged, twang·ing, twangs**) **1.** VIBRATE WITH TWANG to produce a twang, or make something do this **2.** MUSIC STRUM SOMETHING CARELESSLY to play a stringed instrument, or a tune on a stringed instrument, in a rough amateur style **3.** LANGUAGE SPEAK WITH TWANG to speak or say something with a twang [Mid-16C. An imitation of the sound] —**twang·y** *adj*

'twas /twuz, twəz/ *contr* it was (*archaic or literary*)

twat /twot/ *n* **1.** a highly offensive term for a woman's vagina or genital area (*taboo*) **2.** *UK* a highly offensive term for somebody regarded as unintelligent, worthless, or detestable (*taboo insult*) [Mid-17C. Origin ?]

tway·blade /twáy blàyd/ *n* an orchid that has only two leaves, arranged opposite each other, at the base. Genera: *Listera* or *Liparis* or *Ophrys*. [Late 16C. < obsolete variant of TWAIN]

tweak /tweek/ *vt* (**tweaked, tweak·ing, tweaks**) **1.** PINCH SOMEBODY AFFECTIONATELY to pinch somebody gently and usually affectionately or playfully ○ *tweaked the baby on the cheek* **2.** TWIST SOMETHING QUICKLY to take hold of something between the finger and thumb and twist it sharply **3.** ADJUST SOMETHING SLIGHTLY to make a slight adjustment or change to something, especially in order to improve it or fix it (*informal*) ○ *tweaked the engine* **4.** TEASE SOMEBODY to tease somebody, either playfully or maliciously ■ *n* **1.** PINCH a pinch or twist with the finger and thumb **2.** SLIGHT ADJUSTMENT a slight adjustment or change to something, especially in order to improve it or fix it **3.** TEASING REMARK a teasing remark or action [Early 17C. Probably variant of obsolete *twick* < Old English *twiccian* < Germanic]

twee /twee/ *adj* dainty or pretty in an overdone and affected way [Early 20C. Baby-talk alteration of SWEET] —**twee·ly** *adv* —**twee·ness** *n*

tweed /tweed/ *n* a fairly rough, thick woolen fabric often made with several different shades of wool to give it a distinctive flecked appearance. Use: warm clothing. ■ **tweeds** *npl* a tweed suit or outfit [Mid-19C. Alteration of *tweel*, Scottish variant of TWILL, after the river TWEED]

ORIGIN Early accounts date the coinage of ***tweed*** to 1831, and ascribe it to the London cloth merchant James Locke (although Locke himself in his book *Tweed and Don* (1860) does not make any such claim). The term was in general use by 1850, and it was registered as a trademark.

Tweed /tweed/ river of southern Scotland and northeastern England, flowing into the North Sea at Berwick-upon-Tweed. Its lower course runs along the Scottish-English border. Length: 97 mi./160 km.

Tweed, William Marcy (1823–78) US politician. His Tammany Society took control of New York City's politics and finances in the 1850s and 1860s. Known as **Boss Tweed**

tweed·y /twéedee/ (**-i·er, -i·est**) *adj* **1.** *US* CASUAL AND INFORMAL having an appearance or manner that is casual and somewhat disordered, in the manner often associated with academics or people who are fond of the outdoors **2.** WEARING TWEED habitually dressed in tweed **3.** OF TWEED made of or resembling tweed —**tweed·i·ness** *n*

'tween /tween/ *prep, adv* same as **between** (*archaic or literary*) [13C. Shortening]

tweet /tweet/ *n* a light high-pitched note, especially one sung by a small bird ■ *vi* (**tweet·ed, tweet·ing, tweets**) to make the light high-pitched sound of a small bird [Mid-19C. An imitation of the sound]

tweet·er /twéetər/ *n* a loudspeaker used to reproduce high-frequency sounds, e.g., in a hi-fi system

tweeze /tweez/ (**tweezed, tweez·ing, tweez·es**) *vt* to pull out or manipulate something using tweezers [Mid-20C. Back-formation < TWEEZERS]

tweez·er /twéezər/ *n* a pair of tweezers

tweez·ers /twéezərz/ *npl* a metal tool consisting of two narrow slightly curved arms joined at one end, used for extracting or holding small objects [Mid-17C. Alteration of obsolete *tweeze* "tweezer case" < French *étuis*, plural of *étui* (see ÉTUI)]

twelfth /twelfth/ *n* one of twelve equal parts of something [Old English *twelfta*. < Germanic, "twelve"] —**twelfth** *adj, adv*

Twelfth Day *n* CHR same as **Epiphany**

Twelfth Night *n* January 5, the day before Epiphany in the Christian calendar, or the evening of that

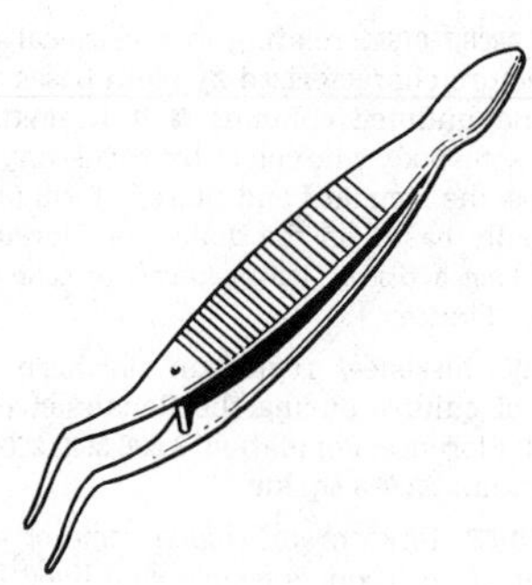

tweezers

day. It was formerly a time of special celebration at the end of the Christmas season.

CULTURAL NOTE ***Twelfth Night*** a play (1600?) by English dramatist William Shakespeare. A comedy set in Illyria, it tells of shipwrecked Viola, who disguises herself as a young man called Cesario and enters the service of Orsino. Orsino loves Olivia, who falls in love with Cesario, while Viola herself is attracted to Orsino. The reappearance of Viola's twin brother Sebastian ultimately brings a happy conclusion to the complicated plot, which also features the colorful characters Malvolio, Sir Andrew Aguecheek, and Sir Toby Belch. The saying "some men are born great, some achieve greatness, and some have greatness thrust upon them" comes from this play.

~~**twelth**~~ incorrect spelling of **twelfth**

twelve /twelv/ *n* **1.** 12 the number 12 **2.** SOMETHING WITH VALUE OF 12 something in a numbered series with a value of twelve **3.** GROUP OF TWELVE a group of twelve people or objects [Old English *twelf* < Germanic, "two left," that is "two left beyond ten"] —**twelve** *adj, pron*

Twelve A·pos·tles, Twelve *npl* according to the Bible, eleven of the twelve followers originally chosen by Jesus Christ, together with Matthias, who was chosen to replace Judas

twelve-mile lim·it *n* an offshore boundary 12 miles from a country's coast, claimed by some countries as marking the territorial limit of their jurisdiction in order to safeguard fishing rights and limit the approach of foreign vessels

twelve·mo /twélv mō/ (*plural* **-mos**) *n* PRINTING same as **duodecimo** [Early 18C. Pronunciation of the printers' abbreviation *12mo*]

twelve·month /twélv mùnth/ *n* a calendar year (*archaic*)

twelve·pen·ny nail /twélv pènnee-/ *n US* a nail that is 3 ¼ in./8.25 cm long [< the original cost per hundred]

twelve-step pro·gram *n* a program for recovery from addiction, based on the methods of Alcoholics Anonymous and involving self-improvement techniques

Twelve Ta·bles *npl* the earliest code of Roman law on civil, criminal, and religious matters, dating back to 451–450 B.C.

~~**twelveth**~~ incorrect spelling of **twelfth**

twelve-tone *adj* relating to or using compositional techniques based on strict sequences of notes selected from the 12 notes of the chromatic scale

twelve-tone row *n* MUSIC same as **tone row**

twen·ti·eth /twéntee əth/ *n* one of twenty equal parts of something [Old English *twentigoþa* < Germanic, "twenty"] —**twen·ti·eth** *adj, adv*

twen·ty /twéntee/ *n* (*plural* **-ties**) **1.** 20 the number 20 **2.** GROUP OF 20 a group of twenty people or objects **3.** $20 BILL a bill worth twenty dollars ■ **twen·ties** *npl* **1.** NUMBERS 20 TO 29 the numbers 20 to 29, particularly as a range of temperature ○ *in the low twenties* **2.** YEARS FROM 20 TO 29 the years from 20 to 29 in a century ○ *in the late twenties* **3.** PERIOD FROM AGE 20 TO 29 the period of somebody's life from the age of 20 to 29 ○ *when I was in my twenties* [Old English *twēntig* < Germanic, "twice ten"] —**twen·ty** *adj, pron*

24/7 /twèntee fawr sévvən/ (*slang*) *adv* constantly or around the clock ○ *now open 24/7* ■ *adj* occurring, happening, or appearing 24 hours a day, 7 days a week

twen·ty-one *n* CARDS same as **blackjack** *n* (senses 1–2)

twen·ty ques·tions *n* a game in which one player thinks of an object and others try to guess what it is by asking questions that can be answered only with "yes" or "no"

twen·ty·some·thing /twéntee sùmthing/ *n* somebody who is between 20 and 30 years old (*informal; usually used in the plural*) —**twen·ty·some·thing** *adj*

twen·ty-twen·ty, 20/20 *adj* describes standard vision or eyesight [< the figures denoting standard eyesight at a distance of 20 feet]

.22 /twèntee to͞o/ *n* a gun or rifle that uses a bullet with a diameter of .22 in., usually used for killing small game.

'twere /twur/ *contr* it were (*archaic or literary*) [Early 17C. Contraction]

twerp /twurp/, **twirp** *n* an offensive term that deliberately insults somebody's seriousness or importance (*slang*) [Late 19C. Origin ?]

Twi /twee/ (*plural same or* **Twis**) *n* **1.** a member of an African people who live in southern Ghana **2.** the language of the Twi people, a dialect of Akan. Native speakers: 1,400,000. [Late 19C. < Kwa] —**Twi** *adj*

twi·bill /twī̀ bìl, twī́b'l/ *n* a double-edged battleax, formerly used as a weapon [Old English *twibil* < *twi-* "two" + *bill* "bladed weapon"]

twice /twīss/ *adv* **1.** on two occasions, or in two instances **2.** double in amount or degree [Old English *twige* < Indo-European]

twice-laid *adj* describes ropes or cables that are made from previously used rope

twice-told *adj* familiar or hackneyed through frequent repetition ○ *"Life is as tedious as a twice-told tale"* (William Shakespeare, *King John*; 1623)

twid·dle /twídd'l/ *vti* (**-dled, -dling, -dles**) **1.** TURN SOMETHING BACK AND FORTH to turn something around or back and forth repeatedly ○ *twiddling the dial on the radio to get better reception* **2.** TWIST OR TURN SOMETHING ABSENT-MINDEDLY to keep twisting something or turning it around in a bored or absent-minded way ○ *sat twiddling his pencil and staring out of the window* ■ *n* TWISTING ACTION a to-and-fro turning or twisting action [Mid-16C. Origin ?] —**twid·dler** *n* —**twid·dly** *adj*

twig[1] /twig/ *n* **1.** a small branch or shoot, especially one from a tree or bush **2.** a structure that resembles a branch, e.g., a minute offshoot of a nerve or blood vessel [Old English *twigge* "forked branch" < Germanic] —**twig·let** *n*

twig[2] /twig/ (**twigged, twig·ging, twigs**) *vti UK* to understand or realize something (*informal*) ○ *finally twigged what was going on* [Mid-18C. Origin ?]

twig·gy /twíggee/ (**-gi·er, -gi·est**) *adj* **1.** very thin or fragile ○ *twiggy legs* **2.** covered in twigs ○ *a twiggy shrub*

twi·light /twī́ lìt/ *n* **1.** TIME AFTER SUNSET OR BEFORE DAWN the time of day just after sunset or before dawn, when the Sun is below the horizon **2.** HALF-LIGHT the faint diffuse light that occurs at twilight **3.** FINAL PERIOD the time when something is declining or approaching its end, especially in a gentle or peaceful way ○ *the twilight of her career* **4.** same as **twilight zone** (sense 1) [15C. < archaic *twi-* "two, half" < Germanic]

Twi·light of the Gods *n* **1.** same as **Götterdämmerung** (sense 1) **2.** same as **Ragnarök** [Translation of German *Götterdämmerung*]

twi·light war *n* a period of ominous inactivity that occurs during a war or leads up to a war

twi·light zone *n* **1.** an ambiguous or unsettled state or condition, especially between two opposing conditions such as life and death or reality and fantasy **2.** the lowest layer of the sea that natural light can reach

CULTURAL NOTE ***The Twilight Zone***, a television series (1959–65) created by US writer Rod Serling. These dramatized fictional tales were the first adult television programs to present paranormal events in a serious and believable way. Staple topics included time travel, accidental journeys, premonitions, and encounters with the dead and with aliens. The series inspired a movie, *Twilight Zone – The Movie* (1983), and was revived sporadically from 1985–87, and run in syndication 1987–88. The expression *twilight zone* has long had the meaning "the lowest layer of the sea that natural light can reach." The show, however, popularized another preexisting meaning, "an ambiguous or unsettled state between two opposing conditions such as life and death or reality and fantasy."

twi·lit /twī́ lìt/ *adj* lit by twilight or a similar kind of half-light, especially so as to create a feeling of mystery [Mid-19C. Past participle of earlier *twilight*, verb]

twill /twil/ *n* **1.** STRONG FABRIC a strong woven material with diagonal ridges or ribs across its surface **2.** TEXTILE WEAVE the weave used to produce twill ■ *vt* (**twilled, twill·ing, twills**) WEAVE TWILL to weave fabric with diagonal ridges or ribs across its surface [14C. < N English dialect variant of Old English *twilic* "having two threads"]

'twill /twil/ *contr* it will (*archaic or literary*)

twin /twin/ *n* **1.** EITHER OF TWO OFFSPRING BORN TOGETHER either of two people or animals born to the same mother at the same time. Fraternal twins arise from different egg cells and are equivalent to ordinary siblings, while identical twins are derived from the same egg cell and are genetically identical. (*often used before a noun*) ○ *twin boys* **2.** EITHER OF TWO SIMILAR THINGS somebody or something similar to or unusually closely associated with another **3.** CHEM COMPOUND CRYSTAL a compound crystal consisting of two mirror-image crystals that share a common plane ■ *v* (**twinned, twin·ning, twins**) **1.** *vti* PAIR PEOPLE OR THINGS to group people or things in pairs, or link people or things very closely, or be paired or closely grouped **2.** *vi* HAVE TWINS to give birth to twins [Old English *twinn* < Indo-European, "two by two"]

twin bed *n* either of a pair of matching single beds

twin·ber·ry /twín bèrree/ (*plural* **-ries**) *n* **1.** PLANTS same as **partridgeberry** (sense 2) **2.** a bush of the honeysuckle family. Flowers: purple. Native to: North America. Latin name: *Lonicera involucrata*.

twin bill *n* **1.** *US* SPORTS same as **double-header 2.** MOVIES same as **double feature**

Twin Cit·ies *npl* the cities of Minneapolis and St. Paul, Minnesota

twine /twīn/ *n* **1.** STRING string or cord made from threads or strands that have been twisted together **2.** SOMETHING MADE BY TWISTING something that is formed by twisting or coiling separate strands together **3.** TWISTING ACTION a twisting or weaving action ■ *v* (**twined, twin·ing, twines**) **1.** *vti* TWIST AROUND SOMETHING to grow, wind, or twist around or together, or make something grow, wind, or twist around something else ○ *the ivy twining around the old oak tree* **2.** *vi* HAVE WINDING COURSE to take or follow a winding route ○ *From the cabin door a path twines through the woods.* **3.** *vt* WEAVE SOMETHING to make something by weaving or twisting separate strands together [Old English *twīn* "double thread." < Germanic] —**twin·er** *n* —**twin·y** *adj*

twin-en·gined, twin-en·gine *adj* powered by two engines ○ *a twin-engined plane*

Twin Falls /twìn fáwlz/ city in southern Idaho, on the southern bank of the Snake River, northeast of Boise. Population: 35,633 (2002 estimate).

twin·flow·er /twín flòwr/ *n* a creeping plant of the honeysuckle family with opposite oval leaves. Flowers: pinkish white, bell-shaped, in pairs. Native to: North America. Latin name: *Linnaea borealis*.

twinge /twinj/ *n* **1.** BRIEF PAIN a sudden brief stab of pain **2.** BRIEF UNCOMFORTABLE EMOTION a sudden brief uncomfortable pang of an emotion such as guilt or fear ■ *vti* (**twinged, twinge·ing** or **twing·ing, twing·es**) FEEL TWINGE to feel a twinge of pain or emotion, or make somebody feel this [Old English *twengan* "pinch" < Germanic]

twi-night dou·ble-head·er /twī̀ nīt dúbb'l hèddər/ *n* two consecutive baseball games between the same teams, the first beginning in late afternoon and the last ending after dark [Blend of TWILIGHT + NIGHT]

twin·kle /twíngk'l/ *vi* (**-kled, -kling, -kles**) **1.** SHINE WITH FLICKER to give out or reflect a bright but unsteady light, especially from a small or distant source **2.** SHINE WITH AMUSEMENT to be bright because of a feeling such as amusement, delight, or mischief (*refers to people's eyes*) ■ *n* **1.** FLICKERING SHINE a bright unsteady light, especially one that is small or seen from a distance **2.** BRIGHTNESS IN SOMEBODY'S EYES a brightness in somebody's eyes, caused by a feeling such as amusement, delight, or mischief **3.** same as **twinkling** [Old English *twinclian* "keep blinking" < *twincan* "blink" < Germanic] —**twin·kler** *n* —**twink·ly** *adj*

twin·kling /twíngkling/ *n* MOMENT an instant of time ■ *adj* **1.** FLICKERING giving out or reflecting light brightly but unsteadily, especially from a small or distant source **2.** SHINING WITH AMUSEMENT shining because of a feeling such as amusement, delight, or mischief (*refers to people's eyes*) ◇ **in the twinkling of an eye** very quickly or very soon

twin-lens re·flex *n* a camera that has two forward-facing lenses, one for focusing through and one for taking pictures

twinned /twind/ *adj* **1.** EXISTING AS MATCHING PAIR linked together as or like a couple **2.** SHARING CULTURAL LINK describes towns or cities in different countries that share cultural and administrative links **3.** CRYSTALS SYMMETRICAL describes a compound crystal consisting of two mirror-image crystals that share a common plane

twin room *n* a hotel room with twin beds

Twins /twinz/ *n* ASTRON, ZODIAC same as **Gemini** (senses 1–2)

twin-screw *adj* describes a ship that has two propellers

twin set *n* a woman's matching short-sleeved pullover and cardigan designed to be worn together

twin-size, twin-sized *adj* made to the size of a standard single bed, usually 39 x 75 in./99 x 190 cm

twin-tip *n* a ski with turned-up points front and back, fatter and softer than a typical downhill ski, designed so that the wearer can move forward and backward on a slope and perform complex moves while engaging in the sport of freeskiing [Late 20C.]

twin-tipped *adj* describes skis, snowboards, or similar pieces of sports equipment that are the same at both ends, e.g., that are rounded or upturned at front and rear

twirl /twurl/ *v* (**twirled, twirl·ing, twirls**) **1.** *vti* SPIN AROUND QUICKLY to turn lightly and rapidly around in a circle, or make something do this ○ *twirled his partner around the dance floor* **2.** *vt* FIDDLE WITH SOMETHING to fiddle with something by turning or spinning it between the fingers **3.** *vi* TURN AND FACE OTHER WAY to turn around suddenly to face somebody or face the other way ○ *She twirled around, her eyes blazing.* **4.** *vti* PITCH BASEBALL in baseball, to pitch the ball ■ *n* **1.** QUICK SPINNING MOVEMENT a quick turning or spinning movement, e.g., when somebody is dancing or modeling clothes **2.** SPIRAL a twisting or spiral shape, pattern, or line, especially something used for decoration [Late 16C. Probably alteration of *tirl*, variant of TRILL, after WHIRL] —**twirl·er** *n* —**twir·ly** *adj*

twirp *n* another spelling of **twerp**

twist /twist/ *v* (**twist·ed, twist·ing, twists**) **1.** *vti* MAKE ENDS TURN IN OPPOSITE DIRECTIONS to make one part or end of something turn in the opposite direction from the other, or turn in this way ○ *I twisted my handkerchief into a knot.* **2.** *vti* DISTORT SOMETHING to distort the shape or position of something, or become distorted ○ *His face was twisted in a grimace of disgust.* **3.** *vti* WIND SOMETHING to wind something around something else or wind things together, or be wound ○ *twisted the strands of fiber into a rope* **4.** *vt* INJURE PART OF BODY to injure part of the body by turning or moving it out of position ○ *I've twisted my ankle.* **5.** *vti* ROTATE SOMETHING to rotate something, or be rotated ○ *The lid just twists and comes off.* **6.** *vt* DISTORT MEANING OF SOMETHING to distort the meaning of something deliberately ○ *keeps twisting what I'm saying to make it sound as if I agree* **7.** *vi* CONSTANTLY CHANGE DIRECTION to change direction constantly instead of continuing in a direct or straight line **8.** *vi* SQUIRM to squirm or wriggle ○ *a child twisting restlessly in her chair* **9.** *vi* DANCE to dance the twist ■ *n* **1.** TWISTING MOVEMENT the action or movement performed when somebody twists something ○ *a twist of the screw* **2.** UNEXPECTED DEVELOPMENT an unexpected development in a narrative or a sequence of events ○ *The story had a strange twist.* **3.** BEND a bend in something such as a road or river ○ *a road full of twists and turns* **4.** PAINFUL WRENCH a painful wrench or pull in a wrist, ankle, or another body part **5.** 1960S DANCE a 1960s dance that involved moving the hips from side to side **6.** SOMETHING SHAPED BY BEING TWISTED something that has been shaped, split, or gathered together by being twisted ○ *a twist of paper* **7.** LENGTH OF YARN OR THREAD a length of yarn or thread whose strands have been twisted together **8.** SLICE OF LEMON a thin slice of lemon, lime, or another peel that is cut and twisted and added to a drink **9.** BREAD OR ROLL a roll or loaf of bread made by twisting pieces of dough **10.** CHEWING TOBACCO tobacco leaves twisted into a roll from which pieces can be cut off and chewed **11.** FORCE CAUSING STRESS a force that causes stress or strain by twisting **12.** SPIN GIVEN TO BALL spin imparted to a hit, thrown, or pitched ball **13.** ROTATION OF BODY a complete turn of the body around a vertical axis, e.g., in gymnastics or diving **14.** DISTORTION a contortion or distortion in the shape of something **15.** QUIRK OF CHARACTER an eccentricity or strange personal characteristic [Mid-16C. < Old English, "something split in two, twisted yarn" < Germanic] —**twist·a·ble** *adj* —**twist·ing·ly** *adv* —**twist·y** *adj*

CULTURAL NOTE ***Oliver Twist***, a novel (1837–39) by the British writer Charles Dickens. It tells the tale of an abandoned child who runs away from his workhouse home to London, where he falls in with a band of criminals led by Fagin and his young assistant, a streetwise pickpocket called the Artful Dodger. The novel inspired a musical, *Oliver!* (1960) and several movies, most notably David Lean's 1948 adaptation.

twist drill *n* a drill bit with one or more helical grooves along its axis to expel cuttings or swarf

twist·ed /twístəd/ *adj* **1.** SUBJECTED TO TWISTING having one part or end turned in the opposite direction to the other ○ *twisted strands of fiber* **2.** DISTORTED IN SHAPE severely distorted in shape or form ○ *The accident left the car a heap of twisted metal.* **3.** CORRUPT morally unacceptable ○ *What kind of twisted mind could think up a thing like that?* **4.** BADLY AFFECTED BY EXPERIENCES badly affected by unpleasant experiences or constant disappointment (*informal*) ○ *The experience left her bitter and twisted.*

twist·er /twístər/ *n* **1.** TORNADO a tornado, cyclone, or whirlwind (*informal*) **2.** SPORTS BALL WITH TWIST a ball that has been thrown or hit with a twist **3.** SOMEBODY OR SOMETHING THAT TWISTS a person or device that twists

twist grip *n* a control mounted in one of the handlebars of a motorcycle or bicycle, allowing the rider to change gear or accelerate by twisting the grip

twist·or /twístər/ *n* any of the solutions to the equations of twistor theory that manifest themselves as matter or energy

twist·or the·o·ry *n* a mathematical theory of space-time that uses four complex numbers to define the three spatial dimensions plus time, rather than the conventional four real numbers, and has applications in relativity, integrable systems, and differential and integral geometry

twist-tie *n* a piece of wire sealed in a paper or plastic strip, used as a fastener, especially for a plastic bag

twit /twit/ *n* an offensive term that deliberately insults somebody's commonsense or consideration for others (*slang insult*) ■ *vt* (**twit·ted, twit·ting, twits**) to make fun of or criticize somebody in a playful friendly way (*dated*) [Mid-16C. Shortening of Old English *ætwītan* "find fault" < *æt-* "at" + *wītan* "reproach" < Germanic]

twitch /twich/ *v* (**twitched, twitch·ing, twitch·es**) **1.** *vi* JERK SLIGHTLY to move with a slight jerk, either once or repeatedly ○ *His eyebrow twitches when he's nervous.* **2.** *vt* PULL SOMETHING LIGHTLY AND QUICKLY to give something a sudden light tug or jerk **3.** *vi* HURT SHARPLY to hurt with a sharp or sudden pain ■ *n* **1.** JERKY MOVEMENT a slight jerky movement **2.** MUSCLE CONTRACTION a brief rapid contraction of a muscle **3.** FEELING OF DISCOMFORT a sharp or sudden feeling of physical or emotional pain **4.** VET HORSE RESTRAINT a restraint used on a horse during a veterinary procedure, consisting of a cord loop that can be pulled tight around the animal's upper lip [12C. Origin ?]

twitch grass *n* PLANTS same as **couch grass** [Alteration of QUITCH GRASS]

twitch·y /twíchee/ (**-i·er, -i·est**) *adj* **1.** nervous and jittery **2.** twitching frequently

twit·ter[1] /twíttər/ *v* (**-tered, -ter·ing, -ters**) **1.** *vi* CHIRP to sing in a succession of light high-pitched chirping sounds (*refers to birds*) **2.** *vi* CHATTER to chatter or giggle in an overexcited or nervous way **3.** *vti* USE SMALL HIGH VOICE to sing or say something in a light shaky high-pitched voice **4.** *vi* TREMBLE to quiver or move about nervously and quickly ■ *n* **1.** REPETITIVE HIGH-PITCHED SONG a continuous string of light high-pitched sounds made by a small bird or animal **2.** HIGH-PITCHED CHATTERING the light high-pitched sound of chattering or laughter **3.** EXCITEMENT a state of great agitation or excitement ○ *all of a twitter* [14C. An imitation of birds chirping] —**twit·ter·y** *adj*

twit·ter[2] /twíttər/ *n* somebody who makes fun of or criticizes somebody in a playful friendly way (*dated*) [Late 16C. < TWIT]

'twixt /twikst/ *prep* same as **between** (*archaic*) [14C. Shortening of BETWIXT]

twiz·zle /twízz'l/ *vt* (**-zled, -zling, -zles**) to twirl or twist something vigorously ■ *n* a vigorous twirl or twist [Late 18C. Probably alteration of TWIST or TWIRL]

two /too/ *n* (*plural* **twos**) **1.** 2 the number 2 **2.** SOMETHING WITH VALUE OF 2 something in a numbered series, e.g., a playing card, with a value of 2 ○ *the two of clubs* **3.** GROUP OF TWO a group of two people or objects ○ *arrived in twos and threes* ■ *prep* **2** ONLINE same as **to**[1] (*used in e-mails and text messages*) ○ *up 2 U* ■ *adv* **2** ONLINE same as **too** (*used in e-mails and text messages*) ○ *me 2* ■ *symbol* **2** TO-, -TO-, OR -TO used to replace "to" within words (*used in e-mails and text messages*) ○ *2day* [Old English *twā* < Indo-European] —**two** *adj, pron* ◇ **it takes two to tango** used to indicate that both of the people involved in an awkward or unpleasant situation are responsible or to blame, not just one ◇ **put two and two together** to work something out from the available evidence ◇ **that makes two of us** used to indicate agreement with something expressed or acknowledgment of something shared

SPELLCHECK See *to*[1].

2,4-D /to͞o fawr dée/ *n* a white crystalline compound. Use: weedkiller. Formula: $C_8H_6Cl_2O_3$. [Mid-20C. *D* < DI-[1]]

2,4,5-T /to͞o fàwr fīv tée/ *n* an insoluble crystalline compound. Use: chemical weedkiller, plant hormone. Formula: $C_8H_5Cl_3O_3$. [Mid-20C. *T* < TRI-]

two-bag·ger *n* BASEBALL same as **double** *n* (sense 13) (*slang*)

two-base hit *n* BASEBALL same as **double** *n* (sense 13)

two-bit *adj* **1.** of very low quality or importance (*informal*) **2.** costing or worth 25 cents (*archaic*)

two-by-four, **2 x 4** *n* wood in lengths that are 4 in. wide and 2 in. thick/10 cm wide and 5 cm thick

two cents plain *n Northeast US* same as **seltzer** (sense 1) [< its price]

two cents worth *n* an opinion, when expressed assertively as one of several ○ *just had to add her two cents worth*

two-cy·cle *adj* describes an internal-combustion engine in which the piston makes two movements, usually one upward and one downward, in each power cycle

two-di·men·sion·al *adj* **1.** HAVING LENGTH AND WIDTH describes a figure that has length and width but no depth, e.g. a geometric figure on a single plane **2.** DONE ON FLAT SURFACE describes works of art such as paintings and drawings that exist on a flat surface, as opposed to art forms such as sculpture that also have depth **3.** HAVING NO DEPTH OF CHARACTER lacking the emotional or psychological depth that creates the impression of realism ○ *a two-dimensional character* —**two-di·men·sion·al·i·ty** *n* —**two-di·men·sion·al·ly** *adv*

two-edged *adj* **1.** having two sharp edges for cutting in opposite directions **2.** having two effects, one positive and one negative, especially two possible and opposite interpretations or meanings

two-faced *adj* **1.** insincere in dealings with people, especially by being outwardly friendly, but secretly disloyal **2.** having two faces or surfaces —**two-fac·ed·ly** /to͞o fáyssədli/ *adv* —**two-fac·ed·ness** /to͞o fáyssədnəss/ *n*

two·fer /to͞ofər/ *n US* (*informal*) **1.** DISCOUNT ENTITLEMENT a coupon entitling somebody to buy two items for the price of one, especially tickets for a play **2.** PAIR OF ITEMS SOLD AT DISCOUNT a set of two items sold together for exactly or approximately the price of each item sold singly **3.** DEAL OFFERING ADDED BENEFIT an offer or a situation in which a single expense or effort yields a benefit additional to the intended return [Late 19C. Alteration of *two for (one)*]

two-fist·ed *adj* characterized by energy, enthusiasm, assertiveness, or aggression (*informal*)

two·fold /to͞o fōld/ *adj* **1.** DOUBLE twice as much or as many **2.** HAVING TWO PARTS consisting of two parts ■ *adv* DOUBLY by the same amount over again

two-four time *n* a rhythm with two quarter-note beats to the measure

two-hand·ed *adj* **1.** USING TWO HANDS using or requiring the use of two hands **2.** DESIGNED FOR TWO designed for two people, especially for two players or operators **3.** AMBIDEXTROUS able to use either the left or right hand with equal skill **4.** WITH TWO HANDS having two hands —**two-hand·ed·ly** *adv*

two-hand·er *n* **1.** TENNIS STROKE a shot in tennis, usually a backhand, made with two hands gripping the handle of the racket **2.** SOMEBODY WHO HITS TWO-HANDERS a tennis player who uses a two-handed backhand **3.** TWO-ACTOR PLAY a play written for and performed by two actors

two-mast·er *n* a sailing ship with two masts

two-name pa·per *n US* a commercial debt whose two signatories are jointly and individually responsible for it

two-pack *n* a set of two identical products packaged together and sold as one

two·pence /túppənss/, **tup·pence** *n UK* the value of two pence, especially two pennies in the predecimal UK monetary system

two·pen·ny /túppənee, to͞o pènnee/, **tup·pen·ny** /túppənee/ *adj* **1.** costing or worth two cents **2.** inexpensive and of the poorest quality

two-phase *adj* describes an electrical system in which there are two alternating voltages of the same frequency, with a phase difference of 90° between them

two-piece *adj* consisting of two parts or pieces, especially pieces of clothing ■ *n* a suit consisting of two garments, e.g., a bikini

two-ply *adj* consisting of two layers or strands

two-seat·er *n* **1.** a vehicle with seats for two people, especially a sports car **2.** a seat for two people, especially a couch

two-shot *n* a movie or television shot in which two people more or less fill the screen

two-sid·ed *adj* **1.** USING TWO SIDES OF PAGE using both sides of a sheet of paper **2.** HAVING TWO CONTESTING SIDES consisting of two contesting sides, e.g., two groups opposing each other or two equally valid opinions **3.** HAVING TWO SURFACES having two sides or surfaces

two·some /to͞ossəm/ *n* **1.** a pair of people, especially two golfers paired to play together, a couple on a date together, or a team consisting of two players **2.** GOLF same as **single** *n* (sense 5)

two-spot *n* **1.** a game piece with two marks on it, e.g., a playing card or a domino **2.** *US* a two-dollar bill (*informal*)

two-step *n* **1.** BALLROOM DANCE a ballroom dance in 2/4 time with sliding steps **2.** DANCE MUSIC the music for a two-step ■ *vi* DANCE **DANCE TWO-STEP** to dance the two-step

two-stroke *adj UK* same as **two-cycle**

two-suit·er /-so͞otər/ *n* **1.** a suitcase designed to hold two suits and their accessories **2.** a hand at bridge with two suits of five or more cards

two-tier *adj* having two levels, especially two levels of administration or two standards of treatment or privilege

two-time *vt* (*informal*) **1.** to be unfaithful to a romantic or sexual partner **2.** to deceive or betray a partner in an undertaking —**two-tim·er** *n* —**two-tim·ing** *adj*

two-toed sloth *n* a mainly nocturnal sloth with two digits on each forefoot. Native to: Central and South America. Latin name: *Choloepus didactylus*.

two-tone *adj* **1.** consisting of two colors or two shades of the same color ○ *two-tone shoes* **2.** consisting of two sounds with different frequencies ○ *a two-tone siren*

'twould /two͝od/ *contr* it would (*archaic or literary*)

two-way *adj* **1.** MOVING IN BOTH DIRECTIONS moving in opposite directions or allowing for movement in opposite directions ○ *a two-way street* **2.** INVOLVING TWO CONTESTANTS involving two people or teams ○ *a two-way race* **3.** ABLE TO TRANSMIT AND RECEIVE able both to transmit and to receive radio signals ○ *two-way radio* **4.** RECIPROCAL requiring cooperation between two people or groups **5.** WORKING IN DIFFERENT WAYS able to operate or be operated in either of two manners **6.** CARDS **AMBIGUOUS AS BID** describes a bid at bridge that may have different meanings, to be clarified by later bids

two-way mir·ror *n UK* same as **one-way mirror**

two-wheel·er *n* a vehicle with two wheels, especially a bicycle

twp. *abbr* township

TWX *abbr* teletypewriter exchange

twy·er *n* ENG same as **tuyère**

TX *abbr* **1.** Texas **2.** ONLINE thanks (*used in e-mails or text messages*)

txt *abbr* a file extension for a text file. Full form **text**

TY *abbr* ONLINE thank you (*used in e-mails or text messages*)

Ty·cho /tī́kō/ *n* a crater on the south of the Moon that is the center of the Moon's most extensive ray system. It is 52 mi./84 km in diameter, 14,750 ft./4500 m high, and is surrounded by terraced walls.

ty·coon /tī ko͞on/ *n* **1.** an amasser of great wealth and power, especially in business **2.** same as **shogun** (*archaic*) [Mid-19C. < Japanese *taikun* "great lord, shogun" < Chinese *dà* "great" + *jūn* "prince"]

ty·iyn /tēe yēen/ (*plural same* or **-iyns**) *n* a subunit of Kyrgyz currency. See table at **currency** [Late 20C. < Kyrgyz]

tyke /tīk/, **tike** *n* **1.** a dog of mixed breed **2.** a little child, especially a boy [14C. < Old Norse *tík* "bitch"]

ty·lec·to·my /tī léktəmee/ (*plural* **-mies**) *n* MED same as **lumpectomy** [Late 20C. < Greek *tulos* "lump"]

Ty·le·nol /tī́lə nàwl/ *tdmk* a trademark for the painkiller acetaminophen

Ty·ler /tī́lər/, **Anne** (*b.* 1941) US writer. Her novels include *Dinner at the Homesick Restaurant* (1982) and *The Accidental Tourist* (1985).

> "I write because I want more than one life; I insist on a wider selection. It's greed, plain and simple."
> [Anne Tyler, *Civilization*; 1995]

Ty·ler, John (1790–1862) 10th president of the United States. He was William Henry Harrison's vice president, and set a controversial historical precedent by assuming the presidency after Harrison's death. As president (1841–45), his greatest achievement was the annexation of Texas (1844). See table at **president**

Library of Congress

John Tyler

Ty·ler, Wat (*d.* 1381) English revolutionary leader. The leader of the Peasants' Revolt of 1381, he secured concessions from Richard II but was killed during negotiations.

> "No man should be a serf, nor do homage or any manner of service to any lord, but should give fourpence rent for an acre of land, and that no one should work for any man but as his own will, and on terms of a regular covenant."
> [Attributed to Wat Tyler. Quoted in *Anonimalle Chronicle*; 14th century]

tym·bal *n* MUSIC another spelling of **timbal**

tym·pan /tímpən/ *n* **1.** PRINTING a piece of padding that fits between the impression cylinder of a printing press and the paper to be printed so as to ensure a uniform image **2.** ARCHIT same as **tympanum** (sense 1) **3.** ACOUSTICS a membrane or diaphragm that vibrates to produce or transmit sound, e.g., the skin on a drum or the diaphragm in a telephone receiver [Pre-12C. < Latin *tympanum* "drum" (see TYMPANUM)]

tym·pa·na plural of **tympanum**

tym·pa·ni MUSIC another spelling of **timpani**

tym·pan·ic /tim pánnik/ *adj* relating to a tympanum

tym·pan·ic bone *n* the part of the temporal bone that supports and partly surrounds the auditory canal

tym·pan·ic mem·brane *n* ANAT same as **eardrum** (*technical*)

tym·pa·ni·tes /tìmpə nī́teez/ *n* swelling of the abdominal wall caused by gas trapped in the intestines or peritoneal cavity [14C. Via late Latin < Greek *tumpanitēs* < *tumpanon* "drum"] —**tym·pa·nit·ic** /-níttik/ *adj*

tym·pa·ni·tis /tìmpə nī́tiss/ *n* inflammation of the eardrum [Mid-19C. < TYMPANUM]

tym·pa·no·plas·ty /tímpənə plàstee/ (*plural* **-ties**) *n* the surgical repair or reconstruction of the eardrum, usually in order to close a perforation [Mid-20C. < TYMPANUM]

tympanum

tym·pa·num /tímpənəm/ (*plural* **-nums** or **-na** /-nə/) *n* **1.** ARCHIT **RECESSED SPACE** a recess, especially the recessed space between the top of a door or window and the arch above it, or between the cornices forming a classical triangular gable (**pediment**) **2.** ANAT **EAR PART** the eardrum or the cavity of the middle ear (*technical*) **3.** INSECTS **INSECT ORGAN** a vibrating membrane in some insects that serves as a hearing organ **4.** ACOUSTICS same as **tympan** (sense 3) [Early 16C. Via Latin < Greek *tumpanon* "drum"]

tym·pa·ny /tímpənee/ *n* MED same as **tympanites** [15C. < Greek *tumpanias* < *tumpanon* "drum"]

Tyn·dale /tínd'l/, **Tin·dal, William** (1492?–1536) English religious reformer. His translation of the Bible into English laid the foundations of the Authorized Version (1611), but he was condemned for heresy and executed by the Church authorities.

Tyn·dall ef·fect /tínd'l-/ *n* the scattering of light by minute particles in its path, such as dust in the air [Early 20C. After John *Tyndall* (1820–93), British physicist]

tyn·dal·lim·e·try /tìnd'l ímmətree/ *n* the measurement of the concentration of suspended particles in a liquid by gauging the amount of light they scatter [See TYNDALL EFFECT]

Tyne /tīn/ river in northeastern England, formed by the union of the North Tyne and South Tyne rivers. It flows through Newcastle upon Tyne shortly before reaching the North Sea. Length: 30 mi./48 km.

Tyne·mouth /tī́n mòwth, tī́nməth/ town at the mouth of the Tyne River, northeastern England. Population: 17,422 (1991).

typ. *abbr* PRINTING **1.** typographer **2.** typographical **3.** typography

type /tīp/ *n* **1.** CATEGORY OR KIND a group made up of individuals or items that have strongly marked and readily defined similarities ○ *What type of decoration did you have in mind?* ○ *People of that type never stay in a job for long.* **2.** PERSON OR THING somebody or something regarded as belonging to a group or category by virtue of having the main qualities associated with it ○ *They sent me a new type of keyboard to try out.* **3.** PARTICULAR KIND OF PERSON a person regarded as having a particular temperament or characteristics (*informal*) ○ *a gathering of bookish types* **4.** SOMEBODY WHO APPEALS somebody with the qualities that appeal to somebody else ○ *He's really not my type.* **5.** PRINTED CHARACTERS printed words, letters, or symbols as they appear on a page ○ *headings in italic type* **6.** PRINTING **BLOCKS** the set of small metal blocks used in printing, especially formerly, each of which has a raised figure that is the mirror image of a number or letter on one of its sides ○ *set up the type* **7.** INDIVIDUAL PRINTING BLOCK an individual piece of type bearing a single character **8.** TEMPLATE something used as a pattern or template for making other things of the same kind **9.** BIOL **REPRESENTATIVE ORGANISM** a plant or animal that most fully represents its genus and whose attributes are used to define the genus as a whole and, usually, give it its name **10.** BIOL **REPRESENTATIVE GENUS OR SPECIES** a genus or species of plant or animal whose attributes serve as the defining characteristics for the next higher level of taxonomic classification **11.** LING **LINGUISTIC UNIT** a letter, word, or other linguistic unit regarded as representing all units that are forms of it, as distinct from an individual form (**token**) **12.** PHILOSOPHY **GENERAL EXPRESSION** an expression regarded not as a physical object but as an abstract pattern that individual expressions can conform to **13.** CHR **SIGN OF SOMETHING TO COME** an event, figure, or sign taken as foreshadowing something in the future ■ *v* (**typed, typ·ing, types**) **1.** *vti* KEY WORDS ON KEYBOARD to key words using a computer keyboard, word processor, or typewriter **2.** *vt* CLASSIFY SOMETHING to classify something, especially blood, according to its type **3.** *vt* TYPECAST SOMEBODY to characterize somebody as being a person who plays a particular kind of role **4.** *vt* CHR **FORESHADOW SOMETHING** to foreshadow a future event or fact [15C. Via Latin *typus* < Greek *tupos* "blow, impression"] —**typ·al** *adj*

USAGE See ***kind***[2].

SYNONYMS ***type, kind, sort, category, class, species, genre***

CORE MEANING: a group having a common quality or qualities

type a group made up of individuals or items that have strongly marked and readily defined similarities ○ *Certain types of bacteria can build up resistance to disinfectants.* ○ *The reactor was of the same type as the one that exploded at Chernobyl in 1986.* **kind** *or* **sort** a group of individuals or items connected by shared characteristics ○ *comparing soils of different kinds* ○ *the kind of music you might have danced to in the 1600s* ○ *leisure activities of various sorts* ○ *What sort of things will you be painting?* **category** a group or set of things, people, or actions that are classified together because of common characteristics ○ *The available courses are broken into two main categories, full-time and part-time.* ○ *People who fall into none of these official categories can still contribute.* **class** a group into which things with at least one characteristic in common are organized ○ *other classes of drugs used in the treatment of cardiac arrest patients* ○ *They swept to eight golds and 11 medals in the 12 weight classes at the world championships.* **species** a type of something ○ *a species of formal public oration rarely heard nowadays* **genre** one of the categories, based on form, style, or subject matter, into which artistic works of all kinds can be divided. ○ *dramatic scenarios that parody genres such as the thriller and the spy novel* ○ *The club promises to feature quality music of all genres.*

type A *n* an anxious, hard-working person who has a strong drive to succeed and finds it hard to delegate or share tasks with colleagues (*often used before a noun*) ○ *type A behavior*

type B *n* a patient and friendly person (*often used before a noun*) ○ *a type B personality*

type·bar /tīp baar/ *n* a lever operated by a typewriter key. Each typebar has one or more printing blocks on the end that print characters on the paper.

type·case /tīp kàyss/ *n* a tray or box for storing printer's type

type·cast /tīp kàst/ (**-cast, -cast·ing, -casts**) *vt* **1.** to give an actor a series of parts of the same type, to the extent that the performer becomes associated with that kind of role and is overlooked for others **2.** to give an actor a part that suits his or her physical or emotional type —**type·cast·er** *n*

type·face /tīp fàyss/ *n* **1.** a style of printed character, e.g., roman or bold **2.** the side of a printing block that has the shape of the printed character on it

type foun·der *n* a manufacturer of metal printing type —**type foun·dry** *n*

type ge·nus *n* the genus within a family or other higher taxonomic category that is most typical of it and usually bears the same name

type-high *adj* as high as the standard height of a block of printer's type, 0.9186 in./23.3 mm

type I er·ror *n* in statistics, the error of rejection of a null hypothesis when it is true

type II er·ror *n* in statistics, the failure to reject a false null hypothesis

type lo·cal·i·ty *n* a place where a rock formation or other geologic feature was first found and described, and after which it is named

type met·al *n* the alloy from which printing type is made, consisting mostly of lead, antimony, and tin

type·script /tīp skrìpt/ *n* a typewritten document or other text [Late 19C. < TYPE + MANUSCRIPT]

type·set /tīp sèt/ (**-set, -set·ting, -sets**) *vt* to prepare text for printing, either by the use of computers or by arranging blocks of type manually

type·set·ter /tīp sèttər/ *n* **1.** somebody who sets type for printing **2.** a mechanical or electronic device that prepares text for printing —**type·set·ting** *n*

type-site *n* an archaeological site that is thought to typify a culture and that gives the culture its name

type spe·cies *n* a species of plant or animal that is most typical of its genus and bears the same name or a related name

type spec·i·men *n* an individual plant or animal that serves as the basis for the description of its species. Its name is usually taken as the name of the species.

type style *n* PRINTING same as **typeface** (sense 1)

type·write /tīp rīt/ (**-wrote** /-ròt/, **-writ·ten** /-ritt'n/, **-writ·ing, -writes**) *vti* to type something using a typewriter [Late 19C. Back-formation < TYPEWRITER]

typewriter

type·writ·er /tīp rītər/ *n* **1.** an electrical or mechanical device with keys that are pressed to print letters or other characters one by one on a sheet of paper inserted into the machine **2.** a printing typeface that looks like characters produced by a typewriter

type·writ·ing /tīp rīting/ *n* **1.** the process or skill of using a typewriter **2.** text produced on a typewriter

type·writ·ten /tīp ritt'n/ *adj* past participle of **typewrite**

type·wrote past tense of **typewrite**

typh·li·tis /ti flītiss/ *n* inflammation of the entrance to the large intestine (**cecum**) [Mid-19C. < Greek *tuphlon* "cecum" < *tuphlos* "sightless"] —**typh·lit·ic** /ti flíttik/ *adj*

typh·lol·o·gy /ti flólləjee/ *n* the scientific study of sightlessness [Late 19C. < Greek *tuphlos* "blind"]

Ty·phoe·us /tī fée əss/ *n* in Greek mythology, a monster with a hundred dragon heads who fought with Zeus and was thrown down into the ground under Mount Etna —**Ty·phoe·an** *adj*

ty·phoid /tī fòyd/, **ty·phoid fe·ver** *n* a serious and sometimes fatal bacterial infection of the digestive system, caused by ingesting food or water contaminated with the bacillus *Salmonella typhi.* It causes fever, severe abdominal pain, and sometimes intestinal bleeding. ■ *adj* relating to typhoid or typhus —**ty·phoi·dal** /tī fóyd'l/ *adj*

Ty·phoid Mar·y *n* **1.** an offensive term for somebody who spreads a disease or is held to be responsible for spreading it **2.** an offensive term for somebody who spreads something undesirable such as pessimism or bad news, and is generally avoided (*insult*) [Early 20C. Nickname of *Mary* Mallon (d. 1938), Irish-born cook in the United States who was found to be a typhoid carrier]

ty·phoon /tī fóon/ *n* a violent tropical storm in the western Pacific and Indian oceans [Late 16C. Partly < Chinese (Cantonese) *taaî fung* "big wind," partly via Portuguese *tufão* < Urdu *ṭūfān* < Arabic < Greek *tuphōn* "whirlwind, hurricane"] —**ty·phon·ic** /tī fónnik/ *adj*

ty·phus /tīfəss/, **ty·phus fe·ver** *n* an infectious disease that causes fever, severe headaches, a rash, and often delirium. It is spread by ticks and fleas carried by rodents. [Late 18C. < Greek *tuphos* "smoke, stupor" < *tuphein* "to smoke"] —**ty·phous** *adj*

typ·i·cal /típpik'l/ *adj* **1.** REPRESENTATIVE having all or most of the characteristics shared by others of the same kind and therefore suitable as an example of it ○ *a typical small Midwestern town* ○ *typical of life in Victorian England* **2.** CHARACTERISTIC characteristic of an individual person or thing ○ *He evaded the question with typical dexterity.* **3.** AS BAD OR ANNOYING AS USUAL in accordance with your worst expectations (*informal*) ○ *That's just typical! There's never a cab when you want one.* **4.** BIOL RESEMBLING OTHERS IN TAXONOMIC GROUP describes an organism, species, or genus that has most of the characteristics that identify the larger taxonomic group to which it belongs [Early 17C. < medieval Latin *typicalis* < late Latin *typicus* < Greek *tupikos* < *tupos* "blow, impression"] —**typ·i·cal·i·ty** /tìppi kállətee/ *n* —**typ·i·cal·ness** *n*

typ·i·cal·ly /típpikəlee/ *adv* **1.** IN USUAL WAY with all or many of the usual or expected characteristics ○ *a typically Mediterranean vista* **2.** AS A RULE in most cases or on most occasions ○ *Political action committees are typically formed by interest groups to raise money for political causes.* **3.** CHARACTERISTICALLY as is to be expected, especially annoyingly expected, of a particular person or thing ○ *The car, typically, refused to start.*

typ·i·fy /típpə fī/ (**-fied, -fy·ing, -fies**) *vt* **1.** to have all or most of the characteristics of a particular type of person or thing and therefore be a suitable example of it ○ *a community that typifies small-town America* **2.** to be a symbolic representation of something [Mid-17C. < Latin *typus* (see TYPE)] —**typ·i·fi·ca·tion** /tìppəfi káysh'n/ *n* —**typ·i·fi·er** *n*

typ·ist /tīpist/ *n* somebody who produces documents using a typewriter or computer keyboard

ty·po /tīpō/ (*plural* **-pos**) *n* PRINTING same as **typographical error** (*informal*) [Early 19C. Shortening]

typo., **typog.** *abbr* PRINTING **1.** typographer **2.** typographical **3.** typography

ty·po·graph·i·cal /tīpə gráffik'l/, **ty·po·graph·ic** /-gráffik/ *adj* **1.** relating to the appearance of printed characters on the page **2.** relating to the activity of preparing texts for printing

ty·po·graph·i·cal er·ror *n* a printing error that results from striking the wrong key on a keyboard, e.g., a misspelled word

ty·pog·ra·phy /tī póggrəfee/ *n* **1.** the appearance of printed characters on the page **2.** the activity or business of preparing texts for printing [Early 17C. Via French < modern Latin *typographia* < Greek *tupos* "blow, impression"] —**ty·pog·ra·pher** *n*

ty·pol·o·gy /tī póllǝjee/ *n* **1.** CLASSIFICATION OF TYPES the study or systematic classification of types **2.** LANGUAGE STUDY the study of syntactic and morphological similarities in languages without regard to their history **3.** STUDY OF RELIGIOUS TEXTS the study of religious texts for the purpose of identifying episodes in them that appear to prophesy later events [Mid-19C. < Greek *typos* "blow, impression"] —**ty·po·log·ic** /tīpə lójjik/ *adj* —**ty·po·log·i·cal** *adj* —**ty·po·log·i·cal·ly** *adv* —**ty·pol·o·gist** *n*

typw. *abbr* **1.** typewriter **2.** typewritten

ty·ra·mine /tīrə meen/ *n* an amine, found in some foods and formed from the breakdown of the amino acid tyrosine, that has the effect of simulating sympathetic nervous system action. Formula: $C_8H_{11}NO$. [Early 20C. Blend of TYROSINE + AMINE]

ty·ran·ni·cal /ti ránnik'l/, **ty·ran·nic** /ti ránnik/ *adj* **1.** ruling with absolute power over a population cruelly kept submissive and fearful **2.** cruelly or irrationally insisting on complete obedience and giving harsh punishment to those who disobey [Mid-16C. < French *tyrannique* < Greek *turannikos* < *turannos* "tyrant"] —**ty·ran·ni·cal·ly** *adv* —**ty·ran·ni·cal·ness** *n*

ty·ran·ni·cide /ti ránni sīd/ *n* **1.** the killing of a tyrant **2.** the killer of a tyrant [Mid-17C. < Latin *tyrannicidium* "tyrant-killing," *tyrannicida* "tyrant-killer" < *tyrannus* (see TYRANT) + *caedere* "kill" (see -CIDE)] —**ty·ran·ni·cid·al** /ti rànni sīd'l/ *adj*

tyr·an·nize /tírrə nīz/ (**-nized, -niz·ing, -niz·es**) *vti* **1.** to govern a people or community with extreme cruelty and harshness **2.** to treat somebody in a cruelly unfair way [15C. < French *tyranniser* < Old French *tyrant* (see TYRANT)] —**tyr·an·niz·er** *n*

ty·ran·no·saur /ti ránnə sàwr/, **ty·ran·no·saur·us** /ti rànnə sáwrəss/, **ty·ran·no·saur·us rex** /-réks/ *n* a large fierce flesh-eating dinosaur that walked on powerful hind legs and had small forelegs. It lived during the Cretaceous Period and was the largest carnivore. [Early 20C. < modern Latin *Tyrannosaurus* < Greek *turannos* "tyrant" + *sauros* "lizard"]

tyr·an·ny /tírrənee/ (*plural* **-nies**) *n* **1.** CRUEL USE OF POWER cruelty and injustice in the exercise of power or authority over others **2.** OPPRESSIVE GOVERNMENT oppressive government by one or more people who exercise absolute power cruelly and unjustly **3.** STATE RULED BY TYRANT a country or state under the power of an oppressive ruler **4.** CRUEL ACT a cruel or oppressive act, especially one committed by a person wielding great power [14C. Via French < late Latin *tyrannia* < Latin *tyrannus* "tyrant"] —**tyr·an·nous** *adj*

ty·rant /tī́rənt/ *n* **1. ABSOLUTE RULER** an absolute ruler who exercises power cruelly and unjustly **2. AUTHORITARIAN PERSON** an unjust and oppressive exerciser of authority **3. ANCIENT GREEK RULER** in ancient Greece, a ruler who took control of a state without legal sanction and governed with absolute power [13C. Via Old French < Latin *tyrannus* < Greek *turannos*]

ty·rant-fly·catch·er *n* BIRDS same as **flycatcher** (sense 2) [Translation of modern Latin *Tyrannidae*, family name]

~~**tyrany**~~ incorrect spelling of **tyranny**

tyre /tīr/ *n* AUTOMOT UK spelling of **tire**[3]

Tyre /tīr/ town in southern Lebanon, on the Mediterranean Sea. It was the most important city of ancient Phoenicia. Population: 120,000 (1988). —**Tyr·i·an** /tírree ən/ *adj*

Ty·ree, Mount /tī rée/ peak in the Ellsworth Mountains, the second highest mountain in Antarctica, first climbed in 1966. Height: 16,290 ft./4,965 m.

Tyr·i·an pur·ple *n* **1.** a deep purple dye extracted from mollusks **2.** a rich crimson-purple color —**Tyr·i·an pur·ple** *adj*

ty·ro /tī́rō/ (*plural* **-ros**), **ti·ro** *n* somebody who is just beginning to learn something [Early 17C. Via medieval Latin, "squire" < Latin *tiro* "young soldier, recruit"] —**ty·ron·ic** /tī rónnik/ *adj*

SYNONYMS See *beginner.*

ty·ro·ci·dine /tīrə sī́d'n, -sī déen/, **ty·ro·ci·din** /tīrə sī́d'n/ *n* an antibiotic polypeptide that is the main constituent of the antibiotic tyrothricin. Source: the soil bacillus *Bacillus brevis.* [Mid-20C. Contraction of TYROTHRICIN + GRAMICIDIN + -INE]

Ty·rol another spelling of **Tirol**

Ty·ro·li·enne /ti rōlee én/ *n* **1.** a lively folk dance of Tirolese origin **2.** the music for a Tyrolienne [Late 19C. < French *tyrolienne*, feminine of *tyrolien* "Tirolean"]

Ty·rone /tī rṓn/ historic county in western Northern Ireland, now divided into four local government districts. It was the largest of the six counties of Northern Ireland.

ty·ros·i·nase /tī róssə nàyss, -nàyz/ *n* a copper-containing enzyme involved in the production of dopa from tyrosine [Late 19C. < TYROSINE]

ty·ro·sine /tī́rə seen/ *n* an amino acid that is the precursor of epinephrine, thyroxine, and melanin. Formula: $C_9H_{11}NO_3$. [Mid-19C. < Greek *turos* "cheese"]

ty·ro·thri·cin /tīrə thrī́ss'n/ *n* an antibiotic drug made from tyrocidine and gramicidin. Use: against gram-positive bacteria in local infections. [Mid-20C. < modern Latin *Tyrothric-* < Greek *turos* "cheese" + *thrix* "hair"]

~~**tyrrany**~~ incorrect spelling of **tyranny**

Tyr·rhe·ni·an Sea /ti réenee ən-/ arm of the Mediterranean Sea, partially enclosed by the Italian Peninsula and the islands of Corsica, Sardinia, and Sicily. Area: 59,800 sq. mi./155,000 sq. km.

Ty·son /tī́ss'n/, **Cicely** (*b.* 1933) US actor. She is best known for her role in the television miniseries *Roots* (1977). She won an Emmy Award for best actress for the television movie *The Autobiography of Miss Jane Pittman* (1974).

Ty·son, Mike (*b.* 1966) US boxer. He is the youngest heavyweight fighter to win a world title (1986). Born **Tyson, Michael Gerald**

> "I'm just a normal guy with heart."
> [Mike Tyson, *Mike Tyson: Money, Myth and Betrayal*, Monteith Illingworth; 1992]

tz *abbr* ONLINE Tanzania (*used in Internet addresses*) See table at **domain name**

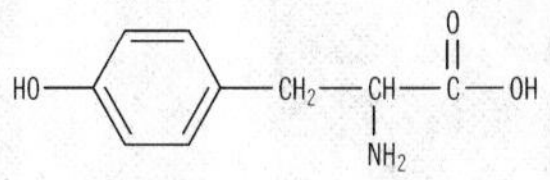

tyrosine

tzad·dik /tsáadik/ (*plural* **-di·kim** /-di kìm/), **tsad·dik, zad·dik** *n* **1.** in Judaism, a righteous man **2.** same as **rebbe** [Late 19C. < Hebrew *ṣaddīq* "righteous"]

tzar *n* POL another spelling of **tsar**

Tza·ra /tsáarə/, **Tristan** (1896–1963) Romanian-born French essayist and poet. A cofounder of the Dada movement, he wrote *Sept Manifestes Dada* (Seven Dada manifestos) (1924).

tzar·ism *n* POL another spelling of **tsarism**

tzet·ze fly *n* INSECTS another spelling of **tsetse fly**

tzi·gane /tsee gáan, see-/ *n* a member of a Roma people, especially one from Hungary [Mid-18C. Via French < Hungarian *czigany*] —**tzi·gane** *adj*

tzim·mes /tsímməss/ (*plural same*), **tsim·mes** *n* **1.** a stew of meat, vegetables, and dried fruits, baked in a casserole **2.** *US* a confused, muddled, or agitated state (*slang*) [Late 19C. < Yiddish *tsimes*]

tzi·tzith /tsítsiss/, **tzi·tzit, tzi·tzes, tsi·tses** *n* the fringes on the corners of a Jewish prayer shawl (**tallis**), a reminder to Jews of God's commandments (Numbers 15:38) [Late 17C. < Hebrew *ṣīṣṯ*]

tzu·ris *n* another spelling of **tsuris**

Uu

u /yoo/ (*plural* **u's**), **U** (*plural* **U's** or **Us**) *n* **1.** the 21st letter of the English alphabet, representing a vowel sound **2.** a written representation of the letter "u"

U[1] /yoo/, **u** *pron* a written form of "you" (*informal*) [Because the letter *U* and *you* are pronounced the same]

U[2] /yoo/ (*plural* **U's** or **Us**) *n* something shaped like a letter "U"

U[3] /oo/ *n* a title of respect for a man used in Myanmar, equivalent to "Mr" [Mid-20C. < Burmese]

U[4] *symbol* **1.** PHYS internal energy **2.** ELEC potential difference **3.** CHEM ELEM uranium

U[5] *abbr* **1.** united **2.** EDUC university **3.** EDUC unsatisfactory

u., **U.** *abbr* **1.** uncle **2.** unit **3.** upper

ua *abbr* ONLINE Ukraine (*used in Internet addresses*) See table at **domain name**

U.A.E *abbr* United Arab Emirates

ua·ka·ri /waa kaáree/ (*plural same*) *n* a short-tailed monkey that lives high in the forest canopy, seldom coming down onto the ground. Native to: South America. Genus: *Cacajao*. [Mid-19C. < Tupi]

UAM *abbr* underwater-to-air missile

UART /yoó aart/ *abbr* COMPUT universal asynchronous receiver/transmitter

UAV *n* an uncrewed aerial vehicle that can fly over combat zones and staging areas, dropping supplies to troops, releasing bombs, and carrying out reconnaissance on enemy forces [Late 20C. Acronym < *uncrewed aerial vehicle*]

UAW, **U.A.W.** *abbr* Automobile, Aerospace, and Agricultural Implement Workers of America

U·ban·gi /yoo báng gee/ river in central Africa. The chief tributary of the Congo River, it is formed by the confluence of the Bomu and Uele rivers. Length: 700 mi./1,130 km.

U·ban·gi-Sha·ri /yoo bàng gee shaáree/ former name for **Central African Republic** (until 1958)

über- *prefix* exceptional of his or her kind (*slang*) ○ *überchef* ○ *übermodel* [< German *über* "over, above, higher," after ÜBERMENSCH]

u·ber·chef /oóbər shèf/ *n* a chef who is considered to be outstandingly talented and successful (*slang*)

Ü·ber·mensch /oóbər mènsh/ (*plural* **-mensch·en** /-mènshən/) *n* a superior kind of human being, especially in Nietzschean philosophy or Nazi ideology [Late 19C. < German, back-formation < *übermenschlich* "superhuman"]

u·ber·mod·el /oóbər mòdd'l/ *n* a fashion model who is regarded as being among the most successful and well-known in the industry (*slang*)

u·bi·e·ty /yoo bí ətee/ *n* the condition of existing in a specific place (*literary*) [Late 17C. < medieval Latin *ubietas* < Latin *ubi* "where"]

u·bi·qui·none /yoóbi kwi nṓn, -kín ōn/ *n* an electron transporter in energy-producing reactions that take place in mitochondria [Mid-20C. Blend of UBIQUITOUS + QUINONE]

u·biq·ui·tar·i·an·ism /yoo bìkwi térree ə nìzzəm/ *n* the Christian belief, held particularly by the Lutheran Church, that Jesus Christ is present in all places and at all times, not just in Communion —**u·biq·ui·tar·i·an** *n, adj*

u·biq·ui·tin /yoo bíkwitin/ *n* a heat-stable protein found in most cellular organisms (eukaryotes) that is involved in many cell processes such as DNA repair and removing metabolic wastes

u·biq·ui·tous /yoo bíkwitəss/ *adj* present everywhere at once, or seeming to be [Mid-19C. < modern Latin *ubiquitas* "presence everywhere" < Latin *ubique* "everywhere" < *ubi* "where"] —**u·biq·ui·tous·ly** *adv* —**u·biq·ui·tous·ness** *n* —**u·biq·ui·ty** *n*

u·bi su·pra /oóbee soópra/ *adv* where mentioned above [Latin, "where above"]

U-boat *n* a German submarine, especially one used during World Wars I and II [Early 20C. Partial translation of German *U-Boot*, shortening of *Unterseeboot* "undersea boat"]

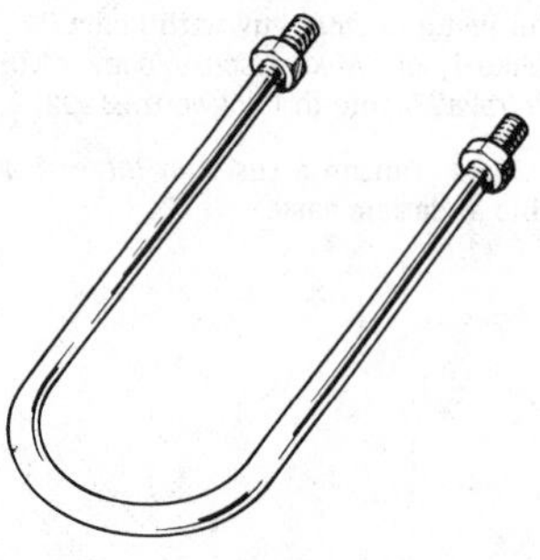

U-bolt

U-bolt *n* a U-shaped bolt, threaded at the two ends

u·bun·tu /oo boóntoo/ *n S Africa* humanity, compassion, and goodness, regarded as fundamental to the way Africans approach life [Late 20C. < Xhosa]

Uc *tdmk* in the United Kingdom, a rating given to a video that is particularly suitable for preschool children

u.c. *abbr* **1.** PRINTING uppercase **2.** CRIME undercover

UCAV /yoó kàv/ *n* an attack aircraft, typically miniaturized, pilotless, and controlled by targeting and weapons systems based both on the ground and in the air. Full form **unmanned combat aerial vehicle**

U·ca·ya·li /oo kaa yaálee/ river in eastern Peru, formed by the confluence of the Apurímac and Urubamba rivers. It is one of the headwaters of the Amazon River. Length: 1,200 mi./1,900 km.

UCC *abbr* **1.** COMM Uniform Commercial Code **2.** United Church of Christ **3.** MED urgent care center

UCE, **uce** *abbr* ONLINE unsolicited commercial e-mail

UCLA *abbr* University of California at Los Angeles

UCMJ *abbr* Uniform Code of Military Justice

U·dai·pur /oo dí poor, yoó dīpoór/ city and administrative headquarters of Udaipur District, Rajasthan State, northwestern India. Population: 308,571 (1991).

ud·der /úddər/ *n* a bag-shaped structure containing two or more milk-secreting glands, each with its own teat, found in mammals such as cows, sheep, and goats [Old English *ūder* < Indo-European]

Ud·jung Pan·dang /oójoòng pan dáng/, **U·jung·pan·dang** city and port on the Makassar Strait, southwestern Sulawesi, Indonesia. Population: 944,372 (1990). Former name **Makassar**

Ud·murt /oód moort/ (*plural same* or **-murts**) *n* **1.** a member of a people who live mainly in Udmurtia in central Russia **2.** the Finno-Ugric language of the Udmurt people. Native speakers: 500,000. [Mid-20C. Via Russian < Udmurt *Ud murt*, < *Ud*, name of a region + *murt* "man"] —**Ud·murt** *adj*

Ud·mur·ti·a /oòd moórtee ə/ autonomous republic in eastern European Russia between Tatarstan and Bashkortostan. Capital: Izhevsk. Population: 1,640,700 (1994). Area: 16,300 sq. mi./42,100 sq. km.

u·do /oó dō/ (*plural* **u·dos**) *n* a perennial plant of the ginseng family whose tender shoots are cooked and eaten as a vegetable. Native to: South Asia. Latin name: *Aralia cordata*. [Late 20C. < Japanese]

u·don /oó dòn/ *n* in Japanese cuisine, pasta in the form of thick wheat strips [Early 20C. < Japanese]

UE *abbr* LEISURE urban exploration

U·fa /oo faá/ industrial city in southeastern European Russia, situated at the confluence of the Ufa and Belaya rivers, on the western slopes of the Ural Mountains. Population: 1,473,912 (1995).

Uf·fi·zi /yoo fítsee/ *n* a museum in Florence that contains one of the world's finest collections of Italian paintings. It is located in 16th-century buildings first used to house the Medici family's art collection, the nucleus of the museum's present holdings. [Mid-19C. < Italian, "offices," because built to house the administrative center of the Florentine state]

UFO /yoó ef ṓ, yoó fṓ/ (*plural* **UFOs**) *n* a flying object that cannot be identified and is thought by some to be an alien spacecraft [Mid-20C. Acronym < *unidentified flying object*]

u·fol·o·gy /yoo fólləjee/ *n* the study of UFOs, especially the investigation of recorded sightings of them

ug *abbr* ONLINE Uganda (*used in Internet addresses*) See table at **domain name**

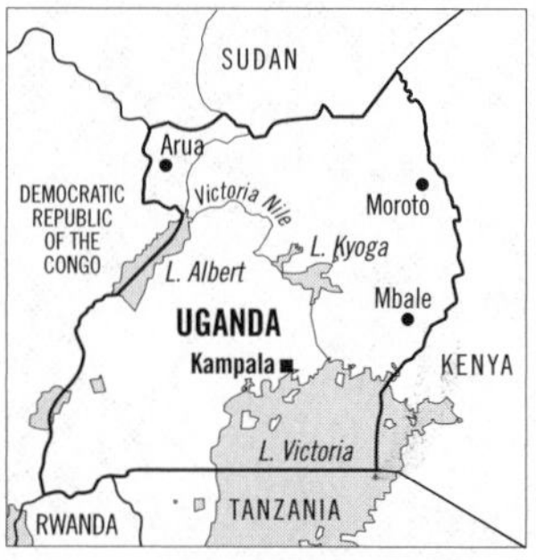

Uganda

U·gan·da /yoo gándə/ country in East Africa. It became a member of the British Commonwealth in 1962 and a republic in 1967. Language: English. Currency: Uganda shilling. Capital: Kampala. Population: 25,632,794 (2003). Area: 93,065 sq. mi./241,038 sq. km. Official name **Republic of Uganda** —**U·gan·dan** *n, adj*

U·ga·rit·ic /oògə ríttik/ *n* an extinct Semitic language of the region that is now northern Syria, closely related to Hebrew and Phoenician [Mid-20C. < *Ugarit*, ancient city in N Syria] —**U·ga·rit·ic** *adj*

ugh /ug, oŏkh, u/ *interj* used as the written form of a grunting exclamation of disgust, strain, or horror [Mid-19C. Representing an involuntary utterance]

ug·li·fy /úgglə fī/ (**-fied, -fy·ing, -fies**) *vt* to make somebody or something physically unappealing —**ug·li·fi·ca·tion** /ùgglәfi káysh'n/ *n* —**ug·li·fi·er** *n*

ug·ly /úgglee/ (**-li·er, -li·est**) *adj* **1. UNATTRACTIVE** lacking appealing physical features, especially facial ones ○ *one of the ugliest cities in Europe* ○ *He was an exceedingly ugly man, and the painter didn't attempt to disguise the fact.* **2. POTENTIALLY VIOLENT** having the potential to result in violence or hostility ○ *an ugly mood* **3. UNPLEASANT** generally unpleasant or objectionable, or morally repulsive ○ *a dull ugly afternoon* ○ *Ugly rumors have been circulating about her private life.* **4.** *Southern US* **ILL-MANNERED** discourteous or rude [13C. < Old Norse *uggligr* "frightful" < *uggr* "fear"] —**ug·li·ly** *adv* —**ug·li·ness** *n*

SYNONYMS See ***unattractive.***

ug·ly A·mer·i·can *n* a loud, boorish, nationalistic American, especially one traveling abroad, who is regarded as conforming to a stereotype that gives Americans a bad reputation

ug·ly duck·ling *n* **1.** somebody or something originally considered ordinary but whose true beauty or value is later revealed or appreciated **2.** somebody or something regarded as physically unappealing in comparison to others [< *The Ugly Duckling*, children's story by Hans Christian Andersen in which a cygnet raised by a duck is considered ugly until it grows into a beautiful swan]

U·gri·an /óogree ən, yóogree ən/ *n* a member of a group of peoples, including the Magyars and Voguls, who live in Hungary and parts of Siberia [Mid-19C. < Russian *Ugry* "Hungarians" < Turkic] —**U·gri·an** *adj*

U·gric /óogrik, yóogrik/ *n* a branch of the Finno-Ugric family of languages that includes Hungarian [Mid-19C. < Russian *Ugry* "Hungarians" (see UGRIAN)] —**U·gric** *adj*

uh /u/ *interj* used as the written form of a grunting exclamation made to express surprise or request something to be said again [Early 17C. Representing an inarticulate sound]

UHF *n* any or all radio frequencies between 300 and 3000 megahertz, typically used for television transmission. Full form **ultrahigh frequency**

uh-huh *interj* used as the written form of a grunting exclamation made to express agreement or to answer affirmatively [Representing an inarticulate sound]

uh-oh *interj* used as the written form of a grunting exclamation made to express apprehension [Representing an articulate sound]

UHT *adj* sterilized and having a long shelf-life as a result of being heated to a very high temperature. Full form **ultra heat treated**

uh-uh *interj* used as the written form of a grunting exclamation made to express disagreement or to answer in the negative [Representing an inarticulate sound]

u·hu·ru /oo hóoroo/ *n* freedom or national independence, especially for the people of eastern Africa [Mid-20C. < Kiswahili]

UI *abbr* **1.** INSUR unemployment insurance **2.** COMPUT user interface

U-ie /yóo ee/ (*plural* **U-ies**) *n UK* same as **U-turn** (*informal*) [Late 20C. Shortening and alteration of U-TURN]

Ui·gur /wée gòor/ (*plural* **Ui·gur** or **Ui·gurs**), **Ui·ghur** *n* **1.** a member of a people who live in western China, mainly in northwestern Xinjiang Uygur Autonomous Region **2.** the Turkic language of the Uigur people. Native speakers: 7 million. [Mid-18C. < E Turkic] —**Ui·gur** *adj* —**Ui·gu·ri·an** /wee góoree ən/ *adj* —**Ui·gu·ric** /-góorik/ *adj*

uil·leann pipes /íllən-/ *npl* Irish bagpipes played by squeezing the bellows under the arm [Early 20C. < Irish *píob uilleann* "elbow pipe" < *uille* "elbow" < Old Irish *uilind*]

u·in·ta·ite /yoo íntə ìt/ *n* a bitumen mined in the Uinta mountains in Utah. Use: manufacturing industries. [Late 19C. < the *Uinta* mountains]

U·jung·pan·dang another spelling of **Udjung Pandang**

uk *abbr* ONLINE United Kingdom (*used in Internet addresses*) See table at **domain name**

U.K., UK *abbr* United Kingdom

u·kase /yoo káyss, yóo kàyss/ *n* **1.** in prerevolutionary Russia, an order from the tsar that had the force of law **2.** any order or ruling, especially one handed down by a self-styled expert or guru [Early 18C. < Russian *ukaz* "edict" < *ukazat'* "show"]

uke /yook/ *n* MUSIC same as **ukulele** (*informal*) [Early 20C. Shortening]

u·ke·le·le *n* MUSIC another spelling of **ukulele**

UK ga·rage *n* a form of garage music developed by bands based in the United Kingdom

u·ki·yo-e /óokee ō áy/, **u·ki·yo-ye** /óokee ō yáy/ *n* a movement in Japanese painting dating from between the 17th and 19th centuries in which scenes and objects from ordinary life were depicted [Late 19C. < Japanese, "transitory-world picture"]

Ukraine

U·kraine /yoo kráyn/ country in eastern Europe, south of Russia, with a coastline on the Black Sea. Language: Ukrainian. Currency: hryvnia. Capital: Kiev. Population: 48,055,439 (2003). Area: 233,100 sq. mi./603,700 sq. km.

U·krain·i·an /yoo kráynee ən/ *n* **1.** somebody who comes from Ukraine **2.** a Balto-Slavic language, the official language of the Ukraine, also spoken in Poland and the Czech Republic. Native speakers: 45 million. —**U·krain·i·an** *adj*

u·ku·le·le /yòokə láylee/, **u·ke·le·le** *n* an instrument like a small guitar with four strings, associated especially with Hawaiian music [Late 19C. < Hawaiian *'ukulele* "jumping flea"]

UL *tdmk* a trademark for a US organization that tests and endorses the safety of products, especially electrical products

U·laan·baa·tar /óo laan baá tàwr/, **U·lan Ba·tor** capital city of the Republic of Mongolia, situated in the north central part of the country, on the Tuul River. Population: 791,000 (2000).

u·la·ma /óolə maá/, **u·le·ma** *npl* a body of Islamic scholars who have jurisdiction over legal and social matters for the people of Islam ■ *n* a member of the ulama [Late 17C. Via Turkish *'ulemā* < Arabic *'ulamā'* "learned men"]

U·lan Ba·tor another spelling of **Ulaanbaatar**

U·lan-U·de /oo laán oo dáy/ port city in southern Siberian Russia, located at the confluence of the Uda and Selenge rivers. Population: 410,359 (1995).

Ul·bricht /óol brìkht/, **Walter** (1893–1973) president of East Germany (1960–73). He was the cofounder and secretary of the Socialist Unity Party (1950–71) and served as deputy premier (1949–50) before becoming head of state in 1960.

ul·cer /úlssər/ *n* **1. INTERNAL SORE** a slow-healing sore on the surface of a mucous membrane, especially the membrane lining the stomach or other part of the digestive tract **2. EXTERNAL SORE** a suppurating sore on the skin that does not heal and results in the destruction of tissue **3. BAD INFLUENCE** a corrupting or debilitating influence [14C. < Latin *ulcer-*, stem of *ulcus* "a sore"] —**ul·cer·ous** *adj*

ul·cer·ate /úlssə ràyt/ (**-at·ed, -at·ing, -ates**) *vti* to cause the formation of an ulcer or ulcers, or undergo the formation of an ulcer or ulcers —**ul·cer·a·tion** /ùlssə ráysh'n/ *n* —**ul·cer·a·tive** *adj*

ul·cer·a·tive co·li·tis *n* inflammation of the walls of the bowel accompanied by the formation of ulcers. The condition can result in permanent bowel damage.

ul·cer·a·tive gin·gi·vi·tis *n* painful inflammation of the gums accompanied by the formation of ulcers. The condition is associated with bacterial infection and malnutrition.

-ule *suffix* small one, miniature ○ *lobule* [Via French < Latin *-ulus*]

u·le·ma *npl* ISLAM another spelling of **ulama**

-ulent *suffix* having a great deal of something ○ *flocculent* [< Latin *-ulentus*]

ul·lage /úllij/ *n* (*formal*) **1.** the amount or volume by which a container, especially one for liquids, is short of being full **2.** the amount of liquid lost from a container through evaporation or leakage [15C. < Anglo-Norman *ulliage* < Old French *ouillier* "fill a barrel to the bunghole" < *oeil* "eye, bunghole" < Latin *oculus* "eye"]

ul·na /úlnə/ (*plural* **-nae** /-nee/ or **-nas**) *n* **1.** the longer of the two bones in the human forearm, situated on the inner side **2.** a bone in the lower forelimb of vertebrate animals, roughly corresponding to the human ulna [Mid-16C. < Latin, "elbow, forearm"] —**ul·nar** *adj*

ul·nar nerve *n* a major nerve of the arm that runs down the inner side of the upper arm and is situated just under the skin at the elbow

u·lot·ri·chous /yoo lóttrikəss/ *adj* having hair that is naturally tightly curled, or belonging to a group of people with this kind of hair [Mid-19C. < Greek *oulos* "crisp, curly" + *trikh-*, stem of *thrix* "hair"]

ul·ster /úlstər/ *n* a man's long heavy double-breasted overcoat [Mid-19C. After ULSTER]

Ul·ster /úlstər/ **1.** historic province in the north of Ireland comprising nine counties, including the six that make up Northern Ireland **2.** an informal name for Northern Ireland —**Ul·ster·man** *n* —**Ul·ster·wom·an** *n*

Ul·ster Un·i·on·ist Par·ty *n* a Northern Ireland political party, formed in 1920. It is the largest and most moderate of the parties committed to the maintenance of the union between Great Britain and Northern Ireland.

ult. *abbr* **1.** ultimate **2.** ultimo

ul·te·ri·or /ul téeree ər/ *adj* **1. UNDERLYING** existing in addition to, or being other than, what is apparent or assumed ○ *ulterior intent* **2. LYING OUTSIDE** lying beyond or outside a point or area **3. HAPPENING IN FUTURE** happening or expected in the future [Mid-17C. < Latin, "further" < assumed *ulter* "beyond"] —**ul·te·ri·or·ly** *adv*

ul·te·ri·or mo·tive *n* a second and underlying motive, usually a selfish or dishonorable one

ul·ti·ma /últimə/ *n* the final syllable of a word [Early 20C. < Latin, form of *ultimus* (see ULTIMATE)]

ul·ti·ma·ta plural of **ultimatum**

ul·ti·mate /últimət/ *adj* **1. FINAL** coming or attained at the end of a series of stages, and often constituting the culmination of something ○ *our ultimate destination* ○ *Their ultimate aim is to introduce a new system of government.* **2. GREATEST** greatest, most nearly perfect, or highest in quality ○ *the ultimate home entertainment system* **3. FUNDAMENTAL** existing as an underlying reality, when all other things are disregarded ○ *the ultimate truth* **4. FARTHEST AWAY** outermost or most remote ■ *n* **GREATEST THING** the greatest or most nearly perfect thing ○ *seats that were the ultimate in passenger comfort* [Mid-17C. < late Latin *ultimatus*, past participle of *ultimare* "be at an end" < Latin *ultimus* "last, final" < assumed *ulter* "beyond"] —**ul·ti·ma·cy** *n*

ul·ti·mate·ly /últimətlee/ *adv* **1.** in the end, as the culmination of a process or event ○ *I ultimately decided not to take part.* **2.** most importantly, when all things are considered ○ *She believes that human beings are ultimately good.*

ul·ti·ma Thu·le /ùltimə thóolee/ *n* (*literary*) **1.** a distant or very remote place **2.** an ultimate or distant goal [Late 18C. < Latin, "farthest Thule," the northernmost part of the inhabited world]

ul·ti·ma·tum /ùltə máytəm/ (*plural* **-tums** or **-ta** /-tə/) *n* a demand accompanied by a threat to inflict some penalty if the demand is not met [Mid-18C. < modern Latin < Latin *ultimatus* (see ULTIMATE)]

ul·ti·mo /últimō/ *adj* used in formal correspondence to refer to the previous month (*dated formal*) ○ *your letter of the 20th ultimo* [Late 16C. < Latin *ultimo (mense)* "in the last (month)" < *ultimus* (see ULTIMATE)]

ul·ti·mo·gen·i·ture /ùltimō jénni chòor, -chər/ *n* the principle of inheritance or succession by the youngest son [Late 19C. < Latin *ultimus* "last," after *primogeniture*]

ul·tra /últrə/ *adj* **1.** **EXTREME** exceeding or going beyond all other of the same kind **2.** **HOLDING EXTREMIST VIEWS** holding extremist views, especially in religious or political matters **3.** **EXCELLENT** excellent or superior (*slang*) ■ *n* **EXTREMIST** somebody with extremist views, especially in religious or political matters [Late 19C. Via French < Latin, "beyond"]

ultra- *prefix* **1.** more than normal, excessively, completely ○ *ultrasophisticated* **2.** outside the range of ○ *ultrasound* [< Latin *ultra* "beyond" < Indo-European]

ul·tra·care·ful *adj*
ul·tra·ca·su·al *adj*
ul·tra·cau·tious *adj*
ul·tra·chic *adj*
ul·tra·clean *adj*
ul·tra·cold *adj*
ul·tra·com·pact *adj*
ul·tra·con·ser·va·tive *adj, n*
ul·tra·con·tem·po·rar·y *adj*
ul·tra·con·ven·ient *adj*
ul·tra·cool *adj*
ul·tra·crit·i·cal *adj*
ul·tra·dense *adj*
ul·tra·dry *adj*
ul·tra·ef·fi·cient *adj*
ul·tra·ex·clu·sive *adj*
ul·tra·fa·mil·iar *adj*
ul·tra·fast *adj*
ul·tra·fas·tid·i·ous *adj*
ul·tra·fine *adj*
ul·tra·glam·or·ous *adj*
ul·tra·heav·y *adj*
ul·tra·high *adj*
ul·tra·hip *adj*
ul·tra·hot *adj*
ul·tra·lib·er·al *adj*
ul·tra·low *adj*
ul·tra·mil·i·tant *adj, n*
ul·tra·min·i·a·ture *adj*
ul·tra·pa·tri·ot *n*
ul·tra·pa·tri·ot·ic *adj*
ul·tra·pow·er·ful *adj*
ul·tra·prac·ti·cal *adj*
ul·tra·pre·cise *adj*
ul·tra·pro·fes·sion·al *adj*
ul·tra·rap·id *adj*
ul·tra·rare *adj*
ul·tra·re·al·is·tic *adj*
ul·tra·re·li·a·ble *adj*
ul·tra·re·lig·ious *adj*
ul·tra·re·spect·a·ble *adj*
ul·tra·rev·o·lu·tion·ar·y *adj*
ul·tra·rich *adj*
ul·tra·roy·al·ist *n*
ul·tra·safe *adj*
ul·tra·sen·si·tive *adj*
ul·tra·sharp *adj*
ul·tra·smart *adj*
ul·tra·smooth *adj*
ul·tra·soft *adj*
ul·tra·so·phis·ti·cat·ed *adj*
ul·tra·sta·ble *adj*
ul·tra·thin *adj*
ul·tra·vi·o·lent *adj*

ul·tra·ba·sic /ùltrə báyssik/ *adj* describes igneous rock that is high in iron and magnesium and contains no free quartz ■ *n* a rock of ultrabasic composition

ul·tra·cen·tri·fuge /ùltrə séntrə fyooj/ *n* a centrifuge for separating microscopic or submicroscopic particles by using a force many times greater than gravity ■ *vt* (**-fuged, -fug·ing, -fuges**) to subject something to the action of an ultracentrifuge —**ul·tra·cen·trif·u·gal** /ùltrə sen trífyəg'l/ *adj* —**ul·tra·cen·trif·u·gal·ly** /-trə fyoogəlee/ *adv*—**ul·tra·cen·trif·u·ga·tion** /-sèntrifyə gáysh'n/ *n*

ul·tra·fiche /últrə feesh/ *n* **1.** a sheet of microfilm of similar size to a microfiche but with a much greater number of documents on it **2.** a device for viewing ultrafiches that has much greater magnification than a microfiche

ul·tra·fil·ter /últrə fíltər/ *n* a filter for separating extremely small particles from a solution or colloid

ul·tra·fil·trate /ùltrə fíl tràyt/ *n* the material that is not filtered out and remains in the liquid phase after ultrafiltration

ul·tra·fil·tra·tion /ùltrəfil tráysh'n/ *n* a filtration process that uses a porous membrane to isolate and remove particles such as bacteria and viruses. The process is used for water purification and in the pharmaceutical industry.

ul·tra·heat·treat·ed *adj* FOOD INDUST full form of **UHT**

ul·tra·high fre·quen·cy /ùltrə hī-/ *n* MEDIA full form of **UHF**

ul·tra·ism /últrə ìzzəm/ *n* religious or political extremism —**ul·tra·ist** *n* —**ul·tra·is·tic** /ùltrə ístik/ *adj*

ul·tra·light /últrə līt/ *adj* extremely light in weight ■ *n* a small single-seat or two-seat aircraft, sometimes resembling a hang glider, constructed of lightweight materials, powered by a small motor, and flown chiefly for recreation

ul·tra·maf·ic /ùltrə máffik/ *adj* describes a dark igneous rock, over 90% of whose content consists of ferromagnesian minerals, including olivine and pyroxenes ■ *n* a rock of ultramafic composition

ul·tra·ma·rine /ùltrəmə reén/ *n* **1.** **BLUE PIGMENT** a deep blue pigment or dye, especially one made from lapis lazuli **2.** **DEEP BLUE COLOR** a brilliant deep blue color ■ *adj* **1.** **DEEP BLUE** ultramarine blue in color **2.** **BEYOND SEA** coming from or lying beyond the sea (*literary*) [Late 16C. < medieval Latin *ultramarinus* "beyond the sea"]

ul·tra·mi·crom·e·ter /ùltrə mī krómmətər/ *n* a measuring device designed to measure spaces and thicknesses more minute than those measurable using a standard micrometer

ul·tra·mi·cro·scope /ùltrə mī́krə skōp/ *n* a microscope that uses scattered light to make submicroscopic objects visible

ul·tra·mi·cro·scop·ic /ùltrə mīkrə skóppik/ *adj* **1.** SCI same as **submicroscopic** **2.** involving the use of an ultramicroscope

ul·tra·mod·ern /ùltrə móddərn/ *adj* more modern than anything comparable, especially in using the very latest designs or making use of the most advanced technology —**ul·tra·mod·ern·ism** *n* —**ul·tra·mod·ern·ist** *n*

ul·tra·mon·tane /ùltrə món tàyn, ùltrə mon táyn/ *adj* **1.** **BEYOND MOUNTAINS** coming from or lying beyond mountains, especially beyond the Alps as viewed from ancient Rome **2.** CHR **SUPPORTING POPE** supporting the power and authority of the pope within the Roman Catholic Church ■ *n* **1.** **DWELLER BEYOND MOUNTAINS** somebody who lives beyond mountains, especially beyond the Alps as viewed from ancient Rome **2.** CHR **PAPAL SUPPORTER** a supporter of the power and authority of the pope in the Roman Catholic Church [Late 16C. < medieval Latin *ultramontanus* "beyond the mountains"]

ul·tra·mon·ta·nism /ùltrə mónt'n ìzzəm/ *n* in the Roman Catholic Church, the policy of investing all power and authority in the pope

ul·tra·mun·dane /ùltrə mun dáyn/ *adj* (*literary*) **1.** coming from or lying beyond Earth or its solar system **2.** belonging or relating to heaven or to the realm of the spirit, and not to the physical world [Mid-16C. < Latin *ultramundanus* "beyond the world" < *ultra* "beyond" + *mundus* "world"]

ul·tra·na·tion·al·ism /ùltrə náshən'l ìzzəm, -náshnə lìzzəm/ *n* nationalism that is so extreme as to be detrimental to international interests or cooperation —**ul·tra·na·tion·al·ist** *n* —**ul·tra·na·tion·al·is·tic** /ùltrə nashən'l ístik, -nashnə lístik/ *adj*

ul·tra·short /ùltrə sháwrt/ *adj* **1.** describes wavelengths that are shorter than 10 m **2.** extremely short in length or duration

ul·tra·son·ic /ùltrə sónnik/ *adj* describes sound waves that have frequencies above the upper limit of the normal range of human hearing, which is about 20 kilohertz —**ul·tra·son·i·cal·ly** *adv*

ul·tra·son·ics /ùltrə sónniks/ *n* the study of sound waves that have frequencies above the upper limit of the normal range of human hearing, which is about 20 kilohertz (*takes a singular verb*)

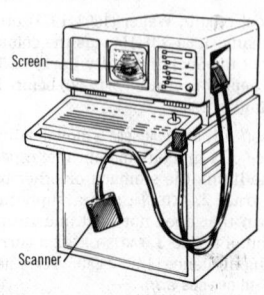

ultrasonic testing

ul·tra·son·ic test·ing *n* the scanning of surfaces with high-frequency sound waves in order to gauge their integrity and check for flaws or to measure the thickness of materials

ul·tra·son·ic weld·ing *n* the bonding of two components by bombarding them with ultrasonic waves to cause vibrations between them

ul·tra·son·o·gram /ùltrə sónnə gràm, -sōnə-/ *n* a picture made with ultrasound for the purpose of medical examination or diagnosis

ul·tra·so·nog·ra·phy /ùltrə sə nóggrəfee/ *n* the use of ultrasound to make images of objects or features that cannot be seen, especially for the purpose of medical examination or diagnosis —**ul·tra·son·o·graph·ic** /ùltrə sonə gráffik, -sōnə-/ *adj*

ul·tra·sound /últrə sòwnd/ *n* **1.** **HIGH-FREQUENCY SOUND** sound of a frequency above the upper limit of the normal range of human hearing, which is about 20 kilohertz **2.** **SOUND WAVES USED IN MEDICINE** a technique that uses high-frequency sound waves for medical diagnosis and treatment, e.g., to create images of internal organs, to treat deep tissue disorders, and to break up kidney stones **3.** *also* **ul·tra·sound scan** MED **MEDICAL EXAM USING ULTRASOUND** an examination of an internal body part, especially a fetus in the womb, using ultrasound technology

ul·tra·struc·ture /últrə strùkchər/ *n* the minute structure of an organic substance or object that becomes evident only under electron microscopy —**ul·tra·struc·tur·al** /ùltrə strúkchərəl/ *adj*

ul·tra·vi·o·let /ùltrə vī́ ələt/ *adj* **RELATING TO INVISIBLE LIGHT** relating to or producing electromagnetic radiation of wavelengths from about 5 to about 400 nanometers, beyond the violet end of the visible light spectrum ■ *n* **1.** **ULTRAVIOLET LAMP** a lamp or bulb that emits ultraviolet radiation **2.** **ULTRAVIOLET RADIATION** radiation with ultraviolet wavelengths. Radiation of this kind is a component of sunlight and is the light that makes exposed skin become darker.

ul·tra vi·res /ùltrə vī́reez/ *adj, adv* beyond the legal capacity of a person, company, or other legal entity [< Latin, "beyond the powers"]

ul·tra·vi·rus /últrə vīrəss/ *n* a virus small enough to pass through an ultrafilter —**ul·tra·vi·ral** /ùltrə vī́rəl/ *adj*

u·lu /oo lòo/ *adj Malaysia, Singapore* rural and not economically or technologically advanced (*informal*) [< Malay *(h)ulu* "the interior," literally "head"]

ul·u·late /yóolyə làyt, úllyə-/ (**-lat·ed, -lat·ing, -lates**) *vi* to howl or wail, in grief or in jubilation [Early 17C. < Latin *ululare*, an imitation of the sound] —**ul·u·la·tion** /yòolyə láysh'n, ùllyə-/ *n*

Ul·u·ru /óolə ròo/ largest individual rock mass in the world, located in the south of the Northern Territory, Australia. Height: 2,848 ft./868 m. Former name **Ayers Rock**

U·lys·ses /yoo lísseez/ *n* the name used by the Romans for the Greek hero Odysseus [Early 17C. < Latin] —**U·lys·se·an** *adj*

um /um/ *interj* a word used in writing to represent the kind of grunting sound that people make when they hesitate in speaking [Early 17C. Representing an inarticulate sound]

U·may·yad /oo mī àd/, **Om·mi·ad, O·may·yad** *n* the family that dominated the politics and commercial economy of Mecca and later established a dynasty as rulers (**caliphs**) of Islam [Mid-18C. < *Umayya*, cousin of Muhammad's grandfather] —**U·may·yad** *adj*

um·bel /úmb'l/ *n* an umbrella-shaped flower head in which the individual flowers are borne on short stems arising from the top of a main stem. It is typical of plants such as parsley, carrot, dill, and fennel. [Late 16C. Directly or via Old French *umbelle* < Latin *umbella* "parasol" < *umbra* "shade"] —**um·bel·lar** /um béllər/ *adj* —**um·bel·late** *adj* —**um·bel·lat·ed** *adj*

um·bel·lif·er·ous /ùmbə líffərəss, -líffrəss/ *adj* with flower heads shaped like an opened umbrella [Mid-17C. < Latin *umbella* "parasol" (see UMBEL)]

um·bel·lule /úmb'l yool, um bél-/ *n* a small umbel that is part of, and has a similar arrangement to, a larger umbel [Late 18C. < modern Latin *umbellula* "little umbel" < Latin *umbella* (see UMBEL)]

um·ber /úmbər/ *n* **1.** **PIGMENT** pigment or dye made from soil that contains oxides of iron and manganese **2.** **SOIL USED FOR PIGMENTS AND DYES** a soil that yields umber.

It is dark yellowish brown in its natural state (**raw umber**), and dark reddish-brown when roasted (**burnt umber**). ■ *adj* **BROWN** colored any shade of brown produced by umber pigment ■ *vt* (**-bered, -ber·ing, -bers**) **PAINT WITH UMBER** to paint or dye something with umber, or color something dark brown [Mid-16C. Via French *terre d'ombre* or Italian *terra di ombre* < Latin *umbra* "shadow"]

Um·ber·to I /oom bértō/ (1844–1900) king of Italy. During his reign (1878–1900), he sought to consolidate Italy as a unified country.

Um·ber·to II (1904–83) king of Italy. He abdicated in 1946, a month after becoming king, when Italians voted in a referendum to establish a republic.

um·bil·i·cal /um bíllik'l/ *adj* **1. OF UMBILICAL CORD** relating to or situated in the umbilical cord, the navel, or the area of the abdomen that surrounds the navel **2. RESEMBLING NAVEL** resembling a navel (**umbilicus**) in appearance **3. PROVIDING LIFELINE** providing a link to something essential, e.g., to supplies or services in wartime, or connecting an astronaut working outside a spacecraft to the spacecraft ■ *n* ANAT same as **umbilical cord** (sense 1) [Mid-16C. < obsolete French, "navel" < Latin *umbilicus* (see UMBILICUS)]

um·bil·i·cal cord *n* **1.** the flexible, often spirally twisted tube that connects the abdomen of a fetus to the mother's placenta in the womb, and through which nutrients are delivered and waste expelled **2.** a cable, tube, or pipe attaching somebody or something to an essential supply, e.g., the tube that connects a deep-sea diver to an oxygen supply on a ship

um·bil·i·cate /um bíllikət, -kàyt/, **um·bil·i·cat·ed** /-kàytəd/ *adj* **1.** with a mark, depression, or perforation that resembles a navel **2.** shaped like a navel [Late 17C. < UMBILICUS]

um·bil·i·cus /um bíllikəss, ùmbi lĭ́kəss/ (*plural* **-ci** /-sī/ or **-cus·es**) *n* **1.** ANAT same as **navel** (*technical*) **2.** a dip or hollow that resembles a navel, e.g., the hollow at each end of the shaft of a feather [Late 17C. < Latin < Indo-European]

um·bo /úmbō/ (*plural* **-bo·nes** /um bṓneez/ or **-bos**) *n* **1. BUMP ON PLANT OR ANIMAL PART** a small protuberance on a plant or animal part, e.g., the hump on the caps of some mushrooms, or the bump just above the hinge of a bivalve shell **2. SMALL HOLLOW IN EARDRUM** a small hollow in the center of the outer surface of the eardrum, at the point where the malleus joins it on the inside **3. KNOB ON SHIELD** a knob at the center of a round shield, especially a Saxon shield [Early 18C. < Latin, "shield boss"] —**um·bo·nal** /úmbən'l, um bṓn'l/ *adj* —**um·bo·nate** /-nàyt, -nət/ *adj*

um·bra /úmbrə/ (*plural* **-bras** or **-brae** /-bree/) *n* **1.** PHYS **COMPLETE SHADOW** an area of complete shadow caused by light from all points of a source being prevented from reaching the area, usually by an opaque object **2.** ASTRON **DARKEST PART OF MOON'S SHADOW** the darkest portion of the shadow cast by an astronomical object during an eclipse, especially that cast on Earth during a solar eclipse **3.** ASTRON **DARK PART OF SUNSPOT** the inner, darker area of a sunspot [Late 16C. < Latin, "shadow"] —**um·bral** *adj*

um·brage /úmbrij/ *n* **1.** resentment or annoyance arising from some offense ○ *took umbrage* **2.** something that gives shade, e.g., a tree (*literary*) [15C. < Old French < Latin *umbra* "shadow"]

ORIGIN The Latin word *umbra* "shadow," from which **umbrage** is derived, is also the source of English *adumbrate, penumbra, somber, sombrero,* and *umbrella.*

um·bra·geous /um bráyjəss/ *adj* **1.** easily offended or likely to become irritated **2.** providing shade and coolness (*literary*) —**um·bra·geous·ly** *adv*

um·brel·la /um bréllə/ *n* **1. COLLAPSIBLE CANOPY THAT PROTECTS FROM WEATHER** a round collapsible canopy of plastic or waterproof material on a frame at the top of a handle, held in the hand to protect somebody from rain, snow, or sun **2. SUPPORT OR AUTHORITY** something that gives support, protection, or authority ○ *under the umbrella of the United Nations* **3. OBJECT LIKE UMBRELLA** an object that looks like an open umbrella, or that collapses like an umbrella, e.g., the folding paper decoration sometimes served in cocktails **4.** ZOOL **JELLYFISH'S BODY** the rounded body of a jellyfish **5.** MIL **AIRCRAFT FLYING OVERHEAD FOR PROTECTION** a group of aircraft patrolling the sky above a place where troops are carrying out operations, to give them protection **6.** MIL **SHIELD OF GUNFIRE** gunfire used to suppress enemy fire and thus shield friendly forces making a movement or attack **7.** *US* MIL same as **parachute** *n* (sense 1) (*slang*) ■ *adj* **1. UNIFYING MEMBER ORGANIZATIONS** acting to coordinate or protect a number of member organizations or bodies **2. INCLUDING SEVERAL THINGS** including or containing a number of things ○ *an umbrella term for a variety of plants* [Early 17C. Via Italian *ombrella* < late Latin *umbrella*, alteration of Latin *umbella* "parasol" (see UMBEL) after *umbra* "shadow"]

umbrella bird

um·brel·la bird *n* a bird of the cotinga family with a large umbrella-shaped crest and a long feathered wattle. Native to: Central and South America. Genus: *Cephalopterus*.

um·brel·la pine *n* TREES same as **stone pine**

um·brel·la plant *n* **1.** a plant of the sedge family that has thin leaves radiating from the top of long stems. Native to: Africa. Latin name: *Cyperus alternifolius*. **2.** *Midwest* same as **May apple**

um·brel·la stand *n* an upright stand or rack for holding walking sticks and folded umbrellas

um·brel·la tree *n* **1.** a magnolia tree with large leaves clustered around the ends of the branches. Native to: southeastern United States. Latin name: *Magnolia fraseri* or *Magnolia tripetala*. **2.** a bush or tree with umbrella-shaped clusters of leaves. Flowers: red, clustered on long spikes. Native to: Australia. Latin name: *Schefflera actinophylla*.

Um·bri·a /úmbree ə/ agricultural region in central Italy, west of the Apennines. Population: 835,488 (2001). Area: 3,265 sq. mi./8,456 sq. km.

Um·bri·an /úmbree ən/ *n* **1.** somebody who comes from Umbria **2.** an extinct Italic language of ancient southern Italy —**Um·bri·an** *adj*

Um·bri·el /úmbree əl/ *n* a large natural satellite of the planet Uranus, discovered in 1851 [After a sprite in the poem "The Rape of the Lock" by Alexander POPE]

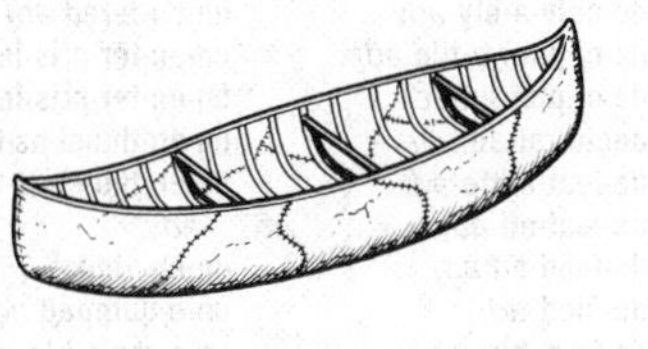

umiak

u·mi·ak /óomee àk/ *n* a large Inuit boat made of animal skins stretched across a wooden frame, larger and more open than a kayak and traditionally paddled by women [Mid-18C. < Inuit *umiaq*]

um·laut /ŏŏm lòwt/ *n* **1. CHANGE IN VOWEL SOUND** in Germanic languages, a change in the way a vowel is pronounced, caused by the influence of another vowel in a syllable immediately after it **2. ACCENT OVER VOWEL** in Germanic languages, the mark (¨) that is placed above a vowel to show that it is pronounced differently from the way the vowel is usually pronounced. See table at **diacritic** ■ *v* (**-laut·ed, -laut·ing, -lauts**) **1.** *vti* **CHANGE VOWEL SOUND** to change a vowel sound because of other vowel sounds close to it, or be changed in this way **2.** *vt* **MARK VOWEL WITH TWO DOTS** to write or print a vowel with an umlaut above it [Mid-19C. < German < *um-* "around, change" + *Laut* "sound"]

um·ma /ŏŏmmə/, **um·mah** *n* within Islam, the community of the faithful that transcended long established tribal boundaries to create a degree of political unity [Late 19C. < Arabic, "people, community"]

um·pire /úm pīr/ *n* **1. OFFICIAL ENFORCING SPORT'S RULES** an official who supervises play and enforces the rules of the game in some sports, e.g., baseball **2. SOMEBODY SETTLING DISPUTE** somebody called in to settle a dispute ■ *vti* (**-pired, -pir·ing, -pires**) **1. SUPERVISE PLAY IN SPORT** to supervise play in a game or sport and enforce the rules **2. SETTLE DISPUTE** to give a ruling on a dispute as an impartial arbitrator [Late 16C. By false division < *noumper* < Old French *nonper* < *non* "not" + *per* "pair"]

ump·teen /úmp teen, úm-/ *adj* a large but unspecified number of (*informal*) [Early 20C Humorous formation after *thirteen, fourteen,* etc] —**ump·teenth** *adj*

um·rah /ŏŏm raa/ *n* a lesser form of pilgrimage to Mecca that is not obligatory for Muslims, unlike the hajj, and that can be performed at any time of year [Early 19C. < Arabic *'umra*]

Um·ta·ta /um taatə/ city in Eastern Cape Province, South Africa. Population: 67,000 (1995 estimate).

u·mun·na /ŏŏ mŏŏnə/ *n W Africa* a social grouping consisting of a person's extended family

UMWA *abbr* POL United Mine Workers of America

un /ən, 'n/, **'un** *pron* a spelling of the pronoun "one" intended to reflect the way it is sometimes pronounced in informal speech (*informal*) [Early 19C. Alteration of ONE]

UN, U.N. *abbr* POL United Nations

un- *prefix* **1.** not ○ *unavoidable* **2.** opposite of, lack of ○ *unrest* **3.** to do the opposite of, reverse ○ *uninstall* **4.** to deprive of, remove something from ○ *unfrock* **5.** to release from ○ *unchain* **6.** completely ○ *unloose* [Old English < Indo-European]

USAGE un- or **non-**? Many adjectives formed with ***un-*** have special (usually unfavorable) meanings, for example, *uncooperative* and *unprofessional.* In these cases neutral equivalents that mean simply "not ..." are formed by means of ***non-***, for example, *noncooperative, nonprofessional.*

un·a·bashed *adj*
un·a·bash·ed·ly *adv*
un·ab·bre·vi·at·ed *adj*
un·a·bridged *adj*
un·ab·sorbed *adj*
un·ab·sorb·ent *adj*
un·ac·a·dem·ic *adj*
un·ac·cent·ed *adj*
un·ac·cept·a·bil·i·ty *n*
un·ac·cept·a·ble *adj*
un·ac·cept·a·bly *adv*
un·ac·cept·ed *adj*
un·ac·cept·ing *adj*
un·ac·com·mo·dat·ing *adj*
un·ac·com·mo·dat·ing·ly *adv*
un·ac·com·plished *adj*
un·ac·count·ed *adj*
un·ac·cred·it·ed *adj*
un·a·chiev·a·ble *adj*
un·a·chiev·a·bly *adv*
un·ac·knowl·edged *adj*
un·a·dapt·a·ble *adj*
un·a·dapt·ed *adj*
un·ad·dict·ed *adj*
un·ad·dressed *adj*
un·ad·ja·cent *adj*
un·ad·just·ed *adj*
un·ad·mired *adj*
un·ad·mit·ted *adj*
un·a·dorned *adj*
un·ad·ven·tur·ous *adj*
un·ad·ver·tised *adj*
un·ad·vis·a·ble *adj*
un·aes·thet·ic *adj*
un·af·fect·ed *adj*
un·af·fect·ed·ly *adv*
un·af·fect·ed·ness *n*
un·af·fect·ing *adj*
un·af·fec·tion·ate *adj*
un·af·fil·i·at·ed *adj*
un·af·ford·a·ble *adj*
un·a·fraid *adj*
un·ag·gres·sive *adj*
un·aid·ed *adj, adv*
un·a·ligned *adj*
un·a·like *adj*
un·a·live *adj*
un·al·le·vi·at·ed *adj*
un·al·lied *adj*
un·al·lo·cat·ed *adj*
un·al·low·a·ble *adj*
un·al·lur·ing *adj*
un·al·ter·a·ble *adj*
un·al·ter·a·bly *adv*
un·al·tered *adj*
un·a·mazed *adj*
un·am·bi·tious *adj*
un·am·biv·a·lent *adj*
un·am·biv·a·lent·ly *adv*
un·a·me·na·ble *adj*
un·a·mend·ed *adj*
un·a·mi·a·ble *adj*
un·am·pli·fied *adj*
un·a·mused *adj*
un·a·mus·ing *adj*
un·an·a·lyz·a·ble *adj*

un·an·chored *adj*
un·an·nounced *adj*
un·an·swered *adj*
un·an·tic·i·pat·ed *adj*
un·a·pol·o·get·ic *adj*
un·a·pol·o·get·i·cal·ly *adv*
un·ap·par·ent *adj*
un·ap·peas·a·ble *adj*
un·ap·peased *adj*
un·ap·pe·tiz·ing *adj*
un·ap·plied *adj*
un·ap·pre·ci·at·ed *adj*
un·ap·pre·cia·tive *adj*
un·ap·pre·hend·ed *adj*
un·ap·pro·pri·at·ed *adj*
un·ap·proved *adj*
un·ar·a·ble *adj*
un·arm *vt*
un·ar·mored *adj*
un·a·roused *adj*
un·ar·rest·ing *adj*
un·ar·rest·ing·ly *adv*
un·ar·tic·u·lat·ed *adj*
un·ar·tis·tic *adj*
un·ar·tis·ti·cal·ly *adv*
un·as·cer·tain·a·ble *adj*
un·as·cer·tained *adj*
un·as·ser·tive *adj*
un·as·ser·tive·ness *n*
un·as·sign·a·ble *adj*
un·as·signed *adj*
un·as·sim·i·lat·ed *adj*
un·as·sist·ed *adj*
un·as·so·ci·at·ed *adj*
un·as·suaged *adj*
un·ath·let·ic *adj*
un·a·toned *adj*
un·at·tain·a·ble *adj*
un·at·test·ed *adj*
un·at·trib·ut·a·ble *adj*
un·at·trib·ut·ed *adj*
un·au·dit·ed *adj*
un·au·then·tic *adj*
un·au·then·ti·cat·ed *adj*
un·au·thor·ized *adj*
un·au·to·mat·ed *adj*
un·a·vail·a·bil·i·ty *n*
un·a·vail·a·ble *adj*
un·a·venged *adj*
un·a·vowed *adj*
un·bait·ed *adj*
un·baked *adj*
un·ban *vt*
un·bap·tized *adj*
un·bat·ed *adj*
un·beau·ti·ful *adj*
un·beau·ti·ful·ly *adv*
un·be·fit·ting *adj*
un·be·fit·ting·ly *adv*
un·be·fit·ting·ness *n*
un·be·hold·en *adj*
un·be·loved *adj*
un·bid·da·ble *adj*
un·bleached *adj*
un·blem·ished *adj*
un·blend·ed *adj*
un·bond·ed *adj*
un·book·ish *adj*
un·bor·dered *adj*
un·bought *adj*
un·branched *adj*
un·brand·ed *adj*
un·breach·a·ble *adj*
un·break·a·ble *adj*
un·breath·a·ble *adj*
un·brib·a·ble *adj*
un·bridge·a·ble *adj*
un·bruised *adj*
un·brushed *adj*
un·buck·le *vti*
un·bud·get·ed *adj*
un·build·a·ble *adj*
un·built *adj*
un·bur·ied *adj*
un·burn·a·ble *adj*
un·burned *adj*
un·busi·ness·like *adj*
un·caged *adj*
un·can·did *adj*
un·ca·non·i·cal *adj*
un·ca·non·i·cal·ly *adv*
un·car·bon·at·ed *adj*
un·car·ing *adj*
un·car·pet·ed *adj*
un·cashed *adj*
un·cas·trat·ed *adj*
un·catch·a·ble *adj*
un·caught *adj*
un·caused *adj*
un·cel·e·brat·ed *adj*
un·cen·sor·ed *adj*
un·cen·sured *adj*
un·cer·ti·fied *adj*
un·chal·lenge·a·ble *adj*
un·chal·lenged *adj*
un·chal·leng·ing *adj*
un·change·a·bil·i·ty *n*
un·change·a·ble *adj*
un·change·a·ble·ness *n*
un·change·a·bly *adv*
un·changed *adj*
un·chang·ing *adj*
un·chan·neled *adj*
un·chap·er·oned *adj*
un·char·ac·ter·is·tic *adj*
un·char·ac·ter·is·ti·cal·ly *adv*
un·charged *adj*
un·char·is·mat·ic *adj*
un·char·i·ta·ble *adj*
un·char·i·ta·ble·ness *n*
un·char·i·ta·bly *adv*
un·chaste *adj*
un·chaste·ly *adv*
un·chaste·ness *n*
un·chic *adj*
un·chiv·al·rous *adj*
un·cho·sen *adj*
un·chron·i·cled *adj*
un·cin·e·mat·ic *adj*
un·cir·cu·lat·ed *adj*
un·cir·cum·cised *adj*
un·cir·cum·ci·sion *n*
un·claimed *adj*
un·clar·i·fied *adj*
un·clas·si·fi·a·ble *adj*
un·cleaned *adj*
un·clear *adj*
un·cleared *adj*
un·clear·ly *adv*
un·clear·ness *n*
un·clench *vti*
un·cloud·ed *adj*
un·co·ag·u·lat·ed *adj*
un·coat·ed *adj*
un·col·lect·ed *adj*
un·col·o·nized *adj*
un·col·ored *adj*
un·combed *adj*
un·com·bined *adj*
un·come·ly *adj*
un·com·pan·ion·a·ble *adj*
un·com·pen·sat·ed *adj*
un·com·pet·i·tive *adj*
un·com·plain·ing *adj*
un·com·plain·ing·ly *adv*
un·com·plet·ed *adj*
un·com·plexed *adj*
un·com·pli·men·ta·ry *adj*
un·com·pound·ed *adj*
un·com·pre·hend·ing *adj*
un·com·pre·hend·ing·ly *adv*
un·con·cealed *adj*
un·con·ceiv·a·ble *adj*
un·con·ceiv·a·bly *adv*
un·con·clud·ed *adj*
un·con·de·scend·ing *adj*
un·con·fessed *adj*
un·con·fi·dent *adj*
un·con·fi·dent·ly *adv*
un·con·firmed *adj*
un·con·fused *adj*
un·con·gen·ial *adj*
un·con·jec·tur·a·ble *adj*
un·con·quer·a·ble *adj*
un·con·quer·a·bly *adv*
un·con·quered *adj*
un·con·se·crat·ed *adj*
un·con·sent·ing *adj*
un·con·sol·i·dat·ed *adj*
un·con·strained *adj*
un·con·strain·ed·ly *adv*
un·con·strict·ed *adj*
un·con·struc·tive *adj*
un·con·sult·ed *adj*
un·con·sum·mat·ed *adj*
un·con·tam·i·nat·ed *adj*
un·con·ten·tious *adj*
un·con·test·ed *adj*
un·con·test·ed·ly *adv*
un·con·tra·dict·ed *adj*
un·con·trived *adj*
un·con·trolled *adj*
un·con·trolled·ly *adv*
un·con·tro·ver·sial *adj*
un·con·tro·ver·sial·ly *adv*
un·con·vert·ed *adj*
un·con·vinced *adj*
un·con·vinc·ing *adj*
un·con·vinc·ing·ly *adv*
un·con·vinc·ing·ness *n*
un·cooked *adj*
un·co·op·er·a·tive *adj*
un·co·op·er·a·tive·ly *adv*
un·co·op·er·a·tive·ness *n*
un·cop·i·a·ble *adj*
un·cor·rect·a·ble *adj*
un·cor·rect·ed *adj*
un·cor·rob·o·rat·ed *adj*
un·cor·rupt·ed *adj*
un·cou·ra·geous *adj*
un·crease *vt*
un·creased *adj*
un·cre·at·ed *adj*
un·cre·a·tive *adj*
un·cre·a·tive·ly *adv*
un·cre·a·tive·ness *n*
un·cropped *adj*
un·crowd·ed *adj*
un·crowd·ed·ness *n*
un·crush·a·ble *adj*
un·crushed *adj*
un·crys·tal·lized *adj*
un·culled *adj*
un·cul·ti·vat·ed *adj*
un·cul·tured *adj*
un·curbed *adj*
un·cured *adj*
un·cur·tailed *adj*
un·cur·tained *adj*
un·cus·tom·ar·y *adj*
un·cut·ta·ble *adj*
un·dam·aged *adj*
un·dam·ag·ing *adj*
un·dat·ed *adj*
un·daunt·a·ble *adj*
un·dealt *adj*
un·de·bat·a·ble *adj*
un·de·bat·a·bly *adv*
un·de·cayed *adj*
un·de·ceiv·a·ble *adj*
un·de·ceiv·a·bly *adv*
un·de·ci·pher·a·ble *adj*
un·de·ci·phered *adj*
un·dec·o·rat·ed *adj*
un·de·feat·a·ble *adj*
un·de·feat·ed *adj*
un·de·fend·ed *adj*
un·de·filed *adj*
un·de·fin·a·ble *adj*
un·de·fin·a·bly *adv*
un·de·fined *adj*
un·de·formed *adj*
un·de·liv·er·a·ble *adj*
un·de·liv·ered *adj*
un·de·lud·ed *adj*
un·de·mand·ing *adj*
un·de·mar·cat·ed *adj*
un·dem·on·strat·ed *adj*
un·de·nied *adj*
un·de·nom·i·na·tion·al *adj*
un·dent·ed *adj*
un·de·pend·a·bil·i·ty *n*
un·de·pend·a·ble *adj*
un·de·pend·a·bly *adv*
un·de·signed *adj*
un·de·sign·ed·ly *adv*
un·de·sired *adj*
un·de·sir·ous *adj*
un·de·stroyed *adj*
un·de·tailed *adj*
un·de·tect·a·ble *adj*
un·de·tect·ed *adj*
un·de·terred *adj*
un·de·vel·oped *adj*
un·di·ag·nosed *adj*
un·dif·fer·en·ti·at·ed *adj*
un·di·gest·i·ble *adj*
un·dig·ni·fied *adj*
un·di·lut·ed *adj*
un·di·min·ished *adj*
un·di·min·ish·ing *adj*
un·dimmed *adj*
un·dis·cern·ing *adj*
un·dis·cern·ing·ly *adv*
un·dis·charged *adj*
un·dis·ci·plined *adj*
un·dis·closed *adj*
un·dis·cov·er·a·ble *adj*
un·dis·cov·ered *adj*
un·dis·crim·i·nat·ing *adj*
un·dis·cussed *adj*
un·dis·mayed *adj*
un·dis·put·a·ble *adj*
un·dis·put·ed *adj*
un·dis·solved *adj*
un·dis·tort·ed *adj*
un·di·vid·a·ble *adj*
un·di·vid·ed *adj*
un·doc·u·ment·ed *adj*
un·do·mes·ti·cat·ed *adj*
un·doubt·ing *adj*
un·drained *adj*
un·dra·mat·ic *adj*
un·draped *adj*
un·drawn *adj*
un·drink·a·ble *adj*
un·dyed *adj*
un·dy·nam·ic *adj*
un·eat·a·ble *adj*
un·eat·en *adj*
un·ed·i·fy·ing *adj*
un·e·lab·o·rate *adj*
un·e·lect·ed *adj*
un·em·bar·rassed *adj*
un·em·bel·lished *adj*
un·em·broi·dered *adj*
un·em·phat·ic *adj*
un·em·phat·i·cal·ly *adv*
un·en·closed *adj*
un·en·cum·bered *adj*
un·en·dowed *adj*
un·en·force·a·bil·i·ty *n*
un·en·force·a·ble *adj*
un·en·forced *adj*
un·en·gaged *adj*
un·en·joy·a·ble *adj*
un·en·light·ened *adj*
un·en·light·en·ing *adj*
un·en·light·en·ment *n*
un·en·tered *adj*
un·en·ter·pris·ing *adj*
un·en·ter·pris·ing·ly *adv*
un·en·thu·si·as·tic *adj*
un·en·thu·si·as·ti·cal·ly *adv*
un·en·vied *adj*
un·e·quipped *adj*
un·e·ras·a·ble *adj*
un·e·rod·ed *adj*
un·e·rot·ic *adj*
un·e·rupt·ed *adj*
un·es·cort·ed *adj*
un·es·tab·lished *adj*
un·e·van·gel·i·cal *adj*
un·ex·am·ined *adj*
un·ex·cit·ing *adj*
un·ex·e·cut·ed *adj*
un·ex·er·cised *adj*
un·ex·haust·ed *adj*
un·ex·pired *adj*
un·ex·plain·a·ble *adj*
un·ex·plained *adj*
un·ex·ploit·ed *adj*
un·ex·plored *adj*
un·ex·posed *adj*
un·ex·pres·sive *adj*
un·ex·tra·or·di·nar·y *adj*
un·fac·et·ed *adj*
un·fad·ing *adj*
un·fad·ing·ly *adv*
un·farmed *adj*
un·fa·ther·li·ness *n*
un·fa·ther·ly *adj*
un·fath·omed *adj*
un·fa·vored *adj*
un·fazed *adj*
un·feath·ered *adj*
un·fed *adj*
un·fed·er·at·ed *adj*
un·feigned *adj*
un·felt *adj*
un·fem·i·nine *adj*
un·fem·i·nin·i·ty *n*
un·fenced *adj*
un·fer·ment·ed *adj*
un·fer·tile *adj*
un·fer·til·ized *adj*
un·filled *adj*
un·fil·tered *adj*
un·fired *adj*
un·flash·y *adj*
un·fla·vored *adj*
un·flawed *adj*
un·fluc·tu·at·ing *adj*
un·flus·tered *adj*
un·flut·ed *adj*
un·force·ful *adj*
un·ford·a·ble *adj*
un·for·est·ed *adj*
un·for·giv·en *adj*
un·for·got·ten *adj*
un·for·mu·lat·ed *adj*
un·for·ti·fied *adj*
un·found *adj*
un·framed *adj*
un·free *adj*
un·fret·ted *adj*
un·ful·fill·ing *adj*
un·fund·ed *adj*
un·fun·ni·ness *n*
un·fur·rowed *adj*
un·fused *adj*
un·fus·si·ly *adv*
un·fuss·y *adj*
un·gain·say·a·ble *adj*
un·gal·lant *adj*
un·gal·lant·ly *adv*
un·gar·nished *adj*
un·geld·ed *adj*
un·gen·er·ous *adj*
un·gen·er·ous·ly *adv*
un·gen·er·ous·ness *n*
un·gen·ial *adj*
un·gen·teel *adj*
un·gen·tle *adj*
un·gen·tle·man·li·ness *n*
un·gen·tle·man·ly *adj*
un·gift·ed *adj*
un·glam·or·ous *adj*
un·glazed *adj*
un·grace·ful *adj*
un·grace·ful·ly *adv*
un·grace·ful·ness *n*
un·grad·ed *adj*
un·grat·i·fied *adj*
un·greased *adj*
un·guess·a·ble *adj*
un·guid·ed *adj*
un·ham·pered *adj*
un·hard·ened *adj*
un·harm·ful *adj*
un·har·mo·ni·ous *adj*
un·hatched *adj*
un·healed *adj*
un·health·ful *adj*
un·heed·ing *adj*
un·heed·ing·ly *adv*
un·hemmed *adj*
un·her·ald·ed *adj*
un·he·ro·ic *adj*
un·he·ro·i·cal·ly *adv*
un·hewn *adj*
un·hip *adj*
un·hon·ored *adj*
un·hope·ful *adj*
un·housed *adj*
un·hu·man *adj*
un·hy·phen·at·ed *adj*
un·i·de·al *adj*
un·i·de·al·ized *adj*
un·i·den·ti·fi·a·ble *adj*
un·id·i·o·mat·ic *adj*
un·ig·nor·a·ble *adj*
un·il·lu·mi·nat·ed *adj*
un·il·lu·mi·nat·ing *adj*
un·il·lus·trat·ed *adj*
un·i·mag·ined *adj*
un·im·pas·sioned *adj*
un·im·pos·ing *adj*
un·im·pos·ing·ly *adv*
un·im·pres·sion·a·ble *adj*
un·im·pres·sive *adj*
un·in·dent·ed *adj*
un·in·dict·ed *adj*
un·in·dus·tri·al·ized *adj*
un·in·fect·ed *adj*
un·in·flamed *adj*
un·in·flat·ed *adj*
un·in·flect·ed *adj*
un·in·flu·enced *adj*
un·in·flu·en·tial *adj*
un·in·su·lat·ed *adj*
un·in·tel·lec·tu·al *adj*
un·in·tend·ed *adj*
un·in·ter·est *n*
un·in·ter·pret·ed *adj*
un·in·tim·i·dat·ed *adj*
un·in·ven·tive *adj*
un·in·ven·tive·ly *adv*
un·in·ven·tive·ness *n*
un·in·ves·ti·gat·ed *adj*
un·i·roned *adj*
un·ir·ri·gat·ed *adj*
un·is·sued *adj*
un·jad·ed *adj*
un·jam *vti*
un·joined *adj*
un·kill·a·ble *adj*
un·knot *vti*
un·knowl·edge·a·ble *adj*
un·la·beled *adj*
un·lad·en *adj*
un·la·dy·like *adj*
un·laid *adj*
un·la·ment·ed *adj*
un·latch *vti*
un·leased *adj*
un·lib·er·at·ed *adj*
un·light·ed *adj*
un·lik·a·ble *adj*
un·lined *adj*
un·link *vti*
un·lit *adj*
un·lock·a·ble *adj*
un·locked *adj*
un·lov·a·ble *adj*
un·loved *adj*
un·lov·ing *adj*
un·lov·ing·ly *adv*
un·lov·ing·ness *n*
un·mailed *adj*
un·man·aged *adj*
un·mapped *adj*
un·mar·ket·a·ble *adj*
un·ma·te·ri·al·is·tic *adj*
un·ma·tured *adj*
un·mea·sur·a·ble *adj*
un·mech·a·nized *adj*
un·me·lod·ic *adj*
un·me·lo·di·ous *adj*
un·me·lo·di·ous·ly *adv*
un·melt·ed *adj*
un·mem·o·ra·ble *adj*
un·mem·o·ra·bly *adv*
un·men·tion·ed *adj*
un·mer·chant·a·ble *adj*
un·mer·it·ed *adj*
un·me·thod·i·cal *adj*
un·me·thod·i·cal·ly *adv*
un·mil·i·tar·y *adj*
un·mind·ful *adj*
un·mind·ful·ly *adv*

un·mind·ful·ness *n*
un·mined *adj*
un·miss·a·ble *adj*
un·mixed *adj*
un·mod·ern·ized *adj*
un·mod·i·fi·a·ble *adj*
un·mod·i·fied *adj*
un·mold·ed *adj*
un·mo·lest·ed *adj, adv*
un·mo·ti·vat·ed *adj*
un·mount·ed *adj*
un·mourned *adj*
un·mov·a·ble *adj*
un·mown *adj*
un·muf·fle *vt*
un·mu·ti·lat·ed *adj*
un·nav·i·ga·ble *adj*
un·nav·i·gat·ed *adj*
un·need·ed *adj*
un·neigh·bor·li·ness *n*
un·neigh·bor·ly *adj*
un·neu·tral *adj*
un·no·tice·a·ble *adj*
un·no·tice·a·bly *adv*
un·ob·jec·tion·a·ble *adj*
un·ob·jec·tion·a·bly *adv*
un·ob·scured *adj*
un·ob·serv·a·ble *adj*
un·ob·ser·vant *adj*
un·ob·ser·vant·ly *adv*
un·ob·served *adj*
un·ob·struct·ed *adj*
un·ob·tain·a·bil·i·ty *n*
un·ob·tain·a·ble *adj*
un·of·fend·ed *adj*
un·of·fend·ing *adj*
un·oiled *adj*
un·o·pen *adj*
un·o·pen·a·ble *adj*
un·o·pened *adj*
un·o·rig·i·nal *adj*
un·o·rig·i·nal·ly *adv*
un·or·na·men·tal *adj*
un·or·na·ment·ed *adj*
un·os·ten·ta·tious *adj*
un·os·ten·ta·tious·ly *adv*
un·os·ten·ta·tious·ness *n*
un·owned *adj*
un·pack·aged *adj*
un·paint·ed *adj*
un·pas·teur·ized *adj*
un·pat·ent·ed *adj*
un·pa·tri·ot·ic *adj*
un·pat·ron·iz·ing *adj*
un·pat·ron·iz·ing·ly *adv*
un·pat·terned *adj*
un·paved *adj*
un·peeled *adj*
un·pe·nal·ized *adj*
un·peo·pled *adj*
un·per·ceived *adj*
un·per·cep·tive *adj*
un·per·cep·tive·ly *adv*
un·per·cep·tive·ness *n*
un·per·fect·ed *adj*
un·per·fo·rat·ed *adj*
un·per·form·a·ble *adj*
un·per·formed *adj*
un·per·fumed *adj*
un·per·suad·a·ble *adj*
un·per·suad·ed *adj*
un·per·sua·sive *adj*
un·per·sua·sive·ly *adv*
un·picked *adj*
un·pic·tur·esque *adj*
un·pig·ment·ed *adj*
un·pit·ied *adj*
un·plant·ed *adj*
un·play·a·ble *adj*
un·played *adj*
un·pleas·ing *adj*
un·pledged *adj*
un·plowed *adj*
un·plucked *adj*
un·plun·dered *adj*
un·point·ed *adj*
un·po·lar·ized *adj*
un·pol·ished *adj*
un·po·lit·i·cal *adj*
un·pol·li·nat·ed *adj*
un·pol·lut·ed *adj*
un·pop·u·lat·ed *adj*
un·posed *adj*
un·pow·ered *adj*
un·prac·ti·cal *adj*
un·pre·dict·ed *adj*
un·prej·u·diced *adj*
un·pre·scribed *adj*
un·pressed *adj*
un·pres·sur·ized *adj*
un·pre·sump·tu·ous *adj*
un·priced *adj*
un·primed *adj*
un·print·ed *adj*
un·prob·lem·at·ic *adj*
un·pro·cessed *adj*
un·pro·claimed *adj*
un·pro·cur·a·ble *adj*
un·pro·fessed *adj*
un·pro·gres·sive *adj*
un·pro·pi·tious *adj*
un·pro·pi·tious·ly *adv*
un·pros·per·ous *adj*
un·pro·test·ing *adj*
un·proud *adj*
un·prov·a·ble *adj*
un·proved *adj*
un·prov·en *adj*
un·pro·voked *adj*
un·pruned *adj*
un·pub·li·cized *adj*
un·pub·lished *adj*
un·punc·tu·al *adj*
un·punc·tu·al·i·ty *n*
un·punc·tu·al·ly *adv*
un·punc·tu·at·ed *adj*
un·pun·ish·a·ble *adj*
un·pun·ished *adj*
un·pu·ri·fied *adj*
un·qual·i·fi·a·ble *adj*
un·quan·ti·fi·a·bil·i·ty *n*
un·quan·ti·fi·a·ble *adj*
un·quelled *adj*
un·quench·a·ble *adj*
un·quench·a·bly *adv*
un·quenched *adj*
un·quot·a·ble *adj*
un·reach·a·bil·i·ty *n*
un·reach·a·ble *adj*
un·reach·a·ble·ness *n*
un·reach·a·bly *adv*
un·reached *adj*
un·re·ac·tive *adj*
un·re·al·ism *n*
un·re·al·is·tic *adj*
un·re·al·is·ti·cal·ly *adv*
un·re·al·iz·a·ble *adj*
un·re·al·ized *adj*
un·re·cep·tive *adj*
un·re·cep·tive·ly *adv*
un·re·cep·tive·ness *n*
un·re·cip·ro·cal *adj*
un·re·cip·ro·cat·ed *adj*
un·rec·og·niz·a·bil·i·ty *n*
un·rec·og·niz·a·ble *adj*
un·rec·og·niz·a·bly *adv*
un·rec·og·nized *adj*
un·rec·om·pensed *adj*
un·rec·on·ciled *adj*
un·re·cord·a·ble *adj*
un·re·cord·ed *adj*
un·rec·ti·fi·a·ble *adj*
un·rec·ti·fied *adj*
un·re·deem·a·ble *adj*
un·re·deem·a·bly *adv*
un·re·deemed *adj*
un·re·dressed *adj*
un·re·formed *adj*
un·reg·is·tered *adj*
un·reg·u·lat·ed *adj*
un·re·hearsed *adj*
un·re·lat·ed *adj*
un·re·lat·ed·ly *adv*
un·re·lat·ed·ness *n*
un·re·laxed *adj*
un·re·lieved *adj*
un·re·lig·ious *adj*
un·rem·e·died *adj*
un·re·mem·bered *adj*
un·re·morse·ful *adj*
un·re·morse·ful·ly *adv*
un·re·mov·a·ble *adj*
un·re·new·a·ble *adj*
un·re·newed *adj*
un·re·pealed *adj*
un·re·peat·ed *adj*
un·re·pent·ant *adj*
un·re·port·ed *adj*
un·rep·re·sen·ta·tive *adj*
un·rep·re·sen·ta·tive·ness *n*
un·rep·re·sent·ed *adj*
un·re·proved *adj*
un·re·quest·ed *adj*
un·re·searched *adj*
un·re·sent·ful *adj*
un·re·sis·tant *adj*
un·re·sist·ed *adj*
un·re·sist·ing *adj*
un·re·sist·ing·ly *adv*
un·re·solv·a·ble *adj*
un·re·solved *adj*
un·res·o·nant *adj*
un·re·spon·sive *adj*
un·re·spon·sive·ly *adv*
un·re·spon·sive·ness *n*
un·rest·ful *adj*
un·re·straint *n*
un·re·strict·ed *adj*
un·re·strict·ed·ly *adv*
un·re·turn·a·ble *adj*
un·re·turned *adj*
un·re·vealed *adj*
un·re·veal·ing *adj*
un·re·vised *adj*
un·re·voked *adj*
un·re·ward·ed *adj*
un·re·ward·ing *adj*
un·rhymed *adj*
un·rhyth·mic *adj*
un·rhyth·mi·cal *adj*
un·rhyth·mi·cal·ly *adv*
un·rid·a·ble *adj*
un·rig *vt*
un·rip·ened *adj*
un·ris·en *adj*
un·ro·man·tic *adj*
un·ro·man·ti·cal·ly *adv*
un·roofed *adj*
un·roy·al *adj*
un·rup·tured *adj*
un·rushed *adj*
un·safe *adj*
un·safe·ly *adv*
un·safe·ness *n*
un·sal·a·ble *adj*
un·salt·ed *adj*
un·sanc·ti·fied *adj*
un·sanc·tioned *adj*
un·san·i·tar·y *adj*
un·sat·is·fied *adj*
un·sat·is·fy·ing *adj*
un·sat·is·fy·ing·ly *adv*
un·scarred *adj*
un·scent·ed *adj*
un·sched·uled *adj*
un·schol·ar·ly *adj*
un·searched *adj*
un·sea·soned *adj*
un·sea·wor·thy *adj*
un·see·ing *adj*
un·see·ing·ly *adv*
un·seg·ment·ed *adj*
un·seg·re·gat·ed *adj*
un·se·lect *adj*
un·se·lect·ed *adj*
un·se·lec·tive *adj*
un·se·lec·tive·ly *adv*
un·self·con·scious *adj*
un·self·con·scious·ly *adv*
un·self·con·scious·ness *n*
un·sent *adj*
un·sen·ti·men·tal *adj*
un·sep·a·rat·ed *adj*
un·se·ri·ous *adj*
un·ser·vice·a·ble *adj*
un·ser·vice·a·ble·ness *n*
un·sewn *adj*
un·sex·y *adj*
un·shad·ed *adj*
un·shak·en *adj*
un·shak·ing *adj*
un·shape·li·ness *n*
un·shape·ly *adj*
un·shared *adj*
un·shaved *adj*
un·shav·en *adj*
un·shed *adj*
un·shell *vt*
un·shel·tered *adj*
un·shield·ed *adj*
un·shock·a·bil·i·ty *n*
un·shock·a·ble *adj*
un·shorn *adj*
un·sift·ed *adj*
un·sink·a·ble *adj*
un·skimmed *adj*
un·slak·a·ble *adj*
un·smoked *adj*
un·soiled *adj*
un·sol·dier·ly *adj*
un·solv·a·bil·i·ty *n*
un·solv·a·ble *adj*
un·solved *adj*
un·sort·ed *adj*
un·soured *adj*
un·sown *adj*
un·spec·i·fi·a·ble *adj*
un·spe·cif·ic *adj*
un·spec·i·fied *adj*
un·spec·tac·u·lar *adj*
un·spir·i·tu·al *adj*
un·spon·ta·ne·ous *adj*
un·sport·ing *adj*
un·sport·ing·ly *adv*
un·sport·ing·ness *n*
un·spun *adj*
un·stained *adj*
un·star·tling *adj*
un·stat·ed *adj*
un·stead·fast *adj*
un·ster·ile *adj*
un·stiff·ened *adj*
un·stim·u·lat·ing *adj*
un·stint·ed *adj*
un·stip·u·lat·ed *adj*
un·strap *vt*
un·stuf·fy *adj*
un·styl·ish *adj*
un·sub·dued *adj*
un·sub·ju·gat·ed *adj*
un·sub·tle *adj*
un·suc·cess *n*
un·sug·ges·tive *adj*
un·suit·ed *adj*
un·sul·lied *adj*
un·sum·moned *adj*
un·su·per·vised *adj*
un·sup·port·ed *adj*
un·sup·pressed *adj*
un·sur·faced *adj*
un·sur·mount·a·ble *adj*
un·sur·pass·a·ble *adj*
un·sur·passed *adj*
un·sur·prised *adj*
un·sus·cep·ti·ble *adj*
un·sus·pi·cious *adj*
un·sus·tain·a·bil·i·ty *n*
un·sus·tain·a·ble *adj*
un·sus·tain·a·bly *adv*
un·swathe *vt*
un·swayed *adj*
un·sweet·ened *adj*
un·sym·met·ri·cal *adj*
un·sym·met·ri·cal·ly *adv*
un·sym·pa·thet·ic *adj*
un·sys·tem·at·ic *adj*
un·sys·tem·at·i·cal·ly *adv*
un·taint·ed *adj*
un·tak·en *adj*
un·tal·ent·ed *adj*
un·tam·a·ble *adj*
un·tamed *adj*
un·tanned *adj*
un·tar·nished *adj*
un·tast·ed *adj*
un·taxed *adj*
un·teach·a·ble *adj*
un·tem·pered *adj*
un·ten·ant·ed *adj*
un·tend·ed *adj*
un·test·ed *adj*
un·thanked *adj*
un·thank·ful *adj*
un·thank·ful·ly *adv*
un·thank·ful·ness *n*
un·themed *adj*
un·threat·ened *adj*
un·throne *vt*
un·tilled *adj*
un·tinged *adj*
un·toast·ed *adj*
un·trace·a·ble *adj*
un·trace·a·bly *adv*
un·traced *adj*
un·tra·di·tion·al *adj*
un·trained *adj*
un·trans·lat·a·ble *adj*
un·trans·lat·ed *adj*
un·trans·port·a·ble *adj*
un·treat·a·ble *adj*
un·treat·a·bly *adv*
un·treat·ed *adj*
un·trend·y *adj*
un·trimmed *adj*
un·trod·den *adj*
un·trust·ing *adj*
un·trust·wor·thi·ly *adv*
un·trust·wor·thi·ness *n*
un·trust·wor·thy *adj*
un·turned *adj*
un·twine *vt*
un·twist *vti*
un·typ·i·cal *adj*
un·typ·i·cal·ly *adv*
un·us·a·ble *adj*
un·u·til·ized *adj*
un·ut·tered *adj*
un·vac·ci·nat·ed *adj*
un·van·quished *adj*
un·var·ied *adj*
un·var·y·ing *adj*
un·var·y·ing·ly *adv*
un·ven·ti·lat·ed *adj*
un·ver·i·fi·a·ble *adj*
un·ver·i·fied *adj*
un·versed *adj*
un·vi·a·bil·i·ty *n*
un·vi·a·ble *adj*
un·vis·it·ed *adj*
un·want·ed *adj*
un·war·like *adj*
un·warmed *adj*
un·watched *adj*
un·watch·ful *adj*
un·waxed *adj*
un·weaned *adj*
un·wea·ry *adj*
un·weath·ered *adj*
un·wed *adj*
un·weight·ed *adj*
un·wel·come *adj*
un·wel·come·ly *adv*
un·wel·come·ness *n*
un·wel·com·ing *adj*
un·wel·com·ing·ly *adv*
un·wet·ted *adj*
un·whipped *adj*
un·willed *adj*
un·win·na·ble *adj*
un·with·ered *adj*
un·wit·nessed *adj*
un·worked *adj*
un·wor·ried *adj*
un·wor·ried·ly *adv*
un·wound·ed *adj*
un·wo·ven *adj*
un·writ·a·ble *adj*
un·yeast·ed *adj*

un·a·bat·ed /ùnnə báytəd/ *adj* still as forceful or intense as before —**un·a·bat·ed·ly** *adv*

un·a·ble /un áyb'l/ *adj* not able to do something

un·ac·com·mo·dat·ed /ùnnə kómmə dàytəd/ *adj* (*formal*) **1.** not adapted to or for something ○ *unaccommodated to the dryness of the desert* **2.** lacking accommodations, equipment, or supplies

un·ac·com·pa·nied /ùnnə kúmpəneed/ *adj, adv* **1.** alone, especially when a companion would be expected **2.** playing or singing alone, without any other instruments or voices

un·ac·count·a·ble /ùnnə kówntəb'l/ *adj* **1.** not answerable or responsible to anyone **2.** impossible to explain or give a reason for —**un·ac·count·a·bil·i·ty** /-kòwntə bílləte̅e/ *n*

un·ac·count·a·bly /ùnnə kówntəblee/ *adv* for some unknown and usually puzzling reason

un·ac·count·ed-for *adj* **1.** missing or absent, for unknown reasons **2.** not explained or understood

un·ac·cus·tomed /ùnnə kústəmd/ *adj* **1.** not used or accustomed to something **2.** not usual or known before

u·na cor·da /o͝onə káwrdə/ *adj, adv* in piano music, using only one string per pitch, achieved by depressing the soft pedal. The effect is a reduction in volume and a change in the quality of the tone. [< Italian, "one string"]

un·ac·quaint·ed /ùnnə kwáyntəd/ *adj* **1.** having no knowledge of something **2.** unknown to somebody or to each other

un·a·dul·ter·at·ed /ùnnə dúltə ràytəd/ *adj* **1.** not mixed or diluted with something else **2.** free from any element that would spoil or detract from it ○ *unadulterated joy*

un·ad·vised /ùnnəd vī́zd/ *adj* **1.** done without being carefully considered **2.** without asking the advice of others —**un·ad·vis·ed·ly** /-vī́zədlee/ *adv*

un·aired /un érd/ *adj* **1.** not broadcast on radio or television **2.** not exposed to the air in order to be dried, have dampness removed, be cooled, or be ventilated

Un·a·las·ka /ùnnə láskə/ island in southwestern Alaska, between the Bering Sea and the Pacific Ocean. It is the most important and second largest of the Aleutian Islands. Population: 4,580 (2002 estimate). Area: 800 sq. mi./1,287 sq. km.

un·al·ien·a·ble /un áylee ənəb'l/ *adj* same as **inalienable**

un·al·lowed /ùnnə lówd/ *adj* **1.** not allowed because illegal, forbidden, or invalid **2.** not allowed as a deduction, e.g., against tax

un·al·loyed /ùnnə lóyd/ *adj* **1.** containing no impurities, and not mixed or alloyed with other metals **2.** not mixed with anything else, especially anything that would dilute it or any other feeling that would diminish it ○ *unalloyed pleasure*

un·am·big·u·ous /ùn am bíggyoo əss/ *adj* completely clear in meaning or intention and unable to be misunderstood —**un·am·big·u·ous·ly** *adv*

un-A·mer·i·can /ùn-/ *adj* **1.** at odds with the customs, traditions, or ways of the people of the United States ○ *It's practically un-American not to like apple pie.* **2.** unpatriotic or disloyal to the United States

un·a·neled /ùnnə néeld/ *adj* in the Roman Catholic Church, not having received the last rites given to people who are dying or very ill (*archaic*) [Early 17C. < UN- + *aneled*, past participle of obsolete *anele* "anoint" < Old English *ele* "oil" < Latin *oleum*]

u·nan·i·mous /yoo nánnəməss/ *adj* **1.** shared as a view by all of the people concerned, with nobody disagreeing **2.** with all members in agreement with each other ○ *Board members were unanimous in their rejection of the proposed merger.* [Early 17C. < Latin *unanimus* < *unus* "one" + *animus* "mind"] —**u·na·nim·i·ty** /yòonə nímmətee/ *n* —**u·nan·i·mous·ly** *adv*

un·an·swer·a·ble /un ánssərəb'l/ *adj* **1.** impossible to answer or solve **2.** so clearly true that nobody could contradict or deny it —**un·an·swer·a·bil·i·ty** /un ànssərə bíllətee/ *n* —**un·an·swer·a·ble·ness** *n* —**un·an·swer·a·bly** *adv*

un·ap·peal·a·ble /ùnnə péeləb'l/ *adj* describes a case or judgment that is not open to appeal —**un·ap·peal·a·bly** *adv*

un·ap·peal·ing /ùnnə péeling/ *adj* not attractive or likely to be enjoyable —**un·ap·peal·ing·ly** *adv*

un·ap·prised /ùnnə prízd/ *adj* not informed or given notice about something

un·ap·proach·a·ble /ùnnə próchəb'l/ *adj* **1.** TOO UNFRIENDLY TO APPROACH OR CONTACT characterized by a formal, unfriendly, or hostile manner that discourages communication **2.** INACCESSIBLE difficult to get to **3.** UNRIVALED so excellent that nothing or nobody else is nearly as good —**un·ap·proach·a·bil·i·ty** /-pròchə bíllətee/ *n* —**un·ap·proach·a·ble·ness** *n* —**un·ap·proach·a·bly** *adv*

un·apt /un ápt/ *adj* **1.** lacking the qualities suitable for or appropriate to a context **2.** not likely or liable to do something (*formal*) ○ *unapt to cause any problems* —**un·apt·ly** *adv* —**un·apt·ness** *n*

un·ar·chive /un aár kīv/ (**-chived, -chiv·ing, -chives**) *vt* to retrieve a computer file from archive storage

un·ar·gu·a·ble /un árgyoo əb'l/ *adj* so clearly true or correct that nobody can argue with it or deny it —**un·ar·gu·a·bly** *adv*

un·armed /un aármd/ *adj* **1.** WITHOUT WEAPONS not carrying or using weapons **2.** BIOL WITH NO OBVIOUS MEANS OF SELF-DEFENSE with no horns, claws, shells, thorns, prickles, or other means of self-protection **3.** MIL UNABLE TO FIRE used to describe a missile or projectile whose fuse or firing mechanism has been disabled

un·ar·ranged /ùnnə ráynjd/ *adj* **1.** not put in order or relative position **2.** not brought about by agreement or planning

u·nar·y /yóonəree/ *adj* describes a mathematical operation that is applied to only one member of a set at a time, e.g., squaring a number [Early 20C. < Latin *unus* "one"]

un·a·shamed /ùnnə sháymd/ *adj* **1.** not ashamed or embarrassed, and not feeling the need to apologize to others **2.** not limited, restrained, or avoided out of a feeling of shame or embarrassment —**un·a·sham·ed·ly** /-sháymədlee/ *adv* —**un·a·sham·ed·ness** /-sháymədnəss/ *n*

un·asked /un áskt/ *adj* **1.** NOT ASKED not having been asked **2.** NOT INVITED coming to a gathering without an invitation **3.** *also* **un·asked-for** NOT ASKED FOR providing something such as assistance that has not been asked for

un·as·pi·rat·ed /un áspə ràytəd/ *adj* describes a letter "h" at the beginning of a word that is not pronounced when the word is spoken, as in "hour" or "honor"

un·as·pir·ing /ùnnə spíring/ *adj* not aspiring to attain a goal

un·as·sail·a·ble /ùnnə sáyləb'l/ *adj* **1.** so sound or well established that it cannot be challenged or overtaken ○ *an unassailable lead* **2.** so strong or impregnable that it cannot be successfully attacked —**un·as·sail·a·bil·i·ty** /-sàylə bíllətee/ *n* —**un·as·sail·a·bly** *adv*

un·as·sum·ing /ùnnə sóoming/ *adj* acting in a way that does not assume superiority —**un·as·sum·ing·ly** *adv* —**un·as·sum·ing·ness** *n*

un·at·tached /ùnnə tácht/ *adj* **1.** WITHOUT SPOUSE OR PARTNER not married and not in a long-term romantic or sexual relationship **2.** NOT JOINED not joined or attached, especially to other or larger organizations or bodies **3.** LAW NOT SEIZED FOR SECURITY describes property that is not taken away from its owner for security under the orders of a court of law

un·at·tend·ed /ùnnə téndəd/ *adj* **1.** WITH NO ONE THERE with no one present to listen, watch, or participate **2.** NOT CARED FOR not taken care of or seen to **3.** NOT ESCORTED not accompanied or escorted (*formal*) **4.** NOT HEEDED not listened to or heeded (*formal*) **5.** NOT HAVING SOMETHING AS CONSEQUENCE not accompanied by something, or not having something as a result or consequence (*formal*)

un·at·trac·tive /ùnnə tráktiv/ *adj* **1.** not having a beautiful, pleasing, or desirable appearance **2.** not having any obvious advantages or interesting aspects ○ *nothing but unattractive prospects* —**un·at·trac·tive·ly** *adv* —**un·at·trac·tive·ness** *n*

SYNONYMS ***unattractive, unsightly, ugly, hideous, homely, plain***

CORE MEANING: not pleasant to look at

unattractive not having a beautiful, pleasing, or desirable appearance ○ *an unattractive combination of colors* ○ *Some find him physically unattractive, but his sense of humor is charming.* **unsightly** not pleasant to look at, or spoiling the appearance of something ○ *unsightly yellow teeth* ○ *an unsightly construction that will mar a beautiful view* **ugly** lacking appealing physical features, especially facial ones ○ *Isn't everyone afraid of getting old and ugly?* ○ *an ugly shape* **hideous** extremely unpleasant to look at ○ *a hideous monster* ○ *It's time to get rid of that hideous orange carpet.* **homely** plain or less than pleasing in appearance ○ *a homely, awkward giant of a man* ○ *Next to her swanlike grace, I'm homely by comparison.* **plain** not pretty or good-looking ○ *a plain woman* ○ *She had a longish, plain face with a straight nose and a small mouth.*

~~unatural~~ incorrect spelling of **unnatural**

u·nau /yóo nòw, -nàw/ (*plural* **u·naus** or *same*) *n* ZOOL same as **two-toed sloth** [Late 18C. Via French < Tupi *unáu*]

un·a·vail·ing /ùnnə váyling/ *adj* done but failing to achieve the desired result —**un·a·vail·ing·ly** *adv*

un·a·void·a·ble /ùnnə vóydəb'l/ *adj* unable to be avoided —**un·a·void·a·bil·i·ty** /-vòydə bíllətee/ *n* —**un·a·void·a·bly** *adv*

un·a·ware /ùnnə wér/ *adj* **1.** not conscious or aware of something **2.** lacking important information or analysis ○ *a politically unaware generation* ■ *adv* same as **unawares** —**un·a·ware·ly** *adv* —**un·a·ware·ness** *n*

un·a·wares /ùnnə wérz/ *adv* **1.** without any warning or anticipation ○ *His question caught me unawares.* ○ *You took me completely unawares.* **2.** without planning or intending to do something ○ *He took the wrong coat, unawares.* [Mid-16C. < UNAWARE + -s, adverbial suffix]

unb. *abbr* PUBL unbound

un·backed /un bákt/ *adj* **1.** NOT SUPPORTED OR BACKED having no support or backing, especially financial backing **2.** FURNITURE WITHOUT BACK describes a chair that has been made without a back **3.** RIDING NEVER RIDDEN describes a horse that has never been ridden ○ *an unbacked mare* **4.** GAMBLING NOT BET ON describes a horse that has had no bets placed on its performance

un·bal·ance /un bálləns/ *vt* (**-anced, -anc·ing, -anc·es**) **1.** KNOCK SOMETHING OFF BALANCE to make something lose its balance or equilibrium **2.** MAKE SOMEBODY PSYCHOLOGICALLY UNSTABLE to make somebody psychologically or emotionally unstable ■ *n* STATE OF INSTABILITY the state of being unstable and out of balance —**un·bal·ance·a·ble** *adj*

un·bal·anced /un bállənst/ *adj* **1.** PSYCHOLOGICALLY UNSTABLE unable to make sound judgments **2.** ONE-SIDED done or provided from only one perspective ○ *unbalanced reporting* **3.** WITHOUT EQUILIBRIUM lacking the proper distribution of weight or forces that would provide balance **4.** ACCT HAVING UNEQUAL DEBITS AND CREDITS in which the totaled debits and credits are not equal

un·bar /un baár/ (**-barred, -bar·ring, -bars**) *vt* **1.** to unlock or open a door or gate **2.** to remove the bars or obstructions from something

unbd. *abbr* PUBL unbound

un·bear·a·ble /un bérrəb'l/ *adj* difficult, unpleasant, or impossible to bear or tolerate —**un·bear·a·ble·ness** *n* —**un·bear·a·bly** *adv*

un·beat·a·ble /un béetəb'l/ *adj* too good or favorable to be beaten or surpassed —**un·beat·a·bly** *adv*

un·beat·en /un béet'n/ *adj* **1.** UNDEFEATED never having been defeated or outdone **2.** COOK NOT WHIPPED OR POUNDED not subjected to pounding, whipping, or beating as part of the preparation for cooking or eating ○ *unbeaten eggs* **3.** ROADS NOT TRAVELED not made smooth from pedestrian or vehicular traffic ○ *an unbeaten path*

un·be·com·ing /ùnbi kúmming/ *adj* **1.** unsuitable or unattractive on the wearer **2.** not suitable, especially as not conforming with accepted attitudes or behavior —**un·be·com·ing·ly** *adv* —**un·be·com·ing·ness** *n*

un·be·known /ùnbi nón/, **un·be·knownst** /-nónst/ *adj* **1.** WITHOUT SOMEBODY KNOWING happening without a particular person knowing about it **2.** NOT KNOWN TO SOMEBODY not known or familiar to somebody ■ *adv* WITHOUT BEING SEEN without being noticed or seen by anybody ○ *slipped away unbeknownst* [Mid-17C. < UN- + *beknown*, past participle of obsolete *beknow* "know thoroughly" < KNOW]

un·be·lief /ùnbi léef/ *n* lack of religious or political belief

un·be·liev·a·ble /ùnbi léevəb'l/ *adj* **1.** too unrealistic or improbable to be believed **2.** used to emphasize that something is very great, or very good, bad, or impressive ○ *reacted with unbelievable agility* —**un·be·liev·a·bil·i·ty** /-leevə bíllətee/ *n* —**un·be·liev·a·bly** *adv*

un·be·liev·er /ùnbi léevər/ *n* somebody who does not believe in an established religious faith or in conventional beliefs

un·be·liev·ing /ùnbi léeving/ *adj* **1.** lacking belief or expressing disbelief about something **2.** with no religious faith or doctrinal beliefs —**un·be·liev·ing·ly** *adv*

un·belt /un bélt/ (**-belt·ed, -belt·ing, -belts**) *vt* **1.** to unfasten the belt on a garment **2.** to remove somebody or something from a supporting or restraining belt

un·bend /un bénd/ (**-bent** /-bént/, **-bend·ing, -bends**) *v* **1.** *vti* MAKE SOMEBODY RELAXED to make somebody become more informal, relaxed, or friendly, or become more informal, relaxed, or friendly **2.** *vti* MAKE SOMETHING STRAIGHT to make something become straight, or become straight, after being bent, twisted, or flexed **3.** *vt* NAUT UNFASTEN SAIL OR ROPE to free a sail, rope, or mooring line that was fastened —**un·bend·a·ble** *adj*

un·bend·ing /un bénding/ *adj* **1.** RESOLUTE not willing to change opinions, beliefs, or attitudes **2.** STRICTLY OBSERVED strictly applied or observed **3.** ALOOF formal or unfriendly in manner or behavior —**un·bend·ing·ly** *adv* —**un·bend·ing·ness** *n*

un·ben·e·fi·cial /ùn bènnə físh'l/ *adj* not advantageous or profitable

un·bent /un bént/ past participle, past tense of **unbend** ■ *adj* **1.** not forced into submitting or giving in **2.** not bent or twisted

un·bi·ased /un bí əst/, **un·bi·assed** *adj* **1.** fair and impartial rather than biased or prejudiced **2.** in statistics, with an expected value that is equal to the parameter being estimated —**un·bi·ased·ly** *adv* —**un·bi·ased·ness** *n*

un·bib·li·cal /un bíbblik'l/ *adj* opposed or in contrast to the teachings of the Bible, or not present or approved in biblical teaching

un·bid·den /un bídd'n/ *adj, adv* (*literary*) **1.** not wished for or willed **2.** not asked for or invited

un·big·ot·ed /un bíggətəd/ *adj* having none of the characteristics of a bigot or of bigotry

un·bind /un bī́nd/ (**-bound** /-bównd/, **-bind·ing, -binds**) *vt* (*literary*) **1.** to free somebody from something restraining or restricting such as a duty or obligation **2.** to untie a person or animal

un·blessed /un blést/ *adj* **1.** WITHOUT BLESSING not given a blessing **2.** UNFORTUNATE unfortunate or wretched (*literary*) **3.** REGARDED AS EVIL in some religions, regarded as behaving in unrighteous ways (*literary*) —**un·bless·ed·ness** /un bléssədnəss/ *n*

un·blink·ing /un blíngking/ *adj* **1.** failing or unable to close and open the eyes in quick succession **2.** showing no emotion, reluctance, or hesitation —**un·blink·ing·ly** *adv*

un·block /un blók/ (**-blocked, -block·ing, -blocks**) *vt* **1.** REMOVE BLOCKAGE FROM SOMETHING to remove an obstruction from something in order to allow free access to it or a passage through it **2.** REMOVE OBSTRUCTION to remove something that is causing an obstruction **3.** RESTART PROCESS to remove an obstacle to the progress of something

un·blush·ing /un blúshing/ *adj* feeling or showing no shame or embarrassment —**un·blush·ing·ly** *adv*

un·bolt /un bṓlt/ (**-bolt·ed, -bolt·ing, -bolts**) *vt* to pull back the bolt or bolts on a door or gate, so that it can be opened

un·bolt·ed /un bṓltəd/ *adj* **1.** not fitted with bolts, or with bolts not fastened **2.** describes flour or grain that has not had the coarse particles sifted from the fine ones

un·born /un báwrn/ *adj* **1.** not yet born, but usually already conceived and gestating ○ *behavior that could benefit the unborn child* **2.** not thought of or begun yet (*literary*)

un·bos·om /un bóozzəm/ (**-omed, -om·ing, -oms**) *v* (*literary*) **1.** *vti* to express something previously suppressed or hidden **2. un·bos·om your·self** *vr* to reveal the thoughts, feelings, or secrets you have been keeping inside yourself ○ *unbosomed himself to us*

un·both·ered /un bó*th*ərd/ *adj* not worried or disturbed by anything or anybody

un·bound /un bównd/ past participle, past tense of **unbind** ■ *adj* **1.** WITHOUT COVER not fastened inside a permanent cover **2.** UNRESTRICTED without restraints or fetters **3.** SCI NOT IN CHEMICAL COMBINATION free from chemical or physical combination **4.** LING CONSTITUTING WORD used to describe a morpheme that can form a word on its own without any added affixes

un·bound·ed /un bówndəd/ *adj* **1.** not controlled or restrained in any way **2.** not subject to limits, boundaries, or restrictions —**un·bound·ed·ly** *adv* —**un·bound·ed·ness** *n*

un·bowed /un bówd/ *adj* **1.** having refused to submit or admit defeat **2.** remaining in an erect position, not bent or bowed

un·brace /un bráyss/ (**-braced, -brac·ing, -brac·es**) *vt* to make something less tense or strained (*literary*)

un·bred /un bréd/ *adj* **1.** NOT TRAINED not given training or instruction (*literary*) **2.** NOT WELL BRED lacking refinement or breeding (*literary*) **3.** AGRIC NOT YET MATED not yet mated with another animal

un·bri·dle /un brī́d'l/ (**-dled, -dling, -dles**) *vt* **1.** to take away the limits, controls, or restraints that apply to something **2.** to take the bridle from a horse

un·bri·dled /un brī́d'ld/ *adj* **1.** freely and openly expressed **2.** not fitted with a bridle —**un·bri·dled·ly** *adv*

un·bro·ken /un brṓkən/ *adj* **1.** WITHOUT GAPS with no gaps or pauses **2.** ONGOING continued without interruption **3.** UNDEFEATED not beaten or subdued **4.** UNTAMED not yet having submitted to human control ○ *an unbroken horse* **5.** NOT FRAGMENTED remaining intact or in one piece **6.** NOT VIOLATED having remained viable or in force —**un·bro·ken·ly** *adv* —**un·bro·ken·ness** *n*

un·bun·dle /un búnd'l/ (**-dled, -dling, -dles**) *vt* to sell or charge for related products and services separately, rather than as a unit

un·bur·den /un búrd'n/ (**-dened, -den·ing, -dens**) *v* **1. un·bur·den your·self** *vr* to relieve yourself of something that has been worrying you by telling somebody about it (*formal*) **2.** *vt* to remove a load from a person or animal (*literary*)

un·but·ton /un bútt'n/ (**-toned, -ton·ing, -tons**) *v* **1.** *vt* to undo a garment by unfastening the buttons **2.** *vi* to relax and become more talkative (*informal*)

un·cal·cu·lat·ed /un kálkyə làytəd/ *adj* done or accepted without careful consideration of the possible results

un·cal·cu·lat·ing /un kálkyə làyting/ *adj* not having or showing a determination to gain the greatest personal advantage —**un·cal·cu·lat·ing·ly** *adv*

un·called-for /un káwld-/ *adj* beyond what is necessary or expected, especially in being unjustifiably unkind or impolite

un·can·ny /un kánnee/ (**-ni·er, -ni·est**) *adj* **1.** too strange or unlikely to seem merely natural or human **2.** unexpectedly accurate or precise ○ *an uncanny resemblance to the president* —**un·can·ni·ly** *adv* —**un·can·ni·ness** *n*

un·can·vassed /un kánvəst/ *adj* **1.** UNASKED not canvassed for orders, opinions, or votes **2.** NOT FULLY CONSIDERED not debated or discussed thoroughly **3.** NOT PROPERLY EXAMINED not examined in detail, e.g., to confirm validity

un·cap /un káp/ (**-capped, -cap·ping, -caps**) *vt* **1.** to remove an upper limit or restriction from something **2.** to remove the cap from a container

un·cared-for /un kérd-/ *adj* neglected and allowed to deteriorate

Un·cas /úngkəss/ (1588?–1683?) Mohegan leader. He sided with the British against other Native American peoples.

un·cat·e·go·rized /un káttəgə rīzd/ *adj* not placed into a category

un·ceas·ing /un seéssing/ *adj* continuing without stopping, pausing, or diminishing —**un·ceas·ing·ly** *adv*

un·cer·e·mo·ni·ous /un sèrrə mṓnee əss/ *adj* **1.** sudden and rude, with no concern for politeness or good manners **2.** done without formality or ceremony —**un·cer·e·mo·ni·ous·ly** *adv* —**un·cer·e·mo·ni·ous·ness** *n*

un·cer·tain /un súrt'n/ *adj* **1.** WITHOUT KNOWLEDGE lacking clear knowledge or a definite opinion **2.** NOT KNOWN OR SETTLED not yet known, or remaining undecided **3.** CHANGEABLE likely to change, and therefore not reliable or stable **4.** LACKING SELF-ASSURANCE lacking self-assurance or confidence —**un·cer·tain·ly** *adv* —**un·cer·tain·ness** *n*

SYNONYMS See ***doubtful***.

un·cer·tain·ty /un súrt'ntee/ (*plural* **-ties**) *n* **1.** the quality or state of being uncertain **2.** something that nobody can predict or guarantee (*often used in the plural*) ○ *economic uncertainties*

un·cer·tain·ty prin·ci·ple *n* a principle in quantum mechanics holding that it is impossible to determine both the position and momentum of a particle at the same time

un·chain /un cháyn/ (**-chained, -chain·ing, -chains**) *vt* **1.** to take off the chain or chains holding a person or animal **2.** to take away the limits, controls, or restraints that apply to something or somebody

un·chart·ed /un chaártəd/ *adj* **1.** not surveyed or recorded on a map **2.** not previously encountered, experienced, or investigated

un·char·tered /un chaártərd/ *adj* not officially authorized or permitted

un·checked /un chékt/ *adj* **1.** not limited or controlled, especially when restraint or control is required **2.** remaining unverified or untested, especially for problems or imperfections

un·chris·tian /un kríschən/ *adj* **1.** unkind or selfish, and therefore against Christian principles and teachings **2.** not belonging to the Christian church

un·church /un chúrch/ (**-churched, -church·ing, -church·es**) *vt* **1.** to expel somebody from a church **2.** to remove the status of being a church from a building

un·ci ANAT plural of **uncus**

uncial

un·cial /únshəl/ *n* **1.** STYLE OF LETTER USED IN MANUSCRIPTS a letter of the kind used in Greek and Latin manuscripts written between the 3rd and 9th centuries that resembles a modern capital letter but is more rounded **2.** MANUSCRIPT IN UNCIALS a manuscript written in uncials ■ *adj* WRITTEN IN UNCIALS relating to or written in uncials [Mid-17C. < late Latin *unciales (litterae)* "inch-high (letters)" < Latin *uncia* "twelfth part, inch"] —**un·cial·ly** *adv*

un·ci·form /únssi fàwrm/ *adj* shaped like a hook ■ *n* ANAT same as **hamate** [Mid-18C. < Latin *uncus* "hook"]

un·ci·nar·i·a·sis /ùnssinə rī́ əssiss/ *n* infestation of the intestines with hookworms [Early 20C. < modern Latin *Uncinaria*, genus of hookworms < Latin *uncus* "hook"]

un·ci·nate /únssinət, -nàyt/ *adj* shaped like a hook at the end [Mid-18C. < Latin *uncinatus* < *uncus* "hook"]

un·ci·nus /un sī́nəss/ (*plural* **-ni** /-nī/) *n* **1.** a small hooked body part, e.g., the hook-shaped tooth of a gastropod or a chitinous hook on the body of an annelid **2.** a cirrus cloud that is curled in a hook shape at one of its elongated ends [Mid-19C. < Latin < *uncus* "hook"]

un·civ·il /un sívv'l/ *adj* behaving in a way that is seen as hostile or indifferent —**un·ci·vil·i·ty** /ùnssi víllətee/ *n* —**un·civ·il·ly** *adv* —**un·civ·il·ness** *n*

un·civ·i·lized /un sívv'l īzd/ *adj* **1.** existing in a condition or behaving in ways that are thought to be socially or culturally undeveloped **2.** far from civilized or settled areas —**un·civ·i·liz·ed·ly** /-īzədlee/ *adv*

un·clad /un klád/ *adj* not wearing any clothes

un·clasp /un klásp/ (**-clasped, -clasp·ing, -clasps**) *vt* **1.** to separate hands previously held together **2.** to unfasten the clasp holding something closed

un·clas·si·fied /un klássə fīd/ *adj* **1.** not arranged or grouped systematically **2.** remaining open for examination by anyone who wishes access

un·cle /úngk'l/ *n* **1.** PARENT'S BROTHER OR BROTHER-IN-LAW the brother of somebody's mother or father, or the husband of somebody's aunt (*capitalized before a name*) **2.** OLDER MALE FAMILY FRIEND a parent's male friend (*capitalized before a name*) **3.** KINDLY OLDER MAN an older male person who gives support, protection, and advice **4.** OCCUPATIONS same as **pawnbroker** (*dated slang*) [13C. Via Old French *oncle* < Latin *avunculus* "maternal uncle"] ◇ **cry uncle** surrender or admit defeat (*informal*)

un·clean /un kleén/ *adj* **1.** DIRTY dirty or insanitary **2.** UNCHASTE sinful, especially involving or guilty of committing a sexual sin **3.** RELIG RELIGIOUSLY OR RITUALLY IMPURE not pure according to religious rules or rituals —**un·clean·ness** *n*

SYNONYMS See ***dirty***.

un·clean·ly *adj* /un klénnlee/ same as **unclean** (*formal or literary*) ■ *adv* /un kleénlee/ in a way that is not clean —**un·clean·li·ness** *n*

Un·cle Sam /úngk'l sám/ *n* **1.** a personification of the government of the United States, shown as a tall thin white man with a white beard, wearing red and white striped trousers, a blue tailcoat, and a stovepipe hat with a band of stars **2.** the United States or the American people [19C. Invented < *US*, abbreviation of *United States*]

Un·cle Tom *n* a highly offensive term for a Black man who is thought to be too solicitous of or subservient to white people (*taboo*) [Mid-19C. After a character in Harriet Beecher Stowe's novel *Uncle Tom's Cabin*] —**Uncle Tom·ism** *n*

un·cloak /un klṓk/ (**-cloaked, -cloak·ing, -cloaks**) *vt* to reveal the identity or true nature of somebody or something

un·clog /un klóg/ (**-clogged, -clog·ging, -clogs**) *vt* to remove a blockage from something such as a pipe

un·close /un klṓz/ (**-closed, -clos·ing, -clos·es**) *vti* **1.** to make something open rather than closed, or become open rather than closed **2.** to reveal something, or be revealed

un·closed /un klṓzd/ *adj* not in a closed condition

un·clothe /un klṓth/ (**-clothed, -cloth·ing, -clothes**) *vt* to remove the clothes or covering from somebody or something —**un·clothed** *adj*

un·clut·ter /un klúttər/ (**-tered, -ter·ing, -ters**) *vt* **1.** to remove the clutter from a place **2.** to remove the complexities, disorganization, or undue busyness from something ○ *Unclutter your life!*

un·clut·tered /un klúttərd/ *adj* not having an excessive amount of objects or details and therefore not appearing messy, obstructed, or cramped

un·co /úngkō/ *Scotland adv* very or extremely ■ *adj* unusual or unfamiliar [15C. Variant of UNCOUTH]

un·coil /un kóyl/ (**-coiled, -coil·ing, -coils**) *vti* to release something from a coiled or wound position, or be released from a coiled or wound position

un·com·fort·a·ble /un kúmfərtəb'l, un kúmftərb'l/ *adj* **1.** feeling a lack of or not providing physical comfort **2.** feeling or making others feel awkward and ill-at-ease —**un·com·fort·a·ble·ness** *n* —**un·com·fort·a·bly** *adv*

un·com·fy /un kúmfee/ *adj* same as **uncomfortable** (*informal*)

un·com·mer·cial /ùnkə múrsh'l/ *adj* **1.** NOT CONCERNED WITH COMMERCE OR BUSINESS not involved in commerce, especially not operated or organized for profit **2.** AGAINST BUSINESS PRINCIPLES OR PRACTICES contrary to the way things are usually done in commerce or business **3.** UNPROFITABLE unappealing to consumers and so not likely to turn a profit

un·com·mit·ted /ùnkə míttəd/ *adj* **1.** not dedicated to a principle, cause, or organization **2.** not pledged to any cause, purpose, or course of action ○ *uncommitted funds*

un·com·mon /un kómmən/ *adj* **1.** appearing or happening infrequently **2.** used to emphasize the great extent of something ○ *showing uncommon wisdom* —**un·com·mon·ness** *n*

un·com·mon·ly /un kómmənlee/ *adv* **1.** not frequently **2.** to a degree or extent that is unusual or rare

un·com·mu·ni·ca·tive /ùnkə myōōnə kàytiv, -kətiv/ *adj* not willing to say much, especially not to reveal information, or tending not to say much —**un·com·mu·ni·ca·tive·ly** *adv* —**un·com·mu·ni·ca·tive·ness** *n*

SYNONYMS See *silent*.

un·com·pli·cat·ed /un kómpli kàytəd/ *adj* readily understood, or easy to deal with —**un·com·pli·cat·ed·ness** *n*

SYNONYMS See *easy*.

un·com·pro·mis·ing /un kómprə mīzing/ *adj* feeling or showing no willingness to compromise or back down —**un·com·pro·mis·ing·ly** *adv* —**un·com·pro·mis·ing·ness** *n*

un·con·cern /ùnkən súrn/ *n* lack of concern or interest, especially where concern would be expected or thought appropriate

un·con·cerned /ùnkən súrnd/ *adj* **1.** not worried or anxious, especially when this seems unexpected or unnatural **2.** lacking concern or interest or unwilling to become involved in something —**un·con·cern·ed·ly** /-súrnədlee/ *adv* —**un·con·cern·ed·ness** /-súrnədnəss/ *n*

un·con·di·tion·al /ùnkən díshən'l, -díshnəl/ *adj* complete or guaranteed, with no conditions, limitations, or provisos attached ○ *unconditional love* —**un·con·di·tion·al·i·ty** /-dìshə nállətee/ *n* —**un·con·di·tion·al·ly** *adv*

un·con·di·tioned /ùnkən dísh'nd/ *adj* **1.** without any conditions or limits restricting or affecting it **2.** arising spontaneously and not as a result of learning or conditioning ○ *an unconditioned reflex* —**un·con·di·tioned·ness** *n*

un·con·di·tioned stim·u·lus *n* a stimulus that evokes a reflexive response without prior conditioning or learning

un·con·fined /ùnkən fīnd/ *adj* **1.** not enclosed or kept within limits or boundaries ○ *in an unconfined space* **2.** expressed naturally and uninhibitedly ○ *Let joy be unconfined!*

un·con·form·a·ble /ùnkən fáwrməb'l/ *adj* **1.** unwilling or unable to follow conventional social customs **2.** describes a layer of rock that lies directly on a much older stratum, indicating a period of erosion —**un·con·form·a·bil·i·ty** /-fàwrmə bíllətee/ *n* —**un·con·form·a·bly** *adv*

un·con·for·mi·ty /ùnkən fáwrmətee/ (*plural* **-form·i·ties**) *n* **1.** LACK OF CONFORMITY behavior or thinking that refuses to follow conventional social prescriptions **2.** GEOL BREAK IN CONTINUITY IN SEDIMENTARY ROCKS a break in the continuity of sedimentary rocks resulting from erosion or cessation of deposition **3.** GEOL SURFACE BETWEEN MISMATCHED STRATA the contact surface between two unconformable strata, often marked by angular discordance

un·con·nect·ed /ùnkə néktəd/ *adj* not related or connected to something else or each other ○ *The two incidents are entirely unconnected.* —**un·con·nect·ed·ly** *adv* —**un·con·nect·ed·ness** *n*

un·con·scion·a·ble /un kónshənəb'l/ *adj* **1.** shocking and morally unacceptable **2.** far beyond what is considered reasonable —**un·con·scion·a·ble·ness** *n* —**un·con·scion·a·bly** *adv*

un·con·scious /un kónshəss/ *adj* **1.** EXPERIENCING LOSS OF SENSES unable to see, hear, or otherwise sense what is going on, usually temporarily and often as a result of an accident or injury **2.** UNAWARE not aware of something **3.** UNINTENTIONAL not intended, or not realized or recognized ○ *unconscious irony* ■ *n* PSYCHOL, PSYCHOANAL MIND'S HIDDEN PART the part of the mind containing memories, thoughts, feelings, and ideas that the person is not generally aware of but that manifest themselves in dreams and dissociated acts —**un·con·scious·ly** *adv* —**un·con·scious·ness** *n*

un·con·sid·ered /ùnkən síddərd/ *adj* done without being adequately thought about beforehand

~~unconsious~~ incorrect spelling of **unconscious**

un·con·sti·tu·tion·al /un kònstə tōōshən'l, -tōōshnəl/ *adj* not allowed by or against the principles set down in a constitution, especially a nation's written constitution —**un·con·sti·tu·tion·al·i·ty** /-tōōsh'n állətee/ *n* —**un·con·sti·tu·tion·al·ly** *adv*

un·con·trol·la·ble /ùnkən trṓləb'l/ *adj* **1.** too strongly felt to be suppressed **2.** too unruly or wild to discipline or control —**un·con·trol·la·bil·i·ty** /-trōlə bíllətee/ *n* —**un·con·trol·la·bly** *adv*

un·con·ven·tion·al /ùnkən vénshən'l/ *adj* different from what is regarded as normal or standard —**un·con·ven·tion·al·i·ty** /-vènshə nállətee/ *n* —**un·con·ven·tion·al·ly** *adv*

un·cool /un kōōl/ *adj* **1.** not suitably relaxed, casual, or self-assured, especially in the opinion of young people (*informal*) **2.** unfashionable, undesirable, or unacceptable, especially in the opinion of young people (*slang*)

un·co·or·di·nat·ed /ùn kō áwrd'n àytəd/ *adj* **1.** awkward when moving or doing something, as if different parts of the body were not acting in harmony **2.** with no organization or proper cooperation between people or groups —**un·co·or·di·nat·ed·ly** *adv*

un·cork /un káwrk/ (**-corked, -cork·ing, -corks**) *vt* **1.** to open a bottle of something, especially wine, by taking out its cork **2.** to release something that has been restrained or repressed, e.g., a strong emotion

un·count·a·ble /un kówntəb'l/ *adj* **1.** too various or great in number to be counted **2.** used to describe a noun that does not refer to a single object

un·count·ed /un kówntəd/ *adj* **1.** too numerous to be counted **2.** not, or not yet, subjected to a count

un·count noun *n* GRAM same as **mass noun**

un·cou·ple /un kúpp'l/ (**-pled, -pling, -ples**) *v* **1.** *vti* to separate two things or one thing from another by undoing a fastening that connects them, or be separated in this way **2.** *vt* to let loose something that has been restrained

un·couth /un kōōth/ *adj* **1.** behaving in an ill-mannered or unrefined way **2.** clumsy and ungraceful [Old English *uncūþ* "unknown" < *cūþ* "known," past participle of *cunnan* "know" (see CAN[2])] —**un·couth·ly** *adv* —**un·couth·ness** *n*

un·cov·e·nant·ed /un kúvvənəntəd/ *adj* not bound, sanctioned, or guaranteed by a covenant

un·cov·er /un kúvvər/ (**-ered, -er·ing, -ers**) *v* **1.** *vti* TAKE COVER OFF SOMETHING to remove a covering from something **2.** *vt* EXPOSE SOMETHING to find, find out about, or reveal something secret or previously hidden ○ *uncover the truth about somebody* **3.** *vti* TAKE OFF YOUR HAT to take off a hat or other head covering (*dated*)

un·cov·ered /un kúvvərd/ *adj* **1.** WITH NO COVERING without any covering or protection **2.** WITH HEAD BARE with a hat or other head covering removed, usually as a sign of respect (*dated*) **3.** INSUR NOT INSURED not protected by insurance or guaranteed by some security

un·crewed /un krōōd/ *adj* not having any personnel, especially not having a pilot or crew

un·crit·i·cal /un kríttik'l/ *adj* accepting or approving something without analyzing or questioning it or discriminating between good and bad —**un·crit·i·cal·ly** *adv*

un·cross /un kráwss, un króss/ (**-crossed, -cross·ing, -cross·es**) *vt* to straighten something out from a crossed position ○ *She sat crossing and uncrossing her arms impatiently.*

un·crowned /un krównd/ *adj* **1.** possessing power, status, or wide respect but without an official title or recognition **2.** with royal rank but not yet crowned

unc·tion /úngkshən/ *n* **1.** ANOINTING WITH OIL the rubbing or sprinkling of oil on somebody as part of a religious ceremony or medical treatment **2.** SUBSTANCE USED IN RITE OR TREATMENT an oil, ointment, or salve used in religious rites or medical treatment **3.** REAL OR PRETENDED EARNESTNESS real or pretended earnestness or fervor, especially with regard to spiritual matters and especially when expressed in suitably solemn language **4.** FLATTERING EFFORTS TO CHARM excessively ingratiating efforts to charm or convince somebody **5.** SOMETHING SOOTHING something that soothes or comforts somebody [14C. < Latin *unction-* < *unguere* "smear, anoint"]

unc·tu·ous /úngkchoo əss/ *adj* **1.** EXCESSIVELY INGRATIATING attempting to charm or convince somebody in an unpleasantly suave, smug, or smooth way **2.** OILY, FATTY, OR GREASY resembling or containing oil, fat, or grease **3.** SOFT AND RICH soft and rich in texture and easily workable, especially through containing a high proportion of organic material [14C. < medieval Latin *unctuosus* < Latin *unctus* "anointing" < *unguere* "smear, anoint"] —**unc·tu·os·i·ty** /ùngkchoo óssətee/ *n* —**unc·tu·ous·ly** *adv* —**unc·tu·ous·ness** *n*

un·curl /un kúrl/ (**-curled, -curl·ing, -curls**) *vti* to straighten something that was previously wound in a curl, coil, or spiral, or become unwound or straight

un·cus /úngkəss/ (*plural* **-ci** /ún sī/) *n* a body part shaped like a hook [Early 19C. Via modern Latin < Latin, "hook"]

un·cut /un kút/ *adj* **1.** NOT CUT with no part removed or divided by cutting **2.** COMPLETE not abridged, shortened, or censored **3.** NOT FACETED describes a gemstone in its original shape, before facets have been cut ○ *uncut diamonds* **4.** PUBL WITH UNSEPARATED PAGES with the edges of the pages not yet trimmed to separate them **5.** DRUGS NOT ADULTERATED in a pure and unadulterated form (*informal*)

un·damped /un dámpt/ *adj* **1.** not subdued or discouraged **2.** describes a scientific instrument or system that is allowed to oscillate unchecked

un·daunt·ed /un dáwntəd/ *adj* not afraid or deterred by the prospect of defeat, loss, or failure —**un·daunt·ed·ly** *adv* —**un·daunt·ed·ness** *n*

un·dead /un déd/ *npl* in fiction, especially vampire stories, people or other beings who are technically dead but still exist, move, and interact with the living in a physical form —**un·dead** *adj*

un·dec·a·gon /un dékə gòn/ *n* a two-dimensional geometric figure formed of eleven sides and eleven angles [Early 18C. < Latin *undecim* "eleven" + -GON, after DECAGON]

un·de·ceive /ùndi séev/ (**-ceived, -ceiv·ing, -ceives**) *vt* to tell the truth to somebody who has been misled (*often passive*) —**un·de·ceiv·er** *n*

un·de·cid·ed /ùndi sídəd/ *adj* **1.** NOT HAVING DECIDED not yet having made a choice or decision **2.** NOT FINALIZED not yet settled or resolved ■ *n* SOMEBODY WITHOUT MIND MADE UP somebody who has not yet made a decision or choice about something ○ *She was counted among the undecideds.* —**un·de·cid·ed·ly** *adv* —**un·de·cid·ed·ness** *n*

unde·clared /ùndə kláird/ *adj* **1.** NOT STATED not stated clearly or announced officially **2.** FIN NOT REVEALED AS DUTIABLE OR TAXABLE not notified to customs or tax authorities **3.** EDUC NOT YET DECIDED ON MAJOR SUBJECT describes students who have not yet chosen or notified the subject in which they wish to major at university or college

un·de·lete /ùndi léet/ (**-let·ed, -let·ing, -letes**) *vt* to reinstate text or a file that has been deleted on a computer

un·dem·o·crat·ic /un dèmmə kráttik/ *adj* not in accordance with or not practicing democracy —**un·dem·o·crat·i·cal·ly** *adv*

un·de·mon·stra·tive /ùndi mónstrətiv/ *adj* tending not to show emotions openly —**un·de·mon·stra·tive·ly** *adv* —**un·de·mon·stra·tive·ness** *n*

un·de·ni·a·ble /ùndi ní əb'l/ *adj* **1.** BEYOND QUESTION unquestionably true or real and beyond dispute **2.** UNABLE TO BE REFUSED not able to be refused because of its importance or impact **3.** INDISPUTABLY WORTHY with worth, merit, or quality that cannot be doubted ○ *a person of undeniable character* —**un·de·ni·a·bly** *adv*

un·der /úndər/ CORE MEANING: a grammatical word used to express the concept of being beneath or below something, e.g., in location, size, age, or price ○ (prep) *Johnny had the book hidden under his blanket.* ○ (prep) *The machine is under a foot high and will fit on top of any work surface.* ○ (prep) *This toy should not be given to children under three years old.* ○ (prep) *It's the best meal you can get for under $10.* ○ (adv) *For one week only, kids five and under eat free.*

1. *prep* BELOW at or to a lower level than something that rests on top or covers and protects ○ *They were sheltering under a huge umbrella.* **2.** *prep* INSIDE inside something that forms a covering outer layer or has an upper surface ○ *He had two sweaters on under his jacket.* ○ *under the water* **3.** *prep* LESS THAN fewer in number than something, or less than something, e.g., in age, quantity, size, or price ○ *We should be finished in under a month.* ○ *There were under a hundred people at the meeting.* **4.** *prep* SUBORDINATE TO lower in rank or status than somebody or something ○ *I was under him in the company hierarchy.* **5.** *prep* SUBJECT TO subject to the control or authority of somebody or something ○ *under existing legislation* ○ *working under a new boss* **6.** *prep* DURING RULE OF during the rule of a person or government ○ *The crime rate had in fact gone down under the new mayor.* **7.** *prep* GIVEN THE EXISTENCE OF while something, especially conditions or circumstances, exists ○ *impossible under these conditions* **8.** *prep* IN THE PROCESS OF used to indicate that somebody or something is going through a particular process or experience ○ *under scrutiny* ○ *under construction* **9.** *prep* USING NAME using a particular name, especially an assumed one ○ *traveling under a false name* **10.** *prep* CLASSIFIED WITHIN classified as or in something ○ *filed under "Miscellaneous"* **11.** *prep* PLANTED WITH planted with a particular crop ○ *a field under rye* **12.** *prep* POWERED BY powered or driven by something ○ *under sail* **13.** *prep* IN SIGN OF ZODIAC during a period in which the Sun is in a particular position in the zodiac ○ *born under Aries* **14.** *adv* BELOW SURFACE OR POINT at or to a point at a lower level, especially one below a surface or covering, or passing through at a lower level ○ *watched from the lifeboats as the ship went under* ○ *lifted the wire and crawled under* **15.** *adv* FEWER OR LESS fewer or less than a previously given figure ○ *Employers with 50 employees or under are exempt.* **16.** *adv, adj* SUBSERVIENT in or into a position of submissiveness or subservience (*informal*) ○ *keeping the masses under* **17.** *adv, adj* UNCONSCIOUS in or into a state of unconsciousness or hypnosis (*informal*) ○ *felt myself going under* [Old English < Indo-European]

under- *prefix* **1.** too little, less than usual ○ *underachiever* ○ *underpay* **2.** below, underneath ○ *underpants* ○ *underscore* **3.** subordinate, of lower rank ○ *undersecretary*

un·der·ac·tive *adj*	**un·der·or·gan·ized** *adj*
un·der·ac·tiv·i·ty *n*	**un·der·pay** *vt*
un·der·ap·pre·ci·at·ed *adj*	**un·der·pay·ment** *n*
un·der·bake *vt*	**un·der·pop·u·lat·ed** *adj*
un·der·booked *adj*	**un·der·pop·u·la·tion** *n*
un·der·bud·get·ed *adj*	**un·der·pow·ered** *adj*
un·der·con·sump·tion *n*	**un·der·pro·duce** *vt*
un·der·cook *vt*	**un·der·pro·duc·tion** *n*
un·der·crewed *adj*	**un·der·pro·vid·ed** *adj*
un·der·eat *vi*	**un·der·pub·li·cized** *adj*
un·der·ed·u·cat·ed *adj*	**un·der·qual·i·fied** *adj*
un·der·em·pha·sis *n*	**un·der·re·act** *vi*
un·der·em·pha·size *vt*	**un·der·ripe** *adj*
un·der·en·dow *vt*	**un·der·served** *adj*
un·der·en·dow·ment *n*	**un·der·staff** *vt*
un·der·ex·er·cise *vi*	**un·der·stock** *v*
un·der·fi·nanced *adj*	**un·der·sub·scribe** *vt*
un·der·fund *vt*	**un·der·sub·scribed** *adj*
un·der·fund·ing *n*	**un·der·sup·ply** *vt, n*
un·der·in·flat·ed *adj*	**un·der·train** *vt*
un·der·in·vest·ment *n*	**un·der·use** *n*
un·der·lay·er *n*	**un·der·used** *adj*
un·der·manned *adj*	**un·der·u·til·i·za·tion** *n*
un·der·mod·u·la·tion *n*	**un·der·u·til·ized** *adj*

un·der·a·chieve /ùndərə chéev/ (**-chieved, -chiev·ing, -chieves**) *vi* to fail to fulfill your potential or somebody's expectations —**un·der·a·chieve·ment** *n*

un·der·a·chiev·er /ùndərə chéevər/ *n* somebody who or something that performs less well than might be expected, especially a student whose academic results are poor, given his or her intelligence and aptitude

un·der·act /ùndər ákt/ (**-act·ed, -act·ing, -acts**) *v* **1.** *vti* to fail to play a dramatic role with enough power or conviction **2.** *vt* to play a role in an understated way deliberately, for dramatic effect

un·der·age /ùndər áyj/ *adj* **1.** below the legal or required age for something **2.** carried on by people who are below the age at which something is legally permitted ○ *underage driving*

un·der·arm /úndər aarm/ *adj* **1.** BELOW ARM below the arm or for use under the arm, especially in the armpit ○ *an underarm deodorant* **2.** FROM WRIST TO ARMPIT relating to the area along the underside of the arm from armpit to wrist **3.** SPORTS same as **underhand** *adj* (sense 2) ○ *an underarm throw* ■ *adv* SPORTS same as **underhand** *adv* (sense 2) ○ *bowl underarm* ■ *n* AREA JUST BELOW ARM the area below the arm on the body or on a garment, especially the armpit

un·der·bel·ly /úndər bèllee/ (*plural* **-lies**) *n* **1.** LOWEST PART OF ANIMAL'S BELLY the underside of an animal, normally the part of the belly that is closest to the ground **2.** LOWER SURFACE the underside of an object, especially an aircraft **3.** WEAK POINT a weak or vulnerable part of something ○ *the soft underbelly of the regime* **4.** SEAMY PART OF SOMETHING a sordid area or aspect of something, especially one regarded as outside the experience of the average person

un·der·bid *v* /ùndər bíd/ (**-bid, -bid·ding, -bids**) **1.** *vti* OFFER LESS to offer a lower price than somebody else in competitive bidding **2.** *vi* MAKE TOO LOW BID to make a very low bid or too low a bid to obtain something **3.** *vti* BID LESS THAN VALUE OF CARDS to bid less than the full value of a hand in cards ■ *n* /úndər bìd/ VERY LOW BID a bid that is lower than somebody else's, or too low to obtain something —**un·der·bid·der** *n*

un·der·bite /úndər bìt/ *n* a dental condition in which the lower incisor teeth overlap the upper

un·der·bod·y /úndər bòddee/ (*plural* **-ies**) *n* the underside of the body of a motor vehicle or of an animal

un·der·boss /úndər bawss, -bòss/ *n* a lesser or deputy boss in a criminal organization, especially the Mafia

un·der·bred /ùndər bréd/ *adj* **1.** not bred from pure stock **2.** not raised well or well-mannered —**un·der·breed·ing** /-brèeding/ *n*

un·der·brush /úndər brùsh/ *n* FORESTRY same as **undergrowth** (sense 1)

un·der·caf·fein·at·ed /ùndər káffə nàytəd/ *adj* very deliberate, unemotional, and neutral in speech and actions (*informal*) ○ *a diplomat whose approach to contentious negotiations was decidedly undercaffeinated*

un·der·cap·i·tal·ize /ùndər káppit'l ìz/ (**-ized, -iz·ing, -iz·es**) *vti* to fail to supply an organization, especially a business, with enough capital to operate efficiently (*often passive*) —**un·der·cap·i·tal·i·za·tion** /ùndər kàppit'li záysh'n/ *n*

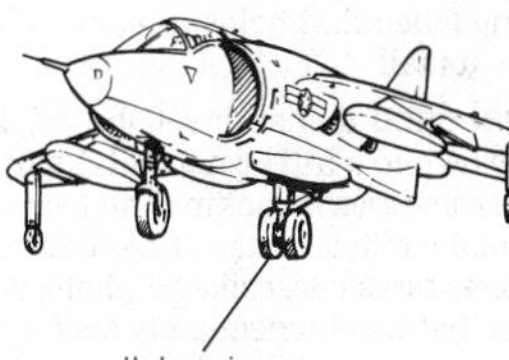

undercarriage

un·der·car·riage /úndər kàrrij/ *n* **1.** the supporting framework underneath a vehicle, to which wheels, tracks, or other means of locomotion are attached **2.** the framework of struts and wheels on which an aircraft runs when it moves on the ground

un·der·charge *v* /ùndər chaarj/ (**-charged, -charg·ing, -charg·es**) **1.** *vti* NOT CHARGE SOMEBODY ENOUGH to charge somebody too low a price for something **2.** *vt* INSERT INSUFFICIENT CHARGE IN SOMETHING to put an inadequate charge in a firearm ■ *n* /úndər chaarj/ EXCESSIVELY LOW PRICE a price charged that is too low

un·der·class /úndər klàss/ *n* a social class consisting of people so underprivileged that they are seen as being excluded from mainstream society

un·der·class·man /ùndər klássmən/ (*plural* **-men** /-mən/) *n* somebody in either of the first two years of high school or college

un·der·clay /úndər klày/ *n* a layer of fine-grained sedimentary clay found beneath a coal seam, containing the fossilized roots of the plants that became the coal

un·der·clothes /úndər klòz, -klò*th*z/ *npl* CLOTHING same as **underwear**

un·der·cloth·ing /úndər klò*th*ing/ *n* CLOTHING same as **underwear**

un·der·coat /úndər kòt/ *n* **1.** COAT BENEATH FINAL PAINT COAT a coat of paint or emulsion applied to a surface before a top coat is applied **2.** PAINT TO BE COVERED paint or emulsion designed to be used as an undercoat **3.** ZOOL SHORT HAIRS UNDER ANIMAL'S COAT a dense layer of short hairs, fur, or wool beneath the longer growth of an animal's outer coat **4.** AUTOMOT same as **undercoating** ■ *vt* (**-coat·ed, -coat·ing, -coats**) **1.** PAINT SOMETHING WITH UNDERCOAT to apply an undercoat to a surface **2.** AUTOMOT APPLY PROTECTIVE COATING TO VEHICLE'S UNDERSIDE to apply a waterproof coating on the underside of a motor vehicle in order to prevent rust and corrosion

un·der·coat·ing /úndər kòting/ *n* a coating of a waterproof material applied to the underside of a motor vehicle as protection against rust and corrosion

un·der·cool /ùndər kóol/ (**-cooled, -cool·ing, -cools**) *vti* CHEM, PHYS same as **supercool** *v*

un·der·cov·er /ùndər kúvvər/ *adj* engaged in or involving the secret gathering of information, especially by somebody who disguises himself or herself as a member of the group whose activities are being investigated ○ *an undercover police officer* —**un·der·cov·er** *adv*

un·der·croft /úndər kròft/ *n* an underground room, especially the crypt of a church

un·der·cur·rent /úndər kùrrənt, -kùr ənt/ *n* **1.** a current in a body of water or air that flows beneath another current or the surface **2.** a feeling, opinion, force, or tendency felt to be present in a person or group, but not openly shown or expressed and often differing markedly from any outwardly expressed reaction ○ *an undercurrent of resentment*

un·der·cut *v* /ùndər kút/ (**-cut, -cut·ting, -cuts**) **1.** *vt* BUSINESS CHARGE LOWER AMOUNT THAN SOMEBODY to charge less for something than somebody else **2.** *vt* REDUCE

SOMETHING'S FORCE to undermine something or detract from its force (*often passive*) **3.** *vt* CUT LOWER PART OF SOMETHING to cut away or cut into the lower part of something, especially in a way that leaves a portion overhanging **4.** *vti* SPORTS HIT BALL WITH BACKSPIN to hit a ball with a downward oblique stroke so that it has backspin, e.g., in golf or tennis ■ *n* /úndər kùt/ **1.** CUT MADE IN LOWER PART a cut made below another cut or into the lower part of something **2.** SOMETHING CUT AWAY a piece of material that has been cut away from the lower part of something **3.** SPORTS STROKE WITH BACKSPIN a stroke that gives backspin to a ball **4.** FORESTRY NOTCH IN TREE TRUNK a notch cut in a tree that is being felled that helps it make a clean break and directs its fall

un·der·de·vel·oped /ùndər di vélləpt/ *adj* **1.** NOT FULLY GROWN not grown to a full or normal extent **2.** WITHOUT MEANS FOR ECONOMIC GROWTH lacking the technology and capital to make efficient use of available resources **3.** NOT DEVELOPED ENOUGH describes a photograph, negative, or film that was inadequately developed during processing, usually through being taken out of the developer too soon, and lacks contrast as a result —**un·der·de·vel·op·ment** *n*

un·der·dog /úndər dàwg, -dòg/ *n* **1.** somebody who is expected to lose a fight or contest **2.** somebody who is unsuccessful

un·der·done /ùndər dún/ *adj* **1.** not cooked as thoroughly as intended or required **2.** *UK* cooked only lightly or partially to achieve a desired flavor or texture

un·der·dress *vi* /ùndər dréss/ (**-dressed, -dress·ing, -dress·es**) to dress less fully or formally than an occasion or circumstance demands, e.g., in cold weather or for a social event (*often passive*) ■ *n* /úndər drèss/ a garment or set of garments worn beneath others, especially if designed to be seen when worn

un·der·em·ployed /ùndər im plóyd/ *adj* **1.** not having enough work to do, or not being used to full capacity in a job **2.** working part-time but preferring full-time employment —**un·der·em·ploy·ment** *n*

un·der·es·ti·mate *v* /ùndər éstə màyt/ (**-mat·ed, -mat·ing, -mates**) **1.** *vti* MAKE TOO LOW ESTIMATE to make an estimate of something that is too low ○ *We underestimated the time it would take.* **2.** *vt* MISJUDGE WORTH OF SOMEBODY OR SOMETHING to judge people or things as being inferior to their real value or ability ○ *Don't underestimate her – she's tougher than she looks.* ■ *n* /ùndər éstəmət/ TOO LOW ESTIMATE an estimate that is too low, or a judgment that is too unfavorable to somebody or something —**un·der·es·ti·ma·tion** /ùndər estə máysh'n/ *n*

un·der·ex·pose /ùndər ik spṓz/ (**-posed, -pos·ing, -pos·es**) *vt* **1.** to expose photographic film to light for too short a time, or expose it to inadequate light **2.** to fail to give somebody or something enough publicity —**un·der·ex·po·sure** *n*

un·der·feed /ùndər féed/ (**-fed** /-féd/, **-feed·ing, -feeds**) *vt* **1.** to fail to give a person or animal enough to eat **2.** to fuel something such as an engine or a furnace from underneath

un·der·floor /úndər flàwr/ *adj* located beneath the flooring of a room or building ○ *underfloor heating*

un·der·flow /úndər flṑ/ *n* **1.** the inability of a location in computer memory to handle data of an excessively small magnitude **2.** a computer error caused by underflow

un·der·foot /ùndər fŏŏt/ *adv* **1.** under the feet of a person or animal, on the ground, or between the feet and the ground ○ *It was muddy underfoot.* **2.** creating an obstacle or obstruction

un·der·fur /úndər fùr/ *n* ZOOL same as **undercoat** *n* (sense 3)

un·der·gar·ment /úndər gaàrmənt/ *n* a piece of clothing worn beneath outer clothes, especially next to the skin, and not normally seen in public

un·der·gird /ùndər gúrd/ (**-gird·ed** or **-girt** /-gúrt/, **-gird·ing, -girds**) *vt* **1.** to support or secure something from below, e.g., by means of ropes passed underneath it **2.** to provide something with support or reinforcement of any kind

un·der·glaze /úndər glàyz/ *adj* describes decoration or pigment applied to a piece of pottery before the glaze is put on ■ *n* something, especially a decoration or pigment, that is applied to a piece of pottery before the glaze is put on

un·der·go /ùndər gṓ/ (**-went** /-wént/, **-gone** /-gáwn, -gón/, **-go·ing, -goes**) *vt* to experience or endure something, or have something happen to you ○ *You'll be obliged to undergo a thorough medical examination.* ○ *The city underwent a period of great change.*

un·der·grad /úndər gràd/ *n* EDUC same as **undergraduate** (*informal*) ○ *undergrad humor* [Early 19C. Shortening]

un·der·grad·u·ate /ùndər grájjoo ət/ *n* a student at a college or university who has not yet received a bachelor's-level degree (*often used before a noun*) ○ *undergraduate courses*

un·der·ground *adj* /úndər gròwnd/ **1.** BENEATH EARTH'S SURFACE located, happening, or operating beneath the surface of the Earth **2.** COVERT concealed and done in secret **3.** CONTRARY TO PREVAILING CULTURE separate from a prevailing social or artistic environment, and often exercising a subversive influence ○ *The story had been circulating in the underground press.* ■ *n* /úndər gròwnd/ **1.** RESISTANCE MOVEMENT a secret movement that aims to overthrow a government or fight against an occupying enemy **2.** MOVEMENT CONTRARY TO PREVAILING CULTURE a movement or group that is separate from the prevailing social or artistic environment and often exerts a subversive influence **3.** *UK* RAIL same as **subway** (sense 1) ■ *adv* /ùndər grównd/ **1.** BELOW GROUND below the surface of the ground **2.** SECRETLY in secret or in hiding

un·der·ground rail·road *n US* a secret network or route by which a fugitive can be smuggled into or out of a country or moved around safely inside it

Un·der·ground Rail·road *n* a secret organization that helped slaves flee from the southern United States to Canada or other places of safety prior to the abolition of slavery

un·der·grown /ùndər grṓn/ *adj* **1.** not grown to the expected size **2.** having or covered with undergrowth

un·der·growth /úndər grṓth/ *n* **1.** bushes, small trees, or other vegetation growing beneath the trees in a forest **2.** growth that is less than expected **3.** ZOOL same as **undercoat** *n* (sense 3)

un·der·hand /úndər hànd/ *adj* **1.** SECRET AND DISHONEST done secretively and dishonestly or with the intention to deceive or cheat somebody **2.** KEEPING ARM BELOW SHOULDER HEIGHT thrown, pitched, or hit with the arm kept below shoulder height and usually close to the body ■ *adv* **1.** SECRETLY AND DISHONESTLY in a secretive and dishonest way **2.** BELOW SHOULDER with the arm kept below shoulder height

un·der·hand·ed /ùndər hándəd/ *adj, adv* same as **underhand** *adj* (sense 1), *adv* (sense 1) —**un·der·hand·ed·ly** *adv* —**un·der·hand·ed·ness** *n*

un·der·hung /ùndər húng/ *adj* **1.** describes a lower jaw that projects beyond the upper jaw **2.** running on a rail or track situated underneath ○ *underhung sliding doors*

un·der·in·sure /ùndərin shŏŏr/ (**-sured, -sur·ing, -sures**) *vt* to take out insufficient insurance to cover the value of something (*often passive*)

un·der·lain past participle of **underlie**

un·der·lay[1] *vt* /ùndər láy/ (**-laid** /-láyd/, **-lay·ing, -lays**) ⚠ PROVIDE WITH SOMETHING UNDERNEATH to lay something underneath something else (*often passive*) ■ *n* /úndər lày/ **1.** LAYER BENEATH CARPET a layer of cushioning and insulating material put down on a floor before a carpet is laid **2.** SUPPORT FOR SOMETHING something laid beneath something else as a base, support, or foundation —**un·der·laid** *adj*

USAGE underlay or **underlie**? Unlike the root words *lay* and *lie*, both verbs are transitive (i.e., take an object). The more common word is ***underlie***, and it has a wider range of meanings including the figurative meaning "be the basis or cause of something": *This trend underlies many of the social changes of recent times.* The primary meaning of ***underlay*** is "to lay something underneath something else" (*We underlaid the carpet with felt*), and in this meaning it also acts as a noun (with the stress on the first syllable).

un·der·lay[2] /ùndər láy/ past tense of **underlie**

un·der·let /ùndər lét/ (**-let, -let·ting, -lets**) *v* **1.** *vt* to let a property for less than its full value **2.** *vti* COMM same as **sublet**

un·der·lie /ùndər lī́/ (**-lay** /-láy/, **-lain** /-láyn/, **-ly·ing, -lies**) *vt* **1.** LIE BENEATH SOMETHING to lie or be put under something else **2.** BE FOUNDATION OF SOMETHING to be the basis or cause of something ○ *the assumptions that underlie this argument* **3.** FIN HAVE FINANCIAL PRIORITY OVER SOMETHING to take priority over other financial rights or securities ○ *This claim underlies yours.*

un·der·line *vt* /úndər lìn, ùndər lī́n/ (**-lined, -lin·ing, -lines**) **1.** PUT LINE BELOW SOMETHING to draw or type a line under something **2.** EMPHASIZE SOMETHING to give emphasis or extra force or prominence to something, or make something appear more important or urgent ○ *The mistake underlines the need for individuals to take responsibility for their own actions.* ■ *n* /úndər lìn/ **1.** LINE BENEATH SOMETHING a line drawn or typed under something **2.** PRINTING CAPTION UNDER ILLUSTRATION a caption placed below an illustration —**un·der·lin·er** *n*

un·der·lin·en /úndər lìnnən/ *n* underwear, especially when made of linen (*archaic*)

un·der·ling /úndərling/ *n* a servant or subordinate, especially one regarded as of little worth or importance

un·der·lip /úndər lìp/ *n* the lower lip of a person or animal

un·der·ly·ing /úndər lī̀ ing/ *adj* **1.** LYING UNDERNEATH positioned beneath something else ○ *the underlying rock strata* **2.** HIDDEN AND SIGNIFICANT present and important but not immediately obvious ○ *the underlying reasons for his odd behavior* **3.** ESSENTIAL basic or fundamental to something ○ *the underlying principles behind the decision* **4.** FIN FINANCIALLY MOST IMPORTANT describes financial obligations or assets that take priority over others

un·der·mine /ùndər mī́n, úndər mī̀n/ (**-mined, -min·ing, -mines**) *vt* **1.** ERODE SOMETHING to weaken something by removing or wearing away material from its base or from beneath it ○ *The chalk cliffs are being gradually undermined by the waves.* **2.** WEAKEN SOMETHING GRADUALLY to diminish or weaken something gradually ○ *undermined her confidence* **3.** SUBVERT SOMEBODY OR SOMETHING to weaken, discredit, or destroy somebody or something by covert and malicious action ○ *The leaked memos undermined the administration's credibility.* **4.** TUNNEL UNDER SOMETHING to dig a tunnel underneath something, especially a fortification, in order to plant explosives or make it collapse

un·der·most /úndər mṑst/ *adj* lowest or last in position, status, or level ■ *adv* in the lowest or last place

un·der·neath /ùndər né͞eth/ CORE MEANING: a grammatical word indicating that something is below or beneath another thing, and may be covered by it ○ (adv) *I lifted up the pile of clothes, and underneath, on the floor, was a dark red stain.* ○ (prep) *I left the key underneath the doormat.*

1. *prep, adv* BENEATH SOMETHING below or beneath something, and perhaps covered by it ○ (prep) *found old paint layers underneath the surface* ○ (adv) *I was wearing a bathrobe and had nothing on underneath.* **2.** *prep, adv* UNDERLYING SOMETHING underlying something that is shown on the surface or openly expressed ○ (prep) *Underneath her confident exterior she was a very shy person.* ○ (adv) *There must be deeper problems underneath.* **3.** *adv, adj* ON LOWER PART OF SOMETHING on the bottom of something or the part that faces toward the ground ○ (adv) *brown with white feathers underneath* ○ (adj) *The underneath part is hard to reach.* **4.** *n* LOWER PART the bottom part of something or the part that faces toward the ground [Old English *underneoþan* < UNDER + *neoþan* "beneath"]

un·der·nour·ish /ùndər núr ish/ (**-ished, -ish·ing, -ish·es**) *vt* to fail to supply somebody with enough food or other resources to provide for proper development (*often passive*) —**un·der·nour·ish·ment** *n*

un·der·pants /úndər pànts/ *npl* briefs or shorts worn as underclothes

un·der·part /úndər paàrt/ *n* **1.** the lower part or underside of an animal or object (*often used in the plural*) **2.** a lesser or subordinate role, e.g., in a play

un·der·pass /úndər pàss/ *n* **1.** a part of a road that crosses under another road or a railroad **2.** a tunnel for pedestrians beneath a road or railroad

un·der·per·form /ùndər pər fáwrm/ (**-formed, -form·ing,**

-forms) *vi* to do less well than expected or than something or somebody else ○ *underperforming investments* —**un·der·per·form·ance** *n* —**un·der·per·form·er** *n*

un·der·pin /ùndər pín/ (**-pinned, -pin·ning, -pins**) *vt* **1.** to support a weakened wall or structure by propping it up from below **2.** to act as a support or foundation for something (*often passive*) ○ *the hard facts that underpin these assumptions*

un·der·pin·ning /úndər pìnning/ *n* **1.** a structure built to support a weakened wall or building **2.** something that supports or acts as a foundation for something (*often used in the plural*)

un·der·play /ùndər pláy/ (**-played, -play·ing, -plays**) *v* **1.** *vt* NOT EMPHASIZE SOMETHING ENOUGH to present something as less important than it actually is, sometimes as a deliberate tactic ○ *I don't wish to underplay the internal conflicts within the organization.* **2.** *vti* ACT ROLE SUBTLY to act a role in a deliberately restrained or subtle way **3.** *vi* PLAY LOWER CARD to play a lower card while holding a higher one

un·der·plot /úndər plòt/ *n* a secondary plot in a play, novel, or other work of fiction

un·der·price /ùndər príss/ (**-priced, -pric·ing, -pric·es**) *vt* **1.** to put a price on something for sale that is less than its actual value **2.** to sell something for a lower price than somebody else

un·der·priv·i·leged /ùndər prívvəlijd/ (*often used euphemistically*) *adj* deprived of many of the rights and privileges enjoyed by most people in society, usually as a result of poverty ■ *npl* underprivileged people considered as a social group

un·der·proof /ùndər pro͞of/ *adj* describes an alcoholic drink that contains less alcohol than is standard or than is legally required

un·der·prop /ùndər próp/ (**-propped, -prop·ping, -props**) *vt* to prop something up from underneath

un·der·quote /ùndər kwṓt/ (**-quot·ed, -quot·ing, -quotes**) *v* **1.** *vti* to offer something for sale at a lower price than the market value **2.** *vt* to quote a lower price than a competitor in tendering for a job

un·der·rate /ùndər ráyt/ (**-rat·ed, -rat·ing, -rates**) *vt* to judge the value, degree, or worth of somebody or something to be less than it really is ○ *a greatly underrated writer*

un·der·re·port /ùndər ri páwrt/ (**-port·ed, -port·ing, -ports**) *vt* to declare or report a number or amount to be smaller than is actually the case

un·der·rep·re·sent /ùndər rèppri zént/ (**-sent·ed, -sent·ing, -sents**) *vt* **1.** to contain a disproportionately small number of representatives of something, e.g., a population group (*often passive*) ○ *reported women were underrepresented at senior levels* **2.** to present something as smaller, less widespread, or less important than it actually is —**un·der·rep·re·sen·ta·tion** /ùndər repri zen táysh'n, -reprizən-/ *n*

un·der·run *v* /ùndər rún/ (**-ran** /-rán/, **-run, -run·ning, -runs**) **1.** *vt* MOVE UNDER to run, pass, or go under something **2.** *vti* NAUT PASS SOMETHING OVER BOAT FOR INSPECTION to haul something in, e.g., a net or cable, and pass it over the deck of a boat so that it can be inspected or repaired, or be hauled in in this way ■ *n* /úndər rùn/ **1.** LOWER-THAN-ESTIMATED COST a cost or expense that is less than anticipated **2.** LOWER-THAN-REQUIRED PRODUCTION RUN a production run of a manufactured or printed item that is less than the quantity ordered **3.** SHORTFALL OF PRODUCTION RUN the amount by which a production run of a manufactured or printed item falls short of the quantity ordered

un·der·sat·u·rat·ed /ùndər sáchə ràytəd/ *adj* **1.** describes igneous rock that contains low levels of combined silica and no free silica **2.** *US* CHEM same as **unsaturated**

un·der·score *vt* /ùndər skáwr/ (**-scored, -scor·ing, -scores**) **1.** DRAW LINE BELOW SOMETHING to draw or incise a line under something **2.** EMPHASIZE SOMETHING to give emphasis or extra force to something ■ *n* /úndər skàwr/ **1.** LINE BENEATH SOMETHING a line drawn or incised under something **2.** BACKGROUND MUSIC a piece of background music accompanying action or dialogue in a movie

un·der·sea /ùndər seé/ *adj* existing, carried out, or designed for use below the surface of the ocean ■ *adv* in or into the area below the surface of the ocean

un·der·seal *UK* AUTOMOT *n* /úndər seèl/ same as **undercoating** ■ *vt* /úndər seèl/ (**-sealed, -seal·ing, -seals**) same as **undercoat** *v* (sense 2)

un·der·seas *adv* OCEANOG same as **undersea**

un·der·sec·re·tar·y /ùndər sékrə tèrree/ (*plural* **-ies**) *n* a secretary who ranks just below a chief secretary in a government or bureaucratic organization —**un·der·sec·re·tar·i·at** /ùndər sekrə térree ət/ *n*

un·der·sell /ùndər sél/ (**-sold** /-sṓld/, **-sell·ing, -sells**) *vt* **1.** SELL SOMETHING BELOW PROPER VALUE to sell something at a price below its full or usual value **2.** SELL MORE CHEAPLY THAN SOMEBODY to sell something more cheaply than a competitor **3.** ADVERTISE SOMETHING WITH TOO LITTLE ENTHUSIASM to present the merits of something or somebody with too little enthusiasm or conviction or in too restrained or understated a way

un·der·set *n* /úndər sèt/ an ocean undercurrent that runs in a direction contrary to the direction of the surface waves ■ *vt* /ùndər sét/ (**-set, -set·ting, -sets**) to support something from below

un·der·sexed /ùndər sékst/ *adj* having less sex drive or less interest in sex than some other people

un·der·shirt /úndər shùrt/ *n* a collarless undergarment for the upper body, usually with short sleeves or no sleeves

un·der·shoot /ùndər sho͞ot/ (**-shot** /-shót/, **-shoot·ing, -shoots**) *vti* **1.** to land an aircraft short of a landing area ○ *The pilot undershot the runway.* **2.** to shoot something such as an arrow so that it lands short of the target

un·der·shorts /úndər shàwrts/ *npl* shorts or briefs worn as underclothes by men and boys

un·der·shot /úndər shòt/ *adj* **1.** MED same as **underhung** (sense 1) **2.** describes a device, especially a water wheel, that is driven by water flowing beneath it

un·der·shrub /úndər shrùb/ *n* BOT same as **subshrub**

un·der·side /úndər sìd/ *n* **1.** the lower side or bottom of something **2.** an aspect of something that is undesirable or unpleasant and usually hidden

un·der·signed /úndər sìnd/ (*formal*) *n* somebody whose signature appears on the document being read ■ *adj* whose signature is written, or whose signatures are written, below

un·der·sized /ùndər sízd/, **un·der·size** /-síz/ *adj* smaller than the prevailing or preferred size

un·der·skirt /úndər skùrt/ *n* a skirt worn under another skirt

un·der·slung /ùndər slúng/ *adj* **1.** suspended or supported from above, like a motor vehicle chassis that is suspended from the axles **2.** built close to the ground with a low center of gravity **3.** MED same as **underhung** (sense 1)

un·der·soil /úndər sòyl/ *n* AGRIC same as **subsoil**

un·der·sold COMM past participle, past tense of **undersell**

un·der·spend /ùndər spénd/ (**-spent** /-spént/, **-spend·ing, -spends**) *vi* to spend less money than is required or expected —**un·der·spend** /úndər spènd/ *n*

un·der·stand /ùndər stánd/ (**-stood** /-sto͝od/, **-stand·ing, -stands**) *v* **1.** *vti* GRASP MEANING OF SOMETHING to know or be able to explain to yourself the nature of somebody or something, or the meaning or cause of something ○ *I can't understand what all the fuss is about.* **2.** *vti* COME TO KNOW SOMETHING to realize or become aware of something ○ *finally understood the urgency of the situation* **3.** *vt* KNOW MEANING OF WORDS IN LANGUAGE to recognize and be able to translate the words of a foreign language ○ *understands Spanish* **4.** *vti* KNOW AND SYMPATHIZE to recognize somebody's character or somebody's situation, especially in a sympathetic, tolerant, or empathetic way ○ *It's such a relief to find someone who understands.* **5.** *vt* TAKE SOMETHING AS MEANT to interpret something in a particular way, or to infer or deduce a particular meaning from something ○ *understood it as a peaceful gesture* **6.** *vt* TAKE SOMETHING AS SETTLED to believe something to be agreed, settled, or firmly communicated ○ *I was given to understand you had agreed.* **7.** *vt* KNOW SOMETHING BY LEARNING OR HEARING to gather or assume something on the basis of having heard or been told it ○ *He is, I understand, expected later.* **8.** *vt* LING INFER IMPLICIT MEANING to assume information or a meaning that is implied but not expressed directly (*usually passive*) [Old English *understandan* < UNDER + *standan* (see STAND)]

un·der·stand·a·ble /ùndər stándəb'l/ *adj* **1.** having a meaning or nature that can be understood ○ *Try to make it understandable to a nonspecialist.* **2.** able to be accepted as normal, reasonable, or forgivable ○ *Under the circumstances it was a perfectly understandable reaction.* —**un·der·stand·a·bil·i·ty** /ùndər stàndə bíllətee/ *n* —**un·der·stand·a·bly** *adv*

un·der·stand·ing /ùndər stánding/ *n* **1.** ABILITY TO GRASP MEANING the ability to perceive and explain the meaning or the nature of somebody or something **2.** KNOWLEDGE OF SOMETHING knowledge of a particular subject, area, or situation ○ *gaining a better understanding of industrial processes* **3.** INTERPRETATION OF SOMETHING somebody's interpretation of something, or a belief or opinion based on an interpretation of or inference from something ○ *It was my understanding that the costs would be shared equally.* **4.** MUTUAL COMPREHENSION an agreement, often an unofficial or unspoken one ○ *I'm sure we can come to an understanding about this.* **5.** KNOWLEDGE OF ANOTHER'S NATURE a sympathetic, empathetic, or tolerant recognition of somebody else's nature or situation ○ *I thought you of all people would show a little understanding.* ■ *adj* SYMPATHETICALLY AWARE sympathetic, empathetic, or tolerant in recognizing somebody's or something's character and situation ○ *fortunate in having understanding parents* —**un·der·stand·ing·ly** *adv*

un·der·state /ùndər stáyt/ (**-stat·ed, -stat·ing, -states**) *vt* **1.** to express something in a deliberately less dramatic, emphatic, or emotional way than it seems to warrant, often to increase its actual impact or for the sake of irony **2.** to describe something as being smaller in quantity or number than it really is ○ *understate the cost*

un·der·stat·ed /ùndər stáytəd/ *adj* achieving its effect through restraint, subtlety, and good taste ○ *understated elegance*

un·der·state·ment /ùndər stáytmənt, úndər stàytmənt/ *n* **1.** a statement, or a way of expressing yourself, that is deliberately less forceful or dramatic than the subject would seem to justify or require **2.** a statement that underrepresents or underreports something

un·der·steer *vi* /ùndər steér/ (**-steered, -steer·ing, -steers**) to turn less sharply than the turning of a steering wheel would lead the driver to expect ■ *n* /úndər steèr/ a motor vehicle's tendency to turn less sharply than expected

un·der·stood /ùndər sto͝od/ past participle, past tense of **understand** ■ *adj* agreed, assumed, or implied, especially without being openly or officially expressed

un·der·sto·ry /úndər stàwree/ (*plural* **-ries**) *n* a layer of small trees and bushes below the level of the taller trees in a forest

un·der·strength /ùndər stréngth/ *adj* having inadequate strength, especially less than the usual or desirable number of personnel

un·der·stud·y /úndər stùddee/ *n* (*plural* **-ies**) **1.** SUBSTITUTE ACTOR an actor who learns the role of another actor in order to be able to act as a replacement if necessary **2.** TRAINED SUBSTITUTE a trained replacement or substitute for somebody ■ *vti* (**-ied, -y·ing, -ies**) BE SUBSTITUTE ACTOR to learn the role of another actor in order to be able to replace him or her if necessary

un·der·take /ùndər táyk/ (**-took** /-to͝ok/, **-tak·en** /-táykən/, **-tak·ing, -takes**) *v* **1.** *vti* to make a commitment to do something ○ *undertook to find out the cost of flights* **2.** *vt* to begin to do something or to set out on something ○ *They are ill-equipped to undertake such a journey.*

un·der·tak·er *n* **1.** /ùndər táykər/ somebody who sets about doing a task **2.** /úndər tàykər/ *Can, UK* somebody whose profession is to prepare the dead for burial or cremation and to arrange funerals. US term **funeral director**

un·der·tak·ing /úndər tàyking/ *n* **1.** TASK a task or project ○ *It was a colossal undertaking.* **2.** PLEDGE TO DO SOMETHING a promise or agreement to do something ○ *She gave an undertaking to serve for a year.* **3.**

FUNERAL BUSINESS the business of preparing the dead for burial or cremation and arranging funerals

un·der-the-count·er *adj* sold or obtained clandestinely or illegally (*not hyphenated after a verb*)

un·der-the-ta·ble *adj* done or organized clandestinely and often illegally (*not hyphenated after a verb*)

un·der·things /úndər thìngz/ *npl* underwear, especially women's underwear

un·der·thrust /úndər thrùst/ *n* a reverse fault in which a lower layer of rock is driven underneath a higher, relatively passive layer

un·der·time /úndər tìm/ *n* time spent by employees during working hours on non-work-related activities, such as shopping or personal appointments [Late 20C. Modeled on OVERTIME] —**un·der·time** *vi*

un·der·tint /úndər tìnt/ *n* a slight or subtle tint

un·der·tone /úndər tōn/ *n* **1. UNDERLYING QUALITY OR ELEMENT** something that is suggested or implied rather than stated openly ○ *undertones of menace* **2. LOW TONE** a quiet, subdued, or background tone, especially of the voice ○ *He spoke in an undertone.* **3. MUTED COLOR** a subdued color

un·der·tow /úndər tō/ *n* **1.** the seaward pull of water away from a shore after a wave has broken **2.** an underlying tendency or force that runs in the opposite direction to the apparent one ○ *an undertow of dissatisfaction*

un·der·trick /úndər trìk/ *n* in bridge, a trick short of the number declared by a player

un·der·trump /úndər trùmp, ùndər trúmp/ (**-trumped, -trump·ing, -trumps**) *vi* in cards, to play a trump that is lower than a trump that has already been played in a hand

un·der·val·ue /ùndər vállyoo/ (**-ued, -u·ing, -ues**) *vt* **1.** to hold too low an opinion of something or somebody **2.** to judge the value of something or somebody as being lower than it really is ○ *buy up stock that is undervalued* —**un·der·val·u·a·tion** /ùndər valyoo áysh'n/ *n*

un·der·wa·ter *adj* /ùndər wáwtər/ **1. BELOW WATER SURFACE** existing, carried out, or designed for use below the surface of water **2.** NAUT **UNDER SHIP'S WATER LINE** below the water line in a ship or boat ■ *adv* /ùndər wáwtər/ **BELOW WATER SURFACE** in or to a place below the surface of a body of water ■ *n* /úndər wàwtər/ **WATER UNDERNEATH SURFACE** the water beneath the surface of a river, lake, or sea

un·der way, un·der·way /ùndər wáy/ *adj, adv* in motion or progress ○ *not long before the project was under way*

USAGE under way or **underway**? Although the form ***underway*** is often seen, and has long been in use, ***under way*** is still widely preferred. The only exception to this is the adjectival use that precedes the noun: *The submarine received underway servicing.*

un·der·wear /úndər wèr/ *n* clothes worn beneath outer clothes, usually next to the skin, and not normally seen in public

un·der weigh *adj, adv* NAUT same as **under way**

un·der·weight /ùndər wáyt, úndər wàyt/ *adj* weighing less than is normal or required

un·der·went past tense of **undergo**

un·der·whelm /ùndər wélm, -hwélm/ (**-whelmed, -whelm·ing, -whelms**) *vt* to fail notably to impress or excite somebody (*humorous*) [Mid-20C. After OVERWHELM] —**un·der·whelm·ing** *adj*

un·der·wing /úndər wìng/ *n* **1. HIND WING OF INSECT** a hind wing of an insect such as a beetle, especially when covered by a forewing while the insect is not in flight **2. MOTH WITH BRIGHT WINGS** a moth that has brightly colored hind wings that become visible only in flight. Genus: *Catocala.* **3. LOWER SIDE OF BIRD'S WING** the underside of a bird's wing

un·der·wire /úndər wìr/ *n* **1.** a brassiere with wire sewn into the lining under each cup to provide support **2.** a wire sewn into the lining under each cup of a brassiere to provide support —**un·der·wired** *adj*

un·der·wood /úndər wòod/ *n* ECOL same as **undergrowth** (sense 1)

un·der·world /úndər wùrld/ *n* **1.** the part of society that lives by crime (*often used before a noun*) ○ *an underworld shooting* **2.** in classical mythology, the place beneath the ground where the souls of the dead go

un·der·write /úndər rìt, ùndər rít/ (**-wrote** /-rōt, -rót/, **-writ·ten** /-rìtt'n, -rítt'n/, **-writ·ing, -writes**) *v* **1.** *vti* **SUBSIDIZE SOMETHING** to agree to provide funds for something and to cover any losses ○ *The tour was underwritten by an electronics company.* **2.** *vti* **ISSUE INSURANCE** to insure somebody or something by accepting liability for designated losses, or to be in the business of doing this **3.** *vti* **AGREE TO BUY UNSOLD SECURITIES** to guarantee the sale of an issue of securities at a fixed price **4.** *vt* **LEND SUPPORT TO SOMEBODY OR SOMETHING** to give support to somebody or something, especially by signing a document **5.** *vt* **WRITE BENEATH OTHER WRITING** to write something, or add a signature, underneath other written matter [15C. After Latin *subscribere* "write underneath, sign"]

un·der·writ·er /úndər rìtər/ *n* **1. INSURER COVERING LIABILITIES** a person, firm, or organization that issues insurance and accepts liability for designated risks **2. SOMEBODY ASSESSING RISKS ON INSURANCE** somebody employed by an insurance company to assess risks and fix premiums **3. GUARANTOR OF SECURITIES ISSUE** a person or organization that agrees to buy at a fixed price any unsold part of an issue of securities

un·de·scend·ed /ùndi séndəd/ *adj* describes a testicle that has remained in the inguinal canal and has not descended into the scrotum

un·de·served /ùndi zúrvd/ *adj* unfairly awarded or unfairly endured, or not merited on the basis of the facts ○ *undeserved punishment* —**un·de·serv·ed·ly** /-zúrvədlee/ *adv*

un·de·serv·ing /ùn di zúrving/ *adj* unworthy of receiving benefits or rewards

un·de·sign·ing /ùndi zìning/ *adj* not trying to deceive or manipulate

un·de·sir·a·ble /ùndi zírəb'l/ *adj* not wanted, liked, or approved of ■ *n* somebody or something regarded as undesirable —**un·de·sir·a·bil·i·ty** /-zìrə bíllətee/ *n* —**un·de·sir·a·bly** *adv*

un·de·ter·mined /ùndi túrmind/ *adj* **1.** not resolved, decided, or fixed **2.** unknown or undiscovered

un·de·vi·at·ing /un deévee àyting/ *adj* not turning or changing, especially remaining constant or true to somebody or something ○ *undeviating loyalty* —**un·de·vi·at·ing·ly** *adv*

un·did past tense of **undo**

un·dies /úndeez/ *npl* underclothes, especially women's underclothes (*informal*) [Late 19C. Shortening]

un·di·gest·ed /ùn dì jéstəd, -di-/ *adj* **1.** not having undergone the process of digestion **2.** not fully analyzed, considered, or understood

un·dine /un deén, ún deèn/ *n* a female spirit that lives in water, especially one that could become human by bearing the child of a human male [Early 19C. < modern Latin *undina* < Latin *unda* "wave"]

un·dip·lo·mat·ic /un dìpplə máttik/ *adj* lacking in tact and diplomacy —**un·dip·lo·mat·i·cal·ly** *adv*

un·di·rect·ed /ùndi réktəd, ùn dì-/ *adj* **1.** without a purpose or object **2.** not marked with an address in the proper way

un·dis·guised /ùndiss gízd/ *adj* expressed fully and openly —**un·dis·guis·ed·ly** /-gízədlee/ *adv*

un·dis·posed /ùndiss pózd/ *adj* **1.** not resolved or dealt with **2.** not prepared or inclined to do something

un·dis·so·ci·at·ed /ùndi sóshee àytəd, -sóssee-/ *adj* describes a molecule not broken down into simpler molecules, atoms, or ions

un·dis·tin·guished /ùndi stíngwisht/ *adj* **1. MEDIOCRE** not very good or ever rising above the ordinary ○ *an undistinguished career* **2. COMMONPLACE** not at all striking or likely to stand out from others ○ *undistinguished appearance* **3. NOT MADE SEPARATE** not differentiated from others

un·dis·trib·ut·ed /ùndi stríbbyətəd/ *adj* **1.** not paid out as a dividend to stockholders, but invested back into the business ○ *undistributed profits* **2.** used to describe a term that does not refer to all members of the class it designates. The term "dogs" is undistributed in the statement "Some dogs are unfriendly."

un·dis·turbed /ùn di stúrbd/ *adj* not interrupted or disrupted by anybody or anything

un·do /un dóo/ (**-did** /-díd/, **-done** /-dún/, **-do·ing, -does** /-dúz/) *v* **1.** *vti* **UNFASTEN** to open, unfasten, untie, or unwrap something, or become unfastened, untied, or unwrapped ○ *I can't undo this button.* **2.** *vt* **NULLIFY SOMETHING** to cancel or reverse the effect of an action ○ *What's done can't be undone.* **3.** *vt* **REVERSE EFFECT OF COMPUTER COMMAND** to cancel the effect of the last command or action done on a computer, restoring the material being worked on to its previous condition **4.** *vt* **RUIN SOMEBODY** to bring somebody or something to ruin or disaster (*literary*)

un·dock /un dók/ (**-docked, -dock·ing, -docks**) *vti* to detach something, or become detached, from a space station or another spacecraft in space

un·do·ing /un dóo ing/ *n* **1. ACT OF BRINGING TO RUIN** the ruin, downfall, or destruction of somebody or something, or something that causes this ○ *Pride was our undoing.* **2. ACT OF UNFASTENING** the opening, unfastening, untying, or unwrapping of something **3. ACT OF NULLIFYING SOMETHING'S EFFECT** the canceling or reversing of the effect of an action

un·done /un dún/ past participle of **undo** ■ *adj* **1. UNCOMPLETED** not yet done or completed **2. UNFASTENED** not tied or fastened **3. BROUGHT TO RUIN** ruined, destroyed, or brought to the brink of collapse (*formal or humorous*)

un·doubt·ed /un dówtəd/ *adj* not subject to doubt or dispute

un·doubt·ed·ly /un dówtədlee/ *adv* without any doubt or question

~~**undoubtly**~~ incorrect spelling of **undoubtedly**

un·draw /un dráw/ (**-drew** /-dróo/, **-drawn** /-dráwn/, **-draw·ing, -draws**) *vt* to draw something such as a curtain back or open

un·dreamed-of, un·dreamt-of *adj* impossible to imagine in advance, usually through being too wonderful or too unlikely

un·dress /un dréss/ *v* (**-dressed, -dress·ing, -dress·es**) **1.** *vti* **TAKE CLOTHES OFF** to remove the clothes from your own or somebody else's body **2.** *vt* **TAKE DRESSING OFF** to remove a dressing from a wound **3.** *vt* **REMOVE ORNAMENTATION** to strip something of its decoration ■ *n* **1. CONDITION OF HAVING NO CLOTHES ON** a condition of nakedness or of being scantily clothed **2. INFORMAL CLOTHING** informal attire or an everyday uniform

un·dressed /un drést/ *adj* **1. WITHOUT CLOTHES** not wearing any or many clothes, or having just removed clothes **2. UNTREATED** not processed or treated in some way ○ *undressed leather* **3. NOT READY FOR TABLE** not fully prepared for cooking or eating **4. WITHOUT DRESSING** not covered with a dressing or sauce **5. INFORMALLY DRESSED** appropriately but not formally dressed for an event or occasion **6. WITHOUT BANDAGE** without a dressing or bandage ○ *an undressed wound*

SYNONYMS See ***naked***.

un·due /un dóo/ *adj* **1.** going beyond the limits of what is proper, normal, justified, or permitted ○ *using undue force to disperse the crowd* **2.** not owed or payable at present

un·du·lant /únjələnt/ *adj* resembling waves in motion or form (*formal*) [Early 19C. < UNDULATE]

un·du·lant fe·ver *n* brucellosis as it affects humans

un·du·late *v* /únjə làyt, úndyə-/ (**-lat·ed, -lat·ing, -lates**) **1.** *vti* **MOVE SINUOUSLY LIKE WAVES** to move in waves or in a movement resembling waves, or cause something to move in this way **2.** *vi* **GO UP AND DOWN GRACEFULLY** to rise and fall gracefully in volume or pitch ■ *adj* /únjələt, -làyt, -làytəd/ *also* **un·du·lat·ed WAVY IN APPEARANCE** with a wavy appearance, edge, or markings [Mid-17C. < Latin *undulatus* "wavy" < *unda* "wave"] —**un·du·la·tion** /ùnjə láysh'n, ùndyə-/ *n*

ORIGIN The Latin word *unda* "wave," from which ***undulate*** is derived, is also the source of English *abound, inundation, redundant, sound*[3], and *surround.*

un·du·ly /un dóolee/ *adv* to a very great extent, or to an excessive, improper, or unjustifiable degree ○ *We were not unduly concerned.*

un·du·ti·ful /un dóotif'l/ *adj* **1.** lacking a sense of moral or legal obligation **2.** unwilling to fulfill moral or legal obligations —**un·du·ti·ful·ly** *adv* —**un·du·ti·ful·ness** *n*

un·dy·ing /un dī́ ing/ *adj* describes an emotion that does not diminish but continues forever —**un·dy·ing·ly** *adv*

un·earned /un úrnd/ *adj* **1.** not acquired by labor or service ○ *unearned income* **2.** not deserved ○ *unearned criticism*

un·earned in·cre·ment *n* an increase in property value resulting from factors other than labor or improvements made by the owner

un·earned run *n* in baseball, a run that in the opinion of the official scorer would not have happened had it not been for errors or passed balls made by the defensive team

un·earth /un úrth/ (**-earthed, -earth·ing, -earths**) *vt* **1. DIG SOMETHING UP** to bring something up out of the ground **2. DISCLOSE SOMETHING** to discover or disclose something, especially after an investigation **3. FIND SOMETHING LOST** to find something that has been lost or hidden

un·earth·ly /un úrthlee/ *adj* **1. NOT FROM THIS WORLD** not being or seeming to be from this world **2. EERIE** looking or sounding so strange as to be frightening **3. UNREASONABLE** completely inappropriate or unreasonable (*informal*) ○ *at this unearthly hour* **4. PERFECT** embodying perfection (*literary*) —**un·earth·li·ness** *n*

un·ease /un éez/ *n* a feeling of anxiety, awkwardness, or discomfort

SYNONYMS See *worry.*

un·eas·y /un éezee/ (**-i·er, -i·est**) *adj* **1. ANXIOUS** anxious or afraid ○ *I always feel slightly uneasy until I know they're safely home.* **2. NOT GUARANTEED TO ENDURE** not sufficiently well established for people to be confident that it will endure ○ *an uneasy truce* **3. ILL AT EASE** awkward or lacking confidence ○ *felt uneasy with strangers* **4. RESTLESS** not restful or not allowing somebody to rest properly ○ *an uneasy sleep* —**un·eas·i·ly** *adv* —**un·eas·i·ness** *n*

~~unecessary~~ incorrect spelling of **unnecessary**

un·ec·o·nom·ic /un èkə nómmik, -èekə-/ *adj* **1.** not making or not likely to make a profit **2.** *also* **un·ec·o·nom·i·cal** not efficient or worth the expense —**un·ec·o·nom·ic·al·ly** *adv*

un·ed·it·ed /un édditəd/ *adj* **1.** not corrected or revised **2.** not adapted for a specific audience, purpose, or medium

un·ed·u·cat·ed /un éjjə kàytəd/ *adj* lacking the learning that is usually acquired in schools

un·e·lect·a·ble /ùnn i léktəb'l/ *adj* certain to be defeated as a candidate for public office, e.g., because of extreme positions on controversial issues

un·e·mo·tion·al /ùnni mṓshən'l, -mṓshnəl/ *adj* **1.** showing little or no feeling **2.** involving reason or intellect rather than feelings —**un·e·mo·tion·al·ly** *adv*

un·em·ploy·a·ble /ùnnim plóyəb'l/ *adj* lacking the skills, education, or ability to get a job

un·em·ployed /ùnnim plóyd/ *adj* **1. JOBLESS** not in paid employment **2. NOT IN USE** not being used ■ *npl* **JOBLESS PEOPLE** people who are out of work

un·em·ploy·ment /ùnnim plóymənt/ *n* **1.** the condition of having no job **2.** the number of people who are unemployed in an area, often given as a percentage of the total labor force **3.** SOC WELFARE same as **unemployment compensation**

un·em·ploy·ment com·pen·sa·tion, **un·em·ploy·ment** *n* regular payments made to somebody who is out of work from a government insurance fund contributed to by employers

un·end·ing /un énding/ *adj* continuing or seeming to continue forever, especially when an end would be welcome

un-En·glish /un íng glish/ *adj* **1.** not characteristic of the English people or their culture **2.** not considered standard English usage

un·en·tan·gle /ùn in táng g'l, -en-/ (**-gled, -gling, -gles**) *vt* **1. FREE SOMETHING FROM TANGLES** to free things that are knotted or tied **2. STRAIGHTEN OUT SOMETHING COMPLEX** to clarify or resolve something that is intricate or puzzling **3. FREE SOMEBODY FROM BAD SITUATION** to release another person, or yourself from a confused, complicated, or undesired situation

un·en·vi·a·ble /un énvee əb'l/ *adj* not pleasant, easy, or likely to be wished for ○ *had the unenviable task of breaking the bad news* —**un·en·vi·a·bly** *adv*

un·e·qual /un éekwəl/ *adj* **1. NOT MEASURABLY SAME** not measurably the same, e.g., in size or number **2. NOT OF SAME SOCIAL POSITION** not of the same status, rank, or position in society **3. UNEVENLY MATCHED** not evenly matched in competition **4. VARIABLE** uneven or variable in quality or character **5. ASYMMETRIC** not evenly balanced **6. UNABLE TO DO SOMETHING** having less than the required ability to do something ○ *unequal to the task* ■ *n* **SOMEBODY NOT EQUAL TO ANOTHER** somebody or something not equal to another —**un·e·qual·ly** *adv*

un·e·qualed /un éekwəld/, **un·e·qualled** *adj* having no equal or parallel among people or things of the same kind

un·e·quiv·o·cal /ùnni kwívvək'l/ *adj* allowing for no doubt or misinterpretation —**un·e·quiv·o·cal·ly** *adv*

un·err·ing /un érring/ *adj* unfailingly accurate or correct —**un·err·ing·ly** *adv*

U·NES·CO /yoo néskō/, **U·nes·co** *n* a United Nations agency that promotes international collaboration on culture, education, and science. Full form **United Nations Educational, Scientific, and Cultural Organization**

un·es·sen·tial /ùnni sénshəl/ *adj* not absolutely needed ■ *n* something that is not absolutely needed

un·eth·i·cal /un éthik'l/ *adj* not conforming to agreed standards of moral conduct, especially within a particular profession ○ *unethical business practices* —**un·eth·i·cal·i·ty** /un èthi kállətee/ *n* —**un·eth·i·cal·ly** *adv* —**un·eth·i·cal·ness** *n*

un·e·ven /un éevən/ *adj* **1. NOT LEVEL** having a surface that is not level or smooth **2. VARYING** varying and inconsistent, e.g., in quality, thoroughness, or duration **3. NOT PARALLEL** not straight or parallel **4. NOT FAIRLY MATCHED** not fairly matched in competition **5. ODD** not divisible by two **6. NOT SAME SIZE** unequal in number or measurement to another —**un·e·ven·ly** *adv* —**un·e·ven·ness** *n*

un·e·vent·ful /ùnni véntfəl/ *adj* not marked by any unusual or important occurrence —**un·e·vent·ful·ly** *adv* —**un·e·vent·ful·ness** *n*

un·ex·am·pled /ùnnig zámp'ld/ *adj* having no similar case or occurrence

un·ex·cep·tion·a·ble /ùnnik sépshənəb'l/ *adj* good enough to provide no reason for criticism or objection —**un·ex·cep·tion·a·bil·i·ty** /ùnnik sepshənə bíllətee/ *n* —**un·ex·cep·tion·a·ble·ness** *n* —**un·ex·cep·tion·a·bly** *adv*

USAGE See *unexceptional.*

un·ex·cep·tion·al /ùnnik sépshən'l/ *adj* **1.** not special or unusual **2.** allowing no exception —**un·ex·cep·tion·al·ly** *adv*

USAGE unexceptional or **unexceptionable**? The distinction in meaning corresponds to that between the positive forms *exceptional* and *exceptionable.* Something is described as ***unexceptional*** when it is not special or unusual, even perhaps a little dull: *Her performance got a good review, but I thought it was unexceptional.* ***Unexceptionable*** comes close to this in meaning, but its strict meaning is "good enough to provide no reason for criticism or objection": *Their behavior has been unexceptionable so far.*

un·ex·cit·ed /ùnnik sī́təd/ *adj* **1.** not emotionally aroused **2.** describes particles that remain at the lowest energy level —**un·ex·cit·ed·ly** *adv*

un·ex·pect·ed /ùnnik spéktəd/ *adj* coming as a surprise —**un·ex·pect·ed·ly** *adv* —**un·ex·pect·ed·ness** *n*

un·ex·pe·ri·enced /ùnnik spéeree ənst/ *adj* **1.** not known or undergone before **2.** lacking experience

un·ex·plod·ed /ùn ik splṓdəd/ *adj* having failed to explode but still capable of exploding ○ *an unexploded bomb*

un·ex·pressed /ùnnik sprést/ *adj* **1.** not spoken or made known **2.** describes a gene that does not have an observable effect on the organism that carries it

un·ex·pur·gat·ed /un ékspər gàytəd/ *adj* not edited to remove words or passages considered offensive or unsuitable

un·fail·ing /un fáyling/ *adj* **1. LIMITLESS** never used up or exhausted **2. ALWAYS RELIABLE** able to be relied on at all times ○ *unfailing good humor* **3. ALWAYS ACCURATE** totally accurate and without fault ○ *an unfailing eye for symmetry and beauty* —**un·fail·ing·ly** *adv* —**un·fail·ing·ness** *n*

un·fair /un fér/ *adj* **1.** not equal or just **2.** not ethical in business dealings —**un·fair·ly** *adv* —**un·fair·ness** *n*

un·faith·ful /un fáythfəl/ *adj* **1. ADULTEROUS** engaging in sexual relations with somebody other than a spouse or partner **2. UNTRUE TO COMMITMENTS** untrue to commitments, duties, beliefs, or ideals **3. NOT LIKE ORIGINAL** not true to the original —**un·faith·ful·ly** *adv* —**un·faith·ful·ness** *n*

un·fal·ter·ing /un fáwltəring/ *adj* strong, steady, and not becoming weaker —**un·fal·ter·ing·ly** *adv*

un·fa·mil·iar /ùnfə míllyər/ *adj* **1.** not previously known or recognized **2.** having no previous knowledge or experience ○ *unfamiliar with the software* —**un·fa·mil·i·ar·i·ty** /ùnfə milee árrətee/ *n* —**un·fa·mil·iar·ly** *adv*

un·fash·ion·a·ble /un fásh'nəb'l/ *adj* **1.** not in the current style **2.** not socially approved of ○ *an unfashionable suburb* —**un·fash·ion·a·ble·ness** *n* —**un·fash·ion·a·bly** *adv*

un·fas·ten /un fáss'n/ (**-tened, -ten·ing, -tens**) *vti* to undo or open something by moving or loosening things that are holding it together, e.g., the buttons of a garment, or be undone or opened in this way

un·fath·om·a·ble /un fáthəməb'l/ *adj* **1.** too deep to be measured ○ *unfathomable ocean depths* **2.** impossible to understand because of being very mysterious or complicated —**un·fath·om·a·bil·i·ty** /un fàthəmə bíllətee/ *n* —**un·fath·om·a·ble·ness** *n* —**un·fath·om·a·bly** *adv*

un·fa·vor·a·ble /un fáyvərəb'l/ *adj* **1.** expressing disapproval or opposition **2.** unlikely to be beneficial —**un·fa·vor·a·ble·ness** *n* —**un·fa·vor·a·bly** *adv*

un·fea·si·ble /un féezəb'l/ *adj* impractical as a goal, or not easily carried out —**un·fea·si·bil·i·ty** /un fèezə bíllətee/ *n* —**un·fea·si·bly** *adv*

un·feel·ing /un féeling/ *adj* **1.** having or expressing no sympathy for somebody else's feelings **2.** unable to experience physical sensation —**un·feel·ing·ly** *adv* —**un·feel·ing·ness** *n*

un·fet·ter /un féttər/ (**-tered, -ter·ing, -ters**) *vt* **1.** to release somebody or something from fetters **2.** to allow somebody to act without restraint

un·fet·tered /un féttərd/ *adj* not subject to limits or restrictions

un·fin·ished /un fínnisht/ *adj* **1. NOT COMPLETED** not completed satisfactorily **2. NOT FINALLY TREATED** not finally processed or treated with dye, varnish, paint, or bleach **3.** TEXTILES **WITH SLIGHT NAP** woven with a slight nap

un·fit /un fít/ *adj* **1. UNSUITABLE** unsuitable for a particular purpose **2. UNQUALIFIED** lacking the necessary skills or qualifications to perform a particular task adequately **3. NOT HEALTHY** not physically or mentally healthy —**un·fit·ly** *adv* —**un·fit·ness** *n*

un·fit·ted /un fíttəd/ *adj* **1.** not suited or adapted for a particular purpose **2.** describes furniture that is not fitted

un·fit·ting /un fítting/ *adj* not suitable or appropriate for somebody or something —**un·fit·ting·ly** *adv*

un·fix /un fíks/ (**-fixed, -fix·ing, -fix·es**) *vt* **1.** to loosen or detach something **2.** to upset the certainty or stability of something

un·flag·ging /un flágging/ *adj* remaining strong and unchanging —**un·flag·ging·ly** *adv*

un·flap·pa·ble /un fláppəb'l/ *adj* able to maintain composure under all circumstances —**un·flap·pa·bil·i·ty** /un flàppə bíllətee/ *n* —**un·flap·pa·bly** *adv*

un·flat·ter·ing /un fláttəring/ *adj* showing or depicting somebody or something in an uncomplimentary or unfavorable way

un·fledged /un fléjd/ *adj* **1.** describes a young bird that has not yet developed the feathers required for flight **2.** young and inexperienced

un·flinch·ing /un flínching/ *adj* strong and unhesitating —**un·flinch·ing·ly** *adv*

un·fo·cused /un fṓkəst/, **un·fo·cussed** *adj* **1.** not adjusted for a clear image **2.** lacking a clear purpose or objective

un·fold /un fṓld/ (**-fold·ed, -fold·ing, -folds**) *v* **1.** *vti* **OPEN OUT** to open something and spread it out, or open and spread out **2.** *vti* MAKE SOMETHING UNDERSTOOD to make something clear and understood by gradual exposure, or become clear and understood in this way **3.** *vi* DEVELOP to develop or expand over time ○ *His talent unfolded as he grew older.*

un·forced /un fáwrst/ *adj* **1.** spontaneous and natural ○ *unforced laughter* **2.** not resulting from compulsion, irresistible pressure, or an opponent's superior skill ○ *made an unforced error and lost the point*

un·fore·see·a·ble /ùn fawr seé əb'l/ *adj* not able to be predicted or planned for in advance —**un·fore·see·a·bly** *adv*

un·fore·seen /ùnfər seén, -fawr-/ *adj* not expected or anticipated

un·for·get·ta·ble /ùnfər géttəb'l/ *adj* remarkable in a way that cannot be forgotten —**un·for·get·ta·bly** *adv*

un·for·giv·a·ble /ùnfər gívvəb'l/ *adj* so bad as to be impossible to forgive —**un·for·giv·a·bly** *adv*

un·for·giv·ing /ùnfər gívving/ *adj* **1.** unwilling or unable to forgive **2.** providing little or no margin for mistakes or weakness ○ *The sea is an unforgiving environment.* —**un·for·giv·ing·ly** *adv*

un·for·mat·ted /un fáwr màttəd/ *adj* describes computer disks that are not formatted into the sectors that are required in order to allow data to be saved and stored

un·formed /un fáwrmd/ *adj* **1.** WITH NO REAL SHAPE lacking a coherent shape or structure ○ *the unformed restless desire in her mind* **2.** UNDEVELOPED not yet fully developed **3.** NOT CREATED not yet created

un·forth·com·ing /ùn fawrth kúmming/ *adj* **1.** UNINFORMATIVE reluctant to talk or to reveal information **2.** UNAVAILABLE not ready when required or requested **3.** FAILING TO HAPPEN not happening despite being expected

un·for·tu·nate /un fáwrchənət/ *adj* **1.** UNLUCKY never experiencing good luck **2.** INVOLVING BAD LUCK accompanied by or bringing bad luck **3.** INAPPROPRIATE not appropriate to a given situation ○ *The unfortunate comment was an example of his lack of social polish.* ■ *n* POOR PERSON somebody who has bad luck or inadequate resources —**un·for·tu·nate·ness** *n*

un·for·tu·nate·ly /un fáwrchənətlee/ *adv* **1.** used when somebody wishes something were not true ○ *I didn't get there before he left, unfortunately.* **2.** in a way that is inappropriate to a given situation ○ *an unfortunately worded critique*

un·found·ed /un fówndəd/ *adj* **1.** not supported by evidence or facts ○ *unfounded allegations* **2.** not yet established

un·freeze /un freéz/ (**-froze** /-frṓz/, **-froz·en** /-frṓz'n/, **-freez·ing**, **-freez·es**) *vt* to remove controls or restrictions on something such as wages, hiring, prices, or rents

un·fre·quent·ed /un freékwəntəd, ùn free kwéntəd/ *adj* not often visited, especially by tourists or travelers

un·friend·ly /un fréndlee/ *adj* **1.** behaving in an obviously cold or hostile way **2.** not beneficial or advantageous ○ *was faced with an array of unfriendly choices* —**un·friend·li·ness** *n*

un·frock /un frók/ (**-frocked, -frock·ing, -frocks**) *vt* **1.** RELIG REMOVE ORDAINED PERSON FROM OFFICE to remove an ordained person from office and duties as a punishment for doing something considered immoral or heretical **2.** TAKE AWAY RIGHT FROM SOMEBODY to take away from somebody the right to practice a profession **3.** REMOVE SOMEBODY FROM POSITION to remove somebody from an honorary or privileged position

un·froze past tense of **unfreeze**

un·froz·en past participle of **unfreeze**

un·fruit·ful /un fróotfəl/ *adj* **1.** not having a successful outcome **2.** not bearing fruit or offspring (*literary*) —**un·fruit·ful·ly** *adv* —**un·fruit·ful·ness** *n*

un·ful·filled /ùn fòol fíld/ *adj* **1.** NOT REALIZED not developed or made use of adequately or to the fullest possible extent **2.** LAW NOT FULLY CARRIED OUT not carried out fully or in accordance with the original requirements or stipulations **3.** NOT SATISFIED not satisfied, especially by not having fully realized ambitions or potential —**un·ful·fill·ment** *n*

un·fun·ny /un fúnnee/ *adj* not amusing, especially when intended to be so —**un·fun·ni·ly** *adv* —**un·fun·ni·ness** *n*

un·furl /un fúrl/ (**-furled, -furl·ing, -furls**) *vti* to unroll or spread out something, or be unrolled or spread out

un·fur·nished /un fúrnisht/ *adj* not furnished, or available to be rented without furniture ○ *an unfurnished apartment*

un·gain·ly /un gáynlee/ *adj* **1.** LACKING GRACE lacking grace in moving **2.** AWKWARD awkward to handle **3.** GANGLY having an awkward long-limbed appearance [Early 17C. < obsolete *gain* "straight, convenient" < Old Norse *gegn*]

Un·ga·va /ŏong gaávə, -gáyvə/ region in northeastern Canada, situated east of Hudson Bay and North of the Eastmain River. Area: 352,100 sq. mi./912,000 sq. km.

Un·ga·va Bay bay in northeastern Quebec, Canada, opening into Hudson Strait

un·glued /un glóod/ *adj* **1.** having become separated or detached **2.** emotionally upset and lacking composure (*informal*)

un·god·ly /un góddlee/ *adj* **1.** NOT REVERING GOD not devoted to or obeying God **2.** WICKED behaving in a way thought to violate moral strictures **3.** UNREASONABLE not meeting standards for reasonableness (*informal*) ○ *woke me up at some ungodly hour* —**un·god·li·ness** *n*

un·gov·ern·a·ble /un gúvvərnəb'l/ *adj* incapable of being governed or restrained —**un·gov·ern·a·bly** *adv*

un·gra·cious /un gráyshəss/ *adj* **1.** inconsistent with good manners **2.** unpleasant or difficult —**un·gra·cious·ly** *adv* —**un·gra·cious·ness** *n*

un·gram·mat·i·cal /ùn grə máttik'l/ *adj* not conforming to the accepted rules of grammar —**un·gram·mat·i·cal·ly** *adv*

un·grasp·able /un graáspəb'l/ *adj* **1.** impossible to catch hold of and retain a grip on ○ *icy deck ropes that were ungraspable* **2.** so complex, difficult, or high-level as to be impossible to understand, reach, or explain ○ *an ungraspable mystery*

un·grate·ful /un gráytfəl/ *adj* **1.** not thankful or appreciative **2.** unpleasant or unrewarding —**un·grate·ful·ly** *adv* —**un·grate·ful·ness** *n*

un·grudg·ing /un grújjing/ *adj* feeling or showing no reluctance or reservations ○ *offered ungrudging support* —**un·grudg·ing·ly** *adv*

un·gual /úng gwəl/ *adj* **1.** relating to or affecting the fingernails or toenails **2.** relating to, occurring in, or supporting a nail, claw, or hoof [Mid-19C. < Latin *unguis* "nail, claw"]

un·guard·ed /un gaárdəd/ *adj* **1.** UNPROTECTED lacking a guard or protection **2.** NATURAL free from pretense or guile **3.** NOT WARY showing a lack of thought or care —**un·guard·ed·ly** *adv* —**un·guard·ed·ness** *n*

un·guent /úng gwənt/ *n* a healing or soothing ointment [15C. < Latin *unguentum* < *unguere* "smear, anoint"]

un·guis /úng gwiss/ (*plural* **-gues** /-gweez/) *n* **1.** a nail, claw, hook, or hoof on a digit or foot of an animal **2.** the claw-shaped base of some petals [Early 18C. < Latin, "nail, claw"]

un·gu·late /úng gyələt, -làyt/ *adj* **1.** WITH HOOVES having hooves **2.** SHAPED LIKE HOOF resembling a hoof in shape or function ■ *n* HOOFED MAMMAL a mammal with hooves, e.g., the horse, rhinoceros, pig, giraffe, deer, or camel [Early 19C. < late Latin *ungulatus* < Latin *ungula* "hoof, claw" < *unguis* "nail, claw"]

un·gu·li·grade /úng gyəli gràyd/ *adj* describes a mammal that walks on hooves [Mid-19C. < Latin *ungula* "hoof" (see UNGULATE)]

un·hal·lowed /un hállōd/ *adj* **1.** NOT CONSECRATED not consecrated or blessed **2.** IRREVERENT lacking religious reverence **3.** NOT ACCEPTABLE TO RELIGION not conforming to the standards of a religion

un·hand /un hánd/ (**-hand·ed, -hand·ing, -hands**) *vt* to let somebody go by releasing a grasp (*archaic or humorous*)

un·hand·y /un hándee/ (**-i·er, -i·est**) *adj* **1.** NOT SKILLED WITH HANDS not skilled at working with the hands or with tools **2.** INCONVENIENTLY LOCATED situated in an inconvenient location **3.** DIFFICULT TO USE not easy to use or handle

un·hap·pi·ly /un háppilee/ *adv* **1.** in a way that expresses or is characterized by unhappiness **2.** used to express a wish that something were not true ○ *Unhappily, she was never able to go there.*

un·hap·py /un háppee/ (**-pi·er, -pi·est**) *adj* **1.** SAD not cheerful or joyful **2.** DISPLEASED not pleased or satisfied with somebody or something **3.** UNFORTUNATE not bringing good luck **4.** INAPPROPRIATE done without proper thought or inappropriate in a specific context ○ *an unhappy choice of words* —**un·hap·pi·ness** *n*

un·harmed /un haármd/ *adj* not hurt or damaged in any way

un·har·ness /un haárnəss/ (**-nessed, -ness·ing, -ness·es**) *vt* **1.** RIDING REMOVE HARNESS FROM HORSE to remove the harness from a horse **2.** RELEASE ENERGY OR PASSIONS to release energy or passions from restraints **3.** ARMS TAKE ARMOR OFF SOMEBODY to remove the armor from somebody (*archaic*)

UNHCR *abbr* United Nations High Commission for Refugees

un·health·y /un hélthee/ (**-i·er, -i·est**) *adj* **1.** SICK affected by ill health **2.** BAD FOR HEALTH not good for the health **3.** SYMPTOMATIC OF ILL HEALTH showing the symptoms of or resulting from ill health **4.** HARMFUL TO CHARACTER harmful to the character of somebody or something **5.** CORRUPT morally corrupt or unwholesome ○ *an unhealthy interest in lurid crimes* **6.** RISKY involving unnecessary risks (*informal*) —**un·health·i·ly** *adv* —**un·health·i·ness** *n*

un·heard /un húrd/ *adj* **1.** not perceived by the ear **2.** not listened to or given a hearing ○ *unheard testimony*

un·heard-of *adj* **1.** UNKNOWN not previously known **2.** UNPRECEDENTED never having happened before **3.** OFFENSIVE extremely offensive or rude

un·heat·ed /un heétəd/ *adj* not supplied or equipped with any form of heating

un·heed·ed /un heédəd/ *adj* not listened to or given serious attention ○ *My warnings went unheeded.*

un·help·ful /un hélpfəl/ *adj* not providing or willing to provide help —**un·help·ful·ly** *adv* —**un·help·ful·ness** *n*

un·hes·i·tat·ing /un hézzi tàyting/ *adj* without pause, indecision, or change —**un·hes·i·tat·ing·ly** *adv*

un·hin·dered /un híndərd/ *adj* not obstructed by any obstacles or difficulties ○ *allowed them to carry on with the work unhindered*

un·hinge /un hínj/ (**-hinged, -hing·ing, -hing·es**) *vt* **1.** REMOVE SOMETHING FROM HINGES to remove something from its hinges **2.** REMOVE HINGES FROM SOMETHING to remove the hinges of something **3.** DISLOCATE SOMETHING to dislodge or detach something **4.** DISRUPT SOMETHING to throw something into confusion **5.** MAKE SOMEBODY PSYCHOLOGICALLY UNSTABLE to cause somebody to become emotionally or mentally unstable

un·hitch /un hích/ (**-hitched, -hitch·ing, -hitch·es**) *vt* **1.** to unfasten something that is connected to something else **2.** to divorce a spouse or each other (*informal; usually passive*)

un·ho·ly /un hṓlee/ (**-li·er, -li·est**) *adj* **1.** NOT BLESSED not blessed or consecrated by a church ritual **2.** DEFYING RELIGIOUS PRECEPTS deliberately defiant of specific religious precepts **3.** EXTREME extremely bad or awful (*used for emphasis*) ○ *This place is an unholy mess!* —**un·ho·li·ness** *n*

un·hook /un hóok/ (**-hooked, -hook·ing, -hooks**) *v* **1.** *vt* REMOVE SOMETHING FROM HOOK to remove something from a hook **2.** *vt* UNDO HOOKS OF SOMETHING to unfasten the hooks of something **3.** *vti US* DETACH to separate somebody from a contract (*informal*)

un·hoped-for /un hṓpt-/ *adj* not expected or anticipated ○ *an unhoped-for victory*

un·horse /un háwrss/ (**-horsed, -hors·ing, -hors·es**) *vt* **1.** to knock or throw somebody from a horse **2.** to bring somebody down from a high office or position

un·hur·ried /un húr eed, -húreed/ *adj* done in a relaxed and deliberate way —**un·hur·ried·ly** *adv*

un·hurt /un húrt/ *adj* having met with no injury or harm ○ *The driver escaped unhurt from the accident.*

un·hy·gi·en·ic /ùn hī jee énnik, -jénnik, -jeénik/ *adj* not clean, sanitary, or healthy

uni- *prefix* one, single ○ *unicellular* [< Latin < *unus* "one." < Indo-European]

U·ni·at /yóonee àt, -ət/, **U·ni·ate** *n* a member of one of the Eastern Christian Churches that recognize papal supremacy, but keep their own liturgy, language, and canon law ■ *adj* relating to the Uniat Churches [Mid-19C. < Russian *uniyat*, Polish *uniat* < *unia* "union" (of the Roman Catholic and Greek churches) < Latin *union-* (see UNION)]

u·ni·ax·i·al /yo͞onee áksee əl/ *adj* **1.** describes a crystal or mineral that has one direction, parallel to the principal axis, along which single refraction occurs **2.** describes a plant with an unbranched main stem —**u·ni·ax·i·al·ly** *adv*

u·ni·cam·er·al /yo͞oni kámmərəl/ *adj* having only one legislative chamber [Mid-19C. < UNI- + Latin *camera* "chamber" (see CAMERA)] —**u·ni·cam·er·al·ism** *n* —**u·ni·cam·er·al·ist** *n* —**u·ni·cam·er·al·ly** *adv*

u·ni·cast /yo͞oni kàst/ *n* a transmission from a single computing terminal to one other terminal

U·NI·CEF /yo͞oni sèf/, **U·ni·cef** *n* a United Nations agency that works for the protection and survival of children around the world. Full form **United Nations Children's Fund**

u·ni·cel·lu·lar /yo͞oni séllyələr/ *adj* consisting of a single cell —**un·i·cel·lu·lar·i·ty** /-sèllyə lárrətee/ *n*

u·ni·col·or /yo͞oni kùllər/ *adj* composed of or containing only one color

unicorn

u·ni·corn /yo͞oni kàwrn/ *n* **1.** a mythical animal usually depicted as a white horse with a single straight spiraled horn growing from its forehead **2.** in the Bible, a horned animal now believed to be a rhinoceros or aurochs [13C. Via French < Latin *unicornis* "one-horned" < *cornu* "horn"]

u·ni·cos·tate /yo͞oni kó stàyt/ *adj* describes a leaf with one main rib

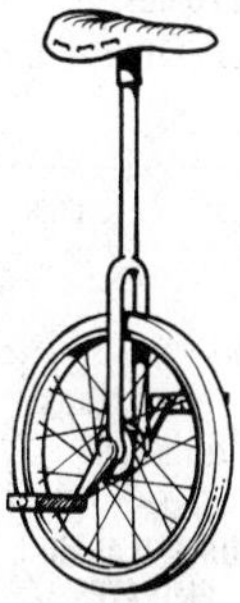

unicycle

u·ni·cy·cle /yo͞oni sìk'l/ *n* a pedal-powered vehicle that has a single wheel with a seat mounted on a frame above it [Mid-19C. After BICYCLE] —**u·ni·cy·clist** *n*

un·i·den·ti·fied /ùn ī déntə fìd/ *adj* **1.** unable to be recognized or given a name **2.** unwilling to be associated with or held responsible for something

u·ni·di·rec·tion·al /yo͞oni di rékshən'l, -dī-/ *adj* thinking, moving, or operating in only one direction

UNIDO /yo͞oni dō/, **Unido** *abbr* United Nations Industrial Development Organization

u·ni·fac·to·ri·al /yo͞onə fak táwree əl/ *adj* describes an inherited characteristic dependent on a single gene

u·ni·fi·ca·tion /yo͞onəfi káysh'n/ *n* **1.** the act or process of uniting or joining together **2.** a result of uniting or joining together

U·ni·fi·ca·tion Church *n* a religious denomination founded in 1954 by the South Korean industrialist Sun Myung Moon

u·ni·fied /yo͞onə fìd/ *adj* brought together to form a single unit or entity

u·ni·fied field the·o·ry *n* a single theory capable of defining the nature of the interrelationships among nuclear, electromagnetic, and gravitational forces

u·ni·fo·li·ate /yo͞oni fólee ət/ *adj* having a single leaf or leaf-shaped part

u·ni·form /yo͞onə fàwrm/ *n* **1.** DISTINCTIVE SET OF CLOTHES a distinctive set of clothes worn to identify somebody's occupation, affiliation, or status **2.** COMPLETE OUTFIT a single outfit of identifying clothes **3.** IDENTIFYING LOOK a distinctive style or other feature that identifies somebody as a member of a group ■ *adj* **1.** UNCHANGING always the same in quality, degree, character, or manner **2.** CONSISTENT conforming to one standard or rule **3.** RESEMBLING ANOTHER OR OTHERS being the same as another or others **4.** UNVARYING IN DESIGN unvarying in color, texture, or design ■ *vt* (**-formed, -form·ing, -forms**) **1.** PROVIDE SOMEBODY WITH UNIFORMS to provide a person or group with a uniform or uniforms **2.** MAKE SOMETHING UNVARYING OR SAME to make something homogeneous, unvarying, or consistent [Mid-16C. Directly or via French < Latin *uniformis* "having one form" < *forma* "shape"] —**u·ni·formed** *adj* —**u·ni·for·mi·ty** /yo͞onə fáwrmətee/ *n* —**u·ni·form·ly** *adv*

U·ni·form *n* a code word for the letter "U," used in international radio communications

U·ni·form Com·mer·cial Code *n* a set of uniform laws governing commercial transactions in the US

u·ni·for·mi·tar·i·an·ism /yo͞onə fawrmi térree ə nìzzəm/ *n* the theory that the same geologic processes occurred in the past as occur today, and that geologic formations and structures can be interpreted by observing present-day actions —**u·ni·for·mi·tar·i·an** *adj, n*

U·ni·form Re·source Lo·ca·tor *n* ONLINE full form of **URL**

u·ni·fy /yo͞onə fì/ (**-fied, -fy·ing, -fies**) *vt* to bring people or things together to form a single unit or entity [Early 16C. Via French *unifier* < Latin *unificare* "make one"] —**u·ni·fi·a·ble** *adj* —**u·ni·fi·er** *n* —**u·ni·fy·ing** *adj*

u·ni·lat·er·al /yo͞onə láttərəl/ *adj* **1.** DECIDED BY ONE PARTY decided or acted on by only one involved party or nation irrespective of what the others do **2.** ACCOUNTING FOR ONE SIDE ONLY taking into account only one side of a subject **3.** BINDING ONLY ONE PARTY binding or at the insistence of only one party to a contract, obligation, or agreement **4.** MED AFFECTING ONLY ONE SIDE affecting or involving only one side of the body, only one of a pair of organs, or only one side of an organ **5.** BOT HAVING PARTS ON ONLY ONE SIDE having parts that are arranged on only one side of a stem or other axis **6.** WITH ONE SIDE having only one side **7.** SOCIOL THROUGH ONE PARENT ONLY tracing lineage through one parent only ■ *n* WAR CORRESPONDENT WORKING ALONE a war correspondent who chooses to work alone rather than being attached officially to a military unit —**u·ni·lat·er·al·ly** *adv*

u·ni·lat·er·al·ism /yo͞onə láttərə lìzzəm/ *n* a foreign policy that takes little or no regard of the views of other nations, including allies, or the implementation of such a policy —**u·ni·lat·er·al·ist** *n*

u·ni·lin·e·al /yo͞oni línnee əl/ *adj* SOCIOL same as **unilateral** *adj* (sense 7)

u·ni·lin·e·ar /yo͞oni línnee ər/ *adj* developing or evolving progressively through defined stages from primitive to advanced and excluding any variation on this course

u·ni·lin·gual /yo͞oni líng gwəl/ *adj* using or knowing only one language

u·ni·lit·er·al /yo͞oni líttərəl/ *adj* having only a single letter ○ *The pronoun "I" is uniliteral.*

u·ni·loc·u·lar /yo͞onə lókyələr/ *adj* having a single loculus, cell, or cavity

un·i·mag·i·na·ble /ùnni májjənəb'l/ *adj* impossible to imagine —**un·i·mag·i·na·bly** *adv*

un·i·mag·i·na·tive /ùnni májjənətiv/ *adj* **1.** unable to think of new or interesting ideas, plans, or situations **2.** boring and ordinary, and showing no evidence of any new or interesting ideas —**un·i·mag·i·na·tive·ly** *adv* —**un·i·mag·i·na·tive·ness** *n*

U·ni·mak Is·land /yo͞onə mak-/ the largest of the Aleutian Islands, lying between the Bering Sea and the Pacific Ocean, in southwestern Alaska. It is about 70 mi./110 km long and 20 mi./32 km wide.

un·im·paired /ùnnim pérd/ *adj* not adversely affected by anything unpleasant, dangerous, or different that happens

un·im·peach·a·ble /ùnnim pe͞echəb'l/ *adj* **1.** impossible to discredit or challenge **2.** so good as to be beyond reproach —**un·im·peach·a·bly** *adv*

un·im·ped·ed /ùnnim pe͞edəd/ *adj* not obstructed, blocked, or held back by anything —**un·im·ped·ed·ly** *adv*

un·im·por·tant /ùnnim páwrt'nt/ *adj* of little or no significance —**un·im·por·tance** *n* —**un·im·por·tant·ly** *adv*

un·im·pressed /ùnnim prést/ *adj* not favorably impressed by somebody or something

un·im·proved /ùnnim pro͞ovd/ *adj* **1.** NOT MADE BETTER not made better or not developed **2.** WITHOUT IMPROVEMENTS describes land that is not modified in a way that would increase value, e.g., by cultivation or the addition of buildings, landscaping, or services ○ *an unimproved lot* **3.** NOT GETTING HEALTHIER not showing improvement in health ○ *Her condition remains unimproved.*

un·in·cor·po·rat·ed /ùnnin káwrpə ràytəd/ *adj* **1.** not organized into a corporation or municipality ○ *an unincorporated township* **2.** not included as a part of something else

un·in·form·a·tive /ùnnin fáwrmətiv/ *adj* not providing adequate information —**un·in·form·a·tive·ly** *adv*

un·in·formed /ùnnin fáwrmd/ *adj* lacking facts or knowledge about something

un·in·hab·it·a·ble /ùnnin hábbitəb'l/ *adj* unfit as a habitation, especially for human beings —**un·in·hab·it·a·bil·i·ty** /-habitə bíllətee/ *n*

un·in·hab·it·ed /ùnnin hábbitəd/ *adj* lacking all human habitation

un·in·hib·it·ed /ùnnin híbbitəd/ *adj* **1.** expressing feelings or views without restraint **2.** not subject to social or other constraints —**un·in·hib·it·ed·ly** *adv* —**un·in·hib·it·ed·ness** *n*

un·in·i·ti·ate /ùnni níshee ət/ *adj* having no experience

un·in·i·ti·at·ed /ùnni níshee àytəd/ *adj* having no experience or knowledge of something ■ *npl* people who have no experience or knowledge of something

un·in·jured /un ínjərd/ *adj* having sustained no injuries

un·in·spired /ùnnin spírd/ *adj* lacking originality or distinction

un·in·spir·ing /ùnnin spíring/ *adj* not arousing interest, enthusiasm, or excitement —**un·in·spir·ing·ly** *adv*

un·in·stall /ùnnin stáwl/ (**-stalled, -stall·ing, -stalls**) *vt* to remove a piece of software from a computer

un·in·struct·ed /ùnnin strúktəd/ *adj* **1.** not educated or informed **2.** natural or instinctive and not acquired by teaching or instruction

un·in·sur·a·ble /ùnnin sho͞orəb'l/ *adj* considered too great a risk to cover by insurance —**un·in·sur·a·bil·i·ty** /-shoorə bíllətee/ *n*

un·in·sured /ùnnin sho͞ord/ *adj* not covered by insurance ■ *n* somebody who is not covered by insurance

un·in·tel·li·gent /ùnnin téllijənt/ *adj* **1.** lacking or showing a lack of intelligence **2.** not having a mind or the ability to think and reason —**un·in·tel·li·gence** *n* —**un·in·tel·li·gent·ly** *adv*

un·in·tel·li·gi·ble /ùnnin téllijəb'l/ *adj* difficult or impossible to understand —**un·in·tel·li·gi·bil·i·ty** /-telijə bíllətee/ *n* —**un·in·tel·li·gi·bly** *adv*

un·in·ten·tion·al /ùnnin ténshən'l/ *adj* not on purpose or by plan —**un·in·ten·tion·al·ly** *adv*

un·in·ter·est·ed /un íntrəstəd/ *adj* having or showing no interest in somebody or something —**un·in·ter·est·ed·ly** *adv* —**un·in·ter·est·ed·ness** *n*

USAGE See ***disinterested.***

un·in·ter·est·ing /un íntrəsting/ *adj* having no interesting qualities —**un·in·ter·est·ing·ly** *adv* —**un·in·ter·est·ing·ness** *n*

SYNONYMS See ***boring***[1].

un·in·ter·rupt·ed /ùnnintə rúptəd/ *adj* **1.** having no interruptions or breaks **2.** free from obstructions ○ *an uninterrupted view* —**un·in·ter·rupt·ed·ly** *adv*

un·in·ter·rupt·i·ble pow·er sup·ply /ùnnintə rúptəb'l-/ *n* a piece of electrical equipment with internal batteries that provides a continuing source of power for a short period of time during a power failure to a computer or electrical appliance that is plugged into it

u·ni·nu·cle·ate /yòoni nóoklee ət/ *adj* describes a cell that has a single nucleus

un·in·vit·ed /ùnnin vítəd/ *adj* not invited or welcome

un·in·vit·ing /ùnnin víting/ *adj* not appealing or pleasant —**un·in·vit·ing·ly** *adv*

un·in·volved /ùnnin vólvd/ *adj* **1.** not connected with or participating in something **2.** not participating in a romantic or sexual relationship with somebody

un·ion /yóonyən/ *n* **1.** ACT OF JOINING TOGETHER the act of joining together people or things to form a whole **2.** RESULT OF JOINING TOGETHER a result of joining together people or things **3.** AGREEMENT agreement or unity of interests or opinions **4.** *also* **Un·ion** EDUC same as **student union 5.** MARRIAGE the state of being married **6.** SEX sexual intercourse **7.** POLITICAL ALLIANCE an alliance formed by the joining of people or organizations for a common political purpose **8.** CONSTR COUPLING a coupling for parts such as pipes and pipe fittings **9.** MATH SET OF MATHEMATICAL ELEMENTS the smallest set that consists of all the elements of any or all of two or more given sets and no other elements. An element is counted only once even if it occurs in more than one of the given sets. **10.** TEXTILES FABRIC OF DIFFERENT YARNS a fabric made of two or more different yarns, e.g., cotton and linen **11.** COMM same as **labor union** [15C. Directly or via French < Latin *union-* "oneness" < *unus* "one"]

Un·ion *n* **1.** NORTHERN SIDE IN CIVIL WAR the side of the northern states in the Civil War, or its armed forces **2.** UNITED STATES OF AMERICA the United States of America **3.** UNION OF BRITAIN AND NORTHERN IRELAND the union of Great Britain and Northern Ireland since 1920

un·ion card *n* a card signifying membership in a labor union

un·ion cat·a·log *n* a library catalog combining the materials in more than one library or in branches of the same library

Un·ion Cit·y /yóonyən-/ **1.** residential and industrial city in western California, on Alameda Creek, near San Francisco Bay. Population: 69,879 (2002 estimate). **2.** city in northeastern New Jersey, on the Hudson River, adjoining Jersey City and opposite New York City. Population: 66,902 (2002 estimate).

Un·ion flag *n* same as **Union Jack**

un·ion·ism /yóonyə nìzzəm/ *n* **1.** the principles or policies of labor unions **2.** the advocacy of forming and joining labor unions —**un·ion·ist** *n, adj*

Un·ion·ism *n* loyalty to the federal union during the Civil War —**Un·ion·ist** *n, adj*

un·ion·ize /yóonyə nìz/ (**-ized, -iz·ing, -iz·es**) *vti* to organize workers into a labor union, or be organized into a labor union —**un·ion·i·za·tion** /yóonyəni záysh'n/ *n* —**un·ion·iz·er** *n*

Un·ion Jack *n* the flag of the United Kingdom, which combines the flags of England, Scotland, and Ireland

un·ion la·bel *n US* a label identifying a product as having been made or produced by members of a labor union

Un·ion of U·trecht *n* a treaty signed at Utrecht in 1579 between the northern provinces of the Netherlands in which they agreed to act as allies in the event of war against Spain

un·ion scale *n* ECON same as **scale**[2] *n* (sense 3)

un·ion shop *n* a place of employment where a contract between the employer and a labor union requires employees to be or become members of the union within a specific time

un·ion suit *n US* a one-piece undergarment covering the entire body, arms, and legs, now considered old-fashioned (*dated*)

Un·ion Ter·ri·to·ry, un·ion ter·ri·to·ry *n* a territory in India ruled directly by the central government

u·nip·a·rous /yoo níppərəss/ *adj* **1.** having given birth to only one child **2.** producing a single offspring at each birth

u·ni·per·son·al /yòoni púrssən'l, -púrssnəl/ *adj* **1.** existing or manifested in the form of only one person **2.** describes a word existing as an inflected form in only one person, especially the third person singular

u·ni·pla·nar /yòoni pláynər/ *adj* in mathematics, occurring or located in a single plane

u·ni·pod /yóoni pòd/ *n* a one-legged stand, e.g., for a camera [Mid-20C. After TRIPOD]

u·ni·po·lar /yòoni pólər/ *adj* **1.** PHYS HAVING SINGLE POLE operating by means of, having, or produced by a single electric or magnetic pole **2.** BIOL BRANCHING OUT AT ONLY ONE END describes a neuron that branches out at only one end **3.** PHYS WITH ONE POLARITY describes a transistor that has carriers with only one polarity —**u·ni·po·lar·i·ty** /yòoni pō lárrətee/ *n*

u·ni·po·tent /yoo níppət'nt/ *adj* describes an embryonic cell that is capable of developing into only one type of cell or tissue

~~**uniqe**~~ incorrect spelling of **unique**

u·nique /yoo néek/ *adj* **1.** ONLY ONE being the only one of a kind **2.** ⚠ SPECIAL different from others in a way that makes somebody or something special and worthy of note ○ *a unique marketing opportunity* **3.** LIMITED TO SOMEBODY OR SOMETHING limited to a particular person or thing ○ *concerns that are unique to resettled refugees* [Early 17C. Via French < Latin *unicus* < *unus* "one"] —**u·nique·ly** *adv* —**u·nique·ness** *n*

USAGE The use of ***unique*** in its sense "worthy of note" is common in marketing and advertising (*Don't miss this unique offer*), as well as in conversation. Many dictionaries and usage guides argue that ***unique*** is an absolute concept and, as such, cannot be used with qualifying words such as *very* and *rather*, but in many cases this stricture seems a pedantic objection to what is a linguistic rather than a philosophical convention. It is, however, best avoided in formal writing.

---

u·nique sell·ing point, u·nique sell·ing prop·o·si·tion *n* MARKETING full form of **USP**

u·ni·sep·tate /yòoni sép tàyt/ *adj* having a single separating wall or membrane [Mid-19C. < UNI- + SEPTUM]

u·ni·ser·i·al /yòoni séeree əl/, **u·ni·se·ri·ate** /-àyt, -ət/ *adj* arranged in or consisting of a single row or series

u·ni·sex /yóoni sèks/ *adj* **1.** designed or suitable for people of either gender ○ *unisex fashions* **2.** not distinctly of either the male or the female gender

u·ni·sex·u·al /yòoni sékshoo əl/ *adj* **1.** related to or limited to one gender **2.** having either only male or only female reproductive organs —**u·ni·sex·u·al·i·ty** /-sèkshoo állətee/ *n* —**u·ni·sex·u·al·ly** *adv*

u·ni·son /yóoniss'n, -z'n/ *n* **1.** two or more notes sharing the same pitch **2.** the performance of two or more parts at the same pitch or an octave apart [Late 16C. Via French < late Latin *unisonus* "having the same sound" < *sonus* "sound"] ◇ **in unison 1.** in perfect agreement or harmony **2.** at the same time as somebody or something else

u·nit /yóonit/ *n* **1.** ONE PERSON, THING, OR GROUP a single person, thing, or group, usually regarded as a whole part of something larger ○ *the family unit* **2.** DISCRETE PART an individual or discrete part or element into which something can be divided, especially for analysis **3.** GROUP WITH PARTICULAR FUNCTION a group of people with a particular function who are part of a larger organization ○ *the cancer research unit* **4.** MIL GROUP OF MILITARY PERSONNEL a group of military personnel organized as a subdivision of a larger body **5.** COMPONENT OR ASSEMBLY OF COMPONENTS a component or assembly of components that performs a specific function ○ *a kitchen unit* **6.** *N Am* RESIDENCE each of a number of similar residences within a building or development **7.** EDUC PART OF ACADEMIC COURSE a part of an academic course that focuses on a specific theme **8.** EDUC MEASURE OF ACADEMIC INSTRUCTION a measure of academic instruction, usually based on the number of hours of classroom and laboratory work **9.** MEASURE MEASUREMENT a standard measurement whose multiples are used in determining quantity, e.g., an inch, degree, calorie, volt, or hour **10.** MED DRUG AMOUNT an amount of an enzyme, hormone, drug, or other agent that produces a given effect, often as specified by an internationally agreed standard **11.** MATH NATURAL NUMBER the lowest positive natural number **12.** MATH NUMBER LESS THAN TEN the first digit to the left of the decimal point in decimal notation, representing a whole number less than ten **13.** LOGIC, MATH SET WITH SINGLE NUMBER a set containing a single number [Late 16C. < Latin *unus* "one," after *digit*]

u·ni·tard /yóoni taàrd/ *n* a one-piece stretchable garment with or without sleeves that covers the body from the neck to the feet [Mid-20C. < UNI- + LEOTARD]

u·ni·tar·i·an /yòoni térree ən/ *n* somebody who supports unity or a unitary system —**u·ni·tar·i·an·ism** *n*

U·ni·tar·i·an /yòoni térree ən/ *n* **1.** MEMBER OF UNITARIAN UNIVERSALIST CHURCH a believer in or practitioner of unitarian universalism **2.** MONOTHEIST WHO IS NOT CHRISTIAN somebody who believes in one god but who is not a Christian **3.** NONBELIEVER IN TRINITY a Christian who does not believe in the doctrine of the Trinity —**U·ni·tar·i·an** *adj*

U·ni·tar·i·an U·ni·ver·sal·ism *n* a religious doctrine that rejects the Christian doctrine of the Trinity, the divinity of Jesus Christ, and formal dogma, but stresses reason and individual conscience in belief and practice —**U·ni·tar·i·an U·ni·ver·sal·ist** *adj, n*

u·ni·tar·y /yóoni tèrree/ *adj* **1.** RELATING TO UNIT relating to or consisting of a unit **2.** CHARACTERIZED BY UNITY based on or characterized by unity **3.** EXISTING AS UNIT undivided and existing as a unit **4.** POL OF CENTRALIZED GOVERNMENT relating to or based on a system of government in which authority is centralized —**u·ni·tar·i·ly** *adv*

u·nit cell *n* the smallest structural unit of a crystal that has all its symmetry and by repetition in three dimensions makes up its full lattice

u·nit cost *n* the cost of producing a single item

u·nite /yoo nít/ (**u·nit·ed, u·nit·ing, u·nites**) *v* **1.** *vti* BRING THINGS TOGETHER to bring things together to form or act as a unit, or be brought together in this way **2.** *vti* UNIFY PEOPLE to unify people by a common interest or concern, or become unified in this way **3.** *vti* MARRY OR GET MARRIED to join a couple in marriage, or be joined in marriage **4.** *vti* ADHERE to adhere, or cause things to adhere **5.** *vt* COMBINE QUALITIES to combine qualities or traits [15C. < Latin *unit-*, past participle of *unire* "make one" < *unus* "one"] —**u·nit·er** *n*

u·nit·ed /yoo nítəd/ *adj* **1.** COMBINED INTO ONE combined into or made one **2.** BY OR FROM UNION formed by or resulting from the union of two or more persons or things **3.** HARMONIOUS in agreement or harmony —**u·nit·ed·ly** *adv* —**u·nit·ed·ness** *n*

U·nit·ed *adj Can* belonging to the United Church of Canada

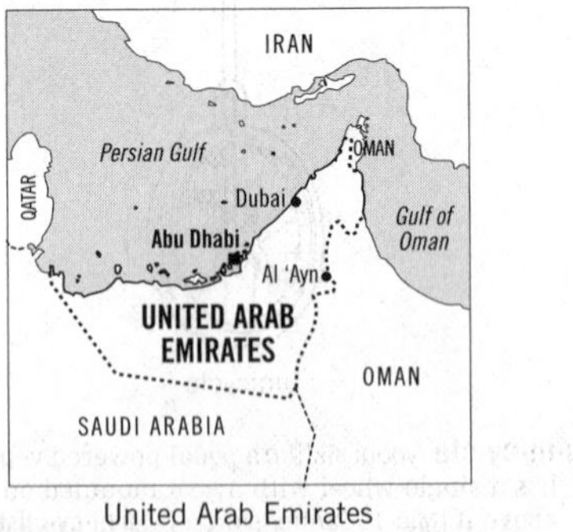

United Arab Emirates

U·nit·ed Ar·ab E·mir·ates /yoo nítəd-/ federation of seven independent states, Abu Dhabi, Ajmān, Dubai, al Fujayrah, Ra's al Khaymah, Sharjah, and Umm al-Qaiwain, located along the southern coast of the Persian Gulf. Language: Arabic. Currency: dirham. Capital: Abu Dhabi. Population: 2,484,818 (2003). Area: 32,300 sq. mi./83,600 sq. km. Former name **Trucial States**

U·ni·ted Ar·ab Re·pub·lic former independent union between Egypt and Syria, founded in 1958. It was disbanded when Syria left the union in 1961, although Egypt retained the name until 1971.

U·nit·ed Church of Can·a·da *n Can* a large Protestant Christian church formed in 1926 by the amalgamation of most Presbyterian, Methodist, and Congregationalist congregations in Canada

United Kingdom

entities to form one **3. SOMETHING WHOLE** something whole or complete formed by combining or joining separate things or entities **4. HARMONY** harmony of opinion, interest, or feeling **5. SINGLENESS AMONG INDIVIDUALS** singleness or constancy among individuals or groups **6.** ARTS **AESTHETIC ARRANGEMENT OF ARTISTIC ELEMENTS** the arranging of separate components in a literary or artistic work to create an overall aesthetic impression **7.** ARTS **AESTHETIC IMPRESSION** the overall aesthetic impression produced by the arrangement of components in an artistic or literary work **8.** THEATER **PRINCIPLE OF DRAMATIC STRUCTURE** one of the three principles of dramatic structure derived from Aristotle's *Poetics.* These state that the action of a play should be limited to one plot **(unity of action)**, one day **(unity of time)**, and one location **(unity of place)**. **9.** MATH **NUMBER ONE** a number by which a given element of a mathematical system can be multiplied with the result being equal to the value of the given element **10.** MATH same as **identity element** [13C. Via French *unite* < Latin *unitas* < *unus* "one"]

univ. *abbr* university

u·ni·va·lent /yo͞oni váylənt/ *adj* **1.** CHEM same as **monovalent** (sense 1) **2.** describes a chromosome that remains unpaired during the cell division **(meiosis)** that precedes sex cell formation —**u·ni·va·len·cy** *n*

u·ni·valve /yo͞oni vàlv/ *adj* **1. WITH SINGLE-PIECE SHELL** having a shell that is a single piece or valve ○ *a univalve gastropod* **2. MADE OF SINGLE PIECE** describes a shell that is made of a single piece ■ *n* **MOLLUSK** a mollusk or shell that is univalve

u·ni·ver·sal /yo͞onə vúrss'l/ *adj* **1. RELATING TO WHOLE WORLD** relating to, affecting, or accepted by the whole world **2. RELATING TO UNIVERSE** relating to the universe or everything **3. RELATING TO THOSE IN PARTICULAR GROUP** relating to, affecting, or including everyone in a group or situation **4. USED BY EVERYONE** used or understood by everyone **5. APPLICABLE TO ALL** applicable to all situations or purposes ○ *a universal solution* **6. PRESENT EVERYWHERE** present or prevalent everywhere **7. KNOWLEDGEABLE** knowledgeable about or encompassing extensive skills, interests, activities, or subjects **8.**

U·nit·ed Church of Christ *n* a Protestant denomination in the United States that was formed in 1957 by the merging of the Evangelical and Reformed Church and the Congregational Church

U·nit·ed King·dom country in northwestern Europe, comprising the historic kingdoms of England and Scotland, the principality of Wales, and the province of Northern Ireland. Language: English. Currency: pound sterling. Capital: London. Population: 60,094,648 (2003). Area: 94,251 sq. mi./244,110 sq. km. Official name **United Kingdom of Great Britain and Northern Ireland**

U·nit·ed Na·tions *n* **1.** an organization of nations that was formed in 1945 to promote peace, security, and international cooperation **2.** an alliance of nations that pledged in January 1942 to defeat the Axis powers in World War II

U·nit·ed States country in central North America, consisting of 50 states (see table on next pages). Language: English. Currency: dollar. Capital: Washington, D.C. Population: 290,342,550 (2001). Area: 3,717,796 sq. mi./9,629,047 sq. km. Official name **United States of America**

u·ni·tive /yo͞onətiv/ *adj* **1.** having the ability to unite or promoting unity **2.** characterized by union or unity [Early 16C. < late Latin *unitivus* < Latin *unit-* (see UNITE)]

u·nit op·er·a·tion *n* an operation that is common to the chemical process industries, e.g., mixing, filtration, chemical reaction, or distillation. The study of unit operations is the basis of chemical engineering.

u·nit price *n* the price of goods per item or measure, e.g., per pound or dozen

u·nit rule *n US* the rule that a state's entire vote for nomination to office must go to the candidate preferred by the majority of its delegation to the political party's national convention

u·nit trust *n UK* same as **mutual fund**

u·ni·ty /yo͞onətee/ (*plural* **-ties**) *n* **1. CONDITION OF BEING ONE** the state or condition of being one **2. COMBINATION INTO ONE** the combining or joining of separate things or

United States

UNITED STATES OF AMERICA

State	Postal code	Capital	Population	Area (sq. mi./sq. km)	State flower	State bird	State tree
Alabama	AL	Montgomery	4,486,508	52,419/135,765	camellia	yellowhammer	Southern longleaf pine
Alaska	AK	Juneau	643,786	663,267/1,717,862	forget-me-not	willow ptarmigan	sitka spruce
Arizona	AZ	Phoenix	5,456,453	113,998/295,255	Saguaro cactus blossom	cactus wren	paloverde
Arkansas	AR	Little Rock	2,710,079	53,179/137,734	apple blossom	mockingbird	pine
California	CA	Sacramento	35,116,033	163,696/423,973	golden poppy	California valley quail	California redwood
Colorado	CO	Denver	4,506,542	104,094/269,604	Rocky Mountain columbine	lark bunting	Colorado blue spruce
Connecticut	CT	Hartford	3,460,503	5,543/14,356	mountain laurel	American robin	white oak
Delaware	DE	Dover	807,385	2,489/6,447	peach blossom	blue hen chicken	American holly
Florida	FL	Tallahassee	16,713,149	65,755/170,306	orange blossom	mockingbird	sabal palmetto palm
Georgia	GA	Atlanta	8,960,310	59,425/153,911	Cherokee rose	brown thrasher	live oak
Hawaii	HI	Honolulu	1,244,898	10,931/28,311	yellow hibiscus	Hawaiian goose	kukui (candlenut)
Idaho	ID	Boise	1,341,131	83,570/216,446	syringa	mountain bluebird	white pine
Illinois	IL	Springfield	12,600,620	57,914/149,997	native violet	cardinal	white oak
Indiana	IN	Indianapolis	6,159,068	36,418/94,323	peony	cardinal	tulip poplar
Iowa	IA	Des Moines	2,936,760	56,272/145,745	wild rose	Eastern goldfinch	oak
Kansas	KS	Topeka	2,715,884	82,277/213,097	native sunflower	Western meadow lark	cottonwood
Kentucky	KY	Frankfort	4,092,891	40,409/104,659	goldenrod	cardinal	tulip poplar
Louisiana	LA	Baton Rouge	4,482,646	51,840/132,266	magnolia	Eastern brown pelican	cypress
Maine	ME	Augusta	1,294,464	35,385/91,647	white pine cone and tassel	chickadee	Eastern white pine
Maryland	MD	Annapolis	5,458,137	12,407/32,134	black-eyed Susan	Baltimore oriole	white oak
Massachusetts	MA	Boston	6,427,801	10,555/27,338	mayflower	chickadee	American elm
Michigan	MI	Lansing	10,050,446	96,716/250,494	apple blossom	robin	white pine
Minnesota	MN	St. Paul	5,019,720	86,939/225,172	pink and white lady's slipper	common loon	red pine
Mississippi	MS	Jackson	2,871,782	48,430/125,434	magnolia	mockingbird	magnolia
Missouri	MO	Jefferson City	5,672,579	69,704/180,533	hawthorn blossom	bluebird	dogwood
Montana	MT	Helena	909,453	147,042/380,839	bitterroot	Western meadowlark	ponderosa pine
Nebraska	NE	Lincoln	1,729,180	77,354/200,347	goldenrod	Western meadowlark	cottonwood
Nevada	NV	Carson City	2,173,491	110,561/286,353	sagebrush	mountain bluebird	single leaf piñon, bristlecone pine
New Hampshire	NH	Concord	1,275,056	9,350/24,217	purple lilac	purple finch	white birch
New Jersey	NJ	Trenton	8,590,300	8,721/22,587	purple violet	Eastern goldfinch	red oak
New Mexico	NM	Santa Fe	1,855,059	121,589/314,916	yucca blossom	roadrunner	piñon
New York	NY	Albany	19,157,532	54,556/141,300	rose	bluebird	sugar maple
North Carolina	NC	Raleigh	8,320,146	53,819/139,391	dogwood blossom	cardinal	pine
North Dakota	ND	Bismark	634,110	70,700/183,113	wild prairie rose	Western meadowlark	American elm
Ohio	OH	Columbus	11,421,267	44,825/116,097	scarlet carnation	cardinal	buckeye
Oklahoma	OK	Oklahoma City	3,493,714	69,898/181,036	mistletoe	scissor-tailed flycatcher	redbud
Oregon	OR	Salem	3,521,516	98,381/254,807	Oregon grape	Western meadowlark	Douglas fir
Pennsylvania	PA	Harrisburg	12,335,091	46,055/119,283	mountain laurel blossom	ruffed grouse	hemlock
Rhode Island	RI	Providence	1,069,725	1,545/4,002	violet	Rhode Island red	red maple
South Carolina	SC	Columbia	4,107,183	32,020/82,931	yellow jessamine	Carolina wren	palmetto
South Dakota	SD	Pierre	761,063	77,116/199,730	pasqueflower	Chinese ring-necked pheasant	Black Hills spruce
Tennessee	TN	Nashville	5,797,289	42,143/109,150	iris	mockingbird	tulip poplar
Texas	TX	Austin	21,779,893	268,581/695,625	bluebonnet	mockingbird	pecan
Utah	UT	Salt Lake City	2,316,256	84,899/219,888	sego lily	seagull	blue spruce
Vermont	VT	Montpelier	616,592	9,614/24,900	red clover blossom	hermit thrush	sugar maple
Virginia	VA	Richmond	7,293,542	42,774/110,785	dogwood blossom	cardinal	dogwood
Washington	WA	Olympia	6,068,996	71,300/184,667	Western rhododendron blossom	willow goldfinch	Western hemlock
West Virginia	WV	Charleston	1,807,873	24,230/62,756	big rhododendron blossom	cardinal	sugar maple
Wisconsin	WI	Madison	5,441,196	65,498/169,640	wood violet	robin	sugar maple
Wyoming	WY	Cheyenne	498,703	97,814/253,338	Indian paintbrush	Western meadowlark	plains cottonwood
FEDERAL DISTRICT:							
District of Columbia	DC	Washington	570,898	68/176	American beauty rose	wood thrush	scarlet oak

* seceded 1860, † seceded 1861, ‡ readmitted 1868, § readmitted 1870

State nickname	Residents	State motto	Statehood	State
Camellia State, Heart of Dixie	Alabamians	We dare defend our rights	12/14/1819†‡ (22nd)	Alabama
Last Frontier (unofficial)	Alaskans	North to the future	01/03/1959 (49th)	Alaska
Grand Canyon State	Arizonans	*Ditat Deus* (God enriches)	02/14/1912 (48th)	Arizona
Natural State, Razorback State	Arkansans	*Regnat Populus* (The people rule)	06/15/1836†‡ (25th)	Arkansas
Golden State	Californians	*Eureka* (I have found it)	09/09/1850 (31st)	California
Centennial State	Coloradans	*Nil Sine Numine* (Nothing without providence)	08/01/1876 (38th)	Colorado
Constitution State, Nutmeg State	Nutmeggers	*Qui Transtulit Sustinet* (He who transplanted still sustains)	01/09/1788 (5th)	Connecticut
Diamond State	Delawareans	Liberty and Independence	12/07/1787 (1st)	Delaware
Sunshine State	Floridians	In God we trust	03/03/1845†‡ (27th)	Florida
Peach State, Empire State of the South	Georgians	Wisdom, justice, and moderation	01/02/1788†§ (4th)	Georgia
Aloha State	Islanders	The life of the land is perpetuated in righteousness	08/21/1959 (50th)	Hawaii
Gem State	Idahoans	*Esto Perpetua* (Let it be perpetual)	07/03/1890 (43rd)	Idaho
Prairie State	Illinoisans	State sovereignty, national union	12/03/1818 (21st)	Illinois
Hoosier State	Hoosiers	Crossroads of America	12/11/1816 (19th)	Indiana
Hawkeye State	Iowans	Our liberties we prize and our rights we will maintain	12/28/1846 (29th)	Iowa
Sunflower State, Jayhawker State	Kansans	*Ad Astra per Aspera* (To the stars through difficulties)	01/29/1861 (34th)	Kansas
Blue Grass State	Kentuckians	United we stand, divided we fall	06/01/1792 (15th)	Kentucky
Pelican State	Louisianans	Union, justice, and confidence	04/30/1812†‡ (18th)	Louisiana
Pine Tree State	Down Easters	*Dirigo* (I lead)	03/15/1820 (23rd)	Maine
Old Line State, Free State	Marylanders	*Fatti Maschii, Parole Femine* (Manly deeds, womanly words)	04/28/1788 (7th)	Maryland
Bay State, Old Colony	Bay Staters	*Ense Petit Placidam Sub Libertate Quietem* (By the sword we seek peace, but peace only under liberty)	02/06/1788 (6th)	Massachusetts
Great Lakes State, Wolverine State	Michiganers	*Amoenam, Circumspice* (If you seek a pleasant peninsula, look about you)	01/26/1837 (26th)	Michigan
North Star State, Gopher State	Minnesotans	*L'Etoile du Nord* (Star of the North)	05/11/1858 (32nd)	Minnesota
Magnolia State	Mississippians	*Virtute et Armis* (By valor and arms)	12/10/1817†§ (20th)	Mississippi
Show Me State	Missourians	*Salus Populi Suprema Lex Est* (The welfare of the people shall be the supreme law)	08/10/1821 (24th)	Missouri
Treasure State	Montanans	*Oro y Plata* (Gold and Silver)	11/08/1889 (41st)	Montana
Cornhusker State	Nebraskans	Equality before the law	03/01/1867 (37th)	Nebraska
Silver State, Sagebrush State, Battle-Born State	Nevadans	All for our country	10/31/1864 (36th)	Nevada
Granite State	New Hampshirites	Live free or die	06/21/1788 (9th)	New Hampshire
Garden State	New Jerseyans	Liberty and Prosperity	12/18/1787 (3rd)	New Jersey
Land of Enchantment	New Mexicans	*Crescit Eundo* (It grows as it goes)	01/06/1912 (47th)	New Mexico
Empire State	New Yorkers	*Excelsior* (Ever Upward)	07/26/1788 (11th)	New York
Tar Heal State, Old North State	North Carolinians	*Esse Quam Videri* (To be rather than to seem)	11/21/1789 (12th)	North Carolina
Peace Garden State	North Dakotans	Liberty and union, now and forever, one and inseparable	11/02/1889 (39th)	North Dakota
Buckeye State	Ohioans	With God, all things are possible	03/01/1803 (17th)	Ohio
Sooner State	Oklahomans, Sooners	*Labor Omnia Vincit* (Labor conquers all things)	11/16/1907 (46th)	Oklahoma
Beaver State	Oregonians	She flies with her own wings	02/14/1859 (33rd)	Oregon
Keystone State	Pennsylvanians	Virtue, Liberty, and Independence	12/12/1787 (2nd)	Pennsylvania
Ocean State, Little Rhody	Rhode Islanders	Hope	05/29/1790 (13th)	Rhode Island
Palmetto State	South Carolinians	*Dum Spiro Spero* (While I breathe, I hope)	05/23/1788*‡ (8th)	South Carolina
Mount Rushmore State, Coyote State	South Dakotans	Under God, the people rule	11/02/1889 (40th)	South Dakota
Volunteer State	Tennesseans	Agriculture and Commerce	06/01/1796 (16th)	Tennessee
Lone Star State	Texans	Friendship	12/29/1845†§ (28th)	Texas
Beehive State	Utahans	Industry	01/04/1896 (45th)	Utah
Green Mountain State	Vermonters	Freedom and Unity	03/04/1791 (14th)	Vermont
Old Dominion	Virginians	*Sic Semper Tyrannis* (Thus always to tyrants)	06/25/1788†§ (10th)	Virginia
Evergreen State	Washingtonians	*Alki* (By and by)	11/11/1889 (42nd)	Washington
Mountain State	West Virginians	*Montani Semper Liberi* (Mountaineers are always free)	06/20/1863 (35th)	West Virginia
Badger State	Wisconsonites	Forward	05/29/1848 (30th)	Wisconsin
Equality State, Cowboy State	Wyomingites	Equal rights	07/10/1890 (44th)	Wyoming
				FEDERAL DISTRICT:
	Washingtonians	*Justitia omnibus* (Justice for all)		District of Columbia

ADAPTABLE TO DIFFERENT SIZES adaptable to many uses or sizes **9.** LOGIC **AFFIRMING OR DENYING EVERY MEMBER** relating to a proposition that is true or false of every member of a class or group ■ *n* **1.** COMMON CHARACTERISTIC a characteristic or behavior pattern common to everyone or all the people in a particular group or situation **2.** LOGIC **PROPOSITION APPLYING TO ALL MEMBERS** a proposition that is true or false for all members of a class or group **3.** PHILOSOPHY **GENERAL TERM OR CONCEPT** a general term or concept, or the thing that it denotes **4.** PHILOSOPHY **UNCHANGING METAPHYSICAL ENTITY** a metaphysical entity that remains unchanged in character through a series of changing relations **5.** PHILOSOPHY **PLATONIC IDEA OR ARISTOTELIAN FORM** a Platonic idea or Aristotelian form **6.** LING **GRAMMATICAL CHARACTERISTIC COMMON TO ALL LANGUAGES** an actual or possible characteristic common to the grammatical description of all human languages —**u·ni·ver·sal·i·ty** /-vur sállətee/ *n* —**u·ni·ver·sal·ly** *adv*

SYNONYMS See ***widespread.***

uni·ver·sal beam *n* a strong steel beam suitable as a support, used either vertically or horizontally

uni·ver·sal class *n* MATH same as **universal set**

uni·ver·sal cou·pling *n* ENG same as **universal joint**

uni·ver·sal do·nor *n* somebody with group O blood who can potentially donate blood to anyone, regardless of the recipient's blood group

uni·ver·sal gram·mar *n* the set of actual or possible rules that form the grammatical description of all human languages

u·ni·ver·sal in·di·ca·tor *n* a solution that undergoes several color changes over a wide range of pH values

u·ni·ver·sal·ism /yoónə vúrss'l ìzzəm/ *n* **1.** a comprehensive range of knowledge, interests, or activities **2.** a universal characteristic or feature — **u·ni·ver·sal·ist** *n* —**u·ni·ver·sal·is·tic** /-vùrss'l ístik/ *adj*

U·ni·ver·sal·ism *n* in Christianity, the doctrine of salvation for all people —**U·ni·ver·sal·ist** *n*

u·ni·ver·sal·ize /yoónə vúrss'l ìz/ (**-ized, -iz·ing, -iz·es**) *vt* **1.** to make something universal in use or distribution, often within a particular field **2.** to generalize a theory, proposition, or idea so that it applies to all people, instances, or situations —**u·ni·ver·sal·iz·a·bil·i·ty** /yoónə vurss'l ìzə bíllətee/ *n* —**u·ni·ver·sal·i·za·tion** /yoónə vùrss'li záysh'n/ *n*

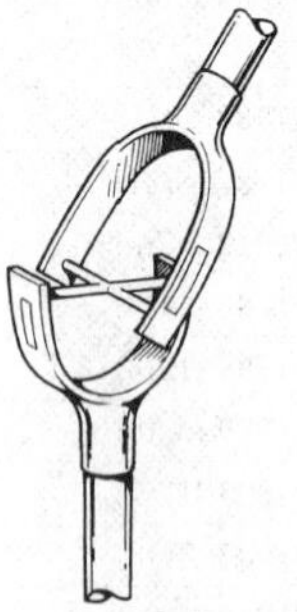

universal joint

u·ni·ver·sal joint, u·ni·ver·sal coup·ling *n* a coupling device between two rotating shafts in line with each other that permits rotation in three planes. It is commonly used in vehicle construction.

u·ni·ver·sal mo·tor *n* an electric motor that runs with a relatively constant output speed on either alternating or direct current

U·ni·ver·sal Prod·uct Code *n* a bar code containing a unique 12-digit number that identifies a commercial product

u·ni·ver·sal quan·ti·fi·er *n* a word that performs the same function in symbolic, mathematical, or predicate logic, e.g., "all" and "every" in English and the logical operator or constant

u·ni·ver·sal re·cip·i·ent *n* a member of the AB blood group who can receive transfusions of blood from any ABO group

U·ni·ver·sal Re·source Lo·cat·or *n* ONLINE same as **URL** (*dated*)

uni·ver·sal ser·i·al bus *n* COMPUT full form of **USB**

u·ni·ver·sal set *n* a mathematical set that contains all of the possible elements and all of the subsets relevant to the solution of a specific problem

U·ni·ver·sal Time, U·ni·ver·sal Time Co·or·di·nat·ed *n* **1.** the time in the zone that includes the 0° meridian of Greenwich, London, England, used as the international standard for calculating the time in other zones **2.** an internationally accepted standard for calculating time based on International Atomic Time

u·ni·verse /yoónə vùrss/ *n* **1.** **ALL MATTER AND ENERGY IN SPACE** the totality of all matter and energy that exists in the vastness of space, whether known to human beings or not **2.** **THE EARTH AND HUMANITY** the Earth along with the human race and the totality of human experience **3.** **SPHERE OF PERSON OR THING** a sphere of activity that is centered on and includes everything associated with a person, place, or thing **4.** LOGIC same as **universe of discourse** **5.** STATS same as **population** (sense 6) [14C. Directly or via French < Latin *universum* "the whole world" < *universus* "whole," < *versus*, past participle of *vertere* "turn"]

u·ni·verse of dis·course *n* in logic, all of a set of objects implied by a specific discussion

u·ni·ver·si·ty /yoónə vúrssətee/ (*plural* **-ties**) *n* **1.** **UNDERGRADUATE AND POSTGRADUATE EDUCATIONAL INSTITUTION** an educational institution for higher learning that typically includes an undergraduate college and graduate schools in various disciplines, as well as medical and law schools and sometimes other professional schools **2.** **BUILDINGS HOUSING UNIVERSITY** the buildings, other facilities, and grounds of a university **3.** **STUDENTS AND FACULTY** the students, teachers, and administrative and other staff of a university [14C. Via French *université* < Latin *universitas* "the whole, society, guild" < *universus* (see UNIVERSE)]

U·ni·vi·sion /yoónee vìzh'n/ *n* a Spanish language television network that broadcasts in the United States

u·niv·o·cal /yoo nívvək'l/ *adj* having only one meaning ■ *n* a word or term with only one meaning [Mid-16C. < late Latin *univocus* "having one voice" < *vox* "voice"] — **u·niv·o·cal·ly** *adv*

UNIX /yoóniks/, **Unix** *tdmk* a trademark for a widely used computer operating system, developed in 1969 at AT&T Bell Laboratories, that can support multitasking in a multiuser environment

un·joint /un jóynt/ (**-joint·ed, -joint·ing, -joints**) *vt* to cut off or dislocate something at a joint —**un·joint·ed** *adj*

un·just /un júst/ *adj* contrary to what is right, just, or fair, or lacking fairness or justice —**un·just·ly** *adv* — **un·just·ness** *n*

un·jus·ti·fi·a·ble /un jústə fī əb'l, ùn justə fī əb'l/ *adj* incapable of being shown to be or defended as being fair, reasonable, or correct —**un·jus·ti·fi·a·bil·i·ty** /un jùstə fī ə bíllətee/ *n* —**un·jus·ti·fi·a·bly** *adv*

un·jus·ti·fied /un jústə fīd/ *adj* **1.** shown to have no good or just reason or explanation **2.** not arranged evenly in such a way that the ends of the lines on a page form a straight vertical line parallel to the margin

un·kempt /un kémpt/ *adj* **1.** **NEEDING GROOMING** tangled and matted and in need of combing or grooming **2.** **MESSY AND NEGLECTED** messy or disorderly as a result of neglect **3.** **UNPOLISHED** lacking in polish or elegance [14C. < UN- + *kempt*, past participle of *kemb* "comb" < Old English *cemban* < Germanic] —**un·kempt·ness** *n*

un·ken·nel /un kénn'l/ (**-neled, -nel·ing, -nels**) *vt* **1.** **RELEASE DOG FROM KENNEL** to let a dog out of a kennel **2.** **FORCE ANIMAL OUT OF LAIR** to make an animal leave its den or lair **3.** **MAKE SOMETHING KNOWN** to reveal something secret or hidden

un·kind /un kínd/ *adj* **1.** lacking kindness, sympathy, or consideration, or resulting from such a lack **2.** severe, harsh, or inclement —**un·kind·ness** *n*

un·kind·ly /un kíndlee/ *adv* in an unkind manner or without showing kindness ■ *adj* lacking in kindliness —**un·kind·li·ness** *n*

un·kink /un kíngk/ (**-kinked, -kink·ing, -kinks**) *v* **1.** *vti* to remove a kink or kinks from something, or have a kink or kinks removed **2.** *vi* to become loose or relaxed

un·knit /un nít/ (**-knit** or **-knit·ted, -knit·ting, -knits**) *vti* **1.** to unravel something, or become unraveled **2.** to allow the eyebrows to move back to a natural position from a position of being drawn together, or be moved apart in this way

un·know·a·ble /un nó əb'l/ *adj* impossible to know, often because of being beyond human experience or understanding ■ *n* something that cannot be known —**un·know·a·bil·i·ty** /un nò ə bíllətee/ *n* —**un·know·a·ble·ness** *n* —**un·know·a·bly** *adv*

un·know·ing /un nó ing/ *adj* **1.** unwitting or lacking awareness **2.** not intended —**un·know·ing·ly** *adv*

un·known /un nṓn/ *adj* **1.** **NOT KNOWN** not forming part of somebody's knowledge or of knowledge in general ○ *an unknown assailant* **2.** **NOT IDENTIFIED** undetermined or undiscovered ○ *Unknown to her family, she left town.* **3.** **NOT WIDELY KNOWN** not known to, or recognized by, many people ○ *An unknown actress was starring in the play.* ■ *n* **1.** **SOMEBODY OR SOMETHING NOT KNOWN** somebody or something that is not part of a person's knowledge or of knowledge in general **2.** **SOMEBODY OR SOMETHING NOT WIDELY KNOWN** somebody or something that is not known or recognized by many people **3.** MATH **VARIABLE TO BE DETERMINED** a variable in an equation whose values are solutions of the equation

un·known quan·ti·ty *n* something or somebody whose nature, behavior, or importance is uncertain and unpredictable

Un·known Sol·dier *n* an unidentified soldier killed in battle and selected for burial with national honors to represent all those who died fighting for their country but remain unidentified

un·la·bored /un láybərd/ *adj* **1.** **DONE WITHOUT EFFORT** done or produced without toil, effort, or difficulty **2.** **NATURAL AND UNSTUDIED** exhibiting a naturalness and ease of accomplishment **3.** **UNCULTIVATED** describes agricultural land that is not being plowed or cultivated

un·la·boured /un láybərd/ *adj* Can, UK spelling of **unlabored**

un·lace /un láyss/ (**-laced, -lac·ing, -lac·es**) *vt* **1.** to loosen or untie the laces of a shoe, piece of clothing, or other item **2.** to remove the shoes or clothes from somebody by undoing the laces

un·lade /un láyd/ (**-lad·ed, -lad·ed** or **-lad·en** /-láyd'n/, **-lad·ing, -lades**) *vt* **1.** to empty a ship or vehicle by removing its cargo **2.** to remove the cargo from a ship or vehicle

un·lash /un lásh/ (**-lashed, -lash·ing, -lash·es**) *vt* to release something by loosening or untying the ropes or other lashing holding or restraining it

un·law·ful /un láwf'l/ *adj* **1.** not permitted by the law **2.** contrary to religious precepts, ethical standards, or the conventions of society —**un·law·ful·ly** *adv* — **un·law·ful·ness** *n*

SYNONYMS ***unlawful, illegal, illicit, wrongful, nonlegal***

CORE MEANING: not in accordance with laws or rules

unlawful not permitted by the law ○ *Possessing a knife was not per se an unlawful act.* ○ *This amendment makes it unlawful for employers to have different compulsory retirement ages for men and women.* **illegal** contravening a specific law, especially a criminal law ○ *drug smuggling and other illegal activities* ○ *Under the new law, refugees whose appeals failed would be declared illegal immigrants.* **illicit** not permitted by the law and considered morally wrong or unacceptable ○ *illicit weapons and drugs* ○ *The divorce papers cited her numerous illicit affairs.* **wrongful** not fair, just, or legal, but not punishable by criminal law ○ *the wrongful use of confidential information* ○ *awarded damages for wrongful arrest* **nonlegal** not established under the law, or by common law or legislation ○ *nonlegal secular holidays*

un·law·ful as·sem·bly *n* a gathering of people that is not sanctioned by law and is therefore illegal

un·law·ful com·bat·ant *n* somebody who undertakes military-style operations but is not a member of a country's regular armed forces, nor responsible to a commander, nor following the rules of war

un·lay /un láy/ (**-laid, -laid** /un láyd/, **-lay·ing, -lays**) *vti* to separate the strands of a rope by untwisting them, or become separated in this way

un·lead /un léd/ (**-lead·ed, -lead·ing, -leads**) *vt* in traditional hot-metal printing, to take out the leading or leads separating lines of type

un·lead·ed /un léddəd/ *adj* **1.** **FREE OF TETRAETHYL LEAD** not containing tetraethyl lead as an antiknock additive and consequently less harmful to the environment ○ *unleaded gas* **2.** PRINTING **NOT SEPARATED BY LEADS** describes lines of type that are not separated by leads ■ *n* **UNLEADED GASOLINE** gasoline that does not contain tetraethyl lead as an antiknock additive

un·learn /un lúrn/ (**-learned** /-lúrnd/ or **-learnt** /-lúrnt/, **-learn·ing, -learns**) *vt* **1.** to rid the mind of the knowledge or memory of something **2.** to break the habit or end the practice of something

un·learn·ed /un lúrnəd/ *adj* **1. LACKING EDUCATION** not having received an education or schooling **2. DISPLAYING LACK OF EDUCATION** showing or resulting from a lack of education **3. UNSKILLED OR UNFAMILIAR** lacking a knowledge of, skills in, or familiarity with, a particular field **4.** *also* **un·learnt NATURAL OR UNSTUDIED** possessed or known without having been practiced, studied, or taught —**un·learn·ed·ly** *adv*

un·leash /un le͞esh/ (**-leashed, -leash·ing, -leash·es**) *vt* **1.** to allow something, especially something previously held in check, to have its full effect **2.** to set a person or animal free from a leash or other form of restraint or confinement

un·leav·ened /un lévvənd/ *adj* made without yeast or other rising agent

un·less /un léss/ *conj* except under the circumstances that ○ *I won't go unless the weather improves.* [15C. < obsolete *on less than* "on a lower condition, except"]

un·let·tered /un léttərd/ *adj* **1. NOT WELL-EDUCATED** lacking a good education or the knowledge and understanding that such an education can provide **2. ILLITERATE** unable to read and write **3. NOT HAVING ANY LETTERING** not containing or inscribed with any lettering

un·li·censed /un lī́ss'nst/ *adj* **1. HAVING NO LICENSE** lacking a required official license **2. UNSANCTIONED** done without authorization or permission **3. WITHOUT ETHICAL INHIBITIONS** lacking ethical or religious constraints

un·licked /un líkt/ *adj* **1.** not licked, e.g., so as to be moistened, cleaned, or dried **2.** *US* not completely or properly formed or shaped (*archaic*)

un·like /un lī́k/ *prep* **1. DISSIMILAR TO** having qualities and characteristics dissimilar to or different from somebody or something ○ *It's unlike anything we've ever seen before.* **2. IN CONTRAST TO** used to indicate a contrast between two things, people, or situations ○ *Unlike my opponent's plan, these reforms will neither impose new costs nor require tax increases.* **3. ATYPICAL OF** used to indicate that somebody's words or actions are not characteristic of him or her ○ *It was so unlike her to speak like that.* ■ *adj* **NOT ALIKE** dissimilar to each other ○ *The boys are very unlike in appearance.* —**un·like·ness** *n*

un·like·ly /un lī́klee/ (**-li·er, -li·est**) *adj* **1. IMPROBABLE** not likely to occur **2. NOT BELIEVABLE** not likely to be true or be believed **3. INCONGRUOUS** not suitable or appropriate **4. PROBABLY NOT SUCCESSFUL** not likely to meet with success —**un·like·li·hood** *n* —**un·like·li·ness** *n*

un·lim·ber[1] /un límbər/ *adj* lacking in flexibility or suppleness ■ *vti* (**-bered, -ber·ing, -bers**) to make something flexible or supple, or become flexible or supple

un·lim·ber[2] /un límbər/ (**-bered, -ber·ing, -bers**) *vti* **1.** to prepare something for action or use **2.** to remove a piece of field artillery from its gun carriage and prepare it for use

un·lim·it·ed /un límmitəd/ *adj* **1. NOT RESTRICTED** without limits, restrictions, or controls **2. INFINITE** lacking or appearing to lack a boundary or end **3. COMPLETE OR TOTAL** not subject to qualification or exception —**un·lim·it·ed·ly** *adv* —**un·lim·it·ed·ness** *n*

un·list·ed /un lístəd/ *adj* **1. NOT PUBLICLY AVAILABLE** not included in a telephone directory available to the public **2. NOT LISTED ON STOCK EXCHANGE** not registered on a stock exchange and consequently not available for trading on that exchange **3. NOT ON LIST** not included on a list

un·liv·a·ble /un lívvəb'l/ *adj* not fit for somebody to live in

un·live /un lív/ (**-lived, -liv·ing, -lives**) *vt* to reverse or undo the effects of an experience, action, or period of life

un·load /un lṓd/ (**-load·ed, -load·ing, -loads**) *vti* **1. REMOVE CARGO FROM CARRIER** to take the load off a ship, truck, or pack animal **2. DISCHARGE** to discharge passengers or cargo **3. REMOVE CHARGE FROM GUN** to remove a charge or cartridge from a gun **4. TAKE FILM OUT OF CAMERA** to remove a roll of film from a camera **5. SHARE TROUBLES** to find an outlet for worries or negative feelings by sharing them with somebody else **6. SELL SOMETHING UNWANTED** to get rid of something, especially by selling a large quantity of it **7. TRANSFER SOMETHING UNWANTED** to pass work, responsibility, or a problem on to somebody else **8.** *US* **HIT SOMETHING FORCEFULLY** to hit something with great force or power

un·lock /un lók/ (**-locked, -lock·ing, -locks**) *v* **1.** *vti* **OPEN OR BECOME OPEN AFTER LOCKING** to open a lock or something locked, or to become open after being locked **2.** *vt* **GIVE ACCESS TO SOMETHING** to provide access to something previously unavailable **3.** *vti* **RELEASE EMOTION** to release or unleash a pent-up feeling or emotion, or be released or unleashed **4.** *vti* **REVEAL SOMETHING, OR BE REVEALED** to expose or explain something, or be exposed or explained **5.** *vt* **MAKE USABLE WITH OTHER SYSTEMS** to program a cell phone so that it can be used with other service providers

un·looked-for /un lo͝okt-/ *adj* not hoped for or expected

un·loose /un lo͞oss/ (**-loosed, -loos·ing, -loos·es**), **un·loos·en** /-lo͞oss'n/ (**-ened, -en·ing, -ens**) *vt* **1. UNFASTEN SOMETHING** to untie or undo something, especially a knot **2. FREE SOMEBODY FROM RESTRAINT** to release somebody or something from restraint or confinement **3. MAKE SOMETHING LOOSER** to relax the tightness of something **4. MAKE SOMETHING LESS INTENSE** to reduce the intensity of something

un·love·ly /un lúvvlee/ (**-li·er, -li·est**) *adj* **1.** not beautiful or pleasing to look at **2.** not producing pleasure or delight —**un·love·li·ness** *n*

un·luck·i·ly /un lúkilee/ *adv* **1.** in an unfortunate manner **2.** in a way characterized by bad luck

un·luck·y /un lúkee/ (**-i·er, -i·est**) *adj* **1. HAVING BAD LUCK** not experiencing good luck **2. FULL OF MISFORTUNE OR FAILURE** full of bad luck or failure **3. BRINGING MISFORTUNE** causing or heralding misfortune **4. DISAPPOINTING** causing disappointment or regret —**un·luck·i·ness** *n*

un·made /un máyd/ past participle, past tense of **unmake** ■ *adj* not restored to a neat state after being slept in ○ *an unmade bed*

un·make /un máyk/ (**-made, -made** /-máyd/, **-mak·ing, -makes**) *vt* **1. UNDO SOMETHING** to undo the effects of something **2. CHANGE SOMETHING COMPLETELY** to make a fundamental change or changes in something **3. REMOVE SOMEBODY FROM POWER** to remove somebody from office or a position of authority

un·man /un mán/ (**-manned, -man·ning, -mans**) *vt* **1.** to cause somebody to lose a quality or qualities traditionally attributed to men, especially courage (*literary*) **2.** to deprive a man or boy of the ability to have intercourse or father children

un·man·age·a·ble /un mánnijəb'l/ *adj* difficult or impossible to deal with —**un·man·age·a·bil·i·ty** /un mànnijə bíllətee/ *n* —**un·man·age·a·bly** *adv*

un·man·ly /un mánnlee/ (**-li·er, -li·est**) *adj* not typical of or appropriate for a man, according to traditional perceptions of masculinity —**un·man·li·ness** *n*

un·manned /un mánd/ *adj* AEROSP same as **uncrewed** (*sometimes considered offensive*)

un·man·nered /un mánnərd/ *adj* **1.** lacking good manners, or displaying such a lack **2.** having an easy unaffected manner —**un·man·nered·ly** *adv*

un·man·ner·ly /un mánnərlee/ *adj* lacking good manners, or displaying such a lack ■ *adv* in a rude or discourteous manner —**un·man·ner·li·ness** *n*

un·marked /un maárkt/ *adj* **1. WITHOUT MARK** not bearing any mark **2. LACKING IDENTIFYING MARKINGS** lacking identifying letters, numbers, or symbols ○ *an unmarked police car* **3. LACKING DISTINGUISHING QUALITY** having no distinguishing quality or character **4. UNSEEN** not seen or spotted **5.** LING **WITHOUT DISTINCTIVE LINGUISTIC FEATURE** not having an extra or less usual distinctive linguistic feature

un·mar·ried /un márreed/ *adj* not joined to another person by marriage ■ *n* somebody who is not married

un·mask /un másk/ (**-masked, -mask·ing, -masks**) *vti* **1.** to reveal the true nature or identity of somebody or something, or reveal your own true nature or identity **2.** to remove a mask, or remove a mask from somebody

un·matched /un mácht/ *adj* **1.** not matching, especially not belonging to a matching pair **2.** having no equal or rival

un·mean·ing /un me͞ening/ *adj* **1. MEANINGLESS** lacking meaning or significance **2. UNINTENTIONAL** not intended or deliberate **3. UNINTELLIGENT** blank and devoid of intelligence ○ *an unmeaning stare* —**un·mean·ing·ly** *adv*

un·meas·ured /un mé*zh*ərd/ *adj* **1. NOT MEASURED** not determined by measuring **2. NOT RESTRAINED** unrestrained, incautious, or ill-considered **3.** MUSIC **NOT DIVIDED INTO BARS** not marked with bar lines and therefore with no set rhythm

un·me·chan·i·cal /ùnmə kánnik'l/ *adj* lacking the skill to work with tools and machinery —**un·me·chan·i·cal·ly** *adv*

un·men·tion·a·ble /un ménshənəb'l/ *adj* not to be mentioned or discussed, especially in polite conversation ■ *n* something that should not be mentioned or discussed, especially in polite conversation ■ **un·men·tion·a·bles** *npl* CLOTHING same as **underwear** (*dated or humorous*) —**un·men·tion·a·ble·ness** *n* —**un·men·tion·a·bly** *adv*

un·mer·ci·ful /un múrssif'l/ *adj* **1.** displaying no mercy, or characterized by a lack of mercy **2.** going beyond what is reasonable —**un·mer·ci·ful·ly** *adv* —**un·mer·ci·ful·ness** *n*

un·met /un mét/ *adj* not satisfactorily fulfilled

un·met·ered /un me͞etərd/ *adj* **1.** not measured using a meter **2.** describes Internet service that is available at a flat rate, typically by the month, rather than by connection time

un·mis·tak·a·ble /ùnmi stáykəb'l/ *adj* easily recognized or understood —**un·mis·tak·a·bil·i·ty** /ùnmi stàykə bíllətee/ *n* —**un·mis·tak·a·bly** *adv*

~~unmistakeable~~ incorrect spelling of **unmistakable**

un·mit·i·gat·ed /un mítti gàytəd/ *adj* **1.** not lessened or eased in any way **2.** absolute and unqualified —**un·mit·i·gat·ed·ly** *adv*

un·mold /un mṓld/ (**-mold·ed, -mold·ing, -molds**) *vt* to remove something from a mold

un·moor /un mo͝or/ (**-moored, -moor·ing, -moors**) *v* **1.** *vti* to free a ship or boat from its moorings, or be freed from moorings **2.** *vt* to leave a ship or boat moored by only one of its anchors

un·mor·al /un máwrəl/ *adj* **1.** lacking a moral sense, or displaying such a lack **2.** not subject to morality or ethics —**un·mo·ral·i·ty** /ùnmə rállətee/ *n* —**un·mor·al·ly** *adv*

un·moved /un mo͞ovd/ *adj* having or showing no emotional reaction to something when it would usually be expected

SYNONYMS See *impassive*.

UNMOVIC /ún mō vìk/ *abbr* United Nations Monitoring, Verification, and Inspection Commission

un·mov·ing /un mo͞oving/ *adj* **1.** not in motion ○ *unmoving vehicles* **2.** failing to arouse deep emotions ○ *an unmoving story*

un·mu·si·cal /un myo͞ozik'l/ *adj* **1.** lacking melodic qualities and consequently unpleasant to hear **2.** having no ability for, or no interest in, music —**un·mu·si·cal·ly** *adv* —**un·mu·si·cal·ness** *n* —**un·mu·si·cal·i·ty** /ùn myo͞ozi kállətee/ *n*

un·muz·zle /un múzz'l/ (**-zled, -zling, -zles**) *vt* **1.** to remove a muzzle from an animal, especially a dog **2.** to restore to a person or organization the right to say, publish, or broadcast something

un·my·e·lin·at·ed /un mī́ əli nàytəd/ *adj* describes a nerve fiber that lacks a myelin sheath. Such fibers transmit nerve impulses more slowly than myelinated ones, and are found mainly in worms, insects, and other invertebrate animals.

un·name·a·ble /un náyməb'l/, **un·nam·a·ble** *adj* incapable of being named, especially too terrible to name

un·named /un náymd/ *adj* **1.** having a name but not identified by it **2.** not yet assigned a name

un·nat·u·ral /un náchərəl/ *adj* **1. CONTRARY TO EXPECTED BEHAVIOR** contrary to habit, custom, or practice ○ *an unnatural tense silence between them* **2. NOT CONFORMING**

TO CONVENTIONS behaving in ways that contradict conventional assumptions about what constitutes normal or acceptable human behavior **3.** ARTIFICIAL affected, artificial, contrived, or strained ○ *an unnatural festive atmosphere* **4.** CONTRARY TO LAWS OF NATURE contrary to the physical laws of nature —**un·nat·u·ral·ly** *adv* —**un·nat·u·ral·ness** *n*

un·nec·es·sar·y /ən néssə sèrree/ *adj* **1.** gratuitous, unjustified, and hurtful **2.** not essential, needed, or required —**un·nec·es·sar·i·ly** *adv*

un·nerve /un núrv/ (**-nerved, -nerv·ing, -nerves**) *vt* **1.** to deprive somebody of courage, resolve, or self-confidence **2.** to cause somebody to feel nervous —**un·nerv·ing** *adj* —**un·nerv·ing·ly** *adv*

un·no·ticed /un nṓtist/ *adv* without being seen or spotted by anybody —**un·no·ticed** *adj*

un·num·bered /un númbərd/ *adj* **1.** not given an identifying number **2.** too many to be counted

UNO, U.N.O. *abbr* United Nations Organization

un·ob·tru·sive /ùnnəb tróossiv/ *adj* not conspicuous, blatant, or assertive —**un·ob·tru·sive·ly** *adv* —**un·ob·tru·sive·ness** *n*

un·oc·cu·pied /un ókyə pīd/ *adj* **1.** NOT IN USE not being used by anybody **2.** NOT DOING ANYTHING not doing anything, or anything important **3.** NOT INHABITED not lived in by anybody **4.** NOT UNDER FOREIGN MILITARY RULE not under the control or military rule of a foreign country

SYNONYMS See *vacant*.

un·of·fi·cial /ùnnə físh'l/ *adj* **1.** UNAUTHORIZED not authorized or sanctioned by the proper authority **2.** NOT ACTING OFFICIALLY not acting or employed in an official capacity or position **3.** NOT DONE OR MADE OFFICIALLY not done or made by somebody acting in an official capacity —**un·of·fi·cial·ly** *adv*

un·op·posed /ùnnə pṓzd/ *adj, adv* **1.** not fought, objected to, or resisted **2.** unchallenged by an official opponent in an election or competition

un·or·gan·ized /un áwrgə nīzd/ *adj* **1.** NOT DONE IN ORGANIZED WAY not arranged or done in an orderly or systematic way **2.** NOT ACTING IN ORGANIZED WAY not acting, thinking, or working in an orderly or systematic manner **3.** NOT UNIONIZED not part of a labor union **4.** NOT LIVING lacking the characteristics of a living organism

un·or·tho·dox /un áwrthə dòks/ *adj* **1.** failing to follow conventional or traditional beliefs or practices **2.** not practicing or conforming to the accepted or established form of a religion —**un·or·tho·dox·ly** *adv* —**un·or·tho·dox·y** *n*

unp. *abbr* PUBL unpaged

un·pack /un pák/ (**-packed, -pack·ing, -packs**) *v* **1.** *vt* TAKE CONTENTS FROM SOMETHING to take the contents out of something ○ *Unpack your suitcase later.* **2.** *vti* TAKE OUT PACKED THINGS to remove something that has been packed from its container or packaging ○ *I had to unpack and repack all my belongings.* **3.** *vt* REMOVE BURDEN FROM SOMEBODY OR SOMETHING to take a pack or other burden from a person or animal that has been carrying it **4.** *vt* COMPUT same as **unzip** **5.** *vt* REVEAL WHAT IS HIDDEN IN to reveal what is hidden, buried, or encoded within something

un·paged /un páyjd/, **un·pag·i·nat·ed** /un pájjə nàytəd/ *adj* not marked with page numbers

un·paid /un páyd/ *adj* **1.** NOT YET SETTLED awaiting payment or settlement ○ *unpaid bills* **2.** NOT HAVING YET RECEIVED PAYMENT not yet in receipt of payment for work done **3.** WORKING FOR NO PAY working without wages or a salary ○ *unpaid volunteers* **4.** NOT PAYING MONEY not paying wages or a salary ○ *unpaid overtime*

un·paired /un pérd/ *adj* **1.** not being one of a pair **2.** characterized by a lack of pairs

un·pal·at·a·ble /un pállətəb'l/ *adj* **1.** not pleasant, agreeable, or acceptable **2.** having an unpleasant taste —**un·pal·at·a·bil·i·ty** /un pàllətə bílletee/ *n* —**un·pal·at·a·bly** *adv*

un·par·al·leled /un párrə lèld/ *adj* not equaled, matched, or paralleled in kind or quality ○ *an unparalleled opportunity*

un·par·don·a·ble /un paard'nəb'l/ *adj* **1.** impossible to pardon **2.** so bad as to merit no forgiveness

un·par·lia·men·ta·ry /ùn paarlə méntəree/ *adj* not acceptable according to parliamentary procedure

un·peg /un pég/ (**-pegged, -peg·ging, -pegs**) *vt* **1.** TAKE PEG FROM SOMETHING to take a peg or pegs from something **2.** RELEASE SOMETHING BY REMOVING PEG to release something by removing a peg or pegs **3.** STOP FIXING LEVEL OF SOMETHING to allow something, especially prices or wages, to fluctuate freely by removing the restrictions holding them at a fixed level

un·per·son /ún pùrss'n/ *n* somebody whose existence is not acknowledged officially, especially a public figure whose existence is, for political or ideological reasons, unrecognized by a totalitarian government and the news media it controls

un·per·turbed /ùnpər túrbd/ *adj* not worried, concerned, or upset —**un·per·turbed·ly** *adv*

un·pho·net·ic /ùn fə néttik/ *adj* using a system of writing that does not represent or correspond to the sounds of human speech

un·pick /un pík/ (**-picked, -pick·ing, -picks**) *vt* to undo something by pulling out a thread or threads

un·pin /un pín/ (**-pinned, -pin·ning, -pins**) *vt* **1.** to take a pin or pins from something **2.** to release or unfasten something by removing a pin or pins

un·pitched /un pícht/ *adj* describes a musical instrument such as a drum, tambourine, or gong that is not set to a particular pitch or key

un·placed /un pláyst/ *adj* not assigned a specific place or position

un·planned /un plánd/ *adj* **1.** NOT INTENDED not happening according to a plan **2.** LACKING PLAN not following or structured according to an overall plan **3.** DONE SPONTANEOUSLY accomplished without advance planning

un·pleas·ant /un plézz'nt/ *adj* **1.** not pleasing, enjoyable, or agreeable **2.** unfriendly and nasty to somebody —**un·pleas·ant·ly** *adv*

un·pleas·ant·ness /un plézz'ntnəss/ *n* **1.** UNPLEASANT CONDITION OR QUALITY the condition or quality of being unpleasant **2.** UNPLEASANT EXPERIENCES OR EVENTS experiences or events that are not pleasing or enjoyable **3.** UNFRIENDLINESS an unfriendly and nasty attitude or behavior **4.** UNPLEASANT SITUATION a situation that is not pleasing or enjoyable **5.** DISAGREEMENT an argument or disagreement

un·pleas·ant·ry /un plézz'ntree/ (*plural* **-ries**) *n* a nasty remark or action (*often used in the plural*)

un·plug /un plúg/ (**-plugged, -plug·ging, -plugs**) *vt* **1.** DISCONNECT ELECTRICAL APPLIANCE to disconnect an electrical appliance by pulling its plug out of a socket **2.** PULL PLUG OUT OF ELECTRIC SOCKET to disconnect an electric plug or wire by pulling it out of a socket **3.** TAKE STOPPER FROM SOMETHING to remove a stopper, cork, or other plug from something **4.** REMOVE BLOCKAGE FROM SOMETHING to remove a blockage, clog, or other obstruction from something

un·plugged /un plúgd/ *adv* without the use of amplified musical instruments, especially guitars ■ *adj* performed without the use of amplified musical instruments, especially guitars

un·plumbed /un plúmd/ *adj* **1.** NOT FULLY EXAMINED not thoroughly understood or investigated **2.** NOT CHECKED FOR VERTICALITY not checked for verticality with a plumb line **3.** NOT MEASURED FOR DEPTH not measured with a plumb line to determine depth

un·polled /un pṓld/ *adj* **1.** NOT INVITED TO PARTICIPATE IN POLL not invited to participate in a survey of public opinion **2.** NOT VOTING not having cast a vote at an election **3.** *US* NOT ON ELECTORAL ROLL not included in a list of electors

un·pop·u·lar /un póppyələr/ *adj* not liked by, approved of, or acceptable to a person, a group of people, or the general public —**un·pop·u·lar·i·ty** /ùn popyə lárrətee/ *n* —**un·pop·u·lar·ly** *adv*

un·prac·ticed /un práktist/ *adj* **1.** UNTRAINED OR INEXPERIENCED lacking in training or experience **2.** NOT DONE FREQUENTLY not done or not commonly done **3.** NOT REHEARSED not prepared and tried out beforehand

un·prec·e·dent·ed /un préssə dèntəd/ *adj* having no earlier parallel or equivalent

un·pre·dict·a·ble /ùnprə díktəb'l/ *adj* not easily foreseen or predicted —**un·pre·dict·a·bil·i·ty** /ùnprə diktə bílletee/ *n* —**un·pre·dict·a·bly** *adv*

un·pre·med·i·tat·ed /ùnprə méddi tàytəd/ *adj* done without advance planning or thought —**un·pre·med·i·tat·ed·ly** *adv*

un·pre·pared /ùnprə pérd/ *adj* **1.** UNREADY not ready for something or not expecting something to happen **2.** NOT MADE READY not having been prepared as required or expected **3.** IMPROVISED done without any preparation —**un·pre·par·ed·ly** /-pérdlee, -pérrədlee/ *adv* —**un·pre·par·ed·ness** /ùnprə pérdnəss, -pérrədnəss/ *n*

un·pre·pos·sess·ing /ùn preepə zéssing/ *adj* not producing a favorable impression —**un·pre·pos·sess·ing·ly** *adv*

un·pre·tend·ing /ùnpri ténding/ *adj* not pretentious or affected

un·pre·ten·tious /ùnprə ténshəss/ *adj* not putting on a false or showy display of importance, wealth, or knowledge —**un·pre·ten·tious·ly** *adv* —**un·pre·ten·tious·ness** *n*

un·prin·ci·pled /un prínssəp'ld/ *adj* lacking, or resulting from a lack of, moral or ethical principles

un·print·a·ble /un príntəb'l/ *adj* not fit for publication, usually because of being obscene, libelous, or otherwise illegal or offensive

un·pro·duc·tive /ùnprə dúktiv/ *adj* **1.** not producing useful results, decisions, or achievements **2.** not producing much work or output —**un·pro·duc·tive·ly** *adv* —**un·pro·duc·tive·ness** *n* —**un·pro·duc·tiv·i·ty** /un prō duk tívvətee/ *n*

un·pro·fes·sion·al /ùnprə féshən'l, -féshnəl/ *adj* **1.** CONTRARY TO PROFESSIONAL STANDARDS contrary to the expected standards of a profession **2.** AMATEURISH unworthy of a professional **3.** NOT BELONGING TO PROFESSION not having membership in a profession —**un·pro·fes·sion·al·ism** *n* —**un·pro·fes·sion·al·ly** *adv*

un·prof·it·a·ble /un próffitəb'l/ *adj* **1.** not producing a profit **2.** not producing a desirable result or having a useful purpose —**un·prof·it·a·bil·i·ty** /un pròffitə bílletee/ *n* —**un·prof·it·a·ble·ness** *n* —**un·prof·it·a·bly** *adv*

UNPROFOR /un prō fàwr/ *abbr* United Nations Protection Force

un·prom·is·ing /un prómmissing/ *adj* **1.** not likely to prove successful **2.** not favorable —**un·prom·is·ing·ly** *adv*

un·prompt·ed /un prómptəd/ *adj* said or done without any encouragement or help

un·pro·nounce·a·ble /ùnprə nównssəb'l/ *adj* very difficult or impossible to pronounce

un·pro·nounced /ùnprə nównst/ *adj* **1.** not clear or easy to notice **2.** not sounded or pronounced

un·pro·tect·ed /ùnprə téktəd/ *adj* **1.** HAVING NO PROTECTION FROM HARM having no protection against harm or damage ○ *With that insurance policy you're still unprotected against accidental damage.* **2.** LACKING SAFETY PRECAUTIONS not provided with something to prevent accident or injury ○ *an unprotected fire* **3.** PERFORMED WITHOUT CONDOM performed without the use of a condom ○ *unprotected sex* **4.** COMPUT NOT LOCKED AGAINST UNAUTHORIZED CHANGES not locked against changes by unauthorized users ○ *an unprotected computer network*

un·pro·vid·ed /ùnprə vídəd/ *adj* not supplied or furnished with something —**un·pro·vid·ed·ly** *adv* ◇ **unprovided for** not provided with money or the means to live adequately

un·pub·lish·a·ble /un púbblishəb'l/ *adj* not fit or feasible to publish, usually because of poor quality or expected poor sales

un·put·down·a·ble /ùn pòot dównəb'l/ *adj* so interesting, entertaining, or exciting that the reader cannot stop reading (*informal*)

un·qual·i·fied /un kwóllə fīd/ *adj* **1.** LACKING REQUIRED QUALIFICATIONS having no academic, professional, or vocational qualifications **2.** GIVEN WITHOUT RESERVATION not limited or modified by any condition or reservation **3.** TOTAL complete and absolute ○ *an unqualified success* —**un·qual·i·fied·ly** *adv*

un·ques·tion·a·ble /un kwéschənəb'l/ *adj* **1.** impossible to doubt, question, or dispute **2.** acknowledged as not subject to doubt or open to question —**un·ques·tion·a·bil·i·ty** /un kwèschənə bílletee/ *n* —**un·ques·tion·a·ble·ness** *n* —**un·ques·tion·a·bly** *adv*

un·ques·tioned /un kwéschənd/ *adj* **1.** not open to questioning, doubt, or dispute **2.** not asked a question or questions

un·ques·tion·ing /un kwéschəning/ *adj* not asking questions, expressing doubt, or hesitating because of questions or doubts —**un·ques·tion·ing·ly** *adv*

un·qui·et /un kwī́ ət/ *adj* **1.** NOISY OR TURBULENT full of noise or unrest **2.** ANXIOUS unsettled or restless, especially in thought or feeling ■ *n* **1.** NOISE OR UNREST a state of noisiness or unrest **2.** ANXIETY restlessness or uneasiness —**un·qui·et·ly** *adv* —**un·qui·et·ness** *n*

un·quote /un kwṓt/ *adv* used when speaking to indicate where the end of a quotation falls ○ *He said, quote, You're fired, unquote.*

un·quot·ed /un kwṓtəd/ *adj* not listed or quoted on a stock exchange

un·raised /ùn ráyzd/ *adj* **1.** made without yeast and therefore fairly flat and firm in consistency **2.** not moved, lifted, or increased to a raised position or level

un·rav·el /un rávv'l/ (**-eled, -el·ing, -els**) *v* **1.** *vti* UNDO KNITTED STRANDS, OR BECOME UNDONE to undo the knitted or woven yarn, thread, or other strands of something, or become undone by having the strands come apart **2.** *vti* BECOME OR MAKE SOMETHING UNDERSTANDABLE to make the complexities of something clear and understandable, or become clear and understandable **3.** *vti* DISENTANGLE OR BECOME DISENTANGLED to separate something out from a tangle or other mass, or become disentangled or separated out **4.** *vi* START TO FAIL to begin to fail or come to an end

un·read /un réd/ *adj* **1.** NOT READ not read, especially by a usual or intended reader **2.** NOT WELL READ having read very little and consequently lacking knowledge acquired from reading **3.** LACKING KNOWLEDGE OF SUBJECT not acquainted with a particular subject through reading

un·read·a·ble /un reédəb'l/ *adj* **1.** NOT ENJOYABLE TO READ impossible to read through being boring, badly written, or intellectually difficult **2.** ILLEGIBLE consisting of letters, words, or symbols that are difficult to identify **3.** IMPOSSIBLE TO INTERPRET impossible to interpret or make sense of ○ *his unreadable face* —**un·read·a·bil·i·ty** /un reédə bíllətee/ *n* —**un·read·a·bly** *adv*

un·read·y /un réddee/ *adj* **1.** UNAVAILABLE not available or prepared for use **2.** NOT PREPARED TO DO SOMETHING not prepared or available to do something or to act **3.** LACKING MENTAL ALERTNESS lacking or displaying a lack of mental alertness or quickness —**un·read·i·ly** *adv* —**un·read·i·ness** *n*

un·re·al /un reé əl/ *adj* **1.** NOT EXISTING having no substance, reality, or existence **2.** FALSE not true or genuine **3.** IMAGINARY imaginary or dreamlike **4.** EXCELLENT excellent or extremely good (*informal*) **5.** INCREDIBLE difficult to believe (*informal*) —**un·re·al·ly** *adv*

un·re·al·i·ty /ùnree állətee/ (*plural* **-ties**) *n* **1.** UNREAL QUALITY an unreal or seemingly unreal state or quality **2.** UNREAL THING something that is not real, genuine, or true, or that lacks substance **3.** INABILITY TO FACE REALITY an inability to accept reality

un·rea·son /un reéz'n/ *n* lack of reason or rationality

un·rea·son·a·ble /un reéz'nəb'l/ *adj* **1.** not acting with or subject to reason **2.** going beyond accepted or reasonable limits —**un·rea·son·a·ble·ness** *n* —**un·rea·son·a·bly** *adv*

un·rea·soned /un reéz'nd/ *adj* not resulting from sound reasoning

un·rea·son·ing /un reéz'ning/ *adj* not guided by sound judgment or reasoning —**un·rea·son·ing·ly** *adv*

un·reck·on·a·ble /un rékənəb'l/ *adj* impossible to calculate

un·re·con·struct·ed /un reèkən strúktəd/ *adj* **1.** retaining outdated beliefs, views, or practices **2.** not rebuilt, restored, or recreated

un·reel /un reél/ (**-reeled, -reel·ing, -reels**) *vti* to unwind something from a reel, or become unwound from it

un·reeve /un reév/ (**-rove** /-rṓv/, **-reeved** or **-rove, -reev·ing, -reeves**) *vti* to pull out a rope or cable from a block or thimble on a ship, or be pulled out from a block or thimble

un·re·fined /ùnri fī́nd/ *adj* **1.** not processed to remove impurities or unwanted substances **2.** not in accord with socially acceptable manners and tastes

un·re·flect·ing /ùnnri flékting/ *adj* showing or resulting from a lack of deep or serious thinking —**un·re·flect·ing·ly** *adv*

un·re·flec·tive /ùnnri fléktiv/ *adj* not thinking or reflecting or resulting from a tendency to not think or reflect —**un·re·flec·tive·ly** *adv*

un·re·gen·er·ate /ùnnri jénnərət/ *adj* **1.** NOT REFORMED not reborn spiritually and not repentant **2.** VIOLATING SOCIAL OR MORAL STRUCTURES behaving in a way regarded as violating social or moral structures **3.** CLINGING TO OUTDATED BELIEFS retaining outdated beliefs, views, or practices **4.** STUBBORN unyielding or stubborn —**un·re·gen·er·a·ble** *adj* —**un·re·gen·er·a·cy** *n* —**un·re·gen·er·ate·ly** *adv*

un·re·lent·ing /ùnnri lénting/ *adj* **1.** unyielding or unswerving in determination or resolve **2.** not weakening, easing up, or otherwise diminishing in strength, speed, or effort —**un·re·lent·ing·ly** *adv* —**un·re·lent·ing·ness** *n*

un·re·li·a·ble /ùnnri lī́ əb'l/ *adj* not able to be relied on or trusted —**un·re·li·a·bil·i·ty** /ùnnri lī̀ ə bíllətee/ *n* —**un·re·li·a·ble·ness** *n* —**un·re·li·a·bly** *adv*

un·re·mark·a·ble /ùnnri maárkəb'l/ *adj* not worthy of special notice or attention because of being ordinary or common

un·re·marked /ùnnri maárkt/ *adj* not noticed or observed

un·re·mit·ting /ùnnri mítting/ *adj* continuing, persisting, or recurring without diminishing or ceasing —**un·re·mit·ting·ly** *adv* —**un·re·mit·ting·ness** *n*

un·re·peat·a·ble /ùnri peétəb'l/ *adj* **1.** too offensive or shocking for the hearer to wish to repeat ○ *His answer was unrepeatable!* **2.** not able to be done or made again ○ *an unrepeatable performance*

un·re·quit·ed /ùnnri kwī́təd/ *adj* **1.** not felt in response, or not returned in the same way or to the same degree **2.** not avenged —**un·re·quit·ed·ly** *adv*

un·re·serve /ùnnri zúrv/ *n* a lack of reserve in showing and expressing feelings or opinions

un·re·served /ùnnri zúrvd/ *adj* **1.** NOT RESERVED FOR SPECIFIC USE not set aside or retained for a specific person or group of people to use **2.** GIVEN WITHOUT QUALIFICATION not limited or modified by any condition or reservation **3.** FRANK OR OPEN not cautious, restrained, or reticent —**un·re·serv·ed·ly** /-zúrvədlee/ *adv* —**un·re·serv·ed·ness** /-zúrvədnəss/ *n*

un·rest /un rést/ *n* **1.** social or political discontent or protest that disrupts the established order **2.** a disturbed, unsettled, or uneasy mental or emotional state

un·re·strained /ùnnri stráynd/ *adj* **1.** not subject to control, restriction, or restraint **2.** natural and uninhibited —**un·re·strain·ed·ly** /ùnri stráynədlee/ *adv* —**un·re·strain·ed·ness** /-stráynədnəss/ *n*

un·rid·dle /un rídd'l/ (**-dled, -dling, -dles**) *vt* to find a solution or explanation for something

un·ri·fled /un rī́f'ld/ *adj* having no spiral grooves (**rifling**) cut on the inside of the barrel

un·right·eous /un rī́chəss/ *adj* **1.** sinful or evil **2.** not just, fair, or right —**un·right·eous·ly** *adv* —**un·right·eous·ness** *n*

un·rip /un ríp/ (**-ripped, -rip·ping, -rips**) *vt* **1.** to open something by ripping **2.** to reveal or divulge something (*archaic*)

un·ripe /un rī́p/ (**-rip·er, -rip·est**) *adj* **1.** not yet ripe or mature **2.** not yet complete or fully developed —**un·ripe·ness** *n*

un·ri·valed /un rī́v'ld/, **un·ri·valled** *adj* having no rival or equal

un·roll /un rṓl/ (**-rolled, -roll·ing, -rolls**) *vti* **1.** to unwind, uncoil, or open up something that is rolled up, or become unwound, uncoiled, or opened up **2.** to disclose something gradually and smoothly, or become disclosed in this way

un·round /un równd/ (**-round·ed, -round·ing, -rounds**) *vt* to pronounce a sound with the lips kept flat —**un·round** *adj*

un·rove NAUT past participle, past tense of **unreeve**

UNRRA *abbr* United Nations Relief and Rehabilitation Administration

un·ruf·fled /un rúff'ld/ *adj* **1.** CALM AND POISED calm and poised, especially in a crisis **2.** SMOOTH having a smooth surface, especially one without ripples **3.** HAVING NO RUFFLE lacking decorative ruffles or ruffling

un·ru·ly /un róolee/ (**-li·er, -li·est**) *adj* difficult to control, manage, discipline, or govern [15C. < archaic *ruly* "disciplined, observing rules" < RULE] —**un·ru·li·ness** *n*

SYNONYMS ***unruly, intractable, recalcitrant, obstreperous, willful, wild, wayward***

CORE MEANING: not submitting to control

unruly difficult to control, manage, discipline, or govern ○ *Police tried to subdue the more unruly elements of the crowd.* ○ *an unruly student who disrupts and unsettles the class* **intractable** stubbornly refusing to be controlled or submit to discipline ○ *Barbara had made up her mind, and she is intractable once she has an idea.* ○ *the problem created by intractable people who refuse to eat the right food to ameliorate their condition* **recalcitrant** stubbornly resisting the authority of another person or group ○ *an armed force sufficient to enforce the law on recalcitrant individuals* ○ *When she spoke, it was in the voice that she reserved for very recalcitrant children.* **obstreperous** noisily and aggressively boisterous ○ *an incident between a shop assistant and an obstreperous customer* **willful** stubbornly determined to act on a desire, regardless of the opinions or advice of others ○ *a willful refusal to answer these specific questions* ○ *the challenge of raising a willful child* **wild** showing a disregard for rules or restraint ○ *We were young, inexperienced, and inclined to be rather wild.* **wayward** disobedient and uncontrollable ○ *The boy's mother found it hard to keep track of her other sometimes wayward children.*

UNRWA *abbr* United Nations Relief and Works Agency

un·sad·dle /un sádd'l/ (**-dled, -dling, -dles**) *v* **1.** *vti* to take a saddle from a horse **2.** *vt* to throw a rider from a saddle

un·said /un séd/ past participle, past tense of **unsay** ■ *adj* not spoken of or discussed, although thought about

un·sat·is·fac·to·ry /un sàtiss fáktəree/ *adj* not adequate, acceptable, or satisfying —**un·sat·is·fac·to·ri·ly** *adv* —**un·sat·is·fac·to·ri·ness** *n*

un·sat·u·rate /un sáchərət/ *n* an unsaturated chemical compound

un·sat·u·rat·ed /un sáchə ràytəd/ *adj* **1.** ABLE TO CONTINUE TO DISSOLVE able to dissolve more of a substance **2.** ABLE TO FORM MORE CARBON BONDS having or able to form double and triple carbon bonds **3.** FOOD HAVING MOLECULES WITH DOUBLE BONDS describes fats with a high proportion of fatty acid molecules with double bonds, that create less cholesterol in the body than saturated fats and are regarded as more healthy in the diet

un·sa·vor·y /un sáyvəree/ *adj* **1.** DISTASTEFUL not pleasant or agreeable **2.** IMMORAL morally unacceptable **3.** UNAPPETIZING tasting or smelling unappetizing —**un·sa·vor·i·ly** *adv* —**un·sa·vor·i·ness** *n*

un·say /un sáy/ (**-said** /-séd/, **-say·ing, -says** /-séz/) *vt* to take back something said as if it has never been said

un·say·a·ble /un sáy əb'l/ *adj* difficult or impossible to say or speak about

un·scathed /un skáy*th*d/ *adj* not hurt, damaged, or harmed in any way

un·schooled /un skóold/ *adj* **1.** not educated or trained **2.** innate and not acquired by education or training

un·sci·en·tif·ic /ùn sī ən tíffik/ *adj* **1.** not following or compatible with the methods and principles of science **2.** not possessing knowledge about science and its methods and principles —**un·sci·en·tif·i·cal·ly** *adv*

un·scram·ble /un skrámb'l/ (**-bled, -bling, -bles**) *vt* **1.** to restore order to something jumbled or confused **2.** to make a message understandable by undoing the effects of scrambling, especially electronic scrambling —**un·scram·bler** *n*

un·screw /un skróo/ (**-screwed, -screw·ing, -screws**) *vti* **1.** REMOVE OR LOOSEN SCREWS OF SOMETHING to remove or loosen a screw or screws holding something in place, or have a screw or screws removed or loosened **2.** OPEN SOMETHING BY REMOVING THREADED LID to open something by turning and removing a threaded lid or cap, or be opened in this way **3.** TURN TO REMOVE OR ADJUST SOMETHING to remove or adjust something by rotating, or be removed or adjusted by rotating

un·script·ed /un skríptəd/ *adj* **1.** not having a script that was written or agreed on in advance **2.** not planned or expected

un·scru·pu·lous /un skrōōpyələss/ *adj* not restrained by moral or ethical principles —**un·scru·pu·lous·ly** *adv* —**un·scru·pu·lous·ness** *n*

un·seal /un seel/ (**-sealed, -seal·ing, -seals**) *vt* **1.** to break or remove the seal of something, or to open something by breaking a seal or closure **2.** to free something from constraint or restriction —**un·seal·a·ble** *adj*

un·seam /un seem/ (**-seamed, -seam·ing, -seams**) *vt* to unpick a seam or seams of something

un·search·a·ble /un súrchəb'l/ *adj* not capable of being searched or investigated —**un·search·a·ble·ness** *n* —**un·search·a·bly** *adv*

un·sea·son·a·ble /un seez'nəb'l/ *adj* **1.** not usual or appropriate for the time of year **2.** not occurring at the right time or at a good time —**un·sea·son·a·ble·ness** *n* —**un·sea·son·a·bly** *adv*

un·seat /un seet/ (**-seat·ed, -seat·ing, -seats**) *vt* **1.** to remove somebody from office or a position, especially by means of an election **2.** to eject somebody from a seat, especially a saddle

un·se·cured /ùnssə kyōōrd/ *adj* **1.** LACKING SECURITY not protected against financial loss **2.** NOT MADE SECURE not fastened, held in place, or otherwise made secure **3.** UNPROTECTED FROM BUGGING not protected against electronic eavesdropping

un·seed·ed /un seedəd/ *adj* not assigned a position in a draw arranged so that the best players or teams can, in theory, avoid meeting until the later rounds

un·seem·ly /un seemlee/ *adj* **1.** NOT IN GOOD TASTE contrary to accepted standards of good taste or appropriate behavior **2.** INCONVENIENT occurring at an inconvenient time or place ■ *adv* IN UNSEEMLY MANNER in an improper or inappropriate manner —**un·seem·li·ness** *n*

un·seen /un seen/ *adj* **1.** not observed, noticed, watched, or examined **2.** done or comprehended without previous study or practice

un·sel·fish /un sélfish/ *adj* putting the general good or the needs or interests of others first —**un·sel·fish·ly** *adv* —**un·sel·fish·ness** *n*

un·sell /un sél/ (**-sold** /-sṓld/, **-sell·ing, -sells**) *vt US* to convince somebody that something is false or worthless

un·set /un sét/ *adj* **1.** NOT HARDENED not hardened or firm **2.** NOT READY not prepared or made ready **3.** NOT MOUNTED not mounted in a jewelry setting

un·set·tle /un sétt'l/ (**-tled, -tling, -tles**) *vt* **1.** to make somebody ill at ease or insecure **2.** to disrupt the orderly, fixed, or established state of something —**un·set·tle·ment** *n*

un·set·tled /un sétt'ld/ *adj* **1.** NOT DECIDED not resolved, determined, or decided ○ *an unsettled issue* **2.** CHANGEABLE changing frequently within a given period of time ○ *unsettled weather* **3.** LACKING ORDER OR STABILITY characterized by a lack of order or stability ○ *an unsettled political climate* **4.** NOT LEGALLY RESOLVED not resolved as required by law ○ *an unsettled lawsuit* **5.** UNCERTAIN not sure, or full of doubt ○ *He was unsettled about his future at the firm.* **6.** MOVING not being in a condition or position of rest ○ *unsettled sediment in the water* **7.** UNINHABITED not inhabited or colonized ○ *unsettled territory* **8.** UNPAID not paid or fulfilled ○ *unsettled debts* **9.** ITINERANT not regular or fixed ○ *an unsettled lifestyle* —**un·set·tled·ness** *n*

un·set·tling /un séttling/ *adj* producing a feeling of unease or insecurity

un·sex /un séks/ (**-sexed, -sex·ing, -sex·es**) *vt* **1.** to strip away from somebody the qualities stereotypically associated with his or her sex ○*"Come, you spirits /That tend on mortal thoughts, unsex me here"* (William Shakespeare, *Macbeth*; c. 1605) **2.** to deprive somebody of the ability to have sex

UNSF *abbr* United Nations Special Fund for Economic Development

un·shack·le /un shák'l/ (**-led, -ling, -les**) *vt* **1.** to release somebody from restrictions or constraints **2.** to release somebody from shackles

un·shak·a·ble /un sháykəb'l/, **un·shake·a·ble** *adj* not subject to doubt or uncertainty —**un·shak·a·bly** *adv*

un·shaped /un sháypt/, **un·shap·en** /un sháypən/ *adj* **1.** not yet shaped, formed, or finished **2.** having a final or finished form or state that is imperfect

un·sheathe /un sheeth/ (**-sheathed, -sheath·ing, -sheathes**) *vt* to remove a sword from a sheath

un·shift /un shíft/ (**-shift·ed, -shift·ing, -shifts**) *vi* to release the depressed shift key on the keyboard of a computer or typewriter

un·ship /un shíp/ (**-shipped, -ship·ping, -ships**) *vti* **1.** to unload something from a ship, or be unloaded **2.** to move something out of its usual position on a ship, or be moved out of the usual position on a ship

un·shod /un shód/ *adj* not wearing shoes or horseshoes

un·shriv·en /un shrívv'n/ *adj* not having confessed sins to a priest and been given absolution

un·sight·ed /un sītəd/ *adj* **1.** UNDETECTED not seen or noticed **2.** NOT FITTED WITH SIGHT FOR AIMING not fitted with a sight or sights to help with aiming **3.** WITHOUT CLEAR VIEW not having a clear view, e.g., because of an obstruction

un·sight·ly /un sītlee/ *adj* not pleasant to look at, or spoiling the appearance of something ○ *an unsightly addition to the building* —**un·sight·li·ness** *n*

SYNONYMS See *unattractive.*

un·signed /un sīnd/ *adj* **1.** LACKING SIGNATURE having no signature **2.** NOT SIGNED TO PLAY FOR TEAM not having signed a contract to join a sports team as a player **3.** MATH, COMPUT LACKING PLUS OR MINUS SIGN having no plus or minus sign, or having no digit in binary notation representing a positive or negative value

un·skil·ful *adj* Can, UK spelling of **unskillful**

un·skilled /un skíld/ *adj* **1.** NOT REQUIRING SPECIAL SKILLS not requiring special training, education, or skill **2.** LACKING SKILL lacking skill or the basic or proper skills **3.** LACKING TRAINING lacking the skills acquired through technical training or higher education **4.** DONE WITHOUT SKILL done without skill, or displaying a lack of the basic or proper skills

un·skill·ful /un skílfəl/ *adj* lacking or done without skill or expertise —**un·skill·ful·ly** *adv* —**un·skill·ful·ness** *n*

un·slaked lime /ún slaykt-/ *n* CHEM same as **calcium hydroxide**

un·sling /un slíng/ (**-slung, -slung** /-slúng/, **-sling·ing, -slings**) *vt* **1.** REMOVE SOMETHING SLUNG to remove something that has been slung, especially over the shoulder or shoulders **2.** REMOVE SOMETHING FROM SLING to take something out of a sling **3.** NAUT REMOVE SUPPORTING ROPES FROM SOMETHING to remove the supporting ropes or chains (**slings**) from something

un·smil·ing /un smīling/ *adj* looking serious and showing no signs of pleasure, amusement, or approval ○ *his grim unsmiling manner*

un·snag /un snág/ (**-snagged, -snag·ging, -snags**) *vt* **1.** to free something caught on an obstruction **2.** to remove a difficulty or difficulties impeding the progress or development of something

un·snap /un snáp/ (**-snapped, -snap·ping, -snaps**) *vt* to release or open something by unfastening a snap or snaps

un·snarl /un snaarl/ (**-snarled, -snarl·ing, -snarls**) *vt* to free something from a snarl or snarls

un·so·cia·ble /un sṓshəb'l/ *adj* **1.** not liking or seeking the company of other people **2.** not favoring or encouraging social interaction —**un·so·cia·bil·i·ty** /un sṓshə bíllətee/ *n* —**un·so·cia·ble·ness** *n* —**un·so·cia·bly** *adv*

USAGE unsociable or **antisocial**? These words can both refer to somebody who avoids the company of others, but ***unsociable*** is less strong in force than ***antisocial***, which often indicates behavior or attitudes that are hostile or indifferent to other people.

un·so·cial /un sṓsh'l/ *adj* **1.** PREFERRING OWN COMPANY not liking or seeking the company of other people **2.** CHARACTERISTIC OF UNSOCIAL PERSON characterized or caused by a dislike of the company of other people **3.** ANTISOCIAL annoying, inconsiderate, or indifferent to the needs of others —**un·so·cial·ly** *adv*

un·sold /ùn sṓld/ COMM past participle, past tense of **unsell** ■ *adj* not bought by anybody

un·so·lic·it·ed /ùnssə líssitəd/ *adj* given, sent, or received without being requested

un·so·phis·ti·cat·ed /ùnssə fístə kàytəd/ *adj* **1.** naive, inexperienced, and not wise in the ways of the world **2.** simple and lacking in refinements —**un·so·phis·ti·cat·ed·ly** *adv* —**un·so·phis·ti·cat·ed·ness** *n* —**un·so·phis·ti·ca·tion** /ùnssə fistə káysh'n/ *n*

un·sought /un sáwt/ *adj* not looked for or asked for

un·sound /un sównd/ *adj* **1.** NOT RELIABLE not based on reliable facts, information, or reasoning ○ *an unsound conclusion* **2.** UNHEALTHY not in a healthy physical or psychological state **3.** NOT SOLID OR FIRM in a structurally poor or dangerous state ○ *unsound foundations* **4.** FINANCIALLY INSECURE not safe or secure financially ○ *an unsound investment* **5.** DISTURBED AND NOT RESTFUL characterized by periods of restlessness ○ *unsound sleep* —**un·sound·ly** *adv* —**un·sound·ness** *n*

un·spar·ing /un spérring/ *adj* **1.** not frugal or stingy with something **2.** harsh or without mercy —**un·spar·ing·ly** *adv* —**un·spar·ing·ness** *n*

un·speak·a·ble /un speekəb'l/ *adj* **1.** EXTREMELY BAD OR AWFUL so bad or awful as to be impossible to describe in words **2.** NOT DESCRIBABLE IN WORDS incapable of being described in words **3.** NOT TO BE SPOKEN OF not allowed to be spoken of, mentioned, or talked about —**un·speak·a·ble·ness** *n* —**un·speak·a·bly** *adv*

un·spe·cial·ized /un spésh'l īzd/ *adj* **1.** not having a special use or purpose **2.** not concerned or involved with just one specialized area of knowledge or skill

un·spoiled /un spóyld/ *adj* **1.** UNCHANGED BY DEVELOPMENT not changed for the worse by modern civilization, industry, or tourism **2.** NOT DAMAGED not damaged or physically harmed **3.** UNFLAWED not lessened or diminished by flaws or imperfections **4.** NOT RUINED IN CHARACTER not ruined in character as a result of success, wealth, or overindulgence

un·spo·ken /un spṓkən/ *adj* not uttered or talked about, although thought about

un·sports·man·like /un spáwrtsmən līk/ *adj* being or acting contrary to fair play or the rules and spirit of a sport or of sports in general

un·spot·ted /un spóttəd/ *adj* **1.** NOT SPOTTED OR STAINED not soiled with spots or stains **2.** MORALLY UNBLEMISHED not marred by moral or ethical lapses or failures **3.** UNOBSERVED not seen or observed —**un·spot·ted·ness** *n*

un·sprung /un sprúng/ *adj* having no springs or having the springs removed

un·sta·ble /un stáyb'l/ *adj* **1.** NOT FIXED not firm, solid, or fixed ○ *unstable ground* **2.** LIKELY TO FALL OR COLLAPSE likely to fall, collapse, or sway ○ *unstable scaffolding* **3.** LACKING EMOTIONAL OR PSYCHOLOGICAL STABILITY lacking, or resulting from a lack of, emotional control or psychological stability ○ *unstable behavior* **4.** CHANGEABLE apt to change ○ *unstable weather* **5.** UNSTEADY IN PURPOSE OR INTENT unsteady or unsure in purpose or intent ○ *political support that is unstable* **6.** PHYS HAVING SHORT HALF-LIFE having a brief existence or half-life **7.** PHYS SUBJECT TO SPONTANEOUS CHANGE describes a particle that is subject to spontaneous change such as radioactive decay —**un·sta·ble·ness** *n* —**un·sta·bly** *adv*

un·stead·y /un stéddee/ *adj* **1.** NOT FIXED not firm, solid, or fixed **2.** TOTTERING staggering or tottering in walking **3.** LIKELY TO MOVE likely to move or shift position ○ *an unsteady ladder* **4.** CHANGEABLE subject to large and frequent changes ○ *unsteady financial markets* **5.** IRREGULAR IN RHYTHM irregular in movement, rhythm, or pitch ○ *a voice that is unsteady* **6.** NOT CONSTANT OR RELIABLE not constant in purpose or actions ■ *vt* (**-ied, -y·ing, -ies**) MAKE SOMETHING UNSTEADY to cause something to become unsteady —**un·stead·i·ly** *adv* —**un·stead·i·ness** *n*

un·steel /un steel/ (**-steeled, -steel·ing, -steels**) *vt* to soften or weaken somebody's harsh attitude or firm resolve

un·step /un stép/ (**-stepped, -step·ping, -steps**) *vt* to take a mast out of its step or socket

un·stick /un stík/ (**-stuck, -stuck** /-stúk/, **-stick·ing, -sticks**) *vt* to cause something to stop sticking

un·stint·ing /un stínting/ *adj* given or giving generously —**un·stint·ing·ly** *adv*

un·stop /un stóp/ (**-stopped, -stop·ping, -stops**) *vt* **1.** TAKE STOPPER FROM SOMETHING to remove a stopper from something **2.** UNBLOCK SOMETHING to remove a blockage from something **3.** MUSIC PULL OUT STOPS OF ORGAN to pull out the stops of an organ

un·stop·pa·ble /un stóppəb'l/ *adj* not capable of being halted, or not easily halted —**un·stop·pa·bly** *adv*

un·stopped /un stópt/ *adj* **1.** NOT BLOCKED OR STOPPERED not blocked, closed, or stoppered **2.** NOT HALTED able to continue without being halted **3.** PHON ARTICULATED WITH VOCAL ORGANS PARTLY OPEN articulated without a complete closure of the vocal organs

un·strained /un stráynd/ *adj* **1.** not put through a strainer to remove lumps **2.** not subjected to strain

un·strat·i·fied /un stráttə fīd/ *adj* **1.** not arranged in or forming layers or strata **2.** not arranged in or forming social classes, grades, or ranks

un·stressed /un strést/ *adj* **1.** not accented or emphasized in pronunciation **2.** not subjected to physical, psychological, or emotional pressure

un·stri·at·ed /un strī àytəd/ *adj* lacking transverse striations

un·string /un stríng/ (**-strung** /-strúng/, **-string·ing, -strings**) *vt* **1.** REMOVE STRINGS OF SOMETHING to remove or loosen a string or strings of something **2.** REMOVE SOMETHING FROM STRING to remove something from a string or wire **3.** UPSET SOMEBODY to make somebody upset or nervous

un·struc·tured /un strúkchərd/ *adj* **1.** NOT ORGANIZED INTO HIERARCHY not organized into a hierarchy or similar system **2.** NOT ORDERED OR CONVENTIONALLY ARRANGED not forced to conform to a specific order or arrangement, especially a conventional one **3.** CLOTHING LOOSE AND FLOWING not tailored to fit tightly, but flowing freely

un·strung /un strúng/ past participle, past tense of **unstring** ■ *adj* **1.** UPSET upset or nervous **2.** LACKING STRINGS having a string or strings missing, removed, or loosened **3.** NOT ON STRING not threaded on a string or wire

un·stuck /un stúk/ past participle, past tense of **unstick** ■ *adj* freed from being stuck or adhering to something

un·stud·ied /un stúddeed/ *adj* **1.** NATURAL natural or casual in manner **2.** NOT LEARNED THROUGH STUDYING not acquired through studying or training **3.** NOT KNOWLEDGEABLE lacking the knowledge and understanding of a particular field that is acquired through studying or training

un·sub·scribe /ùns səb scrīb/ *vi* to end a subscription to or registration with something, especially an e-mail mailing list

un·sub·stan·tial /ùnssəb stánshəl/ *adj* **1.** IMMATERIAL not having physical substance **2.** FLIMSY not strong or firm **3.** NOT TRUE OR BASED ON FACT having no basis in truth or fact —**un·sub·stan·ti·al·i·ty** /ùnssəb stanshee állətee/ *n* —**un·sub·stan·tial·ly** *adv*

un·sub·stan·ti·at·ed /ùnssəb stánshee àytəd/ *adj* not proven factually

un·suc·cess·ful /ùnssək sésfəl/ *adj* **1.** NOT RESULTING IN SUCCESS not resulting in success or turning out favorably **2.** NOT ACHIEVING SUCCESS not achieving an intended objective or goal **3.** LACKING RECORD OF SIGNIFICANT ACHIEVEMENTS not having achieved or gained wealth, fame, or power —**un·suc·cess·ful·ly** *adv* —**un·suc·cess·ful·ness** *n*

un·suit·a·ble /un so͞otəb'l/ *adj* not appropriate or becoming —**un·suit·a·bil·i·ty** /un so͞otə bíllətee/ *n* —**un·suit·a·ble·ness** *n* —**un·suit·a·bly** *adv*

un·sung /un súng/ *adj* **1.** not given the praise or honor that is due **2.** not sung or not to be sung

un·sup·port·a·ble /ùnssə páwrtəb'l/ *adj* **1.** INDEFENSIBLE impossible to defend or excuse **2.** INTOLERABLE impossible to tolerate or endure **3.** IMPOSSIBLE TO SUPPORT PHYSICALLY impossible to support physically in order to prevent collapse

un·sure /un sho͝or/ *adj* **1.** lacking clear knowledge or a definite opinion **2.** lacking in confidence —**un·sure·ly** *adv* —**un·sure·ness** *n*

SYNONYMS See ***doubtful***.

un·sur·pris·ing /ùnssər prīzing/ *adj* not causing surprise, usually because not unexpected —**un·sur·pris·ing·ly** *adv*

un·sus·pect·ed /ùnssə spéktəd/ *adj* **1.** not known or believed to exist **2.** not under suspicion of having done something —**un·sus·pect·ed·ly** *adv*

un·sus·pect·ing /ùnssə spékting/ *adj* not suspicious of somebody or something —**un·sus·pect·ing·ly** *adv*

un·swerv·ing /un swúrving/ *adj* **1.** firm and unchanging in intent or purpose **2.** not turning to the side or otherwise altering the direction of movement —**un·swerv·ing·ly** *adv*

un·tan·gle /un táng g'l/ (**-gled, -gling, -gles**) *vt* **1.** REMOVE TANGLES FROM SOMETHING to undo the tangles in something such as yarn or hair **2.** STRAIGHTEN OUT SOMETHING COMPLEX to clarify or resolve something that is intricate or puzzling **3.** FREE SOMEBODY FROM BAD SITUATION to remove somebody from a difficult or complicated situation

un·tapped /un tápt/ *adj* **1.** not yet in use, but available ○ *untapped talents* **2.** not yet opened or tapped

un·taught /un táwt/ *adj* **1.** past participle, past tense of **unteach** **2.** ignorant or lacking a formal education **3.** arising from innate or natural talent or ability, not from instruction

un·teach /un te͞ech/ (**-taught** /un táwt/, **-teach·ing, -teach·es**) *vt US* **1.** to cause somebody to forget something previously learned **2.** to reverse somebody's opinion or belief about something previously learned

un·ten·a·ble /un ténnəb'l/ *adj* lacking the qualities such as sound reasoning or high ground that make defense possible ○ *an untenable position* —**un·ten·a·bil·i·ty** /un tènnə bíllətee/ *n* —**un·ten·a·ble·ness** *n* —**un·ten·a·bly** *adv*

un·teth·er /un té*th*ər/ (**-ered, -er·ing, -ers**) *vt* **1.** to free a person or animal from a restraining rope or other tie **2.** to give vent to something such as an emotion after keeping it suppressed —**un·teth·ered** *adj*

un·think /un thíngk/ (**-thought** /-tháwt/, **-think·ing, -thinks**) *vt* **1.** to stop thinking about something **2.** to change a view or opinion about something

un·think·a·ble /un thíngkəb'l/ *adj* **1.** OUT OF QUESTION too strange or extreme even to be considered **2.** INCONCEIVABLE impossible even to conceive of **3.** UNLIKELY TO HAPPEN highly unlikely to happen or succeed **4.** TERRIBLE extremely frightening or unpleasant —**un·think·a·bil·i·ty** /un thìngkə bíllətee/ *n* —**un·think·a·ble·ness** *n* —**un·think·a·bly** *adv*

un·think·ing /un thíngking/ *adj* **1.** INCONSIDERATE not thoughtful or considerate of other people **2.** HEEDLESS not giving proper consideration to the possible effects or consequences of what is said or done **3.** UNAWARE unable or unwilling to think deeply about things —**un·think·ing·ly** *adv* —**un·think·ing·ness** *n*

un·thought past participle, past tense of **unthink**

un·thread /un thréd/ (**-thread·ed, -thread·ing, -threads**) *vt* **1.** to remove the thread or threads from something **2.** to remove somebody or something with difficulty from a demanding or complicated situation

un·ti·dy /un tīdee/ *adj* (**-di·er, -di·est**) **1.** NOT NEAT not neat or tidy **2.** DISORDERED not properly organized or ordered ■ *vt* (**-died, -dy·ing, -dies**) MESS SOMETHING UP to mess up something that was tidy —**un·ti·di·ly** *adv* —**un·ti·di·ness** *n*

un·tie /un tī/ (**-tied, -ty·ing, -ties**) *v* **1.** *vti* UNDO KNOT IN SOMETHING to loosen or unfasten a knot or similar fastening in something such as a string, ribbon, or rope, or be loosened or unfastened **2.** *vt* FREE SOMETHING FROM RESTRAINT to release or free somebody or something that is tied up **3.** *vt* RESOLVE DIFFICULTY to resolve a difficult or complicated situation

un·til /un tíl/ *conj, prep* **1.** up to a time or event, but not afterward ○ (conj) *I lived with my grandparents until I was ten.* ○ (prep) *from the late 1980s until 1994* **2.** before a time or event (*used in negative statements*) ○ (conj) *She agreed not to write about the case until a verdict was reached.* ○ (prep) *He did not open his mail until Monday.* [12C. < assumed Old Norse *und* "till" + TILL[1]]

USAGE See ***till***[1].

~~**untill**~~ incorrect spelling of **until**

un·time·ly /un tīmlee/ *adj* **1.** OCCURRING AT BAD TIME happening or done at a bad or inconvenient time ○ *an untimely decision* **2.** PREMATURE happening before the expected time ○ *his untimely death* ■ *adv* **1.** AT INAPPROPRIATE TIME at a bad or inconvenient time **2.** PREMATURELY earlier than wanted or expected —**un·time·li·ness** *n*

un·tir·ing /un tīring/ *adj* **1.** not growing weary or exhausted **2.** continuing in spite of difficulty or frustration ○ *her untiring efforts* —**un·tir·ing·ly** *adv*

un·ti·tled /un tīt'ld/ *adj* **1.** UNNAMED not having a name or title **2.** NOT BELONGING TO NOBILITY possessing no aristocratic title **3.** WITHOUT PROPER CLAIM having no legitimate right or claim

un·to *stressed* /úntoo/; *unstressed* /únto͝o, -tə/ *prep* (*archaic*) **1.** used to indicate that something is said, given, or done to somebody ○ *the elders of Gilead said unto Jephthah* ○ *and they said unto God* **2.** used to indicate that something continues until a particular time ○ *faithful unto death* [13C. < UNTIL, with TO[1] replacing TILL[1]]

un·told /un tōld/ *adj* **1.** too great or numerous to be properly described or counted **2.** not having been revealed or related

un·touch·a·ble /un túchəb'l/ *adj* **1.** NOT TO BE TOUCHED not able or allowed to be touched **2.** OUT OF REACH completely out of reach **3.** ABOVE CRITICISM too well known or important to be investigated or criticized **4.** DISAGREEABLE TO TOUCH unpleasant or disagreeable to touch ■ *n also* **Un·touch·a·ble** OFFENSIVE TERM an offensive term for a member of the hereditary Hindu class that was formerly segregated and regarded as ritually unclean by the four castes, and performed tasks that were considered polluting. Gandhi's alternative term (**Harijan**) meaning "children of God" has also been rejected by many in favor of a term (**Dalit**) meaning "the oppressed." —**un·touch·a·bil·i·ty** /un tùchə bíllətee/ *n* —**un·touch·a·bly** *adv*

un·touched /un túcht/ *adj* **1.** UNINJURED not injured, damaged, or harmed **2.** NOT TOUCHED not touched or handled **3.** UNEATEN not eaten or consumed **4.** UNALTERED not changed or altered **5.** EMOTIONALLY UNAFFECTED emotionally unaffected by something **6.** NOT MENTIONED omitted from mention or discussion

un·to·ward /un táwrd, -tə wáwrd/ *adj* **1.** INAPPROPRIATE not appropriate or fitting ○ *untoward rudeness* **2.** UNEXPECTED unusual or unexpected ○ *an untoward piece of luck* **3.** CAUSING MISFORTUNE causing misfortune or disadvantage ○ *several untoward events* —**un·to·ward·ly** *adv* —**un·to·ward·ness** *n*

un·tram·meled /un trámm'ld/ *adj* not restricted or restrained

un·trav·eled /un trávv'ld/ *adj* **1.** not having wide knowledge or experience of the world **2.** never or rarely traveled along ○ *an untraveled path*

un·tried /un trīd/ *adj* **1.** not tried, tested, or proved **2.** not tried in a court of law

un·trou·bled /un trúbb'ld/ *adj* **1.** not bothered, uneasy, or distracted by something **2.** tranquil and without disturbances ○ *untroubled sleep*

un·true /un tro͞o/ *adj* **1.** WRONG OR FALSE not in accordance with the facts or what is known **2.** UNFAITHFUL not faithful or loyal to somebody **3.** NOT PRECISE not precise or accurate according to a standard or measure —**un·tru·ly** *adv*

un·truth /un tro͞oth/ *n* **1.** something that is presented as being true, but is actually false ○ *accused of telling untruths* **2.** a lack of truth, especially as a result of lying

SYNONYMS See *lie*[2].

un·truth·ful /un tro͞othfəl/ *adj* **1.** not in accordance with the facts or what is known **2.** lying or failing to tell the truth —**un·truth·ful·ly** *adv* —**un·truth·ful·ness** *n*

un·tu·tored /un to͞otərd/ *adj* **1.** not formally educated or trained **2.** lacking any awareness of or interest in what is socially acceptable behavior

un·un·bi·um /ùn un be͞e əm/ *n* a highly unstable radioactive chemical element, produced artificially by nuclear fusion, with an atomic number of 112. Symbol **Uub**. See table at **element** [Late 20C. < Latin *unus* "one" (repeated) + *bi* "two" (see BI-), representing 112, its atomic number]

un·un·hex·i·um /ùn un héksee əm/ *n* a highly unstable, artificially produced radioactive chemical element with an atomic number of 116. Symbol **Uuh**. See table at **element** [Late 20C. < Latin *unus* "one" (repeated) + Greek *hex* "six," representing 116, its atomic number]

un·un·nil·i·um /ùn un íllee əm/ *n* former name for **darmstadtium**. See table at **element** [Late 20C. < Latin *unus* "one" (repeated) + *nil* "nothing," representing 110, its atomic number]

un·un·pen·ti·um /ùn un péntee əm/ *n* a highly unstable radioactive chemical element with an atomic number of 115 reported to have been produced artificially by bombarding americium with calcium atoms. Symbol **Uup**. See table at **element** [Late 20C. < Latin *unus* "one" (repeated) + Greek *pente* "five," representing 115, its atomic number]

un·un·qua·di·um /ùn un kwáydee əm/ *n* a highly unstable radioactive chemical element, produced artificially by nuclear fusion, with an atomic number of 114. Symbol **Uuq**. See table at **element** [Late 20C. < Latin *unus* "one" (repeated) + shortening of *quadri-* "four" (see QUADRI-), representing 114, its atomic number]

un·un·tri·um /ùn un treé əm/ *n* a highly unstable radioactive chemical element with an atomic number of 113 reported to have been produced artificially by bombarding americium with calcium atoms. Symbol **Uut**. See table at **element** [Late 20C. < Latin *unus* "one" (repeated) + *tri-* "three" (see TRI-), representing 113, its atomic number]

un·un·un·i·um /ùn un únnee əm/ *n* a highly unstable radioactive chemical element, produced artificially by nuclear fusion, with an atomic number of 111. Symbol **Uuu**. See table at **element** [Late 20C. < Latin *unus* "one" (repeated), representing 111, its atomic number]

un·used /un yóozd/ *adj* **1.** NOT USED never having been used ○ *unused matches* **2.** NOT IN USE not being put to use ○ *unused land* **3.** /un yóost/ UNFAMILIAR not familiar with or accustomed to something ○ *Our dog is unused to city traffic.*

un·u·su·al /un yóozhoo əl/ *adj* **1.** remarkable or out of the ordinary **2.** not common or familiar —**un·u·su·al·ly** *adv* —**un·u·su·al·ness** *n*

un·ut·ter·a·ble /un úttərəb'l/ *adj* **1.** producing such an intense emotional reaction as to be impossible to express or describe ○ *scenes of unutterable sadness* **2.** impossible to pronounce or say —**un·ut·ter·a·ble·ness** *n* —**un·ut·ter·a·bly** *adv*

un·val·ued /un vállyood/ *adj* **1.** NOT VALUED not regarded as valuable, especially when true value is being overlooked **2.** NOT APPRAISED not assigned a value **3.** PRICELESS so valuable as to have no price in monetary terms (*archaic*)

un·valved /un válvd/ *adj* describes a brass musical instrument that has no valves to extend the range of notes it can play

un·var·nished /un vaárnisht/ *adj* **1.** said or presented without any attempt to disguise the truth ○ *the unvarnished facts* **2.** having no protective or decorative coat of varnish

un·veil /un váyl/ (**-veiled, -veil·ing, -veils**) *v* **1.** *vt* EXPOSE SOMETHING SECRET to reveal something that has been hidden or kept secret **2.** *vt* TAKE COVERING OFF SOMETHING to remove a veil or other covering from something, especially somebody's face or a plaque, monument, or artwork during a formal ceremony **3.** *vi* TAKE OFF VEIL to remove a veil from your face

un·veil·ing /un váyling/ *n* **1.** the formal removal of a covering that has hidden a plaque, monument, or artwork **2.** the revelation of something that has been hidden or kept secret

un·voice /un vóyss/ (**-voiced, -voic·ing, -voic·es**) *vt* PHON same as **devoice**

un·voiced /un vóyst/ *adj* **1.** not spoken or explicitly stated **2.** pronounced without vibration of the vocal chords

un·war·rant·a·ble /un wáwrəntəb'l/ *adj* unable to be justified or condoned —**un·war·rant·a·bly** *adv*

un·war·rant·ed /un wáwrəntəd/ *adj* not justified or deserved —**un·war·rant·ed·ly** *adv*

un·war·y /un wérree/ *adj* failing to be alert and cautious —**un·war·i·ly** *adv* —**un·war·i·ness** *n*

un·washed /un wósht, -wáwsht/ *adj* **1.** not having been washed **2.** an offensive term meaning belonging to the lower social classes ◇ **the great unwashed** an offensive term for the mass of ordinary people

un·watch·a·ble /un wóchəb'l/ *adj* too bad to be worth watching, or too unpleasant and distressing to watch

un·wa·ver·ing /un wáyvəring/ *adj* firm in view or purpose and unable to be swayed or diverted from it —**un·wa·ver·ing·ly** *adv*

un·wea·ried /un weéreed/ *adj* **1.** performing a task or promoting a cause without ceasing **2.** not tired, e.g., from working or playing —**un·wea·ried·ly** *adv*

un·well /un wél/ *adj* not in good health

un·wept /un wépt/ *adj* **1.** held back and not allowed to flow from the eyes ○ *unwept tears* **2.** not cried for or mourned as a loss (*literary*)

un·whole·some /un hṓlssəm/ *adj* **1.** UNHEALTHY harmful to health ○ *unwholesome eating habits* **2.** REGARDED AS HARMFUL TO MORALS regarded as being harmful to character or morals **3.** LOOKING UNHEALTHY unhealthy in appearance ○ *an unwholesome pallor* —**un·whole·some·ly** *adv* —**un·whole·some·ness** *n*

~~**unwieldly**~~ incorrect spelling of **unwieldy**

un·wield·y /un weéldee/ *adj* **1.** hard to handle because of being large, heavy, or awkward **2.** too complex or extensive to be manageable —**un·wield·i·ly** *adv* —**un·wield·i·ness** *n*

USAGE This word is often incorrectly spelled and pronounced *unwieldly*, as if it were formed with the common adjectival ending *-ly*.

un·will·ing /un wílling/ *adj* **1.** not willing to do something ○ *unwilling to participate* **2.** given reluctantly or grudgingly ○ *unwilling assistance* —**un·will·ing·ly** *adv* —**un·will·ing·ness** *n*

SYNONYMS ***unwilling, reluctant, disinclined, averse, hesitant, loath***

CORE MEANING: lacking the desire to do something

unwilling not willing to do something ○ *The authorities seem unable or unwilling to take tough action.* ○ *He viciously put down rebellions, trying to impose his harsh regime on his unwilling subjects* **reluctant** showing no enthusiasm for doing something ○ *Most elderly people value their independence and are often reluctant to accept help.* **disinclined** without a strong motivation to do something ○ *a weapon of last resort that the government is disinclined to use* ○ *The obvious lack of consensus made us disinclined to pursue the matter further.* **averse** (*formal*) strongly opposed to or disliking something ○ *Neither country is averse to using the desperate plight of millions to arouse resentment of the West.* ○ *not averse to marriage* **hesitant** slow to do or say something because of indecision or lack of confidence ○ *Throughout the first set, both players looked tense and were hesitant to attack.* ○ *hesitant about getting involved* **loath** unwilling or reluctant to do something ○ *Today's Hollywood producers are notoriously loath to take chances on newcomers.*

un·wind /un wínd/ (**-wound** /-wównd/, **-wind·ing, -winds**) *v* **1.** *vti* UNCOIL to undo something such as tape or cable by winding, or come undone in this way **2.** *vt* UNTANGLE SOMETHING to remove or undo the tangles in something **3.** *vti* RELAX to relieve somebody of tension or worry, or obtain relief from tension or worry ○ *It's sometimes hard to unwind at the end of a busy day.* —**un·wind·a·ble** *adj*

un·wire /un wír/ (**-wired, -wir·ing, -wires**) *vti* to stop using hard-wired, landline technology in, e.g., a business environment and adopt wireless communication technology ○ *needed to unwire the office system for higher performance ratings* [Early 21C.]

un·wis·dom /un wízdəm/ *n* a lack of wisdom, judgment, or good sense

un·wise /un wíz/ (**-wis·er, -wis·est**) *adj* lacking wisdom, judgment, or good sense —**un·wise·ly** *adv*

un·wish /un wísh/ (**-wished, -wish·ing, -wish·es**) *vt* **1.** to undo or take back a wish **2.** to want something not to be or not to happen

un·wit·ting /un wítting/ *adj* **1.** unaware of what is happening in a situation **2.** said or done unintentionally [Old English *unwitende* < present participle of *witan* "become aware of, learn" < Germanic] —**un·wit·ting·ly** *adv*

un·wont·ed /un wáwntəd, -wṓnt-, -wúnt-/ *adj* unexpected or unusual —**un·wont·ed·ly** *adv* —**un·wont·ed·ness** *n*

un·work·a·ble /un wúrkəb'l/ *adj* **1.** NOT PRACTICAL too complicated or ambitious to be accomplished or established **2.** INDUST NOT ABLE TO BE WORKED unable to be cut, shaped, or otherwise fashioned **3.** AGRIC IMPOSSIBLE TO FARM so hard or rocky as to be impossible to farm —**un·work·a·bil·i·ty** /un wùrkə bíllətee/ *n* —**un·work·a·ble·ness** *n* —**un·work·a·bly** *adv*

un·world·ly /un wúrldlee/ *adj* **1.** NOT MATERIALISTIC not interested in money or material goods **2.** INEXPERIENCED lacking experience of the world **3.** NOT OF THIS WORLD not concerned with or part of the material world —**un·world·li·ness** *n*

un·worn /un wáwrn/ *adj* **1.** NOT WORN not previously or recently worn ○ *an unworn shirt* **2.** LIKE NEW in good condition, and not worn out or ruined ○ *unworn tires* **3.** FRESH original rather than trite or stale

un·wor·thy /un wúr*th*ee/ *adj* **1.** UNDESERVING not deserving something, e.g., a benefit, privilege, or compliment ○ *They proved themselves unworthy of our trust.* **2.** BENEATH SOMEBODY lower than somebody's usual standards of behavior ○ *Such conduct is unworthy of you.* **3.** WITHOUT VALUE lacking value or merit **4.** VILE bad or unpleasant and wholly undeserved —**un·wor·thi·ly** *adv* —**un·wor·thi·ness** *n*

un·wound past participle, past tense of **unwind**

un·wrap /un ráp/ (**-wrapped, -wrap·ping, -wraps**) *vti* to take off the wrapping from something, or have the wrapping removed

un·writ·ten /un rítt'n/ *adj* **1.** ACCEPTED THROUGH TRADITION generally accepted and understood, even though not formally recorded in writing ○ *unwritten laws* **2.** NOT WRITTEN DOWN remaining unprinted or not written down **3.** BLANK not marked or covered with writing

un·yield·ing /un yeélding/ *adj* **1.** not giving in to persuasion, pressure, or force **2.** hard, rigid, or inflexible —**un·yield·ing·ly** *adv* —**un·yield·ing·ness** *n*

un·yoke /un yṓk/ (**-yoked, -yok·ing, -yokes**) *vt* **1.** UNTIE SOMETHING to release an animal such as a horse from a yoke **2.** DISCONNECT SOMETHING to separate two or more connected things **3.** FREE SOMEBODY to set somebody free (*archaic or literary*)

un·zip /un zíp/ (**-zipped, -zip·ping, -zips**) *v* **1.** *vti* to open or unfasten something such as clothing or luggage by means of a zipper, or become open or unfastened by this means **2.** *vt* to decompress a computer file that has been compressed

up /up/ *prep, adv* **1.** AT HIGHER LEVEL in, at, or to a higher level or position ○ (adv) *Put your hand up if you know the answer.* ○ (prep) *We climbed up the hill.* ○ (adv) *Prices are going up all the time.* ○ (prep) *I went up the ladder as far as the second-floor window.* **2.** ALONG in the same direction or way ○ (prep) *Go up the street until you come to a school.* ○ (adv) *You'll find her house up at the top of the street* ■ *adv* **1.** INDICATING COMPLETION used to indicate thoroughness or the completion of an action ○ *I tore up all the photographs.* ○ *drew up a contract* **2.** UPRIGHT in or to an upright position from a lower or prone position ○ *sitting up in bed* **3.** COMING OUT coming through or out of some medium ○ *The whales came up for air.* **4.** OUT in a way that detaches or removes ○ *Pulling up weeds isn't easy.* ○ *We drew up water from the well.* **5.** RISING ABOVE rising, or seeming to rise, above or over something ○ *When does the moon come up?* **6.** INTO CONSIDERATION so as to be discussed or mentioned ○ *The subject just didn't come up.* **7.** IN NORTHERLY POSITION toward or in a northerly position relative to the speaker ○ *Our cousins live up in Alaska.* **8.** TO HIGHER VALUE to or at a higher amount or price ○ *The interest rate is going up again.* **9.** TO GREATER INTENSITY with or to more intensity or higher pitch or volume ○ *His voice goes up when he's nervous.* ○ *Let's turn up the volume.* **10.** NEAR so as to move toward or closer to the speaker ○ *She ran up to me and gave me a big hug.* ○ *They came up to the door and knocked.* **11.** EACH with all participants equal ○ *The score is now 14 up.* ■ *adv, n* AHEAD to the better or ahead ○ (adv) *Our team is up by two.* ○ (n) *Sales are on the up this month.* ■ *adj* **1.** INCREASED more than before ○ *Your grades are up this semester.* **2.** OUT OF BED awake and out of bed ○ *She was already up when I called.* **3.** FACING UPWARD having the face or top side upward **4.** RAISED UPWARD in a raised or lifted position ○ *The switch is in the up position.* **5.** GOING HIGHER OR NORTH located in or moving toward a higher or northern direction ○ *Take the up escalator.* ○ *We're waiting for the up elevator.* **6.** CHEERFUL happy and feeling good ○ *We've been so up since hearing the news.* **7.** HAPPENING going on (*informal*) ○ *What's up with you these days?* **8.** BEING CONSIDERED approaching a deadline for an action ○ *The contract is up for renewal.* **9.** **NOMINATED FOR SOMETHING** in the running for an office or professional achievement ○ *I hear she's up for a promotion.* **10.** **ON TRIAL** charged with an offense or called into a court of law ○ *The accused is up on murder charges.* **11.** **OVER** at an end or finished ○ *Your time is up.* **12.** **HAVING KNOWLEDGE** possessing up-to-date or accurate information ○ *I'm not up on the latest gossip.* ○ *He's well up with recent developments in the field.* **13.** **FUNCTIONING** able to operate or function ○ *Is the computer up?* **14.** BASEBALL **BATTING** taking a turn at bat in baseball ○ *Who's up first in this inning?* ■ *n* **SOURCE OF GOOD FEELING** something that causes excitement or a feeling of euphoria (*informal*) ○ *The news was a real up for her.* ■ *v* (**upped, up·ping, ups**) (*informal*) **1.** *vt* **RAISE SOMETHING** to raise or increase something ○ *The insurance company has upped our premiums again.* **2.** *vt* **PROMOTE SOMEBODY OR SOMETHING** to promote or raise somebody or something to a higher level or position (*usually passive*) ○ *He was upped to manager last week.* **3.** *vi* **ACT SUDDENLY** to act suddenly or impulsively ○ *She just upped and left.* [Old English *up* "upward," *uppe* "on high" < Indo-European] ◇ **be up for something** to be ready or eager to do something (*informal*) ◇ **be up to somebody** to be the duty, responsibility, or job of somebody ◇ **be up to something 1.** to be able to undertake or endure ○ *I don't think I'm up to the journey.* **2.** to be engaged in or doing something, especially something reprehensible (*informal*) ○ *What have you been up to?* ◇ **on the up and up** honest or legitimate (*informal*) ◇ **up against it** facing difficulty or danger ◇ **up and around, up and about** out of bed and moving around after being asleep or sick ◇ **ups and downs** changes of fortune or alternating spells of good and bad experiences ◇ **up to 1.** as many as, or as long as ○ *anything up to 25 miles a day* **2.** until ○ *up to now* ◇ **up yours** an offensive phrase indicating anger, contempt, or strong disagreement ◇ **what's up?** (*informal*) **1.** what is the matter? **2.** what is happening?

USAGE See *back.*

UP *abbr* **1.** underproof **2.** Upper Peninsula

up. *abbr* upper

U·pa·nay·a·na /o͝opə nī́ ə nə/ *n S Asia* a rite of passage into adulthood for Hindi boys that can involve ear piercing, head-shaving, and being doused with milk [Early 19C. < Sanskrit < *upa* "toward" + *nayana* "leading"]

up-and-com·ing *adj* successful or improving, and showing signs of continuing to do so

up-and-down *adj* (*not hyphenated after a verb*) **1.** **GOING UP AND DOWN** moving alternately upward and downward **2.** **VARIABLE** uneven or readily changing **3.** **VERTICAL** in a vertical position or direction ○ *up-and-down stripes*

U·pan·i·shad /oo pa͡ani sha͡ad, -pánni shàd/ *n* a sacred Sanskrit text belonging to a set that forms the basis for Hindu philosophy and doctrine. They date from 400 B.C. and represent the last stage in the tradition of the Vedas, the most ancient of Hindu scriptures. [Early 19C. < Sanskrit *upaniṣad* "a sitting down near (something)" < *upa* "near" + *ni-ṣad* "sit down"] —**U·pan·i·shad·ic** /oo pa͡ani sha͡adik, -pànni sháddik/ *adj*

u·pas /yo͞opəss/ (*plural* **u·pas·es** *or same*) *n* **1.** a tree with white bark and poisonous sap. Native to: Southeast Asia. Latin name: *Antiaris toxicaria.* **2.** a poison made from the sap of the upas. Use: tipping arrows. [Late 18C. < Malay *(pohun) upas* "poison (tree)"]

up·beat /úp bee̅t/ *adj* **OPTIMISTIC** full of optimism or cheerfulness (*informal*) ■ *n* **1.** **IMPROVEMENT** an increase in happiness, prosperity, or favorable activity **2.** MUSIC **UNACCENTED BEAT** an unaccented beat in music, especially one that ends a bar **3.** MUSIC **GESTURE OF BATON** the upward movement of a conductor's baton that indicates an upbeat

up-bow *n* the movement of the bow across the strings of an instrument in which the tip of the bow moves away from the instrument

up·braid /up bráyd/ (**-braid·ed, -braid·ing, -braids**) *vt* to criticize or scold somebody in a harsh manner [Old English *upbrēdan*, origin ?] —**up·braid·er** *n* —**up·braid·ing·ly** *adv*

up·bring·ing /úp brìnging/ *n* the way in which somebody has been brought up, or trained and educated early in life

up·build /up bíld/ (**-built** /up bílt/, **-build·ing, -builds**) *vt* to build up, develop, or enlarge something —**up·build·er** *n*

UPC *abbr* Universal Product Code

up·cast /úp kàst/ *adj* **CAST UPWARD** thrown, propelled, or looking upward ■ *n* **1.** **SOMETHING THROWN UP** material that has been thrown up **2.** MIN EXTRACT **VENTILATION SHAFT** a ventilation shaft in a mine that brings air up

up·chuck /úp chùk/ (**-chucked, -chuck·ing, -chucks**) *vti* to vomit the contents of the stomach (*slang*)

up·com·ing /úp kùmming/ *adj* about to happen or coming soon

up·coun·try /úp kùntree/ *adj* **COMING FROM INTERIOR** coming from, associated with, or located in an inland region of a country ■ *n* **INLAND AREA** an inland region of a country ■ *adv* **TOWARD INTERIOR** in or toward the inland region of a country

up·date *vt* /up dáyt/ (**-dat·ed, -dat·ing, -dates**) to provide somebody or something with the most recent information or with more recent information than was previously available ○ *The website is updated once a month.* ■ *n* /úp dàyt/ the latest available information or more recent information —**up·dat·a·ble** *adj* —**up·dat·er** *n*

Popperfoto

John Updike

Up·dike /úp dìk/, **John** (*b.* 1932) US writer. He is best known for the novel *Rabbit, Run* (1960) and its sequels, two of which won Pulitzer Prizes. Full name **Updike, John Hoyer**. See Cultural note at **rabbit**

> "Truth should not be forced; it should simply manifest itself, like a woman who has in her privacy reflected and coolly decided to bestow herself upon a certain man."
> [John Updike, *Self-Consciousness: Memoirs*; 1989]

up·draft /úp dràft/ *n* a current of air that is moving upward

up·end /up énd/ (**-end·ed, -end·ing, -ends**) *v* **1.** *vti* to place, stand, or turn something upward so that it is standing or resting on one end, or be turned over onto one end **2.** *vt* to upset, disconcert, or disturb somebody or something to a serious degree

up·front, up·front *adj* (*informal*) **1.** frank or straightforward **2.** paid in advance —**up front** *adv* —**up·front·ness** *n*

up·grade *v* /up gràyd, up gráyd/ (**-grad·ed, -grad·ing, -grades**) **1.** *vti* **IMPROVE QUALITY OF SOMETHING** to improve the quality, standard, or performance of something, especially by incorporating new advances ○ *upgrade a computer* **2.** *vti* **EXCHANGE SOMETHING FOR SOMETHING BETTER** to exchange something for another of better quality ○ *upgrade a seat on a flight* **3.** *vt* HR **PROMOTE SOMEBODY** to promote somebody, or increase the status of somebody's job or position **4.** *vt* AGRIC **IMPROVE LIVESTOCK** to improve the quality of livestock by breeding with superior animals in order to introduce desirable traits into the offspring ■ *n* /úp gràyd/ **1.** **IMPROVEMENT OF SOMETHING** an improvement in the quality or performance of something such as computer hardware or software **2.** **SOMETHING THAT IMPROVES** something that improves the performance or quality of something else, or something that has better performance or qualities **3.** TRAVEL **MOVE TO BETTER TRAVEL CLASS** a move to a higher class of travel than that purchased **4.** **UPWARD SLOPE** an upward slope or incline ■ *adj* /úp gràyd/ *US* **SLOPING UPWARD** going or sloping uphill ■ *adv* /úp gràyd/ *US* **UPHILL** up an incline, slope, or hill —**up·grad·a·ble** *adj*

up·growth /úp grṑth/ *n* the process of growing upward, or the result of this process

up·heav·al /up hee̅v'l/ *n* **1.** a strong or sudden change in political, social, or living conditions **2.** a sudden raising of part of the earth's crust

up·heave /up hee̅v/ (**-heaved** *or* **-hove** /-hṓv/, **-heaved, -heav·ing, -heaves**) *vti* to lift something forcefully from underneath, or rise or be thrust upward

up·hill *adv* /up híl/ **1.** **UP SLOPE** up a slope or toward the top of a hill **2.** **WITH DIFFICULTY** against great resistance or in spite of difficulty ■ *adj* /úp hìl/ **1.** **GOING HIGHER ON SLOPE** going upward on a slope or to higher ground **2.** **ON HIGHER GROUND** located farther up on a slope or on higher ground **3.** **DIFFICULT** requiring a lot of effort ○ *an uphill struggle*

up·hold /up hṓld/ (**-held** /-héld/, **-hold·ing, -holds**) *vt* **1.** to maintain or defend something, especially laws or principles, in the face of hostility **2.** to provide somebody with moral support, or inspire somebody with confidence —**up·hold·er** *n*

up·hol·ster /up hṓlstər, ə pṓl-/ (**-stered, -ster·ing, -sters**) *vt* to fit a piece of furniture such as a chair or couch with stuffing, cushions, fabric and other materials [Mid-19C. Back-formation < UPHOLSTERY] —**up·hol·ster·er** *n*

up·hol·ster·y /up hṓlstəree, ə pṓl-/ *n* **1.** the stuffing, cushions, fabric and other materials used to upholster furniture such as chairs and couches ○ *upholstery fabric* **2.** the craft, trade, or business of upholstering furniture [Mid-17C. < obsolete *upholster* "upholsterer" < UPHOLD]

~~**upholstry**~~ incorrect spelling of **upholstery**

UPI *abbr* MEDIA United Press International

Up·john /úp jòn/, **Richard** (1802–78) British-born US architect. He was a leader of the gothic revival style in the United States. Full name **Upjohn, Richard Morris**

up·keep /úp kee̅p/ *n* **1.** the maintenance of somebody or something in proper condition or operation **2.** the financial cost of providing maintenance for somebody or something

up·land /úplənd, úp lànd/ *n* **1.** **HIGH LAND** land that has a high elevation, or a region of such land **2.** **INLAND REGION** a region that lies in the interior of a country ■ *adj* **HIGH OR INLAND** relating to, located in, or native to a region that is at a high elevation or lies in the interior of a country

up·land cot·ton *n* **1.** the wooly fiber of a Central American cotton plant, or fabric made from it **2.** a low, multibranched cotton plant commercially grown as an annual. Native to: Central America. Latin name: *Gossypium hirsutum.*

up·land sand·pi·per, up·land plov·er *n* a large sandpiper with brownish streaked feathers and a short beak. Native to: fields and uplands of eastern North America. Latin name: *Bartramia longicauda.*

up·lift *vt* /up líft/ (**-lift·ed, -lift·ing, -lifts**) **1.** **SPIRITUALLY LIFT SOMEBODY** to help somebody attain a higher intellectual, moral, or spiritual level, or improve the living conditions of somebody **2.** **RAISE SPIRITS OF SOMEBODY** to make somebody feel happier **3.** **PHYSICALLY LIFT SOMETHING** to raise or lift somebody or something ■ *n* /úp lìft/ **1.** **SOMETHING IMPROVING** something that elevates somebody intellectually, morally, or spiritually, or improves somebody's living conditions **2.** **LIFTING UP** the lifting up of something, or the result of doing this **3.** **INCREASE** an increase in the value or amount of something ○ *the recent uplift in land values* **4.** GEOL **UPWARD MOVEMENT OF EARTH'S CRUST** the slow upward movement of large parts of stable areas of the Earth's crust —**up·lift·er** *n*

up·lift·ing /up lífting, úp lìfting/ *adj* raising somebody's intellectual, moral, or spiritual level

up·link /úp lìngk/ *n* a transmitter on the ground that sends radio or other signals to an aircraft or communications satellite ■ *vti* (**up·linked, up·link·ing, up·links**) to transmit a radio or other signal from a ground transmitter to an aircraft or communications satellite

up·load /úp lṑd/ (**-load·ed, -load·ing, -loads**) *vti* to transfer data or programs, usually from a peripheral computer to a central, often remote, computer

up·man·ship /úpmən shìp/ *n* same as **one-upmanship** (*informal*) [Mid-20C. Shortening]

up·mar·ket *adj* /úp maàrkət/ intended or designed for wealthy consumers ■ *adv* /úp maàrkət, ùp maàrkət/ toward a higher and more expensive standard that appeals to wealthy consumers ○ *The hotel seems to have gone upmarket.*

up·most /úp mōst/ *adj* same as **uppermost**

up·on /ə pón/ CORE MEANING: means the same as "on," but is more formal ○ *He stretched out his legs upon the sofa.* ○ *She climbed upon her father's knee.* *prep* **1. ON SURFACE** on or onto the surface of something (*formal*) ○ *The great beast bounced to a halt upon the parapet.* **2. ONE AFTER ANOTHER** used between two occurrences of the same noun to indicate a large amount or number of that noun ○ *They claimed that the report contained "innuendo upon innuendo."* **3. FOLLOWED BY** used to indicate that one event is followed immediately by another event ○ *Upon finding the relevant text, they stored it in their own electronic files.* **4. ABOUT TO HAPPEN** used to indicate that an event is imminent ○ *The holidays are upon us again.* [12C. < UP + ON; after Old Norse *upp á*]

up·per /úppər/ *adj* **1. HIGHER** located above another part of something ○ *the upper deck* ○ *a muscle in the upper arm* **2. MORE IMPORTANT** higher in social position or rank, or greater in importance ○ *upper management* **3. MORE DISTANT** lying farther inland, upstream, or to the north ○ *the upper reaches of the river* **4.** GEOL **LATER** later in a particular geologic formation, period, or system ○ *Upper Jurassic clay formations* **5.** MATH **INDICATING MATHEMATICAL LIMIT** indicating a limit or bound of a set of numbers equal to or greater than every member of the set ■ *n* **1. SOMEBODY OR SOMETHING ABOVE** the higher of two people or objects **2.** CLOTHING **PART OF SHOE** the part of a boot or shoe that covers the upper surface of the foot **3.** DRUGS **STIMULANT** a drug that has a stimulating effect, e.g., an amphetamine (*slang*) **4.** *US* **GOOD EXPERIENCE** an experience that is exciting or produces euphoria (*slang*) ■ **up·pers** *npl* **UPPER TEETH** the teeth of the upper jaw or of a top set of dentures (*informal*)

up·per at·mos·phere *n* the part of the Earth's atmosphere above the troposphere, especially at heights unreachable by balloon

up·per bound *n* in mathematics, a number that is greater than or equal to all the members of a set

Up·per Can·a·da /ùppər-/ former British province in Canada, corresponding to present-day southern Ontario

Up·per Car·bon·if·er·ous *n* GEOL same as **Pennsylvanian** (sense 2) —**Up·per Car·bon·if·er·ous** *adj*

up·per·case /ùppər káyss/ *n* **CAPITAL LETTERS** capital letters used in writing, typing, typesetting, or printing ○ *printed in uppercase* ■ *adj* **IN CAPITAL LETTERS** relating to or written or printed in capital letters ■ *vt* (**-cased, -cas·ing, -cas·es**) **CAPITALIZE SOMETHING** to write, type, typeset, or print something in capital letters [Mid-18C. Because types for capital letters were kept in the upper of two type cases]

up·per cham·ber *n* GOV same as **upper house**

up·per cir·cle *n* the gallery of seats at the top of a theater, above the dress circle

up·per class *n* **1.** the highest social class, or the people in it (*often used in the plural*) **2.** *US* the group of students who belong to the junior or senior class of a high school, college, or university —**up·per-class** *adj*

up·per·class·man /ùppər klássmən/ (*plural* **-men** /-mən/) *n* a student who belongs to the junior or senior class of a high school, college, or university

up·per crust *n* SOC SCI same as **upper class** (*informal*)

up·per·cut /úppər kùt/ *n* a swinging upward blow in which the fist is aimed at an opponent's chin ■ *vt* (**-cut, -cut·ting, -cuts**) to hit or attempt to hit an opponent with an uppercut

up·per hand *n* the controlling position in a situation

up·per house *n* the house in a two-house legislature that is smaller and less representative of the general population, e.g., the US Senate

up·per·most /úppər mōst/ *adj* highest in position, rank, or level ■ *adv* in, at, or toward the highest position, rank, or level

Up·per Pa·le·o·lith·ic *n* the latest of the three periods of the Paleolithic era, about 40,000 to 14,000 years ago, during which modern human beings first appeared —**Up·per Pa·le·o·lith·ic** *adj*

Up·per Pen·in·su·la northern part of Michigan, a peninsula between Lake Superior and Lake Michigan, separated from the Lower Peninsula of Michigan by the Straits of Mackinac

up·per res·pi·ra·to·ry *adj* relating to or affecting any of the air passages or associated structures that connect the lungs with the exterior, including the nasal passages, trachea, and bronchi

Up·per Vol·ta former name for **Burkina Faso**

up·per works *npl* the parts of a ship above the water line when it is fully loaded

up·pi·ty /úppitee/ *adj* behaving in a way that is considered presumptuous and more suited to somebody belonging a higher social class or position (*informal*) [Late 19C. Fancifully < UP] —**up·pi·ty·ness** *n*

Upp·sa·la /up saálə/ city in eastern central Sweden, location of the country's oldest university. Population: 187,302 (1998).

up quark *n* a quark with an electric charge of +2/3 and zero strangeness and charm

up·raise /up ráyz/ (**-raised, -rais·ing, -rais·es**) *vt* to raise something or cause something to rise such as hands, prayers, or voices (*literary*)

up·rear /up reér/ (**-reared, -rear·ing, -rears**) *vti* to rise, or cause something to rise (*archaic or literary*)

up·right /úp rìt/ *adj* **1. ERECT** standing vertically or straight upward **2. RIGHTEOUS** behaving in a moral or honorable manner ■ *adv* **ERECTLY** vertically or straight upward rather than at an angle ■ *n* **1. VERTICAL SUPPORT** something that stands upright, e.g., a stake or post **2.** MUSIC same as **upright piano** —**up·right·ly** *adv* —**up·right·ness** *n*

upright piano

up·right pi·an·o *n* a piano with a rectangular upright case in which the strings are mounted vertically and a keyboard at right angles to the case

up·rise *vi* /up ríz/ (**-rose** /-rṓz/, **-ris·en** /-rízz'n/, **-ris·ing, -ris·es**) **1. RISE UP** to stand or get up (*literary or archaic*) **2. MOVE UPWARD** to stand, go, or move in an upward direction (*literary or archaic*) **3. APPEAR** to rise up or come into view from below a horizon ■ *n* /úp rìz/ **UPWARD SLOPE** an upward slope or incline

up·ris·ing /úp rìzing/ *n* an act of rebellion or revolt against an authority

up·riv·er /úp rìvvər/ *adv, adj* toward or closer to the source of a river

up·roar /úp ràwr/ *n* **1.** a loud or noisy disturbance **2.** a heated or intense controversy [Early 16C. By folk etymology < Middle Low German *uprōr* or Dutch *oproer* "stirring up"]

up·roar·i·ous /up ráwree əss/ *adj* **1. TUMULTUOUS** characterized by noisy confusion **2. HILARIOUS** extremely funny and causing loud laughter **3. VERY LOUD** loud and boisterous —**up·roar·i·ous·ly** *adv* —**up·roar·i·ous·ness** *n*

up·root /up ro͝ot/ (**-root·ed, -root·ing, -roots**) *vt* **1. PULL PLANT FROM SOIL** to pull a plant and its roots from the soil **2. DISPLACE SOMEBODY OR SOMETHING** to displace somebody or something from a home or habitual environment ○ *I don't want to uproot the children until they've finished school.* **3. REMOVE OR DESTROY SOMETHING** to remove or destroy something completely —**up·root·ed·ness** *n* —**up·root·er** *n*

up·rose past tense of **uprise**

up·rush /úp rùsh/ *n* a sudden upward rush of something

UPS *abbr* ELEC uninterruptible power supply

up·sa·dai·sy *interj* same as **upsy-daisy**

up·scale /úp skàyl/ *adj, adv* same as **upmarket**

up·set *adj* /up sét/ **1. DISTRESSED** unhappy, disappointed, or emotionally distressed because of something that has happened **2. DIGESTING POORLY** affected by indigestion or nausea ○ *an upset stomach* **3. OVERTURNED** overturned or spilled ○ *an upset dinghy* ■ *v* /up sét/ (**-set, -set·ting, -sets**) **1.** *vt* **DISTRESS SOMEBODY** to make somebody feel unhappy, disappointed, or emotionally distressed **2.** *vt* **DISTURB ORDER OF SOMETHING** to disrupt the usual order or course of something **3.** *vti* **TURN SOMETHING OVER** to knock or tip something over accidentally, usually scattering its contents, or be knocked or tipped over in this way **4.** *vt* **NAUSEATE SOMEBODY** to make somebody feel nauseous, or cause a disorder of the digestive system ○ *Spicy foods upset my stomach.* **5.** *vt* **DEFEAT SOMEBODY UNEXPECTEDLY** to defeat somebody unexpectedly, e.g., in a sports contest or an election **6.** *vt* METALL **THICKEN RIVET END** to make a heated bolt, rivet, or bar shorter and thicker by hammering one end ■ *n* /úp sèt/ **1. UNEXPECTED RESULT** an unexpected result, e.g., in a sports contest or an election **2. STOMACH ILLNESS** a mild illness of the stomach **3. UNHAPPY EXPERIENCE** an unhappy experience **4. DRAMATIC CHANGE** an unexpected problem that causes distress or a change of plans **5.** METALL **TOOL** a hammering tool used to make a heated bolt, rivet, or bar shorter and thicker at one end **6.** METALL **RIVET** a bolt, rivet, or bar that has been heated and then hammered to make it shorter and thicker at one end —**up·set·ter** *n*

up·set price *n N Am, Scotland* the lowest sale price at which something can be sold or auctioned

up·set·ting /up sétting/ *adj* emotionally distressing or disturbing —**up·set·ting·ly** *adv*

up·shift /úp shìft/ (**-shift·ed, -shift·ing, -shifts**) *vi* to shift a vehicle into a higher gear

up·shot /úp shòt/ *n* the end result of something [Mid-16C. Originally "final shot (in archery)"]

up·side /úp sìd/ *n* **1. POSITIVE SIDE** the most favorable or positive aspect of a situation or event **2. UPPER SIDE** the upper side or part of something **3.** *US* FIN **INCREASE IN VALUE** an increase in business profits or stock prices

up·side down *adv* **1.** turned so that the part that should be higher is lower or the side that should be underneath is on top **2.** in or into total confusion or great disorder ○ *We turned the house upside down looking for the keys.* —**up·side-down** *adj*

up·side-down cake *n* a sponge cake baked with a layer of fruit at the bottom and then inverted before it is served so that the caramelized fruit is on top

up·si·lon /úpsi lòn, yo͞opsi-/ *n* the 20th letter of the Greek alphabet, represented in the English alphabet as "y" or "u." See table at **alphabet** [Mid-17C. < Greek *u psilon* "simple u" (to distinguish it from the diphthong *oi*) < *psilon*, form of *psilos* "simple"]

up·speak /úp speek/ *n* LING same as **uptalk**

up·spring /up spríng/ (**-sprang** /-spráng/, **-sprung** /-sprúng/, **-spring·ing, -springs**) *vi* to come suddenly into existence or become visible (*archaic or literary*)

up·stage *vt* /up stáyj/ (**-staged, -stag·ing, -stag·es**) **1. OUTDO SOMEBODY ELSE** to divert attention from somebody else to yourself by being more impressive or noticeable **2.** THEATER **TURN ACTOR AWAY FROM AUDIENCE** to move toward the back of the stage in order to force another actor to turn his or her back to the audience **3. TREAT SOMEBODY DISDAINFULLY** to treat somebody in a haughty or disdainful manner (*informal*) ■ *adv* THEATER **TOWARD REAR OF STAGE** in, at, or toward the rear part of a stage ■ *adj* **1.** THEATER **LOCATED AT REAR OF STAGE** relating to or located in or at the rear part of a stage **2. ALOOF** distant from and disdainful of other people (*informal*) ■ *n* /úp stàyj/ THEATER **BACK OF STAGE** the rear part of the stage —**up·stag·er** *n*

up·stairs *adv* /up stérz/ **1. TO HIGHER FLOOR** to, toward, or on an upper floor or level in a building or structure **2. MENTALLY** in the mind or brain (*humorous*) ○ *not a lot happening upstairs* **3. TO HIGHER JOB** to a higher level or job in an organization or hierarchy (*informal*) ■ *n* /úp stèrz/ **UPPER FLOOR** an upper floor or the part of a building above the first floor (*often used before a* *noun*) ○ *an upstairs bathroom* ◇ **kick somebody upstairs** to promote somebody to a rank or position that is officially superior, but in fact carries less power and opportunity for influence (*informal*)

up·stand·ing /up stánding, úp stànding/ *adj* **1.** honest and socially responsible **2.** in an erect position (*archaic*) —**up·stand·ing·ness** *n*

up·start /úp staart/ *n* somebody who is newly wealthy, powerful, or famous, but is regarded as not deserving to be so

up·state /up stáyt, úp stàyt/ *US adj* NORTHERN relating to or living in the northern part of a state ■ *adv* NORTHWARD in, to, or toward the northern part of a state ■ *n* NORTHERN AREA the northern part of a state —**up·stat·er** *n*

up·stream /up stréem, úp strèem/ *adv* **1.** TOWARD SOURCE in or toward the source of a river or stream **2.** *US* AGAINST TRADITION contrary to popular opinion and customs (*informal*) **3.** BUSINESS IN EARLY STAGE of, for, or in an early stage of an industrial or commercial operation, e.g., during exploration in the oil industry **4.** GENETICS IN OPPOSITE DIRECTION TO TRANSCRIPTION in a direction along a strand of a DNA molecule counter to that in which transcription takes place ■ *adj* LOCATED NEARER SOURCE located farther toward the source of a river or stream

up·stroke /úp stròk/ *n* **1.** an upward or rising movement of a pen or brush, or the mark it makes **2.** the upward movement of a piston in a reciprocating engine

up·suck·ing *n* sycophantic behavior (*slang*)

up·surge /úp sùrj/ *n* a rapid increase in something

up·sweep *n* /úp swèep/ **1.** UPWARD SWEEP an upward or curving line or motion **2.** *US* HAIRSTYLE a hairstyle in which the hair is swept upward from the neck ■ *vti* /up swéep/ (**-swept** /-swépt/, **-sweep·ing, -sweeps**) MOVE UPWARD to sweep, curve, or brush something upward, or be swept, curved, or brushed upward

up·swing *n* /úp swing/ **1.** INCREASE OR IMPROVEMENT an increase or improvement, e.g., in business profits **2.** UPWARD MOTION a motion or swing upward ■ *vi* /up swíng/ (**-swung** /-swúng/, **-swung, -swing·ing, -swings**) SWING UPWARD to swing or move upward (*archaic*)

up·sy-dai·sy /úpsee dàyzee/, **up·sa·dai·sy** /úpsə-/ *interj* used to reassure a child who is being lifted or who has fallen or stumbled (*baby talk*) [Mid-19C. Alteration of *up-a-daisy* < UP + *a-day*, expressing surprise]

up·take /úp tàyk/ *n* **1.** the process of physically absorbing something into a living organism **2.** a passage that draws up smoke or air, e.g., a pipe or chimney ◇ **be quick** *or* **slow on the uptake** to be quick or slow to understand things or realize what is happening (*informal*)

up·talk /úp tàwk/ *n* the tendency to end sentences with an upward intonation, making a statement sound like a question

up·tem·po /úp témpō/, **up·tem·po** *n* a fast or lively musical tempo ■ *adj* fast-paced, lively, or exciting

up·throw /úp thrò/ *n* the upward movement of one block of rock over another in a low-angle fault

up·thrust /úp thrùst/ *n* **1.** UPWARD PUSH an upward push or thrust **2.** ROCK MOVING UPWARD a block of rock that has moved upward in a low-angle fault ■ *adj* RAISED UP raised or lifted up

up·tick /úp tìk/ *n* a small increase in something, especially in stock or bond prices

up·tight /up tít/ *adj* (*informal*) **1.** tense as a result of anger, fear, or annoyance in a way that is difficult to control **2.** unable or unwilling to show emotion —**up·tight·ness** *n*

up·time /úp tìm/ *n* the time during which a computer or other machine is operating or ready for use

up-to-date *adj* (*not hyphenated after a verb*) **1.** WITH LATEST KNOWLEDGE including or possessing knowledge of the latest information **2.** CURRENT extending up to or reflecting the current time **3.** FASHIONABLE familiar with or knowledgeable about current fashions, styles, or ideas

up-to-the-min·ute *adj* including or relating to the most recent events or things

up·town /úp tòwn/ *adv* TOWARDS UPPER PART OF CITY to, toward, or in the upper or northern part of a city ■ *n* UPPER PART OF CITY the upper or northern part of a city ■ *adv* OF UPPER PART OF CITY relating to or located in the upper or northern part of a city ■ *adj* (*informal*) **1.** *US* CONDESCENDING pretentious or condescending in behavior or attitudes **2.** FASHIONABLE of the latest fashion or style —**up·town·er** /úp tòwnər, up tównər/ *n*

up·trend /úp trènd/ *n* an upward improving trend, especially in business or an economy

up·turn *v* /úp tùrn, up túrn/ (**-turned, -turn·ing, -turns**) **1.** *vti* TURN OVER to turn over, up, or upside down, or make something do this **2.** *vt* TURN FACE UPWARD to turn something such as a face or gaze upward (*usually passive*) ■ *n* /úp tùrn/ IMPROVEMENT an improvement in the economy or in business conditions

up·ward /úpwərd/ *adj* **1.** GOING TOWARD going or directed toward a higher level or position ○ *a steep upward climb* **2.** IMPROVING increasing or becoming better ○ *an upward trend* ■ *adv also* **up·wards** /-wərdz/ **1.** TOWARD HIGHER LEVEL in, to, or toward a higher place, level, or position ○ *She's working her way upward through the company hierarchy.* ○ *Keep going upward and you'll soon see the house.* **2.** TOWARD INTERIOR OR SOURCE toward the interior of a place, or toward an origin or source ○ *The hikers left the path and headed upward along the river.* **3.** FROM SOME LESSER AMOUNT toward a larger amount, degree, or position ○ *Sales have gone steadily upward during the last quarter.* —**up·ward·ly** *adv* ◇ **upward of** more than

USAGE See ***toward.***

up·ward·ly mo·bile *adj* able or desiring to move to a higher social class or to acquire greater wealth, power or status ■ *npl* those who can or desire to move to a higher social class or acquire greater wealth, power or status

up·ward mo·bil·i·ty *n* the ability or desire to move to a higher social class and acquire greater wealth, power, or status

up·well·ing /up wélling/ *n* **1.** ACT OF RISING TO SURFACE an act of rising up from inside the Earth or the body **2.** SURGE a steady surge of something such as an emotion **3.** RISING OF WATER TO SURFACE a process in which cold nutrient-rich water rises to the surface from the ocean depths

up·wind /úp wìnd/; /up wínd/ *adv, adj* **1.** against or into the wind **2.** on the side toward which the wind is blowing

Ur /ur, oor/ ancient city of Mesopotamia, in the southeastern part of present-day Iraq. It was a major city-state of the Sumerian civilization by 2800 B.C.

ur-[1] *prefix* same as **uro-**[1] (*used before vowels*)

ur-[2] *prefix* same as **uro-**[2] (*used before vowels*)

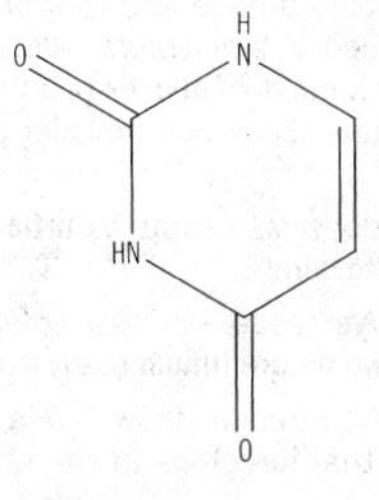

uracil

u·ra·cil /yóorəssil/ *n* a pyrimidine base, one of the four bases in RNA in which it pairs with thymine. Symbol **U** [Late 19C. Origin ?]

u·rae·mi·a *n* MED another spelling of **uremia**

u·rae·us /yoo rée əss/ *n* the sacred serpent found on the headdresses of Egyptian rulers and divinities, representing sovereignty [Mid-19C. Via modern Latin < Greek *ouraios* "cobra"]

U·ral /yóorəl/ river of southern Russia and northwestern Kazakhstan, rising in the southern Ural Mountains and flowing southward into the Caspian Sea. Length: 1,509 mi./2,428 km.

U·ral-Al·ta·ic *n* a hypothetical language group formerly proposed by scholars as containing the Uralic and Altaic language families —**U·ral-Al·ta·ic** *adj*

uraeus

U·ral·ic /yoo rállik/ *n* a family of languages spoken in northern and central Europe and western Siberia, including the branches Finno-Ugric and Samoyed —**U·ral·ic** *adj*

u·ra·lite /yóorə lìt/ *n* a fibrous blue-green mixture of amphibole minerals. Source: metamorphosed pyroxenes. [Mid-19C. < German *Uralit* < *Ural* "Ural Mountains"]

U·ral Moun·tains /yóorəl-/, **U·rals** /yóorəlz/ mountain system running from northern Russia southward to the Kirgiz Steppe in Kazakhstan. It is the traditional dividing line between Asia and Europe. Its highest peak is Mount Narodnaya, 6,214 ft./1,894 m. Length: 1,490 mi./2,400 km.

uran- *prefix* uranium ○ *uranous* [< URANIUM]

U·ra·ni·a /yoo ráynee ə/ *n* in Greek mythology, the Muse of astronomy, one of the nine Muses believed to inspire and nurture the arts

u·ran·ic /yoo ránnik, -ráynik/ *adj* relating to or containing uranium, especially with a high valence [Mid-19C. < Latin *uranus* < Greek *ouranos* "the heavens"]

u·ra·ni·nite /yoo ráynə nìt/ *n* a black uranium oxide mineral containing thorium, radium, and lead. Use: source of uranium. [Late 19C. < German *Uranin* < modern Latin *uranium* (see URANIUM)]

u·ra·nite /yóorə nìt/ *n* a mineral that contains uranium [Late 19C. < URANIUM] —**u·ra·nit·ic** /yóorə níttik/ *adj*

u·ra·ni·um /yoo ráynee əm/ *n* a heavy silvery white radioactive metallic element occurring in three isotopes. Source: uraninite, pitchblende. Use: in one isotope, as fuel in nuclear reactors and weapons. Symbol **U**. See table at **element** [Late 18C. < modern Latin < *Uranus* the planet (discovered eight years before the element was identified)]

u·ra·ni·um 235 /-too thurtee fív/ *n* a uranium isotope with a mass number of 235 that readily undergoes fission when bombarded with neutrons. Use: nuclear energy source.

u·ra·ni·um 238 /-too thurtee áyt/ *n* the most abundant stable isotope of uranium, with a mass number of 238

u·ra·ni·um-lead dat·ing *n* the determination of the age of a uranium-containing mineral by measuring the level of lead isotope produced by the radioactive decay of uranium, which occurs at a known rate

u·ra·nog·ra·phy /yóorə nóggrəfee/ *n* the branch of astronomy that deals with making maps of the constellations [Mid-17C. < Greek *ouranographia* "science of the skies"] —**u·ra·nog·ra·pher** *n* —**u·ra·no·graph·ic** /yóorənə gráffik/ *adj* —**u·ra·nog·ra·phist** *n*

u·ra·nous /yóorənəss/ *adj* relating to or containing uranium, especially with a low valence

U·ra·nus /yóorənəss, yoo ráynəss/ *n* **1.** the seventh smallest planet in the solar system and the seventh planet from the Sun **2.** in Greek mythology, the ruler of the heavens, husband of Gaia, and father of the Titans. He was dethroned by his son Cronus. [Via Latin < Greek *Ouranos*]

u·ra·nyl /yóorə nìl, yoo ráyn'l/ *adj* relating to a chemical group containing uranium and oxygen. Formula: UO_2. [Mid-19C. < URANIUM]

u·rase *n* BIOCHEM same as **urease**

u·rate /yóor àyt/ *n* a salt of uric acid —**u·rat·ic** /yoo ráttik/ *adj*

ur·ban /úrbən/ *adj* relating to or belonging to a city [Early 17C. < Latin *urbanus* < *urbs* "city"]

USAGE urban or **urbane**? Though ultimately from the same Latin form, these words differ in meaning in English. ***Urban*** refers generally to cities (as in *the stress of urban life*); ***urbane*** means "sophisticated" (as in *an urbane manner, He was very urbane.*).

Ur·ban II /úrbən/ (1040?–99) pope. The sermon he preached to the Council of Clermont (1095) led to the First Crusade against the Seljuk Turks. Born **Odo of Lagery**

Ur·ban VIII (1568–1644) pope (1623–44). His reign was marked by diplomatic activity, reform of church affairs, and lavish artistic and architectural patronage. Born **Barberini, Maffeo**

Ur·ban·a /ur bánnə/ city in eastern Illinois, west of Danville and directly east of Champaign. It is home to the University of Illinois. Population: 38,241 (2002 estimate).

ur·ban ad·ven·ture *n* LEISURE same as **urban exploration**

ur·ban blues *n* blues music that has a stronger beat than country blues, often played with electric instruments and featuring songs about life in the city (*takes a singular verb*)

ur·ban cow·girl *n* a woman who wears fashionable clothing that is influenced by the western United States, e.g. fringed skirts and cowboy-style hats and boots

Ur·ban·dale /úrbən dàyl/ city in south-central Iowa, on Walnut Creek. It is a northwestern suburb of Des Moines. Population: 31,152 (2002 estimate).

ur·bane /ur báyn/ (**-ban·er, -ban·est**) *adj* showing sophistication, refinement, or courtesy [Mid-16C. Directly or via Old French *urbaine* "urban" < Latin *urbanus* (see URBAN)] —**ur·bane·ly** *adv* —**ur·bane·ness** *n*

USAGE See ***urban***.

ur·ban ex·plo·ra·tion *n* the recreational activity of secretly exploring urban sites off-limits to the public such as subway tunnels and abandoned buildings

ur·ban guer·ril·la *n* somebody who lives in a city and carries out violent acts there in order to further a political cause

ur·ban·ism /úrbə nìzzəm/ *n* **1.** the typical way of life of people who live in a city or town **2.** the study of life in cities and towns

ur·ban·ist /úrbənist/ *n* a specialist in city planning and the study of cities —**ur·ban·is·tic** /ùrbə nístik/ *adj* —**ur·ban·is·ti·cal·ly** *adv*

ur·ban·ite /úrbə nīt/ *n* somebody who lives in a city or town

ur·ban·i·ty /ur bánnətee/ *n* the quality of being sophisticated, refined, or courteous ■ **ur·ban·i·ties** *npl* polite or courteous actions [Mid-16C. Directly or via French *urbanité* < Latin *urbanitas* < *urbanus* (see URBAN)]

ur·ban·ize /úrbə nīz/ (**-ized, -iz·ing, -iz·es**) *vt* **1. MAKE AREA INTO TOWN** to make an area of countryside or a village into a town or part of one **2. MAKE COUNTRY PERSON MOVE TO CITY** to make somebody who lives in the countryside migrate to a town or city **3. MAKE SOMEBODY URBAN** to accustom somebody to living in a town or city —**ur·ban·i·za·tion** /ùrbəni záysh'n/ *n*

ur·ban leg·end, ur·ban myth *n* a bizarre untrue story that circulates in a society through being presented as something that actually happened, usually to a friend or relative of somebody the speaker knows

ur·ban plan·ning *n* the planning of the physical and social development of a city through the design of its layout and the provision of services and facilities —**ur·ban plan·ner** *n*

ur·ban re·new·al *n* the redevelopment of urban areas that have become run down or impoverished, by demolishing or renovating old buildings or building new ones

ur·ban sprawl *n* the expansion of an urban area into areas of countryside that surround it

ur·ban war·ri·or *n* somebody who copes successfully with the stresses and pace of modern urban living (*slang*)

ur·bi et or·bi /úrbee et áwrbee/ *adv* a phrase used in a papal blessing, meaning "to the city (of Rome) and to the world" [< Latin]

ur·ce·o·late /úrssee ə làyt, ur sée ələt/ *adj* shaped like an urn or pitcher, with a swollen middle and narrowing top [Mid-18C. < Latin *urceolus* "little pitcher" < *urceus* "pitcher"]

ur·chin /úrchin/ *n* **1.** a mischievous child, especially a young one who is unkempt in appearance **2.** MARINE BIOL same as **sea urchin** [13C. Via Old N French *herichon* < Latin *(h)ericius* "hedgehog"]

Ur·du /óor doo, úr-/ *n* the Indic official language of Pakistan, spoken also in Bangladesh and India. It belongs to the Indic group of Indo-European languages and shares basic grammar and vocabulary with Hindi. Native speakers: 40 million. [Late 18C. Via Persian and Urdu *(zabān i) urdū* "(language of the) camp" < Turkish *ordū* "camp"] —**Ur·du** *adj*

LANGUAGE HERITAGE See ***Persian***.

-ure *suffix* **1.** process or condition, or something resulting from an action ○ *erasure* **2.** office or function, or a body performing a particular function ○ *prefecture* ○ *legislature* [Via Old French < Latin *-ura*]

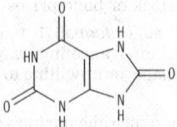

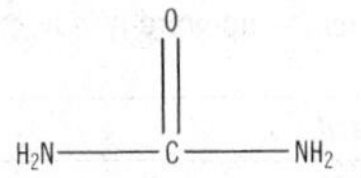

urea

u·re·a /yoo rée ə/ *n* a nitrogenous compound found in the urine of mammals, produced through protein decomposition. It is also produced synthetically. Use: fertilizers, feeds, manufacture of resins. Formula: $CO(NH_2)_2$. [Early 19C. < modern Latin, alteration of French *urée* < Old French *urine* (see URINE)] —**u·re·al** *adj*

u·re·a-for·mal·de·hyde res·in *n* a resin made from urea and formaldehyde. Use: making electrical fittings and in cavity insulation.

u·re·ase /yóoree àyss, -àyz/, **u·rase** /yóor àyss, -àyz/ *n* an enzyme in some bacteria and seeds that breaks down urea to produce carbon dioxide and ammonia [Late 19C. < UREA + -ASE]

u·re·din·i·o·spore /yoorə dínnee ə spàwr/ *n* FUNGI same as **uredospore** [Early 20C. < Latin *uredin-*, stem of *uredo* (see UREDO)]

u·re·din·i·um /yoorə dínnee əm/ (*plural* **-i·a** /-ee ə/), **u·re·di·um** /yoo réedee əm/ (*plural* **-di·a** /-dee ə/) *n* a reddish or black mass of spores produced on a plant by a rust fungus [Early 20C. < Latin *uredin-*, stem of *uredo* (see UREDO)]

u·re·do /yoo réedō/ *n* MED same as **urticaria** [Early 18C. < Latin < *urere* "to burn"]

u·re·do·sor·us /yə rèedə sáwrəss/ (*plural* **-sor·i** /-sáw rī/) *n* FUNGI same as **uredinium** [Early 20C. < UREDO]

u·re·do·spore /yoo réedə spàwr/ *n* a reddish unicellular spore that develops in the uredinia of rust fungi

u·re·ide /yóoree īd, -id/ *n* an acyl derivative of urea

u·re·mi·a /yoo réemee ə/, **u·rae·mi·a** *n* a form of blood poisoning caused by the accumulation in the blood of products that are normally eliminated in the urine [Mid-19C. < modern Latin < Greek *ouron* "urine" + *haima* "blood"] —**u·re·mic** *adj*

u·re·o·tel·ic /yóoree ə téllik/ *adj* producing nitrogen-containing waste in the form of urea [Early 20C. < UREA] —**u·re·o·tel·ism** *n*

u·re·ter /yoo réetər, yóorətər/ *n* either of a pair of ducts that carry urine from the kidneys to the bladder in mammals or to the common cavity for wastes (**cloaca**) in lower vertebrate animals [Late 16C. Via modern Latin < Greek *ourētēr* < *ourein* "urinate" < *ouron* "urine"] —**u·re·ter·al** *adj* —**u·re·ter·ic** /yoorə térrik/ *adj*

u·re·thane /yóorə thàyn/, **u·re·than** /-thàn/ *n* **1.** a colorless odorless crystalline compound, the ethyl ester of carbamic acid. Use: solvents, pesticides, pharmaceuticals. Formula: $C_3H_7NO_3$. **2.** an ester of carbamic acid other than the ethyl ester **3.** CHEM same as **polyurethane** [Mid-19C. < modern Latin *urea* (see UREA) + ETHANE]

u·re·thra /yoo réethrə/ (*plural* **-thras** or **-thrae** /-three/) *n* the tube in mammals that carries urine from the bladder out of the body and in the male also carries semen during ejaculation [Mid-17C. Via late Latin < Greek *ourēthra* < Greek *ourein* "urinate" (see URETER)] —**u·re·thral** *adj*

u·re·thri·tis /yoorə thrítiss/ *n* inflammation of the urethra, usually caused by infection [Early 19C. < URETHRA] —**u·re·thrit·ic** /-thríttik/ *adj*

u·re·thro·scope /yoo réethrə skōp/ *n* a medical instrument for examining the inside of the urethra, consisting of a fine flexible tube fitted with lenses and a light [Mid-19C. < URETHRA] —**u·re·thro·scop·ic** /yoo rèethrə skóppik/ *adj* —**u·re·thros·co·py** /yoori thróskəpee/ *n*

u·ret·ic /yoo réttik/ *adj* relating to, involving, or found in urine [Mid-19C. Via late Latin < Greek *ourētikos* < *ourein* "urinate" (see URETER)]

U·rey /yóoree/, **Harold C.** (1893–1981) US chemist. He discovered the isotope deuterium (**heavy hydrogen**), for which he won the Nobel Prize in chemistry (1934). Full name **Urey, Harold Clayton**

urge /urj/ *vt* (**urged, urg·ing, urg·es**) **1. ADVISE SOMEBODY STRONGLY** to advise somebody strongly to do something ○ *urged his firm to reconsider* **2. ADVOCATE SOMETHING EARNESTLY** to recommend or advocate something earnestly and with persistence ○ *urging restraint* **3. ENCOURAGE SOMEBODY OR SOMETHING** to encourage, drive, or force somebody or something to do something ○ *could hear the crowd urging her on* ■ *n* **STRONG NEED** a strong need, wish, or impulse to do something ○ *the urge to travel* [Mid-16C. < Latin *urgere* "push, press, compel"] —**urg·er** *n*

ur·gent /úrjənt/ *adj* **1.** calling for immediate action or attention **2.** showing earnestness or the desire for something to be done quickly [15C. Via French < Latin *urgent-*, present participle of *urgere* "push, press, compel"] —**ur·gen·cy** *n* —**ur·gent·ly** *adv*

ur·gent care cen·ter *n* a treatment facility for patients with pressing, but not life-threatening, medical problems, staffed by physicians, registered nurses, pharmacists, and other care providers

-urgy *suffix* technique or art of working with something ○ *metallurgy* [Via modern Latin *-urgia* < Greek *-ourgos* "working" < *ergon* "work"]

-uria *suffix* **1.** the condition of having a particular substance in the urine ○ *aciduria* **2.** the condition of having a particular kind of urine ○ *polyuria* [< modern Latin < Greek *ouron* "urine"]

U·ri·ah /yoo rī́ ə/ *n* in the Bible, a Hittite officer deliberately killed in battle to allow King David to marry his wife, Bathsheba (2 Samuel 11:2–16)

U·ri·be /óo rée bày/, **Alvaro** (*b.* 1952) president of Colombia (2002–). A former member of the Liberal Party, he became president as an independent candidate in 2002. Full name **Uribe Velez, Alvaro**

u·ric /yóorik/ *adj* relating to, involving, or found in urine [Late 18C. < French *urine* (see URINE)]

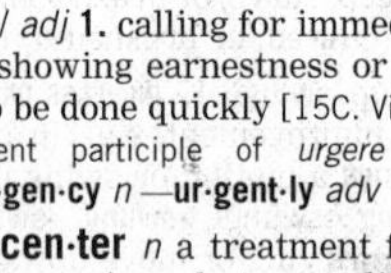

uric acid

u·ric ac·id *n* a slightly soluble compound in urine and blood, made in the breakdown of nitrogenous waste. Crystals of uric acid accumulate in the joints of people affected by gout. Formula: $C_5H_4N_4O_3$.

u·ri·dine /yóorə dīn/ *n* a nucleoside, consisting of uracil and ribose, that plays a role in the metabolism of carbohydrates [Early 20C. < URACIL + -IDINE]

U·rim and Thum·mim /yo͝orim ənd thúmmim/ *npl* oracles on the breastplate of the high priest of ancient Israel [Hebrew *'ūrīm* and *tummīm*]

urin- *prefix* same as **urino-** (*used before vowels*)

u·ri·nal /yo͝orən'l/ *n* **1. RECEPTACLE FOR MEN TO URINATE INTO** a receptacle that is attached to a wall and plumbed in, used for men to urinate into **2. PLACE WITH URINALS** a room or building in which there are urinals **3. PORTABLE CONTAINER FOR URINE** a container used to transport urine [13C. Via French < late Latin *urinalis* "urinary" < Latin *urina* "urine"]

u·ri·nal·y·sis /yo͝orə nálləssiss/ (*plural* **-y·ses** /-ə seez/) *n* the analysis of the physical, chemical, and microbiological properties of urine, carried out to help diagnose disease, monitor treatment, or detect the presence of a specific substance [Late 19C. Blend of URINE + ANALYSIS]

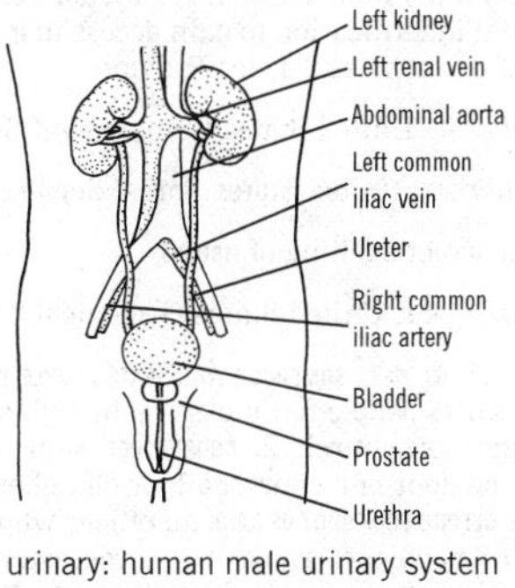

urinary: human male urinary system

u·ri·nar·y /yo͝orə nèrree/ *adj* relating to, involving, or affecting urine or the organs that form and discharge urine [Late 16C. < Latin *urina* "urine"]

u·ri·nar·y blad·der *n* an expanding muscular sac in mammals and some other vertebrates in which urine collects before it is discharged from the body through the urethra

u·ri·nate /yo͝orə nàyt/ (**-nat·ed, -nat·ing, -nates**) *vi* to discharge urine from the body [Late 16C. < medieval Latin *urinat-* past participle of *urinare* < Latin *urina* "urine"] —**u·ri·na·tion** /yo͝orə náysh'n/ *n* —**u·ri·na·tive** *adj* —**u·ri·na·tor** *n*

u·rine /yo͝orin/ *n* the yellowish liquid containing waste products that is excreted by the kidneys and discharged through the urethra. In birds and reptiles it is semisolid. [14C. Directly or via French < Latin *urina*] —**u·ri·nous** *adj*

u·ri·nif·er·ous /yo͝orə nífferəss/ *adj* describes a tube that carries urine, especially the tubules of the kidneys [Mid-18C. < URINE]

urino- *prefix* urine, urinary ○ *urinometer* [< Latin *urina* "urine"]

u·ri·no·gen·i·tal /yo͝orə nō jénnət'l/ *adj* ANAT same as **urogenital**

u·ri·nom·e·ter /yo͝orə nómmətər/ *n* a hydrometer for measuring the specific gravity of urine

URL *n* an address identifying the location of a file on the Internet, consisting of the protocol, the computer on which the file is located, and the file's location on that computer. Full form **Uniform Resource Locator**

URM *abbr* SOCIOL underrepresented minority

Ur·mi·a, Lake /úrmee ə/ large salt lake in northwestern Iran. Area: 1,800 sq. mi./4,700 sq. km.

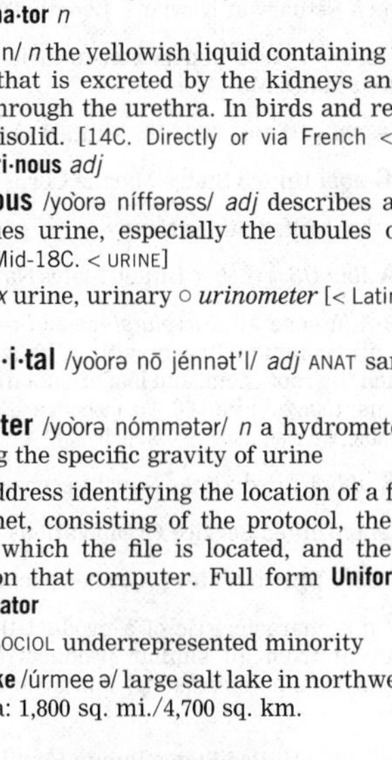
urn (sense 3)

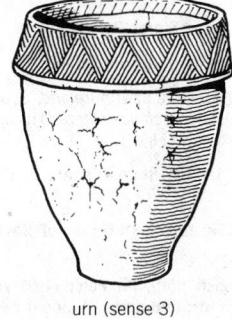

urn /urn/ *n* **1. VESSEL FOR HOT DRINKS** a closed vessel in which a hot drink, especially tea or coffee, is made in a large quantity and poured out through a spigot **2. VASE FOR SOMEBODY'S ASHES** a sealed vase in which the ashes of somebody who has died and been cremated are kept **3. ORNAMENTAL CONTAINER** an ornamental vase that may have a foot or a pedestal **4.** BOT **SPORE-PRODUCING PART OF MOSS CAPSULE** the part of a moss capsule where spores are produced [14C. < Latin *urna*]

CULTURAL NOTE ***Ode on a Grecian Urn***, a poem (1819) by British writer John Keats. It describes the poet's reaction to a Greek vase decorated with reliefs of joyful rural scenes. The urn becomes a symbol of the contrast between the permanence of art and the transience of human life, and inspires the poem's famous proclamation "Beauty is truth, truth beauty."

uro-[1] *prefix* **1.** urine, urinary tract ○ *uroscopy* ○ *urolithiasis* **2.** urea ○ *urease* [< Greek *ouron* "urine"]

uro-[2] *prefix* tail ○ *uropod* [< Greek *oura*]

u·ro·chord /yo͝orə kàwrd/ *n* **1.** a flexible skeletal rod (**notochord**) that supports the posterior part of the body in some sea animals such as sea squirts **2.** MARINE BIOL same as **tunicate** [Late 19C. < URO-[2] + CHORD[2]] —**u·ro·chor·dal** /yo͝orə káwrd'l/ *adj*

u·ro·chor·date /yo͝orə káwr dàyt/ *n* MARINE BIOL same as **tunicate** [Late 19C. < URO-[1] + CHORD[1] + -ATE] —**u·ro·chor·date** *adj*

u·ro·chrome /yo͝orə krōm/ *n* a yellow pigment that gives urine its normal color

u·ro·dele /yo͝orə deel/ *n* an amphibian that has a tail throughout its adult life, a long body, and short limbs, e.g., the salamander or newt. Order: Caudata or Urodela. [Mid-19C. Directly or via French *urodèle* < modern Latin *Urodela*, < Greek *oura* "tail" + *dēlos* "visible"] —**u·ro·dele** *adj*

u·ro·gen·i·tal /yo͝orō jénnit'l/ *adj* relating to or involving the organs of the urinary tract and the reproductive organs [Mid-19C. < URO-[1] + GENITAL]

u·rog·e·nous /yo͞o rójjənəss/ *adj* producing, obtained from, or formed in urine

u·ro·gram /yo͝orə gràm/ *n* an X-ray picture of the urinary tract or a part of it

u·rog·ra·phy /yo͞o róggrəfee/ *n* X-ray photography of all or part of the urinary tract. It is performed after a patient has been given an opaque substance that highlights the various structures, in order to locate and diagnose urinary disorders. —**u·ro·graph·ic** /yo͝orə gráffik/ *adj*

u·ro·ki·nase /yo͝orō kī nàyss, -nàyz, -kí-/ *n* an enzyme, produced by the kidneys, that catalyzes the conversion of plasminogen to plasmin. Use: medicinally, to dissolve blood clots.

urol. *abbr* MED **1.** urological **2.** urology

u·ro·lith /yo͝orə lìth/ *n* a stony mass (**calculus**) in the urinary tract —**u·ro·lith·ic** /yo͝orə líthik/ *adj*

u·ro·lith·i·a·sis /yo͝orəli thī əssiss/ *n* the formation or presence of stony masses in the urinary tract, or the medical condition resulting from this

u·rol·o·gy /yo͞o róllәjee/ *n* the branch of medicine that deals with the study and treatment of disorders of the urinary tract in women and the urogenital system in men —**ur·o·log·ic** /yo͝orə lójjik/ *adj* —**u·ro·log·i·cal** *adj* —**u·rol·o·gist** *n*

u·ro·pod /yo͝orə pòd/ *n* either of a pair of flat appendages on the last abdominal segment of a crustacean such as a lobster or shrimp [Late 19C. < URO-[2]] —**u·ro·po·dal** /yo͞o róppəd'l/ *adj*

u·ro·py·gi·al /yo͝orə píjjee əl/ *adj* relating to the fleshy hindmost part (**uropygium**) of a bird's body from which the tail feathers grow

u·ro·py·gi·al gland *n* a gland in the skin at the base of the tail of most birds that secretes an oil used while preening to condition and waterproof the feathers

u·ro·py·gi·um /yo͝orə píjjee əm/ *n* the fleshy hindmost part of a bird's body from which the tail feathers grow [Late 18C. Via medieval Latin < Greek *ouropugion* < *oura* "tail" + *pugē* "buttocks"]

u·ros·co·py /yo͞o róskəpee/ (*plural* **-pies**) *n* the medical examination of urine in order to make a diagnosis —**u·ro·scop·ic** /yo͝orə skóppik/ *adj* —**u·ros·cop·ist** *n*

-urous *suffix* having a particular kind of tail ○ *anurous* [< Greek *oura* "tail"]

Ur·quhart /úrkərt, -kaart/, **Sir Thomas** (1611?–60) Scottish writer and soldier. A fighter for the royalist cause in the English Civil War, he also wrote on a wide range of subjects and translated Rabelais.

Ur·sa Ma·jor /ùrssə-/ *n* a prominent constellation of the northern hemisphere containing the Big Dipper. See illustration at **constellation**

Ur·sa Mi·nor *n* a small constellation of the northern hemisphere containing the star Polaris. See illustration at **constellation**

ur·sine /úr sīn, -seen/ *adj* **1.** relating to or typical of a bear, or belonging to the bear family **2.** having the characteristics usually associated with a bear [Mid-16C. < Latin *ursinus* < *ursus* "a bear"]

Ur·su·line /úrssəlin, -līn, -leen/ *n* a member of a Roman Catholic order of nuns founded by St. Angela Merici in Brescia, Italy, in the 16th century and dedicated to teaching. [Late 17C. < *Ursula*, patron saint of the order's founder] —**Ur·su·line** *adj*

ur·ti·ca·ceous /ùrti káyshəss/ *adj* describes a plant that belongs to the nettle family [Mid-19C. < Latin *urtica* "nettle" < *urere* "to burn"]

ur·ti·car·i·a /ùrti kérree ə/ *n* a skin rash, usually occurring as an allergic reaction, that is marked by itching and small pale or red swellings, and often lasts for a few days (*technical*) [Late 18C. < modern Latin < Latin *urtica* "nettle"] —**ur·ti·car·i·al** *adj* —**ur·ti·car·i·ous** *adj*

ur·ti·cate /úrti kàyt/ *vi* (**-cat·ed, -cat·ing, -cates**) to be affected by or cause urticaria ■ *adj* producing wheals and itching [Mid-19C. < medieval Latin *urticat-* past participle of *urticare* "sting" < Latin *urtica* "nettle"] —**ur·ti·cant** *adj, n*

ur·ti·ca·tion /ùrti káysh'n/ *n* **1.** the process by which somebody develops urticaria **2.** an intensely itchy or burning sensation

Uru., Urug. *abbr* Uruguay

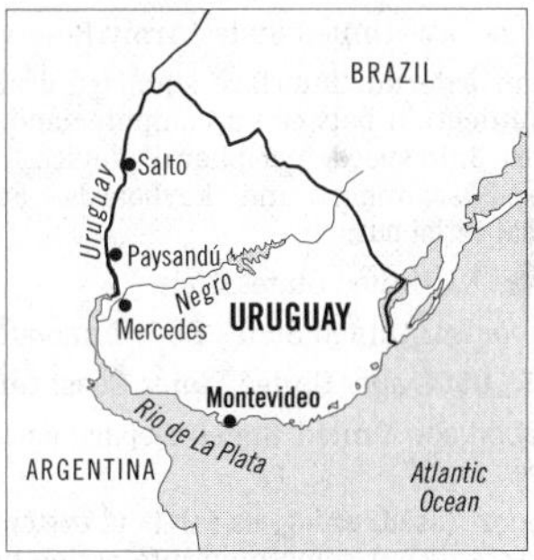

Uruguay

U·ru·guay /yo͝orə gwī, -gwày/ **1.** country in southeastern South America, south of Brazil, bordering the Atlantic Ocean. Language: Spanish. Currency: Uruguayan peso. Capital: Montevideo. Population: 3,413,329 (2003). Area: 68,037 sq. mi./176,215 sq. km. Official name **Oriental Republic of Uruguay 2.** river in southeastern South America, rising in southern Brazil and entering the Atlantic Ocean through the Río de la Plata. Length: 990 mi./1,600 km. —**U·ru·guay·an** /yo͝orə gwī ən, -gwáy-/ *n, adj*

U·rum·qi /o͞o ro͝omchee/ capital city of Xinjiang Uygur Autonomous Region, northwestern China. Population: 1,310,000 (1995).

u·rus /yo͝orəss/ *n* ZOOL same as **aurochs** [Early 17C. Via Latin < Greek *ouros*]

u·ru·shi·ol /o͞o ro͞oshee àwl/ *n* an oily poisonous irritant found in the resin and on the leaves and stems of poison ivy, the lacquer tree, and some related plants [Early 20C. < Japanese *urushi* "lacquer" + -OL[1]]

us[1] *stressed* /uss/; *unstressed* /əss/ *pron* **1. SELF AND OTHER OR OTHERS** a pronoun used to refer to both yourself and another person or other people (*used after a verb or preposition*) ○ *He told us to go away.* ○ *This problem affects all of us.* **2. ROYAL US** used by a king or queen, or the editor of a newspaper, to mean "me" (*formal*) ○ *It gives us great pleasure to declare this building open.* **3.** *UK* **ME** used by a person to refer to himself or herself (*informal*) ○ *Give us a look, then!* **4.** *regional* same as **ourselves** (sense 1) (*informal; used after a verb as the indirect object*) ○ *We'd better find us a place to sleep.* [Old English *ūs* < Germanic]

us² *abbr* United States (*used in Internet addresses*) See table at **domain name**

US *abbr* **1.** Uncle Sam **2.** OPTICS uniform system (*used of lens apertures*) **3.** United States **4.** ROADS United States highway

U.S. *abbr* United States

u.s. *abbr* **1.** ubi supra **2.** ut supra

U/S *abbr* unserviceable

U.S.A., USA *abbr* **1.** United States of America **2.** ARMY United States Army

us·a·ble /yo͝ozəb'l/, **use·a·ble** *adj* capable of being used —**us·a·bil·i·ty** /yo͝ozə bíllətee/ *n* —**us·a·ble·ness** *n* —**us·a·bly** *adv*

USAEUR *abbr* ARMY United States Army, Europe

U.S.A.F., USAF *abbr* United States Air Force

us·age /yo͝ossij, yo͝oz-/ *n* **1. ACT OR WAY OF USING SOMETHING** the act of using something, the way something is used, or the extent to which something is used **2. ACCEPTED PRACTICE** a customary and generally accepted practice or procedure **3.** LANGUAGE **WAY LANGUAGE IS USED** the way in which words and phrases are used in speech or writing **4.** LANGUAGE **EXAMPLE OF LANGUAGE USE** an example of a specific use of language **5. TREATMENT** the handling or treatment of something [13C. < Old French < Latin *usus* (see USE)]

USAID /yo͝o ess áyd/ *n* a US government agency that provides humanitarian aid and assistance for development to other countries. Full form **United States Agency for International Development**

~~usally~~ incorrect spelling of **usually**

us·ance /yo͝oz'nss/ *n* the customary length of time allowed for payment of a bill of exchange in foreign commerce [14C. < Old French < assumed Vulgar Latin *usare* "keep on using" < Latin *uti* "to use"]

USAR *abbr* ARMY United States Army Reserve

USB *n* an external interface standard designed for communication between a computer and attached low- to mid-speed peripheral devices such as printers, scanners, and keyboards. Full form **universal serial bus**

USC *abbr* LAW United States Code

USCA *abbr* LAW United States Code Annotated

U.S.C.G., USCG *abbr* United States Coast Guard

USDA *abbr* GOV United States Department of Agriculture

use *v* /yooz/ (**used, us·ing, us·es**) **1.** *vt* **EMPLOY SOMETHING FOR PURPOSE** to put something into action or service for some purpose ○ *use a hammer* **2.** *vt* **DO SOMETHING HABITUALLY** to do something habitually ○ *use common sense* **3.** *vt* **CONSUME SOMETHING** to expend or consume something, often until none is left ○ *All of the space on the disk has been used.* **4.** *vt* **MANIPULATE OR EXPLOIT SOMEBODY** to exploit or manipulate somebody as a means to an end ○ *the type of person who uses others* **5.** *vti* DRUGS **CONSUME DRUGS OR ALCOHOL REGULARLY** to consume something regularly, especially drugs or alcohol **6.** *vt* **TREAT SOMEBODY IN PARTICULAR WAY** to behave toward somebody or something in a particular way ○ *used his employees poorly* **7.** *vt* **BENEFIT FROM SOMETHING** to benefit or get satisfaction from something ○ *I could use a good night's sleep.* ■ *modal v* /yooss/ **USED** used after "did" in the past tense instead of "used" ○ *Did you use to go there too?* ○ *I didn't use to eat much fruit.* ■ *n* /yooss/ **1. ACT OF USING SOMETHING** the act of using something for a purpose ○ *skilled in the use of computers* **2. STATE OF BEING USED** the state or fact of being used for something ○ *no longer in use* **3. WAY OF USING SOMETHING** a way of using something ○ *We admired the artist's use of color.* **4. RIGHT TO USE SOMETHING** the right to use something, or the benefit of using something ○ *He was denied use of the car as a punishment.* **5. ABILITY TO USE SOMETHING** the power or ability to use something ○ *She lost the use of her left eye.* **6. PURPOSE** the purpose of something ○ *Put your education to good use.* **7. USEFULNESS** the quality of being useful ○ *These empty boxes will be of use when we move.* **8. NEED TO USE SOMETHING** the occasion or need to use something ○ *We may have use for these things later.* **9.** LAW **BENEFIT OF PROPERTY** the benefit or profit of property held by one person for another **10.** LAW **LEGAL ENJOYMENT OF PROPERTY** the legal enjoyment of property, especially by occupying it **11.** RELIG **MODIFIED LOCAL LITURGY** a modified liturgical form or observance practiced in a particular church or religious order [13C. Via Old French *user* "to use" < Latin *usus*, past participle of *uti*] ◇ **have no use for somebody** *or* **something 1.** to have no need or purpose for somebody or something **2.** to have no liking or respect for somebody or something (*informal*) ◇ **make use of something** to use something that is readily available, especially in a sensible or economical way ◇ **what's the use?** used to suggest that doing something is pointless (*informal*)

USAGE See *utilize.*

SYNONYMS *use, employ, make use of, utilize*

CORE MEANING: to put something to use

use to put something into action or service for some purpose ○ *In photography, different lenses are used for different purposes.* ○ *When talking about computers we use the word "hardware" to describe the actual machine and its accessories.* **employ** to make use of something such as a tool or a resource in a particular way ○ *the high-pressure selling techniques sometimes employed by door-to-door salespeople* ○ *There are seven base metals that are commonly employed in the making of coins and artefacts.* **make use of** to use something that is readily available, especially in a sensible or economical way ○ *A split-level bedroom makes maximum use of space.* ○ *All members of staff are encouraged to make use of this facility.* **utilize** to make use of something, or find a practical or effective use for something ○ *Karate is a method of fighting which utilizes all parts of the body as deadly weapons.* ○ *We need to ensure that the country's varied and rich reserves are utilized in the most efficient way.*

use up *vt* to expend or consume something, usually until none is left

use·a·ble *adj* another spelling of **usable**

~~useage~~ incorrect spelling of **usage**

use-by date *n UK* a date displayed on food and other perishable products, after which they should not be used or consumed

used¹ /yoozd/ *adj* **1.** formerly owned by somebody else ○ *bought a used car* **2.** already put to use or expended ○ *a used match*

used² /yoósst-/ *modal v* used in the past tense to say that somebody or something habitually or usually did something ○ *We used to eat out more often.* ○ *He used not to be so grumpy.* ◊ **use** ■ *adj* accustomed to or familiar with somebody or something ○ *We're not used to this weather.*

USAGE used to or **use to**? The spelling ***used to***, with a *-d*, is a form indicating habitual or customary past actions, as in *On Saturdays we used* [not *use*] *to go to ball games.* (People tend to drop the *-d* because it is inaudible in many oral contexts. This practice is unacceptable in writing.) When *did* precedes ***use(d) to***, the correct form is *use to*, as in *Did you use to go to ball games every Saturday? Didn't she use to live in this dorm?*

use·ful /yoósfəl/ *adj* **1.** capable of being put to use or serving a purpose **2.** having value or benefit, or bringing an advantage —**use·ful·ly** *adv* —**use·ful·ness** *n*

~~usefull~~ incorrect spelling of **useful**

use im·mu·ni·ty *n* immunity from prosecution granted to a witness in return for testimony that cannot be used in any manner in any criminal prosecution against him or her

~~useing~~ incorrect spelling of **using**

use·less /yoósslǝss/ *adj* **1. UNUSABLE** not able to be used **2. UNSUCCESSFUL** unsuccessful, or unlikely to be worthwhile **3. INEPT** not able to do something properly (*informal*) —**use·less·ly** *adv* —**use·less·ness** *n*

Use·net /yoóz nèt/ *n* a worldwide system that uses the Internet and other networks to distribute articles of news or information

us·er /yoózər/ *n* **1. PERSON OR THING THAT USES** somebody or something that uses something ○ *computer users* **2. EXPLOITER** somebody who exploits or manipulates others as a means to an end (*informal*) **3. DRUG TAKER** somebody who takes illegal drugs (*informal*) **4.** LAW **EXERCISE OF RIGHT** the exercise of a right to do or use something

us·er-friend·ly *adj* easy to operate, understand, or deal with ○ *user-friendly software* —**us·er-friend·li·ness** *n*

us·er group *n* a group of people with common interests in an aspect of computer hardware or software who share information among themselves and with the hardware manufacturer or software developer

us·er·ID /yoózər ī deé/ *n* an identification name or password used to allow an individual user access to a computer system

us·er in·ter·face *n* the part of the design of a computer or other device or program that accepts commands from and returns information to the user

us·er·name /yoózər nàym/ *n* a unique identifier composed of alphanumeric characters, used as a means of initial identification to gain access to a computer system or Internet Service Provider

USES *abbr* HR United States Employment Service

USFS *abbr* GOV United States Forest Service

~~usful~~ incorrect spelling of **useful**

USGS *abbr* GEOL United States Geological Survey

ush·er /úshər/ *n* **1. SOMEBODY WHO SEATS PEOPLE** somebody who escorts people to their seats in a place such as a theater or church **2. DOORKEEPER** somebody who tends the door of a court, hall, or chamber **3. OFFICER WALKING BEFORE SOMEBODY OF RANK** an officer who walks in front of people of rank in a procession or who introduces strangers at formal events ■ *v* (**-ered, -er·ing, -ers**) **1.** *vt* **ESCORT OR SEAT SOMEBODY** to escort somebody to or from a place or seat **2.** *vi* **ACT AS USHER** to act as an usher [14C. Via Anglo-Norman *usser* < Latin *ostarius* "door-keeper" < *ostium* "door"]

SYNONYMS See *guide.*

usher in *vt* to introduce or lead up to something

USIA *abbr* GOV United States Information Agency

Usk /usk/ river in southeastern Wales. It rises in Brecon Beacons National Park and flows to the Severn Estuary at Newport. Length: 60 mi./97 km.

USM *abbr* **1.** ARMS underwater-to-surface missile **2.** United States Mail

USMA *abbr US* MIL, EDUC US Military Academy

USMC *abbr* United States Marine Corps

USN *abbr* United States Navy

USNA *abbr US* MIL, EDUC United States Naval Academy

us·ne·a /ússnee ə, úz-/ (*plural* **-ne·ae** /-nee eè/ or **-ne·as**) *n* a common lichen with a hanging body in which the root, stem, and leaf are not distinguished. Genus: *Usnea.* [Late 16C. Via modern and medieval Latin < Arabic, Persian *ušna* "moss, lichen"]

USNR *abbr* United States Naval Reserve

USO *abbr* United Service Organizations

USP¹ *abbr* United States Pharmacopoeia

USP² *n* a characteristic of a product that makes it different from all similar products (*used in advertisements and marketing*) Full form **unique selling point**

USPHS *abbr* United States Public Health Service

USPO *abbr* United States Post Office

USPS *abbr* United States Postal Service

us·que·baugh /úskwə bàw/ *n Ireland, Scotland* Scotch or Irish whiskey (*archaic or literary*) [Late 16C. < Gaelic *uisge beatha* "water of life"]

USS *abbr* **1.** United States Senate **2.** United States Ship

U.S.S.R., USSR *abbr* HIST Union of Soviet Socialist Republics

U·sti·nov /yoósti nòff/, **Sir Peter** (1921–2004) British writer, director, and actor. A noted raconteur and mimic, he wrote or directed many plays and movies. He won Academy Awards for supporting actor in *Spartacus* (1960) and *Topkapi* (1964). Full name **Ustinov, Sir Peter Alexander**

Sir Peter Ustinov

"Parents are the bones on which children sharpen their teeth."
[Sir Peter Ustinov, *Dear Me*, 1977]

usu. *abbr* usually

u·su·al /yóo͞zhoo əl/ *adj* **TYPICAL OR NORMAL** characteristic or expected of somebody or something ■ *n* **1. ORDINARY WAY** the ordinary, normal, or customary way of things **2. WHAT SOMEBODY CUSTOMARILY HAS** what somebody customarily has, especially a drink in a bar (*informal*) [14C. Directly or via Old French *usuel* < late Latin *usualis* < Latin *usus* (see USE)] —**u·su·al·ly** *adv* —**u·su·al·ness** *n* ◇ **as usual** in the customary way

SYNONYMS ***usual, customary, habitual, routine, wonted***
CORE MEANING: often done
usual characteristic or expected of somebody or something ○ *He made his way home by his usual route.* ○ *Mom responded in the usual way, with a long-suffering sigh.* **customary** conforming to what is usual or normal ○ *It's customary for us to give presents to everyone in the family.* ○ *done with customary formality* **habitual** done frequently and predictably ○ *a habitual slouch* ○ *He addressed the meeting with his habitual frankness.* **routine** regular or standard, even predictable and monotonous ○ *They found a fault in the fuel supply during a routine check.* ○ *nurses who are engaged in routine work on the floor* **wonted** (*literary*) usual or typical ○ *Briefly overcome with emotion, she soon resumed her wonted composure.*

~~usualy~~ incorrect spelling of **usually**

u·su·fruct /yóo͞zə frùkt, yóo͞ssə-/ *n* the legal right to use and enjoy the advantages or profits of another person's property [Early 17C. < Latin *usufructus*, variant of *ususfructus* "use (and) enjoyment" < *usus* (see USE) + *fructus* "enjoyment"]

u·su·fruc·tu·ar·y /yóo͞zə frúkchoo èrree, yóo͞ssə-/ (*plural* **-ies**) *n* somebody who is entitled by usufruct to the use of somebody else's property —**u·su·fruc·tu·ar·y** *adj*

u·surp /yoo súrp, -zúrp/ (**u·surped, u·surp·ing, u·surps**) *vti* to use something without the right to do so [14C. Via French < Latin *usurpare* "seize for use" <, perhaps, *usus* "use" (see USE) + *rapere* "seize"] —**u·sur·pa·tion** /yóo͞ssər páysh'n, yóo͞zər-/ *n* —**u·surp·er** *n*

u·su·ry /yóo͞zhəree/ (*plural* **-ries**) *n* **1.** the lending of money at an exorbitant rate of interest **2.** an exorbitant rate of interest [14C. Via assumed Anglo-Norman *usurie* < Latin *usura* "use of money lent, interest" < *usus* "use"] —**u·su·rer** *n* —**u·su·ri·ous** /yoo zhóo͞ree əss/ *adj* —**u·su·ri·ous·ly** *adv*

USW *abbr* MEDIA ultrashort wave

ut /ut, oot/ *n* the note C, equivalent to "do" in the solmization system [14C. < Latin, syllable sung to this note in a hymn]

UT *abbr* **1.** Universal Time **2.** *also* **Ut.** Utah

U·tah /yóo͞ taa, -taw/ state in the western United States, bordered by Idaho, Wyoming, Colorado, Arizona, and Nevada. Capital: Salt Lake City. Population: 2,233,169 (2000). Area: 84,904 sq. mi./219,900 sq. km. —**U·tah·an** /yóo͞ taa ən, -tàw ən/ *n, adj*

U·ta·ma·ro /óotaa maárō/ (1753–1806) Japanese artist. He was noted for his delicate portraits of women in

Utah

teahouses, shops, and brothels. Full name **Kitagawa Utamaro**

UTC *n* Universal Time. Full form **Universal Time Co-ordinated**

ut dict. /ŏŏt díkt/ *abbr* as directed (*used on prescriptions*) [Latin *ut dictum*]

Ute /yoot/ (*plural same or* **Utes**) *n* **1.** a member of a Native North American people who mainly live in Colorado, Utah, and New Mexico **2.** the Uto-Aztecan language of the Ute people. Native speakers: 2,500. [Early 19C. < Spanish *Yuta*, Native American language] —**Ute** *adj*

u·ten·sil /yoo ténss'l/ *n* a tool or container, especially one used in a kitchen [14C. Via Old French *utensile* < Latin *utensilis* "usable" < *uti* "to use"]

u·ter·i ANAT, ZOOL plural of **uterus**

u·ter·ine /yóo͞tərin, -rīn/ *adj* **1.** relating to, in, or affecting the womb **2.** related by having the same mother but a different father ○ *a uterine brother* [15C. < late Latin *uterinus* "from the same womb" < Latin *uterus* "womb"]

u·ter·us /yóo͞tərəss/ (*plural* **u·ter·us·es** *or* **u·ter·i** /-rī/) *n* **1.** a hollow muscular organ in the pelvic cavity of female mammals, in which the embryo is nourished and develops before birth (*technical*) **2.** a structure in some animals that is similar to the mammalian womb, in which eggs or young develop [17C. < Latin, "belly, womb"]

UTI *abbr* MED urinary tract infection

U·ti·ca /yóo͞tikə/ city in eastern New York, on the Mohawk River, east of Syracuse. Population: 59,947 (2002 estimate).

util. *abbr* utility

u·til·i·tar·i·an /yoo tìllə térree ən/ *adj* **1. BELIEVING VALUE LIES IN USEFULNESS** relating to, characteristic of, or advocating the doctrine that value is measured in terms of usefulness **2. PRACTICAL** designed primarily for practical use rather than beauty ■ *n* **BELIEVER IN UTILITARIANISM** a believer in the doctrine of utilitarianism

u·til·i·tar·i·an·ism /yoo tìllə térree ə nìzzəm/ *n* **1. ETHICAL DOCTRINE OF GREATEST GOOD** the ethical doctrine that the greatest happiness of the greatest number should be the criterion of the virtue of action **2. DOCTRINE BASED ON VALUE OF USEFULNESS** the doctrine that the value of an action or an object lies in usefulness **3. UTILITARIAN QUALITY** the quality of being designed primarily for practical use rather than beauty

u·til·i·ty /yoo tíllətee/ *n* (*plural* **-ties**) **1.** UTIL same as **public utility 2. SERVICE PROVIDED BY PUBLIC UTILITY** a service such as electricity, gas, or water that is provided by a public utility **3. USEFULNESS** the quality or state of being useful for something **4. SOMETHING USEFUL** something that serves a useful purpose **5. COMPUTER PROGRAM PERFORMING ROUTINE TASKS** a computer program that performs routine tasks and supports operations, as distinct from an applications program **6.** ECON **SATISFACTION DERIVED FROM CONSUMPTION** in economic theory, the amount of satisfaction or pleasure that somebody gains from consuming a commodity, product, or service ■ *adj* **1. INTENDED FOR PRACTICAL USE** designed or intended for practical use rather than for show or appearance **2. DESIGNED FOR STRENGTH** built or designed for performing tasks that require strength and versatility ○ *a utility truck* **3. ABLE TO PLAY SEVERAL POSITIONS** in some sports, able to substitute for other players in several different positions ○ *a utility outfielder* **4.** THEATER **ABLE TO PERFORM ANY SMALL ROLE** able to perform any small role in a theater production ○ *a utility actor* **5.** *US* AGRIC **RAISED FOR FARM USE** grown or raised to be used on a farm ○ *utility livestock* **6.** AGRIC **OF LOWEST GRADE** classified as the lowest grade of beef ■ *n* (*plural* **-ties**) COMPUT **COMPUTER PROGRAM PERFORMING ROUTINE OPERATIONS** a computer program that carries out routine tasks and supports the operation of the computer or another device, as compared to an application program [14C. Via French < Latin *utilitas* < *utilis* "usable" < *uti* "to use"]

u·til·i·ty pro·gram *n* same as **utility**

u·til·i·ty room *n* a room in a house where there are large domestic appliances such as a washing machine or furnace, and where cleaning tools and supplies are sometimes stored

u·til·i·ty ve·hi·cle *n* VEHICLES same as **sport-utility vehicle**

u·til·ize /yóo͞t'l īz/ (**-ized, -iz·ing, -iz·es**) *vt* to make use of something, or find a practical or effective use for something [Early 19C. < French *utiliser* < Latin *utilis* (see UTILITY)] —**u·til·iz·a·ble** *adj* —**u·til·i·za·tion** /yóo͞t'li záysh'n/ *n* —**u·til·iz·er** *n*

USAGE utilize or **use**? ***Utilize*** means "make use of something, or find a practical use for something" and so is more specific than ***use***. ***Utilize*** is more common in technical contexts: *The device utilizes a special plug-in connection.* It can also refer to using things in unusual or unintended ways, as a more formal equivalent of "make use of": *When the fan belt broke they had to utilize a leather belt.* In business jargon and in other contexts, ***utilize*** is often found when the meaning intended is simply "use," a use that should be avoided: *Successful applicants will be able to use* [not *utilize*] *their skills and experience in this field.*

SYNONYMS See ***use***.

ut·most /út mōst/ *adj* **1. OF GREATEST DEGREE** of the greatest degree, number, or amount **2. AT EXTREMITY** at the most distant point or extremity ■ *n* **GREATEST DEGREE OR AMOUNT** the greatest degree, number, or amount of something, especially the greatest effort that somebody is capable of ○ *I did my utmost to persuade her.* [Old English *ūt(e)mest* < OUT + -MOST]

U·to-Az·tec·an /yóo͞tō-/ *n* **1.** a family of Native American languages, including Ute and Nahuatl, spoken in the western United States and in Mexico **2.** a member of a people who speak a Uto-Aztecan language [< UTE] —**U·to-Az·tec·an** *adj*

u·to·pi·a /yoo tṓpee ə/, **U·to·pi·a** *n* an ideal and perfect place or state where everyone lives in harmony and everything is for the best [Mid-16C. < modern Latin, literally "noplace," first used in Sir Thomas More's *Utopia* (1516) < Greek *ou* "not" + *topos* "place"]

CULTURAL NOTE ***Utopia***, a philosophical treatise (1516) by English writer and statesman Sir Thomas More. It contrasts the moral decadence and disunity of contemporary Christian Europe with the tolerance and prosperity of More's imaginary ideal state of Utopia, which is run on secular, communist principles. The term ***utopia*** has spawned a number of derivatives, for example, *utopian, utopianism,* and *utopianist.*

u·to·pi·an /yoo tṓpee ən/ *adj* **1.** *also* **U·to·pi·an IDEAL** belonging to or characteristic of an ideal perfect state or place **2. ADMIRABLE BUT IMPRACTICABLE** admirable but impracticable in real life **3. IMPRACTICALLY IDEALISTIC** tending to deal in admirable but impracticable ideas ■ *n* **PROPOSER OF UTOPIAN REFORMS** a proposer or advocate of visionary but impractical social or political reforms

u·to·pi·an·ism /yoo tṓpee ə nìzzəm/, **U·to·pi·an·ism** *n* **1.** the principles, views, or objectives of a utopian **2.** the belief that an ideal society can be achieved —**u·to·pi·an·ist** *n*

u·to·pi·an so·cial·ism *n* a form of socialism based on the belief that a socialist society can be brought about by peacefully persuading those in power to accept it

U·trecht /yóo͞ trèkt, óo͞ trèkht/ historic university city in the central Netherlands. Population: 234,323 (2000).

u·tri·cle /yóo͞trik'l/, **u·tric·u·lus** /yoo tríkyələss/ (*plural* **-li** /-lī/) *n* **1.** the larger of two fluid-filled sacs in the labyrinth of the inner ear, into which the semicircular canals open **2.** the bladder-shaped fruit of some plants [Mid-18C. Directly or via French *utricule*

< Latin *utriculus* "little leather bottle" < *uter* "leather bottle"] —**u·tric·u·lar** *adj* —**u·tric·u·late** /yoo tríkyələt, -làyt/ *adj*

U·tril·lo /yoo tríllō/, **Maurice** (1883–1955) French artist. The most frequent subject of his paintings was the Parisian urban landscape. His early works show the influence of the impressionist school, whereas later pieces show his interest in the techniques of cubism.

ut su·pra /ŏŏt sŏŏprə/ *adv* as above [< Latin]

Ut·ta·ran·chal /ŏŏttə raán chaál/ state in northern India. Capital: Dehra Dun. Population: 8,479,562 (2001). Area: 21,620 sq. mi./56,000 sq. km.

Ut·tar Pra·desh /ŏŏttər prə dáysh, -désh/ state in N India. Capital: Lucknow. Population: 166,052,859 (2001). Area: 89,288 sq. mi./231,256 sq. km.

ut·ter¹ /úttər/ (**-tered, -ter·ing, -ters**) *vt* **1. SAY SOMETHING** to say or pronounce something **2. EMIT SOMETHING AS VOCAL SOUND** to emit something as a sound made by the voice ○ *uttered a low growl* **3. PUBLISH SOMETHING** to publish something, e.g., in a book or newspaper (*archaic*) **4.** LAW **PUT SOMETHING INTO CIRCULATION** to put something into circulation, especially counterfeit money or a forgery, under the pretense that it is genuine (*formal*) [14C. < Middle Dutch *ūteren* "drive out, announce, speak" < Old Low German *ūt* "out"] —**ut·ter·a·ble** *adj* —**ut·ter·er** *n*

ut·ter² /úttər/ *adj* at the most extreme point or of the highest degree ○ *utter chaos* ○ *utter nonsense* [Old English *ūtera* "farther out" < OUT]

ut·ter·ance /úttərənss/ *n* **1. SOMETHING SAID** something said or emitted as a vocal sound **2. EXPRESSION** the expression of something, especially in speech or vocal sound **3. WAY OF SPEAKING** a style or way of speaking **4. ACT OF SAYING** the act of saying something ◇ **give utterance** to express something, especially in speech

ut·ter·ly /úttərlee/ *adv* in an extreme or complete way

ut·ter·most /úttər mōst/ *adj, n* same as **utmost**

U-turn *n* **1.** a turn in the shape of a "U" made by a vehicle seeking to reverse direction **2.** a complete reversal in opinion, actions, or policy

UU *abbr* **1.** *UK* POL Ulster Unionist **2.** RELIG Unitarian Universalist

UV *abbr* PHYS ultraviolet

UVA *n* ultraviolet radiation, especially from the sun, with a relatively long wavelength

u·va·rov·ite /oo vaárə vīt/ *n* a bright emerald green garnet containing calcium and chromium. Use: gems. [Mid-19C. < Count Sergei Semenovich *Uvarov* (1785–1855), Russian statesman]

UVB *n* ultraviolet radiation, especially from the sun, with a relatively short wavelength

u·ve·a /yŏŏvee ə/ *n* the middle of the three layers of the eyeball, made up of the choroid, ciliary body, and iris surrounding the lens [Early 16C. Via medieval Latin < Latin *uva* "grape"] —**u·ve·al** *adj*

u·ve·i·tis /yŏŏvee ítiss/ *n* inflammation of the uvea of the eye

UV in·dex *n* a scale used to indicate the intensity of the Sun's ultraviolet rays

u·vu·la /yŏŏvyələ/ (*plural* **-las** or **-lae** /-lee/) *n* a small fleshy "V"-shaped extension of the soft palate that hangs above the tongue at the entrance to the throat [14C. < late Latin, "little grape" < Latin *uva* "grape"; from its shape]

u·vu·lar /yŏŏvyələr/ *adj* **1. INVOLVING UVULA** relating to or involving the uvula **2.** PHON **PRONOUNCED VIBRATING UVULA** describes a speech sound pronounced with vibration of the uvula ■ *n* **UVULAR SOUND** a uvular consonant

u·vu·li·tis /yŏŏvyə lítiss/ *n* inflammation of the uvula

UW *abbr* INSUR **1.** underwriter **2.** underwritten

ux. *abbr* wife [Latin *uxor*]

UXB *abbr* unexploded bomb

ux·o·ri·al /uk sáwree əl/ *adj* relating to, involving, or characteristic of a wife [Early 19C. < Latin *uxor* "wife"]

ux·o·ri·cide /uk sáwrə sīd/ *n* **1.** murder of a wife by her husband **2.** a man who murders his wife [Mid-19C. < Latin *uxor* "wife"]

ux·o·ri·ous /uk sáwree əss/ *adj* used to describe a man who is excessively devoted to or submissive to his wife [Late 16C. < Latin *uxoriosus* < *uxor* "wife"] —**ux·o·ri·ous·ly** *adv* —**ux·o·ri·ous·ness** *n*

uy *abbr* ONLINE Uruguay (*used in Internet addresses*) See table at **domain name**

uz *abbr* ONLINE Uzbekistan (*used in Internet addresses*) See table at **domain name**

Uz·bek /ŏŏz bèk, úz bèk/ (*plural same* or **-beks**) *n* **1.** a member of a people who live mainly in Uzbekistan and in neighboring regions **2.** a Turkic language spoken in Uzbekistan and Central Asia. Native speakers: 16 million. [Early 17C. Directly or via Persian or Russian *uzbek* < Turkish, Uzbek *özbek*] —**Uz·bek** *adj*

Uzbekistan

Uz·bek·i·stan /ŏŏz béki stàn, -staán/ country in Central Asia. It was part of the Soviet Union from 1924 to 1991. Language: Uzbek. Currency: som. Capital: Tashkent. Population: 25,981,647 (2003). Area: 172,700 sq. mi./447,400 sq. km. Official name **Republic of Uzbekistan**

U·zi *n* a 9 mm compact submachine gun [Mid-20C. After *Uziel* Gal, its Israeli designer]

Vv

v^{1} /vee/ (*plural* **v's**), **V** (*plural* **V's** or **Vs**) *n* **1. 22ND LETTER OF ENGLISH ALPHABET** the 22nd letter of the English alphabet, representing a consonant sound **2. LETTER "V" WRITTEN** a written representation of the letter "v" **3. ROMAN NUMERAL FOR 5** the Roman numeral for 5

v^{2}, **V** *symbol* PHYS **1.** instantaneous potential difference **2.** instantaneous voltage **3.** specific volume

v^{3} *abbr* **1.** PHYS vacuum **2.** MATH vector **3.** PHYS velocity **4.** ANAT, BOT ventral **5.** GRAM verb **6.** verse **7.** PRINTING verso **8.** versus **9.** vertical **10.** very **11.** vide **12.** MUSIC violin **13.** GRAM vocative **14.** MUSIC voice **15.** MEASURE voltage **16.** LING vowel

V^{1} /vee/ (*plural* **V's** or **Vs**) *n* something shaped like a letter "V"

V^{2} *symbol* **1.** PHYS electric potential **2.** PHYS electromotive force **3.** PHYS potential **4.** PHYS potential efficiency **5.** PHYS potential energy **6.** CHEM ELEM vanadium **7.** MEASURE volt **8.** MEASURE volume

V^{3} *abbr* **1.** PHYS vacuum **2.** MATH vector **3.** CHR Venerable (*used in titles*) **4.** MED ventilator **5.** BOT, ANAT ventral **6.** GRAM verb **7.** verse **8.** version **9.** PRINTING verso **10.** versus **11.** vertical **12.** Very (*used in titles*) **13.** CHEM vibrational quantum number **14.** vice **15.** victory **16.** vide **17.** GRAM vocative **18.** MUSIC voice **19.** MEASURE volt **20.** MEASURE voltage **21.** LING vowel

v. *abbr* PUBL volume

V-1 (*plural* **V-1's**) *n* a German robot bomb used in World War II, mainly against England [Abbreviation of German *Vergeltungswaffe eins* "reprisal weapon one"]

V-2 (*plural* **V-2's**) *n* a German liquid-fueled ballistic missile used in the latter part of World War II, mainly against England [Abbreviation of German *Vergeltungswaffe zwei* "reprisal weapon two"]

V6 (*plural* **V6's**) *n* an internal-combustion engine with six cylinders arranged in a "V" shape

V8 (*plural* **V8's**) *n* an internal-combustion engine with eight cylinders arranged in a "V" shape

va *abbr* **1.** ONLINE Vatican City (*used in Internet addresses*) See table at **domain name** **2.** GRAM verb active **3.** GRAM verbal adjective **4.** MUSIC viola

VA *abbr* **1.** ECON value-added **2.** MED ventricular arrhythmia **3.** MIL Veterans' Administration **4.** CHR vicar apostolic **5.** NAVY Vice Admiral **6.** MAIL Virginia **7.** visual aid **8.** BROADCAST Voice of America **9.** MEASURE volt-ampere **10.** MIL Volunteer Artillery **11.** RELIG, SOC WELFARE Volunteers of America

Va. *abbr* Virginia

Vaal /vaal/ river in northeastern South Africa, a tributary of the Orange River. Length: 720 mi./1,160 km.

Vaa·sa /vaá saa/ capital of Vaasa Province, western Finland. Population: 56,658 (2000).

vac^{1} /vak/ *n* same as **vacation** *n* (sense 2) [Early 18C. Shortening]

vac^{2} /vak/ *n* same as **vacuum cleaner** [Late 20C. Shortening]

vac^{3} *abbr* **1.** vacancy **2.** vacant **3.** PHYS vacuum

va·can·cy /váykənssee/ (*plural* **-cies**) *n* **1. VACANT OFFICE OR POSITION** an office, position, or tenancy that is unfilled or unoccupied **2. MENTAL INACTIVITY** mental inactivity or lack of thought or intelligence **3. VACANT STATE** the state of being vacant **4.** PHYS **EMPTY SITE IN CRYSTAL** an empty site, normally containing an atom or ion, in a crystal [Late 16C. < VACANT or < late Latin *vacantia* < Latin *vacant-* (see VACANT)]

va·cant /váykənt/ *adj* **1. WITHOUT OCCUPANT** with no occupant or contents, often temporarily ○ *There were several vacant seats on the bus.* ○ *a vacant lot* **2. UNOCCUPIED BY INCUMBENT OR OFFICIAL** not occupied by an incumbent, official, or possessor, often temporarily ○ *a vacant ambassadorship* **3. LACKING EXPRESSION** showing no signs of thought, intelligence, or expression ○ *a vacant stare* **4. FREE FROM ACTIVITY** free from activity, business, or work ○ *a vacant afternoon* [13C. Via Old French < Latin *vacant-*, present participle of *vacare* "be empty"] —**va·cant·ly** *adv*

SYNONYMS ***vacant, unoccupied, empty, void***

CORE MEANING: lacking contents or occupants

vacant with no occupant or contents, often temporarily ○ *positions left vacant by teachers* ○ *In this part of the country, there is plenty of vacant land and public support for development.* **unoccupied** not being used or lived in by anybody ○ *The building was unoccupied at the time of the fire.* ○ *You can use the unoccupied desk over there.* **empty** not containing or holding anything, or unoccupied or uninhabited ○ *She took a last hasty gulp of coffee and put the empty cup on the counter.* ○ *Theaters showing the movie were almost empty.* **void** having no contents, or not occupied ○ *void spaces between the particles*

---

va·cate /váy kàyt/ (**-cat·ed, -cat·ing, -cates**) *vt* **1. GIVE UP OCCUPANCY OF SOMETHING** to relinquish the possession or occupancy of something ○ *vacate the premises* **2. EMPTY SOMETHING OF OCCUPANTS** to empty something of incumbents or occupants **3. RESIGN FROM SOMETHING** to withdraw from or surrender possession of an office or post ○ *vacate a congressional seat* **4.** LAW **MAKE SOMETHING INVALID** to make something legally void [Mid-17C. < Latin *vacat-*, past participle of *vacare* "be empty"]

va·ca·tion /vay káysh'n, və-/ *n* **1. BREAK FROM WORK** a period of time devoted to rest, travel, or recreation **2. FIXED HOLIDAY PERIOD** a scheduled period during which the activities of courts, schools, or other regular businesses are suspended **3. ACT OR INSTANCE OF VACATING** an act or an instance or vacating something ■ *vi* (**-tioned, -tion·ing, -tions**) LEISURE **TAKE VACATION** to take or spend a vacation [14C. Directly or via French < Latin *vacation-* < *vacat-* (see VACATE)]

va·ca·tion·er /vay káysh'nər, və-/, **va·ca·tion·ist** /vay káysh'nist, və-/ *n* a person who takes or is on a vacation

va·ca·tion·land /vay káysh'n lànd, və-/ *n* an area with many attractions and facilities for vacationers

vac·ci·nate /váksə nàyt/ (**-nat·ed, -nat·ing, -nates**) *vt* to inoculate a person or animal with a vaccine to produce immunity to a disease —**vac·ci·na·tion** /vàksə náysh'n/ *n*

vac·cine /vak seén, vák seèn/ *n* **1.** a preparation containing weakened or dead microbes of the kind that cause a disease, administered to stimulate the immune system to produce antibodies against that disease **2.** a software program that protects a system against a computer virus [Late 18C. < Latin *vaccinus* "of a cow" < *vacca* "cow," because originally the cowpox virus used to prevent smallpox]

ORIGIN ***Vaccine*** was used by the British physician Edward Jenner at the end of the 18th century in the terms *vaccine disease*, meaning "cowpox," and hence *vaccine inoculation*, meaning the technique he developed of preventing smallpox by injecting people with cowpox virus. There is no evidence of the use of ***vaccine*** as a noun to denote the inoculated material until the 1840s.

---

vac·ci·nee /vàksə neé/ *n* somebody who is vaccinated [Late 19C. < VACCINATE]

vac·cin·i·a /vak sínnee ə/ *n* a skin eruption in reaction to inoculation with the weakened cowpox virus that was once used to vaccinate people against smallpox [Early 19C. < modern Latin < Latin *vaccinus* (see VACCINE)] —**vac·cin·i·al** *adj*

~~**vaccum**~~ incorrect spelling of **vacuum**

va·cher·in /vásh ràN, vash ráN/ *n* a soft cheese from France or Switzerland [Mid-20C. < French]

vac·il·late /vássə làyt/ (**-lat·ed, -lat·ing, -lates**) *vi* **1.** to be indecisive or irresolute, changing between one opinion and another **2.** to sway from side to side [Late 16C. < Latin *vacillat-*, past participle of *vaccillare* "sway, totter"] —**vac·il·la·tion** /vàssə láysh'n/ *n* —**vac·il·la·tor** *n*

SYNONYMS See ***hesitate***.

---

vac·u·a PHYS plural of **vacuum**

va·cu·i·ty /va kyoó ətee/ (*plural* **-ties**) *n* **1. LACK OF IDEAS** a lack of intelligent or serious content **2. EMPTINESS** the condition or quality of being empty of all contents (*formal*) **3. EMPTY SPACE** an empty area or space (*formal*) **4. MEANINGLESS STATE OR THING** a thing or condition that is inane or devoid of any meaningful content (*formal*) ○ *legislative vacuity* [Mid-16C. Directly or via French *vacuité* < Latin *vacuitas* < *vacuus* "empty"]

vac·u·o·lar mem·brane /vàkyoo ōlər-, vàkyoo ələr-/ *n* a membrane containing fluid in the cytoplasm of a cell

vac·u·o·late /vákyoo ō làyt, -ōlit/, **vac·u·o·lat·ed** /vákyoo ō làytəd/ *adj* having small holes —**vac·u·o·la·tion** /vàkyoo ō láysh'n/ *n*

vac·u·ole /vákyoo ōl/ *n* **1.** a membrane-bound compartment containing fluid that is found in the cytoplasm of a cell **2.** a small cavity in tissue [Mid-19C. < French, "little empty (space)" < Latin *vacuus* "empty"] —**vac·u·o·lar** /vàkyoo ōlər, vákyoo ələr/ *adj*

vac·u·ous /vákyoo əss/ *adj* **1. INANE** lacking ideas or intelligence, or showing such a lack ○ *a vacuous remark* **2. IDLE** lacking attention, concentration, or serious thought ○ *a vacuous stare* **3. LACKING CONTENT** having no content or substance (*archaic*) [Mid-17C. < Latin *vacuus* "empty"] —**vac·u·ous·ly** *adv* —**vac·u·ous·ness** *n*

vac·u·um /vákyoo əm, vákyoom, vákyəm/ *n* (*plural* **-u·ums** or **-u·a** /-yoo ə/) **1.** PHYS **SPACE EMPTY OF MATTER** a space completely empty of matter but not achievable in practice on Earth **2.** PHYS **SPACE WITH ALL GAS REMOVED** a space from which all air or gas has been extracted **3. EMPTINESS CAUSED BY ABSENCE** an emptiness caused by somebody or something's absence or removal ○ *Inconclusive elections created a political vacuum until a runoff ballot could be held.* **4. ISOLATION FROM OUTSIDE WORLD** isolation from external influences ○ *You can't live in a vacuum.* **5.** (*plural* **vac·u·ums**) HOUSEHOLD same as **vacuum cleaner** ■ *vti* (**-u·umed, -u·um·ing, -u·ums**) **CLEAN SOMETHING USING VACUUM CLEANER** to clean an area or object using a vacuum cleaner [Mid-16C. < modern Latin < neuter of Latin *vacuus* "empty"]

vac·u·um bot·tle *n US* a bottle with two walls enclosing a vacuum, used for keeping the contents at a constant temperature

vac·u·um brake *n* a train or vehicle brake system in which a reservoir-maintained vacuum, under the control of the driver, operates the brake cylinder

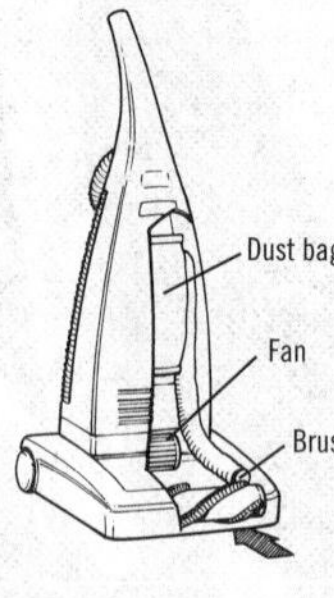

vacuum cleaner

vac·u·um clean·er *n* an electrical appliance that cleans surfaces such as carpets and upholstery by sucking dirt and other material into a bag or cylinder

vac·u·um dis·til·la·tion *n* a process of distilling liquid at low pressure so that it boils at a lower boiling point

vac·u·um dry·ing *n* the removal of liquid from a solution or mixture at reduced air pressure so that it dries at a lower temperature than it would at full pressure

vac·u·um flask *n UK* same as **vacuum bottle**

vac·u·um form·ing *n* the process of shaping sheets of heated thermoplastic by placing them in a mold and removing air by suction

vac·u·um gauge *n* an instrument that measures pressures below atmospheric pressure

vac·u·um-packed *adj* packed in an airtight container or package under low pressure in order to prevent the contents from spoiling or corroding

vac·u·um pan *n* a device with a vacuum pump that removes moisture quickly by boiling a substance at a low temperature under reduced pressure

vac·u·um pump *n* **1.** a device that creates a partial vacuum **2.** ENG same as **pulsometer**

vac·u·um tube *n* an electron tube that is either evacuated or filled with low-pressure gas and in which electrons are pulled from the cathode by an applied anode voltage

va·da *n S Asia* FOOD another spelling of **wada**

va·de me·cum /vàydee meékəm, vaàdee máykəm/ *n* **1.** a guidebook, handbook, or manual, especially one carried around or designed to be carried around constantly and referred to often **2.** an object that a person carries constantly because it is useful [Early 17C. < Latin, "go with me"]

V.Adm., **VADM** *abbr* Vice Admiral

Va·do·da·ra /və dṓdə raà/ industrial city in Gujarat State, western India. Population: 1,492,398 (2001).

va·dose /váy dṑss/ *adj* describes water in the unsaturated zone of the Earth's crust that is above the level of ground water, or relating to such water [Late 19C. < Latin *vadosus* < *vadum* "shallow piece of water"]

va·dose zone *n* the unsaturated zone between the ground surface and the water table through which ground water can percolate

Va·duz /vaa doòts, faa-/ capital of Liechtenstein, on the Rhine River. Population: 4,927 (2001).

Va·fa /vaàfə/, **Cumrun** (*b.* 1960) Iranian physicist. A professor of physics at Harvard University, he made important advances in string theory as a unified description of gravity and other forces.

vag- *prefix* same as **vago-** (*used before vowels*)

vag·a·bond /vággə bònd/ *n* **1.** HOMELESS WANDERER a wanderer who has no permanent place to live **2.** BEGGAR a beggar for food or money ■ *adj* **1.** OF VAGABONDS relating to or characteristic of a vagabond **2.** UNPREDICTABLE wayward or capricious by nature ■ *vi* (**-bond·ed, -bond·ing, -bonds**) BE VAGABOND to wander from place to place [15C. Via French < Latin *vagabundus* < *vagari* "wander"] —**vag·a·bond·age** *n*

va·gal /váyg'l/ *adj* relating to the tenth pair of cranial nerves (**vagi**) —**va·gal·ly** *adv*

va·ga·ry /váygəree/ (*plural* **-ries**) *n* an unpredictable or eccentric change, action, or idea ○ *the vagaries of the weather* [Late 16C. < Latin *vagari* "wander"]

va·gi ANAT plural of **vagus**

vag·ile /vájjəl/ *adj* able to move around within a specific environment [Early 20C. < VAGUS] —**va·gil·i·ty** /və jíllətee/ *n*

va·gi·na /və jī́nə/ (*plural* **-nas** or **-nae** /-nee/) *n* **1.** in female mammals, a lubricated muscular tube that connects the cervix of the womb to the vulva **2.** a plant or animal part that forms a sheath, e.g., that formed by a leaf around a stem [Late 17C. < Latin, "sheath, scabbard"] —**vag·i·nal** /vájjən'l/ *adj* —**vag·i·nal·ly** *adv*

vag·i·nate /vájjənət, vájjə nàyt/, **vag·i·nat·ed** /vájjə nàytəd/ *adj* having, forming, or resembling a sheath

vag·i·nec·to·my /vàjjə néktəmee/ (*plural* **-mies**) *n* **1.** surgical removal of all or part of the vagina **2.** surgical removal of all or part of the smooth moist membrane that encloses the testis and epididymis

vag·i·nis·mus /vàjjə nízməss/ *n* a painful and often prolonged contraction of the vagina in response to touching of the vulva or vagina [Mid-19C. < modern Latin < VAGINA]

vag·i·ni·tis /vàjjə nī́tiss/ *n* inflammation of the vagina

vago- *prefix* vagus ○ *vagotomy* [< VAGUS]

va·got·o·my /və góttəmee/ (*plural* **-mies**) *n* the surgical cutting of the tenth pair of cranial nerves (**vagi**) or any of their branches, performed to control duodenal ulcers by decreasing acid secretion of the stomach

va·go·to·ni·a /vàygə tṓnee ə/ *n* a pathological condition in which overactivity of the tenth pair of cranial nerves (**vagi**) affects bodily functions controlled by these nerves, e.g., those in blood vessels and the gut [Early 20C. < VAGO- + Greek *tonos* "stretching, tension"] —**va·go·ton·ic** /-tónnik/ *adj*

va·go·tro·pic /vàygə trṓpik, -tróppik/ *adj* describes a drug that has an effect on the tenth pair of cranial nerves (**vagi**)

va·grant /váygrənt/ *n* **1.** HOMELESS WANDERER a wanderer who has no permanent place to live **2.** WANDERER somebody who never stays in one place for long **3.** LAW SOMEBODY ILLEGALLY LIVING ON STREETS somebody guilty of the legal offense of living on the streets and, in some jurisdictions, begging ■ *adj* **1.** HOMELESS wandering from one place to another and having no permanent place to live **2.** WANDERING never staying in one place for long **3.** WAYWARD wayward or capricious in nature **4.** RANDOM acting or done in a random way ○ *a vagrant breeze* [15C. < Anglo-Norman *varagarant*] —**va·gran·cy** *n*

vague /vayg/ (**vagu·er, vagu·est**) *adj* **1.** NOT EXPLICIT not clear in meaning or intention ○ *a vague proposal* **2.** NOT DISTINCTLY SEEN not having a clear or perceptible form ○ *a vague form in the shadows* **3.** NOT CLEARLY PERCEIVED IN MIND not clearly felt, understood, or recalled ○ *I have a vague recollection of it.* **4.** UNCLEAR IN THINKING unclear or incoherent in thinking or expression ○ *made vague mutterings in his sleep* [Mid-16C. Directly or via French < Latin *vagus* "wandering, inconstant"] —**vague·ly** *adv* —**vague·ness** *n*

va·gus /váygəss/ (*plural* **-gi** /-gī, -jī/), **va·gus nerve** *n* either of the tenth pair of cranial nerves that carry sensory and motor neurons serving the heart, lungs, stomach, intestines, and various other organs [Mid-19C. < Latin *vagus* "wandering, inconstant"]

VAH *abbr* Veterans' Administration Hospital

vai·dy·a /vídee ə/ *n S Asia* an Ayurvedic Hindu physician [Mid-20C. < Hindi < *vaidy* "expert on Ayurvedic medicine"]

vain /vayn/ *adj* **1.** EXCESSIVELY PROUD excessively proud, especially of personal appearance **2.** UNSUCCESSFUL failing to have or unlikely to have the intended or desired result ○ *a vain attempt to escape* **3.** EMPTY OF SUBSTANCE devoid of substance or meaning [14C. Via Old French < Latin *vanus* "empty, without substance"] —**vain·ly** *adv* —**vain·ness** *n* ◇ **in vain 1.** fruitlessly, pointlessly, or unsuccessfully ○ *We searched in vain for a solution.* **2.** in a disrespectful or blasphemous way

SPELLCHECK vain, **vane**, or **vein**? Do not confuse the spelling of ***vain***, ***vane***, and ***vein***, which sound similar. ***Vain*** is an adjective meaning "excessively proud," "unsuccessful," or "devoid of meaning," as in *a vain man, a vain hope, vain threats*; it is also used in the phrase *in vain*, as in *trying in vain to reach them.* ***Vane*** is a noun denoting a flat rotating blade or the flat part of a feather; a *weather vane* indicates the direction of the wind. ***Vein*** is chiefly used as a noun, denoting a blood vessel, a similar structure in a leaf or an insect's wing, a layer of ore in rock, or a streak in somethng such as marble, wood, or cheese.

vain·glo·ri·ous /vayn gláwree əss/ *adj* excessively proud or boastful (*literary*) —**vain·glo·ri·ous·ly** *adv* —**vain·glo·ri·ous·ness** *n*

vain·glo·ry /váyn glàwree/ (*plural* **-ries**) *n* (*literary*) **1.** excessive pride in or boastfulness about personal abilities or achievements **2.** an excessive display of something in order to draw attention to it [12C. Via French < Latin *vana gloria* "empty glory"]

vair /ver/ *n* **1.** fur used as a trimming on medieval robes **2.** a blue-and-white fur used on heraldic shields [14C. Via French < Latin *varius* "speckled, changeable"]

Vais·a·kha /vī́ss aàkə/ *n* in the Hindu calendar, the second month of the year, lasting 31 days and falling about the same time as April to May. See table at **calendar**

Vaish·na·va /vī́shnəvə/ *n* a member of a group devoted to the worship of the Hindu god Vishnu or one of his incarnations [Late 18C. < Sanskrit *vaiṣṇava* "relating to Vishnu"] —**Vaish·na·vism** *n*

Vais·ya /vī́ssyə, vī́sh-/, **Vaish·ya** *n* **1.** the third of the four Hindu castes, the members of which were traditionally merchants and farmers **2.** a member of the Vaisya caste [Mid-17C. < Sanskrit *vaiśya* "farm laborer, tradesman"]

Vaj·pa·yee /vàj páy ee/, **Atal Bihari** (*b.* 1924) Indian prime minister. He was the first leader of the Hindu nationalist party Bharatiya Janata Party (1980). He was briefly prime minister (1996) but was forced to resign due to lack of support from other parties. He was prime minister of a coalition government (1998–2004).

va·kil /və keél/, **va·keel, wa·kil** *n S Asia* a lawyer or legal representative in a court of law [Early 17C. Via Persian and Urdu *wakīl*, Turkish *vakīl* < Arabic *wakīl*]

val. *abbr* **1.** GEOL valley **2.** COMM value

Va·lais Alps /vaa lày-/ ➧ **Pennine Alps**

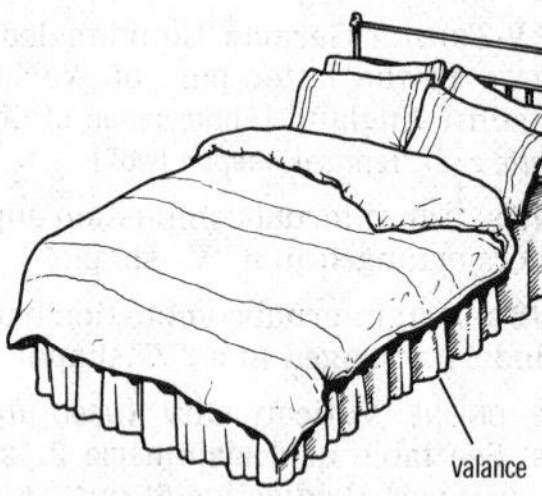

valance (sense 2)

val·ance /vállənss, váyl-/ *n* **1.** a short decorative piece of drapery or wood hung across a window to cover the rod from which curtains hang **2.** a plain, pleated, or gathered fabric cover that hangs from a shelf or from the base of a bed to the floor [15C. Origin ?]

Val·dez /val deéz/ city in southeastern Alaska, on the shore of an inlet of Prince William Sound. Population: 4,109 (2002 estimate).

Val-d'Or /vàl dáwr/ city in southwestern Quebec, Canada. It was a gold-rush town in the 1930s. Population: 24,942 (2001).

vale[1] /vayl/ *n* a valley or dale, often one that has a stream running through it (*often used in place names*) [14C. Via French < Latin *valles* "valley"] ◇ **vale of tears** the world considered as a place full of sadness or unhappiness

SPELLCHECK vale or **veil**? Do not confuse the spelling of ***vale*** and ***veil***, which sound similar. The word ***vale***, meaning "valley," is chiefly found in place names or in the phrase *vale of tears.* ***Veil*** is a noun or verb referring to a covering for the face or something that conceals in a similar way, as in *a bridal veil, a veil of mist, veiled in secrecy.*

va·le[2] /vaá lày, váylee/ *interj* a Latin expression of farewell ■ *n* an act of saying farewell or adieu [Mid-16C. < Latin, "be well!", form of *valere* "be strong or well"]

val·e·dic·tion /vàllə díkshən/ *n* (*formal*) **1.** the act of saying goodbye or an instance of leave-taking **2.** a statement, speech, or letter of farewell [Mid-17C. < Latin *valedicere* "say goodbye," after BENEDICTION]

val·e·dic·to·ri·an /vàllə dik táwree ən/ *n* a student in a graduating class who is highest in academic ranking and is usually required to give a valedictory address at the graduation ceremony

val·e·dic·to·ry /vàllə díktəree/ *n* (*plural* **-ries**) **1.** a statement or speech of farewell (*formal*) **2.** EDUC same as **valedictory address** ■ *adj* performing the function of saying farewell (*formal*)

val·e·dic·to·ry ad·dress *n* a speech delivered at graduation, usually by the graduating student with the highest academic ranking

va·lence /váylənss/, **va·len·cy** /-see/ (*plural* **-cies**) *n* **1.** COMBINING POWER OF ATOMS the combining power of atoms or groups measured by the number of electrons the atom or group will receive, give up, or share in forming a compound **2.** COMBINING ANTIGENIC DETERMINANTS the number of different antigenic determinants with which a single antibody molecule can combine **3.** COMBINING POWER OF VERB the ability of a verb to combine grammatically with noun phrases in a given clause [Late 19C. Variant of VALENCY]

va·lence e·lec·tron *n* an electron in an outer shell of an atom that can be lost to or shared with another atom to form a molecule

va·lence shell *n* the outer electron shell of an atom, containing one or more electrons (**valence electrons**) that are available to form bonds with other atoms to create molecules

Va·len·ci·a /və lénshee ə, -see ə/ **1.** capital of the autonomous region of Valencia in E Spain. The city was founded in Roman times. Population: 761,871 (2002). **2.** city in northern Venezuela, on the Cabriales River. Population: 1,034,033 (1992 estimate).

Va·len·ci·a or·ange *n* an orange with sweet juicy flesh and a thin skin

Va·len·ci·ennes[1] /və lènssee én, va laaN syén/ *n* a fine cotton lace made with bobbins in a floral design, originally made of linen [Early 18C. After VALENCIENNES[2]]

Va·len·ci·ennes[2] /və lènssee én, va laaN syen/ city in the Nord-Pas-de-Calais Region of northern France and administrative center of the Nord Department. Population: 41,278 (1999).

va·len·cy *n* CHEM, IMMUNOL, GRAM same as **valence**

-valent *suffix* having a particular valence or valences ○ *divalent* [< VALENCE]

val·en·tine /vállən tīn/ *n* **1.** a greeting card or gift sent, traditionally anonymously, to somebody on Valentine's Day as a token of love **2.** the person to whom somebody sends a card or gift on Valentine's Day as a token of love [15C. After St. VALENTINE]

Val·en·tine /vállən tīn/, **St.** (*d.* A.D. 269?) Roman priest and martyr. He is thought to have been killed during the persecution of Christians by Emperor Claudius II.

Val·en·tine's Day *n* the Christian feast day of St. Valentine and the traditional day for sending a romantic card or gift, especially anonymously, to somebody you love. Date: February 14.

Rudolph Valentino

Val·en·ti·no /vàllən teénō/, **Rudolph** (1895–1926) Italian-born US actor. His passionate roles in silent movies made him a romantic screen idol. Born **d'Antonguolla, Rodolpho Guglielmi di Valentina**

Va·le·ra ▸ **De Valera, Eamon**

va·le·ri·an /və leéree ən/ (*plural* **-ans** or *same*) *n* **1.** PLANTS PLANT WITH MEDICINAL ROOT an herbaceous perennial plant. Flowers: small, sweet-smelling, white or pinkish. Native to: Europe, Asia. Genus: *Valeriana*. **2.** FLOWERING PLANT a bushy perennial plant. Flowers: red, pink, or white. Native to: Mediterranean. Latin name: *Centranthus ruber*. **3.** MED SEDATIVE MADE FROM VALERIAN an herbal medicine made from the dried roots of valerian. Use: mild sedative, tranquilizer. [15C. Via French < medieval Latin *valeriana*, after *Valeria*, Roman province]

va·ler·ic ac·id /və leérik-, və lèrrik-/ *n* a pungent colorless liquid. Use: flavorings, perfumes, pharmaceuticals. Formula: $C_5H_{10}O_2$. [< VALERIAN]

Va·lé·ry /và le reé, vaa lay reé/, **Paul** (1871–1945) French poet and critic. He was considered to be one of France's greatest 20th-century poets and his prolific early output was followed by a 20-year silence, during which he worked mainly on mathematics and philosophical meditations. His later work was heavily influenced by the symbolists. Full name **Valéry, Paul Ambroise**

> "God made everything out of nothing. But the nothingness shows through."
> [Paul Valéry, *Mauvaises pensées et autres (Wicked and Other Thoughts)*; 1942]

val·et *n* /vállət, vá lày, va láy/ **1.** SOMEBODY PERFORMING CAR PARKING SERVICE somebody employed to park the cars of people arriving at a hotel, restaurant, or airport and bring the cars back for them on departure **2.** MALE HOTEL OR PASSENGER SHIP EMPLOYEE a male employee whose duties include cleaning the clothes of hotel guests or passengers on ships **3.** MALE SERVANT a male personal servant of a man, whose duties include taking care of his employer's clothes and providing his meals ■ *v* /vállət/ (**-et·ed, -et·ing, -ets**) **1.** *vti* WORK AS VALET to work as a valet or provide valet services to somebody **2.** *vt* CLEAN CAR to clean somebody's car in return for payment **3.** *vi* USE VALET PARKING to use the services of a valet to park a car ○ *We valeted our car and entered the casino.* [15C. < French < assumed medieval Latin *vassus* "servant to a knight"]

va·le·ta *n* DANCE another spelling of **veleta**

val·et de cham·bre /và lay də shaáNbrə/ (*plural* **val·ets de cham·bre** /*pronunc. same*/) *n* OCCUPATIONS same as **valet** *n* (sense 3) [French, "valet of the room"]

val·et park·ing *n* a service provided by some hotels, restaurants, and airports whereby an employee parks people's cars for them on arrival and brings the cars back for them on departure

val·e·tu·di·nar·i·an /vàllə tood'n érree ən/, **val·e·tu·di·nar·y** /vàllə tood'n èrree/ *n* (*plural* **-ans**; *plural* **-ies**) **1.** SOMEBODY WITH POOR HEALTH somebody who has persistent ill health **2.** SOMEBODY OBSESSED WITH HEALTH somebody who is excessively concerned with his or her own health ■ *adj* **1.** OF VALETUDINARIAN relating to or being a valetudinarian **2.** OF POOR HEALTH relating to, characterized by, or arising from poor health [Late 16C. < Latin *valetudinarius* "in ill health" < *valetudo* "state of health" < *valere* "be well"] —**val·e·tu·di·nar·i·an·ism** *n*

~~**valey**~~ incorrect spelling of **valley**

Val·hal·la /val hállə, vaal haálə/, **Wal·hal·la**, **Wal·hall** /vaál haál/ *n* in Norse mythology, the great hall where the souls of heroes killed in battle spend eternity [Late 17C. Via modern Latin < Old Norse *valhall* "hall of the slain" < *valr* "those slain in battle"]

val·iant /vállyənt/ *adj* **1.** COURAGEOUS brave and steadfast ○ *a valiant warrior* **2.** DONE COURAGEOUSLY characterized by or performed with bravery but often ending in failure ○ *a valiant attempt at rescue* ■ *n* SOMEBODY COURAGEOUS a brave and steadfast person [14C. Via Old French < Latin *valent-*, present participle of *valere* "be strong"] —**val·iance** *n* —**val·iant·ly** *adv*

val·id /vállid/ *adj* **1.** UNEXPIRED usable or acceptable until a fixed expiration date or under specific conditions of use ○ *a valid passport* **2.** JUSTIFIABLE reasonable or justifiable in the circumstances ○ *That's a valid question.* **3.** EFFECTIVE bringing about the results or ends intended ○ *regards the test as a valid measure of student performance* **4.** LAW LEGALLY BINDING having binding force in law **5.** LOGIC LOGICAL having premises from which the conclusion follows logically ○ *It's a perfectly valid argument.* [Late 16C. Directly or via French < Latin *validus* "strong" < *valere* "be strong"] —**va·lid·i·ty** /və líddətee/ *n* —**val·id·ly** *adv*

SYNONYMS *valid, cogent, convincing, reasonable, sound*

CORE MEANING: worthy of acceptance or credence

valid reasonable or justifiable in the circumstances ○ *Mrs. Smith raises a valid point in her letter.* ○ *We are required to notify all other parties unless there is a valid reason why such notice should not be given.* **cogent** forceful and convincing to the intellect and reason ○ *a cogent analysis of the situation* ○ *Their rationale is neither logical nor cogent.* **convincing** likely to overcome doubts and win the support of those who hear it ○ *Your explanation is not wholly convincing.* ○ *He needs to see convincing evidence before he can accept this theory.* **reasonable** acceptable and according to common sense ○ *must show reasonable grounds for his actions* ○ *It seemed like a reasonable assumption at the time.* **sound** based on good sense and acceptable reasoning and worthy of approval ○ *Her portfolio is diversified in accordance with sound investment policy.* ○ *offers some sound advice on road safety*

val·i·date /válli dàyt/ (**-dat·ed, -dat·ing, -dates**) *vt* **1.** CONFIRM TRUTHFULNESS OF SOMETHING to confirm or establish the truthfulness or soundness of something **2.** LAW MAKE SOMETHING LEGAL to declare or render something legal or binding ○ *validate a passport* **3.** REGISTER SOMETHING FORMALLY to register something formally and have its use officially sanctioned **4.** MAKE SOMEBODY FEEL VALUED to make somebody feel valued as a person, or feel that his or her ideas or opinions are worthwhile [Mid-17C. < Latin *validare* "render legally valid" < *validus* (see VALID)] —**val·i·da·tion** /vàlli dáysh'n/ *n*

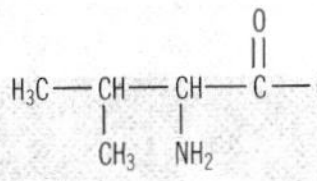

valine

val·ine /vá leèn, váy-/ *n* an essential amino acid, required for normal growth. Formula: $C_5H_{11}NO_2$. [Early 20C. < VALERIC ACID]

va·lise /və leéss/ *n* a small piece of luggage [Early 20C. Via French < Italian *valigia*]

Val·i·um /vállee əm/ *tdmk* a trademark for diazepam, a tranquilizer

Val·kyr·ie /val keéree, válkəree/, **Wal·kyr·ie**, **Val·kyr** /válkər/ *n* in Norse mythology, one of the twelve handmaids of Odin who ride their horses over the field of battle and escort the souls of slain heroes to Valhalla [Mid-18C. < Old Norse *Valkyrja* "chooser of the slain" < *valr* "those slain in battle"] —**Val·kyr·i·an** /val keéree ən/ *adj*

val·la ANCIENT HIST, BUILDINGS plural of **vallum**

Val·la·do·lid /vaàlə do líd/ capital of Valladolid Province, northern Spain. It was the capital of Spain before Madrid. Population: 318,576 (2002).

val·late /vá làyt/ (**-lat·ed, -lat·ing, -lates**) *vt* to plan or build earthworks to defend a position [Late 19C. Back-formation < VALLATION]

val·la·tion /va láysh'n/ *n* **1.** a defensive fortification or embankment made of earth **2.** the planning or building of defensive fortifications or embankments made of earth [Mid-17C. < Latin *vallation-* < *vallare* "protect" < *vallum* SEE VALLUM]

val·lec·u·la /və lékyələ/ (*plural* **-lae** /-leè/) *n* a shallow groove, depression, or furrow in an animal or plant body, e.g., that between the hemispheres of the cerebellum in the brain [Mid-19C. < Latin *vallicula* < *valles* "valley"] —**val·lec·u·lar** *adj*

Val·le d'A·os·ta /vaa lay daa ōstə/ region in northern Italy, on the border with France and Switzerland. It contains the Alpine peaks of the Matterhorn and Mont Blanc. Population: 120,343 (2000). Area: 1,260 sq. mi./3,264 sq. km.

Val·les Ma·ri·ner·is /và less màrri nérriss/ system of valleys and canyons in the equatorial region of Mars, 2,500 mi./4,000 km long, up to 150 mi./240 km wide, and 4 mi./6.5 km deep

Val·let·ta /və léttə/ capital and chief port of Malta. Population: 7,048 (2000).

val·ley /vállee/ (*plural* **-leys**) *n* **1.** **LOW-LYING AREA** a long low area of land, often with a river or stream running through it, that is surrounded by higher ground **2.** **LOW-LYING LAND AROUND RIVER** a large area of low-lying land around a river and its tributaries **3.** **VALLEY-SHAPED HOLLOW** a long sunken area or groove shaped like a valley **4.** ARCHIT **ANGLE BETWEEN ROOF SLOPES** the angle formed where two slopes of a roof intersect [13C. Via Old French *valee* < Latin *valles* "valley"] —**val·leyed** *adj*

val·ley fe·ver *n* MED same as **coccidioidomycosis** [After the San Joaquin *Valley*, California]

Val·ley Forge /vàllee fáwrj/ historic site in Pennsylvania, northwest of Philadelphia on the Schuylkill River. During the winter of 1777–78, George Washington and 12,000 troops of the Continental Army endured a season of intense deprivation and demoralization that came to be seen as the bleakest period of the American Revolution.

Val·ley of the Kings gorge on the western bank of the Nile River, southern Egypt. It was the burial site of pharaohs of the New Kingdom (1570–1070 B.C.).

Val·lis Al·pes /vàlliss ál pèz/ valley on the Moon northeast of mare imbrium, running approximately from west to east and cutting across Montes Alpes

val·lum /vállәm/ (*plural* **-lums** or **-la** /-lə/) *n* an ancient Roman fortification or embankment, built for military defense [Early 17C. < Latin < *vallus* "palisade, stake"]

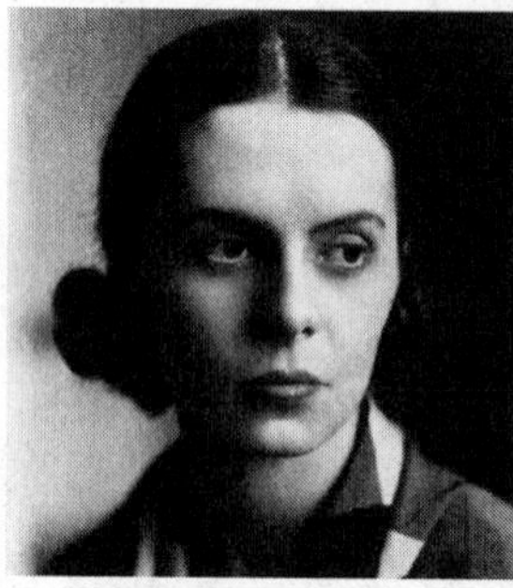
Hulton-Deutsch Collection/Corbis

Dame Ninette de Valois

Val·ois /vál waa/, **Dame Ninette de** (1898–2001) Irish-born British dancer and choreographer. She founded the Sadler's Wells Ballet (1931) in London, England, which became the Royal Ballet in 1956. Born **Stannus, Edris**

> "Ladies and gentleman, it takes more than one to make a ballet."
> [Dame Ninette de Valois, *New Yorker*; 1950]

va·lo·ni·a /və lṓnee ə/ *n* the dried acorn cups and unripe acorns of an oak. Use: tanning, inks, dyes. [Early 18C. Via Italian < Greek *balanos* "acorn"]

val·or /vállər/ *n* courage, especially that shown in war or battle [Late 16C. Via Italian *valore* < Latin *valor* < *valere* "be strong"]

val·or·ize /vállə rīz/ (**-ized, -iz·ing, -iz·es**) *vt* to set and maintain the price of a commodity at an artificially high level through government action [Early 20C. Via Portuguese *valorizar* < *valor* "value" < late Latin (see VALOR)] —**val·or·i·za·tion** /vàlləri záysh'n/ *n*

val·or·ous /vállərəss/ *adj* having or showing courage, especially in war or battle —**val·or·ous·ly** *adv*

val·our *n* Can, UK spelling of **valor**

Val·pa·rai·so /vàlpə ráyzō, -rīzō/ **1.** *also* **Val·pa·ra·í·so** /bàlpara éessō/ capital of Valparaiso Region in central Chile. Population: 293,800 (1998). **2.** city in northwestern Indiana, south of Lake Michigan and southwest of Michigan City. Population: 28,185 (2002 estimate).

Val·po·li·cel·la /vàl pōlə chéllə/ *n* a light red wine from northwestern Italy [Early 20C. After a district]

val·pro·ate /val prṓ àyt/, **val·pro·ic ac·id** /val prṑ ik-/ *n* a synthetic crystalline compound with anticonvulsant properties. Use: treatment of epilepsy. [Late 20C. < *valproic acid* (< VALERIC ACID + PROPYL)]

Val·sal·va ma·neu·ver /val sálvə-/ *n* **1.** the action of attempting to breathe out when the mouth is closed and the nostrils are held shut, thereby forcing air into the middle ear via the eustachian tubes **2.** the action of attempting to breathe out against a closed glottis, which increases pressure in the thoracic cavity and hinders the return of venous blood to the heart [After Antonio Maria *Valsalva* (1666–1723), Italian anatomist]

valse /vaalss/ *n* a waltz, especially one of French origin [Late 18C. Via French < German *Walzer* (see WALTZ)]

val·u·a·ble /vállyoo əb'l, -yəb'l/ *adj* **1.** **WORTH GREAT DEAL OF MONEY** having significant monetary value **2.** **USEFUL** having great importance or usefulness ○ *a valuable insight* **3.** **HELD DEAR** cherished or esteemed because of personal qualities **4.** **RARE** highly prized because of being in short or limited supply **5.** **ABLE TO BE VALUED** capable of being assigned a value ■ *n* **VALUABLE ITEM** a possession, especially a piece of jewelry, that has significant monetary value (*often used in the plural*) —**val·u·a·ble·ness** *n* —**val·u·a·bly** *adv*

val·u·a·ble con·sid·er·a·tion *n* in English contract law, something given or undertaken as part of an agreement between two parties that has some objective value and so makes the agreement a valid contract. For example, in the sale of a car, valuable consideration is the money paid to the person selling the car.

val·u·ate /vállyoo àyt/ (**-at·ed, -at·ing, -ates**) *vt* to determine the price or cost of something

val·u·a·tion /vàllyoo áysh'n/ *n* **1.** **APPRAISAL OF COST** the act of determining the value or price of something, especially property **2.** **PRICE** the price of something established by appraisal of its quality, condition, and desirability, or of the cost of replacement **3.** **ESTIMATE OF IMPORTANCE** an estimate of the importance or usefulness of something —**val·u·a·tion·al** *adj*

val·u·a·tor /vállyoo àytər/ *n* somebody who assesses the value of objects such as jewelry or works of art

~~valuble~~ incorrect spelling of **valuable**

val·ue /vállyoo/ *n* **1.** **MONETARY WORTH** an amount expressed in money or another medium of exchange that is thought to be a fair exchange for something ○ *goods to the value of $500* **2.** **FULL RECOVERED WORTH** the adequate or satisfactory return on or recompense for something ○ *It's value for money.* **3.** **WORTH OR IMPORTANCE** the worth, importance, or usefulness of something to somebody ○ *a ring with great sentimental value* **4.** LING **MEANING** the exact meaning or significance of a word **5.** MATH **NUMERICAL QUANTITY** a numerical quantity assigned to a mathematical symbol **6.** MUSIC **LENGTH OF NOTE** in music, the length of time that a note or pause is held **7.** ART **SHADE OF COLOR** in painting and drawing, the lightness or darkness of a color **8.** PHON **SOUND REPRESENTED** the quality or tone of a speech sound that a letter or written character represents ■ **val·ues** *npl* **PRINCIPLES OR STANDARDS** the accepted principles or standards of a person or a group ■ *vt* (**-ued, -u·ing, -ues**) **1.** **ESTIMATE VALUE OF SOMETHING** to estimate or determine the value of something ○ *the painting was valued at $5,000* **2.** **RATE SOMETHING** to rate something according to its perceived worth, importance, or usefulness ○ *a car valued at $30,000* **3.** **REGARD SOMEBODY OR SOMETHING HIGHLY** to regard somebody or something as important or useful ○ *I value her as a friend.* [14C. < Old French < *valoir* "be worth" < Latin *valere* "be powerful"] —**val·u·er** *n*

val·ue add·ed *n* the amount by which the value of a product increases as it proceeds through the various stages of its manufacture and distribution

val·ue-add·ed *adj* relating to the increasing value of a product as it proceeds through the various stages of its manufacture and distribution

val·ue-add·ed net·work *n* ONLINE full form of **VAN**

val·ue-add·ed tax *n* FIN full form of **VAT**

val·ue date *n* in the calculation of exchange rates, the date on which a transaction is judged to have occurred

val·ued pol·i·cy /vàllyood-/ *n* an insurance policy in which the amount payable for a valid claim is established when the policy is issued and is independent of the value of a loss subsequently incurred

val·ue-free *adj* not affected by or based on value judgments

val·ue judg·ment *n* a judgment of the worth, appropriateness, or importance of somebody or something made on the basis of personal beliefs, opinions, or prejudices rather than facts

val·ue·less /vállyooləss/ *adj* having no value —**val·ue·less·ness** *n*

val·ue sys·tem *n* a set of personal principles and standards

val·u·ta /və lóotə/ *n* the value of one nation's currency in terms of its exchange rate with another currency [Late 19C. < Italian, "value"]

val·val, **val·var** *adj* ANAT same as **valvular**

val·vate /vál vàyt/ *adj* **1.** **EQUIPPED WITH VALVES** having valves or parts similar to valves **2.** BOT **NOT OVERLAPPING IN BUD** describes sepals or petals that touch but do not overlap in the bud **3.** BOT **TAKING PLACE BY MEANS OF VALVES** describes the splitting open of the seed capsules of the iris or lily that takes place by means of valves [Early 19C. < Latin *valvatus* "having folding doors" < *valva* "leaf of a folding door"]

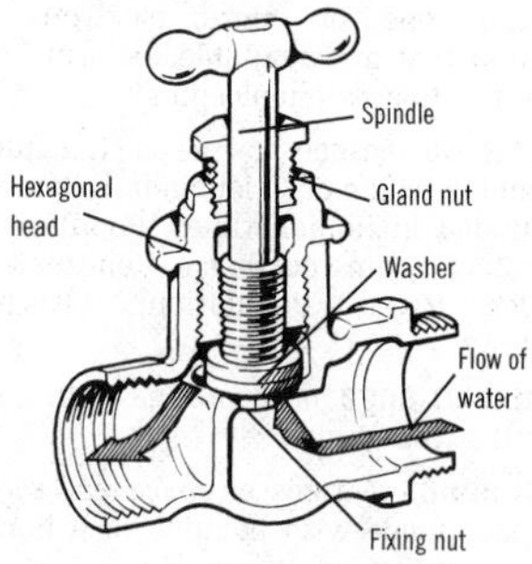

valve

valve /valv/ *n* **1.** ENG **DEVICE THAT CONTROLS LIQUID FLOW** a device that controls the movement of liquids or gases through pipes or other passages by opening or closing ports and channels **2.** MUSIC **PART ON BRASS INSTRUMENT** a device in some brass instruments that diverts air down tubes of varying length, thereby altering the pitch **3.** *UK* ELECTRONICS same as **vacuum tube** **4.** ANAT **CLOSABLE FLAP IN ORGAN** a membranous structure in a hollow organ or vessel such as the heart or a vein that prevents the return flow of fluid passing through it by folding or closing **5.** BOT **PART OF SEED POD** a segment of the wall of a seed pod or other fruit that splits apart to reveal the contents **6.** BOT **ANTHER FLAP** a flap that acts like a lid in some types of anthers **7.** BOT **PART OF CELL WALL** either of the two parts of the silica-impregnated cell wall of a type of alga (**diatom**) that fit together like the lid and base of a box **8.** ZOOL **SEPARABLE PART OF SHELL** a hinged part of the shell of a brachiopod or some mollusks **9.** ZOOL **SINGLE-UNIT SHELL** the single-unit shell of a snail and some other mollusks [15C. < Latin *valva* "leaf of a folding door"] —**valved** *adj* —**valve·less** *adj*

valve gear *n* a mechanical device that controls the valves of a reciprocating engine

valve-in-head en·gine *n UK* same as **overhead-valve engine**

valve spring *n* **1.** a spiral spring that holds a valve closed in the cylinder head of an internal-combustion engine **2.** a spring that closes an opened valve

val·vu·la /válvyələ/ (*plural* **-lae** /-lèe/) *n* BIOL, ANAT same as **valvule** [Early 17C. < modern Latin < Latin *valva* "leaf of a folding door"]

val·vu·lar /válvyələr/, **val·val** /válvəl/, **val·var** /válvər/ *adj* **1.** relating to, having, or acting like a valve or set of valves **2.** involving or affecting a valve or set of valves

val·vule /vál vyo͞ol/ *n* a small valve or a part that functions or looks like one [Mid-18C. Variant of VALVULA]

val·vu·li·tis /vàlvyə lī́tiss/ *n* inflammation of a valve in the body, especially one in the heart, often caused by rheumatic fever

val·vu·lo·plas·ty /válvyələ plàstee/ (*plural* **-ties**) *n* plastic surgery performed to repair a valve in the body, especially one in the heart [Mid-20C. < VALVULE]

vam·brace /vám bràyss/ *n* a piece of armor formerly worn over the forearm as protection [14C. Via Anglo-Norman *vauntbras* < Old French *avantbras* < *avant* "before" + *bras* "arm"]

va·moose /va mo͞oss, və-/ (**-moosed, -moos·ing, -moos·es**) *vi* to leave in a hurried way (*slang*) [Mid-19C. < Spanish *vamos* "let us go"]

REGIONAL NOTE The term ***vamoose*** is now widespread through the United States. It spread into general currency from Texas to California and has been further strengthened by the accelerated influx of Mexican Americans across the country.

vamp[1] /vamp/ (*sometimes considered offensive*) *n* **SEDUCTIVE WOMAN** a woman who is believed to use her sexual attractiveness for the seduction and manipulation of others ■ *v* (**vamped, vamp·ing, vamps**) **1.** *vti* **SEDUCE SOMEBODY** to seduce and manipulate somebody by appearing to offer sexual intercourse **2.** *vi* **ACT LIKE VAMP** to act like or play the role of a vamp [Early 20C. Shortening of VAMPIRE] —**vamp·ish** *adj* —**vamp·ish·ly** *adv* —**vamp·y** *adj*

vamp[2] /vamp/ *n* **1. SOMETHING PATCHED UP** something repaired so as to appear new **2. REHASHING OF SOMETHING** a reworking of something already used or available, especially a book or article **3.** CLOTHING **UPPER PART OF SHOE** the upper part of a shoe that covers the front part of the foot **4.** MUSIC **IMPROVISED MUSICAL INTRODUCTION** an improvised musical introduction or accompaniment that is repeated as necessary until the entry of the solo line ■ *v* (**vamped, vamp·ing, vamps**) **1.** *vt* CLOTHING **PUT VAMP ON SHOE** to put a vamp on a shoe **2.** *vti* MUSIC **IMPROVISE MUSICAL INTRODUCTION OR ACCOMPANIMENT** to improvise a musical introduction or accompaniment for a solo line [14C. Shortening of Old French *avantpié* < *avant* "before" + *pié* "foot"] —**vamp·er** *n*

vamp up *vt* **1.** to rework or renovate something ○ *vamp up an old deck* **2.** to make something up or improvise something

vam·pire /vám pīr/ *n* **1. BLOODSUCKING EVIL SPIRIT** in European folklore, a dead person believed to rise each night from the grave and suck blood from the living for sustenance **2. PREDATORY PERSON** somebody who preys on other people for financial or emotional gain **3.** ZOOL same as **vampire bat** **4.** THEATER **TRAP DOOR** a trap door on the floor of a stage (*technical*) [Mid-18C. Via French or German < Serbo-Croatian *vampir*] —**vam·pir·ic** /vam pírrik/ *adj* —**vam·pir·i·cal** *adj* —**vam·pir·ish** *adj*

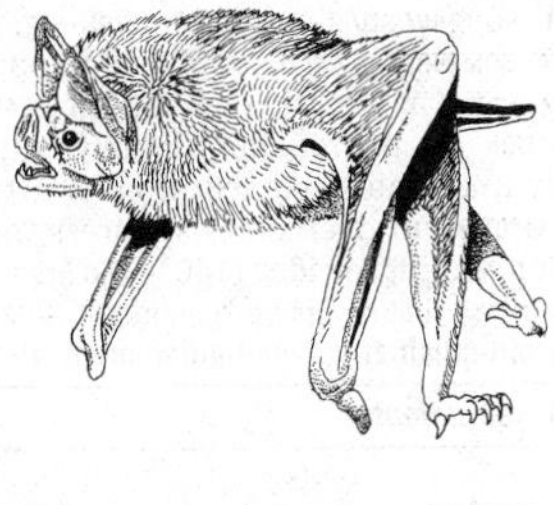

vampire bat

vam·pire bat *n* a bat that bites the skin of birds or other mammals and laps the blood. Native to: tropical and subtropical Central and South America. Family: Desmodontidae.

vam·pir·ism /vám pī rìzzəm/ *n* **1. BELIEF IN VAMPIRES** the belief that some corpses can leave their graves at night and suck the blood of living people **2. STATE OF BEING VAMPIRE** the supposed state or practices of a vampire **3. FINANCIAL OR EMOTIONAL EXPLOITATION** the act of preying on other people for financial or emotional gain

van[1] /van/ *n* **1. ENCLOSED MOTOR VEHICLE** a motor vehicle that has rear or side doors or sliding side panels and is used for transporting goods or people **2.** *UK* RAIL **RAILROAD CAR** a closed railroad car for goods, or the section of the car for the conductor, luggage, packages, or mail ■ *v* (**vanned, van·ning, vans**) *US* TRANSP **1.** *vt* **TRANSPORT SOMETHING BY VAN** to move something from one place to another by van **2.** *vi* **TRAVEL IN VAN** to drive or travel in a van [Early 19C. Shortening of CARAVAN]

van[2] /van/ *n* **1.** a device used for winnowing grain (*archaic*) **2.** a bird's wing (*archaic or literary*) [15C. Variant of FAN[1]]

van[3] /van/ *n* same as **vanguard** (sense 1) (*informal*) [Early 17C. Shortening]

van[4], **Van** see also under surname

Van /van, vaan/ city in eastern Turkey, the capital of Van Province. It lies on the eastern shore of Lake Van, about 50 mi./80 km west of the Turkish-Iranian border. Population: 219,319 (1997).

Van, Lake /van, vaan/ saltwater lake in eastern Turkey, between the sources of the Euphrates and Tigris rivers, at an altitude of 5,643 ft./1,720 m. Area: 1,453 sq. mi./3,763 sq. km.

VAN /van/ *n* a computer network that enables private companies to exchange information with other registered subscribers. Full form **value-added network**

van. *abbr* vanilla

van·a·date /vánnə dàyt/ *n* a salt or ester of vanadium [Mid-19C. < VANADIUM]

va·na·dic /və náydik, -náddik/ *adj* relating to or containing vanadium, especially with a high valence [Mid-19C. < VANADIUM]

va·na·di·nite /və náyd'n ìt, və nádd'n-/ *n* a rare brown, red, or yellow mineral. Source: lead minerals. Use: source of vanadium. [Mid-19C. < VANADIUM]

va·na·di·um /və náydee əm/ *n* a poisonous silvery white metallic element. Source: carnotite, vanadinite. Use: manufacture of tough steel alloys, catalyst. Symbol **V**. See table at **element** [Mid-19C. < modern Latin < Old Norse *Vanadis*, Scandinavian goddess]

va·na·di·um pent·ox·ide *n* a yellow or red crystalline compound. Use: catalyst, manufacture of glass. Formula: V_2O_5.

va·na·di·um steel *n* a low-alloy steel containing the element vanadium for added strength

va·na·dous /və náydəss, vánnədəss/ *adj* relating to or containing vanadium, especially with a low valence [Mid-19C. < VANADIUM]

Van Al·len /van állən/, **James** (*b.* 1914) US physicist. A pioneer in high altitude and space research, he discovered (1958) two radiation belts that encircle the Earth. Full name **Van Allen, James Alfred**

Van Al·len belt, **Van Al·len ra·di·a·tion belt** *n* either of two belts surrounding Earth and containing charged particles held there by the Earth's magnetic field

van·as·pa·ti /və náspətee/ *n* a hydrogenated vegetable oil commonly used in South Asian cooking instead of butter [Mid-20C. < Sanskrit *vanas-pati* "lord of the plants"]

Corbis

Martin Van Buren

Van Bu·ren /-byo͞orən/, **Martin** (1782–1862) 8th president of the United States (1837–41). During his presidency, he supported the war against the Seminoles in Florida but opposed the annexation of Texas. Known as **Little Magician, Red Fox of Kinderhook**. See table at **president**

"I tread in the footsteps of illustrious men, whose superiors it is our happiness to believe are not found on the executive calendar of any country."
[Martin Van Buren, *Inaugural presidential address*; March 4, 1837]

Vance /vanss/, **Cyrus** (1917–2002) US government official. He resigned as Jimmy Carter's secretary of state (1977–80) after a failed attempt to rescue US hostages in Iran. He subsequently worked as an international peace negotiator, notably in Bosnia (1992–93). Full name **Vance, Cyrus Roberts**

van·co·my·cin /vàngkə mī́ssən/ *n* an antibiotic that is effective against some bacteria that are resistant to other antibiotics. Strains of bacteria resistant to vancomycin have now developed. [Mid-20C. < *vanco-*, origin?]

van·co·my·cin in·ter·me·di·ate Staph·y·lo·coc·cus au·re·us *n* MICROBIOL full form of **VISA**

van·co·my·cin re·sis·tant Staph·y·lo·coc·cus au·re·us *n* MICROBIOL full form of **VRSA**

Van·cou·ver /van ko͞ovər/ city and port in southwestern British Columbia, Canada, opposite Vancouver Island. Population: 545,671 (2001).

Van·cou·ver, Mount peak of St. Elias Range in southwestern Yukon Territory, Canada. Height: 15,840 ft./4,828 m.

Van·cou·ver /van ko͞ovər/, **George** (1757–98) British naval officer and explorer. He sailed with Captain James Cook and later was the first European to circumnavigate Vancouver Island, during a surveying expedition.

Van·cou·ver Is·land island off the southwestern coast of British Columbia, Canada. It is the largest island off western North America. Population: 702,000. Area: 12,079 sq. mi./31,285 sq. km.

van·da /vándə/ (*plural* **-das** or *same*) *n* an orchid with strap-shaped leaves. Flowers: flattened with a spur on the lip. Native to: East Asia, Australia. Genus: *Vanda*. [Early 19C. Via modern Latin < Sanskrit *vandā*]

van·dal /vánd'l/ *n* somebody who intentionally defaces or destroys somebody else's property [Mid-16C. < Latin *Vandalus* "Vandal" < Germanic] —**van·dal·ish** /vánd'lish/ *adj*

Van·dal /vánd'l/ *n* a member of an ancient Germanic people who came from Jutland, conquering Gaul, Spain, Rome, and parts of North Africa during the 3rd and 4th centuries A.D., before being defeated at Carthage in 533 [Old English *Wendlas* (plural) "Vandals" < Germanic] —**Van·dal·ic** /van dállik/ *adj* —**Van·dal·ism** *n*

van·dal·ism /vánd'l ìzzəm/ *n* the malicious and deliberate defacement or destruction of somebody else's property —**van·dal·is·tic** /vànd'l ístik/ *adj*

van·dal·ize /vánd'l īz/ (**-ized, -iz·ing, -iz·es**) *vt* to deface, destroy, or otherwise damage private or public property maliciously and deliberately —**van·dal·i·za·tion** /vànd'li záysh'n/ *n*

van·da or·chid *n* PLANTS same as **vanda**

van de Graaff gen·er·a·tor /ván də graf-/ *n* an electrostatic machine that produces electrical discharges at extremely high voltages, used in particle accelerators and for testing electrical insulators. The electric charge from a source of direct current accumulates on a high-speed belt inside an insulated metal sphere filled with Freon™ or nitrogen gas under high pressure. [After R. J. *van de Graaff* (1901–67), US physicist]

Van·den·berg /vándən bùrg/, **Arthur H.** (1884–1951) US politician. A US senator from 1928, he was influential in setting up the United Nations (1945). Full name **Vandenberg, Arthur Hendrick**

Van·der·bilt /vándər bìlt/, **Cornelius** (1794–1877) US industrialist. He made a fortune from his steamship company. In 1862 he began investing in the railroads and established a rail link between New York and Chicago in 1873. He was reputed to be the richest man in the United States when he died. Known as **Commodore Vanderbilt**

"You have undertaken to cheat me. I won't sue you, for the law is too slow. I'll ruin you."
[Cornelius Vanderbilt, *Letter to former business associates*; 1853]

van der Post, Sir Laurens (1906–96) South African writer, farmer, and explorer. His many books include *The Lost World of the Kalahari* (1958) and *The Heart of the Hunter* (1961), which brought international attention to the Kalahari and the Bushmen.

> "Human beings are perhaps never more frightening than when they are convinced beyond doubt that they are right."
> [Laurens van der Post, *The Lost World of the Kalahari*; 1958]

van der Waals' e·qua·tion /vàn dər waálz-, -wáwlz-/ *n* a modified equation of state describing the physical behavior of gases that takes into account the volumes of molecules and the interactions between them. It explains the difference in behavior between a real gas and an ideal gas that obeys the gas laws. [After Johannes *van der Waals* (1837–1923), Dutch physicist]

van der Waals' force *n* a weak attractive force between atoms or molecules resulting from the positioning of the electrons within the interacting particles [See VAN DER WAALS' EQUATION]

Van Die·men's Land /van deémənz-, vaan-/ former name for **Tasmania** (1642–1856)

Van Dor·en /-dáwrən/, **Mark** (1894–1972) US poet and critic. His *Collected Poems 1928–38* (1939) won a Pulitzer Prize. Full name **Van Doren, Mark Albert**

Van·dyke /van dík/ *n* **1.** HAIR same as **Vandyke beard 2.** CLOTHING same as **Vandyke collar 3.** a V-shape forming part of a decorative border on material or clothing **4.** a decorative border on material or clothing made up of V-shaped points [Mid-18C. After Sir Anthony van DYCK] —**van·dyked** *adj*

Van·dyke beard *n* a short, neatly trimmed, pointed beard

Van·dyke brown *n* a deep rich brown color or pigment —**Van·dyke brown** *adj*

Van·dyke col·lar *n* a large white collar of linen or lace that has a deeply indented edge

Van Dy·ken /van díkən/, **Amy** (*b.* 1973) US swimmer. She won four gold medals in the 1996 summer Olympics, exceeding the record for multiple gold medals won by a woman in a single Olympics.

Van·dyke stitch *n* a V-shaped variation of cross stitch, used as a filling stitch to form a solid decoration

vane /vayn/ *n* **1.** ENG **ROTATING BLADE** a flat blade mounted as part of a set in a circle so as to rotate under the action of wind or liquid. Windmill sails and turbine blades are examples. **2.** METEOROL same as **weather vane 3.** ARMS **STABILIZER ON MISSILE** a stabilizing or guiding blade on a missile **4.** BIRDS **BLADE OF BIRD'S FEATHER** the flat part of a feather, consisting of interlocking rows of barbs. Each feather has two vanes, one on each side. **5. PART OF LEVELING ROD** the moving part on a leveling rod **6.** COMPASS **COMPASS OR QUADRANT SIGHT** a sight on a compass or quadrant [15C. Variant of *fane* "temple"] —**vaned** *adj*

SPELLCHECK See *vain*.

Vä·nern, Lake /vénnərn, váynərn/ the largest lake in Sweden, situated in the southwest of the country. Area: 2,156 sq. mi./5,584 sq. km.

Van Fleet /-fleét/, **James A.** (1892–1992) US general. A veteran of World War I and World War II, he was field commander (1951–53) of United Nations forces during the Korean War. Full name **Van Fleet, James Alward**

vang /vang/ *n* a guy rope forming part of a pair that extend from a gaff to the deck of a boat [Mid-18C. Variant of FANG]

van Gogh /van gó, -gáwkh, vaan kháwkh/, **Vincent** (1853–90) Dutch painter. His highly expressive canvases are characterized by their bright colors and vigorous brushstrokes. Among his best known works is *Starry Night* (1889). Full name **van Gogh, Vincent Willem**

> "The Mediterranean has the color of mackerel, changeable I mean. You don't always know if it is green or violet, you can't even say it's blue, because the next moment the changing reflection has taken on a tint of rose or gray."
> [Vincent van Gogh, *The Letters of Vincent Van Gogh*, M. Roskill (ed.); 1927]

van·guard /ván gaard/ *n* **1.** the leading position of a movement, field, or cultural trend, or the people who are foremost in a movement, field, or cultural trend **2.** the military divisions of an army or navy that lead the advance into battle [15C. Shortening of French *avant-garde* < *avant* "before" + *garde* "guard"] —**van·guard·ism** *n* —**van·guard·ist** *n*

Van·ha·nen /vánhənən/, **Matti** (*b.* 1955) prime minister of Finland (2003–). A member of the Center Party, he entered parliament in 1991 and was briefly minister of defense before becoming prime minister.

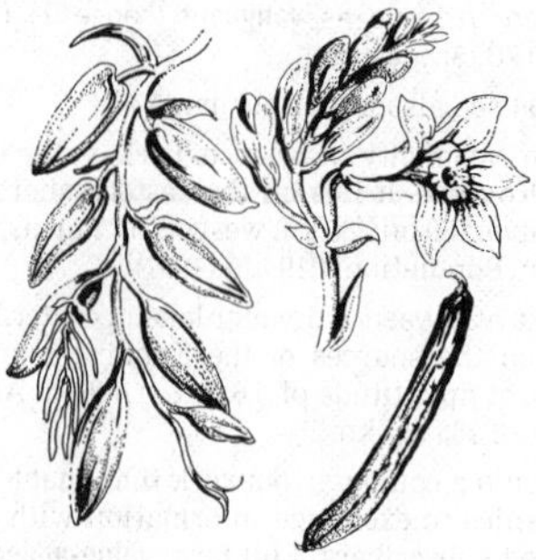

vanilla

va·nil·la /və níllə/ *n* **1.** *also* **va·nil·la bean VANILLA POD** the long narrow fleshy seedpod of a tropical climbing orchid. Use: food flavoring. **2. VANILLA FLAVORING** a substance with a mild taste extracted from vanilla seedpods or produced artificially. Use: food flavoring, perfumes. **3. CLIMBING PLANT** a climbing plant of the orchid family that produces seedpods from which vanilla is extracted. Native to: tropical America. Genus: *Vanilla*. ■ *adj* **1. FLAVORED WITH VANILLA** flavored with vanilla, or having a flavor of vanilla **2. PLAIN OR DULL** lacking outstanding or interesting characteristics ○ *a vanilla rendition of the concerto* **3.** COMPUT **OF BASIC SOFTWARE OR HARDWARE** relating to the most basic version of a hardware device or software program that does not have the refinements of the full-featured version (*slang*) [Mid-17C. < Spanish *vainilla* "small sheath" < *vaina* "sheath" < Latin *vagina*]

va·nil·lic /və níllik/ *adj* resembling, containing, or derived from vanilla or vanillin

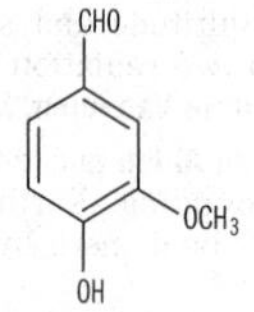

vanillin

va·nil·lin /və níllin, vánnəlin/ *n* a white aldehyde obtained from vanilla or prepared synthetically. Use: food flavorings, perfumes. Formula: $C_8H_8O_3$.

Va·nir /vaá neér/ *npl* in Norse mythology, a race of peace-loving gods [< Old Norse]

van·ish /vánnish/ (**-ished, -ish·ing, -ish·es**) *vi* **1. DISAPPEAR SUDDENLY** to disappear suddenly or inexplicably ○ *It can't just have vanished!* **2. STOP EXISTING** to cease to exist **3.** MATH **BECOME ZERO** to assume or be given the value of zero (*refers to a function or variable*) [14C. < Old French *esvaniss-* < *esvanir* < Latin *evanescere* "die out, pass away" < *vanus* "empty"] —**van·ish·er** *n* —**van·ish·ing·ly** *adv* —**van·ish·ment** *n*

van·ish·ing point *n* **1.** a point in a drawing or painting at which parallel lines seem to meet as represented in perspective **2.** a point at which something disappears or ceases to exist

van·i·ty /vánnətee/ (*plural* **-ties**) *n* **1. EXCESSIVE PRIDE** excessive pride, especially in personal appearance ○ *She is entirely free of personal vanity.* **2. SOMETHING SOMEBODY IS VAIN ABOUT** an instance or source of excessive pride **3. FUTILITY** the state or fact of being futile, worthless, or empty of significance **4. SOMETHING FUTILE** something that is considered futile, worthless, or empty of significance **5.** *US* COSMETICS same as **vanity case 6.** FURNITURE same as **dressing table 7. CABINET HOLDING SINK** a cabinet that holds a sink and its plumbing, usually with drawers or shelves under the sink for storage [13C. Via French < Latin *vanitas* < *vanus* "empty"]

van·i·ty case *n* **1.** a small case or bag for carrying cosmetics and toiletries **2.** *US* same as **compact**[1] *n* (sense 1) (*dated*)

Van·i·ty Fair, van·i·ty fair *n* a place, especially a very large city or the world in general, considered to be frivolous and full of idle worthless amusements (*literary*) [Coined by John BUNYAN in his *Pilgrim's Progress* (1678)]

CULTURAL NOTE *Vanity Fair*, a novel (1847–48) by British writer William Makepeace Thackeray. Thackeray's first major novel, it is a story of English society at the time of the Napoleonic Wars. The central characters are the penniless orphan Becky Sharp and Amelia Sedley, the daughter of a rich merchant. The fortunes in life and love of the two young women remain in distinct contrast throughout the complex plot, as Amelia descends into poverty and widowhood while the sharp-witted and unscrupulous Becky enjoys an extravagant lifestyle with a series of lovers.

van·i·ty plate *n* a license plate for a motor vehicle for which the owner has paid extra to be able to choose its numbers and letters

van·i·ty pub·lish·er, van·i·ty press *n* a publishing house that publishes an author's work in return for payment from the author. Vanity publishers typically do not market or distribute their publications.

van·i·ty pub·lish·ing *n* the business of publishing books at the author's expense

van·i·ty ta·ble *n* FURNITURE same as **dressing table**

van·i·ty tel·e·phone num·ber *n US* a telephone number consisting of numbers chosen by the customer, usually so as to spell a mnemonic on the standard telephone dial

van·load /ván lōd/ *n* the amount of goods or passengers that a van can transport at one time

Van Loon /-lóon, -lōn/, **Hendrick Willem** (1882–1944) Dutch-born US historian. He is known for his bestselling *The Story of Mankind* (1921) and other works of popular history.

van·pool /ván pool/ *n* an arrangement by which a number of people travel together to and from work in a shared van ■ *vi* (**-pooled, -pool·ing, -pools**) to convey somebody to and from work in a shared van, or to be conveyed in this way

van·quish /vángkwish/ (**-quished, -quish·ing, -quish·es**) *vt* **1. DEFEAT SOMEBODY IN BATTLE** to defeat an opponent or opposing army in a battle or fight **2. DEFEAT SOMEBODY IN COMPETITION** to prove convincingly superior to somebody in a contest, competition, or argument **3. OVERCOME EMOTION** to overcome, suppress, or subdue an emotion, feeling, or idea [14C. < Old French *venquis*, form of *veintre* < Latin *vincere* "conquer"] —**van·quish·a·ble** *adj* —**van·quish·er** *n* —**van·quish·ment** *n*

SYNONYMS See *defeat*.

Van Rens·se·laer /-rènssə leér, -rénssələr/, **Stephen** (1764–1839) US soldier and politician. A major landowner in New York State, he commanded the New York militia during the War of 1812 and also promoted educational and development projects.

van·tage /vántij/ *n* **1.** a position that provides an advantage **2.** superiority in a contest or competition **3.** same as **vantage point** (sense 1) [14C. < Old French *avantage* (see ADVANTAGE)] —**van·tage·less** *adj*

van·tage point *n* **1.** a position or location that provides a broad view or perspective of something **2.** a personal point of view

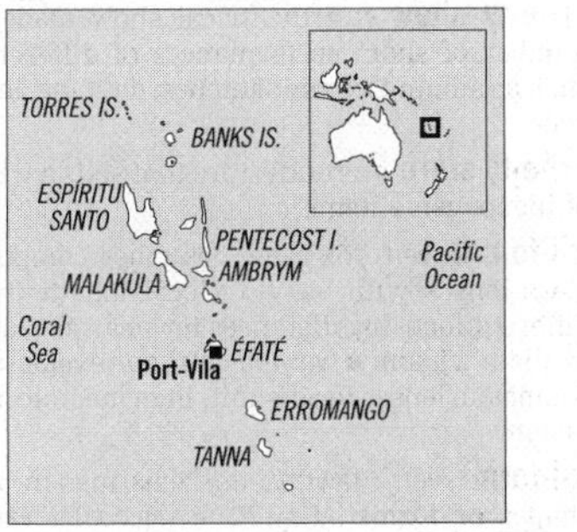

Vanuatu

Van·u·a·tu /vaanoo aatoo/ country in the southwestern Pacific Ocean, comprising approximately 80 islands. It became an independent member of the British Commonwealth in 1980. Language: English, French. Currency: vatu. Capital: Port-Vila. Population: 199,414 (2003). Area: 4,707 sq. mi./12,190 sq. km. Official name **Republic of Vanuatu**. Former name **New Hebrides** (until 1980). **—Van·u·a·tan** *n, adj*

Van Vleck /van vlék/, **John Hasbrouck** (1899–1980) US physicist. He shared the 1977 Nobel Prize in physics for his contributions to the study of semiconductors.

van·ward /vánnwərd/ *adj* in or at the vanguard of something ■ *adv* to or toward the vanguard of something

Van·zet·ti /van zéttee/, **Bartolomeo** (1888–1927) Italian-born US anarchist. With Nicola Sacco, he was convicted of murder in 1921 and executed in 1927 despite a lengthy appeal and worldwide protests that the verdict was politically motivated The case continued to generate controversy, and modern scholars believe that Vanzetti was probably innocent.

> "Sacco's name will live in the hearts of the people...when your name,...your laws, institutions and your false god are but a dim remembering of a cursed past in which man was wolf to the man."
> [Bartolomeo Vanzetti, *Statement disallowed at his trial*; April 1927]

vap·id /váppid/ *adj* **1.** lacking interest or liveliness **2.** lacking strength, taste, or flavor [Mid-17C. < Latin *vapidus* "insipid"] **—va·pid·i·ty** /və píddətee/ *n* **—vap·id·ly** *adv* **—vap·id·ness** *n*

va·por /váypər/ *n* **1.** PHYS **MOISTURE PARTICLES** moisture or another type of matter visible in the air as mist, clouds, fumes, or smoke **2.** PHYS **GASEOUS SUBSTANCE** a gaseous substance at a temperature lower than that at which it can be liquefied or solidified by an appropriate increase in pressure alone **3.** PHYS **GASEOUS STATE OF SUBSTANCE** the gaseous state of a liquid or solid at a temperature below its boiling point **4.** CHEM **VAPORIZED SUBSTANCE** a substance prepared for military, industrial, or medical use in vaporized form **5.** ENG **GAS AND AIR MIXTURE** a combination of air with a gaseous substance such as that of air and gasoline in an internal-combustion engine ■ **va·pors** *npl* **LOW SPIRITS** a bout of low spirits or sadness (*literary; usually used ironically*) ■ *v* (**-pored, -por·ing, -pors**) **1.** *vti* **EVAPORATE** to change into a vapor, or cause something to change into a vapor **2.** *vi* **EMIT VAPOR** to give off or send up vapor **3.** *vi* **BRAG** to talk boastfully [14C. Directly or via Old French < Latin *vapor* "steam, heat"] **—va·por·a·bil·i·ty** /vàypərə bíllətee/ *n* **—va·por·a·ble** *adj* **—va·por·er** *n* **—va·por·y** *adj*

va·por bar·ri·er *n* a protective layer of material used in building to keep out moisture

va·por den·si·ty *n* the density of a gas or vapor in relation to that of hydrogen

va·por·es·cence /vàypə réss'nss/ *n* the formation or creation of vapor **—va·por·es·cent** *adj*

va·por·et·to /vaapə réttō/ (*plural* **-ti** /-réttee/ or **-tos**) *n* a motorboat for transporting passengers along the canals in Venice, Italy [Early 20C. < Italian, "small steamboat" < *vapore* "steam" < Latin *vapor* (see VAPOR)]

va·por·if·ic /vàypə ríffik/ *adj* **1. PRODUCING VAPOR** producing, causing, or becoming vapor **2. BEING VAPOR** being, containing, or resembling vapor **3.** PHYS **VOLATILE** capable of changing easily from a liquid or solid state into vapor

va·por·ize /váypə rīz/ (**-ized, -iz·ing, -iz·es**) *vti* **1. CHANGE INTO VAPOR** to change into vapor, or cause something to change into vapor **2. VANISH OR MAKE VANISH** to vanish, or cause somebody or something to vanish **3. ANNIHILATE OR BE ANNIHILATED** to destroy somebody or something so completely that the person or object is turned into a gas or vapor, or be destroyed in this way **—va·por·iz·a·ble** *adj* **—va·por·i·za·tion** /vàypəri záysh'n/ *n*

va·por·iz·er /váypə rīzər/ *n* something used to produce a vapor, especially a device used to vaporize a medication so that it can be inhaled

va·por lock *n* a bubble of vaporized gasoline that blocks the normal flow of fuel in the line that supplies the carburetor of an internal-combustion engine

va·por·ous /váypərəss/ *adj* **1. BEING VAPOR** being, containing, or resembling vapor **2. PRODUCING VAPOR** producing, causing, or becoming vapor **3. VOLATILE** capable of changing easily from a liquid or solid state into vapor **4. UNSUBSTANTIAL** lacking material existence or permanence **5. FANCIFUL** of a fanciful, ridiculous, or implausible nature **6. OBSCURED BY VAPOR** made hard to see because of being obscured by mist or vapor **—va·por·os·i·ty** /vàypə róssətee/ *n* **—va·por·ous·ly** *adv* **—va·por·ous·ness** *n*

va·por pres·sure, va·por ten·sion *n* the pressure exerted by a vapor, particularly a vapor in contact with its liquid form

va·por trail *n* a visible trail of condensed vapor left by an aircraft flying at high altitude

va·por·ware /váypər wèr/ *n* new software that has been announced or advertised but has not yet been, and may never be, produced [Late 20C. After SOFTWARE]

va·pour *n, vti* PHYS, CHEM, ENG Can, UK spelling of **vapor**

va·que·ro /vaa kérrō/ (*plural* **-ros**) *n Hispanic* same as **cowboy** (sense 1) [Early 19C. < Spanish < *vaca* "cow"]

REGIONAL NOTE ***Vaquero*** is primarily a Texas word, where it contrasts in social usage with two other terms, the Anglicized *buckaroo* and the Mexican-Spanish loan *charro* (in Spain this meant "a rude, tasteless farm laborer," but in Mexico it referred to "a landowner who employed vaqueros"). In Texas, ***vaquero*** applies mainly to a working cowboy, especially a bachelor, *buckaroo* to a married working cowboy, and *charro* to an ostentatiously dressed pretender, a dude.

var *abbr* MEASURE volt-ampere reactive

VAR[1] /vaar/ *n* a retail seller of computers who adds products to computers produced by manufacturers or performs services such as product integration or customization before selling the computers to customers. Full form **value-added reseller**

VAR[2] *abbr* **1.** NAVIG visual aural range **2.** ELEC volt-ampere reactive

var. *abbr* **1.** variable **2.** variant **3.** variation **4.** variety

va·ra /vaarə/ *n* a unit of length used in Spain, Portugal, and Latin America that can be from 32 in./80 cm to 43 in./108 cm in length [Late 17C. Via Spanish, "rod, yardstick" < Latin, "forked pole, trestle" < *varus* "bent"]

va·rac·tor /və ráktər/ *n* a semiconductor diode with a capacitance that varies according to the voltage applied to it, used to regulate the frequency of electronic circuits in amplifiers [Mid-20C. Blend of VARIABLE + REACTOR]

Va·ra·na·si /və raanəssee/, **Vā·rā·na·si** city in Uttar Pradesh State, northern India, on the Ganges River. It was a center of Hindu learning and is an important place of pilgrimage for Hindus. Population: 1,100,748 (2001). Former name **Benares**

Va·rang·i·an /və ránjee ən/ *n* a member of a Scandinavian people who invaded and settled in Russia between the 8th and the 11th centuries [Late 18C. < medieval Latin *Varangus* < medieval Greek *baraggos* < Old Norse *Væringi* < *vár* "pledge"] **—Va·rang·i·an** *adj*

Va·rang·i·an Guard *n* **1.** the body of Scandinavian soldiers who were the Byzantine emperor's bodyguard in the 10th and 11th centuries **2.** a Scandinavian soldier in the Varangian Guard

var·ec /várrək/ *n* PLANTS same as **kelp** [Late 17C. < French]

~~**vareity**~~ incorrect spelling of **variety**

AKG London
Mario Vargas Llosa

Var·gas Llo·sa /vaargəss yōssə/, **Mario** (*b.* 1936) Peruvian writer and critic. Many of his works deal with issues of social change and political corruption. Full name **Vargas Llosa, Jorge Mario Pedro**

> "Since it is impossible to know what's really happening, we Peruvians lie, invent, dream...Because of these strange circumstances, Peruvian life, a life in which so few actually do read, has become literary."
> [Mario Vargas Llosa, *The Real Life of Alejandro Mayta*; 1984]

vari- *prefix* same as **vario-** (*used before vowels*)

var·i·a /vérree ə/ *npl* a collection, especially one of diverse literary works [Mid-20C. < Latin, "various things"]

var·i·a·ble /vérree əb'l/ *adj* **1. ABLE TO CHANGE** able or liable to change, especially suddenly and unpredictably **2. INCONSISTENT** inconsistent or uneven in quality or performance **3. FICKLE** inconstant and capricious in nature or character **4.** METEOROL **LIKELY TO BLOW DIFFERENTLY** describes a wind that is likely to change direction or intensity **5.** ELECTRONICS **HAVING VARYING RESISTANCE** describes an electrical device that has a resistance that varies **6.** BIOL **DIFFERING FROM SPECIES NORM** describes a species that tends to differ in some characteristic from a recognized or known type **7.** MATH **HAVING NO FIXED NUMERICAL VALUE** not having a fixed numerical value ■ *n* **1. SOMETHING THAT CAN VARY** something capable of changing or varying **2.** ENG **FLUCTUATING DESIGN CRITERION** a parameter of an engineering design criterion whose value may fluctuate over a wide range, e.g., the dynamic load on a bridge caused by traffic **3.** MATH **SYMBOL FOR UNSPECIFIED QUANTITY** a symbol that represents an unspecified or unknown quantity, e.g., "a," "b," or "x" **4.** MATH **RANGE OF VALUES** a range of values, any one of which is a solution to an algebraic expression **5.** LOGIC **LOGIC SYMBOL** a symbol, especially "x," "y," or "z," that is used usually in connection with quantifiers to represent individuals in a universe of discourse **6.** ASTRON same as **variable star 7.** METEOROL **VARIABLE WIND** a wind that is likely to change in direction or intensity ■ **var·i·a·bles** *npl* METEOROL **REGION OF VARIABLE WINDS** a region where variable winds are likely to be encountered [14C. Via French < Latin *variabilis* < *variare* (see VARY)] **—var·i·a·bil·i·ty** /vèrree ə bíllətee/ *n* **—var·i·a·ble·ness** *n* **—var·i·a·bly** *adv*

var·i·a·ble cost *n* a cost that varies directly in relation to output

var·i·a·ble-ge·om·e·try *adj* describes an aircraft with wings that are hinged so that in flight they can move backward or forward. The wings are swept back to give low drag in supersonic flight and are moved forward for takeoff and landing.

var·i·a·ble-in·ter·val sched·ule *n US* in operant conditioning, a rule for delivering reinforcements after varying amounts of time, e.g., at intervals averaging one minute

var·i·a·ble-rate mort·gage *n UK* FIN same as **adjustable-rate mortgage**

var·i·a·ble-ra·tio sched·ule *n US* in operant conditioning, a rule for delivering reinforcement after a varying number of responses, e.g., after every 10 responses on average

var·i·a·ble star *n* a star whose brightness changes at regular or irregular intervals

var·i·a·ble-sweep *adj* AVIAT same as **variable-geometry**

var·i·ance /vérree ənss/ *n* 1. CHANGE IN SOMETHING a change that occurs in something 2. DIFFERENCE BETWEEN THINGS a difference between two or more things 3. DISAGREEMENT a difference of opinion or attitude 4. LAW DISCREPANCY IN SOMETHING a discrepancy between two statements, documents, or steps in a legal proceeding 5. LAW LEGAL DISPENSATION a dispensation to ignore a rule or law ○ *a zoning variance* 6. ACCT DIFFERENCE IN COST a difference between actual costs and the usual costs of production 7. STATS SQUARE OF STANDARD DEVIATION a statistical measure of the spread or variation of a group of numbers in a sample, equal to the square of the standard deviation. Other measures are the ratio of the squared standard deviation to the sample size (**population variance**), and the ratio of the squared standard deviation to the sample size minus one (**sample variance**). [14C. Via Old French < Latin *variantia* < *variare* (see VARY)]

var·i·ant /vérree ənt/ *adj* 1. DIFFERING SLIGHTLY having or showing a difference from the norm ○ *variant pronunciations of common words* 2. CHANGEABLE tending or likely to change ■ *n* 1. SLIGHTLY DIFFERENT FORM something that differs slightly from the norm 2. LING DIFFERENT FORM OR SPELLING OF WORD a form or spelling of a word or phrase that differs from the standard one 3. STATS same as **random variable** [14C. French, < *varier* "vary" < Latin *variare* (see VARY)]

va·ri·ant CJD *n* a form of Creutzfeldt-Jakob disease that has a much shorter incubation period than previously recognized types but is clinically identical. It first appeared in the late 1980s. Full form **variant Creutzfeldt-Jakob disease**

var·i·ate /vérree it, -àyt/ *n* STATS same as **random variable** [Late 19C. < Latin *variatus*, past participle of *variare* (see VARY)]

var·i·a·tion /vérree áysh'n/ *n* 1. ACT OF VARYING the act or a result of varying 2. STATE OF DIFFERING the state or fact of differing, e.g., from a former state or value, from others of the same type, or from a standard 3. DEGREE OF DIFFERENCE the degree to which something differs, e.g., from a former state or value, from others of the same type, or from a standard ○ *There is a variation of several points in the test scores.* 4. SOMETHING DIFFERING SLIGHTLY something that differs slightly from the norm 5. MUSIC ALTERED VERSION OF MUSICAL THEME an altered version of an original musical theme or melody, such that the rhythm or harmony is varied or melodic embellishment is added. Variations are often found in sets, where a theme is followed by several variations. 6. MUSIC REPETITION OF MUSICAL THEME the repetition of a musical theme with modifications of melody, rhythm, or harmony 7. MATH MATHEMATICAL FUNCTION a mathematical function that relates the values of one variable to those of other variables 8. BIOL BIOLOGICAL DEVIATION a significant deviation from the normal biological form, function, or structure 9. BIOL LIVING ORGANISM THAT DIFFERS a living organism that differs from the normal form for its kind 10. BALLET SOLO DANCE a dance performed by a single dancer 11. ASTRON CHANGE IN ORBIT a change in or deviation from the average motion or orbit of an astronomical object 12. ASTRON TERM IN EQUATION DESCRIBING MOON'S MOTION a term representing the gravitational attraction of the Sun on the Earth-Moon system in the mathematical equation for the Moon's motion 13. PHYS same as **magnetic declination** 14. LING LINGUISTIC CHANGE a change in conjugation, declension, inflection, or vowel form [14C. Directly or via French < Latin *variation-* < *variare* (see VARY)] —**var·i·a·tion·al** *adj* —**var·i·a·tion·al·ly** *adv*

~~**variaty**~~ incorrect spelling of **variety**

varic- *prefix* same as **varico-** (*used before vowels*)

var·i·cel·la /vàrri séllə/ *n* MED same as **chickenpox** (*technical*) [Late 18C. < modern Latin, "lesser smallpox" < late Latin *variola* (see VARIOLA)] —**va·ri·cel·lar** *adj* —**var·i·cel·lous** *adj*

var·i·cel·la-zos·ter vi·rus /vàrri sèllə zóstər-/ *n* a herpes virus that is responsible for chickenpox and shingles

var·i·ces MED, MARINE BIOL plural of **varix**

varico- *prefix* varix, varicose vein ○ *varicotomy* [< Latin *varic-*, stem of *varix*]

var·i·co·cele /várrikō seèl/ *n* a swelling of the veins in the spermatic cord of the scrotum. It may cause only slight discomfort but can affect fertility, so that surgical correction is required.

var·i·col·ored /vérri kùllərd/ *adj* consisting of or having many colors

var·i·col·oured *adj* Can, UK spelling of **varicolored**

var·i·cose /várri kòss/, **var·i·cosed** /várri kòst/ *adj* 1. MED SWOLLEN swollen, knotted, or distended to a greater extent than normal 2. MED WITH VARICOSE VEINS affected with or having varicose veins 3. MED PRODUCING SWELLING relating to or producing swelling 4. ZOOL RIDGED LIKE GASTROPOD SHELL resembling a small longitudinal ridge (**varix**) on the shell of some gastropods [15C. < Latin *varicosus* < *varix* "dilated vein, varicose vein"]

var·i·cos·es MED, ZOOL plural of **varicosis**

var·i·cose vein *n* a vein that has become swollen and knotted as a result of faulty valves ■ **var·i·cose veins** *npl* a condition in which the surface veins, especially of the legs, become knotted and swollen, as a result of flaws in the valves of the affected veins. The tendency to develop the condition may be inherited, while other causes include injury, inflammation, or thrombosis.

var·i·co·sis /vàrri kóssiss/ (*plural* **-co·ses** /-kō seèz/) *n* 1. a condition in which a vein or veins become swollen or knotted 2. the formation of small longitudinal ridges on the surface of a gastropod shell

var·i·cos·i·ty /vàrri kóssətee/ (*plural* **-ties**) *n* MED 1. the state of being swollen or knotted 2. same as **varicose vein** (*technical*) 3. the condition of suffering from or having swollen or enlarged veins

var·i·cot·o·my /vàrri kóttəmee/ (*plural* **-mies**) *n* a surgical incision into a swollen vein, usually performed to treat varicose veins

var·ied /vérreed/ *adj* 1. DIVERSE showing or characterized by many different forms or kinds 2. CHANGED having undergone change or alteration 3. MULTICOLORED consisting of or having many colors —**var·ied·ly** *adv* —**var·ied·ness** *n*

var·ied thrush *n* a thrush that looks like a robin but has a black band on its breast. Native to: North America. Latin name: *Ixoreus naevius*.

var·i·e·gate /vérree ə gàyt, vérri gàyt/ (**-gat·ed, -gat·ing, -gates**) *vt* 1. to change the way something looks, especially by adding different colors 2. to add variety to something [Mid-17C. < Latin *variegare* "make varied" < *varius* "diverse"] —**var·i·e·ga·tion** /vèrri ə gáysh'n, vèrri gáysh'n/ *n* —**var·i·e·ga·tor** *n*

var·i·e·gat·ed /vérree ə gàytəd, vérri gàytəd/ *adj* 1. HAVING PATCHES OF DIFFERENT COLORS marked with or containing patches of different colors 2. HAVING PATCHES OF LIGHTER COLOR marked with or containing patches of lighter color ○ *variegated leaves* 3. DIVERSE showing or characterized by many different forms or kinds

va·ri·e·tal /və rī́ ət'l/ *adj* 1. TYPICAL OF BIOLOGICAL VARIETY relating to, typical of, or being a variety of something, especially a biological variety 2. MADE FROM SINGLE GRAPE VARIETY describes wine made entirely or principally from a single variety of grape ■ *n* WINE MADE FROM SINGLE GRAPE VARIETY a wine that is made entirely or principally from a single variety of grape, and is usually known by the name of the grape variety —**va·ri·e·tal·ly** *adv*

va·ri·e·ty /və rī́ ətee/ (*plural* **-ties**) *n* 1. QUALITY OF BEING VARIED the quality of being varied or diversified ○ *It's easy to get bored if there's no variety in your work.* 2. SPECIFIC TYPE a specific type or kind within a general group ○ *a new variety* 3. COLLECTION OF VARIED THINGS a collection of varied things, often belonging to the same general group 4. THEATER ENTERTAINMENT MADE UP OF DIFFERENT ACTS entertainment made up of a number of different types of acts 5. BOT SUBDIVISION OF SPECIES a taxonomic category of related organisms, especially plants, of a rank below a species. Varieties of a species generally have distinguishing characteristics such as a flower color and may arise naturally or through deliberate plant breeding. [Mid-16C. Via French < Latin *varietas* < *varius* "variegated, diverse"]

va·ri·e·ty meat *n US* 1. a meat taken from a slaughtered animal other than flesh removed from the skeleton, especially organ meat 2. a meat that is processed, e.g., sausage

va·ri·e·ty show *n* a theatrical show made up of a number of short performances of different kinds, such as singing, comic sketches, dancing, and magic acts

va·ri·e·ty store *n* a retail store that sells a wide range of inexpensive items

var·i·fo·cal /vèrri fṓk'l/ *adj* describes composite eyeglass lenses with varying focal length that allow different focusing distances for near, far, and intermediate vision ■ **var·i·fo·cals** *npl* eyeglasses with composite lenses for distant, intermediate, and near vision

var·i·form /vérri fàwrm/ *adj* existing in different shapes or forms [Mid-17C. < VARIOUS] —**var·i·form·ly** *adv*

~~**varigate**~~ incorrect spelling of **variegate**

vario- *prefix* variation, variance, difference ○ *variolite* [< Latin *varius* "variegated, diverse"]

va·ri·o·la /vərree ṓlə/ *n* MED same as **smallpox** (*technical*) [Early 19C. < late Latin, "pustule" < Latin *varius* "variegated, diverse"] —**var·i·o·loid** /vérree ə lòyd/ *adj, n*

var·i·o·late /vèrree ə làyt/ *adj* with a pitted or scarred appearance, like the skin of somebody who has had smallpox ■ *vt* (**-lat·ed, -lat·ing, -lates**) to inoculate somebody with the smallpox virus (*dated*) —**var·i·o·la·tion** /vèrree ə láysh'n/ *n*

var·i·ole /vérree ṑl/ *n* a small rounded mass that causes the pockmarked surface in the rock variolite [Early 19C. < late Latin *variola* (see VARIOLA)]

var·i·o·lite /vérree ə lī̀t/ *n* a rock that has a pockmarked surface caused by rounded fibrous crystalline masses that are embedded in it [Late 18C. < VARIOLA] —**var·i·o·lit·ic** /vèrree ə líttik/ *adj*

va·ri·o·lous /və rī́ ələss/ *adj* relating to, like, or affected by smallpox

var·i·om·e·ter /vèrree ómmətər/ *n* 1. an instrument used to measure magnetic fields, especially variations in the Earth's magnetic field 2. an instrument used to measure the rate of climb of an aircraft such as a glider

var·i·o·rum /vèrree áwrəm/ *adj* 1. CONTAINING VARIOUS ANNOTATIONS having commentary or notes written by various editors or scholars 2. HAVING DIFFERENT VERSIONS OF TEXT containing different versions or readings of a text ■ *n* VARIORUM EDITION an edition of a text with commentary or notes written by various editors or scholars, or with various different versions or readings [Early 18C. < Latin genitive plural of *varius* "variegated, diverse," in *editio cum notis variorum* "edition with notes of various (commentators)"]

var·i·ous /vérree əss/ *det* ASSORTED many different ○ *after various attempts* ■ *adj* 1. OF DIFFERENT KINDS of different kinds or categories ○ *declined the invitation for various reasons* 2. INDIVIDUAL individual or separate ○ *The various arguments all have their strong and weak points.* [Mid-16C. < Latin *varius* "variegated, diverse"] —**var·i·ous·ly** *adv* —**var·i·ous·ness** *n*

var·i·sized /vérri sī̀zd/ *adj US* being or consisting of different sizes

var·is·tor /və rístər/ *n* a two-element semiconductor with nonlinear resistance in which the resistance drops as the applied voltage increases. Varistors are often used as a safety device to short-circuit transient high voltages in electronic circuits. [Mid-20C. < VARIABLE + RESISTOR]

var·ix /várriks/ (*plural* **-i·ces** /-seèz/) *n* 1. a swollen or knotted bodily vessel, especially a vein 2. a ridge along the length of the shell of a gastropod mollusk [14C. < Latin, "dilated vein, varicose vein"] —**var·i·ce·al** /vèrri seé əl/ *adj*

var·let /vaárlət/ *n* (*archaic*) 1. a rogue or rascal 2. a servant or attendant [15C. < Old French, variant of *valet* (see VALET)]

var·mint /vaármint/ *n* a person or an animal regarded as troublesome, unpleasant, or despicable (*regional*; *offensive when used of people*) [Mid-16C. Variant of VERMIN]

REGIONAL NOTE Used of animals, the term *varmint* is found across the rural South, the Lower Southwest, and even into the middle Rocky Mountain states.

var·na /vaárnə/ *n* a social caste in Hindu society. The four castes are the priests (**Brahmans**), warriors

(**Kshatriyas**), merchants (**Vaisyas**), and workers (**Sudras**), with, below these, the untouchables (**Dalits**). [Mid-19C. < Sanskrit, "color, cover, class, sort"]

Var·na /vaárnə/ city, port, and tourist center in eastern Bulgaria, on the Black Sea. Population: 301,421 (1996).

var·nish /vaárnish/ *n* **1. TRANSPARENT RESIN SOLUTION** a solution of a resin in oil or spirits, applied to a surface to give it a protective gloss **2. SMOOTH COATING OF VARNISH** a coating of varnish, applied to something to give it a protective gloss **3. SUPERFICIALLY ATTRACTIVE MANNER OR APPEARANCE** a superficially or deceptively attractive manner or appearance ■ *vt* (**-nished, -nish·ing, -nish·es**) **1. APPLY VARNISH TO SOMETHING** to coat something with varnish **2. GIVE SOMETHING SMOOTH SURFACE** to give something a smooth and usually glossy surface **3. MAKE SOMETHING SUPERFICIALLY ATTRACTIVE** to make something superficially or deceptively attractive [14C. Via Old French *vernis* < medieval Latin *vernicium* "sandarac" < Greek *Bereníkē* "Berenice," city in Cyrenaica] —**var·nish·er** *n*

Var·ro /várrō/, **Marcus Terentius** (116–27 B.C.) Roman scholar. He was one of the most learned Romans of his day, and the author of more than 70 known works on a variety of subjects from farming to the Latin language. Little of his work survives.

var·si·ty /vaárssətee/ *n* (*plural* **-ties**) **1.** the principal team representing a university, college, or high school, especially in sports competitions **2.** *UK* EDUC same as **university** (*dated*) ■ *adj* belonging to or involving a university, e.g., a sports competition or team [Mid-19C. Dialectal variant of *versity*, shortening of UNIVERSITY]

var·us /vérrəss/ *adj* used to describe a condition in which a body part such as the foot is turned or displaced inward toward the midline of the body or limb (*technical*) [Late 18C. < Latin, "bent, crooked"]

varve /vaarv/ *n* a layer or series of layers of sediment deposited annually in a still body of water, e.g., by a glacier. Varves can be counted back to date a specific layer. [Early 20C. < Swedish *varv* "layer, turn"]

var·y /vérree/ (**-ied, -y·ing, -ies**) *v* **1.** *vti* **UNDERGO CHANGE OR CHANGE SOMETHING** to change within a range of possibilities, or in connection with something else, or make something undergo such a change **2.** *vi* **BE DIFFERENT** to be different **3.** *vt* **GIVE VARIETY TO SOMETHING** to give variety or diversity to something [14C. Via Old French *varier* < Latin *variare* < *varius* "variegated, diverse"] —**var·y·ing** *adj* —**var·y·ing·ly** *adv*

SYNONYMS See ***change***.

var·y·ing hare *n* ZOOL **1.** *US* same as **snowshoe hare 2.** *Can* same as **arctic hare**

vas /vass/ (*plural* **va·sa** /vaázə/) *n* a vessel or duct in the body of a person or animal [Mid-17C. < Latin, "vessel"] —**va·sal** /váyss'l, váyz'l/ *adj*

vas- *prefix* same as **vaso-** (*used before vowels*)

va·sa ANAT plural of **vas**

Va·sa·ré·ly /vaázə ráylee/, **Victor** (1908–97) Hungarian-born French painter, sculptor, and graphic artist. He was the creator of Op Art and one of the most important artists in the movement.

Va·sa·ri /və saáree/, **Giorgio** (1511–74) Italian painter, architect, and art historian. He is famed for his book of biographies, *Lives of the Most Eminent Italian Architects, Painters, and Sculptors* (1550), which is the basic source of our knowledge about the artists of the Renaissance.

vas·cu·la BOT plural of **vasculum**

vas·cu·lar /váskyələr/ *adj* relating to fluid-carrying vessels, e.g., blood vessels in animals or the sap-carrying vessels in plants [Mid-17C. < modern Latin *vascularis* < Latin *vasculum* (see VASCULUM)] —**vas·cu·lar·i·ty** /vàskyə lárrətee/ *n* —**vas·cu·lar·ly** *adv*

vas·cu·lar bun·dle *n* a strand of plant tissue containing the xylem and phloem vessels, responsible for conducting sap through the stems and branches of a plant. They are most prominent in annual and young plants, and in perennial and woody plants they become part of an inner cylinder of vascular tissue.

vas·cu·lar cyl·in·der *n* BOT same as **stele** (sense 2)

vas·cu·lar·i·za·tion /vàskyələri záysh'n/ *n* the development of vessels, especially blood vessels, in an organism or tissue

vas·cu·lar plant *n* any plant that possesses specialized sap-conducting tissues, particularly phloem and xylem. Vascular plants include all flowering plants and conifers, as well as ferns, club mosses, and horsetails, but not mosses and liverworts.

vas·cu·lar tis·sue *n* plant tissue that is specialized for conducting sap. It comprises phloem, which conveys chiefly dissolved sugars, and xylem, which conveys water and dissolved minerals.

vas·cu·la·ture /váskyələ chòor, -ləchər/ *n* the arrangement of blood vessels in the body or in an organ or tissue

vas·cu·li·tis /vàskyə lítiss/ *n* inflammation of a blood vessel or lymph vessel

vas·cu·lum /váskyələm/ (*plural* **-la** /-lə/) *n* a small box or case used by botanists in the field for storing collected plants or other specimens [Mid-19C. < Latin, "little vessel" < vas "vessel"]

vas def·er·ens /vàss déffərənz, -rènz/ (*plural* **va·sa def·er·en·ti·a** /vaázə deffə rénshə, -deffə rénshee ə/) *n* either of a pair of ducts that carry sperm from the testes to the urethra during ejaculation. Contraction of its thick muscular wall propels sperm rapidly through the duct, which forms part of the spermatic cord. [Late 19C. < Latin, "carrying-away vessel"]

vase /vayss, vayz, vaaz/ *n* an open container, usually tall and rounded, used for displaying cut flowers or as an ornament [Mid-16C. Via French < Latin *vas* "vessel"]

va·sec·to·mize /və séktə mīz/ (**-mized, -miz·ing, -miz·es**) *vt* to perform a vasectomy on somebody

va·sec·to·my /və séktəmee/ (*plural* **-mies**) *n* a surgical operation in which the vas deferens from each testis is cut and tied to prevent transfer of sperm during ejaculation. It is the most common form of male sterilization. [Late 19C. < VAS DEFERENS]

Vas·e·line /vássə leen/ *tdmk* a trademark for medical petroleum jelly and various skin-care products

vaso- *prefix* **1.** blood vessels, vascular ○ *vasodilation* **2.** vas deferens ○ *vasectomy* [< Latin *vas* "vessel"]

va·so·ac·tive /vàyzō áktiv/ *adj* making blood vessels contract or dilate —**va·so·ac·tiv·i·ty** /vàyzō ak tívvətee/ *n*

va·so·con·stric·tion /vàyzō kən stríksh'n/ *n* narrowing of the blood vessels with consequent reduction in blood flow or increased blood pressure

va·so·con·stric·tor /vàyzō kən stríktər/ *n* an agent that narrows the blood vessels, which in turn increases resistance to blood flow and raises blood pressure, e.g., a nerve or hormone. Vasoconstrictors such as the hormone epinephrine and various drugs are used medically to maintain or raise blood pressure in circulatory disorders or during surgery, or to counteract shock. ■ *adj* causing narrowing of the blood vessels —**vas·o·con·stric·tive** *adj*

va·so·dil·a·tion /vàyzō dī láysh'n, -di-/, **va·so·dil·a·ta·tion** /vàyzō dìlə táysh'n, -dìllə-/ *n* widening of the blood vessels, especially the arteries, leading to increased blood flow or reduced blood pressure

va·so·di·la·tor /vàyzō dī láytər, -di-/ *n* an agent that widens the blood vessels, which in turn decreases resistance to blood flow and lowers blood pressure, e.g., a nerve or hormone. Drugs that act as vasodilators are used medically to treat high blood pressure and various other circulatory disorders. ■ *adj* causing widening of the blood vessels —**va·so·di·la·to·ry** /vàyzō dìllə tàwree/ *adj*

va·so·in·hib·i·tor /vàyzō in híbbitər/ *n* something that depresses or stops the activity of the nerves that control widening or narrowing of the blood vessels —**va·so·in·hib·i·to·ry** *adj*

va·so·mo·tor /vàyzə mṓtər/ *adj* causing or influencing changes in the diameter of blood vessels

va·so·pres·sin /vàyzō préssin/ *n* a hormone produced by the pituitary gland that causes narrowing of the arteries and raises blood pressure. It also reduces the volume of urine excreted by the kidneys.

va·so·pres·sor /vàyzō préssər/ *adj* causing or promoting the narrowing of blood vessels, which in turn raises blood pressure ■ *n* something that has the effect of raising blood pressure

va·so·spasm /váyzō spàzzəm/ *n* sustained contraction of the muscular walls of the blood vessels with a resultant reduction in blood flow. In Raynaud's disease there is vasospasm of the arteries of the fingers, which causes cold or numb fingers. —**va·so·spas·tic** /vàyzō spástik/ *adj*

va·so·va·gal /vàyzō váyg'l/ *adj* relating to or involving the influence of the vagus nerve on circulation. Stimulation of the vagus reduces heart rate and, consequently, the amount of blood being pumped by the heart.

vas·sal /váss'l/ *n* **1. DEPENDENT LANDHOLDER IN FEUDAL SOCIETY** somebody who gave loyalty and homage to a feudal lord and received the right to occupy the lord's land and be protected by him **2. SLAVE** a bondman or slave **3. PERSON OR NATION DEPENDENT ON ANOTHER** a person, nation, or group that is dependent on or subordinate to another [14C. Via French < medieval Latin *vassallus* < *vassus* "servant" < Celtic, "young man, squire"] —**vas·sal** *adj*

vas·sal·age /váss'lij/ *n* **1.** the dependent condition of being somebody's vassal **2.** a condition of being dependent on or subordinate to somebody or something else (*literary*)

Vas·sar /vássər/, **Matthew** (1792–1868) US merchant and philanthropist. An advocate for higher education for women, he endowed Vassar College in Poughkeepsie, New York (1861).

vast /vast/ *adj* very great in number, size, amount, extent, or degree ■ *n* the immense expanse of space (*literary*) [Late 16C. < Latin *vastus* "immense, empty"] —**vast·ly** *adv* —**vast·ness** *n* —**vas·ti·tude** *n* —**vas·ti·ty** *n*

vast·y /vástee/ (**-i·er, -i·est**) *adj* same as **vast** (*archaic or literary*)

vat /vat/ *n* **1. LARGE CONTAINER FOR LIQUID** a large container used to hold or store liquid **2. PREPARATION OF DYE** a preparation of weakly colored soluble dye (**vat dye**) ■ *vt* (**vat·ted, vat·ting, vats**) **TREAT OR PUT IN VAT** to treat, store, or put something in a vat [12C. Alteration of *fat* < Old English *fæt* "vessel" < Germanic]

VAT /vee ay tee, vat/, **V.A.T** *n* a tax on the increased value of a product or service added at each stage of its production or distribution, paid by the consumer. Full form **value-added tax**

Vat. *abbr* Vatican

vat dye *n* a dye that is made insoluble and fixed by oxidation after being taken up by fibers —**vat-dyed** *adj*

vat·ic /váttik/ *adj* relating to, involving, or characteristic of a prophet (*formal*) [Early 17C. < Latin *vates* "prophet, seer"]

Vat·i·can /váttikən/ *n* **1.** the palace in the Vatican City that is used as the official residence of the pope and the administrative center of the papacy **2.** the authority and jurisdiction of the pope [Mid-16C. < Latin *(mons) Vaticanus* "Vatican (hill)"]

Vatican City

Vat·i·can Cit·y world's smallest independent nation and headquarters of the Roman Catholic Church. Language: Italian, Latin. Currency: euro. Population: 1000 (2001). Area: 110 acres/44 hectares. Official name **State of Vatican City**

Vat·i·can·ism /váttikə nìzzəm/ *n* the policies and authority of the pope, especially the idea of absolute papal authority

va·tic·i·nate /və tíss'n àyt/ (**-nat·ed, -nat·ing, -nates**) *vti* same as **prophesy** (*formal*) [Early 17C. < Latin *vaticinari* < *vates* "prophet, seer" + *canere* "sing"] —**va·tic·i·nal** *adj* —**va·tic·i·na·tion** /və tìss'n áysh'n/ *n* —**va·tic·i·na·tor** *n*

va·tu /vaá to͞o/ (*plural same*) *n* a unit of currency in Vanuatu. See table at **currency** [< Bislama]

Vau·ban /vō baáN/, **Sebastien le Prestre de** (1633–1707) French marshal of France. He was a specialist in sieges and fortifications during the reign of Louis XIV. He directed the sieges of Mons (1691) and Namur (1692).

vaude·ville /váwd vil, váwdə-/ *n* **1.** THEATER, MUSIC **POPULAR ENTERTAINMENT** a type of entertainment popular in the late 19th and early 20th centuries consisting of a variety of singing, dancing, and comic acts **2. VAUDEVILLE SHOW** a vaudeville show **3. COMIC PLAY WITH SONGS** a comic play with songs and dances **4.** MUSIC **SATIRICAL POPULAR SONG** a satirical popular song of the type performed in cabarets in the 19th and 20th centuries [Mid-18C. < Old French *vaudevire*, shortening of *chanson du Vau de Vire* "song of the Valley of Vire," region of Normandy noted for satirical folksongs] —**vaude·vil·lian** /vàwd víllee ən, vàwdə-/ *adj, n*

ORIGIN In 15th-century France there was a fashion for songs from the valley of the Vire, in the Calvados region of Normandy (particularly popular, apparently, were the satirical songs composed by a local fuller, Olivier Basselin). The geographic connection had been lost by the time English acquired the word, and the element *-vire* had been replaced with *-ville* "town." The semantic transition from "popular song" to "light theatrical entertainment" is not recorded until the early 19th century.

Vau·dreu·il /vō drő ee/, **Pierre de Rigaud de Vaudreuil de Cavagnal, marquis de** (1698–1778) French soldier and colonial administrator. He was governor of New France (now Canada) from 1755 to 1760, when he was forced to surrender to British forces during the French and Indian War.

Sarah Vaughan

Vaughan /vawn/, **Sarah** (1924–90) US jazz singer. Performing with Earl Hines, Billy Eckstine, Count Basie, and other leading jazz musicians, she was known for her complex harmonization and vocal improvisation. Full name **Vaughan, Sarah Lois**

Ralph Vaughan Williams

Vaughan Wil·liams /vawn wíllyəmz/, **Ralph** (1872–1958) British composer. He developed a British national style of music from choral tradition and folk song. His works include nine symphonies and many choral pieces.

vault[1] /vawlt/ *n* **1. STRENGTHENED ROOM FOR VALUABLES** a strengthened room or compartment used for the safe storage of valuables, especially one in a bank **2. ARCHED CEILING** an arched structure of stone, brick, wood, or plaster that forms a ceiling or roof **3. ROOM WITH ARCHED CEILING** a room, especially an underground room, with an arched ceiling **4. BURIAL CHAMBER** a burial chamber, usually underground **5. SOMETHING ARCHING OVERHEAD** something that arches overhead, especially the sky (*literary*) ○ *the great vault of the sky* **6.** ANAT **ARCHED PART OF BODY** a part of the body with an arched shape ■ *v* (**vault·ed, vault·ing, vaults**) **1.** *vi* **FORM VAULT** to arch or curve like a vault **2.** *vt* ARCHIT **PUT ARCHED STRUCTURE OVER SOMETHING** to cover a building with an arched ceiling or roof **3.** *vt* ARCHIT **BUILD SOMETHING AS VAULT** to build something in the shape of a vault [14C. < Old French *vaute* < assumed Vulgar Latin *volvita* "turn, vault" < Latin *voluta*, feminine past participle of *volvere* "turn, roll"] —**vault·ed** *adj*

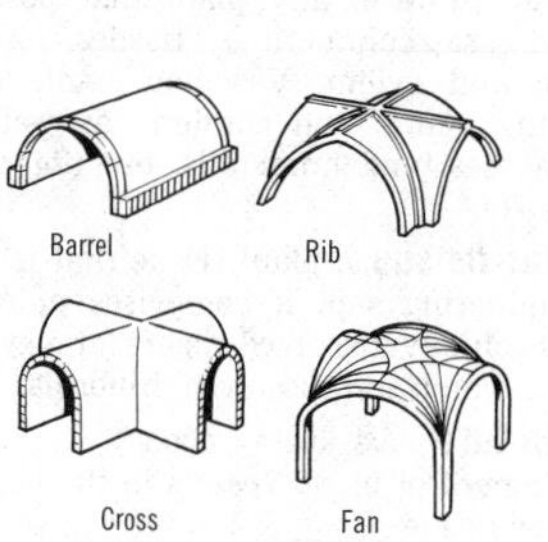

vault (sense 2)

vault[2] /vawlt/ *v* (**vault·ed, vault·ing, vaults**) **1.** *vti* **SPRING OVER OBJECT** to leap or spring over something, especially by pushing on it with the hands or using a pole **2.** *vi* **MOVE WITH BOUND** to move with a leap or bound **3.** *vi* **RISE SUDDENLY TO PROMINENCE** to arrive somewhere or achieve something suddenly ○ *She vaulted to fame with the publication of her first novel.* **4.** *vti* RIDING same as **curvet** ■ *n* **1. ACT OF VAULTING** an act of vaulting **2.** RIDING same as **curvet** [Mid-16C. Via Old French *volter* < assumed Vulgar Latin *volvitare* "roll repeatedly" < Latin *volvere* "turn, roll"] —**vault·er** *n*

vault·ing[1] /váwlting/ *n* the structural use of brick, stone, or reinforced concrete to form a ceiling or roof over a space [15C. < VAULT[1]]

vault·ing[2] /váwlting/ *adj* aspiring or confident, especially in an excessive way (*literary*) ○ *vaulting ambition* [Late 16C. < VAULT[2]]

vault·ing horse *n* a piece of gymnastic equipment with four legs and a solid leather-covered oblong body, used for exercises and especially for vaulting over

vaunt /vawnt/ *v* (**vaunt·ed, vaunt·ing, vaunts**) **1.** *vt* **BE BOASTFUL ABOUT SOMETHING** to boast or act boastfully about something such as achievements or possessions **2.** *vi* **BOAST** to boast or brag (*literary*) ■ *n* **BOASTFUL STATEMENT OR DISPLAY** a boast, or display of boasting [14C. Via Old French *vanter* < late Latin *vanitare* "be vain" < *vanus* "empty"] —**vaunt·er** *n* —**vaunt·ing·ly** *adv*

vaunt-cour·i·er *n* somebody or something sent in advance of another (*archaic or literary*) [Mid-16C. < French *avant* "before" + COURIER, after French *avant-coureur*]

vaunt·ed /váwntəd/ *adj* boasted about or praised in an ostentatious way ○ *their vaunted home and car*

vav /vaav/, **waw** /waw/ *n* the sixth letter in the Hebrew alphabet, represented in the English alphabet as "v" or "w." See table at **alphabet** [Early 19C. < Hebrew *wāw* "hook"]

vav·a·sor /vávvə sàwr, vávvə so͞or/, **vav·a·sour** *n* a feudal lord or knight who has power over vassals but is himself a vassal of a more powerful lord [14C. Via French < medieval Latin *vavassor*]

vb. *abbr* LING **1.** verb **2.** verbal

VBAC /veé bàk/ *n* a vaginal delivery of a baby by a woman whose first baby was delivered by cesarean section. Full form **vaginal birth after cesarean (delivery)**

VC *abbr* ONLINE St. Vincent and the Grenadines (*used in Internet addresses*) See table at **domain name**

VC *abbr* Vietcong

V.C. *abbr* **1.** FIN, BUSINESS venture capital **2.** FIN venture capitalist **3.** vice chairman **4.** vice chancellor **5.** POL vice consul **6.** MIL Victoria Cross

V-chip *n* an electronic chip in a television that enables parents to block programs with sexual or violent content

vCJD *abbr* MED variant CJD

VCR *n* a tape recorder that can record and play videocassettes through a standard television receiver. Full form **videocassette recorder**

VCT *abbr UK* venture capital trust

VD *abbr* MED venereal disease

v.d. *abbr* **1.** PHYS vapor density **2.** various dates

VDR *abbr* **1.** videodisk recorder **2.** videodisk recording

VDRL *abbr* venereal disease research laboratory

VDSL *abbr* TELECOM, ONLINE **1.** Very-High-Bit-Rate Digital Subscriber Line **2.** Very-High-Data-Rate Digital Subscriber Line

VDT *abbr* video display terminal

ve *abbr* ONLINE Venezuela (*used in Internet addresses*) See table at **domain name**

've /v, əv/ *contr* have

USAGE See ***of***.

veal /veel/ *n* **1.** meat from a calf **2.** AGRIC same as **veal calf** [14C. Via Anglo-Norman, Old French *veel* < Latin *vitellus*, diminutive of *vitulus* "calf"]

veal calf *n* a calf raised for veal

veal·er /veélər/ *n* AGRIC same as **veal calf**

Veb·len /vébblən/, **Thorstein** (1857–1929) US economist. An unorthodox thinker, he criticized modern industrial society in works such as *The Theory of the Leisure Class* (1899). He coined the expression "conspicuous consumption." Full name **Veblen, Thorstein Bunde**

> "All business sagacity reduces itself in the last analysis to a judicious use of sabotage."
> [Thorstein Veblen, *The Nature of Peace*; 1917]

vec·tor /véktər/ *n* **1.** MATH **QUANTITY WITH DIRECTION AND MAGNITUDE** a quantity that has both direction and magnitude, e.g., force or velocity, usually represented by an arrow **2.** MATH **ITEM IN SET OF VECTORS** an element of a vector space **3.** AVIAT **COURSE OF AIRCRAFT** the course taken by an aircraft or a missile **4.** BIOL **DISEASE-TRANSMITTING ORGANISM** an organism such as a mosquito or tick that transmits disease-causing microorganisms from an infected person or animal to another **5.** GENETICS **GENE TRANSFER AGENT** an agent such as a plasmid or bacteriophage that is used in genetic modification to transfer a segment of foreign DNA into a bacterium or other cell. The foreign DNA is spliced into the vector's DNA, which contains the genes necessary for switching on replication and transcription of the foreign DNA in its new setting. **6.** COMPUT **COMPUTER ARRAY** in computing, an array of any length, but only one dimension ■ *vt* (**-tored, -tor·ing, -tors**) AVIAT **1. DIRECT AIRCRAFT BY RADIO** to direct an aircraft or pilot by radio, often from the ground **2. CHANGE THRUST DIRECTION OF AIRCRAFT ENGINE** to change the direction of the thrust of an aircraft engine as a means of steering the aircraft [Early 18C. < Latin, "carrier" < *vectus*, past participle of *vehere* "carry"] —**vec·to·ri·al** /vek táwree əl/ *adj* —**vec·to·ri·al·ly** *adv*

vec·tor graph·ics *npl* COMPUT same as **object-oriented graphics**

vec·tor prod·uct *n* the result of multiplying two vectors. It is perpendicular to the vectors and its magnitude equals the product of their magnitudes multiplied by the sine of the included angle.

vec·tor space *n* a mathematical set of vectors associated with a field of scalars comprising a commutative group under addition and in which multiplication of a vector and a scalar is a vector

vec·tor sum *n* the result of adding two vectors, obtained graphically as the directed diagonal of the parallelogram whose sides are the given vectors

Ve·da /váydə, veédə/ *n* any or all of the collections of Aryan hymns, originally transmitted orally, but written down in sacred books from the 6th century B.C. [Mid-18C. < Sanskrit, "knowledge, sacred book" < Indo-European, "know"] —**Ve·da·ic** /vi dáy ik, vay-/ *adj*

Ve·da·ism /váydə ìzzəm/ *n* HINDUISM same as **Vedism**

Ve·dan·ta /vi daántə/ *n* one of the six philosophical

schools of Hinduism [Late 18C. < Sanskrit *vedānta* < *veda* (see VEDA) + *anta* "end"] —**Ve·dan·tic** *adj* —**Ve·dan·tism** *n* —**Ve·dan·tist** *n*

V-E Day *n* the day after the German surrender, designated by the Allies to mark their victory in Europe in World War II. May 8, 1945.

Ved·da /véddə/ (*plural same* or **-das**), **Ved·dah** (*plural same* or **-dahs**) *n* a member of an indigenous forest people of Sri Lanka [Late 17C. < Sinhalese *vaddā* "hunter"] —**Ved·doid** *adj*

ve·dette /və dét/ *n* **1.** a mounted soldier positioned ahead of a force of soldiers to serve as a scout **2.** *also* **ve·dette boat** a small fast boat that serves as a scout for a seaborne force [Late 17C. Via French < Italian *vedetta*, alteration (after *vedere* "see") of *veletta* < Spanish *vela* "watch" < Latin *vigilare* (see VIGILANT)]

Ve·dic /váydik, véedik/ *adj* **1.** RELIG **OF VEDAS** relating to the Vedas **2.** HINDUISM **OF CULTURE THAT PRODUCED VEDAS** relating to the Hindu culture that produced the Vedas **3.** LANG **IN ANCIENT SANSKRIT** relating to the ancient form of Sanskrit in which the Vedas are written ■ *n* LANG **ANCIENT SANSKRIT** the ancient form of Sanskrit in which the Vedas are written

Ve·dism /váy dìzzəm/ *n* the Hindu religious theory and practice contained in, or based on, the Vedas

vee /vee/ *n* the letter "V," or something with a similar shape [Late 19C. < the pronunciation of the letter's name]

vee·na /vée naa/, **vi·na** *n* a South Asian musical instrument with seven strings that has a long fretted fingerboard with resonating gourds at both ends and is played by plucking [Late 18C. < Sanskrit *vīnā*]

veep /veep/ *n* same as **vice president** (*slang*) [Mid-20C. < VP]

veer[1] /veer/ *v* (**veered, veer·ing, veers**) **1.** *vti* **CHANGE DIRECTION SUDDENLY** to change direction, especially suddenly, or make something do this **2.** *vi* **CHANGE FROM ONE OPINION TO ANOTHER** to change from one opinion or state of mind to another, especially suddenly or radically **3.** *vi* METEOROL **MOVE CLOCKWISE** to shift in a clockwise direction (*refers to winds*) **4.** *vti* NAUT, SAILING **SAIL AWAY FROM WIND** to change course in a sailing vessel away from the wind, or make a vessel do this ■ *n* **CHANGE IN DIRECTION** a change in direction or course [Late 16C. < French *virer* "turn"]

veer[2] /veer/ (**veered, veer·ing, veers**) *vt* to let out a cable or chain, or make it go slack [15C. < Middle Dutch *vieren* "let out"]

vee·ry /véeree/ (*plural* **-ries**) *n* a woodland thrush with tawny upper parts and a spotted breast. Native to: eastern United States. Latin name: *Catharus fuscescens*. [Mid-19C. Origin ?]

veg[1] /vej/ (*plural same*) *n UK* vegetables, or a vegetable (*informal*) [Mid-20C. Shortening]

veg[2] /vej/ (**vegged, veg·ging, veg·ges**) *vi* same as **veg out** (*informal*) [Late 20C. < VEGETATE]

veg out *vi* to relax, be idle, or loaf, e.g., while watching television (*informal*)

Ve·ga /véegə, váygə/ *n* the brightest star in the constellation Lyra and one of the brightest in the northern hemisphere

Ve·ga /véegə, váygə/ /váygə/ ♦ **Lope de Vega**

ve·gan /véegən, véjjən/ *n* somebody who does not eat meat, fish, dairy products, or eggs [Mid-20C. Contraction of VEGETARIAN] —**ve·gan** *adj* —**ve·gan·ism** *n*

veg·e·ta·ble /véjjətəb'l/ *n* **1.** **EDIBLE PLANT** a plant with edible parts, especially leafy or fleshy parts that are used mainly for soups or salads, or to accompany main courses **2.** PLANTS **PLANT** a member of the plant kingdom **3.** **HAVING REDUCED MENTAL FUNCTIONS** used to describe somebody in whom the usual mental and physical functions are severely reduced or absent, often as a result of injury to the brain (*offensive*) ○ *in a vegetative state* **4.** **SOMEBODY INACTIVE** somebody regarded as lacking in vitality, alertness, or drive (*insult*) ■ *adj* **CONSISTING OF VEGETABLES** consisting of, made from, using, or resembling vegetables [14C. Via Old French < medieval Latin *vegetabilis* "animating, able to grow" < Latin *vegetare* (see VEGETATE)]

veg·e·ta·ble i·vor·y *n* **1.** a hard pale material like ivory, used to make decorative items and accessories. It comes from the endosperm of a South American palm nut (**ivory nut**). **2.** TREES same as **ivory nut**

veg·e·ta·ble oil *n* an oil that has been extracted from a plant or the seeds of a plant, e.g., olive oil, sunflower oil, sesame oil, or canola oil

veg·e·ta·ble oy·ster *n* FOOD same as **salsify**

veg·e·ta·ble wax *n* a waxy material that forms part of the thin film covering the surfaces of most plants and helps reduce their loss of water through evaporation. It is obtained commercially from some palms such as the carnauba.

veg·e·tal /véjjət'l/ *adj* **1.** relating to plants **2.** BIOL same as **vegetative** (sense 2) [14C. < medieval Latin *vegetalis* < Latin *vegetare* (see VEGETATE)]

veg·e·tal pole *n* the end of an animal egg that contains the greatest concentration of yolk, lying opposite to the animal pole

veg·e·tar·i·an /vèjjə térree ən/ *n* somebody who eats vegetables, fruits, grains, seeds, and usually eggs and dairy products, but not meat or fish ■ *adj* eating or including vegetables, fruits, grains, seeds, and usually eggs and dairy products, but not meat or fish [Mid-19C. < VEGETABLE] —**veg·e·tar·i·an·ism** *n*

veg·e·tate /véjjə tàyt/ (**-tat·ed, -tat·ing, -tates**) *vi* **1.** **BEHAVE IN DULL OR INACTIVE WAY** to live or behave in a dull, inactive, or undemanding way **2.** BOT **DEVELOP LIKE PLANT** to grow or sprout like a plant **3.** MED **PRODUCE FLESHY OUTGROWTHS** to grow or spread, especially by producing fleshy outgrowths (*refers to warts or polyps*) [Early 17C. < Latin *vegetat-*, past participle of *vegetare* "grow" < *vegere* "quicken"]

veg·e·ta·tion /vèjjə táysh'n/ *n* **1.** **PLANTS IN GENERAL** plants in general or the mass of plants growing in a particular place **2.** **VEGETATING** the process of vegetating **3.** MED **OUTGROWTH** an outgrowth from a body part, e.g., on the membranes surrounding the heart —**veg·e·ta·tion·al** *adj*

veg·e·ta·tive /véjjə tàytiv/ *adj* **1.** **OF PLANTS** relating to or typical of vegetation, plants, or plant growth **2.** **INVOLVING GROWTH, NOT SEXUAL REPRODUCTION** relating to, involving, or typical of the growth and maintenance of an organism, rather than its sexual reproduction **3.** **REPRODUCING ASEXUALLY** describes reproduction, especially in plants, in which new individuals develop asexually from specialized structures such as bulbs, rhizomes, or runners rather than from specialized sex cells **4.** **HAVING SEDENTARY LIFESTYLE** leading a physically or mentally inactive life **5.** MED **RELATING TO PERSISTENT COMA** characterized by the reduction or absence of the usual mental or physical functions, often as a result of injury to the brain —**veg·e·ta·tive·ly** *adv* —**veg·e·ta·tive·ness** *n*

veg·e·ta·tive nerv·ous sys·tem *n* the part of the body's nervous system that controls involuntary functions such as the beating of the heart

veg·gie /véjjee/, **veg·ie** *n* FOOD (*informal*) **1.** same as **vegetable** **2.** same as **vegetarian** [Mid-20C. Shortening] —**veg·gie** *adj*

veg·gie·bur·ger /véjjee bùrgər/ *n* a flat patty made from vegetables, grains, or legumes, often served in the same way as a hamburger

veg·ie *n* FOOD another spelling of **veggie** (*informal*)

~~**vegtable**~~ incorrect spelling of **vegetable**

ve·he·ment /vée əmənt/ *adj* **1.** expressed with or showing conviction or intense feeling **2.** done with vigor or force [15C. Via Old French < Latin *vehement-* "forceful, violent"] —**ve·he·mence** *n* —**ve·he·ment·ly** *adv*

~~**vehical**~~ incorrect spelling of **vehicle**

ve·hi·cle /vée ik'l, -hik'l/ *n* **1.** **MEANS OF LAND TRANSPORTATION** a usually wheeled conveyance used on land for carrying people or goods **2.** **STRUCTURE FOR TRANSPORT IN SPACE** a powered structure, device, or rocket used to transport a payload or another craft through space **3.** **COMMUNICATION MEDIUM** a medium for communicating, expressing, or accomplishing something **4.** ARTS **PERFORMANCE FOR PARTICULAR PERFORMER** a film, play, show, or other performance designed or used to show off the talents of a particular performer **5.** ART **MIXTURE FOR PAINT PIGMENT** a substance such as linseed oil or an acrylic vinyl polymer in which a pigment is mixed for painting **6.** PHARM **SUBSTANCE BLENDED WITH DRUG** an inactive substance with which a drug is blended to make it easier to apply, administer, or take [Early 17C. Via French *véhicule* < Latin *vehiculum* < *vehere* "carry"]

ve·hic·u·lar /vee híkyələr/ *adj* relating to, involving, or for use by vehicles, especially motor vehicles [Early 17C. < late Latin *vehicularis* < Latin *vehiculum* (see VEHICLE)]

veil /vayl/ *n* **1.** **FACE COVERING WORN BY WOMEN** a length of fabric, usually sheer, worn by women over the head and face as a concealment or for protection **2.** **NETTING ATTACHED TO WOMAN'S HAT** a piece of netting or other sheer fabric attached to a woman's hat and covering the eyes **3.** **NUN'S HEADDRESS** a part of a nun's headdress covering the sides and back of the head **4.** **NUN'S VOWS OR LIFE** the vows that a nun takes, or the life that she leads **5.** **MEANS OF CONCEALMENT** something that hides, disguises, or obscures something, or separates one thing from another **6.** BOT **MEMBRANE COVERING YOUNG MUSHROOM** a thin membrane that covers the cap and stalk of an immature mushroom **7.** ANAT same as **caul** (sense 1) **8.** CHR same as **humeral veil** ■ *v* (**veiled, veil·ing, veils**) **1.** *vt* **COVER SOMETHING WITH VEIL** to cover something such as somebody's face with a veil **2.** *vt* **HIDE SOMETHING** to hide or disguise something, or separate one thing from another **3.** *vi* **WEAR VEIL** to put on or wear a veil [12C. Via Old French *veile* < Latin *vela* "covering," plural of *velum* "sail"] ◇ **draw a veil over something** to ignore something deliberately or refrain from mentioning it, in order to be discreet ◇ **take the veil** to become a nun (*literary*)

SPELLCHECK See *vale*[1].

veiled /vayld/ *adj* **1.** not open or direct, but disguised or suggested **2.** covered with or wearing a veil —**veil·ed·ly** /váylədlee/ *adv*

veil·ing /váyling/ *n* **1.** fabric used for veils **2.** a veil

vein /vayn/ *n* **1.** **VESSEL CARRYING BLOOD TO HEART** a blood vessel that carries blood to the heart **2.** **BLOOD VESSEL** a vessel that carries blood around the body (*not in technical use*) **3.** INSECTS **SUPPORTING STRUCTURE IN INSECT WING** a hollow supporting structure in the wing of an insect that carries blood vessels, nerves, and air tubes supplying the wing **4.** BOT **SAP-CONDUCTING LEAF STRAND** a distinct strand of tissue in a leaf that contains the sap-conducting vessels. It comprises one of several bundles of vessels and associated tissues (**vascular bundles**) and forms part of a network, arranged in a characteristic pattern. **5.** GEOL **LAYER OF MINERAL** a layer of a mineral in rock, especially an ore or a metal **6.** GEOL **FISSURE FILLED WITH MATERIAL** a fissure, crack, or channel in rock or ice that has been filled with a crystallized mixture of minerals **7.** **STREAK OF DIFFERENT COLOR** a streak of different color or material within a substance such as marble, wood, or cheese **8.** **PARTICULAR QUALITY** a particular recurrent quality or characteristic **9.** **DISPOSITION** a disposition, tone, or mood ○ *continued his speech in a more light-hearted vein* ■ *vt* (**veined, vein·ing, veins**) **1.** **FORM VEINS IN SOMETHING** to form veins, streaks, or layers in something **2.** **STREAK SOMETHING** to streak or suffuse something of one color or material with another ○ *green marble veined with white* [13C. Via Old French *veine* < Latin *vena* "blood vessel, vein of metal, mine"] —**vein·al** *adj* —**veined** *adj*

SPELLCHECK See *vain*.

vein·ing /váyning/ *n* a distribution or pattern of veins or streaks

vein·let /váynlət/ *n* a small vein

vein·stone /váyn stōn/ *n* MIN EXTRACT same as **gangue**

vel. *abbr* **1.** vellum **2.** PHYS velocity

ve·la BIOL plural of **velum**

Ve·la /véelə/ *n* a constellation of the southern hemisphere. See illustration at **constellation** [Mid-19C. Latin, literally "sails," from the shape of the constellation]

ve·la·men /və láymən/ (*plural* **-la·m·i·na** /-lámmənə/) *n* a spongy absorbent and protective layer that covers the aerial roots of some plants such as tree-dwelling orchids [Late 19C. < Latin, "covering" < *velare* "to cover" < *velum* "sail"]

ve·lar /véelər/ *adj* **1.** **WITH TONGUE NEAR SOFT PALATE** pronounced with the back of the tongue close to, or in contact with, the soft palate **2.** **OF VELUM** relating to, involving, or typical of a velum ■ *n* PHON **VELAR CONSONANT** a consonant pronounced with the back of the tongue close to, or in contact with, the soft palate [Early 18C. < modern Latin *velaris* < Latin *velum* "sail"]

ve·lar·i·a ANCIENT HIST plural of **velarium**

ve·lar·i·um /və lérree əm/ (*plural* **-i·a** /-ee ə/) *n* in ancient Rome, a large awning used in amphitheaters to shade the audience [Mid-19C. < Latin, "awning, curtain" < *velum* "sail"]

ve·lar·ize /veélə rīz/ (**-ized, -iz·ing, -iz·es**) *vt* to pronounce a speech sound by bringing the back of the tongue close to or against the soft palate —**ve·lar·i·za·tion** /veéləri záysh'n/ *n*

ve·late /veélət, -làyt/ *adj* having or covered by a velum [Mid-19C. < VELUM]

Ve·láz·quez /və laáss kèss/, **Diego** (1599–1660) Spanish painter. Court painter to Philip IV, he is noted for his portraits, kitchen scenes, and interior schemes. *Las Meninas* (1656) is considered to be his masterpiece. Full name **Velázquez, Diego Rodríguez de Silva y**

Vel·cro /vélkrō/ *tdmk* a trademark for a fastener consisting of two strips, one with a dense layer of tiny nylon hooks and the other of loops that interlock with them. Use: outerwear, athletic shoes, luggage.

veld /felt/, **veldt** /velt/ *n* an area of open grassland, especially in southern Africa [Early 19C. Via Afrikaans < Dutch, "field"]

Vel·de /véldə/, **Henry van de** (1863–1957) Belgian architect. He was the most influential architect of the Art Nouveau style. After designing integrated buildings and furniture in Belgium, France, and Germany, he founded the Weimar School of Arts and Crafts (1907), which later became the Bauhaus.

veldt *n* GEOG another spelling of **veld**

ve·le·ta /və leétə/, **va·le·ta** *n* a ballroom dance in triple time in which partners sometimes dance side by side and sometimes do a quick waltz [Early 20C. < Spanish, literally "weather vane"]

vel·le·i·ty /və leé ətee, ve-/ (*plural* **-ties**) *n* **1.** volition or desire at its weakest level (*literary*) **2.** a vague wish or desire [Early 17C. < medieval Latin *velleitas-* < Latin *velle* "to wish"]

vel·lum /vélləm/ *n* **1.** ANIMAL SKIN PARCHMENT high quality parchment made from calfskin, kidskin, or lambskin **2.** VELLUM MANUSCRIPT a manuscript written or printed on vellum **3.** PAPER RESEMBLING VELLUM an off-white heavy paper resembling vellum [15C. < French *vélin* "of a calf" < Old French *veel* "calf" (see VEAL)] —**vel·lum** *adj*

ve·lo·ce /və lṓchee/ *adv* to be played or performed rapidly (*used as a musical direction*) [Early 19C. Via Italian < Latin *veloc-* "quick, swift"] —**ve·lo·ce** *adj*

ve·lo·cim·e·ter /vèllə símmətər, veèlō-/ *n* an instrument used to measure the speed of a fluid or sound

ve·loc·i·pede /və lóssə peèd/ *n* an early form of bicycle or tricycle, including those that had pedals attached to the front wheel or were propelled by pushing the feet along the ground [Early 19C. < French *vélocipède* "bicycle" < Latin *veloc-* "quick, swift" + *ped-* "foot"] —**ve·loc·i·pe·dist** *n*

vel·o·ci·rap·tor /və lóssə ràptər/ *n* a small two-legged carnivorous dinosaur

ve·loc·i·ty /və lóssətee/ (*plural* **-ties**) *n* **1.** the speed at which something moves or happens **2.** the rate of change in the position of an object as it moves in a particular direction [Mid-16C. < Latin *velocitas-* < *veloc-* "quick, swift"]

ve·loc·i·ty of cir·cu·la·tion *n* the rate at which money circulates throughout an economy during a particular period, usually a year

ve·lo·drome /véllə drṑm/ *n* a stadium that has a banked track for bicycle races [Late 19C. < French *vélodrome* < *vélocipède* (see VELOCIPEDE) + -DROME < Greek *dromos* (see -DROME)]

ve·lour /və lóor/, **ve·lours** *n* a fabric with a thick pile, similar to velvet. Use: upholstery, clothing. [Early 18C. Via Old French *velous* < Latin *villosus* "shaggy" < *villus* "shaggy hair, wool"]

ve·lou·té /və loo táy/ *n* a creamy white sauce based on chicken, veal, or fish stock that is often used on poultry or vegetables [Mid-19C. < French, "velvety" < Old French *vellute* < *velous* (see VELOUR)]

ve·lum /veéləm/ (*plural* **-la** /-lə/) *n* **1.** a thin layer of tissue that covers or separates something **2.** ANAT same as **soft palate 3.** BOT same as **veil** *n* (sense 6) [Late 18C. < Latin, "sail, covering"]

ve·lu·ti·nous /və lóot'nəss/ *adj* densely covered with short soft hairs [Early 19C. < modern Latin *velutinus* "velvety" < medieval Latin *velutum* "velvet" < *villutus* (see VELVET)]

vel·vet /vélvət/ *n* **1.** FABRIC WITH SOFT LUSTROUS PILE a cotton, silk, or nylon fabric with a dense, soft, usually lustrous pile and a plain underside **2.** SOMETHING LIKE VELVET something that is smooth and soft like velvet **3.** ZOOL FURRY COVERING ON DEER ANTLERS the furry layer that covers the growing antlers of deer and is sloughed off when the antlers stop growing and harden **4.** *US* GAMBLING GAMBLING WINNINGS winnings from gambling (*slang*) **5.** *US* FIN UNEXPECTEDLY LARGE GAIN a gain or profit that is unexpectedly large (*slang*) ■ *adj* **1.** MADE OF VELVET made of or covered with velvet **2.** LIKE VELVET like velvet, especially in being or looking soft, smooth, or lustrous [14C. < Old French *veluotte* < *velu* "shaggy (cloth)" < medieval Latin *villutus* < Latin *villus* "shaggy hair, wool"]

vel·vet ant *n* a wasp whose body is covered in soft hair. The female is generally wingless and has a potent sting. Family: Mutillidae.

vel·vet·een /vèlvə teén/ *n* a brushed fabric with a soft pile like velvet [Late 18C. < VELVET + variant of -INE]

vel·vet glove *n* kind, careful, or gentle treatment, often disguising strength or determination

vel·vet shank *n* an edible mushroom that grows in clusters on hardwood trees and has a yellow cap and a velvety dark brown stalk. Native to: Europe, North Africa. Latin name: *Flammulina velutipes.*

vel·vet·y /vélvətee/ *adj* **1.** soft and smooth in a way that suggests the feel of velvet **2.** smooth and mellow

Ven. *abbr* **1.** CHR Venerable **2.** Venezuela

ven- *prefix* same as **veno-** (*used before vowels*)

ve·na /veénə/ (*plural* **-nae** /-nee/) *n* ANAT same as **vein** *n* (sense 1) (*technical*) [14C. < Latin]

ve·na ca·va /-káyvə, -kaávə/ (*plural* **ve·nae ca·vae** /-káyvee, -kaávee/) *n* either of two major veins that carry circulating blood into the right atrium of the heart. One carries blood returning from the upper body and head (**superior vena cava**) and the other brings that from below the chest (**inferior vena cava**). [Late 16C. < Latin, "hollow vein"] —**ve·na·ca·val** *adj*

ve·nal /veén'l/ *adj* **1.** ⚠ OPEN TO BRIBERY open to persuasion by corrupt means, especially bribery **2.** CORRUPT characterized by corruption **3.** ABLE TO BE BOUGHT able to be obtained for a price [Mid-17C. < Latin *venalis* < *venum* "something for sale"] —**ve·nal·i·ty** /vee nállətee/ *n* —**ve·nal·ly** *adv*

USAGE venal or **venial**? The two words are derived from entirely different Latin roots: ***venal*** comes from *venum* meaning "something for sale" and ***venial*** from *venia* meaning "forgiveness." ***Venal***, meaning "open to or characterized by corruption," describes people as well as processes and organizations: *The political system is so venal that bribery is commonplace.* ***Venial***, meaning "easily forgiven," is used in connection with minor faults or transgressions: *He was inclined to be thoughtless, but that was a venial fault in one so young.* In Roman Catholic theology, a *venial sin* is one that does not deprive the soul of divine grace, as opposed to a *mortal sin*, which does.

---

ve·na·tion /vee náysh'n/ *n* **1.** the pattern formed by the network of veins in an insect's wing or in a leaf **2.** all the veins making up a network [Mid-17C. < Latin *vena* "vein"] —**ve·na·tion·al** *adj*

vend /vend/ (**vend·ed, vend·ing, vends**) *v* **1.** *vt* to sell something from a vending machine **2.** *vti* to sell something, especially in the street, or make a living doing this [Early 17C. Directly or via French *vendre* < Latin *vendere* "sell"]

Ven·da[1] /véndə/ (*plural same* or **-das**) *n* **1.** a member of a people who live in northern South Africa and southern Zimbabwe **2.** a Bantu language spoken mainly in northern South Africa. Native speakers: 750,000. [Early 20C. < Bantu] —**Ven·da** *adj*

Ven·da[2] /véndə/ former homeland in South Africa. Abolished in 1994, it is now part of Limpopo Province.

vend·a·ble *adj* COMM another spelling of **vendible**

ven·dace /véndəss/ (*plural* **-dac·es** or *same*) *n* a whitefish with a streamlined body and protruding lower jaw. Native to: freshwater lakes of northwestern Europe, Russia. Genus: *Coregonus.* [Late 17C. Probably < Old French *vendoise* < Celtic]

vend·ee /ven deé/ *n* somebody who buys something

vend·er *n* COMM another spelling of **vendor**

ven·det·ta /ven déttə/ *n* **1.** a prolonged bitter feud or quarrel **2.** a feud between families started by the killing of a member of one family that is then avenged by the killing of a member of the other family [Mid-19C. Via Italian < Latin *vindicta* "vengeance"]

vend·i·ble /véndəb'l/, **vend·a·ble** *adj* suitable or fit to be sold ■ *n* something that can be sold or is available for sale —**vend·i·bil·i·ty** /vèndə bíllətee/ *n* —**vend·i·ble·ness** *n*

vend·ing ma·chine /vénding-/ *n* a machine from which items such as packaged food or drinks can be bought by inserting money

Ven·dôme /vaaN dṓm/, **Louis Joseph, duc de** (1654–1712) French soldier. He commanded forces in a number of battles during the War of the Spanish Succession (1701–14).

ven·dor /véndər/, **vend·er** *n* **1.** somebody who sells something **2.** COMM same as **vending machine**

ven·due /vén doò, ven doó/ *n US* a public sale or auction [Late 17C. Via Dutch *vendu* < French *vendue*, form of *vendre* "sell" (see VEND)]

ve·neer /və neér/ *n* **1.** THIN LAYER AS SURFACE a thin layer of a material bonded to the surface of a less attractive or inferior material **2.** LAYER OF PLYWOOD a thin layer of wood that is glued together with others to make plywood **3.** OUTER LAYER an outer layer applied to a surface for decoration or protection, e.g., a facing of stone on a brick building **4.** DECEPTIVE APPEARANCE a superficial appearance or show put on to please or impress others ○ *a thin veneer of civility* ■ *vt* (**-neered, -neer·ing, -neers**) **1.** FIX VENEER TO SOMETHING to bond or apply a veneer to a surface **2.** GLUE LAYERS OF WOOD to glue layers of wood together to make plywood **3.** HIDE SOMETHING BEHIND DECEPTIVELY PLEASANT APPEARANCE to hide or disguise something behind a deceptively pleasant or impressive appearance [Early 18C. < German *Fournier* "inlay, veneer" < French *fournir* "furnish, provide"] —**ve·neer·er** *n*

ve·ne·punc·ture *n* MED another spelling of **venipuncture**

ven·er·a·ble /vénnərəb'l/ *adj* **1.** WORTHY OF RESPECT worthy of respect as a result of great age, wisdom, remarkable achievements, or similar qualities **2.** RELIG REVERED revered for qualities such as great age or holiness **3.** ANCIENT extremely old **4.** CHR USED AS TITLE BEFORE CANONIZATION used by the Roman Catholic Church to describe somebody who has died and attained the first of the three degrees of canonization **5.** CHR USED AS ARCHDEACON'S TITLE used in the Church of England as a title for an archdeacon [15C. Directly or via French < Latin *venerabilis* < *venerari* (see VENERATE)] —**ven·er·a·bil·i·ty** /vènnərə bíllətee/ *n* —**ven·er·a·bly** *adv*

ven·er·ate /vénnə ràyt/ (**-at·ed, -at·ing, -ates**) *vt* **1.** to regard somebody with profound respect or reverence **2.** to honor somebody or something as sacred or special [Early 17C. < Latin *venerat-*, past participle of *venerari* < *vener-*, stem of *venus* "love, desire"] —**ven·er·a·tor** *n*

ven·er·a·tion /vènnə ráysh'n/ *n* **1.** FEELING OF RESPECT feelings of deep respect or awe **2.** EXPRESSING OF RESPECT the expression of profound respect or reverence for somebody or something **3.** CONDITION OF BEING RESPECTED the condition of being respected or revered —**ven·er·a·tion·al** *adj*

SYNONYMS See *regard.*

---

ve·ne·re·al /və neéree əl/ *adj* **1.** PASSED ON THROUGH SEX describes an infection or disease that is caught or transmitted through sexual intercourse **2.** ASSOCIATED WITH SEXUALLY TRANSMITTED DISEASE associated with, symptomatic of, or infected with a sexually transmitted disease **3.** GENITAL affecting or originating in the genitals **4.** ABOUT SEX relating to sex acts or sexual desire (*archaic* or *literary*) [15C. < Latin *venereus* < *vener-*, stem of *venus* "love, desire"]

ve·ne·re·al dis·ease *n* MED same as **sexually transmitted infection** (*dated*)

ve·ne·re·ol·o·gy /və neéree óllәjee/ *n* the branch of medicine involving the study and treatment of sexually transmitted diseases [Late 19C. < VENEREAL] —**ve·ne·re·o·log·i·cal** /və neéree ə lójjik'l/ *adj* —**ve·ne·re·ol·o·gist** *n*

ven·er·y[1] /vénnəree/ *n* the pursuit of or indulgence in sexual pleasure (*archaic*) [15C. < medieval Latin *veneria* < Latin *vener-*, stem of *venus* "love, desire"]

ven·er·y[2] /vénnəree/ *n* the sport or practice of hunting, or the animals hunted (*archaic*) [14C. Via French *vénerie* < Latin *venari* "to hunt"]

ven·e·sec·tion /vènnə sékshən, vénnə sèk-/ *n* SURG same as **phlebotomy** [Mid-17C. < medieval Latin *venae sectio* "cutting of a vein"]

Ven·e·ti /vénnə tī/ *npl* an ancient people who lived in northeastern Italy and neighboring areas from about the 10th century B.C. The Veneti allied themselves with the Romans during the 1st century B.C. [Early 17C. < Latin]

Ve·ne·tian /və neésh'n/ *adj* relating to the Italian city of Venice, or its people or culture ■ *n* somebody who comes from Venice [15C. < Old French *Venicien* < Latin *Venetia* "Venice"]

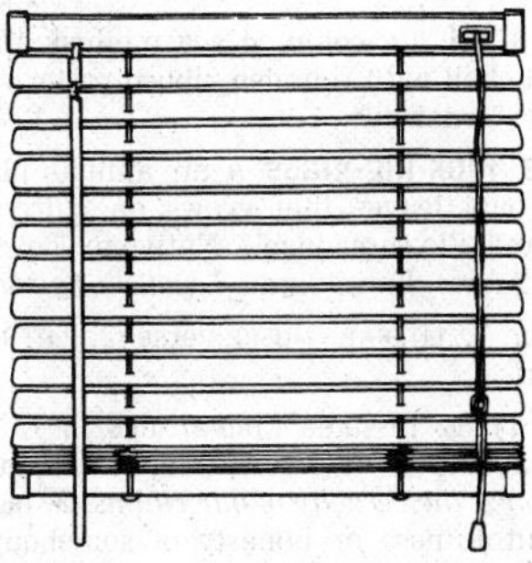

Venetian blind

Ve·ne·tian blind, **ve·ne·tian blind** *n* a window blind consisting of narrow horizontal slats whose angle can be adjusted to let in more or less light

Ve·ne·tian glass *n* delicate glassware, often with colorful ornamentation, made in or around Venice, especially at Murano

ve·ne·tian red *n* **1.** a dark red pigment. Source: hematite, synthetic iron oxide. **2.** a strong reddish brown color —**ve·ne·tian red** *adj*

Ve·net·ic /və néttik/ *n* the extinct language spoken in northwestern Italy by the Veneti people —**Ve·net·ic** *adj*

Venez. *abbr* Venezuela

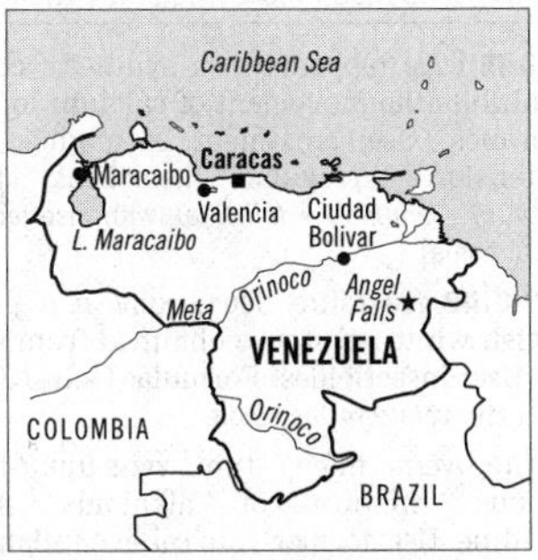

Venezuela

Ven·e·zue·la /vènnə zwáylə/ country in northeastern South America, north of Brazil, on the Caribbean Sea and the Atlantic Ocean. Language: Spanish. Currency: bolivar. Capital: Caracas. Population: 24,654,694 (2003). Area: 352,144 sq. mi./912,050 sq. km. Official name **Republic of Venezuela** —**Ven·e·zue·lan** *n, adj*

Ven·e·zue·la, Gulf of inlet of the Caribbean Sea in northwestern Venezuela. It is connected to Lake Maracaibo to the south by a narrow strait.

~~vengance~~ incorrect spelling of **vengeance**

ven·geance /vénjənss/ *n* punishment that is inflicted in return for a wrong [13C. Via French < Latin *vindicare* "avenge" (see VINDICATE)] ◇ **with a vengeance** in an extreme or intense manner

venge·ful /vénjfəl/ *adj* **1.** having or showing a strong desire for revenge **2.** serving the purpose of revenge or resulting from somebody's desire for revenge —**venge·ful·ly** *adv* —**venge·ful·ness** *n*

V-en·gine *n* an internal-combustion engine with cylinders arranged in two rows to form a V-shaped angle

veni- *prefix* same as **veno-**

ve·ni·al /veénee əl, veényəl/ *adj* easily forgiven or excused [13C. Via French < late Latin *venialis* < Latin *venia* "forgiveness"] —**ve·ni·al·i·ty** /veènee állətee/ *n* —**ve·ni·al·ly** *adv*

USAGE See *venal*.

ve·ni·al sin *n* in the Roman Catholic Church, a sin that does not deprive the soul of divine grace, either because it was not serious or because it was committed without intent or without understanding its seriousness

Ven·ice /vénniss/ historic city and seaport in northeastern Italy, built on islands in a lagoon on the coast of the Adriatic Sea. Population: 271,073 (2001).

ven·i·punc·ture /vénni pùngkchər, veéni-/, **ve·ne·punc·ture** *n* the puncturing of a vein for any medical purpose, e.g., to take blood, to feed somebody intravenously, or to administer a drug

ve·ni·re /və nīree, və neéree/, **ve·ni·re fa·ci·as** /və nīree fáyshəss, -neéree-/ *n* a judicial writ ordering the summoning of jurors [Mid-17C. < medieval Latin *venire facias* "you should cause to come"]

ve·ni·re·man /və nīreemən, -neéreemən/ (*plural* **-men** /-mən/) *n* a citizen, especially a man, summoned for jury duty under a venire

ve·ni·re·per·son /və nīree pùrss'n, -neéree-/ *n* a citizen summoned for jury duty under a venire

ven·i·son /vénniss'n, -z'n/ *n* the meat of a deer used as food [13C. Via Old French < Latin *venation-* "hunting" < *venari* "to hunt"]

Ve·ni·te /və nītee, -neétee/ *n* **1.** the 95th Psalm from the Bible, sung as an invitation to morning prayer **2.** a musical setting of the 95th Psalm [13C. < Latin, "come ye," the first word of the psalm]

Ven·lo /vénnlō/ city in Limburg Province, in the southeastern Netherlands. Population: 64,775 (2000).

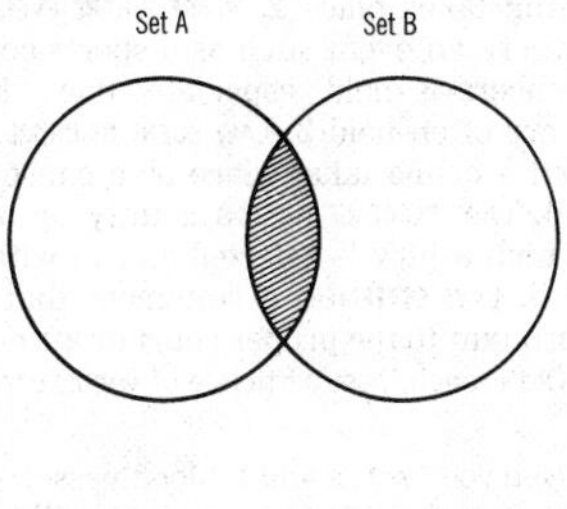

Venn diagram

Venn di·a·gram /vén-/ *n* a mathematical diagram representing sets as circles, with their relationships to each other expressed through their overlapping positions, so that all possible relationships between the sets are shown [Early 20C. After John *Venn* (1834–1923), British logician]

veno-, **veni-** *prefix* vein, venous ○ *venogram* [< Latin *vena* "vein"]

ve·no·gram /veénə gràm/ *n* an X-ray photograph of a vein or network of veins, taken after injecting a substance that absorbs X-rays and so makes the veins visible

ve·nog·ra·phy /vi nóggrəfee/ *n* the examination of somebody's veins by taking an X-ray photograph (**venogram**) after injecting a substance that absorbs X-rays

ven·om /vénnəm/ *n* **1.** a poisonous fluid produced by an animal and injected into prey or attackers by a bite or sting. Venoms are produced by a wide range of animals, including snakes, scorpions, spiders, and fish. **2.** malice, spite, or vicious hostility [13C. Via Old French *venim* < Latin *venenum* "poison"] —**ven·om·ous** *adj*

ve·nose /veé nōss/ *adj* describes something such as an insect's wing or the leaf of a plant that contains veins, especially many branched veins [Mid-17C. < Latin *venosus* < *vena* "vein"]

ve·nos·i·ty /vi nóssətee/ *n* **1.** EXCESSIVE AMOUNT OF BLOOD an excessive amount of blood in the veins, or in an organ or other body part **2.** HIGH NUMBER OF VEINS an unusually large number of veins in an organ or other body part **3.** QUALITY OF VENOUS BLOOD the deoxygenated state of venous blood **4.** VEINED CONDITION the presence or possession of veins, especially many branched veins

ve·nous /veénəss/ *adj* **1.** OF VEINS relating to or involving the veins **2.** RELATING TO BLOOD IN VEINS describes blood in the veins, which is returning to the heart, as opposed to blood in the arteries, which is leaving the heart **3.** WITH VEINS containing or full of veins [Early 17C. < Latin *vena* "vein"] —**ve·nous·ly** *adv* —**ve·nous·ness** *n*

vent[1] /vent/ *n* **1.** OPENING FOR AIR a small opening that allows fresh air to enter or stale air, gas, smoke, or steam to escape **2.** RELEASE OF STRONG FEELINGS a release or expression of strong feelings or emotions, or a chance to do this ○ *gave vent to his anger* **3.** GEOL OPENING IN EARTH'S CRUST an opening in the Earth's crust from which gases or volcanic material escape **4.** ZOOL OPENING IN ANIMAL'S BODY the external opening through which all waste material and eggs pass in fish, amphibians, reptiles, birds, and primitive mammals **5.** ARMS OPENING IN GUN BREECH a small opening in the breech of an old muzzle-loading gun through which the charge is ignited ■ *vt* (**vent·ed, vent·ing, vents**) **1.** RELEASE EMOTIONS to release or forcefully express strong feelings or emotions ○ *She vented her frustration on her family.* ○ *He's just venting.* **2.** LET OUT AIR to let out stale air, gas, smoke, or steam through a vent **3.** MAKE VENT FOR SOMETHING to provide a vent for something [14C. Via Old French *esventer* "let out air" < assumed Vulgar Latin *exventare* < Latin *ventus* "wind"] —**vent·less** *adj*

vent[2] /vent/ *n* a vertical slit at the bottom of a seam in a jacket or other garment that provides room for movement ■ *vt* (**vent·ed, vent·ing, vents**) to put a vent in a jacket or other garment [15C. Old French *fente* "slit" < Latin *findere* "to split"] —**vent·ed** *adj* —**vent·less** *adj*

vent·age /véntij/ *n* **1.** a finger hole in a recorder or other wind instrument **2.** a small opening or vent [Early 17C. < VENT[1]]

ven·tail /vén tàyl/ *n* a movable covering for the neck or lower face on a medieval helmet [14C. < Old French < Latin *ventus* "wind"]

ven·ter /véntər/ *n* **1.** ANAT, ZOOL BELLY OF ANIMAL WITH BACKBONE the abdomen of a vertebrate **2.** ZOOL BODY PART RESEMBLING ABDOMEN the part of the body in invertebrates that corresponds to the abdomen in vertebrates **3.** ANAT SOFT PART OF MUSCLE the soft fleshy area that forms the main part of a muscle **4.** ANAT HOLLOW OR CAVITY a hollow or cavity, e.g., on a bone **5.** BOT FEMALE PLANT PART in plants such as mosses and ferns, the swollen lower part of the female sex organ (**archegonium**) where the ovum develops **6.** LAW WOMB a woman's womb (*technical*) [Mid-16C. Directly or via French *ventre* < Latin *venter* "stomach, abdomen"]

ven·ti·fact /véntə fàkt/ *n* a rock, stone, or pebble that has been shaped, cut, or polished by wind-blown sand [Early 20C. < Latin *ventus* "wind," after ARTIFACT]

ven·ti·late /vént'l àyt/ (**-lat·ed, -lat·ing, -lates**) *vt* **1.** PROVIDE ROOM WITH FRESH AIR to provide a room or other enclosed space with fresh air or a current of air **2.** PROVIDE ENCLOSED SPACE WITH VENT to provide an enclosed space with a vent or other means of letting fresh air in and stale air out **3.** EXPOSE SOMETHING TO MOVING AIR to expose something to moving fresh air, e.g., in order to dry, cool, or preserve it **4.** PUBLICLY EXAMINE SOMETHING to state, examine, or discuss publicly something such as an opinion, question, or grievance **5.** PHYSIOL SUPPLY OXYGEN TO BLOOD to oxygenate or aerate the blood through the blood vessels of the lungs [15C. < Latin *ventilat-*, past participle of *ventilare* "to fan" < *ventilus* "fan" < *ventus* "wind"]

ven·ti·la·tion /vènt'l áysh'n/ *n* **1.** CIRCULATION OF AIR the movement or circulation of fresh air **2.** MEANS OF SUPPLYING FRESH AIR the means of supplying fresh air to an enclosed space, e.g., an opening or equipment installed in a building **3.** PUBLIC DISCUSSION the public announcement, examination, or discussion of something such as an opinion, question, or grievance

ven·ti·la·tor /vént'l àytər/ *n* **1.** a machine that keeps air moving in and out of the lungs of a patient who cannot breathe unaided **2.** a device that circulates fresh air in an enclosed space

ven·ti·la·to·ry /vént'lə tàwree/ *adj* relating to or used for breathing or for oxygenating the blood

ventr- *prefix* same as **ventro-** (*used before vowels*)

ven·trad /vén tràd/ *adv* toward the ventral surface or side

ven·tral /véntrəl/ *adj* **1.** ZOOL **OF LOWER BODY AT FRONT** located on or affecting the lower surface of an animal's body, or the front of the human body ○ *ventral fin* **2.** ANAT **OF OR CLOSE TO ABDOMEN** relating to or situated in, on, or near the abdomen **3.** BOT **FACING STEM** describes the upper side of a leaf or other surface that faces toward the stem ■ *n* FISH same as **ventral fin** [Mid-18C. < Latin *ventr-* "stomach, abdomen"] —**ven·tral·ly** *adv*

ven·tral fin *n* a fin on the underside of a fish, especially a pelvic fin or anal fin

ven·tral root *n* the spinal nerve root emerging from the lower surface of the spinal cord in animals and from the front surface in humans and mammals, consisting of motor nerve fibers

ven·tri·cle /véntrik'l/ *n* **1.** PHYSIOL **HEART CHAMBER** either of the two lower chambers of the heart that receive blood from the upper chambers **(atria)** and pump it into the arteries by contraction of their thick muscular walls **2.** PHYSIOL **BRAIN CAVITY** a cavity in the brain that is an enlargement of the central canal of the spinal cord and contains cerebrospinal fluid **3. HOLLOW IN BODY PART** a small cavity or chamber in the body or in an organ [14C. < Latin *ventriculus* (see VENTRICULUS)]

ven·tri·cose /véntri kòss/ *adj* **1.** describes a body part or plant part that is swollen, distended, or protruding on one side **2.** corpulent and fleshy, especially around the middle of the body (*formal*) [Mid-18C. < modern Latin *ventricosus* < Latin *venter* "stomach, abdomen"] —**ven·tri·cos·i·ty** /vèntri kóssətee/ *n*

ven·tric·u·lar /ven tríkyələr/ *adj* relating to, involving, or affecting a ventricle or a ventriculus

ven·tric·u·lar fib·ril·la·tion *n* an often fatal heartbeat irregularity in which the muscle fibers of the ventricles work without coordination and cause a loss of effective pumping action of the heart

ven·tric·u·lus /ven tríkyələss/ (*plural* **-li** /-lī/) *n* **1.** the part of an insect's gut where digestion takes place **2.** the part of a bird's stomach where digestion takes place [Early 18C. < Latin, "little stomach" < *venter* "stomach, abdomen"]

ven·tril·o·quism /ven trílla kwìzzəm/, **ven·tril·o·quy** /-kwee/ *n* the art or skill of producing vocal sounds that seem to come from somewhere other than the speaker [Late 18C. < modern Latin *ventriloquium* "speaking from the stomach" < Latin *venter* "stomach, abdomen" + *loqui* "speak"] —**ven·tri·lo·qui·al** /vèntri lṓkwee əl/ *adj* —**ven·tril·o·quist** *n*

ven·tril·o·quize /ven trílla kwìz/ (**-quized, -quiz·ing, -quiz·es**) *vi* to produce vocal sounds that seem to come from somewhere other than the speaker

ven·tril·o·quy *n* ARTS same as **ventriloquism**

Ven·tris /véntriss/, **Michael** (1922–56) British linguist. He is known for his decipherment of the Linear B script of ancient Crete, revealing it to be a form of Greek. Full name **Ventris, Michael George Francis**

ventro- *prefix* ventral, having to do with the stomach or abdomen ○ *ventromedial* [< Latin *venter* "stomach, abdomen"]

ven·tro·dor·sal /vèntrō dáwrss'l/ *adj* ANAT same as **dorsoventral** (sense 1) —**ven·tro·dor·sal·ly** *adv*

ven·tro·lat·er·al /vèntrō láttərəl/ *adj* relating to or extending between the ventral and lateral surfaces of something such as an animal or organ —**ven·tro·lat·er·al·ly** *adv*

ven·tro·me·di·al /vèntrō meédee əl/ *adj* located near or facing the middle of a ventral surface of something such as an animal or organ —**ven·tro·me·di·al·ly** *adv*

ven·ture /vénchər/ *n* **1. NEW BUSINESS ENTERPRISE** a business enterprise that involves risk, but could lead to profit **2. RISKY PROJECT** a risky or daring undertaking that has no guarantee of success **3. MONEY RISKED** the money or property risked in a business venture ■ *v* (**-tured, -tur·ing, -tures**) **1.** *vi* **MAKE DANGEROUS TRIP** to make a trip that is unpleasant or dangerous ○ *I ventured out into the storm to close the barn doors.* **2.** *vt* **RISK DANGERS OF SOMETHING** to undertake the risks or dangers of a particular task or project **3.** *vt* **MAKE SUGGESTION** to offer or express something tentatively at the risk of being contradicted, embarrassed, or ignored ○ *ventured a suggestion* **4.** *vi* **DARE TO DO SOMETHING** to presume or dare to do something **5.** *vt* FIN **PUT MONEY AT RISK** to expose money or property to risk [15C. Shortening of ADVENTURE] —**ven·tur·er** *n* ◇ **nothing ventured, nothing gained** if you take no risks, you will achieve nothing

ven·ture cap·i·tal *n* money used for investment in enterprises that involve high risk, but offer the possibility of large profits —**ven·ture cap·i·tal·ist** *n*

ven·ture·some /vénchərssəm/ *adj* (*formal*) **1.** willing to take risks or have new experiences **2.** involving risk or danger —**ven·ture·some·ly** *adv* —**ven·ture·some·ness** *n*

ven·tu·ri /ven tŏŏree/ (*plural* **-ris**) *n* **1.** a constriction in a tube designed to cause a pressure drop when a liquid or gas flows through it **2.** a restricted air inlet in a carburetor that produces a drop in pressure, causing fuel vapor to be drawn out of the carburetor bowl [Late 19C. After Giovanni Battista *Venturi* (1746–1822), Italian physicist]

Ven·tu·ri /ven tŏŏree/, **Robert** (*b.* 1925) US architect. He led a reaction as both theorist and practitioner against modernist architecture, and is regarded as the founder of postmodernism. He won the Pritzker Prize in 1991. He worked in partnership with his wife, Denise Scott Brown (*b.* 1931). Full name **Venturi, Robert Charles**

> "In iconographic terms, the cathedral is a decorated shed."
> [Robert Venturi, "Historical and Other Precedents," *Learning from Las Vegas*; 1972]

ven·tu·ri tube, Ven·tu·ri tube *n* a tube containing a constriction **(venturi)** that is placed in a fluid to measure its rate of flow. The measurement is based on the pressure drop in the fluid as it travels from one end of the tube to the other.

ven·tur·ous /vénchərəss/ *adj* same as **venturesome** (sense 1) —**ven·tur·ous·ly** *adv* —**ven·tur·ous·ness** *n*

ven·ue /vén yōō/ *n* **1. SCENE** a scene or setting in which something takes place **2. PLACE WHERE EVENT IS HELD** a place where an event such as a sports competition or a concert is held, especially one where such events are often held **3.** LAW **SCENE OF CRIME** the place at which a crime takes place or a cause of action arises **4.** LAW **PLACE OF TRIAL** a county or other area from which a jury is selected and in which a trial is held **5.** LAW **STATEMENT** a statement that a case is being brought to the proper court or authority [Mid-16C. < Old French, past participle of *venir* "come" < Latin *venire*]

ven·ule /vén yōōl/ *n* **1.** a small blood vessel, especially one that transfers blood from the capillaries to the veins **2.** a small branching vein in a leaf or an insect's wing [Mid-19C. < Latin *venula* "small vein" < *vena* "vein"] —**ven·u·lar** *adj*

Ve·nus /veénəss/ *n* **1.** in Roman mythology, the goddess of love and beauty. Greek equivalent **Aphrodite 2.** the fourth smallest planet in the solar system and the second planet from the Sun, seen from Earth as a bright morning or evening star [Pre-12C. < Latin < *venus* "love, desire"] —**Ve·nu·sian** /və nŏŏsh'n, vi nŏŏshee ən/ *adj, n*

Ve·nus fly·trap *n* PLANTS same as **Venus's flytrap**

Ve·nus·hair *n* PLANTS same as **Venus's-hair**

Ve·nus's flow·er bas·ket *n* a deep-sea sponge with a skeleton of glassy slender pointed structures **(spicules)** that intersect to form a geometrically patterned surface. Native to: western Pacific and Indian oceans. Genus: *Euplectella.*

Ve·nus's fly·trap, Ve·nus fly·trap *n* an insect-eating plant that has leaves ending in hinged lobes that spring shut, entrapping the insect. Native to: North and South Carolina. Latin name: *Dionaea muscipula.*

Ve·nus's gir·dle *n* a ctenophore that lives in warm seas and has a long almost transparent belt-shaped body with rows of cilia along the top and bottom edges. Latin name: *Cestum veneris.*

Ve·nus's-hair /veénəss hér/, **Ve·nus·hair** *n* a delicate fan-shaped fern that is widely grown as an ornamental plant. Native to: southern United States and tropical America. Latin name: *Adiantium capillus-veneris.*

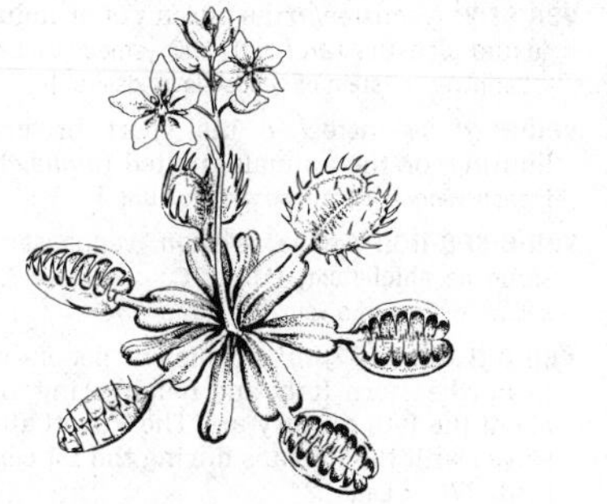

Venus's flytrap

Ve·nus shell *n* a common sea mollusk that has a hinged shell with rounded ribbed patterning on it. Family: Veneridae.

Ve·nus's look·ing-glass *n* an annual plant with hairy oval leaves that grows on cultivated and bare land. Flowers: purple. Native to: Europe, Asia, North Africa. Latin name: *Legousia hybrida.*

ver. *abbr* **1.** LITERAT, MUSIC verse **2.** LITERAT, BIBLE version

ve·rac·i·ty /və rássətee/ (*plural* **-ties**) *n* **1. TRUTH** the truth, accuracy, or precision of something ○ *They questioned the veracity of our claims.* **2. TRUTHFULNESS** the truthfulness or honesty of somebody **3. TRUE STATEMENT** a truth or true statement [Early 17C. Directly or via French < medieval Latin *veracitas* < Latin *verax* "truthful" < *verus* "true"] —**ve·ra·cious** /və ráyshəss/ *adj*

Ve·ra·cruz /vèrrə krŏŏz/ city and port in eastern Mexico, located on the Gulf of Mexico. Population: 457,377 (2000).

ve·ran·da /və rándə/, **ve·ran·dah** *n* a porch, usually roofed and sometimes partly enclosed, that extends along an outside wall of a building [Early 18C. Via Hindi *varaṇḍā* < Portuguese *varanda* "railing, balcony"] —**ve·ran·daed** *adj*

REGIONAL NOTE To refer to a large porch, especially with a suggestion of luxury, ***veranda*** is most common in the Middle and South Atlantic states. In the Gulf States *piazza*, especially in Lower Alabama, and *gallery*, which dominates the Lower Mississippi Valley out of New Orleans, are used much more frequently than ***veranda.***

ve·ra·pa·mil /və ráppəmil/ *n* a synthetic compound that inhibits the movement of calcium ions across membranes. Use: treatment of angina pectoris, hypertension, irregular heartbeat. [Mid-20C. < *v(al)er(ic)* + *am(ino-)* + *(nitr)il(e)* (with inserted "p"), its chemical name]

ve·rat·ri·dine /və ráttrə deèn, -din/ *n* a poisonous yellowish white substance obtained from sabadilla seeds. Use: insecticides. Formula: $C_{36}H_{51}NO_{11}$. [Early 20C. < Latin *veratrum* "hellebore"]

ver·a·trine /vérrə treèn, -trin/, **ver·a·trin** /-trin/ *n* a poisonous mixture of alkaloids including veratridine. Use: formerly, to relieve inflammation. [Early 19C. < Latin *veratrum* "hellebore"]

verb /vurb/ *n* **1.** a word used to show that an action is taking place or to indicate the existence of a state or condition, or the part of speech to which such a word belongs **2.** the part of a clause or sentence that includes the verb, but excludes the subject of the verb [14C. Via Old French < Latin *verbum* "word"]

ver·bal /vúrb'l/ *adj* **1. USING WORDS AS OPPOSED TO PICTURES** using words or language, especially as opposed to pictorial representation ○ *a verbal picture of the scene outside* **2. USING WORDS AS OPPOSED TO ACTION** relating to or consisting of words, as opposed to physical action or confrontation ○ *verbal protest* **3. ORAL AS OPPOSED TO WRITTEN** relating to or consisting of spoken words, as opposed to written words ○ *They made a verbal agreement.* **4. RELATING TO WORDS ALONE** relating to words alone, as opposed to their meaning ○ *a purely verbal distinction* **5. INVOLVING SKILL WITH WORDS** involving skill in the use and understanding of words and language ○ *verbal dexterity* **6.** GRAM **RELATING TO VERBS** relating to or derived from a verb or verbs in general **7.** GRAM **FORMING VERBS** used to form verbs ■ *n* GRAM **WORD FORMED FROM VERB** a word formed from a verb, especially one used as a noun or an adjective, e.g., a gerund or participle [15C. Via Old French < late Latin *verbalis* < Latin *verbum* "word"] —**ver·bal·ly** *adv*

SYNONYMS *verbal, spoken, oral*

CORE MEANING: expressed in words

verbal using words, especially spoken words, as opposed to pictures or physical action ○ *a stream of verbal abuse* ○ *the sort of eye contact that transmits messages more effectively than any verbal communication* **spoken** expressed with the voice ○ *the development of students' understanding of the spoken word* ○ *Written language is sometimes viewed as more "correct" than spoken language.* **oral** expressed in spoken form as distinct from written form ○ *Assessment is by written essays and an oral examination.* ○ *The committee's findings relied on oral histories and genealogical records.*

ver·bal ad·jec·tive *n* a verb participle ending in -ing or -ed that is used as an adjective

ver·bal·ism /vúrb'l ìzzəm/ *n* **1. PHRASE** something expressed in words **2. LONG-WINDED EXPRESSION** a wordy expression that has little meaning or relevance **3. USE OF TOO MANY WORDS** the uncritical or undisciplined use of words, especially without any attempt to analyze their meaning or value **4.** *US* **WAY SOMETHING IS EXPRESSED** the manner in which something is expressed or communicated

ver·bal·ist /vúrb'list/ *n* **1.** somebody who is skilled in the use of words and language **2.** somebody who concentrates on words or language rather than on facts, feelings, or ideas —**ver·bal·is·tic** /vùrb'l ístik/ *adj*

ver·bal·ize /vúrb'l ìz/ (**-ized, -iz·ing, -iz·es**) *v* **1.** *vt* **EXPRESS SOMETHING IN WORDS** to express feelings, thoughts, or ideas in words **2.** *vt* GRAM **MAKE WORD INTO VERB** to make a word that is another part of speech, e.g., a noun or adjective, into a verb **3.** *vi* **BE VERBOSE** to speak or write in a way that uses too many words —**ver·bal·i·za·tion** /vùrb'li záysh'n/ *n* —**ver·bal·iz·er** *n*

ver·bal noun *n* a form of a verb ending in "-ing" used as a noun, e.g., "dancing" in "he teaches dancing"

ver·ba·tim /vər báytim/ *adj* corresponding word for word with something else ■ *adv* repeated, written down, or copied word for word [15C. < medieval Latin < Latin *verbum* "word"]

ver·be·na /vər beénə/ *n* a common ornamental herbaceous plant. Flowers: colorful, in clusters. Native to: North and South America. Genus: *Verbena.* [Mid-16C. < Latin]

ver·bi·age /vúrbee ij/ *n* **1.** an excess of words that add little or nothing to the meaning **2.** the style of language in which something is expressed ○ *bureaucratic verbiage* [Early 18C. < French < Latin *verbum* "word"]

ver·bid /vúrbid/ *n* LING same as **verbal**

verb·i·fy /vúrbə fì/ (**-fied, -fy·ing, -fies**) *vt* GRAM same as **verbalize** (sense 2) (*archaic or formal*) —**verb·i·fi·ca·tion** /vùrbəfi káysh'n/ *n*

ver·big·er·ate /vər bíjjə ràyt/ (**-at·ed, -at·ing, -ates**) *vi* to repeat the same words or phrases obsessively as a symptom of a psychiatric disorder [Late 19C. < Latin *verbigerat-*, past participle of *verbigerare* "chat" < *verbum* "word" + *gerare* "keep carrying on"] —**ver·big·er·a·tion** /vər bìjjə ráysh'n/ *n*

ver·bose /vər bṓss/ *adj* expressed in or using too many words [Late 17C. < Latin *verbosus* < *verbum* "word"] —**ver·bose·ly** *adv* —**ver·bose·ness** *n* —**ver·bos·i·ty** *n*

SYNONYMS See *wordy.*

ver·bo·ten /vər bṓt'n, fər-/ *adj* forbidden or prohibited [Early 20C. < German]

verb phrase *n* a grammatical construction that includes a verb and any direct and indirect objects and modifiers linked to it, but excludes the subject of the verb

Ver·cheres /ver shér/, **Marie-Madeleine Jarret de** (1678–1747) French-Canadian colonist. She is known for defending her family's fort against an attack by the Iroquois in 1692.

Ver·cin·get·o·rix /vùrssin jéttəriks, -géttəriks/ (*d.* 46 B.C.) Gaulish leader. He led a revolt of Gallic tribes against Roman rule, but was eventually captured by Julius Caesar in 52 B.C.

ver·dant /vúrd'nt/ *adj* **1. WITH LUSH GREEN GROWTH** green with vegetation or foliage **2. GREEN** green in color **3. NAIVE** lacking experience or sophistication (*literary*) [Late 16C. < Old French *verdeant* "becoming green" < Latin *viridis* "green"] —**ver·dan·cy** *n* —**ver·dant·ly** *adv*

verd an·tique /vùrd an teék/, **verde an·tique** *n* **1.** a dark-green mottled or veined variety of serpentine marble that is used in decoration **2.** a green marble or stone that resembles verd antique **3.** CHEM same as **verdigris** (sense 1) [< obsolete French, "antique green"]

Verde, Cape /vurd/ **1.** ➧ **Cape Vert 2.** ➧ **Cape Verde**

verde antique *n* MINERALS, CHEM another spelling of **verd antique**

Ver·di /vérdee/, **Giuseppe** (1813–1901) Italian composer. He was one of the greatest operatic composers of all time. His works include *Rigoletto* (1851), *La Traviata* (1853), *Aïda* (1871), *Otello* (1887), and *Falstaff* (1893). Full name **Verdi, Giuseppe Fortunino Francesco**

> "Our mistake, you see, was to write interminable large operas, which had to fill an entire evening...And now along comes someone with a one- or two-act opera without all that pompous nonsense...that was a happy reform."
> [Attributed to Giuseppe Verdi]

ver·dict /vúrdikt/ *n* **1.** the finding of a jury on the matter that has been submitted to it in a trial **2.** a judgment, opinion, or conclusion about something ○ *Power companies are being asked for their verdict on wind power as an energy source.* [13C. < Anglo-Norman *verdit* "true speech" < *ver* "true" + *dit* "speech, saying"]

ver·di·gris /vúrdi greèss, -griss, -greè/ *n* **1.** a green or greenish blue deposit (**patina**) of copper carbonates on copper, brass, and bronze that is caused by atmospheric corrosion **2.** a green or greenish blue poisonous powder formed by the action of acetic acid on copper and consisting of one or more basic copper acetates. Use: paint pigment, fungicide. [14C. < Old French *vert de Grece* "green of Greece"]

ver·din /vúrd'n/ *n* a small bird with gray feathers, a white breast, and a yellow head and throat. Native to: southwestern United States, Mexico. Latin name: *Auriparus flaviceps.* [Late 19C. < French < Latin *viridis* "green"]

ver·di·ter /vúrditər/ *n* either of two basic copper carbonates, of which one is blue and the other green. Use: pigments. [Early 16C. < Old French *verd de terre* "green of the earth"]

Ver·dun /vur dún/ town in northeastern France. One of the longest and bloodiest battles of World War I was fought around the town during 1916. Population: 19,624 (1999).

ver·dure /vúrjər/ *n* **1. VIVID GREEN OF PLANTS** the green color associated with lush vegetation **2. VEGETATION** extremely lush vegetation **3. FRESHNESS** a fresh, healthy, or flourishing condition (*literary*) [14C. < French < Latin *viridis* "green"] —**ver·dured** *adj* —**ver·dure·less** *adj* —**ver·dur·ous** *adj* —**ver·dur·ous·ness** *n*

Ve·ree·nig·ing /və reéniking/ industrial city in Gauteng Province, South Africa. Population: 71,255 (1991).

Ver·en·drye ➧ **La Vérendrye, Sieur Pierre Gaultier de Varennes de**

verge[1] /vurj/ *n* **1. POINT BEYOND WHICH SOMETHING HAPPENS** the point beyond which something happens or begins ○ *He was on the verge of tears.* **2. BOUNDARY** a line, belt, or strip that acts as a boundary or edge **3. EDGE** the edge, rim, or margin of something **4.** *UK* ROADS **ROADSIDE BORDER** a narrow border that runs alongside a road **5.** ARCHIT **ROOF EDGE** the edge of a sloping roof where it extends beyond the gable **6. CLOCK SPINDLE** the spindle of a balance wheel in early clock and watch mechanisms **7.** HIST **ROD HELD BY TENANT** a rod held by a feudal tenant when swearing an oath of loyalty to his or her lord **8. ROD AS SYMBOL OF OFFICE** a rod or staff carried as a symbol of authority or an emblem of office [14C. Via French, "rod" (symbolizing office) < Latin *virga*]

verge on (**verged on, verging on, verges on**), **verge upon** *vt* **1.** to border on or be on the edge of a particular place or area ○ *Their property verged on ours.* **2.** to approach or come close to a particular quality or condition ○ *The whole performance verged on the ridiculous.*

verge[2] /vurj/ (**verged, verg·ing, verg·es**) *vi* **1. MOVE IN PARTICULAR DIRECTION** to move or lean in a particular direction or toward a particular condition **2. CHANGE GRADUALLY** to change gradually from one thing to another (*literary*) **3. SINK FROM VIEW** to descend toward the horizon (*literary*) [Early 17C. < Latin *vergere* "to bend, incline"]

ver·gence /vúrjənss/ *n* the inward or outward turning of both eyes when they are focusing on an object [Early 20C. Back-formation < CONVERGENCE and DIVERGENCE]

verg·er /vúrjər/ *n UK* **1.** a church official who carries the staff of office (**verge**) in front of somebody such as a bishop or dean during ceremonies and processions **2.** a church official who acts as a caretaker and attendant and looks after the inside of a church, usually including the furnishings and the vestments [15C. < Anglo-Norman < Old French *verge* "rod of office" (see VERGE[1])]

Ver·gil another spelling of **Virgil**

ver·glas /ver glaá/ *n* a thin coating of ice found on rock or exposed ground [Early 19C. < French < *verre* "glass" + *glas* "ice"]

ve·rid·i·cal /və ríddik'l/ *adj* (*formal*) **1.** telling the truth **2.** corresponding to facts or to reality, and therefore genuine or real [Mid-17C. < Latin *veridicus* "truth-speaking" < *verus* "true" + *dicere* "say"] —**ve·rid·i·cal·i·ty** /və rìddi kállətee/ *n* —**ve·rid·i·cal·ly** *adv*

ver·i·fi·ca·tion /vèrrəfi káysh'n/ *n* **1. ESTABLISHMENT OF TRUTH** the establishment of the truth or correctness of something by investigation or evidence **2. EVIDENCE** the evidence that proves something is true or correct **3.** LAW **CONFIRMATION OF PROCEDURES** in international law, the process of confirming that procedures laid down in an agreement such as a weapons limitation treaty are being followed **4.** LAW **AFFIDAVIT** in law, an affidavit swearing to the truth of a pleading **5.** LAW **CONFIRMATORY EVIDENCE** evidence or testimony that confirms something —**ver·i·fi·ca·tive** /vérrəfi kàytiv/ *adj*

ver·i·fi·ca·tion·ism /vèrrəfi káysh'n ìzzəm/ *n* the view that every meaningful proposition is capable of being shown to be true or false

ver·i·fi·ca·tion prin·ci·ple *n* the principle that a proposition or sentence is meaningful only if it is possible to establish whether it is true or false by experience or observation

ver·i·fy /vérrə fì/ (**-fied, -fy·ing, -fies**) *vt* **1. PROVE SOMETHING** to prove that something is true **2. CHECK WHETHER SOMETHING IS TRUE** to check whether or not something is true by examination, investigation, or comparison **3.** LAW **SWEAR SOMETHING UNDER OATH** in law, to swear or affirm under oath that something is true **4.** LAW **ATTEST TO TRUTH BY AFFIDAVIT** in law, to support the truth of a pleading by affidavit [14C. Via French *verifier* < medieval Latin *verificare* "make true" < Latin *verus* "true" + *facere* "make"] —**ver·i·fi·a·bil·i·ty** /vèrrə fì ə bíllətee/ *n* —**ver·i·fi·a·ble** /vérrə fì əb'l, vèrrə fí əb'l/ *adj* —**ver·i·fi·a·bly** *adv* —**ver·i·fi·er** *n*

ver·i·ly /vérrəlee/ *adv* in truth (*archaic*) ○ *Verily, he has admitted it.* [13C. < VERY "true"]

ver·i·sim·i·lar /vèrrə símmilər/ *adj* appearing to be true or real (*archaic*) [Late 17C. < Latin *verisimilis* "like the truth" < *verus* "true" + *similis* "like"] —**ver·i·sim·i·lar·ly** *adv*

ver·i·si·mil·i·tude /vèrrə si míllə tood/ *n* (*formal*) **1.** the appearance of being true or real **2.** something that only appears to be true or real, e.g., a statement that is not supported by evidence [Early 17C. < Latin *verisimilitudo* < *verisimilis* (see VERISIMILAR)] —**ver·i·si·mil·i·tu·di·nous** /vèrrə similə tood'nəss/ *adj*

ver·ism /vé rizzəm/ *n* strict realism or naturalism in art and literature [Late 19C. < Latin *verus* or Italian *vero* "true"] —**ver·ist** *n* —**ve·ris·tic** /və rístik/ *adj*

ve·ris·mo /və rízmō/ *n* a late 19th-century movement in Italian opera that advocated the use of themes drawn from real life and naturalistic portrayal of characters and events. Puccini was one of the principal members of this movement. [Early 20C. < Italian, "verism"]

ver·i·ta·ble /vérrətəb'l/ *adj* used to emphasize a figurative concept ○ *The business is a veritable gold* *mine.* [15C. < French < Latin *veritas* "truth" (see VERITY)] —**ver·i·ta·ble·ness** *n* —**ver·i·ta·bly** *adv*

ver·i·ty /vérrətee/ (*plural* **-ties**) *n* (*formal*) **1.** the quality of being true or real **2.** something that is true, especially a statement or principle that is accepted as a fact [14C. Via French < Latin *veritas* < *verus* "true"]

ver·juice /vúr jooss/ *n* **1.** an acid liquid made from crab apples or other sour or unripe fruit. Use: formerly, in cooking or as a condiment instead of vinegar. **2.** sourness of temper, attitude, or expression [14C. < Old French *vertjus* < *verd* "green" + *jus* "juice"]

Ver·laine /ver láyn, -lén/, **Paul** (1844–96) French poet. He wrote *Songs Without Words* (1874) while in prison for shooting his friend Arthur Rimbaud. His later symbolist verse influenced the development of French poetry. Full name **Verlaine, Paul Marie**

"The drawn-out sobs of the violins of autumn wound my heart with a monotonous languor."
[Paul Verlaine, "Chanson d'Automne (Song of Autumn)," *Poèmes Saturniens (Saturnine Poems)*; 1866]

ver·lan /ver láN/ *n* a form of French slang, used commonly in some ethnic working-class French neighborhoods and among young people, that involves reversing the order of syllables [20C. < French, reversal of syllables of *l'envers* "reverse side"]

Ver·meer /vər méer, -mér/, **Jan** (1632–75) Dutch artist. A major painter of the Dutch Golden Age, he painted domestic interiors of great serenity. Only 35 of his paintings survive.

ver·meil /vúrm'l, vúr màyl/ *n* **1.** gilded silver, bronze, or copper **2.** COLORS same as **vermilion** (*literary*) [14C. Via Old French < late Latin *vermiculus*, kermes insect from which red dye was made (see VERMICULAR)] —**ver·meil** *adj*

vermi- *prefix* worm ○ *vermivorous* [< Latin *vermis* "worm" < Indo-European]

ver·mi·cel·li /vùrmə séllee, -chéllee/ *n* pasta in long fine threads [Mid-17C. < Italian, "little worms" < Latin *vermis* "worm"]

ver·mi·cide /vúrmi sīd/ *n* **1.** a substance used to kill worms **2.** a chemical substance that expels parasitic worms from the small intestine —**ver·mi·cid·al** /vùrmi sīd'l/ *adj*

ver·mi·com·post·er /vúrmi kòmpōstər/ *n* a container in which specially bred worms are used to convert organic matter into compost

ver·mi·com·post·ing /vúrmi kòmpōsting/ *n* GARDENING same as **vermiculture**

ver·mic·u·lar /vər míkyələr/ *adj* **1.** in wavy lines like the movements, shape, or tracks of worms **2.** relating to worms [Late 17C. < medieval Latin *vermicularis* < Latin *vermiculus* "little worm" < *vermis* "worm"] —**ver·mic·u·lar·ly** *adv*

ver·mic·u·late *vt* /vər míkyə làyt/ (**-lat·ed, -lat·ing, -lates**) DECORATE SOMETHING WITH WAVY LINES to decorate something with wavy lines or patterns (*formal*) ■ *adj* /vər míkyələt, -làyt/ **1.** WITH WAVY LINES with wavy lines like the movements, shape, or tracks of a worm **2.** SINUOUS with many twists and turns (*formal*) **3.** LOOKING WORM-EATEN with a worm-eaten appearance (*literary*) [Early 17C. < Latin *vermiculat-*, past participle of *vermiculari* "be full of worms" < *vermiculus* (see VERMICULAR)]

ver·mic·u·la·tion /vər mìkyə láysh'n/ *n* **1.** MOVEMENT IN WAVES movement in waves, e.g., the muscular contractions of the intestines (**peristalsis**) **2.** WAVY DECORATION decorative wavy lines, patterns, or carvings **3.** WORM INFESTATION infestation by worms, or the resulting worm-eaten condition

ver·mic·u·lite /vər míkyə līt/ *n* a hydrous silicate of aluminum, magnesium, or iron. Source: altered basic rocks. Use: insulation, lubricant, growing medium in horticulture. [Early 19C. < Latin *vermiculus* "little worm" (see VERMICULAR), because of the way flakes of it expand and writhe in long shapes when heated]

ver·mi·cul·ture /vúrmi kùlchər/ *n* the use of specially bred worms to convert organic matter into compost

ver·mi·form /vúrmi fàwrm/ *adj* resembling a worm in shape

ver·mi·form ap·pen·dix, ver·mi·form proc·ess *n* same as **appendix** (sense 1)

ver·mi·fuge /vúrmi fyooj/ *n* a drug or other substance that causes worms or other parasites to be expelled from the intestines —**ver·mif·u·gal** /vər míffyəg'l, vùrmi fyoog'l/ *adj*

ver·mil·ion /vər míllyən/, **ver·mil·lion** *n* **1.** a bright red pigment made from mercuric sulfide or synthetically **2.** a bright red color, sometimes tinged with orange [13C. < Old French *vermeillon* < *vermeil* (see VERMEIL)] —**ver·mil·ion** *adj*

ver·min /vúrmin/ *n* **1.** small animals or insects that harm people, livestock, property, or crops and are difficult to control, e.g., rats, weasels, fleas, or cockroaches **2.** an offensive term for a person or group considered to be extremely unpleasant or undesirable [13C. Via Old French < assumed Vulgar Latin *verminum* "noxious life forms" < Latin *vermis* "worm"]

ver·mi·na·tion /vùrmi náysh'n/ *n* the spreading of or infestation with vermin, especially parasites

ver·min·ous /vúrminəss/ *adj* **1.** OF VERMIN relating to or infested with vermin **2.** CAUSED BY VERMIN caused by vermin or parasitic worms **3.** DISGUSTING extremely unpleasant or offensive —**ver·min·ous·ly** *adv* —**ver·min·ous·ness** *n*

ver·mis /vúrmiss/ *n* the middle lobe of the brain that connects the two hemispheres of the cerebellum [Late 19C. < Latin, "worm"]

ver·miv·o·rous /vər mívvərəss/ *adj* used to describe birds or other animals that feed on worms

Vermont

Ver·mont /vər mónt/ state in the northeastern United States, bordered by Canada, New Hampshire, Massachusetts, and New York State. Capital: Montpelier. Population: 616,592 (2002 estimate). Area: 9,615 sq. mi./24,903 sq. km. —**Ver·mon·ter** *n*

ver·mouth /vər mooth/ *n* a wine flavored with aromatic herbs [Early 19C. Via French < German *Wermut* "wormwood," with which it was originally flavored]

ver·nac·u·lar /vər nákyələr/ *n* **1.** ORDINARY LANGUAGE the everyday language of the people in a country or region, as distinct from official or formal language **2.** SPOKEN LANGUAGE the common spoken language of a people, as distinct from formal written or literary language **3.** LANGUAGE OF GROUP the distinctive vocabulary or language of a profession, group, or class **4.** BIOL COMMON NAME a common name of a plant, animal, or other organism, as distinct from its scientific name **5.** ARCHIT ORDINARY BUILDING STYLE the local architecture of a place or people, especially the architectural style that is used for ordinary houses as opposed to large official or commercial buildings [Early 17C. < Latin *vernaculus* "native" < *verna* "native-born slave"] —**ver·nac·u·lar** *adj* —**ver·nac·u·lar·ly** *adv*

ver·nac·u·lar·ism /vər nákyələ rìzzəm/ *n* **1.** a word or phrase from the everyday language of a country or region, as distinct from official or formal language **2.** the use of everyday language, as distinct from official or formal language

ver·nac·u·lar·ize /vər nákyələ rīz/ (**-ized, -iz·ing, -iz·es**) *vt* to make a word or phrase part of ordinary everyday language

ver·nal /vúrn'l/ *adj* **1.** appearing or happening in the season of spring **2.** having the freshness or energy associated with youth (*literary*) [Mid-16C. < Latin *vernalis* < *vernus* "of the spring" < *ver* "spring"]

ver·nal e·qui·nox *n* **1.** the time when the Sun crosses the celestial equator and day and night are of equal length, marking the beginning of spring. In the northern hemisphere this is around March 21, in the southern hemisphere around September 23. **2.** the point on the celestial sphere where the path of the Sun (**ecliptic**) crosses the celestial equator, in the constellation Pisces

ver·nal·ize /vúrn'l īz/ (**-ized, -iz·ing, -iz·es**) *vt* to expose plant seeds or seedlings to artificially cold temperatures in order to promote subsequent development and flowering —**ver·nal·i·za·tion** /vùrn'li záysh'n/ *n*

ver·na·tion /vər náysh'n/ *n* the way that young leaves are arranged in a bud [Late 18C. < modern Latin *vernation-* < Latin *vernare* "grow in the spring" < *vernus* (see VERNAL)]

Verne /vurn/, **Jules** (1828–1905) French writer. His novels, which include *20,000 Leagues Under the Sea* (1870) and *Around the World in Eighty Days* (1872), anticipated later scientific developments.

ver·ni·cle /vúrnək'l/ *n* CHR same as **veronica**[2] [14C. < Old French *veronicle*, variant of *veronique* < medieval Latin *veronica* (see VERONICA[2])]

ver·ni·er /vúrnee ər/ *n* **1.** SMALL SCALE FOR PRECISE READINGS a small movable graduated scale parallel to a larger graduated scale, calibrated to obtain more precise readings from the larger scale **2.** DEVICE FOR MAKING FINE ADJUSTMENTS an auxiliary device used to make fine adjustments to a precision instrument ■ *adj* WITH VERNIER relating to or fitted with a vernier [Mid-18C. After Pierre *Vernier* (1580–1637), French mathematician]

ver·ni·er rock·et *n* AEROSP same as **thruster** (sense 2) [Mid-20C. See VERNIER]

ver·nis·sage /vùrni saazh/ *n* a private showing or preview before the public opening of an art exhibition [Early 20C. < French, "varnishing," because originally the day before a public exhibition, when exhibitors varnished paintings after they were in place]

Ver·non /vúrnən/ city in southern British Columbia, Canada. Population: 39,995 (2001).

Ver·ny /vúrnee/ former name for **Almaty** (1855–1921)

Ve·ro·na /və rṓnə/ capital city of Verona Province, Veneto Region, northern Italy. Population: 253,208 (2001). —**Ver·o·nese** /vèrrə néez, -néess/ *n, adj*

Ve·ro·ne·se /vèrrə náyzee/, **Paolo** (1528–88) Italian artist. A painter of the Venetian school, he made dramatic use of color and perspective in his large-scale religious and secular compositions. Born **Caliari, Paolo**

ve·ron·i·ca[1] /və rónnikə/ *n* a perennial or annual plant or bush of the figwort family, e.g., the speedwell. Flowers: small, typically blue, in clusters. Genus: *Veronica*. [Early 16C. < modern Latin]

ve·ron·i·ca[2] /və rónnikə/ *n* **1.** IMPRESSION OF JESUS CHRIST'S FACE the impression of Jesus Christ's face believed by some to have been miraculously left on the cloth with which Saint Veronica wiped it on his way to his crucifixion **2.** CLOTH THAT WIPED JESUS CHRIST'S FACE the cloth with which Saint Veronica is said to have wiped Jesus Christ's face on his way to his crucifixion **3.** CLOTH WITH JESUS CHRIST'S FACE a cloth bearing a representation of Jesus Christ's face, sometimes worn by pilgrims [Late 17C. < medieval Latin, perhaps alteration (after the saint Veronica) of *vera iconica* "true image"]

ve·ron·i·ca[3] /və rónnikə/ *n* in bullfighting, a move in which the bullfighter stands in place and slowly swings the cape away from the bull as it charges [Mid-19C. < Spanish *verónica*, after Saint *Veronica*; from the gesture involved in wiping Jesus Christ's face]

Ver·raz·za·no /vèrrə zaánō, vè raa tsaá-/, **Ver·ra·za·no, Giovanni da** (1480?–1527?) Italian explorer. He explored the eastern coast of North America and was the first European to sail into New York Bay.

ver·ru·ca /və rookə/ (*plural* **-cae** /-kee/) *n* **1.** a wart that grows on the foot, usually on the sole **2.** a wart-shaped growth or projection on a plant or the skin of an animal [Mid-16C. < Latin, "wart"]

ver·ru·cose /vérrə kòss/, **ver·ru·cous** /-kəss/ *adj* covered with warts or similar growths or projections [Late 17C. < Latin *verrucosus* < *verruca* "wart"] —**ver·ru·cos·i·ty** /vèrrə kóssətee/ *n*

vers *abbr* MATH versed sine

Ver·sailles /vər sī/ *n* a large and elaborately decorated palace near Paris, France, built for Louis XIV in the mid-17th century. It is now a museum. The

Treaty of Versailles was signed there in 1919, ending World War I.

ver·sant /vúrss'nt/ *n* **1.** the slope of a mountain or mountain range **2.** the slope of a large area of land [Mid-19C. < French, present participle of *verser* "turn over" < Latin *versare* (see VERSATILE)]

ver·sa·tile /vúrssət'l/ *adj* **1. WITH MANY USES** able or meant to be used in many different ways **2. MOVING EASILY BETWEEN TASKS** able to move easily from one subject, task, or skill to another **3. CHANGEABLE** subject to rapid or unpredictable change **4.** ZOOL **FREE-MOVING** describes a body part or joint that can turn or move freely in more than one direction, e.g., an insect's antenna **5.** BOT **ATTACHED LOOSELY** describes an anther that is attached to the filament by a small area, allowing it to move more freely [Early 17C. < Latin *versatilis* < *versat-*, past participle of *versare* "keep turning or changing" < *vertere* "to turn"] —**ver·sa·tile·ly** *adv* —**ver·sa·til·i·ty** /vùrssə tíllətee/ *n*

vers de so·cié·té /vèr də sōssyə táy/ *n* verse or poetry written in a light witty sophisticated style [< French, "society verse"]

verse[1] /vurss/ *n* **1. GROUP OF LINES** a section of a poem or song consisting of a number of lines arranged together to form a single unit **2.** BIBLE **NUMBERED DIVISION OF BIBLE CHAPTER** a numbered subdivision into which each chapter of the Bible is divided **3.** LITERAT **POETRY** poetry, as distinct from prose **4.** LITERAT **BAD POETRY** poetry that is trivial in content or inferior in quality ○ *It's not poetry at all, it's just verse.* **5.** LITERAT **SHORT POEM** a poem, especially a short one **6.** LITERAT **LINE OF POEM** a single line of a poem, arranged rhythmically in metrical feet ■ *vt* (**versed, vers·ing, vers·es**) **VERSIFY PROSE CONTENT** to turn something from prose into poetry (*archaic*) [Pre-12C. Directly and via Old French *vers* < Latin *versus* "turning (of a plow), furrow, line" < *vertere* "to turn"]

ORIGIN The Latin word *vertere* "to turn," from which *verse* is derived, is also the source of the English words *adverse, advertise, controversy, converse*[1] ("to talk"), *convert, divert, inverse, obverse, pervert, prose, reverse, subvert, universe, versatile, version, versus, vertebra, vertical*, and *vertigo*.

verse[2] /vurss/ (**versed, vers·ing, vers·es**) *vt* to instruct somebody in something (*archaic or literary*) [Back-formation < VERSED]

versed /vurst/ *n* very knowledgeable about or skilled in something ○ *well versed in the art of flattery* [Early 17C. Directly or via French *versé* < Latin *versatus*, past participle of *versari* "occupy yourself with" < *versare* (see VERSATILE)]

versed co·sine *n* a trigonometric function equal to one minus the sine of an angle [After VERSED SINE]

versed sine *n* a trigonometric function equal to one minus the cosine of an angle [Translation of modern Latin *sinus versus* "turned sine"]

ver·set /vúrssət/ *n* a short verse, especially one from a sacred book [Early 17C. < French, "short verse" < *vers* "line" (see VERSE[1])]

ver·si·cle /vúrssik'l/ *n* **1.** a short sentence spoken or chanted by the minister during a liturgical service and responded to by the congregation or choir **2.** a short verse (*literary or archaic*) [14C. < Latin *versiculus* "short verse" < *versus* "line" (see VERSE[1])] —**ver·sic·u·lar** /vər síkyələr/ *adj*

ver·si·col·or /vúrssi kùllər/, **ver·si·col·ored** /-kùllərd/ *adj* **1.** having various colors **2.** varying or changing in color [Early 17C. < Latin *versicolor* < *versus*, past participle of *vertere* "turn, change" + *color* "color"]

ver·si·col·our *adj* Can, UK spelling of **versicolor**

ver·si·fi·ca·tion /vùrssəfi káysh'n/ *n* **1. ART OF VERSE-WRITING** the art or practice of writing verse **2. METRICAL FORM** the metrical form or structure of a poem **3. TURNING PROSE INTO VERSE** the conversion of prose into verse, or the recounting of something in verse **4. VERSION IN POETRY** a poetic or metrical version of a prose work

ver·si·fy /vúrssə fì/ (**-fied, -fy·ing, -fies**) *v* **1.** *vt* **CHANGE PROSE INTO POETRY** to turn prose into verse, e.g., by introducing rhyme and a metrical structure **2.** *vt* **TELL STORY IN POETRY** to recount something in verse **3.** *vi* **WRITE POETRY** to compose verse [14C. Via French < Latin *versificare* "make verses" < *versus* "line" (see VERSE[1])] —**ver·si·fi·er** *n*

ver·sine /vúr sīn/ *n* MATH same as **versed sine**

ver·sion /vúrzh'n/ *n* **1. ACCOUNT OF SOMETHING** an account of something, given from a specific point of view **2. SPECIFIC VARIETY** a form or variety of something that is different from others or from the original ○ *a later version of the text* **3. ADAPTATION OF SOMETHING** an adaptation of something for another medium, e.g., a book made into a play or film **4. TRANSLATION OF SOMETHING** a translation of something into another language **5.** *also* **Ver·sion BIBLE TRANSLATION** a particular translation of the Bible **6.** MED **MANIPULATION OF FETUS** the manipulation of a fetus to change its position in the womb, e.g., so that it can be delivered safely **7.** MED **TILTED CONDITION OF ORGAN** a condition in which an internal organ, especially the womb, is tilted or turned ■ *vt* COMPUT **IDENTIFY PREVIOUS VERSIONS OF DATA** to attach versioning information to data, especially for security or diagnostic purposes [Late 16C. Via French < Latin *version-* < *vers-*, past participle of *vertere* "turn"] —**ver·sion·al** *adj*

ver·sion·ing /vúrsh'ning, vúrzh'ning/ *n* the storage and management of previous versions of data, especially for security or diagnostic purposes

vers li·bre /vèr léebrə/ *n* LITERAT same as **free verse** [< French]

ver·so /vúrsō/ (*plural* **-sos**) *n* **1.** PUBL the back of a page or other printed sheet **2.** PUBL any left-hand page of a book, usually printed with an even page number **3.** COINS same as **reverse** *n* (sense 6) [Mid-19C. < Latin *verso (folio)* "(with the page) turned" < *versus*, past participle of *vertere* "turn"]

verst /vurst/ *n* a Russian measure of length equal to 0.66 mi./1.07 km [Mid-16C. Via French *verste* or German *Werst* < Russian *versta* "line"]

ver·sus /vúrssəss/ *prep* **1.** against, especially in a competition or court case ○ *the United States versus Canada* **2.** as opposed to or contrasted with ○ *such considerations as money versus job satisfaction* [15C. < medieval Latin, "against" < past participle of Latin *vertere* "turn"]

vert /vurt/ *n* **1.** HERALDRY **GREEN COLOR** in heraldry, the color green **2.** LAW **RIGHT TO CUT WOOD OR VEGETATION** formerly, the right to cut living wood or green vegetation in a forest **3.** HIST **WOOD OR VEGETATION** formerly, living wood or green vegetation in a forest [15C. Via Old French, "green" < Latin *viridis*] —**vert** *adj*

Vert, Cape ➧ **Cape Vert**

vert. *abbr* vertical

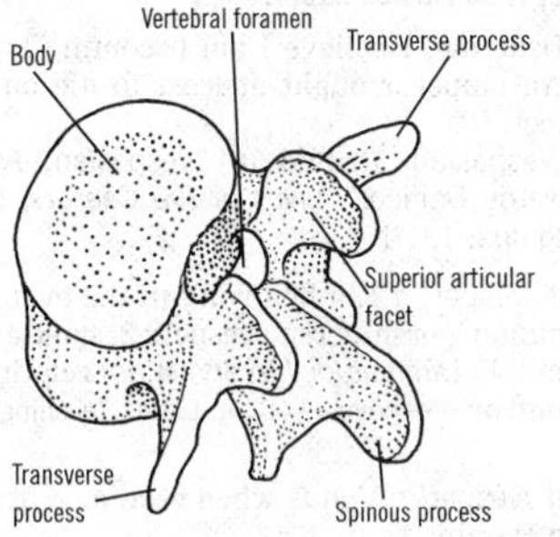

vertebra

ver·te·bra /vúrtəbrə/ (*plural* **-brae** /-brày, -bree/ or **-bras**) *n* a bone of the spinal column, typically consisting of a thick body, a bony arch enclosing a hole for the spinal cord, and stubby projections that connect with adjacent bones [Early 17C. < Latin < *vertere* "to turn"] —**ver·te·bral** *adj* —**ver·te·bral·ly** *adv*

ver·te·bral ca·nal *n* ANAT same as **spinal canal**

ver·te·bral col·umn *n* ANAT same as **spinal column**

ver·te·brate /vúrtəbrət, -bràyt/ *n* an animal with a segmented spinal column and a well-developed brain, e.g., a mammal, bird, reptile, amphibian, or fish [Early 19C. < Latin *vertebratus* "having joints" < *vertebra* (see VERTEBRA)] —**ver·te·brate** *adj*

~~**verternarian**~~ incorrect spelling of **veterinarian**

ver·tex /vúr tèks/ (*plural* **-ti·ces** /-ti seez/ or **-tex·es**) *n* **1. APEX** the highest point of something **2.** ANAT **TOP OF HEAD** the highest point of a body part, especially the top or crown of the head **3.** MATH **POINT OPPOSITE BASE** the point of a geometric figure that is opposite the base **4.** MATH **POINT WHERE SIDES OF ANGLE MEET** the point where two sides of a plane figure or an angle intersect **5.** MATH **POINT WHERE PLANES OF SOLID MEET** the point where three or more planes of a solid figure intersect **6.** ASTRON **POINT TOWARD WHICH STARS MOVE** a point on the celestial sphere toward which or from which a group of stars appears to move [Late 16C. < Latin, "whirl, spiral of hair at the top of the head" < *vertere* "to turn"]

ver·ti·cal /vúrtik'l/ *adj* **1. AT RIGHT ANGLE TO HORIZON** positioned at a right angle to the horizon **2. UPRIGHT** in an upright position, or running lengthwise up or down **3. OVERHEAD** at the vertex or directly overhead **4.** ECON **INVOLVING ALL STAGES OF PRODUCTION** relating to or involving all the consecutive stages in the production of goods, from design to sale **5.** ANAT **AT TOP OF HEAD** at or relating to the highest point of a body part, especially the top or crown of the head **6. MADE UP OF MANY LEVELS** involving or made up of successive or many levels ○ *a vertical management structure* ■ *n* **1. SOMETHING VERTICAL** a vertical structure, line, surface, or part **2. VERTICAL POSITION** a position that is upright or at a right angle to the horizon [Mid-16C. Directly or via French < late Latin *verticalis* "overhead" < Latin *vertex* (see VERTEX)] —**ver·ti·cal·i·ty** /vùrti kállətee/ *n* —**ver·ti·cal·ly** *adv*

ver·ti·cal an·gle *n* either of a pair of equal angles formed on opposite sides of the point at which two lines intersect

ver·ti·cal cir·cle *n* a great circle on the celestial sphere whose plane is perpendicular to the horizon and passes through the zenith and the nadir

ver·ti·cal file *n US* a collection of miscellaneous resource materials stored separately from the main collection, e.g., in a library [Because stored vertically, in suspension files]

ver·ti·cal mo·bil·i·ty *n* the movement of people or groups in society either upward or downward in terms of class or status

ver·ti·cal sta·bi·liz·er *n* AEROSP same as **fin**[1] *n* (sense 4)

ver·ti·cal un·ion *n US* HR same as **industrial union**

ver·ti·ces ANAT, MATH, ASTRON plural of **vertex**

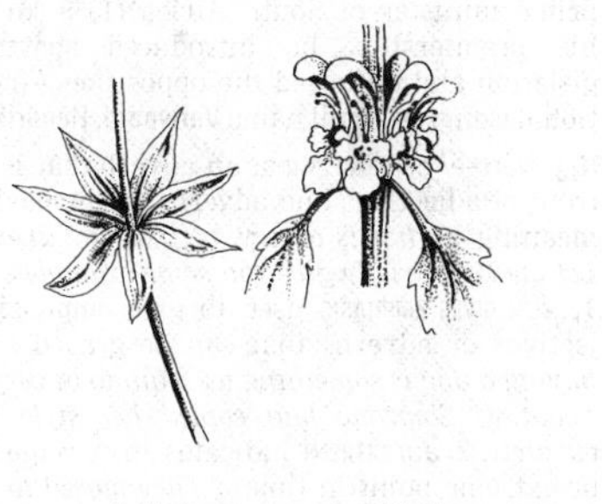

verticil: two types of verticil

ver·ti·cil /vúrtə sìl/ *n* a circular arrangement of similar parts around a central point [Early 18C. < Latin *verticillus* "whorl of a spindle"]

ver·ti·cil·las·ter /vùrtəssi lástər/ *n* a flower cluster that looks like a whorl of flowers but actually consists of two crowded clusters (**cymes**) arising opposite each other, as in many mints [Mid-19C. < Latin *verticullus* "whorl of a spindle"] —**ver·ti·cil·las·trate** *adj*

ver·ti·cil·late /vùrtə síllət, -làyt/ *adj* arranged in whorls, or forming a whorl —**ver·ti·cil·late·ly** *adv* —**ver·ti·cil·la·tion** /vùrtəssi láysh'n/ *n*

ver·tig·i·nes HEALTH plural of **vertigo**

ver·tig·i·nous /vur tíjjənəss/ *adj* **1. DIZZYING** causing dizziness, especially because of being very high or exposed ○ *the mountain's vertiginous summit* **2. SUFFERING FROM VERTIGO** relating to or suffering from the whirling or tilting sensation of vertigo **3. ROTARY** whirling or spinning on an axis **4. FICKLE** tending to change frequently or suddenly (*formal*) —**ver·tig·i·nous·ly** *adv* —**ver·tig·i·nous·ness** *n*

ver·ti·go /vúrti gō/ (*plural* **-ti·goes** or **-ti·gos** or **-tig·i·nes** /-tíjjə neez/) *n* **1.** a condition in which somebody feels a sensation of whirling or tilting that causes a loss of balance **2.** an instance or episode of vertigo [15C. < Latin (stem *vertigin-*), "whirling about, giddiness" < *vertere* "to turn"]

CULTURAL NOTE ***Vertigo***, a movie (1958) by British director Alfred Hitchcock. One of Hitchcock's most highly regarded films, it is both a typically suspenseful thriller and a powerful study of obsession. When former policeman Scottie Fergusson is asked to shadow a friend's wife, he first falls in love with her and then, after her suicide, becomes infatuated with a woman who appears to be her double.

ver·tu *n* ARTS another spelling of **virtu**

Ver·tum·nus /vur túmnəss/ *n* in Roman mythology, the god of gardens

ver·vain /vúr vàyn/ *n* a herbaceous plant that grows wild in temperate regions. Flowers: small, blue, white, or purple. Genus: *Verbena*. [14C. Via French *verveine* < Latin *verbena* "verbena"]

verve /vurv/ *n* **1.** enthusiasm, energy, or spirit, especially in the expression of artistic ideas **2.** lively vigorous spirit [Late 17C. Via French, "vigor, fanciful expression" < Latin *verba* "whimsical words," plural of *verbum* "word"]

vervet

ver·vet /vúrvət/, **ver·vet mon·key** *n* an African monkey that lives in large groups in savanna woodlands and has a long tail and black face, hands, and feet. Latin name: *Cercopithecus aethiops*. [Late 19C. < French]

Ver·woerd /fər vóort/, **Hendrik** (1901–66) Dutch-born prime minister of South Africa (1958–66). During his premiership, he introduced apartheid legislation and outlawed the opposition African National Congress. Full name **Verwoerd, Hendrik Frensch**

ver·y /vérree/ CORE MEANING: an adverb that is used in front of adjectives and adverbs to emphasize their meaning ○ *That is a very, very strong argument.* ○ *Let me very briefly give you some examples.*
1. *adv* **GIVES EMPHASIS** used to give emphasis to adjectives or adverbs that can be graded ○ *I think buying a dog is something we want to be very careful about.* ○ *Someone had copied her style very accurately.* **2.** *adj* **EXTREME** indicates an extreme position or extreme point in time ○ *They moved to the very back of the set, smiling at the technicians.* **3.** *adj* **RIGHT** exactly the right or appropriate person or thing, or exactly the same person or thing ○ *Hello! The very person I wanted to see!* ○ *He died this very day in 1986.* **4.** *adj* **EMPHASIZES IMPORTANCE** used before nouns to emphasize seriousness or importance ○ *An event like this can't help but shake the boxing world to its very foundation.* [13C. Via Old French *verrai* < Latin *verax* "truthful" < *verus* "true"] ◇ **very much so** an emphatic way of saying yes to something or indicating that it is true or correct ○ *"He was a good man, brave and honest." – "Yes, very much so."* ◇ **very well** indicates that somebody agrees to do something or accepts what somebody has said

ver·y high fre·quen·cy *n* the radio frequency band between 30 and 300 megahertz, reserved for the transmission of television and FM radio signals

Ver·y light /vérree lìt/ *n* a colored flare fired from a pistol, used as a signal [Early 20C. After Edward W. *Very* (1847–1910), US naval officer]

ver·y low fre·quen·cy *n* the radio frequency band between 3 and 30 kilohertz

Ver·y pis·tol /vérree-, véeree-/ *n* a pistol used for firing colored flares [Early 20C. See VERY LIGHT]

Ver·y Rev·er·end *n* the title of religious officials of a rank below bishop, abbot, or abbess

Ve·sey /véezee/, **Denmark** (1767?–1822) US abolitionist leader. Having purchased his own freedom, he planned an uprising to free all the slaves in South Carolina (1822), but the plot was discovered and he was hanged.

> "We are free but the white people here won't let us be so, and the only way is to rise up and fight the whites."
> [Denmark Vesey, *A Documentary History of the Negro People in the United States*, Herbert Aptheker; 1951]

ve·si·ca /və sìkə, və séekə, véssikə/ (*plural* **-si·cae** /və sìkee, -sìssee, -séekee, -séessee/) *n* **1.** a bladder, especially the urinary bladder (*technical*) **2.** a pointed oval shape used in medieval art and sculpture, especially to enclose a figure of Jesus Christ or the Virgin Mary [Mid-17C. < Latin, "bladder, blister"]

ves·i·cal /véssik'l/ *adj* occurring in or relating to a bladder, especially the urinary bladder ○ *vesical veins*

ves·i·cant /véssikənt/, **ves·i·ca·to·ry** /véssikə tàwree/ *n* (*plural* **-ries**) a substance that causes blisters, especially a substance such as mustard gas used in chemical warfare ■ *adj* causing blisters to form

ves·i·cate /véssi kàyt/ (**-cat·ed, -cat·ing, -cates**) *vti* to cause blisters, or be affected by blisters —**ves·i·ca·tion** /vèssi káysh'n/ *n*

ves·i·ca·to·ry *n* CHEM same as **vesicant**

ves·i·cle /véssik'l/ *n* **1.** MED **FLUID-FILLED CYST** a small sac or hollow organ in the body, especially one containing fluid **2.** MED **FLUID-FILLED BLISTER** a very small blister filled with clear fluid **(serum) 3.** GEOL **SPHERICAL CAVITY WITHIN ROCK** a bubble-shaped cavity in an igneous rock, formed by the expansion of gases trapped in lava and often later filled with minerals deposited from percolating solutions **4.** BOT **CAVITY IN WATER PLANT** a cavity filled with air in a seaweed or water plant [Late 16C. Directly or via French *vésicule* < Latin *vesicula* "small vesica" < *vesica* "bladder, blister"]

ve·sic·u·lar /və síkyələr/ *adj* resembling, having, or made up of vesicles —**ve·sic·u·lar·ly** *adv*

ve·sic·u·late *vti* /və síkyə làyt/ (**-lat·ed, -lat·ing, -lates**) to form blisters or vesicles in something, or take on the form of a blister or vesicle ■ *adj* /və síkyələt, -làyt/ having or resembling blisters or vesicles —**ve·sic·u·la·tion** /və sìkyə láysh'n/ *n*

Ves·pa·sian /ve spáyzh'n/ (A.D. 9–79) Roman emperor. His reign (69–79) saw the destruction of Jerusalem and the construction of the Colosseum. Born **Vespasianus, Titus Flavius Sabinus**

> "Dear me, I believe I am becoming a god. An emperor ought at least to die on his feet."
> [Vespasian. Quoted in "Vespasian, Afterwards Deified," *Lives of the Caesars*, Suetonius; 121?]

ves·per /véspər/ *n* **1.** a bell rung in the evening, e.g., to summon worshipers to vespers **2.** same as **evening** *n* (sense 1) (*archaic or literary*) ■ *adj* relating to the evening or vespers [14C. < Latin, "evening, evening star"]

Ves·per /véspər/ *n* Venus when seen as a bright star in the evening sky

ves·per·al /véspərəl/ *n* **1.** a book that contains the prayers and hymns used at vespers **2.** a covering for an altar cloth

ves·per bell *n* RELIG same as **vesper** *n* (sense 1)

ves·pers /véspərz/, **Ves·pers** *n* (*takes a singular or plural verb*) **1.** an evening church service, particularly evensong **2.** in the Roman Catholic Church, the sixth of the seven separate hours **(canonical hours)** that are set aside for prayer each day, or a service held on Sundays and holy days at this time [14C. Via Old French *vespres* (plural) < Latin *vespera* (singular) "evening" < *vesper* "evening, evening star"]

ves·per spar·row *n* a sparrow with white outer feathers on a notched tail, known for its evening song. Native to: grasslands of North America. Latin name: *Pooecetes gramineus*.

ves·per·til·i·o·nid /vèspər tíllee ənid/ *n* an insect-eating long-tailed bat. Family: Vespertilionidae. [Late 19C. < modern Latin *Vespertilionidae* < Latin *vespertilio* "bat" < *vesper* "evening"]

ves·per·tine /véspər tìn/ *adj* **1.** BOT **OPENING IN EVENING** describes a flower that opens in the evening **2.** ZOOL **ACTIVE IN EVENING** describes an animal that tends to be most active in the evening **3.** ASTRON **APPEARING IN EVENING** describes an astronomical object that appears or sets in the evening

ves·pi·ar·y /véspee èrree/ (*plural* **-ies**) *n* a nest or colony of social wasps or hornets [Early 19C. < Latin *vespa* "wasp," after APIARY]

ves·pid /véspid/ *n* an insect of the family that includes wasps and hornets. Family: Vespidae. ■ *adj* belonging or related to the family of insects that includes wasps and hornets [Early 20C. < Latin *vespa* "wasp"]

ves·pine /vé spìn/ *adj* relating to or resembling wasps [Mid-19C. < Latin *vespa* "wasp"]

Ves·puc·ci /vess póochee, -pyóochee/, **Amerigo** (1454–1512) Italian explorer. He claimed to be the first European to reach the mainland of the Americas (1497–98). America is named for him.

> "These new regions of America which we found and explored with the fleet...we may rightly call a New World...a continent more densely peopled and abounding in animals than our Europe or Asia or Africa."
> [Amerigo Vespucci, *Letter to Lorenzo de' Medici*; 1503]

ves·sel /véss'l/ *n* **1. RECEPTACLE** a hollow receptacle, especially one that is used as a container for liquids **2. LARGE WATERCRAFT** a ship or large boat **3. AIRSHIP** a flying craft, especially an airship **4.** ANAT **TUBULAR STRUCTURE CONDUCTING BODY FLUID** a duct that carries fluid, especially blood or lymph, around the body **5.** BOT **TUBE CONDUCTING WATER IN PLANT** a tube found in most flowering plants and some ferns that carries water and dissolved minerals through the plant, forming part of the sap-conducting tissue **(xylem) 6. SOMEBODY WHO EMBODIES QUALITY** somebody seen as the recipient or embodiment of a quality (*literary*) [14C. Via Anglo-Norman < Latin *vascellum* "small dish or vase, ship" < *vas* "dish, vase"]

vest /vest/ *n* **1.** CLOTHING **SLEEVELESS GARMENT** a man's or woman's sleeveless and collarless waist-length garment, usually with buttons down the front, worn over a shirt and traditionally worn by men under a suit jacket **2.** *UK* same as **undershirt** ■ *v* (**vest·ed, vest·ing, vests**) **1.** *vt* **CONFER POWER ON SOMEBODY OR SOMETHING** to bestow a power on somebody or something (*usually passive*) ○ *The governor was vested with powers* **2.** *vti* **CONFER RIGHTS, OR EXIST AS RIGHT** to settle or confer property, power, or rights on somebody, or be a part of somebody's property, power, or rights ○ *by the authority vested in me* **3.** *vti* **CLOTHE SOMEBODY, OR PUT ON CLOTHES** to clothe somebody, or put on clothes, especially vestments [15C. < Old French *vestu*, past participle of *vestir* "clothe" < Latin *vestire* < *vestis* "clothing, garment"]

Ves·ta /véstə/ *n* **1.** in Roman mythology, the goddess of the hearth. Greek equivalent **Hestia 2.** the brightest and third largest of the asteroids that orbit the Sun [< Latin]

ves·tal /vést'l/ *adj* **1. CHASTE** chaste, or not having experienced sexual intercourse **2.** MYTHOL **OF VESTA** relating to the Roman goddess Vesta ■ *n* **1. VIRGIN** a woman who is a virgin (*literary*) **2.** same as **nun**[1] (sense 1) (*literary*) **3.** RELIG, ANCIENT HIST same as **vestal virgin**

ves·tal vir·gin *n* in ancient Rome, a celibate woman who tended the sacred fire in the temple of Vesta. There were originally four, and later six vestal virgins, who were vowed to 30 years of service.

vest·ed /véstəd/ *adj* **1. HAVING RIGHTS TO SOMETHING** having an unquestionable right to the possession of property or a privilege **2. CLOTHED** wearing clothes, especially religious vestments **3. INCLUDING VEST** coming with a vest as part of the whole ○ *a vested suit*

vest·ed in·ter·est *n* **1. SPECIAL INTEREST** a special concern in maintaining or promoting an issue or situation for reasons of private gain **2. PERSON OR GROUP HAVING SPECIAL INTEREST** a person or group with a vested interest in maintaining or promoting something (*often used in the plural*) **3.** LAW **RIGHT TO POSSESS SOMETHING** a right to the present or future possession of property

vest·ee /ve stée/ *n* **1.** a decorative, detachable piece of material that is worn under a man's jacket and is intended to look like a vest **2.** a piece of clothing that is worn under a dress, jacket, or sweater and fills only the neckline

ves·ti·ar·y /véstee èrree/ *n* (*plural* **-ies**) a dressing room or storeroom for clothes ■ *adj* relating to clothes (*formal*) [13C. Via Old French *vestiarie* < Latin *vestiarium* "clothes chest, wardrobe," later "vestry" < *vestis* "clothing, garment"]

ves·tib·u·lar /ve stíbbyələr/ *adj* relating to a vestibule

ves·tib·u·lar nerve *n* a branch of the acoustic nerve that carries nerve impulses from the semicircular canals and other organs in the inner ear, conveying information about posture and balance

ves·ti·bule /vésti byoo̅l/ *n* **1. ENTRANCE HALL** a small room or hall between an outer door and the main part of a building **2.** ANAT **BODY CAVITY** a cavity or space in the body that serves as the entrance to another cavity or canal, e.g., the part of the mouth between the teeth and lips **3.** ANAT **MIDDLE CAVITY OF INNER EAR** the middle cavity of the inner ear between the cochlea and the semicircular canals **4.** RAIL **ENCLOSED AREA AT RAIL CAR ENTRANCE** an enclosed area at the entrance to a railroad car [Early 17C. Directly or via French < Latin *vestibulum*]

ves·ti·bule school *n* a school organized in a factory where workers can go to learn specific skills

ves·ti·bu·lo·coch·le·ar nerve /ve stìbbyəlō kòklee ər-/ *n* either of the eighth pair of cranial nerves, critical to the sense of hearing [< Latin *vestibulum* "entrance"]

ves·tige /véstij/ *n* **1. TRACE OF SOMETHING GONE** a trace or sign of something that is no longer present **2. SMALL AMOUNT** the slightest amount ○ *There wasn't a vestige of truth in what she wrote.* **3.** BIOL **RUDIMENTARY BODY PART** an organ or part of the body that is now rudimentary and no longer functions, but was formerly fully developed [Early 17C. Via French < Latin *vestigium* "sole of the foot, footprint, trace"]

ves·tig·i·al /ve stíjjee əl/ *adj* **1.** remaining after nearly all the rest has disappeared or dwindled ○ *a vestigial stirring of passion* **2.** having become degenerate or functionless in the course of time ○ *the vestigial muscles of the ear* —**ves·tig·i·al·ly** *adv*

vest·ing /vésting/ *n* the granting of pension rights to an employee, usually after a fixed period of employment, with the pension given either when the job is terminated or at retirement

vest·ment /véstmənt/ *n* **1.** a garment, especially a robe worn to show rank or office **2.** a ceremonial robe worn by members of the clergy during a religious ceremony [13C. Via Old French *vestiment* < Latin *vestimentum* < *vestire* (see VEST)] —**vest·men·tal** /vest mént'l/ *adj* —**vest·ment·ed** *adj*

vest-pock·et *adj* small enough to fit into the pocket of a vest ○ *a vest-pocket edition*

vest-pock·et park *n* a small park in an urban area

ves·try /véstree/ (*plural* **-tries**) *n* **1. ROOM FOR VESTMENTS** a room attached to a church, where vestments or sacred objects are kept **2. MEETING ROOM** a room in a church where meetings or classes are held **3. CHURCH COMMITTEE** in the Anglican Church, a committee of parishioners elected by the congregation to manage the temporal affairs of the parish **4. MEETING OF CHURCH MEMBERS** in the Anglican Church, a meeting of church members or their representatives [14C. < Anglo-Norman variant of Old French *vestiarie* (see VESTIARY)] —**ves·tral** *adj*

ves·try·man /véstreemən/ (*plural* **-men** /-mən/) *n* somebody, especially a man, who is a member of a church vestry

ves·try·per·son /véstree pùrss'n/ *n* a member of a church vestry

ves·try·wom·an /véstree wo̅o̅mmən/ (*plural* **-wom·en** /-wìmmin/) *n* a woman who is a member of a church vestry

ves·ture /véschər/ (*archaic*) *n* clothing, or something that covers in the way that clothing does ■ *vt* (**-tured, -tur·ing, -tures**) to clothe or cover somebody or something [14C. < Old French < Latin *vestire* (see VEST)] —**ves·tur·al** *adj*

Ve·su·vi·al /və so̅o̅vee əl/ *adj* resembling in force or degree the consequences of a huge volcanic eruption ○ *in a Vesuvial rage*

ve·su·vi·an /və so̅o̅vee ən/ *n* a slow-burning match used especially for lighting cigars (*archaic*) [Late 17C. After MOUNT VESUVIUS]

Ve·su·vi·an /və so̅o̅vee ən/ *adj* **1.** relating to or like the volcano Vesuvius **2.** *also* **ve·su·vi·an** marked by volatile sudden outbursts [Late 17C. After MOUNT VESUVIUS in S Italy]

ve·su·vi·an·ite /və so̅o̅vee ə nīt/ *n* a semiprecious stone that is a green, brown, or yellow silicate of aluminum containing calcium, magnesium, and iron. Source: marble. Use: gems. [Late 19C. After MOUNT VESUVIUS]

Ve·su·vi·us, Mount /və so̅o̅vee əss/ active volcano overlooking the Bay of Naples, southern Italy. An eruption in A.D. 79 destroyed the Roman cities of Pompeii and Herculaneum. Height: 4,190 ft./1,277 m.

vet[1] /vet/ *n* same as **veterinarian** ■ *v* (**vet·ted, vet·ting, vets**) **1.** *vt* **CHECK UP ON SOMEBODY OR SOMETHING** to subject somebody or something to a careful examination or scrutiny, especially when this involves determining suitability for something **2.** *vt* VET **EXAMINE ANIMAL** to examine or treat an animal **3.** *vi US* VET **PRACTICE VETERINARY MEDICINE** to practice as a veterinarian [Mid-19C. Shortening of VETERINARY or VETERINARIAN]

vet[2] /vet/ *n* a former member of the armed forces, especially in a particular conflict (*informal*) ○ *Vietnam vets* [Mid-19C. Shortening of VETERAN]

vet. *abbr* **1.** MIL veteran **2.** VET veterinarian **3.** VET veterinary

vetch /vech/ (*plural* **vetch·es** or *same*) *n* **1.** a leguminous plant with small flowers. Use: silage, fodder. Genus: *Vicia.* **2.** a plant related to or similar to vetch, e.g., the kidney vetch [14C. Via Old N French *veche* < Latin *vicia*]

vetch·ling /véchling/ *n* a creeping wild plant that is related to vetch. Genus: *Lathyrus.*

vet·er·an /véttərən/ *n* **1.** MIL **SOMEBODY FORMERLY IN ARMED FORCES** a former member of the armed forces **2.** MIL **EXPERIENCED SOLDIER** a long-serving member of the military who has had much active service ○ *a veteran of three foreign wars* **3. SOMEBODY WITH EXPERIENCE** somebody who is considerably experienced in something [Early 16C. Directly or via French *vétéran* < Latin *veteranus* < *vetus* "old"] —**vet·er·an** *adj*

Vet·er·ans Day *n* in the United States, a legal holiday honoring former members of the armed forces. Date: November 11.

vet·er·i·nar·i·an /vèttərə nérree ən, vèttrə-/ *n* somebody trained and qualified in the medical treatment of animals [Mid-17C. < Latin *veterinarius* (see VETERINARY)]

vet·er·i·nar·y /véttərə nèrree, véttrə-/ *adj* relating to diseases of animals and their treatment [Late 18C. < Latin *veterinarius* < *veterinus* "relating to (mature) cattle" < *veter-*, stem of *vetus* "old"]

vet·er·i·nar·y med·i·cine *n* the branch of medicine dealing with the health of animals and the diagnosis and treatment of their diseases and injuries

vet·er·i·nar·y sur·geon *n UK* same as **veterinarian**

~~vetinary~~ incorrect spelling of **veterinary**

vet·i·ver /véttəvər/ *n* **1.** a tall grass, the leaves of which are used to make screens and fans. Native to: South Asia. Latin name: *Vetiveria zizanioides.* **2.** the roots of the vetiver, which produce an oil that is used to make perfume [Mid-19C. Via French *vétiver* < Tamil *veṭṭivēr* < *vēr* "root"]

ve·to /vēetō/ *n* (*plural* **-toes**) **1. RIGHT TO REJECT LEGISLATION** the power of one branch of government to reject the legislation of another **2. EXERCISE OF RIGHT TO REJECT MEASURES** the exercise of the right to reject something, especially a political measure **3. PROHIBITION** an order prohibiting something ■ *vt* (**-toed, -to·ing, -toes**) **1. REJECT SOMETHING** to reject something such as a measure or government bill by veto **2. PROHIBIT SOMETHING** to refuse to consent to or approve something ○ *My teacher vetoed the idea.* [Early 17C. < Latin, "I forbid"] —**ve·to·er** *n*

vex /veks/ (**vexed, vex·ing, vex·es**) *vt* **1. ANNOY SOMEBODY** to make somebody slightly annoyed or upset, especially over a relatively unimportant matter **2. AGITATE SOMEBODY** to cause somebody anxiety or distress (*archaic*) **3. CONFOUND SOMEBODY** to confuse or puzzle somebody [15C. Via French *vexer* < Latin *vexare* "shake, disturb"] —**vex·ing·ly** *adv*

SYNONYMS See ***annoy.***

vex·a·tion /vek sáysh'n/ *n* **1. STATE OF BEING VEXED** the state of being provoked to slight annoyance, anxiety, or distress **2. ACT OF VEXING** the act of provoking somebody to irritability or anxiety **3. SOMETHING THAT VEXES** something that provokes irritability or anxiety

vex·a·tious /vek sáyshəss/ *adj* **1.** provoking irritation or anxiety by causing trouble **2.** describes legal proceedings put forward on insufficient grounds and with the intention of causing annoyance to the defendant —**vex·a·tious·ly** *adv* —**vex·a·tious·ness** *n*

vexed /vekst/ *adj* **1.** provoked to slight annoyance, anxiety or distress **2.** being the subject of much debate ○ *a vexed issue such as global warming* ○ *the vexed question of the next budget* —**vex·ed·ly** /véksədlee/ *adv* —**vex·ed·ness** *n*

vex·il·la ANCIENT HIST plural of **vexillum**

vex·il·lol·o·gy /vèksə lóllajee/ *n* the study of flags — **vex·il·lo·log·ic** /vèksələ lójjik/ *adj* —**vex·il·lo·log·i·cal** *adj* —**vex·il·lol·o·gist** *n*

vex·il·lum /vek sílləm/ (*plural* **-la** /-lə/) *n* in ancient Rome, a military standard, or the troops serving under a separate standard [Early 18C. < Latin, "flag, banner" < *vex-*, a stem of *vehere* "carry"]

VF, V.F. *abbr* **1.** MEDIA video frequency **2.** visual field

VFD *abbr* volunteer fire department

VFR *abbr* AEROSP visual flight rules

VFW *abbr* MIL Veterans of Foreign Wars

vg *abbr* **1.** very good **2.** ONLINE British Virgin Islands (*used in Internet addresses*) See table at **domain name**

V.G. *abbr* CHR Vicar General

VGA *n* a specification for video display controllers used in personal computers. Full form **video graphics array**

VHF, vhf *abbr* COMMUNICATION very high frequency

vi *abbr* **1.** GRAM verb intransitive **2.** ONLINE Virgin Islands of the United States (*used in Internet addresses*) See table at **domain name**

VI, V.I. *abbr* Vancouver Island

v.i., vi *abbr* vide infra

vi·a /vī ə, vēe ə/ *prep* **1.** by way of or through ○ *Can you come home via the post office?* **2.** using the means or agency of ○ *removed the obstruction via surgery* [Early 17C. < Latin, "by way of," form of *via* "way, road"]

vi·a·ble /vī əb'l/ *adj* **1. PRACTICABLE OR WORTHWHILE** able to be done or worth doing ○ *a viable proposition* **2.** BIOL **ABLE TO GROW** able to germinate or develop normally **3.** MED **ABLE TO SURVIVE OUTSIDE WOMB** describes a fetus that can survive outside the womb [Early 19C. < French *vie,* < Latin *vita* "life"] —**vi·a·bil·i·ty** /vī ə bíllətee/ *n* —**vi·a·bly** *adv*

USAGE The word ***viable*** was originally restricted to the senses of "able to grow" and "able to survive," as in *a viable fetus.* However, its extended sense of "able to be done or worth doing," as in *viable alternatives,* is well established in the language.

Vi·a Do·lo·ro·sa /vēe ə dòllə rṓssə, -dōlə-/ *n* **1.** the route taken by Jesus Christ to Calvary to be crucified **2.** *also* **vi·a do·lo·ro·sa** a difficult or distressing experience or series of events [< Latin, "sorrowful way"]

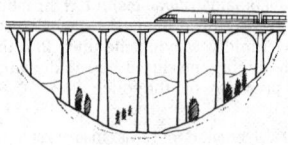

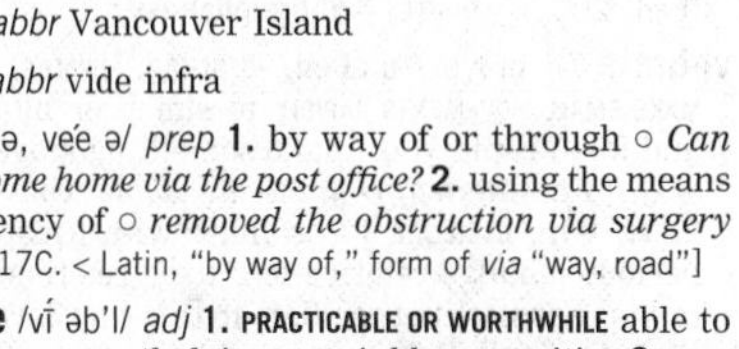

viaduct

vi·a·duct /vī ə dùkt/ *n* a bridge that consists of a series of short masonry or concrete arched spans supported on towers [Early 19C. < Latin *via* "way, road," after AQUEDUCT]

vi·al /vī əl/ *n* a small glass bottle, especially one for medicines [14C. Alteration of PHIAL]

vi·a me·di·a /vī ə méedee ə, -méddee ə/ *n* a middle course or choice between extreme possibilities [< Latin]

vi·and /vī ənd/ *n* (*formal*) **1.** a store or collection of food, especially the food that makes up a meal or a feast (*often used in the plural*) **2.** an item of food [14C. Via French *viande* "food" (now "meat") < Latin *vivenda* "things for living" < *vivere* "to live"]

vi·at·i·cum /vī áttikəm, vee-/ (*plural* **-ca** /-kə/ or **-cums**) *n* **1.** Communion given to somebody who is dying or in danger of dying **2.** provisions or money for a journey (*literary*) [Mid-16C. < Latin, "provision for a journey" < *via* "way, road"]

vibe /vīb/ *n* a particular kind of feeling or ambience (*slang; often used in the plural*) ○ *The new decor has a kind of 50s vibe to it.* [Mid-20C. Shortening of VIBRATION]

vibes /vībz/ (*plural same*) *n* same as **vibraphone** (*slang*) [Shortening]

vib·ist /víbist/ *n* somebody who plays the vibraphone (*slang*)

Vi·borg /vée bàwrg/ capital city of Viborg County, north central Jutland, Denmark. Population: 31,239 (1996).

vi·bra·harp /víbrə haàrp/ *n US* MUSIC same as **vibraphone** [Mid-20C. After VIBRAPHONE]

vi·brant /víbrənt/ *adj* **1. ENERGETIC** full of liveliness or energy **2. PULSATING WITH ENERGY** seeming to quiver or pulsate with energy or activity **3. RESONANT** having a full rich sound that tends to continue for some time **4. BRIGHT** dazzling or radiantly bright ○ *awash in vibrant reds and oranges* **5. VIBRATING** vibrating very rapidly [Mid-16C. < Latin *vibrant-*, past participle of *vibrare* "shake"] —**vi·bran·cy** *n* —**vi·brant·ly** *adv*

vi·bra·phone /víbrə fōn/ *n* a percussion instrument with electrically driven resonators beneath a set of metal bars that are struck with small mallets or sometimes played with a bow, causing vibration [Early 20C. < VIBRATE] —**vi·bra·phon·ist** *n*

vi·brate /vī bràyt/ (**-brat·ed, -brat·ing, -brates**) *v* **1.** *vti* **MAKE SMALL MOVEMENTS RAPIDLY** to shake or move back and forth rapidly, or make something move in this way ○ *Passing trains make the whole room vibrate.* **2.** *vti* PHYS **OSCILLATE** to oscillate with a continuing periodic change relative to a fixed reference point, or make something oscillate in this way **3.** *vi* **RESONATE** to make a full rich sound that tends to continue for some time **4.** *vi* **THRILL** to experience a rush of emotion in response to something [Early 17C. < Latin *vibrat-*, past participle of *vibrare* "shake"] —**vi·bra·to·ry** /víbrə tàwree/ *adj*

vi·bra·tile /víbrət'l/ *adj* **1.** showing vibration **2.** capable of vibrating, or operating by means of vibration [Early 19C. Alteration of *vibratory* after PULSATILE] —**vi·bra·til·i·ty** /víbrə tíllətee/ *n*

vi·bra·tion /vī bráysh'n/ *n* **1. INSTANCE OF VIBRATING** an instance of shaking or moving back and forth very rapidly **2. PROCESS OF VIBRATING** the process of moving or being moved back and forth very rapidly **3.** PHYS **REPETITIVE PERIODIC OSCILLATION** a continuing periodic oscillation relative to a fixed reference point, or a single complete oscillation **4. ATMOSPHERE OF PLACE** the atmosphere or aura given off by a place or situation (*informal; often used in the plural*) **5. FEELING COMMUNICATED SUBCONSCIOUSLY** a feeling communicated from one person to another (*informal; often used in the plural*) —**vi·bra·tion·al** *adj*

vi·bra·to /vi braátō/ (*plural* **-tos**) *n* **1.** a throbbing effect in the playing of a stringed or wind instrument, made by rapidly varying the pitch **2.** a throbbing effect in singing, produced by rapidly varying the breath pressure or the pitch [Mid-19C. < Italian, "vibrated"]

vi·bra·tor /vī bràytər/ *n* **1. VIBRATING DEVICE** an electric device that vibrates, e.g., one used to give a massage or as a sexual aid **2. SOMETHING THAT VIBRATES** something that vibrates or makes something vibrate **3.** ELEC ENG **DEVICE CONVERTING DIRECT TO ALTERNATING CURRENT** an electromechanical device, often used in bells and buzzers, that interrupts a direct current to convert it into an alternating current

vib·ri·o /víbbree ō/ (*plural* **-os** or **-on·es** /vìbbree óneez/) *n* a bacterium shaped like a comma or like the letter S. Genus: *Vibrio.* [Mid-19C. < modern Latin < Latin *vibrare* "shake"] —**vib·ri·oid** /víbbree òyd/ *adj*

vib·ri·o·sis /vìbbree óssiss/ *n* an infectious disease, especially of sheep, cattle, and goats, characterized by the death of a developing fetus and caused by a vibrioid bacterium *Vibrio fetus*

vi·bris·sa /vī brísslə/ (*plural* **-sae** /-see/) *n* **1.** a mammal's hair or whisker, usually on the face or limbs, that vibrates when touched, stimulating nervous tissue in the animal's skin **2.** a feather that is like a bristle, near the beak of an insect-eating bird [Late 17C. < Latin < *vibrare* "shake"] —**vib·ris·sal** *adj*

vi·bron·ic /vī brónnik/ *adj* relating to the electronic and vibrational energy states of elementary particles and atoms [Mid-20C. < *vibrational* + ELECTRONIC]

vi·bro·tron /víbrə tròn/ *n* a triode electron tube in which the anode can be vibrated by an external force

vi·bur·num /vī búrnəm/ (*plural* **-nums** or *same*) *n* a bush or small tree with flat or rounded flower clusters, e.g., the guelder rose. Flowers: white, sometimes tinged with pink. Genus: *Viburnum.* [Mid-18C. Via modern Latin < Latin, "wayfaring tree"]

vic. *abbr* **1.** RELIG vicar **2.** vicinity

Vic. *abbr* Victoria

vic·ar /víkər/ *n* **1.** *US* **EPISCOPAL CHURCH CLERIC** a cleric in the Episcopal Church who is in charge of a chapel **2. ANGLICAN PRIEST** a priest in the Church of England who is in charge of a parish. Vicars, unlike rectors, were not formerly entitled to receive the tithes, which went to a religious house, chapter, or lay person, and were paid a stipend. **3. MEMBER OF ANGLICAN CLERGY** a member of the Anglican clergy who acts in place of a rector or bishop at Communion **4. ROMAN CATHOLIC PRIEST** a Roman Catholic priest who represents or deputizes for a bishop [14C. Via Anglo-Norman *vicare* < Latin *vicarius* "substitute" < *vic-* "change, place"; because the vicar acted as a substitute for the rector] —**vic·ar·ly** *adj* —**vic·ar·ship** *n*

vic·ar·age /víkərij/ *n* **1.** the residence of a vicar **2.** the office or duties of a vicar

vic·ar ap·os·tol·ic (*plural* **vic·ars ap·os·tol·ic**) *n* a titular bishop or missionary in the Roman Catholic Church

vic·ar·ate *n* CHR same as **vicariate**

vic·ar gen·er·al (*plural* **vic·ars gen·er·al**) *n* **1.** a priest acting as an assistant to a Roman Catholic bishop **2.** a lay official assisting an Anglican bishop with administrative or judicial duties

vi·car·i·al /vī kérree əl, vi-/ *adj* **1.** being or acting as a vicar **2.** relating to a vicar **3.** same as **vicarious** (sense 3)

vi·car·i·ate /vī kérree ət, -àyt, vi-/, **vic·ar·ate** /víkərət, víkə ràyt/ *n* **1.** the office or authority of a vicar **2.** the district that falls under the care of a vicar

vi·car·i·ous /vī kérree əss, vi-/ *adj* **1. EXPERIENCED THROUGH ANOTHER BY IMAGINING** experienced through somebody else rather than at first hand, by using sympathy or the power of the imagination ○ *vicarious pleasure* **2. ENDURED FOR SOMEBODY ELSE** done or endured by somebody as a substitute for somebody else ○ *vicarious suffering* **3. DELEGATED** delegated to somebody else or performing a function that has been delegated ○ *vicarious authority* **4.** MED **IN UNEXPECTED PART OF BODY** occurring in a part of the body remote from the usual site, e.g., menstrual bleeding in the breasts, nose, or sweat glands [Mid-17C. < Latin *vicarius* (see VICAR)] —**vi·car·i·ous·ly** *adv* —**vi·car·i·ous·ness** *n*

Vic·ar of Christ *n* in Roman Catholicism, the pope

vice[1] /vīss/ *n* **1. IMMORAL HABIT** an immoral or wicked habit or characteristic ○ *Lying is the least of her vices.* **2. DEPRAVITY** immoral conduct **3. PROSTITUTION, GAMBLING, AND DRUGS** criminal activity connected with prostitution and other sexual offenses, gambling, and illegal drugs (*often used before a noun*) **4. MILD FAILING IN CHARACTER** a mild failing or flaw in somebody's behavior or character **5. FAULT IN ANIMAL** a fault or undesirable habit in a horse or other domestic animal [13C. Via French < Latin *vitium*]

vi·ce[2] /víssee, víssə/ *prep* in place of or instead of somebody or something [Late 18C. < Latin *vice* "in place of" < *vic-* "change, place"]

vice[3] *n, vt* MECH ENG UK spelling of **vise**

vice ad·mi·ral *n* an officer in the US Navy or Coast Guard of a rank above rear admiral —**vice-ad·mi·ral·ty** *n*

vice chair *n* somebody who takes the place of a chairperson in his or her absence

vice chair·man *n* somebody, especially a man, who takes the place of a chairperson in his or her absence

vice chair·per·son *n* same as **vice chair**

vice chair·wo·man *n* a woman who takes the place of a chairperson, especially a woman, in his or her absence

vi·ce chan·cel·lor *n* **1. ASSISTANT CHANCELLOR OF UNIVERSITY** a deputy or assistant chancellor in a university **2. DEPUTY CHANCELLOR** a deputy for the chancellor of a country **3. JUDGE** a US judge ranking below a chancellor, or an English judge who runs the Chancery Division of the High Court —**vice-chan·cel·lor·ship** *n*

vice con·sul *n* an officer who acts as the deputy for the official representing a country's commercial interest in an overseas country —**vice-con·su·lar** *adj*

vice·ge·rent /vīss jéerənt/ *n* a deputy appointed to act on the authority of a ruler or magistrate, especially in administrative duties [Mid-16C. < medieval Latin, "deputy" < Latin *gerent-*, present participle of *gerere* "carry on"] —**vice·ge·ral** *adj* —**vice·ge·ren·cy** *n*

vic·e·nar·y /víss'n èrree/ *adj* **1.** being or relating to the number 20 **2.** using 20 as a basis for counting or ordering [Early 17C. < Latin *vicenarius* < *viginti* "twenty"]

vi·cen·ni·al /vī sénnee əl/ *adj* lasting for or occurring every 20 years [Mid-18C. < Latin *vicennium* "period of twenty years" < *vic-*, stem of *vicies* "twenty times"]

Vi·cen·za /vi chénzə/ capital of Vicenza Province, Veneto Region, northern Italy. Population: 107,223 (2001).

vice pres·i·dent *n* an official of a rank below a president, who can take the president's place if necessary —**vice-pres·i·den·cy** *n* —**vice-pres·i·den·tial** *adj*

vice·re·gal /vīss rée̋g'l/ *adj* relating to a viceroy —**vice·re·gal·ly** *adv*

vice·re·gent /vīss réejənt/ *n* a deputy for the regent of a country —**vice·re·gen·cy** *n*

vice·reine /víss ràyn/ *n* a viceroy who is a woman, or the wife of a viceroy [Early 19C. < French, "vice-queen"]

vice·roy /víss ròy/ *n* **1.** a governor who represents a sovereign in a province, colony, or country **2.** a brightly colored orange-and-black butterfly of North America that resembles the monarch butterfly. Latin name: *Limenitis archippus.* [Early 16C. < French, "vice-king"] —**vice·roy·ship** *n*

vice·roy·al·ty /vīss róy əltee, vīss ròy əltee/ (*plural* **-ties**) *n* **1.** the office, term of office, or authority of a viceroy **2.** a district that is governed by a viceroy

vice squad *n* a police division in charge of enforcing laws relating to prostitution, gambling, and drugs

vi·ce ver·sa /vīss vúrssə, vīssə-/ *adv* the other way around [< Latin, "the position being reversed"]

Vi·chy[1] /véeshee/ *n* same as **Vichy water** [Mid-19C. < VICHY[2]]

Vi·chy[2] /véeshee/ city in central France, the site of important mineral springs. It was the seat of a French government that collaborated with the Germans during World War II. Population: 26,528 (1999).

vi·chys·soise /vìshee swaáz, vèeshee-/ *n* a creamy soup made from leeks, potatoes, and onions, often served chilled [Mid-20C. Shortening of French *crème vichyssoise glacée* "iced cream soup from Vichy"]

Vi·chy wa·ter *n* a natural sparkling mineral water from Vichy, France, or a similar sparkling water

vic·i·nage /víss'nij/ *n* **1.** a neighborhood, or the people living in it (*archaic*) **2.** the area immediately surrounding a place [14C. < Old French *vis(e)nage*, < Latin *vicinus* (see VICINITY)]

vic·i·nal /víssən'l/ *adj* **1. NEIGHBORING** adjacent or neighboring **2. LOCAL** relating to or restricted to a local area **3.** CHEM **OF CONSECUTIVE POSITIONS ON CARBON CHAIN** relating to two or more adjacent positions on a carbon ring or chain [Early 17C. Directly or via French < Latin *vicinalis* < *vicinus* (see VICINITY)]

vi·cin·i·ty /və sínnətee/ (*plural* **-ties**) *n* (*formal*) **1.** a neighborhood, or the area surrounding a particular place ○ *The fire threatened to spread, and all the houses in the vicinity had to be evacuated.* **2.** the fact of being close either in space or relationship [Mid-

16C. < Latin *vicinitas* < *vicinus* "neighbor" < *vicus* "village, homestead"] ◇ **in the vicinity of 1.** close to, neighboring, or surrounding **2.** roughly or approximately

vi·cious /víshəss/ *adj* **1. FEROCIOUS AND VIOLENT** carried out with intense violence and an apparent desire to inflict serious harm, or acting in an aggressive, cruel, and violent way ○ *a vicious attack* ○ *Her husband's a vicious brute.* **2. DANGEROUS AND AGGRESSIVE** aggressive and liable to attack or bite ○ *a vicious dog* **3. MALICIOUS** intended to cause somebody mental anguish or to defame somebody **4. SEVERE** extremely severe or powerful and damaging in its effects ○ *a vicious frost* **5. GOING FROM BAD TO WORSE** involving a chain of cause and effect or action and reaction in which things get progressively worse ○ *a vicious spiral* **6. UNSOUND** incorrect or showing faulty logic **7. WICKED AND IMMORAL** displaying or given to immoral behavior (*formal*) [14C. < VICE[1]] —**vi·cious·ly** *adv* —**vi·cious·ness** *n*

vi·cious cir·cle, **vi·cious cy·cle** *n* **1. SITUATION WORSENED BY ATTEMPTED SOLUTIONS** a situation in which attempts to solve one problem lead to further problems that only make the original position worse **2.** LOGIC **REASONING BASED ON UNPROVEN ASSUMPTION** a form of reasoning that bases a conclusion on a statement assumed to be true but not proven independently **3.** MED **LINKING OF TWO DISEASES** a situation in which two diseases or conditions are linked so that each leads to or aggravates the other

USAGE vicious circle or **vicious cycle**? Until quite recently the invariable choice was ***vicious circle***. Perhaps influenced by such phrases as *the cycle of welfare dependency*, however, the variant ***vicious cycle*** has been gaining ground, to the point that it is now seen almost as frequently as ***vicious circle***, in virtually indistinguishable contexts.

vi·cis·si·tude /vi síssi to͞od/ *n* the fact of being variable (*literary*) ■ **vi·cis·si·tudes** *npl* unexpected changes, especially in somebody's fortunes [Mid-16C. Directly or via French < Latin *vicissitudo* < *vicissim* "by turns" < *vic-* (see VICAR)] —**vi·cis·si·tu·di·nar·y** /vi sìssi to͞od'n èrree/ *adj* —**vi·cis·si·tu·di·nous** /vi sìssi to͞od'nəss/ *adj*

Vick·ers /víkərz/, **Jonathan Stewart** (*b.* 1926) Canadian opera singer. He is known especially for his roles in operas by Verdi and Wagner. Known as **Vickers, Jon**

Vicks·burg /víks bùrg/ city in western Mississippi. In 1863, during the Civil War, the city was besieged for 47 days before falling to Union forces led by General Ulysses S. Grant. Population: 26,226 (2002 estimate).

vi·comte /vee káwNt/ *n* a French nobleman who is equal in rank to a British viscount [Mid-19C. Via French < Old French *vi(s)conte* (see VISCOUNT)]

vi·com·tesse /vee kawN téss/ *n* a French noblewoman who is equal in rank to a British viscountess [Late 18C. < French < *vicomte* (see VICOMTE)]

vic·tim /víktim/ *n* **1. SOMEBODY HURT OR KILLED** somebody who is hurt or killed by somebody or something, especially in a crime, accident, or disaster ○ *a murder victim* **2. SOMEBODY OR SOMETHING HARMED** somebody who or something that is adversely affected by an action or circumstance ○ *a victim of her own success* **3. SOMEBODY DUPED** somebody who is tricked or exploited **4. LIVING BEING USED FOR SACRIFICE** a live human or animal used as a sacrifice or in a religious rite **5. HELPLESS PERSON** somebody who experiences misfortune and feels helpless to remedy it [15C. < Latin *victima* "animal offered as a sacrifice"] —**vic·tim·hood** *n* ◇ **fall victim to somebody** *or* **something** to be affected, harmed, or deceived by somebody *or* something

vic·tim·ize /víktə mīz/ (**-ized, -iz·ing, -iz·es**) *vt* **1.** to single somebody out unfairly for punishment or ill treatment **2.** to cause somebody to become a victim —**vic·tim·i·za·tion** /vìktəmi záysh'n/ *n* —**vic·tim·iz·er** *n*

vic·tim·less crime /vìktəmləss-/ *n* an illegal act in which there is no obvious injured party, e.g., prostitution or drug use

vic·tor /víktər/ *n* a winner in a contest or battle [14C. Directly or via Anglo-Norman < Latin < *vic-* past participle of *vincere* "conquer"]

Vic·tor /víktər/ *n* a code word used for the letter "v" in telecommunications

Vic·tor Em·man·u·el I /víktər i mánnyoo əl/ (1759–1824) king of Sardinia. His family possessions in northern Italy were occupied by French forces for much of his reign. He abdicated in 1821 following an uprising.

Vic·tor Em·man·u·el II (1820–78) king of Sardinia (1849–61) and king of Italy (1861–78). He became the first king of a united Italy and, in the course of his reign, established the Italian capital in Rome after it was annexed in 1870.

vic·to·ri·a /vik táwree ə/ *n* **1.** *UK* a large red-and-yellow variety of plum **2.** a horse-drawn carriage with four wheels and a folding hood, accommodating two passengers [Mid-19C. After Queen VICTORIA]

Vic·to·ri·a /vik táwree ə/ **1.** state in southeastern Australia. Capital: Melbourne. Population: 4,917,400 (2003). Area: 87,880 sq. mi./227,600 sq. km. **2.** capital city of British Columbia, Canada, on the southern tip of Vancouver Island. Population: 288,346 (2001). **3.** capital city of the Republic of Seychelles, situated on the northeastern coast of Mahé Island. Population: 30,000 (2001). **4.** capital city of the Hong Kong Special Administrative Region, situated on the north coast of Hong Kong Island. Population: 1,183,621 (2000).

Vic·to·ri·a (1819–1901) queen of the United Kingdom. She reigned longer than any other British monarch (1837–1901), and was empress of India (1876–1901).

> "Please understand that there is no one depressed in *this* house; we are not interested in the possibilities of defeat; they do not exist."
> [Victoria. Quoted in *Life of Robert, Marquis of Salisbury*, Gwendolen Cecil; 1931]

Vic·to·ri·a, Lake largest lake in Africa, with shorelines in Tanzania, Uganda, and Kenya. Area: 26,830 sq. mi./69,490 sq. km.

Vic·to·ri·a Cross *n* a decoration in the form of a bronze cross, given to members of British and Commonwealth armed forces for conspicuous bravery. It was instituted by Queen Victoria in 1856.

Vic·to·ri·a Day *n* in Canada, a statutory holiday marking the birthday of Queen Victoria. Date: May 24 or preceding Monday.

Victoria Falls

Vic·to·ri·a Falls falls on the Zambezi River in south central Africa, on the border between Zambia and Zimbabwe. Height: 355 ft./108 m.

Vic·to·ri·a Is·land the second largest island in Canada, located in the Arctic Archipelago, divided between Nunavut and the Northwest Territories. Area: 83,897 sq. mi./217,291 sq. km.

Vic·to·ri·a Land region of Antarctica, west of Ross Sea and east of Wilkes Land

Vic·to·ri·an /vik táwree ən/ *adj* **1. CHARACTERISTIC OF TIME OF QUEEN VICTORIA** relating to, belonging to, or characteristic of the reign of the British Queen Victoria **2. CONVENTIONAL, HYPOCRITICAL, OR PRUDISH** characterized by attitudes commonly considered to be prevalent during the Victorian era, especially prudery or conventionalism **3. ARCHITECTURALLY ELABORATE** in, or typical of, the elaborate style of architecture popular in Victorian Britain **4. FROM VICTORIA** relating to or coming from the state of Victoria in Australia, or the cities of Victoria in Canada or the Seychelles ■ *n* **1. SOMEBODY LIVING IN VICTORIA'S REIGN** somebody who lived in the reign of Queen Victoria **2. SOMEBODY FROM VICTORIA** somebody who comes from the state of Victoria in Australia, or the cities of Victoria in Canada or the Seychelles **3.** *US* **VICTORIAN HOUSE** a house in Victorian architectural style —**Vic·to·ri·an·ism** *n*

Vic·to·ri·a·na /vik tàwree ánnə, -áanə/ *npl* collectable objects dating from the time of Queen Victoria

Vic·to·ri·a Nile section of the upper Nile River in Uganda, between lakes Victoria and Albert

Vic·to·ri·a Peak mountain on Hong Kong Island, overlooking Hong Kong Harbor. Height: 1,818 ft./554 m.

vic·to·ri·ous /vik táwree əss/ *adj* **1.** having won something such as a contest or a battle **2.** resulting in victory, or characteristic of victors, victory, or the joy of winning —**vic·to·ri·ous·ly** *adv* —**vic·to·ri·ous·ness** *n*

vic·to·ry /víktəree/ (*plural* **-ries**) *n* **1.** success in a contest against an enemy or opponent, or a particular contest or battle that is won **2.** success in overcoming a difficult situation or an obstacle ○ *Being able to get out of bed was a small victory in her struggle against the illness.* [14C. Via Anglo-Norman *victorie* < Latin *victoria* < *victor* (see VICTOR)]

vict·ual /vítt'l/ *v* (*archaic or formal*) **1.** *vt* to provide something or somebody, e.g., a ship or its crew, with a supply of food **2.** *vi* to collect a store of food [14C. < Old French *vitaillier* < *vitaille* (see VICTUALS)]

vict·ual·er /vítt'lər/, **vict·ual·ler** (*plural* **-ers** or **-lers**) *n* (*archaic or formal*) **1. SUPPLIER OF PROVISIONS** somebody who supplies food or other provisions **2. INNKEEPER** an innkeeper, especially one licensed to sell spirits **3. SHIP CARRYING STORES** a ship carrying food or other provisions

vict·uals /vítt'lz/ *npl* food or other provisions (*archaic or humorous*) [14C. Via Old French *vitaille* < Latin *victualia* (which later influenced the English spelling) < *victus* "livelihood, food" < *vivere* "to live"]

vicuña

vi·cu·ña /vī ko͞onyə, vī ko͞onə, vi-/, **vi·cu·na** *n* **1.** a tawny colored mammal with a silky fleece, related to the llama. Native to: Andes. Latin name: *Vicugna vicugna*. **2.** cloth made from the wool of the vicuña, or an imitation of it [Early 17C. Via Spanish < Quechua *wikúña*]

vid /vid/ *n* same as **videocassette** (*informal*) [Late 20C. Shortening]

Vi·dal /vi dáal/, **Gore** (*b.* 1925) US writer. His novels, critical works, and essays are often sharply critical of US politics and culture. They include *The City and the Pillar* (1948) and the fictionalized study *Lincoln* (1984). Full name **Vidal, Eugene Luther Gore**

> "Unless drastic reforms are made, we must accept the fact that every four years the United States will be up for sale, and the richest man or family will buy it."
> [Gore Vidal, *Reflections upon a Sinking Ship*; 1969]

Vi·dal·ia on·ion /vi dáylyə-/ *n* a large sweet onion that has a delicate flavor and is grown in Georgia [After the city of *Vidalia* in Georgia]

vi·da·ra·bine /vī dárrə bīn/ *n* an antiviral drug. Use: treatment of herpes, chickenpox, shingles, hepatitis B. [Late 20C. Probably < VIRUS + *-d-* for euphony + ARABINOSE]

vid·clip /víd klìp/ *n* a short excerpt from a movie or television production, used for news or promotion (*informal*) [Late 20C. Shortening of *video clip*]

vi·de /vídee, veé dày/ *vt* a word used to refer a reader to another place in a text, or tell a musician to skip to a place farther ahead in the score [Mid-16C. < Latin, "see!", form of *videre* "see"]

vi·de in·fra *vt* a term used to refer a reader to a place farther on in a text [< Latin, "see below!"]

vi·del·i·cet /və déllə sèt/ *adv* full form of **viz.** [15C. < Latin < *vide* stem of *videre* "to see" + *licet* "it is permissible"]

vid·e·o /víddee ō/ *n* (*plural* **-os**) **1. VISUAL PART OF TELEVISION** the visual part of a television broadcast **2. SOMETHING RECORDED ONTO VIDEOTAPE** something that has been recorded on videotape, especially a movie or music performance ○ *a video of my brother's wedding* **3. VIDEOCASSETTE** videotape, or a videocassette (*informal*) ○ *now available to rent or buy on video* **4.** COMPUT **IMAGES ON COMPUTER SCREEN** the text and graphics images that appear on a computer screen **5. IMAGE REPRODUCTION INDUSTRY** the industry of recording and broadcasting visual information and entertainment, especially that which can be viewed on a television ○ *a star of stage, screen, and video* ■ *adj* **1. RELATING TO VISUAL IMAGE REPRODUCTION** relating to the recording or broadcasting of visual information or entertainment by means of videotape or television **2. RELATING TO VIDEO FREQUENCIES** relating to or using video frequencies [Mid-20C. < Latin *videre* "to see," after AUDIO]

vid·e·o a·dapt·er *n* COMPUT same as **graphics card**

vid·e·o ar·cade *n* a place where people pay to play video games

vid·eo blog *n* a weblog that uses video as a means of communication, e.g., to conduct an interview or illustrate a story (*informal*)

vid·e·o cam·er·a *n* a camera that records onto videotape

vid·e·o card *n* COMPUT same as **graphics card**

vid·e·o·cas·sette /víddee ō kə sét/ *n* a flat rectangular plastic cassette containing two tape reels and a magnetic videotape

vid·e·o·cas·sette re·cord·er *n* HOUSEHOLD full form of **VCR**

vid·e·o·con·fer·enc·ing /víddee ō kònfərənssing/ *n* the holding of meetings in which the participants are in different places but are connected by audio and video links —**vid·e·o·con·fer·ence** *n*

vid·e·o·disk /víddee ō disk/, **vid·e·o·disc** *n* an optical disk that can store full-motion video and audio

vid·e·o dis·play ter·mi·nal *n* a device used to display data from and enter data into a computer, consisting of a visual display such as a cathode-ray tube and a keyboard, mouse, or touch-screen

vid·e·o fre·quen·cy *n* a frequency in the range of signals used to carry the image and synchronizing pulses in a television broadcasting system. Video frequencies range from the very high to the ultra high in the United States and are found in two ultra high bands in Europe.

vid·e·o game *n* an electronic or computerized game, usually controlled by a microprocessor, played by making images move on a computer or television screen or, for hand-held games, on a liquid-crystal display

vid·e·og·ra·phy /vìddee óggrəfee/ *n* the art or practice of using a video camera to make films or programs —**vid·e·og·ra·pher** *n*

vid·e·o jock·ey *n* somebody who plays videos, especially music videos, on television

vid·e·o·phile /víddee ō fīl/ *n* somebody who enjoys watching or making video recordings

vid·e·o·phone /víddee ō fōn/ *n* a communications device that can transmit and receive both video and audio signals using a camera, receiver, and screen

vid·e·o·tape /víddee ō tàyp/ *n* magnetic tape on which pictures and sound can be recorded ■ *vt* (**-taped, -tap·ing, -tapes**) to make a recording of something on videotape

vid·e·o·tape re·cord·er *n* a tape recorder that can record and play back images and sound using magnetic tape

vid·e·o ter·mi·nal *n US* MEDIA same as **video display terminal**

vid·e·o·text /víddee ō tèkst/ *n* a communications service linked to an adapted television receiver or video display terminal by telephone or cable television lines to allow access to pages of information. Systems can be one-way, allowing only for the display of selected information, or on-line or interactive, allowing for two-way communication.

vid·e·o vér·i·té /vìddee ō vèrri táy/ *n* the use in video documentaries of the realistic unrehearsed portrayal of people and situations [After CINÉMA VÉRITÉ]

vi·de su·pra /veédee sōōprə/ *vi* a term used to refer a reader to an earlier place in a text [< Latin, "see above!"]

vi·dette *n* ARMY another spelling of **vedette** (sense 1)

vid·i·con /víddi kòn/ *n* a light-sensitive television camera tube in which an image is stored on a photoconductive plate as an electric charge pattern that is scanned by an electron beam and transmitted. These tubes have been replaced by more reliable solid-state television cameras using semiconductor charge-coupled devices. [Mid-20C. < VIDEO + ICONOSCOPE]

~~vidio~~ incorrect spelling of **video**

Vi·dor /veé dàwr/, **King** (1894–1982) US movie director. His movies spanned the period from the silent era to the television age. Full name **Vidor, King Wallis**

> "Marriage isn't a word…it's a *sentence*!"
> [King Vidor, *The Crowd*; 1928]

vie /vī/ (**vied, vy·ing, vies**) *vi* to strive for superiority or compete with somebody or something [Mid-16C. Shortening of obsolete *envie* < Old French *envier* "raise the bid (at cards), challenge" < Latin *invitare* "entertain, feast"] —**vi·er** *n*

~~viel~~ incorrect spelling of **veil**

Vi·en·na /vee énnə/ capital city of Austria, located in the east of the country, on the Danube River. Population: 1,562,482 (2001). —**Vi·en·nese** /veè ə neéz, -neéss/ *n, adj*

Vi·en·na cir·cle /vee ènnə-/ *n* the leading school of logical positivists of the 1920s and 1930s [Because based at Vienna University]

Vi·en·na sau·sage *n* a small spicy sausage like a frankfurter, often served as a snack or hors d'oeuvre

Vien·tiane /vyen tyaán/ capital city of Laos, in the central part of the country, on the Mekong River. Population: 640,000 (2000).

Vi·e·quen·se /veè ay kénssay/ *n* somebody who was born in or lives in Vieques, Puerto Rico

Vi·e·ques, Is·la de /vee áy kayss/ island of Puerto Rico off the eastern coast of the main island, used until May of 2003 as a bombing test range by the US Navy. Area: 52 sq. mi./135 sq. km. Population: 8,602 (1990). Official name **Isla de Vieques**

Viet. *abbr* **1.** Vietnam **2.** PEOPLES, LANG Vietnamese

Vi·et·cong /vee èt kóng, vyèt-/ (*plural same*), **Vi·et Cong** *n* **1.** a member or supporter of the Communist-led armed forces of the National Liberation Front of South Vietnam that fought to unite the country with North Vietnam between 1954 and 1976 **2.** somebody, especially a guerrilla soldier, who belonged to or supported the Vietcong during the Vietnam War [Mid-20C. < Vietnamese *Việt-công*, shortening of *Việt-Nam Công Sam* "Vietnamese Communist"]

Vi·et kieu /vee ət kyóo, vyet-/ (*plural same*) *n SE Asia* a Vietnamese person who does not live in Vietnam, especially one born or living in the United States who sometimes returns to Vietnam [Late 20C. *Kieu* modeled on Chinese *qiao* "person living overseas, to live overseas"]

Vi·et·minh /vee èt mín, vyèt-/ (*plural same*), **Viet Minh** *n* **1.** the Vietnamese armed forces led by Ho Chi Minh that resisted and defeated first the Japanese and then the French between 1941 and 1954. The Vietminh operated from a base in southern China during World War II and employed guerrilla tactics similar to the Maoists in China. **2.** a member or supporter of the Vietminh [Mid-20C. < Vietnamese *Việt Minh*, shortening of *Việt-Nam Dôc-Lâp Dông-Minh* "Vietnam Independence Federation"]

Vietnam

Vi·et·nam /vee èt naám, vyèt-/ country in Southeast Asia, on the South China Sea, south of China and east of Cambodia and Laos. Language: Vietnamese. Currency: new dong. Capital: Hanoi. Population: 81,624,716 (2003). Area: 128,066 sq. mi./331,690 sq. km. Official name **Socialist Republic of Vietnam**

Vi·et·nam·ese /vee ètnə meéz, vyètnə-, -meéss/ *adj* **1. OF VIETNAM** relating to Vietnam, or its people or culture **2. OF VIETNAMESE LANGUAGE** relating to the official language of Vietnam ■ *n* (*plural same*) **1. SOMEBODY FROM VIETNAM** somebody who comes from Vietnam **2. OFFICIAL LANGUAGE OF VIETNAM** the Austroasiatic official language of Vietnam. Native speakers: 60 million.

Vi·et·nam·ese pot·bel·lied pig *n* ZOOL same as **potbellied pig**

Vi·et·nam War *n* a conflict in which the Communist forces of North Vietnam and guerrillas in South Vietnam fought against the non-Communist forces of South Vietnam and the United States. It began in 1954 and ended in 1975 in a Communist victory.

view /vyoo/ *n* **1. RANGE OF VISION** the range or extent of somebody's ability to see something ○ *As we rounded the bend the mountains came into view.* **2. SCENE** a scene or an area that can be seen, especially one that is pleasing or impressive ○ *We have a wonderful view of the ocean from our porch.* **3. OPINION** somebody's opinion or judgment on something or particular way of interpreting or thinking about something (*often used in the plural*) ○ *His superiors took the view that he had made an error.* ○ *a person with strong political views* **4. ACT OF LOOKING AT SOMETHING** an act of looking at or inspecting something **5. PERSPECTIVE** a particular position or angle from which something is seen ○ *a bird's eye view* **6. PICTORIAL REPRESENTATION** a painting, drawing, or photograph of a scene or building **7. SURVEY** a general survey of a subject ■ *v* (**viewed, view·ing, views**) **1.** *vt* **REGARD SOMETHING IN PARTICULAR WAY** to have a particular opinion of or attitude to somebody or something, or interpret something in a particular way ○ *She viewed his motives with suspicion.* ○ *The committee views this proposal as an attempt to undermine its authority.* **2.** *vt* **OBSERVE SOMETHING** to see or look at something, especially from a particular angle or location or using a particular device ○ *viewed from above* ○ *viewed the specimen through a microscope* **3.** *vt* **INSPECT SOMETHING** to make an inspection or examination of something, often with the intention of buying it ○ *The prospective buyers have arranged to view the house tomorrow morning.* **4.** *vti* **WATCH TELEVISION** to watch television, or watch something on television **5.** *vt* **REVIEW SOMETHING** to make a mental survey of something or of a range of things [15C. < Old French *vëue*, past participle of *vëoir* "see" < Latin *videre*] —**view·less** *adj* ◇ **in view of something** because of something, or bearing something in mind ◇ **on view** put somewhere so as to be seen ◇ **take a dim view of somebody** *or* **something** to consider somebody or something with disapproval ◇ **with a view to something** with the aim, intention, or hope of doing or achieving something

CULTURAL NOTE *A Room with a View*, a novel (1908) by British writer E. M. Forster. It describes how a young Englishwoman's visit to Italy and her encounter there with a young unconventional expatriate encourage her to rebel against the emotionally stifling conventions of her upper-class background. It was made into a movie by Ismail Merchant and James Ivory in 1985.

view·a·ble /vyóo əb'l/ *adj* **1.** able to be seen or inspected **2.** of a good enough standard, or in a good enough condition, to be watched

view·er /vyoó ər/ *n* **1.** SPECTATOR somebody who watches something such as television, a movie, or an event **2.** OPTICAL DEVICE an optical device for illuminating and magnifying a photographic transparency, videotape, or motion picture film **3.** SOMEBODY WHO MAKES FORMAL INSPECTION somebody appointed, especially by a court, to inspect something such as property —**view·er·ship** *n*

view·find·er /vyoó fìndər/ *n* a device on a camera that lets the user see what is being photographed

view hal·loo /vyoó hə lóo/ *interj* used during a fox hunt as a shout to signal that the fox has been seen breaking cover ■ *n* a shout of "view halloo!"

view·ing /vyoó ing/ *n* **1.** ACT OF LOOKING the act or an act of looking at, seeing, or inspecting something, or an opportunity to look at or inspect something **2.** WATCHING TELEVISION the act of watching television programs **3.** TV SHOWS COLLECTIVELY television programs considered collectively or with respect to their nature or quality

view·point /vyoó pòynt/ *n* **1.** a personal perspective from which somebody considers something **2.** a place or position from which people can look at something

view·screen /vyoó skreen/ *n* the screen on a digital camera on which the user can view the image he or she has just recorded

vig /vig/ *n US* same as **vigorish** (*slang*)

vi·ges·i·mal /vī jéssəm'l, vi-/ *adj* based on or reckoned in units of the number twenty [Mid-17C. < Latin *vigesimus*, variant of *vicesimus* "twentieth" < *viginti* "twenty"]

vi·gi·a /vi jée ə, vee hée ə/ *n* something marked on a chart as a hazard to navigation, although its existence, position, and nature are unconfirmed [Mid-19C. < Portuguese, "lookout" < Latin *vigilia* (see VIGIL)]

vig·il /víjjəl/ *n* **1.** NIGHT WATCH a period spent in doing something through the night, e.g., watching, guarding, or praying **2.** FESTIVAL EVE the eve of some festivals and holy days, spent in prayer ■ **vig·ils** *npl* RELIGIOUS SERVICES AT NIGHT religious services or prayers at night, especially on the eve of a festival or holy day [13C. Via Old French *vigile* < medieval Latin *vigilia* "eve of a holy day" < Latin, "watchfulness" < *vigil* "awake, alert"]

vig·i·lance /víjjələnss/ *n* the condition of being watchful and alert, especially to danger

vig·i·lance com·mit·tee *n US* a group of people who pursue and punish suspected or alleged criminals without having the legal authority to do so

vig·i·lant /víjjələnt/ *adj* watchful and alert, especially to guard against danger, difficulties, or errors [15C. < Latin *vigilant-*, present participle of *vigilare* "keep awake" < *vigil* "awake, alert"] —**vig·i·lant·ly** *adv*

SYNONYMS See ***cautious***.

vig·i·lan·te /vìjjə lántee/ *n* **1.** somebody who punishes lawbreakers personally rather than relying on the legal authorities **2.** *US* a member of a vigilance committee [Mid-19C. < Spanish, "watchman" < Latin *vigilant-* (see VIGILANT)] —**vig·i·lan·tism** *n*

Vi·gneaud ➧ **du Vigneaud, Vincent**

vig·ne·ron /veenyə ráwn, -ráwN/ *n* a grower of grapes for use in making wine [15C. < French < *vigne* (see VINE)]

vi·gnette /vin yét/ *n* **1.** SHORT ESSAY a short descriptive piece of literary writing **2.** BRIEF SCENE a brief scene from a movie or play **3.** DESIGN ON BOOK PAGE a small decorative design printed at the beginning or end of a book or chapter of a book, or in the margin of a page **4.** UNBORDERED PICTURE a painting, drawing, or photograph that has no border but is gradually faded into its background at the edges **5.** ARCHITECTURAL ORNAMENTATION a carved architectural decoration in the form of tendrils and leaves ■ *vt* (**-gnet·ted, -gnet·ting, -gnettes**) **1.** FINISH PICTURE OFF BY SOFTENING EDGES to finish a painting, drawing, or photograph by gradually fading it into its background at the edges rather than giving it a border **2.** DESCRIBE SOMETHING BRIEFLY to describe something in a brief but elegant way [Mid-18C. < French, "small vine" (from such decorations in margins in early books) < *vigne* (see VINE)] —**vi·gnet·ter** *n* —**vi·gnet·tist** *n*

Vi·go /veégō/ city and port in the autonomous region of Galicia, northwestern Spain, on the Atlantic Ocean. Population: 288,324 (2002).

vig·or /víggər/ *n* **1.** VITALITY great physical or mental strength and energy **2.** INTENSITY intensity or forcefulness in the way something is done **3.** ABILITY TO GROW the ability of plants or animals to survive, grow, and thrive **4.** *US* LEGAL VALIDITY legal validity or force [14C. Via Old French < Latin, "liveliness, energy" < *vigere* "be lively"]

vig·o·rish /víggərish/ *n US* (*slang*) **1.** any additional payment that somebody is forced to make, e.g., a bribe or interest paid to a usurer **2.** a sum of money that a bookmaker or gambling establishment charges a customer for accepting a bet [Early 20C. Origin ?]

vig·o·ro·so /vìggə róssō/ *adv* to be played with intensity and liveliness (*used as a musical direction*) [Early 18C. < Italian, "vigorous" < medieval Latin *vigorosus* < Latin *vigor* (see VIGOR)] —**vi·go·ro·so** *adj*

vig·or·ous /víggərəss/ *adj* **1.** extremely strong and active, physically or mentally **2.** displaying or using great energy ○ *vigorous exercise* —**vig·or·ous·ly** *adv* —**vig·or·ous·ness** *n*

vig·our *n* Can, UK spelling of **vigor**

Vi·ja·ya·wa·da /vee jī yə waadə/ city in Krishna District, Andhra Pradesh State, southern India. Population: 1,011,152 (2001).

Vi·king /vīking/ *n* **1.** MEMBER OF ANCIENT SCANDINAVIAN PEOPLE a member of a Scandinavian people who carried out seaborne raids of northwestern Europe between the 8th and 11th centuries A.D., often settling in the areas they invaded, as in Britain. They usually came in longships and raided mainly coastal regions. **2.** LANG same as **Old Norse** **3.** *also* **vi·king** SEAFARER any plundering seafarer or pirate **4.** SPACE PROBE TO MARS either of two identical highly instrumented uncrewed US space probes to Mars, launched in 1975. The probes' orbiters photographed the surface of Mars and its satellites and mapped water vapor and surface temperature variations while the landers transmitted color pictures and meteorological and soil data. [Early 19C. < Old Norse *víkingr*, either < *vík* "creek, inlet" or < Old English *wīc* "camp"]

vil. *abbr* village

~~**vilage**~~ incorrect spelling of **village**

vile /vīl/ (**vil·er, vil·est**) *adj* **1.** DISGUSTING causing disgust or abhorrence ○ *vile smell* **2.** WICKED despicable or shameful ○ *vile crimes* **3.** VERY UNPLEASANT extremely unpleasant to experience ○ *vile weather* **4.** WORTHLESS of little or no worth (*archaic*) [13C. Via French < Latin *vilis* "of little value, cheap, base"] —**vile·ly** *adv* —**vile·ness** *n*

SYNONYMS See ***mean***[2].

vil·i·fy /víllə fī/ (**-fied, -fy·ing, -fies**) *vt* to make malicious and abusive statements about somebody [15C. < late Latin *vilificare* "hold cheap" < Latin *vilis* "worthless"] —**vil·i·fi·ca·tion** /vìlləfi káysh'n/ *n* —**vil·i·fi·er** *n*

SYNONYMS See ***malign***.

vil·i·pend /víllə pènd/ (**-pend·ed, -pend·ing, -pends**) *vt* (*literary*) **1.** to treat or view somebody with contempt **2.** to make malicious or contemptuous statements about somebody [15C. Via Old French *vilipender* < Latin *vilipendere* "consider base" < *vilis* "base, cheap"]

vill, **vill.** *abbr* village

vil·la /víllə/ *n* **1.** VACATION HOME a house rented for a vacation, especially one rented abroad **2.** EXPENSIVE HOUSE a large luxurious house in the country **3.** ROMAN HOUSE in ancient Rome or one of its colonies, a country house with living quarters, farm buildings, and a courtyard [Early 17C. Via Italian < Latin, "country home, farm"]

Vil·la /veé yə/, **Pancho** (1878–1923) Mexican revolutionary. He helped overthrow two Mexican dictators in 1911 and 1914. He was later assassinated. Born **Villa, Francisco, Doroteo Arango**

vil·lage /víllij/ *n* **1.** RURAL COMMUNITY a group of houses and other buildings in a rural area, smaller than a town **2.** INHABITANTS OF VILLAGE all of the people who live in a village **3.** SMALL INCORPORATED COMMUNITY in some US states, a community that is smaller than a town but that is similarly incorporated **4.** TEMPORARY COMMUNITY a place where people live temporarily as a community, e.g., an apartment complex for the use of athletes taking part in the Olympic Games **5.** ANIMAL DWELLINGS a group of bird or animal dwellings [14C. Via French < Latin *villaticum* "farmstead" < *villa* "country home, farm"] —**vil·lag·er** *n*

Vi·lla·her·mo·sa /veè ə her mṓssə/ city and capital of Tabasco State, southeastern Mexico. Population: 536,498 (2000). Former name **San Juan Bautista**

vil·lain /víllən/ *n* **1.** an evil character in a novel, movie, play, or other story, especially one who is the main enemy of the hero **2.** any person regarded as evil or otherwise contemptible (*archaic or humorous*) **3.** HIST same as **villein** [14C. Via Old French *vilein* "feudal serf" < medieval Latin *villanus* "farm hand" < Latin *villa* "country home, farm"]

vil·lain·age /víllənij/ *n* HIST same as **villeinage**

vil·lain·ess /víllənəss/ *n* **1.** an evil woman character in a novel, movie, play, or other story, especially one who is the main enemy of the hero **2.** any woman regarded as evil or otherwise contemptible (*archaic or humorous*)

vil·lain·ous /víllənəss/ *adj* **1.** characteristic of an evil or contemptible person **2.** obnoxious or unpleasant —**vil·lain·ous·ly** *adv* —**vil·lain·ous·ness** *n*

vil·lain·y /víllənee/ *n* **1.** EVIL CONDUCT behavior characteristic of an evil or contemptible person **2.** STATE OF BEING EVIL the state of being evil or contemptible **3.** (*plural* **vil·lain·ies**) EVIL ACT an evil or immoral act

Vil·la-Lo·bos /veèlə lṓ boss, -lṓbōosh/, **Heitor** (1887–1959) Brazilian composer. His prolific output was much influenced by popular Brazilian and Native South American music. His work includes the nine suites entitled *Bachianas brasileiras* (1930–45).

~~**villan**~~ incorrect spelling of **villain**

vil·la·nelle /vìllə nél/ *n* a 19-line poem, originally French, that uses only two rhymes and consists of five three-line stanzas and a final quatrain. The first and third lines of the first stanza are alternately repeated as a refrain that closes the following stanzas, and are joined as a final couplet of the quatrain. [Late 16C. Via French < Italian *villanella* "old rustic (Italian) song" < *villano* "peasant" < medieval Latin *villanus* (see VILLAIN)]

Vil·la·no·van /vìllə nṓvən/ *adj* belonging to or characteristic of an early Iron Age culture that existed near Bologna, Italy, in which bronze was used and also, in a simple way, iron ■ *n* a member of the Villanovan culture [Early 20C. After *Villanova*, town in NE Italy]

Vil·la Park /víllə paárk/ village in northeastern Illinois, west of Elmhurst. It is a western suburb of Chicago. Population: 23,120 (2002 estimate).

Vil·lar·ri·ca /vìllə reékə/ city in southern Paraguay. Population: 21,203 (1982).

~~**villege**~~ incorrect spelling of **village**

vil·lein /víllən/ (*plural* **-leins** or **-lains**) *n* a feudal serf who had the status of a freeman except in relation to his lord, to whom he owed dues and services in exchange for land [14C. Variant of VILLAIN]

vil·lein·age /víllənij/ *n* **1.** the status of being a villein in feudal society **2.** the form of feudal tenure by which a villein held land

vil·li BIOL plural of **villus**

vil·li·form /víllə fàwrm/ *adj* in the form of or resembling a minute projection (**villus**) [Mid-19C. < VILLUS]

Vil·lon /vee yóN/, **François** (1431?–63?) French poet. He wrote lyric poetry notable for its fresh interpretation of medieval verse forms and its frank expression of feeling. He was repeatedly arrested for criminal acts, and nothing is known of him after he was banished from Paris in 1463. Born **Montcorbier, François de** *or* **Loges, François des**

> "I know everything except myself."
> [François Villon, "Ballade of Small Talk"; 1460?]

vil·lose *adj* BIOL same as **villous** [Early 18C. < Latin *villosus* (see VILLOUS)]

vil·los·i·ty /vi lóssətee/ (*plural* **-ties**) *n* BIOL **1.** HAIRINESS the condition of being covered in long shaggy hairs **2.** BEING COVERED WITH PROJECTIONS the state of being covered with minute projections **3.** COATING OF

PROJECTIONS a surface or coating of very fine projections resembling hairs **4. PART RESEMBLING HAIR** a fine projection that resembles a hair [Late 18C. < Latin *villosus* (see VILLOUS)]

vil·lous /víllǝss/ *adj* **1.** covered with long shaggy hairs **2.** relating to, resembling, or covered with minute projections [14C. < Latin *villosus* "shaggy" < *villus* "shaggy hair"] —**vil·lous·ly** *adv*

vil·lus /víllǝss/ (*plural* **-li** /-lī/) *n* **1. MINUTE PROTUBERANCE** a vascular protuberance growing out from some mucous membranes, e.g., from that of the small intestine of some vertebrates or from the chorion that surrounds an embryo **2.** ZOOL, ANAT **PLACENTAL GROWTH** a finger-shaped protuberance that contributes to the formation of the placenta in mammals **3. OUTGROWTH ON PLANT** a fine part resembling a hair, growing from the surface of a plant [Early 18C. < Latin, "shaggy hair"]

Vil·ni·us /vílnee ǝss/ capital city of Lithuania, situated in the southeast of the country, near the border with Belarus. Population: 577,970 (2000).

vim /vim/ *n* exuberant vitality and energy (*informal*) [Mid-19C. Probably < Latin, form of *vis* "power, strength"]

VIN /vin/ *abbr US* AUTOMOT vehicle identification number

vin. *abbr* FOOD vinegar

vin- *prefix* same as **vini-** (*used before vowels*)

vi·na *n* MUSIC another spelling of **veena**

vi·na·ceous /vī náyshǝss, vi-/ *adj* **1.** of the nature of or containing wine **2.** of the color of red wine [Late 17C. < Latin *vinaceus* < *vinum* "wine"]

~~vinagrette~~ incorrect spelling of **vinaigrette**

vin·ai·grette /vìnnǝ grét/ *n* **1.** a salad dressing made with vinegar, oil, salt, pepper, and sometimes other seasonings **2.** a small bottle or box with a perforated cap, used to hold aromatic substances such as smelling salts or vinegar [Late 17C. < French, "little vinegar" < *vinaigre* < Old French *vyn egre* (see VINEGAR)]

vi·nasse /vi náss, vī-/ *n* the residue left in a still after the distillation of an alcoholic beverage, especially brandy. It is used as a fertilizer and is a source of potassium salts. [Via French < Provençal *vinassa* < Latin *vinaceus* (see VINACEOUS)]

vin·blas·tine /vin bláss teen/ *n* an alkaloid drug from the Madagascar periwinkle. Use: cancer treatment. Formula: $C_{46}H_{58}N_4O_9$. [Mid-20C. < modern Latin *Vinca* (see VINCA) + LEUKOBLAST]

vin·ca /víngkǝ/ *n* PLANTS same as **periwinkle**[2] [Mid-19C. < modern Latin *Vinca* < late Latin *pervinca* (see PERIWINKLE[2])]

Vin·cennes /vin sénz/ city in southwestern Indiana, on the Wabash River. Population: 18,246 (2002 estimate).

Vin·cent de Paul /vaN saaN dǝ páwl, vínssǝnt-/, **St.** (1581–1660) French priest. He was the founder of the Congregation of the Mission (1625), also called the Vincentians.

Vin·cen·tian /vin sénsh'n/ *n* a member of the Congregation of the Mission, a Roman Catholic order of missionary priests founded by St. Vincent de Paul. [Mid-19C. After St. VINCENT DE PAUL] —**Vin·cen·tian** *adj*

Vin·cent's an·gi·na /vínssǝnts-/, **Vin·cent's in·fec·tion** *n* a painful mouth inflammation with ulcers and gum damage. Two organisms that are normally present cause the condition only when somebody has a vitamin B deficiency or an immune deficiency. [Early 20C. After Jean Hyacinthe *Vincent* (1862–1950), French physician]

Vin·ci ♦ **Leonardo da Vinci**

vin·cris·tine /vin kríss teen/ *n* an alkaloid drug similar to vinblastine. It works by blocking cell division (**mitosis**) and is highly toxic. Use: cancer treatment. Formula: $C_{46}H_{56}N_4O_{10}$. [Mid-20C. < modern Latin *Vinca* (see VINCA) + Latin *crista* "crest"]

vin·cu·lum /víngkyǝlǝm/ (*plural* **-lums** or **-la** /-lǝ/) *n* **1.** a horizontal line above two or more members of a compound mathematical expression, used to show that the expression is to be treated as a single term. Parentheses, brackets, and braces are used more frequently for this purpose than is the vinculum. **2.** a band of tissue, especially a ligament [Mid-17C. < Latin, "fetter, bond" < *vincire* "tie, fasten"]

vin·da·loo /vìndǝ lóo/ *n* a very hot curry sauce made with coriander, red chili, ginger, and other spices, or a dish cooked in this [Late 19C. Via Konkani *vindalu* < Portuguese *vinho de alho*, a wine and garlic sauce, literally "wine of garlic"]

vin·di·cate /víndi kàyt/ (**-cat·ed, -cat·ing, -cates**) *vt* **1. SHOW SOMEBODY TO BE BLAMELESS** to clear somebody or something of blame, guilt, suspicion, or doubt **2. JUSTIFY SOMEBODY OR SOMETHING** to show that somebody or something is justified or correct **3. UPHOLD SOMETHING** to defend or maintain something such as a cause or rights [Mid-16C. < Latin *vindicat-*, past participle of *vindicare* "claim, set free, avenge" < *vindic-* "avenger"] —**vin·di·ca·ble** *adj* —**vin·di·ca·tor** *n* —**vin·di·ca·to·ry** /víndikǝ tàwree/ *adj*

vin·di·ca·tion /vìndi káysh'n/ *n* **1.** the act of vindicating somebody or something, or the condition of being vindicated **2.** evidence or an argument used to vindicate somebody or something

vin·dic·tive /vin díktiv/ *adj* **1. VENGEFUL** looking for revenge or done through a desire for revenge **2. SPITEFUL** feeling, showing, or done through a desire to hurt somebody **3.** LAW **MEANT TO PUNISH** describes damages awarded by a court that are set higher than the amount necessary to compensate the victim, in order to punish the defendant [Early 17C. < Latin *vindicta* "revenge"] —**vin·dic·tive·ly** *adv* —**vin·dic·tive·ness** *n*

vine /vīn/ *n* **1. CLIMBING PLANT** a plant that supports itself by climbing, twining, or creeping along a surface **2. STEM** the weak flexible stem of a vine **3.** PLANTS same as **grapevine** (sense 1) **4. GRAPEVINES** grapevines considered collectively ■ *vi* (**vined, vin·ing, vines**) **GROW LIKE VINE** to form or grow like a vine [13C. Via French < Latin *vinea* "vine, vineyard" < *vinum* "wine"] —**vin·y** *adj*

vine·dress·er /vīn drèssǝr/ *n* somebody who tends and prunes grapevines

vin·e·gar /vínnǝgǝr/ *n* **1. SOUR-TASTING LIQUID** a sour-tasting liquid that is used to flavor and preserve foods. It is a dilute acetic acid made by fermenting beer, wine, or cider. **2. ILL TEMPER** sourness or ill-tempered behavior or speech **3. VITALITY** exuberant energy and enthusiasm [13C. < Old French *vyn egre* "sour wine" < Latin *vinum acre*] —**vin·e·gar·ish** *adj*

vin·e·gar eel, **vin·e·gar worm** *n* a very small nematode worm that feeds on bacteria that cause fermentation, especially in vinegar. Latin name: *Anguillula aceti.*

vin·e·gar·y /vínnǝgǝree/ *adj* **1.** with a sour taste or smell like vinegar **2.** showing an unpleasant irritable disposition

vin·er·y /vīnǝree/ (*plural* **-ies**) *n* an area or building, especially a greenhouse, in which grapevines are grown

vine wee·vil *n* a black flightless weevil that produces adult females only and has creamy-white larvae that destroy the roots of many different plants. Latin name: *Otiorhycus sulcatus.*

vine·yard /vínnyǝrd/ *n* **1.** a piece of land where grapevines are grown **2.** *US* any sphere of mental, physical, or spiritual endeavor

vingt-et-un /vàN tay ŏN/ *n* CARDS same as **blackjack** [Late 18C. < French, "twenty-one"]

vini- *prefix* wine, grapes ○ *viniculture* [< Latin *vinum*]

vin·i·cul·ture /vínni kùlchǝr/ *n* AGRIC same as **viticulture** —**vin·i·cul·tur·al** /vìnni kúlchǝrǝl/ *adj* —**vin·i·cul·tur·ist** /-kúlchǝrist/ *n*

vin·i·fy /vínnǝ fī/ (**-fied, -fy·ing, -fies**) *vt* to ferment grape juice, or another liquid, into wine —**vin·i·fi·ca·tion** /vìnnǝfi káysh'n/ *n*

Vin·land /vínnlǝnd/ part of North America, now northern Newfoundland, first seen by the Norse voyager Bjarni Herjólfsson during a voyage from Iceland to Greenland in about A.D. 986. The Icelandic explorer Leif Ericson explored the Newfoundland and Labrador coasts several years later.

vi·no /veenō/ *n* wine, especially cheap wine (*informal*) [Late 19C. < Italian, "wine"]

vin or·di·naire /vàN áwrdee nér/ *n* cheap table wine, especially from France [Early 19C. < French, "ordinary wine"]

vi·nos·i·ty /vī nóssǝtee/ *n* the distinctive and essential character of wine, including qualities such as body, color, and taste

vi·nous /vīnǝss/ *adj* **1. OF WINE** relating to, typical of, or containing wine **2. WINE-DRINKING** tending to drink a lot of wine, or caused by wine-drinking **3.** *US* **WINE-COLORED** of the color of red wine [Mid-17C. < Latin *vinum* "wine"] —**vi·nous·ly** *adv* —**vi·nous·ness** *n*

Vin·son /vínssǝn/, **Frederick M.** (1890–1953) chief justice of the US Supreme Court (1946–53). He served as a Democrat in the House of Representatives (1924–29 and 1931–38) and was appointed as chief justice by President Harry S. Truman. Full name **Vinson, Frederick Moore**

> "Wars are not 'acts of God.' They are caused by man, by manmade institutions, by the way in which man has organized his society. What man has made, man can change."
> [Frederick Moore Vinson, *Speech at Arlington National Cemetery*, Memorial Day 1945]

Vin·son Mas·sif /vìnssǝn máss eef/ highest mountain in Antarctica, in the central Ellsworth Mountains. Height: 16,066 ft./4,897 m.

vin·tage /víntij/ *n* **1. WINE PRODUCTION YEAR** the year in which the grapes used in making a specific wine were harvested **2. WINE FROM PARTICULAR YEAR** wine made from a particular harvest of grapes **3. GRAPE HARVESTING** the harvesting of grapes for wine **4. WINE** a wine, especially an excellent one **5. PERIOD** the period of time when something appeared or began, or when somebody was born or flourished ○ *Depression-vintage furniture* **6. GROUP SHARING CHARACTERISTICS** a group of people or things that are similar or belong to the same period of time (*informal*) ■ *adj* **1. GOOD FOR WINE** produced from or characterized by a good harvest of grapes for wine-making, so that the wine does not have to be improved by blending with wine from another harvest ○ *a vintage year* **2. OF BEST** representing what is best or most characteristic of somebody or something ○ *a vintage performance* **3. CLASSIC** recognized as being of high quality and lasting appeal ○ *a series of vintage Laurel and Hardy comedies* **4. OUT OF DATE** no longer fashionable or modern [14C. Alteration (influenced by VINTNER) of *vendage* < Old French *vendange* < Latin *vindemia* "grape-gathering" < *vinum* "wine" + *demere* "take away"] —**vin·tag·er** *n*

vin·tage car *n* an old car, especially one built between 1919 and 1930

vin·tage year *n* **1.** a year in which the wine that is made is of excellent quality **2.** a year of extraordinary accomplishment or success

vint·ner /víntnǝr/ *n* **1.** a dealer in wines **2.** a maker of wine [15C. Via Old French *vinetier* < medieval Latin *vinetarius* < Latin *vinetum* "vineyard" < *vinum* "wine"]

vi·nyl /vīn'l/ *n* **1. CHEMICAL GROUP** a univalent unsaturated chemical group or radical that is formed when one hydrogen atom is removed from ethylene. Formula: CH_2CH. **2. COMPOUND USED IN PLASTICS** a reactive compound that contains the vinyl group, usually in polymerized form. Use: plastics. **3. PLASTIC MATERIAL** a plastic material, made from a vinyl polymer **4. PLASTIC RECORDS** phonograph records made of a vinyl polymer, as opposed to compact disks [Mid-19C. < VINI- + -YL] —**vi·nyl** *adj* —**vi·nyl·ic** /vī níllik/ *adj*

vi·nyl chlo·ride *n* a colorless carcinogenic explosive flammable gas. Use: manufacture of polyvinyl chloride, adhesives, organic chemicals. Formula: CH_2:CHCl.

vi·nyl·i·dene /vī nílli deen/ *n* a bivalent chemical group or radical, made when two hydrogen atoms are removed from one carbon atom of ethylene. Formula: CH_2:C.

vi·nyl pol·y·mer, **vi·nyl res·in** *n* an odorless tasteless thermoplastic material made by polymerizing compounds containing vinyl groups, e.g., PVC

Vi·og·nier /vee ànn yáy/ *n* **1.** a typically dry white wine made from a variety of grape originally grown mainly in the Rhône valley of France but now cultivated elsewhere **2.** a white grape variety. Use: to make Viognier.

vi·ol /vī ǝl/ *n* **1.** a member of a family of stringed instruments popular during the 16th and 17th centuries. Viols have a fretted fingerboard, a flat-backed body, six strings, and are played with a curved bow. They were the precursors of the violin family. **2.** MUSIC same as **viola da gamba** [15C. Via Old French *viole* < Old Provençal *viola*]

vi·o·la[1] /vee ṓlə/ *n* **1.** a stringed instrument slightly larger and lower in pitch than a violin. It is held under the chin and played with a bow. The viola is tuned an octave above the cello and is the alto of the violin family. **2.** MUSIC same as **viola da gamba** [Late 18C. Via Italian < Old Provençal]

vi·o·la[2] /vī́ ōlə, vee-, vī́ ələ/ *n* a plant related to violets and pansies, especially one with small, white, yellow, or purple flowers. Genus: *Viola*. [15C. < Latin, "violet"]

vi·o·la·ceous /vī̀ ə láyshəss/ *adj* relating to, belonging to, or typical of the family of plants that includes violets and pansies [Mid-17C. < Latin *violaceus* "violet-colored" < *viola* "violet"]

vi·o·la da brac·cio /vee ṓlə də braáchō/ (*plural* **vi·o·las da brac·cio**) *n* an old stringed instrument of the viol family, held against the shoulder when played [Mid-19C. < Italian, "viol for (the) arm"]

vi·o·la da gam·ba /vee ṓlə də gaámbə, -gámbə/ (*plural* **vi·o·las da gam·ba**) *n* an old stringed bass instrument of the viol family, with a range similar to a cello [Late 16C. < Italian, "viol for (the) leg"]

vi·o·la d'a·mo·re /vee ṓlə daa máw rày/ (*plural* **vi·o·las d'a·mo·re**) *n* a fretless stringed instrument of the viol family with six or seven strings and a second set of strings that are not played but are made to vibrate by the first set **(sympathetic strings)** [Late 17C. < Italian, "viol of love"]

~~violance~~ incorrect spelling of **violence**

vi·o·late /vī́ ə làyt/ (**-lat·ed, -lat·ing, -lates**) *vt* **1.** DISREGARD SOMETHING to act contrary to something such as a law, contract, or agreement, especially in a way that produces significant effects **2.** DISTURB SOMETHING to disturb or interrupt something in a rude or violent way **3.** DEFILE SOMETHING to treat something sacred with a lack of respect **4.** RAPE SOMEBODY to rape or sexually assault somebody (*formal*) [15C. < Latin *violatus*, past participle of *violare* "treat with violence, injure"] —**vi·o·la·ble** *adj* —**vi·o·la·tive** *adj* —**vi·o·la·tor** *n*

vi·o·la·tion /vī̀ ə láysh'n/ *n* **1.** the act or an example of violating somebody or something **2.** a crime or infringement of a law or rules, especially one less serious than a misdemeanor or a foul in sports

vi·o·lence /vī́ ələnss/ *n* **1.** PHYSICAL FORCE the use of physical force to injure somebody or damage something ○ *threats of violence* **2.** DESTRUCTIVE FORCE extreme, destructive, or uncontrollable force, especially of natural events ○ *the violence of the storm* **3.** FERVOR intensity of feeling or expression ○ *the violence of her response to our suggestion* **4.** LAW ILLEGAL FORCE the illegal use of unjustified force, or the intimidating effect created by the threat of this ○ *robbery with violence* ◇ **do violence to something** to violate, harm, or damage something

vi·o·lent /vī́ ələnt/ *adj* **1.** USING PHYSICAL FORCE using physical force to injure somebody or damage something ○ *violent crime* **2.** EMOTIONALLY INTENSE showing emotional intensity or strong feeling ○ *his violent objections to the plan* **3.** SHOWING DESTRUCTIVE FORCE showing extreme, destructive, or uncontrollable force ○ *a violent thunderstorm* **4.** INTENSE very intense or severe ○ *a violent headache* ○ *violent passion* **5.** CAUSED BY FORCE caused by force rather than natural causes ○ *met a violent death* [14C. < Latin *violentus* "forcible, vehement"] —**vi·o·lent·ly** *adv*

vi·o·lent storm *n* a storm that causes widespread damage with winds of force 11 on the Beaufort scale, reaching speeds of 64–72 mph/103–117 kph

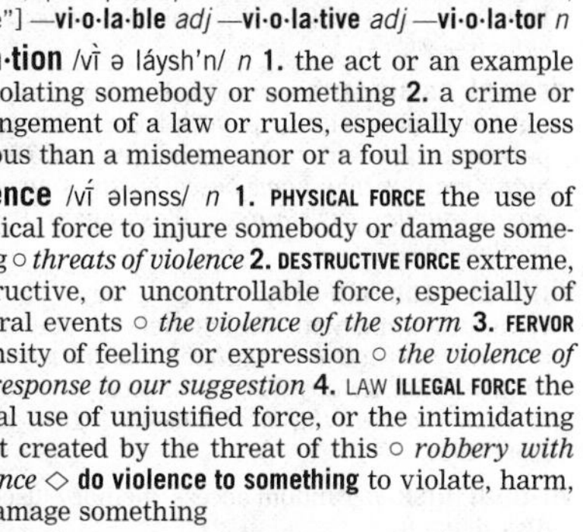

violet

vi·o·let /vī́ ələt/ *n* **1.** FLOWERING PLANT a low-growing perennial plant. Flowers: irregular, usually purplish blue. Genus: *Viola*. **2.** PLANT RESEMBLING VIOLET a plant that looks like a violet but is not necessarily related to it, e.g., an African violet **3.** PURPLISH BLUE COLOR a deep purplish blue color [14C. < Old French *violete*, diminutive of *viole* < Latin *viola* "violet"] —**vi·o·let** *adj*

vi·o·lin /vī̀ ə lín/ *n* **1.** a wooden musical instrument with four strings and an unfretted fingerboard, held under the player's chin and played with a bow. The violin has the highest range in the family of stringed instruments to which it gives its name. **2.** a musician who plays a violin, especially in an orchestra [Late 16C. < Italian *violino*, diminutive of *viola* (see VIOLA[1])] —**vi·o·lin·ist** *n*

vi·o·list[1] /vee ṓlist, vī́ əlist/ *n* somebody who plays the viola [Late 20C. < VIOLA[1]]

vi·o·list[2] /vī́ əlist/ *n* somebody who plays the viol [Mid-17C. < VIOL]

vi·o·lon·cel·lo /vèe ələn chéllō, vī̀-/ (*plural* **-los**) *n* MUSIC same as **cello** (*formal*) [Early 18C. < Italian, diminutive of *violone* (see VIOLONE)]

vi·o·lo·ne /vèe ə lṓ này/ *n* the double-bass viol, larger and with a deeper range than the viola da gamba [Early 18C. < Italian, "large viola" < *viola* (see VIOLA[1])]

VIP *abbr* very important person

vi·pas·sa·na /vi paássənə/, **Vi·pas·sa·na** *n* Theravada Buddhist meditation that aims at concentrating the mind on the body

viper

vi·per /vī́pər/ *n* **1.** POISONOUS SNAKE a snake with hollow fangs that it uses to inject venom into its victim when it bites. Native to: Europe, Asia, Africa. Family: Viperidae. **2.** REPT same as **adder**[2] **3.** POISONOUS SNAKE NOT OF VIPER FAMILY a poisonous snake belonging to a family other than that of the true viper, e.g., the horned viper **4.** ZOOL same as **pit viper** **5.** OFFENSIVE TERM an offensive term for somebody who is considered to be malicious, treacherous, or ungrateful (*offensive literary*) [Early 16C. Via Old French *vipere* < Latin *vipera* "snake," contraction of assumed *vivipera* "live-bearing" (from the ancient belief that snakes bore live young) < *vivus* "alive"] —**vi·per·ous** *adj*

vi·per·ish /vī́pərish/ *adj* **1.** malicious or spiteful **2.** characteristic of or resembling a viper —**vi·per·ish·ly** *adv*

vi·per's bu·gloss *n* a widely naturalized weed with rough foliage. Flowers: blue, tubular, in spikes. Native to: Europe, Asia. Latin name: *Echium vulgare*.

Vir. *abbr* **1.** LITERAT Virgil **2.** ASTRON Virgo

vir- *prefix* same as **viro-** (*used before vowels*)

vi·ra·go /vi raágō/ (*plural* **-goes** or **-gos**) *n* **1.** an offensive term that deliberately insults a woman by implying that her temperament or behavior is violent **2.** a woman who is strong and brave (*archaic*) [Pre-12C. < Latin < *vir* "man, husband"] —**vi·rag·i·nous** /vi rájjənəss/ *adj*

vi·ral /vī́rəl/ *adj* **1.** CAUSED BY VIRUS relating to, typical of, or caused by a virus **2.** OF UNWANTED FORWARDED E-MAIL of or using unsolicited e-mails that are forwarded spontaneously from one user to another ■ *n* MESSAGE INTENDED TO BE SPREAD an e-mail message, usually in the form of advertising, that contains elements that make recipients want to forward it to others (*informal*) —**vi·ral·ly** *adv*

vi·ral load *n* the amount of HIV in a person's blood, usually measured by a test that determines the number of copies of HIV in one milliliter of blood

vi·ral mar·ket·ing *n* **1.** the distribution over the Internet of a service that becomes so immediately desirable that it leads to an enormous growth in traffic **2.** a form of marketing in which an organization's customers, wittingly or unwittingly, act as advertisers for its products by spreading knowledge of them by word of mouth [< the idea of a virus spreading rapidly]

vi·ral pneu·mo·nia *n* an infection of the lungs caused by a virus

Vir·chow /féerkō/, **Rudolf** (1821–1902) German pathologist and anthropologist. His textbook on cellular pathology (1850) was the foundation text of the field. He also published significant works in anthropology and archaeology. Full name **Virchow, Rudolf Carl**

> "As long as vitalism and spiritualism are open questions so long will the gateway of science be open to mysticism."
> [Rudolf Virchow. Quoted in *Bulletin of the New York Academy of Medicine*, F. H. Garrison; 1928]

vir·e·lay /véerə lày/ *n* an old French verse form consisting of short lines arranged in stanzas with two rhymes, the end rhyme being repeated in the first line of the next stanza [14C. < French *virelai*]

vi·re·mi·a /vī réemee ə/ *n* the presence of viruses in the bloodstream [Mid-20C. < modern Latin < VIRUS] —**vi·re·mic** *adj*

Vi·ren /véerən/, **Lasse** (*b.* 1949) Finnish athlete. An Olympic gold medalist in the 5,000 and 10,000 meters (1972 and 1976), he set several world records in both events. Full name **Viren, Lasse Artturi**

vir·e·o /véeree ṑ/ (*plural* **-os**) *n* a small songbird with grayish or greenish feathers that eats insects. Native to: Americas. Genus: *Vireo*. [Mid-19C. Via modern Latin < Latin, a bird (probably the greenfinch) < *virere* "be green"]

vi·res plural of **vis**

vi·res·cence /vi réss'nss, vī-/ *n* the state of being green or the process of becoming green, especially the development of green coloration in plant parts that are not normally green, as a result of disease

vi·res·cent /vi réss'nt, vī-/ *adj* **1.** being or becoming green **2.** used to describe plant parts that are not normally green but are turned green by disease [Early 19C. < Latin *virescent-*, present participle of *virescere* "become green"]

vir·ga /vúrgə/ *n* vertical trails of rain, snow, or ice from the underside of a cloud that evaporate before reaching the ground [Mid-20C. < Latin, "rod, staff, twig"]

vir·gate /vúrgət, vúr gàyt/ *adj* describes plant parts that are long and thin like a rod (*technical*) [Early 19C. < Latin *virgatus* < *virga* "rod, staff"]

Vir·gil /vúrjəl/, **Ver·gil** (70–19 B.C.) Roman poet. Regarded as the finest Latin poet of his age, he wrote pastoral verse before composing his great mythological epic *The Aeneid*, which tells the story of the seven-year wanderings of Aeneas after the fall of Troy. Full name **Publius Vergilius Maro** —**Vir·gil·i·an** /vur jíllee ən/ *adj*

> "I sing of arms and the man...."
> [Virgil, *The Aeneid*; 19 B.C.]

> "Do not trust the horse, Trojans. Whatever it is, I / fear the Greeks even when they bring gifts."
> [Virgil, *The Aeneid*; 19 B.C.]

vir·gin /vúrjin/ *n* **1.** SOMEBODY WHO HAS NEVER HAD SEX somebody who has never had sexual intercourse **2.** RELIG RELIGIOUS WOMAN COMMITTED TO CHASTITY a woman who has taken a vow of chastity for religious reasons **3.** ZOOL FEMALE ANIMAL a female animal that has never copulated **4.** INSECTS FEMALE INSECT a female insect that produces fertile eggs without the help of a male ■ *adj* **1.** OF VIRGIN relating to or characteristic of a virgin **2.** PURE in a pure, natural, or clean state ○ *virgin snow* **3.** ENVIRON NOT TOUCHED BY HUMANS describes a natural area that has never been explored or exploited by humans **4.** OCCURRING FOR FIRST TIME happening or carried out first or for the first time ○ *The freshman senator delivered his virgin speech* *yesterday.* **5.** FOOD **FROM FIRST PRESSING** describes vegetable oils that come from the first pressing of fruit, leaves, or seeds without the use of heat **6.** METALL **PRODUCED DIRECTLY FROM ORE** describes metals produced directly from an ore, not from scrap metal **7.** MINERALS **UNALLOYED** found in a pure unmixed state **8.** PHYS **NEVER HAVING COLLIDED** describes a neutron that has never been in a collision and therefore retains the energy with which it started **9. WITH NO ALCOHOL** nonalcoholic (*slang*) [12C. Via Old French *virgine* < Latin *virgin-*, stem of *virgo* "maiden"]

Vir·gin /vúrjən/ *n* **1.** CHR same as **Virgin Mary 2.** ZODIAC, ASTRON same as **Virgo**

vir·gin·al[1] /vúrjin'l/ *adj* **1. CHASTE** relating to, characteristic of, or appropriate for somebody, especially a woman, who has never had sexual intercourse **2. LIVING CHASTELY** living in a state of virginity **3. PURE** not corrupted or spoiled in any way [15C. Directly or via French < Latin *virginalis* < *virgin-* (see VIRGIN)] —**vir·gin·al·ly** *adv*

vir·gin·al[2] /vúrjin'l/ *n* a smaller, often legless, oblong version of the harpsichord, popular in the 16th and 17th centuries [Early 16C. Directly or via French < Latin *virginalis* < *virgin-* (see VIRGIN)] —**vir·gin·al·ist** *n*

Vir·gin Birth *n* in Christianity, the doctrine that Jesus Christ was born as the son of God, not of a human father, and that his mother was a virgin

Vir·gin·ia[1] /vər jínnyə/, **vir·gin·ia** *n* tobacco of a type originally grown in the state of Virginia [Early 17C. < VIRGINIA[2]]

Virginia

Vir·gin·ia[2] /vər jínnyə/ state in the eastern United States, bordered by Maryland, the Atlantic Ocean, North Carolina, Tennessee, Kentucky, and West Virginia. Capital: Richmond. Population: 7,293,542 (2002 estimate). Area: 42,326 sq. mi./109,624 sq. km. Official name **Commonwealth of Virginia** —**Vir·gin·ian** *n, adj*

Vir·gin·ia Beach largest city in Virginia, situated in the southeastern part of the state, on the Atlantic Ocean and the Chesapeake Bay, near the border with North Carolina. Population: 433,934 (2002 estimate).

Vir·gin·ia cow·slip, Vir·gin·ia blue·bell *n* a plant with clusters of blue flowers. Native to: eastern North America. Latin name: *Mertensia virginica.*

Vir·gin·ia creep·er *n* a climbing plant with leaves made up of five leaflets and bluish black berries. Latin name: *Parthenocissus quinquefolia.*

Vir·gin·ia deer *n* ZOOL same as **white-tailed deer**

Vir·gin·ia fence *n regional* same as **worm fence**

Vir·gin·ia ham *n* lean hickory-smoked ham with dark reddish meat

Vir·gin·ia rail *n* a small bird of the rail family with a long slender beak. Native to: North America. Latin name: *Rallus limicola.*

Vir·gin·ia reel *n* a US country dance in which a caller instructs couples facing each other in long rows

Vir·gin Is·lands, British /vùrjin-/ ◆ **British Virgin Islands**

Vir·gin Is·lands Na·tion·al Park national park on the islands of St. John and Hassel, in the US Virgin Islands. It was established in 1956. Area: 23 sq. mi./59 sq. km.

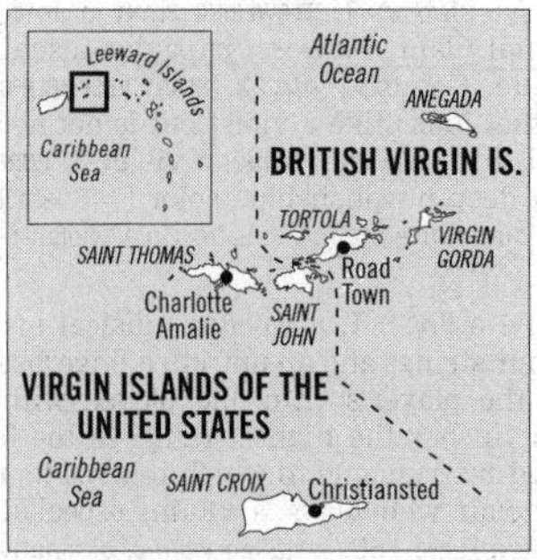

Virgin Islands of the United States and British Virgin Islands

Vir·gin Is·lands of the U·ni·ted States unincorporated external territory of the United States in the eastern Caribbean Sea, consisting of three main islands and over 60 smaller islands and islets. Capital: Charlotte Amalie. Population: 122,211 (2001). Area: 134 sq. mi./347 sq. km.

vir·gin·i·ty /vər jínnətee/ *n* **1.** the state of being a virgin **2.** the state of being untouched, unexplored, or unspoiled

Vir·gin Mar·y *n* in Christianity, Mary, the mother of Jesus Christ

Vir·gin Queen *n* Elizabeth I, queen of England

vir·gin's bow·er *n* a clematis that produces silky glistening seeds. Flowers: small, white, in clusters. Native to: eastern North America. Latin name: *Clematis virginiana.*

vir·gin soil *n* soil that has not yet been used for cultivation

vir·gin wool *n* wool that has not already been used to make something

Vir·go /vúrgō/ (*plural* **-gos**) *n* **1.** ZODIAC **SIXTH SIGN OF ZODIAC** the sixth sign of the zodiac, represented by a virgin and lasting from approximately August 23 to September 22. Virgo is classified as an earth sign and its ruling planet is Mercury. **2.** ASTROL **SOMEBODY BORN UNDER VIRGO** somebody whose birthday falls between August 23 and September 22 **3.** ASTRON **CONSTELLATION ON CELESTIAL EQUATOR** a zodiacal constellation on the celestial equator. The Virgo cluster, which lies near the north galactic pole about 16 billion light-years from the Earth, contains about 3,000 galaxies. See illustration at **constellation** [Pre-12C. < Latin, "maiden"] —**Vir·go** *adj* —**Vir·go·an** *n, adj*

vir·go in·tac·ta /vùrgō in táktə/ *n* a girl or woman whose hymen remains unbroken [< Latin, "intact virgin"]

vir·gu·late /vúrgyələt, -làyt/ *adj* shaped like a rod (*technical*) [Mid-19C. < Latin *virgula*, diminutive of *virga* "rod, staff, twig"]

vir·gule /vúr gyool/ *n US* a diagonal mark used to separate alternatives, as in "and/or," to stand for the word per, as in "miles/hours," and to show the line breaks in verse printed continuously. For example, "The expense of spirit in a waste of shame/Is lust in action." (*technical*) Can term **solidus** [Mid-19C. Via French, "comma, little rod" < Latin *virgula* (see VIRGULATE)]

vi·ri·cide /vîrə sīd/, **vi·ru·cide** *n* a drug or other agent that neutralizes or destroys a virus or viruses [Mid-20C. < VIRUS] —**vi·ri·cid·al** /vîrə sīd'l/ *adj*

vir·i·des·cent /vèeri déss'nt/ *adj* green or becoming green [Mid-19C. < late Latin *viridescent-*, present participle of *viridescere* "become green" < Latin *viridis* "green"] —**vir·i·des·cence** *n*

vi·rid·i·an /və ríddee ən/ *n* **1.** a green pigment made from a hydrated chromic oxide **2.** a bluish green color [Late 19C. < Latin *viridis* "green"] —**vi·rid·i·an** *adj*

vi·rid·i·ty /və ríddətee/ *n* (*literary*) **1.** the state of being green **2.** the state of being inexperienced [15C. < Latin *viridis* "green"]

vir·ile /véerəl, ví rīl/ *adj* **1. MASCULINE** relating to or having the characteristics of an adult male **2. FORCEFUL** showing energy, power, and forcefulness **3. SEXUALLY POTENT** able to carry out the male sexual function [15C. < Latin *virilis* < *vir* "man, husband"]

vir·il·ism /véerə lìzzəm/ *n* the development of male secondary sex characteristics culturally considered to be unusual in a woman, e.g., body hair or a deep voice

vi·ril·i·ty /vi rílləte/ *n* the state of being male, having male characteristics, or male sexual potency

vir·i·lo·cal /vèeree lṓk'l/ *adj* describes a form of marriage or the custom where, after the wedding, the bride moves to her new husband's family home [Mid-20C. < Latin *virilis* "of a man" (see VIRILE)]

vi·ri·on /vîree òn, vée-/ *n* the form taken by a virus when it is outside living cells and capable of causing infection. It consists of a core of DNA or RNA surrounded by a protein coat, sometimes covered by an outer envelope. [Mid-20C. < French < *virien* "viral" + -ON[1]]

viro- *prefix* virus, viral ○ *virology* [< VIRUS]

vi·roid /vī ròyd/ *n* an infectious RNA particle that resembles a virus, but is smaller. It causes diseases in plants. [Mid-20C. < VIRUS]

vi·rol·o·gy /vī róllәjee/ *n* the branch of science and medicine that deals with the study of viruses and the diseases caused by them —**vi·ro·log·ic** /vīrə lójjik/ *adj* —**vi·ro·log·i·cal** *adj* —**vi·ro·log·i·cal·ly** *adv* —**vi·rol·o·gist** *n*

vir·tu /vər tóo/, **ver·tu** *n* a love of or taste for fine-art objects or curios [Early 18C. < Italian, "virtue"]

vir·tu·al /vúrchoo əl/ *adj* **1. BEING SOMETHING IN PRACTICE** being something in effect even if not in reality or not conforming to the generally accepted definition of the term **2. GENERATED BY COMPUTER** simulated by a computer for reasons of economics, convenience, or performance **3.** PHYS **HYPOTHETICAL** describes a particle whose existence is suggested to explain observed phenomena, but is not proven or directly observable **4.** COMPUT **RELATING TO DATA STORAGE MANAGEMENT TECHNIQUE** describes a technique of moving data between storage areas or media to create the impression that a computer has a storage capacity greater than it actually has [14C. < medieval Latin *virtualis* < Latin *virtus* (see VIRTUE)]

vir·tu·al as·sis·tant *n* somebody who uses a computer and phone links to work from a distance as a personal assistant to somebody else ○*"There are many reasons why home-based business owners are hiring virtual assistants."* (*Washington Post*; December 1998)

vir·tu·al com·mu·ni·ty *n* a group of people communicating with each other via the Internet ○*"... an interactive virtual community where local residents can do anything from look for local work to book seats at the local cinema."* (*BBC website*; April 1999)

vir·tu·al disk *n* random-access memory used as a disk drive

vir·tu·al fo·cus *n* the point from which divergent reflected or refracted light rays seem to originate

vir·tu·al im·age *n* an image from which reflected or refracted light rays appear to diverge. It cannot be projected onto a screen or photographic emulsion.

vir·tu·al·i·ty /vùrchoo állətee/ *n* **1.** the inherent ability or potential to come into existence **2.** COMPUT same as **virtual reality**

vir·tu·al·ly /vúrchoo əlee/ *adv* almost, but not quite ○ *At that time he was virtually unknown as a writer.*

vir·tu·al ma·chine *n* a program running on a computer that creates a self-contained operating environment and presents the appearance to the user of a different computer. A virtual machine simulates at a minimum the instruction set of the computer it emulates.

vir·tu·al mem·o·ry *n* a technique for creating the illusion that a computer has more memory than it really has by swapping blocks or pages of data between memory and external storage

vir·tu·al pri·vate net·work *n* COMPUT full form of **VPN**

vir·tu·al re·al·i·ty *n* **1.** a technique by which a computer simulates a three-dimensional physical environment using visual and auditory stimuli with and within which somebody can interact to affect what happens in the simulation **2.** a computer-generated environment that simulates three-dimensional reality

Vir·tu·al Re·al·i·ty Mod·el·ing Lan·guage *n* COMPUT full form of **VRML**

vir·tu·al stor·age *n* COMPUT same as **virtual memory**

~~**virtualy**~~ incorrect spelling of **virtually**

vir·tue /vúrchoo/ *n* **1. GOODNESS** the quality of being morally good or righteous ○ *a paragon of virtue* **2. GOOD QUALITY** a quality that is morally good ○ *Patience is a virtue.* **3. ADMIRABLE QUALITY** a quality that is good or admirable, but not necessarily in terms of morality **4.** CHR **CARDINAL OR THEOLOGICAL MORALITY** a cardinal virtue, e.g., justice or moderation, or theological virtue, e.g., hope or charity **5. CHASTITY** the moral quality of being chaste, especially in a woman **6. WORTH** the worth, advantage, or beneficial quality of something ○ *knew the virtue of thrift* **7.** CHR **ANGEL OF FIFTH HIGHEST ORDER** in the traditional Christian hierarchy, an angel of the fifth of the nine orders of angels [12C. Via Old French *vertu* < Latin *virtus* "manliness, excellence, worth" < *vir* "man, husband"] —**vir·tue·less** *adj* ◇ **by virtue of** because of, through the power of, or by the authority of something ◇ **make a virtue of necessity** to do something with good grace, when you are obligated to do it anyway

vir·tu·o·sa /vùrchoo óssə, -ṓzə/ *n* a female musician who shows exceptional ability, technique, or artistry [Mid-17C. < Italian, feminine of *virtuoso* (see VIRTUOSO)]

vir·tu·o·si ARTS plural of **virtuoso**

vir·tu·os·i·ty /vùrchoo óssətee/ *n* **1.** great skill or technique shown by somebody who excels at doing something, especially performing music **2.** interest in, or knowledge and appreciation of, fine-art objects

vir·tu·o·so /vùrchoo óssō, -ṓzō/ (*plural* **-sos** *or* **-si** /-see/) *n* **1. EXCEPTIONAL PERFORMER** a musician who shows exceptional ability, technique, or artistry **2. TALENTED PERSON** somebody who shows exceptional technique or ability in something **3. CONNOISSEUR** somebody who is knowledgeable and cultivated in appreciating the fine arts [Early 17C. < Italian, "skilful, versed" < late Latin *virtuosus* "good" < Latin *virtus* (see VIRTUE)] —**vir·tu·o·sic** /-óssik, -ṓzik/ *adj* —**vir·tu·o·si·cal·ly** *adv*

vir·tu·ous /vúrchoo əss/ *adj* **1.** having or showing moral goodness or righteousness **2.** not having sexual intercourse with anyone except a partner in marriage, especially a husband —**vir·tu·ous·ly** *adv* —**vir·tu·ous·ness** *n*

vir·tu·ous cir·cle *n* a chain or cycle of events, the opposite of a vicious circle, in which one event with a beneficial outcome brings about further events with increasingly beneficial outcomes

vi·ru·cide *n* PHARM another spelling of **viricide**

vir·u·lence /veéryələnss, veérə-/, **vir·u·len·cy** /veéryələnssee, veérə-/ *n* **1.** the quality of being extremely poisonous, infectious, or damaging, or the extent to which a disease or toxin possesses this quality **2.** the quality of being bitter, malicious, or hostile

vir·u·lent /veéryələnt, veérə-/ *adj* **1. VERY POISONOUS** extremely poisonous, infectious, or damaging to organisms **2. MALICIOUS** showing great bitterness, malice, or hostility ○ *virulent criticism* **3. IRRITATING** extremely obnoxious or harsh [14C. < Latin *virulentus* "poisonous" < *virus* "poison, venom"] —**vir·u·lent·ly** *adv*

vir·u·lif·er·ous /veéryə líffərəss, veérə-/ *adj* describes an organism that contains or carries a virus [Mid-20C. < VIRULENT]

vi·rus /vírəss/ *n* **1. SUBMICROSCOPIC PARASITE** a submicroscopic parasitic particle of a nucleic acid surrounded by protein that can only replicate within a host cell. Viruses are not considered to be independent living organisms. **2. VIRAL DISEASE** a disease caused by a virus **3. CONTAGIOUS COMPUTER PROGRAM** a computer program that is part of another and inserts copies of itself, often damaging the integrity of stored data. It travels with the program that contains it. ◊ **Trojan horse** (sense 3), **worm** *v* (sense 1) **4. SOMETHING THAT CORRUPTS** something that has a corrupting or poisonous effect, especially on the mind [Late 16C. < Latin, "poison, venom, medicinal liquid"]

vis[1] /viss/ (*plural* **vi·res** /ví reez/) *n* force or power (*literary*) [Early 17C. < Latin]

vis[2] *abbr* **1.** PHYS viscosity **2.** *also* **VIS** visibility **3.** visible **4.** visual

Vis. *abbr* **1.** Viscount **2.** Viscountess

vi·sa /veézə/ *n* **1. PASSPORT INSERTION** an official endorsement in a passport authorizing the bearer to enter or leave, and travel in or through, a specific country or region **2. AUTHORIZATION** a mark of official authorization ■ *vt* (**-saed, -sa·ing, -sas**) **1. SUPPLY DOCUMENT WITH VISA** to insert a visa in a passport or other document **2. GIVE SOMEBODY VISA** to provide somebody with a visa [Mid-19C. Via French < Latin *visa* "things seen" < past participle of *videre* "see"]

VISA *n* a strain of a common infection-causing bacterium that shows some resistance to treatment by the antibiotic vancomycin. Full form **vancomycin intermediate Staphylococcus aureus**

~~**visable**~~ incorrect spelling of **visible**

vis·age /vízzij/ *n* (*literary*) **1.** somebody's face or facial expression **2.** the appearance or look of something [13C. < Old French < *vis* "face, appearance" < Latin *visus* past participle of *videre* "see"]

vis-à-vis /veézə veé/ *prep* **1. REGARDING** in relation to **2. OPPOSITE** opposite to or face to face with ■ *adv* **FACE TO FACE** face to face, or opposite each other ■ *n* (*plural same*) **1. SOMEBODY OR SOMETHING FACING** somebody or something that is face to face with another person or thing **2. COUNTERPART** somebody who is the counterpart of somebody else **3. HORSE-DRAWN CARRIAGE** a horse-drawn carriage in which people sit facing each other [Mid-18C. < French, "face to face" < Old French *vis* (see VISAGE)]

Vi·sa·yan /vi sí ən/ *n* **1.** a member of a people of the central and southern islands of the Philippines **2.** the Austronesian language of the Visayan people. Native speakers: 15,000,000. [Early 20C. < a language of the central Philippines] —**Vi·sa·yan** *adj*

Vis·by /vízbee/ port on the western coast of the island of Gotland, Sweden. It was an important member of the Hanseatic League in the Middle Ages. Population: 20,986 (1994).

visc *abbr* viscosity

Visc. *abbr* **1.** Viscount **2.** Viscountess

visc- *prefix* same as **visco-** (*used before vowels*)

vis·ca·cha /vi skaáchə/, **viz·ca·cha** *n* a burrowing gregarious rodent with black and white markings on its face, related to and resembling the chinchilla. Native to: South America. Latin name: *Lagostomus maximus*. [Early 17C. Via Spanish < Quechua *(h)uiscacha*]

vis·cer·a /víssərə/ *npl* the internal organs of the body, especially those of the abdomen such as the intestines [Early 18C. < Latin, "internal organs, entrails"]

vis·cer·al /víssərəl/ *adj* **1. INSTINCTUAL** proceeding from instinct rather than from reasoned thinking **2. EMOTIONAL** characterized by or showing basic emotions **3.** ANAT **OF INTERNAL ORGANS** relating to or affecting one or more internal organs of the body —**vis·cer·al·ly** *adv*

vis·cer·o·mo·tor /vìssərō mṓtər/ *adj* relating to the nervous control of gut movements, especially to disorders of bowel movement

vis·cid /víssid/ *adj* **1.** thick and sticky in consistency **2.** describes a leaf or other plant part that is covered with a sticky substance [Mid-17C. < late Latin *viscidus* < Latin *viscum* (see VISCOUS)] —**vis·cid·i·ty** /vi síddətee/ *n* —**vis·cid·ly** *adv* —**vis·cid·ness** *n*

visco- *prefix* viscosity ○ *viscoelastic* [< VISCOUS]

vis·co·e·las·tic /vìskō i lástik/ *adj* describes asphalt and many polymers that exhibit both viscous and elastic properties —**vis·co·e·las·tic·i·ty** /-ee lass tíssətee/ *n*

vis·com·e·ter /vi skómmətər/ *n* an instrument used to measure the viscosity of a substance —**vis·co·met·ric** /vìskə méttrik/ *adj* —**vis·co·met·ri·cal** /-méttrik'l/ *adj* —**vis·com·e·try** *n*

Vis·con·ti /viss kṓntee/, **Luchino** (1906–76) Italian movie and theater director. He is noted for his neorealist films and literary adaptations. He also directed plays, ballets, and operas. Full name **Visconti, Don Luchino, Conte di Modrone**

vis·cose /vís kòss/ *n* **1.** a rayon with a soft silky feel, made from a cellulose solution **2.** a cellulose solution of thick consistency. Use: rayon manufacture. [Late 19C. < late Latin *viscosus* (see VISCOUS)]

vis·co·sim·e·ter /vìskō símmətər/ *n* PHYS same as **viscometer** —**vis·cos·i·met·ric** /-si méttrik/ *adj* —**vis·cos·i·met·ri·cal** *adj* —**vis·cos·i·me·try** *n*

vis·cos·i·ty /viss kóssətee/ (*plural* **-ties**) *n* **1. THICKNESS AND STICKINESS** a thick and sticky consistency or quality **2.** PHYS **PROPERTY OF FLUID THAT RESISTS FLOWING** the property of a fluid or semifluid that causes it to resist flowing **3.** PHYS **MEASURE OF SUBSTANCE'S RESISTANCE TO MOTION** a measure of the resistance of a substance to motion under an applied force

vis·cos·i·ty in·dex *n* an arbitrary scale for lubricating oils that is used to indicate how much the viscosity of the oil varies according to its temperature

vis·count /ví kòwnt/ *n* **1. BRITISH NOBLEMAN** a British nobleman of a rank above baron **2. COUNT'S SON OR YOUNGER BROTHER** in European countries other than the United Kingdom, especially France, somebody whose father or elder brother is a count **3. COUNT'S REPRESENTATIVE** in medieval Europe, somebody acting for or representing a count [14C. Via Anglo-Norman *viscounte*, Old French *vi(s)conte* < medieval Latin *vicecomes* < Latin *vice* "in place of" (see VICE[2]) + *comes* "companion"] —**vis·count·cy** *n* —**vis·count·y** *n*

vis·count·ess /ví kòwntəss/ *n* **1.** a woman who holds a rank equivalent to viscount **2.** the wife or widow of a viscount

vis·cous /vískəss/ *adj* **1.** thick and sticky, reluctant to flow, and difficult to stir **2.** describes a fluid that has a relatively high resistance to flow [14C. < late Latin *viscosus* "sticky" < Latin *viscum* "mistletoe, birdlime made from mistletoe berries"] —**vis·cous·ly** *adv* —**vis·cous·ness** *n*

Visct. *abbr* **1.** Viscount **2.** Viscountess

vis·cus /vískəss/ *n* ANAT singular of **viscera**

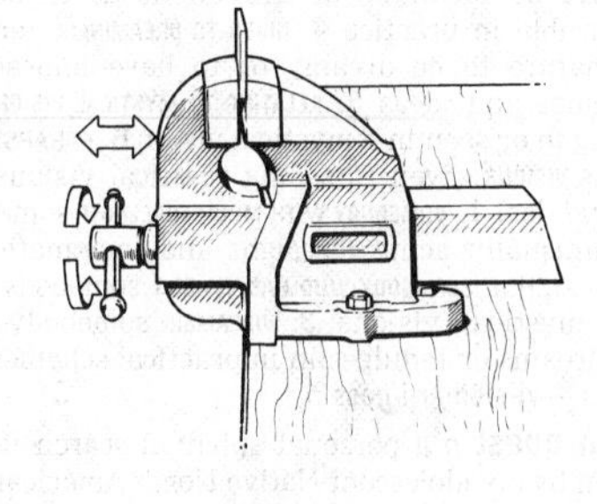

vise

vise /víss/ *n* a tool with two jaws that can be closed by a lever or screw, used to hold an object immobile so that it can be worked on ■ *vt* (**vised, vis·ing, vi·ses**) to hold something tightly in a vise [13C. Via Old French *vis* "screw" < Latin *vitis* "vine"] —**vise·like** *adj*

Vi·sha·kha·pat·nam /vi shaákə pútnəm/ city and port on the Bay of Bengal, in Andhra Pradesh State, southeastern India. Population: 1,329,472 (2001).

Vish·nu /vísh noo/ *n* in Hinduism, a god called the Preserver, the second member of the triad that includes Brahma the Creator and Shiva the Destroyer [Mid-17C. < Sanskrit *Viṣṇu*]

vis·i·bil·i·ty /vìzzə bíllətee/ *n* **1. ABILITY TO BE SEEN** the fact of being able to be seen **2. DISTANCE IT IS POSSIBLE TO SEE** the distance it is possible to see under the prevailing atmospheric or weather conditions **3. CLEAR VIEW** the ability to provide somebody, especially the driver of a vehicle, with a good view of what is around him or her, or the view obtained from a fixed position **4. PUBLIC PROMINENCE** the degree to which somebody or something is easily noticed by and catches the attention of the public or a group of people ○ *the comparatively low visibility of the board of directors*

vis·i·ble /vízzəb'l/ *adj* **1. ABLE TO BE SEEN** capable of being seen by, or perceptible to, the human eye ○ *the visible spectrum* **2. IN SIGHT** in somebody's sight at a particular time ○ *The building became visible again as soon as she turned the corner.* **3. OBVIOUS** easily noticeable ○ *the very visible results of the recent floods* **4. DETECTABLE** capable of being discovered by means of the mental faculties ○ *no visible prospect of a solution to the problem* **5. OFTEN SEEN PUBLICLY** frequently in the public eye ○ *the company's very visible head of public relations* **6. DESIGNED TO KEEP SOMETHING IN VIEW** designed to keep information or an item in view or able to be readily brought to view

○ *a visible index* [14C. < Latin *visibilis* < *vis-*, past participle of *videre* "see"] —**vis·i·ble·ness** *n* —**vis·i·bly** *adv*

vis·i·ble ra·di·a·tion *n* radiation that falls within the range of wavelengths that can be detected by the human eye, e.g., sunlight

vis·i·ble speech *n* **1.** a set of phonetic symbols intended to represent the position of the lips, tongue, and other speech organs in creating sounds **2.** a visual representation of speech using a spectrograph that disperses radiation into a spectrum and photographs it

Vis·i·goth /vízzi gòth/ *n* a member of an ancient Germanic people who conquered parts of the Roman Empire during the 5th century. They destroyed Rome in 410 and took over parts of Spain and southern France, where they established a powerful kingdom that lasted until the beginning of the 8th century. [Mid-16C. < late Latin *Visigothi* "Visigoths"] —**Vis·i·goth·ic** /vìzzi góthik/ *adj*

vi·sion /ví<u>zh</u>'n/ *n* **1.** EYESIGHT the ability to see **2.** MENTAL PICTURE an image or concept in the imagination ○ *visions of power and wealth* **3.** PARAPSYCHOL SOMETHING SEEN IN DREAM OR TRANCE an image or series of images seen in a dream or trance, often interpreted as having religious, revelatory, or prophetic significance **4.** FAR-SIGHTEDNESS the ability to anticipate possible future events and developments **5.** SOMEBODY OR SOMETHING BEAUTIFUL a beautiful or pleasing sight [13C. < Latin *vision-* < *vis-* (see VISIBLE)] —**vi·sion·al** *adj* —**vi·sion·al·ly** *adv* —**vi·sion·less** *adj*

vi·sion·ar·y /ví<u>zh</u>'n èrree/ *adj* **1.** FULL OF FORESIGHT characterized by unusually acute foresight and imagination **2.** IMAGINARY produced by, resulting from, or originating in the imagination **3.** INCAPABLE OF BEING REALIZED so idealistic or unrealistic as to be unrealizable in practice **4.** GIVEN TO DREAMINESS tending by nature to be dreamy or to have impractical schemes and ideas **5.** RELATING TO MYSTICAL VISIONS relating to or seen in a mystical vision **6.** PARAPSYCHOL HAVING VISIONS given to seeing mystical visions ■ *n* (*plural* **-ies**) **1.** SOMEBODY WITH MUCH FORESIGHT somebody of unusually acute foresight and imagination **2.** PARAPSYCHOL SOMEBODY WHO HAS VISIONS somebody who has mystical visions **3.** DREAMER somebody who daydreams or indulges in impractical schemes and ideas —**vi·sion·ar·i·ness** *n*

vi·sion quest *n* a personal spiritual search undertaken by an adolescent Native North American boy in order to learn by means of a trance or vision the identity of his guardian spirit

vis·it /vízzit/ *v* (**-it·ed, -it·ing, -its**) **1.** *vti* GO TO SEE SOMEBODY to go to see and spend time with somebody, especially as an act of affection or friendship ○ *Nobody visited him in hospital.* **2.** *vt* STAY WITH SOMEBODY to go to stay with somebody for a time as a guest in his or her home ○ *I'm going to visit my family over the vacation.* **3.** *vti* GO TO SEE PLACE to go to see or stay at a place for a time, e.g., as a tourist **4.** *vt* GO TO INSPECT PLACE to go to a place as an official inspector **5.** *vti* ONLINE GO TO WEBSITE to view a website **6.** *vi* CHAT WITH SOMEBODY to engage in amiable or casual conversation with somebody **7.** *vt* INFLICT SOMETHING ON SOMEBODY to inflict something unpleasant such as punishment or vengeance on somebody (*literary or formal*) ○ *visited them with plagues* ■ *n* **1.** SOCIAL CALL a trip to see somebody and a period of time spent in his or her company **2.** EXTENDED STAY IN PLACE an extended temporary stay in a place, e.g., as somebody's guest or as a tourist **3.** CONVERSATION an amiable or casual conversation **4.** OFFICIAL INSPECTION an official call paid for the purpose of inspection ○ *a visit to the ship by the admiral* **5.** LAW BOARDING OF SHIP the boarding of a ship on the high seas to carry out a search for contraband [12C. Directly or via French < Latin *visitare* "go to see," < *visare* "to view" < *vis-* (see VISIBLE)] —**vis·it·a·ble** *adj*

vis·i·tant /vízzit'nt/ *n* **1.** BIRDS same as **visitor** (sense 2) **2.** same as **visitor** (sense 1) (*archaic*) **3.** PARANORMAL a being thought to visit from the spirit world ■ *adj* paying a visit to somebody or something

vis·i·ta·tion /vìzzi táysh'n/ *n* **1.** *US* LAW RIGHT OF PARENTAL ACCESS the right of a divorced parent to have access to a child for a set period of time, or a period of time with the child granted by this right **2.** OFFICIAL VISIT an official visit for inspection or examination **3.** SOCIAL VISIT a social visit to somebody's home, especially if it is unwelcome or lasts too long (*humorous*) **4.** RELIG PUNISHMENT FROM GOD a punishment or, sometimes, a benefit received, especially one believed to be sent by God **5.** PARAPSYCHOL APPEARANCE FROM SPIRIT WORLD a supposed appearance made by a supernatural being —**vis·i·ta·tion·al** *adj*

Vis·i·ta·tion /vìzzi táysh'n/ *n* **1.** according to the Bible, the visit made by the Virgin Mary after the Annunciation to her cousin Elizabeth **2.** a Christian festival celebrating the Visitation of the Virgin Mary to Elizabeth. Date: July 2.

vis·it·ing card /vízziting-/ *n UK* same as **calling card**

vis·it·ing fire·man *n* an important visitor who is entertained lavishly and impressively (*informal*)

vis·it·ing hours *npl* the period of time during which patients in a hospital may have visitors

vis·it·ing nurse *n* a registered nurse who provides medical care to sick people in their homes

vis·it·ing pro·fes·sor *n* a professor from one college or university who teaches at another for a semester or academic year

vis·it·ing teach·er *n US* a teacher employed by a public school system to teach children in their homes if they have medical conditions that prevent them from attending school

vis·i·tor /vízzitər/ *n* **1.** SOMEBODY VISITING somebody who visits a person or place **2.** BIRDS MIGRATORY BIRD APPEARING TEMPORARILY a migratory bird that regularly spends a season or part of a season in a place **3.** ONLINE WEBSITE VIEWER an Internet user who views a website ■ **vis·i·tors** *npl* SPORTS OUT-OF-TOWN TEAM an out-of-town team that travels to an opponent's stadium or sports field to play ○ *We lost 14–7 to the visitors.* ○ *The scoreboard read: Visitors 13; Home 7.*

vis·i·tor cen·ter *n* a building offering information and services to visitors in a city or at a historical or archaeological site, park, or nature reserve

vis·i·tors' book *n* a book in which visitors, e.g., to a house, guesthouse, hotel, or art gallery, write their names, their home addresses, and often their comments on the visit

vis·i·tor·ship /vízzitər shìp/ *n* the total number of tourists visiting a specific place

vis·na /víssnə/ *n* a chronic progressive pneumonia of sheep and goats [Mid-20C. < Old Norse, "wither"]

visor

vi·sor /vízər/, **vi·zor** *n* **1.** TRANSPARENT FRONT OF HELMET a hinged front part of a helmet, made of transparent or tinted plastic and designed to protect the face or eyes, especially on helmets worn by motorcyclists or welders **2.** FLAP OVER WINDSHIELD FOR GLARE a flap mounted above the windshield inside an automobile used to shield the eyes from glare **3.** EYESHADE a shade for the eyes attached to a band worn around the head **4.** CAP BRIM the front brim of a cap **5.** FRONT OF MEDIEVAL HELMET a hinged metal front part of a medieval helmet in a suit of armor, designed to protect the face and fitted with slits for the eyes to see through [13C. < Anglo-Norman *viser* < French *vis* (see VISAGE)] —**vi·sored** *adj*

vis·ta /vístə/ *n* **1.** SCENIC VIEW a scenic or panoramic view **2.** VIEW SEEN THROUGH NARROW OPENING a view seen through a long narrow opening, e.g., between rows of trees **3.** MENTAL PICTURE a mental picture covering a wide range of objects or a long succession of events in the past or future ○ *open up vistas of expansion into untapped markets* [Mid-17C. < Italian, "view" < past participle of *vedere* "see" < Latin *videre*]

VISTA /vístə/ *abbr* Volunteers in Service to America

Vis·tu·la /víschələ, vísch∞̆lə/ longest river of Poland, flowing northward from the Carpathian Mountains in the southwest of the country, through Cracow, Warsaw, and Torun, before emptying into the Baltic Sea at the Gulf of Gdansk. Length: 675 mi./1,090 km. Polish name **Wisła**

vi·su·al /ví<u>zh</u>oo əl/ *adj* **1.** OF VISION relating to vision or sight **2.** VISIBLE able or intended to be seen by the eyes, especially as opposed to being registered by one of the other senses or by a machine ○ *visual humor* **3.** PERCEPTIBLE BY MIND'S EYE able to be perceived as a picture in the mind rather than as an abstract idea ○ *a visual memory* **4.** DONE BY SIGHT ONLY describes direction-finding done by sight only and without the use of scientific instruments or equipment ○ *visual navigation* ○ *made a visual landing* ■ *n* **1.** COMMUNICATION same as **visual aid 2.** MARKETING PIECE OF ILLUSTRATIVE MATERIAL a photograph, picture, chart, or graph that displays information or promotional material in a way that appeals to the eye [15C. < late Latin *visualis* < Latin *visus* "sight" < past participle of *videre* "see"] —**vi·su·al·ly** *adv* —**vi·su·al·ness** *n*

vi·su·al a·cu·i·ty *n* acuteness of vision as determined by a comparison with the normal ability to identify letters at a distance of 20 ft./6 m

vi·su·al aid *n* something that is looked at as a complement to a lesson or presentation, e.g., a model, chart, or movie

vi·su·al arts *npl* arts that are perceived by sight, e.g., painting or sculpture

vi·su·al bi·na·ry *n* a star that can be seen to be a double star either with the naked eye or when viewed through a telescope

vi·su·al field *n* OPTICS same as **field of vision**

vi·su·al·ize /ví<u>zh</u>oo ə lìz/ (**-ized, -iz·ing, -iz·es**) *v* **1.** *vti* IMAGINE SOMETHING to form a visual image of something in the mind **2.** *vti* PSYCHOL CREATE POSITIVE MENTAL PICTURE OF SOMETHING to create a vivid positive mental picture of something such as a desired outcome to a problem, in order to promote a sense of well-being **3.** *vt* MED MAKE IMAGE OF INTERNAL ORGANS to produce an image of an internal organ or other part of the body by using X-rays or other means such as magnetic resonance imaging —**vi·su·al·i·za·tion** /vì<u>zh</u>oo əli záysh'n/ *n* —**vi·su·al·iz·er** *n*

vi·su·al·ly im·paired *adj* having reduced vision, especially having eyesight so poor that it interferes with the ability to perform day-to-day activities effectively

vi·su·al-mo·tor co·or·di·na·tion *n* the co-ordination of the body's visual and motor systems, as occurs when somebody reaches out for something that is being looked at

vi·su·al pur·ple *n* BIOL same as **rhodopsin**

vi·su·o·mo·tor /vì<u>zh</u>oo ō mṓtər/ *adj* relating to or involving body motor processes that are linked to vision, e.g., the coordination of movements

vi·ta /veétə/ (*plural* **-tae** /-tee/) *n* **1.** HR same as **résumé** (sense 1) **2.** a brief account of somebody's life (*formal*) [Mid-20C. < Latin, "life"]

USAGE The correct plural form of ***vita*** is *vitae*, not *vitas*. The plural *vitae* is sometimes incorrectly used as a singular, perhaps because it is thought to be a short form of *curriculum vitae*. In Latin *vitae* means "of life" or "lives" (plural).

vi·tal /vít'l/ *adj* **1.** CRUCIAL extremely important and necessary, or indispensable to the survival or continuing effectiveness of something **2.** NEEDED FOR LIFE required for the continuation of life ○ *vital body organs* **3.** LIVELY full of animation or vigor ○ *a vital neighborhood* **4.** OF LIFE relating to life ○ *vital records of a population* [14C. < Latin *vitalis* < *vita* "life"] —**vi·tal·ness** *n*

SYNONYMS See ***necessary***.

vi·tal ca·pac·i·ty *n* a measure of the air that can be exhaled from the lungs after maximum inhalation

vi·tal force *n* **1.** FORCEFUL VITALIZING PERSON OR THING somebody or something infusing vitality or strength into somebody or something else ○ *She was the vital force behind passage of the law.* **2.** ANIMATING SOUL OR SPIRIT the animating or vitalizing spirit, soul, or source of energy believed by some to be inherent in living beings **3.** NATURAL FORCE FOR HEALTH in alternative medicine, the natural mechanism or force that keeps somebody healthy and that, when weakened, makes the person susceptible to illness

vi·tal·ism /vít'l ìzzəm/ *n* a doctrine that maintains that life and the functions of a living organism depend on a nonmaterial force or principle separate from physical and chemical processes —**vi·tal·is·tic** /vít'l ístik/ *adj* —**vi·tal·is·ti·cal·ly** *adv*

vi·tal·i·ty /vī tállətee/ *n* **1.** LIVELINESS abundant physical and mental energy, usually combined with a wholehearted and joyous approach to situations and activities **2.** DURABILITY the ability of something to live and grow or to continue in existence ○ *the vitality of cherished traditions* **3.** PHILOSOPHY VITAL PRINCIPLE the nonmaterial force that, according to vitalism, distinguishes the living from the nonliving

vi·tal·ize /vít'l ìz/ (-ized, -iz·ing, -iz·es) *vt* **1.** to cause somebody or something to live **2.** to make somebody or something lively —**vi·tal·i·za·tion** /vīt'li záysh'n/ *n* —**vi·tal·iz·er** *n*

vi·tal·ly /vít'lee/ *adv* extremely or indispensably

vi·tals /vít'lz/ *npl* **1.** PHYSIOL ORGANS ESSENTIAL TO LIFE the internal organs of the body that are essential to life, especially the stomach and intestines **2.** MED same as **vital signs** (*informal*) **3.** GENITALS the genitals, especially those of a man (*humorous*) **4.** ESSENTIALS the essential parts of something [Early 17C. < Latin *vitalia* "vital things" < form of *vitalis* (see VITAL)]

vi·tal signs *npl* the signs that indicate life, e.g., pulse, body temperature, breathing, and blood pressure

vi·tal stain·ing *n* the process of using a substance that colors only live cells in order to study the fate of cells in embryonic development

vi·tal sta·tis·tics *npl* **1.** statistics of human births, deaths, marriages, and health **2.** the measurements of a woman's bust, waist, and hips (*dated informal*)

vi·ta·min /vítəmin/ *n* an organic substance essential in small quantities to the metabolism in most animals. Vitamins are found in minute quantities in food, in some cases are produced by the body, and are also produced synthetically. [Early 20C. < German *Vitamine* < Latin *vita* "life" + AMINE] —**vi·ta·min·ic** /vìtə mínnik/ *adj*

vi·ta·min A, **vi·ta·min A_1** *n* a fat-soluble vitamin found in some vegetables, fish, milk, and eggs, important for vision. Vitamin A is important to the health of the outer layer of cells in the skin and organs. A deficiency leads to roughening of the skin and night blindness.

vi·ta·min A_2 *n* a form of vitamin A obtained from fish liver

vi·ta·min B *n* BIOCHEM **1.** same as **vitamin B complex** **2.** same as **thiamine**

vi·ta·min B_1 *n* BIOCHEM same as **thiamine**

vi·ta·min B_2 *n* BIOCHEM same as **riboflavin**

vi·ta·min B_6 *n* BIOCHEM same as **pyridoxine**

vi·ta·min B_{12} *n* a water-soluble vitamin obtained only from fish and other animal products, important for blood formation. A deficiency of it causes pernicious anemia.

vi·ta·min B com·plex *n* a group of water-soluble coenzyme vitamins found in many foods

vi·ta·min C *n* a water-soluble vitamin found in fruits and leafy vegetables or made synthetically and used as an antioxidant. Lack of vitamin C causes scurvy.

vi·ta·min D *n* a fat-soluble vitamin that occurs in fish-liver oils and eggs, essential for the formation of bones and teeth. Lack of vitamin D causes rickets.

vi·ta·min D_2 *n* a form of vitamin D made by plants

vi·ta·min D_3 *n* a form of vitamin D formed by the action of sunlight on the skin

vi·ta·min E *n* a mixture of fat-soluble vitamins found in seed oils, essential for reproduction

vi·ta·min H *n US* BIOCHEM same as **biotin**

vi·ta·min K *n* a fat-soluble vitamin essential for blood clotting

vi·ta·min K_1 *n* a form of vitamin K found in green vegetables

vi·ta·min K_2 *n* a form of vitamin K found in fish

vi·ta·min P *n* BIOCHEM same as **bioflavonoid**

vi·tel·li BIOL plural of **vitellus**

vi·tel·lin /vi téllin, vī-/ *n* a protein in egg yolk [Mid-19C. < *vitellus*]

vi·tel·line /vi téllin, vī-, -té leen/ *adj* **1.** relating to egg yolk **2.** of the yellow color of egg yolk [< medieval Latin *vitellinus* < Latin *vitellus* "egg yolk"]

vi·tel·line mem·brane *n* the membrane that encloses a fertilized egg

vi·tel·lus /vi télləss, vī-/ (*plural* **-lus·es** or **-li** /-lī/) *n* the yolk of an egg (*technical*) [Early 18C. < Latin, "egg yolk"]

vi·ti·ate /víshee àyt/ (**-at·ed, -at·ing, -ates**) *vt* (*formal*) **1.** MAKE SOMETHING INEFFECTIVE to destroy or drastically reduce the effectiveness of something, or make it invalid **2.** MAKE SOMETHING FAULTY to cause something to become faulty **3.** DEBASE SOMETHING to degrade something morally [Mid-16C. < Latin *vitiare* < *vitium* "fault, vice"] —**vi·ti·a·ble** *adj* —**vi·ti·a·tion** /vìshee áysh'n/ *n* —**vi·ti·a·tor** *n*

vit·i·cul·ture /vítti kùlchər, víti-/ *n* the science or practice of growing grapevines, especially for winemaking [Late 19C. < Latin *vitis* "vine"] —**vit·i·cul·tur·al** /vìtti kúlchərəl/ *adj* —**vit·i·cul·tur·al·ly** *adv* —**vit·i·cul·tur·ist** *n*

vit·i·li·go /vìtt'l ígō/ *n* a skin disorder in which smooth whitish patches appear on the skin [Late 16C. < Latin, "skin eruption"]

Vi·to·ri·a /vi táwree ə/ capital city of the Basque Country in northern Spain. Population: 221,270 (2002).

Vi·tó·ri·a /vi táwree ə/ island city and capital of Espírito Santo State, eastern Brazil. Population: 265,874 (1996).

vitr- *prefix* same as **vitri-** (*used before vowels*)

vit·rain /ví tràyn/ *n* a narrow glassy band found in bituminous coal [Early 20C. < VITREOUS + *-ain* after FUSAIN]

vit·rec·to·my /vi tréktəmee/ (*plural* **-mies**) *n* a surgical operation to remove some or all of the vitreous humor of the eye

vit·re·ous /víttree əss/ *adj* **1.** SIMILAR TO GLASS having the characteristics or appearance of glass **2.** OF GLASS relating to, consisting of, or derived from glass **3.** MED OF VITREOUS HUMOR relating to the vitreous humor of the eye [Mid-17C. < Latin *vitreus* < *vitrum* "glass"] —**vit·re·os·i·ty** /vìttree óssətee/ *n* —**vit·re·ous·ness** *n*

vit·re·ous bod·y *n* the transparent gel that fills the main cavity of the eye between the lens and the retina

vit·re·ous e·nam·el *n* an opaque glassy coating applied to steel or other metals through firing

vit·re·ous hu·mor *n* the fluid component of the gel (**vitreous body**) that fills the main cavity of the eye between the lens and the retina

vit·re·ous sil·i·ca *n* glass made solely from silica

vi·tres·cent /vi tréss'nt/ *adj* capable of being made into glass [Mid-18C. < Latin *vitrum* "glass"]

vitri- *prefix* glass ○ *vitrify* [< Latin *vitrum*]

vit·ric /víttrik/ *adj* having the characteristics or appearance of glass [Early 20C. < Latin *vitrum* "glass"]

vit·ri·fi·ca·tion /vìttrəfi káysh'n/ *n* **1.** the process of converting materials to glass **2.** in pottery, the point at which a pot loses its porosity during a firing

vit·ri·form /víttrə fàwrm/ *adj* having the form or appearance of glass [Late 18C. < Latin *vitrum* "glass"]

vit·ri·fy /víttrə fì/ (**-fied, -fy·ing, -fies**) *vti* to become changed into glass, or change materials into glass [Late 16C. < French *vitrifier* or directly < Latin *vitrum* "glass"] —**vit·ri·fi·a·bil·i·ty** /vìttrə fì ə bílləte e/ *n* —**vit·ri·fi·a·ble** *adj*

vi·trine /vi tréen/ *n* a cabinet or case with glass walls for displaying specimens or art objects [Late 19C. < French < *vitre* "glass" < Latin *vitrum* "glass"]

vit·ri·ol /víttree ōl/ *n* **1.** extreme bitterness and hatred toward somebody or something, or an expression of this feeling in speech or writing **2.** a glassy metallic sulfate such as that of copper or iron **3.** CHEM same as **sulfuric acid** (*archaic or literary*) [14C. < medieval Latin *vitriolum* < Latin *vitrum* "glass"]

vit·ri·ol·ic /vìttree óllik/ *adj* **1.** filled with or expressing extreme bitterness and hatred toward somebody or something **2.** CHEM resembling a glassy metallic sulfate —**vit·ri·ol·i·cal·ly** *adv*

Vi·tru·vi·us /vi tróovee əss/ (*fl* 1st century B.C.) Roman architect and engineer. His book *De Architectura* provides valuable information about architecture and engineering in classical times. Full name **Vitruvius Pollio, Marcus**

> "Pictures should not be given approbation which are not likenesses of reality; even if they are refined creations executed with artistic skill."
> [Vitruvius, *Vitruvius, The Ten Books on Architecture*; 1960 (tr. M H Morgan)]

vit·ta /víttə/ (*plural* **-tae** /-tee/) *n* **1.** a tube or cavity containing oil in the carpels of the family of plants that includes carrot, parsley, and celery **2.** a stripe or band of color on the body of an animal [Late 17C. < Latin, "headband"] —**vit·tate** *adj*

vit·tles /vítt'lz/ *npl* food or other provisions (*dated or regional*) [Variant of VICTUALS]

vi·tu·line /víchə lìn, víchəlin/ *adj* relating to or resembling a calf or veal (*technical*) [Mid-17C. < Latin *vitulinus* < *vitulus* "calf"]

vi·tu·per·ate /vī tóopə ràyt, vi-/ (**-at·ed, -at·ing, -ates**) *vti* to attack somebody in violently abusive or harshly critical language [Mid-16C. < Latin *vituperare* < *vitium* "fault, vice" + *parare* "make ready"] —**vi·tu·per·a·tive** /vī tóopərətiv, -ràytiv, vi-/ *adj* —**vi·tu·per·a·tive·ly** *adv* —**vi·tu·per·a·tive·ness** *n* —**vi·tu·per·a·tor** *n* —**vi·tu·per·a·to·ry** *adj*

vi·tu·per·a·tion /vī tóopə ráysh'n, vi-/ *n* **1.** an outburst of violently abusive or harshly critical language **2.** the use of violent abuse or extremely harsh criticism

vi·va[1] /véevə, vée vàa/ *interj* used to express enthusiastic support for somebody ○ *Viva the president!* [Mid-17C. < Italian, "may he, she, or it live," form of *vivere* "to live" < Latin]

vi·va[2] /vívə, véevə/ *n UK* an examination, especially one taken as part of a university or college degree, in which a student is asked and answers questions in a spoken interview instead of on paper [Late 19C. Shortening of VIVA VOCE]

vi·va·ce /vi vaá chày, -vaáchee/ *adv* in a lively and spirited manner (*used as a musical direction*) ■ *n* a piece of music, or a section of a piece, played vivace [Late 17C. < Italian, "lively" < Latin *vivac-* (see VIVACIOUS)] —**vi·va·ce** *adj*

vi·va·cious /vi váyshəss/ *adj* exhibiting or characterized by liveliness and high-spiritedness [Mid-17C. < Latin *vivac-* "lively, long-lived" < *vivus* (see VIVID)] —**vi·va·cious·ly** *adv* —**vi·va·cious·ness** *n*

vi·vac·i·ty /vi vássətee/ *n* liveliness and high-spiritedness

Vi·val·di /vi vaáldee, -váwl-/, **Antonio** (1678–1741) Italian composer. His music epitomizes the Italian baroque style, his concertos being particularly influential on later composers. Full name **Vivaldi, Antonio Lucio**

vi·van·dière /vee vaaN dyér/ *n* in former times, a woman who followed an army and sold food and drink to the soldiers [Late 16C. < French, feminine of *vivandier* < late Latin *vivenda* (see VIAND)]

vi·var·i·um /vī vérree əm/ (*plural* **-i·a** /-ee ə/ or **-i·ums**) *n* a transparent enclosure in which small animals are kept so that their behavior can be studied [Early 17C. < Latin, "game preserve, fish pond" < form of *vivarius* "of living things" < *vivus* (see VIVID)]

vi·va vo·ce /vívə vṓssee, véevə-/ *adv* by word of mouth (*formal*) [Mid-16C. < medieval Latin, "with the living voice"]

vi·vax ma·lar·i·a /vī vaks-/, **vi·vax** *n* a form of malaria marked by convulsions that occur every 48 hours and caused by the parasite *Plasmodium vivax* [< modern Latin *vivax* taxonomic name < Latin, "long lived"]

vi·ver·rid /vī vérrid, vi-/ *n* a civet, mongoose, or other similar small carnivorous mammal with a long slender body. Family: Viverridae. [Early 20C. < modern Latin *Viverridae* (plural) < *Viverra* (singular) < Latin, "ferret"] —**vi·ver·rid** *adj*

viv·id /vívvid/ *adj* **1.** VERY BRIGHT strikingly bright or intense in color **2.** GRAPHIC producing strong and distinct mental images **3.** INVENTIVE active and inventive ○ *a vivid imagination* **4.** EXTREMELY CLEAR AND FRESH characterized by striking clarity, distinctness, or truth to life when perceived either by the eye or the mind ○ *a vivid image* **5.** LIVELY characterized by spirit and animation [Mid-17C. < Latin *vividus* < *vivus* "alive" < *vivere* "to live"] —**viv·id·ly** *adv* —**viv·id·ness** *n*

viv·i·fy /vívvə fì/ (**-fied, -fy·ing, -fies**) *vt* **1.** to cause somebody or something to come to life **2.** to give liveliness or vividness to something [14C. Via French *vivifier* < late Latin *vivificare* "make alive" < Latin *vivus* (see VIVID)] —**viv·i·fi·ca·tion** /vìvvəfi káysh'n/ *n* —**viv·i·fi·er** *n*

vi·vip·a·rous /vī vípparəss, vi-/ *adj* **1.** ZOOL **BEARING LIVE YOUNG** bearing live young, not eggs **2.** BOT **PRODUCING PLANTLETS** describes a plant that produces plantlets or bulbils from the flower stem, e.g., the spider plant **3.** BOT **PRODUCING SEEDLINGS ON PLANT** describes a plant with seeds that germinate and develop into seedlings before being shed from the parent plant, e.g., a mangrove [Mid-17C. < Latin *viviparus* "bringing forth alive" < *vivus* (see VIVID)] —**vi·vip·a·rous·ly** *adv*

viv·i·sect /vívvi sèkt/ (**-sect·ed, -sect·ing, -sects**) *vti* to perform operations on living animals that involve cutting into their bodies in order to gain knowledge of pathological or physiological processes [Mid-19C. Back-formation < VIVISECTION] —**viv·i·sec·tive** *adj* —**viv·i·sec·tor** *n*

viv·i·sec·tion /vìvvi séksh'n/ *n* the practice of operating on living animals in order to gain knowledge of pathological or physiological processes [Early 18C. < Latin *vivus* (see VIVID) after DISSECTION] —**viv·i·sec·tion·al** *adj*—**viv·i·sec·tion·al·ly** *adv*—**viv·i·sec·tion·ist** *n*

viv·i·sec·to·ri·um /vìvvi sek táwree əm/ (*plural* **-ri·ums** or **-ri·a** /-ree ə/) *n* an establishment where vivisection is practiced [Late 20C. < VIVISECTION after EMPORIUM]

vi·vo /véevō/ *adv* in a lively and energetic manner (*used as a musical direction*) [Mid-18C. Via Italian < Latin *vivus* (see VIVID)] —**vi·vo** *adj*

vix·en /víksən/ *n* **1.** a female fox **2.** an offensive term that deliberately insults a woman regarded as vindictive and bad-tempered (*insult*) [15C. Variant of *fixen* < Old English *fyxe*, feminine of *fox* (see FOX)] —**vix·en·ish** *adj* —**vix·en·ish·ly** *adv* —**vix·en·ish·ness** *n* —**vix·en·ly** *adj, adv*

viz. /viz/ *adv* namely. Full form **videlicet**

viz·ca·cha *n* ZOOL another spelling of **viscacha**

Víz·ca·í·no /vìz kaa éenō, bèeth-/, **Sebastián** (1550?–1615) Spanish explorer. He was the first European to explore the Pacific coast of North America systematically.

vi·zier /vi zéer/ *n* in some Islamic countries and especially in the former Ottoman Empire, a high-ranking government officer [Mid-16C. Via French or Spanish *visir* < Turkish *vezir* < Arabic *wazīr* "vizier," earlier "helper, assistant"] —**vi·zier·ate** /vi zéerət, vi zéer àyt/ *n* —**vi·zier·i·al** *adj* —**vi·zier·ship** *n*

vi·zor *n* CLOTHING, AUTOMOT, HIST another spelling of **visor**

vizsla

vizs·la /vízhlə, vízh láa/ *n* a medium-sized hunting dog with a short smooth reddish coat, belonging to a Hungarian breed [Mid-20C. Origin ?]

VJ *abbr* video jockey

V-J day *n* the day of the Japanese surrender in World War II. Date: August 15, 1945. [Abbreviation of *victory over Japan*]

vl *abbr* variant reading [Latin *varia lectio*]

VL *abbr* Vulgar Latin

VLA *n* a system of radio telescopes at the National Radio Astronomy Observatory, New Mexico. Full form **Very Large Array**

Vlach /vlaak, vlak/ *n* **1.** a member of a southeastern European people who in the 13th century founded the principalities of Walachia and Moldavia, later merged to become Romania. Vlachs now live mainly in the mountainous regions of the Balkans, the Former Yugoslav Republic of Macedonia, Albania, or northern Greece. **2.** a language of the Romance family that is spoken in southeastern Europe, especially by the Vlach people. Native speakers: 300,000. [Mid-19C. < Bulgarian and Serbo-Croatian < Germanic, "foreign"] —**Vlach** *adj*

Vla·di·mir /vláddə mèer, vlə dyée meer/ city and capital of Vladimir Oblast in western Russia. Population: 349,899 (1995).

Vla·di·vos·tok /vlàddəvə stók, vlàddə vóss tòk/ city and major port in southeastern Russia, on Golden Horn Bay, an inlet of the Sea of Japan. It is the eastern terminus of the Trans-Siberian Railway. Population: 640,672 (1995).

Vla·minck /vlámmingk, vlaa máNk/, **Maurice de** (1876–1958) French painter. Greatly influenced by the work of van Gogh, he was a leading light of the Fauvist movement. The bright colors and strong contrasts of his early works give way to a more subdued palette in his later landscapes.

> "Painting was an abscess which drained off the evil in me. Without a gift for painting I would have gone to the bad...What I could only have achieved in a social context by throwing a bomb...I have tried to express in art."
> [Maurice de Vlaminck. Quoted in *Fauvism*, Joseph Emile Muller; 1967]

VLCC *abbr* INDUST very large crude carrier

VLDL *abbr* MED very low density lipoprotein

VLF, vlf *abbr* MEDIA very low frequency

VLSI *adj* made using technology that allows hundreds of thousands of components to exist on a single microchip. Full form **very large-scale integration**

v-mail /vée màyl/, **v·mail** *n* an e-mail message with a video clip as an attachment [Late 20C. < *v* for VIDEO after E-MAIL]

V.M.D. *abbr* EDUC Doctor of Veterinary Medicine

vn *abbr* Vietnam (*used in Internet addresses*) See table at **domain name**

V-neck *n* **1.** a neckline shaped like a letter "V" **2.** a garment, especially a sweater or T-shirt, with a V-shaped neckline —**V-necked** *adj*

VO *abbr* **1.** verbal order **2.** very old (*used on labels for bottles of brandy, whiskey, or port*) **3.** voiceover

vo. *abbr* PRINTING verso

VOA *abbr* BROADCAST Voice of America

VOC *abbr* CHEM volatile organic compound

voc. *abbr* **1.** EDUC vocational **2.** GRAM vocative

vo·cab /vṓ kàb/ *n* LANGUAGE same as **vocabulary** (sense 3) (*informal*) [Early 20C. Shortening]

vo·ca·ble /vṓkəb'l/ *n* a single word considered only as a grouping of sounds or letters, not in terms of its meaning (*dated formal*) ■ *adj* capable of being pronounced or spoken (*formal*) [Mid-16C. Directly or via French < Latin *vocabulum* "name" < *vocare* "call, name"] —**vo·ca·bly** *adv*

vo·cab·u·lar·y /vō kábbyə lèrree, və-/ (*plural* **-ies**) *n* **1.** **WORDS OF LANGUAGE** all the words used in a language as a whole **2.** **WORDS OF SUBJECT AREA** the set of words associated with a subject or area of activity, or used by an individual person ○ *the vocabulary of international diplomacy* ○ *The program encourages students to develop a wide scientific vocabulary.* **3.** **LIST OF WORDS** an alphabetical list of words and phrases supplied with definitions or translations **4.** ARTS **RANGE OF EXPRESSIVE TECHNIQUES** a repertoire of expressive forms or techniques used by an artist or in an art form [Mid-16C. < medieval Latin *vocabularium* "of words" < Latin *vocabulum* (see VOCABLE)]

SYNONYMS See ***language*** and ***jargon***[1].

vo·cal /vṓk'l/ *adj* **1.** **SPOKEN** uttered with the voice **2.** **OF VOICE** relating to the voice **3.** **HAVING VOICE** having a voice or using a voice to produce speech or sound **4.** **OUTSPOKEN** using frank, forthright, or insistent speech ○ *a vocal critic of the plan* **5.** MUSIC **OF OR FOR SINGING** composed or arranged for singing, or relating to the art or techniques of singing **6.** **NOISY WITH VOICES** full of the sound of voices ○ *vocal enthusiasm* **7.** PHON same as **vocalic** ■ *n* **1.** **SUNG PART** the sung part of a piece of pop music or jazz **2.** MUSIC **POP OR JAZZ SONG** a song in the pop or jazz style [14C. < Latin *vocalis* < *voc-*, stem of *vox* "voice"] —**vo·cal·i·ty** /vō kállətee/ *n* —**vo·cal·ly** *adv*

vo·cal cords *npl* a pair of fibrous sheets of tissue that span the cavity of the larynx and produce sounds by vibrating

vo·cal folds *npl* a pair of folds in the wall of the larynx situated just above the vocal cords

vo·cal·ic /vō kállik/ *adj* **1.** relating to or containing vowels **2.** used or acting as a vowel —**vo·cal·i·cal·ly** *adv*

vo·cal·ise /vṑk'l éez/ *n* **1.** a voice training exercise in which a singer sings using only vowel sounds, especially one single vowel sound **2.** a passage or composition for performance in which a singer sings only vowel sounds, especially one single vowel sound [Late 19C. < French < *vocaliser* "vocalize"]

vo·cal·ism /vṓk'l ìzzəm/ *n* **1.** **USE OF VOICE** the use of the voice in producing speech, singing, or other sounds **2.** MUSIC **ART OF SINGING** the art or technique of singing **3.** PHON **VOWELS OF LANGUAGE** the range of vowels used in a language **4.** PHON **VOWEL** a vowel sound

vo·cal·ist /vṓk'list/ *n* a singer, especially of pop music or jazz

vo·cal·ize /vṓk'l ìz/ (**-ized, -iz·ing, -iz·es**) *v* **1.** *vti* **EXPRESS SOMETHING WITH VOICE** to use the voice to express something **2.** *vt* **ARTICULATE SOMETHING** to use words to express something ○ *vocalized their concerns* **3.** *vti* PHON **TRANSFORM INTO VOWEL** to transform a consonant into a vowel sound in speaking, or be transformed into a vowel **4.** *vt* PHON same as **voice** *v* (sense 2) **5.** *vt* LING same as **vowelize** **6.** *vi* MUSIC **SING WITHOUT WORDS** to sing without words, using only one or more vowel sounds, especially as a vocal exercise to warm up the voice —**vo·cal·i·za·tion** /vṑk'li záysh'n/ *n* —**vo·cal·iz·er** *n*

vo·cal score *n* the score of a vocal work, especially an opera, that gives the vocal parts in full with the orchestral parts transcribed for piano

vo·cal tic *n* a sudden noise or shout produced involuntarily, especially as a symptom of Tourette's syndrome or a similar neurological condition

vocat. *abbr* GRAM vocative

vo·ca·tion /vō káysh'n/ *n* **1.** somebody's work, job, or profession, especially a type of work demanding special commitment **2.** a strong feeling of being destined or called to undertake a specific type of work, especially a sense of being chosen by God for religious work or a religious life [15C. < Latin *vocation-* < *vocat-*, past participle of *vocare* "call, name"]

ORIGIN The Latin word *vocare* "to call, name," from which ***vocation*** is derived, is also the source of the English words *advocate, convoke, evoke, invoke, provoke, revoke, vocable, vocabulary, vocative,* and *vouch.*

vo·ca·tion·al /vō káyshən'l, -káyshnəl/ *adj* **1.** relating to education designed to provide the necessary skills for a specific job or career **2.** relating to somebody's vocation —**vo·ca·tion·al·ly** *adv*

vo·ca·tion·al guid·ance *n* guidance in the form of interviews and tests to see which job or career would best suit somebody's individual abilities and personality

vo·ca·tion·al·ism /vō káyshən'l ìzzəm, -káyshnə lìzzəm/ *n* an emphasis on vocational training in education

vo·ca·tion·al school *n* a secondary school at which students are trained in a trade or skill to be pursued as a career

voc·a·tive /vókətiv/ *n* **1.** **GRAMMATICAL CASE OF SOMEBODY ADDRESSED** a grammatical case that indicates that somebody or something is being directly addressed by the speaker. In Julius Caesar's dying words to Brutus "et tu, Brute," "Brute" is in the vocative. **2.** **WORD IN VOCATIVE** a word or form in the vocative case ■ *adj* **INDICATING SOMEBODY OR SOMETHING ADDRESSED** in or relating to the vocative [15C. < Latin *vocativus* < *vocat-* (see VOCATION)]

Voc Ed /vòk éd/ *abbr* vocational education

vo·cif·er·ate /vō síffə ràyt/ (**-at·ed, -at·ing, -ates**) *vti* to shout something out loudly [Late 16C. < Latin *vociferari* "carry voice" < *voc-* (see VOCAL) + *ferre* "carry"] —**vo·cif·er·a·tion** /vō sìffə ráysh'n/ *n*

vo·cif·er·ous /vō síffərəss/ *adj* **1.** shouting in a noisy and determined way **2.** characterized by noisy and determined shouting [Early 17C. < Latin *vociferari* (see VOCIFERATE)] —**vo·cif·er·ous·ly** *adv* —**vo·cif·er·ous·ness** *n*

vo·cod·er /vō kōdər/ *n* an electronic device or computer program that converts speech into digital form and resynthesizes it at a later time or after transmission as artificial speech [Mid-20C. < VOICE + CODE]

vod·ka /vódkə/ *n* a colorless distilled liquor originally from Russia that is made from a grain such as rye or wheat or from potatoes [Early 19C. < Russian, "small water" < *voda* "water"]

vod·ka·ti·ni /vòdkə teénee/ *n* a cocktail consisting of vodka mixed with dry vermouth and ice, often served in a frosted glass [Late 20C. Blend of VODKA + MARTINI]

vo·doun /vō dóon/, **vo·dun** *n* RELIG same as **voodoo** *n* (sense 1) [Late 19C. < Fon *vodũ* "fetish"]

vog /vog/ *n* air pollution in the form of sulfur dioxide emitted from Kilauea volcano on the island of Hawaii [Blend of VOLCANO + SMOG or FOG]

vogue[1] /vōg/ *n* **1.** PREVAILING FASHION the prevailing fashion at a particular time **2.** POPULARITY the state of being widely popular and fashionable at a particular time ○ *in vogue* ■ *adj* FASHIONABLE currently popular or fashionable [Late 16C. < French, literally "rowing" < *voguer* "to row"]

vogue[2] /vōg/ (**vogued, vogu·ing** or **vogue·ing, vogues**) *vi* to dance by imitating the poses struck by fashion models [Late 20C. After *Vogue*, fashion magazine] —**vogu·ing** *n*

vogu·ish /vōgish/ *adj* **1.** elegantly fashionable and stylish in appearance **2.** enjoying brief or sudden popularity —**vogu·ish·ly** *adv* —**vogu·ish·ness** *n*

Vo·gul /vō gòol/ (*plural same* or **-guls**) *n* a member of a people who live along the western tributaries of the Ob River and the central and northern Ural Mountains in Russia [Late 18C. < Russian *vogul*] —**Vo·gul** *adj*

voice /voyss/ *n* **1.** SOUND MADE USING VOCAL ORGANS the sound produced by using the vocal organs, especially the sound used in speech **2.** SOUND OF SINGING the musical sound produced in singing **3.** ABILITY TO USE VOICE the ability to produce vocal sounds for speaking or singing ○ *have a good voice* **4.** SOUND LIKE HUMAN VOICE a sound similar to a human voice ○ *listening to the voice of the wind* **5.** RIGHT TO STATE OPINION a right to express an opinion ○ *sections of society that feel they have no voice* **6.** EXPRESSED OPINION an expressed opinion or desire ○ *hear the voice of the people* **7.** REPRESENTATIVE EXPRESSION a medium of communication or expression for somebody or something ○ *the voice of reason* **8.** MUSIC SINGER a singer taking a part in a musical composition **9.** MUSIC SINGING PART a sung part in a musical composition **10.** PHON VIBRATION OF VOCAL CORDS IN SPEAKING the passing of air across the vocal cords so as to create audible vibrations **11.** GRAM FORM OF VERB the form of a verb that indicates the relation of the subject to the verb. In the active voice, the subject performs the action, as in "I hit him," while in the passive voice the subject suffers the effect of the action, as in "he was hit." ■ *v* (**voiced, voic·ing, voic·es**) **1.** *vt* SPEAK SOMETHING to express a sentiment or opinion verbally **2.** *vt* PHON PRONOUNCE SOMETHING USING VOCAL CORDS to pronounce a consonant or vowel by passing air across the vocal cords so as to create audible vibrations **3.** *vt* MUSIC REGULATE TONE OF ORGAN to regulate the tone of an organ pipe in order to produce the desired sound **4.** MEDIA DO VOICEOVER FOR to provide the voiceover for a character in a cartoon or a radio or television advertisement [13C. Via Old French *vois* < Latin *vox*] —**voic·er** *n* ◇ **be in (good) voice** to be singing well or speaking well ◇ **with one voice** simultaneously or unanimously

voice-ac·ti·vat·ed *adj* operated by the user's spoken commands, rather than by physical input

voice box *n* ANAT same as **larynx**

voiced /voyst/ *adj* **1.** having or conducted in a voice of a particular kind (*often used in combination*) ○ *a low-voiced conversation* **2.** describes a consonant or vowel pronounced by passing air across the vocal cords to create audible vibrations, as is the "s" sound in the word "his"

voice·ful /vóysfəl/ *adj* having a loud or ringing voice (*literary*)

voice·less /vóyssləss/ *adj* **1.** SAYING NOTHING maintaining a silence **2.** HAVING NO SAY having no vote or influence ○ *the voiceless people in a dictatorship* **3.** HAVING NO VOICE not endowed with a voice **4.** PHON PRONOUNCED WITHOUT VIBRATION OF VOCAL CORDS describes a consonant or vowel pronounced without passing air across the vocal cords and creating audible vibrations, as is the "s" sound in the word "hiss" —**voice·less·ly** *adv* —**voice·less·ness** *n*

voice mail *n* an electronic communications system that stores digitized recordings of telephone messages for later playback (*hyphenated before a noun*)

voice-o·ver /vóyss ōvər/ *n* the voice of, or the words spoken by, an unseen narrator, commentator, or character in a motion picture or television program

voice o·ver In·ter·net pro·to·col *n* ONLINE full form of **VoIP**

voice-over-the-Net *adj* describes voice communication using VoIP technology

voice·print /vóyss print/ *n* a representation in graph form of the frequencies that make up somebody's voice [Mid-20C. < VOICE + FINGERPRINT]

voice·print i·den·ti·fi·ca·tion *n* the use of the sound frequencies of speech as a method of identifying somebody

voice rec·og·ni·tion *n* **1.** COMPUT same as **speech recognition** **2.** a computer function that enables the machine to recognize the voice of a person speaking into a microphone attached to it

voice vote *n* a vote taken in a parliament or other legislative body in which voters cry out "aye" or "no," or "yea" and "nay," with the louder cry winning the vote

voice writ·er *n* somebody who records proceedings by voice, speaking into a device that silences and records the spoken words for subsequent transcription by hand or voice recognition software —**voice·writ·ing** *n*

void /voyd/ *adj* **1.** NOT LEGALLY VALID having no legal force ○ *declared the will null and void* **2.** DEVOID totally lacking in something (*formal*) ○ *a personality void of all compassion* **3.** NOT CONTAINING ANYTHING having no contents **4.** VACANT not occupied **5.** POINTLESS ineffective or useless **6.** CARDS HAVING NO CARDS IN SUIT lacking any cards in a particular suit in a hand dealt in a card game ■ *n* **1.** EMPTY SPACE a large empty space **2.** PRIVATION a state of loss or privation **3.** FEELING OF LOSS a feeling of loneliness and emptiness **4.** GAP a gap or opening **5.** CARDS LACK OF CARDS IN SUIT a complete lack of cards in a particular suit in a hand dealt in a card game ○ *a void in spades* ■ *v* (**void·ed, void·ing, voids**) **1.** *vt* MAKE SOMETHING LEGALLY INVALID to deprive something of legal force **2.** *vt* EMPTY CONTENTS OF SOMETHING to empty out the contents of something, or empty something of its contents **3.** *vti* EMPTY BOWELS OR BLADDER to empty the bowels or bladder [13C. < Old French *voide* "empty" < assumed Vulgar Latin *vocitus*, alteration of Latin *vocivus*] —**void·a·ble** *adj* —**void·er** *n* —**void·ness** *n*

SYNONYMS See ***vacant***.

void·ance /vóyd'nss/ *n* **1.** INVALIDATION OF CONTRACT the act of depriving a contract of legal force **2.** ACT OF EMPTYING the act of voiding or emptying something **3.** VACANCY the situation of having no incumbent or occupant, e.g., no bishop in a diocese

void deck *n* in Malaysia and Singapore, the empty ground floor of an apartment block, used for social events by people living in the block

void·ed /vóydəd/ *adj* **1.** having been deprived of legal force ○ *a voided check* **2.** in heraldry, having the center and a narrow surrounding area removed or left empty

voi·là /vwaa laá/ *interj* used to bring somebody's attention to something, especially in order to elicit appreciation or approval [Mid-18C. < French < *voi* "see!" + *là* "there"]

voile /voyl/ *n* a crisp lightweight translucent fabric made from cotton, synthetic fiber, or wool [Late 19C. < French, "veil" < Latin *vela* (see VEIL)]

VoIP /voyp/ *n* a technology that enables voice messages to be sent via the Internet, often simultaneously with data in text or other forms. Full form **voice over Internet protocol**

voir dire /vwaar deér/ *n* the preliminary examination of a witness or juror to determine his or her competency to give or hear evidence [Late 17C. < Law French < Old French *voir* "truth" + *dire* "speak"]

voix cé·leste /vwaa say lést/ *n* an organ stop that gives a light wavering otherworldly quality to the notes played [Late 19C. < French < *voix* "voice" + *céleste* "heavenly"]

vol. *abbr* **1.** GEOG volcano **2.** MEASURE volume **3.** volunteer

Vo·lans /vō lànz/ *n* a small constellation of the southern hemisphere. See illustration at **constellation** [Mid-20C. Shortening of modern Latin *Piscis Volans* "flying fish," earlier name of the constellation]

vo·lant /vōlənt/ *adj* **1.** ABLE TO FLY flying or having the power of flight **2.** NIMBLE moving quickly, lightly, and easily (*literary*) **3.** HERALDRY HAVING WINGS SPREAD in heraldry, having the wings outspread as in flight [Early 16C. < French, present participle of *voler* "fly" < Latin *volare*]

Vo·la·pük /vōlə pòok, vóllə-/ *n* a synthetic language based on English and German, invented by Johann Martin Schleyer in 1880 [Late 19C. < *vol*, alteration of WORLD + *pük* "speech," alteration of SPEAK] —**Vo·la·pük** *adj*

vo·lar /vōlər/ *adj* relating to the palm of the hand or the sole of the foot [Early 19C. < *vola* "hollow of the hand or foot" < Latin, "sole, palm"]

vol·a·tile /vóllət'l/ *adj* **1.** UNSTABLE AND POTENTIALLY DANGEROUS apt to become suddenly violent or dangerous **2.** UNPREDICTABLE OR FICKLE changeable in mood, temper, or desire **3.** CHANGING SUDDENLY characterized by or prone to sudden change **4.** SHORT-LIVED continuing for only a short time **5.** CHEM PRONE TO EVAPORATION evaporating at a relatively low temperature **6.** COMPUT LOSING DATA WHEN POWER IS OFF describes a computer memory that does not store data when the power is turned off ■ *n* CHEM VOLATILE SUBSTANCE a substance that evaporates at a relatively low temperature [Late 16C. < Latin *volatilis* < *volat-*, past participle of *volare* "fly"] —**vol·a·til·i·ty** /vòllə tíllətee/ *n*

vol·a·tile or·gan·ic com·pound *n* an organic compound that evaporates at a relatively low temperature and contributes to air pollution, e.g., ethylene, propylene, benzene, or styrene

vol·a·til·ize /vóllət'l ìz/ (**-ized, -iz·ing, -iz·es**) *vti* to change into a vapor, or cause a solid or liquid to be changed into a vapor —**vol·a·til·iz·a·ble** *adj* —**vol·a·til·i·za·tion** /vòllət'li záysh'n/ *n*

vol-au-vent /vàwlə vaáN/ *n* a small light pastry shell traditionally filled with meat or fish in a sauce [< French, literally "flight in the wind"]

vol·can·ic /vol kánnik/ *adj* **1.** OF VOLCANOES relating to or originating from a volcano **2.** CONSISTING OF VOLCANOES characterized by or made up of volcanoes **3.** SUDDEN AND VIOLENT characterized by sudden violent outbursts ○ *a volcanic temper* [Late 18C. < French *volcanique* < *volan* "volcano"] —**vol·can·i·cal·ly** *adv*

vol·can·ic arc *n* GEOG same as **island arc**

vol·can·ic bomb *n* a lump of lava ejected from a volcano that has acquired a characteristic form as a result of its solidification while traveling through the air

vol·can·ic cone *n* a cone-shaped mass of material that has built up around the crater of a volcano

vol·can·ic dust *n* fine particles of ash that are suspended in the atmosphere after a volcanic eruption

vol·can·ic glass *n* natural glass formed when molten lava from a volcano cools too quickly to crystallize

vol·can·ic·i·ty /vòlkə níssətee/ *n* the tendency or likelihood of a volcano or group of volcanoes to erupt [Mid-19C. < French *volcanicité* < *volcan* "volcano"]

vol·can·ic plug, **vol·can·ic neck** *n* a massive cylindrical formation of solidified lava that once blocked the vent of a volcano, now exposed after erosion of softer surrounding material

vol·ca·nism /vólkə nìzzəm/ *n* the processes involved in the formation of volcanoes, and in the transfer of magma and volatile material from the interior of the Earth to its surface [Mid-19C. < French *volcanisme* < *volcan* "volcano"]

vol·ca·nize /vólkə nīz/ (**-nized, -niz·ing, -niz·es**) *vt* to cause something to change as a result of volcanic activity —**vol·ca·ni·za·tion** /vòlkəni záysh'n/ *n*

MAJOR VOLCANOES OF THE WORLD

Cotopaxi *Ecuador*
Elevation [**19,347 ft / 5,897 m**]
World's highest active volcano

Mauna Loa *Hawaii*
Elevation [**13,680 ft / 4,170 m**]
Major eruption 1984

Erebus *Antarctica*
Elevation [**12,448 ft / 3,794 m**]
Major eruptions 1970s

Cameroon *Cameroon*
Elevation [**13,435 ft / 4,095 m**]
Major eruption 1982

Etna *Italy*
Elevation [**10,902 ft / 3,323 m**]
Over 90 recorded eruptions

Ruapehu *New Zealand*
Elevation [**9,177 ft / 2,797 m**]
Major eruptions 1995, 1996

St. Helens *United States*
Elevation [**8,365 ft / 2,550 m**]
Major eruption 1980

Vesuvius *Italy*
Elevation [**4,190 ft/1,277 m**]
Major eruption 79 AD—destroying Roman Pompeii

Soufriere Hills *Montserrat*
Elevation [**3,002 ft / 915 m**]
Major eruption 1997—much of island left uninhabitable

Krakatau *Indonesia*
Elevation [**2,667 ft / 813 m**]
Major eruption 1883—tidal waves from eruption estimated to have caused over 30,000 deaths

vol·ca·no /vol káynō/ (*plural* **-noes** or **-nos**) *n* **1.** a naturally occurring opening in the surface of the Earth through which molten, gaseous, and solid material is ejected **2.** a mountain created by the deposition and accumulation of materials ejected from a vent in a central crater [Early 17C. Via Italian < Latin *Volcanus, Vulcanus* "Vulcan"]

CULTURAL NOTE ***Under the Volcano***, a novel (1947) by British writer Malcolm Lowry. Set in Mexico on the annual Day of the Dead, it describes the last hours of British consul Geoffrey Firman, who, depressed by the failure of his marriage and the onset of war, slowly drinks himself to death. A harrowing psychological study, it can also be read as an allegory of the disintegration of Western values.

vol·ca·nol·o·gy /vòlkə nóllǝjee/ *n* the scientific study of volcanoes, including their formation, signs of an eruption, and other aspects of volcanic activity —**vol·ca·no·log·ic** /vòlkənə lójjik/ *adj* —**vol·ca·no·log·i·cal** *adj* —**vol·ca·nol·o·gist** *n*

vole

vole[1] /vōl/ (*plural* **voles** or *same*) *n* a small rodent similar to a mouse but with a shorter tail and legs and a stocky body. Native to: North America, Europe, Asia. Genus: *Microtus*. [Early 19C. < Norwegian *voll mus* "field mouse"]

vole[2] /vōl/ *n* in a card game such as bridge, a taking of all the tricks in a single hand [Late 17C. < French, probably < *voler* "to fly" < Latin *volare*]

Vol·ga /vólgə, váwlgə/ longest river of Europe, in western Russia. It rises northwest of Moscow and flows southeast and south before emptying into the Caspian Sea. Length: 2,300 mi./3,700 km.

Vol·go·grad /vólgə gràd, vólgə-/ industrial and port city in southwestern Russia on the Volga River. It is an important rail junction and inland port. In World War II, the city was subjected to a long siege by German forces that proved to be one of the turning points of the war. Population: 1,260,171 (1995). Former name **Stalingrad** (1925–61)

vol·i·tant /vóllət'nt/ *adj* **1.** flying, or capable of flight **2.** moving about rapidly or constantly [Early 17C. < Latin *volitare* "keep on flying" < *volare* "to fly"]

vo·li·tion /və lísh'n/ *n* **1.** the act of exercising the will **2.** the ability to make conscious choices or decisions [Early 17C. Directly or via French < Latin *volition-* < *vol-* (see VOLUNTARY)] —**vo·li·tion·al** *adj* —**vo·li·tion·al·ly** *adv*

vol·i·tive /vóllətiv/ *adj* **1.** relating to or beginning in the will **2.** GRAM same as **desiderative** (sense 2) [15C. < medieval Latin *volitivus* < Latin *volition-* (see VOLITION)]

Volks·lied /fáwlks leed, fóks-/ (*plural* **-lie·der** /-leedər/) *n* a traditional German folk song [Mid-19C. < German, "people's song"]

vol·ley /vóllee/ *n* **1. SIMULTANEOUS EXPRESSION OF SOMETHING** a simultaneous rapid expression of something such as curses or protests **2. MISSILES FIRED** a discharge of missiles or other projectiles fired simultaneously **3. FIRING OF WEAPONS** a simultaneous discharge of several weapons, especially firearms **4. SWING AT BALL** in tennis or soccer, a swing, kick, or hit at a ball before it touches the ground ■ *v* (**-leyed, -ley·ing, -leys**) **1.** *vti* **STRIKE BALL BEFORE IT LANDS** to hit or kick a ball before it reaches the ground, e.g., in tennis or soccer **2.** *vti* **FIRE SIMULTANEOUSLY** to fire weapons simultaneously, or be fired simultaneously **3.** *vti* **SAY RAPIDLY** to say something forcefully or loudly and rapidly, or be spoken forcefully or loudly and rapidly **4.** *vi* **MOVE RAPIDLY** to move rapidly or loudly [Late 16C. < French *volée* < Latin *volare* "to fly"] —**vol·ley·er** *n*

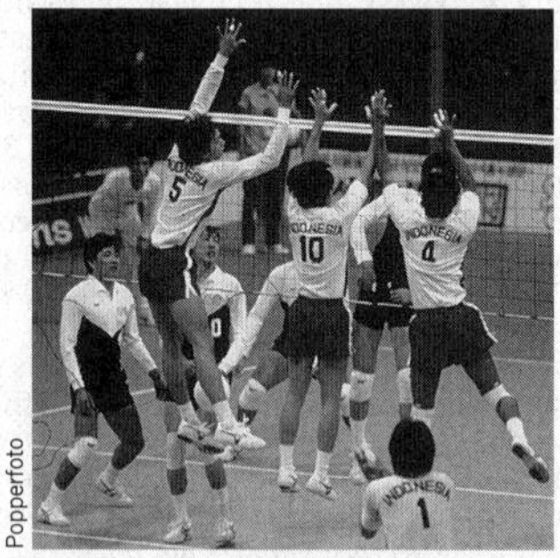

volleyball: players jump to block a smash

vol·ley·ball /vóllee bàwl/ *n* **1.** a sport in which two teams hit a large ball over a high net using their hands, played on a rectangular court **2.** a large, usually white inflated ball used to play volleyball —**vol·ley·ball·er** *n*

vol·plane /vól plàyn/ *vi* (**-planed, -plan·ing, -planes**) **1. GLIDE TO GROUND** to glide toward the ground in an airplane with the engine turned off **2. MOVE BY GLIDING** to travel or move by gliding ■ *n* **ACT OF GLIDING** a glide toward the ground in an aircraft with the engine turned off [Early 20C. < French *vol plané* "planed flight"]

vols. *abbr* volumes

Vol·sci /váwlskee, vól sī, vólshee/ *npl* an ancient people who lived in Latium, a region of central Italy that was taken over by the Romans during the 5th and 4th centuries B.C. —**Vol·sci·an** *n, adj*

volt[1] /vōlt/ *n* the unit of electromotive force and electric potential difference equal to the difference between two points in a circuit carrying one ampere of current and dissipating one watt of power. Symbol **V** [Late 19C. After Alessandro VOLTA]

volt[2] /vōlt, vawlt/, **volte** *n* **1.** in dressage, a circular movement executed by a horse **2.** in fencing, a sudden leap made to elude an opponent's thrust [Late 16C. Via French *volte* < Italian *volta* (see VOLTA)]

vol·ta /vóltə, vóltə/ (*plural* **-te** /-tày/) *n* **1. ITALIAN DANCE** a fast Italian dance of the 16th and 17th centuries **2. VOLTA MUSIC** the music for a volta **3. ONE PLAYING OF MUSICAL PASSAGE** a single playing of a passage of music that may then be repeated [Late 16C. < Italian, "a turn" < *volgere* "to turn" < Latin *volvere* "to roll"]

Vol·ta /vóltə, vóltə/ river in southeastern Ghana, formed by the confluence of the Black Volta and White Volta rivers and emptying into the Atlantic Ocean. Length: 930 mi./1,500 km.

Vol·ta /vóltə/, **Alessandro, Count** (1745–1827) Italian physicist. He developed the first electric battery (1800).

volt·age /vóltij/ *n* electric potential expressed in volts

volt·age di·vid·er *n* a resistor or series of resistors used to provide various voltages that are fractions of the source voltage

vol·ta·ic /vol táy ik, vōl-/ *adj* relating to or denoting direct electric current produced by chemical action [Early 19C. < After Alessandro VOLTA]

Vol·ta·ic /vol táy ik/ *adj* **1.** relating to Burkina-Faso, or to its people or culture **2.** relating to the Gur group of languages, spoken chiefly in Burkina-Faso and Ghana [Mid-20C. < the River VOLTA]

vol·ta·ic bat·ter·y *n* an electric battery made up of one or more primary cells

vol·ta·ic cell *n* ELEC same as **primary cell**

vol·ta·ic cou·ple *n* two different metals immersed in an electrolyte that produce a potential difference by chemical action

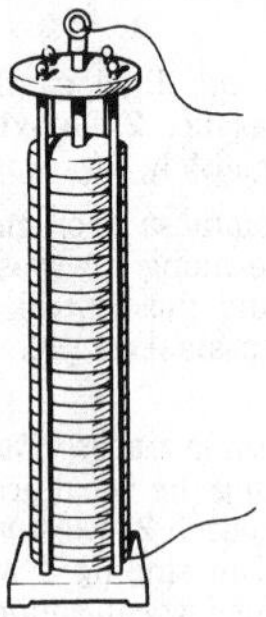

voltaic pile

vol·ta·ic pile *n* a source of electricity consisting of a stack of dissimilar metal disks separated by a porous material soaked in electrolyte that acts as a battery

Vol·taire /vōl tér/ (1694–1778) French writer and philosopher. A leading figure in the Enlightenment, he produced a range of literary works embodying his radical spirit and religious ideas. They include *Philosophical Letters* (1734), *Candide* (1759), and the *Dictionnaire philosophique* (*Philosophical Dictionary*) (1764). Born **Arouet, François Marie**

"In this best of possible worlds...all is for the best."
[Voltaire, *Candide*; 1759]

"If God did not exist, it would be necessary to invent Him."
[Voltaire, "À l'auteur du livre des trois Imposteurs (To the Author of The Three Impostors)," *Épîtres (Epistles)*; 1769]

vol·ta·ism /vóltə ìzzəm, vóltə-/ *n* PHYS same as **galvanism** (sense 1)

volte[1] /vōlt, vawlt/ *n* RIDING, FENCING another spelling of **volt**[2]

vol·te[2] /vóltay/ DANCE, MUSIC plural of **volta**

volte-face /vàwlt fáass, vàwltə-/ *n* **1.** a sudden reversal in opinion or policy **2.** a change in position so as to be facing the opposite direction [Early 19C. Via French < Italian *voltafaccia* "turn of the face"]

volt·me·ter /vólt meetər/ *n* an instrument calibrated in volts that measures the electromotive force or potential difference between two points in a circuit

vol·u·ble /vóllyəb'l/ *adj* **1.** talking easily and at length, or involving lengthy talking **2.** twining or twisting [14C. Directly or via French < Latin *volubilis* < *volvere* "to roll"] —**vol·u·bil·i·ty** /vòllyə bíllətee/ *n* —**vol·u·bly** *adv*

vol·ume /vóllyəm, -yoom/ *n* **1. SPACE INSIDE OBJECT** the size of a three-dimensional space enclosed within or occupied by an object. Symbol **V 2. AMOUNT** the total amount of something **3.** LOUDNESS the loudness of a sound **4.** SOUND CONTROL the knob or button on a radio, television, or audio player that controls loudness **5.** BOOK a bound collection of printed or written pages **6.** BOOK OF SET a single book that belongs to a set of books **7.** PUBL CONSECUTIVE MAGAZINE ISSUES a set of issues of a periodical spanning one calendar year **8.** THICKNESS the thick quality or appearance of somebody's hair ■ *adj* INVOLVING LARGE QUANTITIES using or involving large amounts or quantities ○ *offering volume discounts on carpeting* [14C. Via Old French < Latin *volumen* "roll, scroll, book" < *volvere* "to roll"] ◇ **speak volumes** to be highly expressive or significant

vol·umed /vóllyəmd, -yo͞omd/ *adj* **1.** published in a series or set of a number of books (*usually used in combination*) ○ *a three-volumed set* **2.** forming or rolling in a rounded mass (*literary*)

vol·u·me·ter /vóllyə meetər/ *n* an instrument used to measure the volume of a solid, liquid, or gas

vol·u·met·ric /vòllyə méttrik/ *adj* relating to volume, or using measurement by volume —**vol·u·met·ri·cal·ly** *adv*

vol·u·met·ric a·nal·y·sis *n* **1.** an analysis of liquids using measured volumes of standard chemical reagents **2.** an analysis of gas by volume

vo·lu·mi·nous /və lo͞omənəss/ *adj* **1.** LARGE having great size, capacity, or fullness ○ *a voluminous cloak* **2.** EXTREMELY LONG very lengthy and taking up many pages or books ○ *a voluminous report* **3.** PROLIFIC producing a large amount of creative work ○ *a voluminous writer* [Early 17C. < late Latin *voluminosus* "with many coils" < Latin *volumen* (see VOLUME)] —**vo·lu·mi·nous·ly** *adv* —**vo·lu·mi·nous·ness** *n*

vol·un·ta·rism /vóllәntә rizzәm/ *n* **1.** RELIANCE ON VOLUNTEERS the use of or dependence on the work of volunteers rather than paid employees to do the work of an organization or to achieve something **2.** PHILOSOPHICAL THEORY the philosophical theory that regards the will rather than the intellect as the essential principle of humankind or the cosmos **3.** RELIANCE ON VOLUNTARY CONTRIBUTIONS the use of or dependence on voluntary contributions rather than government funds to keep an institution such as a school or church in existence —**vol·un·ta·rist** *n* —**vol·un·ta·ris·tic** /vòllәntә rístik/ *adj*

vol·un·tar·y /vóllən tèrree/ *adj* **1.** OF FREE WILL arising, acting, or resulting from somebody's own choice or decision rather than because of external pressure or force **2.** WITHOUT PAY performing, working, or done without financial reward ○ *voluntary work* **3.** USING VOLUNTEERS composed of, functioning with or requiring volunteers ○ *voluntary organizations* **4.** UK NOT PART OF GOVERNMENT not part of statutory provision such as that of social services, and usually maintained at least in part by private charitable donations rather than by government or other official support ○ *a voluntary organization* **5.** HAVING WILL having the capacity required to make conscious choices or decisions **6.** LAW WITHOUT LEGAL OBLIGATION not involving legal obligation, coercion, or persuasion ○ *a voluntary agreement* **7.** LAW DONE ON PURPOSE performed or carried out with intention rather than by accident ○ *voluntary manslaughter* **8.** LAW GIVEN WITHOUT PAYMENT IN RETURN done or given freely with no promise of money or other recompense ■ *n* (*plural* **-ies**) **1.** SHORT COMPOSITION a short musical composition, often played on a solo instrument, that introduces a longer work **2.** MUSIC CHURCH MUSIC a piece of music or improvisation for the organ, played before, during, or at the end of a church service [14C. < Latin *voluntarius* < *voluntas* "will, choice" < *vol-*, stem of *velle* "to wish"] —**vol·un·tar·i·ly** /vòllən térrəlee, vóllən tèrrəlee/ *adv* —**vol·un·tar·i·ness** *n*

vol·un·tar·y·ism /vóllən teree ìzzəm/ *n* PUBLIC ADMIN same as **voluntarism** (sense 3) —**vol·un·tar·y·ist** *n*

vol·un·tar·y mus·cle *n* a muscle, usually made up of striated fibers, that is consciously controlled

vol·un·teer /vòllən te͞er/ *n* **1.** SOMEBODY WHO WORKS FOR NOTHING somebody who works without being paid **2.** SOMEBODY ACTING VOLUNTARILY somebody who does something voluntarily, especially something undesirable **3.** VOLUNTARY RECRUIT TO ARMED FORCES somebody who has freely offered to serve in the armed services **4.** BOT CULTIVATED PLANT GROWING NATURALLY a cultivated plant, especially a crop plant, that grows without having been intentionally sown or planted **5.** LAW SOMEBODY ACTING WITHOUT LEGAL OBLIGATION a participant in something who is not legally bound to participate and does not expect to be paid **6.** LAW SOMEBODY GIVEN PROPERTY a recipient of property who does not have to pay for it or give anything in return **7.** *Southeast US* AGRIC SECOND CROP IN SAME SEASON a second crop or growth of grass in the same season, after the first harvest or mowing ■ *v* (**-teered, -teer·ing, -teers**) **1.** *vti* OFFER FREE HELP to do charitable or helpful work without receiving pay for it ○ *volunteers his time* ○ *Many companies now encourage their staff to volunteer.* **2.** *vti* DO SOMETHING BY CHOICE to perform, or offer to perform, work of your own free will ○ *volunteered to work the night shift* **3.** *vt* TELL SOMETHING WITHOUT BEING ASKED to tell somebody something or give information without being asked ○ *volunteering information* **4.** *vt* OFFER SOMEBODY ELSE'S HELP to suggest somebody else as a helper (*informal*) ○ *volunteered her secretary for a few days* **5.** *vi* OFFER TO DO MILITARY SERVICE to offer to serve in one of the armed services without being required by law to join ■ *adj, adv Southeast US* AGRIC AS VOLUNTEER CROP as a crop that is the second crop or growth of grass in the same season, after the first harvest or mowing [Late 16C. Via French *volontaire* < Latin *voluntarius* (see VOLUNTARY)]

REGIONAL NOTE ***Volunteer*** is used of a second or unplanted crop, often one that develops from seed left the year before, throughout the Mid-Atlantic rural South. It can be a noun (*harvest the volunteers*), adjective (*volunteer tomatoes*), or adverb (*came up volunteer*). See also ***aftermath***.

vol·un·teer ar·my *n* an army that relies on recruiting people who enlist voluntarily, rather than conscripting recruits by law

vol·un·teer crop *n Southeast US* AGRIC same as **volunteer** *n* (sense 7)

vol·un·teer·ism /vòllən te͞er ìzzəm/ *n* the practice of using volunteer workers, especially in community service or educational organizations and programs

Vol·un·teers of A·mer·i·ca *n* a religious organization that provides community service programs

Vol·un·teer State *n* a nickname for Tennessee

vol·un·teer va·ca·tion *n US* a vacation during which somebody does volunteer work such as cleaning up the environment or housing construction and repair

~~**voluptious**~~ incorrect spelling of **voluptuous**

vo·lup·tu·ar·y /və lúpchoo èrree/ (*plural* **-ies**) *n* somebody whose life is devoted to enjoying luxury and the pleasures of the senses [Early 17C. < Latin *voluptuarius* < *voluptas* "pleasure"]

vo·lup·tu·ous /və lúpchoo əss/ *adj* **1.** sensual in appearance, or providing sensual pleasure **2.** inclined or devoted to a life of sensual pleasure [14C. Directly or via French *voluptueux* < Latin *voluptuosus* < *voluptas* "pleasure"] —**vo·lup·tu·ous·ly** *adv* —**vo·lup·tu·ous·ness** *n*

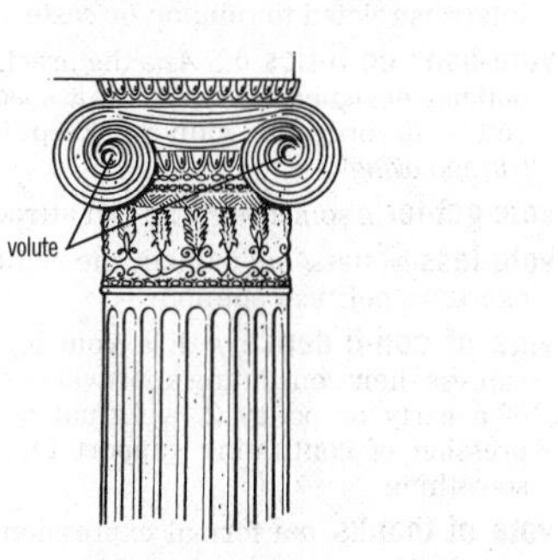

volute (sense 2)

vo·lute /və lo͞ot/ *n* **1.** SPIRAL SHAPE a spiral form or structure, e.g., the whorl in the shell of a snail **2.** ARCHIT DECORATIVE SCROLL a carved spiral decoration, usually on an Ionic capital **3.** MARINE BIOL TROPICAL MOLLUSK a gastropod mollusk with a colorful spiral shell. Native to: tropical waters. Family: Volutidae. ■ *adj* SPIRALING moving in or following a spiral path [Mid-16C. Directly or via French < Latin *voluta*, feminine past participle of *volvere* "to roll"]

ORIGIN The Latin word *volvere* "to roll," from which ***volute*** is derived, is also the source of the English words *convolute, convolvulus, devolution, evolution, involve, revolt, revolution, revolve, vault*[1], *voluble*, and *volume*.

vol·u·tin /vóllyətin, və lo͞ot'n/ *n* an easily stained substance found in the cytoplasm of some bacterial and fungal cells that serves to store phosphates for the energy needs of the cell [Early 20C. < modern Latin *Spirillum volutans* "rolling spirillum," bacterium in which first found < Latin *volutare* "wallow"]

vo·lu·tion /və lo͞osh'n/ *n* **1.** a shape that coils, twists, or turns around a center **2.** a spiral segment of a gastropod's shell [15C. < late Latin *volution-* < Latin *volvere* "to roll"]

vol·va /vólvə/ *n* a cup-shaped structure that encircles the base of the stalk of some mushrooms [Mid-18C. < modern Latin < Latin *volvere* "to roll"]

vol·vox /vól vòks/ *n* freshwater green algae that form communities made up of hollow multicellular spheres. Genus: *Volvox*. [Late 18C. < modern Latin < Latin *volvere* "to roll"]

vol·vu·lus /vólvyələss/ (*plural* **-li** /vólvyə lī/) *n* a twisting of the digestive tract that leads to partial or complete obstruction and a reduction in blood supply [Late 17C. < medieval Latin < Latin *volvere* "to roll"]

vo·mer /vómər/ *n* a thin plate of bone that forms part of the septum dividing the nasal passages inside the nose [Early 18C. < Latin, "plowshare"; because of its shape] —**vo·mer·ine** /vómə rīn/ *adj*

vom·it /vómmit/ *vti* (**-it·ed, -it·ing, -its**) **1.** THROW UP STOMACH CONTENTS to expel the contents of the stomach through the mouth as a result of a series of involuntary spasms of the stomach muscles **2.** GUSH FORTH to send something out in a forceful stream, or be ejected forcefully ○ *to vomit curses* ■ *n* **1.** EXPELLED STOMACH CONTENTS the stomach contents expelled through the mouth. Technical name **vomitus** **2.** ACT OF VOMITING the act of expelling the stomach contents through the mouth [15C. Directly or via Anglo-French < Latin *vomitus*, past participle of *vomere* "eject, vomit"] —**vom·it·er** *n*

vom·i·to·ry /vómmi tàwree/ *n* (*plural* **-ries**) **1.** OPENING an opening through which matter is ejected (*formal*) **2.** BUILDINGS, ANCIENT HIST ANCIENT ROMAN PASSAGEWAY a passageway, usually in an ancient Roman amphitheater or stadium, connecting a tier of seats with an outside entrance ■ *adj also* **vom·i·tive** /vómmitiv/ MED CAUSING VOMITING causing the vomiting of stomach contents (*dated*) [Early 17C. < Latin *vomitorius* < *vomitus* (see VOMIT)]

vom·i·tus /vómmitəss/ *n* vomited contents of the stomach (*technical*) [Early 20C. < Latin (see VOMIT)]

von, Von see also under surname

von Braun /von brówn/, **Wernher** (1912–77) German engineer. He developed the V-2 rocket for Germany during World War II. After 1945, he worked in the United States developing the launch vehicle used in the Moon landing program.

> "Everything in space obeys the laws of physics. If you know these laws and obey them, space will treat you kindly. And don't tell me that man doesn't belong out there. Man belongs wherever he wants to go; and he'll do plenty well when he gets there."
> [Wernher von Braun, *Time*; February 17, 1958]

Vo Ngu·yen Giap /vŏ no͝o yen yáp, -záp, -ngo͝o yen-/ (*b.* 1912) Vietnamese military leader. In Vietnam, he led Communist fighters against the Japanese (1945), the French (1954), and the United States (1964–73).

Von·ne·gut /vónnigət/, **Kurt** (*b.* 1922) US writer. He is known for his satirical novels, including *Slaughterhouse Five* (1969). Full name **Vonnegut, Jr., Kurt.** See Cultural note at **slaughterhouse**

> "Beware of the man who works hard to learn something, learns it, and finds himself no wiser than before, Bokonon tells us. He is full of murderous resentment of people who are ignorant without having come by their ignorance the hard way."
> [Kurt Vonnegut, *Cat's Cradle*; 1963]

> "A flaw in the human character is that everybody wants to build and nobody wants to do maintenance."
> [Kurt Vonnegut, *Hocus Pocus*; 1969]

von Neu·mann /von nóy maàn/, **John** (1903–57) Hungarian-born US mathematician. He developed game theory and quantum mechanics and was a pioneer in computer theory and design. Born **János von Neumann**

> "In mathematics you don't understand things. You just get used to them."
> [John von Neumann. Quoted in *The Dancing Wu Li Masters*, Gary Zukav; 1979]

von Stern·berg /von stúrn bùrg/, **Josef** (1894–1969) Austrian-born US movie director. His interest in visual style is a notable element in his movies, most notably *The Blue Angel* (1930). Born **Sternberg, Jonas**

> "The only way to succeed is to make people hate you. That way, they remember you."
> [Josef von Sternberg, *Fun in a Chinese Laundry*; 1965]

von Stro·heim /von strō hìm/, **Erich** (1885–1957) Austrian-born US actor and movie director. In Hollywood after 1914, he directed movies of unparalleled realism and psychological intensity, including his masterpiece, *Greed* (1925). Born **Stroheim, Erich Oswald**

voo·doo /vóo dòo/ *n* (*plural* **voo·doos**) **1. CARIBBEAN RELIGION** a religion practiced throughout Caribbean countries, especially Haiti, that is a combination of Roman Catholic rituals and animistic beliefs, involving magic and communication with ancestors **2. PRACTITIONER OF VOODOO** a practitioner, priest, or priestess of voodoo **3. SUPPOSED MAGIC CHARM** a charm, spell, or fetish regarded by those who practice voodoo as having magical powers **4.** *US* **SOMETHING WITHOUT BASIS** a belief, theory, or method that lacks sufficient evidence or proof ■ *vt* (**voo·dooed, voo·doo·ing, voo·doos**) **CAST SPELL ON SOMEBODY** to cast a voodoo spell on somebody [Early 19C. Via Louisiana French *voudou* < Fon *vodū* "fetish"]

voo·doo·ism /vóodoo ìzzəm/ *n* **1.** the practices and beliefs of voodoo **2.** an attempt to control or affect the world using magic or sorcery —**voo·doo·ist** *n* —**voo·doo·is·tic** /vòodoo ístik/ *adj*

VOR *abbr* very-high-frequency omnidirectional radio range

vo·ra·cious /vaw ráyshəss, və-/ *adj* **1.** desiring or consuming food in great quantities ○ *a voracious appetite* **2.** unusually eager or enthusiastic about an activity ○ *a voracious reader* [Mid-17C. < Latin *vorac-* < *vorare* "devour"] —**vo·ra·cious·ly** *adv* —**vo·ra·cious·ness** *n* —**vo·rac·i·ty** /vaw rássətee, və-/ *n*

Vor·la·ge /fáwr laàgə/, **vor·la·ge** *n* a skiing position in which a skier leans forward from the ankle but keeps his or her heels on the skis [Mid-20C. < German, "forward position"]

Vo·ro·nezh /və ráwnish/ city and capital of Voronezh Oblast in western Russia. Population: 1,084,734 (1995).

-vorous *suffix* eating, having a particular kind of food ○ *herbivorous* [< Latin *-vorus* < *vorare* "to swallow"]

Vor·ster /fáwrstər/, **John** (1915–83) South African politician. During his premiership (1966–78) and presidency (1978–79), he reinforced the apartheid legislation introduced by his predecessor and mentor, Hendrik Verwoerd. His career ended after he was implicated in a financial scandal. Born **Vorster, Balthazar Johannes**

vor·tal /váwrt'l/ *n* a portal website devoted to one specific industry that enables business-to-business e-commerce transactions by bringing together businesses at different points in the supply chain [Late 20C. Blend of VERTICAL + PORTAL]

vor·tex /váwr tèks/ (*plural* **vor·tex·es** or **vor·ti·ces** /-tə seèz/) *n* **1.** a whirling mass of something, especially water or air, that draws everything near it toward its center **2.** a situation or feeling that seems to swamp or engulf everything else [Mid-17C. < Latin, variant of *vertex* (see VERTEX)]

vor·ti·cal /váwrtik'l/, **vor·ti·cose** /váwrti kòss/ *adj* relating to or moving in a vortex [Mid-17C. < Latin *vortic-*, stem of *vortex* (see VORTEX)] —**vor·ti·cal·ly** *adv*

vor·ti·cel·la /vàwrti séllə/ (*plural* **-lae** /-lee/ or **-las**) *n* an underwater protozoan with a bell-shaped body. It is usually attached to something such as a plant by a slender stalk. Genus: *Vorticella*. [Late 18C. < modern Latin, "little vortex" < Latin *vortic-* (see VORTICAL)]

vor·ti·ces plural of **vortex**

vor·ti·cism /váwrti sìzzəm/ *n* a short-lived early-20th-century British movement in art and literature that used abstract forms to express concern about the future and the machine age [Early 20C. < Latin *vortic-* (see VORTICAL)] —**vor·ti·cist** *n*

vor·tic·i·ty /vawr tíssətee/ *n* the state of a fluid moving in a vortex [Late 19C. < Latin *vortic-* (see VORTICAL)]

vor·ti·cose *adj* PHYS same as **vortical**

Vosges /vōzh/ mountain range in northeastern France. Length: 120 mi./190 km. Highest peak: Grand Ballon 4,672 ft./1424 m.

vo·ta·ry /vṓtəree/ (*plural* **-ries**), **vo·ta·rist** /-rist/ *n* **1.** somebody who has sworn to dedicate his or her life to religious worship or service **2.** a dedicated follower of something such as a religion or cause [Mid-16C. < Latin *vot-*, past participle of *vovere* "vow"]

vote /vōt/ *n* **1. FORMAL CHOICE FOR OR AGAINST SOMETHING** a formal indication of somebody's choice or opinion, especially in an election or referendum **2. ACT OF CHOOSING** the act of making a choice or of stating a preference to determine the outcome of something **3. BALLOTS CAST** the total number of ballots cast by eligible voters ○ *They got 83 percent of the vote.* **4. SUFFRAGE** the right to express opinions and preferences by casting a ballot ○ *Women struggled for many years to get the vote.* **5. MEANS OF EXPRESSING VOTE** the ticket, ballot, or other method by which somebody expresses a vote **6. RESULT OF BALLOTING** the outcome of an election or referendum **7. GROUP OF VOTERS** a group of voters who are considered to have significant common interests or views ○ *the youth vote* **8.** *US* **POTENTIAL VOTERS** all the people eligible to cast their ballots in an election or for a referendum ○ *working hard to get out the vote* ■ *v* (**vot·ed, vot·ing, votes**) **1.** *vti* **INDICATE FORMAL PREFERENCE** to express an opinion or preference in an election or for a referendum ○ *How did you vote in the last election?* **2.** *vt* **VOTE FOR OR AGAINST SOMEBODY** to decide the outcome of an election by voting for or against somebody ○ *was voted out of office* **3.** *vt* **VOTE TO MAKE SOMETHING AVAILABLE** to create something or make something available by casting a vote ○ *refused to vote additional funds for the new building* **4.** *vt* **DECLARE WINNER BY VOTING** to declare somebody to be the winner of a competition by voting ○ *He was voted "Employee of the Year."* **5.** *vt* **SHOW OPINION ON SOMETHING** to express agreement on something with regard to its degree of success (*informal*) ○ *The meal was voted a great success.* **6.** *vt* **SUGGEST SOMETHING** to make a suggestion ○ *I vote that we eat out.* **7.** *vt* *US* **USE SOMETHING AS GUIDE** to use something such as the conscience to determine how to vote ○ *Citizens often vote their pocketbooks, not their conscience.* [13C. < Latin *votum* "vow" < *vovere* "to vow," later "desire"] —**vot·a·ble** *adj*

vote down *vt* to defeat a proposal or candidate in a vote

vote bank *n S Asia* a group of voters whose votes can be won by offering policies that meet their special interests related to religion or caste

vote-bank po·li·tics *n S Asia* the practice of making policies designed to appeal to a specific group of voters in order to gain or keep their support (*disapproving*)

vote get·ter *n* somebody who can attract many votes

vote·less /vṓtləss/ *adj* without the right to choose or express a political opinion

vote of con·fi·dence *n* **1.** a vote in which voters express their continuing approval of the leadership of a party or policy **2.** a formal or informal expression of continuing support for somebody or something

vote of thanks *n* a formal expression of thanks to somebody, proposed as a motion at a meeting

vot·er /vṓtər/ *n* somebody who votes or is eligible to vote

vot·ing booth *n US* a booth where a voter casts a vote in an election. Can term **polling booth**

vo·tive /vṓtiv/ *adj* **1.** given, done, or offered in fulfillment of an oath or vow ○ *a votive offering* **2.** showing or symbolizing a wish or desire ○ *a votive prayer* [Late 16C. < Latin *votivus* < *votum* (see VOTE)] —**vo·tive·ly** *adv*

Vot·yak /vṓtee àk/ (*plural same* or **-yaks**) *n* **1.** a member of a Finnish people living in east central European Russia, especially in the Udmurt Autonomous Region **2.** LANG same as **Udmurt** (sense 2) [Mid-19C. < Russian] —**Vot·yak** *adj*

vouch /vowch/ (**vouched, vouch·ing, vouch·es**) *v* **1.** *vi* **PROVIDE SUPPORTING EVIDENCE** to provide supporting evidence for the quality of somebody or something ○ *testimony that vouches for the defendant's credibility* **2.** *vt* **CITE AUTHORITY** to cite somebody such as an authority in support of something (*archaic*) **3.** *vt* **DECLARE SOMETHING** to assert or declare something (*archaic*) [14C. Via French *voucher* "summon" < Latin *vocare* "to call"]

vouch·ee /vow cheé/ *n* somebody for whom another person vouches

vouch·er /vówchər/ *n* **1. SUBSTITUTE FOR MONEY WHEN BUYING SOMETHING** a card, token, or other document that can be exchanged for goods and services in place of money **2. DOCUMENTARY EVIDENCE** a document that provides supporting evidence for a claim, e.g., a receipt proving that a purchase was made **3. GUARANTOR** somebody or something that guarantees something or provides proof of something

vouch·safe /vòwch sáyf, vówch sàyf/ (**-safed, -saf·ing, -safes**) *vt* to promise, give, or allow something (*formal*)

vous·soir /voo swaár/ *n* a wedge-shaped brick or stone used to form the curved parts of an arch or vault [14C. < French < Latin *volvere* "to roll"]

Vou·vray /voo vráy/ *n* a still or sparkling white wine from west central France [Late 19C. After a village in Indre-et-Loire, France]

vow /vow/ *n* **SOLEMN PLEDGE** a solemn promise to perform an act, carry out an activity, or behave in a given way ■ **vows** *npl* **RELIGIOUS PROMISE** a solemn promise to join a religious order and live in accordance with its rules ■ *v* (**vowed, vow·ing, vows**) **1.** *vt* **PLEDGE SOMETHING** to promise something solemnly and seriously **2.** *vti* **DEDICATE SOMEBODY** to promise somebody to a pledge or task, or to somebody such as a deity **3.** *vt* **ASSERT SOMETHING** to assert or declare something [13C. Via Old French *vou* < Latin *votum* (see VOTE)] —**vow·er** *n*

vow·el /vów əl/ *n* **1.** a speech sound produced by the passage of air through the vocal tract, with relatively little obstruction **2.** a letter of the alphabet that represents a vowel. In English, the vowels are "a," "e," "i," "o," "u," and sometimes "y." [14C. Via Old French *vouel* < Latin *vocalis* (see VOCAL)]

vow·el gra·da·tion *n* LING same as **ablaut**

vow·el·ize /vów ə lìz/ (**-ized, -iz·ing, -iz·es**) *vt* to mark the vowel points in a Hebrew or Arabic text —**vow·el·i·za·tion** /vòw əli záysh'n/ *n*

vow·el mu·ta·tion *n* LING same as **umlaut** *n* (sense 1)

vow·el point *n* a diacritical mark placed above or below a consonant to show a preceding or following vowel, used especially in languages such as Arabic and Hebrew that lack symbols for vowel sounds

vox an·gel·i·ca /vòks an jéllikə/ *n* a quiet organ stop, usually with vibrato, that enriches the tone of other quiet stops [< Latin, "angelic voice"]

vox·el /vóksəl, vók sèl/ *n* the smallest unit of three-dimensional space in a computer image, equivalent to a three-dimensional pixel [Blend of VOLUME + PIXEL]

vox hu·ma·na /-hyoo maánə, -máynə/ *n* an organ reed stop that produces a tone resembling the human voice [< Latin, "human voice"]

vox pop /vòks póp/ *n* the impromptu opinions of ordinary members of the public as gathered by a radio or television interviewer (*hyphenated when used before a noun*) [Shortening of VOX POPULI]

vox pop·u·li /-póppyə lì, -leè/ *n* popular public opinion ○ *Let's see if we can detect the vox populi.* [< Latin, "voice of the people"]

voy·age /vóy ij/ *n* **1. LONG TRIP** a long journey, especially one by sea or through space **2. NARRATIVE** a story of an exploratory trip ■ *vti* (**-aged, -ag·ing, -ag·es**) **TRAVEL** to make a long journey to or through a place [13C. Via Old French *voiage* < Latin *viaticus* "of a road or journey" < *via* "road"]

voy·a·ger /vóyijər/ *n* somebody who makes a long journey to or through a place

voy·a·geur /vòy ə júr, vwaàyə zhúr/ *n Can* a boatman, woodsman, trapper, or explorer formerly hired by fur companies to carry furs and supplies from one remote station to another, especially in Canada and the northwestern United States [Late 18C. < French, "voyager"]

Voy·a·geurs Na·tion·al Park /vòy ə jùrz-/ national park in Northern Minnesota, established in 1975. Area: 341 sq.mi./883 sq. km.

voy·eur /voy yúr, vwaá yúr/ *n* **1.** somebody who gains pleasure from watching, especially secretly, other people's bodies or the sexual acts in which they participate **2.** a fascinated observer of distressing, sordid, or scandalous events [Early 20C. < French, "somebody who sees" < *voir* "see" < Latin *videre*] —**voy·eur·ism** *n* —**voy·eur·is·tic** /vòy yə rístik, vwaà yə-/ *adj* —**voy·eur·is·ti·cal·ly** *adv*

Voz·ne·sen·sky /vòzne sénskee/, **Andrey** (*b.* 1933) Russian poet. One of the most important of the young poets to emerge after the Stalinist era, he experimented with changes in meter and rhyme and projected in his poems a strong moral resonance. His best-known poems are "Parabola" and "Goya" (both 1960), the latter of which exposes the stark horrors of war.

> "I am Goya / of the bare field, by the enemy's beak gouged / till the craters of my eyes gape, / I am grief, / I am the tongue / of war, the embers of cities / on the snows of the year 1941 / I am hunger."
> [Andrey Voznesensky, "Goya"; 1960]

VP, **V.P.** *abbr* **1.** GRAM verb phrase **2.** vice president

VPL *abbr* visible panty line

VPN *n* a network that provides remote offices or users with secure access to their organization's network using the Internet or other public telecommunications system. Full form **virtual private network**

vr *abbr* GRAM verb reflexive

VR[1] *abbr* **1.** variant reading **2.** COMPUT virtual reality **3.** MIL Volunteer Reserve

VR[2] *abbr* Queen Victoria [Latin *Victoria Regina*]

vrai·sem·blance /vrày saaN blaáNss/ *n* the quality of seeming to be true or likely [Early 19C. < French, "true appearance"]

Vree·land /vreéland/, **Diana** (1906–89) US fashion magazine editor. She was the editor-in-chief of *Vogue* magazine and for many years an influential arbiter of fashion and design. Born **Dalziel, Diana**

> "Style! It helps you get up in the morning!"
> [Diana Vreeland. Quoted in *New York Times*; October 15, 1995]

Vries ◆ **De Vries, Hugo**

VRM *abbr* variable-rate mortgage

VRML *n* a computer-graphics programming language used to create images of three-dimensional scenes. Full form **Virtual Reality Modeling Language**

vroom /vroom/ *n* **LOUD ENGINE NOISE** the loud noise of an engine when it is being revved up or is running at high speed (*informal*) ■ *vi* (**vroomed, vroom·ing, vrooms**) **MOVE NOISILY** to move noisily at high speed ■ *interj* **USED TO IMITATE NOISY ENGINE** used to imitate an engine running at high speed [Mid-20C. An imitation of the sound]

VRSA *n* a strain of a common infection-causing bacterium that has become resistant to treatment by the antibiotic vancomycin and is therefore a hazard in places such as hospitals. Full form **vancomycin-resistant Staphylococcus aureus**

vs. *abbr* versus

v.s. *abbr* vide supra

V-shaped *adj* having the shape of a "V"

V sign, **V-sign** *n* a hand sign that indicates victory, approval, or solidarity, made by holding up the index and middle fingers so that they form a "V" with the palm facing outward

VSO *adj* used to indicate that brandy or port is between 12 and 17 years old. Full form **very superior old**

VSOP /veé sòp/ *adj* used to indicate that brandy or port is between 20 and 25 years old. Full form **very special old pale, very superior old pale**

vss. *abbr* **1.** verses **2.** versions

V/STOL[1] /veé stàwl/ *abbr* vertical and short takeoff and landing

V/STOL[2] /veé stàwl/ *n* **1.** a system used by some aircraft that enables them to take off and land vertically or using a short runway. Full form **vertical/short takeoff and landing 2.** an aircraft capable of taking off and landing vertically or using a short runway

vt *abbr* GRAM verb transitive

VT *abbr* **1.** PHYS vacuum tube **2.** variable time **3.** Vermont

Vt. *abbr* Vermont

VTOL /veé tàwl/ (*plural* **VTOLs**) *n* **1.** a system used by some aircraft that enables them to take off and land vertically. Full form **vertical takeoff and landing 2.** an aircraft capable of vertical takeoff and landing

VTR *abbr* HOUSEHOLD videotape recorder

vu *abbr* Vanuatu (*used in Internet addresses*) See table at **domain name**

vug /vug, vŏŏg/ *n* a small hole in a rock or vein that often contains a mineral lining that differs from that of the surrounding matrix [Early 19C. < Cornish *vooga*] —**vug·gy** *adj*

Vuil·lard /vwee yaár/, **Édouard** (1868–1940) French painter. He designed theater sets and textiles in addition to the intricately patterned paintings of domestic interiors for which he is best known. Full name **Vuillard, Jean Édouard**

Vul. *abbr* BIBLE Vulgate

Vul·can /vúlkən/ *n* in Roman mythology, the god of fire. Greek equivalent **Hephaestus** —**Vul·ca·ni·an** /vul káynee ən/ *adj*

vul·ca·ni·an /vul káynee ən/ *adj* **1.** relating to or caused by a type of explosive volcanic eruption resulting when the pressure of gases trapped in viscous magma is sufficient to blow off overlying solidified material **2.** relating to or consisting of metalworking or metal craft

vul·can·ic·i·ty /vùlkə níssətee/ *n* GEOL same as **volcanicity** [Late 18C. < French *vulcanicité*, variant of *volcanicité* (see VOLCANICITY)]

vul·ca·nism *n* GEOL another spelling of **volcanism**

vul·ca·nite /vúlkə nīt/ *n* a hard rubber produced by vulcanizing natural rubber with large amounts of sulfur [Mid-19C. After VULCAN]

vul·ca·nize /vúlkə nīz/ (**-nized, -niz·ing, -niz·es**) *vt* to strengthen a material such as rubber by combining it with sulfur and other additives and then applying heat and pressure —**vul·ca·niz·a·ble** *adj* —**vul·can·i·za·tion** /vùlkəni záysh'n/ *n* —**vul·ca·niz·er** *n*

vul·ca·nol·o·gy /vùlkə nóllǝjee/ *n* GEOL same as **volcanology** [Mid-19C. < French *vulcanique*, variant of *volcanique* (see VOLCANIC)] —**vul·ca·no·log·ic** /vúlkənə lójjik/ —**vul·ca·no·log·i·cal** *adj* —**vul·ca·nol·o·gist** *n*

vulg. *abbr* **1.** vulgar **2.** vulgarly

Vulg. *abbr* BIBLE Vulgate

vul·gar /vúlgər/ *adj* **1. CRUDE OR INDECENT** crude or obscene, particularly with regard to sex or bodily functions ○ *vulgar language* **2. TASTELESS OR OSTENTATIOUS** showing a lack of taste or reasonable moderation **3. LACKING REFINEMENT** lacking in courtesy and manners **4.** LANGUAGE **OF ORDINARY PEOPLE'S LANGUAGE** relating to a form of a language spoken by people generally **5. OF ORDINARY PEOPLE** relating to the majority of people (*archaic*) ■ *npl* **ORDINARY PEOPLE** ordinary people in society regarded as a group (*disapproving*) ○ *She believes that fine food and wine are beyond the taste of the vulgar.* [14C. < Latin *vulgaris* < *vulgus* "the common people"] —**vul·gar·ly** *adv*

vul·gar frac·tion *n* MATH same as **simple fraction**

vul·gar·i·an /vul gérree ən/ *n* somebody who is a wealthy but lacks taste or a sense of reasonable moderation

vul·gar·ism /vúlgə rìzzəm/ *n* **1.** a crude or indecent word or phrase **2.** a word or phrase from the language spoken by people generally, as contrasted with a more formal or refined usage **3.** same as **vulgarity**

vul·gar·i·ty /vul gárrətee/ (*plural* **-ties**) *n* **1.** a vulgar state or way of behaving **2.** a crude or tasteless joke, remark, or act

vul·gar·ize /vúlgə rīz/ (**-ized, -iz·ing, -iz·es**) *vt* **1.** to make something less refined or lower in quality **2.** to present or treat something in a way that makes it accessible to ordinary people —**vul·gar·i·za·tion** /vùlgəri záysh'n/ *n* —**vul·gar·iz·er** *n*

Vul·gar Lat·in *n* the form of Latin that was the common spoken language of the western Roman Empire

vul·gate /vúl gàyt, -gət/ *n* **1.** the everyday informal use of a language **2.** a text generally accepted among experts as being the best or most accurate version [Early 16C. < Latin *vulgatus*, past participle of *vulgare* "make public or common" < *vulgus* "the common people"]

Vul·gate /vúl gàyt, vúlgət/ *n* a Latin version of the Bible, produced by Saint Jerome in the 4th century [Early 17C. < Latin *vulgata editio* "edition made public, edition for ordinary people" < *vulgatus* (see VULGATE)]

vul·ner·a·ble /vúlnərəb'l/ *adj* **1. WITHOUT ADEQUATE PROTECTION** open to physical or emotional harm **2. EXTREMELY SUSCEPTIBLE** easily persuadable or liable to give in to temptation **3. PHYSICALLY OR PSYCHOLOGICALLY WEAK** unable to resist illness, debility, or failure **4.** MIL **OPEN TO ATTACK** exposed to an attack or possible damage **5.** CARDS **LIABLE TO INCREASED STAKES** in bridge, liable to higher penalties as well as bonuses after winning one game of a rubber [Early 17C. < late Latin *vulnerabilis* < Latin *vulnerare* "to wound" < *vulnus* "wound, injury"] —**vul·ner·a·bil·i·ty** /vùlnərə bíllətee/ *n* —**vul·ner·a·ble·ness** *n* —**vul·ner·a·bly** *adv*

vul·ner·ar·y /vúlnə rèrree/ (*archaic*) *adj* capable of or used for treating and healing wounds ■ *n* (*plural* **-ies**) a drug or other agent used in treating and healing wounds [Late 16C. < Latin *vulnerarius* < *vulnus* "wound, injury"]

Vul·pec·u·la /vul pékyələ/ *n* a constellation of the northern hemisphere [< Latin, diminutive of *vulpes* "fox"]

vul·pine /vúl pīn/ *adj* **1.** typical of or resembling a fox **2.** having or displaying a trait such as cunning that is commonly associated with foxes [Early 17C. < Latin *vulpes* "fox"]

vulture

vul·ture /vúlchər/ *n* **1.** a large bird of prey with usually dark feathers and broad wings that feeds on carrion. Native to: Europe, Asia, Africa, the Americas. Family: Accipitridae or Cathartidae. **2.** somebody who waits for the chance to exploit somebody else when that person is vulnerable [14C. Via French < Latin *vultur*]

vul·tur·ine /vúlchə rīn/ *adj* **1.** typical of or resembling a vulture **2.** *also* **vul·tur·ous** /vúlchərəss/ having a trait such as opportunism or greed that is commonly associated with vultures

vul·va /vúlvə/ (*plural* **-vae** /-vee/ or **-vas**) *n* the external female genitals. These include the clitoris and the two pairs of fleshy folds, the labia majora and labia minora, that surround the opening of the vagina. [14C. < Latin, variant of *volva* "womb" < *volvere* "to roll"] —**vul·val** *adj* —**vul·var** *adj* —**vul·vi·form** /vúlvə fàwrm/ *adj*

vul·vec·to·my /vul véktəmee/ (*plural* **-mies**) *n* the surgical removal of all or part of a woman's external genitals

vul·vi·tis /vul vītiss/ *n* painful swelling and redness of the vulva

vul·vo·vag·i·ni·tis /vùlvō vajə nītiss/ *n* painful swelling and redness of the vulva and vagina

vum /vum/ *interj New England* used to express surprise or puzzlement (*dated*) [Late 18C. Alteration of VOW]

vv. *abbr* **1.** verses **2.** MUSIC (first and second) violins **3.** volumes

v.v. *abbr* vice versa

VW *abbr* very worshipful

VX, **VX gas** *n* a deadly human-made nerve agent that is odorless and tasteless and occurs as an amber oily liquid that evaporates slowly [Mid-20C. < code letters, *V* indicating that it is very persistent]

vy. *abbr* very

Vyat·ka /vyaátkə/ former name for **Kirov** (1780–1934)

Ww

W /dúbb'l yo͞o/ (*plural* **w's**), **W** (*plural* **W's** or **Ws**) *n* **1.** the 23rd letter of the English alphabet, representing a consonant or sometimes a vowel **2.** a written representation of the letter "w"

W[1] *abbr* women's (*used of clothing sizes*)

W[2] /dúbb'l yo͞o/ (*plural* **W's** or **Ws**) *n* something shaped like a letter "W"

W[3] *symbol* **1.** CHEM ELEM tungsten **2.** ELEC watt **3.** PHYS weight **4.** PHYS work

W[4] /dúbb'l yo͞o/ *abbr* **1.** Wales **2.** Warden **3.** COMMUNICATION web (address) **4.** Wednesday **5.** Welsh **6.** *also* **W.** West **7.** Western

W. *abbr* **1.** TIME week **2.** MEASURE width **3.** wife **4.** with

w/ *abbr* with

W-2 *n* a form given to an employee by January 31 of each year showing the amounts of income and money withheld for taxes for the previous calendar year

W3 *abbr* ONLINE World Wide Web

W3C *n* a consortium of organizations, programmers, developers, industry executives, and users that seeks to guide the future development of the World Wide Web and ensure that all web technologies are compatible with one another. Full form **World Wide Web Consortium**

W8 *abbr* wait (*used in e-mails or text messages*)

W8ING *abbr* waiting (*used in e-mails or text messages*)

WA *abbr* **1.** Washington (State) **2.** Western Australia **3.** INSUR with average

Waal /vaal/ largest and southernmost of the three branches of the Rhine River in the Netherlands. Length: 52 mi./84 km.

Wa·bash /wáw bàsh/ river in the north-central United States. It rises in Ohio, and forms the Indiana-Illinois border before flowing into the Ohio River. Length: 512 mi./824 km.

wab·bit /wábbit/ *adj Scotland* tired, weak, or feeling slightly sick [Late 19C. Origin ?]

wab·ble *vti, n US* another spelling of **wobble**

wab·bly *adj US* another spelling of **wobbly**

WAC[1] /wak/ (*plural* **WACs**) *n* a member of the Women's Army Corps, a division of the United States Army that existed between 1942 and 1978

WAC[2] *abbr* Women's Army Corps

wack[1] /wak/ *n US* an offensive term that deliberately insults somebody who is regarded as unconventional or unpredictable (*slang*) [Mid-20C. Back-formation < WACKY]

wack[2] /wak/, **wack·er** *adj* in snowboarding, bad or unlucky (*slang*) [Mid-20C. Origin ?]

wack·o /wákō/ (*plural* **wack·os** or **wack·oes**), **whack·o** /wákō, hwákō/ (*plural* **-os** or **-oes**) *n* an offensive term that deliberately insults somebody regarded as unconventional, unpredictable, or unusual (*slang*) [Late 20C. < WACKY]

wack·y /wákee/ (**-i·er, -i·est**), **whack·y** /wákee, hwákee/ *adj* **1.** an offensive term meaning unconventional, unpredictable, or unusual (*slang*) **2.** entertainingly silly (*informal*) [Mid-19C. Probably < *out of whack* "out of order"] —**wack·i·ly** *adv* —**wack·i·ness** *n*

Wa·co /wáykō/ city on the Brazos River in central Texas. In 1993, 84 people were killed when federal agents stormed the compound of a religious group just outside the city. Population: 115,749 (2002 estimate).

wad /wod/ *n* **1.** PIECE OF SOFT MATERIAL a small rounded mass of soft material, usually used to pack or stuff something ○ *The vase was carefully packed in wads of cotton.* **2.** BUNDLE a roll or small bundle of paper money ○ *a wad of notes* **3.** LUMP OF COMPRESSED MATERIAL a rounded compressed lump of something soft, especially tobacco or gum for chewing **4.** *US* LARGE QUANTITY a large number or amount of people or things (*informal*) ○ *She has a wad of friends.* **5.** LOT OF MONEY a large amount of money (*informal*) **6.** ARMS POWDER PLUG a plug of material such as paper or cloth used to hold the powder charge in a muzzle-loading gun or cannon **7.** ARMS DISK IN SHOTGUN CARTRIDGE a disk made of felt or paper, used to hold the powder or shot in a shotgun cartridge **8.** MINERALS MINERAL MIXTURE IN BOGGY GROUND a fine-grained mixture of hydrated barium manganese oxide and other hydrated oxide minerals. Source: poorly drained boggy ground. ■ *v* (**wad·ded, wad·ding, wads**) **1.** *vti* COMPRESS TIGHTLY to compress something into a small mass, or be compressed in this way ○ *He wadded up the speeding ticket and threw it away.* **2.** *vt* PUT WADDING INTO SOMETHING to stuff or plug something with wadding ○ *She wadded her ears so she wouldn't hear the noise.* **3.** *vt* ARMS KEEP CHARGE IN PLACE to hold a charge of powder or shot in place **4.** *vt* ARMS INSERT WADDING INTO GUN to insert a piece of wadding into a gun [Mid-16C. Origin ?] —**wad·der** *n* ◇ **shoot your wad** to use all your resources in achieving something and be unable to achieve anything more

wa·da /waádə/, **va·da** *n S Asia* a fried lentil ball eaten as a snack, especially in southern India [< Hindi *vaḍā*]

wad·die *n* another spelling of **waddy**

wad·ding /wódding/ *n* **1.** SOFT PROTECTIVE MATERIAL soft material used to protect something, especially in packaging **2.** ARMS GUN WADS material used to hold powder or shot in a gun or cartridge **3.** TEXTILES PADDING MATERIAL USED IN SEWING a bonded fiber material produced in different thicknesses. Use: interlining, patchwork quilt padding.

wad·dle /wódd'l/ *vi* (**-dled, -dling, -dles**) to walk with short steps while causing the body to tilt slightly from one side to the other, especially because of having short legs and being overweight ■ *n* a way of walking, taking short steps with the body tilting slightly from one side to the other with each step [Late 16C. < WADE] —**wad·dler** *n* —**wad·dly** *adj*

wad·dy /wóddee/ (*plural* **-dies**), **wad·die** *n regional* **1.** same as **cowboy** (sense 1) **2.** a cattle thief [Late 19C. Origin ?]

wade /wayd/ *v* (**wad·ed, wad·ing, wades**) **1.** *vti* WALK IN WATER to walk against the pressure of water or mud **2.** *vi* READ THROUGH SOMETHING WITH DIFFICULTY to read through something with difficulty, especially because it is very long or boring ○ *wading through a tome on Greek philosophy* ■ *n* WALK TAKEN IN WATER an act or instance of walking against the pressure of water or mud [Old English *wadan* < Indo-European, "go"] —**wad·a·ble** *adj*

wade in *v* **1.** *vi* to interrupt forcefully or with determination **2.** *vti* to intervene in a situation in an attempt to help or restore order

Wade /wayd/, **Virginia** (*b.* 1945) British tennis player. She won the US Open (1968), Italian Open (1971), French Open (1972), Australian Open (1972), and Wimbledon (1977). Full name **Wade, Sarah Virginia**

wad·er /wáydər/ *n* **1.** a person or animal that wades through something **2.** BIRDS same as **wading bird** ■ **wad·ers** *npl* waterproof boots or combined boots and pants that reach to the hips or chest, worn as protection while fishing

wa·di /waádee/ (*plural* **wa·dis** or **wa·dies**), **wa·dy** (*plural* **-dies**) *n* **1.** a steep-sided watercourse in dry regions of North Africa and southern Asia through which water flows only after heavy rainfalls **2.** an oasis, especially in North Africa [Early 17C. < Arabic *wādī* "valley, river bed"]

wad·ing bird /wáyding-/ *n* a long-legged bird such as a crane, heron, or stork that walks in water and hunts for food such as fish, frogs, invertebrates, carrion, or algae

wad·ing pool *n* a shallow pool, sometimes near a larger pool, for small children's water play

Wad Me·da·ni /waád mi daánee/ capital city of El Gezira Province, central Sudan. Population: 218,714 (1993).

wa·dy *n* GEOG another spelling of **wadi**

WAF /waf/, **Waf** *n* formerly, a member of the women's section of the Air Force [Acronym < *Women in the Air Force*]

Wafd /waaft/ *n* an Egyptian nationalist party that emerged after an Egyptian delegation was refused a hearing at the Versailles Treaty negotiations following World War I. Negotiations eventually led to limited Egyptian independence beginning in 1922. [Early 20C. < Arabic, "delegation," shortening of *al-wafd, al-misrī* "the Egyptian delegation"]

wa·fer /wáyfər/ *n* **1.** THIN CRISP COOKIE a thin, crisp, and sometimes sweetened cookie, usually in a rectangular, fan, or cone shape, often eaten with ice cream **2.** DISK OF ADHESIVE MATERIAL a small thin disk of adhesive material, used to seal a letter or formal document **3.** CHR BREAD DISK IN CHRISTIAN COMMUNION SERVICE a very thin disk of unleavened bread used to represent the body of Jesus Christ in the Christian Communion **4.** ELECTRONICS same as **chip** *n* (sense 4) ■ *vt* (**-fered, -fer·ing, -fers**) FASTEN SOMETHING WITH WAFER to fasten something such as a letter or formal document with a wafer [14C. Via Anglo-Norman *wafre*, variant of French *gaufre* < Middle Low German *wāfel* < Germanic]

wa·fer-thin *adj* extremely thin or narrow

waf·fle[1] /wóff'l/ *n* a thick light pancake, crisp on the outside, that is baked in a waffle iron to give a pattern of indentations on both sides [Mid-18C. < Dutch *wafel* "wafer"]

waf·fle[2] /wóff'l/ (*informal*) *vi* (**-fled, -fling, -fles**) to be unable to make a decision ■ *n* speech or writing that is indecisive and vague [Late 17C. < *waff* "yelp or bark," an imitation of the sound] —**waf·fly** *adj*

waf·fle i·ron *n* an appliance used to bake waffles that has hinged indented plates that press a grid design into both sides of the waffle as it cooks

waft /woft/ *vti* (**waft·ed, waft·ing, wafts**) FLOAT GENTLY to float gently through the air, or move something gently through the air ■ *n* **1.** SOMETHING CARRIED THROUGH AIR something carried on the air or by a breeze, e.g., a scent **2.** WAVING MOTION a gentle waving or fluttering motion **3.** LIGHT BREEZE a brief gentle gust of air [Early

16C. Back-formation < *wafter* "armed ship used to guard a convoy" < Dutch *wachter* < *wachten* "to guard"]

wag[1] /wag/ *v* (**wagged, wag·ging, wags**) **1.** *vti* MOVE SOMETHING RAPIDLY TO AND FRO to move part of the body to and fro, or move to and fro ○ *The dog wagged its tail.* **2.** *vi* GOSSIP to gossip about somebody or something, especially disapprovingly ○ *Tongues are wagging.* ■ *n* MOTION GOING TO AND FRO a motion that goes to and fro rapidly [Old English *wagian* "move backward and forward" < Germanic]

CULTURAL NOTE See ***Wag the Dog syndrome.***

wag[2] /wag/ *n* a humorous or witty person (*informal*) [Mid-16C. Origin ? Originally an affectionate term for a mischievous boy] —**wag·ger·y** *n* —**wag·gish** *adj* —**wag·gish·ly** *adv* —**wag·gish·ness** *n*

wa·ga·ma·ma /waágaa maámaa/ *adj* exhibiting a willful selfishness [Late 20C. < Japanese]

wage /wayj/ *n* a sum of money paid to a worker in exchange for services, especially for work performed on an hourly, daily, or weekly basis, or by the piece (*often used in the plural*) ■ *vt* (**waged, wag·ing, wag·es**) to engage in war or in a serious fight to achieve an end ○ *wage war* [14C. < Anglo-Norman or Old N French < Germanic, "pledge"] —**wage·less** *adj* —**wage·less·ness** *n*

SYNONYMS ***wage, salary, pay, fee, remuneration, emolument, honorarium, stipend***

CORE MEANING: money given for work done

wage a sum of money paid to a worker in exchange for services, especially for work performed on an hourly, daily, or weekly basis, or by the piece ○ *hired at a low wage* ○ *The club pays my wages weekly.* **salary** a fixed annual sum, paid at regular intervals, usually monthly, to an employee, especially for professional or clerical work ○ *teachers' salaries* ○ *The successful candidate was to be paid an annual salary approaching $1 million.* **pay** money that is given in return for work or services provided, especially in the form of a salary or wages ○ *a month-long strike for better pay and conditions* ○ *"Equal pay for equal work" was the battle cry of the feminist movement.* **fee** a payment for professional services ○ *Such lawyers charged high fees and served only the elite.* ○ *The expert's fees are to be borne equally by the parties concerned.* **remuneration** a payment or reward for goods or services or for losses sustained or inconvenience caused ○ *a review body to advise on the proper remuneration for teachers* ○ *a need to investigate the levels of remuneration paid to daycare workers* **emolument** (*formal*) a payment for work done ○ *Unfortunately, his fame was accompanied by only a small emolument.* **honorarium** an amount of money paid to somebody, especially a professional or famous person, for providing a service such as addressing a conference ○ *Group members receive a small honorarium on the principle that their time is valued.* **stipend** a fixed amount of money paid at regular intervals as a salary or to cover living expenses, especially one paid to a member of the clergy ○ *The priest's yearly stipend was barely sufficient to live on.*

wage curve *n* a graphic representation showing the relationship between the average wage rate in a region or industry and the unemployment rate in that region or industry

waged /wayjd/ *adj* working and in receipt of a wage

wage dif·fer·en·tial *n* a difference in wages between workers with different skills working in the same industry or workers with similar skills working in different industries or regions

wage earn·er *n* **1.** somebody in a family or household who is earning a wage or salary **2.** somebody who works by the hour, day, or week for wages and not for a fixed salary

wage in·cen·tive *n* an additional sum of money paid to a worker in order to improve that person's productivity

wa·ger /wáyjər/ *n* **1.** BET ON OUTCOME an agreement between two people that whoever loses a bet on an uncertain outcome will pay the other a specific amount or another form of compensation **2.** AMOUNT BET a sum of money, piece of property, or other compensation to be paid to the person who wins a bet **3.** HIST PLEDGE in former times, a pledge to engage in combat, especially in order to establish guilt or innocence by single combat ■ *vt* (**-gered, -ger·ing, -gers**) BET MONEY to risk or bet money or property on the outcome of a game, event, or uncertain situation [14C. < Anglo-Norman *wageure* < *wagier* "to pledge" < *wage* "pledge"] —**wa·ger·er** *n*

wag·es /wáyjəz/ *n* a just reward or recompense for something (*literary; takes a singular verb*) ○ *the wages of sin*

wage scale *n* a scale of the different wages paid to employees who are performing different jobs within a single company or industry

wage slave *n* somebody who depends completely on earning money from work in order to live (*informal*)

wag·gle /wágg'l/ *vti* (**-gled, -gling, -gles**) to move rapidly back and forth, or make something do this ■ *n* a rapid motion back and forth [Late 16C. < WAG[1]] —**wag·gly** *adj*

AKG London

Richard Wagner

Wag·ner /vaágnər/, **Richard** (1813–83) German composer. He developed both the form and content of opera, notably in his opera cycle *The Ring of the Nibelung* (1852–76), and was a major influence on orchestral composers of the late romantic period. Full name **Wagner, Wilhelm Richard** —**Wag·ner·i·an** /vaag neéree ən/ *adj, n*

> "It is a truth forever, that where the speech of man stops short there Music's reign begins."
> [Richard Wagner, "A Happy Evening"; 1841]

Wag·ner /wágnər/, **Robert F.** (1877–1953) German-born US politician. He took the lead in passing progressive legislation while representing New York in the US Senate (1927–49). Full name **Wagner, Robert Ferdinand**

wag·on /wággən/ *n* **1.** WHEELED VEHICLE FOR CARRYING LOADS a rectangular vehicle that is used to carry heavy loads and is pulled by an animal or tractor or is motor-powered **2.** *US* DELIVERY VEHICLE a light automotive vehicle used to sell or deliver something **3.** POLICE TRANSPORT VEHICLE a van or truck used by the police to transport suspects or criminals **4.** CHILD'S FOUR-WHEELED CART a low four-wheeled cart with a long handle a child can use to pull the cart or to control the direction of the front wheels **5.** SERVING CART a four-wheeled rectangular cart used to display or serve food or drink **6.** *UK* FREIGHT CAR a railroad car for goods, particularly an open one [15C. < Dutch *wagen* < Germanic] —**wag·on·er** *n* ◇ **be off the wagon** to resume drinking alcoholic beverages after a period of abstinence ◇ **be on the wagon** to abstain from drinking any alcoholic beverage

wag·on·ette /wàggə nét/ *n* a light four-wheeled horse-drawn vehicle with two lengthwise seats facing each other behind a crosswise driver's seat

wag·on-lit /vaa gawN leé/ (*plural* **wag·on-lits** /*pronunc. same*/ or **wag·ons-lits** /*pronunc. same*/) *n* **1.** a sleeping car on a European railroad **2.** an individual compartment in a railroad sleeping car [< French < *wagon* "railroad coach" + *lit* "bed"]

wag·on·load /wággən lōd/ *n* the amount that a wagon holds

wag·on train *n* a line of two or more animal-drawn wagons traveling cross-country and carrying people, food supplies, or goods

wag·on vault *n* ARCHIT same as **barrel vault**

Wa·gram /vaág raam/ village in northeastern Austria. It was the site of the Battle of Wagram in which Napoleon's army defeated the Austrians in July 1809.

wag·tail /wág tàyl/ *n* a songbird with a long tail that bobs up and down when it walks and especially when it lands. Native to: Europe, Asia, Africa. Family: Motacillidae.

Wag the Dog syn·drome *n US* a situation in which a US president uses military attacks on other nations as a diversionary tactic to deflect intense public and media scrutiny from a personal scandal (*slang*) ○ *"Was the bombing of Iraq really a result of Wag the Dog syndrome?"* (*Vanity Fair*; March 1999) [Late 20C. *Wag the Dog* < a movie title]

Wah·ha·bi /wə haábee, waa-/ (*plural* **-bis**), **Wa·ha·bi** *n* a member of a very conservative Islamic group that rejects any innovation that occurred after the 3rd century of Islam. It flourishes primarily in Arabia. [Early 19C. < Arabic *wahhābī*, after Muhammad ibn bd-al-*Wahhāb* (1703–92), its founder] —**Wah·ha·bism** *n*

wa·hi·ne /waa heénee, -này/ *n* **1.** *Hawaii* a Hawaiian or Maori woman or wife **2.** *Hawaii* a young woman surfer (*informal*) [Late 18C. < Hawaiian or Maori]

wa·hoo[1] /waa hoó, waá hoó/ *n* a deciduous bush with pink to purple fruit capsules that split open to reveal scarlet seeds. Native to: eastern North America. Latin name: *Euonymus atropurpureus.* [Mid-19C. < Dakota *wa hu* "arrow-wood"]

wa·hoo[2] /waa hoó, waá hoó/ (*plural* **-hoos**) *n* a small elm tree with hairy reddish fruits and twigs with corky projections resembling wings. Native to: southeastern United States. Latin name: *Ulmus alata.* [Late 18C. Origin ?]

wa·hoo[3] /waa hoó, waá hoó/ (*plural* **-hoos**) *n* a large fast-swimming fish of the mackerel family that weighs up to 120 lb./54.4 kg. Native to: tropical seas. Latin name: *Acanthocybium solanderi.* [Early 20C. Origin ?]

wa·hoo[4] /waa hoó/ *US interj* used to express happy excitement ■ *n* (*plural* **-hoos**) a rowdy cry of excitement [Mid-20C. Combining natural exclamations]

wah-wah /waá waá/, **wa-wa** *n* **1.** WAVERING SOUND OF WIND INSTRUMENT the wavering sound made by alternately covering and uncovering the bell of a brass instrument **2.** ELECTRONIC SOUND a sound resembling a wah-wah, created for electronic instruments **3.** ELECTRONIC DEVICE an electronic device that is attached to a musical instrument and produces a wah-wah sound [Early 20C. An imitation of the sound]

wah-wah ped·al *n* a foot pedal attached to an electronic musical instrument, used to create a wavering sound

waif /wayf/ *n* **1.** ABANDONED CHILD a homeless or friendless person, especially an abandoned child **2.** STRAY ANIMAL a stray animal whose owner is unknown **3.** THIN YOUNG PERSON somebody, usually a young person, with a thin fragile appearance who looks needy **4.** UNCLAIMED ITEM an item that has been found whose owner is unknown (*literary*) [14C. < Anglo-Norman *weyf*, earlier *gwayf* "lost property" < N Germanic] —**waif·like** *adj*

Wai·ka·to[1] /wī kaátō/ administrative region in the northern part of the North Island, New Zealand. Population: 357,726 (2001). Area: 13,472 sq. mi./34,892 sq. km.

Wai·ka·to[2] longest river in New Zealand. It rises in Lake Taupo in the center of the North Island and empties into the Tasman Sea south of Waiuku. Length: 264 mi./425 km.

Wai·ki·ki /wī kee keé/ beach resort northeast of Honolulu, Oahu Island, Hawaii

wail /wayl/ *v* (**wailed, wail·ing, wails**) **1.** *vti* MAKE MOURNFUL CRY to express pain, grief, or misery in a long mournful high-pitched cry or in words uttered in a mournful way ○ *He could only wail when he heard the news.* **2.** *vi* MAKE LONG HIGH-PITCHED NOISE to make a long loud high-pitched sound ○ *The sirens wailed.* **3.** *vt* LAMENT SOMEBODY OR SOMETHING to express grief over somebody or something (*archaic*) ■ *n* **1.** LONG MOURNFUL SOUND a long mournful high-pitched cry or sound **2.** PROTEST a loud plaintive expression of protest, resentment, or disappointment [13C. < Old Norse < *vei* "woe"] —**wail·er** *n* —**wail·ful** *adj* —**wail·ful·ly** *adv*

SPELLCHECK wail, wale, or **whale**? Do not confuse the spelling of ***wail***, ***wale***, and ***whale***, which sound similar. ***Wail*** is a noun or verb denoting a long loud high-pitched sound, as in *the wail of a siren, wailing children.* The word ***wale***, which is less frequently encountered in general usage, denotes a raised mark on the skin caused by a blow or a ridge (for example, on fabric). A ***whale*** is a large ocean mammal or something similarly impressive, as in *having a whale of a time.*

Wail·ing Wall *n* JUDAISM same as **Western Wall**

wain /wayn/ *n* a farm wagon or cart (*archaic or literary*) [Old English *wæ(g)n* < Germanic]

wain·scot /wáynskət, -skòt/ *n* **1. WOODEN PANELS LINING ROOM** a lining for the walls of a room, especially one made of wood paneling **2. LOWER PART OF WALL OF ROOM** the lower part of the wall of a room, especially when it is paneled in wood or finished differently from the upper part **3. OAK PANELING** a fine grade of oak used as wall paneling ■ *vt* (**-scot·ed** or **-scot·ted, -scot·ing** or **-scot·ting, -scots**) **COVER WALL WITH PANELING** to cover a wall, especially with wood paneling [14C. < Middle Dutch *waghenscote* or Middle Low German *wagenschot* "wagon-boarding"]

wain·scot·ing /wáynskəting, -skòtting/, **wain·scot·ting** *n* **1.** the material, especially wood, used to cover a wall **2.** CONSTR same as **wainscot** *n* (sense 1)

wain·wright /wáyn rìt/ *n* somebody who makes and repairs wagons

Wai·ra·ra·pa, Lake /wī raa ráapə/ lake in the southern part of the North Island, New Zealand. Area: 50 sq. mi./80 sq. km.

Wai·rau /wī row/ river in the northern part of the South Island, New Zealand. It rises in the Southern Alps and empties into the Cook Strait near Blenheim. Length: 105 mi./169 km.

waist /wayst/ *n* **1. BODY AREA BETWEEN RIBS AND HIPS** the part of the human trunk between the rib cage and the hips, usually narrower than the rest of the trunk **2. PART OF CLOTHING** the part of a garment that fits around the waist of the body **3. NARROW PART** the narrow middle part of something, e.g., the middle of a violin **4.** NAUT **MIDDLE OF SHIP** the middle part of a ship or of a ship's deck between the raised sections at the bow and stern **5.** AVIAT **MIDDLE OF AIRPLANE** the middle section of an aircraft's fuselage **6.** INSECTS **MIDDLE OF INSECT** the narrow part of an insect's body between the thorax and the abdomen [14C. Origin ?] —**waist·ed** *adj* —**waist·less** *adj*

SPELLCHECK waist or **waste**? Do not confuse the spelling of ***waist*** and ***waste***, which sound similar. ***Waist*** is only used as a noun, denoting the narrow part of the body between the rib cage and the hips, or a part of a garment that fits around it. ***Waste*** can be used as a noun, denoting a failure to use something wisely or inwanted or unusable remains (as in *a waste of money, industrial waste*), or as a verb, meaning "fail to make use of something" or "become gradually weaker or thinner": *You're wasting your time. They were wasting away from malnutrition.*

waist·band /wáyst bànd/ *n* a band of fabric that circles the waist at the top of a garment such as a skirt or pair of pants

waist·cloth /wáyst klàwth, -klòth/ *n* CLOTHING same as **loincloth** (*archaic*)

waist·coat /wáyst kōt/ *n* **1.** a man's sleeveless garment reaching to the hips or knees, worn under a doublet in the 16th century **2.** *UK* a man's or woman's sleeveless and collarless waist-length garment, usually with buttons down the front, worn over a shirt and traditionally worn by men under a suit jacket —**waist·coat·ed** *adj*

waist·line /wáyst lìn/ *n* **1.** the measurement around the narrowest part of the waist **2.** the level, usually near the waist, where the bodice and skirt of a dress meet ○ *a low waistline*

wait /wayt/ *v* (**wait·ed, wait·ing, waits**) **1.** *vi* **DO NOTHING EXPECTING SOMETHING TO HAPPEN** to stay in one place or do nothing for a period of time until something happens or in the expectation or hope that something will happen ○ *I'll wait for you here until noon.* **2.** *vi* **STOP SO SOMEBODY CAN CATCH UP** to stop or slow down in order to allow somebody else to catch up ○ *Wait for me!* **3.** *vi* **BE HOPING FOR SOMETHING** to be hoping for something or on the lookout for something ○ *He is waiting for a job opportunity.* **4.** *vi* **BE DELAYED OR IGNORED FOR NOW** to be postponed or put off until later ○ *Fame would just have to wait.* **5.** *vi* **BE READY OR AVAILABLE** to be ready or available for somebody to take or use ○ *Your mail is waiting for you.* **6.** *vt* **DELAY SOMETHING** to delay something, especially a meal, because somebody is expected to arrive soon (*informal*) ○ *We waited dinner for you.* **7.** *vti* **BE WAITER** to serve at restaurant tables as a waiter ○ *She waits tables at the hotel.* ■ *n* **TIME SPENT WAITING** a period of time spent while expecting something to happen ○ *The wait seemed to go on forever.* ■ **waits** *npl* **BAND OF MUSICIANS** a band of musicians who play and sing Christmas carols in the streets (*archaic*) [12C. Via Old N French *waitier* "spy, prepare to ambush" < Frankish] ◇ **lie in wait for somebody** *or* **something** to be waiting to catch or attack somebody or something

SPELLCHECK wait or **weight**? Do not confuse the spelling of ***wait*** and ***weight***, which sound similar. ***Wait*** refers to a period of time before doing something or before something happens: *Wait until it stops raining. We had a long wait for the train.* ***Weight*** refers to heaviness, importance, or arranging something so that it either favors or disadvantages a particular person or group, as in *the weight of the suitcase, weighted it down with a stone, opinions that carry little weight, weighted in their favor.*

USAGE See ***await***.

CULTURAL NOTE ***Waiting for Godot***, a play (1954) by Irish writer Samuel Beckett. A classic drama of the theater of the absurd, it has two main characters, the tramps Estragon and Vladimir. They indulge in idle conversation and games while waiting for Godot, who they hope will give some meaning to their futile existence. Godot does not arrive, and the tramps decide to go, but they do not leave the stage.

wait on *v* **1.** *vt* **SERVE SOMEBODY BY BRINGING REQUESTED ITEMS** to go and get the things that somebody asks for, usually continuously for a period of time ○ *It's nice to be waited on for a change.* **2.** *vt* **SERVE SOMEBODY AT TABLE** to bring food and drink to somebody sitting at a table, usually in a restaurant **3.** *vt* **SERVE RETAIL CUSTOMER** to attend to the purchasing needs of a customer **4.** *vi* **WAIT FOR SOMEBODY OR SOMETHING** to wait for somebody or something (*informal*) **5.** *vt* **VISIT SOMEBODY** to pay a formal visit to somebody (*archaic*)

wait out *vt* to stay in one place or do nothing until something ends ○ *We decided to wait out the storm.*

wait up *vi* **1.** to delay going to bed to await an event or somebody's arrival ○ *I'll be home late; don't wait up.* **2.** to wait for somebody or something (*informal; usually used as a command*) ○ *Wait up! I won't be a minute.*

wait upon *vt* same as **wait on** (senses 1–3, 5)

Wai·ta·ki /wī tákee/ river in the southeastern part of the South Island, New Zealand. It rises in Lake Benmore and empties into the Pacific Ocean near the town of Waitaki. Length: 130 mi./209 km.

Wai·tang·i /wī taángee/ historic site in the northern part of the North Island, New Zealand. A treaty between the Maori people and the British government was signed there in February 1840.

Waite /wayt/, **Morrison Remick** (1816–88) chief justice of the US Supreme Court (1874–88)

Wai·te·ma·ta Har·bour /wìtə màttə-/ arm of the Pacific Ocean on the northeastern coast of the North Island, New Zealand. Auckland is situated on part of it.

wait·er /wáytər/ *n* **1.** somebody employed to bring food and drink to people, usually in a restaurant **2.** a tray for carrying dishes or serving food [14C. Via Anglo-Norman, "attendant, watchman" < Old N French, or directly < WAIT]

wait·ing game /wáyting-/ *n* a tactic whereby somebody delays taking any action or making a move in a contest or negotiation, hoping that his or her position will improve with the passage of time

wait·ing list *n* a list of people waiting for something that is not immediately available such as a table in a restaurant, a place in a school, or an out-of-stock product

wait·ing room *n* a room in which people may wait, e.g., for a doctor's appointment

Wai·to·mo Caves /wī tōmō-/ limestone cave system in the western part of the North Island, New Zealand, noted for its large colonies of glowworms

wait·per·son /wáyt pùrss'n/ (*plural* **-peo·ple** /-peep'l/ or **-per·sons**) *n* OCCUPATIONS same as **waiter** (sense 1)

wait·ress /wáytrəss/ *n* a woman employed to bring food or drink to people, usually in a restaurant

wait·ron /wáytrən/ *n US* OCCUPATIONS same as **waiter** (sense 1) (*slang*) [Late 20C. Blend of WAITER or WAITRESS and AUTOMATON, suggesting mechanical repetitive work]

wait·staff /wáyt stàf/ *n US* the waitpersons in a café or restaurant

wait state *n* a period of time during which a central processing unit in a computer sits idle while a slower component such as a memory or bus functions

waive /wayv/ (**waived, waiv·ing, waives**) *vt* **1. SURRENDER CLAIM** to give something up voluntarily, especially a right or claim ○ *She waived her right to remain silent.* **2. NOT ENFORCE SOMETHING** to refrain from enforcing or applying something ○ *They decided to waive the restrictions.* **3. TEMPORARILY DELAY SOMETHING** to put off something for a time **4. MAKE PLAYER AVAILABLE TO OTHER TEAM** to remove a professional ball player from a team's roster, thereby making the player available to other teams [13C. < Anglo-Norman *weyver* "make a waif of, abandon" < *weyf* (see WAIF)]

SPELLCHECK ***waive*** or ***wave***? Do not confuse the spelling of ***waive*** and ***wave***, which sound similar. ***Waive*** is a verb meaning "surrender or refrain from enforcing something": *She waived her right to remain silent. They decided to waive the restrictions.* The related noun is spelled *waiver.* ***Wave*** is a noun and verb with various meanings, usually involving ridge-shaped or undulating motion, as in *the waves of the ocean, radio waves, waved goodbye.* The noun *waver* is unrelated to ***wave***: it corresponds to the verb *waver* meaning "go back and forth between possibilities."

waiv·er /wáyvər/ *n* **1. RELINQUISHING OF RIGHT** the voluntary surrender of a right or claim **2. DOCUMENT CONTAINING WAIVER** a document or formal statement giving up a right or claim, or an action indicating an intention to waive something **3. ACT OF GIVING UP CLAIM ON PLAYER** the act of a sports team in giving up the right to claim a professional ball player who has been removed from another team's roster

SPELLCHECK See ***waive***.

Waj·da /vídə/, **Andrzej** (*b.* 1926) Polish movie director. Much of his work focuses on Poland during and after World War II and on Polish nationalism of the 1970s and 1980s.

wa·ka·me /waa kaámee/ (*plural* **-mes** or *same*) *n* an edible brown seaweed. Use: dried, in Japanese and Chinese cooking. Native to: coasts of Japan, China, and Korea. Latin name: *Undaria pinnatifida.* [Mid-20C. < Japanese]

wa·kan·da /waa kaándə/ *n* in the religion of the Sioux people, the great supernatural power that lies behind the whole of the natural world

Wa·kash·an /waa kásh'n, waákə shàn/ *n* a family of languages spoken by Native North American peoples in British Columbia and Washington State. Native speakers: 3,000. [Late 19C. < Nootka *waukash* "good"] —**Wa·kash·an** *adj*

Wa·ka·ti·pu /waákə típpoo/ lake in the southwestern part of the South Island, New Zealand. The town of Queenstown is located on its northern shore. Area: 113 sq. mi./293 sq. km.

Wa·ka·ya·ma /waákə yaámə/ seaport and capital city of Wakayama Prefecture, southwest of Osaka, Japan. Population: 391,008 (2002).

wake[1] /wayk/ *v* (**woke** /wōk/ or **waked, wok·en** /wōkən/ or **waked, wak·ing, wakes**) **1.** *vti* **STOP SLEEPING** to come back to a conscious state after sleeping, or make somebody do this ○ *I woke suddenly at dawn.* **2.** *vti* **STOP BEING INACTIVE** to become alert and active after being inactive, in a daydream, or preoccupied, or make somebody do this **3.** *vti* **REALIZE OR MAKE SOMEBODY REALIZE SOMETHING** to become aware of something, or make somebody aware ○ *Their pleas woke us to the* *situation.* **4.** *vi* **WATCH OVER CORPSE** to hold a vigil over the body of somebody who has died **5.** *vi* **STAY AWAKE** to be or remain awake ○ *"Fled is that music — Do I wake or sleep?"* (John Keats, *Ode to a Nightingale*; 1819) **6.** *vti* **KEEP WATCH** to keep watch over somebody or something (*archaic*) ■ *n* **1. WATCH KEPT OVER CORPSE** a vigil held over a corpse before burial or cremation **2. FESTIVE GATHERING ASSOCIATED WITH DEATH** a social gathering held after a funeral or, in Ireland, often after the death but before the funeral. Traditionally people drink and talk about the dead person, and there is a happy jovial atmosphere. [Old English *wacan* "become awake" < Indo-European, "be active or lively"] —**wak·er** *n*

USAGE See *awake.*

CULTURAL NOTE ***Finnegans Wake***, a novel (1939) by Irish writer James Joyce. Joyce's last novel recounts a single night in the life of a Dublin barkeeper, Humphrey Chimpden Earwicker, and his family. An extraordinary multilayered work consisting chiefly of extended interior monologues, it is crammed with multilingual puns, poetry, and literary and historical allusions that emphasize the universal and cyclic nature of human experience.

wake up *v* **1.** *vti* same as **wake**[1] *v* (senses 1–3) **2.** *vt* to make something look more interesting or attractive

wake[2] /wayk/ *n* **1. TRACK IN WATER** the track left in water by a vessel or another body moving through it **2. DISTURBED AIR BEHIND VEHICLE** the stream of turbulence in the air left by an aircraft or land vehicle passing through it **3. POSITION BEHIND SOMEBODY** the position or area behind somebody or something that is moving ahead fast ○ *left the rest of the field trailing in her wake* **4. AFTEREFFECTS** the aftermath or aftereffects of a dramatic event or powerful thing ○ *The bomb left destruction in its wake.* [15C. Via Middle Low German < Old Norse *vok* "hole in ice (made by a boat)"] ◇ **in the wake of something** immediately after and usually as a result of something

wake·board·ing /wáyk bàwrding/ *n* a water sport in which somebody riding a single board is pulled behind a motor boat and performs jumps while crisscrossing the wake of the boat [Late 20C. After SKATEBOARDING] —**wake·board** *vi* —**wake·board·er** *n*

Wake·field /wáyk feèld/ **1.** town in northeastern Massachusetts, southeast of Lake Quannapowitt, east of Woburn, and north of Boston. Population: 24,817 (2002 estimate). **2.** city in West Yorkshire, northern England, on the Calder River. Population: 315,172 (2001).

wake·ful /wáykfəl/ *adj* **1. NOT SLEEPING** unable to sleep **2. SLEEPLESS** passed without sleep ○ *a wakeful night* **3. ALERT** awake, especially while watching or guarding something ○ *promised to remain wakeful* —**wake·ful·ly** *adv* —**wake·ful·ness** *n*

Wake Is·land /wáyk-/ group of three islets constituting a coral atoll in the central Pacific Ocean. It was occupied by the United States in 1898 and held by the Japanese in World War II between 1941 and 1945. Population: 126 (1997). Area: 3 sq. mi./8 sq. km.

wake·less /wáykləss/ *adj* uninterrupted by waking, or spent in uninterrupted sleep

wak·en /wáykən/ (**-ened, -en·ing, -ens**) *vti* to become conscious, active, or aware after sleeping, being inactive, or being unaware, or make a person or animal do this —**wak·en·er** *n*

USAGE See *awake.*

wake-rob·in (*plural* **wake-rob·ins** or *same*) *n* **1.** a member of a group of early-blooming arums such as the arrow arum. Native to: North America. **2.** PLANTS same as **trillium 3.** PLANTS same as **cuckoopint**

wake-up call *n* **1.** a telephone call or a personal visit made to awaken somebody, especially a telephone call from or arranged by hotel staff made at an agreed-upon time to awaken a guest **2.** a frightening experience that is interpreted as a sign that a major change is needed in the way somebody lives or conducts business

wa·kil LAW another spelling of **vakil**

Waks·man /wáksmən/, **Selman A.** (1888–1973) Russian-born US microbiologist. He was the pioneer researcher of streptomycin, and was the first person to use the term "antibiotics." He was awarded a Nobel Prize in physiology or medicine (1952). Full name **Waksman, Selman Abraham**

Wa·la·chi·a /wə láykee ə/, **Wal·la·chi·a** former region in southeastern Europe, in present-day southern Romania. Founded as a principality toward the end of the 13th century, it was ruled by Turkey from 1387 until it joined Moldavia to form Romania in 1861. —**Wa·la·chi·an** *n, adj*

Wal·cott /wáwl kòt/, **Derek** (*b.* 1930) St. Lucian writer. His Caribbean-based novels and plays are characterized by a vivid use of language. He won the Nobel Prize in literature (1992).

> "I who have cursed / The drunken officer of British rule, how choose / Between this Africa and the English tongue I love? / Betray them both, or give back what they give? / How can I face such slaughter and be cool? / How can I turn from Africa and live?"
> [Derek Walcott, "A Far Cry From Africa," *In a Green Night*; 1962]

Wald /wawld/, **George** (1906–97) US biologist. He shared the Nobel Prize in physiology or medicine (1967) for his work on vision. He was an outspoken opponent of the arms race and the Vietnam War.

Wald, Lillian D. (1867–1940) US nurse and social worker. She founded the Henry Street Settlement for social work (1893) in New York City and promoted the need for public health services.

Wal·de·mar I /vaáldə maàr/ (1131–82) **king of Denmark** Having gained sole control of the Danish throne (1157–82), he established a dynastic rule in Denmark. Known as **Waldemar the Great**

Wal·de·mar II (1170–1241) **king of Denmark** He was the son of Waldemar I. As king (1202–41), he extended Danish territory and instituted legal and administrative reforms. Known as **Waldemar the Conqueror**

Wal·den·ses /wol dén seèz/ *npl* the members of a small Christian denomination, originating in southern France, that broke with the Roman Catholic Church in the 12th century and experienced much persecution. In the 16th century the Waldenses joined the Reformation and adopted Calvinist doctrines. [Mid-16C. < medieval Latin < *Waldensis*, variant of Peter *Valdes* (d. 1205), who founded the movement] —**Wal·den·si·an** *adj*

Wald·heim /wáwld hìm, vaált-/, **Kurt** (*b.* 1918) secretary general of the United Nations (1972–81) and president of Austria (1986–92). During his presidency it was alleged he had been complicit in Nazi war crimes.

Wal·dorf sal·ad /wáwl dawrf-/ *n* a salad made of diced raw apples, celery, and walnuts with a mayonnaise dressing [Early 20C. After the *Waldorf*-Astoria Hotel in New York]

Wal·dorf School /wáwl dawrf-/ *n* a school belonging to a movement that emphasizes a holistic approach to education and a broad curriculum linked to knowledge of child development. The movement is based on the ideas of Rudolph Steiner. [After the *Waldorf* cigarette factory in Stuttgart, Germany, whose chief executive initiated such a school for its workers' children in 1919]

wale /wayl/ *n* **1. SKIN WELT** a raised red swollen mark on the skin made by a blow, especially with a whip **2.** TEXTILES **RIDGE ON FABRIC** a ridge on the surface of a woven fabric such as corduroy **3.** TEXTILES **WEAVE OF FABRIC** the weave or texture of a fabric with ribs **4.** HANDICRAFT **VERTICAL ROW OF KNITTING** a vertical row of stitches in knitting **5.** NAUT **WOOD FORMING SIDES OF SHIP** a strong horizontal plank forming part of the side of a wooden ship ■ *vt* (**waled, wal·ing, wales**) **1. RAISE WELT ON SKIN** to raise a red swollen mark on the skin by striking a blow, especially with a whip **2.** TEXTILES **WEAVE RIDGED FABRIC** to weave fabric with ridges [Old English *walu* "ridge" < Germanic]

SPELLCHECK See *wail.*

Wales /waylz/ principality in Great Britain, part of the United Kingdom. Once a separate kingdom, it was united with England in 1536. It voted in 1997 to have its own assembly, and as a result has a degree of self-government. Capital: Cardiff. Population: 2,903,085 (2001). Area: 8,015 sq. mi./20,760 sq. km.

Wal·hal·la, **Wal·hall** *n* MYTHOL same as **Valhalla**

walk /wawk/ *v* (**walked, walk·ing, walks**) **1.** *vi* **MOVE ON FOOT** to move or travel on legs and feet, alternately putting one foot a comfortable distance in front of, or sometimes behind, the other, and usually proceeding at a moderate pace. When walking, as opposed to running, one of the feet is always in contact with the ground, the one being put down as or before the other is lifted. ○ *a toddler just learning to walk* **2.** *vt* **TRAVEL THROUGH PLACE ON FOOT** to travel along or through something on foot ○ *walking the coastal path* **3.** *vt* **TAKE ANIMAL FOR EXERCISE BY WALKING** to take an animal for exercise by walking, usually a dog on a leash ○ *walked the dog* **4.** *vt* **WALK WITH SOMEBODY TO PLACE** to accompany somebody on foot as far as a particular place such as a home or car ○ *I'll walk you home.* **5.** *vt* **CAUSE SOMEBODY TO WALK** to help or force somebody to walk by holding and pushing from behind ○ *We kept walking him until he was able to stand on his own.* **6.** *vti* **MOVE LARGE OBJECT BY ROCKING** to move something in a way that suggests walking, e.g., by pivoting a large heavy object alternately on its corners and swinging the other side forward, or be moved in this way ○ *The bureau's too heavy to lift; we'll have to walk it into the bedroom.* **7.** *vt* **MEASURE SOMETHING BY WALKING** to measure or inspect something by walking over or along it, especially the boundaries of an area or piece of property ○ *walk the west property line* **8.** *vi* **BE STOLEN** to disappear or be stolen (*informal*) ○ *The petty cash seems to have walked.* **9.** *vi US* **GO OUT ON STRIKE** to take strike action (*slang*) ○ *threatened to walk* **10.** *vi US* **LEAVE IN PROTEST** to quit a job, event, or meeting in order to express disagreement (*slang*) ○ *You better apologize, or I'm walking!* **11.** *vi* **BE FREED FROM JAIL OR ACQUITTED** to be released from prison or found innocent of a crime (*slang*) ○ *I couldn't believe they walked after what they did!* **12.** *vi* **LIVE IN PARTICULAR WAY** to conduct your life in a particular way (*archaic*) ○ *walk with God* **13.** *vi* BASEBALL **GO TO FIRST BASE** in baseball, to proceed to first base on four balls **14.** *vt* BASEBALL **ALLOW BATTER ON FIRST** in baseball, to allow a batter to go to first base on four balls **15.** *vi* BASKETBALL **TAKE STEPS ILLEGALLY** in basketball, to take more than two steps without dribbling while holding the ball, in contravention of the rules ■ *n* **1. JOURNEY MADE ON FOOT** a journey made on foot, especially for pleasure or exercise ○ *a walk in the woods* **2. DISTANCE OR TIME OF FOOT JOURNEY** the distance traveled or the time it takes to go somewhere on foot ○ *a four-mile walk* ○ *a ten-minute walk from home* **3. WAY OF WALKING** somebody's characteristic way of walking ○ *She's got a graceful walk.* **4. PLACE FOR PEDESTRIANS** a place designed or set aside for the use of people on foot **5. ROUTE FOR PEOPLE WALKING** a route or path for travelers on foot ○ *The miners' trail is an easy scenic walk.* **6. RACE** a race in which the competitors walk a particular distance as quickly as possible **7. AREA FOR ANIMALS** an enclosed area for exercising or pasturing domestic animals such as horses **8. ROWS OF TREES** a plantation of widely spaced trees or shrubs **9. SPACE BETWEEN ROWS** the space between rows of widely spaced trees or shrubs **10.** *US* **SOMETHING VERY EASY** something that is very easy to do (*informal*) **11.** RIDING **SLOW GAIT OF HORSE** a relatively slow-paced way of moving for a horse or other four-legged animal, in which two feet are always on the ground ○ *The mare started at a walk before breaking into a trot.* **12.** BASEBALL **ACT OF REACHING FIRST BASE** in baseball, the act of reaching first base on four balls **13.** BASKETBALL **ILLEGAL MOVEMENT WHILE HOLDING BALL** in basketball, the taking of more than two steps without dribbling while holding the ball, in contravention of the rules [Old English *wealcan* "roll, toss," *wealcian* "roll up" < Germanic] —**walk·a·ble** *adj* ◇ **walk all over somebody 1.** to ignore the rights or feelings of somebody **2.** to defeat somebody easily ◇ **walk tall** to feel and display self-confidence and pride in your achievements

walk away *vi* **1. ABANDON PROBLEM** to avoid becoming or refuse to become involved in a situation or problem **2. HAVE MINOR INJURIES** to survive an accident uninjured or with only minor injuries and be able to walk from the scene **3. WIN SOMETHING** to win or achieve something ○ *She walked away with the first prize.*

4. **DEFEAT SOMEBODY** to defeat or outdo another person or team easily

walk in on *vt* to interrupt or intrude on somebody or something by entering a place without warning ○ *She walked in on them in the middle of an argument.*

walk off *v* **1.** *vi* to leave a place abruptly ○ *She walked off without a word.* **2.** *vt* to get rid of something such as an injury or feeling of sickness by walking

walk off with *vt (informal)* **1.** to steal something ○ *walked off with all the jewels* **2.** to win something effortlessly

walk out *vi* **1. LEAVE WITHOUT EXPLANATION** to leave, especially in anger or protest, without explanation **2. GO OUT ON STRIKE** to take strike action **3. LEAVE** to leave, abandoning a spouse, partner, or family permanently

walk out on *vt* to abandon a spouse, partner, or family permanently (*informal*) ○ *My wife walked out on me last summer.*

walk through *vt* **1. GIVE SOMEBODY STEP-BY-STEP EXPLANATION** to go through the various stages of something with somebody in advance in order to make it familiar and understandable ○ *They walked their client through the whole cross-examination procedure.* **2.** ARTS **REHEARSE OR PERFORM PLAY PERFUNCTORILY** to rehearse something in a simple unelaborate way, without props or costumes, mainly practicing basic moves and positions, or perform something in a perfunctory uncommitted way that resembles a rehearsal **3.** MEDIA **REHEARSE PROGRAM WITHOUT CAMERAS** to rehearse a television program without cameras

walk·a·bout /wáwkə bòwt/ *n* an extended journey on foot through a remote area made by an Australian Aboriginal wishing to experience or return to a traditional way of life and to traditional beliefs ◇ **go walkabout** to go for an extended journey on foot through a remote area in order to experience or return to a traditional Australian Aboriginal way of life and beliefs (*informal*)

walk·a·way /wáwkə wày/ *n US* **1.** an easily won contest or victory (*slang*) ○ *The election was a walkaway.* **2.** something that can be easily done or accomplished (*informal*)

walk·er /wáwkər/ *n* **1. SOMEBODY WHO WALKS** somebody who walks, especially for exercise or in races **2. SUPPORT FOR BABY** a lightweight framework on wheels that surrounds a baby, used to help a baby learn to walk **3. WALKING SUPPORT** a lightweight waist-high framework, usually with four legs and rubber feet, used to help somebody who cannot walk without support **4.** *US* CLOTHING **WALKING SHOE** a shoe designed for walking

Alice Walker

Wal·ker /wáwkər/, **Alice** (*b.* 1944) US writer. Her novels, including the Pulitzer Prize-winning *The Color Purple* (1982), are concerned largely with the experience of African American women. Full name **Walker, Alice Malsenior**. See Cultural note at **purple**

"People think pleasing God is all God cares about. But any fool living in the world can see it always trying to please us back."
[Alice Walker, *The Color Purple*; 1982]

"Expect nothing. Live frugally / on surprise."
[Alice Walker, "Expect Nothing"; 1973]

Wal·ker, John (*b.* 1952) New Zealand athlete. He won the 1,500 meters at the 1976 Olympic Games and was the first person to run a mile in less than 3 minutes 50 seconds (1975). Full name **Walker, John George**

Wal·ker, Sarah Breedlove (1867–1919) US businesswoman and philanthropist. She developed a hair-straightening product (1905) and went on to establish and run the most successful African American-owned-and-managed company of that period. Known as **Madame C. J. Walker**

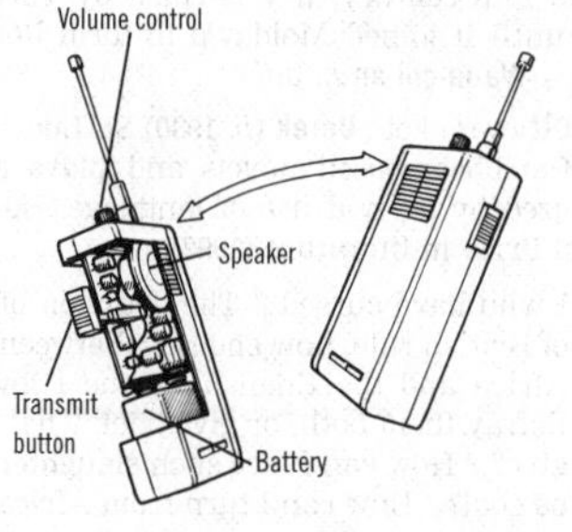

walkie-talkie

walk·ie-talk·ie /wàwkee táwkee/, **walk·y-talk·y** (*plural* **walk·y-talk·ies**) *n* a handheld battery-operated radio transmitter and receiver often used by emergency personnel to communicate with one another [Mid-20C. Playful variant of WALK + TALK]

walk-in /wáwk ìn/ *adj* **1. LARGE ENOUGH TO ENTER** large and spacious enough to enter ○ *a walk-in closet* **2. LOCATED ON STREET** having direct access from the street ○ *a walk-in apartment* ■ *n* **1.** *US* **COLD STORAGE ROOM** a cold storage room or a refrigerator or freezer large enough to enter **2. CUSTOMER WITHOUT APPOINTMENT** a customer, patient, or interviewee who is served or seen without an appointment, e.g., at a barber shop or doctor's office (*informal*) **3.** *US* **DEFECTOR** somebody who walks into a foreign embassy or consulate wanting to leave his or her country **4.** *US* **EASY VICTORY** an easily won victory

walk·ing /wáwking/ *adj* **1. ABLE TO WALK** capable of walking **2. FOR WALKING** used or designed for the purpose of walking ○ *walking shoes* **3. OF WALKING** involving traveling on foot ○ *a walking tour* ◇ **a walking dictionary** *or* **encyclopedia** somebody who is very knowledgeable

walk·ing bass /-bàyss/ *n* a bass musical accompaniment, usually consisting of small steps or intervals up and down the scale in 4/4 time

walk·ing boot *n* a lightweight rigid knee-length boot with a reinforced sole and straps that fasten around the leg. Use: support after a sprain or fracture.

walk·ing cat·fish *n* a freshwater catfish with special organs that enable it to breathe on land for short periods while it moves to another body of water. Native to: tropical Asia. Latin name: *Clarius batrachus.*

walk·ing del·e·gate *n US* a labor-union representative appointed to visit local unions and their employers to insure compliance with contracts and sometimes to represent the local union in negotiations

walk·ing fern *n* a fern whose long arching fronds take root at the tip and sprout new plants. Native to: eastern North America. Latin name: *Camptosorus rhizophyllus.*

walk·ing horse *n* ZOOL same as **Tennessee Walking Horse**

walk·ing leaf *n* **1.** PLANTS same as **walking fern 2.** *US* INSECTS same as **leaf insect**

walk·ing pa·pers *npl* official notification that somebody has been fired from a job or dismissed from military service (*informal*)

walk·ing stick *n* **1.** a cane or stick used to assist in walking **2.** *US* a long brown or green insect that resembles a twig, especially a North American species that feeds on leaves. Latin name: *Diapheromera femorata.*

walk·ing wound·ed *npl* **1.** casualties of war, terrorism, or disaster who are able to walk despite their injuries **2.** people who continue to be affected by great emotional pain experienced during their lives

Walk·man /wáwkmən/ *tdmk* a trademark for a small portable cassette player with earphones

walk of life *n* somebody's occupation or social or economic class ○ *people from all walks of life*

walk-on *n* **1.** a small part, usually a nonspeaking one, in a stage or movie production **2.** an actor who has a small part, usually a nonspeaking one, in a stage or movie production

walk·out /wáwk òwt/ *n* **1.** an organized strike by employees in which workers walk out of the building or off the premises **2.** a departure in protest or anger about something

walk·o·ver /wáwk ōvər/ *n* **1.** an easy victory or one that is obtained without a contest, e.g., because the opposing side did not show (*informal*) **2.** a horse race in which only one horse is entered

walk·through /wáwk thrōō/ *n* **1.** an early play rehearsal without props or costumes, or a television rehearsal without cameras, usually to practice basic moves and positions **2.** a set of instructions on how to use a piece of software or complete a computer game, including advice on how to proceed if problems are encountered

walk-up *n* **1.** a building of several stories without an elevator (*informal*) **2.** an apartment in a building of several stories without an elevator

walk·way /wáwk wày/ *n* a specially constructed path for pedestrians

Wal·kyr·ie *n* MYTHOL another spelling of **Valkyrie**

walk·y-talk·y *n* COMMUNICATION another spelling of **walkie-talkie**

wall /wawl/ *n* **1. FLAT SIDE OF BUILDING OR ROOM** a vertical structure forming an inside partition or an outside surface of a building **2. STANDING STRUCTURE THAT SURROUNDS OR BLOCKS** a narrow upright structure, usually built of stone, wood, plaster, or brick, that acts as a boundary or keeps something in or out **3. DEFENSIVE STRUCTURE** a structure of earth or stone built for defensive purposes **4. PHYSICAL OR PSYCHOLOGICAL OBSTACLE** something similar to a wall in appearance or impenetrability ○ *met with a wall of reporters* **5. SOMETHING THAT PREVENTS COMMUNICATION** an obstacle to understanding or communication between people **6.** CLIMBING **ROCK FACE** a vertical or nearly vertical rock face ○ *a sheer wall of granite* **7.** CIV ENG **BARRIER TO FLOODING** a structure built as a barrier to flooding **8.** ANAT **BODY MEMBRANE OR LINING** a membrane or lining enclosing or bounding an organ, blood vessel, or cavity of the body ○ *the uterine wall* **9.** BIOL **RIGID COVERING FOR SOME CELLS** a rigid covering over the outer membranes of plant cells and of some prokaryotic animal cells **10.** SOCCER **LINE OF DEFENSIVE PLAYERS** in soccer, a line of defensive players who must stand at least ten yards from a free kick and who try to block a shot on goal ■ **walls** *npl* **BARRIERS TO INTIMACY** protective behavior used by somebody to keep others from getting too close ■ *vt* (**walled, wall·ing, walls**) **1. SURROUND SOMETHING WITH WALLS** to fortify or surround somebody or something with a wall ○ *They walled in the back yard.* **2. SEPARATE SOMETHING WITH WALLS** to put up a wall to separate one area from another **3. CLOSE SOMETHING WITH WALL** to close an opening with a wall ○ *wall up the passage* **4. TRAP OR BURY SOMEBODY BEHIND WALL** to seal somebody or something in a space with a wall [Pre-12C. < Latin *vallum* "rampart" < *vallus* "stake"] —**walled** *adj* ◇ **be climbing the wall** *or* **walls** to be extremely bored or frustrated (*informal*) ◇ **drive somebody up the wall** to annoy or irritate somebody to an extreme degree (*informal*) ◇ **go to the wall** to be destroyed or ruined, especially financially (*informal*) ◇ **hit a brick wall** to encounter an insurmountable difficulty or obstacle ◇ **hit the wall** to reach a point at which no more can be done or achieved, e.g., a state of total exhaustion during a marathon run (*informal*)

wal·la *n* another spelling of **wallah** (*dated informal*)

wal·la·by /wóllәbee/ (*plural* **-bies**) *n* a marsupial that resembles a small kangaroo. Native to: Australia, New Guinea. Family: Macropodidae. See illustration on next page [Early 19C. < Dharuk *walabi, waliba*]

wal·la·by grass *n* PLANTS same as **danthonia**

Wal·lace /wólliss/, **Alfred Russel** (1823–1913) British naturalist. He formulated a theory of natural selection independently of Charles Darwin, and his rec-

wallaby

ognition of the distinctions between the fauna of Asia and Australia led him to define Wallace's line.

"Why do some die and some live?...The answer was clearly, that on the whole the best fitted live...This self-acting process would necessarily *improve the race...the fittest would survive.*"
[Alfred Russel Wallace, *My Life: A Record of Events and Opinions*; 1905]

Barnaby's

Edgar Wallace

Wal·lace, Edgar (1875–1932) British writer. He wrote more than 170 popular crime novels and thrillers, beginning with *The Four Just Men* (1905). Full name **Wallace, Richard Horatio Edgar**

Wal·lace, Henry A. (1888–1965) US agriculturalist and politician. With his father, Henry Cantwell Wallace, he developed the first successful hybrid seed corn. He became vice president during Franklin D. Roosevelt's third term (1941–45), and ran unsuccessfully for president as a progressive in 1948. Full name **Wallace, Henry Agard**

"The century on which we are entering—the century which will come out of this war—can be and must be the century of the common man."
[Henry A. Wallace, *Address,* "The Price of Free World Victory"; May 8, 1942]

Wal·lace, Lew (1827–1905) US writer, politician, and diplomat. A veteran of the Mexican War and the Civil War, he was governor of New Mexico (1878–81) and minister to Turkey (1881–85). He wrote *Ben Hur* (1880). Full name **Wallace, Lewis**

"Would you hurt a man keenest, strike at his self-love."
[Lew Wallace, *Ben Hur: A Tale of the Christ*; 1880]

Barnaby's

Sir William Wallace: commemorative statue near Melrose, Scotland

Wal·lace, Sir William (1272?–1305) Scottish patriot. He led a rebellion against the English (1297), but was defeated by Edward I (1298). He was later captured and executed.

Wal·lace's line /wóllissəz-/ *n* a hypothetical boundary separating the southwestern Pacific into two biogeographic regions with distinctive types of wildlife. The line runs between Bali and Lombok in the Indonesian island chain and north through the Makassar Strait, passing south of the Philippines. [Mid-19C. After Alfred Russel WALLACE]

Wal·la·chi·a another spelling of **Walachia**

wal·lah /wóllə/, **wal·la** *n* somebody in charge of something or associated with a particular service or occupation (*dated informal*) ○ *a legal wallah* [Late 18C. Via Hindi *-vālā* "(somebody) responsible for something or some duty" < Sanskrit *pālaka* "keeper"]

wal·la·roo /wòllə ro͞o/ (*plural* **-roos** or *same*) *n* a large and sturdy kangaroo. Native to: rocky upland areas of Australia. Latin name: *Macropus robustus* or *Macropus bernardus.* [Early 19C. < Dharuk *walāru*]

Wal·la Wal·la /wóllə wòllə/ city in southeastern Washington, near the border with Oregon. It is home to Whitman College and Washington State Penitentiary. Population: 29,818 (2002 estimate).

wall bars *npl* a series of horizontal bars attached to a wall and used for exercise

wall·board /wáwl bàwrd/ *n* BUILDINGS same as **drywall**

wall·chart /wáwl chaàrt/ *n* a chart designed to be displayed on a wall to provide information or aid in instruction

wall·cov·er·ing *n* something such as wallpaper used as a decorative covering for a wall

wall·creep·er *n* a songbird with a long slender beak and black wings with scarlet markings. Native to: mountains of Europe and Asia. Latin name: *Tichodroma muraria.*

walled gar·den *n* **1.** a garden surrounded on all sides by a high wall **2.** a browsing environment for viewing websites that provides a means of controlling the information and websites that a user is able to access. It may either protect users such as children from unsuitable information or direct users to specific, often paid content supported by an Internet service provider.

Wal·ler /wóllər/, **Fats** (1904–43) US singer, pianist, and composer. He wrote and performed many jazz classics such as "Ain't Misbehavin" (1929). Born **Waller, Thomas Wright**

"Jazz isn't *what* you do, it's *how* you do it."
[Fats Waller. Quoted in *The Jazz Book,* Joachim E. Berendt; 1983]

wal·let /wóllət/ *n* **1.** POCKET-SIZED FOLDED CASE FOR MONEY a small flat folding case, usually made of leather or plastic, that holds paper money and credit cards and is usually carried in a pocket or purse **2.** FOLDER a folder for holding items such as papers, photographs, or maps **3.** SOFTWARE PROGRAM FOR ONLINE PURCHASES a software program used to carry out transactions for purchases made on the Internet (*used in e-commerce*) [14C. Probably via Anglo-Norman, "traveling pack" < Germanic, "roll"]

wall·eye /wáwl ī/ (*plural same* or **-eyes**) *n* **1.** FRESHWATER FISH OF N AMERICA a large predatory freshwater fish with large eyes that is related to the perch. Native to: northeastern North America. Latin name: *Stizostedion vitreum.* **2.** EYE THAT APPEARS WHITE an eye with a white or streaked iris that gives the appearance of a pale ring around the pupil **3.** WHITE IN CORNEA an eye with an opaque white cornea, or the condition that causes this opacity **4.** SQUINT a squint (**strabismus**) in which one or both eyes turn outward [Early 16C. Back-formation < WALLEYED]

wall·eyed /wáwl īd/ *adj* **1.** affected by walleye **2.** having bulging or staring eyes [14C. < N Germanic, "speckle-eyed"]

wall·eyed pike *n* FISH same as **walleye** (sense 1)

wall·eyed pol·lack *n* a fish of the cod family resembling a pollack. Native to: northern Pacific. Latin name: *Theragra chalcogramma.*

wall·flow·er /wáwl flòwr/ *n* **1.** SPRING-FLOWERING GARDEN PLANT a common spring-blooming garden plant with rather woody erect stems. Flowers: fragrant, yellow, orange, or brownish, clustered at top of stem. Genera: *Cheiranthus* or *Erysimum.* **2.** PLANT WITH FRAGRANT COLORFUL FLOWERS a wild plant often found growing on walls, rocks, and cliffs. Flowers: fragrant, colorful. Native to: southern Europe. Latin name: *Cheiranthus cheiri.* **3.** SOMEBODY UNNOTICED AT SOCIAL EVENT a shy or retiring person who remains unnoticed at social events, especially a woman without a dance partner (*informal*)

wall hang·ing *n* a tapestry or other large flat object hung on a wall as a decoration

Wal·lis /wólliss/, **Sir Barnes** (1887–1979) British aeronautical engineer. He designed the Wellington bomber and the "bouncing bombs" that destroyed two dams in a raid on Germany during World War II. Full name **Wallis, Sir Barnes Neville**

Wal·lis and Fu·tu·na Is·lands /-foo to͞onə-/ island group situated in the southwestern Pacific Ocean, northeast of Fiji. It is an overseas territory of France. Capital: Mata Utu. Population: 15,734 (2003). Area: 106 sq. mi./274 sq. km.

wall mus·tard *n* PLANTS same as **wall rocket**

wall of sound *n* a recorded musical effect on pop records achieved by overdubbing or layering many different instruments around a pop tune

Wal·loon /wo lo͞on, wə-/ *n* **1.** a member of a French-speaking people living in southern Belgium, mainly in the autonomous region of Wallonia, and in neighboring parts of France **2.** a dialect of French spoken in southern Belgium and neighboring parts of France [Mid-16C. Via French *Wallon* < medieval Latin *wallo(n)-* "foreigner" < Germanic] —**Wal·loon** *adj*

wal·lop /wólləp/ (*informal*) *vt* (**-loped, -lop·ing, -lops**) **1.** HIT SOMEBODY OR SOMETHING VERY HARD to strike somebody or something with great force ○ *She can really wallop the ball.* **2.** BEAT SOMEBODY to give somebody a sound physical beating **3.** DEFEAT SOMEBODY DECISIVELY to defeat a person or team decisively ■ *n* **1.** HARD HIT a powerful blow **2.** ABILITY TO HIT HARD the ability to strike a powerful blow ○ *He's got a wallop that could make him heavyweight champion.* **3.** ABILITY TO IMPRESS the ability to create a powerful impression on others ○ *The play's final revelations pack the emotional wallop of the most sublime of Shakespearean comedies.* [14C. < Old French *waloper,* variant of *galoper* "gallop, run well" < Germanic]

wal·lop·ing /wólləping/ (*informal*) *n* **1.** BEATING a sound physical beating **2.** DECISIVE DEFEAT a decisive defeat or victory ■ *adj* BIG very large or impressive ○ *The fishermen came back with a walloping catch.* ■ *adv* ADDS EMPHASIS used to emphasize the size or extent of something ○ *a walloping big lie*

wal·low /wóllō/ *vi* (**-lowed, -low·ing, -lows**) **1.** ROLL IN SOMETHING to lie down and roll around in something ○ *hogs wallowing in mud* **2.** INDULGE IN SOMETHING EXCESSIVELY to take pleasure or be immersed in something in a self-indulgent way ○ *wallowed in memories of the long-gone glory days* **3.** HAVE HUGE AMOUNT OF SOMETHING to have an ample or excessive supply of something ○ *a family wallowing in money* **4.** WALK WITH DIFFICULTY to move clumsily or with difficulty ■ *n* **1.** ACT OF WALLOWING an instance of wallowing in something such as mud, emotion, or material luxury **2.** ZOOL PLACE WHERE ANIMALS ROLL a muddy, wet, or dusty place used by animals for rolling around in **3.** ZOOL DEPRESSION FORMED BY ANIMAL a sunken area in the ground made by a rolling animal **4.** *US* CONDITION OF DEPRAVITY a state of degradation or moral corruption [Old English *wealwian* "to roll" < Indo-European] —**wal·low·er** *n*

wall·pa·per /wáwl pàypər/ *n* **1.** PAPER TO DECORATE WALLS paper, usually printed with a pattern, that is pasted on walls and sometimes ceilings as a covering and decoration **2.** BACKGROUND PATTERN FOR SCREEN the background pattern for a computer screen, composed of graphics ■ *vti* (**-pered, -per·ing, -pers**) PUT WALLPAPER ON SOMETHING to cover a surface with wallpaper

wall plug *n* a receptacle in a wall, connected to an electric circuit, into which appliances can be plugged

wall rock *n* the rock that surrounds a vein, mineral deposit, or fault

wall rock·et *n* a cruciferous plant that grows on

walls and waste ground. Flowers: yellow. Native to: Europe. Latin name: *Diplotaxis muralis* or *Diplotaxis tenuifolia*.

wall rue *n* a small delicate fern that grows in fan-shaped clusters on walls or in rocky crevices. Latin name: *Asplenium ruta-muraria*.

Wall Street /wáwl-/ *n* **1.** the street in Manhattan, New York City, where the New York Stock Exchange and many major financial institutions of the United States are located **2.** the US financial market, especially as represented by the publicly traded companies comprising the stock markets

wall-to-wall *adj* **1. FROM ONE WALL TO ANOTHER** completely covering a floor ○ *wall-to-wall carpeting* **2. FILLING SOMETHING COMPLETELY** completely filling, covering, or pervading something (*informal*) ○ *fed up with wall-to-wall pop music* **3. ALL-INCLUSIVE** including everyone or everything (*informal*) ○ *wall-to-wall insurance coverage* ■ *n* **FITTED CARPET** a carpet that completely covers a floor

wal·ly /wóllee/ (*plural* **-lies**) *n UK* an offensive term that deliberately insults somebody's intelligence or common sense (*slang*) [Mid-20C. Origin ?]

wal·nut /wáwl nùt, -nət/ *n* **1. EDIBLE NUT** a deeply wrinkled nut that is enclosed in a hard shell and a thick leathery husk **2. VALUABLE WOOD** a hard dark brown wood. Use: cabinetwork, paneling, veneers. (*often used before a noun*) **3. TREE VALUED FOR NUTS AND WOOD** a deciduous tree with fragrant compound leaves and drooping catkins, grown worldwide for its shade, wood, and walnuts. Genus: *Juglans*. **4. DARK BROWN COLOR** a dark brown color like that of walnut wood [14C. < Old English *wealhnutu* "foreign nut," < *wealh* "foreign, Welsh, Celtic"] —**wal·nut** *adj*

ORIGIN The prehistoric Germanic peoples regarded the ***walnut*** as the "foreign nut" because it did not originally grow in northern Europe, but was introduced from Gaul and Italy, the lands of the Celts and the Romans (the Germans' own native nut was the hazel).

Wal·pole /wáwl pōl, wól-/ town in eastern Massachusetts, west of Stoughton and southwest of Boston. Population: 3,632 (2002 estimate).

Wal·pole, Horace (1717–97) British writer. The son of Sir Robert Walpole, he wrote one of the first Gothic novels *The Castle of Otranto* (1764) and engaged in extensive and celebrated literary correspondence.

> "This world is a comedy to those who think, a tragedy to those who feel."
> [Horace Walpole, *Letter to Anne, Countess of Upper Ossory*; August 16, 1776]

Wal·pole, Robert, 1st Earl of Orford (1676–1745) English political leader. He became a Whig member of Parliament in 1701. From 1721 to 1742 he wielded considerable political power as chief minister to George I and George II. Although he himself repudiated the title, which did not become official until much later, he is regarded as Britain's first prime minister.

> "Anything but history, for history must be false."
> [Robert Walpole, *Walpoliana*; 1781]

Wal·pur·gis Night /vaal pŏŏrgiss-/ *n* **1.** in German folklore, the witches' feast night on the Brocken in the Harz Mountains. Date: April 30. **2.** a nightmarish situation [Early 19C. Translation of German *Walpurgisnacht*, after *Walpurga*, 8C Anglo-Saxon saint]

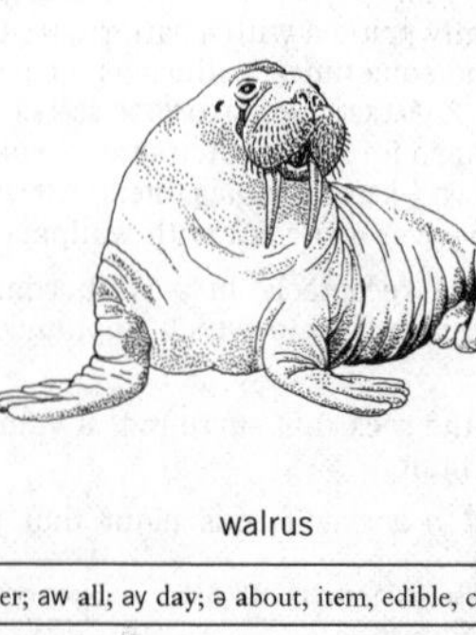

walrus

wal·rus /wáwlrəss/ (*plural same* or **-rus·es**) *n* a large sea mammal related to seals and sea lions, with tough wrinkled skin, large tusks, and bristly whiskers. Native to: Arctic. Latin name: *Odobenus rosmarus*. [Early 18C. < Dutch *walrus, walros* "whale-horse" < *walvis(ch)* "whale"]

wal·rus mus·tache *n* a thick drooping mustache resembling a walrus's whiskers

Wa·łę·sa /waa lénssə, vaa wénssə/, **Lech** (*b.* 1943) labor leader and president of Poland (1990–95). At the head of Solidarity after 1980, he led Poland's independent labor movement and was instrumental in ending Communist rule there. He was awarded the Nobel Peace Prize (1983).

> "SOLIDARITY was born at that precise moment when the shipyard strike evolved from a local success in the shipyard, to a strike in support of other factories and business enterprises, large and small, in need of our protection."
> [Lech Wałęsa, "The Strike and the August Agreements," *A Path of Hope*; 1987]

Wal·sall /wáwl sàwl/ industrial city near Birmingham, in central England. Population: 174,739 (1991).

Wal·ter /vaaltər, wáwl-/, **Bruno** (1876–1962) German-born US conductor. He was best known for his interpretations of the music of Mozart, Bruckner, and Mahler. Born **Schlesinger, Bruno Walter**

Wal·ter Mit·ty /wàwltər míttee/ (*plural* **Wal·ter Mit·ties**) *n* somebody with a very ordinary dull life who daydreams about having great adventures and success [Mid-20C. After the hero of "The Secret Life of Walter Mitty," a 1939 short story by James Thurber] —**Wal·ter Mit·ty·ish** *adj*

Barbara Walters

Wal·ters /wáwltərz/, **Barbara** (*b.* 1931) US television journalist. As a reporter and host of television news magazines and celebrity interview shows, she established a reputation for eliciting candid answers to difficult questions from public figures.

Wal·tham /wáwlthəm/ city in eastern Massachusetts, southwest of Arlington. Founded in 1636, it is a western suburb of Boston. Population: 59,073 (2002 estimate).

Wal·ton /wáwlt'n/, **Ernest T. S.** (1903–95) Irish physicist. He helped develop a particle accelerator, which led to the first artificial nuclear reaction. He shared the Nobel Prize in physics (1951). Full name **Walton, Ernest Thomas Sinton**

Wal·ton, Izaak (1593–1683) English writer. He is remembered for his book on fishing and the charms of pastoral life, *The Compleat Angler* (1653).

> "No man can lose what he never had."
> [Izaak Walton, *The Compleat Angler*; 1653]

Wal·ton, Sir William (1902–83) British composer. He wrote orchestral works, an opera, and movie scores, including the music for Laurence Olivier's adaptations of Shakespeare's plays. Full name **Walton, Sir William Turner**

waltz /wawlts/ *n* (*plural* **waltz·es**) **1. DANCE FOR COUPLES IN TRIPLE TIME** a ballroom dance in triple time in which a couple turn continuously while moving around **2. MUSIC FOR WALTZ** the music for a waltz **3. SOMETHING EASY** something that can be accomplished effortlessly (*informal*) ■ *v* (**waltzed, waltz·ing, waltz·es**) **1.** *vti* **DANCE WALTZ** to dance a waltz, or lead somebody in a waltz ○ *waltzed me around the room* **2.** *vi* **MOVE WITH SELF-CONFIDENCE** to move quickly with ease and self-assurance (*informal*) ○ *She just waltzed right in and demanded more money*. **3.** *vi* **SUCCEED EASILY** to achieve success effortlessly in an activity [Late 18C. < German *Walzer* < *walzen* "waltz, roll, revolve"]

Wal·vis Bay /wàwlviss-/ town and port in western Namibia, on the Atlantic coast. It was a former enclave of South Africa until 1994. Population: 50,000 (1997).

Wam·pa·no·ag /wòmpə nṓ ag/ (*plural same* or **-ags**) *n* a member of an Algonquian people who lived in Rhode Island and Massachusetts [Late 17C. < Narraganset, "easterners"] —**Wam·pa·no·ag** *adj*

wam·pum /wómpəm/, **wam·pum·peag** /-pèeg/ *n* **1.** small polished beads made from shells, threaded on string, and used by some Native North Americans as decoration, for ceremonial purposes, or in former times for money **2.** same as **money** (*dated slang*) [Mid-17C. Shortening of *wampumpeag* < Massachusett, "white strings"]

wan /won/ *adj* (**wan·ner, wan·nest**) **1. PALE** unhealthily pale, especially from illness or grief **2. INDICATIVE OF LOW SPIRITS** suggesting ill health or unhappiness ○ *He gave me a wan look*. **3. FAINT** lacking brightness ○ *a wan star* ■ *vti* (**wanned, wan·ning, wans**) **MAKE OR BECOME PALE OR ILL** to become pale or unhealthy, or make somebody or something do this (*literary*) [Old English *wann* "dark, dusky, gray," origin ?] —**wan·ly** *adv* —**wan·ness** *n*

WAN /wan/ *abbr* COMPUT wide-area network

Wan·a·ma·ker /wónnə mâykər/, **John** (1838–1922) US merchant. He began a clothing business in Philadelphia (1861), which expanded to become one of the leading department store chains in the United States.

wand /wond/ *n* **1. ROD WITH SUPPOSED MAGICAL POWERS** a thin rod believed to possess magical powers, used by supposed magicians, wizards, and supernatural beings **2. STAFF SHOWING AUTHORITY** a thin staff carried as a symbol of office **3. VACUUM CLEANER PART** an attachment between the hose and cleaning tool of a vacuum cleaner that resembles a pipe **4.** COMPUT **BAR-CODE SCANNER** a hand-held optical scanning device used to read and enter bar-code information into a computer **5.** MUSIC same as **baton** [12C. < Old Norse *vondr* "straight flexible stick" < Germanic, "to turn"]

wan·der /wóndər/ *v* (**-dered, -der·ing, -ders**) **1.** *vti* **TRAVEL WITHOUT DESTINATION** to move from place to place, either without a purpose or without a known destination ○ *They wander the countryside looking for work*. **2.** *vi* **LEAVE FIXED PATH** to stray from a place, path, or course ○ *Don't wander far from home*. **3.** *vi* **DAYDREAM** to lose the ability to concentrate or pay attention ○ *My mind was wandering*. **4.** *vi* **MEANDER** to follow a winding course ○ *The river wandered through the meadows*. **5.** *vi* **STROLL SOMEWHERE** to go somewhere at a leisurely pace **6.** *vi* **FAIL TO THINK OR SPEAK CLEARLY** to lose the ability to think, speak, or write in an organized and coherent way ■ *n* **AIMLESS STROLL** an act of moving from place to place in an aimless or leisurely way [Old English *wandrian* < Germanic, "to turn"] —**wan·der·er** *n* —**wan·der·ing** *adj* —**wan·der·ing·ly** *adv*

SPELLCHECK wander or **wonder**? Do not confuse the spelling of ***wander*** and ***wonder***, which sound similar. ***Wander*** means "move from p,lace to place without a purpose or destination" or "stray": *We wandered along the beach. Try not to let your thoughts wander.* ***Wonder*** is a noun denoting "amazed admiration or awe" or "something marvelous" (as in *a feeling of wonder, one of the wonders of the world, no wonder he doesn't trust her*), and also a verb meaning "speculate about something" (as in *I wonder how much it costs.*).

wan·der·ing Jew *n* a trailing plant widely grown as a houseplant for its variegated foliage. Flowers: white, rose-red. Native to: tropical America. Latin name: *Tradescantia fluminensis* or *Tradescantia albiflora* or *Zebrina pendula*.

Wan·der·ing Jew *n* in medieval legend, a Jewish man who was condemned to remain alive and wandering the world until Judgment Day for having mocked Jesus Christ on the day of the Crucifixion

wan·der·lust /wóndər lùst/ *n* a strong desire to travel [Early 20C. < German, "desire to travel"]

wane /wayn/ *vi* (**waned, wan·ing, wanes**) **1.** SHOW LESS LIGHTED AREA to show a decreasing illuminated surface between a full moon and new moon **2.** GET SMALLER OR LESS to decrease gradually in intensity or power ○ *His interest was waning.* **3.** FINISH to draw to a close ○ *Winter is waning at last.* ■ *n* **1.** LESSENING IN INTENSITY a gradual lessening of power or intensity **2.** TIME DURING WANING OF MOON the period during which the Moon's visible illuminated surface is decreasing in size **3.** PERIOD OF LESSENING a period of gradual decrease **4.** END OF PERIOD the conclusion of a time or season ○ *the wane of summer* **5.** WOODWORK IRREGULARITY ON PLANK EDGE a flawed edge left on a rough-sawn plank [Old English *wanian* "lessen" < Germanic, "lacking"] ◇ **be on the wane** to be decreasing or passing out of fashion

Wang /waang/, **Vera** (*b.* 1949) US fashion designer. She was a senior editor at Vogue before opening her own design studio (1990), creating luxury clothes and becoming known especially for her wedding dresses.

Wang·a·nu·i /wòngə nōō ee/ river in the southwestern part of the North Island, New Zealand. It rises on Mount Tongariro and flows southward through the city of Wanganui to the Cook Strait. Length: 180 mi./290 km.

wan·gle /wáng g'l/ (*informal*) *vt* (**-gled, -gling, -gles**) **1.** GET SOMETHING DEVIOUSLY to get something using indirect and sometimes deceitful methods ○ *I'm trying to wangle some time off work.* **2.** FALSIFY ACCOUNTS to manipulate accounts or records, usually deceitfully ■ *n* DEVIOUS METHOD an indirect and sometimes deceitful means of accomplishing something [Late 19C. Origin ?] —**wan·gler** *n*

wan·i·gan /wónnigən/ *n* **1.** *Northern US* BOAT OR CHEST OF LUMBER SUPPLIES a watertight boat or chest equipped with supplies for a lumber camp **2.** *Northeast US, Northwest US* CAMP SUPPLIES supplies for a camp or cabin **3.** *regional* LIVING QUARTERS ON RUNNERS a cabin on runners towed behind a trailer, used as living quarters in Alaska for a work crew **4.** *regional* TRAILER HOUSE ADDITION an addition built on a trailer house in Alaska for extra space [Mid-19C. < Montagnais *atawangan* < *atawan* "buy or sell"]

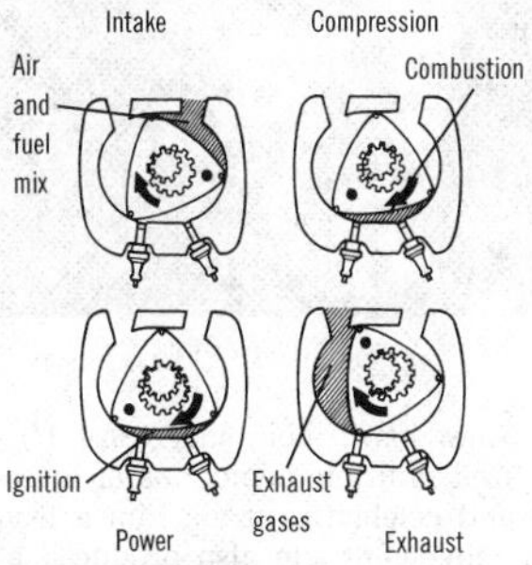

Wankel engine

Wan·kel en·gine /wángk'l-/ *n* an internal-combustion engine in which an approximately triangular rotor inside an elliptical combustion chamber replaces the pistons of a conventional engine, thus reducing the number of moving parts [Mid-20C. After Felix *Wankel* (1902–88), German engineer]

wan·na /wónnə/ *contr* want to (*nonstandard*) ○ *I wanna go!*

wan·na·be /wónnəbee/ *n* somebody who tries to be like somebody else or to belong to a specific group (*informal disapproving*) [Late 20C. Alteration of *want to be*]

want /wont/ *vt* (**want·ed, want·ing, wants**) **1.** DESIRE SOMETHING to feel a need or desire for something ○ *We want a new car.* **2.** WISH SOMETHING DONE to desire to do something or that something be done ○ *I don't want you being late.* ○ *He wants his steak well done.* **3.** MISS SOMETHING to feel the lack of something ○ *After a week on the road, I want my own bed.* **4.** WISH SOMEBODY TO BE PRESENT to wish to see or speak to somebody ○ *He's wanted on the phone.* ○ *Someone wants you at the door.* **5.** SEEK SOMEBODY AS CRIME SUSPECT to seek somebody in connection with a crime (*usually passive*) ○ *wanted for two felonies* **6.** NEED SOMETHING to have a need for something (*informal*) ○ *What that kid wants is some discipline!* ○ *The closets want cleaning.* **7.** DESIRE SOMEBODY SEXUALLY to feel sexual desire for somebody (*informal*) ■ *n* **1.** NEED something that somebody desires or needs (*usually used in the plural*) ○ *All your wants can be easily supplied.* **2.** LACK OF SOMETHING an absence or scarcity of something ○ *no want of snow for the skiers this winter* ○ *If we fail, it won't be for want of trying.* **3.** POVERTY the state of being poor ○ *Freedom from want is a fundamental human right.* [12C. < Old Norse *vanta* "be lacking" < Germanic, "lacking"] —**want·er** *n*

SYNONYMS ***want, desire, wish, long, yearn, covet, crave***
CORE MEANING: to seek to have, do, or achieve something
want to feel a need or desire for something ○ *What do you want for your birthday?* ○ *All I really wanted was to buy a house and settle down.* **desire** to want something very strongly ○ *He had everything that a man could desire – looks, talent, wealth.* ○ *She needed to conquer her phobia if she was to lead the normal happy life she so desired.* **wish** to have a strong feeling of wanting something to happen or wanting to have something. ○ *We wished there was more time to arrange everything.* ○ *"I do wish we could help her somehow," sighed Christine.* **long** to have a strong desire for a person, place, or thing, especially somebody or something unattainable or not within immediate reach ○ *We've all been longing to see him.* ○ *She'd been longing for peace and quiet so that she could finish her book.* **yearn** to have a strong desire for somebody or something, especially when the desire is tinged with sadness ○ *peoples who yearn for freedom, democracy, equality, and human rights* **covet** to have a strong desire to possess something that belongs to somebody else, or (*formal*) to want to have something very much ○ *This is his third failure to win the post he so covets.* **crave** to have a strong desire for something ○ *She openly craves publicity.* ○ *Will craved fame and fortune.*

want for *vt* to experience the lack of something ○ *The family wants for nothing.*
want in *vi* (*informal*) **1.** to wish to be included in something, especially a business deal ○ *Do you want in?* **2.** to wish to go inside a place ○ *See if the cat wants in.*
want out *vi* (*informal*) **1.** to wish to be excluded from or to leave something, especially a business deal ○ *We want out before we get into trouble.* **2.** to wish to go outside a building ○ *The dog wants out.*

want ad *n* a classified advertisement in a newspaper or magazine (*informal*)

want·ing /wónting/ *adj* not meeting expectations or requirements ○ *found wanting in the area of security*

wan·ton /wóntən/ *adj* **1.** SEXUALLY INDISCRIMINATE lacking restraint or inhibition, especially in sexual behavior **2.** RANDOM lacking reason or provocation ○ *wanton violence and destruction* **3.** DESIRING TO DO HARM done out of a desire to cause harm **4.** EXCESSIVE unrestrained, heedless of reasonable limits, or characterized by greed and extravagance ○ *wanton indulgence* **5.** UNRULY lacking discipline **6.** LUSH growing luxuriantly (*archaic*) **7.** PLAYFUL engaged in play that is carefree (*archaic*) ■ *n* SOMEBODY WITHOUT SEXUAL RESTRAINT a lascivious or sexually uninhibited person ■ *vi* (**-toned, -ton·ing, -tons**) BE WANTON to behave in a wanton manner (*archaic*) [14C. < Old English *wan-* "un-" + *togen* "disciplined" < *tēon* "train, discipline, pull"] —**wan·ton·ly** *adv* —**wan·ton·ness** *n*

WAP /wap/ *n* a standard protocol for the transmission of electronic data between handheld narrowband devices such as cellular phones and pagers and other sources of digital information such as the Internet. Full form **wireless application protocol**

wa·pee /wóppee/ *n Carib* a card game similar to poker, usually played for money (*informal*) [Possibly from a form of WHOP in the sense of "defeat somebody"]

wap·i·ti /wóppitee/ (*plural* **-tis** or *same*) *n* a large deer that has tall branched antlers and lives in herds. Native to: mountains of western North America. Latin name: *Cervus elaphus.* [Early 19C. < Shawnee *wapiti* "white rump"]

Wap·pin·ger /wóppinjər/ (*plural same* or **-gers**) *n* a member of a Native North American people who lived along the Hudson River in New York State, and whose members dispersed following wars with Dutch settlers in the 17th century

war /wawr/ *n* **1.** ARMED FIGHTING BETWEEN GROUPS a period of hostile relations between countries, states, or factions that leads to fighting between armed forces, especially in land, air, or sea battles ○ *The two countries are at war.* **2.** PERIOD OF ARMED FIGHTING a period of armed conflict between countries or groups ○ *during the Vietnam War* **3.** METHODS OF WARFARE the techniques or the study of the techniques of armed conflict **4.** CONFLICT a serious struggle, argument, or conflict between people ○ *The candidates are at war.* **5.** SERIOUS EFFORT TO END SOMETHING an effort to combat or eradicate something harmful ○ *a war against drugs* ■ *vi* (**warred, war·ring, wars**) **1.** MAKE WAR to engage in an armed conflict with somebody **2.** BE IN STRUGGLE to be involved in a serious struggle, argument, or conflict with somebody or an effort to combat or eradicate something harmful [12C. Via Old N French *werre*, Old French *guerre* < Germanic, "strife, confusion"]

CULTURAL NOTE ***War and Peace***, a novel (1865–69) by Russian writer Leo Tolstoy. This monumental work is set in Russia during and after the Napoleonic Wars (1805–14). Though it focuses on five fictional families, the story incorporates historical accounts and philosophical essays to create an extraordinarily comprehensive portrait of Russian society that touches on almost every aspect of human experience, from love and happiness to grief and war.

SYNONYMS See ***fight***.

war. *abbr* warrant

~~**waranty**~~ incorrect spelling of **warranty**

war ba·by *n* a baby born or conceived during a war

War Be·tween the States *n* HIST same as **Civil War** (sense 1)

war·ble[1] /wáwrb'l/ *vti* (**-bled, -bling, -bles**) **1.** SING WITH CHANGING NOTES to sing with trills and often changing notes (*refers to birds*) **2.** SING SOMETHING to sing in a quavering or trilling way, or express something in such song ○ *warble a tune* ■ *n* **1.** SINGING WITH OFTEN CHANGING NOTES singing with trills or other vocal modulations **2.** TRILLING SOUND a sound with trills or quavers [14C. < Old N French *werbler* "sing with trills" < Frankish, "whirl, trill"]

war·ble[2] /wáwrb'l/ *n* **1.** SWELLING IN HORSES AND CATTLE a swelling under the skin, usually on the back, of horses and cattle, caused by the warble fly maggot **2.** WARBLE FLY OR ITS LARVA the warble fly, or the maggot of the warble fly **3.** LUMP ON HORSE'S BACK FROM SADDLE a hard lump of tissue on the back of a riding horse, caused by the rubbing of the saddle [Late 16C. Origin ?]

war·ble fly *n* a large hairy fly, the larvae of which form painful swellings under the skin of cattle and horses. Family: Oestridae.

war·bler /wáwrblər/ *n* **1.** SMALL INSECT-EATING BIRD a small songbird of the wood warbler family that eats insects and is often brightly colored. Native to: North and South America. Family: Parulidae. **2.** BIRD RELATED TO THRUSH a songbird that is related to the thrush. Native to: Europe, Asia. Family: Sylviidae. **3.** SOMEBODY WHO SINGS somebody who sings, especially in a quavering or trilling way

war·bling vir·e·o *n* a small gray bird with a distinctive warbling song. Native to: North America. Latin name: *Virio gilvus.*

war·blog /wáwr blòg/ *n* a weblog concerned with terrorism, war, and conflict, often with a promilitary stance [Late 20C. After WEBLOG] —**war·blog·ger** *n*

war bon·net *n* a ceremonial headdress decorated with feathers, worn by some Native North American warriors

war bride *n* a woman who meets and marries a serviceman during wartime, especially one from another country

war·chalk·ing /wáwr chàwking/ *n* the act of scrawling symbols on sidewalks or building walls indicating to others the presence of unprotected private or corporate high-speed Internet connections, for use in obtaining free access (*slang*) —**war·chalk·er** *n*

war chest *n* an amount of funds collected to pay for a war or something such as a political campaign

war clouds *npl* signs of impending war

war cor·re·spon·dent *n* a journalist reporting from a war

war crime *n* a crime committed during wartime that is in violation of international agreements concerning the conventions of war, e.g., the mistreatment of prisoners or genocide (*often used in the plural*) —**war crim·i·nal** *n*

war cry *n* MIL same as **battle cry** (sense 1)

ward /wawrd/ *n* **1. CITY DIVISION** an administrative or electoral division of an area such as a city, town, or county **2. ROOM IN HOSPITAL** a room in a hospital, especially one for several patients being given similar treatment **3. PRISON DIVISION** a division in a prison **4.** LAW **SOMEBODY UNDER OFFICIAL CARE** somebody, especially a child or young person, who is under the care of a guardian or a court **5.** BUILDINGS **AREA IN CASTLE** an open area within the walls of a castle **6.** LAW **CUSTODY** a state of official custody or protection **7. DEFENSE MOVEMENT** a movement or stance used as a means of protection, e.g., in fencing **8.** CHR **LATTER-DAY SAINTS' ADMINISTRATIVE DIVISION** in the Church of Jesus Christ of Latter-Day Saints, an administrative division presided over by a bishop and two counselors **9. RIDGE IN KEY OR LOCK** a ridge or groove in a key or a lock that makes one fit the other ■ *vt* (**ward·ed, ward·ing, wards**) **PROTECT SOMEBODY OR SOMETHING** to guard or protect somebody or something (*archaic*) [Old English *weard* < Germanic, "be on guard"]

ward off *vt* **1.** to parry or repel a blow or attack **2.** to keep away or avert something bad

Ward /wawrd/, **Aaron Montgomery** (1843–1913) US merchant. He pioneered mail-order merchandising (1872) with a catalog offering low-cost goods to people in rural areas.

Ward, Artemus (1834–67) US humorist. In the persona of an uneducated traveling showman, he wrote newspaper pieces and lectures combining humor, satire, and basic common sense. Pseudonym of **Browne, Charles Farrar**

> "It is a pity that Chawcer, who had geneyus, was so unedicated. He's the wuss speller I know of."
> [Artemus Ward, *Artemus Ward in London*; 1867]

Ward, Sir Joseph (1856–1930) Australian-born prime minister of New Zealand (1906–12 and 1928–30). After serving as a Liberal prime minister, he was again elected to the premiership in 1928 as the leader of the United Party. See table at **prime minister**. Full name **Ward, Joseph George**

-ward, -wards *suffix* **1.** moving in a particular direction or directed toward a particular place ○ *earthward* **2.** lying or occurring in a particular direction ○ *rightward* ○ *windward* [Old English *-weard* < Germanic, "to turn"]

USAGE See *toward.*

war dance *n* a dance performed as a ceremony before a battle or to celebrate victory, e.g., by Native North Americans

ward·ed /wáwrdəd/ *adj* describes keys or locks that have ridges or grooves

war·den /wáwrd'n/ *n* **1.** CRIME **PRINCIPAL PRISON OFFICER** the principal officer in charge of a prison **2. OFFICIAL CONCERNED WITH REGULATIONS** an official who makes sure that regulations are enforced ○ *game warden* ○ *forest fire warden* **3.** *UK* **SOMEBODY IN CHARGE OF INSTITUTION** somebody who is in charge of an institution such as a college or school **4.** CHR same as **churchwarden** (sense 1) [12C. < Anglo-Norman *wardein* < Germanic, "be on guard"] —**war·den·ship** *n*

ward·er /wáwrdər/ *n UK* a prison officer [14C. < Anglo-Norman < Old N French *warder* "to guard," variant of French *garder*]

ward heel·er *n* somebody who does minor tasks for a local or city politician (*informal*)

war·driv·ing /wáwr drìving/ *n* the act of driving around an area in search of an unprotected wireless network in order to take advantage of a high-speed Internet connection belonging to somebody else and avoid paying a fee (*slang*)

ward·robe /wáwr drōb/ *n* **1. PLACE FOR CLOTHES** a large closet or freestanding cupboard with a rail or shelves for clothes and shoes **2. CLOTHES COLLECTION** all the clothes that belong to somebody **3. CLOTHES FOR PARTICULAR PURPOSE** a collection of clothes for a particular season or purpose **4. THEATER COSTUMES** the costumes used by a theatrical company **5. PLACE FOR COSTUMES** a place in a theater where costumes are kept **6. ROYAL DEPARTMENT** the department in a royal or noble household in charge of robes and jewels [14C. < Old N French *warderobe*, variant of French *garderobe* < French *garder* "to guard" + *robe* "robe"]

ward·robe mis·tress *n* the woman in charge of the costumes in a theater or on a movie set

ward·robe trunk *n* a large upright trunk with a rail on which clothes can be hung

ward·room /wáwrd ròom, -ròom/ *n* **1.** a room on a warship used by all the officers except the captain **2.** the officers on a ship who can use the wardroom

-wards *suffix* same as **-ward**

ward·ship /wáwrd shìp/ *n* **1.** the state of being in the care of a guardian appointed by parents or a court **2.** the state of being a ward in the church of Jesus Christ of Latter-Day Saints

ware[1] /wer/ *n* **1. SIMILAR THINGS** similar things, or things that are made of the same material (*usually used in combination*) ○ *flatware* **2. CERAMICS** ceramic articles of a particular kind or made by a particular manufacturer (*often used in combination*) ○ *delftware* ■ **wares** *npl* **1. THINGS FOR SALE** articles offered for sale **2. MARKETABLE SKILLS** skills or talents offered as a service or a commodity [Old English *waru*]

SPELLCHECK ware, wear, were, or **where**? Do not confuse the spelling of ***ware, wear, were,*** and ***where,*** which sound similar. ***Ware*** (referring to similar things, or things made of the same material), is most likely to be confused with ***wear*** (referring to clothing) in compound words such as *software, tableware, footwear,* and *knitwear.* ***Were*** is the past tense of *are* (as in *We were all young once.*), and ***where*** is used to ask about or indicate the place that somebody or something is in, at, going to, or coming from: *Where were you last night? They still live in the town where they were born.*

ware[2] /wer/ (*archaic*) *vti* (**wared, war·ing, wares**) same as **beware** ■ *adj* wary or prudent [Old English *warian* < Germanic, "be on guard"]

Ware·ham /wérrəm/ town in southeastern Massachusetts, on an inlet of Buzzards Bay, south of Plymouth and northeast of New Bedford. Population: 20,935 (2002 estimate).

ware·house *n* /wér hòwss/ (*plural* **-hous·es** /-hówzəz/) **1. STORAGE BUILDING** a large building in which goods, raw materials, or commodities are stored **2. BIG STORE** a large store, especially one where goods are sold wholesale ■ *vt* /wér hòwz, -hòwss/ (**-housed** /-hòwzd/, **-hous·ing** /-hòwzing/, **-hous·es** /-hòwzəz/) **1. STORE SOMETHING IN WAREHOUSE** to store goods, raw materials, or commodities in a warehouse **2. ABANDON IN INSTITUTION** to leave somebody in an institution that does not provide adequate care or treatment (*informal*) —**ware·hous·er** /-hòwzər/ *n*

ware·house·man /wér hòwssmən/ (*plural* **-men** /-mən/) *n* somebody, especially a man, who works in or owns a warehouse

ware·house·per·son /wér howss pùrss'n/ *n* somebody who works in or owns a warehouse

ware·hous·ing /wér hòwzing/ *n* the accumulation of a security in the hope that demand will push the price up as a result of the reduced supply on the open market

ware·room /wér ròom, -ròom/ *n US* a room where goods are kept or displayed for sale

warez /wérz/ *n* a commercial game or application that has been stripped of its copy protection and made available on the Internet by software pirates (*slang*) [Late 20C. Respelling of *wares*, the *-z* suffix being typically used to indicate the plural of terms for pirated software]

~~warf~~ incorrect spelling of **wharf**

war·fare /wáwr fèr/ *n* **1.** the act or fact of engaging in a war **2.** conflict or struggle ○ *economic warfare*

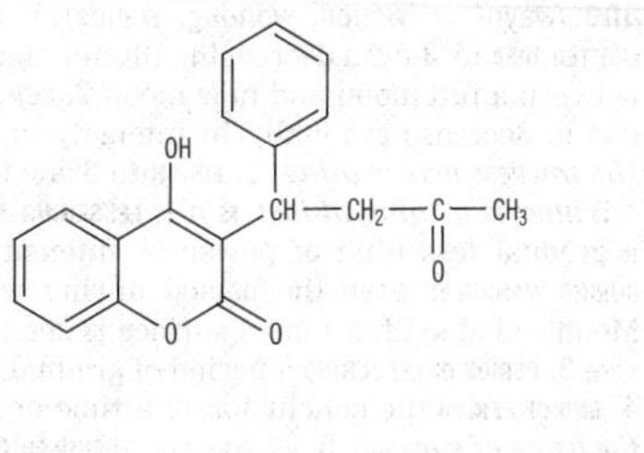

warfarin

war·fa·rin /wáwrfərin/ *n* a colorless crystalline compound. Use: rodenticide, anticoagulant in medicine. Formula: $C_{19}H_{16}O_4$. [Mid-20C. < initial letters of *Wisconsin Alumni Research Foundation* + COUMARIN]

war·fight·er /wáwr fìtər/ *n* a soldier, sailor, Marine, or airman who is engaged in combat against an enemy force

war·fight·ing /wáwr fìting/ *n* armed combat between the armed forces of nations engaged in war

war game *n* **1.** a military exercise that simulates battle conditions **2.** a game in which models of soldiers, battlefields, and equipment are used to refight historical battles

war-game (**war-gamed, war-gam·ing, war-games**) *v* **1.** *vi* to take part in a war game **2.** *vt US* to try out a military operation or strategy using simulation —**war-gam·er** *n*

war·head /wáwr hèd/ *n* the part of a bomb, ballistic or guided missile, rocket, or torpedo that contains the biological, chemical, explosive, incendiary, or nuclear material intended to damage the enemy

AKG London
Andy Warhol

War·hol /wáwr hàwl, -hōl/, **Andy** (1928–87) US artist. His stylized multiple depictions of mass-produced objects and celebrities made him a leader of the pop art movement. He also produced a series of movies that reproduced the banalities of life. Born **Wahola, Andrew**

> "An artist is someone who produces things that people don't need to have but that he—for *some reason*—thinks it would be a good idea to give them."
> [Andy Warhol, "Atmosphere," *The Philosophy of Andy Warhol: From A to B and Back Again*; 1975]

> "In the future everybody will be world-famous for 15 minutes."
> [Andy Warhol, *Andy Warhol*; 1968]

war·horse /wáwr hàwrss/ *n* **1. HORSE IN BATTLE** a horse ridden in battle **2. SURVIVOR OF CONFLICT** somebody who has taken part in and survived many conflicts (*informal*) **3. STANDARD WORK** a play or a piece of music that is familiar and hackneyed because of too frequent performance (*informal*)

War in I·raq *n* the invasion of Iraq in 2003 by forces led by the United States, the United Kingdom, Spain, and some other nations, during which Saddam Hussein and his Baath Party were overthrown

war·i·son /wárrəss'n/ *n* a note played on a bugle as a

sign for soldiers to attack [13C < Old French, variant of *garison* "provision" (see GARRISON)]

war·like /wáwr lìk/ *adj* **1.** HOSTILE hostile and inclined to fight **2.** RELATING TO WAR relating to war or warfare **3.** RELATING TO WARRIORS relating to the armed forces or military

war·lock /wáwr lòk/ *n* a man who is supposed to be a sorcerer or wizard [Old English *wærloga* "oath-breaker" < *wær* "oath, pledge" + *-loga* "liar" < Indo-European, "true"]

war·lord /wáwr làwrd/ *n* a military leader, especially a powerful one, operating outside the control of government —**war·lord·ism** *n*

warm /wawrm/ *adj* **1.** FAIRLY HOT moderately or comfortably hot ○ *a warm climate* **2.** PROVIDING WARMTH providing warmth or protection against cold ○ *a warm scarf* **3.** WITH TOO MUCH HEAT having or feeling an undesirable amount of heat, from exertion or ambient temperature **4.** FRIENDLY showing or feeling kindness and friendliness ○ *a warm person* **5.** PASSIONATE showing passion or liveliness ○ *a warm debate* **6.** ENTHUSIASTIC OR ARDENT showing or feeling great enthusiasm ○ *Warm congratulations!* **7.** QUICK TO ANGER excitable or easily angered ○ *a warm temper* **8.** SUGGESTING WARMTH having a color suggesting warmth, especially yellow or red **9.** PHYSIOL HEATED BY METABOLISM giving off the heat that arises naturally in warm-blooded animals **10.** HUNTING FRESH describes a scent in hunting that is fresh and strong **11.** CLOSE close to the hidden object in a game or to guessing a secret (*informal*) ○ *You're getting warm.* **12.** UNCOMFORTABLE uncomfortable because of danger (*informal*) ■ *v* (**warmed, warm·ing, warms**) **1.** *vti* MAKE SOMETHING OR BECOME WARM to increase the temperature of something to a desirable or comfortable level, or become warm **2.** *vt* MAKE SOMEBODY HAPPY to make somebody or something cheerful or happy ○ *were warmed by the presence of all their children* **3.** *vi* BECOME ENTHUSIASTIC to become enthusiastic about something ○ *warmed to the idea of buying a new car* **4.** *vi* BECOME FRIENDLY to become fond of somebody ○ *She warmed to him.* ■ *n* (*informal*) **1.** WARM PLACE a warm environment **2.** ACT OF WARMING an act of making somebody or something warm or becoming warm [Old English *wearm* < Indo-European] —**warm·er** *n* —**warm·ish** *adj* —**warm·ness** *n*

warm down *vi* to gradually return to the body's usual level of activity after strenuous physical exertion (*informal*)

warm over *vt* **1.** COOK same as **reheat** **2.** to suggest something again, without having greatly altered it

warm up *v* **1.** *vi* PREPARE FOR EXERCISE to prepare for physical exercise by stretching or practicing **2.** *vi* PREPARE FOR SOMETHING to prepare for something that is going to happen **3.** *vti* GET WARM to become warm or warmer, or make something become warm or warmer **4.** *vti* GET TO OPERATING TEMPERATURE to run something such as an engine to bring it to a temperature at which it works efficiently, or reach this condition **5.** *vti* GET ANIMATED to become enthusiastic, animated, or eager, or make somebody enthusiastic, animated, or eager

war ma·chine *n* the combined military resources with which a country can fight a war

warm-blood·ed *adj* **1.** maintaining a nearly constant body temperature, usually higher than and independent of the environment **2.** passionate, impetuous, and enthusiastic —**warm-blood·ed·ness** *n*

warm·boot /wáwrm bo͞ot/ (**-boot·ed, -boot·ing, -boots**) *vt* to restart a computer without switching it off, e.g., by pressing the control, Alt, and delete keys together

warm front *n* the gently sloping advancing edge of a warm air mass that displaces colder air, bringing a temperature increase and heavy rain where the front makes contact with the ground

warm fuz·zies *npl* a warm feeling of contentment and well-being (*informal*)

warm-heart·ed *adj* having or showing a kind and sympathetic nature —**warm-heart·ed·ly** *adv* —**warm-heart·ed·ness** *n*

warm·ing pan /wáwrming-/ *n* in former times, a long-handled metal pan that was filled with hot coals and placed in a bed to warm it

warm·ly /wáwrmlee/ *adv* **1.** with enthusiasm, fondness, or passion **2.** in a way that will keep somebody warm ○ *dressed warmly*

war·mon·ger /wáwr mùng gər, -mòng-/ *n* somebody who is eager for war or tries to start a war —**war·mon·ger·ing** *n*

war·mouth /wáwr mòwth/ (*plural* **-mouths** /-mòwthz, -mòwths/), **war·mouth bass** /-báss/ *n US* an olive-colored freshwater sunfish with a large mouth. Native to: midwestern and eastern United States. Latin name: *Lepomis gulosus.* [Late 19C. Origin ?]

warm sec·tor *n* a wedge of warm air within the low-pressure region between the cold front and warm front of a storm

warmth /wawrmth/ *n* **1.** WARM STATE the feeling, quality, or state of being warm **2.** AFFECTION affection and kindness **3.** AMOUNT OF HEAT a moderate amount of heat present in something **4.** EXCITEMENT strong emotion, especially anger or zeal **5.** EFFECT OF COLOR the effect gained from using colors such as red and yellow

warm-up, **warm·up** /wáwrm ùp/ *n* **1.** an exercise or a period spent exercising before a contest or event **2.** *US* an outfit worn while warming up, e.g., a track-suit (*often used in the plural*)

warn /wawrn/ (**warned, warn·ing, warns**) *v* **1.** *vti* TELL SOMEBODY OF RISK to tell somebody about something that might cause injury or harm **2.** *vt* TELL SOMEBODY IN ADVANCE to tell somebody about something in advance **3.** *vt* ADVISE SOMEBODY AGAINST SOMETHING to advise somebody against a potentially risky or damaging course of action ○ *The doctor warned him against traveling.* ○ *were warned against complacency* [Old English *war(e)nian* < Germanic, "be cautious"] —**warn·er** *n*

SPELLCHECK warn or **worn**? Do not confuse the spelling of ***warn*** and ***worn***, which sound similar. ***Warn*** is a verb meaning "tell somebody about something that may cause injury or harm": *I warned them not to set sail.* ***Worn*** is the past participle of the verb *wear* or an adjective derived from this, as in *clothes that are worn for comfort rather than fashion, worn down by rubbing, worn out after a hard day's work.*

---

warn off *vt* **1.** to tell somebody to leave or keep away from a place, usually in an authoritative or forceful manner ○ *Sightseers were warned off by security guards.* **2.** to advise somebody to avoid something, usually in an authoritative manner ○ *warned customers off buying cheap imitations*

warn·ing /wáwrning/ *n* **1.** SIGN OF SOMETHING BAD COMING a threat or a sign that something bad is going to happen **2.** ADVICE TO BE CAREFUL a piece of advice given to somebody to be careful or to stop doing something ○ *If you're late again, you'll get a written warning.* ■ *adj* MEANT TO WARN intended to warn somebody —**warn·ing·ly** *adv*

warn·ing col·or·a·tion *n* markings on an animal warning predators that it is poisonous or dangerous. Many insects and amphibians have warning coloration.

warn·ing shot *n* a shot fired deliberately off target as a warning to somebody to stop doing something

war of nerves *n* a conflict in which psychological tactics are used against an opponent

War on Ter·ror *n* the US response to the September 11, 2001 attacks by Islamic terrorists on the World Trade Center, the Pentagon, and other targets, involving coordinated action domestically and internationally by the armed forces, the intelligence community, law enforcement, the criminal justice system, and the banking community

warp /wawrp/ *v* (**warped, warp·ing, warps**) **1.** *vti* GET TWISTED to become twisted or out of shape, or make something become twisted or out of shape ○ *warped wood* **2.** *vti* DEVIATE FROM COURSE to make something deviate from its usual or correct course, or deviate from a usual or correct course ○ *Funny how the thought of huge profits can warp your judgment.* **3.** *vti* NAUT MOVE SHIP BY PULLING ON ROPES to move a ship by pulling on ropes fastened to a dock or fixed buoy, or be moved in this way **4.** *vt* TEXTILES ARRANGE THREADS to arrange threads to form the warp in a loom ■ *n* **1.** DISTORTION a twist or distortion in something, e.g., in wood that curls when dried **2.** PERVERSION a deviation or perversion of mind or character **3.** TEXTILES THREADS RUNNING LENGTHWISE the threads that run lengthwise on a loom or in a piece of fabric **4.** NAUT ROPE FOR TOWING a rope used to warp a vessel [Old English *weorpan* < Germanic, "to throw"] —**warp·age** *n* —**warp·er** *n*

war paint *n* **1.** paint used to decorate the body before a battle, e.g., that used in former times by some Native North American peoples **2.** COSMETICS same as **makeup** (*informal*)

warp and woof *n US* the foundation or base of something

war par·ty *n US* **1.** a group of people, especially formerly Native North Americans, engaged in fighting or attacking an enemy **2.** a political party that supports or wants war

war·path /wáwr pàth/ *n* in former times, a route taken by Native North Americans on the way to war ◇ **on the warpath** angry and in the mood for a confrontation (*informal*)

war·plane /wáwr plàyn/ *n* an aircraft used in war

Warr ➧ **De la Warr, Thomas West**

war·rant /wáwrənt/ *n* **1.** AUTHORIZATION something that authorizes somebody to do something **2.** WRITTEN AUTHORIZATION a written authorization or certifying document **3.** DOCUMENT AUTHORIZING POLICE TO DO SOMETHING a document that gives police specific rights or powers such as the right to search or arrest somebody **4.** FIN OPTION TO BUY STOCK a document authorizing a stockholder to buy shares from a company at a later date and at a specific price **5.** MIL WARRANT OFFICER'S CERTIFICATE a warrant officer's certificate of appointment ■ *vt* (**-rant·ed, -rant·ing, -rants**) **1.** SERVE AS REASON FOR SOMETHING to serve as a justifiable reason to do, believe, or think something **2.** GUARANTEE SOMETHING to guarantee something such as the truth or dependability of somebody or something **3.** AUTHORIZE SOMEBODY to give authority to somebody **4.** LAW GUARANTEE TITLE to guarantee the title to property [12C. < Old N French *warant*, variant of Old French *guarant* < Germanic, "be on guard"] —**war·rant·er** *n*

war·rant·a·ble /wáwrəntəb'l/ *adj* able to be justified or permitted —**war·rant·a·bil·i·ty** /wàwrəntə bíllətee/ *n* —**war·rant·a·bly** *adv*

war·ran·tee /wàwrən tée/ *n* somebody to whom a warrant is given or a warranty is made

war·rant of·fi·cer *n* an officer in the US Army or Marine Corps who holds a warrant as opposed to a commission, of a rank above the highest grade of noncommissioned officer but below the lowest grade of commissioned officer

war·ran·tor /wáwrəntər, -tàwr/ *n* somebody who gives a warranty to somebody else

war·ran·ty /wáwrəntee/ (*plural* **-ties**) *n* **1.** GUARANTEE a guarantee on purchased goods that they are of the quality represented and will be replaced or repaired if found to be faulty **2.** LAW INSURED PERSON'S UNDERTAKING a condition in an insurance contract in which the insured person guarantees that something is the case **3.** LAW GUARANTEE OF TITLE a covenant guaranteeing the security of the title to property being sold **4.** JUSTIFICATION a justification or authorization for an action

war·ran·ty deed *n US* a deed that binds a seller of property to defend the security of the title against any claims that may arise against the buyer

war·ren /wáwrən/ *n* **1.** RABBIT HABITAT a group of connected burrows where rabbits live and breed **2.** RABBITS IN WARREN a group of rabbits living in a warren **3.** CROWDED BUILDING OR AREA an area or building that is crowded or has a complicated layout **4.** AREA FOR GAME ANIMALS a piece of ground where game animals are kept and bred [14C. < Anglo-Norman *warenne* "enclosed area for breeding game"]

War·ren /wáwrən/, **Earl** (1891–1974) chief justice of the US Supreme Court (1953–69). As Supreme Court chief justice he presided over a liberal court that desegregated public schools and articulated the rights of criminal suspects.

> "We conclude that in the field of public education the doctrine of 'separate but equal' has no place. Separate educational facilities are inherently unequal."
> [Earl Warren, *Opinion in Brown v. Board of Education of Topeka, 347 US 483*; 1954]

> "The freedom to marry has long been rec-

ognized as one of the vital personal rights essential to the orderly pursuit of happiness by free men."
[Earl Warren, *Unanimous opinion striking down a Virginia law prohibiting interracial marriages, Loving v. Virginia*; June 12, 1967]

War·ren, Joseph (1741–75) American patriot. A noted leader among the anti-British protesters in pre-Revolutionary Boston, he died in the Battle of Bunker Hill.

War·ren, Robert Penn (1905–89) US author and poet. He is best known for the Pulitzer Prize-winning political novel *All the King's Men* (1946). He became the first US Poet Laureate (1986) but stepped down the following year because of ill health.

"I am not dead yet, though in years, / And the world's way is yet long to go, / And I love the world even in my anger, / And that's a hard thing to outgrow."
[Robert Penn Warren, "America Portrait: Old Style," *Now and Then: Poems 1976–78*; 1978]

war·ren·er /wáwrənər/ *n* a gamekeeper, or the keeper of a rabbit warren

War·ren Re·port *n* the 1964 report of the Commission, headed by Chief Justice Earl Warren, that officially investigated the assassination of President John F. Kennedy.

~~**warrent**~~ incorrect spelling of **warrant**

War·ring·ton /wáwringtən/ city in Cheshire, northwestern England. Population: 181,080 (2001).

war·ri·or /wáwree ər/ *n* **1.** somebody who takes part in or is experienced in warfare **2.** somebody who takes part in a struggle or conflict [13C. < Old N French *werreior* < *werre* "war" (see WAR)]

Warr·nam·bool /wáwrnəm bo͝ol/ city in southwestern Victoria, Australia. It is a commercial and industrial center. Population: 30,115 (2002 estimate).

War·rum·bun·gle Range /wàwrəm bung g'l-/ range of volcanic peaks in northern New South Wales, Australia

war·saw /wáwr sàw/ *n US* a large sea bass. Native to: southeastern United States. Latin name: *Epinephelus nigritus*. [Mid-20C. Alteration of American Spanish *guasa*]

War·saw /wáwr sàw/ capital city of Poland, located in the center of the country, on the Vistula River. Population: 1,618,468 (1999).

war·ship /wáwr shìp/ *n* an armored ship that is equipped with weapons and is used in war

war sto·ry *n US* a narrative of personal experience involving conflict or hardship ○ *frightening the interns with emergency-room war stories*

wart /wawrt/ *n* **1.** a small benign rough lump that grows, usually, on the hands, feet, or genitals, caused by a virus **2.** a growth on a plant that looks like a wart [Old English *wearte* < Indo-European, "raised spot"] —**wart·ed** *adj* —**wart·y** *adj* ◇ **warts and all** including any flaws, faults, or disadvantages (*hyphenated when used before a noun*)

wart hog

wart hog *n* a wild hog that has tusks, a coarse mane, and warty growths on its face. Native to: Africa south of the Sahara. Latin name: *Phacochoerus aethiopicus*.

war·time /wáwr tìm/ *n* the period during which a war is being fought

war-torn *adj* disrupted by war, especially war between different groups from one country

war whoop *n* a yell made when attacking, formerly used by Native North American warriors

War·wick /wáwr wìk/ city in eastern Rhode Island on Narragansett Bay, at the mouth of the Providence River. Population: 87,039 (2002 estimate).

War·wick·shire /wórrik shèer, -shər/ county in central England. It is largely agricultural with some light industry. Warwick is the administrative center. Population: 505,860 (2001). Area: 765 sq. mi./1,981 sq. km.

war wid·ow *n* a woman whose husband was killed in a war, especially while serving as a member of a country's armed forces

war·y /wérree/ (**-i·er, -i·est**) *adj* **1.** cautious and alert for problems ○ *wary of hidden rocks in the water* **2.** showing watchfulness or suspicion ○ *a wary approach* [15C. < WARE[2]] —**war·i·ly** *adv* —**war·i·ness** *n*

SYNONYMS See ***cautious***.

was /stressed woz, wuz, unstressed wəz/ past tense of **be**[1] (*used with I, he, she, it, and singular nouns*) [Old English *wæs*, form of *wesan* "be" < Indo-European, "stay, dwell"]

wa·sa·bi /wáassə bee/ (*plural* **-bis** or *same*) *n* **1.** a strong-tasting green powder or paste from a plant root. Use: condiment in Japanese cooking. **2.** a plant whose root is ground to make wasabi powder or paste. Native to: Asia. Latin name: *Eutrema wasabi*. [Early 20C. < Japanese]

Wa·satch Range /wáw sach-/ mountain range in the western United States, forming part of the Rocky Mountain system, in southeastern Idaho and central Utah. Its highest point is Mount Timpanogos (12,008 ft./3,662 km).

wash /wosh, wawsh/ *v* (**washed, wash·ing, wash·es**) **1.** *vt* **CLEAN SOMETHING** to clean something with water, usually with added soap or detergent ○ *He washed his hair.* **2.** *vti* **CLEAN YOURSELF** to clean yourself, especially your hands or face, with soap and water ○ *went upstairs to wash before supper* **3.** *vi* **WASH CLOTHES** to clean clothes in soap and water or in a washing machine ○ *spent the morning washing* **4.** *vi* **BE WASHABLE** to be capable of being washed without fading or being damaged (*refers to garments or fabrics*) ○ *curtains that wash well* **5.** *vti* **LICK SOMETHING CLEAN** to clean something by licking ○ *The cat washed her kittens.* **6.** *vti* **REMOVE SOMETHING BY WASHING** to remove something with water and usually with soap, or be removed in this way ○ *couldn't get the stain to wash out* **7.** *vt* **MOISTEN SOMETHING** to wet or moisten something (*literary*) ○ *lashes washed with tears* **8.** *vt* **FLOW OVER SOMETHING** to flow over the surface of something ○ *washed by the tides* **9.** *vt* **ERODE SOMETHING WITH WATER** to erode something by the action of water **10.** *vt* **MOVE SOMETHING ON WATER** to carry something along or away on water, or in a way that resembles the action of water ○ *A huge wave washed her over the side.* ○ *He was washed along by the huge crowd.* **11.** *vt* **PURIFY SOMETHING** to remove something corrupting ○ *the power to wash away sins* **12.** *vt* MIN EXTRACT **SEPARATE SOMETHING BY WASHING** to separate something such as precious stones or valuable minerals by sifting ore or gravel through water **13.** *vt* **APPLY THIN COATING TO SOMETHING** to brush a thin coating or layer over something **14.** *vi* **BE CONVINCING** to be convincing or believable (*informal*) ○ *That story won't wash.* **15.** *vt* CHEM **PUT GAS THROUGH LIQUID** to pass a gas or vapor through a liquid to remove contaminants ■ *n* **1. ACT OF WASHING** the act or process of washing somebody or something **2. QUANTITY OF CLOTHES** a quantity of clothes that have been or are to be washed **3. SKIN TREATMENT** a lotion, antiseptic, or cosmetic that is applied to the skin **4.** MANUF **THIN LIQUID COATING** a thin or weak liquid, especially one used to rinse or coat something **5.** ART **LAYER OF COLOR** a thin layer of color applied with a brush **6.** ART **PAINTING TECHNIQUE** the technique of using washes in painting **7.** ART same as **wash drawing 8. FLOW OF WATER** the flow of water against a surface, or the sound made by this **9. SURGE OF DISTURBED WATER OR AIR** the surge of disturbed water, air, or other fluid caused by something such as an oar, propeller, or jet engine moving through the fluid **10.** AGRIC **REMOVAL OF SOIL** the removal of soil by the action of flowing water **11.** GEOL **SEDIMENT** alluvial material carried and left by the movement of water. When washed down the side of a mountain, the sediment forms fans and cone-shaped deposits. **12.** GEOG **LAND PERIODICALLY COVERED BY WATER** land that is periodically covered by a sea or river, e.g., by a tide **13.** MIN EXTRACT **ORE** material from which precious stones and valuable minerals can be extracted by washing, e.g., gravel **14.** *UK* AGRIC same as **swill** *n* (sense 1) **15.** BEVERAGES **FERMENTED MALT** the liquor from fermented malt before it is distilled **16.** *Southwest US* **DRY STREAM BED** the dry bed of a stream that flows only after heavy rains, often found at the bottom of a canyon **17.** *US* **EVEN OUTCOME** a situation in which the losses and gains are balanced (*informal*) ○ *We sold a lot at the crafts fair, but our expenses were so high that in the end it was a wash.* [Old English *wæscan* < Germanic]

wash down *vt* **1.** to wash something thoroughly and completely ○ *had to wash down the kitchen walls afterward* **2.** to follow something drunk or eaten with another drink ○ *washed down the cake with a glass of milk*

wash out *v* **1.** *vt* **CLEAN INSIDE OF SOMETHING** to clean something by washing the inside **2.** *vti* **REMOVE SOMETHING BY WASHING** to come out by washing, or get something out by washing **3.** *vt* **CANCEL SOMETHING** to cancel an event because of rain **4.** *vti* **MOVE SOMETHING AWAY ON WATER** to carry away something on water, or be carried away on water ○ *washed out to sea* **5.** *vti* **WEAR SOMETHING AWAY** to wear something away by water, or be worn away by water **6.** *vt US* **EXHAUST SOMEBODY** to make somebody exhausted (*informal*) **7.** *vt* **END SOMETHING** to bring something to an end (*informal*) ○ *"Baltimore washed out the Indians' six-game win streak with an 8–3 win."* ("Major League Baseball News," *ESPN Sports Zone*; 1997)

wash over *vt* **1. FLOW OVER SOMETHING** to flow over and cover something **2. FILL SOMEBODY WITH EMOTION** to well up in and affect somebody emotionally ○ *A wave of homesickness washed over him.* **3. FAIL TO AFFECT SOMEBODY DEEPLY** to fail to make an impression on somebody

wash up *v* **1.** *vi* **WASH FACE AND HANDS** to wash your face and hands **2.** *vti* **ARRIVE BY WATER** to deposit something on the shore as a result of tidal or wave action, or be deposited in this way ○ *Look what the tide washed up!* **3.** *vt US* **ELIMINATE SOMETHING BY WASHING** to get rid of something by washing ○ *wash up that spilled coffee* **4.** *vti UK* **WASH DISHES** to wash the dishes after a meal

Wash /wosh, wawsh/ shallow inlet of the North Sea, on the eastern coast of England, between Lincolnshire and Norfolk. Area: 330 sq. mi./855 sq. km.

Wash. *abbr* Washington

wash·a·ble /wóshəb'l, wáwsh-/ *adj* capable of being washed without being damaged —**wash·a·bil·i·ty** /wòshə bíllətee, wàwshə-/ *n*

wash-and-wear *adj* easily washed and dried and needing little or no ironing

wash·ba·sin /wósh bàyss'n, wáwsh-/ *n* a bowl or basin for washing the face and hands or small articles

washboard

wash·board /wósh bàwrd, wáwsh-/ *n* **1. RIDGED BOARD** a board with a corrugated surface on which clothes being washed can be rubbed to help get them clean **2. MUSICAL INSTRUMENT** a board resembling a washboard, used as a musical instrument to produce a scratching sound **3.** ROADS **ROUGH ROAD** a road or section of road with bumpy ridges **4.** *US* BUILDINGS same as **baseboard** (sense 2) **5.** NAUT **PROTECTIVE FEATURE ON BOAT** a thin plank on the gunwale of a boat to stop water from splashing over the side ■ *adj* **MUSCULAR** describes a stomach that is flat with well-defined muscles

wash·bowl /wósh bōl, wáwsh-/ *n* HOUSEHOLD same as **washbasin**

wash·cloth /wósh klàwth, wáwsh-, -klòth/ *n US* a small piece of absorbent fabric, usually terry cloth, for washing the face or body

wash·day /wósh dày/ *n* a day when clothes are washed, especially the same day each week

wash draw·ing *n* a drawing made in ink to which a wash of color is applied, or a painting made using washes

washed-out *adj* (*not hyphenated after a verb*) **1.** faded or lacking color **2.** exhausted or lacking vitality and strength

washed-up *adj* no longer likely to continue or succeed (*informal; not hyphenated after a verb*)

wash·er /wóshər, wáwshər/ *n* **1. SMALL RING** a small disk or ring used to keep a screw or bolt secure or prevent leakage at a joint **2. WASHING APPLIANCE** an appliance used for washing, especially a washing machine **3. SOMEBODY WASHING SOMETHING** somebody who washes something

wash·er-up (*plural* **wash·ers-up**) *n UK* somebody who is employed to wash dishes (*informal*)

wash·er·wom·an /wóshər wŏŏmmən, wáwshər-/ (*plural* **-wom·en** /-wìmmin/), **wash·wom·an** /wósh wŏŏmmən, wáwsh-/ *n* a woman employed to wash clothes

wash house *n* a building where laundry or other washing is done

wash·ing /wóshing, wáwsh-/ *n* **1. CLOTHES FOR WASHING** clothes that are to be washed, are being washed, or have just been washed **2. DOING OF LAUNDRY** the act or process of washing clothes **3.** MANUF **THIN COAT** a thin coat of something ○ *a washing of silver* **4. LIQUID USED FOR WASHING** the liquid that has been used to wash something (*often used in the plural*)

wash·ing ma·chine *n* a machine for washing clothes, usually an electric one

wash·ing so·da *n* a crystalline form of sodium carbonate. Use: washing and cleaning.

Washington

Wash·ing·ton /wóshingtən, wáwsh-/ state in the northwestern United States, bordered by British Columbia, Idaho, Oregon, and the Pacific Ocean. Capital: Olympia. Population: 6,068,996 (2002 estimate). Area: 70,637 sq. mi./182,949 sq. km. —**Wash·ing·to·ni·an** /wòshing tṓnee ən/ *n, adj*

Wash·ing·ton, Booker T. (1856–1915) US educator. As the first principal of Alabama's Tuskegee Institute (1881–1915), he urged African Americans to attempt to gain advancement through educational attainments. Full name **Washington, Booker Taliaferro**

> "When freedom came, the slaves were almost as well fitted to begin life anew as the master, except in the matter of book learning and ownership of property. The slave owner and his sons had mastered no special industry."
> [Booker T. Washington, *Up from Slavery*; 1901]

Washington, D.C. capital city of the United States. The city of Washington has the same boundaries as the District of Columbia, a federal territory established in 1790 as the site of the new nation's permanent capital. Located at the confluence of the Potomac and Anacostia rivers, it is bordered by Maryland and Virginia. Population: 570,898 (2002 estimate).

Wash·ing·ton, Denzel (*b.* 1954) US actor. His movies include *Malcolm X* (1992) and *Training Day* (2001), for which he won the Academy Award for best actor.

Library of Congress

George Washington

Wash·ing·ton, George (1732–99) 1st president of the United States (1789–97). Commander in chief of the American forces during the American Revolution (1775–83) and president of the second Constitutional Convention, he was the first president of the newly independent United States. See table at **president**

> "Discipline is the soul of an army. It makes small numbers formidable; procures success to the weak, and esteem to all."
> [George Washington, *Letter of Instructions to the Captains of the Virginia Regiments*; July 29, 1759]

> "The preservation of the sacred fire of liberty, and the destiny of the republican model of government, are justly considered as deeply, perhaps as finally staked, on the experiment entrusted to the hands of the American people."
> [George Washington, *First inaugural address*; April 30, 1789]

Wash·ing·ton, Martha Dandridge Custis (1731–1802) US First Lady. The widow of Daniel Parke Custis, she married George Washington in 1759 and as his wife later became the first of a long line of first ladies.

Wash·ing·ton's birth·day *n US* the birthday of George Washington. Date: February 22.

wash·ing-up liq·uid *n UK* same as **dishwashing liquid**

wash-off *adj* removable by washing or by the use of water with soap or a detergent

wash·out /wósh òwt, wáwsh-/ *n* **1. FAILURE** a complete failure or fiasco (*informal*) **2. INEFFECTUAL PERSON** somebody regarded as lacking in competence or effectiveness (*informal insult*) **3.** GEOL **EROSION CAUSED BY RUNNING WATER** erosion caused by running water, e.g., during a flash flood **4.** GEOL **CHANNEL WASHED OUT** a hole or channel made by floodwater

wash·room /wósh ròŏm, -ròŏm, wáwsh-/ *n* a room, especially in a public place, with a toilet and washing facilities

wash sale *n US* **1.** the illegal practice of buying and selling a stock almost simultaneously in order to give the impression that the stock is being actively traded **2.** the repurchase of stock sold within 30 days of the time it was sold. Capital losses on such a sale are not tax deductible.

wash·stand /wósh stànd, wáwsh-/ *n* a stand on which a basin and jug can be placed for washing the face and hands

wash·tub /wósh tùb, wáwsh-/ *n* a large container in which clothes can be washed

wash-up *n* the final phase or summing up of a process (*informal*) ○ *In the wash-up on TV after the election, the senator admitted that government policy was out of step with the public.*

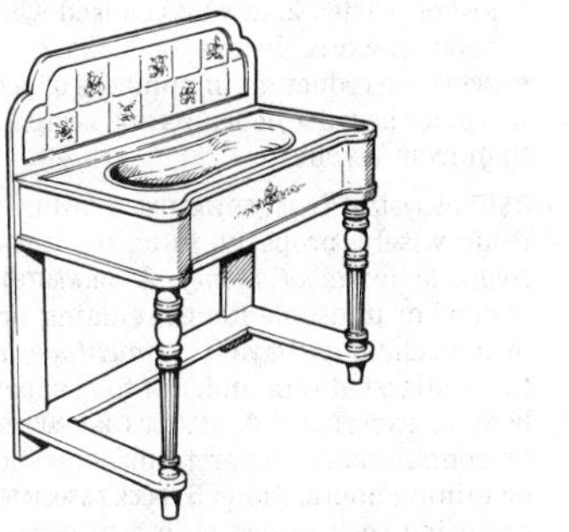

washstand

wash·wom·an *n* OCCUPATIONS same as **washerwoman**

wash·y /wóshee, wáwshee/ (**-i·er, -i·est**) *adj* **1. WEAK** watery or weak **2. PALE** faint or faded **3. NOT FORCEFUL** lacking intensity or vitality —**wash·i·ly** *adv* —**wash·i·ness** *n*

was·n't /wúzz'nt, wózz'nt/ *contr* was not

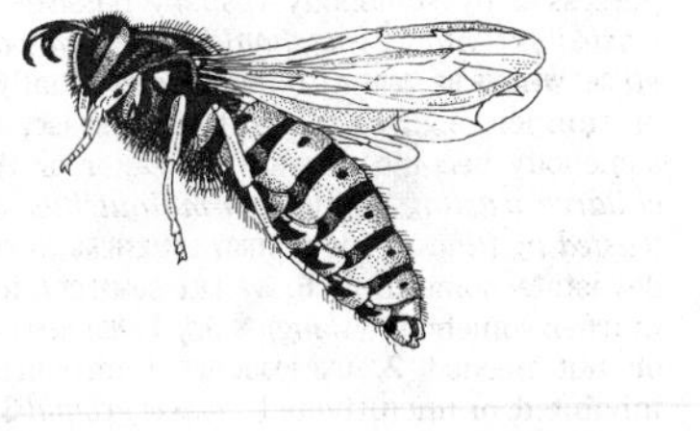

wasp

wasp /wosp/ *n* a slender black-and-yellow-striped social stinging insect that typically has well-developed wings, biting mouthparts, and a narrow stalk connecting the abdomen and thorax. Families: Vespidae or Sphecidae. [Old English *wæsp* < Indo-European, "to weave"]

Wasp /wosp/, **WASP** *n* an offensive term for a white person who has a Protestant Anglo-Saxon background and is viewed as belonging to the dominant and most powerful level of society (*informal insult*) [Mid-20C. Acronym < *White Anglo-Saxon Protestant*] —**Wasp** *adj* —**Wasp·ish·ness** *n* —**Wasp·y** *adj*

wasp·ish /wóspish/, **wasp·y** /wóspee/ (**-i·er, -i·est**) *adj* **1. OF WASPS** like a wasp, or relating to wasps **2. EASILY IRRITATED** easily irritated or annoyed **3. SPITEFUL** showing spite or bad temper —**wasp·ish·ly** *adv* —**wasp·ish·ness** *n*

wasp moth *n* INSECTS same as **clearwing**

wasp waist *n* a very slender waist, or one that is corseted to make it appear slender —**wasp-waist·ed** *adj*

wasp·y *adj* same as **waspish**

was·sail /wóss'l, wó sàyl/ (*archaic*) *n* **1. FESTIVE SALUTATION** a salutation or drinking toast made during festivities **2. FESTIVE OCCASION** a festive occasion at which people drink a great deal **3. ALCOHOLIC DRINK** an alcoholic drink, usually mulled wine or ale, drunk on a festive occasion **4. DRINKING OR CHRISTMAS SONG** a drinking song or a song sung at Christmas ■ *v* (**-sailed, -sail·ing, -sails**) **1.** *vi* **DRINK IN CELEBRATION** to celebrate by drinking alcohol **2.** *vi UK regional* **SING CHRISTMAS SONGS** to go from house to house at Christmas, singing carols and greeting people **3.** *vt* **TOAST SOMEBODY** to drink to somebody's health [12C. < Old Norse *ves heill* "be healthy," *heill* < Germanic] —**was·sail·er** *n*

Was·ser·mann test /waássərmən-/, **Was·ser·mann re·ac·tion** *n* a test for syphilis infection, based on determining the presence in a blood sample of antibodies to the syphilis bacterium [After August Paul *Wassermann* (1866–1925), German bacteriologist]

wast *stressed* /wost/; *unstressed* /wəst/ 2nd person singular past of **be**[1] (*archaic*)

wast·age /wáystij/ *n* **1. AMOUNT WASTED** an amount that is lost or wasted **2.** LOSS loss caused when something is used, is worn, decays, or leaks **3.** *UK* REDUCTION IN NUMBERS the reduction in numbers of people working in a place because of deaths and resignations, rather than from layoffs

waste /wayst/ *n* **1.** ACT OF WASTING a failure to use something wisely, properly, fully, or to good effect ○ *a complete waste of money* **2.** UNWANTED MATERIAL unwanted or unusable items, remains, or byproducts, or household garbage ○ *chemical waste* **3.** EXCREMENT the undigested remainder of food expelled from the body as excrement **4.** USED OR CONTAMINATED WATER used or contaminated water from domestic, industrial, or mining applications **5.** ROCK ASSOCIATED WITH MINERAL enclosing rock mined with a mineral, or ore with insufficient mineral content to justify further processing **6.** WILD AREA an uncultivated, desolate, or wild area (*often used in the plural*) ○ *the frozen wastes of Antarctica* **7.** DESTROYED AREA a place or region that has been destroyed or ruined ■ *v* (**wast·ed, wast·ing, wastes**) **1.** *vt* USE SOMETHING CARELESSLY to use something or use something up carelessly, extravagantly, or ineffectively ○ *She wasted the whole morning daydreaming.* ○ *Don't waste your arguments on her; she's already made up her mind!* **2.** *vt* FAIL TO USE SOMETHING to fail to make use of something such as an opportunity **3.** *vt* NOT EXPLOIT POTENTIAL OF SOMEBODY to fail to make full use of the abilities or talents possessed by somebody (*usually passive*) ○ *You're wasted as a nurse, you should have been a doctor.* **4.** *vti* GET WEAKER OR MORE ILL to become gradually weaker or thinner, e.g., as a result of disease, or make somebody become gradually weaker or thinner ○ *children wasting away from malnutrition* ○ *a body wasted by illness* **5.** *vt* DESTROY SOMETHING to ravage or devastate something **6.** *vt* KILL SOMEBODY to kill or murder somebody (*slang*) ■ *adj* **1.** NOT NEEDED useless or not needed **2.** UNPRODUCTIVE unproductive, uninhabited, or uncultivated ○ *waste ground* **3.** EXCRETED expelled from the body as indigestible ○ *waste matter* **4.** FOR WASTE used to carry off or store waste [12C. Via Old N French < Latin *vastus* "empty"] —**wast·a·ble** *adj* ◇ **be wasted on somebody** to be directed at somebody who is unable or unwilling to understand or heed it ○ *I'm afraid all her good advice was wasted on me.* ◇ **go to waste** to be unused or underutilized and therefore discarded or lost ○ *This pie will just go to waste if we don't eat it.* ○ *Don't let your talent go to waste.* ◇ **lay something (to) waste** to destroy or devastate something

SPELLCHECK See *waist.*

waste·bas·ket /wáyst bàskət/ *n* HOUSEHOLD, COMM a small container into which people can throw trash, especially paper

wast·ed /wáystəd/ *adj* **1.** USED TO NO PURPOSE used without achieving any purpose or in an extravagant or careless manner ○ *wasted efforts* **2.** NOT USED not used or exploited when available ○ *a wasted opportunity* **3.** VERY THIN emaciated or shrunken as a result of disease **4.** EXHAUSTED exhausted from exertion (*slang*) **5.** INTOXICATED under the influence of drink or drugs (*slang*)

waste dis·pos·al, waste dis·pos·al u·nit *n UK* same as **garbage disposal**

waste·ful /wáystfəl/ *adj* **1.** using resources unwisely **2.** causing waste or devastation —**waste·ful·ly** *adv* —**waste·ful·ness** *n*

waste heat re·cov·er·y *n* the reclaiming of otherwise wasted heat from furnaces, kilns, engines, or similar sources, for use in another process, e.g., preheating air or water

waste·land /wáyst lànd/ *n* **1.** an area of land that is desolate or barren and not used **2.** an environment that is thought to be spiritually or intellectually barren ○ *the wasteland of daytime TV*

CULTURAL NOTE ***The Waste Land***, a poem by US-born British poet T. S. Eliot (1922). One of the 20th century's major poetic works, it portrays the disintegration of Western values, the soullessness of modern society, and humankind's desperate search for salvation. It consists of five seemingly disconnected sections made up of fragmented verses written in a variety of styles but linked by imagery, symbols, and diverse literary and historical references.

waste·lot /wáyst lòt/ *n Can* an area of wasteland in a city

waste man·age·ment *n* activities that deal with waste before and after it is produced, including its minimization, transfer, storage, separation, recovery, recycling, and final disposal

waste·pa·per /wáyst pàypər/ *n* paper that is not needed and has been thrown away

waste·pa·per bas·ket *n UK* same as **wastebasket**

waste pipe *n* a pipe that carries excess or used fluids from a container such as a sink or bathtub

waste prod·uct *n* a useless or unwanted byproduct of a process

wast·er /wáystər/ *n* **1.** somebody or something that wastes something, especially somebody who is careless with money or resources **2.** an object that has been spoiled during manufacture, especially a ceramic piece

waste·wa·ter /wáyst wàwtər/ *n* water that has been used ○ *a wastewater treatment plant*

waste·weir /wáyst wèer/ *n* GEOG same as **spillway**

wast·ing /wáysting/ *adj* gradually taking away strength and energy and emaciating the body ○ *a wasting disease* —**wast·ing·ly** *adv*

wast·ing as·set *n* an asset, especially a natural resource such as a mine, that cannot be renewed and that loses its value over time

wast·rel /wáystrəl/ *n* somebody regarded as wasteful, spendthrift, or lazy (*insult*) [Late 16C. < WASTE + *-rel*, ending indicating "little" or a derogatory sense]

wat /wot/ *n* a Buddhist monastery or temple in Thailand, Cambodia, or Laos [Mid-19C. Via Thai < Sanskrit *vāṭa* "enclosure"]

wa·tap /wa taáp/ *n* a stringy thread used for sewing and weaving, formerly made by some Native North Americans from conifers [Mid-18C. Via N American French < Ojibwa]

watch /woch/ *v* (**watched, watch·ing, watch·es**) **1.** *vti* OBSERVE to look at and keep your attention on something or somebody over a period of time ○ *Are you coming to watch the game?* ○ *I watched him as he walked off down the street.* ○ *Would you mind doing that again? I wasn't watching.* **2.** *vi* KEEP LOOKOUT to keep a lookout for something that might appear or happen ○ *Your job is to watch for anyone coming.* **3.** *vti* MONITOR SOMETHING OR SOMEBODY to keep something or somebody under observation as a protective measure, to gather information, or to exert control ○ *Can you watch the baby while I go upstairs?* **4.** *vt* EXERCISE CARE ABOUT SOMETHING to be careful about something (*often used as a command*) ○ *Watch your language!* ○ *Watch where you're going!* **5.** *vi* KEEP VIGIL to stay awake and keep a vigil ■ *n* **1.** PERSONAL CLOCK a small clock worn on the wrist or carried in a pocket **2.** TIME SPENT OBSERVING a period of time spent observing something closely **3.** PEOPLE WATCHING a person or group that guards or observes something, especially at night ○ *posted a watch around the house, day and night* **4.** GUARD'S DUTY the period during which a guard is on duty **5.** DUTY ON SHIP a fixed period of a day spent on duty on board a ship **6.** PERSON'S PERIOD IN CHARGE a period when a particular person is in charge of something (*informal*) ○ *didn't want anything going wrong on his watch* **7.** CREW ON DUTY the members of a ship's crew who are on duty at a particular time **8.** DIVISION OF NIGHT one of the periods of time into which the night was formerly divided **9.** *US* WEATHER ALERT an official notice from meteorological authorities that weather of a particular kind is likely to develop in an area ○ *a tornado watch* [Assumed Old English *wæccan* "keep watch, be awake" < Germanic] —**watch·er** *n* ◇ **be on the watch for somebody** *or* **something** to look out for somebody or something ◇ **watch it** to be careful (*informal*)

watch out *vi* **1.** to be careful, alert, or wary **2.** to look and wait for somebody or something

watch over *vt* to look after, supervise, or guard somebody or something

watch·a·ble /wóchəb'l/ *adj* **1.** capable of being observed **2.** interesting and enjoyable to watch ○ *a very watchable detective series* —**watch·a·bil·i·ty** /wòchə bíllətee/ *n*

watch·band /wóch bànd/ *n* a strap for a wristwatch

watch cap *n* a dark-blue close-fitting knitted woolen cap worn in cold weather, especially by sailors in the Navy

watch·case /wóch kàyss/ *n* the protective casing for a watch mechanism

watch·dog /wóch dàwg, -dòg/ *n* **1.** same as **guard dog** **2.** a person or organization guarding against illegal practices, unacceptable standards, or inefficiency ○ *a government watchdog* ■ *vti* (**-dogged, -dog·ging, -dogs**) to act as a watchdog on something

watch·eye /wóch ì/ *n* an eye with a white or streaked iris, especially of a dog

watch fire *n* a fire kept burning at night either as a signal or for the comfort of somebody keeping watch

watch·ful /wóchfəl/ *adj* **1.** carefully observant or alert ○ *watchful for signs of recovery* **2.** not asleep (*archaic*) —**watch·ful·ly** *adv* —**watch·ful·ness** *n*

watch glass *n* **1.** *UK* same as **crystal** *n* (sense 8) **2.** a shallow round glass dish used to evaporate liquids or to cover something

watch·mak·er /wóch màykər/ *n* a maker or repairer of watches

watch·man /wóchmən/ (*plural* **-men** /-mən/) *n* somebody, especially a man, employed to patrol or guard buildings or an area

watch night *n* **1.** the last night of the year, marked in some churches by a service that spans the midnight transition from the old year to the new one. Date: night of December 31. **2.** the night before Christmas Day, marked in some churches by a service that spans midnight. Date: night of December 24.

watch·per·son /wóch pùrss'n/ *n* somebody employed to patrol or guard buildings or an area

watch pock·et *n* a small pocket for a watch in a vest or pants

watch·strap /wóch stràp/ *n UK* same as **watchband**

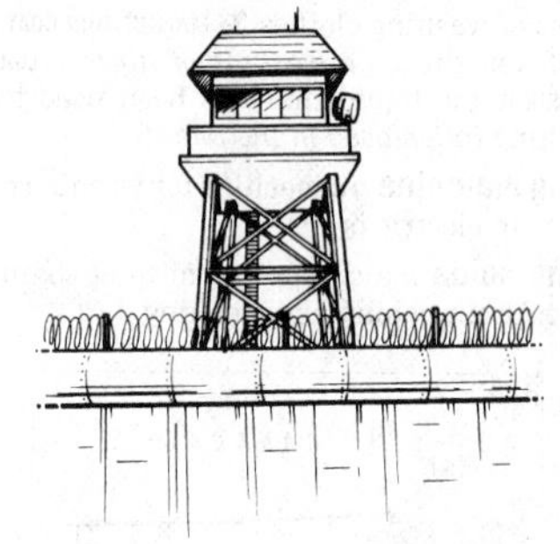

watchtower

watch·tow·er /wóch tòw ər/ *n* a high tower in which sentries keep watch for the approach of an enemy

watch·wom·an /wóch wŏŏmən/ (*plural* **-wom·en** /-wìmmin/) *n* a woman employed to patrol or guard buildings or an area

watch·word /wóch wùrd/ *n* **1.** a word or slogan that encapsulates a mode of action, a set of beliefs, or membership of a group **2.** a word or phrase that somebody has to say to prove a right to be in a place with restricted access

wa·ter /wáwtər/ *n* **1.** LIQUID OF RAIN AND RIVERS the clear colorless liquid, odorless and tasteless when pure, that occurs as rain, snow, and ice, forms rivers, lakes, and seas, and is essential for life. Naturally occurring water picks up color and taste from substances in its environment. Formula: H_2O. **2.** AREA OF WATER an area or body of water, e.g., a river, stream, lake, or sea ○ *We went down to the water to feed the ducks.* **3.** SURFACE OF WATER the surface of a body of water ○ *swim under water* **4.** ELEMENT in ancient and medieval philosophy, water as one of the four elements **5.** TRANSPORTATION OVER WATER transportation by ship, boat, or some other means of travel over or through water ○ *can only get there by water* **6.** WATER SUPPLY a supply of water to a house, town, or region ○ *Our water's been turned off.* **7.** SOLUTION OF SUBSTANCE IN WATER a solution of a particular chemical or substance in water ○ *lavender water* **8.** BODY FLUID any watery fluid present in or secreted by the body, e.g., urine, sweat, saliva, or tears **9.** *US* FLUID

SURROUNDING FETUS the amniotic fluid that surrounds the fetus in the womb (*often used in the plural*) **10.** WAVY PATTERN a lustrous wavy pattern on the surface of some fabrics such as silk **11.** BRIGHTNESS the quality of brightness of a gem ■ **wa·ters** *npl* **1.** PARTICULAR AREA OF SEA a particular region of sea, e.g., that belonging to a specific nation ○ *territorial waters* **2.** WATER CONTAINING MINERALS naturally occurring water containing minerals, e.g., that found at a spa and used for health reasons ○ *take the waters* ■ *v* (**-tered, -ter·ing, -ters**) **1.** *vt* SPRINKLE OR SOAK SOMETHING WITH WATER to sprinkle, wet, or soak something with water **2.** *vt* IRRIGATE LAND to take water to crops or fields **3.** *vti* GIVE OR GET WATER to give drinking water to an animal, or get or take water as an animal does **4.** *vi* FILL WITH TEARS WHEN IRRITATED to fill with tears, especially because of irritation (*refers to eyes*) **5.** *vi* PRODUCE SALIVA to produce saliva, particularly in pleasant anticipation of food (*refers to the mouth*) **6.** *vi* NAUT TAKE ON WATER SUPPLY to take on a supply of water **7.** *vt* TEXTILES GIVE FABRIC WAVY SHEEN to give a lustrous wavy pattern to fabric, especially silk [Old English *wæter* < Indo-European, "water"] —**wa·ter·er** *n* ◇ **be dead in the water** to have no chance of success or survival ◇ **be water under the bridge** to be something that is in the past and that cannot be altered ◇ **hold water** to be well-founded, or stand up under scrutiny ◇ **in deep water** in a difficult or complicated situation ◇ **in hot water** in trouble or in an embarrassing situation ◇ **muddy the waters** to cause confusion or trouble ◇ **pour** *or* **throw cold water on** *or* **onto** *or* **over something** to discourage a plan or idea by showing a lack of interest in it or rejecting it as impractical ◇ **throw water** *W Africa* to offer somebody a bribe ◇ **tread water 1.** to keep afloat without moving forward, by moving the legs and arms **2.** to make no progress but manage to keep a situation the same for a period of time ◇ **water off a duck's back** words or actions that have absolutely no effect on the attitude or behavior of the person to whom they are said or done

CULTURAL NOTE ***Water Music***, an orchestral suite (1717) by German-born British composer George Frederick Handel. It consists of three separate suites for strings and wind instruments. The exact circumstances of its composition are not known, but it was first performed to accompany a royal barge trip along the Thames River from Whitehall to Chelsea on July 17, 1717.

water down *vt* **1.** to weaken or dilute something by adding water to it **2.** to moderate or attenuate something in order to make it less difficult, offensive, or controversial ○ *The producers want to water down her original script.* —**wa·tered-down** *adj*

wa·ter ar·um *n* a water plant cultivated for its glossy heart-shaped leaves and large white funnel-shaped cone surrounding the flower spike. Native to: northern temperate regions. Latin name: *Calla palustris*.

wa·ter ash *n* TREES same as **stinking ash**

wa·ter bag *n* **1.** a bag made of leather, canvas, or similar material used for carrying water **2.** ANAT, MED same as **amnion** (sense 2)

wa·ter bal·let *n* the performance of dance movements in water

wa·ter bear *n* ZOOL same as **tardigrade**

Wa·ter Bear·er *n* ZODIAC same as **Aquarius** (sense 2)

wa·ter bed *n* a bed with a special mattress filled with water

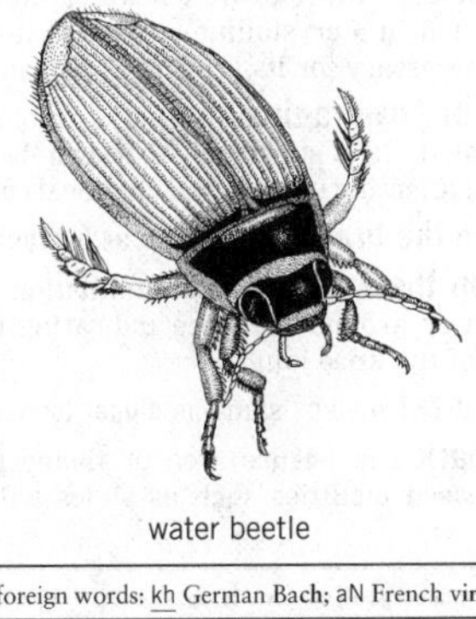

water beetle

wa·ter bee·tle *n* a member of a group of beetles that live mainly in water. Some have broad hind legs for swimming; others crawl over vegetation. Family: Hydrophilidae.

wa·ter bird *n* a bird that lives mainly near and wades in or swims on water, especially fresh water

wa·ter bis·cuit *n* a thin plain cracker made from flour and water, often served with cheese

wa·ter blis·ter *n* a blister that contains clear watery fluid without blood or pus

wa·ter bloom *n* a growth of algae on a body of water such as a lake

wa·ter boat·man *n* **1.** any bug that lives mainly at the bottom of ponds and has oar-shaped flattened hind legs used for swimming. Most water boatmen are good fliers. Family: Corixidae. **2.** INSECTS same as **backswimmer**

wa·ter·borne /wáwtər bàwrn/ *adj* **1.** traveling on or transported by water ○ *a waterborne vessel* **2.** transmitted or transported by water, as some infectious agents are

wa·ter boy *n* somebody who supplies drinking water to a group of people such as athletes

wa·ter brash *n* the sudden filling of the mouth with acidic juices from the stomach, usually accompanied by heartburn and often resulting from indigestion. It is common in pregnancy but may also be an indication of a disorder of the digestive tract.

wa·ter·buck /wáwtər bùk/ (*plural* **-bucks** or *same*) *n* a large antelope with a shaggy dark-gray or reddish coat, found in grassland and woodland near open water. Native to: southern Africa. Latin name: *Kobus ellipsiprymnus*.

wa·ter buf·fa·lo *n* **1.** LARGE ASIAN BUFFALO a large buffalo with a gray-black coat and long backward-curving horns that is domesticated in many countries. Raised for: haulage, milk. Native to: Southeast Asia. Latin name: *Bubalus bubalis*. **2.** MIL AMPHIBIOUS TANK an amphibious tank, especially one used in World War II **3.** MIL DRINKING WATER CONTAINER a water storage container hauled by truck into an operational area without potable water

wa·ter bug *n* an insect that lives in water, e.g., the water boatman or water strider

wa·ter·bus /wáwtər bùss/ *n* a boat carrying passengers in a regular service across or along a river or lake

wa·ter cal·trop *n* PLANTS same as **water chestnut** (sense 3)

wa·ter can·non *n* an apparatus, usually mounted on a truck, that produces a jet of high-pressure water and is used to disperse crowds

Wa·ter Car·ri·er *n* ZODIAC same as **Aquarius** (sense 2)

wa·ter chest·nut *n* **1.** CRUNCHY NUT-SHAPED CORM a round white crunchy stem base (**corm**) of a Chinese water plant, often used in Asian cooking. Water chestnuts are sometimes used in food manufacture to add crunchiness to processed foods. **2.** CHINESE PLANT WITH EDIBLE STEM a Chinese water plant that produces water chestnuts. Latin name: *Eleocharis tuberosa*. **3.** WATER PLANT an annual water plant that forms rosettes of diamond-shaped floating leaves, has feathery underwater leaves, and bears hard spiny dark-gray fruit containing edible seeds. Native to: Europe, Asia. Latin name: *Trapa natans*.

wa·ter chin·qua·pin *n* a water plant with shield-shaped leaves and edible seeds. Flowers: fragrant, cup-shaped, pale yellow. Native to: North America. Latin name: *Nelumbo lutea*.

wa·ter clock *n* TIME same as **clepsydra**

wa·ter clos·et *n* **1.** a small room with a toilet and, often, a sink **2.** a flush toilet (*archaic*)

wa·ter clo·ver *n* PLANTS same as **pepperwort**

wa·ter·col·or /wáwtər kùllər/ *n* **1.** PAINTING a painting created with pigments mixed with water rather than oil **2.** PIGMENT MIXED WITH WATER an individual painting pigment mixed with water for use rather than oil, or such pigments collectively (*often used in the plural*) **3.** METHOD OF PAINTING the art or technique of painting with pigments mixed with water rather than oil —**wa·ter·col·or·ist** *n*

wa·ter·col·our *n* ART Can, UK spelling of **watercolor**

wa·ter-cool *vt* to cool an engine or machine by means of water, typically by circulating water in a water jacket or by pipes

wa·ter cool·er *n* a device that dispenses cooled drinking water and often serves as a focal point in a workplace where colleagues meet and gossip ■ *adj* popular enough to be the subject of everyday conversation, especially between colleagues around the water cooler in the workplace (*informal*) ○ *water cooler TV*

wa·ter·course /wáwtər kàwrss/ *n* **1.** a natural or artificial channel through which water flows **2.** the water of a river or stream that flows along a watercourse

wa·ter·craft /wáwtər kràft/ (*plural same*) *n* **1.** skill in swimming, handling boats, or other water-related activities **2.** a vessel used for traveling on water (*formal*)

watercress

wa·ter·cress /wáwtər krèss/ *n* a perennial water plant, widely cultivated for its peppery-flavored leaves and stems, used in salads. Native to: Europe, Asia. Latin name: *Nasturtium officinale*.

wa·ter cure *n* a session of treatment by hydrotherapy or hydropathy

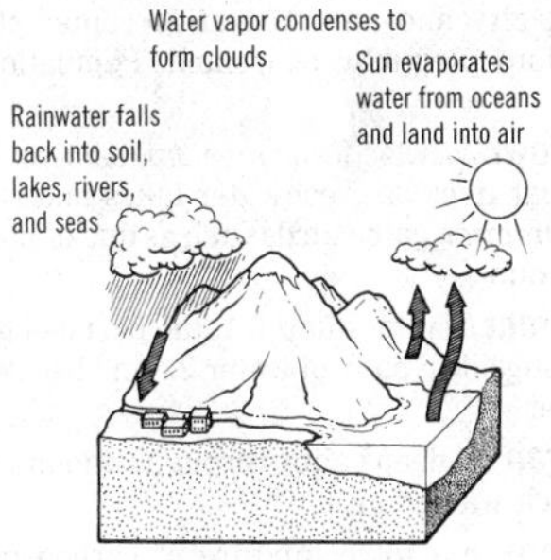
Water vapor condenses to form clouds
Sun evaporates water from oceans and land into air
Rainwater falls back into soil, lakes, rivers, and seas

water cycle

wa·ter cy·cle *n* the constant circulation of water between atmosphere, land, and sea by evaporation, precipitation, and percolation through soils and rocks

wa·ter di·vin·er *n* same as **dowser**

wa·ter dog *n* **1.** a dog that likes water, especially one trained to hunt or retrieve game in water **2.** somebody who likes being in, on, or near water, e.g., a sailor or swimmer (*informal*)

wa·ter·fall /wáwtər fàwl/ *n* a vertical stream of water that occurs where a river or stream falls over the edge of a steep place. See table on next page

wa·ter fea·ture *n* a small fountain or pond, used for aesthetic effect in landscape gardening

wa·ter fern *n* PLANTS same as **mosquito fern**

wa·ter fil·ter *n* an appliance or fitting for removing unwanted matter from water, especially bacteria or harmful chemicals from drinking water

wa·ter·find·er /wáwtər fìndər/ *n* PARANORMAL same as **dowser**

wa·ter flea *n* a tiny crustacean that swims with rapid jerky movements, using its large forked antennae. Suborder: Cladocera.

WORLD'S HIGHEST WATERFALLS

1		Angel Falls
	Height	[3,212 ft / 979 m*] (also single largest drop, [2,647 ft / 807 m*])
	Location	*Venezuela*
2		Tugela Falls
	Height	[3,110 ft / 948 m*]
	Location	*South Africa*
3		Mtarazi Falls
	Height	[2,500 ft / 762 m*]
	Location	*Zimbabwe*
4		Yosemite Falls
	Height	[2,425 ft / 739 m*]
	Location	*United States*
5		Cuquenán Waterfall
	Height	[2,000 ft / 610 m*]
	Location	*Venezuela*
6		Sutherland Falls
	Height	[1,904 ft / 580 m*]
	Location	*New Zealand*
7		Kile Waterfall
	Height	[1,840 ft / 561 m*]
	Location	*Norway*
8		Kahiwa Waterfall
	Height	[1,748 ft / 533 m*]
	Location	*Hawaii, United States*
9		Mardal Waterfall
	Height	[1,696 ft / 517 m*]
	Location	*Norway*
10		Takakkaw Falls
	Height	[1,223 ft / 373 m*]
	Location	*Canada*

* Total height may include more than one drop

Wa·ter·ford /wáwtərfərd/ **1.** county in Munster Province, in the southern part of the Republic of Ireland. Population: 94,680 (2002). Area: 710 sq. mi./1,838 sq. km. **2.** city and administrative center of County Waterford, Republic of Ireland. Population: 44,000 (1996).

wa·ter·fowl /wáwtər fòwl/ *n* (*plural same* or **-fowls**) a bird that lives on freshwater lakes and streams ■ *npl* swimming game birds such as ducks, considered as a group

wa·ter·front /wáwtər frùnt/ *n* **1.** the part of a town that lies alongside a body of water **2.** land beside an area of water

wa·ter gap *n* a deep valley through a mountain ridge, in which water flows

wa·ter gas *n* a toxic mixture of carbon monoxide and methane generated by passing air and steam over hot glowing coals. Use: fuel for heating, lighting, and power.

wa·ter gate *n* **1.** CIV ENG same as **floodgate 2.** a gate that gives access to an area of water

Wa·ter·gate /wáwtər gàyt/ *n* **1.** a political scandal stemming from a break-in by Republican operatives at the 1972 US Democratic National Committee headquarters, which were in the Watergate complex in Washington, D.C. The scandal led to the resignation of President Nixon and the conviction and imprisonment of a number of his closest aides. **2.** a public scandal involving politicians or officials abusing power, especially if a cover-up is also attempted

wa·ter gauge *n* a device that indicates the quantity or level of water in a tank, boiler feed, reservoir, or stream

wa·ter glass *n* **1.** DRINKING GLASS a drinking glass, especially for water **2.** THICK CHEMICAL SOLUTION an extremely viscous solution of sodium silicate. Use: cement, waterproofing and fireproofing agent, egg preservative. **3.** GLASS GAUGE a water gauge consisting of a glass tube **4.** DEVICE FOR EXAMINING UNDERWATER OBJECTS an instrument used for looking at objects under the water's surface, e.g., an open box or tube with a glass bottom

wa·ter gum *n* a deciduous tree that is a species of tupelo. Native to: southeastern United States. Latin name: *Nyssa aquatica*.

wa·ter gun *n* *US* a water pistol, or a larger toy gun capable of shooting a stream of water a long distance. Can term **water pistol**

wa·ter ham·mer *n* a hammering or stuttering sound in a pipeline that sometimes accompanies a sudden and significant change in the flow rate of the fluid through the pipeline

wa·ter hem·lock *n* any of various poisonous highly scented plants found in marshy areas. Flowers: small, white, in dense flat-topped clusters. Native to: northern hemisphere. Genus: *Cicuta*.

wa·ter hen *n* a bird that lives near water, e.g., a rail or a coot. Family: Rallidae.

wa·ter hole *n* a natural hollow in the ground containing water, especially one where animals drink

wa·ter hy·a·cinth *n* a perennial water plant that has glossy rounded leaves with bulbous stalks. Flowers: lilac-blue. Native to: subtropical America. Latin name: *Eichhornia crassipes*.

wa·ter ice *n* a frozen dessert of sweet flavored ice

wa·ter·ing can /wáwtəring-/, **wa·ter·ing pot** *n* a container with a handle and a spout, often with a perforated nozzle, used to water plants

wa·ter·ing hole *n* **1.** a place where people meet socially to drink, e.g., a bar (*informal*) **2.** GEOG same as **water hole**

wa·ter·ing place *n* **1.** GEOG same as **water hole 2.** a place where people go to drink or bathe in the local water for health reasons **3.** LEISURE same as **watering hole** (sense 1) (*informal*)

wa·ter·ing pot *n* *US* GARDENING same as **watering can**

wa·ter·ish /wáwtərish/ *adj* somewhat watery

wa·ter jump *n* a place in a race where the runners or horses have to jump over an obstacle that includes a stream, ditch, or pool

wa·ter·leaf /wáwtər lèef/ *n* a woodland plant with deeply toothed leaves. Flowers: bell-shaped, white or purple. Native to: western North America. Genus: *Hydrophyllum*.

wa·ter·less /wáwtərləss/ *adj* **1.** lacking water **2.** able to be made or used without water

wa·ter lev·el *n* **1.** the level of the surface of a body of water **2.** NAUT same as **water line** (sense 1) **3.** GEOL same as **water table** (sense 1)

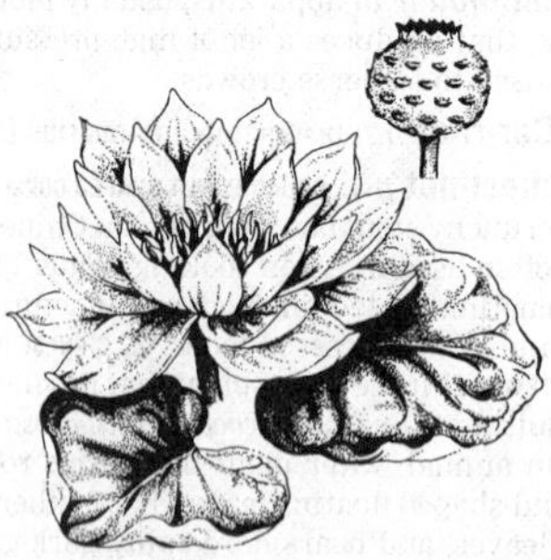

water lily

wa·ter lil·y *n* a perennial water plant with rounded leaves that float on the water. Flowers: cup-shaped, often fragrant. Family: Nymphaeaceae.

CULTURAL NOTE ***Water Lilies***, the title of a number of paintings (1899–1925) by French artist Claude Monet. In his later years, Monet retired to his house at Giverny near Paris, where he painted numerous studies of the water lilies in his garden pond. While tending toward abstraction, many of these works, for example, the enormous panels now in the Orangerie in Paris, succeed brilliantly in capturing the evanescent quality of natural phenomena.

wa·ter line *n* **1.** a line on a ship's hull indicating the level to which the ship can sink into the water under various conditions **2.** the line to which a body of water rises or reaches

wa·ter·logged /wáwtər lògd/ *adj* **1.** having absorbed so much water as to become spongy or marshy and difficult to walk or play on ○ *a waterlogged field* **2.** filled with water and therefore hard to steer ○ *a waterlogged boat* —**wa·ter·log** *vt* —**wa·ter·log·ging** *n*

Wa·ter·loo /wáwtər lòo/ **1.** town in central Belgium, about 10 mi./16 km south of Brussels. It was the site of the Battle of Waterloo on June 18, 1815, where Napoleon was decisively defeated by British and Prussian forces. Population: 28,111 (1995). **2.** city in northeastern Iowa, northwest of Cedar Rapids and southeast of Cedar Falls. Population: 67,742 (2002 estimate). ◇ **meet your Waterloo** to be decisively defeated or overcome

wa·ter main *n* a large underground pipe supplying water

wa·ter·man /wáwtərmən/ (*plural* **-men** /-mən/) *n* somebody who works on or rents out boats

wa·ter·mark /wáwtər màark/ *n* **1.** HIDDEN MARK IN PAPER a design or mark in paper that can be seen when the paper is held up to the light, or the metal tool used to make such a design **2.** NAUT same as **water line** (sense 1) **3.** LINE LEFT BY WATER a line showing where the edge or surface of water has been **4.** COMPUT EMBEDDED PATTERN IN DATA FILE a pattern of bits digitally embedded in a data file, used in detecting unauthorized copies ■ *vt* (**-marked, -mark·ing, -marks**) **1.** PUT WATERMARK OR PATTERN IN PAPER to put a watermark into paper while it is being made, or impress a pattern as a watermark **2.** COMPUT EMBED IDENTIFYING PATTERN IN DATA FILE to embed a pattern of bits in a data file for identification and detection of unauthorized copies

wa·ter·mel·on /wáwtər mèllən/ *n* **1.** a large oval or round fruit with a hard green skin and sweet and juicy pink, red, or yellow flesh, usually with many black seeds **2.** a climbing plant that produces watermelons. Native to: Africa. Latin name: *Citrullus lanatus*.

wa·ter me·ter *n* a device that records the amount of water that passes through a pipe, usually for billing purposes

wa·ter mil·foil *n* a perennial water plant that has submerged leaves made up of many feathery segments and bears slender spikes of tiny flowers above the water surface. Genus: *Myriophyllum*.

wa·ter mill *n* a mill that has machinery powered by moving water

wa·ter mint *n* a perennial plant of swampy areas with toothed hairy leaves and a hairy stem, that emits a strong scent when crushed. Flowers: lilac-pink, in whorls. Latin name: *Mentha aquatica*.

wa·ter moc·ca·sin *n* **1.** a venomous snake belonging to the pit viper family that has an olive to brownish back and indistinct black bars and lives partly on land, partly in water. Native to: southern United States. Latin name: *Agkistrodon piscivorus*. **2.** a snake that resembles the venomous water moccasin but is harmless. Genus: *Nerodia*.

wa·ter mold *n* a fungus that inhabits fresh or brackish water and feeds mainly on dead organic material but is sometimes parasitic on fish, plants, and other living organisms. Order: Saprolegniales.

wa·ter nymph *n* in folklore and classical mythology, a nymph that lives in water

wa·ter oak *n* an oak that grows in wet locations. Native to: southern United States. Latin name: *Quercus nigra*.

wa·ter of crys·tal·li·za·tion *n* water molecules incorporated in a crystalline substance that are typically necessary for its properties and structure

wa·ter of hy·dra·tion *n* water molecules incorporated in a substance that can be removed without affecting its essential chemical composition

wa·ter on the brain *n* MED same as **hydrocephalus**

wa·ter on the knee *n* the accumulation of watery fluid in or around the knee indicating disease or injury of the knee joint

wa·ter ou·zel *n* BIRDS same as **dipper** (sense 2)

wa·ter park *n* a leisure area or theme park with water-based facilities such as slides with flowing water

wa·ter part·ing *n* GEOG same as **divide** *n* (sense 2)

wa·ter pen·ny·wort *n* a creeping plant that grows in water or moist places. Genus: *Hydrocotyle.*

wa·ter pep·per *n* an annual plant widely distributed in damp places that has lance-shaped leaves and a hot peppery taste. Flowers: inconspicuous, pink or greenish, in slender spikes. Latin name: *Polygonum hydropiper.*

wa·ter pipe *n* **1.** a pipe for transporting water from one place to another **2.** a pipe for smoking tobacco or marijuana that incorporates a water container through which the smoke is drawn and cooled

wa·ter pis·tol *n* a toy pistol that squirts out water

wa·ter plan·tain *n* a perennial plant found in water or wet places, with a rosette of pointed oval leaves. Flowers: pinkish or white, in branching heads. Genus: *Alisma.*

wa·ter po·lo *n* a game played in a swimming pool by two teams of seven players whose object is to score by sending a large ball into the opposing team's goal

wa·ter pow·er *n* energy contained in moving water, or derived from the weight of standing water, used to drive machinery or to generate electricity through the use of hydraulic turbines

wa·ter·proof /wáwtər proof/ *adj* **IMPERVIOUS TO WATER** treated or constructed so as to be impenetrable or unaffected by water ■ *n* **1. TEXTILE IMPERVIOUS TO WATER** a textile that has been made or treated so as to be impenetrable by water **2.** *UK* **ITEM OF WATERPROOF CLOTHING** an item of waterproof clothing, e.g., a plastic cape ■ *vt* **(-proofed, -proof·ing, -proofs) MAKE SOMETHING WATERPROOF** to make something such as a surface or an item of clothing impenetrable by water —**wa·ter·proof·ness** *n*

wa·ter purs·lane *n* a creeping annual plant growing in moist places with fleshy rounded leaves. Flowers: small, purplish, growing at leaf base. Latin name: *Lythrum portula.*

wa·ter rat *n* **1.** ZOOL same as **muskrat** (sense 1) **2.** a large amphibious rat with broad paddle-shaped hind feet for swimming. Native to: Australia, New Guinea, Philippines. Subfamily: Hydromyinae. **3.** *US* a criminal, loafer, or hooligan who often frequents waterfront areas (*slang*)

wa·ter-re·pel·lent, wa·ter-re·sis·tant *adj* treated or constructed so as to prevent water being absorbed or passing through

wa·ter right *n* **1.** the right to use a water source, especially for irrigation (*often used in the plural*) **2.** the right to sail on specific rivers, lakes, or seas

Wa·ters /wáwtərz/, **Ethel** (1900–77) US singer and actor. A noted blues singer, she was one of the most prominent African American performers of stage and screen in the 1930s and 1940s.

> "Poverty works like a steamroller, crushing a lot of people. But, like the steam roller, it's also a great leveler."
> [Ethel Waters, *His Eye Is On The Sparrow*; 1951]

Wa·ters, Muddy (1915–83) US guitarist and singer. He was a country blues singer who originated the Chicago blues style in the 1950s, and was a leading figure in the revival of folk-blues music in the 1960s. Born **Morganfield, McKinley**

> "All my life I was having trouble with women...Then after I quit having trouble with them, I could feel in my heart that somebody would always have trouble with them, so I kept writing those blues."
> [Muddy Waters. Quoted in *All You Need is Love*, Tony Palmer; 1977]

wa·ter sap·phire *n* a blue precious stone that is a variety of cordierite. Source: river gravel. Use: gems.

wa·ter·scape /wáwtər skàyp/ *n* a view or picture of an expanse of water

wa·ter scor·pi·on *n* an insect that lives in water and uses a long tubular siphon for breathing. It catches prey with its front pair of legs. Family: Nepidae.

wa·ter seal *n* water that lies in a waste pipe and forms a seal that prevents the escape of unpleasant smells

wa·ter·shed /wáwtər shèd/ *n* **1.** the land area that drains into a particular lake, river, or ocean **2.** *UK* GEOG same as **divide** *n* (sense 2) **3.** an important period, time, event, or factor that marks a change or division ○ *Becoming a mother was a watershed in her life.* [Early 19C. Anglicization of German *Wasserscheide* "water divide"]

wa·ter shield *n* **1.** a perennial water plant with floating leaves that are purple underneath and covered in a layer of clear jelly. Flowers: purple. Latin name: *Brasenia schreberi.* **2.** a water plant with roundish floating leaves or finely divided needle-shaped submerged leaves. Genus: *Cabomba.* [Because the leaves are shaped like shields]

wa·ter-sick *adj* describes land that has been made unproductive by excessive irrigation

wa·ter·side /wáwtər sìd/ *n* land alongside an area of water ■ *adj* living or working beside an area of water

wa·ter sign *n* each of the three signs of the zodiac, Pisces, Cancer, and Scorpio, traditionally associated with emotional sensitivity

wa·ter ski *n* a ski designed for skiing over water

waterski

wa·ter·ski /wáwtər skee/ **(-skied, -ski·ing, -skis)** *vi* to ski over water while being towed by a boat —**wa·ter·ski·er** *n* —**wa·ter·ski·ing** *n*

wa·ter skip·per *n US* INSECTS same as **water strider**

wa·ter slide *n* a slide with water flowing down it at a swimming pool or an amusement park

wa·ter snake *n* **1.** a snake that lives in or near water **2.** a nonvenomous snake that lives in marshes and other wet places. Native to: North America, Europe, Southeast Asia. Genus: *Natrix.*

wa·ter soft·en·er *n* **1.** a device that removes or reduces hardness in water, usually by means of ion-exchange resins **2.** a substance used to reduce water hardness, e.g., by precipitating out the minerals causing the hardness

wa·ter-sol·u·ble *adj* capable of being dissolved completely by water

wa·ter span·iel *n* a dog with a thick curly water-resistant coat, belonging to a breed developed for retrieving game from water

wa·ter sports *npl* **1.** sports carried out on or in water **2.** an offensive term for sexual activity in which urine or the act of urination provides gratification (*slang*)

wa·ter·spout /wáwtər spòwt/ *n* **1.** a funnel-shaped tornado, sometimes hundreds of feet wide, extending from the surface of the sea or a lake to the cloud base and caused by violent circulation of air **2.** a hole or spout through which water flows, e.g., from the gutter of a building

wa·ter sprite *n* in folklore and classical mythology, a sprite that lives in water

wa·ter strid·er, wa·ter skip·per *n* an insect that walks on water with long legs and feeds on dead insects. Family: Gerridae.

wa·ter sup·ply *n* **1.** the water distributed to a town, community, or region **2.** the source or delivery system supplying water to an area, e.g., reservoirs, pipes, or purification plants

wa·ter sys·tem *n* **1.** a river with all its tributaries **2.** a system for delivering water to a group of users or a town or region

wa·ter ta·ble *n* **1.** the upper surface of ground water, below which pores in the rocks are filled with water **2.** a molding or band that projects from a wall and is intended to divert rainwater

wa·ter tax·i *n* a motorboat used to ferry passengers between destinations separated by water for a fare

wa·ter·thrush *n* a small songbird of the wood warbler family with markings similar to a thrush, found near streams, ponds, and swampy ground. Native to: North America. Genus: *Seiurus.*

wa·ter·tight /wáwtər tìt/ *adj* **1.** not allowing water to pass in, out, or through **2.** without loopholes or flaws ○ *a watertight argument*

Wa·ter·ton-Gla·cier In·ter·na·tion·al Peace Park /wàwtərtən-/ national park established in 1932 by linking the US Glacier National Park with the Canadian Waterton Lakes National Park. Area: 1,787 sq. mi./4,628 sq. km.

wa·ter tor·ture *n* a form of torture in which water is used, especially one in which water is dripped steadily onto somebody's forehead

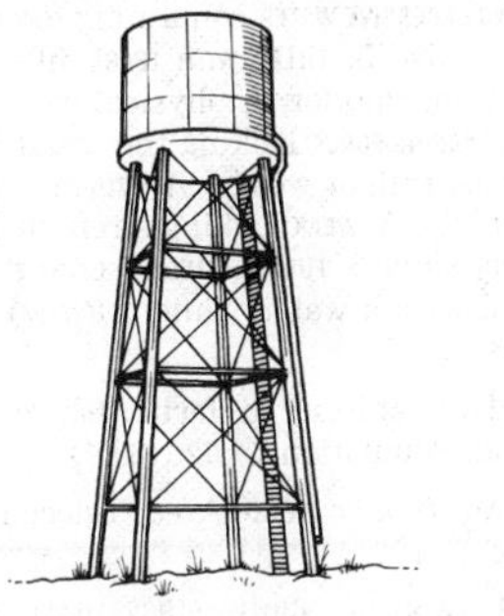
water tower

wa·ter tow·er *n* **1.** a tower for water storage where the prevailing water pressure is not sufficient for either firefighting or general distribution **2.** a fire-fighting apparatus for lifting hoses to high levels

Wa·ter·town /wáwtər tòwn/ **1.** city in eastern Massachusetts, on the Charles River. Founded in 1630, it is a western suburb of Boston. Population: 32,857 (2002 estimate). **2.** city in northern New York, on the Black River, northeast of Syracuse. Population: 25,581 (2002 estimate). **3.** city in eastern South Dakota, on the Big Sioux River, north of Sioux Falls. Population: 20,191 (2002 estimate).

wa·ter turk·ey *n* BIRDS same as **anhinga**

wa·ter va·por *n* water in vapor form, but usually below boiling point

wa·ter-vas·cu·lar sys·tem *n* a system of water-filled vessels connecting the tube feet of echinoderms such as starfish

Wa·ter·ville /wáwtər vìl/ city in southwestern Maine, on the western bank of the Kennebec River, southwest of Bangor and northeast of Augusta. It is home to Colby College. Population: 15,629 (2002 estimate).

wa·ter·way /wáwtər wày/ *n* **1.** a navigable channel used by boats or ships, e.g., a river or canal **2.** a drain for water at the edge of the deck of a boat

wa·ter·weed /wáwtər weed/ *n* any of various plants that grow profusely in ponds, rivers, and other areas of fresh water, e.g., pondweed

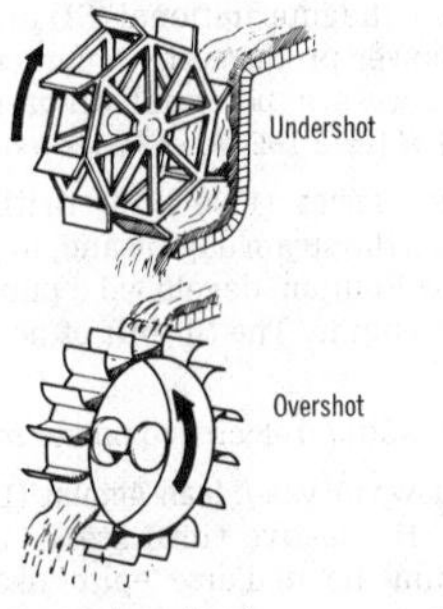

water wheel

wa·ter wheel *n* **1.** a simple wheel driven by water flowing or falling onto vanes or into buckets on the edges of the wheel, used to power machinery. See illustration on previous page **2.** a wheel with buckets fixed to its rim, used for lifting water

wa·ter wings *npl* a pair of air-filled supports that fit closely around the upper arms of a swimmer, especially a child learning to swim

wa·ter witch *n* PARANORMAL same as **dowser**

wa·ter·works /wáwtər wùrks/ *n* (*plural same*) **1.** **SYSTEM FOR SUPPLYING WATER** the entire system of treating, storing, supplying, and managing the distribution networks of pumps and pipes that provide water to a community or region (*takes a singular or plural verb*) **2.** **COMPONENT OF WATER SYSTEM** a single component of a waterworks system, e.g., a pumping station ■ *npl* **1.** **FOUNTAINS** a display of fountains, cascades, and other mechanically driven water-moving devices, or the equipment that produces such a display **2.** **TEARS** a display of crying (*informal*)

wa·ter·worn /wáwtər wàwrn/ *adj* smoothed or eroded by the action of water

wa·ter·y /wáwtəree/ *adj* **1.** **RELATING TO OR CONTAINING WATER** relating to, containing, soaked with, or like water **2.** **HAVING EXCESSIVE WATER** containing too much water ○ *watery coffee* **3.** **FILLED WITH TEARS** filled with tears, either from emotion or physical irritation ○ *watery eyes* **4.** **LACKING FORCE** lacking the usual full force and appearing thin or weak ○ *A watery sun hung in the autumn sky.* **5.** **WEAK** lacking strength or sincerity ○ *a watery smile* **6.** **FULL OF FLUID** discharging, secreting, or filled with a watery fluid ○ *watery blister* —**wa·ter·i·ness** *n*

Wat·ford /wótfərd/ city in Hertfordshire, south central England. Population: 79,726 (2001).

WATS /wots/ *abbr* Wide-Area Telecommunications Service

Wat·son /wóts'n/, **Chris** (1867–1941) Chilean-born prime minister of Australia (1904). He was involved in the labor movement during the 1890s and became the leader of the Labour Party in 1901. He was Australia's first Labour prime minister. See table at **prime minister**

Wat·son, James D. (*b.* 1928) US biochemist. He worked with Francis Crick and Maurice Wilkins in exploring the structure of the DNA molecule, for which they shared the Nobel Prize in physiology or medicine (1962). Full name **Watson, James Dewey**

> "Biology has at least 50 more interesting years."
> [James D. Watson, *Remark*; December 31, 1984]

Wat·son, Thomas J., Jr. (1914–93) US computer industry executive. He was president (1952–61), chairman (1961–71), and chairman of the executive board (1972–79) of IBM, and US ambassador to the Soviet Union (1979–81). Full name **Watson, Thomas John Jr.**

> "The beliefs that mold great organizations frequently grow out of the character, the experience, and the convictions of a single person."
> [Thomas J. Watson Jr. Quoted in *Key Management Ideas*, Stuart Crainer; 1996]

Wat·son-Crick mod·el *n* the three-dimensional double-helix model of the DNA molecule proposed by James Watson and Francis Crick in 1953 [Mid-20C. After J. D. WATSON and F. H. C. CRICK]

watt /wot/ *n* the international (**SI**) unit of power equal to the power produced by a current of one ampere acting across a potential difference of one volt. Symbol **W** [Late 19C. After James WATT]

Watt /wot/, **James** (1736–1819) British inventor. He improved the steam engine and, in partnership with Matthew Boulton, developed a pumping engine and rotative engine. The SI unit of power is named for him.

watt·age /wóttij/ *n* electrical power measured in watts

Wat·teau /wo tṓ, vaa-/, **Jean-Antoine** (1684–1721) French painter. His festive rural scenes and figures from the commedia dell'arte epitomize French rococo painting.

watt-hour *n* a unit of electrical energy equal to that of one watt operating for one hour

wat·tle /wótt'l/ *n* **1.** **STAKES INTERWOVEN WITH BRANCHES** stakes or poles interwoven with branches and twigs, used for walls, fences, and roofs **2.** **MATERIAL FOR WATTLE** material used to make wattle, e.g., branches or stakes **3.** **SKIN HANGING FROM ANIMAL'S THROAT** a loose, often highly colored fold of bare skin hanging from the throat or cheek of birds and lizards. It is used in courtship and other displays. **4.** **AUSTRALIAN ACACIA TREE** a drought-resistant tree or bush, often planted for shade or ornament, whose feathery-looking leaves are sometimes replaced by flattened green leaf stalks in maturity. Native to: Australia. Genus: *Acacia.* ■ *vt* (**-tled, -tling, -tles**) **1.** **MAKE SOMETHING FROM WATTLE** to construct something from wattle **2.** **WEAVE BRANCHES INTO WATTLE** to weave branches or twigs into wattle [Old English *watul*, origin ?] —**wat·tled** *adj*

wat·tle and daub *n* building material consisting of wattle covered with mud or clay, often containing lime, dung, or straw

wat·tle·bird /wótt'l bùrd/ *n* a slender-bodied gray-brown or olive-brown bird with a long beak, a brush-tipped tongue for lapping nectar, and wattles on the cheeks. Native to: Australia. Genus: *Anthochaera.*

watt·me·ter /wótt meetər/ *n* an instrument designed to measure the magnitude of the power in an electric circuit. It may be scaled in watts, kilowatts, or megawatts.

Popperfoto

Evelyn Waugh

Waugh /waw/, **Evelyn** (1903–66) British novelist. His early novels satirizing high society gave way to the more serious later work such as *Brideshead Revisited* (1945) that reflected his preoccupation with Roman Catholicism. Full name **Waugh, Evelyn Arthur St. John**. See Cultural note at **handful**

> "You never find an Englishman among the underdogs-except in England, of course."
> [Evelyn Waugh, *The Loved One*; 1948]

Wau·ke·gan /waw kéegən/ city in northeastern Illinois, on the shore of Lake Michigan, north of North Chicago. Population: 91,323 (2002 estimate).

wav /wav/ *abbr* a file extension for a sound file. Full form **waveform**

wave /wayv/ *n* **1.** **LARGE RIPPLE ON LIQUID OR OCEAN** a raised ridge-shaped formation moving across the surface of a liquid, especially the ocean, or an ocean wave curling over and falling as it reaches the shore **2.** **UNDULATING MOTION** a movement through, or over the surface of or along the edge of something that is similar in its appearance or effects to a wave ○ *The wind made waves across the field of grain.* **3.** **ACT OF WAVING HAND** an instance of moving the hand or arm as a signal or greeting **4.** **LINE CURVING IN ALTERNATING DIRECTIONS** a line, shape, surface, or pattern that curves in one direction and then another, especially one with repeated curves **5.** **SURGE IN ACTIVITY** a sudden occurrence of or increase in a particular phenomenon or activity ○ *a crime wave* ○ *a wave of strikes* **6.** **BURST OF FEELING** a sudden and often overwhelming experience of a particular feeling ○ *a wave of sorrow* ○ *Relief came over me in waves.* **7.** **INCOMING GROUP** a large number or body of people moving together or doing the same thing at the same time ○ *a wave of immigrants* ○ *attack in waves* **8.** **LOOSE CURVE IN HAIR** a soft, usually large curve or ripple in the hair where the lie of the hair changes direction, either naturally or after setting **9.** **RIPPLED PATTERN** a rippled pattern in material such as silk **10.** PHYS **OSCILLATION OF ENERGY** an oscillation that travels through a medium by transferring energy from one particle or point to another without causing any permanent displacement of the medium ○ *sound waves* **11.** LEISURE **CONTINUOUS RIPPLING MOVEMENT BY SPORTS CROWD** the rippling effect produced by rows of spectators at a sporting event standing up, raising their arms, and then sitting down again ■ **waves** *npl* **SEA** the waves of the ocean, or the ocean itself ■ *v* (**waved, wav·ing, waves**) **1.** *vti* **MOVE HAND REPEATEDLY AS SIGNAL** to move the hand or arm from side to side or up and down as a greeting, farewell, or signal **2.** *vti* **MOVE SOMETHING REPEATEDLY IN AIR** to move from side to side or up and down, or cause something such as a flag to move from side to side or up and down ○ *The flag waved in the wind.* **3.** *vt* **DIRECT SOMEBODY OR SOMETHING BY WAVING** to direct somebody or something by waving a hand, arm, or object ○ *The police waved the traffic around the procession.* **4.** *vti* **MAKE INTO OR BE IN UNDULATIONS** to make something into swells, ridges, or swirls, or be in the form of swells, ridges, or swirls ○ *a field of grain waving in the wind* **5.** *vi* **MOVE IN WAVES** to move in a series of swells (*refers to water*) **6.** *vti* **BE OR MAKE SLIGHTLY CURLED** to be slightly curled, or make hair slightly curled **7.** *vt* **GIVE MATERIAL RIPPLED PATTERN** to create a rippled pattern in a fabric such as silk [Old English *wafian* < Germanic, "move back and forth"] ◇ **catch a wave** to find or launch yourself onto a wave of the type that can be enjoyably ridden on a surfboard (*slang*) ◇ **make waves** to cause a disturbance or trouble, e.g., by suggesting or introducing changes or making criticisms

SPELLCHECK See *waive.*

wave aside *vt* to dismiss something or somebody as trivial or inconsequential

wave down *vt* to stop a vehicle by waving to the driver to halt

wave off *vt* to watch and wave to somebody who is leaving

Wave /wayv/ *n US* a member of the WAVES [Back-formation]

wave·band /wáyv bànd/ *n* a range of radio frequencies within which transmissions occur

wave e·qua·tion *n* in physics, an equation, usually a partial differential equation, that defines the propagation of a wave through a medium. The form of the equation is determined by the medium, the method by which the wave is transmitted, and the circumstance of its propagation.

wave file *n* a computer file containing a digitized representation of sound waves

wave·form /wáyv fàwrm/ *n* in physics, the profile or shape of a wave, especially the graphic representation of one of its characteristics such as frequency or amplitude relative to time

wave·front /wáyv frùnt/ *n* in physics, a line or surface that joins points of the same phase in a wave traveling through a medium

wave func·tion *n* in quantum physics, an equation that shows how a wave's amplitude varies in space and time

wave·guide /wáyv gīd/ *n* in electronics, a transmission line consisting of a hollow metal conductor used as a path to convey microwave energy along its length. It is used in radar systems to convey transmitted energy from the transmitter to the antenna and received energy from the antenna back to the receiver.

wave·length /wáyv lèngth/ *n* **1.** in physics, the distance between two points on adjacent waves that have the same phase, e.g., the distance between two consecutive peaks or troughs. Symbol λ **2.** in broadcasting, the wavelength of the fundamental radio wave used by a broadcasting station ◇ **be on the same wavelength** to be able to understand each other, or to have similar opinions, attitudes, or tastes

wave·let /wáyvlət/ *n* a small wave, e.g., a ripple

wa·vel·lite /wáyvə līt/ *n* a soft light gray, yellow, or brown hydrated aluminum phosphate mineral, forming clusters of radiating crystals. Source: slates and shales. [Early 19C. After William *Wavell* (d. 1829), British physician]

wave me·chan·ics *n* a form of quantum theory in which happenings on the atomic scale are explained in terms of interactions between systems of waves, represented by wave functions (*takes a singular verb*)

wave·me·ter /wáyv meetər/ *n* an instrument for measuring wavelengths

wave num·ber *n* in physics, the number of waves in a given unit distance. Wave number is the reciprocal of wavelength. Symbol σ

wave·off /wàyv awf, -of/ *n* a signal or instruction to an aircraft that it is not to land

wave-par·ti·cle du·al·i·ty *n* a fundamental concept of quantum theory holding that energy sometimes behaves like particles and sometimes behaves like waves, so that descriptions of energy as one or the other are inadequate

wave pool *n* a public swimming pool equipped with a device to produce waves

wa·ver /wáyvər/ *vi* (**-vered, -ver·ing, -vers**) **1.** FLUCTUATE BETWEEN POSSIBILITIES to go back and forth between possibilities, or be indecisive in making a choice **2.** BEGIN TO CHANGE OPINION to become unsure or begin to change from a previous opinion **3.** MOVE IN DIFFERENT DIRECTIONS to move one way and then another in an irregular pattern **4.** FLUCTUATE, ESPECIALLY IN TONE to vary or fluctuate, e.g., as the voice does from emotion **5.** FLICKER to go on and off, especially when burning unsteadily (*refers to lights or flames*) ■ *n* ACT OF WAVERING an instance or act of wavering [14C. < Old Norse *vafra*] —**wa·ver·er** *n* —**wa·ver·ing·ly** *adv*

SPELLCHECK See ***waive***.

SYNONYMS See ***hesitate***.

WAVES /wayvz/ *n* the women's branch of the US Naval Reserve that was organized in World War II. It no longer exists as a separate entity. Full form **Women Accepted for Volunteer Emergency Service**

wave the·o·ry *n* the theory that the behavior of light or any other electromagnetic radiation can be explained by assuming that it travels in waves

wave train *n* in physics, a series of similar waves produced at equal intervals and traveling in the same direction

wav·y /wáyvee/ (**-i·er, -i·est**) *adj* **1.** REPEATEDLY CURVING forming a series of smooth curves that go in one direction and then another **2.** HAVING SOFT CURVES having loose open waves ○ *wavy hair* **3.** CONTAINING WAVES full of waves or having a surface covered by waves **4.** MOVING LIKE WAVE moving with an up-and-down or side-to-side motion **5.** WAVERING wavering or changeable —**wav·i·ly** *adv* —**wav·i·ness** *n*

waw *n* same as **vav**

wa-wa *n* MUSIC another spelling of **wah-wah**

wax[1] /waks/ *n* **1.** INDUST NATURALLY-OCCURRING GREASY SUBSTANCE a moldable substance of animal, plant, or mineral origin that feels slightly greasy or oily to the touch **2.** HOUSEHOLD PREPARATION FOR POLISHING a preparation containing wax used to polish floors, cars, and other surfaces **3.** INDUST same as **beeswax** *n* (sense 2) **4.** MED same as **earwax 5.** INDUST RESINOUS MIXTURE USED IN SHOEMAKING a resinous mixture rubbed onto thread used in shoemaking **6.** SOMEBODY OR SOMETHING EASILY MOLDED somebody or something that is easily molded, shaped, or manipulated ■ *vt* (**waxed, wax·ing, wax·es**) **1.** POLISH SOMETHING WITH WAX to coat or polish something such as a floor or car with wax **2.** COSMETICS REMOVE HAIR WITH WAX to remove unwanted hair from the skin using heated wax that is left to dry and then removed [Old English *wæx* < Germanic] —**wax·er** *n*

wax[2] /waks/ (**waxed, wax·ing, wax·es**) *vi* **1.** to show a gradually increasing illuminated surface, as does the Moon between its new and full phases **2.** to increase in size, power, or intensity (*literary*) **3.** same as **become** (*literary*) ○ *waxed lyrical* [Old English *weaxan* < Indo-European, "to increase"]

wax bean *n* a variety of string bean that is yellow

wax·bill /wáks bìl/ *n* a small brightly colored bird of the finch family with a conical beak. Waxbills feed on seeds and insects and build roofed nests of grass. Native to: Africa, Arabia. Genus: *Estrilda*.

wax cap *n* a mushroom with a cap that has waxy gills. Family: Hygrophoraceae.

waxed pa·per *n* HOUSEHOLD same as **wax paper**

wax·en /wáks'n/ *adj* **1.** PALE AND UNHEALTHY-LOOKING lacking the rosy glow of life or health ○ *a waxen complexion* **2.** MADE OF WAX covered with, permeated with, or made of wax **3.** LIKE WAX resembling wax in texture and appearance **4.** EASY TO SHAPE easily shaped, changed, or manipulated [Pre-12C. Old past participle of WAX[1]]

wax in·sect *n* a scale insect that secretes wax. Superfamily: Coccoidea.

wax moth *n* a small brownish moth whose larvae develop inside beehives, feeding on the wax of the honeycombs and often damaging the honey and the honey bee larvae. Latin name: *Galleria mellonella*.

wax mu·se·um *n* a museum containing wax models of famous people

wax myr·tle *n* TREES same as **bayberry** (sense 2)

wax palm *n* TREES same as **carnauba** (sense 1)

wax pa·per *n* paper that does not allow oil or grease to soak into it or pass through it and is used especially in cooking, preparing, or wrapping food

wax plant *n* an evergreen climbing plant or bush that is related to milkweed. Flowers: waxy, white. Native to: Asia, Australia. Genus: *Hoya*.

wax vine *n* PLANTS same as **wax plant**

wax·wing /wáks wìng/ *n* a bird with a crest, buff-brown feathers, and waxy-looking red tips on the edges of the wings. Native to: northern regions. Genus: *Bombycilla*.

wax·work /wáks wùrk/ *n* **1.** WAX MODEL a realistic model, usually of a famous person, made from wax **2.** WAX OBJECT an object made of wax, especially an ornament **3.** ART OF USING WAX FOR MODELING the art of using wax as a modeling or expressive medium

wax·y /wáksee/ (**-i·er, -i·est**) *adj* **1.** LIKE WAX resembling wax in texture, appearance, or pliability **2.** COVERED WITH WAX covered with, containing a lot of, or made of wax **3.** MED HAVING HARD DEPOSITS LIKE WAX containing deposits of a hard substance resembling wax (**amyloid**) resulting from tissue degeneration [15C. < WAX[1]] —**wax·i·ness** *n*

way /way/ *n* **1.** MANNER OR METHOD a means, manner, or method of doing something ○ *I'll do it my way.* **2.** RESPECT a feature, aspect, or example of something ○ *In some ways, they're very similar.* **3.** PATH a path or physical means of getting from one place to another ○ *The way out is through here.* **4.** DOOR OR OPENING a door or opening leading or providing access to or from somewhere ○ *came in the front way* **5.** JOURNEY OR ROUTE a journey or the route followed or to be followed ○ *on my way home* **6.** PROGRESS THROUGH LIFE progress or a path through life and its experiences or difficulties **7.** *also* **Way** STREET a street (*often used in place names*) **8.** DIRECTION a direction, e.g., left, right, up, or down **9.** MANNER OF PLACING the manner in which something is placed, packed, or arranged, or the direction it faces **10.** SPACE FOR ACTION path, room, territory, or space allowing movement, progress, or action ○ *got out of the way* **11.** AREA an area or district, e.g., around somebody's home (*informal*) ○ *out our way* **12.** DISTANCE a distance away in space or time ○ *a long way off* **13.** AMOUNT the extent or amount to which somebody does something or to which something happens ○ *He's fallen for her in a big way.* **14.** PART OF SOMETHING each of a particular number of parts into which something divides or is split ○ *split the money four ways* **15.** CONDITION the state or condition of somebody or something, especially with regard to health or finances ○ *He's in a bad way.* **16.** PREFERENCE something that somebody wants to do or to happen ○ *always wants his own way* **17.** TRADITION OR CUSTOM the customary practice of a person or group **18.** TYPICAL OCCURRENCE the usual occurrence or pattern of events ○ *It's always the way when you're in a hurry.* **19.** MECH ENG GUIDE OR SUPPORT a surface used to guide or provide support for moving parts of a machine tool such as a lathe (*often used in the plural*) ■ *adv* **1.** VERY MUCH to a considerable degree or at a considerable distance (*informal*) ○ *way out of our price range* **2.** ⚠ VERY extremely (*slang*) ○ *That's way cool!* [Old English *weg* < Indo-European, "to go"] ◇ **by the way** used to introduce something that is not strictly part of the subject at hand ◇ **by way of something** as a means of or for the purpose of something ◇ **every which way 1.** in all directions **2.** in every way possible (*informal*) ◇ **give way 1.** to become useless, break, or otherwise fail, especially under weight or pressure or from age or wear **2.** TRANSP to slow down or stop in order to let another vehicle pass ◇ **give way to somebody** *or* **something** to be replaced or superseded by somebody or something ○ *The rain gave way to patchy sunshine.* ◇ **give way to something** to be overcome by an emotion that you have been trying to resist ◇ **go out of your way to do something** to make an exceptional effort or take exceptional steps in order to do something ◇ **have a way with somebody** *or* **something** to be good at dealing with somebody or something ◇ **have it both ways** to have the benefits of opposing situations or actions ◇ **in a way** from a certain point of view ◇ **(in) the worst way** very much, very badly, or very intensely ◇ **make way (for somebody** *or* **something)** to move aside in order to make room for somebody or something ◇ **make your way 1.** to go somewhere, especially when getting there requires overcoming some obstacle, e.g., finding the route or some transportation **2.** to become successful ◇ **nine ways from Sunday** *US* in every possible way and to the greatest extent (*informal*) ○ *The potential cross-examination questions were covered nine ways from Sunday during pretrial preps.* ◇ **no way** used as an emphatic negative (*informal*) ◇ **out of the way** in a remote location ◇ **pay your way** to pay your share of expenses ◇ **see your way (clear) to doing something** to be willing and able to oblige somebody by doing something ○ *Could you see your way clear to lending me $100?* ◇ **there are no two ways about it** there is no room for dispute ◇ **way to go** used to congratulate somebody on something that he or she has done (*informal*)

SPELLCHECK **way, weigh,** or **whey?** Do not confuse the spelling of ***way***, ***weigh***, and ***whey***, which sound similar. ***Way*** is a noun in frequent use, with meanings including "means, manner, or method," "journey or route," and "direction," as in *a different way to do it, on the way home, going the wrong way.* ***Weigh*** is a verb meaning "find out the weight of something," "be of a particular weight," or "consider or evaluate something," as in *weigh the ingredients, weighs five pounds, weigh up the pros and cons.* ***Whey*** is a much less usual noun denoting the watery liquid that separates from the solid part of milk, as in *curds and whey.*

USAGE **Way** or **ways?** The plural noun ***ways*** is informally used in place of ***way*** in expressions such as *a long ways to go down this old trail; a long ways to go to capture the tennis title.* Such usages are not appropriate in formal speaking and writing: *Researchers have a long way* [not *ways*] *to go before they can validate the safety of this drug for public consumption.* As an adverb, ***way*** is used informally to mean "to a considerable degree," where *far* is preferable in formal speaking and writing. In formal contexts *a synopsis that was far too long* should be used rather than *a synopsis that was way too long.* Another meaning of the adverb ***way***, "extremely," is slang, and usages like the following are inappropriate in formal spoken and written English: *way scared, way cool, way mean,* and *way wrong,* where *quite scared, extremely cool, very mean,* and *totally wrong* are appropriate substitutes.

way·bill /wáy bìl/ *n* a document that gives information about goods being shipped or carried

way·far·er /wáy fèrrər/ *n* a traveler, especially somebody who makes a journey on foot (*literary*) —**way·far·ing** *n, adj*

way·far·ing tree *n* a bush with red berries that turn black as they ripen. Flowers: white, in flat-topped clusters. Native to: Europe, western Asia. Latin name: *Viburnum lantana*.

way·lay /wáy lày/ (**-laid** /-làyd/, **-lay·ing, -lays**) *vt* **1.** to lie in wait for somebody, especially as part of an attack or ambush **2.** to stop or accost somebody, e.g., in order to talk —**way·lay·er** *n*

way·leave /wáy leev/ *n* the right of way over somebody else's property, for which payment is usually made

Wayne /wayn/, **Anthony** (1745–96) American soldier. As a general in the American Revolution (1775–83), he led a brilliant victory at Stony Point (1779) and contributed to the British defeat at Yorktown (1781). Known as **Mad Anthony**

John Wayne

Wayne, John (1907–79) US actor. He starred as the rugged hero in numerous westerns, including *True Grit* (1969), for which he won an Academy Award. Born **Morrison, Marion Michael**. Known as **the Duke**

> "Courage is being scared to death and saddling up anyway."
> [John Wayne. Quoted in *Never Let Them See You Cry*, Edna Buchanan; 1992]

way of life *n* **1.** the habits and behavior that characterize a person or group of people ○ *had an increasingly sedentary way of life* **2.** something commonly used, done, or experienced by a person or group of people ○ *Smart cards are a way of life for most of us.*

Way of the Cross *n* a series of pictures representing Jesus Christ's progress on the road to Calvary, according to the Bible

way-out *adj* **1.** unusual, peculiar, or unconventional (*informal*) **2.** excellent or exciting (*dated informal*)

way·point /wáy pòynt/ *n* a point on a journey or route where a traveler can stop or change course

ways /wayz/ *n* **1.** ⚠ a distance traveled or to be traveled (*informal; takes a singular verb*) ○ *The next gas station is quite a ways from here.* **2.** the tracks a ship slides down to be launched (*takes a singular or plural verb*)

USAGE See ***way.***

-ways *suffix* in a particular direction or position ○ *edgeways* [Old English *weges*, form of *weg* "way, of (such a) way"]

ways and means *npl* **1.** methods of accomplishing or achieving something, especially finding a way of paying for something **2.** methods used by a government to raise money, e.g., legislation

Ways and Means *n* a legislative committee in charge of methods of raising money for government

way·side /wáy sīd/ *n* the side of a road or path ■ *adj* situated at the side of a road or path ◇ **fall by the wayside** to fail to continue or complete something ○ *Several students fell by the wayside after the first few weeks.* ◇ **go by the wayside** *US* to be abandoned because of other commitments or interests

way sta·tion *n US* **1.** a station between the major stations on a railroad **2.** a point or stopping place on a route or process

way·ward /wáywərd/ *adj* **1.** disobedient and uncontrollable **2.** behaving in an erratic, apparently perverse, or unpredictable manner [14C. Alteration of *awayward*] —**way·ward·ly** *adv* —**way·ward·ness** *n*

SYNONYMS See ***unruly.***

way·worn /wáy wàwrn/ *adj* worn out or weary from traveling

wa·zoo /waa zoō/ (*plural* **-zoos**) *n US* an offensive term for the anus or buttocks (*slang*) [Origin ?] ◇ **up the wazoo** used to indicate an abundance of something (*sometimes considered offensive*)

Wb *symbol* MEASURE weber

WB *abbr* **1.** water ballast **2.** waybill **3.** westbound

WBA *abbr* World Boxing Association

WBC *abbr* **1.** BIOL white blood cell **2.** BOXING World Boxing Council

WbN *abbr* COMPASS west by north

W bo·son *n* PHYS same as **W particle**

WbS *abbr* COMPASS west by south

w.c. *abbr* without charge

W.C. *n* HOUSEHOLD full form **water closet**

WCC, W.C.C. *abbr* World Council of Churches

WCTU, W.C.T.U. *abbr* Women's Christian Temperance Union

wd. *abbr* **1.** HEALTH SERVICES ward **2.** wood **3.** word

WDM, wdm *abbr* wavelength division multiplex

WDYT *abbr* what do you think (*used in e-mails or text messages*)

we /wee/ *pron* **1. REFERS TO SPEAKER AND OTHERS** used to refer to the speaker or writer and at least one other person (*first person plural personal pronoun, used as the subject of a verb*) ○ *We are going on vacation.* ○ *We all want our children to have a better future.* **2. REFERS TO PEOPLE IN GENERAL** used to refer to all people or to people in general, including the speaker or writer ○ *We're getting closer to the election.* **3. USED INSTEAD OF "I"** used by a writer or speaker to include the listener or speaker in what is being said, especially to talk about how a book or talk is organized ○ *We will now consider the causes of the Civil War.* **4. USED INSTEAD OF "YOU"** used sarcastically or condescendingly by a speaker ○ *And how are we today?* [Old English *wē* < Indo-European]

weak /week/ *adj* **1. NOT STRONG OR FIT** not physically fit or mentally strong **2. EASILY DEFEATED** easily overcome or defeated **3. LACKING STRENGTH OF CHARACTER** not having strength of character **4. NOT INTENSE** not powerful or intense ○ *weak winter sunshine* **5. LACKING SKILLS OR ABILITIES** not having particular skills or abilities ○ *weak in math* **6. WATERY OR TASTELESS** watery or lacking flavor ○ *weak coffee* **7. NOT WORKING TO FULL CAPACITY** not working as well as usual or desirable **8. UNCONVINCING** not persuasive or convincing ○ *a weak excuse* **9. NOT STRONG POLITICALLY** not politically strong or powerful ○ *a weak country* **10.** LITERAT **UNSTRESSED** describes a syllable or word that is not stressed or accented **11.** LITERAT **HAVING ACCENT ON UNSTRESSED SYLLABLE** describes verse that has the accent on a syllable that is usually unstressed **12.** GRAM **CHARACTERIZED BY REGULAR INFLECTIONAL ENDINGS** describes a verb whose forms are characterized by regular inflectional endings, not by vowel changes **13.** FIN **CHARACTERIZED BY FALLING PRICES** falling in price, or characterized by falling prices ○ *a weak market* [13C. < Old Norse *veikr* "pliant" < Germanic]

SPELLCHECK weak or **week**? Do not confuse the spelling of ***weak*** and ***week***, which sound similar. ***Weak*** is an adjective meaning "not strong," as in *weak legs, weak tea, a weak argument.* ***Week*** is a noun denoting a period of seven days, as in *three weeks ago.*

SYNONYMS *weak, feeble, frail, infirm, debilitated, decrepit, enervated*

CORE MEANING: lacking physical strength or energy

weak not physically fit or mentally strong ○ *He felt too weak to climb the stairs.* ○ *He's a weak man who can't resist the chance of what seems like easy money.* **feeble** lacking physical or mental strength or health ○ *Her father grew bent and feeble, but still walked his dog every day.* ○ *feeble, incompetent people who were easily persuaded by her promises* **frail** in a physically weakened state and vulnerable to injury ○ *a slight old man with the light, frail bones of a child* ○ *He looked frail but happy as he descended the hospital steps.* **infirm** lacking strength and vitality, especially because of sickness or age ○ *elderly and infirm people* ○ *Their aunt was becoming increasingly infirm and was unable to visit them this year.* **debilitated** with reduced strength or energy as a result of illness or physical exertion ○ *feeling thoroughly debilitated after his surgery* ○ *Rescuers found the pair in a half-frozen and debilitated condition.* **decrepit** (*informal*) with strength lessened by the effects of age ○ *The president wasn't always the decrepit old man of his last years in office.* **enervated** weakened or exhausted physically, mentally, or morally ○ *The intense heat made us feel faint and enervated.* ○ *She's been enervated by her long ordeal.*

weak·en /wéekən/ (**-ened, -en·ing, -ens**) *vti* to make somebody or something weak or weaker, or become weak or weaker —**weak·en·er** *n*

weak·er sex /wéekər-/ *n* an offensive term for women considered as a group (*dated*)

weak·fish /wéek fish/ (*plural same or* **-fish·es**) *n* FISH same as **sea trout** (sense 1) [Late 18C. < obsolete Dutch *weekvisch* "soft fish" < *week* "soft" + *visch* "fish"]

weak in·ter·ac·tion, weak force *n* the fundamental interaction between elementary particles that is mediated by the W and Z particles. It is involved in radioactive decay, which occurs by electron production, and particle decay. One of the four fundamental interactions, it is only effective at distances of less than 10^{-15} m and is a trillion times weaker than the strong interaction.

weak-kneed *adj* easily persuaded or intimidated

weak·ling /wéekling/ *n* somebody who lacks physical strength or a strong character

weak·ly /wéeklee/ *adj* (**-li·er, -li·est**) sickly or delicate ■ *adv* with little strength or force ○ *She nodded weakly.* —**weak·li·ness** *n*

weak-mind·ed *adj* **1.** easily persuaded or convinced (*disapproving*) **2.** an offensive term meaning of low intelligence —**weak-mind·ed·ness** *n*

weak·ness /wéeknəss/ *n* **1. LACK OF STRENGTH OR DETERMINATION** lack of strength, power, or determination **2. WEAK POINT** a weak point in the structure or arrangement of something ○ *Unfortunately, the escape plan had a serious weakness.* **3. CHARACTER FLAW** a feature of somebody's character regarded as unfavorable **4. FONDNESS** a strong liking for something ○ *a weakness for chocolate* **5. OBJECT OF DESIRE** an irresistible object of desire ○ *My weakness is action movies.*

SYNONYMS See ***flaw***[1].

weak sis·ter *n* **1.** an offensive term for somebody regarded as a weak or unreliable member or component of a group (*insult*) **2.** an offensive term for somebody regarded as timid or cowardly

weak-willed *adj* not having a strong will

weal[1] /weel/ *n* a general state of well-being, prosperity, and happiness (*literary*) [Old English *wela* < Indo-European, "to wish"]

weal[2] /weel/ *n* MED same as **wheal**

wealth /welth/ *n* **1. LARGE AMOUNT OF MONEY** a large amount of money or possessions **2. STATE OF HAVING MUCH MONEY** the state of having plenty of money or possessions ○ *came from a background of great wealth* **3. ABUNDANCE OF SOMETHING** an abundance or great quantity of something ○ *quoted a wealth of statistics to prove the point* **4.** ECON **VALUE OF ASSETS** the value of assets owned by a person or a community ○ *need to determine the family's wealth* [13C. < WEAL[1]]

CULTURAL NOTE *The Wealth of Nations*, a philosophical treatise (1776) by Scottish economist and philosopher Adam Smith. One of the earliest and most comprehensive analyses of economic systems, it began as a study of the relationship between human nature and social evolution. Smith's assertion that the natural outcome of this evolution is an economy based on open markets and driven by competition inspired many modern-day laissez-faire capitalist philosophies.

wealth·y /wélthee/ (**-i·er, -i·est**) *adj* **1.** having a large amount of money or possessions **2.** enjoying an abundance or great quantity of something —**wealth·i·ly** *adv* —**wealth·i·ness** *n*

wean /ween/ (**weaned, wean·ing, weans**) *v* **1.** *vti* **STOP FEEDING BABY WITH MOTHER'S MILK** to start feeding a baby or young animal food other than its mother's milk **2.** *vt* **STOP SOMEBODY FROM HAVING SOMETHING** to cause somebody to go without something that has become a habit or that is much liked ○ *weaning her gradually off the medication* **3.** *vt* **ACCUSTOM SOMEBODY TO SOMETHING FROM CHILDHOOD** to accustom somebody to something from an early age ○ *children weaned on computer games and videos* [Old English *wenian* "accustom" < Germanic]

wean·er /wéenər/ *n* **1.** a young animal that has recently been weaned, especially a hog **2.** somebody who weans animals, or something used in weaning animals

wean·ling /wéenling/ *n* a child or young animal that has just been weaned ■ *adj* newly weaned ○ *a weanling lamb*

weap·on /wéppən/ *n* **1.** DEVICE DESIGNED TO INJURE OR KILL a device designed to inflict injury or death on an opponent **2.** SOMETHING USED TO GAIN ADVANTAGE something used as a way of getting an advantage in a situation ○ *A teacher's best weapon can be humor.* **3.** ZOOL ANIMAL'S PROTECTIVE PART an animal part used for defense or attack, e.g., claws ■ *vt* (**-oned, -on·ing, -ons**) GIVE ARMS TO SOMEBODY to provide somebody with weapons [Old English *wǣpen* < Germanic] —**weap·oned** *adj* —**weap·on·less** *adj*

weap·on·eer /wèppə néer/ *n* **1.** somebody who prepares a nuclear weapon for detonation **2.** somebody who designs nuclear weapons

weap·on·ize /wéppə nìz/ (**-ized, -iz·ing, -iz·es**) *vt* to process chemical, nuclear, or biological material so that it can be deployed as or integrated into a weapon —**weap·on·i·za·tion** /wèppəni záysh'n/ *n*

weap·on of mass de·struc·tion *n* a weapon, usually nuclear, biological, or chemical, that causes overwhelming devastation and loss of life

weap·on·ry /wéppənree/ *n* **1.** all the weapons possessed by a person, group, or nation **2.** techniques for producing weapons

weap·ons-grade *adj* describes plutonium, uranium, or other material in a form suitable for manufacturing weapons

weap·ons sys·tem *n* a weapon consisting of two or more major components, e.g., a missile and its ground-based radar guidance

wear[1] /wer/ *v* (**wore** /wawr/, **worn** /wawrn/, **wear·ing, wears**) **1.** *vt* HAVE SOMETHING ON BODY to have something on all or part of the body as clothing, jewelry, protection, or for another purpose, e.g., to aid sight or hearing, either temporarily or habitually **2.** *vt Malaysia, Singapore* PUT SOMETHING ON to put on a piece of clothing **3.** *vt* DISPLAY FACIAL EXPRESSION to display, show, or present an expression or physical manifestation of an emotion on the face ○ *wearing a smile* **4.** *vti* DAMAGE SOMETHING BY USING OR RUBBING to damage or alter something by using or rubbing it, or be damaged or altered in this way ○ *The lettering had been worn away by years of use.* **5.** *vti* PRODUCE SOMETHING BY USING OR RUBBING to produce something, especially a hole, through continued use, pressure, or friction, or be produced in this way ○ *had worn a hole in his sweater* **6.** *vti* RUB OFF to rub something off or away, or be rubbed off or away **7.** *vti* TIRE OUT to tire somebody out, or become tired out **8.** *vi* MAINTAIN SAME CONDITION to last in the same, especially good condition with much use or through time ○ *The carpet's wearing well.* **9.** *vti* PASS SLOWLY to pass time slowly, or be passed slowly ○ *as the evening wore on* **10.** *vt* NAUT FLY FLAG to fly a particular flag or colors as a ship's identification ■ *n* **1.** ACT OF WEARING the act of wearing something, or the condition of being worn **2.** DAMAGE FROM BEING USED damage or deterioration that results from being used **3.** ABILITY TO LAST the ability to last without deteriorating **4.** CLOTHING CLOTHING OF PARTICULAR KIND clothing, especially clothing of a particular kind (*often used in combination*) ○ *children's wear* [Old English *werian* < Germanic] —**wear·er** *n* ◇ **the worse for wear 1.** in a poor condition because of much use **2.** looking or feeling unwell, especially because of being tired ◇ **wear thin 1.** to weaken or fail ○ *My patience is wearing thin.* **2.** to become unacceptable or implausible because of excessive use ○ *That excuse is beginning to wear a little thin.* **3.** to become thinner or disappear because of abrasion or heavy use

SPELLCHECK See *ware*[1], *warn*.

wear down *vti* **1.** to overcome or weaken somebody or something by a gradual process, or be overcome or weakened in this way **2.** to rub or use something so much that it becomes thinner or disappears, or be rubbed or used in this way

wear off *vi* to lose effectiveness or strength gradually ○ *Let me know when the anesthetic wears off.*

wear out *v* **1.** *vti* to use something heavily or for a long time until it is no longer useful, or be used in this way **2.** *vt* to tire somebody out

wear[2] /wer/ (**wore** /wawr/, **worn** /wawrn/, **wear·ing, wears**) *vti* to bring a ship about by turning the stern to windward, or come about in this way [Early 17C. Origin ?]

-wear *suffix* clothing of a particular kind or for a particular context or activity ○ *swimwear*

wear·a·ble /wérrəb'l/ *adj* suitable and in a condition to be worn ■ *n* (*often used in the plural*) **1.** CLOTHING an item of clothing in a condition to be worn **2.** COMPUT same as **wearable computer** —**wear·a·bil·i·ty** /wèrrə bíllətee/ *n*

wear·a·ble com·put·er *n* a battery-powered computer small enough to be worn on the body —**wear·a·ble com·put·ing** *n*

wear and tear /-tér/ *n* damage caused by using something over a period of time

wea·ri·ful /wéerif'l/ *adj* **1.** tedious and causing annoyance or fatigue **2.** tired and weary

wea·ri·less /wéereeləss/ *adj* not feeling or showing tiredness

wear·ing /wérring/ *adj* **1.** tiring or tedious ○ *found the long journey very wearing* **2.** made or designed to be worn ○ *wearing apparel* —**wear·ing·ly** *adv*

wear·ing course *n* the upper layer of an asphalt or bitumen roadway

wea·ri·some /wéereessəm/ *adj* physically or mentally tiring and tedious ○ *a wearisome task* —**wea·ri·some·ly** *adv* —**wea·ri·some·ness** *n*

wear·proof /wér proof/ *adj* able to withstand ordinary wear or use

wea·ry /wéeree/ *adj* (**-ri·er, -ri·est**) **1.** TIRED tired, especially in having run out of strength, patience, or endurance **2.** TIRING tiring or exhausting **3.** SHOWING TIREDNESS showing or characterized by tiredness ■ *vti* (**-ried, -ry·ing, -ries**) BECOME OR MAKE SOMEBODY TIRED to become tired or impatient, or make somebody do this [Old English *wērig* < Germanic] —**wea·ri·ly** *adv* —**wea·ri·ness** *n* —**wea·ry·ing** *adj* —**wea·ry·ing·ly** *adv*

weasel

wea·sel /wéez'l/ *n* (*plural* **-sels** or *same*) **1.** SMALL ANIMAL WITH LONG BODY a small carnivorous animal with a long body and tail, short legs, and brown fur that in northern species may turn white in winter. Genus: *Mustela.* **2.** SOMEBODY SLY a sly or underhanded person (*informal insult*) **3.** VEHICLES VEHICLE USED ON SAND OR SNOW a vehicle designed for use on sand, snow, or ice ■ *vi* (**-seled** or **-selled, -sel·ing** or **-sel·ling, -sels**) BE EVASIVE to be evasive or try to mislead [Old English *wesule* < Germanic] —**wea·sel·ly** *adj*

weasel out *vi* to try to get out of an obligation or commitment, especially in a cowardly way (*informal*)

wea·sel words *npl* deliberately misleading or ambiguous language (*informal*) —**wea·sel-word·ed** *adj*

weath·er /wéthər/ *n* **1.** STATE OF ATMOSPHERE the state of the atmosphere with regard to temperature, cloudiness, rainfall, wind, and other meteorological conditions **2.** BAD WEATHER adverse weather, e.g., a storm, or the effects of this ○ *protection from the weather* ■ *adj* **1.** METEOROL USED IN WEATHER FORECASTING relating to or used in weather forecasting **2.** NAUT WINDWARD toward the wind ■ *v* (**-ered, -er·ing, -ers**) **1.** *vti* EXPOSE SOMETHING TO WEATHER to expose something to the weather, or be exposed to it **2.** *vti* CHANGE BECAUSE OF EXPOSURE TO WEATHER

WEATHER SYMBOLS

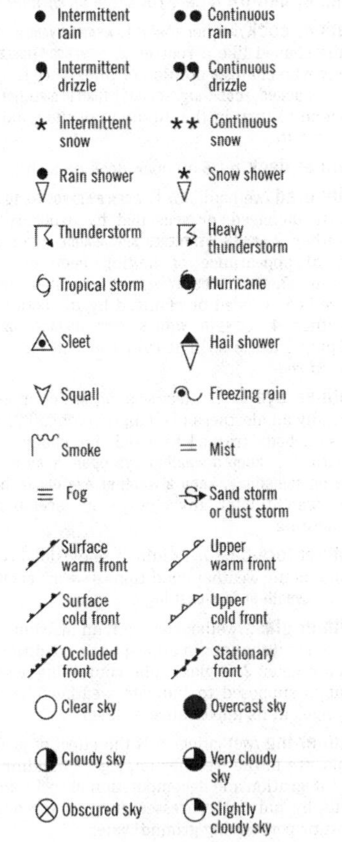

weather symbols

to change color or become worn because of prolonged exposure to the weather, or make something do this **3.** *vi* ENDURE EFFECTS OF WEATHER to endure the damaging effects of the weather **4.** *vt* SURVIVE CRISIS to come safely through a crisis or difficult time **5.** *vt* NAUT SAIL WINDWARD OF SOMETHING to sail on the windward side of something **6.** *vt* CONSTR SLANT SOMETHING TO KEEP OFF RAIN to give a slope to something such as a roof to keep off rain [Old English *weder* < Indo-European, "to blow"] ◇ **make heavy weather of something** to make a task that is fairly easy to do seem more difficult than it is ◇ **under the weather** slightly unwell

SPELLCHECK weather, wether, or **whether**? Do not confuse the spelling of ***weather, wether,*** and ***whether,*** which sound similar. ***Weather*** is a noun referring to meteorological conditions such as rain, sunshine, wind, or clouds (as in *stormy weather, the weather forecast*) or a verb meaning "expose something to the weather" or "come safely through a difficult time" (as in *weathered lumber, weather the storm*). The word ***wether,*** which is not frequently encountered in general usage, denotes a castrated sheep or goat. ***Whether*** introduces an alternative or indirect question: *whether you want to or not*; *Ask her whether she wants some coffee.*

weath·er bal·loon *n* a balloon used to carry meteorological instruments

weath·er-beat·en *adj* damaged, worn, or marked by exposure to the weather ○ *a weather-beaten face*

weath·er·board /wéthər bàwrd/ *n* **1.** *US* CONSTR same as **clapboard 2.** the windward side of a ship

weath·er·board·ing /wéthər bàwrding/ *n* clapboards collectively

weath·er·bound /wéthər bòwnd/ *adj* delayed or kept from functioning by bad weather ○ *a weatherbound plane*

weath·er bu·reau *n US* an agency that collects meteorological information and provides weather forecasts. Can term **weather centre**

weath·er·cast /wéthər kàst/ *n US* METEOROL same as

zh vision. In foreign words: kh German Bach; aN French vin; aaN French blanc; ö German schön, French feu; öN French bon; öN French un; ü as in French rue. Stress marks: ´ as in secret /séekrət/ ` as in secretary /sékrə tèrree/

weather forecast [Mid-19C. Contraction of WEATHER FORECAST] —**weath·er·cast·er** *n* —**weath·er·cast·ing** *n*

weath·er cen·tre *n Can, UK* same as **weather bureau**

weath·er·cock /wéthər kòk/ *n* **1. WEATHER VANE** a weather vane shaped like a rooster **2. SOMEBODY FICKLE** somebody who changes opinion or allegiance frequently ■ *vi* (**-cocked, -cock·ing, -cocks**) **TURN IN DIRECTION OF WIND** to tend to turn in the direction of the wind (*refers to aircraft*)

weath·er deck *n US* an open deck on a ship

weath·ered /wéthərd/ *adj* **1. WORN BY EXPOSURE TO WEATHER** worn, damaged, or seasoned by exposure to the weather **2. GIVEN WEATHERED APPEARANCE** given an artificial appearance of having been exposed to weather **3.** GEOL **ERODED BY WEATHER** describes rocks that have been eroded or changed by the action of the weather **4.** CONSTR **WITH SLOPING SURFACE** having a sloping surface so that rain can run off ○ *a weathered roof*

weath·er eye *n* **1.** alertness or watchfulness, especially an alertness to change (*informal*) **2.** the eye of somebody trained to watch for changes in the weather ◇ **keep a weather eye open, keep a weather eye on something, keep a weather eye out** to be alert and watchful for any change or development in something

weath·er fore·cast *n* a radio or television broadcast announcing weather conditions —**weath·er fore·cast·er** *n* —**weath·er fore·cast·ing** *n*

weath·er·glass /wéthər glàss/ *n* **1.** an instrument used to indicate changes in atmospheric conditions, e.g., a barometer **2.** a glass tube containing a solution that is supposed to indicate weather changes by changes in its appearance or level

weath·er·ing /wéthəring/ *n* **1.** the effect of prolonged exposure to the weather on, e.g., a building **2.** the disintegration and decomposition of rocks and minerals by natural processes such as the action of frost or percolating ground water

weath·er·ize /wéthə rìz/ (**-ized, -iz·ing, -iz·es**) *vt* to take action to protect something such as a building against cold weather

weath·er·ly /wéthərlee/ *adj* capable of sailing close to the wind

weath·er·man /wéthər màn/ (*plural* **-men** /-mèn/) *n* a man who works as a professional weather forecaster (*dated*)

weath·er map *n* a map or chart showing the meteorological conditions over a large area

weath·er·per·son /wéthər pùrss'n/ (*plural* **-per·sons** or **-peo·ple** /-peep'l/) *n* somebody who works as a professional weather forecaster

weath·er·proof /wéthər proof/ *adj* able to withstand exposure to rain or bad weather ■ *vt* (**-proofed, -proof·ing, -proofs**) to make something able to withstand exposure to rain or bad weather

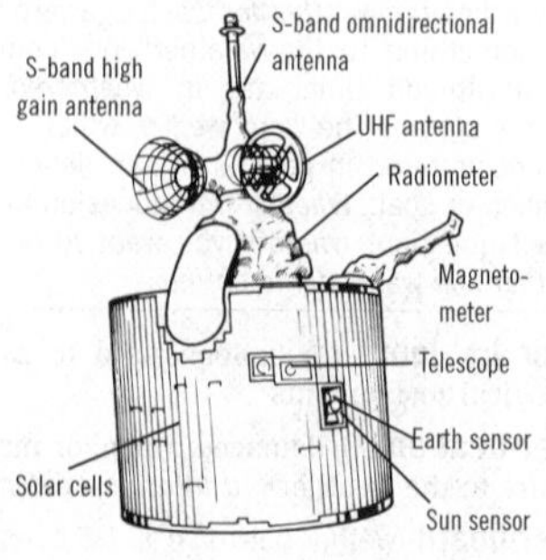

weather satellite

weath·er sat·el·lite *n* a satellite that records cloud distribution and temperature to help in predicting weather patterns

weath·er ship *n* a ship that collects meteorological information

weath·er sta·tion *n* an observation post where meteorological conditions are observed and recorded

weath·er·strip /wéthər strìp/ (**-stripped, -strip·ping, -strips**) *vt* to put weather stripping around a door or window

weath·er strip·ping *n* a thin piece of material fastened around a door or window to stop wind, rain, and cold from coming through

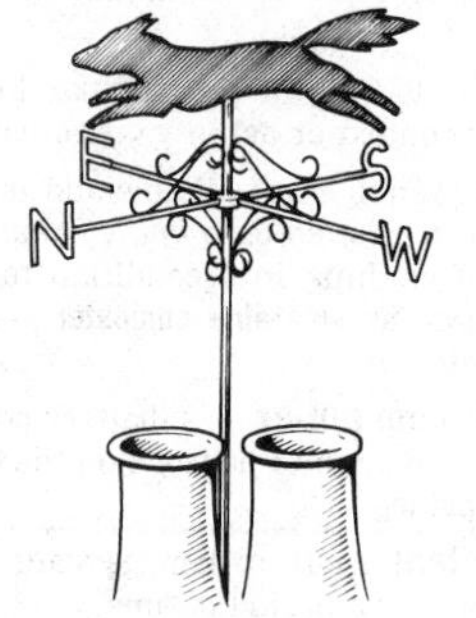

weather vane

weath·er vane *n* a device, usually mounted on a roof, that turns to point in the direction that the wind is blowing

weath·er win·dow *n* a period of time in which weather conditions are suitable for an activity

weath·er-wise *adj* **1.** good at predicting what the weather will be **2.** good at predicting what public opinion will be

weath·er·wom·an /wéthər wòommən/ (*plural* **-wom·en** /-wìmmin/) *n* a woman who works as a professional weather forecaster

weath·er·worn /wéthər wàwrn/ *adj* worn or damaged by exposure to the weather

weave[1] /weev/ *v* (**wove** /wōv/ or **weaved, wo·ven** /wṓvən/ or **weaved, weav·ing, weaves**) **1.** *vti* **MAKE CLOTH** to make cloth by interlacing threads vertically and horizontally, especially on a loom **2.** *vt* **MAKE SOMETHING BY INTERLACING STRANDS** to make something by interlacing strands or strips of any material **3.** *vti* **SPIN WEB** to spin something such as a spider's web **4.** *vt* **CONSTRUCT STORY** to construct something such as a story by combining separate parts **5.** *vt* **INTRODUCE PARTS INTO SOMETHING LARGER** to introduce separate parts into something larger ○ *weaving new characters into the plot* ■ *n* **WAY IN WHICH SOMETHING IS WOVEN** the way in which something is woven and the pattern formed by it ○ *a fabric with an open weave* [Old English *wefan* < Germanic]

weave[2] /weev/ (**weaved, weav·ing, weaves**) *vi* to move forward on a zigzag course [Late 16C. Origin ?]

weav·er /weevər/ *n* **1.** somebody who weaves, especially professionally **2.** BIRDS same as **weaverbird**

weav·er·bird /weevər bùrd/, **weav·er finch** *n* a gregarious finch known for its communal woven nest. Native to: Africa, Asia. Family: Ploceidae.

web /web/ *n* **1. SPIDER'S CONSTRUCTION** a delicate structure of threads woven by a spider or other arachnid to catch prey **2. MEMBRANE BETWEEN ANIMAL TOES** a membrane of skin joining the digits of an animal's foot, especially the foot of a bird or amphibian **3. COMPLEX NETWORK** a complex structure, network, or design ○ *a web of interconnecting wires* ○ *a web of deceit* **4. WOVEN FABRIC** a piece of fabric created by weaving **5. THIN METAL PLATE** a thin plate or strip of metal, e.g., the blade of a saw **6.** BIRDS **PART OF BIRD'S FEATHER** the vanes on either side of the shaft of a feather **7.** ARCHIT **RIBBED SURFACE IN VAULT** a ribbed surface within a vaulted structure **8.** PRINTING **PRINTING PAPER** a roll of paper that is used on a rotary printing press **9.** *also* **Web** ONLINE same as **World Wide Web** (*informal*) ■ *vi* (**webbed, web·bing, webs**) **FORM WEB** to form or produce a web [Old English, < Indo-European, "weave"]

webbed /webd/ *adj* **1. JOINED BY SKIN MEMBRANE** joined by a membrane or membranes of skin ○ *webbed feet* **2. HAVING WEB** formed of, covered by, or connected with a web **3. DESIGNED FOR INTERNET USE** optimized for use on the Internet, e.g., by minimizing the loading time of webpages

web·bing /wébbing/ *n* **1. STRONG COARSE FABRIC** a strong coarse fabric. Use: belts, harnesses, upholstery support. **2. SKIN OF FOOT** the membrane of skin joining the digits of an animal's foot, especially the foot of a bird or amphibian **3. SOMETHING FORMING WEB** something that forms a web

web brows·er *n* a program used for displaying and viewing pages on the World Wide Web

web bug *n* a minute inclusion in a webpage or e-mail message designed to record information about the person reading it

Web·by /wébbee/ (*plural* **-bys**) *n* an annual award made by the International Academy of Digital Arts and Sciences for the best Internet website (*informal*)

web·cam /wéb kàm/, **Web·cam** *n* a video camera recording pictures that are broadcast live on the Internet [Late 20C. < WEB + CAMERA]

web·cast /wéb kàst/, **Web·cast** *n* a broadcast made on the World Wide Web ○ *"...they spent $5 million promoting the live Webcast of their Spring Fashion Show ..."* (*The New York Times*; April 1999) [Late 20C. < WEB + BROADCAST]

web·cast·ing /wéb kàsting/, **Web·cast·ing** *n* the use of the World Wide Web as a medium for broadcasting information [Late 20C. < WEB + BROADCASTING]

web crawl·er *n* a program used to search through pages on the World Wide Web for documents containing a specific word, phrase, or topic

web de·sign·er *n* somebody who designs websites

web-en·a·ble *vt* to make an electronic device or a software application capable of accessing the Internet

web·er /wébbər, váybər/ *n* the SI unit of magnetic flux, equal to 1 joule per ampere or 1 volt-second. Symbol **Wb** [Late 19C. After Wilhelm Eduard *Weber* (1804–91), German physicist]

We·ber /váybər/, **Carl Maria von** (1786–1826) German composer. His orchestral works and operas were important for the growth of early romanticism. Full name **Weber, Carl Maria Friedrich Ernst von**

We·ber, Max (1864–1920) German economist and sociologist. He was a major influence in modern sociological theory and the author of *The Protestant Ethic and the Spirit of Capitalism* (1904–05).

Web·er /wébbər/, **Max** (1881–1961) Russian-born US artist. His vivid pictures combine cubist, expressionist, and fauvist styles.

> "The earning of money within the modern economic order is, so long as it is done legally, the result and the expression of virtue and proficiency in a calling."
> [Max Weber, *The Protestant Ethic and the Spirit of Capitalism*; 1930]

We·bern /váybərn/, **Anton** (1883–1945) Austrian composer. He extended the 12-tone system of Arnold Schoenberg and influenced a generation of post-World War II composers. Full name **Webern, Anton Friedrich Wilhelm von**

web farm *n* E-COMMERCE same as **web server farm**

web fo·li·o *n* a collection of webpages with an underlying defining theme, e.g., the pages of an electronic book or the electronic images of an artist's portfolio

web·foot /wéb fòot/ (*plural* **-feet** /-feet/) *n* **1.** a foot that has the toes joined by a membrane of skin **2.** an animal with webbed feet —**web-foot·ed** *adj*

web·head /wéb hèd/, **Web·head** *n* a frequent user of the World Wide Web (*slang*)

web host·ing *n* the business of supplying server space for storage of websites on the Internet, and sometimes the provision of ancillary services such as website creation

web·i·sode /wébbi sōd/, **Web·i·sode** *n* an episode, preview, or promotion of a movie, television program, or music video on a website (*slang*) [Late 20C. Blend of WEB + EPISODE]

web·li·og·ra·phy /wèbblee óggrəfee/ (*plural* **-phies**), **Web·li·og·ra·phy** *n* **1.** a list of documents available on the World Wide Web **2.** a list or catalog of all the web-based material relating to a specific subject [Late 20C. Blend of WEB + BIBLIOGRAPHY]

web·lish /wébblish/, **Web·lish** *n* the form of English used globally online, with characteristic features such as the omission of apostrophes and capital letters, the use of abbreviations, and the rapid absorption of new words [Late 20C. Blend of WEB + ENGLISH]

web·log /wéb lòg/, **Web log** *n* a frequently updated personal journal chronicling links at a website, intended for public viewing —**web·log·ger** *n*

web·mas·ter /wéb màstər/, **Web·mas·ter** *n* somebody who creates, organizes, or updates information on a website

web·meis·ter /wéb mìstər/, **Web·meis·ter** *n* ONLINE same as **webmaster** (*informal*)

web mem·ber *n* a brace that links the top and bottom flanges of a lattice girder or truss

web off·set *n* offset printing carried out on a web press

web·page /wéb pàyj/, **Web page** *n* a computer file, encoded in HyperText Markup Language (**HTML**) and containing text, graphics files, and sound files, that is accessible through the World Wide Web

web·phone /wéb fòn/, **Web·phone** *n* a phone that uses the Internet to make connections and carry voice messages

web press *n* a printing press that is fed paper from a large roll

web ring *n* a series of interlinked websites that are visited one after the other until the first is reached again

web serv·er *n* a program that serves up webpages when requested by a client, e.g., a web browser

web serv·er farm *n* a business with a group of interconnected servers engaged in web hosting

web·site /wéb sìt/, **Web site** *n* a computer program that runs a web server that provides access to a group of related webpages

web spin·ner *n* an insect that spins a web, especially one with glands that produce silk for constructing a web. Order: Embioptera.

Web·ster /wébstər/ town in southern Massachusetts, north of the Connecticut border and south of Worcester. Population: 16,736 (2002 estimate).

Web·ster, Daniel (1782–1852) US lawyer and politician. In a political career spanning over four decades, he served twice as secretary of state (1841–43 and 1850–52). Considered one of the most effective orators of his time, he represented New Hampshire in the House of Representatives and then Massachusetts in the House of Representatives and the Senate.

Web·ster, John (1578?–1632?) English playwright. His plays *The White Devil* (1612?) and *The Duchess of Malfi* (1614?) are outstanding examples of the revenge tragedy.

> "We think caged birds sing, when indeed they cry."
> [John Webster, *The White Devil*; 1612]

Web·ster, Noah (1758–1843) US lexicographer. He is known for institutionalizing the differences between American and British English grammar, pronunciation, and spelling in his *American Dictionary of the English Language* (1828).

> "This Dictionary, like all others of the kind, must be left, in some degree, imperfect; for what individual is competent to trace the source, and define in all their various applications, popular, scientific, and technical, seventy or eighty thousand words!"
> [Noah Webster. Author's Preface, *An American Dictionary of the English Language*; 1828]

web store·front *n US* a virtual store on the Internet providing information about the retailer, a product catalog, and secure payment facilities

web-toed *adj* having a membrane of skin tissue between the toes

web·worm /wéb wùrm/ (*plural* **-worms** or *same*) *n* a caterpillar, especially a tiger moth caterpillar, that spins a web in which it feeds or rests

web·zine /wéb zèen/, **Web·zine** *n* ONLINE same as **e-zine**

Wechs·ler A·dult In·tel·li·gence Scale-Re·vised /wèkslər-/ *n US* an individually administered IQ test for adults, measuring both verbal and performance abilities [After David *Wechsler* 1896–1981, US psychologist]

Wech·sler In·tel·li·gence Scale for Chil·dren *n US* an individually administered IQ test for children, measuring a wide variety of abilities [See WECHSLER ADULT INTELLIGENCE SCALE-REVISED]

wed /wed/ (**wed·ded** or **wed, wed·ding, weds**) *v* **1.** *vt* MARRY SOMEBODY to marry somebody (*formal or literary*) ○ *wanted to wed a princess* **2.** *vi* GET MARRIED to become united in marriage ○ *They wed in April.* **3.** *vt* JOIN COUPLE IN MARRIAGE to join two people in marriage **4.** *vt* UNITE THINGS to bring two things together or regard them as linked ○ *The two concepts had become wedded in his mind.* [Old English *weddian* < Indo-European, "pledge"]

we'd /weed/ *contr* **1.** we had **2.** we would

Wed. *abbr* Wednesday

wed·ded /wéddəd/ *adj* **1.** MARRIED united in marriage **2.** OF MARRIAGE relating to marriage ○ *wedded bliss* **3.** COMMITTED TO SOMETHING strongly attached or committed to something ○ *wedded to the idea of reform*

Wed·dell Sea /wédd'l-, wə dél-/ arm of the South Atlantic Ocean, south of Cape Horn and the Falkland Islands

wed·ding /wédding/ *n* **1.** MARRIAGE CEREMONY a ceremony in which two people get married (*often used before a noun*) ○ *Their rabbi will perform the wedding service.* **2.** ACT OF MARRYING the act or an instance of marrying somebody (*often used before a noun*) ○ *a wedding veil* **3.** WEDDING ANNIVERSARY the anniversary of a marriage (*used in combination*) ○ *a silver wedding* **4.** UNITING OF TWO THINGS the bringing together of two things ○ *the wedding of form and function*

wed·ding band *n* JEWELRY same as **wedding ring**

wed·ding cake *n* a cake decorated with icing, usually white, and arranged in tiers, served at a wedding reception

wed·ding-cake *adj* characterized by an extremely ornate style of architecture

wed·ding dress *n* a dress worn by a bride at her wedding

wed·ding march *n* a piece of music in march time played during a marriage ceremony, usually when the bride enters

wed·ding ring *n* a ring, usually a gold band, worn on the third finger of the left hand by somebody who is married

We·de·kind /váydə kìnt/, **Frank** (1864–1918) German playwright. His work, often dealing with sexual themes, anticipates expressionism and the theater of the absurd. Full name **Wedekind, Benjamin Franklin**

~~Wedensday~~ incorrect spelling of **Wednesday**

wedge

wedge /wej/ *n* **1.** TAPERING BLOCK a solid block that is thick at one end and thin at the other, used to secure or separate two objects **2.** WEDGE-SHAPED OBJECT an object that has a wedge shape ○ *a wedge of cake* **3.** SOMETHING ACTING AS WEDGE something that acts as a wedge, e.g., by causing division ○ *drove a wedge between the two families* **4.** CLOTHING same as **wedge heel** **5.** GOLF GOLF CLUB a golf club with a markedly slanted head, used to hit the ball along a high arcing trajectory **6.** STROKE IN CUNEIFORM WRITING a wedge-shaped stroke used in cuneiform writing ■ *v* (**wedged, wedg·ing, wedg·es**) **1.** *vt* SECURE SOMETHING WITH WEDGE to secure or tighten something with a wedge **2.** *vti* SQUEEZE to squeeze or pack something into a small space, or be squeezed or packed in this way ○ *Hundreds of people were wedged into the room.* **3.** *vt* FORCE SOMETHING APART WITH WEDGE to force something apart or open with a wedge [Old English *wecg* < Germanic, probably < Indo-European, "plowshare, wedge"] —**wedg·y** *adj*

wedge heel *n* **1.** a shoe heel shaped like a wedge, forming a solid extension of the shoe so that there is no gap under the instep **2.** a shoe with a wedge heel

wedge is·sue *n US* a controversial political issue that divides the loyalty of a constituency, electorate, or political party

wedg·ie /wéjjee/, **wed·gy** (*plural* **-gies**) *n* **1.** same as **wedge heel** **2.** an uncomfortable intrusion of clothing, usually briefs, up into the crack between the buttocks (*slang*)

Wedg·wood /wéj wòod/, **Josiah** (1730–95) British potter. He developed a distinctive pottery inspired by ancient Greek ware, and established a highly successful pottery business.

wed·lock /wéd lòk/ *n* the state of being married [12C. < *wedlac* "action of pledging" < *wed* "pledge," after LOCK[1]] ◇ **born** *or* **conceived out of wedlock** born to *or* conceived by parents who are not married (*formal*)

Wednes·day /wénz dày, -dee/ *n* the third day of the traditional working week, coming after Tuesday and before Thursday [Old English *wōdnesdæg* "Woden's day" < WODEN + *dæg* "day," translation of Latin *Mercurii dies* "Mercury's day"]

Wednes·days /wénz dàyz, -deez/ *adv* every Wednesday ○ *Wednesdays I leave a little early.*

~~Wednsday~~ incorrect spelling of **Wednesday**

wee /wee/ *adj* very small ■ *n Scotland* a brief period of time ○ *bide a wee* [Old English *wēg* "weight"]

weed[1] /weed/ *n* **1.** UNWANTED PLANT a plant, especially a wild plant, growing where it is not wanted **2.** UNWANTED PLANTS weeds in general (*often used before a noun*) ○ *weed control* **3.** PLANT GROWING IN WATER a plant that grows in water, especially seaweed **4.** MARIJUANA marijuana for smoking as a drug (*slang*) **5.** TOBACCO tobacco or cigarettes (*slang*) **6.** INFERIOR ANIMAL an inferior animal, especially a horse that cannot be bred ■ *v* (**weed·ed, weed·ing, weeds**) **1.** *vt* REMOVE WEEDS FROM GROUND to clear an area of weeds ○ *to weed the garden* **2.** *vi* PULL UP WEEDS to pull up and remove weeds ○ *spent several hours weeding* [Old English *wēod* < Germanic] —**weed·er** *n*

weed out *vt* to separate out or remove somebody or something undesirable or unwanted ○ *a test to weed out unsuitable candidates*

weed[2] /weed/ *n* something worn as a sign of mourning, especially a black band around a sleeve or hat ■ **weeds** *npl* the black clothes once traditionally worn by widows (*archaic or literary*) [Old English *wǣd* < Germanic, "garment"]

weed·kill·er /wéed kìllər/ *n* a chemical that kills plants by attacking the root, leaf, or vascular system

weed·y /wéedee/ (**-i·er, -i·est**) *adj* **1.** FULL OF WEEDS filled with or containing many weeds ○ *a weedy patch of ground* **2.** LIKE WEED resembling or having the characteristics of a weed ○ *weedy plants* **3.** THIN considered strikingly thin and weak-looking (*insult*) —**weed·i·ly** *adv* —**weed·i·ness** *n*

wee hours *npl* same as **wee small hours**

week /week/ *n* **1.** 7-DAY PERIOD a period of seven consecutive days **2.** CALENDAR WEEK a period of seven days beginning from a specific day, usually Sunday ○ *the middle of the week* **3.** WORKING WEEK the days of the week or the time every week during which somebody usually works ○ *goes to bed early during the week* **4.** SPECIAL WEEK a week containing a particular holiday or dedicated to a particular cause ○ *Easter week* ■ *adv UK* ONE WEEK AFTER PARTICULAR DAY one week after or before a particular day ○ *arranged to meet on Thursday week* [Old English *wice* < Germanic, "series, succession"]

SPELLCHECK See *weak*.

week·day /wéek dày/ *n* a day of the week other than Saturday or Sunday ○ *only open on weekdays*

week·end /wéek ènd/ *n* the end of the week, from Friday evening, or sometimes Saturday morning, until Sunday evening ■ *vi* (**-end·ed, -end·ing, -ends**) to spend a weekend or weekends in a particular place

week·end bag *n* a bag or small suitcase used to carry clothes and other items needed for a short trip or vacation

week·end break *n* a short vacation away from home lasting for a weekend

week·end·er /wéek èndər/ *n* **1.** somebody spending a weekend somewhere, especially on a regular basis **2.** same as **weekend bag**

week·ends /wéek èndz/ *adv* on or during the weekend (*informal*)

week·long /wéek làwng, -lòng/ *adj* lasting for a whole week

week·ly /wéeklee/ *adj* **1.** HAPPENING ONCE EACH WEEK happening, produced, or done once a week or every week **2.** CALCULATED BY WEEK worked out by the week ○ *weekly pay* ■ *adv* **1.** ONCE EACH WEEK once each week ○ *does the shopping weekly* **2.** EVERY WEEK every single week **3.** BY WEEK by the week ○ *paid weekly* ■ *n* (*plural* **-lies**) SOMETHING PUBLISHED ONCE EACH WEEK a newspaper or magazine published once a week

week·night /wéek nìt/ *n* the evening or night of a weekday ○ *I'm not letting you go out on a weeknight.*

Weems /weemz/, **Parson** (1759–1825) US cleric and writer. His fictionalized biography of George Washington (1800) was a bestseller for decades. Full name **Weems, Mason Locke**

ween /ween/ (**weened, ween·ing, weens**) *vti* to think, believe, or suppose something (*archaic*) [Old English *wēnan* < Indo-European, "to desire"]

ween·ie /wéenee/ *n* **1.** FOOD another spelling of **wiener** (*informal*) **2.** an offensive term for somebody regarded as weak or insignificant (*slang insult*) **3.** an offensive term for a penis (*slang*)

wee·ny /wéenee/ (**-ni·er, -ni·est**), **ween·sy** /wéenssee/ (**-si·er, -si·est**) *adj* very small (*informal*) [Late 18C. < WEE after *tiny*]

wee·ny-bop·per /wéenee bòppər/ *n* a child, especially a young girl, who is fond of pop music and the latest fashions (*informal*) [After TEENYBOPPER]

weep /weep/ *v* (**wept** /wept/, **weep·ing, weeps**) **1.** *vti* CRY to shed tears, especially as a sign of sorrow for something or somebody ○ *They walked behind the coffin, weeping silently.* ○ *It's no use weeping over him, that won't bring him back.* ○ *weep bitter tears* **2.** *vt* EXPRESS SOMETHING WHILE WEEPING to say something while crying or express something by crying tears **3.** *vti* LEAK FLUID to leak, drip, or ooze drops of liquid ○ *The area around the wound was inflamed and weeping.* **4.** *vt* MOURN SOMEBODY to lament or cry tears for somebody or something (*literary*) ■ *n* SPELL OF CRYING a period of time spent crying ○ *When they'd had a little weep, they both felt better.* [Old English *wēpan* < Germanic]

weep·er /wéepər/ *n* **1.** SOMEBODY WHO WEEPS somebody who weeps **2.** CONSTR HOLE FOR WATER TO ESCAPE a hole in a wall or foundation that allows accumulated water to escape **3.** *US* MOVIES, LITERAT same as **weepie** (*informal*) ■ **weep·ers** *npl* SIDEBURNS long sideburns (*informal*)

weep·ie /wéepee/, **weep·er** /wéepər/ *n* a movie, play, or book that tends to move people to tears, especially one that is blatantly sentimental in tone (*informal*)

weep·ing /wéeping/ *adj* **1.** CRYING shedding tears **2.** LEAKING FLUID leaking, dripping, or oozing drops of liquid **3.** WITH DROOPING BRANCHES having slender drooping branches ○ *a weeping birch* —**weep·ing·ly** *adv*

weep·ing fig *n* a small fig tree with glossy leaves, often grown as a houseplant. Latin name: *Ficus benjamina.*

weep·ing wil·low *n* a popular ornamental willow tree with long drooping branches and narrow leaves. Native to: China. Latin name: *Salix babylonica.*

weep·y /wéepee/ (**-i·er, -i·est**) *adj* (*informal*) **1.** weeping frequently, or feeling sad and liable to weep **2.** tending to make people cry —**weep·i·ly** *adv* —**weep·i·ness** *n*

wee small hours *npl* the early hours of the morning, especially those just after midnight

weeping willow

wee·ver /wéevər/, **wee·ver·fish** /wéevər fìsh/ (*plural* **-fish·es** or *same*) *n* a small ocean fish with a venomous spine on each gill cover and several on its back. Family: Trachinidae. [Early 17C. Probably < Old N French *wivre* (see WYVERN)]

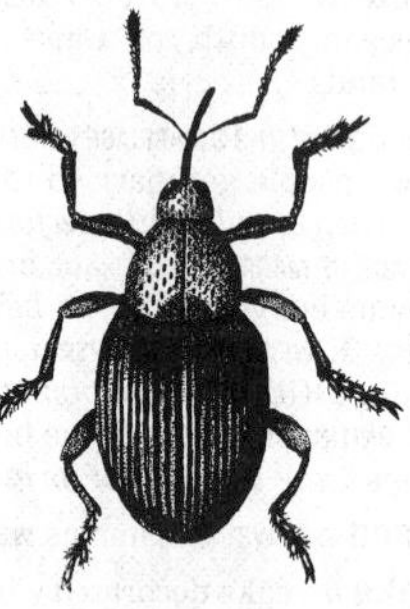

weevil

wee·vil /wéev'l/ *n* **1.** DESTRUCTIVE BEETLE WITH SNOUT a member of a family of beetles that have an elongated downward-curving snout (**rostrum**). Many weevils are pests, destroying plants and grain. Family: Curculionidae. **2.** PEA OR BEAN PEST a beetle whose larvae live in the seeds of peas and beans. Family: Bruchidae or Lariidae. **3.** BEETLE RESEMBLING WEEVIL a beetle similar to a weevil, especially in being likely to eat stored grain. Family: Rhynchophora. [Old English *wifel* "beetle" < Indo-European, "move quickly"] —**wee·vi·ly** *adj*

wee-wee /wée wee/ (*informal or baby talk*) *n* **1.** an act or instance of urinating **2.** same as **urine** ■ *vi* (**wee-weed, wee-wee·ing, wee-wees**) same as **urinate** [An imitation of the sound of urinating]

weft /weft/ *n* **1.** HORIZONTAL THREADS the horizontal threads of a woven fabric or a tapestry **2.** YARN FOR WEFT yarn used for the weft **3.** SOMETHING WOVEN a piece of woven fabric [Old English, < Indo-European, "weave"]

We·ge·ner /váygənər/, **Alfred** (1880–1930) German meteorologist. His *Origin of Continents and Oceans* (1915) introduced the theory of continental drift.

Wehr·macht /vér maàkt, -maàkht/ *n* the German armed forces, especially the army between 1935 and 1945 [Mid-20C. < German, "defense force"]

wei·ge·la /wī jéelə, -géelə, wíjələ, wígələ/ *n* a deciduous bush. Flowers: bell-shaped, pink, white, or red. Native to: Asia. Genus: *Weigela.* [Mid-19C. < modern Latin *Weigela*, after Christian E. *Weigel* (1748–1831), German physician]

weigh /way/ (**weighed, weigh·ing, weighs**) *v* **1.** *vt* FIND WEIGHT OF SOMETHING to find out the weight of somebody or something ○ *He weighed himself regularly.* **2.** *vi* BE PARTICULAR WEIGHT to be of a particular weight ○ *The baby weighed seven pounds three ounces at birth.* **3.** *vt* MEASURE BY WEIGHT to measure or distribute something by weight ○ *weighed out two pounds of onions* **4.** *vt* EVALUATE to consider or evaluate something, especially so as to be able to come to a decision or choice ○ *had to weigh all possible options* **5.** *vi* HAVE IMPORTANCE to have importance or be influential ○ *Her advice weighs heavily with him.* **6.** *vt* GUESS WEIGHT OF to hold something in the hand in order to assess its weight **7.** *vi* BE BURDENSOME to be burdensome, oppressive, or worrying to somebody ○ *The problem weighed heavily on my mind.* **8.** *vti* NAUT RAISE ANCHOR to raise the anchor of a vessel [Old English *wegan* "weigh, carry" < Indo-European, "carry"] —**weigh·a·ble** *adj* —**weigh·er** *n*

SPELLCHECK See *way.*

weigh against *vt* **1.** to assess the relative importance of one thing in relation to another ○ *had to weigh the added costs against the gain in speed* **2.** to have a negative part in influencing a decision with regard to somebody or something ○ *Her lack of experience weighed against her in the final selection.*

weigh down *vt* **1.** to be oppressive or burdensome to somebody ○ *weighed down by grief* ○ *weighed down with extra paperwork* **2.** to press or pull somebody or something down by being heavy ○ *trees weighed down with fruit*

weigh in *vi* **1.** BE WEIGHED FOR RACE OR CONTEST to be weighed before or after a boxing match, a horserace, or a similar contest **2.** HAVE BAGGAGE WEIGHED to have baggage weighed before a flight **3.** CONTRIBUTE COMMENT to contribute or produce something such as an argument or comment, especially in an assertive way (*informal*) ○ *Then Sarah weighed in with some candid observations on Melanie's dress sense.*

weigh-in *n* the weighing of the competitors before or after a boxing match or a race

weight /wayt/ *n* **1.** HEAVINESS the quality of heaviness in things, determined by their mass or quantity of matter as acted on by the force of gravity, that counteracts efforts to lift or move them ○ *Just feel the weight of it!* **2.** AMOUNT SOMEBODY OR SOMETHING WEIGHS the heaviness of a particular object or person, especially as measured by a particular system of weight ○ *She'll have to watch her weight.* **3.** SYSTEM FOR MEASURING HEAVINESS a system of standard measures of weight ○ *troy weight* **4.** UNIT OF WEIGHT a unit used as a measure of weight **5.** WEIGHTED COUNTER USED ON SCALES an object of known weight, usually one of a set, placed on one side of a pair of scales to counterbalance another object that is being weighed **6.** HEAVY OBJECT a heavy object used to hold something down **7.** OBJECT USED IN WEIGHTLIFTING a heavy object, often a bar with a heavy metal disk at each end, used in weightlifting or for exercise (*often used in the plural*) **8.** HEAVY LOAD a heavy load to carry ○ *had to put the trunk down since it was too heavy a weight* **9.** MENTAL BURDEN a mental or moral burden or load ○ *That's a weight off my mind.* **10.** IMPORTANCE importance, or power to influence or persuade ○ *a motion that did not carry much weight with the judge* **11.** GREATER PART the preponderance or greater part of something ○ *the weight of exculpatory evidence* **12.** PRINTING HEAVINESS OF TYPEFACE the heaviness or thickness of a typeface **13.** TEXTILES THICKNESS OF CLOTH the heaviness or thickness of cloth (*often used in combination*) **14.** PHYS FORCE CAUSED BY GRAVITY the vertical force experienced by a mass because of gravity. Symbol *W* ■ *vt* (**weight·ed, weight·ing, weights**) **1.** MAKE SOMETHING HEAVIER to add weight or weights to something **2.** KEEP SOMETHING IN PLACE WITH WEIGHTS to hold something in position by placing a heavy object on it ○ *weighted the papers down with an ashtray to stop them blowing away* **3.** SLANT SOMETHING IN SOMEBODY'S FAVOR to arrange something in such a way that it either favors or disadvantages a specific person or group (*often passive*) ○ *The criteria governing the choice of candidate were heavily weighted in her favor.* **4.** GIVE ADDITIONAL IMPORTANCE TO SOMETHING to assign additional importance to something, e.g., a test or part of one **5.** TEXTILES INCREASE DENSITY OF FABRIC to treat fabric so as to increase its density **6.** HORSERACING ASSIGN HORSE HANDICAP WEIGHT to assign a handicap weight to a horse [Old English *wiht* < Indo-European] —**weight·er** *n* ◇ **be worth its** *or* **your weight in gold** to be extremely valuable ◇ **gain** *or* **lose weight** ◇ **pull your weight** to do your fair share of work or take your fair share of responsibility ◇ **throw your weight around** to be domineering (*informal*)

SPELLCHECK See *wait.*

weight·ed /wáytəd/ *adj* adjusted by the addition of a statistical value

weight·less /wáytləss/ *adj* having no weight, especially by virtue of being in an atmosphere in which there is no gravitational pull —**weight·less·ly** *adv* —**weight·less·ness** *n*

weight·lift·ing /wáyt lifting/ *n* the sport of lifting heavy weights, either for exercise or in competition —**weight·lift·er** *n*

weight train·ing *n* physical training using weights to strengthen the muscles

weight·y /wáytee/ (**-i·er, -i·est**) *adj* **1.** HEAVY weighing a great deal **2.** IMPORTANT of an important or serious nature ○ *discussing weighty matters* **3.** INFLUENTIAL able to exert influence **4.** OPPRESSIVE oppressive or burdensome ○ *a weighty responsibility* —**weight·i·ly** *adv* —**weight·i·ness** *n*

Weil /vayl/, **Simone** (1909–43) French philosopher and mystic. Her major writings, reflecting her Christian mysticism, were published posthumously and include *Waiting for God* (1950).

> "The word 'revolution' is a word for which you kill, for which you die, for which you send the laboring masses to their death, but which does not possess any content."
> [Simone Weil, "Reflections Concerning the Causes of Liberty and Social Oppression," *Oppression and Liberty*; 1958]

~~**weild**~~ incorrect spelling of **wield**

Weill /vīl, wīl/, **Kurt** (1900–50) German-born US composer. His work, including *The Threepenny Opera* (1928) which he wrote with Bertolt Brecht, was banned by the Nazis. After settling in the United States (1935) he wrote successful Broadway musicals. Full name **Weill, Kurt Julian**

> "Musical theater is the highest, the most expressive and the most imaginative form of theater...a composer who has a talent and a passion for the theater can express himself completely in this branch of musical creativeness."
> [Kurt Weill. Quoted in *American Composers*, David Ewen; 1982]

Weil's dis·ease /vílz-, wílz-/ *n* a severe form of leptospirosis, usually resulting from contact with the urine of infected animals such as rats. Symptoms include jaundice, anemia, hemorrhaging, fever, and meningitis. [Late 19C. After H. Adolf *Weil* (1848–1916), German physician]

Wei·mar /wí maar/ city in Thuringia State, east central Germany, southwest of Leipzig. It was a major cultural center in the 18th and 19th centuries. Population: 62,233 (1997).

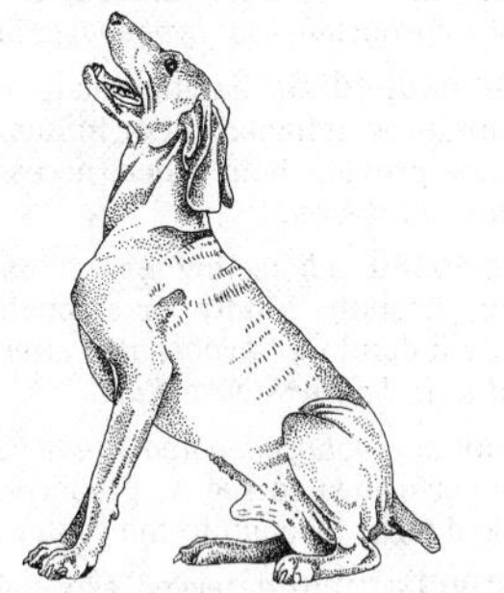

Weimaraner

Wei·mar·an·er /wímə raanər/ *n* a large hunting dog with a shorthaired silver-gray coat, belonging to a breed originating in Germany [Mid-20C. After WEIMAR]

Wei·mar Re·pub·lic *n* the government of Germany between 1919 and 1933, so named because the National Assembly met in Weimar in 1919 to establish a new republic and draw up a constitution

Wei·ner /wéenər/, **Lawrence** (*b.* 1942) US conceptual artist. He has been a central figure of conceptual art since the 1960s. Many of his installations consist solely of words in a nondescript lettering painted on walls.

weir /weer/ *n* **1.** a dam built across a river to regulate the flow of water, divert it, or change its level **2.** a fence placed in a stream to catch fish [Old English *wer* < Indo-European, "cover"]

Weir /weer/, **Peter** (*b.* 1944) Australian movie director. After achieving international success with the Australian-made *Picnic at Hanging Rock* (1975), he established himself as a leading Hollywood director. Full name **Weir, Peter Lindsay**

weird /weerd/ *adj* **1.** ODD strange or unusual **2.** SUPERNATURAL belonging to or suggesting the supernatural **3.** OF FATE relating to or influenced by fate (*archaic*) [Old English *wyrd* "fate" < Indo-European, "turn"] —**weird·ly** *adv* —**weird·ness** *n*

weird·ie /wéerdee/, **weird·y** (*plural* **-ies**) *n* an offensive term for somebody who is regarded as strange or unconventional (*slang*)

weird·o /wéerdō/ (*plural* **-os**) *n* (*slang*) **1.** an offensive term for somebody who behaves in a way regarded as strange or unconventional, especially somebody whose sexual tastes or habits are regarded as unusual **2.** an offensive term for somebody who is regarded as prone to dangerous behavior because of a psychiatric disorder

weird sis·ters, Weird Sisters *npl* **1.** MYTHOL same as **Fates 2.** the three witches in Shakespeare's play *Macbeth* [*Weird* in the meaning of "having the power to control fates"]

weird·y *n* another spelling of **weirdie** (*slang offensive*)

weis·en·heim·er *n US* another spelling of **wisenheimer** (*informal*)

Weis·mann /vī́ssmən/, **August** (1834–1914) German biologist. He was the first to propose that genetic variability results from the recombination of chromosomes during reproduction. Full name **Weissman, August Friedrich Leopold**

Weis·mann·ism /wī́ssmə nìzzəm/ *n* the principle that the inherited characteristics of any organism are determined solely by material (**germplasm**) contained in the male and female sex cells from which the organism develops. This theory excludes any role for the body cells in inheritance and rules out the inheritance of characteristics acquired during an organism's lifetime. It remains a fundamental tenet of modern genetics. [Late 19C. After August WEISMANN]

Weiz·mann /vī́ts maan, wī́tsmən/, **Chaim** (1874–1952) Russian-born chemist and first president of Israel (1949–52). He helped to secure the Balfour Declaration (1917) which committed Britain to Zionism and was president of the World Zionist Organization (1921–29). Full name **Weizmann, Chaim Azriel**

we·ka /wéekə, wáykə/ *n* a fast-running flightless bird of the rail family with mainly brown and black feathers. Native to: scrubland and forest margins of New Zealand. Latin name: *Gallirallus australis*. [Mid-19C. < Maori, an imitation of bird's call]

welch *vi* another spelling of **welsh** (*sometimes offensive*)

Welch /welch/, **Jack** (*b.* 1936) US business executive. He introduced new management techniques as chairman and chief executive officer of General Electric (1981–2001), and helped it to grow into the world's largest company. Full name **Welch, John Francis, Jr.**

> "People always overestimate how complex business is. This isn't rocket science; we've chosen one of the world's more simple professions."
> [Jack Welch, *Harvard Business Review*; September-October 1989]

wel·come /wélkəm/ *adj* **1.** ADMITTED GLADLY received, especially into somebody's home, or entertained gladly ○ *a welcome guest* ○ *She's no longer welcome in this house.* **2.** EAGERLY AND DELIGHTEDLY ACCEPTED accepted or anticipated with delight and eagerness, often because it answers a need ○ *It was a welcome break after two solid weeks of writing.* **3.** FREELY INVITED OR PERMITTED freely and willingly invited or permitted ○ *You're welcome to stay for dinner.* **4.** WITH NOTHING EXPECTED IN RETURN used to respond to expressions of thanks and indicate that something such as a courtesy, favor, or gift was gladly done or given ○ *"Thank you for giving me a lift." – "You're very welcome, it was no trouble."* ■ *n* **1.** GREETING a greeting or reception, especially a friendly or celebratory one, given to somebody who arrives or is being met ○ *gave a warm welcome to their guests* **2.** REACTION a positive response or reaction to something, or a response of the kind specified ○ *Local authorities have extended a cautious welcome to the new proposals.* ■ *vt* (**-comed, -com·ing, -comes**) **1.** RECEIVE SOMEBODY IN FRIENDLY WAY to greet, receive, or entertain somebody, especially in a friendly way ○ *There was nobody there to welcome us when we arrived.* **2.** ACCEPT SOMETHING WITH PLEASURE to accept or receive something with pleasure ○ *We welcome any feedback from our customers.* ■ *interj* USED AS GREETING used to express a friendly or courteous greeting to somebody who has just arrived or is a stranger [Old English *wilcuma* "welcome guest" (influenced by WELL[2] and either Old Norse *velkominn* or Old French *bien venu*)] —**wel·come·ly** *adv* —**wel·come·ness** *n* —**wel·com·er** *n* ◇ **be welcome to something** used to indicate that the speaker is happy for somebody to have something (*often used ironically*) ◇ **make somebody welcome** to show that you are pleased to see somebody or treat somebody hospitably ◇ **wear out** *or* **outstay** *or* **overstay your welcome** to stay longer than is polite or accept somebody's hospitality for too long

wel·come mat *n* a doormat, especially one with the word "welcome" on it ◇ **put out** *or* **roll out the welcome mat for somebody** to make somebody feel very welcome (*informal*)

wel·come page *n* ONLINE same as **homepage** (sense 1)

wel·com·ing /wélkəming/ *adj* providing a warm and friendly greeting ○ *a welcoming smile* —**wel·com·ing·ly** *adv*

weld[1] /weld/ *v* (**weld·ed, weld·ing, welds**) **1.** *vti* FUSE MATERIAL BY HEATING to join together pieces or parts of some material by heating them and hammering or using other pressure to make them fuse, or be joined in this way ○ *to weld two pieces of iron together* **2.** *vt* MAKE SOMETHING BY WELDING to construct or repair something by welding separate pieces or parts together ○ *to weld a metal sculpture* **3.** *vti* FORM ASSOCIATION OR BECOME ASSOCIATED to form a union or a close association, or become joined in a union or a close association ○ *weld an alliance* ■ *n* **1.** JOINT FORMED BY FUSION a joint where pieces or parts have been fused together **2.** FUSION OF PARTS the union or fusion of parts or pieces [Late 16C. Alteration of WELL[1] (verb) in the obsolete meaning of "liquefy by heating"; influenced by its past participle *welled*] —**weld·a·bil·i·ty** /wèldə bíllətee/ *n* —**weld·a·ble** *adj* —**weld·er** *n*

weld[2] /weld/ *n* **1.** a yellow dye extracted from the dyer's rocket plant. Use: colorant for wool and other fabrics. **2.** PLANTS same as **dyer's rocket** [14C. Ultimately < Germanic]

weld·ment /wéldmənt/ *n* something that has been assembled by welding its parts or pieces together

wel·fare /wél fèr/ *n* **1.** WELL-BEING somebody's state or condition with respect to whether he or she is healthy, safe, happy, or prospering ○ *concerned about the welfare of prisoners held in solitary confinement* **2.** WORK TO IMPROVE PEOPLE'S WELFARE efforts, especially on the part of government and institutions, to ensure that the physical, social, and financial conditions under which people live are satisfactory **3.** AID TO PEOPLE IN NEED financial aid and other benefits for people who are unemployed, below a specific income level, or otherwise requiring assistance, especially when provided by a government agency or program **4.** same as **welfare work** ■ *adj* **1.** AIDING PEOPLE IN NEED concerning or designed to aid people who are poor, unemployed, or in need of assistance in some other way ○ *a welfare agency* **2.** RECEIVING GOVERNMENT AID OWING TO NEED receiving government financial aid or benefits because of income level, unemployment, or other conditions that create a need for assistance ○ *welfare clients* [14C. Contraction of *well fare*]

wel·fare state *n* **1.** a political system in which a government assumes the primary responsibility for assuring the basic health, education, and financial well-being of all its citizens through programs and direct assistance **2.** a nation whose government assumes primary responsibility for the social welfare of its citizens

wel·fare work *n US* the efforts of an organization, community, or agency to improve the living conditions and economic status of its socially disadvantaged members, residents, or citizens —**wel·fare work·er** *n*

wel·far·ism /wél fer ìzzəm/ *n* the policies, practices, and beliefs that characterize the welfare state (*disapproving*) —**wel·far·ist** *n*

wel·kin /wélkin/ *n* the sky, heaven, or the upper air (*archaic or literary*) [Old English *weolcen, wolc(e)n* "cloud, firmament" < Germanic]

Wel·kom /wélkəm, vélk-/ city in Free State, central South Africa. It is the center of a gold-mining region. Population: 68,111 (1991).

well

well[1] /wel/ *n* **1. HOLE MADE TO DRAW UP FLUIDS** a hole or shaft that is dug or drilled into the ground in order to obtain water, brine, petroleum, or natural gas ○ *an oil well* ○ *get their water from a well* **2. SOURCE OF SOMETHING** a source providing a freely and abundantly available supply of something ○ *a well of information* **3. CONTAINER FOR LIQUID** a container or sunken area for holding ink or another liquid ○ *a well on a cutting board* **4. VERTICAL PASSAGE IN BUILDING** a vertical space within or enclosed by a building, often used as a passageway for stairs or elevators or for air and light **5. ENCLOSURE FOR SHIP'S PUMPS** an enclosed area in the hold of a ship in which the pumps are located **6. SHIPBOARD CONTAINER FOR FISH** a compartment in a fishing boat in which freshly caught fish are held **7. ENCLOSING COMPARTMENT** a compartment that encloses or is used to store something temporarily such as the retracted wheels of an aircraft in flight **8. SPRING OF WATER** a place where water comes out of the ground as a natural spring or forms a natural pool (*often used in place names*) ■ *v* (**welled, well·ing, wells**) **1.** *vti* **RISE OR BRING TO SURFACE** to rise or flow to the surface from inside the ground or the body, or cause something to do this ○ *Tears welled up in his eyes.* ○ *The fountain welled a stream of clear water into the basin below.* **2.** *vi* **GROW STRONGER** to surge from within or grow stronger so as to threaten to burst forth ○ *Fear welled up inside me.* [Old English *wella* "spring of water," *wellan* "boil" < Indo-European, "turn"]

well[2] /wel/ (**bet·ter** /béttər/, **best** /best/) CORE MEANING: a grammatical word indicating that something is satisfactory or is performed in a satisfactory way ○ *She did very well on her test.*

1. *adv* **PLEASINGLY OR DESIRABLY** in an efficient, satisfying, or otherwise desirable way (*often used in combination*) ○ *I thought the party went very well.* **2.** *adv* **ETHICALLY OR PROPERLY** in an ethical, proper, or courteous way ○ *He always treated the children very well.* **3.** *adv* **SKILLFULLY OR EXPERTLY** with proficiency, skill, or expertise (*often used in combination*) ○ *She plays tennis really well.* **4.** *adv* **JUSTLY AND APPROPRIATELY** with justice and good reason ○ *I could not very well refuse her request.* **5.** *adv* **COMFORTABLY** in ease and comfort (*often used in combination*) ○ *I just want to be rich enough to live well.* **6.** *adv* **ADVANTAGEOUSLY** in a way that promotes somebody's advantage and well-being (*often used in combination*) ○ *She married well.* **7.** *adv* **CONDUCIVE TO GOOD HEALTH** in a way that promotes health and physical well-being (*often used in combination*) ○ *Both mother and baby are doing well.* **8.** *adv* **CONSIDERABLY** to a considerable extent, distance, or degree (*often used in combination*) ○ *I was well prepared for the exams.* **9.** *adv* **FULLY AND THOROUGHLY** in a complete and thorough way (*often used in combination*) ○ *Stir the mixture well, then turn it out onto a baking sheet.* **10.** *adv* **WITH CERTAINTY** with no doubt whatever about something ○ *As you well know, I will not tolerate any laziness.* **11.** *adv* **FAMILIARLY AND INTIMATELY** in a familiar and intimate way ○ *I knew them well when they were students.* **12.** *adv* **GOOD-NATUREDLY** taking something in a tolerant or good-humored way ○ *I teased him but he took it well.* **13.** *adj* **IN GOOD HEALTH** mentally and physically healthy ○ *I don't feel very well.* **14.** *adj* **PROPER OR APPROPRIATE** suitable, proper, or appropriate in the circumstances ○ *It is as well that you apologized to her.* **15.** *adj* **HIGHLY SATISFACTORY** in a good, pleasing, or satisfying condition ○ *Is everything well with you?* **16.** *interj* **EXPRESSING EMOTION** expresses surprise, agreement, indignation, disapproval, or some other emotion ○ *Well! You've finally come back!* **17.** *interj* **INTRODUCING OR RESUMING** introduces a comment or statement, or resumes a conversation ○ *Well, it looks as if we'll be waiting a while.* [Old English *wel(l)* < Indo-European, "to wish"] ◇ **as well** in addition to something ○ *The members were mostly young couples, but there were several grandparents as well.* ◇ **as well as** to an equal degree or extent ○ *Banking, as well as other businesses, will take the demographics into consideration.* ◇ **be as well to do something** to be advisable or sensible to do something ○ *It would be as well to look at a variety of mutual funds before investing your savings.* ◇ **be well** used to wish somebody well on parting (*informal*) ◇ **be well out of something** to be fortunate in having escaped from a difficult or unhappy situation (*informal*) ○ *You're well out of it – they weren't treating you very nicely in that job.* ◇ **that's** *or* **it's (just) as well** used to indicate that something is fortunate ○ *It's just as well that she's going to be a little late, because we're not quite ready.* ◇ **well and good** indicating qualified approval ○ *If he wants to come with us, well and good, but he'll have to pay his share.*

USAGE as well or **aswell**? ***As well***, as in *You know as well as I do that the answer is wrong*, is spelled as two words.

USAGE See ***good***.

well-ac·cept·ed *adj*
well-ac·cus·tomed *adj*
well-ac·quaint·ed *adj*
well-act·ed *adj*
well-a·dapt·ed *adj*
well-ad·just·ed *adj*
well-ad·min·is·tered *adj*
well-ad·ver·tised *adj*
well-aimed *adj*
well-aired *adj*
well-ar·gued *adj*
well-armed *adj*
well-ar·ranged *adj*
well-as·sort·ed *adj*
well-at·tend·ed *adj*
well-at·test·ed *adj*
well-au·then·ti·cat·ed *adj*
well-a·ware *adj*
well-be·haved *adj*
well-be·lov·ed *adj, n*
well-blessed *adj*
well-cal·cu·lat·ed *adj*
well-clothed *adj*
well-con·cealed *adj*
well-con·di·tioned *adj*
well-con·duct·ed *adj*
well-con·sid·ered *adj*
well-con·struct·ed *adj*
well-con·trolled *adj*
well-cooked *adj*
well-co·or·di·nat·ed *adj*
well-cov·ered *adj*
well-cul·ti·vat·ed *adj*
well-cut *adj*
well-de·fend·ed *adj*
well-de·fined *adj*
well-dem·on·strat·ed *adj*
well-de·scribed *adj*
well-de·served *adj*
well-de·signed *adj*
well-de·vel·oped *adj*
well-dis·ci·plined *adj*
well-dis·guised *adj*
well-doc·u·ment·ed *adj*
well-drained *adj*
well-dressed *adj*
well-drilled *adj*
well-ed·u·cat·ed *adj*
well-e·quipped *adj*
well-es·tab·lished *adj*
well-ex·pressed *adj*
well-fa·vored *adj*
well-filled *adj*
well-fi·nanced *adj*
well-fin·ished *adj*
well-fit·ted *adj*
well-fixed *adj*
well-for·ti·fied *adj*
well-fought *adj*
well-fur·nished *adj*
well-gov·erned *adj*
well-grown *adj*
well-guard·ed *adj*
well-hid·den *adj*
well-honed *adj*
well-il·lus·trat·ed *adj*
well-in·te·grat·ed *adj*
well-in·tend·ed *adj*
well-judged *adj*
well-jus·ti·fied *adj*
well-liked *adj*
well-lit *adj*
well-loved *adj*
well-main·tained *adj*
well-man·aged *adj*
well-man·i·cured *adj*
well-marked *adj*
well-matched *adj*
well-mer·it·ed *adj*
well-mixed *adj*
well-mo·ti·vat·ed *adj*
well-nour·ished *adj*
well-or·ga·nized *adj*
well-paid *adj*
well-placed *adj*
well-planned *adj*
well-played *adj*
well-pleased *adj*
well-prac·ticed *adj*
well-pre·pared *adj*
well-pre·sen·ted *adj*
well-pro·duced *adj*
well-pro·por·tioned *adj*
well-pro·tect·ed *adj*
well-pro·vid·ed *adj*
well-pub·li·cized *adj*
well-qual·i·fied *adj*
well-rea·soned *adj*
well-re·ceived *adj*
well-rec·om·mend·ed *adj*
well-re·gard·ed *adj*
well-reg·u·lat·ed *adj*
well-re·hearsed *adj*
well-re·mem·bered *adj*
well-rep·re·sent·ed *adj*
well-re·searched *adj*
well-re·spect·ed *adj*
well-rest·ed *adj*
well-re·ward·ed *adj*
well-run *adj*
well-sat·is·fied *adj*
well-schooled *adj*
well-sea·soned *adj*
well-se·cured *adj*
well-shaped *adj*
well-si·tu·at·ed *adj*
well-spaced *adj*
well-spent *adj*
well-stocked *adj*
well-struck *adj*
well-struc·tured *adj*
well-suit·ed *adj*
well-sup·plied *adj*
well-sup·port·ed *adj*
well-taught *adj*
well-tend·ed *adj*
well-thumbed *adj*
well-tim·bered *adj*
well-timed *adj*
well-trained *adj*
well-trav·eled *adj*
well-treat·ed *adj*
well-trod·den *adj*
well-un·der·stood *adj*
well-used *adj*
well-versed *adj*
well-wood·ed *adj*
well-worked *adj*
well-writ·ten *adj*
well-wrought *adj*

we'll /weel, wil/ *contr* **1.** "we shall" **2.** "we will"

well-ad·vised *adj* acting with or showing good sense (*not hyphenated after a verb*) ○ *You would be well advised to leave before the storm hits.*

Wel·land Ca·nal /wèllənd-/, **Wel·land Ship Ca·nal** canal system in Ontario, Canada, linking Lake Ontario and Lake Erie. It is part of the St. Lawrence Seaway, and bypasses Niagara Falls. Length: 28 mi./44 km.

well-ap·point·ed *adj* equipped, furnished, or arranged with whatever is necessary or desired (*not hyphenated after a verb*)

well-bal·anced *adj* **1.** organized, conducted, or constructed so that all the parts are appropriately and sensibly proportioned or coordinated (*not hyphenated after a verb*) ○ *a well-balanced diet* **2.** psychologically or emotionally stable (*not hyphenated after a verb*)

well-be·ing *n* a good, healthy, or comfortable state

well·born /wèl báwrn, wél bàwrn/ *adj* born into an aristocratic, highly respected, or wealthy family ■ *npl* people who are born in aristocratic, highly respected, or wealthy families

well-bred *adj* (*not hyphenated after a verb*) **1.** possessing or displaying good manners or other marks of a good upbringing **2.** born from a good breed or of good stock

well-built *adj* (*not hyphenated after a verb*) **1.** having a sturdy and strong physique **2.** of strong or sound construction

well-cho·sen *adj* selected carefully so as to be suitable or appropriate (*not hyphenated after a verb*)

well-con·nect·ed *adj* having relatives, friends, or acquaintances in important or influential positions who can provide help when necessary (*not hyphenated after a verb*)

well-dis·posed *adj* feeling or inclined to be approving, friendly, kindly, or sympathetic and potentially helpful (*not hyphenated after a verb*) ○ *She seemed well disposed toward us.*

well-done *adj* (*not hyphenated after a verb*) **1.** carried out or performed correctly, properly, or skillfully **2.** cooked right through to the center

well-earned *adj* fully deserved, especially as a result of hard work or effort (*not hyphenated after a verb*) ○ *sat down for a well-earned rest*

well-en·dowed *adj* **1. AFFLUENT** provided with substantial property, a sizable income, or a good source of income (*not hyphenated after a verb*) **2. NATURALLY EXCELLENT** talented or capable as a result of a natural gift (*not hyphenated after a verb*) **3. OFFENSIVE TERM** an offensive term meaning having a large penis or large breasts (*slang*)

Welles /welz/, **Orson** (1915–85) US actor and director. He starred in and directed *Citizen Kane* (1941), which garnered enormous critical respect. His other movies include *Touch of Evil* (1958) and *The Trial* (1962), but Hollywood's mistrust of his maverick talents prevented him from producing more than a handful of movies. Full name **Welles, George Orson**. See illustration on next page

"There are only two emotions in a plane: boredom and terror."
[Orson Welles, *Interview*, *Times (London)*; May 6, 1985]

Orson Welles

Welles·ley /wélzlee/ town in eastern Massachusetts, southwest of Boston. It is home to Wellesley College. Population: 26,671 (2002 estimate).

~~**wellfare**~~ incorrect spelling of **welfare**

well-fed *adj* (*not hyphenated after a verb*) **1.** having a diet that provides proper nourishment **2.** overweight, especially as a result of having eaten a great deal of good or rich food

well-formed *adj* fully conforming to the rules of grammar and syntax in a language (*not hyphenated after a verb*)

well-found *adj* properly and fully fitted out or equipped (*not hyphenated after a verb*)

well-found·ed *adj* based on sound reasons, information, or evidence or on undisputable facts (*not hyphenated after a verb*)

well-groomed *adj* (*not hyphenated after a verb*) **1.** clean, neat, and well-dressed **2.** carefully cleaned, brushed, or tended

well-ground·ed *adj* (*not hyphenated after a verb*) **1.** encompassing or thoroughly familiar with the essential details or knowledge of a subject **2.** same as **well-founded**

well-han·dled *adj* (*not hyphenated after a verb*) **1.** managed or conducted properly and efficiently **2.** handled many times or by many people, especially showing wear or other signs of having been handled in this way

well·head /wél hèd/ *n* **1. SOURCE OF SPRING OR STREAM** the place where a spring emerges from the earth or a stream begins **2. SOURCE OF SOMETHING** a principal or primary source of something **3. STRUCTURE ON TOP OF WELL** a structure or enclosure at the upper end of a water, oil, or natural-gas well, e.g., one containing pipes and pumping equipment

well-heeled *adj* having a large income or substantial property (*informal*; *not hyphenated after a verb*)

SPELLCHECK See *heal*.

well-hung *adj* (*not hyphenated after a verb*) **1. OFFENSIVE TERM** an offensive term meaning having a large penis or a large penis and testicles (*slang*) **2. HANGING AS DESIRED OR REQUIRED** suspended or attached so as to hang in a way that is desired or required **3. HUNG FOR PROPER TIME** hung up long enough to mature and be good to eat ○ *He liked his venison well hung.*

well-in·formed *adj* having a broad and detailed knowledge, either of things in general, or of a specific subject, or of recent events and developments (*not hyphenated after a verb*)

wel·ling·ton /wéllingtən/ *n UK* CLOTHING same as **wellington boot**

Wel·ling·ton /wéllingtən/ capital city of New Zealand, built around a deep harbor at the southern end of the North Island. Population: 162,981 (2001).

Wel·ling·ton, Mount mountain near Hobart in southern Tasmania, Australia. Height: 4,167 ft./1,270 m.

Wel·ling·ton /wéllingtən/, **Arthur Wellesley, 1st Duke of** (1769–1852) British general and prime minister (1828–30). He led the British forces that helped defeat Napoleon at the Battle of Waterloo (1815).

> "I always say that, next to a battle lost, the greatest misery is a battle gained."
> [Arthur Wellesley Wellington. Quoted in *Recollections by Samuel Rogers,* William Sharpe; 1859]

wel·ling·ton boot *n UK* **1.** a loose waterproof rubber boot extending to the knee or just below it and worn in wet weather or muddy conditions **2.** a leather boot that reaches to the top of or above the knee in the front but is cut lower in the back [Early 19C. After the 1st Duke of WELLINGTON]

well-in·ten·tioned *adj* intended to be helpful or useful in some way, but producing a negative effect or result (*not hyphenated after a verb*)

well-kept *adj* (*not hyphenated after a verb*) **1.** carefully maintained or looked after **2.** not revealed to anyone or to only a few people ○ *a well-kept secret*

well-knit *adj* (*not hyphenated after a verb*) **1. BOUND BY CLOSE TIES** bound or joined together by close relationships or ties **2. FIRMLY CONSTRUCTED** constructed or produced in such a way that the parts are firmly joined together or are integrated well **3. COMPACT IN PHYSIQUE** with a compact and strong physique

well-known *adj* (*not hyphenated after a verb*) **1.** known to many people **2.** fully known or understood

well-made *adj* (*not hyphenated after a verb*) **1. STRONGLY CONSTRUCTED** built or constructed strongly or skillfully **2. WITH STRONG PHYSIQUE** with a strong and sturdy physique **3. SKILLFULLY DEVISED** skillfully contrived or executed **4. WELL-PLOTTED** skillfully plotted or structured

well-man·nered *adj* behaving with politeness and courtesy (*not hyphenated after a verb*)

well-mean·ing *adj* trying to be helpful or useful in some way, but often producing a negative effect or result (*not hyphenated after a verb*)

well-meant *adj* arising from a desire to be helpful or useful, but often producing a negative effect (*not hyphenated after a verb*)

well·ness /wélnəss/ *n US* physical well-being, especially when maintained or achieved through good diet and regular exercise

well-nigh *adv* nearly or almost ○ *well-nigh impossible*

well-off (**bet·ter-off, best-off**) *adj* **1. FAIRLY WEALTHY** having a good income or enough money to live comfortably (*not hyphenated after a verb*) ○ *They were well off, certainly, but not millionaires.* **2. FAVORABLY PLACED** in a good or favorable situation or circumstances ○ *It's not a good idea to change jobs; you're better off where you are.* **3. WITH PLENTY** having a good supply of something ○ *well off for fuel right now*

well-oiled *adj* (*not hyphenated after a verb*) **1.** functioning, operating, or carried out efficiently **2.** having drunk too much alcohol (*informal*)

well-or·dered *adj* (*not hyphenated after a verb*) **1.** arranged or organized so that things are in the proper place or run smoothly **2.** in mathematics, having the property that every subset with members has an element that precedes all other elements in that subset

well-pad·ded *adj* (*not hyphenated after a verb*) **1.** having a greater body weight than is desirable or advisable (*informal*) **2.** having money or access to a ready source of it

well-pre·served *adj* in good condition or maintaining a good appearance or good health in spite of advanced age (*not hyphenated after a verb*)

well-read *adj* knowing much about many things or a particular field from having read widely and thoroughly (*not hyphenated after a verb*)

well-round·ed *adj* (*not hyphenated after a verb*) **1. WITH EXPERIENCE IN MANY AREAS** having abilities, experience, or achievements in a wide and balanced variety of fields **2. COMPREHENSIVE AND VARIED** encompassing or including a wide, desirable, and balanced variety of subjects or activities **3. SHAPELY** having a rounded or otherwise pleasingly shaped body

Wells /welz/, **H. G.** (1866–1946) British writer. A prolific writer of history and science books, he is remembered for his science fiction novels, including *The Time Machine* (1895), *The War of the Worlds* (1898), and *The Shape of Things to Come* (1933). Full name **Wells, Herbert George**

> "Moral indignation is jealousy with a halo."
> [H. G. Wells, *The Wife of Sir Isaac Harman*; 1914]

Wells, Ida B. (1862–1931) US teacher, journalist, and reformer. She campaigned against lynching in the 1890s and served as secretary of the National Afro-American Council (1898–1902). She became the founder and president of the Negro Fellowship League in 1910. Full name **Wells-Barnett, Ida Bell**

well-set *adj* (*not hyphenated after a verb*) **1.** strong and solid in physique **2.** solidly established or fixed

Wells no·tice *n* a notice from the US Securities and Exchange Commission that informs the recipient of the enforcement staff's recommendation to file a lawsuit against him or her, outlining the charges and evidence supporting them

well-spo·ken *adj* (*not hyphenated after a verb*) **1.** speaking clearly, articulately, and in a refined accent **2.** selected or expressed appropriately

well·spring /wél spring/ *n* **1.** a source of a spring or stream **2.** a plentiful source or supply of something ○ *a wellspring of artistic talent*

well-stacked *adj* an offensive term meaning having large breasts (*slang*)

well-tak·en *adj* based on sound reasons, information, or evidence (*not hyphenated after a verb*) ○ *The point is well taken.*

well-tem·pered *adj* tuned so as to permit playing in any key (*not hyphenated after a verb*)

well-thought-of *adj* regarded with respect or esteem or enjoying a good reputation (*not hyphenated after a verb*)

well-thought-out *adj* carefully and skillfully planned (*not hyphenated after a verb*)

well-to-do *adj* having a good income or enough money to live comfortably

well-tried *adj* thoroughly tested or used and so known from experience to be reliable (*not hyphenated after a verb*) ○ *a well-tried publishing formula*

well-turned *adj* (*not hyphenated after a verb*) **1. GRACEFULLY OR ATTRACTIVELY SHAPED** having a graceful or attractive shape ○ *a well-turned ankle* **2. SKILLFULLY STATED** skillfully expressed or worded ○ *a well-turned phrase* **3. MANUFACTURED WITH GRACEFUL SHAPE** turned on a lathe or formed so as to have a pleasing, graceful shape

well-wish·er *n* somebody who wishes success or good luck to another or good will toward somebody or something —**well-wish·ing** *adj, n*

well-worn *adj* (*not hyphenated after a verb*) **1. SHOWING WEAR** showing signs of wear as a result of much use **2. OVERUSED** trite or hackneyed as result of being used too often in speech or writing **3. CARRIED BECOMINGLY** becomingly worn or borne, especially with grace, style, or dignity ○ *well-worn celebrity*

wels /velss/ (*plural* **wels**) *n* a large freshwater catfish. Native to: central and eastern Europe. Latin name: *Silurus glanis*. [Late 19C. < German]

welsh /welsh, welch/ (**welshed, welsh·ing, welsh·es**), **welch** /welch/ (**welched, welch·ing, welch·es**) *vi* to fail to fulfill or honor an obligation entered into or incurred (*sometimes offensive*) [Mid-19C. Probably < WELSH] —**welsh·er** *n*

Welsh /welsh/ *npl* the people of Wales ■ *n* a Celtic language spoken in Wales. Native speakers: 50,000. [Old English *Wēlisc*, *Wǣlisc*. < *W(e)alh* "Briton, Celt, Welshman" ("foreigner"), via Germanic "foreign." < Latin *Volcae* "Celtic people of southern Gaul"] —**Welsh** *adj*

Welsh cob *n* a horse with a strong neck, powerful shoulders, and compact body, used as a saddle and harness horse. It is descended from the Welsh mountain pony.

Welsh cor·gi *n* BREED same as **corgi**

Welsh Eng·lish *n* the variety of English spoken in Wales. See panel on next page

Welsh harp *n* a harp with three rows of strings that allow the production of a chromatic scale

Welsh·man /wélshmən/ (*plural* **-men** /-mən/) *n* a man who comes from Wales [Old English]

Welsh moun·tain po·ny *n* a pony of a breed that has tiny pointed ears and a compact body. Native to: Wales.

WORLD ENGLISH ***Welsh English*** is the variety of English used in Wales, where it is the majority language, coexisting with Welsh, the surviving Celtic language with the largest number of speakers but a minority language in its homeland. ***Welsh English*** has three main influences: the Welsh language (mainly in the northern counties, often referred to as "Welsh Wales"; dialects in neighboring counties of England; and school and the media. The Welsh are often said to have a singsong accent, perhaps because of their use of a rising-and-falling tone at the end of sentences (rather than a simple fall), and because of their full vowels and stress on usually weak syllables such as the "den" in *garden*. ***Welsh English*** tends not to pronounce *r* in words such as *art, door,* and *worker.* Two sounds from Welsh are common, especially in names: the "ll" of *Llangollen*, pronounced as /hl/, and the "ch" in *bach* (dear), pronounced as /kh/. Native speakers of English in South Wales, like some dialect speakers in England, generally do not pronounce an initial "h" (as in *hat* and *home*), whereas residents of North Wales do, because it occurs in Welsh. A general influence from Welsh is notable in such usages as *Coming back soon she is* for *She's coming back soon* and *there* in exclamations such as *There's kind he is!* for *How kind he is!* The catchall question tag *isn't it?* has long been common, as in *They'll be here soon, isn't it?* (as opposed to standard *won't they?*). Some words of Welsh origin are *bugaboo, corgi, crag, flannel,* and *flummery.*

Welsh po·ny *n* a pony belonging to a breed developed from crosses between Welsh cobs and Welsh mountain ponies, slightly larger than the latter. It is used for jumping and riding.

Welsh rare·bit /-rérbit/, **Welsh rab·bit** /-rábbit/ *n* a dish made of hard cheese melted with seasoning, then spread on toast and grilled until bubbling and golden

Welsh spring·er span·iel *n* a spaniel with a thick silky coat that is chiefly white with large reddish patches, belonging to a breed that is smaller than the English springer spaniel

Welsh ter·ri·er *n* a wirehaired terrier that has a long thick, typically black-and-tan coat, belonging to a breed originally developed for hunting

Welsh·wom·an /wélsh wòomman/ (*plural* **-wom·en** /-wìmmin/) *n* a woman who comes from Wales

welt /welt/ *n* **1. RIDGE ON SKIN** a raised ridge or bump on the skin caused by a lash from a whip, a scratch, or a similar blow **2. LASH FROM A WHIP CAUSING RIDGE** a lash from a whip or a similar blow that causes a raised ridge or bump on the skin **3. STRIP SEWN INTO SHOE** a strip of leather or other material that is sewn into a shoe or boot between the upper and the sole in order to strengthen the seam **4. REINFORCEMENT FOR SEAM** a folded strip of cloth, sometimes wrapped around a cord, that is sewn into a seam in a garment or pillow as a reinforcement or decoration ■ *vt* (**welt·ed, welt·ing, welts**) **1. BEAT SOMEBODY SEVERELY** to beat or hit somebody severely, especially with a whip or switch **2. RAISE SMALL RIDGES ON SKIN** to cause raised ridges or bumps on the skin as a result of a lash from a whip or switch **3. STITCH SOMETHING REINFORCING OR DECORATIVE** to stitch or supply something with a strip of material as a reinforcement or decoration [15C. Origin ?]

Welt·an·schau·ung /vélt aan shòw òong/ (*plural* **-ung·en** /-òongən/) *n* PHILOSOPHY same as **world view** [Mid-19C. < German, "world view" < *Welt* "world" + *Anschauung* "view"]

wel·ter /wéltər/ *n* **1. CONFUSED MASS** a confused or jumbled mass of something **2. CONFUSED CONDITION** a state of confusion or chaos or a disorderly or chaotic situation **3. SURGING MOTION OF WATER** a surging, rolling, or heaving motion made by the sea or waves **4.** BOXING same as **welterweight** (*informal*) ■ *vi* (**-tered, -ter·ing, -ters**) **1. WALLOW IN SOMETHING** to wallow or roll around in something **2. LIE DRENCHED WITH LIQUID** to lie soaked or bathed in water, blood, or some other liquid **3. BE COMPLETELY IMMERSED IN SOMETHING** to be completely or deeply involved, absorbed, or entangled in something **4. SURGE OR ROLL IN WATER** to surge, roll, or heave in the sea or waves [14C. < Middle Dutch or Middle Low German *welteren* "roll"]

wel·ter·weight /wéltər wàyt/ *n* BOXING **1. WEIGHT CATEGORY IN PROFESSIONAL BOXING** in professional boxing, a weight category for competitors who weigh between 135 lb./61 kg and 147 lb./66.5 kg **2. WEIGHT CATEGORY IN AMATEUR BOXING** in amateur boxing, a weight category for competitors who weigh between 135 lb./61 kg and 147 lb./66.5 kg **3. BOXER AT WELTERWEIGHT LEVEL** a professional or amateur boxer who competes at welterweight **4. BOXER BETWEEN LIGHTWEIGHT AND MIDDLEWEIGHT** a sports contestant ranked by body weight between a lightweight and a middleweight [Early 19C. < *welter* "heavyweight rider or boxer," origin ?]

Welt·schmerz /vélt shmèrts/, **welt·schmerz** *n* sadness felt at the imperfect state of the world, especially at the behavior of human beings [Late 19C. < German < *Welt* "world" + *Schmerz* "pain"]

CORBIS/Philip Gould

Eudora Welty

Wel·ty /wéltee/, **Eudora** (1909–2001) US writer. Her novels, set in her native Mississippi, include the Pulitzer Prize-winning *The Optimist's Daughter* (1969).

> "Fiction has, and must keep, a private address."
> [Eudora Welty, *The Eye of the Story*; 1977]

wen[1] /wen/ *n* a cyst containing material secreted by a sebaceous gland of the skin, usually on the scalp or genitals. It may grow to an appreciable size and become infected. [Old English *wen(n)*, origin ?]

wen[2] /wen/ *n* ALPHA same as **wynn**

Wen·ces·las /wénsəss làwss, -làss/, **Wen·ces·laus** (1361–1419) Holy Roman Emperor and king of Germany (1378–1400) and, as Wenceslas IV, king of Bohemia (1378–1419). A weak ruler, he was deposed by the German Electors and imprisoned by his own relatives in Bohemia.

Wen·ces·las /wénssəss làwss/, **Wen·ces·laus, St.** (907?–929) duke of Bohemia. He encouraged Bohemia's conversion to Christianity during his reign (925?–929), but was murdered by his brother. He is the patron saint of the Czech Republic. Known as **Good King Wenceslas**

wench /wench/ *n* **1. SERVANT GIRL** formerly, a girl or young woman who worked at a paid job, usually as a servant or on a farm (*archaic*) **2. OFFENSIVE TERM** an offensive term for a prostitute or a woman who is regarded as sexually promiscuous **3. OFFENSIVE TERM** an offensive term for a young woman ■ *vi* (**wenched, wench·ing, wench·es**) **OFFENSIVE TERM** an offensive term meaning to engage in sex with prostitutes or with women considered to be promiscuous [13C. Shortening of obsolete *wenchel* "child, enslaved laborer, prostitute" < Old English *wencel* "child" < Germanic, "to falter"] —**wench·er** *n*

wend /wend/ (**wend·ed, wend·ing, wends**) *vti* to proceed along a course or route ○ *The boat wended its way through the reefs.* [Old English *wendan* "turn, proceed" < Germanic, "turn"]

Wend /wend/ *n* a member of a Slavic people who lived in northeastern Germany in medieval times [Late 18C. < German *Wende*]

wen·di·go /wéndi gō/ (*plural* **-gos** or **-goes**), **win·di·go** /wíndi gō/ *n Can* in Cree and Algonquian folklore, a demonic being who eats people or possesses them and turns them into cannibals [Early 18C. < Ojibwa *wintiko*]

Wend·ish /wéndish/ *n* a Slavic language spoken in eastern Germany. Native speakers: 100,000. —**Wend·ish** *adj*

Wen·dy house /wéndee-/ *n UK* same as **playhouse** (sense 2) [Mid-20C. After the house built around the character *Wendy* in the play *Peter Pan* (1904) by J. M. Barrie]

wen·ge /wéng gày/ *n* the dark brown wood of an African tree. Use: veneer for furniture. Latin name: *Millettia laurentii*. [Mid-20C. < a Congolese language]

Wen Jia·bao /wèn jyaa bów/ (1942–) Chinese premier (2003–). A former geologist, he was vice premier (1998–2003), when he was involved in agricultural reform.

Wens·ley·dale /wénzlee dàyl/ *n* **1.** a white crumbly hard English cheese with a slightly tangy flavor **2.** a sheep with a blue-gray head and ears and dark mottled legs, belonging to a breed originating in northern England and raised for its wool [Late 19C. After a valley in N Yorkshire, England]

went past tense of **go**[1]

wen·tle·trap /wént'l tràp/ *n* an ocean gastropod mollusk with a spiral prominently ribbed shell that is typically white but is sometimes tinged with brown. Family: Epitoniidae. [Mid-18C. < Dutch *wenteltrap* "winding stair," from the appearance of the shells]

wept past participle, past tense of **weep**

were *stressed* /wur/; *unstressed* /wər/ past tense of **be**[1] [Old English *wǣron* (plural past indicative), *wǣren* (plural past subjunctive), and *wǣre* (2nd person singular past indicative and singular past subjunctive), forms of *wesan* "be" (see WAS)]

we're /weer/ *contr* we are

were·gild *n* LAW, HIST another spelling of **wergild**

weren't /wurnt/ *contr* were not

were·wolf /wér wòolf, wúr-/ (*plural* **-wolves** /-wòolvz/) *n* somebody believed to have been transformed into a wolf, or to be able to change into a wolf and then back into a human being [Old English *werewulf* < *were-* "man" + *wulf* "wolf" < Indo-European, "man"]

wer·gild /wúr gild/, **were·gild** /wúr-/, **wer·geld** /-gèld/ *n* in Anglo-Saxon and Germanic law, the amount of compensation paid to the relatives of somebody slain, calculated on the basis of the person's rank in society [Old English *wergeld* < *wer* "man" + *gield* "payment" < Germanic]

wer·ner·ite /wúrnə rìt/ *n* MINERALS same as **scapolite** [Early 19C. After Abraham Gottlob *Werner* (1750–1817), German mineralogist]

Wer·nick·e-Kor·sa·koff syn·drome /vèrnikee káwrssə kàwf-, vèrnikə-/ *n* a form of brain damage occurring in long-term alcoholics that results from severe nutritional deficiencies [Mid-20C. After Karl *Wernicke* (1848–1905), German neurologist, and Sergei Sergeevich *Korsakov* (1854–1900), Russian psychiatrist]

wert /wurt/ past tense of **be**[1] (*archaic*)

Wert·heim·er /vért hìmər/, **Max** (1880–1943) Czech-born US psychologist. He taught at the New School for Social Research (1933–43) and was one of the founders of Gestalt theory.

We·ser /váyzər/ river in northwestern Germany. Formed by the confluence of the Werr and Fulda rivers, it flows northwestward through Lower Saxony and empties into the North Sea near Bremerhaven. Length: 273 mi./439 km.

wes·kit /wéskit/ *n* same as **waistcoat** (sense 2) (*archaic*) [Mid-19C. Alteration]

Wes·ley /wésslee, wéz-/, **Charles** (1707–88) British religious leader. He cofounded Methodism with his brother John in 1739 and wrote many hymns.

Wes·ley, John (1703–91) British religious leader. He cofounded Methodism with his brother Charles in 1739, and thereafter preached tirelessly to huge crowds and published hymns and other religious works for mass distribution.

> "An ounce of love is worth a pound of knowledge."
> [John Wesley. Quoted in *Life of Wesley*, R. Southey; 1820]

Wes·ley·an /wésslee ən, wéz-/ *adj* based on, consisting of, or resembling the teachings, practices, and beliefs of the Christian preacher John Wesley and his brother Charles, or of Methodism ■ *n* a follower of the Christian preacher John Wesley and his brother Charles, or a believer in their teachings or those of Methodism —**Wes·ley·an·ism** *n*

Wes·sex /wéssiks/ former Anglo-Saxon kingdom in southern England

west /west/ *n* **1.** DIRECTION IN WHICH SUN SETS the direction that lies directly ahead of somebody facing the setting Sun or that is located toward the left-hand side of a conventional map of the world **2.** COMPASS POINT OPPOSITE EAST the compass point that lies directly opposite east **3.** AREA IN WEST the part of an area, region, or country that is situated in or toward the west **4.** POSITION EQUIVALENT TO WEST the position equivalent to west in any diagram consisting of four points at 90-degree intervals ■ *adj* **1.** IN WEST situated in, facing, or coming from the west of a place, region, or country **2.** BLOWING FROM WEST describes a wind that blows from the west ○ *a west wind* ■ *adv* TOWARD WEST in or toward the west [Old English, < Indo-European, "evening, night"] ◇ **go west** to die, disappear, or be destroyed (*informal*)

West *n* **1.** EUROPE AND AMERICAS the countries of Europe and North and South America **2.** COUNTRIES WITH GRECO-ROMAN AND CHRISTIAN TRADITIONS the countries of the world, especially in Europe and North and South America, whose culture and society are most influenced by traditions rooted in Greek and Roman culture and in Christianity **3.** NON-COMMUNIST COUNTRIES IN COLD WAR the non-Communist countries of Europe and North and South America during the Cold War **4.** W UNITED STATES the part of the United States west of the Mississippi River or west of the Allegheny Mountains, especially during early phases of the country's history

West /west/, **Benjamin** (1738–1820) US artist. His historical and portrait paintings include *The Death of General Wolfe* (1771).

AKG London

Mae West

West, Mae (1892–1980) US actor and comedian. She was known for her irreverent wit and disdain for conventional morals. Her movies include *She Done Him Wrong* (1933), *I'm No Angel* (1933), and *Klondike Annie* (1936).

> "Too much of a good thing can be wonderful."
> [Mae West, *The Wit and Wisdom of Mae West*; 1967]

West, Nathanael (1903–40) US writer. His four novels, which include *The Day of the Locust* (1939), satirize contemporary society. Born **Weinstein, Nathan Wallenstein**

> "The Miss Lonelyhearts are the priests of twentieth-century America."
> [Nathanael West, *Miss Lonelyhearts*; 1933]

West, Dame Rebecca (1892–1983) British writer. She wrote noted studies of the Nuremberg war crimes trials, *Black Lamb and Grey Falcon* (1941), a study of Yugoslavia and Nazism, and novels including *The Thinking Reed* (1936). Born **Fairfield, Cicily Isabel**

> "But there are other things than dissipation that thicken the features. Tears, for example."
> [Dame Rebecca West, "Serbia," *Black Lamb and Grey Falcon*; 1941]

West, Thomas, 3rd Baron De La Warr ♦ **De la Warr, Thomas West**

West Af·ri·ca region in sub-Saharan western Africa including Ghana and Nigeria —**West Af·ri·can** *adj, n*

West Bank

West Bank territory in Southwest Asia on the western bank of the Jordan River, bordered by Israel and Jordan. Once part of Palestine, it was annexed by Jordan in 1950 and occupied by Israel in 1967. As a result of peace agreements between 1993 and 1997 some of it was transferred to Palestinian National Authority administration, with further negotiations under way. Population: 2,237,194 (2003). Area: 2,350 sq. mi./6,080 sq. km.

West Ben·gal former name for **Bangla**[2]

West Ber·lin western part of the city of Berlin. It was officially part of West Germany between 1945 and 1990, when the rest of the city was designated East German territory. —**West Ber·lin·er** *n*

west·bound /wést bòwnd/ *adj* leading, going, or traveling toward the west

West Brom·wich /-brómmich, -ij/ industrial city in west central England, near Birmingham. Population: 146,386 (1991).

west by north *n* the direction or compass point midway between west and west-northwest —**west by north** *adj, adv*

west by south *n* the direction or compass point midway between west and west-southwest —**west by south** *adj, adv*

West·ches·ter /wést chèstər/ town on Salt Creek in northeastern Illinois. It is a suburb of Chicago. Population: 16,862 (2002 estimate).

West Ches·ter borough in southeastern Pennsylvania, west of Philadelphia. Population: 17,837 (2002 estimate).

West Coast 1. region comprising the coastal areas of California, Oregon, and Washington on the Pacific coast of the United States **2.** region comprising the western area of British Columbia between the mountains and the sea, including coastal areas, Vancouver Island, the Gulf Islands, and the Queen Charlotte Islands

West Coun·try southwestern part of England, comprising the counties of Cornwall, Devon, and Somerset

West Des Moines town in south central Iowa. It is a western suburb of Des Moines. Population: 49,961 (2002 estimate).

West End *n* the western part of central London, England, and its commercial and entertainment center

west·er /wéstər/ *n* a wind that blows from the west, especially one blowing ahead of or with a storm ■ *vi* (**-ered, -er·ing, -ers**) to move, or appear to move, across the sky to the west (*refers to the Sun, Moon, or other astronomical objects*)

west·er·ly /wéstərlee/ *adj* **1.** IN WEST situated in or toward the west **2.** BLOWING FROM WEST describes a wind that blows from the west ■ *n* (*plural* **-lies**) WIND FROM WEST a wind that blows from the west ■ *adv* **1.** FROM WEST coming from the west **2.** TOWARD WEST moving toward the west

Wes·ter·ly /wéstərlee/ town in southwestern Rhode Island, on its border with Connecticut, southwest of South Kingstown. Population: 23,623 (2002 estimate).

west·ern /wéstərn/ *adj* **1.** IN WEST situated in the west of a region or country **2.** FACING WEST situated in or facing the west ○ *The house has a western aspect.* **3.** COMING FROM WEST blowing from the west ○ *a western wind* **4.** WEST OF PRIME MERIDIAN lying west of the prime meridian **5.** OF WEST characteristic of or native to the west of a region or country **6.** *also* **West·ern** another spelling of **Western** ■ *n* COWBOY MOVIE OR NOVEL a movie, novel, or radio or television program set in the western United States, usually during the late 19th century [Old English *westerne* < WEST + a suffix denoting direction] —**west·ern·ness** *n*

West·ern, west·ern *adj* **1.** INFLUENCED BY GRECO-ROMAN AND CHRISTIAN TRADITIONS found in or characteristic of countries, especially in Europe and North and South America, whose culture and society are greatly influenced by traditions rooted in Greek and Roman culture and in Christianity **2.** OF NON-COMMUNIST COUNTRIES IN COLD WAR found in or belonging to the non-Communist countries of Europe and North and South America during the Cold War **3.** CHARACTERISTIC OF AMERICAN WEST found in or relating to the part of the United States west of the Mississippi River or west of the Allegheny Mountains, especially during early phases of the country's history **4.** FOUND IN EUROPE AND AMERICAS located in or relating to Europe and North and South America **5.** CHR CATHOLIC AND PROTESTANT based on, consisting of, or resembling the teachings, practices, and beliefs of Roman Catholicism and Protestantism, as opposed to those of the Eastern Orthodox Church ■ *n* LITERAT, MOVIES, MEDIA another spelling of **western**

West·ern Aus·tra·lia /wèstərn-/ state occupying the western part of Australia. Founded as a British colony in 1829, it is the largest state in Australia. Capital: Perth. Population: 1,527,400 (2003). Area: 975,100 sq. mi./2,525,500 sq. km.

West·ern blot, West·ern blot·ting *n* a technique that analyzes mixtures of proteins by separating them and then binding them to specific antibodies [After SOUTHERN BLOT]

West·ern Can·a·da region comprising the Canadian provinces of Manitoba, Saskatchewan, Alberta, and British Columbia

West·ern Cape province in South Africa, in the southwestern part of the country. Capital: Cape Town. Population: 4,524,316 (2001). Area: 49,950 sq. mi./129,370 sq. km.

West·ern Church *n* the Christian Church as found in or influenced by that of Europe, especially the Roman Catholic Church

west·ern·er /wéstərnər/, **West·ern·er** *n* **1.** SOMEBODY FROM WESTERN NATION somebody who comes from Europe or the Americas or from a country that is culturally aligned with Europe and, particularly, North America **2.** SOMEBODY FROM WEST somebody who comes from the western part of a country or region **3.** SOMEBODY FROM WESTERN CANADA somebody who comes from Western Canada

West·ern Eu·ro·pe·an Time *n* the standard time in the time zone centered on 0° longitude (**the prime meridian**), which includes the United Kingdom. It is the same time as Universal Time.

West·ern Eur·o·pe·an Un·ion *n* an association of European countries, inaugurated in 1955, whose main function is to coordinate defense, economic, and social policy

West·ern Front *n* the battle line between the French and British armies and the German armies in western Europe during World War I. It extended from Belgium to the Swiss border.

West·ern Ghats /-gaàts/ mountain range in southern India, forming the western edge of the Deccan plateau. The highest peak is Doda Betta, 8,652 ft./2,637 m.

west·ern hem·i·sphere *n* the half of Earth that is to the west of the prime meridian, including North and South America and portions of western Europe and Africa

west·ern hem·lock *n* a coniferous tree with drooping foliage, widely grown for ornament and lumber. Native to: western North America. Latin name: *Tsuga heterophylla.*

west·ern hon·ey mes·quite *n* a mesquite with sugar-rich pods. Native to: southwestern United States, Mexico. Latin name: *Prosopis glandulosa.*

west·ern·ism /wéstər nìzzəm/, **West·ern·ism** *n* **1.** a custom or practice characteristic of the countries of Europe and North and South America **2.** a word or idiom chiefly used in the western part of a country or region, especially the western United States

west·ern·ize /wéstər nīz/ (**-ized, -iz·ing, -iz·es**), **West·ern·ize** *v* **1.** *vti* to adopt the customs, practices, or beliefs of the people of Europe or North and South America, or cause a person, country, or culture to adopt the customs, practices, or beliefs of the people of Europe or North and South America **2.** *vt* to change a law, custom, practice, or belief so that it resembles or is replaced by its European or North American counterpart —**west·ern·i·za·tion** /wèstərni záysh'n/ *n*

West·ern mead·ow·lark *n* BIRDS a meadowlark with a yellow throat and black V on the breast and a sharply pointed beak. Native to: central and western United States and Canada. Latin name: *Sturnella neglecta*.

west·ern·most /wéstərn mōst/ *adj* situated farthest west

west·ern om·e·let *n* an omelet made with diced ham, green pepper, and onion

west·ern red ce·dar *n* **1.** the wood of the red cedar tree of western North America **2.** TREES same as **red cedar** (sense 2)

West·ern rho·do·den·dron *n* a species of rhododendron. Flowers: pink, white. Native to: Pacific coast from northern California to British Columbia. Latin name: *Rhododendrum macrophyllum*.

west·ern roll *n* a high jump in which the body is half-turned over the bar

west·ern sad·dle, West·ern sad·dle *n UK* same as **stock saddle**

West·ern Sa·ha·ra region in northwestern Africa formerly ruled by Spain. It was partitioned between Morocco and Mauritania in 1976 and fully occupied by Morocco in 1979. While currently under United Nations mediation, the territory is disputed between Morocco and internal independence movements. Area: 97,344 sq. mi./252,120 sq. km. Former name **Spanish Sahara**

West·ern Sa·mo·a former name for **Samoa**

west·ern sand·wich *n* a sandwich with a filling of an omelet made with diced ham, green pepper, and onion

West·ern Stan·dard Time *n* the standard time in the time zone centered on longitude 120° W, which includes the whole of Western Australia. It is seven to nine hours ahead of Universal Time.

west·ern swing *n* country and western music played on guitars, steel guitars, fiddles, and other instruments and incorporating aspects of swing music

West·ern Wall *n* a wall in Jerusalem believed to be part of the Second Temple, destroyed in A.D. 70 by the Romans. It is used by some Jews as a place for prayer and lamentation.

West·ford /wéstfərd/ town in northeastern Massachusetts, southwest of Chelmsford and northwest of Bedford. Population: 21,249 (2002 estimate).

West Ger·man·ic *n* **1.** a subgroup of Germanic languages that consists of English, German, Yiddish, Dutch, Flemish, Afrikaans, and Frisian **2.** the language that is the ancestor of modern languages belonging to West Germanic —**West Ger·man·ic** *adj*

West Ger·ma·ny former republic of western Europe from 1945 to 1990, formed from the territories of Germany occupied by the US, British, and French forces at the end of World War II. In 1990 it was reunited with East Germany. Area: 95,976 sq. mi./248,577 sq. km. Official name **Federal Republic of Germany** —**West Ger·man** *n, adj*

West Goth *n* PEOPLES, HIST same as **Visigoth**

West High·land ter·ri·er, West High·land white ter·ri·er *n* a small hardy terrier with a pure white longhaired coat, belonging to a breed originally developed for hunting small animals but now kept as a pet [< its having originated in the western Highlands of Scotland]

west·ie /wéstee/ *n* BREED same as **West Highland terrier**

West In·dies /-índeez/ former name for the islands of the Caribbean, now used only in specific contexts, such as the West Indies cricket team —**West In·di·an** *adj, n*

west·ing /wésting/ *n* **1.** the distance due west between two points on a course heading in a westward direction **2.** travel or progress in a westward direction

West·ing·house /wésting hòwss/, **George** (1846–1914) US engineer and industrialist. He invented the air brake (1869), which revolutionized the railroad industry, and founded the Westinghouse Electric Company (1886).

West I·ri·an former name for **Irian Jaya**

Westm. *abbr* Westminster

West Mem·phis town in eastern Arkansas near the Mississippi River, a western suburb of Memphis, Tennessee. Population: 28,030 (2002 estimate).

West·min·ster[1] /wést mìnstər/ **1.** borough in central London, England. Many notable buildings including the Houses of Parliament, Buckingham Palace, and Westminster Abbey are located there. Population: 181,286 (2001). Official name **City of Westminster** **2.** town in north central Maryland on the northern branch of the Monocacy River, northwest of Baltimore. Population: 17,128 (2002 estimate).

West·min·ster[2] /wést mìnstər/ *n* the British parliament or parliamentary system (*often used before a noun*)

West·min·ster Ab·bey *n* a large Gothic church in London, England, originally a Benedictine abbey, in which British monarchs are traditionally crowned

West·mont /wést mònt/ town in northeastern Illinois, southwest of La Grange. It is a western suburb of Chicago. Population: 24,747 (2002 estimate).

West·more·land /wèst máwr lənd/, **William Childs** (*b.* 1914) US general. He was commander of US forces in Vietnam (1964–68).

West New Gui·nea former name for **Irian Jaya**

West Nile fe·ver, West Nile dis·ease, West Nile en·ceph·a·li·tis *n* a mosquito-borne viral infection affecting birds, horses, and humans that causes fever, rash, headache, muscle pain, enlarged lymph nodes, and, in some cases, inflammation of the brain [Because first identified in the West Nile district of Uganda]

West Nile vi·rus *n* **1.** a virus, carried by mosquitoes, that causes West Nile fever **2.** MED same as **West Nile fever**

west-north·west *n* the direction or compass point midway between west and northwest ■ *adj, adv* in, from, facing, or toward the west-northwest —**west-north·west·er·ly** *adj, adv*

Edward Weston: photographed in 1923 by Tina Modotti

Wes·ton /wést'n/, **Edward** (1886–1958) US photographer. His sharp, semiabstract photographs often magnify details of natural objects.

Wes·ton stan·dard cell *n* a portable, highly accurate, voltage source used as a standard for calibration purposes [Early 20C. After Edward *Weston* (1850–1936), British-born electrical engineer]

West Pak·i·stan one of the two areas that made up Pakistan following the partition of British India in 1947, comprising the provinces of Baluchistan, North-West Frontier Province, Punjab, and Sind. It became the Islamic Republic of Pakistan in 1971 after East Pakistan seceded to become the independent nation of Bangladesh.

West Palm Beach city opposite Palm Beach, on the Atlantic Intracoastal Waterway and Lake Worth in southeastern Florida. It is a manufacturing, trade, and tourist center. Population: 86,517 (2002 estimate).

West·pha·lia /west fáylyə, -fáylee ə/ former province in northeastern Germany, in the present-day state of North-Rhine Westphalia. The Peace of Westphalia, signed at Münster and Osnabrück in 1648, marked the end of the Thirty Years' War. —**West·pha·lian** *n, adj*

West·pha·lian ham *n* German ham that is cured and eaten raw, very thinly sliced

West Point *n* the site of the US Military Academy, on the Hudson River in New York State, or the Academy itself

West·port /wést pàwrt/ town on Long Island Sound in southwestern Connecticut, near Norwalk. It is a residential and resort community. Population: 26,171 (2002 estimate).

West Sax·on *n* **1.** a dialect of Old English used in Wessex during Anglo-Saxon times as the main literary dialect **2.** somebody who came from Wessex during Anglo-Saxon times —**West Sax·on** *adj*

west-south·west *n* the direction or compass point midway between west and southwest ■ *adj, adv* in, from, facing, or toward the west-southwest —**west-south·west·er·ly** *adj, adv*

West Sus·sex county in southeastern England, formed in 1974 from the former county of Sussex. Chichester is the administrative center. Population: 753,614 (2001). Area: 768 sq. mi./1,989 sq. km.

West Virginia

West Vir·gin·ia state in the eastern United States, bordered by Ohio, Pennsylvania, Maryland, Virginia, and Kentucky. Capital: Charleston. Population: 1,801,873 (2002 estimate). Area: 24,231 sq. mi./62,758 sq. km. —**West Vir·gin·ian** *n, adj*

west·ward /wéstwərd/ *adj* IN WEST toward or in the west ■ *n* POINT IN WEST a direction toward or a point in the west ■ *adv also* **west·wards** /-wərdz/ TOWARD WEST in a westerly direction —**west·ward·ly** *adv, adj*

West War·wick town in Rhode Island, southwest of Providence and west of Warwick. Population: 29,941 (2002 estimate).

West Wing *n US* the president's senior staff and advisers [Because the Oval Office is located in the West Wing of the White House]

Vivienne Westwood

West·wood /wést wŏŏd/, **Vivienne** (*b.* 1941) British fashion designer. She was a pioneer of punk fashion in the late 1970s and is known for her unconventional clothing designs. See illustration on previous page

wet /wet/ *adj* **1.** SOAKED WITH WATER covered, soaked, or dampened with water or some other liquid **2.** NOT YET DRY not completely dry **3.** NOT YET SET not yet firm or solidified ○ *wet cement* **4.** RAINY, SHOWERY, MISTY, OR FOGGY characterized by rain, showers, mist, or fog ○ *a wet weekend* **5.** WITH RAINY WEATHER subject to frequent heavy rain, showers, mist, or fog ○ *a wet climate* **6.** USING OR DONE WITH LIQUID using or done in water or another liquid **7.** ALLOWING LIQUOR SALES allowing the legal manufacture, storage, transportation, and sale of alcoholic beverages (*informal*) ○ *a wet town* **8.** *US* FAVORING LIQUOR SALES favoring the legal manufacture, storage, transportation, and sale of alcoholic beverages (*informal*) ○ *a wet representative* **9.** *UK* OFFENSIVE TERM an offensive term used to indicate somebody regarded as weak and lacking resolution or decisiveness (*informal insult*) ■ *n* **1.** LIQUID OR MOISTURE water or another liquid, or moisture from it **2.** RAINY OR DAMP WEATHER rainy, showery, misty, or foggy weather ○ *Come in out of the wet.* **3.** *US* SUPPORTER OF LEGAL LIQUOR SALES a supporter of the legal manufacture, storage, transportation, and sale of alcoholic beverages (*informal*) **4.** *UK* OFFENSIVE TERM an offensive term for somebody regarded as weak, irresolute, or indecisive (*informal insult*) **5.** *UK* LIBERAL CONSERVATIVE a Conservative politician whose policies some other Conservatives consider not to be sufficiently pure or doctrinaire (*informal*) ■ *v* (**wet** or **wet·ted, wet·ting, wets**) **1.** *vti* MAKE OR BECOME WET to become damp or soaked with water or some other liquid, or cause something to become damp or soaked **2.** *vt* MAKE WET BY URINATING to cause something to be damp or soaked with urine [Old English *wǣt, wǣta* (noun), *wǣt* (adjective), and *wǣtan* (verb) < Indo-European, "water, wet"] —**wet·ly** *adv* —**wet·ness** *n* —**wet·ta·ble** *adj* —**wet·ter** *n* —**wet·tish** *adj* ◇ **all wet** completely mistaken or wrong (*slang*)

SPELLCHECK wet or **whet**? Do not confuse the spelling of ***wet*** and ***whet***, which sound similar. ***Wet*** is chiefly used as an adjective, meaning "not dry" (as in *a wet towel, wet paint, wet weather*); as a verb it usually means "make something wet": *I wetted my handkerchief and wiped the dirt from my face.* ***Whet*** is chiefly used as a verb, meaning "stimulate" or "sharpen," as in *recipes to whet your appetite,whet the blade on a stone.*

SYNONYMS *wet, damp, moist, dank, humid, sodden, saturated, soaking, sopping*

CORE MEANING: not dry

wet covered, soaked, or dampened with water or some other liquid ○ *a wet sponge* ○ *It can be dangerous driving on wet roads.* **damp** slightly wet, especially undesirably so ○ *The mattress was too damp to sleep on.* **moist** slightly wet, especially pleasantly so ○ *rich moist gardening soil* **dank** unpleasantly damp and cold ○ *Inside the hut, the walls were cold, dank, and rather slimy.* **humid** with a relatively high level of moisture in the air ○ *the humid swamps of Florida* ○ *unpleasantly hot and humid weather* **sodden** extremely wet and heavy with retained moisture ○ *Emergency workers watched warily over the weak and sodden dike.* **saturated** soaked with moisture. ○ *There is no indication that farmers would be able to get into the saturated fields even if the weather is becoming drier.* **soaking** very wet, especially because of being rained on ○ *He came in from the downpour with soaking clothes and shoes.* ○ *I'm soaking – there's never a cab to be had when it's raining.* **sopping** (*informal*) thoroughly and unpleasantly wet ○ *a tangle of sopping hair*

wet·back /wét bàk/ *n* a highly offensive term for a Mexican person recently arrived in the United States, especially somebody who has entered the country illegally to work as a laborer (*taboo*) [Early 20C. < Mexican immigrants having waded or swum across the Rio Grande to enter the United States]

wet bar *n* a small bar equipped with a sink in a house or hotel room, used for mixing alcoholic drinks

wet blan·ket *n* somebody who spoils or diminishes other people's enthusiasm or enjoyment (*informal*) [< the use of wet blankets to smother small fires]

wet-bulb ther·mom·e·ter *n* a thermometer that records the temperature at which pure water must be evaporated to saturate a given volume of air

wet cell *n* a primary cell that contains a free-flowing electrolyte

wet dream *n* **1.** a dream that has sexual content and leads to the ejaculation of semen (*sometimes offensive*) **2.** an overly optimistic and highly unrealistic idea or image (*slang*)

wet fish *n UK* fresh fish for sale, as distinguished from frozen or cooked fish

wet fly *n* a fishing lure resembling a fly that slips beneath the surface of the water after it is cast

weth·er /wéthər/ *n* a male sheep or goat that has been castrated before becoming sexually mature [Old English *weþer* < Germanic]

SPELLCHECK See ***weather.***

wet·land /wét lànd/ *n* a marsh, swamp, or other area of land where the soil near the surface is saturated or covered with water, especially one that forms a habitat for wildlife (*often used in the plural*)

wet look *n* **1.** a glossy finish on a material that gives an appearance of wetness **2.** a glossy sheen given to the hair by the use of a special hair gel that gives an appearance of wetness —**wet-look** *adj*

wet nurse *n* a woman who breast-feeds and takes care of another woman's baby

wet-nurse *vt* **1.** to breast-feed and take care of another woman's baby **2.** to bestow excessive care or attention on somebody (*informal*)

wet pack *n* a piece or pieces of material dampened with hot or cold water and wrapped around a patient's body for therapeutic purposes

wet suit *n* a tight-fitting garment worn by a diver, made of foam neoprene rubber or a similar material. It traps a thin insulating layer of water near the skin.

wet·ting a·gent /wétting-/ *n* a chemical agent that allows a liquid to spread more easily across or into a surface by lowering the liquid's surface tension

wet·ware /wétwàir/ *n* the human brain or human thought processes, regarded as data-processing devices comparable with, or in contrast to, computer systems

we've /weev/ *contr* shortening of "we have"

We·wak /wé wak/ coastal town on northern New Guinea island, Papua New Guinea. Population: 23,224 (1990).

Wex·ford /wéksfərd/ **1.** county in Leinster Province, in the southeastern part of the Republic of Ireland. Population: 104,371 (2002). Area: 908 sq. mi./2,351 sq. km. **2.** town, port, and administrative center of Wexford County, in the Republic of Ireland. Population: 16,000 (1996).

Wey·den /wáyd'n/, **Rogier van der** (1399?–1464) Flemish painter. His predominantly religious oeuvre, characterized by elegant, flowing lines and the use of cold colors, influenced other European painters of the 15th century.

Wey·mouth /wáyməth/ city in eastern Massachusetts, south of Boston. Population: 54,754 (2002 estimate).

wf, w.f. *abbr* **1.** Wallis and Futuna Islands (*used in Internet addresses*) See table at **domain name 2.** PRINTING wrong font

wff *abbr* LOGIC well-formed formula

WFTU *abbr* World Federation of Trade Unions

w.g., WG *abbr* **1.** water gauge **2.** wire gauge

Wh, wh *abbr* watt-hour

wh. *abbr* white

whack /wak, hwak/ *v* (**whacked, whack·ing, whacks**) **1.** *vti* HIT SOMEBODY WITH LOUD SHARP BLOW to hit somebody or something with a swift sharp blow that produces a loud noise **2.** *vti* CUT OR CHOP SOMETHING to cut or chop something with a swift sharp blow **3.** *vt* same as **murder** (*slang*) ■ *n* **1.** LOUD SHARP BLOW a swift sharp blow that produces a loud noise **2.** LOUD SOUND OF SHARP BLOW the loud sound made by a swift sharp blow **3.** ATTEMPT AT SOMETHING an attempt at doing something (*informal*) ○ *That looks like fun – can I take a whack at it?* **4.** SHARE OF SOMETHING a share or portion of something, especially one deserved or due (*informal*) [Early 18C. Probably an imitation of the sound] —**whack·er** *n* ◇ **at one** *or* **a (single) whack** *US* quickly and on a single occasion (*informal*) ◇ **out of whack** not working properly, especially because of being out of order or alignment (*informal*)

whack off *vti* **1.** a highly offensive term meaning to masturbate, or masturbate somebody (*taboo*) **2.** to remove or separate something suddenly and forcefully (*informal*)

whacked /wakt, hwakt/ *adj* **1.** relaxed, excited, or euphoric as a result of taking drugs, especially marijuana (*slang*) **2.** *Can, UK* very tired or exhausted (*informal*)

whacked-out *adj* **1.** very tired after physical or mental exertion (*informal*) **2.** *US* same as **whacked** (sense 1) (*slang*)

whack·ing /wáking, hwáking/ *UK* (*informal*) *adj* very large or impressive ■ *adv* to an extreme degree

whack·o *n* same as **wacko** (*slang offensive*)

whack·y *adj* same as **wacky** (*informal*)

Wha·ka·ta·ne /fàakə taa nay/ coastal town in the northeastern part of the North Island, New Zealand. It is a commercial center for agriculture and timber from the surrounding region. Population: 17,778 (2001).

whale[1] /wayl, hwayl/ *n* **1.** BIG OCEAN MAMMAL a large ocean mammal that breathes through a blowhole on the top of its head and has front flippers, no hind limbs, and a flat horizontal tail. Its body is insulated by a thick layer of fatty blubber beneath the skin, and many species live in social groups, communicating by sound. Order: Cetacea. **2.** IMPRESSIVE EXAMPLE OF SOMETHING an impressive, very large, or very enjoyable example of something (*informal*) ○ *a whale of a party* ■ *vi* (**whaled, whal·ing, whales**) HUNT WHALES to hunt for and kill whales [Old English *hwæl* < Germanic]

SPELLCHECK See ***wail.***

whale[2] /wayl, hwayl/ (**whaled, whal·ing, whales**) *v* **1.** *vt* THRASH SOMEBODY to beat somebody severely as a punishment **2.** *vt* HIT SOMETHING FORCEFULLY to hit or strike somebody or something with great force **3.** *vi US* BE HIGHLY CRITICAL to be critical of somebody or something in a severe way (*informal*) ○ *whaling away at her detractors* **4.** *vt* DEFEAT SOMEBODY CONVINCINGLY to defeat somebody soundly or completely (*informal*) [Late 18C. Origin ?]

whale·back /wáyl bàk, hwáyl-/ *n* **1.** something large and rounded like the back of a whale, e.g., an ocean wave or a small hill **2.** a cargo vessel with a rounded bow and arched upper deck designed to allow the water from waves breaking on it to run off more easily

whale·boat /wáyl bōt, hwáyl-/ *n* a long, narrow, easily maneuvered boat with a pointed bow and stern, originally rowed in pursuit of whales, but now often powered and used as a lifeboat

whale·bone /wáyl bōn, hwáyl-/ *n* **1.** MARINE BIOL same as **baleen 2.** a piece or strip of a hard elastic material found in some whales. Use: formerly, corset stays, whips.

whale·bone whale *n* MARINE BIOL same as **baleen whale**

whale catch·er *n* a boat with a harpoon launcher mounted in its bow, used for pursuing and catching whales

Whale Is·land /wàyl-, hwàyl-/ uninhabited volcanic island in the Bay of Plenty off the northeastern coast of the North Island, New Zealand. Area: 2 sq. mi./4 sq. km.

whale oil *n* a yellowish oil manufactured by rendering the blubber of whales. Use: formerly, lamp fuel, soap, candles.

whal·er /wáylər, hwáylər/ *n* **1.** same as **whaleboat 2.** a ship used for hunting whales or processing killed whales **3.** somebody who hunts or harpoons whales, or who processes killed whales

whale shark *n* the largest of all sharks, with a white-spotted dark body up to 50 ft./15 m in length. Native to: warm oceanic waters. Latin name: *Rhincodon typus.*

whal·ing /wáyling, hwáyling/ *n* the activity or industry of hunting and processing whales

wham /wam, hwam/ (*informal*) *n* **1. FORCEFUL BLOW** a solid forceful blow or impact **2. SOUND OF FORCEFUL BLOW** the loud noise produced by a solid forceful blow or impact ■ *vti* (**whammed, wham·ming, whams**) **HIT SOMETHING WITH LOUD NOISE** to hit or crash into somebody or something forcefully with a loud noise ○ *The car whammed into the brick wall.* ■ *interj* **INDICATES SOUND OF BLOW** used to imitate the loud sound of a forceful blow or impact ■ *adv* **SUDDENLY AND FORCEFULLY** with a startling or jarring suddenness ○ *I ran wham right into my ex-husband.* [Early 20C. An imitation of the sound]

wham·mo /wámmō, hwámmō/ *adv US* with a startling or jarring suddenness (*informal*)

wham·my /wámmee, hwámmee/ (*plural* **-mies**) *n* (*informal*) **1.** a jinx or hex on somebody or something **2.** something with unpleasant or damaging consequences [Mid-20C. Origin ?]

whang[1] /wang, hwang/ *n* **1. RESOUNDING BLOW** a heavy blow that resounds loudly when it hits something **2. SOUND OF RESOUNDING BLOW** the loud sound produced by a heavy blow when it hits something ■ *vti* (**whanged, whang·ing, whangs**) **HIT WITH RESOUNDING SOUND** to hit something heavily and produce a loud resounding sound [Early 19C. An imitation of the sound]

whang[2] /wang, hwang/ *n* **1. THONG** a thong, especially one made from leather **2. UNTANNED ANIMAL HIDE** untanned hide from cattle or other animals **3.** *US* **OFFENSIVE TERM** an offensive term for a penis (*slang*) ■ *vt* (**whanged, whang·ing, whangs**) **1. HIT SOMEBODY SEVERELY** to beat, whip, or thrash somebody severely **2. HIT SOMETHING WITH FORCE** to hit or kick something with enough force to dislodge it (*informal*) [Early 16C. Alteration of *thwang*, a variant of THONG]

Whang·a·rei /fàangə ráy/ coastal town in the northern part of the North Island, New Zealand. It is a commercial and tourist center. Population: 46,047 (2001).

whang·ee /wang gée, hwang-/ *n* **1.** a walking stick or cane made from a piece of bamboo **2.** a bamboo plant whose stems are used to make whangees. Native to: China. Genus: *Phyllostachys*. [Late 18C. < Chinese *huang* "bamboo sprouts too old for eating"]

whap *n, vt* another spelling of **whop**

wharf /wawrf, hwawrf/ *n* (*plural* **wharves** /wawrvz, hwawrvz/ or **wharfs**) **LANDING PLACE FOR SHIPS** a structure built alongside or out into the water as a landing place for boats and ships, sometimes with a protective covering or enclosure ■ *v* (**wharfed, wharf·ing, wharfs**) **1.** *vti* **MOOR BOAT AT WHARF** to moor a vessel at a wharf, or be moored there **2.** *vt* **UNLOAD OR STORE CARGO ON WHARF** to unload cargo onto or store it on a wharf **3.** *vt* **EQUIP PLACE WITH WHARF** to provide a place with a wharf or wharves [Old English *hwearf* "embankment, wharf" < Germanic, "turn"]

wharf·age /wáwrfij, hwáwrfij/ *n* **1. USE OF WHARF** the use of a wharf or wharves **2. FEE TO USE WHARF** a fee that is paid for the use of a wharf or wharves **3. WHARVES** wharves collectively, especially the wharves in a particular location

wharf·in·ger /wárfinjər, hwárfinjər/ *n* somebody who owns or supervises the running of a wharf or group of wharves [Mid-16C. Alteration of obsolete *wharfager*]

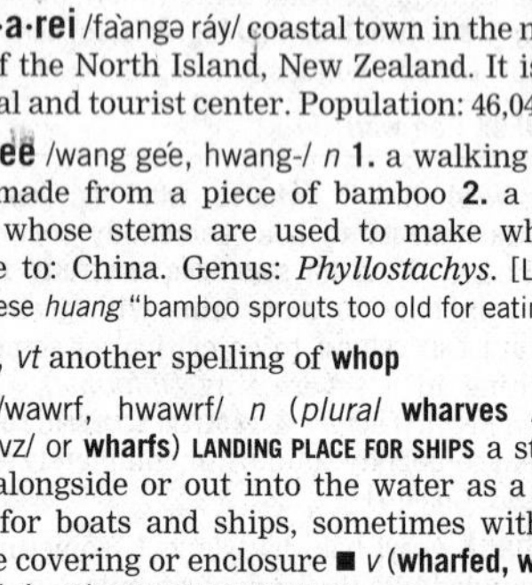

Edith Wharton

Whar·ton /wáwrt'n, hwáwrt'n/, **Edith** (1862–1937) US writer. She wrote on everything from interior decorating to the art of writing, but is best known for her novels, particularly the Pulitzer Prize-winning *The Age of Innocence* (1920). Born **Jones, Edith Newbold**. See Cultural note at **innocence**

> "The worst of doing one's duty was that it apparently unfitted one for doing anything else."
> [Edith Wharton, *The Age of Innocence*; 1920]

wharve /wawrv, hwawrv/ *n* a wheel or similar part on a spindle that operates as a pulley on a spinning machine or as a flywheel on a spinning wheel [Old English *hweorfa* < *hweorfan* "turn" < Germanic]

wharves NAUT plural of **wharf**

what /wot, hwot/ CORE MEANING: a grammatical word used in direct and indirect questions to request information, e.g., about the identity or nature of somebody, or about the purpose of something ○ (adj) *What time will you be back?* ○ (adj) *I'm not sure what kind of sauce goes best with this dish.* ○ (pron) *What are they doing?* ○ (pron) *Do you know what she does for a living?*
1. *adj, pron* **REQUESTS INFORMATION** used to request information, e.g., about the identity or nature of somebody or something ○ *What time is it?* ○ *What are they doing?* **2.** *adj, pron* **THAT WHICH** the person or persons who, or the thing or things that ○ (adj) *We spent what money we did have.* ○ (pron) *picking their way through what remained of the house* **3.** *adj* **EMPHASIZING REACTION** used in exclamations to emphasize a reaction or opinion ○ *What fantastic news!* ○ *What a miserable day it's been.* **4.** *adv* **HOW** in what respect or to what degree ○ *What does it matter now that they've gone?* **5.** *adv* **AT GUESS** used to indicate a guess or approximation of an amount or value ○ *It must be, what, ten years since we first met.* **6.** *interj* **EXCLAMATION** used as an exclamation when expressing an emotion such as surprise, anger, or disappointment ○ *What? The plane will be delayed by two hours.* [Old English *hwæt* < Indo-European] ◇ **give somebody what for** to scold or punish somebody severely (*informal*) ◇ **what about ... 1.** used to suggest that somebody or something be taken into consideration ○ *What about all the money we already paid then?* **2.** used to suggest that somebody might like to do something ○ *What about going on a fishing trip?* ◇ **what for** used to ask the reason for or the purpose of something ◇ **what have you** other things similar to those just mentioned ◇ **what if 1.** used to make a suggestion about a possible course of action **2.** used to ask what might or would happen in a given situation ◇ **what of it?** used to suggest that something is not important ◇ **what's what** the true facts or actual situation (*informal*) ◇ **what with** used to introduce the reason or reasons for something ○ *I didn't get there until ten, what with all the traffic and setting out late.* ◇ **what's to** what is there to

USAGE As a pronoun, the word ***what*** means "the thing that," as in *This is much nicer than what he gave me last Christmas. Remember what I told you.* Beware of adding ***what*** where it is not needed: *It was a lot more difficult than* [not *than what*] *I thought it would be.*

what all *pron US* something of the same or a similar kind (*informal*)

what·cha·ma·call·it /wòchəmə káwlit, hwòch-/ *n* something whose name is forgotten or is not known (*informal*) [Early 20C. < a pronunciation of *what you may call it*]

what·ev·er /wot évvər, hwot-/ CORE MEANING: a grammatical word used to refer to everything of a particular type, without limitation ○ (pron) *Feel free to say whatever you like.* ○ (adj) *He lost whatever interest he may have had in it.*
1. *pron, adj* **NO MATTER WHAT** used to indicate that something is the case in all circumstances ○ (pron) *She always seems to succeed, whatever she does.* ○ (adj) *Whatever problem you come up with they'll deal with.* **2.** *pron* **EMPHATIC "WHAT"** an emphatic form of "what" used to express an emotion such as surprise or perplexity ○ *Whatever is the matter now?* **3.** *adv* **OF ANY KIND** used for emphasis ○ *I can see no reason whatever why you shouldn't go.* **4.** *adv* **EXPRESSING MILD DISAGREEMENT** used to indicate that the speaker disagrees with what has just been said, but is not prepared to argue (*informal*) ○ *OK, if that's what you think, whatever.* ◇ **or whatever** used to refer generally to something else of the same kind ○ *any tool such as a hoe, fork, spade, or whatever*

what-if *n* a situation, difficulty, or obstacle that could arise in the future (*informal*)

what·not /wót nòt, hwót-/ *n* **1. SOMETHING SAME OR SIMILAR** something of the same or a similar kind **2. FURNITURE SET OF SHELVES** a set of light shelves for displaying small ornamental items **3. SOMETHING UNIMPORTANT** something nondescript, trivial, or unimportant

what's /wots, hwots/ *contr* **1.** what does **2.** what has **3.** what is

whats·her·name /wótsər nàym, hwótsər-/ *pron* a woman or girl whose name has been forgotten or is not known (*informal*)

whats·his·name /wótsiz nàym, hwótsiz-/ *pron* a man or boy whose name has been forgotten or is not known (*informal*)

what·sis /wótsiss, hwótsiss/ *n US* something whose name you have forgotten or do not know (*informal*) [Contraction and alteration of *what-is-it*]

whats·it /wótsit, hwótsit/, **whats·is** /wótsiss, hwótsiss/ *n* something whose name is not known or has been forgotten (*informal*) [Contraction of *what-is-it*]

whats·its·name /wótsits nàym, hwótsits-/ *pron* something whose name is not known or has been forgotten (*informal*)

what·so·ev·er /wòtsō évvər, hwòt-/ *adv* used to emphasize a negative statement, after words such as "none," "no one," and "anyone" ○ *"Did you have any doubts?" – "None whatsoever."* ■ *pron, adj* same as **whatever**

wheal /weel, hw-/, **weal** /weel/ *n* **1.** a raised or reddened area on the skin, caused by being hit with something **2.** a short-lived raised area on the skin, often red and itchy, caused by something such as a nettle or insect sting or by exposure to an allergen [Early 19C. Alteration of WALE under the influence of WHEAL]

wheat /weet, hweet/ *n* **1. EDIBLE GRAIN** a grain harvested in temperate regions from a widely cultivated annual grass. Use: making flour for bread, pasta, and other foods. **2. CEREAL PLANT** an annual grass of a genus that includes types cultivated for their grain for making flour. The numerous varieties of cultivated wheat belong to three main species: bread wheat, durum or hard wheat, and emmer. Native to: southwestern Asia. Genus: *Triticum*. **3. PALE YELLOW COLOR** a pale yellow color [Old English *hwǣte* "that which is white" < Indo-European, "white"] —**wheat** *adj*

wheat bread *n* a bread that is made from a blend of white flour and whole-wheat flour

wheat·ear /wéet èer, hwéet-/ *n* a small thrush with a white rump and black face. Native to: Europe, Asia, Africa, North America. Genus: *Oenanthe*. [Late 16C. Back-formation < *wheatears*, probably by folk etymology < WHEAT + EAR[1]]

wheat·en /wéet'n, hwéet'n/ *adj* **1.** made from or with wheat or milled wheat flour **2.** pale yellow in color —**wheat·en** *n*

wheat germ *n* the embryonic center of the wheat grain, rich in B vitamins, that is milled finely and sometimes toasted, and is used for sprinkling over cereals or in cooking

wheat·grass /wéet gràss, hwéet-/ *n* wheat grains sprouted to a height of around 7 in./17 cm, cut, and pulped to produce a highly nutritious juice that is drunk in very small quantities

wheat·ish /wéetish, hwéetish/ *adj S Asia* light creamy brown, or having a light brown complexion

Wheat·ley /wéetlee, hwéet-/, **Phillis** (1753?–84) African-born US poet. Sold into slavery to the Wheatley family as a child, she started writing poetry at an early age and gained recognition in the United States and Britain for her neoclassical verse. She is regarded as the first important African American poet.

> "Some view our sable race with scornful eye; / Their color is a diabolic dye. / Remember, *Christians*, *Negroes*, black as *Cain*, / May be refined, and join th' angelic train."
> [Phillis Wheatley, "On Being Brought from

Africa to America," *Poems on Various Subjects, Religious and Moral*; 1773]

Whea·ton /wéet'n, hwéet'n/ city in northeastern Illinois, southwest of Addison. It is a western suburb of Chicago and home to Wheaton College. Population: 55,352 (2002 estimate).

wheat rust *n* **1.** a disease of wheat caused by various fungi and marked by blackish, brownish, or yellowish streaks on the leaves and stems **2.** a fungus that causes rust in wheat

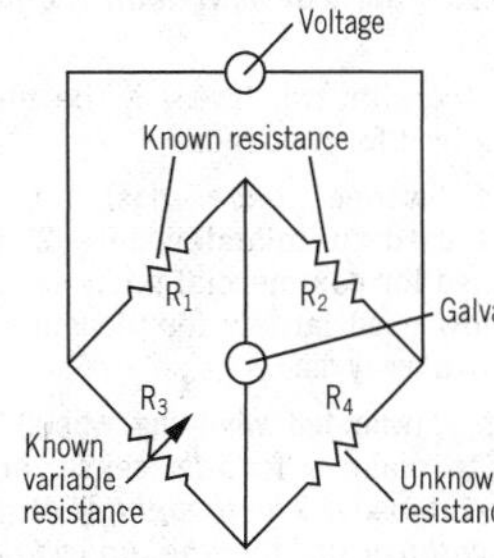

Wheatstone bridge

Wheat·stone bridge /wéet stōn-, hwéet-/ *n* a device consisting of an electrical circuit, three known resistances, and a galvanometer, used for measuring an unknown resistance [Late 19C. After Sir Charles *Wheatstone* (1802–75), English physicist]

wheat·worm /wéet wùrm, hwéet-/ (*plural* **-worms** or *same*) *n* a small nematode worm that lives as a parasite on and is destructive to wheat. Latin name: *Anguina tritici*.

whee /wee, hwee/ *interj* used to express exhilarating or unrestrained joy, pleasure, or excitement [Early 20C. Natural exclamation]

whee·dle /wéed'l, hwéed'l/ (**-dled, -dling, -dles**) *v* **1.** *vti* to coax or try to persuade somebody to do something using flattery, guile, or other indirect means **2.** *vt* to obtain something from somebody by coaxing, persuasion, flattery, guile, or other indirect means [Mid-17C. Origin ?] —**whee·dler** *n* —**whee·dling·ly** *adv*

wheel /weel, hweel/ *n* **1.** ROTATING ROUND PART a ring or disk that revolves or is turned by a central shaft or pin, sometimes with a central hub that has radiating spokes attached to a circular rim (*often used in combination*) ○ *a wagon wheel* **2.** SOMETHING RESEMBLING WHEEL something that resembles a wheel in shape, form, or function **3.** MECH ENG ROUND MACHINE PART THAT TURNS ANOTHER a rotating circular part of a mechanism, often with projections on the outer edge, used to turn another part **4.** AUTOMOT same as **steering wheel** ○ *He fell asleep at the wheel.* **5.** HANDICRAFT same as **spinning wheel 6.** FURNITURE **CASTER** a small rotating or swiveling circular part fitted to the base of something such as a piece of furniture or luggage to make it easier to move **7.** CERAMICS same as **potter's wheel** (*informal*) **8.** ROTATING FIREWORK a flat round or coiled firework that spins as it burns (*often used in combination*) **9.** WHEEL OF FORTUNE an imaginary wheel said to be spun by fate **10.** GAMBLING ROUND FRAME SPUN IN GAMBLING a circular device that is spun in games of chance such as roulette in order to determine who wins in a random way **11.** HIST MEDIEVAL TORTURE DEVICE a medieval instrument of torture in the form of a large wheel to which the victim was tied. The outstretched arms and legs of the victim were usually broken with a metal bar. **12.** TURN a turn or revolution **13.** MOVEMENT IN CIRCLE a turning, spinning, pivoting, or circular movement **14.** MIL MILITARY FORMATION a military formation in which the inner unit remains in one place, as a pivot, while the outer units change direction and make an arc around it. It is used in marching performances by a troop of soldiers and displays by a fleet of ships. **15.** *US* MIL ROUND MILITARY CAP a round cap with a visor, worn by members of the armed forces (*slang*) **16.** LITERAT SET OF RHYMING LINES a group of rhyming lines that end a stanza of verse. They are usually shorter than the other lines and often occur in a group of four. **17.** same as **bicycle** (*informal*) ■ **wheels** *npl* **1.** CAR a car, especially for personal use (*slang*) **2.** DRIVING FORCE OR WORKINGS the system or influences controlling the way something functions or operates ○ *the wheels of justice* ■ *v* (**wheeled, wheel·ing, wheels**) **1.** *vt* MOVE ON WHEELS to push something that has wheels ○ *wheeled her bicycle up the steep hill* **2.** *vt* TRANSPORT SOMEBODY IN WHEELED OBJECT to move or carry somebody or something in a conveyance with wheels such as a cart or wheelchair ○ *wheeled the patient out of the room* **3.** *vi* TURN QUICKLY to move quickly in a circle **4.** *vi* MAKE CIRCULAR MOVEMENT to do something with a circular or curving movement ○ *Her arms wheeled frantically in the air as she tried to signal for help.* **5.** *vi* MOVE SMOOTHLY to move smoothly and easily ○ *He wheeled through the gathering, making all his appointed stops.* **6.** *vt* PROVIDE SOMETHING WITH WHEELS to fit something with a wheel or wheels [Old English *hwēol* < Indo-European, "go around"] —**wheeled** *adj* —**wheel·less** *adj*
◇ **reinvent the wheel 1.** to waste time recreating something that already exists in a perfectly usable and acceptable form **2.** to produce a new version of something very basic and familiar ◇ **wheel and deal** to use complex, skillful and sometimes slightly dishonest negotiating techniques in order to secure something (*informal*)

wheel about *vi* same as **wheel around**

wheel around *vi* **1.** to turn around quickly or suddenly **2.** to reverse or radically change an opinion, position, or belief

wheel in *vi* to approach or enter a place quickly and confidently (*informal*)

wheel out *v* **1.** *vt* to present somebody or use something readily or repeatedly **2.** *vi* to leave a place quickly (*informal*)

wheel and ax·le *n* a simple machine, often used to raise or lower loads, usually consisting of a cylindrical drum and wheel mounted on the same axle with ropes wound around each

wheel·arch /wéel àarch, hwéel-/ *n UK* AUTOMOT same as **wheel well**

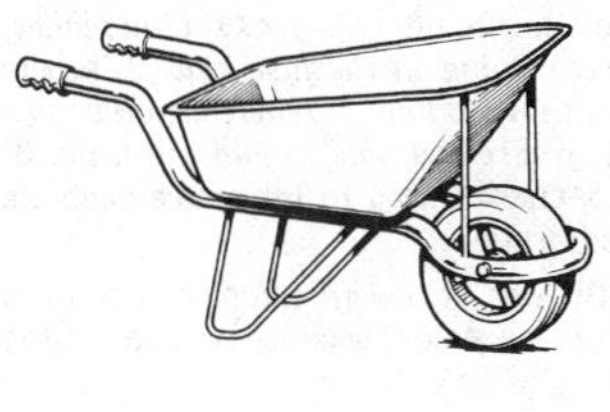
wheelbarrow

wheel·bar·row /wéel bàrrō, hwéel-/ *n* a small cart used to transport things, usually in the form of an open container with a single wheel at the front and two handles at the back ■ *vt* (**-rowed, -row·ing, -rows**) to move or transport something in a wheelbarrow

wheel·base /wéel bàyss, hwéel-/ *n* the distance between the front axle and the rear axle of a motor vehicle, usually measured in inches. It determines how sharply the vehicle can turn in a given direction.

wheel bug *n* a large and powerful insect belonging to the assassin bug family that preys on other insects and has an outgrowth on its back resembling a gear. Latin name: *Arilus cristatus*.

wheel·chair /wéel chèr, hwéel-/ *n* a chair with two small wheels at the front and two large wheels at the sides, used as a way of moving around by somebody who cannot walk. Wheelchairs may be propelled by turning the large wheels, by somebody pushing from behind, or by a small motor.

wheel·chair hous·ing *n Can, UK* houses and apartments designed or adapted for people who use wheelchairs to enable them to move around easily

wheel clamp *n UK* same as **Denver boot** —**wheel-clamp** *vt*

wheel·er /wéelər, hwéelər/ *n* **1.** WHEELED VEHICLE a vehicle that has a particular number of wheels (*used in combination*) ○ *He hauled it in a ten-wheeler.* **2.** SOMEBODY WHO WHEELS somebody or something that wheels or pushes something with wheels **3.** MAKER AND REPAIRER OF WHEELS somebody who makes and repairs wheels, especially the wheels of carriages or wagons

Wheel·er /wéelər, hwéelər/, **William A.** (1819–87) vice president of the United States (1877–81). He served in the US House of Representatives (1869–77) and formulated the Wheeler Compromise to settle a disputed Louisiana election (1874) before becoming vice president to Rutherford B. Hayes (1877).

wheel·er-deal·er *n* an adroit negotiator who uses complex or sometimes dishonest techniques to obtain what he or she wants, especially in business or politics (*informal*) —**wheel·er-deal·ing** *n*

wheel horse *n* a steady, diligent, and reliable worker, especially in a political organization

wheel·house /wéel hòwss, hwéel-/ (*plural* **-hous·es** /-hòwzəz/) *n* NAUT same as **pilothouse**

wheel·ie /wéelee, hwéelee/ *n* a maneuver performed on a moving or stationary bicycle or motorcycle in which the rider raises the front wheel off the ground and balances on the back wheel (*informal*)

wheel·ing /wéeling, hwéel-/ *n* the transmission by an electric utility of electricity produced by another utility or generating company along its own distribution network

Wheel·ing /wéeling, hwéeling/ city in northern West Virginia, on its border with Ohio. Population: 30,367 (2002 estimate).

wheel lock *n* in some old firearms, a firing mechanism in which a steel spring-wound wheel strikes sparks from a piece of iron pyrite

wheel·man /wéelmən, hwéel-/ (*plural* **-men** /-mən/), **wheels·man** /wéelzmən/ *n* **1.** a driver of a motor vehicle, especially in criminal activity (*slang*) **2.** somebody, especially a man, who rides a bicycle or motorcycle **3.** NAUT same as **helmsman** (sense 1)

wheel of for·tune, Wheel of For·tune *n* an imaginary revolving wheel said to determine random changes in the course of somebody's life, used as a symbol of the inconstancy of fortune

wheel·per·son /wéel pùrss'n, hwéel-/ (*plural* **-peo·ple** /-peèp'l/ or **-per·sons**) *n* somebody who rides a bicycle

wheels·man *n* NAUT, AUTOMOT, CYCLING, MOTORCYCLES same as **wheelman**

wheel·spin /wéel spin, hwéel-/ *n* the rapid revolving of a vehicle's wheels without sufficient contact with the ground to produce forward or backward motion

wheels up *adj* airborne after having taken off from a runway ◇ **go wheels up** to take off from a runway and become airborne

wheel-thrown *adj* made by being turned on a potter's wheel

wheel well *n US* a semicircular cavity in the body of a vehicle that fits over a wheel

wheel·wom·an /wéel wòommən, hwéel-/ (*plural* **-wom·en** /-wìmmin/) *n* a woman who rides a bicycle

wheel·work /wéel wùrk, hwéel-/ *n* an arrangement of interlocking wheels or gears within a machine or other device, e.g., the gear train in a mechanical timepiece

wheel·wright /wéel rìt, hwéel-/ *n* somebody who makes and repairs wheels, especially the wheels of carriages and wagons

wheesht *vti, n Scotland* same as **whisht**

wheeze /weez, hweez/ *v* (**wheezed, wheez·ing, wheez·es**) **1.** *vi* BREATHE WITH HOARSE WHISTLING SOUND to breathe with an audible whistling sound and with difficulty, usually because of a respiratory disorder such as asthma **2.** *vt* SAY SOMETHING WITH HOARSE WHISTLING SOUND to say or express something while breathing with an audible whistling sound and with difficulty **3.** *vi* MAKE WHISTLING OR PUFFING SOUND to make a noisy whistling or puffing sound that resembles wheezing ○ *The old locomotive wheezed and puffed up the steep slope.* ■ *n* **1.** NOISY BREATHING SOUND noisy and difficult breathing, or the hoarse whistling sound of this **2.** OFTEN REPEATED JOKE a hackneyed story, joke, or saying (*informal*) [15C. Origin ?] —**wheez·er** *n* —**wheez·i·ly** *adv* —**wheez·i·ness** *n* —**wheez·y** *adj*

whelk[1] /welk, hwelk/ (*plural same* or **whelks**) *n* an invertebrate sea animal with a conical spiraling shell. Some kinds of whelk are edible. Family: Buccinidae. [Old English *weoloc*, altered perhaps by association with WHELK2]

whelk2 /welk, hwelk/ *n* a raised spot or mark on the skin, e.g., a pimple, boil, or wheal [Old English *hwylca* "pustule, tumor"] —**whelk·y** *adj*

whelm /welm, hwelm/ (**whelmed, whelm·ing, whelms**) *vt* (*literary*) **1.** to engulf or submerge something in water **2.** to overpower or overburden somebody or something [14C. Probably alteration of Old English *āhwylfan* "cover over, submerge," influenced by *helmian* "to cover"]

whelp /welp, hwelp/ *n* **1.** YOUNG ANIMAL a young animal, especially the young of carnivorous mammals such as wolves, lions, bears, and dogs **2.** CHILD a child or young person **3.** RUDE YOUNG MAN a boy or young man regarded as showing inappropriate boldness or lack of deference (*insult*) **4.** NAUT RIDGE ON CAPSTAN OR WINDLASS a projection on the barrel of a capstan or windlass **5.** MECH ENG TOOTH ON WHEEL a tooth on a sprocket wheel ■ *vti* (**whelped, whelp·ing, whelps**) BEAR YOUNG to give birth to young, especially baby carnivores [Old English *hwelp* < Germanic]

when /wen, hwen/ CORE MEANING: an adverb used to ask at what time or at what point something happens ○ *When can we expect you?* ○ *When should you use your rearview mirror?*

1. *conj* WHILE at or during the time that ○ *When I was a child, I lived in the country.* **2.** *conj* AS SOON AS as soon as somebody does something or something happens ○ *Call me when you get home.* **3.** *conj* AT SOME POINT at some point during an activity, event, or circumstance ○ *We got him when he was still a pup.* **4.** *conj* EACH TIME THAT each time that something happens ○ *When I dial, I get a busy signal.* **5.** *conj* IF considering the fact that ○ *Why walk when you can ride?* **6.** *conj* ALTHOUGH in spite of the fact that ○ *They think I'm really easygoing, when in fact I'm not.* **7.** *adv* AT OR DURING WHICH TIME used to indicate a time at or during which something happens ○ *When did it happen?* ○ *Since when has that been a problem?* ○ *He remembered a time when he could run a mile without any difficulty.* **8.** *n* UNSPECIFIED TIME PERIOD used to refer to the time that something happened or will happen (*often used in the plural*) ○ *We're having trouble determining the whens and hows of the thing.* [Old English *hwonne, hwænne* < Indo-European]

USAGE See *if*.

when·as /wen áz, hwen-/ *conj* (*archaic*) **1.** WHENEVER at such time as **2.** WHILE at or during the time that **3.** ALTHOUGH in spite of the fact that

whence /wenss, hwenss/ *adv* **1.** FROM WHERE from what place or source (*archaic or literary*) ○ *Can we know whence comes this good luck?* **2.** FROM WHICH PLACE from the place or thing previously referred to (*archaic or literary*) ○ *that envy whence comes hate* **3.** AS RESULT from which cause or origin (*formal*) ○ *You have treated her badly, whence her anger.* [13C. < *whennes* "of or from when"]

USAGE whence or **from whence** Though the expression ***from whence*** is regarded by some critics as redundant because ***whence*** by itself means "from where," it has occurred over the centuries many times, most notably in the Bible. Nonetheless, it is best, if one wants to avoid possible criticism, to avoid use of the *from*.

whence·so·ev·er /wènssō évvər, hwènssō-/ *adv, conj* from whatever cause, origin, or source (*archaic*) ○ *accept the gifts whencesoever they come*

when·e'er /wen ér, hwen-/ *adv, conj* same as **whenever** (*literary*)

when·ev·er /wen évvər, hwen-/ *conj* **1.** NO MATTER WHEN at whatever time that ○ *Whenever you need me I'll be there.* **2.** EACH TIME THAT each and every time that ○ *Whenever you're around, the dog growls.* ■ *adv* WHEN INDEED used as an emphatic form of "when" (*informal*) ○ *Whenever will you learn?*

when·so·ev·er /wènssō évvər, hwèn-/ *adv, conj* used as an intensive form of "whenever"

where /wer, hwer/ CORE MEANING: an adverb used to ask a question about the place that somebody or something is in, at, coming from, or going to ○ *Where are my keys?* ○ *Where are you going?* ○ *"Guess where I've been." – "Where?"*

1. *adv* IN OR TO PLACE used to indicate the place in which something is located or happens ○ *I want to live where it's warm.* ○ *Nobody really knew where she had gone.* ○ *They went to the beach, where they spent the afternoon.* **2.** *adv* WHAT PURPOSE used to ask a question about the purpose or goal of something ○ *Where will all your hard work get you?* ○ *Where do you want to be after five years in this job?* **3.** *adv* IN SITUATION IN WHICH in a or any situation in which ○ *Where there's life, there's hope.* ○ *They're at a stage where they can now talk about their problems.* **4.** *n* UNKNOWN PLACE used to refer to an unspecified place or event (*usually used in the plural*) ○ *Let us know the wheres and whens of your itinerary.* [Old English *hwær, hwar* < Indo-European]

SPELLCHECK See *ware*1.

USAGE It is best to avoid usages in which ***where*** follows nouns that are unrelated to the ideas of place and space: *This is a case where we must confer with a specialist. This is a situation where the accountants are wrong.* In formal writing, *in which* would be more appropriate than ***where*** in both these sentences. The preposition *from* is needed with ***where*** when the context involves a point of origin: *Where did that cat come from? From where we sit, we can see the stage clearly.* In formal writing, the redundant, dangling use of *at* with ***where*** should also be avoided. Thus: *He doesn't know where the car is* not *He doesn't know where the car is at.* The preposition *to* is superfluous with ***where*** when ***where*** is used in contexts involving destination. Thus: *Where are you going?* not *Where are you going to?*

where·a·bouts /wér ə bòwts, hwér-/ *adv* in, at, or near what location ○ *Do you know whereabouts the hotel is?* ○ *I've forgotten whereabouts I parked the car.* ■ *n* the approximate place where somebody or something is (*takes a singular or plural verb*) ○ *Could you give us any information regarding the whereabouts of your brother?*

where·af·ter /wer áftər, hwer-/ *adv* after which time or event (*formal*) ○ *She left, whereafter he also departed.*

where·as /wer áz, hwer-/ *conj* **1.** WHILE IN CONTRAST while on the other hand ○ *She was saving money, whereas you were living in the fast lane.* **2.** BECAUSE for the reason that (*formal*) ○ *Whereas you've proven your worth, you're welcome to join the team.* **3.** CONNECTS SERIES OF CLAUSES used to introduce each clause in a series (*formal*)

where·at /wer át, hwer-/ (*archaic*) *adv* toward or at which place ■ *conj* because or as a consequence of which

where·by /wer bī́, hwer-/ *adv* by means of or through which ○ *the invention whereby he made his millions*

where'er /wer er, hwer-/ *adv* same as **wherever** (*literary*)

~~whereever~~ incorrect spelling of **wherever**

where·fore /wer fàwr, hwer-/ *n* REASON a reason or purpose for something ○ *I don't want to know the whys or the wherefores of your decision.* ■ *adv* **1.** BECAUSE OF WHICH for which reason **2.** FOR WHAT REASON for what reason or purpose (*archaic*)

where·from /wer fróm, hwer-/ *adv* from what place or origin (*archaic*) ○ *Do we know wherefrom this stranger comes?*

where·in /wer ín, hwer-/ *adv* **1.** HOW in what way or respect ○ *Wherein did I misspeak myself?* **2.** WHERE in which place (*archaic*) ○ *the country wherein they dwelled* **3.** DURING WHICH during the time that (*archaic*) ○ *the years wherein we were ignorant and happy*

where·in·to /wer íntoo, hwer-/ *adv* into which place or thing (*archaic*)

where·of /wer óv, hwer-/ *adv* of or about what person or thing ○ *Do you know whereof you speak?*

where·on /wer ón, hwer-/ on which thing or place (*archaic or formal*) ○ *the couch whereon she lay*

where·so·ev·er /wèrssō évvər, hwèr-/ *adv, conj* used as an emphatic form of "wherever"

where·to /wer to͝o, hwer-/, **where·un·to** /-úntoo/ *adv* where or to which ○ *the place whereto you've brought me*

where·up·on /wérə pòn, hwérə-/ *conj* at which time or as a result of ○ *The rain began to come down hard, whereupon we ran for the house.* ■ on or upon which (*archaic or formal*) ○ *the pillow whereupon she laid her head*

wher·ev·er /wer évvər, hwer-/ *conj* **1.** TO ANY PLACE in, at, or to any place ○ *I'll go wherever you go.* **2.** EVERY TIME OR PLACE THAT on every occasion or in every place that ○ *Take exercise wherever possible.* ○ *I crossed the fields wherever there was a gate.* ■ *adv* **1.** NO MATTER WHERE at or in an indefinite place ○ *I'll sleep on the couch, the floor, wherever.* **2.** AT UNKNOWN PLACE to, in, or at an unknown or unidentified place or position **3.** *also* **where ev·er** WHERE INDEED used as an emphatic form of "where" ○ *Wherever have my glasses gone?*

where·with /wer wíth, hwer-/ *adv* with or by means of which (*archaic*) ○ *the tool wherewith the deed was done*

where·with·al /wérwith àwl, hwér-/ *n* the money or resources required for a purpose

wher·ry /wérree, hwérree/ (*plural* **-ries**) *n* **1.** a small light rowboat used in inland waters **2.** a small barge, once used for commercial purposes in parts of England, now used largely for pleasure cruises [15C. Origin ?] —**wher·ry·man** *n*

whet /wet, hwet/ *vt* (**whet·ted, whet·ting, whets**) **1.** STIMULATE SOMETHING to make a feeling, sense, or desire more keen or intense ○ *The thought of easy money whetted my enthusiasm for the undertaking.* **2.** SHARPEN TOOL OR WEAPON to sharpen the cutting edge or blade of a tool or weapon, usually by rubbing it on a stone ■ *n* **1.** SHARPENING OR INTENSIFYING OF SOMETHING an act of sharpening, intensifying, or stimulating something **2.** SHARPENING BLOCK something that sharpens a cutting edge **3.** SOMETHING THAT STIMULATES SENSES something that stimulates a feeling, sense, or desire, especially a small amount that makes somebody want more (*informal*) [Old English *hwettan* "sharpen" < Germanic, "sharp"] —**whet·ter** *n*

SPELLCHECK See ***wet***.

wheth·er /wéthər, hwéthər/ *conj* **1.** INTRODUCES ALTERNATIVES used to indicate alternatives in an indirect question or a clause following a verb that expresses or implies doubt or the possibility of choice ○ *We should try to meet them whether it's raining or not.* **2.** INTRODUCES INDIRECT QUESTION used to introduce an indirect question ○ *I wonder whether it's worth the effort.* **3.** EITHER used to introduce doubt regarding two equal possibilities ○ *She said she'd get here whether by car or by train.* [Old English *hwæþer, hweþer* < Indo-European] ◇ **whether or no** whatever the circumstances might be (*archaic*)

SPELLCHECK See ***weather***.

whet·stone /wét stōn, hwét-/ *n* a stone used to sharpen the cutting edge or blade of a tool or weapon by rubbing

whew /fyoo, hyoo/ *interj* used to express great relief, surprise, or discomfort [15C. Natural exclamation]

whey /way, hway/ *n* the watery liquid that separates from the solid part of milk when it turns sour or when enzymes are added in cheese making [Old English *hwæg, hweg* < Germanic] —**whey·ey** *adj*

SPELLCHECK See ***way***.

whey·face /wáy fàyss, hwáy-/ *n* **1.** a very pale face (*informal*) **2.** somebody whose face is regarded as too pale (*insult*) —**whey·faced** *adj*

whf. *abbr* wharf

which /wich, hwich/ CORE MEANING: used to ask for something to be identified from a known larger group or range of possibilities ○ (adj) *Which part of it don't you understand?* ○ (pron) *Which would you like?* ○ (pron) *Which of the colors do you prefer?* ○ (adj) *At which stage do we start to cut our losses?*

1. *def art, pron* ASKS QUESTION asks for something to be identified from a known group or range ○ *Which hat should I wear?* **2.** *adj, pron* ONE FROM KNOWN SET one of a range of things or possibilities specified or implied by the immediate context ○ (adj) *I can't decide which activity would be the most fun.* ○ (pron) *He decided which to buy and paid the money.* **3.** *adj, pron* same as **whichever** ○ (adj) *Use which method best suits you.* ○ (pron) *Take which you prefer.* **4.** *pron* INTRODUCES RELATIVE CLAUSE used to introduce a clause that provides additional information about something previously mentioned ○ *The cabin, which we bought last spring, sits high on the dunes.* ○ *A success for which she is to be congratulated.* **5.** *pron*

THAT used to introduce a relative clause that provides necessary information about its antecedent ○ *Please return the money which I loaned to you.* **6.** *pron* **REFERS BACK TO PHRASE OR SENTENCE** used to refer back to an entire verb phrase or sentence ○ *Swimming after eating, which I've told you not to do, can be very dangerous.* [Old English *hwilc* "of what form, like what" < Germanic]

SPELLCHECK which or **witch**? Do not confuse the spelling of ***which*** and ***witch***, which sound similar. The word ***which*** is used to ask about or identify one or more of a larger group (as in *decide which car to use, Which are your children?*) or to introduce additional information: *The house, which was built in the 18th century, is now in ruins.* A ***witch*** is a person, especially a woman, with supposed magical powers.

USAGE See ***that***.

which·ev·er /wich évvər, hwich-/ *adj, pron* used to refer to any one or any number of items in a class ○ (adj) *Whichever job you take, starting out will be hard.* ○ (pron) *I'll buy whichever you think best.*

which·so·ev·er /wìchsō évvər, hwìchsō-/ *pron, adj* same as **whichever** (*archaic*)

whick·er /wíkər, hwíkər/ (**-ered, -er·ing, -ers**) *vi* to neigh softly [Mid-17C. An imitation of the sound] —**whick·er** *n*

whid·ah *n* BIRDS another spelling of **whydah**

whiff /wif, hwif/ *n* **1. SLIGHT OR BRIEF ODOR** a faint smell of something, pleasant or unpleasant, usually perceived briefly ○ *a whiff of disinfectant* **2. TRACE OF SOMETHING** a slight sign or trace of something ○ *a whiff of corruption* **3. GENTLE GUST OR PUFF** a short light gust, puff, or breath of wind or smoke **4. SNIFF OF SOMETHING** a sniff, smell, or brief inhalation of something ○ *took one whiff of the concoction and started coughing* **5.** *UK* NAUT **SMALL SKIFF** a narrow skiff for one rower **6.** *US* BASEBALL **STRIKE-OUT** in baseball, an instance of swinging at and missing the third strike in a turn at bat **7.** GOLF **COMPLETE MISS** in golf, a swing that completely misses the ball ■ *v* (**whiffed, whiff·ing, whiffs**) **1.** *vti* **WAFT OR PUFF** to come in short light gusts or puffs, or send something out in short light gusts or puffs ○ *The smoke whiffed and curled around the room.* **2.** *vt* **SNIFF SOMETHING** to sniff, smell, or inhale something ○ *The hyena whiffed the night air for predators.* **3.** *vti US* BASEBALL **STRIKE OUT** in baseball, to strike out a batter, or strike out ○ *That pitcher whiffed all the batters this inning.* **4.** *vi* GOLF **FAIL TO HIT BALL** in golf, to swing at and miss a ball completely [Late 16C. Thought to suggest a light puff of wind that carries a smell] —**whiff·er** *n*

whif·fle /wíff'l, hwíff'l/ (**-fled, -fling, -fles**) *v* **1.** *vi* **BEHAVE ERRATICALLY** to be indecisive or unpredictable in thought or action **2.** *vti* **BLOW GENTLY** to blow or move in short light variable gusts or puffs, or make something do this **3.** *vi* **WHISTLE** to whistle softly [Late 17C. < WHIFF] —**whif·fler** *n*

whif·fle·tree /wíff'l trèe, hwíff'l-/ *n* a horizontal crossbar used to attach the harness traces of a draft animal, that is then attached to a vehicle or device [Mid-19C. Variant of WHIPPLETREE]

Whig /wig, hwig/ *n* **1.** *US* **SUPPORTER OF REVOLUTION AGAINST BRITISH** a supporter of the American side against the British in the American Revolution **2.** *US* **MEMBER OF 19C US POLITICAL PARTY** a member of a 19th-century US political party that favored a loose interpretation of the Constitution and opposed the Democratic Party **3.** *UK* **MEMBER OF FORMER BRITISH POLITICAL PARTY** a member of a reforming British political party that supported the aristocracy and later the business community, finally becoming the core of the Liberal Party **4.** *UK* **CONSERVATIVE IN BRITISH LIBERAL PARTY** a conservative member of the Liberal Party in the United Kingdom **5.** *UK* **SUPPORTER OF FREE ENTERPRISE** an opponent of government intervention in commerce and the economy **6.** *Scotland* **SCOTTISH PRESBYTERIAN** a 17th-century Presbyterian in Scotland [Mid-17C. Shortening of obsolete Scots dialect *whiggamaire* "horse driver"] —**Whig·ger·y** *n* —**Whig·gish** *adj* —**Whig·gish·ly** *adv* —**Whig·gish·ness** *n* —**Whig·gism** *n*

ORIGIN The Scots word ***Whig*** seems originally to have been used as a contemptuous term for a country dweller, but by the middle of the 17th century it was being applied to Presbyterian supporters in Scotland. It was later adopted as a name for those who opposed the succession of the Catholic King James II of England, and by 1689 it had established itself as the title of one of the two main British political parties, opposed to the Tories.

while /wīl, hwīl/ *conj* **1. AT OR DURING SAME TIME** at or during the same time that ○ *We can talk while I fix supper.* **2. EVEN THOUGH** in spite of the fact that ○ *While I admire your tenacity, I cannot support your aims.* **3. BUT IN CONTRAST** but on the contrary ○ *An older car would be cheaper to buy while a newer one might be more reliable.* ■ *n* **PERIOD OF TIME** a period of time or an interval ○ *It's been a while since I saw her.* [Old English *hwīl* "period of time" < Indo-European, "rest, period of rest"] ◇ **once in a while** very occasionally ◇ **worth somebody's while 1.** deserving somebody's time, money, or support **2.** rewarding in terms of money or advantage

SPELLCHECK while or **wile**? Do not confuse the spelling of ***while*** and ***wile***, which sound similar. ***While*** indicates a time or an additional consideration: *took it while I was not looking, While I applaud the motive, the result might be disastrous.* ***Wile***, or more often the plural ***wiles***, refers to cunning behavior.

while away (**whiled away, whiling away, whiles away**) *vt* to pass time in an idle, leisurely, and usually pleasant way

whiles /wīlz, hwīlz/ *conj* same as **while** (*archaic*)

whi·lom /wīləm, hwīləm/ (*archaic*) *adv* same as **formerly** ■ *adj* same as **former**[1] *adj* (sense 1) ○ *his whilom friend* [Old English *hwīlom*, form of *hwīl* (see WHILE)]

whim /wim, hwim/ *n* **1.** a sudden thought, idea, or desire, especially one based on impulse rather than reason or necessity **2.** a winch used to lift ore or water from a mine, drawn by a horse [Mid-17C. Origin ?]

whim·brel /wímbrəl, hwímbrəl/ (*plural same* or **-brels**) *n* a large shorebird with a long downward-curving beak, related to the curlew. Latin name: *Numenius phaeopus*. [Mid-16C. < obsolete dialect *whimp* "whimper" (with reference to the bird's cry), or < WHIMPER]

~~**whimp**~~ incorrect spelling of **wimp**

whim·per /wímpər, hwím-/ *v* (**-pered, -per·ing, -pers**) **1.** *vi* **SOB SOFTLY** to make repeated weak plaintive crying or whining sounds of pain, distress, or fear **2.** *vt* **SAY SOMETHING PLAINTIVELY** to say something in a plaintive crying or whining voice **3.** *vi* **COMPLAIN PEEVISHLY** to complain in a weak, whining, or irritated manner ■ *n* **1. WHINE** a weak plaintive cry or whine **2. COMPLAINT** a weak, whining, or irritated complaint [Early 16C. < *whimp* "whimper," an imitation of the sound] —**whim·per·ing·ly** *adv*

whim·sey another spelling of **whimsy**

whim·si·cal /wímzik'l, hwím-/ *adj* **1. FANCIFUL** imaginative and impulsive **2. AMUSING** slightly odd or playfully humorous, especially in an endearing way ○ *He gave me that whimsical smile of his.* **3. ERRATIC OR UNPREDICTABLE** behaving in a way that is impossible to predict ○ *She distrusted his whimsical nature.* [Mid-17C. < WHIMSY] —**whim·si·cal·i·ty** /wìmzi kálləteе, hwìm-/ *n* —**whim·si·cal·ly** *adv* —**whim·si·cal·ness** *n*

whim·sy /wímzee, hwímzee/ (*plural* **-sies**), **whim·sey** (*plural* **-seys**) *n* **1.** the quality of being slightly odd or playfully humorous, especially in an endearing way ○ *There's a touch of whimsy about the old cottage.* **2.** an idea that has no immediately obvious reason to exist ○ *We can't always be catering to their whimsies.* [Early 17C. Probably based on WHIM-WHAM, perhaps after words like *dropsy*]

whim-wham *n* a quaint, odd, or fanciful object, e.g., an ornament, toy, or device (*archaic*) ○ *some whim-wham he bought somewhere* [Origin ?]

whin[1] /win, hwin/ (*plural same* or **whins**) *n* PLANTS same as **gorse** [15C. Probably < a N Germanic word related to Old Danish *hvinegræs* "rough grass"]

whin[2] /win, hwin/ *n* MINERALS same as **whinstone** [13C. Origin ?]

whin·chat /wín chàt, hwín-/ (*plural same* or **-chats**) *n* a small songbird of the thrush family with mottled brown and white feathers and a streaky reddish brown breast. Native to: Asia, Europe. Latin name: *Saxicola rubetra*. [Late 17C. < WHIN[2] + CHAT "warbler"]

whine /wīn, hwīn/ *v* (**whined, whin·ing, whines**) **1.** *vi* **COMPLAIN PEEVISHLY** to complain in an unreasonable, repeated, or irritating way **2.** *vi* **MAKE HIGH SORROWFUL SOUND** to cry, moan, or plead with a long, plaintive, high-pitched sound **3.** *vt* **UTTER SOMETHING IN WHINING VOICE** to say something in a plaintive high-pitched voice **4.** *vi* **MAKE HIGH-PITCHED SOUND** to make a continuous high-pitched sound ○ *The wind whined and moaned through the trees.* ■ *n* **1. HIGH-PITCHED CRY** a long, plaintive, high-pitched cry **2. PEEVISH COMPLAINT** a complaint or protest, especially one made repeatedly in an annoyingly plaintive voice **3. CONTINUOUS HIGH-PITCHED SOUND** a long or continuous high-pitched sound ○ *The whine of the jet engines woke me up.* [Old English *hwīnan* "(of an arrow) to whistle through the air," of imitative origin] —**whin·er** *n* —**whin·ing·ly** *adv* —**whin·y** *adj*

SPELLCHECK whine or **wine**? Do not confuse the spelling of ***whine*** and ***wine***, which sound similar. ***Whine*** is a noun and verb referring to a long plaintive high-pitched sound or a peevish complaint, as in *the whine of the engines, customers whining about poor service.* ***Wine*** is a noun denoting an alcoholic drink made from grapes or other fruit; it is occasionally used as a verb in the phrase *wine and dine.*

SYNONYMS See ***complain***.

whinge /winj, hwinj/ (**whinged, whinge·ing, whing·es**) *vi UK* to complain annoyingly or continuously about something relatively unimportant (*informal*) [Old English *hwinsian* "whine," an imitation of the sound of a whining dog] —**whing·er** *n* —**whin·gy** *adj*

whin·ny /wínnee, hwínnee/ *v* (**-nied, -ny·ing, -nies**) **1.** *vi* **NEIGH** to neigh softly **2.** *vi* **MAKE SOUND LIKE NEIGHING HORSE** to make a neighing sound, especially when laughing **3.** *vt* **UTTER SOMETHING WITH NEIGHING SOUND** to say or express something with a sound like a neighing horse ■ *n* (*plural* **-nies**) **NEIGHING SOUND** a soft neigh, or a sound like a neighing horse [Mid-16C. An imitation of the sound]

whin·stone /wín stōn, hwín-/ *n* a hard, dark, fine-grained rock, e.g., basalt or chert [Early 16C. < WHIN[2]]

whip /wip, hwip/ *v* (**whipped, whip·ping, whips**) **1.** *vt* **LASH SOMEBODY OR SOMETHING** to strike a person or animal repeatedly with a flexible rod, length of rope, thin strip of leather attached to a handle, or something similar, especially as a punishment **2.** *vti* **STRIKE AGAINST SOMETHING SHARPLY** to strike somebody or something very hard, sharply, or repeatedly ○ *The icy rain whipped our faces.* **3.** *vt* **CRITICIZE SOMEBODY SEVERELY** to criticize or reproach somebody very strongly or severely **4.** *vti* **MOVE RAPIDLY** to move very quickly, forcefully, or suddenly, or make something do this ○ *She whipped around guiltily as I came in.* **5.** *vt* **DO SOMETHING WITH RAPID ACTION** to do something very quickly, suddenly, or forcefully ○ *She whipped out her camera and took a photo.* **6.** *vt* **BIND END OF ROPE** to wind thread, cord, or twine around the end of a rope or cable to keep it from fraying **7.** *vt* **DEFEAT SOMEBODY** to defeat, overcome, or outdo somebody (*informal*) **8.** *vt* COOK **BEAT LIQUID UNTIL STIFF** to make food such as batter or cream stiff and creamy by adding air to it with short quick movements, using a fork, whisk, or electric beater **9.** *vt* NAUT **LIFT SOMETHING BY ROPE AND PULLEY** to lift something by means of a device consisting of a rope passed through a single pulley **10.** *vt* HANDICRAFT **SEW SOMETHING IN WHIPSTITCH** to sew the edge of a piece of fabric using whipstitch ■ *n* **1. INSTRUMENT FOR INFLICTING PAIN** a flexible rod, length of rope, or thin strip of leather attached to a handle, used to strike people or animals repeatedly **2. LASHING STROKE OR BLOW** a stroke or blow with a whip or something similar ○ *a whip across the face* **3. SOMETHING RESEMBLING WHIP** something that resembles a whip in form, motion, or flexibility **4. SOMEBODY WHO USES WHIP** somebody who is experienced or skilled in using a whip, e.g., the driver of a horse-drawn carriage **5.** POL **SOMEBODY IN CHARGE OF PARTY DISCIPLINE** an elected representative in a legislative body such as Congress or the UK Parliament who has special responsibility for ensuring discipline and attendance among his or her party's representatives **6.** POL **CALL FOR PARTY SOLIDARITY** a call issued to a political party's elected legislators to ensure they attend for an important vote and vote the party line **7.** FOOD **SWEET DISH** a light creamy dessert made from whipped cream with added sweetening and flavoring **8.** HOUSEHOLD same as **whisk** *n* (sense 1) **9.** NAUT **HOISTING**

APPARATUS a device that consists of a rope, a pulley, and a snatch block. Use: raising heavy cargo. **10.** MUSIC FLEXIBLE PERCUSSION INSTRUMENT a percussion instrument with two flexible strips of wood attached in the shape of a V that make a loud clapping sound when they are waved in the air **11.** INDUST WINDMILL VANE a sail or arm of a windmill **12.** LEISURE FAIRGROUND AMUSEMENT a ride at an amusement park with small cars that travel with sudden rapid jerking movements around a track **13.** WRESTLING WRESTLING THROW in wrestling, a throw in which an opponent is seized by an outstretched arm and thrown to the floor **14.** *US* LONG FLEXIBLE BRANCH a long, slender, flexible branch of some trees such as willows ○ *furniture made of willow whips* [13C. Probably < Middle Low German or Middle Dutch *wippen* "swing," < Germanic, "move quickly"] ◇ **crack the whip** a game in which children join hands in a line and pull each other around sharply **whip in** *vt* to keep the members of a political party in line with the party's aims

whip through *vt* to do something very quickly (*informal*)

whip up *vt* **1.** EXCITE SOMEBODY OR SOMETHING to arouse or provoke a strong feeling or reaction in a group of people **2.** MAKE SOMETHING RISE UP to stir or disturb something with force so that it rises or flies up **3.** PREPARE SOMETHING RAPIDLY to make something quickly, especially an impromptu meal (*informal*)

whip·cord /wíp kàwrd, hwíp-/ *n* **1.** a strong cotton or woolen fabric woven with diagonal ribs **2.** a tough twisted cord used for whips

whip graft *n* a way of grafting two plants by inserting the cut end of a scion into a similar cut in a rootstock and tying them securely together until they join

whip hand *n* **1.** the most powerful or advantageous position in a situation ○ *She has the whip hand.* **2.** the hand that holds a whip, especially when driving horses

whip·lash /wíp làsh, hwíp-/ *n* **1.** MED INJURY TO NECK an injury to the muscles, ligaments, vertebrae, or nerves of the neck caused when the head is suddenly thrown forward and then sharply back **2.** LASHING BLOW a stroke or blow from a whip **3.** LASHING MOVEMENT OR IMPACT something that resembles a stroke or blow from a whip in motion, speed, or force **4.** FLEXIBLE PART OF WHIP the flexible part of a whip

whip·per-in (*plural* **whip·pers-in**) *n US* POL same as **whip** *n* (sense 5)

whip·per·snap·per /wíppər snàppər, hwíppər-/ *n* an impudent and unimportant person, especially somebody who is young (*dated*) [Late 17C. Origin ?]

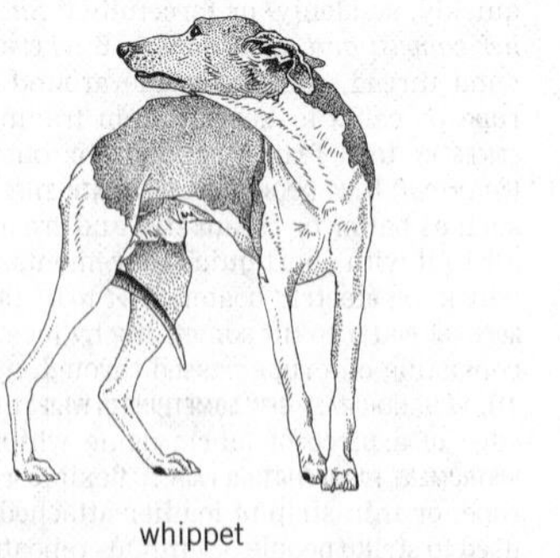

whippet

whip·pet /wíppət, hwíppət/ *n* a fast slender short-haired dog belonging to a breed that resembles, but is smaller than, a greyhound. They are bred in the British Isles for racing. [Mid-16C. < WHIP]

whip·ping /wípping, hwípping/ *n* **1.** PUNISHMENT a beating, spanking, or flogging with a whip or something similar **2.** BINDING CORD thread, cord, or twine wound around the end of a rope or cable to keep it from fraying **3.** DEFEAT a convincing defeat (*informal*) ○ *They really gave us a whipping in that last game.*

whip·ping boy *n* somebody who gets the blame or punishment for the mistakes or wrongdoings of more important people [Originally, this referred to a boy raised and educated with a prince. If the prince misbehaved, the boy would be punished in his place]

whip·ping cream *n* a heavy cream containing a high proportion of butterfat, which causes it to stiffen when whipped

Whip·ple /wípp'l, hwípp'l/, **William** (1730–85) American patriot. Representing New Hampshire, he was a signatory of the Declaration of Independence (1776) and fought in the American Revolution.

whip·ple·tree /wípp'l trèe, hwípp'l-/ *n* AGRIC same as **whiffletree** [Mid-18C. < WHIP]

whip·poor·will /wíppər wìl, hwíppər-/ *n* a common nocturnal bird of the nightjar family, with spotted dark feathers and a distinctive song. Native to: North America. Latin name: *Caprimulgus vociferus.* [An imitation of its call]

whip·saw /wíp sàw, hwíp-/ *n* NARROW CROSSCUT SAW a narrow crosscut saw for use by two people ■ *vt* (**-sawed** or **-sawn** /-sàwn/, **-saw·ing, -saws**) **1.** CUT WITH WHIPSAW to saw something with a whipsaw **2.** MAKE SOMETHING MOVE BACK AND FORTH to cause something to move or alternate back and forth sharply ○ *was whipsawed by criticism from two sides* **3.** *US* DEFEAT IN TWO WAYS SIMULTANEOUSLY to defeat somebody or win in two ways at the same time **4.** *US* WIN TWO BETS AT ONCE to win two bets simultaneously from one person

whip scor·pi·on *n* a terrestrial invertebrate related to the scorpion, but with a whip-shaped appendage at the end of its abdomen. Native to: tropics, subtropics. Order: Uropygi.

whip snake *n* a nonpoisonous snake that can pursue its prey at a fast speed. Native to: North America, Asia, Europe, Africa. Genus: *Coluber.*

whip·stall /wíp stàwl, hwíp-/ *n* a maneuver in a small aircraft in which it goes into a vertical climb, pauses briefly, and then drops toward the earth, nose first

whip·stitch /wíp stich, hwíp-/ *n* a small stitch that passes over the edge of a piece of fabric, used to finish the edge or baste two pieces of fabric together ■ *vt* (**-stitched, -stitch·ing, -stitch·es**) to sew the edge of a piece of fabric using a whipstitch

whip·stock /wíp stòk, hwíp-/ *n* the handle of a whip

whip·tail /wíp tàyl, hwíp-/ *n* a lizard with a long thin tail. Native to: South America, Mexico. Genus: *Cnemidophorus.*

whip·worm /wíp wùrm, hwíp-/ *n* a nematode worm found in human intestines. Its presence usually produces no symptoms, but a severe infection with this parasite can cause diarrhea. Latin name: *Trichuris trichiura.*

whir /wur, hwur/, **whirr** *vti* (**whirred, whir·ring, whirs; whirred, whir·ring, whirrs**) to make a continuous soft buzzing or humming sound, usually by vibrating or turning very quickly, or make something do this ■ *n* a continuous soft buzzing or humming sound like that of something vibrating or turning very quickly [14C. Probably < N Germanic]

whirl /wurl, hwurl/ *v* (**whirled, whirl·ing, whirls**) **1.** *vti* TURN OR SPIN RAPIDLY to turn or spin very quickly, or make something do this **2.** *vti* MOVE WHILE TURNING QUICKLY to move along while turning or spinning very quickly, or make something do this ○ *The dancers whirled around the floor.* **3.** *vi* FEEL DIZZY OR CONFUSED to seem to spin with dizziness, confusion, or excitement ○ *So much information at one time made my head whirl.* **4.** *vti* MOVE VERY FAST to move very quickly on a straight or curved course, or make something do this ○ *Cars whirled past on the highway.* ■ *n* **1.** SPINNING MOTION a rapid turning or spinning movement ○ *The whirl of the top was mesmerizing.* **2.** SOMETHING THAT WHIRLS something that moves or is moved with a rapid circular or spiral motion ○ *Whirls of dust filled the air.* **3.** SENSATION OF SPINNING a spinning sensation caused, e.g., by dizziness, confusion, or excitement ○ *So much good luck had my head in a whirl.* **4.** QUICK SUCCESSION OF EVENTS the bustling activity of an endless series of events or engagements ○ *the whirl and bustle of a large city* **5.** BRIEF TRIP OR RIDE a short trip, ride, or dance (*informal*) ○ *Let's go for a whirl in my new car.* [13C. Probably < Old Norse *hvirfla* < Indo-European, "turn around"] —**whirl·er** *n* —**whirl·y** *adj* ◇ **give something a whirl** to have a try at something (*informal*)

whirl·a·bout /wúrl ə bòwt, hwúrl-/ *n* a turn, spin, or revolution

whirl·i·gig /wúrli gìg, hwúrli-/ *n* **1.** SPINNING TOY a toy that spins or turns very quickly **2.** MERRY-GO-ROUND a merry-go-round or carousel **3.** SOMETHING THAT WHIRLS something that revolves rapidly or changes continuously ○ *Her life's a whirligig since she took over the business.* **4.** INSECTS same as **whirligig beetle** [15C. < *whirling* or *whirly* + *gig* "spinning top"]

whirl·i·gig bee·tle *n* an insect with a smooth oval flattened body, usually seen spinning around in groups on the surface of calm fresh water. Family: Gyrinidae.

whirl·ing der·vish *n* **1.** somebody who busily does many things in quick succession **2.** a member of an ascetic Muslim religious group known for very energetic whirling

whirl·pool /wúrl pòol, hwúrl-/ *n* **1.** SPIRALING CURRENT OF WATER a spiraling current of water in a stream or river **2.** SOMETHING RESEMBLING WHIRLPOOL something that has or seems to have the action, motion, or power of a whirlpool ○ *a whirlpool of despair* **3.** *US* POOL OR TUB WITH WATER JETS a bathtub or pool with underwater jets that keep the water constantly moving or swirling

whirl·pool bath *n UK* same as **whirlpool** (sense 3)

whirl·wind /wúrl wìnd, hwúrl-/ *n* **1.** SOMETHING HAPPENING OR CHANGING SWIFTLY something that happens very quickly, or a rapid succession of events (*often used before a noun*) ○ *a whirlwind romance* ○ *a whirlwind visit* **2.** SOMETHING VERY DESTRUCTIVE something that has a terrible destructive force ○ *swept up in the whirlwind of war* **3.** METEOROL SPINNING COLUMN OF AIR a column of air rotating rapidly around a core of low pressure [14C. < Old Norse *hvirfilwindr*]

whirl·y·bird /wúrlee bùrd, hwúrlee-/ *n* AVIAT same as **helicopter** (*informal*)

whirr *vti, n* another spelling of **whir**

whish /wish, hwish/ *v* (**whished, whish·ing, whish·es**) **1.** *vi* MAKE OR MOVE WITH RUSHING SOUND to make a soft whistling or rushing sound, or move with such a sound ○ *Water whished along the boat as we rowed upstream.* **2.** *vt* MOVE SOMETHING WITH WHISHING SOUND to make something move with a whishing sound ○ *The dog whished its tail.* ■ *n* WHISHING SOUND OR MOVEMENT a soft whistling or rushing sound, or a movement that makes such a sound ○ *the whish of the windshield wipers* ■ *adv* WITH WHISHING SOUND moving or falling with a whishing sound ○ *Whish, the branch came down.* [Early 16C. An imitation of the sound]

whisht /wisht, hwisht/, **whist** /wist, hwist/, **wheesht** /weesht, hweesht/ *Scotland vti* (**whisht·ed, whisht·ing, whishts; whist·ed, whist·ing, whists; wheesht·ed, wheesht·ing, wheeshts**) to silence somebody or something, or become or remain silent ■ *n* the state or condition of being silent [Mid-16C. An imitation of the sound made by someone calling for silence]

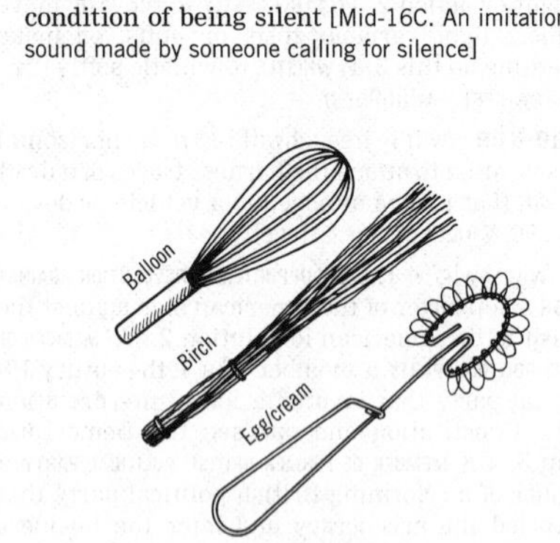

whisk

whisk /wisk, hwisk/ *n* **1.** UTENSIL FOR WHIPPING LIQUIDS a kitchen utensil, formed of curved or coiled wires attached to a handle, or a bundle of twigs, used to whip soft or liquid substances **2.** BRUSHING MOVEMENT a quick light brushing or sweeping movement ○ *He wiped the table with a whisk of his hand.* **3.** BRUSH a bundle of twigs, straw, or grass attached to a handle used to sweep things ■ *v* (**whisked, whisk·ing, whisks**) **1.** *vt* WHIP LIQUID WITH WHISK to whip a soft or liquid substance with a fork, whisk, or other utensil **2.** *vt* BRUSH SOMETHING AWAY LIGHTLY to remove something with a quick light brushing or sweeping movement ○ *He whisked the crumbs from the table.* **3.** *vt* MOVE SOMETHING

WITH SWEEPING MOTION to move something or put something somewhere with a quick light sweeping motion **4.** *vti* MOVE QUICKLY to move somewhere quickly or suddenly, or make somebody or something do this ○ *They whisked her off to the hospital.* [14C. < N Germanic]

whisk·broom /wísk bro͝om, hwísk-/ *n US* a small short-handled broom with stiff bristles, used to clean small areas

whisk·er /wískər, hwískər/ *n* **1.** HAIR ON SOMEBODY'S FACE a short stiff hair growing on somebody's face, especially on the cheeks, chin, or upper lip **2.** HAIR NEAR ANIMAL'S MOUTH a long stiff hair growing near the mouth of some mammals such as cats, mice, and rabbits **3.** SMALL MARGIN a very small amount or margin ○ *We came within a whisker of losing everything.* **4.** *also* **whisk·er boom** NAUT LIGHT POLE a light pole used for extending the corners of a sail **5.** CHEM THIN CRYSTAL a strong thin hair-shaped crystal of a metal or mineral ■ **whisk·ers** *npl* SOMEBODY'S FACIAL HAIR a short growth of hair growing on somebody's cheeks, chin, or upper lip [15C. < WHISK] —**whisk·ered** *adj* —**whisk·er·y** *adj*

whis·key /wískee, hwískee/ (*plural* **-keys**), **whis·ky** (*plural* **-kies**) *n* **1.** an alcoholic beverage made from a fermented grain such as rye or barley and sometimes aged or blended **2.** a drink or measure of whiskey [Early 18C. < Scottish Gaelic *usquebea, usque beatha* "water of life" < *usque* "water" and *bethu* "life"]

USAGE whiskey or **whisky**? ***Whisky*** is the spelling used for the Scottish drink and in British English generally; ***whiskey*** is used for the drink produced in Ireland and in American English generally.

Whis·key *n* a code word for the letter "W," used in international radio communications

whis·key jack *n* BIRDS same as **gray jay** [< *whiskey john*, by folk etymology < Cree *wiskatjan*]

whisk fern *n* a simple plant with slender branching stems and tiny scale-shaped leaves that reproduces by means of spores. Native to: tropical and subtropical regions. Latin name: *Psilotum nudum.*

whis·ky *n* BEVERAGES another spelling of **whiskey**

USAGE See ***whiskey.***

whis·per /wíspər, hwís-/ *v* (**-pered, -per·ing, -pers**) **1.** *vti* BREATHE WORDS VOICELESSLY to speak or say something very softly, without using the vocal cords **2.** *vti* SPEAK OR SUGGEST SOMETHING SECRETLY to speak or say something in a confidential or furtive manner, e.g., in order to reveal a secret or conspire with somebody ○ *Whisper so that no one else hears.* **3.** *vi* RUSTLE SOFTLY to make a soft rustling sound ■ *n* **1.** VERY LOW VOICE a soft speaking sound that uses the breath but not the vocal cords ○ *She spoke in a whisper.* **2.** SOMETHING SAID IN SOFT VOICE something said in a whisper **3.** RUMOR a rumor expressed confidentially or furtively ○ *There have been whispers of a romance.* **4.** RUSTLING SOUND a soft rustling sound **5.** FAINT HINT a hint or trace of something ○ *a whisper of interest* [Old English *hwisprian* < Germanic] —**whis·per·er** *n*

whis·per·ing cam·paign /wíspəring-, hwís-/ *n* a concerted effort to spread scandalous rumors in order to damage or destroy the reputation of a person or group

whis·per·ing gal·ler·y *n* a space or gallery beneath a dome or vault with acoustic properties that enable a faint sound made at one point to travel around the entire circumference and be audible at any point on it

whis·per mi·cro·phone *n* a small highly sensitive microphone with headphones, used especially by military or security personnel

whist /wist, hwist/ *n* a card game in which two pairs of people try to take a majority of the tricks and the trump suit is determined by the last card dealt. Whist is a forerunner of bridge. [Mid-17C. Origin ?]

whis·tle /wíss'l, hwíss'l/ *v* (**-tled, -tling, -tles**) **1.** *vi* MAKE SHRILL SOUND THROUGH PURSED LIPS to make a shrill or musical sound by forcing the breath through a small gap between the lips or the teeth **2.** *vi* PRODUCE SHRILL SOUND to produce a shrill sound or signal by forcing steam or air through a narrow opening (*refers to trains, kettles, etc.*) ○ *heard the train whistle as it came around the bend* **3.** *vi* EMIT SHRILL CALL to make a shrill call or cry (*refers to birds and animals*) **4.** *vi* MOVE WITH SHRILL SOUND to move at great speed through the air, making a shrill sound ○ *traffic whistling by* **5.** *vi* PRODUCE SOUND WHEN WIND RUSHES BY to make a sound, especially a high-pitched one, when moving through a narrow opening ○ *wind whistling through the rafters* **6.** *vt* MAKE MUSICAL SOUND BY WHISTLING to produce music or give a signal by whistling ○ *whistling a tune* **7.** *vti* ISSUE CALL OR ORDER BY WHISTLING to summon, order, or signal to a person or animal by whistling ■ *n* **1.** DEVICE PRODUCING SHRILL SOUND a device or instrument that produces a shrill or musical sound when air or breath is forced through it **2.** WHISTLING SOUND a sound or signal made by a person, animal, or object whistling ○ *He let out a low whistle.* **3.** ACT OF WHISTLING an act of whistling [Old English *hwistlian* < Germanic, "whistle, hiss"] —**whis·tling** *adj* ◇ **blow the whistle (on somebody** *or* **something)** to report somebody for doing something wrong or illegal, or reveal something wrong or illegal that is being done, especially within an organization (*informal*) ◇ **wet your whistle** to have a drink, especially of alcohol (*informal*)

whis·tle-blow·er *n* somebody who exposes wrongdoing, especially within an organization (*informal*) [< the idea of a police officer sounding the alarm when witnessing a crime] —**whis·tle-blow·ing** *n*

whis·tle pig *n regional* same as **woodchuck** [< the chirping sound it makes when threatened]

whis·tler /wísslər, hwísslər/ *n* **1.** WHISTLING PERSON OR OBJECT somebody or something that whistles **2.** MEDIA RADIO DISTURBANCE an interference signal in a radio receiver, resembling a whistling sound of decreasing pitch and caused by lightning or other electromagnetic disturbance **3.** BIRDS WHISTLING SONGBIRD an often brightly colored songbird with a particularly melodious whistling call. Native to: Indonesia, New Guinea, Australia, western Pacific. Family: Pachycephalidae. **4.** VET HORSE WITH RESPIRATORY PROBLEM a horse with a respiratory condition that causes it to make a whistling noise when it breathes in

AKG London

James Abbott McNeill Whistler

Whis·tler /wísslər, hwíss-/, **James McNeill** (1834–1903) US artist. Influenced by both European and Japanese art, he was renowned for his etchings, subtle landscapes, and portraits such as the one popularly known as *Whistler's Mother* (1871). Full name **Whistler, James Abbott McNeill**

> "As music is the poetry of sound so painting is the poetry of sight, and the subject matter has nothing to do with harmony of sound or color."
> [James McNeill Whistler, *The Gentle Art of Making Enemies*; 1890]

whis·tle stop *n* **1.** SMALL RAILROAD STATION a town or railroad station where trains stop only when signaled to do so **2.** SMALL TOWN a small town or community (*slang*) **3.** SHORT CAMPAIGN STOP a brief stop by a political candidate in a small town during an election campaign

whis·tle-stop *adj* conducted very rapidly with frequent brief stops in order to make public appearances or deliver election speeches ○ *a whistle-stop tour of the state* ■ *vi* to make a series of brief stops in small towns as part of a political campaign

whis·tling duck /wíssling-, hwíss-/ *n* a long-legged duck with an upright stance and often a whistling call. Native to: tropical wetlands. Genus: *Dendrocygna.*

whit /wit, hwit/ *n* the smallest imaginable degree or amount ○ *I don't care a whit whether they succeed or fail.* [15C. Alteration of WIGHT]

white /wīt, hwīt/ *adj* (**whit·er, whit·est**) **1.** SNOW-COLORED having the color of fresh snow or milk, as a result of the reflection of nearly all light from visible wavelengths **2.** WITHOUT COLOR lacking color or hue **3.** *also* **White** PALE-SKINNED relating to or belonging to a people with naturally pale skin, especially one of European ancestry **4.** COMPARATIVELY LIGHT light in color in comparison with others of the same kind ○ *white cabbage* **5.** WINE MADE FROM WHITE GRAPES describes wine made from pale-skinned grapes **6.** LACKING PIGMENT describes hair that has lost most or all of its pigment, usually as a result of aging **7.** HAVING VERY PALE COMPLEXION unusually pale in the face, e.g., from fright or shock **8.** ZOOL, BOT HAVING WHITE PARTS OR COLORINGS describes plants or animals with light or white parts or colorings ○ *white bass* **9.** FOOD INDUST WITHOUT BRAN OR GERM describes wheat flour that has had the bran and germ removed **10.** COOK MADE FROM WHITE FLOUR made using white flour **11.** BEVERAGES SERVED WITH MILK served with milk added ○ *white coffee* **12.** UNMARKED BY WRITING not written on or printed on **13.** PURE unblemished, especially in character **14.** WEARING WHITE dressed in white, or characterized by the wearing of white **15.** INCANDESCENT heated to such a high degree that the substance turns white in color **16.** HAVING SNOW accompanied or characterized by the presence of snow **17.** MUSIC LACKING TONAL WARMTH relating to a pure musical tone that lacks warmth, color, and resonance **18.** *also* **White** HIST, POL POLITICALLY CONSERVATIVE conservative in political outlook ■ *n* **1.** COLORS COLOR OF SNOW the color of fresh snow or milk **2.** ART WHITE PAINT a paint or dye that is or is near to the color of fresh snow **3.** WHITE FABRIC OR AREA a white substance or fabric, or the part of something that is white, e.g., an unprinted area on a page **4.** WHITE THING a white object **5.** *also* **White** PALE-SKINNED PERSON a member of a people with pale skin, especially one of European ancestry **6.** FOOD PART OF EGG the transparent liquid that surrounds the yolk of an egg and turns white when the egg is cooked **7.** ANAT PART OF EYE the part of the eyeball surrounding the iris **8.** BOARD GAMES GAME PIECE OR PLAYER a white or light-colored piece or set of pieces in a game such as chess or checkers, or the player using them **9.** INSECTS BUTTERFLY a butterfly that is predominantly white in color. Family: Pieridae. **10.** ARCHERY PART OF TARGET the white outermost ring of an archery target, or a shot that lands in it ■ *npl* **1.** WHITE LAUNDRY white or light-colored laundry, usually washed separately from colored laundry items **2.** SPORTS CLOTHES white or off-white sports clothing, especially as worn by tennis players **3.** WHITE DRESS MILITARY UNIFORM the white dress uniform of a military service, e.g., that of the US Navy or Coast Guard **4.** MED same as **leukorrhea** (*informal*) **5.** WHITE-COLORED PRODUCTS products that are white in color, e.g., flour, sugar, or salt ■ *v* (**whit·ed, whit·ing, whites**) **1.** *vt* LEAVE BLANK SPACES IN SOMETHING to put or leave blank spaces in something, especially something printed **2.** *vti* WHITEN to become white, or cause something to become white (*archaic*) [Old English *hwīt* < Indo-European, "shine"] —**white·ness** *n* —**whit·ish** *adj*

white out *v* **1.** *vt* to cover a mistake in written, printed, or typed material using white correction fluid **2.** *vi* to lose visibility in daylight because of snow or fog

White /wīt, hwīt/, **Byron** (1917–2002) associate justice of the US Supreme Court (1962–93). A former professional football player, he was appointed by John F. Kennedy to the US Supreme Court. Full name **White, Byron Raymond**

White, E. B. (1899–1985) US writer and humorist. The author of popular essays, children's fiction, and light verse, he is best known for the children's classic *Charlotte's Web* (1952) and for his revision of a writing guide originally published in 1918, *The Elements of Style* (1959), regarded as a classic to this day. Full name **White, Elwyn Brooks**

> "It is easier for a man to be loyal to his club than to his planet; the bylaws are shorter, and he is personally acquainted with the other members."
> [E. B. White, *One Man's Meat*; 1944]

"Democracy is the recurrent suspicion that more than half of the people are right more than half of the time."
[E. B. White, *The Wild Flag*; 1946]

White, Edward Douglass (1845–1921) chief justice of the US Supreme Court (1910–21)

White, Stanford (1853–1906) US architect. A specialist in adapting older styles, especially Italian Renaissance, he designed Madison Square Garden (1889) and the Washington Arch in Washington Square Park (1895), both in New York. His murder by millionaire Harry Kendall Thaw, with whose wife he was having an affair, was a social cause célèbre.

White, Theodore Harold (1915–86) US political journalist. He is noted for his coverage of presidential election campaigns, most notably John F. Kennedy's, described in *The Making of the President 1960* (1961).

White, William Allen (1868–1944) US writer and newspaper editor. The small-town paper he owned and edited, the *Emporia Gazette*, became known across the United States and enjoyed great political influence. Known as **the Sage of Emporia**

"Reason never has failed men. Only force and oppression have made wrecks of the world."
[William Allen White, *Emporia Gazette*; July 27, 1922]

white ad·mi·ral *n* **1.** a butterfly that has brown wings with white marks. Native to: Europe, Asia. Latin name: *Limenitis camilla.* **2.** a butterfly that has bluish black wings with a large white band on them. Native to: North America. Latin name: *Limenitis arthemis.*

white al·ka·li *n* a whitish deposit of mineral salts that is sometimes seen on the surface of very alkaline soils

white ant *n* INSECTS same as **termite**

white ash *n* **1.** the strong resilient wood of an ash tree whose leaves have a pale silvery underside. Use: oars. **2.** an ash tree that has leaves with a pale silvery underside and yields white ash. Native to: North America. Latin name: *Fraxinus americana.* [< the pale color of the undersides of its leaves]

white ba·con *n regional* same as **fatback**

REGIONAL NOTE See ***fatback***.

white·bait /wīt bàyt, hwīt-/ (*plural same*) *n* a small young fish fried and eaten whole, especially a young herring [Mid-18C. *White* < the silvery color of most of the fish]

white·bark pine /wīt baärk-, hwīt-/ *n* a pine tree with small purplish cones. Native to: northwestern United States. Latin name: *Pinus albicaulis.* [< its whitish gray bark]

white bass /-báss/ *n* an edible silvery freshwater fish of the bass family. Native to: Great Lakes, Mississippi valley. Latin name: *Morone chrysops.*

white bear *n* ZOOL same as **polar bear**

white belt *n* **1.** the belt worn by a beginner in a martial art such as karate or judo **2.** a beginner in a martial art such as karate or judo who wears a white belt

white birch *n* a birch tree with whitish or grayish bark, e.g., the European silver birch or the North American paper birch. Genus: *Betula.*

white blood cell *n* an unpigmented large cell in blood that helps protect the body against infection and also plays a role in inflammation and allergic reactions

white·board /wīt bàwrd, hwīt-/ *n* a board with a white plastic surface that is written on with erasable marker pens, used in teaching and in giving presentations [Mid-20C. < WHITE, after *blackboard*]

white book *n* in some countries, an official government report published in a white binding

white bread *n* bread made from flour that has had the bran and wheat germ removed

white-bread *adj* **1.** relating to, belonging to, or considered characteristic of white middle-class North America (*informal*) **2.** bland, conventional, and unimaginative

white bry·o·ny *n* a climbing plant with lobed leaves and reddish-black berries. Native to: Europe, Asia, North Africa. Genus: *Bryonia.* [< its greenish-white flowers]

white·cap /wīt kàp, hwīt-/ *n* the white crest of a breaking wave

white ce·dar *n* **1.** a light-colored durable wood from either of two coniferous trees. Use: building boats, telephone poles. **2.** a coniferous tree that has leaves resembling scales and yields white cedar. Native to: eastern North America. Latin name: *Chamaecyparis thyoides* or *Thuja occidentalis.* [< the light color of their wood]

white cell *n* PHYSIOL same as **white blood cell**

white chip *n* **1.** a betting chip with the lowest possible value **2.** something of little value

white choc·o·late *n* a cream-colored confection containing the same ingredients as chocolate but lacking cocoa powder

white Christ·mas *n* a Christmas when there is snow, especially on Christmas day

white cloud, **white cloud moun·tain fish** *n* a small brightly colored freshwater fish of the minnow family that is often kept in aquariums. Native to: Asia. Latin name: *Tanichthys albonubes.* [Mid-20C. After *White Cloud*, English name of a mountain northeast of Guangzhou (Canton), China]

white clo·ver *n* a perennial plant grown with grass as pasture for livestock. Flowers: small, white, attractive to honey bees. Native to: Europe, Asia, naturalized in North America. Latin name: *Trifolium repens.*

white coal *n* flowing water considered as a source of hydroelectric power

white·coat /wīt kōt, hwīt-/ *n Can* a young harp seal, before its fine white coat has turned brown

white-col·lar *adj* relating to jobs that are usually salaried and do not involve manual labor [< the white shirts traditionally worn by people in such jobs]

white-col·lar crime *n* theft, fraud, embezzlement, or some other nonviolent lawbreaking act perpetrated by somebody who is a salaried employee or a member of the higher management of a company or an organization

white cor·pus·cle *n* PHYSIOL same as **white blood cell**

white crab *n* MARINE BIOL same as **ghost crab**

white crap·pie *n* an edible silvery fish of the sunfish family. Native to: muddy waters of North America. Latin name: *Pomoxis annularis.*

white-crowned spar·row *n* a sparrow with black-and-white bands on its head. Native to: western and northern North America. Latin name: *Zonotrichia leucophrys.*

white cur·rant *n* **1.** a greenish white berry, usually eaten raw **2.** a variety of the red currant bush that produces white currants. Latin name: *Ribes sativum.*

whit·ed sep·ul·cher /wītəd-, hwītəd-/ *n* a hypocrite, especially somebody who is falsely righteous or pious [< the Bible (Matthew 23:27), which compares such people to whitewashed tombs]

white dwarf *n* a small, dim, extremely dense star that has collapsed on itself and is in the final stages of its evolution [< its color]

white el·e·phant *n* **1.** SOMETHING COSTLY TO MAINTAIN an expensive and often rare or valuable possession whose upkeep is a considerable financial burden **2.** POSSESSION OF QUESTIONABLE VALUE something with a questionable or at least very limited value **3.** CONSPICUOUS FAILED VENTURE a much publicized or eagerly anticipated venture that proves to be a spectacular flop **4.** DISCARDED OBJECT an unwanted object of possible use to somebody else (*hyphenated before a noun*) **5.** ALBINO ELEPHANT a rare albino Indian elephant regarded as sacred in parts of South and Southeast Asia [In sense 1 and related senses < the reputed practice of the King of Siam (Thailand) of giving a white elephant to troublesome courtiers, who would be ruined by the cost of keeping it]

white-eye *n* a small green or greenish brown songbird with a ring of white feathers around the eye. Native to: tropical and subtropical regions. Family: Zosteropidae.

white·face /wīt fàyss, hwīt-/ *n* white makeup for the face, particularly as used by clowns

white-faced *adj* **1.** having an unusually pale face **2.** having white markings on the face, especially as a distinguishing feature between similar species

white feath·er ◇ **show the white feather** to behave in a cowardly way (*dated*)

White·field /wīt fèeld, wīt-, hwīt-, hwīt-/, **George** (1714–70) British-born US evangelist. As leader of the Calvinist Methodists, he ignited the Great Awakening religious revival of the late 1730s.

white fish *n UK* an edible ocean fish with whitish flesh such as the cod, hake, or whiting, as distinct from a flat fish such as the plaice and an oily fish such as the mackerel

white·fish /wīt fìsh, hwīt-/ (*plural* **-fish·es** or *same*) *n* **1.** a freshwater fish with large scales and a small mouth. Native to: North America. Family: Coregonidae. **2.** the pale flesh of a whitefish eaten as food

white flag *n* a white cloth or improvised flag waved as an international sign of truce or surrender

white flight *n* the movement of white people that sometimes occurs from neighborhoods where members of other groups are settling, especially because of racism

white·fly /wīt flī, hwīt-/ (*plural* **-flies** or *same*) *n* a minute insect with a white waxy coating on the body. Many species suck the sap from garden and house plants. Family: Aleyrodidae.

white-foot·ed mouse *n* a mouse with small white feet and undersides. Native to: North and Central America. Latin name: *Peromyscus leucopus.*

white fox *n* the arctic fox in its white winter coat. Its coat is dark gray in summer.

white fri·ar, **White Fri·ar** *n* a member of the Carmelite order of monks [< the white habits of the monks]

white frost *n* METEOROL same as **hoar frost**

white gas·o·line *n US* gasoline that contains no tetraethyl lead, used especially as a fuel in stoves in the early 20th century [Because it lacks the yellow color of regular gasoline]

white-glove *adj* offering, involving, or treated with exceptional care and attention ○*"Even everyday moving companies are offering white-glove features, from picking up prescriptions to designing the den."* (Paula Szuchman "The Pampered Move," *Wall Street Journal*)

white gold *n* a silvery-looking gold alloy that contains gold mixed with palladium, nickel, or sometimes zinc and is usually used in jewelry

white goods *npl* **1.** household goods made of fabric, e.g., bed linens, towels, and tablecloths **2.** large household appliances typically finished with white enamel, e.g., refrigerators, stoves, and dishwashers

white-haired *adj* having hair that has become white with advanced age

White·hall /wīt hàwl, hwīt-/ *n* **1.** CENTRAL LONDON STREET a street in central London, England, between Trafalgar Square and the Houses of Parliament, containing the main offices of the British civil service **2.** BRITISH GOVERNMENT a collective term for the administration and civil service departments of the British government, many of which are located on Whitehall **3.** TRINIDADIAN PRIME MINISTER'S RESIDENCE the official residence of the prime minister of Trinidad

white·head /wīt hèd, hwīt-/ *n* a small pimple with a whitish top formed when a sebaceous gland becomes blocked. Technical name **milium** [Mid-20C. After *blackhead*]

White·head /wīt hèd, hwīt-/, **Alfred North** (1861–1947) British mathematician and philosopher. He wrote *Principia Mathematica* (1910–13) with Bertrand Russell.

"Civilization advances by extending the number of important operations which we

can perform without thinking about them."
[Alfred North Whitehead, *An Introduction to Mathematics*; 1948]

white-head·ed *adj* **1.** having white markings on the feathers, hair, or fur of the head, especially as a distinguishing feature between similar species **2.** favored over others and considered blessed by luck

white heat *n* **1.** an extremely high degree of heat characterized by the emission of white light **2.** a state of intense excitement or activity

white hole *n* a hypothetical region in space from which stars, light, and other forms of energy emerge explosively [After *black hole*]

White·horse /wīt hàwrss, hwīt-/ capital city of the Yukon Territory, Canada, located on the Yukon River, just off the Alaska Highway. Population: 16,843 (2001).

white-hot *adj* **1.** so hot that white light is emitted **2.** characterized by intense excitement or activity

Barnaby's
White House, Washington, D.C.

White House *n* **1.** OFFICIAL RESIDENCE OF US PRESIDENT the large white mansion in Washington, D.C. that is the official residence of the president of the United States. It was built between 1792 and 1800 in the classical Palladian style. **2.** EXECUTIVE BRANCH OF US GOVERNMENT the executive branch of the US government **3.** RUSSIAN PARLIAMENT BUILDING the Russian parliament building in central Moscow

white hunt·er *n* especially formerly in Africa, a white man hunting big game professionally or working as a safari guide

white knight *n* **1.** somebody who rescues a person or situation from disaster **2.** a person or organization that rescues a company, especially from an undesirable takeover

white-knuck·le, white-knuck·led *adj* causing or characterized by fear, apprehension, nervousness, or uncertainty (*slang*) [< the appearance of nervously clenched fists]

white-knuck·le ride *n* **1.** a situation, experience, or encounter that causes fear, anxiety, or uncertainty **2.** a frightening or exhilarating fairground ride, especially a roller coaster

white la·dy *n* a cocktail made with gin, Cointreau, and lemon juice

white lead *n* **1.** lead carbonate in the form of a poisonous heavy white powder. Use: pigment in paints and in putty. Formula: $2PbCO_3.Pb(OH)_2$. **2.** putty made from white lead suspended in boiled linseed oil

white leath·er *n* a soft leather treated with salt and alum for a white finish

white lie *n* a lie not intended to harm, but told in order to avoid distress or embarrassment

SYNONYMS See ***lie***[2].

white light *n* light that contains all the wavelengths from red to violet at approximately equal intensity, e.g., sunlight

white light·ning *n Can, Southern US* BEVERAGES same as **moonshine** (sense 1) [*White* because it is usually colorless]

white line *n* a usually broken line of white paint along the middle or edge of a road, used to mark the edge of a road or to separate lanes of traffic, especially those moving in opposite directions

white list *n* **1.** a list of people, organizations, or items deemed acceptable **2.** a list of e-mail addresses, e.g., from friends or customers, to which somebody wants to permit access. ◊ **blacklist** [After *blacklist*] —**white-list·ed** *adj*

white-liv·ered *adj* same as **lily-livered** (*archaic or literary*)

white·ly /wītlee, hwītlee/ *adv* showing a face pale with anger, fear, or shock

white mag·ic *n* supposed magic practiced for good purposes or to counteract evil [After *black magic*]

white ma·hog·a·ny *n US* INDUST same as **primavera**[1] (sense 1)

White·man /wītmən, hwītmən/, **Paul** (1891?–1967) US bandleader. He was an exponent of "sweet jazz," and became celebrated for commissioning *Rhapsody in Blue* (1924) from George Gershwin.

white man's bur·den *n* the supposed responsibility of Europeans and their descendants to impose their allegedly advanced civilization on the nonwhite original inhabitants of the territories they colonized

white mar·lin *n* a large ocean fish with a light-colored belly. It is one of the smaller species of marlin. Native to: western Atlantic. Latin name: *Tetrapturus albidus*.

white mat·ter *n* the whitish nerve tissue of the brain and spinal cord, consisting mostly of myelinated nerve fibers

white meat *n* light-colored meat, especially chicken, turkey, or pork

white met·al *n* a light-colored alloy, especially one with a high tin or lead content such as pewter or babbitt

white mi·ca *n* MINERALS same as **muscovite**

White Moun·tain /wīt-, hwīt-/ peak in the Sierra Nevada, east central California. Height: 14,246 ft./4,345 m.

White Moun·tains /wīt-, hwīt-/ mountain range in northern New Hampshire and southwestern Maine, forming part of the Appalachian Mountains. The highest peak is Mount Washington, 6,288 ft./1,917 m.

white mul·ber·ry *n* **1.** the edible berry of a Chinese mulberry tree **2.** a mulberry tree that produces white mulberries. Native to: China. Latin name: *Morus alba*.

whit·en /wīt'n, hwīt'n/ (**-ened, -en·ing, -ens**) *vti* to become white or lighter in color, or make something do this

whit·en·er /wīt'nər, hwīt'nər/ *n* **1.** a substance such as bleach used to color something white or enhance its whiteness **2.** a substance added to tea or coffee as a substitute for milk, usually in powder form and lower in calories or with a longer shelf life than milk

White Nile section of the Nile river from near the Sudan-Uganda border to its junction with the Blue Nile at Khartoum. Length: 1,295 mi./2,084 km.

white noise *n* low-volume electrical or radio noise of equal intensity over a wide range of frequencies [By analogy with white light, which contains light from the whole range of visible frequencies]

white oak *n* **1.** an oak tree with evenly lobed hairless leaves and pale wood. Native to: eastern North America. Latin name: *Quercus alba*. **2.** TREES same as **roble** (sense 1)

white·out /wīt òwt, hwīt-/ *n* **1.** an atmospheric condition in which low clouds merge with a snow-covered landscape, greatly restricting visibility, so that only darker objects are discernible **2.** a blizzard that is so severe it reduces visibility almost to zero [Mid-20C. After BLACKOUT]

white pag·es *npl* the part of a telephone book that alphabetically lists names, brief addresses, and telephone numbers of people and groups

white pa·per *n* **1.** in many countries, an official report setting out government policy on an issue to be voted on by the country's legislature **2.** an official, authoritative, or heavily researched report on a topic, e.g., a report produced by a group of journalists [Because such reports are customarily printed as white pamphlets]

white pep·per *n* a light-colored pepper made from peppercorns that have had their dark husk removed

white perch *n* a silver-colored edible fish that is a variety of sea bass. Native to: western Atlantic, freshwater streams of eastern North America. Latin name: *Morone americana*.

white pine *n* **1.** SOFT DURABLE PINE WOOD the soft durable wood of a North American pine tree (*hyphenated before a noun*) **2.** N AMERICAN PINE TREE a fast-growing pine tree that is grown for its soft durable wood. Native to: eastern North America. Latin name: *Pinus strobus*. **3.** PINE SIMILAR TO WHITE PINE a pine that resembles the white pine, particularly in having five-needle clusters [< its light-colored wood]

White Plains city in southeastern New York, northeast of Yonkers. It is a northern suburb of New York City. Population: 55,392 (2002 estimate).

white pop·lar *n* **1.** the straight-grained wood of a poplar tree that has white wooly leaves (*hyphenated before a noun*) **2.** a poplar tree that has white wooly leaves and yieldswhite poplar. Native to: Europe, Asia. Latin name: *Populus alba*.

white po·ta·to *n* **1.** a potato with whitish flesh **2.** a plant whose tubers are white potatoes

white rat *n* an albino strain of brown rat, used widely in scientific research. Latin name: *Rattus norvegicus*.

white rice *n* a rice that has had both the outer husk and the bran layer removed

white room *n* SCI same as **clean room**

White Rus·sian *n* **1.** a cocktail made from vodka, coffee liqueur, and cream **2.** PEOPLES same as **Belarusian** (sense 1)

white sale *n* a sale of household linen

white sap·phire *n* a colorless precious stone that is a variety of corundum. Use: gems.

white sauce *n* a pale milk sauce, thickened with butter and flour or cornstarch, and variously seasoned or flavored

White Sea arm of the Barents Sea, forming an indentation in the coast of northwestern Russia and partly enclosed on the north by the Kola Peninsula. Area: 30,000 sq. mi./90,000 sq. km.

white shark *n* FISH same as **great white shark**

white sheep *n* BREED same as **Dall sheep**

white slave *n* a white girl or woman sold into prostitution against her will —**white slav·er** *n* —**white slav·er·y** *n*

white·smith /wīt smìth, hwīt-/ *n* **1.** somebody who makes or repairs objects made from white metals **2.** somebody whose job is polishing forged metal articles [14C. After BLACKSMITH]

white snake·root *n* a poisonous plant with heart-shaped leaves. Flowers: small, white, in clusters. Native to: eastern North America. Latin name: *Eupatorium rugosum*.

white space *n* an area of a page or other printed surface where no text or pictures appear

white spruce *n* **1.** the soft wood of a North American spruce tree **2.** a spruce tree that has short blue-gray needles and whitish shoots and yields a white spruce. Native to: northern North America. Latin name: *Picea glauca*. [< its silvery brown bark]

white squall *n* a violent tropical or subtropical storm that stirs up the surface of the sea into whitecaps, but is limited to a very localized area, often with no storm clouds present

white stur·geon *n* the largest freshwater fish in the United States, caught commercially and for sport. Native to: North American Pacific coast. Latin name: *Acipenser transmontanus*. [< its grayish white color]

white su·prem·a·cy *n* the view that white people are supposedly genetically and culturally superior to all other people or races and should therefore rule over them —**white su·prem·a·cist** *n*

white-tailed deer, white·tail /wīt tàyl, hwīt-/ *n* a deer with a grayish or reddish brown coat and a tail that is white on the underside. Native to: North America. Latin name: *Odocoileus virginianus.*

white·throat /wīt thrōt, hwīt-/ *n* **1.** BIRDS same as **white-throated sparrow 2.** a small songbird with a white throat. Native to: Europe, Asia, North Africa. Genus: *Sylvia.*

white-throat·ed spar·row *n* a sparrow with a prominent white throat and black-and-white bands on its head. Native to: North America. Latin name: *Zonotrichia albicollis.*

white tie *n* **1.** a white bow tie worn as part of a man's formal evening dress **2.** a man's full formal evening clothes, consisting of a black suit with a tailcoat and a white bow tie —**white-tie** *adj*

white trash *n* an offensive term for a white person or group of white people considered as possessing the stereotypical characteristics of members of a lower-income group in society (*slang*)

white vit·ri·ol *n* CHEM same as **zinc sulfate**

white·wall /wīt wàwl, hwīt-/, **white·wall tire** *n* a vehicle tire with a band of white on the outside sidewall

white wal·nut *n* TREES same as **butternut** [*White* < because its wood is lighter in color than that of the black walnut]

white·wash /wīt wòsh, hwīt-/ *n* **1.** COVER-UP a coordinated attempt to hide unpleasant facts, especially in a political context (*informal*) **2.** WHITE PAINTING SOLUTION lime suspended in water, often with glue or sizing, and used like paint for whitening walls **3.** THOROUGH DEFEAT a resounding defeat, especially one in which the losing player or team does not score (*informal*) ■ *v* (**-washed, -wash·ing, -wash·es**) **1.** *vti* HIDE TRUTH ABOUT SOMETHING to conceal the unpleasant facts about something **2.** *vt* PAINT SOMETHING WITH WHITEWASH to paint something, usually a wall, with whitewash **3.** *vt* DEFEAT SOMEBODY DECISIVELY to defeat an opposing player or team resoundingly, especially by preventing the player or team from scoring —**white·wash·er** *n* —**white·wash·ing** *n*

white wa·ter *n* **1.** fast-flowing water with a foamy choppy surface **2.** lighter-colored sea water visible in shallow areas

white-wa·ter raft·ing /wīt wawtər-, hwīt-/ *n* the outdoor leisure pursuit of floating on a raft down a fast-flowing river

white wed·ding *n* a wedding for which the bride wears a traditional white dress, often taking place in church

white whale *n* a small white fish-eating whale with a bulbous head. Native to: Arctic waters. Latin name: *Delphinapterus leucas.*

white-winged dove *n* a dove with white patches on its wings. Native to: southern United States, Mexico. Latin name: *Zenaida asiatica.*

white-winged sco·ter *n* a ocean duck that is mostly black with a white patch on each wing. Native to: North America. Latin name: *Melanitta fusca.*

white witch *n* a witch whose supposed magic is designed to do good or to counteract evil [*White* because such a witch practices supposed white magic]

white·wood /wīt wòod, hwīt-/ *n* **1.** the pale wood of some deciduous trees **2.** a deciduous tree whose wood is pale in color, e.g., the tulip tree, cottonwood, or basswood

whit·ey /wītee, hwītee/ (*plural* **-eys**), **whit·y** (*plural* **-ies**) *n* an offensive term for a white person (*slang*)

whith·er /wi<u>th</u>ər, hwi<u>th</u>ər/ *adv* **1.** to what place **2.** to what state, condition, outcome, or degree [Old English *hwider* < Germanic]

whit·ing[1] /wīting, hwīting/ (*plural same*) *n* **1.** EUROPEAN FISH a small edible sea fish with a silvery underside, related to the cod, commercially important throughout Europe. Native to: Europe. Latin name: *Merlangus merlangus.* **2.** PACIFIC AND ATLANTIC FISH a commercially important fish that is similar to the European whiting, e.g., the silver hake or corbina. Native to: Pacific and Atlantic oceans. Genera: *Merluccius* or *Menticirrhus.* **3.** FOOD WHITING AS FOOD the white flesh of the whiting as food [15C. < Dutch *wijting*, < *wijt* "white"]

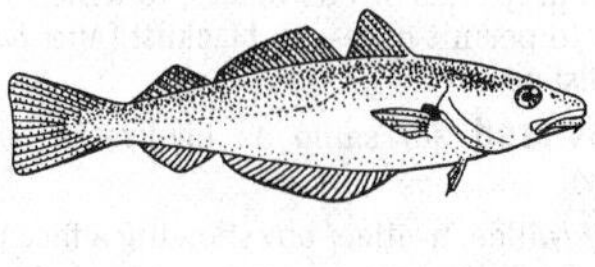

whiting

whit·ing[2] /wīting, hwīting/ *n* pure powdered chalk used as an ingredient in various commercial preparations such as putty and whitewash [15C. < WHITE]

Whit·lam /wítləm, hwítləm/, **Gough** (*b.* 1916) prime minister of Australia (1972–75). He became leader of the Labor Party in 1967 and introduced a wide-ranging reform program during his premiership. His government was controversially dismissed by the governor-general, Sir John Kerr. Full name **Whitlam, Edward Gough.** See table at **prime minister**

whit·low /wítlō, hwítlō/ *n* a pus-filled infection on the skin at the side of a fingernail or toenail [14C. Alteration of earlier *whitflawe* < WHITE + FLAW[1]]

Library of Congress

Walt Whitman

Whit·man /wítmən, hwít-/, **Walt** (1819–92) US poet and essayist. He is known for his free verse, best exemplified in the stylistically revolutionary collection *Leaves of Grass* (1855–91). Born **Whitman, Walter.** See Cultural note at **grass**

> "The United States themselves are essentially the greatest poem..."
> [Walt Whitman. Preface, *Leaves of Grass, 1st edition*; 1855]

> "I hear America singing, the varied carols I hear."
> [Walt Whitman, "I hear America Singing," *Leaves of Grass, 1st edition*; 1855]

Whit·mon·day /wít mùndee, -day, hwít-, -/ *n* formerly, a public holiday in England, Ireland, and Wales. Date: the Monday after Pentecost. [After WHITSUNDAY]

Whit·ney, Mount /wítnee, hwít-/ mountain in eastern California, in the Sierra Nevada. Height: 14,494 ft./4,418 m.

Whit·ney /wítnee, hwít-/, **Eli** (1765–1825) US inventor. His cotton gin, a machine for separating the seeds from the fiber of the cotton plant, revolutionized the cotton industry.

Whit·sun /wíts'n, hwíts'n/ *adj* relating to or happening on Whitsuntide or Whitsunday [13C. Back-formation < WHITSUNDAY, understood as "Whitsun day"]

Whit·sun·day /wíts'ndee, -dày, hwíts'n-/ *n US* CHR same as **Pentecost** (sense 1) [Old English *hwīta sunnandæg* "white Sunday," because of the white robes the priests wear on this day]

Whit·sun·tide /wíts'n tīd, hwíts'n-/ *n* the days around and including the Christian festival of Pentecost [13C. < WHITSUN + TIDE in obsolete sense of "period of time"]

Whit·ta·ker /wíttəkər, hwít-/, **Charles Evans** (1901–73) US Supreme Court associate justice (1957–62)

Whit·tier /wíttee ər, hwíttee-/, **John Greenleaf** (1807–92) US poet and abolitionist. His strong Quaker beliefs, which underlie his poetry, prompted him to oppose slavery.

> "For of all sad words of tongue or pen, / The saddest are these: 'It might have been!'"
> [John Greenleaf Whittier, "Maud Muller"; 1856]

Whit·ting·ton /wíttingtən, hwít-/, **Dick** (1358?–1423) English merchant and Lord Mayor of London (1397–98, 1406–07, 1419–20). The legend of his beginnings as an orphaned country boy who went to London with his cat is a popular source of English folk tales and pantomimes.

whit·tle /wítt'l, hwítt'l/ (**-tled, -tling, -tles**) *vti* to carve something out of wood, usually something small enough to hold in the hand, by cutting away small pieces of wood [Mid-16C. < *whyttel* "knife," variant of *thwitel*, "tool for paring" < Old English *þwītan* "pare, cut"] —**whit·tler** *n* —**whit·tling** *n*

whittle away *vt* to deplete something by using or spending a little of it at a time

whittle down *vt* to reduce or diminish something gradually by taking away a little of it at a time

Whit·tle /wítt'l, hwítt'l/, **Sir Frank** (1907–96) British engineer. He invented and developed the turbojet engine (1936), first used to power British fighter aircraft during World War II.

whit·tlings /wíttlingz, hwítt-/ *npl* pieces of wood that have been whittled off a larger piece and discarded

Whit·worth-Ayl·mer /wìt wurth áylmər, hwìt \wurth áylmər/, **Matthew** (1775–1850) British-born American colonial administrator. He was governor-general (1830–35) of British North America (now Canada).

whit·y *n* another spelling of **whitey** (*slang*; *offensive*)

whiz /wiz, hwiz/, **whizz** *v* (**whizzed, whiz·zing, whiz·zes**) **1.** *vi* HUM to make a humming, hissing, or buzzing noise **2.** *vti* MOVE WITH HUMMING NOISE to move swiftly with a humming, hissing, or buzzing noise, or make something do this ○ *bullets whizzing past* **3.** *vi* MOVE QUICKLY to move or travel somewhere rapidly ○ *whizzed down to the store* **4.** *vt* THROW SOMETHING to throw something, especially with a spin, or make something spin (*informal*) ○ *He whizzed the ball right past the catcher.* **5.** *vi* OFFENSIVE TERM an offensive term meaning to urinate (*slang*) ■ *n* (*plural* **whiz·zes**) **1.** EXPERT somebody who is very skilled at something (*informal*) ○ *a computer whiz* **2.** HUMMING SOUND a humming, hissing, or buzzing sound **3.** FAST MOVEMENT a fast movement, often accompanied by a humming, hissing, or buzzing sound **4.** OFFENSIVE TERM an offensive term for an act of urinating (*slang*) [Mid-16C. An imitation of the sound]

whiz-bang (*informal*) *n* **1.** SOMEBODY OR SOMETHING EXCELLENT somebody or something that is outstandingly successful or effective, loud, or fast **2.** ARMS, HIST ARTILLERY SHELL a lightweight artillery shell used in World War I ■ *adj* EXCELLENT, FAST, OR LOUD outstandingly successful or effective, loud, or fast ○ *a whiz-bang presentation*

whiz kid *n* a young and exceptionally talented and successful person in a field of activity (*informal*)

whizz, etc. *vti, n* another spelling of **whiz, etc.**

whiz·zo /wízzō, hwízzō/ *adj* ingeniously clever (*humorous or dated*) ○ *a whizzo plan*

who /hoo/ *pron* **1.** used to introduce a question asking about the name or identity of a person or people ○ *Who's that at the door?* ○ *Who did you see there?* **2.** used to introduce a relative clause giving information about a person or people ○ *meals for people who are too busy to cook* [Old English *hwā* < Indo-European, "who, what"]

SPELLCHECK See *who's.*

USAGE who or whom? ***Whom*** has fallen into disuse in everyday speech, with ***who*** taking its place, especially in British English. *Do you remember whom you saw?* is more usually expressed as *Do you remember who you saw?*, and ***whom*** is omitted when it is associated with a preposition: *the man I was talking to* rather than *the man to whom I was talking*. However, in formal contexts, ***whom*** is still preferred by careful writers. Note that ***whom*** is incorrect in sentences such as *The woman who we thought was dead is still alive*: ***who*** is the subject of *was*, not the object of *thought* (*We thought that she was dead...*).

USAGE See *that*.

WHO *abbr* World Health Organization

whoa /wō, hwō/ *interj* used to order an animal or, humorously, a person, to stop [Mid-19C. Variant of HO[2]]

who'd /hood/ *contr* **1.** who had **2.** who would

who·dun·it /hoo dúnnit/, **who·dun·nit** *n* a novel, movie, or play centering on the solving of a crime, usually a murder [Mid-20C. Alteration of "who done it?"]

who·ev·er /hoo évvər/ *pron* **1. INTRODUCES EMPHATIC QUESTION** used to introduce an emphatic question indicating surprise or disbelief ○ *Whoever would do such a thing?* **2. ANY PERSON WHO** used to indicate a person or people whose identity is not known ○ *Whoever takes over from her will have difficult decisions to make.* **3. NO MATTER WHO** used to indicate a person or people whose identity is not important ○ *You can bring whoever you like to the party.*

whole /hōl/ *adj* **1. ENTIRE** complete, including all parts or aspects, with nothing left out **2. UNDIVIDED** not divided into parts or not regarded as consisting of separate parts **3. RELATING TO DURATION OR EXTENT** relating to or representing the full duration or extent of something ○ *stayed up the whole night* **4. UNBROKEN** not damaged or broken ○ *not a single item of furniture left whole* **5. UNIMPAIRED** not wounded, impaired, or incapacitated ○ *no longer a whole man* **6. HEALED OR HEALTHY** healed or restored to health physically or psychologically ○ *made him whole again* **7. HAVING PARENTS IN COMMON** having both parents in common with your siblings ○ *a whole sister* **8. NOT FRACTIONAL** containing no fractions or decimals ■ *adv* **1. AS SINGLE PIECE** in a single piece ○ *Many snakes swallow their food whole.* **2. COMPLETELY** completely and in every way (*informal*) ○ *a whole different approach* ■ *n* **1. SOMETHING COMPLETE** something that is complete and has no parts missing **2. SINGLE ENTITY OR UNIT** something regarded as a single and complete unit or entity, as opposed to a set of components [Old English *hāl* < Indo-European, "sound, propitious"] —**whole·ness** *n* ◇ **as a whole** as a single and complete entity ◇ **on the whole 1.** as a rule or in general **2.** taking all relevant factors into account

SPELLCHECK See *hole*.

ORIGIN The prehistoric Germanic word from which *whole* is derived, is also the source of English *hale*[1], *hallow*, *heal*, *health*, and *holy*.

whole cloth *n* complete fiction or fabrication ○ *an explanation made out of whole cloth* [< the underlying meaning "cut from new material, in any shape you please"]

whole en·chi·la·da *n* the entirety of something (*slang*)

whole food /hōl food/ *n* food that has undergone very little processing and has been grown or produced without the use of synthetic pesticides or fertilizers

whole gale *n* a wind of between 55 mi./87 km and 63 mi./102 km per hour, classified as force ten on the Beaufort scale and capable of causing considerable structural damage

whole·grain /hōl gràyn/ *adj* describes food containing whole unprocessed grains of something ○ *wholegrain muffins* ○ *wholegrain mustard*

whole·heart·ed /hōl haártəd/ *adj* characterized by unreserved enthusiasm, passion, or commitment —**whole·heart·ed·ly** *adv* —**whole·heart·ed·ness** *n*

whole hog *adv* in every way or to the fullest extent (*informal*) [Origin ?]

~~**wholely**~~ incorrect spelling of **wholly**

whole·meal /hōl meel/ *adj UK* same as **whole-wheat**

whole milk *n* cow's milk from which no fat has been removed

whole note *n* the longest musical note in common use, equal in length to four quarter notes or two half notes. It is written as an open note-head with no stem or tail. [*Whole* < because it lasts for one full measure]

whole num·ber *n* a positive or negative number, including zero, that does not contain a fraction or decimal

whole rest *n* the longest musical rest in common use, equal in length to a **whole note**

whole·sale /hōl sàyl/ *n* **SALE OF GOODS TO RETAILERS** the business of buying goods in large quantities and selling them especially to retailers for resale ■ *adj* **1. OF TRADE IN QUANTITY** relating to the wholesale business **2. DONE ON LARGE SCALE** done on a large scale and indiscriminately ○ *wholesale destruction* ■ *adv* **1. IN BULK** in large quantities, especially for resale by retailers ○ *Buy wholesale and save yourself money.* **2. INDISCRIMINATELY** as a whole, without exercising judgment or taking individual cases into account ■ *v* (**-saled, -sal·ing, -sales**) **1.** *vti* **BUY AND SELL GOODS WHOLESALE** to buy goods in large quantities and sell them especially to retailers for resale **2.** *vi* **TO BE SOLD WHOLESALE** to participate in selling things wholesale, or to be sold in such a way [15C. < the phrase "by whole sale," that is, sold in a single lot for redistribution at retail] —**whole·sal·er** *n*

whole·some /hōlssəm/ *adj* **1. HEALTH-GIVING** beneficial to physical health, usually by virtue of being fresh and naturally produced **2. MORALLY BENEFICIAL** leading to or promoting improved moral well-being **3. SENSIBLE** based on openness, honesty, and common sense **4. HEALTHY AND FIT** having a fit healthy appearance that suggests clean living —**whole·some·ly** *adv* —**whole·some·ness** *n*

whole step *n US* a musical interval consisting of two half steps, e.g., between the notes D and E or A and B. Can term **whole tone**

whole tone *n Can, UK* same as **whole step**

whole-wheat *adj* **1.** not having had the bran and wheat germ taken out **2.** made using whole-wheat flour

who'll /hool/ *contr* **1.** who shall **2.** who will

whol·ly /hōlee, hōl lee/ *adv* **1.** totally and in every way or to the fullest extent **2.** solely and to the exclusion of all other things

whom /hoom/ *pron* (*formal*) **1.** used to introduce a question asking about the name or identity of a person or people ○ *Whom did you expect to see?* **2.** used to introduce a relative clause giving information about a person or people ○ *Birch and her colleagues studied 162 infants, none of whom were born prematurely.* [Old English *hwǣm* < Germanic]

USAGE See *who*.

whom·ev·er /hoom évvər/ *pron* a form of "whoever" when used as the object of a verb or preposition

whomp /womp, hwomp/ *v* (**whomped, whomp·ing, whomps**) **1.** *vti* **STRIKE SOMEBODY OR SOMETHING** to hit somebody or something with great force, especially noisily **2.** *vt US* **DEFEAT SOMEBODY RESOUNDINGLY** to subject somebody to a crushing defeat (*informal*) ■ *n* **BLOW OR NOISE OF BLOW** a heavy blow, or the loud deep sound it makes [Early 20C. An imitation of the sound]
whomp up *vt US* to arouse, incite, or stir up interest or enthusiasm (*dated*)

whom·so·ev·er /hoom sō évvər/ *pron* an emphatic form of "whomever" (*formal*)

whoop /hoop, hwoop/ *v* (**whooped, whoop·ing, whoops**) **1.** *vi* **CRY OUT IN EXCITEMENT OR JOY** to make a loud howling cry of excitement or joy **2.** *vt* **EXCLAIM SOMETHING** to exclaim something loudly and with great excitement **3.** *vt* **URGE OR DRIVE SOMEBODY FORWARD** to urge, chase, or drive a person or animal forward with a whooping call **4.** *vi* **MED WHEEZE** to breathe in with the sharp wheezing sound associated with whooping cough ■ *n* **1. EXCITED OR JOYFUL CRY** a loud howling cry of excitement or joy **2. BATTLE CRY** a cry uttered before a battle or hunt, by a warrior, soldier, or hunter **3. CALL MADE BY BIRD OR ANIMAL** a loud call or hoot, e.g., from a bird or animal **4. MED WHEEZING SOUND** a sharply wheezing inhalation associated with whooping cough [14C. An imitation of the sound] ◇ **whoop it up** (*informal*) **1.** to have fun or celebrate in an extravagant or noisy way **2.** to express and try to arouse enthusiasm for somebody or something

whoop-de-do /hoop dee doo, hwoop-/, **whoop-de-doo** (*informal*) *n* (*plural* **whoop-de-dos**; *plural* **whoop-de-doos**) **1. PARTY** a large-scale party or celebration that is lively or noisy **2. US PUBLICITY** noisy activity meant to attract attention ○ *the whoop-de-do surrounding the movie's release* **3. FUSS** a noisy public commotion or outcry ■ *interj* **EXPRESSING EXCITEMENT** used to express excitement (*often used ironically*) [Mid-20C. Expressive alteration of WHOOP]

whoop·ee /wooppee, woopee, hwooppee, hwoopee/ *interj* used to express great and sudden excitement (*informal*; *often used ironically*) [Mid-19C. Alteration of WHOOP] ◇ **make whoopee** (*dated informal*) **1.** to engage in sexual activity **2.** to celebrate noisily and exuberantly

whoop·ee cush·ion *n* a practical joker's toy in the form of an inflatable cushion with a small opening, designed to make a noise resembling flatulence when somebody sits on it

whoop·er /hoopər, hwoopər/ *n* BIRDS **1.** same as **whooping crane 2.** same as **whooper swan**

whoop·er swan *n* a large white swan with a yellow and black beak, straight neck, and loud whooping cry in flight. Native to: Europe, Asia. Latin name: *Cygnus cygnus*.

whoop·ie pie /wooppee-, woopee-, hw-/ *n* a cake consisting of two layers with a moist filling [< variant of WHOOPEE]

whoop·ing cough /hooping-, hwooping-/ *n* an infectious bacterial disease that causes violent coughing spasms followed by sharp, shrill inhalations. It mainly affects children. Latin name: *Bordetella pertussis*. Technical name **pertussis**

whoop·ing crane *n* a large white crane with black wing tips that makes a loud whooping cry in flight. It is now an endangered species. Native to: North America. Latin name: *Grus americana*.

whoops /woops, hwoops/, **woops** /woops/ *interj* used to express surprise, concern, or embarrassment at making a mistake or having a slight accident [Mid-20C. Origin ?]

whoosh /woosh, hwoosh/ *n* **1. NOISE OF RUSHING AIR OR WATER** the sound made by rushing air or water **2. SWIFT MOTION OR RUSH** a swift motion, spurt, or rush ■ *vi* (**whooshed, whoosh·ing, whoosh·es**) **1. MAKE RUSHING SOUND** to make the sound of rushing air or water **2. MOVE FAST** to move rapidly, with a whooshing sound ○ *whooshed into the room* [Mid-19C. An imitation of the sound]

whop /wop, hwop/, **whap** *vt* (**whopped, whop·ping, whops; whapped, whap·ping, whaps**) (*informal*) **1. HIT SOMEBODY OR SOMETHING** to strike somebody or something forcefully **2. DEFEAT SOMEBODY DECISIVELY** to subject an opponent to a crushing defeat ■ *n* **BLOW OR NOISE OF BLOW** a heavy blow or the loud dull sound it makes [14C. Variant of *wap* "strike, slap," also "a blow," origin ?]

whop·per /wóppər, hwóppər/ *n* (*informal*) **1.** something that is much bigger than others of its kind **2.** a blatant and outrageous lie [Late 18C. < WHOPPING]

whop·ping /wópping, hwópping/ (*informal*) *adj* very big or great ■ *adv* extremely [Early 18C. < WHOP]

whore /hawr/ *n* (*insult*) **1.** an offensive term for a prostitute **2.** an offensive term for somebody regarded as being sexually indiscriminate **3.** an offensive term for somebody who is regarded as willing to set aside principles or personal integrity in order to obtain something, usually for selfish motives ■ *vi* (**whored, whor·ing, whores**) **1.** an offensive term meaning to be a regular customer of prostitutes **2.** an offensive term meaning to work as a prostitute [Old English *hōre* < Indo-European, "to desire"] —**whore·dom** *n*
whore after *vt* an offensive term meaning to pursue something desperately, making whatever sacrifices of principles or personal integrity are necessary

whore·house /háwr hòwss/ (*plural* **-hous·es** /-hòwzəz/) *n* an offensive term for a brothel or other place of prostitution

whore·mon·ger /háwr mùng gər, -mòng-/ *n* an offensive term for a sexually indiscriminate man, especially one who frequents prostitutes (*archaic*) —**whore·mon·ger·y** *n*

whore·son /háwrss'n/ *n* an offensive term for a man regarded as dishonest, treacherous, or otherwise disreputable (*archaic insult*) ■ *adj* an offensive term meaning contemptible or loathsome (*archaic*) [14C. Translation of Anglo-Norman *fiz a putain*]

Whorf hy·poth·e·sis *n* PSYCHOL same as **Sapir-Whorf hypothesis**

whor·ish /háwrish/ *adj* **1.** an offensive term meaning characteristic of the behavior stereotypically ascribed to prostitutes **2.** an offensive term meaning relating to prostitutes or prostitution —**whor·ish·ly** *adv* —**whor·ish·ness** *n*

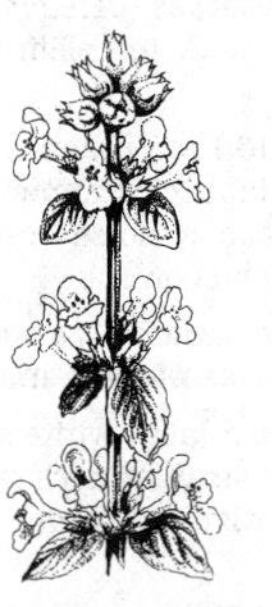

whorl (sense 3)

whorl /wawrl, wurl, hwawrl, hwurl/ *n* **1.** SOMETHING SPIRAL-SHAPED something in the shape of a spiral, coil, or curl **2.** ANAT, CRIME PATTERN ON FINGER a series of concentric circular or elliptical ridges in the pattern of lines on the gripping surface of a finger or thumb, or this shape seen in a fingerprint **3.** BOT CIRCLE OF PLANT PARTS a circular arrangement of three or more leaves, petals, or other plant parts arising at the same level on a stem or other axis, like spokes on a wheel **4.** ZOOL SPIRAL IN SHELL a turn or coil in a mollusk's shell [15C. Alteration of WHIRL] —**whorled** *adj*

whor·tle·ber·ry /wúrt'l bèrree, hwúrt'l-/ (*plural* **-ries**) *n* **1.** EDIBLE BERRY a small sweet edible blue-black fruit **2.** PLANT WITH EDIBLE BERRIES a low-growing plant found in heath and mountainous areas that produces whortleberries. Flowers: greenish pink. Native to: Europe. Latin name: *Vaccinium myrtillus.* **3.** PLANT RELATED TO WHORTLEBERRY a plant related to the whortleberry that has edible berries, e.g., the blueberry [Late 16C. Dialect variant of *hurtleberry,* origin?]

who's /hooz/ *contr* **1.** who has **2.** who is

SPELLCHECK whose or **who's**? ***Who's*** is a contraction of *who is* or *who has*: *She's the one who's* [not *whose*] *coming to dinner next week. Who's* [not *Whose*] *got my pen?* ***Whose*** means "of whom" or "of which" and indicates or asks about belonging: *These are the children whose* [not *who's*] *father we saw yesterday. Whose* [not *Who's*] *coat is that?*

whose /hooz/ *pron, adj* a grammatical word used to talk or ask about the person or thing something belongs to ○ *Whose are these boots?* ○ *"It wasn't my idea." – "Well, whose was it then?"* ○ *a theatre whose doors will always be open to such a talented performer* ○ *Whose car shall we use?* ○ *He wanted to know whose the scarf was.* [Old English *hwæs*, genitive of the pronouns *hwa* (masculine) "who" and *hwæt* (neuter) "what." Influenced in Middle English by *who* and *whom*]

SPELLCHECK See *who's*.

USAGE Some people dislike the use of ***whose*** to mean "of which" (as in *There was a church whose steeple had been struck by lightning.*), but it is a well-established use and the alternatives are usually awkward.

who·so·ev·er /hòossō évvər/ *pron* an emphatic form of "whoever" (*formal*)

Who's Who *tdmk* a trademark for a reference work giving brief biographical sketches of notable people

WH-ques·tion *n* a question that starts with *who, what, where, when, why,* or *how.* It cannot be answered by "yes" or "no."

whs. *abbr* COMM warehouse

whsle. *abbr* COMM wholesale

whump /wump, hwump/ *n* the sound of a dull thump or muffled explosion ■ *vti* (**whumped, whump·ing, whumps**) to make the sound of a dull thump or muffled explosion, or hit somebody or something with such a sound [Late 19C. An imitation of the sound]

whup /wup, wo͝op, hwup, hwo͝op/ (**whupped, whup·ping, whups**) *vt* **1.** STRIKE SOMEBODY to beat somebody (*informal*) **2.** *US* DEFEAT SOMEBODY to subject an opponent to a crushing defeat (*informal*) **3.** *Southern US* WHIP SOMEBODY to beat somebody with a whip [Late 19C. Dialect variant of WHIP]

why /wī, hwī/ CORE MEANING: an adverb used to ask or talk about the reason, purpose, or cause of something ○ *Why didn't you call?* ○ *I wish you'd tell me why you're so unhappy.* ○ *He couldn't say why he'd done it.* ○ *It seems clear to me why.*

1. *adv* ASKING REASON for what reason ○ *Why didn't you call?* **2.** ⚠ *adv* BECAUSE OF for or on account of which ○ *There's no reason why you shouldn't go.* **3.** *interj* EXCLAMATION an exclamation used to express surprise, shock, or indignation ○ *Why, John, how could you!* **4.** *n* REASON a reason or purpose for something ○ *the whys and wherefores of the case* [Old English *hwȳ*, instrumental case form of *hwæt* "what"] ◇ **why not** used to express agreement with a suggestion or proposed course of action ○ *"Would you like another coffee?" – "Why not?"*

USAGE Since people disagree as to whether *reason why* is redundant, the safest course is to avoid using it in formal writing: *The reason the experiment failed is that our test procedures were flawed,* rather than *The reason why the experiment failed is that our test procedures were flawed.*

Why·al·la /wī állə, hwī-/ city and port on the Spencer Gulf in South Australia. It is a center of iron and steel production. Population: 21,903 (2002 estimate).

whyd·ah /wíddə, hwíddə/ (*plural same* or **-ahs**), **whid·ah** *n* a songbird, the male of which has long black tail feathers during the breeding season. Native to: Africa. Genus: *Vidua.* [Late 18C. After *Ouidah*, West African town]

whys and where·fores *n* all the reasons and explanations for something ○ *Without going into all the whys and wherefores, let's just say the wedding's off.*

WI *abbr* MAIL Wisconsin

W.I. *abbr* **1.** West Indian **2.** West Indies

WIA *abbr* wounded in action

Wic·ca /wíkə/ *n* a religious practice involving nature-worship and witchcraft [Mid-20C. Revival of Old English *wicca* "wizard"] —**Wic·can** *n, adj*

Wich·i·ta[1] /wíchi tàw/ (*plural same* or **-tas**) *n* a member of a Native North American people who lived in Kansas, Oklahoma, and Texas, and now live mainly in Oklahoma [Mid-19C. < Caddo] —**Wich·i·ta** *adj*

Wich·i·ta[2] /wíchi tàw/ city in south central Kansas, on the Arkansas River, southwest of Emporia. Population: 355,126 (2002 estimate).

wick /wik/ *n* **1.** MATERIAL HOLDING FUEL THAT BURNS a string or piece of fabric that uses capillary action to draw the fuel to the flame in a candle, oil lamp, or cigarette lighter **2.** MED MATERIAL THAT DRAWS UP LIQUID any piece of material that draws liquid up by capillary action, e.g., a strip of gauze put into a wound to drain it ■ *vti* (**wicked, wick·ing, wicks**) MOVE LIQUID BY CAPILLARY ACTION to take in or transfer liquid by capillary action, or be taken in or transferred in this way [Old English *wēoc*, origin ?]

wick·ed /wíkid/ *adj* **1.** EVIL very wrong or very bad **2.** MISCHIEVOUS playfully mischievous without intending to upset people seriously ○ *a wicked sense of humor* **3.** MEAN expressing very unpleasant things to people ○ *She has a really wicked tongue sometimes!* **4.** DANGEROUS capable of causing harm to somebody ○ *a knife with a wicked blade* **5.** DISGUSTING tasting or smelling disgusting and repulsive **6.** DISTRESSING causing discomfort, distress, or disappointment (*informal*) ○ *I've got a wicked headache.* **7.** VERY GOOD very impressive or very skillful (*slang*) ○ *He plays a wicked game of tennis.* ■ *adv* VERY extremely (*slang*) ○ *It was wicked good!* ■ *npl* BAD PEOPLE people who do very bad things [13C. Related to Old English *wicca* "sorcerer" (see WITCH)] —**wick·ed·ly** *adv* —**wick·ed·ness** *n*

wick·er /wíkər/, **wick·er·work** /wíkər wùrk/ *n* **1.** objects made of twigs, canes, or reeds, e.g., baskets **2.** twigs, canes, or reeds woven together to make such things as baskets or chairs [14C. < N Germanic < Indo-European, "bend"]

wick·er·work /wíkər wùrk/ *n* **1.** same as **wicker** (sense 1) **2.** objects made by weaving together thin twigs, canes, or reeds, e.g., baskets and chairs

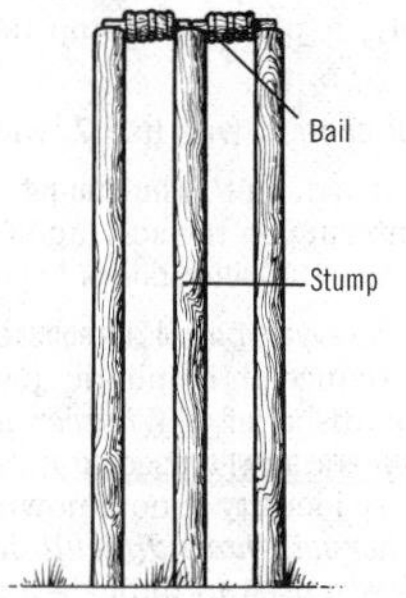

wicket (sense 4)

wick·et /wíkit/ *n* **1.** SMALL DOOR OR GATE a small door or gate, especially one close to or forming part of a larger one **2.** *US* SMALL OPENING FOR COMMUNICATION a small opening or window in a wall or door through which people can communicate. Wickets are often fitted with glass, a grating, or a sliding panel. **3.** GATE CONTROLLING WATER FLOW a gate used to control the flow of water at a lock or water wheel **4.** UPRIGHT STICKS DEFENDED BY CRICKET BATSMAN in cricket, either of two sets of three upright sticks (**stumps**) on which are balanced two shorter sticks (**bails**) and in front of which the batsman or batswoman stands **5.** PART OF CRICKET PITCH the part of a cricket pitch between the two sets of stumps, which are placed 22 yd./20 m apart **6.** TURN OF BATTING in cricket, a batsman's or batswoman's turn of batting, or that of a pair of batsmen or batswomen **7.** ENDING OF TURN OF BATTING in cricket, the ending of somebody's turn of batting, effected, e.g., by knocking down the stumps or catching the ball **8.** CROQUET HOOP a hoop through which the ball is hit in croquet [13C. < Old N French *wiket* < Germanic < Indo-European, "bend"]

wick·et·keep·er /wíkit kēepər/ *n* in cricket, the player positioned behind the wicket to catch the ball or knock the bails off the stumps —**wick·et·keep·ing** *n*

wick·ing /wíking/ *n* material used to make wicks

wick·i·up /wíkee ùp/, **wik·i·up** *n* a hut made by Native North Americans of the southwestern United States by covering a framework of arched poles with mats of bark, grass, or branches [Mid-19C. < Fox *wikiyapi*]

Wick·low /wíklō/ **1.** county in Leinster Province in the southeastern part of the Republic of Ireland. Population: 102,683 (2002). Area: 782 sq. mi./2,025 sq. km. **2.** town and administrative center of County Wicklow in the Republic of Ireland. Population: 6,215 (1991).

wick·y /wíkee/ (*plural* **-ies**) *n* TREES same as **sheep laurel**

Wi·cliff ♦ **Wycliffe, John**

wic·o·py /wíkəpee/ (*plural* **-pies**) *n* TREES same as **leatherwood** (sense 1) [Late 18C. < Algonquian]

wid·der·shins /wíddər shìnz/, **with·er·shins** /wíthər-/ *adv Scotland* (*literary*) **1.** counterclockwise or in a direction opposite to that of the apparent movement of the Sun **2.** in the direction that is contrary to the natural course [Early 16C. Alteration of Middle Low German *weddersinnes* < Middle High German *widersinnes* < *wider* "against, opposite" + *sin* "sense, direction"]

wide /wīd/ *adj* (**wid·er, wid·est**) **1.** WITH SIDES OR EDGES FAR APART having a relatively large distance or space between one side or edge and the other **2.** BEING PARTICULAR DISTANCE APART having a particular distance between one side or edge and the other ○ *three inches wide* **3.** OPENED TO GREAT EXTENT opened to a great extent or as far as possible ○ *staring at him with wide eyes* **4.** WITH MANY TYPES OR CHOICES including many varieties, offering many choices, or having a large range ○ *a wide selection of cheeses* **5.** INVOLVING MANY PEOPLE from, involving, or given to many people ○ *wide support for the plan* **6.** LARGE IN SCOPE with a large scope ○ *a very wide gap between living standards here and in developing countries* **7.** NOT HITTING TARGET going some distance away from the intended, expected, or correct place **8.** GOING BEYOND DETAILS looking beyond the issue toward the more general aspects of something rather than the details ○ *We need to look at the wider implications of these proposals.* **9.** FITTING LOOSELY not fitting tightly round the body **10.** BASEBALL same as **outside** (sense 6) **11.** PHON same as **lax** (sense 4) ■ *adv* (**wid·er, wid·est**) **1.** TO GREAT EXTENT to a great extent or as much as possible ○ *Stand with your legs wide apart.* **2.** OVER LARGE AREA over an extensive area ○ *scattered far and wide* **3.** TO SIDE OF TARGET to one side of the intended target ○ *A few shots were fired but they all went wide.* ■ *n* BALL BOWLED BEYOND BATSMAN'S REACH in cricket, a ball bowled beyond the reach of the batsman or batswoman, for which one run is awarded to the batting side [Old English *wīd* < Indo-European, "apart"] —**wide·ness** *n* —**wid·ish** *adj*

-wide *suffix* effective throughout a particular place ○ *statewide* ○ *storewide* [< WIDE]

wide-an·gle *adj* **1.** describes a camera lens that gives an unusually wide field of view by making things appear smaller or further away than they really are **2.** relating to or using a camera lens with an unusually wide field of view ○ *a wide-angle shot*

wide-ar·e·a net·work *n* a network of computers and peripheral devices linked by cable and satellite over a broad geographic area

wide-a·wake *adj* **1.** FULLY AWAKE completely awake and alert (*not hyphenated after a verb*) **2.** ALERT very aware of surroundings and watching for advantageous possibilities (*informal*) ○ *a wide-awake young go-getter* ■ *n also* **wide-a·wake hat** FELT HAT a soft felt hat with a wide brim and a low crown —**wide-a·wake·ness** *n*

wide ball *n* CRICKET same as **wide**

wide-bod·ied, **wide-bod·y** *adj* describes a jet airliner with a fuselage wide enough to have three sets of passenger seats in a row, separated by two long aisles

wide·bod·y /wīd bòddee/ *n* a commercial jet aircraft with a fuselage wide enough to accommodate three rows of seats and two aisles

wide-eyed *adj* **1.** with eyes that are wide open, e.g., in amazement or fear **2.** lacking experience, wisdom, or common sense and therefore easily fooled by other people

wide·ly /wídlee/ *adv* **1.** BY MANY PEOPLE by a large number of people ○ *It is not widely known that he was once an acrobat.* **2.** OVER LARGE RANGE so as to cover an extensive range ○ *The conversation ranged widely, from politics to bee-keeping.* **3.** GREATLY to a great degree ○ *widely different examples of this phenomenon* **4.** OVER LARGE AREA over an extensive area ○ *She is very widely travelled.* **5.** WITH SPACE BETWEEN with a relatively large distance between ○ *Plant them fairly widely apart.* **6.** MAKING SOMETHING SPREAD OR OPEN WIDE in such a way as to make something open or spread as much as possible or to a great extent ○ *smiling a little too widely*

wide-mouthed *adj* **1.** with a mouth that is notably wider than average **2.** with the mouth open wide, e.g., in surprise

wid·en /wíd'n/ (**-ened, -en·ing, -ens**) *vti* to become wider, or make something wider —**wid·en·er** *n*

wide-o·pen *adj* (*not hyphenated after a verb*) **1.** OPEN TO GREAT EXTENT open to a great extent, or as much as possible ○ *The door was wide open.* **2.** UNPREDICTABLE not as yet decided or even predictable in outcome ○ *The match is still wide open.* **3.** VULNERABLE TO ATTACK unprotected and therefore able to be attacked easily **4.** *US* WITHOUT LAWS OR LAW ENFORCEMENT with few laws regulating such things as prostitution, gambling, or the sale of alcohol, or not stringently enforcing the laws that do exist (*informal*)

wide-rang·ing *adj* **1.** dealing with a great variety of matters **2.** affecting a large number of people or things ○ *a decision that has wide-ranging implications*

wide re·ceiv·er *n* in football, a player who positions himself to the side of the offensive formation, and whose role is to catch long passes from the quarterback

wide-screen *adj* **1.** describes a type of film projection in which the image is substantially wider than it is tall **2.** describes a television whose screen is notably wider than average —**wide screen** *n*

wide·spread /wīd spréd/ *adj* **1.** existing or happening in many places, or affecting many people **2.** spread or extending far apart ○ *with arms widespread*

SYNONYMS *widespread, prevalent, rife, epidemic, universal*

CORE MEANING: occurring in many situations

widespread existing or happening in many places, or affecting many people ○ *This semi-desert antelope was once widespread in North Africa.* ○ *The report claims that drugs in sports are becoming a much more widespread problem.* **prevalent** occurring, accepted or practiced, commonly or widely ○ *the prevalent public mood* ○ *Depression is the most prevalent of all psychiatric disorders.* **rife** extremely widespread, or occurring over a wide area, in great numbers, or very frequently ○ *Prostitution is rife in the area.* ○ *Wall Street at the time was rife with insider trading scandals.* **epidemic** spreading more quickly and more extensively than would usually be expected ○ *Bribery in the country was reported to have reached epidemic proportions.* **universal** applicable to all situations or purposes ○ *His suggestions met with almost universal derision.* ○ *Divorce has become an almost universal feature of modern life.*

---

wid·geon /wíjjən/ (*plural* **-geons** or *same*), **wi·geon** *n* **1.** a freshwater duck, the male of which has a white crown. Native to: North America. Latin name: *Anas americana.* **2.** a freshwater duck with a white patch on each wing. Native to: Europe, Asia. Latin name: *Anas penelope.* [Early 16C. Origin ?]

wid·get /wíjjit/ *n* **1.** a little device or mechanism, especially one whose name is unknown or forgotten (*humorous*) **2.** a hypothetical manufactured object, considered to represent the typical product of a manufacturer [Early 20C. Origin ?]

Wid·nes /wídnəss/ city near Liverpool, northwestern England, on the Mersey River. Population: 57,162 (1991).

wid·ow /wíddō/ *n* **1.** WOMAN WHOSE HUSBAND HAS DIED a woman whose husband has died, especially when she has not remarried **2.** WOMAN LEFT BEHIND a woman whose partner regularly goes away from her to take part in a particular activity (*only used in combination*) ○ *a golf widow* **3.** PRINTING SHORT FINAL LINE OF PARAGRAPH a short line at the end of a paragraph, especially when occurring as the top line of a page or column of text. The text is usually altered so that this is removed. **4.** CARDS EXTRA HAND OF CARDS an extra hand of cards dealt out in some card games ■ *vt* (**-owed, -ow·ing, -ows**) MAKE SOMEBODY WIDOW OR WIDOWER to cause somebody to become a widow or widower (*usually passive*) [Old English *widuwe* < Indo-European, "to separate"] —**wid·ow·hood** *n*

wid·ow·bird /wíddō bùrd/ (*plural* **-birds** or *same*) *n* BIRDS same as **whydah** [Late 18C. Alteration]

wid·ow·er /wíddō ər/ *n* a man whose wife has died, especially when he has not remarried —**wid·ow·er·hood** *n*

wid·ow·mak·er /wíddō màykər/ *n* something that is so dangerous that it might kill anyone who uses it or tries it

wid·ow's cruse *n* a source that provides an unending supply of something [< the biblical story of the widow's cruse of oil that supplies Elijah during a famine (I Kings 17:8–16)]

wid·ow's mite *n* a contribution that, although small, is generous because it comes from somebody who has very little to give [< the poor widow's contribution of two copper coins to the treasury in the Bible (Mark 12:42)]

wid·ow's peak *n* a V-shaped hairline across the top of somebody's forehead behind which the hair grows [< the superstition that this feature portends early widowhood]

wid·ow's walk *n* a walkway with a rail around it on the rooftop of a house, especially one that was used to keep watch for incoming ships [Because, while pacing along it, wives commonly looked for signs of their husbands returning from sea]

wid·ow's weeds *npl* the black clothes once traditionally worn by widows (*archaic or literary*)

width /width, witth/ *n* **1.** DISTANCE ACROSS the distance from one side or edge of something to the other **2.** STATE OF BEING WIDE the fact of being wide, or how wide something is **3.** HANDICRAFT MATERIAL OF FULL WIDTH a piece of material of its full width

width·wise /wídth wīz, wítth-/, **width·ways** /-wàyz/ *adv* from one side or edge to the other

~~**wiegh**~~ incorrect spelling of **weigh**

~~**wieght**~~ incorrect spelling of **weight**

wield /weeld/ (**wield·ed, wield·ing, wields**) *vt* **1.** to have and be able to use something, especially power or authority ○ *the immense economic power wielded by large companies* **2.** to hold and use a weapon or tool [Old English *wielden* "rule," variant of *wealden* < Indo-European, "be strong"] —**wield·a·ble** *adj* —**wield·er** *n*

wield·y /wéeldee/ (**-i·er, -i·est**) *adj* easily handled or used, or easy enough to manage

wie·ner /wéenər/ *n* FOOD same as **frankfurter** [Late 19C. Shortening of WIENERWURST]

Wie·ner /wéenər/, **Norbert** (1894–1964) US mathematician. His work on the mathematics and theories underlying communication and electronic machines founded the science of cybernetics.

> "The world of the future will be an ever more demanding struggle against the limits of our intelligence, not a comfortable hammock in which we can lie down to be waited upon by our robot slaves."
> [Norbert Wiener, *God and Golem, Inc.*; 1964]

Wie·ner schnit·zel /véenər shnìts'l/ *n* a thin slice of veal coated in egg and breadcrumbs and fried [< German *Wiener* "of Vienna"]

wie·ner·wurst /wéenər wùrst, -wŏorst/ *n* FOOD same as **frankfurter** [Late 19C. < German < *Wiener* "of Vienna" + *Wurst* "sausage"]

wie·nie /wéenee/ *n* same as **frankfurter** (*informal*) [Mid-19C. Alteration of WIENER]

~~**wier**~~ incorrect spelling of **weir**

~~**wierd**~~ incorrect spelling of **weird**

Wies·ba·den /véess baàd'n, véez-/ industrial city and spa resort in west central Germany. It is the capital city of Hesse State. Population: 266,081 (1997).

Wie·schaus /wée shòwss, vée-/, **Eric F.** (*b.* 1947) US geneticist. He shared the Nobel Prize in physiology or medicine (1995) with Christiane Nüsslein-Volhard and Edward B. Lewis for his research on embryonic development.

Wie·sel /véess'l/, **Elie** (*b.* 1928) Romanian-born US writer. He survived the Holocaust, and after settling in the United States in 1956 devoted himself to writing and speaking about it. His first book *And the World Remained Silent* (1956), abridged as *Night* (1958), is regarded as one of the most important works in the Holocaust literary canon. He won a Nobel Peace Prize (1986). Full name **Wiesel, Eliezer**

> "No one is as capable of gratitude as one who has emerged from the kingdom of night...."
> [Elie Wiesel, *On accepting the Nobel Peace Prize, New York Times*; December 11, 1986]

> "Take sides. Neutrality helps the oppressor, never the victim. Silence encourages the tormentor, never the tormented."
> [Elie Wiesel, *On accepting the Nobel Peace Prize, New York Times*; December 11, 1986]

Wie·sen·thal /véez'n taàl, wéez'n thàwl/, **Simon** (*b.* 1908) Polish-born Austrian war-crimes investigator. He founded the Jewish Documentation Center, Linz (1947) and Vienna (1961), and is thought to have tracked down about 1,000 Nazi war criminals.

wife /wīf/ (*plural* **wives** /wīvz/) *n* **1.** the woman to whom a man is married **2.** *UK regional* a woman, especially a mature or married one (*archaic*) [Old English *wīf* "woman, wife," origin ?] —**wife·hood** *n*

wife·ly /wíflee/ (**-li·er, -li·est**) *adj* showing the attitudes or behavior stereotypically expected of a wife —**wife·li·ness** *n*

Wi-Fi *tdmk* a certification trademark used to certify

the interoperability of wireless local area network products

wig[1] /wig/ *n* **1.** a covering of hair or something resembling hair worn on the head for adornment, ceremony, or to cover baldness **2.** same as **toupee** (*informal*) [Late 17C. Shortening of PERIWIG] —**wigged** *adj*

wig[2] /wig/ (**wigged, wig·ging, wigs**) *vt UK* to speak sternly to somebody who has done something wrong (*dated informal*) [Early 19C < WIG[1]]

wig out *vti US* to become enthusiastic or anxious about something, or make somebody enthusiastic or anxious (*slang*) ○ *He wigged out from the stress of his new job.*

wig·an /wíggən/ *n* a tough fabric used for stiffening clothes [Mid-19C. After the town in Lancashire, England, where the material was first made]

Wig·an /wíggən/ industrial city near Manchester, northwestern England. Population: 301,415 (2001).

wi·geon *n* BIRDS another spelling of **widgeon**

wigged-out *adj US* experiencing an extreme emotional or psychological state such as nervousness or anxiety (*slang*) ○ *wigged-out from staying up all night*

wig·gle /wígg'l/ *vti* (**-gled, -gling, -gles**) **MAKE SMALL MOVEMENTS** to move side to side in small quick movements, or make something move in this way ■ *n* **1. INSTANCE OF WIGGLING** a small quick side to side movement **2. WAVY LINE** a line with irregular curves in it [13C. < Low German or Dutch *wiggelen* < Germanic]

wig·gler /wígglər/ *n* **1.** somebody or something that moves side to side in small quick movements **2.** *US* the larva or pupa of a mosquito

wig·gle room *n* freedom or latitude, e.g., in making decisions or achieving a goal ○ *The contract terms leave little wiggle room.*

wig·gly /wígglee/ (**-gli·er, -gli·est**) *adj* **1.** moving side to side with small quick movements, or able to be moved in this way (*informal*) **2.** with many irregular curves ○ *a wiggly line*

wig·gy /wíggee/ (**-gi·er, -gi·est**) *adj US* (*slang*) **1.** tending to behave in an unconventional or unpredictable way **2.** behaving in an extremely excited and uninhibited way [Mid-20C. < WIG[2], as in *wig out*]

wight /wīt/ *n* a living being, especially a human being (*archaic*) [Old English *wiht* < Germanic]

Wight, Isle of /wīt/ ➧ **Isle of Wight**

wig·let /wígglət/ *n* a small hairpiece for a woman, worn as an addition to a hairstyle rather than to cover the head

wig·mak·er /wíg màykər/ *n* a professional maker of wigs

Wig·ner /wígnər/, **Eugene Paul** (1902–95) Hungarian-born US physicist. He shared the Nobel Prize in physics (1963) for his research on the structure of the atom and its nucleus.

wig·wag /wíg wàg/ *vti* (**-wagged, -wag·ging, -wags**) **1. MOVE FROM SIDE TO SIDE** to wave or swing from side to side in an arc around a fixed point, or make something such as a flag move in this way **2.** NAUT **SIGNAL BY WAVING SOMETHING** to send a message by waving something such as an arm or a flag ■ *n* NAUT **1. PROCESS OF WIGWAGGING** the method of communicating by waving an arm or a flag **2. MESSAGE SENT BY WIGWAGGING** a message communicated by the moving of arms or flags [Late 16C. Reduplication of WAG[1]] —**wig·wag·ger** *n*

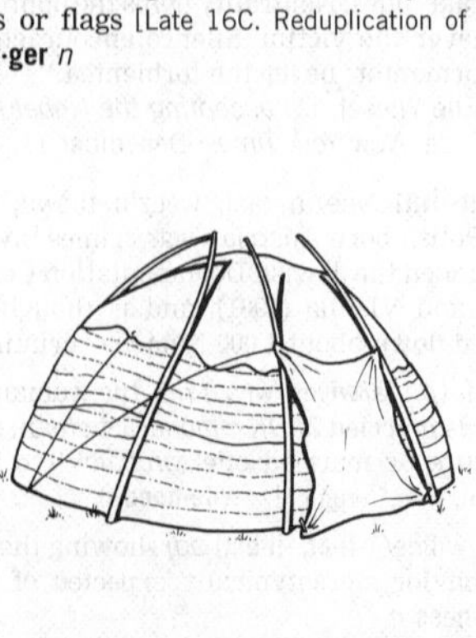

wigwam

wig·wam /wíg wòm/ *n* **1.** a Native North American hut made by covering a conical or dome-shaped framework of poles with woven rush mats or sheets of bark. Wigwams were used by the Algonquian-speaking Native North Americans of the northeastern United States. **2.** a light tent in the shape of a wigwam for a child to play in [Early 17C. < Abenaki *wikewam* "house"]

wik·i·up *n* BUILDINGS another spelling of **wickiup**

wik·i·wik·i /wíkee wìkee/ *adv Hawaii* quickly [< Hawaiian]

Wil·ber·force /wílbər fàwrss/, **William** (1759–1833) British politician and political reformer. His campaign to end the slave trade resulted in its abolition in the Atlantic in 1807, and in the Slave Abolition Act of 1833.

> "They charge me with fanaticism. If to be feelingly alive to the sufferings of my fellow-creatures is to be a fanatic, I am one of the most incurable fanatics ever permitted to be at large."
> [William Wilberforce, *Speech in the British Parliament*; June 19, 1816]

wil·co /wílkō/ *interj* used to indicate that you understand what has just been said in a radio message and will do what is necessary [Mid-20C. Blend and shortening of *will comply*]

Wil·cox·on test /wíl kòks'n-/ *n* a statistical test of the equality of similar or matched groups of data to determine whether they differ significantly from one another, without any assumptions about the underlying distribution patterns [Mid-20C. After Frank *Wilcoxon* (1892–1965), Irish statistician]

wild /wīld/ *adj* **1. NOT TAME OR DOMESTICATED** not kept as a pet or used for display, work, or experimentation, but living freely in a natural habitat **2. NOT CULTIVATED** growing in a natural state rather than being cultivated in fields, parks, or gardens ○ *wild strawberries* **3. PRODUCED BY WILD ANIMALS** produced by animals living freely rather than by domesticated animals ○ *wild honey* **4. REMOTE AND BARREN** describes territory that is not inhabited or able to be inhabited by humans because of being remote and barren **5. ENTHUSIASTIC OR EAGER** feeling enthusiastic or eager or showing enthusiasm or eagerness ○ *I'm not wild about the idea.* **6. OVERWHELMED BY EMOTION** overwhelmed by or showing a strong emotion such as anger, grief, or desire ○ *wild with grief* **7. STORMY** rough and stormy, with a strong wind ○ *wild winds and seas* **8. UNRULY** lively and showing a disregard for rules ○ *The kids next door are really wild.* **9. UNRESTRAINED** marked by a lack of restraint or prudence, especially in things considered to be vices ○ *a really wild party* **10. MESSY** not neat or well-groomed ○ *His hair was wild.* **11. NOT CAREFULLY THOUGHT OUT** not based on rational thought, evidence, or probability ○ *I just made a wild guess.* **12. OFFENSIVE TERM** an offensive term meaning supposedly culturally inferior **13. UNCONVENTIONAL** unconventional, exciting, and slightly irrational (*informal*) ○ *a wild idea* **14. EXCELLENT** very good or admirable (*dated slang*) ○ *Hey, man, that's really wild!* **15. POORLY AIMED** not carefully aimed ○ *throwing wild punches* **16.** CARDS **WITH VALUE ASSIGNED BY PLAYER** describes a playing card that has any value that the player using it wishes to give it ○ *Jokers are wild.* ■ *adv* **1. IN UNCULTIVATED WAY** in a natural state rather than being cultivated in fields, parks, or gardens ○ *flowers that grow wild in the fields* **2. IN UNCONTROLLED WAY** in an uncontrolled, unpredictable, or unplanned way ○ *He just lets his kids run wild.* **3.** *Ireland* **EXTREMELY** to an extreme degree (*informal*) ○ *That was wild stupid.* ■ *n* **UNDOMESTICATED STATE** the natural, free state of an undomesticated animal ○ *Most people have never actually seen a panda in the wild.* ■ **wilds** *npl* **UNINHABITED AREA** an area that is completely uninhabited or only very sparsely populated because it is remote and barren ○ *They live somewhere out in the wilds.* [Old English *wilde* < Indo-European, "wild, woods"] —**wild·ish** *adj* —**wild·ness** *n*

SYNONYMS See *unruly.*

wild ber·ga·mot *n* a North American mint with fragrant leaves. Flowers: purple, in a round cluster. Latin name: *Monarda fistulosa.*

wild boar *n* a wild pig with a coat ranging from pale gray to black, dense bristles, a thin body, and small tusks. Native to: Europe, Asia. Latin name: *Sus scrofa.*

wild card *n* **1. SOMEBODY OR SOMETHING UNPREDICTABLE** somebody or something that is important to a plan or course of action but whose behavior cannot be predicted (*informal*) **2. EXTRA PLAYER OR TEAM IN COMPETITION** an extra player or team selected to take part in a competition although not technically qualified to do so **3.** CARDS **CARD OF NO FIXED VALUE** in card games, a card that can have whatever value its player assigns it **4.** COMPUT **COMPUTER SYMBOL REPRESENTING ANY CHARACTER** a symbol that can be used to represent any character that may appear in the same position in a computer search argument. A single character is usually represented by ? and multiple characters by *.

wild car·rot *n* PLANTS same as **Queen Anne's lace**

wildcat

wild·cat /wīld kàt/ *n* (*plural* **-cats** or *same*) **1. UNDOMESTICATED CAT** a wild cat that resembles the domestic tabby but is heavier and has a bushy tail. Native to: Europe, Asia, Africa. Latin name: *Felis sylvestris.* **2. MEDIUM-SIZED WILD FELINE** any medium-sized wild feline, e.g., the bobcat or caracal **3. QUICK-TEMPERED PERSON** an easily angered person **4.** INDUST **EXPLORATORY OIL OR GAS WELL** an exploratory or speculative well drilled in an area not yet known to be productive of oil or gas **5.** COMM **FINANCIALLY UNSOUND BUSINESS** a financially unsound business ■ *adj* **NOT FINANCIALLY SAFE** practicing unethical or financially risky business methods, or characteristic of such methods ○ *wildcat stocks* ■ *vti* (**-cat·ted, -cat·ting, -cats**) *US* **DRILL EXPLORATORY WELL** to drill an exploratory well in, or take samples in, an area not yet known to have any reserves of what is being sought, especially oil or gas

wild·cat strike *n* a sudden strike not authorized by the labor union that the strikers belong to

wild·cat·ter /wīld kàttər/ *n* **1. PROSPECTOR** a prospector for oil in areas not yet known to be productive **2. UNETHICAL BUSINESSPERSON** a developer or promoter of risky or fraudulent business ventures **3. WILDCAT STRIKE PARTICIPANT** a participant in a sudden strike not authorized by the labor union that he or she belongs to

wild cel·er·y *n* PLANTS same as **tape grass**

wild child *n* a reckless, impulsive, and undisciplined person, usually a young adult (*informal*)

wild dog *n* any wild member of the dog family, especially the dingo, the African hunting dog, or the dhole

Wilde /wīld/, **Oscar** (1854–1900) Irish writer. His works include the plays *Lady Windermere's Fan* (1892) and *The Importance of Being Earnest* (1895) and the novel *The Picture of Dorian Gray* (1891). His flamboyance and legendary wit made him a leading figure in society, but he was convicted of sodomy and sentenced to two years' hard labor in 1895. Full name **Wilde, Oscar Fingal O'Flahertie Wills**. See illustration on next page

> "We have really everything in common with America nowadays, except, of course, language."
> [Oscar Wilde, *The Canterville Ghost*; 1887]

> "I can resist everything except temptation."
> [Oscar Wilde, *Lady Windermere's Fan*; 1892]

AKG London
Oscar Wilde

wil·de·beest /wíldə bèest/ (*plural* **-beests** or *same*) *n* ZOOL same as **gnu** [Early 19C. < Afrikaans, "wild beast"]

wil·der /wíldər/ (**-dered, -der·ing, -ders**) *vti* (*archaic*) **1.** to go astray, or lead somebody or something astray **2.** to become confused by a number of complex options, or confuse somebody in this way [Early 17C. Origin ?] —**wil·der·ment** *n*

Wil·der /wíldər/, **Billy** (1906–2002) Austrian-born US movie director. At home in a wide variety of movie genres, he made several Hollywood classics, including *Sunset Boulevard* (1950) and *Some Like It Hot* (1959). Born **Wilder, Samuel**

> "An audience is never wrong. An individual member of it may be an imbecile, but a thousand imbeciles together in the dark—that's critical genius."
> [Billy Wilder, *Arena (BBC Television)*; January 24, 1992]

Wil·der, Laura Ingalls (1867–1957) US writer. She is famed for her "Little House" books, including *Little House in the Big Woods* (1932) and *Little House on the Prairie* (1935), which were based on her childhood experiences on the western frontier in the 1870s and 80s.

Wil·der, Thornton (1897–1975) US writer. His Pulitzer-Prize-winning works include the novel *The Bridge of San Luis Rey* (1927) and the play *Our Town* (1938). Full name **Wilder, Thornton Niven**. See Cultural note at **town**

> "The best part of married life is the fights. The rest is merely so-so."
> [Thornton Wilder, *The Matchmaker*; 1954]

wil·der·ness /wíldərnəss/ *n* **1.** NATURAL UNCULTIVATED LAND a mostly uninhabited area of land in its natural uncultivated state, sometimes deliberately preserved like this, e.g., a forest or mountainous region **2.** BARREN AREA an area that is empty or barren ○ *in the vast wilderness of outer space* **3.** DELIBERATELY UNCULTIVATED LAND a piece of land that is deliberately not cultivated but is left to grow wild, e.g., in a garden **4.** UNCOMFORTABLE SITUATION a place, situation, or multitude of people or things that makes somebody feel confused, overwhelmed, or desolate ○ *the wilderness of the big city* [Old English *wilddēornes* < *wilddēor* "wild beast" < *wilde* "wild" + *dēor* "animal"] ◇ **be (a voice) crying in the wilderness** to be giving advice or suggestions that are very unlikely to be followed

wil·der·ness ar·e·a *n US* a protected area set aside for preservation in as natural a state as possible, with restrictions on most human activity except for nonmotorized forms of outdoor recreation ○ *backpacking in the wilderness areas*

wild-eyed *adj* **1.** with eyes that are wide and glaring because of fear, anger, or a psychological disorder **2.** marked by or advocating ideas that are so extreme and far-fetched as to be completely impracticable

wild·fire /wíld fìr/ *n* **1.** RAPIDLY SPREADING FIRE a fierce fire that spreads rapidly, especially in an area of wilderness **2.** PHYS same as **will-o'-the-wisp** (sense 1) **3.** LIGHTNING WITHOUT THUNDER lightning that occurs without audible thunder **4.** INFLAMMABLE MATERIAL AS WEAPON any inflammable material formerly used in warfare ◇ **like wildfire** very rapidly

wild·flow·er /wíld flòwr/ *n* a flowering plant growing in a natural, uncultivated state, or the flower of such a plant

wild·fowl /wíld fòwl/ (*plural same*) *n* a bird that is hunted for food or sport, e.g., a duck, goose, pheasant, or quail —**wild·fowl·er** *n* —**wild·fowl·ing** *n*

wild ge·ra·ni·um *n* a geranium with deeply divided leaves. Flowers: rosy purple. Native to: North America. Latin name: *Geranium maculatum*.

wild gin·ger *n* an herb with two heart-shaped leaves and an aromatic root. Flowers: single, reddish brown. Native to: North America. Latin name: *Asarum canadense*.

wild-goose chase *n* a futile search for something that there is no chance of finding, especially because it does not exist [Originally of an irregular course, like the patterned flight of wild geese]

wild hy·a·cinth *n* PLANTS same as **bluebell** (sense 2)

wild in·di·go *n* a perennial plant that is tall and branching with leaves similar to clover leaves. Flowers: bright yellow in clusters. Native to: dry, open areas of North America. Latin name: *Baptisia tinctoria*.

wild·ing /wílding/ *n* **1.** WILD PLANT OR TREE a plant that grows wild, or one that has escaped from cultivation, especially a wild crab-apple tree **2.** FRUIT the fruit of a plant that grows wild or that has escaped from cultivation, especially a wild crab apple **3.** WILD ANIMAL a wild animal ■ *adj* UNCULTIVATED uncultivated or undomesticated

wild·land /wíld lànd/ *n* land that is in a natural uncultivated state, especially when it forms a habitat for wildlife (*often used in the plural*)

wild·life /wíld lìf/ *n* wild animals, birds, and other living things, sometimes including vegetation, living in a natural undomesticated state

wild·life park *n* LEISURE same as **safari park**

wild·life ref·uge *n US* a protected area set aside to preserve the habitats of some types of wild animals, especially migratory waterfowl, and in which people are allowed to view wildlife in a natural setting

wild·ling /wíldling/ *n* BIOL same as **wilding**

wild·ly /wíldlee/ *adv* **1.** WITH ENTHUSIASM in a very enthusiastic way ○ *cheering wildly* **2.** WITHOUT CAREFUL THOUGHT not considering something carefully **3.** VERY to a great extent (*informal*) ○ *not wildly enthusiastic about the idea* **4.** IN WAY THAT SHOWS FEAR in an uncontrolled way that betrays fear or anxiety, and often with eyes that are wide and staring ○ *looking wildly in all directions* **5.** STRONGLY in a fierce and rough way ○ *The wind blew wildly through the trees.*

wild mus·tard *n* PLANTS same as **charlock**

wild oat *n* a weedy annual grass of temperate regions that resembles cultivated oats. Latin name: *Avena fatua*. ◇ **sow your wild oats** to behave in an uncontrolled way, especially sexually, while young

wild ol·ive *n* same as **devilwood**

wild pink *n* a small perennial plant. Flowers: pink or white in hairy clusters. Native to: dry woods of the eastern United States. Latin name: *Silene caroliniana*.

wild pitch *n* a baseball pitch that a catcher could not have caught and that results in a runner advancing to the next base

wild prai·rie rose *n* PLANTS a species of wild rose. Flowers: pink, with a central cluster of yellow stamens. Native to: central US and south central Canada. Latin name: *Rosa arkansana*.

wild rice *n* **1.** the dark grain of a grass, traditionally used as food by Native Americans **2.** a tall perennial grass that grows in water and produces edible seeds. Native to: North America. Latin name: *Zizania aquatica*.

wild rose *n* any wild-growing rose, e.g., the dog rose and sweetbriar

wild rub·ber *n* rubber obtained from uncultivated rubber trees

wild rye *n* a perennial tall grass. Native to: temperate regions of the northern hemisphere. Genus: *Elymus*.

wild silk *n* **1.** silk fiber obtained from wild silkworms **2.** fabric woven from the silk of wild silkworms, or an imitation of this made with short silk fibers

wild type *n* the form of an organism, strain, or gene that results from natural breeding, as distinct from mutant forms or those resulting from selective breeding

Wild West *n* the western United States in the second half of the 19th century, regarded as a place of lawlessness

Wild West show *n* a form of entertainment involving the demonstration of skills associated with the Wild West, e.g., shooting, riding, and roping cattle, especially performed by people dressed as cowboys

wild·wood /wíld wòod/ *n* natural uncultivated woodland

wile /wīl/ *n* CUNNING STRATEGY a trick or cunning ruse ■ **wiles** *npl* CUNNING BEHAVIOR cunning behavior intended to persuade somebody to do something, especially in the form of insincere charm or flattery ■ *vt* (**wiled, wil·ing, wiles**) PERSUADE SOMEBODY BY WILES to trick or entice somebody into doing or not doing something [12C. Origin ?]

SPELLCHECK See *while*.

Wil·frid /wílfrid/, **Wil·frith** /wílfrith/, **St.** (634–709?) English prelate. At the Synod of Whitby (664), he successfully argued for the replacement of Celtic forms of worship with Roman ones in the English Church.

wil·ful *adj* another spelling of **willful**

SYNONYMS See *unruly*.

Wil·helm /wíl hèlm/ highest mountain in Papua New Guinea. Height: 14,793 ft./4,509 m.

Wil·helm I /víl hèlm/ (1797–1888) king of Prussia. He became the first emperor of Germany in 1871, and is noted for the repression of the later part of his reign.

Wil·helm II (1859–1941) emperor of Germany. A grandson of Queen Victoria, he succeeded his grandfather Wilhelm I in 1888 and presided over a rise in German militarism. After defeat in World War I he went into exile.

Wil·hel·mi·na /wìl hel méenə/ (1880–1962) **queen of the Netherlands** In the course of her reign (1890–1948) she supported Dutch neutrality during World War I and established a government in exile in England during World War II. Full name **Wilhelmina Helena Pauline Maria**

Wil·helms·ha·ven /vìl helmz haávən, -helms haáfən/ city and port in northwestern Germany. It was formerly an important naval base. Population: 91,230 (1997).

Wilkes /wilks/, **Charles** (1798–1877) US naval officer and explorer. He charted the coastlines of northwestern North America, the Antarctic, and numerous South Pacific islands (1838–42). As a Union officer during the Civil War, his interception and removal of Confederate commissioners aboard a neutral British ship caused an international crisis.

Wilkes-Bar·re /wilks bàrree, -bàrrə/ city on the Susquehanna River in northeastern Pennsylvania. A center of coal-mining until the 1940s, it is now an industrial city. Population: 42,021 (2002 estimate).

Wil·kie /wílkee/, **Wendell Lewis** (1892–1944) US lawyer and politician. Although he ran (unsuccessfully) against Franklin D. Roosevelt for president in 1940, after the election he became a supporter of some of FDR's most controversial programs. At Roosevelt's request, he toured Britain and the Soviet Union (1941–42), reporting on wartime conditions. Upon his return he wrote *One World* (1943), in which he made the case for establishing a postwar international peacekeeping organization.

Wil·kins /wílkinz/, **Maurice** (*b.* 1916) New Zealand-born British biophysicist. He worked with James D. Watson and Francis H. Crick in exploring the structure of DNA, for which they shared the Nobel Prize in physiology or medicine (1962). Full name **Wilkins, Maurice Hugh Frederick**

Wil·kins, Roy (1901–81) US civil rights leader. He headed the National Association for the Advancement of Colored People (NAACP) (1955–77).

will[1] /wil/ CORE MEANING: a modal verb used to indicate future time ○ *Delegates from all over Europe will*

attend the forum. ○ *Will you ever be able to forgive him?* ○ *Your suit will be ready for collection tomorrow.*
modal v **1.** **POLITE QUESTIONS** used in questions to make polite invitations or offers ○ *Will you sit down, please?* ○ *Will you have more coffee?* **2.** **REQUESTS** used in questions to make requests ○ *Will you take the washing out for me please?* ○ *Phone the garage, will you?* **3.** **COMMANDS** used when ordering somebody to do something ○ *You will do exactly as I say.* **4.** **CUSTOMARY BEHAVIOR** used to indicate the way that something usually happens or the way that somebody usually does something ○ *The wetter the road conditions, the harder it will be for a vehicle to stop.* ○ *When they're out together they will shop till they drop!* **5.** **WILLINGNESS** used to indicate that somebody is willing to do something ○ *I will mail your letters for you.* ○ *I will not tolerate this kind of behavior.* **6.** **ABILITY** used to indicate the ability or capacity of something ○ *That wardrobe will not fit in your bedroom.* ○ *The truck will carry loads of up to 10 tons.* **7.** **EXPECTATION** used to express surmise or likelihood ○ *That will be them at the door now.* ○ *He will have left the country by now.* **8.** **INCLUSION** used to indicate the inevitability of something happening or being true ○ *She will stay up till all hours in front of the TV.* [Old English *wyllan* < Indo-European]

USAGE See ***shall.***

will² /wil/ *n* **1.** **PART OF MIND THAT MAKES DECISIONS** the part of the mind with which somebody consciously decides things **2.** **POWER TO DECIDE** the power to make decisions ○ *This lawn mower seems to have a will of its own!* **3.** **PROCESS OF MAKING DECISIONS** the use of the mind to make decisions about things ○ *It's a matter of will as much as opportunity.* **4.** **DETERMINATION** the determination to do something ○ *She has lots of ability but she lacks the will to succeed.* **5.** **DESIRE OR INCLINATION** a desire or inclination to do something **6.** **ATTITUDE TOWARD SOMEBODY ELSE** the attitude or feelings somebody has toward somebody or something ○ *I bear you no ill will.* **7.** **SOMETHING THAT SOMEBODY WANTS TO HAPPEN** what a person or group, especially one in authority, wants to happen (*formal*) ○ *It was her will that he should never be told the truth.* **8.** LAW **STATEMENT OF DISTRIBUTION OF DECEASED'S PROPERTY** a statement of what somebody wants to happen to his or her property after he or she dies, or a legal document containing this statement ■ *vt* (**willed, will·ing, wills**) **1.** **TRY TO CAUSE SOMETHING BY THOUGHTS** to try to make something happen by the power of the mind ○ *He willed himself to stay awake.* ○ *Her parents were watching her run, willing her on.* **2.** LAW **LEAVE SOMEBODY SOMETHING IN WILL** to give something officially to somebody by declaring it in a will **3.** **WANT OR DECIDE SOMETHING** to want something to happen or to decide that something will happen (*archaic or formal*) ○ *It shall be as God wills.* [Old English *willa* (noun), *wyllan* (verb), and *willian* (verb < noun) < Indo-European, "to will, wish"] —**will·able** *adj* —**will·er** *n* ◇ **at will** when somebody wishes (*formal*) ○ *They are free to come and go at will.* ◇ **with a will** with energy and enthusiasm ○ *He set about the task with a will.* ◇ **with the best will in the world** used to indicate that somebody cannot do something however much he or she wishes or tries to do it ○ *With the best will in the world we won't be able to supervise her all the time.*

Wil·lad·sen /wí làdsən/, **Steen** (*b.* 1944) Danish geneticist. He was responsible for the first cloning of a mammal from embryo cells.

Wil·lam·ette /wə lámmit/ river in western Oregon flowing north into the Columbia River near Portland. Length: 309 mi./497 km.

Wil·lard /wíllərd/, **Frances** (1839–98) US reformer and educator. She headed the Women's Christian Temperance Union (1879–98) and the National Council of Women (1890–98). Full name **Willard, Frances Elizabeth Caroline**

Wil·lard, Jess (1881–1968) US boxer. He beat Jack Johnson for the heavyweight world title (1915), which he held until he was defeated by Jack Dempsey (1919).

wil·lem·ite /wíllə mìt/ *n* a colorless fluorescent brown, green, or red zinc sulfate mineral [Mid-19C. After *Willem* I (1772–1843), king of the Netherlands]

Wil·lem·stad /víllәm staat/ capital and port of the Netherlands Antilles, on southern Curaçao. Population: 125,000 (1985).

wil·let /willit/ *n* a large gray shorebird with a long straight beak, long legs, and a distinctive black and white wing pattern. Native to: North America. Latin name: *Catoptrophorus semipalmatus.* [Mid-19C. An imitation of its call]

will·ful /wílfəl/, **wil·ful** *adj* **1.** done deliberately, especially with the intention of harming somebody or in spite of knowing that it will harm somebody **2.** stubbornly determined to act on a desire, regardless of the opinions or advice of others —**will·ful·ly** *adv* —**will·ful·ness** *n*

SYNONYMS See ***unruly.***

Wil·liam /wíllyəm/, (*b.* 1982) Prince. He is the first child of Prince Charles and Diana, Princess of Wales. Full name **Prince William Arthur Philip Louis**

Wil·liam I, (1028?–87) king of England. A Norman, he invaded England and defeated Harold II at the Battle of Hastings (1066), subsequently imposing a new ruling aristocracy on England. The *Domesday Book* was compiled during his reign. Known as **William the Conqueror**

Wil·liam I (1533–84) prince of Orange. He led the Dutch rebellion against the imperial rule of Philip II that culminated in the Pacification of Ghent (1576) and the Union of Utrecht (1579). Known as **William the Silent**

Wil·liam II (1056?–1100) king of England. The son and successor of William I, he seized territory in Normandy and Scotland. He was killed, probably accidentally, while hunting in the New Forest. Known as **William Rufus**

Wil·liam III (1650–1702) king of England, Scotland, and Ireland. Dutch-born, he was the grandson of Charles I and the husband of James II's daughter, Mary. He and Mary replaced James II on the English throne after the Revolution of 1689. Known as **William of Orange**

Wil·liam IV (1765–1837) king of the United Kingdom. He succeeded his brother George IV on the throne after a 50-year naval career, and during his reign (1830–37) was the last monarch to exercise the royal prerogative. Known as **the Sailor King**

Wil·liams /wíllyəmz/ (*plural same*), **Wil·liams pear** *n UK* same as **Bartlett**¹ [Early 19C. After *William's* Nursery of Middlesex]

Wil·liams /wíllyəmz/, **Eric** (1911–81) Trinidadian politician and historian. Having led his country to independence from the United Kingdom, he then became its first prime minister (1962–81). He wrote *Capitalism and Slavery* (1944).

Wil·liams, Hank (1923–53) US musician. He developed a wide audience for country music through his recordings and performances on radio and at the Grand Ole Opry. His songs include "Your Cheatin' Heart." Born **Williams, Hiram**

> "You got to have smelled a lot of mule manure before you can sing like a hillbilly."
> [Hank Williams. Quoted in *Look*; July 13, 1971]

Wil·liams, Jody (*b.* 1950) US political activist. She shared the 1997 Nobel Peace Prize for her efforts to ban landmines worldwide.

Wil·liams, John (*b.* 1932) US composer and conductor. He is known especially for his movie scores, including the Academy Award-winning scores for the movies *Jaws* (1975), *Star Wars* (1977), *E.T. the Extra-Terrestrial* (1982), and *Schindler's List* (1993).

Wil·liams, Robin (*b.* 1952) US comedian and actor. Originally known for his standup comedy, he went on to perform both comic and serious roles in Hollywood movies, and won an Academy Award for *Good Will Hunting* (1997).

> "[Psychotherapy is] open-heart surgery in installments."
> [Robin Williams, *New York Times*; January 25, 1988]

Wil·liams, Roger (1603–83) American colonial cleric. A Puritan who advocated religious freedom, he left Massachusetts to establish a colony (1636) in present-day Rhode Island.

Wil·liams, Serena (*b.* 1981) US tennis player. She and her sister Venus Williams came to dominate international women's tennis after 1999.

Wil·liams, Shirley, Baroness Williams of Crosby (*b.* 1930) British politician. She held various ministerial posts in the Labor governments of the 1970s before cofounding the Social Democratic Party in 1981. She served as the party's president from 1982 to 1988. Born **Brittain, Shirley Vivien Teresa**

Wil·liams, Ted (*b.* 1918) US baseball player. A Boston Red Sox outfielder (1939–60), he was one of the game's greatest hitters, batting.406 in 1941 and compiling a lifetime average of .344. Full name **Williams, Theodore Samuel**

> "Nothing has as many variables and as few constants."
> [Ted Williams, on the techniques used in batting a baseball, *The Science of Hitting*; 1971]

New Directions Publishing Corp.
Tennessee Williams

Wil·liams, Tennessee (1911–83) US playwright. His plays are largely set in the American South, and he won Pulitzer Prizes for *A Streetcar Named Desire* (1947) and *Cat on a Hot Tin Roof* (1955). Born **Williams, Thomas Lanier**. See Cultural note at **roof**

> "A vacuum is a hell of a lot better than some of the stuff that nature replaces it with."
> [Tennessee Williams, *Cat on a Hot Tin Roof*; 1955]

> "Humanity is just a work in progress."
> [Tennessee Williams, *Camino Real*; 1953]

Wil·liams, Venus (*b.* 1980) US tennis player. She has recorded the fastest ever women's serve, and with her sister Serena Williams came to dominate international women's tennis after 1999.

Wil·liams, William (1731–1811) American patriot. Representing Connecticut, he was a signatory of the Declaration of Independence (1776), and raised funds and equipment for the Continental Army.

Wil·liams, William Carlos (1883–1963) US writer and physician. While practicing medicine (1910–51), he produced poetry and novels concerned with everyday American life, including the epic poem *Paterson* (1946–58).

> "Minds like beds always made up, / (more stony than a shore) / unwilling or unable."
> [William Carlos Williams, *Paterson*; 1946–58]

> "A cool of books / will sometimes lead the mind to libraries / of a hot afternoon, if books can be found / cool to the sense to lead the mind away."
> [William Carlos Williams, *Paterson*; 1946–58]

Wil·liams·burg /wíllyəmz bùrg/ city in southeastern Virginia. The central part of the city has been restored along colonial lines and is an important tourist center. Population: 11,693 (2002 estimate).

Wil·liam Tell /wìlyəm tél/ *n* in Swiss legend, a patriot who liberated Switzerland from Austrian rule in the 14th century. He was forced by the Austrian governor to shoot an arrow through an apple on his son's head and later killed the governor.

wil·lie *n* another spelling of willy (*informal offensive*)

wil·lies /wílleez/ *npl* an uncomfortable, anxious, or fearful feeling (*informal*) [Late 19C. Origin ?]

will·ing /wílling/ *adj* **1. READY TO DO SOMETHING VOLUNTARILY** ready to do something without being forced **2. HELPFUL** cooperative and enthusiastic **3. OFFERED VOLUNTARILY** offered or given by somebody readily and enthusiastically —**will·ing·ly** *adv* —**will·ing·ness** *n*

wil·li·waw /wíllee wàw/ *n* **1. GUST OF WIND** a sudden gust of wind **2. COLD WIND BLOWING SEAWARD** a violent gust of cold wind that blows down from a mountainous region to the coast and out to sea, especially in the Straits of Magellan and in Alaska **3. TURMOIL** a state of confusion or turmoil [Mid-19C. Origin ?]

will-o'-the-wisp /wíllə thə wísp/ *n* **1.** a phosphorescent light sometimes seen at night over marshy ground, caused by the spontaneous combustion of gases given off by rotting organic matter **2.** somebody or something that is misleading or elusive, e.g., a false hope [< *Will*, shortening of the forename *William*, + OF + THE + WISP]

wil·low /wíllō/ *n* **1. TREE WITH LONG FLEXIBLE BRANCHES** a tree or bush with long flexible branches, narrow leaves, and catkins containing small flowers without petals. Some species are valued for their wood, twigs, and tanbark. Genus: *Salix*. **2. WILLOW WOOD** the wood of a willow tree **3.** INDUST **MACHINE WITH SPIKES** a machine with a revolving spiked cylinder inside a box that is also fitted with spikes. Use: cleaning or loosening fibrous materials such as cotton, wool, or rags. [Old English *welig* < Germanic] —**wil·low·ish** *adj*

CULTURAL NOTE ***The Wind in the Willows***, a children's story (1908) by British writer Kenneth Grahame. Originally written as a bedtime story for Grahame's son, it recounts the mishaps that befall four animals – Mole, Ratty, Toad, and Badger – when they venture outside their natural habitats. Much loved by children, the tales are also enjoyed by adults as entertaining allegories of human behavior.

wil·low gold·finch *n* BIRDS same as **American goldfinch**

wil·low grouse *n* UK same as **willow ptarmigan**

wil·low herb *n* PLANTS same as **fireweed**

wil·low oak *n* an oak with narrow leaves and hard wood. Native to: North America. Latin name: *Quercus phellos*.

wil·low pat·tern *n* a pattern used to decorate china, usually blue on a white background, featuring a Chinese landscape with a willow tree, pagoda-style buildings, a bridge, and two swallows

wil·low ptar·mi·gan *n US* a plump ground bird of the grouse family that turns from mottled brown to white in the winter. Native to: Arctic regions. Latin name: *Lagopus lagopus*.

willowware

wil·low·ware /wíllō wèr/ *n* china decorated with the willow pattern

wil·low·y /wíllō ee/ (**-i·er, -i·est**) *adj* **1. GRACEFUL** describes somebody who is slim, graceful, and elegant, partly because of being tall **2. FLEXIBLE** able to be bent easily, and springing back into place **3. COVERED BY WILLOWS** covered or shaded by willow trees

will·pow·er /wíl pòwr/ *n* a combination of determination and self-discipline that enables somebody to do something despite the difficulties involved

Wills /wilz/, **Helen Newington** (1905–98) US tennis player. She won the US women's singles title seven times between 1923 and 1931, and was eight times Wimbledon singles champion. Also known as **Moody, Helen Wills**

wil·ly /wíllee/ (*plural* **-lies**), **wil·lie** *n* an offensive term for a penis (*informal*) [Early 20C. < shortening of the proper name *William*]

wil·ly-nil·ly /wíllee níllee/ *adv* **1. WITHOUT WANTING TO** whether or not somebody wants it to happen ○ *He won't be rushed willy-nilly into a quick decision.* **2. HAPHAZARDLY** in a disorganized or unplanned way ○ *Totally confused by now, I handed out the invitations willy-nilly.* ■ *adj* **1. HAPPENING WITHOUT CHOICE** happening or existing without plan or choice **2. HAPHAZARD** lacking direction or organization [Early 17C. < *will I, nill I* "whether I wish it or do not wish it"]

Wil·mette /wil mét/ village in northeastern Illinois on the shore of Lake Michigan, north of Evanston. It is a northern suburb of Chicago. Population: 27,531 (2002 estimate).

Wil·ming·ton /wílmingtən/ **1.** city in northern Delaware. Situated on the Delaware River, it is the largest city in the state. Population: 72,503 (2002 estimate). **2.** city in southeastern North Carolina on the Cape Fear River. It is the state's principal seaport and an important commercial center. Population: 90,644 (2002 estimate).

Wil·mut /wílmət/, **Ian** (*b.* 1944) British embryologist. With Keith Campbell, he was responsible for the first successful cloning of a mammal from adult cells.

Wil·son, Mount /wílss'n/ mountain in southern California. It is home to Mount Wilson Observatory, an astronomical observatory. Height: 5,710 ft./1,740 m.

Wil·son /wílss'n/, **Alexander** (1766–1813) British-born US ornithologist. He conducted the first major studies of North American birds and wrote and illustrated *American Ornithology* (1808–13).

Wil·son, August (*b.* 1945) US playwright. He won Pulitzer prizes for his plays *Fences* (1985) and *The Piano Lesson* (1987) which portray the lives of African Americans.

> "You all line up at the door with your hands out. I give you the lint from my pockets. I give you my sweat and my blood. I ain't got no tears. I done spent them."
> [August Wilson, *Fences*; 1985]

Wil·son, Edith (1872–1961) US first lady (1915–21). The second wife of Woodrow Wilson, she took over many presidential duties after her husband suffered a severe stroke in 1919. Full name **Wilson, Edith Bolling Galt**

Wil·son, Edmund (1895–1972) US literary critic. One of the leading essayists of his generation, he wrote critical studies across a broad spectrum of literature and social thought, including a volume on the Civil War, *Patriotic Gore* (1962).

> "The taking over by the state of the means of production and the dictatorship in the interests of the proletariat can by themselves never guarantee the happiness of anybody but the dictators themselves... Lenin and Trotsky...founded a dictatorship which perpetuated itself as an autocracy."
> [Edmund Wilson, "Old Antichrist's Sayings," *Letters on Literature and Politics 1912–72*; 1977]

Wil·son, Ellen (1860–1914) US first lady (1913–14). The first wife of Woodrow Wilson and a professional artist, she pursued social reforms including the improvement of slum housing. She died during her husband's first term in office. Full name **Wilson, Ellen Louise Axson**

Harold Wilson

Wil·son, Harold, Baron Wilson of Rievaulx (1916–95) British prime minister (1964–70 and 1974–76). During his premierships, he sought to bolster Britain's economy and introduced the first antiracist legislation. See table at **prime minister**. Full name **Wilson, James Harold**

> "He who rejects change is the architect of decay. The only human institution which rejects progress is the cemetery."
> [Harold Wilson, *Speech to the House of Commons on US involvement in the Vietnam War*; January 5, 1966]

Wil·son, Henry (1812–75) vice president of the United States (1873–75). He joined the Republican Party (1856) because of its opposition to slavery and became Ulysses S. Grant's vice president in 1873. Born **Colbath, Jeremiah Jones**

Wil·son, James (1742–98) British-born US lawyer, patriot, and judge. One of the signatories of the Declaration of Independence, he was elected to the Continental Congress in 1775 and appointed associate justice of the US Supreme Court (1789–98).

Wil·son, Robert (1936–2002) US astrophysicist. He and coresearcher Arno Penzias discovered background radiation in the Milky Way, which supported the "big bang" theory. They shared the Nobel Prize in physics (1978). Full name **Wilson, Robert Woodrow**

Woodrow Wilson

Wil·son, Woodrow (1856–1924) 28th president of the United States (1913–21). A Democratic president, he brought the United States into World War I in 1917 and negotiated the peace treaty in 1918, making the League of Nations a part of the treaty. He was awarded the Nobel Peace Prize (1919). Full name **Wilson, Thomas Woodrow**. See table at **president** —**Wil·so·ni·an** /wil sṓnee ən/ *adj*

> "A general association of nations must be formed under specific covenants for the purpose of affording mutual guarantees of political independence and territorial integrity to great and small states alike."
> [Woodrow Wilson, *Speech to Congress*, "Fourteen Points"; January 8, 1918]

> "The world must be made safe for democracy."
> [Woodrow Wilson, *Speech to Congress*; April 2, 1917]

Wil·son's dis·ease /wílss'nz-/ *n* a rare hereditary disease resulting from an inability to metabolize copper and marked by cirrhosis of the liver, damage to other organs, and psychiatric disorder [Early 20C.

After S. A. Kinnier *Wilson* (1878–1937), British neurologist]

Wil·son's phal·a·rope *n* a small swimming shorebird with a long thin beak. Native to: western North American wetlands. Latin name: *Phalaropus tricolor*. [Early 19C. After Alexander *Wilson*]

Wil·son's Prom·on·to·ry /wilss'nz-/ peninsula in southeastern Victoria, Australia. It is the most southerly point on the Australian mainland.

wilt[1] /wilt/ *v* (**wilt·ed, wilt·ing, wilts**) **1.** *vti* **DROOP OR SHRIVEL** to droop or shrivel through lack of water, too much heat, or disease, or make a plant droop or shrivel **2.** *vi* **BECOME WEAK** to become weak and tired, e.g., because of heat **3.** *vti* **LOSE SPIRIT** to lose confidence, composure, or enthusiasm, or make somebody do this ■ *n* **1. DROOPING OR SHRIVELING** the drooping of plants or shriveling of leaves because of a lack of water, too much heat, or disease **2. PLANT DISEASE** a plant disease caused by fungi, bacteria, or viruses that make plants droop and leaves shrivel **3. ACT OF WILTING** an instance of wilting or the condition of having wilted [Late 17C. Origin ?]

wilt[2] /wilt/ *vti* 2nd person singular present of **will**[1] (*archaic*)

Wil·ton /wílt'n/ *n* carpet with a thick velvety pile [Late 18C. After a town in Wiltshire, England]

Wilt·shire /wílt sheer, -shər/ county in southwestern England. Trowbridge is the administrative center. Population: 432,973 (2001). Area: 1,344 sq. mi./3,486 sq. km.

wi·ly /wílee/ (**-li·er, -li·est**) *adj* skilled at using clever tricks to deceive people —**wil·i·ly** *adv* —**wil·i·ness** *n*

wim·ble /wímb'l/ *n* a handheld tool used for boring holes ■ *vt* (**-bled, -bling, -bles**) to bore a hole with a wimble [13C. < Anglo-Norman, probably < Middle Dutch *wimmel* "augur"]

Wim·ble·don /wímb'ldən/ southern suburb of London, England. It is the home of the All England Lawn Tennis Club, the site of annual international tennis championships.

wimp /wimp/ *n* an offensive term that deliberately insults somebody regarded as weak, timid, unassertive, or ineffectual (*informal insult*) ■ *vi* (**wimped, wimp·ing, wimps**) [Early 20C. Origin ?] —**wimp·ish** *adj* —**wimp·y** *adj*

wimp out (**wimped out, wimping out, wimps out**) *vi* to fail to do or finish doing something because of fear or a weakness of character (*slang*)

WIMP[1] /wimp/ *n* a graphical user interface for computers, designed to make them more user-friendly, that includes windows, icons, mice, and pull-down menus. Full form **windows, icons, mice, and pull-down menus**

WIMP[2] /wimp/ *n* a hypothetical nonbaryonic subatomic particle that has been proposed as a possible form of dark matter. Full form **weakly interacting massive particle**

wim·ple /wímp'l/ *n* **1. WOMAN'S HEAD COVERING** a cloth covering for a woman's head and neck. The wimple was common in medieval Europe and it is still worn by some orders of nuns. **2. FOLD IN CLOTH** a fold or pleat in a piece of cloth ■ *v* (**-pled, -pling, -ples**) **1.** *vi* **RIPPLE** to form small undulating waves **2.** *vt* **DRESS SOMEBODY IN WIMPLE** to put a wimple on somebody (*archaic*) [Old English *wimpel* < Germanic]

win /win/ *v* (**won** /wun/, **win·ning, wins**) **1.** *vti* **ACHIEVE VICTORY** to beat any or every opponent or enemy in a competition or fight **2.** *vt* **GET SOMETHING FOR DEFEATING OTHERS** to get something as a prize by beating other competitors ○ *proud of the cups he had won for swimming* **3.** *vt* **MAKE SOMEBODY SUCCEED IN GETTING SOMETHING** to be the reason that somebody is first in something or receives something as a prize ○ *That photo is sure to win you a prize.* **4.** *vt* **GAIN SOMETHING** to gain something such as respect or friendship, e.g., because of something done or said or an ability shown, or to make somebody do this ○ *His attitude won him few friends in the company.* **5.** *vt* **GET SOMETHING** to obtain something by hard work (*literary*) ○ *winning his livelihood by the sweat of his brow* **6.** *vt* **REACH PLACE WITH EFFORT** to arrive somewhere by great effort or with difficulty (*literary*) **7.** *vt* **CAPTURE SOMETHING USING FORCE** to capture something such as a city using force (*formal*) **8.** *vt* **GAIN SUPPORT** to persuade somebody to do something or agree to something, or to gain somebody's sympathy or support **9.** *vt* **EARN LOVE OF SOMEBODY** to persuade somebody to love or marry you **10.** *vt* MIN EXTRACT **GET SOMETHING BY MINING** to mine coal, oil, or ore from a source **11.** *vt* MIN EXTRACT **PREPARE LODE FOR MINING** to discover a source of coal, oil, or ore and prepare it for mining **12.** *vt* MIN EXTRACT **EXTRACT SOMETHING FROM ORE** to extract a metal or mineral from its ore ■ *n* **1. VICTORY** success in a competition, game, or bet ○ *The team has had six wins in a row.* **2. AMOUNT OF MONEY WON** the amount of money won, e.g., in a bet **3. FIRST PLACE** the position of first place in a race [Old English *winnan* < Indo-European, "to desire"] —**win·less** *adj* —**win·na·ble** *adj* ◇ **(you) win some, (you) lose some** used to indicate philosophically or humorously that in life everyone has some successes and some failures

win out *vi* to be successful or dominant after a struggle

win over *vt* to persuade somebody to agree with you, support you, or give you permission

wince /winss/ *vi* (**winced, winc·ing, winc·es**) **1. MAKE PAINED EXPRESSION** to make an expression of pain with the face because of seeing or thinking of something unpleasant or embarrassing **2. MOVE BODY BACK SLIGHTLY** to make an involuntary movement away from something because of pain or fear ■ *n* **1. EXPRESSION OF PAIN** a facial expression of pain or fear **2. EXPRESSION OF DISPLEASURE OR EMBARRASSMENT** a facial reaction to seeing or thinking of something unpleasant or embarrassing **3. SLIGHT MOVEMENT AWAY** a slight movement away from something because of pain or fear [13C. < Anglo-Norman, variant of Old French *guencir* "turn aside" < Germanic] —**winc·er** *n*

SYNONYMS See ***recoil***.

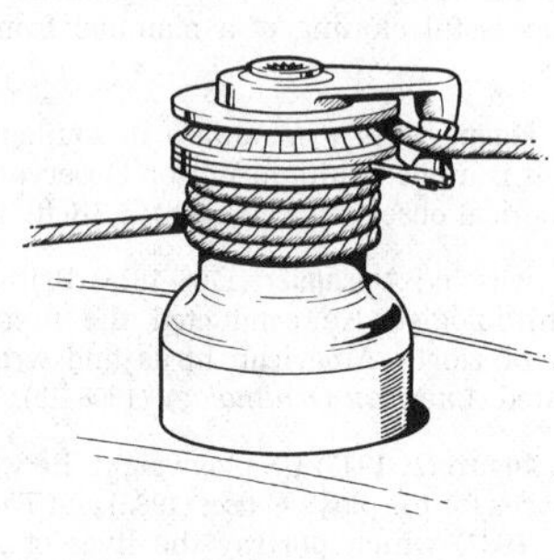

winch

winch /winch/ *n* **1. LIFTING MACHINE** a machine for lifting loads by means of a rope or chain that is wound around a cylinder turned by an engine or by hand **2. CRANK OR HANDLE** the handle used to turn a machine ■ *vt* (**winched, winch·ing, winch·es**) **MOVE SOMETHING WITH WINCH** to lift or pull something by means of a winch [Old English *wince* < Germanic] —**winch·er** *n* —**winch·man** *n*

Win·ches·ter /wín chèstər, -chistər/ city in Hampshire, southern England. It was the capital of the Anglo-Saxon kingdom of Wessex. Population: 102,222 (2001).

Win·ches·ter ri·fle /wín chèstər-/ *tdmk* a trademark for a rifle first produced in the late 19th century that can fire several shots before it has to be reloaded

Win·ckel·mann /vínkəl màn/, **Johann Joachim** (1717–68) German archaeologist and art historian. He made the first scientific reports on the excavations at Pompeii and Herculaneum, and his theories concerning Greek art and aesthetics influenced many writers and philosophers.

wind[1] /wind/ *n* **1. MOVING AIR** air moving across the surface of the planet or through the atmosphere at a speed fast enough to be noticed **2. AIR MOVED ARTIFICIALLY** air that is being made to move by a device such as a fan **3. SOCIAL OR ECONOMIC FORCE** a force or movement bringing something such as change or destruction ○ *the winds of change* **4. BREATH** the breath of normal breathing and talking **5. POWER TO BREATHE** the power to breathe, especially when making an effort such as running **6.** MUSIC **MUSICAL INSTRUMENTS** a group of musical instruments that requires a flow of air to produce a sound, including both woodwind and brass instruments ○ *the wind section of the orchestra* **7. HINTING INFORMATION** news that brings information of something intended to be secret ○ *If wind of this gets out, we've had it.* **8.** PHYSIOL **STOMACH GAS** gas that builds up in the stomach and intestines while food is being digested **9. IDLE TALK** talk that is empty and meaningless **10. DIRECTION OF WIND** the direction from which the wind blows (*literary*) **11. VANITY** boastful vanity or self-importance **12.** ASTRON **FLOW OF PARTICLES INTO SPACE** a flow of particles ejected into space from the surface of the Sun or a star **13.** HUNTING **AIR CARRYING SCENT** the air on which a scent such as that of a hunter is carried ■ **winds** *npl* MUSIC **PLAYERS OF WIND INSTRUMENTS** the musicians in an ensemble, especially an orchestra, who play wind instruments ■ *v* (**wind·ed, wind·ing, winds**) **1.** *vt* **MAKE SOMEBODY SHORT OF BREATH** to make somebody temporarily unable to breathe properly, e.g., because of too much exertion or by a blow to the abdomen **2.** *vt* **LET HORSE REST** to allow a horse to rest after exertion **3.** *vt* **EXPOSE SOMETHING TO WIND** to expose something to the wind, e.g., in order to dry it **4.** *vti* **SMELL SOMEBODY OR SOMETHING** to get a scent of somebody or something in the air **5.** *vt* **PURSUE ANIMAL BY SCENT** to pursue an animal in a hunt by following its scent [Old English, < Indo-European, "to blow"] —**wind·ed** *adj* ◇ **be in the wind** to be about to happen or be likely to happen ◇ **break wind** to pass intestinal gas through the anus ◇ **get wind of something** to hear indirectly about something ◇ **get your** *or* **a second wind** to recover your natural breathing pattern, and your usual energy levels, after a period of breathlessness and great effort ◇ **it's an ill wind (that blows nobody any good)** somebody somewhere will benefit from an unfortunate event ◇ **piss in the wind** an offensive phrase meaning to do something that is likely to have little or no effect (*slang*) ◇ **sail close to the wind** to come very close to breaking the law or a rule ◇ **see which way** *or* **how the wind blows** to wait and find out the nature of a situation before making a decision ◇ **swing** *or* **twist in the wind** to be left in a difficult or unpleasant situation without any help or support from other people (*informal*) ◇ **take the wind out of somebody's sails** to make somebody feel deflated, silly, or embarrassed, or put somebody at a disadvantage

CULTURAL NOTE ***Gone With the Wind***, a movie (1939) by US director Victor Fleming and producer David O. Selznick. Based on Margaret Mitchell's popular novel (1936), this idealized portrait of the American South focuses on the relationship between dashing rake Rhett Butler (Clark Gable) and resourceful, prewar plantation belle and formidable postwar southern woman Scarlett O'Hara (Vivien Leigh).

wind[2] /wīnd/ *v* (**wound** /wownd/, **wind·ing, winds**) **1.** *vti* **GO OR PUT SOMETHING AROUND** to go around something in a coil or coils, or wrap something around something else in a coil or coils ○ *winding the thread onto the bobbin* **2.** *vt* **WRAP SOMETHING WITH COILS** to cover or decorate something by wrapping something else around it in coils ○ *She wound the injured arm with a scarf.* **3.** *vt* **MOVE SOMETHING UP OR DOWN** to move or lift something by turning a handle or pressing a button ○ *wound the window up* **4.** *vti* **MOVE SOMETHING BACKWARD OR FORWARD** to move something such as film or tape forward or backward by turning a handle or pressing a button, or be moved in this way **5.** *vt* **MAKE SOMETHING REVOLVE** to turn something such as a crank with a circular motion **6.** *vt* **MAKE CLOCKWORK MECHANISM WORK** to turn a key or handle in a clock or clockwork device in order to make the mechanism operate, usually by means of a spring that tightens on being wound **7.** *vti* **GO ALONG PATH WITH BENDS** to move along a course with many bends and twists in it ○ *The river winds lazily through the valley.* ○ *The procession wound its way slowly up the hill.* **8.** *vi* **FOLLOW SPIRAL PATH** to go in a spiral path ○ *smoke winding slowly up into the air* **9.** *vt* US **INTRODUCE SOMETHING SLYLY** to introduce something into something else in a sly way ○ *She wound an insinuation into her testimony.* ■ *n* **1. CURVE OR BEND** a bend or twist in something such as a river or a path **2. ACT OF WINDING SOMETHING** the act of winding something such as a clock or motor **3. TURN IN WINDING SOMETHING** a single turn in the process of winding something [Old English *windan* < Germanic]

wind down *v* **1.** *vi* **GO MORE SLOWLY** to operate more and more slowly and then stop because the spring by which a mechanism works is losing or has lost its tension **2.** *vi* **RELAX** to relax after a period of feeling stressed or tense **3.** *vti* **STEADILY REDUCE WORK** to reduce gradually the amount of work done before stopping completely, or bring a business or activity gradually to an end

wind up *v* **1.** *vt* **FINISH ACTIVITY** to conclude something or to bring an activity to an end **2.** *vi* **END UP** to come to be in a particular place or situation as a result of, or at the end of, a series of earlier events (*informal*) **3.** *vt* **MAKE SOMEBODY TENSE** to make somebody nervous or irritated, usually deliberately (*informal; often passive*) **4.** *vi* BASEBALL **PREPARE TO PITCH** in baseball, to make a windup in preparation for pitching the ball

wind[3] /wīnd, wind/ (**wind·ed** or **wound** /wownd/, **wind·ing, winds**) *v* **1.** *vti* to blow a horn or bugle to create a sound **2.** *vt* to make a signal by blowing a horn [14C. < WIND[1]] ◇ **leave somebody swinging in the wind** to desert somebody during a time of crisis (*informal*) ○ *left victims of the attack swinging in the wind*

wind·age /wíndij/ *n* **1.** **DEFLECTION CAUSED BY WIND** the amount of deflection the wind will produce in a projectile **2.** **ALLOWANCE MADE FOR WIND DEFLECTION** the amount of adjustment needed in the aim of a projectile to counter wind deflection **3.** ARMS **DIFFERENCE BETWEEN BORE AND PROJECTILE** the amount by which the bore of a gun is larger than the bullet or shell it fires, so that gases can escape **4.** NAUT **PART OF SHIP ABOVE WATER** the part of a ship's body that is above the water and consequently causes wind resistance **5.** MECH ENG **FRICTION BETWEEN AIR AND MOVING PARTS** the friction between air and the moving parts of a machine, which tends to slow the machine

wind·bag /wínd bàg/ *n* **1.** a talkative person who is thought to have little of interest or value to say (*informal insult*) **2.** the bag in a set of bagpipes into which air is forced by the player's lungs or a set of bellows and from which it flows to produce sound

wind·bell /wínd-/ *n* a light bell that rings when the wind moves it ■ **wind-bells** *npl* a set of wind chimes

wind·blast /wínd blàst/ *n* the harmful effect of air friction on a pilot who has ejected from an aircraft traveling at high speed

wind·blown /wínd blōn/ *adj* **1.** blown about by the wind ○ *They came back from their walk looking windblown.* **2.** growing in a shape caused by the action of the prevailing winds

wind-borne /wínd-/ *adj* carried or dispersed by the wind

wind·bound /wínd bòwnd/ *adj* unable to sail because the wind is blowing in the wrong direction

wind·break /wínd bràyk/ *n* something that breaks the force of the prevailing wind, e.g., a wall or a line of trees

wind·break·er /wínd bràykər/ *n* a warm windproof outer jacket with tight-fitting neck, cuffs, and waistband, and sometimes with a hood

wind-bro·ken /wínd-/ *adj* describes a horse that has impaired breathing, e.g., because of heaves

wind·burn /wínd bùrn/ *n* redness and inflammation of the skin caused by exposure to harsh wind —**wind·burned** *adj*

Wind Cave Na·tion·al Park /wìnd kàyv-/ national park in the Black Hills of southwestern South Dakota, established in 1903. It is noted for its limestone caverns. Area: 44 sq. mi./115 sq. km.

wind·cheat·er /wínd chèetər/ *n UK* same as **windbreaker**

wind chest /wínd-/ *n* a compartment in a pipe organ that stores wind from the bellows under pressure before it goes to the pipes

wind·chill fac·tor /wínd chil-/, **wind·chill** *n* the combined effect on exposed skin of air temperature and wind speed, usually given as an equivalent temperature in calm conditions

wind chime /wínd-/ *n* a musical decoration consisting of objects such as beads or metal tubes suspended on strings so that they will make a pleasant noise when moved by the wind

wind cone /wínd-/ *n* AVIAT same as **windsock**

win·der /wīndər/ *n* **1.** **SOMETHING THAT WINDS UP** a key, knob, or other device that is used to wind up a spring-powered mechanism such as a clock **2.** **SOMEBODY OR SOMETHING THAT WINDS SOMETHING** a person or device that winds something such as thread or textiles around a spool, cone, or tube **3.** **OBJECT FOR WINDING SOMETHING AROUND** a spool or bobbin around which something such as thread is wound **4.** **STEP IN SPIRAL STAIRCASE** a step in a spiral staircase or at the turn of a staircase that is narrower at the inside

Win·der·mere, Lake /wíndər meer/ largest lake in England, in the Lake District in the northwest of the country. Area: 6 sq. mi./16 sq. km.

wind·fall /wínd fàwl/ *n* **1.** something good that is received unexpectedly, especially a sum of money **2.** something that the wind has blown down, especially a piece of ripe fruit blown off a tree

wind farm /wínd-/ *n* an area of land with a large number of electricity-generating windmills or wind turbines

wind·flaw /wínd flàw/ *n* METEOROL same as **flaw**[2] (sense 1)

wind·flow·er /wínd flòwr/ *n* PLANTS same as **anemone** (sense 1)

wind·gall /wínd gàwl/ *n* a fluid-filled swelling around the fetlock joint of a horse, usually not associated with loss of function or lameness

wind gap /wínd-/ *n* a shallow pass or gap in a mountain ridge, often originally a water gap

wind gauge /wínd-/ *n* **1.** METEOROL same as **anemometer** **2.** an attachment to the sight on a musket or rifle showing how much the aim should be adjusted to allow for the effect of the wind on the bullet

wind harp /wínd-/ *n* MUSIC same as **aeolian harp**

Wind·hoek /wínd hòok, wínt-, vínt-/ capital city of Namibia, located in the center of the country. Population: 202,000 (1999).

win·di·go *n Can* same as **wendigo**

wind·ing /wīnding/ *adj* **1.** **TWISTING AND CURVING** made up of many consecutive curves or twists **2.** **SPIRALING** arranged or moving in a spiral ■ *n* **1.** **SOMETHING WOUND** something wound or coiled around an object **2.** **SINGLE COIL** a single turn of something coiled or wound around an object **3.** **ACT OF COILING** the act or process of coiling something **4.** **CURVING COURSE** the bending or curving course that something follows **5.** ELEC ENG **WIRE COIL CARRYING ELECTRICITY** a wire coil designed to have an electric current passing through it, forming part of numerous electrical devices such as electric motors and transformers

wind·ing drum *n* a revolving drum with a wire rope coiled around it that acts as the lifting mechanism of a hoist or winch

wind·ing sheet *n* a sheet that a corpse is wrapped in before it is buried

wind in·stru·ment /wìnd-/ *n* a musical instrument played by causing air to vibrate by blowing into or across a tube, e.g., a trumpet or flute

wind·jam·mer /wínd jàmmər/ *n* a large sailing ship, especially a large and fast merchant ship

wind·lass /wíndləss/ *n* a device that uses a rope or cable wound around a revolving drum to pull and lift things, especially the mechanism on a ship to raise and lower the anchor ■ *vt* (**-lassed, -lass·ing, -lass·es**) to raise or pull something using a windlass [14C. Alteration of Old Norse *vindáss* < *vinda* "wind" + *áss* "pole"]

win·dle·straw /wínd'l stràw/ *n* **1.** a thin dry stalk of grass **2.** *UK regional* somebody who is regarded as lacking in strength of character (*archaic or literary*) [Old English *windelstrēaw* < *windan* "wind" + *strēaw* "straw"]

wind ma·chine /wínd-/ *n* **1.** a device used to simulate the sound or effects of wind, e.g., a machine used backstage in a theater **2.** a machine that creates a strong current of air, e.g., a device that produces warm air to protect crops from frost

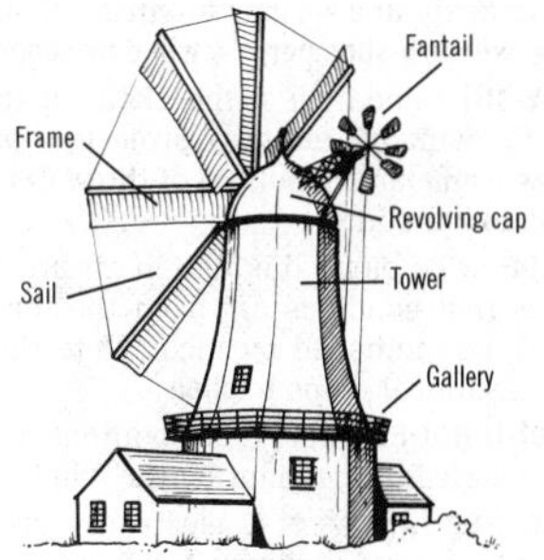

windmill

wind·mill /wínd mìl/ *n* **1.** **BUILDING WITH REVOLVING BLADES** a building with a set of wind-driven revolving sails or blades attached to the side of its roof that drive a grinding machine inside **2.** **DEVICE HARNESSING WIND POWER** a building or device fitted with a set of revolving blades designed to harness the power of the wind, e.g., to pump water or generate electricity **3.** *UK* LEISURE same as **pinwheel** (sense 1) ■ *v* (**-milled, -mil·ling, -mills**) **1.** *vti* **SPIN LIKE WINDMILL** to spin or turn like the sails of a windmill, or be spun or turned in this way **2.** *vi* **ROTATE UNPOWERED** to rotate solely by wind force and with no engine power ◇ **tilt at windmills** to struggle against imagined enemies or opponents

win·dow /wíndō/ *n* **1.** **GLASS-COVERED OPENING IN BUILDING** an opening in a wall of a building, usually with an inner frame of wood or metal with glass fitted in it, to let in light or, when opened, air **2.** **GLASS-COVERED OPENING IN VEHICLE** a glass-covered opening designed to let in light or, when opened, air, e.g., in a vehicle **3.** BUILDINGS same as **windowpane** **4.** COMPUT **SECTION ON COMPUTER SCREEN** a rectangular frame on a computer screen in which images output by application programs can be displayed, moved around, or resized **5.** **OPENING SIMILAR TO WINDOW** an opening that makes it possible to see something behind or underneath, e.g., the opening on some envelopes **6.** **OPENING WHERE SOMETHING IS DISPENSED** an opening above a counter where somebody provides information, goods, or services to customers **7.** **DISPLAY IN STORE WINDOW** the area immediately behind a large window in the wall of a store, where merchandise is put on display **8.** **PERIOD OF AVAILABLE TIME** a period of time available for a particular activity or during which conditions are right for something to take place **9.** **OPPORTUNITY TO EXPERIENCE SOMETHING** an opportunity to see or experience something **10.** PHYS **PART OF ELECTROMAGNETIC SPECTRUM** the range of the electromagnetic spectrum that a given medium will allow to pass through it **11.** AIR FORCE same as **chaff**[1] (sense 3) [Pre-12C. < Old Norse *vindauga* < *vindr* "wind" + *auga* "eye"] ◇ **be** *or* **go out the window** to be lost for good (*informal*)

win·dow box *n* **1.** a box in which plants can be grown or displayed on a window ledge **2.** either of the spaces in the sides of the frame of a sash window that conceal the weights, ropes, and pulleys that raise and lower the window's separate sections

win·dow dress·ing *n* **1.** a deceptively appealing presentation of something, intended to conceal flaws **2.** the arrangement of a display of merchandise for sale in a store window —**win·dow dress·er** *n*

win·dow en·ve·lope *n* an envelope with a transparent panel at the front through which the address of the recipient, printed or written on the material inside, can be seen

win·dow of op·por·tu·ni·ty *n* a brief opportunity to do something, especially something that will be beneficial or profitable in some way

win·dow·pane /wíndō pàyn/ *n* a sheet of glass that forms part of a window

win·dow seat *n* **1.** a seat by a window in an airplane, train, or bus **2.** an indoor seat attached to a wall under a window, especially a window that is set into a recess

win·dow shade *n* a shade for a window, e.g., a flexible fabric shade on a roller

win·dow-shop *vi* to look at goods displayed in store

windows without a serious intention of buying anything —**win·dow-shop·per** *n* —**win·dow-shop·ping** *n*

win·dow·sill /wíndō sìl/ *n* the shelf on the bottom edge of a window, either a projecting part of the window frame or the bottom of the wall recess that the window fits into

wind·pipe /wínd pìp/ *n* the tube in air-breathing vertebrates that conducts air from the throat to the bronchi, strengthened by incomplete rings of cartilage. Technical name **trachea**

wind-pol·li·nat·ed /wínd-/ *adj* pollinated by pollen that is carried to the plant by the wind

wind pow·er /wínd-/ *n* **1.** electricity produced by windmills or wind turbines **2.** the force of the wind harnessed by windmills and wind turbines for conversion into electricity

wind·proof /wínd proof/ *adj* resisting the force of the wind

wind·puff /wínd pùff/ *n* VET same as **windgall**

wind rose /wínd-/ *n* a circular diagram indicating the range of wind speeds and directions for a location over a given time period

wind·row /wínd rō/ *n* **1.** ROW OF DRYING HAY a long thin pile of cut hay or grain designed to catch the wind and dry quickly **2.** PILE BLOWN TOGETHER BY WIND a long thin pile of things, especially leaves or snow, heaped up by the wind ■ *vt* (**-rowed, -row·ing, -rows**) GATHER HAY INTO WINDROWS to gather cut grass, hay, or other crop material into windrows for drying —**wind·row·er** *n*

wind·sail /wínd sàyl/; *nautical* /wíndss'l, wínss'l/ *n* **1.** a tube or funnel of sailcloth rigged over a companionway or hatch to catch breezes and provide ventilation for a ship **2.** a sail on a windmill

wind scale /wínd-/ *n* a scale for measuring the strength of a wind, e.g., the beaufort scale

wind·screen /wínd skreen/ *n* **1.** a screen used to protect somebody or something from the wind, used, e.g., by sunbathers on a beach or gardeners protecting plants **2.** *UK* AUTOMOT same as **windshield** (sense 1)

wind shake /wínd-/ *n* a crack between the growth rings of a tree, thought to be caused when the tree bends violently in the wind

wind shear /wínd-/ *n* the amount by which the speed of the wind varies at different altitudes, often causing difficulties for aircraft

wind·shield /wínd sheeld/ *n* **1.** the pane of glass or plastic that forms the front window of a motor vehicle **2.** *UK* same as **windscreen** (sense 1)

wind·shield wip·er *n* a motorized device consisting of a rubber blade on a metal arm that is attached just below a vehicle's windshield, used for wiping rain and snow off the windshield

wind·sock /wínd sòk/ *n* a fabric tube or cone attached at one end to the top of a pole, so that it blows like a flag to show which way the wind is blowing

Wind·sor[1] /wínzər/ **1.** town in southern England, on the Thames River. Windsor Castle, located in the town, has been a royal residence for over 900 years. Population: 30,832 (1991). **2.** town in northern Connecticut. Established in 1633, it was the first English settlement in Connecticut. Population: 28,519 (2002 estimate). **3.** city in southern Ontario, Canada, on the border opposite Detroit, Michigan. It is Canada's southernmost city. Population: 263,204 (2001).

Wind·sor[2] *n* the royal house of the United Kingdom from 1917, when George V changed the family name to Windsor

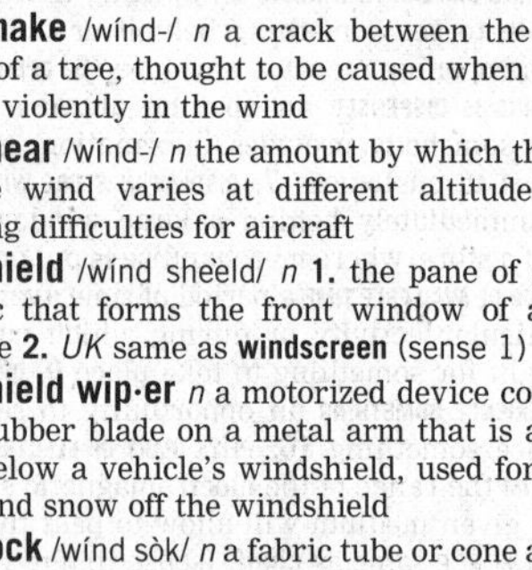
AKG London

Duke and Duchess of Windsor

Wind·sor, Duke of title granted to Edward VIII after his abdication from the British throne in 1936 and subsequent marriage to Wallis Simpson in June 1937

Wind·sor chair *n* a wooden chair that traditionally has a back formed of spindles, a saddle-shaped seat, and splayed legs [Mid-18C. After WINDSOR[1] in England]

Wind·sor knot *n* a large triangular knot in a man's necktie, made by putting an extra turn on each side of the loop that lies beneath the knot [Mid-20C. Probably after the Duke of WINDSOR, DUKE OF]

Wind·sor tie *n* a broad necktie loosely knotted with a double bow

wind·storm /wínd stàwrm/ *n* a storm consisting of very strong winds and little or no rain or other precipitation

wind·suck·ing /wínd-/ *n* the habit some horses have of biting the edge of a stall or fence while gulping air or sucking in air by moving their head and neck

wind·surf /wínd sùrf/ (**-surfed, -surf·ing, -surfs**) *vi* to ride and steer a sailboard fitted with a movable sail —**wind·surf·er** *n*

Wind·surf·er /wínd sùrfər/ *tdmk* a trademark for a type of sailboard

Popperfoto

windsurfing

wind·surf·ing /wínd sùrfing/ *n* the sport of riding and steering a sailboard

wind·swept /wínd swèpt/ *adj* **1.** exposed to the wind and usually very windy **2.** disheveled in appearance as a result of exposure to the wind

wind tee /wínd-/ *n* a T-shaped weather vane at an airfield that shows which way the wind is blowing

wind tun·nel /wínd-/ *n* a tunnel-shaped chamber through which air can be passed at a known speed in order to test the aerodynamic properties of an object such as an aircraft or automobile placed inside it

wind tur·bine *n* a turbine with vanes that are rotated by the wind to generate electricity, usually similar in appearance to a giant aircraft propeller and mounted on a tall slim tower

wind-up /wínd ùp/ *adj* OPERATED BY TURNING HANDLE made to work by turning a handle or key that winds an internal spring ■ *n* **1.** ENDING OF SOMETHING the bringing to a close of an activity such as a meeting, discussion, or electoral campaign **2.** BASEBALL PITCHER'S PREPARATION TO THROW in baseball, a pitcher's preparation to pitch, including pulling the arm back just before releasing the ball

wind·ward /wíndwərd/ *adj* FACING WIND facing the wind, or on the side of something, especially a boat, that is facing the wind ■ *adv* INTO WIND toward the direction the wind is blowing from ■ *n* PLACE FACING WIND a place or direction facing, toward, or exposed to the direction the wind is blowing from

Wind·ward Is·lands /wíndwərd-/ group of islands in the eastern Caribbean Sea, at the southern end of the Lesser Antilles. It includes Martinique and the independent island states of Barbados, Dominica, St. Lucia, Grenada, and St. Vincent and the Grenadines. Area: 1,412 sq. mi./3,657 sq. km.

wind·way /wínd wày/ *n* an opening or passage allowing air through, e.g., a ventilation shaft in a mine

wind·y /wíndee/ (**-i·er, -i·est**) *adj* **1.** WITH WIND BLOWING with strong winds blowing ○ *a windy day* **2.** WHERE WINDS BLOW where strong winds tend to blow ○ *a high and windy hill* **3.** FULL OF EMPTY WORDS full of long and important-sounding though largely meaningless words designed to impress people (*informal*) **4.** FLATULENT suffering from flatulence (*informal*) —**wind·i·ly** *adv* —**wind·i·ness** *n*

wine /wīn/ *n* **1.** ALCOHOL FERMENTED FROM GRAPES an alcoholic drink made by fermenting the juice of grapes **2.** ALCOHOL FERMENTED FROM OTHER FRUIT an alcoholic drink made by fermenting the juice or an infusion of another fruit, a flower, or a vegetable ○ *dandelion wine* **3.** SOMETHING STIMULATING OR INTOXICATING something that has a stimulating or intoxicating effect resembling that of wine (*literary*) **4.** DARK PURPLISH RED COLOR a dark purplish red color, like that of red wine [Old English *wīn* < Latin *vinum* < Indo-European] —**wine** *adj* ◇ **wine and dine** (**wined and dined, wining and dining**) to enjoy, be treated, or treat somebody to an expensive meal out

SPELLCHECK See *whine.*

wine bar *n* a bar that specializes in serving wine, although beer and liquor may also be served

wine cel·lar *n* **1.** a dark cool room used for storing wine, especially in a cellar **2.** a stock of wine

wine cool·er *n* **1.** a mixture of wine and fruit juice, sometimes with carbonated water, sold in bottles **2.** a container filled with ice or a refrigerant and used to keep one or more bottles of wine cool

wine·glass /wīn glàss/ *n* a glass suitable for drinking wine, with a bowl mounted on a stem and usually a rounded base

wine grow·er *n* a grower of grapes for making wine, especially the owner or manager of a vineyard who also oversees the winemaking

wine·mak·ing /wīn màyking/ *n* the art or business of producing wine, from the growing of the grapes to the finished product —**wine·mak·er** *n*

wine palm *n* a palm tree whose fermented sap is used to make palm wine

wine·press /wīn prèss/ *n* a piece of winemaking equipment that squeezes the juice from grapes

win·er·y /wīnəree/ (*plural* **-ies**) *n* a place where wine is made

wine·skin /wīn skìn/ *n* a container for wine made from the skin of a sheep or goat sewn into a bag

wine·tast·ing /wīn tàysting/ *n* **1.** a gathering of people to sample, learn about, and enjoy drinking a variety of wines **2.** the sampling of a variety of wines, either as a preliminary to buying wine or as instruction in the appreciation of wine

wi·ney /wīnee/ *adj* another spelling of **winy**

Win·frey /wínfree/, **Oprah** (*b.* 1954) US talk show host and actor. Hosting *The Oprah Winfrey Show* from 1985, she pioneered television programs in which people publicly discuss their intimate problems. Full name **Winfrey, Oprah Gail**

> "I am the product of every other black woman before me who has done or said anything worthwhile. Recognizing that I am a part of history is what allows me to soar."
>
> [Oprah Winfrey, *I Dream a World: Portraits of Black Women Who Changed America*, Brian Lanker; 1989]

wing /wing/ *n* **1.** BIRD'S LIMB FOR FLYING either of a bird's feather-covered limbs that are typically used for flying **2.** INSECT'S OR BAT'S LIMB FOR FLYING a large membrane-covered limb on an insect or a bat that is used for flying. Many insects have two pairs of wings. **3.** AIRCRAFT STRUCTURE either of the large flat surfaces sticking out from the sides of an aircraft's body that provide the main source of lift **4.** FLAT PROJECTING PART either of a pair of flat parts that stick out from the main body of something, e.g., the outgrowths of a wind-dispersed seed case or the ends of an old-fashioned collar **5.** PART OF BUILDING PROJECTING FROM MIDDLE one of the parts of a building that project from the main part **6.** LONGER SIDE OF SPORTS FIELD in some sports, either of the longer sides of the field of play, at right angles to the sides where the goals are **7.** OFFENSIVE PLAYER ON SIDE OF FIELD in some team sports such as soccer and field hockey, an offensive player who plays down one side of the field **8.**

OFFENSIVE FIELD POSITION in some sports, the position played by a wing **9.** SUBSIDIARY GROUP a group attached and subordinate to a parent organization **10.** POL SUBDIVISION OF POLITICAL GROUP a faction within a political party or movement, especially either of two broad factions, one more conservative, the other more liberal **11.** AIR FORCE AIR FORCE UNIT an air force unit that is larger than a group but smaller than a division **12.** MIL PART OF MILITARY FORMATION the left or right part of a large military formation such as a field army or a fleet **13.** THEATER SCENERY PIECE AT SIDE OF STAGE a piece of scenery at the side of the stage **14.** *UK* AUTOMOT same as **fender** (sense 1) ■ **wings** *npl* **1.** THEATER SIDE OF THEATER STAGE the areas of a theater to the sides of the stage, unseen by the audience **2.** AVIAT QUALIFIED PILOT'S BADGE a badge with a design in the shape of wings, worn by a trained and qualified pilot ■ *v* (**winged, wing·ing, wings**) **1.** *vti* MOVE SWIFTLY to move or travel somewhere swiftly, or send something with great speed **2.** *vt* THROW SOMETHING to throw or propel something **3.** *vt* WOUND BIRD BY HITTING WING to wound a bird superficially by hitting it on its wing **4.** *vt* WOUND OR DAMAGE SOMEBODY SUPERFICIALLY to wound somebody superficially, especially in the arm or leg, or cause only superficial damage to something [12C. < N Germanic < Indo-European, "to blow"] ◇ **be (waiting) in the wings** to be ready and prepared to do something, or available for use when needed ◇ **on the wing** flying or in flight (*refers to birds*) ◇ **take somebody under your wing** to take care of or protect somebody ◇ **wing it** to improvise (*informal*) ◇ **with wings** to be taken away rather than consumed on the premises (*informal*) ○ *one cappuccino with wings*

wing and wing *adv* with sails extended on either side when sailing with the wind directly behind the boat

wing·back /wíng bàk/ *n* **1.** OFFENSIVE BACK IN FOOTBALL in football, an offensive back who lines up outside an end **2.** SOCCER DEFENDER WHO ALSO ATTACKS in soccer, an essentially defensive player who also makes attacking runs and who plays close to the touchlines on either side of the defense **3.** POSITION OF WINGBACK the position played by a wingback

wing bar *n* a short white band on the wing of a bird, visible when the wing is folded

wing case *n* INSECTS same as **elytron**

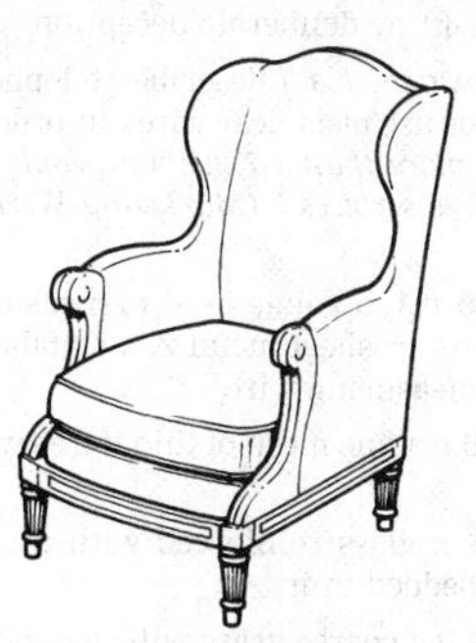

wing chair

wing chair *n* an armchair with a high back and large side panels

wing col·lar *n* a high stiff collar on a man's shirt, worn with the points at the upper corner turned down over the tie as part of formal dress

wing com·mand·er *n* a commissioned officer in the British Royal Air Force of a rank above squadron leader and below group captain

wing cov·ert *n* BIRDS same as **covert** *n* (sense 3)

wing·ding /wíng dìng/ *n* a party or celebration, especially a noisy and boisterous one (*dated*) [Early 20C. Origin ?]

winged /wingd/ *adj* **1.** CAPABLE OF FLIGHT able to fly because of having wings **2.** WITH PARTICULAR WINGS having wings of a particular kind ○ *broad-winged* **3.** /wingd, wíngəd/ MOVING SWIFTLY moving swiftly in a manner resembling flying (*literary*) **4.** /wingd, wíngəd/ FLYING moving using or as if using wings (*literary*)

wing·er /wíngər/ *n* SPORTS same as **wing** (sense 7)

wing·less /wíngləss/ *adj* used to describe insects without wings or having only very small wings that are not used for flying

wing·man /wíng màn/ (*plural* **-men** /-mèn/) *n* a pilot who flies in a position behind, and to the side of, the leader of a flying formation

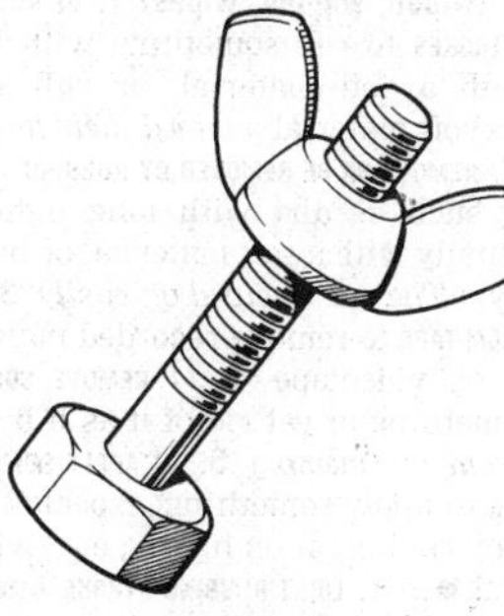

wing nut

wing nut *n* a nut that has flat projections on its sides for the fingers to grip

wing·o·ver /wíng ṑvər/ *n* a flying maneuver to turn an aircraft in which the pilot puts the aircraft into a steep banking climb to a near stall and then allows the nose to fall

wing·span /wíng spàn/, **wing·spread** /-sprèd/ *n* **1.** the distance from tip to tip of an aircraft's wings **2.** the distance from tip to tip of the outstretched wings of a bird or insect

wing·tip /wíng tìp/, **wing tip** *n* **1.** a shoe with a leather cap on the toe and along the sides that has a decorative pattern of tiny holes **2.** the tip of the wing of a bird, insect, or aircraft that is the point farthest away from the center of its body

wink /wingk/ *v* (**winked, wink·ing, winks**) **1.** *vti* GESTURE BY CLOSING ONE EYE BRIEFLY to close one eye briefly, usually as a friendly greeting or to show that something just done or said is a joke or a secret **2.** *vi* SHINE INTERMITTENTLY to shine intermittently or faintly ■ *n* **1.** BRIEF CLOSING OF ONE EYE a brief closing of one eye as a gesture, greeting, or signal **2.** TWINKLING LIGHT a twinkling or faintly flashing light **3.** SHORT TIME the briefest period of time [Old English *wincian* "close your eyes" < Germanic, "move from side to side" < Indo-European] ◇ **not sleep a wink, not get a wink of sleep** to be unable to sleep

wink at *vt* to pretend not to notice an offense or wrongdoing (*informal*)

wink·er /wíngkər/ *n* **1.** SOMEBODY WHO WINKS somebody or something that winks **2.** *US* EYE OR PART OF EYE an eye, or a part of the eye such as an eyelid or eyelash (*informal*) ■ **win·kers** *npl* BLINKERS a racehorse's blinkers

win·kle /wíngk'l/ *n* a small edible mollusk with a spiral shell. Native to: coastal waters. Genus: *Littorina*. [Late 16C. Shortening of PERIWINKLE[1]]

Win·ne·ba·go /wìnnə báygō/ (*plural same* or **-gos** or **-goes**) *n* **1.** a member of a Siouan people who lived in Wisconsin and Illinois, and now live mainly in Wisconsin and Nebraska **2.** the Siouan language of the Winnebago people. Native speakers: 250. [Mid-18C. < Algonquian *wi:nepye:ko:ha* "person of the dirty water"] —**Win·ne·ba·go** *adj*

Win·ne·ba·go, Lake /wìnnə báy gō/ lake in eastern Wisconsin, forming part of the course of the Fox River. Area: 206 sq. mi./534 sq. km.

win·ner /wínnər/ *n* **1.** SOMEBODY OR SOMETHING WINNING COMPETITION somebody or something that wins a competition or contest **2.** SOMEBODY OR SOMETHING SUCCESSFUL somebody or something that is or seems likely to become very successful or popular **3.** WINNING SHOT in some sports, a shot that wins a point

win·ner's cir·cle *n* an enclosure at a racetrack where the winning horses are unsaddled and prizes awarded to owners, trainers, and jockeys

Win·net·ka /wi nétkə/ village in northeastern Illinois, on the shore of Lake Michigan, north of Wilmette. It is a northern suburb of Chicago. Population: 12,468 (2002 estimate).

win·ning /wínning/ *adj* **1.** VICTORIOUS victorious or bringing victory **2.** CHARMING very charming, to the extent that people are won over ■ *n* VICTORY the act of earning a victory or succeeding in a competition ■ **win·nings** *npl* MONEY WON money or other valuables that are won, especially from gambling —**win·ning·ly** *adv*

win·ning·est /wínningəst/ *adj* winning the highest number of victories or prizes, or the most prize money (*informal*) ○ *a list of the all-time winningest baseball coaches*

win·ning gal·ler·y *n* an opening in a side wall of a court-tennis court into which the ball is hit from the other side of the net in order to win a point

Win·ni·peg /wínni pèg/ capital city of Manitoba, Canada, located in the southern part of the province. Population: 626,685 (2001).

Win·ni·peg, Lake freshwater lake in central Manitoba, Canada. Depth: 60 ft./18 m. Area: 9,417 sq. mi./24,390 sq. km.

Win·ni·peg couch *n Can* a couch with no back or arms that opens out to form a double bed [Mid-20C. After WINNIPEG]

Win·ni·pe·go·sis, Lake /wìnnipi góssiss/ lake in western Manitoba, southern Canada, that drains into Lake Manitoba. Area: 2,103 sq. mi./5,447 sq. km.

Win·ni·pe·sau·kee, Lake /wìnnəpi sáwkee/ lake in central New Hampshire, near the southern extremity of the White Mountains. Area: 72 sq. mi./190 sq. km.

win·now /wínnō/ *v* (**-nowed, -now·ing, -nows**) **1.** *vti* REMOVE CHAFF FROM GRAIN to separate grain from its husks (**chaff**) by tossing it in the air or blowing air through it **2.** *vt* EXAMINE SOMETHING TO REMOVE BAD PARTS to examine something in order to remove the bad, unusable, or undesirable parts ■ *n* **1.** DEVICE FOR WINNOWING a device used to winnow grain **2.** PROCESS OF WINNOWING the process of separating grain from chaff [Old English *windwian* < *wind* "wind"] —**win·now·er** *n*

win·o /wínō/ (*plural* **-os**) *n* an offensive term for somebody who is addicted to alcohol, especially wine, and is usually also homeless (*informal insult*)

win·some /wínssəm/ *adj* charming, especially because of a naive, innocent quality [Old English *wynsum* "pleasant" < *wynn* "joy" < Indo-European, "to desire"] —**win·some·ly** *adv* —**win·some·ness** *n*

Win·ston-Sa·lem /wìnstən-/ city in northern North Carolina, an important center of manufacturing and tobacco production. Population: 188,934 (2002 estimate).

win·ter /wíntər/ *n* **1.** YEAR'S COLDEST SEASON the coldest season of the year, which runs in the northern hemisphere from around November or December to February or March and in the southern hemisphere from June to August **2.** CLOSING PERIOD OR PERIOD OF INACTIVITY a period in which something is declining, inactive, or ending **3.** YEAR one of a number of years, especially a great number (*literary*) ○ *a man of many winters* ■ *v* (**-tered, -ter·ing, -ters**) **1.** *vi* SPEND WINTER SOMEWHERE to spend the winter in a particular place, especially away from home **2.** *vt* KEEP SOMETHING SOMEWHERE IN WINTER to keep something, especially farm animals, in a particular place during the winter [Old English, < Indo-European, "wet"]

win·ter ac·o·nite *n* a low-growing plant with a single yellow flower that blooms in winter or early spring. Native to: Europe, Asia. Latin name: *Eranthis hyemalis*.

win·ter·ber·ry /wíntər bèrree/ (*plural* **-ries** or *same*) *n* a deciduous holly with bright red berries and leaves that turn black in the fall. Native to: eastern North America. Latin name: *Ilex verticillata*.

win·ter·bourne /wíntər bàwrn/ *n* a stream that flows only or mostly in winter, after heavy rains

win·ter cher·ry *n US* a plant of the nightshade family that has red berries enclosed in papery orange cases resembling Chinese lanterns. Native to: Europe, Asia. Latin name: *Physalis alkekengi*. Can term **Chinese lantern**

win·ter·cress /wíntər krèss/ *n* a bitter-tasting plant of the mustard family. Flowers: yellow. Genus: *Barbarea*.

win·ter·feed /wíntər fèed/ (**-fed** /-fed/, **-feed·ing, -feeds**) *vt* to feed livestock in winter, e.g., on hay or silage, when there is little or no grazing

win·ter floun·der *n* a reddish brown flounder that is a popular food fish in winter. Native to: northwestern Atlantic. Latin name: *Pseudopleuronectes americanus.*

win·ter gar·den *n* **1.** a garden planted with evergreens and other plants that give color and interest in winter **2.** a greenhouse or conservatory where plants are kept or grown during the winter

win·ter·green /wíntər grèen/ (*plural* **-greens** or *same*) *n* **1.** a low-growing evergreen bush with red berries and fragrant leathery leaves from which an oil (**oil of wintergreen**) is distilled. Native to: eastern North America. Latin name: *Gaultheria procumbens.* **2.** same as **oil of wintergreen** [Mid-16C. Translation of Dutch *wintergroen*]

win·ter·ize /wíntə rīz/ (**-ized, -iz·ing, -iz·es**) *vt* to prepare something, especially a house or an automobile, to withstand cold winter conditions —**win·ter·i·za·tion** /wìntəri záysh'n/ *n*

win·ter·kill /wíntər kìl/ *vti* (**-killed, -kill·ing, -kills**) to die from lack of adequate protection from winter weather conditions, or cause a plant to die in these conditions ■ *n* exposure to harsh winter weather that kills unprotected plants

win·ter mel·on *n* a large gourd with an unusually smooth skin that keeps for a long time when stored. Latin name: *Benincasa hispida.*

Win·ter O·lym·pics, Win·ter O·lym·pic Games *n* an international gathering for athletes competing in a variety of winter sports, taking place every four years (*takes a singular or plural verb*)

win·ter purs·lane *n* a flowering plant whose fleshy leaves are sometimes used in salad. Native to: North America. Latin name: *Montia perfoliata.*

win·ter sports *npl* sports performed on snow and ice, e.g., skiing and ice skating

win·ter squash *n* a slow-maturing squash that grows on long trailing vines, has a tough skin, and stores well

win·ter·time /wíntər tìm/ *n* the season of winter

win·ter·weight /wíntər wàyt/ *adj* made of thick heavy fabric and designed to protect somebody or something from cold weather

win·ter wheat *n* a variety of wheat planted in autumn, left in the ground over winter, and harvested the following spring or early summer

win·ter wren *n US* a very small brownish bird with a short tail and a powerful warbling call. Latin name: *Troglodytes troglodytes.*

win·ter·y *adj* another spelling of **wintry**

Win·throp /wínthrəp/, **John** (1587–1649) English-born American colonial governor. For most of the years between 1629 and 1649, he presided over the Massachusetts Bay Colony, exerting a decisive influence in shaping it as a Puritan commonwealth.

Win·throp, John (1605–76) English-born American colonial governor. The son of John Winthrop, he followed his father to Massachusetts and was commissioned to settle Saybrook Colony, Connecticut. He was governor of Connecticut (1657–76).

> "For we must consider that we shall be as a city upon a hill. The eyes of all people are upon us, so that if we shall deal falsely with our God in this work...and so cause Him to withdraw His present help from us, we shall be made a story and a byword through the world."
> [John Winthrop, *Sermon*, "A Model of Christian Charity"; 1630]

win·try /wíntree/ (**-tri·er, -tri·est**), **win·ter·y** /wíntəree/ (**-i·er, -i·est**) *adj* **1.** relating to or typical of winter, especially in being cold **2.** cheerless or unfriendly ○ *She gave him a wintry smile.* —**win·tri·ly** *adv* —**win·tri·ness** *n*

win-win *adj* describes a situation in which all parties benefit in some way (*informal*) ○ *a win-win move for both companies*

win·y /wínee/ (**-i·er, -i·est**) *adj* like wine in taste or appearance

winze /winz/ *n* a steeply inclined or vertical shaft between levels in a mine [Mid-18C. Alteration of obsolete *winds*, origin ?]

wipe /wīp/ *v* (**wiped, wip·ing, wipes**) **1.** *vt* **RUB SOMETHING WITH LIGHT STROKES** to rub something with long light strokes with a soft material, or rub something lightly on a soft material ○ *wiped their hands on the towel* **2.** *vti* **REMOVE OR BE REMOVED BY RUBBING** to remove something such as dirt with long light rubbing strokes, usually with a soft material, or be removed in this way ○ *The mark wiped off easily.* **3.** *vt* **REMOVE RECORDING FROM TAPE** to remove recorded material from an audio- or videotape **4.** *vt* **REMOVE SOMETHING** to remove something or get rid of it as if by wiping ○ *wiped it from my memory* **5.** *vt* **APPLY SOMETHING WITH LIGHT RUBBING** to apply something, especially a liquid or cream, by rubbing it on lightly, e.g., with a cloth or the hand ■ *n* **1. LIGHT RUBBING STROKE** one or more long light rubbing strokes **2. DISPOSABLE CLEANING CLOTH** a soft disposable cloth or tissue soaked with a cleansing liquid, used for cleaning something such as the skin ○*"Remember trash bags, wipes, and napkins. It's no fun sitting next to banana peel for five hours."* (*Washington Post*; July 1998) **3.** MOVIES, MEDIA **ONE PICTURE PUSHING OTHER OFF SCREEN** a cinematic scene-changing device in which one picture appears to push the other off the screen, often used to move from scene to scene [Old English *wīpian* < Indo-European, "move back and forth"]

wipe out *v* **1.** *vt* **DESTROY SOMETHING IN LARGE NUMBERS** to destroy large numbers of things or kill large numbers of people, especially suddenly and violently (*informal*) **2.** *vt* **TIRE SOMEBODY** to make somebody feel thoroughly exhausted (*informal*) **3.** *vi* **FALL FROM SURFBOARD** to fall from a surfboard, either because of losing control or because of being knocked off by a wave, or fall or crash in some other sport (*informal*) **4.** *vt* **MURDER SOMEBODY** to murder or assassinate somebody (*slang*)

wiped out /wīpt-/ *adj* (*slang*) **1.** thoroughly exhausted **2.** *US* intoxicated by drugs or alcohol

wipe·out /wīp òwt/ *n* (*informal*) **1. FALL IN SURFING** a fall from a surfboard, or a fall or crash in other sports such as skiing and cycling **2. FAILURE OR DEFEAT** a total failure or a crushing defeat **3.** MEDIA **RECEIVING OF RADIO SIGNAL MASKING OTHERS** the receiving of a radio signal that is so strong it makes receiving other signals impossible

wip·er /wīpər/ *n* **1.** AUTOMOT same as **windshield wiper** **2. SOMEBODY WHO WIPES** somebody or something that wipes **3. SOMETHING USED FOR WIPING** something such as a cloth or sponge that is used for wiping **4.** MECH ENG **CAM PROJECTING FROM SHAFT** a cam that projects from a rotating shaft and is designed to move, dislodge, or lift another component **5.** ELEC ENG **ELECTRICAL DEVICE MOVING CONDUCTING ARM** an electrical device in which a conducting arm may be rotated or moved over a row of contacts, e.g., a rheostat

WIPO /wīpō/, **Wipo** *abbr* World Intellectual Property Organization

Wi·rad·hu·ri /wi ráajəree/, **Wi·rad·ju·ri** *n* an Australian Aboriginal language of New South Wales and southern Queensland, now extinct [Late 19C. < an Aboriginal language < Wiradhuri *wirai* "no"] —**Wi·rad·hu·ri** *adj*

wire /wīr/ *n* **1. STRAND OF METAL** metal in the form of thin flexible strands, or a single strand of it **2. METAL STRAND CARRYING ELECTRIC CURRENT** a strand of metal, usually copper, that is encased in plastic or another insulating material and is used to carry an electric current **3. MESH STRUCTURE** a mesh made of strands of metal, or a structure made of the mesh, e.g., a fence **4.** SPORTS **RACETRACK FINISH LINE** the finish line on a racetrack **5.** *US* **END OR FINISH** the end of something, or the time when something ends (*informal*) ○ *writing in their blue books right down to the wire* **6.** *US* **ELECTRONIC LISTENING DEVICE** a small electronic listening device concealed in somebody's clothes (*slang*) **7.** TELECOM **CABLE PROVIDING TELECOMMUNICATIONS LINK** a cable that provides a telecommunications link **8.** TELECOM **TELEGRAM OR TELEGRAPH** a telegram, or the telegraph system ■ *v* (**wired, wir·ing, wires**) **1.** *vt* **FASTEN SOMETHING WITH WIRE** to use wire to fasten or secure something **2.** *vti* **EQUIP PLACE WITH ELECTRICAL WIRES** to install a system of electrical wires in a building or an area **3.** *vt* **CONNECT ELECTRICAL EQUIPMENT** to connect a piece of electrical equipment to a power source or to another piece of equipment **4.** *vt* **SEND TELEGRAM** to send a telegram to somebody, or send something to somebody by means of a telegram **5.** *vt* **PROVIDE PLACE WITH NECESSARY EQUIPMENT** to provide a place with the equipment, especially electrical or electronic equipment, needed to give it a particular facility or capability **6.** *vt US* **FIT SOMEBODY WITH LISTENING DEVICE** to fit somebody or a place with a concealed electronic listening device (*slang*) **7.** *vt* PHYSIOL **DETERMINE FUNCTION WITH PHYSIOLOGICAL STRUCTURE** to control a function in the body by means of a neurological or physiological structure or process ○ *This is learned behavior; it's not wired into the genes.* [Old English *wīr* "metal thread" < Indo-European, "twist"] ◇ **go to the wire** to risk your reputation, job, or life in order to help somebody (*informal*) ◇ **have** *or* **get your wires crossed** have a misunderstanding

wire brush *n* a brush with short stiff wires instead of bristles

wire cloth *n* a flexible mesh of soft fine wires woven closely together, used to make strainers and some types of screening

wired /wīrd/ *adj* **1. SUPPORTED BY WIRE** supported or strengthened by wire **2. EQUIPPED FOR INTERNET** having computer equipment that allows use of the Internet (*informal*) ○*"Ireland has seen Dublin go wired."* (*Newsweek*; November 1998) **3. FITTED WITH LISTENING DEVICES** fitted with one or more concealed electronic listening devices (*slang*) **4. OVERSTIMULATED** full of nervous energy or excitement (*slang*)

wire·draw /wīr dràw/ (**-drew** /-dròo/, **-drawn** /-dràwn/, **-draw·ing, -draws**) *vt* **1.** to reduce the diameter of a wire by pulling it through successively smaller dies **2.** to spin something out to great lengths, overrefining it and treating it with excessive subtlety [Late 16C. Back-formation < *wiredrawer* "somebody skilled in drawing metal into threads"]

wire en·tan·gle·ment *n* a barrier of barbed wire used to keep enemy troops back

wire fox ter·ri·er *n US* a fox terrier with a wirehaired coat

wire fraud *n* the crime of using interstate telecommunications wires to obtain money or some other benefit by deliberate deception

wire·free /wīr frèe/ *adj* describes telephone systems that do not use electrical wires in order to operate ○*"Today, more than 1.7 million people subscribe to our wirefree services."* (*Marketing Week*; December 1998)

wire gauge *n* **1.** a gauge used to measure the thickness of wire or sheet metal **2.** a standard system of sizes for measuring wire

wire gauze *n* a fine mesh of thin wires woven closely together

wire glass *n* glass reinforced with a sheet of wire mesh embedded in it

wire grass *n* a coarse grass with tough wiry roots

wire·hair /wīr hèr/ *n* VERTEB same as **wire fox terrier**

wire·haired /wīr hèrd/ *adj* having a coat of coarse stiff hair

wire·less /wīrləss/ *adj* **1. WITHOUT WIRES** lacking wires **2. USING RADIO SIGNALS** using radio signals rather than wires **3. USING CELL PHONE TECHNOLOGY** describes communications systems and devices that make use of cell phone technology ○ *wireless networks* ○ *wireless headphones* ■ *n* **RADIO** a radio or a radio set (*dated*) —**wire·less·ly** *adv*

wire·less lo·cal ar·e·a net·work *n* a local area network that uses high-frequency radio signals to communicate between computers over relatively short distances

wire·less mark·up lan·guage *n* a standardized system for tagging text files, based on XML, that specifies the interfaces of narrowband wireless devices

wire·less te·leg·ra·phy *n* a system that sends telegrams using radio signals rather than wires

wire·line /wīr līn/ *adj* operating or transmitting by means of a connecting wire, as opposed to using a wireless system

wire·man /wī́rmən/ (*plural* **-men** /-mən/) *n US* **1.** somebody, especially a man, who installs or repairs electrical or telecommunications cables **2.** an expert at installing and operating electronic listening devices (*slang*)

wire net·ting *n* mesh made of medium to thick wire that is stronger, is less flexible, and has larger spaces than wire gauze

wire·per·son /wī́r pùrss'n/ (*plural* **-peo·ple** /-pēep'l/ or **-per·sons**) *n* an installer or repairer of electrical or telecommunications cables

wir·er /wī́rər/ *n* **1.** an electrician who installs and maintains electrical circuits and wiring systems **2.** somebody who snares animals (*informal*)

wire re·cord·er *n* an early type of magnetic recorder that used stainless steel wire instead of magnetic tape to record sound

wire rope *n* strong thick rope made of twisted strands of wire

wire ser·vice *n* a news agency that sends out syndicated news items to various media by means of wire or satellite

wire·tap /wī́r tàp/ *n* **1. SECRET CONNECTION TO TELEPHONE LINE** a connection made to a telephone line in order to listen secretly to somebody's conversations **2. INSTALLATION OR USE OF WIRETAP** the act of installing or using a wiretap ■ *vti* (**-tapped, -tap·ping, -taps**) **1. TAP TELEPHONE LINE** to make a wire connection to a telephone line in order to listen in secret to somebody's conversations **2. LISTEN IN SECRET TO TELEPHONE COMMUNICATIONS** to listen in secret to somebody's conversations on a telephone line by means of a wire connection —**wire·tap·per** *n*

wire wheel *n* **1.** a motor vehicle wheel that has wire spokes connecting the hub to the rim **2.** a disk of coarse wires designed to be attached to a power tool and used for rubbing down metal

wire·work /wī́r wùrk/ *n* **1. LAYOUT OF WIRES** an arrangement or system of wires **2. SOMETHING MADE OF WIRE** something made by shaping or weaving wire **3. TIGHTROPE ACROBATICS** acrobatics performed on a tightrope

wire·works /wī́r wùrks/ *n* a factory where wire is made, or where wire articles are made

wire·worm /wī́r wùrm/ *n* the long thin hard-bodied larva of various kinds of beetle that feeds on plant roots and is a serious agricultural pest

wir·ing /wī́ring/ *n* **1. INSTALLATION OF ELECTRICAL WIRES** the act or process of installing a system of electrical wires **2. SYSTEM OF ELECTRICAL WIRES** a network of electrical wires **3. PHYSIOLOGICAL STRUCTURE DETERMINING FUNCTION** a neurological or physiological structure or process that controls a function in the body ○ *A certain degree of anxiety may simply be built into our wiring.*

wir·y /wī́ree/ (**-i·er, -i·est**) *adj* **1. SLIM BUT STRONG** slim but muscular and strong **2. COARSE** stiff and coarse like wire ○ *a dog with wiry hair* **3. PRODUCED BY VIBRATING WIRES** produced by or sounding as though produced by vibrating wires —**wir·i·ly** *adv* —**wir·i·ness** *n*

wis /wiss/ (**wissed** or **wist** /wist/, **wiss·ing, wiss·es**) *vti* to know, think, or suppose something (*archaic*) [Old English *wissian*]

Wis. *abbr* Wisconsin

Wisc. *abbr* Wisconsin

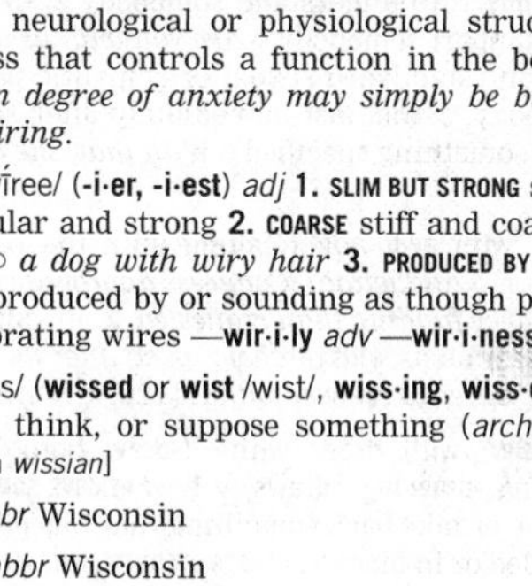

Wisconsin

Wis·con·sin /wiss kónssin/ state of the north central United States, bordered by Lake Superior, Michigan, Lake Michigan, Illinois, Iowa, and Minnesota. Capital: Madison. Population: 5,441,196 (2002 estimate). Area: 65,499 sq. mi./169,642 sq. km. —**Wis·con·sin·ite** *n*

Wisd. *abbr* BIBLE Wisdom of Solomon

wis·dom /wízdəm/ *n* **1. GOOD SENSE** the ability to make sensible decisions and judgments based on personal knowledge and experience **2. WISE DECISION** good sense shown in a way of thinking, judgment, or action **3. ACCUMULATED LEARNING** accumulated knowledge of life or of a sphere of activity that has been gained through experience **4. OPINION WIDELY HELD** an opinion that almost everyone seems to share or express **5. SAYINGS** ancient teachings or sayings [Old English *wīsdōm* < *wīs* (see WISE[1])]

SYNONYMS See ***knowledge***.

Wis·dom lit·er·a·ture *n* a speculative or didactic form of religious writing, exemplified by the books of Job, Proverbs, and Ecclesiastes in the Bible, and the Wisdom of Solomon and Ecclesiasticus in the Apocrypha

Wis·dom of Je·sus, the Son of Sir·ach /-sī́ raàk/ *n* BIBLE same as **Ecclesiasticus**

Wis·dom of Sol·o·mon *n* a book of the Roman Catholic Bible and Protestant Apocrypha that expounds Jewish doctrines in the terminology of Greek philosophy. It was probably written in the 1st century B.C. See table at **Bible**

wis·dom tooth *n* one of the four teeth at the back of either side of the upper and lower jaw of human beings. They are the last teeth to come in. [Translation of Latin *dens sapientiae*]

Wis·dom writ·ings *npl* works of Wisdom literature

wise[1] /wīz/ (**wis·er, wis·est**) *adj* **1. KNOWING MUCH FROM EXPERIENCE** able to make sensible decisions and judgments on the basis of personal knowledge and experience **2. SENSIBLE** showing good sense or good judgment **3. LEARNED** knowledgeable about many subjects **4. SHREWD** capable of achieving some purpose or goal by cunning **5. DISRESPECTFUL** behaving in a way that is perceived as disrespectful or impudent (*informal*) ○ *Don't get wise with me!* [Old English *wīs* < Indo-European, "see, know"] —**wise·ly** *adv* ◇ **be** or **get wise (to something)** to be or become aware of something, usually something dishonest or secret (*informal*) ◇ **put somebody wise (to something)** to let somebody know about something, or give somebody information about something (*informal*)

wise up (wised up, wising up, wises up) *vti* to become aware or informed, or make somebody aware or informed (*informal*)

wise[2] /wīz/ *n* a way or manner (*archaic*) [Old English *wīse* < Germanic, "shape, form, something seen"]

Wise /wīz/, **Isaac Mayer** (1819–1900) Bohemian-born US rabbi. A leader in establishing Reform Judaism in the United States, he formed the Central Conference of American Rabbis (1889).

Wise, Stephen Samuel (1874–1949) Hungarian-born US Zionist. Outspoken on behalf of labor and other liberal causes, he was one of the founders of the Federation of American Zionists (1893).

-wise *suffix* **1.** in a particular manner or direction ○ *clockwise* **2.** ⚠ with regard to, with respect to (*informal*) ○ *salary-wise* [Old English *-wīsan* < *wīse* "manner" (see WISE[2])]

USAGE Is it wise to overextend **-wise**? Many critics object to words ending in the suffix ***-wise*** when the meaning is "with regard to, with respect to," as in these controversial examples: *moneywise, timewise,* and *politicswise,* as in *Politicswise, this has been an exciting year.* The use of words ending in **-wise** is acceptable when the meaning of the suffix is "in a particular manner or direction," as in *clockwise, counterclockwise,* and *lengthwise.*

wise·a·cre /wī́z àykər/ *n* (*informal*) **1.** somebody who speaks with irritating authority or self-assurance, especially when not truly knowledgeable **2.** an insolent person who likes to make wisecracks [Late 16C. Alteration of Middle Dutch *wijsseggher* "soothsayer"]

wise·ass /wī́z àss/ (*plural* **-ass·es** *informal*) *n* a person who tries to tell others what to do, especially in an impudent or sarcastic way, or somebody who makes impudent or sarcastic remarks generally (*slang*)

wise·crack /wī́z kràk/ (*informal*) *n* a flippant or sarcastic remark ■ *vi* (**-cracked, -crack·ing, -cracks**) to make flippant or sarcastic remarks —**wise·crack·er** *n*

wise guy *n* **1.** somebody inclined to make impudent or sarcastic remarks (*informal*) **2.** *also* **wise·guy** /wī́z gī/ *US* a member of the Mafia (*slang*)

wise man *n* **1. LEARNED MAN** a scholar or a very learned man **2. SPECIAL ADVISER** a man chosen as a special senior adviser to a government or other authority (*informal*) **3. ONE OF MAGI** in the Bible, a Magi who came with two others to pay homage to the infant Jesus Christ **4. ANCIENT PRACTITIONER OF OCCULT ARTS** a man who, in ancient times, practiced any of the occult arts such as magic or astrology (*archaic*)

wis·en·heim·er /wī́z'n hīmər/, **weis·en·heim·er** *n US* somebody inclined to make impudent or sarcastic remarks (*informal*) [Early 20C. < WISE[1], after surnames such as *Oppenheimer* and *Guggenheimer*]

wi·sent /vēe zènt, vēez'nt/ *n* a bison with a head that is smaller and higher than that of the North American bison. Native to: Europe. Latin name: *Bison bonasus*. [Mid-19C. Via German < Old High German *wisunt* < Indo-European]

wise·wom·an /wī́z wòommən/ (*plural* **-wom·en** /-wimmin/) *n* a woman who is skilled in the art of using herbs to heal people and ease the pains of childbirth

wish /wish/ *v* (**wished, wish·ing, wish·es**) **1.** *vt* **HAVE STRONG DESIRE** to have a strong feeling of wanting something to happen or wanting to have something ○ *I wish she'd say yes.* ○ *What do you wish for?* **2.** *vt* **WANT SOMETHING** to want something or want to do something ○ *Stay longer, if you wish.* **3.** *vti* **EXPRESS DESIRE** to express or feel a desire that something is true or will come to pass ○ *They wished me a safe journey.* ○ *We only wish for peace.* **4.** *vt* **REGRET SOMETHING** used for expressing regret about something ○ *I wish I'd never mentioned it.* **5.** *vt* **GREET SOMEBODY** to greet somebody in a particular way ○ *She wished me good afternoon as I left.* ■ *n* **1. A DESIRE** a desire to do or have something ○ *I had no wish to offend you.* **2. SOMETHING WISHED** something that is desired ○ *He finally got his wish.* **3. HOPE** a hope for somebody's welfare or health (*usually plural*) ○ *Give him our best wishes.* **4. POLITE REQUEST** a polite request (*formal; often plural*) ○ *They honored our wishes and changed the date of the meeting.* [Old English *wȳscan* < Indo-European, "to desire"] —**wish·er** *n*

SYNONYMS See ***want***.

wish on *vt* to wish that something, usually something unpleasant, would happen to somebody ○ *I wouldn't wish that on my worst enemy.*

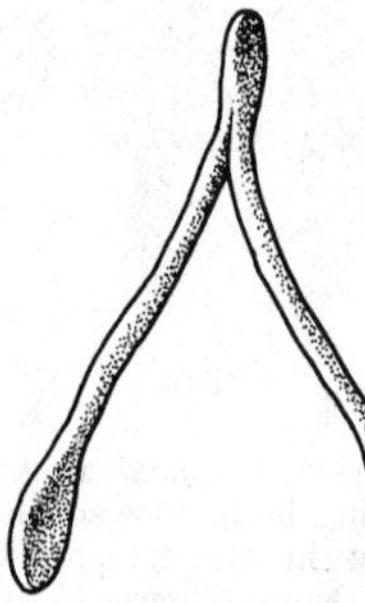
wishbone

wish·bone /wísh bòn/ *n* **1.** the V-shaped bone found between the breasts of a chicken or other bird. Technical name **furcula** **2.** a Y-shaped component connecting the wheels to the frame in a vehicle or aircraft suspension, the single end usually attaching to the wheel and the double end to the frame [Mid-19C. < a tradition of pulling the bone from a cooked bird between two people to break it, the person left with the larger part then making a wish]

wish·bone boom *n* the boom on a sailboat that a

windsurfer holds onto. It has two curving arms, one on either side of the sail, joined at the ends.

wish·bone-T *n* in football, a variant of the T-formation in which the halfbacks line up further from the line of scrimmage than the fullback

wish·ful /wíshfəl/ *adj* wishing for something, or expressing a wish or longing —**wish·ful·ly** *adv* —**wish·ful·ness** *n*

wish ful·fill·ment *n* in psychoanalytic theory, the process by which unconscious desires are realized in the imagination, mainly through dreams and fantasies

wish·ful think·ing *n* the unrealistic belief that something that is wished for is actually true or will be realized

wish·ing well *n* a well or representation of a well, supposed to grant the wish of somebody who makes a wish while dropping a coin into the well

wish list *n* an often informal list of things somebody would like to have or would like to happen

wish-wash *n* (*informal*) **1.** an unpleasantly weak or tasteless drink **2.** uninteresting and uninspiring talk or writing [Late 18C. Doubling of WASH, in the sense "thin, weak"]

wish·y-wash·y /wìshee wóshee, -wáwshee/ *adj* (*informal*) **1.** changeable or fluctuating in character, especially unable to make firm decisions or develop clear opinions **2.** weak, lacking taste, or unattractively pale [Late 17C. Doubling of *washy* "thin, watery" < WASH] —**wish·y-wash·i·ly** *adv* —**wish·y-wash·i·ness** *n*

Wis·ła /víssWə/ Polish name for **Vistula**

wisp /wisp/ *n* **1.** SOMETHING RESEMBLING THREAD something that is thin and delicate like thread, especially a lock of hair, a piece of straw, or a streak of smoke **2.** SOMEBODY SLENDER AND DELICATE somebody or something that is slender and delicate ○ *a wisp of a child* **3.** SOMETHING INSUBSTANTIAL something that is vague and fleeting ○ *a wisp of a memory* **4.** BUNDLE a bundle of something, especially a bundle of hay or straw ■ *v* (**wisped, wisp·ing, wisps**) **1.** *vt* BUNDLE UP STRAW OR HAY to make a handful of straw or hay into a bundle **2.** *vi* MOVE LIKE WISP to float like something delicate or faint [14C. Origin ?] —**wisp·i·ly** *adv* —**wisp·i·ness** *n* —**wisp·y** *adj*

wist[1] past participle, past tense of **wis** (*archaic*)

wist[2] past participle, past tense of **wit**[2] (*archaic*)

Wis·ter /wístər/, **Owen** (1860–1938) US writer. His novel about cowboy life, *The Virginian* (1902), became the archetype for the Western.

wisteria

wis·ter·i·a /wi stéeree ə/ (*plural* **-as** or *same*) *n* a deciduous climbing bush. Flowers: blue, pink, or white, hanging in clusters. Native to: North America, Asia. Genus: *Wisteria*. [Early 19C. < modern Latin, after Caspar *Wistar* (1761–1818), US anatomist]

wist·ful /wístfəl/ *adj* deep in sad thoughts, especially thoughts of something yearned for or lost, or expressing this sad yearning [Early 17C. < obsolete *wistly* "intently"] —**wist·ful·ly** *adv* —**wist·ful·ness** *n*

wit[1] /wit/ *n* **1.** INGENIOUS HUMOR the apt, clever, and often humorous association of words or ideas, or a capacity for it **2.** SPEECH OR WRITING SHOWING WIT speech or writing that shows an apt, clever, and often humorous association of words **3.** WITTY PERSON somebody known for using wit **4.** INTELLIGENCE mental acumen, intelligence, or reasoning power ■ **wits** *npl* SHREWDNESS mental acumen, shrewdness, or reasoning power [Old English *wit* "mind, understanding" < Indo-European, "see, know"] —**wit·ted** *adj* ◇ **be at your wits' end** to be in despair as to how to cope with something ◇ **live by your wits** to use cunning and ingenuity in order to survive ◇ **pit your wits against somebody** to compete with somebody in an intellectual exercise ◇ **scare** *or* **frighten somebody out of his** *or* **her wits** to fill somebody with sudden terror

wit[2] /wit/ (**wist** /wist/, **wist, wit·ting, wits** or **wot** /wot/) *vti* to know or become aware of something (*archaic*) [Old English *witan* < Germanic] ◇ **to wit** that is to say

wit·an /wí taan/ *n* in Anglo-Saxon England, an assembly of the king's counselors [Early 19C. Revival of Old English, "counselors" < *wita* "counselor, person who knows"]

Wit·bank /wít bàngk/ city in Mpumalanga Province, northeastern South Africa. Population: 83,400 (1998).

witch /wich/ *n* **1.** SOMEBODY WITH ALLEGED MAGIC POWERS somebody, especially a woman, who is supposed to have magical or wonder-working powers that are most often used malevolently **2.** FOLLOWER OF NATURE RELIGION a follower of Wicca, a pre-Christian natural religion **3.** OFFENSIVE TERM an offensive term that deliberately insults a woman regarded as ugly, vicious, or malicious (*insult*) **4.** SEDUCTIVE WOMAN a woman who is regarded as alluring or seductive (*informal; sometimes offensive*) ■ *vt* (**witched, witch·ing, witch·es**) AFFECT SOMETHING USING WITCHCRAFT to cause or change something by use of the supposedly magical powers of witchcraft [Old English *wicce* "witch" and *wicca* "wizard"]

SPELLCHECK See ***which***.

witch·craft /wích kràft/ *n* **1.** EXERCISE OF ALLEGEDLY MAGICAL POWERS the art of using allegedly magical powers **2.** ALLEGED EFFECT OF MAGICAL POWERS the alleged effect or influence of magical powers **3.** SEDUCTIVE CHARM alluring or seductive charm or influence (*informal*)

witch doc·tor *n* **1.** in tribal societies, somebody who practices healing, divining, or other magical powers **2.** in some African cultures, somebody who detects or identifies supposed witches

witch elm *n* TREES another spelling of **wych elm**

witch·er·y /wíchəree/ *n* **1.** the practice of witchcraft or magic (*dated or literary*) **2.** charm or influence that has a bewitching quality or effect

witch·es' brew *n* **1.** a malevolent or diabolical mixture of different things ○ *an article that was a witches' brew of spite and innuendo* **2.** a potion concocted by a witch

witch·es' broom *n* a tufted growth of shoots on a tree or woody plant, usually caused by parasitic fungi. The fungi usually responsible are of the genus *Taphrina*.

witch·es' but·ter *n* FUNGI same as **jelly fungus**

witch·es' Sab·bath *n* an assembly to celebrate Wicca rites

witch grass *n* **1.** a grass with creeping roots. Native to: North America. Latin name: *Panicum capillare*. **2.** PLANTS same as **couch grass** [Probably alteration of QUITCH GRASS]

witch ha·zel *n* **1.** a tree or bush that has toothed egg-shaped leaves and blooms in fall or winter. Flowers: small, yellow with strap-shaped petals. Genus: *Hamamelis*. **2.** a mixture of water, alcohol, and extract from the bark and dried leaves of the witch hazel. Use: astringent, embrocation. [< Old English *wice* (see WYCH ELM)]

witch-hunt *n* **1.** an intensive systematic campaign directed against those who have done something wrong or who hold different views **2.** a persecution of people believed to be witches —**witch-hunt·er** *n*

witch·ing /wíching/ *adj* **1.** suitable for or resembling witchcraft (*archaic*) **2.** same as **bewitching** (*literary*) ■ *n* witchcraft or sorcery (*archaic*)

witch·ing hour *n* midnight, said to be the time when witches allegedly appear

witch·weed /wích weed/ *n* a parasitic weed. Flowers: small, red. Native to: South Africa, introduced into the southern United States. Genus: *Striga*. [Probably < alteration of 1st element of QUITCH GRASS]

wit·e·na·ge·mot /wítt'nəgə mòt/ *n* HIST same as **witan** [Old English *witena gemōt* "assembly of wise men" < *wita* "counselor" + *gemōt* "assembly"]

Wite-Out /wít òwt/ *tdmk* a trademark for a white fluid used to cover up mistakes in writing, typing, or printing

with /with, with/ *prep* **1.** IN COMPANY OF used to indicate that somebody is accompanying or is in the company of another person or people, or that something is accompanying something else ○ *at the amusement park with their children* ○ *Do you still want me to go with you?* **2.** USED TOGETHER used together or at the same time ○ *ordered tea with cream* **3.** INVOLVING involving that person or people ○ *He organized the meeting together with a professor from the university.* **4.** AGAINST in opposition to ○ *students competing with one another for a limited number of spaces* **5.** BY MEANS OF by the means of or using a particular object, substance, or system ○ *After 18 months, all the rats treated with the altered virus were healthy.* **6.** ON ONE'S PERSON carrying or having in one's possession ○ *He came into the office with a box full of files.* **7.** HAVING having as a possession, attribute, or feature ○ *The movie is in French with English subtitles.* **8.** BECAUSE OF in a particular condition as a result of something ○ *I felt heartsick and faint with anxiety.* **9.** ON OR IN used to indicate that something has a substance or things on or in it ○ *brightly painted walls covered with photographs of Italy* **10.** CONCERNING used to indicate the person or thing that a state, quality, or action relates to or affects ○ *not happy with the service provided* **11.** IN THIS WAY used to indicate the way something is done, or the degree to which it is done ○ *sitting with her head on his shoulder* **12.** ACCOMPANIED BY used to indicate the feeling, gesture, sound, or facial expression that accompanies or causes an action ○ *walks with a limp* **13.** IN LIGHT OF in the light of or given the situation mentioned ○ *With all the problems you have, the last thing you need is a lawsuit.* **14.** IN SPITE OF in spite of the situation mentioned ○ *With all his charm and good breeding, he's a man not to be trusted.* **15.** AT TIME OF at the same time as ○ *He woke with the alarm and hurriedly dressed.* **16.** FOLLOWING DIRECTION OF in the same direction as ○ *They were to sail with the tide the next day.* **17.** ACCORDING TO used to indicate that something happens or is true according to something else ○ *how much the risk of death increases with age* **18.** AFTER following on from ○ *With a final wave goodbye she turned the corner.* [Old English *wiþ* "with, against" < Indo-European, "apart"] ◇ **be with it 1.** to be fashionable or up to date with fashion (*informal dated*) **2.** to be able to understand what is going on in a situation (*informal*) ◇ **be with somebody 1.** to understand somebody **2.** to approve of or support somebody ○ *Are you with us or not?* **3.** to be an established sexual or romantic partner of somebody ◇ **with that** immediately after saying or doing something specified ○ *With that, she turned to go.*

with·al /with áwl/ *adv* **1.** along with the rest or in addition ○ *And withal, Congress approved even more emergency funding than requested.* **2.** in spite of that ■ *prep* same as **with** (*archaic; used after its object*) ○ *all the better to see you withal* [12C. < WITH + ALL]

with·draw /with dráw, with-/ (**-drew** /-dróo/, **-drawn** /-dráwn/, **-draw·ing, -draws**) *v* **1.** *vt* REMOVE SOMETHING to remove or take back something that was previously provided or in place **2.** *vt* RETRACT STATEMENT to deny the truth or validity of something that was previously stated **3.** *vi* MIL RETREAT FROM POSITION to retreat or retire from a position, especially during a battle **4.** *vt* BANKING TAKE MONEY FROM ACCOUNT to take money out of an account —**with·draw·able** *adj* —**with·drawer** *n*

with·draw·al /with dráw əl, with-/ *n* **1.** TAKING MONEY FROM BANK the act of taking money from a bank account, or the amount of money taken out **2.** TAKING SOMETHING AWAY the act or condition of taking something away or no longer taking part in something **3.** DRUGS PERIOD OF FIGHTING ADDICTION a period during which somebody addicted to a drug or other addictive substance stops taking it, causing the person to experience painful or uncomfortable symptoms **4.** MIL RETREAT OF ARMY retreat or retirement of an army or other military force from an area in which it was fighting

with·drawn /with dráwn, with-/ past participle of

withdraw ■ *adj* **1.** not friendly or sociable but quiet and thoughtful, especially to an unusual or worrying degree **2.** removed from circulation, competition, or activity —**with·drawn·ness** *n*

with·drew past tense of **withdraw**

withe /with, with, wi̲th/ *n* **1.** CONSTR **FLEXIBLE STEM** a strong flexible twig or stem used to bind something **2. FLEXIBLE TOOL HANDLE** a shock-absorbing flexible handle for a tool ■ *vt* (**withed, with·ing, withes**) **BIND SOMETHING WITH WITHES** to bind something with strong flexible twigs or stems [Old English *wiþþe* < Indo-European, "twist, bend"]

with·er /wíthər/ (**-ered, -er·ing, -ers**) *v* **1.** *vti* **SHRIVEL** to shrivel or dry up as part of the process of dying, or make something, especially a plant or part of a plant, shrivel in this way **2.** *vi* **FADE AWAY** to fade or lose freshness or vitality **3.** *vti* **BECOME OR MAKE SOMEBODY LESS CONFIDENT** to make somebody feel embarrassed, foolish, or incapable of activity as the object of scorn or contempt, or lose confidence in the face of somebody's scorn [14C. Probably variant of WEATHER "expose to the elements"] —**with·ered** *adj* —**with·er·er** *n*

with·er·ing /wíthəring/ *adj* expressing scorn or contempt with the intention of causing somebody to feel embarrassed or foolish ○ *"When he assumed this attitude in the courtroom, ears were always pricked up, as it usually foretold a flood of withering sarcasm."* (Willa Cather, *The Troll Garden*; 1905) —**with·er·ing·ly** *adv*

with·er·ite /wíthə rìt/ *n* a rare grayish white barium carbonate mineral. Source: lead ores. Use: source of barium. [Late 18C. After William *Withering* (1741–99), British scientist]

withe rod *n* a small tree or bush that produces tough flexible shoots. Native to: eastern North America. Latin name: *Viburnum nudum* var. cassinoides.

with·ers /wíthərz/ *npl* the ridge between the shoulder bones of a horse, sheep, ox, or similar four-legged animal, forming the highest part of its back [Early 16C. Probably < Old English *wiþer* "against"]

with·er·shins *adv Scotland* another spelling of **widdershins** (*literary*)

With·er·spoon /wíthər spòon/, **John** (1723–94) British-born US cleric and educator. As president of the College of New Jersey, now Princeton University (1768–94), he expanded the college. He was a signatory of the Declaration of Independence (1776).

with·hold /with hṓld, with-/ (**-held** /-héld/, **-hold·ing, -holds**) *v* **1.** *vti* to refuse to do or give something until something else is done **2.** *vt* to collect or deduct tax from a salary —**with·hold·er** *n*

with·hold·ing tax /with hṓlding-/ *n US* part of an employee's wage or salary withheld and remitted to the government by an employer in payment of taxes

with·in /with ín/ *prep, adv* **1. INSIDE PLACE** used to indicate that somebody or something is inside or enclosed by a place, area, or object ○ (prep) *goods manufactured within a country* ○ (prep) *A natural pool lay within a grove of young trees.* ○ (adv) *The door was locked from within.* **2. INSIDE ORGANIZATION** happening inside an organization, system, or society ○ (prep) *keeping companies within a given industry technologically competitive* ○ (adv) *Much of our Internet development activity is coming from within.* **3. INSIDE YOURSELF** inside the body or mind ○ (adv) *Her new-found happiness was from within.* ○ (prep) *He needed to find the strength within him to persevere.* ■ *prep* **1. NOT BEYOND** not beyond the scope, experience, range, time, or distance of ○ *regulations requiring that all accidents be reported within 48 hours* **2. INSIDE LIMITS OF** inside the limits or rules of ○ *Try to keep within your budget and avoid overspending.* ■ *adv* same as **indoors** (*literary*) [Old English *wiþinnan* "on the inside" < WITH + *innan* "from within"]

USAGE See *inside.*

with-it *adj* fashionable and modern in dress and behavior (*dated informal*)

~~**withold**~~ incorrect spelling of **withhold**

with·out /with ówt/ *prep* **1. NOT HAVING** used to indicate that somebody or something does not have the thing mentioned ○ *left without proper tools to finish the job* **2. LACKING** lacking a feeling of ○ *The accused committed perjury without remorse.* **3. NOT ACCOMPANIED BY** not with somebody, or not having the involvement of somebody ○ *We can't really make any decisions without him.* **4. NOT HAPPENING** used to indicate that something does not happen or occur ○ *The bill was passed without a dissenting vote.* ■ *prep, adv* **OUTSIDE** on, at, or to the outside of somewhere (*archaic or literary*) ○ (prep) *Without the town the air was fresher.* ○ (adv) *She knocked and waited without.* ■ *conj* same as **unless** (*nonstandard*) [Old English *wiþūtan* "on the outside of," < WITH + *ūtan* "from the outside"] ◇ **be** *or* **do without** to manage in spite of not having something considered necessary or desirable ○ *a form of power he could not buy or do without*

with·stand /with stánd, with-/ (**-stood** /-stóod/, **-stand·ing, -stands**) *vti* to be strong enough to stand up to somebody or remain unchanged by something such as extremes of heat or pressure —**with·stand·er** *n*

with·y /wíthee/ *n* (*plural* **-ies**) **1.** CONSTR same as **withe** *n* (sense 1) **2.** TREES a willow tree, especially an osier ■ *adj* tough and pliable, like withes (*dated*) [Old English *wīþig* "willow" < Indo-European, "twist, bend"]

wit·less /wíttləss/ *adj* lacking intelligence or common sense ○ *a witless comment* —**wit·less·ly** *adv* —**wit·less·ness** *n*

wit·ling /wíttling/ *n* somebody who wishes to be witty (*archaic*)

wit·ness /wítnəss/ *n* **1. SOMEBODY WHO SEES OCCURRENCE** somebody who gives evidence after seeing or hearing something **2. SIGNATORY OF DOCUMENT** somebody who signs a document to show that it, or another signature, is genuine **3. SOMEBODY WHO TESTIFIES TO CHRISTIAN BELIEFS** somebody who publicly states his or her strong Christian beliefs **4. PUBLIC STATEMENT OF CHRISTIAN BELIEFS** a public statement of strong personal Christian beliefs ■ *v* (**-nessed, -ness·ing, -ness·es**) **1.** *vt* **SEE SOMETHING HAPPEN** to see something happen, especially a crime or an accident **2.** *vt* **COUNTERSIGN DOCUMENT** to affirm the authenticity of a document or a signature on a document by signing it **3.** *vt* **EXPERIENCE IMPORTANT EVENTS** to experience important events or changes, or be the time in which they occur **4.** *vt* **BE SIGN OF SOMETHING** to be a sign or proof of something that is happening **5.** *vi* **SPEAK PUBLICLY ABOUT RELIGIOUS BELIEFS** to talk in public about strong personal Christian beliefs [Old English *witnes* < *wit* (see WIT[1])] —**wit·ness·a·ble** *adj* —**wit·ness·er** *n* ◇ **bear witness (to something)** to prove or be evidence that something is true or that something happened

wit·ness stand *n* the enclosed place in a courtroom where witnesses give evidence

Witt ▸ **De Witt, Jan**

Wit·ten·berg /vítt'n bùrg/ city in east central Germany where Martin Luther began his campaign for the reform of the Roman Catholic Church in 1517. Population: 53,400 (1989).

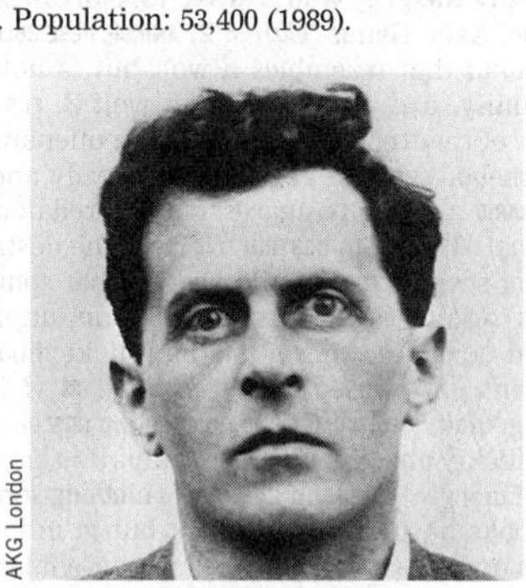

AKG London

Ludwig Wittgenstein

Witt·gen·stein /vítgən shtīn, -stīn/, **Ludwig** (1889–1951) Austrian-born British philosopher. He is considered one of the most important thinkers of the 20th century. His *Tractatus Logico-philosophicus* (1921) and *Philosophical Investigations* (1953) represent distinct phases in his work in analytic and linguistic philosophy. Full name **Wittgenstein, Ludwig Josef Johann**

> "The world is everything that is the case."
> [Ludwig Wittgenstein, *Tractatus Logico-philosophicus*; 1921]

> "Philosophy is a battle against the bewitchment of our intelligence by means of language."
> [Ludwig Wittgenstein, *Philosophical Investigations*; 1953]

wit·ti·cism /wítti sìzzəm/ *n* a witty or clever remark [Late 17C. Blend of WITTY + CRITICISM]

wit·ting /wítting/ *adj* (*formal*) **1.** done deliberately or intentionally **2.** responsible and fully aware —**wit·ting·ly** *adv*

wit·ty /wíttee/ (**-ti·er, -ti·est**) *adj* **1.** using words in an apt, clever, and amusing way **2.** strikingly clever, stylish, or original in design or execution —**wit·ti·ly** *adv* —**wit·ti·ness** *n*

SYNONYMS See *funny.*

Wit·wa·ters·rand /wit wáwtərz rànd/ rocky ridge in northeastern South Africa. Commonly known as "the Rand," it is the most productive gold-mining area in the world. Johannesburg is located near its center. Length: 60 mi./100 km.

wive /wīv/ (**wived, wiv·ing, wives**) *v* (*archaic*) **1.** *vti* to marry a woman **2.** *vt* to supply somebody with a wife [Old English *wīfian* < *wīf* "woman, wife"]

wi·vern *n* HERALDRY another spelling of **wyvern**

wives plural of **wife**

wiz /wiz/ (*plural* **wiz·zes**) *n* same as **whiz** *n* (sense 1) (*informal*) [Early 20C. Partly shortening of WIZARD; partly variant of WHIZ]

wiz·ard /wízzərd/ *n* **1.** a man who is supposed to have magical or wonder-working powers **2.** somebody who is extremely skilled in or knowledgeable about something (*informal*) [15C. < WISE[1]] —**wiz·ard·ly** *adj*

CULTURAL NOTE ***The Wizard of Oz***, a movie (1939) by US producer David O. Selznick and director Victor Fleming. This enchanting musical, based on a novel by L. Frank Baum (1900), tells the story of Dorothy, a young Kansas girl who dreams she is transported to the magical world of Oz, a utopian place without disease, poverty, or political discussion "except in the outlying districts." Evading the Wicked Witch of the West, she sets off along the yellow brick road in search of the mysterious Wizard. The words *Oz* (a magical, unreal, even bizarre place or situation), *Wicked Witch of the West* (evil person), and *munchkin* (from the elflike Munchkins in the movie, now meaning also an elflike person, a young child, or a minor government official) have established a place in the English language.

wiz·ard·ry /wízzərdree/ *n* **1.** the art, activities, or alleged accomplishments of a wizard **2.** extreme skill, ability, or accomplishment

wiz·ened /wízz'nd/ *adj* looking wrinkled, shriveled, or dried up [Early 16C. Past participle of *wizen* < Old English *wisnian* < Germanic] —**wiz·en** *adj, vi*

wiz kid *n* same as **whiz kid** (*informal*)

wk. *abbr* **1.** weak **2.** week **3.** work

wkly *abbr* weekly

WL *abbr* **1.** *also* **w.l.** NAUT water line **2.** ELEC wavelength

WLAN *abbr* COMPUT wireless local area network

WLTM *abbr* ONLINE would like to meet (*informal*)

WMD *abbr* MIL weapons of mass destruction

wmk. *abbr* watermark

WML *abbr* COMPUT wireless markup language

WMO *abbr* World Meteorological Organization

WNF *abbr* MED West Nile fever

WNV *abbr* MED West Nile virus

WNW *abbr* west-northwest

W.N./W.D. *abbr* HEALTH well-nourished and well-developed

WO, **W.O.** *abbr* MIL warrant officer

w/o *abbr* without

woad /wōd/ *n* **1.** a blue dye obtained from the leaves of a European plant. Use: formerly, body paint. **2.** a plant formerly cultivated for woad. Native to: Europe. Latin name: *Isatis tinctoria.* [Old English *wād* < Germanic]

woad·wax·en /wṓd wàks'n/ (*plural* **-ens** *or* **same**) *n*

PLANTS same as **dyer's greenweed** [14C. Alteration (influenced by *woad*) of *woodwaxen* < Old English *wuduweaxe* < *wudu* "wood" + *weaxan* "grow"]

w.o.b. *abbr* INSUR washed overboard

wob·ble /wóbb'l/, **wab·ble** *v* (**-bled, -bling, -bles**) **1.** *vti* **MOVE FROM SIDE TO SIDE** to move in a swaying, shaking, or trembling way, or cause something to move in a swaying, shaking, or trembling way **2.** *vi* **QUAVER** to vary uncertainly in pitch or volume ○ *a voice wobbling with emotion* **3.** *vi* **BE UNABLE TO DECIDE** to be unable or unwilling to reach a decision ■ *n* **WOBBLING EFFECT** a wobbling movement or sound [Mid-17C. Probably < Low German *wabbeln* < Germanic] —**wob·bler** *n* —**wob·bling·ly** *adv*

wob·bler syn·drome *n* a condition in horses and dogs characterized by an unsteady gait and sometimes falling, as a result of a misalignment of vertebrae in the neck, which press on the spinal cord

wob·bly /wóbblee/ (**-bli·er, -bli·est**), **wab·bly** /wábblee/ *adj* **1. UNSTEADY** moving unsteadily from side to side **2. FEELING WEAK** feeling weak and unable to keep balanced (*informal*) **3. WISHY-WASHY** unable or unwilling to make firm decisions and stand by them in the face of opposition (*informal*) ○ *a wobbly leader with a vacillating foreign policy* [Mid-19C. < WOBBLE] —**wob·bli·ness** *n*

Wob·bly /wóbblee/ (*plural* **-blies**) *n US* a member of the Industrial Workers of the World (*informal*) [Early 20C. Origin ?]

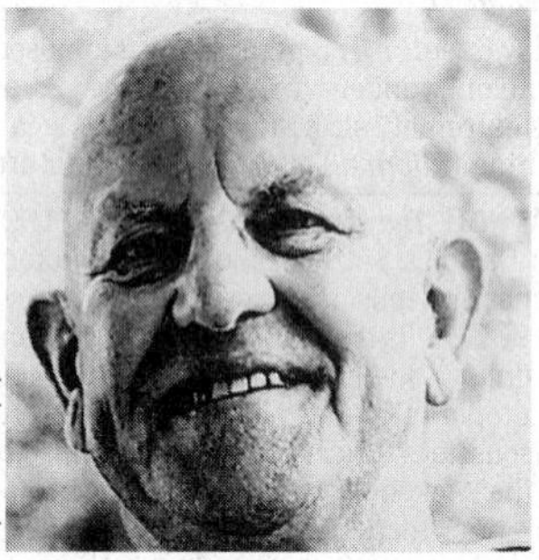
Express Newspapers

P. G. Wodehouse

Wode·house /wo͝od hòwss/, **P. G.** (1881–1975) British writer. He wrote over 100 novels, many of which feature the fictional characters Bertie Wooster and his "gentleman's gentleman," Jeeves. He became a US citizen in 1955. Full name **Wodehouse, Sir Pelham Grenville**

> "Fate was quietly slipping the lead into the boxing glove."
> [P. G. Wodehouse, *Very Good, Jeeves*; 1930]

> "Has anyone ever seen a dramatic critic in the daytime? Of course not. They come out after dark, up to no good."
> [P. G. Wodehouse, *New York Mirror*; May 27, 1955]

Wo·den /wṓd'n/ *n* in Anglo-Saxon mythology, the equivalent of the Norse god Odin

wodge /woj/ *n UK* a large lump or chunk of something (*informal*) ○ *They caught him stuffing wodges of banknotes into his pockets.* [Mid-19C. Blend of WAD + WEDGE]

woe /wō/ *n* **1.** a serious affliction or misfortune **2.** grief or distress resulting from a serious affliction or misfortune [Old English *wā* < Germanic < Indo-European] ◇ **woe betide somebody** used as a threat to indicate that somebody is going to regret something or be punished in some way ○ *Woe betide him if he turns up late for work again.* ◇ **woe is me** used to indicate that the speaker is in distress or feels unhappy or unfortunate (*literary or humorous*)

woe·be·gone /wṓ bi gòn/ *adj* feeling or looking distressed or sorrowful [13C. < WOE + *begon* "beset" (< Old English *gān*)]

woe·ful /wṓf'l/ *adj* **1. UNHAPPY** feeling or expressing great distress or sorrow **2. CAUSING GRIEF** bringing or causing great distress or sorrow **3. PATHETICALLY BAD** pitifully or regrettably bad —**woe·ful·ly** *adv* —**woe·ful·ness** *n*

wog /wog/ *n UK* a highly offensive term for a member of any people who have dark skin (*taboo insult*) [Early 20C. Probably shortening of GOLLIWOG]

wok

wok /wok/ *n* a large thin metal pan with a curved base, used for stir-frying, steaming, and braising food, especially in Chinese and other East Asian styles of cooking [Mid-20C. < Chinese (Cantonese)]

woke past tense of **wake**[1]

wok·en past participle of **wake**[1]

Wok·ing /wṓking/ city in Surrey, southeastern England. Population: 89,840 (2001).

wold /wōld/ *n* upland or rolling country, especially when treeless [Old English *wald, weald* "forest" < Indo-European, "wild"]

Wolds /wōldz/ range of chalk hills in eastern England. It is divided by the Humber estuary into the Yorkshire Wolds and the Lincolnshire Wolds.

wolf

wolf /wo͝olf/ *n* (*plural* **wolves** /wo͝olvz/) **1. CARNIVORE THAT HUNTS IN PACKS** any one of several predatory animals that are related to the dog and hunt in packs, especially the gray wolf. Native to: North America, Europe, Asia. Genus: *Canis*. **2. ANIMAL RESEMBLING WOLF** an animal that resembles a wolf but is not of the dog family, e.g., the Tasmanian wolf **3. FUR OF WOLF** the fur of the wolf **4. OFFENSIVE TERM** an offensive term for somebody who is regarded as greedy and cruel **5. LOTHARIO** a sexually aggressive or predatory man (*informal*) **6.** INSECTS **DESTRUCTIVE LARVA** the destructive larva of several moths and beetles that sometimes infests granaries **7.** MUSIC **DISCORD** an unpleasant discord produced on a string or keyboard instrument (*often used before a noun*) ■ *vt* (**wolfed, wolf·ing, wolfs**) **EAT SOMETHING QUICKLY AND GREEDILY** to eat food quickly and greedily or in gulps [Old English *wulf* < Indo-European] ◇ **a wolf in sheep's clothing** somebody who looks harmless or pleasant but is in fact dangerous or unpleasant ◇ **cry wolf** to give a false alarm or cry for help too many times, so that when help is really needed, no one will give it ◇ **keep the wolf from the door** to be enough to prevent hunger or starvation ◇ **the wolf is at the door** somebody, especially a bill collector, is close at hand, demanding something of you ◇ **throw somebody to the wolves** to abandon somebody to be destroyed by enemies in order to save yourself

Wolf *n* ASTRON same as **Lupus**

Wolf /vawlf/, **Hugo** (1860–1903) Austrian composer. He wrote nearly 300 songs exploring a wide range of themes and moods. Full name **Wolf, Hugo Philipp Jakob**

wolf dog *n* **1.** a dog that is used to hunt wolves **2.** an offspring of a wolf and a dog

Barnaby's

James Wolfe

Wolfe /wo͝olf/, **James** (1727–59) British general. The second in command of British troops in North America, he is most famous for his capture of Quebec (1759) from the French in the French and Indian War (1756–63). He was fatally wounded in the attack.

Wolfe, Thomas (1900–38) US writer. His novels, including *Look Homeward, Angel* (1929) and *You Can't Go Home Again* (1940), are heavily autobiographical. Full name **Wolfe, Thomas Clayton**

> "Which of us has known his brother? Which of us has looked into his father's heart? Which of us has not remained forever prison-pent? Which of us is not forever a stranger and alone?"
> [Thomas Wolfe. Foreword, *Look Homeward, Angel*; 1929]

Wolfe, Tom (*b.* 1930) US journalist and writer. A leading proponent of New Journalism, he is the author of *The Right Stuff* (1979) and *Bonfire of the Vanities* (1987). He established his reputation as a satirist of American society with his first collection of essays entitled *The Kandy-Colored Flake Streamline Baby* (1964). Full name **Wolfe, Thomas Kennerly Jr.** See Cultural note at **bonfire**

> "He was learning for himself the truth of the saying, 'A liberal is a conservative who has been arrested.'"
> [Tom Wolfe, *The Bonfire of the Vanities*; 1987]

> "Status is an influence at every level...all part of what I call plutography: depicting the acts of the rich."
> [Tom Wolfe, *Time*; February 13, 1989]

wolf eel *n* a large long fish with a pointed tail. Native to: Pacific coastal waters of North America. Latin name: *Anarrhicthys ocellatus*. [Because it is a species of wolffish]

wolf·er *n* HUNTING same as **wolver**

wolf·fish /wo͝olf fìsh/ (*plural same* or **-fish·es**) *n* a large fish with sharp teeth and no pelvic fins. Native to: northern Atlantic. Genus: *Anarhichas*. [< its voracious appetite]

wolf·hound /wo͝olf hòwnd/ *n* a large dog belonging to a breed originally developed to hunt wolves

wolf·ish /wo͝olfish/ *adj* resembling or characteristic of a wolf —**wolf·ish·ly** *adv*

wolf pack *n* **1.** a group of wolves that hunt together **2.** a group of submarines, especially German ones, that engaged in hunting and attacking enemy convoys during World War II

wolf·ram /wo͝olfrəm/ *n* CHEM ELEM same as **tungsten** (*archaic*) [Mid-18C. < German, "wolframite" < *Wolf* "wolf" + German dialect *Rahm* "soot, dirt"]

wolf·ram·ite /wo͝olfrə mìt/ *n* a brownish black crystalline mineral consisting of iron manganese tungstate. Use: source of tungsten. [Mid-19C. < German (see WOLFRAM)]

wolfs·bane /wo͝olfs bàyn/ (*plural* **-banes** or *same*) *n* a wild or cultivated poisonous plant. Flowers: yellow or purplish blue. Use: medicines. Genus: *Aconitum*. [Mid-16C. Translation of Greek *lukoktonon* "wolf-killer," from the poison found in the plants]

Wolfs·burg /wŏŏlfs bùrg, váwlfs bŏŏrk/ industrial city in Lower Saxony State, north central Germany. Population: 126,965 (1997).

wolf spi·der *n* a ground spider that hunts its prey rather than using a web. Family: Lycosidae.

wolf whis·tle *n* a whistle given to signal sexual interest in or admiration of somebody —**wolf-whis·tle** *vti*

wol·las·ton·ite /wŏŏllǝstǝ nīt/ *n* a fibrous gray-white calcium silicate mineral. Source: metamorphosed limestone. [Early 19C. After William Hyde *Wollaston* (1766–1828), British physicist]

Wol·lon·gong /wŏŏllǝng gòng/ coastal city in eastern New South Wales, Australia. It is an industrial center and the site of a university. Population: 191,254 (2002 estimate).

Mary Wollstonecraft: Portrait (1790) by John Opie

Woll·stone·craft /wŏŏlstǝn kràft/, **Mary** (1759–97) British feminist. Her *A Vindication of the Rights of Woman* (1792), advocating the equality of the sexes, is an important early document of modern feminism.

> "Virtue can only flourish amongst equals."
> [Mary Wollstonecraft, *A Vindication of the Rights of Men*; 1790]

> "Till women are more rationally educated, the progress in human virtue and improvement in knowledge must receive continual checks."
> [Mary Wollstonecraft, *A Vindication of the Rights of Women*; 1792]

Wo·lof /wŏ lòf/ (*plural same* or **-lofs**) *n* **1.** a member of a people who live in West Africa, mainly in Senegal but also in Gambia and Mauritania **2.** a Niger-Congo language spoken in Senegal and the Gambia. Native speakers: 2 million. [Early 19C. < Wolof] —**Wo·lof** *adj*

Wol·sey /wŏŏlzee/, **Thomas** (1475–1530) English cleric and political leader. As Henry VIII's Lord Chancellor (1515–29), he exercised great power both in England and abroad. He was impeached for failing to secure Henry's divorce from Catherine of Aragon. Known as **Wolsey, Cardinal**

wol·ver /wŏŏlvǝr/, **wol·fer** /wŏŏlfǝr/ *n* somebody who hunts wolves

Wol·ver·hamp·ton /wŏŏlvǝr hámptǝn/ industrial city in west central England. Population: 236,582 (2001).

wol·ver·ine /wŏŏlvǝ reén/ (*plural* **-ines** or *same*) *n* a strong dark-furred, usually solitary carnivore of the weasel family. Native to: forests of northern Europe, Asia, North America. Latin name: *Gulo gulo*. [Late 16C. Probably < WOLF]

Wol·ver·ine State *n* a nickname for Michigan

wolves plural of **wolf**

wom·an /wŏŏmmǝn/ (*plural* **wom·en** /wímmin/) *n* **1.** FEMALE ADULT an adult female human being **2.** WOMEN AS GROUP women collectively or in general **3.** FEMININITY feminine qualities or feelings **4.** DOMESTIC EMPLOYEE a woman who is a domestic employee (*sometimes offensive*) **5.** WIFE OR GIRLFRIEND a wife, female lover, or girlfriend (*informal; sometimes offensive*) [Old English *wimman*, variant of *wīfman*, < *wīf* "woman, wife" + *man* "person"] ◇ **to a woman** used to indicate that every one of a group of women does or thinks something, without any exceptions

USAGE See *girl, person.*

CULTURAL NOTE ***Little Women***, a novel (1868–69) by Louisa May Alcott. An abidingly popular family saga set in 1860s New England, it recounts the emotional and intellectual development of four sisters – Meg, Jo, Beth, and Amy – as they progress through adolescence to adulthood. It was followed by two sequels, *Little Men* (1871) and *Jo's Boys* (1886).

wom·an·ful·ly /wŏŏmmǝnfǝlee/ *adv* in a way that shows or is characteristic of womanly spirit or energy [Early 19C. After *manfully*]

wom·an·hood /wŏŏmmǝn hŏŏd/ *n* **1.** the state or condition of being a woman **2.** women in general, or as a group

wom·an·ish /wŏŏmmǝnish/ *adj* an offensive term meaning having qualities stereotypically attributed to women such as weakness or fussiness —**wom·an·ish·ly** *adv* —**wom·an·ish·ness** *n*

wom·an·ist /wŏŏmmǝnist/ *adj* having a respect for and a belief in the abilities and talents of women [Late 20C. After *humanist*]

wom·an·ize /wŏŏmmǝ nīz/ (**-ized, -iz·ing, -iz·es**) *vi* to be constantly in search of casual sex with women (*disapproving; refers to men*) —**wom·an·iz·er** *n*

wom·an·kind /wŏŏmmǝn kīnd/, **wom·en·kind** /wímmin-/ *n* women collectively or in general

wom·an·ly /wŏŏmmǝnlee/ *adj* having positive characteristics or qualities, especially warmth, calmness, and competence, attributed to mature women —**wom·an·li·ness** *n*

wom·an of the hour (*plural* **wom·en of the hour**) *n* a woman, often a public figure, who is currently publicly admired because of her accomplishments or actions ○ *Because of her bravery in enemy captivity the army nurse was the woman of the hour.*

wom·an of the house *n* a woman who is in charge of or who is the primary woman of a household

wom·an of the world (*plural* **wom·en of the world**) *n* a socially experienced and sophisticated woman

wom·an·pow·er /wŏŏmmǝn pòwr/ *n* **1.** women as part of the work force in society **2.** the influence and impact of women in society [Early 20C. After MANPOWER]

wom·an suf·frage *n* POL same as **women's suffrage**

wom·an-to-wom·an *adj* **1.** marked by directness and candor between women **2.** in sports such as women's basketball, having each defensive player of one team guard a corresponding offensive player of the other team —**wom·an-to-wom·an** *adv*

womb /woom/ *n* **1.** UTERUS OF WOMAN a uterus, especially a woman's (*not in technical use*) **2.** PLACE OF ORIGIN a place where something is conceived and nurtured **3.** PLACE OF SECURITY a place that offers protection and shelter, or a state of mind that provides comfort [Old English *wamb* < Germanic]

wombat

wom·bat /wóm bàt/ *n* a burrowing marsupial that is short, robust, covered in dense wiry hair, and has a stumpy tail and wide blunt snout. Native to: Australia. Latin name: *Vombatus ursinus* or *Lasiorhinus latifrons*. [Late 18C. < Dharuk *wambaty*]

womb·like /wóom līk/ *adj* resembling a womb, especially in being reassuring, all-enclosing, and giving a feeling of security

wom·en plural of **woman**

wom·en·folk /wímmin fōk/, **wom·en·folks** *npl* women collectively, or a particular group of women, especially those belonging to the same family or society (*dated*)

wom·en·kind *n* same as **womankind**

wom·en's lib *n* SOC SCI same as **women's liberation** (*informal*) —**wom·en's lib·ber** *n*

wom·en's lib·er·a·tion *n* a political movement intended to free women from oppression, or the act of a woman's freeing herself

wom·en's move·ment *n* a movement seeking to promote and improve the position of women in society

wom·en's ref·uge *n UK* same as **women's shelter**

wom·en's room *n* a public toilet for women and girls to use

wom·en's shel·ter *n* a place where women and children can stay after leaving home to escape domestic violence

wom·en's stud·ies *n* a course of study examining the historical, economic, and cultural roles and achievements of women (*takes a singular or plural verb*)

wom·en's suf·frage *n* the right of women to vote in elections

wom·ens·wear /wímminz wèr/ *n* clothing and accessories for women

wom·er·a *n* ARMS another spelling of **woomera**

won¹ /won/ (*plural same*) *n* the main unit of currency in North and South Korea. See table at **currency** [Mid-20C. < Korean *wǎn*]

won² /wun/ past participle, past tense of **win**

won·der /wúndǝr/ *n* **1.** AMAZED ADMIRATION amazed admiration or awe, especially at something very beautiful or new **2.** SOMETHING MARVELOUS a miracle or other cause of intense admiration or awe ■ *adj* EXTRAORDINARILY GOOD exciting admiration or amazement by virtue of being outstandingly good, effective, or unusual ■ *v* (**-dered, -der·ing, -ders**) **1.** *vti* SPECULATE ABOUT SOMETHING to speculate or be curious to know about something **2.** *vi* BE AMAZED to be in a state of amazed admiration or awe [Old English *wundor* < Germanic] —**won·der·er** *n* ◇ **no** *or* **small** *or* **little wonder** used to indicate that something is not surprising ◇ **wonders (will) never cease** used, often ironically, to express astonishment or incredulity ○ *I hear he managed to get to work on time today – wonders will never cease!* ◇ **work** *or* **perform** *or* **do wonders** to achieve remarkable results or be very effective in solving a problem

SPELLCHECK See *wander.*

Won·der /wúndǝr/, **Stevie** (*b.* 1950) US singer and songwriter. He released his first album at age 13, began an international career, and won numerous Grammy awards for a succession of recordings of Motown rhythm and blues. Born **Judkins, Steveland**

> "Pride is like a perfume. When it is worn, it radiates a sense of self the world reacts to."
> [Stevie Wonder, *Essence*; January 1975]

won·der drug *n* MED same as **miracle drug**

won·der·ful /wúndǝrf'l/ *adj* **1.** of a quality that excites admiration or amazement **2.** suiting somebody perfectly —**won·der·ful·ly** *adv* —**won·der·ful·ness** *n*

won·der·land /wúndǝr lànd/ *n* a land where wonderful things happen or exist

CULTURAL NOTE ***Alice's Adventures in Wonderland***, a children's story (1865) by British writer Lewis Carroll. This extraordinarily inventive and immensely popular tale was based on stories that the author made up to entertain his friends' children. A girl called Alice dreams that she falls down a rabbit hole into a surreal world inhabited by eccentric characters including the Mad Hatter, the March Hare, and the King and Queen of Hearts. The expressions "Curiouser and curiouser!" and "Oh my fur and whiskers!" are direct quotations from this book. The often-used expressions "grin like a Cheshire cat," "wild as a March hare," and "mad as a hatter" have associations with characters in the book.

won·der·ment /wúndərmənt/ *n* **1.** amazed admiration or awe **2.** puzzled surprise

won·der·work /wúndər wùrk/ *n* something made or done that arouses amazed admiration or awe —**won·der·work·er** *n*

won·drous /wúndrəss/ (*literary*) *adj* so good or admirable as to inspire wonder or awe ■ *adv* wondrously or extraordinarily [15C. Alteration (influenced by MARVELOUS) of obsolete *wonders* < WONDER] —**won·drous·ly** *adv*—**won·drous·ness** *n*

wonk /wongk/ *n* **1.** an expert in matters of policy, especially in government, the economy, or diplomacy (*informal*) ○ *The dinner conversation was dominated by deep discussions among the Administration's policy wonks.* **2.** a student who works unduly hard or long (*informal disapproving*) [Early 20C. Origin ?]

won·ky[1] /wóngkee/ *adj* (**-ki·er, -ki·est**), *adv UK* not to be relied on to be steady or secure or to function correctly (*informal*) [Early 20C. Origin ?] —**won·ki·ly** *adv*—**won·ki·ness** *n*

wonk·y[2] /wóngkee/ (**-i·er, -i·est**) *adj* (*informal disapproving*) **1.** expert in matters of policy, especially in government, the economy, or diplomacy ○ *a wonky Vice President who delved deep into economic policies* **2.** studying too hard or too much [< WONK] —**wonk·i·ness** *n*

wont /wawnt, wōnt/ *adj* **ACCUSTOMED TO SOMETHING** accustomed or likely to do something (*formal*) ○ *He is wont to be rather quick of temper when tired.* ■ *n* **SOMEBODY'S CUSTOM** a habit or custom followed by a person or group of people (*formal*) ○ *It is her wont to surf the Internet every night.* ■ *vti* (**wont** or **wont·ed, wont·ing, wonts**) **BE ACCUSTOMED** to have the habit of doing something, or give somebody the habit of doing something (*archaic*) [12C. < past participle of Old English *wunian* "be accustomed"]

SYNONYMS See ***habit***.

won't /wōnt/ *contr* a shortening of "will not"

wont·ed /wáwntəd, wṓntəd/ *adj* usual or typical (*literary*) —**wont·ed·ly** *adv* —**wont·ed·ness** *n*

SYNONYMS See ***usual***.

won ton /wòn tón/ *n* **1.** in Chinese cooking, a small dumpling made from a square of noodle dough with a little filling in the middle, boiled in soup or deep-fried **2.** *also* **won ton soup** Chinese soup with boiled small dumplings in it [Mid-20C. < Chinese (Cantonese) *wān t'ān*]

woo /woo/ (**wooed, woo·ing, woos**) *vti* **1.** to seek the affection or love of a woman in order to marry her (*literary*) **2.** to try to please somebody in order to gain something, especially acceptance, fame, or approval [Old English *wōgian*, origin ?] —**woo·ing·ly** *adv*

wood /wŏŏd/ *n* **1. SUBSTANCE OF TREES** a hard fibrous substance that chiefly composes trees and bushes and is found beneath their bark **2. FUEL OR BUILDING MATERIAL** wood from trees, cut and dried for use as a fuel or a building material or in other areas of craft and manufacture **3. AREA WITH TREES** an area of land covered by trees or bushes. A wood is usually smaller than a forest. **4. GOLF CLUB** a golf club with a head formerly made of wood, but now usually made of stainless steel or titanium ■ **woods** *npl* **1. FORESTED AREA** a forested or wooded area or region **2. WOODWIND** the woodwind instruments or players of an orchestra ■ *adj* **1. OF WOOD** made of or used for wood **2. AMONG TREES** located or living in a forested area ■ *v* (**wooded, wood·ing, woods**) **1.** *vt* **COVER AREA WITH TREES** to cover an area of land with trees **2.** *vti* **FUEL SOMETHING WITH WOOD** to supply somebody or something with wood as fuel, or be supplied with wood as fuel [Old English *wudu* < Germanic] —**wood·ed** *adj* ◇ **knock on wood** used to express a wish for good fortune in a particular respect to continue ○ *Sunny skies for the picnic, knock on wood.* ◇ **out of the woods** out of danger or difficulty (*informal*) ◇ **touch wood** used, whether you are actually touching wood or not, to try to avoid the bad luck that is supposed to come from being too confident or hopeful

SPELLCHECK wood or **would**? Do not confuse the spelling of ***wood*** and ***would***, which sound similar. ***Wood*** refers to the hard substance that chiefly composes trees, or to an area covered by trees, as in *boats made of wood, a path through the wood.* ***Would*** indicates a conditional statement or introduces a polite request: *I would write to her if I knew her address. Would you close the door, please.*

CULTURAL NOTE *Stopping by Woods on a Snowy Evening*, a poem (1923) by Robert Frost. In this much-anthologized poem, the narrator pauses on horseback, drawn into the dark beauty of the woods in snow. He lingers, attracted by the quiet, the solitude, and, according to many critics, the prospect of death, while yet considering the practical obligations of society. It ends with the famous lines, "But I have promises to keep,/ And miles to go before I sleep,/ And miles to go before I sleep.".

ORIGIN The ancestral meaning of ***wood*** is probably "collection of trees, forest." The meanings "tree" (now obsolete) and "substance from which trees are made" are secondary developments. It has been suggested that the word ***wood*** may go back to an Indo-European source meaning "separate," in which case it would originally have denoted a "separated" or "remote" piece of territory, near the outer edge or borders of known land. Since such remote, uninhabited areas were usually wooded, the word came to denote "forest."

Wood /wŏŏd/, **Grant** (1892–1942) US artist. His paintings of his native Iowa are influenced by the formal early Dutch and Flemish style. His best known work is "American Gothic" (1930).

Wood, Leonard (1860–1927) US general. He was the military governor (1899–1902) of Cuba after the Spanish-American War (1898) and governor-general of the Philippines (1921–27). As army chief of staff (1910–14), he advocated US military preparedness on the eve of World War I.

wood al·co·hol *n* CHEM same as **methanol**

wood a·nem·o·ne *n* a spring-flowering anemone that grows in shady places. Flowers: single, white to crimson. Native to: North America, Europe. Latin name: *Anemone quinquefolia* or *Anemone nemorosa.*

Wood·ard /wŏŏdərd/, **Alfre** (*b.* 1953) US actor. She won Emmy awards for her work on the television series *L.A. Law* and *Hill Street Blues* and in the movie *Miss Evers' Boys* (1997).

wood bet·o·ny *n* a plant related to lousewort that grows in woods and clearings. Flowers: yellow, red, or both. Native to: eastern North America. Latin name: *Pedicularis canadensis.*

wood·bine /wŏŏd bīn/ (*plural* **-bines** or *same*) *n* **1.** a honeysuckle with fragrant yellow flowers. Native to: Europe, Asia, North Africa. Latin name: *Lonicera periclymenum.* **2.** PLANTS same as **Virginia creeper** [Old English *wudubinde*, < *wudu* "wood" + *bindan* "bind"; because the plant grows around trees]

wood·block /wŏŏd blòk/ *n* **1.** HANDICRAFT same as **woodcut** (sense 1) **2.** MUSIC a hollow block of wood used as a percussion instrument in an orchestra or band **3.** CONSTR a small flat piece of wood laid in a pattern with others to make a floor surface

wood·bor·er /wŏŏd bàwrər/ *n* a medium-sized moth with a stocky body that, as a large fleshy larva, bores into wood, causing considerable damage. Family: Cossidae.

Wood·bridge /wŏŏd brìj/ township in northeastern New Jersey. Population: 100,421 (2002 estimate).

Wood Buf·fa·lo Na·tion·al Park /wŏŏd búffəlō-/ national park and preserve in central Canada, on the Alberta-Northwest Territories border, established in 1922. Area: 17,300 sq. mi./44,807 sq. km.

wood·carv·ing /wŏŏd kaarving/ *n* **1.** the art of carving wood **2.** a decorative object carved from wood

wood·chat /wŏŏd chàt/ (*plural* **-chats** or *same*), **wood·chat shrike** *n* a songbird of the shrike family with black and white feathers and a reddish brown crown. Native to: Europe, North Africa. Latin name: *Lanius senator.*

wood·chip·per /wŏŏd chìppər/ *n* a machine with a hopper into which large pieces of wood are fed and then shredded into small pieces

wood·chop /wŏŏd chòp/ *n* in Australia, a wood-chopping competition held at country fairs

wood·chop·per /wŏŏd chòppər/ *n* somebody who chops wood, especially somebody who chops down trees

wood·chuck /wŏŏd chùk/ (*plural* **-chucks** or *same*) *n* a heavy-set short-legged marmot with brownish fur streaked with gray. Native to: northern North America. Latin name: *Marmota monax.* [Late 17C. By folk etymology < Algonquian]

wood coal *n* INDUST **1.** same as **brown coal 2.** same as **charcoal** (sense 1)

wood·cock /wŏŏd kòk/ (*plural* **-cocks** or *same*) *n* a medium-sized ground-dwelling game bird related to the snipe, with short legs and rounded wings, a stocky body and a long beak. Native to: North America, Europe, Asia. Genus: *Scolopax.*

wood·craft /wŏŏd kràft/ *n* **1.** skill in carving or making objects from wood **2.** skill in traveling, living, or working in woods or forests —**wood·craft·er** *n* —**wood·crafts·man** *n*

wood·creep·er /wŏŏd kreepər/ (*plural* **-ers** or *same*) *n* a brown bird that clings to tree trunks with its short strong legs and probes for insects with its long beak. Native to: forests of Central and South America. Family: Dendrocolaptidae.

wood·cut /wŏŏd kùt/ *n* **1.** a block of wood carved with a picture or design from which prints are made **2.** a print made by pressing a woodcut into a coloring substance and then onto paper

wood·cut·ter /wŏŏd kùttər/ *n* **1.** somebody who cuts down trees **2.** somebody who makes and prints from woodcuts

wood duck *n* a crested duck that nests in tree cavities near water, the male of which has black, chestnut, green, purple, and white feathers. Native to: North America. Latin name: *Aix sponsa.*

wood·en /wŏŏdd'n/ *adj* **1. MADE OF WOOD** made or consisting of wood **2. UNGAINLY** lacking flexibility, relaxation, and grace ○ *a ballet dancer with wooden movements* **3. INEXPRESSIVE** lacking animation, emotion, or responsiveness ○ *a wooden prose style* **4. DULL IN SOUND** making a dull unresonant sound ○ *spoke in a toneless, wooden voice* —**wood·en·ly** *adv*—**wood·en·ness** *n*

wood en·grav·ing *n* **1.** the art or process of engraving a picture or design with a burin on a block of wood **2.** an engraving made with a burin on a block of wood, or a print made from such an engraving —**wood en·grav·er** *n*

wood·en·head /wŏŏdd'n hèd/ *n* an offensive term for a person considered to be unintelligent (*informal insult*) —**wood·en·head·ed** *adj* —**wood·en·head·ed·ly** *adv* —**wood·en·head·ed·ness** *n*

Wood·en Horse *n* MYTHOL same as **Trojan horse** (sense 1)

wood·en In·di·an *n* a carved wooden figure of a Native American, formerly used as an advertisement outside tobacco shops

wood·en·ware /wŏŏdd'n wèr/ *n* dishes or utensils made from wood

wood frog *n* a frog that lives in woodland and is light brown with darker markings on the head. Native to: eastern North America. Latin name: *Rana sylvatica.*

wood·grain /wŏŏd gràyn/ *n* a material or finish that imitates the natural grain of wood

wood grouse *n* BIRDS same as **capercaillie**

wood hoo·poe (*plural* **wood hoo·poes** or *same*) *n* a bird that has dark glossy feathers, a long tail, and a slender curved beak. Native to: tropical Africa. Genus: *Phoeniculus.*

Wood·hull /wŏŏd hùl/, **Victoria** (1838–1927) US feminist. She was the first woman to run for the US presidency (1872). Born **Claflin, Victoria**

wood hy·a·cinth *n* PLANTS same as **bluebell** (sense 2)

wood·ie *n* **1.** CARS another spelling of **woody** *n* (sense 1) **2.** *US* another spelling of **woody** *n* (sense 2) (*slang offensive*)

wood·land /wŏŏddlənd/, **wood·lands** *n* land that is covered with trees, shrubs, or bushes —**wood·land** *adj* —**wood·land·er** *n*

wood·lark /wŏŏd laark/ (*plural* **-larks** or *same*) *n* a small lark noted for its song in flight. Native to: Europe, Asia. Latin name: *Lullula arborea*.

wood·lot /wŏŏd lòt/ *n* a privately owned tract of woodland where trees are grown for fuel, posts, timber, or pulpwood

wood louse *n* a small land-dwelling crustacean that lives in damp woody places and is capable of rolling into a ball. Genera: *Oniscus* or *Porcellio*.

wood·man *n* same as **woodsman**

wood mouse *n* a small mouse. Native to: woodlands in western and central Europe and North Africa. Latin name: *Adopdemus sylvaticus*.

wood·note /wŏŏd nòt/ *n* a natural musical note, call, or song, e.g., that made by a wild bird (*literary*)

wood nymph *n* **1.** MYTHOL **WOODLAND NYMPH** a nymph that lives in woodland, e.g., a dryad **2.** INSECTS **BUTTERFLY** a brown butterfly, especially one with a broad yellow band and black-and-white eyespots on each front wing. Family: Satyridae. **3.** *also* **wood·nymph** /wŏŏd nìmf/ BIRDS **HUMMINGBIRD** a tropical hummingbird. Native to: Central and South America. Genus: *Thalurania*.

wood o·pal *n* wood impregnated and fossilized by silica, preserving the grain

wood owl *n* BIRDS same as **tawny owl**

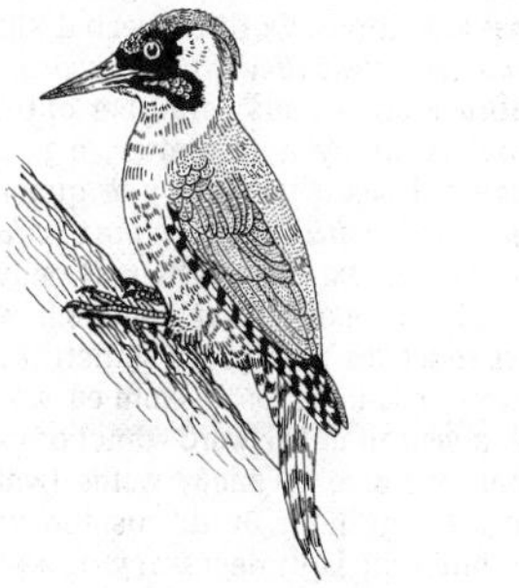

woodpecker

wood·peck·er /wŏŏd pèkər/ *n* a bird with boldly patterned feathers, a stiff tail used in climbing or clinging to tree trunks, and a hard beak for hammering into wood to extract insects or create a nest hole. Family: Picidae.

wood pi·geon *n* a large pigeon that has a white patch on each side of the neck and lives in parks, fields, and woodland. Latin name: *Columba palumbus*.

wood·pile /wŏŏd pìl/ *n* a heap or stack of firewood

wood pitch *n* the sticky residue left after wood tar has been distilled

wood·print /wŏŏd prìnt/ *n* HANDICRAFT same as **woodcut** (sense 1)

wood pulp *n* wood that has been mechanically and chemically broken down for use in making paper and paper products

wood puss·y *n US* same as **skunk** *n* (sense 1) (*informal humorous*)

wood rab·bit *n US* ZOOL same as **cottontail**

wood rat *n* ZOOL same as **pack rat**

Wood·ridge /wŏŏddrij/ town in northeastern Illinois, northeast of Naperville. It is a western suburb of Chicago. Population: 33,734 (2002 estimate).

Wood·roffe, Mount /wŏŏddrəf/ mountain in South Australia, the highest peak in the state. Height: 4,724 ft./1,440 m.

wood·ruff /wŏŏd rùf/ (*plural* **-ruffs** or *same*) *n* a plant with sweet-scented flowers. Use: perfumery, flavoring for wines and liqueurs. Genera: *Asperula* or *Galium*. [Old English *wudurofe*, < *wudu* "wood" + *rofe*, origin ?]

Wood·ruff key /wŏŏd ruff-/ *n* a self-aligning key that is semicircular in cross-section, designed to fit into the recess of a shaft [Late 19C. After the *Woodruff* Manufacturing Co. in Hartford, Connecticut]

wood·rush /wŏŏd rùsh/ *n* a plant with flat leaves fringed with hairs. Native to: cold and temperate areas of the northern hemisphere. Genus: *Luzula*.

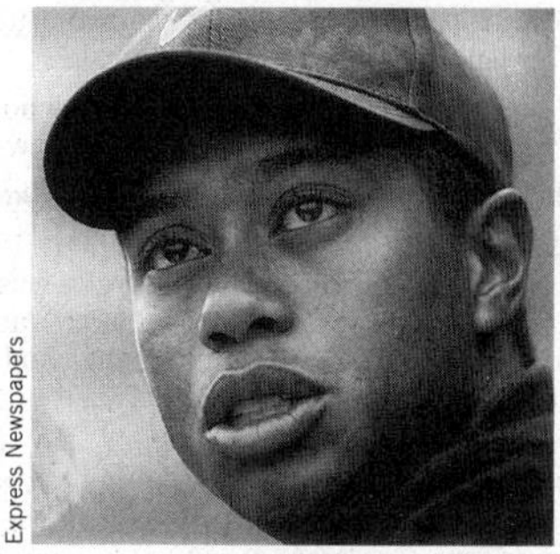

Express Newspapers

Tiger Woods

Woods /wŏŏdz/, **Tiger** (*b.* 1975) US golfer. At 21, he became the youngest player ever to win the US Masters championship (1997). Born **Woods, Eldrick**

wood·screw /wŏŏd skrōō/ *n* a tapered metal screw that can be driven into wood by a screwdriver

wood·shed /wŏŏd shèd/ *n* an outbuilding or connected room in which firewood and tools are stored

wood·si·a /wŏŏdzee ə/ (*plural* **-as** or *same*) *n* a small fern that has wiry fronds. Native to: northern, often mountainous regions. Genus: *Woodsia*. [Mid-19C. < modern Latin, after Joseph *Woods* (1776–1864), British botanist]

woods·man /wŏŏdzmən/ (*plural* **-men** /-mən/), **wood·man** /wŏŏdmən/ *n* somebody who is skilled at living, working, or traveling in the woods

wood sor·rel *n* an herb with a creeping stem and heart-shaped leaves. Flowers: white, with colored veins. Genus: *Oxalis*.

wood spir·it *n* CHEM same as **methanol**

Wood·stock /wŏŏd stòk/ **1.** town in New York State. It is best known for a rock music festival in 1969, although the site of the festival was moved beforehand to nearby Bethel. Population: 6,261 (2002 estimate). **2.** town in southern Ontario, Canada, on the Thames River. Population: 33,061 (2001). **3.** town in Oxfordshire, England. Blenheim Palace, home of the Dukes of Marlborough, is located there. Population: 2,898 (1991).

wood sug·ar *n* CHEM same as **xylose**

Woods·worth /wŏŏdz wùrth/, **James Shaver** (1874–1942) Canadian cleric and politician. He led the Co-operative Commonwealth Federation and, as a gospel minister, advocated democratic socialism.

> "I do not believe in moral issues being settled by physical force."
> [James Shaver Woodsworth, *Speech, Winnipeg*; June 4, 1916]

woods·y /wŏŏdzee/ (**-i·er, -i·est**) *adj* relating to or reminiscent of the woods, especially in scent (*informal*)

wood tar *n* a black viscous tar produced as a by-product in the destructive distillation of wood, used as a protective coating for rope and timber

wood thrush *n* a large thrush with a reddish brown head and a pale spotted breast. Native to: woods of eastern North America. Latin name: *Hylocichla mustelina*.

wood tick *n* a tick that transmits the pathogenic microorganism that causes Rocky Mountain spotted fever. Native to: western North America. Genus: *Dermacentor*.

wood vin·e·gar *n* CHEM same as **pyroligneous acid**

wood war·bler *n* **1.** a small, insect-eating, often brightly colored songbird. Native to: North and South America. Family: Parulidae. **2.** a small yellowish green songbird that lives in woods. Native to: Europe. Latin name: *Phylloscopus sibilatrix*.

Wood·ward /wŏŏdwərd/, **Robert B.** (1917–79) US chemist. He is noted for his work in chemical synthesis, especially quinine (1944), cholesterol (1951), and cortisone (1951). He won the Nobel Prize in chemistry (1965). Full name **Woodward, Robert Burns**

Wood·ward, Roger (*b.* 1944) Australian pianist. He is noted for his renditions of works by Beethoven and Chopin. Full name **Woodward, Roger Robert**

wood·wax·en /wŏŏd wàks'n/ *n* PLANTS same as **dyer's greenweed**

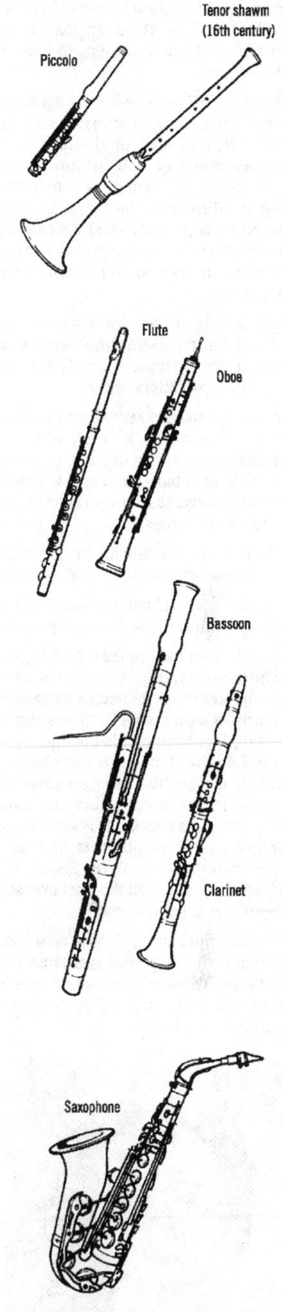

woodwind: woodwind instruments

wood·wind /wŏŏd wìnd/ *n* **MUSICAL INSTRUMENT** a wind musical instrument that produces sound by vibration of mouthpiece reeds, e.g., the bassoon, clarinet, oboe, or saxophone, or by passage of air over the mouthpiece, e.g., the flute ■ *npl* **1. MUSICAL INSTRUMENTS** wind instruments belonging to the family that includes the flute, clarinet, oboe, and bassoon, instruments originally made of wood **2. PLAYERS IN ORCHESTRA** the players of woodwind instruments in an orchestra, considered collectively (*often used with "the"*) —**wood·wind** *adj*

wood·work /wŏŏd wùrk/ *n* **1.** items or components made from wood, especially the interior parts of a building, e.g., the frames of windows, staircases, and doors **2.** *UK* HANDICRAFT same as **woodworking** —**wood·work·er** *n* ◇ **crawl** *or* **come out of the woodwork** to appear suddenly and unexpectedly in large numbers (*slang*)

wood·work·ing /wŏŏd wùrking/ *n US* the skill or craft of making items or parts out of wood ■ *adj* relating to woodworking, or used in making things from wood

wood·worm /wŏŏd wùrm/ *n* **1.** the damaged condition of wood from its infestation by wood-boring insects, especially larvae **2.** a worm or insect larva that bores into and weakens wood, e.g., in joists or stairs inside a building

wood·y /wŏŏddee/ *adj* (**-i·er, -i·est**) **1. HAVING MANY TREES** containing or covered with many trees **2. RELATING TO WOODS** relating to, typical of, or situated in the woods **3. MADE OF WOOD** made of or containing wood or a material resembling wood **4. RESEMBLING WOOD** resembling wood in some way, e.g., in appearance, texture, or smell ■ *n* (*plural* **-ies**) *also* **wood·ie** *US* **1.** CARS **WOOD-PANELED CAR** a wood-paneled station wagon (*dated*) **2. OFFENSIVE TERM** an offensive term for an erect penis (*slang*)

wood·y night·shade *n Can, UK* a woody plant with poisonous red fruits resembling berries. Flowers: purple. Native to: Europe, Asia. Genus: *Solanum dulcamara.* US term **bittersweet**

woof[1] /wŏŏf, woof/ *n* **SOUND OF BARKING DOG** the sound made by a dog when it barks ■ *interj* **REPRESENTATION OR IMITATION OF BARKING** a representation or imitation of the sound made by a barking dog ■ *vi* (**woofed, woof·ing, woofs**) **MAKE BARKING SOUND** to produce a woof [Early 19C. An imitation of the sound]

woof[2] /wŏŏf/ *n* a woven fabric, or its texture [Old English *owef* "weave on" < *wefan* "weave" < Indo-European]

woof·er /wŏŏffər/ *n* a loudspeaker used to reproduce low-frequency sounds [Mid-20C. As a metaphor < WOOF[1]]

wool /wŏŏl/ *n* **1. YARN USED TO MAKE CLOTHES** yarn spun from the short curly hair of sheep or other animals. Use: knitting, weaving. **2. WOOLEN MATERIAL** material knitted or woven using wool **3. SHEEP'S HAIR** the short curly overlapping hair of sheep and some other animals such as the llama and the alpaca, used to make wool **4.** INSECTS **HAIR OF INSECT LARVA** the furry hair of some insect larvae such as caterpillars (*informal*) **5.** BOT **HAIRS GROWING ON PLANT** a mass of soft hairs that grows on some plants ■ *adj* **MADE FROM WOOL** knitted or woven using wool [Old English *wull* < Indo-European] —**wooled** *adj* ◇ **pull the wool over somebody's eyes** to deceive or trick somebody

wool·en /wŏŏllən/, **wool·len** *adj* **1. MADE FROM WOOL** knitted or woven using wool **2. OF WOOL PRODUCTION** relating to the production of wool or items made from wool ■ *n* **WOOLEN GARMENT** a garment made from wool, especially one with a fleecy surface

Virginia Woolf

Woolf /wŏŏlf/, **Virginia** (1882–1941) British novelist and critic. The psychological depth of her stream-of-consciousness technique and the poetic language of novels such as *To the Lighthouse* (1927) profoundly influenced the 20th-century English novel. Born **Stephen, Virginia Adeline**

> "If we didn't live venturously, plucking the wild goat by the beard, and trembling over precipices, we should never be depressed, I've no doubt; but already should be faded, fatalistic and aged."
> [Virginia Woolf, *A Writer's Diary,* Leonard Woolf ed.; 1953]

wool fat *n* PHARM same as **lanolin**

wool·gath·er·ing /wŏŏl ga̱thəring/ *n* daydreaming or absent-mindedness [Mid-16C. Originally "gathering the bits of wool torn from sheep by bushes"]

wool grease *n* a fatty wax that coats the fibers of sheep's wool and yields lanolin

wool·grow·er /wŏŏl grō ər/ *n* somebody who keeps sheep in order to sell their wool —**wool·grow·ing** *n*

wool·len *adj, n* TEXTILES another spelling of **woolen**

Wool·ley /wŏŏllee/, **Mary Emma** (1863–1947) US educator. A leading educator of women, she was president of Mount Holyoke College (1901–37) and was a leading advocate for women's rights and world peace.

wool·ly /wŏŏllee/, **wool·y** *adj* (**-li·er, -li·est; -i·er, -i·est**) **1. MADE OF WOOL** knitted or woven using wool **2. CONFUSED** confused, vague, and lacking focus ○ *woolly thinking* **3.** *US* **UNCIVILIZED AND UNRULY** rough and boisterous in a way that is reminiscent of the frontier days of the American West (*informal*) ○ *wild and woolly* **4.** INSECTS **COVERED WITH INSECT HAIR** describes an insect larva such as a caterpillar that is covered with furry hair resembling wool **5.** BOT **COVERED WITH PLANT HAIRS** describes a stem, leaf, or other plant part that is covered with long, soft, white hairs ■ *n* (*plural* **-lies;** *plural* **-ies**) CLOTHING same as **woolen** (*informal*) ■ **wool·lies** *npl US* **LONG WOOLEN UNDERWEAR** long underwear made of wool —**wool·li·ly** *adv* —**wool·li·ness** *n*

wool·ly a·phid *n* a tiny insect that secretes a waxy substance in long filaments that give it a woolly appearance. Family: Aphididae.

wool·ly bear *n* the caterpillar of various moths, especially the tiger moth, that has a coat of dense woolly hairs

wool·ly-head·ed *adj* **1.** having thick curly hair that looks or feels like wool **2.** confused, vague, and lacking focus

wool·ly mam·moth *n* an extinct mammoth with a shaggy coat that lived during the Ice Age. Native to: cold regions of North America, Europe, and Asia. Genus: *Mammuthus primigenius.*

Wool·ner /wŏŏlnər/, **Thomas** (1825–92) British sculptor and poet. A founder of the Pre-Raphaelite Brotherhood, he is best known for his portrait sculptures of leading intellectuals, poets, and scientists, including Wordsworth, Tennyson, Gladstone, and Darwin.

wool·pack /wŏŏl pàk/ *n* **1.** the coarse material, usually jute or canvas, used to wrap a bale of wool **2.** a package in which a bale of raw wool is transported

wool·sack /wŏŏl sàk/ *n* a sack for holding wool

wool·skin /wŏŏl skìn/ *n US* the skin of a sheep with the wool still on it

wool sort·er *n* somebody who sorts wool into different grades

wool-sort·er's dis·ease *n* pulmonary anthrax resulting from the inhalation of spores of an anthrax bacterium that contaminates wool

wool sta·pler *n* **1.** somebody who deals in wool **2.** OCCUPATIONS same as **wool sorter**

Wool·worth /wŏŏl wùrth/, **Frank W.** (1852–1919) US retailer. In 1879 he opened what was to prove the first of a chain of more than 1,000 five-and-dime stores across the United States and Great Britain. Full name **Woolworth, Frank Winfield**

wool·y *adj, n* TEXTILES another spelling of **woolly**

woom·er·a /wŏŏmmərə, wŏŏm-/, **woom·er·ah, wom·er·a** *n* a wooden stick with a notch at one end, used by Australian Aboriginals to launch a spear. The stick provides extra leverage and force. [Early 19C. < Dharuk]

Woon·sock·et /woon sókit/ city in northeastern Rhode Island, on its border with Massachusetts, northwest of Providence. Population: 43,879 (2002 estimate).

woops *interj* another spelling of **whoops** (*informal*)

Woot·ton /wŏŏtt'n/, **Barbara Frances, Baroness Wootton of Abinger** (1897–1988) British social scientist. Her writings include *Testament for Social Science* (1950), a pioneering study of the nature of social science. Born **Adam, Barbara Frances**

wooz·y /woozee/ (**-i·er, -i·est**) *adj* **1.** weak and unsteady or dizzy **2.** confused or unable to think clearly [Late 19C. Origin ?] —**wooz·i·ly** *adv* —**wooz·i·ness** *n*

wop /wop/ *n* a highly offensive term for an Italian person (*taboo*) [Early 20C. < Italian dialect *guappo* "tough, bold" < Spanish *guapo* "dandy"]

Worces·ter /wŏŏstər/ **1.** city in central Massachusetts, west of Boston. Population: 174,962 (2002 estimate). **2.** city and administrative center of Worcestershire, west central England. Population: 93,353 (2001).

Worces·ter chi·na, Worces·ter por·ce·lain, Worces·ter *n* a fine china made in Worcester, England, since 1751, or the articles made from this china

Worces·ter sauce *n UK* same as **Worcestershire sauce**

Worces·ter·shire /wŏŏstər sheèr, -shər/ county of west central England. Area: 670 sq. mi./1735 sq. km.

Worces·ter·shire sauce *n* a thin pungent table sauce flavored with soy, tamarind, and spices, originally made in Worcestershire, England

word /wurd/ *n* **1. MEANINGFUL UNIT OF LANGUAGE SOUNDS** a meaningful sound or combination of sounds that is a unit of language or its representation in a text **2. BRIEF UTTERANCE** a brief comment, announcement, discussion, or conversation ○ *Could I have a word with you in my office, please?* **3. INFORMATION** information or news about somebody or something ○ *Is there any word on your daughter?* **4. RUMOR** rumor or gossip ○ *The word is that she's leaving the company.* **5. PROMISE** a promise, assurance, or guarantee ○ *I give you my word.* **6. COMMAND** a command, order, or authorization ○ *He gave the word to attack.* **7. PASSWORD** a password or verbal signal ○ *Don't let anyone in unless they give the word.* **8.** COMPUT **FIXED NUMBER OF PROCESSED BITS** a number of bits processed as a single unit by a computer, e.g., 32, 48, or 64 ■ **words** *npl* **1. ANGRY TALK** angry or quarrelsome speech ○ *had words with him over the shoddy merchandise he sold us* **2. TEXT OF SONG** the text or lyrics of a song, musical, or opera ■ *vt* (**word·ed, word·ing, words**) **PHRASE SOMETHING** to express something in words [Old English < Indo-European] —**word·ed** *adj* ◇ **a man of his word, a woman of her word** somebody who keeps his or her promise ◇ **bandy words (with somebody)** to have an argument or discussion with somebody, often one that is unnecessary or a waste of time ◇ **be as good as your word** to do as promised ◇ **eat your words** to admit humbly that you were wrong or mistaken (*informal*) ◇ **get a word in edgewise** to succeed in speaking when other people are talking nonstop (*usually used in negative statements*) ◇ **in a word** briefly or very concisely expressed ◇ **my word** used to express surprise or astonishment (*dated*) ◇ **put in** *or* **say a good word for somebody** to speak well of or recommend somebody ◇ **put something into words** to express something such as a feeling or emotion clearly ◇ **put words in somebody's mouth** to say that somebody has said something when in fact he or she did not say it ◇ **the ... word** used after a letter of the alphabet to indicate a word beginning with that letter that you wish to avoid actually saying but that can be understood from the context ○ *the F word*

Word *n* **1.** in Christian theology, the divine rational principle as epitomized by Jesus Christ **2.** in Christianity, the Bible or Scriptures, considered as revealing divine truth

word·age /wúrdij/ *n* **1. NUMBER OF WORDS** the number of words in a text **2. WORDS COLLECTIVELY** words considered as a group **3. WORDINESS** the use of too many words to express something **4. WORDING OF SOMETHING** the choice of words made by a writer or speaker

word as·so·ci·a·tion *n* a method of assessing somebody's mental state or personality by asking the person to respond with the first word that comes to mind when a given word is heard

word blind·ness *n* MED same as **alexia** —**word-blind** *adj*

word·book /wúrd bŏŏk/ *n* a dictionary, vocabulary, or lexicon

word·break /wúrd bràyk/ *n* the point in a word where it can be divided if there is insufficient room at the end of a line for the entire word

word class *n* a category of words that have the same form or function, e.g., parts of speech

word count *n* the calculation of the number of words in a piece of text, or the result of such a calculation

word deaf·ness *n* the loss of the capacity to understand spoken words, especially when caused by a cerebral lesion —**word-deaf** *adj*

word find·er *n* a book that lists words according to meaning or subject, designed to help users find the word that best expresses the meaning they want to convey

word for word *adv* **1.** in exactly the same words as originally used **2.** by translating each word used in a spoken or written piece of foreign language individually —**word-for-word** *adj*

word game *n* **1.** a game in which players have to construct, find, or change the form of words **2.** a piece of disingenuous language intended to mislead, misrepresent, conceal, or put a spin on a usually awkward situation or issue (*slang; often used in the plural*) ○ *Please stop the word games and give me a truthful answer.*

word-hoard *n* the total number of words that somebody is able to use or understand

word·ing /wúrding/ *n* the choice of words made by a writer or speaker

word·less /wúrdləss/ *adj* **1.** communicating without the use of speech **2.** incapable of speech, especially temporarily —**word·less·ly** *adv* —**word·less·ness** *n*

Word of God *n* CHR same as **Word** (sense 2)

word of hon·or *n* a solemn promise or undertaking to do something

word of mouth *n* communication using the spoken word —**word-of-mouth** *adj*

word-per·fect *adj* **1.** accurate in every detail **2.** *UK* same as **letter-perfect**

word pic·ture *n* a vivid description of something in words

word·play /wúrd plày/ *n* the witty, subtle, or ingenious use of words, e.g., in taking advantage of their multiple meanings

word proc·ess·ing *n* the creation, retrieval, modification, storage, and printing of text using a computer or other electronic equipment (*hyphenated before a noun*)

word proc·es·sor *n* **1.** MACHINE FOR MANIPULATING TEXT a piece of electronic equipment that has a keyboard and video display unit and is used to create, retrieve, modify, store, and print text. It is usually not as advanced as a personal computer. **2.** COMPUTER PROGRAM FOR MANIPULATING TEXT a computer program that is used to create, retrieve, modify, store, and print text **3.** SOMEBODY PROCESSING WORDS somebody who does word processing

word·smith /wúrd smìth/ *n* somebody who uses words skillfully, e.g., a professional writer or journalist —**word·smith** *vti*

word square *n* a puzzle consisting of a square grid to be constructed of words that read the same vertically and horizontally

word stress *n* the placing of stress on the syllables of a word, or an instance of this

Words·worth /wúrdz wùrth/, **Dorothy** (1771–1855) British writer. She was the sister and companion of William Wordsworth. Her journals, which are literary documents in their own right, shed valuable light on her brother's life and work.

Words·worth, William (1770–1850) British poet. *Lyrical Ballads* (1798), written with Samuel Taylor Coleridge, was the seminal work of English romantic poetry. His greatest work is the autobiographical epic *The Prelude* (1850). —**Words·worth·i·an** /wùrdz wúrthee ən/ *adj*

> "I wandered lonely as a cloud / That floats on high o'er vales and hills, / When all at once I saw a crowd, / A host, of golden daffodils."
> [William Wordsworth, "I Wandered Lonely as a Cloud," *Poems in Two Volumes*; 1807]

> "Poetry is the spontaneous overflow of powerful feelings: it takes its origin from emotion recollected in tranquility."
> [William Wordsworth, *Lyrical Ballads (2nd ed.)*; 1800]

> "Our birth is but a sleep and a forgetting: / The Soul that rises with us, our life's Star, / Hath had elsewhere its setting, / And cometh from afar: / Not in entire forgetfulness, / And not in utter nakedness, / But trailing clouds of glory do we come / From God, who is our home."
> [William Wordsworth, "Ode: Intimations of Immortality from Recollections of Early Childhood," *Poems in Two Volumes*; 1807]

word wrap, word wrap·ping *n* a feature of word-processing programs in which a word that exceeds a preset line length is moved automatically to the next line

word·y /wúrdee/ (-i·er, -i·est) *adj* **1.** using an excessive number of words in writing or speech **2.** relating to or consisting of words —**word·i·ly** *adv* —**word·i·ness** *n*

SYNONYMS ***wordy, verbose, long-winded, rambling, prolix, diffuse***

CORE MEANING: not concisely expressed

wordy using an excessive number of words in writing or speech ○ *I need a clear concise summary of the relevant material rather than an exhaustive and wordy report.* ○ *He has played some of the theater's wordiest parts, including Prospero and King Lear.* **verbose** expressed in or using too many words ○ *His memoirs, at 1088 pages, are as long and verbose as his political speeches.* ○ *a verbose and self-pitying excuse* **long-winded** tediously wordy in speech or writing ○ *a very long-winded question* ○ *The records were infuriatingly terse about important things, and long-winded about trivial ones.* **rambling** continuing for too long and with many changes of subject ○ *a rambling 15-page letter* ○ *He told a series of long, rambling stories to which he forgot the punch lines.* **prolix** tiresomely wordy ○ *His lengthy and prolix instructions are no help at all.* **diffuse** lacking organization and conciseness, especially in writing or speech ○ *Section 4 of the 1938 Act has been described as being turgid and diffuse.*

wore past tense of **wear**[1]

work /wurk/ *n* **1.** PAID JOB paid employment at a job **2.** DUTIES OF JOB the duties or activities that are part of a job or occupation ○ *Much of my work involves talking on the phone.* **3.** SOMEBODY'S PLACE OF EMPLOYMENT the place where somebody is employed ○ *spends all her time at work* **4.** TIME SPENT AT PLACE OF EMPLOYMENT the time that somebody spends carrying out his or her job ○ *I'll meet you after work.* **5.** PURPOSEFUL EFFORT the physical or mental effort directed at doing or making something ○ *It was a lot of work, but it was worth it.* **6.** FUNCTION the function of completing a process or carrying out a task ○ *Computers have taken over the work of filing.* **7.** SOMETHING DONE OR MADE something that has been done or made as part of a job or as a result of effort or activity requiring skill (*often used in combination*) ○ *Your work is satisfactory.* **8.** SOMETHING MANUFACTURED something that has been or is in the process of being worked on or manufactured **9.** ARTISTIC OR INTELLECTUAL CREATION an artistic or intellectual composition, e.g., a book, treatise, painting, sculpture, film, or piece of music (*often used in the plural*) **10.** PHYS MEANS FOR ENERGY TRANSFER the transfer of energy, measured as the product of the force applied to a body and the distance moved by that body in the direction of the force. Symbol *W* ■ *v* (**worked, work·ing, works**) **1.** *vi* HAVE JOB to have a paid job **2.** *vti* EXERT EFFORT to exert physical or mental effort in order to do, make, or accomplish something, or make somebody do this ○ *worked without a break until evening* ○ *He works his staff hard.* **3.** *vti* FUNCTION to function or operate, or make something do this ○ *The television doesn't work.* ○ *Do you know how to work the burglar alarm?* **4.** *vi* BE SUCCESSFUL to be effective or achieve a desired result ○ *Our relationship just isn't working.* **5.** *vti* WORK IN SPECIFIC PLACE to carry on an operation or activity in a particular place or area ○ *You'll be working the southern region.* **6.** *vi* EXERT INFLUENCE to produce results or exert an influence ○ *Everything seemed to be working against them.* **7.** *vti* SHAPE SOMETHING to shape, bend, form, or forge a material, or be shaped, bent, formed, or forged ○ *worked the malleable metal* **8.** *vt* CULTIVATE LAND to cultivate land in order to grow crops on it **9.** *vt* ACHIEVE SOMETHING to effect something or bring something about ○ *Attention to detail can work wonders.* **10.** *vti* ATTAIN PARTICULAR CONDITION to attain a particular condition slowly or gradually, or cause something to do this ○ *The screw worked itself loose.* **11.** *vti* MOVE SLOWLY AND WITH EFFORT to move or progress slowly and with effort, or make something do this ○ *He worked his way through the crowd.* **12.** *vt* SOLVE MATHEMATICAL PROBLEM to solve a mathematical problem or puzzle **13.** *vti* EXERCISE to move or exercise a muscle or part of the body, or be moved or exercised **14.** *vt* PROVOKE EMOTIONAL RESPONSE IN SOMEBODY to arouse or stir up emotions in somebody ○ *worked the crowd into a frenzy* **15.** *vt* CHARM SOMEBODY to use charm and personal influence on somebody in order to attain popularity or acclaim ○ *a politician who really knew how to work a crowd* **16.** *vt* ARRANGE SOMETHING to arrange or exploit something in order to gain an advantage (*informal*) ○ *He managed to work it so that he got every other Friday off.* **17.** *vti* FERMENT to ferment, or make something ferment **18.** *vt* HANDICRAFT MAKE SOMETHING IN NEEDLEWORK to make or decorate something by hand in needlework or embroidery **19.** *vi* MECH ENG MOVE LOOSELY to move in a loose way that results in friction and wear (*refers to machinery*) **20.** *vi* NAUT STRAIN SLIGHTLY IN ROUGH WATER to give slightly in rough water so that the joints move slightly and the fastenings become looser (*refers to boats*) **21.** *vi* SAILING SAIL INTO WIND to sail against the wind [Old English *weorc* < Indo-European] ◇ **at work 1.** engaged in employment **2.** in operation ◇ **have your work cut out (for you)** to be faced with a difficult task ◇ **make short work of somebody** *or* **something** to dispose of or deal with somebody or something very quickly ◇ **work to rule** *Can, UK* to take part in a labor protest in which workers make a point of adhering strictly to the rules of the workplace so that work will slow down

USAGE See ***wrought***.

SYNONYMS ***work, labor, toil, drudgery***

CORE MEANING: sustained effort required to achieve something

work the physical or mental effort directed at doing or making something, or the function of completing a process or carrying out a task ○ *You will have general managers to coordinate your work.* ○ *Most installation programs will do all the work for you.* **labor** work done using the strength of the body ○ *Antony did casual manual labor in his vacations.* ○ *A group spent the day cleaning up the beach, and the results of their labor was a truckload of trash.* **toil** hard exhausting work or effort ○ *His rough hands bore testimony to a life of toil.* **drudgery** exhausting, boring, unpleasant work ○ *the drudgery of filing, coding, and organizing reams of documents*

work back *vi* to stay on late at work, with or without payment

work in *vt* **1.** to add something gradually while blending it with another substance **2.** to arrange a time or place for somebody or something in a particular situation ○ *I'll see if I can work you in on Friday.*

work off *vt* **1.** to pay back a debt by doing work instead of paying the money owed **2.** to use up or get rid of something by the effort of working ○ *worked off the extra fat*

work on *vt* **1.** AFFECT SOMEBODY OR SOMETHING to influence or attempt to influence somebody or something ○ *He's been working on her to change her decision.* **2.** MAKE OR FIX SOMETHING to spend time making, improving, or fixing something **3.** USE SOMETHING AS BASIS to use something as a starting point for further investigation or inquiry ○ *We've nothing to work on in this case.*

work out *v* **1.** *vi* EXERCISE to train or take part in strenuous physical exercise as a way of keeping in shape ○ *How do you find the time for working out?* **2.** *vi* END SATISFACTORILY to have a satisfactory or successful result **3.** *vi* END IN PARTICULAR WAY to have a particular result **4.** *vt* RESOLVE DIFFICULTY to resolve differences or find a way of dealing with a difficulty **5.** *vt* THINK SOMETHING UP to devise something, especially a course of action **6.** *vt* SOLVE OR CALCULATE SOMETHING to solve a problem or find an answer to a question by reasoning or calculation **7.** *vi* MAKE TOTAL to come to a particular amount ○ *That works out to $100 each.* **8.** *vt* COMPREHEND SOMEBODY OR SOMETHING to understand somebody or something fully **9.** *vt* ACHIEVE SOMETHING BY EFFORT to succeed in doing something after working long and hard at it **10.** *vt* same as **work off**

(sense 1) **11.** *vt* EXHAUST MINE BY EXTRACTION to extract all the valuable material from a mine or deposit

SYNONYMS See *deduce.*

work over *vt* **1.** GIVE SOMEBODY BEATING to give somebody a severe beating or physical punishment (*informal*) **2.** REDO SOMETHING to do something again **3.** EXAMINE SOMETHING THOROUGHLY to work at or examine something thoroughly and in detail

work through *vt* to deal with an emotional problem by thinking about it often until it is understood or its impact is lessened

work up *v* **1.** *vt* EXCITE EMOTIONS IN SOMEBODY to arouse or stir up emotions in somebody **2.** *vt* CREATE SOMETHING to create something or cause it to grow ○ *working up a sweat* **3.** *vt* IMPROVE SOMETHING to develop, refine, or improve something **4.** *vi* BECOME MORE INTENSE to grow or develop in intensity **5.** *vt* MED EXAMINE PATIENT THOROUGHLY to subject a patient to a thorough diagnostic examination

work up to *vt* to gradually reach a particular level by effort

work·a·ble /wúrkəb'l/ *adj* **1.** able to be accomplished or carried out ○ *The plan is not workable.* **2.** capable of being operated, handled, or shaped ○ *workable steel* —**work·a·bil·i·ty** /wùrkə bíllətee/ *n* —**work·a·ble·ness** *n* —**work·a·bly** *adv*

work·a·day /wúrkə dày/ *adj* **1.** ordinary or forming part of the experience of most people **2.** suitable for work or for a working day [Mid-16C. Origin ?]

work·a·hol·ic /wùrkə háwlik/ *n* somebody who has a compulsive need to work hard and for very long hours (*informal*) —**work·a·hol·ism** *n*

work·a·round /wúrkə rὸwnd/ *n* a technique that enables somebody to overcome a fault in a computer program or system without actually putting the fault or defect right

work·bag /wúrk bàg/ *n* a bag for holding materials and tools for work, especially sewing or knitting

work·bas·ket /wúrk bàskit/ *n* a basket for holding materials and tools for work, especially sewing or knitting

work·bench /wúrk bènch/ *n* a table or surface on which work is done, e.g., by a carpenter or mechanic

work·boat /wúrk bōt/ *n* a boat used solely for work, e.g., for fishing or transporting cargo

work·book /wúrk bŏŏk/ *n* **1.** STUDENT'S EXERCISE BOOK a book of exercises and questions for students, usually with spaces in which answers can be written **2.** INSTRUCTION BOOK a book of instructions on how to do or operate something **3.** RECORD OF WORK a book in which a record is kept of work done or to be done

work·book slow·down *n US* INDUST same as **rulebook slowdown**

work camp *n* **1.** a camp where volunteers, especially young people or members of a religious organization, work on a project of benefit to the community **2.** a camp in which prisoners are forced to work

work·day /wúrk dày/ *n* **1.** a day on which people work, usually but not always a weekday **2.** the part of a day during which somebody works

worked /wurkt/ *adj* produced, decorated, or treated with craft and skill

worked up *adj* full of anger or another strong emotion (*informal*)

work·er /wúrkər/ *n* **1.** PERSON OR THING THAT WORKS a person, animal, or device that is engaged in or used for a task of some kind **2.** EMPLOYEE an employee of a person, company, or organization **3.** MEMBER OF WORKING CLASS a member of the working class, especially a factory employee or manual laborer **4.** INSECTS INSECT THAT WORKS a member of a colony of social insects, especially sterile females, that carry out all the work such as gathering food or feeding larvae

work·er par·tic·i·pa·tion *n* the involvement of ordinary employees in making decisions at all levels in a business

work·er-priest *n* a Roman Catholic priest who also has a secular job

work·ers' com·pen·sa·tion *n* **1.** a form of insurance required from employers that provides money as compensation for workers who are injured at work or contract an occupational disease **2.** money paid as compensation to a worker who is injured at work or contracts an occupational disease

work eth·ic *n* a dedication to work, or belief in the moral value of hard work ○ *doesn't have much of a work ethic*

work ex·pe·ri·ence *n* time spent by a student doing a job in an ordinary work environment in order to give him or her experience of employment

work·fare /wúrk fèr/ *n* a government program that obliges unemployed people to do community work or attend training courses in return for welfare payments [Mid-20C. Blend of WORK + WELFARE]

work farm *n* a farm on which short-term prisoners are confined and forced to work

work·flow /wúrk flō/ *n* the progress or rate of progress of work done by a business, department, or person

work force, **work·force** /wúrk fàwrss/ *n* **1.** all of the workers employed in a company or industry **2.** all of the people who are employed or able to work, e.g., in a country

work func·tion *n* the minimum energy needed to remove an electron from within a solid to a point outside its surface in a vacuum. Symbol Φ

work-hard·en *vt* to increase the hardness or strength of a metal by subjecting it to compression, tension, or another mechanical process

work·horse /wúrk hàwrss/ *n* **1.** HARD-WORKING PERSON somebody who works hard and diligently, often assuming extra duties (*informal*) **2.** RELIABLE TOOL OR MACHINE something that performs well over long periods, e.g., a machine **3.** HORSE USED FOR HEAVY WORK a horse used for heavy work such as hauling

work·house /wúrk hòwss/ (*plural* **-hous·es** /-hòwzəz/) *n* **1.** formerly, a publicly run institution in Great Britain in which people living in poverty were given food and accommodations in return for unpaid work **2.** *US* a prison in which prisoners guilty of minor violations work at manual labor

work·ing /wúrking/ *adj* **1.** FUNCTIONING capable of being used or operated **2.** WORN AT WORK suitable for use while at work **3.** HAVING PAID JOB engaged in doing paid work **4.** SPENT AT WORK taken up with work ○ *all his working life* **5.** GIVEN OVER TO WORK spent doing work at a time when work is not normally done ○ *a working lunch* **6.** ADEQUATE good enough for a purpose, though not perfect or complete ○ *a working knowledge of Italian* **7.** PROVIDING BASIS usable as a basis for further work ○ *a working theory* ■ *n* **1.** PROCESS OF SHAPING SOMETHING the shaping, bending, forming, or forging of a material **2.** JERKING MOTION the convulsive involuntary motion of a part of the body, caused by excitement or tension (*formal*) ■ **work·ings** *npl* **1.** FUNCTIONING OF SOMETHING the operation of something, or the way in which it operates ○ *the workings of the government* **2.** MECHANISM INSIDE DEVICE the internal mechanism of a device **3.** PARTS OF MINE BEING WORKED the parts of a mine or quarry in which work is carried on

work·ing cap·i·tal *n* **1.** the money that a business has available for use **2.** the amount of current assets that remains after current liabilities are deducted

work·ing class *n* **1.** the part of society made up of people who work for hourly wages, not salaries, especially manual or industrial laborers **2.** in Marxist theory, the proletariat or revolutionary class

work·ing-class *adj* relating to or belonging to the part of society made up of people who work for hourly wages, not salaries, especially manual or industrial laborers ○ *a working-class neighborhood*

work·ing day *n UK* same as **workday** (sense 1)

work·ing dog *n* a dog that is kept in order to do work such as herding, guarding, or guiding. Among breeds of working dogs are the collie, Doberman pinscher, German shepherd, and husky.

work·ing draw·ing *n* a detailed scale drawing of something, used as a guide in building or manufacturing

work·ing girl *n* **1.** a young woman who works for a living (*informal*) **2.** a woman who is a prostitute (*slang*)

work·ing group *n US* a group of people appointed to study and report back on a subject

work·ing hours *npl* the part of the day during which most people usually work and stores and offices are open

work·ing·man /wúrking màn/ *n* a man who works for wages, especially at manual labor

work·ing mem·o·ry *n* the contents of somebody's consciousness at the present moment

work·ing pa·per *n* a document created as a basis for discussion rather than as an authoritative text

work·ing pa·pers *npl US* official documents showing that somebody such as an alien or a minor is legally permitted to work

work·ing par·ty *n UK* same as **working group**

work·ing stor·age *n* the amount of storage in a computer's memory that is assigned for data stored only while a program is running

work·ing sub·stance *n* a substance, especially a fluid, that undergoes changes in form or degree that are used to operate something such as an engine

work·ing ti·tle *n* the provisional title by which a project, especially a movie or novel, is known while it is still being worked on

work·ing week *n UK* same as **workweek**

work·ing·wom·an /wúrking wŏŏmmən/ (*plural* **-wom·en** /-wìmmin/) *n* a woman who works for wages, not a salary, especially in a manual job

work in pro·gress *n* an incomplete ongoing piece of work, especially an artistic work

work·load /wúrk lōd/ *n* **1.** the amount of work that a machine does or can do in a specific period **2.** the amount of work assigned to a person or group to do in a specific period

work·man /wúrkmən/ (*plural* **-men** /-mən/) *n* **1.** a man described or judged according to his skill or diligence as a worker ○ *a tidy workman* **2.** a craftsman or artisan

work·man·like /wúrkmən līk/, **work·man·ly** /-lee/ *adj* done in a way that is thorough and satisfactory, but not imaginative or exciting

work·man·ship /wúrkmən shìp/ *n* **1.** ART OR SKILL OF WORKER the skill or craft of a worker or artisan **2.** QUALITY OF SKILL the level of skill used in making or doing something **3.** PRODUCT OR RESULT OF WORKER'S SKILL the product or result of the skill of a worker or artisan

work·mate /wúrk màyt/ *n* somebody who works with or in the same place as another

work of art *n* **1.** a piece of fine art, e.g., a painting or sculpture **2.** something made or done exceptionally well ○ *The second touchdown was an absolute work of art.*

work·out /wúrk òwt/ *n* **1.** a session of strenuous physical exercise or of practicing physical skills as a way of keeping in shape or as practice for a game or athletic competition **2.** a tough practical test of the capability or performance of a person, animal, or device

work·peo·ple /wúrk pèep'l/ *npl UK* people who work for wages, not a salary, especially in manual jobs

work·piece /wúrk pèess/ *n* something that has been, or is in the process of being, worked on or manufactured

work·place /wúrk plàyss/ *n* the place where somebody works, e.g., a factory or office

work plane *n* a simple, wheeled desk that can be used in various work sites by several employees using the same desk at different times in a flexible workplace

work print *n* a print of a movie used in various stages of editing and as a guide in cutting the original negative from which the final commercial prints are made

work rage *n* feelings of violent anger experienced by people as a result of stress or frustration at work and often leading to outbursts of violent or destructive behavior

work-re·lease *n US* a system of allowing prisoners to perform paid work outside prison while serving their sentences

work·room /wúrk ro͝om, -ro͞om/ *n* a room in which work is done, especially one equipped for manual work

works /wurks/ *n* (*plural same*) PLACE FOR INDUSTRIAL PRODUCTION a place where industrial work, especially manufacturing, is done ○ *an engineering works* ■ *npl* **1.** INNER MECHANISM the interior moving parts of a mechanism ○ *The works of the clock are rusty.* **2.** ACTS deeds or actions **3.** EVERYTHING all things that are available (*informal*) ○ *a hot dog with the works* **4.** SYRINGE FOR INJECTING NARCOTICS a syringe used to inject narcotics (*slang*) **5.** *US* BAD BEATING a severe beating or punishment (*slang*) ◇ **in the works** being prepared or worked on

work·sheet /wúrk sheet/ *n* **1.** SHEET OF QUESTIONS FOR STUDENTS a sheet of questions or tasks for students on a recent lesson **2.** SHEET RECORDING WORK a sheet of paper used for keeping a record of work done or scheduled **3.** SHEET FOR DRAFT a sheet of paper used for making a rough draft or preliminary notes

work·shop /wúrk shòp/ *n* **1.** a place where manual work is done, especially manufacturing or repairing **2.** a group of people working on a creative project, discussing a topic, or studying a subject ○ *a song-writing workshop*

work song *n* a song sung by people working, usually with a repetitive rhythm that guides the rhythm of the work being done

work·space /wúrk spàyss/ *n* an area set aside for an individual worker or a business

work·sta·tion /wúrk stàysh'n/ *n* **1.** WORKING AREA a small area in a workplace assigned to one worker, especially a desk with a computer **2.** TERMINAL OF NETWORK OR MAINFRAME a computer terminal, usually connected to a network in a business environment, that runs application programs and serves as an access point to the network **3.** POWERFUL SPECIALIZED COMPUTER a powerful stand-alone computer, often with a high-resolution display, used for computer-aided design and other complex and specialized applications

work stop·page *n* an occasion when a group of employees stop work, often as a protest or as a bargaining tool

work-stud·y *adj* combining an academic program with paid employment in which a student gains practical experience in the workplace

work sur·face *n* a rigid flat area on which work is done, e.g., a tabletop or kitchen counter

work·ta·ble /wúrk tàyb'l/ *n* a table at which work such as writing or drawing is done

work·top /wúrk tòp/ *n UK* same as **work surface**

work-to-rule *n Can, UK* a labor protest in which workers make a point of adhering strictly to the rules of the workplace so that work will slow down. US term **rulebook slowdown**

work·up /wúrk ùp/ *n* a complete diagnostic medical examination

work·wear /wúrk wèr/ *n* clothes worn at work, especially at manual work

work·week /wúrk week/, **work week** *n* the amount of hours or days worked in a week

work·wom·an /wúrk wo͝omman/ (*plural* **-wom·en** /-wìmmin/) *n* SOC SCI same as **workingwoman**

world /wurld/ *n* **1.** PLANET EARTH the planet Earth **2.** EARTH AND EVERYTHING ON IT the Earth, including all of its inhabitants and the things upon it **3.** HUMAN RACE all of the human inhabitants of Earth ○ *Soon, the world would know the truth.* **4.** SOCIETY human society ○ *in the eyes of the world* **5.** PART OF EARTH a particular part of the Earth, considered in terms of time or space ○ *the western world* **6.** AREA OF ACTIVITY a particular area of human activity and the people involved in it ○ *the world of fashion* **7.** UNIVERSE all the galaxies that are known or thought to exist in space **8.** DOMAIN a sphere, realm, or domain ○ *the world of reptiles* **9.** INHABITED BODY an astronomical body considered to be inhabited, e.g., a planet ○ *the alien worlds of science fiction* **10.** EVERYTHING IN SOMEBODY'S LIFE all that relates to or makes up somebody's life ○ *Her entire world collapsed.* **11.** CONDITION OF EXISTENCE a condition or state of existence ○ *the world of tomorrow* **12.** GREAT DEAL OR AMOUNT a very large amount, degree, or distance ○ *They're still worlds apart.* **13.** SECULAR EXISTENCE secular life and its ways ○ *a woman of the world* ■ *adj* **1.** OF ENTIRE WORLD relating to the entire world ○ *the world champions* **2.** EXERTING INFLUENCE GLOBALLY exerting influence over the whole of the world ○ *a world figure* **3.** AFFECTING WHOLE WORLD involving or affecting the whole of the Earth ○ *a world crisis* [Old English *woruld* "human existence, age, Earth" < Germanic, "age of man"] ◇ **come down in the world** to have less money or power than previously ◇ **for all the world** exactly and in every detail ◇ **have the best of both worlds** to have the advantage of the best features of two different situations ◇ **in the world** used to add intensity to a question, often indicating surprise or disbelief on the part of the questioner ○ *What in the world have you done?* ◇ **it's a small world** used to express surprise at a coincidence such as unexpectedly meeting somebody you know in a distant place ◇ **not for the world** no matter what happens ○ *Not for the world would I think of doing such a thing.* ◇ **out of this world** extraordinarily good (*informal*) ◇ **the world is your oyster** there are limitless opportunities available for you to be successful ◇ **think the world of somebody** to be extremely fond of somebody

World Bank *n* a specialized agency of the United Nations, established in 1944, that guarantees loans to member nations for the purpose of reconstruction and development. Official name **International Bank for Reconstruction and Development**

world-beat·ing *adj* surpassing all others in a particular field —**world-beat·er** *n*

world-class *adj* ranked among the best or most prominent in the world ○ *a world-class downhill racer*

World Coun·cil of Church·es *n* an international ecumenical organization, founded in 1948, that links Protestant and Eastern churches from around the world for the purpose of coordinated and cooperative action in religious and secular areas

World Court *n* LAW same as **International Court of Justice**

World Cup *n* a sports tournament, especially in soccer, contested by the national teams of qualifying countries, that has been held every four years in a different country of a different continent

world e·con·o·my *n* the economy of the world, considered as an international exchange of goods and services

World Eng·lish *n* the English language in all its varieties as it is spoken and written throughout the world

world-fa·mous *adj* renowned throughout the world

World Health Or·gan·i·za·tion *n* a specialized agency of the United Nations that helps countries to improve their health services and coordinates international action against diseases

World Her·i·tage Site *n* an area or structure designated by UNESCO as being of global significance and conserved by a country that has signed a United Nations convention pledging its protection

world lan·guage *n* **1.** a language that is used in many countries, e.g., English, Spanish, or Arabic **2.** a language created for international use, e.g., Esperanto or Interlingua

world lead·er *n* **1.** the leader of a politically and economically powerful country **2.** a company, organization, or country that is the biggest or best in a particular field

world line *n* the path of a particle in time and space, which is straight if the particle moves in a uniform way

world·ling /wúrldling/ *n* somebody more interested in everyday material things than in spiritual matters

world·ly /wúrldlee/ *adj* **1.** EXPERIENCED IN LIFE experienced in and knowledgeable about human society and its ways **2.** BELONGING TO PHYSICAL WORLD relating to everyday material existence ○ *all my worldly goods* **3.** MATERIALISTIC much more interested in everyday materialistic concerns than in the spiritual side of life —**world·li·ness** *n*

world·ly-mind·ed *adj* same as **worldly** (senses 1, 3)

world·ly-wise *adj* same as **worldly** (sense 1)

world mu·sic *n* popular music from or influenced by countries outside the Western world and its traditions

world pow·er *n* a country or alliance of countries powerful enough to influence events on a global scale

World Se·ries *tdmk* a trademark for a series of baseball games played between the winners of the American League and the National League to decide the major league championship

world's fair *n* an exhibition of commercial and cultural products from many different countries

world-shak·ing, **world-shat·ter·ing** *adj* same as **earth-shaking**

world soul *n* in some beliefs, a spirit that animates the world in the same way that the human soul is believed to animate the body

World Trade Cen·ter *n* a complex of buildings featuring two skyscrapers in New York City, destroyed with great loss of life in a terrorist attack using two hijacked aircraft on September 11, 2001. The complex was completed in 1972, and the twin towers, 110 stories high, were at one time the tallest in the world.

World Trade Or·gan·i·za·tion *n* an international organization founded in 1995 to promote and regulate trade between countries. It was created to replace GATT.

world view, **world·view** /wúrld vyo͞o/ *n* a comprehensive and usually personal conception or view of humanity, the world, or life [Translation of German *Weltanschauung*]

world war *n* a war involving a number of countries on each side, with fighting spread over much of the world

World War I *n* a war fought mainly in Europe from 1914 to 1918, in which an alliance including Great Britain, France, Russia, Italy, and the United States defeated the alliance of Germany, Austria-Hungary, Turkey, and Bulgaria

World War II *n* a war fought in Europe, Africa, and Asia from 1939 to 1945, in which an alliance including Great Britain, France, the Soviet Union, and the United States defeated the alliance of Germany, Italy, and Japan

world-wea·ry *adj* tired of or bored with life —**world-wea·ri·ness** *n*

world·wide /wúrld wíd/ *adj* affecting or found throughout the entire world ■ *adv* all over the world

World Wide Web *n* a system for accessing, manipulating, and downloading a very large set of hypertext-linked documents and other files located on computers connected through the Internet

World Wide Web Con·sor·ti·um *n* ONLINE full form of **W3C**

worm /wurm/ *n* **1.** LONG CYLINDRICAL INVERTEBRATE an invertebrate that has a slender, soft, cylindrical or flat body and no apparent appendages, especially an annelid, nematode, or flatworm (*often used in combination*) **2.** INSECT LARVA the larva of an insect, e.g., a caterpillar, grub, or maggot **3.** ANIMAL LOOKING OR MOVING LIKE WORM an animal that looks or moves like a worm, e.g., the shipworm or the slowworm **4.** OFFENSIVE TERM an offensive term for somebody regarded as contemptible, especially because of behaving in a groveling way (*insult*) **5.** SOMETHING THAT TORMENTS something that torments, undermines, or corrupts somebody from within ○ *a worm of discontent* **6.** COMPUT INVASIVE COMPUTER PROGRAM a computer program that invades computers on a network, replicates itself to prevent deletion, and interferes with the host computer's operation **7.** SPIRAL CONDENSER IN STILL a spiral pipe in a still in which alcohol condenses **8.** MECH ENG THREADED SHAFT a shaft with a helical thread that is the part of a gear that meshes with a toothed wheel ■ *v* (**wormed, worm·ing, worms**) **1.** *vt* PROCEED DEVIOUSLY to make your way or advance yourself deviously or obsequiously ○ *wormed her way out of trouble* **2.** *vt* OBTAIN SOMETHING DEVIOUSLY to obtain something from somebody by devious or underhand means ○ *They wormed his secret out of him.* **3.** *vt* WIND YARN AROUND ROPE to wind yarn around a rope so as to give it a smooth surface **4.** *vi* MOVE LIKE WORM to move in a slow, slithering way **5.** *vi* SEARCH FOR WORMS to search for worms, especially for use as fishing bait **6.** *vt* VET, MED TREAT SOMEBODY FOR PARASITIC WORMS to treat a person or animal in order to prevent or remove an infestation of parasitic worms [Old English *wurm* < Indo-European] —**worm·er** *n* —**worm·ish** *adj*

WORM /wurm/ *n* a computer storage medium, usually optical, in which data cannot be changed after it is stored but can be read. Full form **write once read many (times)**

worm burn·er *n* (*slang*) **1.** a shot in golf that stays close to the surface of the ground **2.** a sailboarding maneuver that involves swinging the mast through 360 degrees while balancing on the tail of the board

worm·cast /wúrm kàst/ *n* a small spiral mound of earth or sand that has been excreted by a burrowing earthworm or lugworm

worm-eat·en *adj* **1.** EATEN INTO BY WORMS weakened by burrowing worms **2.** DECAYED affected by decay or rot **3.** DILAPIDATED old or worn out

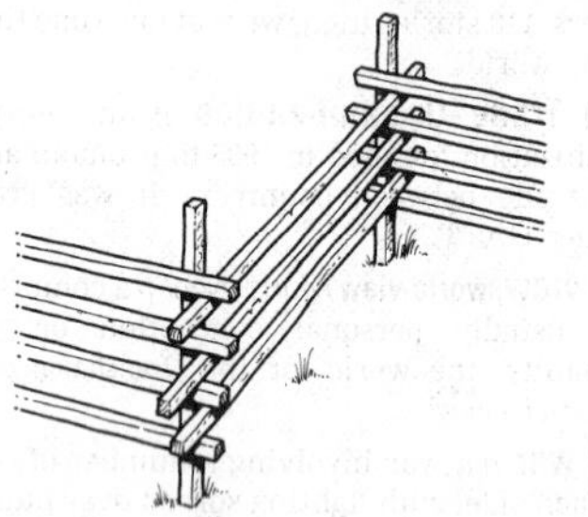

worm fence

worm fence *n* a fence consisting of crossed poles that support interlocking rails in a zigzag pattern

REGIONAL NOTE See ***zigzag fence.***

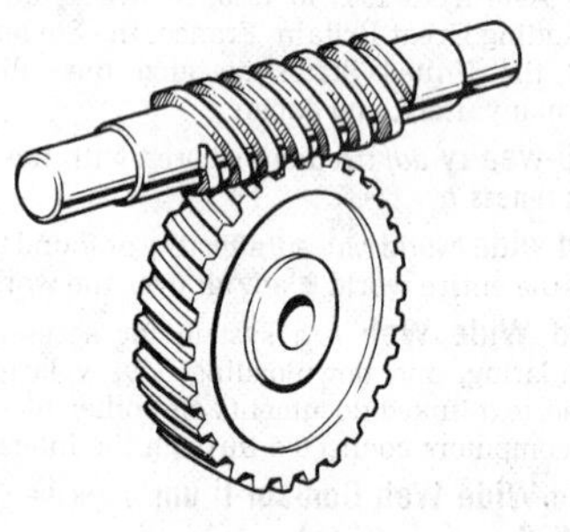

worm gear

worm gear *n* **1.** a gear consisting of a shaft with a helical thread that meshes with a toothed wheel to transfer rotary motion between two shafts at right angles to one another **2.** MECH ENG same as **worm wheel**

worm grass *n* PLANTS same as **pinkroot** (sense 2)

worm·hole /wúrm hōl/ *n* **1.** a hypothetical passage in space-time connecting widely separated parts of the universe **2.** a hole made by a burrowing worm, e.g., in wood —**worm·holed** *adj*

worm liz·ard *n* REPT same as **amphisbaena** (sense 1)

worms /wurmz/ *n* an infestation of parasites, especially pinworms or tapeworms, affecting the intestines or other parts of a person's or animal's body (*takes a singular verb*)

Worms /wurmz, vawrmz/ historic city in Rhineland-Palatinate State, southwestern Germany. Population: 79,521 (1997).

worm·seed /wúrm sēed/ *n* a plant whose seeds or other parts are used as a treatment for infestation by parasitic worms

worm's-eye view *n* a view of somebody or something from a lower or inferior position

worm snake *n* a small nonvenomous snake with vestigial eyes. Native to: central and eastern United States. Genus: *Carphophis.*

worm wheel *n* the toothed wheel that meshes with the threaded shaft in a worm gear

worm·wood /wúrm wòod/ *n* **1.** a plant that yields a bitter extract. Use: flavoring for absinthe, formerly, medicine for intestinal worms. Genus: *Artemisia.* **2.** something that causes somebody to feel bitter (*literary*) ○ *Her ingratitude was wormwood to him.* [14C. By folk etymology < Old English *wermod*, by association with WORM, because the plant was used as medicine for intestinal worms]

worm·y /wúrmee/ *adj* **1.** full of or eaten into by worms **2.** resembling or characteristic of a worm —**worm·i·ness** *n*

worn /wawrn/ past participle of **wear**[1] ■ *adj* **1.** SHOWING EFFECTS OF WEAR weakened or frayed by use **2.** SHOWING EFFECTS OF FATIGUE showing the effects of fatigue, worry, illness, or age **3.** HACKNEYED used so much as to have lost meaning ○ *trite, worn phrases* —**worn·ness** *n*

SPELLCHECK See *warn.*

worn-out *adj* (*not hyphenated after a verb*) **1.** DAMAGED OR WEAKENED BY LONG USE so damaged or affected by prolonged use as to be no longer usable **2.** EXHAUSTED very tired **3.** OUTDATED no longer relevant, useful, or fashionable

wor·ri·ment /wúr eemənt/ *n US* anxiety or something that causes anxiety (*archaic*)

wor·ri·some /wúr eessəm/ *adj* **1.** causing worry, anxiety, or distress **2.** having a tendency to worry —**wor·ri·some·ly** *adv*

wor·ry /wúr ee/ *v* (**-ried, -ry·ing, -ries**) **1.** *vti* BE OR MAKE ANXIOUS to feel anxious about something unpleasant that may have happened or may happen, or make somebody do this **2.** *vt* ANNOY SOMEBODY to annoy somebody by making insistent demands or complaints **3.** *vt* TRY TO BITE ANIMAL to try to wound or kill an animal by biting it ○ *a dog suspected of worrying sheep* **4.** *vt* same as **worry at 5.** *vi* PROCEED DESPITE PROBLEMS to proceed persistently despite problems or obstacles **6.** *vt* TOUCH SOMETHING REPEATEDLY to touch, move, or interfere with something repeatedly ○ *Stop worrying that button or it'll come off.* ■ *n* (*plural* **-ries**) **1.** ANXIOUSNESS a troubled unsettled feeling **2.** CAUSE OF ANXIETY something that causes anxiety or concern **3.** PERIOD OF ANXIETY a period spent feeling anxious or concerned [Old English *wyrgan* "strangle"] —**wor·ried** *adj* —**wor·ried·ly** *adv* —**wor·ried·ness** *n* —**wor·ri·er** *n* —**wor·ry·ing** *adj* —**wor·ry·ing·ly** *adv* ◇ **not to worry** used to tell somebody that something is not important and need not be a cause of concern (*informal*) ○ *Not to worry. We'll do better next time.* ◇ **no worries** *UK* used to say that something is no trouble or is not worth mentioning (*informal*)

SYNONYMS ***worry, unease, care, anxiety, angst, stress***

CORE MEANING: a troubled state of mind

worry a troubled unsettled feeling ○ *I was beside myself with worry.* ○ *Unemployment was his major source of worry.* **unease** a feeling of anxiety, awkwardness, or discomfort ○ *The announcement provoked considerable unease among U.N. officials.* ○ *There was a silence, laden with unease.* **care** (*literary or formal*) a troubled state of mind arising from worry or concern ○ *worn down with care and grief* **anxiety** nervousness or agitation, often about something that is going to happen ○ *Although she has been teaching for eight years, she always feels a twinge of anxiety at the beginning of a new term.* **angst** any feeling of dread or anxiety ○ *suffering from loneliness, insecurity and general teenage angst* **stress** mental, emotional, or physical strain caused, for example, by anxiety or overwork ○ *a class in breathing techniques to help control the stress of everyday life*

worry at *vt* to shake or tear at something with the teeth ○ *a dog worrying a bone*

wor·ry beads *npl* a string of beads for fingering or playing with when feeling tense

wor·ry·guts /wúrree gùts/ (*plural same*) *n UK* same as **worrywart** (*informal*)

wor·ry·wart /wúr ee wàwrt/ *n US* somebody who tends to worry needlessly (*informal*)

worse /wurss/ comparative of **bad, badly, ill** ■ *adj* **1.** LESS GOOD THAN SOMETHING ELSE less good in quality or effect than before or than somebody or something else ○ *did a worse job on the painting than the previous workers* **2.** MORE SEVERE more severe than before or than something else of the same kind ○ *Her fever is worse this morning.* **3.** SICKER more ill than before ○ *The patient is worse today.* ■ *adv* TO WORSE DEGREE to a degree worse than before ■ *n* SOMETHING WORSE somebody or something that is worse than another ○ *Of the two of them, this one's the worse.* [Old English *wyrsa* < Germanic] ◇ **be none the worse for something** to experience no harm or ill effects from something ◇ **if worse comes to worst** if the situation reaches an intolerable state

USAGE In *If worse comes to worst, we can declare bankruptcy, worse* plus the following form *worst* clearly shows a progression from an awful situation to a dreadful one. Variant but illogical wordings include *if worse comes to worse* and *if worst comes to worst.*

wors·en /wúrss'n/ (**-ened, -en·ing, -ens**) *vti* to become worse, or cause something to become worse

wors·er /wúrssər/ comparative of **bad** (*nonstandard*)

wor·ship /wúrship/ *v* (**-shiped** or **-shipped, -ship·ing** or **-ship·ping, -ships**) **1.** *vti* TREAT SOMEBODY OR SOMETHING AS DEITY to treat somebody or something as divine and show respect by engaging in acts of prayer and devotion **2.** *vi* TAKE PART IN RELIGIOUS SERVICE to take part in a religious service **3.** *vt* LOVE SOMEBODY DEEPLY to love, admire, or respect somebody or something greatly and perhaps excessively or unquestioningly ■ *n* **1.** RELIGIOUS ADORATION the adoration, devotion, and respect given to a deity **2.** RELIGIOUS RITES the rites or services through which people show their adoration, devotion, and respect for a deity **3.** GREAT DEVOTION great or excessive love, admiration, and respect felt for somebody or something [Old English *weortscipe* "condition of worth" < *weorth* "worth"] —**wor·ship·er** *n*

Wor·ship *n Can, UK* a title of respect for a mayor, magistrate, or other similar dignitary ○ *His Worship, the Mayor*

wor·ship·ful /wúrshipfəl/ *adj* **1.** showing or expressing deep reverence and devotion **2.** *also* **Wor·ship·ful** *UK* used as the honoring adjective in the titles of some dignitaries such as mayors, and of the ancient guild companies of the City of London —**wor·ship·ful·ly** *adv* —**wor·ship·ful·ness** *n*

worst /wurst/ superlative of **bad, badly, ill** ■ *adj* LEAST GOOD least good, most unpleasant, or most unfavorable ○ *your worst enemy* ■ *adv* LEAST WELL in the least good, most unpleasant, or most unfavorable way ■ *n* LEAST GOOD THING the least good, least pleasant, or least favorable aspect or part of something, or the worst thing that could happen or be done ○ *fear the worst* ○ *The worst was over.* ■ *vt* (**worst·ed, worst·ing, worsts**) DEFEAT SOMEBODY to get the better of or defeat an opponent ○ *We were worsted by the visiting team.* [Old English *wyrsta* < Indo-European, "confuse"] ◇ **get the worst of it** to be defeated, or get the least benefit from something

worst case *n* the least desirable, most disastrous situation or result that can be envisioned (*hyphenated before a noun*) ○ *the worst-case scenario*

wor·sted /wúrstəd/ *n* **1.** smooth closely-woven woolen cloth without a nap, made from tightly twisted yarn **2.** the tightly twisted yarn, made from long-fibered wool, from which worsted cloth is made [13C. After the village of *Worstead* in Norfolk, England]

wort[1] /wurt, wawrt/ *n* a medicinal plant. This word survives mainly in plant names such as "liverwort" and "woundwort." (*usually used in combination*) [Old English *wyrt* < Indo-European, "branch, root"]

wort[2] /wurt, wawrt/ *n* a sugary liquid produced from crushed malted grain and water, to which yeast and hops are added in the brewing of beer [Old English *wyrt* < Germanic]

worth /wurth/ *n* **1.** VALUE IN MONEY the value of something, especially in terms of money **2.** AMOUNT EQUALING GIVEN VALUE the amount of something that can be bought for a particular sum of money or that will last for a particular length of time ○ *get your money's worth* **3.** MORAL OR SOCIAL VALUE the goodness, usefulness, or importance of something or somebody, irrespective of financial value or wealth ○ *A diploma from that place has little worth.* **4. WEALTH** the wealth of a person, group, organization, or other entity ○ *your aunt's net worth* ■ *adj* **1. EQUAL TO PARTICULAR AMOUNT** equivalent in value to a particular amount ○ *How much is it worth?* ○ *a painting worth thousands* **2. IMPORTANT ENOUGH TO JUSTIFY SOMETHING** important, large, or good enough to justify something ○ *His friendship is not worth having.* [Old English *weorþ* < Indo-European, "turn"] ◇ **for all you are worth** as fast, energetically, or enthusiastically as possible ◇ **for what it's worth** used to suggest that what you say may not be true or of much value ○ *Here's my opinion on the issue, for what it's worth.*

Wor·thing /wúrthing/ seaside resort in West Sussex, southeastern England. Population: 97,568 (2001).

worth·less /wúrthləss/ *adj* **1.** having no financial or other value or usefulness **2.** having no good, attractive, or admirable qualities at all —**worth·less·ly** *adv* —**worth·less·ness** *n*

worth·while /wùrth wīl, wúrth wīl, -hwīl, wúrth hwīl/ *adj* rewarding or beneficial enough to justify the time taken or the effort made [Mid-17C. Shortening of *worth the while*] —**worth·while·ness** *n*

wor·thy /wúrthee/ *adj* (**-thi·er, -thi·est**) **1. DESERVING** fully deserving something, usually as a suitable reward for merit or importance ○ *That remark is not worthy of a reply.* **2. RESPECTABLE** morally upright, good, and deserving respect ○ *a worthy person* **3. GOOD BUT DULL** having good qualities, good intentions, or the best of motives, but being boring and pedestrian ○ *a worthy attempt at playing the concerto* ■ *n* (*plural* **-thies**) **SOMEBODY GOOD OR MORAL** a good, morally upright, or reputable person (*often ironic*) ○ *colonial governors and other 18th-century worthies* —**wor·thi·ly** *adv* —**wor·thi·ness** *n*

wot 1st person singular present of **wit**². 3rd person singular present of **wit**² (*archaic*)

Wo·tan /vō taan/ *n* in Germanic mythology, the supreme god and the god of war. He corresponds to Odin in Norse mythology.

would /wood/ CORE MEANING: used to express the sense of "will" in reported speech or when referring to an event that has not happened yet ○ *Susan didn't think she would pass.* ○ *It would be wrong to suggest otherwise.*

modal v **1. USED WITH "IF" CLAUSES** used in stating what will or suggesting what might happen under the circumstances described in the conditional clause ○ *You would know him if you saw him.* ○ *My mother would be annoyed if I were to come home late.* **2. POLITE REQUEST** used in making polite requests or offers ○ *Would you mind closing the window?* ○ *Would you like more coffee?* **3. HABITUAL ACTION** used to indicate that a past action was habitual ○ *Every Sunday we would drive out to Coney Island.* ◇ **would that** used to introduce a strong desire or wish, usually one that is not expected to be fulfilled (*formal*) ○ *Would that we had never met.*

SPELLCHECK See *wood.*

USAGE See *should.*

would-be *adj* desiring or aspiring to do or be something ○ *a would-be poet* ■ *n* somebody who is hoping or trying to become something or achieve the status of something (*informal*) ○ *The reception was attended by all the major candidates for office and other would-bes.*

would·n't /wood'nt/ *contr* would not

wouldst /woodst, wootst/ 2nd person singular past of **will** (*archaic*)

would've /wooddəv/ *contr* would have (*informal*)

USAGE See *of.*

Woulfe bot·tle /woolf-/ *n* a container with more than one neck. Use: bubbling gases through liquids. [After Peter *Woulfe* (1727?–1803), English chemist]

wound¹ /woond/ *n* **1. INJURY TO BODY** an injury in which the skin, tissue, or an organ is broken by some external force such as a blow or surgical incision, with damage to the underlying tissue **2. EMOTIONAL INJURY** a lasting emotional or psychological injury ○ *still recovering from the wounds of a bitter divorce* **3. INJURY TO PLANT** damage to plant tissue caused by an external agent such as wind or frost ■ *vti* (**wound·ed, wound·ing, wounds**) **1. INJURE** to cause a wound in the body of somebody or something, especially using a knife, gun, or other weapon ○ *He was wounded in the leg.* **2. CAUSE EMOTIONAL WOUND** to cause somebody emotional or psychological distress by saying or doing something ○ *cutting remarks intended to wound* [Old English *wund* < Indo-European, "to beat"] —**wound·a·ble** *adj* —**wound·ed** *adj* —**wound·er** *n* —**wound·ing** *adj* —**wound·ing·ly** *adv* —**wound·less** *adj*

SYNONYMS See *harm.*

wound² /wownd/ past participle, past tense of **wind**³

Wound·ed Knee /woondəd née/ village in South Dakota. In 1890 it was the site of a massacre of Native North Americans in which between 150 and 370 Sioux people were killed, most of them unarmed.

wound up /wòwnd úp/ *adj* extremely tense, nervous, and agitated (*informal*) ○ *a litigator who is really wound up the night before trial*

wound·wort /woond wùrt, -wàwrt/ (*plural* **-worts** or *same*) *n* **1.** betony or a related plant of the mint family. Use: formerly, to treat wounds. Genus: *Stachys.* **2.** any plant formerly used to treat wounds

wove HANDICRAFT past tense of **weave**¹

wo·ven /wṓvən/ HANDICRAFT past participle of **weave**¹ ■ *adj* made or manufactured by the process of weaving ○ *woven synthetic textiles* ■ *n* a textile or other material that is created by weaving ○ *a factory making cotton and other wovens*

wove pa·per *n* paper made using a roller with a fine mesh that leaves a faint mesh imprint

Wo·vo·ka /wō vṓkə/ (1856?–1932) US prophet. A member of the Paiute people, he developed the ritual of the Ghost Dance. Many of his followers were killed by federal troops at Wounded Knee (1890). Known as **Wilson, Jack**

wow¹ /wow/ (*informal*) *interj* **EXPRESSING SURPRISE** used to express surprise, admiration, wonder, or pleasure ■ *vt* (**wowed, wow·ing, wows**) **IMPRESS SOMEBODY GREATLY** to impress or delight somebody greatly ○ *The acrobats wowed the audience with their daring moves.* ■ *n* **GREAT SUCCESS** a great success or an object of great admiration [Early 16C. Natural exclamation]

wow² /wow/ *n* a distortion in recorded sound in the form of slow fluctuations in the pitch of long notes, caused by variations in the speed of the reproducing or recording equipment [Mid-20C. An imitation of the acoustic effect]

wow·ser /wówzər/ *n* somebody who disapproves of activities such as drinking and dancing (*informal*) [Late 19C. Origin ?]

WP *abbr* **1.** weather permitting **2.** LAW without prejudice **3.** word processing **4.** word processor

WPA *abbr* HIST Work Projects Administration

W par·ti·cle *n* an elementary particle with a relatively large mass and a positive or negative charge, believed to mediate weak interactions between other particles in which the charges on the particles change

WPGA *abbr* Women's Professional Golfers' Association

WPI *abbr* FIN wholesale price index

wpm, w.p.m. *abbr* MEASURE words per minute

wpn. *abbr* ARMS weapon

wrack¹ /rak/ *n* another spelling of **rack**⁶

SPELLCHECK See *rack*¹.

wrack² /rak/ *n* **1. OCEAN VEGETATION** seaweed floating in the sea or growing on the shoreline **2. BROWN SEAWEED** any brown seaweed, e.g., bladder wrack. Family: Fucaceae. **3. WRECKED SHIP** a wrecked ship, especially one driven onto the shore (*archaic*) **4. WRECKAGE** wreckage, or a piece of wreckage (*archaic*) ■ *vti* (**wracked, wrack·ing, wracks**) **WRECK OR BE WRECKED** to wreck something, or be wrecked [14C. < Dutch *wrak* "wreck"]

SPELLCHECK See *rack*¹.

wraith /rayth/ *n* **1.** the supposed ghost of a dead person, or any ghostly and insubstantial apparition **2.** a vision of a person still alive, said to appear as a premonition of that person's death [Early 16C. Origin ?]

Wran·gel Is·land /ráng g'l-/ island in the Arctic Ocean, northeastern Russia, between the East Siberian Sea and the Chukchi Sea. Area: 1,800 sq. mi./4,662 sq. km.

Wran·gell Moun·tains /ráng g'l-/ mountain range in southeastern Alaska, near the border with the Yukon Territory, Canada. The highest peak is Mount Blackburn, 16,390 ft./4,996 m.

Wran·gell-St. E·li·as Na·tion·al Park and Pre·serve /ràng g'l saynt i lī əss-/ the largest national park in the United States, in southeastern Alaska, established in 1980. It is noted for its high peaks, glaciers, and wildlife. Area: 20,588 sq. mi./53,323 sq. km.

wran·gle /ráng g'l/ *v* (**-gled, -gling, -gles**) **1.** *vi* **ARGUE PERSISTENTLY** to argue persistently and angrily ○ *wrangled for hours over the wording of the agreement* **2.** *vt* **GET SOMETHING BY PERSISTENT ARGUMENT** to obtain something or persuade somebody by arguing persistently (*informal*) ○ *managed to wrangle a commitment to peace out of the opposing side* **3.** *vt* **HERD ANIMALS** to herd horses or cattle ■ *n* **LONG ARGUMENT** a lengthy or noisy and bad-tempered argument or dispute [14C. Ultimately < Germanic]

wran·gler /ráng glər/ *n* **1.** a worker who takes care of saddle horses on a ranch **2.** a noisy and persistent arguer, or a participant in a lengthy argument

wrap /rap/ *v* (**wraps, wrapped, wrap·ping**) **1.** *vt* **COVER SOMETHING UP** to cover something up by winding or folding a pliable material such as cloth or paper around it ○ *The package was wrapped in plain brown paper.* **2.** *vti* **COIL AROUND SOMETHING** to wind, fold, or clasp something round somebody or something else, or be wound round somebody or something ○ *He wrapped his arms around the pole and wouldn't let go.* **3.** *vt* **FOLD SOMETHING UP** to fold or roll something up into a compact bundle ○ *linen napkins neatly wrapped* **4.** *vt* **ENVELOP SOMETHING** to envelop and obscure or conceal something ○ *Fog wrapped the harbor.* **5.** *vt* **GIVE SOMETHING AURA** to surround something with a particular type of atmosphere or quality such as secrecy or scandal ○ *The whole affair was wrapped in secrecy.* **6.** *vt* **ENGROSS SOMEBODY** to occupy the mind and attention of somebody fully ○ *was wrapped in thought* **7.** *vi* MOVIES **FINISH FILMING** to finish filming or videotaping something ○ *We're scheduled to wrap at the end of the month.* **8.** *vi* **FINISH** to come to an end ○ *"The government's antitrust case ... was supposed to wrap by the end of the year."* (*Newsweek*; November 1998) **9.** *vti* COMPUT **TAKE SOMETHING OVER TO NEXT LINE** to take a word or piece of text over to the next line automatically on reaching the margin, or be taken over in this way ■ *n* **1. OUTER GARMENT** an outer garment to be wrapped or folded around the wearer, e.g., a shawl, cloak, or coat **2.** INDUST **MATERIAL FOR WRAPPING** material, or a piece of material, used to wrap something **3.** MOVIES **COMPLETION OF FILMING** the completion of filming or videotaping something ○ *All right, everybody, that's a wrap!* **4.** FOOD **FILLED TORTILLA SANDWICH** a sandwich consisting of fillings enclosed in a tortilla ○ *a ham and cheese wrap* ■ *adj* CLOTHING same as **wraparound** *adj* (sense 1) [14C. Origin ?] ◇ **keep something under wraps** to keep something secret ○ *Our new product is being kept under wraps for the moment.*

SPELLCHECK See *rap*¹.

wrap up *vt* **1. COMPLETE SOMETHING** to complete something or bring it to an end (*informal*) ○ *We'll wrap up the editing phase of the project next week.* **2.** *US* **SUMMARIZE SOMETHING** to give a short final summary of something such as the news **3. COVER SOMETHING WITH MATERIAL** to cover something completely with material such as paper, plastic, or foil ◇ **wrapped up in somebody** *or* **something** completely absorbed by or preoccupied with somebody or something ○ *She is completely wrapped up in her career.*

wrap·a·round /ráppə ròwnd/ *adj* **1. DESIGNED FOR WRAPPING AROUND BODY** designed to be worn wrapped around the body and tied in position with one edge overlapping the other, rather than fastened with buttons or a zipper **2. CURVING AROUND SIDES** curving around the sides of whatever it is attached to ○ *a wraparound porch* ■ *n* **1. WRAPAROUND GARMENT** a wraparound skirt or other piece of clothing **2.** **WRAPAROUND CABINET** a cabinet that is shaped to curve around the sides of something **3.** COMPUT **COMPUTER FUNCTION AUTOMATICALLY STARTING NEW LINE** a function of a computer program or visual display unit that makes text automatically begin a new line as soon as the last character space in the previous line is filled **4.** PUBL **PAPER STRIP AROUND BOOK'S DUST JACKET** a strip of paper fastened around the dust jacket of a book, e.g., to announce a price reduction **5.** PRINTING **PLATE FOR ATTACHING TO PRESS CYLINDER** a plate of flexible material that can be attached to the cylinder of a rotary press

wrap·per /ráppər/ *n* **1.** **MATERIAL WRAPPED AROUND SOMETHING** the paper, plastic, or other material wrapped around something that is sold **2.** **PAPER AROUND MAGAZINE OR NEWSPAPER** a piece of paper wrapped around a magazine or newspaper sent through the mail **3.** **TOBACCO LEAF FORMING OUTSIDE OF CIGAR** a tobacco leaf wrapped around a cigar to form its outer skin **4.** PUBL same as **dust jacket** **5.** *US* **LOOSE LOUNGING GARMENT** a garment that wraps loosely around the body, e.g., a dressing gown **6.** *US* **SOMEBODY WHO WRAPS PACKAGES IN STORE** an employee whose job is to wrap up packages in a store or to wrap manufactured products in a factory

wrap·ping /rápping/ *n* the paper, plastic, or other material used to wrap something

wrap·ping pa·per *n* specially decorated paper used for wrapping gifts

wrap-up *n US* a short summary at the end of something such as a news bulletin

wrasse /rass/ (*plural* **wrass·es** or *same*) *n* a fish with protruding lips and well developed canine teeth. Native to: temperate and tropical seas. Family: Labridae. [Late 17C. < Cornish *wrah* "old woman"]

wrath /rath, raath/ *n* **1.** **GREAT ANGER** strong anger, often with a desire for revenge **2.** **DIVINE RETRIBUTION** in some beliefs, God's punishment for sin **3.** **VENGEANCE** the vengeance, punishment, or destruction wreaked by somebody in anger (*literary*) [Old English *wrǣþþu* < *wrāþ* "angry"] —**wrath·ful** *adj* —**wrath·less** *adj*

SYNONYMS See *anger.*

Wrath, Cape /rath/ the most northwesterly point of mainland Scotland

Wray /ray/, **Fay** (*b.* 1907) Canadian-born US actor. She starred in several movies of the early sound era, most notably *King Kong* (1933). Full name **Wray, Vina Fay.**

wreak /reek/ (**wreaked, wreak·ing, wreaks**) *vt* **1.** **CAUSE DESTRUCTION** to cause havoc or destruction ○ *a storm that wreaked vast destruction* **2.** **INFLICT REVENGE** to inflict revenge or punishment on somebody **3.** **EXPRESS ANGER OR HATRED** to express anger, hatred, or another violent emotion in action against somebody (*literary*) [Old English *wrecan* "drive out" < Indo-European] —**wreak·er** *n*

SPELLCHECK See *reek.*

USAGE See *wrought.*

wreath /reeth/ (*plural* **wreaths** /reeths, reeth͟z/) *n* **1.** **CIRCULAR ARRANGEMENT OF FLOWERS** a circular arrangement of flowers or greenery placed as a memorial on a grave, hung up as a decoration, or put on somebody's head as a sign of honor **2.** **REPRESENTATION OF WREATH** a representation of a circular arrangement of flowers, vines, or other things, e.g., in a carving or on a coat of arms **3.** **CIRCULAR SHAPE** a hollow circular shape formed by something such as smoke [Old English *wriþa* < *wrīþan* (see WRITHE)] —**wreath·less** *adj*

SPELLCHECK wreath or **wreathe**? Do not confuse the spelling of ***wreath*** and ***wreathe***. ***Wreath*** is a noun, meaning "a circular arrangement of flowers or greenery" or "a holllow circular shape," as in *lay a wreath at the base of the monument, wreaths of smoke.* ***Wreathe*** is a verb, meaning "encircle," "intertwine," or "coil": *Mist wreathes the mountains in the early morning.*

wreathe /ree͟th/ (**wreathed, wreath·ing, wreathes**) *v* **1.** *vt* **PUT WREATH ON OR AROUND SOMETHING** to encircle, surround, or cover something with a wreath or wreaths or a similar type of decoration **2.** *vt* **MAKE SOMETHING INTO WREATH BY INTERTWINING** to make things into a wreath by twisting and intertwining them **3.** *vti* **WRITHE OR COIL** to move in coils, curves, or spirals, or cause something to move in coils, curves, or spirals [Mid-16C. Partly < WREATH, partly back-formation < *wrethen* "twisted," obsolete past participle of WRITHE]

SPELLCHECK See *wreath.*

wreck /rek/ *vt* (**wrecked, wreck·ing, wrecks**) **1.** **DESTROY OR DAMAGE SOMETHING** to destroy something completely or damage it beyond repair **2.** **DESTROY SHIP** to cause a ship to sink or run aground and be destroyed ■ *n* **1.** same as **crash**[1] *n* (sense 1) **2.** **SOMETHING BADLY DAMAGED** something that is in very poor condition, damaged, or dilapidated **3.** **REMAINS OF SOMETHING DESTROYED** something that has been totally destroyed, or its shattered remains **4.** **BADLY DAMAGED SHIP** a very badly damaged or sunken ship **5.** **DESTRUCTION OF SHIP** the sinking or destruction at sea of a ship from accidental causes **6.** **CARGO FROM WRECKED SHIP** cargo or other goods that are washed ashore after a shipwreck **7.** **DESTRUCTION** the ruin or destruction of something **8.** **SOMEBODY LOOKING OR FEELING TERRIBLE** somebody who is physically or emotionally exhausted or broken down [13C. Via Anglo-Norman *wrec* < N Germanic]

wreck·age /rékij/ *n* **1.** the broken pieces left after something has been extremely badly damaged or destroyed **2.** the ruin or destruction of something (*formal*)

wrecked /rekt/ *adj* **1.** very tired or exhausted (*informal*) **2.** in an intoxicated or drugged state (*slang*)

wreck·er /rékər/ *n* **1.** AUTOMOT **TRUCK FOR TOWING** a truck with a hoisting mechanism used to tow away damaged cars or other vehicles **2.** **SOMEBODY DEMOLISHING BUILDINGS OR DISMANTLING CARS** somebody whose job is to demolish buildings or dismantle old cars for salvage **3.** **DESTROYER OR SPOILER** somebody who destroys or spoils something, especially deliberately, maliciously, or with pleasure **4.** **SOMEBODY LURING SHIPS TO DESTRUCTION** in former times, somebody who lured ships onto rocks in order to steal the cargo or other goods on board

wreck·er's ball *n* URBAN PLAN same as **wrecking ball**

wreck·fish /rék fish/ (*plural same* or **-fish·es**) *n* FISH same as **stone bass** [Late 19C. < its habit of following wreckage]

wreck·ing ball /réking-/ *n* a heavy ball attached by a cable to a crane and swung to knock down parts of buildings that are being demolished

wreck·ing bar *n* a short crowbar forked at one end and bent at the other to provide leverage

wren

wren /ren/ *n* a small songbird with a slender downturned beak, usually brown feathers, and a short upright tail. Native to: Europe, Asia, North and South America. Family: Troglodytidae. [Old English *wrenna*]

Wren /ren/ *n* a member of the former British Women's Royal Naval Service [Early 20C. < WRNS]

Wren /ren/, **Sir Christopher** (1632–1723) English architect, scientist, and mathematician. The founder of the English baroque style, he designed St. Paul's Cathedral, London (1675–1710) and some 50 other London churches as well as residences and public buildings. He is credited with the design of the main building at the College of William and Mary in Williamsburg, VA.

"Architecture has its political use; public buildings being the ornament of a country; it establishes a nation, draws people and commerce; makes the people love their native country."
[Sir Christopher Wren, *Parentalia*; 1750]

Sir Christopher Wren: portrait medal by G. D. Gaab

wrench /rench/ *v* (**wrenched, wrench·ing, wrench·es**) **1.** *vti* **PULL AND TWIST SOMETHING AWAY** to pull something away forcefully, often using a twisting movement **2.** *vt* **INJURE SOMETHING BY TWISTING** to injure part of the body by twisting it suddenly and forcibly **3.** *vi* **MOVE WITH TWISTING MOVEMENT** to move with a forceful twisting movement **4.** *vt* **DISTRESS SOMEBODY** to make somebody feel very sad or distressed **5.** *vt* **SKEW MEANING OR FUNCTION** to distort something in order to make it mean or appear to be something different ■ *n* **1.** CONSTR **TOOL USED TO GRASP AND TURN** a hand or power tool with fixed or movable jaws, used to seize, turn, or twist objects such as nuts and bolts **2.** **SPRAIN CAUSED BY TWISTING** a sprain caused by a sudden forceful twisting movement of a part of the body **3.** **FORCEFUL TWISTING PULL** a forceful twisting pull at something, especially to free it **4.** **SURGE OF EMOTION** a sudden surge of emotion such as pity or empathy ○ *the wrench we felt when viewing film footage of the flood's devastation* **5.** **SADNESS AND LOSS ON PARTING** a difficult parting from a person or place, or the feelings of sadness and loss that accompany such a parting ○ *Leaving New York was a terrible wrench after having lived there for 30 years.* [Old English *wrencan* < Indo-European, "to turn"]

wrest /rest/ *vt* (**wrest·ed, wrest·ing, wrests**) **1.** **GAIN CONTROL OR POWER** to take something such as control or power from somebody in the face of opposition or resistance **2.** **PULL SOMETHING AWAY FORCIBLY** to seize something with the hands and take it away from somebody using physical force **3.** **GET SOMETHING WITH EFFORT** to get or extract something with an effort or struggle **4.** **ALTER SOMETHING'S MEANING** to change or twist the meaning of something ■ *n* **FORCEFUL PULL** a sharp wrench or pull at something [Old English *wrǣstan* < Germanic] —**wrest·er** *n*

wres·tle /réss'l/ *v* (**-tled, -tling, -tles**) **1.** *vti* **FIGHT BY GRIPPING AND PUSHING** to fight somebody using special holds and moves in an attempt to force his or her shoulders onto a mat **2.** *vti* **HAVE STRUGGLING FIGHT** to fight with somebody by gripping and pushing rather than hitting **3.** *vi* **HAVE DIFFICULTY** to struggle to deal with something difficult or intractable ○ *I spent the evening wrestling with my accounts.* **4.** *vti* **MANEUVER SOMETHING AWKWARD** to struggle to lift or move something ○ *We wrestled the trunk down the hall.* ■ *n* **1.** **FIGHT BETWEEN WRESTLERS** a wrestling match, or a fight in which people wrestle rather than hit each other **2.** **DIFFICULT STRUGGLE** a struggle to deal with something difficult or intractable [Old English. < *wrǣstan* (see WREST)] —**wres·tler** *n*

wres·tling /réssling/ *n* **1.** a sport in which two contestants fight by gripping each other using special holds, each trying to force the other's shoulders onto a mat **2.** the action of having a struggling fight with somebody

wretch /rech/ *n* **1.** **SOMEBODY WHO IS PITIED** a troubled or distressed person who evokes pity in others **2.** **ANNOYING PERSON** somebody who causes mild irritation or annoyance (*humorous*) **3.** **DESPICABLE PERSON** somebody viewed with contempt or disapproval [Old English *wrecca* < W Germanic]

SPELLCHECK See *retch*.

wretch·ed /réchəd/ *adj* **1. UNHAPPY OR ILL** feeling very unhappy or ill **2. APPEARING MISERABLE OR DEPRIVED** in a state of great hardship, deprivation, and hopelessness and arousing sympathy in others ○ *living in wretched conditions* **3. INADEQUATE OR OF LOW QUALITY** seriously inadequate or of very low quality **4. IRRITATING** provoking irritation or anger ○ *The wretched car won't start!* —**wretch·ed·ly** *adv* —**wretch·ed·ness** *n*

wrig·gle /rígg'l/ *v* (**-gled, -gling, -gles**) **1.** *vti* **TWIST AND TURN** to make small quick twisting and turning movements with the body, or cause the body to move in this way **2.** *vi* **MOVE WHILE TWISTING AND TURNING** to move by making quick twisting and turning movements ○ *managed to wriggle out of the sleeping bag* ■ *n* **1. TWISTING OR TURNING MOVEMENT** a small quick twisting or turning movement **2. TWISTING PASSAGE OR COURSE** a twisting passage or line [14C. Probably < Middle Low German *wriggelen* < *wriggen* "to turn"] —**wrig·gly** *adj*

wriggle out of *vt* to avoid doing something or suffering the consequences of something by making excuses or using deception

wrig·gler /rígglər/ *n* INSECTS same as **wiggler** (sense 2)

Wright /rīt/, **Fanny** (1795–1852) British-born US social reformer. Her interest in the abolition of slavery included the founding of a controversial and short-lived settlement in Tennessee in the 1820s intended to demonstrate the practicality of emancipation. Full name **Wright, Frances**

Library of Congress

Frank Lloyd Wright

Wright, Frank Lloyd (1867–1959) US architect. The clean lines of his designs, his use of new materials, and his consideration of the environment around his buildings made him one of the most influential modern architects. Fallingwater (1937), a house that extends over a waterfall in Bear Run, Pennsylvania, is one of his best known designs.

> "No house should be ever on a hill or on anything. It should be of the hill, belonging to it, so hill and house could live together each the happier for the other."
> [Frank Lloyd Wright, *Autobiography*; 1932]

Wright, Richard (1908–60) US writer. A campaigner against racism, he achieved considerable success with his autobiographical novel, *Black Boy* (1945). Full name **Wright, Richard Nathaniel**

> "Injustice which lasts for three long centuries and which exists among millions of people over thousands of square miles of territory, is injustice no longer; it is an accomplished fact of life."
> [Richard Wright, *Native Son*; 1940]

Library of Congress

Wilbur (right) and Orville Wright

Wright Broth·ers US inventors and aviation pioneers. Wilbur (1867–1912) and Orville (1871–1948) made the first successful flight of a powered aircraft at Kitty Hawk, North Carolina (1903).

> "The airplane stays up because it doesn't have the time to fall."
> [Attributed to Wright Brothers]

wring /ring/ *vt* (**wrung** /rung/, **wring·ing, wrings**) **1. TWIST AND COMPRESS SOMETHING** to twist and compress something in order to force liquid out of it ○ *Wring the towel out and hang it up to dry.* **2. FORCE OUT LIQUID BY TWISTING** to force liquid out of something by twisting and compressing it **3. EXTRACT SOMETHING WITH DIFFICULTY** to extract something from somebody with great difficulty ○ *finally managed to wring an answer out of him* **4. TWIST SOMETHING FORCIBLY AND PAINFULLY** to twist something such as an animal's neck forcefully, usually causing pain or death **5. CAUSE DISTRESS** to cause somebody emotional pain and distress ■ *n* **TWIST GIVEN TO WET MATERIAL** a twist or squeeze given to wet material in order to force out water or other liquid [Old English *wringen* < Germanic]

SPELLCHECK See *ring*[1].

wring·er /ríngər/ *n* a machine with two rollers set close together that can be turned by a handle so that wet clothes fed between them have the water forced out of them ◇ **put somebody through the wringer** to subject somebody to a very difficult or stressful experience (*informal*)

wring·ing wet *adj* extremely wet

wrin·kle /ríngk'l/ *n* **1. FACIAL LINE FROM AGING** a line or crease between small folds of skin that forms on the face as a result of aging or exposure to the sun **2. SMALL FOLD IN MATERIAL** a small messy or unintentional fold in cloth or paper **3. PROBLEM** something that causes trouble or inconvenience ○ *We need to iron out the wrinkles in the plan before implementing it.* **4. NEW FEATURE** an ingenious trick, method of doing something, or feature of something (*informal*) ○ *We've added a couple of new wrinkles to the policy.* ■ *vti* (**-kled, -kling, -kles**) **1. MAKE OR GET SMALL MESSY FOLDS** to make small messy or unintentional folds in something, or come to have messy folds ○ *This fabric wrinkles easily.* **2. MAKE OR GET LINES ON SKIN** to develop lines in the skin as a result of aging or exposure to the sun, or to cause such lines to develop **3. CONTRACT PART OF FACE** to tighten the muscles in part of the face so that it contracts or creases, or be tightened in this way ○ *wrinkled her nose* [14C. Origin ?] —**wrin·kled** *adj*

wrin·kly /ríngklee/ (**-kli·er, -kli·est**) *adj* covered with wrinkles

wrist /rist/ *n* **1. JOINT AT BASE OF HAND** the lower end of the forearm or the joint between the forearm and the hand together with the tissue surrounding it **2. PART OF GARMENT OVER WRIST** the part of a sleeve or glove that covers the wrist ■ *vt* SPORTS **HIT WITH TWISTING STROKE** to hit a ball with a lot of wrist movement to make the ball spin [Old English, < Germanic]

wrist·band /ríst bànd/ *n* **1. ABSORBENT BAND WORN AROUND WRIST** an absorbent band of material worn around the wrist to keep sweat from running onto the hand **2. WATCH STRAP** the strap of a wristwatch **3. IDENTIFICATION BAND WORN AROUND WRIST** an identification band worn around the wrist, e.g., when in the hospital **4.** CLOTHING **PART OF SOMETHING COVERING WRIST** a band of material that fits over the wrist, e.g., at the end of a long sleeve or on a glove

wrist-drop *n* inability to move the muscles that raise the wrist and move the fingers, caused by damage to or compression of the radial nerve

wrist·let /rístlət/ *n* a close-fitting band of material worn around the wrist, especially a decorative one that is attached to the top of a glove or the end of a sleeve

wrist·lock /ríst lòk/ *n* a hold in wrestling in which the wrist is held and twisted, rendering an opponent helpless

wrist pin *n* a pin in a piston of an internal-combustion engine attaching to the little end of a connecting rod

wrist sup·port, wrist rest *n* a long rectangular pad in front of a keyboard on which a keyboarder's wrists can rest, designed to help prevent cumulative trauma disorder

wrist·watch /ríst wòch/ *n* a watch on a band that is worn around the wrist

wrist·y /rístee/ (**-i·er, -i·est**) *adj* using a lot of wrist movement when hitting a ball

writ[1] /rit/ *n* a written court order demanding that the addressee do or stop doing whatever is specified in the order [Old English, "something written" < *wrītan* (see WRITE)]

writ[2] /rit/ past participle, past tense of **write** (*archaic*)

write /rīt/ (**wrote** /rōt/, **writ·ten** /rítt'n/, **writ·ing, writes**) *v* **1.** *vti* **PUT WORDS ON PAPER** to put words, letters, numbers, or musical notation on a surface using a pen, pencil, or similar instrument **2.** *vti* **CREATE BOOK, POEM, OR MUSIC** to create or compose something for others to read or listen to such as a letter or note, an article, a poem, or a piece of music **3.** *vt* **SPELL SOMETHING** to spell a word or words ○ *two words that are written the same but mean different things* **4.** *vti* **COMPOSE AND SEND LETTER** to compose and send a letter to somebody ○ *I wrote her a long letter.* **5.** *vi* **COMPOSE MATERIAL FOR PUBLICATION** to create books, poems, or newspaper articles for publication, often as part of a job ○ *writes for a newspaper* **6.** *vt* **FILL IN FORM** to fill in the details on a form such as a check, prescription, or other document and, usually, sign it ○ *I had to write 20 checks this morning.* **7.** *vt* **EXPRESS SOMETHING IN WORDS** to express something in a letter, book, or article ○ *He wrote that he would be home on Tuesday.* **8.** *vi* **WORK AS WRITING TOOL** to function as a writing instrument, or function in a particular way ○ *There's something wrong with this pen: it won't write.* **9.** *vti* **USE CURSIVE SCRIPT** to employ a cursive script when setting down words **10.** *vt* **DISPLAY SOMETHING** to reveal or exhibit something clearly ○ *She had glee written all over her face.* **11.** *vt* INSUR same as **underwrite** (sense 3) **12.** *vt* **PREDETERMINE SOMETHING** to ordain or prophesy what will happen in the future (*usually passive*) ○ *It is written in the stars.* **13.** *vt* COMPUT **STORE COMPUTER DATA** to transfer data to a storage medium such as a magnetic or optical disk or tape **14.** *vt* COMPUT **DISPLAY SOMETHING ON SCREEN** to display text or images on a computer monitor [Old English *wrītan* "score, draw, write" < Germanic, "to tear"]

SPELLCHECK See *right*.

ORIGIN The notion underlying ***write*** is of "cutting" or "scratching" (it is related to German *reissen* "to tear"). The earliest form of writing involved cutting marks on hard materials such as stone and wood, and the same word was carried over when the technique of writing moved on to pen and ink.

write away *vt* to send off an order for goods of some kind to a distant supplier ○ *wrote away for new upholstery materials*

write down *vt* **1. RECORD SOMETHING IN WORDS** to record something in writing, usually so that the information is not lost or forgotten ○ *I wrote down her address.* **2. OVERSIMPLIFY SOMETHING FOR UNSOPHISTICATED AUDIENCE** to write something in excessively simplified language for the benefit of an audience considered to be unsophisticated, inexperienced, or unintelligent **3. WRITE DISPARAGINGLY ABOUT SOMEBODY** to write slightingly or disparagingly about somebody **4. REDUCE ENTERED VALUE OF SOMETHING** to reduce the price or value of something, especially the value of an asset as entered in the accounts of a business

write in *v* **1.** *vi* **WRITE TO ORGANIZATION** to send a letter to an organization **2.** *vt* **ADD NAME TO BALLOT** to add somebody's name to a ballot in an election in order to vote for that person **3.** *vt* **WRITE DETAILS IN FORM** to write additional words into a text or document ○ *wrote in all the personal health data required*

write off *vt* **1. DECIDE SOMEBODY OR SOMETHING IS WORTHLESS** to dismiss somebody or something as worthless or unsuccessful and not worth continued attention (*informal*) **2.** *UK* **DAMAGE VEHICLE TOO BADLY TO REPAIR** to damage a vehicle so badly that it is not economical to repair it **3. REDUCE VALUE OF SOMETHING** to reduce the estimated value of an asset for accounting purposes **4. REMOVE BAD DEBT OR VALUELESS ASSET** to remove a debt considered irrecoverable or an asset with no value from the accounts of a business

write out *vt* **1. WRITE SOMETHING IN COMPLETE FORM** to write something in its complete form ○ *write out your* *name* 2. EXPRESS SOMETHING IN WRITING to express something in written form 3. REMOVE SOMEBODY FROM SERIES to remove a regular character from a radio or television series ○ *He's been written out of the show.* **write up** *vt* 1. WRITE SOMETHING FROM EARLIER NOTES to write a report or account of something from notes made earlier 2. WRITE REVIEW OF SOMETHING to write a review of something such as a new play or book 3. UPDATE JOURNAL OR DIARY to bring something such as a journal or log up to date by writing additional entries 4. *US* REPORT SOMEBODY FOR UNLAWFUL ACT to report somebody in writing for violating a law or rule ○ *wrote the motorist up for illegal parking* 5. *US* OVERVALUE ASSETS to overvalue corporate assets

write-down *n* a reduction in the value of an asset as entered in the books of a business

write-in *n* 1. a vote cast in an election by adding somebody's name to the ballot 2. a candidate added to a ballot by a voter

~~**writeing**~~ incorrect spelling of **writing**

~~**writen**~~ incorrect spelling of **written**

write-off *n* 1. REDUCTION IN VALUE a reduction in the estimated value of an asset 2. SOMETHING REDUCED IN VALUE an asset that has had its estimated value reduced 3. AMOUNT OF REDUCTION IN VALUE the monetary amount by which something such as a corporate asset has been reduced in value ○ *The corporation took a $5 million write-off in the second quarter.* 4. *UK* VEHICLE DAMAGED BEYOND REPAIR a vehicle that is so badly damaged that it is not economical to repair it

write-pro·tect·ed *adj* describes computer storage space that cannot be altered or erased

writ·er /rītər/ *n* 1. SOMEBODY WHO WRITES AS PROFESSION somebody who writes books or articles professionally 2. PERSON WHO WROTE DOCUMENT the person who wrote a specific text or document 3. SOMEBODY WHO CAN WRITE somebody who can write, who writes well, or who enjoys writing

writ·er's block *n* an inability on the part of a writer to start a new piece of writing or continue an existing one

writ·er's cramp *n* a muscular spasm that results from a prolonged period of writing and affects the muscles of the forearm, hand, and fingers, causing temporary cramping and pain

write-up *n* 1. a written account of material, especially a published review of a new play, book, or movie 2. *US* a deliberate overvaluation of company assets

writhe /rīth/ *v* (**writhed, writh·ing, writhes**) 1. *vi* TWIST OR SQUIRM to make violent twisting and rolling movements with the body, especially as a result of severe pain ○ *writhing in agony* 2. *vti* MOVE IN TWISTING WAY to move in a twisting squirming way, or cause the body to move in this way 3. *vi* EXPERIENCE STRONG EMOTION to feel a strong emotion, especially embarrassment or shame, and experience internal stress as a result of it ■ *n* WRITHING MOVEMENT a twisting or squirming movement [Old English *wrīþan* < Germanic] —**writh·er** *n*

writ·ing /rīting/ *n* 1. WORDS WRITTEN DOWN words or other symbols such as hieroglyphics written down as a means of communication 2. WRITTEN MATERIAL written material, especially considered as the product of a writer's skill 3. ACTIVITY OF CREATING BOOKS the activity of creating written works, especially as a job 4. same as **handwriting** (sense 2) ■ **writ·ings** *npl* ALL AUTHOR'S WRITTEN OUTPUT all the publications and written work of a writer ○ *Churchill's writings on the war* ◇ **the writing on the wall** an omen of somebody's unpleasant fate or of impending disaster ◇ **see the writing on the wall** to foresee the decline or demise of something or somebody ○ *She should have seen the writing on the wall when her boss suggested a change of career.*

writ·ing desk *n* 1. a desk with a surface for writing on and compartments for holding paper, envelopes, and other writing materials 2. a portable case used for carrying writing materials, often with a hard surface for writing

writ·ing pa·per *n* paper of a quality good enough to write on with ink

Writ·ings /rītingz/ *npl* BIBLE same as **Hagiographa**

writ of e·lec·tion *n US* an order to hold an election, particularly a special election to fill a vacancy, issued by a governor or other controlling authority

writ of er·ror *n US* a writ that directs and empowers an appellate court to review, and if necessary correct, a prior proceeding or ruling of a lower court

writ of pro·hi·bi·tion *n* a writ made by a higher court to a lower court ordering the lower court to stop proceeding in a matter outside its jurisdiction

writ·ten past participle of **write**

Writ·ten Law *n* JUDAISM same as **Torah** (sense 2)

~~**writting**~~ incorrect spelling of **writing**

WRNS, W.R.N.S. *abbr* HIST Women's Royal Naval Service

wrnt. *abbr* LAW warrant

Wroc·law /vráwt slaaf/ city and port in southwestern Poland, on the Oder River. Population: 639,400 (1997).

wrong /rawng/ *adj* 1. INCORRECT not correct or accurate ○ *That's the wrong answer.* 2. MISTAKEN holding an incorrect opinion about a person, thing, or matter ○ *I thought it would be fun, but I was wrong.* 3. NOT MEANT not the intended or desired one ○ *It was sent to the wrong address.* 4. NOT IN NORMAL STATE not in the normal satisfactory state ○ *What's wrong with you today?* 5. NOT CONFORMING TO ACCEPTED STANDARDS not in accordance with law, morality, or with people's sense of what is acceptable behavior ○ *It's wrong to steal.* 6. UNSUITABLE unsuitable, or showing poor judgment on the part of the person who chooses, does, or says it ○ *It's the wrong time of year to be planting seeds.* 7. NOT WORKING not functioning correctly ○ *Something's wrong with the TV.* 8. REVERSED OR INVERTED opposite to the normal, proper, or intended side, way, or direction ○ *This picture is the wrong way up.* ■ *adv* 1. INCORRECTLY incorrectly or in a way that leads to failure or a different result from the one intended ○ *You've spelled that wrong.* 2. IN WRONG DIRECTION in a direction that is different from or opposite to the right or intended direction ■ *n* 1. ACTION NOT CONSIDERED MORAL an action or situation that does not conform to ideas of morality or justice 2. UNACCEPTABLE BEHAVIOR behavior that is morally or socially unacceptable ○ *Children have to be taught the difference between right and wrong.* 3. LAW same as **tort** 4. LAW INFRINGEMENT OF SOMEBODY'S LEGAL RIGHTS an infringement, abridgment, or violation of another party's rights under the law ■ *vt* (**wronged, wrong·ing, wrongs**) 1. TREAT SOMEBODY UNJUSTLY to judge or treat somebody unjustly ○ *He felt he had been wronged.* 2. DISCREDIT SOMEBODY to discredit somebody by saying malicious but untrue things about him or her [Old English *wrange* "wrongful act." The adjective *wrang* probably existed in Old English, but is not found before the 12C] —**wrong·er** *n* —**wrong·ly** *adv* —**wrong·ness** *n* ◇ **get somebody wrong** to misunderstand somebody ◇ **get something wrong** 1. to make a mistake in an answer or calculation 2. to misunderstand something ◇ **go wrong** 1. to go badly or not according to plan 2. to make a mistake 3. to fail to conform to ideas of morality or justice ◇ **in the wrong** 1. at fault for something 2. mistaken ◇ **two wrongs don't make a right** an act of retaliation cannot be justified

wrong·do·ing /ráwng dòo ing/ *n* behavior or an action that fails to conform to standards of law or morality —**wrong·do·er** *n*

wrong-foot *vt* in sports, to cause an opponent to anticipate wrongly the direction in which you are going to move or hit, kick, or pass a ball

wrong·ful /ráwngfəl/ *adj* not fair, just, or legal, but not punishable by criminal law ○ *brought a suit alleging wrongful arrest* —**wrong·ful·ly** *adv* —**wrong·ful·ness** *n*

SYNONYMS See ***unlawful***.

wrong·ful death ac·tion *n US* an action provided by statute or constitution to recover or obtain remedy from a party that is judged to have contributed to or caused the death of another person

wrong-head·ed *adj* 1. completely contrary to reason or good sense ○ *a wrong-headed notion* 2. obstinately sticking to a false belief, opinion, or course of action —**wrong-head·ed·ly** *adv* —**wrong-head·ed·ness** *n*

wrong num·ber *n* an incorrectly dialed telephone number that connects the caller with the wrong person

wrote past tense of **write**

wroth /roth/ *adj* extremely angry (*archaic or literary*) [Old English *wrāþ* < Germanic]

wrought /rawt/ past participle, past tense of **work** (*archaic*) ■ *adj* 1. made in a skillful or decorative way (*often used in combination*) ○ *a delicately wrought ebony screen* 2. describes decorative metalwork shaped by hammering and welding

USAGE ***Wrought*** is an old past tense and past participle not of *wreak* (for which the past tense is *wreaked*) but of *work*: it is the equivalent of modern *worked*. ***Wrought*** survives mainly as an adjective in a few, rather specialized contexts such as *wrought iron*; it is seen also in the set phrase *What hath God wrought* (used by Samuel Morse in the first successful test of the telegraph). *Wrought havoc* is not correct; it should be *wreaked havoc*.

wrought iron

wrought i·ron *n* a highly refined form of iron that is easy to shape but is strong and fairly resistant to rust. Use: decorative metalwork. —**wrought-i·ron** *adj*

wrought-up *adj* tensely nervous, agitated, or excited

WRT *abbr* POL (*used in e-mails or text messages*) 1. with regard to 2. with respect to

wrung past participle, past tense of **wring**

wry /rī/ (**wri·er** or **wry·er, wri·est** or **wry·est**) *adj* 1. AMUSING AND IRONIC combining or expressing a mixture of mild amusement and irony ○ *a wry remark* 2. CHARACTERIZED BY IRONIC ACCEPTANCE characterized by or showing a slightly ironic acceptance of something that is not particularly pleasant or desirable ○ *a wry grin* 3. TWISTED out of shape or twisted to one side [Old English *wrīgian* "to turn" < Indo-European] —**wry·ly** *adv* —**wry·ness** *n*

wry·bill /rī bìl/ *n* a shorebird of the plover family whose beak is bent to one side allowing it to search for food beneath pebbles. Native to: New Zealand. Latin name: *Anarhynchus frontalis.*

wry·neck /rī nèk/ *n* 1. a bird of the woodpecker family that has mottled gray-brown feathers and a short sharp beak, eats insects and lives in holes, but does not drill into trees. Native to: Europe, Asia. Latin name: *Jynx torquilla* or *Jynx ruficollis.* 2. MED same as **torticollis**

WS *abbr* ONLINE Samoa (*used in Internet addresses*) See table at **domain name**

WSW *abbr* COMPASS west-southwest

wt. *abbr* MEASURE weight

WTC *abbr* World Trade Center

WTO *abbr* COMM World Trade Organization

Wu /woo/ *n* a group of Chinese dialects spoken mainly in the Jiangsu and Zhejiang provinces of China, the colloquial language of Shanghai. Native speakers: 90 million. [Early 20C. < Chinese *wú*] —**Wu** *adj*

Wu·han /wòo haán/ capital city of Hubei Province, central China. Population: 4,250,000 (1995).

wul·fen·ite /wŏŏlfə nīt/ *n* an orange, yellow, or brown mineral consisting of lead molybdate. Use: source of molybdenum. [Mid-19C. After F. X. von *Wulfen* (1728–1805), Austrian scientist]

wun·der·kind /vŏŏndər kìnd, wúndər-/ (*plural* **-kind·er** /-kìndər/ or **-kinds**) *n* **1.** somebody who is extremely successful at a young age **2.** a child who is unusually talented at something [Late 19C. < German, "wonder child"]

Wup·per·tal /vŏŏppər taal/ city in North Rhine-Westphalia State, northwestern Germany. It is situated about 20 mi./32 km east of Düsseldorf. Population: 383,776 (1997).

Wurl·itz·er /wúrlitsər/ *tdmk* **1.** a trademark for an electric organ **2.** a trademark for a jukebox

wurst /wurst, woorst/ *n* **1.** *US* sausage of any kind **2.** *UK* a sausage made in Germany and Austria, especially a large sausage intended to be sliced and eaten cold [Mid-19C. < German *Wurst* "sausage" < Indo-European, "confuse"]

Würz·burg /vúrts burg, vŭrts bòork/ city in northeastern Bavaria State, southern Germany. Population: 127,946 (1997).

wu·shu /wòo shòo/, **wu shu** *n* Chinese martial arts considered collectively [Late 20C. < Chinese *wǔ shù* "military technique"]

wuss /wuss/ *n* an offensive term that deliberately insults somebody regarded as weak or ineffectual (*slang insult*) [Late 20C. Origin ?] —**wuss·y** *adj*

wuth·er·ing /wúthəring/ *adj N England* describes a wind that blows strongly and makes a loud roaring sound [Late 18C. < obsolete *wuther* "to rush"]

W. Va., **WV** *abbr* West Virginia

WWF *abbr* **1.** ENVIRON World Wide Fund for Nature **2.** WRESTLING World Wrestling Federation

WWI *abbr* HIST World War One

WWII *abbr* HIST World War Two

WWW *abbr* ONLINE World Wide Web

Wy·an·dot /wī́ ən dòt/ (*plural same* or **-dots**), **Wy·an·dotte** (*plural same* or **-dottes**) *n* a member of an Iroquois people who lived west of Lake Huron, and now live mainly in Oklahoma [Mid-18C. Via French *Ouendat* < Huron *Wendat*]

Wy·an·dotte /wī́ ən dòt/ *n* **1.** a bird belonging to a North American medium-sized breed of domestic chicken **2.** PEOPLES another spelling of **Wyandot** [Late 19C. Variant of WYANDOT]

Wy·att /wī́ ət/, **Sir Thomas** (1503–42) English courtier and poet. His service at Henry VIII's court included diplomatic missions. His poems, published in 1557, introduced Italian verse forms into England.

> "Now is this song both sung and past: / My lute, be still, for I have done."
> [Sir Thomas Wyatt, "My Lute Awake!"; 1542?]

wych elm /wích èlm/, **witch elm** *n* an elm with prominently tipped leaves and clusters of winged green fruit. Latin name: *Ulmus glabra*. [Old English *wice* < Indo-European, "bend, be pliant"]

Wych·er·ley /wíchərlee/, **William** (1640?–1716) English playwright. His comedies include *The Country Wife* (1675) and *The Plain Dealer* (1677).

> "A man without money needs no more fear a crowd of lawyers than a crowd of pick-pockets."
> [William Wycherley, *The Plain Dealer*; 1677]

Wy·cliffe /wíklif/, **Wy·clif**, **Wi·cliff**, **John** (1330?–84) English philosopher and religious reformer. He supervised the first English translation of the Bible, published posthumously in 1388. He rejected the doctrine of transubstantiation and denounced abuses in the Roman Catholic Church, anticipating the Protestant Reformation. —**Wy·cliff·ite** *n, adj*

wye /wī/ *n* **1.** the letter "Y" **2.** something shaped like the letter "Y" [Mid-19C. Probably representing the letter's pronunciation]

Wye /wī/ river of southwestern Wales and western England. It flows into the estuary of the Severn River. Length: 130 mi./209 km.

Andrew Wyeth (right)

Wy·eth /wī́ əth/, **Andrew** (*b.* 1917) US artist. The son of N. C. Wyeth, he typically depicted rural scenes with a strong emotional charge in paintings such as *Christina's World* (1948). Full name **Wyeth, Andrew Newell**

Wy·eth, N. C. (1882–1945) US artist. A leading illustrator and muralist, he produced illustrations for many children's classics, notably *Treasure Island* (1924). Full name **Wyeth, Newell Convers**

Wy·ler /wílər/, **William** (1902–81) German-born US movie director. His Academy Award-winning movies include *Mrs. Miniver* (1942) and *Ben-Hur* (1959).

Wy·lie /wílee/, **Elinor** (1885–1928) US writer. She achieved success with both poetry and fiction, especially *The Orphan Angel* (1926), a fantasy on the life of the poet Shelley. Full name **Wylie, Elinor Morton**

wyn *n* another spelling of **wynn**

wynd /wīnd/ *n N England* a narrow lane in a town [15C. Probably < WIND²]

wynn /win/, **wyn**, **wen** /wen/ *n* a runic letter used in Old and early Middle English, representing a "w" sound [Old English *wyn* "joy." Runes were named using words beginning with their sound]

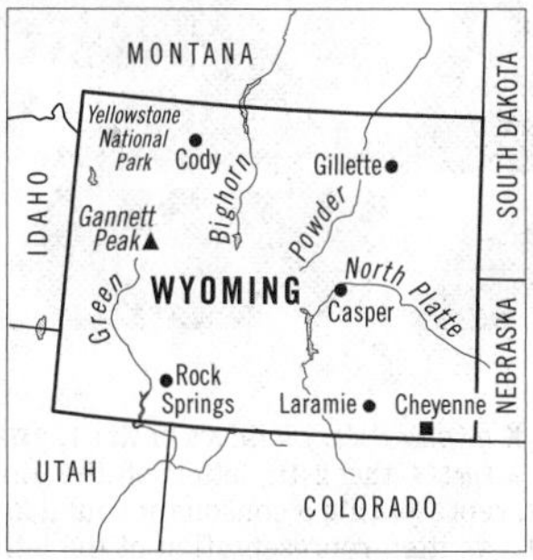

Wyoming

Wy·o·ming /wī ṓming/ state in the northwestern United States, bordered by Montana, South Dakota, Nebraska, Colorado, Utah, and Idaho. Capital: Cheyenne. Population: 498,703 (2002 estimate). Area: 97,818 sq. mi./253,347 sq. km. —**Wy·o·ming·ite** *n*

WYSIWYG /wízzee wìg/ *adj* describes a technology that enables the user to see an image of text and graphics on a computer display exactly as it will appear when printed [Late 20C. Acronym < *what you see is what you get*]

Wythe /with/, **George** (1726–1806) American patriot and lawyer. Representing Virginia, he was a signatory of the Declaration of Independence (1776). His greatest influence came through his work training lawyers at the College of William and Mary (1779–90).

wyvern

wy·vern /wī́vərn/, **wi·vern** *n* in heraldry, a mythical being depicted as having two legs, a dragon's head, wings, and a long tail [Late 16th C. Via Old French *wivre* < Latin *vipera* "snake"]

Xx

X[1] /eks/, **X** *n* (*plural* **X's**; *plural* **X's** or **Xs**) **1. 24TH LETTER OF ENGLISH ALPHABET** the 24th letter of the English alphabet, representing a consonant sound **2. LETTER "X" WRITTEN** a written representation of the letter "x" **3. "X" INDICATING SOMETHING** an x-shaped mark used for indicating a vote, showing that something is incorrect, representing a kiss, or representing a signature by somebody who cannot write **4. ROMAN NUMERAL** the Roman numeral for 10 ■ *vt* (**x-ed** or **x'ed, x-ing** or **x'ing, x-es** or **x's; X-ed** or **X'ed, X-ing** or **X'ing, X-es** or **X'es**) **MARK SOMETHING WITH "X"** to mark or sign something with an "x"

x out, X out *vt US* to cross something out

x[2] *symbol* **1. SYMBOL USED TO REPRESENT UNKNOWN** a letter "x" or an "x"-shaped mark used to represent something or somebody unknown or unspecified **2.** by (*used in dimensions*) **3.** TELECOM, BUSINESS extension **4.** MATH multiplied by **5.** MATH an algebraic variable **6.** MATH a Cartesian coordinate along the x-axis **7.** CARDS a card that is not an honor **8.** COMM ex

X[1] /eks/ (*plural* **X's** or **Xs**) *n* **1.** something shaped like a letter "X" **2.** a movie rating used until 1990 in the United States to indicate that a movie could not be shown publicly to anyone under the age of 17. Now called **NC-17**

X[2] *symbol* PHYS, ELECTRONICS reactance

Xan·a·du /zánnə doo/ (*plural* **-dus**) *n* a beautiful idyllic place [Mid-20C. After the residence of KUBLAI KHAN in Samuel Taylor Coleridge's poem *Kubla Khan* (1816)]

xanth- *prefix* same as **xantho-** (*used before vowels*)

xan·than gum /zánthən-/ *n* a natural gum with a high molecular weight. Source: bacterial fermentation of glucose. Use: food stabilizer. [Mid-20C. < modern Latin *Xanthomonas*, a bacterium < Greek *xanthos* "yellow" + late Latin *monas* (stem *monad-*): see MONAD)]

xan·thate /zán thàyt/ *n* a salt or ester of xanthic acid. Use: extraction of metals, manufacture of rayon. [Mid-19C. < XANTHIC ACID]

xan·thene /zán theen/ *n* a yellow crystalline compound. Use: fungicide, basis of some organic dyes. Formula: $CH_2(C_6H_4)_2O$.

xan·thic ac·id /zànthik-/ *n* an unstable organic sulfur-containing acid. Formula: ROC(S)SH where R is an organic group.

xan·thine /zán theen, -thin/ *n* **1.** a yellow-white crystalline compound, the precursor of uric acid, found in blood, urine, and some plants. Formula: $C_5H_4N_4O_2$. **2.** a derivative of xanthine, e.g., caffeine, theophylline, or theobromine

xantho- *prefix* **1.** yellow ○ *xanthophyll* **2.** xanthic acid ○ *xanthate* [< Greek *xanthos* "yellow"]

xan·tho·ma /zan thṓmə/ (*plural* **-mas** or **-ma·ta** /-mətə/) *n* a yellow lipid-filled lesion on the skin, especially on the eyelids, that indicates a disorder of fat metabolism —**xan·thom·a·tous** /zan thómmətəss/ *adj*

xan·tho·ma·to·sis /zànthəmə tṓssiss/ *n* the presence of multiple xanthomas on the skin

xan·thone /zán thōn/ *n* a colorless crystalline compound. Use: basis of some yellow dyes. Formula: $C_{13}H_8O_2$.

xan·tho·phyll /zánthə fil/ *n* a yellow or brown oxygenated carotenoid pigment that colors autumn leaves —**xan·tho·phyl·lic** /zànthə fíllik/ *adj*

Xan·thus /zánthəss/ ancient capital city of Lycia in southern Asia Minor, in present-day southwestern Turkey. It was destroyed by the Persians in 546 B.C. and again by the Romans in 42 B.C. The remains of the city and numerous artworks were discovered by Sir Charles Fellows in 1838. —**Xan·th·i·an** *n, adj*

Xa·vi·er /záyvee ər, záv-/, **St. Francis** (1506–52) Spanish missionary. He helped St. Ignatius Loyola to found the Society of Jesus and established missions in India, Japan, and parts of Southeast Asia. Known as **the Apostle of the Indies**

x-ax·is *n* **1.** the horizontal axis in a two-dimensional coordinate system **2.** an axis in the three-dimensional Cartesian coordinate system, conventionally the horizontal one

XC, X-C *abbr* SPORTS cross-country

X-cer·tif·i·cate *adj UK* same as **X-rated** (sense 2)

X-chro·mo·some *n* a chromosome present in both sexes that plays a role in determining the sex of an individual. Female mammals carry two X chromosomes and males carry one.

x-co·or·di·nate *n* the position of a point in space with reference to the x-axis in the Cartesian coordinate system, defined in conjunction with the y- and z-coordinates

XD *abbr* FIN ex dividend

x-div. *abbr* FIN ex dividend

Xe *symbol* CHEM ELEM xenon

xe·bec /zée bèk/, **ze·bec** *n* a small Mediterranean ship with three masts rigged with both square and triangular sails [Mid-18C. Via French *chebec* < Arabic *šabbāk*]

xen- *prefix* same as **xeno-** (*used before vowels*)

Xe·na·kis /zə naákiss/, **Iannis** (1922–2001) Romanian-born Greek composer. Originally an engineer and architect, he used mathematical ideas in his "stochastic music."

xe·ni·a /zéenee ə, zéenyə/ *n* the effect of genes carried by pollen on the food storage tissue (**endosperm**) of the pollinated seed [Late 19C. Via modern Latin < Greek, "hospitality" < *xenos* "stranger, foreigner"]

xeno- *prefix* foreign, strange, different ○ *xenophile* ○ *xenolith* [Via modern Latin < Greek *xenos* "stranger, foreigner"]

xen·o·bi·ot·ic /zènnə bī óttik, zéenə-/ *adj* describes a chemical compound such as a drug or pesticide that is foreign to the body of a living organism —**xen·o·bi·ot·ic** *n*

xen·o·cryst /zénnə krìst, zéenə-/ *n* a crystal in an igneous rock introduced from an external source and not crystallized from the magma [Late 19C. < XENO- + CRYSTAL]

xen·o·di·ag·no·sis /zènnō dī əg nṓssiss, zéenō-/ (*plural* **-no·ses** /-nṓ séez/) *n* the diagnosis of a parasitic infection by allowing a noninfected disease-carrying organism such as a mosquito to feed on an infected person's blood and then examining the organism for infection —**xen·o·di·ag·nos·tic** /-dī əg nóstik/ *adj*

xen·o·ge·ne·ic /zènnəjə née ik, -náy ik, zéenə-/ *adj* coming from or derived from a different species [Mid-20C. After SYNGENEIC]

xen·o·gen·e·sis /zènnə jénnəssiss, zéenə-/ *n* **1.** the supposed production of offspring completely different from both parents **2.** the existence in the life cycle of an organism of two or more alternating forms or reproductive modes, e.g., sexual and asexual cycles —**xen·o·ge·net·ic** /zènnə jə néttik, zéenə-/ *adj*

xen·o·graft /zénnə gràft, zéenə-/ *n* MED same as **heterograft**

xen·o·lith /zénnə lìth, zéenə-/ *n* a fragment of rock that is different in origin from the igneous rock in which it occurs —**xen·o·lith·ic** /zènnə líthik, zéenə-/ *adj*

xe·non /zée nòn/ *n* a heavy colorless odorless gaseous element that is relatively inert. Source: in minute quantities in air. Use: electronic tubes, specialized lamps. Symbol **Xe**. See table at **element** [Late 19C. < Greek *xenon*, neuter of *xenos* "stranger, foreigner"]

Xe·noph·a·nes /zə nóffə néez/ (*fl* late 6th–early 5th centuries B.C.) Greek philosopher and poet. He ridiculed the polytheistic beliefs of earlier Greek poets and is considered the founder of the Eleatic school of philosophy.

> "But if cattle and horses or lions had hands …horses would draw the forms of the gods like horses, and cattle like cattle."
> [Xenophanes. Quoted in *The Presocratic Philosophers*, G. S. Kirk, J. E. Raven, and M. Schofield; 1983]

xen·o·phile /zénnə fīl, zéenə-/ *n* somebody who likes the people, customs, and culture of other countries, or things from abroad —**xen·o·phil·i·a** /zènnə fíllee ə, zéenə-/ *n* —**xe·noph·i·lous** /ze nóffələss, zə-/ *adj*

xen·o·pho·bi·a /zènnə fṓbee ə, zéenə-/ *n* an intense fear or dislike of foreign people, their customs and culture, or foreign things —**xe·no·phobe** /zénnə fōb, zéenə-/ *n* —**xen·o·pho·bic** *adj*

Xen·o·phon /zénnəfən, -fòn/ (430?–355? B.C.) Greek historian and soldier. A pupil of Socrates, he participated in the attack on Persia by Cyrus the Younger (401 B.C.) and led a 10,000-strong Greek force back to safety on the Black Sea, an episode he described in his *Anabasis*.

xe·no·pus /zénnəpəss/ (*plural same* or **-pi** /-pī/) *n* a water frog. Native to: southern Africa. Genus: *Xenopus*. [Late 19C. < modern Latin < Greek *xeno-* "stranger, foreigner" + *pous* "foot"]

xe·no·trans·plant *vt* /zènnə transs plánt, zéenə-/ (**-plant·ed, -plant·ing, -plants**) **TRANSPLANT SOMETHING TO DIFFERENT SPECIES** to transfer a tissue or organ between members of different species ■ *n* /zènnə tránss plànt, zéenə-/ **1. OPERATION TRANSPLANTING TISSUE TO DIFFERENT SPECIES** a surgical operation in which a tissue or organ is transferred between members of different species **2. SOMETHING TRANSPLANTED TO DIFFERENT SPECIES** a tissue or organ that is transferred between members of different species —**xe·no·trans·plan·ta·tion** /zènnə tránss plan táysh'n, zéenə-/ *n*

xer- *prefix* same as **xero-** (*used before vowels*)

xer·ic /zérrik, zír-/ *adj* relating to or living in a dry habitat —**xer·i·cal·ly** *adv*

Xe·ri·scape /zéerə skàyp, zérrə-/ *tdmk US* a trademark for a method of landscaping that emphasizes water conservation in its use of drought-resistant plants

xero- *prefix* dry, dryness ○ *xerothermic* [< Greek *xēros* "dry"]

xer·o·der·ma /zéerō dúrmə/, **xe·ro·der·mi·a** /-dúrmee ə/ *n* a mild form of the hereditary disorder ichthyosis, marked by discolored dry hard scaly skin —**xe·ro·der·mat·ic** /-dur máttik/ *adj* —**xe·ro·der·ma·tous** *adj*

xer·o·der·ma pig·men·to·sum /-pìgmən tṓssəm/ *n* a rare and often fatal hereditary condition beginning in infancy in which the skin and eyes are damaged by sunlight. It results in freckles, discolored patches, and skin cancers.

xe·ro·der·mi·a *n* MED same as **xeroderma**

xe·rog·ra·phy /zi róggrəfee/ *n* a method of photocopying in which an image is formed by attracting a resinous powder to an electrostatically charged plate, and is then transferred to paper and fixed by heating —**xe·rog·ra·pher** *n* —**xe·ro·graph·ic** /zeérə gráffik/ *adj* —**xe·ro·graph·i·cal·ly** *adv*

xe·ro·mor·phic /zeérə máwrfik/ *adj* describes plants or plant parts that are adapted for survival in dry conditions, e.g., spiny leaves that reduce surface area and therefore water loss

xe·roph·i·lous /zi róffələss/ *adj* thriving in or adapted for a hot dry habitat —**xe·ro·phile** /zeérə fīl/ *n* —**xe·roph·i·ly** *n*

xer·oph·thal·mi·a /zeèrəf thálmee ə/ *n* an eye disease caused by vitamin A deficiency, marked by dryness and ulceration of the conjunctiva and cornea. If untreated, it may cause blindness. —**xer·oph·thal·mic** *adj*

xer·o·phyte /zeérə fīt/ *n* a plant that is adapted for a dry habitat, e.g., a cactus —**xer·o·phyt·ic** /zeérə fíttik/ *adj* —**xer·o·phyt·i·cal·ly** *adv* —**xe·ro·phyt·ism** *n*

xe·ro·ra·di·og·ra·phy /zeérə ràydee óggrəfee/ *n* a high-definition X-ray photography in which the image is first made on a specially coated metal plate and then transferred to paper. It is often used in screening for breast cancer.

xe·ro·sis /zi róssiss/ *n* excessive dryness of the skin and mucous membranes of the eye, caused by thickening of the membranes —**xe·rot·ic** /zi róttik/ *adj*

xe·ros·to·mi·a /zeérə stómee ə/ *n* a lack of saliva in the mouth, caused by disease, poisoning, or some drugs

xe·ro·ther·mic /zeérə thúrmik/ *adj* very hot and having little rainfall ○ *a xerothermic climate*

Xer·ox /zeér ròks/ *tdmk* a trademark for a photocopying process that uses xerography

Xer·xes I /zúrk seèz/ (519?–465 B.C.) **king of Persia** As king (486–465 B.C.), he led a huge army into Greece (480 B.C.), defeating the Greeks at Thermopylae and burning Athens, but his fleet was defeated at Salamis. He was assassinated by his palace guard. Known as **Xerxes the Great**

> "I am moved to pity, when I think of the brevity of human life, seeing that of all this host of men not one will still be alive in a hundred years' time."
> [Xerxes I, *Remark*; 480? B.C.]

x-height *n* the height of the lowercase letter "x" in a typeface, used as a measure of the height of the main body of all lowercase letters in that typeface

Xho·sa /kó saa, kózə/ (*plural same* or **-sas**), **Xo·sa** *n* **1.** a member of a Bantu-speaking people of South Africa **2.** the Bantu language of the Xhosa people. Native speakers: 7 million. [Early 19C. < Nguni] —**Xho·sa** *adj*

xi /zī, ksī/ (*plural* **xis**) *n* the 14th letter of the Greek alphabet, represented in the English alphabet as "x." See table at **alphabet**

Xia·men /shyaá mén/ city and seaport on Xiamen Island in Fujian Province, southeastern China. It lies in the Taiwan Strait, west of Taiwan. Population: 357,290 (1991).

Xi'an /shee aán/ capital city of Shaanxi Province in eastern China. One of China's oldest cities, it is home to some major archaeological sites, including one found to contain a vast army of life-size soldiers made of terra cotta, known as "The Terra cotta Warriors." Population: 2,970,000 (1995).

Xiang·tan /shyaáng taán/ city in southern China, in Hunan Province. It is an inland port and industrial center on the Xiang River. Population: 525,448 (1991).

xi hy·per·on *n* a neutral or negatively charged elementary particle present in cosmic rays and in high-energy collisions in particle accelerators

Xi Jiang /sheé jyaáng/ river in southern China that rises in Yunnan Province and flows east to the South China Sea. Length: 1,300 mi./2,100 km.

Xin·gu /sheéng goó/ river in northwestern Brazil. It flows north through the states of Mato Grosso and Pará and empties into the Amazon delta. Length: 1,230 mi./1,980 km.

Xi·ning /sheé níng/ capital city of Qinghai Province, in western China, northeast of Lanzhou. Population: 777,983 (1991).

Xin·jiang Uy·gur /shìn jyaáng weégər/ autonomous region in northwestern China. With one sixth of China's land, it is the country's largest region. Capital: Urumqi. Population: 16,890,000 (1997). Area: 635,833 sq. mi./1,646,800 sq. km.

xi par·ti·cle *n* PHYS same as **xi hyperon**

xiph·i·ster·num /zìffi stúrnəm/ (*plural* **-na** /-nə/) *n* the third and lowest segment of the breastbone (**sternum**) in humans. It consists of a flat plate of cartilage that gradually changes into bone during life.

xiph·oid /zí fòyd/ *adj* **1.** shaped like a sword **2.** relating to the xiphisternum ■ *n* ANAT same as **xiphisternum**

xiph·oid proc·ess *n* ANAT same as **xiphisternum**

Xi·zang /sheé dzaáng/ Chinese name for **Tibet**

XL *abbr* extra large (*clothing size*)

X·mas /krísməss, éksməss/ *n* CHR, CALENDAR same as **Christmas** (*informal*) [Mid-16C. *X* represents the Greek letter *chi*, in *Khristos* "Christ"]

XML *n* a programming language designed for web documents that allows for the creation of customized tags for individual information fields. Full form **Extensible Markup Language**

X·mo·dem /éks mō dem/ *n* a file transfer protocol for asynchronous communications in which data is sent in 128-byte blocks

Xn. *abbr* CHR Christian

Xnty. *abbr* CHR Christianity

xo·a·non /zó ə nòn/ (*plural* **-a·na** /-ənə/) *n* an image of a god that has been carved out of wood [Early 18C. < Greek, "carved statue"]

Xo·chi·mil·co /sòchee meélkō/ city in south central Mexico. It is a suburb of Mexico City and is famous for its precolonial canals and floating gardens. Population: 356,833 (2000).

Xo·sa *n, adj* PEOPLES, LANG another spelling of **Xhosa**

X-ra·di·a·tion *n* **1.** exposure to or medical treatment by X-rays **2.** radiation in the form of X-rays

X-rat·ed *adj* **1.** containing explicit sex scenes or descriptions of sex (*informal*) **2.** formerly used to describe a movie not allowed to be viewed by people under the age of 17, usually because of its sexual or violent content

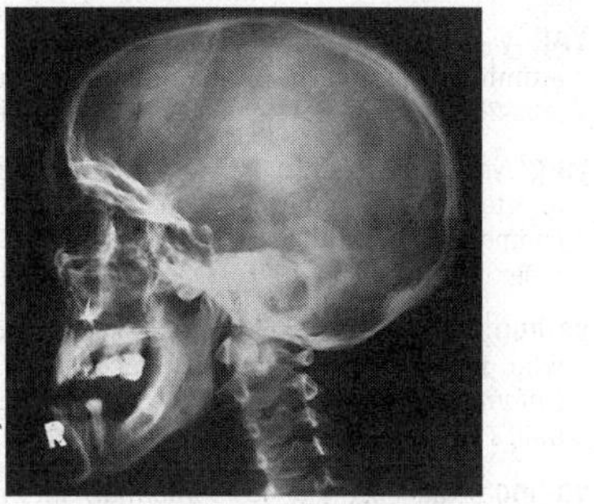

X-ray: image of a human skull

X-ray, X ray, x-ray, x ray *n* **1.** ELECTROMAGNETIC RADIATION a high-energy electromagnetic radiation that can penetrate solids and ionize gas. It has a wavelength between 0.01 and 10 nanometers, which is between gamma rays and ultraviolet light. **2.** PHOTOGRAPHIC IMAGE USING X-RAYS an image produced on photographic film by X-rays passing through objects or parts of the body, often used in medicine and science as a diagnostic tool **3.** COMMUNICATION CODE WORD FOR LETTER "X" a code word for the letter "X," used in international radio communications ■ *vt* (**X-rayed, X-ray·ing, X-rays**) **1.** PHOTOGRAPH SOMETHING USING X-RAYS to expose something such as a part of the body to X-rays in order to obtain a photographic image of it **2.** EXAMINE SOMETHING WITH X-RAYS to examine something, e.g., baggage or freight, using X-rays [Late 19C. Translation of German *X-Strahl*, *X* signifying "unknown"]

X-ray as·tron·o·my *n* the branch of astronomy in which the properties of astronomical objects are determined using the X-rays they emit

X-ray crys·tal·log·ra·phy *n* the study of crystal structures using the diffraction patterns produced by scattered X-rays

X-ray dif·frac·tion *n* the diffraction of X-rays produced by the atoms within a crystal, used to determine information about the crystal's structure

X-ray star, X-ray source *n* an astronomical object that emits X-rays in addition to other types of radiation

X-ray ther·a·py *n* the medical application of X-rays in treating illnesses such as cancer

X-ray tube *n* a vacuum tube in which a stream of high-energy electrons is made to strike a metal target to produce X-rays

XS *abbr* extra small (*clothing size*)

Xt. *abbr* CHR Christ

Xtian. *abbr* CHR Christian

Xty. *abbr* CHR Christianity

xu /soo/ (*plural same*) *n* a subunit of Vietnamese currency. See table at **currency** [Mid-20C. Via Vietnamese < French *sou* (see SOU)]

Xu·zhou another spelling of **Suzhou**

xyl- *prefix* same as **xylo-** (*used before vowels*)

xy·lan /zī làn, zīlən/ *n* a polysaccharide (**pentosan**) found in plant cell walls and woody tissue

xy·lem /zīləm/ *n* the woody supportive plant tissue that carries water and dissolved minerals from the roots through the stem and leaves [Late 19C. Via German < Greek *xulon* "wood"]

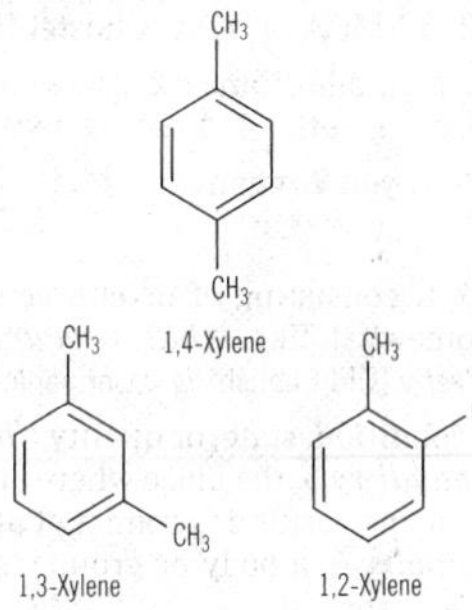

xylene

xy·lene /zī leèn/ *n* a flammable volatile colorless liquid hydrocarbon in three forms. Source: petroleum, natural gas, coal tar. Use: solvents, manufacture of aviation fuel, resins, and dyes. Formula: C_8H_{10}.

xy·li·dine /zīlə deèn, zíllə-, zīlədin, zíllədin/ *n* a toxic amine in six forms derived from xylene. Use: manufacture of dyes, organic synthesis. Formula: $C_8H_{11}N$.

xylo- *prefix* **1.** wood ○ *xylograph* **2.** xylene ○ *xylidine* [< Greek *xulon* "wood"]

xy·log·e·nous /zī lójjənəss/ *adj* adapted to or living in or on wood

xy·lo·graph /zīlə gràf/ *n* **1.** WOOD ENGRAVING an engraving made on wood **2.** PRINT FROM WOOD ENGRAVING a print made from an engraving made on wood ■ *vt* (**-graphed, -graph·ing, -graphs**) MAKE XYLOGRAPH to take a print from an engraving made on wood —**xy·log·ra·pher** /zī lóggrəfər/ *n* —**xy·lo·graph·ic** /zīlə gráffik/ *adj* —**xy·lo·graph·i·cal** *adj* —**xy·lo·graph·i·cal·ly** *adv* —**xy·log·ra·phy** /zī lóggrəfee/ *n*

xy·loid /zī lòyd/ *adj* relating to or resembling wood

xy·lol /zī làwl, -lòl/ *n* CHEM same as **xylene**

xy·loph·a·gous /zī lóffəgəss/ *adj* feeding on or living in wood —**xy·lo·phage** /zīlə fàyj/ *n*

xy·lo·phone /zīlə fōn/ *n* a musical instrument with a row of wooden bars of different lengths that are laid out like a keyboard and produce a tone when struck with a mallet —**xy·lo·phon·ist** *n*

xy·lose /zī lōss/ *n* a sugar with five carbon atoms in each molecule, found in the cell walls of many plants. As it cannot be broken down in humans, it does not increase blood sugar levels, so is used in sugar-free foods for people with diabetes or a need to control their weight. Formula: $C_5H_{10}O_5$.

xys·tus /zístəss/ (*plural* **-tus·es**), **xyst** /zist/ *n* **1.** in ancient Greece, a long walkway with a roof supported by pillars, used for athletics **2.** in ancient Rome, a covered or open path in a garden, lined with trees or pillars [Mid-17C. Via Latin < Greek *xustos* "covered colonnade," literally "smooth" (from its polished floor) < *xuein* "to scrape"]

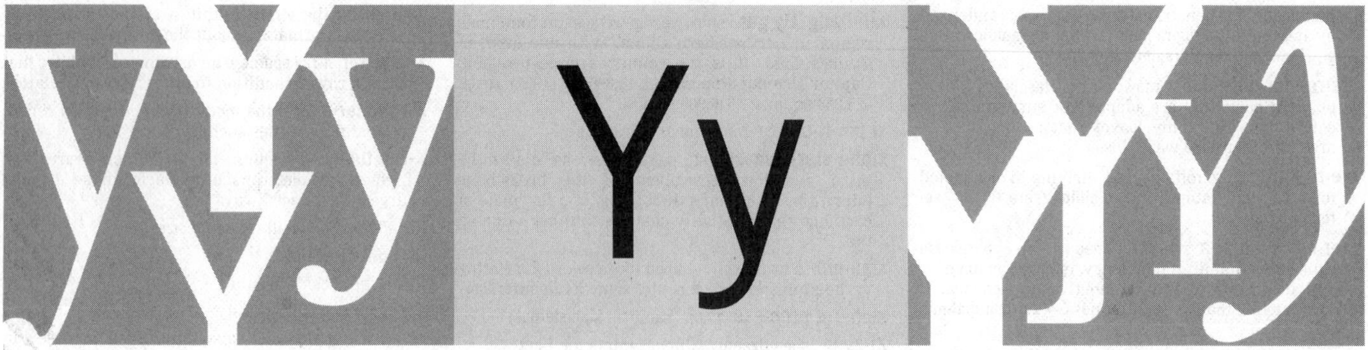

y[1] /wī/ (*plural* **y's**), **Y** (*plural* **Y's** or **Ys**) *n* **1.** the 25th letter of the English alphabet, representing a consonant sound or sometimes a vowel **2.** a written representation of the letter "y"

y[2] *symbol* **1.** MATH an algebraic variable **2.** MATH a Cartesian coordinate along the y-axis **3.** MATH y-axis **4.** MEASURE yocto-

y[3] *abbr* NAVY yeoman

Y[1] /wī/ (*plural* **Y's** or **Ys**) *n* **1.** something shaped like a letter "Y" **2.** a YMCA or YWCA hostel (*informal*)

Y[2] *symbol* **1.** ELEC admittance **2.** MATH an unknown factor **3.** MEASURE yotta- **4.** CHEM ELEM yttrium

Y[3] *abbr* MONEY **1.** yen **2.** yuan

y. *abbr* year

-y[1], **-ey** *suffix* **1.** consisting of or characterized by ○ *muddy* **2.** somewhat, like ○ *chilly* ○ *wintry* **3.** tending toward ○ *sleepy* [Old English *-ig* < Germanic]

-y[2] *suffix* **1.** a condition, state, or quality ○ *infamy* **2.** an activity ○ *chandlery* **3.** the place where an activity is carried on, or the result or product of an activity ○ *colliery* ○ *laundry* **4.** a body or group ○ *soldiery* [Via Old French *-ie* < Latin *-ia*]

-y[3] *suffix* same as **-ie**

Y2K *n* used to refer to the year 2000, especially with regard to the millennium bug and its anticipated damaging effects on software ○ *Y2K-compliant software* [Abbreviation]

YA *abbr* young adult

yaar /yaar/ *n S Asia* used as a familiar or affectionate form of address, especially among young people (*informal*) [Via Hindi < Arabic *yar*]

yab·ber /yábbər/ *UK* (*informal*) *vti* (**-bered, -ber·ing, -bers**) to talk a lot or say something rapidly, often so that it is incomprehensible ■ *n* rapid speech that is often incomprehensible [Mid-19C. < an Aboriginal language]

YAC /yak/ *abbr* GENETICS, BIOTECH yeast artificial chromosome

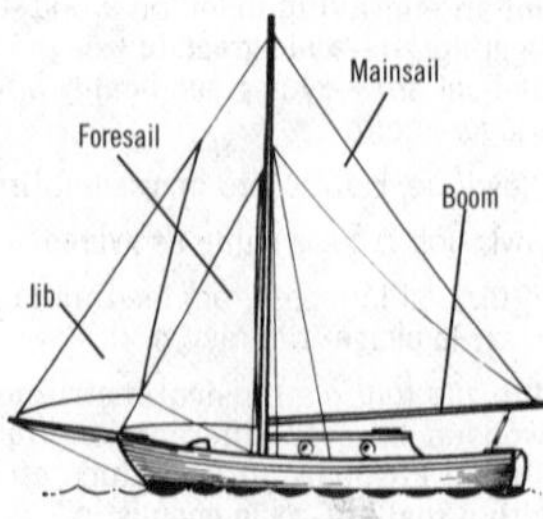

yacht

yacht /yot/ *n* **1.** SAILBOAT a sailboat, often one that has living quarters and is used for cruising or racing **2.** MOTORBOAT FOR CRUISING a large motorboat used for cruising ■ *vi* (**yacht·ed, yacht·ing, yachts**) SAIL IN YACHT to sail in a yacht for leisure or sport [Mid-16C. < obsolete Dutch *jaghte*, shortening of *jaghtschip* "chasing ship"]

yacht·ie /yóttee/ *n* somebody who owns a yacht or enjoys sailing, cruising, or racing in yachts (*informal*)

yacht·ing /yótting/ *n* the sport or pastime of sailing a yacht

yachts·man /yótsmən/ (*plural* **-men** /-mən/) *n* somebody, especially a man, who owns or sails a yacht —**yachts·man·ship** *n*

yachts·per·son /yóts pùrss'n/ (*plural* **-peo·ple** /-peep'l/ or **-per·sons**) *n* somebody who owns or sails a yacht

yachts·wom·an /yóts wòommən/ (*plural* **-wom·en** /-wìmmin/) *n* a woman who owns or sails a yacht

yack *vi, n* ZOOL another spelling of **yak**[2] (*informal*)

yack·e·ty-yak /yàkkətee yák/ *v* (**yack·e·ty-yakked, yack·e·ty-yak·king, yack·e·ty-yaks**), *n* same as **yak**[2] (*informal*) [Mid-20C. An imitation of the sound]

yad·da yad·da yad·da /yaádə yaádə yaádə/, **ya·da ya·da ya·da** *US* (*slang*) *n* boring trite superficial unending talk ○ *just a lot of yadda yadda yadda on the talk shows tonight* ■ *interj* used in speaking as a filler for unstated material or to indicate boredom or distaste for things others are saying or have said ○ *We chewed it over forever ... yadda yadda yadda, nothing important.* [Late 20C. Origin ?]

Yad·kin /yádkin/ river in central North Carolina. It joins the Uharie to form the Pee Dee River, flows through South Carolina, and empties into the Atlantic Ocean. Length: 202 mi./325 km.

YAG /yag/ *n* a synthetic mineral containing yttrium, aluminum, and garnet. Use: infrared lasers, gems. [Mid-20C. Acronym < *yttrium, aluminum, garnet*]

ya·gi /yaágee, yággee/ (*plural* **-gis**) *n* a directional radio or television antenna consisting of several components arranged in line [Mid-20C. After Hidetsugu *Yagi* (1886–1976), Japanese electrical engineer]

ya·hoo[1] /yaá hòo, yaa hóo/ (*plural* **-hoos**) *n* somebody who is regarded as unruly, crude, or brutish (*informal insult*) [Early 18C. After the *Yahoos* in Jonathan Swift's *Gulliver's Travels* (1726)] —**ya·hoo·ism** *n*

ya·hoo[2] /yaá hòo, yaa hóo/ (*informal*) *interj* used to express enthusiasm, approval, or celebration ○ *Yahoo! Let's go!* ■ *n* (*plural* **-hoos**) a cry of enthusiasm, approval, or celebration [Late 20C. Natural exclamation]

Yahr·zeit /yaár tsīt/ *n* in Judaism, the anniversary of somebody's death, celebrated by near relatives with the lighting of a memorial candle and the saying of the Kaddish [Mid-19C. < Yiddish *yortsayt* "year's time"]

Yah·veh, etc. *n* JUD-CHR same as **Yahweh, etc.**

Yah·weh /yaá wày/, **Jah·weh, Yah·veh** /-vày/, **Jah·veh** *n* a name of God, expanded from the four letters YHWH (**Tetragrammaton**) that form the name of God in Hebrew [Late 19C. < Hebrew]

Yah·wism /yaá wìzzəm/, **Yah·vism** /-vìzzəm/ *n* the use of the four letters YHWH (**Tetragrammaton**) to represent the name of God or to worship God

Yah·wist /yaáwist/, **Yah·vist** /-vist/ *n* the unknown writer of the parts of the Bible in which the set of four letters YHWH (**Tetragrammaton**) is used to refer to God

Yah·wis·tic /yaa wístik/, **Yah·vis·tic** /-vístik/ *adj* relating to Yahweh, Yahwism, or the Yahwist

yak

yak[1] /yak/ (*plural* **yaks** or *same*) *n* a large longhaired ox that has long curved horns and is found both wild and domesticated. Native to: Tibetan highlands. Latin name: *Bos grunniens*. [Late 18C. < Tibetan *gyag*]

yak[2] /yak/, **yack** (*informal*) *vi* (**yakked, yak·king, yaks; yacked, yack·ing, yacks**) to talk continuously, usually about unimportant matters ■ *n* continuous talking, usually about unimportant matters, or an instance of this [Mid-20C. An imitation of the sound]

Ya·ka·ma /yákəmə/ (*plural same* or **-mas**) *n* **1.** a member of a Native North American people of south central Washington **2.** the Penutian language of the Yakama people. Native speakers: 3,000. [Mid-19C. < Sahaptin] —**Ya·ka·ma** *adj*

ya·ki·to·ri /yaákə táwree/ *n* a dish of Japanese origin consisting of small pieces of grilled chicken that are basted on skewers with a sauce of soy, stock, sugar, and mirin [Mid-20C. < Japanese, "grilling fowl"]

Ya·kut /yaa kóot, yə-/ (*plural same* or **-kuts**) *n* **1.** a member of a people who live in northeastern Siberia, mainly in the Russian republic of Sakha **2.** the Turkic language of the Yakut people. Native speakers: 300,000. [Mid-18C. Via Russian < Yakut] —**Ya·kut** *adj*

Ya·kutsk /yə kóotsk/ capital city of the autonomous region of Sakha, northeastern Russia. Population: 240,743 (1995).

ya·ku·za /yaá koo zaa, yaa kóozə/ (*plural same*) *n* **1.** a Japanese criminal organization involved in illegal activities such as drug-dealing, extortion, and prostitution **2.** a member of the yakuza [Mid-20C. < Japanese, "gambler" < *ya* "eight" + *ku* "nine" + *-za* "three," the worst hand in a card game]

Yale /yayl/, **Elihu** (1649–1721) English merchant and philanthropist. He grew wealthy as an East India Company agent in India (1670–99), and made large gifts to the Collegiate School in Connecticut, which later became Yale University (1887).

Yale lock *tdmk* a trademark for a padlock operated with a key

Ya·lie /yáylee/ *n* a graduate or student of Yale University, New Haven, Connecticut (*informal*)

y'all *pron Southern US* same as **you-all**

Yal·lourn /yál àwrn/ town in southern Victoria, Australia. It is a major coal-mining center. Population: 15,512 (1996).

Yal·ta /yáwltə/ resort city in Crimea Region, southern Ukraine. Situated on the Black Sea, it was the site of a conference in 1945 between Joseph Stalin, Franklin Roosevelt, and Winston Churchill that determined the administration of Germany after World War II. Population: 115,548 (1993).

Ya·lu /yaá loó/ river in East Asia, forming most of the boundary between North Korea and China. Length: 490 mi./790 km.

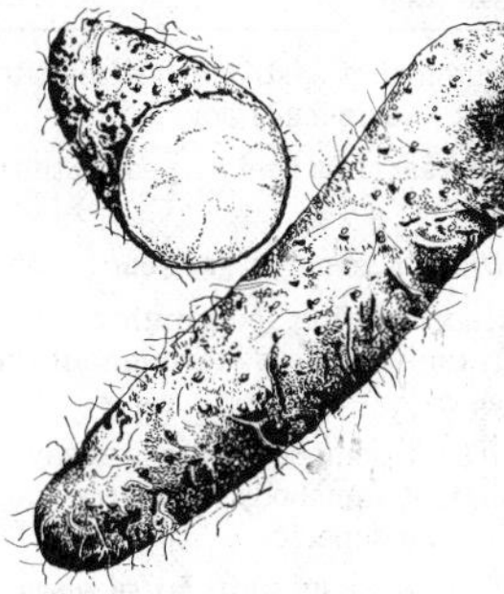

yam

yam /yam/ *n* 1. PLANTS, FOOD same as **sweet potato** (senses 1–2) **2.** a vine root that resembles a large white floury potato and is eaten cooked as a vegetable **3.** a tropical plant that produces yams. Genus: *Dioscorea*. [Late 16C. Via Portuguese *inhame* or Spanish *iñame* < a W African language]

REGIONAL NOTE In the sense "sweet potato," **yam** was formerly largely restricted to the South, where its use was universal. Now, through commercial usage, the term is found virtually everywhere in the United States.

ya·men /yaámən/ *n* in the Chinese Empire, the home or office of a mandarin or other public official [Early 19C. < Chinese *yámen* < *yá* "office" + *mén* "gate"]

yam·mer /yámmər/ (*informal*) *vi* (**-mered, -mer·ing, -mers**) **1.** TALK LOUDLY AND AT LENGTH to talk, chat, or chatter noisily and continuously **2.** WHINE to whine or complain persistently about something **3.** HOWL OR WAIL to make repeated howling sounds of pain or distress ■ *n* **1.** NOISY CHATTERING noisy continuous talk, chat, or chattering **2.** COMPLAINT a whine or complaint [15C. Probably < Middle Dutch *jammeren* "mourn"] —**yam·mer·er** *n*

Ya·mous·sou·kro /yàmmoo soókrō/ capital city of Côte d'Ivoire, in the central part of the country. Population: 120,000 (1990).

Ya·mu·na /yúmmənə/ river in northern India flowing south through Delhi into the Ganges River at Allahabad. Length: 870 mi./1,400 km. Former name **Jumna**

Ya·na·ma·mi /yaánə maámee/ *npl* a South American people indigenous to the rain forests of Brazil in areas close to the Colombian and Venezuelan borders [< a Native South American language] —**Ya·na·ma·mi** *adj*

Yan'an /yàn án/ city in northern Shaanxi Province, northeastern China. The terminus of the Long March, Yan'an was used by Communist forces as a base between 1936 and 1949. Population: 113,277 (1991).

yang /yang/, **Yang** *n* in Chinese philosophy, the principle of light, heat, motivation, and masculinity that is the counterpart of yin and is thought to exist along with yin in all things [Late 17C. < Chinese *yáng* "sun, positive"]

Yan·gon /yàng gón/ capital city of Myanmar, in the south of the country. Population: 4,196,000 (2000). Former name **Rangoon** (until 1989)

Yang·tze /yáng see, -tseé/, **Yang·zi** longest river in China. It rises in the Kunlun Mountains, and flows southward and then eastward to enter the East China Sea directly north of Shanghai. Length: 3,900 mi./6,300 km.

yank /yangk/ *v* (**yanked, yank·ing, yanks**) **1.** *vti* PULL SOMEBODY OR SOMETHING SHARPLY to pull somebody or something suddenly and sharply **2.** *vt* REMOVE SOMEBODY OR SOMETHING SWIFTLY to remove somebody or something suddenly and quickly ■ *n* SHARP PULL a sudden sharp pull or jerk [Early 19C. Origin ?]

SYNONYMS See *pull*.

Yank /yangk/ *n* same as **Yankee** (senses 1–3) (*informal; offensive in some contexts*) [Late18C. Shortening of YANKEE]

Yan·kee /yángkee/ *n* **1.** PEOPLES SOMEBODY FROM UNITED STATES somebody who is from the United States (*informal; offensive in some contexts*) **2.** *US* SOMEBODY FROM NORTHERN STATE somebody who comes from a Northern state of the United States, especially a soldier fighting on the side of the Union during the Civil War (*offensive in some contexts*) **3.** *US* SOMEBODY FROM NEW ENGLAND somebody who comes from one of the states of New England (*offensive in some contexts*) **4.** CODE WORD FOR LETTER "Y" a code word for the letter "Y," used in international radio communications [Mid-18C. Origin ?] —**Yan·kee·dom** *n*

Yan·kee Doo·dle *n* **1.** a song first popular during the American Revolutionary War **2.** *US* same as **Yankee** (senses 1–3) (*informal; offensive in some contexts*)

Yan·kee·ism /yángkee ìzzəm/ *n* something such as an expression that is considered characteristic of Yankees

Yank·ton /yángktən/ city in southeastern South Dakota, southwest of Sioux Falls and northwest of Sioux City, Iowa. Population: 13,440 (2002 estimate).

yan·qui /yaángkee/ (*plural* **-quis**) *n Hispanic* an offensive term used by some Latin Americans to refer disparagingly to an English-speaking US citizen [Early 20C. Spanish-style spelling of YANKEE]

Yao /yow/ (*plural same*) *n* **1.** PEOPLES a member of a people who live in the mountains of southern People's Republic of China **2.** LANG the language of the Yao people, belonging to the Miao-Yao group of languages. Native speakers: 1 million. [Mid-19C. < Chinese, literally, "precious jade"] —**Yao** *adj*

Ya·oun·dé /yaà oon dáy/ capital city of Cameroon, in the southwestern part of the country. Population: 1,000,000 (1997).

yap /yap/ *vi* (**yapped, yap·ping, yaps**) **1.** MAKE HIGH BARKING SOUND to make a short loud high-pitched barking noise **2.** CHATTER ANNOYINGLY to talk continuously about trivial things, often in a loud or high-pitched voice (*informal*) ■ *n* **1.** SHORT HIGH-PITCHED BARK a short loud high-pitched bark **2.** TRIVIAL CONVERSATION a trivial or meaningless conversation (*informal*) **3.** ANAT same as **mouth** *n* (senses 1–2) (*slang*) **4.** *US* OFFENSIVE TERM an offensive term that deliberately insults somebody regarded as vulgar and unintelligent (*slang*) [Early 19C. An imitation of a dog's bark] —**yap·per** *n* —**yap·py** *adj*

Yap /yap/ group of islands, islets, and atolls in the western Pacific Ocean. Part of the Caroline Islands, the group is one of the states of Micronesia. Population: 10,886 (1991). Area: 46 sq. mi./119 sq. km.

ya·pok /yə pók/ (*plural* **-poks** or *same*) *n* an amphibious nocturnal opossum that has dense fur, webbed hind feet, a long tail, and feeds on water organisms such as shrimp. Native to: Central and South America. Latin name: *Chironectes minimus*. [Early 19C. After the River *Oyapok*, which forms the border between N Brazil and French Guiana]

ya·pon *n* TREES another spelling of **yaupon**

Ya·qui /yaákee/ (*plural same* or **-quis**) *n* **1.** a member of a Native North American people of Arizona and Sonora, a state in northwestern Mexico **2.** the Uto-Aztecan language of the Yaqui people. Native speakers: 20,000. [Early 19C. Via Spanish < Yaqui *Hiaki*] —**Ya·qui** *adj*

yar·bor·ough /yaárbərō, -bərə/, **Yar·bor·ough** *n* in bridge or whist, a hand consisting of 13 cards, each of which has a value lower than ten [Late 19C. After Charles Anderson Worsley (1809–97), 2nd Earl of *Yarborough*]

yard[1] /yaard/ *n* **1.** UNIT OF LENGTH a unit of length equal to 3 ft./0.9144 m **2.** SPAR SUPPORTING SAIL a long spar that supports the head of a square sail, lugsail, or lateen **3.** *US* ONE HUNDRED DOLLARS one hundred dollars (*slang*) **4.** A BILLION one billion in foreign-exchange currency (*slang*) ○ *a yard of yen* [Old English *gerd* "rod" < W Germanic] ◇ **the whole nine yards** the totality or full extent of something (*informal*)

yard[2] /yaard/ *n* **1.** LAND AROUND HOUSE the area of land immediately surrounding a house, often covered with grass or landscaping **2.** ENCLOSED PAVED PIECE OF LAND an area of ground that is usually paved and enclosed, and is next to or surrounded by a building or buildings ○ *a prison yard* **3.** AREA USED FOR BUSINESS OR ACTIVITY an area of ground, sometimes with associated buildings, used for a particular purpose (*often used in combination*) ○ *a shipbuilding yard* **4.** RAILROAD STORAGE AREA an area of railroad tracks used for storing cars or locomotives and for making up trains **5.** LIVESTOCK ENCLOSURE an enclosed area of land for livestock **6.** WINTER GRAZING AREA an area of land where deer, moose, or other animals graze in winter ■ *vt* (**yard·ed, yard·ing, yards**) KEEP LIVESTOCK IN YARD to put or keep livestock in a yard [Old English *geard* "enclosure, garden" < Germanic]

yard·age[1] /yaárdij/ *n* measurement in yards, or an amount measured in yards [Late 19C. < YARD[1]]

yard·age[2] /yaárdij/ *n* **1.** the use of a livestock yard for storing animals before transporting them **2.** a fee charged for storing livestock in a yard [Mid-19C. < YARD[2]]

yard·arm /yaárd aàrm/ *n* an end of the yard used to support a sail [15C. < YARD[1]]

yard·bird /yaárd bùrd/ *n US* **1.** CONVICT a convict or prisoner (*slang*) **2.** SOLDIER ASSIGNED MENIAL DUTIES a soldier who is assigned menial tasks or is confined to a limited area, usually as a punishment (*informal*) **3.** INEPT RECRUIT an untrained and inept military recruit (*dated informal*) [Mid-19C. < YARD[2], after JAILBIRD]

yard broom *n Southern US* a push broom that is strong enough to use outdoors

REGIONAL NOTE The term ***yard broom*** is mainly Southern. The Coastal Southern term is *stick broom*; the Northern and Western term is *corn broom*.

yard goods *npl* COMM same as **piece goods** [< YARD[1]]

yard grass *n* a coarse annual grass with ground-hugging leaves and grouped spikes that grows widely as a weed. Latin name: *Eleusine indica*. [< YARD[2]]

Yard·ie /yaárdee/ *n* **1.** a member of a criminal syndicate that originated in Jamaica **2.** *Carib* somebody who lives in a building with a shared yard [Late 20C. < YARD[2] in the Jamaican sense "house, home"]

yard-long bean *n* the long thin edible pod produced by a type of cowpea. Native to: South Asia. Latin name: *Vigna unguiculata sesquipedalis*. [Because it reaches up to a yard (nearly a meter) in length]

yard·man /yaárdmən/ (*plural* **-men** /-mən/) *n* **1.** somebody, especially a man, who works in a yard, especially a railroad yard or a lumberyard **2.** *US* somebody, especially a man, hired to care for a lawn or yard [Early 19C. < YARD[2]]

yard·mas·ter /yaárd màstər/ *n US* somebody in charge of a railroad yard

yard of ale *n* **1.** a long narrow drinking glass, sometimes shaped like a horn, approximately one yard long and holding two to three pints of beer **2.** the contents of a yard of ale [< YARD[1]]

yard·per·son /yaárd pùrss'n/ *n* **1.** somebody who works in a yard, especially a railroad yard or a lumberyard **2.** *US* somebody hired to care for a lawn or yard [Late 20C. < YARD[2]]

yard sale *n* a sale at which personal possessions and household items are sold, usually held in the yard of somebody's house [< YARD[2]]

yard·stick /yaárd stìk/ *n* **1.** a measuring stick one yard long, usually marked in feet and inches **2.** a standard used to judge the quality, value, or success of something [Early 19C. < YARD[1]]

yard work *n* tending a yard as a chore or hobby

yare /yer/ *adj* **1.** EASY TO HANDLE describes a ship that is easy to handle and responsive **2.** READY ready or prepared (*archaic*) **3.** QUICK quick or lively (*archaic*) ■ *adv* QUICKLY quickly or nimbly (*archaic*) [Old English *gearo* "ready" < Germanic] —**yare·ly** *adv*

yar·mul·ke /yaárməlkə, yaáməlkə/, **yar·mel·ke, yar·mul·ka, yar·mul·kah** *n* a small round cap worn by Jewish men and boys. Orthodox Jews wear the yarmulke at all times, while Conservative Jews wear it for prayer or on ceremonial occasions only. [Mid-20C. Via Yiddish < Polish *jarmułka*]

yarn /yaarn/ *n* **1. STRAND OF FIBER** a continuous twisted strand of wool, cotton, or synthetic fiber. Use: knitting, weaving. **2. STRAND OF GLASS OR METAL** a continuous strand of a material such as glass or metal **3. LONG STORY** a long or involved tale, especially one that relates exciting or incredible events (*informal*) ■ *vi* (**yarned, yarn·ing, yarns**) **TELL STORY** to relate a long tale full of incredible events (*informal*) [Old English *gearn* < Indo-European, "entrail"]

yarn-dyed *adj* dyed in the form of yarn before being woven or knitted

Ya·ro·slavl /yaàrə slaáv'l/ city and capital of Yaroslavl Oblast, central European Russia. It is situated on the Volga River. Population: 763,175 (1995).

Yar·ra /yárrə/ river in southern Victoria, Australia. Length: 155 mi./250 km.

yar·row /yárrō/ (*plural* **-rows** or *same*) *n* a plant of the daisy family with leaves like ferns. Flowers: usually white, in broad flat clusters. Native to: Europe, Asia. Latin name: *Achillea millefolium*. [Old English *gearwe* < W Germanic]

yash·mak /yásh màk, yaash maák/, **yash·mac** *n* a veil covering the face except for the eyes worn by some Muslim women in public [Mid-19C. < Turkish *yaşmak*]

yat·a·ghan /yáttə gàn, -gən/, **yat·a·gan, at·a·ghan** /áttə gàn, -gən/ *n* a Turkish sword with no handle guard and a single-edged blade that curves inward then outward [Early 19C. < Turkish *yatağan*]

ya·tra /yáttrə/ *n* a holy pilgrimage for Hindus [Early 19C. < Sanskrit *yātrā* < *yā* "undertake a trip"]

yaup *vi, n US* another spelling of **yawp**

yau·pon /yáw pòn/ (*plural* **-pons** or *same*), **ya·pon** /yá pòn/ *n* an evergreen holly with red fruit and smooth bitter leaves that have emetic and purgative properties. Native to: southeastern United States. Latin name: *Ilex vomitoria*. [Early 18C. < Catawba *yápa* "tree leaf"]

yau·ti·a /yow teé ə/ (*plural* **-as** or *same*) *n* **1.** a brown starchy tuber, cooked and eaten as a vegetable **2.** a plant of the arum family that produces yautias. Native to: Caribbean. Genus: *Xanthosoma*. [Early 20C. Via Spanish < Taino]

yaw /yaw/ *vti* (**yawed, yaw·ing, yaws**) **1. GO OR PUT SHIP OFF COURSE** to deviate from a straight course, or make a boat or ship do this **2. TURN AROUND VERTICAL AXIS** to turn around the vertical axis, or make an aircraft do this **3. ZIGZAG** to move unsteadily on a zigzag course, or make somebody or something do this ■ *n* **DEVIATION FROM COURSE** the deviation of a boat or ship from a straight course [Mid-16C. Origin ?]

yawl /yawl/ *n* **1.** a sailing vessel rigged fore-and-aft with a large mainmast and a smaller mizzenmast toward the stern **2.** a small boat kept on a ship, rowed by four or six people [Mid-17C. < Dutch *jol*]

Yawm Ar·a·fat /yàwm árrə fàt/, **Yom Ar·a·fat** *n* an Islamic festival during which people on the hajj gather at the plain of Arafat near Mecca and Muslims elsewhere remember them in prayer. Date: 9th day of Dhu al-Hijjah.

yawn /yawn/ *v* (**yawned, yawn·ing, yawns**) **1.** *vi* **OPEN MOUTH WIDE** to open the mouth wide and take a long deep breath, usually involuntarily, because of tiredness or boredom **2.** *vt* **SAY SOMETHING WHILE YAWNING** to say something while yawning, or in a tired or bored voice **3.** *vi* **GAPE** to open wide or be a wide open space in front of somebody or something ■ *n* **1. ACT OF YAWNING** an involuntary response to tiredness or boredom in which the mouth is opened wide and a long deep breath is taken **2. SOMEBODY OR SOMETHING BORING** a boring person, thing, or event (*informal*) [Old English *ginian*] —**yawn·ing** *adj* —**yawn·ing·ly** *adv*

yawn·er /yáwnər/ *n* **1.** somebody who yawns **2.** same as **yawn** *n* (sense 2) (*informal*)

yawp /yawp/, **yaup** (*informal*) *vi* (**yawped, yawp·ing, yawps; yauped, yaup·ing, yaups**) **1. TALK COARSELY** to talk or complain loudly, coarsely, and sometimes meaninglessly **2. UTTER YELP** to utter a sharp loud yelp ■ *n* **1. COARSE TALK** loud, coarse, and sometimes meaningless talk **2. YELP** a sharp loud yelp [14C. Origin ?] —**yawp·er** *n*

yaws /yawz/ *n* an infectious tropical disease marked initially by red skin eruptions and later by joint pains. It mainly affects children and is caused by the bacterium *Treponema pertenue*. (*takes a singular or plural verb*) [Late 17C. < Carib *yaya*]

y-ax·is *n* **1.** the vertical axis in a two-dimensional coordinate system such as a graph **2.** one of the axes in the three-dimensional Cartesian coordinate system, conventionally the vertical one

Yb *symbol* CHEM ELEM ytterbium

YB *abbr* yearbook

Y-chro·mo·some *n* the sex chromosome that determines the male sex in humans and other mammals. The body cells of males each possess one Y chromosome paired with one X chromosome.

y·clept /i klépt/ *adj* called by the name of (*archaic or humorous*) [Old English *geclipod*, past participle of *geclipian* "to call"]

yd. *abbr* MEASURE yard

YDT *abbr* TIME Yukon Daylight Time

ye[1] /yee/; *unstressed* /yə/ *pron* plural of **thou** (*archaic or regional*) [Old English *gē*]

ye[2] *abbr* Yemen (*used in Internet addresses*) See table at **domain name**

yea /yay/ (*archaic*) *adv, n* same as **yes** ■ *adv* same as **indeed** (sense 1) ○ *"Yea, though I walk through the valley of the shadow of death, I will fear no evil" (Psalm 23, King James Bible)* [Old English *gēa* "yes" < Germanic]

Yea·ger /yáygər/, **Chuck** (*b.* 1923) US aviator. He was the first person to fly faster than the speed of sound. Full name **Yeager, Charles Elwood**

yeah /yé ə, yaa/ *adv, interj* **1.** same as **yes** (*informal*) **2.** used to express skepticism about what somebody has just said (*informal*) ○ *Yeah, yeah, I've heard that before!* [Early 20C. Variant of YEA]

year /yeer/ *n* **1. TWELVE-MONTH PERIOD FROM JANUARY 1** a period of 365 days (or 366 in a leap year), measured from January 1 to December 31 **2. TWELVE-MONTH PERIOD FROM ANY DATE** a period of 365 or 366 days, measured exactly or approximately from any date ○ *The company's financial year ends on July 31.* **3. SOLAR YEAR** the time it takes Earth to orbit the Sun, approximately 365.25 days **4. TIME OF PLANET'S ORBIT AROUND SUN** the time taken for a planet to orbit the Sun once **5. PERIOD OF PARTICULAR ACTIVITY** the time occupied by a particular activity within a twelve-month period ○ *academic year* **6. AGE BAND IN SCHOOL OR COLLEGE** a group of students, usually of approximately the same age, who start school or college at the same time and study together in one or more classes ○ *in my year in college* ■ **years** *npl* **1. LONG TIME** a very long time (*informal*) ○ *It's years since I last saw him.* ○ *We haven't been back for years.* **2. AGE** age, especially advanced age ○ *a man of his years* **3. TIME IN GENERAL** time in the past, present, or future ○ *in years to come* **4. PARTICULAR PERIOD OF TIME** a particular period of time, usually in the past ○ *her early years* [Old English *gēar* < Indo-European] ◇ **year in, year out** in a regular or repeated way over a long period of time, especially when this is seen as monotonous (*informal*)

year·book /yeér bòok/ *n* **1.** a book compiled by members of a graduating class of a high school or college, commemorating their school year and usually including photographs of the students **2.** a book published annually containing details of events in the previous year, usually within a particular organization or field of interest

year-end *n* the end of a financial year or calendar year ■ *adj* occurring or done at the end of a financial year or calendar year

year·ling /yeérling/ *n* **1.** an animal between one and two years of age, e.g., a calf or deer **2.** a racehorse that is one year old, as calculated from January 1 in the year after it was born

year·long /yeer láwng, -lóng, yeér làwng, -lòng/ *adj* lasting for a year or continuing throughout a year

year·ly /yeérlee/ *adj* **1. ANNUAL** happening, done, appearing, or published once a year or every year **2. RELATING TO ONE YEAR** relating to or lasting for a period of twelve months ■ *adv* **1. ANNUALLY** once every year **2. PER YEAR** during a period of a year ■ *n* (*plural* **-lies**) **ANNUAL EVENT OR ISSUE** something that happens or appears once a year, especially an annual publication

yearn /yurn/ (**yearned, yearn·ing, yearns**) *vi* **1.** to have a strong desire for somebody or something, especially when the desire is tinged with sadness **2.** to feel affection, tenderness, or compassion [Old English *giernan* < Indo-European, "to want"] —**yearn·er** *n*

SYNONYMS See *want.*

yearn·ing /yúrning/ *n* a strong desire, often tinged with sadness —**yearn·ing·ly** *adv*

year of grace, year of our Lord *n* a year of the Christian era

year out *n UK* EDUC same as **gap year**

year-round *adj* existing, continuing, or operating throughout the year ■ *adv* throughout the year —**year-round·er** *n*

yea-say·er *n US* **1.** somebody who is always confident and optimistic **2.** somebody who always agrees submissively with a superior

yeast /yeest/ *n* **1. SMALL SINGLE-CELLED FUNGUS** a small single-celled fungus that ferments sugars and other carbohydrates and reproduces by budding. Genus: *Saccharomyces*. **2. PREPARATION FOR BAKING** a commercial preparation of yeast cells. Use: brewing, baking, food supplement. **3. FROTH** the yellowish froth that forms on the surface of a fermenting liquid such as beer, contains yeast cells and carbon dioxide, and promotes fermentation **4. FOAM** a foam or froth, e.g., on sea waves **5. CAUSE OF UNREST OR ACTIVITY** somebody or something that causes ferment, activity, or unrest ■ *vi* (**yeast·ed, yeast·ing, yeasts**) **FERMENT** to ferment, froth, or foam [Old English *gist* < Germanic]

yeast ar·ti·fi·cial chro·mo·some *n* a sequence of DNA taken from another organism and inserted in a yeast to reveal its function

yeast ex·tract *n* a thick sticky brown food obtained from yeast and eaten as a spread or used in cooking

yeast in·fec·tion *n* an overgrowth of a fungus in the vagina, intestines, skin, or mouth, causing irritation and swelling. Technical name **candidiasis**

yeast·y /yeéstee/ (**-i·er, -i·est**) *adj* **1. RELATING TO YEAST** relating to, containing, or tasting or smelling of yeast **2. CAUSING FERMENTATION** fermenting, or causing fermentation **3. FROTHY** full of foam or froth **4. RESTLESS** marked by or causing agitation or restlessness **5. ENERGETIC** full of vitality, productivity, or creativity **6. FRIVOLOUS** light and frivolous —**yeast·i·ly** *adv* —**yeast·i·ness** *n*

Barnaby's

William Butler Yeats

Yeats /yayts/, **W. B.** (1865–1939) Irish poet and dramatist. A leader of the Irish Renaissance, he is considered to be one of the greatest poets of the 20th century. His poetry incorporates a complex personal mythology and includes "The Wild Swans at Coole" (1919) and "The Second Coming" (1922). He wrote plays for Dublin's Abbey Theatre, which he cofounded. He won the Nobel Prize in literature (1923). Full name **Yeats, William Butler**

"All changed, changed utterly: / A terrible beauty is born."
[W. B. Yeats, "Easter 1916," *Michael Robartes and the Dancer*, 1921]

"Things fall apart; the center cannot hold; / Mere anarchy is loosed upon the world, / The blood-dimmed tide is loosed, and everywhere / The ceremony of innocence

is drowned; / The best lack all conviction,
while the worst / Are full of passionate
intensity."
[W. B. Yeats, "The Second Coming," *Michael Robartes and the Dancer*; 1921]

yech /yek, yekh/, **yecch** *interj US* used to express disgust (*informal*) [Mid-20C. Natural exclamation]

yee·haw /yeé hàw/ (*slang*) *interj* used as an expression of enthusiastic approval or high spirits, associated especially with the cowboy culture of the southern United States ■ *adj* extremely aggressive, especially in an unrefined, rustic manner [Late 20C]

yegg /yeg/ *n* a burglar, especially a safecracker (*slang*) [Early 20C. Origin ?]

~~**yeild**~~ incorrect spelling of **yield**

Ye·ka·ter·in·burg /yə káttərin bùrg/ industrial city in central Russia, on the Iset River, on the eastern slopes of the Ural Mountains. Population: 1,398,774 (1995).

Ye·kat·e·rin·o·dar /yə kàttə reénə daár/ former name for **Krasnodar**

yell /yel/ *vti* (**yelled, yell·ing, yells**) **SHOUT LOUDLY** to shout or scream something, or speak in a very loud voice ○ *Stop yelling at me!* ■ *n* **1. LOUD CRY** a loud shout, scream, or cry **2. CHEER OF SUPPORT** a rhythmic word or phrase chanted by a group of people to give support or encouragement [Old English *giellan* < Indo-European, "to call"] —**yell·er** *n*

yel·low /yéllō/ *adj* **1. OF COLOR OF BUTTER** having or being near the color of butter or ripe lemons **2. COWARDLY** cowardly or afraid (*insult*) **3. SENSATIONALIST** using scandalous or sensational material, often greatly exaggerating or distorting the truth ○ *yellow journalism* **4. OFFENSIVE TERM** a highly offensive term meaning from or born in East or Southeast Asia (*dated taboo*) ■ *n* **1. YELLOW COLOR** a color that lies between orange and green on the visible spectrum, e.g., that of butter or ripe lemons. It is one of the three primary colors of pigment. Yellow is also one of the three primary colors used in printing and photographic processing. **2. YELLOW PIGMENT** a yellow pigment or dye **3. YELLOW FABRIC** yellow clothing or fabric ○ *dressed in yellow* **4. YELLOW THING** a yellow object **5.** *regional* **EGG YOLK** the yolk of an egg ■ *vti* (**-lowed, -low·ing, -lows**) **BECOME YELLOW** to become, or make something, yellow or yellowish, especially as a result of age [Old English *geolu* < Indo-European, "to shine"] —**yel·low·ish** *adj* —**yel·low·ly** *adv* —**yel·low·ness** *n* —**yel·low·y** *adj*

yel·low-bel·lied *adj* **1.** cowardly or afraid (*informal insult*) **2.** describes organisms having a yellow underside

yel·low-bel·lied sap·suck·er *n* a small woodpecker that feeds on sap and insects, the male of which has a yellowish belly and bright red crown and throat. Native to: North America. Latin name: *Sphyrapicus varius*.

yel·low·bel·ly /yéllō bèllee/ *n* an offensive term that deliberately insults somebody's courage (*informal insult*)

yel·low bile *n* MED, HIST same as **choler** (sense 2)

yel·low birch *n* **1.** a hard, light reddish-colored birch wood. Use: building, furniture-making. **2.** a birch that has yellowish peeling bark and yields yellow birch. Native to: North America. Latin name: *Betula alleghaniensis*.

yel·low brain fun·gus *n* FUNGI same as **jelly fungus**

yel·low-breast·ed chat *n* a songbird with a bright yellow breast and white marks over the eyes. Native to: North America. Latin name: *Icteria virens*.

yel·low·cake /yéllō kàyk/ *n* the concentrated semi-refined oxide of uranium ore

yel·low card *n* in soccer, a card shown by the referee to a player guilty of serious or persistent foul play as an indication that the player has been cautioned

yel·low-dog *adj US* an offensive term meaning so cowardly and mean as to be beneath contempt (*informal insult*)

yel·low-dog con·tract *n US* an illegal employment contract in which the employee agrees not to join a labor union

yel·low fe·ver *n* an infectious, often fatal viral disease of warm climates, transmitted by mosquitoes and marked by high fever, hemorrhaging, vomiting of blood, liver damage, and jaundice

yel·low·fin tu·na /yèllō fìn-/, **yel·low·fin** (*plural* **-fins** or *same*) *n* a small tuna with yellowish anal and dorsal fins. Native to: warm regions. Latin name: *Thunnus albacares*.

yel·low flag *n* NAUT same as **quarantine flag**

yel·low-green al·ga *n* an alga that lives in soil and other moist environments and contains brown and bright yellow pigments that mask the chlorophyll. Division: *Chrysophyta*.

yel·low·ham·mer /yéllō hàmmər/ *n* a songbird of the bunting family, the male of which has a bright yellow head, neck, and breast. Native to: Europe. Latin name: *Emberiza citrinella*. [Mid-16C. < *hammer*, origin ?]

yel·low jack *n* **1.** MED same as **yellow fever** (*archaic*) **2.** NAUT same as **quarantine flag 3. yel·low jack** (*plural* **yel·low jacks** or *same*) FISH a large yellowish food fish. Native to: Atlantic coast of North, South, and Central America. Latin name: *Caranx bartholomaei*.

yel·low jack·et *n* a social wasp with black-and-yellow bands on its body that nests in the ground or in the hollows of trees, and can sting repeatedly. Family: Vespidae.

yel·low jas·mine *n* TREES same as **Carolina jasmine**

yel·low jer·sey *n* in the Tour de France, the jersey awarded to the cyclist with the fastest elapsed time at a completed stage of the race

yel·low jes·sa·mine *n* same as **Carolina jasmine**

yel·low jour·nal·ism *n* a style of journalism that makes unscrupulous use of scandalous, lurid, or sensationalized stories to attract readers [Late 19C. After the *Yellow Kid* cartoons, in yellow ink, in the sensationalistic *New York World*]

Yel·low·knife /yéllō nīf/ capital city of the Northwest Territories, Canada. It is situated on the northern shore of the Great Slave Lake. Population: 16,055 (2001).

yel·low·legs /yéllō lègz/ (*plural same*) *n* a large shorebird of the sandpiper family with bright yellow legs, mottled brown feathers, and white underparts. Native to: Americas. Latin name: *Tringa melanoleuca* or *Tringa flavipes*.

yel·low o·cher *n* a yellow brown pigment containing iron. Use: artists' colors.

yel·low perch *n* a bony freshwater fish with a yellow body, greenish brown vertical bars and orange fins that is valued as a food and sport fish. Native to: North America. Latin name: *Perca flavescens*.

yel·low per·il *n* a highly offensive term referring to the perceived threat to Western nations posed by the nations of East Asia, especially China (*dated taboo*)

yel·low pine *n* **1.** a strong yellowish pine wood **2.** a North American pine that yields yellow pine, e.g., the longleaf pine, shortleaf pine, or ponderosa pine

yel·low pop·lar *n* **1.** TREES same as **tulip tree 2.** INDUST same as **tulipwood**

yel·low press *n* collectively, the newspapers that make unscrupulous use of scandalous, lurid, or sensationalized stories to attract readers

yel·low rain *n* a fungal toxin that occurs as a form of precipitation in Southeast Asia. It has been attributed by different sections of the scientific community to residue from chemical warfare or to the excrement of wild honeybees.

yel·low rat·tle *n* a plant with yellow flowers whose seeds rattle in their pouches when they are shaken. Native to: Europe, North America. Latin name: *Rhinanthus minor*.

Yel·low Ri·ver /yèllō-/ ♦ **Huang He**

yel·lows /yéllōz/ *n* a plant disease marked by a yellowing of foliage that may be caused by a mineral deficiency, virus, or some other infectious agent (*takes a singular verb*)

Yel·low Sea /yèllō-/ arm of the Pacific Ocean bordered on the west and north by China and on the east by the Korean Peninsula. It merges with the East China Sea to the south. Chinese name **Huang Hai**

yel·low-shaft·ed flick·er *n* a large woodpecker with streaks of yellow on the underside of its wings and tail and a red spot on its nape. Native to: eastern North America. Latin name: *Colaptes auratus*.

yel·low spot *n* OPHTHALMOL same as **macula** (sense 2)

Yel·low·stone /yéllō stōn/ river in the western United States, rising in northwestern Wyoming, and flowing into the Missouri River in North Dakota. Length: 692 mi./1,110 km.

Yel·low·stone Na·tion·al Park world's first national park, established in 1872 in parts of Wyoming, Montana, and Idaho. It is noted for its geysers, hot springs, and the Yellowstone Falls. Area: 3,468 sq. mi./8,983 sq. km.

yel·low·tail /yéllō tàyl/ (*plural same* or **-tails**) *n* **1.** an ocean game fish with a yellowish tail. Native to: coastal waters of California and Mexico. Latin name: *Seriola lalandei*. **2.** a small greenish fish with silver underparts and a yellow tail and fins that is commonly used as bait. Native to: southern Australian and New Zealand waters. Latin name: *Trachurus novaezelandiae*.

yel·low·throat /yéllō thrōt/ *n* a small songbird of the warbler family that nests in dense undergrowth and has a yellow breast and throat, a black mask, and a brownish back. Native to: North America. Latin name: *Geothlypis trichas*.

yel·low-throat·ed war·bler *n* a small songbird of the warbler family that has a bright yellow throat. Native to: eastern United States. Latin name: *Dendroica dominica*.

yel·low war·bler *n* a common songbird of the warbler family that has bright yellow feathers with brown streaks along its sides. Native to: North America. Latin name: *Dendroica petechia*.

yel·low·wood /yéllō wòod/ (*plural* **-woods** or *same*) *n* **1. YELLOWISH WOOD OF N AMERICAN TREE** the yellowish wood of a leguminous North American tree. Use: source of yellow dye. **2. YELLOWISH WOOD OF S AFRICAN TREE** the yellowish wood of a southern African coniferous tree **3. N AMERICAN TREE** a leguminous tree that yields yellowwood. Native to: southern United States. Latin name: *Cladastris lutea*. **4. S AFRICAN TREE** a coniferous tree that yields yellowwood. Native to: southern Africa. Latin name: *Podocarpus falcatus*.

yelp /yelp/ *v* (**yelped, yelp·ing, yelps**) **1.** *vi* **BARK OR CRY SHARPLY** to utter a short sharp high-pitched bark or cry, usually of pain **2.** *vt* **UTTER SOMETHING WITH YELPING SOUND** to say something in a sharp high-pitched voice ■ *n* **SHORT BARK OR CRY** a short high-pitched bark or cry [Old English *gielpan* "to boast" < Indo-European, "to call"] —**yelp·er** *n*

Yel·tsin /yéltsin/, **Boris** (*b.* 1931) Russian president (1991–99). He was the first democratically elected Russian president, and was instrumental in planning the country's transition from Communism to a market economy. Full name **Yeltsin, Boris Nikolayevich**

"Europe has not yet freed itself from the heritage of the Cold War and is in danger of plunging into a Cold Peace."
[Boris Yeltsin, *Independent (London)*; December 6, 1994]

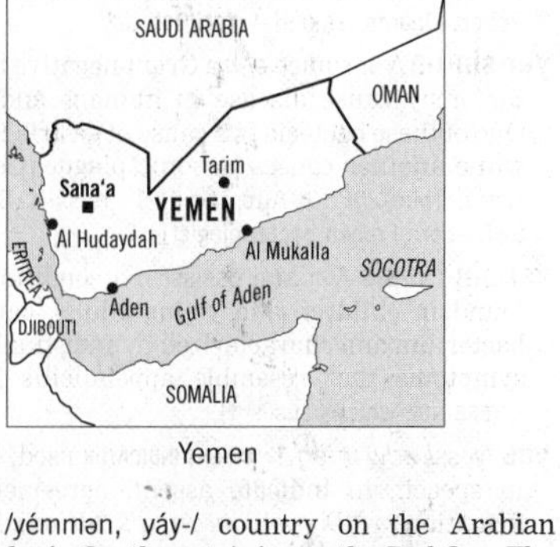

Yemen

Ye·men /yémmən, yáy-/ country on the Arabian peninsula, in Southwest Asia, on the Red Sea. The country was created in 1990 by the unification of the Yemen Arab Republic, or North Yemen, and the People's Democratic Republic of Yemen, or South Yemen. Language: Arabic. Currency: Yemeni riyal. Capital: Sana'a. Population: 19,349,881 (2003). Area: 203,850 sq. mi./527,970 sq. km. Official name **Republic of Yemen** —**Ye·me·ni** *n, adj*

yen[1] /yen/ (*plural same*) *n* the main unit of currency in Japan, worth 100 sen. See table at **currency** [Late 19C. Via Japanese *en* < Chinese *yuán* "round"]

yen[2] /yen/ *n* a strong yearning for something ■ *vi* (**yenned, yen·ning, yens**) to have a strong yearning for something [Early 20C. Probably < Chinese (Cantonese) *yăn*]

Ye·ni·sey /yènnə sáy/ river in central Siberian Russia. It is formed in the Sayan Mountains in southern Siberia by the union of the Greater Yenisey and the Little Yenisey, and flows northward into the Kara Sea. Length: 2,540 mi./4,090 km.

yen·ta /yéntə/, **yen·te** *n* somebody, often a woman, known as a meddler or a gossip (*slang; sometimes offensive*) [Mid-20C. Via Yiddish *yente* < woman's name *Yente* < Latin *gentilis* "of the same family"]

yeo. *abbr* NAVY yeoman

yeo·man /yṓmən/ *n* (*plural* **-men** /-mən/) **1.** ENLISTED NAVY CLERK an enlisted member of the US Navy whose duties are mostly clerical **2.** *US* LOYAL WORKER a loyal, reliable, or diligent worker **3.** FARMER WITH SMALL FREEHOLD a member of a former class of English commoners who owned and cultivated their own land **4.** SHERIFF'S ASSISTANT formerly, an assistant to a sheriff or other official **5.** ATTENDANT TO NOBILITY OR ROYALTY formerly, a servant or minor official employed in a royal or noble household **6.** MIL same as **yeoman of the guard** ■ *adj* PERFORMED DILIGENTLY characterized by loyalty, diligence, and reliability ○ *performed yeoman service in completing the task on time* [13C. Origin ?]

yeo·man·ly /yṓmənlee/ *adj* **1.** RELATING TO YEOMAN relating to or characteristic of a yeoman or yeomen **2.** STAUNCH AND DEPENDABLE dependable, loyal, and brave (*archaic or literary*) ■ *adv* BRAVELY in a brave and loyal way

yeo·man of the guard (*plural* **yeo·men of the guard**) *n* a member of a British royal guards unit that performs ceremonial duties, especially as guards of the Tower of London

yeo·man·ry /yṓmənree/ *n* **1.** in England in former times, a class of commoners who owned and cultivated their own land **2.** a British cavalry force, organized as a home guard in 1761, that became part of the Territorial Army in 1907

yep /yep/ *adv, interj* same as **yes** (*informal*) [Late19C. Alteration]

YER *abbr* BANKING yearly effective rate

yer·ba /yérbə, yúrbə/, **yer·ba ma·té** *n* BEVERAGES, TREES same as **maté** [Early 19C. < Spanish, "herb"]

Ye·re·van /yèrrə vaán/ capital and largest city of Armenia, on the Hrazdan River, in the west of the country. Population: 1,250,000 (2000).

Yer·kes /yúrkeez/, **Robert Mearns** (1876–1956) US psychobiologist. He developed intelligence tests and was an authority on experimental primate psychology.

Yerk·ish /yúrkish/ *n* an artificial language of visual symbols created for experimental communication between chimpanzees and humans [Late 20C. After Robert Mearns YERKES] —**Yerk·ish** *adj*

yer·sin·i·a /yur sínnee ə/ *n* a Gram-negative bacterium that may cause disease in humans and animals. One of these bacteria is a cause of gastric infections, while another causes bubonic plague. Genus: *Yersinia*. [Mid-20C. < After A. E. J. *Yersin* (1863–1943), Swiss-born French bacteriologist]

yer·sin·i·o·sis /yur sìni óssiss/ *n* a condition, mainly found in children and young adults, caused by a bacterium and characterized by intestinal pain and symptoms that resemble appendicitis [Late 20C. < YERSINIA, which causes it]

yes /yess/ *adv, interj* **1.** ASSENT INDICATOR used, especially in speech, to indicate assent, agreement, or affirmation ○ *"Do you mean it's all over?" "Yes, I suppose I do."* ○ *97 percent of respondents answered yes.* **2.** INDICATES CONTRADICTION used to indicate contradiction in response to a negative proposition ○ *"He won't believe you." "Oh yes he will."* **3.** MARK OF ATTENTION used to indicate that somebody is ready to give his or her attention to somebody who has asked for it ○ *"Doctor?" "Yes?"* **4.** ACCEPTANCE used to accept an offer or a request ○ *"Would you like some tea?" "Yes, please."* ■ *n* (*plural* **yes·es** or **yes·ses**) **1.** AFFIRMATIVE RESPONSE an affirmative response to a question ○ *Was that a yes or a no?* **2.** AFFIRMATIVE VOTER somebody who votes in the affirmative ○ *The yeses have 65 percent and the noes 35 percent, so the motion is carried.* ■ *interj* EXCLAMATION OF JUBILATION used as a loud exclamation to express triumph, jubilation, or extreme excitement and pleasure (*informal*) ○ *Our team won the championship–yes!!!* [Old English *gēse* < *gēa* (see YEA) + *sīe* "may it be (so)," form of the verb *to be*] ◇ **say yes** to express agreement or consent

ye·shi·va /yə sheévə/ (*plural* **-vas** or **-vot** /-vot, -vōt/ or **-voth**), **ye·shi·vah** (*plural* **-vahs** or **-vot** or **-voth**) *n* **1.** a seminary for orthodox Jewish, usually unmarried, men where they study the primary source of Jewish law, the Talmud **2.** a secondary school for Jewish students with a curriculum including religious and cultural, as well as academic, studies [Mid-19C. < Hebrew *yĕšīḇāh* < *yāšaḇ* "sit"]

yes man, yes-man *n* somebody, especially a man, who enthusiastically and uncritically agrees with the ideas and views of a superior

yes/no ques·tion *n* a question that can be answered with "yes" or "no" and that in English begins with an actual or implied verb

yes·sir /yéssər/, **yess·ir·ee** /yèssə reé/ *interj* used, often ironically or humorously, to express submissive assent or obedience (*informal*) [Early 20C. Representing a casual pronunciation of *yes, sir*]

yester- *prefix* used to refer to a time in the past denoted by the suffix ○ *yestermorning* [Old English *geostran* < Germanic]

yes·ter·day /yéstər day, -dee/ *n* **1.** DAY BEFORE TODAY the day before this one **2.** PAST a time in the past ■ *adv* **1.** ON PREVIOUS DAY on the day before today **2.** IN PAST at a time in the past

yes·ter·eve·ning /yéstər eévning/ (*archaic or literary*) *adv* yesterday in the evening ■ *n* the evening of yesterday

yes·ter·morn·ing /yéstər màwrning/ (*archaic or literary*) *adv* yesterday in the morning ■ *n* the morning of yesterday

yes·ter·night /yéstər nīt/ (*archaic or literary*) *adv* yesterday at night ■ *n* the night of yesterday

yes·ter·year /yéstər yeér/ *n* **1.** the not very recent past **2.** the year before this one

yet /yet/ *adv* **1.** SO FAR up to now or a particular time in the past or future (*often used with a negative or interrogative*) ○ *The information had not yet been analyzed.* ○ *Have you finished eating yet?* ○ *This study is the most comprehensive yet.* **2.** NOW now, as opposed to later (*often used with a negative*) ○ *I can't come over just yet.* **3.** EVEN even or still (*often used with a comparative*) ○ *This spurred her on to yet greater efforts.* ○ *Yet again, we find the same reluctance to act.* **4.** IN SPITE OF EVERYTHING used to stress that it remains possible that something will happen or that you are still determined to do something despite present difficulties ○ *We'll solve this problem yet.* **5.** FOR LONGER used to indicate that something will go on happening for a particular length of time ○ *It will take hours yet for the space telescope photos to arrive on Earth and be processed.* **6.** NEVER UP TO NOW used to indicate that somebody has not done something up to now ○ *She's been there several weeks and we've yet to hear from her.* ■ *conj* NEVERTHELESS however or nevertheless ○ *Her problems are increasing, yet she keeps smiling.* [Old English *gīet*, origin ?]

USAGE *Did she go yet?* In the simple past tense ***yet*** is used in this way in informal English rather than the perfect tense: *Has she gone yet?* In some meanings, ***yet*** and *still* are largely interchangeable: *This has still to be decided* or *This has yet to be decided.*

ye·ti /yéttee/ (*plural* **-tis**) *n* a mysterious hairy humanoid animal said to live in the Himalaya range [Mid-20C. Origin ?]

yet·tie /yéttee/ *n* a young, technologically knowledgeable entrepreneur who is involved in e-commerce and who typically buys and sells technology stock (*slang*) [Late 20C. Acronym < *young, entrepreneurial, tech(nology)-based*, after YUPPIE and similar words]

Yev·tu·shen·ko /yèvtə shéngkō/, **Yevgeny Aleksandrovich** (*b.* 1933) Russian poet. His works such as *Zima Junction* (1956) and *Babi Yar* (1961) were critical of the former Soviet Union during its post-Stalinist years, and, although officially condemned by the Soviets, were widely read in both his own country and the West.

> "Over Babi Yar / There are no memorials. / The steep hillside like a rough inscription."
> [Yevgeny Aleksandrovich Yevtushenko, *Babi Yar*; 1961]

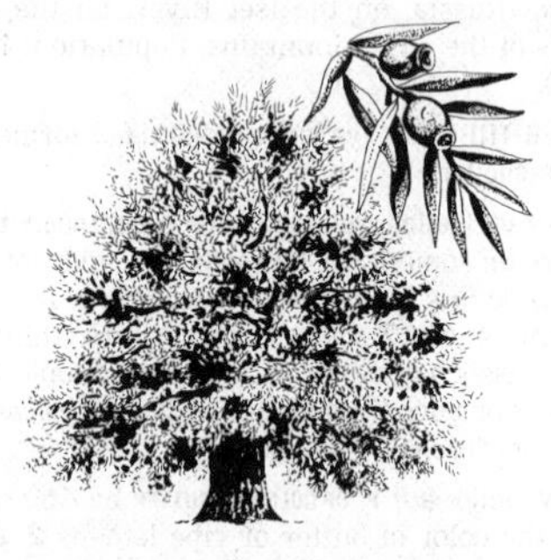

yew

yew /yoo/ *n* **1.** EVERGREEN TREE an evergreen tree or bush that has flat dark green needles and scarlet fruits (**arils**) that resemble berries. Most parts of the tree are considered poisonous. Genus: *Taxus*. **2.** WOOD the fine-grained wood of a poisonous evergreen tree. Use: cabinetmaking and, especially formerly, making bows. **3.** YEW BOW an archer's bow made of yew wood [Old English *īw* < Germanic]

Yez·i·di /yézzədee/ *n* a member of a Kurdish religious group founded by an Muslim mystic in the 12th century but incorporating Iranian myth and tradition. The group has been declared as heretical by orthodox Muslims and has been the object of intense persecution. [Early 19C. Origin ?] —**Yez·i·dism** *n*

Ygg·dra·sil /ígdrəss'l/, **Yg·dra·sil** *n* in Norse mythology, the great ash tree that overshadows the world, binding together earth, heaven, and hell [< Old Norse]

YHWH, YHVH, JHVH, JHWH *n* the transliteration of the four letters (**Tetragrammaton**) representing the name of God in the Bible. This transliteration was only ever pronounced by the high priest in the Temple.

Yi /yee/ *n* a Korean dynasty that ruled Korea from 1392, following a period of Mongol invasions, until 1910, and that restored aristocratic dominance and Chinese influence

yid /yid/ *n* a highly offensive term for a Jew (*taboo insult*) [Late 19C. Via Yiddish < Middle High German *jüde* "Jew" (see YIDDISH)]

Yid·dish /yíddish/ *n* a language derived from a medieval German dialect and written in Hebrew script, spoken by some Jews in Europe, Israel, and North and South America. It reflects the influence of Hebrew, Aramaic, and other languages, especially Slavonic languages. See panel on next page [Late 19C. Via Yiddish *yidish (daytsh)* "Jewish (German)" < Middle High German *jüdisch diutsch* < *jüde* "Jewish person" < Latin *Judaeus* (see JEW)] —**Yid·dish** *adj*

yield /yeeld/ *v* (**yield·ed, yield·ing, yields**) **1.** *vt* PRODUCE SOMETHING to produce something naturally or as a result of cultivation ○ *The field yields a good crop.* **2.** *vt* GIVE SOMETHING AS RESULT to produce something as the result of work, activity, or calculation ○ *The research has yielded some interesting results.* **3.** *vt* FIN GIVE PROFIT to gain an amount as a return on an investment ○ *bonds that yield 9 percent* **4.** *vi* NOT BE FIRM OR SOLID to move or bend under pressure or when force is applied ○ *The window was painted shut and wouldn't yield.* **5.** *vi* STOP RESISTING to stop opposing or resisting and agree to somebody's demands or

LANGUAGE HERITAGE ***Yiddish*** Much of English is made up of words from other languages, and Yiddish is an important contributor in this respect, making English all the more richly textured and colorful. Words migrating into English directly from Yiddish alone are, for example, ***mazuma***, ***shlemiel***, and ***tush***. Many others came into English via Yiddish but have other ancestral roots, for example, ***bagel*** (from Old High German), ***chutzpah*** (from Aramaic), ***nudge*** (from Polish), and ***yenta*** (from Latin). And the word ***Yiddish*** itself is an émigré from Middle High German and Latin. Yiddish words derived from Hebrew include, for example, ***matzo***, ***maven***, and ***schmooze***.
Yiddish also has given English two colorful affixes. The first is the suffix ***-nik***, "somebody associated with or characterized by," for example, ***peacenik*** and ***refusenik***, along with creative forms such as "real-estatenik," "noshnik," "Freudnik," "nogoodnik," and "allrightnik." Yiddish acquired this form from Russian, and some early words containing it may be directly from that language, but its creativity stems from Yiddish use. The second is ***schm-*** or ***shm-***, "somebody or something purported or purporting to be genuine, real, or of the expected high quality but really not." This prefix creates hyphenated rhyming compounds by replacing the initial consonants or consonant clusters in English words, yielding, for example, "doctor-schmoctor," "fancy-schmancy," or by preceding initial vowels ("Elvis-Schmelvis," "opera-shmopera").
In some instances Yiddish has fused with English to yield familiar compounds like ***gefilte fish*** and ***matzo balls***. What is more, certain English grammatical constructions and idioms are traceable to Yiddish constructions, for example, "Be well," a loose translation of Yiddish *zay gezunt*. Other English expressions originally associated with Yiddish speakers are these verb commands, a good many opening with *so*: "So stop it already!" "So sit." "Enjoy." "Go know." "Get lost!" "Eat your heart out." Others are inversions, for example, "He is a boy is all." "A fashion model she is not." Still others are rhetorical questions opening with "What's to" followed by a verb, for example, "What's to like?" "What's not to like?" "What's to forgive?" See also ***Hebrew***.

requests ○ *She refused to yield despite our pleas.* **6.** *vi* **SURRENDER** to admit defeat and surrender ○ *The commander finally yielded after a long siege.* **7.** *vt* **PASS SOMETHING ON TO SOMEBODY** to give something up to somebody else or allow somebody else to take it over ○ *He eventually yielded control of the company to his daughter.* **8.** *vi* **BE REPLACED BY SOMETHING** to be replaced by something else ○ *Older houses and gardens were gradually yielding to modern apartments.* **9.** *vi* ROADS **LET ANOTHER PASS** to slow down or stop in order to let another vehicle pass ○ *yield to traffic on the right* ■ *n* **1. AMOUNT PRODUCED** the amount of something, especially a crop, produced by cultivation or labor ○ *Yields per acre were slightly lower than last year.* **2. RETURN ON INVESTMENT** a return on an investment in the form of interest or dividends ○ *The yield on the account was disappointing.* **3. PRODUCT FROM CHEMICAL REACTION** the quantity of product resulting from a chemical reaction or process, often expressed as a percentage of the amount that is theoretically obtainable **4. EXPLOSIVE FORCE** the amount of energy released in a nuclear explosion expressed as the amount of TNT that would have the same explosive force [Old English *geldan* "pay" < Germanic] —**yield·a·ble** *adj* —**yield·er** *n*

SYNONYMS ***yield, capitulate, submit, succumb, surrender, give in***

CORE MEANING: to stop resisting

yield to stop opposing or resisting and agree to somebody's demands or requests ○ *The government would not yield to public pressure.* **capitulate** to accept an argument, request, pressure, or something unavoidable ○ *We cannot afford the gains we have made to be lost by capitulating to the demands of special interest groups.* **submit** to accept somebody else's authority or will, especially reluctantly or under pressure ○ *We don't intend to submit meekly to the proposed changes.* **succumb** to be unable to resist or oppose something ○ *For all her good intentions, she soon succumbed to the temptation of another cigarette.* **surrender** to declare to an opponent that he or she has won so that fighting or conflict can cease ○ *Still the enemy refused to surrender.* **give in** to accept demands or conditions ○ *Governments can't be seen to give in to terrorist threats.*

yield up *vt* to reveal something formerly hidden or secret

yield·ing /yéelding/ *adj* **1. SOFT AND BENDING** inclined to give or bend under pressure **2. COMPLIANT** tending to obey others **3. PRODUCING** productive of a good or bad yield or crop —**yield·ing·ly** *adv* —**yield·ing·ness** *n*

yikes /yīks/ *interj* used when suddenly startled (*informal*) [Late 20C. Origin ?]

yin /yin/ *n* the principle of darkness, negativity, and femininity in Chinese philosophy that is the counterpart of yang. The dual, opposite, and complementary principles of yin and yang are thought to exist in varying proportions in all things. [Late 17C. < Chinese *yīn* "shade, feminine, moon"]

Yin·chuan /yìn chwaán/ capital city of Ningxia Hui Autonomous Region in north central China. Population: 337,855 (1991).

Ying·lish /yíng glish/ *n* a type of English influenced by Yiddish words and syntax, spoken by early Jewish immigrants to the United States [Mid-20C. Blend of YIDDISH + ENGLISH] —**Ying·lish** *adj*

yip /yip/ *vi* (**yipped, yip·ping, yips**) to give a high-pitched bark ■ *n* a high-pitched bark [An imitation of the sound]

yipe /yīp/ *interj US* used to express fear or alarm (*informal*) [Mid-20C. Origin ?]

yip·ee /yi pée/, **yip·pee** *interj* used to express joy and excitement (*usually used by children*) [Early 20C. A natural exclamation]

yip·pie /yíppee/ *n US* a politically radical hippie during the late 1960s and early 1970s in the United States [Mid-20C. < *Y(outh) I(nternational) P(arty)*, after HIPPIE]

yips /yips/ *npl* nervousness that impairs the performance of a sportsman or sportswoman, especially a golfer [Mid-20C. Origin ?]

Yiz·kor /yíz kàwr/ *n* in Judaism, a memorial prayer for deceased relatives recited in synagogues on festivals and Yom Kippur [Mid-20C. < Hebrew *yizkōr* "may He remember"]

-yl *suffix* a group of atoms forming a radical ○ *carbonyl* [Via French *-yle* < Greek *hulē* "wood, organic matter"]

y·lang-y·lang /ée laáng ée laáng/, **i·lang-i·lang** *n* a tree with flowers that yield a fragrant oil used in perfumery. Native to: tropical Asia, northern Australia. Latin name: *Cananga odorata*. [Late 19C. < Tagalog *ilang-ilang*]

y·lem /īləm/ *n* hypothetical matter that, according to the big bang theory of the origin of the universe, was the substance from which the chemical elements were formed [Mid-20C. < medieval Latin *hylem* "universal matter" < Greek *hulē* "wood, matter"]

Y-lev·el *n* a rotatable level mounted on a Y-shaped frame, used in surveying

YMCA[1] *n* a building or other center where social, sports, or educational facilities are provided by the YMCA for its members

YMCA[2], **Y.M.C.A.** *abbr* Young Men's Christian Association

YMHA, **Y.M.H.A.** *abbr* Young Men's Hebrew Association

Y·mir /ée méer/ *n* in Norse mythology, the forefather of all the giants. Ymir was killed by Odin and his brothers, and the world was formed from his body, the sky from his skull, and the water from his blood.

Y·mo·dem /wī́ mō dem/ *n* a variation of the Xmodem file transfer protocol in which data is sent in 1-kilobyte blocks

yo /yō/ *interj* used as a greeting or to get somebody's attention (*slang*) [15C. Natural exclamation]

yob /yob/, **yob·bo** /yóbbō/ (*plural* **-bos**) *n UK* a young hooligan (*slang*) [Mid-19C. Backward spelling of BOY] —**yob·ber·y** *n* —**yob·bish** *adj*

YOB *abbr* year of birth

yob·bo *n* same as **yob**

yocto- *prefix* indicates 10^{-24} in measurements ○ *yoctojoule* [Late 20C. Modeled on OCTO-]

yod /yod/, **yodh** *n* the tenth letter of the Hebrew alphabet, represented in the English alphabet as "y." See table at **alphabet** [Mid-18C. < Hebrew *yōḏ*]

yo·del /yṓd'l/, **yo·dle** *vi* (**-deled, -del·ing, -dels; -dled, -dling, -dles**) to sing, changing rapidly between a normal and falsetto voice. It is a feature of Alpine folk music and of some US country and western music. ■ *n* a song or passage that features yodeling [Early 19C. < German *jodeln* an imitation of the sound] —**yo·del·er** *n*

yodh *n* another spelling of **yod**

yo·dle *vi, n* MUSIC another spelling of **yodel**

Tony Arruza/Corbis

yoga: half spinal twist position

yo·ga /yṓgə/ *n* **1.** a Hindu discipline that promotes spiritual unity with a supreme being through a system of postures and rituals **2.** a system or set of breathing exercises and postures derived from or based on Hindu yoga [Late 18C. < Sanskrit *yogaḥ* "union"]

Yo·ga·la·tes /yōgə laátayz/ *tdmk* a trademark for a holistic form of exercise that combines the breathing techniques of yoga with the body movements of Pilates [Late 20C]

yogh /yōg/ *n* a letter ʒ used in Middle English, usually represented in modern English as "gh" or "y" [13C. Origin ?]

yo·ghurt *n* FOOD another spelling of **yogurt**

yo·gi /yṓgee/ (*plural* **-gis**), **yo·gin** /yṓgən/ *n S Asia* **1.** somebody who has mastered yoga **2.** a guru or other spiritual teacher of religion [Early 17C. < Sanskrit *yogī* < *yogaḥ* "yoga"]

yo·gurt /yṓgərt/, **yo·ghurt**, **yo·ghourt** *n* milk fermented by bacteria to give a tangy or slightly sour flavor and a lightly set or thick and creamy consistency. It is sometimes sweetened and flavored, usually with fruit. [Early 17C. < Turkish *yoğurt*]

Yog·ya·kar·ta /yòggyə kaártə, jàwk yaa-/ city in southwestern Indonesia, on the island of Java. Population: 477,073 (1997).

yo-heave-ho *interj* formerly used by sailors as a rhythmic accompaniment to hauling work

Yo·ho Na·tion·al Park /yṓhō-/ national park in the Rocky Mountains of southeastern British Columbia, Canada. Area: 507 sq. mi./1,313 sq. km.

yoicks /yoyks/ *interj* used to encourage hounds in a foxhunt [Mid-18C. Origin ?]

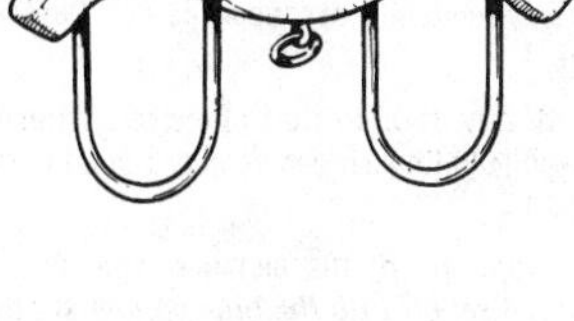

yoke

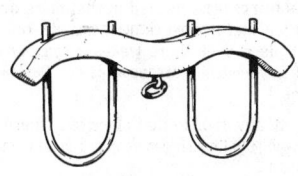

yoke /yōk/ *n* **1. ANIMAL HARNESS** a wooden frame for harnessing two draft animals to whatever they had to pull **2. JOINED ANIMALS** two animals joined by a yoke ○ *a yoke of oxen* **3. FRAME FOR CARRYING LOADS** a frame designed to fit across somebody's shoulders with balanced loads suspended at each end **4.** CLOTHING **FITTED PART OF GARMENT** the fitted part of a garment, usually around the shoulders or waist, from which an unfitted part is suspended **5. RESTRICTIVE BURDEN** something that is felt to be oppressive and restrictive ○ *throw off the tyrant's yoke* **6. BOND KEEPING PEOPLE CLOSE** a bond or tie that keeps people together ○ *the yoke of marriage* **7. CROSSED SPEARS** an archway made of crossed spears under which defeated enemies of the ancient Romans were forced to march **8.** NAUT **RUDDER CROSSBAR** a crossbar attached to the top of a rudder and connected to the front of a boat by ropes or cables for steering **9.** ELECTRONICS **CATHODE RAY DEVICE** a device attached to the neck of a cathode ray tube to control the scanning motion of the electron beam **10.** RECORDING **EQUIPMENT FOR MULTITRACK RECORDING** equipment for recording or reproducing sounds or music on more than one track simultaneously, by joining together two or more magnetic recording heads **11.** AVIAT **AIRCRAFT PART** the handle of the steering mechanism for an airplane's ailerons ■ *vt* (**yoked, yok·ing, yokes**) **1. FIT ANIMALS WITH YOKE** to put a yoke on two draft animals **2. CONNECT ANIMAL TO VEHICLE** to connect a draft animal to a plow or vehicle **3. LINK THINGS TOGETHER** to join or link two things forcibly or surprisingly ○ *Ranchers were yoked together with farmers on the issue.* [Old English *geoc* < Indo-European, "join"]

SPELLCHECK Do not confuse the spelling of ***yoke*** and ***yolk***, which sound similar. ***Yoke*** refers to a frame for pulling or carrying a load, or something oppressive or restrictive: *put the yoke on the oxen, the yoke of tyranny, yoked them to the plow.* The ***yolk*** is the yellow portion of an egg.

yo·kel /yṓk'l/ *n* an offensive term that deliberately insults a country dweller by suggesting that he or she lacks the sophistication, education, or other qualities thought characteristic of city dwellers (*insult*) [Early 19C. Origin ?] —**yo·kel·ish** *adj*

Yo·ko·ha·ma /yṑkō haámə/ capital city and port of Kanagawa Prefecture, in southeastern Honshu Island, Japan. Population: 3,433,612 (2002).

yolk /yōk/ *n* **1.** the round yellow portion of a bird's or reptile's egg, containing protein and fats that provide nourishment for the developing young. The eggs of mammals, whose embryos absorb nutrients from the mother, contain very little yolk. **2.** a greasy substance from the skin of sheep that collects in wool [Old English *geol(o)ca* < *geolu* (see YELLOW)] —**yolk·y** *adj*

SPELLCHECK See ***yoke***.

yolk sac *n* a thin membrane surrounding the embryo in birds, fish, reptiles, and mammals. In birds, fish, and reptiles, it encloses the yolk.

Yom A·ra·fat another spelling of **Yawm Arafat**

Yom Kip·pur /yàwm kíppər, -kee poór/ *n* the holiest day of the Jewish year, on which Jews fast and say prayers of penitence. Date: 10th day of Tishri. [< Hebrew *Yōm Kippūr* "day of atonement"]

yom tov /yáwm tàwv/ (*plural* **ya·mim to·vim** /yaa meém taw veém/) *n* any Jewish religious festival [Directly and via Yiddish *yontef* < Hebrew *yōm ṭōḇ* "good day"]

yon /yon/ *adv* **OVER THERE** in or to that place over there (*regional or literary*) ○ *wandered hither and yon* ■ *adj regional* **THAT OR THOSE** located in that place over there ■ *pron regional* **THAT ONE OR THOSE ONES** the one or ones in that place over there (*takes a singular or plural verb*) [Partly shortening of YONDER, partly < Old English *geon* "that one"]

yond /yond/ *adv* in or to that place over there (*archaic or literary*) [Old English *geond, geondan* < Indo-European, "that one"]

yon·der /yóndər/ *n* **THE DISTANCE** the far distance (*informal*) ○ *set off into the blue yonder* ■ *adv regional* **OVER THERE** in or to that place over there ■ *adj Southern US* **THAT OR THOSE** located in that place over there ■ *pron Southern US* **THAT ONE OR THOSE ONES** the one or ones in that place over there (*takes a singular or plural verb*)

yo·ni /yṓnee/ (*plural* **-nis**) *n* in Hinduism, a representation of the female genitals regarded as a manifestation of the feminine principle [Late 18C. < Sanskrit *yoniḥ* "womb"]

Yon·kers /yóngkərz/ city in southeastern New York, on the Hudson River. It is a northern suburb of New York City. Population: 197,234 (2002 estimate).

yoo-hoo /yoȯ hoȯ/ *interj* used to get somebody's attention, especially when the speaker is at a distance ■ *vti* (**yoo-hooed, yoo-hoo·ing, yoo-hoos**) to say or shout "yoo-hoo" to somebody [Early 20C. Natural exclamation]

Yor·ba Lin·da /yàwrbə líndə/ city in the Santa Ana Mountains of southwestern California. President Richard M. Nixon was born there, and it is home to his presidential library. Population: 61,065 (2002 estimate).

yore /yawr/ [Old English *geāra*, origin ?] ◇ **of yore** in the far distant past (*literary*) ○ *in days of yore*

York /yawrk/ city in Yorkshire, northern England. Originally a Celtic settlement, under the Romans it became an important regional center. Population: 181,094 (2001).

York, Alvin Cullum (1887–1964) US soldier. He is famed for his successful, almost single-handed, attack on a German machine-gun nest during World War I (November 1, 1918). He was awarded the Congressional Medal of Honor and the Croix de Guerre. Known as **Sergeant York**

Yorke Pen·in·su·la /yàwrk-/ peninsula in South Australia, situated between the Gulf of St. Vincent and the Spencer Gulf.

york·ie /yáwrkee/, **York·ie** *n* BREED same as **Yorkshire terrier** (*informal*) [Early 19C. Shortening]

York·ist /yáwrkist/ *n* a supporter or member of the House of York during the Wars of the Roses and when it ruled England from 1461 to 1485

York rite *n* a masonic ceremony that confers different degrees at different levels of the membership [Late 19C. After YORK in England]

York·shire /yáwrk sheér, -shər/ former county in northern England, at one time the largest in the country. Traditionally divided into the East, West, and North Ridings, it has been a historically important region since Roman times.

York·shire Dales area of wild moorlands divided by fertile valleys in the mid-Pennines, Northern England

York·shire pud·ding *n* a flour-based batter pudding that is traditionally served with roast beef. It was originally served with gravy before roast meat with the intention of satisfying appetites so that a small amount of meat would go a long way.

Yorkshire terrier

York·shire ter·ri·er *n* a very small longhaired terrier with a long silky brown-and-gray coat

York·ton /yáwrktən/ town in Saskatchewan, Canada, northeast of Regina. Population: 15,107 (2001).

York·town /yáwrk tòwn/ historic site in southeastern Virginia, situated on the York River near Chesapeake Bay. It was the site of the final battle of the Revolution and of the British general Cornwallis's surrender to George Washington on October 19, 1781, and of the earliest engagement of George McClellan's Peninsular Campaign during the Civil War in the spring of 1862.

Yo·ru·ba /yáwrəbə/ (*plural same* or **-bas**) *n* **1. MEMBER OF W AFRICAN PEOPLE** a member of a West African people living mostly in Nigeria **2. W AFRICAN LANGUAGE** a Niger-Congo language spoken in southwestern Nigeria, Benin, and Togo. Native speakers: 20 million. **3. REGION OF CITY-STATES IN NIGERIA** a region of city-states that developed in northern Nigeria around A.D. 1200, notable for the population's animistic religion and their artistic work, in particular wood and bronze pieces [Mid-19C. < Yoruba] —**Yo·ru·ba** *adj* —**Yo·ru·ban** *adj*

Yo·sem·i·te Falls /yō sèmmətee-/ falls in the Yosemite National Park, California. Consisting of the Upper Yosemite Falls and the Lower Yosemite Falls, it is one of the highest falls in the world, with a total drop of 2,425 ft./739 m.

Yo·sem·i·te Na·tion·al Park national park in central California in the Sierra Nevada, established in 1890. It is noted for its giant sequoia trees and falls. Area: 1,189 sq. mi./3,081 sq. km.

yotta- *prefix* indicates 10^{24} in measurements ○ *yottabyte* [Late 20c. Probably < Italian *otto* "eight"]

you *stressed* /yoo/; *unstressed* /yə/ *pron* **1. PERSON BEING ADDRESSED** refers to the person or people being addressed or written to ○ *I'm fine – how about you?* **2. PERSON OR PEOPLE UNSPECIFIED** refers to an unspecified person or people in general ○ *You have to see it to believe it.* ○ *You mix all the dry ingredients together in a bowl.* **3. THOSE BEING REFERRED TO** used to refer to the person you are talking to, as well as other people of the same type or class (*used before a pl*) ○ *Isn't it time you kids were in bed?* **4. PERSONALITY OF PERSON ADDRESSED** refers to the personality of the person addressed or something's suitability to express it (*informal*) ○ *Don't buy that suit; it's really not you!* **5.** *US* same as **yourself** (sense 1) (*informal; used as an indirect object*) ○ *You'll have to get you a job.* [Old English *ēow* < *gē* (see YE[1])]

USAGE See ***yourself***.

you-all, **y'all** /yawl/ *pron Southern US* used to address more than one person (*informal*)

REGIONAL NOTE The pronoun ***you-all*** is Southern usage. Unlike Northern *youse*, which is limited to nonstandard usage, the Southern form ***you-all*** is found among all social groups. It is virtually never used in the singular except in bad imitations by people of other regions.

you'd /yood/ *contr* **1.** you had **2.** you would

you'll /yool/ *contr* **1.** you shall **2.** you will

young /yung/ *adj* (**young·er, young·est**) **1. NOT VERY OLD** having lived or been in existence a relatively short time ○ *a young person* **2. OF YOUTH** relating to somebody's youth ○ *my younger days* **3. YOUTHFUL** looking or behaving like a young or younger person ○ *very young for her age* **4. FOR YOUNG PEOPLE** designed for or appropriate to young people ○ *young fashions* **5. RECENTLY BEGUN** recently begun or in an early stage ○ *The night is still young.* **6.** GEOL **NOT SIGNIFICANTLY ERODED** in a relatively early stage of landscape formation and therefore steep and largely uneroded ■ *npl* **1. OFFSPRING** offspring, especially when still completely dependent on parents ○ *watching her young* **2. YOUNG PEOPLE** young people in general ○ *a club for the young* [Old English *geong* < Indo-European, "youth, vigor"] — **young·ish** *adj* —**young·ness** *n* ◇ **in your younger days** when you were younger than you are now ◇ **the Younger** used after a person's name to indicate that he or she is the second-born person of that name ○ *Pitt the Younger*

Young /yung/, **Andrew Jackson, Jr.** (*b.* 1932) US civil rights activist, diplomat, and politician. A close associate of Martin Luther King, he helped draft the Civil Rights Act of 1964 and the Voting Rights Act of 1965. He was elected a US congressman from Georgia (1972, 74, 76) and appointed US ambassador to the United Nations (1976), He later also served as mayor of Atlanta, GA (1981–89).

Young, Brigham (1801–77) US religious leader. He succeeded Joseph Smith as the leader of the Church of Jesus Christ of Latter-Day Saints (1844–77). He organized the church members' migration from Illinois to Utah (1846–47), where he founded Salt Lake City.

> "I am here to answer. I shall be on hand to answer when I am called upon, for all the counsel and for all the instruction that I

have given to this people."
[Brigham Young. Quoted in *Journal of Discourses*, John A. Widtsoe (ed.); 1954]

Young, Cy (1867–1955) US baseball player. He was the first player in major league history to pitch a perfect game (1904), and an annual award for the best major league pitcher was established in his honor. Born **Young, Denton True**

Young, Thomas (1773–1829) British physicist and Egyptologist. He was noted for his work in optics, in particular his discovery of the phenomenon of interference. He helped decipher the Egyptian hieroglyphics on the Rosetta stone.

Young, Whitney M., Jr. (1921–71) US civil rights leader and social worker. He directed the National Urban League (1961–71) and advised President Lyndon B. Johnson on antipoverty programs. Full name **Young, Whitney Moore, Jr.**

"White is ugly when it oppresses Blacks—and so is Black ugly when Black people exploit other Blacks. No race has a monopoly on vice or virtue."
[Whitney M. Young, Jr, *Beyond Racism: Building an Open Society*; 1969]

young·ber·ry /yúng bèrree/ (*plural* **-ries**) *n* **1.** a large, sweet, dark-purple fruit, a hybrid of the blackberry and dewberry **2.** the trailing bramble that produces youngberries. Native to: southwestern United States. [Early 20C. After B. M. *Young*, US horticulturist]

young blood *n* fresh, new, and vigorous ideas or people

Young·er Ed·da *n* LITERAT same as **Edda** (sense 2)

young·ling /yúngling/ *n* a young person or a young animal

young of·fend·er *n* **1.** *Can* in Canada, somebody between the ages of 12 and 18 who has committed a crime and must be treated according to the terms of the Young Offenders Act, 1984 **2.** *UK* same as **youthful offender**

young of·fend·er in·sti·tu·tion, young of·fend·ers in·sti·tu·tion *n* in the United Kingdom, a place where somebody between the ages of 14 and 20 can be detained to serve a court sentence or while on remand accused of a crime

young·ster /yúngstər/ *n* **1. CHILD** a child or young person **2.** somebody who is younger than other people ○ *All you youngsters in your 40s don't think too seriously about retirement.* **3.** *US* NAVY **SECOND-YEAR NAVAL CADET** a second-year midshipman at the US Naval Academy **4. YOUNG HORSE** a young horse

SYNONYMS See *youth.*

Youngs·town /yúngz tòwn/ city on the Mahoning River in northeastern Ohio. It is an industrial center, and was formerly a major iron and steel producer. Population: 80,026 (2002 estimate).

Young Turk *n* **1.** a young person, especially one of a group, who attempts to wrest control of an organization from an older, established, more conservative group **2.** a member of a liberal prodemocratic Turkish nationalist movement in the early 20th century that brought about a short-lived revolution in 1908

young'un /yúngən/ *n* an infant or child (*informal*)

youn·ker /yúngkər/ *n* (*archaic*) **1.** a young man **2.** same as **child** (sense 1) [Early 16C. < Middle Dutch *jonckher* < *jonc* "young" + *hēre* "lord"]

your *stressed* /yawr, yoor/; *unstressed* /yər/ *adj* **1. BELONGING TO PERSON SPOKEN TO** refers to something that belongs to or relates to the person who is being spoken to ○ *What's your phone number?* **2. BELONGING OR RELATING TO SOMEBODY** refers to something that belongs or relates to an unspecified person or people in general ○ *The house is on your left as you come down the street.* **3. INDICATES TYPICALITY** refers to somebody or something as a typical example of a familiar type (*informal*) ○ *your typical neighborhood park* [Old English *ēower* < *gē* (see YE[1])]

SPELLCHECK your or **you're**? Do not confuse the spelling of **your** and **you're** which sound similar. The word **your** indicates possession: *Your* [not *You're*] *e-mail password must be protected.* **You're** is a contraction of "you are": *You're* [not *Your*] *protecting your e-mail password, aren't you?*

Popperfoto

Marguerite Yourcenar

Your·ce·nar /yoórssə naár/, **Marguerite** (1903–87) Belgian-born French and US writer. Many of her works, including *Memoirs of Hadrian* (1951), follow historical themes. Pseudonym of **Crayencour, Marguerite de**

"A man who reads, who thinks, or who calculates, belongs to the species and not to the sex; in his better moments, he even escapes being human."
[Marguerite Yourcenar, *Memoirs of Hadrian*; 1951]

you're *stressed* /yoor, yawr/; *unstressed* /yər/ *contr* you are

SPELLCHECK See *your.*

yours /yawrz, yoorz/ *pron* **1.** refers to something that belongs or relates to the person or people being addressed ○ *This idea of yours is very interesting.* **2.** *also* **Yours** used at the end of letters before somebody signs his or her name ○ *Sincerely yours, Marcia Klein*

your·self /yawr sélf, yoor-, yər-/ (*plural* **yourselves** /-sélvz/) *pron* **1. SOMEBODY BEING ADDRESSED** refers to the person or people being addressed or written to ○ *Be careful not to hurt yourself.* **2. MAKING REFERENCE TO SOMEBODY SPOKEN TO** refers emphatically or politely to the person or people being addressed or written to ○ *"Consider," he replied, "how you yourself really feel about such things."* **3. YOUR NORMAL SELF** your normal or usual self ○ *You are not yourself tonight.*

USAGE The primary uses of *yourself* are as a reflexive pronoun (*Don't hurt yourself*) and as an emphatic pronoun (*Can you do it yourself?*). In formal writing it should not be used as an alternative for *you* in sentences of the type: *That's up to you* [not *up to yourself*].

yours tru·ly *pron* me, myself, or I (*informal*) ○ *Of course, everyone's going to be there except yours truly.*

youse /yooz/, **yous** *pron regional* used to address more than one person (*nonstandard*) [Late 19C. < YOU]

youth /yooth/ *n* **1. TIME WHEN SOMEBODY IS YOUNG** the period of human life between childhood and maturity **2. TIME OF BEING YOUNG** the state of being young **3. YOUNG MAN** a boy or young man in his teens or early twenties **4. EARLY STAGE** an early stage of something **5.** GEOL **EROSION STAGE** the first stage in landscape formation in which fast-flowing streams travel down steep mountain valleys ■ *npl* **YOUNG PEOPLE** young people in general [Old English *geogup* < Germanic]

SYNONYMS *youth, child, kid, teenager, youngster*

CORE MEANING: somebody who is young

youth a boy or young man in his teens or early twenties. ○ *youths who regularly attend rock concerts* **child** a young person between birth and the onset of puberty ○ *In these early years, children grow and learn within their families.* **kid** (*informal*) a child or young person ○ *a happily married bank manager with four lovely kids* **teenager** somebody between the ages of 13 and 19 ○ *the problems and pressures facing teenagers today* **youngster** a child or young person, or somebody who is younger than others mentioned or present ○ *a club for youngsters aged between 6 and 11* ○ *veterans in their 70s and 80s, with a few youngsters in their 60s*

youth·an·ize /yoóthə nīz/ (**-iz·ed, -iz·ing, -izes**) *vt US* to design or alter something such as a clothing line so that it will appeal to youth culture or to youthful buyers (*informal*)

youth-cen·tric /yoóth séntrik/ *adj* specifically focused on and directed toward the interests of young people ○ *a youth-centric website*

Youth Court *n* in Canada, a provincial court with jurisdiction over all cases involving offenders under the age of 18

youth·ful /yoóthf'l/ *adj* **1. LIKE YOUTH** characteristic of or possessing youth **2. VIGOROUS** vigorous and energetic **3. NOT FULLY DEVELOPED** in early development and not yet mature **4.** GEOL **MILDLY ERODED** steep, rugged, and relatively uneroded **5.** GEOG **NEAR SOURCE** describes a fast-flowing stream close to its source —**youth·ful·ly** *adv* —**youth·ful·ness** *n*

youth·ful of·fend·er *n US* somebody under 18 who has committed a criminal act

youth hos·tel *n* an establishment offering cheap lodging for travelers, especially young travelers

you-uns /yoó ənz/ *pron Southern US* used to address more than one person (*nonstandard*)

you've /yoov/ *contr* you have

yow /yow/ *interj* used to express pain, surprise, or alarm (*informal*) [Mid-19C. Natural exclamation]

yowl /yowl/ *vi* (**yowled, yowl·ing, yowls**) to cry out mournfully or as an expression of pain ■ *n* a long mournful wail [12C. Probably an imitation of the sound] —**yowl·er** *n*

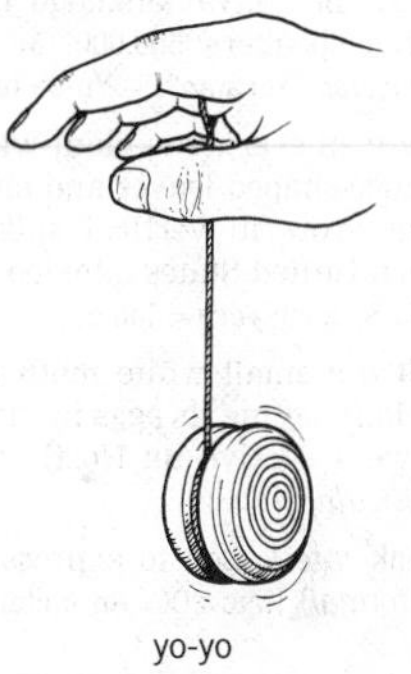

yo-yo

yo-yo /yṓ yṑ/ *n* (*plural* **yo-yos**) **1. TOY WITH STRING WOUND ON SPOOL** a toy consisting of a long string wound onto a spool that is dropped and raised repeatedly using the force of gravity and momentum to unwind and rewind the string **2. FLUCTUATING THING** something that repeatedly goes up and down or fluctuates between one extreme and another **3. OFFENSIVE TERM** an offensive term that deliberately insults a person's intelligence or judgment (*slang insult*) ■ *vi* (**yo-yoed, yo-yo·ing, yo-yos**) **FLUCTUATE** to fluctuate between two extremes or directions [Early 20C. Origin ?]

yo-yo di·et·ing *n* a situation in which somebody repeatedly loses weight through dieting and then regains the weight that he or she has lost

Y·pres /eéprə/ town in southwestern Belgium, in West Flanders Province, near the border of France. During World War I, the town was the site of several major battles and was almost completely destroyed. Population: 35,409 (1995).

yr. *abbr* **1.** year **2.** younger **3.** your

YST *abbr* Yukon Standard Time

yt *abbr* Mayotte (*used in Internet addresses*) See table at **domain name**

YT *abbr also* **Y.T.** Yukon Territory

YTD *abbr* year to date

yt·ter·bi·a /i túrbee ə/ *n* CHEM same as **ytterbium oxide** [Late 19C. After *Ytterby* (see YTTERBIUM)]

yt·ter·bi·um /i túrbee əm/ *n* a soft silvery metal of the lanthanide group of rare-earth elements. Source: monazite, bastnaesite. Use: strengthening steel, in laser devices and portable X-ray units. Symbol **Yb.** See table at **element** [Late 19C. After *Ytterby*, a Swedish quarry] —**yt·ter·bic** *adj*

yt·ter·bi·um ox·ide *n* a colorless oxide of ytterbium. Use: alloys, ceramics. Formula: Yb_2O_3.

yt·tri·a /íttree ə/ *n* CHEM same as **yttrium oxide** [Early 19C. After *Ytterby*, a Swedish quarry]

yt·trif·er·ous /i tríffərəss/ *adj* yielding or containing yttrium

yt·tri·um /íttree əm/ *n* a silvery gray metallic element. Source: uranium, rare-earth ores. Use: superconducting alloys, permanent magnets. Symbol **Y**. See table at **element** [Early 19C. < YTTRIA] —**yt·tric** *adj*

yt·tri·um met·al *n* a metal in the group that includes yttrium and related rare-earth elements such as holmium, erbium, thulium, ytterbium, and lutetium

yt·tri·um ox·ide *n* a yellowish powder. Use: optical glass, ceramics, lasers, microwave components. Formula: Y_2O_3.

yu *abbr* Yugoslavia (*used in Internet addresses*) See table at **domain name**

yu·an /yoo a̋an/ (*plural same*) *n* the main unit of currency in China, worth 10 jiao. See table at **currency** [Early 20C. < Chinese *yuán* "round"]

Yu·ca·tán /yo͝okə tán, -ta̋an/ **1.** peninsula in Central America consisting of three Mexican states, Belize, and part of northern Guatemala. Area: 70,000 sq. mi./181,300 sq. km. **2.** state in southeastern Mexico on the northern coast of the Yucatán Peninsula. Capital: Mérida. Population: 1,686,500 (2000). Area: 16,700 sq. mi./43,257 sq. km.

Yuc·a·tec /yo͝okə tèk/ (*plural same* or **-tecs**) *n* **1.** a member of a Maya people living in the Yucatán Peninsula **2.** the Maya language of the Yucatec people. Native speakers: 500,000. [Mid-19C. < Spanish *yucateco* < *Yucatán* "Yucatan"] —**Yu·ca·tec** *adj*

yuc·ca /yúkə/ *n* an evergreen plant widely grown for its sharp lance-shaped leaves and clusters of white flowers that grow in vertical spikes. Native to: southwestern United States, Mexico. Genus: *Yucca*. [Mid-16C. Via Spanish *yuca* < Taino]

yuc·ca moth *n* a small white moth that pollinates the yucca plant, laying its eggs in the ovaries of the yucca's flowers. Native to: North America. Latin name: *Tegeticula alba*.

yuck /yuk/, **yuk** *interj* used to express disgust or revulsion (*informal*) [Mid-20C. An imitation of the sound of vomiting]

yuck·y /yúkee/ (**-i·er, -i·est**), **yuk·ky** (**-ki·er, -ki·est**) *adj* disgusting or unpleasant (*informal*) —**yuck·i·ness** *n*

Yug. *abbr* Yugoslavia

yu·ga /yo͝ogə/ *n* in Hinduism, any of the four stages in each cycle of history, each worse than the one before [Late 18C. < Sanskrit *yugam* "yoke, era"]

Yugo. *abbr* Yugoslavia

Yu·go·sla·via /yo͝ogō sla̋avee ə/ former name for **Serbia and Montenegro** —**Yu·go·slav** /yo͝ogō sla̋av/ *n, adj* —**Yu·go·sla·vi·an** *adj, n*

yuk[1] /yuk/ *interj* another spelling of **yuck** (*informal*)

yuk[2] /yuk/ *US* (*slang*) *n* a laugh or chortle ■ *vi* (**yukked, yuk·king, yuks**) to produce a laugh [Mid-20C. Origin ?]

yu·ka·ta /yo͞o káttə/ (*plural same* or **-tas**) *n* a light cotton kimono, worn typically after a bath [Early 19C. < Japanese < *yu* "hot water" + *kata(bira)* "light kimono"]

yuk·ky *adj* another spelling of **yucky** (*informal*)

Yu·kon /yo͞o kòn/ river in North America, flowing through Canada and Alaska and into the Bering Sea. Length: 1,980 mi./3,190 km.

Yukon Territory

Yu·kon Ter·ri·to·ry territory in northwestern Canada. It was the site of the Klondike gold rush between 1896 and 1899. Capital: Whitehorse. Population: 28,674 (2001). Area: 186,272 sq. mi./482,443 sq. km.

Yu·kon Time *n* the time observed in the Yukon Territory and in a section of more or less equivalent longitude extending southward from there, being nine hours behind Universal Coordinated Time

Yule /yool/, **yule** *n* Christmas day or the Christmas season (*archaic or literary*) [Old English *gēol* "mid-winter festival, Christmas" < Germanic]

yule log *n* a large log traditionally placed on the hearth fire on Christmas Eve

Yule·tide /yo͞ol tīd/ *n* the Christmas season (*archaic or literary*)

Yu·ma[1] /yo͞omə/ *n* a member of a Native North American people of southwestern Arizona and neighboring areas [Early 19C. < Pima *yumí*] —**Yu·ma** *adj*

Yu·ma[2] /yo͞omə/ city in the southwestern corner of Arizona, on the Arizona-California border, southwest of Phoenix. Population: 80,358 (2002 estimate).

Yu·man /yo͞omən/ *n* a family of languages spoken in the southwestern United States and in northern Mexico. Native speakers: 4,000. —**Yu·man** *adj*

yum·my /yúmmee/ (**-mi·er, -mi·est**) *adj* very appealing to taste or smell (*informal*) [Late 19C. < *yum*, an imitation of the sound of smacking the lips] —**yum·mi·ness** *n*

Yun·nan /yo͞o na̋an, yŭn na̋an/ province in southern China, on the southwestern border of the country. Capital: Kunming. Population: 40,420,000 (1997). Area: 152,124 sq. mi./394,000 sq. km.

Yun Shou·ping /yŭn shō píng/ (1633–90) Chinese artist. He is known for his landscapes and flower paintings.

yup[1] /yup/ *adv* same as **yes** (*informal*) [Early 20C. Representing a casual pronunciation of YES]

yup[2] /yup/ *n* same as **yuppie** (*informal*) [Late 20C. Shortening]

Yu·pik /yo͞opik/ (*plural same* or **-piks**) *n* **1.** a member of an aboriginal people of western Alaska and parts of coastal Siberia, related to the Inuit of the Canadian Arctic and Greenland **2.** the group of Eskimo-Aleut languages spoken by the Yupik people. Native speakers: 3,000. [Mid-20C. < Alaskan Yupik *Yup'ik* "real person"] —**Yu·pik** *adj*

yup·pie /yúppee/ *n* a young educated city-dwelling professional, especially when regarded as materialistic and snobbish [Late 20C. < *y(oung) u(rban) p(rofessional)*, after HIPPIE and YIPPIE]

yup·pie flu, yup·pie disease *n* MED same as **chronic fatigue syndrome** (*informal*)

yup·pi·fy /yúppə fī/ (**-fied, -fy·ing, -fies**) *vt* to cause an area to be increasingly populated by young educated city-dwelling professionals or to modify something with the values ascribed to yuppies (*disapproving*) —**yup·pi·fi·ca·tion** /yùppəfi káysh'n/ *n*

Yu·rok /yo͞or ok/ (*plural same* or **-roks**) *n* a member of a Native North American people that live in California, mainly along the northwestern coast and in the lower Klamath River valley [Mid-19C. < Karok *yúruk* "downstream"] —**Yu·rok** *adj*

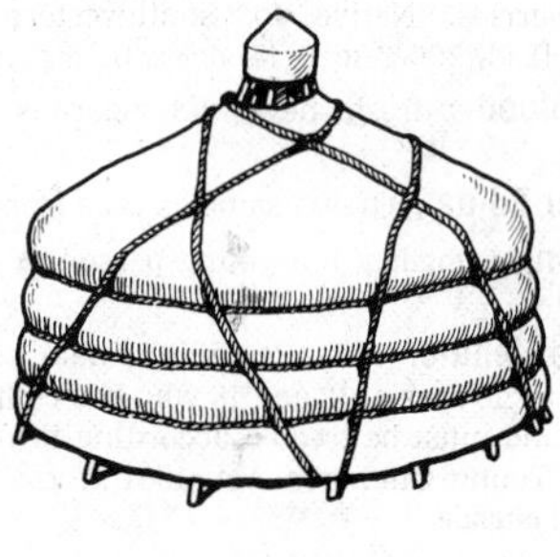

yurt

yurt /yurt/ *n* **1.** a collapsible circular tent of felt or skins stretched over a pole frame, originally used by Central Asian nomadic peoples and now used more widely **2.** a circular structure with a tight, fitted roofing material, used especially by highway departments to store road salt and sand for winter use [Late 18C. Via Russian *yurta* < Turkic *jurt*]

Yu·waa·la·raay /yoo wa̋alə rī/ *n* an extinct Australian Aboriginal language of New South Wales, now being revived —**Yu·waa·la·raay** *adj*

yu·zu /yo͞o zo͞o/ *n* a citrus fruit, about the size of a mandarin with a rough skin and very sour flesh, mainly used for its peel [< Japanese]

YWCA[1], **Y.W.C.A.** *abbr* Young Women's Christian Association

YWCA[2] *n* a building or other center where social, sports, or educational facilities are provided by the YWCA for its members

YWHA, Y.W.H.A. *abbr* Young Women's Hebrew Association

Z z

z[1] /zee/, **Z** *n* (*plural* **z's**; *plural* **Z's** or **Zs**) **1. 26TH LETTER OF ENGLISH ALPHABET** the 26th and final letter of the English alphabet, representing a consonant sound **2. LETTER "Z" WRITTEN** a written representation of the letter "z" ■ **z's** *npl* **SLEEP** sleep, from the traditional transcription of the sound of snoring (*informal*) ○ *I need to catch some z's.*

z[2] *symbol* **1.** MATH an algebraic variable **2.** CHEM atomic number **3.** MATH a Cartesian coordinate along the z-axis **4.** MEASURE zepto- **5.** MEASURE zetta-

z[3] *abbr* **1.** MONEY zaïre **2.** GEOG zone

Z[1] /zee/ (*plural* **Z's** or **Zs**) *n* something shaped like a letter "Z"

Z[2] *abbr* GEOG zone

Z[3] *symbol* **1.** CHEM atomic number **2.** PHYS impedance **3.** MEASURE zetta-

za *abbr* South Africa (*used in Internet addresses*) See table at **domain name**

Zaan·stad /zaan shtát/ city in North Holland Province, western Netherlands. Population: 135,621 (2000).

za·ba·gli·o·ne /zaàb'l yṓnee/ *n* a dessert made of egg yolks, sugar, and Marsala wine beaten over hot water until pale and foamy. It is served hot with sponge finger biscuits. [Late 19C. < Italian]

Za·ca·te·cas /zàkə táykəss/ capital city of Zacatecas State in central Mexico. It is an important mining center. Population: 125,258 (2000).

Zach·a·rias /zàkə rī́ əss/ *n* in Christian tradition, the father of John the Baptist

zad·dik *n* JUDAISM another spelling of **tzaddik**

zaf·fer /záffər/, **zaf·fre** *n* an impure form of cobalt oxide. Use: blue coloring agent in enamels and glass. [Mid-17C. Via Italian *zaffera* < French *safre*]

zaf·tig /zaáftig/ *adj* with a full-figured body [Mid-20C. Via Yiddish < Middle High German *saftec* "juicy" < *saft* "juice"]

zag /zag/ *n* a direction or segment of a course running opposite to a zig ■ *vi* (**zagged, zag·ging, zags**) to change direction quickly [Late 18C. < ZIGZAG]

Za·greb /zaá grèb/ capital city of Croatia, situated in the north of the country, approximately 15 mi./25 km from the border with Slovenia. Population: 682,598 (2001).

Zag·ros Moun·tains /zàg ross-/ mountain range in southwestern Iran, extending from the borders with Turkey and Azerbaijan in the north to the Persian Gulf in the south. The highest peak is Zard Kuh, 14,921 ft./4,548 m. Length: 1,000 mi./1,600 km.

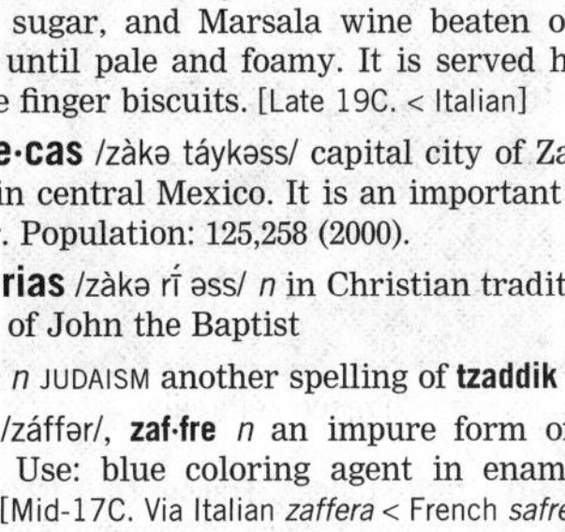

Popperfoto

Babe Didrikson Zaharias

Za·har·i·as /zə hárree əss/, **Babe Didrikson** (1913–56) US athlete. She excelled in basketball, swimming, track and field, and golf. She won two gold medals, in javelin and 80-meter hurdles, at the summer Olympics (1932). In golf, she also won the US Open three times (1948, 1950, and 1954). Born **Didrikson, Mildred**

zai·bat·su /zī baat so͞o/ (*plural same*) *n* a large industrial combine created in Japan in the 1890s, usually by a single family, as part of the process of industrialization [Mid-20C. < Japanese *zai* "wealth" + *batsu* "clique"]

zai·kai /zī kī/ *n* the business and financial community of Japan [Mid-20C. < Japanese *zai* "wealth" + *kai* "world"]

za·ïre /zī eér, zaa-/ (*plural same* or **-ïres**) *n* a former unit of currency in the Democratic Republic of Congo [Mid-20C. After *Zaire*, local name for the Congo River]

Za·ire /zī eér, zaa-/ **1.** former name for **Congo, Democratic Republic of the 2.** former name for **Congo** —**Za·ir·e·an** /zī eéree ən, zaa-/ *adj*

za·kat /zə kaát/ *n* a tax that goes to charity, obligatory for all Muslims, set traditionally at 2.5 percent of somebody's annual income and capital [Early 19C. Via Persian and Urdu *zakā(t)* or Turkish *zekât* < Arabic *zakā(t)* "the giving of alms"]

Za·kin·thos /zákin thòss, zə kín thòss/, **Za·kyn·thos** most southerly of the Ionian Islands, in southwestern Greece. Population: 38,680 (2001). Area: 155 sq. mi./401 sq. km.

za·kus·ki /zə ko͝oskə/ *npl* blinis and breads of various kinds with toppings, especially caviar, served in Russia with vodka. Traditionally, zakuski are an alternative to the first course of a meal, but they sometimes provide a pretheater supper, followed by the main meal after the show. [Late 19C. < Russian, plural of *zakuska* "hors d'oeuvre"]

Za·kyn·thos another spelling of **Zakinthos**

Zam·be·zi /zam beézee/ river in southern Africa, flowing through Zambia, Angola, Botswana, Zimbabwe, and Mozambique, and into the Indian Ocean. Length: 1,650 mi./2,650 km.

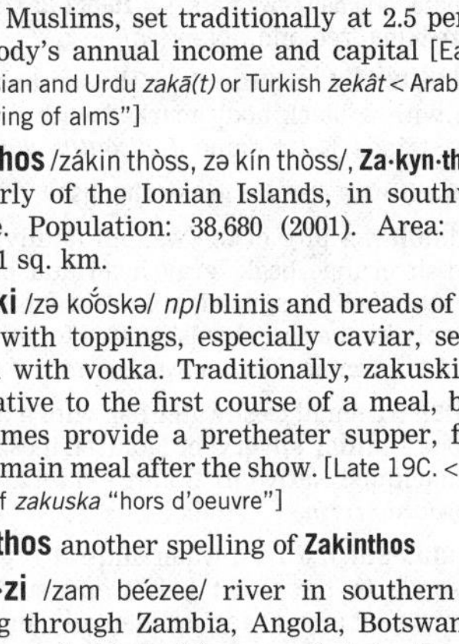

Zambia

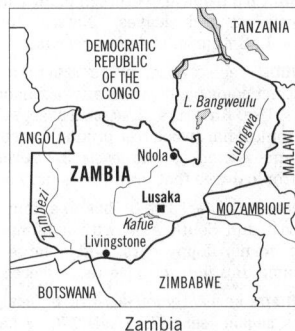

Zam·bi·a /zámbee ə/ country in south central Africa. It became an independent member of the British Commonwealth in 1964. Language: English. Currency: kwacha. Capital: Lusaka. Population: 10,307,333 (2003). Area: 290,586 sq. mi./752,614 sq. km. Official name **Republic of Zambia**. Former name **Northern Rhodesia** (until 1964) —**Zam·bi·an** *n, adj*

za·mi·a /záymee ə/ *n* a small tropical tree (**cycad**) that resembles a palm tree, with a short thick trunk, spiky leaves, and upright woody cones that contain seeds. It is a modern representative of a group of trees that are largely extinct. Genus: *Zamia.* [Early 19C. < modern Latin, misreading of Latin *azaniae* "pine cones"]

za·min·dar /zàmmən daár/, **ze·min·dar** /zè-/ *n* in South Asia, somebody who has traditionally owned land [Late 17C Via Urdu < Persian *zamīndār* < *zamīn* "land" + *dār* "holder"]

zam·in·dar·i /zàmmən daáree, zə meén-/ (*plural* **-is**), **zem·in·dar·y** /zèmmən daáree, zə meén-/ (*plural* **-ies**) *n* in South Asia, the system of traditional land ownership, or the area of land owned [Mid-18C. Via Urdu < Persian *zamīndārī* < *zamīndār* (see ZAMINDAR)]

za·na·na *n* ISLAM, TRANSP another spelling of **zenana**

zan·der /zándər/ (*plural same* or **-ders**) *n* a freshwater fish of the perch family, harvested for food. Native to: central Europe. Latin name: *Stizostedion lucioperca.* [Mid-19C. Via German < Low German *sandāt*]

zang /zang, dzaang/ *npl* in traditional Chinese medicine, the five organs, the heart, lungs, kidneys, liver, and spleen, that control the yin-yang bodily balance and the main body functions [< Chinese]

Zan·tac /zán tàk/ *tdmk* a trademark for the drug ranitidine. Use: to treat peptic ulcers.

Zan·te /zán tay/ ➧ **Zakinthos**

za·ny /záynee/ *adj* (**-ni·er, -ni·est**) **AMUSINGLY UNCONVENTIONAL** entertainingly strange or amusingly unusual ■ *n* (*plural* **-nies**) **1. CLOWN** a fool, buffoon, or clown **2. STOCK CHARACTER** a stock character in Renaissance comedies who mimicked other characters [Late 16C. Via French *zani* < Italian dialect *Zanni*, variant of *Gianni*, pet form of *Giovanni*, character in the commedia dell'arte who tried to mimic the clown] —**za·ni·ly** *adv* —**za·ni·ness** *n* —**za·nism** *n*

Zan·zi·bar /zánzi baár/ island of Tanzania, in the Indian Ocean, approximately 22 mi./35 km off the eastern coast of Africa. Population: 456,934 (1995). Area: 641 sq. mi./1,660 sq. km.

zap /zap/ (*informal*) *v* (**zapped, zap·ping, zaps**) **1.** *vt* **DESTROY SOMEBODY OR SOMETHING** to kill or finish somebody or something off with sudden force **2.** *vti* **CHANGE TV CHANNELS USING REMOTE CONTROL** to change channels on a television set using a remote control device, especially to change channels rapidly **3.** *vi* **MOVE QUICKLY** to move about or accomplish something very rapidly **4.** *vt* **COOK SOMETHING IN MICROWAVE** to cook something in a microwave oven ○ *I'll just zap this for a minute and then we can eat.* **5.** *vt Malaysia, Singapore* **PHOTOCOPY SOMETHING** to make a photocopy of something ■ *n* **1. ENERGY** energy and excitement **2. TIME IN MICROWAVE** a short period of time in a microwave oven ■ *interj* **EXPRESSION OF FORCEFUL ACTION** used especially in comic books to indicate sudden and violent force [Early 20C. An imitation of the sound of a lightning strike or electric sparks]

Za·pa·ta /zə paátə, saa paá taa/, **Emiliano** (1879–1919) Mexican revolutionary. He took part in a number of uprisings, and redistributed land among the Native Central Americans in southern Mexico.

Za·pa·ta mus·tache *n* a thick mustache that curves down around the edges of the mouth

za·pa·te·a·do /zàppətee aádō/ (*plural* **-dos**), **za·pa·te·o** /zàppə táy ō/ (*plural* **-os**) *n Hispanic* a Spanish or Latin American dance involving rhythmic tapping of the feet [Mid-19C. < Spanish < *zapatear* "tap with the shoe" < *zapato* "shoe"]

Za·pa·te·ro /zàppə térrō/, **José Luis** (*b.* 1960) Spanish politician. A member of the Socialist Party, he was Spain's youngest member of parliament (1986) and went on to become leader of his party (2000). He became prime minister following the general election of 2004. Full name **Zapatero, José Luis Rodríguez**

Za·pa·tis·ta /zaapə téestə/ *n Hispanic* a member of the Zapatista National Liberation Army, a rebel group of Native Americans from southern Mexico. The Zapatistas launched a military revolt against the Mexican government in 1994, briefly occupying several cities in the state of Chiapas. [Late 20C. After Emiliano ZAPATA]

Za·po·pan /zaapō pan/ city in southwestern Mexico near Guadalajara. Population: 1,001,021 (2000).

Za·po·rizh·zhya /zaapə reezhyə/ city in southeastern Ukraine. It is situated about 135 mi./217 km west of Donets'k. Population: 863,000 (1998).

Za·po·tec /zàppə ték/ (*plural same* or **-tecs**) *n* **1.** a member of a Native Central American people who founded a Mesoamerican civilization in the region of Oaxaca, Mexico, between the 7th century B.C. and the 11th century A.D., and now live in the highlands of the same region **2.** the Oto-Manguean language of the Zapotec people. Native speakers: 500,000. [Late 18C. Via Spanish *zapoteco* < Nahuatl *tzapotecatl* "person from the place of the sapodilla"] —**Za·po·tec·an** *adj*

zap·per /záppər/ *n* (*informal*) **1.** a remote control for a television or other home entertainment device **2.** *US* a device that attracts and electrocutes insects

zap·py /záppee/ (**-pi·er, -pi·est**) *adj* lively and forcefully impressive (*informal*)

Za·ra·go·za /zàrrə gózə/ capital of Zaragoza Province in the autonomous region of Aragon, northeastern Spain. Population: 620,419 (2002).

Za·ra·thu·stra /zàrrə thóostrə/ ➧ **Zoroaster**

za·ra·tite /zárrə tīt/ *n* an amorphous green mineral consisting of hydrated nickel carbonate [Mid-19C. < Spanish *zaratita* < the surname *Zarate*]

za·re·ba /zə reebə/ *n* an outdoor enclosure, especially one made of thorn bushes and used as protection around a campsite or village in various parts of North Africa [Mid-19C. < Arabic *zarība* "cattle pen"]

zarf /zaarf/ *n* a metal frame for holding a cup, used in Southwest Asia [Mid-19C. < Arabic *ẓarf* "vessel"]

za·ri /zaaree/ *n S Asia* gold brocade used to decorate clothes [Mid-20C. Via Urdu < Persian *zarī* < *zar* "gold"]

Za·ri·a /zaaree ə/ city in Kaduna State, north central Nigeria. Population: 369,800 (1995).

zar·zue·la /zaar zwáylə/ *n* Spanish musical theater, usually comic, combining dialogue, music, and dance [Late 19C. < Spanish]

zax /zaks/ *n* a tool similar to a hatchet used for cutting and shaping slate [Mid-17C. Representing Old English *seax* "knife" < Indo-European]

z-ax·is *n* one of the axes of the Cartesian coordinate system that provides a reference in three-dimensional space

za·yin /zaa yìn/ *n* the seventh letter of the Hebrew alphabet, represented in the English alphabet as "z." See table at **alphabet** [Early 19C. < Hebrew, "weapon"]

za·zen /zaa zèn/ *n* a form of meditation in Zen, practiced sitting in a prescribed position [Early 18C. < Japanese, "sitting Zen"]

ZBB *abbr* zero-based budgeting

Z bo·son *n* PHYS same as **Z particle**

Z chart *n* a chart used in business and industry to illustrate production data

z-co·or·di·nate *n* one of three numbers that provide a reference to a position in three-dimensional space, conventionally the vertical one

zeal /zeel/ *n* energetic and unflagging enthusiasm, especially for a cause or idea [14C. Via late Latin *zelus* < Greek *zēlos* "eager rivalry"]

Zea·land /zeelənd/ ➧ **Sjælland**

zeal·ot /zéllət/ *n* a zealous supporter of a cause, especially a religious cause [Mid-16C. Via late Latin < Greek *zēlōtēs* < *zēloun* "be jealous" < *zēlos* "eager rivalry"] —**zeal·ot·ry** *n*

Zeal·ot *n* a member of a group of Jewish rebels who attempted the military overthrow of Roman rule in Palestine in the 1st and 2nd centuries A.D.

zeal·ous /zélləss/ *adj* actively and unreservedly enthusiastic [Early 16C. < medieval Latin *zelosus* < *zelus* (see ZEAL)] —**zeal·ous·ly** *adv* —**zeal·ous·ness** *n*

ze·a·tin /zee ətin/ *n* a naturally occurring growth promoter found in many plants, first isolated from kernels of corn [Mid-20C. < modern Latin *Zea* (see ZEIN) + -IN]

ze·bec *n* another spelling of **xebec**

Ze·be·dee /zébbə dee/ *n* in the Bible, a fisherman, and the father of the apostles James and John (Matthew 4:21)

zebra

ze·bra /zeebrə/ *n* **1.** an animal resembling a horse that has a black-and-white or brown-and-white striped hide. Native to: Africa. Genus: *Equus.* **2.** INSECTS same as **zebra butterfly** [Early 17C. < Italian, Spanish, or Portuguese, originally "wild ass"] —**ze·bra·ic** /zə bráy ik/ *adj* —**ze·brine** /zee brīn, -brən/ *adj*

ze·bra but·ter·fly *n* a butterfly of the southern United States with a black body marked with distinctive yellow stripes. Latin name: *Heliconius chairtonius.*

ze·bra da·ni·o *n* FISH same as **zebra fish**

ze·bra finch *n* a bird of the waxbill family that has a reddish orange beak, gray head and back, and a black-and-white striped tail. Zebra finches are commonly kept as cagebirds. Native to: inland Australia. Latin name: *Taeniopygia guttata.*

ze·bra fish *n* a small freshwater fish with a blue body and longitudinal silvery or gold stripes, popular for aquariums. Native to: South Asia. Latin name: *Brachydanio rerio.*

ze·bra mus·sel *n* a freshwater mussel regarded as a nuisance in the Great Lakes and surrounding waterways where it was accidentally introduced. Native to: Europe, Asia. Latin name: *Dreissena polymorpha.*

ze·bra plant *n* a tropical evergreen plant with green-and-purple striped leaves. Native to: South America. Latin name: *Calathea zebrina.*

ze·bra·wood /zeebrə wòod/ *n* **1.** STRIPED WOOD wood in two distinct color bands, from any of various tropical trees. Use: furniture. **2.** HARDWOOD TREE WITH STRIPED WOOD a tropical hardwood tree producing zebrawood. Latin name: *Connarus guianensis.* **3.** TREE WITH STRIPED WOOD a tropical tree that produces zebrawood

ze·bu /zeeboo/ (*plural same* or **-bus**) *n* a domesticated ox of East and South Asia with a humped back, curving horns, floppy ears, and a large dewlap. Latin name: *Bos indicus.* [Late 18C. < French *zébu*]

zec·chi·no /ze keenō/ (*plural* **-ni** /-nee/ or **-nos**) *n* MONEY same as **sequin** (sense 2) [Early 17C. < Italian (see SEQUIN)]

Zech·a·ri·ah /zèkə rī ə/ *n* **1.** in the Bible, a Hebrew priest and prophet of the 6th century B.C. **2.** a book of the Bible that contains the prophecies traditionally attributed to Zechariah, including his visions of the rebuilding of the Temple in a restored Jerusalem. See table at **Bible**

zech·in /zékən/ *n* MONEY same as **sequin** (sense 2) [Late 16C. < Italian *zecchino* (see SEQUIN)]

zed /zed/ *n UK* same as **zee** [15C. Via French *zède* < Greek *zēta* (see ZETA)]

Zed·e·ki·ah /zèddə kī ə/ *n* in the Bible, the last king of Judah (597–586 B.C.). After rebelling against Nebuchadnezzar II, he was imprisoned in Babylon, where he died in captivity (2 Kings 24–25, 2 Chronicles 36).

zed·o·ar·y /zéddō èrree/ (*plural* **-ies**) *n* **1.** an aromatic powder obtained from crushing the dried roots of a South Asian tree **2.** a plant with starchy aromatic rhizomes that yield zedoary. Use: as a condiment, in cosmetics, perfume, medicinally as a stimulant. Flowers: yellow. Native to: South Asia. Latin name: *Curcuma zedoaria.* [15C. < medieval Latin *zedoarium* < Persian *zadwār*]

ze·donk /zə dóngk/ *n* the offspring of a male zebra and a female donkey [Late 20C. < ZEBRA + DONKEY]

zee /zee/ *n* a written representation of the sound of the letter "Z" [Late 17C Alteration of Latin *zeta* (< Greek *zēta*: see ZETA) after *b, p,* etc]

Zee·brug·ge /záy bròoggə/ port in northwestern Belgium, in northwestern Flanders Province. Population: 4,500 (1996).

Zee·land /zeelənd/ province in the southwestern Netherlands. Population: 371,686 (2000). Area: 692 sq. mi./1,792 sq. km.

Zee·man /záy maan/, **Pieter** (1865–1943) Dutch physicist. He discovered the zeeman effect, which confirmed the electromagnetic theory of light, and was awarded the Nobel Prize in physics (1902).

Zee·man ef·fect /záy maan-/ *n* the splitting of single lines in a spectrum into two, three, or more polarized lines when the source of the spectrum is placed in a magnetic field

Express Newspapers

Franco Zeffirelli

Zef·fi·rel·li /zèffə réllee/, **Franco** (*b.* 1923) Italian movie, stage, and opera director. His movies include versions of Shakespeare and adaptations of operas.

ze·in /zee in/ *n* a powder of proteins obtained from corn, with various applications in industry and manufacturing [Early 19C. < modern Latin *Zea* via Latin *zea* "emmer" < Greek *zeia,* kind of wheat]

Zeit·geist /zīt gīst, tsīt-/, **zeit·geist** *n* the ideas prevalent in a period and place, particularly as expressed in literature, philosophy, and religion [Mid-19C. < German, "spirit of the time"]

zel·ko·va /zélkəvə/ *n* a tree of the elm family cultivated for its resistance to Dutch elm disease. Native to: Asia. Genus: *Zelkova.* [Late 19C. Via modern Latin < a Caucasian language]

zem·in·dar another spelling of **zamindar**

zem·stvo /zém stvō/ (*plural* **-stvos**) *n* an elected provincial legislature that existed in Russia between 1864 and 1917 [Mid-19C. < Russian < obsolete *zem* "land"]

Zen /zen/ *n* a major school of Buddhism originating in 12th-century China that emphasizes enlightenment through meditation and insight [Early 18C. Via Japanese *zen* and Chinese *chán* < Sanskrit *dhyānam* "meditation"]

ze·na·na /zə naanə/, **za·na·na** *n* **1.** in parts of northern South Asia, an area reserved for women in some trains and waiting rooms in railroad stations **2.** in Muslim households in parts of South and Southwest Asia, the area of the house reserved for women and girls [Mid-18C. < Persian, Urdu *zanānah* < *zan* "woman"]

Zen Bud·dhism *n* BUDDHISM same as **Zen**

Zend /zend/ *n* **1.** RELIG same as **Zend-Avesta** **2.** LANG same as **Avesta** —**Zend** *adj*

Zend-A·ves·ta /-ə véstə/ *n* the canonical writings of Zoroastrianism, preserved in the Pahlavi language [Mid-17C. Via French < Persian *zand-awastā* "Avesta with interpretation"]

ze·ner di·ode /zeénər-/ *n* a semiconductor used as a voltage regulator because of its ability to maintain a constant voltage during fluctuating current conditions [Mid-20C. After Clarence M. *Zener* (1905–93), US physicist]

Zeng·er /zéng ər, zéng gər/, **John Peter** (1697–1746) German-born US newspaper publisher. His acquittal on a charge of sedition libel (1735) was a milestone for freedom of the press.

Zen·i·ca /zénnitsə/ city in central Bosnia and Herzegovina. Before the Bosnian-Croatian-Serbian War, Zenica was a major center for heavy industry. Population: 145,577 (1991).

ze·nith /zeénith/ *n* **1.** HIGHEST POINT the high point or climax of something **2.** POINT STRAIGHT UP the point of the celestial sphere that is directly over the observer and 90 degrees from all points on that person's horizon **3.** HIGHEST POINT OF ASTRONOMICAL OBJECT the highest point reached by an astronomical object [14C. Via Old French and medieval Latin < Arabic *samt (ar-ra's)* "path (over the head)"] —**ze·nith·al** *adj*

ze·nith·al pro·jec·tion *n* a map projection of the Earth onto a plane tangential to a point on the surface of the Earth such as the North Pole or the equator

Ze·no of Cit·i·um /zeénō əv síttee əm/ (*fl* late 4th-early 3rd centuries B.C.) Greek philosopher. He founded a school of philosophy, stoicism, in Athens in about 300 B.C.

> "The reason why we have two ears and one mouth is that we may listen the more and talk the less."
> [Zeno of Citium. Quoted in "Zeno," *Lives of the Philosophers*; Diogenes (3rd century A.D.)]

Ze·no of E·le·a /-éelee ə/ (*fl* 5th century B.C.) Greek mathematician and philosopher. The paradoxes for which his philosophy is known were designed to discredit the information conveyed by the senses. Aristotle regarded him as the inventor of dialectical reasoning.

ze·o·lite /zeé ə lìt/ *n* one of a large group of amorphous hydrated aluminum silicate minerals containing various other elements. Source: weathered igneous rocks, hydrothermal veins. Use: water purification. [Late 18C. < Greek *zein* "to boil"] —**ze·o·lit·ic** /zeé ə líttik/ *adj*

Ze·pa /zé paà/ town in eastern Bosnia and Herzegovina, overrun by Bosnian Serb forces during the Bosnian-Croatian-Serbian War. Population: 15,000 (1995).

Ze·pha·ni·ah /zèffə nī ə/ *n* **1.** in the Bible, a minor Hebrew prophet of the 7th century B.C. **2.** a book in the Bible, traditionally attributed to Zephaniah. It urges repentance by the people of Judah, and predicts a day of judgment. See table at **Bible**

zeph·yr /zéffər/ *n* **1.** a light warming breeze **2.** a delicate usually woolen fabric or garment [Pre-12C. Via Latin < Greek *zephuros* "west wind"]

zeph·yr lil·y *n* a plant that grows from clump-forming bulbs and has narrow grassy leaves. Flowers: funnel-shaped, colorful. Native to: tropical America. Genus: *Zephyranthes.*

Zeph·y·rus /zéffərəss/ *n* in Greek mythology, the god who personified the west wind and was always mild and gentle in character

zep·pe·lin /zéppələn/ *n* a rigid cylindrical airship consisting of a covered frame and a suspended compartment for engines and passengers [Early 20C. After Count Ferdinand von *Zeppelin* (1838–1917), German inventor]

zepto- *prefix* indicates 10^{-21} in measurements ○ *zeptosecond* [Late 20C. After SEPTI-]

zep·to·sec·ond /zéptō sèkənd/ *n* a unit of time equal to one-sextillionth of a second

Zer·matt /zúr màt, tser maát/ town and ski resort in Valais Canton, southwestern Switzerland. Population: 4,225 (1996).

ze·ro /zeérō/ *n* (*plural* **-ros** or **-roes**) **1.** SYMBOL 0 the numerical symbol 0, representing the absence of any quantity or magnitude **2.** NUMBER WITH VALUE OF 0 the number that, when added to another number, results in that number, e.g., 0 + 4 = 4 **3.** STARTING POINT FOR VALUES ON GAUGE the starting or center point for values on a counter, scale, or gauge ○ *Set the odometer to zero.* **4.** LOW TEMPERATURE the temperature indicated by 0 on a thermometer scale ○ *It got down to zero last night.* **5.** LOW POINT the lowest possible point or degree ○ *Her spirits are at zero.* **6.** NOTHING nothing or nil ○ *They beat us five to zero.* **7.** US FAILURE somebody who is regarded as a complete failure (*informal insult*) **8.** LING ABSTRACT REALIZATION OF MORPHEME a variant form of a morpheme (**allomorph**) that is purely abstract and does not exist in any physical phonetic form. An example of a zero allomorph in English is the plural marker of "sheep." **9.** ARMS SETTING ON GUN SIGHT a setting on a gun sight indicating the center of a target ■ *vt* (**-roed, -ro·ing, -roes**) SET SOMETHING TO ZERO to set an instrument, gauge, counter, or similar measuring device to zero ■ *adj* **1.** NIL having no quantity or magnitude ○ *zero inflation* **2.** MINIMAL very small in amount or extent (*informal*) ○ *Our chances of winning are zero.* ○ *had zero confidence* **3.** METEOROL WITH LIMITED VISIBILITY describes a level of visibility limited to 50 ft./15 m vertically or 165 ft./50 m horizontally **4.** LING LACKING USUAL EXPRESSION OF FEATURE characterized by the absence of a form or feature that exists elsewhere in the same linguistic context, e.g., an inflection or vowel change [Early 17C. Via French and Italian < Arabic *ṣifr* "emptiness"]

zero in *vi* **1.** to identify something precisely and concentrate all efforts on dealing with it ○ *The report zeroed in on the weaknesses in the current policy.* **2.** to find the precise position of a target and move toward it or aim a weapon at it, threateningly or inexorably [< the technique of setting a gun sight exactly on a target by canceling out the effects of elevation and wind deflection]

zero out *vt* **1.** ELIMINATE SOMETHING to eliminate something or reduce it to zero ○ *That round zeroes out your score.* **2.** CUT OFF FUNDING FOR SOMETHING to cut off funding for a project or activity so that it cannot go forward ○ *zeroing out after-school programs* **3.** SET SOMETHING TO ZERO to set something such as a gauge or counter to zero

ze·ro-base, **ze·ro-based** *adj* relating to a budget or budgeting that considers each item on its merits without reference to previous practice or expenditure

ze·ro-cou·pon *adj* not paying interest but sold at a discount and redeemable at maturity ○ *a zero-coupon bond*

ze·ro-de·fect *adj* with no flaws or errors

ze·ro·fill /zeérō fìl/ (**-filled, -fill·ing, -fills**) *vti* in computing, to fill empty storage space with zeros

ze·ro grav·i·ty *n* a condition of apparent weightlessness resulting from the centrifugal force on an object counterbalancing the gravitational force attracting it

ze·ro growth *n* no increase in the growth or development of something, especially when an increase might have been expected and where any increase is measured as a percentage ○ *predictions of zero growth in the economy*

ze·ro hour *n* **1.** the time set for the start of a military operation **2.** the time or date when something important is due to happen

ze·ro·ize /zeérō ìz/ (**-ized, -iz·ing, -izes**) *vti* COMPUT same as **zerofill**

ze·ro op·tion *n* an offer to limit the number of short-range nuclear missiles or remove them altogether if an opposing side agrees to do the same

ze·ro pop·u·la·tion growth *n* a situation in which the number of new births is no greater than the number of people dying, so that the overall population size remains the same

ze·ro-sum *adj* relating to a situation in which a gain by one side or person requires any other side or person involved in it to sustain a corresponding loss

ze·roth /zí rōth/ *adj* preceding number one in a series

ze·ro tol·er·ance *n* the absence of any leniency or exception in the enforcement of a law, rule, or regulation, especially a law against antisocial behavior

ze·ro-ze·ro *adj* describes flying conditions in which cloud is so thick and low that the pilot can see nothing ahead and nothing above or below the aircraft [Shortening of *zero ceiling, zero visibility*]

ze·ro-ze·ro op·tion *n* MIL same as **double-zero option**

zest /zest/ *n* **1.** HEARTY ENJOYMENT lively enjoyment and enthusiasm ○ *zest for life* **2.** EXCITING AND ENJOYABLE QUALITY an exciting or interesting aspect of something that makes it particularly enjoyable **3.** COOK CITRUS PEEL USED AS FLAVORING the thin outer rind of the peel of a citrus fruit that is cut, scraped, or grated to yield a sharp fruity flavoring for foods and drinks **4.** PIQUANT FLAVOR a pleasantly sharp flavor ■ *vt* (**zest·ed, zest·ing, zests**) **1.** COOK GRATE SKIN OF CITRUS FRUIT to cut, grate, or scrape the rind of a citrus fruit for use as a flavoring in foods and drinks **2.** MAKE SOMETHING MORE STIMULATING AND ENJOYABLE to make an experience more enjoyable by adding excitement or interest to it [15C. < French] —**zest·ful** *adj* —**zest·y** *adj*

zest·er /zéstər/ *n* a small utensil with a row of tiny sharpened holes or edges at its tip for cutting strips of zest from oranges, lemons, or other citrus fruits

ze·ta /záytə, zeétə/ *n* the sixth letter of the Greek alphabet, written in the English alphabet as "z." See table at **alphabet** [Early 18C. < Greek *zēta*, of Phoenician origin]

Ze·thus /zeéthəss/ *n* in Greek mythology, a son of Zeus and Antiope and the twin of Amphion. The brothers became joint kings of Thebes.

zetta- *prefix* indicates 10^{21} in measurements ○ *zettabyte* [Late 20C. Probably < Italian *sette* "seven"]

zet·ta·byte /zéttə bìt/ *n* a unit of computer memory or disk storage space equal to one sextillion bytes

zeug·ma /zoógmə/ *n* a figure of speech in which an adjective or verb is used with two nouns but is appropriate to only one of them or has a different sense with each, as in "During the race he broke the record and his leg" [Late 16C. Via Latin < Greek, "joining"]

Zeus /zooss/ *n* in Greek mythology, the god of the sky, ruler of the Olympian gods, and spiritual father of gods and mortals. Roman equivalent **Jupiter** (sense 1)

Zhang·jia·kou /jaàng jyaà kṓ/ city in northeastern China in Hebei Province, situated at one of the gates of the Great Wall of China. Population: 673,901 (1991).

Zhang Zhi·dong /jaàng jee dáwng/ (1837–1909) Chinese reformer and provincial governor. A modernizer at the end of the Manchu dynasty, he held several provincial governorships (1884–1907) and reformed the Chinese educational system.

Zhao Meng·fu /jòw məng foó/ (1254–1322) Chinese artist. He is known for his realistic animal pictures and for his expressive landscapes and studies of bamboo.

Zhe·jiang /jè jyaàng/ province in eastern China, on the East China Sea. Capital: Hangzhou. Population: 43,430,000 (1997). Area: 39,382 sq. mi./102,000 sq. km.

Zheng·zhou /jùng jṓ/ capital of Henan Province, eastern China, on the Huang He between Taiyuan and Wuhan. Population: 1,990,000 (1995).

zhlub /shlub/ *n* an offensive term for a person who is regarded as lacking in social skills and refinement (*slang insult; offensive*) [Alteration of SCHLUB] —**zhlub·by** /shlúbbee/ *adj*

zho *n* ZOOL another spelling of **dzo**

Zhou /jō/ *n* a Chinese dynasty that ruled between the 12th and the 3rd centuries B.C., during which China was divided into feudal states and the religions of Confucianism and Taoism arose [Late 18C. < Chinese *zhōu*]

Zhou En·lai /jō en lì/ (1898–1976) premier of the People's Republic of China (1949–75). He became the first premier of Communist China and also served as the country's foreign minister (1949–58). Toward the end of his premiership, he increased contact with Japan and the United States.

Zi·a /zée ə/, **Khaleda** (*b.* 1945) prime minister of Bangladesh (1991–96, 2001–). The widow of the murdered military ruler Zia ur-Rahman and leader of the Bangladesh Nationalist Party, she came to power in 1991 after a series of coups and assassinations. She was reelected in 2001.

Zi·a ul-Haq /zée ə ōōl haák/, **Muhammad** (1924–88) Pakistani general and national leader. He overthrew Prime Minister Zulfikar Ali Bhutto (1977), and as president of Pakistan (1978–88) imposed martial law and introduced the Islamic legal code. He approved Bhutto's execution (1979) over international protests.

zib·e·line /zíbbə leen, -līn/, **zib·el·line** *n* a thick soft fabric with a long nap, made of wool, especially mohair or alpaca, or of the hair of another animal such as a camel [Late 16C. Via French < Italian *zibellino* "sable" < Slavic]

zib·et /zíbbit/ *n* a species of civet that is eaten in China. Native to: Southeast Asia. Latin name: *Viverra zibetha*. [Late 16C. Via medieval Latin *zibethum* or Italian *zibetto* < Arabic *zabād* "musky perfume obtained from civets"]

zi·do·vu·dine /zi dṓvyoo deen/ *n* an antiviral drug. Use: AIDS treatment. [Late 20C. < AZIDE + *-vudine*, INN stem]

Florenz Ziegfeld

Zieg·feld /zíg fèld/, **Florenz** (1869–1932) US theater producer. He launched the Ziegfeld Follies, an annual musical revue (1907), and produced extravagant musicals in New York.

zig /zig/ *n* a sharp line, direction, movement, or course that forms part of a zigzag ■ *vi* (**zigged, zig·ging, zigs**) to move in a sharp line, direction, movement, or course that forms part of a zigzag [Mid-20C. < ZIGZAG]

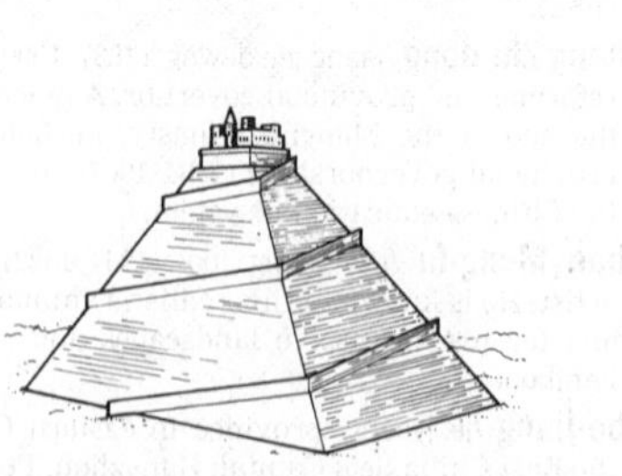
ziggurat

zig·gu·rat /zíggə ràt/ *n* an ancient Mesopotamian pyramid-shaped tower with a square base, rising in stories of ever-decreasing size, with a terrace at each story and a temple at the very top [Late 19C. < Assyrian *ziqquratu* "pinnacle"]

zig·zag /zíg zàg/ *n* **1.** LINE TAKING ALTERNATING TURNS a line going at an angle first one way, then sharply the opposite way, then back the first way, and so on, like the outline of a saw's teeth **2.** SOMETHING REPEATEDLY SWITCHING DIRECTIONS SHARPLY something that follows a sharply alternating line or course, e.g., a road with sharp bends alternating right and left ■ *adv* IN SHARPLY ALTERNATING DIRECTIONS along a sharply alternating line or course ■ *v* (**-zagged, -zag·ging, -zags**) **1.** *vti* PROCEED IN SHARPLY ALTERNATING PATH to follow a sharply alternating line or course, or cause something to move in this way ○ *They zigzagged across the field, dodging enemy bullets.* **2.** *vt* HANDICRAFT MAKE SHARPLY ALTERNATING PATTERN to make a pattern of sharply alternating lines or directions on something, e.g., with herringbone stitches [Early 18C. Via French < German *Zickzack*]

zig·zag fence *n Northeast US* a fence made of split rails each resting on and set at angles to the next, forming a zigzag

REGIONAL NOTE The term ***zigzag fence*** belongs to Upper New England. It occupies much the same territory as *snake fence*; together, they contrast with the Pennsylvania and North Midland *worm fence*. In the South and the West, *rail fence* prevails, with scattered instances of the Eastern forms, as well as *log fence*, *split-rail fence*, and *stake-and-rider fence*.

zilch /zilch/ *pron* zero or nothing at all (*informal*) ○ *They take all the profits and we're left with zilch.* [Mid-20C. Origin ?]

zill /zil/ *n* either of a pair of tiny cymbals that belly dancers hold in their fingers and play in time to their dancing [< Turkish *zil* "cymbals"]

zil·lion /zíllyən/ *n* a number of people or a quantity of things so huge it cannot be counted or determined (*informal*) ○ *The new stadium must seat zillions!* [Mid-20C. After MILLION and BILLION, with *z* representing the last in a series] —**zil·lion** *adj*

zil·lion·aire /zìllyə nér, zíllyə nèr/ *n* an extremely wealthy person (*informal*) [Mid-20C. After MILLIONAIRE]

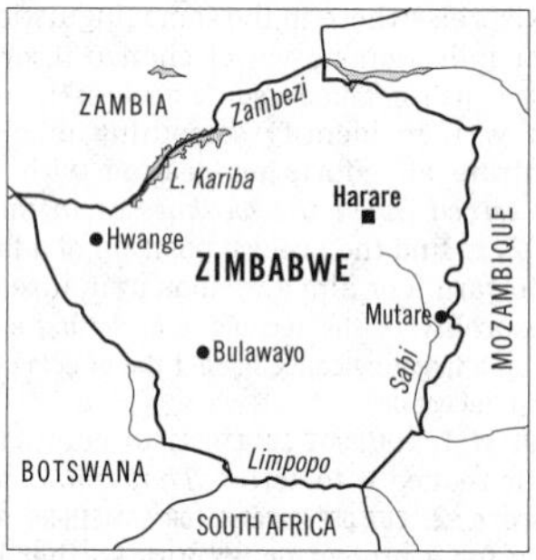

Zimbabwe

Zim·bab·we /zim baábwee, -way/ country in southern Africa. Language: English. Currency: Zimbabwe dollar. Capital: Harare. Population: 12,576,742 (2003). Area: 150,873 sq. mi./390,759 sq. km. Official name **Republic of Zimbabwe**. Former name **Rhodesia** (1964–79), **Southern Rhodesia** (1923–64) —**Zim·bab·we·an** *n, adj*

zinc /zingk/ *n* a bluish white metallic element. Source: calamine, sphalerite, franklinite. Use: in alloys such as brass and German silver, as a protective corrosion-resistant coating for other metals, especially steel and iron. Symbol **Zn**. See table at **element** ■ *vt* (**zinced** or **zincked, zinc·ing** or **zinck·ing, zincs**) to cover a metal, especially iron or steel, with a protective corrosion-resistant coating of zinc [Mid-17C. < German *Zink*]

zinc·ate /zíng kàyt/ *n* a salt derived from zinc hydroxide

zinc blende *n* MINERALS same as **sphalerite**

zinc chlo·ride *n* a poisonous soluble salt. Use: wood preservative, antiseptic, catalyst. Formula: $ZnCl_2$.

zinc hy·drox·ide *n* a colorless crystalline compound. Use: in chemical synthesis, as an absorbent.

zinc·if·er·ous /zing kíffərəss/ *adj* containing or yielding zinc, especially as an ore

zinc·ite /zíng kīt/ *n* a reddish orange zinc oxide mineral

zinck·en·ite *n* MINERALS another spelling of **zinkenite**

zinc·o·graph /zíngkə gràf/ *n* **1.** a printing plate made of zinc that has the design to be printed etched into its surface **2.** a print taken from a zincograph —**zinc·og·ra·phy** /zing kóggrəfee/ *n*

zinc oint·ment *n* an antiseptic ointment containing zinc oxide in a base of petroleum jelly or lanolin. Use: treatment of skin disorders.

zinc ox·ide *n* an odorless water-insoluble white powder. Use: pigment, astringent, antiseptic. Formula: ZnO.

zinc sul·fate *n* a colorless crystalline powder. Use: pigment, emetic, wood preservative, crop spray. Formula: $ZnSO_4$.

zinc sul·fide *n* a crystalline white or yellowish powder. Use: pigment, phosphor on X-ray and television screens. Formula: ZnS.

zinc white *n* zinc oxide used as a white pigment in paint

Zin·der /zíndər/ city in south central Niger. Situated about 70 mi./113 km north of the border with Nigeria, it was Niger's capital until 1926. Population: 120,900 (1988).

zine /zeen/ *n* a self-published paper, Internet magazine, or other periodical, issued at irregular intervals with and usually appealing to a specialist readership (*informal*) [Mid-20C. Shortening of MAGAZINE]

zin·fan·del /zínfən dèl/, **Zin·fan·del** *n* **1.** a typically light fruity red or rosé wine made from a black variety of grape grown mainly in California **2.** a black grape variety. Use: to make zinfandel. [Mid-19C. Origin ?]

zing /zing/ *n* **1.** LIVELY AND EXCITING QUALITY a lively exciting aspect of something that makes it particularly enjoyable (*informal*) ○ *The rhythm guitar gives the tune extra zing.* **2.** SHARP SINGING SOUND a short high-pitched humming or buzzing sound, e.g., the sound of a bullet whizzing through the air ■ *v* (**zinged, zing·ing, zings**) (*informal*) **1.** *vi* MAKE HUMMING NOISE to make or move with a short high-pitched humming or buzzing noise **2.** *vi* SPEED to move very quickly ○ *kids zinging by on skates* **3.** *vi* BE LIVELY to be very energetic and animated ○ *The production zings with energy.* **4.** *vt* ATTACK SOMEBODY WITH WORDS to criticize somebody sharply, especially in a swift and clever way [Early 20C. An imitation of the sound] —**zing·y** *adj*

zing·er /zíngər/ *n* (*informal*) **1.** CLEVER REMARK SKILLFULLY DELIVERED a remark delivered with great skill and speed, especially a sharp and perfectly timed witticism or criticism **2.** SHOCKING AND UNEXPECTED HAPPENING a shocking and unexpected turn of events, e.g., an abrupt shift in the plot of a movie, play, or book **3.** SOMEBODY OR SOMETHING ENERGETIC AND SURPRISING an energetic person or thing that produces startling results

~~**zink**~~ incorrect spelling of **zinc**

zink·en·ite /zíngkən īt/, **zinck·en·ite** *n* a dark gray lead antimony sulfide mineral [Mid-19C. After J. K. L. *Zincken* (1790–1862), German mineralogist]

zinnia

zin·ni·a /zínnee ə/ (*plural* **-as** or *same*) *n* a plant of the daisy family with large colorful flowers that is widely grown as a garden plant. Native to: Mexico. Genus: *Zinnia*. [Mid-18C. < modern Latin, after J. G. *Zinn* (1727–59), German botanist]

Zins·ser /zínssər/, **Hans** (1878–1940) US bacteriologist. A pioneer in immunology, he worked on typhus, cholera, and other bacterial diseases.

> "The scientist takes off from the manifold observations of predecessors, and shows his intelligence...by selecting here and there the significant stepping stones that will lead across the difficulties to new understanding."
> [Hans Zinsser, *As I Remember Him*; 1940]

Zi·on /zī ən/ *n* **1.** one of the hills of Jerusalem, in biblical times emblematic of the house or household of God and later by extension the Jews and their religion **2.** in Christian belief, the place where God lives and is worshiped on Earth or in the kingdom of heaven [Pre-12C. Via late Latin and Greek < Hebrew *ṣīyôn*]

Zi·on·ism /zī ə nìzzəm/ *n* a worldwide movement, originating in the 19th century, that sought to establish and develop a Jewish nation in Palestine. Since 1948 its function has been to support the state of Israel.

Zi·on·ist /zī ənist/ *n* **1.** a supporter of Zionism **2.** *S Africa* a member of an independent Christian church in South Africa that incorporates traditional African beliefs and forms of worship —**Zi·on·ist** *adj* —**Zi·on·is·tic** /zì ə nístik/ *adj*

Zi·on Na·tion·al Park /zī ən-/ national park in southwestern Utah. Noted for its canyons, mesas, and cliffs, its main feature is Zion Canyon. Area: 229 sq. mi./593 sq. km.

zip[1] /zip/ *n* **1.** US MAIL same as **ZIP Code** **2.** *UK* CLOTHING same as **zipper** **3.** BRIEF HISSING SOUND a brief sibilant sound, e.g., the sound of a bullet whizzing through the air **4.** LIVELY AND EXCITING QUALITY a lively exciting aspect of something that makes it particularly enjoyable (*informal*) **5.** *US* ZERO nothing at all (*slang*) ○ *worked hard and got zip for my efforts* ■ *v* (**zipped, zip·ping, zips**) **1.** *vti* FASTEN WITH ZIPPER to fasten something with a zipper, or be fastened with a zipper **2.** *vt* COMPUT COMPRESS FILE to compress a computer file for storage or transmission **3.** *vti* GO OR MOVE VERY FAST to go somewhere very fast, or move something somewhere very fast (*informal*) **4.** *vi* MAKE OR MOVE WITH HISSING SOUND to make or move with a rapid sibilant sound (*informal*) [Late 19C. An imitation of the sound]

zip[2] /zip/ *abbr* a file extension for a zip file

ZIP Code /zíp-/ *tdmk US* a trademark for a mail delivery system using a set of numbers to identify a postal district. Can term **postal code**

ZIP drive /zíp-/ *tdmk* a trademark for a piece of computer equipment that compresses large computer files for easier storage or faster transmission

zip file *n* a computer file with the extension .zip containing data that has been compressed for storage or transmission.

zip gun *n* a homemade pistol, especially one that uses a spring or a rubber band as the firing mechanism (*slang*)

zip·less /zípləss/ *adj* **1.** not fitted with a zipper, or not fastened using a zipper **2.** passionate and lasting only a short time [Late 20C. In the sense "passionate" from the idea of clothes coming off without the awkward undoing of zippers]

zip·per /zíppər/ *n* a fastener for clothes, bags, or garments consisting of two rows of interlocking metal or plastic teeth with an attached sliding tab pulled to open or close the fastener ■ *vti* (**-pered, -per·ing, -pers**) to fasten or unfasten a zipper, or become fastened or unfastened in this way

zip·pered /zíppərd/ *adj* fitted with or fastened using a zipper

zip·po /zíppō/ *n* nothing at all (*informal*)

zip·py /zíppee/ (**-pi·er, -pi·est**) *adj* showing or having spirit or energy (*informal*)

zip-up *adj UK* same as **zippered**

zir·con /zúr kòn/ *n* a very hard zirconium silicate mineral. Use: source of zirconium, gems. [Late 18C. < German *Zirkon*]

zir·co·ni·a /zur kṓnee ə/ *n* CHEM same as **zirconium oxide**

zir·co·ni·um /zur kṓnee əm/ *n* **1.** a grayish white, corrosion-resistant, metallic element. Source: zircon, zirconia. Use: coating fuel rods in nuclear reactors. Symbol **Zr**. See table at **element** **2.** the mineral zircon used as a gemstone, often as a substitute diamond —**zir·con·ic** /-kónnik/ *adj*

zir·co·ni·um ox·ide *n* a heavy water-insoluble white powder. Use: pigment, abrasive, manufacture of heat-resistant materials and ceramics. Formula: ZrO_2.

zit /zit/ *n* a pimple on the skin (*slang*) [Mid-20C. Origin ?]

zither

zith·er /zíthər, zíthər/ *n* a musical instrument consisting of a flat shallow soundbox with metal strings stretched across it that are plucked [Mid-19C. Via German < Latin *cithara* (see CITHARA)] —**zith·er·ist** *n*

zi·ti /zeé teè/ *n* pasta in the form of medium-sized tubes, longer and thicker than macaroni [Mid-19C. < Italian, plural of *zito* "boy"]

Z line *n* a narrow dark line across striated muscle fibers that marks the boundaries between adjacent segments [< abbreviation of German *Zwischenscheibe* "intervening disk"]

zlo·ty /zlóttee/ (*plural* **-ties** or *same*) *n* the main unit of currency in Poland, worth 100 groszy. See table at **currency** [Early 20C. < Polish *złoty* "golden" < *złoto* "gold"]

zm *abbr* Zambia (*used in Internet addresses*) See table at **domain name**

Z-mo·dem /zeé mō dem/ *n* a variation of the Ymodem file transfer protocol in which data is sent in 512-byte blocks without waiting for acknowledgment from the recipient between blocks

Zn *symbol* CHEM ELEM zinc

zo *n* ZOOL another spelling of **dzo**

zo- *prefix* same as **zoo-** (*used before vowels*)

zo·ar·i·um /zō érree əm/ (*plural* **-i·ums** or **-i·a** /-ee ə/) *n* a collection of distinct organisms that together form a compound organism [Late 19C. < Greek *zōion* "animal" (see -ZOON)]

zod. *abbr* zodiac

zo·di·ac /zṓdee àk/ *n* **1.** ASTROLOGICALLY SIGNIFICANT PART OF SKY a narrow band in the sky in which the movements of the major planets, Sun, and Moon take place, astrologically divided into twelve sections named for the major constellations **2.** ASTROLOGER'S CHART a chart linking twelve constellations to twelve divisions of the year, used as the astrologer's main tool for analyzing character and predicting the future **3.** RECURRING SET a set of things or a sequence of events that repeats itself cyclically (*literary*) [14C. Via French and Latin < Greek *zōidiakos kuklos* "circle of animal figures" < *zōidion* "small animal" < *zōion* (see -ZOON)] —**zo·di·a·cal** /zō dī ək'l/ *adj*

zo·di·a·cal con·stel·la·tion *n* a constellation that a sign of the zodiac is named for

zo·di·a·cal light *n* a faint glow in the sky, seen before sunrise to the east and after sunset to the west, and caused by small particles reflected in sunlight

zof·tig /zóftig/ *adj US* same as **zaftig** (*slang*) [Mid-20C. Variant]

Zo·har /zō haar/ *n* a 13th-century Jewish mystical text that is the primary text of Kabbalistic writings [Late 17C. < Hebrew *zōhar* "light, splendor"]

-zoic *suffix* **1.** relating to a particular geologic era ○ *Mesozoic* **2.** having a particular kind of animal existence ○ *epizoic* [< Greek *zōē* "life" < Indo-European, "to live"]

zoi·site /zóy sīt/ *n* a gray or green hydrated calcium aluminosilicate mineral. Source: metamorphic rocks. [Early 19C. After Baron Sigismund *Zois* von Edelstein (1747–1819), Slovenian scholar]

AKG London

Émile Zola

Zo·la /zṓlə, zō laa/, **Émile** (1840–1902) French novelist. One of the leading French novelists of the 19th century, he employed a scientifically based technique of naturalism in his epic 20-novel cycle *Les Rougon-Macquart* (1871–93). He is also known for "J'Accuse" (1898), a defense of Alfred Dreyfus. Full name **Zola, Émile Édouard Charles Antoine**

> "One forges one's style on the terrible anvil of daily deadlines."
> [Emile Zola, *Le Figaro*; 1881]

Zoll·ver·ein /tsáwlfə rīn, záwl-/ *n* **1.** a customs union formed in the 19th century by a number of German states to establish uniform import tariffs from other countries and free trade among themselves **2.** a customs union formed to establish uniform import tariffs [Mid-19C. < German, "tariff union"]

zom·bie /zómbee/, **zom·bi** *n* **1.** OFFENSIVE TERM an offensive term for a person considered to lack energy, enthusiasm, or the ability to think independently (*insult*) **2.** DEAD BODY GIVEN LIFE BY VOODOO in voodoo, a dead body supposedly brought back to life again without a soul **3.** VOODOO SPIRIT REVIVING DEAD BODY in voodoo, a spirit that supposedly brings a dead body back to life again **4.** RELIG SNAKE GOD OF VOODOO in Caribbean, Brazilian, and West African voodoo religions, a snake god **5.** BEVERAGES STRONG RUM COCKTAIL a very strong alcoholic cocktail made with various kinds of rum **6.** HIST ARMY CONSCRIPT ASSIGNED FOR HOME DEFENSE in Canada, a conscripted soldier assigned to home defense during World War II (*slang*) **7.** COMPUT PROGRAM ALLOWING REMOTE CONTROL a hidden software program that is installed on another computer by means of a virus, allowing it to be accessed remotely and used to access or attack another computer **8.** COMPUT REMOTELY CONTROLLED COMPUTER a computer that has been infected with a zombie [Early 19C. Via Caribbean Creole < Kimbundu *n-zumbi* "ghost, snake god"] —**zom·bi·ism** *n*

zom·bie drone *n* COMPUT same as **zombie** (senses 7–8) (*slang*)

zom·bi·fy /zómbə fī/ (**-fied, -fy·ing, -fies**) *vt* to convert somebody into a zombie —**zom·bi·fi·ca·tion** /zòmbəfi káysh'n/ *n*

zo·nal /zṓn'l/, **zo·na·ry** /zṓnəree/ *adj* **1.** relating to a zone or zones **2.** divided up into zones —**zo·nal·ly** *adv*

zo·nal soil *n* soil whose nature is established by the action of the climate and vegetation of the area in which it is found

zo·na pel·lu·ci·da /zṓnə pə lóossidə/ *n* a thick transparent envelope that surrounds a developing ovum, allowing only one sperm cell through to fertilize the ovum [< modern Latin, "transparent band"]

zo·na·ry *adj* same as **zonal**

zo·nate /zō nàyt/, **zo·nat·ed** /zō nàytəd/ *adj* **1.** divided up into zones **2.** distinguished by zones, e.g., of color or texture —**zo·na·tion** /zō náysh'n/ *n*

zone /zōn/ *n* **1.** SEPARATE AREA WITH PARTICULAR FUNCTION an area regarded as separate or kept separate, especially one with a particular use or function ○ *a loading zone* **2.** SUBSECTION OF PARTICULAR AREA one of the smaller, usually named or numbered sections that an area is divided into, e.g., those of a transportation network or an athletic field **3.** METEOROL HORIZONTAL CLIMATIC BAND AROUND EARTH one of the five horizontal belts across the Earth's surface, separated by the Arctic Circle, the Tropic of Cancer, the Tropic of Capricorn, and the Antarctic Circle, that marks out a climatic region. The zones are called the North Frigid Zone, the North Temperate Zone, the South Frigid Zone, the South Temperate Zone, and the Torrid Zone. **4.** TIME same as **time zone** **5.** ECOL **AREA WITH DISTINCT PLANTS AND ANIMALS** an area with characteristic types of organisms determined largely by its environment, e.g., a belt of vegetation on a mountain **6.** GEOL **UNIT OF ROCK FORMATION WITH FOSSILS** a unit of a rock formation characterized by its fossil content **7.** MATH **PART OF SPHERE** the portion of a sphere included between two parallel planes meeting the sphere, one of which may be tangent to the sphere or both of which may intersect it ■ *v* **(zoned, zon·ing, zones) 1.** *vt* **SPLIT AREA INTO ZONES** to divide an area into zones **2.** *vti* **DESIGNATE AREA FOR SOMETHING** to declare officially that an area is to be used for a particular purpose, or be developed in a particular way (*often passive*) ○ *The canal areas have been zoned for recreation.* [15C. Via French and Latin < Greek *zōnē* "belt, girdle"] —**zon·ing** *n* ◇ **in the zone** performing an action, especially playing a sport, extremely well with intense focus (*informal*)

zone out *vi US* to lose focus or concentration (*slang*)

zone de·fense *n* a system of defense in sports, especially in basketball and football, in which each defender is responsible for guarding a portion of the playing area

zone melt·ing *n* METALL same as **zone refining**

zone of sat·u·ra·tion *n* an area of soil or rock below the level of the water table where all the voids are filled with water

zone re·fin·ing *n* a technique for greatly purifying metals in which a molten area is made to pass along an otherwise solid bar so that impurities become concentrated at one end

zone·time /zṓn tìm/ *n* the standard time that exists throughout a time zone

zonk /zongk/ **(zonked, zonk·ing, zonks)** *v* (*slang*) **1.** *vti* to lose consciousness or become stupefied from exhaustion or an intake of alcohol or narcotic drugs, or make somebody do this **2.** *vt* to hit somebody very hard [Early 20C. An imitation of the sound of a heavy blow]

zonked /zongkt/, **zonked out** *adj* **1.** exhausted to the point of hardly being able to function (*informal*) **2.** unconscious, stupefied, or sleeping, especially as a result of the effects of alcohol or a drug (*slang*)

zon·ule /zṓn yool/ *n* a small zone, band, or belt —**zon·u·lar** *adj*

zoo /zoo/ (*plural* **zoos**) *n* **1.** a park where live wild animals from different parts of the world are kept in cages or enclosures for people to come and see, and where they are bred and studied by scientists **2.** a place characterized as being full of noisy obstreperous people creating confusion and disorder (*informal*) [Mid-19C. Shortening of ZOOLOGICAL GARDEN]

zoo- *prefix* **1.** animal, animal kingdom ○ *zoology* **2.** motile organism ○ *zoospore* [< Greek *zōion* (see -ZOON)]

zo·o·flag·el·late /zṑ ə flájjələt, -làyt/ *n* a colorless protozoan that ingests organic matter, is often parasitic, and has one or more flagella

zo·o·ge·og·ra·phy /zṑ ə jee óggrəfee/ *n* the scientific study of the areas where different animals live and the causes and effects of such distribution, especially distributions on a large or global scale —**zo·o·ge·og·ra·pher** *n* —**zo·o·ge·o·graph·ic** /zṑ ə jee ə gráffik/ *adj*

zo·o·gle·a /zṑ ə glée ə/ (*plural* **-as** or **-ae** /-ee/), **zo·o·gloe·a** *n* a colony of microbes embedded in a gelatinous matrix [Late 19C. < modern Latin *zoogloea*, < Greek *zōion* "animal" + *gloios* "glutinous substance"] —**zo·o·gle·al** *adj*

zo·og·ra·phy /zō óggrəfee/ *n* a branch of zoology that deals with describing animals and their habitats —**zo·og·ra·pher** *n* —**zo·o·graph·ic** /zṑ ə gráffik/ *adj*

zo·oid /zṓ òyd/ *n* an individual invertebrate animal that reproduces nonsexually by budding or splitting, especially one that lives in a colony in which each member is joined to others by living material, e.g., a coral [Mid-19C. < ZOO- + -OID] —**zo·oid·al** /zo óyd'l/ *adj*

zoo·keep·er /zóo keepər/ *n* somebody whose job is taking care of the animals in a zoo

zool. *abbr* **1.** zoological **2.** zoology

zo·ol·a·try /zō óllətree, zə wól-/ *n* **1.** in some ancient cultures, the worshiping of animals **2.** an excessive devotion to animals, especially domestic pets (*humorous*)

zo·o·log·i·cal /zṑ ə lójjik'l/ *adj* **1.** relating to the scientific study of animals **2.** relating to animals —**zo·o·log·i·cal·ly** *adv*

zo·o·log·i·cal gar·den *n* same as **zoo** (sense 1) (*dated*)

zo·ol·o·gy /zō óllәjee, zə wól-/ (*plural* **-gies**) *n* **1.** **SCIENTIFIC STUDY OF ANIMALS** the branch of biology that involves the scientific study of animals and all aspects of animal life **2.** **ANIMALS LIVING IN REGION** the animal life of a particular region **3.** **CHARACTERISTICS OF ANIMAL OR GROUP** the physical and biological characteristics of a particular animal or group of animals [Mid-17C. Via modern Latin < Greek *zōologia* "the study of life" < *zōion* (see -ZOON)] —**zo·ol·o·gist** *n*

zoom /zoom/ *v* **(zoomed, zoom·ing, zooms) 1.** *vi* **MOVE SPEEDILY** to move very fast, especially while emitting a loud low-pitched buzzing noise **2.** *vi* **INCREASE SUDDENLY** to rise or increase suddenly and significantly **3.** *vi* **SIMULATE MOVEMENT WITH CAMERA LENS** to simulate movement toward or away from an object with a camera lens that allows various focal lengths **4.** *vi* **MAKE LOUD BUZZING NOISE** to emit a loud low-pitched buzzing or humming noise **5.** *vti* AVIAT **CARRY OUT STEEP CLIMB IN AIRCRAFT** to make an aircraft climb rapidly at a very steep angle, or be piloted in this way ■ *n* **1.** PHOTOGRAPHY, MOVIES same as **zoom lens** **2.** PHOTOGRAPHY, MOVIES **SHOT WITH ZOOM LENS** a shot in which a zoom lens is used to make the object in focus appear to move closer or farther away while the camera itself stays still **3.** **LOUD BUZZING NOISE** a loud low-pitched buzzing noise, especially one caused by rapid movement **4.** **ACT OF VERY RAPID MOVEMENT** an act of moving or performing an activity at great speed [Late 19C. An imitation of a buzzing sound]

zoom in *vi* to make an object appear bigger or closer, or to decrease the area in view, by use of a zoom lens or a graphic imaging device

zoom out *vi* to make an object appear smaller or farther away, or to increase the area in view, by use of a zoom lens or a graphic imaging device

zo·om·e·try /zō ómmətree/ *n* the branch of zoology that deals with the sizes and proportions of animals —**zo·o·met·ric** /zṑ ə méttrik/ *adj* —**zo·o·met·rist** *n*

zoom lens *n* a camera lens assembly with adjustable focal lengths, facilitating transitions between long shots and close-ups

zo·o·mor·phism /zṑ ə máwr fìzzəm/ *n* **1.** the attribution of animal forms or characteristics to gods **2.** the use of animal figures in art and design, or of animal symbols in literature —**zo·o·mor·phic** *adj*

-zoon *suffix* animal, zooid ○ *epizoon* [Via modern Latin < Greek *zōion* "living being, animal" < Indo-European, "to live"]

zo·on·o·sis /zō ónnəssiss/ (*plural* **-o·no·ses** /-nə seez/) *n* a disease that can be transmitted from vertebrate animals to humans, e.g., rabies, anthrax, or ringworm [Late 19C. < ZOO- + Greek *nosos* "disease"] —**zo·on·o·tic** /zṑ ə nóttik/ *adj*

zo·oph·a·gous /zō óffəgəss/ *adj* feeding on animals

zo·o·phil·i·a /zṑ ə fíllee ə/ *n* a sexual attraction to animals

zo·o·phil·ic /zṑ ə fíllik/ *adj* ZOOL same as **zoophilous**

zo·oph·i·lism /zō óffə lìzzəm/ *n* a strong affinity for animals and a devotion to protecting or rescuing them from human activities such as vivisection that exploit or endanger them

zo·oph·i·lous /zō óffələss/ *adj* **1.** very fond of animals **2.** using the actions of animals other than insects in pollinating a plant

zo·o·pho·bi·a /zṑ ə fóbee ə/ *n* an unusually intense fear of animals —**zo·o·phobe** /zṓ ə fòb/ *n*

zo·o·phyte /zṓ ə fìt/ *n* an invertebrate animal that looks like a plant, e.g., a sea anemone, coral, or sponge [Early 17C. Via modern Latin < Greek *zōiophuton* "animal-plant" < *zōion* "animal" + *phuton* "plant"] —**zo·o·phyt·ic** /zṑ ə fíttik/ *adj*

zo·o·plank·ton /zṑ ə plángktən/ *n* plankton that is made up of microscopic animals such as protozoans

zo·o·plas·ty /zṓ ə plàstee/ *n* the surgical transplantation of an animal organ such as a pig's heart into a human body —**zo·o·plas·tic** /zṑ ə plástik/ *adj*

zo·o·sperm /zṓ ə spùrm/ *n* BIOL same as **spermatozoon** —**zo·o·sper·mat·ic** /zṑ ə spur máttik/ *adj*

zo·o·spo·ran·gi·um /zṑ əspə ránjee əm/ (*plural* **-gi·a** /-jee ə/) *n* an organ of a fungus or plant that produces spores that can swim —**zo·o·spo·ran·gi·al** *adj*

zo·o·spore /zṓ ə spàwr/ *n* a spore of some algae and fungi that is capable of independent movement —**zo·o·spor·ic** /zṑ ə spáwrik/ *adj*

zo·os·ter·ol /zō óstə ràwl/ *n* a sterol produced by an animal

zo·ot·o·my /zō óttəmee/ *n* **1.** the study of the anatomy of animals, especially comparative anatomy **2.** the dissection of animals [Mid-17C. < ZOO-, after ANATOMY]

zo·o·tox·in /zṑ ə tóksin/ *n* a poisonous substance produced by an animal, e.g., snake venom

zoot suit /zóot-/ *n* a man's suit, popular in the 1940s, that had a long jacket heavily padded at the shoulders and baggy high-waisted trousers tapering to narrow bottoms [Mid-20C. Rhyming formation] —**zoot suit·er** *n*

zoo TV *n* a genre of television program that encourages emotional and often uncontrolled reactions from the participants, featuring debates or personal disclosures in front of live audiences (*slang*)

zo·o·xan·thel·la /zṑəzən théllə/ (*plural* **-lae** /-lee/) *n* a microscopic yellow-green alga that lives symbiotically within the cells of some ocean invertebrates, especially corals [Late 19C. < modern Latin, "small yellow animal" < Greek *zōion* "animal" + *xanthos* "yellow"]

zo·ri /záwree/ (*plural same* or **-ris**) *n* a simple Japanese sandal with a flat sole and a single thong, originally made of straw but now also made of rubber or felt [Early 19C. < Japanese *sō* "grass, straw" (< Middle Chinese *tsaw*) + *ri* "sole" (< Middle Chinese *li*)]

zo·ril·la /zə ríllə/, **zor·ille** /záwril/, **zor·il** *n* a carnivorous mammal of the weasel family that looks like a skunk and has long black-and-white fur. Native to: Africa. Latin name: *Ictonyx striatus.* [Late 18C. Via French and modern Latin < Spanish *zorilla* "little fox" < *zorro* "fox"]

Zo·ro·as·ter /záwrō àstər/, **Za·ra·thu·stra** /zàrrə thóostrə/ (630?–550? B.C.) Persian prophet. He founded Zoroastrianism, a religion based on revelations he received from Ahura Mazda, the "Lord Wisdom."

Zo·ro·as·tri·an·ism /zàwrō ástree ə nìzzəm/ *n* an ancient religion founded by the Persian prophet Zoroaster, the principal belief of which is in a supreme deity and a cosmic contest between two spirits, one good and one evil —**Zo·ro·as·tri·an** *n, adj*

zos·ter /zóstər/ *n* **1.** MED same as **shingles** (*technical*) **2.** a belt worn by men, especially soldiers, in ancient Greece [Early 18C. Via Latin < Greek *zōstēr* "girdle"]

Zou·ave /zoo áav, zwaav/ *n* **1.** a member of a former French infantry unit composed of Algerian soldiers, noted for their colorful uniforms and precision drill **2.** a member of an army unit whose uniforms imitate those of the French Zouaves, especially such a soldier on the Union side during the Civil War [Mid-19C. Via French < Kabyle *Zouaoua*, tribe in Algeria]

zouk /zook/ *n* a style of dance music originating in Guadeloupe and Martinique and played with guitars and synthesizers, combining a strong fast disco beat and Caribbean rhythms [Late 20C. Via French < French Creole of the Antilles]

zounds /zowndz/ *interj* a mild expression of surprise or annoyance (*archaic*) [Late 16C. Contraction of *by God's wounds!*]

Zo·vi·rax /zō vī ràks/ *tdmk* a trademark for an antiviral drug. Use: treatment of herpes infections.

zow·ie /zów ee/ *interj* used to express surprise, admiration, or pleasure (*dated informal*) [Early 20C. Natural exclamation]

zoy·si·a /zóyssee ə/ *n* a low-growing grass plant often used for lawns. Native to: Asia. Genus: *Zoysia.* [Mid-

20C. < modern Latin, after Carl von *Zoys* zu Laubach (1756–1800?), Austrian botanist]

Z par·ti·cle *n* a short-lived electrically neutral elementary particle considered to mediate the weak interaction between other elementary particles

ZPG *abbr* zero population growth

Zr *symbol* CHEM ELEM zirconium

zuc·chet·to /zoo kéttō/ (*plural* **-tos**) *n* a small round skullcap worn by members of the Roman Catholic clergy, the color of which depends on the rank of the person wearing it [Mid-19C. Alteration of Italian *zucchetta* "small head" < *zucca* "gourd, head" (see ZUCCHINI)]

zuc·chi·ni /zoo keénee/ (*plural same* or **-nis**) *n* **1.** a small summer squash that is shaped like a cucumber with a smooth thin dark-green or yellow skin and is eaten cooked as a vegetable **2.** the plant that produces zucchini [Early 20C. < Italian, plural of *zucchino* "zucchini" < *zucca* "gourd" < late Latin *cucutia*, variant of Latin *cucurbita*]

~~zuchini~~ incorrect spelling of **zucchini**

zug·zwang /tsoók tsvaàng/ *n* a chess situation in which a player is forced into making a disadvantageous move, especially one that involves the loss of a piece ■ *vt* (**-zwanged, -zwang·ing, -zwangs**) to force a chess opponent into a disadvantageous situation, especially one that involves the loss of one of the opponent's pieces [Early 20C. < German, "being forced to move"]

Zui·der Zee /zídər zeé, zàydər-/ former inlet of the North Sea in the northern Netherlands. After completion of the IJsselmeer Dam in 1932, parts of it were drained, and the remainder now forms the IJsselmeer.

Zuk·er·man /zoókər mən, zoókər-/, **Pinchas** (*b.* 1948) Israeli-born US violinist and conductor. His performance of both the classical repertoire and 20th-century works established his reputation as one of the outstanding violinists of his generation.

Zu·lu /zoóloo/ (*plural same* or **-lus**) *n* **1.** MEMBER OF S AFRICAN PEOPLE a member of a people of South Africa who live mainly in northern KwaZulu-Natal Province **2.** S AFRICAN LANGUAGE a Bantu language spoken in eastern South Africa, closely related to Xhosa. Native speakers: 8 million. **3.** COMMUNICATION CODE WORD FOR LETTER "Z" a code word for the letter "Z," used in international radio communications [Early 19C. < Zulu *umzulu*] —**Zu·lu** *adj*

Zu·lu·land /zoóloo lànd/ historic region in South Africa. Now incorporated into KwaZulu-Natal Province, it is the homeland of the Zulu people.

Zu·lu time *n* TIME same as **Universal Time**

Zu·ni /zoónee/ (*plural same* or **-nis**), **Zu·ñi** /zoónyee, zoónee/ (*plural same* or **-ñis**) *n* **1.** a member of a Pueblo people of western New Mexico **2.** the language of the Zuni people, unrelated to other languages. Native speakers: 5,000. [Mid-19C. < American Spanish < Keresan] —**Zu·ni** *adj*

Zu·rich /zoórik/, **Zü·rich** largest city in Switzerland, in the north of the country. It is the capital of Zurich Canton and an important financial, commercial, and manufacturing center. Population: 337,900 (2001).

Zu·rich, Lake lake in northern Switzerland. Area: 34 sq. mi./88 sq. km.

ZW *abbr* ONLINE Zimbabwe (*used in Internet addresses*) See table at **domain name**

Zwick·au /zwík ow, tsvík ow/ city in Saxony, eastern Germany. Population: 104,921 (1997).

zwie·back /zweé bàk, sweé bàk/ *n* a piece of bread, sliced and baked again until crisp and dry [Late 19C. < German, "twice-bake"]

Zwing·li /zwínglee, swínglee/, **Huldreich** (1484–1531) Swiss religious reformer. Using his own translations of the Christian Scriptures, he questioned many Roman Catholic practices, held that the Communion wafer and wine were only symbolic of Christ's body and blood, and became the leader of the Reformation in Switzerland.

Zwing·li·an /zwínglee ən, swínglee ən/ *adj* relating to the life, works, or beliefs of the Swiss Protestant theologian Huldreich Zwingli ■ *n* a follower of Huldreich Zwingli or his beliefs —**Zwing·li·an·ism** *n*

zwit·ter·i·on /zwíttə rī ən, swíttə-/ *n* an ion that has both a negative and a positive pole [Early 20C. < German, "hybrid ion"]

Zwol·le /zwóllə/ capital city of Overijssel Province, in the north central Netherlands. Population: 105,819 (2000).

Zwor·y·kin /zwáwri kìn/, **Vladimir** (1889–1982) Russian-born US inventor. He was largely responsible for the development of the television camera and television tube during the 1920s and 1930s. Full name **Zworykin, Vladimir Kosma**

zy·de·co /zídə kō/ *n* a style of dance music originating in Louisiana that is usually played on accordion, guitar, and violin and combines traditional French melodies with Caribbean and blues influences [Mid-20C. Probably < Louisiana creole *Les haricots (sont pas salés)* "the beans (are not salted)," a well-known dance tune]

zyg- *prefix* same as **zygo-** (*used before vowels*)

zygo- *prefix* **1.** yoke, pair ○ *zygomorphic* **2.** union, reproduction ○ *zygogenesis* [< Greek *zugon* "yoke, pair" < Indo-European, "join"]

zy·go·dac·tyl /zígə dákt'l/ *adj also* **zy·go·dac·ty·lous** /zīgə dáktələss/ describes the feet of birds in which the second and third toes face forward and the first and fourth toes face backward. ◊ **heterodactylous** ■ *n* a bird that has two pairs of toes facing in different directions, e.g., a woodpecker —**zy·go·dac·tyl·ism** *n*

zy·go·gen·e·sis /zìgō jénnəssiss/ *n* reproduction involving the fusion of male and female nuclei —**zy·go·ge·net·ic** /zīgōjə néttik/ *adj*

zy·go·ma /zī gṓmə/ (*plural* **-ma·ta** /-mətə/ or **-mas**) *n* ANAT **1.** same as **cheekbone** (*technical*) **2.** same as **zygomatic arch 3.** same as **zygomatic process** [Late 17C. < Greek *zugōma* "joining" < *zugoun* "to join"] —**zy·go·mat·ic** /zīgə máttik/ *adj*

zy·go·mat·ic arch *n* a slender bar of bone connecting the cheekbone with the temporal bone on the side of the skull

zy·go·mat·ic bone *n* ANAT same as **cheekbone** (*technical*)

zy·go·mat·ic proc·ess *n* a bony projection that forms part of the zygomatic arch and is joined to the cheekbone

zy·go·mor·phic /zìgə máwrfik/ *adj* producing identical halves only when divided along a vertical axis —**zy·go·mor·phism** *n* —**zy·go·mor·phy** /zígə màwrfee/ *n*

zy·go·sis /zī gṓssiss/ *n* BIOL same as **conjugation** (sense 6) [Late 19C. < Greek *zugōsis* < *zugoun* "to join"] —**zy·gose** /zí gōss/ *adj*

zy·gos·i·ty /zī góssətee/ *n* a characterization of a

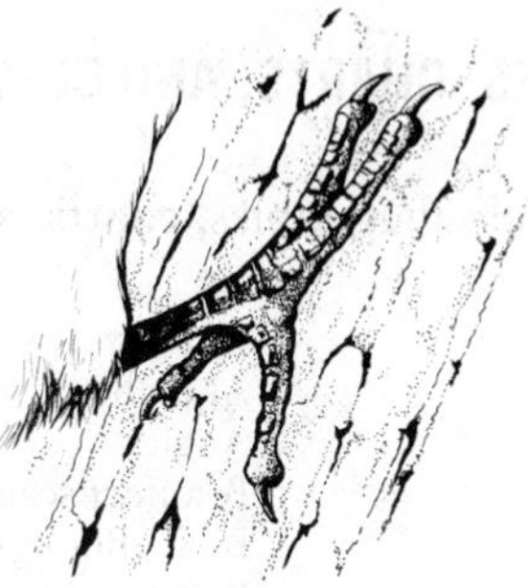

zygodactyl

genetic trait, zygote, or embryo, e.g., whether twins have resulted from the division of one zygote or from two different zygotes (*often used in combination*) [Mid-20C. < ZYGOSIS]

zy·go·spore /zígə spàwr/ *n* a thick-walled sexual spore formed from the union of two gametes in some fungi and green algae

zy·gote /zí gōt/ *n* an ovum that has been fertilized by a spermatozoon [Late 19C. < Greek *zugōtos* "joined" < *zugoun* "to join"] —**zy·got·ic** /zī góttik/ *adj* —**zy·got·i·cal·ly** *adv*

zy·go·tene /zígə teén/ *n* a stage of the first meiotic cell division in which homologous chromosomes are paired [Early 20C. < French *zygotène* < *zygo-* "zygo-" + *-tène* "ribbon" (< Latin *taenia*)]

-zygous *suffix* having a particular kind of zygotic constitution ○ *hemizygous* [< Greek *zugos* "yoked, paired," < *zugon* (see ZYGO-)]

zym- *prefix* same as **zymo-** (*used before vowels*)

zy·mase /zí màyss, -màyz/ *n* an enzyme or enzyme complex obtained from yeast that ferments sugars [Late 19C. < Greek *zumē* "leaven" (see ZYMO-)]

zymo- *prefix* **1.** fermentation ○ *zymology* **2.** enzyme ○ *zymogen* [Via modern Latin < Greek *zumē* "leaven" < Indo-European, "to mix"]

zy·mo·gen /zímə jən/ *n* BIOCHEM same as **proenzyme**

zy·mo·gen·e·sis /zìmə jénnəssiss/ *n* the transformation of a zymogen into an enzyme

zy·mo·gen·ic /zìmə jénnik/, **zy·mo·ge·net·ic** /zìməjə néttik/, **zy·mog·e·nous** /zī mójjənəss/ *adj* **1.** relating to a zymogen **2.** causing or producing fermentation

zy·mol·o·gy /zī mólləjee/ *n* the study of fermentation and the action of enzymes as it takes place —**zy·mo·log·ic** /zìmə lójjik/ *adj* —**zy·mol·o·gist** *n*

zy·mol·y·sis /zī mólləssiss/ *n* the action of enzymes in the process of fermentation (*technical*) —**zy·mo·lyt·ic** /zìmə líttik/ *adj*

zy·mom·e·ter /zī mómmətər/, **zy·mo·scope** /zímə skōp/ *n* an instrument that measures degrees of fermentation

zy·mo·sis /zī mṓssiss/ *n* BIOCHEM same as **zymolysis** [Early 18C. < Greek *zumōsis* "fermentation" < *zumoun* "to leaven" < *zumē* (see ZYMO-)]

zy·mot·ic /zī móttik/ *adj* relating to, producing, or produced by fermentation [Mid-19C. < Greek *zumōtikos* "causing fermentation" < *zumōsis* (see ZYMOSIS)] —**zy·mot·i·cal·ly** *adv*

zy·mur·gy /zí mùrjee/ *n* the scientific study of fermentation processes involved in the production of alcoholic drinks [Mid-19C. < ZYMO-, after METALLURGY]

zzz /zz/ *n* a representation of the sound made by somebody sleeping or snoring, often used in cartoons (*humorous*)

TABLES, CHARTS, AND COMPOSITE PICTURES

The following tables, charts, and composite pictures can be found at their alphabetical entry: